2017

JANUARY

M	T	W	T	F	S	S
						1
2	3	4	5	6	7	8
9	10	11	12	13	14	15
16	17	18	19	20	21	22
23	24	25	26	27	28	29
30	31					

FEBRUARY

M	T	W	T	F	S
		1	2	3	4
6	7	8	9	10	11
13	14	15	16	17	18
20	21	22	23	24	25
27	28				

APRIL

M	T	W	T	F	S	S
					1	2
3	4	5	6	7	8	9
10	11	12	13	14	15	16
17	18	19	20	21	22	23
24	25	26	27	28	29	30

MAY

M	T	W	T	F	S	S
1	2	3	4	5	6	7
8	9	10	11	12	13	14
15	16	17	18	19	20	21
22	23	24	25	26	27	28
29	30	31				

JUNE

M	T	W	T	F	S	S
			1	2	3	4
5	6	7	8	9	10	11
12	13	14	15	16	17	18
19	20	21	22	23	24	25
26	27	28	29	30		

JULY

M	T	W	T	F	S	S
					1	2
3	4	5	6	7	8	9
10	11	12	13	14	15	16
17	18	19	20	21	22	23
24	25	26	27	28	29	30
31						

AUGUST

M	T	W	T	F	S	S
	1	2	3	4	5	6
7	8	9	10	11	12	13
14	15	16	17	18	19	20
21	22	23	24	25	26	27
28	29	30	31			

SEPTEMBER

M	T	W	T	F	S	S
				1	2	3
4	5	6	7	8	9	10
11	12	13	14	15	16	17
18	19	20	21	22	23	24
25	26	27	28	29	30	

OCTOBER

M	T	W	T	F	S	S
						1
2	3	4	5	6	7	8
9	10	11	12	13	14	15
16	17	18	19	20	21	22
23	24	25	26	27	28	29
30	31					

NOVEMBER

M	T	W	T	F	S	S
		1	2	3	4	5
6	7	8	9	10	11	12
13	14	15	16	17	18	19
20	21	22	23	24	25	26
27	28	29	30			

DECEMBER

M	T	W	T	F	S	S
				1	2	3
4	5	6	7	8	9	10
11	12	13	14	15	16	17
18	19	20	21	22	23	24
25	26	27	28	29	30	31

2018

JANUARY

M	T	W	T	F	S	S
1	2	3	4	5	6	7
8	9	10	11	12	13	14
15	16	17	18	19	20	21
22	23	24	25	26	27	28
29	30	31				

FEBRUARY

M	T	W	T	F	S	S
			1	2	3	4
5	6	7	8	9	10	11
12	13	14	15	16	17	18
19	20	21	22	23	24	25
26	27	28				

MARCH

M	T	W	T	F	S	S
			1	2	3	4
5	6	7	8	9	10	11
12	13	14	15	16	17	18
19	20	21	22	23	24	25
26	27	28	29	30	31	

APRIL

M	T	W	T	F	S	S
						1
2	3	4	5	6	7	8
9	10	11	12	13	14	15
16	17	18	19	20	21	22
23	24	25	26	27	28	29
30						

MAY

M	T	W	T	F	S	S
	1	2	3	4	5	6
7	8	9	10	11	12	13
14	15	16	17	18	19	20
21	22	23	24	25	26	27
28	29	30	31			

JUNE

M	T	W	T	F	S	S
				1	2	3
4	5	6	7	8	9	10
11	12	13	14	15	16	17
18	19	20	21	22	23	24
25	26	27	28	29	30	

JULY

M	T	W	T	F	S	S
						1
2	3	4	5	6	7	8
9	10	11	12	13	14	15
16	17	18	19	20	21	22
23	24	25	26	27	28	29
30	31					

AUGUST

M	T	W	T	F	S	S
		1	2	3	4	5
6	7	8	9	10	11	12
13	14	15	16	17	18	19
20	21	22	23	24	25	26
27	28	29	30	31		

SEPTEMBER

M	T	W	T	F	S	S
					1	2
3	4	5	6	7	8	9
10	11	12	13	14	15	16
17	18	19	20	21	22	23
24	25	26	27	28	29	30

OCTOBER

M	T	W	T	F	S	S
1	2	3	4	5	6	7
8	9	10	11	12	13	14
15	16	17	18	19	20	21
22	23	24	25	26	27	28
29	30	31				

NOVEMBER

M	T	W	T	F	S	S
			1	2	3	4
5	6	7	8	9	10	11
12	13	14	15	16	17	18
19	20	21	22	23	24	25
26	27	28	29	30		

DECEMBER

M	T	W	T	F	S	S
					1	2
3	4	5	6	7	8	9
10	11	12	13	14	15	16
17	18	19	20	21	22	23
24	25	26	27	28	29	30
31						

THE FAMILY COURT PRACTICE 2017

THE FAMILY COURT PRACTICE 2017

Published by LexisNexis
LexisNexis
Regus
Terrace Floor
Castlemead
Lower Castle Street
Bristol BS1 3AG

British Library Cataloguing-in-Publication Data
A catalogue record for this book is available from the British Library.

ISSN 1350–1860

ISBN 978 1 78473 253 0

The publishers are grateful to the Secretariat of the Principal Registry of the Family Division for providing updated texts of a number of practice directions issued by the Division, which are set out in Part V of this work.

The kind permission of the President of the Family Division to reproduce certain materials from the *Handbook of Best Practice in Children Act Cases* is gratefully acknowledged.

This volume is typeset by Letterpart Ltd, Caterham on the Hill, Surrey CR3 5XL.

SENIOR EDITOR: Jonathan Cailes BA (Hons)

FAMILY LAW PSL: Amy Royce-Greensill, Solicitor
Amy Sanders, Solicitor
Paula Tanner, Solicitor

COMMISSIONING EDITOR: Gregory Woodgate LLB, LLM, Barrister

The Index is researched and compiled by Kim Harris

Printed in the UK by CPI William Clowes, Beccles, NR34 7TL

EDITOR-IN-CHIEF
The Rt Hon Lord Wilson of Culworth
Justice of the Supreme Court

GENERAL EDITOR
His Honour Judge Anthony Cleary

CONSULTING EDITOR
The Rt Hon Lady Justice Black
Head of International Family Justice for England and Wales

CONTRIBUTORS
District Judge Michael Anson
Preston Combined Court Centre and Nominated Judge of the Court of Protection

David Burrows BA, Solicitor Advocate

Andrew Commins MA, LLM, Barrister
St John's Chambers

Ruth Henke QC

Neil Hickman
Former District Judge

Robert Hill
Recorder, Deputy District Judge, Regional Costs Judge
North Eastern Circuit

Elizabeth Isaacs QC
Deputy High Court Judge

The Hon Mr Justice Keehan

The Hon Mr Justice MacDonald

The Rt Hon Lord Justice McFarlane

Her Honour Nasreen Pearce

David Salter MA, LLM, Solicitor
Recorder and Deputy High Court Judge

Maggie Silver BA, Solicitor
Family Legal Team Manager,
East London Family Court

Preface

When first published in 1993, *The Family Court Practice* was new and innovative, designed to meet the need for a definitive work of reference covering the entire range of family proceedings at every level of court. It was hoped then that it might stand alongside *The Supreme Court Practice* and *The County Court Practice* as the comprehensive and authoritative guide for practitioners.

Over the ensuing years the hope has become reality and as civil procedure has changed so *The Family Court Practice* has been updated annually to reflect developments in law and procedure. The work is now universally accepted as a standard book of reference for judges and practitioners throughout the jurisdiction.

Congratulations are due to the team of contributors who have achieved so much in just a few years.

The Hon Mrs Justice Bracewell
Family Division

February 2001

Foreword

Nine years ago, when I became Editor-in-Chief of *The Family Court Practice*, I wrote a Foreword to it. It is time to write another one. The themes are the same – my pride at being associated with something now essential for family practitioners and my admiration for those who combine year after year to create it for them.

But the circumstances are different. For this 2017 edition of the book is the 25th edition. It calls for a celebration.

In 1993, the choice of title was prescient, anticipating as it did the creation of the Family Court by 21 years. Bound in the arresting colour which was to precipitate its popular name, it then ran to 1773 pages. This year's edition, however, has 2982 pages. Much of the book's success has been achieved by the comprehensive inclusion of the texts of all manner of instruments relating to family law (indeed it seems no longer to have significant competition in that regard) and every year brings a net accretion of such material to which practitioners must have access.

When I compare the first edition with this 25th, there is one remarkable feature: there has been no change in the identity of the General Editor. Anthony Cleary, then a District Judge and now a Circuit Judge, represents the pivot around which the assembly of each year's edition revolves. Within days of one year's publication, his work begins on the volume for the following year. He reads the mass of new material generated each week (yes, I accept that there is a real problem about the length of our family judgments) and he reaches a provisional decision as to whether, and if so where and to what extent, it should be accommodated in the book. He invites the relevant contributor to address it accordingly; appraises the response; and of course carries the burden of ultimate responsibility for the book's treatment of it. His contribution has been … just brilliant.

Anthony's introduction to the first edition intriguingly highlights the longevity of the book. He there referred to two challenges. First, the 'considerable' challenge presented by the Child Support Act 1991. That was to put it mildly. Secondly, the fact that Lord Mackay, then the Lord Chancellor, 'has challenged the profession to consider mediation as a route to the resolution of disputes'. There we see the first articulation of an idea (do I detect some circumspection in Anthony's reference to it?) which has developed into a mainstream feature of the system. In this year's Introduction, by contrast, the challenges are very different (and, I am sure, more intractable): underfunded children's services; a mass of self-represented parties; overcrowded court lists; and demoralised judges.

The praise for the Red Book consistently given by Sir James Munby, President of the Family Division, has been of profound value to all of us who are associated with it. In his address to the Family Law Bar Association at its dinner last year, he described it as 'a remarkable monument of legal publishing'. But his reference to it was in the context of a visionary presentation of a future digital family court where the necessary forms and rules, all much simplified, would be embedded in its software; and in which applications would be not only issued online but mostly determined online by videolink or even just in writing. At that point, the President's vision became apocalyptic and he foresaw a day when this, our monument of legal publishing, would be 'fit only for the bonfire'. One day the President's prophecy may come true. But I would respectfully urge our readers to try to resist the temptation to fling their Red Books onto a fire quite yet.

Nicholas Wilson
Justice of the Supreme Court

February 2017

Introduction

Family practitioners and the Family Court face troubling times. The legal landscape is increasingly populated by alarming metaphors: from the measured words of the Lord Chief Justice, the crisis in courts is 'unprecedented' (third annual report to Parliament); then to 'Justice in Freefall' (Legal Action Group, January 2017); 'Public confidence in the "secret" family justice system is "shaky"' (Association of Lawyers for Children, January 2017); 'crisis in the Family Court on the horizon' (*Family Law*, November 2016); '[w]e are approaching a crisis for which we are ill-prepared and where there is no clear strategy to manage the crisis' (15th View from the President's Chambers); 'Fed-up judges on the edge' (*Law Society Gazette*, February 2017). The debate, if there is one, was exacerbated in January 2017 by the assertion by the International Red Cross that the provision of social care in the UK now faces a 'humanitarian crisis'.

The hyperbole, if that is what it was, sought to address or expose the poor state of funding for the elderly in the community and the manning of overworked and under-resourced Accident and Emergency departments, but it hides a darker truth. A good proportion of the community will have occasion, perhaps more than once, to visit hospital. A larger number will have experience of the provision (or lack of it) of care in the community. The description by the Red Cross, described as 'unhelpful' by at least one commentator, may still not resonate with the Government until more attention is paid to the issue. What appears to be overlooked, however, is the funding crisis which presents itself to local authorities in the poorest areas of the country, struggling as they are to make provision for children's services in the face of an inexorable rise in care applications. The tensions facing councils which have to respond positively to central Government demands for only modest and even negligible rises in council tax, while addressing the increased cost of elderly care, educational provision, policing and even highway repair – all in plain sight of constituents – result in inevitable shortfalls, leading to local outcry.

That community outcry, however, is notable for its silence when it comes to the provision of services for children at risk of harm. Until a child is murdered.

But it seems that assistance from Whitehall simply will not be considered, while an innovative suggestion by a council in the Home Counties that there be a local referendum to test the willingness of the public to accept an increase in council tax appears to have been quietly shelved. And so another local authority, the latest being a cathedral city to the west of the country, is singled out for its failures.

One might wonder whether, let alone when, anyone will listen. As an example, the 16th View from Sir James Munby's chambers makes sobering reading. The President writes of his attempts, which now stretch back over 2 years, to alert Government to the issue of vulnerable witnesses. Having expressed his increasing dissatisfaction with the apparent inertia of the legislature, both by reference to case-law emerging from the Division, and in addresses to the FLBA, his View draws together the alerts of the Children and Vulnerable Witnesses Working Group, the All-Party Parliamentary Group on Domestic Violence, Women's Aid ('Nineteen Child Homicides'), his presentation to Swansea University ('Unheard voices: the involvement of children and vulnerable people in the family justice system'), Parliamentary debate and even the BBC. The flavour of what might be described as a remarkable response to the BBC, to whom the Ministry provided a prepared statement, can be judged from the opening sentence: 'We have a generous legal aid system that provides support to a range of cases.'

It seems that the combination of criticism, comment and continued endeavour might at last be producing some response. The President's View was published in January 2017, and this Introduction was prepared 2 months later. We shall see.

Meanwhile, local authorities, Cafcass and the Family Court all struggle with a tsunami of applications. One of the consequences of the withdrawal of legal aid from private law proceedings has been a mushrooming of unrepresented parties making without notice (and therefore unlisted) applications for personal protection or for relief across the s 8 Children Act menu. It appears that a number of family hearing centres do not have a full judicial complement, and District Judges in particular can be presented with applications which somehow have to be shoehorned into lists which are already running at over-capacity. All tiers of court face a seemingly inexorable rise in demand without a parallel increase in resourcing. Thus, in September 2016, the Ministry of Justice published the then latest legal aid and family court statistics: in over 30% of cases in the Family Court, neither side is represented; applications for care orders increase at a rate which is likely to extend beyond 20% per year; private law applications increased in the second quarter of 2016 by 16%; and applications relating to deprivation of liberty doubled in the same quarter. Worryingly, the only downward movement was seen in the take-up of MIAMS, which reduced by 12%, while adoption applications reduced by 4%.

The Court of Appeal has been so overburdened that appeals in private family law cases are now to be fielded by the High Court, a device which will in all probability cause further difficulties downstream when ultimately the delegation of work will meet such an accumulation that hearing dates and lists will stretch into the far distance. That the time taken to conclude care cases averages just 27 weeks is testament to the personnel who man the barricades, but it is unlikely that the timetable can be maintained without an increasing counterbalance against other court business, which is already exemplified by the average time for the disposal of divorce cases with financial remedies steadily increasing from a reported 20.5 weeks in early 2015 to 24.9 weeks a year later.

Readers might search in vain for a cure. In the public domain, two examples stand out: PAUSE and Settlement Conferences (SCs), both of which have found favour with the President. But significant doubts have been expressed, which might be shared by practitioners who are troubled by the suggestion that a Judge (in SCs) can change from adjudicator to facilitator – or even negotiator – with all the appearance of seeking to persuade a parent to abandon opposition to an application to remove his or her child and perhaps to agree to a change in that child's legal and familial identity. The legal representatives of the parent(s) might find themselves in professional difficulty when they introduce their client(s) to the process, while the parent(s) could be forgiven for wondering whether they now face an alliance of local authority and Judge, with limited assistance of legal personnel to whom they have turned for advice and representation. In financial remedy applications, the Financial Dispute Resolution appointment is universally accepted as a significant help in the reduction of conflict and costs, and indeed in the empowerment of the parties who experience the return of their lives to their own control rather than that of their lawyers and the Court. But observers might not easily identify where it is that a parent is equally empowered by the surrender of their child.

Readers might, in general, welcome the motives which underpin PAUSE, provided that coercion is not part of the plan. The guiding principle will receive greater support if it is not a cost-saving exercise but rather a helping hand to young mothers who out of ignorance or desperation seek comfort in or simply cannot avoid conception of another child. The conundrum is that entry to PAUSE requires a degree of insight and commitment, both of which are often missing when a family comes to the attention of the local authority and then the Court.

And then there is Brexit. Contrary to some public opinion, European jurisprudence is not confined to sovereignty or to the curvature of bananas, and in its more helpful form has been gently woven into UK statute- and case-law. If we are to throw out the bathwater, we must take great care to observe what might go with it, let alone what might replace it. As yet, one might be forgiven for the impression that family lawyers are getting on with the business of representing and protecting the most vulnerable in our society, and have little time, let alone the appetite, for looking into the unknown.

Anthony Cleary

March 2017

Contents

Calendars	Inside front cover
Preface	vii
Foreword	ix
Introduction	xi
Table of Statutes	xv
Table of Statutory Instruments	xlvii
Table of Cases	lxxxi
Table of Practice Directions	cxlix
Table of CPR, FPR and Supreme Court Practice Directions	cliii
Abbreviations	clxvii
PART I: Procedural Guides	1
PART II: Statutes	239
PART III: Procedure Rules	1267
PART IV: Statutory Instruments	2367
PART V: Practice Guidance	2531
PART VI: European Material	2725
Index	2893
Summary of Fees	Inside back cover

Table of Statutes

References are to page numbers.

Access to Justice Act 1999 243
s 10 2074
s 24 340, 368, 511, 1254
s 31 1248
s 54 1234, 1235, 2198
s 55 197, 198, 211, 1866, 1870
s 64 250
s 72 626
s 76 1079
s 90 341, 343, 349, 611, 652, 669, 821, 824, 825, 1068, 1071, 1073, 1076, 1077, 1078, 1079, 1083, 1093, 1094, 1096, 1104, 1106, 1110, 1111, 1112, 1211
s 106 250, 354, 655, 799, 825, 1081, 1207, 1235
Sch 4
para 8 340
para 31 368
para 45 511
para 48 1254
Sch 10
para 22 1079
Sch 13
para 7 1083
para 13 1068
para 14 1071
para 15 1073
para 26 1076
para 27 1076
para 28 1077
para 29 1078
para 31 1079
para 65 341
para 66 343
para 68 349
para 72 1093
para 73 1094
para 74 1096
para 75 1104
para 77 1106
para 78 1106
para 79 1110
para 80 1111
para 81 1112
para 82 1211
para 91 821
para 92 824
para 93 825
para 160 611
para 161 652
para 162 669
Sch 15 250, 354, 655, 799, 825, 1071, 1076, 1077, 1078, 1079, 1081, 1083, 1096, 1207, 1235
Administration of Estates Act 1925 702
s 4 1015
Administration of Justice Act 1920 1929, 2299
s 9(1) 84, 85
Administration of Justice Act 1920—*continued*
s 9(2) 84, 85, 2299
s 10(1) 83
s 12(1) 83, 84
Administration of Justice Act 1960 244, 1040, 1481
s 2 2354
s 12 626, 627, 1040, 1249, 1544, 1564, 1837
s 12(1) 1543
s 12(4) 1564, 1755
s 13 352, 796
s 13(4) 2354
Administration of Justice Act 1969
s 12 197, 198, 199
s 13 198, 2355
Administration of Justice Act 1970 250
s 1(6) 1080
s 11 118, 1930, 1983
s 27(3) 1075
s 28 1930
s 48 1077
s 54(3) 1079
Sch 2
para 2 1080
Sch 8 118, 1930, 1983
Sch 11 1077, 1079
Administration of Justice Act 1977
s 3 1064, 1065, 1068, 1069, 1071, 1073, 1075, 1076, 1077, 1078
s 19(5) 343
s 32 1077
Sch 3 1077
para 1 1075
para 2 1076
para 4 1078
para 6 1068
para 7 1069
para 8 1071
para 9 1073
para 11 1064
para 12 1065
Sch 5 1077
Administration of Justice Act 1982
s 16 1168
s 34(3) 359
s 51 1202
s 52 1037
s 53(1) 348
s 53(2) 352
s 54 357
s 55 1245
Sch 4
Pt I 1245
Administration of Justice Act 1985
s 52 803, 1245
s 67(2) 803

Administration of Justice Act 1985—*continued*
Sch 8
Pt II 803
Adoption Act 1976 281, 1650
Pt IV 291, 427
s 39 826
s 65(1) 807
s 65(2) 807
s 73(2) 1057, 1058
Sch 3
para 23 1057
para 24 1058
Adoption (Inter-Country Aspects) Act 1999 280
Adoption (Intercountry Aspects) Act 1999 328, 1015
s 15(1) 871
Sch 1 292
Sch 2
para 5 871
Adoption (Scotland) Act 1978
s 18 1668
Adoption and Children Act 2002 186, 255, 989, 1016, 1289, 1650, 1704, 2593
s 1 261, 267, 282, 289
s 1(2) 530
s 1(4) 160, 530, 539
s 1(4)(c) 256
s 1(7) 256, 282
s 1(8) 256
s 4 188
s 18 184, 1670
ss 18–29 530
s 18(3) 258
s 18(5) 258
s 19 184, 258, 259, 260, 262
s 19(1) 258, 259
s 19(1)(a) 258
s 19(1)(b) 258
s 19(2) 258
s 19(3) 259
s 19(4) 258
s 20 281, 1651
s 20(1) 260
s 20(2) 260
s 20(3) 260
s 20(4) 260
s 20(4)(a) 187, 1668, 1673
s 21 184, 186, 258, 1644, 1663, 1668
s 21(1) 185, 260
s 21(3) 185
s 21(4) 264
s 22 185, 262
s 22(1)–(3) 262
s 22(2) 259
s 22(6) 264
s 23 1644, 1663
s 24 184, 264, 265, 478, 1663
s 24(3) 455
s 24(5) 265
s 25 184, 186, 258, 260
s 25(4) 477
s 26 184, 258, 259, 261, 267, 1644, 1664, 1673
s 26(1) 266, 267
s 26(2) 267
s 26(3) 267

Adoption and Children Act 2002—*continued*
s 26(4) 267
s 26(5) 267
s 27 1644, 1664
s 27(1) 267
s 27(2) 267
s 27(4) 267
s 28(1) 258, 261
s 28(2) 259, 1644, 1664
s 28(3) 259, 1644
s 28(4) 259
s 29(1) 261
s 29(2) 261
s 29(3) 261
s 29(5) 261, 476
s 29(6) 153, 476
s 29(7) 477
ss 30–35 258
ss 30–40 277
s 30(2)(b) 270
ss 36–40 279
s 41 277
s 41(2) 1641, 1664
s 42 187
s 42(2)–(5) 277
s 42(6) 187
s 42(7) 278
s 43 279
s 44 187, 278, 279, 301, 1670
s 44(2) 187, 279
s 46 189, 293, 1644, 1663
s 46(1) 186
s 46(2) 186, 280
s 46(2)(b) 280
s 46(3)(b) 186, 286, 293
s 46(6) 280
s 47 184, 258, 283, 289, 290, 301, 1650, 1656
s 47(2) 281
s 47(2)(c) 283
s 47(3) 281
s 47(4) 282
s 47(4)(b)(i) 258
s 47(5) 282
s 47(7) 281, 282
s 47(8) 187
s 47(9) 187, 283
s 48 187, 284
s 49 187, 284
s 49(2) 187, 284
s 49(3) 187, 284
s 49(4) 187, 283, 284
s 49(5) 284
s 50 187, 283, 284, 285, 286
s 50(1) 285
s 50(2) 285
s 50(2)(a) 285
s 51 187, 284, 286
s 51(1) 187
s 51(2) 293
s 51(3) 187
s 51(3A) 187
s 51(4) 286
s 51A 1644
s 52 185, 260, 281, 283, 665, 1656

Adoption and Children Act 2002—*continued*
s 52(1) 185, 188, 289
s 52(1)(b) 289
s 52(3) 185, 188, 259, 285
s 52(4) 258, 260
s 52(5) 258, 1656
s 52(6) 259, 282, 283, 285
s 52(7) 259
s 55 186, 280, 291, 1644
s 66 292, 296, 1015
ss 66–76 280
s 66(1)(c) 292, 1644
s 66(1)(d) 292
s 66(1)(e) 292
s 67 186, 454, 1015
s 67(1) 826, 991
s 67(2) 286, 293
s 67(3) 293
s 67(4) 286
s 77(3)(b) 296
s 83 186
s 83(1) 1664, 1665
s 83(1)(a) 300
s 83(4) 1670
s 83(5) 1670
s 83(6) 1670
s 83(7) 300, 1670
s 83(8) 300
s 84 290, 301, 303, 1663, 1664, 1665, 1673
s 84(3) 1670
s 84(6) 1670
s 85 303
s 87 186, 1644
s 87(1) 292, 1015
s 88 293, 1644, 1664
s 89 304, 1321, 1661, 1664
s 92 186, 306, 989
s 92(1) 306
s 92(2) 306
s 92(3) 306
s 93 186, 306, 989
s 94 186, 307
s 94(2) 307
s 95 186, 308
s 95(1) 308
s 95(3) 308
s 96 186
s 97(b) 308
s 97(c) 306, 307, 308
s 100 1863
s 101(2) 626
s 101(3) 626
s 103 1653
s 104(1) 283
s 107 296
s 110 279
s 111 375, 425, 426, 427, 634
s 112 431
s 113 451
s 114 470
s 114(2) 451
s 114(5) 619
s 115 422, 432, 474, 477, 478, 480
s 116(1) 485

Adoption and Children Act 2002—*continued*
s 116(2) 497
s 116(3) 508
s 117 510, 517
s 118 517, 530, 552
s 119 518
s 120 522
s 121 522, 545
s 122 569, 1514
s 122(1) 568
s 122(2) 622
s 123 306
s 139 470, 517
s 139(1) 329, 453, 493, 508, 509, 549, 551, 619, 633, 653, 664, 807, 898
s 139(3) 493, 633
s 144 187, 256
s 144(1) 185, 278, 279, 283, 318
s 144(2) 702
s 144(4)–(6) 186, 285
s 144(7) 286
Sch 1 296
para 3 296
para 3(5) 292
para 4 1644
Sch 3
para 17 1057
para 18 1058
para 45 398
para 47 838
para 49 871
para 51 925
para 52 926
para 54 453, 470, 493, 508, 509, 549, 551, 619, 633, 664
para 55 439
para 56 453
para 57 470
para 58 482
para 59 493
para 60 508
para 61 508
para 62 509
para 63 549
para 64 551
para 65 609
para 68 619
para 69 633
para 70 637
para 71 645, 652, 653
para 72 664
para 73 678
para 85 898
para 86 897
para 87 897
para 88 898
para 96 329
para 97(a) 329
para 118 807
Sch 4 281
Sch 5 291, 493, 549
Sch 6 261
Age of Legal Capacity (Scotland) Act 1991
s 10 848

Age of Legal Capacity (Scotland) Act 1991—*continued*
s 10(1) 838
Sch 1
para 44 838
para 45 848
para 46 848
Air Force Act 1955
s 144 812
s 150 812
s 151 812
s 152 812
s 203(1),(2) 1170
Anti-social Behaviour Act 2003
s 88 496
Sch 2
para 5 496
Anti-Social Behaviour, Crime and Policing Act 2014 35, 337
s 120 902, 903, 904, 905
s 121 899, 901
s 122A 899
Sch 6A 899
Arbitration Act 1996
s 107(1) 1235, 1250
s 107(2) 696
Sch 3
para 37(1) 1250
para 37(2) 1235
para 37(3) 1250
Sch 4 696
Armed Forces Act 2001
s 23 1237
Armed Forces Act 2011
s 26 1250
Sch 2
para 5 1250
Army Act 1955
s 144 812
s 150 812
s 151 812
s 152 812
s 203(1),(2) 1170
Attachment of Earnings Act 1971 339
s 1(1) 105
s 2 2015
s 3 105
s 3(4) 1933
s 6(5) 107
s 8(2)(b) 2280
s 11(1)(a) 104
s 14 106, 1062
s 14(1) 2016
s 14(1)(b) 107
s 23 106
s 23(1A) 107, 2018
s 23(2) 2020
s 23(2)(c) 107, 2016
s 23(3) 107
s 23(4) 107
s 23(11) 107
s 24 2015
s 25 2015
Sch 1 359
Attachment of Earnings Act 1971—*continued*
Sch 5 1079
Bail Act 1976 1474
Bankers' Book Evidence Act 1879 2115
s 7 1757
Banking Act 1987
s 108(1) 806, 1244
Sch 6
para 11 1244
para 15 806
Bankruptcy Act 1914 343
Births and Deaths Registration Act 1953 142, 446
s 2 448
s 10 380, 427
s 10A 427, 428, 446
s 14A 870
Borders, Citizenship and Immigration Act 2009
s 53 1239
British Nationality Act 1981 863, 868
British Overseas Territories Act 2002
s 1(2) 840, 863, 868
Broadcasting Act 1990
s 203(1) 626
Sch 20
para 53 626
Building Societies Act 1986
s 120(1) 362
Sch 18
para 14 362

Care Act 2014
s 66 492
Care Act 20140
s 9 225
Care Standards Act 2000
s 79(1) 599, 600, 601, 602, 603, 604, 605, 606, 607
s 79(2) 685
s 105 615
s 105(5) 593
s 106(1) 616
s 106(2) 616
s 107 617
s 108 617
s 109 609
s 110 681
s 116 329, 585, 591, 593, 594, 595, 609, 610, 611, 613, 637, 671, 672, 677, 678, 681
s 117 590, 593, 609, 634
Sch 3 685
Sch 4
para 14(1) 585, 591, 593, 594, 595, 609, 610, 611, 613
para 14(7) 585
para 14(8) 591
para 14(9) 591
para 14(10) 593
para 14(11) 593
para 14(12) 594
para 14(13) 595
para 14(14) 595
para 14(15) 595
para 14(16) 609
para 14(18) 610

Care Standards Act 2000—*continued*
Sch 4—*continued*
para 14(19) 611
para 14(20) 613
para 14(23) 637
para 14(24) 671, 672
para 14(25) 677
para 14(27) 678, 681
para 14(28) 678
para 27 329
Sch 6 590, 591, 593, 609, 634
Charging Orders Act 1979 358
s 1 2022
s 1(1) 412
s 1(2)(b) 108
s 1(2)(ba) 108
s 1(2)(c) 108
s 1(5)(b) 2024
s 2 1255
s 3(1) 110, 2025
s 3(2) 2023
s 3(3) 2023
Child Abduction and Custody Act 1985 176, 363, 1554
s 4 177
s 5 178, 179, 1553
s 6 1553
s 12(1) 1557
s 16 1557
s 17 1557
s 19 178, 1553
s 21 1553
s 24A 178, 181, 184, 365, 1557
s 50 1553
Sch 1 178, 1532, 1550, 2732, 2735
Art 3 177
Art 4 177, 284, 415, 522, 841, 1545
Art 5 1610
Art 7 1553
Art 8 177
Art 10 1553
Art 11 1554
Art 12 1553, 1639, 1697, 2735
Art 13 1707
Sch 2 1550
Art 1 177
Art 1(a) 1557
Art 4 177
Art 5 1553
Art 9 1554
Art 10 1554
Art 10(1)(a) 2009
Art 12 177, 178
Art 13 178, 1554
Child Care Act 1980
s 89 1064, 1065
s 89(3) 1063
Sch 5
para 2 1064
para 3 1065
Sch 6 1063
Child Maintenance and Other Payments Act 2008 400, 403, 406, 411
s 13(4) 401, 403, 406, 409, 410, 412, 413, 415

Child Maintenance and Other Payments Act 2008—*continued*
s 35(1) 403
s 35(3) 408
s 42 416
s 57(1) 406, 1254
s 58 403, 406, 408, 410, 1252
Sch 3
para 1 406, 409, 410, 412, 413, 415
para 6 406
para 7 409
para 18 410
para 19 410
para 36 412
para 41 413
para 46 415
Sch 7
para 1(2) 406
para 1(10) 412
para 1(25),(26) 416
para 2(1) 1254
Sch 8 403, 406, 408, 410, 412, 1252
Child Support Act 1991 12, 25, 400, 481, 645, 821, 1243
s 4 652, 1169, 1195
s 8 645, 648, 1198
s 8(1) 645
s 8(3) 645, 1856
s 8(6) 815
s 9(5) 1856
s 17(4) 407
s 20 870, 1422, 1676, 1863, 2431
s 26 1421, 1422, 2431
s 27 226, 870, 1422, 2486
s 27(2) 1421
ss 28A–28F 404
s 28J 407
ss 32E–32H 198
ss 33–40 2431
s 39A 1762, 2492
s 40B 2492
s 41C 407
s 44 860, 861, 864, 865, 869, 870, 871
s 50 1853
s 50(6) 1853
s 55 648, 815, 1198, 1285
s 58(14) 647
Sch 1 403
para 7 404
para 16(1)(d) 406
Sch 4A 404
Sch 4B 404
Child Support Act 1995
s 18 403, 406, 408
s 30 412, 416
Sch 3
para 10 412
para 16 416
Child Support, Pensions and Social Security Act 2000 400, 403, 1422
s 1(2) 401, 402, 403, 406, 408, 409, 415, 416
s 2 403
s 2(1),(2) 403
s 16(1) 413

Child Support, Pensions and Social Security Act 2000—*continued*
s 22 415
s 26 402, 403, 406, 408, 412, 415, 648, 652, 657, 815, 820, 825, 1198, 1202, 1215
s 82(1) 920, 922, 923
s 82(2) 920
s 82(3) 922
s 82(4) 923
s 83 869, 871
s 83(1) 870
s 83(2) 870
s 83(3) 872
s 83(5) 410
s 85 415, 416, 648, 810, 815, 1198
Sch 3
para 3 1198, 1202, 1215
para 4 815, 820, 825
para 10 648, 652, 657
para 11 415, 416
para 11(1) 402, 406, 412
para 11(2) 401, 402, 406, 408
para 11(6) 408
para 11(17) 412
Sch 8
para 4 869
para 5 871
para 6 871
para 7 872
para 8 872
para 9 920
para 13 410
Sch 9 648, 810, 815, 871, 872, 1198
Pt I 415
Childcare Act 2006 1289
s 102(1) 683
s 102(2)(a) 683
s 102(2)(b) 683
s 103 599, 600, 601, 602, 603, 604, 605, 606, 607, 682, 683, 684, 685
Sch 2
para 3 1251
para 5 599
para 6 600, 601, 602, 603, 604, 605, 606, 607, 682, 683, 684
para 7 600
para 8 601
para 9 601
para 14 606
para 15 606
para 16 607
para 18 682, 683, 684, 685
Sch 3 600
Pt 2 599, 601, 606, 682
Children Act 1975
s 108(1) 1064, 1065
s 108(1)(b) 826, 1215
Sch 3
para 10 1064
para 11 1065
para 76 355
Sch 4 1215
Pt I 826
Children Act 1989 245, 263, 282, 387, 422, 847, 1289, 1539
Pt II 184, 186, 457, 1507, 1519, 1525
Pt III 258, 485, 497, 2592
Pt IV 156, 158, 160, 164, 166, 169, 246, 263, 1507, 1508, 1509, 1517, 1519, 1533, 2539, 2544, 2552, 2588
Pt V 156, 158, 1519
Pt VII 497
Pt VIII 497
s 1 256, 289, 1795, 2603
s 1(1) 159, 163, 1500, 1853, 2431
s 1(1)(a) 650, 842
s 1(2) 159, 1322, 1508, 1517
s 1(2A) 144
s 1(3) 159, 160, 163, 256, 530, 1285, 1832
s 1(3)(a)–(f) 1713
s 1(5) 134, 159, 162, 163, 166, 168, 170, 173
s 2 1543
s 2(1A) 701
s 2(2A) 701
s 3 142, 270, 275, 402, 1526
s 3(5) 380
s 4 142, 163, 166, 282, 283
s 4(1) 143, 282
s 4(1)(a) 142, 144, 147
s 4(1)(b) 549, 1642, 2504, 2740
s 4(1)(c) 1503
s 4(2) 1642, 2504
s 4(3) 142
s 4(3)(b) 1290
s 4(4) 1520
s 4A 142, 701
s 4A(1) 144
s 4A(1)(a) 1642
s 4A(2) 1642
s 4ZA 142
s 4ZA(1) 143, 144
s 4ZA(1)(b) 1642
s 5 402
s 5(2) 147, 162, 166, 168, 171
s 6(7)(c) 162, 166, 168, 171
s 7 555, 1290, 1505, 1515, 1696
s 7(1)(a) 807
s 8 125, 147, 148, 152, 156, 157, 158, 159, 166, 173, 184, 186, 259, 261, 266, 280, 283, 373, 514, 829, 839, 856, 857, 858, 921, 982, 984, 1501, 1503, 1505, 1508, 1509, 1514, 1517, 1520, 1541, 1546, 1978, 2431, 2539
s 8(1) 145, 148, 150, 269, 270, 272, 273, 443
s 8(2) 145, 150, 1525, 1541
s 8(4) 186, 188
s 9 226, 280
s 9(1) 147, 162, 166, 168, 170
s 9(2) 145, 162, 166, 168, 170
s 9(3) 145, 1501
s 9(5) 162
s 9(6B) 147
s 10 145, 150, 280, 1289, 1502, 1540, 1831
s 10(1) 142, 146, 149, 151, 162, 166, 168, 170
s 10(1)(a) 146, 149, 151
s 10(1)(b) 146, 151
s 10(2) 146, 149, 151

Children Act 1989—*continued*

s 10(3) 1501
s 10(5) 153
s 10(6) 145
s 10(8) 152, 153, 1520
s 10(9) 152, 153, 475, 478, 982, 984, 1501
s 10(10) 153
s 11(1) 282, 1508, 1517
s 11(3) 1289
s 11(4) 148
s 11(7) 145, 147, 149, 152, 155, 158
s 11A 145, 147
ss 11A–11P 145, 458
s 11A(3) 145
s 11C 145, 147
ss 11D–11G 442
ss 11E–11M 1712
s 11G 145, 442
s 11H 145, 147, 442
s 11I 145, 147, 148, 149, 443
ss 11I–11P 148
s 11J 1632, 2584
ss 11J–11L 158
ss 11J–11N 145, 148, 443, 1713
s 11J(2) 148
s 11J(3) 148
s 11J(5) 149
s 11J(5)(a)–(d) 443
s 11K 148
s 11L 148
s 11M 148
s 11O 145, 148, 150, 1713
s 11P 145, 148, 149, 150, 1713
s 12(1) 142, 143, 144
s 12(1A) 144
s 12(2) 144
s 12(2A) 144
ss 14A–14F 152
s 14A(2) 153
s 14A(3) 153
s 14A(3)–(7) 153
s 14A(5)(d) 153
s 14A(5)(e) 153
s 14A(6)(b) 153
s 14A(8) 195, 1853
s 14A(9) 195, 1853
s 14A(11) 152
s 14A(12) 152
s 14A(13) 153
s 14B(1) 155
s 14B(2)–(4) 155
s 14C(1) 152
s 14C(3) 153
s 14C(4) 152
s 14D 152, 154
s 14D(1) 155
s 14D(3) 155
s 14D(4) 153, 155
s 14D(5) 155, 478
s 14E(1) 154
s 14E(1)–(3) 154
s 14E(4) 155
s 14E(5) 155
s 14F 152

Children Act 1989—*continued*

s 15 162, 166, 923, 1262, 1849, 2036
s 16 147, 1539, 1712
s 16(1) 162, 166, 168, 171
s 16(1)(a) 807, 808
s 16A 1542, 1712
s 17 2595
s 17(1) 2593
s 17(4A) 2599
s 20 630, 1006, 1544, 2595, 2598, 2602, 2607
s 20(3) 171
s 20(6) 2599
s 21 480
s 22 402
s 22(1) 2434, 2435
s 22(4) 545
s 23 2598
s 23(3) 275, 277
s 25 171, 173, 1540, 1706, 1865, 2433
s 25(6) 172, 1520
s 26A 1704
s 27 181
s 29(4)(b) 153
s 29(5)(b) 153
s 29(6) 498
s 31 159, 259, 629, 1507, 1508, 1524, 1533, 1534, 1535, 2588, 2589, 2590, 2591, 2592, 2593, 2594, 2604, 2605
s 31(1) 160, 161, 162, 1537
s 31(1)(b) 147
s 31(2) 163, 199, 203, 260, 262, 1008, 1043, 1871, 2205, 2602
s 31(4) 161
s 31(5) 161, 162
s 31(9) 160, 267
s 31(11) 261, 270, 1537
s 31A 1508
s 32(1) 1508
s 32(1)(a) 160, 1533, 1534
s 32(5) 160, 533
s 33 160, 501
s 33(1) 160
s 34 162, 166, 169, 259, 266, 283
s 34(1) 166
s 34(2) 166, 167
s 34(3) 166, 167
s 34(4) 166, 167
s 34(5) 162, 166, 167, 169
s 34(7) 166
s 34(9) 169
s 34(11) 159
s 35 147, 160
s 36(1) 147
s 37 1505, 1514, 1524, 1696, 1697
s 37(1) 160, 1289, 1505, 1524, 1525, 1538
s 37(5) 1524
s 38 147, 261, 1290, 1508, 1537, 1832, 2737
s 38(1) 160, 162, 194, 195, 210, 1289
s 38(2) 160
s 38(4) 160, 1517
s 38(6) 160, 162, 264, 922, 1537, 1705
s 38(7) 160
s 38(7A) 533
s 38(8) 160, 1537

Children Act 1989—*continued*
s 38A 160, 163, 1537, 1538, 1539, 1540
s 38A(2) 163
s 38A(2)(b) 1538
s 38A(2)(b)(ii) 1539
s 39 160, 163, 1539
s 39(1) 164
s 39(2) 164
s 39(3) 164
s 39(3A) 163, 1538
s 39(3B) 163, 1538
s 39(4) 163
s 39(6) 166
s 41 263, 1502, 1505, 1514, 1530, 1536, 1706
s 41(1) 134, 136, 139, 141, 162, 165, 168, 170, 172, 807, 1505, 1696
s 41(1)(b) 1705
s 41(2) 807
s 41(2)(b) 1704
s 41(3) 1515, 1709
s 41(4) 1709
s 41(6) 12, 1505
s 41(6)(b) 1505, 1697
s 41(6)(e) 1505
s 41(6)(hh) 186
s 42 1512, 1653, 1705, 1706
s 43(2) 270
s 43(3) 133
s 43(4) 133
s 43(8) 922, 1520, 1705
s 44 132, 1290, 1537
s 44(1) 132, 133, 1289
s 44(6) 137
s 44(7) 922
s 44(9) 137, 138
s 44(9)(b) 137, 138, 139
s 44(14) 134
s 44A 132, 134, 1538, 1539, 1540
s 44A(2) 134
s 44A(2)(b) 1538
s 45 132, 1539
s 45(4) 137, 138
s 45(4)–(6) 137
s 45(8) 134, 135
s 45(8A) 135, 136, 1538
s 45(8B) 135, 136, 1538
s 45(9) 135
s 45(10) 134, 136, 139
s 45(11) 135, 136
s 46(3)(f) 496
s 46(7) 132, 133
s 47 2600, 2601
s 47(1)(b) 132
s 47(5A) 2599
s 48 132, 1290, 1757
s 48(9) 137, 138, 139, 1289
s 48(13) 138, 139
s 50 140, 156, 158, 1757
s 50(4) 140, 1289
s 50(5) 141
s 51 133, 135, 138, 141, 161, 165, 168, 170, 172
s 51(1) 1540
s 51(2) 1540
s 70 989

Children Act 1989—*continued*
s 75 1522
s 83 1678
s 89 920
s 91(1) 160, 162, 164, 166, 168, 170
s 91(2) 166
s 91(3) 160
s 91(14) 1246, 1324
s 91(15) 165
s 91(17) 168, 170
s 92 825
s 92(2) 173
s 92(7) 146, 149, 151, 153
s 92(11) 1251
s 93(2)(i) 134, 136, 139, 141, 162, 166, 170
s 94 2545
s 95 1519
s 96(2) 1684
s 97 245
s 97(2) 246, 1040, 1481, 1543, 1837
s 98 373, 2093
s 100 181, 1544
s 100(2) 1421
s 100(3) 297, 918
s 100(4) 1547
s 102(1) 1289
s 105(1) 260, 261, 270, 401, 650, 1537, 2431
s 105(10) 1285
s 108 245, 838, 845, 846, 847, 848, 850, 852
s 108(4) 1215
s 108(5) 355, 367, 372, 374, 398, 817, 819, 820, 822, 825, 834, 838, 840, 841, 842, 844, 852, 853, 854, 856, 857, 860, 863, 1145, 1235, 1245, 1251, 1256
s 108(7) 374, 819, 820, 822, 825, 834, 841, 863, 1215
s 110(6) 149
Sch A1
para 4 150
para 8(8) 150
para 9 1632, 2584
Pt I 148
Pt II 148
Sch 1 12, 16, 19, 25, 50, 162, 166, 407, 415, 702, 1044, 1165, 1170, 1262, 1434, 1541, 1685, 1742, 1744, 1848, 1849, 1856, 2036, 2048, 2810
para 1 18, 147
para 1(1) 12
para 1(2) 13
para 1(2)(c) 406
para 1(6) 12
para 2 923, 1285
para 2(1)(a),(b) 12
para 2(3),(6) 12
para 2(4) 12
para 3 407
para 3(2)(b) 1198
para 3(4) 406
para 3(5) 407
para 3(6) 407
para 4 1165
para 5(1) 406
para 6 1285

Children Act 1989—*continued*
Sch 1—*continued*
para 6(4) 13
para 9 13, 407
para 10 408
para 10(2) 13
para 11(1) 13
Sch 2
para 19 301, 303, 1539, 1540
para 19(9) 302
para 19B 503, 507
para 21 11
para 22 11
para 23 11
para 23(6) 11
para 23(8) 11
para 23(11) 12
Pt III 498
Sch 3
para 6(3) 164
Pt I 160
Pt II 160
Sch 11
para 6 825
para 9 1251
Sch 12
para 33 1215
Sch 13
para 14 245
para 29 355
para 33 834
para 36 817
para 37 819
para 38 820
para 39 822
para 41 822
para 43 825
para 45 1251
para 45(1) 1235
para 45(2) 1245
para 45(3) 1251
para 51 1145
para 56 1256
para 57(1) 367, 372
para 57(2) 374
para 57(3) 398
para 62 838, 841, 842, 844, 845, 846, 847, 848, 850, 852, 853, 854, 856, 857, 860, 863
para 63 838
para 64 838, 840
para 65 841
para 66 844
para 67 844
para 68 845, 846, 850, 852
para 69 850, 852
para 70 857
para 71 863
Sch 14
para 11(4) 1290
Sch 15 367, 372, 374, 819, 820, 822, 825, 834, 838, 841, 863, 1215
Children Act 2004 497, 2593
s 10 1755
Children Act 2004—*continued*
s 11 486, 1755, 1756
s 40 310, 311, 435, 482, 517, 568, 637, 823
s 44 596, 680
s 48 600, 602, 682, 683, 684
s 49(4) 591
s 52 497
s 53 485, 493, 582, 2599
s 54 611
s 62(1) 626
s 62(2) 245
s 62(6) 315
s 64 602
Sch 3
para 1 823
para 3 366
para 4 374
para 5 435, 482, 517, 568, 637
para 6 435
para 7 482
para 8(1) 517
para 8(2) 517
para 8(3) 517
para 9 568
para 11 637
para 15 310, 311
para 16 310
para 17 311
Sch 4
para 1 600, 602, 682, 683, 684
para 2 600
para 2(2) 602
para 3(1) 602
para 3(2) 602
para 4 602
para 4(2)(b) 684
para 6 600
para 7 682
para 8 683
para 9 684
Sch 5 602
Children (Leaving Care) Act 2000
s 1 665, 666
s 2(1) 497, 502, 503, 505
s 2(2) 497
s 2(4) 502, 503, 505
s 3 506, 507
s 4(1) 508, 509, 510
s 5 510
s 7 520
s 7(2) 485
s 7(4) 657
Children (Scotland) Act 1995
s 105(4) 367, 372, 374, 398, 402, 416, 522, 585, 678, 838, 856, 863
s 105(5) 847, 848
Sch 4
para 37 367, 372
para 37(1),(4) 374
para 37(5) 374
para 37(6)(a) 398
para 37(6)(b) 398
para 41 838
para 41(1) 856

Children (Scotland) Act 1995—*continued*
Sch 4—*continued*
para 41(1),(9) 863
para 41(7) 856
para 48(1),(2) 522
para 48(1),(3) 585
para 48(1),(5) 678
para 52 402, 416
Sch 5 847, 848
Children and Adoption Act 2006
Pt 2 300
s 1 459, 460, 461, 462, 463, 464, 465, 466, 467, 468, 469
s 4(2) 644
s 6 443
s 6(1) 482
s 6(2) 482, 483
s 6(3) 482, 483
s 6(4) 482, 483
s 6(5) 482, 483
s 9 300
s 13 305
s 14(1) 300
s 14(2) 300
s 14(3) 678
s 15 477
s 15(1) 266, 619, 634, 637, 834, 842, 854, 855
Sch 1 644
Sch 2
para 1 834
para 2 842, 854, 855
para 3 842
para 4 854
para 5 855
para 6 855
para 7 477, 619, 634
para 8 477
para 9 619
para 10 634
para 11 637
para 12 834
para 13 266
para 14 266
Sch 3 477
Children and Families Act 2014 134, 136, 139, 141, 142, 144, 147, 150, 152, 155, 157, 159, 163, 166, 169, 171, 423, 440, 441, 442, 459, 470, 547, 558, 560, 1533, 1534
s 1 309
s 2 499
s 3 256
s 4 315
s 7 315, 316, 318, 320, 626
s 8 551
s 9 256, 280, 287, 288, 308, 439, 451, 838
s 10(1) 12, 13, 20, 25, 50, 52, 811, 1443
s 11 422
s 12 266, 269, 272, 273, 328, 398, 402, 432, 439, 451, 453, 457, 459, 460, 461, 462, 463, 464, 465, 466, 467, 469, 470, 471, 474, 477, 478, 482, 493, 499, 551, 558, 568, 572, 574, 579, 619, 637, 641, 642, 643, 644, 645, 653, 656, 834, 842, 844
s 13 457, 478, 541, 558, 1793, 1794, 1796

Children and Families Act 2014—*continued*
s 13(6) 533, 1794
s 13(8) 1795
s 14 313, 547
s 15 522
s 16 634
s 17 705, 713, 1154, 1159
s 37 491
s 50 490
s 82 507, 658
s 96 488, 489, 634
s 97 490, 634
s 98 505, 666
s 99 497
s 105 595
Sch 1 316, 318, 320
Sch 2 266, 269, 272, 273, 328, 398, 402, 432, 439, 451, 453, 457, 459, 460, 461, 462, 463, 464, 465, 466, 467, 469, 470, 471, 474, 477, 478, 482, 493, 499, 551, 558, 568, 572, 574, 579, 619, 637, 641, 642, 643, 644, 645, 653, 656, 834, 842, 844
Sch 3 507, 658
Children and Young Persons Act 1933
s 39 245, 246, 247, 627
Children and Young Persons Act 1969
s 25 1540
Children and Young Persons Act 2008 497
s 8 591
s 8(1) 498, 499, 500
s 8(2) 662
s 8(3) 328, 485, 637, 667, 681, 682
s 9 501
s 10 513, 514
s 15 501
s 16 502
s 17 612, 613
s 18 613
s 19 659
s 21 505
s 22 503, 506, 507, 509
s 23(1) 506
s 24 485
s 25 658
s 30 135, 578
s 33 611
s 36 453
s 37(1) 451
s 37(2) 470
s 37(3) 619
s 38 474
s 39 485, 496, 497, 502, 503, 506, 507, 508, 509, 510, 511, 517, 518, 520, 591, 593, 634, 665, 666, 670
s 42 634
Sch 1
para 1 485
para 2 591
para 3 637
para 4 662
para 5 667
para 6 681
para 7 682
para 14 328

Children and Young Persons Act 2008—*continued*
Sch 3
para 1 485, 496, 497, 502, 503, 506, 507, 508, 509, 510, 511, 517, 518, 520, 591, 593, 634, 665, 666, 670
para 2 485
para 5 496
para 6 497
para 8 502
para 9 503
para 10 506
para 11 507
para 12 508
para 13 509
para 14 510
para 15 511
para 16 517
para 18 518
para 19 518
para 20 520
para 21 520
para 23 591
para 24 593
para 25 634
para 26 634
para 27 665, 666, 670
Sch 4 634
Sch 6
para 31 619
Civil Evidence Act 1968 2431
s 11 1763
s 11(2)(a) 1763
s 12 1763
Civil Evidence Act 1972 1794
s 3 1793, 1794
s 3(1) 2128
s 3(2) 2128
Civil Evidence Act 1995 2432
s 1(1) 1778, 1779
s 1(2) 1778, 1779
s 2(1) 1761, 1778
s 4 1778, 1779
s 11 1778
s 15(1) 623
Sch 1
para 16 623
Civil Jurisdiction and Judgments Act 1982 93, 95, 688, 1446, 2299, 2436, 2446, 2834
Pt I 1126
s 5(4) 93
s 11 91
s 12 90
s 15(4) 251, 355, 1075
s 16(5) 1064
s 23(2) 1064
s 25(1) 1242
s 36 69
s 36(6) 1068, 1069, 1073
s 37(1) 1068, 1076, 1088, 1091, 1094, 1096, 1097, 1103, 1104, 1117, 1118
s 54 1065, 1117, 1118
Sch 1
Art 1 1126
Art 27 96
Civil Jurisdiction and Judgments Act 1982—*continued*
Sch 1—*continued*
Art 28 96
Art 31 91, 95
Art 32 91
Sch 6 98
para 2(1) 97, 98
para 5 99
para 6 99
para 7 99
para 8 99
para 9 99
para 10 99
Sch 7 98
para 2(1) 97, 98
para 5(3) 98
para 5(4) 99
para 5(5) 99
para 6 99
para 7 99
para 8 99
para 9 99
Sch 11 1076
para 1 1068
para 2 1076
para 4 1096, 1103
para 5 1068
para 6 1076
para 9 1088
para 10 1091
para 11 1094
para 12 1096
para 13 1097
para 15 1103
para 16 1104
para 17 1117
para 18 1118
Sch 12
para 1 1068, 1073
para 1(3) 1069
para 2 1064
para 3 1075
para 5 251
para 6 355
Sch 14 1065, 1117, 1118
Civil Jurisdiction and Judgments Act 1991 93
s 2 689
s 3 690, 691, 694, 695, 696
Sch 2
para 2 690
para 3 691
para 6 694
para 7 695
para 10 695
para 12 696
Civil Partnership Act 2004 22, 25, 57, 407, 415, 701, 1121, 1165, 1285, 1286, 1379, 1435
Pt 2
Ch 1 701
Ch 5 701
Pt 7 702
s 1 260
s 2 701

Civil Partnership Act 2004—*continued*

s 2(5) 701
s 3 701
s 4 701, 1380
s 6 701
s 6A 701
s 7 701
s 8 701
s 10 701
s 11 701
s 12 701
s 14 701
s 17 701
s 18 701
s 19 701
s 20 701
ss 21–27 701
s 37(1) 1380
s 37(2) 46
s 38 47
s 38(1) 46, 47, 1403
s 38(4) 1403
s 38A 406
s 38B 406
s 39 1401
s 40(1) 1401
s 40(2) 47, 48, 1403, 1405
s 40(3) 1405
s 42 1381
s 44(1) 45, 46
s 44(2) 1393, 1394
s 44(3) 1393, 1394
s 44(4) 1393, 1394
s 44(4)(a) 1382
s 44(5) 46, 1386
s 44(5)(a) 1395
s 44(5)(b) 1382, 1386
s 44(5)(c) 1387
s 44(5)(d) 1395
s 45 1382, 1404
s 46 1380, 1394
s 47 49, 1380
s 47(1) 1380
s 48(1) 1380, 1400
s 48(2) 1400
s 48(5) 1400
s 49 46
s 50 46
s 50(1)(d) 1384
s 50(1)(e) 1384
s 56 46
s 58 1421
s 62 1389
s 63(1) 1404
s 64 1383
s 66 14, 1123, 1418
s 71 22, 702, 1014, 1020, 1022, 1027, 1033, 1034, 1035, 1036, 1037, 1039
s 72 50
s 72(3) 25
s 73 27
s 74(2) 1744
s 75(1) 431, 637, 701
s 75(2) 431, 701

Civil Partnership Act 2004—*continued*

s 75(3) 637, 702
s 75(4) 637
s 76 434
s 77 453, 702
s 78 702
s 78(1) 647, 656, 657
s 78(2) 647
s 78(3) 656
s 78(4) 657
s 79 702
s 79(1) 281, 286, 295, 298, 299, 309, 318
s 79(3) 281
s 79(4),(5) 286
s 79(7) 295
s 79(8) 298
s 79(9) 299
s 79(10) 309
s 79(11),(12) 318
s 81 702
s 82 702, 875, 876, 877, 878, 879, 881, 883, 884, 887, 889, 894, 897, 898, 907, 908, 909, 911, 912, 913, 914, 915, 916
s 83 702
ss 219–223 828
s 221 2776
s 250(1) 946, 948, 951, 952, 953, 956, 958
s 250(2) 946, 948
s 250(3) 951
s 250(4) 951
s 250(5) 952, 953, 958
s 250(6) 956
s 250(7) 958
s 251 702
s 254 702
s 254(1) 406, 416, 1252
s 255 702
s 256 702
s 257 702
s 261(1) 251, 355, 373, 439, 583, 584, 629, 790, 810, 813, 825, 866, 1040, 1065, 1077, 1125, 1144, 1145, 1157, 1159, 1173, 1196, 1207, 1211, 1215, 1235, 1251
s 261(4) 406, 898, 914, 1040
Sch 1
para 154 790
Sch 2 131
para 1 131
para 3 131, 1426
para 3(3) 131
para 4 131, 1426
para 4(3) 131
para 10 131, 1426
para 10(1) 131
Sch 4 22, 702, 1015
para 15(1)–(6) 1014
para 15(4) 1016
para 16 1020
para 17(1)–(5) 1022
para 18 1022
para 19 1027
para 20 1033
para 21 1034
para 22 1035

Civil Partnership Act 2004—*continued*
Sch 4—*continued*
para 23 1035
para 24 1036
para 25 1037
para 26 1037
para 27 1039
Sch 5 50, 1165
para 48 50
para 63 108, 118
para 74 56
Sch 6 25
para 1 25
para 9 25
para 15 25
para 39 26
Pt 4 26
Sch 7 1418
para 15 1744
Sch 8 702
Sch 9 702
para 1(1)–(11) 875
para 2(1)–(12) 876
para 3 877
para 4(1)–(7) 878
para 5 879
para 6(1)–(10) 881
para 7 883
para 8(1)–(4) 884
para 9 887
para 10(1)–(4) 889
para 11 894
para 12 894
para 13(1)–(4) 897
para 13(1)–(5) 898
para 15(1) 907, 909
para 15(1)–(8) 908
para 15(2) 907
para 15(3) 907
para 15(9)–(11) 909
para 15(12) 909
para 16(1) 911, 912, 913, 914, 915, 916
para 16(2) 911
para 16(3),(4) 912
para 16(5) 912
para 16(6) 912
para 16(7) 913
para 16(8)–(11) 914
para 16(12),(13) 914
para 16(14) 914, 915
para 16(15),(16) 915
para 16(17) 916
para 16(18) 916
para 16(19),(20) 916
Sch 24
para 1 406
para 3 416
paras 23–33 702
para 51 702
para 61(1)–(4) 1252
Pt 3 702
Sch 25 702
Sch 26 702

Civil Partnership Act 2004—*continued*
Sch 27
para 8(1)–(3) 1040
para 18(1)–(4) 1065
para 22 1077
para 29 810
para 34 251
para 35 355
para 40 1157
para 41(1)–(3) 1159
para 42 1173
para 43(1)–(5) 1196
para 44 1207
para 45(1)–(4) 1211
para 46 1215
para 57 813
para 58(1) 825
para 68 1235
para 70 1251
para 90(1)–(3) 1125
para 91 1144
para 93 1145
para 94 1145
para 110 373
para 125 866
para 129 439
para 130 583
para 131 584
para 132 629
Sch 30 406, 898, 1040
Sch 41
paras 16–22 702
Civil Procedure Act 1997 2146
s 7 55, 1135, 1240, 1741, 1744
s 7(1) 2087
s 7(1)(b) 1744
s 10 799, 800, 801, 803, 805, 806, 1235, 1250
Sch 2
para 1(1) 1235
para 1(2) 1235
para 2(1) 799, 800, 801, 803, 805, 806, 1250
para 2(2) 799, 801, 803, 805, 806
para 2(7) 799, 1250
para 2(8) 800
para 2(9) 806
Commissioners for Oaths Act 1889 2119
s 2 2119
Commissioners for Oaths Act 1891 2119
Communications Act 2003
s 406 1259
Schs 17, 19 1259
Companies Act 2006
s 1139 1347
ss 1139–1143 115
Companies Consolidation (Consequential Provisions) Act 1985
s 30 1245
Sch 2 1245
Constitutional Reform Act 2005
s 12(2) 796
s 15(1) 406, 435, 621, 623, 626, 651, 796, 812, 896, 1073, 1156, 1250
s 40(2) 199, 209
s 146 796, 812

Constitutional Reform Act 2005—*continued*
Sch 1
para 17 796
Sch 4
para 76 1156
para 96 812
para 114 1250
para 116 1250
para 160 796
para 167 796
para 203 435, 621, 623, 626, 651
para 204 435
para 205 621
para 207 623
para 208 626
para 209 651
para 218 406
para 219 406
para 252 896
para 253 896
para 365 1073
Sch 9
para 13(7) 250
para 35(2) 794
para 36(3) 1234
para 39 691
para 66(2) 995
para 66(3) 996
para 66(4) 997
para 68(2) 244
Sch 11
para 1 1233
para 1(2) 787, 1133, 1144, 2033, 2087, 2088, 2191, 2203, 2253, 2254, 2260, 2269, 2291
para 4(1) 806
para 19(2) 1066
para 19(3) 1068
para 26(2) 1250
Sch 18
Pt 1 796
Pt 2 812
Contempt of Court Act 1981 789, 790, 896, 906, 910, 1471, 1473, 1483, 1984
s 2 246
s 11 1040, 1249
s 12 1543
s 14 130, 466, 893, 1474
s 14(4B) 2468
s 41(5) 352
Sch 2 352
County Courts Act 1984 795, 1134
s 14 250
s 23 16, 18, 2043
s 23(c) 110, 2298
s 24 2298
s 25 22, 1016, 2269
s 38 37, 112, 127, 543, 631, 1135, 1231, 1243, 1744, 2253, 2254
s 38(1) 1929
s 38(3) 1135
s 58 2119
s 63 1801
s 71(2) 112
s 76 112

County Courts Act 1984—*continued*
s 77 207, 209, 535
ss 83, 84 189
s 92 250
s 108 2291
s 109 117
s 110 119
s 110(2) 1932
s 111(1) 2335
s 118 250, 792
s 133 2286
s 142 1989
s 147 158, 858
s 147(1) 1348
s 148(1) 250, 352, 354, 362
Sch 2
para 25 250
para 41 352
para 42 354
para 72 362
County Courts (Penalties for Contempt) Act 1983
s 1 791
Courts Act 1971
s 56 809
s 56(1),(4) 250
Sch 8
para 40(1),(2) 250
para 58 809
Sch 11 809
Pt II 250
Courts Act 2003
s 75 1043
s 75(1) 1279
s 75(4) 46
s 75(5)(b) 1379
s 76(3) 1331
s 88(1),(2)(a) 2354
s 109 806
s 109(1) 291, 315, 318, 341, 343, 349, 354, 611, 626, 652, 655, 669, 1066, 1081, 1083, 1084, 1093, 1101, 1111, 1250
s 109(3) 1250
Sch 8
para 68 1081
para 69 1083
para 70 1084
para 87 1066
para 88 1068
para 89 1071
para 90 1073
para 91 1073
para 98 1076
para 99 1076
para 101 1078
para 103 1079
para 104 1079
para 141 341
para 142 343
para 143 349
para 145 354
para 151 1093
para 152 1094
para 153 1096
para 154 1100

Courts Act 2003—*continued*
Sch 8—*continued*
para 155 1101
para 156 1103
para 159 1106
para 160 1106
para 162 1111
para 163 1112
para 164 1118
para 169 1207
para 170 1211
para 191 816
para 192 821
para 194 823
para 195 824
para 196 825
para 197 825
para 265 1250
para 268 690
para 269 695
para 336 611
para 337 626
para 338(1)–(4) 652
para 339 655
para 340 669
para 412 291
para 413 315
para 414 318
Sch 10 315, 806, 1250
Courts and Legal Services Act 1990 1046
s 1 1016
s 3 796
s 4(1) 1248
s 7(1)–(3) 1235
s 27 1529
s 28 1529
s 58C(5) 2070
s 74(3) 801
s 74(4) 795
s 74(6) 804
s 116 251, 355, 496, 518, 519, 555, 568, 570, 578, 582, 622, 626, 639, 645, 662, 920, 1064
s 119(1) 2160
s 125(2) 352, 799
s 125(3) 799, 806, 1250
s 125(7) 518, 570, 639, 823
Sch 16 1065
para 3 920
para 6 251
para 10(1) 481
para 10(2) 645
para 11 496
para 14 518
para 15 519
para 16 555
para 17 568
para 18 570
para 19 578
para 20 582
para 22 622
para 24 626
para 25 639
para 26 662
para 34 1064

Courts and Legal Services Act 1990—*continued*
Sch 16—*continued*
para 37 251
para 38 355
Sch 17 352
para 15 799
Sch 18
para 41 1250
para 49(1) 806
para 49(3) 799
Sch 20 518, 570, 639, 823, 1065, 1235
Crime and Courts Act 2013
Pt 1 1279
Pt 2 1279
s 17 243, 244, 245, 250, 291, 306, 308, 310, 315, 318, 340, 341, 343, 344, 345, 346, 347, 349, 350, 352, 354, 359, 361, 362, 409, 465, 481, 563, 576, 611, 621, 622, 626, 645, 651, 652, 655, 656, 669, 690, 691, 692, 693, 695, 699, 704, 708, 714, 716, 724, 729, 756, 758, 760, 761, 764, 767, 768, 769, 770, 773, 774, 775, 776, 777, 778, 787, 791, 795, 796, 798, 799, 800, 801, 804, 805, 806, 809, 811, 816, 817, 819, 820, 821, 822, 823, 824, 825, 828, 869, 870, 871, 890, 892, 896, 898, 906, 907, 909, 911, 953, 989, 1034, 1035, 1039, 1041, 1054, 1059, 1062, 1063, 1064, 1066, 1068, 1069, 1071, 1073, 1075, 1076, 1077, 1078, 1079, 1080, 1081, 1083, 1084, 1089, 1091, 1093, 1094, 1096, 1097, 1099, 1100, 1101, 1103, 1104, 1105, 1106, 1107, 1108, 1110, 1111, 1112, 1114, 1115, 1116, 1117, 1118, 1122, 1134, 1144, 1145, 1150, 1204, 1205, 1207, 1208, 1211, 1214, 1215, 1216, 1231, 1237, 1240, 1243, 1246, 1248, 1251, 1252, 2468
s 17(3) 1134, 1279
s 17(6) 1135, 1136, 1138, 1139, 1141, 1142, 1143, 1144
s 22 1239
Sch 9 243, 244, 245, 250, 340, 341, 343, 344, 345, 347, 352, 354, 361, 362, 791, 795, 796, 798, 799, 800, 801, 804, 805, 806, 809, 1039, 1059, 1231, 1237, 1248
Sch 10 243, 244, 250, 340, 341, 343, 344, 345, 346, 349, 350, 352, 359, 361, 362, 626, 791, 796, 809, 1034, 1035, 1054, 1062, 1075, 1076, 1077, 1078, 1079, 1134, 1214, 1240, 1243, 1246, 1248, 1251, 1279, 2468
para 1 1135, 1136, 1138, 1139, 1141, 1142, 1143, 1144
Sch 11 291, 306, 308, 310, 315, 318, 409, 465, 481, 563, 576, 611, 621, 622, 645, 651, 652, 655, 656, 669, 690, 691, 692, 693, 695, 699, 704, 708, 714, 716, 724, 729, 756, 758, 760, 761, 764, 767, 768, 769, 770, 773, 774, 775, 776, 777, 778, 787, 811, 816, 817, 819, 820, 821, 822, 823, 824, 825, 828, 869, 870, 871, 890, 892, 896, 898, 906, 907, 909, 911, 953, 989, 1041, 1063, 1064, 1066, 1068, 1069,

Crime and Courts Act 2013—*continued*
Sch 11—*continued* 1071, 1073, 1080, 1081, 1083, 1084, 1089, 1091, 1093, 1094, 1096, 1097, 1099, 1100, 1101, 1103, 1104, 1105, 1106, 1107, 1108, 1110, 1111, 1112, 1114, 1115, 1116, 1117, 1118, 1122, 1134, 1144, 1145, 1150, 1204, 1205, 1207, 1208, 1211, 1215, 1216, 1252
para 110 1289
Crime and Disorder Act 1998
s 15(4) 582
s 119 439, 582
Sch 8
para 68 439
para 69 582
Criminal Appeal Act 1968
s 52(1) 250
Sch 5
Pt I 250
Criminal Defence Service Act 2006
s 4(1) 340
Criminal Justice Act 1982
s 37 352
s 37(2) 352, 690, 824, 1068
s 38 352, 1058
s 46 352, 690, 824, 1058, 1094
s 46(1) 1040
s 77 791
s 78 791
Sch 14
para 60 791
Sch 16 791
Criminal Justice Act 1988
s 33A 625
Criminal Justice Act 1991
s 17 352, 791
s 17(3)(a) 804
s 60(3) 513
s 100 617
Sch 4 804
Pt I 352, 791
Pt V
para 4 791
Sch 11
para 40 617
Criminal Justice Act 1993
s 65(3) 791
Sch 3
para 6(5) 791
Criminal Justice Act 2003 130
s 119 629
s 258 792, 1996
s 258(2) 793
s 304 597
s 332 597
Sch 32
para 59 597
para 60 597
para 61 683
Sch 37
Pt 7 597
Criminal Justice and Court Services Act 2000 806
s 11 435, 1505, 1696
Criminal Justice and Court Services Act 2000—*continued*
s 11(3) 435, 482, 2585
s 12 1505, 1696, 2574
s 12(5)(b) 1704
s 13 1678
s 16 438
s 74 366, 372, 374, 435, 482, 522, 568, 570, 590, 597, 637, 673, 823
s 75 482, 522, 568, 590, 673
Sch 7
para 57 823
para 80 366, 372
para 81 374
para 87 482, 522, 568, 570, 590, 673
para 88 435
para 89 482
para 90 522
para 91 568
para 92 570
para 93 590
para 94 597
para 95 637
para 96 673
Sch 8 482, 568, 590, 673
Criminal Justice and Courts Act 2015
s 63(3) 198
s 84 1239
s 87 191
s 88 191
s 89 191
s 90 191
Criminal Justice and Immigration Act 2008
s 6(2) 496, 522, 637, 674, 675, 678
s 6(3) 496
s 149 496, 522, 637, 674, 675, 678
Sch 4
para 34 496
para 35 522
para 36 637
para 37 674, 675
para 38 678
para 105 496
Sch 28
Pt 1 496
Criminal Justice and Police Act 2001
s 44 1232
Criminal Justice and Public Order Act 1994
s 22 587
s 156(1),(2) 964
Criminal Law Act 1977
s 6 875
s 12A 875, 877
Criminal Procedure (Consequential Provisions) (Scotland) Act 1995
s 4 1259
s 5 1259
Sch 4
para 57 1259
Criminal Procedure and Investigations Act 1996
s 53 341
Crown Proceedings Act 1947 2087
s 17 996, 1347, 1855, 2057, 2258, 2262
s 18 1347

Crown Proceedings Act 1947—*continued*
s 27 2291

Debtors Act 1869 125
s 5 118, 119, 413, 797, 805, 1142, 1762, 1930, 1932, 1933, 1934, 1983
s 6 1236
Debtors Act 1878 125
Deregulation Act 2015
s 99(3) 1121
Deregulation and Contracting Out Act 1994
s 38 616
Disability Living Allowance and Disability Working Allowance Act 1991
s 7(2) 485, 519, 667
Sch 3
para 13 485
para 14 519
para 15 667
Divorce (Religious Marriages) Act 2002
s 1 1156
Divorce (Scotland) Act 1976
s 12(1) 1065
Sch 1
para 1 1065
Dock Work Act 1989
Sch 1
Pt I 354
Domestic and Appellate Proceedings (Restriction of Publicity) Act 1968 808
s 2(3) 1041
Domestic and Matrimonial Proceedings Act 1973
Sch 1
para 9 2776
Domestic Proceedings and Magistrates' Courts Act 1978 25, 718, 811
Pt I 647
s 1 25
s 2 25
s 2(1)(b) 25
s 2(1)(d) 25
s 3 25
s 4 25
s 5 25
s 6 25, 408
s 6(1) 25
s 6(2)(b) 25
s 6(2)(d) 25
s 7 25
s 7(1) 25
s 19 26
s 20 26
s 20(12) 26
s 20A 26
s 20ZA 26
s 26 26
s 30(5) 25
s 32(5) 103
s 54 1091, 1094, 1096
s 60(3) 1115
s 62 1150
s 63 1195
s 88 25
s 89 251

Domestic Proceedings and Magistrates' Courts Act 1978—*continued*
s 89(2) 1065, 1071, 1081, 1100, 1118, 1215
s 89(2)(a) 1064, 1150, 1214
s 89(2)(b) 1195
Sch 2
para 2 1081
para 12 1064
para 13 1065
para 14 1071
para 26 251
para 28 1215
para 32 355
para 37 1118
para 38 1150
para 39 1214
Sch 3 1100, 1195, 1215
Domestic Violence, Crime and Victims Act 2004 891
s 1 445, 888
s 2(2) 883
s 3 897
s 10 445
s 58(1) 884, 887, 890, 892, 894, 897, 898, 912
s 58(2) 887
Sch 10
para 34 883
para 35 884
para 36(1)–(3) 887
para 37(1)–(4) 890
para 38 888
para 38(1)–(5) 892
para 39 894
para 40 897
para 41 898
para 42(1) 912
para 42(2) 912
para 42(3) 912
Sch 11 887
Domicile and Matrimonial Proceedings Act 1973 826, 829
s 5 284
s 5(2) 46, 2776
s 5(2)(b) 415, 2776, 2777
s 5(3(b)(ii)) 46
s 5(3) 2776
s 5(5A) 2776
s 5(6) 1398
s 5(6A) 829
s 6(1) 1195
Sch A1 2776
Sch 1 725
para 2 1398
para 8 843, 1358
para 9 842, 1398
para 9(4) 1398
para 10(1) 1399
Sch 3
para 8 855

Education Act 1993
s 307 518
s 307(1) 554
s 307(3) 554

Education Act 1993—*continued*
Sch 19
para 147 518
para 149 554
Sch 21
Pt II 518, 554
Education Act 1996 1666, 1671
Pt IV 494
s 576 675
s 582(1) 554, 593, 615, 616, 619, 637, 658, 674, 676, 815, 1198
Sch 37
para 85 554
para 86 593
para 87 615
para 89 616
para 90 619
para 91 637
para 92 658
para 93 674, 676
para 136 1198
para 138 815
Education Act 2002
s 148 605
s 152 600, 606
s 155 605
s 215 605
s 215(1) 685
s 215(2) 606
Sch 13
para 1 600
para 3 605
para 5 606
Sch 14
para 3 605
Sch 21 685
Sch 22
Pt 3 605, 606
Education Act 2005
s 53 606
s 117 554
Sch 7
para 6 606
Sch 18
para 1 554
Education Act 2011
s 43 615, 616, 617
s 54 593, 609, 615
Sch 13
para 6 593, 609, 615
Education and Inspections Act 2006
s 184 615
Sch 14
para 12 595
para 13 600
para 16 615
para 17 666
para 76 310
Sch 18
Pt 5 615
Employment Rights Act 1996
s 240 357
Sch 1
para 3 357
Enduring Powers of Attorney Act 1985 1685
Equality Act 2010 541, 2063
Sch 9
para 18(1) 702
European Communities Act 1972
s 2(2) 2487
Evidence (Proceedings in Other Jurisdictions) Act 1975 2753
s 1 1782
s 8(1) 1118
Sch 1 1118
Evidence Amendment Act 1853
s 1 1214
Extradition Act 2003 2267
Family Law Act 1986 428, 836
Ch 1 990
Pt I 156, 157, 158, 439
Pt II 1125
Pt III 1041
Pt 3 1421
s 2A 839
s 3(2) 1545
s 3(6) 1545
s 25 156, 158
ss 25–31 1919
s 25(3) 156, 158
s 27 180, 181
s 27(1) 156, 158
s 28 1921
s 28(2) 1922
s 29 1922
s 29(1) 156, 158
s 32 1921, 1922, 1923
s 32(1) 156, 158
s 33 155, 156, 157, 159, 181, 184, 623, 1549, 1757
s 33(1) 156, 157
s 33(2) 157
s 34 157, 158, 450, 458, 1549
s 34(1) 158
s 37 181, 184
s 41 378
s 55 45, 714
s 55(1) 45
s 55(3) 45
s 55A 400, 411, 428, 870, 920, 921, 922, 979, 1421, 1422, 1424, 1698
s 55A(1) 428
s 55A(2) 428
s 55A(3) 411, 428, 920, 1422
s 55A(4) 411
s 56 921
s 56(1)(b) 1422
s 56(2) 1422
s 57 292, 1422
s 57(1) 292
s 57(2) 292
s 58(1) 45
s 58(2) 45
s 59 1424
s 59(2) 45
s 63 45
s 67(2),(3) 372
s 67(4) 373

Family Law Act 1986—*continued*
s 67(5) 374
s 68 810
s 68(1) 367, 372, 374, 398, 823, 1144, 1214, 1251
Sch 1
para 9 810
para 14 1214
para 24 823
para 26 1251
para 27 1144
para 28 367
para 29 372
para 30 374
para 31 398
Sch 2 810
Family Law Act 1996 37, 792, 797, 874, 1172, 1230, 1289, 1472, 1473
Pt IV 27, 41, 125, 126, 129, 184, 186, 702, 797, 916, 1429, 1469, 1539, 1741, 1744, 2458
Pt 4A 31, 129, 387, 899, 1741, 1744
Pt 33 2458
s 30 28
s 33 27, 28, 29, 31, 718, 1170, 2025
s 33(6) 14, 1122
s 33(10) 30
s 35 27, 28, 29, 31
s 35(3) 30
s 35(4) 30
s 35(5) 30
s 35(10) 30
s 36 27, 28, 29, 31
s 36(3) 30
s 36(4) 30
s 36(6) 30
s 36(10) 30
s 37 27, 28
s 37(3) 30
s 37(5) 30
s 38 27, 28
s 38(3) 30
s 38(6) 30
s 39 27
s 40 27, 29, 30
s 42 27, 718
s 42(1) 27
s 42(6) 29
s 42(7) 30
s 42A 27, 30, 126, 130, 1472
s 42A(3) 128, 1984
s 42A(4) 128, 1984
s 43 27
s 45 1469, 1745
s 45(1) 28
s 45(2) 28
s 45(3) 28, 1745
s 46 563, 576, 1473
s 46(1) 30
s 46(2) 797
s 46(3) 30
s 46(3A) 30
s 46(4) 31, 797
s 47 128, 129, 797, 1471, 1472, 1473, 1474, 1483
s 47(2) 30
s 47(3) 30, 125

Family Law Act 1996—*continued*
s 47(6) 1983
s 47(7) 126, 128, 129, 1473
s 47(7)(a) 1983
s 47(7)(b) 128, 1984
s 47(8) 126, 127, 128
s 47(9) 126, 128
s 47(10) 128, 129, 1984
s 47(11) 126, 128, 1984
s 47(12) 128, 1984
s 48 126, 128, 793, 1474, 1484, 1984
s 48(1) 1984
s 48(4) 1984
s 49 1472
s 52 562, 563, 564, 576, 578, 637
s 53 911, 1425
s 55A(7) 1424
s 58 129, 1473, 1483
s 62(3) 27, 28, 36
s 62(3)(eza) 718
s 62(4) 27
s 63(1) 27, 127, 129, 1473
s 63(2) 27, 186, 188
s 63A 932, 1513
s 63B 31, 32, 35, 632, 932
s 63C 32
s 63C(6) 31
s 63CA 35, 36
s 63D 32, 935, 1477, 1481, 1745
s 63D(3) 33, 1745
s 63D(4) 33
s 63E 35
s 63F 35
s 63G 35, 1482
s 63J 126, 127, 128
s 63J(2) 36, 1483
s 63J(3) 1483
s 63J(4) 1483
s 63K 936, 1483
s 63L 936, 1483
s 63L(4) 1484
s 63L(5) 1484
s 63M 32
s 63O 129
s 63S 129
s 66(1) 439, 1132, 1251
s 66(3) 439, 823
Sch 5 126, 129, 793, 905, 936, 1472, 1473, 1483, 1485, 1984
para 2(1)(a) 1984
para 2(1)(b) 1474, 1984
para 2(1),(2) 936
para 2(2) 1473
para 2(3) 937
para 2(5) 128
para 3 1473
Sch 6
para 1 562, 563
para 2 564
para 3 576
para 4 578
para 5 637
Sch 7 894, 1171, 1425
para 2(2) 41

Family Law Act 1996—*continued*
Sch 7—*continued*
para 3 41
para 7 1171
paras 7–9 41
para 10 41
para 11 42
para 13 41
Sch 8
para 16(5)(a) 1202
para 16(6)(b) 1202
para 16(7) 1202
para 51 1251
para 52 1132
para 60(1) 439
Sch 10 439, 823
Family Law (Scotland) Act 1985
s 28(1) 1065
Sch 1
para 3 1065
Family Law Reform Act 1969 917
Pt III 2085
s 1 217, 1245
s 9 793
s 9(1) 285
s 12 217
s 20 411, 426, 440, 870, 1422, 1742
s 20(1) 226, 2085
s 20(1A) 226
s 20(2) 227
s 20(3) 227
s 20(6) 227
s 21(1) 226
s 21(3) 226, 1016
s 22 227
s 23 410
s 23(1) 226
s 25 2085
Family Law Reform Act 1987 282, 924, 1016
s 1 426, 454
s 1(2) 142, 427
s 1(3) 427
s 1(4) 427
ss 15, 16 481
s 22 871
s 23(1) 920
s 23(2) 924
s 27(1)(b) 1016
s 28 1055
s 33 810, 820, 1111
s 33(1) 251, 690, 822, 824, 920, 922, 923, 1094, 1195
s 33(4) 1079, 1089, 1251
Sch 2 355, 825, 1065, 1068, 1076
para 19 810
para 21 920
para 22 922
para 23 923
para 24 923
para 25 923
para 27 251
para 45 1094
para 50 1111
para 52 1195

Family Law Reform Act 1987—*continued*
Sch 2—*continued*
para 69 822
para 70 824
para 89 690
Sch 3 355
Sch 4 251, 810, 820, 1065, 1079, 1089, 1251
Family Provision Act 1966 702
Fatal Accidents Act 1976 1666, 1671, 2071, 2073
Female Genital Mutilation Act 2003 532, 927, 1744
s 5 1745
s 5(3) 1745
Sch 2
para 1(3) 631, 934
para 2(2) 1478
para 5 1477
para 6 1482
para 7 1483
para 8 1483
para 9 1483
paras 10–14 1483
Finance Act 2005
s 103 702
Finance Act 2006
Sch 23
para 2 2520
Forced Marriage (Civil Protection) Act 2007 632
s 1 899, 900, 901, 903, 904, 905, 906, 907
s 3(1) 898, 1251
Sch 2
para 1 1251
para 3 898
Foreign Judgments (Reciprocal Enforcement) Act 1933 83, 93, 1929, 2299
s 1(1)(c) 89
s 2(1) 87, 89
s 4 87, 88
s 6 2299
s 10(2) 86
s 11(1) 86
Forfeiture Act 1982 1024
Fraud Act 2006
s 13 2093
s 13(4) 2093

Gender Recognition Act 2004 720, 944, 1010, 1015
ss 1–8 944
s 1(1) 944, 946, 949
s 1(1)(a) 946
s 1(2) 710, 1384
s 4 1157, 1158
s 4(1) 951
s 4(2) 949, 951, 1384
s 4(3) 951, 1384
s 4(4) 948
s 5 951
s 5(2) 944, 949
s 5A(2) 944, 949
s 6 949, 1418
s 6(1) 944, 949
s 8 949
s 8(5) 949, 1384
s 9 955
ss 9–21 944

Gender Recognition Act 2004—*continued*
s 10 949
s 11 949, 954, 1157, 1158
s 12 953
s 13 944
s 14 944
s 15 953, 956, 957
s 16 953
s 17 955
s 17(1) 955
s 17(2) 955
s 17(3) 955
s 18 955
s 18(2) 956
s 18(3) 956
s 18(4),(5) 956
s 19 953
s 20 953
s 21(1) 957
s 21(3) 957
s 21(4) 957
s 21(5) 957
s 22 944
s 22(4) 944
s 22(5) 944, 958
s 22(7) 944, 958
s 25 710, 951, 1384
Sch 1 944, 945
Sch 2 944, 948
para 2 1157
para 3 1158
Sch 3 944, 949, 954
Sch 4 944, 954
para 5 949, 1157
para 6 1158
Sch 5 944
Sch 6 944
Government of Wales Act 2006 2262
Sch 9
para 1 2262
Sch 10
para 56 1004
Guardianship Act 1973
s 9 355
s 9(3) 1065
s 14 1065
s 15(3) 1065
Sch 5
para 4 1065
Guardianship of Minors Act 1971
s 18(1) 1065
Sch 1 1065

Health and Social Care Act 2008
Sch 15 251, 355, 1063
Pt 5 1065
Health and Social Care Act 2012
s 55(2) 496, 508, 510, 518, 520, 582, 609, 612, 637
s 213(8) 958
Sch 5
para 48 496
para 49 508
para 50 510
para 51 518

Health and Social Care Act 2012—*continued*
Sch 5—*continued*
para 52 520
para 53 582
para 54 609
para 55 612
para 56 637
Health and Social Care (Community Health and Standards) Act 2003
s 34 508, 510, 518, 582, 609, 612
s 117 517
s 147 310, 595, 615, 666
Sch 4
para 75 508, 510, 609, 612
para 76 508
para 77 510
para 78 518
para 79 582
para 80 609
para 81 612
Sch 9
para 10 595, 615, 666
para 32 310
Health Authorities Act 1995
s 2 496, 518, 519, 582, 609, 612, 637
s 5 637
Sch 1
para 118 496, 518, 519, 582, 609, 612, 637
Sch 3 637
House of Lords Act 1999 1679
Housing Act 1985 875
s 91(3) 914
Housing Act 1988
Pt I 875
s 140(1) 799
Sch 17
para 35(2) 799
Housing Act 1996 875
Pt VII 912
s 153C 797
s 189(1)(b) 442
Housing (Consequential Provisions) Act 1985
s 4 799
Sch 2
para 57(3) 799
Human Fertilisation and Embryology Act 1990 807, 959, 980, 1016
s 27 870
s 28 870
s 30 1016
ss 33–48 427
s 36 1256
s 49(5) 924
Sch 4
para 1 924
Human Fertilisation and Embryology Act 2008 380, 456, 978, 1256
s 1 960
s 2 962
s 3 963
s 3(5) 963
s 4(1) 964
s 4(2) 965
s 11(1) 966

Human Fertilisation and Embryology Act 2008—*continued*
s 12 967
s 14(2)–(4) 969
s 15(2)–(5) 970
s 26 972
s 27 973
ss 33–45 1016, 1056
ss 33–48 454
s 35 43
s 36 43
s 42 43, 456
ss 42–45 701
s 43 43, 142, 144, 430, 470
s 45 456
s 48 456
s 54 42, 43, 996, 1016, 1634, 2058
s 54(1) 42
s 54(1)–(8) 1639
s 54(2) 42
s 54(3) 42
s 54(6) 1636
s 54(8) 1636
s 56 425, 430, 470, 619, 637, 871, 924, 925, 1056, 1058, 1059
s 59(2) 1256
s 59(3)–(8) 1258
s 59(7) 1259
Sch 2
para 2 973
para 3 974, 975
para 4 975
Sch 6
para 13(a) 924
para 16 1056
para 17 1056
para 18(b) 1058
para 19 1059
para 23 871
para 24(1)–(3) 925
para 25(1) 925
para 25(3) 925
para 26(1)–(3) 425
para 27 430
para 28(1),(2) 470
para 34 971
para 35 972
para 39 286
Sch 7
para 2 962
para 5 969
para 6 971
para 12 971
Human Fertilisation and Embryology (Deceased Fathers) Act 2003 980
s 2(1) 286
Sch
para 18 286
Human Reproductive Cloning Act 2001 963
Human Rights Act 1998 189, 620, 992, 1240, 1377, 1657, 1930, 1931, 2043, 2063, 2261, 2263
s 1 234, 2057
s 3 234
s 4 234, 235, 236, 989, 1854, 2043, 2258

Human Rights Act 1998—*continued*
s 5 201, 236
s 6 234, 529, 530
s 7 529, 530, 1141, 1513, 1545, 1855, 2048, 2142
s 7(1) 204, 235
s 7(1)(a) 234, 235
s 7(1)(b) 234, 529
s 7(5) 235
s 8 164, 236, 529, 530, 1141, 2048, 2135, 2142
s 8(1) 529, 1043, 2049
s 8(2) 1043
s 9 1141, 1854, 2258
s 9(1) 235
Sch 1
Pt I
Art 2 960, 1481
Art 3 1481
Art 5 1547
Art 5(1) 511
Art 6 383, 448, 528, 529, 530, 582, 624, 792, 795, 804, 903, 1210, 1320, 1481, 1501, 1512, 1516, 1639, 2289
Art 6(1) 414, 2068, 2116
Art 8 235, 247, 248, 256, 283, 285, 381, 383, 428, 443, 448, 529, 530, 624, 999, 1481, 1501, 1510, 1512, 1516, 1639, 2025, 2294, 2298, 2743
Art 8(1) 528, 1853
Art 8(2) 445, 528, 1853
Art 9 256, 996, 2057
Art 9(2) 996, 2058
Art 10 247, 248, 448, 627
Art 12 996, 1531, 2057
Art 13 448, 999
Pt II 1256
Art 1 2294
Human Tissues Act 2004 1421
Immigration Act 2016
s 89 1121
Sch 15 1121
Immigration and Asylum Act 1999
s 4 486
s 15 392
Industrial Tribunals Act 1996
s 45 794
Sch 3
Pt I 794
Inheritance (Provision for Family and Dependants) Act 1975 226, 702, 1013, 1134, 1165, 1429, 2048, 2135, 2146, 2158, 2274, 2823
s 1 22, 2048, 2269, 2271
s 1(1)(a) 702
s 1(1)(ba) 22
s 1(1)(c) 22
s 1(1)(d) 22
s 1(1)(e) 22
s 1(a) 22
s 1(b) 22
s 1A 22
s 1B 22
s 2 54, 2271
s 2(1) 2271
s 2(1)(a) 24

Inheritance (Provision for Family and Dependants) Act 1975—*continued*
s 2(1)(b) 24
s 2(1)(c) 24
s 2(1)(d) 24
s 2(1)(e) 24
s 2(1)(f) 24
s 2(1)(g) 24
s 2(1)(h) 24
s 2(4) 24
s 3 2272
s 4 22, 23, 2270
s 5 24, 2271
s 6 2271
s 7 2271
s 9 24
s 10 24, 2271
ss 10–13 2271
s 11 24, 2271
s 15 54
s 16 24, 2271
s 17 24, 2271
s 19(3) 2275
s 25(1) 1285, 2274
s 26(1) 1208
Inheritance and Trustees' Powers Act 2014 1016, 1023, 1028
s 4 294
s 5 925
s 6 653, 655, 755, 1014, 1020, 1022, 1024, 1028, 1202
Sch 2 653, 655, 755, 1014, 1020, 1022, 1024, 1028, 1202
Insolvency Act 1985
s 235(1) 1211
Sch 8
para 23 1211
Insolvency Act 1986 343, 1173
s 281(5) 1170
s 310 1173
s 335A 1262, 1264
s 339 1173, 1211
s 340 1211
s 421 1028
s 439(2) 803, 1211, 1245
Sch 14 803, 1211, 1245
Intestates' Estates Act 1952 702

Jobseekers Act 1995
s 41 416, 485, 519, 637, 667, 1252
Sch 2
para 19 485, 519, 637, 667
para 20 416
para 51 1252
Judgments Act 1838 54
Judicature (Northern Ireland) Act 1978
s 122(1) 1073
Sch 5
Pt II 1073
Judicial Proceedings (Regulation of Reports) Act 1926 1039, 1543
Justice (Northern Ireland) Act 2002
Sch 4
para 39 1001
Justices of the Peace Act 1949
s 46(2) 1084
Sch 7
Pt II 1084
Justices of the Peace Act 1979
s 71 1081
Sch 2
para 1 1081
Justices of the Peace Act 1997
s 73(2) 655, 825, 1081, 1207
Sch 5
para 2 1081
para 14 1207
para 18 825
para 27 655

Land Charges Act 1972 876
Land Registration Act 2002 876
s 29 2023
s 34(2) 876
s 34(3) 908
s 42 877
s 46 798, 877, 1243
s 66 1172
s 133 361
Sch 11 361
Sch 13 361, 876
Law of Property Act 1925
s 2 2023
s 27 2023
Law Reform (Miscellaneous Provisions) Act 1970 1041
s 2(2) 14, 1123
Law Reform (Succession) Act 1995
s 2 1014, 1022
s 4 434
Legal Aid Act 1974
s 9(6) 1042
Legal Aid Act 1988
s 45(1),(3) 368
Sch 5
para 3 354
para 16 368
Legal Aid, Sentencing and Punishment of Offenders Act 2012 440, 646, 796, 1165, 1166, 1984
s 4 130
s 6 1985
s 8(1)(b) 1043
s 10 440
s 12(1)(b) 1043
s 14(g) 130
s 18 1985
s 23 1043
s 24 1043
s 25 1255, 2539
s 25(1) 2139
s 29 228
s 39 340, 368, 511, 1254
s 49 406, 1163, 1165
s 50 406, 1166
s 51 1173
s 52 745, 746
s 53 746
s 54 733

Legal Aid, Sentencing and Punishment of Offenders Act 2012—*continued*
s 104 2433
s 105 496
Sch 1 130
Sch 3 130
Sch 5
para 6 340
para 26 368
para 38 511
para 41 1254
Sch 12
para 24 496
Legal Services Act 2007 1046, 1470
s 12 2119
s 18 1347, 2119
s 177 1255
s 208(1) 706, 806, 808, 907, 909, 1152
Sch 2 2119
Sch 4 2119
Sch 16
para 1 1255
para 68 1255
Sch 21
para 29 1152
para 61 806
para 121 907, 909
para 133 808
para 150 706
Legitimacy Act 1976 1016, 1055
s 1 426
s 2 282, 1016
s 9 446
s 10 427
Sch 1 1016
Life Assurance Act 1774
s 1 718
Limitation Act 1980 2045
s 9 414
Local Authority Social Services Act 1970
s 2(1) 570
s 7 475, 480, 486, 497, 1755, 2593
Sch 1 570
Local Government Act 1985
s 12 825
Local Government Act 2000
s 103 520
s 107(1) 497, 570, 637
Sch 5
para 19 497
para 20 570
para 22 637
Local Government (Wales) Act 1994
s 22 637
s 66 637
Sch 10
para 13 637
Sch 18 637
Local Government etc (Scotland) Act 1994
s 180(1) 374
Sch 13
para 139 374
Magistrates' Courts Act 1980 1059, 2834
s 32(2) 923
s 60 1063
s 63(3) 130, 157, 250, 450, 458
s 76 414, 1076
s 77 414
s 93 1076
s 97(1) 2161
s 111A 198, 400, 411, 412, 414, 1863, 1867, 2844
s 111A(2) 198
s 111A(4) 198
s 122 578
s 128 126, 910
s 129 126, 910
s 154 250, 341, 344, 354, 823, 824, 825, 1073, 1079, 1099, 1101, 1103, 1116
Sch 7
para 8 1073
para 24 1079
para 37 250
para 97 341
para 98 344
para 101 354
para 105 1099
para 106 1101
para 107 1103
para 109 1116
para 163 823
para 164 824
para 167 825
Sch 9 1079, 1103
Maintenance Enforcement Act 1991 69, 1060
s 1 25, 341, 342, 348, 812, 1933, 2295
s 1(1) 105, 120
s 1(2) 119
s 1(3) 105, 120
s 1(4)(a) 1204, 1933
s 1(6) 120
s 1(7) 120
s 1(8) 120
s 1(10) 119
s 5 821
s 6 652
s 10 690, 1068, 1071, 1073, 1076, 1077, 1078, 1083, 1084, 1093, 1094, 1096, 1111, 1112
s 11(1) 341, 481, 824
Sch 1
para 1 1083
para 2 1084
para 3 1068
para 4 1068
para 5 1071
para 6 1073
para 7 1076
para 8 1076
para 9 1077
para 10 1077
para 11 1078
para 12 1093
para 13 1094
para 14 1096
para 18 1111
para 19(1) 1111
para 19(2) 1112

Maintenance Enforcement Act 1991—*continued*
Sch 1—*continued*
para 21 690
Sch 2
para 1 341
para 3 824
para 10 481
Maintenance Orders Act 1950 1063
s 17 68
s 17(1) 68
s 17(1)(b),(c) 69
s 17(3)(b) 69
s 17(4) 69
s 17(4),(5) 68
s 18 69
s 18(1) 69
s 18(1A) 69
s 20(3) 69
s 21 70
s 22 70
s 23 70
s 24 70
s 24(2) 70
Maintenance Orders Act 1958 102, 1074, 1917
s 1(1) 104
s 2(1) 1916
s 2(2) 104
s 2(5) 104
s 3 104
s 4 104, 1917
s 5 105
Maintenance Orders (Facilities for Enforcement) Act 1920 1080, 2487, 2847
s 1 65
s 1(1) 65
s 2 64
s 3 66
s 3(1),(2) 66
s 3(3),(4) 66
s 3(6) 67
s 4 67
s 4(1) 67
s 4(2)–(5) 67
s 4(6) 68
s 10 66
Maintenance Orders (Reciprocal Enforcement) Act 1972 63, 78, 90, 1087, 1946, 1949
Pt I 63, 71, 72, 78, 2847
Pt II 82
s 2 71, 72
s 2(1) 71
s 2(3) 71
s 3 75
s 3(1) 74, 75
s 3(2) 75
s 3(5) 75, 76
s 3(6) 76
s 3(6A) 76
s 3(6B) 76
s 3(6C) 76
s 3(6D) 76
s 5 78
s 5(3) 79
s 5(4) 79, 80

Maintenance Orders (Reciprocal Enforcement) Act 1972—*continued*
s 5(5) 79, 80
s 5(6) 79, 80
s 5(7) 79, 80
s 5(8) 80
s 5(9) 80
s 6 73, 74, 77, 78
s 6(2) 72
s 6(3) 73
s 6(4) 73
s 7(2) 76, 77
s 7(5) 77
s 8 73, 78
s 9 78, 79, 80
s 12(1) 79
s 16 74, 78
s 21 76
s 22(1) 251, 355, 1075
s 22(2) 1080
s 26 81
s 27A 81
s 27B 81
s 27B(3) 82
s 27B(4) 82
s 27C 82
s 34(1) 82
s 34(2) 82
s 34(3) 82
s 34(4) 83
s 34A 82
s 35(3) 83
s 36 82
s 40 74, 75, 77
s 42(3) 1215
Sch
para 4 1075
para 6 251
para 7 355
Maintenance Orders (Reciprocal Enforcement) Act 1992
s 1 1081, 1083, 1084, 1089, 1091, 1093, 1096, 1100, 1101, 1103, 1106, 1107, 1108, 1111, 1114, 1115, 1117
Sch 1
para 1 1081
para 2 1083
para 3 1083
para 4 1084
para 6 1089
para 7 1091
para 8 1093
para 9 1096
para 10 1100
para 11 1101
para 12 1103
para 13 1106, 1107, 1108
para 14 1111
para 16 1114
para 17 1115
para 18 1117
para 19 1117
Marriage Act 1949 954
s 3 131, 1426

Marriage Act 1949—*continued*
s 3(1) 131
s 3(1)(b) 131
s 3(1A) 131
s 3(5) 131
Marriage (Prohibited Degrees of Relationship) Act 1986
s 5 1251
s 6(4) 1157
Marriage (Same Sex Couples) Act 2013 701, 944, 1119
s 9 701
s 10 720
s 11 828, 831, 1148, 1157, 1635
s 12 945, 946, 947, 948, 950, 952, 953, 954, 955, 956, 958
s 13 703, 720
s 17 978, 981, 982, 985, 1157
Sch 2 720
Sch 3 1635
Sch 4
para 3 1148
para 4 1157
para 6 828
para 8 831
Sch 5
para 2 946
para 3 948
para 4 950
para 5 952
para 6 952
para 7 952
para 8 953
para 9 954
para 10 955
para 11 955
para 13 958
para 14 958
para 17 947, 948
para 18 946
Sch 6 720
Sch 7
para 27 1157
para 34 703, 720
para 38 978
para 39 981
para 40 982
para 41 985
Marriage and Civil Partnership (Amendment) Act 2016 701
Married Women's Property Act 1882 1122, 1429
s 11 718
s 17 14, 15, 716, 797, 1122, 1170, 1418
Married Women's Property Act 1964 1123
Matrimonial and Family Proceedings Act 1984 1124, 1856
Pt III 718, 778, 1165, 1387, 1418, 1424, 2857, 2867
s 1 1150
s 2 1158
s 3 1178, 1185
s 4 1195
s 5 1196, 1198
s 6 1202
Matrimonial and Family Proceedings Act 1984—*continued*
s 7 1205
s 8(1) 1034
s 9 813
s 9(2) 815
s 9(3) 820
s 10 816
s 11 820
s 12 57
ss 12–27 57
s 13 58, 1164
s 13(1) 58
s 13(2) 58
s 14 1286
s 14(1) 59
s 15 57
s 15(1A) 57
s 16 1164
s 16(2) 1425
s 17 59
s 20 59
s 21 59
s 22 59
s 23 59, 1744
s 23(2)(a) 59
s 24 57
s 24(1)(a) 59
s 24(1)(b) 59
s 25 1034
ss 31A–31P 1279, 2468
s 31C(1)(a)–(i) 1743
s 31E 103
s 31E(1) 1757, 1929
s 31E(1)(a) 212, 1421, 1741
s 31E(2) 112, 2320, 2331
s 31F(2) 1741
s 31F(2)(b) 215, 790, 1286
s 31F(5) 812, 816
s 31F(6) 212, 1399
s 31G 1760, 1782
s 31G(6) 1762, 1765, 2563
s 31J 1757
s 31N 1782
s 31P(1) 1332
s 32 1279
s 38 1527
s 38(2) 182
s 40 2193
s 43 1122
s 46(1) 251, 811, 817, 819, 820, 828, 1065, 1068, 1077, 1148, 1173, 1195, 1207, 1214, 1215
s 46(3) 806
Sch 1 1076
para 1 1065
para 2 1068
para 5 1077
para 8 251
para 10 1148
para 11 1173
para 12 1195
para 13 1207
para 15 1214
para 16 1215

Matrimonial and Family Proceedings Act 1984—*continued*
Sch 1—*continued*
para 17 828
para 21 811
para 22 817
para 24 819
para 25 820
Sch 3 806
Matrimonial Causes Act 1973 57, 415, 645, 655, 953, 1020, 1147, 1261, 1262, 1285, 1286, 1379, 1435, 2026
Pt II 125, 340, 718, 730, 1930, 2514
s 1 1380
s 1(1) 45, 46
s 1(2) 46, 1386
s 1(2)(a) 1395
s 1(2)(b) 1395
s 1(2)(c) 1395
s 1(2)(d) 51, 1382, 1386, 1389, 1404
s 1(2)(e) 51, 1380, 1387, 1404
s 1(3) 1393, 1394
s 1(4) 1393, 1394
s 1(5) 46, 47, 1403
s 1(6) 46
s 2 1382, 1394
s 2(5) 1404
s 2(6) 1404
s 2(7) 1382, 1386
s 4 708
s 5 709
s 5(1) 49, 1380
s 6 1381
s 7 408, 706, 1442, 2037
s 8 1401
ss 8–10(1) 1380
s 8(6) 407
s 8(7)(a) 407
s 9(1) 1401, 1405
s 9(2) 47, 48, 1148, 1403, 1405
s 10 710
s 10(1) 1400
s 10(2) 47, 50, 1400, 1404
s 10(3) 50, 1404
s 10(4) 1400, 1404
s 10A 48
s 10A(1) 48, 1401
s 10A(2) 48, 1401
s 10A(4) 48
s 11 46, 1014, 1380
s 12 46, 949, 1380
s 12(1)(g) 1384
s 12(1)(h) 1384
s 12(e) 710
s 12(f) 710
s 12(h) 949
s 13(2A) 949
s 15 46, 47
s 17 1380
s 17(1) 46
s 20 715, 1389
s 21 50, 1128
s 21A 50, 54, 702, 734, 1173, 1453, 1454
s 21A(2)(a) 2452

Matrimonial Causes Act 1973—*continued*
s 21B 50, 734, 1459, 2456
s 21B(1) 54
s 21C 50, 730, 734
s 22 50, 730, 1125, 1161
ss 22–24G 51
s 22ZA 406, 730, 1042
s 22ZA(1) 215
s 22ZB 406, 730
s 23 12, 14, 50, 481, 647, 1033, 1035, 1043, 1125, 1161, 1172
s 23(1)(a) 54
s 23(1)(b) 54, 359
s 23(1)(c) 54
s 23(1)(d) 54
s 23(1)(e) 54, 359
s 23(1)(f) 54, 406
s 23(3)(b) 406
s 23(6) 54, 1131, 2283
s 24 12, 14, 50, 54, 481, 894, 914, 1033, 1043, 1125, 1161, 1440
s 24A 50, 54, 1125
s 24A(2) 1453
s 24B 50, 734, 1161
s 24B(2) 1454, 2519
s 24C 50, 734, 1453, 1454, 2457
s 24C(1) 2519
s 24D 50, 734
s 24E 50
s 24F 50
s 24G 50, 734
s 25 50, 813, 1018, 1023, 1122, 1161, 1179, 1447, 2105
s 25(1) 1129
s 25(2) 730, 1129
s 25(2)(a) 1191
s 25(2)(h) 1191
s 25(3) 730
s 25(4) 730
s 25A 50, 730, 1161
s 25A(3) 54, 1131
s 25B 50, 734
s 25B(5) 54, 1454
s 25B(7) 54
s 25C 50, 734
s 25D 734
s 25D(1) 2454
s 25D(3) 2452
s 25E 730, 734, 1459, 2456, 2511
s 25E(1) 734
s 25E(7) 734
s 25E(9) 734
s 25F 50, 730, 734, 1459
s 25F(3) 55
s 25F(5) 55
s 25G 730, 734
s 26 730
s 27 12, 50, 481, 647, 730, 1041, 1161, 2865, 2869
s 28 730, 1431
s 28(1A) 50, 54, 1131
s 28(3) 50, 730, 1125
s 29 730
s 29(2)–(4) 648
s 29(3)(b) 648

Matrimonial Causes Act 1973—*continued*
s 29(5) 407
s 29(6) 407
s 30 730
s 31 50, 730, 1168, 1169, 1183, 1184
s 31(1) 404
s 32 103, 105, 108, 112, 118, 120, 730
s 33 730
ss 33A–36 730
s 33A(1) 1129
s 34(2) 21, 408, 1419
s 35 20, 50, 408, 481, 655
s 35(1) 20
s 35(2) 21
s 36 481, 656, 1036
s 37 55, 481, 730, 797, 1133, 2454
s 37(1) 56
s 37(2) 56
s 37(2)(a) 797, 1133, 1286, 1744, 1848
s 39 730, 1173
s 40 217, 730, 1685
s 40A 730, 2520
s 40B 730, 2520
s 41 1404
s 49 715, 1383
s 49(1) 1383
s 49(3) 1383
s 49(5) 1383
s 52 1160, 1285
s 52(1) 401
s 53 355, 810
s 54 810, 1065, 1391
s 54(1) 251
Sch 1 810
para 11 949
para 11(1)(e) 1384
para 11(3A) 949
Sch 2
para 3(1) 1065
para 7(1) 810
para 10(2) 251
para 13 355
Sch 3 810
Matrimonial Causes (Property and Maintenance) Act 1958
s 7 717, 1122
s 7(7) 15, 1122
s 8 1122
Matrimonial Homes Act 1983
s 1 875
s 7 894
s 8(2) 895
s 12 1150
Sch 1 894, 1125
Sch 2 1150
Matrimonial Homes and Property Act 1981
s 7 1173
s 8(2) 1202
s 8(3) 834
Matrimonial Proceedings (Transfer) Act 1988
s 1(1) 1145
Matrimonial Proceedings and Property Act 1970 1215
s 37 716
Matrimonial Proceedings and Property Act 1970—*continued*
s 39 14, 1123
s 42(1) 251, 810
Sch 2
para 3 810
para 5 251
Mental Capacity Act 2005 215, 217, 219, 223, 225, 227, 338, 901, 1212, 1216, 1220, 1680, 1685, 1686, 2062, 2063, 2085, 2275, 2576
Pt 1 223, 2060
s 1 1638, 1680, 2060
s 1(2) 224
s 2 289, 1680, 1681, 2060
s 2(1) 216, 219, 224, 1008, 1131, 1212, 1221, 1547, 1638, 1681, 2060
s 2(4) 224
s 3 1547, 1680, 2060
s 3(1) 216, 219, 224, 1681
s 4 1009, 1546, 1680, 2060, 2065
s 15 225
s 16 225
s 16(2)(b) 1686
ss 24–26 1547
s 48 225
s 49 225, 226
s 67(1) 245, 289, 922, 995, 1212
Sch 4 1685
Sch 6
para 10 245
para 15 922
para 19 1212
para 43 995
para 45 289
Mental Health Act 1983 494, 630, 1350, 1474, 1666, 1671, 1681, 1687
s 1(2) 407, 487, 1157, 1158
s 35 130, 793, 1484
s 37 130, 793
s 38 130, 793
s 148 791, 922, 1157
Sch 4
para 25 922
para 34 1157
para 57 791
Mental Health Act 2007 1220, 1350
s 1(4) 791, 893
s 50(2) 1218, 1219
s 50(4)(a) 1220
Sch 1
para 19 791
para 20 893
Mental Health (Amendment) Act 1982
s 65(1) 791
Sch 3
paras 59, 60 791
Merchant Shipping Act 1979
s 39(1) 353
Merchant Shipping Act 1995
s 314(2) 353
Sch 13
para 46 353
Ministry of Social Security Act 1966
s 39(3) 1068

Ministry of Social Security Act 1966—*continued*
Sch 8 1068
National Health Service and Community Care Act 1990
s 66(1) 496, 519, 609, 612
Sch 9
para 36 496, 612
para 36(3) 519
para 36(4) 609
Naval Discipline Act 1957
s 128G(1),(2) 1170
Northern Ireland Act 1998 2262
Sch 10
para 1 2262
Offender Rehabilitation Act 2014
s 14 641
Sch 4
para 9 641
Partnership Act 1890
s 23 360
Pension Schemes Act 1993
s 159(4),(4A) 1170
s 190 353
Sch 8
para 4 353
Pension Schemes Act 2015 2516
Pensions Act 1995 953
s 166 1170, 1178, 1187, 1188, 1189, 1202, 1210
s 166(4) 1170, 1187
s 166(5) 1170, 1187
s 166(6) 1170, 1187
Pensions Act 2004
s 160 1191
s 161 1191
s 220 734, 1191, 1192
s 286 1191
Sch 7 734
Sch 12
para 3 1191
Pensions Act 2008
Sch 6
Pt 1 1162, 1163, 1176, 1177, 1178, 1185, 1191, 1193, 1202, 1213
Pt 2 1128, 1129, 1131
Pt 3 736, 737, 738, 739, 740, 742, 744, 745, 752, 753, 754, 763, 782, 785
Pensions Act 2014 2524
s 2 2525
s 4 2525
s 8 2525
ss 16–19 2525
s 22 2525
s 54 2525
Sch 8
para 4 2525
Sch 10
para 4 2525
Police and Criminal Evidence Act 1984 629
s 24(1) 445
s 38(6) 171, 496, 513, 2433
Police and Magistrates' Courts Act 1994
s 91 823
Sch 8
para 29 823
Police Reform Act 2002
s 107(2) 1230
Sch 8 1230
Policing and Crime Act 2009
s 34 2201, 2202
s 41 2202
s 112 496
Sch 7
para 21 496
Powers of Criminal Courts (Sentencing) Act 2000
s 96 130, 793
s 165 341, 496, 522, 637, 667, 674, 675, 678, 791, 794
Sch 9
para 44 341
para 84 791
para 85 794
para 126 496
para 127 522
para 129 637
para 130 667
para 131 674, 675
para 132 678
Presumption of Death Act 2013 1014, 1222, 2271
s 1 725
s 1(3) 828
s 1(4) 828
s 16 725, 828
Sch 2
para 2 828
para 3 725
Prevention of Social Housing Fraud Act 2013
s 10 875
Sch
para 6 875
Private International Law (Miscellaneous Provisions) Act 1995
s 8 1157, 1214
Sch
para 2 1157, 1214
Probation Service Act 1993
s 32 590, 673
Sch 3
para 9 590, 673
Proceeds of Crime Act 2002 1161, 2267
Prosecution of Offences Act 1985
s 24 1246
Protection from Harassment Act 1997 27, 36, 37, 125, 126, 1229, 1741, 2060, 2823
s 3 31, 37, 39, 40, 797
s 3(1) 37
s 3(3) 37, 39, 126, 128, 129, 797
s 3(3)(a) 2004
s 3(4) 39, 40, 126, 128, 129
s 3(5) 40, 126, 128, 129
s 3(5)(a) 2117
Protection of Trading Interests Act 1980
s 5 84, 88
Public Trustee Act 1906 702

Registered Homes (Amendment) Act 1991
s 2(6) 591, 593, 615, 637, 678

Scotland Act 1998 2262
Sch 6
para 1 2262
Senior Courts Act 1981 1210, 1233, 2087
s 9 533, 1544, 1859, 2254
s 15 202, 2193, 2204
s 16 197, 207, 209, 212, 2193
s 17 212, 384, 2193, 2204
s 17(1) 212
s 18 2193
s 18(1)(d) 1395, 1399
s 19 1243, 1744, 2087
s 29 400
ss 29–31 189, 2253, 2254
s 30 192
s 31 2252, 2261
s 31(2) 1421
s 31(3) 189
s 31(4) 192
s 34 1744, 1757
s 37 55, 631, 798, 1133, 1187, 1544, 1545, 1743, 2087, 2254
s 37(1) 55, 1743
s 37(3) 1209
s 39 1174
s 40 2291
s 40A 117
s 41(2) 183
s 51 230, 1042, 1165, 2136, 2146
s 51(1) 227, 228, 1395, 1846, 2145, 2146, 2150
s 51(3) 227, 228, 1795, 1849, 2145, 2157
s 51(6) 231, 2146, 2160
s 51(7) 228, 231, 2151, 2160
s 51(13) 2160
s 61(1) 1279
s 61(1)(iii) 714
s 61(1),(3) 250
s 70 1801
s 72 2093
s 90 1683, 2070
s 128 2269
s 139(2) 2291
s 152(1) 362
s 152(4) 250, 794
Sch 1 182
para 1 2043
para 2(a),(b) 2043
para 3 714, 1043, 1134, 1279
para 3(d) 250
para 3(f)(iv) 42
Sch 5 362
Sch 7 250, 794
Serious Crime Act 2015
s 70 928, 929
s 71 929
s 72 929
s 73 929, 943
s 74 931
s 75 931
s 76 887
s 85 898, 1251

Serious Crime Act 2015—*continued*
Sch 4
para 5 1251
para 17 898
Serious Organised Crime and Police Act 2005
s 125(2) 1230
s 125(3) 1230
s 125(4) 1231
s 125(5) 1231
s 125(7) 1232
Sex Discrimination Act 1975 702, 944
Sexual Offences Act 2003
s 139 295
Sch 6 295
Social Security Act 1985
s 21 353
Sch 4
para 1 353
Social Security Act 1986
s 86 251
s 86(1) 353, 355, 1063
Sch 10 1065
para 35 1063
para 42 251
para 43 355
para 102 353
Social Security Act 1998 400
s 86 401, 403
s 86(1) 406, 409, 410, 415, 416
s 86(2) 416
Sch 7
para 18 401
para 19 403
para 22 406
para 23 409
para 31 410
para 41 415
para 47 416
Sch 8 401, 403
Social Security (Consequential Provisions) Act 1975
s 1(3) 357
Sch 2
para 43 357
Social Security (Consequential Provisions) Act 1992
s 4 251, 355, 416, 485, 519, 667, 1063, 1065
Sch 2
para 3 1063, 1065
para 7 251, 355
para 108 485, 519, 667
para 114 416
Social Security Administration Act 1992 1251
Social Security and Housing Benefit Act 1982
s 48(5) 1065
Sch 4
para 2 1065
Social Security Contributions and Benefits Act 1992 702
ss 55A–55C 2525
s 175 2525
Social Security Pensions Act 1975
s 65(1) 353
s 65(3) 357
Sch 4
para 15 353

Social Security Pensions Act 1975—*continued*
Sch 5 357
Social Services and Wellbeing (Wales) Act 2014 484
Social Work (Scotland) Act 1968
s 95(1) 1065
Sch 8
para 34 1065
Solicitors Act 1974 1255
s 50 158, 1989
s 65(2) 1827
s 73 858, 1042
South Africa Act 1995
s 1 1103
Sch
para 7(2) 1103
State Immunity Act 1978
s 12 1347
State Pension Credit Act 2002
s 14 520
Sch 2
para 30 520
Statute Law (Repeals) Act 1969 1122
Statute Law (Repeals) Act 1986 795, 799, 804
Statute Law (Repeals) Act 1993 806, 1076, 1259
Suicide Act 1961 1024
Supplementary Benefits Act 1976
s 35(2) 251, 355, 1063, 1065
Sch 7
para 8 1063
para 13 1065
para 17 251
para 20 355
Surrogacy Arrangements Act 1985 1256

Tax Credits Act 1999
s 1(2) 416, 519, 667
Sch 1
paras 1, 6(d)(ii) 519
paras 1, 6(d)(iii) 667
paras 1, 6(f)(ii) 416
Tax Credits Act 2002
s 47 353, 485, 520, 634, 667
Sch 3 634
para 1 353
para 15 485, 520, 667
para 16 485
para 18 520
para 20 667
Taxation of Pensions Act 2014 1187, 2454
Theft Act 1968
s 31 2093
Tribunals, Courts and Enforcement Act 2007 400, 1134
Pt 3 2338
s 11 400
s 13 400
s 19(1) 1239
s 26 416
s 62(3) 341, 413, 801, 806, 1084
s 67 801
s 93(2) 359
s 93(3) 361
s 93(4) 362
s 94 361
Tribunals, Courts and Enforcement Act 2007—*continued*
s 141 1239
Sch 12 2338
Sch 13
para 22 1084
para 36 341
para 69 801
para 70 801
para 82 806
para 95 413
Sch 23
Pt 2 416
Trustee Act 1925
s 44(vii) 1244
Trusts of Land and Appointment of Trustees Act 1996 646, 1134, 1170, 1260, 1429, 2135, 2146, 2823, 2857, 2869
s 14 15, 110, 226, 359, 1044, 1744, 2036, 2048, 2298
s 14(2)(a) 18
s 14(2)(b) 16, 18, 19
s 15 17, 18
s 25(1) 926
s 25(2) 1040, 1059
s 25(4),(5) 1059
Sch 3
para 25 926
Sch 4 1059

Wages Act 1986
s 32(1) 357
Sch 4
para 4 357
Welfare Reform Act 2007
s 28(1) 416, 485, 520, 637, 667
Sch 3
para 6 520
para 6(1) 485, 637, 667
para 6(2) 485
para 6(5) 637
para 6(6) 667
para 7(1) 416
para 7(7) 416
Welfare Reform Act 2009
s 9(3)(b) 416
s 58(1) 416
s 136 408
Sch 7 416
Welfare Reform Act 2012
s 31 485, 520, 667, 1252, 1254
s 91 406
s 137 403
Sch 2
para 1 485, 520, 667
para 9 1252
para 11 1252
para 12 1254
Sch 9
para 2 406
Welfare Reform and Pensions Act 1999 1192, 1264
s 19 1161, 1171, 1174, 1175, 1178, 1185, 1202, 1205, 1209, 1213, 1215
ss 19–46 1161

Welfare Reform and Pensions Act 1999—*continued*
s 21 1187, 1188, 1189
s 22(2),(3) 1129
s 23 2525
s 23(1)(a) 2514
s 29 1175, 1454
s 29(1) 1162
s 34(1) 1454, 2519
s 35(2) 2520
s 38(2)(c) 2514
s 41 1175
s 41(2)(a) 2514
s 41(3)(b) 1175, 1454
s 47 1161
ss 47–51 2525
ss 47(3),(4) 2524
ss 49 2524
ss 49A 2525
s 84(1) 1128, 1131, 1251
s 85(3)(b) 1203
s 88 1187, 1189
Sch 3
para 2 1161
para 3 1171
para 4 1174, 1175

Welfare Reform and Pensions Act 1999—*continued*
Sch 3—*continued*
para 5 1178
para 6 1185
para 7 1202
para 8 1205
para 9 1209
para 10 1213
para 11 1215
Sch 4
para 1 1187
para 2 1188
para 3 1189
Sch 12
para 1 1251
para 3 1128
para 4 1131
Sch 13
Pt II 1187, 1189
Wills Act 1837 702
s 18B(1) 702
s 18C 702

Youth Justice and Criminal Evidence Act 1999 1684
Pt 2 1138, 1763
s 29 625

Table of Statutory Instruments

References are to page numbers.

A chronological list of statutory instruments referred to in this work appears at the end of the alphabetical list below.

Access to Justice Act 1999 (Destination of Appeals) (Family Proceedings) (Amendment) Order 2016, SI 2016/891 202, 1865, 2373
Access to Justice Act 1999 (Destination of Appeals) (Family Proceedings) Order 2009, SI 2009/871 1059
Access to Justice Act 1999 (Destination of Appeals) (Family Proceedings) Order 2011, SI 2011/1044 2371
Access to Justice Act 1999 (Destination of Appeals) (Family Proceedings) Order 2014, SI 2014/602 1863, 2371
Access to Justice Act 1999 (Destination of Appeals) Order 2000, SI 2000/1071 799, 1234
Access to Justice Act 1999 (Destination of Appeals) Order 2016, SI 2016/917 799, 1234
Access to Justice (Northern Ireland) Order 2003, SI 2003/435 368
Act of Sederunt (Rules for the Registration of Custody Orders of the Sheriff Court) 1988, SI 1988/613 180, 853
Act of Sederunt (Rules of the Court of Session 1994) 1994, SI 1994/1443
- r 260V 181
- r 260V(4) 181

Administration of Insolvent Estates of Deceased Persons Order 1986, SI 1986/1999 1028
Adopted Children and Adoption Contact Registers Regulations 2005, SI 2005/924 292, 296
- reg 9 298

Adoption Agencies (Miscellaneous Amendments) Regulations 2013, SI 2013/985 2376, 2377, 2381, 2382, 2383, 2384
Adoption Agencies (Panel and Consequential Amendments) Regulations 2012, SI 2012/1410 2380, 2389, 2392
Adoption Agencies Regulations 2005, SI 2005/389 2606
- Pt 6 258
- reg 3 1678
- reg 14 283
- reg 14(1)(a) 283
- reg 14(1)(b)(i) 283
- reg 14(1)(b)(iii) 283
- reg 14(1)(c) 283
- reg 19 262
- reg 19A 261
- reg 20 259
- reg 23(3) 1669
- reg 35(4) 259
- reg 41 1657
- reg 42 1657
- reg 45(4)(a) 592

Adoption Agencies Regulations 2005, SI 2005/389—*continued*
- reg 45(4)(b),(c) 592
- reg 46 267
- reg 47 267
- reg 47(2) 267

Adoption Agencies (Wales) Regulations 2005, SI 2005/1313
- reg 3 1678

Adoption Agency Regulations 1983, SI 1983/1964
- reg 14 571

Adoption and Care Planning (Miscellaneous Amendments) Regulations 2014, SI 2014/1556 2402, 2407, 2420, 2423
Adoption and Children Act 2002 (Commencement No 9) Order 2005, SI 2005/2213 245
Adoption and Children (Miscellaneous Amendments) Regulations 2005, SI 2005/3482 2383, 2386, 2394
Adoption and Children (Scotland) Act 2007 (Consequential Modifications) Order 2011, SI 2011/1740 281, 302, 308, 314, 324, 329, 398, 460, 838
Adoption and Children (Scotland) Act 2007 (Consequential Provisions) Order 2010, SI 2010/2469 281
Adoption (Designation of Overseas Adoptions) Order 1973, SI 1973/19 1015
Adoption (Northern Ireland) Order 1987, SI 1987/2203
- art 17(1) 1668
- art 18(1) 1668

Adoption (Recognition of Overseas Adoptions) Regulations 2013, SI 2013/1801 292, 1015
Adoption Rules 1984, SI 1984/265
- r 5(1) 807
- r 6(1),(2) 807
- r 17(1) 807
- r 18(1),(2) 807
- r 53(2) 1657
- r 53(4 1661

Adoptions with a Foreign Element (Amendment) Regulations 2009, SI 2009/2563 2384
Adoptions with a Foreign Element Regulations 2005, SI 2005/392 280, 300, 1664, 1670, 2375
- Pt 3
  - Ch 1 292
- reg 3 300
- reg 5 300
- reg 11(1) 301
- reg 11(1)(a) 301

Allocation and Transfer of Proceedings Order 2008, SI 2008/2836 2458

Apprenticeships, Skills, Children and Learning Act 2009 (Consequential Amendments) (England and Wales) Order 2010, SI 2010/1080 609, 615
Armed Forces (Forfeitures and Deductions) Regulations 2009, SI 2009/1109 105, 353, 2015
Arrangements for Placement of Children by Voluntary Organisations and others (England) Regulations 2011, SI 2011/582 497
Pt 2 497
Pt 3 497
Pt 4 498
Pt 5 498
Pt 6 498
Attachment of Debts (Expenses) Order 1996, SI 1996/3098 803, 1245
Attachment of Earnings (Employer's Deduction) Order 1991, SI 1991/356 344
Blood Tests (Evidence of Paternity) Regulations 1971, SI 1971/1861 920, 923
Care Act 2014 and Children and Families Act 2014 (Consequential Amendments) Order 2015, SI 2015/914 488, 490
Care Leavers (England) Regulations 2010, SI 2010/2571 503
reg 3 503
reg 4 503
reg 5 503
reg 6 507
reg 7 507
reg 8 503
reg 8(1) 506
reg 9(2) 503
Sch 2 503
Care Planning and Care Leavers (Amendment) Regulations 2014, SI 2014/1917 2401, 2415, 2427
Care Planning and Fostering (Miscellaneous Amendments) (England) Regulations 2015, SI 2015/495 2399, 2408, 2411, 2413, 2414, 2422, 2427
Care Planning, Placement and Case Review and Fostering Services (Miscellaneous Amendments) Regulations 2013, SI 2013/984 2409, 2422
Care Planning, Placement and Case Review (England) (Miscellaneous Amendments) Regulations 2013, SI 2013/706 2399, 2417, 2418, 2420, 2423
Care Planning, Placement and Case Review (England) Regulations 2010, SI 2010/959 497, 501, 503, 507, 509, 514, 545, 549, 551, 552, 2398
Pt 5 501
Pt 6 500
Pt 8 502
reg 8 552, 553
reg 25A 262
reg 44 506
reg 45 514
Care Planning, Placement and Case Review (England) Regulations 2010, SI 2010/959—*continued*
reg 45(3) 514
reg 46 514
Care Planning, Placement and Case Review (Wales) Regulations 2015, SI 2015/1818
reg 8 552
reg 9 552
Charging Orders (Orders for Sale Financial Thresholds) Regulations 2013, SI 2013/491 361
Child Abduction and Custody Act 1985 (Isle of Man) Order 1994, SI 1994/2799 375
Child Abduction and Custody (Cayman Islands) Order 1997, SI 1997/2574 375
Child Abduction and Custody (Parties to Conventions) (Amendment) (No 2) Order 2011, SI 2011/1081 2430
Child Abduction and Custody (Parties to Conventions) (Amendment) Order 2009, SI 2009/702 2430
Child Abduction and Custody (Parties to Conventions) Order 1986, SI 1986/1159 364, 2427
Child Abduction and Custody (Parties to Conventions) Order 1993, SI 1993/3144 369
Child Arrangements Order (Consequential Amendments to Subordinate Legislation) Order 2014, SI 2014/852 2399
Child Maintenance and Other Payments Act 2008 (Commencement) Order 2008, SI 2008/1476 404
Child Maintenance (Written Agreements) Order 1993, SI 1993/620 408
art 2 407
Child Support Act 1991 (Consequential Amendments) Order 1994, SI 1994/731 652, 821
Child Support Appeals (Jurisdiction of Courts) Order 2002, SI 2002/1915 411, 1422, 2431
Child Support (Applications: Prescribed Date) Regulations 2003, SI 2003/194 404
Child Support (Collection and Enforcement) Regulations 1992, SI 1992/1989
Pt IV 411, 2492
reg 22 411
reg 25B 400
reg 31 411
reg 34(3),(4) 414
Child Support Information Regulations 2008, SI 2008/2551
reg 3(1) 1852
reg 4(1) 1852
reg 4(2) 1853
reg 4(2)(a) 1852
reg 6(2)(a) 1852
Child Support (Maintenance Arrangements and Jurisdiction) Regulations 1992, SI 1992/2645
reg 2 407
reg 3(2) 410
reg 4(1) 409
reg 7 815

Child Support (Maintenance Calculation Procedure) Regulations 2000, SI 2001/157
Pt VII 407
reg 21 402
reg 26 410
reg 28 410
Child Support Maintenance Calculation Regulations 2012, SI 2012/2677 403, 404
reg 12 410
Child Support (Variations) Regulations 2000, SI 2000/156 404
Children Act 1989 Representations Procedure (England) Regulations 2006, SI 2006/1738
reg 8(1) 517
Children Act (Miscellaneous Amendments) (England) Regulations 2002, SI 2002/546 2432, 2434, 2435
Children (Admissibility of Hearsay Evidence) Order 1993, SI 1993/621 623, 2431, 2632
Art 2 1778
Children (Allocation of Proceedings) Order 1991, SI 1991/1677
art 3 669
art 3C(2) 265, 267, 269
art 4(1) 673
art 4(2) 673
art 5 669
arts 5–13 673
art 7(2) 669
art 17 264
Children and Families Act 2014 (Transitional Proceedings) Order 2014, SI 2014/1042 134, 136, 139, 141, 144, 147, 150, 152, 155, 157, 159, 163, 166, 169, 171
Children and Family Court Advisory and Support Service (Reviewed Case Referral) Regulations 2004, SI 2004/2187 514
Children (Leaving Care) (England) Regulations 2001, SI 2001/2874 503
Children (Northern Ireland Consequential Amendments) Order 1995, SI 1995/756 367, 372, 374, 399, 410, 838, 840, 841, 844, 845, 846, 863, 1064, 1065, 1068, 1073, 1106
Children (Northern Ireland) Order 1995, SI 1995/755 690, 699, 849, 850, 852, 857, 1083, 1089, 1091, 1093, 1096, 1100, 1101, 1108, 1109, 1111, 1114, 1115, 1117, 1256
Children (Prescribed Orders – Northern Ireland, Guernsey and Isle of Man) Regulations 1991, SI 1991/2032 632
Children (Secure Accommodation) Amendment Regulations 1992, SI 1992/2117 2432, 2433
Children (Secure Accommodation) Amendment Regulations 1995, SI 1995/1398 2432, 2435
Children (Secure Accommodation) (Amendment) (England) Regulations 2012, SI 2012/3134 2433
Children (Secure Accommodation) (Amendment) (England) Regulations 2015, SI 2015/188 171
Children (Secure Accommodation) (Amendment) (England) Regulations 2015, SI 2015/1883 513, 1540, 2433
Children (Secure Accommodation) (No 2) Regulations 1991, SI 1991/2034 171, 511, 1540, 2435
reg 2(1) 171
reg 2(2) 171
Children (Secure Accommodation) Regulations 1991, SI 1991/1505 171, 511, 1540, 2432
reg 6 513
reg 6(1)(a) 513
reg 6(2)(a) 513
reg 6(2)(b) 513
reg 8 171
reg 10 511
reg 11 511
reg 12 511
reg 14 172
Children (Secure Accommodation) (Wales) Regulations 2015, SI 2015/1988 2432, 2435
Children's Hearings (Scotland) Act 2011 (Consequential and Transitional Provisions and Savings) Order 2013, SI 2013/1465 280, 372, 398, 522, 585, 678, 1555
Children's Homes and Looked after Children (Miscellaneous Amendments) (England) Regulations 2013, SI 2013/3239 2404, 2405, 2412, 2422, 2426
Civil Jurisdiction and Judgments Act 1982 (Amendment) Order 1989, SI 1989/1346 689
Civil Jurisdiction and Judgments Act 1982 (Amendment) Order 1990, SI 1990/2591 689
Civil Jurisdiction and Judgments Act 1982 (Amendment) Order 2000, SI 2000/1824 689
Civil Jurisdiction and Judgments (Amendment) Regulations 2014, SI 2014/2947 689
Civil Jurisdiction and Judgments (Hague Convention on Choice of Court Agreements 2005) Regulations 2015, SI 2015/1644 689, 692, 693, 694, 695, 696
Civil Jurisdiction and Judgments (Maintenance) and International Recovery of Maintenance (Hague Convention 2007 etc) (Amendment) Order 2015, SI 2015/1489 2444, 2491, 2493
Civil Jurisdiction and Judgments (Maintenance) Regulations 2011, SI 2011/1484 91, 251, 340, 355, 415, 655, 656, 696, 747, 760, 778, 780, 781, 823, 1064, 1071, 1075, 1077, 1126, 1127, 1195, 1207, 1215, 1254, 2436, 2857, 2858
reg 2(1)(a) 2879
reg 3 2871, 2875
Sch 1
Pt 2 2871
Pt 3 2875
Civil Jurisdiction and Judgments (Maintenance) (Rules of Court) Regulations 2011, SI 2011/1215 689
Civil Jurisdiction and Judgments Order 2001, SI 2001/3929 251, 355, 689, 696, 1075, 1126, 1254, 2436
Civil Jurisdiction and Judgments (Protection Measures) Regulations 2014, SI 2014/3298 1251, 2003
Civil Jurisdiction and Judgments Regulations 2007, SI 2007/1655 251, 355, 689, 1075, 1126, 1254

Civil Jurisdiction and Judgments Regulations 2009, SI 2009/3131 689, 690, 691, 692, 693, 694, 695, 696
Civil Legal Aid (General) Regulations 1989, SI 1989/339
reg 94(d)(i) 21
Civil Legal Aid (Merits Criteria) Regulations 2013, SI 2013/104
reg 18(2) 2486
Civil Legal Aid (Procedure) Regulations 2012, SI 2012/3098 2137
reg 33 440
reg 37(3) 1043
Civil Legal Aid (Remuneration) (Amendment) Regulations 2013, SI 2013/2877 2450
Civil Legal Aid (Remuneration) Regulations 2013, SI 2013/422 686, 2448
Civil Legal Aid (Statutory Charge) Regulations 2013, SI 2013/503 1044
reg 2(1) 1043
reg 5 1044
reg 5(1)(b)(i) 1187
reg 9 1044
reg 13(1) 1044
reg 14 1044
reg 22 1044
Civil Partnership Act 2004 (Amendments to Subordinate Legislation) Order 2005, SI 2005/2114 2455
Civil Partnership Act 2004 (International Immunities and Privileges, Companies and Adoption) Order 2005, SI 2005/3542 298
Civil Partnership Act 2004 (Overseas Relationships and Consequential, etc Amendments) Order 2005, SI 2005/3129 520, 720, 789
Civil Partnership Act 2004 (Overseas Relationships) Order 2005, SI 2005/3135 720, 789
Civil Partnership Act 2004 (Overseas Relationships) Order 2012, SI 2012/2976 720, 789
Civil Partnership Act 2004 (Tax Credits, etc) (Consequential Amendments) Order 2005, SI 2005/2919 702
Civil Partnership (Amendments to Registration Provisions) Order 2005, SI 2005/2000 710, 711
Civil Partnership (Contracted-out Occupational and Appropriate Personal Pension Schemes) (Surviving Civil Partners) Order 2005, SI 2005/2050 702
Civil Partnership (Family Proceedings and Housing Consequential Amendments) Order 2005, SI 2005/3336 402, 838, 840, 841, 844, 849, 852, 860, 863, 1145
Civil Partnership (Jurisdiction and Recognition of Judgments) Regulations 2005, SI 2005/3334 46, 704, 723, 828, 1897, 2776
Civil Partnership (Miscellaneous and Consequential Provisions) Order 2005, SI 2005/3029 702
Civil Partnership (Pensions and Benefit Payments) (Consequential, etc Provisions) Order 2005, SI 2005/2053 702
Civil Partnership (Pensions, Social Security and Child Support) (Consequential, etc Provisions) Order 2005, SI 2005/2877 702, 2513, 2514, 2516, 2524, 2525, 2526
art 2(5) 751, 756
Sch 5
para 1 751, 756
para 2(1) 751, 756
para 2(2) 751
para 2(3) 756
Civil Partnership (Registration Provisions) Regulations 2005, SI 2005/3176 701
Civil Partnership (Supplementary Provisions Relating to the Recognition of Overseas Dissolutions, Annulments or Legal Separations) (England and Wales and Northern Ireland) Regulations 2005, SI 2005/3104 726, 727, 728, 729
Civil Partnership (Treatment of Overseas Relationships) (No 2) Order 2005, SI 2005/3284 721
Civil Partnership (Treatment of Overseas Relationships) Order 2005, SI 2005/3042 721
Civil Procedure (Modification of Enactments) Order 2002, SI 2002/439 362, 803, 804, 806, 1245
Civil Procedure (Modification of Supreme Court Act 1981) Order 2004, SI 2004/1033 1237, 1239
Civil Procedure Rules 1998, SI 1998/3132 1221, 1261, 2031
Pt 1 544
r 1.1 1879
r 1.1(1) 2350
r 1.1(2)(c) 2286
r 1.3 1879, 2350
r 1.4 17
r 2.1(2) 1279
r 2.3(1) 1285, 1722, 2123
r 2.8 39
r 2.8(2) 115, 122
r 2.9 1858
r 3.1 17, 1320
r 3.1(2) 2290
r 3.1(2)(a) 39
r 3.1(3) 2290
r 3.1(7) 212
r 3.3(5) 212
r 3.9 1324
r 3.11 1324, 2080
r 5.4C 1755
r 5.5 2351, 2353
Pt 6 115, 2292
r 6 2273
r 6.6 23
r 6.13 221
r 6.13(1) 221
r 6.13(2) 222
r 6.13(4) 222
r 6.13(6) 222
r 6.15 122, 2288, 2352
r 6.17 221
rr 6.17–6.31 2823
r 6.21(2) 131
r 6.25(2) 222

Civil Procedure Rules 1998, SI 1998/
3132—*continued*
r 6.25(3) 222
r 6.25(5) 222
r 6.25(6) 222
r 6.27 122, 2288
r 6.32 23
r 6.33 23
r 6.35 23
Pt 7 17, 18, 19, 37, 2042
r 7.6 23
r 7.11 235, 999, 2057
Pt 8 37, 235, 999, 1001, 1422, 2051, 2273, 2299
r 8.2 22, 37, 38, 236
r 8.3 37, 39
r 8.3(1) 23
r 8.4 37, 39
r 8.5 37, 39
r 8.5(1) 23
r 8.5(2) 23
r 8.5(5),(6) 24
r 8.6 37
r 8.9 236
r 10.3(1) 23
r 10.3(2) 23
Pt 16 17, 18, 20
Pt 18 2055
r 18.1 17, 19, 1390
r 18.2 17, 19
Pt 19 2322
r 19.1 387
r 19.2 19, 387
r 19.2(2) 17, 1439
r 19.4A 191, 235, 236, 995, 996, 1546
r 19.4A(2) 995, 996
r 19.7 23
r 20.3(1) 221
Pt 21 219, 223, 1680, 2070
r 21.1 1681
r 21.1(1) 220
r 21.1(2) 1285
r 21.1(2)(b) 219
r 21.1(2)(d) 219, 223, 1638
r 21.1(2)(e) 222, 223
r 21.2(2) 220
r 21.2(3) 220
r 21.2(4) 220
r 21.2(5) 220
r 21.3 223
r 21.3(2) 220, 223
r 21.3(3) 220, 223
r 21.3(4) 220, 224
r 21.4(2) 220, 225
r 21.4(3) 220, 221, 224, 225
r 21.5 220, 224
r 21.5(4)(a) 221
r 21.5(4)(b) 221
r 21.6 220, 221
r 21.6(4) 221
r 21.6(5) 221
r 21.7 221
r 21.8(1) 222
r 21.8(2) 222
r 21.8(3) 222

Civil Procedure Rules 1998, SI 1998/
3132—*continued*
r 21.8(4) 221
r 21.9(1) 221
r 21.9(2) 221
r 21.9(6) 223
r 21.10(1) 222
r 21.10(2) 222
r 21.11 1684
r 21.11(1) 222
r 21.11(2) 222
r 21.11(3) 223
r 21.13 222
Pt 22 1722, 2055, 2084, 2089, 2117, 2122
r 22.1(1) 38
r 22.19 1768
Pt 23 37, 83, 84, 85, 86, 87, 88, 94, 95, 96, 98, 100, 102, 124, 125, 127, 128, 191, 213, 234, 2008, 2009, 2087, 2117, 2160, 2167, 2172
r 23.2(1) 1331
r 23.3(2)(b) 38
r 23.7(1) 131, 2089
r 23.7(1)(a) 39
r 23.7(1)(b) 226
r 23.7(2) 2089
r 23.7(3)(b) 39
r 23.7(4) 2089
r 23.8 39
r 23.10 39, 212
r 23.10(1) 38
r 23.10(2) 38
Pt 25 37, 191, 1741, 1744, 1747
r 25.1 39
r 25.1(1) 1742
r 25.1(1)(a) 37
r 25.1(1)(f) 2088
r 25.1(1)(h) 2088
r 25.2 39
r 25.2(1) 37, 38
r 25.2(2) 37, 38
r 25.2(3) 2090
r 25.3(1) 37, 38
r 25.3(2) 37, 38
r 25.3(3) 38
r 25.4 214
r 25.10 40
r 26.5(3)–(5) 2054
rr 26.6–26.10 2054
rr 29.6–29.8 24
Pt 30 2043
r 30.6 796
Pt 31 19
r 31.1 1752
r 31.2 17, 1753
r 31.3 17
r 31.3(1) 1753
rr 31.5–31.15 1755
r 31.5(1) 1755
r 31.6 17
r 31.8 17
r 31.10(3) 1754
r 31.11 1439
r 31.15 1755

Civil Procedure Rules 1998, SI 1998/3132—*continued*
r 31.19 1755
r 31.22(1) 1755
Pt 32 2089
r 32.1(3) 2119
r 32.2 1763
r 32.4(3)(b) 2119
r 32.6(1) 2117
r 32.6(2) 2117
r 32.6(2)(a) 2123
r 32.13(2) 2123
r 32.13(4) 2123
r 32.14 1934
r 32.15(2) 2117
r 35.1 17
r 35.4 17
r 35.8 1798
r 35.8(1) 1799
r 35.14 1800
r 35.15 1825
Pt 36 1021
r 39.2 17, 129, 791
r 39.2(1) 39
r 39.3 128, 129, 1834
Pt 40 1857
r 40.6 233
r 40.12 212, 1234
Pt 44 227, 1021, 1846
r 44.1 232, 1285, 1395, 1848
r 44.2 22, 48, 50, 55, 232, 234, 481, 911, 1042, 1164, 1196, 1210, 1248, 1264, 1795, 1848, 1849
r 44.2(1) 228
r 44.2(2) 227, 1277, 1846
r 44.2(2)(b) 227
r 44.2(3) 1248
r 44.2(4) 227, 229
r 44.2(5) 227, 229
r 44.2(6) 229
r 44.2(8) 230
r 44.3 228, 232
r 44.3(1)–(5) 230
r 44.3(1)(a) 230
r 44.3(1)(b) 230
r 44.3(2) 230
r 44.3(3) 230
r 44.3(4) 230
r 44.4 228
r 44.4(1)(a) 230
r 44.4(1)(b) 230
r 44.4(3) 230
r 44.6 231, 232, 1164
r 44.7 229, 234
r 44.8 229
r 44.11 1248
r 45.6 2026
r 45.8 227, 801, 1846, 2018
Pt 46 227, 1846
r 46.3 228
r 46.4 222
r 46.8 231
r 46.15 191
r 46.16 191

Civil Procedure Rules 1998, SI 1998/3132—*continued*
r 46.17 191
r 46.18 191
r 46.19 191
Pt 47 227, 1846
r 47.1 232
r 47.2 232
r 47.6(1) 233
r 47.6(2) 232, 233
r 47.7 233
r 47.8 233
r 47.9(1) 233
r 47.9(2) 233
r 47.9(4) 233
r 47.10 233
r 47.12(1) 233
r 47.12(2) 233
r 47.12(3) 233
r 47.13 233
r 47.14(1) 233
r 47.14(2) 233
r 47.14(3),(4) 233
r 47.14(6) 234
r 47.14(7) 234
r 47.16 234
r 47.17 234
r 47.20 234
r 47.21–47.24 234
Pt 50 512
Pt 52 203, 400, 799, 1234, 1848, 1863, 1871
r 52.1(3) 208
r 52.3 207, 243, 799, 1234, 1235, 1243, 1865
r 52.3(1)(a) 793
r 52.3(2) 207
r 52.3(3) 207, 243
r 52.3(6) 455
r 52.4 207, 566
r 52.4(2)(b) 1224
r 52.5(4) 205, 207
r 52.6(2) 205, 207
r 52.7 211, 566, 802
r 52.8 192
r 52.9(2) 1387
r 52.10 1234
r 52.10(2) 535, 800, 1234
r 52.10(2)(a) 212
r 52.11 204, 1871
r 52.11(2) 800
r 52.12 192
r 52.12(2)(a) 205
r 52.12(3) 208
r 52.13 197, 208, 244
r 52.14(2) 244
r 52.15 190
r 52.17 212, 214, 1235
r 52.17(1) 213
r 52.17(4) 213
r 52.17(5) 213
r 52.17(6) 213
r 52.18 205
r 52.20(1) 209
r 52.20(2) 209
r 52.21(2) 209

Civil Procedure Rules 1998, SI 1998/3132—*continued*
Pt 54 189, 400, 412, 800, 1001, 1237, 1239, 2048
r 54.1 189
r 54.1A 191
r 54.2 192, 1237, 1239
r 54.3 192, 1237, 1239
r 54.4 800, 1239
r 54.5 189, 1239
r 54.7 191
r 54.7A 189
r 54.8 191
r 54.8(2)(a) 190
r 54.8(2)(b) 190
r 54.8(4) 190
r 54.10 191
r 54.12 190, 1387
r 54.14 191
r 54.15 191
r 54.17 191
Pt 57 22
r 57.15 22
r 57.16 22, 1025
r 57.16(1) 22
r 57.16(3) 23
r 57.16(3A) 23, 24
r 57.16(4) 23, 24
r 57.16(4A) 23
r 57.16(5) 23, 24, 1025
rr 57.17–57.23 1014, 1222
r 57.18(2) 1222
Pt 65 37, 1231
r 65.28 37
r 65.29 40, 126, 128
r 65.30 128
r 66.7(1)(a) 2291
Pt 69 802
Pt 70 1928
r 70.2(2)(b) 103
Pt 71 121, 1928
r 71.1 121
r 71.2(2)(a) 122
r 71.2(2)(b)(i) 122
r 71.2(6) 103, 120
r 71.2(7) 120
r 71.3 122
r 71.5(1)(a) 122
r 71.5(1)(b) 123
r 71.5(1)(c) 123
r 71.6(2) 122
r 71.6(3)(b) 123
r 71.8 121, 1929
r 71.8(1) 123
r 71.8(2) 123
r 71.8(4) 123
Pt 72 803, 1244, 1723, 1928
r 72.1(1) 113
r 72.2(1) 117
r 72.3 114
r 72.3(1)(b) 114
r 72.3(2)(a) 1928
r 72.4(2)(a) 114
r 72.4(2)(b) 114
r 72.4(4) 115

Civil Procedure Rules 1998, SI 1998/3132—*continued*
r 72.4(5) 114
r 72.5(1)(a) 115
r 72.5(1)(b) 115
r 72.5(2) 115
r 72.6(1) 115
r 72.6(2) 115
r 72.6(3) 115
r 72.6(4) 115
r 72.7(1) 116
r 72.7(2)(a) 116
r 72.7(2)(b) 116
r 72.7(3) 116
r 72.7(4)(a) 116
r 72.7(4)(b) 116
r 72.7(5) 116
r 72.7(6) 116
r 72.8(1) 116
r 72.8(3) 117
r 72.8(4) 116, 117
r 72.8(5) 117
r 72.8(6)(a) 117
r 72.8(6)(b) 117
r 72.8(6)(c) 117
r 72.8(6)(d) 117
r 72.9(1) 117
r 72.9(2) 117
Pt 73 108, 413, 2022, 2023
r 73.1 2022
r 73.10 361
r 73.10C 110, 2022
Pt 74 83, 93
r 74.1 83
r 74.3 84, 96
r 74.4(1) 84, 87
r 74.4(1)(a) 96
r 74.4(1)(b) 96
r 74.4(2) 84, 87, 96
r 74.4(4) 87
r 74.4(5)(a) 96
r 74.4(5)(b) 96
r 74.4(5)(c) 96
r 74.4(6) 96
r 74.6 85, 88, 96, 99
r 74.7 99
r 74.7(1),(2) 85
r 74.7(3) 100
r 74.7A 95
r 74.7B 95
r 74.7C 95
r 74.8 96, 97, 99
r 74.9 85, 88, 99
r 74.9(1) 95
r 74.12 83, 86, 94
r 74.13(1) 83, 86, 94
r 74.13(2) 83, 86, 94
r 74.15 98
r 74.16 98
r 74.16(4) 99
r 74.16(5) 99, 100
r 74.17 97
r 74.18 97, 98
rr 74.27–74.33 2811

Civil Procedure Rules 1998, SI 1998/ 3132—*continued*
r 74.27(d) 101
r 74.28 100
r 74.31 101
r 74.31(1) 101
r 74.32 102
rr 74.34–74.41 2004
r 74.34(f)(i)–(iv) 2004
r 74.37 2005
r 74.38 2005
rr 74.38–74.50 2004
r 74.39 2005
r 74.41 2006
r 74.42 2006
r 74.44 2007
r 74.45 2008
r 74.46 2008
r 74.47 2008
r 74.49 2009
Pt 81 124, 125, 1231, 1983
S 9 795
r 81.1 1983
r 81.2 1985
r 81.3 127, 1986
r 81.4 797, 857, 1986
rr 81.4–81.11 40
r 81.4(1)(a) 124
r 81.5 40, 125, 127, 1987, 2005
r 81.5(1) 858
r 81.6 1987
r 81.7 40, 127, 1987
r 81.8 1987, 2005
r 81.9 797, 1988
r 81.10 125, 127, 1988
r 81.11 1989
r 81.12 1990
r 81.13 1990
r 81.14 1990
r 81.16 792, 804, 1989
r 81.17 1991
r 81.18 1991
r 81.19 130, 179, 1992
r 81.20 130, 1992
r 81.21 130, 1992
r 81.22 130, 1993
r 81.23 130, 1993
r 81.24 130, 1993
r 81.25 130, 1993
r 81.26 130, 1994
r 81.27 1994
r 81.28 128, 129, 1995
r 81.29 130, 1995
r 81.29(2) 131
r 81.30 131, 1995
r 81.31 131
r 81.32 1996
r 81.33 1996
r 81.34 805, 1997
r 81.35 1997
r 81.36 1997
r 81.37 1997
r 81.38 1997
r 82.7 130

Civil Procedure Rules 1998, SI 1998/ 3132—*continued*
Pt 83 801, 1928
r 83.2(3) 111, 124, 801
r 83.2(4) 124
r 83.3 111
r 83.7 112, 802
r 83.9 112, 124
r 83.9(5) 111
r 83.9(5)(b) 112
r 83.13(2) 124
r 83.13(3) 124
r 83.13(5) 124
r 83.13(6) 124
r 83.14 111
r 83.15 111, 113
r 83.15(6)(b)(i) 112
r 83.15(9) 112
r 83.23 111
r 83.24 111
r 83.25 111
r 83.26 124
Pt 84 801
Pt 87 1550
Pt 89 340, 345, 2015
r 89.3 106
r 89.5(1) 107
r 89.5(2) 107
r 89.5(4) 107
r 89.6 107
r 89.7(1) 107
r 89.7(7) 107
r 89.7(9) 107
r 89.7(14) 106, 340
r 89.8(2) 107
r 89.8(4) 107
r 89.8(5) 107
r 89.9(1) 107
r 89.14(3) 345
Sch 1 512, 2051
RSC Ord 99
r 4 2271
Sch 2 2051
Civil Procedure (Amendment) Rules 1999, SI 1999/ 1008 2033, 2036
Civil Procedure (Amendment) Rules 2000, SI 2000/ 221 2050, 2054, 2058, 2079, 2111, 2193, 2194, 2197, 2198, 2199, 2200, 2201, 2202, 2203
Civil Procedure (Amendment No 3) Rules 2000, SI 2000/1317 2039, 2048, 2049, 2050
Civil Procedure (Amendment No 4) Rules 2000, SI 2000/2092 2034, 2042, 2057, 2252, 2253, 2254, 2255, 2256, 2257, 2258, 2259, 2260, 2261
Civil Procedure (Amendment) Rules 2001, SI 2001/ 256 2050
Civil Procedure (Amendment No 2) Rules 2001, SI 2001/1388 2269
Civil Procedure (Amendment No 4) Rules 2001, SI 2001/2792 2280, 2281, 2284, 2285, 2286, 2287, 2291, 2292, 2293, 2294, 2295
Civil Procedure (Amendment No 5) Rules 2001, SI 2001/4015 2034, 2050, 2110, 2130, 2131, 2287, 2291, 2293

Civil Procedure (Amendment) Rules 2002, SI 2002/2058 2059, 2087, 2260, 2269, 2270, 2280
Civil Procedure (Amendment) Rules 2003, SI 2003/364 2252, 2253, 2254, 2260, 2261
Civil Procedure (Amendment No 2) Rules 2003, SI 2003/1242 2033
Civil Procedure (Amendment No 4) Rules 2003, SI 2003/2113 2203
Civil Procedure (Amendment No 5) Rules 2003, SI 2003/3361 2042, 2060, 2203, 2252, 2254
Civil Procedure (Amendment) Rules 2004, SI 2004/1306 2270, 2278, 2279
Civil Procedure (Amendment No 2) Rules 2004, SI 2004/2072 2034, 2037, 2080
Civil Procedure (Amendment No 4) Rules 2004, SI 2004/3419 2067
Civil Procedure (Amendment No 2) Rules 2005, SI 2005/656 2032
Civil Procedure (Amendment No 3) Rules 2005, SI 2005/2292 2036, 2037, 2070, 2080
Civil Procedure (Amendment No 4) Rules 2005, SI 2005/3515 2033, 2087, 2088
Civil Procedure (Amendment) Rules 2006, SI 2006/1689 2039
Civil Procedure (Amendment No 3) Rules 2006, SI 2006/3435 2036
Civil Procedure (Amendment) Rules 2007, SI 2007/2204 219, 2033, 2034, 2059, 2060, 2061, 2062, 2063, 2064, 2065, 2066, 2067, 2068, 2070, 2142, 2203, 2204
Civil Procedure (Amendment No 2) Rules 2007, SI 2007/3453 2260
Civil Procedure (Amendment) Rules 2008, SI 2008/2178 2034, 2039, 2040, 2041, 2048, 2060, 2063, 2066, 2270
Civil Procedure (Amendment No 2) Rules 2008, SI 2008/3085 2032
Civil Procedure (Amendment No 3) Rules 2008, SI 2008/3327 2036, 2040
Civil Procedure (Amendment No 4) Rules 2008, SI 2014/867 2306, 2308, 2313, 2322, 2323
Civil Procedure (Amendment) Rules 2009, SI 2009/2092 2128, 2129, 2130, 2131, 2203
Civil Procedure (Amendment No 2) Rules 2009, SI 2009/3390 2034, 2035, 2039, 2040, 2042, 2049, 2050, 2057, 2128, 2130, 2255, 2269, 2270, 2280, 2285, 2292
Civil Procedure (Amendment) Rules 2010, SI 2010/621 2067
Civil Procedure (Amendment No 2) Rules 2010, SI 2010/1953 2111
Civil Procedure (Amendment No 3) Rules 2010, SI 2010/2577 2258, 2259
Civil Procedure (Amendment) Rules 2011, SI 2011/88 2039, 2048, 2105, 2109
Civil Procedure (Amendment No 3) Rules 2011, SI 2011/2970 2032
Civil Procedure (Amendment No 4) Rules 2011, SI 2011/3103 2034, 2078
Civil Procedure (Amendment) Rules 2012, SI 2012/505 2285, 2292
Civil Procedure (Amendment No 2) Rules 2012, SI 2012/2208 2111, 2253, 2257, 2285, 2287, 2313
Civil Procedure (Amendment) Rules 2013, SI 2013/262 2031, 2036, 2067, 2070, 2107, 2116, 2128, 2143, 2144, 2145, 2148, 2149, 2150, 2151, 2157, 2158, 2159, 2160, 2161, 2166, 2167, 2168, 2169, 2170, 2171, 2172, 2173, 2174, 2175, 2176, 2255
Civil Procedure (Amendment No 2) Rules 2013, SI 2013/515 2148
Civil Procedure (Amendment No 4) Rules 2013, SI 2013/1412 2255, 2259
Civil Procedure (Amendment No 5) Rules 2013, SI 2013/1571 2032
Civil Procedure (Amendment No 6) Rules 2013, SI 2013/1695 2168
Civil Procedure (Amendment No 7) Rules 2013, SI 2013/1974 2036, 2039, 2049, 2050, 2060, 2070, 2107, 2159
Civil Procedure (Amendment) Rules 2014, SI 2014/407 2033, 2034, 2048, 2060, 2078, 2144, 2160, 2167, 2173, 2176, 2191, 2205, 2269, 2278, 2280, 2281, 2285, 2287, 2292, 2294, 2302, 2305, 2308, 2312, 2313, 2321, 2322, 2323, 2324, 2325, 2326, 2327, 2328, 2329, 2330, 2331, 2332, 2333, 2334, 2335, 2336, 2338, 2339, 2340, 2341, 2342, 2343
Civil Procedure (Amendment No 2) Rules 2014, SI 2014/482 2343, 2344
Civil Procedure (Amendment No 6) Rules 2014, SI 2014/2044 2128, 2269, 2270, 2272, 2273, 2274, 2307, 2325, 2327
Civil Procedure (Amendment No 8) Rules 2014, SI 2014/3299 2004, 2070, 2135, 2136, 2137, 2138, 2139, 2140, 2141, 2175, 2304, 2347, 2348, 2349
Civil Procedure (Amendment) Rules 2015, SI 2015/406 2032
Civil Procedure (Amendment No 2) Rules 2015, SI 2015/670 2258
Civil Procedure (Amendment No 4) Rules 2015, SI 2015/1569 2036, 2040, 2168
Civil Procedure (Amendment) Rules 2016, SI 2016/234 2149, 2168, 2280, 2298
Civil Procedure (Amendment No 3) Rules 2016, SI 2016/788 2172, 2192, 2193, 2194, 2197, 2198, 2199, 2200, 2201, 2202, 2203, 2204, 2205, 2206, 2207, 2208, 2255
Civil Proceedings and Family Proceedings (Amendment) Order 2015, SI 2015/576 38
Civil Proceedings Fees Order 2008, SI 2008/1053
Sch 1
fee 1.4 17, 18, 19
fee 1.5 19, 24, 38
fee 1.9(a) 2254
fee 1.9(a)–(d) 190
fee 1.9(b) 191, 2254
fee 1.9(c) 2254
fee 8.7 108
fee 13.1(a) 207
fee 13.1(b) 207
fee 13.1(c) 208
fee 13.2 208

Civil Proceedings, Family Proceedings and Upper Tribunal Fees (Amendment) Order 2016, SI 2016/402 2479, 2481
Collection of Fines (Final Scheme) Order 2006, SI 2006/1737 340, 341, 343, 344, 345, 348, 354, 357
Community Legal Service (Financial) Regulations 2000, SI 2000/516
reg 52 1169
Companies Act 2006 (Consequential Amendments, Transitional Provisions and Savings) Order 2009, SI 2009/1941 415
Competition Act 1998 (Consequential Provisions) Order 2013, SI 2013/294 809
Contact with Children Regulations 1991, SI 1991/891 169
County Court Jurisdiction Order 2014, SI 2014/503 359, 2298
Art 3 16
County Court Remedies Regulations 2014, SI 2014/982 797, 1135, 1241, 2451, 2458
County Court Rules 1981, SI 1981/1687 2052
Ord 20
r 12 2431
County Court Rules (Northern Ireland) 1991, SI 1981/225
Ord 51
rr 6–11 853
County Courts (Interest on Judgment Debts) Order 1991, SI 1991/1184 2283
art 4(3) 107
Court of Protection Rules 2007, SI 2007/1744 2063
r 3A 1899
Pt 13
rr 90–93 248
Courts Act 2003 (Consequential Amendment) Order 2006, SI 2006/1001 412
Courts Act 2003 (Consequential Amendments) Order 2004, SI 2004/2035 1117, 1250
Courts and Tribunals Fee Remissions Order 2013, SI 2013/2302 2485, 2529
Courts and Tribunals Fees (Miscellaneous Amendments) Order 2014, SI 2014/590 2485
Crime and Courts Act 2013 (Family Court: Consequential Provision) (No 2) Order 2014, SI 2014/879 2438, 2439, 2441, 2444, 2488, 2489, 2490, 2491, 2493, 2494, 2495
Crime and Courts Act 2013 (Family Court: Consequential Provision) Order 2014, SI 2014/605 251, 355, 359, 823, 1094, 1100, 1111, 1114, 1115
Crime and Courts Act 2013 (Family Court: Transitional and Saving Provision) Order 2014, SI 2014/956
para 6 102
Criminal Defence Service (Financial Eligibility) Regulations 2006, SI 2006/2492 2266
reg 2 2486
Criminal Legal Aid (Financial Resources) Regulations 2013, SI 2013/471
reg 20(2)(b) 2486
Criminal Penalties etc. (Increase) Order 1984, SI 1984/447 791
Criminal Procedure Rules 2014, SI 2014/1610 1762
Cross-Border Mediation (EU Directive) Regulations 2011, SI 2011/1133 1976
Disclosure of Adoption Information (Post-Commencement Adoption) Regulations 2005, SI 2005/888
Pt 2 1657
Dissolution etc (Pension Protection Fund) Regulations 2006, SI 2006/1934 734
Dissolution etc (Pensions) Regulations 2005, SI 2005/2920 734, 742
Divorce and Dissolution etc (Pension Protection Fund) Regulations 2011, SI 2011/780 734, 1459, 2452
reg 3 1177
reg 5 54
Divorce etc (Pension Protection Fund) Regulations 2006, SI 2006/1932 741, 1191, 2456
Divorce etc (Pensions) Regulations 2000, SI 2000/1123 1190, 2452, 2456
reg 3 54, 1175, 1265, 2516
reg 8 2456
reg 9 54, 1174, 1175
Education (School Records) Regulations 1989, SI 1989/1261 449
Emergency Protection Order (Transfer of Responsibilities) Regulations 1991, SI 1991/1414 578, 585
Enrolment of Deeds (Change of Name) Regulations 1994, SI 1994/604 447
European Communities (Jurisdiction and Judgments in Matrimonial and Parental Responsibility Matters) Regulations 2005, SI 2005/265 363, 369, 838, 840, 841, 842, 849, 850, 863, 868, 1251
European Communities (Matrimonial Jurisdiction and Judgments) (Northern Ireland) Regulations 2001, SI 2001/660 849, 850, 863
European Communities (Matrimonial Jurisdiction and Judgments) Regulations 2001, SI 2001/310 369, 828, 832, 838, 842, 863, 868
Family Court (Composition and Distribution of Business) (Amendment) Rules 2014, SI 2014/3297 2462, 2463, 2466, 2468
Family Court (Composition and Distribution of Business) (Amendment) Rules 2015, SI 2015/1421 2463
Family Court (Composition and Distribution of Business) Rules 2014, SI 2014/840 29, 32, 34, 42, 142, 146, 149, 151, 153, 157, 158, 159, 621, 1139, 1477, 1502, 1515, 1544, 1634, 1859, 1863, 1881, 2005, 2009, 2458, 2715
rr 2–7 193
r 3 160, 162, 166, 167, 168, 170
r 4 900
rr 5–7 194
r 6(3) 411
r 14 11, 12, 106, 116, 118, 171, 172, 1929
r 15(1) 1425

Family Court (Composition and Distribution of Business) Rules 2014, SI 2014/840—*continued*
r 15(2) 1425
r 16 27, 1743
r 16(1),(3)(a)(iii) 134
r 16(1),(3)(a)(iv),(ix) 139
r 16(1),(3)(a)(vi) 136
r 16(1),(3)(a)(x) 141
r 16(2),(3)(a)(iii) 133
r 16(2),(3)(a)(x) 140
r 16(3)(a)(ix) 137
r 16(4),(5)(b) 899
r 16(5) 889
r 17 27, 1743, 1930, 2023, 2291, 2320, 2323
r 17(1) 135, 167, 270
r 17(1),(2) 164, 169
r 17(5) 118, 1932
r 18 137
r 20 11, 12, 27, 160, 161, 162, 165, 166, 167, 168, 170, 171, 172, 900
r 20(2) 160, 471, 522
Sch 1 1644
para 1 1634
para 1(a) 65, 66, 67
para 1(c) 69, 70
para 1(e) 73, 74, 76, 79, 81, 82
para 1(f),(m) 25
para 1(g),(k),(p) 93
para 2 14
para 2(a) 14, 49
para 2(b) 20, 52, 1439
para 2(c) 58
para 2(d) 12, 13, 25, 549, 812
para 4(a) 58, 59, 1425
para 4(f) 42, 1634
para 5 263, 2552
Sch 2 104, 110, 111, 113, 114, 1323, 2023, 2291, 2320, 2323
para 16 124
Table 1 56
Table 3 2087
Family Court (Contempt of Court) (Powers) Regulations 2014, SI 2014/833 126, 127, 129, 130, 541, 563, 796, 805, 893, 896, 2468
reg 4 2287
reg 5 1985
Family Law Act 1986 (Dependent Territories) (Amendment) Order 1994, SI 1994/2800 863
Family Law Act 1986 (Dependent Territories) Order 1991, SI 1991/1723 180, 838, 840, 841, 844, 845, 846, 847, 850, 852, 853, 854, 855, 856, 859, 860, 861, 863, 1919, 2469
art 2 852, 853, 854
Sch 1 838
Sch 3 838, 863
Family Law Act 1996 (Commencement No 2) Order 1997, SI 1997/1892 912, 914, 1132
Family Law Act 1996 (Commencement No 3) Order 1998, SI 1998/2572 1202
Family Law Act 1996 (Dependent Territories) (Amendment) Order 2006, SI 2006/1456 2470, 2472
Family Law Act 1996 (Forced Marriage) (Relevant Third Party) Order 2009, SI 2009/2023 32, 901
Family Law (Northern Ireland Consequential Amendments) Order 1993, SI 1993/1577 1068, 1071, 1073
Family Law (Northern Ireland) Order 1993, SI 1993/1576 690, 699, 1093, 1094, 1096, 1111, 1113
Family Procedure (Adoption) Rules 2005, SI 2005/2795
r 5(3) 1854
Family Procedure (Civil Partnership: Staying of Proceedings) Rules 2010, SI 2010/2986 725, 831
Family Procedure (Modification of Enactments) Order 2011, SI 2011/1045 2033, 2269, 2452, 2454, 2455, 2456, 2472
Family Procedure Rules 2010, SI 2010/2955 25, 816, 1261, 1264, 1277, 2031, 2032
Pt 1 21, 53, 1979
r 1.1 527, 544, 1500, 1760
r 1.1(2)(c) 528, 2196
r 1.4 1745, 1761, 2036, 2037
r 1.4(2)(c) 1422
r 1.4(2)(e) 1760
Pt 2 1636
r 2.3 12, 20, 50, 56, 215, 217, 223, 481, 570, 1125, 1210, 1424, 1477, 1539, 1548, 1550, 1552, 1555, 1556, 1557, 1636, 1637, 1686, 1713, 2033, 2548
r 2.3(1) 1289, 1290, 1291, 1331, 1380, 1381, 1383, 1386, 1391, 1392, 1393, 1398, 1399, 1403, 1405, 1422, 1505, 1507, 1537, 1634, 1638, 1642, 1644, 1645, 1650, 1651, 1652, 1654, 1655, 1656, 1657, 1658, 1659, 1660, 1661, 1662, 1663, 1680, 1722, 1747, 1764, 1846, 1848, 1852, 1856, 1919, 1920, 1923
r 2.5 12, 75, 79, 172, 797, 2618
r 2.6 12, 136, 166, 170, 172, 857, 858, 2618
r 2.6(1)(a) 134, 141, 633
r 2.6(1)(c) 139, 168
r 2.6(2) 162
r 2.7 75, 79, 2618
r 2.8 1682, 1745, 1782
r 2.9 49, 1517, 1541
r 2.9(2) 109, 119
r 2.9(3) 1291
r 2.9(4) 1175, 1177
r 2.10 1858
r 2.10(3) 1291
r 2.31(1) 1406
Pt 3
Ch 3 811
r 3.1 1553
r 3.2 1553
r 3.3 1553
r 3.6(2)(b) 25, 1443
r 3.8 12, 25, 142, 144, 150, 152
Pt 4 12, 172, 1136, 1553, 1761
r 4.1 26, 1507, 1553, 1556, 1745, 1765, 2036
r 4.1–4.8 1553
r 4.1(1) 1722
r 4.1(3) 437, 1397

Family Procedure Rules 2010, SI 2010/2955—*continued*
r 4.1(3)(a) 146, 149, 151, 154, 161
r 4.1(3)(c) 2025
r 4.1(3)(h) 1151
r 4.1(3)(i) 1151
r 4.1(3)(o) 1479
r 4.1(6) 212, 384, 1137, 1684
r 4.3 26, 44, 134, 136, 139, 141, 143, 146, 150, 151, 154, 162, 165, 168, 170, 457, 1291, 1397, 1507, 1797
r 4.3(2)–(7) 1636
r 4.3(5) 212
r 4.4 1178, 1422, 1724
r 4.5(3) 526, 1533
r 4.7(b) 1724
r 4.8 1246, 2080
Pt 5 12, 19, 172, 182, 185, 187, 583, 1285, 1286, 1470
r 5 621, 633
r 5.1 13, 20, 46, 52, 146, 152, 263, 453, 603, 673, 857, 858, 1504, 1656
r 5.1(1) 46
r 5.2 13, 20, 46, 52, 603, 673, 1504
r 5.3 13, 20, 52, 603, 673, 1477, 1504
r 5.3(1) 1745
Pt 6 15, 33, 45, 47, 56, 132, 183, 1402, 1470, 1477, 1478, 1552, 1638, 1651, 1688, 1832
Ch 1 49
Ch 2 47
Ch 3 49
Ch 4 2823
r 6.5 1688, 1703
r 6.8 47
r 6.14 34
r 6.14(1) 219, 1703
r 6.14(2) 217
r 6.14(7) 1688, 1703
r 6.14(8) 1688, 1703
r 6.15 1387
r 6.16 1387
r 6.18 47
r 6.23 67, 77, 1470
rr 6.23–6.39 1541
r 6.28 217, 219, 1688, 1703
r 6.29 217, 219
r 6.34 67, 77, 1387
r 6.37 29, 34, 1479, 1552
r 6.42 2823
r 6.42(2) 183
r 6.42(3) 183
r 6.44 2823
Pt 7 1148, 1157, 1159, 1768
r 7.6 46, 706, 1152
r 7.7(1) 1159
r 7.7(2) 1150, 1160
r 7.8 46
r 7.10 47
r 7.10(3) 1148
r 7.11 944
r 7.12 47
r 7.12(1) 47
r 7.12(4),(6),(12) 707
r 7.12(8) 49

Family Procedure Rules 2010, SI 2010/2955—*continued*
r 7.13 52
r 7.13(1) 47
r 7.14(1) 49
r 7.14(2) 49
r 7.16 49, 1214
r 7.16(3) 49
r 7.18 47
r 7.19 1351
r 7.19(4) 47
r 7.19(5) 47
r 7.20 47, 1148
r 7.20(2) 47, 48
r 7.20(2)(a) 47, 48, 1148, 1159
r 7.20(2)(b) 47
r 7.20(2)(b)(ii) 48
r 7.20(3) 48
r 7.20(4) 49, 1151
r 7.21(1) 48
r 7.22 1148, 1151
r 7.22(2)(a) 49
r 7.22(2)(b) 49
r 7.22(2)(c) 49
r 7.22(2)(d) 49
r 7.22(3) 48
r 7.26 1157
r 7.27 725, 829, 2787
r 7.27(4) 2785
r 7.28 212, 1155
r 7.30 48, 1156
r 7.30(1)(a) 48
r 7.30(1)(b) 48
r 7.30(1)(c) 49
r 7.30(1)(d) 49
r 7.31 705, 1154
r 7.31(6) 705
r 7.32 47, 1148
r 7.32(2) 1148
r 7.32(3) 48, 1149
r 7.33 47, 48
r 7.33(2)(c) 1148, 1154
Pt 8 1421, 2271
Ch 2 944, 952
Ch 3 1036
Ch 4 716, 797
Ch 5 45, 411, 714
Ch 6 778
Ch 9 131
r 8.1 131
rr 8.1–8.13 429
r 8.4 15
r 8.5 15
r 8.6 15
rr 8.6–8.11 20, 1036, 1208, 2271
r 8.7 15
rr 8.12–8.17 1122
r 8.13 14
r 8.14 14, 1122
r 8.15 15
r 8.15(1) 1122
r 8.15(2) 15, 1122
r 8.16 15
r 8.18 226, 292, 428, 870

Family Procedure Rules 2010, SI 2010/2955—*continued*
r 8.18(b) 400
r 8.19 400, 428
r 8.20 45, 226, 292, 428, 870, 921, 922, 1698
r 8.20(1) 45, 1422
r 8.20(3) 1422
r 8.20(4) 921
r 8.20(5) 921
r 8.21 45, 292, 428, 870
r 8.22 428, 870
r 8.23 57
r 8.24 57, 58, 1125
r 8.25 57, 58, 1125
r 8.26 57, 1125
r 8.27 57, 1125
r 8.28 57, 58, 59
r 8.29 41, 894, 911, 916
r 8.30 41, 894, 911, 916
r 8.31 41, 894, 911, 916
r 8.32 41, 894, 911, 916
r 8.33 41, 894, 911, 916
r 8.34 41, 894, 911, 916
r 8.42 131
r 8.43 131
Pt 9 19, 20, 55, 57, 59, 407, 811, 1161, 1163, 1168, 1171, 1173, 1195, 1205, 1207, 1211, 1425, 1856, 2036, 2834
Ch 4 50, 52, 53
Ch 5 12, 50, 52, 53
Ch 9 1162
r 9.3 1210, 1285
r 9.4 19, 1194, 1197, 1209, 1286, 1453
r 9.5(1) 52
r 9.5(2) 13, 58, 656
r 9.5(3) 58
r 9.6(1) 56, 1209
r 9.6(2) 56, 1209
r 9.7 26, 50, 52, 59, 407, 1136, 1331, 1741, 2087
r 9.7(1) 1286
r 9.7(2) 13
r 9.8 1163
r 9.9A 212, 213, 214, 215, 1448, 1849
r 9.9A(1)(b) 212
r 9.9A(2) 213
r 9.9A(3) 214
r 9.9A(4) 214
r 9.9A(5) 215
r 9.10 12
r 9.12 21, 53
r 9.12(1) 13, 21
r 9.12(2) 13, 21, 52
r 9.13 52, 53, 1172
r 9.14 53, 1153
r 9.14(1) 19, 1744
r 9.14(4) 21, 53
r 9.14(5) 21, 53
r 9.15 21, 53, 1856
r 9.15(2)(a) 19
r 9.15(7)(c) 1454
r 9.16 21, 53
r 9.17 21, 53
r 9.17(2) 1165
r 9.18 13, 26, 52, 53, 1202

Family Procedure Rules 2010, SI 2010/2955—*continued*
r 9.18(1) 13, 53
r 9.18(1)(a) 25
r 9.18(1)(b) 26
r 9.18(2) 26
r 9.18(3) 25
r 9.18A 13, 52, 53, 1202
r 9.19 13, 26, 52, 53, 481, 1202
r 9.19(1) 26
r 9.19(2) 26
r 9.19(3) 26
r 9.19(4) 13, 54
r 9.20 13, 14, 26, 52, 53, 54, 481, 1202
r 9.21 26
r 9.21A 823
r 9.24 54
r 9.24(2) 1174
r 9.25(1) 1978
r 9.25(1)(a) 1978
r 9.26 26, 816, 821, 1129, 1205, 1978
r 9.26(2) 1723
r 9.26(3) 1723
r 9.26(6) 58
r 9.26B 45, 1424, 1439, 1450
r 9.30 1453
r 9.30(1) 1459
r 9.31 1453, 1454, 1456, 2518
r 9.32 1453, 1454
r 9.33 1162, 1454
r 9.33(1) 1453, 1454
r 9.33(2)–(4) 1453
r 9.33(5) 1453
r 9.33(6) 1453
r 9.34 1454
r 9.34(3) 1454
r 9.35 55, 1453, 1454, 2518
r 9.36 55, 1453, 1454
r 9.36(5) 55
r 9.37 1192, 2456
rr 9.38–9.45 1453
r 9.42 1162
r 9.44 55
r 9.45 55
r 9.45(2) 55
Pt 10 792, 888, 893, 910, 1741, 1984
r 10.2 28, 1289
r 10.2(4) 28
r 10.3 29, 888, 890
r 10.3(1)(b)(ii) 29
r 10.3(3) 29
r 10.5 29
r 10.6 28, 31, 888
r 10.6(2) 31, 1538
r 10.6(3) 31
r 10.8 30
r 10.9 36
r 10.10 31, 36, 1538
r 10.11 36, 126, 1538
r 10.11(3) 128
r 10.12 30, 36, 1538
r 10.13 36, 903, 1538
r 10.14 36, 1538
r 10.15 36, 893, 1538

Family Procedure Rules 2010, SI 2010/2955—*continued*
r 10.16 36, 1538
r 10.17 911, 1539
Pt 11 31, 934, 935, 1741
r 11.1(1) 33
r 11.2(2) 32
r 11.2(3) 32
r 11.3(1) 32
r 11.3(3) 33
r 11.4 33, 34, 625, 903
r 11.4(1) 34
r 11.4(1A) 33
r 11.4(2) 33, 34
r 11.4(3) 33, 34
r 11.4(4) 34
r 11.4(5) 34
r 11.4(6) 34
r 11.6(5) 1480
r 11.7 35, 903
r 11.7(1) 34
r 11.7(2) 903
r 11.7(3) 35
r 11.7(3A) 33
r 11.7(4) 33
r 11.8 31, 34, 901
r 11.9 35
r 11.10 35
r 11.13 36, 905
r 11.15 35
Pt 12 264, 423, 454, 526, 555, 558, 1524, 1553, 1980, 2588
Ch 6 370
r 12.2 139, 141, 155, 157, 159, 171, 857, 858
r 12.2(c) 133
r 12.2(d),(e),(i) 137
r 12.2(f) 135
r 12.3 11, 12, 133, 135, 137, 138, 140, 143, 146, 149, 151, 153, 154, 161, 165, 168, 170, 171, 172, 178, 182, 455, 562, 673
r 12.3(1) 578, 859
r 12.3(2) 572
r 12.3(3) 11, 134, 136, 141, 143, 146, 151, 162, 165, 168, 170, 172, 387
r 12.4 2740
r 12.5 11, 172, 183, 603, 2347
r 12.5(2)(b) 162
r 12.6 568, 2347
r 12.7 11, 172, 568, 2347
r 12.8 11, 172, 2347
r 12.8(2) 146
r 12.12 12, 134, 136, 139, 141, 143, 144, 146, 147, 149, 150, 151, 152, 154, 162, 165, 168, 170, 172, 423, 437, 438, 457, 543, 547, 628, 857, 888, 900, 1838, 2347, 2539, 2552
r 12.12(2) 437, 552, 555, 556, 1524
r 12.13 144, 147, 150, 152, 154, 183, 423, 437, 457, 2347
r 12.13(1) 555, 556, 1524
r 12.13(3) 139
r 12.14 144, 147, 150, 152, 154, 454, 564, 578, 622, 2347
r 12.14(3) 512

Family Procedure Rules 2010, SI 2010/2955—*continued*
r 12.15 2347
r 12.16 11, 133, 136, 139, 141, 146, 151, 156, 157, 159, 162, 165, 168, 170, 172, 458, 633, 857, 1289, 1517, 2347
r 12.16(2) 857, 858
r 12.16(3) 857
r 12.16(4) 857, 858
r 12.16(5) 134, 857, 858
r 12.17 555
r 12.17(4)(a) 556
r 12.17(4)(b) 556
r 12.18(4) 163
r 12.18(6) 163
r 12.19 157, 159, 857, 858
r 12.21 457, 551, 2347, 2578
r 12.22 132, 135, 137, 140, 423, 436
r 12.23 134, 136, 139, 141
r 12.24 134, 136, 139, 141, 162, 165, 168, 170, 457, 547, 548
r 12.25 457, 534, 545, 2539, 2545, 2552
r 12.26A 548
r 12.26B 548
r 12.26C 548
r 12.27 12, 570, 1505
r 12.27(1)(d) 673
r 12.27(2) 562
r 12.27(3) 574
r 12.28 563, 576
r 12.28(2) 134, 163
r 12.28(3) 134, 163
r 12.28(4) 136
r 12.28(5) 136, 163
r 12.28(6) 136
r 12.29 134, 163
r 12.31 436, 2539
r 12.32 143, 147, 149, 152, 154, 2539
r 12.33 148, 464
r 12.34 445
r 12.35 150
r 12.36 1552
rr 12.36–12.42 181, 630
r 12.36(1) 182
r 12.36(2) 182
r 12.37 182
r 12.39 2347
r 12.43 365
r 12.44 364
rr 12.44–12.57 373, 381, 393
r 12.45 177, 365
r 12.46 177
r 12.47 178, 179, 365, 371
r 12.48 179, 365, 387, 1507, 1552, 1553, 1556
r 12.48(1) 178
r 12.49 178
r 12.50(1) 178
r 12.50(2) 178
r 12.51 365, 1553
rr 12.51–12.57 368
r 12.52 365, 367, 1556, 1919
r 12.53 367
r 12.54 179
r 12.54(4) 365

Family Procedure Rules 2010, SI 2010/2955—*continued*
r 12.55 371
r 12.57 373
r 12.58 179
rr 12.58–12.71 370, 385
r 12.60 2736
r 12.61 2736
rr 12.61–12.66 524
r 12.62 2736
r 12.63 2736
r 12.64 2736
r 12.65 2736
r 12.66 2736
r 12.66(3) 526
r 12.71(1)(b) 2740
r 12.72 246
r 12.73 246, 247, 1488
r 12.75 246, 247, 311, 475, 538, 1488
Pt 13 42, 989, 990
r 13.1 807, 1637, 1638
rr 13.1–13.14 1641
r 13.3 42
r 13.3(2) 43
r 13.3(3) 43
r 13.3(4) 43
r 13.5 43, 1637
r 13.5(1)(b) 43
r 13.6 43
r 13.7 43
r 13.8 43, 1636
r 13.9 807, 1636
r 13.9(1) 44
r 13.9(1)(f) 1637
r 13.9(3) 44
r 13.9(4) 44
r 13.9(4)(b) 1637
r 13.9(5) 44
r 13.10(2) 43
r 13.11 43, 44
r 13.12 44
r 13.13 44
r 13.14(a) 44
r 13.14(b) 44
r 13.15(2)(a) 43
r 13.20(1) 44
r 13.20(2) 44
r 13.21 44
Pt 14 184, 186, 263, 264, 265, 267, 280, 293, 304, 1330
r 14.1 1650
r 14.1(2) 1654, 1660
r 14.2 187
r 14.3 154, 263, 265, 267, 293
r 14.3(1) 185, 188
r 14.3(2) 185, 188, 267
r 14.3(3) 185, 188, 267, 283
r 14.6 568
r 14.6(1) 263
r 14.6(1)(a)(i) 284
r 14.6(1)(b) 186, 188
r 14.6(3) 186, 263
r 14.6(4) 263, 1654
r 14.7 186, 263

Family Procedure Rules 2010, SI 2010/2955—*continued*
r 14.8 186, 188
r 14.8(1) 263
r 14.8(1)(b) 1650
r 14.9 263, 290
r 14.10 1639
r 14.10(1) 283
r 14.10(1)(a) 259
r 14.11 185, 188
r 14.11(1) 278
r 14.11(2) 278
r 14.11(4) 278
r 14.11(6) 278
r 14.12 188
r 14.16 263
r 14.16(6) 186, 189
r 14.16(7) 186, 189
r 14.16(8) 189
r 14.16(9) 186
r 14.20 1641
r 14.21 283
Pt 15 223, 226, 290, 901, 1212, 1479, 1654, 2060
r 15.1 625, 921, 1212, 1479
r 15.2 216, 223
r 15.3 216
r 15.3(1) 223
r 15.3(3) 216, 224
r 15.4(2) 216, 225
r 15.4(3) 216, 225
r 15.4(4) 216
r 15.5 216
r 15.5(3) 224
r 15.6 217
r 15.6(3) 1636
r 15.7 217
r 15.8(1) 217
r 15.8(2) 217
r 15.9 217
Pt 16 182, 449, 568, 569, 570, 807, 889, 901, 1501, 1505, 1530, 1553, 2573
Ch 5 1422, 1680
rr 16.1–16.15 1548
r 16.2 11, 154, 172, 386, 455, 487, 569, 1502, 1553
r 16.3 186, 188, 263, 568, 808, 1553, 1653
r 16.4 154, 156, 435, 446, 556, 569, 1553
r 16.5 31, 217, 1553
r 16.6 31, 1553
rr 16.6–16.21 1653
r 16.6(1) 217, 901
r 16.6(1)(c) 182
r 16.6(2) 217
r 16.6(3) 901
r 16.6(5) 568
r 16.8 218
r 16.8(3) 218
r 16.9(2) 218
r 16.9(3) 218
r 16.10(1) 218
r 16.10(4) 218
r 16.11 218
r 16.12 218
r 16.13(1) 219

Family Procedure Rules 2010, SI 2010/ 2955—*continued*
r 16.13(2) 219
r 16.14 454
r 16.15 218
r 16.18 808
r 16.19 568, 569
r 16.20 622
r 16.24 569
r 16.27 569
r 16.29 429, 455, 569, 622, 625
r 16.30 186, 188
r 16.33 186, 188, 435, 436, 437, 445, 808
r 16.34 1640
r 16.35 807, 1640
r 16.38 435, 483
r 16.39 465, 469
Pt 17 1444, 1469, 1724, 1765, 1920, 1922
r 17 32
r 17.1 1722
r 17.2 182, 1479, 1552, 1554, 1636
Pt 18 12, 13, 14, 19, 26, 32, 36, 49, 50, 52, 56, 57, 59, 70, 125, 131, 183, 187, 212, 213, 214, 226, 231, 291, 385, 407, 621, 630, 829, 1136, 1153, 1158, 1163, 1209, 1285, 1286, 1291, 1331, 1382, 1386, 1387, 1389, 1390, 1391, 1394, 1395, 1397, 1398, 1399, 1400, 1401, 1402, 1403, 1405, 1418, 1420, 1421, 1422, 1423, 1425, 1432, 1433, 1450, 1477, 1478, 1480, 1483, 1549, 1552, 1636, 1637, 1641, 1722, 1724, 1741, 1744, 1745, 1746, 1747, 1758, 1760, 1765, 1779, 1783, 1797, 1863, 1867, 2087, 2158, 2160, 2167, 2172, 2754
r 18.1 103, 108, 112, 120, 1243, 1636
rr 18.1–18.13 143, 147, 149, 154, 429, 434, 453, 455, 456, 471, 544, 549, 551, 1502, 1519, 1526
r 18.1(1) 183
r 18.1(2) 1741
r 18.1(2)(a) 226
r 18.2 103, 108, 112, 120, 183
r 18.3 15, 56, 103, 108, 112, 120
r 18.3(b)(ii) 32
r 18.3(c) 32
r 18.4 32, 52, 58, 103, 108, 112, 120
rr 18.4–18.7 56
r 18.5 103, 108, 112, 120
r 18.5(1) 58
r 18.5(10)(b) 33
r 18.7 32, 58, 103, 108, 112, 120, 183, 1724
r 18.7(1) 52
r 18.7(2) 52
r 18.8 15, 53, 56, 103, 108, 112, 120, 131, 147
r 18.8(1)(b)(ii) 226
r 18.8(3) 183
r 18.9 15
r 18.10 15, 56
r 18.10(2) 33
r 18.10(3) 32, 33
r 18.11 15, 33, 58, 212, 802, 903, 935, 1477
r 18.12 34

Family Procedure Rules 2010, SI 2010/ 2955—*continued*
Pt 19 14, 45, 131, 173, 283, 292, 870, 1152, 1153, 1331, 1418, 1421, 1422, 1423, 1547, 1723, 1760, 1765, 1898, 1922
r 19.3 131, 1422
r 19.3(b) 1422
r 19.5 45, 183, 1422
r 19.5(3) 1422, 1723
r 19.5(3)(a) 1422
r 19.7(1) 1422
r 19.7(3) 1422
r 19.7(4) 183
r 19.7(5) 183
r 19.7(6) 183
r 19.8 183
Pt 20 57, 59, 790, 1285, 1286, 1331, 1741, 1742, 2087
r 20.2 2087
r 20.2(1) 1741, 1742
r 20.2(1)(c)(v) 54, 1122, 1170
r 20.2(1)(f) 1241
r 20.2(1)(h) 1240
r 20.2(3) 1741
r 20.3 59, 790, 1745
r 20.3(2)(b) 1746
r 20.3(3) 1745
r 20.3(4) 1745
r 20.4 790, 1743, 1745, 1746
r 20.4(1) 1741, 1746
r 20.4(3) 1746
Pt 21 1390, 1397
r 21.1 19, 1513
r 21.2 900, 1481
r 21.3 900, 903, 935, 1513
r 21.3(1)–(8) 35
Pt 22 49
r 22.1 183, 214, 857, 858
r 22.2 75, 79
r 22.2(1) 1136, 1741
r 22.3 1291
r 22.4 75, 79, 156, 157, 158, 159, 1554, 1922
r 22.5 75, 79, 1554
r 22.6 1554
r 22.7 1554
r 22.7(1) 1724
r 22.7(2) 1724
r 22.12 156, 159
r 22.13 156, 159
Pt 23 49, 1724, 1765
rr 23.2–23.5 1724
r 23.9 75, 79
r 24 1557
r 24.2 1423, 2431
rr 24.2–24.6 1781
r 24.3(2) 1781
r 24.3(3) 1781
r 24.5 1781
r 24.5(3) 1781
r 24.6 1781
r 24.7 1781
r 24.8 1781
r 24.9 1781
r 24.10 1781

Family Procedure Rules 2010, SI 2010/2955—*continued*
r 24.11 1781
r 24.12 1781, 1782, 1786, 2753
r 24.13 1781
r 24.14 1781
r 24.16 1786, 2754
Pt 25 49, 437, 541, 686, 1136, 1397, 1513, 1514, 1528, 1760
r 25.1 390
Pt 27 791, 1554
r 27.2 75, 79, 1533
r 27.3 75, 79
r 27.4 75, 79
r 27.4(1) 512
r 27.4(3) 512
r 27.10 45, 157, 626, 1527, 2142
r 27.10(1) 132
r 27.10(2) 626, 1391
r 27.11 45, 248, 626, 628, 1040, 1481, 2142
r 27.11(1)(a) 1442
r 27.11(2) 628
Pt 28 450, 1277, 1286, 1848, 1979, 2143
r 28.1 26, 1548
r 28.1(1) 2145, 2146
r 28.2 48, 227, 1395
r 28.2(1) 227, 1846, 1848, 1849
r 28.3 55, 227, 228, 481, 646, 911, 1165, 1166, 1196, 1210, 1848, 2143
r 28.3(1) 1848
r 28.3(2) 230
r 28.3(3) 229, 1443
r 28.3(3)(b) 1848
r 28.3(4)(a) 1164
r 28.3(4)(b) 1848
r 28.3(4)(b)(i) 1848
r 28.3(4)(b)(ii) 1125
r 28.3(5) 215, 229, 1443, 1849
r 28.3(6) 229, 1125, 1164, 1443, 1848
r 28.3(6),(7) 1849
r 28.3(7) 230, 1849
r 28.3(7)(d) 1849
r 28.3(7)(e) 1849
r 28.3(8) 229, 1848
r 28.3(9) 215
r 28.8 1125
r 29.4 147, 149, 154, 217, 219, 544, 1684
r 29.4(3) 544
r 29.4(4) 544
r 29.4(6) 544
r 29.5 235, 443, 529, 530, 995, 1545
r 29.5(3) 236, 995, 996, 1855, 2057
r 29.5(4) 236, 995, 996, 1855, 2057
r 29.5(5) 235, 1855, 2057
r 29.5(6) 1855
r 29.6 944
r 29.8 407, 1857
r 29.8(1) 1856
r 29.8(7) 1857
r 29.9 1856
r 29.16 212
r 29.17 133, 135, 137, 140, 160, 164, 167, 169
r 29.17(3) 140, 2715
r 29.17(3),(4) 133, 135, 138, 161, 164, 167, 169

Family Procedure Rules 2010, SI 2010/2955—*continued*
r 29.17(3)(b) 106, 109, 119
r 29.17(4) 2715
r 29.18 133, 135, 140, 161, 164, 167, 169
r 29.19 133, 135, 137, 140, 160, 164, 167, 169
Pt 30 12, 50, 192, 198, 250, 400, 411, 799, 1059, 1236, 1395, 1399, 1848, 2146, 2545
r 30.1 194, 198, 210
r 30.1(3) 195
r 30.2 198
r 30.3 194, 352, 1060
r 30.3(1) 194
r 30.3(1B) 209
r 30.3(2) 194, 799
r 30.3(4) 209
r 30.3(5) 209
r 30.3(5A) 211
r 30.3(8) 209
r 30.4 198, 1175, 1177, 2457
r 30.4(2) 194, 210, 566
r 30.4(3) 194, 198, 210, 566
r 30.4(4) 194, 210
r 30.4(5) 194, 195
r 30.5 195
r 30.5(4) 211
r 30.5(5) 211
r 30.6 198
r 30.7(1) 566
r 30.8 197, 198, 566, 802, 2877
r 30.9 195, 198
r 30.11 197, 211, 450
r 30.11(2) 198
r 30.11(2)(a) 212
r 30.11(4) 211
r 30.11(5) 211
r 30.12 211
r 30.12(1) 192, 197
r 30.12(2) 197
r 30.12(3) 197
r 30.12(3)(a) 1060
r 30.13 197
r 30.14 197, 212, 214
r 30.14(1) 213
r 30.14(4) 213
r 30.14(5) 213
r 30.14(6) 213
Pt 31 173, 369, 1866, 2742, 2743, 2790
r 31.1 2788
r 31.3(1) 173
r 31.4(1) 173
r 31.4(2)(a) 173
r 31.5(c) 2742
r 31.6 175
r 31.8(2)(a) 174
r 31.8(3)(a) 174
r 31.8(3)(b) 175
r 31.8(4) 175
r 31.8(5) 175
r 31.8(7) 175
r 31.9 176
r 31.10 175
r 31.11 2790
r 31.11(2) 175

Family Procedure Rules 2010, SI 2010/
2955—continued
r 31.11(3) 175
r 31.11(5)(a) 176
r 31.11(5)(b) 176
r 31.11(5)(c) 176
r 31.11(5)(d) 176
r 31.12 2788
r 31.14(2) 175
r 31.14(4)(a) 176
r 31.14(4)(b) 176
r 31.14(4)(c) 176
r 31.14(4)(d) 176
r 31.15(1) 176
r 31.15(2) 176
r 31.16 176
r 31.17 2798
r 31(2) 113
rr 32.2–32.12 1066, 1069
r 32.3 68, 1073
r 32.3(2) 68
r 32.3(3) 68
r 32.4 1073
r 32.5 1071, 1073
r 32.6 68, 1071
r 32.7 69, 1071
r 32.8 70
r 32.9A 70
r 32.10 69, 70
r 32.11 69
r 32.14 104, 1076
r 32.15 104
r 32.19 1077
r 32.23 180, 838, 852, 853, 854, 856, 863, 1920, 1921, 1922, 1923
rr 32.23–32.32 853, 854
r 32.24 1921, 1922
r 32.25 180, 853
r 32.25(1) 180
r 32.25(1)(c) 180
r 32.25(4) 180
r 32.25(5) 180
r 32.26 180, 853
r 32.27 854
r 32.28 854
r 32.29 181, 854
r 32.30 855
r 32.33 103
Pt 33 125, 903, 1137, 1849
Ch 7 400
Ch 8 400
r 33.1(2) 111, 553
r 33.2 2279
r 33.3 103, 112, 113, 120
r 33.3(1) 103, 106, 121, 122
r 33.3(1)(a) 109, 114, 2296
r 33.3(1)(b) 1723
r 33.3(2) 103
r 33.3(2)(b) 120, 121
r 33.3(3) 103
r 33.4 112
r 33.7 458
r 33.9 2282
rr 33.9–33.17 413, 1204

Family Procedure Rules 2010, SI 2010/
2955—continued
rr 33.10–33.14 104
r 33.10(1) 118
r 33.10(2) 118
r 33.11 118
r 33.11(3) 104
r 33.11(3)(b) 119
r 33.11(4) 119
r 33.11(5) 119
r 33.13(2) 119
r 33.14(1) 119
r 33.14(2) 121
r 33.14(3) 119
r 33.14(3)(a) 119
r 33.14(4) 119
r 33.14A 804
r 33.14A(1) 119
r 33.16 104
r 33.16(1) 119
r 33.16(2) 119
r 33.19 103
r 33.20 112
r 33.24 803, 1723, 1928, 2291
r 33.24(1A) 114
r 33.24(3)(a) 116
r 33.24(3)(b) 116
Pt 34 2834, 2875
Ch 3 2436, 2858
r 34.2 65, 1088, 1089, 1091, 1093, 1094, 1096, 1097, 1099
r 34.2(2) 71, 90
r 34.3 65, 67, 73, 92, 1091, 1093, 1097, 1104
rr 34.4–34.11 1085
r 34.5 67
r 34.6 65
r 34.7 65, 68
r 34.8 66
r 34.9 65, 1080
r 34.10 64, 1080
r 34.10(3) 64
r 34.10(4) 64
r 34.11 1080
r 34.14 71, 1088
r 34.15 75, 79, 1089, 1091
r 34.16 77
r 34.17 1091
r 34.18 1091, 1096
r 34.19 77, 79, 1096
r 34.20 1099
r 34.22 71, 72, 79, 1091
r 34.23 74, 1100
r 34.24 73, 78, 1094
r 34.25 73, 78
r 34.27 71, 73, 77
r 34.28 72, 74
r 34.28ZD 82
r 34.28ZF 82
r 34.28ZG 82
r 34.28ZH 82
r 34.28ZI 82
r 34.28ZJ 82
r 34.30 91, 92
r 34.31 93

Family Procedure Rules 2010, SI 2010/2955—*continued*
r 34.32 93
r 34.33(2) 93
r 34.33(4) 93
r 34.36C 91
r 34.39 90, 695, 2874, 2876
r 34.39(3) 90
r 34.39(5) 90
r 34.39(6) 90
r 34.39(7) 90
r 34.40 90, 2874, 2877
r 35.2 1978
Pt 37 125, 795, 893, 906, 910, 935, 1142, 1478, 1484, 2301
Ch 2 903
r 37.3 127
r 37.4 150, 158
r 37.5 31, 125, 127
r 37.7 30, 127, 891
r 37.8 127
r 37.9 30, 152, 157, 797
r 37.10 125, 127
r 37.10(3) 127
r 37.12 792, 804
r 37.25 130
r 37.27 128, 129
r 37.27(3) 129
r 37.28 130, 131
r 37.29 131
r 37.30 131
r 37.33 805
37.4(1) 2287
Pt 38 2300
Pt 39 103, 340, 345
r 39.1 340
r 39.2 359
r 39.4 106
r 39.5 1062
r 39.5(1) 105
r 39.5(2)(a)5 1723
r 39.6(2) 106
r 39.7(2) 343
r 39.9 106
r 39.10 106
r 39.16(3) 345
r 39.20 105
r 39.21 106
Pt 40 108
Ch 2 1255
r 40.4 109
r 40.4(2) 108
r 40.4(4)(b) 1723
r 40.5(1) 109
r 40.5(2)(b) 109
r 40.6 109
r 40.6(1) 109
r 40.6(2) 109
r 40.6(3)(a) 110
r 40.6(3)(b) 110
r 40.6(3)(c) 110
r 40.6(3)(d) 110
r 40.6(3)(e) 110
r 40.6(3)(f) 110

Family Procedure Rules 2010, SI 2010/2955—*continued*
r 40.8(1) 110
r 40.8(2)(a) 110
Family Procedure (Amendment) Rules 2011, SI 2011/1328 1285, 1330, 1359, 1431, 1436, 1437, 1444, 1446, 1449, 1722, 1747, 1910, 1939, 1940, 1942, 1943, 1945, 1952, 1953, 1954, 1955, 1956, 1958, 1959, 2872
Family Procedure (Amendment) Rules 2012, SI 2012/679 1285, 1320, 1330, 1351, 1381, 1383, 1386, 1392, 1393, 1398, 1403, 1406, 1423, 1437, 1444, 1450, 1458, 1479, 1482, 1563, 1712, 1747, 1858, 1910, 1940, 1953, 1959
Family Procedure (Amendment No 2) Rules 2012, SI 2012/1462 1903
Family Procedure (Amendment No 3) Rules 2012, SI 2012/2046 1285, 1558, 1559, 1560, 1561, 1562
Family Procedure (Amendment No 4) Rules 2012, SI 2012/2806 1285, 1330, 1331, 1431, 1436, 1437, 1444, 1449, 1722, 1723, 1747, 1765, 1939, 1940, 1952, 1953, 1954, 1955, 1956, 1958, 1959, 2834
Family Procedure (Amendment No 5) Rules 2012, SI 2012/3061 1278, 1485, 1550, 1562, 1793
Family Procedure (Amendment) Rules 2013, SI 2013/530 1846, 1848, 1865
Family Procedure (Amendment No 2) Rules 2013, SI 2013/1472 1285, 1433, 1730, 1848
Family Procedure (Amendment No 3) Rules 2013, SI 2013/3204 1279, 1285, 1289, 1322, 1324, 1332, 1351, 1352, 1380, 1393, 1405, 1420, 1424, 1425, 1426, 1431, 1432, 1435, 1436, 1443, 1444, 1445, 1446, 1452, 1469, 1470, 1472, 1474, 1477, 1478, 1479, 1480, 1481, 1482, 1483, 1484, 1485, 1522, 1541, 1542, 1543, 1555, 1634, 1638, 1640, 1641, 1642, 1654, 1659, 1660, 1725, 1729, 1731, 1766, 1782, 1786, 1834, 1846, 1859, 1903, 1910, 1911, 1912, 1913, 1914, 1915, 1916, 1917, 1918, 1919, 1920, 1921, 1923, 1930, 1931, 1932, 1933, 1935, 1939, 1940, 1941, 1943, 1944, 1945, 1946, 1948, 1949, 1950, 1951, 1952, 1953, 1954, 1955, 1956, 1958, 1959
Family Procedure (Amendment) Rules 2014, SI 2014/524 1119, 1384, 1397, 1896, 1897, 1898, 1900, 1902
Family Procedure (Amendment No 2) Rules 2014, SI 2014/667 1285, 1289, 1290, 1437, 1444, 1445, 1451, 1452, 1471, 1473, 1484, 1780, 1801, 1831, 1860, 1863, 1865, 1867, 1868, 1872, 1915, 1927, 1928, 1929, 1931, 1935, 1936, 1981, 1983, 1985, 1986, 1987, 1988, 1989, 1990, 1991, 1992, 1993, 1994, 1995, 1996, 1997, 1998
Family Procedure (Amendment No 3) Rules 2014, SI 2014/843 1278, 1285, 1308, 1309, 1311, 1312, 1504, 1505, 1506, 1518, 1521,

Family Procedure (Amendment No 3) Rules 2014, SI 2014/843—*continued* 1533, 1534, 1535, 1536, 1541, 1564, 1634, 1644, 1645, 1650, 1654, 1657, 1660, 1661, 1662, 1712, 1713, 1723, 1794, 1795, 1796, 1797, 1800, 1988
Family Procedure (Amendment No 4) Rules 2014, SI 2014/3296 1285, 1309, 1382, 1388, 1425, 1472, 1550, 1865, 1983, 1988, 2003, 2004, 2005, 2006, 2007, 2008, 2009
Family Procedure (Amendment) Rules 2015, SI 2015/913 1285, 1380, 1384, 1386, 1393, 1395, 1403, 1482, 1855, 1956
Family Procedure (Amendment No 2) Rules 2015, SI 2015/1420 1476, 1477
Family Procedure (Amendment No 3) Rules 2015, SI 2015/1868 1308, 1332, 1353, 1354, 1461, 1858
Family Procedure (Amendment) Rules 2016, SI 2016/355 1322, 1935, 1936, 1996, 1997, 2014, 2015, 2016, 2017, 2018, 2019, 2020, 2021, 2022, 2023, 2024, 2025, 2026, 2027, 2028
Family Procedure (Amendment No 2) Rules 2016, SI 2016/901 1423, 1434, 1697, 1698, 1699, 1848
Family Procedure (Amendment No 3) Rules 2016, SI 2016/1013 1645
Family Procedure (Amendment) Rules 2017, SI 2017/413 1470, 1471, 1477, 1479, 1481, 1699
Family Proceedings Courts (Child Support Act 1991) Rules 1993, SI 1993/627 400
Family Proceedings Courts (Children Act 1989) Rules 1991, SI 1991/1395
r 17(1)(a) 158
Family Proceedings Courts (Matrimonial Proceedings etc) Rules 1991, SI 1991/1991
rr 2–16 1469
Family Proceedings Fees (Amendment No 2) Order 2005, SI 2005/3443 850
Family Proceedings Fees (Amendment No 2) Order 2015, SI 2015/1419 2472, 2479
Family Proceedings Fees (Amendment) Order 2013, SI 2013/1407 161
Family Proceedings Fees (Amendment) Order 2014, SI 2014/877 1470, 2472, 2479
Family Proceedings Fees (Amendment) Order 2015, SI 2015/687 933, 2472, 2479, 2481
Family Proceedings Fees Order 2008, SI 2008/1054 2472
Sch 1
fee 1.1 15, 20, 41, 59, 84, 88, 95, 96, 98, 131, 159, 173, 177
fee 1.2 45, 46
fee 1.5 47
fee 1.6 49
fee 2.1(a) 143
fee 2.1(b) 143
fee 2.1(d) 145, 151
fee 2.1(e) 149, 153
fee 2.1(i) 172
fee 2.1(k) 168, 170
fee 2.1(m) 165
Family Proceedings Fees Order 2008, SI 2008/1054—*continued*
Sch 1—*continued*
fee 2.1(o) 133, 135, 138
fee 2.1(p) 138
fee 2.1(q) 140
fee 2.1(v) 13
fee 2.2 161
fee 2.2(b) 161
fee 2.3 195
fee 2.4 195
fee 3.1 187
fee 3.2 185
fee 3.3 182
fee 5.1 26, 70, 86, 94, 98, 100, 101, 156, 159, 182, 821
fee 5.3 26, 28, 47, 48, 56, 70, 85, 88, 100, 106, 120, 127, 182, 214, 821
fee 5.4 52
fee 6 195
fee 6.1 198
fee 6.2 2504
fee 10.1 122
fee 10.2 68, 104
fee 11.1 25, 811, 816, 817
fee 12.1 121
fee 12.2 117
fee 12.3 109
fee 12.4 118
fee 12.5 106
fee 13.1 113
fee 13.3 111, 124
fee 14.1 111, 113, 124
fee 14.2 84, 86, 94, 98, 100, 101
Sch 2 46
Family Proceedings Rules 1991, SI 1991/1247
r 2.6A 1384
r 2.12(1) 1380
r 2.12A 1384
r 2.12B 1384
r 2.24 1392
r 2.42 1399
r 2.45A 1401
r 2.51B 1420
r 2.71(1) 1848
r 2.71(1)(b) 1848
r 2.71(5)(c) 1849
r 2.71(5)(d) 1849
r 3.8 1469
r 3.9 1469
r 3.9A 1469
r 3.9(A) 1472
r 3.10 1469
r 4.12 512
r 9.2 454
r 9.2A 386
r 10.28(4) 248
Financial Assistance Scheme Regulations 2005, SI 2005/1986 1191
Financial Services and Markets Act 2000 (Consequential Amendments and Repeals) Order 2001, SI 2001/3649 803, 806, 1245
art 290 1244

Fostering Services (England) Regulations 2011, SI 2011/581 497, 2399, 2401, 2407, 2408, 2409, 2422, 2427
Pt 2 497
Pt 3 497
Pt 4 497
Pt 5 497
Pt 6 497
Pt 7 497
Fostering Services Regulations 2002, SI 2002/57 630

Gender Recognition Act 2004 (Commencement) Order 2005, SI 2005/54 944, 958
art 2 955, 956
Gender Recognition (Application Fees) Order 2006, SI 2006/758 952
Gender Recognition (Approved Countries and Territories) Order 2011, SI 2011/1630 945
Gender Recognition (Disclosure of Information) (England, Wales and Northern Ireland) (No 2) Order 2005, SI 2005/916
art 3 958
art 4 958
art 5 958
art 6 958
art 7 958
Gender Recognition Register (Marriage and Civil Partnership) Regulations 2015, SI 2015/50 944
Gender Recognition Register Regulations 2005, SI 2005/912 954

Health Act 1999 (Consequential Amendments) (Nursing and Midwifery) Order 2004, SI 2004/1771 578, 583, 633
Health Act 1999 (Supplementary, Consequential etc Provisions) (No 2) Order 2000, SI 2000/694 2434, 2435
Health Act 1999 (Supplementary, Consequential etc Provisions) Order 2000, SI 2000/90 496, 518, 520, 582, 609, 612, 637
Health and Social Care Act 2012 (Consequential Provision – Social Workers) Order 2012, SI 2012/1479 2416
Health and Social Care (Community Health and Standards) Act 2003 (Supplementary and Consequential Provision) (NHS Foundation Trusts) Order 2004, SI 2004/696 2434, 2435
Health Care and Associated Professions (Miscellaneous Amendments and Practitioner Psychologists) Order 2009, SI 2009/1182 946, 958
High Court and County Courts Jurisdiction Order 1991, SI 1991/724 796, 801
art 2(1) 1016
art 2(1)(a) 110
art 7 1016
art 7(5) 1016
art 8 101, 2332
art 8(1) 2320
art 8(2) 2320
art 9 2042
art 12(a) 801
High Court (Distribution of Business) Order 1991, SI 1991/1210 1251
High Court (Distribution of Business) Order 1993, SI 1993/622 1251, 2486
High Court (Distribution of Business) Order 2004, SI 2004/3418 949
High Court (Distribution of Business) Order 2014, SI 2014/3257 1251
Housing Act 1996 (Consequential Amendments) Order 1997, SI 1997/74 875, 911, 914
Human Fertilisation and Embryology Act 2008 (Commencement No 3) Order 2010, SI 2010/987 989
Human Fertilisation and Embryology (Consequential Amendments and Transitional and Saving Provisions) Order 2009, SI 2009/1892 634
Human Fertilisation and Embryology (Mitochondrial Donation) Regulations 2015, SI 2015/572 989
Human Fertilisation and Embryology (Parental Orders) (Consequential, Transitional and Saving Provisions) Order 2010, SI 2010/986 989
Human Fertilisation and Embryology (Parental Orders) Regulations 2010, SI 2010/985 989, 991
Human Fertilisation and Embryology (Quality and Safety) Regulations 2007, SI 2007/1522 960, 962, 963, 964, 966, 967, 969, 970, 971, 975, 977
Human Fertilisation and Embryology (Quality and Safety) Regulations 2014, SI 2014/2884 960
Human Fertilisation and Embryology (Statutory Storage Period for Embryos and Gametes) Regulations 2009, SI 2009/1582 970
Human Rights Act 1998 (Amendment) Order 2004, SI 2004/1574 992, 1004

Insolvency Rules 1986, SI 1986/1925 15, 16
r 12.3 343
Intercountry Adoption (Hague Convention) Regulations 2003, SI 2003/118 329
International Recovery of Maintenance (Hague Convention 2007 etc) Regulations 2012, SI 2012/2814 251, 340, 341, 355, 656, 1075, 1081, 1083, 1089, 1100, 1106, 1108, 1114, 1254, 2439, 2444, 2448, 2488, 2834, 2849
Sch 2 2848, 2849
International Recovery of Maintenance (Hague Convention 2007) (Rules of Court) Regulations 2012, SI 2012/1770 689, 2834

Judgment Debts (Rate of Interest) Order 1993, SI 1993/564 2283
Justices' Clerks and Assistants (Amendment) Rules 2014, SI 2014/841 2503
Justices' Clerks and Assistants (Amendment) Rules 2015, SI 2015/890 2503
Justices' Clerks and Assistants Rules 2014, SI 2014/603 26, 134, 136, 139, 141, 162, 166, 168, 170, 2498
r 2 1290

Justices' Clerks and Assistants Rules 2014, SI 2014/603—*continued*
r 3 1290
r 4 1290
Sch 1290
Justices of the Peace Rules 2016, SI 2016/709 2461

Land Registration Rules 2003, SI 2003/1417
r 82 876
Legal Aid, Sentencing and Punishment of Offenders Act 2012 (Children Act 1989) (Children Remanded to Youth Detention Accommodation) Regulations 2012, SI 2012/2813 2433
Legal Aid, Sentencing and Punishment of Offenders Act 2012 (Consequential, Transitional and Saving Provisions) Regulations 2013, SI 2013/534 1563, 1658, 1826, 2161, 2169, 2174
Legal Services Act 2007 (Designation as a Licensing Authority) (No 2) Order 2011, SI 2011/2866
Art 8(1) 568
Sch 2 568
Local Authorities (Executive and Alternative Arrangements) (Modification of Enactments and Other Provisions) (England) Order 2001, SI 2001/2237 2434
Local Education Authorities and Children's Services Authorities (Integration of Functions) (Local and Subordinate Legislation) Order 2010, SI 2010/1172 2379, 2385, 2434, 2435
Local Education Authorities and Children's Services Authorities (Integration of Functions) Order 2010, SI 2010/1158 508, 510, 518, 520, 554, 582, 609, 612, 615, 616, 637, 676, 682
Lord Chancellor (Transfer of Functions and Supplementary Provisions) (No 2) Order 2006, SI 2006/1016 778

Magistrates' Courts (Adoption) Rules 1984, SI 1984/611
r 32(4) 1661
Magistrates' Courts (Attachment of Earnings) Rules 1971, SI 1971/809
rr 10, 11 350
Magistrates' Courts (Family Law Act 1986) Rules (Northern Ireland) 1988, SI 1988/113 853
Magistrates' Courts (Increase of Lump Sums) Order 1988, SI 1988/1069 812
Magistrates' Courts (Northern Ireland) Order 1981, SI 1981/1675 1068, 1094, 1099, 1100, 1101, 1103, 1116, 1118
Magistrates' Courts Rules 1981, SI 1981/552 400
r 66 1073
Maintenance Orders (Backdating) Order 1993, SI 1993/623 648, 652, 654, 657, 815, 819, 820, 825, 1198, 1202, 1215
Maintenance Orders (Northern Ireland Consequential Amendments) Order 1980, SI 1980/564 1064, 1065, 1118
Marriage (Same Sex Couples) Act 2013 (Consequential and Contrary Provisions and Scotland) and Marriage and Civil Partnership (Scotland) Act 2014 (Consequential Provisions) Order 2014, SI 2014/3168 832, 1055, 1157
Marriage (Same Sex Couples) Act 2013 (Consequential and Contrary Provisions and Scotland) Order 2014, SI 2014/560 720, 925, 1055, 1056
Marriage (Same Sex Couples) (Jurisdiction and Recognition of Judgments) Regulations 2014, SI 2014/543 46, 828, 1119, 2776
Marriages and Civil Partnerships (Approved Premises) (Amendment) Regulations 2011, SI 2011/2661 701
Matrimonial Causes (Decree Absolute) General Order 1972, SI 1972/1900 46
Mental Health (Care and Treatment) (Scotland) Act 2003 (Consequential Provisions) Order 2005, SI 2005/2078 611

National Health Service Reform and Health Care Professions Act 2002 (Supplementary, Consequential etc Provisions) Regulations 2002, SI 2002/2469 520, 637
National Treatment Agency (Abolition) and the Health and Social Care Act 2012 (Consequential, Transitional and Saving Provisions) Order 2013, SI 2013/235 1500, 2379, 2385, 2405, 2434, 2435
Non-Contentious Probate Rules 1987, SI 1987/2024
r 43 1025
Non-Domestic Rating (Collection and Enforcement) (Local Lists) Regulations 1989, SI 1989/1058
reg 22 400
Northern Ireland Act 1998 (Devolution of Policing and Justice Functions) Order 2010, SI 2010/976 364, 366, 369, 370, 372, 373, 690, 691, 723, 958, 1099, 1116
Northern Ireland (Modification of Enactments – No 1) Order 1973, SI 1973/2163 1099, 1116
Nursing and Midwifery Order 2001, SI 2002/253 578, 583, 633

Occupational and Personal Pension Schemes (Disclosure of Information) Regulations 2013, SI 2013/2734 2453, 2524
Occupational and Personal Pension Schemes (Prescribed Bodies) Regulations 2007, SI 2007/60 2516
reg 3(1)(d)(iv) 2516
Occupational Pension Schemes (Disclosure of Information) Regulations 1996, SI 1996/1655 2453
Occupational Pension Schemes (Transfer Values and Miscellaneous Amendments) Regulations 2003, SI 2003/1727 2518
Occupational Pension Schemes (Transfer Values) (Amendment) Regulations 2008, SI 2008/1050 2513, 2518
Occupational, Personal and Stakeholder Pensions (Miscellaneous Amendments) Regulations 2009, SI 2009/615 2513, 2523
reg 15 1174

Parental Responsibility Agreement (Amendment) Regulations 2005, SI 2005/2808 2503, 2504
Parental Responsibility Agreement (Amendment) Regulations 2009, SI 2009/2026 2503
Parental Responsibility Agreement Regulations 1991, SI 1991/1478 2503
reg 2 429
reg 3 429
Sch 429
Parental Responsibility and Measures for the Protection of Children (International Obligations) (England and Wales and Northern Ireland) Regulations 2010, SI 2010/1898 173, 365, 367, 838, 842, 849, 850, 863, 1251, 1545, 1550, 2505
reg 3(2) 2736
reg 4 524, 525
reg 5 2737
reg 5(2) 558
reg 5(3) 522, 545, 568
reg 7 1898, 2739, 2740
reg 10 2744
reg 12 2745
reg 13 2745
reg 14 2745
reg 16 2746, 2747
Pension Protection Fund and Occupational Pension Schemes (Levy Ceiling and Compensation Cap) Order 2017, SI 2017/50 1191
Pension Protection Fund (Pension Compensation Sharing and Attachment on Divorce etc) Regulations 2011, SI 2011/731 734, 1459, 2511
reg 3 54, 1177
reg 4 54, 1177
reg 9 55
reg 16 55, 1177
reg 17 1177
Pension Protection Fund (Pension Sharing) Regulations 2006, SI 2006/1690 734, 1192
reg 2(2)(b) 1192
Pension Protection Fund (Provision of Information) Regulations 2005, SI 2005/674 1192, 1459, 2511
reg 2(1) 1192
Pension Sharing (Consequential and Miscellaneous Amendments) Regulations 2000, SI 2000/2691 2513, 2518, 2520
Pension Sharing (Excepted Schemes) Order 2001, SI 2001/358 1161
Pension Sharing (Implementation and Discharge of Liability) Regulations 2000, SI 2000/1053
reg 6 2520
reg 6(4) 2520
Pension Sharing (Miscellaneous Amendments) Regulations 2016, SI 2016/289 2453, 2513, 2514, 2516, 2518
Pensions Act 2014 (Consequential, Supplementary and Incidental Amendments) Order 2017, SI 2017/422 2481, 2483, 2529
Pensions Act 2014 (Pension Sharing on Divorce etc) (Transitional Provision) Order 2016, SI 2016/39 2524
Pensions on Divorce etc (Charging) Regulations 2000, SI 2000/1049 1175
reg 2 2514
reg 3(1) 2514
reg 3(2) 2514
reg 4(1)(b) 2514
reg 7 2514
reg 9 2514
Pensions on Divorce etc (Provision of Information) Regulations 2000, SI 2000/1048 1190, 2511
reg 2 1175, 2511
reg 2(2) 1454
reg 2(7) 1453
reg 3 54, 1175, 1189, 1453, 1454, 2453, 2511
reg 4 1453, 2511
reg 5 55, 1174, 1453, 1454, 2511
reg 7 55, 1454, 2511
reg 8 55, 1454, 2511
reg 10 2511
reg 11 2453
Personal Pension Schemes (Disclosure of Information) Regulations 1987, SI 1987/1110 2453
Prison Rules 1999, SI 1999/728 793
Protection of Freedoms Act 2012 (Disclosure and Barring Service Transfer of Functions) Order 2012, SI 2012/3006 1285
Public Bodies (Child Maintenance and Enforcement Commission: Abolition and Transfer of Functions) Order 2012, SI 2012/2007 401, 403, 406, 408, 409, 410, 412, 413, 415, 416, 1285, 1852
art 5(3) 2444
Public Contracts Regulations 2015, SI 2015/102 2255

Railways (Convention on International Carriage by Rail) Regulations 2005, SI 2005/2092 2059
Reciprocal Enforcement of Judgments (India) Order 1958, SI 1958/425 64
Sch 86, 2299
Reciprocal Enforcement of Maintenance Orders (Designation of Reciprocating Countries) Order 1974, SI 1974/556 1087
Reciprocal Enforcement of Maintenance Orders (Hague Convention Countries) Order 1993, SI 1993/593 63, 71, 73, 75, 77
Sch 1 1946
Reciprocal Enforcement of Maintenance Orders (Hague Convention Countries) (Variation) Order 1999, SI 1999/1318 63, 71, 73, 75, 77, 79
Reciprocal Enforcement of Maintenance Orders (United States of America) Order 2007, SI 2007/2005 72, 74, 80, 1949
Recovery Abroad of Maintenance (Convention Countries) Order 1975, SI 1975/423 1105
Recovery of Maintenance (United States of America) Order 2007, SI 2007/2006 1949
References to Health Authorities Order 2007, SI 2007/961 496, 508, 510, 518, 520, 582, 609, 612, 637

Regulation and Inspection of Social Care (Wales) Act 2016 (Consequential Amendments to Secondary Legislation) Regulations 2017, SI 2017/52 2416
Reserve Forces Act 1996 (Consequential Provisions etc) Regulations 1988, SI 1998/3086 353
Road Safety Act 2006 (Consequential Amendments) Order 2015, SI 2015/583 2493
Rules of the Court of Judicature (NI) 1980, SR 1980/346
  Ord 90
    rr 26–35 853
Rules of the Supreme Court 1965, SI 1965/1776 2052
  Ord 15
    r 6 1439
  Ord 55 2193
  Ord 58 2193

Secretary of State for Constitutional Affairs Order 2003, SI 2003/1887 992, 993, 999
Sharing of State Scheme Rights (Provision of Information and Valuation) (No 2) Regulations 2000, SI 2000/2914 1162, 1190, 2512, 2524
  reg 2 1454
Social Care (Self-directed Support) (Scotland) Act 2013 (Consequential Modifications and Savings) Order 2014, SI 2014/513 2481
Social Services and Well-being (Wales) Act 2014 (Consequential Amendments) Regulations 2016, SI 2016/413 251, 270, 273, 274, 275, 276, 291, 328, 355, 480, 484, 485, 488, 490, 492, 493, 496, 497, 499, 500, 501, 502, 503, 505, 506, 507, 508, 509, 510, 511, 513, 514, 517, 518, 520, 549, 551, 570, 582, 591, 612, 613, 634, 637, 657, 658, 659, 660, 662, 663, 665, 666, 669, 670, 1142, 1251
Social Services and Well-being (Wales) Act 2014 (Consequential Amendments) (Secondary Legislation) Regulations 2016, SI 2016/211 2432, 2434, 2479
Special Educational Needs (Consequential Amendments to Subordinate Legislation) Order 2014, SI 2014/2103 2385, 2399
Special Guardianship (Amendment) Regulations 2016, SI 2016/111 152, 474, 475, 476
Special Guardianship Regulations 2005, SI 2005/1109 480
  regs 3–5 475
  reg 5 475, 480
  regs 6–10 475, 480
  regs 11–16 475
  regs 12, 13 480
  regs 17, 18 475
  reg 21 475, 476
  reg 22 475
  Sch 152, 153, 474, 475, 476
State Pension Regulations 2015, SI 2015/173 2525, 2526, 2527, 2528
  reg 14 2524
  Sch 2524
Statement of Changes in Immigration Rules 2003 (HC 538)
  paras 310–313 301
Suitability of Adopters Regulations 2005, SI 2005/1712 285
Supplementary Benefits etc (Consequential Provisions) (Northern Ireland) Order 1977, SI 1977/2158 1065, 1073
Supreme Court Fees (Amendment) Order 2011, SI 2011/1737 2529
Supreme Court Fees Order 2009, SI 2009/2131 2528
  Sch 1
    fee 1.1 200
    fee 1.2 200
    fee 2.1 200
    fee 2.2 200
    fee 2.4 200
    fee 2.5 201
Supreme Court Rules 2009, SI 2009/1603 176, 199, 2350
  r 10 199
  rr 10–17 201
  r 11 199
  r 11(1) 199, 209
  r 13 200
  r 14 199
  r 15 200
  r 16 200
  r 18 200
  r 19 200
  r 21 200
  r 22 201
  r 22(4) 201
  rr 23, 24 201
  r 25(1) 201
  r 25(2) 201
  r 26 201
  r 27 202
  r 28 202

Taking Control of Goods (Fees) Regulations 2014, SI 2014/1 2338, 2343
  reg 6(1)(a) 2338
Taking Control of Goods Regulations 2013, SI 2013/1894 2338
  reg 9(3) 2324
Tax and Civil Partnership Regulations 2007, SI 2007/493 702
Transfer of Functions (Children, Young People and Families) Order 2003, SI 2003/3191 426
Transfer of Functions (Equality) Order 2007, SI 2007/2914 720
Transfer of Functions (Equality) Order 2010, SI 2010/1839 720
Transfer of Functions (Lord Chancellor and Secretary of State) Order 2005, SI 2005/3429 993, 999
Transfer of Functions (Magistrates' Courts and Family Law) Order 1992, SI 1992/709 626, 651, 690, 812, 923, 1080, 1081, 1083, 1084, 1088, 1089, 1091, 1093, 1097, 1103, 1105, 1110, 1111, 1115, 1116
Transfer of Functions (Miscellaneous) Order 2001, SI 2001/3500 992

Transfer of Functions (Registration) Order 2008, SI 2008/678 297, 298, 299, 309, 316, 320, 322, 324
Transfer of Functions (Science) Order 1992, SI 1992/1296 350
Transfer of Functions (Science) Order 1995, SI 1995/2985 350
Transfer of Tribunal Functions Order 2008, SI 2008/2833 245, 416, 595, 600, 603, 605
Treaty of Lisbon (Changes in Terminology or Numbering) Order 2012, SI 2012/1809 689, 2363
Tribunal Procedure (First-tier Tribunal) (Social Entitlement Chamber) Rules 2008, SI 2008/2685 1423
Universal Credit (Consequential, Supplementary, Incidental and Miscellaneous Provisions) Regulations 2013, SI 2013/630 1063

Chronological List of Statutory Instruments

1958 Reciprocal Enforcement of Judgments (India) Order 1958, SI 1958/425
1965 Rules of the Supreme Court 1965, SI 1965/1776
1971 Magistrates' Courts (Attachment of Earnings) Rules 1971, SI 1971/809
Blood Tests (Evidence of Paternity) Regulations 1971, SI 1971/1861
1972 Matrimonial Causes (Decree Absolute) General Order 1972, SI 1972/1900
1973 Adoption (Designation of Overseas Adoptions) Order 1973, SI 1973/19
Northern Ireland (Modification of Enactments – No 1) Order 1973, SI 1973/2163
1974 Reciprocal Enforcement of Maintenance Orders (Designation of Reciprocating Countries) Order 1974, SI 1974/556
1975 Recovery Abroad of Maintenance (Convention Countries) Order 1975, SI 1975/423
1977 Supplementary Benefits etc (Consequential Provisions) (Northern Ireland) Order 1977, SI 1977/2158
1980 Rules of the Court of Judicature (NI) 1980, SR 1980/346
Maintenance Orders (Northern Ireland Consequential Amendments) Order 1980, SI 1980/564
1981 County Court Rules (Northern Ireland) 1991, SI 1981/225
Magistrates' Courts Rules 1981, SI 1981/552
Magistrates' Courts (Northern Ireland) Order 1981, SI 1981/1675
County Court Rules 1981, SI 1981/1687
1983 Adoption Agency Regulations 1983, SI 1983/1964
1984 Adoption Rules 1984, SI 1984/265
Criminal Penalties etc. (Increase) Order 1984, SI 1984/447
Magistrates' Courts (Adoption) Rules 1984, SI 1984/611
1986 Child Abduction and Custody (Parties to Conventions) Order 1986, SI 1986/1159
Insolvency Rules 1986, SI 1986/1925
Administration of Insolvent Estates of Deceased Persons Order 1986, SI 1986/1999
1987 Personal Pension Schemes (Disclosure of Information) Regulations 1987, SI 1987/1110
Non-Contentious Probate Rules 1987, SI 1987/2024
Adoption (Northern Ireland) Order 1987, SI 1987/2203
1988 Magistrates' Courts (Family Law Act 1986) Rules (Northern Ireland) 1988, SI 1988/113
Act of Sederunt (Rules for the Registration of Custody Orders of the Sheriff Court) 1988, SI 1988/613
Magistrates' Courts (Increase of Lump Sums) Order 1988, SI 1988/1069
1989 Civil Legal Aid (General) Regulations 1989, SI 1989/339
Non-Domestic Rating (Collection and Enforcement) (Local Lists) Regulations 1989, SI 1989/1058
Education (School Records) Regulations 1989, SI 1989/1261
Civil Jurisdiction and Judgments Act 1982 (Amendment) Order 1989, SI 1989/1346
1990 Civil Jurisdiction and Judgments Act 1982 (Amendment) Order 1990, SI 1990/2591
1991 Attachment of Earnings (Employer's Deduction) Order 1991, SI 1991/356
High Court and County Courts Jurisdiction Order 1991, SI 1991/724
Contact with Children Regulations 1991, SI 1991/891
County Courts (Interest on Judgment Debts) Order 1991, SI 1991/1184
High Court (Distribution of Business) Order 1991, SI 1991/1210
Family Proceedings Rules 1991, SI 1991/1247
Family Proceedings Courts (Children Act 1989) Rules 1991, SI 1991/1395
Emergency Protection Order (Transfer of Responsibilities) Regulations 1991, SI 1991/1414
Parental Responsibility Agreement Regulations 1991, SI 1991/1478
Children (Secure Accommodation) Regulations 1991, SI 1991/1505
Children (Allocation of Proceedings) Order 1991, SI 1991/1677
Family Law Act 1986 (Dependent Territories) Order 1991, SI 1991/1723
Family Proceedings Courts (Matrimonial Proceedings etc) Rules 1991, SI 1991/1991
Children (Prescribed Orders – Northern Ireland, Guernsey and Isle of Man) Regulations 1991, SI 1991/2032
Children (Secure Accommodation) (No 2) Regulations 1991, SI 1991/2034
1992 Transfer of Functions (Magistrates' Courts and Family Law) Order 1992, SI 1992/709
Transfer of Functions (Science) Order 1992, SI 1992/1296
Child Support (Collection and Enforcement) Regulations 1992, SI 1992/1989
Children (Secure Accommodation) Amendment Regulations 1992, SI 1992/2117
Child Support (Maintenance Arrangements and Jurisdiction) Regulations 1992, SI 1992/2645

1993 Judgment Debts (Rate of Interest) Order 1993, SI 1993/564
Reciprocal Enforcement of Maintenance Orders (Hague Convention Countries) Order 1993, SI 1993/593
Child Maintenance (Written Agreements) Order 1993, SI 1993/620
Children (Admissibility of Hearsay Evidence) Order 1993, SI 1993/621
High Court (Distribution of Business) Order 1993, SI 1993/622
Maintenance Orders (Backdating) Order 1993, SI 1993/623
Family Proceedings Courts (Child Support Act 1991) Rules 1993, SI 1993/627
Family Law (Northern Ireland) Order 1993, SI 1993/1576
Family Law (Northern Ireland Consequential Amendments) Order 1993, SI 1993/1577
Child Abduction and Custody (Parties to Conventions) Order 1993, SI 1993/3144
1994 Enrolment of Deeds (Change of Name) Regulations 1994, SI 1994/604
Child Support Act 1991 (Consequential Amendments) Order 1994, SI 1994/731
Act of Sederunt (Rules of the Court of Session 1994) 1994, SI 1994/1443
Child Abduction and Custody Act 1985 (Isle of Man) Order 1994, SI 1994/2799
Family Law Act 1986 (Dependent Territories) (Amendment) Order 1994, SI 1994/2800
1995 Children (Northern Ireland) Order 1995, SI 1995/755
Children (Northern Ireland Consequential Amendments) Order 1995, SI 1995/756
Children (Secure Accommodation) Amendment Regulations 1995, SI 1995/1398
Transfer of Functions (Science) Order 1995, SI 1995/2985
1996 Occupational Pension Schemes (Disclosure of Information) Regulations 1996, SI 1996/1655
Attachment of Debts (Expenses) Order 1996, SI 1996/3098
1997 Housing Act 1996 (Consequential Amendments) Order 1997, SI 1997/74
Family Law Act 1996 (Commencement No 2) Order 1997, SI 1997/1892
Child Abduction and Custody (Cayman Islands) Order 1997, SI 1997/2574
1998 Family Law Act 1996 (Commencement No 3) Order 1998, SI 1998/2572
Reserve Forces Act 1996 (Consequential Provisions etc) Regulations 1988, SI 1998/3086
Civil Procedure Rules 1998, SI 1998/3132
1999 Prison Rules 1999, SI 1999/728
Civil Procedure (Amendment) Rules 1999, SI 1999/1008
Reciprocal Enforcement of Maintenance Orders (Hague Convention Countries) (Variation) Order 1999, SI 1999/1318
2000 Health Act 1999 (Supplementary, Consequential etc Provisions) Order 2000, SI 2000/90
Child Support (Variations) Regulations 2000, SI 2000/156
Civil Procedure (Amendment) Rules 2000, SI 2000/221
Community Legal Service (Financial) Regulations 2000, SI 2000/516
Health Act 1999 (Supplementary, Consequential etc Provisions) (No 2) Order 2000, SI 2000/694
Pensions on Divorce etc (Provision of Information) Regulations 2000, SI 2000/1048
Pensions on Divorce etc (Charging) Regulations 2000, SI 2000/1049
Pension Sharing (Implementation and Discharge of Liability) Regulations 2000, SI 2000/1053
Access to Justice Act 1999 (Destination of Appeals) Order 2000, SI 2000/1071
Divorce etc (Pensions) Regulations 2000, SI 2000/1123
Civil Procedure (Amendment No 3) Rules 2000, SI 2000/1317
Civil Jurisdiction and Judgments Act 1982 (Amendment) Order 2000, SI 2000/1824
Civil Procedure (Amendment No 4) Rules 2000, SI 2000/2092
Pension Sharing (Consequential and Miscellaneous Amendments) Regulations 2000, SI 2000/2691
Sharing of State Scheme Rights (Provision of Information and Valuation) (No 2) Regulations 2000, SI 2000/2914
2001 Child Support (Maintenance Calculation Procedure) Regulations 2000, SI 2001/157
Civil Procedure (Amendment) Rules 2001, SI 2001/256
European Communities (Matrimonial Jurisdiction and Judgments) Regulations 2001, SI 2001/310
Pension Sharing (Excepted Schemes) Order 2001, SI 2001/358
European Communities (Matrimonial Jurisdiction and Judgments) (Northern Ireland) Regulations 2001, SI 2001/660
Civil Procedure (Amendment No 2) Rules 2001, SI 2001/1388
Local Authorities (Executive and Alternative Arrangements) (Modification of Enactments and Other Provisions) (England) Order 2001, SI 2001/2237
Civil Procedure (Amendment No 4) Rules 2001, SI 2001/2792
Children (Leaving Care) (England) Regulations 2001, SI 2001/2874
Transfer of Functions (Miscellaneous) Order 2001, SI 2001/3500
Financial Services and Markets Act 2000 (Consequential Amendments and Repeals) Order 2001, SI 2001/3649

Civil Jurisdiction and Judgments Order 2001, SI 2001/3929
Civil Procedure (Amendment No 5) Rules 2001, SI 2001/4015
2002 Fostering Services Regulations 2002, SI 2002/57
Nursing and Midwifery Order 2001, SI 2002/253
Civil Procedure (Modification of Enactments) Order 2002, SI 2002/439
Children Act (Miscellaneous Amendments) (England) Regulations 2002, SI 2002/546
Child Support Appeals (Jurisdiction of Courts) Order 2002, SI 2002/1915
Civil Procedure (Amendment) Rules 2002, SI 2002/2058
National Health Service Reform and Health Care Professions Act 2002 (Supplementary, Consequential etc Provisions) Regulations 2002, SI 2002/2469
2003 Intercountry Adoption (Hague Convention) Regulations 2003, SI 2003/118
Child Support (Applications: Prescribed Date) Regulations 2003, SI 2003/194
Civil Procedure (Amendment) Rules 2003, SI 2003/364
Access to Justice (Northern Ireland) Order 2003, SI 2003/435
Civil Procedure (Amendment No 2) Rules 2003, SI 2003/1242
Land Registration Rules 2003, SI 2003/1417
Occupational Pension Schemes (Transfer Values and Miscellaneous Amendments) Regulations 2003, SI 2003/1727
Secretary of State for Constitutional Affairs Order 2003, SI 2003/1887
Civil Procedure (Amendment No 4) Rules 2003, SI 2003/2113
Transfer of Functions (Children, Young People and Families) Order 2003, SI 2003/3191
Civil Procedure (Amendment No 5) Rules 2003, SI 2003/3361
2004 Health and Social Care (Community Health and Standards) Act 2003 (Supplementary and Consequential Provision) (NHS Foundation Trusts) Order 2004, SI 2004/696
Civil Procedure (Modification of Supreme Court Act 1981) Order 2004, SI 2004/1033
Civil Procedure (Amendment) Rules 2004, SI 2004/1306
Human Rights Act 1998 (Amendment) Order 2004, SI 2004/1574
Health Act 1999 (Consequential Amendments) (Nursing and Midwifery) Order 2004, SI 2004/1771
Courts Act 2003 (Consequential Amendments) Order 2004, SI 2004/2035
Civil Procedure (Amendment No 2) Rules 2004, SI 2004/2072
Children and Family Court Advisory and Support Service (Reviewed Case Referral) Regulations 2004, SI 2004/2187
High Court (Distribution of Business) Order 2004, SI 2004/3418
Civil Procedure (Amendment No 4) Rules 2004, SI 2004/3419
2005 Gender Recognition Act 2004 (Commencement) Order 2005, SI 2005/54
European Communities (Jurisdiction and Judgments in Matrimonial and Parental Responsibility Matters) Regulations 2005, SI 2005/265
Adoption Agencies Regulations 2005, SI 2005/389
Adoptions with a Foreign Element Regulations 2005, SI 2005/392
Civil Procedure (Amendment No 2) Rules 2005, SI 2005/656
Pension Protection Fund (Provision of Information) Regulations 2005, SI 2005/674
Disclosure of Adoption Information (Post-Commencement Adoption) Regulations 2005, SI 2005/888
Gender Recognition Register Regulations 2005, SI 2005/912
Gender Recognition (Disclosure of Information) (England, Wales and Northern Ireland) (No 2) Order 2005, SI 2005/916
Adopted Children and Adoption Contact Registers Regulations 2005, SI 2005/924
Special Guardianship Regulations 2005, SI 2005/1109
Adoption Agencies (Wales) Regulations 2005, SI 2005/1313
Suitability of Adopters Regulations 2005, SI 2005/1712
Financial Assistance Scheme Regulations 2005, SI 2005/1986
Civil Partnership (Amendments to Registration Provisions) Order 2005, SI 2005/2000
Civil Partnership (Contracted-out Occupational and Appropriate Personal Pension Schemes) (Surviving Civil Partners) Order 2005, SI 2005/2050
Civil Partnership (Pensions and Benefit Payments) (Consequential, etc Provisions) Order 2005, SI 2005/2053
Mental Health (Care and Treatment) (Scotland) Act 2003 (Consequential Provisions) Order 2005, SI 2005/2078
Railways (Convention on International Carriage by Rail) Regulations 2005, SI 2005/2092
Civil Partnership Act 2004 (Amendments to Subordinate Legislation) Order 2005, SI 2005/2114
Adoption and Children Act 2002 (Commencement No 9) Order 2005, SI 2005/2213
Civil Procedure (Amendment No 3) Rules 2005, SI 2005/2292
Family Procedure (Adoption) Rules 2005, SI 2005/2795

Parental Responsibility Agreement (Amendment) Regulations 2005, SI 2005/2808
Civil Partnership (Pensions, Social Security and Child Support) (Consequential, etc Provisions) Order 2005, SI 2005/2877
Civil Partnership Act 2004 (Tax Credits, etc) (Consequential Amendments) Order 2005, SI 2005/2919
Dissolution etc (Pensions) Regulations 2005, SI 2005/2920
Civil Partnership (Miscellaneous and Consequential Provisions) Order 2005, SI 2005/3029
Civil Partnership (Treatment of Overseas Relationships) Order 2005, SI 2005/3042
Civil Partnership (Supplementary Provisions Relating to the Recognition of Overseas Dissolutions, Annulments or Legal Separations) (England and Wales and Northern Ireland) Regulations 2005, SI 2005/3104
Civil Partnership Act 2004 (Overseas Relationships and Consequential, etc Amendments) Order 2005, SI 2005/3129
Civil Partnership Act 2004 (Overseas Relationships) Order 2005, SI 2005/3135
Civil Partnership (Registration Provisions) Regulations 2005, SI 2005/3176
Civil Partnership (Treatment of Overseas Relationships) (No 2) Order 2005, SI 2005/3284
Civil Partnership (Jurisdiction and Recognition of Judgments) Regulations 2005, SI 2005/3334
Civil Partnership (Family Proceedings and Housing Consequential Amendments) Order 2005, SI 2005/3336
Transfer of Functions (Lord Chancellor and Secretary of State) Order 2005, SI 2005/3429
Family Proceedings Fees (Amendment No 2) Order 2005, SI 2005/3443
Adoption and Children (Miscellaneous Amendments) Regulations 2005, SI 2005/3482
Civil Procedure (Amendment No 4) Rules 2005, SI 2005/3515
Civil Partnership Act 2004 (International Immunities and Privileges, Companies and Adoption) Order 2005, SI 2005/3542

2006 Gender Recognition (Application Fees) Order 2006, SI 2006/758
Courts Act 2003 (Consequential Amendment) Order 2006, SI 2006/1001
Lord Chancellor (Transfer of Functions and Supplementary Provisions) (No 2) Order 2006, SI 2006/1016
Family Law Act 1996 (Dependent Territories) (Amendment) Order 2006, SI 2006/1456
Civil Procedure (Amendment) Rules 2006, SI 2006/1689
Pension Protection Fund (Pension Sharing) Regulations 2006, SI 2006/1690
Collection of Fines (Final Scheme) Order 2006, SI 2006/1737
Children Act 1989 Representations Procedure (England) Regulations 2006, SI 2006/1738
Divorce etc (Pension Protection Fund) Regulations 2006, SI 2006/1932
Dissolution etc (Pension Protection Fund) Regulations 2006, SI 2006/1934
Criminal Defence Service (Financial Eligibility) Regulations 2006, SI 2006/2492
Civil Procedure (Amendment No 3) Rules 2006, SI 2006/3435

2007 Occupational and Personal Pension Schemes (Prescribed Bodies) Regulations 2007, SI 2007/60
Tax and Civil Partnership Regulations 2007, SI 2007/493
References to Health Authorities Order 2007, SI 2007/961
Human Fertilisation and Embryology (Quality and Safety) Regulations 2007, SI 2007/1522
Civil Jurisdiction and Judgments Regulations 2007, SI 2007/1655
Court of Protection Rules 2007, SI 2007/1744
Reciprocal Enforcement of Maintenance Orders (United States of America) Order 2007, SI 2007/2005
Recovery of Maintenance (United States of America) Order 2007, SI 2007/2006
Civil Procedure (Amendment) Rules 2007, SI 2007/2204
Transfer of Functions (Equality) Order 2007, SI 2007/2914
Civil Procedure (Amendment No 2) Rules 2007, SI 2007/3453

2008 Transfer of Functions (Registration) Order 2008, SI 2008/678
Occupational Pension Schemes (Transfer Values) (Amendment) Regulations 2008, SI 2008/1050
Civil Proceedings Fees Order 2008, SI 2008/1053
Family Proceedings Fees Order 2008, SI 2008/1054
Child Maintenance and Other Payments Act 2008 (Commencement) Order 2008, SI 2008/1476
Civil Procedure (Amendment) Rules 2008, SI 2008/2178
Child Support Information Regulations 2008, SI 2008/2551
Tribunal Procedure (First-tier Tribunal) (Social Entitlement Chamber) Rules 2008, SI 2008/2685
Transfer of Tribunal Functions Order 2008, SI 2008/2833
Allocation and Transfer of Proceedings Order 2008, SI 2008/2836
Civil Procedure (Amendment No 2) Rules 2008, SI 2008/3085
Civil Procedure (Amendment No 3) Rules 2008, SI 2008/3327

2009 Occupational, Personal and Stakeholder Pensions (Miscellaneous Amendments) Regulations 2009, SI 2009/615
Child Abduction and Custody (Parties to Conventions) (Amendment) Order 2009, SI 2009/702
Access to Justice Act 1999 (Destination of Appeals) (Family Proceedings) Order 2009, SI 2009/871
Armed Forces (Forfeitures and Deductions) Regulations 2009, SI 2009/1109
Health Care and Associated Professions (Miscellaneous Amendments and Practitioner Psychologists) Order 2009, SI 2009/1182
Human Fertilisation and Embryology (Statutory Storage Period for Embryos and Gametes) Regulations 2009, SI 2009/1582
Supreme Court Rules 2009, SI 2009/1603
Human Fertilisation and Embryology (Consequential Amendments and Transitional and Saving Provisions) Order 2009, SI 2009/1892
Companies Act 2006 (Consequential Amendments, Transitional Provisions and Savings) Order 2009, SI 2009/1941
Family Law Act 1996 (Forced Marriage) (Relevant Third Party) Order 2009, SI 2009/2023
Parental Responsibility Agreement (Amendment) Regulations 2009, SI 2009/2026
Civil Procedure (Amendment) Rules 2009, SI 2009/2092
Supreme Court Fees Order 2009, SI 2009/2131
Adoptions with a Foreign Element (Amendment) Regulations 2009, SI 2009/2563
Civil Jurisdiction and Judgments Regulations 2009, SI 2009/3131
Civil Procedure (Amendment No 2) Rules 2009, SI 2009/3390

2010 Civil Procedure (Amendment) Rules 2010, SI 2010/621
Care Planning, Placement and Case Review (England) Regulations 2010, SI 2010/959
Northern Ireland Act 1998 (Devolution of Policing and Justice Functions) Order 2010, SI 2010/976
Human Fertilisation and Embryology (Parental Orders) Regulations 2010, SI 2010/985
Human Fertilisation and Embryology (Parental Orders) (Consequential, Transitional and Saving Provisions) Order 2010, SI 2010/986
Human Fertilisation and Embryology Act 2008 (Commencement No 3) Order 2010, SI 2010/987
Apprenticeships, Skills, Children and Learning Act 2009 (Consequential Amendments) (England and Wales) Order 2010, SI 2010/1080
Local Education Authorities and Children's Services Authorities (Integration of Functions) Order 2010, SI 2010/1158
Local Education Authorities and Children's Services Authorities (Integration of Functions) (Local and Subordinate Legislation) Order 2010, SI 2010/1172
Transfer of Functions (Equality) Order 2010, SI 2010/1839
Parental Responsibility and Measures for the Protection of Children (International Obligations) (England and Wales and Northern Ireland) Regulations 2010, SI 2010/1898
Civil Procedure (Amendment No 2) Rules 2010, SI 2010/1953
Adoption and Children (Scotland) Act 2007 (Consequential Provisions) Order 2010, SI 2010/2469
Care Leavers (England) Regulations 2010, SI 2010/2571
Civil Procedure (Amendment No 3) Rules 2010, SI 2010/2577
Family Procedure Rules 2010, SI 2010/2955
Family Procedure (Civil Partnership: Staying of Proceedings) Rules 2010, SI 2010/2986

2011 Civil Procedure (Amendment) Rules 2011, SI 2011/88
Fostering Services (England) Regulations 2011, SI 2011/581
Arrangements for Placement of Children by Voluntary Organisations and others (England) Regulations 2011, SI 2011/582
Pension Protection Fund (Pension Compensation Sharing and Attachment on Divorce etc) Regulations 2011, SI 2011/731
Divorce and Dissolution etc (Pension Protection Fund) Regulations 2011, SI 2011/780
Access to Justice Act 1999 (Destination of Appeals) (Family Proceedings) Order 2011, SI 2011/1044
Family Procedure (Modification of Enactments) Order 2011, SI 2011/1045
Child Abduction and Custody (Parties to Conventions) (Amendment) (No 2) Order 2011, SI 2011/1081
Cross-Border Mediation (EU Directive) Regulations 2011, SI 2011/1133
Civil Jurisdiction and Judgments (Maintenance) (Rules of Court) Regulations 2011, SI 2011/1215
Family Procedure (Amendment) Rules 2011, SI 2011/1328
Civil Jurisdiction and Judgments (Maintenance) Regulations 2011, SI 2011/1484
Gender Recognition (Approved Countries and Territories) Order 2011, SI 2011/1630
Supreme Court Fees (Amendment) Order 2011, SI 2011/1737
Adoption and Children (Scotland) Act 2007 (Consequential Modifications) Order 2011, SI 2011/1740

Marriages and Civil Partnerships (Approved Premises) (Amendment) Regulations 2011, SI 2011/2661
Legal Services Act 2007 (Designation as a Licensing Authority) (No 2) Order 2011, SI 2011/2866
Civil Procedure (Amendment No 3) Rules 2011, SI 2011/2970
Civil Procedure (Amendment No 4) Rules 2011, SI 2011/3103
2012 Civil Procedure (Amendment) Rules 2012, SI 2012/505
Family Procedure (Amendment) Rules 2012, SI 2012/679
Adoption Agencies (Panel and Consequential Amendments) Regulations 2012, SI 2012/1410
Family Procedure (Amendment No 2) Rules 2012, SI 2012/1462
Health and Social Care Act 2012 (Consequential Provision – Social Workers) Order 2012, SI 2012/1479
International Recovery of Maintenance (Hague Convention 2007) (Rules of Court) Regulations 2012, SI 2012/1770
Treaty of Lisbon (Changes in Terminology or Numbering) Order 2012, SI 2012/1809
Public Bodies (Child Maintenance and Enforcement Commission: Abolition and Transfer of Functions) Order 2012, SI 2012/2007
Family Procedure (Amendment No 3) Rules 2012, SI 2012/2046
Civil Procedure (Amendment No 2) Rules 2012, SI 2012/2208
Child Support Maintenance Calculation Regulations 2012, SI 2012/2677
Family Procedure (Amendment No 4) Rules 2012, SI 2012/2806
Legal Aid, Sentencing and Punishment of Offenders Act 2012 (Children Act 1989) (Children Remanded to Youth Detention Accommodation) Regulations 2012, SI 2012/2813
International Recovery of Maintenance (Hague Convention 2007 etc) Regulations 2012, SI 2012/2814
Civil Partnership Act 2004 (Overseas Relationships) Order 2012, SI 2012/2976
Protection of Freedoms Act 2012 (Disclosure and Barring Service Transfer of Functions) Order 2012, SI 2012/3006
Family Procedure (Amendment No 5) Rules 2012, SI 2012/3061
Civil Legal Aid (Procedure) Regulations 2012, SI 2012/3098
Children (Secure Accommodation) (Amendment) (England) Regulations 2012, SI 2012/3134
2013 Civil Legal Aid (Merits Criteria) Regulations 2013, SI 2013/104
National Treatment Agency (Abolition) and the Health and Social Care Act 2012 (Consequential, Transitional and Saving Provisions) Order 2013, SI 2013/235
Civil Procedure (Amendment) Rules 2013, SI 2013/262
Competition Act 1998 (Consequential Provisions) Order 2013, SI 2013/294
Civil Legal Aid (Remuneration) Regulations 2013, SI 2013/422
Criminal Legal Aid (Financial Resources) Regulations 2013, SI 2013/471
Civil Legal Aid (Statutory Charge) Regulations 2013, SI 2013/503
Civil Procedure (Amendment No 2) Rules 2013, SI 2013/515
Family Procedure (Amendment) Rules 2013, SI 2013/530
Legal Aid, Sentencing and Punishment of Offenders Act 2012 (Consequential, Transitional and Saving Provisions) Regulations 2013, SI 2013/534
Universal Credit (Consequential, Supplementary, Incidental and Miscellaneous Provisions) Regulations 2013, SI 2013/630
Care Planning, Placement and Case Review (England) (Miscellaneous Amendments) Regulations 2013, SI 2013/706
Care Planning, Placement and Case Review and Fostering Services (Miscellaneous Amendments) Regulations 2013, SI 2013/984
Adoption Agencies (Miscellaneous Amendments) Regulations 2013, SI 2013/985
Family Proceedings Fees (Amendment) Order 2013, SI 2013/1407
Civil Procedure (Amendment No 4) Rules 2013, SI 2013/1412
Children's Hearings (Scotland) Act 2011 (Consequential and Transitional Provisions and Savings) Order 2013, SI 2013/1465
Family Procedure (Amendment No 2) Rules 2013, SI 2013/1472
Civil Procedure (Amendment No 5) Rules 2013, SI 2013/1571
Civil Procedure (Amendment No 6) Rules 2013, SI 2013/1695
Adoption (Recognition of Overseas Adoptions) Regulations 2013, SI 2013/1801
Taking Control of Goods Regulations 2013, SI 2013/1894
Civil Procedure (Amendment No 7) Rules 2013, SI 2013/1974
Courts and Tribunals Fee Remissions Order 2013, SI 2013/2302
Occupational and Personal Pension Schemes (Disclosure of Information) Regulations 2013, SI 2013/2734
Civil Legal Aid (Remuneration) (Amendment) Regulations 2013, SI 2013/2877

Family Procedure (Amendment No 3) Rules 2013, SI 2013/3204
Children's Homes and Looked after Children (Miscellaneous Amendments) (England) Regulations 2013, SI 2013/3239
2014 Taking Control of Goods (Fees) Regulations 2014, SI 2014/1
Civil Procedure (Amendment) Rules 2014, SI 2014/407
Civil Procedure (Amendment No 2) Rules 2014, SI 2014/482
County Court Jurisdiction Order 2014, SI 2014/503
Social Care (Self-directed Support) (Scotland) Act 2013 (Consequential Modifications and Savings) Order 2014, SI 2014/513
Family Procedure (Amendment) Rules 2014, SI 2014/524
Marriage (Same Sex Couples) (Jurisdiction and Recognition of Judgments) Regulations 2014, SI 2014/543
Marriage (Same Sex Couples) Act 2013 (Consequential and Contrary Provisions and Scotland) Order 2014, SI 2014/560
Courts and Tribunals Fees (Miscellaneous Amendments) Order 2014, SI 2014/590
Access to Justice Act 1999 (Destination of Appeals) (Family Proceedings) Order 2014, SI 2014/602
Justices' Clerks and Assistants Rules 2014, SI 2014/603
Crime and Courts Act 2013 (Family Court: Consequential Provision) Order 2014, SI 2014/605
Family Procedure (Amendment No 2) Rules 2014, SI 2014/667
Family Court (Contempt of Court) (Powers) Regulations 2014, SI 2014/833
Family Court (Composition and Distribution of Business) Rules 2014, SI 2014/840
Justices' Clerks and Assistants (Amendment) Rules 2014, SI 2014/841
Family Procedure (Amendment No 3) Rules 2014, SI 2014/843
Child Arrangements Order (Consequential Amendments to Subordinate Legislation) Order 2014, SI 2014/852
Civil Procedure (Amendment No 4) Rules 2008, SI 2014/867
Family Proceedings Fees (Amendment) Order 2014, SI 2014/877
Crime and Courts Act 2013 (Family Court: Consequential Provision) (No 2) Order 2014, SI 2014/879
Crime and Courts Act 2013 (Family Court: Transitional and Saving Provision) Order 2014, SI 2014/956
County Court Remedies Regulations 2014, SI 2014/982
Children and Families Act 2014 (Transitional Proceedings) Order 2014, SI 2014/1042
Adoption and Care Planning (Miscellaneous Amendments) Regulations 2014, SI 2014/1556
Criminal Procedure Rules 2014, SI 2014/1610
Care Planning and Care Leavers (Amendment) Regulations 2014, SI 2014/1917
Civil Procedure (Amendment No 6) Rules 2014, SI 2014/2044
Special Educational Needs (Consequential Amendments to Subordinate Legislation) Order 2014, SI 2014/2103
Human Fertilisation and Embryology (Quality and Safety) Regulations 2014, SI 2014/2884
Civil Jurisdiction and Judgments (Amendment) Regulations 2014, SI 2014/2947
Marriage (Same Sex Couples) Act 2013 (Consequential and Contrary Provisions and Scotland) and Marriage and Civil Partnership (Scotland) Act 2014 (Consequential Provisions) Order 2014, SI 2014/3168
High Court (Distribution of Business) Order 2014, SI 2014/3257
Family Procedure (Amendment No 4) Rules 2014, SI 2014/3296
Family Court (Composition and Distribution of Business) (Amendment) Rules 2014, SI 2014/3297
Civil Jurisdiction and Judgments (Protection Measures) Regulations 2014, SI 2014/3298
Civil Procedure (Amendment No 8) Rules 2014, SI 2014/3299
2015 Gender Recognition Register (Marriage and Civil Partnership) Regulations 2015, SI 2015/50
Public Contracts Regulations 2015, SI 2015/102
State Pension Regulations 2015, SI 2015/173
Children (Secure Accommodation) (Amendment) (England) Regulations 2015, SI 2015/188
Civil Procedure (Amendment) Rules 2015, SI 2015/406
Care Planning and Fostering (Miscellaneous Amendments) (England) Regulations 2015, SI 2015/495
Human Fertilisation and Embryology (Mitochondrial Donation) Regulations 2015, SI 2015/572
Civil Proceedings and Family Proceedings (Amendment) Order 2015, SI 2015/576
Road Safety Act 2006 (Consequential Amendments) Order 2015, SI 2015/583
Civil Procedure (Amendment No 2) Rules 2015, SI 2015/670
Family Proceedings Fees (Amendment) Order 2015, SI 2015/687
Justices' Clerks and Assistants (Amendment) Rules 2015, SI 2015/890
Family Procedure (Amendment) Rules 2015, SI 2015/913
Care Act 2014 and Children and Families Act 2014 (Consequential Amendments) Order 2015, SI 2015/914

Family Proceedings Fees (Amendment No 2) Order 2015, SI 2015/1419
Family Procedure (Amendment No 2) Rules 2015, SI 2015/1420
Family Court (Composition and Distribution of Business) (Amendment) Rules 2015, SI 2015/1421
Civil Jurisdiction and Judgments (Maintenance) and International Recovery of Maintenance (Hague Convention 2007 etc) (Amendment) Order 2015, SI 2015/1489
Civil Procedure (Amendment No 4) Rules 2015, SI 2015/1569
Civil Jurisdiction and Judgments (Hague Convention on Choice of Court Agreements 2005) Regulations 2015, SI 2015/1644
Care Planning, Placement and Case Review (Wales) Regulations 2015, SI 2015/1818
Family Procedure (Amendment No 3) Rules 2015, SI 2015/1868
Children (Secure Accommodation) (Amendment) (England) Regulations 2015, SI 2015/1883
Children (Secure Accommodation) (Wales) Regulations 2015, SI 2015/1988

2016 Pensions Act 2014 (Pension Sharing on Divorce etc) (Transitional Provision) Order 2016, SI 2016/39
Special Guardianship (Amendment) Regulations 2016, SI 2016/111
Social Services and Well-being (Wales) Act 2014 (Consequential Amendments) (Secondary Legislation) Regulations 2016, SI 2016/211
Civil Procedure (Amendment) Rules 2016, SI 2016/234
Pension Sharing (Miscellaneous Amendments) Regulations 2016, SI 2016/289
Family Procedure (Amendment) Rules 2016, SI 2016/355
Civil Proceedings, Family Proceedings and Upper Tribunal Fees (Amendment) Order 2016, SI 2016/402
Social Services and Well-being (Wales) Act 2014 (Consequential Amendments) Regulations 2016, SI 2016/413
Justices of the Peace Rules 2016, SI 2016/709
Civil Procedure (Amendment No 3) Rules 2016, SI 2016/788
Access to Justice Act 1999 (Destination of Appeals) (Family Proceedings) (Amendment) Order 2016, SI 2016/891
Family Procedure (Amendment No 2) Rules 2016, SI 2016/901
Access to Justice Act 1999 (Destination of Appeals) Order 2016, SI 2016/917
Family Procedure (Amendment No 3) Rules 2016, SI 2016/1013

2017 Pension Protection Fund and Occupational Pension Schemes (Levy Ceiling and Compensation Cap) Order 2017, SI 2017/50
Regulation and Inspection of Social Care (Wales) Act 2016 (Consequential Amendments to Secondary Legislation) Regulations 2017, SI 2017/52
Family Procedure (Amendment) Rules 2017, SI 2017/413
Pensions Act 2014 (Consequential, Supplementary and Incidental Amendments) Order 2017, SI 2017/422

Table of Cases

References are to page numbers.

(1) Blight (2) Meredith (3) Lewis v Brewster [2012] EWHC 165 (Ch), [2012] 1 WLR 2841, [2012] BPIR 476 1242, 2279, 2291
(1) KE (2) TB Appellants v SE Respondent & others [2011] EWCA Civ 361, [2011] 2 FLR 724; *sub nom* Re E (Children) 389, 391

A & L (Children), Re [2011] EWCA Civ 1205, [2012] 1 WLR 595, [2012] 1 FLR 134 203
A (A Child) (Adoption), Re [2007] EWCA Civ 1383, [2008] 1 FLR 959; *sub nom* Re A; Coventry City Council v CC and A 278
A (A Child) (Residence Order), Re [2007] EWCA Civ 899 204, 1235, 1522
A (A Child) v Chief Constable of Dorset Police [2010] EWHC 1748 (Admin), [2011] 1 FLR 11 903, 1481
A (A Child), Re [2010] EWCA Civ 1413 535
A (A Child), Re [2013] EWCA Civ 543 445, 551
A (A Child), Re [2014] EWCA Civ 1577, [2015] 1 Fam 277, [2015] 2 FLR 625 650
A (A Child), Re [2015] EWHC 1709 (Fam) 512
A (A Child), Re [2016] EWCA Civ 572, [2016] 4 WLR 111 1546, 1552, 2721, 2787, 2800
A (A Child: Application for leave to apply for a child arrangements order), Re [2015] EWCA Civ 910 446
A (A Child: Financial Provision), Re [2014] EWCA Civ 1577, [2015] 1 Fam 277, [2015] 2 FLR 625 1440
A (A Minor) (Abduction), Re [1988] 1 FLR 365, CA 389
A (A Minor) (Paternity: Refusal of Blood Test), Re [1994] 2 FLR 463, CA 410, 921, 923
A (A Minor) (Residence Order: Leave to Apply), Re [1993] 1 FLR 425, FD 1501
A (A Patient) v A Health Authority; Re J; The Queen on the Application of S v Secretary of State for the Home Department [2002] EWHC 18 (Fam/Admin), [2002] Fam 213, [2002] 1 FLR 845; *sub nom* A v A Health Authority and Others; Re J and Linked Applications 1239, 1513, 1545
A (Abduction: Children's Objections: Domestic Violence), Re [2013] EWCA Civ 1256, [2014] 1 FLR 1433 391
A (Abduction: Habitual Residence), Re [1996] 1 WLR 25, [1996] 1 FLR 1, FD; *sub nom* Re A (Minors) (Abduction: Habitual Residence) 379
A (Abduction: Habitual Residence: Consent), Re [2005] EWHC 2998 (Fam), [2006] 2 FLR 1 378
A (Abduction: Interim Directions: Accommodation by Local Authority), Re [2010] EWCA Civ 586, [2011] 1 Fam 179, [2011] 1 FLR 1 366, 1553
A (Abduction: Rights of Custody: Imprisonment), Re [2004] 1 FLR 1, FD 379
A (Adoption of a Russian Child), Re [2000] 1 FLR 539 289
A (Adoption: Removal), Re [2009] EWCA Civ 41, [2010] 1 Fam 9, [2009] 2 FLR 597 278, 301, 664
A (Application for Care and Placement Orders: Local Authority Failings), Re [2015] EWFC 11, [2016] 1 FLR 1; *sub nom* Darlington Borough Council v M, F, GM and GF 532, 534, 536, 543
A (Application for Leave), Re [1998] 1 FLR 1, CA 620, 1514, 1528
A (Area of Freedom, Security and Justice), Re (Case C-523/07) [2009] ECR I-2805, [2010] Fam 42, [2009] 2 FLR 1, ECJ 377, 522, 524, 2733, 2774, 2778, 2787, 2869
A (Care Plan), Re [2008] EWCA Civ 650, [2008] 2 FLR 1183 545
A (Care Proceedings: Learning Disabled Parent), Re [2013] EWHC 3502 (Fam), [2014] 2 FLR 591 541, 625
A (Care: Discharge Application by Child), Re [1995] 1 FLR 599, FD 564
A (Child Abuse), Re [2007] EWCA Civ 1058, [2008] 1 FLR 1423 203, 2194
A (Child of the Family), Re [1998] 1 FLR 347, CA 1016
A (Children) (Interim Care Order), Re [2001] 3 FCR 402, FD 559
A (Children: Scottish Adoptions), Re [2017] EWHC 35 (Fam) 282
A (Children: Split Hearing), Re [2006] EWCA Civ 714, [2007] 1 FLR 905 204, 566, 1508, 2200, 2205
A (Conjoined Twins: Medical Treatment) (No 2), Re [2001] 1 FLR 267, CA 1704, 2065, 2068
A (Contact: Section 91(14)), Re [2009] EWCA Civ 1548, [2010] 2 FLR 151 620
A (Contact: Separate Representation), Re [2001] 1 FLR 715, CA 2573
A (Custody Decision after Maltese Non-Return Order), Re [2006] EWHC 3397 (Fam), [2007] 1 FLR 1923 384, 2794

A (Fact-Finding Hearing: Judge Meeting with Child), Re [2012] EWCA Civ 185, [2012] 2 FLR 369 1531
A (Family Proceedings: Electronic Tagging), Re [2009] EWHC 710 (Fam), [2009] 2 FLR 891 446
A (Father: Knowledge of Child's Birth), Re [2011] EWCA Civ 273, [2011] 2 FLR 123 448, 1502, 1530
A (Foreign Access Order: Enforcement), Re [1996] 1 FLR 561, CA 394, 396
A (Foreign Contact Order: Jurisdiction), Re [2003] EWHC 2911 (Fam), [2004] 1 FLR 641 395, 2783
A (Intractable Contact Dispute: Human Rights Violations), Re [2013] EWCA Civ 1104 443
A (Joint Residence: Parental Responsibility), Re [2008] EWCA Civ 867, [2008] 2 FLR 1593 429, 442
A (Jurisdiction: Return of Child), Re [2013] UKSC 60, [2014] AC 1, [2014] 1 FLR 111 377, 379, 522, 523, 838, 839, 841, 1545, 2778, 2783
A (Male Sterilisation), Re [2000] 1 FLR 549, CA 1547
A (Medical Treatment: Removal of Artificial Ventilation), Re [2015] EWHC 443 (Fam), [2016] 1 FLR 241 1546
A (Minors) (Abduction: Acquiescence) (No 2), Re [1993] Fam 1, [1993] 1 FLR 396, CA; *sub nom* Re A (Minors) (Abduction: Custody Rights) (No 2) 389
A (Minors) (Abduction: Acquiescence), Re [1992] Fam 106, [1992] 2 FLR 14, CA; *sub nom* Re A (Minors) (Abduction: Custody Rights) 391
A (Minors) (Abduction: Custody Rights) (No 2), Re [1993] Fam 1, [1993] 1 FLR 396, CA; *sub nom* Re A (Minors) (Abduction: Acquiescence) (No 2) 389
A (Minors) (Abduction: Custody Rights), Re [1992] Fam 106, [1992] 2 FLR 14, CA; *sub nom* Re A (Minors) (Abduction: Acquiescence) 391
A (Minors) (Abduction: Habitual Residence), Re [1996] 1 WLR 25, [1996] 1 FLR 1, FD; *sub nom* Re A (Abduction: Habitual Residence) 379
A (Placement Order: Imposition of Conditions on Adoption), Re [2013] EWCA Civ 1611, [2014] 1 WLR 2139, [2014] 2 FLR 351 264, 290
A (Removal from Jurisdiction), Re [2012] EWCA Civ 1041, [2014] 1 FLR 1 472, 2196
A (Removal Outside Jurisdiction: Habitual Residence), Re [2011] EWCA Civ 265, [2011] 1 FLR 2025 379, 838, 844, 2782, 2783
A (Residence Order), Re [2009] EWCA Civ 1141, [2010] 1 FLR 1083 444
A (Section 8 Order: Grandparent Application), Re [1995] 2 FLR 153, CA 455
A (Secure Accommodation Order), Re [2001] Fam Law 806, FD 512
A (Security for Return to the Jurisdiction) (Note), Re [1999] 2 FLR 1, FD 472
A (Sexual Abuse: Disclosure), Re [2012] UKSC 60, [2013] 2 AC 66, [2013] 1 FLR 948 1512, 1753, 1763
A (Specific Issue Order: Parental Dispute), Re [2001] 1 FLR 121, CA 449
A (Supervised Contact Order: Assessment of Impact of Domestic Violence), Re [2015] EWCA Civ 486, [2016] 1 FLR 689 444, 445
A (Supervision Order: Extension), Re [1995] 1 WLR 482, [1995] 1 FLR 335, CA 672, 673
A (Temporary Removal from Jurisdiction), Re [2004] EWCA Civ 1587, [2005] 1 FLR 639 473
A (Termination of Parental Responsibility), Re [2013] EWHC 2963 (Fam), [2014] 1 FLR 1305 429
A (Vulnerable Witness), Re [2013] EWHC 1694 (Fam), [2013] 2 FLR 1473 625
A (Vulnerable Witness: Fact Finding), Re [2013] EWHC 2124 (Fam), [2014] 1 FLR 146 625
A and Another v C and Another [2016] EWFC 42 42
A and Anr v C [2016] EWFC 4 990
A and B (Children: Brussels II Revised: Article 15), Re [2014] EWFC 40 2754
A and B (Children: Restrictions on Parental Responsibility: Radicalisation and Extremism), Re [2016] EWFC 40, [2016] 2 FLR 977 425, 448
A and B (Contact) (No 4), Re [2015] EWHC 2839 (Fam), [2016] 2 FLR 429 424, 443
A and B (Minors) (No 2), Re [1995] 1 FLR 351, FD 423, 436, 437, 543, 547, 556, 1514, 1515, 2543
A and B (One Parent Killed by the Other: Guidance), Re [2010] EWHC 3824 (Fam), [2011] 1 FLR 783 534
A and B (Parental Order), Re [2015] EWHC 2080 (Fam), [2016] 2 FLR 446 990
A and B (Parental Order: Domicile), Re [2013] EWHC 426 (Fam), [2014] 1 FLR 169 990
A and D (Local Authority: Religious Upbringing), Re [2010] EWHC 2503 (Fam), [2011] 1 FLR 615 549
A and L (Children), Re [2011] EWCA Civ 1205, [2012] 1 WLR 595, [2012] 1 FLR 134 1533, 1865, 2194
A and L (Fact-Finding Hearing: Extempore Judgment), Re [2011] EWCA Civ 1611, [2012] 1 FLR 1243 2196
A and Others (Minors) (Residence Order: Leave to Apply), Re [1992] Fam 182, [1992] 2 FLR 154, CA; *sub nom* Re A and W (Minors) (Residence Order: Leave to Apply) 451, 454
A and S v Lancashire County Council [2012] EWHC 1689 (Fam), [2013] 2 FLR 803 514, 1000
A and S v London Borough of Enfield [2008] EWHC 1886 (Admin), [2008] 2 FLR 1945 1513
A and W (Minors) (Residence Order: Leave to Apply), Re [1992] Fam 182, [1992] 2 FLR 154, CA; *sub nom* Re A and Others (Minors) (Residence Order: Leave to Apply) 451, 454
A B and C (Surrogacy Expenses), Re [2016] EWFC 33 991

A Barrister (Wasted Costs Order) (No 1 of 1991), Re [1993] QB 293, CA 231, 2160
A Chief Constable v YK and Others [2010] EWHC 2438 (Fam), [2012] Fam 102, [2011] 1 FLR 1493 903, 1481, 1758
A City Council v T, J and K [2011] EWHC 1082 (Fam), [2011] 2 FLR 803 512, 622, 1519
A Council v M and Others (No 3) (Reporting Restriction Order; Adoption; Artificial Insemination) [2012] EWHC 2038 (Fam), [2013] 2 FLR 1270 628, 1040
A County Council v A Mother, A Father and X, Y and Z (by their Guardian) [2005] EWHC 31 (Fam), [2005] 2 FLR 129 1532
A County Council v DP, RS, BS by his Children's Guardian [2005] EWHC 1593 (Fam), [2005] 2 FLR 1031 540
A County Council v K, D and L [2005] EWHC 144 (Fam), [2005] 1 FLR 851 1532
A County Council v K, T and C [2011] EWHC 1672 (Fam), [2011] 2 FLR 817 531
A County Council v M and Others (No 4) (Foreign Adoption: Refusal of Recognition) [2013] EWHC 1501 (Fam), [2014] 1 FLR 881 1015
A County Council v SB, MA and AA [2010] EWHC 2528 (Fam), [2011] 1 FLR 651 903, 1481
A Health Authority v X (Discovery: Medical Conduct) [2001] 2 FLR 673 1757
A Local Authority v A [2009] EWCA Civ 1057, [2010] 2 FLR 1757 1795
A Local Authority v A [2009] EWHC 1574 (Fam), [2010] 1 FLR 545 1510
A Local Authority v A, B and E [2011] EWHC 2062 (Fam), [2012] 2 FLR 601 549, 552
A Local Authority v D and Others [2015] EWHC 3125 (Fam), [2016] 1 WLR 1160, [2016] 2 FLR 601 487, 494, 558, 1547
A Local Authority v DG and Others [2014] EWHC 63 (Fam), [2014] 2 FLR 713 543, 1762, 1766
A Local Authority v DL & Ors [2012] EWCA Civ 253, [2013] Fam 1, [2012] COPLR 504 2576
A Local Authority v DL, RL, and ML [2010] EWHC 2675 (Fam), [2011] Fam 189, [2011] 1 FLR 957 1548
A Local Authority v E and Others [2012] EWHC 1639 (COP), [2012] COPLR 441 1008
A Local Authority v GC [2008] EWHC 2555 (Fam), [2009] 1 Fam 83, [2009] 1 FLR 299 258, 259, 283
A Local Authority v H [2012] EWHC 49 (COP, [2012] COPLR 305 338
A Local Authority v K and N [2011] EWHC 1156 (Fam), [2011] 2 FLR 1165 534
A Local Authority v K and Others [2011] EWHC 2581 (Fam), [2012] 1 FLR 765 530
A Local Authority v M (Funding of Residential Assessments) [2008] EWHC 162 (Fam), [2008] 1 FLR 1579 561
A Local Authority v M and F; The Children (by their Guardian) [2009] EWHC 3172 (Fam), [2010] 1 FLR 1355 1502
A Local Authority v SB, AB & MB [2010] EWHC 1744 (Fam), [2010] 2 FLR 1203 559, 631, 1546, 1547
A Local Authority v W, L, W, T and R (by the Children's Guardian) [2005] EWHC 1564 (Fam), [2006] 1 FLR 1 247, 628
A Local Authority v Y, Z and Others [2006] 2 FLR 41, FD 474
A Local Health Board v Y (A Child) [2016] EWHC 206 (Fam) 1546
A London Borough Council v K and Others [2009] EWHC 850 (Fam) 624, 1510, 1794
A v (1) SSWP and (2) G [2017] UKUT 9 2049
A v A (A Minor: Financial Provision) [1994] 1 FLR 657, FD 648
A v A (Abduction: Jurisdiction) [1995] Fam 96, [1995] 1 FLR 341, FD; *sub nom* Re N 365
A v A (Child Abduction) [1993] 2 FLR 225, FD 379
A v A (Financial Provision) [1998] 2 FLR 180, FD 1020
A v A (forum conveniens) [1999] 1 FLR 1, FD 828
A v A (Maintenance Pending Suit: Provision for Legal Fees) [2001] 1 FLR 377, FD 215
A v A [1997] Fam Law 301, CA 56
A v A [2004] EWHC 2818 (Fam), [2006] 2 FLR 115 1181
A v A [2007] EWHC 99 (Fam), [2007] 2 FLR 467 1181
A v A [2012] All ER (D) 108 (Dec), FD 1184
A v A (No 2) (Ancillary Relief: Costs) [2007] EWHC 1810 (Fam), [2008] 1 FLR 1428 1439, 1849, 2146
A v A (Reporting Restriction) [2012] EWHC 4226 (Fam), [2013] 2 FLR 947 1040
A v A (Return Order on the Basis of British Nationality) [2013] EWHC 3298 (Fam), [2014] 2 FLR 244 841
A v A (Shared Residence) [2004] EWHC 142 (Fam), [2004] 1 FLR 1195 441, 2573
A v A Health Authority and Others; J and Linked Applications, Re [2002] EWHC 18 (Fam/Admin), [2002] Fam 213, [2002] 1 FLR 845; *sub nom* A (A Patient) v A Health Authority; Re J; The Queen on the Application of S v Secretary of State for the Home Department 1239, 1513, 1545
A v B (Abduction: Declaration) [2008] EWHC 2524 (Fam), [2009] 1 FLR 1253 367, 375, 379
A v B (Case C-184/14) [2015] 2 FLR 637, CJEU 2866
A v B (Case C-489/14) [2016] 1 FLR 31, CJEU 2785, 2786, 2787
A v B (Jurisdiction) [2011] EWHC 2752 (Fam), [2012] 1 FLR 768 524, 843, 2786

A v B and C (Lesbian Co-Parents: Role of Father) [2012] EWCA Civ 285, [2012] 1 WLR 3456, [2012] 2 FLR 607 427, 428, 441, 455, 702
A v British Broadcasting Corporation [2014] UKSC 25, [2015] 1 AC 558 2142
A v East Sussex County Council and Chief Constable of Sussex [2010] EWCA Civ 743, [2010] 2 FLR 1596 574, 580
A v Essex County Council [2010] UKSC 33, [2011] AC 280 1012
A v H (Presumption of Death) [2016] EWHC 762 (Fam) 1222
A v L (Jurisdiction: Brussels II) [2002] 1 FLR 1042, FD 2783
A v L [2011] EWHC 3150 (Fam), [2012] 1 FLR 985 1017, 1179
A v M (Family Proceedings: Publicity), Re [2000] 1 FLR 562, FD 1544
A v M and Walsall Metropolitan Borough Council [1993] 2 FLR 244, FD 551
A v P (Surrogacy: Parental Order: Death of Applicant) [2011] EWHC 1738 (Fam), [2012] 2 FLR 145 990
A v United Kingdom (1999) 27 EHRR 611, [1998] 2 FLR 959 1005
A v Ward [2010] EWHC 16 (Fam), [2010] 1 FLR 1497 246, 1040
A, B & C v Ireland [2010] ECHR 2032 1004
A, Re; Coventry City Council v CC and A [2007] EWCA Civ 1383, [2008] 1 FLR 959; *sub nom* Re A (A Child) (Adoption) 278
A, Re; HA v MB (Brussels II Revised: Article 11(7) Application) [2007] EWHC 2016 (Fam), [2008] 1 FLR 289 385, 2734, 2779, 2781
A-H (Contact Order), Re [2008] EWCA Civ 630, [2008] 2 FLR 1188 435
AA v BB and Children (Through their Children's Guardian) [2013] EWHC 227 (Fam), [2014] 1 FLR 178 448
AA v NA and KAB [2010] 2 FLR 1173, FD 445
AAA v ASH, Registrar-General for England and Wales and The Secretary for Justice Intervening [2009] EWHC 636 (Fam), [2010] 1 FLR 1 380
AB (BIIR: Care Proceedings), Re [2012] EWCA Civ 978, [2013] 1 WLR 308, [2013] 1 FLR 168 524, 2745, 2798
AB (Care Proceedings: Disclosure of Medical Evidence to Police) [2002] EWHC 2198 (Fam), [2003] 1 FLR 579 629
AB (Care Proceedings: Service on Husband Ignorant of Child's Existence), Re [2003] EWCA Civ 1842, [2004] 1 FLR 527 1502
AB (Surrogacy: Consent), Re [2016] EWHC 2643 (Fam) 991
AB and CD v CT (Parental Order: Consent of Surrogate Mother) [2015] EWFC 12, [2016] 1 FLR 41 989, 991
AB v CB (Financial Remedy: Variation of Trust) [2014] EWHC 2998 (Fam), [2015] 2 FLR 25 1172
AB v CD (Financial Remedy Consent Order: Non- Disclosure) [2016] EWHC 10 (Fam), [2017] 1 FLR 13 1758
AB v CD and the Z Fertility Clinic [2013] EWHC 1418 (Fam), [2013] 2 FLR 1357 702, 983
AB v JJB [2015] EWHC 192 (Fam), [2015] 2 FLR 1143 93, 2440, 2868, 2882
AB v JLB (Brussels II Revised: Article 15) [2008] EWHC 2965 (Fam), [2009] 1 FLR 517 524, 525
Abbassi v Abbassi and another [2006] EWCA Civ 355, [2006] 2 FLR 415 869
Abbot v Abbot [2007] UKPC 53, [2008] 1 FLR 1451 1181, 1262
ABC v PM and Another [2015] EWFC 32 1210
Abdulaziz & Others v United Kingdom (1985) 7 EHRR 471 1010
Abram (Deceased), Re [1996] 2 FLR 379, ChD 1019, 1023
AC v DC (No 2) [2012] EWHC 2420 (Fam), [2013] 2 FLR 1499 1180
AC v DC and Eight Others [2012] EWHC 2032 (Fam), [2013] 2 FLR 1483 1209
AD and AM (Fact-Finding Hearing) (Application for Re-Hearing), Re [2016] EWHC 326 (Fam), [2016] 2 FLR 1247 535
AD v CD and AD [2007] EWCA Civ 1277, [2008] 1 FLR 1003 2794
Adam v Germany [2009] 1 FLR 560, ECHR 1007
Adams v Innovene Trustees Ltd (2013) 18 September, ref PO823, Pensions Ombudsman 2517
Adams v Schofield [1983] CLY 594, CA 1025
Adetola v First-Tier Tribunal (Immigration and Asylum Chamber) and SSHD [2010] EWHC 3197 (Admin), [2011] 2 FLR 611 1015
Adoption Application (Adoption of Non-Patrial), Re An [1992] 1 WLR 596, [1992] 1 FLR 341, FD; *sub nom* Re an Adoption Application 301
Adoption Application, Re An [1990] 1 WLR 520, [1990] 1 FLR 412, FD 1657
Adoption Application, Re An [1992] 1 WLR 596, [1992] 1 FLR 341, FD; *sub nom* Re An Adoption Application (Adoption of Non-Patrial) 301
AF v T and Another (Brussels II Revised: Art 11(7) Application) [2011] EWHC 1315 (Fam), [2011] 2 FLR 891 385, 2781
Agbaje v Agbaje [2010] UKSC 13, [2010] 1 AC 628, [2010] 1 FLR 1813 57, 58, 1125, 1127, 1128, 1387, 1394, 1425, 2857

AGN (Adoption: Foreign Adoption), Re [2000] 2 FLR 431, FD; *sub nom* Re N (A Minor) (Adoption: Foreign Guardianship) 282, 283
Aguilar v Secretary of State for the Home Department [2010] EWCA Civ 1482, [2011] 1 FLR 1187 996, 1010
AH v PH (Scandinavian Marriage Settlement) [2013] EWHC 3873 (Fam), [2014] 2 FLR 251 650, 1440
Ahmed v Mustafa [2014] EWCA Civ 277, [2015] 1 FLR 139 1209
AI v MT (Alternative Dispute Resolution) [2013] EWHC 100 (Fam), [2013] 2 FLR 371 179, 366, 1307, 1448
Aintree University Hospitals NHS Foundation Trust v James [2013] UKSC 67, [2014] 1 AC 591, [2013] COPLR 492 1546
Air Ministry v Harris [1951] 2 All ER 862, CA 2335
AJ (Adoption Order or Special Guardianship Order), Re [2007] EWCA Civ 55, [2007] 1 FLR 507 256, 474
AJ (Brussels II Revised), Re [2011] EWHC 3450 (Fam), [2012] 2 FLR 689 382, 2750, 2780
AJ (Contact: Brussels II Revised), Re [2012] EWHC 931 (Fam), [2012] 2 FLR 1065 382, 2780
AK (Medical Treatment: Consent), Re [2001] 1 FLR 129, FD 1547
AK (Secure Accommodation Order), Re [2000] NI 205, [2000] 1 FLR 317, FD (NI) 511
Al Hassan-Daniel v Revenue and Customs Commissioners [2010] EWCA Civ 1443, [2011] QB 866 999
Al Hilli (Children Reporting Restrictions), Re [2013] EWHC 2190 (Fam), [2014] 1 FLR 403 247, 1002, 1543, 1563
Al Nahkel for Contracting and Trading v Lowe [1986] QB 235, QBD 1236
Al Skeini v UK (2011) 53 EHRR 18 993
Al-Baker v Al-Baker [2016] EWHC 2510 (Fam) 1321
Al-Jeffery v Al-Jeffery (Vulnerable adult; British citizen) [2016] EWHC 2151 (Fam) 1545
Al-Khatib v Masry [2004] EWCA Civ 1353, [2005] 1 FLR 381 2193
Al-Saedy v Musawi (Presumption of Marriage) [2010] EWHC 3293 (Fam), [2011] 2 FLR 287 1014
Albert v Albert [1997] 2 FLR 791, [1996] BPIR 232, CA 2158
Alcott, Re [2016] EWHC 2414 (Fam) 628
Ali & Others v Birmingham City Council & Others [2010] UKSC 8, [2010] 2 AC 39 1006
Ali v Headteacher and Governors of Lord Grey School [2006] UKHL 14, [2006] 2 AC 363 1012
Allan v Clibbery [2002] EWCA Civ 45, [2002] Fam 261, [2002] 1 FLR 565; *sub nom* Clibbery v Allan 1040, 1248, 1249, 1391, 1755, 2111
Allard v Sweden (2004) 39 EHRR 321 1011
Allied Arab Bank Ltd v Hajjar [1988] QB 787, QBD 1236
Alltrans Express v CVA Holdings [1984] 1 WLR 394, CA 1235
AM v News Group Newspapers Ltd & Persons Unknown [2012] EWHC 308 (QB) 1010
AM v SS (Legal Services Order) [2013] EWHC 4380 (Fam), [2015] 1 FLR 1237 1166
Amberley Construction Ltd v Beamish [2003] EWCA Civ 1267 804
American Cyanamid Co v Ethicon Ltd [1975] AC 396, HL 1743
Ampthill Peerage Case [1977] 1 AC 547, HL 211
AMR (Adoption: Procedure), Re [1999] 2 FLR 807, FD 282, 283
AMV v RM (Children: Judge's Visit to Private Home) [2012] EWHC 3629 (Fam), [2013] 2 FLR 150 1528
An NHS Foundation Trust v Mr and Mrs R [2013] EWHC 2340 (Fam), [2014] 2 FLR 955 1547
An NHS Trust v SR (Radiotherapy and Chemotherapy) [2012] EWHC 3842 (Fam), [2013] 1 FLR 1297 1546
Anderson v Bank of British Columbia (1876) 2 Ch D 644, CA 1753
Andreson v Lovell [2009] EWHC 3397 (QB) 37
Ansari v Ansari [2008] EWCA Civ 1456, [2010] Fam 1, [2009] 1 FLR 1121 1210
Anufrijeva v Southwark London Borough Council; R (N) v Secretary of State for the Home Department); R (M) v Secretary of State for the Home Department) [2003] EWCA Civ 1406, [2004] QB 1124, [2004] 1 FLR 8 1001, 1043, 2048, 2049, 2136, 2137, 2254
AO (Care Proceedings), Re [2016] EWFC 36 533
AP v TD (Relocation: Retention of Jurisdiction) [2010] EWHC 2040 (Fam), [2011] 1 FLR 1851 840, 2782
Appleton and Gallagher v News Group Newspapers and PA [2015] EWHC 2689 (Fam), [2016] 2 FLR 1 1858
Application to commit Muhammed Nawaz Chaudry [2015] EWHC 2655 (Fam); *sub nom* Re Dad 30, 902, 1473, 1984, 1988
AR (A Child: Relocation), Re [2010] EWHC 1346 (Fam), [2010] 2 FLR 1577 442, 472
AR v AR (Treatment of Inherited Wealth) [2011] EWHC 2717 (Fam), [2012] 2 FLR 1 1181
AR v AS (Abduction: Non-Convention Country) [2015] EWHC 3440 (Fam), [2016] 2 FLR 1280 385
AR v RN (Habitual Residence) [2015] UKSC 35, [2016] 1 AC 76, [2015] 2 FLR 503 377, 2778
Arab Monetary Fund v Hashim [1989] 1 WLR 565, ChD 1242
Arbili v Arbili [2015] EWCA Civ 542, [2016] 1 FLR 473 1183, 1440
Archer v Archer [1999] 1 FLR 327, CA 1152

Arena Corp Ltd v Schroeder [2003] EWHC 1089 (Ch) 1241
Arif v Anwar and anor [2013] EWHC 624 (Fam) 20
Arif v Anwar and Rehan [2015] EWHC 124 (Fam), [2016] 1 FLR 359 1762
Arif v Zar and anor [2012] EWCA Civ 986 384, 1044, 1321
Arros Invest Ltd v Rafik Nishanov [2004] EWHC 576 (Ch), [2004] ILPr 22 1359
AS (Secure Accommodation Order), Re [1999] 1 FLR 103, FD 511, 512, 578, 1520, 1833
Asia Islamic Trade Finance Fund Ltd v Drum Risk Management Ltd & Ors [2015] EWHC 3748 (Comm) 795
Askew Page v Page [2001] Fam Law 794, Cty Ct 406, 410
Aspden v Elvy [2012] EWHC 1387 (Ch), [2012] 2 FLR 807 1263
Aston Cantlow and Wilmcote with Billesley Parochial Church Council v Wallbank [2003] UKHL 37, [2004] 1 AC 546 997
Aston v Aston [2007] WTLR 1349, [2008] CL 348, Cty Ct 1017
AT v SS (No 2) [2015] EWHC 3328 (Fam), [2016] 2 FLR 1122 382
Atkinson v Atkinson [1988] Fam 88, [1988] 2 FLR 353, CA 1184, 1203
Attorney-General v Barker [2000] 1 FLR 759, QBD 1246
Attorney-General v Guardian Newspapers Ltd (No 2) [1990] AC 109, HL 1753
Attorney-General v Leveller Magazine [1979] AC 440, HL 790
Attorney-General v Vernazza [1960] AC 965, HL 1233
Austin-Fell v Austin-Fell [1990] Fam 172, [1989] 2 FLR 497, FD 359, 2025
AV v RM (Appeal) [2012] EWHC 1173 (Fam), [2012] 2 FLR 709 193, 1866
AVH v SI & Anr (Abduction: Child's Objection) [2014] EWHC 2938 (Fam), [2015] 2 FLR 269 391
Avis v Turner [2007] EWCA Civ 748, [2008] Ch 2183 1264

B (A Child by her Guardian), Re [2017] EWHC 488 (Fam) 377, 386
B (A Child) (Disclosure of Evidence in Care Proceedings), Re [2012] 1 FLR 142, FD 1563
B (A Child) (Disclosure), Re [2004] EWHC 411 (Fam), [2004] 2 FLR 142 245, 246, 247, 2586
B (A Child) (Habitual Residence: Inherent Jurisdiction), Re [2016] UKSC 4, [2016] 1 AC 606, [2016] 1 FLR 561 377, 378, 839, 841, 1543, 1545, 2778
B (A Child) (Immunisation), Re [2003] EWCA Civ 1148, [2003] 2 FLR 1095; *sub nom* Re C (Welfare of Child: Immunisation) 559, 1795
B (A Child), Re [2006] EWCA Civ 716 435, 1707
B (A Child), Re [2009] UKSC 5, [2009] 1 WLR 2496, [2010] 1 FLR 551 205, 441, 472, 566, 1869, 2203
B (A Child), Re [2013] EWCA Civ 1434, [2014] 1 Fam 139, [2014] 1 FLR 900 2684
B (A Child), Re [2014] EWCA Civ 565, [2014] 1 WLR 4344, [2015] 1 FLR 884 206, 1870, 2204
B (A Child), Re [2014] EWCA Civ 843, [2015] 1 Fam 209, [2015] 1 FLR 871 373, 859, 1008
B (A Child), Re [2015] EWCA Civ 974 527
B (A Child), Re [2015] EWCA Civ 1053 206, 1865
B (A Minor) (Abduction), Re [1994] 2 FLR 249, CA 379, 380, 389
B (A Minor) (Care Order: Review), Re [1993] 1 FLR 421, FD; *sub nom* Chester County Council v B 551
B (A Minor) (Child Abduction: Habitual Residence), Re [1994] 2 FLR 915, FD; *sub nom* Re B (Child Abduction: Habitual Residence) 377
B (A Minor) (Disclosure of Evidence), Re [1993] Fam 142, [1993] 1 FLR 191, CA 157, 1509, 1510
B (A Minor) (Habitual Residence), Re [2016] EWHC 2174 (Fam) 377, 379, 1551, 2778
B (A Minor) (Residence Order: Ex Parte), Re [1992] Fam 162, [1992] 2 FLR 1, CA; *sub nom* Re B (Minors) (Residence Order) 449, 450, 1523
B (A Minor) (Secure Accommodation Order), Re [1995] 1 WLR 232, [1994] 2 FLR 707, CA; *sub nom* Re B (A Minor) (Secure Accommodation) 512
B (A Minor) (Secure Accommodation), Re [1995] 1 WLR 232, [1994] 2 FLR 707, CA; *sub nom* Re B (A Minor) (Secure Accommodation Order) 512
B (A Minor) (Split Hearings: Jurisdiction), Re [2000] 1 WLR 790, [2000] 1 FLR 334, CA; *sub nom* Re B (Split Hearings: Jurisdiction) 535, 1234, 1508
B (Abduction: Article 13 Defence), Re [1997] 2 FLR 573, FD 389
B (Abduction: Children's Objections), Re [1998] 1 FLR 667, FD 379
B (Adoption: Jurisdiction to Set Aside), Re [1995] Fam 239, [1995] 2 FLR 1, CA 280, 1651
B (Adoption: Natural Parent), Re [2001] UKHL 70, [2002] 1 WLR 258, [2002] 1 FLR 196; *sub nom* B v P (Adoption by Unmarried Father); B (A Child) v RP 286
B (Adult: Refusal of Medical Treatment), Re [2002] EWHC 429 (Fam), [2002] 1 FLR 1090; *sub nom* Re B (Consent to Treatment: Capacity) 1547
B (Agreed Findings of Fact), Re [1998] 2 FLR 968, CA; *sub nom* Re B (Threshold Criteria) 540
B (Appeal: Lack of Reasons), Re [2003] EWCA Civ 881, [2003] 2 FLR 1035 2196
B (Care or Supervision Order), Re [1996] 2 FLR 693, FD 539

B (Care Order: Jurisdiction), Re [2013] EWCA Civ 1434, [2014] 1 Fam 139, [2014] 1 FLR 900 522, 524, 525, 2778, 2785, 2787
B (Care Proceedings: Appeal), Re [2013] UKSC 33, [2013] 1 WLR 1911, [2013] 2 FLR 1075 193, 199, 203, 282, 289, 528, 530, 532, 538, 539, 1008, 1871, 2205
B (Care Proceedings: Diplomatic Immunity), Re [2002] EWHC 1751 (Fam), [2003] 1 Fam 16, [2003] 1 FLR 241 522
B (Care Proceedings: Interim Care Order), Re [2009] EWCA Civ 1254, [2010] 1 FLR 1211 559
B (Care Proceedings: Notification of Father Without Parental Responsibility) [1999] 2 FLR 408, FD 1501
B (Care Proceedings: Standard of Proof), Re [2008] UKHL 35, [2008] 2 FLR 141; *sub nom* Re B (Children) 445, 532, 536, 924, 1761, 2048
B (Care: Expert Witnesses), Re [1996] 1 FLR 667, CA 1532, 1832
B (Care: Interference with Family Life), Re [2003] EWCA Civ 786, [2003] 2 FLR 813 528, 1008
B (Case Management), Re [2012] EWCA Civ 1742, [2013] 1 FLR 963 527, 1278, 1528
B (Change of Surname), Re [1996] 1 FLR 791, CA; *sub nom* Re B (Minors) (Change of Surname) 447, 471
B (Child Abduction: Habitual Residence), Re [1994] 2 FLR 915, FD; *sub nom* Re B (A Minor) (Child Abduction: Habitual Residence) 377
B (Children Act Proceedings: Issue Estoppel), Re [1997] Fam 117, [1997] 1 FLR 285, FD; *sub nom* Re B (Minors) (Care Proceedings: Evidence); *sub nom* Re B (Minors) (Care Proceedings: Issue Estoppel) 1528, 1762, 1763
B (Children), Re [2002] EWCA Civ 1225 560
B (Children), Re [2008] UKHL 35, [2008] 2 FLR 141; *sub nom* Re B (Care Proceedings: Standard of Proof) 445, 532, 536, 924, 1761, 2048
B (Confiscation Order), Re [2008] EWHC 690 (Admin), [2008] 2 FLR 1 1173
B (Consent to Treatment: Capacity), Re [2002] EWHC 429 (Fam), [2002] 1 FLR 1090; *sub nom* Re B (Adult: Refusal of Medical Treatment) 1547
B (Contact: Stepfather's Hostility), Re [1997] 2 FLR 579, CA; *sub nom* Re B (Contact: Stepfather's Opposition) 1514, 1528
B (Contact: Stepfather's Opposition), Re [1997] 2 FLR 579, CA; *sub nom* Re B (Contact: Stepfather's Hostility) 1514, 1528
B (Contempt: Evidence), Re [1996] 1 WLR 627, [1996] 1 FLR 239, FD 1985
B (Court's Jurisdiction), Re [2004] EWCA Civ 681, [2004] 2 FLR 741 841, 861
B (Disclosure to Other Parties), Re [2001] 2 FLR 1017, FD 1007, 1511, 1512, 1513, 1657
B (Habitual Residence: Inherent Jurisdiction), Re [2015] EWCA Civ 886, [2016] 1 AC 606 1545
B (Hague Convention Proceedings), Re [2014] EWCA Civ 375, [2015] 1 FLR 389 382, 522, 523
B (Interim Care Order), Re [2010] EWCA Civ 324, [2010] 2 FLR 283 559
B (Interim Care Order: Directions), Re [2002] EWCA Civ 25, [2002] 1 FLR 545 560
B (Litigants In Person: Timely Service of Documents), Re [2016] EWHC 2365 (Fam) 527, 542, 1515, 1838
B (Local Authorities: Representation) (Note), Re [1996] 1 FLR 56, CA 1502
B (Looked After Child), Re [2013] EWCA Civ 964, [2014] 1 FLR 277 2714
B (Medical Treatment), Re [2008] EWHC 1996 (Fam), [2009] 1 FLR 1264 1547
B (Minors) (Abduction) (No 1), Re [1993] 1 FLR 988, FD 378
B (Minors) (Care Proceedings: Evidence), Re; *sub nom* Re B (Minors) (Care Proceedings: Issue Estoppel) [1997] Fam 117, [1997] 1 FLR 285, FD; *sub nom* Re B (Children Act Proceedings: Issue Estoppel) 1528, 1762, 1763
B (Minors) (Care Proceedings: Issue Estoppel), Re [1997] Fam 117, [1997] 1 FLR 285, FD; *sub nom* Re B (Children Act Proceedings: Issue Estoppel); *sub nom* Re B (Minors) (Care Proceedings: Evidence) 1528, 1762, 1763
B (Minors) (Care: Procedure), Re [1994] Fam Law 72, FD 1509, 1519, 1522
B (Minors) (Change of Surname), Re [1996] 1 FLR 791, CA; *sub nom* Re B (Change of Surname) 447, 471
B (Minors) (Custody), Re [1991] 1 FLR 137, CA 1870
B (Minors) (Parentage), Re [1996] 2 FLR 15, FD; *sub nom* Re B (Parentage) 1016
B (Minors) (Residence Order), Re [1992] Fam 162, [1992] 2 FLR 1, CA; *sub nom* Re B (A Minor) (Residence Order: Ex Parte) 449, 450, 1523
B (Parentage), Re [1996] 2 FLR 15, FD; *sub nom* Re B (Minors) (Parentage) 1016
B (Paternal Grandmother: Joinder as Party), Re [2012] EWCA Civ 737, [2012] 2 FLR 1358 455, 1501
B (Private Law Proceedings: Child's Evidence), Re [2014] EWCA Civ 1015, [2015] 1 FLR 1381 624
B (Procedure: Family Proceedings Court), Re [1993] Fam Law 209, CA 1831
B (Removal from Jurisdiction), Re; S (Removal from Jurisdiction), Re [2003] EWCA Civ 1149, [2003] 2 FLR 1043 472
B (Role of Biological Father), Re [2007] EWHC 1952 (Fam), [2008] 1 FLR 1015 428, 702
B (Section 91(14) Order: Duration), Re [2003] EWCA Civ 1966, [2004] 1 FLR 871 619

B (Secure Accommodation) (No 2), Re [2013] EWHC 4655 (Fam) 630
B (Secure Accommodation: Inherent Jurisdiction) (No 1), Re [2013] EWHC 4654 (Fam) 630
B (Split Hearings: Jurisdiction), Re [2000] 1 WLR 790, [2000] 1 FLR 334, CA; *sub nom* Re B (A Minor) (Split Hearings: Jurisdiction) 535, 1234, 1508
B (Supervision Order: Parental Undertaking), Re [1996] 1 WLR 716, [1996] 1 FLR 676, CA 544, 671, 1832
B (Threshold Criteria), Re [1998] 2 FLR 968, CA; *sub nom* Re B (Agreed Findings of Fact) 540
B and G (Children) (No 2), Re [2015] EWFC 3, [2015] 1 FLR 905; *sub nom* Leeds City Council v M, F, B, G (B and G by their Children's Guardian) 532, 534, 539, 927
B and H (Children), Re [2003] EWCA Civ 1818 535
B and H (Children), Re [2012] EWCA Civ 1359 534
B and H (Minors) (Costs: Legal Aid), Re [1994] 1 FLR 327, FD 1501, 1502
B and T (Care Proceedings: Legal Representation), Re [2001] 1 FLR 485, CA 1529
B and W (Threshold Criteria), Re [1999] 2 FLR 833, CA 537
B Borough Council v S (by the Official Solicitor) [2006] EWHC 2584 (Fam), [2007] 1 FLR 1600 1743
B County Council v L and Others [2002] EWHC 2327 (Fam) 561
B decd, Re [2000] Ch 662, [2000] 1 FLR 363, CA; [1999] Ch 206, [1999] 2 FLR 466, ChD; *sub nom* Bouette v Rose 1017, 1025
B Metropolitan Borough Council v H (Goodman Project: Concurrent Planning) [2000] Fam Law 237, Cty Ct 531
B v A (Wasted Costs Order) [2012] EWHC 3127 (Fam), [2013] 2 FLR 958 38, 368, 1523, 1743
B v A [2006] EWHC 2 (Fam); *sub nom* Re D (Contact and Parental Responsibility: Lesbian Mothers and Known Father) (No 2) 428, 702
B v B (Abduction) [1993] Fam 32, [1993] 1 FLR 238, CA; *sub nom* B v B (Abduction: Custody Rights) 390, 391
B v B (Abduction: Child with Learning Difficulties) [2011] EWHC 2300 (Fam), [2012] 1 FLR 881 390, 391
B v B (Abduction: Custody Rights) [1993] Fam 32, [1993] 1 FLR 238, CA; *sub nom* B v B (Abduction) 390, 391
B v B (Ancillary Relief) [2009] EWHC 3422 (Fam), [2010] 2 FLR 887 1181
B v B (Ancillary Relief: Distribution of Assets) [2008] EWCA Civ 284, [2008] 1 WLR 2362, [2008] 2 FLR 1627 1179
B v B (Ancillary Relief: Post-Separation Income) [2010] EWHC 193 (Fam), [2010] 2 FLR 1214 1183
B v B (Assessment of Assets: Pre-Marital Property) [2012] EWHC 314 (Fam), [2012] 2 FLR 22 2516
B v B (Brussels II Revised: Jurisdiction) [2010] EWHC 1989 (Fam), [2011] 1 FLR 54; *sub nom* Butt v Butt 2783
B v B (Child Abuse: Contact) [1994] 2 FLR 713, FD 423, 1514, 1705
B v B (Court Bundles: Video Evidence), (Note) [1994] 1 FLR 323; *sub nom* B v B (Sexual Abuse: Procedural Delay) 2543
B v B (Foreign Hague Convention Proceedings: Costs) [2015] EWCA Civ 1166, [2016] 2 FLR 1019 368
B v B (Injunction: Restraint on Leaving Jurisdiction) [1998] 1 WLR 329, [1997] 2 FLR 148, FD 57, 1236
B v B (Interim Contact with Grandparents) [1993] Fam Law 393, FD 457, 558
B v B (Mesher Order) [2002] EWHC 3106 (Fam), [2003] 2 FLR 285 1183
B v B (Minors) (Interviews and Listing Arrangements) [1994] 2 FLR 489, CA; *sub nom* B v B (Minors) (Residence and Care Disputes) 423, 437, 457, 1531, 1709
B v B (Minors) (Residence and Care Disputes) [1994] 2 FLR 489, CA; *sub nom* B v B (Minors) (Interviews and Listing Arrangements) 423, 437, 457, 1531, 1709
B v B [2010] EWHC 543 (Fam), [2012] COPLR 480 1684
B v B [2014] EWHC 1804 (Fam) 205, 366, 2738, 2781
B v B (Relinquishment of Jurisdiction: Brussels II Revised Art 12) [2012] EWHC 1924 (Fam), [2013] 2 FLR 1145 2783
B v B (Residence Order: Reasons for Decision) [1997] 2 FLR 602, CA 423
B v B (Residence: Condition Limiting Geographical Area) [2004] 2 FLR 979, FD 473
B v B (Scottish Contact Order: Jurisdiction to Vary) [1996] 1 WLR 231, [1996] 1 FLR 688, FD 839
B v B (Sexual Abuse: Procedural Delay) [1994] 1 FLR 323; *sub nom* B v B (Court Bundles: Video Evidence), (Note) 2543
B v C (Surrogacy: Adoption) [2015] EWFC 17 (Fam), [2015] 1 FLR 1392 989
B v Croydon Health Authority (No 2) [1996] 1 FLR 253, CA 2147
B v D (Abduction: Inherent Jurisdiction) [2008] EWHC 1246 (Fam), [2009] 1 FLR 1015 377, 2779
B v El-B (Abduction: Sharia Law: Welfare of Child) [2003] 1 FLR 811, FD 390
B v Kirklees Metropolitan Council [2010] EWHC 467 (Admin), [2010] 2 FLR 405 480
B v Lewisham Borough Council [2008] EWHC 738 (Admin), [2008] 2 FLR 523 475, 480
B v M [2015] EWHC 2941 (Fam); *sub nom* Re G (A Child) 859
B v P (Access) [1992] 2 FCR 576, FD 1870

B v P (Adoption by Unmarried Father); B (A Child) v RP [2001] UKHL 70, [2002] 1 WLR 258, [2002] 1 FLR 196; *sub nom* Re B (Adoption: Natural Parent) 286
B v R [2009] EWHC 2026 (Fam), [2010] 1 FLR 563 2869
B v S (Financial Remedy: Marital Property Regime) [2012] EWHC 265 (Fam), [2012] 2 FLR 502 1180
B v UK (2004) 39 EHRR 30 1010
B v UK (Case 39067/97) [2000] 1 FLR 1, ECHR 428, 1007
B v UK; P v UK [2001] 2 FLR 261, ECHR 1516
B, Re; RB v FB and MA (Forced Marriage: Wardship: Jurisdiction) [2008] EWHC 1436 (Fam), [2008] 2 FLR 1624 839, 2783
B, Re; X Council v B [2007] EWHC 1622 (Fam), [2008] 1 FLR 482 627, 2586
B, Re; X Council v B (No 2) [2008] EWHC 270 (Fam), [2008] 1 FLR 1460 248, 627, 1040, 1543, 2586
B-C (A Child), Re [2016] EWCA Civ 970 132, 205, 575
B-G (Parental Orders: Domicile), Re [2014] EWHC 444 (Fam), [2014] 2 FLR 968 990
B-G v B-G [2008] EWHC 688 (Fam), [2008] 2 FLR 965 388, 389
B-J (Power of Arrest), Re [2001] Fam 415, [2000] 2 FLR 443, CA 893
B-S (Adoption: Application of s 47(5)), Re [2013] EWCA Civ 1146, [2014] 1 WLR 563, [2014] 1 FLR 1035 282, 289, 531, 539, 547, 1008, 1535
B-T v B-T (Divorce: Procedure) [1990] 2 FLR 1, FD 1234
Babanaft International Co SA v Bassatne and Another [1990] Ch 13, CA 797, 1242
Bagum v Hafiz and Another [2015] EWCA Civ 801, [2016] 1 Ch 241, [2016] 2 FLR 337 1261
Bailey v Warren [2006] EWCA Civ 51 1683
Baker Tilly (A Firm) v Makar [2013] EWHC 759 (QB), [2013] COPLR 245 225, 1683
Baker v Baker [2008] EWHC 977 (Ch), [2008] 2 FLR 1956 1017, 1018
Baker v Rowe [2009] EWCA Civ 1162, [2010] 1 FLR 761 227, 1847, 1849, 2146
Balabel v Air India [1988] Ch 317, CA 1753
Baldwin v Baldwin [2014] EWHC 4857 (Fam) 2866, 2867
Balogh v St Albans Crown Court [1975] QB 73, CA 1989
Banco Nacional de Comercio Exterior v Empresa de Telecomunucaciones de Cuba SA [2007] EWHC 2322 (Comm) 96
Banik v Banik [1973] 1 WLR 860, (1973) FLR Rep 65, CA 1152
Bank Mellat v Her Majesty's Treasury (No 1) [2013] UKSC 38, [2014] 1 AC 700 1511, 1754, 2359
Bank Mellat v Kazmi [1989] QB 541, CA 1242
Bank Mellat v Nikpour (Mohammad Ebrahim) [1985] FSR 87, CA 1241
Banyard v Banyard [1984] FLR 643, CA 1169
Barcham (A Bankrupt), Re [2008] EWHC 1505 (Ch), [2009] 1 WLR 1124, [2008] BPIR 857 1264
Barder v Barder (Caluori Intervening) [1988] AC 20, [1987] 2 FLR 480, HL; *sub nom* Barder v Caluori 211, 212, 1205, 1434, 1448, 1865
Barder v Caluori [1988] AC 20, [1987] 2 FLR 480, HL; *sub nom* Barder v Barder (Caluori Intervening) 211, 212, 1205, 1434, 1448, 1865
Barefoot v Clarke [1949] 2 KB 97, CA 1933
Barlow Clowes International Limited v Henwood [2008] EWCA Civ 577, [2008] BPIR 778 828, 2777
Barnes v Phillips [2015] EWCA Civ 1056, [2016] 2 FLR 1292 1263
Barnett v Barnett [2014] EWHC 2678 (Fam) 58, 59, 1425
Barnett v Hassett [1982] 1 WLR 1385, CA 877
Barnish v Barnish (1976) Fam Law 174, FD 812
Barrass v Harding and Newman [2001] 1 FLR 138, CA 1015
Barrell Enterprises, Re [1973] 1 WLR 19, CA 212, 1857
Barrister (Wasted Costs Order) (No 1 of 1991), Re A [1993] QB 293, CA 2160
Barron v Woodhead [2008] EWHC 810 (Ch), [2009] 1 FLR 747 1017, 1023
Barry v Barry [1992] Fam 140, [1992] 2 FLR 233, FD 1170
Bartley (t/a Lundy) v Wilson [2004] EWCA Civ 1338 792
Basham (dec'd), Re [1986] 1 WLR 1498, [1987] 2 FLR 264, ChD 1023
Bater and Bater v Greenwich London Borough Council [1999] 2 FLR 993, CA 41, 894, 1210
Bater v Bater [1951] P 35, CA 1761
Bayer AG v Winter [1986] 1 WLR 497, CA 57
Baynes v Hedger [2008] EWHC 1587 (Ch), [2008] 2 FLR 1805 702
Baynes v Hedger [2009] EWCA Civ 374, [2009] 2 FLR 767 1017
BBC v Coventry CC and Others (Care Proceedings: Costs: Identification of Local Authority [2011] 1 FLR 977, FD 1543
BBC v Rochdale Metropolitan Borough Council and X and Y [2005] EWHC 2862 (Fam), [2007] 1 FLR 101 246, 247
BC v DE [2016] EWHC 1806 (Fam) 440
BCC v FZ, AZ, HZ and TVP [2012] EWHC 1154 (Fam), [2013] 1 FLR 974 903, 1512
BE v DE [2014] EWHC 2318 (Fam) 2776

Beaumont (dec'd), Re; Martin v Midland Bank Trust Co [1980] Ch 444, ChD 1017
Beaumont, Re [1893] 3 Ch 490, ChD 826
Beddoe, Re; Downes v Cottam [1893] 1 Ch 547, CA 228, 2158
Bedford Police Constabulary v RU & FHS [2013] EWHC 2350 (Fam) 36
Begum v Anam [2004] EWCA Civ 578 126, 129
Behbehani v Salem (Note) [1989] 1 WLR 723, CA 1242
Behzadi v Behzadi [2008] EWCA Civ 1070, [2009] 2 FLR 649 1174, 1179, 1180, 1182
Belgian Linguistic Case (1979–80) 1 EHRR 252 1011
Bellinger v Bellinger [2003] UKHL 21, [2003] 2 AC 467, [2003] 1 FLR 1043 944, 953, 954, 1010
Ben Hashem v Al Shayif [2008] EWHC 2380 (Fam), [2009] 1 FLR 115 1172
Ben Hashem v Ali Shayif and Radfan Ltd [2009] EWHC 864 (Fam), [2009] 2 FLR 896 2146
Benson v Benson (Deceased) [1996] 1 FLR 692, FD 2196
Benson v Richards [2002] EWCA Civ 1402 1987
Bentinck v Bentinck [2007] EWCA Civ 175, [2007] 2 FLR 1 1359
Berkovits v Grinberg (Attorney-General Intervening) [1995] Fam 142, [1995] 1 FLR 477, FD 865
Berkshire County Council v C and Others [1993] Fam 203, [1993] 1 FLR 569, FD 561
Besharova v Berezovsky [2016] EWCA Civ 161 1205
Besterman (dec'd), Re; Besterman v Grusin [1984] Ch 458, [1984] FLR 503, CA; *sub nom* Re Besterman (Deceased) 1020
Besterman (Deceased), Re [1984] Ch 458, [1984] FLR 503, CA; *sub nom* Re Besterman (dec'd); Besterman v Grusin 1020
Bexley LBC v V, W and D [2014] EWHC 2187 (Fam) 526
Bezeliansky v Bezelianskaya [2016] EWCA Civ 76 1434, 1934
Bheekun v Williams [1999] 2 FLR 229, CA 1023
Bhura v Bhura [2012] EWHC 3633 (Fam), [2013] 2 FLR 44 1236, 1934
Bibby (James) Ltd v Woods (Howard, Garnishee) [1949] 2 KB 449, KBD 2295
Bibi v Chief Adjudication Officer [1998] 1 FLR 375, CA 1015
Biggs v Biggs and Wheatley [1977] Fam 1, FD 1404
Billington v Billington [1974] Fam 24, FD 343
Birch v Birch [2015] EWCA Civ 833, [2016] 2 FLR 467 1174, 1447
Bird Precision Bellows Ltd, Re [1984] 1 Ch 419, CA 1181
Bird v Secretary of State for Work and Pensions [2008] EWHC 3159 (Admin), [2009] 2 FLR 660 412
Birmingham CC v SK [2016] EWHC 310 (Fam) 533
Birmingham City Council v H (A Minor) [1994] 2 AC 212, [1994] 1 FLR 224, HL; *sub nom* Birmingham City Council v H (No 3) 1502
Birmingham City Council v H [1992] 2 FLR 323, FD 458
Birmingham City Council v H (No 3) [1994] 2 AC 212, [1994] 1 FLR 224, HL; *sub nom* Birmingham City Council v H (A Minor) 1502
Birmingham City Council v H and ors [2005] EWHC 2885 (Fam) 535
Birmingham City Council v M [2008] EWHC 1085 (Fam), [2008] 2 FLR 542 171, 512, 1540, 2434
Birmingham City Council v R [2006] EWCA Civ 1748, [2007] Fam 41, [2007] 1 FLR 564 476
Birmingham City Council v Riaz and Others [2014] EWHC 4247 (Fam), [2015] 2 FLR 763 627, 1002, 1135, 1421, 1563
Birmingham City Council v S, R and A [2006] EWHC 3065 (Fam), [2007] 1 FLR 1223 448
Bishop v Plumley [1991] 1 WLR 582, [1991] 1 FLR 121, CA 1017
BJ (Care: Third Party Intervention), Re [1999] Fam Law 613, CA 1502
BJ v MJ (Financial Order: Overseas Trust) [2011] EWHC 2708 (Fam), [2012] 1 FLR 667 2517
Black v Pastouna [2005] EWCA Civ 1389 1291, 1773, 1865, 1879
Blackburn v Bowering [1994] 1 WLR 1324, CA 795
Blight v Brewster [2012] EWHC 165 (Ch) 1187
Blunt v Park Lane Hotels [1942] 2 KB 253, CA 629
BM-Bank JSC v Chernyakov & ors, Lawtel 24 November 2016 2294
BN v MA (MPS: Pre Nuptial Agreement) [2013] EWHC 4250 (Fam) 1163, 1166
Board (Board Intervening) v Checkland [1987] 2 FLR 257, CA 1168
Bohez v Wiertz (Case C-4/14) [2016] 1 FLR 1159, CJEU 2774
Bokor-Ingram v Bokor-Ingram [2009] EWCA Civ 412, [2009] 2 FLR 922 1439
Bolsom v Bolsom (1983) 4 FLR 21, CA 1170
Bolton NHS Foundation Trust v C (by her Guardian) and LB & BT [2015] EWHC 2920 (Fam) 1546
Boso v Italy [2002] ECHR 846 1010
Bothe v Amos [1976] Fam 46, CA 15, 1123
Bouette v Rose [2000] Ch 662, [2000] 1 FLR 363, CA; [1999] Ch 206, [1999] 2 FLR 466, ChD; *sub nom* Re B decd 1017, 1025
Boughton v Punter Southall (2009) 22 September, ref 74851/1, Pensions Ombudsman 1265, 2519
Bove v Italy (Application No 30595/02) [2005] Fam Law 752, ECHR 443

Boylan v Boylan [1988] 1 FLR 282, FD 1203
BP, KP and NI (Financial Remedy Proceedings: Res Judicata) [2012] EWHC 2995 (Fam), [2013] 1 FLR 1310 1180
BR (Proof of Facts), Re [2015] EWFC 41 537
BR and C (Care: Duty of Disclosure: Appeals), Re [2002] EWCA Civ 1825 1510
BR v VT (Financial Remedies: Interim) [2015] EWHC 2727 (Fam), [2016] 2 FLR 519 14, 54, 877, 1136, 1170, 1172, 1173, 2025
Bracknell Forest Borough Council v N [2006] EWCA Civ 1562 2205
Bradbury and Others v Paterson and Others [2014] EWHC 3992 (QB), [2015] COPLR 425 2065
Bradford, Re; O'Connell, Re [2006] EWCA Civ 1199, [2007] 1 FLR 530 620
Brauer v Germany (Application No 3545/04) (2009) 51 EHRR 574 1015
Brazil v Brazil [2002] EWCA Civ 1135 1834
Breuning v Breuning [2002] EWHC 236 (Fam), [2002] 1 FLR 888 2776
Briers v Briers [2017] EWCA Civ 15 1168, 1432
Briffett v DPP [2001] EWHC 841 (Admin) 790
Brighton and Hove Bus and Coach Co. Ltd v Brooks [2011] EWHC 806 (Admin) 1991
Bristol City Council v NGN Ltd and Others [2012] EWHC 3748 (Fam), [2013] 1 FLR 1205 1040
Bristol-Myers Squibb Co v (1) Baker Norton Pharmaceuticals Inc (2) Napro Biotherapeutics Inc [2001] EWCA Civ 414 1859
British Arab Commercial Bank Plc & Ors v Algosaibi & Ors [2011] EWHC 2444 (Comm), [2011] BPIR 1568 2025
British Broadcasting Corporation v CAFCASS Legal & Ors [2007] EWHC 616 (Fam), [2007] 2 FLR 765 246, 1543, 2586
Brockwell v Brockwell (1975) 6 Fam Law 46, CA 706
Bromiley v Bromiley [1987] 2 FLR 207, FD; *sub nom* Bromilley v Bromilley 1077
Bromilley v Bromilley [1987] 2 FLR 207, FD; *sub nom* Bromiley v Bromiley 1077
Broniowski v Poland (2005) 40 EHRR 495 1011
Brookes v Secretary of State for Work and Pensions [2010] EWCA Civ 420, [2010] 1 WLR 2448, [2010] 2 FLR 1038 401, 411
Broomleigh Housing Association Ltd v Okonkwo [2010] EWCA Civ 1113 123, 352, 2287, 2694
Brough v Law [2011] EWCA Civ 1183, [2012] 1 WLR 1021, [2012] 1 FLR 375 406
Brown v British Airways Pension Trustees Limited (2012), 13 January, ref 83320/1, Deputy Pensions Ombudsman 2517
Brown v London Borough of Haringey [2015] EWCA Civ 483 130, 1984, 1985
Brown v Rice and anor [2007] EWHC 625 (Ch) 1153
Brown v Stott [2003] 1 AC 681, PC 1007, 1753
BT v JRT (Abduction: Conditional Acquiescence and Consent) [2008] EWHC 1169 (Fam), [2008] 2 FLR 972 389
Buckinghamshire County Council v M [1994] 2 FLR 506, CA; *sub nom* Re M and C (Minors) (Interim Care Order) 1529
Buckley v Crawford [1893] 1 QB 105, QBD 1930
Bulled v Khayat and Another [2002] EWCA Civ 804 243, 1235, 2198
Bunning (dec'd), Re; Bunning v Salmon [1984] Ch 480, [1985] FLR 1, ChD 1017
Burden v United Kingdom [2008] ECHR 357, (2008) 47 EHRR 857, [2008] 2 FLR 787 702, 996
Burgess v Burgess [1996] 2 FLR 34, CA 1240
Burnet v Francis Industries plc [1987] 1 WLR 802, CA 2326
Burns v Burns [2004] EWCA Civ 1258 1448
Burris v Azadani [1995] 1 WLR 1372, [1996] 1 FLR 266, CA 29, 36, 39, 797, 1231
Burrow v Burrow [1999] 1 FLR 508, FD 1187
Burton v Earl of Darnley (1869) LR 8 Eq 576 857
Bush v Bush [2008] EWCA Civ 865, [2008] 2 FLR 1437 839, 2782, 2783
Butcher v Wolfe and Wolfe [1999] 1 FLR 334, CA 2136, 2137, 2148
Butler v Butler (Nos 1 and 2) [1998] 1 WLR 1208, [1997] 2 FLR 311, CA 828
Butler v Butler, The Queen's Proctor Intervening [1990] 1 FLR 114, FD 1150, 1151, 1382
Butt v Butt [2010] EWHC 1989 (Fam), [2011] 1 FLR 54; *sub nom* B v B (Brussels II Revised: Jurisdiction) 2783
Butterworth v Butterworth [1997] 2 FLR 336, CA 1390, 1396
Button v Salama [2013] EWHC 2474 (Fam), [2014] 2 FLR 471 388

C (A Child) (Application by Dr X and Y), Re [2015] EWFC 79, [2017] 1 FLR 82 247
C (A Child) v Plymouth County Council [2000] 1 FLR 875, CA; *sub nom* Plymouth County Council v C 540, 638
C (A Child) v XYZ County Council, Re [2007] EWCA Civ 1206, [2008] Fam 54, [2008] 1 FLR 1294 283, 448, 660

C (A Child), Re [2001] EWCA Civ 718 457
C (A Child), Re [2005] EWCA Civ 300 435
C (A Child), Re [2012] EWCA Civ 535 2197
C (A Child), Re [2013] EWCA Civ 1412, [2014] 1 WLR 2182, [2014] 1 FLR 1239 1523, 1529
C (A Child), Re [2016] EWCA Civ 798 247, 627, 628, 1321
C (A Minor) (Adopted Child: Contact), Re [1993] Fam 210, [1993] 2 FLR 431, FD 287, 454
C (A Minor) (Care Order: Appeal), Re [1996] 1 FCR 332, FD 540
C (A Minor) (Care: Child's Wishes), Re [1993] 1 FLR 832, FD 1519
C (A Minor) (Contempt), Re [1986] 1 FLR 578, CA 130
C (A Minor) (Contribution Notice), Re [1994] 1 FLR 111, FD 669
C (A Minor) (Disclosure of Adoption Reports), Re [1994] 2 FLR 525, FD 1657
C (A Minor) (Interim Care Order: Residential Assessment), Re [1997] AC 489, [1997] 1 FLR 1, HL; *sub nom* Re C (Interim Care Order: Residential Assessment) 560
C (A Minor) (Medical Treatment: Court's Jurisdiction), Re [1997] 2 FLR 180, FD; *sub nom* Re C (Detention: Medical Treatment) 511
C (A Minor) (Secure Accommodation: Bail), Re [1994] 2 FLR 922, FD; *sub nom* Re C (Secure Accommodation: Bail) 511, 2434
C (A Minor) (Secure Accommodation: Bail), Re [1994] 2 FLR 922, FD; *sub nom* RE C (Secure Accommodation: Bail) 2435
C (A Minor) (Wardship: Jurisdiction), Re [1991] 2 FLR 168, CA 1548
C (Abduction: Consent), Re [1996] 1 FLR 414, FD 389
C (Abduction: Grave Risk of Psychological Harm), Re [1999] 1 FLR 1145, CA 391
C (Abduction: Interim Directions: Accommodation by Local Authority), Re [2003] EWHC 3065 (Fam), [2004] 1 FLR 653 381, 446, 1553
C (Abduction: Residence and Contact), Re [2005] EWHC 2205 (Fam), [2006] 2 FLR 277 386
C (Abduction: Separate Representation of Children), Re [2008] EWHC 517 (Fam), [2008] 2 FLR 6 388, 391, 2781
C (Abduction: Setting Aside Return Order: Remission), Re [2012] EWCA Civ 1144, [2013] 1 FLR 403 384, 388
C (Abduction: Settlement), Re [2004] EWHC 1245 (Fam), [2005] 1 FLR 127 386
C (Abduction: Wrongful Removal), Re [1999] 2 FLR 859, FD 380, 381
C (Adoption Proceedings: Change of Circumstances), Re [2013] EWCA Civ 431, [2013] 1 WLR 3720, [2013] 2 FLR 1393 193, 203, 263, 2195
C (Adoption: Disclosure to Father), Re [2005] EWHC 3385 (Fam), [2006] 2 FLR 589 283
C (Adoption: Notice), Re [1999] 1 FLR 384, FD 451
C (Adult Patient: Publicity), Re [1996] 2 FLR 251, FD 2569
C (Adult) (Refusal of Treatment), Re [1994] 1 WLR 290, [1994] 1 FLR 31, FD; *sub nom* Re C (Refusal of Medical Treatment) 1681, 2577
C (Appeal from Care and Placement Orders), Re [2013] EWCA Civ 1257, [2014] 1 WLR 2247, [2014] 2 FLR 131 530
C (Breach of Human Rights: Damages), Re [2007] EWCA Civ 2, [2007] 1 FLR 1957 235, 1000, 2254
C (Care or Supervision Order), Re [1999] 2 FLR 621, FD 539, 1831
C (Care Order or Supervision Order), Re [2001] 2 FLR 466, FD 540
C (Care Order: Appropriate Local Authority), Re [1997] 1 FLR 544, FD; *sub nom* Re C (Minors) (Care Proceedings: Ordinary Residence) 541, 545, 638, 1509
C (Care Plan: Human Rights Challenge), Re [2002] Fam Law 790, FD 529, 530
C (Care Proceedings: Parents with Disabilities), Re [2014] EWCA Civ 128, [2014] 1 WLR 2495, [2015] 1 FLR 521 541
C (Care: Consultation with Parents Not in Child's Best Interests), Re [2005] EWHC 3390 (Fam), [2006] 2 FLR 787 498, 517, 611, 1501
C (Change of Surname), Re [1998] 1 FLR 549, CA 448
C (Change of Surname), Re [1998] 2 FLR 656, CA 446, 447, 449
C (Child Abduction) (Unmarried Father: Rights of Custody), Re [2002] EWHC 2219 (Fam), [2003] 1 WLR 493, [2003] 1 FLR 252 380
C (Child Abduction: Settlement), Re [2006] EWHC 1229 (Fam), [2006] 2 FLR 797 382, 386
C (Children Act 1989: Expert Evidence), Re [1995] 1 FLR 204, FD; *sub nom* Re C (Expert Evidence: Disclosure: Practice) 570, 1512, 1705
C (Children) (Residential Assessment), Re [2001] EWCA Civ 1305 561
C (Children), Re [2011] EWCA Civ 1230 792
C (Children), Re [2016] EWCA Civ 356 206
C (Children: Power to Choose Forenames), Re [2016] EWCA Civ 374, [2017] 1 Fam 137, [2017] 1 FLR 487 448
C (Contact), Re [2007] EWHC 3495 (Fam), [2008] 1 FLR 1151 267
C (Contact: Conduct of Hearings), Re [2006] EWCA Civ 144, [2006] 2 FLR 289 1527

C (Contact: Jurisdiction), Re [1996] Fam 79, [1995] 1 FLR 777, CA 451, 453
C (Contact: Moratorium: Change of Gender), Re [2006] EWCA Civ 1765, [2007] 1 FLR 1642 435
C (Costs: Enforcement of Foreign Contact Order), Re [2007] EWHC 1993 (Fam), [2008] 1 FLR 619 2794
C (Deceased) (Leave to Apply for Provision), Re [1995] 2 FLR 24, FD 1025
C (Detention: Medical Treatment), Re [1997] 2 FLR 180, FD; *sub nom* Re C (A Minor) (Medical Treatment: Court's Jurisdiction) 511
C (Direct Contact: Suspension), Re [2011] EWCA Civ 521, [2011] 2 FLR 912 443, 446
C (Disclosure), Re [1996] 1 FLR 797, FD 1509, 1510, 1519, 1706
C (Divorce: Financial Relief), Re [2007] EWHC 1911 (Fam), [2008] 1 FLR 625 1181
C (Domestic Violence: Fact-finding Hearing), Re [2009] EWCA Civ 994, [2010] 1 FLR 1728 534, 2614
C (Due Process), Re [2013] EWCA Civ 1412, [2014] 1 WLR 2182, [2014] 1 FLR 1239 449, 2721
C (Expert Evidence: Disclosure: Practice), Re [1995] 1 FLR 204, FD; *sub nom* Re C (Children Act 1989: Expert Evidence) 570, 1512, 1705
C (Family Assistance Order), Re [1996] 1 FLR 424, FD 483
C (Family Proceedings: Case Management), Re [2012] EWCA Civ 1489, [2013] 1 FLR 1089 1278, 1527, 2196
C (Financial Provision), Re [2007] 2 FLR 13, FD 650
C (Financial Provision: Leave to Appeal), Re [1993] 2 FLR 799, FD 2196
C (Interim Care Order: Residential Assessment), Re [1997] AC 489, [1997] 1 FLR 1, HL; *sub nom* Re C (A Minor) (Interim Care Order: Residential Assessment) 560
C (Internal Relocation), Re [2015] EWCA Civ 1305, [2016] 1 Fam 253, [2017] 1 FLR 103 471, 472
C (Leave to Remove from Jurisdiction), Re [2000] 2 FLR 457, CA 1870
C (Litigant in Person: s 91(14) Order), Re [2009] EWCA Civ 674, [2009] 2 FLR 1461 621
C (Minors) (Care Proceedings: Ordinary Residence), Re [1997] 1 FLR 544, FD; *sub nom* Re C (Care Order: Appropriate Local Authority) 541, 545, 638, 1509
C (Minors) (Wardship: Adoption), Re [1989] 1 WLR 61, [1989] 1 FLR 222, CA 318
C (Older Children: Relocation), Re [2015] EWCA Civ 1298, [2016] 2 FLR 1159; *sub nom* H v C & E (A Child by his solicitor, Anne-Marie Hutchinson) 471
C (Permission to Relocate), Re [2014] EWCA Civ 705 472
C (Prohibition on Further Applications), Re [2002] EWCA Civ 292, [2002] 1 FLR 1136 619
C (Publication of Judgment), Re [2015] EWCA Civ 500, [2016] 1 FLR 495 628
C (Refusal of Medical Treatment), Re [1994] 1 WLR 290, [1994] 1 FLR 31, FD; *sub nom* Re C (Adult) (Refusal of Treatment) 1681, 2577
C (Residence Order), Re [2007] EWCA Civ 866, [2008] 1 FLR 211 444
C (Residence: Child's Application for Leave), Re [1995] 1 FLR 927, FD 454
C (Section 8 Order: Court Welfare Officer), Re [1995] 1 FLR 617, CA 438
C (Secure Accommodation Order: Representation), Re [2001] EWCA Civ 458, [2001] 2 FLR 169 512
C (Secure Accommodation: Bail), Re [1994] 2 FLR 922, FD; *sub nom* Re C (A Minor) (Secure Accommodation: Bail) 511, 2434, 2435
C (Sterilisation: Mental Patient: Procedure), Re [1990] 1 WLR 1248, [1990] 2 FLR 527, FD 183
C (Transcripts: Permission to Appeal), Re [2013] EWCA Civ 1158, [2014] 2 FLR 147 205, 244, 2202
C (Welfare of Child: Immunisation), Re [2003] EWCA Civ 1148, [2003] 2 FLR 1095; *sub nom* Re B (A Child) (Immunisation) 559, 1795
C (Welfare of Child: Immunisation), Re [2003] EWHC 1376 (Fam), [2003] 2 FLR 1054 559
C and D (Children) (Fact Finding Hearing), Re [2015] EWHC 1059 (Fam) 990
C and V (Minors) (Contact: Parental Responsibility Order), Re [1998] 1 FLR 392, CA 427
C v B (Abduction: Grave Risk) [2005] EWHC 2988 (Fam), [2006] 1 FLR 1095 389, 390
C v Bury Metropolitan Council [2002] EWHC 1438 (Fam), [2002] 2 FLR 868 999
C v C (Abduction: Jurisdiction) [1994] 1 FCR 6, FD 390
C v C (Access Order: Enforcement) [1990] 1 FLR 462, CA 1548
C v C (Ancillary Relief: Trust Fund) [2009] EWHC 1491 (Fam), [2010] 1 FLR 337 1181
C v C (Contempt: Evidence) [1993] 1 FLR 220, CA 2431
C v C (Divorce: Stay of English Proceedings) [2001] 1 FLR 624, FD 1179
C v C (Financial Relief: Short Marriage) [1997] 2 FLR 26, CA 1169, 1185
C v C (International Relocation: Shared Care Arrangement) [2011] EWHC 335 (Fam), [2011] 2 FLR 701 472
C v C (Minors) (Child Abduction) [1992] 1 FLR 163, FD 376, 379
C v C [2001] EWCA Civ 1625 887
C v C [2007] EWHC 2033 (Fam), [2009] 1 FLR 8 1182
C v C (Non-Molestation Order: Jurisdiction) [1998] Fam 70, [1998] 1 FLR 554, FD 887
C v C (Without Notice Orders) [2005] EWHC 2741 (Fam), [2006] 1 FLR 936 1210
C v D (Abduction: Grave Risk of Harm) [2013] EWHC 2989 (Fam), [2014] 2 FLR 724 390
C v F (Disabled Child: Maintenance Orders) [1998] 2 FLR 1, CA 648, 1198

C v Finland [2006] 2 FLR 597, ECHR 528
C v H (Abduction: Consent) [2009] EWHC 2660 (Fam), [2010] 1 FLR 225 389
C v Humberside County Council and Another [1994] 2 FLR 759, FD 512
C v K (Children: Application for Temporary Removal to Algeria) [2014] EWHC 4125 (Fam), [2015] 2 FLR 791 473
C v K (Inherent Powers: Exclusion Order) [1996] 2 FLR 506, FD 631
C v M (Case C-376/14 PPU) [2015] 1 FLR 1, CJEU 2775
C v S (A Minor) (Abduction) [1990] 2 AC 562, [1990] 2 FLR 442, HL; *sub nom* Re J (A Minor) (Abduction: Custody Rights) 376, 392, 415, 839
C v S (Divorce: Jurisdiction) [2010] EWHC 2676 (Fam), [2011] 2 FLR 19 2785, 2786
C v Salford City Council and Others [1994] 2 FLR 926, FD 451
C v Secretary of State for Work and Pensions and B [2002] EWCA Civ 1854, [2003] 1 FLR 829 402
C v Solihull Metropolitan Borough Council [1993] 1 FLR 290, FD 423, 457, 547, 1290, 1508
C, Re (Case C-435/06) [2007] ECR I-10141, [2008] Fam 27, [2008] 1 FLR 490, ECJ 522, 2774
C, Re [2016] EWHC 3171 (Fam) 1757
C-P (A Child), Re (2006) Lawtel 24 January, CA 1528
C-W (A Child) (Contact Overseas), Re [2015] EWCA Civ 1272, [2017] 1 FLR 131 473, 859
Calderbank v Calderbank [1976] Fam 93, (1975) FLR Rep 113, CA 1453, 1848, 2135, 2136, 2140, 2146
Calderdale MBC v S and Legal Services Commission [2004] EWHC 2529 (Fam), [2005] 1 FLR 751 1799
Callaghan (dec'd), Estate of, Re [1985] Fam 1, [1985] FLR 116, FD 1016
Cambra v Jones (Contempt Proceedings: Child Joined as Party) [2014] EWHC 913 (Fam), [2015] 1 FLR 263 387, 1695
Cambra v Jones [2013] EWHC 88 (Fam), [2014] 1 FLR 5 387, 388, 2793
Cambra v Jones [2014] EWHC 2264 (Fam) 1985
Camden LBC v PC, GM, YC, PC and KM) [2013] EWHC 2336 (Fam), [2014] 1 FLR 605; *sub nom* Re C, PC and KM (Children) 526
Camden London Borough Council v R (A Minor) (Blood Transfusion) [1993] 2 FLR 757, FD; *sub nom* Re R (A Minor) (Blood Transfusion) 449, 1522, 1547
Campbell & Cosans v UK (1982) 4 EHRR 293 1012
Campbell v Campbell [2016] EWHC 1828 (Ch) 2158
Campbell v Mirror Group Newspapers Ltd. [2004] UKHL 22, [2004] 2 AC 457 994, 997, 1008
Cannon v Cannon [2004] EWCA Civ 1330, [2005] 1 WLR 32, [2005] 1 FLR 169 386
Capehorn v Harris [2015] EWCA Civ 955, [2016] 2 FLR 1026 1263
Caras (Iosub) v Romania (Application No 7198/04) [2007] 1 FLR 661, ECHR 381, 383
Carmarthenshire County Council v Lewis [2010] EWCA Civ 1567 224, 1683
Carpenter v Carpenter [1988] 1 FLR 121, CA 797
Carpenter v Secretary of State for Justice [2012] EWHC 4421 (Fam) 953
Carpenter v Secretary of State for Justice [2015] EWHC 464 (Admin), [2015] 1 WLR 4111 944, 946
Carron v Carron [1984] FLR 805, CA 1161
Carson v Carson [1983] 1 WLR 285, (1981) 2 FLR 352, CA 1172
Cart v The Upper Tribunal [2011] UKSC 28, [2012] 1 AC 663, [2012] 1 FLR 997 1134, 2257
Cattle v Evans [2011] EWHC 945 (Ch), [2011] 2 FLR 843 1016
Cavendish Square Holdings BV-v-Makdessi [2013] EWCA Civ 1540 1990, 1991, 2306
Cavendish-Bentinck v Cavendish-Bentinck [1949] P 203, CA 1233
Cawdrey Kaye Fireman & Taylor v Minkin [2012] EWCA Civ 546 1827
CB (A Child) (No 2) (Adoption Proceedings: Vienna Convention), Re [2015] EWCA Civ 888, [2016] 1 Fam 123, [2016] 1 FLR 1286 289
CB (A Minor) (Parental Responsibility Order), Re [1993] 1 FLR 920, FD 428
CB (Access: Attendance of Court Welfare Officer), Re [1995] 1 FLR 622, CA 438
CB and JB (Care Proceedings: Guidelines), Re [1998] 2 FLR 211, FD 1507, 1509
CBS United Kingdom v Lambert [1983] Ch 37, CA 1242, 1243
CC v NC (Maintenance Pending Suit) [2014] EWHC 703 (Fam), [2015] 1 FLR 404 1163, 2776, 2787
CE (Section 37 Direction), Re [1995] 1 FLR 26, FD 556, 569, 1515, 1697
Centre for Reproductive Medicine v U [2002] EWHC 36 (Fam), [2002] 1 FLR 927 969
CF v KM (Financial Provision for Child: Costs of Legal Proceedings) [2010] EWHC 1754 (Fam), [2011] 1 FLR 208 407, 646
CF v Secretary of State for the Home Department [2004] EWHC 111 (Fam), [2004] 2 FLR 517 528, 999, 1239
CG v CW [2006] UKHL 43, [2006] 1 WLR 2305, [2006] 2 FLR 629; *sub nom* Re G (Children); *sub nom* Re G (Children) (Residence: Same Sex Partner) 423, 441, 472, 702, 982
CG v IF (MFPA 1984 Part III: Lugano Convention) [2010] EWHC 1062 (Fam), [2010] 2 FLR 1790 1125
CH (Care or Interim Care Order), Re [1998] 1 FLR 402, CA 560, 1532
Chachani Misti v Hostplanet Limited and Finn Grimpe [2016] EWHC 983 (Ch) 2817, 2818

Chadwick v Chadwick [2014] EWHC 3055 (Ch) 1024
Chai v Peng [2014] EWHC 750 (Fam), [2014] 2 FLR 1189 1163
Chai v Peng [2014] EWHC 3518 (Fam), [2015] 2 FLR 424 828, 2776
Chai v Peng [2014] EWHC 3519 (Fam), [2015] 2 FLR 412 828, 2776
Chalal v UK [1996] ECHR 54, (1996) 23 EHRR 413 1005
Chalmers v Johns [1999] 1 FLR 392, CA 879, 890
Chandler v Chandler [2011] EWCA Civ 143 2776
Chandless-Chandless v Nicholson [1942] 2 KB 321, CA 1832
Chapman v Honig [1963] 2 QB 502, CA 804
Chapman, Re (2002) Lawtel, 9 April 1511
Charles & Ors v Fraser [2010] EWHC 2154 (Ch) 1024
Charman v Charman [2005] EWCA Civ 1606, [2006] 1 WLR 1053, [2006] 2 FLR 422 1440
Charman v Charman (No 2) [2006] EWHC 1879 (Fam), [2007] 1 FLR 593 1181
Charman v Charman (No 3) [2006] EWCA Civ 1791, [2007] 1 FLR 1237 1747, 2147
Charman v Charman (No 4) [2007] EWCA Civ 503, [2007] 1 FLR 1246 1178, 1181, 1184
Chartwell Estate Agents Ltd v Fergies Properties SA & Anor [2014] EWCA Civ 506 1766
Chaudry v Chaudry [1976] Fam 148, [1976] 1 WLR 221, CA 1123
Chaundy v James Hay Pension Trustees Limited [2007] (22 May), ref Q00060, Pensions Ombudsman 1265
Chechi v Bashier [1999] 2 FLR 489, CA 891, 892, 897
Chekov v Fryer & Fryer [2015] EWHC 1642 (Ch) 1015
Chelmsford County Court v Ramet [2014] EWHC 56 (Fam), [2014] 2 FLR 1081 130, 792, 796, 1997, 2313
Cherwayko v Cherwayko (No 3) (Contempt in financial remedy proceedings and costs) [2015] EWHC 2482 (Fam) 1934
Cheshire County Council v C [1995] 2 FLR 862, FD 571
Cheshire County Council v M [1993] 1 FLR 463, FD 1527
Chessum & Sons v Gordon [1901] 1 KB 694, CA 798
Chester County Council v B [1993] 1 FLR 421, FD; *sub nom* Re B (A Minor) (Care Order: Review) 551
Chester v Secretary of State for Justice & Anthr [2010] EWCA Civ 1439 998
Chief Constable of Greater Manchester v KI and KW (by their guardian) and PN [2007] EWHC 1837 (Fam), [2008] 1 FLR 504 449
Chief Constable of West Yorkshire Police v S [1999] 1 WLR 1716, [1998] 2 FLR 973, CA; *sub nom* S v S (Chief Constable of West Yorkshire Police Intervening) 155, 156, 856, 857
Child and Family Agency v JD (Case C-428/15), CJEU 524, 525
Child Maintenance and Enforcement Commission v Mitchell [2010] EWCA Civ 333, [2010] 2 FLR 622 414
Child X (Residence and Contact: Rights of Media Attendance: FPR r 10.28(4)), Re [2009] EWHC 1728 (Fam), [2009] 2 FLR 1467 248, 1040, 1837, 1844, 1845, 1846, 2586, 2588
Children Act 1989 (Taxation of Costs), Re [1994] 2 FLR 934, FD 2148
Chiltern District Council v Keane [1985] 1 WLR 619, CA 129
Chiva v Chiva [2014] EWCA Civ 1558 1185
Chorley v Chorley [2005] EWCA Civ 68, [2005] 2 FLR 38 2786
Christofi v National Bank of Greece [2015] EWHC 986 (QB) 96
CIBC Mellon Trust Co v Stolzenberg [2004] EWCA Civ 827 1324
Ciccone v Ritchie (No 1) [2016] EWHC 608 (Fam), [2017] 1 FLR 795 387
Ciccone v Ritchie (No 2) [2016] EWHC 616 (Fam), [2016] 1 WLR 3545, [2017] 1 FLR 812 384, 544
Ciliz v The Netherlands (Case 29192/95) [2000] 2 FLR 469, ECHR 443
City and County of Swansea v XZ and YZ [2014] EWHC 212 (Fam), [2014] 2 FLR 1091 247, 628, 1002, 1563
City of London v Tammy Samede (Representative of those Persons Taking Part in a Protest Camp at St Paul's Churchyard, London EC4) & Othrs [2012] EWHC 34 (QB) 1009
CJ v Flintshire Borough Council [2010] EWCA Civ 393, [2010] 2 FLR 1224 131, 466, 792
CL v East Riding Yorkshire Council, MB and BL (A Child) [2006] EWCA Civ 49, [2006] 2 FLR 24 534
Clark v Cabinet Office and Paymaster (1836) Limited (2007) 19 November, ref R00408, Pensions Ombudsman 2517
Clark v Clark (No 2) [1991] 1 FLR 179, FD 2161
Clarke v Chadburn [1985] 1 WLR 78, ChD 36
Clarke v Clarke [1990] 2 FLR 115, CA 131
Clarke v Harlowe [2005] EWHC 3062 (Ch), [2007] 1 FLR 1, [2006] BPIR 636 1262
Clarkson v Gilbert [2000] 2 FLR 839, CA 1046
Clayton v Clayton [2006] EWCA Civ 878, [2006] Fam 83, [2007] 1 FLR 11 245, 627, 1543, 1844, 2586
Cleveland County Council v F [1995] 1 WLR 785, [1995] 1 FLR 797, FD 629

Cleworth v Teacher's Pension Scheme (2012) 21 December, ref 87725 /2, Deputy Pensions Ombudsman 1175
Clibbery v Allan [2002] EWCA Civ 45, [2002] Fam 261, [2002] 1 FLR 565; *sub nom* Allan v Clibbery 1040, 1248, 1249, 1391, 1755, 2111
Clifford v Clifford [1985] FLR 732, CA 1352
Clifford v Tanner [1987] CLY 3881, CA 1030
CM v Blackburn with Darwen Borough Council [2014] EWCA Civ 1479, [2015] 1 WLR 2441, [2015] 2 FLR 290 531
CM v The Executor of the Estate of EJ (Deceased) and Her Majesty's Coroner [2013] EWHC 1680 (Fam), [2013] 2 FLR 1410 236, 1421
CO v CO (Ancillary Relief: Pre-marriage Cohabitation) [2004] EWHC 287 (Fam), [2004] 1 FLR 1095 1183
Coleman v Coleman [1973] Fam 10, FD 1169
Coles v Coles [1957] P 68, PDAD 1992
Coles v Perfect [2013] EWHC 1955 (QB) 2068
Collins (dec'd), Re [1990] Fam 56, [1990] 2 FLR 72, FD 1016, 1019
Collinson v NHS Pension Scheme (2013) 28 March, ref PO-128, Pensions Ombudsman 1175
Collister v Collister [1972] 1 WLR 54, FD 66
Colt Industries Inc v Sarlie (No 2) [1966] 1 WLR 1287, CA 2299
Columbia Picture Industries and Others v Robinson and Others [1987] Ch 38, ChD 1240
Comet Products UK v Hawkex Plastics [1971] 2 QB 67, CA 1985
Commissioner of Police of the Metropolis v A Local Authority and Ors [2016] EWHC 2400 (Fam) 246, 527, 1510, 1564
Compagnie Noga d'Importation et d'Exportation SA v Abacha (No 3) [2002] EWCA Civ 1142, [2003] 1 WLR 307 535
Constantinides v Constantinides [2013] EWHC 3688 (Fam), [2014] 1 WLR 1934, [2014] 2 FLR 736 1933
Continental Transfert Technique Ltd v Federal Government of Nigeria & ors [2009] EWHC 2898 (Comm) 2291
Conway v Rimmer [1968] AC 910, HL 1754
Cook v Plummer [2008] EWCA Civ 484, [2008] 2 FLR 989 1870
Cooper-Hohn v Hohn [2014] EWCA Civ 896 526
Cooper-Hohn v Hohn [2014] EWHC 2314 (Fam), [2015] 1 FLR 19 1040, 1440
Cooper-Hohn v Hohn [2014] EWHC 4122 (Fam), [2015] 1 FLR 745 1179, 1183
Corbett v Corbett [2003] EWCA Civ 559, [2003] 2 FLR 385 121, 1928, 1934
Corbett v Corbett (otherwise Ashley) [1971] P 83, PDAD 954
Cordle v Cordle [2001] EWCA Civ 1791, [2002] 1 WLR 1441, [2002] 1 FLR 207 1866
Cornick v Cornick [1994] 2 FLR 530, FD 1448
Cossey v United Kingdom (1990) 13 EHRR 622, [1991] 2 FLR 492 949
Cotton v Official Solicitor [1989] 6 CL 385, ChD 2271
Council of Civil Service Unions v Minister for the Civil Service [1985] AC 374, HL 401, 1239
County Durham and Darlington NHS Foundation Trust v SS [2016] EWHC 535 (Fam) 1546
Court v Despallieres; Re Ikin (Deceased) [2009] EWHC 3340 (Ch), [2010] 1 FLR 1734 702
Coventry (dec'd), Re; Coventry v Coventry [1980] Ch 461, (1979) FLR Rep 142, CA 1019, 1023
Coventry CC v O (Adoption) [2011] EWCA Civ 729, [2011] 2 FLR 936 265, 1000, 1545, 1855, 2058
Coventry City Council v C, B, CA and CH [2012] EWHC 2190 (Fam), [2012] COPLR 658 494
Coventry City Council v X, Y and Z (Care Proceedings: Costs) [2011] 1 FLR 1045, FD 533
Coventry City Council v X, Y and Z (Identification of Local Authority) [2010] EWHC B22 (Fam), [2011] 1 FLR 977 1040
Cowan v Cowan [2001] EWCA Civ 679, [2002] Fam 97, [2001] 2 FLR 192 1017, 2516
Cowl & Ors v Plymouth City Council [2001] EWCA Civ 1935, [2002] Fam Law 265 2136
Cowland v Capita SIPP Services [2007] (3 April), ref Q00244, Pensions Ombudsman 1265
CR v CR [2007] EWHC 3206 (Fam), [2008] 1 FLR 323 1180
CR v MZ (Financial Remedies: Beneficial Ownership) [2013] EWHC 295 (Fam), [2014] 1 FLR 22 1439
CR v SR (Financial Remedies: Permission to Appeal) [2013] EWHC 1155 (Fam), [2014] 1 FLR 186 193, 1866
Crabtree v BAE Executive Pension Scheme (2008) 19 May, ref S00522, Pensions Ombudsman 1265
Cramer v Cramer [1987] 1 FLR 116, CA 828
Crawford (dec'd), Re (1983) 4 FLR 273, FD 1028
Credit Suisse Fides Trust SA v Cuoghi [1998] QB 818, CA 696
Critchell v Critchell [2015] EWCA Civ 436, [2016] 1 FLR 400 1448
Crossley v Crossley [2007] EWCA Civ 1491, [2008] 1 FLR 1467 1179, 1439
Croydon London Borough Council v A (No 1) [1992] 2 FLR 341, FD 448

Croydon London Borough Council v A (No 2) (Note) [1992] 1 WLR 984, [1992] 2 FLR 348, FD 566
Croydon London Borough Council v A (No 3) [1992] 2 FLR 350, FD 671, 1523
Crystall v Crystall [1963] 1 WLR 564, CA 1235
CS v ACS (Consent Order: Non-Disclosure: Correct Procedure) [2015] EWHC 1005 (Fam), [2015] 1 WLR 4592, [2016] 1 FLR 131 212, 384, 1321, 1434, 1684
CSC (An Infant), Re [1960] 1 WLR 304, ChD 277
CT (A Minor) (Wardship: Representation), Re [1994] Fam 49, [1993] 2 FLR 278, CA; *sub nom* Re T (A Minor) (Wardship: Representation) 182, 1285, 1699
Cumbria CC v M & Ors [2014] EWHC 2596 (Fam) 628, 1040
Cumbria County Council, Petitioner [2016] CSIH 92 513
Curling v Law Society [1985] 1 WLR 470, [1985] FLR 831, CA 1043
Currey v Currey (No 2) [2006] EWCA Civ 1338, [2007] 1 FLR 946 646, 1166
CW v SG (Parental Responsibility: Consequential Orders) [2013] EWHC 854 (Fam), [2013] 2 FLR 655 429
Cyganik v Agulian [2006] EWCA Civ 129 1014
CZ (Human Rights Claim: Costs) [2017] EWFC 11 1043

D (A Child) (International Recognition), Re [2016] EWCA Civ 12, [2016] 1 WLR 2469, [2016] 2 FLR 347 424, 569, 1697, 2789
D (A Child) (Supreme Court: Jurisdiction), Re [2016] UKSC 34, [2016] 2 FLR 379 199, 523, 839, 2789, 2792, 2802
D (A Child), Re [2014] EWCA Civ 1057 443
D (A Child), Re [2014] EWFC 39, [2015] 1 FLR 531 997
D (A Child: Deprivation of Liberty), Re [2015] EWHC 922 (Fam), [2015] COPLR 209 1547
D (A Child: Habitual Residence: Consent and Acquiescence), Re [2015] EWHC 1562 (Fam), [2016] 1 FLR 937 377, 389
D (A Minor) (Adoption Order: Validity), Re [1991] Fam 137, [1991] 2 FLR 66, CA 619
D (A Minor) (Care or Supervision Order), Re [1993] 2 FLR 423, FD 539, 540
D (A Minor) (Child Abduction), Note, Re [1989] 1 FLR 97, FD 389, 1553, 1554, 1557
D (A Minor) (Child: Removal from Jurisdiction), Re [1992] 1 WLR 315, [1992] 1 FLR 637, CA 448, 449, 1520
D (Abduction: Rights of Custody), Re [2006] UKHL 51, [2007] 1 AC 619, [2007] 1 FLR 961 364, 375, 379, 380, 387, 1697, 2781
D (Adoption) (No 3), Re [2016] EWFC 1, [2017] 1 FLR 237 541
D (Appeal: Procedure: Evidence), Re [2015] EWCA Civ 409, [2016] 1 FLR 249 206, 1324, 1863
D (Article 13B: Non-Return), Re [2006] EWCA Civ 146, [2006] 2 FLR 305 390
D (Brussels II Revised: Contact), Re [2007] EWHC 822 (Fam), [2008] 1 FLR 516 2789, 2790
D (Care or Supervision Order), Re [2000] Fam Law 600, FD 539
D (Care Order: Evidence), Re [2010] EWCA Civ 1000, [2011] 1 FLR 447 532
D (Care Proceedings: Legal Privilege), Re [2011] EWCA Civ 684, [2011] 2 FLR 1183 542, 1510, 1754
D (Care Proceedings: Preliminary Hearing), Re [2009] EWCA Civ 472, [2009] 2 FLR 668 536
D (Child: Threshold Criteria), Re [2001] 1 FLR 274, CA 540, 1508
D (Children) (Child Abduction: Practice), Re [2016] EWHC 504 (Fam) 383, 1553
D (Children) (Shared Residence Orders), Re [2001] 1 FLR 495, CA; *sub nom* D v D (Shared Residence Order) 441
D (Children), Re [2009] EWCA Civ 1467 444
D (Children), Re [2012] EWCA Civ 1584 535, 2196
D (Children), Re [2015] EWCA Civ 749 541, 1685
D (Children), Re [2016] EWCA Civ 89 440
D (Contact and Parental Responsibility: Lesbian Mothers and Known Father) (No 2), Re [2006] EWHC 2 (Fam); *sub nom* B v A 428, 702
D (Contact: Interim Order), Re [1995] 1 FLR 495, FD 1527, 1528, 1831
D (Costs), Re [2012] EWHC 886 (COP), [2012] COPLR 499 228, 1847
D (Evidence: Facilitated Communication), Re [2001] 1 FLR 148, FD 1529
D (Leave to Remove: Shared Residence), Re [2006] Fam Law 1006, FD 442
D (Local Authority Responsibility), Re [2012] EWCA Civ 627, [2013] 1 Fam 34, [2013] 2 FLR 673 541, 638
D (Minors) (Adoption Reports: Confidentiality), Re [1996] AC 593, [1995] 2 FLR 687, HL; [1995] 1 WLR 356, [1995] 1 FLR 631, CA 527, 1509, 1653, 1657, 1795
D (Minors) (Conciliation: Disclosure of Information), Re [1993] Fam 231, [1993] 1 FLR 932, CA; *sub nom* Re D (Minors) (Conciliation: Privilege) 436, 1513, 1754
D (Minors) (Conciliation: Privilege), Re [1993] Fam 231, [1993] 1 FLR 932, CA; *sub nom* Re D (Minors) (Conciliation: Disclosure of Information) 436, 1513, 1754
D (Minors) (Residence: Imposition of Conditions), Re [1996] 2 FLR 281, CA; *sub nom* Re D (Residence: Imposition of Conditions) 449, 556

D (Paternity), Re [2006] EWHC 3545 (Fam), [2007] 2 FLR 26 448
D (Recognition and enforcement of Romanian Order), Re [2014] EWHC 2756 (Fam), [2015] 1 FLR 1272; *sub nom* MD v AA 2742
D (Residence: Imposition of Conditions), Re [1996] 2 FLR 281, CA; *sub nom* Re D (Minors) (Residence: Imposition of Conditions) 449, 556
D (Safeguarding Checks), Re [2014] EWHC 2376 (Fam), [2015] 1 WLR 818, [2015] 1 FLR 991 437
D (Secure Accommodation Order) (No 1), Re [1997] 1 FLR 197, FD 511
D (Sexual Abuse Allegations: Evidence of Adult Victim), Re [2002] 1 FLR 723, FD 538
D (Surrogacy), Re [2014] EWHC 2121 (Fam) 979, 991
D (Unborn Baby), Re [2009] EWHC 446 (Fam), [2009] 2 FLR 313 529, 1544
D (Withdrawal of Parental Responsibility), Re [2014] EWCA Civ 315, [2015] 1 FLR 166 424, 425, 427, 429
D and G v ED and DD [2015] EWHC 911 (Fam), [2016] 2 FLR 530 990
D and K (Care Plan: Twin Track Planning), Re [2000] 1 WLR 642, [1999] 2 FLR 872, FD 531
D and L (Surrogacy), Re [2012] EWHC 2631 (Fam), [2013] 2 FLR 275 990, 991, 1638, 1639, 1640
D McG v Neath Talbot County Borough Council [2010] EWCA Civ 821, [2010] 2 FLR 1827 261
D O'H (Parenting Assessment), Re [2011] EWCA Civ 1343, [2012] 2 FLR 713 531
D v A & Co [1900] 1 Ch 484, ChD 1987
D v D (Application for Contact) [1994] 1 FCR 694, FD 1832
D v D (County Court Jurisdiction: Injunctions) [1993] 2 FLR 802, CA 449, 543, 797
D v D (Custody: Jurisdiction) [1996] 1 FLR 574, FD 861
D v D (Divorce: Media Presence) [2009] EWHC 946 (Fam), [2009] 2 FLR 324 1439
D v D (Financial Provision: Periodical Payments) [2004] EWHC 445 (Fam), [2004] 1 FLR 988 1169, 1196
D v D (Recognition of Foreign Divorce) [1994] 1 FLR 38, FD 864
D v D (Shared Residence Order) [2001] 1 FLR 495, CA; *sub nom* Re D (Children) (Shared Residence Orders) 441
D v K and B (By Her Guardian) [2014] EWHC 700 (Fam) 439
D v N and D (by her Guardian Ad Litem) [2011] EWHC 471 (Fam), [2011] 2 FLR 464 385, 387, 2781
D v National Society for the Prevention of Cruelty to Children [1978] AC 171, (1977) FLR Rep 181, HL 1512, 1754
D v S (Abduction: Acquiescence) [2008] EWHC 363 (Fam), [2008] 2 FLR 293 386, 388, 389
D v S [1996] EWCA Civ 1341, [1997] 1 FLR 724 1046
D, L and LA (Care: Change of Forename), Re [2003] 1 FLR 339, FD 448, 549
D-R (Adult: Contact), Re [1999] 1 FLR 1161, CA 440
Dad, Re [2015] EWHC 2655 (Fam); *sub nom* Application to commit Muhammed Nawaz Chaudry 30, 902, 1473, 1984, 1988
Danchevsky v Danchevsky [1975] Fam 17, CA 2336
Daniels v Walker (Practice Note) [2000] 1 WLR 1382, CA 1798, 2129
Darlington Borough Council v M, F, GM and GF [2015] EWFC 11, [2016] 1 FLR 1; *sub nom* Re A (Application for Care and Placement Orders: Local Authority Failings) 532, 534, 536, 543
Dart v Dart [1996] 2 FLR 286, CA 1155, 1432, 1440, 2146
Daryananii v Kumar and Gerry (2000) (unreported) 12 December, CA 1324
Daubney v Daubney [1976] Fam 267, CA 1182
Davila v Davila and another [2016] EWHC B14 (Ch) 2063, 2065
Davis v Johnson [1979] AC 264, HL 887
Davis v Smith [2011] EWCA Civ 1603, [2012] 1 FLR 1177 1029
Davis v Windsor Life Assurance Co Ltd (2012) 6 March, ref 80998/1, Deputy Pensions Ombudsman 1175
Dawkins (dec'd), Re; Dawkins v Judd [1986] 2 FLR 360, FD 1024
Dawson v Wearmouth [1999] 2 AC 308, [1999] 1 FLR 1167, HL; [1998] Fam 75, [1997] 2 FLR 629, CA 446, 447, 449, 528
Day v Day [1980] Fam 29, (1980) 1 FLR 341, CA 1386, 1387, 1393, 1394, 1395, 1399
DB v AB and CB [2014] EWHC 384 (Fam), [2014] 2 FLR 1197 702
DB v CMEC [2010] UKUT 356 407
DB v DLJ (Challenge to Arbitral Award) [2016] EWHC 324 (Fam), [2016] 2 FLR 1308 212, 1153, 1308, 1448
DB v PB [2016] EWHC 3431 (Fam) 1180
DE (A Child), Re [2014] EWFC 6, [2015] Fam 145, [2015] 1 FLR 1001 564, 565
De Bruyne v De Bruyne [2010] EWCA Civ 519, [2010] 2 FLR 1240 1181
De Dampierre v De Dampierre [1988] AC 92, [1987] 2 FLR 300, HL 828
De L v H [2009] EWHC 3074 (Fam), [2010] 1 FLR 1229 376, 389, 391
DE v AB (Financial Provision for Child) [2010] EWHC 3792 (Fam), [2012] 2 FLR 1396 1866
DE v AB (No 2) Permission Hearing: Publicity Protection) [2014] EWCA Civ 1064, [2015] 1 FLR 1119 1040
Deak v Romania and UK (Application No 19055/05) [2008] 2 FLR 994, ECHR 381
Dean v Dean [1987] 1 FLR 517, CA 896

Dean v Stout (the Trustee in Bankruptcy of Dean) [2005] EWHC 3315 (Ch), [2006] 1 FLR 725, [2005] BPIR 1113 1264
Debenham (dec'd), Re [1986] 1 FLR 404, FD 1023
Delaney v Delaney [1996] QB 387, [1996] 1 FLR 458, CA 792, 1474
Dennis (Deceased), Re [1981] 2 All ER 140 1018
Department of Social Security v Butler [1995] 1 WLR 1528, [1996] 1 FLR 65, CA 1243
Detičekv v Sgueglia (Case C–403 /09) [2009] ECR I-12193, [2010] Fam 104, [2010] 1 FLR 1381, ECJ 385, 524, 2787, 2870
Deutsche Bank AG v Sebastian Holdings Inc & Anor [2016] EWCA Civ 23 1849, 2157
Deutsche Bank AG v Sebastian Holdings Inc [2016] EWHC 3222 (Comm) 124, 2287
Devjee v Patel [2006] EWCA Civ 1211 1984
Devon County Council and Others v S and Others [1993] 1 FLR 842, FD 1547
Devon County Council v B [1997] 1 FLR 591, CA 543
Devon County Council v Kirk [2016] EWCA Civ 1221 793
Devon County Council v S and Others [1992] Fam 176, [1992] 2 FLR 244, FD 540, 1527, 1831
DH v CL and Others [2014] EWHC 1836 (Fam) 472
Dickson v Rennie [2014] EWHC 4306 (Fam), [2015] 2 FLR 978 645, 646
Dietz v Lennin Chemicals Ltd [1969] 1 AC 170, HL 2068
Dinch v Dinch [1987] 1 WLR 252, [1987] 2 FLR 162, HL 1172
Dingmar v Dingmar [2006] EWCA Civ 942, [2007] Ch 109, [2007] 1 FLR 210 1029
Director General of Fair Trading v Smiths Concrete [1992] QB 213, CA; *sub nom* Re Supply of Ready Mixed Concrete 129
Director of Legal Aid Casework and Another v IS [2016] EWCA Civ 464, [2016] 1 WLR 4733, [2016] 2 FLR 392 440
Director of Public Prosecutions v P (No 2) (Note) [2007] EWHC 1144 (Admin) 207
Divall v Divall [2014] EWHC 95 (Fam), [2014] 2 FLR 1104 828, 1014, 2777
Dixon v Marchant [2008] EWCA Civ 11, [2008] 1 FLR 655 1448
DL and ML v Newham London Borough Council and Secretary of State for Education [2011] EWHC 1127 (Admin), [2011] 2 FLR 1033 273
DL v EL (Hague Abduction Convention: Effect of Reversal of Return Order on Appeal) [2013] EWHC 49 (Fam), [2013] 2 FLR 163 384
DL v SL [2015] EWHC 2621 (Fam) 1756, 1835
DM & LK v SJ & OJ [2016] EWHC 270 (Fam) 990, 1256
DN v HN [2014] EWHC 3435 (Fam), [2016] 1 FLR 1171 1442
Dodd v Dodd [1906] P 189, PDAD 812
Doherty v Birmingham City Council [2008] UKHL 57, [2009] AC 367 993
Doherty v Doherty [1976] Fam 71, CA 1197
Dolhamre v Sweden [2010] 2 FLR 912, ECHR 528, 559
Doncaster MBC v Haigh, Tune and X (by the Children's Guardian) [2012] 1 FLR 577, FD 248, 1563
Doncaster MBC v Watson and Haigh [2012] 1 FLR 599, FD 466
Doncaster Metropolitan Borough Council v Haigh & Ors [2011] EWHC 2412 (Fam) 627
Doncaster Metropolitan Borough Council v Watson (No 2) [2011] EWHC 2498 (Fam), [2012] 1 FLR 619 466
Doncaster Metropolitan District Council v Watson [2011] EWHC 2376 (Fam), [2012] 1 FLR 613 466
Donsland Ltd v Van Hoogstraten [2002] EWCA Civ 253 1827
Dorney-Kingdom v Dorney-Kingdom [2000] 2 FLR 855, CA 406, 1169, 1183
Down Lisburn Health and Social Services Trust v H [2006] UKHL 36, [2007] 1 FLR 121 287
DR v GR and Others (Financial Remedy: Variation of Overseas Trust) [2013] EWHC 1196 (Fam), [2013] 2 FLR 1534 1172, 1450
Drinkall v Whitwood [2003] EWCA Civ 1547, [2004] 1 WLR 462 2068
DS (Removal from Jurisdiction), Re [2009] EWHC 1594 (Fam), [2010] 1 FLR 576 473
DT v LBT [2010] EWHC 3177 (Fam), [2011] 1 FLR 1215 389, 390, 391
Duer (Anne-Margaret) v Frazer (Peter Nigel) [2001] 1 WLR 919, QBD 89, 97
Duhur-Johnson v Duhur-Johnson (Attorney-General intervening) [2005] 2 FLR 1042, FD 867
Dukali v Lamrani (Attorney-General Intervening) [2012] EWHC 1748 (Fam), [2012] 2 FLR 1099 1014, 1125
Dunbar v Plant [1998] Ch 412, [1998] 1 FLR 157, CA 1024
Duncan v Cammell Laird [1942] AC 624, HL 1758
Dunhill (A Protected Party By Her Litigation Friend Tasker) v Burgin (Nos 1 and 2) [2014] UKSC 18, [2014] 1 WLR 933, [2014] COPLR 199 1681, 1682, 1683, 2062, 2068
Dunhill (An Infant), Re (1967) 111 SJ 113, ChD 1548
Durham County Council v Dunn [2012] EWCA Civ 1654 1754
Durrant v Avon & Somerset Constabulary [2013] EWCA Civ 1624, [2014] 1 WLR 4313 1766

Duxbury v Duxbury [1987] 1 FLR 7, CA 1169

E & Others v United Kingdom (2002) 36 EHRR 519, [2003] 1 FLR 348 1005
E (A Child) (Northern Ireland), Re [2008] UKHL 66, [2009] AC 536 1005
E (A Child), Re [2013] EWCA Civ 1592 538
E (A Child), Re [2014] EWHC 6 (Fam) 2681, 2683
E (A Child), Re [2016] EWCA Civ 473 386, 542, 624, 625
E (A Minor) (Abduction), Re [1989] 1 FLR 135, CA 390, 1554
E (A Minor) (Child Abuse: Evidence), Re [1991] 1 FLR 420, FD 248, 619
E (A Minor) (Wardship: Medical Treatment), Re [1993] 1 FLR 386, FD 1547
E (Abduction: Intolerable Situation), Re [2008] EWHC 2112 (Fam), [2009] 2 FLR 485 382, 383, 388, 391
E (Abduction: Rights of Custody), Re [2005] EWHC 848 (Fam), [2005] 2 FLR 759 375, 376
E (Adopted Child: Contact: Leave), Re [1995] 1 FLR 57, FD 455
E (Adoption Order: Proportionality of Outcome to Circumstances), Re [2013] EWCA Civ 1614, [2014] 2 FLR 514 423, 1008
E (An Alleged Patient), Re; Sheffield City Council v E and S [2004] EWHC 2808 (Fam), [2005] Fam 326, [2005] 1 FLR 965 901
E (Brussels II Revised: Vienna Convention: Reporting Restrictions), Re [2014] EWHC 6 (Fam), [2014] 1 WLR 2670, [2014] 2 FLR 151 248, 522, 523, 524, 2778, 2785, 2797
E (Care Proceedings: Social Work Practice), Re [2000] 2 FLR 254, FD 531
E (Children) (Abduction: Custody Appeal), Re [2011] UKSC 27, [2012] 1 AC 144, [2011] 2 FLR 758 383, 389, 2781
E (Children) (Female Genital Mutilation Protection Orders), Re [2015] EWHC 2275 (Fam), [2015] 2 FLR 997 631, 932, 934, 1478
E (Children), Re [2011] EWCA Civ 361, [2011] 2 FLR 724; *sub nom* (1) KE (2) TB Appellants v SE Respondent & others 389, 391
E (Family Assistance Order), Re [1999] 2 FLR 512, FD 483
E (Female Genital Mutilation and Permission to Remove), Re [2016] EWHC 1052 (Fam) 932
E (Mental Health Patient), Re [1984] 1 WLR 320 2718
E (Minors), Re [1991] TLR 300, CA 1529
E (Relocation: Removal from Jurisdiction), Re [2012] EWCA Civ 1893, [2013] 2 FLR 290 471
E (Wardship Order: Child in Voluntary Accommodation), Re [2012] EWCA Civ 1773, [2013] 2 FLR 63 493, 630
E v B (Case C-436/13) [2015] Fam 162, [2015] 1 FLR 64, CJEU 2783
E v C (Child Maintenance) [1996] 1 FLR 472, FD 813
E v E (BIIA: Arts 16 and 19) [2015] EWHC 3742 (Fam), [2017] 1 FLR 658 1352, 2785, 2786
E v E (Child Abduction: Intolerable Situation) [1998] 2 FLR 980, FD 391
E v Humberside County Council and S [1996] Fam Law 444, FD 457, 548
E-R (Child Arrangements Order), Re [2015] EWCA Civ 405, [2016] 1 FLR 521 441, 476
E-R (Child Arrangements), Re [2016] EWHC 805 (Fam) 444
EA v AP [2013] EWHC 2344 (Fam) 2866, 2869, 2870
EC (Child Abduction: Stayed Proceedings), Re [2006] EWCA Civ 1115, [2007] 1 FLR 57 204, 524, 2200
EC (Disclosure of Material), Re [1997] Fam 76, [1996] 2 FLR 725, CA; [1996] 2 FLR 123, FD 629, 1534
ECC (The Local Authority) v SM [2010] EWHC 1694 (Fam), [2011] 1 Fam 110, [2011] 1 FLR 234 303
ECC v M [2008] EWHC 332 (Fam) 277
EDG v RR (Enforcement of Foreign Maintenance Order) [2014] EWHC 816 (Fam), [2015] 1 FLR 270 2440, 2871, 2882
Edgar v Edgar [1980] 1 WLR 1410, (1981) 2 FLR 19, CA 1152, 1206, 1442
Edgcome, Re, ex parte Edgcome [1902] 2 KB 403, CA 1932, 1934
Edgerton v Edgerton and Shaikh [2012] EWCA Civ 181, [2012] 1 WLR 2655, [2012] 2 FLR 273 20, 1024, 1168, 1763
Edmonds v Edmonds [1965] 1 WLR 58, PDAD 353
Edwards v Edwards [1986] 1 FLR 205, CA affirming [1986] 1 FLR 187, QBD & FD 2193
Edwards v Golding [2007] EWCA Civ 416 1321
Egan v Motor Services (Bath) Ltd [2007] EWCA Civ 1002, [2008] 1 FLR 1346 203
El Fadl v El Fadl [2000] 1 FLR 175, FD 864, 867
El Gamal v Al-Maktoum [2012] 2 FLR 387, FD 1014
Elder v Elder [1986] 1 FLR 610, CA 1532
Elgindata (No 2), Re [1992] 1 WLR 1207, CA 2146
Ella v Ella [2007] EWCA Civ 99, [2007] 2 FLR 35 828, 1358
Elliot v Elliot [2001] 1 FCR 477, CA 1183
Elsholz v Germany (Case 2573/943) [2000] 2 FLR 486, ECHR 443
Elsholz v Italy [2000] Fam Law 680, ECHR 443

EM (Lebanon) v Secretary of State for the Home Department [2008] UKHL 64, [2008] 2 FLR 2067, [2009] AC 1198 1010
Emailgen Systems Corp v Exclaimer Ltd & Anor [2013] EWHC 167 (Comm), [2013] 1 WLR 2132 1242
Emanuel v Emanuel [1982] 1 WLR 669, (1982) 3 FLR 319, FD 1240
Emin v Yeldag (Attorney-General and Secretary of State for Foreign & Commonwealth Affairs Intervening) [2002] 1 FLR 956, FD 867
Emson v Teachers' Pensions (2013) 10 September, ref PO-168, Deputy Pensions Ombudsman 1175
Enfield London Borough Council v Mahoney [1983] 1 WLR 749, CA 792
Engel and Others v The Netherlands (No 1) (1979) 1 EHRR 647 413, 1762
English v Emery Reimbold & Strick Ltd [2002] EWCA Civ 605, [2002] 1 WLR 2409 1007, 1533, 2194
Eroglu v Eroglu [1994] 2 FLR 287, FD 867
Erskine Trust, Re [2012] EWHC 732 (Ch), [2012] 2 FLR 725 1015
Escritt v Escritt (1982) 3 FLR 280, CA 1025
Espinosa v Bourke [1999] 1 FLR 747, CA 1023
Essex County Council v B [1993] 1 FLR 866, FD 569, 1514
Essex County Council v F [1993] 1 FLR 847, FD 578, 1831
ET v TZ (Recognition and Enforcement of Foreign Residence Order) [2013] EWHC 2621 (Fam), [2014] 2 FLR 373 2789, 2800
ET, BT, CT v Islington London Borough Council [2013] EWCA Civ 323 486, 582
Evans v Amicus Healthcare and Others; Hadley v Midland Fertility Services Ltd and others [2003] EWHC 2161 (Fam), [2005] Fam 1, [2004] 1 FLR 67 960, 963, 969
Evans v Evans [2012] EWCA Civ 1293, [2013] 2 FLR 295 1404
Evans v Evans [2013] EWHC 506 (Fam), [2013] 2 FLR 999 1179, 1180, 1181, 1183
Evans v HSBC Trust Co (UK) Ltd [2005] WTLR 1289, ChD 1023
Evans v United Kingdom (Application No 6339/05) (2007) 46 EHRR 728, [2007] 1 FLR 1990 1004, 1008
Evans v Wills (1876) 1 CPD 229 1934
Everitt v Everitt [1948] WN 237, CA 1235
Ezair v Ezair [2012] EWCA Civ 893, [2013] 1 FLR 281 1184

F (A Child) (International Relocation Cases), Re [2015] EWCA Civ 882, [2017] 1 FLR 979 290, 442, 471, 472
F (A Child) (International Relocation Cases), Re [2015] EWCA Civ 882 472
F (A Child), Re [2014] EWCA Civ 789 522, 523, 841, 2778
F (A Minor) (Care Order: Procedure), Re [1994] 1 FLR 240, FD 1528
F (A Minor) (Care Order: Withdrawal of Application), Re [1993] 2 FLR 9, FD 1831, 1853
F (A Minor) (Care Proceedings: Directions), Re [1995] 3 FCR 601, FD 1514
F (A Minor) (Child Abduction: Rights of Custody Abroad), Re [1995] Fam 224, [1995] 2 FLR 31, CA; *sub nom* Re F (Child Abduction: Risk if Returned) 376
F (A Minor) (Custody: Consent Order: Procedure), Re [1992] 1 FLR 561, CA 1235
F (Abduction: Art 13(b): Psychiatric Assessment), Re [2014] EWCA Civ 275, [2014] 2 FLR 1115 390
F (Abduction: Child's Wishes), Re [2007] EWCA Civ 468, [2007] 2 FLR 697 382, 385, 391, 2781
F (Abduction: Consent), Re [2014] EWHC 484 (Fam) 389
F (Abduction: Joinder of Child as Party), Re [2007] EWCA Civ 393, [2007] 2 FLR 313 387, 2781
F (Abduction: Refusal to Return), Re [2009] EWCA Civ 416, [2009] 2 FLR 1023 385, 2781
F (Abduction: Removal Outside Jurisdiction), Re [2008] EWCA Civ 842, [2008] 2 FLR 1649 1516
F (Abduction: Rights of Custody), Re [2008] EWHC 272 (Fam), [2008] Fam 75, [2008] 2 FLR 1239 375, 376, 380, 382
F (Abduction: Unborn Child), Re [2006] EWHC 2199 (Fam), [2007] 1 FLR 627 376, 378
F (Abduction: Unmarried Father: Sole Carer), Re [2002] EWHC 2896 (Fam), [2003] 1 FLR 839 380
F (Adoption: Natural Parents), Re [2006] EWCA Civ 1345, [2007] 1 FLR 363 1650, 1658
F (Adult: Court's Jurisdiction), Re [2001] Fam 38, [2000] 2 FLR 512, CA 440
F (Care Proceedings), Re [2007] EWCA Civ 810 1508
F (Care Proceedings: Contact), Re [2000] Fam Law 708, FD 552
F (Care Proceedings: Interim Care Order), Re [2010] EWCA Civ 826, [2010] 2 FLR 1455 559
F (Care: Party Status: Directions), Re [1999] Fam Law 294, FD 1501
F (Child Abduction: Risk if Returned), Re [1995] Fam 224, [1995] 2 FLR 31, CA; *sub nom* Re F (A Minor) (Child Abduction: Rights of Custody Abroad) 376
F (Child's Objections), Re [2015] EWCA Civ 1022 391, 424
F (Children), Re [2013] EWCA Civ 726 1530
F (Children), Re [2015] EWCA Civ 1315 423, 446
F (Children), Re [2016] EWCA Civ 353 1847
F (Children), Re [2016] EWCA Civ 546 206, 386, 542, 623
F (Children), Re [2016] EWCA Civ 1253 384
F (Contact), Re [2007] EWHC 2543 (Fam), [2008] 1 FLR 1163 448, 1532

F (Contact: Child in Care), Re [1995] 1 FLR 510, FD 451
F (Family Proceedings: Section 37 Investigation), Re [2005] EWHC 2935 (Fam), [2006] 1 FLR 1122 556
F (Habitual Residence), Re [2014] EWFC 26, [2015] 1 FLR 1303 2783
F (In Utero) (Wardship), Re [1988] Fam 122, [1988] 2 FLR 307, CA 960, 1544
F (Infants) (Adoption Order: Validity), Re [1977] Fam 165, CA 285
F (Interim Care Order), Re [2007] EWCA Civ 516, [2007] 2 FLR 891 560
F (Interim Care Order), Re [2011] EWCA Civ 258, [2011] 2 FLR 856 537
F (Mental Health Act: Guardianship), Re [2000] 1 FLR 192, CA 630
F (Minors) (Custody: Foreign Order: Enforcement) [1989] Fam 1, [1989] 1 FLR 335, FD 395
F (Paternity: Jurisdiction), Re [2007] EWCA Civ 873, [2008] 1 FLR 225 448, 449
F (Paternity: Registration), Re [2011] EWCA Civ 1765, [2013] 2 FLR 1036 870, 1424
F (Placement Order), Re [2008] EWCA Civ 439, [2008] 2 FLR 550 265
F (Relocation), Re [2012] EWCA Civ 1364, [2013] 1 FLR 645 442
F (Residence Order: Jurisdiction), Re [1995] 2 FLR 518, FD 844
F (Shared Residence Order), Re [2003] EWCA Civ 592, [2003] 2 FLR 397 441
F (Special Guardianship Order: Contact with Birth Family), Re [2015] EWFC 25, [2016] 1 FLR 593 475
F (Supervised Contact: Disputed Evidence), Re [2012] EWCA Civ 828, [2013] 1 FLR 665 2197
F and F v AG and F [1980] Fam Law 60, FD 1055
F and X (Female Genital Mutilation), Re [2015] EWHC 2653 (Fam), [2016] 2 FLR 1032 932
F v Cambridgeshire County Council [1995] 1 FLR 516, FD 556, 1501
F v Child Support Agency [1999] 2 FLR 244, QBD 2431
F v Cumbria County Council [2016] EWHC 14 (Fam) 536
F v F (Divorce: Jurisdiction) [2009] EWHC 1448 (Fam), [2009] 2 FLR 1496 2777
F v F (Duxbury Calculation: Rate of Return) [1996] 1 FLR 833, FD 1169
F v F (Financial Remedies: Premarital Wealth) [2012] EWHC 438 (Fam), [2012] 2 FLR 1212 1206
F v F (MMR Vaccine) [2013] EWHC 2683 (Fam), [2014] 1 FLR 1328 559
F v F (Pre-nuptial Agreement) [2009] EWHC 2485 (Fam), [2010] 1 FLR 1743 1180
F v G (Child: Financial Provision) [2004] EWHC 1848 (Fam), [2005] 1 FLR 261 650
F v M (Abduction: Grave Risk of Harm) [2008] EWHC 1467 (Fam), [2008] 2 FLR 1263 384, 390, 2781
F v M and N (Abduction: Acquiescence: Settlement) [2008] EWHC 1525 (Fam), [2008] 2 FLR 1270 382, 386
F v R (Contact: Justices' Reasons) [1995] 1 FLR 227, FD 449, 1831
F v Y (Abduction: Acquiescence) [2014] 2 FLR 875, FD 388
F-H (Dispensing with Fact-Finding Hearing), Re [2008] EWCA Civ 1249, [2009] 1 FLR 349 445
Fabris v France (Application No 16574/08) [2013] ECHR 16574/08 1015
Fallon v Fallon [2008] EWCA Civ 1653, [2010] 1 FLR 910 1184, 1870
Farley v Secretary of State for Department of Work and Pensions and Another [2006] UKHL 31, [2006] 1 WLR 1817, [2006] 2 FLR 1243 412
Farley v Secretary of State for Work and Pensions (No 2) [2005] EWCA Civ 869, [2005] 2 FLR 1075 2202
Farm Assist Ltd v Secretary of State for the Environment, Food and Rural Affairs (No 2) [2009] EWHC 1102 (TCC) 1754
Farrant v Farrant [1957] P 188, PDAD 1930
Farrell v Long [1998] 1 FLR 559, ECJ 2866
FAS v Secretary of State for the Home Department and Another [2015] EWCA Civ 951, [2016] 1 WLR 407, [2016] 2 FLR 1035 256
Felton v Callis [1969] 1 QB 200, QBD 1236
Fengl v Fengl [1914] P 274, DC 812
Ferrari v Romania (Application No 1714/10) [2015] 2 FLR 303, ECHR 381
FG Hemisphere Associates LLC v The Republic of Congo [2005] EWHC 3103 (Comm) 2295
FG v MBW (Financial Remedy for Child) [2011] EWHC 1729 (Fam), [2012] 1 FLR 152 646
FGMPO, Re (2016) *The Times*, 1 March 932
Field v Leeds City Council [2001] CPLR 129, CA 687, 1799
Fielden v Cunliffe [2005] EWCA Civ 1508, [2006] Ch 361, [2006] 1 FLR 745 1017, 1020, 1025
Fielding v Fielding [1977] 1 WLR 1146, CA 1122
Fields v Fields [2015] EWHC 1670 (Fam), [2016] 1 FLR 1186 1185
Fisher Meredith v JH and PH (Financial Remedy: Appeal: Wasted Costs) [2012] EWHC 408 (Fam), [2012] 2 FLR 536 1439, 2160
Fisher-Aziz v Aziz [2010] EWCA Civ 673, [2010] 2 FLR 1053 1171
Fitzroy Robinson v Mentmore Towers [2009] EWHC 3070 (TCC) 1320
FK v ML & A [2016] EWHC 517 (Fam) 391
Flavell v Flavell [1997] 1 FLR 353, CA 1169

Fleet Mortgage and Investment Co v Lower Maisonette, 46 Eaton Place; Lower Maisonette, 46 Eaton Place v Crown Lodge (Belgravia) [1972] 1 WLR 765, ChD 2322
Fleming v Fleming [2003] EWCA Civ 1841, [2004] 1 FLR 667 1202, 1203
Flintshire County Council v K [2001] 2 FLR 476, FD 664
FM & KAH v SU & SA (by their guardian) [2017] EWHC 441 (Fam) 378
Folks v Faizey [2006] EWCA Civ 381 1683, 2065
Foster v Foster [2003] EWCA Civ 565, [2003] 2 FLR 299 1183
Fowler v Barron [2008] EWCA Civ 377, [2008] 2 FLR 831 1263
Fowler v Fowler (1981) 2 FLR 141, FD 414
Foxon v Gascoigne (1874) LR 9 Ch App 654 1043
French v Groupama Insurance Company Ltd [2011] EWCA Civ 1119 2136
Fuld's Estate (No 3), Re [1968] P 675, PDAD 1014
Fullard (dec'd), Re [1982] Fam 42, CA 1017
FZ v SZ and Others (Ancillary Relief: Conduct: Valuations) [2010] EWHC 1630 (Fam), [2011] 1 FLR 64 1180, 1184, 1241

G & Others (HFEA 2008), Re [2016] EWHC 729 (Fam) 982, 983
G (A Child) (Special Guardianship Order), Re [2010] EWCA Civ 300, [2010] 2 FLR 696 478
G (A Child), Re [2013] EWCA Civ 965, [2014] 1 FLR 670 193, 203, 290, 538
G (A Child), Re [2014] EWCA Civ 1365 204, 2193
G (A Child), Re [2015] EWCA Civ 834 526
G (A Child), Re [2015] EWHC 2941 (Fam); *sub nom* B v M 859
G (A Child), Re [2016] EWCA Civ 297 383, 2206
G (A Minor) (Child Abduction: Enforcement), Re [1990] 2 FLR 325, FD 394, 395
G (A Minor) (Enforcement of Access Abroad), Re [1993] Fam 216, [1993] 1 FLR 669, CA; *sub nom* Re G (A Minor) (Hague Convention: Access) 379
G (A Minor) (Hague Convention: Access), Re [1993] Fam 216, [1993] 1 FLR 669, CA; *sub nom* Re G (A Minor) (Enforcement of Access Abroad) 379
G (A Minor) (Parental Responsibility Order), Re [1994] 1 FLR 504, CA 428
G (A Minor) (Role of the Appellate Court), Re [1987] 1 FLR 164, CA 2160
G (A Minor) (Social Worker: Disclosure), Re [1996] 1 WLR 1407, [1996] 1 FLR 276, CA; *sub nom* Re G (Social Worker: Disclosure) 629
G (A Minor) (Wardship: Access), Re [1988] 1 FLR 305, CA 1870
G (Abduction: Children's Objections), Re [2010] EWCA Civ 1232, [2011] 1 FLR 1645 386, 391
G (Abduction: Rights of Custody), Re [2001] EWCA Civ 1624, [2002] 2 FLR 703 367, 379
G (Abduction: Withdrawal of Proceedings), Re [2007] EWHC 2807 (Fam), [2008] 2 FLR 351 376, 378, 388, 389
G (Adoption Proceedings: Representation of Children) [2001] 1 FCR 353, CA 1529
G (Adoption: Contact), Re [2002] EWCA Civ 761, [2003] 1 FLR 270 287, 552
G (Adoption: Leave to Oppose), Re [2014] EWCA Civ 432, [2015] 1 Fam 223, [2014] 2 FLR 525 283
G (Adult Patient: Publicity), Re [1995] 2 FLR 528, FD 790, 1248
G (Care Proceedings: Split Trials), Re [2001] 1 FLR 872, CA 535, 1507, 1508
G (Care Proceedings: Threshold Conditions), Re [2001] EWCA Civ 968, [2001] 1 WLR 2100, [2001] 2 FLR 1111, CA; *sub nom* Re G (Children) (Care Order: Threshold Criteria) 532
G (Care: Challenge to Local Authority's Decision), Re [2003] EWHC 551 (Fam), [2003] 2 FLR 42 529, 1008
G (Celebrities: Publicity), Re [1999] 1 FLR 409, CA 248, 1544
G (Children) (Care Order: Threshold Criteria), Re [2001] EWCA Civ 968, [2001] 1 WLR 2100, [2001] 2 FLR 1111, CA; *sub nom* Re G (Care Proceedings: Threshold Conditions) 532
G (Children) (Residence: Same Sex Partner), Re [2006] UKHL 43, [2006] 1 WLR 2305, [2006] 2 FLR 629; *sub nom* Re G (Children); *sub nom* CG v CW 423, 441, 472, 702, 982
G (Children), Re [2005] EWCA Civ 1283, [2006] 1 FLR 771 424
G (Children), Re [2006] UKHL 43, [2006] 1 WLR 2305, [2006] 2 FLR 629; *sub nom* Re G (Children) (Residence: Same Sex Partner); *sub nom* CG v CW 423, 441, 472, 702, 982
G (Children), Re [2015] EWCA Civ 1091 547
G (Contempt: Committal), Re [2003] EWCA Civ 489, [2003] 1 WLR 2051, [2003] 2 FLR 58 620, 2194
G (Decree Absolute: Prejudice), Re [2002] EWHC 2834 (Fam), [2003] 1 FLR 870 1148, 1405
G (Domestic Violence: Direct Contact), Re [2000] 2 FLR 865, FD 552
G (Foreign Adoption: Consent), Re [1995] 2 FLR 534, FD 1651
G (Foreign Contact Order: Enforcement), Re [2003] EWCA Civ 1607, [2004] 1 WLR 521, [2004] 1 FLR 378 394, 396
G (Interim Care Order), Re [2011] EWCA Civ 745, [2011] 2 FLR 955 559, 560
G (Interim Care Order: Residential Assessment), Re [2005] UKHL 68, [2006] 1 AC 576, [2006] 1 FLR 601 558, 559, 561

G (Intractable Contact Dispute), Re [2013] EWHC B16 (Fam), [2014] 1 FLR 1185 443
G (Jurisdiction: Art 19, BIIR), Re [2014] EWCA Civ 680, [2015] 1 FLR 276 2783, 2786, 2787
G (Leave to Appeal: Jurisdiction), Re [1999] 1 FLR 771, CA 664
G (Minors) (Care: Leave to Place Outside Jurisdiction), Re [1994] 2 FLR 301, FD 664, 665
G (Minors) (Ex Parte Interim Residence Order), Re [1993] 1 FLR 910, CA; *sub nom* Re G (Minors) 146, 1522
G (Minors) (Interim Care Order), Re [1993] 2 FLR 839, CA 1290, 1501
G (Minors) (Wardship: Costs), Re [1982] 1 WLR 438, CA 2147
G (Minors) (Welfare Report: Disclosure), Re [1993] 2 FLR 293, CA 438, 1509
G (Minors), Re [1993] 1 FLR 910, CA; *sub nom* Re G (Minors) (Ex Parte Interim Residence Order) 146, 1522
G (Parental Responsibility Order), Re [2006] EWCA Civ 745, [2006] 2 FLR 1092 428
G (Recognition of Brazilian Adoption), Re [2014] EWHC 2605 (Fam), [2015] 1 FLR 1402 292
G (Residence: Restrictions on Further Applications), Re [2008] EWCA Civ 1468, [2009] 1 FLR 894 619, 620
G (Secure Accommodation Order), Re [2001] 1 FLR 884, FD 513
G (Secure Accommodation), Re [2000] 2 FLR 259, CA 513
G (Shared Residence Order: Biological Mother of Donor Egg), Re [2014] EWCA Civ 336, [2014] 2 FLR 897 427, 430, 441, 978, 985
G (Shared Residence), Re [2012] EWCA Civ 1434, [2013] 1 FLR 1323 702, 1505
G (Social Worker: Disclosure), Re [1996] 1 WLR 1407, [1996] 1 FLR 276, CA; *sub nom* Re G (A Minor) (Social Worker: Disclosure) 629
G (Surrogacy: Foreign Domicile), Re [2007] EWHC 2814 (Fam), [2008] 1 FLR 1047 990
G and A (Care Order: Freeing Order: Parents with a Learning Disability), Re [2006] NIFam 8 541
G and B (Fact-Finding Hearing), Re [2009] EWCA Civ 10, [2009] 1 FLR 1145 534, 535
G v A (Financial Remedy: Enforcement) (No 1) [2011] EWHC 2380 (Fam), [2012] 1 FLR 389 646
G v A (Financial Remedy: Enforcement) (No 2) [2011] EWHC 968 (Fam), [2012] 1 FLR 402 646
G v A (Financial Remedy: Enforcement) (No 3) [2011] EWHC 2377 (Fam), [2012] 1 FLR 415 646
G v A (Financial Remedy: Enforcement) (No 4) [2011] EWHC 2377 (Fam), [2012] 1 FLR 427 646
G v A Borough Council [2000] Fam Law 11, Cty Ct 1705
G v B (Financial Remedies: Asset Beneficiaries) [2013] EWHC 3414 (Fam), [2014] 2 FLR 292 1181
G v F (Contact and Shared Residence: Applications for Leave), Re [1998] 2 FLR 799, FD 455
G v F (Non-Molestation Order) [2000] Fam 186, [2000] 2 FLR 533, FD; *sub nom* G v F (Non-Molestation Order: Jurisdiction) 897
G v F (Non-Molestation Order: Jurisdiction) [2000] Fam 186, [2000] 2 FLR 533, FD; *sub nom* G v F (Non-Molestation Order) 897
G v G (Child Maintenance: Interim Costs Provision) [2009] EWHC 2080 (Fam), [2010] 2 FLR 1264 646
G v G (Financial Provision: Discovery) [1992] 1 FLR 40, FD 1440
G v G (Financial Provision: Equal Division) [2002] EWHC 1339 (Fam), [2002] 2 FLR 1143 1181, 1184
G v G (Financial Provision: Separation Agreement) [2004] 1 FLR 1011, CA 1184
G v G (Financial Remedies: Short Marriage: Trust Assets) [2012] EWHC 167 (Fam), [2012] 2 FLR 48 1169
G v G (Interim Custody: Appeal) (1983) 4 FLR 327, CA 2193
G v G (Minors: Custody Appeal) [1985] 1 WLR 647, [1985] FLR 894, HL 193, 203, 1870, 1871, 2205
G v G [2007] EWCA Civ 680, [2007] 2 FLR 1127 2196
G v G [2012] EWHC 167 (Fam) 1183, 1184
G v G [2015] EWHC 2101 (Fam) 2857
G v G (Ouster: Ex Parte Application) [1990] 1 FLR 395, CA 39, 890
G v G (Parental Order: Revocation) [2012] EWHC 1979 (Fam), [2013] 1 FLR 286 989, 990, 991, 1639, 1640
G v G (Role of FDR Judge) [2006] EWHC 1993 (Fam), [2007] 1 FLR 237 1202, 1442
G v Hertfordshire County Council [2000] Fam Law 883, CA 582
G v M [2011] EWHC 2651 (Fam) 47
G v N County Council [2009] 1 FLR 774, FD 528
G v S [2017] EWHC 365 (Fam) 650
G, Re; Re Z (Children: Sperm Donors: Leave to Apply for Children Act Orders) [2013] EWHC 134 (Fam), [2013] 1 FLR 1334 455, 456, 982
G, S and M (Wasted Costs), Re [2000] Fam 104, [2000] 1 FLR 52, FD 1534
Gadd v Gadd [1984] 1 WLR 1435, [1985] FLR 220, CA 828
Gadhavi v Gadhavi [2015] EWCA Civ 520 1181
Galan v Galan [1985] FLR 905, CA 888
Galbraith v Grimshaw & Baxter [1910] AC 5082, HL 2293
Galloway v Goldstein [2012] EWHC 60 (Fam), [2012] Fam 129, [2012] 1 FLR 1254 869
Gandolfo v Gandolfo (Standard Chartered Bank, Garnishee) [1981] QB 359, CA 797

Garcia v Garcia [1992] Fam 83, [1992] 1 FLR 256, CA 1155
Garland v Morris [2007] EWHC 2 (Ch), [2007] 2 FLR 528 1023
Gaskin v United Kingdom (1989) 12 EHRR 36, [1990] 1 FLR 167 1009
Gay v Sheeran [2000] 1 WLR 673, [1999] 2 FLR 519, CA 912
GB (Children), Re [2013] EWCA Civ 164 205, 528, 2196, 2202
GD and BD (Children) and ors v Wakefield MDC and West Yorks Police [2016] EWHC 3312 (Fam) 1756
GE v KE & AE (Nigerian Customary Marriage and Divorce) [2013] EWHC 1938 (Fam) 1015
Ghaidan v Godin-Mendoza [2004] UKHL 30, [2004] 2 AC 557, [2004] 2 FLR 600 992, 994, 1010
Ghandi v Patel [2002] 1 FLR 603, ChD 1014
Ghoth v Ghoth [1992] 2 FLR 300, CA 797
Gill and Aui v Spain (Application No 56673 /00) [2005] 1 FLR 190, ECHR 383
Gillick v West Norfolk and Wisbech Area Health Authority and Another [1986] 1 AC 112, [1986] 1 FLR 224, HL; *sub nom* Gillick v West Norfolk and Wisbech Area Health Authority and the DHSS 448, 918, 919, 922, 1285, 1421, 1754, 1756, 2061, 2087, 2743
Gillick v West Norfolk and Wisbech Area Health Authority and the DHSS [1986] 1 AC 112, [1986] 1 FLR 224, HL; *sub nom* Gillick v West Norfolk and Wisbech Area Health Authority and Another 448, 918, 919, 922, 1285, 1421, 1754, 1756, 2061, 2087, 2743
Gillingham v Gillingham [2001] EWCA Civ 906 1870
Giltinane v Child Support Agency [2006] EWHC 423 (Fam), [2006] 2 FLR 857 1060
GIO Personal Investment Services Ltd v Liverpool and London Steamship Protection and Indemnity Association Ltd [1999] 1 WLR 984, CA 1843
Gissing v Gissing [1970] UKHL 3, [1971] 1 AC 886 1263
Glaser v UK (Case 32346 /96) [2001] 1 FLR 153, ECHR 443, 852
Gloucestershire County Council v P [2000] Fam 1, [1999] 2 FLR 61, CA 451, 453
Gluhakovic v Croatia [2011] 2 FLR 294, ECHR 443
GN v MA (Child Maintenance: Children Act Sch 1) [2015] EWHC 3939 (Fam), [2017] 1 FLR 285 1077, 1323
Gogova v Iliev (Case C-215 /15) [2016] 1 FLR 158, CJEU 2775, 2783
Gohil v Gohil [2015] UKSC 61, [2015] 2 FLR 1289 211, 214, 384, 1017, 1448
Gojkovic v Gojkovic (No 2) [1992] Fam 40, [1991] 2 FLR 233, CA 227, 1164, 1210, 1286, 1846, 1848, 1849, 2145, 2146
Golder v United Kingdom (1975) 1 EHRR 524 1007
Goldstone v Goldstone [2011] EWCA Civ 39, [2011] 1 FLR 1926 1439, 1450
Goodchild (Deceased) and Another, Re [1997] 1 WLR 1216, [1997] 2 FLR 644, CA; *sub nom* Goodchild v Goodchild 1023
Goodchild v Goodchild [1997] 1 WLR 1216, [1997] 2 FLR 644, CA; *sub nom* Re Goodchild (Deceased) and Another 1023
Goodwin v United Kingdom (2002) 35 EHRR 18, [2002] 2 FLR 487 944, 953, 1010
Goodwin, Re; Goodwin v Goodwin [1969] 1 Ch 283, ChD 1020
Gora v Treasury Solicitor [2003] Fam Law 93, Cty Ct 1019, 1023
Gordon (formerly Stefanou) v Stefanou [2010] EWCA Civ 1601, [2011] 1 FLR 1582 1182
Gowers v Gowers [2011] EWHC 3485 (Fam), [2012] 1 FLR 1040 1172
Goyal v Goyal [2016] EWCA Civ 792 1182, 1209
Goyal v Goyal [2016] EWFC 50 54, 1162, 1182, 1187, 1190, 1209
GR (Care Order), Re [2010] EWCA Civ 871, [2011] 1 FLR 669 559
Graham v Murphy and Another [1997] 1 FLR 860, ChD 1017, 1018, 1021
Grant & Another v Baker [2016] EWHC 1782 (Ch) 1264
Grant v United Kingdom (2007) 44 EHRR 1 953
Gray v Going Places Leisure Travel Ltd [2005] EWCA Civ 189 2205
Green (A Bankrupt), Re, ex parte Official Receiver v Cutting [1979] 1 WLR 1211, ChD; *sub nom* Re Green; Official Receiver v Cutting 343
Green, Re; Official Receiver v Cutting [1979] 1 WLR 1211, ChD; *sub nom* Re Green (A Bankrupt), ex parte Official Receiver v Cutting 343
Gregory v Goodenough [1970] 1 WLR 1455, CA; *sub nom* Re Gregory 1023
Gregory v Turner; R (Morris) v North Somerset Council [2003] EWCA Civ 183, [2003] 1 WLR 1149 1046, 2063
Gregory, Re [1970] 1 WLR 1455, CA; *sub nom* Gregory v Goodenough 1017, 1023
Grenfell v Grenfell [1978] Fam 128, CA 1152
Grepe v Loam (1887) 37 Ch D 168 620
Grey v Grey [2009] EWCA Civ 1424, [2010] 1 FLR 1764 1178, 1183, 1203
Grigson v Grigson [1974] 1 WLR 228, CA 1156
Grocholewska-Mullins v Mullins [2014] EWCA Civ 148 1203
Group Seven Ltd v Allied Investment Corp Ltd [2013] EWHC 1509 (Ch), [2014] 1 WLR 735 1242

GS v Georgia (Application No 2361/13) [2015] 2 FLR 647, ECHR 376
GS v L (Financial Remedies: Pre-Acquired Assets: Needs) [2011] EWHC 1759 (Fam), [2013] 1 FLR 300 1180
Guardian News and Media Ltd, Re [2010] UKSC 1, [2010] 2 AC 697 2142
Guerroudj v Rymarczyk [2015] EWCA Civ 743, [2016] 1 FLR 1349 912
Gull v Gull [2007] EWCA Civ 900, [2008] 1 FLR 232 875
Gully v Dix [2004] EWCA Civ 139, [2004] 1 WLR 1399, [2004] 1 FLR 918 1016
Gustafson v Sweden (1996) 22 EHRR 409 1011
GW v RW (Financial Provision: Departure from Equality) [2003] EWHC 611 (Fam), [2003] 2 FLR 108 645, 1183
Gwynedd Council v Grunshaw [2000] 1 WLR 494, CA 1326

H (A Child) (Analysis of Realistic Options and SGOs), Re [2015] EWCA Civ 406, [2016] 1 FLR 286 475, 526
H (A Child) (Interim Care Order), Re [2002] EWCA Civ 1932 558
H (A Child), Re (29 June 2016, CA, McFarlane, Lindblom LJJ, unreported 423
H (A Child), Re [2002] EWCA Civ 2005 458
H (A Child), Re [2011] EWCA Civ 762 193, 205, 458, 1863, 2193
H (A Child), Re [2014] EWCA Civ 232 538
H (A Child), Re [2014] EWCA Civ 271 424, 443, 1529
H (A Child), Re [2016] EWCA Civ 988 384, 385, 386, 392
H (A Minor) (Abduction), Re [1990] 2 FLR 439, FD 376
H (A Minor) (Blood Tests: Parental Rights), Re [1997] Fam 89, [1996] 2 FLR 65, CA; *sub nom* Re H (Paternity: Blood Test) 226, 921, 923
H (A Minor) (Care Proceedings: Child's Wishes), Re [1993] 1 FLR 440, FD 1515, 1705, 1709
H (A Minor) (Contact), Re [1994] 2 FLR 969, CA; *sub nom* Re H (Contact: Principles) 453
H (A Minor) (Foreign Custody Order: Enforcement), Re [1994] Fam 105, [1994] 1 FLR 512, CA 394
H (A Minor) (Guardian ad Litem: Requirement), Re [1994] Fam 11, [1993] 2 FLR 552, FD; *sub nom* Re H (A Minor) (Role of Official Solicitor) 568
H (A Minor) (Role of Official Solicitor), Re [1994] Fam 11, [1993] 2 FLR 552, FD; *sub nom* Re H (A Minor) (Guardian ad Litem: Requirement) 568
H (A Minor) (Section 37 Direction), Re [1993] 2 FLR 541, FD 556
H (A Minor) v Northamptonshire County Council & Anor [2017] EWHC 282 (Fam) 1043, 2049, 2157
H (A Minor: Wardship) (Challenging Ex Parte Order), Re [1994] 2 FLR 981, CA; *sub nom* Re H (Wardship: Ex Parte Orders) 1524
H (Abduction), Re [2006] EWCA Civ 1247, [2007] 1 FLR 242 388, 1707
H (Abduction), Re [2009] EWHC 1735 (Fam), [2009] 2 FLR 1513 385, 524
H (Abduction: Acquiescence), Re [1998] AC 72, [1997] 1 FLR 872, HL; *sub nom* Re H (Minors) (Abduction: Acquiescence), HL; H v H (Abduction: Acquiescence) [1996] 2 FLR 570, CA 388
H (Abduction: Child of 16), Re [2000] 2 FLR 51, FD 376
H (Abduction: Dominica: Corporal Punishment), Re [2006] EWCA Civ 871, [2007] 1 FLR 72 385
H (Abduction: Grave Risk), Re [2003] EWCA Civ 355, [2003] 2 FLR 141 390
H (Abduction: Habitual Residence: Agreement), Re [2013] EWCA Civ 148, [2013] 2 FLR 1426 377, 379
H (Abduction: Habitual Residence: Consent), Re [2000] 2 FLR 294, FD 392
H (Abduction: Non-Convention Application), Re [2006] EWHC 199 (Fam), [2006] 2 FLR 314 385
H (Abduction: Rights of Custody), Re [2000] 2 AC 291, [2000] 1 FLR 374, HL 364, 380
H (Abduction: Whereabouts Order to Solicitors), Re [2000] 1 FLR 766, FD 365
H (Appeal: Case Management Decisions), Re [2012] EWCA Civ 1797, [2013] 1 FLR 1234 1530
H (Care Order: Appropriate Local Authority), Re [2003] EWCA Civ 1629, [2004] Fam 89, [2004] 1 FLR 534 541, 638
H (Care Plan), Re [2008] EWHC 327 (Fam), [2008] 2 FLR 21 627
H (Care Plan: Human Rights), Re [2011] EWCA Civ 1009, [2012] 1 FLR 191 529, 1000, 2058
H (Care Proceedings: Foster Care Placement for Mother and Baby), Re [2012] EWCA Civ 1700, [2013] 1 FLR 1445 560, 2196
H (Care Proceedings: Intervener), Re [2000] 1 FLR 775, CA 1501
H (Care: Change in Care Plan), Re [1998] 1 FLR 193, CA 2431
H (Child Abduction) (Unmarried Father: Rights of Custody), Re [2003] EWHC 492 (Fam), [2003] 2 FLR 153 380
H (Child Abduction), Re [2012] EWCA Civ 913 2750, 2779, 2785
H (Child Abduction: Mother's Asylum), Re [2003] EWHC 1820 (Fam), [2003] 2 FLR 1105 176, 383
H (Child's Name: First Name), Re [2002] EWCA Civ 190, [2002] 1 FLR 973 448
H (Children) (Application to Extend Time: Merits of Proposed Appeal), Re [2015] EWCA Civ 583, [2015] 1 WLR 5085, [2016] 1 FLR 952 206, 1865, 2196

H (Children) (Care Proceedings: Sexual Abuse), Re [2000] 2 FCR 499, CA 1501
H (Children) (Residence Order: Condition), Re [2001] EWCA Civ 1338, [2001] 2 FLR 1277 472, 473
H (Children) (Summary Determination of Issues), Re [2002] EWCA Civ 1692 540
H (Children), Re [2007] EWCA Civ 529 1311
H (Children), Re [2011] EWCA Civ 1218 560
H (Children), Re [2012] EWCA Civ 743 1710
H (Conciliation: Welfare Reports), Re [1986] 1 FLR 476, FD 436
H (Contact Order) (No 2), Re [2002] 1 FLR 22, FD 437, 446
H (Contact Order: Permissibility of Judge's Actions), Re [2012] EWCA Civ 714, [2012] 2 FLR 1114 1528
H (Contact with Biological Father), Re [2012] EWCA Civ 281, [2012] 2 FLR 627 428
H (Contact: Adverse Findings of Fact), Re [2011] EWCA Civ 585, [2011] 2 FLR 1201 442
H (Contact: Principles), Re [1994] 2 FLR 969, CA; *sub nom* Re H (A Minor) (Contact) 453
H (Criminal Proceedings: Disclosure of Adoption Records), Re [1995] 1 FLR 964, FD 1512, 1657
H (Freeing Orders: Publicity), Re [2005] EWCA Civ 1325, [2006] 1 FLR 815 248
H (Interim Contact: Domestic Violence Allegations), Re [2013] EWCA Civ 72, [2014] 1 FLR 41 193, 205, 444, 445, 1870, 2205
H (Jurisdiction), Re [2009] EWHC 2280 (Fam), [2010] 1 FLR 598 2781
H (Jurisdiction), Re [2014] EWCA Civ 1101, [2015] 1 WLR 863, [2015] 1 FLR 1132 377, 379, 2778, 2780
H (Leave to Apply for Residence Order), Re [2008] EWCA Civ 503, [2008] 2 FLR 848 456
H (Mental Patient: Diagnosis), Re [1993] 1 FLR 28, FD 1547
H (Minors) (Abduction: Custody Rights), Re; S (Minors) (Abduction: Custody Rights), Re [1991] 2 AC 476, [1991] 2 FLR 262, HL; *sub nom* Re H; Re S (Abduction: Custody Rights) 376
H (Minors) (Injunction: Public Interest), Re [1994] 1 WLR 1141, [1994] 1 FLR 519, CA; *sub nom* Re H-S (Minors) (Protection of Identity) 1543
H (Minors) (Prohibited Steps Order), Re [1995] 1 WLR 667, [1995] 1 FLR 638, CA; *sub nom* Re H (Prohibited Steps Order) 446, 448, 449, 451, 458, 671, 1501
H (Minors) (Sexual Abuse: Standard of Proof), Re [1996] 1 FLR 80, [1996] AC 563, HL; *sub nom* Re H and Others (Minors) (Sexual Abuse: Standard of Proof); *sub nom* Re H and R (Child Sexual Abuse: Standard of Proof) 532, 536, 537
H (Minors) (Terms of Supervision Order), Re [1994] 2 FLR 979, FD; *sub nom* Re H (Supervision Order) 671
H (Minors) (Welfare Reports), Re [1990] 2 FLR 172, CA 437
H (Minors), Re [1993] 1 FLR 958, FD; *sub nom* H v H (Minors) (Forum Conveniens) (Nos 1 and 2) 842
H (National Youth Advocacy Service), Re [2006] EWCA Civ 896, [2007] 1 FLR 1028 435, 1707
H (Parental Responsibility), Re [1998] 1 FLR 855, CA 427
H (Paternity: Blood Test), Re [1997] Fam 89, [1996] 2 FLR 65, CA; *sub nom* Re H (A Minor) (Blood Tests: Parental Rights) 226, 921, 923
H (Prohibited Steps Order), Re [1995] 1 WLR 667, [1995] 1 FLR 638, CA; *sub nom* Re H (Minors) (Prohibited Steps Order) 446, 448, 449, 451, 458, 671, 1501
H (Residence Order: Placement Out of Jurisdiction), Re [2004] EWHC 3243 (Fam), [2006] 1 FLR 1140 844
H (Supervision Order), Re [1994] 2 FLR 979, FD; *sub nom* Re H (Minors) (Terms of Supervision Order) 671
H (Wardship: Ex Parte Orders), Re [1994] 2 FLR 981, CA; *sub nom* Re H (A Minor: Wardship) (Challenging Ex Parte Order) 1524
H and A (Paternity: Blood Tests), Re [2002] EWCA Civ 383, [2002] 1 FLR 1145 921, 1016
H and L (Abduction: Acquiescence), Re [2010] EWHC 652 (Fam), [2010] 2 FLR 1277 382, 383, 386, 389
H and Others (Minors) (Sexual Abuse: Standard of Proof), R [1996] AC 563, [1996] 1 FLR 80, HL; *sub nom* Re H and R (Child Sexual Abuse: Standard of Proof); *sub nom* Re H (Minors) (Sexual Abuse: Standard of Proof) 532, 536, 537
H and R (Child Sexual Abuse: Standard of Proof), Re [1996] AC 563, [1996] 1 FLR 80, HL; *sub nom* Re H (Minors) (Sexual Abuse: Standard of Proof); *sub nom* Re H and Others (Minors) (Sexual Abuse: Standard of Proof) 532, 536, 537
H v A (No 2) [2015] EWHC 2630 (Fam), [2016] 2 FLR 723 627, 628, 1321, 2656
H v C & E (A Child by his solicitor, Anne-Marie Hutchinson) [2015] EWCA Civ 1298, [2016] 2 FLR 1159; *sub nom* Re C (Older Children: Relocation) 471
H v C [2009] EWHC 1527 (Fam), [2009] 2 FLR 1540 407, 650
H v City and Council of Swansea and Others [2011] EWCA Civ 195 537
H v Dent and Others [2015] EWHC 2228 (Fam), [2016] 2 FLR 566 483
H v G (Adoption: Appeal) [2013] EWHC 2136 (Fam), [2014] 1 FLR 691 193, 1866
H v H (A Minor) (No 2) (Forum Conveniens) [1997] 1 FCR 603, FD 842

H v H (Abduction: Acquiescence) [1996] 2 FLR 570, CA; Re H (Abduction: Acquiescence), Re [1998] AC 72, [1997] 1 FLR 872, HL; *sub nom* Re H (Minors) (Abduction: Acquiescence) 388
H v H (Child Abduction: Stay of Domestic Proceedings) [1994] 1 FLR 530, FD 376
H v H (Child: Judicial Interview) [1974] 1 WLR 595, CA; *sub nom* Hayes v Hayes 1532
H v H (Financial Provision) [2009] EWHC 494 (Fam), [2009] 2 FLR 795 1180
H v H (Financial Relief) [2010] EWHC 158 (Fam), [2010] 1 FLR 1864 1183, 1184
H v H (Financial Relief: Attempted Murder as Conduct) [2005] EWHC 2911 (Fam), [2006] 1 FLR 990 1184
H v H (Financial Relief: Pensions) [2009] EWHC 3739 (Fam), [2010] 2 FLR 173 54, 1162, 1453, 1454
H v H (Jurisdiction to Grant Wardship) [2011] EWCA Civ 796, [2012] 1 FLR 23 379, 841, 1545, 2783
H v H (Minors) (Forum Conveniens) (Nos 1 and 2) [1993] 1 FLR 958, FD; *sub nom* Re H (Minors) 842
H v H [2007] EWHC 459 (Fam), [2007] 2 FLR 548 1180
H v H [2008] EWHC 935 (Fam), [2008] 2 FLR 2092 1181
H v H [2014] EWCA Civ 1523, [2015] 2 FLR 447 1169, 1857
H v H [2014] EWHC 760 (Fam), [2014] 2 FLR 1338 1179, 1203
H v H (Residence Order: Leave to Remove from Jurisdiction) [1995] 1 FLR 529, CA 423
H v H (Talaq Divorce) [2007] EWHC 2945 (Fam), [2008] 2 FLR 857 864
H v H (The Queen's Proctor Intervening) (Validity of Japanese Divorce) [2006] EWHC 2989 (Fam), [2007] 1 FLR 1318 864
H v L and R [2006] EWHC 3099 (Fam), [2007] 2 FLR 162 1138, 1762, 2563
H v S (Disputed Surrogacy Agreement) [2015] EWFC 36, [2016] 1 FLR 723 991
H v W (Cap on Wife's Share of Bonus Payments) [2013] EWHC 4105 (Fam), [2015] 1 FLR 75 1183
H v W (Cap on Wife's Share of Bonus Payments) (No 2) [2014] EWHC 2846 (Fam), [2015] 2 FLR 161 1307
H v West Sussex County Council [1998] 1 FLR 862, FD 1528
H, Barhanu and B v London Borough of Wandsworth, London Borough of Hackney, London Borough of Islington and Secretary of State for Education and Skills (Interested Party) [2007] EWHC 1082 (Admin), [2007] 2 FLR 822 493
H, R and E (Abduction: Consent: Acquiescence), Re [2013] EWHC 3857 (Fam), [2014] 2 FLR 385 388
H, Re; G, Re (Adoption: Consultation of Unmarried Fathers) [2001] 1 FLR 646, FD 283
H, Re; S (Abduction: Custody Rights), Re [1991] 2 AC 476, [1991] 2 FLR 262, HL; *sub nom* Re H (Minors) (Abduction: Custody Rights); Re S (Minors) (Abduction: Custody Rights) 376
H-B (Contact), Re [2015] EWCA Civ 389 426, 440
H-C (Children), Re [2014] EWCA Civ 536 534, 541
H-K (Habitual Residence), Re [2011] EWCA Civ 1100, [2012] 1 FLR 436 378
H-L (Expert Evidence: Test for Permission), Re [2013] EWCA Civ 655, [2014] 1 WLR 1160, [2013] 2 FLR 1434 527, 547, 560, 686, 1795
H-S (Minors) (Protection of Identity), Re [1994] 1 WLR 1141, [1994] 1 FLR 519, CA; *sub nom* Re H (Minors) (Injunction: Public Interest) 1543
Haase v Germany [2004] 2 FLR 39, ECHR 528
Habib Bank v Central Bank of Sudan [2006] EWHC 1767 (Comm), [2007] 1 WLR 470 1359
Hackney Borough Council v John Williams and Adineke Williams [2017] EWCA Civ 26 494
Hackney London Borough Council v Driscoll [2003] EWCA Civ 1037, [2003] 1 WLR 2602 1834
Hadjimilitis (Tsavliris) v Tsavliris (Divorce: Irretrievable Breakdown) [2003] 1 FLR 81, FD; *sub nom* Hadjimilitis (Tsavliris) v Tsavliris 2146
Hadjimilitis (Tsavliris) v Tsavliris [2003] 1 FLR 81, FD; *sub nom* Hadjimilitis (Tsavliris) v Tsavliris (Divorce: Irretrievable Breakdown) 2146
Halden v Halden [1966] 1 WLR 1481, CA 1123
Hale v Tanner [2000] 1 WLR 2377, [2000] 2 FLR 879, CA 130, 466, 792
Haley v Barry (1868) 3 Ch App 452, CA 2025
Hallmark Cards Inc v Image Arts Ltd [1977] FSR 150, CA 1241
Halsey v Milton Keynes General NHS Trust [2004] EWCA Civ 576, [2004] 1 WLR 3002 1307, 2141
Hamilton v Hamilton [2013] EWCA Civ 13, [2013] 1 Fam 292, [2014] 1 FLR 55 1169
Hamlin v Hamlin [1986] Fam 11, [1986] 1 FLR 61, CA 797, 1171, 1209
Hammersmith and Fulham London Borough Council v Monk; Barnet London Borough Council v Smith [1992] 1 AC 478, [1992] 1 FLR 465, HL 41
Hammerton v Hammerton [2007] EWCA Civ 248, [2007] 2 FLR 1133 124, 466
Hampshire County Council v S [1993] Fam 158, [1993] 1 FLR 559, FD 551, 558, 1526, 1530, 1831
Hancock (dec'd), Re [1998] 2 FLR 346, CA; *sub nom* Snapes v Aram 1019
Hand and Anr v George and Anr [2017] EWHC 533 (Ch) 1015
Hanlon v Law Society [1981] AC 124, HL 1042, 1043
Hannigan v Hannigan & ors [2000] 2 FCR 650, CA 1324

Hansen v Turkey (Application No 36141/97) [2004] 1 FLR 142, ECHR 443
Harb v King Fahd Bin Abdul Aziz [2005] EWCA Civ 1324, [2006] 1 WLR 578, [2006] 1 FLR 825 1196
Harbin v Masterman [1896] 1 Ch 351, CA 225, 1683, 2716, 2720
Harcourt v Griffin [2007] EWHC 1500 (QB) 1390
Hardwick, Re [1995] Jersey LR 245 1929
Hargood (formerly Jenkins) v Jenkins [1978] Fam 148, FD 1197
Haringey London Borough Council v MA, JN, IA [2008] EWHC 1722 (Fam), [2008] 2 FLR 1857 278, 301
Harker-Thomas's Application, Re [1969] P 28, CA; Harker-Thomas v Harker-Thomas; *sub nom* Re Harker-Thomas 1023
Harker-Thomas, Re [1969] P 28, CA *sub nom* Harker-Thomas's Application, Re; Harker-Thomas v Harker-Thomas 1023
Harman v Glencross [1986] Fam 81, [1986] 2 FLR 241, CA 359, 361, 2024, 2025
Harman v Secretary of State for the Home Department [1983] 1 AC 280 1755, 1756
Harmsworth v Harmsworth [1987] 1 WLR 1676, [1988] 1 FLR 349, CA 127
Haroutunian v Jennings (1980) 1 FLR 62, FD 650
Harrington v Gill (1983) 4 FLR 265, CA 1017
Harris v Harris [1949] WN 290, PDAD 1083, 1093
Harris v Harris [2001] 1 FCR 68, CA 1203
Harris v Harris [2001] EWCA Civ 1645, [2002] Fam 253, [2002] 1 FLR 248 131, 792, 1996
Harris v Harris; Attorney General v Harris [2001] 2 FLR 895, FD 246, 620, 1543
Harris v Manahan [1997] 1 FLR 205, CA 213
Harrison v Harrison [2008] EWHC 362 (QB), [2008] 2 FLR 35 1210
Harrop v Harrop [1920] 3 KB 386, KBD 83, 2299
Hashtroodi v Hancock [2004] EWCA Civ 652, [2004] 1 WLR 3206 1025
Hayes v Hayes [1974] 1 WLR 595, CA; *sub nom* H v H (Child: Judicial Interview) 1532
Hayes v Hayes [2012] EWHC 1240 (Ch), [2012] BPIR 739 1170
Hayes v Transco plc [2003] EWCA Civ 1261 1761
HB v A Local Authority & Anor (Wardship – Costs Funding Order) [2017] EWHC 524 (Fam) 533, 1042
Healey v Brown [2002] EWHC 1405 (Ch) 1024
Health Authority, Re A v X [2001] EWCA Civ 2014, [2002] 1 FLR 1045, CA 1507
Health Service Executive v SC and AC (Case C-92/12) [2012] 2 FLR 1040, CJEU 524, 2798
Heathcote v Crackles [2002] EWCA Civ 222 620
Heatons Transport (St Helens) Ltd v Transport and General Workers' Union, Craddock Brothers v Same, Panalpina Services v Same [1973] AC 15, HL 1985
Hellyer v Sheriff of Yorkshire [1975] Ch 16, CA 1235
Henderson v Henderson (1843) 3 Hare 100 1762
Henderson v Henderson [1967] P 77, PDAD 826
Hendriks v The Netherlands (1982) 5 EHRR 223 544
Hentrich v France (1994) 18 EHRR 440 1011
Her Majesty's Attorney-General v Pelling [2005] EWHC 414 (Admin), [2006] 1 FLR 93 245, 248
HG (Specific Issue Order: Procedure), Re [1993] 1 FLR 587, FD; *sub nom* Re HG (Specific Issue Order: Sterilisation) 449, 454, 455
HG (Specific Issue Order: Sterilisation), Re [1993] 1 FLR 587, FD; *sub nom* Re HG (Specific Issue Order: Procedure) 449, 454, 455
HH & PH v Italy; FK v Poland [2012] UKSC 25, [2013] 1 AC 338 687, 1008
HH v BLW (Appeal: Costs: Proportionality) [2012] EWHC 2199 (Fam), [2013] 1 FLR 420 450, 1870
HH v SH [2016] EWHC 1252 (Fam) 857
Hickey v Marks (2000) 6 July (unreported), [2000] CA Transcript 1469 1870
High Tech International AG & Ors v Deripaska [2006] EWHC 3276 (QB) 378
Hildebrand v Hildebrand [1992] 1 FLR 244, FD 1390, 1440, 1849, 2105
Hill v Haines [2007] EWCA Civ 1284, [2008] Ch 412, [2008] 1 FLR 1192 1173
Hill v Hill (1972) 116 SJ 565, DC 812
Hillingdon London Borough Council v H [1993] Fam 43, [1992] 2 FLR 372, FD 1831
Hinckley and South Leicestershire Permanent Benefit Building Society v Freeman [1941] Ch 32, ChD 1247
Hinds v Liverpool County Court and Ors [2008] EWHC 665 (QB), [2008] 2 FLR 63 999, 1001
Hipgrave and Hipgrave v Jones [2004] EWHC 2901 (QB) [2005] 2 FLR 174 39
HK v Finland (Application No 36065/97) [2007] 1 FLR 633, ECHR 528
HM (Vulnerable Adult: Abduction), Re [2010] EWHC 870 (Fam), [2010] 2 FLR 1057 1757
HM Revenue and Customs v Benchdollar Ltd & others [2009] EWHC 1310 (Ch) 1023
HMRC v Charman and Charman [2012] EWHC 1448 (Fam), [2012] 2 FLR 1119 2111
Hoffman v Krieg (No 145/86) [1988] ECR 645, ECJ 2789, 2871
Holliday v Musa [2010] EWCA Civ 335, [2010] 2 FLR 702 828, 1014
Holman v Howes [2007] EWCA Civ 877, [2008] 1 FLR 1217 1263

Holmes-Moorhouse v Richmond-upon-Thames London Borough Council [2009] UKHL 7, [2009] 1 WLR 413, [2009] 1 FLR 904 442
Holt v Heatherfield Trust Ltd [1942] 2 KB 1, KBD 2293
Holtby v Hodgson (1889) 24 QBD 103, 59 LJQB 46, 62 LT 145, CA 2291
Hoppe v Germany (Application 28422/95) [2003] 1 FLR 384, ECHR 443
Horgan v Horgan [2002] EWCA Civ 1371 888, 890, 2721
Horn v Horn [1985] FLR 984, FD 1091
Horton v Henry [2016] EWCA Civ 989 1173
Hounslow LBC v Powell [2011] UKSC 8, [2011] 2 AC 186 994
Hounslow London Borough Council v A [1993] 1 WLR 291, [1993] 1 FLR 702, FD 423, 457, 1508
Howell v Montey (1990) 61 P & CR 18, CA 2025
HSE Ireland v SF (A Minor) [2012] EWHC 1640 (Fam), [2012] 2 FLR 1131 2745, 2798
Human Fertilisation and Embryology Act 2008 (Case I), Re [2016] EWHC 791 (Fam) [2017] 1 FLR 998 983
Human Fertilisation and Embryology Act 2008 (Cases A, B, C, D, E, F, G and H), Re [2015] EWHC 2602 (Fam), [2016] 1 WLR 1325, [2017] 1 FLR 366 980, 982, 983
Hunter v Chief Constable of West Midlands [1982] AC 529, HL 1763
Hunter v Murrow (Abduction: Rights of Custody) [2005] EWCA Civ 976, [2005] 2 FLR 1119 392
Huntingdon Life Sciences v Stop Huntingdon Animal Cruelty [2003] EWHC 1139 (QB) 37, 1231
Hussain & Qutb v Bank of Scotland [2012] EWCA Civ 264 2062
Hussain v Hussain [1986] Fam 134, [1986] 2 FLR 271, CA 40, 127, 1987
Hvorostovsky v Hvorostovsky [2009] EWCA Civ 791, [2009] 2 FLR 1574 1179, 1203

I (A Child) (Contact Application: Jurisdiction), Re [2009] UKSC 10, [2010] 1 AC 319, [2010] 1 FLR 361 524, 839, 2778, 2782, 2783
I (Adoption: Appeal: Special Guardianship), Re [2012] EWCA Civ 1217 475
I and H (Contact: Right to Give Evidence), Re [1998] 1 FLR 876, CA 1528
I v I (Ancillary Relief: Disclosure) [2008] EWHC 1167 (Fam), [2009] 1 FLR 201 1440
Ian Roberts (Trustee in Bankruptcy of Jonathan Elichaoff, Deceased) v Woodall [2016] EWHC 2987 (Ch) 1171
Iberian Trust Ltd v Founders Trust and Investment Co Ltd [1932] 2 KB 87, KBD 1988
II (A Child) (Contact Application: Jurisdiction), Re [2009] UKSC 10, [2010] 1 AC 319, [2010] 1 FLR 361 2783
IJ (Foreign Surrogacy Agreement: Parental Order), Re [2011] EWHC 921 (Fam), [2011] 2 FLR 646 989, 991
Illott v The Blue Cross & Others [2017] UKSC 17 1018, 1019, 1022, 1023
Imerman v Imerman [2012] EWHC 4047 (Fam), [2014] 1 FLR 232 1754
Imerman v Tchenguiz [2009] EWHC 2902 (QB) 1440
Imerman v Tchenguiz and Others [2010] EWCA Civ 908, [2011] Fam 116, [2010] 2 FLR 814 1240, 1744, 1752, 1755, 1758, 1761, 2087, 2105, 2109
Imutran Ltd v Uncaged Campaigns [2001] 2 All ER 385, ChD 1240
In the Matter of the Children of Mr O'Connell, Mr Whelan and Mr Watson [2005] EWCA Civ 759, [2006] Fam 1, [2005] 2 FLR 967 1530
Independent News & Media v A [2010] EWCA Civ 343, [2010] 1 WLR 2262, [2010] COPLR Con Vol 686 1009
Independent News Media Ltd & Ors v A (by the Official Solicitor) [2009] EWHC 2858 (Fam), [2010] 1 FLR 916, [2009] COPLR Con Vol 702 248
Inland Revenue Commissioners v National Federation of Self-Employed and Small Businesses Ltd [1982] AC 617, HL 1239
Inplayer Ltd v Thorogood [2014] EWCA Civ 1511 125
International Sports Tours Ltd v Shorey [2015] EWHC 2040 (QB) 2308
Interpool Ltd v Galani [1988] QB 738, CA 2285
Inventors Friend Limited v Leathes Prior [2011] EWHC 711 (QB) 1827
Iqbal v Ahmed [2011] EWCA Civ 900, [2012] 1 FLR 31 1023
Iqbal v Iqbal [2017] EWCA Civ 19 413, 1321, 1932
IRC v Duchess of Portland [1982] Ch 314, (1982) 3 FLR 293, ChD 826
Ireland v UK [1978] ECHR 1, (1978) 2 EHRR 25 1005
Irvine v Irvine [2006] EWHC 583 (Ch) 1181
Irving v Askew (1870) LR 5 QB 208 798
IS v DBS [2015] EWHC 219 (Fam) 839
Isayeva v Russia (2005) 41 EHRR 847 1011
Islington LBC v EV [2010] EWHC 3240 (Fam), [2011] 1 FLR 1681 664

J (A Child) (1996 Hague Convention) (Morocco), Re [2015] EWCA Civ 329, [2015] 2 FLR 513 2749

J (A Child) (Custody Rights: Jurisdiction), Re [2005] UKHL 40, [2006] 1 AC 80, [2005] 2 FLR 802; *sub nom* Re J (Child Returned Abroad: Convention Rights) 193, 203, 386, 2193
J (A Child) (Finland) (Habitual Residence), Re [2017] EWCA Civ 80 377, 379, 384, 1551, 2779
J (A Child), Re [2015] EWCA Civ 222 534, 535, 536
J (A Child: Brussels II Revised: Art 15 – Practice and Procedure), Re [2014] EWFC 41 524
J (A Minor) (Abduction), Re [1989] Fam 85, [1990] 1 FLR 276, FD; *sub nom* Re J (A Minor) (Abduction: Ward of Court) 390
J (A Minor) (Abduction: Custody Rights), Re [1990] 2 AC 562, [1990] 2 FLR 442, HL; *sub nom* C v S (A Minor) (Abduction) 376, 392, 415, 839
J (A Minor) (Abduction: Ward of Court), Re [1989] Fam 85, [1990] 1 FLR 276, FD; *sub nom* Re J (A Minor) (Abduction) 390
J (A Minor) (Change of Name), Re [1993] 1 FLR 699, FD 549, 568, 1505
J (A Minor) (Child in Care: Medical Treatment), Re [1993] Fam 15, [1992] 2 FLR 165, CA; *sub nom* Re J (A Minor) (Medical Treatment) 1547
J (A Minor) (Medical Treatment), Re [1993] Fam 15, [1992] 2 FLR 165, CA; *sub nom* Re J (A Minor) (Child in Care: Medical Treatment) 1547
J (A Minor) (Property Transfer), Re [1993] 2 FLR 56, FD; *sub nom* J v J (A Minor: Property Transfer) 454
J (A Minor), Re [2016] EWHC 2430 (Fam) 532
J (A Minor), Re [2016] EWHC 2595 (Fam) 627, 628, 1135
J (Abduction: Acquiring Custody Rights by Caring For Child), Re [2005] 2 FLR 791, FD 376, 391
J (Abduction: Declaration of Wrongful Removal), Re [1999] 2 FLR 653, FD 845
J (Abduction: Wrongful Removal), Re [2000] 1 FLR 78, CA 383
J (Adoption: Consent of Foreign Public Authority), Re [2002] EWHC 766 (Fam), [2002] 2 FLR 618 283
J (Appeal from Care Order), Re [2013] EWCA Civ 1685, [2014] 2 FLR 1351 206, 1834
J (Care Proceedings: Disclosure), Re [2003] EWHC 976 (Fam), [2003] 2 FLR 522 571
J (Care Proceedings: Past Possible Perpetrators in a New Family Unit), Re [2012] EWCA Civ 380, [2012] 2 FLR 842 538
J (Care Proceedings: Possible Perpetrators), Re [2013] UKSC 9, [2013] 1 AC 680, [2013] 1 FLR 1373 537
J (Care: Assessment: Fair Trial), Re [2006] EWCA Civ 545, [2007] 1 FLR 77 1008
J (Child Returned Abroad: Convention Rights), Re [2005] UKHL 40, [2006] 1 AC 80, [2005] 2 FLR 802; *sub nom* Re J (A Child) (Custody Rights: Jurisdiction) 193, 203, 385, 386, 2193
J (Child Returned Abroad: Human Rights), Re [2004] EWCA Civ 417, [2004] 2 FLR 85 383, 999
J (Children) (Residence: Expert Evidence), Re [2001] 2 FCR 44, CA 438
J (Children), Re [2012] EWCA Civ 1457 2196
J (Children), Re [2015] EWCA Civ 1019, [2016] 2 FLR 1207 129, 795
J (Children: Ex Parte Orders), Re, Note [1997] 1 FLR 606, FD 1522
J (Expert Evidence: Hearsay), Re [1999] 2 FLR 661, FD 1532, 1832
J (Jurisdiction: Abduction), Re [2015] UKSC 70, [2016] 1 FLR 170 375, 376, 382, 2735, 2737, 2781, 2787
J (Leave to Issue Application for Residence Order), Re [2002] EWCA Civ 1346, [2003] 1 FLR 114 455, 1501
J (Minors) (Care: Care Plan), Re [1994] 1 FLR 253, FD 545, 560, 1290
J (Paternity: Welfare of Child), Re [2006] EWHC 2837 (Fam), [2007] 1 FLR 1064 448
J (Refusal of Contact), Re [2012] EWCA Civ 720, [2013] 2 FLR 1042 424
J (Reporting Restriction: Internet: Video), Re [2013] EWHC 2694 (Fam), [2014] 1 FLR 523 247, 544, 1002, 1009, 1543, 1563
J (Residence and Contact Dispute), Re [2012] EWCA Civ 1231, [2013] 1 FLR 716 1278, 1528
J (Specific Issue Orders: Child's Religious Upbringing and Circumcision), Re [2000] 1 FLR 571, CA 449
J and K (Children: Private Law), Re [2014] EWHC 330 (Fam), [2015] 1 FLR 86 439, 440
J and S (Children), Re [2014] EWFC 4, [2015] 1 FLR 850 524, 2798
J v C (Child: Financial Provision) [1999] 1 FLR 152, FD 650
J v C (Void Marriage: Status of Children) [2006] EWCA Civ 551, [2007] Fam 1, [2006] 2 FLR 1098 953, 1016
J v G (Parental Orders) [2013] EWHC 1432 (Fam), [2014] 1 FLR 297 991
J v J (A Minor: Property Transfer) [1993] 2 FLR 56, FD; *sub nom* Re J (A Minor) (Property Transfer) 454
J v J [1955] P 215, CA 1439, 1440
J v J [2009] EWHC 2654 (Fam) 1442
J v J [2014] EWHC 3654 (Fam) 1762
J v J (Relinquishment of Jurisdiction) [2011] EWHC 3255 (Fam), [2012] 1 FLR 1259 524
J v Merthyr Tydfil County Borough Council [1997] Fam Law 522, FD 512

J v P [2007] EWHC 704 (Fam 2869
J, R (on Application of) v Worcestershire County Council [2014] EWCA Civ 1518, [2015] 1 WLR 2825, [2015] 2 FLR 1053 486
J, Re [2016] EWHC 1330 (Fam) 980
J-L (Findings of Fact: Schedule of Allegations), Re [2012] EWCA Civ 1832, [2013] 1 FLR 1240 534, 2197
J-M (A Child), Re [2014] EWCA Civ 434, [2015] 1 FLR 838 446
Jaffray v Society of Lloyd's [2007] EWCA Civ 586, [2008] 1 WLR 75 212
Jake (Withholding of Medical Treatment), Re [2015] EWHC 2442 (Fam) 559, 1546
Jamaa v Italy (2012) 55 EHRR 627 993
James v Thomas [2007] EWCA Civ 1212, [2008] 1 FLR 1598 1262, 1263
Jarvis Field Press Ltd v Chelton [2003] EWHC 2674 (Ch) 1242
JB (Child Abduction) (Rights of Custody: Spain), Re [2003] EWHC 2130 (Fam), [2004] 1 FLR 796 380
JB v KS and E (Contact: Parental Responsibility) [2015] EWHC 180 (Fam), [2015] 2 FLR 1180 427, 428
JB v MB [2015] EWHC 1846 (Fam) 1183
JC (Care Proceedings: Procedure), Re [1995] 2 FLR 77, FD 548, 1509
JC and RT v Central Criminal Court, CPS, BBC & Just For Kids Law [2014] EWHC 1041 (QB), [2014] 1 WLR 3697 627
Jefferson v O'Connor [2014] EWCA Civ 38, [2014] 2 FLR 759 829, 2786
JEG v IS and Another (Sexual Abuse Allegations) [2014] EWHC 287 (Fam) 445
Jelley v Iliffe [1981] Fam 128, CA 1017
Jennings (deceased), Re, Harlow v National Westminster Bank plc and Others [1994] Ch 286, [1994] 1 FLR 536, CA; *sub nom* Re Jennings, deceased 1018, 1019, 1023
Jennings, deceased, Re [1994] Ch 286, [1994] 1 FLR 536, CA; *sub nom* Re Jennings (deceased), Harlow v National Westminster Bank plc and Others 1018, 1019, 1023
Jessop v Jessop [1992] 1 FLR 591, CA 1020, 1028, 1029
Jevremović v Serbia (Application No 3150/05) [2008] 1 FLR 550, ECHR 448
JG v The Lord Chancellor and Others [2014] EWCA Civ 656, [2014] 2 FLR 1218 440
JIH v News Group Newspapers [2011] EWCA Civ 42, [2011] 1 WLR 1645 2142, 2689
JKN v JCN (Divorce: Forum) [2010] EWHC 843 (Fam), [2011] 1 FLR 826 828, 2776
JL v SL (No 2) (Appeal: Non-Matrimonial Property) [2015] EWHC 360 (Fam), [2015] 2 FLR 1202 1182
JL v SL (No 3) (Post-Judgment Amplification) [2015] EWHC 555 (Fam), [2015] 2 FLR 1220 2517
JM (A Child) (Medical Treatment), Re [2015] EWHC 2832 (Fam), [2016] 2 FLR 235 1546
JMcB v Le (Case C-400/10) [2010] ECR I-08965, [2011] Fam 364, [2011] 1 FLR 518, ECJ 380, 384, 2775
Johansen v Norway (1996) 23 EHRR 33, [1996] ECHR 31 528
John Fox v Bannister, King & Rigbeys [1988] QB 925, CA 1137
Johnson v Diamond (1855) 11 Exch 73, 24 LJ Ex 217, 3 WR 407 2291
Johnson v Walton [1990] 1 FLR 350, CA 1230
Jones & Anor v Persons Unknown & Anor [2014] EWHC 4691 (Ch) 2325
Jones (Deceased), Re, Jones v Midland Bank Trust Co Ltd and Others [1998] 1 FLR 246, CA 1024
Jones v Jones [1997] Fam 59, [1997] 1 FLR 27, CA 1171
Jones v Jones [2001] Fam 96, [2000] 2 FLR 307, CA 1197, 1202
Jones v Jones [2011] EWCA Civ 41, [2012] Fam 1, [2011] 1 FLR 1723 1179, 1180, 1182
Jones v Kernott [2011] UKSC 53, [2012] 1 AC 776, [2012] 1 FLR 45, [2011] BPIR 1653 1263
Jones v McKie [1964] 1 WLR 960, CA; *sub nom* Jones v McKie and Mersey Docks and Harbour Board 1235
Jones v McKie and Mersey Docks and Harbour Board [1964] 1 WLR 960, CA; *sub nom* Jones v McKie 1235
Jones v Roberts [1995] 2 FLR 422, ChD 1024
Joy v Joy-Morancho (Rev 1) [2015] EWHC 2507 (Fam) 1849
JP v LP and Others (Surrogacy Arrangement: Wardship) [2014] EWHC 595 (Fam), [2015] 1 FLR 307 989, 1258
JP v NP [2014] EWHC 1101 (Fam), [2014] 1 WLR 4607, [2015] 1 FLR 659 236, 1136, 1137, 2701
JR v Merton London Borough [1992] 2 FCR 174, FD & CA 451
JRG v EB (Abduction: Brussels II Revised) [2012] EWHC 1863 (Fam), [2013] 1 FLR 203 2750, 2781, 2789, 2790
JS (A Minor) (Wardship: Boy Soldier), Re [1990] Fam 182, [1991] 1 FLR 7, FD 1548
JS (Disposal of Body), Re [2016] EWHC 2859 (Fam) 424
JS v An NHS Trust; JA v An NHS Trust [2002] EWHC 2734 (Fam), [2003] Fam 83, [2003] 1 FLR 879; *sub nom* Simms v Simms 1548
JS v RS [2015] EWHC 2921 (Fam), [2016] 2 FLR 839 1453
JSC BTA Bank v Ablyazov [2015] EWCA Civ 70 1242
JSC BTA Bank v Solodchenko & Ors [2011] EWCA Civ 1241, [2012] 1 WLR 350 2287
JSC Mezhdunarodniy Promyshlenniy Bank & Anor v Pugachev [2016] EWHC 192 (Ch) 2304

Jucius and Juciuvienė v Lithuania [2009] 1 FLR 403, ECHR 529
Judge v Judge [2008] EWCA Civ 1458, [2009] 1 FLR 1287 228, 229, 1183, 1286, 1448, 1847, 1848, 1849
Justice for Families Ltd v Secretary of State for Justice [2014] EWCA Civ 1477, [2015] 2 FLR 321 1858
JXMX v Dartford and Gravesham NHS Trust [2015] EWCA Civ 96, [2015] 1 WLR 3647 2049

K (A Child), Re [2011] EWCA Civ 1075, [2012] 2 FLR 635 879
K (A Child), Re [2013] EWCA Civ 895, [2014] 1 Fam 130, [2014] 1 FLR 749; *sub nom* Re T (A Child: Article 15 of Brussels II Revised) 524, 525, 2783
K (A Child), Re [2016] EWCA Civ 931 472
K (A Minor) (Abduction), Re [1990] 1 FLR 387, FD 395
K (Abduction: Case Management), Re [2010] EWCA Civ 1546, [2011] 1 FLR 1268 391, 1554, 2781
K (Abduction: Child's Objections), Re [1995] 1 FLR 977, FD 1554
K (Abduction: Inchoate Rights), Re [2014] UKSC 29, [2014] 1 AC 1401, [2014] 2 FLR 629 375, 380, 2732, 2775
K (Abduction: Psychological Harm), Re [1995] 2 FLR 550, CA 383
K (Adoption and Wardship), Re [1997] 2 FLR 221, CA 280, 282, 989
K (Adoption: Disclosure of Information), Re [1997] 2 FLR 74, FD 1510
K (Adoption: Permission to Advertise), Re [2007] EWHC 544 (Fam), [2007] 1 WLR 2531, [2007] 2 FLR 326 261, 628
K (Breakdown of Arrangements: Urgent Hearing), Re [2014] EWCA Civ 1195, [2015] 1 FLR 95 1531, 1532
K (Care Order or Residence Order), Re [1995] 1 FLR 675, FD 539
K (Care Proceedings: Care Plan), Re [2007] EWHC 393 (Fam), [2008] 1 FLR 1 560
K (Children with Disabilities: Wardship), Re [2012] 2 FLR 745, FD 630
K (Children), Re [2012] EWCA Civ 1549 555
K (Contact Order: Condition Ousting Parent from Family Home), Re [2011] EWCA Civ 1075, [2012] 2 FLR 635 449, 458
K (Contact), Re [2008] EWHC 540 (Fam), [2008] 2 FLR 581 552
K (Contact), Re [2016] EWCA Civ 99, [2017] 1 FLR 530 444
K (Contact: Psychiatric Report), Re [1995] 2 FLR 432, CA 436
K (dec'd), Re [1985] Ch 85, [1985] FLR 558, ChD 1024
K (Foreign Surrogacy), Re [2010] EWHC 1180 (Fam), [2011] 1 FLR 533 990
K (Non-accidental Injuries: Perpetrator: New Evidence), Re [2004] EWCA Civ 1181, [2005] 1 FLR 285 535, 536
K (Order Delay), Re [2007] EWHC 2090 (Fam), [2008] 1 FLR 572 1509
K (Removal From Jurisdiction: Practice), Re [1999] 2 FLR 1084, CA 472
K (Replacement of Guardian ad Litem), Re [2001] 1 FLR 663, CA 1707
K (Rights of Custody: Spain), Re [2009] EWHC 1066 (Fam), [2010] 1 FLR 57 380, 382
K (Secure Accommodation Order: Right to Liberty), Re [2001] Fam 377, [2001] 1 FLR 526, CA 511
K (Shared Residence Order), Re [2008] EWCA Civ 526, [2008] 2 FLR 380 441
K (Special Guardianship Order), Re [2011] EWCA Civ 635, [2012] 1 FLR 1265 531
K (Supervision Orders), Re [1999] 2 FLR 303, FD 540, 1705, 1706
K (Wardship: Publicity) (No 2), Re [2013] EWHC 3748 (Fam), [2014] 2 FLR 310 628
K (Wardship: Publicity), Re [2013] EWHC 2684 (Fam), [2014] 1 FLR 548 1543
K and Another v A Local Authority [2008] EWCA Civ 103, [2008] 1 FLR 1229; *sub nom* Lambeth London Borough Council v TK and KK 556
K and D (Wardship Without Notice Return Order), Re [2017] EWHC 153 (Fam) 377, 379, 384, 631, 1543, 1545, 1546, 1552, 1745, 2780
K and H (Children), Re [2015] EWCA Civ 543, [2015] 1 WLR 3801, [2016] 1 FLR 754; *sub nom* Re K and H (Private Law: Public Funding) 439, 1041, 1042, 1138, 2563
K and H (Children: unrepresented father: cross-examination of child), Re [2015] EWFC 1, [2015] 2 FLR 802 625
K and H (Private Law: Public Funding), Re [2015] EWCA Civ 543, [2015] 1 WLR 3801, [2016] 1 FLR 754; *sub nom* Re K and H (Children) 439, 1041, 1042, 1138, 2563
K and H, Re [2006] EWCA Civ 1898, [2007] 1 FLR 2043 559
K and Others (Minors) (Disclosure of Privileged Material) Re [1994] 1 WLR 912, [1994] 1 FLR 377, FD; *sub nom* Kent County Council v K; *sub nom* Re K and Others (Minors) (Disclosure) 629
K and Others (Minors) (Disclosure), Re [1994] 1 WLR 912, [1994] 1 FLR 377, FD; *sub nom* Re K and Others (Minors) (Disclosure of Privileged Material); *sub nom* Kent County Council v K 629
K v A (Marriage: Validity) [2014] EWHC 3850 (Fam), [2015] 2 FLR 461 1014
K v B (Abduction: Child's Objection to Return) [2014] EWHC B7 (Fam) 391
K v D and others [1998] 1 FLR 700, Cty Ct 1323
K v K (1983) 4 FLR 515, FD; *sub nom* Kepa v Kepa 1240

K v K (Abduction) (No 1) [2009] EWHC 2721 (Fam), [2010] 1 FLR 1295 389, 1554
K v K (Ancillary Relief: Deed of Appointment) [2007] EWHC 3485 (Fam), [2009] 2 FLR 936 1172
K v K (Financial Relief: Management of Difficult Cases) [2005] EWHC 1070 (Fam), [2005] 2 FLR 1137 1320
K v K (Hague Convention: Adjournment) [2009] EWHC 3378 (Fam), [2010] 1 FLR 1310 1554
K v K (Minors: Property Transfer) [1992] 1 WLR 530, [1992] 2 FLR 220, CA 645
K v K [2006] EWHC 2685 (Fam) 2781
K v K [2015] EWHC 1064 (Fam) 1322, 1324
K v K [2016] EWHC 2002 (Fam) 227, 1847, 2145, 2148, 2149
K v K (Periodical Payments: Cohabitation) [2005] EWHC 2886 (Fam), [2006] 2 FLR 468 1203
K v K (Relocation: Shared Care Arrangement) [2011] EWCA Civ 793, [2012] 1 Fam 134, [2012] 2 FLR 880 471, 472
K v L (Non-Matrimonial Property: Special Contribution) [2011] EWCA Civ 550, [2012] 1 WLR 306, [2011] 2 FLR 980 1181, 1182, 2142
K v LBX and Others [2012] EWCA Civ 79, [2012] COPLR 411 1009
K v London Borough of Brent and others [2013] EWCA Civ 926 539
K, Re; Re F (Enduring Powers of Attorney) [1988] Ch 310, [1988] 2 FLR 15, ChD 1682
KA v Finland (Application No 27751/95) [2003] 1 FLR 696, ECHR 528
Kamarah Kathleen Inessah Graham-York v Adrian York (Personal Representative of the Estate of Norton Brian York) and Others [2015] EWCA Civ 72, [2016] 1 FLR 407 1263
Kanev-Lipinski v Aharon Lipinski [2016] EWHC 475 (QB) 1242
Karadzic v Croatia (Application No 35030/04) [2006] 1 FCR 36, ECHR 381
Kaur v Dhaliwal [2014] EWHC 1991 (Ch) 1016
Kaur v Matharu [2010] EWCA Civ 930, [2011] 1 FLR 698 244
Kaur v Randhawa [2015] EWHC 1592 (Fam) 121, 1928
Kay and Others v London Borough of Lambeth and Others; Leeds City Council v Price and Others [2006] UKHL 10, [2006] 2 AC 465 994, 1008
Keegan v Ireland (Application No 16969/90) (1994) Series A No 290, (1994) 18 EHRR 342 283
Keller v Keller and Legal Aid Board [1995] 1 FLR 259, CA 227
Kellman v Kellman [2000] 1 FLR 785, FD 864, 867
Kennedy (dec'd), Re; Kennedy v Official Solicitor to the Supreme Court [1980] CLY 2820, Cty Ct 1030
Kennedy v Cordia (Services) LLP [2016] UKSC 6, [2016] 1 WLR 597 686, 1795
Kennedy v Kennedy [2009] EWCA Civ 986, [2010] 1 FLR 782 380
Kent County Council v A Mother, F and X, X and Z (IR Intervener) [2011] EWHC 402 (Fam) 527
Kent County Council v C [1993] Fam 57, [1993] 1 FLR 308, FD 551, 552, 1704, 1705
Kent County Council v C, G and A [2014] EWHC 604 (Fam), [2015] 1 FLR 115 383, 392, 523
Kent County Council v IS and others [2013] EWHC 2308 (Fam), [2014] 1 FLR 787 2798
Kent County Council v K [1994] 1 WLR 912, [1994] 1 FLR 377, FD; *sub nom* Re K and Others (Minors) (Disclosure); *sub nom* Re K and Others (Minors) (Disclosure of Privileged Material) 629
Kent County Council v M and K [2016] EWFC 28 495, 1001
Kent County Council v PA-K and IA (A Child) [2013] EWHC 578 (Fam), [2014] Fam 1, [2013] 2 FLR 541 664
Kepa v Kepa (1983) 4 FLR 515, FD; *sub nom* K v K 1240
Kerai v Patel [2008] EWCA Civ 600, [2008] 2 FLR 2137 130, 793, 910
Kerbel v Southwark Council (2009) 26 January, ref 725771, Pensions Ombudsman 1174
KH (Medical Treatment: Advanced Care Plan), Re [2013] 1 FLR 1471, FD 1546
Khanna v Lovell White Durrant (A Firm) [1995] 1 WLR 121, ChD 1290, 1762, 1782, 2115
Khans Solicitors (a Firm) v Chifuntwe [2013] EWCA Civ 481, [2014] 1 WLR 1185 1255
Khawaja v Popat [2016] EWCA Civ 362 2304
Khorasandjian v Bush [1993] QB 727, [1993] 2 FLR 66, CA 36, 1231
Kiam v MGN Ltd (No 2) [2002] EWCA Civ 66, [2002] 1 WLR 2810 2148
Kim v Morris [2012] EWHC 1103 (Fam), [2013] 2 FLR 1197 48, 1149, 1404
Kinderis v Kineriene [2013] EWHC 4139 (Fam) 382
King v King [1942] P 1, PDAD 875, 1126
King v Read and Slack [1999] 1 FLR 425, CA 352, 804
King v Telegraph Group Ltd [2004] EWCA Civ 613, [2005] 1 WLR 2282 1390
Kingdon v Kingdon [2010] EWCA Civ 1251, [2011] 1 FLR 1409 1440
Kirklees Metropolitan Borough Council v London Borough of Brent [2004] 2 FLR 800, FD 638
KJ v Poland (Application No 30813/14) [2017] 1 FLR 1006, ECHR 381, 383
Kjeldsen & Othrs v Denmark (1979–80) 1 EHRR 711 1012
KL (A Child), Re [2013] UKSC 75, [2014] 1 AC 1017, [2014] 1 FLR 772 377, 388, 841, 2778

KL (Abduction: Habitual Residence: Inherent Jurisdiction), Re [2013] UKSC 75, [2014] 1 AC 1017, [2014] 1 FLR 772 384
Klentzeris v Klentzeris [2007] EWCA Civ 533, [2007] 2 FLR 996 382, 390, 392, 2200
KM v Lambeth MBC [2011] EWCA Civ 1125, [2012] 1 FLR 1278 1510
Kosmopoulou v Greece [2004] 1 FLR 800, ECHR 443
Kotke v Saffarini [2005] EWCA Civ 221, [2005] 2 FLR 517 1016
Kourkgy v Lusher (1983) 4 FLR 65, FD 1017, 1029
KP (Abduction: Child's Objections), Re [2014] EWCA Civ 554, [2014] 1 WLR 4326, [2014] 2 FLR 660 387, 1531, 1700
KR (Abduction: Forcible Removal by Parents), Re [1999] 2 FLR 542, FD 1543
Kremen v Agrest (Financial Remedy: Non-Disclosure: Post Nuptial Agreement) [2012] EWHC 45 (Fam), [2012] 2 FLR 414 1180
Kremen v Agrest [2013] EWCA Civ 41, [2013] 2 FLR 187 2025
Kremen v Agrest and Fishman [2010] EWHC 2571 (Fam), [2011] 2 FLR 478 1210
Krenge v Krenge [1999] 1 FLR 969, FD 829, 1398
Krombach v Bamberski (Case C-7-98) [2000] ECR I-1935, [2001] 1 QB 709, ECJ 2873
Krubert (Deceased), Re [1997] Ch 97, [1997] 1 FLR 42, CA; *sub nom* Krubert v Rutherford Davies 1024
Krubert v Rutherford Davies [1997] Ch 97, [1997] 1 FLR 42, CA; *sub nom* Re Krubert (Deceased) 1024
KS v MK [2015] EWHC 3276 (Fam) 390
KS v ND (Schedule 1: Appeal: Costs) [2013] EWHC 464 (Fam), [2013] 2 FLR 698 646
KS v Neath Port Talbot Borough Council [2014] EWCA Civ 941 455
KSO v MJO, JMO and PSO [2008] EWHC 3031 (Fam), [2009] 1 FLR 1036 1762, 1848, 1849
KT (Adoption Application), Re [1993] Fam Law 567, FD 277
Kusminow v Barclays Bank Trust Co Ltd and Sokolow and Sitnikova [1989] Fam Law 66, FD 1022, 1024
KY v DD [2011] EWHC 1277 (Fam), [2012] 2 FLR 200 1523, 1546, 1743

L & B (Children) (Specific Issues: Temporary Leave to Remove from the Jurisdiction; Circumcision), Re [2016] EWHC 849 (Fam) 424, 449, 473
L (A Child), Re [2005] EWHC 1237 (Fam), [2006] 1 FLR 843 379
L (A Child), Re [2012] EWCA Civ 1157, [2013] 1 Fam 94, [2013] 1 FLR 430 2742, 2789
L (A Child), Re [2016] EWCA Civ 146 859
L (A Child), Re [2016] EWCA Civ 821 525
L (A Child), Re [2016] EWCA Civ 871 1528
L (A Child), Re; Re Oddin [2016] EWCA Civ 173, [2017] 1 FLR 1135 125, 250, 1995
L (A Minor) (Adoption: Procedure), Re [1991] 1 FLR 171, CA 283
L (Abduction: Child's Objections to Return), Re [2002] EWHC 1864 (Fam), [2002] 1 WLR 3208, [2002] 2 FLR 1042 391
L (Abduction: Future Consent), Re [2007] EWHC 2181 (Fam), [2008] 1 FLR 914 389
L (Abduction: Pending Criminal Proceeding), Re [1999] 1 FLR 433, FD 390
L (Adoption: Contacting Natural Father), Re [2007] EWHC 1771 (Fam), [2008] 1 FLR 1079 448
L (Application Hearing: Legal Representation), Re [2013] EWCA Civ 267, [2013] 2 FLR 1444 1007, 2196
L (Care Proceedings: Disclosure to Third Party), Re [2000] 1 FLR 913, FD 1705
L (Care Proceedings: Human Rights Claims), Re [2003] EWHC 665 (Fam), [2003] 2 FLR 160 529, 1854, 2048, 2049
L (Care Proceedings: Removal of Child), Re [2008] 1 FLR 575, FD 559
L (Care Proceedings: Risk Assessment), Re [2009] EWCA Civ 1008, [2010] 1 FLR 790 534
L (Care: Assessment: Fair Trial), Re [2002] EWHC 1379 (Fam), [2002] 2 FLR 730 526, 529, 1007, 1507, 1509, 1526, 1534
L (Care: Confidentiality), Re [1999] 1 FLR 165, FD 629
L (Case Management: Child's Evidence), Re [2013] EWCA Civ 1778, [2014] 2 FLR 972 204, 1866, 2193
L (Child Abduction: European Convention), Re [1992] 2 FLR 178, FD 394, 396
L (Child Abduction: Psychological Harm), Re [1993] 2 FLR 401, FD 390
L (Children), Re [2016] EWCA Civ 1110 205
L (Commercial Surrogacy), Re [2010] EWHC 3146 (Fam), [2011] Fam 106, [2011] 1 FLR 1423 991
L (Contact: Domestic Violence), Re; V (Contact: Domestic Violence), Re; M (Contact: Domestic Violence), Re; H (Contact: Domestic Violence), Re [2001] Fam 260, [2000] 2 FLR 334, CA 444, 445, 552
L (Family Proceedings Court) (Appeal: Jurisdiction), Re [2003] EWHC 1682 (Fam), [2005] 1 FLR 210 870
L (Interim Care Order: Extended Family), Re [2013] EWCA Civ 179, [2013] 2 FLR 302 555
L (Interim Care Order: Power of Court), Re [1996] 2 FLR 742, CA 457, 559, 560

L (Minors) (Parties), Re [1994] 1 FLR 156, CA; *sub nom* L v L (Minors) (Separate Representation) 436, 1502, 1514
L (Occupation Order), Re [2012] EWCA Civ 721, [2012] 2 FLR 1417 879
L (Police Investigation: Privilege), Re [1997] AC 16, [1996] 1 FLR 731, HL; [1995] 1 FLR 999, CA 686, 1502, 1514, 1532, 1753
L (Procedure: Bundles: Translation), Re [2015] EWFC 15, [2015] 1 FLR 1417 205, 527, 1513, 1837, 2704
L (Residence: Jurisdiction), Re [2006] EWHC 3374 (Fam), [2007] 1 FLR 1686 840
L (Section 37 Direction), Re [1999] 1 FLR 984, CA 556
L (Sexual Abuse: Standard of Proof), Re [1996] 1 FLR 116, CA 560
L (Shared Residence Order), Re [2009] EWCA Civ 20, [2009] 1 FLR 1157 442, 473
L (Special Guardianship: Surname), Re [2007] EWCA Civ 196, [2007] 2 FLR 50 474
L and H (Residential Assessment), Re [2007] EWCA Civ 213, [2007] 1 FLR 1370 561
L and M (Children: Private Law), Re [2014] EWHC 939 (Fam) 482
L and Others, The Queen OTA v Manchester City Council; The Queen OTA of R and another v Manchester City Council [2001] EWHC 707 (Admin), [2002] 1 FLR 43 498
L v C (Applications by Non-Biological Mother) [2014] EWFC 1280, [2015] 1 FLR 674 430, 2785
L v Finland (Case 25651/94) (2001) 31 EHRR 30, [2000] 2 FLR 118 528
L v L (Access: Contempt) [1991] 1 WLR 235, [1991] 2 FLR 43, CA 1532
L v L (Financial Remedies: Deferred Clean Break) [2011] EWHC 2207 (Fam), [2012] 1 FLR 1283 1185
L v L (Minors) (Separate Representation) [1994] 1 FLR 156, CA; *sub nom* Re L (Minors) (Parties) 436, 1502, 1514
L v L [2006] EWHC 956 (Fam), [2008] 1 FLR 26 1448
L v L [2007] EWHC 140 (QB), [2007] 2 FLR 171 1440, 2087
L v L [2008] 1 FLR 142, FD 1178
L v London Borough of Bexley [1996] 2 FLR 595, FD 541, 545, 553
L v London Borough of Bromley [1998] 1 FLR 709, FD 552, 663
L v M (R Intervening) (Case C-656/13), [2015] Fam 173, CJEU 2782
L-A (Care: Chronic Neglect), Re [2009] EWCA Civ 822, [2010] 1 FLR 80 559
L-B (Reversal of Judgment), Re [2012] EWCA Civ 984, [2013] 1 FLR 209 2196
L-B (Reversal of Judgment), Re [2013] UKSC 8, [2013] 1 WLR 634, [2013] 2 FLR 859 203, 212, 1136, 1533, 1857, 1865, 2195
L-K (Children), Re [2015] EWCA Civ 830 532, 537
L-K v K (Brussels II Revised: Maintenance Pending Suit) [2006] EWHC 153 (Fam), [2006] 2 FLR 1113 2785, 2787, 2870
L-K v K (No 2) [2006] EWHC 3280 (Fam), [2007] 2 FLR 729 2776
L-K v K (No 3) [2006] EWHC 3281 (Fam), [2007] 2 FLR 741 2785
L-M (Transfer of Irish Proceedings), Re [2013] EWHC 646 (Fam), [2013] 1 Fam 308, [2013] 2 FLR 708 526
L-R (Children), Re [2013] EWCA Civ 1129 541
L-W (Enforcement and Committal: Contact), Re; CPL v CH-W and Others [2010] EWCA Civ 1253, [2011] 1 FLR 1095 443, 466
La Chemise Lacoste SA v Sketchers USA Ltd [2006] EWHC 3642 (Ch) 1389
La Grange v McAndrew (1879) 4 QBD 210 1247
LAB v KB (Abduction: Brussels II Revised) [2009] EWHC 2243 (Fam), [2010] 2 FLR 1664 2789
Lachaux v Lachaux [2017] EWHC 385 (Fam) 378, 839, 1137, 1148, 1321, 1398
Ladd v Marshall [1954] 1 WLR 1489, (1954) FLR Rep 422, CA 205, 1448, 1554, 1866, 1870
Lake v Lake [1955] P 336, CA 1234
Lake v Lake [2006] EWCA Civ 1250, [2007] 1 FLR 427 879, 912
Lambert v Lambert [2002] EWCA Civ 1685, [2003] Fam 103, [2003] 1 FLR 139 1440
Lambeth LBC v JO [2014] EWHC 3597 (Fam) 522, 2783
Lambeth London Borough Council v TK and KK [2008] EWCA Civ 103, [2008] 1 FLR 1229; *sub nom* K and Another v A Local Authority 556
Lancashire County Council v B [2000] UKHL 16, [2000] 2 AC 147, [2000] 1 FLR 583 537
Land (Deceased), Re; Land v Land [2006] EWHC 2069 (Ch), [2007] 1 WLR 1009 1024
Langley v Langley [1994] 1 FLR 383, CA 1242
Langley v Liverpool City Council [2005] EWCA Civ 1173, [2006] 1 WLR 375, [2006] 1 FLR 342 580
Langley v North West Water Authority [1991] 1 WLR 697, CA 2151
Langley v Police Pension Scheme [2006] (21 January), Pensions Ombudsman ref P00586 1174
Laskar v Laskar [2008] EWCA Civ 347, [2008] 1 WLR 2695, [2008] 2 FLR 589 1263
Lauder v Lauder [2007] EWHC 1227 (Fam), [2007] 2 FLR 802 1179, 1203
Law v Ahumuda & ors [2010] EWCA Civ 1145, [2011] 1 FLR 708 1422
Lawlor v Lawlor [1995] 1 FLR 269, CA 1387
Lawrence v Gallagher [2012] EWCA Civ 394, [2012] 2 FLR 643 730, 1181

Layton v Martin [1986] 2 FLR 227, ChD 1017
LB of Waltham Forest v AD [2014] EWHC 1985 (Fam) 628
LBL v RYJ and VJ [2010] EWHC 2665 (COP), [2011] 1 FLR 1279, [2010] COPLR Con Vol 795 1548
LC (Reunite: International Child Abduction Centre Intervening), Re [2014] UKSC 1, [2014] 1 AC 1038, [2014] 1 FLR 1486 377, 378, 386, 841, 1553, 2778
LCC v A & Ors [2011] EWHC 4033 (Fam) 559, 1421
LCG v RL (Abduction: Habitual Residence and Child's Objections) [2013] EWHC 1383 (Fam), [2014] 1 FLR 307 2781
Le Marchant v Le Marchant [1977] 1 WLR 559, CA 1152
Leach (dec'd), Re; Leach v Lindeman [1986] Ch 226, [1985] FLR 1120, CA; [1984] FLR 590, ChD 1016, 1023
Leadbetter v Leadbetter [1985] FLR 789, FD 1452
Leader, The (1868) LR 2 A&E 314, Admlty 2293
Lebbink v The Netherlands (2004) 40 EHRR 417, [2004] 2 FLR 463 1008
Lee (Geo) & Sons (Builders) Ltd v Olink [1972] 1 WLR 214, CA 2295
Lee v Lee [1952] 2 QB 489, CA 1123
Leeds City Council v M, F, B, G (B and G by their Children's Guardian) [2015] EWFC 3, [2015] 1 FLR 905; *sub nom* Re B and G (Children) (No 2) 532, 534, 539, 927
Leeds County Council & Others v Channel 4 Television Corporation [2007] 1 FLR 678, FD 1544
Leeds Teaching Hospitals NHS Trust v A and B [2003] 1 FLR 412, QBD 969, 2569
Leffler v Berlin Chemie AG (Case C-443 /03) [2005] ECR I-9611, ECJ 2829
Leicester City Council v Chhatbar [2014] EWHC 830 (Fam), [2014] 2 FLR 1365 378
Leicester City Council v S [2014] EWHC 1575 (Fam), [2015] 1 FLR 1182 2684, 2754
Levene v Maton (1907) 51 SJ 532 2293
Levy (Trustee in Bankruptcy of Ellis-Carr) v Ellis-Carr and Another [2012] EWHC 63 (Ch), [2012] BPIR 347 1519
Lewis v Warner [2016] EWHC 1787 (Ch) 1017, 1022, 1023
Lewisham LBC v D (Local Authority Disclosure of DNA Samples to Police) [2010] EWHC 1238 (Fam), [2011] 1 FLR 895 1563, 1564
LG v DK [2011] EWHC 2453 (COP), [2012] COPLR 80 922, 1424
Li Quan v Stuart Bray & Save China's Tigers [2015] EWCA Civ 1253 1533
Li Quan v William Stuart Bray [2014] EWHC 3340 (Fam), [2015] 2 FLR 546 1172
Liden v Burton [2016] EWCA Civ 275, [2017] 1 FLR 310, CA 1262
Lifely v Lifely [2008] EWCA Civ 904 1752, 1755, 1761
Lilleyman v Lilleyman [2012] EWHC 821 (Ch), [2013] 1 FLR 47 1021
Lim v Walia [2014] EWCA Civ 1076, [2015] Ch 375, [2015] 2 FLR 339 1028, 1029
Lindop v Agus, Bass and Hedley [2009] EWHC 1795 (Ch), [2010] 1 FLR 631 1016
Lindsay v Wood [2006] EWHC 2895 (QB) 1682, 1683
Liverpool City Council v B [1995] 1 WLR 505, [1995] 2 FLR 84, FD 513
Livesey (formerly Jenkins) v Jenkins [1985] AC 424, [1985] FLR 813, HL 214, 1205, 1447, 1448, 2105
Livock v Livock [2011] EWHC 3040 (Fam), [2012] 1 FLR 776 193, 204, 1866, 2197
LLBC v TG, JG and KR [2007] EWHC 2640 (Fam), [2009] 1 FLR 414 1501
Lloyd v Bow Street Magistrates' Court [2003] EWHC 2294 (Admin) 414
Lloyd-Davies v Lloyd-Davies [1947] P 53, CA 1235
Lloyds Bank plc v Byrne and Byrne [1993] 1 FLR 369, CA 359
Lloyds Bank plc v Dix & anor [2000] EWCA Civ 269 1320
Lloyds Bank plc v Rosset [1991] 1 AC 107, [1990] 2 FLR 155, HL 16, 1018, 1263
Lloyds Investment (Scandinavia) Ltd v Ager Handerssen [2003] EWHC 1740 (Ch) 384
LM (Reporting Restrictions: Coroner's Inquest), Re [2007] EWHC 1902 (Fam), [2008] 1 FLR 1360 247, 627, 1543
LM v Essex County Council [1999] 1 FLR 988, FD 512
Locabail (UK) Ltd v Bayfield Properties Ltd & Anor [1999] EWCA Civ 3004, [2000] QB 451 212
Local Authority X v HI and Ors [2016] EWHC 1123 (Fam) 527
Lock ex parte Poppleton, Re (No 1) (1891) 8 Morr 44, DC 799
Lock International plc v Beswick [1989] 1 WLR 1268, ChD 1240
Lomas v Parle [2003] EWCA Civ 1804, [2004] 1 WLR 1642, [2004] 1 FLR 812 27, 31, 40, 130, 792, 1231, 1984
London Borough of Barking and Dagenham v SS [2014] EWHC 3338 (Fam), [2015] 2 FLR 181 377, 2783
London Borough of Croydon v R [1997] 2 FLR 675, FD 1831
London Borough of Redbridge v A, B and E (Failure to Comply with Directions) [2016] EWHC 2627 (Fam) 423, 526, 1509, 1517
London Borough of Redbridge v Newport City Council [2003] EWHC 2967 (Fam), [2004] 2 FLR 226 540, 638
London Borough of Redbridge v SNA [2015] EWHC 2140 (Fam), [2015] 1 Fam 335, [2016] 1 FLR 994 1421

London Borough of Southwark v B [1993] 2 FLR 559, CA 533, 638
London Borough of Southwark v Onayamoke [2007] EWCA Civ 1426 1324
London Borough of Sutton v Davis (Costs) (No 2) [1994] 1 WLR 1317, [1994] 2 FLR 569, FD; *sub nom* Sutton London Borough Council v Davis (No 2) 1533, 1847
London Borough of Sutton v MH, RH and NH (No 2) [2016] EWHC 1371 (Fam) 626, 628, 1040
London Borough of Tower Hamlets v Ali [2014] EWHC 845 (Fam), [2015] 1 FLR 205 630
London Borough of Tower Hamlets v B [2015] EWHC 2491 (Fam), [2016] 2 FLR 877 533
London Borough of Tower Hamlets v M and Others [2015] EWHC 869 (Fam), [2015] 2 FLR 1431 630, 1543, 1544
London Borough of Tower Hamlets v R (X) [2013] EWCA Civ 904, [2014] 1 FLR 1076 498
London County Council v Boot (Henry) & Sons [1959] 1 WLR 1609, HL 353
Longley (dec'd), Re; Longley and Longley v Longley [1981] CLY 2885 1025
Lowery v Walker [1911] AC 10, HL 798
Lownds v Home Office (Practice Note) [2002] EWCA Civ 365, [2002] 1 WLR 2450 2148
Lowsley v Forbes (t/a LE Design Services) [1998] 1 AC 329, HL 693, 2283
LR (A Child), Re [2014] EWCA Civ 1624, [2015] 2 FLR 1066 2782, 2783
Lucas v Lucas [1992] 2 FLR 53, CA 858
Luckwell v Limata [2014] EWHC 502 (Fam), [2014] 2 FLR 168 1180, 1835
Lumba (Congo) v SSHD; Mighty (Jamaica) v SSHD [2011] UKSC 12, [2012] AC 245 580
Lumsden v Lumsden (unreported) (1998) 11 November, CA 1204
Lykiardopulo v Lykiardopulo and Lykiardopulo [2010] EWCA Civ 1315, [2011] 1 FLR 1427 1040, 1178

M & F (Covert Recording of Children), Re [2016] EWFC 29; *sub nom* M v F & C (A Child by her Children's Guardian) 624
M (A Child), Re [2012] EWCA Civ 1905 535
M (A Child), Re [2014] EWCA Civ 1755 442, 458
M (A Child), Re [2015] EWCA Civ 1296 1527
M (A Child: Long Term Foster Care), Re [2014] EWCA Civ 1406, [2015] 2 FLR 197 539
M (A Minor) (Appeal: Interim Order) (No 1), Re [1994] 1 FLR 54, CA 567
M (A Minor) (Care Order: Threshold Conditions), Re [1994] 2 AC 424, [1994] 2 FLR 577, HL 532
M (A Minor) (Care Orders: Jurisdiction), Re [1997] Fam 67, [1997] 1 FLR 456, FD; *sub nom* M (Care Orders: Jurisdiction) 522
M (A Minor) (Disclosure of Material), Re [1990] 2 FLR 36, CA; *sub nom* Re M (A Minor) (Discovery: Wardship Proceedings) 1511, 1512, 1754
M (A Minor) (Discovery: Wardship Proceedings), Re [1990] 2 FLR 36, CA; *sub nom* Re M (A Minor) (Disclosure of Material) 1511, 1512, 1754
M (A Minor) (Habitual Residence), Re [1996] 1 FLR 887, CA; *sub nom* Re M (Abduction: Habitual Residence) 377
M (Abduction) (Consent: Acquiescence), Re [1999] 1 FLR 171, FD 389
M (Abduction: Acquiescence), Re [1996] 1 FLR 315, FD 390
M (Abduction: Appeals), Re [2007] EWCA Civ 1059, [2008] 1 FLR 699 2195
M (Abduction: Child's Objections), Re [2007] EWCA Civ 260, [2007] 2 FLR 72 391, 392
M (Abduction: Child's Objections: Appeal), Re [2014] EWCA Civ 1519, [2016] 1 FLR 296 387
M (Abduction: Habitual Residence), Re [1996] 1 FLR 887, CA; *sub nom* Re M (A Minor) (Habitual Residence) 377
M (Abduction: Intolerable Situation), Re [2000] 1 FLR 930, FD 390
M (Abduction: Undertakings), Re [1995] 1 FLR 1021, CA 391
M (Abduction: Zimbabwe), Re [2007] UKHL 55, [2008] AC 1288, [2008] 1 FLR 251 383, 386, 388, 1553, 1697, 2781
M (Adoption: Leave to Oppose), Re [2009] EWHC 3643 (Fam), [2010] 1 FLR 238 265
M (Assessment: Official Solicitor), Re [2009] EWCA Civ 315, [2009] 2 FLR 950 561
M (Brussels II Revised: Art 15), Re [2014] EWCA Civ 152, [2014] 2 FLR 1372 523, 524, 525, 2783
M (Care Disclosure to Police), Re [2008] 2 FLR 390, FD 249, 629
M (Care Orders: Jurisdiction), Re [1997] Fam 67, [1997] 1 FLR 456, FD; *sub nom* M (A Minor) (Care Orders: Jurisdiction) 522
M (Care: Challenging Decisions made by Local Authority), Re [2001] 2 FLR 1300, FD 1000
M (Care: Contact: Grandmother's Application for Leave), Re [1995] 2 FLR 86, CA 454, 455, 551, 1501
M (Care: Leave to Interview Child), Re [1995] 1 FLR 825, FD 451
M (Child Abduction) (European Convention), Re [1994] 1 FLR 551, FD 394, 395
M (Child Abduction: Delay), Re (2007) *The Times*, August 28, CA 1554
M (Child Abduction: Existence of Undertakings), Re [2000] 3 FCR 693, FD 390, 1553
M (Child Abuse: Disclosure), Re [2011] EWCA Civ 1035, [2012] 1 FLR 205 558
M (Children) (Sexual Abuse), Re [2008] EWCA Civ 3 2194
M (Children), Re [2007] EWCA Civ 177 2194

M (Children), Re [2013] EWCA Civ 1170 204, 535, 1235, 1871, 2193
M (Children), Re [2015] EWCA Civ 280 446
M (Children), Re [2015] EWCA Civ 994 424
M (Children), Re [2016] EWCA Civ 937 540, 630
M (Children), Re [2016] EWCA Civ 942 383
M (Contact), Re [1995] 1 FLR 1029, FD 1528
M (Contact), Re [2012] EWHC 1948 (Fam), [2013] 1 FLR 1403 444, 458
M (Disclosure), Re [1998] 2 FLR 1028, CA 1509, 1510
M (Disclosure: Children and Family Reporter), Re [2002] EWCA Civ 1199, [2003] Fam 26, [2002] 2 FLR 893 626
M (Fact-Finding Hearing: Burden of Proof), Re [2008] EWCA Civ 1261, [2009] 1 FLR 1177 535, 2194
M (Fact-Finding Hearing: Burden of Proof), Re [2012] EWCA Civ 1580, [2013] 2 FLR 874 535
M (Freezing Injunction), Re [2006] 1 FLR 1031, FD 1209
M (HFEA 2008), Re [2016] EWHC 1572 (Fam) 980
M (Interim Care Order: Removal), Re [2005] EWCA Civ 1594, [2006] 1 FLR 1043 559
M (Intractable Contact Dispute: Interim Care Order), Re [2003] EWHC 1024 (Fam), [2003] 2 FLR 636 437, 446, 556, 569
M (Judge's Discretion), Re [2001] EWCA Civ 1428, [2002] 1 FLR 730 1520
M (Local Authority's Costs), Re [1995] 1 FLR 533, FD 534
M (Minors) (Adoption), Re [1991] 1 FLR 458, CA 280, 989
M (Minors) (Custody: Jurisdiction), Re [1992] 2 FLR 382, CA 854, 855
M (Minors) (Disclosure of Evidence), Re [1994] 1 FLR 760, CA; *sub nom* Re M (Minors) (Disclosure of Welfare Report) 448, 1509
M (Minors) (Disclosure of Welfare Report), Re [1994] 1 FLR 760, CA; *sub nom* Re M (Minors) (Disclosure of Evidence) 448, 1509
M (Minors) (Interim Residence Order), Re [1997] 2 FCR 28, CA 457
M (Minors) (Sexual Abuse: Evidence), Re [1993] 1 FLR 822, CA 1502
M (Official Solicitor's Role), Re [1998] 2 FLR 815, CA 556
M (Prohibited Steps Order: Application for Leave), Re [1992] Fam 182, [1993] 1 FLR 275, FD 455, 1831
M (Republic of Ireland) (Child's Objections) (Joinder of Children as Parties to Appeal), Re [2015] EWCA Civ 26, [2016] 1 Fam 1, [2015] 2 FLR 1074 391, 424, 1553, 1697
M (Residence Order), Re [2008] EWCA Civ 66, [2008] 1 FLR 1087 442
M (Residence), Re [2002] EWCA Civ 1052, [2002] 2 FLR 1059 1532
M (Section 91(14) Order), Re [2012] EWCA Civ 446, [2012] 2 FLR 758 620
M (Section 94 Appeals), Re [1995] 1 FLR 546, CA 1831
M (Secure Accommodation Order), Re [1995] Fam 108, [1995] 1 FLR 418, CA 512
M (Sexual Abuse: Evidence), Re [2010] EWCA Civ 1030 624
M (Threshold Criteria: Parental Concessions), Re [1999] 2 FLR 728, CA 540
M (Wardship: Jurisdiction and Powers), Re [2015] EWHC 1433 (Fam), [2016] 1 FLR 1055 630, 1481, 1543, 1544
M and C (Minors) (Interim Care Order), Re [1994] 2 FLR 506, CA; *sub nom* Buckinghamshire County Council v M 1529
M and M v Croatia (Application No 10161 /13) [2016] 2 FLR 18, ECHR 387
M and N (Parallel Family and Immigration Proceedings), Re [2008] EWHC 2281 (Fam), [2008] 2 FLR 2030 543, 1516
M and R (Child Abuse: Evidence), Re [1996] 2 FLR 195, CA; *sub nom* Re M and R (Minors) (Sexual Abuse: Expert Evidence) 536, 537, 1794
M and R (Minors) (Sexual Abuse: Expert Evidence), Re [1996] 2 FLR 195, CA; *sub nom* Re M and R (Child Abuse: Evidence) 536, 537, 1794
M v B (Residence: Forum Conveniens) [1994] 2 FLR 819, FD 842
M v C (Children Orders: Reasons) [1993] 2 FLR 584, FD 449, 451
M v C and Calderdale Metropolitan Borough Council [1994] Fam 1, [1993] 1 FLR 505, CA 280
M v F & C (A Child by her Children's Guardian) [2016] EWFC 29; *sub nom* Re M & F (Covert Recording of Children) 624
M v F and H (Legal Paternity) [2013] EWHC 1901 (Fam), [2014] 1 FLR 352 978
M v H (Education Welfare) [2008] EWHC 324 (Fam), [2008] 1 FLR 1400 448
M v M (Abduction: England and Scotland) [1997] 2 FLR 263, CA 843
M v M (Abduction: Settlement) [2008] EWHC 2049 (Fam), [2008] 2 FLR 1884 386, 2780
M v M (Defined Contact Application) [1998] 2 FLR 244, FD 424, 1832
M v M (Financial Provision) [2010] EWHC 2817 (Fam), [2011] 1 FLR 1773 1126
M v M (Maintenance Pending Suit: Enforcement on Dismissal of Suit) [2009] 1 FLR 790, FD 1163
M v M (Minor: Custody Appeal) [1987] 1 WLR 404, [1987] 2 FLR 146, CA; *sub nom* M v M (Transfer of Custody: Appeal) 1870
M v M [2007] EWHC 1404 (Fam), [2007] 2 FLR 1010 389

M v M [2011] EWHC 3574 (Fam) 1026
M v M [2013] EWCA Civ 1255, [2014] 1 Fam 102, [2014] 1 FLR 1514; *sub nom* Mittal v Mittal 828, 2776
M v M [2015] EWFC B63 2517
M v M (Parental Responsibility) [1999] 2 FLR 737, FD 427
M v M (Residence Order: Ancillary Injunction) [1994] Fam Law 440, FD 448
M v M (Stay of Proceedings: Return of Children) [2005] EWHC 1159 (Fam), [2006] 1 FLR 138 842
M v M (Third Party Subpoena: Financial Conduct) [2006] 2 FLR 1253, FD 1184, 1440
M v M (Transfer of Custody: Appeal) [1987] 1 WLR 404, [1987] 2 FLR 146, CA; *sub nom* M v M (Minor: Custody Appeal) 1870
M v M and Others [2013] EWHC 2534 (Fam), [2014] 1 FLR 439 1023, 1129
M v Revenue and Customs Commissioners [2010] UKFTT 356 (TC) 945, 954
M v T (Abduction) [2008] EWHC 1383 (Fam), [2009] 1 FLR 1309 389, 390, 391
M v T (Abduction: Brussels II Revised, Art 11(7)) [2010] EWHC 1479 (Fam), [2010] 2 FLR 1685 385, 2781
M v V (Child Maintenance: Jurisdiction: Brussels I) [2010] EWHC 1435 (Fam), [2011] 1 FLR 109 1432
M v W (Application after New Zealand Financial Agreement) [2014] EWHC 925 (Fam), [2015] 1 FLR 465 2866
M v W (Declaration of Parentage) [2006] EWHC 2341 (Fam), [2007] 2 FLR 270 292
M v Warwickshire County Council [1994] 2 FLR 593, FD 672, 1527
M v Warwickshire County Council [2007] EWCA Civ 1084, [2008] 1 WLR 991, [2008] 1 FLR 1093 265, 278, 282, 454, 455, 478
M'P-P (Children), Re [2015] EWCA Civ 584 538, 539
M, GP and AK v Suffolk County Council [2014] EWCA Civ 942 539
M, T, P, K and B (Care: Change of Name), Re [2000] 2 FLR 645, FD 549
M-B (Children), Re [2015] EWCA Civ 1027 535
M-F (Children), Re [2014] EWCA Civ 991, [2015] 1 WLR 909 547
M-H (Children), Re [2006] EWCA Civ 499 205, 566, 2200
M-J (Adoption Order or Special Guardianship Order), Re [2007] EWCA Civ 56, [2007] 1 FLR 691 474
M-M (Schedule 1 Provision), Re [2014] EWCA Civ 276, [2014] 2 FLR 1391 645, 650
M-T v T (Marriage: Strike-Out) [2013] EWHC 2061 (Fam), [2014] 1 FLR 1352 1015
M-T v T [2006] EWHC 2494 (Fam), [2007] 2 FLR 925 645, 646
M-W (Care Proceedings: Expert Evidence), Re [2010] EWCA Civ 12, [2010] 2 FLR 46 205, 2196
MA (Care Threshold), Re [2009] EWCA Civ 853, [2010] 1 FLR 431 532
MA v DB (Inherent Jurisdiction) [2011] 1 FLR 724, FD 2793, 2794
MA v JA and the Attorney-General [2012] EWHC 2219 (Fam), [2013] 2 FLR 68 1014, 2271
MA v RS (Contact: Parenting Roles) [2011] EWHC 2455 (Fam), [2012] 1 FLR 1056 702
Mabon v Mabon [2005] EWCA Civ 634, [2005] Fam 366, [2005] 2 FLR 1011 1531, 1699, 1709
MacDonald & Anor v Frost [2009] EWHC 2276 (Ch) 1023
Macdonald v Taree Holdings Ltd [2001] CPLR 439, CA 232
Macey v Macey (1982) 3 FLR 7, FD 813
MacLeod v MacLeod [2008] UKPC 64, [2010] 1 AC 298, [2009] 1 FLR 641 1179, 1207
Magiera v Magiera [2016] EWCA Civ 1292 359, 2022
Maher v Gower (formerly Kubilius) (1982) 3 FLR 287, FD 2286
Maire v Portugal (Application No 48206/99) [2004] 2 FLR 653, ECHR 381
Malone v Harrison [1979] 1 WLR 1353, FD 1022
Maltez v Lewis (2000) 16 Const LJ 65, ChD 1277
Manchanda v Manchanda [1995] 2 FLR 590, CA 1154, 1405
Manchester CC v Pinnock [2010] UKSC 45, [2011] 2 AC 104 993, 1000
Manchester City Council v F (Note) [1993] 1 FLR 419, FD 1508
Manchester City Council v T [1994] Fam 181, [1994] 1 FLR 632, CA; *sub nom* Re T (A Minor) (Guardian ad litem: Case Record) 571, 1706
Manda (Wardship: Disclosure of Evidence), Re [1993] Fam 183, [1993] 1 FLR 205, CA 1544
Manley v Law Society [1981] 1 WLR 335, CA 1043, 1044, 1255
Mann v Mann [2014] EWCA Civ 1674, [2015] 2 FLR 1116 1203
Mann v Mann [2014] EWHC 537 (Fam), [2014] 1 WLR 2807, [2014] 2 FLR 928 1307, 1309
Manor Electronics Ltd v Dickson [1988] RPC 618, QBD 1241
Mansfield v Mansfield [2011] EWCA Civ 1056, [2012] 1 FLR 117 1182
Mansour v Mansour [1989] 1 FLR 418, CA 829, 1398
MAP v MFP (Financial Remedies: Add-Back) [2015] EWHC 627 (Fam), [2016] 1 FLR 70 1181
MAP v RAP [2013] EWHC 4784 (Fam), [2015] 2 FLR 67 1684
Marano v Marano [2010] EWCA Civ 119, [2010] 1 FLR 1903 1180
Marcan Shipping (London) Ltd v George Kefalas & Candida Corporation [2007] EWCA Civ 463, [2007] 1 WLR 1864 1323

Marckx v Belgium (1979) 2 EHRR 330 1010, 1015
Mareva Compania Naviera SA v International Bulk Carriers SA, The Mareva [1980] 1 All ER 213, CA 790, 1241
Marinos v Marinos [2007] EWHC 2047 (Fam), [2007] 2 FLR 1018 828, 2776
Marley v Rawlings & Anor [2014] UKSC 2 1024
Marley v Rawlings [2012] EWCA Civ 61, [2012] 2 FLR 556 1024
Marley v Rawlings (No 2) (Costs) [2014] UKSC 51, [2015] AC 15, [2015] 1 FLR 1063 1024
Maronier v Larmer [2002] EWCA Civ 774, [2003] QB 620 97
Martin v Williams [2017] EWHC 491 (Ch) 1018
Martin-Dye v Martin-Dye [2006] EWCA Civ 681, [2006] 1 WLR 3448, [2006] 2 FLR 901 2516
Masefield v Alexander (Lump Sum: Extension of Time) [1995] 1 FLR 100, CA 1169, 1202
Masich v Masich (1977) Fam Law 245, CA 890
Maskell v Maskell [2001] EWCA Civ 858, [2003] 1 FLR 1138 2516
Mason v Lawton [1991] 1 WLR 322, [1991] 2 FLR 50, CA 793
Masri v Consolidated Contractors [2011] EWCA Civ 898, [2012] 1 WLR 223 793
Masterman-Lister v Brutton & Co and Jewell & Home Counties Dairies [2002] EWCA Civ 1889, [2003] 1 WLR 1511 223, 1680, 1681, 1682, 1683, 1700, 2061, 2062, 2064, 2068
Masterman-Lister v Jewell & Another [2002] EWHC 417 (QB) 1682, 1683, 1684, 1685
Matthews v Matthews [2013] EWCA Civ 1874, [2014] 2 FLR 1259 1185
Maughan v Wilmot [2016] EWHC 29 (Fam), [2016] 2 FLR 1349 1352, 1358
Mawson v Mawson [1994] 2 FLR 985, FD 1196
Mayeka v Belgium (Application 13178/03) (2006) 46 EHRR 449, [2007] 1 FLR 1726 1005
MB (Caesarean Section), Re, Re L (Patient: Non-Consensual Treatment), Re L (An Adult: Non-Consensual Treatment) [1997] 2 FLR 426, CA; *sub nom* Re MB (Medical Treatment) 960, 1681, 1682
MB (Medical Treatment), Re [1997] 2 FLR 426, CA; *sub nom* Re MB (Caesarean Section), Re L (Patient: Non-Consensual Treatment), Re L (An Adult: Non-Consensual Treatment) 960, 1681, 1682
MB v GK [2014] EWHC 963 (Fam) 378
MB v KB [2007] EWHC 789 (Fam), [2007] 2 FLR 586 645
MB v Secretary of State for Work and Pensions [2016] UKSC 53 944
McC (Care Proceedings: Fresh Evidence of Foreign Expert), Re [2012] EWCA Civ 165, [2012] 2 FLR 121 204, 1871, 2205
McCartney v Mills McCartney [2008] EWHC 401 (Fam), [2008] 1 FLR 1508 1180
McFarlane v McFarlane [2009] EWHC 891 (Fam), [2009] 2 FLR 1322 1203
McFarlane v McFarlane; Parlour v Parlour [2004] EWCA Civ 872, [2005] Fam 171, [2004] 2 FLR 893 244
McGonnell v United Kingdom [2000] ECHR 62 1007
McHugh v McHugh [2014] EWCA Civ 1671 206, 1865, 2196
McLoughlin v Grovers (A Firm) [2001] EWCA Civ 1743, [2002] QB 1312 1320
McMichael v United Kingdom (1995) 20 EHRR 205 1008
McMinn v McMinn (Ancillary Relief: Death of Party to Proceedings: Costs) [2003] 2 FLR 839, FD 2146
McNare, Re; McNare v McNare [1964] 1 WLR 1255, ChD 1025
McNicholas v Scottish Widows (2013) 11 April, ref PO408, Pensions Ombudsman 2517
McPhilemy v Times Newspapers Ltd & Ors [2001] EWCA Civ 933, [2002] 1 WLR 934 2141
McRoberts v McRoberts [2012] EWHC 2966 (Ch), [2013] 1 WLR 1601, [2013] BPIR 77 1170
McShane v UK [2002] ECHR 469, (2002) 35 EHRR 593 1004
McV v B [1988] Fam 69, [1988] 2 FLR 67, FD; *sub nom* McVeigh v Beattie 923
McVeigh v Beattie [1988] Fam 69, [1988] 2 FLR 67, FD; *sub nom* McV v B 923
MD and TD (Minors) (No 2), Re [1994] Fam Law 489, FD 565
MD v AA [2014] EWHC 2756 (Fam), [2015] 1 FLR 1272; *sub nom* Re D (Recognition and enforcement of Romanian Order) 2742
MD v CT (Parental Responsibility Order: Recognition and Enforcement) [2014] EWHC 871 (Fam), [2015] 1 FLR 213 2742, 2789
MD v D [2008] EWHC 1929 (Fam), [2009] 1 FLR 810 1179, 1183
Medcalf v Mardell [2002] UKHL 27, [2003] 1 AC 120; *sub nom* Medcalf v Weatherhill 214, 1754, 2161
Medcalf v Weatherhill [2002] UKHL 27, [2003] 1 AC 120; *sub nom* Medcalf v Mardell 214, 1754, 2161
Medway Council v G and Ors [2008] EWHC 1681 (Fam), [2008] 2 FLR 1687 248, 627
Medway Council v JB and Others [2015] EWHC 3064 (Fam), [2016] 2 FLR 1360 525
Mercantile Credit Co Ltd v Ellis (1987) *The Times*, 1 April, CA 359
Mercredi v Chaffe (Case C-497/10) [2010] ECR I-14309, [2012] Fam 22, [2011] 1 FLR 1293, CJEU 376, 379, 380, 2734, 2778, 2783, 2785
Mercredi v Chaffe [2011] EWCA Civ 272, [2011] 2 FLR 515 377, 524
Merrick & Wellington [2014] Fam CA 514 2742

Merton London Borough Council v K; Re K (Care: Representation: Public Funding) [2005] EWHC 167 (Fam), [2005] 2 FLR 422 1502
MET v HAT (Interim Maintenance) [2013] EWHC 4247 (Fam), [2014] 2 FLR 692 1164, 1165, 2787
MET v HAT (No 2) [2014] EWHC 717 (Fam), [2015] 1 FLR 576 1164, 2787
Metropolitan Council, A v DB [1997] 1 FLR 767, FD 511
MG and JG v JF (Child Maintenance: Costs Allowance) [2015] EWHC 564 (Fam), [2016] 1 FLR 424 1165
MH (A Child), Re; and SB and MB (Children), Re [2002] 1 WLR 189, [2001] 2 FLR 1334, FD 543, 569, 1704
MH v MH (Case C-173/16) (2016) 22 June, CJEU 2785
Michael Wilson & Partners v Sinclair [2017] EWCA Civ 55 2326
Middleton v Middleton [1998] 2 FLR 821, CA 2193
MIG and MEG, Re [2010] EWHC 785 (Fam), [2010] COPLR Con Vol 850 1006
Migliaccio v Migliaccio (Rev 2) [2016] EWHC 1055 (Fam) 1933
Miles v Bull [1969] 1 QB 258, QBD 877
Miles v Miles [1979] 1 WLR 371, CA 353
Millburn-Snell v Evans [2011] EWCA Civ 577, [2012] 1 WLR 41 2062
Miller v Allied Sainif (UK) (2000) *The Times*, 31 October, ChD 1827
Miller v Miller [1961] P 1, PDAD 1077
Miller v Miller; McFarlane v McFarlane [2006] UKHL 24, [2006] 2 AC 618, [2006] 1 FLR 1186 1023, 1169, 1178, 1181, 1183, 1184, 1185, 1186, 1202, 1203, 1440
Miller-Smith v Miller-Smith [2009] EWCA Civ 1297, [2010] 1 FLR 1402 1261, 1262
Milne v Milne (1981) 2 FLR 286, (1981) 125 SJ 375, CA 1187
Milton v Milton [2008] EWCA Civ 926, [2009] 1 FLR 661 1169
Minkin v Landsberg [2015] EWCA Civ 1152, [2016] 1 WLR 1489 1449, 1827
Minton v Minton [1979] AC 593, (1978) FLR Rep 461, HL 1185
Mitchell v Alasia [2005] EWHC 11 (QB) 1682
Mitchell v Mitchell [1984] Fam 1, [1984] FLR 50, CA 1394, 1399
Mitchell v News Group Newspapers Ltd [2013] EWCA Civ 1537, [2014] 1 WLR 795 1320, 1324
Mittal v Mittal [2013] EWCA Civ 1255, [2014] 1 Fam 102, [2014] 1 FLR 1514; *sub nom* M v M 828, 2776
ML (Use of Skype Technology), Re [2013] EWHC 2091 (Fam) 1636
MN and KN v Hackney Borough Council [2013] EWHC 1205 (Admin) 485
MO v RO & Anor [2013] EWHC 392 (Fam) 1015
Moat Housing Group-South Ltd v Harris [2005] EWCA Civ 287, [2005] 2 FLR 551 1743
Mohan v Mohan [2013] EWCA Civ 586, [2014] 1 FLR 717 1929, 1933, 1983, 2285
Monroe v Hopkins [2017] EWHC 645 (QB) 1865
Monte Developments Ltd v Court Management Consultants Ltd and others [2010] EWHC 3071 (Ch), [2011] 1 WLR 1579 359
Moon v Moon (1980) 1 FLR 115, FD 1077
Moore v Holdsworth [2010] EWHC 683 (Ch), [2010] 2 FLR 1501 1017
Moore v Moore [2007] EWCA Civ 361, [2007] 2 FLR 339 1127, 2857, 2869, 2870
Moore v Moore [2009] EWCA Civ 1427, [2010] 1 FLR 1413 1163
Moore v Moore [2016] EWHC 2202 (Ch) 1024
Morgan v Hill [2006] EWCA Civ 1602, [2007] 1 WLR 855, [2007] 1 FLR 1480 408, 645, 655
Morgan v Morgan [1977] Fam 122, (1976) FLR Rep 473, FD 1783
Morris v Morris [2008] EWCA Civ 257 1262, 1263
Morris v Morris [2016] EWCA Civ 812 1202, 1933
Moser v Austria (Application No 12643/02) [2007] 1 FLR 702, ECHR 529
Moses-Taiga v Taiga [2005] EWCA Civ 1013, [2006] 1 FLR 1074 2787
Motorola Credit Corp v Uzan (No 2) [2003] EWCA Civ 752, [2004] 1 WLR 113 1240, 1242
Moynihan v Moynihan (Nos 1 and 2) [1997] 1 FLR 59, FD 1041
MP (Fact-Finding Hearing: Care Proceedings: Art 15), Re [2013] EWHC 2063 (Fam), [2014] 1 FLR 702 524
Mr R v Mrs R [2014] EWFC 48, [2015] 1 WLR 2743 29, 887, 890, 1324
Mrs R v Central Independent Television plc [1994] Fam 192, [1994] 2 FLR 151, CA; *sub nom* R v Central Independent Television plc 1544
MS v PS (Case C-283/16) [2017] 1 FLR 1163, CJEU 91, 2440, 2877, 2882
MS v PS (Enforcement Procedure Under the Maintenance Regulation: Reference to CJEU) [2016] EWHC 88 (Fam), [2017] 1 FLR 394 2882
MT v OT (Financial Provision: Costs) [2007] EWHC 838 (Fam), [2008] 2 FLR 1311 406, 648, 650
Mubarak v Mubarak [2001] 1 FLR 698, CA 118, 1930, 1931
Mubarak v Mubarik [2006] EWHC 1260 (Fam), [2007] 1 WLR 271, [2007] 1 FLR 722 118, 797
Mulholland v Mitchell [1971] AC 666, HL 1753
Munro v Munro [2007] EWHC 3315 (Fam), [2008] 1 FLR 1613 828, 2776
Murphy v Murphy & Others [2003] EWCA Civ 1862 1028

Murphy v Murphy [2014] EWHC 2263 (Fam) 1168, 1186
Murray v Robinson [2005] EWCA Civ 935, [2006] 1 FLR 365 130, 792
Musa v Holliday [2012] EWCA Civ 1268, [2013] 1 FLR 806 1016
Muscovitch, Re, ex parte M [1939] Ch 694, CA 853
Mutch v Mutch [2016] EWCA Civ 370, [2017] 1 FLR 408 1202
MW and Hertfordshire County Council v A & V and Mr & Mrs J [2014] EWCA Civ 405 228, 527, 531, 538, 1696, 1706
MXB v East Sussex Hospitals Trust [2012] EWHC 3279 (QB), [2013] 1 FLR 1152 1040
Myers v Myers [2004] EWHC 1944 (Fam) 1018, 1023
Myerson v Myerson [2008] EWCA Civ 1376, [2009] 1 FLR 826 1442
Myerson v Myerson (No 2) [2009] EWCA Civ 282, [2010] 1 WLR 114, [2009] 2 FLR 147 1448

N (A Child), Re [2016] EWHC 3085 (Fam) 292
N (A Child: Religion: Jehovah's Witness), Re [2011] EWHC 3737 (Fam), [2012] 2 FLR 917 448
N (A Minor) (Adoption: Foreign Guardianship), Re [2000] 2 FLR 431, FD; *sub nom* Re AGN (Adoption: Foreign Adoption) 282, 283
N (A Minor), Re (unreported) 25 September 1997, CA 455, 1502
N (Abduction: Appeal), Re [2012] EWCA Civ 1086, [2013] 1 FLR 457 839, 1545, 2783
N (Abduction: Brussels II Revised), Re [2014] EWHC 749 (Fam), [2015] 1 FLR 227 2742, 2789
N (Adoption: Jurisdiction), Re [2015] EWCA Civ 1112, [2016] 1 FLR 621 256, 260, 280, 494, 522, 524
N (Adoption: Jurisdiction), Re [2016] UKSC 15, [2016] 1 FLR 1082 525
N (Care Proceedings: Adoption), Re [2012] EWCA Civ 1563, [2013] 1 FLR 1244 558
N (Children), Re [2016] EWCA Civ 656 455
N (Contact: Minor Seeking Leave to Defend and Removal of Guardian), Re [2003] 1 FLR 652, FD 454, 1699
N (Family Proceedings: Disclosure), Re [2009] EWHC 1663 (Fam), [2009] 2 FLR 1152 1563, 1564
N (Infants) (No 2), Re [1967] Ch 512, ChD 1245
N (Jurisdiction), Re [2007] EWHC 1274 (Fam), [2007] 2 FLR 1196 2776
N (Leave to Remove from the Jurisdiction) (No 2), Re [2014] EWHC B16 (Fam) 472
N (Leave to Withdraw Care Proceedings), Re [2000] 1 FLR 134, FD 534, 544, 1706, 1853
N (McKenzie Friend: Rights of Audience), Re [2008] EWHC 2042 (Fam), [2008] 1 WLR 2743, [2008] 2 FLR 1899 1529
N (Minors) (Abduction), Re [1991] 1 FLR 413, FD 383, 390
N (Payments for Benefit of Child), Re [2009] EWHC 11 (Fam), [2009] 1 WLR 1621, [2009] 1 FLR 1442 359, 648, 650, 1170
N (Recognition of Foreign Adoption Order), Re [2009] EWHC 29 (Fam), [2010] 1 FLR 1102 293
N (Residence: Appointment of Solicitor: Placement with Extended Family), Re [2001] 1 FLR 1028, CA 1707
N (Section 91(14) Order), Re [1996] 1 FLR 356, CA 620
N and N v Newham London Borough Council and Essex Borough Council [2013] EWHC 2475 (Admin) 486
N v C (Financial Provision; Schedule 1 Claims Dismissed) [2013] EWHC 399 (Fam) 645
N v D (Customary Marriage) [2015] EWFC 28 1015
N v D [2008] 1 FLR 1629, PRFD 649, 650
N v F (Financial Orders: Pre-Acquired Wealth) [2011] EWHC 586 (Fam), [2011] 2 FLR 533 1182
N v K (Jurisdiction: International Liaison) (No 2) [2014] EWHC 507 (Fam), [2014] 2 FLR 1147 525, 2736, 2778
N v K [2013] EWHC 2774 (Fam) 2778
N v N (Abduction: Article 13 Defence) [1995] 1 FLR 107, FD 390
N v N (Child Maintenance: Res Judicata and Strike Out) [2015] EWHC 514 (Fam), [2015] 2 FLR 1441 1762
N v N (Divorce: Agreement not to Defend) [1992] 1 FLR 266, CA 1386
N v N [2014] EWCA Civ 314, [2015] 1 FLR 241 1753
N v N (Stay of Maintenance Proceedings) [2012] EWHC 4282 (Fam), [2014] 1 FLR 1399 2787, 2869
N, Re [1995] Fam 96, [1995] 1 FLR 341, FD; *sub nom* A v A (Abduction: Jurisdiction) 365
N, Re [2016] EWHC 1329 (Fam) 980
N, Re; A v G and N [2009] EWHC 1807 (Fam), [2010] 1 FLR 272 1527
NA (Applicant) v ZA and ors [2015] EWHC 2188 (Fam) 553
NA v MA [2006] EWHC 2900 (Fam), [2007] 1 FLR 1760 1181, 1207
NAB v Serco Ltd & Anor [2014] EWHC 1225 (QB) 1755, 1756
Nanglegan v Royal Free Hampstead NHS Trust [2001] EWCA Civ 127, [2002] 1 WLR 1043 1348
Natasha Armes v Notts County Council [2016] EWHC 2864 (QB) 627
National Commercial Bank of Jamaica Ltd v Olint Corp Ltd (Jamaica) [2009] UKPC 16, [2009] 1 WLR 1405 1743, 1745, 1746

National Justice Compania Naviera SA v Prudential Assurance Co; the Ikarian Reefer [1993] 2 Lloyd's Rep 68, Comm Ct 1795
National Westminster Bank Plc v King [2008] EWHC 280 (Ch), [2008] Ch 385 2298
National Westminster Bank Plc v Rushmer [2010] EWHC 554 (Ch), [2010] 2 FLR 362 1264
Nationwide Building Society v Wright [2009] EWCA Civ 811, [2010] Ch 318, [2009] BPIR 1047 359
NB v Haringey LBC [2011] EWHC 3544 (Fam), [2012] 2 FLR 125 193, 566
ND v KP (Freezing Order: Ex Parte Application) [2011] EWHC 457 (Fam), [2011] 2 FLR 662 1209, 1241, 1242, 1744
Negus v Bahouse [2007] EWHC 2628 (Ch), [2008] 1 FLR 381 1018, 1022
Nesheim v Kosa [2006] EWHC 2710 (Ch) 2271
Neulinger and Shuruk v Switzerland [2011] 1 FLR 122, ECHR 389, 528, 2781
Newlon Housing Trust v Alsulaimen [1999] 1 AC 313, [1998] 2 FLR 690, HL 1171
Newman (t/a Mantella Publishing) v Modern Bookbinders Ltd [2000] 1 WLR 2559, CA 124, 804, 1473, 2289
NG v OG [2014] EWHC 4182 (Fam) 2742, 2775, 2781
NG v SG (Appeal: Non-Disclosure) [2011] EWHC 3270 (Fam), [2012] 1 FLR 1211 204, 1178, 1180, 1440, 1871, 2206
Nguyen v Phung [1984] FLR 773, CA 130
NHS Foundation Trust v AB & Ors [2014] EWHC 1031 (Fam) 1547
NHS Trust v A [2007] EWHC 1696 (Fam), [2008] 1 FLR 70 1547
NHS Trust v Baby X [2012] EWHC 2188 (Fam), [2013] 1 FLR 225 1546
NHS Trust v MB (A Child Represented by CAFCASS as Guardian ad Litem), An [2006] EWHC 507 (Fam), [2006] 2 FLR 319 1547
NHS Trust v T (Adult Patient: Refusal of Medical Treatment) [2004] EWHC 1279 (Fam) 2577
Nicholls v Nicholls [1997] 1 WLR 314, [1997] 1 FLR 649, CA 125, 1984
Nightingale v Nightingale [2014] EWHC 77 (Fam), [2014] COPLR 397 1210
Nixon v Fox [1978] Fam 173, FD 1197
NL (Appeal: Interim Care Order: Facts and Reasons), Re [2014] EWHC 270 (Fam), [2014] 1 WLR 2795, [2014] 1 FLR 1384 547, 558, 559, 1533, 1831, 2659
NLW v ARC [2012] EWHC 55 (Fam), [2012] 2 FLR 129 193, 1866
NN v ZZ and ors [2013] EWHC 2261 (Fam) 1764
Norfolk County Council v Webster [2006] EWHC 2898 (Fam), [2007] 2 FLR 415 246, 247, 1543, 1755, 1756, 2586
Norman v Norman [2017] EWCA Civ 49 2049, 2142
Norman v Norman [2017] EWCA Civ 120 212, 1137, 1321, 1762
Norris v Norris [2002] EWHC 2996 (Fam), [2003] 1 FLR 1142 1180
Norris v United States [2010] UKSC 9, [2010] 2 AC 487 1008
North Shore Ventures Limited v Anstead Holdings Inc [2012] EWCA Civ 11 1753
North Somerset Council v LW & Others (Care & RRO) [2014] EWHC 1670 (Fam) 630
North v North [2007] EWCA Civ 760, [2008] 1 FLR 158 1183
North Yorkshire CC v SA [2003] EWCA Civ 839, [2003] 2 FLR 849 537
North Yorkshire County Council v B [2008] 1 FLR 1645, FD 535, 1528
North Yorkshire County Council v G [1993] 2 FLR 732, FD 1500, 1502
Northampton Health Authority v The Official Solicitor and the Governors of St Andrews Hospital [1994] 1 FLR 162, CA 2147
Northamptonshire County Council v AS, KS and DS [2015] EWHC 199 (Fam) 235, 526, 999
Northamptonshire County Council v Islington Borough Council [2001] Fam 364, [1999] 2 FLR 881, CA 540, 638
Norwich Pharmacal v Commissioners of Customs & Excise [1974] AC 133 1757
Nottingham City Council v LM and Others [2016] EWHC 11 (Fam), [2016] 1 WLR 2995, [2016] 2 FLR 1221 529
Nottinghamshire County Council v H [1995] 1 FLR 115, FD 571, 1511, 1512
Nottinghamshire County Council v P [1994] Fam 18, [1993] 2 FLR 134, CA 449, 451, 539, 555
Noueiri v Paragon Finance plc [2001] EWCA Civ 1402, [2001] 1 WLR 2357 1530
NRA and Others, Re [2015] EWCOP 59, [2015] COPLR 690 2065
NS-H v Kingston upon Hull City Council and MC [2008] EWCA Civ 493, [2008] 2 FLR 918 261, 265
Nwogbe v Nwogbe [2000] 2 FLR 744, CA 886, 1930
Nzolameso v Westminster City Council [2015] UKSC 22 486

O (A Child) v Doncaster Metropolitan Borough Council [2014] EWHC 2309 (Admin) 493
O (A Minor) (Abduction: Habitual Residence), Re [1993] 2 FLR 594, FD 379
O (A Minor) (Costs: Liability of Legal Aid Board), Re [1997] 1 FLR 465, CA; *sub nom* Re O (Costs: Liability of Legal Aid Board) 1502
O (A Minor) (Medical Treatment), Re [1993] 2 FLR 149, FD 449, 631, 1547
O (Abduction: Settlement), Re [2011] EWCA Civ 128, [2011] 2 FLR 1307 382

O (Care Proceedings: Evidence), Re [2003] EWHC 2011 (Fam), [2004] 1 FLR 161 541, 629
O (Care: Delay), Re [2001] Fam Law 339, Cty Ct 547
O (Child Abduction: Competing Orders), Re [1997] 2 FLR 712, FD; *sub nom* Re O (Child Abduction: Re-Abduction) 392
O (Child Abduction: Re-Abduction), Re [1997] 2 FLR 712, FD; *sub nom* Re O (Child Abduction: Competing Orders) 392
O (Costs: Liability of Legal Aid Board), Re [1997] 1 FLR 465, CA; *sub nom* Re O (A Minor) (Costs: Liability of Legal Aid Board) 1502
O (Proposed Wardship Proceedings), Re [1990] FCR 599, FD 1245
O (Residence), Re [2012] EWCA Civ 1955, [2014] 1 FLR 89 472
O (Supervision Order), Re [2001] EWCA Civ 16, [2001] 1 FLR 923 540
O (Transracial Adoption: Contact), Re [1995] 2 FLR 597, FD 569
O and J (Paternity: Blood Tests), Re [2000] Fam 139, [2000] 1 FLR 418, FD 922
O and N (Children) (Non Accidental Injury), Re [2003] UKHL 18, [2004] 1 AC 523, [2003] 1 FLR 1169; *sub nom* Re O and N; Re B 535, 537
O and N, Re; Re B [2003] UKHL 18, [2004] 1 AC 523, [2003] 1 FLR 1169; *sub nom* Re O and N (Children) (Non Accidental Injury) 535, 537
O v O (Procedure for Listing Applications for Permission to Appeal to the High Court) [2011] EWHC 14 July 2011 (unreported) 1865, 1866
O v P (Jurisdiction under Children Act 1989 Sch 1) [2011] EWHC 2425 (Fam), [2012] 1 FLR 329 415
O v P (No 2) (Sch 1 Application: Stay: Forum Conveniens) [2014] EWHC 2225 (Fam), [2015] 2 FLR 77 649
O'Brien v Ministry of Justice; Walker v Innospec [2015] EWCA Civ 1000, [2016] ICR 182 702
O'Driscoll v Manchester Insurance Committee [1915] 3 KB 499, CA 2291
O'Farrell v O'Farrell [2012] EWHC 123 (QB), [2013] 1 FLR 77 1204, 1242, 1744, 2299
O'Regan v Iambic Productions Ltd (1989) 139 NLJ 1378, HC 1241
O-C (Children), Re [2013] EWCA Civ 162 558
Oaktree Financial Services Ltd v Higham [2004] EWHC 2098 (Ch) 1241
OB (Private Law Proceedings: Costs), Re [2013] EWHC 1956 (Fam), [2016] 1 FLR 92 227, 556, 1524
Oceanica Castelana Armadora SA v Mineralimportexport (Barclays Bank International Intervening), The Theotokos [1983] 1 WLR 1302, CA 1242
Official Solicitor to the Senior Courts v Yemoh and others [2010] EWHC 3727 (Ch), [2011] 1 WLR 1450, [2011] 2 FLR 371 1015
Official Solicitor v K [1965] AC 201, (1963) FLR Rep 520, HL 1509, 1510
Olafisoye v Olafisoye (Jurisdiction) [2010] EWHC 3539 (Fam), [2011] 2 FLR 553 1014, 2776
Oldham Metropolitan Borough Council v GW and PW [2007] EWHC 136 (Fam), [2007] 2 FLR 597 2586
Omotajo v Omotajo [2008] All ER (D) 156 (Oct), QBD 1260
Oral Contraceptive Group Litigation XYZ & Ors v Schering Health Care Ltd & Ors [2004] EWHC 823 (QB) 1290
Orwell Steel (Erection and Fabrication) Ltd v Asphalt and Tarmac (UK) Ltd [1984] 1 WLR 1097, QBD 1240
OS v DS (Oral Disclosure: Preliminary Hearing) [2004] EWHC 2376 (Fam), [2005] 1 FLR 675 1439, 1762
Osman v United Kingdom [1999] 1 FLR 193, ECHR 1004
Otkritie International Investment Management Ltd v Olessia Jemai [2016] EWCA Civ 1316 791
Otobo v Otobo [2002] EWCA Civ 949, [2003] 1 FLR 192 828
Owens v Owens [2017] EWCA Civ 182 1148
Owusu v Jackson (Case C-281 /02) [2005] ECR I-1383, [2005] QB 801, ECJ 828, 2776
Oxfordshire County Council v L (Care or Supervision Order) [1998] 1 FLR 70, FD 539, 540
Oxfordshire County Council v L and F [1997] 1 FLR 235, FD 569, 629
Oxfordshire County Council v M [1994] Fam 151, [1994] 1 FLR 175, CA 1532
Oxfordshire County Council v P [1995] Fam 161, [1995] 1 FLR 552, FD 629
Oxfordshire County Council v R [1992] Fam 150, [1992] 1 FLR 648, FD; *sub nom* R v Oxfordshire County Council (Secure Accommodation Order) 1540, 1831
Oxfordshire County Council v R [1997] Fam Law 828, FD 1832
Oxfordshire County Council v S [2000] Fam Law 20, FD 619
Oxfordshire County Council v S [2003] EWHC 2174 (Fam), [2004] 1 FLR 426 1832
Oxfordshire County Council v X, Y and J [2010] EWCA Civ 581, [2011] Fam 31, [2011] 1 FLR 272 206, 287, 1502, 1871, 2205
Oxley v Hiscock [2004] EWCA Civ 546, [2005] Fam 211, [2004] 2 FLR 669 1262, 1263

P (A Child) (Mirror Orders), Re [2000] 1 FLR 435, FD; *sub nom* Re P (Jurisdiction: Mirror Order) 839
P (A Child), Re [2013] EWCA Civ 963, [2014] 1 FLR 824 538, 1871, 2205

P (A Child), Re [2014] EWCA Civ 888 204, 527, 2195
P (A Minor) (Ex Parte Interim Residence Order), Re [1993] 1 FLR 915, CA 146, 1235, 1522, 1524
P (A Minor) (Wardship: Sterilisation), Re [1989] 1 FLR 182, FD 1547
P (A Minor), Re [1986] 1 FLR 272, FD 1547
P (Abduction: Consent), Re [2004] EWCA Civ 971, [2005] 1 Fam 293, [2004] 2 FLR 1057 379, 388
P (Abduction: Declaration), Re [1995] 1 FLR 831, CA 376, 392
P (Adoption: Breach of Care Plan), Re [2004] EWCA Civ 355, [2004] 2 FLR 1109 999
P (Adoption: Leave Provisions), Re [2007] EWCA Civ 616, [2007] 1 WLR 2556, [2007] 2 FLR 1069 265, 282
P (By His Litigation Friend the Official Solicitor) v Cheshire West and Chester Council and Another; P and Q (By Their Litigation Friend the Official Solicitor) v Surrey County Council [2014] UKSC 19, [2014] 1 AC 896, [2014] COPLR 313 494, 1006, 1547
P (Care Orders: Injunctive Relief), Re [2000] 2 FLR 385, FD 544, 632
P (Care Proceedings: Appeal), Re [2016] EWCA Civ 3, [2017] 1 FLR 417 539
P (Care Proceedings: Father's Application to be Joined as Party), Re [2001] 1 FLR 781, FD 1501
P (Care Proceedings: Split Hearings), Re [2007] EWCA Civ 1265 534, 1508
P (Change of Surname: Parent's Rights), Re [1997] 2 FLR 730, FD; *sub nom* Re PC (Change of Surname) 447, 448, 449
P (Child: Financial Provision), Re [2003] EWCA Civ 837, [2003] 2 FLR 865 406, 407, 649, 650
P (Children Act 1989, ss 22 and 26: Local Authority Compliance), Re [2000] 2 FLR 910, FD 498, 517, 619
P (Contact: Disclosure), Re [1998] 2 FLR 696, FD; *sub nom* Re P (Contact: Discretion) 1831
P (Contact: Discretion), Re [1998] 2 FLR 696, FD; *sub nom* Re P (Contact: Disclosure) 1831
P (Contact: Supervision), Re [1996] 2 FLR 314, CA 446
P (Custody of Children: Split Custody Order), Re [1991] 1 FLR 337, CA 438
P (Emergency Protection Order), Re [1996] 1 FLR 482, FD 578
P (Enforced Caesarean: Reporting Restrictions), Re [2013] EWHC 4048 (Fam), [2014] 2 FLR 410 628, 1543, 2568
P (Findings of Fact), Re [2014] EWCA Civ 89 537
P (Forced Marriage), Re [2011] EWHC 3467 (Fam), [2011] 1 FLR 2060 899
P (GE) (An Infant), Re [1965] Ch 568, CA 638
P (Jurisdiction: Mirror Order), Re [2000] 1 FLR 435, FD; *sub nom* Re P (A Child) (Mirror Orders) 839
P (Minors) (Adoption by Step-Parent), Re [1989] 1 FLR 1, CA; *sub nom* Re P (Minors) (Adoption) 1659
P (Minors) (Adoption), Re [1989] 1 FLR 1, CA; *sub nom* Re P (Minors) (Adoption by Step-Parent) 1659
P (Minors) (Contact with Children in Care), Re [1993] 2 FLR 156, FD 552, 663
P (Minors) (Interim Order), Re [1993] 2 FLR 742, CA 560, 664
P (Parental Dispute: Judicial Determination), Re [2002] EWCA Civ 1627, [2003] 1 FLR 286 450
P (Placement Orders: Parental Consent), Re [2008] EWCA Civ 535, [2008] 2 FLR 625 261, 267, 287, 289
P (Recognition and Registration of Orders under the Hague Child Protection Convention), Re [2014] EWHC 2845 (Fam) 1898, 1899, 2742, 2743
P (Representation), Re [1996] 1 FLR 486, CA 1705
P (Residence: Appeal), Re [2007] EWCA Civ 1053, [2008] 1 FLR 198 205, 566
P (Section 91(14) Guidelines) (Residence and Religious Heritage), Re [2000] Fam 15, [1999] 2 FLR 573, CA 619, 620
P (Shared Residence Order), Re [2005] EWCA Civ 1639, [2006] 2 FLR 347 442
P (Step-Parent Adoption), Re [2014] EWCA Civ 1174, [2015] 1 WLR 2927, [2015] 1 FLR 1327 285
P (Witness Summons), Re [1997] 2 FLR 447, CA 1530, 2431
P and B v Z [2016] EWHC 1594 (Fam) 990
P and L (Contact), Re [2011] EWHC 3431 (Fam), [2012] 1 FLR 1068 702
P and Ors (Adoption: Unmarried Couple), Re [2008] UKHL 38, [2009] 1 AC 173, [2008] 2 FLR 1084 996
P v A Local Authority [2016] EWHC 2779 (Fam) 1043, 1044
P v G (Family Law Act 1986: Jurisdiction) [2010] EWHC 1311 (Fam), [2010] 2 FLR 1888 855
P v G, P and P (Family Provision: Relevance of Divorce Provision) [2004] EWHC 2944 (Fam), [2006] 1 FLR 431 1017, 1020
P v P (Financial Relief: Illiquid Assets) [2004] EWHC 2277 (Fam), [2005] 1 FLR 548 1179, 1181
P v P (Financial Relief: Procedure) [2008] EWHC 2953 (Fam) [2009] 1 FLR 696 1439
P v P (Financial Remedies: Disclosure) [2012] EWHC 1733 (Fam), [2013] 1 FLR 1003 1440
P v P (Post-Separation Accruals and Earning Capacity) [2007] EWHC 2877 (Fam), [2008] 2 FLR 1135 1180
P v P (Variation of Post-Nuptial Settlement) [2015] EWCA Civ 447, [2016] 1 FLR 437 1172
P, C and S v UK (2002) 35 EHRR 1075, [2002] 2 FLR 631 1007, 1529

P, Re (Case C-455/15) [2016] 1 FLR 337, CJEU 2789
P-B (Placement Order), Re [2006] EWCA Civ 1016, [2007] 1 FLR 1106 264
P-J (Abduction: Habitual Residence: Consent), Re [2009] EWCA Civ 588, [2010] 1 WLR 1237, [2009] 2 FLR 1051 389, 841
P-M (Parental Order: Payments to Surrogacy Agency), Re [2013] EWHC 2328 (Fam), [2014] 1 FLR 725 991
P-S, Re [2013] EWCA Civ 223, [2013] 1 WLR 3831, [2014] 2 FLR 27 424, 570
Packman Lucas Ltd v (1) Mentmore Towers Ltd (2) Charles Street Holdings Ltd [2010] EWHC 1037 (TCC) 2298
Pakhomova v Russia (Application No 22935/11) [2014] 2 FLR 44, ECHR 1007
Palmer (dec'd) (a debtor), Re [1994] Ch 316, [1994] 2 FLR 609, CA; *sub nom* Re Palmer (Deceased) (Insolvent Estate) 1029
Palmer (Deceased) (Insolvent Estate), Re [1994] Ch 316, [1994] 2 FLR 609, CA; *sub nom* Re Palmer (dec'd) (a debtor) 1029
Papamichalopoulos v Greece (1993) 16 EHRR 440 1011
Park, Re, ex parte Koster (1885) 14 QBD 597, CA 1933
Parkes v Legal Aid Board [1997] 1 WLR 1547, [1997] 1 FLR 77, CA 1043
Parra v Parra [2002] EWCA Civ 1886, [2003] 1 FLR 942 1440
Parris v Williams [2008] EWCA Civ 1147, [2009] BPIR 96 1263
Parry-Jones v Law Society [1969] 1 Ch 1, CA 1753
Parsons v Nasar [1990] 2 FLR 103, CA 797
Paton v United Kingdom (Application 8416/78) (1980) 3 EHRR 408; *sub nom* X v UK 960
Paulin v Paulin [2009] EWCA Civ 221, [2010] 1 WLR 1057, [2009] 2 FLR 354 1173, 1209, 1211, 1241, 1857
Payne v Payne [2001] EWCA Civ 166, [2001] Fam 473, [2001] 1 FLR 1052 442, 471, 472, 473, 528
PB v SE [2013] EWHC 647 (Fam), [2013] 2 FLR 1584; *sub nom* Re S (Jurisdiction: Prorogation) 524, 2782, 2783
PC (Change of Surname), Re [1997] 2 FLR 730, FD; *sub nom* Re P (Change of Surname: Parent's Rights) 447, 448, 449
Peagram v Peagram [1926] 2 KB 165 1093
Pearce (Deceased), Re [1998] 2 FLR 705, CA 1019
Pearce v Pearce (1980) 1 FLR 261, CA 1203
Pearce v Pearce [2003] EWCA Civ 1054, [2004] 1 WLR 68, [2003] 2 FLR 1144 1203
Peek v Peek [1948] P 46 212, 213, 1400
Pelling v Bruce-Williams (Secretary of State for Constitutional Affairs Intervening) [2004] EWCA Civ 845, [2004] Fam 155, [2004] 2 FLR 823 248, 1516, 2586
Peng v Chai [2015] EWCA Civ 1312, [2017] 1 FLR 318 828, 2776
Penrose v Penrose [1994] 2 FLR 621, CA 1202
Pepper v Pepper [1960] 1 WLR 131, PDAD 343
Perdoni v Curati [2011] EWHC 3442 (Ch) 1014
Perez-Adamson v Perez-Rivas [1987] Fam 89, [1987] 2 FLR 472, CA 877
Peyman-Fard v Peyman-Fard [2011] EWCA Civ 959 1210, 1242
PG v TW (No 1) (Child: Financial Provision: Legal Funding) [2012] EWHC 1892 (Fam), [2014] 1 FLR 508 646, 1165
PG v TW (No 2) (Child: Financial Provision) [2014] 1 FLR 923, FD 645
PGF II SA v OMFS Company 1 Ltd [2013] EWCA Civ 1288, [2014] 1 WLR 1386 1307, 2141
Phillips v Peace [1996] 2 FLR 230, FD 648
Phillips v Symes [2004] EWHC 2330 (Ch), [2005] 1 WLR 2043 1795
Pidduck v Molloy [1992] 2 FLR 202, CA 130
Piglowska v Piglowski [1999] 1 WLR 1360, [1999] 2 FLR 763, HL 192, 203
Pike v Teachers Pension Scheme (2008) 26 March, ref 26355, Pensions Ombudsman 1175
Pilcher v Pilcher [1955] P 318, PDAD 65, 1080
Piller (Anton) KG v Manufacturing Processes Ltd [1976] Ch 55, CA 790, 1240
Pine Valley Developments Ltd v Ireland (1992) 14 EHRR 319 1011
PJ (Adoption: Practice on Appeal), Re [1998] 2 FLR 252, CA 2869
PJS v News Group Newspapers Ltd [2016] UKSC 26, [2016] 1 AC 1081, [2016] 2 FLR 251 2049, 2142
PJSC Vseukrainskyi v Aktsionernyi Bank [2014] EWHC 3771 (Comm) 129, 1243
PK v BC (Financial Remedies: Schedule 1) [2012] EWHC 1382 (Fam), [2012] 2 FLR 1426 645
Pla and Puncernau v Andorra (Application No 69498/01) [2004] 2 FCR 630, ECHR 1015
Plumex v Young Sports NV (Case C-473/04) [2006] ECR I-1417, ECJ 2822, 2828
Plummer v IRC [1988] 1 WLR 292, ChD 826
Plymouth County Council v C [2000] 1 FLR 875, CA; *sub nom* C (A Child) v Plymouth County Council 540, 638
Polanski (Roman) v Conde Nast Publications Ltd [2005] UKHL 10, [2005] 1 WLR 637 1763
Poole BC v Hambridge [2007] EWCA Civ 990 793
Poon v Poon [1994] 2 FLR 857, FD 877

Portsmouth NHS Trust v Wyatt [2005] EWHC 2293 (Fam), [2006] 1 FLR 652 1546
Pounds v Pounds [1994] 1 WLR 1535, [1994] 1 FLR 775, CA 1152, 1153, 1168, 1395
Povse v Alpago (Case C-211/10) [2010] ECR I-06673, [2011] Fam 199, [2010] 2 FLR 1343, ECJ 384, 2780, 2782, 2795
Prazic v Prazic [2006] EWCA Civ 497, [2006] 2 FLR 1128 1261, 1358, 2857, 2869
Prest v Petrodel Resources Ltd & Others [2013] UKSC 34, [2013] 2 AC 415, [2013] 2 FLR 732 1023, 1171
Prest v Prest (Judgment Summons: Appeal) [2015] EWCA Civ 714, [2016] 1 FLR 773 413, 1762
Prest v Prest [2014] EWHC 3430 (Fam) 1933, 1934
Pretty v UK [2002] ECHR 427, (2002) 35 EHRR 1, [2002] 2 FLR 45 1004
Price v Price [2014] EWCA Civ 655, [2015] 1 FLR 1202 1324
Pritchard v Cobden Ltd and Another (No 1) [1988] Fam 22, [1987] 2 FLR 30, CA 1182
Purrucker v Vallés Pérez (No 1) (Case C-256/09) [2010] ECR I-7353, [2011] Fam 254, [2012] 1 FLR 903, CJEU 369, 2787
Purrucker v Vallés Pérez (No 2) (Case C-296/10) [2010] ECR I-11163, [2011] Fam 312, [2012] 1 FLR 925, CJEU 2786

Q (Implacable Contact Dispute), Re [2015] EWCA Civ 991, [2016] 2 FLR 287 444, 445, 1323
Q (Parental Order), Re [1996] 1 FLR 369, FD 1016
Q (Parental Order: Domicile), Re [2014] EWHC 1307 (Fam), [2015] 1 FLR 704 989, 990
Q v Q (Contact: Undertakings) (No 3) [2016] EWFC 5, [2017] 1 FLR 438, FD 445
Q v Q (Funding of Representation and Expert Attendance) [2014] EWFC 7, [2015] 1 FLR 318 439
Q v Q [2008] EWHC 1874 (Fam), [2009] 1 FLR 935 1262
Quigley v Masterson [2011] EWHC 2529 (Ch) 1029

R (A Child), Re [2003] EWCA Civ 182, [2003] Fam 129, [2003] 1 FLR 1183; *sub nom* Re R (Paternity: IVF Baby); *sub nom* Re R (IVF: Paternity of Child) 870
R (A Child), Re [2013] EWCA Civ 899 536
R (A Child), Re [2014] EWCA Civ 270 203
R (A Child), Re [2014] EWCA Civ 597 194, 207, 1871, 2206
R (A Minor) (Abduction), Re [1992] 1 FLR 105, FD 391
R (A Minor) (Adoption: Parental Agreement), Re [1987] 1 FLR 391, CA 799
R (A Minor) (Blood Transfusion), Re [1993] 2 FLR 757, FD; *sub nom* Camden London Borough Council v R (A Minor) (Blood Transfusion) 449, 1522, 1547
R (A Minor) (Contempt), Re [1994] 1 WLR 487, [1994] 2 FLR 185, CA 792
R (A Minor) (Court Welfare Report), Re [1993] Fam Law 722, CA 437
R (A Minor) (Residence: Religion), Re [1993] 2 FLR 163, CA 1531
R (A Minor) (Wardship: Consent to Treatment), Re [1992] Fam 11, [1992] 1 FLR 190, CA; *sub nom* Re R (A Minor) (Wardship: Medical Treatment) 918, 919, 1547
R (A Minor) (Wardship: Medical Treatment), Re [1992] Fam 11, [1992] 1 FLR 190, CA; *sub nom* Re R (A Minor) (Wardship: Consent to Treatment) 918, 919, 1547
R (A Minor) (Wardship: Restrictions on Publication), Re [1994] Fam 254, [1994] 2 FLR 637, CA; *sub nom* Re R (Wardship: Restrictions on Publication) 247
R (A) v Coventry City Council [2009] EWHC 34 (Admin), [2009] 1 FLR 1202 493
R (A) v Croydon London Borough Council; R (M) v Lambeth London Borough Council [2008] EWCA Civ 1445, [2009] 1 FLR 1324 1006
R (A) v London Borough of Croydon [2008] EWHC 2921 (Admin), [2009] 2 FLR 173 486
R (A) v London Borough of Croydon; R (M) v London Borough of Lambeth [2009] UKSC 8, [2009] 1 WLR 2557, [2010] 1 FLR 959 486, 658
R (AB and SB) v Nottingham City Council [2001] EWHC Admin 235 486
R (AB) v Secretary of State for Justice and another [2009] EWHC 2220 (Admin) 953
R (Abduction: Hague and European Conventions), Re [1997] 1 FLR 663, CA 394, 395
R (Abduction: Immigration Concerns), Re [2004] EWHC 2042 (Fam), [2005] 1 FLR 33 383
R (AC) v Birmingham City Council [2008] EWHC 3036 (Admin), [2009] 1 FLR 838 1516
R (Adoption: Contact), Re [2005] EWCA Civ 1128, [2006] 1 FLR 373 287
R (Adoption: Disclosure), Re [1999] 2 FLR 1123, FD 1653
R (Al Jedda) v Secretary of State for Defence [2007] UKHL 58, [2008] 1 AC 332 993
R (Axon) v The Secretary of State for Health and the Family Planning Association [2006] EWHC 37 (Admin), [2006] QB 539, [2006] 2 FLR 206 919
R (B) v Merton London Borough Council [2003] EWHC 1689 (Admin), [2003] 2 FLR 888 486
R (Baiai & Others) v Secretary of State for the Home Department [2008] UKHL 53, [2009] 1 AC 287, [2008] 2 FLR 1462 996, 1010, 2057
R (Bewry) v Norfolk County Council [2010] EWHC 2545 (Admin), [2011] 1 FLR 945 498
R (Bizzy B Management Ltd) v Stockton-on-Tees Borough Council) [2011] EWHC 2325 (Admin) 1011

R (C) v Knowsley Metropolitan Borough Council [2008] EWHC 2551 (Admin), [2009] 1 FLR 493 493
R (C) v Secretary of State for Work and Pensions [2016] EWCA Civ 47 944
R (Care Proceedings: Appeal), Re [2011] EWCA Civ 1795, [2013] 1 FLR 467 2196
R (Care Proceedings: Disclosure), Re [2000] 2 FLR 751, FD 571
R (Care: Disclosure: Nature of Proceedings), Re [2002] 1 FLR 755, FD 526, 534, 570, 1507, 1511, 1512, 1526, 1534, 1754
R (Casey) v Restormel Borough Council [2007] EWHC 2554 (Admin) 449, 2721
R (Child Abduction: Acquiescence), Re [1995] 1 FLR 716, CA 389, 2781
R (Child of a Teenage Mother), Re [2000] 2 FLR 660, FD 531
R (Children), Re [2014] EWCA Civ 1110 205, 2196
R (Children), Re [2015] EWCA Civ 167 536, 542, 625
R (Children: Peremptory Return), Re [2011] EWCA Civ 558, [2011] 2 FLR 863 194, 205, 1522, 1870, 2198
R (CJ) v Cardiff City Council [2011] EWCA Civ 1590 534
R (Contact: Consent Order), Re [1995] 1 WLR 184, [1995] 1 FLR 123, CA 1235
R (Court of Appeal: Order Against Identification), Re [1999] 2 FLR 145, CA 1516
R (Dinjan Hysaj) v The Home Secretary [2014] EWCA Civ 1633 1324
R (E) v Governing Body of JFS and the Admissions Appeal Panel of JFS and others [2009] UKSC 1, [2009] 1 WLR 2353 199, 2194
R (Equality & Human Rights Commission) v Secretary of State for Justice and anor [2010] EWHC 147 (Admin) 411
R (Eunice Johns & Owen Johns) v Derby City Council & Othrs [2011] EWHC 375 (Admin), [2011] 1 FLR 2094 1009
R (F) v Lewisham London Borough Council; R (D) v Manchester City Council; Secretary of State (Interested Party) and Others [2009] EWHC 3542 (Admin), [2010] 1 FLR 1463 486
R (Fact-Finding Hearing), Re [2009] EWCA Civ 1619, [2009] 2 FLR 83 445
R (Family Proceedings: No Case to Answer), Re [2008] EWCA Civ 1619, [2009] 2 FLR 83 1528
R (Faulkner) v Director of Legal Aid Casework [2016] EWHC 717 (Admin) 1043
R (G) v Barnet London Borough Council; R (W) v Lambeth London Borough Council; R (A) v Lambeth London Borough Council [2003] UKHL 57, [2004] 2 AC 208, [2004] 1 FLR 454 485
R (G) v Nottingham City Council [2008] EWHC 152 (Admin), [2008] 1 FLR 1660 559
R (G) v Nottingham City Council and Nottingham University Hospital [2008] EWHC 400 (Admin), [2008] 1 FLR 1668 507, 528, 529, 665
R (G) v Southwark London Borough Council [2009] UKHL 26, [2009] 1 WLR 1299, [2009] 2 FLR 380 493
R (Green) v Secretary of State for Work and Pensions [2010] EWHC 1278 (Admin) 407
R (Greenfield) v Secretary of State for the Home Department [2005] UKHL 14, [2005] 1 WLR 673 1001
R (Guardian News and Media Ltd) v City of Westminster Magistrates' Court [2012] EWCA Civ 420, [2013] QB 618 1755, 1756
R (Gunn) v Secretary of State for the Home Department [2001] EWCA Civ 891, [2001] 1 WLR 1634 2150
R (H) v Kingston upon Hull City Council [2013] EWHC 388 (Admin), [2014] 1 FLR 1094 189, 234, 999, 2254
R (Habitual Residence), Re [2014] EWCA Civ 1032, [2015] 2 FLR 124 377
R (Hooper) v Secretary of State for Work & Pensions [2005] UKHL 29, [2005] 1 WLR 1681 997
R (Hussain) v Birmingham City Council [2002] EWHC 949 (Admin) 2063
R (Identification: Restrictions on Publication), Re [2007] EWHC 2742 (Fam), [2008] 1 FLR 1252 627
R (Inter-Country Adoptions: Practice), Re [1999] 1 WLR 1324, [1999] 1 FLR 1042, FD 279, 1654
R (Internal Relocation: Appeal), Re [2016] EWCA Civ 1016 472
R (IVF: Paternity of Child), Re [2003] EWCA Civ 182, [2003] Fam 129, [2003] 1 FLR 1183; *sub nom* R (A Child), Re; *sub nom* Re R (Paternity: IVF Baby) 870
R (IVF: Paternity of Child), Re [2003] EWCA Civ 182, [2003] Fam 129, [2003] 1 FLR 1183; *sub nom* Re R (A Child), Re; *sub nom* Re R (Paternity: IVF Baby) 870
R (J) v Caerphilly County Borough Council [2005] EWHC 586 (Admin), [2005] 2 FLR 860 507, 666
R (Kadri) v Birmingham City Council & Othrs [2012] EWCA Civ 1432, [2013] 1 WLR 1755 658
R (Kehoe) v Secretary of State for Work and Pensions [2005] UKHL 48, [2006] 1 AC 42, [2005] 2 FLR 1249 407, 412, 1006
R (Kelly) v Warley Magistrates Court [2007] EWHC Admin 1836, [2008] 1 WLR 2001 1753
R (L) v Commissioner of the Metropolis [2009] UKSC 3, [2010] 1 AC 410, [2010] 1 FLR 643 994
R (Leave to Remove: Contact), Re [2010] EWCA Civ 1137, [2011] 1 FLR 1336 471
R (LH and MH) v London Borough of Lambeth [2006] EWHC 1190 (Admin), [2006] 2 FLR 1275 658
R (Lydia Playfoot) v Millais School Governing Body [2007] EWHC 1698 (Admin), [2007] ELR 484 996, 2057

R (M and MM) v Human Fertilisation and Embryology Authority [2015] EWHC 1706 (Admin), [2016] 1 FLR 1211 967
R (M) v Birmingham City Council [2008] EWHC 1863 (Admin), [2009] 1 FLR 1068 656
R (M) v Gateshead Council [2006] EWCA Civ 221, [2006] QB 650, [2006] 2 FLR 379 496
R (M) v Hammersmith and Fulham London Borough Council [2008] UKHL 14, [2008] 1 WLR 535, [2008] 1 FLR 1384 497
R (M) v Human Fertilisation and Embryology Authority [2016] EWCA Civ 611, [2017] 1 FLR 452 967
R (M) v London Borough of Barnet [2008] EWHC 2354 (Admin), [2009] 2 FLR 725 494
R (M) v London Borough of Bromley [2002] EWCA Civ 1113, [2002] 2 FLR 802 605, 1239
R (Mazim Jumaa Gatteh Al Skeina & Others) v The Secretary of State for Defence [2007] UKHL 26, [2008] 1 AC 153 992
R (Minors) (Abduction), Re [1994] 1 FLR 190, FD 376
R (Minors) (Custody), Re [1986] 1 FLR 6, CA 437, 2204
R (Mount Cook Land Ltd) v Westminster City Council [2003] EWCA Civ 1346 2146
R (O) v East Riding of Yorkshire County Council (Secretary of State for Education Intervening) [2011] EWCA Civ 196, [2011] 2 FLR 207 494
R (O) v London Borough of Barking and Dagenham (SSHD and the Children's Society Intervening) [2010] EWCA Civ 1101, [2011] 1 WLR 1283, [2011] 1 FLR 734 505
R (O) v London Borough of Hammersmith and Fulham [2011] EWCA Civ 925, [2012] 1 WLR 1057, [2012] 2 FLR 290 2254
R (on the application of (1) C (2) T (3) M (4) U) (Appellant) v Southwark London Borough Council (Respondent) & Coram Children's Legal Centre (Intervener) [2016] EWCA Civ 707 486
R (on the application of JK) v Registrar General for England & Wales & Ors [2015] EWHC 990 (Admin) 448, 944
R (Parental Responsibility), Re [2011] EWHC 1535 (Fam), [2011] 2 FLR 1132 428, 431
R (Pretty) v DPP [2001] UKHL 61, [2002] 1 AC 800, [2002] 1 FLR 268 1004
R (Prohibited Steps Order), Re [2013] EWCA Civ 1115, [2014] 1 FLR 643 473
R (Purdy) v DPP [2009] UKHL 45, [2010] 1 AC 345 1005, 1007
R (Quila); R (Bibi) v Secretary of State for the Home Department [2011] UKSC 45, [2012] 1 AC 621, [2012] 1 FLR 788 1008
R (Quintavelle) v Human Fertilisation and Embryology Authority [2005] UKHL 28, [2005] 2 AC 561, [2005] 2 FLR 349 962, 963
R (Quintavelle) v Human Fertilisation and Embryology Authority (Secretary of State for Health Intervening) [2003] EWCA Civ 667, [2004] QB 168, [2003] 2 FLR 335 974
R (Quintavelle) v Secretary of State for Health [2002] EWCA Civ 29, [2002] QB 628 960
R (Razgar) v Secretary of State for the Home Department [2004] UKHL 27, [2004] 2 AC 368 1007
R (Recovery Orders), Re [1998] 2 FLR 401, FD 585
R (Residence Order), Re [2009] EWCA Civ 445, [2010] 1 FLR 509 438
R (Residence: Contact: Restricting Applications), Re [1998] 1 FLR 749, CA 620
R (Residence: Shared Care: Children's Views), Re [2005] EWCA Civ 542, [2006] 1 FLR 491 441
R (Rights of Women) v Secretary of State for Justice [2016] EWCA Civ 91, [2016] 1 WLR 2543, [2017] 1 FLR 615 440
R (Rusbridger) v Attorney General [2003] UKHL 38, [2004] AC 35 995
R (S) v Sutton London Borough Council [2007] EWHC 1196 (Admin), [2007] 2 FLR 849 494, 665
R (Secure Editing of Documents), Re [2007] EWHC 876 (Fam), [2007] 1 WLR 1654, [2007] 2 FLR 759 627, 1526
R (Sinclair Collis Ltd) v Secretary of State for Health [2011] EWCA Civ 437, [2012] 1 QB 394, [2011] LLR 592 1011
R (Sivasubramaniam) v Wandsworth County Court [2002] EWCA Civ 1738, [2003] 1 WLR 475 1134
R (Smith) v Secretary of State for Defence and Secretary of State for Work and Pensions [2004] EWCA Civ 1664 (unreported); [2004] EWHC 1797 (Admin), [2005] 1 FLR 97 1174
R (Surname: Using Both Parents'), Re [2001] EWCA Civ 1344, [2001] 2 FLR 1358 447
R (Teresa Gudanaviciene & 5 Ors) (Claimants /Respondents) v (1) Director of Legal Aid Casework (2) Lord Chancellor (Defendants /Appellants) & British Red Cross Society (Intervener) [2014] EWCA Civ 1622, [2015] 1 WLR 2247 439
R (TG) v Lambeth Borough Council [2011] EWCA Civ 526, [2011] 2 FLR 1007 485
R (Thomas) v Ministry of Defence [2008] EWHC 1119 (Admin), [2008] 2 FLR 1385 1174
R (Translation of Documents in Proceedings), Re [2015] EWFC B112; *sub nom* Suffolk County Council v M, F and child 1511
R (TT) v London Borough of Merton [2012] EWHC 2055 (Admin) 480
R (VC) v Newcastle City Council and Secretary of State for the Home Department [2011] EWHC 2673 (Admin), [2012] 1 FLR 944 485, 486

R (W) v North Lincolnshire Council [2008] EWHC 2299 (Admin), [2008] 2 FLR 2150 493
R (Wardship: Child Abduction) (No 2), Re [1993] 1 FLR 249, FD 378
R (Wardship: Child Abduction), Re [1992] 2 FLR 481, CA 378
R (Wardship: Restrictions on Publication), Re [1994] Fam 254, [1994] 2 FLR 637, CA; *sub nom* Re R (A Minor) (Wardship: Restrictions on Publication) 247
R (Wright & others) v Secretary of State for Health [2009] UKHL 3, [2009] 1 AC 739 995
R (Wright) v Secretary of State of the Home Department [2006] EWCA Civ 67 234
R (X) v Governors of Y School [2007] EWHC 298 (Admin), [2007] ELR 278 996, 2058
R and H v United Kingdom (Application No 35348/06) [2011] 2 FLR 1236, ECHR 528
R and Others v Cafcass [2012] EWCA Civ 853, [2013] 1 WLR 163, [2012] 2 FLR 1432 808, 1696
R and R v A (Costs in Children Proceedings) [2011] EWHC 1158 (Fam), [2011] 2 FLR 672 1548
R and S v T (Surrogacy: Service, Consent and Payments) [2015] EWFC 22 991
R v A (AJ) [2013] EWCA Crim 591, [2013] 2 FLR 1383 36, 1230, 1231
R v A [2001] UKHL 25, [2002] 1 AC 45 994, 1006
R v B County Council ex parte P [1991] 1 WLR 221, [1991] 1 FLR 470, CA 437, 541, 624, 625, 626
R v Barker [2010] EWCA Crim 4 624, 2635
R v Barnet Borough Council ex parte Shah [1983] 2 AC 309, HL 2778
R v Boness; R v Bebbington [2005] EWCA Crim 2395 29, 887
R v Bow Street Metropolitan Stipendiary Magistrate, ex p Pinochet Ugarte (No 2) [2000] 1 AC 119, HL 212
R v Central Criminal Court ex parte Godwin and Crook [1995] 1 WLR 139, [1995] 1 FLR 132, CA 247
R v Central Independent Television plc [1994] Fam 192, [1994] 2 FLR 151, CA; *sub nom* Mrs R v Central Independent Television plc 1544
R v Chief Constable of Cheshire ex parte K [1990] 1 FLR 70, QBD 158, 858
R v Chief Constable of West Midlands Police ex parte Wiley; R v Chief Constable of Nottinghamshire, ex parte Sunderland [1995] 1 AC 274, HL 1511, 1512, 1754
R v Children and Family Court Advisory and Support Service [2003] EWHC 235 (Admin), [2003] 1 FLR 953 569, 1505
R v Cornwall County Council ex parte Cornwall and Isles of Scilly Guardians ad Litem and Reporting Officers Panel [1992] 1 WLR 427, [1992] 1 FLR 270, QBD; *sub nom* R v Cornwall County Council ex parte G 1704
R v Cornwall County Council ex parte G [1992] 1 WLR 427, [1992] 1 FLR 270, QBD; *sub nom* R v Cornwall County Council ex parte Cornwall and Isles of Scilly Guardians ad Litem and Reporting Officers Panel 1704
R v Cornwall County Council ex parte LH [2000] 1 FLR 236, QBD 531
R v Cripps ex parte Muldoon [1984] 1 QB 686, CA 1859
R v Derby Magistrates Court ex parte B [1996] AC 487, [1996] 1 FLR 513, HL 1753
R v Derby Magistrates' Court ex parte B [1996] AC 487, [1996] 1 FLR 513, HL 625
R v Director of Serious Fraud Office, ex parte Smith [1993] AC 1, HL 1753
R v E and F (Female Parents: Known Father) [2010] EWHC 417 (Fam), [2010] 2 FLR 383 428, 702
R v East Sussex County Council, ex parte W [1998] 2 FLR 1082, QBD 517, 611
R v F (Schedule One: Child Maintenance: Mother's Costs of Contact Proceedings) [2011] 2 FLR 991, FD 646
R v Farooqi & Ors [2013] EWCA Crim 1649 2704
R v Hampshire County Council, ex parte H [1999] 2 FLR 359, CA 611
R v Hayes [1977] 1 WLR 234, CA 625
R v Hereford and Worcester County Council ex p D [1992] 1 FLR 448, QBD 498
R v Hills [2001] 1 FLR 580, CA 1230
R v Horncastle [2009] UKSC 14, [2010] 2 AC 373 993
R v Human Fertilisation and Embryology Authority ex parte Blood [1999] Fam 151, [1997] 2 FLR 742, CA 963, 1016
R v Hurst (Judge Sir Donald) ex parte Smith; R v Oxford Electoral Registration Officer ex parte Smith [1960] 2 QB 133, QBD 800
R v K (Abduction: Return Order) [2009] EWHC 132 (Fam), [2010] 1 FLR 1456 383, 390
R v Kensington Income Tax Commissioners, ex p Princess Edmond de Polignac [1917] 1 KB 486, CA 1743, 1746
R v Lambert [2001] UKHL 37, [2002] 2 AC 545 994
R v Leicestershire Education Authority ex parte C [1991] Fam Law 302, QBD 449
R v London Borough of Barking and Dagenham ex parte Bilkisu Mohammed [2002] EWHC 2663 (Admin) 486
R v London Borough of Brent ex parte S [1994] 1 FLR 203, CA 611, 659
R v London Borough of Islington ex parte Rixon [1996] EWHC 399 (Admin), [1997] ELR 66, QBD 486, 531

R v Lubemba & Ors [2014] EWCA (Crim) 2064, [2015] 1 WLR 1579 1763
R v Lucas [1981] QB 720, CA 543
R v Luton Magistrates' Court ex parte Sullivan [1992] 2 FLR 196, FD 413
R v M (Wasted Costs Order) [1996] 1 FLR 750, QBD 2161
R v North & East Devon District Health Authority, ex p Coughlan [2001] QB 213, CA 1008
R v North Yorkshire County Council ex parte M [1989] QB 411, [1989] 1 FLR 203, QBD 1653
R v North Yorkshire County Council ex parte M (No 2) [1989] 2 FLR 79, QBD 1653
R v Nottinghamshire County Council [1993] Fam Law 625, FD 1509, 1517, 1526, 2151
R v Nottinghamshire County Court ex parte Byers [1985] 1 WLR 403, [1985] FLR 695, QBD 1393, 1394
R v Oxfordshire County Council (Secure Accommodation Order) [1992] Fam 150, [1992] 1 FLR 648, FD; *sub nom* Oxfordshire County Council v R 1540, 1831
R v R (Children Cases: Costs) [1997] 2 FLR 95, CA; *sub nom* R v R (Costs: Child Case) 227, 1847
R v R (Costs: Child Case) [1997] 2 FLR 95, CA; *sub nom* R v R (Children Cases: Costs) 227, 1847
R v R (Divorce: Hemain Injunction) [2003] EWHC 2113 (Fam), [2005] 1 FLR 386 828
R v R (Divorce: Jurisdiction: Domicile) [2006] 1 FLR 389, FD 828, 2776
R v R (Divorce: Stay of Proceedings) [1994] 2 FLR 1036, FD 2785, 2823
R v R (Financial Relief: Company Valuation) [2005] 2 FLR 365, FD 1181
R v R (Financial Remedies) [2012] EWHC 2390 (Fam), [2013] 1 FLR 106 1179
R v R (Financial Remedies: Needs and Practicalities) [2011] EWHC 3093 (Fam), [2013] 1 FLR 120 1184
R v R (Jurisdiction and Acquiescence) [2016] EWHC 1339 (Fam) 389, 392, 453, 1503
R v R (Private Law Proceedings: Residential Assessment) [2002] 2 FLR 953, FD 458
R v R (Residence Order: Child Abduction) [1995] Fam 209, [1995] 2 FLR 625, FD 392, 393
R v R and S (Bankruptcy Jurisdiction Concerning Real Property Abroad: Setting Aside Consent Order) [2007] EWHC 2589 (Fam), [2008] 2 FLR 474 1212
R v Rastelli [2008] EWCA Crim 373 1173
R v Reading Justices, ex parte Berkshire County Council [1996] 1 FLR 149, QBD 2161
R v Registrar General ex parte Smith [1991] 2 QB 393, [1991] 1 FLR 255, CA; affirming [1990] 2 QB 253, [1990] 2 FLR 79 297
R v Rose ex parte McGibbon (1959) 123 JP 374, QBD 65, 1080
R v Secretary of State for Social Security, ex parte Biggin [1995] 1 FLR 851, QBD 401
R v Selby Justices ex parte Frame [1992] QB 72, QBD 130, 793
R v Shane Tony P [2004] EWCA Crim 28 887
R v Sheffield County Court Judge (1889) 5 TLR 303, QBD 799
R v St Albans Magistrates' Court ex parte J [1993] Fam Law 518, QBD 604, 1522
R v Tameside Metropolitan Borough Council ex parte J [2000] 1 FLR 942, QBD 428, 493
R v Wandsworth County Court ex parte Wandsworth London Borough Council [1975] 1 WLR 1314, QBD 2335
R v Wandsworth London Borough Council; Hammersmith & Fulham London Borough Council and Lambeth London Borough Council ex parte Stewart [2001] EWHC 709 (Admin), [2002] 1 FLR 469 486
R v Westminster City Council ex parte Castelli; R v Same ex parte Tristran-Garcia [1996] 1 FLR 534, QBD 790
R v Widdows [2011] EWCA Crim 1500, [2011] 2 FLR 869 1230
R, Re [2014] EWCA Civ 1625, [2015] 1 WLR 3273, [2015] 1 FLR 715 289, 528, 530, 539, 1008
R-J (Minors) (Fostering: Person Disqualified), Re [1999] 1 WLR 581, [1999] 1 FLR 605, CA; *sub nom* Re RJ (Fostering: Person Disqualified) 458, 560
RA (Baby Relinquished for Adoption: Case Management), Re [2016] EWFC 25 533
RAB v MIB [2008] CSIH 52, [2009] 1 FLR 602, IH 843
Rabone & Othrs v Pennine Care NHS Trust [2012] UKSC 2, [2012] 2 AC 72 1004
Radmacher (formerly Granatino) v Granatino [2010] UKSC 42, [2011] 1 AC 534, [2010] 2 FLR 1900 1153, 1179, 1180
Radmacher v Granatino [2008] EWCA Civ 1304, [2009] 1 FLR 1566 206, 1869, 2196, 2203
Raja v Van Hoogstraten [2004] EWCA Civ 968 1243
Ralphs, Re, Ralphs v District Bank [1968] 1 WLR 1522, ChD 1026
Ramadani v Ramadani [2015] EWCA Civ 1138 1168, 1432, 2865
Ramsbotham v Senior (1869) LR 8 Eq 575, (1869) FLR Rep 591, CE 857, 1549, 1757
Rawlings v Rawlings [1964] P 398, CA 1123
Ray v Sekhri [2014] EWCA Civ 119, [2014] 2 FLR 1168 204, 828, 1014
RB v DB [2015] EWHC 1817 (Fam) 366, 389, 2738
RBS v Etridge (No 2) [2001] UKHL 44, [2002] 2 AC 773, [2001] 2 FLR 1364 1180
RC and BC (Child Abduction) (Brussels II Revised: Article 11(7)), Re [2009] 1 FLR 574, FD 385, 2781
RD (Child Abduction) (Brussels II Revised: Arts 11(7) and 19), Re [2009] 1 FLR 586, FD 385, 2781, 2786

RE v North Yorkshire County Council, LO and A (A Child) [2015] EWCA Civ 1169, [2016] 1 WLR 512 457, 527, 1527, 2714, 2715
Redbridge LBC v B and C and A (through his Children's Guardian) [2011] EWHC 517 (Fam), [2011] 2 FLR 117 544
Rees v Newbery and the Institute of Cancer Research [1998] 1 FLR 1041, ChD 1017
Rees v United Kingdom (1986) 9 EHRR 56, [1987] 2 FLR 111 949
Reeve v Plummer [2014] EWHC 4695 (QB) 95
Regency Rolls Ltd v Carnall [2000] EWCA Civ 379 1834
Reid Minty (a Firm) v Taylor [2002] EWCA Civ 1723, [2002] 1 WLR 2800, CA 2148
Republic of Costa Rica v Strousberg (1880) 16 Ch D 8, CA 2285
Republic of Haiti v Duvalier [1990] 1 QB 202, CA 1242
Richards v Secretary of State for Work and Pensions (Case C-423/04) [2006] ECR I-3585, [2006] 2 FLR 487, ECJ 953
Richardson v Richardson [1994] 1 WLR 186, [1994] 1 FLR 286, FD 1196
Richardson v Richardson [2011] EWCA Civ 79, [2011] 2 FLR 244 1202, 1448
Rickards v Rickards [1990] Fam 194, [1990] 1 FLR 125, CA 1235
Ridehalgh v Horsefield, and Watson v Watson (Wasted Costs Order) [1994] Ch 205, [1994] 2 FLR 194, CA 228, 231, 2160
Riley v Riley [1986] 2 FLR 429, CA 821
Rinau, Re (Case C-195/08) [2008] ECR I-05271, [2009] Fam 51, [2008] 2 FLR 1495, ECJ 2791, 2794
RJ (Fostering: Person Disqualified), Re [1999] 1 WLR 581, [1999] 1 FLR 605, CA; *sub nom* Re R-J (Minors) (Fostering: Person Disqualified) 458, 560
RK and AK v UK [2009] 1 FLR 274, ECHR 999
Roberts Petroleum Ltd v Bernard Kenny Ltd [1983] 2 AC 192, CA 359, 2025, 2295
Roberts v Roberts [1970] P 1, PDAD 1203
Robertson v Canadian Imperial Bank of Commerce [1994] 1 WLR 1493, PC 1757, 2115
Robertson v Robertson [2016] EWHC 613 (Fam), [2017] 1 FLR 1174 1182
Robin v Robin (1983) 4 FLR 632, CA 1197
Robson v Robson [2010] EWCA Civ 1171, [2011] 1 FLR 751 1170, 1180, 1181, 1182, 1183, 1185
Roche v Roche (1981) Fam Law 243, CA 1240
Roddy (A Child) (Identification: Restriction on Publication), Re [2003] EWHC 2927 (Fam), [2004] 2 FLR 949 1754
Rodway v Landy [2001] EWCA Civ 471, [2001] Ch 703 1261
Rogers-Headicar v Headicar [2004] EWCA Civ 1867 2776
Roker International Properties Inc [2000] 2 FLR 976, FD 1782
Rolls-Royce plc v Unite the Union [2009] EWCA Civ 387, [2010] 1 WLR 318 1421
Roocroft v Ball [2016] EWCA Civ 1009 1018, 1023
Ropaigealach v Allied Irish Bank plc [2001] EWCA Civ 1790 359
Rose v Laskington [1990] 1 QB 562, QBD 1985
Rose v Rose [2002] EWCA Civ 208, [2002] 1 FLR 978 1152, 1442
Rossi v Rossi [2006] EWHC 1482 (Fam), [2007] 1 FLR 790 1180, 1183
Rothwell v Rothwell [2008] EWCA Civ 1600, [2009] 2 FLR 96 1442, 2193
Roult (by his mother and litigation friend) v North West Strategic Health Authority [2009] EWCA Civ 444, [2010] 1 WLR 487 2068
Rowe & Ors v Fryers & Anor [2003] EWCA Civ 655, [2003] 1 WLR 1952 1757
Rowlands (dec'd), Re [1984] FLR 813, CA 1017, 1023
RP and Others v UK (Application No 38245/08) [2013] 1 FLR 744, ECHR 997
RP v Nottingham CC and the Official Solicitor (Mental Capacity of Parent) [2008] EWCA Civ 462, [2008] 2 FLR 1516 1682, 1683, 2597
RP v RP [2006] EWHC 3409 (Fam), [2007] 1 FLR 2105 1179
RS v Entry Clearance Officer (New Delhi) [2005] EWCA Civ 89, [2005] 2 FLR 219 301
RS v KS (Abduction: Wrongful Retention) [2009] EWHC 1494 (Fam), [2009] 2 FLR 1231 376, 382, 383, 390
RS v Poland (Application No 63777/09) [2015] 2 FLR 848, ECHR 376, 381, 383
Rubin v Rubin [2014] EWHC 611 (Fam), [2014] 2 FLR 1018 1166
Ruiz-Mateos v Spain (1993) 16 EHRR 505 1007
Rush & Tompkins Ltd v Greater London Council [1989] AC 1280, HL 1452
Ruttie, Re; Ruttie v Saul [1970] 1 WLR 89, ChD 1025
Ryan v Friction Dynamics [2001] CP Rep 75, ChD 696
Rybak v Langbar International Ltd [2010] EWHC 2015 (Ch) 790

S & Marper v United Kingdom [2008] ECHR 1581 1010
S (A Child Acting by the Official Solicitor) v Rochdale Metropolitan Borough Council and the Independent Reviewing Officer [2008] EWHC 3283 (Fam), [2009] 1 FLR 1090 514, 627
S (A Child) (Abduction: Rights of Custody) [2012] UKSC 10, [2012] 2 AC 257, [2012] 2 FLR 442 390, 391, 392

S (A Child) (Child Arrangements Order: Effect of Long-Term Supervised Contact on Welfare), Re [2015] EWCA Civ 689, [2016] 2 FLR 217 446, 553
S (A Child) (Costs: Care Proceedings), Re [2015] UKSC 20, [2015] 1 WLR 1631, [2015] 2 FLR 208 199, 544, 1248, 1847
S (A Child) (Family Division: Without Notice Orders), Re [2001] 1 WLR 211, [2001] 1 FLR 308, FD; *sub nom* Re S (Ex Parte Orders) 38, 1522
S (A Child) (Residence Order: Condition) (No 2), Re [2002] EWCA Civ 1795 473
S (A Child), Re [2013] EWCA Civ 771, [2014] 1 FLR 739 537
S (A Child), Re [2014] EWCC B44 (Fam) 547, 560
S (A Child: Abduction), Re [2002] EWCA Civ 1941, [2003] 1 FLR 1008 378, 389, 861
S (A Minor) (Adoption), Re [1993] 2 FLR 204, CA 553
S (A Minor) (Care: Contact Order), Re [1994] 2 FLR 222, CA 551, 552
S (A Minor) (Guardian ad Litem /Welfare Officer), Re [1993] 1 FLR 110, CA; *sub nom* Re S (A Minor) 436
S (A Minor) (Independent Representation), Re [1993] Fam 263, [1993] 2 FLR 437, CA 1514, 1699
S (A Minor) (Medical Treatment), Re [1993] 1 FLR 376, FD 448, 631
S (A Minor) (Stay of Proceedings), Re [1993] 2 FLR 912, CA 842
S (A Minor), Re [1993] 1 FLR 110, CA; *sub nom* Re S (A Minor) (Guardian ad Litem /Welfare Officer) 436
S (Abduction: Acquiescence), Re [1998] 2 FLR 115, CA 389
S (Abduction: Children's Representation), Re [2008] EWHC 1798 (Fam), [2008] 2 FLR 1918 386
S (Abduction: Children: Separate Representation), Re [1997] 1 FLR 486, FD 388
S (Abduction: Custody Rights), Re [2002] EWCA Civ 908, [2002] 1 WLR 3355, [2002] 2 FLR 815 390
S (Abduction: Hague and European Convention), Re [1998] AC 750, [1998] 1 FLR 122, HL; [1997] 1 FLR 958, CA; [1996] 1 FLR 660, FD; *sub nom* Re S (Custody: Habitual Residence) 373, 376, 379, 380, 394, 396, 839
S (Abduction: Hearing the Child), Re [2014] EWCA Civ 1557, [2015] 1 Fam 263, [2015] 2 FLR 588 387, 623, 1532
S (Abduction: Intolerable Situation: Beth Din), Re [2000] 1 FLR 454, FD 391, 1554
S (Abduction: Sequestration), Re [1995] 1 FLR 858, FD 388
S (Adoption and Contact Applications: Representation of the Child), Re [2015] EWCA Civ 649, [2016] 2 FLR 81 1650
S (Adoption Order or Special Guardianship Order) (No 2), Re [2007] EWCA Civ 90, [2007] 1 FLR 855 476
S (Adoption Order or Special Guardianship Order), Re [2007] EWCA Civ 54, [2007] 1 FLR 819 256, 474
S (Adoption: Annex A Report), Re [2015] EWCA Civ 1345 1656
S (Authorising Children's Immediate Removal), Re [2010] EWCA Civ 421, [2010] 2 FLR 873 559, 1522
S (Brussels II Revised: Enforcement of Contact Order), Re [2008] 2 FLR 1358, FD 394, 2794
S (Brussels II: Recognition: Best Interests of Child) (No 1), Re [2003] EWHC 2115 (Fam), [2004] 1 FLR 571 2789
S (Care and Placement Orders), Re [2012] EWCA Civ 847, [2013] 1 FLR 354 2202
S (Care or Supervision Order), Re [1996] 1 FLR 753, CA 539, 671
S (Care Order: Criminal Proceedings), Re [1995] 1 FLR 151, CA 543
S (Care Proceedings: Evaluation of Grandmother), Re [2015] EWCA Civ 325, [2016] 1 FLR 109 290
S (Care Proceedings: Human Rights), Re [2010] EWCA Civ 1383, [2012] 2 FLR 209 559, 1000, 1044
S (Care Proceedings: Split Hearing), Re [1996] 2 FLR 773, FD 423, 534, 1508, 2613
S (Care: Jurisdiction), Re [2008] EWHC 3013 (Fam), [2009] 2 FLR 550 523, 524, 2787
S (Care: Parental Contact), Re [2004] EWCA Civ 1397, [2005] 1 FLR 469 552
S (Care: Residence: Intervener), Re [1997] 1 FLR 497, CA 1501
S (Change of Surname), Re [1999] 1 FLR 672, CA 447
S (Child Abduction: Asylum Appeal), Re [2002] EWCA Civ 843, [2002] 1 WLR 2548, [2002] 2 FLR 465; *sub nom* S v K (Return to Wardship Jurisdiction: India) 392
S (Child Abduction: Delay), Re [1998] 1 FLR 651, FD 386
S (Child Abduction: Joinder of Sibling: Child Objections), Re [2016] EWHC 1227 (Fam) 387
S (Child Proceedings: Urgent Appeals), Re [2007] EWCA Civ 958, [2007] 2 FLR 1044 204, 566, 1235, 2203
S (Child: Financial Provision), Re [2004] EWCA Civ 1685, [2005] Fam 316, [2005] 2 FLR 94 645
S (Children) (Contact: Fact-finding Hearing), Re [2007] EWCA Civ 694 203
S (Children), Re [2016] EWCA Civ 83 625, 1138
S (Children), Re [2016] EWCA Civ 1020 534
S (Contact Order), Re [2012] EWCA Civ 617, [2013] 1 FLR 825 1528
S (Contact: Application by Sibling), Re [1999] Fam 283, [1998] 2 FLR 897, FD 455
S (Contact: Evidence), Re [1998] 1 FLR 798, CA 1533

S (Contact: Promoting Relationship with Absent Parent), Re [2004] EWCA Civ 18, [2004] 1 FLR 1279 528, 619
S (Custody: Habitual Residence), Re [1998] AC 750, [1998] 1 FLR 122, HL; *sub nom* Re S (Abduction: Hague and European Convention); [1997] 1 FLR 958, CA; [1996] 1 FLR 660, FD 373, 376, 379, 380, 394, 396, 839
S (Deceased) (Forfeiture Rule), Re [1996] 1 WLR 235, [1996] 1 FLR 910, ChD 1024
S (Discharge of Care Order), Re [1995] 2 FLR 639, CA 565
S (Ex Parte Orders), Re [2001] 1 WLR 211, [2001] 1 FLR 308, FD; *sub nom* Re S (A Child) (Family Division: Without Notice Orders) 38, 1522
S (Expert Evidence), Re [2008] EWCA Civ 365, [2008] 2 FLR 1163 1511
S (Findings of Fact: Honour Based Violence), Re [2013] EWHC 15 (Fam) 445
S (Foreign Contact Order), Re [2009] EWCA Civ 993, [2010] 1 FLR 982 2742, 2791, 2792, 2802
S (Habeas Corpus), Re: S v Haringey London Borough Council [2003] EWHC 2734 (Admin), [2004] 1 FLR 590 1513
S (Habitual Residence and Child's Objections: Brazil), Re [2015] EWCA Civ 2, [2015] 2 FLR 1338 377, 391
S (Habitual Residence), Re [2009] EWCA Civ 1021, [2010] 1 FLR 1146 378, 385
S (Identification: Restrictions on Publication), Re [2004] UKHL 47, [2005] 1 AC 593, [2005] 1 FLR 591 247, 687, 1009, 1040, 1543, 1755, 2049, 2142, 2586
S (Jurisdiction to Stay Application), Re [1995] 1 FLR 1093, FD 840
S (Jurisdiction: Prorogation), Re [2013] EWHC 647 (Fam), [2013] 2 FLR 1584; *sub nom* PB v SE 524, 2782, 2783
S (Minors) (Abduction), Re [1993] 1 FCR 789, CA 1554
S (Minors) (Abduction: Wrongful Retention), Re [1994] Fam 70, [1994] 1 FLR 82, FD; *sub nom* Re S (Minors) (Child Abduction: Wrongful Retention) 376
S (Minors) (Care Order: Implementation of Care Plan), Re; W (Minors) (Care Order: Adequacy of Care Plan), Re [2002] UKHL 10, [2002] 2 AC 291, [2002] 1 FLR 815 529, 530, 559, 994, 996
S (Minors) (Child Abduction: Wrongful Retention), Re [1994] Fam 70, [1994] 1 FLR 82, FD; *sub nom* Re S (Minors) (Abduction: Wrongful Retention) 376
S (Parental Order), Re [2009] EWHC 2977 (Fam), [2010] 1 FLR 1156 991
S (Parental Responsibility), Re [1995] 2 FLR 648, CA 427
S (Parental Responsibility: Jurisdiction), Re [1998] 1 WLR 1701, [1998] 2 FLR 921, CA 428
S (Permission to Seek Relief), Re [2006] EWCA Civ 1190, [2007] 1 FLR 482 620
S (Placement Order: Revocation), Re [2008] EWCA Civ 1333, [2009] 1 FLR 503 265
S (Practice: Muslim Women Giving Evidence), Re [2007] 2 FLR 461, FD 1529
S (Relocation: Interests of Siblings), Re [2011] EWCA Civ 454, [2011] 2 FLR 678 472
S (Relocation: Parental Responsibility), Re [2013] EWHC 1295 (Fam), [2013] 2 FLR 1453 1636
S (Reporting Restriction Order), Re [2015] EWHC 4159 (Fam) 1040
S (Residence Order: Forum Conveniens), Re [1995] 1 FLR 314, FD 844
S (Split Hearing), Re [2014] EWCA Civ 25, [2014] 1 FLR 1421 534, 537, 547
S (Sterilisation: Patient's Best Interests), Re [2000] 2 FLR 389, CA 1547
S (Transfer of Residence), Re [2011] 1 FLR 1789, FD 444
S (Unco-operative Mother), Re [2004] EWCA Civ 597, [2004] 2 FLR 710 435, 2573
S (Unmarried Parents: Financial Provision), Re [2006] EWCA Civ 479, [2006] 2 FLR 950 650
S (Wardship: Peremptory Return), Re [2010] EWCA Civ 465, [2010] 2 FLR 1960 1544, 1545
S (Wardship: Stranded Spouses), Re [2010] EWHC 1669 (Fam), [2011] 1 FLR 305 1516
S (Wardship: Summary Return: Non-Convention Country), Re [2015] EWHC 176 (Fam) 385
S and D (Children: Powers of Court), Re [1995] 2 FLR 456, CA 451, 543
S and G v Italy (Cases 39221 /98 and 41963 /98) [2000] 2 FLR 771, ECHR 443
S and O (Temporary Removal from Jurisdiction), Re [2009] Fam Law 114, FD 473
S and P (Discharge of Care Order), Re [1995] 2 FLR 782, FD 1528
S and W (Care Proceedings), Re [2007] EWCA Civ 232, [2007] 2 FLR 275 999, 1239, 1513
S v AG (Financial Orders: Lottery Prize) [2011] EWHC 2637 (Fam), [2012] 1 FLR 651 1181
S v B and Newport City Council; Re K [2007] 1 FLR 1116, FD 620
S v E (A Minor) (Contact) [1993] Fam Law 407, FD; *sub nom* S v E (Access to Child) 1527
S v E (Access to Child) [1993] Fam Law 407, FD; *sub nom* S v E (A Minor) (Contact) 1527
S v H (Abduction: Access Rights) [1998] Fam 49, [1997] 1 FLR 971, FD 376, 379
S v H and another [2015] EWHC 3313 (Fam) 627
S v K (Return to Wardship Jurisdiction: India) [2002] EWCA Civ 843, [2002] 1 WLR 2548, [2002] 2 FLR 465; *sub nom* Re S (Child Abduction: Asylum Appeal) 392
S v Knowsley Borough Council [2004] EWHC 491 (Fam), [2004] 2 FLR 716 512
S v Oxfordshire County Council [1993] 1 FLR 452, FD 1706
S v P (Settlement by Collaborative Law Process) [2008] 2 FLR 2040, FD 1153

S v R (Parental Responsibility) [1993] 1 FCR 331, FD 424, 1832
S v S (Ancillary Relief after Lengthy Separation) [2006] EWHC 2339 (Fam), [2007] 1 FLR 2120 1180, 1182
S v S (Ancillary Relief) [2008] EWHC 2038 (Fam), [2009] 1 FLR 254 1179
S v S (Ancillary Relief: Consent Order) [2002] EWHC 223 (Fam), [2003] Fam 1, [2002] 1 FLR 992 1448
S v S (Ancillary Relief: Importance of FDR) [2007] EWHC 1975 (Fam), [2008] 1 FLR 944 1181, 1442
S v S (Brussels II Revised: Art 19(1) and (3): Reference to CJEU) [2014] EWHC 3613 (Fam), [2015] 2 FLR 364 2784, 2787
S v S (Chief Constable of West Yorkshire Police Intervening) [1999] 1 WLR 1716, [1998] 2 FLR 973, CA; *sub nom* Chief Constable of West Yorkshire Police v S 155, 156, 856, 857
S v S (Children: Periodical Payments) [1993] Fam 200, [1993] 1 FLR 606, FD 1831
S v S (Custody: Jurisdiction) [1995] 1 FLR 155, FD 847
S v S (Divorce: Staying Proceedings) [1997] 1 WLR 1200, [1997] 2 FLR 100, FD 1179
S v S (Family Proceedings: Reserved Costs Order) [1995] 1 FLR 739, FD; *sub nom* S v S (Reserved Costs Order) 2145
S v S (Financial Remedies: Arbitral Award) [2014] EWHC 7 (Fam), [2014] 1 WLR 2299, [2014] 1 FLR 1257 236, 1153, 1308, 1448, 1531, 2699
S v S (Interim Contact) [2009] EWHC 1575 (Fam), [2009] 2 FLR 1586 445
S v S (Maintenance Pending Suit) [2012] EWHC 4109 (Fam), [2013] 1 FLR 1173 1163
S v S [2008] EWHC 519 (Fam), [2008] 2 FLR 113 1184
S v S [2008] EWHC 2288 (Fam), [2009] 1 FLR 241 1548
S v S (Reserved Costs Order) [1995] 1 FLR 739, FD; *sub nom* S v S (Family Proceedings: Reserved Costs Order) 2145
S v Slough Borough Council and others [2009] All ER (D) 182 (Apr), FD 523
S v T (Permission to Relocate to Russia) [2012] EWHC 4023 (Fam), [2013] 2 FLR 457 471
S, Re; Newcastle City Council v Z [2005] EWHC 1490 (Fam), [2007] 1 FLR 861 256
S-B (Children), Re [2009] UKSC 17, [2010] 1 AC 678, [2010] 1 FLR 1161 532, 536, 537
S-C (Contempt), Re [2010] EWCA Civ 21, [2010] 1 WLR 1311, [2010] 1 FLR 1478; *sub nom* Shadrokh-Cigari v Shadrokh-Cigari 1988
S-L, Re [2011] EWCA Civ 1022 535
S-R (Jurisdiction: Contact), Re [2008] 2 FLR 1741, FD 2782
S-W (Children), Re [2015] EWCA Civ 27, [2015] 1 WLR 4099, [2015] 2 FLR 136 527, 545, 1761
SA v PA [2014] EWHC 392 (Fam) 1179
Sahin v Germany; Sommerfeld v Germany (Application Nos 30943 /96 and 31871 /96) [2003] 2 FLR 671, ECHR 443
Sahin v Germany; Sommerfeld v Germany; Hoffmann v Germany [2002] 1 FLR 119, ECHR 443
Salmon (dec'd), Re; Coard v National Westminster Bank [1981] Ch 167, ChD 1025
Salomon v Salomon and Co Ltd [1897] AC 22, HL 1172
Sandford v Sandford [1986] 1 FLR 412, CA 1172
Saulle v Nouvet [2007] EWHC 2902 (QB) 1682, 2060, 2067
Savage v Norton [1908] 1 Ch 290, ChD 1243
Savings & Investment Bank v Gasco Investments (Netherlands) BV (No 2) [1988] Ch 422, CA, reversing in part (1986) 136 New LJ 657, ChD 125, 1985, 2431
Saward v Saward [2013] EWCA Civ 1060 2776
SB (India) v Secretary of State for the Home Department [2016] EWCA Civ 451 1119
SB v MB (Costs in Hague Convention proceedings) [2014] EWHC 3721 (Fam) 1847
SC (A Minor) (Leave to Seek Residence Order), Re [1994] 1 FLR 96, FD 454, 455
SC v BH (Passport Order) [2014] EWHC 1584 (Fam) 859
Scherer v Counting Instruments Ltd [1986] 1 WLR 615, CA 1235
Schofield v Schofield [2011] EWCA Civ 174, [2011] 1 FLR 2129 1125
Scott v Scott [1913] AC 417, (1913) FLR Rep 657, HL 790, 1248, 2142
Scott v UK (Case 34745 /97) [2000] 1 FLR 958, ECHR 528
Seagrove v Sullivan [2014] EWHC 4110 (Fam), [2015] 2 FLR 602 1513, 1837
Sears Tooth (A Firm) v Payne Hicks Beach (A Firm) and others [1997] 2 FLR 116, FD 1166, 1255
Secretary of State for Work and Pensions v Jones [2003] EWHC 2163 (Fam), [2004] 1 FLR 282 410, 923
Sehota, (dec'd), Re; Kaur v Kaur [1978] 1 WLR 150, ChD 1015
Sekhri v Ray [2013] EWHC 2290 (Fam), [2014] 1 FLR 612 2777
Sen v Headley [1991] Ch 425, [1991] 2 FLR 449, CA 1028
Senior-Milne v Secretary of State [2012] EWHC 3062 (Admin) 1325
Serious Organised Crime Agency v Hymans [2011] EWHC 3599 (QB) 1987
SH (Care Order: Orphan), Re [1995] 1 FLR 746, FD 432
Shadrokh-Cigari v Shadrokh-Cigari [2010] EWCA Civ 21, [2010] 1 WLR 1311, [2010] 1 FLR 1478; *sub nom* Re S-C (Contempt) 1988
Sharbatly v Shagroon [2012] EWCA Civ 1507, [2013] 1 Fam 267, [2013] 1 FLR 1493 1014, 1125

Sharbatly v Shagroon [2013] EWHC 3756 (Fam), [2014] 2 FLR 209 1848
Sharland v Sharland [2014] EWCA Civ 95, [2014] 2 FLR 89 1447
Sharland v Sharland [2015] UKSC 60, [2015] 2 FLR 1367 211, 212, 214, 384, 1018, 1134, 1136, 1137, 1205, 1448
Shaw v Fitzgerald [1992] 1 FLR 357, FD 1123
Sheffield CC v Bradford CC [2013] 1 FLR 1027, FD 541, 638
Sheffield City Council v V (Legal Services Commission Intervening) [2006] EWHC 1861 (Fam), [2007] 1 FLR 279 561
Shemshadford v Shemshadford [1980] Fam Law 189, FD 828
Shepherd v Trustees of the Air Products plc Pension Plan [2006] (21 September), Pensions Ombudsman ref Q00278 1175
Shield v Shield [2014] EWHC 23 (Fam), [2014] 2 FLR 1422 1441, 1762
Shipman v Shipman [1991] 1 FLR 250, FD 797, 1240, 1744, 1848, 2087
Shoreditch County Court Bailiffs v de Madeiros (1988) *The Times*, 24 February, CA 1984
Silverton v Gravett [2001] All ER (D) 282 (Oct), QBD 36, 39, 1231
Simms v Simms [2002] EWHC 2734 (Fam), [2003] Fam 83, [2003] 1 FLR 879; *sub nom* JS v An NHS Trust; JA v An NHS Trust 1548
Singer (formerly Sharegin) v Sharegin [1984] FLR 114, CA 1849, 2145
Singh v Bhakar [2007] 1 FLR 880, Cty Ct 36, 40, 1231
Singh v Entry Clearance Officer, New Delhi [2004] EWCA Civ 1075, [2005] QB 608, [2005] 1 FLR 308 1008
SJ (A Child) (Habitual Residence: Application to Set Aside), Re [2014] EWHC 58 (Fam) 2778, 2782
SJ v RA [2014] EWHC 4054 (Fam) 2516
SK (By his Litigation Friend, the Official Solicitor), Re [2012] EWHC 1990 (COP), [2012] COPLR 712 2067
SK v WL (Ancillary Relief: Post-Separation Accrual) [2010] EWHC 3768 (Fam), [2011] 1 FLR 1471 1182
SL (Adoption: Home in Jurisdiction), Re [2004] EWHC 1283 (Fam), [2005] 1 FLR 118 278, 279
SL (Permission to Vaccinate), Re [2017] EWHC 125 (Fam) 559
Slade v Slade [2009] EWCA Civ 748, [2010] 1 WLR 1262, [2010] 1 FLR 160 130, 466, 1984
Slattery v Cabinet Office (Civil Service Pensions) [2009] EWHC 226 (Ch), [2009] 1 FLR 1365 1265, 2517
Slot v Isaac [2002] EWCA Civ 481 1235, 2198
Smallwood v UK (29779 /96) (1999) 27 EHRR CD 155 428
SMBC v PR (SR Intervening) (Care Proceedings: Children's Evidence) (No 1) [2012] 1 FLR 842, FD 624
SMBC v PR (SR Intervening) (Care Proceedings: Children's Evidence) (No 2) [2012] 1 FLR 852, FD 625
SMC Engineering (Bristol) Limited v Fraser (2001) *The Times*, 26 January, CA 1827
Smith & Ors v Ministry of Defence [2013] UKSC 41, [2014] 1 AC 52 993
Smith (Letitia) v Smith (Richard) [2000] 3 FCR 374, CA 1206
Smith v Doncaster Metropolitan Borough Council [2014] EWCA Civ 16 1996
Smith v Huertas [2015] EWHC 3745 (Comm) (Brussels I) 2873
Smith v McInerney [1994] 2 FLR 1077, FD 1152, 1442
Smith v Smith [1990] 1 FLR 438, FD 1405
Smith v Smith [2007] EWCA Civ 454, [2007] 2 FLR 1103 1179
Smith v Smith and others [2011] EWHC 2133 (Ch), [2012] 2 FLR 230 1026
Smithkline Beecham Biologicals SA v Connaught Laboratories Inc [1999] EWCA Civ 1781 1756
Snapes v Aram [1998] 2 FLR 346, CA; *sub nom* Re Hancock (dec'd) 1019
Snoek (dec'd), Re (1983) Fam Law 18, FD 1023
SO (Wardship: Extension of Protective Injunction Orders), Re [2015] EWHC 935 (Fam), [2016] 1 FLR 1144 1545
Société Eram Shipping Co Ltd v Compagnie Internationale de Navigation [2003] UKHL 30, [2004] 1 AC 260 2291
Söderbäck v Sweden [1999] 1 FLR 250, ECHR 285
Solomon v Solomon and Ors [2013] EWCA Civ 1095 1164, 1210, 1849
Somerset County Council v D & Others [2007] EWCA Civ 722, [2008] 1 FLR 399 1508
Sorrell v Sorrell [2005] EWHC 1717 (Fam), [2006] 1 FLR 497 1184
South Carolina Insurance Co v Assurantie Maatschappij 'De Zeven Provincien' NV; Same v Al Ahlia Insurance Co [1987] AC 24, HL 1231
South Glamorgan County Council v W and B [1993] 1 FLR 574, FD 631
South Tyneside Borough Council v Wickes Building Supplies Ltd [2004] EWHC 2428 (Comm) 1783
Southam, Re ex parte Lamb (1881) 19 Ch D 169, CA 853
Southampton City Council v IB [2014] EWFC 16 2754
Southwark London Borough Council v B [1998] 2 FLR 1095, FD 532
SP v EB and KP [2014] EWHC 3964 (Fam), [2016] 1 FLR 228 382, 383, 386, 390, 391, 392, 2781, 2782

Spelman (A Child by his Litigation Friends) v Express Newspapers [2012] EWHC 239 (QB) 1010
Spence (dec'd), Re; Spence v Dennis [1990] Ch 652, [1990] 2 FLR 278, CA 1016, 1055
Spencer v Barclays Bank plc [2009] EWHC 2832 (Ch) 1323
Spencer v Spencer [2009] EWHC 1529 (Fam), [2009] 2 FLR 1416 1439, 1564
Spiliada Maritime Corpn v Cansulex, The Spiliada [1987] AC 460, HL 828, 842, 1358
Sports Direct v Rangers Football Club [2016] EWHC 85 (Ch) 2304
Spurling v Broadhurst [2012] EWHC 2883 (Ch) 1686, 1701, 2063
SR v CR (Ancillary Relief: Family Trusts) [2008] EWHC 2329 (Fam), [2009] 2 FLR 1083 1181
SS v NS (Spousal Maintenance) [2014] EWHC 4183 (Fam), [2015] 2 FLR 1124 1169, 1183, 1185, 1202
St George's Healthcare NHS Trust v S; R (S) v Collins and Others [1999] Fam 26, [1998] 2 FLR 728, CA 2577
Stack v Dowden [2007] UKHL 17, [2007] 2 AC 432, [2007] 1 FLR 1858 17, 1181, 1262, 1263, 1439
Staley v Marlborough Investment Management Limited Retirement Scheme (2012) 31 July, ref 81482/2, Pensions Ombudsman 1265
Stead v Stead [1985] FLR 16, CA 1022
Steel & Morris v United Kingdom [2005] ECHR 103, [2005] 18 EHRR 545 1007
Steele v Mooney & ors [2005] EWCA Civ 96, [2005] 1 WLR 2819 1324
Steinfeld v Secretary of State for Education [2017] EWCA Civ 81 701
Stevenson v Police Pension Scheme [2004] (30 April), Pensions Ombudsman ref M00258 1174
Stewart v Engel & Anor [2000] EWCA Civ 362, [2000] 1 WLR 2268 1857
Stilwell v Williamson (1986) *The Times*, 1 September, CA 1985
Stock v Brown [1994] 1 FLR 840, FD 1025
Stockport Metropolitan Borough Council v D [1995] 1 FLR 873, FD 540
Stocks v Hornbuckle Mitchell Trustee Limited (2012) 13 November, ref 84269/1, Deputy Pensions Ombudsman 1265
Stodgell v Stodgell [2009] EWCA Civ 243, [2009] 2 FLR 244 1161
Storck v Germany (2006) 43 EHRR 6 1006
Stringer v Stringer [2006] EWCA Civ 1617, [2007] 1 FLR 1532 620
Sucden Financial v Fluxo-Cane Overseas Ltd [2009] EWHC 3555 (QB) 2285
Suffolk CC v Nottinghamshire CC [2012] EWCA Civ 1640, [2013] 2 FLR 106 475, 480, 541
Suffolk County Council v M, F and child [2015] EWFC B112; *sub nom* Re R (Translation of Documents in Proceedings) 1511
Suggitt v Suggitt [2011] EWHC 903 (Ch), [2011] 2 FLR 875 1024
Sulaiman v Juffali [2001] EWHC 556 (Fam), [2002] 1 FLR 479 864, 2776
Sunday Times v United Kingdom (No 1) (1979) 2 EHRR 245 1009
Sundelind Lopez v Lopez Lizazo (Case C-68/07) [2007] ECR I-10403, [2008] Fam 21, [2008] 1 FLR 582, ECJ 2777
Superior Composite Structures LLC v Parrish [2015] EWHC 3688 (Admin) 2873
Supply of Ready Mixed Concrete, Re [1992] QB 213, CA; *sub nom* Director General of Fair Trading v Smiths Concrete 129
Surrey County Council v Al-Hilli and Others [2013] EWHC 3404 (Fam), [2014] 2 FLR 217 475
Surrey County Council v M, F and E [2013] EWHC 2400 (Fam) 531
Surrey County Council v ME and Others [2014] EWHC 489 (Fam), [2014] 2 FLR 1267 248, 544, 628, 1040, 1544
Surrey County Council v S [2014] EWCA Civ 601 530, 531, 538, 539, 1857
Sutton London Borough Council v Davis (No 2) [1994] 1 WLR 1317, [1994] 2 FLR 569, FD; *sub nom* London Borough of Sutton v Davis (Costs) (No 2) 1533, 1847
SW & TW (Human Rights Claim: Procedure) (No 1) [2017] EWHC 450 (Fam) 2049, 2135, 2136, 2137
SW (A Minor) (Care Proceedings), Re [1993] 2 FLR 609, FD 552, 1508, 1520
SW v RC [2008] EWHC 73 (Fam), [2008] 1 FLR 1703 645, 650
Swindale v Forder (Forder Intervening) [2007] EWCA Civ 29, [2007] 1 FLR 1905 1202
Swindon BC v Webb [2016] EWCA Civ 152 2312
Sylvester v Austria (Application Nos 36812/97 and 40104/98) (2003) 37 EHRR 17, [2003] 2 FLR 210 383, 443
Symmons v Symmons [1993] 1 FLR 317, FD 797, 1930, 1983
Symphony Group plc v Hodgson [1994] QB 179, CA 227, 2157

T (A Child) (Suspension of Contact: Section 91(14) CA 1989), Re [2015] EWCA Civ 719, [2016] 1 FLR 916 423, 620
T (A Child), Re (19 November 2015, Elias LJ, Beatson LJ, Baker J, unreported) 424, 471
T (A Child), Re [2001] EWCA Civ 1067 472
T (A Child), Re [2016] EWCA Civ 1210 423
T (A Child), Re [2017] EWFC 19 289

T (A Child: Article 15 of Brussels II Revised), Re [2013] EWCA Civ 895, [2014] 1 Fam 130, [2014] 1 FLR 749; *sub nom* Re K (A Child) 524, 525, 2783
T (A Minor) (Care Order: Conditions), Re [1994] 2 FLR 423, CA 545, 671
T (A Minor) (Contact Order), Re [1995] TLR 7, [1995] 2 FLR 251, CA; *sub nom* Re T (Adoption: Contact) 287
T (A Minor) (Guardian ad litem: Case Record), Re [1994] Fam 181, [1994] 1 FLR 632, CA; *sub nom* Manchester City Council v T 571, 1706
T (A Minor) (Procedure: Alleged Sexual Abuse) (No 1), Re [1996] 2 FCR 370, CA 1508
T (A Minor) (Wardship: Medical Treatment), Re [1997] 1 WLR 242, [1997] 1 FLR 502, CA; *sub nom* Re T (Wardship: Medical Treatment) 631
T (A Minor) (Wardship: Representation), Re [1994] Fam 49, [1993] 2 FLR 278, CA; *sub nom* Re CT (A Minor) (Wardship: Representation) 182, 1285, 1699
T (Abduction: Appointment of Guardian ad Litem), Re [1999] 2 FLR 796, FD 395, 396
T (Abduction: Child's Objection to Return), Re [2000] 2 FLR 192, CA 391
T (Abduction: Rights of Custody), Re [2008] EWHC 809 (Fam), [2008] 2 FLR 1794 375
T (Adopted Children: Contact), Re [1996] Fam 34, [1995] 2 FLR 792, CA 287
T (Adoption Order), Re [2012] EWCA Civ 191, [2013] 1 FLR 360 282
T (Adoption Order: Leave to Appeal), Re [1995] 3 FCR 299 289
T (Adoption: Contact), Re [1995] TLR 7, [1995] 2 FLR 251, CA; *sub nom* Re T (A Minor) (Contact Order) 287
T (Adoption: Contact), Re [2010] EWCA Civ 1527, [2011] 1 FLR 1805 287
T (Care Order), Re [2009] EWCA Civ 121, [2009] 2 FLR 574 539
T (Change of Surname), Re [1998] 2 FLR 620, CA 447, 448, 449
T (Children), Re [2015] EWCA Civ 606, [2016] 1 WLR 14 548
T (Contact: Alienation: Permission to Appeal), Re [2002] EWCA Civ 1736, [2003] 1 FLR 531 1533, 2194, 2195
T (Costs: Care Proceedings: Serious Allegation Not Proved), Re [2012] UKSC 36, [2012] 1 WLR 2281, [2013] 1 FLR 133 199, 228, 1248, 1847
T (Divorce: Interim Maintenance: Discovery), Re [1990] 1 FLR 1, FD; *sub nom* T v T (Financial Provision) 1383
T (Interim Care Order: Removal of Children Where No Immediate Emergency), Re [2015] EWCA Civ 453, [2016] 1 FLR 347 193, 205, 566
T (Judicial Review: Local Authority Decisions Concerning Child in Need), Re [2003] EWHC 2515 (Admin) [2004] 1 FLR 601 1239
T (Minors) (Termination of Contact: Discharge of Order), Re [1997] 1 WLR 393, [1997] 1 FLR 517, CA; *sub nom* Re T (Termination of Contact: Discharge of Order) 552, 663
T (Paternity: Ordering Blood Tests), Re [2001] 2 FLR 1190, FD 922
T (Placement Order), Re [2008] EWCA Civ 248, [2008] 1 FLR 1721 261
T (Residential Parenting Assessment), Re [2011] EWCA Civ 812, [2012] 2 FLR 308 561
T (Staying Contact in Non-Convention Country), Re [1999] 1 FLR 262, FD 472
T (Termination of Contact: Discharge of Order), Re [1997] 1 WLR 393, [1997] 1 FLR 517, CA; *sub nom* Re T (Minors) (Termination of Contact: Discharge of Order) 552, 663
T (Wardship: Impact of Police Intelligence), Re [2009] EWHC 2440 (Fam), [2010] 1 FLR 1048 1481, 1510, 1512, 1757, 1758
T (Wardship: Medical Treatment), Re [1997] 1 WLR 242, [1997] 1 FLR 502, CA; *sub nom* Re T (A Minor) (Wardship: Medical Treatment) 631
T and E (Proceedings: Conflicting Interests), Re [1995] 1 FLR 581, FD 1505, 1696
T and M (Adoption), Re [2010] EWHC 964 (Fam), [2011] 1 FLR 1487 319
T v B (Parental Responsibility: Financial Provision) [2010] EWHC 1444 (Fam), [2010] Fam 193, [2010] 2 FLR 1966 441, 657
T v B and Revenue and Customs Prosecutions Office [2008] EWHC 3000 (Fam), [2009] 1 FLR 1231 481
T v P (Jurisdiction: Lugano Convention and Forum Conveniens) [2012] EWHC 1627 (Fam), [2013] 1 FLR 478 828
T v R (Abduction: Forum Conveniens), Re [2002] 2 FLR 544, FD 371, 395
T v R (Maintenance After Remarriage – Agreement) [2016] EWFC 26 1206
T v S [2013] EWHC 2521 (Fam) 426
T v T (An Agreement not embodied in a consent order) [2013] EWHC B3 1017
T v T (Brussels II Revised: Art 15) [2010] EWHC 3928 (Fam), [2013] 2 FLR 1326 2784
T v T (Custody: Jurisdiction) [1992] 1 FLR 43, FD 847
T v T (Financial Provision) [1988] 1 FLR 480, FD 1197
T v T (Financial Provision) [1990] 1 FLR 1, FD; *sub nom* Re T (Divorce: Interim Maintenance: Discovery) 1383
T v T (Financial Provision: Private Education) [2005] EWHC 2119 (Fam), [2006] 1 FLR 903 1170
T v T (Financial Relief: Pensions) [1998] 1 FLR 1072, FD 1187

T v T (Interception of Documents) [1994] 2 FLR 1083, FD 1440
T v T (Jurisdiction) [2012] EWHC 2877 (Fam), [2013] 1 FLR 1419 2782, 2783
T v T [2010] EWCA Civ 1366 441, 702
T v T (Occupation Orders, Brussels I and Protective Measures) [2010] EWHC 3776 (Fam), [2013] 1 FLR 364 2857, 2869, 2870
T v W (Contact: Reasons for Refusing Leave) [1996] 2 FLR 473, FD 1831
Tameside Metropolitan Borough Council v Grant [2002] Fam 194, [2002] 1 FLR 318, FD 605
Tameside Metropolitan Borough Council v M (Injunctive Relief: County Courts: Jurisdiction), Re [2001] Fam Law 873, Cty Ct 543
Tan v Choy [2014] EWCA Civ 251, [2015] 1 FLR 492 828, 2776
Tarasag a Szabadsagjogokert v Hungary (App No 37374/05) (2009) 53 EHRR 130 1543
Tarn Insurance Services Ltd (in Administration) v Kirby [2009] EWCA Civ 19 1324
Tattersall v Tattersall [2013] EWCA Civ 774, [2014] 1 FLR 997 1179
Tavoulareas v Tsavliris [2004] EWCA Civ 48 2779, 2823, 2828
Tavoulareas v Tsavliris (The Atlas Pride) [2006] EWCA Civ 1772, [2007] 1 WLR 1573 2828
Taylor v Lawrence [2002] EWCA Civ 90, [2003] QB 528 212, 213
Taylor v UKF Fertilizers Ltd and Harvey Plant Ltd (1988) *The Independent*, 14 November, CA 1235
TB (Care Proceedings: Criminal Trial), Re [1995] 2 FLR 801, CA 423, 543
TB v DB (Change of Residence) [2013] EWHC 2275 (Fam) 444
Tchenguiz-Imerman v Imerman (Disclosure) [2013] EWHC 3627 (Fam), [2014] 2 FLR 939 1440
Tchenguiz-Imerman v Imerman [2012] EWHC 4047 (Fam), [2014] 1 FLR 232 1137, 1752, 1758
Tchenguiz-Imerman v Imerman [2012] EWHC 4277 (Fam) 1450
Tebbutt v Haynes [1981] 2 All ER 238, CA 16, 19, 1172
Teeling v Teeling [1984] FLR 808, CA 1160
Terry Navarro Peart v Secretary of State for Transport, Local Government & Regions [2003] EWCA Civ 295 1011
TF v PJ [2014] EWHC 1780 (Fam), [2014] 1 WLR 4375, [2015] 1 FLR 861 384, 1554
TG (Care Proceedings: Case Management: Expert Evidence), Re [2013] EWCA Civ 5, [2013] 1 FLR 1250 527, 547, 560, 1502, 2195
Thaha v Thaha [1987] 2 FLR 142, FD 1236
Thakkar v Thakkar [2016] EWHC 2488 (Fam) 1148, 1155, 1404
The Prospective Adopters v IA and Croydon LBC [2014] EWHC 331 (Fam), [2014] 2 FLR 1158 265
Third Chandris Shipping Corpn v Unimarine SA; Aggelikai Ptera Compania Maritima SA v Same, Western Sealanes Corpn v Same, The Genie, The Pythia, The Angelic Wings [1979] QB 645, CA 1241
Thomas v Thomas [1995] 2 FLR 668, CA 1181
Thompson and Venables v News Group Newspapers, Associated Newspapers Ltd and MGN Ltd [2001] Fam 430, [2001] 1 FLR 791, CA; *sub nom* Venables v News Group Newspapers Ltd and Others; Thompson v News Group Newspapers Ltd and Others 997, 1545, 2569
Thompson v Hurst [2012] EWCA Civ 1752, [2014] 1 FLR 238 1263
Thompson v Thompson [1986] Fam 38, [1986] 1 FLR 212, CA 438
Thomson v Humphrey [2009] EWHC 3576 (Ch), [2010] 2 FLR 107 1262, 1263
Thomson v Mitchell [2004] EWCA Civ 1271 792, 1996
Thorner v Majors [2009] UKHL 18, [2009] 1 WLR 776, [2009] 2 FLR 405 1023, 1262
Thum v Thum [2016] EWHC 2634 (Fam) 1322
Thwaite v Thwaite (1981) 2 FLR 280, [1982] Fam 1 1434
Thyssen-Bornemisza v Thyssen-Bornemisza [1985] FLR 670, CA 1440
Tibbles v SIG plc [2012] EWCA Civ 518, [2012] 1 WLR 2591 212, 384, 1321
Tibbs v Dick [1998] 2 FLR 1118, CA 1235, 2196
Ticketus LLP & anor v Whyte, Lawtel 29 September 2014 2285, 2288, 2290
Tickle v Council of the Borough of North Tyneside and others [2015] EWHC 2991 (Fam) 628
Timbrell v Secretary of State for Work & Pensions [2010] EWCA Civ 701, [2011] 1 FLR 332 953, 954
TJB v RJB [2016] EWHC 1171 (Fam) 340
TL v ML and Others (Ancillary Relief: Claim against Assets of Extended Family) [2005] EWHC 2860 (Fam), [2006] 1 FLR 1263 16, 20, 1163, 1181, 1439, 1452, 2048
TM (Medical Treatment), Re [2013] EWHC 4103 (Fam) 1546
Tomlin v Standard Telephones [1969] 1 WLR 1378, CA 1153
Topping v Topping [2008] EWCA Civ 1142 1932, 1933
Tovey & Othrs v Ministry of Justice [2011] EWHC 271 (QB) 998
Tower Hamlets London Borough Council v MK and Others [2012] EWHC 426 (Fam), [2012] 2 FLR 762 523, 2780
TP and KM v United Kingdom [2001] 2 FLR 549, ECHR 1513
Traversa v Freddi (Part III Application following Italian divorce) [2011] EWCA Civ 81, [2011] 2 FLR 272 57, 58, 1125, 1387, 1425, 2857, 2869

Trott, Re; Trott v Miles [1958] 1 WLR 604, ChD 1025
Truex v Kitchin [2007] EWCA Civ 618, [2007] 2 FLR 1203 1684
TT (Surrogacy), Re [2011] EWHC 33 (Fam), [2011] 2 FLR 392 991, 1256
Tuohy v Bell [2002] EWCA Civ 423, [2002] 1 WLR 2703, [2003] BPIR 749 2336
Tuppen and anor v Microsoft Corporation Ltd and anor (2000) *The Times*, 15 November, QBD 1231
Turkington & Others v Times Newspapers Ltd (Northern Ireland) [2000] UKHL 57, [2001] 2 AC 277 1009
Turner v Avis and Avis [2009] 1 FLR 74, [2008] BPIR 1143, ChD 1264
TW v A City Council [2011] EWCA Civ 17, [2011] 1 WLR 819, [2011] 1 FLR 1597 624
TW v PL (Agreement) [2013] EWHC 3078 (Fam), [2014] 2 FLR 106 1442
TW v TM (Minors) (Child Maintenance: Jurisdiction and Departure from Formula) [2015] EWHC 3054 (Fam), [2016] 2 FLR 1386 1928

U (Abduction: Nigeria), Re [2010] EWHC 1179 (Fam), [2011] 1 FLR 354 385
U (Application to Free for Adoption), Re [1993] 2 FLR 992, CA 318
U (Re-opening of Appeal), Re [2005] EWCA Civ 52, [2005] 1 WLR 2398, [2005] 2 FLR 444 1235, 1871, 1872, 2208
UCB Bank plc v Hedworth [2003] EWCA Civ 945 1827
UL v BK (Freezing Orders: safeguards: Standard Examples) [2013] EWHC 1735 (Fam), [2014] 1 Fam 35 56, 1209, 1240, 1241, 1242, 1743, 1744, 1752, 1755, 2723
Ulrich v Ulrich and Felton [1968] 1 WLR 180, CA 1172
Unilever PLC v Chefaro Properties Ltd (Practice Note); Chiron Corp v Organon Teknika; Henderson v Merrett Syndicate; Brown v KMR Services [1995] 1 WLR 243, [1995] 1 FLR 1102, CA 2206
Unilever PLC v The Procter & Gamble Company [1999] EWCA Civ 3027, [2000] 1 WLR 2436 1753

V (A Child) (Inadequate Reasons for Findings of Fact), Re [2015] EWCA Civ 274, [2015] 2 FLR 1472 444
V (A Child), Re [2013] EWCA Civ 1649 444
V (Abduction: Habitual Residence), Re [1995] 2 FLR 992, FD 378
V (Care or Supervision Order), Re [1996] 1 FLR 776, CA 539, 670
V (Care Proceedings: Human Rights Claim), Re [2004] EWCA Civ 54, [2004] 1 WLR 1433, [2004] 1 FLR 944 234, 529, 996, 2048, 2254
V (Care: Pre-Birth Actions), Re [2004] EWCA Civ 1575, [2005] 1 FLR 627 235, 1008
V (European Maintenance Regulation), Re [2016] EWHC 668 (Fam), [2017] 1 FLR 1083 2446, 2857, 2869
V (Forum Conveniens), Re [2004] EWHC 2663 (Fam), [2005] 1 FLR 718 842
V (Long-Term Fostering or Adoption), Re [2013] EWCA Civ 913, [2014] 1 FLR 1009 280, 539
V (Residence: Review), Re [1995] 2 FLR 1010, CA 438
V v V (Child Maintenance) [2001] 2 FLR 799, FD 406, 1202
V v V (Divorce: Jurisdiction) [2011] EWHC 1190 (Fam), [2011] 2 FLR 778 828, 2776
V v V (Financial Relief) [2005] 2 FLR 697, FD 1181
V v V (Financial Relief) [2009] EWHC 2901 (Fam), [2010] 2 FLR 516 1440
V v V (Pre-Nuptial Agreement) [2011] EWHC 3230 (Fam), [2012] 1 FLR 1315 1153, 1180
V-B (Abduction: Custody Rights), Re [1999] 2 FLR 192, CA 379
V-Z (Children), Re [2016] EWCA Civ 475 526
Van Colle v Chief Constable of Hertfordshire Police [2008] UKHL 50, [2009] 1 AC 225 1004
Van den Boogaard v Laumen (Case C-220/95) [1997] ECR I-01147, [1997] QB 759, [1997] 2 FLR 399, ECJ 1432, 2857
Van Hoorn v Law Society [1985] QB 106, [1984] FLR 203, QBD 1043
Vasey v Vasey [1985] FLR 596, CA 813
Vaughan v Vaughan [1973] 1 WLR 1159, CA 887
Vaughan v Vaughan [2007] EWCA Civ 1085, [2008] 1 FLR 1108 203, 1180, 1182, 2193, 2516
Vaughan v Vaughan [2010] EWCA Civ 349, [2011] Fam 46, [2010] 2 FLR 242 1203
VB v JP [2008] EWHC 112 (Fam), [2008] 1 FLR 742 1168, 1179, 1203
VC v GC (Jurisdiction: Brussels II Revised Art 12) [2012] EWHC 1246 (Fam), [2013] 1 FLR 244 2782
Venables v News Group Newspapers Ltd and Others; Thompson v News Group Newspapers Ltd and Others [2001] Fam 430, [2001] 1 FLR 791, CA; *sub nom* Thompson and Venables v News Group Newspapers, Associated Newspapers Ltd and MGN Ltd 997, 1545, 2569
Venema v The Netherlands (Application No 35731/97) [2003] 1 FLR 552, ECHR 528, 529
Vernon v Bosley (No 2) [1999] QB 18, [1998] 1 FLR 304, CA 1752, 1794, 2109
Vernon v Spoudeas [2010] EWCA Civ 666 1324
Vigreux v Michel [2006] EWCA Civ 630, [2006] 2 FLR 1180 381, 384, 1551, 2781
Villars, ex parte (1874) LR 9 Ch 432, CA 2341
Ville de Bauge v China [2014] EWHC 3975 (Fam), [2015] 2 FLR 873 2786, 2787

Villiers v Villiers [1994] 1 WLR 493, [1994] 1 FLR 647, CA 792
Viner (dec'd), Re; Kreeger v Cooper [1978] CLY 3091 1017
Virgin Atlantic Airways Ltd v Zodiac Seats UK Ltd [2013] UKSC 46, [2014] AC 160 1762
VK v JV (Abduction: Consent) [2012] EWHC 4033 (Fam), [2013] 2 FLR 237 389
Vo v France [2004] ECHR 326 1004
Vodanas v Kriaris [2012] VSC 248 1025
Vogel v Lothschütz [2012] EWHC 3411 (QB) 92, 102, 1946, 1955, 2816
Vogel v Lothschütz [2013] EWCA Civ 664 92
Vogel v Lothschütz [2014] EWHC 473 (QB) 102

W (A Child) (Care Order), Re [2005] EWCA Civ 649 1794
W (A Child) (Secure Accommodation), Re [2016] EWCA Civ 804 171
W (A Child), Re [2001] All ER (D) 348 (Nov), CA 446
W (A Child), Re [2013] EWCA Civ 314 551
W (A Child), Re [2014] EWCA Civ 772 556
W (A Child), Re [2016] EWCA Civ 793 290, 538, 539
W (A Child), Re [2016] EWCA Civ 804 512, 2434, 2435
W (A Child), Re [2016] EWCA Civ 1140 204, 1286
W (A Child:Separate representation), Re [2016] EWCA Civ 1051 387
W (A Minor) (Consent to Medical Treatment), Re [1993] Fam 64, [1993] 1 FLR 1, CA; *sub nom* Re W (A Minor) (Medical Treatment: Court's Jurisdiction) 918, 1705
W (A Minor) (Contact), Re [1994] 1 FLR 843, FD 569, 1515, 1831
W (A Minor) (Interim Care Order), Re [1994] 2 FLR 892, CA 551, 1290, 1520, 1527
W (A Minor) (Medical Treatment: Court's Jurisdiction), Re [1993] Fam 64, [1993] 1 FLR 1, CA; *sub nom* Re W (A Minor) (Consent to Medical Treatment) 918, 1705
W (A Minor) (Secure Accommodation Order), Re [1993] 1 FLR 692, FD 1540, 1831
W (A Minor) (Welfare Reports: Appeals), Re [1995] 2 FLR 142, CA; *sub nom* Re W (Welfare Reports) 423, 436, 457
W (Abduction: Acquiescence: Children's Objections), Re [2010] EWHC 332 (Fam), [2010] 2 FLR 1150 377, 391
W (Abduction: Child's Objections), Re [2010] EWCA Civ 520, [2010] 2 FLR 1165 391, 2781
W (Abduction: Committal), Re [2011] EWCA Civ 1196, [2012] 1 WLR 1036, [2012] 2 FLR 133 792
W (Abduction: Domestic Violence), Re [2004] EWCA Civ 1366, [2005] 1 FLR 727 389
W (Abduction: Procedure), Re [1995] 1 FLR 878, FD 376
W (Adoption Details: Disclosure), Re [1998] 2 FLR 625, FD 297
W (Adoption Order: Leave to Oppose), Re; Re H (Adoption Order: Application for Permission for Leave to Oppose) [2013] EWCA Civ 1177, [2014] 1 WLR 1993, [2014] 1 FLR 1266 282, 2583
W (Adoption Order: Set Aside and Leave to Oppose), Re [2010] EWCA Civ 1535, [2011] 1 FLR 2153 280, 282
W (Adoption: Procedure: Conditions), Re [2015] EWCA Civ 403, [2016] 1 FLR 454 282, 2583
W (Application for Leave: Whether Necessary) (Case Note), Re [1996] Fam Law 665, FD 454
W (Assessment of Child), Re [1998] 2 FLR 130, CA 561
W (B) (An Infant), Re [1969] 2 Ch 50, CA 2290
W (Care Order: Sexual Abuse), Re [2009] EWCA Civ 644, [2009] 2 FLR 1106 543, 2614
W (Care Proceedings: Functions of Court and Local Authority), Re [2013] EWCA Civ 1227, [2014] 1 WLR 1611, [2014] 2 FLR 431 234, 529, 530, 532, 534, 539, 545, 1853
W (Care Proceedings: Leave to Apply), Re [2004] EWHC 3342 (Fam), [2005] 2 FLR 468 455, 551
W (Care Proceedings: Litigation Capacity), Re [2008] EWHC 1188 (Fam), [2010] 1 FLR 1176 1528
W (Care Proceedings: Witness Anonymity), Re [2002] EWCA Civ 1626, [2003] 1 FLR 329 544, 1530
W (Children) (Abduction: Striking Out), Re [2015] EWHC 4002 (Fam) 383
W (Children) (Abuse: Oral Evidence), Re [2010] EWCA Civ 57, [2010] 2 FLR 256 2632
W (Children) (Abuse: Oral Evidence), Re [2010] UKSC 12, [2010] 1 WLR 701, [2010] 1 FLR 1485 542, 623, 624, 625, 1519, 1684, 2632
W (Children) (Contact Dispute) (No 2), Re [2014] EWCA Civ 401 424, 443, 446
W (Children) (Education: Choice of School), Re [2002] EWCA Civ 1411 449
W (Children) (Strict Compliance with Court Orders), Re [2014] EWFC 22, [2015] 1 FLR 1092 526, 1323
W (Children) (Threshold Criteria: Parental Concessions), Re [2001] 1 FCR 139, CA 540
W (Children), Re [2003] EWCA Civ 116 441
W (Children), Re [2016] EWCA Civ 113 247, 627, 628
W (Children: Abducton:Striking Out, Re [2015] EWHC 4002 (Fam) 382
W (Children: Domestic Violence), Re [2012] EWCA Civ 528, [2014] 1 FLR 260 445
W (Contact: Application by Grandparent), Re [1997] 1 FLR 793, FD 455
W (Contact: Application: Procedure), Re [2000] 1 FLR 263, FD 1528
W (Contact: Joining Child as Party), Re [2001] EWCA Civ 1830, [2003] 1 FLR 681 446

W (Contact: Permission to Appeal), Re [2012] EWCA Civ 1214, [2013] 1 FLR 609 440
W (dec'd), Re (1975) 119 SJ 439, ChD 1023
W (Direct Contact), Re [2012] EWCA Civ 999, [2013] 1 FLR 494 425, 426, 440, 1504
W (Discharge of Party to Proceedings), Re [1997] 1 FLR 128, FD 1500
W (Disclosure to Police), Re [1999] 1 WLR 205, [1998] 2 FLR 135, CA 1512
W (Ex Parte Orders), Re [2000] 2 FLR 927, FD 56, 57, 1523
W (Exclusion: Statement of Evidence), Re [2000] 2 FLR 666, FD 1538
W (Fact Finding Hearing: Hearsay Evidence), Re [2013] EWCA Civ 1374, [2014] 2 FLR 703 1540, 2431
W (Family Proceedings: Applications), Re [2011] EWHC 76 (Fam), [2011] 1 FLR 2163 466
W (Inherent Jurisdiction: Permission Application), Re [2013] EWHC 1957 (Fam) 630
W (Interim Care Order), Re [2012] EWCA Civ 106, [2012] 2 FLR 240 558
W (Leave to Remove), Re [2008] EWCA Civ 538, [2008] 2 FLR 1170 1531, 1709
W (Minors) (Abduction: Father's Rights), Re; Re B (A Minor) (Abduction: Father's Rights) [1999] Fam 1, [1998] 2 FLR 146, FD; *sub nom* Re W; Re B (Child Abduction: Unmarried Father) 380
W (Minors), Re (unreported) 15 December 1998, CA 1514
W (Parental Responsibility Order: Inter-Relationship with Direct Contact), Re [2013] EWCA Civ 335, [2013] 2 FLR 1337 427
W (Permission to Appeal), Re [2007] EWCA Civ 786, [2008] 1 FLR 406 203, 1870, 2195
W (Relocation: Removal Outside Jurisdiction), Re [2011] EWCA Civ 345, [2011] 2 FLR 409 203, 206, 1866, 2205
W (Section 34(2) Orders), Re [2000] Fam 130, [2000] 1 FLR 502, CA 552
W (Secure Accommodation Order: Attendance at Court), Re [1994] 2 FLR 1092, FD 512, 1519, 1706
W (Shared Residence Order), Re [2009] EWCA Civ 370, [2009] 2 FLR 436 441
W (Welfare Reports), Re [1995] 2 FLR 142, CA; *sub nom* Re W (A Minor) (Welfare Reports: Appeals) 423, 436, 457
W and B v H (Child Abduction: Surrogacy) [2002] 1 FLR 1008, FD 379
W and D (Secure Accommodation), Re [1995] 2 FLR 807, FD 513
W and P (Children), Re (2002) Lawtel 30 April 1532
W and V v X (2017) (Case C-499/15), CJEU 2778, 2866
W and W v H (Child Abduction: Surrogacy) No 2 [2002] 2 FLR 252, FD 379
W and X (Wardship: Relatives Rejected as Foster Carers), Re [2003] EWHC 2206 (Fam), [2004] 1 FLR 415 630
W v Ealing London Borough Council [1993] 2 FLR 788, CA 1527
W v Egdell [1990] Ch 359, CA 1513, 1754
W v H [2001] 1 All ER 300, FD 38
W v J (Child: Variation of Financial Provision) [2003] EWHC 2657 (Fam), [2004] 2 FLR 300 645
W v M (TOLATA Proceedings: Anonymity) [2012] EWHC 1679 (Fam), [2013] 1 FLR 1513 1040
W v UK (1987) Series A No 121, (1988) 10 EHRR 29 552
W v W (Divorce Proceedings) [2010] EWHC 1843 (Fam), [2011] 1 FLR 372 2785
W v W (Financial Relief: Enforcement) [2010] EWHC 3825 (Fam), [2011] 2 FLR 1268 792, 1243
W v W (Financial Remedies: Confiscation Order) [2012] EWHC 2469 (Fam), [2013] 2 FLR 359 1161
W v W (Joinder of Trusts of Land Act and Children Act 1989 Applications) [2003] EWCA Civ 924, [2004] 2 FLR 321 18, 2036
W v W (Periodical Payments: Variation) [2009] EWHC 3076 (Fam), [2010] 2 FLR 985 1203
W v W (Residence: Enforcement of Order) [2005] EWHC 1811 (Fam) 2789
W v Wakefield City Council [1995] 1 FLR 170, FD 436, 1501, 1515, 1706
W, Re [1997] Fam Law 766, CA 449
W, Re, Re A, Re B (Change of Name) [2001] Fam 1, [1999] 2 FLR 930, CA 203, 446, 447, 1870
W, Re; B (Child Abduction: Unmarried Father), Re [1999] Fam 1, [1998] 2 FLR 146, FD; *sub nom* Re W (Minors) (Abduction: Father's Rights); Re B (A Minor) (Abduction: Father's Rights) 380
W, Re; Re F (Children) [2015] EWCA Civ 1300 624
W, X, Y, and Z (Withdrawal of Care Proceedings), Re [2010] EWHC 1914 (Fam), [2011] 1 FLR 188; *sub nom* WSCC v M, F, W, X, Y and Z 544
W-B (Family Proceedings: Appropriate Jurisdiction Within the UK), Re [2012] EWCA Civ 592, [2013] 1 FLR 394 526, 853
W-M (Children), Re [2015] EWCA Civ 1201 1509, 1526
Wagstaff v Wagstaff [1992] 1 WLR 320, [1992] 1 FLR 333, CA 1182
Wakefield Metropolitan District Council v T [2008] EWCA Civ 199, [2009] Fam 1, [2008] 1 FLR 1569 672, 673
Wakolo v DPP [2012] EWHC 611 (Admin) 875, 877
Walkden v Walkden [2009] EWCA Civ 627, [2010] 1 FLR 174 1448
Walker v Walker [1983] Fam 68, (1983) 4 FLR 779, CA 1170

Walley v Walley [2005] EWCA Civ 910 2193
Walsh v Singh [2009] EWHC 3219 (Ch), [2010] 1 FLR 1658 1262
Walton v Allman [2015] EWHC 3325 (Ch), [2016] 1 WLR 2053 2023
Ward v Shakeshaft [1860] 1 Dr & Sm 269, 8 WR 335 359
Wardle Fabrics Ltd v G Myristis Ltd [1984] FSR 263, ChD 1240
Warren v CARE and the HFEA [2014] EWHC 602 (Fam), [2015] 1 Fam 1, [2014] 2 FLR 1284 969, 970
Waterhouse v Barker [1924] 2 KB 759, CA 1757, 2115
Watkins v Ross (1893) 68 LT 423, CA 2285
Watkinson v Legal Aid Board [1991] 2 FLR 26, CA 1043, 1044
Watson (Deceased), Re [1999] 1 FLR 878, ChD 1016
Watson v Chief Constable of Cleveland Police [2001] EWCA Civ 1547 1761
Watson v Sadiq [2015] EWHC 3403 (QB) 2285
Waugh v British Railways Board [1980] AC 521, HL 1753, 1794
Wayling v Jones [1995] 2 FLR 1029, CA 1023
WB (Residence Orders), Re [1995] 2 FLR 1023, FD 1831
WBC (Local Authority) v Z and others [2016] EWCOP 4 225, 1683
WD v HD [2015] EWHC 1547 (Fam), [2017] 1 FLR 160 1453
WEA Records v Visions Channel 4 [1983] 1 WLR 721, CA 1234, 1235, 1241
Webb v Webb (Case C-294/92) [1994] QB 696, ECJ 2857
Webb v Webb [1986] 1 FLR 541, CA 858
Webber v Webber [2006] EWHC 2893 (Fam), [2007] 1 WLR 1052, [2007] 2 FLR 116 1161
Webster v Webster [2008] EWHC 31 (Ch), [2009] 1 FLR 1240 1018
Webster, Re [1907] 1 KB 623, KBD 2293
Webster, Re; Norfolk County Council v Webster and Ors [2006] EWHC 2733 (Fam), [2007] 1 FLR 1146 627, 2586
Wells v Wells [2002] EWCA Civ 476, [2002] 2 FLR 97 1179
Wermuth v Wermuth (No 1) [2002] EWHC 3049 (Fam), [2003] 1 FLR 1022 2786
Wermuth v Wermuth (No 2) [2003] EWCA Civ 50, [2003] 1 WLR 942, [2003] 1 FLR 1029 828, 2786, 2787, 2869, 2870
West Glamorgan County Council v P (No 1) [1992] 2 FLR 369, FD 551
West London Pipeline and Storage Ltd v Total UK Ltd [2008] EWHC 1729 (Comm) 1758
West Sussex CC v H [2014] EWHC 2550 (Fam) 2778
Westwood v Knight [2012] EWPCC 14 103, 1929
WF v FJ, BF and RF (Abduction: Child's Objections) [2010] EWHC 2909 (Fam), [2011] 1 FLR 1153 386, 391, 2781, 2782
Whaley v Whaley [2011] EWCA Civ 617, [2012] 1 FLR 735 1181
Wheat, Re [1932] 2 KB 716 1083, 1093
Wheeldon v Wheeldon [1998] 1 FLR 463, CA 126
Wheeler v Somerfield [1966] 2 QB 94, CA 1235
White v Fell (1987) 12 November, QBD (unreported) 1682
White v White [2001] 1 AC 596, [2000] 2 FLR 981, HL 1017, 1153, 1178, 1183, 1185, 1440
White v Withers LLP and Dearle [2009] EWCA Civ 1122, [2010] 1 FLR 859 1440
White, Son & Pill v Stennings [1911] 2 KB 418, CA 2292
Whitehead v Whitehead (orse Vasbor) [1963] P 117, CA 1234
Whitehouse-Piper v Stoke [2008] EWCA Civ 1049, [2009] 1 FLR 983 1197
Whittingstall v Whittingstall [1990] 2 FLR 368, FD 812
Whitton v Devizes Justices [1985] Fam Law 125, QBD 821
Wicken v Wicken [1999] Fam 224, [1999] 1 FLR 293, FD 864
Wickler v Wickler [1998] 2 FLR 326, FD 1405
Wicks v Wicks [1999] Fam 65, [1998] 1 FLR 470, CA 14, 1122, 1136, 1170
Wigan Borough Council v M and Others (Veracity Assessments) [2015] EWFC 8, [2016] 1 FLR 126 624, 1794
Wilcox v Wilcox (1902) 66 JP 166, DC 812
Wilkinson (dec'd), Re [1978] Fam 22, FD 1017
Wilkinson v Kitzinger [2006] EWHC 2022 (Fam), [2007] 1 FLR 295 720, 869, 1010
Wilkinson v Kitzinger and Her Majesty's Attorney-General (the Lord Chancellor Intervening) [2006] EWHC 835 (Fam), [2006] 2 FLR 397 720, 1010
Wilkinson v S [2003] EWCA Civ 95, [2003] 1 WLR 1254 792, 804, 1989, 2194
Williams v Johns [1988] 2 FLR 475, ChD 1017
Wilson v First County Trust Ltd (No 2) [2001] EWCA Civ 633, [2002] QB 74 996
Wilson v Wilson [1976] Fam 142, CA 1197
Wiltshire County Council v Frazer [1986] 1 WLR 109, QBD 2335
Winchester Cigarette Machinery Ltd v Payne (No 2) (1993) *The Times*, December 15, CA 2326
Wintle v Williams (1858) 3 H & N 288, Exch 2295

Witkowska v Kaminski [2006] EWHC 1940 (Ch), [2007] 1 FLR 1547 1016
WM (Adoption: Non-Patrial), Re [1997] 1 FLR 132, FD 285
Wolfe v Marshall and Harding (Garnishee) [1997] EWCA Civ 1329 2291
Wood v Collins [2006] EWCA Civ 743 792, 2195
Wood, Re; Wood v Wood (1982) LS Gaz 774 1023
Woodley v Woodley [1992] 2 FLR 417, CA 1932
Woodley v Woodley (No 2) [1994] 1 WLR 1167, [1993] 2 FLR 477, CA 1933
Wooldridge v Wooldridge (Case No 3CL1022132) [2016] Fam Law 451 1018
Wright v Wright [2015] EWCA Civ 201 1185
WS v WS [2015] EWHC 3941 (Fam) 1182, 2517
WSCC v M, F, W, X, Y and Z [2010] EWHC 1914 (Fam), [2011] 1 FLR 188; *sub nom* Re W, X, Y, and Z (Withdrawal of Care Proceedings) 544
WT (Foreign Surrogacy), Re [2014] EWHC 1303 (Fam), [2015] 1 FLR 960 991, 1638
WW v HW (Prenuptial Agreement: Needs: Conduct) [2015] EWHC 1844 (Fam), [2016] 2 FLR 299 1180
Wyatt v Vince [2013] EWCA Civ 495, [2013] 1 WLR 3525, [2014] 1 FLR 246 1848
Wyatt v Vince [2015] UKSC 14, [2015] 1 WLR 1228, [2015] 1 FLR 972 1165, 1168, 1178, 1323, 1431
Wyatt, Re [2006] EWHC 319 (Fam), [2006] 2 FLR 111 1546

X (A Child by His Litigation Friend), Re [2011] EWCA Civ 555, [2011] 2 FLR 793 466, 1549
X (A Child) (Surrogacy: Time Limit), Re [2014] EWHC 3135 (Fam), [2015] 1 Fam 186, [2015] 1 FLR 349 42, 989, 990
X (A Child), Re [2011] EWHC 3401 (Fam), [2012] 2 FLR 456 625, 1479, 1684
X (A Child), Re [2014] EWHC 1871 (Fam) 424
X (A Child), Re [2016] EWHC 1668 (Fam) 626, 628
X (A Child), Re, Re Y (A Child) [2016] EWHC 2271 (Fam) 513
X (A Minor) (Adoption Details: Disclosure), Re [1994] Fam 174, [1994] 2 FLR 450, CA 297
X (A Woman formerly known as Mary Bell) v O'Brien [2003] EWHC 1101 (QB) 2569
X (Adoption Application: Gateway Requirements), Re [2013] EWHC 689 (Fam), [2014] 1 FLR 1281 277
X (Adoption Child: Access to Court File), Re [2014] EWFC 33, [2015] 1 FLR 375 1661
X (Adoption: Confidential Procedure), Re [2002] EWCA Civ 828, [2002] 2 FLR 476 1510, 1657
X (Children) and Y (Children) (No 1), Re [2015] EWHC 2265 (Fam), [2015] 2 FLR 1487 533, 859, 1545, 2690
X (Children) and Y (Children) (No 2), Re [2015] EWHC 2358 (Fam), [2015] 2 FLR 1515 179, 184, 366, 1545
X (Children), Re [2007] EWHC 1719 (Fam), [2008] 1 FLR 589 248, 629
X (Disclosure for Purposes of Criminal Proceedings), Re [2008] EWHC 242 (Fam), [2008] 2 FLR 944 629
X (Emergency Protection Orders), Re [2006] EWHC 510 (Fam), [2006] 2 FLR 701 132, 533, 575
X (Minors) (Care Proceedings: Parental Responsibility), Re [2000] Fam 156, [2000] 1 FLR 517, FD; *sub nom* Re X (Parental Responsibility Agreement: Children in Care) 428, 549
X (No 2) (Application for contact by the biological father), Re [2015] EWFC 84 441
X (Parental Responsibility Agreement: Children in Care), Re [2000] Fam 156, [2000] 1 FLR 517, FD; *sub nom* Re X (Minors) (Care Proceedings: Parental Responsibility) 428, 549
X and Y (Bundles), Re [2008] EWHC 2058 (Fam), [2008] 2 FLR 2053 1513, 1837
X and Y (Disclosure of Judgment to Police), Re [2014] EWHC 278 (Fam), [2015] 1 FLR 1218 1755
X and Y (Executive Summary of Serious Case Review: Reporting Restrictions), Re [2012] EWCA Civ 1500, [2013] 2 FLR 628 1040
X and Y (Foreign Surrogacy), Re [2008] EWHC 3030 (Fam), [2009] Fam 71, [2009] 1 FLR 733 990, 991
X and Y (s 54 HFEA 2008), Re [2011] EWHC 3147 (Fam), [2012] 1 FLR 1347 991
X and Y v A Local Authority (Adoption: Procedure) [2009] EWHC 47 (Fam), [2009] 2 FLR 984 287, 1650
X and Y v St Bartholomew's Hospital Centre for Reproductive Medicine) [2015] EWFC 13, [2016] 1 FLR 544 979
X Council v B (Emergency Protection Orders) [2004] EWHC 2015 (Fam), [2005] 1 FLR 341 132, 574
X County Council v B (Abduction: Rights of Custody in the Court) [2009] EWHC 2635 (Fam), [2010] 1 FLR 1197 380
X County Council v M & Others [2014] EWHC 2262 (Fam) 630, 1543, 1544
X Local Authority v Trimega Laboratories [2013] EWCC 6 (Fam), [2014] 2 FLR 232 227
X v Dartford and Gravesham NHS Trust (Personal Injury Bar Association and another intervening) [2015] EWCA Civ 96, [2015] 1 WLR 3647 790, 2049, 2068, 2142
X v Latvia (Application No 27853/09) [2014] 1 FLR 1135, ECHR 381
X v UK (1980) 3 EHRR 408; *sub nom* Paton v United Kingdom (Application 8416/78) 960
X v X (Y and Z intervening) [2002] 1 FLR 508, FD 1442
X v Y (Repayment of Overpaid Maintenance) [2012] EWCC 2 (Fam) 1849
X v Y and Another [2014] EWHC 2147 (Fam), [2015] 1 FLR 1463 2782

X v Y and Z Police Force, A, B and C (By Their Children's Guardian) [2012] EWHC 2838 (Fam), [2013] 1 FLR 1277 390
X, Re [2015] EWHC 3651 (Fam) 533, 536
X, Re; Barnet London Borough Council v Y and X [2006] 2 FLR 998, Cty Ct 545
X, Y and Z (Disclosure to the Security Service), Re [2016] EWHC 2400 (Fam) 1755, 1756
X, Y and Z (Expert Witness), Re [2011] EWHC 1157 (Fam), [2012] 1 WLR 182, [2011] 2 FLR 1437 246, 1543, 1563
XCC v AA and Others [2012] EWHC 2183 (COP), [2012] COPLR 730 899
Xydhias v Xydhias [1999] 1 FLR 683, CA 1153, 1442

Y (A Child), Re [2013] EWCA Civ 1337 539, 543
Y (A Minor) (Ex parte Interim Orders), Re [1994] 1 FLR 172, FD; *sub nom* Re Y (A Minor) (Ex parte Residence Order) 1522
Y (A Minor) (Ex parte Residence Order), Re [1994] 1 FLR 172, FD; *sub nom* Re Y (A Minor) (Ex parte Interim Orders) 1522
Y (Abduction: Undertakings Given for Return of Child), Re [2013] EWCA Civ 129, [2013] 2 FLR 649 366, 389, 2738
Y (Children), Re [2016] EWCA Civ 1091 206, 542
Y (Leave to Remove from Jurisdiction), Re [2004] 2 FLR 330, FD 472
Y (Private Law: Interim Change of Residence), Re [2014] EWHC 1068 (Fam) 444
Y (Risk of Young Person Travelling to Join IS) (No 1), Re [2015] EWHC 2098 (Fam), [2016] 2 FLR 225 1544
Y (Risk of Young Person Travelling to Join IS) (No 2), Re [2015] EWHC 2099 (Fam), [2016] 2 FLR 229 1544
Y and K (Minors) (Split Hearing: Evidence), Re [2003] EWCA Civ 669, [2003] 2 FLR 273; *sub nom* Re Y and K (Split Hearing: Evidence) 541, 1508
Y and K (Split Hearing: Evidence), Re [2003] EWCA Civ 669, [2003] 2 FLR 273; *sub nom* Re Y and K (Minors) (Split Hearing: Evidence) 541, 1508
Y v Y (Financial Orders: Inherited Wealth) [2012] EWHC 2063 (Fam), [2013] 2 FLR 924 1181
Yager v Musa [1961] 2 QB 214, CA 1996
YC v United Kingdom (Application No 4547/10) [2012] 2 FLR 332, ECHR 256, 528
YC, PC and KM (Children), Re [2013] EWHC 2336 (Fam), [2014] 1 FLR 605; *sub nom* Camden LBC v PC, GM, YC, PC and KM 526
Yianni v Yianni [1966] 1 WLR 120, ChD 1985
YL v Birmingham City Council [2007] UKHL 27, [2008] 1 AC 95 234, 997
Yorke v Katra [2003] EWCA Civ 867 1799
Young v Young [2012] EWHC 138 (Fam), [2012] 2 FLR 470 57, 1210, 1236, 1243, 1744
Young v Young [2013] EWHC 3637 (Fam), [2014] 2 FLR 786 1178, 1439, 1762, 1932
Yousef v The Netherlands (Application No 33711/96) [2003] 1 FLR 210, ECHR 528, 1008, 1853
Yukon Consolidated Gold Corporation Ltd v Clark [1938] 2 KB 241, CA 2299

Z & Others v News Group Newspapers Ltd & Others [2013] EWHC 1150 (Fam) 1040
Z & Others v News Group Newspapers Ltd & Others [2013] EWHC 1371 (Fam) 1040
Z (A Child) (No 2), Re [2016] EWHC 1191 (Fam), [2016] 2 FLR 327 989, 996, 2058
Z (A Child: Human Fertilisation and Embryology Act: Parental Order), Re [2015] EWFC 73, [2015] 1 WLR 4993 989
Z (Abduction), Re [2008] EWHC 3473 (Fam), [2009] 2 FLR 298 378
Z (Children) (Care Proceedings: Review of Findings), Re [2014] EWFC 9, [2015] 1 WLR 95 535
Z (Foreign Surrogacy: Allocation of Work: Guidance on Parental Order Reports), Re [2015] EWFC 90, [2016] 2 FLR 803 42, 989, 990, 1634
Z (Recognition of Foreign Order), Re [2016] EWHC 784 (Fam), [2016] 1 Fam 375, [2017] 1 FLR 1236 1543, 1545, 1899
Z (Surrogacy Agreements: Child Arrangements Orders), Re [2016] EWFC 34, [2017] 1 FLR 946 991, 1256
Z (Unsupervised Contact: Allegations of Domestic Violence), Re [2009] EWCA Civ 430, [2009] 2 FLR 877 444, 445
Z County Council v R [2001] 1 FLR 365, FD 660
Z County Council v TS, DES, ES and A [2008] EWHC 1773 (Fam), [2008] 2 FLR 1800 248, 627
Z Ltd v A-Z and AA-LL [1982] QB 558, CA 1241, 1242
Z v A (Financial Remedy after Overseas Divorce) [2012] EWHC 1434 (Fam), [2014] 2 FLR 109 1129
Z v United Kingdom (2002) 34 EHRR 3, [2001] 2 FLR 612 1005
Z v Z (Divorce: Jurisdiction) [2009] EWHC 2626 (Fam), [2010] 1 FLR 694 2776
Z v Z (No 2) (Financial Remedy: Marriage Contract) [2011] EWHC 2878 (Fam), [2012] 1 FLR 1100 1153, 1180

ZA and PA v NA (Abduction: Habitual Residence) [2012] EWCA Civ 1396, [2013] 1 Fam 232, [2013] 1 FLR 1041 377, 378
Zakharov v White [2003] EWHC 2463 (Ch) 1242
Zarbafi v Zarbafi [2014] EWCA Civ 1267, [2014] 1 WLR 4122 2065
Zawadka v Poland (Application No 48542/99) [2005] 2 FLR 897, ECHR 443
Zeeland Navigation Company Ltd v Banque Worms (1995) *The Times*, 26 December, QBD 858
Zehentner v Austria (Application 20082/02) [2009] ECHR 1119 2298
ZM and OS (Sterilisation: Patient's Best Interests), Re [2000] 1 FLR 523, FD 1547
Zuk v Zuk [2012] EWCA Civ 1871, [2013] 2 FLR 1466 118, 792, 1934, 1983

Table of Practice Directions

References are to page numbers.

1963	Lord Chancellor's Direction of 29 May	131
1981	Secretary's Circular of 28 September (Contempt of Court)	131
1983	Practice Direction of 25 July (Contempt of Court) [1983] 1 WLR 998, (1983) 4 FLR 640	131
1991	Practice Direction of 19 August (Statutory Charge: Form of the Order of the Court) [1991] 1 WLR 955, [1991] 2 FLR 384	54, 1441, 1442, 2539
	Practice Direction of 26 September (Grants of Representation: Children Act 1989) [1991] 2 FLR 462	2270
1997	Best Practice Guidance of June (Handbook of Best Practice in Children Act Cases)	546, 1290, 1507, 1524, 1525, 1526, 1832, 2539
	Practice Note of 14 October (Hague Convention: Applications by Fathers Without Parental Responsibility) [1998] 1 FLR 491	376, 380, 381, 1610
1998	Practice Direction of 31 August (Judgments and Orders: County Court: Enforcement in High Court) [1998] 4 All ER 63	2332
	Practice Statement of 22 April (Supreme Court: Judgments) [1998] 1 WLR 825, [1998] 1 FLR 1102	2552
	Practice Statement of 25 November (Supreme Court: Judgments (No 2)) [1999] 1 FLR 314	2555
1999	Practice Direction of 12 January (Names of Deceased: Death Certificates) [1999] 1 FLR 503	1025
2000	Practice Direction of 2 October (Justices: Clerk to Court)	2557
	Practice Direction of 10 March (Family Proceedings: Court Bundles) [2000] 1 WLR 737, [2000] 1 FLR 536	1861
	Practice Direction of 24 July (Human Rights Act 1998) [2000] 2 FLR 429	2556
2001	Attorney-General's Memorandum of 19 December (Requests for the Appointment of an Advocate to the Court) [2002] Fam Law 229	1138, 1530, 1758, 2562, 2686
	Practice Direction of 9 April (Citation of Authorities)	2560, 2566
	Practice Direction of 11 January (Judgments: Form and Citation)	2559
	Practice Note of 2 April (Official Solicitor: Appointment in Family Proceedings) [2001] 2 FLR 155	2564, 2574
	Practice Note of March (CAFCASS Practice Note – Officers of CAFCASS Legal Services and Special Casework: Appointment in Family Proceedings) [2001] 2 FLR 151	2564
2003	President's Office Guidance of November (Disclosure Orders Against the Inland Revenue)	106, 109, 113, 119, 120, 1377
	Protocol of January (Child Abduction Cases Between the UK and Pakistan) [2003] Fam Law 199	176, 383, 2564, 2707
2004	President's Direction of 5 April (Representation of Children in Family Proceedings Pursuant to Family Proceedings Rules 1991, Rule 9.5) [2004] 1 FLR 1188	2573
	President's Guidance of 21 January (UK Passport Applications on Behalf of Children in the Absence of the Signature of a Person with Parental Responsibility) [2004] 1 FLR 746	2566
2005	CAFCASS Practice Note of 18 March (Applications for Reporting Restriction Orders) [2005] 2 FLR 111	1002, 2567
	Cairo Declaration Resulting from Anglo-Egyptian Meetings on Judicial Co-operation in International Child Abduction Matters between Egypt and the United Kingdom	176, 2567
	Practice Note of 18 March (Official Solicitor: Deputy Director of Legal Services: Cafcass: Applications for Reporting Restriction Orders) [2005] 2 FLR 111	247, 1544, 1846
	Protocol of December (Between the National Youth Advocacy Service and the Children and Family Court Advisory and Support Service) [2006] Fam Law 243	435, 2573

2006	CAFCASS and the National Assembly for Wales Practice Note of June (Appointment of Guardians in Private Law Proceedings) [2006] 2 FLR 143	1697, 1707
	Practice Direction of 27 July (Family Proceedings: Court Bundles) (Universal Practice to be Applied in All Courts other than the Family Proceedings Court) [2006] 2 FLR 199	1861
	Practice Note of 28 July (Official Solicitor, CAFCASS and the National Assembly for Wales: Urgent and Out of Hours Cases in the Family Division of the High Court) [2006] 2 FLR 354	2576
	Practice Note of 28 July (Official Solicitor: Declaratory Proceedings Medical and Welfare Decisions for Adults who Lack Capacity) [2006] 2 FLR 373	2576
2007	JSB's Equal Treatment Advisory Committee Guidance on Religious Dress	1529, 2578
	Practice Direction of 3 September (Children Act 1989: Risk Assessments under Section 16A) [2007] 2 FLR 625	1631
	Practice Direction of 3 September (Family Assistance Orders: Consultation) [2007] 2 FLR 626	1632
	Protocol of July (Generic Template) (ACPO Pilots: Disclosure of Information in Family Proceedings)	437
2008	Practice Direction of 1 April (Guide to Case Management in Public Law Proceedings) [2008] 2 FLR 668	2589, 2591, 2603, 2605, 2608
	Practice Direction of 6 November (Enforcement of Children Act 1989 Contact Orders: Disclosure of Information to Officers of the National Probation Service) [2009] 1 FLR 373	2584
	President's Guidance of 3 October (Listing Final Hearings in Adoption Cases)	2582
2009	Best Practice Guide of August (Preparing for Care and Supervision Proceedings)	1505
	President's Guidance of 22 April (Applications Consequent upon the Attendance of the Media in Family Proceedings) [2009] 2 FLR 167	248, 1040, 1836, 1837, 2585
2010	Guidelines of April (Judges Meeting Children who are Subject to Family Proceedings)	387, 1531, 1709
	Practice Guidance of 12 July (McKenzie Friends (Civil and Family Courts)) [2010] 2 FLR 962	1046, 1529, 1586, 2158, 2618
	Practice Guidance of June (Re S (Wardship) Guidance in Cases of Stranded Spouses) [2011] 1 FLR 319	2614
	Practice Note of April (Guidelines for Judges Meeting Children who are Subject to Family Proceedings) [2010] 2 FLR 1872	2611
	President's Guidance of 18 November (Out of Hours Hearings) [2011] 1 FLR 303	2621
	President's Guidance of May (Split Hearings (Bulletin Number 1)) [2010] 2 FLR 1897	445, 534, 1508, 2612
	President's Joint Guidance of December (Cases Involving Protected Parties in which the Official Solicitor is Being Invited to Act as Guardian Ad Litem or Litigation Friend) [2011] 1 FLR 943	1515, 2622
	Revised Protocol of 2 July (Referrals of Families to Supported Child Contact Centres by Judges and Magistrates)	2615
2011	Domestic Abuse Committee of the Family Justice Council Protocol of November (Protocol for Process Servers: Non-Molestation Orders) [2012] 1 FLR 1226	28, 31, 33, 40, 127, 134, 163, 563, 893, 903, 1231, 1471, 1472, 1481, 2631
	Experts Committee of the Family Justice Council Guidelines of December (Instruction of Medical Experts from Overseas in Family Cases) [2012] 1 FLR 889	204, 1871, 2205, 2638
	Guidance Note of 16 June (In-Court Family Mediation Services)	2628
	Practice Direction of April (Cafcass and the Work of Independent Reviewing Officers)	514, 2623
	Practice Direction of August (Interim Non-Disclosure Orders)	1010
	President's Joint Message of 29 July (Joint Message from Sir Nicholas Wall, President of the Family Division and Anthony Douglas CBE, the Chief Executive of Cafcass)	2629
	Working Party of the Family Justice Council Guidance of December (MARACs and Disclosure into Court Proceedings) [2012] 1 FLR 980	888, 900, 1513, 2636
	Working Party of the Family Justice Council Guidelines of December (Children Giving Evidence in Family Proceedings) [2012] Fam Law 79	387, 624, 625, 1531, 2632
2012	Practice Direction of 24 March (Citation of Authorities)	206, 1513, 1867, 2200, 2206, 2560, 2562, 2641
	Practice Guidance of 19 April (Litigants in Person)	1529
2013	Practice Guidance of March (Terminology for Litigants in Person)	2643

Year	Direction	Page
2013—*continued*	Practice Note of 9 January (Attendance of Solicitors at Local Authority Children Act Meetings)	529
	President's Guidance of 19 July (Communications Between Judges of the Family Court and Immigration and Asylum Chambers of the First-tier Tribunal and Upper Tribunal)	543, 2643
	Protocol and Good Practice Model of October (Disclosure of information in cases of alleged child abuse and linked criminal and care directions hearings)	423, 484, 1511, 2645
2014	Practice Guidance of 16 January (Transparency in the Family Courts: Publication of Judgments)	1481, 1543
	President's Guidance of 10 November (The International Child Abduction and Contact Unit (ICACU))	365, 2679, 2736
	President's Guidance of 22 April (Allocation and Gatekeeping for Care, Supervision and other Proceedings under Part IV of the Children Act 1989 (Private Law))	2715
	President's Guidance of 22 April (Allocation and Gatekeeping for Care, Supervision and other Proceedings under Part IV of the Children Act 1989 (Public Law))	160, 161, 165, 167, 170, 177, 522, 1515, 1859, 1881, 2661, 2715
	President's Guidance of 22 April (Allocation and Gatekeeping for Proceedings under Part II of the Children Act 1989 (Private Law))	142, 146, 149, 151, 153, 157, 158, 471, 1502, 1504, 1515, 2670
	President's Guidance of 22 April (Allocation and Gatekeeping for Proceedings under Part II of the Children Act 1989 (Public Law))	1832
	President's Guidance of 22 April (Continuity and Deployment (Private Law))	1504, 2676
	President's Guidance of 22 April (Continuity and Deployment (Public Law))	522, 2666
	President's Guidance of 22 April (Use of Prescribed Documents (Private Law))	1504, 2677
	President's Guidance of 22 April (Use of Prescribed Documents (Public Law))	2669
	Revised Guidance of 16 January (Transparency in the Family Courts Publication of Judgments)	247, 626, 627, 1040, 2656
	Revised Guidance of March (Provision of Justices' Reasons in Uncontested Cases)	1533, 1831, 2659
2015	Guidance Note of June (Financial Remedies Unit at the Central Family Court)	51, 2692
	Legal Aid Agency Guidance of April (Remuneration of Expert Witnesses)	562, 686
	Practice Direction of 26 March (Committal for Contempt of Court – Open Court)	125, 129, 250, 541, 1040, 1472, 2687
	Practice Guidance of 24 June (Committal for Contempt of Court – Open Court)	2687, 2693
	Practice Guidance of April (Tagging or Electronic Monitoring in Family Cases)	366, 533, 859, 1545, 2690
	President's Guidance of 8 October (Radicalisation Cases in the Family Courts)	472, 533, 1544, 1859, 2695
	President's Guidance of 26 March (The Role of the Attorney General in Appointing Advocates to the Court or Special Advocates in Family Cases)	1758, 2562, 2563, 2686
	President's Practice Guidance of 23 November (Arbitration in the Family Court)	1448, 2697
	para 2	1307, 1308
	Protocol of 19 January (Between the Association of Chief Police Officers, the Crown Prosecution Service and Her Majesty's Courts & Tribunals Service to Expedite Cases Involving Witnesses under 10 Years)	543
2016	Guidance for the Judiciary of April (Transfer of proceedings under Article 15 of Brussels IIa and Articles 8 and/or 9 of the 1996 Hague Convention)	525, 2709, 2784
	Guidance from the President's Office of April (Liaison between Courts in England and Wales and British Embassies and High Commissions Abroad)	526, 938, 2706, 2712
	Local Direction of 17 October (Electronic Filing at the Central Family Court: Pilot Scheme)	51, 2712
	Mr Justice Mostyn's Statement of 1 February (Efficient Conduct of Financial Remedy Hearings Allocated to a High Court Judge Whether Sitting at the Royal Courts of Justice or Elsewhere)	51, 1145, 1432, 1446, 2702
	President's Guidance of December (Allocation of Work to Section 9 Judges)	1859, 1860, 1862, 2464, 2675, 2714
	Special guardianship guidance of February (Statutory guidance for local authorities on the Special Guardianship Regulations 2005 (as amended by the Special Guardianship (Amendment) Regulations 2016))	475

2017 Practice Guidance of 18 January (Family Court – Duration of Ex Parte (Without Notice) Orders) 890, 1745, 2721
Practice Note of January (The Official Solicitor to the Senior Courts Appointment in Family Proceedings and Proceedings under the Inherent Jurisdiction in Relation to Adults) 1688, 1697, 1707, 2574, 2716

Table of CPR, FPR and Supreme Court Practice Directions

References are to page numbers.

CPR Pt 2	Allocation of Cases to Levels of Judiciary (PD2B)	
	para 4.1	17
	para 11.1(b),(d)	17
CPR Pt 3	Civil Restraint Orders (PD3C)	2035, 2080
	para 2.1	1323
	Sanctions for Non-Payment of Fees (PD3B)	2035
	Striking out a Statement of Case (PD3A)	2035
CPR Pt 5	Court Documents (PD5A)	
	Appendix	447
	para 6.1	447
	Electronic Communication and Filing of Documents (PD5B)	2353
	Electronic Working Scheme (PD5C)	2351
CPR Pt 6	Service Out of the Jurisdiction (PD6B)	23
CPR Pt 7	How to Start Proceedings – The Claim Form (PD7A)	2042
	para 2.5	16, 18
CPR Pt 8	Alternative Procedure for Claims (PD8A)	22, 2052
	para 3	39
	para 4.1	24
	para 4.2	24
	para 5	39
CPR Pt 10	Acknowledgment of Service (PD10)	
	para 5.4	2257
CPR Pt 16	Statements of Case (PD16)	
	para 3	17, 18, 19, 20
	para 7.4	17, 18, 19, 20
	para 7.5	17, 18, 19, 20
	para 8	17, 18, 19, 20
	para 10	17, 18, 19, 20
	para 15.1	190, 214, 2255
CPR Pt 17	Amendments to Statements of Case (PD17)	1389
CPR Pt 18	Further Information (PD18)	2055
	para 1.1	17, 19
CPR Pt 19	Addition and Substitution of Parties (PD19A)	996, 2057
	para 6.1	236
	para 6.4(1)	2057, 2258
	Group Litigation (PD19B)	2057
CPR Pt 21	Children and Protected Parties (PD21)	219, 223, 2070
	para 1.1	220
	para 1.2	220
	para 2.1	1686
	paras 3.1–3.4	221
	para 3.4	221
	paras 4.2–4.4	221
	para 4.5	221
	para 4.6	221
	paras 5.1–5.6	222
	paras 8.1–8.4	222
	paras 9.1–9.8	222
	paras 10.1–10.7	222
	para 12	222
	para 13.1	222
	para 13.4	222

CPR Pt 22	Statements of Truth (PD22)	
	para 2.2	221
CPR Pt 23	Applications (PD23A)	37, 2080
	para 4.2	38
	para 9.1	2109
	Applications under Particular Statutes (PD23B)	1742, 2085
	para 1.1(3)	226, 921
	para 1.2	226, 921
	para 1.4(1)	227
	para 1.4(2)	227
	para 1.5	227
CPR Pt 25	Interim Injunctions (PD25A)	37, 1010, 1242, 1744, 2088
	Annex	1240
	para 2.1	37
	para 2.2	39
	para 2.4	39
	para 3	37
	para 3.2	38
	para 3.3	38
	para 3.4	38
	para 4.2	38
	para 4.3	38, 39
	para 4.3(3)	39
	para 4.4	37
	para 4.4(3)	38
	para 4.5	38
	para 5.1(2)	38
	para 5.1(3)	38, 39
	para 5.1(4)	38
	para 5.1(5)	38
	para 5.2	40
CPR Pt 31	Disclosure and Inspection (PD31A)	2111
	Annex	2109
	para 3.1	1754
	para 3.2	2104
	para 3.3	2109
	para 4.1	1754
	paras 4.1–4.4	2104
	paras 4.2–4.6	2109
	para 4.5	2109
	para 5	2104
	para 5.3	2109
	para 5.4	2109
	Disclosure of Electronic Documents (PD31B)	2115
	para 1	2106
	para 2	2106
	para 5(3)	2106
	para 6	2106
	para 8	2106
	para 9	2106
	para 10	2106
	para 15	2106
	para 17	2106
	para 20	2106
	Sch	2106
CPR Pt 32	Evidence (PD32)	2117
	Annex 3	1291, 1865
	paras 17.1–22.2	2116
CPR Pt 35	Experts and Assessors (PD35)	
	para 10	1825
CPR Pt 36	Practice Direction B Supplementing CPR Part 36 (PD36B)	1753
CPR Pt 39	Court Sittings (PD39B)	791

CPR Pt 39—*continued*	Miscellaneous Provisions Relating to Hearings (PD39A)	
	para 1.5	1391
	para 1.11	1391, 1400
CPR Pt 40	Judgments and Orders (PD40B)	
	para 3.3(2)	1857
	Reserved Judgments (PD40E)	207
CPR Pt 44	General Rules About Costs (PD44)	2151
	para 1.2	232
	para 4.1	228
	para 4.2	229
	para 9.1	232
	para 9.2	232
	para 9.5	232
	para 9.6	232
	para 9.8	232
	para 9.9	232
CPR Pt 46	Costs Special Cases (PD46)	2162
	para 5.2	231
	para 5.3	231
	para 5.4	231
	para 5.6	231
	para 5.9	231
CPR Pt 47	Procedure for Detailed Assessment of Costs and Default Provisions (PD47)	2176
	paras 1.1–1.4	232
	para 2	232
	para 5.2	233
	para 5.5	232
	para 6.1	233
	para 8.2	233
	para 13.2	233
	para 13.4	234
	para 13.6	234
	para 15	234
	paras 16.3–16.8	234
CPR Pt 52	Appeals by way of Case Stated (PD52E)	207, 243, 1235, 1863, 2194
	Appeals in the County Court and High Court (PD52B)	207, 243, 1235, 1863, 2194

CPR Pt 52—*continued*

	Appeals to the Court of Appeal (PD52C)	203, 206, 207, 243, 1235, 1863, 2194
	para 3	207, 208
	para 3.3(h)	799
	para 4	207
	para 8	208
	para 9	206, 208
	para 10	208
	para 13	206
	para 14	206
	para 15	207
	para 15.1	2195
	para 15.2	2195
	para 16	206, 207
	para 17	206
	para 18	2196
	para 18(3)	2196
	para 19	206, 207, 1865
	para 20	207
	para 21	208, 209
	para 21–24	206
	para 23	208
	para 26	204, 566, 1235
	para 27	206, 208, 209
	para 29	206, 208
	para 29(2)	206
	para 29(4)	206
	para 31	206, 207
	para 32	206
	Appeals: General Provisions (PD52A)	203, 206, 207, 243, 1235, 1863, 2194
	para 4.1	207
	para 4.1(a)	2195
	para 4.1(b)	2195
	para 4.6	2195
	para 4.7	2195
	para 5.1	206
	para 5.2	206
	para 5.3	206
	para 7.1	213
	para 7.2	213
	para 7.3	213
	para 7.4	213
	para 8.1	2192
	para 8.2	2192
	Statutory Appeals and Appeals Subject to Special Provision (PD52D)	203, 207, 243, 1235, 1863, 2194
	para 6.1	2194
	para 9.1	2194
CPR Pt 54	Administrative Court (Venue) (PD54D)	2266

CPR Pt 54—*continued*	Judicial Review (PD54A)	189, 2261
	para 3.1	2253
	para 5.1	191
	para 5.6	189, 2254, 2255
	para 5.7	190
	para 5.9	192
	para 5.10	190
	para 6.1	191, 2256
	para 8.4	190, 2254, 2259
	para 8.5	2254
	para 8.6	2150
	para 9.1	190
	para 10.1	2259
	para 13	2260
	para 14.2	2261
	para 15.1	192, 2260
	para 15.3	192
	para 16	2260
	para 16.1	2260
	para 19	189
	References by the Legal Services Commission (PD54C)	2266
CPR Pt 57	Probate (PD57A)	22, 23, 2274
	para 15	2271
	para 16	24, 1025, 2271
	para 17	2271
	Proceedings under the Presumption of Death Act 2013 (PD57B)	1014, 1222, 2275
CPR Pt 65	Anti-Social Behaviour and Harassment (PD65)	2278
CPR Pt 66	Crown Proceedings (PD66)	996, 1855
	Annex 1	191, 236, 2057, 2258
CPR Pt 70	Enforcement of Judgments and Orders (PD70)	2281
	para 6	107
	para 7.1	2280
	para 7.2	2280
CPR Pt 71	Orders to Obtain Information from Judgment Debtors (PD71)	2287
	para 1.2	122, 2285
	para 2.1	122
	para 2.2	122, 2286
	para 4.1	123
	para 4.2(2)	122
	para 6	123
	para 7.1	2287
	para 8.1	123
	para 8.2	123
	para 8.3	123
	para 8.4	123, 2287
CPR Pt 72	Third Party Debt Orders (PD72)	1928, 2296
	para 1.2	114
	para 2	115
	para 3.1	115
	para 3.2	115
	para 4	116
	para 5.1	116
	para 5.2	116
	para 5.3(1)	116
	para 5.3(2)	116
	para 5.5	116
	para 5.6	116
CPR Pt 73	Charging Orders, Stop Orders and Stop Notices (PD73)	
	paras 4.1–4.5	110

CPR Pt 74	Enforcement of Judgments in Different Jurisdictions (PD74A)	2299
	para 4.1	84
	para 4.1(1)	84, 87, 96
	para 4.1(2)	98
	para 4.2	83, 86, 94
	para 4.2(2)	86
	para 4.3	97
	para 4.3(2)	86
	paras 7.1–7.3	84
	para 8.1	99
	European Enforcement Orders (PD74B)	100, 2299, 2300, 2811
	Annex	100
	para 2.1	100, 101
	para 2.2	101
	para 5.1	101
	para 5.2	101
	para 6.1	102
	para 7.1	102
CPR Pt 81	Applications and Proceedings in relation to Contempt of Court (PD81)	857, 2005
	para 1	40, 797
	para 2	40
	para 2.2	127
	para 4	792, 804
	para 4.5	804
	para 6	130
	para 7	130
	para 10	127
	para 10.2(2)	129
	para 12(2)	129
	para 13.2	129
	para 15	129
	para 15.2	129
	para 16	129
	para 16.2	125
CPR Schedules	Application for Writ of Habeas Corpus (PDRSC54)	512
FPR	Practice Directions relating to Family Proceedings in force before 6 April 2011 which support the Family Procedure Rules 2010	1292
FPR Pt 2	Functions of the Court in the Family Procedure Rules 2010 and Practice Directions which may be Performed by a Single Lay Justice (PD2A)	172, 1297, 2618
	References in the Rules to Actions done by the Court or by a Court Officer (PD2B)	1306
FPR Pt 3	Family Mediation Information and Assessment Meetings (MIAMS) (PD3A)	1396, 2628
	Annex A	143, 146, 151, 153, 429
	para 12(c)	433
	para 13(1)(b)	1443
	para 13(1)(e)	25, 811, 1443
	paras 17–21	142, 144, 150
FPR Pt 4	Civil Restraint Orders (PD4B)	1326, 1731
	Striking Out a Statement of Case (PD4A)	1325
FPR Pt 5	Forms (PD5A)	13, 20, 21, 25, 32, 34, 36, 42, 43, 44, 45, 46, 52, 53, 54, 58, 105, 125, 133, 135, 136, 138, 139, 140, 141, 143, 146, 147, 149, 151, 152, 153, 154, 156, 158, 161, 165, 167, 168, 170, 180, 181, 182, 183, 185, 187, 198, 283, 285, 453, 583, 603, 621, 633, 673, 706, 857, 858, 1148, 1285, 1332, 1392, 1436, 1437, 1477, 1479, 1480, 1482, 1504, 1526, 1541, 1551, 1635, 1639, 1656, 1687, 1701, 1728, 1736, 1832, 2539
FPR Pt 6	Disclosure of Addresses by Government Departments (PD6C)	106, 109, 113, 119, 120, 824, 857, 1349, 1373, 1549

FPR Pt 6—*continued*

FPR Pt 6—*continued*	Service out of the Jurisdiction (PD6B)	1368, 2823
	para 2	1359, 2823
	para 5.1	1358
	para 7.1	1358
	Service within the Jurisdiction (PD6A)	1362
	para 3.1	47
	para 6.4	1932
	para 9.1	1688, 1703
	para 11	1348
	para 11.3	1348
	para 12	1348
FPR Pt 7	Medical Examinations on Applications for Annulment of a Marriage (PD7B)	1411
	Polygamous Marriages (PD7C)	1214, 1411
	Procedure for Applications in Matrimonial and Civil Partnership Proceedings (PD7A)	46, 1148, 1406
	para 2.1	1383
	para 3	2785
	para 3.1	46
	para 3.2	47
	para 3.3	47
	para 5	47
	para 6	49
	para 6.1	1390
	para 6.2	1390
	para 7	49
	paras 8.1–8.4	1148
	The Gender Recognition Act 2004 (PD7D)	1412
FPR Pt 8	Where to Start Certain Proceedings (PD8A)	1427
	para 1.1(a)	14, 41
FPR Pt 9	Application for a Financial Remedy (PD9A)	13, 21, 50, 52, 53, 811, 1431, 1436, 1438, 1439, 1462
	para 1.2	1202
	para 1.2(a)(ii)	481
	para 4	53
	para 6	53
	paras 13.1–13.8	1448
	paras 13.1–13.9	1434
	para 13.2	212
	para 13.5	212, 1434
	para 13.8	1434
	para 13.9	214
FPR Pt 10	Part 4 of the Family Law Act 1996 (PD10A)	1040
	para 4.1	1483
	para 6	905
	paras 6.1–6.5	1483
	para 7	1484
	para 7.1	905
FPR Pt 12	Applications for Reporting Restriction Orders (PD12I)	1002, 1544, 1623
	Care, Supervision and Other Part 4 Proceedings	
	Guide to Case Management (PD12A)	132, 133, 135, 136, 137, 138, 139, 140, 161, 162, 164, 165, 166, 167, 168, 169, 170, 423, 435, 436, 457, 526, 535, 541, 547, 555, 558, 575, 585, 673, 1500, 1505, 1507, 1508, 1509, 1513, 1514, 1524, 1533, 1534, 1535, 1565, 1684, 1837, 1980, 2539, 2541, 2544, 2552, 2592, 2629
	para 3.1	168
	Child Arrangements & Contact Order: Domestic Violence and Harm (PD12J)	437, 444, 445, 552, 1508, 1624, 2612, 2613
	para 33	444
	para 34	444

FPR Pt 12—*continued*

Child Arrangements Programme (PD12B) 144, 146, 147, 149, 150, 151, 152, 153, 154, 155, 156, 157, 158, 159, 183, 423, 436, 437, 440, 453, 457, 555, 1504, 1507, 1513, 1519, 1525, 1529, 1541, 1577, 2539, 2548, 2614, 2628
- para 8.8 143, 146, 148, 151
- para 12.2 146
- para 14.3 147, 149, 152
- paras 17–21 152
- para 21 150

Child: Arrival by Air (PD12O) 1633

Children Act 1989: Exclusion Requirement (PD12K) 134, 163, 1538, 1631
- para 1 563
- para 2 563
- para 3 563

Children Act 1989: Risk Assessments under Section 16A (PD12L) 445, 483, 1631

Communication of Information (PD12G) 246, 247, 1488, 1564, 1618, 1705, 1756, 1837

Contribution Orders (PD12H) 1623

Enforcement of Children Act 1989 Child Arrangements Orders: Disclosure of Information to Officers of the National Probation Service (High Court and County Court) (PD12N) 148, 442, 467, 468, 1632

Family Assistance Orders: Consultation (PD12M) 482, 1632

Inherent Jurisdiction (Including Wardship) Proceedings (PD12D) 181, 182, 368, 630, 857, 858, 1602
- para 1.1 1543, 1544
- para 1.2 184
- para 1.3 1543
- para 2 1544
- para 2.3 1544, 1545
- para 3.1 182, 1546
- para 4.1 1543
- para 5 1543
- para 6 1543
- para 7.1 1549

FPR Pt 12—*continued*

International Child Abduction (PD12F) 365, 368, 370, 373, 381, 1606
- Annex 1 1515, 1614
- para 1.4 177
- para 1.5 177
- para 2.10 1551
- para 2.11 1551
- para 2.12 177, 1551
- para 2.13 177, 1551
- para 2.14 178, 179, 381, 385
- para 2.15 367
- paras 2.16–2.19 375
- para 2.17 380
- para 2.20 370
- paras 2.21–2.24 1554
- paras 2.22, 2.23 178
- para 2.24 178
- para 3.1 179, 385
- para 3.2 179
- para 3.3 179
- para 3.4 179
- para 3.5 179
- paras 4.2–4.8 179
- para 4.9 179
- para 4.10 178
- para 4.14 178
- para 4.15 179, 365, 1549, 1553
- para 4.16 1549, 1553
- paras 5.1–5.6 370
- para 20 393
- Pt 2 177
- Pt 3 179

Removal from Jurisdiction: Issue of Passports (PD12P) 859, 1633

Service of Application in Certain Children Proceedings (PD12C) 133, 136, 138, 141, 146, 149, 151, 154, 157, 161, 162, 163, 165, 168, 170, 1506, 1515, 1523, 1524, 1525, 1526, 1540, 1541, 1598, 1713
- Annex 143
- Annex B 146, 159
- para 1.1 11, 172
- para 2.1 11, 138, 149, 1520
- para 2.1(1) 172
- para 2.1(6) 172
- para 3.1 11, 133, 135, 136, 138, 141, 143, 146, 149, 151, 154, 165, 170, 172
- para 3.1(1) 172

Urgent Business (PD12E) 133, 136, 139, 368, 458, 857, 858, 1509, 1517, 1522, 1544, 1547, 1552, 1605, 2546
- para 1.4 184
- para 1.5 184
- para 2.2 184
- para 3.1 1543, 1548
- para 3.2 182, 1543
- para 4.1 181
- para 4.4 1547

FPR Pt 14

Communication of Information Relating to Proceedings (PD14E) 1675

Disclosing Information to an Adopted Adult (PD14F) 1679

Reports by a Registered Medical Practitioner ('Health Reports') (PD14D) 1673

Reports by the Adoption Agency or Local Authority (PD14C) 185, 188, 278, 285, 1665

The First Directions Hearing – Adoptions with a Foreign Element (PD14B) 1654, 1664

Who Receives a Copy of the Application Form for Orders in Proceedings (PD14A) 1663

FPR Pt 15	Adults Who May Be Protected Parties and Children Who May Become Protected Parties in Family Proceedings (PD15B)	1680, 1691
	Protected Parties (PD15A)	223, 1680, 1684, 1689
	para 1.1	216
	para 1.2	216
	para 2.1	216, 1686
	para 3.1	216
	para 4	217
	para 5	217
	para 6	217
FPR Pt 16	Representation of Children (PD16A)	186, 263, 435, 436, 437, 446, 449, 454, 469, 487, 568, 569, 807, 1501, 1515, 1518, 1530, 1542, 1548, 1653, 1705, 1713, 2552
	para 1.1	218
	para 2.1	218
	para 3	218
	para 3.1	218
	para 4	218
	para 5	218
	paras 6.1–6.11	1505, 1705, 1707, 1708
	para 6.2	188
	para 6.2(a)	1515
	para 6.6	622, 1520
	para 6.8(b)	1653
	para 6.10	1653
	para 6.11	1653
	para 7.1	1697
	paras 7.1–7.5	1502, 1695
	paras 7.1–7.19	1502, 1706
	para 7.2	386
	para 7.3	386
	para 7.6	1707, 1708
	para 7.7	1707, 1708
	paras 7.17–7.19	1708
	paras 9.1–9.4	1711
	para 9.4(a)	808
	paras 10.1–10.5	1640
	paras 11.1–11.7	445, 483, 1712
	Pt 3	568
	Pt 4	568
FPR Pt 17	Statements of Truth (PD17A)	177, 179, 1444, 1554, 1725, 1922
	para 1	1920
	paras 2–4.4	1920
FPR Pt 18	Other Applications in Proceedings (PD18A)	183, 1433, 1478, 1522, 1549, 1636, 1637, 1641, 1728, 1732
	para 3.5	1502
	para 4.2	1503
	paras 4.7–4.9	1503
	para 5.1	1209, 1477, 1552
FPR Pt 19	Alternative Procedure for Applications (PD19A)	1737, 1739
	para 1.5	1152
FPR Pt 20	Interim Remedies (PD20A)	1240, 1241, 1242, 1745, 1748
	para 1.1	1742
	para 2.2	1745
	para 3.1	1722, 1746
	para 3.2	1746
	para 3.3	1746
	para 4.3	146, 151
	para 4.3(c)	56
	para 4.4	146, 151
	para 4.5	146, 151
	paras 6.1–6.9	1744
FPR Pt 21	Disclosure and Inspection (PD21A)	1759
FPR Pt 22	Written Evidence (PD22A)	156, 157, 158, 159, 857, 858, 1509, 1554, 1768, 1922
	Annex 3	1291, 1865

FPR Pt 24	Witnesses, Depositions and Taking of Evidence in Member States of the European Union (PD24A)	1781, 1786, 1787
	Annex C	2753
	para 1	1557
	para 5	2753
	paras 6–9	2754
	para 7	2753
	para 8	2753
FPR Pt 25	Assessors in Family Proceedings (PD25F)	437, 529, 1439, 1513, 1514, 1528, 1801, 1825, 2545
	Children Proceedings – The Use of Single Joint Experts and the Process Leading to an Expert Being Instructed or Expert Evidence Being Put Before the Court (PD25C)	437, 529, 1439, 1513, 1514, 1528, 1812, 2545
	Discussions Between Experts in Family Proceedings (PD25E)	437, 529, 1439, 1513, 1514, 1528, 1823, 2545
	Experts – Emergencies and Pre Proceedings Instructions (PD25A)	437, 529, 993, 1397, 1439, 1513, 1514, 1528, 1801, 2545
	para 3.3	1797
	para 3.3(i)	529, 1724
	para 7.1	1800
	Financial Remedy Proceedings and Other Family Proceedings (Except Children Proceedings) – The Use of Single Joint Experts and the Process Leading to Expert Evidence Being Put Before the Court (PD25D)	437, 529, 1439, 1513, 1514, 1528, 1818, 2545
	The Duties of an Expert, the Expert's Report and Arrangements for an Expert to Attend Court (PD25B)	437, 529, 1439, 1513, 1514, 1528, 1803, 2545, 2601
FPR Pt 26	Change of Solicitor (PD26A)	1828
FPR Pt 27	Attendance of Media Representatives at Hearings in Family Proceedings (Family Proceedings Court) (PD27C)	
	para 6.2	1837
	Attendance of Media Representatives at Hearings in Family Proceedings (High Court and County Courts) (PD27B)	248, 1040, 1836, 1837, 1843
	para 6.2	1837
	Family Proceedings: Court Bundles (Universal Practice to be applied in the High Court and Family Court) (PD27A)	527, 542, 791, 993, 1442, 1513, 1525, 1526, 1554, 1838, 1861, 2548, 2556
	para 12	1513
FPR Pt 28	Costs (PD28A)	481, 911, 1196, 1210, 1443, 1849
	para 4.6	1165
FPR Pt 29	Human Rights Act 1998 (PD29B)	1861
	Human Rights, Joining the Crown (PD29A)	235, 995, 1860, 1867
	paras 1.1–1.6	1855
	paras 2.1–2.3	1855
	Transfer of Proceedings from the Family Court to the High Court (PD29C)	106, 109, 119, 133, 135, 138, 140, 161, 164, 167, 169, 544, 1862, 2715

FPR Pt 30	Appeals (PD30A)	192, 193, 194, 250, 799, 1059, 1236, 1863, 1867, 1868, 1872
	para 2.1	243, 2545
	para 4.6	194
	paras 4.7–4.9	194
	para 4.10	209
	paras 4.10–4.13	58
	para 4.14	1387
	para 4.15	58, 209
	para 4.18	209
	para 4.22	58
	para 4.23	58, 2355
	para 4.24	58
	para 5.8	195
	paras 5.9–5.12	196
	para 5.10A	209, 210
	para 5.10B	210
	para 5.10C	210
	para 5.12	195
	para 5.13	210
	paras 5.13–5.22	196
	para 6.2	210
	para 6.4(a)–(d)	210
	para 7.1	211
	paras 7.1–7.4	195
	para 7.2	211
	paras 7.7–7.12	197
	para 7.14	197, 211
	para 7.15	197, 211
	para 7.16	196
	para 7.17	196
	para 9.1	198
	paras 9.1–9.12	198
	paras 9.3–9.5	1059
	para 9.4	198
	para 9.8	197
	para 9.30	1871
	paras 12.1–12.3	1422
	para 13.1	1423
	para 13.2	1423
	para 14.1	1684
	para 18.3	213
	para 18.4	213
	para 18.5	213
	para 18.6	213
	para 18.7	213
FPR Pt 31	Registration of Orders under the Council Regulation, the Civil Partnership (Jurisdiction and Recognition of Judgments) Regulations 2005, the Marriage (Same Sex Couples) (Jurisdiction and Recognition of Judgments) Regulations 2014 and under the 1996 Hague Convention (PD31A)	173, 1905, 2742, 2743, 2790
	para 1.1	173
	para 1.2	173
	para 2.2	173
	para 4.2(a)	174
	para 4.2(b)	174
	para 4.2(c)	174
	para 4.2(d)	174
	para 4.2(e)	174
	para 4.2(f)	174
	para 4.3	174
	para 4.3(b)	174
	para 4.4	174
FPR Pt 32	Forms Relating to Part 32 (PD32A)	1924
FPR Pt 33	Enforcement of Undertakings (PD33A)	125, 1447, 1473, 1936, 1983

FPR Pt 34 Applications for Recognition and Enforcement To or From European Union Member States (PD34C) 1970, 2436, 2858
para 3.1 91
para 3.2 91
para 5.1 91
Form Relating to Part 34 (PD34D) 1973
Reciprocal Enforcement of Maintenance Orders – Designated Family Judge Areas (PD34E) 73, 76, 77, 82, 1973, 2834
para 4.2 92
para 4.3 92
para 4.4 92
para 4.5 92
para 7.1 91
para 7.2 91
para 7.3 2882
Reciprocal Enforcements of Maintenance Orders (PD34A) 64, 72, 74, 78, 90, 93, 1087, 1088, 1959, 2834
Annex 2 1948
Annex 3 1949
paras 1.1–2.3 2875
para 3.3 64
para 4.2 71
paras 4.5–4.7 71
para 4.9 72
para 4.10 72
para 4.11 72
para 8.1 1094
Tracing Payers Overseas (PD34B) 64, 71, 1969
FPR Pt 35 Mediation Directive (PD35A) 1979
FPR Pt 36 Pilot Scheme
Care and Supervision Proceedings and Other Proceedings Under Part 4 of the Children Act 1989 (PD36C) 1980
Annex 170, 2588
para 6.1 2588
Procedure for Using an Online System to Generate Applications in Certain Proceedings for a Matrimonial Order (PD36D) 46, 1330, 1331, 1379, 1406, 1407, 1408, 1409, 1980
Transitional Arrangements (PD36A) 1980
para 1.2 1979
para 2.1 1979
para 4.1 1979
para 4.2 1979
para 4.4 1979
para 4.5 1979
FPR Pt 37 Applications and Proceedings in Relation to Contempt of Court (PD37A) 35, 125, 797, 902, 906, 1473, 1478, 1483, 1484, 1998
para 1.1 30
para 2.1 903
paras 2.1–2.3 903
para 2.2 903
para 3 792, 804
para 12.2 129
para 12.3 129
para 13.2 125
FPR Pt 38 Recognition and Enforcement of Protection Measures (PD38A) 2009, 2300
FPR Pt 40 Charging Orders, Stop Orders and Stop Notices (PD40A) 2028
para 1.2 109
para 1.3 109
para 1.3(8) 109
para 3.1 109

SCPD 1 General Note and the Jurisdiction of the Supreme Court
para 1.2.17 197, 199

SCPD 3	Applications for Permission to Appeal	
	para 3.1.2	2354
	para 3.1.8	2355
	paras 3.1.8–3.1.10	200
	para 3.2.1	199, 2355
	paras 3.3.1–3.4.8	200
	para 3.3.17	200
	paras 3.6.1–3.6.16	197, 199
SCPD 4	Notice of Appeal	200
SCPD 5	Papers for the Appeal Hearing	
	paras 5.1.2–5.1.5	201
SCPD 6	The Appeal Hearing	
	para 6.2.2	2359
	paras 6.3.1–6.3.13	201
	paras 6.4.1–6.4.4	201
	para 6.5.1	201
SCPD 7	Applications, Documents, Forms and Orders	200
	Annex 1	2354, 2355
	Form 1	199
	Form 3	200
	para 7.2.3	2355
SCPD 8	Miscellaneous Matters	
	paras 8.3.1–8.3.8	201

Abbreviations

AA 1976	Adoption Act 1976
ACA 2002	Adoption and Children Act 2002
AFER 2005	Adoptions with a Foreign Element Regulations 2005
AJA 1920/1960/1969/1970/1982/1985	Administration of Justice Act 1920/1960/1969/1970/1982/1985
AJA 1999	Access to Justice Act 1999
CA 1989/2004	Children Act 1989/2004
CAA 2006	Children and Adoption Act 2006
CACA 1985	Child Abduction and Custody Act 1985
CAO	child arrangements order
CAP	Child Arrangements Programme
C(AP)O 1991	Children (Allocation of Proceedings) Order 1991
CCA 1981	Contempt of Court Act 1981
CCA 1984	County Courts Act 1984
CCA 2013	Crime and Courts Act 2013
CCR	County Court Rules 1981
CCRR 2014	County Court Remedies Regulations 2014
CFA 2014	Children and Families Act 2014
CJA 2003	Criminal Justice Act 2003
CJCSA 2000	Criminal Justice and Court Services Act 2000
CJJA 1982/1991	Civil Jurisdiction and Judgments Act 1982/1991
CJJ(M)R 2011	Civil Jurisdiction and Judgments (Maintenance) Regulations 2011
CLA(G)R 1989	Civil Legal Aid (General) Regulations 1989
CLSA 1990	Courts and Legal Services Act 1990
CLS(F)R 2000	Community Legal Service (Financial) Regulations 2000
CMOPA 2008	Child Maintenance and Other Payments Act 2008
COA 1979	Charging Orders Act 1979
CPA 2004	Civil Partnership Act 2004
CPFO 2008	Civil Proceedings Fees Order 2008
CPR 1998	Civil Procedure Rules 1998
CPR 1998, Sch 1, RSC	Rules taken from the Rules of the Supreme Court 1965 and set out (as amended) in Schedule 1 to CPR
CPR 1998, Sch 2, CCR	Rules taken from the County Court Rules 1981 and set out (as amended) in Schedule 2 to CPR
CRA 2005	Constitutional Reform Act 2005
CSA 1991	Child Support Act 1991
C(SA)R 1991	Children (Secure Accommodation) Regulations 1991
C(SA)(No 2)R 1991	Children (Secure Accommodation) (No 2) Regulations 1991
CS(CE)R 1992	Child Support (Collection and Enforcement) Regulations 1992
CSPSSA 2000	Child Support, Pensions and Social Security Act 2000
CYPA 1933/1969/2008	Children and Young Persons Act 1933/1969/2008
DA 1869	Debtors Act 1869
DAP(RP)A 1968	Domestic and Appellate Proceedings (Restriction of Publicity) Act 1968
DMPA 1973	Domicile and Matrimonial Proceedings Act 1973
DPMCA 1978	Domestic Proceedings and Magistrates' Courts Act 1978
D(P)R 2000	Divorce etc (Pensions) Regulations 2000
ECHR 1950	European Convention for the Protection of Human Rights and Fundamental Freedoms 1950
ECtHR	European Court of Human Rights
FC(CDB)R 2014	Family Court (Composition and Distribution of Business) Rules 2014

FGMA 2003	Female Genital Mutilation Act 2003
FJ(RE)A 1933	Foreign Judgments (Reciprocal Enforcement) Act 1933
FLA 1986/1996	Family Law Act 1986/1996
FLA 1986(DT)O 1991	Family Law Act 1986 (Dependent Territories) Order 1991
FLA 1996(FM)(RTP)O 2009	Family Law Act 1996 (Forced Marriage) (Relevant Third Party) Order 2009
FLRA 1969/1987	Family Law Reform Act 1969/1987
FMPO	Forced marriage protection order
FPC(CA 1989)R 1991	Family Proceedings Courts (Children Act 1989) Rules 1991
FPC(CSA 1991)R 1993	Family Proceedings Courts (Child Support Act 1991) Rules 1993
FPC(MP etc)R 1991	Family Proceedings Courts (Matrimonial Proceedings etc) Rules 1991
FPFO 2008	Family Proceedings Fees Order 2008
FPR 1991	Family Proceedings Rules 1991
FPR 2010	Family Procedure Rules 2010
GRA 2004	Gender Recognition Act 2004
HCCCJO 1991	High Court and County Courts Jurisdiction Order 1991
HFEA 1990/2008	Human Fertilisation and Embryology Act 1990/2008
I(PFD)A 1975	Inheritance (Provision for Family and Dependants) Act 1975
JA 1838	Judgments Act 1838
JCAR 2014	Justices' Clerks and Assistants Rules 2014
LASPOA 2012	Legal Aid, Sentencing and Punishment of Offenders Act 2012
LPA 1925	Law of Property Act 1925
LRA 2002	Land Registration Act 2002
LR(MP)A 1970	Law Reform (Miscellaneous Provisions) Act 1970
MA 1949	Marriage Act 1949
MCA 1973	Matrimonial Causes Act 1973
MCA 1980	Magistrates' Courts Act 1980
MCA 2005	Mental Capacity Act 2005
MC(AE)R 1971	Magistrates' Courts (Attachment of Earnings) Rules 1971
MCR 1981	Magistrates' Courts Rules 1981
MEA 1991	Maintenance Enforcement Act 1991
MFPA 1984	Matrimonial and Family Proceedings Act 1984
MOA 1950/1958	Maintenance Orders Act 1950/1958
MO(FE)A 1920	Maintenance Orders (Facilities for Enforcement) Act 1920
MO(RE)A 1972/1992	Maintenance Orders (Reciprocal Enforcement) Act 1972/1992
MoJ	Ministry of Justice
MPPA 1970	Matrimonial Proceedings and Property Act 1970
MWPA 1882	Married Women's Property Act 1882
PACE 1984	Police and Criminal Evidence Act 1984
PD	Practice Direction, Registrar's Direction, Secretary's Circular etc
PD[number]	Practice Direction which supplements Part [number] of CPR 1998 or FPR 2010
PD(PI)R 2000	Pensions on Divorce etc (Provision of Information) Regulations 2000
PHA 1997	Protection from Harassment Act 1997
PLO	Public Law Outline
PRMPC(IO)(EWNI)R 2010	Parental Responsibility and Measures for the Protection of Children (International Obligations) (England and Wales and Northern Ireland) Regulations 2010
REMO(HCC)O 1993	Reciprocal Enforcement of Maintenance Orders (Hague Convention Countries) Order 1993

REMO(USA)O 2007	Reciprocal Enforcement of Maintenance Orders (United States of America) Order 2007
RRCOSC 1988	Act of Sederunt (Rules for the Registration of Custody Orders of the Sheriff Court) 1988
RSC	Rules of the Supreme Court 1965
SCA 1981	Senior Courts Act 1981
SCFO 2009	Supreme Court Fees Order 2009
SCR 2009	Supreme Court Rules 2009
TCEA 2007	Tribunals, Courts and Enforcement Act 2007
TLATA 1996	Trusts of Land and Appointment of Trustees Act 1996
WRA 2009/2012	Welfare Reform Act 2009/2012
WRPA 1999	Welfare Reform and Pensions Act 1999
****/...	Some of the text from the statutory provision is not included in this work

PART I

Procedural Guides

PART I: Procedural Guides

Contents

SECTION A: APPLICATIONS FOR RELIEF OTHER THAN DIVORCE

A1: Contribution Order 11

A2: Financial Relief for a Child under Children Act 1989, Sch 1 12

A3: Declaration of Proprietary Rights under Married Women's Property Act 1882, s 17 or Civil Partnership Act 2004, s 66 14

A4: Order under Trusts of Land and Appointment of Trustees Act 1996, s 14 15

A5: Variation of a Maintenance Agreement under Matrimonial Causes Act 1973, s 35 20

A6: Claim for Financial Provision under the Inheritance (Provision for Family and Dependants) Act 1975 22

A7: Lay Justices' Powers to Make Orders for Financial Provision 25

A8: Non-molestation and/or Occupation Order under Family Law Act 1996, Pt IV 27

A9: Order for Forced Marriage Protection Order under Family Law Act 1996, Pt 4A 31

A10: Claims under the Protection from Harassment Act 1997 36

A11: Transfer of a Tenancy under Family Law Act 1996, Pt IV, s 53 and Sch 7 41

A12: Parental Order under Human Fertilisation and Embryology Act 2008, s 54 42

SECTION B: APPLICATION FOR MATRIMONIAL AND CIVIL PARTNERSHIP PROCEEDINGS AND RELATED ORDERS

B1: Declaration as to Marital Status 45

B2: Applications for Divorce, Judicial Separation or Nullity in Undefended Cases 45

B3: Staying Grant of Decree Absolute under Matrimonial Causes Act 1973, s 10A 48

B4: Applications for Divorce, Judicial Separation or Nullity Orders and Equivalent Civil Partnership Orders in Defended Case 49

B5: Financial applications in the Family Court under MCA 1973 for Orders for Maintenance Pending Suit (s 22), Financial Provision and Property Adjustment (ss 23–24), Pension Orders (ss 21B, 21C, 24B–24D and 24E–24G), Variation (s 31) and Consideration of Respondent's Financial Position (s 10(2)) and under CPA 2004, s 72 and Sch 5 50

PART I

B6: Injunctions to Restrain Future Disposals and Avoidance of Disposition Orders under Matrimonial Causes Act 1973, s 37 55

B7: Financial Relief after Overseas Proceedings under Matrimonial and Family Proceedings Act 1984, Pt III, Including Injunctions under s 24 to Restrain Anticipated Dealings 57

SECTION C: ENFORCEMENT OF ORDERS

C1: Reciprocal Enforcement 59

C1(1): Maintenance Order having been Made in England or Wales, Payee Seeks to Enforce it Abroad, and Vice Versa (not designated under MO(RE)A 1972) 64

C1(2): Application in England and Wales for a Provisional Maintenance Order against a Respondent Abroad, and Vice Versa (under MO(FE)A 1920) 66

C1(3): Maintenance Order having been Made in England or Wales, Payee Seeks to Enforce it in Scotland or Northern Ireland, and Vice Versa 68

C1(4): Variation or Discharge of Registered Maintenance Orders and Cancellation of Registration (Scotland and Northern Ireland) 70

C1(5): Maintenance Order having been Made in England or Wales, Payee Seeks to Enforce it Abroad, and Vice Versa (designated under MO(RE)A 1972) 71

C1(6): Application in England and Wales for a Maintenance Order against a Respondent Abroad, and Vice Versa (under MO(RE)A 1972) 74

C1(7): Application to Vary, Discharge or Revoke an Order Registered under Maintenance Orders (Reciprocal Enforcement) Act 1972, Pt I 78

C1(8): Applicant in England or Wales Makes Maintenance Claim for Transmission Abroad for Determination There against Respondent, and Vice Versa 81

C1(9): Variation and Revocation of Orders Registered under Maintenance Orders (Reciprocal Enforcement) Act 1972, Pt II 82

C1(10): Money Judgment or Order having been Made in England or Wales, Payee Seeks to Enforce it in Certain Commonwealth Countries, and Vice Versa 83

C1(11): Enforcement in Certain Foreign Countries of an English or Welsh Judgment or Order for Payment of a Sum of Money, and Vice Versa 86

C1(12): Enforcement in a European Union Member State, Non-European Union Contracting State to the 2007 Hague Convention or EFTA Country of a Maintenance Order Made in England and Wales, and Vice Versa 89

C1(13): Enforcement in a European Union or EFTA Country of a Judgment or Order (other than a Maintenance Order) Made in England or Wales, and Vice Versa 93

C1(14): Enforcement in Scotland or Northern Ireland of a Judgment or Order (other than a Maintenance Order) of an English or Welsh Court other than a Magistrates' Court, and Vice Versa 97

C1(15): Enforcement of an Uncontested Claim as a European Enforcement Order 100

C2: Lay Justices' Power to Enforce Orders for Financial Provision 102

C3: Registration in the Family Court of a Maintenance Order Made in the High Court 104

C4: Attachment of Earnings Order (High Court or Family Court) 105

C5: Charging Order 108

C6: Writ or Warrant of Delivery 111

C7: Execution against Goods 112

C8: Application for a Third Party Debt Order 113

C9: Committal by way of Judgment Summons 118

C10: Means of Payment Order 119

C11: Seeking 'Such Method of Enforcement as the Court Considers Appropriate' 120

C12: Obtaining Information from the Debtor 121

C13: Writ or Warrant of Possession of Land 124

C14: Committal and Arrest for Disobedience of an Injunctive Order or Breach of an Undertaking in the Family Court, the High Court and the County Court 125

SECTION D: CHILDREN

D1: Consent to Marriage of a Minor 131

D2: Emergency Protection Order 132

D3: Discharge of an Emergency Protection Order 134

D4: Extension of an Emergency Protection Order, Warrant under Children Act 1989, s 48(9) or Variation of Directions as to Contact or Assessment under Children Act 1989, s 44(9)(b) 137

D5: Recovery Order 140

D6: Parental Responsibility Order or Agreement (or Discharge of the Same) 142

D7: Child Arrangements Orders (or Discharge or Variation of the Same) 144

D8: Enforcement of Child Arrangements Orders 148

D9: Specific Issue Order or Prohibited Steps Order (or Discharge or Variation of the Same) 150

D10: Special Guardianship Order (or Discharge or Variation of the Same) 152

D11: Private Law Proceedings for the Disclosure of Information as to the Whereabouts of a Child 155

D12: Private Law Proceedings for an Order Authorising the Taking Charge of, and Delivery of, a Child 157

D13: Care or Supervision Order 159

D14: Discharge etc of a Care or Supervision Order, Substitution of a Supervision Order for a Care Order or Variation or Extension of a Supervision Order 163

D15: Regulating Contact with Children in Care 166

D16: Discharge or Variation of an Order Regulating Contact with Children in Care 169

D17: Secure Accommodation Order 171

D18: Applications for Recognition, Non-Recognition and Enforcement of Court Orders under the 1996 Convention 173

D19: Application in Respect of an Abducted Child under the Hague Convention 1980 or European Convention 1980 176

D20: Application for Registration of an Order under the Family Law Act 1986 in Respect of an Abducted Child 180

D21: Application to Enforce a Registered Order in Respect of an Abducted Child under the Family Law Act 1986 181

D22: Applications under the Inherent Jurisdiction of the High Court, including Wardship 181

D23: Placement Order 184

D24: Adoption Order 186

SECTION E: JUDICIAL REVIEWS AND APPEALS

E1: Application for Judicial Review 189

E2: Family Court – Appeal from Lay Justice or a Judge of District Judge Level to a Judge of Circuit Judge Level or from a District Judge of the High Court to a Judge of High Court Level 192

E3: Appeal from Magistrates under Child Support Act 1991 198

E4: Appeal from a Judge of the High Court or from the Court of Appeal to the Supreme Court 198

E5: Family Court – Appeal from Judge of Circuit Judge Level or a Judge of High Court Level to the Court of Appeal 202

E6: Family Court – Appeal from Judge of Circuit Judge Level in Private Law Cases to a Judge of the High Court 209

E7: Applications to Re-open or Set Aside Final Court Orders 211

E7(1): Application to Re-Open a Final Appeal 213

E7(2): Setting Aside a Financial Relief Order 213

SECTION F: MISCELLANEOUS

F1: Proceedings involving a Protected Party 215

F1(1): Family Proceedings involving a Protected Party 215

F1(2): Family Proceedings involving a Child 217

F1(3): Non-family Proceedings involving a Child or a Protected Party 219

F1(4): Resolving Doubt about Capacity 223

F2: Scientific Test Direction 226

F3: Withdrawal of Treatment in Persistent Vegetative State etc Cases where the Patient is an Adult 227

F4: Costs in Family Proceedings (High Court and Family Court) 227

F4(1): Order for Costs Against Another Party to the Proceedings 228

F4(2): Order for Wasted Costs 231

F4(3): Summary Assessment of Costs 231

F4(4): Detailed Assessment of Costs 232

F5: Application in Respect of the Human Rights Act 1998 234

F6: Alternative Procedure for Applications in Family Proceedings (FPR 2010, Pt 19) 236

Notes to Procedural Guides

(1) Index

Application	*Guide No*
abducted child	
enforcement (FLA 1986)	D21
Hague/European Convention 1980, under	D19
information as to whereabouts of	D11
registration order (FLA 1986)	D20
taking charge/delivery of	D12
adoption order	D24
placement order	D23
appeals	
Family Court	E2/E6
from magistrates (under CSA 1991)	E3
High Court judge/circuit judge to Court of Appeal	E5
High Court judge/Court of Appeal to Supreme Court	E4
to re-open or set aside final court orders	E7
attachment of earnings order	C4
care/supervision order	D13
discharge etc	D14
charging order	C5
child arrangements order	D7
enforcement	D8
committal	
breach of injunctive order etc	C14
judgment summons, by way of	C9
contact with child in care	D15
discharge etc	D16
contribution order	A1
costs (family proceedings)	F4
decree of divorce etc	
defended cause	B4
religious marriage	B3
undefended cause	B2
emergency protection order	D2
discharge	D3
extension etc	D4
enforcement	
lay justices' powers	C2
execution against goods	C7
family proceedings	
alternative procedure (FPR 2010, Pt 19)	F6
financial provision etc	B5
lay justices' powers	A7
overseas proceedings, in	B7
financial relief for child (CA 1989, Sch 1)	A2
forced marriage protection order (FLA 1996, Pt 4A)	A9
Hague Convention 1996	D18
human rights, declaration of	F5
inherent jurisdiction/wardship	D22
inheritance claim (I(PFD)A 1975)	A6
judicial review	E1
maintenance agreement, variation (MCA 1973, s 35)	A5
maintenance order, registration in the Family Court	C3
marital status, declaration of	B1
marriage of minor, consent to	D1
means of payment order	C10
non-molestation/occupation order (FLA 1996, Pt IV)	A8
obtaining information from debtor/seeking enforcement	C12

parental order
HFEA 2008, s 54, under A12
parental responsibility agreement/order D6
discharge D6
personal protection (PHA 1997) A10
proprietary rights, declaration of
MWPA 1882, s 17/CPA 2004, s 66, under A3
TLATA 1996, s 14, under A4
protected party, by or against F1
PVS patient, withdrawal of treatment F3
reciprocal enforcement C1
recovery order D5
restraining dealings with property
MCA 1973, s 37, under B6
scientific test, direction for F2
secure accommodation order D17
special guardianship D10
specific issue/prohibited steps order D9
tenancy transfer (FLA 1996, Pt IV) A11
third party debt order C8
writ/warrant, of
delivery C6
possession of land C13

(2) Fees

Information concerning fees payable is included, where appropriate, in the Guides that follow. However, **no** fee is payable where Schedule 2 to each of the Fees Orders applies (see annotations to both Fees Orders in Part IV).

A1: Contribution Order

Legal background

Where a local authority is looking after a child, it has to consider whether it should recover contributions towards that child's maintenance from either of his parents (where he is under 16) or from the child himself (where he is 16 or over) (CA 1989, Sch 2, para 21). If the local authority decides that it is reasonable to recover a contribution, it will first serve a contribution notice on the proposed contributor specifying the weekly sum he should contribute and the arrangements for payment (CA 1989, Sch 2, para 22). An agreement may then be reached between the authority and the contributor, but if no agreement is reached within one month from the service of the contribution notice, or if the contributor subsequently serves a notice withdrawing his agreement, the authority may apply to the court for a contribution order (CA 1989, Sch 2, para 23). The court may make an order requiring the contributor to contribute a weekly sum towards the child's maintenance. In fixing the sum, the court must have regard to the contributor's means and must not specify a sum greater than that specified in the local authority's contribution notice. A contribution order may be varied or revoked by the court (CA 1989, Sch 2, para 23(8)). Alternatively, a subsequent contribution agreement between the local authority and the contributor in accordance with Sch 2, para 23(6) will have the effect of discharging the order.

Procedure

Who may apply	Local authority looking after child	CA 1989, Sch 2, para 23
Which court	The Family Court	FC(CDB)R 2014, rr 14, 20
Which proceedings	Freestanding application	
Variation or discharge of order by which court	Court by which original order made	
Application	*Initial application* On Form C1, with sufficient copies for each respondent Copy of contribution notice Copy of any contributor's notice under CA 1989, Sch 2, para 22(8) withdrawing agreement	FPR 2010, rr 12.5, 12.7, 12.8 and 12.16; PD12C, para 2.1
	Variation/revocation application On Form C1, with sufficient copies for each respondent Copy of contribution order	FPR 2010, rr 12.5, 12.7, 12.8 and 12.16
Respondents	*Initial application* Contributor *Variation/revocation application* Where local authority is applicant, contributor Where contributor is applicant, local authority	FPR 2010, r 12.3
Additional persons to whom notice in Form C6A is to be given	Local authority providing accommodation for child Person caring for child at commencement of proceedings Person providing a s 51 refuge for child	FPR 2010, rr 12.3, 12.5, 12.7, 12.8 and 12.16; PD12C, para 3.1
Service	Copy of application, together with Form C6, to be served on respondents at least 14 days before date of hearing or directions appointment	FPR 2010, r 12.8; PD12C, paras 1.1, 2.1
	Form C6A to be served on additional persons at same time as application etc served on respondents	FPR 2010, r 12.8; PD12C, paras 1.1, 3.1
Ex parte	Not available	FPR 2010, r 12.16
Joinder or removal of parties	By court order, of its own motion or on written request	FPR 2010, rr 12.3(3), 16.2

Answer to application	No provision either forbidding or permitting an answer	
Directions	As to the powers of the justices' clerk or the court, see –	FPR 2010, rr 2.5, 2.6, 12.12 and Pt 4
Children's guardian	Not 'specified proceedings'	CA 1989, s 41(6); FPR 2010, r 12.27
Who has power to make the order	The Family Court	FC(CDB)R 2014, rr 14, 20; FPR 2010, r 12.3
Order	Form C21	FPR 2010, Pt 5
Appeals	See Guide E2	CA 1989, Sch 2, para 23(11); FPR 2010, Pt 30

A2: Financial Relief for a Child under Children Act 1989, Sch 1

Legal background

CA 1989, Sch 1 provides the legal basis for financial orders made for the benefit of a child of (unmarried) parents. Broadly, the orders available are for periodical payments (subject to the provisions of the CSA 1991), transfer or settlement of property and lump sums. For married parents, MCA 1973 provides a standalone legal basis for claims under MCA 1973, ss 23, 24 and 27.

An application under CA 1989, Sch 1 is defined as a financial remedy under FPR 2010, r 2.3. The procedure under FPR 2010, Pt 9, Ch 5 applies, envisaging a shorter procedure with the aim of early resolution. Applications are to the Family Court, to be dealt with at district judge level: FC(CDB)R 2014, Sch 1, para 2(d).

Applicants under Sch 1 are required to attend a mediation information and assessment meeting (MIAM) before making the application: CFA 2014, s 10(1); FPR 2010, Ch 3; PD3A, para 13(1)(b), subject to exemptions (FPR 2010, r 3.8).

Form E calculation errors

Subscribers should note that HMCTS recently became aware of calculation errors in the automatic calculators used in Form E1 (net assets not fully deducting certain liabilities). HMCTS is writing to those individuals who may be affected. Applications can be made to set aside or vary the original order if the order was materially affected by the calculation error. The application is made pursuant to FPR 2010, Pt 18 using Form D651; court fees will be waived.

Procedure

Who may apply	*Application for child under 18* Parent or guardian or special guardian of child or holder of child arrangements order The order will be made either on the application of the above or without an application on the making, varying or discharging of a child arrangements order *Application by child over 18* The child who is over 18 and: – who is or will be undergoing education or training or where there are special circumstances – who has not had in force a periodical payments order immediately before he was 16 – whose parents are not living together	CA 1989, Sch 1, para 1(1); FPR 2010, r 9.10 CA 1989, Sch 1, para 1(6) CA 1989, Sch 1, para 2(1)(a),(b) CA 1989, Sch 1, para 2(3),(6) CA 1989, Sch 1, para 2(4)

	Variation application Any of the persons set out above, with, additionally on an application under CA 1989, Sch 1, para 1, the child himself if he has reached 16	CA 1989, Sch 1, para 6(4)
	Application to alter maintenance agreement Either party to the agreement or a personal representative	CA 1989, Sch 1, paras 10(2), 11(1)
Level of judge	District judge	FC(CDB)R 2014, Sch 1, para 2(d)
Application	Preliminary requirement for proposed parties to attend a MIAM before application, subject to exemptions	CFA 2014, s 10(1); FPR 2010, Ch 3; PD3A, para 13(1)(b); FPR 2010, r 3.8
	To the Family Court	FPR 2010, r 9.5(2)
	The application is on Form A1 together with any documents stated to be required or referred to in the application. Proceedings start when a court officer issues an application, and are issued on that date	FPR 2010, rr 5.1–5.3; PD5A
	The application is dealt with by the shorter procedure in FPR 2010, Pt 9, Ch 5	FPR 2010, rr 9.18–9.20; PD9A
	On application, the court may direct that the longer procedure in FPR 2010, Pt 9, Ch 4 is followed, for example where there are contested issues about the settlement of property. This is determined on paper without notice to the parties before the first hearing	FPR 2010, r 9.18A
Fee	£215	FPFO 2008, fee 2.1(v)
Service	Within 4 days of the date on which the application was filed, a court officer will serve a copy of the application on the respondent and give notice of the date of the first hearing to both parties. Alternatively, the applicant must serve the respondent within 4 days, beginning with the date on which the copy of the application was received from the court, and file a certificate of service on or before the first appointment	FPR 2010, r 9.12(1),(2)
Respondents	Any parent who is not an applicant, or both parents, where the holder of a child arrangements order or special guardianship order makes an application	CA 1989, Sch 1, para 1(2)
Directions/Interim orders	The court may make an interim order for periodical payments. FPR 2010, Pt 18 procedure applies to applications for interim orders	CA 1989, Sch 1, para 9; FPR 2010, r 9.7(2)
Procedure	The shorter procedure under FPR 2010, Pt 9, Ch 5 applies	
	The court will fix a first hearing not less than 4 weeks and not more than 8 weeks after the filing of the application	FPR 2010, r 9.18(1)
	Not more than 14 days after the issue of the application, parties must simultaneously exchange and file with the court a financial statement	FPR PD5A
	No disclosure or inspection of the parties' documents may be given between the filing of the application and the first hearing, save as laid down in FPR 2010, r 9.19(4)	FPR 2010, r 9.19(4)

	Unless the court is able to determine the application at the first hearing, the court may direct further evidence and set a date for a directions hearing or final hearing	FPR 2010, r 9.20
Order	*Application for child under 18* Periodical payments Secured periodical payments Lump sum Settlement of property or transfer of property *Application by child over 18* Periodical payments Lump sum *Application to alter maintenance agreement* Varying or revoking any financial arrangements contained in the maintenance agreement, including inserting provision for periodical payments or for security for increasing or decreasing the level of periodical payments	
Appeals	See Guides E2 and E5	

A3: Declaration of Proprietary Rights under Married Women's Property Act 1882, s 17 or Civil Partnership Act 2004, s 66

Legal background

The High Court and the Family Court have jurisdiction on an application by a spouse, fiancé(e) to declare and enforce their proprietary rights in respect of any property that they possess or control at the time of the application or, as extended by s 7 of the Matrimonial Causes (Property and Maintenance) Act 1958, that they formerly possessed or controlled. The use of MWPA 1882, s 17 has been strongly disapproved when MCA 1973, ss 23 and 24 are available but it is useful in two circumstances: (i) where a declaration of beneficial ownership is needed if there are doubts about the solvency of one of the parties; (ii) as suggested in *Wicks v Wicks* [1998] 1 FLR 470, CA where an order for sale [of property] is required before the making of a financial order: only if, in an applicable case, the court is also satisfied that the other party's home rights should be terminated after applying and balancing the factors in FLA 1996, s 33(6): see *BR v VT (Financial Remedies: Interim)* [2016] 2 FLR 519, FD and commentary to MWPA 1882, s 17.

Where a claim for title or possession of property under MWPA 1882, s 17 or CPA 2004, s 66 is made in any proceedings for a financial order, the procedure under FPR 2010, Pt 18 applies. An application under MWPA 1882 or CPA 2004 is not a claim for a financial order or financial remedy.

Procedure

Who may apply	Spouse, civil partner, fiancé(e), provided application made within 3 years of decree absolute or termination of engagement	MPPA 1970, s 39; LR(MP)A 1970, s 2(2)
Level of judge	District judge	FC(CDB)R 2014, Sch 1, para 2(a)
Application	The application may be made to the Family Court or the same court as matrimonial/civil partnership proceedings	FC(CDB)R 2014, Sch 1, para 2; FPR 2010, r 8.14, PD8A, para 1.1(a)
	Application must be made using Pt 18 procedure if it is made in the course of existing proceedings. If there are no existing proceedings then Pt 19 applies	FPR 2010, r 8.13

	Application is by notice of application on Form D50, stating what order is sought and why, with a draft order attached. Application to transfer tenancy under MWPA 1882, s 17 is on Form D50B	FPR 2010, rr 8.4–8.7
Fee	£245	FPFO 2008, fee 1.1
Service	A copy of the application notice must be served in accordance with the provisions of FPR 2010, Pt 6, at least 7 days before the hearing, with any written evidence in support and the draft order sought Where there is a mortgage, the applicant must serve the mortgagee	FPR 2010, r 18.8 FPR 2010, r 8.15
Respondents	Spouses, fiancé(e)s, parties to concluded proceedings and any other person the court may direct A mortgagee who requests joinder must be made a party	FPR 2010, r 18.3 FPR 2010, r 8.15(2)
Procedure	Application may be dealt with without a hearing, if the court considers it appropriate and the parties agree. There is power to proceed in the absence of the parties Order may be made without notice to the respondent, subject to his right to apply to set aside or vary	FPR 2010, rr 18.9, 18.11 FPR 2010, r 18.10
Orders	The court may make interim orders, give directions, grant injunctions ancillary to the claim and make final orders Power to grant injunctions ancillary to claim Power to declare and enforce proprietary rights of both parties, including power to order sale; power to order lump sum equal in value to assessed interest	FPR 2010, r 8.16 Matrimonial Causes (Property and Maintenance) Act 1958, s 7(7); *Bothe v Amos* [1976] Fam 46
Appeals	See Guides E2, E4 and E5	

A4: Order under Trusts of Land and Appointment of Trustees Act 1996, s 14

Legal background

TLATA 1996, s 14 provides the procedural means whereby parties who assert that they have an interest in land as trustees can apply to the court to exercise its powers (eg if their powers are being opposed by fellow trustee(s), or by others who have an interest in land subject to their trust interests). Section 14(2) provides accordingly that on application for an order, in this case generally to the High Court or the County Court, the court may make 'such order' as

- Declares – that is, defines – the 'nature or extent of a person's interest in [the trust] property'; or
- Relates to any functions of the trustees (eg to sell property).

A trust may be express (the trusts are defined in writing), implied (constructive or resulting trusts) or imposed by law (eg by bankruptcy).

Mostly, claims will be dealt with on family breakdown under CPR 1998. However, there will be cases where parallel family property proceedings may be in progress (governed by FPR 2010) or family proceedings under FPR 2010 may be the lead proceedings and, for example, the trust property is a former matrimonial home and a third party (eg one spouse's parent or parents) has a trust claim on that home. If the former matrimonial home is made subject to a bankruptcy order, the case will almost certainly proceed under Insolvency Rules 1986.

In proceedings under MCA 1973, in *Tebbutt v Haynes* [1981] 2 All ER 238, CA, the Court of Appeal held that the family courts can dispose of all issues relevant to matrimonial assets in the family proceedings, with the trustees joined as interveners: 'If there is a dispute between a respondent spouse and a third party as to the ownership of a particular item of property which stands in the respondent spouse's name, that dispute must be resolved before the judge can make an effective final order under [MCA 1973, s 24]'. (See also case management directions (often later commended by senior courts judges) in *TL v ML (Ancillary Relief: Claim against Assets of Extended Family)* [2006] 1 FLR 1263, FD.)

The County Court (but not the Family Court) has the same equity jurisdiction as the High Court (CCA 1984, s 23):

23 Equity jurisdiction

The county court shall have all the jurisdiction of the High Court to hear and determine –

[…]

(b) proceedings –

(i) for the execution of any trust, or

(ii) for a declaration that a trust subsists,

where the estate or fund subject, or alleged to be subject, to the trust does not exceed in amount or value the county court limit; [which now stands at £350,000]

[…]

The main forms of process in family proceedings that will be considered here are where the application is made for the following:

(1) Declaration of an implied (resulting or constructive) trust;
(2) An application for an order for sale of a trust interest;
(3) An application under TLATA 1996, s 14 alongside CA 1989, Sch 1 proceedings;
(4) An intervener 'chancery' claim by trustees in MCA 1973 proceedings.

Crossover procedural rules

It will be appreciated that (3) and (4) above (and the same will apply if an application is made by a trustee in bankruptcy) involve parallel procedural rules, namely CPR 1998 and FPR 2010 (and could involve also Insolvency Rules 1986). Yet, there is no practice direction that assists courts or parties to know how they are to deal with cases where separate rules and court administrative arrangements conflict. What follows is a suggested solution to this problem.

Procedure

(1) Declaration of an implied (resulting or constructive) trust

Who may apply	The claimant who seeks to assert: (a) an implied trust interest in the land held in the name of another or others; or (b) a share other than that shown on the legal title, eg: (i) *Constructive trust* Thus a cohabitant who claims an agreement with her cohabitee that she was to have a share; (ii) *Resulting trust* Parents or other relatives who claim a trust results to them for their investment into a couple's home (see **(4)**, below) (iii) *Joint ownership* Where an owner wishes to assert as at (b), above	*Lloyds Bank plc v Rosset* [1990] 2 FLR 155, HL
Application	For a declaration as to how the property is held	TLATA 1996, s 14(2)(b)
Court	High Court, Chancery Division County Court (marked 'Chancery Business') – subject to County Court equity jurisdiction limit, i e £350,000	CPR PD7A, para 2.5 CCA 1984, s 23; County Court Jurisdiction Order 2014, Art 3
Defendant	Legal owner	

Fee	High Court: £480 County Court: £355	CPFO 2008, fee 1.4
Procedure	CPR 1998, Pt 7 (generally)	
Pleading the claim	Particulars of claim should be either included in the claim form (unlikely in TLATA 1996 claim) or served separately within 14 days after service of the claim form	CPR 1998, Pt 16; PD16, paras 3, 8
	Content of particulars will include pleaded information (but not actual evidence at this stage) including, for example submissions arising from: • TLATA 1996, s 15 • *Stack v Dowden* [2007] 1 FLR 1858, HL, at [69] • Details of any oral or other agreement	CPR PD16, paras 7.4, 7.5
Defence		CPR PD16, para 10
Case management issues that may arise (for more detail on CPR 1998 proceedings, see Civil Court Service (LexisNexis))		
Disclosure	'Disclosure' means stating that a document exists and providing a list accordingly	CPR 1998, r 31.2
	'Standard disclosure' must be provided as defined by r 31.6, limited to documents in a party's control	CPR 1998, r 31.8
	The right to inspect, save for exceptions in r 31.3	CPR 1998, r 31.3
Information	Preliminary request for 'clarification or information'	CPR PD18, para 1.1
	Order for information	CPR 1998, r 18.1
	Restriction on use of information	CPR 1998, r 18.2
Evidence	The court may control evidence	CPR 1998, r 31.2
Expert (i e opinion) evidence	Use only with permission	CPR 1998, r 35.4
	Limited to that which is 'reasonably required to resolve' an application	CPR 1998, r 35.1
Case management	(1) Definition of issues (2) Control of evidence (3) Definition of preliminary issues (if any) for split trial	CPR 1998, rr 1.4, 3.1
Adding or substituting a party	A party may be added: – to resolve all issues – to resolve issues which involve that party	CPR 1998, r 19.2(2)
Hearing	Open court unless otherwise ordered	CPR 1998, r 39.2
Level of judge	High Court (Chancery Division): by judge; only by a Master or district judge if the parties agree	CPR PD2B, para 4.1
	County Court: by judge; only by a district judge if the parties agree and DCJ consent; or if proceedings for recovery of land	CPR PD2B, para 11.1(b) and (d)
(2) An order for sale of a trust interest		
Who may apply	The claimant who is one of two or more trustees (e g a joint owner, i e one of two cohabitants); trustee in bankruptcy	

Application	For an order for sale (an 'exercise by [a trustee] of any of [his/her] functions')	TLATA 1996, s 14(2)(a)
Court	High Court, Chancery Division	CPR PD7A, para 2.5
	County Court (marked 'Chancery Business') subject to 'County Court limit'	CCA 1984, s 23
Defendant	The other owner(s)	
Fee	High Court: £480	
	County Court: £355	CPFO 2008, fee 1.4
Procedure	CPR 1998, Pt 7 (generally)	
Pleading the claim	Particulars of claim should be either included in the claim form (unlikely in TLATA 1996 claim) or served separately within 14 days after service of the claim form	CPR 1998, Pt 16; PD16, paras 3, 8
	Content of particulars will include pleaded information (but not evidence at this stage) including, for example: • TLATA 1996, s 15 • Details of any oral or other agreement • If children or other purpose of trust not exhausted: justification for exercising power of sale	CPR PD16, paras 7.4, 7.5
Defence		CPR PD16, para 10
Steps in proceedings (as in (1), above)		
(3) An application under TLATA 1996, s 14 alongside Children Act 1989, Sch 1 proceedings		
Who may apply	A parent who is not married to the parent of his/her children and who owns or otherwise claims a trust interest in the parties and their child(ren)'s home	*W v W (Joinder of Trusts of Land Act and Children Act 1989 Applications)* [2004] 2 FLR 321, CA (both sets of proceedings should be dealt with together)
Application	By the carer parent, e g for orders under: (1) CA 1989, Sch 1 for lump sum or property adjustment (e g adjustment of shares), perhaps carer allowance etc (2) TLATA 1996 (a) Non-owner parent: per **(1)** (b) Absent parent: perhaps per **(2)**, above	CA 1989, Sch 1, para 1 TLATA 1996, s 14(2)(a),(b)
Court	(1) (i) High Court, Family Division (ii) Family Court (2) (i) High Court, Chancery Division (ii) County Court subject to 'County Court limit' **Note:** (1) files can be consolidated at High Court level (as with bankruptcy in family proceedings: transferred to High Court); but no longer are CA 1989 and TLATA 1996 both in the same County Court (2) There still remains the problem (as before April 2014) of how files which proceed under CPR 1998 and FPR 2010 are to be dealt with in parallel	CPR PD7A, para 2.5 CCA 1984, s 23

Defendant/ respondent	The other parent	
Fee	(1) Family courts: £308	CPFO 2008, fee 1.5
	(2) High Court: £480 County Court: £355	CPFO 2008, fee 1.4
Procedure	(1) FPR 2010, Pt 9	
	(2) CPR 1998, Pt 7 (generally: as at **(1)**, above)	
Pleading the claim	(1) Form E	FPR 2010, Pt 5, r 9.4
	(2) As at **(1)** and **(2)**, above **Note:** if an oral agreement: see requirements of CPR PD16, paras 7.4, 7.5	CPR PD16, paras 3, 8
Defence	(1) Reply by simultaneous Form E	FPR 2010, r 9.14(1)
	(2) Per CPR 1998 as at **(1)**, above	CPR PD16, para 10
Disclosure	Parties are urged to follow the common law as codified in CPR 1998, Pt 31 and touched upon in FPR 2010; and see 'Disclosure' under (1), above	FPR 2010, r 21.1; CPR 1998, Pt 31
Information	(1) By direction on application to district judge only (i e CPR 1998, Pt 18 voluntary provision of information not permitted)	FPR 2010, r 9.15(2)(a)
	(2) Preliminary request for 'clarification or information' Order for information Restriction on use of information	CPR PD18, para 1.1 CPR 1998, r 18.1 CPR 1998, r 18.2
(4) An intervener claim by trustees in MCA 1973 proceedings		
Application by intervener as preliminary issue in MCA 1973 financial relief proceedings	Parties claiming an interest in parties' property, such as their former matrimonial home (e g person(s) who provided capital to buy the property claiming a resulting trust)	
Application	For a declaration as to how the property is held	TLATA 1996, s 14(2)(b); *Tebbutt v Haynes* [1981] 2 All ER 238, CA
Making the application	(1) By freestanding Chancery application: e g where no existing MCA 1973 proceedings	CPR 1998, Pt 7, r 19.2
	(2) Intervene in MCA 1973 or CA 1989, Sch 1 proceedings; parties can be added on FPR 2010, Pt 18 application	*Tebbutt v Haynes*
Court	County Court (or if transferred: Family Court), but if CPR 1998 proceedings are already underway proceedings can only proceed in parallel in the High Court	
Defendant	The (other) owner(s)	
Fee	If free-standing CPR 1998 proceedings High Court: £480 County Court: £355	CPFO 2008, fee 1.4

Procedure	Neither rules nor practice guidance indicate whether courts will proceed under FPR 2010 or CPR 1998 (where procedures differ, e g on disclosure, information, valuation, evidence etc) **Note:** in general terms CPR 1998 is likely to be more economical: (a) not so prescriptive in terms of information and irrelevant documents to be disclosed (b) where needed, clearer rules on information and disclosure (c) clarity of rules and law on whether proceedings are in private or in open court (see CPR 1998, r 39.2)	
Case management	Preliminary issue for trial must be defined and directions given for its separate trial	*Edgerton v Edgerton and Shaikh* [2012] 2 FLR 273, CA; *Arif v Anwar and anor* [2013] EWHC 624 (Fam), FD
Pleading the claim	Must be pleaded as if a 'Chancery' claim: *TL v ML (Ancillary Relief: Claim against Assets of Extended Family)* [2006] 1 FLR 1263, FD	CPR 1998, Pt 16; PD16, paras 3, 8; any oral agreement: PD16, paras 7.4, 7.5
Defence	Pleaded as for the claim, above	CPR PD16, para 10

A5: Variation of a Maintenance Agreement under Matrimonial Causes Act 1973, s 35

Legal background

The court's power to vary a maintenance agreement during the lives of the parties (MCA 1973, s 35) is exercised by the Family Court.

An application under s 35 is defined as a financial remedy under FPR 2010, r 2.3. The procedure under Pt 9 applies. For the procedure to vary a maintenance agreement on the death of one of the parties, see FPR 2010, rr 8.6–8.11.

Applicants under MCA 1973, s 35 are required to attend a mediation information and assessment meeting (MIAM) before making the application: CFA 2014, s 10(1); FPR 2010, Ch 3; PD3A, para 13(1)(d), subject to exemptions (FPR 2010, r 3.8).

Procedure

Who may apply	Either spouse	MCA 1973, s 35(1)
Level of judge	District judge	FC(CDB)R 2014, Sch 1, para 2(b)
Application	Preliminary requirement for proposed parties to attend a MIAM before application, subject to exemptions	CFA 2014, s 10(1); FPR 2010, Ch 3; PD3A, para 13(1)(d); FPR 2010, r 3.8
	The application is on Form D50H, together with any documents stated to be required, or referred to in the application. Proceedings start when a court officer issues an application and are issued on that date	FPR 2010, rr 5.1–5.3; PD5A
Fee	£245	FPFO 2008, fee 1.1

Service	Within 4 days of the date on which the application was filed, a court officer will serve a copy of the application on the respondent and give notice of the date of first hearing to both parties Alternatively, the applicant must serve the respondent within 4 days, beginning with the date on which the copy of the application was received from the court, and file a certificate of service on or before the first appointment	FPR 2010, r 9.12(1),(2)
Procedure	The court will fix a first appointment not less than 12 weeks and not more than 16 weeks after the filing of the application	FPR 2010, r 9.12
	By 35 days before the first appointment, the parties must simultaneously exchange a financial statement on Form E1, accompanied by a limited category of documents. No disclosure or inspection of the parties' documents may be given between the filing of the application and the first appointment, save as laid down in FPR 2010, r 9.14(4)	FPR PD5A; FPR 2010, r 9.14(4)
	By 14 days before the first appointment, each party must file and serve a concise statement, a chronology, a questionnaire and a notice stating whether that party will be in a position to use the hearing as a FDR appointment. In addition, the parties should if possible exchange an agreed case summary, a schedule of assets and a draft of directions sought by the parties	FPR 2010, r 9.14(5); PD9A
	At the first appointment, the court in pursuance of the overriding objective in FPR 2010, Pt 1 will case manage the financial application in relation to defining the issues and saving costs. The court will approve the content of questionnaires and make directions in respect of replies, requests for documents and expert evidence. The next hearing, normally the FDR, will be timetabled. Both parties must attend in person. Costs will be considered. After the first appointment, there is no further provision for the disclosure of documents, save with the leave of the court	FPR 2010, rr 9.15, 9.16
	At the FDR appointment, the parties are to meet for discussion and negotiation. 7 days before the FDR appointment, the applicant must file details of all offers and proposals and the responses to them. If the court cannot make a consent order, the court must give direction for final hearing. Both parties must personally attend the FDR hearing, unless the court directs otherwise	FPR 2010, r 9.17; PD9A
Order	Vary or revoke financial arrangements contained in the agreement, or insert new financial arrangements into the agreement for the benefit of spouse or child	MCA 1973, ss 34(2), 35(2)
	Statutory charge may be rolled over on MCA 1973, s 35	CLA(G)R 1989, reg 94(d)(i)
Appeals	See Guides E2, E4 and E5	

A6: Claim for Financial Provision under the Inheritance (Provision for Family and Dependants) Act 1975

Legal background

Certain members of the deceased's family and dependants may make a claim for financial provision out of the net estate of the deceased, on the ground that the disposition of the deceased's estate effected by his will and/or under the laws of intestacy is not such as to make reasonable financial provision for the applicant (I(PFD)A 1975, s 1 and CPA 2004). Unless the court gives permission extending the time limit, the application must be made within 6 months of the date on which representation is first granted (s 4) but an application may be made before the grant is issued.

The procedure for both the High Court and County Court is governed by CPR 1998, Pt 57. Rule 57.16 (as amended) takes account of applications made before the grant is issued. See also CPR PD57 and CPR PD8A in Part III. Before issuing proceedings practitioners must comply with the CPR Protocol and paras 24.5–24.10 of the Chancery Guide 2002, Ch 24. Non-compliance could result in the court making an order for costs against the non-complying party (CPR 1998, r 44.2).

Procedure

Who may apply	The spouse (which includes the surviving spouse of a same-sex marriage) of the deceased	I(PFD)A 1975, s 1(a); Marriage (Same Sex Couples) Act 2013, s 11, Sch 3, para 5(1)(a),(b)
	The registered civil partner of the deceased	I(PFD)A 1975, s 1(a); CPA 2004, s 71, Sch 4
	The former spouse (which includes the surviving spouse of a same-sex marriage) of the deceased who has not remarried	I(PFD)A 1975, s 1(b); Marriage (Same Sex Couples) Act 2013, s 11, Sch 3, para 5(1)(a),(b)
	The former civil partner of the deceased who has not formed a subsequent civil partnership	I(PFD)A 1975, s 1(b); CPA 2004, s 71, Sch 4
	A cohabitant of the deceased	I(PFD)A 1975, ss 1(1)(ba), 1A
	A person who lived in the same household as the deceased as his/her civil partner	I(PFD)A 1975, s 1(1)(ba), s 1B; CPA 2004, s 71, Sch 4
	A child of the deceased	I(PFD)A 1975, s 1(1)(c)
	Any person who in relation to any marriage or civil partnership to which the deceased was at any time a party, or otherwise in relation to any family to which the deceased at any time stood in the role of a parent, was treated by the deceased as a child of the family	I(PFD)A 1975, s 1(1)(d), as amended; Marriage (Same Sex Couples) Act 2013, s 11, Sch 3, para 5
	Any other person who immediately before the death of the deceased was being maintained either wholly or partly by him	I(PFD)A 1975, s 1(1)(e); CPA 2004
Which court	High Court (Chancery or Family Division) or County Court. The County Court has unlimited jurisdiction to hear claims under the Act	CPR 1998, r 57.15; CCA 1984, s 25
	District judges (including district judges of the Principal Registry of the Family Division) have jurisdiction to hear such applications	CPR 1998, r 57.15
Application	*High Court/County Court*	
	By Pt 8 claim form, which should be entitled 'In the estate of . . . deceased' and 'In the matter of I(PFD)A 1975' and set out the remedy sought and the grounds for the same	CPR 1998, rr 8.2, 57.16(1)

Time limit	The claim must be issued within 6 months of the date on which representation is taken out (unless extended by the court) but an application can and should be made before such representation is first taken out. Application to extend the time limit must be included in the claim form	I(PFD)A 1975, s 4, as amended
Documents	The applicant must file with the claim form a witness statement/affidavit in support exhibiting an official copy of the grant of probate or letters of administration and of every testamentary document admitted to proof. Where an application is made before a grant has been obtained, the written evidence must: (a) explain the reasons why it has not been possible for a grant to be obtained; and (b) be accompanied by the original or copy (if either is available) of the will or other testamentary document in respect of which probate or letters of administration are to be granted; (c) contain (so far as known) (i) brief details of the property comprised in the estate with an approximate estimate of its capital value and of any income received from it, (ii) details of the liabilities of the estate, (iii) names and addresses of the persons who are in possession of documents relating to the estate and (iv) names of the beneficiaries and their respective interests in the estate. The statement must be accompanied by the original or a copy of the will (if available) or other testamentary document	CPR 1998, rr 8.5(1),(2), 57.16(3),(3A)
Defendants	Personal representatives Beneficiaries Other persons affected by the claim Any other person directed by the court to be added Where no grant has been obtained, the claim may be made without naming a defendant	CPR 1998, rr 19.7, 57.16(3A)
Service	The claim form must be served within 4 months after date of issue Extension of time must be sought under CPR 1998, r 7.6	
Acknowledgement of service	Acknowledgement of service must be filed within 21 days after service of the claim form and served on the claimant and other parties if served within the jurisdiction If served outside the jurisdiction under CPR 1998, r 6.32 or 6.33, this period is extended by 7 days longer than that specified in r 6.35 or PD6B A personal representative who wishes to remain neutral and agrees to abide by the decision of the court should state this in section A of the acknowledgement of service For service on children and patients see CPR 1998, r 6.6 otherwise, in accordance with CPR 1998, r 10.3(2)	CPR 1998, r 57.16(4) CPR 1998, r 57.16(4A). See also, rr 8.3(1), 10.3(1) CPR 1998, rr 57.16(5); PD57A, para 15 CPR 1998, r 10.3(2)

Statement/Affidavit in answer	Must be filed by the personal representatives within 21 days after service of the claim form (it should include the matters set out in CPR PD57, para 16) May be filed by other defendants within 21 days after service of the claim form	CPR 1998, r 57.16(4),(5); PD57, para 16 CPR 1998, r 57.16(4)
Service of answer	Every defendant who files any written evidence within 21 days in answer must serve a copy on the claimant and every other defendant who is not represented by the same solicitor	CPR 1998, r 57.16(4)
Reply	A claimant may file and serve a statement in reply on all other parties within 14 days of service of the defendant's evidence on him	CPR 1998, r 8.5(5),(6)
Directions/case management conference pre-trial hearing	At the same time as issuing the claim form a directions hearing may be requested. Where a claim is made before a grant is obtained, application for directions may be made as to the representation of the estate The court will in any event give directions after the defendant has filed the acknowledgement of service or after the time for filing it has expired Parties must complete the listing questionnaire in Form N170 and provide (unless the court otherwise orders) a costs budget, following which the court will consider whether to hold a case-management conference or a pre-trial review, set a timetable and fix the date for the trial	CPR PD8A, para 4.1; r 57.16(3A) CPR PD8A, para 4.2; CPR 1998, rr 29.6–29.8
Fee	High Court: £528 County Court: £308	CPFO 2008, fee 1.5 CPFO 2008, fee 1.5
Order	Periodical payments Lump sum Transfer of property Settlement of property Acquisition, transfer and settlement of property Variation of antenuptial and post-nuptial settlement, including settlement made during the subsistence of or in anticipation of the formation of a civil partnership Variation for the applicant's benefit of the trusts on which the deceased's estate is held whether arising under the will or the law of intestacy or both Variation or discharge of secured periodical payments Variation or revocation of maintenance agreements Order setting aside disposition intended to defeat a claim under the Act Treatment of deceased's former beneficial interest in joint property as part of his estate and not passing by survivorship Interim order Consequential orders	I(PFD)A 1975, s 2(1)(a) I(PFD)A 1975, s 2(1)(b) I(PFD)A 1975, s 2(1)(c) I(PFD)A 1975, s 2(1)(d) I(PFD)A 1975, s 2(1)(e) I(PFD)A 1975, s 2(1)(f),(g) I(PFD)A 1975, s 2(1)(h) I(PFD)A 1975, s 16 I(PFD)A 1975, s 17 I(PFD)A 1975, ss 10, 11 I(PFD)A 1975, s 9 I(PFD)A 1975, s 5 I(PFD)A 1975, s 2(4)
Appeals	See Guides E2, E4 and E5	

A7: Lay Justices' Powers to Make Orders for Financial Provision

Legal background

Three separate forms of application for financial provision may be made under DPMCA 1978: an application under DPMCA 1978, s 2 based on the grounds in s 1 (failure to provide reasonable maintenance for the applicant or for any child of the family, behaviour or desertion); an application under DPMCA 1978, s 6 based on agreed financial provision; or an application under DPMCA 1978, s 7 based on the level of maintenance paid in the 3 months preceding the date of the application while the parties have been living apart by agreement.

There is provision for the 'conversion' of an application under DPMCA 1978, s 2 to an application under s 6, and for the 'conversion' of an application under s 7 to an application under s 2.

Financial provision may be made for either party to the marriage and for any child of the family (as defined in DPMCA 1978, s 88). The court is required to have regard to the matters contained in DPMCA 1978, s 3 in assessing the amount of any order.

A lump sum order is available under DPMCA 1978, s 2(1)(b) for the benefit of a spouse and under s 2(1)(d) for the benefit of a child of the family. The amount of any lump sum order under s 2 is limited to £1000. Lump sum orders are also available under DPMCA 1978, s 6(2)(b) to a spouse and s 6(2)(d) for a child of the family. There is no limit to the amount of a lump sum order under s 6.

The term of a periodical payments order to a spouse is governed by DPMCA 1978, s 4; the term of an order to or for a child of the family is governed by DPMCA 1978, s 5. Financial provision for children under CA 1989, Sch 1 is now allocated to judges at District Judge level (FC(CDB)R 2014, Sch 1, para 2(d)) and financial applications under that Act will no longer be heard by lay justices.

Periodical payments and lump sum orders payable by instalments may be ordered to be paid under MEA 1991, s 1 either directly between the parties, through the court, by standing order or by an attachment of earnings order.

CPA 2004, s 72(3) and Sch 6 make provision for financial relief in connection with civil partnerships (civil partners and children of the family) by lay justices corresponding to the provisions in DPMCA 1978.

Proceedings under DPMCA 1978 and CPA 2004 are governed by FPR 2010 and defined as an application for a financial remedy under FPR 2010, r 2.3. The procedure under Pt 9, Ch 5 applies with the aim of early resolution. Applicants are required to attend a mediation and information assessment meeting (MIAM) before making the application: CFA 2014, s 10(1); FPR 2010, r 3.6(2)(b) and PD3A, para 13(1)(e), subject to exemptions (FPR 2010, r 3.8).

The jurisdiction of the lay justices to make orders for financial relief in respect of a child under DPMCA 1978 is limited by the provisions of CSA 1991. A claim for child maintenance against a step-parent or civil partner is unaffected by CSA 1991.

Procedure

Who may apply	Either party to a marriage	DPMCA 1978, ss 1, 6(1), 7(1)
	Either party to a civil partnership	CPA 2004, Sch 6, paras 1, 9, 15
Which court	Application is made to the Family Court and that court has jurisdiction even if one of the parties is not domiciled in England	DPMCA 1978, ss 1, 30(5)
	The proceedings will be allocated for hearing before lay justices	FC(CDB)R 2014, Sch 1, para 1(f),(m)
Application	The application must be made on Form A1 with financial statement on Form E1	FPR PD5A
Hearing date	The court will fix a first hearing date not less than 4 weeks and not more than 8 weeks after the date that the application was filed Hearing dates may only be cancelled with the permission of the court and, if cancelled, a new date must immediately be fixed	FPR 2010, r 9.18(1)(a),(3)
	Fee: £215	FPFO 2008, fee 11.1
Respondent	The other party to the marriage The other party to a civil partnership	DPMCA 1978 CPA 2004

Service	Within 4 days of the date on which the application was filed, the court will serve a copy of the application on the respondent, give notice of the date of first hearing to both parties and send a copy of a blank financial statement to the respondent and also to the applicant	FPR 2010, r 9.18(1)(b)
	Alternatively, the applicant may choose to serve the application on the respondent. In which case, the issued application will be returned to the applicant and, within 4 days of receipt, the applicant must serve the application, notice of first hearing and a blank financial statement on the respondent. The applicant must also file a certificate of service at or before the first hearing	FPR 2010, r 9.18(2)
Financial statements	Within 14 days of issue of the application, the parties must serve their financial statements on each other and file a copy with the court The financial statement must be verified by statement of truth and be accompanied by any documents referred to in the statement or that clarify information contained in the statement. Any party unavoidably prevented from sending such documents must, at the earliest opportunity, serve a copy on the other party and file a copy with the court, together with an explanation	FPR 2010, r 9.19(1)–(3)
Consent orders	Applicant files two copies of draft order endorsed with statement signed by respondent signifying agreement and each party files with the court and serves on the other a statement of information	FPR 2010, r 9.26
Directions	May be given by the justices' clerk or court, on a party's written request filed and served, or on written request by consent or (in an urgent case) orally without notice or on the court's own initiative Directions for the conduct of the proceedings may include the timetable for the proceedings, variation of the time within which or by which an act is required to be done, the service of documents, the submission of evidence and attendance at a directions appointment or hearing	FPR 2010, rr 4.1, 4.3, 9.20; JCAR 2014
Additional or alternative orders	The court may make an interim order for periodical payments; FPR 2010, Pt 18 procedure applies to applications for interim orders	DPMCA 1978, s 19; CPA 2004, Sch 6, Pt 4; FPR 2010, r 9.7
	Costs	FPR 2010, r 28.1
	Adjournment for reconciliation and report	DPMCA 1978, s 26
Variation, revival and revocation	Application may be made by either party, or by a child who has attained the age of 16 on Form A1 with financial statement on Form E1, following the procedure for the making of an order set out above	DPMCA 1978, ss 20, 20A, 20ZA, 20(12); CPA 2004, Sch 6, para 39; FPR 2010, rr 9.18–9.21
Fee	Applications on notice: £155	FPFO 2008, fee 5.3
	Applications by consent: £50	FPFO 2008, fee 5.1
Appeals	See Guide E3	

A8: Non-molestation and/or Occupation Order under Family Law Act 1996, Pt IV

Legal background

An application under FLA 1996, Pt IV can be made to the Family Court either as a freestanding application or within existing proceedings. By FC(CDB)R 2014, r 17, an application within existing proceedings will be allocated to the level of judge dealing with the existing proceedings.

An application by a person under the age of 18, or for leave under s 43 (applications by children under 16) will be allocated to the first available judge other than a lay justice (FC(CDB)R 2014, r 16).

Applications without notice are allocated to 'the first available judge of the Family Court'. In practice, this is usually a district judge although the full hearing may be listed before justices. Applications on notice are allocated in accordance with FC(CDB)R 2014, r 20.

Personal protection in the form of a 'non-molestation order' is available to 'associated persons', a term widely defined in s 62(3). 'Molestation' is not defined in the Act. It includes violence and threats of violence but is not confined to such acts (see s 42). It includes controlling, coercive or threatening behaviour and all forms of abuse.

'Occupation orders' are available under ss 33, 35, 36, 37 and 38. Each section is self-contained, setting out who may apply and the court's powers. In practice, most applications will be under s 33. If an application is made under the wrong section, the court can make an order under another section (s 39). The court can include ancillary provisions (s 40). Lay justices cannot deal with an occupation order that requires determination of property ownership (FC(CDB)R 2014, r 16).

Power of arrest may be attached to an occupation order. However, it is not possible to attach a power of arrest to a non-molestation order (s 42A). A breach of a non-molestation order is a criminal offence.

Where injunctive relief from harassment within the meaning of PHA 1997 is sought, see Guide A10. Thus a person who is not an 'associated person' within FLA 1996, Pt IV may need to sue under PHA 1997. Compensatory damages can be awarded under PHA 1997 and thus that Act (and/or proceedings in tort for, eg, assault) should be used where such a claim is pursued. Concurrent proceedings under FLA 1996 and PHA 1997 can be brought and should be consolidated (see *Lomas v Parle* [2004] 1 FLR 812, CA).

The Legal Aid Agency has published a guide to assist parties and professionals with applications for legal aid where domestic abuse is alleged to have occurred and protection is sought (see *www.gov.uk/legal-aid/domestic-abuse-or-violence*).

Procedure

What is a 'non-molestation' order?	An order prohibiting the respondent from molesting another person who is associated with the respondent and/or a relevant child	FLA 1996, s 42(1)
Who may apply for a 'non-molestation' order?	An associated person; a person is associated with another person if: – they are or have been married to each other – they are or have been civil partners of each other – they are cohabitants or former cohabitants – they live or have lived in the same household, otherwise than merely by reason of one of them being the other's employee, tenant, lodger or boarder – they are relatives (as defined) – they have agreed to marry one another (whether or not that agreement has been terminated) – they have entered into a civil partnership agreement (whether or not that agreement has been terminated) – they have or have had an intimate personal relationship with each other which is or was of significant duration – in relation to a child both persons are parents or have or have had parental responsibility for the child – they are parties to the same family proceedings	FLA 1996, s 62(3) FLA 1996, s 63(1) CPA 2004, s 73 FLA 1996, s 62(3) FLA 1996, s 62(4) FLA 1996, s 63(1),(2)

Who may apply for an 'occupation order' under s 33?	An applicant who is entitled to occupy a dwelling-house by virtue of a beneficial estate or interest or contract or by virtue of any enactment giving him the right to remain in occupation or who has home rights	FLA 1996, s 30
	The respondent is an 'associated person'	FLA 1996, s 62(3)
	The dwelling-house must be, have been, or have been intended to be, the home of the applicant and respondent	FLA 1996, s 33
Who may apply for an 'occupation order' under s 35?	An applicant former spouse or former civil partner who is not entitled to occupy; the respondent is entitled to occupy; the dwelling-house was or was intended to be their home	FLA 1996, s 35
Who may apply for an 'occupation order' under s 36?	An applicant cohabitant or former cohabitant who is not entitled to occupy; the respondent is entitled to occupy; the dwelling-house is, was, or was intended to be the home where they live(d) together	FLA 1996, s 36
Who may apply for an 'occupation order' under s 37?	An applicant spouse former spouse, civil partner or former civil partner where neither applicant nor respondent is entitled to occupy; the dwelling-house must be or have been their home	FLA 1996, s 37
Who may apply for an 'occupation order' under s 38?	An applicant cohabitant or former cohabitant where neither applicant nor respondent is entitled to occupy. The dwelling-house must be or have been the home in which they live(d) together	FLA 1996, s 38
How is the application made?	In all cases, on Form FL401 supported by a witness statement (which must state the grounds)	FPR 2010, r 10.2
Fee	No fee is payable on an application for a non-molestation or occupation order Similarly, no fee is payable by an applicant who applies to vary, extend or discharge an order An application to vary etc by the respondent attracts a fee of £155	FPFO 2008, fee 5.3
Without notice applications	In any case where it considers it is 'just and convenient' to do so the court can make a non-molestation order or an occupation order on a without notice basis. The court must have regard to 'all the circumstances', including the criteria in s 45(2)	FLA 1996, s 45(1),(2)
	The witness statement must state the reasons why notice was not given	FPR 2010, r 10.2(4)
	If a without notice order is made there **must** be a 'full hearing' as soon as just and convenient	FLA 1996, s 45(3)
Form of order	An occupation order is in Form FL404 A non-molestation order is in Form FL404A	
Service of without notice order	Respondent must be personally served with: – a copy of the order made – a copy of the application in Form FL401 – a copy of the witness statement in support of the application – notice of the date of the full hearing in Form FL402	FPR 2010, r 10.6; FJC Protocol of November 2011: *Process Servers: Non-Molestation Orders*

Application on notice	Notice in Form FL402, together with a copy of the application in Form FL401 and the witness statement in support must be served on the respondent personally not less than 2 days before the application is to be heard Before the application is served, the court can abridge time for service If the application is for an occupation order under ss 33, 35 or 36 a copy of the application and notice in Form FL416 must be served by first class post on the mortgagee or landlord	FPR 2010, r 10.3 FPR 2010, r 10.3(1)(b)(ii) FPR 2010, r 10.3(3)
Proof of service	After service, the applicant must file a statement in Form FL415	FPR 2010, r 6.37
Response	Respondent may, but is not required to, serve a statement in reply and/or make a cross-application	
Hearing	An application for a non-molestation order or an occupation order is dealt with in private unless the court otherwise directs The application in the Family Court may be heard by a District Judge (magistrates' court), a lay bench, a District Judge or a Circuit Judge where they are co-located. If the Family Court is in a County Court hearing centre then the application should be heard by a District Judge or Circuit Judge The court keeps a record of the hearing in Form FL405	FPR 2010, r 10.5 FC(CDB)R 2014
Orders available	*Non-molestation order* An order may forbid molestation in general or particular acts of molestation or both The better practice is to make the order as clear and specific as possible whether or not it also includes a clause forbidding molestation in general The order can include an 'exclusion zone' if this is proportionate and is necessary to protect the applicant Such an exclusion zone can be included in an occupation order but it is not necessary to make an occupation order solely for this purpose and the term can be included in a non-molestation order provided the evidence justifies it *Occupation order under s 33* An order may: – enforce the applicant's entitlement to remain in occupation as against the respondent – require the respondent to permit the applicant to enter and remain in the dwelling-house or part of the dwelling-house – regulate the occupation of the dwelling-house by either or both of the parties – if the respondent is entitled to occupy, prohibit, suspend or restrict the exercise by him of his right to occupy the dwelling-house – if the respondent has home rights in relation to the dwelling-house, restrict or terminate those rights – require the respondent to leave the dwelling-house or part of the dwelling-house – exclude the respondent from a defined area in which the dwelling-house is included For additional provisions, see s 40	FLA 1996, s 42(6) *Boness v R* [2005] EWCA Crim 2395 *Burris v Azadani* [1996] 1 FLR 266, CA *Mr R v Mrs R* [2014] EWFC 48

	Occupation orders under ss 35, 36 Mandatory provisions are set out in ss 35(3), (4), 36(3), (4), and discretionary provisions in ss 35(5), 36(6) For additional provisions, see s 40 *Occupation orders under ss 37, 38* See ss 37(3), 38(3)	
Duration of non-molestation orders	For a specified period or until further order Application for extension of the order is made in Form FL403	FLA 1996, s 42(7); FPR 2010, r 10.8
Duration of occupation orders	*Applicant with estate or interest etc or with home rights* for a specified period until the occurrence of a specified event or until further order	FLA 1996, s 33(10)
	Application for extension of the order is made in Form FL403	FPR 2010, r 10.8
	Spouse, former spouse, civil partner or former civil partner not entitled to an interest for a maximum of 6 months, but can be renewed any number of times	FLA 1996, ss 35(10), 37(5)
	Application for extension of the order is made in Form FL403	FPR 2010, r 10.8
	Cohabitant or former cohabitant not entitled to an interest for a maximum of 6 months, but can be renewed only once	FLA 1996, ss 36(10), 38(6)
	Application for extension of the order is made in Form FL403	FPR 2010, r 10.8
Penal notice	A penal notice must be endorsed on an order before it can be enforced by committal	FPR 2010, rr 10.12, 37.9; PD37A; *Re Dad* [2015] EWHC 2655 (Fam)
	The prescribed forms of order (Form FL404 and Form FL404A) include an appropriately worded penal notice. Because the sanction for breach is different, the wording of the penal notice for breach of a non-molestation order is unique to that form of order. Thus two separate orders are required if the court makes both types of order	FPR 2010, r 10.12; PD37A
Power of arrest	The court '*shall* attach a power of arrest to one or more provisions of an occupation order unless satisfied that ... the applicant ... will be adequately protected without [it]' if the respondent has used or threatened violence	FLA 1996, s 47(2)
	If the order is made without notice, the court *may* attach a power of arrest to an occupation order if 'the respondent has used or threatened violence' and 'there is a risk of significant harm ... if the power of arrest is not attached'	FLA 1996, s 47(3)
	It is not possible to attach a power of arrest to a non-molestation order. Breach of such an order is a criminal offence	FLA 1996, s 42A
Undertakings	The court may accept an undertaking. The court 'shall not accept an undertaking ... instead of making an occupation order in any case where ... a power of arrest would be attached' nor instead of making a non-molestation order where 'it is necessary ... that any breach may be punishable under s 42A'	FLA 1996, s 46(1),(3), (3A)
	The court must deliver a copy of the undertaking to the party giving the undertaking	FPR 2010, r 37.7

	A warrant of arrest can be issued to enforce an undertaking	FLA 1996, s 46(4)
Damages	It is not possible to claim damages under FLA 1996. However, damages can be claimed under PHA 1997, s 3. If concurrent proceedings are brought they should be consolidated	*Lomas v Parle* [2004] 1 FLR 812, CA
Service of injunction	Personal service of an order is required The applicant's solicitor should endeavour to effect service as soon as possible	FPR 2010, r 10.6; FJC Protocol of November 2011: *Process Servers: Non-Molestation Orders*
	A litigant in person can require the court to effect personal service	FPR 2010, r 10.6(2)
	An injunction directing an act to be done cannot be enforced unless it is served before the time within which the act is to be done has expired; an injunction cannot be enforced unless the respondent knows about it. Service should be effected in accordance with the terms of the Protocol	FPR 2010, r 37.5; FJC Protocol of November 2011: *Process Servers: Non-Molestation Orders*
	Form FL404A (non-molestation order) and/or Form FL406 (containing only those provisions of the occupation order to which a power of arrest has been attached) must be delivered to the officer in charge of any police station for the applicant's address or such other police station as the court may specify. The form must be served together with a statement showing that the respondent has been served with the order(s) or otherwise informed of its terms	FPR 2010, r 10.10
	A copy of an occupation order made under s 33, 35 or 36 must be served by the applicant by first class post on the mortgagee or landlord	FPR 2010, r 10.6(3)

A9: Order for Forced Marriage Protection Order under Family Law Act 1996, Pt 4A

Legal background

An application for a forced marriage protection order (FMPO) may be made as a freestanding application or in other family proceedings in the High Court, the Principal Registry of the Family Division (Central Family Court), or in one of the 11 family courts specified. The definition of family proceedings has been extended to include applications under FLA 1996, Pt 4A. An order may also be made by the court of its own motion (FPR 2010, r 11.8) in circumstances set out in s 63C(6).

There is no age restriction for applicants for a forced marriage protection order. A child does not require leave of the court but the provisions of FPR 2010, rr 16.5 and 16.6 apply to applications for a FMPO. Procedure generally is governed by FPR 2010, Pt 11.

Any order which is appropriate to protect a person being forced into marriage, or to protect a person who has been forced into a marriage may be made. The terms of such an order may relate to conduct outside England and Wales, and persons who are or may be involved or become involved in the forced marriage or in any other respects (s 63B).

A power of arrest cannot be attached to a FMPO. A breach of an order is a criminal offence. On the breach being reported to the police, they will take the appropriate action. It is only if they fail or decide not to take any action that it will be possible for committal proceedings to be issued in the Family Court, as is the case for breach of a non-molestation order.

Procedure

Who may apply	The person who is to be protected (PTBP) by the order A relevant third party, i e a local authority that is now specified as a relevant third party Any other person with permission of the court	FLA 1996, s 63C FLA 1996 (FM)(RTP)O 2009
Application for permission to apply	Where permission to apply is required, the applicant must use the Pt 18 procedure and file (a) an application on Form FL430, setting out the reasons for the application, the applicant's connection with the PTBP and the applicant's knowledge of the person's circumstances and of the person's wishes and feelings; and (b) a draft of the substantive application with sufficient copies for service on each respondent and the PTBP The application or the statement in support should be verified by statement of truth The application notice must have attached to it a draft of the order sought and must state: (a) what order the applicant is seeking; and (b) the reasons for seeking the order It must be verified by a statement of truth	FLA 1996, s 63C; FPR 2010, r 11.3(1) and Pt 18; PD5A Table 2 FPR 2010, Pt 17 and r 18.7
Substantive application	A draft of the substantive application in Form FL401A with sufficient copies for service Sworn statement in support and documents as on without notice application	
Which court	The High Court The Family Court (including the Central Family Court) other than lay justices	FLA 1996, s 63M; FC(CDB)R 2014
Fee	Nil	
Respondent	Parents of the applicant or PTBP The PTBP Any person who is involved in forcing or is attempting to force a person to enter into a marriage Any person who is or may become involved in other respects as well as respondents of any kind (see s 63B(3) for examples of 'involvement in other respects') Any other person as the court may direct	FLA 1996, s 63B; see also FPR 2010, rr 18.3(b)(ii),(c)
Without notice application	In any case where it is considered 'just and convenient' to do so, the court may make a FMPO. The court must have regard to all the circumstances including the matters set out in s 63D(2)	FLA 1996, s 63D; FPR 2010, r 18.4
Documents to be filed when a without notice application is made	Pt 18 application notice A sworn statement in support must be made explaining why notice was not given. Where the application is made by an organisation, it must state the name and address of the person submitting the application and the position that person holds in the organisation The substantive application on Form FL401A	FPR 2010, rr 11.2(2),(3) FPR 2010, r 18.10(3)

	Draft of the order that must contain a penal notice and a statement of the respondent's right to make an application to set aside or vary the order within 7 days of service If an order is made without notice the respondent must be given an opportunity to make representation at a hearing on notice as soon as 'just and convenient' Emergency/notice of legal aid certificate, if any	FLA 1996, s 63D(3),(4)
Service of without notice and on notice proceedings	*Who should serve the notice* The applicant is required to serve a copy of the application and the notice of the proceedings **except** where the applicant is an individual, ie a person (whether legally represented or not) who is not applying for an order on behalf of an organisation and includes the PTBP. In this case, the application must not be served personally by the applicant himself/herself. If the applicant is an individual acting in person, application should be made for service to be effected by the court or for substituted service. If legally represented, a process server should be instructed to effect service	FPR 2010 rr 11.1(1), 11.4(1A),(3)
	Documents to be served Unless otherwise directed, the respondent, the PTBP (if not the applicant) and any other person directed by the court must be personally served in accordance with the FJC's November 2011 Protocol on service (see Part V) with: • a copy of any order made; • a copy of the application in Form FL401A; • a copy of any statement in support; • notice of the date of the next hearing in Form FL402A not less than 2 days before the next hearing A sworn statement of service containing all the information set out in the FJC's Protocol must be prepared and filed	FPR 2010, rr 11.3(3), 11.4 and 18.5(10)(b) FJC Protocol of November 2011: *Process Servers: Non-Molestation Orders*
Service of order made on application without notice	*Who should be served* An order made without notice must be served personally on all the parties and the PTBP in accordance with the FJC's Protocol of November 2011. The order must contain a penal notice and a statement of the right of the respondent and the PTBP to make an application for the order to be set aside or to be varied within 7 days of service of the order The court may abridge time for service or make an order for substituted service	FPR 2010, rr 11.4(2),(3), 18.10(2),(3), 18.11 and Pt 6; FJC Protocol of November 2011: *Process Servers: Non-Molestation Orders*
	By whom should the order be served The applicant is required to serve the order **except** where the applicant is an individual (as defined in r 11.1(1)); service **must not** be effected personally by the applicant himself/herself. In this case, the court should be asked to direct for service by the court or for substituted service under r 11.7(4). If the individual is legally represented, a process server should be instructed to effect service	FPR 2010, rr 11.1(1), 11.7(3A),(4)

Service on person to be protected of application on notice	Where the application is served on the PTBP, it must be accompanied by a notice informing that person of how to apply to become a party to the proceedings and of that person's right to make representations in writing or orally at any hearing For service on a child or a protected person, see FPR 2010, r 6.14 but in either case it may be inappropriate to serve a parent or a person in whose care the PTBP is, so a direction from the court should be applied for when making the application or obtaining the FMPO	FPR 2010, r 11.4(4),(5)
Documents to be served	A copy of the order Copy of Form FL401A Copy of statement in support Notice of the hearing in Form FL402A Copy of draft order sought at the next hearing where appropriate	FPR 2010, rr 11.4 and 18.8
Time for service of substantive application	The application in Form FL401A and all documents set out above must be served personally on the respondent/s unless otherwise directed by the court, not less than 2 days before the application is to be heard The court may abridge time for service The court may make an order for substituted service	FPR 2010, r 11.4(1)–(3)
Proof of service	Where the application is served by the applicant, the applicant must file a certificate of service on Form FL415 stating the date and time of personal service and details required under r 6.37	FPR 2010, rr 6.37, 11.4(6)
Hearing	An application for a FMPO is dealt with in private unless the court otherwise directs The court may deal with the application notwithstanding that the applicant or any respondent is absent from the hearing The application in the Family Court is dealt with by: • a circuit judge or deputy circuit judge nominated for private or public family law proceedings; • a recorder nominated for private or public family law proceedings; • a district judge of the PRFD or Central Family Court; • a district judge nominated for private or public family law proceedings	FPR 2010, rr 11.7(1), 18.12 FC(CDB)R 2014
Form of order	Form FL404B	FPR PD5A
Substantive orders	See Form FL404B. The order may include: • prohibitions, restrictions and other requirements preventing a forced marriage taking place; • provision forbidding the named respondent/s from entering into any arrangement in relation to the engagement or marriage whether civil or religious of the PTBP whether in this jurisdiction or overseas and from arranging or holding any celebration for such a marriage; • order prohibiting the removal of the PTBP from the jurisdiction;	

	• order prohibiting the named respondent from applying for a passport or other travel documents for the PTBP; • order for surrender of passports and order for the Identity and Passport Service to cancel any passport issued and not to issue any further or new passport without leave of the court; • non molestation orders; • disclosure of whereabouts order; • where appropriate, for the local authority, the police and the legal representatives of the PTBP to have access to the PTBP; • for the PTBP to be interviewed by a member of the British High Commission in (a named country) (where the PTBP is outside the jurisdiction); • order for the return of the PTBP; • order for disclosure of the case papers to the Foreign and Commonwealth Office FMU; • any other order that may be appropriate, e g that the FMPO be served on the FMU and the UK Border Agency via the FMU and requests to the appropriate foreign government/department	FLA 1996, s 63B; FPR 2010, r 11.7(3)
Interlocutory order	The court may direct non-disclosure of information to protect the PTBP or any other person or for any good reason. Where such an order is made it may also list a further hearing to consider representations by the respondent, PTBP or any other person. A copy of the order, record of the hearing and (if the order is made without notice) a copy of the application statement in support must be served personally on the respondent, the PTBP (if neither the applicant nor a respondent) and any other person named in the order as soon as practicable	FPR 2010, rr 11.7 and 11.9 and 21.3(1)–(8)
Penal notice	Breach of a FMPO is a criminal offence. Consequently, the form of the penal notice is the same or similar to that which applies on a non-molestation order. A power of arrest is not available	FLA 1996, s 63CA; FPR 2010, r 11.15; PD37A, para 1.1
Undertakings	The court may accept an undertaking but not if it appears to the court that the respondent has used or threatened violence against the PTBP and it is necessary to make a FMPO so that any breach may be punishable as an offence under s 63CA	FLA 1996, s 63E as amended by the Anti-Social Behaviour, Crime and Policing Act 2014; see FPR PD37A on form of undertaking
Duration of orders	A FMPO may be made for a specified period or until varied or discharged	FLA 1996, s 63F
Variation/ Discharge of orders	The court may vary or discharge a FMPO on the application of: • any party to the proceedings; • the PTBP by the order if not a party to the proceedings; • any person affected by the order	FLA 1996, s 63G; see also FPR 2010, r 11.10
Application to vary extend or discharge FMPO	Must be made on Form FL403A setting out the facts relied on and if the application is not verified by a statement of truth	

	A statement in support that is verified by a statement of truth must be filed Pt 18 procedure will apply to such an application	FPR PD5A
Enforcement	Breach of a FMPO is a criminal offence. The breach should therefore be reported to the police to take action. A person convicted of an offence under FLA 1996, s 63CA cannot be committed for contempt unless a prosecution is not pursued	
Warrant of arrest	In certain circumstances the court may issue a warrant for arrest of a person if there has been a breach of the order, but the application must be supported by a sworn statement and the court must have reasonable grounds for believing that the person to be arrested has failed to comply with the order or is otherwise in contempt of court The warrant must be in Form FL408	FLA 1996, s 63J(2); FPR 2010, r 11.13; PD5A
Application for warrant of arrest	The application must be in Form FL407A accompanied by a sworn statement	FPR PD5A; FPR 2010, rr 10.9–10.16
Committal for breach	Only if a prosecution is not pursued. If the contemnor is charged and convicted, he cannot be committed for contempt. Contempt proceedings may be issued in relation to orders made before 16 June 2014 See under Guide C14 but note that application may be made by: (a) The police, but only if they were the applicant for the FMPO; (b) Any party who obtained the FMPO; (c) The Attorney-General, if the public interest requires it; (d) The court, in exceptional circumstances and where there is an urgent need to take immediate action to be taken immediately	FLA 1996, s 63CA *Bedford Police Constabulary v RU & FHS* [2013] EWHC 2350 (Fam) *Clarke v Chadburn* [1985] 1 WLR 78, ChD

A10: Claims under the Protection from Harassment Act 1997

Legal background

The High Court and the County Court have jurisdiction to grant an injunction for personal protection by forbidding harassment under PHA 1997 or any conduct which amounts to a recognised form of tort (*Khorasandjian v Bush* [1993] 2 FLR 66, CA). Such proceedings are not 'family proceedings' but unlike FLA 1996, the court can award damages under PHA 1997 (see *Singh v Bhakar* [2007] 1 FLR 880, Cty Ct, where damages of £35,000 were awarded). In *Burris v Azadani* [1996] 1 FLR 266, CA, the Court of Appeal held that, where it is necessary to make the injunction effective for the protection of the applicant, an 'exclusion zone' can be ordered forbidding the defendant to go within a specified area around the applicant's home. In *Silverton v Gravett* [2001] All ER (D) 282 (Oct), QBD, the 'exclusion zone' included also the claimant's place of work. There must be a 'course of conduct' amounting to harassment (*AJR v Regina* [2013] 2 FLR 1383, CA), which requires two or more incidents within a reasonably limited time.

Where the victim and the perpetrator of harassment or molestation are 'associated persons' within FLA 1996, s 62(3), the remedies under that Act are more comprehensive, particularly if occupation of the family home is an issue. See Guide A8.

For precedents, see *Emergency Remedies in the Family Courts* (Family Law).

Injunctions under Protection from Harassment Act 1997

An injunction can be granted in the County Court (as in the High Court) with or without a claim for damages or other relief, by virtue of CCA 1984, s 38. An application for an injunction under PHA 1997 is governed by CPR 1998, Pt 65 which requires the claim to be brought under CPR, Pt 8. By r 8.5, the claimant must file written evidence with the claim form.

Generally, a Pt 8 claim form (N208) should not contain the same amount of detail as in a Pt 7 claim. A Pt 8 claim form should set out in summary form the issue which the claimant wants the court to decide and the remedy sought (see r 8.2). If an interim remedy is also sought (eg a without notice injunction) see also CPR 1998, Pt 25 and in particular CPR PD25A (see Part III) which supplements Pt 25. Best practice is to file N208 incorporating short particulars of claim, which can, but need not, include a claim for damages, together with an application in Form N16A (County Court) or Application Notice in Form N244 (High Court), provided that the evidence setting out the relevant facts is given in Form N16A or Form N244, or in witness statement(s), verified by a statement of truth (see para 3 of PD25A).

Assault and battery

If protection is required but is not available under the FLA 1996 (eg because the parties are not 'associated persons') nor under the PHA 1997 (eg because there is no 'course of conduct': in *Andreson v Lovell* [2009] EWHC 3397 (QB) a 'one-off unwanted grope' was an isolated incident and not harassment, but it would be an assault) it may be possible to sue in tort and seek an injunction in those proceedings. Such actions are beyond the scope of this work.

Procedure

Who may apply	A person who is or may be the victim of a course of conduct prohibited by PHA 1997, s 1	PHA 1997, s 3(1)
	Application for an interim injunction may be made by the defendant to the claim	*Huntingdon Life Sciences v Stop Huntingdon Animal Cruelty* [2003] EWHC 1139 (QB); CPR 1998, rr 25.1(1)(a), 25.2(1)
Which court?	High Court or the County Court at the hearing centre for the area where the claimant or defendant resides	
	A District Judge has jurisdiction to deal with all claims under PHA 1997	PHA 1997, s 3(3); CPR 1998, r 65.28
Application	Claim Form N208 must be issued, unless the court allows the application to be made before proceedings are started because the matter is urgent or there are good reasons for not giving notice	
	A claimant must file any written evidence relied on with the claim form. A claimant may rely on the matters set out in the claim form if it is verified by a statement of truth	CPR 1998, rr 65.28, 25.2(1),(2), 25.3(1); PD25A, para 4.4; rr 8.5 and 8.6
	An urgent application for an injunction should be made as an interim application in pending proceedings by application notice in Form N16A (County Court) or Form N244 (High Court)	CPR 1998, Pt 23; PD23A; r 25.1(1)(a); PD25A, para 2.1
	A form of acknowledgement of service (Form N210) must be served with the claim form. The defendant must file an acknowledgement of service: a defendant who does not do so may attend the hearing but may not take part unless the court gives permission	CPR PD8A, para 3; CPR 1998, rr 8.3 and 8.4
	Damages can be claimed, but need not be	PHA 1997, s 3; CCA 1984, s 38; CPR PD2, para 8.1(d)(ii)
	An application for an interim injunction must be supported by evidence, i e a witness statement, unless the court orders otherwise	CPR 1998, r 25.3(2)

Fee	High Court: £528 County Court: £308 (non-money claim) payable on issue of application in Form N16A or Form N244 together with Claim Form N208	CPFO 2008 (as amended), fee 1.5
	If damages are claimed, the fee is based on the sum claimed which, for claims exceeding £10,000 but not exceeding £200,000 is 5% of that sum	Civil Proceedings and Family Proceedings (Amendment) Order 2015
Oral application without documents	Although it is rare, the court can dispense with the requirement for an application notice and in cases of extreme urgency can grant an interim injunction by telephone. However, the court will require an undertaking to file evidence, verified by a statement of truth, notice of application and, if not yet done, to issue a claim form	CPR 1998, r 23.3(2)(b); PD25A, paras 4.2, 4.5, 5.1(2)
	Such an undertaking must be strictly complied with	*Re S (A Child) (Family Division: Without Notice Orders)* [2001] 1 FLR 308, FD
Application begun without notice	An interim injunction can be granted without notice of the application having been given, where the matter is urgent and the court considers that there are good reasons for not giving notice	CPR 1998, rr 25.2(1),(2), 25.3(1)
	Any applicant without notice is under a duty to give full and frank disclosure of all relevant facts	*W v H* [2001] 1 All ER 300, FD; *B v A (Wasted Costs Order)* [2013] 2 FLR 958, FD
	In an urgent case informal notice, i e short notice, of application for a personal protection injunction is better practice than no notice, unless the circumstances require secrecy	CPR PD23A, para 4.2
	If a claim form has already been served, the applicant should take steps to tell the respondent that the application is being made without full notice unless secrecy is essential	CPR PD25A, para 4.3
	The reasons for not giving notice must be stated in the evidence in support	CPR 1998, r 25.3(3); PD25A, para 3.4
	If the application is made before the application notice has been issued, the notice and evidence in support and fee must be filed on the same or next working day (or as ordered by the court), as should the claim form and fee, if not already issued	CPR PD25A, paras 4.4(3), 5.1(4),(5)
	The respondent against whom an interim injunction is granted may apply to have it set aside or varied, but must apply within 7 days after it is served or at the return date provided in the order	CPR 1998, r 23.10(1),(2); PD25A, para 5.1(3)
Evidence	Applications for interim injunctions must be supported by evidence, i e set out in a document verified by a statement of truth, which may be in a witness statement or the statement of case or the application itself	CPR 1998, r 25.3(2); PD25, para 3.2
	The evidence must set out the facts on which the applicant relies for the claim including all material facts of which the court should be made aware	CPR PD25A, para 3.3
	The witness statement must be verified by a statement of truth	CPR 1998, rr 8.2 and 22.1(1)

Service of notice	The application and evidence in support must be served as soon as practicable after it is filed and at least 3 working days before the hearing to give valid notice; unless the court shortens the time	CPR 1998, rr 2.8, 3.1(2)(a), 23.7(1)(a); PD25A, para 2.2
	Informal notice (i e less than 3 days) is better than no notice	*G v G* [1990] 1 FLR 395, CA
	Where proceedings have commenced, informal notice should be given unless secrecy is essential	CPR PD25A, para 4.3(3)
Response	The defendant must file an acknowledgment of service. A defendant who intends to rely on written evidence must file it with the acknowledgment of service. (A claimant may file further written evidence in reply.) A defendant who fails to acknowledge service may attend the hearing but may not take part unless the court gives permission	CPR 1998, rr 8.3–8.5; PD8A, para 3
	Defendant to application for injunction may: (i) elect not to oppose (ii) oppose in whole or in part by filing and serving evidence (iii) make an application in like form	CPR PD8A, para 5
Hearing	CPR 1998 do not require the hearing of an interim application to be conducted in open court in public	CPR 1998, rr 23.8, 25.1, 25.2, 39.2(1)
	The applicant should submit a draft of the injunction in typescript (in Form N16 in the County Court) and on disk (in a format compatible with the word processing format used by the court)	CPR 1998, r 23.7(3)(b); PD25A, paras 2.4, 4.3
	Breach of an order under PHA 1997, s 3 is both a crime and a contempt of court. The facts on which the order is obtained need to be proven to the civil standard	*Hipgrave and Hipgrave v Jones* [2005] 2 FLR 174, QBD
Orders available	The court may grant an injunction restraining the defendant from pursuing any conduct which amounts to harassment. The order may prohibit specific conduct and/ or harassment in general. Where necessary for the protection of the applicant, an exclusion zone can be provided around a home or place of work	*Burris v Azadani* [1996] 1 FLR 266, CA; *Silverton v Gravett* [2001] All ER (D) 282 (Oct), QBD
	Power of arrest is not available (though a warrant of arrest can be granted after the event)	PHA 1997, s 3(3),(4)
Order made without notice: duration and review	If an injunction is granted at a hearing of which the respondent has not been given notice: a return date must (unless the court orders otherwise) be given for a hearing at which the respondent can be present	CPR PD25A, para 5.1(3)
	the respondent is in any event entitled within 7 days of service on him to apply to have the order set aside	CPR 1998, r 23.10; Form N16
	Where an injunction is granted without notice having been given, it is good practice for the court to order that it runs to a date later than the return date, so that there is no hiatus until an injunction granted on notice can be served	

Damages	The court can award damages under PHA 1997 Concurrent proceedings under FLA 1996 and PHA 1997 should be consolidated and tried together	PHA 1997, s 3, eg, *Singh v Bhakar* [2007] 1 FLR 880, Cty Ct *Lomas v Parle* [2004] 1 FLR 812, CA
Undertakings	An enforceable undertaking can be accepted by the court	*Hussain v Hussain* [1986] 2 FLR 271, CA; CPR 1998, rr 81.4–81.11
Form of injunction order or undertaking: penal notice and clear instructions	To be enforceable, when served an injunction order must have prominently displayed on the front a warning notice of the consequences of disobedience Any order for an injunction must set out clearly what the respondent must do or not do (in the County Court the injunction should be issued in Form N138) An undertaking given to the County Court must be recorded in Form N117	CPR PD81, paras 1, 2; Form N16A CPR PD25A, para 5.2
Service of injunction or delivery of form of undertaking	Before an injunction can be enforced it must have been personally served on the respondent, before any alleged breach, unless the court has dispensed with service or the respondent was present when the order was made or has been notified of the terms of the order. Service should be effected in accordance with the Protocol (see 'Introduction' in the Protocol, which extends it to 'harassment') An undertaking becomes enforceable when and because it is given to the court; however, unless a record of it is given to the person who gave it, difficulties can arise on enforcement proceedings, and in the County Court a copy is required to be delivered to the giver by the court or, failing that, served by the applicant	CPR 1998, r 81.5; Family Justice Council *Protocol for Process Servers*, November 2011 CPR 1998, r 81.7; *Hussain v Hussain* [1986] 2 FLR 271, CA
Duration of interim injunction made on notice	An interim injunction granted on notice can be ordered to last until a fixed date or trial or further order If the claim is stayed other than by agreement between the parties, an interim injunction shall be set aside unless the court orders that it should continue to have effect	CPR PD25A, para 5.2 CPR 1998, r 25.10
Warrant for arrest	Application for a warrant of arrest in respect of disobedience of an injunction prohibiting harassment should be made in the High Court if the order was made there or, if the order was made in the County Court, the application may be made to any County Court office The formal requirements upon making application for a warrant are provided by rules; see Guide C14 for practice	PHA 1997, s 3(4),(5) CPR 1998, r 65.29

A11: Transfer of a Tenancy under Family Law Act 1996, Pt IV, s 53 and Sch 7

Legal background

Since the coming into force of FLA 1996, Pt IV on 1 October 1997, the court is empowered to transfer tenancies, both contractual and statutory, between cohabitants who no longer live together as husband and wife, as well as between a spouse/civil partner and a former spouse/civil partner. As set out in FLA 1996, Sch 7, para 10, the person to whom the tenancy is transferred can be ordered to pay compensation to the other party. The power to transfer the tenancy to a former spouse/civil partner arises on decree nisi; the order becomes effective on decree absolute; and there is a prohibition on applying if that former spouse/civil partner has remarried. If there is a decree of judicial separation, the power to transfer arises after the decree is pronounced. A tenancy in the other spouse/civil partner's name, or in joint names, can be destroyed by the unilateral surrender or giving of notice to quit by one tenant without consultation with the other (*Hammersmith and Fulham London Borough Council v Monk* [1992] 1 FLR 465, HL). A party should ask for an undertaking that the tenancy will not be surrendered and then serve that undertaking on the landlord. If the undertaking is not given the applicant should apply for an injunction and serve the order on the landlord (*Bater v Greenwich London Borough Council* [1999] 2 FLR 993, CA).

An application under FLA 1996, s 53 and Sch 7 is governed by the procedure in FPR 2010, rr 8.29–8.34.

Procedure

Who may apply	Either spouse/civil partner, but a matrimonial/civil partnership order must be granted before the order is made	FLA 1996, Sch 7, para 2(2)
	Either former spouse/civil partner, but a decree nisi must be granted before the order is made and the applicant must not have remarried; if application is for the transfer of a statutory tenancy or contractual tenancy containing a prohibition on assignment, it must be made before decree absolute	FLA 1996, Sch 7, para 13
	A cohabitant who is no longer living with the other cohabitant as husband and wife	FLA 1996, Sch 7, para 3
Application	To the Family Court or the same court as existing matrimonial/civil partnership proceedings	FLA 1996, Sch 7, para 2(2); FPR 2010, r 8.30, PD8A, para 1.1(a)
Fee	£245	FPFO 2008, fee 1.1
Service	The court will serve the respondent and the landlord unless the applicant is directed to serve	FPR 2010, r 8.31
	A landlord will be made a party to proceedings if the landlord requests to be one	FPR 2010, r 8.32
Respondent	The other spouse/civil partner or cohabitant	
Interlocutory injunction	The court may grant an injunction if ancillary or incidental to the assistance sought; an application for an injunction must be in accordance with procedure under FPR 2010, r 20.4	FPR 2010, r 8.34
Orders for disclosure	Any party may apply to the court under r 21.2 for any person to attend a production appointment to produce documents specified or described in the order	FPR 2010, r 8.33
Order	Transfer of tenancy or statutory tenancy	FLA 1996, Sch 7, paras 7–9
	Payment by the spouse/civil partner or cohabitant to whom the tenancy is transferred, to the other; deferment of payment or payment by instalments if transferee's financial hardship greater than transferor's	FLA 1996, Sch 7, para 10

	Order that both liable to discharge obligations before date of transfer and indemnity	FLA 1996, Sch 7, para 11
Appeals	See Guides E2, E4 and E5	

A12: Parental Order under Human Fertilisation and Embryology Act 2008, s 54

Legal background

HFEA 2008, s 54 deals with applications for a parental order. Provisions under HFEA 2008 extend the categories of applicants who may make an application for a parental order to heterosexual married couples, married same-sex couples (see Marriage (Same Sex Couples) Act 2013), civil partners who have entered into a civil partnership and unmarried heterosexual and same-sex couples who are living in an enduring relationship, but not by a single person. The procedure is governed by FPR 2010, Pt 13. The following Guide is provided as a guide only. Practitioners should refer to s 54 of the Act and FPR 2010 when making applications for a parental order.

Procedure

Who may apply	Married heterosexual couples and married same-sex couples Civil partners of each other Two persons who are living as partners in an enduring family relationship and are not within the prohibited degrees of relationship in relation to each other. A single intended parent is outside the requirement of HFEA 2008, s 54(1),(2)	See HFEA 2008, s 54(2); Marriage (Same Sex Couples) Act 2013, s 11, Sch 3, para 5; FPR 2010, r 13.3
Which court	Proceedings must be commenced in the Family Court before lay justices Proceedings may be transferred or allocated to other levels of the Family Court depending on the complexity of issues to be determined All cases where the child was born outside England and Wales must be allocated to be heard by a High Court Judge of the Family Division (not a deputy or s 9 judge). In London, all cases should if possible be allocated to Pauffely J, Theis J or Russell J. On circuit, it should be allocated to a High Court Judge of the Family Division in consultation with the judge in charge of HEFA cases (currently Theis J)	FC(CDB)R 2014 *Re Z (Foreign Surrogacy: Allocation of Work: Guidance on Parental Order Reports)* [2016] 2 FLR 803, FD; FC(CDB)R 2014, Sch 1, para 4(f); SCA 1981, Sch 1, para 3(f)(iv)
Time limit	Although HFEA 2008, s 54(3) contains mandatory provision that the application should be made within 6 months of the child's birth, an application outside this period may be accepted to protect the child's Art 8 rights	*Re X (A Child) (Surrogacy: Time Limit)* [2015] 1 FLR 349, FD; *A and Another v C and Another* [2016] EWFC 42
Application	Freestanding in Form C51 for each child (if more than one) with sufficient copies for each respondent	FPR PD5A

Documents to be filed with application	Marriage certificate if the applicants are married Civil partnership certificate if applicants are civil partners Child's birth certificate Any relevant orders Agreement (if any) to the making of a parental order in Form A101A	FPR PD5A; FPR 2010, rr 13.5(1)(b), 13.11, 13.15(2)(a)
Grounds for application	Consent of the birth mother and any other person who is a parent of the child but is not one of the applicants (including any man who is the father of the child pursuant to s 35 or 36 or any woman who is a parent pursuant to s 42 or 43) in Form A101A	FPR PD5A; HFEA 2008, s 54
	or birth parent(s) cannot be found or birth parent(s) are incapable of giving consent and in either case this should be stated in the application with a statement in supporting setting out a summary of the history	FPR 2010, r 13.10(2)
Respondent	The woman who carried the child The other parent (if any) Any person for whom provision is made in a child arrangements order Any other person or body with parental responsibility for the child Any other person with parental responsibility on the direction of the court and on request by that person	FPR 2010, r 13.3(2)
	Any other person or body on the direction of the court	FPR 2010, r 13.3(3),(4)
Appointment of parental order reporter	As soon as is practicable after issue the court will consider the appointment of a parental order reporter	FPR 2010, r 13.5
Service	Respondent/s must be served with: • a copy of the application • notice of hearing and first direction hearing (Form C6) and • Form C52 must be served on each respondent within 14 days before the hearing or first directions hearing; notice of proceedings must be served on any local authority or voluntary organisation who has accommodated the child	FPR PD5A; FPR 2010, r 13.6
Acknowledgement	Each respondent must file and serve an acknowledgement of service within 7 days of service on all other parties	FPR 2010, r 13.7
First direction hearing	Must take place within 4 weeks of issue of the application unless the court otherwise directs	FPR 2010, r 13.8
Directions	(a) Fix a timetable for filing of: – parental order reporter's report and give directions relating to the report – statement of fact or amendment to it – any other evidence (b) Directions relating to the parental order reporter's report and other evidence (c) Consider whether any other person should be made a party and give appropriate directions in relation thereto	

	(d) Consider the appointment of a litigation friend for a protected person unless one has already been appointed (e) Consider transfer of proceedings and if so give directions in relation thereto in accordance with the allocation order (f) Give direction for: tracing the other parent or the woman who carried the child; service of documents; disclosure; and final hearing Other directions may be given at any stage of the proceedings The parties or their legal representatives must attend the first hearing unless otherwise directed by the court Further directions may be given of the court's own motion or on the application of a party or the parental order reporter	FPR 2010, r 13.9(1),(3),(4) FPR 2010, r 13.9(4),(5); see also r 4.3(2)–(7)
Consent of birth parent(s)	May be given on Form A101 or a form to like effect Any form of agreement executed in Scotland must be witnessed by a Justice of the Peace or sheriff Any form of agreement executed in Northern Ireland must be witnessed by a Justice of the Peace Any form of agreement executed outside the UK must be witnessed by: (a) any person currently authorised by law in the place where the document is executed to administer an oath for any judicial or other legal process (b) a British Consular officer (c) a notary public (d) an officer holding a commission in any of the armed forces if the person executing the document is serving in the regular armed forces	FPR PD5A; FPR 2010, r 13.11
Disclosure of parental order reporter's report	Only on the direction of the court. Before giving such directions the court should consider whether the report needs redacting	FPR 2010, r 13.12
Notice of final hearing	Must be by the court on the parties and the parental order reporter, stating the date and place of the hearing	FPR 2010, r 13.13
Final hearing	Any person who has been given notice of the hearing may attend and be heard on the question of whether an order should be made The court may direct that any person may attend the hearing	FPR 2010, r 13.14(a),(b)
Order	A parental order takes effect on the date when it is made or such later date as the court may specify If the proceedings are in Wales a party may request the order to be drawn up in Welsh as well as in English	FPR 2010, rr 13.20(1),(2)
Service of order	Within 7 days of the order being made or such shorter time as the court may direct, the court must send a copy of the order to the persons and court referred to in FPR 2010, rr 13.3, 13.21	

B1: Declaration as to Marital Status

Legal background

FLA 1986, s 55 allows the court to make a declaration that a marriage: (a) was valid at its inception; (b) subsisted on a particular date; or (c) did not subsist on a particular date. If the truth of the proposition sought to be declared is established, the court is obliged to make the declaration, unless to do so would manifestly be contrary to public policy (FLA 1986, s 58(1)). If made, a declaration binds the world and not just the parties (FLA 1986, s 58(2)). Procedure for a declaration is at FPR 2010, Pt 8, Ch 5, by the Pt 19 procedure.

Procedure

Who may apply	A party to the marriage in question and any other person who has a sufficient interest	FLA 1986, s 55(1),(3); see also under FPR 2010, Pt 8, Ch 5
Which court	High Court or Family Court	FLA 1986, ss 55(1), 63
Pre-application requirement	The application must be served on Attorney-General at least 1 month before it is filed	FPR 2010, r 8.21
Application	By application on Form D70 Fee: £550	FPR PD5A FPFO 2008, fee 1.2
Documents to accompany petition	Any marriage certificate or divorce/annulment/legal separation decree where relevant (and with an authenticated English translation where relevant)	Per Form D70
Respondents	The parties (or other party) to the marriage in question	FPR 2010, r 8.20(1)
Other parties	The Attorney-General has the right to intervene in accordance with – Addition of other parties	FLA 1986, s 59(2) No specific provision: see, for example, FPR 2010, r 9.26B
Service		FPR 2010, Pt 6
Acknowledgment of service	14 days after service of the application	FPR 2010, r 19.5
Other interim procedures		FPR 2010, Pt 18
Hearing		FPR 2010, rr 27.10, 27.11
Order	A declaration that the marriage: – was valid at its inception – subsisted on a particular date – did not subsist on a particular date	FLA 1986, s 55
Appeals	See Guide E5	

B2: Applications for Divorce, Judicial Separation or Nullity in Undefended Cases

Legal background

A marriage (heterosexual or same-sex) or civil partnership may be dissolved on the ground that it has broken down irretrievably (MCA 1973, s 1(1); CPA 2004, s 44(1): references to MCA 1973 and 'marriage' apply also to same-sex couples). Application is made to the Family Court (by petition: MCA 1973, s 1(1)) for a matrimonial or civil partnership order or decree.

To prove that the marriage or civil partnership has broken down irretrievably, the applicant (petitioner) must prove one or more of five facts set out in MCA 1973, s 1(2) or, in the case of a civil partnership, four facts in CPA 2004, s 44(5) (adultery cannot apply to single-sex couples: MCA 1973, s 1(6)). If satisfied on the fact(s), the court grants an order, which in the first instance is a decree nisi or conditional order. This cannot be made absolute/final for 6 weeks (MCA 1973, s 1(5), as varied by Matrimonial Causes (Decree Absolute) General Order 1972; CPA 2004, s 38(1)).

A marriage or civil partnership may be annulled on the ground that either it is void as set out in MCA 1973, s 11 or CPA 2004, s 49, or that it is voidable as set out in MCA 1973, s 12 or CPA 2004, s 50. Any order is a decree nisi or conditional order, which cannot be made absolute/final for 6 weeks (MCA 1973, s 15 which applies s 1(5) to nullity cases; CPA 2004, ss 37(2), 38(1)).

Parties to a marriage may be judicially separated on the ground that one or more of the facts set out in MCA 1973, s 1(2) or CPA 2004, s 44(5) is proved (MCA 1973, s 17(1); CPA 2004, s 56). The procedure is the same as for dissolution of a marriage or civil partnership, save that no final order is made: the marriage or civil partnership is not finally dissolved.

Jurisdiction to apply: habitual residence or domicile

The court can only entertain proceedings (1) if it has jurisdiction under Brussels II (EC No 2201/2003) Art 3 (i e that a party is habitually resident in England and Wales); or (2) no court of a Contracting State has jurisdiction under Art 3 and either of the parties to the marriage is domiciled in England and Wales on the date when the proceedings are begun (DMPA 1973, s 5(2); but see s 5(3)(b)(ii) in the event of the death of a party to nullity proceedings). In the case of civil partnerships and same-sex marriages, jurisdiction is based on Civil Partnership (Jurisdiction and Recognition of Judgments) Regulations 2005 or Marriage (Same Sex Couples) (Jurisdiction and Recognition of Judgments) Regulations 2014.

Pilot scheme for online divorce

FPR PD36D introduces a pilot scheme (per Courts Act 2003, s 75(4)) for divorces only filed after 25 January 2017. The application procedure for a divorce is altered by PD36D by introduction, where the scheme applies, to a modified FPR 2010, r 5.1 and omission of r 5.2. PD7A is modified to make clear the forms and documentation required for filing a divorce petition.

With the introduction of the Family Court, HMCTS has resolved to introduce divorce centres as follows:

Region	*Divorce centre*
North East	Durham, Bradford, Doncaster
Wales	Neath & Port Talbot, Newport (Gwent), Wrexham
North West	Liverpool
Midlands	Nottingham, Stoke-on-Trent
South West	Southampton
London and South East	Bury St Edmunds

'Urgent applications' can still be issued at 'local hearings centres'. It is understood that the FPR Committee will be considering changes to the petition form and Form A (so that applicants can indicate where they would prefer hearings to take place, if one is required).

Procedure

Who may apply	To the Family Court by either party to the marriage or civil partnership	MCA 1973, s 1(1); CPA 2004, s 44(1)
Application on line	In the case of divorce petitions issued online where so required under the divorce pilot scheme	FPR 2010, r 5.1 and PD7A, para 3.1 (as modified by PD36D; and see note above
Application	By prescribed application form	FPR 2010, rr 5.1(1), 5.2;PD5A
	The application form must be accompanied by:	FPR 2010, r 7.8
	– copies for service on all other parties	
	– marriage (civil partnership) certificate	
	– reconciliation statement (if solicitor acting)	FPR 2010, r 7.6
	– court fee or 'fee exempt' form	FPFO 2008, Sch 2
	Fee: £550	FPFO 2008, fee 1.2

Filing without marriage certificate	Application (normally without notice) with explanation for the absence of a certificate Proof of urgency (as indicated by PD7A) is not a prerequisite for an application	FPR PD7A, paras 3.2, 3.3 *G v M* [2011] EWHC 2651 (Fam)
Parties	As respondent, other party to the marriage As co-respondent, anyone with whom respondent is alleged to have committed adultery or had improper association	FPR 2010, r 7.10
Service	The application and relevant documents (as above) are served personally or by post on respondent and co-respondent Service may be by the court by post, DX or alternative service provider or as further set out in FPR 2010, Pt 6	FPR 2010, Pt 6, Ch 2 FPR 2010, rr 6.8, 6.18; PD6A, para 3.1
Jurisdiction	The ability of a party to file a petition depends on habitual residence in England or Wales, or domicile	See 'Jurisdiction to apply …', above
Acknowledgement of service	A party served (mostly a respondent) may acknowledge service on Form M6 stating no intention to defend Notice of intention to defend must be given within 7 days of service	FPR 2010, r 7.12 FPR 2010, r 7.12(1)
Amended petitions	Filed as of right before answer filed; thereafter, filing only with leave Fee: £95	FPR 2010, r 7.13(1); PD7A, para 5 FPFO 2008, fee 1.5
Directions for trial	Directions may be: – in the undefended list or – as a cause to be treated as defended (see Guide B4)	FPR 2010, r 7.20 FPR 2010, r 7.20(2)(a) FPR 2010, r 7.20(2)(b)
Decree, conditional order in undefended list		FPR 2010, r 7.18
Undefended application procedure	In the case of undefended petitions/applications for divorce, nullity or judicial separation, the applicant files a statement verified by a statement of truth A judge considers the evidence If satisfied on consideration of evidence filed, the court certifies satisfaction as to entitlement to decree nisi or conditional order If not satisfied, court directs (1) further evidence or (2) listing for case management hearing If entitlement to a decree/order certified, court fixes date for formal pronouncement	FPR 2010, r 7.19(4),(5) FPR 2010, r 7.20(2) FPR 2010, r 7.20(2)(a) FPR 2010, r 7.20(2)(b) FPR 2010, r 7.18
Decree nisi/ conditional order application by petitioner/ applicant	Application for decree nisi or conditional order Subject to MCA 1973, ss 10(2) , application for the decree nisi to be made absolute can be made by the applicant (petitioner) after 6 weeks	MCA 1973, ss 1(5), 15; CPA 2004, s 38 MCA 1973, s 1(5); CPA 2004, s 38(1); FPR 2010, r 7.32
Decree nisi/ conditional order application by respondent	Application by a respondent by application on notice 3 months after that 6-week period Fee: £155	MCA 1973, s 9(2); CPA 2004, s 40(2); FPR 2010, r 7.33 FPFO 2008, fee 5.3

Decree nisi/ conditional order application by petitioner/ applicant after 12 months	If application is made by petitioner/applicant more than 12 months after decree nisi or conditional order, it must be supported by a document stating: (1) the reasons for the delay; (2) whether parties lived together since decree; and (3) whether a child has been born to the couple and, if so, whether a child of the family If the delay is substantial, the court may have power to set aside a decree nisi	FPR 2010, r 7.32(3) *Kim v Morris* [2013] 2 FLR 1197, FD
Costs	The court can deal with costs when dealing with a FPR 2010, r 7.20(2) certificate If a party wishes to be heard on costs claimed against them notice should be given to the court; decided on family proceedings costs award principles Note: a respondent who applies under MCA 1973, s 9(2); CPA 2004, s 40(2); or FPR 2010, r 7.33 should apply for costs in any event	FPR 2010, r 7.20(3) FPR 2010, r 7.21(1) FPR 2010, r 28.2, applying CPR 1998, r 44.2
Case management hearing	If the court is not satisfied that an applicant is entitled to a decree or conditional order (per FPR 2010, r 7.20(2)(a)) it may list the application for a case management hearing	FPR 2010 rr 7.20(2)(b)(ii), 7.22(3)

B3: Staying Grant of Decree Absolute under Matrimonial Causes Act 1973, s 10A

Legal background

MCA 1973, s 10A provides that, where a couple were married in accordance with 'the usages of the Jews' or other religious usages which prescribe final dissolution, the grant of a decree absolute can be stayed. No decree absolute will be granted until the court is satisfied by a declaration of both parties that the marriage is also dissolved in accordance with 'those [Jewish or other] usages'. FPR 2010, r 7.30 provides the regulatory framework for an application under s 10A.

Procedure

Who may apply	Either party to the marriage, although it is more likely to be the wife (whether respondent or petitioner)	MCA 1973, s 10A(2)
Time for application	After decree nisi, but before grant of decree absolute NB: Because of the time-frame from grant of decree nisi, prompt application is essential	MCA 1973, s 10A(1)
Application	On notice with affidavit in support setting out grounds of application	FPR 2010, r 7.30
Fee on application	£155	FPFO 2008, fee 5.3
Effect of order	Stay on grant of decree absolute until parties jointly declare that they have co-operated in arranging dissolution of their marriage in accordance with their religious usages	
Stay lifted	Upon filing declaration containing: – signature of both parties – particulars of MCA 1973 proceedings	MCA 1973, s 10A(4) FPR 2010, r 7.30(1)(a) FPR 2010, r 7.30(1)(b)

	– confirmation of necessary religious steps being taken	FPR 2010, r 7.30(1)(c)
	Declaration should be accompanied by documents listed in FPR 2010, r 7.30(1)(d)	FPR 2010, r 7.30(1)(d)

B4: Applications for Divorce, Judicial Separation or Nullity Orders and Equivalent Civil Partnership Orders in Defended Case

Legal background

See Guide B2.

Procedure

Answer to petition	An answer to the petition/application must be filed by any respondent who: – wishes to defend the application or to dispute any of the facts in it	FPR 2010, r 7.12(8)
	– wishes to oppose the grant of a decree under MCA 1973, s 5(1); CPA 2004, s 47	
	The answer must be filed 7 days plus 21 days (note: this is not necessarily 28 days – see commentary to FPR 2010, r 2.9)	FPR 2010, r 7.12(8)
	Fee: £245	FPFO 2008, fee 1.6
Petition/ application by a respondent	A respondent to a petition who seeks his/her own decree, must file a separate petition/application (as in Guide B2)	FPR 2010, r 7.14(1)
	Note: the application/petition is treated as an application in the first decree proceedings	FPR 2010, r 7.14(2)
Service of answer	There are no special rules for service of an answer as there are for divorce etc proceedings: normal service rules apply	FPR 2010, Pt 6, Chs 1, 3
Case management hearing	Case management hearing is listed by the district judge as directed on application for a decree nisi or conditional order	FPR 2010, r 7.20(4)
	At the hearing the court decides: – place of hearing	FPR 2010, r 7.22(2)(a)
	– timetable for filing and service of evidence; and for attendances of witnesses	FPR 2010, r 7.22(2)(b),(d)
	– documents disclosure – as appropriate; and see FPR 2010, r 7.15 for further information	FPR 2010, r 7.22(2)(c); PD7A, paras 6, 7
Hearing	In public	FPR 2010, r 7.16
	Application for hearing in private:	FPR 2010, Pt 18 procedure
	Factors or decision as to publicity	FPR 2010, r 7.16(3)
	Witness statements and other requirements as to evidence	FPR 2010, Pts 22, 23, 25
Level of judge	Family Division: High Court judge	
	Family Court: Judge of district judge level and above	FC(CDB)R 2014, Sch 1, para 2(a)
Decree	As for undefended cases, per Guide B2	

Costs	In the discretion of the court	CPR 1998, r 44.2
Appeals	See Guides E2, E4 and E5	FPR 2010, Pt 30

B5: Financial applications in the Family Court under MCA 1973 for Orders for Maintenance Pending Suit (s 22), Financial Provision and Property Adjustment (ss 23–24), Pension Orders (ss 21B, 21C, 24B–24D and 24E–24G), Variation (s 31) and Consideration of Respondent's Financial Position (s 10(2)) and under CPA 2004, s 72 and Sch 5

Legal background

MCA 1973, s 10(2) enables the court to consider the financial position of a respondent to a petition based on 5 years' separation or 2 years' separation with consent before allowing the decree to be made absolute. MCA 1973, ss 22 (maintenance pending suit), 23 (periodical payments and lump sum for a party to the marriage and the children, including pension attachment under ss 25B and 25C and pension compensation attachment under s 25F), 24 (property adjustment), 21A and 24B–24D (pension sharing) and 21B, 21C and 24E–24G (pension compensation sharing) enable the court in an application for divorce, judicial separation or nullity to make wide-ranging orders allocating the income and capital of both parties between themselves and in respect of any children. There are restrictions on the availability of pension sharing/attachment and pension compensation sharing/attachment (see further under MCA 1973, ss 24B, 24E, 25B, 25C and 25F). Further, neither pension sharing nor pension compensation sharing may be ordered on an application for judicial separation.

CPA 2004, s 72 and Sch 5 provides for financial relief for civil partners on dissolution, nullity or separation, which corresponds to the provision made for financial relief in connection with marriages under MCA 1973, Pt II.

The court's power to impose a clean break does not apply to judicial separation (MCA 1973, s 25A). The court has power to order the sale of property, when making a secured periodical payments order, a lump sum order or a property adjustment order (MCA 1973, s 24A), and will exercise its discretion in accordance with MCA 1973, ss 25 and 25A.

If a party remarries before making an application for a financial provision or property adjustment order (but not a pension (compensation) sharing order), that party is barred by MCA 1973, s 28(3) from making the application for himself or herself (although an application for children is unaffected by the s 28(3) bar). The corresponding provision for civil partners is found in CPA 2004, Sch 5, para 48. Remarriage after an application has been made, but before it is heard, is not a bar to jurisdiction, although a periodical payments or secured periodical payments order ends on the remarriage of the payee.

Orders that can be varied under MCA 1973, s 31 include those for maintenance pending suit, periodical payments, lump sum by instalments and deferred pension attachment lump sums. A pension sharing order may be varied where the order has not taken effect. The court's powers under MCA 1973, s 31 are extensive and include the power to extend the term of a fixed term order in the absence of a s 28(1A) bar.

All of the applications to which this Guide relates are defined as 'financial orders' with the exception of an order under MCA 1973, s 10(2), which is defined as a 'financial remedy' (FPR 2010, r 2.3). A financial order is within the definition of a financial remedy (FPR 2010, r 2.3). The definition of 'financial remedy' covers a wide range of other applications, including MCA 1973, ss 10(2), 27 and 35, and CA 1989, Sch 1. The procedure relating to all financial remedy applications, including financial orders, is governed by the longer procedure under FPR 2010, Pt 9, Ch 4. Applications for variation of a financial order are governed by the shorter procedure in FPR 2010, Pt 9, Ch 5 (see PD9A). An application may be made at any stage of the proceedings for interim orders, such as maintenance pending suit, interim periodical payments or legal costs orders. Applications for interim orders are governed by FPR 2010, Pt 18 procedure, to be read with r 9.7.

Applicants for orders under MCA 1973, ss 10(2), 21, 22, 23, 24 and 31 and equivalent provision under CPA 2004 are required to attend a mediation information and assessment meeting (MIAM) before making the application: CFA 2014, s 10(1); FPR 2010, Ch 3; PD3A, para 13(1)(a),(f), subject to exemptions (FPR 2010, r 3.8).

Divorce Centres, the Central Family Court (Financial Remedies Unit) and High Court applications

Issuing Forms A in Divorce Centres

The Family Court is divided into regional Divorce Centres (see Procedural Guide B2). Petitions for divorce and financial remedy applications should be made and issued in the appropriate Divorce Centre, which can be determined by using the facility at *https://courttribunalfinder.service.gov.uk/search/*. The proceedings will then be allocated to a local court (the Form A and petition (Form D8) will, in future, be amended to allow a location preference to be indicated). Urgent applications, for example, those involving jurisdictional issues or injunctions can still be issued in a local court with a district judge. Changes have not yet been implemented for issuing applications for financial relief after dissolution of a civil partnership, but these are likely to follow the scheme for applications on divorce.

The Central Family Court (Financial Remedies Unit)

The Financial Remedies Unit (FRU) has been established to ensure the efficient handling of complex financial cases. An application issued within the FRU at the Central Family Court (rather than through the Bury St Edmunds Divorce Centre designated for London and South East claims) requires completion of the Certificate of Financial Complexity (see *www.familylaw.co.uk/news_and_comment/how-to-refer-cases-to-the-financial-remedies-unit*). The Certificate is annexed to the Guidance Note on the Financial Remedies Unit at the Central Family Court, which is set out in Part V. Complexity is determined according to the level of assets involved and case-specific issues such as offshore trusts and conduct. If the Certificate is not clear as to the appropriateness of the case proceeding in the FRU, a judge at the FRU will make the allocation decision. Applications inappropriately issued in the FRU may be subject of delay while being returned or re-allocated to a local court. Forms A and petitions can still be issued at the Central Family Court if, for example, there is a 'jurisdictional race' to issue or urgent relief is required. Note that Local Direction of 17 October 2016: *Electronic Filing at the Central Family Court* (see Part V) provides for the option of electronic (email) filing of applications for financial order and Forms E. This is a pilot scheme; it applies to all applications issued after 1 January 2016 and will be reviewed in April 2017.

Financial Remedy Hearings in the High Court

On 1 February 2016, Mostyn J issued a revised *Statement on the Efficient Conduct of Financial Remedy Hearings Allocated to a High Court Judge* (set out in Part V). The Statement also includes Guidance as to the allocation of cases to a judge of the High Court by means of self-certification. The Guidance applies to all cases commenced after 1 July 2015 and, as far as practicable, to cases commenced before that date. The Statement provides for a governing principle that a case will only be allocated to a High Court judge if it is 'exceptionally complex or there is another substantial ground for the case being heard at that level, and that allocation is proportionate'. Allocation is (1) rarely likely to be appropriate unless the net asset value exceeds £7.5m, (2) likely (but not necessarily appropriate) in cases in which the net assets exceed £15m and/or the overall annual net income exceeds £1m, (3) in cases not falling within (2) above, dependent on the existence of certain issues of complexity in the case, such as a dispute over a nuptial agreement and (4) in cases in which the assets, on any view, do not exceed £7.5m, only likely if the application involves a novel and important point of law. The Statement also includes important direction as to the management of High Court cases including FDR listings, judicial continuity and the requirement for a pre-trial review. Where parties seek the allocation of proceedings to a High Court judge before an allocation decision has been made, i e self-certification, both counsel (or solicitors if counsel has not been instructed) must complete and file a Certificate explaining why and how the case falls within the governing principle and is suitable for allocation.

Form E calculation errors

See Guide A2.

Procedure

Who may apply	*Under MCA 1973, s 10(2)* The respondent to a petition under MCA 1973, s 1(2)(d) or (e) in the court where the application is proceeding at any time after the petition is filed but before the decree is made absolute *Under MCA 1973, ss 22–24G* Either spouse/civil partner, provided (in the case of financial provision and property adjustment orders) the applicant has not remarried at the time of application	

Level of judge	District judge	FC(CDB)R 2014, Sch 1, para 2(b)
Application	Preliminary requirement for proposed parties to attend a MIAM before application, subject to exemptions	CFA 2014, s 10(1); FPR 2010, Ch 3; PD3A, para 13(1)(a),(f); FPR 2010, r 3.8
	To the appropriate Divorce Centre (see Guide B2 and notes above). If issuing in the FRU (London), a Certificate of Complexity must be filed	FPR 2010, r 9.5(1)
	The application is on Form A, or Form B for an application under s 10(2), together with any documents stated to be required, or referred to in the application. Proceedings start when a court officer issues the application and are issued on that date	FPR 2010, rr 5.1–5.3; PD5A
	If claim omitted from petition or answer claiming relief, permission is needed to make claim. If application for permission is made before decree nisi, apply on notice to other party with supporting statement	FPR 2010, r 7.13, Pt 18 (Form D11)
	Applications for variations are governed by the shorter procedure in FPR 2010, Pt 9, Ch 5. However, the court may direct that the longer procedure under FPR 2010, Pt 9, Ch 4 is followed, for example where an application proposes a capital payment or pension sharing order. This is determined on paper, without notice to the parties, before the first hearing	FPR 2010, rr 9.18–9.20; PD9A
	Applications for interim orders, as defined in r 9.7(1)(a)–(e), are governed by Pt 18 and are by notice of application, unless dispensed with by the court	FPR 2010, r 18.4
	Applications for interim orders should state what order is sought and why, and attach a draft order	FPR 2010, r 18.7(1),(2)
	Where an application is made before a financial statement is filed, written evidence in support must explain why the order is necessary and give up-to-date financial information	FPR 2010, r 9.7
Fee	£255	FPFO 2008, fee 5.4
Service	Within 4 days of the date on which the application was filed, a court officer will serve a copy of the application upon the respondent and give notice of the date of the first hearing to both parties	
	Alternatively, the applicant must serve the respondent within 4 days, beginning with the date on which the copy of the application was received from the court, and file a certificate of service on or before the first appointment	FPR 2010, r 9.12(2)
	Where an application is for a variation of settlement, an avoidance of disposition or an application relating to land, the relevant trustees, mortgagees etc must be served. A person so served may file a statement in answer within 14 days of service. A certificate of service must be filed on or before the first appointment	FPR 2010, r 9.13
	An application for a legal services payment order is 'any other form of interim order' under r 9.7(1)(e) and therefore may be made without notice	FPR 2010, r 9.7

	Applications for maintenance pending suit and other orders defined under r 9.3(1)(a)–(d) are governed by Pt 18 procedure as to service	FPR 2010, r 18.8
Respondent	The other spouse/civil partner	
Procedure	Financial applications (save for variations) are dealt with by the longer procedure in FPR 2010, Pt 9, Ch 4	FPR 2010, rr 9.12–9.17; PD9A
	The court will fix a first appointment not less than 12 weeks and not more than 16 weeks after the filing of the application	FPR 2010, r 9.12
	By 35 days before the first appointment, the parties must simultaneously exchange and file at court a financial statement on Form E, or Form E1 for applications under s 10(2) and other financial remedies such as MCA 1973, ss 27 and 35, accompanied by a limited category of documents. No disclosure or inspection of the parties' documents may be given between the filing of the application and the first appointment, save as laid down in r 9.14(4)	FPR PD5A; FPR 2010, r 9.14(4)
	By 14 days before the first appointment, each party must file and serve a concise statement of issues, a chronology, a questionnaire and a notice stating whether that party will be in a position to use the hearing as a FDR appointment. In addition, the parties should (if possible) exchange an agreed case summary, a schedule of assets and a draft of directions sought by the parties	FPR PD9A, para 4; FPR 2010, r 9.14(5)
	At the first appointment, the court in pursuance of the overriding objective in Pt 1 will case manage the financial application seeking to define issues and saving costs. The court will approve the content of questionnaires and make direction in respect of replies, requests for documents and expert evidence (subject to compliance with Pt 25). In applications for pension (compensation) sharing/attachment orders, the court may direct the filing and service of Form P (Pension Inquiry Form) or Form PPF (PPF Inquiry Form). Both parties must attend in person.	
	The next hearing, normally the FDR, will be timetabled. Alternatively, the court may list for further directions, the making of an interim order, a final hearing or treat the First Appointment as an FDR. Costs will be considered. After the first appointment, there is no further provision for the disclosure of documents, save with the permission of the court	FPR 2010, rr 9.15, 9.16
	At the FDR appointment, the parties are to meet for discussion and negotiation. 7 days before the FDR appointment, the applicant must file details of all offers and proposals and the responses to them. If the court cannot make a consent order, the court must give direction for a final hearing. Both parties must personally attend the FDR hearing, unless the court directs otherwise	FPR PD9A, para 6; FPR 2010, r 9.17
Variation applications	Variation applications are dealt with by the shorter procedure under FPR 2010, Pt 9, Ch 5	FPR 2010, rr 9.18–9.20; PD9A
	The court will fix a first hearing not less than 4 weeks and not more than 8 weeks after the filing of the application	FPR 2010, r 9.18(1)

	Not more than 14 days after the issue of the application, parties must simultaneously exchange and file with the court a financial statement	FPR PD5A
	No disclosure or inspection of the parties' documents may be given between the filing of the application and the first hearing, save as laid down in FPR 2010, r 9.19(4)	FPR 2010, r 9.19(4)
	Unless the court is able to determine the application at the first hearing, the court may direct further evidence and set a date for a directions hearing or final hearing	FPR 2010, r 9.20
Interim orders	The power to make interim orders is governed by the statute. There is no power to make interim lump sum orders, property adjustment orders or pension sharing orders. However, an interim order for sale of property may be ordered	MCA 1973, ss 23(1)(c), 24; FPR 2010, r 20.2(1)(c)(v); *BR v VT (Financial Remedies: Interim)* [2016] 2 FLR 519, FD
Orders	Periodical payments and/or secured periodical payments for spouse/civil partner and/or children (by standing order or by direct debit)	MCA 1973, s 23(1)(a), (b),(d),(e)
	Lump sum for spouse/civil partner and/or children; for wording of roll-over of statutory charge, see –	MCA 1973, s 23(1)(c),(f); *PD of 19 August 1991*
	Interest on lump sum before and after payment due	MCA 1973, s 23(6); JA 1838
	Order for sale of property (where order also made for secured periodical payments, lump sum or property adjustment), with a direction that vacant possession be given	MCA 1973, s 24A; FPR 2010, r 9.24
	If there is to be a complete, clean break (divorce/dissolution or nullity only), a direction preventing an application to extend the term of the periodical payments order or to make any future application in relation to the marriage. A dismissal of Inheritance Act claims should also be made	I(PFD)A 1975, ss 2, 15; MCA 1973, ss 28(1A), 25A(3)
	A pension sharing order (divorce/dissolution or nullity only) is for a percentage of the Cash Equivalent	MCA 1973, s 21A; PD(PI)R 2000, reg 3; D(P)R 2000, reg 3; *H v H (Financial Relief: Pensions)* [2010] 2 FLR 173, FD
	A pension sharing order may not be made against an overseas pension	*Goyal v Goyal* [2016] EWFC 50
	A pension sharing order cannot take effect until the later of decree absolute and 7 days after the time for appealing has expired	D(P)R 2000, reg 9
	A pension compensation sharing order (divorce/dissolution or nullity only) is for a percentage of the Cash Equivalent of the PPF compensation	MCA 1973, s 21B(1); Pension Protection Fund (Pension Compensation Sharing and Attachment on Divorce etc) Regulations 2011, regs 3 and 4
	A pension compensation sharing order cannot take effect until the later of decree absolute and 7 days after the time for appealing has expired	Divorce and Dissolution etc (Pension Protection Fund) Regulations 2011, reg 5
	A pension attachment order is for a percentage of the benefit and, if the benefit is for a lump sum, the pension member can be required to commute	MCA 1973, s 25B(5),(7)

	A pension compensation attachment order is for a percentage of the payment that becomes due to the party with compensation rights and, where the party with compensation rights has a right to commute, he/she may be required to exercise that right to any extent	MCA 1973, s 25F(3),(5)
	A pension (compensation) sharing or attachment order must contain appropriate annexes and should direct whether the court or one of the parties is to serve the order and accompanying documents on the pension arrangement/PPF	FPR 2010, rr 9.35, 9.36, 9.44 and 9.45
	Costs including payment on account and interest	CPR 1998, r 44.2; FPR 2010, r 28.3
Service and implementation of pension orders	Within 7 days of making the order or decree absolute, whichever is the later, the court or one of the parties (as directed) serves order for pension (compensation) sharing or attachment on pension provider together with copy of the decree absolute	FPR 2010, rr 9.36(5) and 9.45(2)
	Parties serve on the pension provider formal information	PD(PI)R 2000, reg 5; Pension Protection Fund (Pension Compensation Sharing and Attachment on Divorce etc) Regulations 2011, reg 9
	4-month period that the pension provider/PPF has to implement the order then starts. Within 3 weeks of receiving pension (compensation) sharing order pension provider/PPF gives notice of charges	PD(PI)R 2000, reg 7; Pension Protection Fund (Pension Compensation Sharing and Attachment on Divorce etc) Regulations 2011, reg 9
Pension provider's/PPF's obligations on pension (compensation) sharing	Percentage debited from member's share and transferred to applicant by way of pension credit either by internal or external transfer. Alternatively, percentage debited from member's rights to PPF compensation and transfer to applicant by way of pension credit by internal transfer. Pension arrangement/PPF then gives notice of completion of this process (notice of discharge)	PD(PI)R 2000, reg 8; Pension Protection Fund (Pension Compensation Sharing and Attachment on Divorce etc) Regulations 2011, reg 16
Appeals	See Guides E2, E4 and E5	

B6: Injunctions to Restrain Future Disposals and Avoidance of Disposition Orders under Matrimonial Causes Act 1973, s 37

Legal background

There are two separate jurisdictions that enable the court to grant injunctions to protect or recover assets subject of a claim for a financial order. The first, MCA 1973, s 37 enables an applicant for financial relief on divorce to apply to the court under s 37(1) to restrain anticipated dealings that may defeat the applicant's financial claim. Under s 37(2)(b),(c), the court may also set aside a reviewable disposition or order where there was a transaction for valuable consideration without notice to the applicant. This power may be exercised by the court at the final hearing of the financial applications under MCA 1973, under FPR 2010, Pt 9 procedure. Before this, injunction orders may be made to prevent a third party disposing of an asset acquired in such a way, under SCA 1981, s 37 and Civil Procedure Act 1997, s 7 (see below).

The second jurisdiction is the general framework that is available in all civil claims. It has two separate bases: (i) the court's inherent jurisdiction to freeze assets where the balance of convenience justifies such a course; and (ii) under SCA 1981, s 37(1) as fortified by Civil Procedure Act 1997, s 7. Under these Acts the court can make injunctions, including freezing injunctions (formerly called *Mareva* injunctions) against assets in England and Wales or worldwide, and make search orders (formerly called *Anton Piller* orders) whereby a home or business premises is searched under the auspices of a supervising solicitor. Search orders may only be made in exceptional circumstances in family cases (*A v A* [1997] Fam Law 301, CA) and must be made in the High Court. Other orders may be made in the Family Court.

Where the applicant shows good grounds for no notice, the application may be made without notice. The application for an injunction without notice carries with it a strict obligation to give full disclosure of facts that may militate against an order being made (*Re W (Ex Parte Orders)* [2000] 2 FLR 927, FD). The exceptional nature of a without notice application was highlighted in *UL v BK (Freezing Orders: safeguards: Standard Examples)* [2013] EWHC 1735 (Fam), which provides a useful summary of applicable principles and safeguards (at [51]), as well as a specimen order. Regard should also be had to FPR PD20A, para 4.3(c), which requires an applicant to take steps to notify a respondent informally of an application except in a case where it is essential that the respondent must not be aware of the application. If an order is made without notice, the on notice hearing should be listed and the absent respondent is entitled to copies of the material presented to the court and a note of what was said at the hearing.

An application under MCA 1973, s 37 for the avoidance of a disposition is defined as a financial remedy under FPR 2010, r 2.3. By FPR 2010, r 9.6(1), the procedure under Pt 18 applies in an application for an order preventing a disposition.

CPA 2004, Sch 5, para 74 provides a corresponding jurisdiction to the court in cases of financial relief on the dissolution of a civil partnership.

Procedure

Who may apply	A spouse/civil partner, where proceedings for financial relief under MCA 1973 have been brought	MCA 1973, s 37(1),(2)
Level of judge	May not be granted by Justices in the Family Court	FC(CDB)R 2014, Sch 2, Table 1
Application	The application may be made to the High Court or Family Court Application may be made using FPR 2010, Pt 18 procedure in the course of existing matrimonial proceedings or in connection with concluded proceedings Application is by an application notice, stating what order is sought and why the applicant is seeking the order, with a draft order attached	FPR 2010, r 9.6(1) FPR 2010, rr 18.4–18.7
Fee	£155	FPFO 2008, fee 5.3
Service	A copy of the application notice must be served in accordance with the provisions of Pt 6 at least 7 days before the hearing, with any written evidence in support and the draft order	FPR 2010, r 18.8
Respondents	Spouses/civil partners, parties to existing or concluded proceedings and any other person as the court may direct	FPR 2010, r 18.3
Procedure	The application may be made without notice to the respondent. The evidence in support of the application must state why notice has not been given. It is then usual to list a return date Consider whether informal notice can be given The order, application notice and evidence in support must normally be served on all parties. The order must state the respondent's right to apply to set aside or vary Where a disposition has been made in favour of a third party, the third party may be joined to the proceedings and an order made under the court's inherent jurisdiction restraining any disposition by him of the property	FPR 2010, r 9.6(2) FPR PD20A, para 4.3(c) FPR 2010, r 18.10

Orders	The injunction order must set out clearly what the respondent must and must not do. The court may make whatever order is necessary to protect the claim, including a freezing injunction and orders for the surrender of the respondent's passport and restraining him from leaving the jurisdiction	*Bayer AG v Winter* [1986] 1 WLR 497, CA
	A respondent cannot be restrained from leaving the jurisdiction as a means of enforcement in its own right; the court may exercise the power to impound a respondent's passport	*B v B (Injunction: Restraint on Leaving Jurisdiction)* [1997] 2 FLR 148, FD; *Young v Young* [2012] 2 FLR 470, FD
	The applicant may be required to give an undertaking as to damages, if the order may affect third party rights	*Re W (Ex parte Orders)* [2000] 2 FLR 927, FD
	On an application to set aside a disposition, the court may give consequential directions, including the making of payment or for the disposal of any property,	MCA 1973, s 37(3)
Appeals	See Guides E2, E4 and E5	

B7: Financial Relief after Overseas Proceedings under Matrimonial and Family Proceedings Act 1984, Pt III, Including Injunctions under s 24 to Restrain Anticipated Dealings

Legal background

MFPA 1984, ss 12–27 allow a party to a marriage that has been ended by overseas proceedings that are recognised in England and Wales to apply for financial relief in the same way as if the marriage had been ended here. FPR 2010 define the relief as 'financial remedy'. The court can make the same order available under MCA 1973/CPA 2004, subject to permission to proceed being granted. Jurisdiction to grant permission depends on domicile, habitual residence for 1 year or the existence of a matrimonial home within the jurisdiction: if this is the sole ground, the court can only make capital orders in respect of that property and cannot make income or other capital orders for the applicant or children. If the application, or part of it, is for the payment of maintenance, jurisdiction is determined in accordance with the Maintenance Regulation (EC) No 4/2009 (MFPA 1984, s 15(1A)).

At the permission stage, the application will be dealt with on a without notice basis following the Pt 18 procedure supplementing rr 8.23–8.28: see Lord Collins in *Agbaje v Agbaje* [2010] 1 FLR 1813, SC (at [33]) and Munby LJ in *Traversa v Freddi* [2011] 2 FLR 272, CA (at [49]–[58]).

Under MFPA 1984, s 24, the court may restrain anticipated dealings with property where the sole ground on which the applicant may claim jurisdiction is habitual residence for 1 year, and that year has not been completed. Once permission is granted, the applicant may apply to restrain anticipated dealings and set aside past dealings where the intention was to defeat the claim for financial relief.

When applying for permission to apply for a financial remedy after an overseas divorce, the procedure under FPR 2010, rr 8.23–8.28 applies. If permission is granted, the application proceeds as an application for a financial order under FPR 2010, Pt 9. When applying for an injunction under MFPA 1984, s 24, the procedures under FPR 2010, Pts 18 and 20 apply.

Procedure

Who may apply for leave	A party whose marriage has been ended by overseas proceedings (judicial or otherwise) recognised in England and Wales and who can establish domicile, 1 year's habitual residence or the existence of a matrimonial home within the jurisdiction. Remarriage bars an application	MFPA 1984, ss 12, 15

Level of judge	Judge of High Court level where (i) parties do not consent to permission being granted; or (ii) parties consent to permission but do not consent to the substantive order sought	FC(CDB)R 2014, Sch 1, para 4(a)
Application for permission (leave)	To a High Court judge where no consent to permission, or consent to permission but not to substantive order. To a district judge of the Family Court, where parties consent to permission being granted and to the substantive order	*Barnett v Barnett* [2014] EWHC 2678 (Fam); FC(CDB)R 2014, Sch 1, paras 2(c), 4(a)
Issue of application	The application will be by Forms D50E (application for permission) and Form D50F (substantive application), accompanied by: (1) a statement (as outlined in Form D50F) by the applicant (2) a draft order (3) documents, including in relation to existing court proceedings and financial documents	FPR PD5A
	Where the application is by consent, Form D50E and Form D50F should be filed (together with evidence of the respondent's consent) in the Family Court (rr 8.24, 9.5(2), 9.26(6))	FPR 2010, r 8.24, read in conjunction with rr 18.4 and 18.7
Service	Issue and permission dealt with on notice; no rules are provided for service in that event	FPR 2010, rr 8.25 and 18.5(1); *Traversa v Freddi* [2011] 2 FLR 272, CA, at [56]
Test for permission	'Substantial ground', not high, but higher than 'serious issue to be tried'. May be made if order made in another jurisdiction	MFPA 1984, s 13(1) and (2); *Agbaje v Agbaje* [2010] 1 FLR 1813, SC, at [33]
Disposal of application	The application for leave should be listed ex parte for a hearing before a judge, time estimate: 30 mins	*Agbaje* (above) at [33]; *Traversa* (above) at [56]–[58] (for permission to appeal, see FPR PD30A, paras 4.10–4.13, 4.15, 4.22–4.24)
Order made without notice		FPR 2010, r 8.25
Setting aside leave granted without notice	A person who was not served with a copy of the application notice before an order was made may apply within 7 days beginning with the date on which the order was served to have the order set aside or varied An application to set aside leave, if not dismissed then and there, should be adjourned to be heard with the substantive application	
	It will succeed only if compelling reason ('knock-out' blow: per Lord Collins; and see CPR 1998, r 52.9(2))	FPR 2010, r 18.11; *Agbaje* (above) at [33]; *Traversa* (above) at [58]
Order on leave application	Grant or refusal of leave, with or without conditions. A judge may direct that substantive application may be heard by a district judge of the Family Court	MFPA 1984, s 13; FPR 2010, rr 8.28, 9.5(3)
Costs	As for Court of Appeal permission, the respondent should not normally have costs, even on an attended permission hearing	FPR PD30A, paras 4.22, 4.23

Application for substantive order	Following the granting of leave, a High Court judge may direct that the application be heard by a district judge of the PRFD (exercising High Court jurisdiction). It may also be heard by an appropriate judge of the Family Court, including a district judge, where there is consent to the substantive order, or as directed by the court as envisaged in *Barnett*	*Barnett v Barnett* [2014] EWHC 2678 (Fam); FPR 2010, r 8.28; FC(CDB)R 2014, Sch 1, para 4(a)
Fee	On an application to start proceedings where no other fee is specified: £245	FPFO 2008, fee 1.1
Procedure	As in Guide B5 for a financial remedy	FPR 2010, Pt 9
Interim order	Where leave has been granted under MFPA 1984, s 13 and it appears that an applicant or child is in immediate need of financial assistance, the court may make an interim order for maintenance	MFPA 1984, s 14(1)
Application for interim order	Pt 18 procedure	FPR 2010, r 9.7
Injunctions	Applications to restrain the respondent from disposing of assets may be applied for before the conclusion of 1 year's habitual residence. Once leave is granted, the applicant can apply for an injunction to restrain anticipated dealings	MFPA 1984, s 24(1)(a),(b)
	The application for an injunction is governed by FPR 2010, Pt 18 and Pt 20 procedures The without notice order, application notice and evidence in support must normally be served on all parties. The order must state the respondent's right to apply to set aside or vary	FPR 2010, r 20.3
Orders	Injunction restraining any disposition, transfer out of the jurisdiction or any other dealing with the property	MFPA 1984, s 23(2)(a)
	Periodical payments, secured periodical payments and lump sum for the applicant and the children, but no power to award interest on lump sum	MFPA 1984, ss 17, 21
	Property adjustment order for the spouse and/or children, and an order for sale	MFPA 1984, ss 17, 21
	Transfer of a statutory or contractual tenancy	MFPA 1984, s 22
	Setting aside a disposition made with the intention of defeating a claim for financial relief	MFPA 1984, s 23
	If only fact establishing jurisdiction is existence of matrimonial home in England and Wales, the court can only make orders in relation to that asset and cannot make any income order for applicant or children	MFPA 1984, s 20
Appeals	See Guides E2, E4 and E5	

C1: Reciprocal Enforcement

Legal background

The provisions for enforcing in other countries judgments and orders (including maintenance orders) made in England and Wales, and vice versa, and for making in England and Wales claims for maintenance against persons resident in other countries, and vice versa, are complex. The Table and Procedural Guides that follow constitute an outline of the relevant procedures and their availability. However, reference should always be made to the text of the rules, statutes and, where appropriate, international conventions from which the remedies derive. Moreover, no attempt is made to provide a comprehensive account of the particular requirements of individual countries. Before expense is undertaken in attempting to pursue a remedy abroad, enquiry should be made of a local lawyer as to any requirements of a particular territory and, indeed, as to the likelihood of the remedy being effective, for example because of stringent exchange control regulation. For enforcement abroad of residence (custody) and contact (access) orders and recovery of children abducted abroad, see Guides D19–D21.

How to use the Table

Identify from the list below the activity to be undertaken. The letter (A to F) associated with it is the number of a vertical column in the Table. Locate the territory concerned on the left-hand side of the Table and note the number reference(s) given (1 to 15) in the chosen column beside it. Find the number reference(s) in the Guides (C1(1) to C1(15)) that follow the Table. Each Guide deals with the English (and Welsh) aspect of 'outward' enforcement (i e an applicant in England pursuing a remedy abroad) and, so far as appropriate, 'inward' enforcement (i e a foreign applicant pursuing the equivalent remedy in England).

The presence of more than one number reference indicates that alternative remedies may be available to the applicant. The absence of any indicates that no appropriate remedy has been discovered by the authors. However, the information has had to be gathered from a wide range of sources and international arrangements are constantly changing. It is always worth checking the up-to-date position: in the case of maintenance orders, assistance can usually be obtained from the REMO (Reciprocal Enforcement of Maintenance Orders) Unit, Official Solicitor & Public Trustee, Victory House, 30–34 Kingsway, London WC2B 6EX, DX 141423 Bloomsbury 7, telephone 020 3681 2757, email remo@offsol.gsi.gov.uk. The website at *www.gov.uk/remo-unit-helpline* offers useful guidance and a number of international links.

In the Table, lower case letters in parentheses refer to notes given at the foot of the Table.

The cases to which the Table refers

- A A maintenance order having been made in England or Wales, the payee seeks to enforce it abroad, and vice versa
- B Application in England and Wales for a provisional maintenance order against a respondent abroad, and vice versa
- C Applicant in England or Wales makes a maintenance claim for transmission abroad for determination there against a respondent there, and vice versa
- D Application to vary, discharge or revoke an order which has been registered or made under Case A, B or C
- E A money judgment having been given in England or Wales, the creditor seeks to enforce it abroad, and vice versa
- F A judgment or order including a non-monetary provision having been given or made in England or Wales, the person entitled to the benefit of that provision seeks to enforce it abroad, and vice versa

Table

CASE	A	B	C	D	E	F
Scotland and Northern Ireland	3			4	14	14
Akrotiri (Sovereign Base Area)					10	
Albania	12					
Algeria			8	9		
Anguilla	5	6		7	10	
Antigua and Barbuda	1	2			10	
Antilles (n)						
Aruba (n)						
Australia	5(h)	6(h)	8	7(h),9	11	
Austria	12		8		13, 15(aa)	13
Bahamas	1	2			10	
Barbados	5	6	8	7,9	10	
Belgium	12		8		13, 15(aa)	13
Belize	1	2			10	
Bermuda	5	6		7	10	
Bosnia and Herzegovina	12					
Botswana	1	2			10	

CASE	A	B	C	D	E	F
Brazil			8	9		
British Indian Ocean Territory					10	
British Virgin Islands	1	2				
Brunei Darussalam	5(l)	6(l)		7(l)		
Bulgaria	12	6(h)	8		13, 15(aa)	
Burkina Faso			8	9		
Canada:						
Federal Court					11	
Alberta	5(ab)	6(abc)		7(ab)	11	
British Columbia	5	6		7	11	
Manitoba	5	6		7	11	
New Brunswick	5(abc)	6(abc)		7(abc)	11	
Newfoundland and Labrador	5	6		7	11	
Northwest Territories	5(abc)	6(abc)		7(abc)	11	
Nunavut	5(abc)	6(abc)		7(abc)	11	
Nova Scotia	5(ab)	6(ab)		7(ab)	11	
Ontario	5(b)	6(b)		7(b)	11	
Prince Edward Island	1	2			11	
Saskatchewan	5(b)	6(bc)		7(b)	11	
Yukon	1	2			11	
Cape Verde Islands			8	9		
Cayman Islands	1	2			10	
Central African Republic			8	9		
Chile			8	9		
Christmas Island	1	2			10	
Cocos (Keeling) Islands	1	2			10	
Comoro Archipelago			8	9		
Croatia			8	9		
Cyprus	12		8		10, 13, 15(aa)	
Czech Republic, The	12		8		13, 15(aa)	
Denmark	12		8		13	13
Dhekelia (Sovereign Base Area)					10	
Dominica	1	2			10	
Ecuador			8	9		
Estonia	12				13, 15(aa)	
Falkland Islands	5	6		7	10	
Fiji	5	6		7	10	
Finland	12		8		13, 15(aa)	13
France (f)	12		8		13, 15(aa)	13
French Guiana (f)			8	9		
French Polynesia			8	9		
Gambia	1	2			10	
Germany	12		8		13, 15(aa)	13
Ghana	5(bc)	6(bc)		7(bc)	10	
Gibraltar	5,12	6		7	13	13
Greece	12		8		13, 15(aa)	13

CASE	A	B	C	D	E	F
Grenada	1	2			10	
Guadeloupe (f)			8	9		
Guatemala			8	9		
Guernsey	1	2			11	
Guyana	1	2			10	
Haiti			8	9		
Holy See *see* Vatican						
Hong Kong	5	6		7	10	
Hungary	12		8		13, 15(aa)	
Iceland	12				13	13
India	5(abc)	6(abc)		7(abc)	10(z)	
Ireland, Republic of	12		8		13, 15(aa)	13
Isle of Man	5	6		7	11(d)	
Israel			8	9	11	
Italy	12		8		13, 15(aa)	13
Jamaica	1	2			10	
Jersey	5	6			11(e)	
Kenya	5(bc)	6(bc)		7(bc)	10	
Kiribati	1	2			10	
Latvia	12		8		13, 15(aa)	
Lesotho	1	2			10	
Lithuania	12				13, 15(aa)	
Luxembourg	12		8		13, 15(aa)	13
Macedonia (former Yugoslav republic)			8	9		
Malawi	1	2			10	
Malaysia	1	2			10	
Malta and Gozo (g)	12				10,13, 15(aa)	
Martinique (f)			8	9		
Mauritius	1	2			10	
Mexico			8	9		
Monaco			8	9		
Montenegro	12					
Montserrat	1	2			10	
Morocco			8	9		
Nauru	5	6		7		
Netherlands (n)	12		8		13, 15(aa)	13
New Caledonia and Dependencies			8	9		
New Zealand	5	6	8	7,9	10	
Niger			8	9		
Nigeria	1	2			10	
Norfolk Island	5(a)	6(a)	8	7(a),9	10	
Norway	12				13	13
Pakistan			8	9	11	
Papua New Guinea	5	6(c)		7	10	
Philippines			8	9		
Poland	12		8		13, 15(aa)	
Polynesia, French *see* French Polynesia						
Portugal	12		8		13, 15(aa)	13

CASE	A	B	C	D	E	F
Réunion (f)			8	9		
Romania	12		8			
St Helena	5	6		7	10	
St Kitts and Nevis	1	2			10	
St Lucia	1	2			10	
St Pierre et Miquelon			8	9		
St Vincent and the Grenadines	1	2			10	
Serbia			8	9		
Seychelles	1	2			10	
Sierra Leone	1	2			10	
Singapore	5	6		7	10	
Slovakia	12		8		13, 15(aa)	
Slovenia	12		8		13, 15(aa)	
Solomon Islands	1	2			10	
South Africa	5(bc)	6(bc)		7(bc)		
Spain	12		8		13, 15(aa)	13
Sri Lanka	1	2	8	9	10	
Surinam			8	9	11	
Swaziland	1	2			10	
Sweden	12		8		13, 15(aa)	13
Switzerland	5(h),12	6(h)	8	7(h),9	13	13
Tanzania (except Zanzibar)	5(abc)	6(abc)		7(abc)	10	
Tonga					11	
Trinidad and Tobago	1	2			10	
Tunisia			8	9		
Turkey	5(h),12	6(h)	8	7(h),9		
Turks and Caicos Islands	5(abc)	6(abc)		7(abc)	10	
Tuvalu	1	2			10	
Uganda	1	2			10	
USA	5,12		8	7,9		
Uruguay			8	9		
Vatican			8	9		
Virgin Islands (UK) *see* British Virgin Islands						
Zambia	1	2			10	
Zanzibar	1	2			10	
Zimbabwe	5(bc)	6(bc)		7(bc)	10	

Notes

(a) Other than orders obtained by or in favour of a public authority
(aa) An alternative procedure for the enforcement of uncontested claims is available, at the creditor's option, under Council Regulation (EU) No 805/2004
(b) Other than orders for the payment of birth and funeral expenses of child
(c) Other than affiliation orders
(d) Family Court judgments and orders must have first been transferred to the High Court
(e) High Court judgments and orders only
(f) For some purposes, France includes the overseas departments of Guadeloupe, Guiana, Martinique and Réunion
(g) Malta is a 'reciprocating country' for the purpose of MO(RE)A 1972, but the Maintenance Regulation (EC) No 4/2009 takes precedence
(h) MO(RE)A 1972, Pt I applies to the Hague Convention countries as modified by SI 1993/593 and SI 1999/1318
(l) Other than lump sum orders

(n) For most purposes, the Netherlands include the Netherlands Antilles and Aruba
(z) The territories named in SI 1958/425

C1(1): Maintenance Order having been Made in England or Wales, Payee Seeks to Enforce it Abroad, and Vice Versa (not designated under MO(RE)A 1972)

OUTWARD

Registration abroad of maintenance order made in England or Wales

Who may apply	The payee under a maintenance order made in England or Wales where the payer resides in a Commonwealth country which is not designated as a reciprocating country under MO(RE)A 1972, Pt I	MO(FE)A 1920, s 2
Which court	*High Court order* The Principal Registry or the district registry if the cause is proceeding there	FPR 2010, r 34.10(3),(4)
	All other orders Application should be made to the Family Court for the area where the order was made	MO(FE)A 1920, s 2
Documents required	*High Court order* A certified copy of the maintenance order A sworn written statement stating the reason for believing that the payer is residing in the territory in question So far as known, his address and occupation Any other information required by the law of that territory for the purpose of enforcement of the order	FPR PD34A
	It is therefore necessary to enquire in advance as to the particular requirements of the territory and to disclose the result in the sworn written statement	FPR 2010, r 34.10
	In the case of Yukon, Prince Edward Island, the Solomon Islands, Kiribati and Tuvulu, if the payer's address is unknown the court can cause enquiries to be made	FPR PD34B
	All other orders A certified copy of the order and signed certificate of arrears	MO(FE)A 1920, s 2; Home Office Circular 469, 726/4 dated 15 June 1925
	Information sufficient to ascertain the whereabouts of the payer (including his last known address) Information sufficient to identify the payer (including where possible a photograph) A certificate of marriage A certificate of the birth of the child (where maintenance is payable in respect of a child)	
Fee	None	
What happens next	If satisfied, the court sends the documents to the Lord Chancellor for transmission to the governor of that part of Her Majesty's dominions and records the fact of transmission in the court records	MO(FE)A 1920, s 2; FPR PD34A, para 3.3

Variation or discharge	MO(FE)A 1920 contains no provisions affecting the court's power to vary or discharge a maintenance order, but enforcement will be subject to any equivalent powers which the corresponding legislation in the country of registration may accord to its courts	
Appeals	See relevant Guides in Appeals section	

INWARD

Registration in England of maintenance order made abroad

Who may apply	The Lord Chancellor, on receipt of a maintenance order made in a Commonwealth country which is not designated as a reciprocating country under MO(RE)A 1972, Pt I	MO(FE)A 1920, s 1
Which court	If the maintenance order was made by a court of superior jurisdiction, the Principal Registry of the Family Division; otherwise, the Maintenance Enforcement Business Centre for the Family Court for the area where the defendant resides	FPR 2010, r 34.9; MO(FE)A 1920, s 1
Fee	None	
What happens next	The Senior District Judge in the Principal Registry or court officer for the Family Court as the case may be enters the order in the register. In the Family Court, unless it is satisfied that it is undesirable to do so, the court will order payments due to be made through the court	FPR 2010, rr 34.2, 34.3, 34.6
	The order has full retrospective effect from the date specified in the order Registration is an administrative act and the defendant cannot appeal against registration of the order	MO(FE)A 1920, s 1
Enforcement	*High Court* The order is enforceable as a High Court maintenance order and all proceedings may be taken on it as if it had been made by the High Court (including further registration in the Family Court)	MO(FE)A 1920, s 1(1)
	Family Court The order is enforceable as a maintenance order made by the Family Court	
	Enforcement proceedings will be allocated for hearing before lay justices	FC(CDB)R 2014, Sch 1, para 1(a)
	Monies collected are to be sent to the court which made the order or to such other person or authority as that court or the Lord Chancellor may from time to time direct	FPR 2010, r 34.7
Variation	A registered order cannot be varied or revoked by a court in England and Wales. Application must be made to the foreign court	*Pilcher v Pilcher* [1955] P 318, PDAD; *R v Rose ex parte McGibbon* (1959) 123 JP 374, QBD

C1(2): Application in England and Wales for a Provisional Maintenance Order against a Respondent Abroad, and Vice Versa (under MO(FE)A 1920)

OUTWARD

Confirmation abroad of provisional maintenance order made in England and Wales

Who may apply	An applicant for maintenance against a person who lives in one of the countries to which the Act is extended by Order in Council; there is no power under the Act to make a provisional affiliation order	MO(FE)A 1920, ss 3, 10
Which court	The Family Court acting for the area in which the applicant resides	*Collister v Collister* [1972] 1 WLR 54, FD
	The proceedings will be allocated for hearing before lay justices	FC(CDB)R 2014, Sch 1, para 1(a)
Fee	None	
What happens next	The court must hear an application for a maintenance order as if the respondent had received reasonable notice of the date of the hearing and the respondent had failed to appear; if satisfied of the justice of the application, the court may make a maintenance order but the order is provisional only and will have no effect unless and until confirmed in the foreign court The evidence of any witnesses must be taken down as a deposition	MO(FE)A 1920, s 3(1),(2)
Documents required	Where a provisional maintenance order is made, the court must send to the Lord Chancellor (in practice, the Reciprocal Enforcement of Maintenance Unit (REMO), Office of the Official Solicitor and Public Trustee, Victory House, 30–34 Kingsway, London WC2B 6EX, DX 141423 Bloomsbury 7; tel: 020 3681 2757; email: remo@offsol.gsi.gov.uk), for transmission to the appropriate authority of the relevant country, the following documents: – the depositions – a certified copy of the order – a statement of possible grounds of opposition – information for facilitating the identification of the person and ascertaining his whereabouts – a photograph, where available – a marriage certificate – the birth certificate(s) of any child(ren) for whom maintenance has been ordered, where appropriate There is provision for the taking of further evidence and for the rescission of the provisional order on the remittal of the case to the original court by the foreign court	MO(FE)A 1920, s 3(3),(4); FPR 2010, r 34.8

Confirmation of provisional order	If the provisional order is confirmed by the foreign court in the same or different terms, it should be treated as a maintenance order made by the Family Court and registered in the foreign court for enforcement	
Appeal	The applicant can appeal against refusal to make a provisional order	MO(FE)A 1920, s 3(6)

INWARD

Confirmation in England and Wales of provisional maintenance order made abroad

Application	The application for confirmation is sent by the Lord Chancellor to the Family Court on receipt of the relevant documents from the foreign court	MO(FE)A 1920, s 4
Which court	The documents are to be sent to the Maintenance Enforcement Business Centre for the Family Court for the area within which the respondent is alleged to be living The proceedings will be allocated for hearing before lay justices	 FC(CDB)R 2014, Sch 1, para 1(a)
Documents required	The following documents should be sent to the officer of the court: – the depositions – a certified copy of the order – a statement of possible grounds of opposition – information for facilitating the identification of the person and ascertaining his whereabouts – a photograph, where available – a marriage certificate – the birth certificate(s) of any child(ren) for whom maintenance has been ordered, where appropriate – a requisition for the notice to be served	MO(FE)A 1920, s 4(1)
Fee	None	
What happens next	The order will be registered by way of memorandum in the court register A notice should be issued and served setting a hearing date for the payer to attend to show cause why the order should not be confirmed At the hearing, it is open to the respondent only to oppose the confirmation of the order on any grounds on which he might have opposed the making of the original order If the respondent does not appear, it is open to the court to confirm the order with or without modifications and to make an order that payments be made directly to the Family Court by a specified method of payment If the respondent appears and the court is satisfied that it is necessary to obtain further evidence, it may adjourn the proceedings and/or remit the case to the court which made the original order	FPR 2010, rr 6.23, 6.34, 34.3, 34.5 MO(FE)A 1920, s 4(2)–(5)

Enforcement	The order is enforceable as a maintenance order made by the Family Court Monies collected are to be sent to the Maintenance Enforcement Business Centre for the court that made the order or to such other person or authority as that court or the Lord Chancellor may from time to time direct	FPR 2010, r 34.7
Variation	An order registered as a result of confirmation of a provisional order made by a foreign court can be varied or revoked by application to the confirming Family Court and any order made is final, not provisional	MO(FE)A 1920, s 4(6)

C1(3): Maintenance Order having been Made in England or Wales, Payee Seeks to Enforce it in Scotland or Northern Ireland, and Vice Versa

OUTWARD

Registration in Scotland or Northern Ireland of maintenance order made in England or Wales

Who may apply	The person entitled to payments under the order or on that person's behalf	
Which court	The appropriate court is the court which made the order or to which the proceedings have since been transferred	MOA 1950, s 17(1)
Application	*High Court or Family Court* The applicant files in the court or registry that made the order a certified copy of the order and a statement (verified by a statement of truth) that contains: – the address and occupation of the payer – the date the order was served on him or the reason why service has not been effected – the reason why it is convenient that the order should be enforceable in Scotland or Northern Ireland – the amount of any arrears – that the order is not already registered	FPR 2010, rr 32.3, 32.6
Fee	£50	FPFO 2008, fee 10.2
What happens next	*High Court or Family Court* If the court is satisfied that it is convenient for the order to be enforced in Scotland or Northern Ireland, the court sends the documents filed to (in the case of a High Court order) the Court of Session or the Court of Judicature of Northern Ireland or (in the case of a Family Court order) the Sheriff Court or the court of summary jurisdiction in whose area the payer resides, and the order is registered in that court The court officer of the original court must enter a memorandum of the proceedings in the register and, on receipt of notice of registration, must enter particulars in the register	MOA 1950, s 17; FPR 2010, rr 32.3(2),(3), 32.6 MOA 1950, s 17(4),(5)

Transfer of registration	Once an order has been registered in the High Court in Northern Ireland or in a court of summary jurisdiction there, either party may apply to the court which made the order for its registration in a court of summary jurisdiction or the High Court in Northern Ireland instead	CJJA 1982, s 36
Enforcement	The order is enforceable as if it had been made in the court in which the order is registered. In Northern Ireland, enforcement is undertaken by the court. In Scotland, proceedings for enforcement must be taken in the payee's own name and legal representation is advisable	MOA 1950, ss 18, 20(3)
Appeals	See relevant Guides in Appeals section	

INWARD

Registration in England and Wales of maintenance order made in Scotland or Northern Ireland

Application	Application for registration is made by the original court sending prescribed documents to the Maintenance Enforcement Business Centre for the court in England or Wales	MOA 1950, s 17(1)(b),(c)
Which court	If the order was made by the Court of Session or the Court of Judicature of Northern Ireland, it is transmitted to the Principal Registry for registration; otherwise, the court of registration is the Family Court for the area in which the defendant appears to be	MOA 1950, s 17(3)(b); FPR 2010, r 32.7
	Proceedings under MOA 1950 are allocated to lay justices	FC(CDB)R 2014, Sch 1, para 1(c)
Fee	None	
What happens next	On receipt of the certified copy of the maintenance order, the proper officer of the Principal Registry or a court officer in the Family Court must cause the order to be registered in that court and gives written notice of the registration of the order to the original court	MOA 1950, s 17(4); FPR 2010, r 32.7
Enforcement	The order may be enforced in all respects as if it had been made by the court in which it is registered and as if that court had had jurisdiction to make it	MOA 1950, s 18(1); FPR 2010, r 32.11
	A Scottish order which carries interest will continue to do so if registered in the High Court, but not if registered in a Family Court	MOA 1950, s 18(1A)
	The Senior District Judge of the Principal Registry may, on written application, order that an order registered there may be enforced in a district registry	
Payment of money	On registration in the Family Court, the court may order payments to be made through the collecting officer of the court or through any means set out in MEA 1991	FPR 2010, r 32.10
	An alternative means of payment order may be made on enforcement of the order (see Guide C10).	

C1(4): Variation or Discharge of Registered Maintenance Orders and Cancellation of Registration (Scotland and Northern Ireland)

Variation or discharge	*Maintenance order made by or registered in the High Court* The court which made the order retains the exclusive jurisdiction to vary or discharge it. However, in the case of a Scottish order registered in the High Court, the payer on application may adduce in the High Court evidence for the purpose of variation or discharge proceedings in the original court. The application is made by lodging in the Principal Registry a request for an appointment before a district judge. Notice of the appointment is given by post to both parties	FPR 2010, r 32.8 and Pt 18; MOA 1950, s 21
	Any other case Application to vary the rate of payments must be made to the court in which the order is registered; however, application to vary it in any other respect or to discharge it must be made to the court that made it	
	Proceedings under MOA 1950 are allocated to lay justices	FC(CDB)R 2014, Sch 1, para 1(c)
	Either party may, on application to the other court, adduce his evidence there for transmission to the court hearing the variation or discharge application	MOA 1950, s 22
	If the order is varied, notice of the variation is to be given to the prescribed officer of the court which made the order and any court in which the order is registered. The notice must consist of a certified copy of the order of variation	MOA 1950, s 23; FPR 2010, r 32.9A
Fee	Applications on notice: £155	FPFO 2008, fee 5.3
	Applications by consent: £50	FPFO 2008, fee 5.1
Cancellation	The payee may apply, using the Pt 18 procedure without notice to the payer, to the court where the order is registered to cancel the registration. The court of registration gives notice of the cancellation to the original court	FPR 2010, r 32.10 and Pt 18; MOA 1950, s 24
	The payer may apply to the original court if he has ceased to reside in the jurisdiction of the court where the order is registered; if satisfied, the court sends notice to the court of registration which cancels the registration	MOA 1950, s 24(2)
Fee	None	

C1(5): Maintenance Order having been Made in England or Wales, Payee Seeks to Enforce it Abroad, and Vice Versa (designated under MO(RE)A 1972)

OUTWARD

Registration abroad of maintenance order made in England

Who may apply	The payee under the order	MO(RE)A 1972, s 2(1)
Which court	*High Court or Family Court*	
	The Family Court or registry in which the order was made	MO(RE)A 1972, s 2(3); FPR 2010, r 34.2(2)
Application	The following must be filed: – an affidavit stating the reasons for believing that the payer resides in the country in question, and the current arrears, the date to which they are calculated and the date the next payment falls due – a certified copy of the maintenance order – a statement giving all known information as to the payer's whereabouts – all known information to help identify the payer (including employer, occupation and date and place of issue of passport) – if possible, a photograph of the payer In the cases of Australia, Canada, New Zealand and South Africa, if the payer's address is unknown the court can cause enquiries to be made The court, if satisfied that the payer is residing in a reciprocating country, will send the relevant documents to the Lord Chancellor with a view to their being transmitted to the responsible authority in the reciprocating country If the applicant relies on the alternative ground (added into MO(RE)A 1972 by CJJA 1982, Sch 11, Pt III, paras 8, 9(a)) that the payer has assets in the foreign country, the affidavit or application should also give reasons for believing that fact and set out the nature and location of the assets	FPR 2010, r 34.14; PD34A, para 4.2 FPR PD34B MO(RE)A 1972, s 2; FPR 2010, r 34.22
Fee	None	
Applicability to Hague Convention countries	MO(RE)A 1972, Pt I applies to Hague Convention countries as modified by SI 1993/593 and SI 1999/1318. In addition to the basic requirements, the affidavit must state whether the time for appealing against the order has expired and whether an appeal is pending. The applicant files in addition a statement as to whether the payer appeared in the proceedings and, if not, a document (or certified copy) establishing that notice of the proceedings including notice of the substance of the claim was served on him, a document which establishes that notice of the order was sent to him and a statement whether the payee had legal aid for those proceedings or the instant application with a certified copy of any such legal aid certificate	MO(RE)A 1972, s 2; FPR 2010, r 34.27; PD34A, paras 4.5, 4.6, 4.7

	The procedure for registration on the basis of assets in the foreign country is not available in Hague Convention countries. In the case of the EU and EFTA countries, reference should be made to Guide C1(12)	
Applicability to USA	MO(RE)A 1972, Pt I, as modified by SI 2007/2005, applies to the USA. The application follows the procedure for Hague Convention countries, except that the address of the payee, information as to the whereabouts of the payer and a description of the nature and location of any assets available for execution is to be set out in the affidavit and that three certified copies of the maintenance order must be lodged These provisions apply to applications made before 1 January 2017. From that date, the 2007 Hague Convention came into effect for the USA and Art 10 of that Convention should be used for applications for recognition and enforcement of orders from the UK (See Guide C1(12))	MO(RE)A 1972, s 2, as modified by REMO(USA)O 2007; FPR 2010, r 34.28; PD34A, paras 4.9. 4.10, 4.11 Hague Convention 2007, Art 48
Restrictions	In the case of territories indicated (a), (b) or (c) in the Table, the facility does not exist to enforce respectively (a) orders obtained by or in favour of a public authority, (b) orders for the payment of birth or funeral expenses of a child, or (c) affiliation orders	
What happens next	If satisfied, the court officer sends the relevant documents to the Lord Chancellor with a view to their being transmitted to the responsible authority in the reciprocating country, provided the Lord Chancellor is satisfied that there is sufficient information. He has a discretion to transmit them or not The relevant documents are: – a certified copy of the maintenance order (or, for the USA, three certified copies) – a certificate signed by the proper officer certifying that the order is enforceable in the UK – a certificate of arrears so signed – a statement giving such information as the officer possesses as to the whereabouts of the payer and the nature and location of his assets in that country – a statement giving such information as the officer possesses for facilitating the identification of the payer – where available, a photograph of the payer	FPR 2010, r 34.22; PD34A
Appeals	See relevant Guides in Appeals section	

INWARD

Registration in England of maintenance order made abroad

Who may apply	Where the Lord Chancellor receives a certified copy of a maintenance order made by a court in a reciprocating country and it appears that the payer is residing or has assets in the UK, he must send it to the prescribed officer of the appropriate court	MO(RE)A 1972, s 6(2)

Which court	The appropriate court is the Family Court where the payer resides or where the payer has assets. If the court officer receives a certified order and, after taking such steps as he considers appropriate, is satisfied that the payer is not residing and has no assets within the area covered by the Maintenance Enforcement Business Centre for the appropriate court, he will return the order to the Lord Chancellor with a statement giving such information as he possesses as to the whereabouts of the payer and the nature and location of his assets	MO(RE)A 1972, s 6(4); FPR PD34E
	Proceedings under MO(RE)A 1972 are allocated to lay justices	FC(CDB)R 2014, Sch 1, para 1(e)
Fee	None	
What happens next	Unless the court officer returns the order to the Lord Chancellor under MO(RE)A 1972, s 6(4), the order is registered by means of a signed entry in the register and the statutory provision or international instrument under which the order is registered is specified At the same time, the court officer must send written notice to the payer stating that the order has been registered and that payments under the order should be made to the court	MO(RE)A 1972, s 6(3); FPR 2010, rr 34.3, 34.25
Enforcement	The order is enforceable as if it were a maintenance order made by the Family Court. The court officer is under a duty, in any case where the order is in arrears to an amount equal to four weekly payments, to take enforcement proceedings in his own name. The court officer is also under a duty to take reasonable steps to notify the payee of the steps available for the enforcement of the order	MO(RE)A 1972, s 8; FPR 2010, r 34.24
Applicability to Hague Convention countries	The provisions outlined above apply equally to orders made in a Hague Convention country, except for the modifications made by REMO(HCC)O 1993 and REMO(HCC)(V)O 1999. The main differences are that: – registration may be refused if there was an error of jurisdiction in the court which made the order, if registration is manifestly contrary to public policy, if the order was obtained by fraud in connection with a matter of procedure, if there are similar proceedings pending between the same parties in the UK and those proceedings were the first to be instituted or if the order is incompatible with a similar order between the parties in the UK or in another country and the latter order fulfils the conditions necessary for registration – the court officer will refuse to register the order if the payer did not appear in the proceedings in which the order was made and there was a defect of service – an appeals procedure is prescribed and forms are prescribed for the purposes of giving notices under the modified Act and for the purposes of any appeal	MO(RE)A 1972, s 6, as modified by REMO(HCC)O 1993, REMO(HCC)(V)O 1999, FPR 2010, r 34.27 and the Hague Convention 2007, Art 23

Applicability to USA	The provisions outlined above apply equally to orders from the USA where the application was made before 1 January 2017 Now that the USA is a Contracting State to the 2007 Hague Convention, application for recognition and enforcement should be made under Art 10 of that Convention (see Guide C1(12))	MO(RE)A 1972, s 6, as modified by REMO(USA)O 2007, FPR 2010, r 34.28 Hague Convention 2007, Art 48
Payment of money	The sum to be paid, if expressed in a foreign currency, is calculated on the basis of the rate of exchange prevailing at the date of registration of the order or the date of last variation. A written certificate of a bank officer in the UK is evidence of the rate of exchange prevailing at that time Payments under the order are to be made to the court officer at the Maintenance Enforcement Business Centre of the registering court. The court officer is required to send the payments to the court which made the order or to such other person or authority as the Secretary of state may direct If the court that made the order is in one of the countries listed in FPR PD34A any such sums must be sent to the Crown Agents for Overseas Governments and Administrations for transmission to the person to whom they are due	MO(RE)A 1972, s 16; FPR 2010, r 34.23; PD34A

C1(6): Application in England and Wales for a Maintenance Order against a Respondent Abroad, and Vice Versa (under MO(RE)A 1972)

OUTWARD

Where there is no existing order in force, there is a two-stage process whereby a provisional order is made at the hearing in one country and confirmation of that order with or without modification at a subsequent hearing in the other country. MO(RE)A 1972, s 40 applies a modified procedure to countries reciprocating under the Hague Convention 1973, whereby notice of the hearing is provided to the respondent abroad and any order made is not subject to confirmation.

Confirmation abroad of provisional maintenance order made in England and Wales

Who may apply	Any person entitled to make an application for a maintenance order under DPMCA 1978 or CA 1989 if the respondent was habitually resident in England and Wales	
Which court	A Family Court has jurisdiction as if the respondent resided in England and Wales and as if notice of hearing had been duly served on him Proceedings under MO(RE)A 1972 are allocated to lay justices	MO(RE)A 1972, s 3(1) FC(CDB)R 2014, Sch 1, para 1(e)
Fee	None	

What happens next	The court hears the application and may make a provisional maintenance order For procedure, see –	MO(RE)A 1972, s 3(2) FPR 2010, rr 2.5, 2.7, 22.2, 22.4, 22.5, 23.9, 27.2–27.4
	If a provisional maintenance order is made, the court officer sends the following documents to the Lord Chancellor (in practice, the Reciprocal Enforcement of Maintenance Unit (REMO), Office of the Official Solicitor and Public Trustee, Victory House, 30–34 Kingsway, London WC2B 6EX, DX 141423 Bloomsbury 7; tel: 020 3681 2757; email: remo@offsol.gsi.gov.uk) for transmission to the responsible authority in the reciprocating country: – a certified copy of the maintenance order – a document authenticated in accordance with FPR 2010, r 34.15, setting out or summarising the evidence given in the proceedings – a certificate setting out possible grounds of opposition – a statement giving such information as was available to the court as to the whereabouts of the payer – a statement giving such information as the court officer possesses for facilitating the identification of the payer – where available, a photograph of the payer	MO(RE)A 1972, s 3(5)

Hague Convention countries

Making an application	A separate procedure under MO(RE)A 1972, s 3 exists for making maintenance orders against payers resident in a Hague Convention country to which the Maintenance Regulation (EC) No 4/2009 does not apply, namely Australia, Switzerland and Turkey (but Turkey is a Contracting State to the 2007 Hague Convention and from 1 February 2017 the provisions of that Convention replaced this procedure)	MO(RE)A 1972, s 40; MO(RE)A 1972, s 3, as modified by REMO(HCC)O 1993 and REMO(HCC)(V)O 1999; Hague Convention 2007, Art 48
	An applicant who is habitually resident in England and Wales may make application for a maintenance order	MO(RE)A 1972, s 3(1), as modified
	The application is made to the court which would have jurisdiction to make a maintenance order if the respondent were residing in England and Wales and a notice of hearing had been duly served on him	
	On hearing an application, the court may make a maintenance order For procedure, see –	MO(RE)A 1972, s 3(1), as modified FPR 2010, rr 2.5, 2.7, 22.2, 22.4, 22.5, 23.9, 27.2–27.4
	On the making of an application the following documents must be sent to the Lord Chancellor (in practice, the Reciprocal Enforcement of Maintenance Unit (REMO), Office of the Official Solicitor and Public Trustee, Victory House, 30–34 Kingsway, London WC2B 6EX, DX 141423 Bloomsbury 7; tel: 020 3681 2757; email: remo@offsol.gsi.gov.uk) for transmission to the appropriate authority in the Hague Convention country:	

	– notice of the institution of the proceedings, including notice of the substance of the application – a statement signed by the court officer giving such information as he possesses as to the whereabouts of the respondent – a statement giving such information as the officer possesses for facilitating the identification of the respondent – where available, a photograph of the respondent The notice mentioned above must be served in accordance with the laws of the Hague Convention country or in such other manner as the Lord Chancellor may authorise at least 6 weeks before the hearing at which any order is made	MO(RE)A 1972, s 3(5), (6C), as modified
	The court is obliged to take into account any representations made or evidence adduced by or on behalf of the respondent, and a copy of any representations or evidence must be served by the court officer on the applicant before the hearing	MO(RE)A 1972, s 3(6), (6A), as modified
	The court officer must give the respondent notice in writing of the date fixed for the hearing	MO(RE)A 1972, s 3(6B), as modified
	Where a maintenance order has been made, the court officer must send the following documents to the Lord Chancellor for transmission to the appropriate authority in the Hague Convention country with a view to recognition and enforcement of the order: – a certified copy of the order – a certificate signed by the court officer certifying that the order is enforceable and that it is no longer subject to the ordinary forms of review – a written statement signed by the court officer as to whether the respondent appeared and, if not, the original or a certified copy of a document that establishes that the notice of the institution of the proceedings and substance of the application was duly served – a document that establishes that notice of the order was sent to the respondent – a written statement signed by the court officer as to whether or not the applicant received legal aid in the proceedings	MO(RE)A 1972, s 3(6D), as modified

INWARD

Confirmation in England and Wales of maintenance order made abroad

Who may apply	Where the Lord Chancellor receives a certified copy of a provisional order from a reciprocating country and it appears that the payer under the order is residing in the UK, he must send the relevant documents to the court officer	MO(RE)A 1972, s 7(2)
Which court	The Family Court having jurisdiction where the payer resides or where the payer has assets	MO(RE)A 1972, s 21; FPR PD34E
	Proceedings under MO(RE)A 1972 are allocated to lay justices	FC(CDB)R 2014, Sch 1, para 1(e)

Documents required	The Lord Chancellor must send to the court officer a certified copy of the order, a duly authenticated document setting out or summarising the evidence and a statement of possible grounds of opposition	MO(RE)A 1972, s 7(2)
Fee	None	
What happens next	The court officer must fix the date, time and place for a hearing or directions appointment in not less than 21 days and send notice to the payer together with a copy of the order and accompanying documents. The court then proceeds as if an application for a maintenance order had been made against the payer	FPR 2010, rr 6.23, 6.34, 34.16
	If the payer establishes any defence he might have raised in the proceedings in which the order was made, the court will refuse to confirm the order. In any other case, the court confirms the order either with or without such alteration as the court thinks reasonable	
	If the court confirms the order, the court officer registers the order. Written notice of confirmation or otherwise is also sent to the relevant court in the reciprocating country	
	At the same time as confirming the order, the court will make an order as to the method of payment (payment by standing order or otherwise through the court or payment under an attachment of earnings order)	MO(RE)A 1972, s 7(5); FPR 2010, r 34.19
	If the court refuses to confirm the order, the court officer must return the documents to the Lord Chancellor. If the application cannot be served, the court officer returns the documents to the Lord Chancellor, together with a statement giving such information as he possesses as to the whereabouts of the payer	MO(RE)A 1972, s 7(5); FPR PD34E

Registration of orders made in Hague Convention countries

	A separate procedure exists for the registration in a UK court of an order made in a Hague Convention country to which the Maintenance Regulation (EC) No 4/2009 does not apply	MO(RE)A 1972, s 40; MO(RE)A 1972, s 6, as modified by REMO(HCC)O 1993, REMO(HCC)(V)O 1999 and FPR 2010, r 34.27
	The following differences are of importance: – registration may be refused if there was an error of jurisdiction in the court which made the order, if registration is manifestly contrary to public policy, if the order was obtained by fraud in connection with a matter of procedure, if there are similar proceedings pending between the same parties in the UK and those proceedings were the first to be instituted or if the order is incompatible with a similar order between the parties in the UK or in another country and the latter order fulfils the conditions necessary for registration – the court will refuse to register the order if the payer did not appear in the proceedings in which the order was made and there was a defect in service	

	– an appeals procedure is prescribed and forms are prescribed for the purposes of giving notices under the modified Act and for the purposes of any appeal – partial registration and enforcement, on request, is permissible	MO(RE)A 1972, s 6, as modified

Enforcement of maintenance orders made abroad

Procedure	The order is enforceable as if it were a maintenance order made by the Family Court	MO(RE)A 1972, s 8
	The court officer is under a duty, in any case where the order is in arrears to an amount equal to four weekly payments, to take enforcement proceedings in his own name. The court officer is also under a duty to take reasonable steps to notify the payee of the steps available for the enforcement of the order	FPR 2010, rr 34.24, 34.25
Payment of money	The sum to be paid, if expressed in a foreign currency, is calculated on the basis of the rate of exchange prevailing at the date of registration of the order or the date of last variation. A written certificate of a bank officer in the UK is evidence of the rate of exchange prevailing at that time Payments under the order are to be made to the court officer of the registering court. The court officer is required to send the payments to the court which made the order or to such other person or authority as the Lord Chancellor may direct If the court which made the order is in one of the countries listed in FPR PD34A, any such sums must be sent to the Crown Agents for Overseas Governments and Administrations for transmission to the person to whom they are due	MO(RE)A 1972, s 16; FPR 2010, r 34.24; PD34A

C1(7): Application to Vary, Discharge or Revoke an Order Registered under Maintenance Orders (Reciprocal Enforcement) Act 1972, Pt I

Legal background

Where a maintenance order has been registered abroad under MO(RE)A 1972 for enforcement, the power of the court of origin to vary or revoke the order is contained in MO(RE)A 1972, s 5. Provision is made for variation and revocation of foreign maintenance orders registered in the UK by MO(RE)A 1972, s 9. Both sections apply in a modified form in respect of orders registered in or made by courts in the USA. The 2007 Hague Convention should be used for applications made on or after 1 January 2017 concerning the UK and the USA (see Guide C1(12)).

Procedure

General position	In addition to its usual powers, the court may vary a maintenance order made in the UK and registered abroad by a provisional order. If the court proposes to increase the payments, the order varying *must* be a provisional order, unless both the payer and payee appear or the applicant appears and the process has been duly served on the other party	MO(RE)A 1972, s 5(3)
	Proceedings under MO(RE)A 1972 are allocated to lay justices	FC(CDB)R 2014, Sch 1, para 1(e)
	For procedure, see –	FPR 2010, rr 2.5, 2.7, 22.2, 22.4, 22.5, 23.9, 27.2–27.4, 34.19
	If the order is a provisional order, the court sends a certified copy of it and a note or a summary of the evidence taken, authenticated in accordance with the rules, to the foreign court for confirmation	MO(RE)A 1972, s 5(4); FPR 2010, rr 34.15, 34.22
	The court in the reciprocating country may, under powers given to it by its own laws, transmit to the original court in England and Wales which made the order a provisional order varying or revoking it, together with an authenticated note or summary of the evidence which it heard. The court must then proceed as if the application to vary or revoke had been made to it and may confirm or refuse to confirm the order. If it confirms a variation order, it may do so with or without alteration	MO(RE)A 1972, s 5(5), (6)
	The order, whether provisional or not, must state the date from which it takes effect; in the case of a provisional order, it does so in the form in which it is confirmed (i e subject to any alteration made by the confirming court)	MO(RE)A 1972, s 5(7)
	There is no right of appeal against the making of a provisional order	MO(RE)A 1972, s 12(1)
	Similar provision exists to vary/revoke foreign registered orders by way of provisional order unless the payer and payee are both resident in the UK or the application is made by the payee or variation is for reduction in the rate of payments on the grounds of change in the payer's circumstances	MO(RE)A 1972, s 9
Fee	None prescribed	
Applicability to orders made by Hague Convention countries	Article 12 of the Hague Convention states: 'There shall be no review by the authority of the state addressed of the merits of the decision' and the Permanent Bureau in the Hague has confirmed that the intention of Art 12 is to prevent receiving countries from varying orders except for the method of payment	REMO(HCC)(V)O 1999
	Any request by a payer living in the UK for variation of an order made by a Hague Convention country and registered in the UK should be sent to the Reciprocal Enforcement of Maintenance Orders (REMO) Section at the office of the Official Solicitor & Public Trustee, Victory House, 30–34 Kingsway, London WC2B 6EX, DX 141423 Bloomsbury 7; tel: 020 3681 2757; email: remo@offsol.gsi.gov.uk for onward transmission to the overseas authority	

Applicability to USA	The provisional order procedure does not apply. The UK retains power to vary/revoke its own orders. When a UK maintenance order has been sent to the USA under MO(RE)A 1972, s 2 for enforcement and the payee applies for variation or revocation, the court officer sends to the Lord Chancellor notice of the institution of proceedings, including notice of the substance of the application, with a view to its being transmitted to the appropriate authority in the USA for service on the payer and also sends to the payer notice in writing of the date fixed for the hearing by post to his last known or usual place of abode	MO(RE)A 1972, s 5(4), as modified by REMO(USA)O 2007
	The order may not be varied or revoked unless the notice is served by the appropriate authority, and any representations and evidence adduced by the payer must be served on the payee before the hearing and taken into account by the court	MO(RE)A 1972, s 5(5), as modified by REMO(USA)O 2007
	Where the application is made by the payer, the court officer is required to arrange for the service of notice of institution of the proceedings, including notice of the substance of the application, on the payee	MO(RE)A 1972, s 5(6), as modified by REMO(USA)O 2007
	Where the order is varied or revoked, the court officer must send to the Lord Chancellor three certified copies of the order and a written statement as to whether both parties appeared in the proceedings and, if only the applicant appeared, the original or certified copy of the document establishing proof of service of the notice of the proceedings upon the other party. The Lord Chancellor will send these documents to the appropriate authority in the USA for registration and enforcement of the order of variation/revocation	MO(RE)A 1972, s 5(7), as modified by REMO(USA)O 2007
	The variation or revocation takes effect as from the date of the order but, in the case of revocation, arrears continue to be enforceable	MO(RE)A 1972, s 5(8), (9), as modified by REMO(USA)O 2007
	A maintenance order made in the USA may not be varied or revoked in the UK and application should be made to the court in the USA. The variation or revocation takes effect from the date of the order. Any arrears remain recoverable and any variation must be registered by the UK court	MO(RE)A 1972, s 9, as modified by REMO(USA)O 2007

C1(8): Applicant in England or Wales Makes Maintenance Claim for Transmission Abroad for Determination There against Respondent, and Vice Versa

OUTWARD

Application by person in England or Wales for recovery etc of maintenance in a Convention country

General position	A person in the UK who claims to be entitled to recover, in a Convention country, maintenance from another person is required to make an application to the Lord Chancellor The application must be made through the court officer of the Family Court acting for the area in which the applicant resides and the court officer is under a duty to assist the applicant complete the relevant forms The Lord Chancellor is under a duty to forward the application to the appropriate authority in the Convention country unless he is satisfied that the application is not made in good faith or that it does not comply with the requirements of the law applied in that country. If the Lord Chancellor requires further information, he can request the court officer to obtain the information from the court, and the court is under a duty to furnish the information	MO(RE)A 1972, s 26
Fee	None	
Applicability to USA	On 1 January 2017, the 2007 Hague Convention came into effect for the USA and applications to establish a maintenance order should be made under Art 10 of that Convention (see Guide C1(12))	Hague Convention 2007, Art 49

INWARD

Pursuit in England and Wales of a claim for maintenance made in a convention country

General position	Where the Lord Chancellor receives an application from the appropriate authority in a Convention country for the recovery of maintenance, he sends the claim to the officer of the Maintenance Enforcement Business Centre for the Family Court for the area in which the respondent is residing. The claim is to be treated as an application for an appropriate order made at a time when the application was received by the Lord Chancellor Proceedings under MO(RE)A 1972 are allocated to lay justices	MO(RE)A 1972, ss 27A, 27B FC(CDB)R 2014, Sch 1, para 1(e)

	If a notice of hearing cannot be served, the officer of the court is required to return the application and documents to the Lord Chancellor, together with such information he may have as to the whereabouts of the respondent or, if the court officer is satisfied that the respondent is residing in the DFJ area of another Family Court, he may send the documents to the officer of the Maintenance Enforcement Business Centre for that court and notify the Lord Chancellor accordingly	MO(RE)A 1972, s 27B(3), (4); FPR PD34E
	For procedure, see –	FPR 2010, r 34.28ZD
	If the court makes an order, the court officer must register the order and, at the time of making the order, the court orders payments to be made through the court by standing order or otherwise, or by an attachment of earnings order	FPR 2010, r 34.28ZH
	The court officer must also notify the Lord Chancellor that the order has been registered	MO(RE)A 1972, s 27C; FPR 2010, r 34.28ZF
	Payments received by the court officer under the order must be sent to the Lord Chancellor by post	FPR 2010, r 34.28ZG
Fee	None	

C1(9): Variation and Revocation of Orders Registered under Maintenance Orders (Reciprocal Enforcement) Act 1972, Pt II

General position	Jurisdiction to vary or revoke an order registered under MO(RE)A 1972, Pt II may only be exercised by the registering court and, where the registering court revokes an order, it must cancel the registration	MO(RE)A 1972, s 34(1), (2)
	Application is made through the appropriate authority in the Convention country and transmitted to the Lord Chancellor (in practice, the Reciprocal Enforcement of Maintenance Unit (REMO), Office of the Official Solicitor and Public Trustee, Victory House, 30–34 Kingsway, London WC2B 6EX, DX 141423 Bloomsbury 7; tel: 020 3681 2757; email: remo@offsol.gsi.gov.uk), who then sends it together with any accompanying documents (which may include evidence taken in the Convention country and which is admissible under MO(RE)A 1972, s 36) to the court officer of the registering court	MO(RE)A 1972, s 34(3)
	Proceedings under MO(RE)A 1972 are allocated to lay justices	FC(CDB)R 2014, Sch 1, para 1(e)
	For procedure, see –	FPR 2010, rr 34.28ZI, 34.28ZJ
	On the variation of a registered order, if the court is satisfied that payment has not been made in accordance with the order, the court may also order that payments are made through the officer of that court or of any other Family Court, either directly or by standing order, or the court may order payment by attachment of earnings	MO(RE)A 1972, s 34A

	The application is treated as if an application for variation had been made, and the court must proceed as if the applicant were before the court	MO(RE)A 1972, s 35(3)
	Where the respondent does not appear, if the court is satisfied that the respondent is residing outside England and Wales and that notice of the proceedings has been given in the prescribed form, the court may nevertheless proceed	MO(RE)A 1972, s 35(3)
	Where the court makes or refuses to make an order, any person has the same right of appeal as they would have if the registered order had been made by that court	MO(RE)A 1972, s 34(4)
Fee	None	

C1(10): Money Judgment or Order having been Made in England or Wales, Payee Seeks to Enforce it in Certain Commonwealth Countries, and Vice Versa

Legal background

A judgment of a foreign court cannot be directly enforced in England and Wales, but a judgment other than a maintenance order (*Harrop v Harrop* [1920] 3 KB 386, KBD) can be made the basis of an action in the English courts. Four pieces of legislation – AJA 1920, FJ(RE)A 1933 and CJJA 1982 and Council Regulation (EU) No 1215/2012 on Jurisdiction and the Recognition and Enforcement of Judgments in Civil and Commercial Matters (the recast Judgments Regulation, herein JR) – allow foreign judgments to be registered in the High Court for enforcement, without the claimant needing to bring a fresh action. A fifth, Council Regulation (EC) No 805/2004, creating the European enforcement order, allows certain judgments from EU countries to be enforced in the High Court or the County Court. Unless the case falls within the scope of one of them, there is no power to register a foreign judgment for enforcement and a fresh action is necessary.

As amendments to CPR 1998, Pt 74 have inadvertently done away with the procedures that were necessary to give effect to the previous Judgments Regulation No 44/2001, which continues to apply to judgments given in proceedings commenced before 10 January 2015, it is unclear how such judgments will be dealt with by the courts until the Civil Procedure Rule Committee remedies the position.

OUTWARD

Enforcement in certain Commonwealth countries of a High Court judgment or order for payment of a sum of money

What countries	Countries to which AJA 1920 was applied by Order in Council before 1933	See notes to CPR 1998, r 74.1 for the full list
Who may apply	The judgment creditor under a judgment or order given or made by the High Court	AJA 1920, ss 10(1), 12(1)
To whom application made	A district judge of the Family Division presumably (PD74 is silent on the point) in the PRFD	CPR PD74A, para 4.2
Documents required	Application without notice under CPR 1998, Pt 23 supported by written evidence exhibiting copies of: – the claim form; – evidence of service; – the statements of case; – where relevant, notice that the applicant was an assisted person or LSC funded client.	CPR 1998, rr 74.12, 74.13(1)
	The written evidence must:	CPR 1998, r 74.13(2)

	(a) identify the grounds on which the judgment was obtained; (b) state whether the defendant objected to the jurisdiction, and if so, on what grounds; (c) show that the judgment has been served and is not subject to a stay of execution; (d) give details of any possible appeal; (e) state the amount in respect of which the judgment remains unsatisfied; (f) give particulars of interest recoverable	
Fee	£60	FPFO 2008, fee 14.2
What happens next	The court issues a certified (office) copy of the judgment accompanied by a certificate signed by a district judge in Form 110 The creditor must transmit this to the country in question and attempt enforcement in accordance with that country's procedures	CPR PD74A, paras 7.1–7.3
Limitations	The 1920 Act only applies to High Court judgments. Not all countries will recognise a County Court judgment which has been transferred to the High Court for enforcement, and advice should be sought in the country in which enforcement is desired	

INWARD

Enforcement in England and Wales of a money judgment or order of the courts of certain Commonwealth countries

What countries	As above	
Who may apply	A judgment creditor under a judgment or order obtained in a superior court in a country to which AJA 1920 applies	AJA 1920, ss 9(1), 12(1)
Which court	The Queen's Bench Division of the High Court (even in family-related cases). Application is made in the Action Department at the Royal Courts of Justice, not in a district registry	CPR PD74A, para 4.1(1)
Documents required	Application without notice under CPR 1998, Pt 23 to a master supported by written evidence exhibiting: (a) the judgment or a certified copy of it; (b) where the judgment is not in English, a certified translation The written evidence must state: – the name and address of the judgment creditor and judgment debtor; – the grounds on which the creditor is entitled to enforce the judgment; – the amount unsatisfied; – particulars of interest; and confirm the creditor's entitlement to enforce the judgment or order, the amount outstanding under it and that it does not contravene AJA 1920, s 9(2) (see Limitations below) and verify that Protection of Trading Interests Act 1980, s 5 does not apply	CPR 1998, r 74.3; PD74A, para 4.1 CPR 1998, r 74.4(1) CPR 1998, r 74.4(2)
Fee	£245	FPFO 2008, fee 1.1

What happens next	A registration order must be drawn up by the judgment creditor and served on the debtor It must state: – full particulars of the judgment registered; – the name of the judgment creditor and his address for service within the jurisdiction; – the right of the judgment debtor to apply to have the registration set aside; – the period within which such an application may be made; – that no enforcement measures (other than for preservation of property) will be taken before the end of that period	CPR 1998, r 74.6 CPR 1998, r 74.9
Setting aside	The debtor may apply to set aside the registration within the period stated in the registration order, which may be extended Application is made under CPR 1998, Pt 23 to a master The court may order an issue to be tried. The registration may be set aside if the court finds that the judgment or order contravenes AJA 1920, s 9(2) (see Limitations below), that it is not just or convenient that it be enforced in England and Wales or that there is some other sufficient reason to set aside the registration Fee: £155	CPR 1998, r 74.7(1),(2) FPFO 2008, fee 5.3
Limitations	The application must generally be made within 12 months of the date of the judgment or order, although the court has power to allow a later application A judgment or order cannot be registered for enforcement in England and Wales under this provision if: – the original court acted without jurisdiction – the debtor did not live or carry on business within that court's jurisdiction and did not appear or submit to the court's jurisdiction – the debtor (being the defendant) was not duly served with the court's process and did not appear – the judgment or order was obtained by fraud – the debtor satisfies the court that an appeal is pending or that he is entitled to, and intends to, appeal – the action would not have been entertained by the High Court for some public policy or similar reason	AJA 1920, s 9(1) AJA 1920, s 9(2)
Security for costs	Note that the procedures under the 1920 and 1933 Acts effectively require the claimant to give security for costs	

C1(11): Enforcement in Certain Foreign Countries of an English or Welsh Judgment or Order for Payment of a Sum of Money, and Vice Versa

Legal background

CPR 1998 provides (see CPR PD74A, paras 4.2(2) and 4.3(2)) for the reciprocal enforcement of money judgments or orders arising in family proceedings, other than maintenance orders, as to which see the appropriate Guides elsewhere in this work.

OUTWARD

Enforcement in certain foreign countries of a judgment or order for payment of a sum of money

Which countries	Australia including the Australian Capital Territory, the Federal Court of Canada and courts of all provinces except Quebec, Island of Guernsey, Isle of Man, Bailiwick of Jersey, certain territories of the Republic of India named in the Schedule to the Reciprocal Enforcement of Judgments (India) Order 1958, Israel, Pakistan, Surinam and Tonga	
Who may apply	The judgment creditor under a judgment or order for payment or a sum of money given or made by a court in England or Wales in civil proceedings or, if for compensation or damages to an injured party, in criminal proceedings, but not taxes etc or a fine or other penalty	FJ(RE)A 1933, ss 10(2), 11(1)
Which court	A district judge of the Family Division in the case of a judgment in that Division; a district judge in the case of a County Court judgment	CPR PD74A, para 4.2
Documents required	Application without notice under CPR 1998, Pt 23 supported by written evidence exhibiting copies of: – the claim form; – evidence of service; – the statements of case; – where relevant, notice that the applicant was an assisted person or LSC funded client The written evidence must: (a) identify the grounds on which the judgment was obtained; (b) state whether the defendant objected to the jurisdiction, and if so, on what grounds; (c) show that the judgment has been served and is not subject to a stay of execution; (d) give details of any possible appeal; (e) state the amount in respect of which the judgment remains unsatisfied; (f) give particulars of interest recoverable As to County Court judgments, note under Limitations below. There are no provisions applying the 1933 Act to the orders of magistrates' courts or the Family Court	CPR 1998, rr 74.12, 74.13(1) CPR 1998, r 74.13(2)
Fee	High Court: £60 County Court: £50	FPFO 2008, fee 14.2 FPFO 2008, fee 5.1

What happens next	In the High Court or the County Court, the creditor receives from the court a sealed copy of the judgment or order appropriately certified by the district judge and a sealed certificate signed by him setting out, in essence, the information required to be given in the affidavit and any other particulars which it may be necessary to give to the foreign court The creditor must then apply to the relevant court or authority in the foreign state in accordance with its law and procedures for enforcement of the judgment there	
Limitations	If the judgment or order was given or made by a court other than the High Court, its enforceability in a particular country depends on the terms of the individual arrangements made with that country. Reference to the Statutory Instrument enabling that country's judgments to be enforced here will give an indication, as the reciprocal arrangements will be equivalent. Further enquiry may be made of the Ministry of Justice, 102 Petty France, London SW1H 9AJ (Tel 020 3334 3555) The foreign country's relevant provisions may impose conditions similar to those which the Act applies in the case of foreign judgments sought to be enforced in the UK (see INWARD section below)	

INWARD

Enforcement in England and Wales of a judgment or order for payment of a sum of money given in certain foreign countries

Who may apply	The judgment creditor under a judgment or order	FJ(RE)A 1933, s 2(1)
Which court	The Queen's Bench Division of the High Court (even in family-related cases). Application is made in the Action Department at the Royal Courts of Justice, not in a district registry	CPR PD74A, para 4.1(1)
Documents required	Application without notice under CPR 1998, Pt 23 to a master supported by written evidence exhibiting: (a) the judgment or a certified copy of it; (b) where the judgment is not in English, a certified translation	CPR 1998, r 74.4(1)
	The written evidence must state: – the name and address of the judgment creditor and judgment debtor; – the grounds on which the creditor is entitled to enforce the judgment; – the amount unsatisfied; – particulars of interest	CPR 1998, r 74.4(2)
	It must also: – state that the judgment is a money judgment, that it can be enforced by execution in the original country and that any registration is not liable to be set aside under FJ(RE)A 1933, s 4 (see Setting aside below) – specify the interest (if any) then due on it under the law of the original country and	CPR 1998, r 74.4(4)

	– verify that the Protection of Trading Interests Act 1980, s 5 does not apply If there are several provisions in the judgment, it must be made clear which ones are to be registered The Order in Council applying FJ(RE)A 1933 to the country may also require further evidence to be given as to the enforceability of the judgment or the accrual of interest	
Fee	£245	FPFO 2008, fee 1.1
Note	Security may be required for the costs of registration and of any application by the debtor to set the registration aside	
What happens next	A registration order must be drawn up by the judgment creditor and served on the debtor It must state: – full particulars of the judgment registered; – the name of the judgment creditor and his address for service within the jurisdiction; – the right of the judgment debtor to apply to have the registration set aside; – the period within which such an application may be made; – that no enforcement measures (other than for preservation of property) will be taken before the end of that period	CPR 1998, r 74.6 CPR 1998, r 74.9
Setting aside	The debtor may apply to set aside the registration within the period stated in the registration order, which may be extended Application is made under CPR 1998, Pt 23 to a master The court may order an issue to be tried. The registration must be set aside if the court finds that: – the Act does not apply to the judgment, or was contravened in effecting the registration – the original court acted without jurisdiction – the debtor (being the defendant) had insufficient notice to enable him to defend and did not appear – the judgment was obtained by fraud – enforcement would be contrary to public policy or – the benefit of the judgment is not vested in the applicant The registration *may* be set aside if, before the judgment, another court of competent jurisdiction had already decided the issue; it may also be set aside if there is an appeal pending against the judgment or if the debtor is entitled to and intends to appeal Fee: £155	FJ(RE)A 1933, s 4 FPFO 2008, fee 5.3

Limitations	FJ(RE)A 1933 applies only to the judgments and orders of the courts identified in the Statutory Instruments applying it to the particular country. (Statutory Instruments made before the Act was amended, with effect from 1 January 1987, by CJJA 1982 applied the Act only to superior courts.) A judgment or order cannot be registered if it could not be enforced by execution in the original country, if it is fully paid (though if partly paid it can be registered as to the balance), or if it was given or made more than 6 years before the application for registration	FJ(RE)A 1933, ss 1(1)(c), 2(1)
	Enforcement more than 6 years after the judgment is registered will not be allowed except in a special case, notwithstanding that a longer limitation period applies in the country where the judgment was given	*Duer v Frazer* [2001] 1 WLR 919, QBD
Appeals	See relevant Guides in Appeals section	

C1(12): Enforcement in a European Union Member State, Non-European Union Contracting State to the 2007 Hague Convention or EFTA Country of a Maintenance Order Made in England and Wales, and Vice Versa

Legal background

The 2007 Hague Convention for the International Recovery of Child Support and Other Forms of Family Maintenance came into force for the UK on 1 August 2014. Although the EU is a Contracting State to the 2007 Hague Convention, EU Member States will continue to use the EU Maintenance Regulation (No 4/2009) between Member States. The non-EU Contracting States to the 2007 Hague Convention are Albania, Bosnia and Herzegovina, Montenegro, Norway, Turkey, Ukraine and the USA. The EFTA countries that reciprocate with the EU Member States under the Lugano Convention 2007 are Iceland, Norway and Switzerland. In addition to governing the recognition and enforcement of foreign judgments between EU Member States and those three countries, the Lugano Convention contains detailed rules as to jurisdiction for hearings.

The EU Maintenance Regulation (No 4/2009) and 2007 Hague Convention enable application to be made for a maintenance order in another Member State/Contracting State in certain circumstances, as well as setting out a regime for recognition and enforcement of maintenance orders. Article 10 of the 2007 Hague Convention and Art 56 of the Maintenance Regulation make identical provision for the following applications to be made by a creditor seeking to recover maintenance:

(a) Recognition or recognition and enforcement of a decision
(b) Enforcement of a decision made or recognised in the requested state
(c) Establishment of a decision where there is no existing decision
(d) Establishment of a decision where recognition and enforcement of an existing decision is not possible
(e) Modification of a decision made in the requested State/Member State
(f) Modification of a decision made in a State other than the requested State/Member State.

Articles 10 and 56, respectively, provide for the following applications to be made by a debtor against whom there is an existing decision in force:

(a) Recognition of a decision or equivalent procedure leading to suspension or limiting enforcement of a previous decision
(b) Modification of a decision given in the requested State/Member State
(c) Modification of a decision given in a state other than the requested State/Member State

Application is made by the applicant, by way of prescribed form through the Central Authority for the State/Member State in question (Arts 11 and 57, respectively) and Arts 12 and 58 make provision for transmission, receipt and processing of the application, including timescales for updating on progress.

FPR 2010, Pt 9 (Financial Remedy) and PD9A (see Part III) apply to incoming applications from a Contracting State/Member State under Art 10 of the 2007 Hague Convention and Art 56 of the EU Maintenance Regulation.
The recognition/recognition and enforcement process is set out below.

OUTWARD

Enforcement in a European Union Member State, non-European Union Contracting State to the 2007 Hague Convention or EFTA country of a maintenance order

General position	If the order has been made or registered in the Family Court, application must be made for a certified copy of the order, a certificate as to the payments made and arrears accrued under it while it has been registered and certificate giving particulars relating to the judgment	FPR 2010, r 34.39; PD34A
Who may apply	Any interested party	CJJA 1982, s 12
Which court	The Family Court which made the order or where the order is registered	FPR 2010, r 34.39
Application for a certified copy order	Application for a certified copy of the order is made in writing to the officer of the Family Court. The application must give: – the names of the parties to the proceedings in which the order was made – the date or approximate date and the nature of those proceedings – the State in which application for recognition and enforcement has been or is to be made and the postal address of the applicant	FPR 2010, rr 34.2(2), 34.39(3)
	The court officer sends to the applicant a copy of the order with a certificate certifying that it is a true copy and giving particulars of the proceedings in which it was made and, where the Maintenance Regulation (Council Regulation (EC) No 4/2009) applies, a completed extract from the decision in the form of Annex II to that Regulation	FPR 2010, rr 34.39(3), 34.40
Application for a certificate of payments made or arrears accrued under a registered order	Application for a certified copy of the order is made in writing to the court officer for the registering court	FPR 2010, r 34.39(5),(6)
	The officer must send the applicant a certificate giving the information requested	FPR 2010, r 34.39(7)
What happens next	The applicant must then deliver these documents to the Lord Chancellor (in practice, the Reciprocal Enforcement of Maintenance Unit (REMO), Office of the Official Solicitor and Public Trustee, Victory House, 30–34 Kingsway, London WC2B 6EX, DX 141423 Bloomsbury 7; tel: 020 3681 2757; email: remo@offsol.gsi.gov.uk) for transmission to the Central Authority in the state in question	FPR 2010, r 34.39
Alternative procedures	The procedures afforded by MO(RE)A 1972 (see Guides C1(5) and C1(8)) continue to be available in respect of the countries where they are indicated in the Table	

INWARD

Enforcement in England and Wales of a maintenance order made in a European Union Member State, non-European Union Contracting State to the 2007 Hague Convention or EFTA country

Who may apply	Any interested party	CJJA 1982, Sch 1, Art 31
Which court	The appropriate court is the Family Court Jurisdiction for enforcement is based on (a) the residence of the paying party, (b) the location of the paying party's assets or (c) where any other matter relevant to enforcement arises but provision is made for the application to be heard in the Designated Family Court area in which the applicant resides in prescribed circumstances	FPR 2010, r 34.36C; PD34E, paras 7.1, 7.2
Application	The application (including the documents supplied by the foreign court) is forwarded by the Central Authority in the state in question to the Lord Chancellor (in practice, the Reciprocal Enforcement of Maintenance Unit (REMO), Office of the Official Solicitor and Public Trustee, Victory House, 30–34 Kingsway, London WC2B 6EX, DX 141423 Bloomsbury 7; tel: 020 3681 2757; email: remo@offsol.gsi.gov.uk) for transmission to the appropriate court. Authenticated copy orders are deemed to be true copies, and other documents required to be produced are admissible in evidence Alternatively, the applicant may choose to make the application directly to the appropriate court without going through the Central Authority (i e REMO)	CJJA 1982, s 11, Sch 1, Art 32 CJJ(M)R 2011, Sch 1, para 4; *MS v PS* (Case C-283/16) [2017] 1 FLR 1163, CJEU
What happens next	Orders made in EU countries (other than Denmark) in proceedings commenced on or after 18 June 2011 are recognised automatically (unless any of provisions of Council Regulation (EC) No 4/2009, Art 24 apply) and enforced directly as if the order had been made by that court. The court officer will cause the order to be recognised by way of register entry Transitional provisions preserve a registration process for outstanding applications and orders made prior to 18 June 2011 If the order was made in Denmark, the court officer must determine an application for enforceability, but given the mandatory nature of the Regulation this is a formality, provided that the requirements of Art 28 have been complied with. The paying party is not entitled to make any submissions at this stage; but see 'Challenge by paying party' below If the order was made in an EFTA country bound by the Lugano Convention or non-EU Contracting State to the 2007 Hague Convention, the order may be registered for enforcement and if registered is treated as having been declared enforceable Grounds for refusing recognition and enforcement are set out in Art 34 of the Lugano Convention and Art 22 of the 2007 Hague Convention	FPR PD34C, para 3.1 FPR PD34C, para 5.1 Council Regulation (EC) No 4/2009, Art 30; FPR 2010, r 34.30; PD34C, para 3.2 FPR 2010, r 34.30

	If the registration process applies, the officer of the court must consider whether the payer resides within the area of the Maintenance Enforcement Business Centre to which the application has been sent or has assets against which the order could be enforced	FPR PD34E, para 4.2
	If the payer is not resident in area covered by the Maintenance Enforcement Business Centre but does have assets in that area against which the order could be enforced, the court officer must either register or, if he believes that the payer is resident in an area covered by a different Maintenance Enforcement Business Centre, refuse the application and return the documents to the Lord Chancellor (in practice, the Reciprocal Enforcement of Maintenance Unit (REMO), Office of the Official Solicitor and Public Trustee, Victory House, 30–34 Kingsway, London WC2B 6EX, DX 141423 Bloomsbury 7; tel: 020 3681 2757; email: remo@offsol.gsi.gov.uk) with a view to registration in the other area, stating the information that the court officer has as to the whereabouts of the payer and the location of assets	FPR PD34E, paras 4.4, 4.5
	If the payer is not resident and does not have assets in that area against which the order could be enforced, the court officer must refuse the application	FPR PD34E, para 4.3
	If the court officer refuses the application, he notifies the applicant. If he recognises/registers the order, he notifies the Lord Chancellor, the applicant and the payer. He also enters a memorandum of the order in the register and specifies the statutory provision or international instrument under which the order is registered	FPR 2010, rr 34.3, 34.30
Challenge by paying party	Where the Maintenance Regulation (EC) No 4/2009 applies, or the decision was made by a non-EU Contracting State to the 2007 Hague Convention, the decision may not be reviewed as to its substance in the enforcing court	Reg (EC) No 4/2009, Art 42; 2007 Hague Convention, Art 28
	It appears, however, that obvious arithmetical errors may be corrected provided that the sum due is not increased	*Vogel v Lothschütz* [2012] EWHC 3411 (QB) (a decision on a European Enforcement Order); *Vogel v Lothschütz* [2013] EWCA Civ 664 (application for permission to appeal)
	In addition to resisting enforcement on its merits, the paying party may challenge enforcement only by:	
	– applying for review in the state of origin. Note the strict time limit and that 'no extension may granted on account of distance';	Reg (EC) No 4/2009, Art 19
	– applying to the enforcing court for the refusal or suspension of enforcement on the grounds that:	
	– enforcement is time-barred;	Reg (EC) No 4/2009, Art 21(2)
	– enforcement would be inconsistent with another decision;	
	– an application for review has been made in the state of origin	Reg (EC) No 4/2009, Art 21(3)

	For all registrations in respect of orders made in Denmark, non-EU Contracting States bound by the 2007 Hague Convention and EFTA countries bound by the Lugano Convention, the payer can appeal against registration within 30 days of receiving notice of it or within 60 days if registered only on the basis of assets being located in the Designated Family Judge Area	Reg (EC) No 4/2009, Art 32; FPR 2010, r 34.31
Enforcement	On registration, the order is enforceable as if it had been made by the Family Court. Payments may be directed to be made through the court, in which case they are sent by the court officer to the original court (or to such other person or authority as that court or the Lord Chancellor may direct);	CJJA 1982, s 5(4); FPR 2010, r 34.32
	If the order is payable through the court, the court officer may, or, if at least 4 weeks' arrears accrue, must (unless it appears unreasonable to do so), take steps in his own name to enforce the order whether or not the payee so requests	FPR 2010, r 34.33(4); PD34A
	In all other circumstances, the payee must apply to enforce the order	
	The court officer is also under a duty to take reasonable steps to notify the payee of the methods of enforcement available	FPR 2010, r 34.33(2)
	Enforcement proceedings are allocated to lay justices	FC(CDB)R 2014, Sch 1, para 1(g),(k),(p)
Modification of a decision	Jurisdiction to vary a decision lies with the Member State/Contracting State where the decision was made if the creditor remains habitually resident in the State of origin.	Reg (EC) No 4/2009, Art 3; Hague Convention 2007, Art 18
	Where the Maintenance Regulation (EC) No 4/2009 applies, any application to vary has to be issued through the Central Authority of the Member States concerned and not direct to the court in England and Wales	Reg (EC) No 4/2009, Art 56; *AB v JJB* [2015] 2 FLR 1143, FD

C1(13): Enforcement in a European Union or EFTA Country of a Judgment or Order (other than a Maintenance Order) Made in England or Wales, and Vice Versa

Legal background

The CJJA 1982 gave effect to the Brussels Convention 1968 (to which the EEC countries were parties); CJJA 1991 gave effect to the similar Lugano Convention of 1988 signed by the Member States of EFTA. As with FJ(RE)A 1933, a registrable judgment cannot be made the subject of an action. The grounds on which registration may be set aside are very limited. The JR applied a uniform regime, similar though not identical to that under the Brussels Convention, to all the Member States of the European Union. It has applied to Denmark from 1 July 2007. The Lugano Convention 2007 applies with effect from 1 January 2010 in relation to Norway (and Denmark, although this is academic as Denmark is subject to the JR), with effect from 1 January 2011 in relation to Switzerland and with effect from 1 May 2011 in relation to Iceland. Denmark's ratification of the Lugano Convention 2007 does not apply to its overseas territories of Greenland and the Faroe Islands.

Recent amendments to CPR 1998, Pt 74, removing the procedures to give effect to the former JR No 44/2001 and defining the JR only as Regulation No 1215/2012, have created potential difficulties with the enforcement of EU judgments given in proceedings instituted before 10 January 2015.

OUTWARD

Enforcement in a European Union or EFTA country of any High Court or County Court judgment or order

Who may apply	Any interested party	JR Art 36, para 2
To whom application made	A district judge of the Family Division in the case of a judgment in that Division; a district judge in the case of a County Court judgment	CPR PD74A, para 4.2
Application	Application without notice under CPR 1998, Pt 23 supported by written evidence exhibiting copies of: – the claim form; – evidence of service; – the statements of case; – where relevant, notice that the applicant was an assisted person or LSC funded client The written evidence must: (a) identify the grounds on which the judgment was obtained; (b) state whether the defendant objected to the jurisdiction, and if so, on what grounds; (c) show that the judgment has been served and is not subject to a stay of execution; (d) give details of any possible appeal; (e) state the amount in respect of which the judgment remains unsatisfied; (f) give particulars of interest recoverable	CPR 1998, r 74.12 CPR 1998, r 74.13(1) CPR 1998, r 74.13(2)
Fee	High Court: £60 County Court: £50	FPFO 2008, fee 14.2 FPFO 2008, fee 5.1
What happens next	If the district judge is satisfied, the court issues a certified copy of the judgment and a certificate in Form 110 prescribed by RSC, adapted as necessary and signed by the district judge. The applicant must apply to the relevant court or authority in the foreign state in accordance with its law and procedures for enforcement of the judgment there	
Appeals	See relevant Guides in Appeals section	

INWARD

Enforcement in England or Wales of a judgment or order (other than a maintenance order) made in a European Union or EFTA country

Judgment enforceable under the JR	A judgment of the courts of a Member State in proceedings commenced after 10 January 2015 is directly enforceable in the English courts 'without any special procedure being required'	JR Art 36.1
	The judgment creditor must serve the certificate issued pursuant to Art 53, accompanied by the judgment, if not already served	JR Art 43.1; CPR 1998, r 74.9(1)
	Unless the judgment debtor is domiciled in the Member State of origin, he may request a translation of the judgment into either a language that he understands or an official language of the Member State in which he is domiciled	JR Art 43.2
	Where a translation of the judgment is requested, no enforcement measures (other than protective measures) may be taken until that translation has been provided	
Application for refusal of recognition under the JR	A judgment may not be reviewed as to its substance	JR Art 52
	Recognition may be refused if: – it would be manifestly contrary to public policy; – the judgment was obtained by default, if the defendant was not served in sufficient time to arrange for his defence; or – it is irreconcilable with another judgment between the same parties	JR Arts 45 and 46 But cf *Reeve v Plummer* [2014] EWHC 4695 (QB)
Application for relief against enforcement under the JR	The court may: (a) limit the enforcement proceedings to protective measures; (b) make enforcement conditional on the provision of such security as it shall determine; or (c) suspend, either wholly or in part, the enforcement proceedings Enforcement must be suspended where the enforceability of the judgment is suspended in the Member State of origin	JR Art 42
Application for suspension of enforcement proceedings under the JR	The court may suspend enforcement proceedings where the judgment is being challenged in the Member State of origin, or where an application has been made for recognition to be refused	JR Art 38
Which court	To the court in which the judgment is being enforced or, if the debtor is not aware of enforcement proceedings, the High Court	CPR 1998, r 74.7A
Application	Application under CPR 1998, Pt 23 supported by written evidence	CPR 1998, rr 74.7A, 74.7B, 74.7C
Fee	£245	FPFO 2008, fee 1.1
Judgment enforceable under CJJA 1982 or the Lugano Convention		
Who may apply	Any interested party	CJJA 1982, Sch 1, Art 31

Which court	High Court, Queen's Bench Division. Application should be made to the Action Department of the Royal Courts of Justice, not a district registry	CPR 1998, r 74.3; PD74A, para 4.1(1)
Application	Ex parte application under CPR Pt 23 supported by written evidence which must exhibit an authenticated translation of the judgment, if not in English, and give particulars of interest due The evidence in support of an application under the 1982 Act must exhibit: – the judgment or order or an authenticated copy; – documents to show that the judgment is enforceable in the country of origin and has been served; – if a default judgment, evidence that the proceedings were served; – where appropriate, evidence of the judgment creditor's legal aid and must state: (a) the judgment creditor's name and address for service within England and Wales; (b) the name and address (if known) of the judgment debtor; (c) the grounds on which the judgment creditor is entitled to enforce the judgment; (d) the amount unsatisfied; (e) details of interest payable	CPR 1998, rr 74.4(1)(b), 74.4(6) CPR 1998, r 74.4(1)(a) CPR 1998, r 74.4(5)(a) CPR 1998, r 74.4(5)(b) CPR 1998, r 74.4(5)(c) CPR 1998, r 74.4(2)
Fee	£245	FPFO 2008, fee 1.1
Order	Drawn up by the applicant, stating the period for appeal against it and that the judgment or order will not be enforced by execution until that period has expired	CPR 1998, r 74.6
Service	Notice of the registration of the judgment or order must be served on the debtor, stating full particulars of the judgment or order registered and of the order for registration, the name and address for service of the applicant, the right of the debtor to appeal against the registration and the time for such an appeal (1 month from service, or 2 months in the case of a debtor not domiciled within the jurisdiction) which may be extended in the case of a debtor not domiciled in a convention country on application made within 2 months after service	There is no general power to extend the mandatory time limit in relation to a debtor domiciled in a convention country. There is only a residual power to extend the time limit in the rare case where its application would impair the very essence of the right of appeal: *Christofi v National Bank of Greece* [2015] EWHC 986 (QB)
Appeal by judgment debtor	The debtor has a right of appeal but, since the court is not permitted to review the foreign judgment as to its substance, the appeal may extend only to the grounds on which registration could have been refused, i e that the judgment is one which would not be recognised here for the reasons set out in CJJA 1982, Sch 1, Arts 27, 28, principally: – if recognition of the judgment is manifestly contrary to public policy – in the case of a default judgment, if the defendant was not served and failed to challenge the judgment when it was possible for him to do so;	CPR 1998, r 74.8 and see *Banco Nacional de Comercio Exterior v Empresa de Telecomunucaciones de Cuba SA* [2007] EWHC 2322 (Comm)

	– if it is irreconcilable with certain other judgments between the same parties. The appeal is by summons to a judge – an application to a master to set aside a registration under CJJA 1982 is a nullity	*Maronier v Larmer* [2003] QB 620, CA
Appeal by judgment creditor	Appeal from refusal to register, see relevant Guides in Appeals section	CPR 1998, r 74.8
Enforcement	Execution may not be issued, nor may the judgment or order be otherwise enforced, until the time for appeal (including any extension) has expired and any appeal has been disposed of. This does not prevent an application, for example, to prevent the disposal of assets	
Limitation	Enforcement more than 6 years after the judgment is registered will not be allowed except in a special case, notwithstanding that a longer limitation period applies in the country where the judgment was given	*Duer v Frazer* [2001] 1 WLR 919, QBD

C1(14): Enforcement in Scotland or Northern Ireland of a Judgment or Order (other than a Maintenance Order) of an English or Welsh Court other than a Magistrates' Court, and Vice Versa

Legal background

CPR 1998 apply to the reciprocal enforcement of money judgments or orders arising in family proceedings, other than maintenance orders, as to which see the appropriate Guides in this volume.

OUTWARD

Enforcement in Scotland or Northern Ireland of an existing High Court or County Court judgment or order (other than a maintenance order)

Who may apply	Any interested party	CJJA 1982, Sch 6, para 2(1), Sch 7, para 2(1)
Which court	The Principal Registry, district registry or County Court in which the judgment or order was given or made Application is made to a master or district judge	CPR 1998, rr 74.17, 74.18 CPR PD74A, para 4.3
Documents required	*Money judgments* The judgment creditor may obtain a certificate to enable the money provisions of a judgment to be enforced in another part of the UK by filing written evidence stating: – the name and address of the judgment creditor and (if known) the debtor; – the sums payable and unsatisfied; – details of interest recoverable; – that the judgment is not stayed; – the date on which the time for appealing expired or will expire, and whether an appeal or application for permission to appeal is current (in practice, confirming that it is not)	CPR 1998, r 74.17

	Non-monetary provisions of a judgment or order The judgment creditor may obtain a certificate by filing written evidence which must: – give particulars of the judgment – confirm that the judgment is not stayed; – the date on which the time for appealing expired or will expire, and whether an appeal or application for permission to appeal is current (in practice, confirming that it is not) – give the usual or last known addresses of the creditor and the debtor	CPR 1998, r 74.18
Fee	High Court: £60 County Court: £50	FPFO 2008, fee 14.2 FPFO 2008, fee 5.1
What happens next	*Monetary provisions* The certificate is completed by the proper officer and issued to the creditor, who uses it to found the appropriate steps in Scotland or Northern Ireland	CJJA 1982, Sch 6
	Non-monetary provisions The court provides a certified copy of the judgment and a certificate annexed to it in Form 112 prescribed by RSC adapted as necessary. The applicant uses these documents to found the appropriate application in Scotland or Northern Ireland	CJJA 1982, Sch 7
Appeals	Not applicable	

INWARD

Enforcement in England and Wales of a judgment or order (other than a maintenance order) of a Scottish or Northern Irish court other than a magistrates' court

Who may apply	Any interested party	CJJA 1982, Sch 6, para 2(1), Sch 7, para 2(1)
Which court	High Court. Applications to register Scottish or Northern Irish judgments are assigned to the Queen's Bench Division	CPR PD74A, para 4.1(2)
Application	*Monetary provisions* No application as such is made. The certificate issued by the Scottish or Northern Ireland court is filed in the Central Office of the Senior Courts	CPR 1998, r 74.15
	Non-monetary provisions Application is made without notice under CPR Pt 23	CPR 1998, r 74.16
Documents required	*Monetary provisions* A certificate of the judgment or order issued within the preceding 6 months by the Scottish or Northern Irish court, together with a copy certified by written evidence (usually that of the applicant's solicitor) to be a true copy	CPR 1998, r 74.15
	Non-monetary provisions A certified copy of the judgment or order and the prescribed form of certificate issued within the previous 6 months by the Scottish or Northern Irish court	CJJA 1982, Sch 7, para 5(3); CPR 1998, r 74.16
Fee	£245	FPFO 2008, fee 1.1

What happens next	*Monetary provisions* The certified copy is sealed by the court and returned as evidence of the registration of the judgment or order, which may then be enforced as a judgment or order of the High Court	CJJA 1982, Sch 6, paras 5, 6; CPR PD74A, para 8.1
	Non-monetary provisions The judgment or order must not be registered if compliance would breach the law in England and Wales; otherwise, the court must order it to be registered. If the order is granted, the applicant must draw it up. The order must state the period within which an application may be made to set aside the order for registration and that execution will not be issued on the judgment or order until that period has expired. No period is in fact specified in the Act or Rules, but it seems likely that the court would apply by analogy the 1-month period applicable under CPR 1998, r 74.8 in the case of an order made in a convention country	CJJA 1982, Sch 7, para 5(4),(5); CPR 1998, rr 74.6, 74.7, 74.9, 74.16(4),(5)
Service	*Monetary provisions* There is no requirement for notice of the registration to be served	
	Non-monetary provisions Notice of the registration must be served on the person against whom the order was made, giving full particulars of the judgment or order registered and the order for registration, the name of the applicant and his address for service within England and Wales. It must state the right of that person to apply to set aside the registration and the period within which that application must be made. The order is then enforceable as if made by the High Court	CJJA 1982, Sch 7, para 6; CPR 1998, rr 74.6, 74.7, 74.16(4) and (5)
Costs and interest	*Monetary provisions* The costs of obtaining and registering the certificate are added to the judgment debt. Interest continues to accrue at the rate stated in the certificate, including interest from the date of registration on the added costs. No other interest is recoverable	CJJA 1982, Sch 6, paras 7, 8
	Non-monetary provisions The costs of obtaining the copy order and certificate and of registration are recoverable as if the original order included an order for their payment, but interest is recoverable on those costs as if, on registration, the High Court had ordered their payment	CJJA 1982, Sch 7, para 7
Stay and setting aside	If satisfied that the debtor is entitled to and intends to appeal against or apply to have set aside the judgment or order, the court may stay enforcement on such terms as it thinks fit and for such period as appears to be sufficient. On the application of any interested party, the court *must* set aside the registration if satisfied that registration was contrary to the provisions of the relevant Schedule, and it *may* set the registration aside if the issue in the original proceedings had previously been decided by another court of competent jurisdiction	CJJA 1982, Sch 6, paras 9, 10, Sch 7, paras 8, 9

	Any application to set aside the registration must be made under CPR Pt 23, supported by written evidence. The court may order an issue to be tried Fee: £155	CPR 1998, rr 74.7(3), 74.16(5) FPFO 2008, fee 5.3
Appeals	Appeal against master's refusal; appeal from application to set aside	See relevant Guide in Appeals section

C1(15): Enforcement of an Uncontested Claim as a European Enforcement Order

Legal background

Regulation (EC) No 805/2004 of 21 April 2004 (see Part VI) introduces an optional procedure for the enforcement of uncontested claims within the European Union. The rules relating to this procedure are in CPR rr 74.28 and PD74B, to which the (lengthy) text of the Regulation is annexed. Whereas the Judgments Regulation applies to Denmark, the European Enforcement Order (EEO) does not.

Note that the EEO procedure also applies to 'court settlements and authentic instruments'.

OUTWARD

Registration of an Uncontested Judgment as an EEO

What claims	The EEO procedure does not apply to, inter alia, 'rights in property arising out of a matrimonial relationship'	EC Reg 805/2004, Art 2(2)(b)
What judgments	Judgments on uncontested claims, i e where the debtor has: – expressly agreed to the claim; or – failed to object to the claim; or – failed to attend a hearing as a result of which judgment has been entered If the creditor relies on default of defence or objection, it must be shown that the debtor was aware of the proceedings	Regulation 805/2004, Art 3
Service of proceedings	If the debtor's default of defence or objection is relied upon, the proceedings must have been served with proof of receipt by the debtor; or served without proof of receipt e g by delivery to the debtor's address, but only if the debtor's address is known with certainty Postal service is only acceptable if the debtor's address is in England and Wales	Regulation 805/2004, Art 13 Regulation 805/2004, Art 14(1) Regulation 805/2004, Art 14(1)(e),(2)
Documents needed	The judgment; Costs certificate (if debtor has not objected to the principle of bearing the costs); Document attesting service (if relevant); Completed draft EEO Certificate; Practice Form N219 (express agreement) or Form N219A (default)	CPR PD74B, para 2.1 Annex to CPR PD74B (not printed in this work – see *Civil Court Service* (LexisNexis)
Fee	High Court: £60 County Court: £50	FPFO 2008, fee 14.2 FPFO 2008, fee 5.1

Which judge	In the County Court, a district judge; in the Chancery or Queen's Bench Divisions of the High Court, or in a District Registry, a master or a district judge No express provision is made for money judgments in the Family Division – it is submitted that application should be made to a district judge of the Principal Registry	CPR PD74B, para 2.1 See Regulation 805/2004, Art 4, para 1
What happens next	If the application is granted, the court will send the EEO certificate and a sealed copy of the judgment to the applicant. Enforcement proceedings may then be taken in another Regulation State	CPR PD74B, para 2.2

INWARD

Enforcement of an Uncontested Claim which has been registered as an EEO

Which court	High Court or County Court; judgments in excess of £5000 may only be enforced by execution against goods in the High Court; judgments for less than £600 shall only be enforced in the County Court	CPR r 74.31; HCCCJO 1991, art 8
From which country	Any Regulation State, i e any Member State other than Denmark	CPR 1998, r 74.27(d)
Documents required	Authentic copy of the judgment, court settlement or authentic instrument; Authentic copy of the EEO certificate issued by the foreign court; (An official copy issued by the court of the Member State of origin will be acceptable) Certified translation of each of the above documents into English	Regulation 805/2004, Arts 20, 24, 25 CPR 1998, r 74.31(1) CPR PD74B, para 5.2 Form C20(2)(c)
Fee	High Court: £60 County Court: £50	FPFO 2008, fee 14.2 FPFO 2008, fee 5.1
What happens next	The EEO will be assigned a case number in the court in which it is lodged Enforcement proceedings may be taken without further formality	CPR PD74B, para 5.1
Review of decision	Neither a judgment nor its certification as an EEO may be reviewed as to its substance	Regulation 805/2004, Art 21(2)
Refusal of enforcement	In the case of an EEO based on a judgment, the debtor may apply under Pt 23 to the court in which the EEO is being enforced for an order that the court should refuse to enforce an EEO but the only grounds on which this can be done are that the EEO is irreconcilable with an earlier judgment and that the irreconcilability was not, and could not have been, raised in the court proceedings in the Member State of origin But a court settlement or authentic instrument that has been certified as an EEO in the Member State of origin shall be enforced 'without any possibility of opposing its enforceability'	Regulation 805/2004, Art 21 Regulation 805/2004, Arts 24(2), 25(2)

	Clerical errors (e g an authentic instrument being wrongly described as a judgment debt) are not a ground for setting aside registration. It appears that obvious errors of calculation may be corrected, but the fact that an EEO is rescinded in the Member State of origin does not nullify steps (and specifically orders for costs) already taken in the Member State of enforcement	*Vogel v Lothschütz* [2012] EWHC 3411 (QB); *Vogel v Lothschütz* [2014] EWHC 473 (QB)
Documents required	Application notice under CPR Pt 23 Official copy of earlier judgment; Written evidence showing why the judgment is irreconcilable and why this could not have been raised in the proceedings in the court of origin	CPR 1998, r 74.32; PD74B, para 6.1
Stay or limitation of enforcement	Before the debtor can ask the court not to enforce an EEO based on a judgment he must first apply for a stay to the court of origin, unless the court otherwise orders	CPR PD74B, para 7.1; Regulation 805/2004, Art 23
Documents required	Application notice under CPR Pt 23; Evidence of application in the court of origin; Certified translation of that application; Written evidence stating that an application has been made to the court of origin, the nature of that application and the grounds for it, and the date on which it was filed and the date by which it is believed it will be determined	CPR PD74B, paras 7.1, 7.2

C2: Lay Justices' Power to Enforce Orders for Financial Provision

Legal background

From 22 April 2014, with the establishment of the single Family Court, the process of registering a maintenance order in the magistrates' court for enforcement under MOA 1958 is now obsolete. However, Crime and Courts Act 2013 (Family Court: Transitional and Saving Provision) Order 2014, para 6 allows for decisions, warrants or other acts made or ordered before 22 April 2014 to continue as if they had been issued or made by the Family Court. The effect is that orders already registered remain registered and the court can take enforcement action on behalf of the creditor where consent has been established for the court to consider the method of enforcement.

Any application to enforce a maintenance order that is not already registered should be made to the Family Court for the area where the original order was made, for hearing by the level of judiciary who made that order. Where the order was made by magistrates, any enforcement application will be allocated to them if lay justices have the jurisdiction to deal with it. Certain methods of enforcement are not available to magistrates, i e order to obtain information, charging order, third party debt order and warrant of control.

Procedure

Application	The creditor or the court officer for the relevant Maintenance Enforcement Business Centre on behalf of the creditor (with the creditor's consent) applies to the Family Court for the area where the order was made for an order seeking a specific enforcement method or more than one method of enforcement or an order for such method of enforcement as the court may consider appropriate (the Form D50K procedure)	FPR 2010, rr 32.33, 33.3(2) CPR 1998, r 70.2(2)(b), as applied by FPR 2010, r 33.3
	Where the creditor is making the application, it must be accompanied by a statement setting out the amount due and how it is arrived at, verified by a statement of truth	FPR 2010, r 33.3(1)
What happens next	Under the Form D50K procedure, for an attachment of earnings hearing or if the court is dealing with an application to obtain information from the debtor, the debtor is ordered to attend court for a means enquiry at the time and place specified, to produce at court any financial document requested and to answer on oath such questions as the court may require in relation to non-payment	FPR 2010, r 33.3(3); CPR 1998, r 71.2(6)
	If the court officer proceeds in the officer's own name to recover any sums due, the creditor does not need to attend	FPR 2010, rr 32.33
Failure to attend	If it is not possible or appropriate to proceed in the absence of the debtor, the court may adjourn to a contempt hearing. The notice, incorporating a penal notice, should be served personally. If the debtor then fails to attend the contempt hearing it appears that a bench warrant may be issued	MFPA 1984, s 31E, *Westwood v Knight* [2012] EWPCC 14
Powers of the court	Leave is required to enforce arrears that are over 12 months old	MCA 1973, s 32; DPMCA 1978, s 32(5); CPA 2004, Sch 5, para 63
	The application for permission is made on notice using the Pt 18 procedure	FPR 2010, rr 18.1–18.5, 18.7, 18.8
	The court has power to remit or reduce arrears accrued under domestic maintenance orders only when considering an application for permission to enforce arrears of more than 12 months and when considering whether to vary or discharge such a maintenance order. There is no power to remit arrears accrued under international orders to which the reciprocal enforcement provisions are applicable	
	The power of lay justices to issue a distress warrant is no longer available, but see Guide C7	
	Enforcement options available to lay justices are: – To require payment of the amount of the order plus an amount in respect of arrears – Means of payment order to require a standing order to be set up	MEA 1991, s 1
	– To order an attachment of earnings order (see Guide C4)	FPR 2010, r 33.19, Pt 39

	– Committal by way of Judgment Summons, but see Guide C9. Specific application must be made for enforcement by this method and it is not available under the Form D50K procedure by way of enforcement as the court may consider appropriate	FPR 2010, rr 33.10–33.14, 33.16
	Reasonable travelling expenses must be paid or offered to the debtor	FPR 2010, r 33.11(3)
	If it appears that one of the enforcement remedies not available to lay justices is suitable, the case must be re-allocated to a District Judge	FC(CDB)R 2014, Sch 2

C3: Registration in the Family Court of a Maintenance Order Made in the High Court

Legal background

The person entitled to receive payment under a maintenance order made by the High Court may apply to that court for its registration in the Family Court and, provided that it remains registered, it is treated as a Family Court order for the purpose of enforcement and (broadly) variation.

Procedure

Availability	Only 'maintenance orders' may be registered, but this expression includes lump sum orders. Although an application may be made and granted while enforcement process is outstanding in the original court, the registration will not be effected until that process has been completed	MOA 1958, s 1(1)
	The grant of the application will become void if the enforcement process is not completed within 14 days	MOA 1958, s 2(2); FPR 2010, rr 32.14, 32.15
Application	Two copies of the application form and a certified copy of the order are lodged in the court which made the order If the application is granted, the order is registered in the Family Court. The rules are silent as to location but it is suggested that the appropriate court is Designated Family Court for the Designated Family Judge area where the payer resides	FPR 2010, rr 32.14, 32.15
	The Family Court has no discretion to decline registration	MOA 1958, s 2(5)
Fee	£50	FPFO 2008, fee 10.2
Effect	Any attachment of earnings order ceases to have effect	AEA 1971, s 11(1)(a)
	The order is enforceable only as if it were an order made by the Family Court	MOA 1958, s 3
	Variation proceedings must be in the Family Court, unless there is an application to vary some provision (e g extension of the term of the order) other than merely the rate of payment or the payer is outside England and Wales; in either of those cases, the application is to the High Court. In any event, the Family Court may remit a variation application made to it to the High Court for hearing	MOA 1958, s 4

Cancellation	The person entitled to receive payment may simply give notice to the Family Court. The High Court may give such a notice, but only where it varies or discharges the maintenance order The notice has the effect of cancelling the registration as soon as any outstanding enforcement process or variation application has been concluded Fee: none prescribed	MOA 1958, s 5
Form	Form D151	FPR PD5A
Appeals	See relevant Guide in Appeals section	

C4: Attachment of Earnings Order (High Court or Family Court)

Legal background

Where the debtor is in employment, the court may order his employer to deduct periodic amounts from his earnings and remit them to the court against the amount(s) due under the order to be enforced. The position varies according to whether the attachment of earnings order is to secure (a) a qualifying periodical maintenance order (including some lump sum orders), (b) some other maintenance order (including a lump sum order) or (c) an order which is not a maintenance order.

The procedure for attachment of earnings orders other than in respect of maintenance orders changed with effect from 6 April 2016.

This procedural guide deals separately with the procedure relating to maintenance orders (as defined) and orders that are not maintenance orders (such as orders for costs in decree proceedings).

Procedure

Maintenance order		
Availability	Leave is required if it is sought to enforce arrears more than 12 months old under a financial provision or similar order The application for leave is made to the court on notice to the debtor must be made in the attachment of earnings application itself	MCA 1973, s 32; CPA 2004, Sch 5, para 63 FPR 2010, r 39.20
	An attachment of earnings order cannot be made against a member of HM Forces, but a deduction from pay may be sought	Armed Forces (Forfeitures and Deductions) Regulations 2009
	Qualifying periodical maintenance order The person to whom the payments are to be made, the person (if different) who applied for the maintenance order or the debtor may apply at any time; otherwise, the court may make an order of its own motion on making the maintenance order or in the course of any proceedings relating to it	MEA 1991, s 1(1),(3)
	Other maintenance order The person to whom the payments are to be made may apply at any time The debtor may apply on the making or variation of the maintenance order	AEA 1971, s 3 FPR 2010, r 39.5(1)
Application	*High Court* The High Court has power to make an attachment of earnings order only to secure a High Court maintenance order	AEA 1971, s 1(1)

	Application is made to the District Registry for the district in which the debtor resides	FPR 2010, r 39.21
	Family Court The application is made to the Family Court in the Designated Family Judge area within which the order was made	FPR 2010, r 39.4 and notes thereunder
	The creditor must file a statement, verified by a statement of truth, showing how the amount due and any interest claimed are calculated	FPR 2010, r 33.3(1)
	If the application is to enforce a maintenance order, a return date is given before the court, which the applicant should attend	
	The debtor must file a reply in the form provided, giving particulars of his means, within 8 days of being served	FPR 2010, r 39.6(2)
Fee	High Court: £155	FPFO 2008, fee 5.3
	Family Court: £100 for each person against whom the order is sought (NB it appears that no fee is payable if the order is made of the court's own motion, and it is not payable when an attachment of earnings order is made on the hearing of a judgment summons)	FPFO 2008, fee 12.5
Debtor's address	It is for the creditor to provide the address of the debtor. In case of difficulty, assistance may sometimes be obtained from certain Government departments However, it may be necessary to obtain a High Court order authorising the disclosure	FPR PD6C *President's Office Guidance of November 2003*; FPR 2010, r 29.17(3)(b); PD29C
Composition of court	Any level of judge in the Family Court, including lay justices, may grant an attachment of earnings order	FC(CDB)R 2014, r 14
Powers of the court	The court has wide powers to require the debtor to provide the information needed to deal with the application	AEA 1971, s 14
	Provision is also made for where a debtor fails to attend or provide information	AEA 1971, s 23; FPR 2010, rr 39.9, 39.10
Order	The debtor's employer must make periodic deductions from his pay and remit them to CAPS (Central Attachment of Earnings Payment System), PO Box 464, Northampton NN1 2ZY, which passes them on to the creditor Where the payee is receiving income support, this enables the payee to divert the payments to the Department for Work and Pensions enabling her (or him) to receive full benefit, regardless of any irregularity in payment	
Forms	Form FE15 should be used for a maintenance order, County Court Form N337 for other debts. The court prepares Notice to the debtor in Form N55 (debt) or Form FE17 (maintenance)	
Judgment or order other than a maintenance order		
Availability	The balance due under the judgment or order must be at least £50	CPR 1998, r 89.7(14)
Which court	Application is made to the County Court Money Claims Centre, not to a hearing centre	CPR 1998, r 89.3

	Note that the High Court's jurisdiction to make attachment of earnings orders is limited to the enforcement of High Court maintenance orders	
	If interest is claimed, details of the calculation must be filed	CPR PD70, para 6
	Note that interest will cease to accrue while an attachment of earnings order is in force	County Courts (Interest on Judgment Debts) Order 1991, art 4(3)
What happens next	The court serves notice of the application on the debtor, together with a reply form	CPR 1998, r 89.5(1)
	The debtor is required to complete and return the reply Form N56 (giving details of his means and his employment) within 8 days of service (unless he pays the judgment debt)	CPR 1998, r 89.5(2)
	A copy of the reply is sent to the creditor	CPR 1998 r 89.5(4)
Failure by debtor	If the debtor fails to comply, the court will make a further order requiring compliance, which will contain a warning of the consequences of disobedience and will be served personally. It will also direct that any future payments be made to the court	CPR 1998, r 89.8(2)
	If the debtor continues to fail to comply, the application will be transferred to the debtor's home court, which may give him notice to show cause why he should not be imprisoned, giving him at least 5 days' notice of the hearing. Failure to comply is punishable by up to 14 days' imprisonment or a fine of up to £500. Such proceedings may be heard by the District Judge. A suspended order may be made, on terms that the debtor provide the information	CPR 1998, rr 89.8(4),(5), 89.9(1); AEA 1971, s 23(2)(c),(3),(4) and (11)
	Alternatively, a warrant may be issued for the debtor's arrest	AEA 1971, s 23(1A)
	If the court has information as to the employer's identity, it may request details of the debtor's pay from the employer. Should it prove necessary, it can order the employer to provide it	CPR 1998, r 89.6; AEA 1991, s 14(1)(b)
The order	On the debtor replying, the proper officer may make an attachment of earnings order, which will be based on the information given by the debtor and the use of a table of allowances similar to that applied to the assessment of income support	CPR 1998, 89.7(1)
	If the proper officer is unable to make an order, the application is referred to a District Judge, who may deal with it without a hearing or direct that it be transferred to the debtor's home court for hearing	CPR 1998, 89.7(7)
	Where an order is made without a hearing, either party may apply within 14 days of service that it be reconsidered, and a hearing will be fixed for that application	CPR 1998, 89.7(9)
	An attachment of earnings order fixes the amount to be deducted in each period (the normal deduction rate) provided that the debtor's net pay for the period is not reduced below a specified amount (the protected earnings rate). The employer remits the amounts deducted to a central accounting point maintained by the Court Service, which passes them on to the creditor	AEA 1991, s 6(5)

Court fees	On application, in respect of each respondent: £110	CPFO 2008, fee 8.7
Form	Request for issue: Form N337	

C5: Charging Order

Legal background

The court may impose a charge on the debtor's interest in land or securities. The effect of this remedy is to provide security for the debt, rather than enforce it but, having made a charging order, the court may appoint a receiver of the income generated by the property charged, as to which see the relevant Guide in *Civil Court Service* (LexisNexis), and/or may order its sale.

There is a two-stage procedure, with an interim charging order made without notice to the debtor, followed by a hearing on notice at which the interim order may be made 'final' (i e confirmed, with or without variation).

Changes in the civil courts

The procedure for charging orders over interests in land in the County Court changed with effect from 6 April 2016. The procedure in the Family Court and the Family Division of the High Court now differs substantively from that in the County Court. The text of the new CPR 1998, Pt 73, which now applies to the grant of charging orders in the County Court, differs appreciably from that of FPR 2010, Pt 40, notably that:

- such applications are processed at the County Court Money Claims Centre;
- the interim order will be made by a court officer;
- the interim order will provide that unless within 10 days of service the debtor objects, the court will proceed to consider making a final order (which will be made by a District Judge or Deputy District Judge);
- if the debtor objects to the making of a final charging order, the application will be transferred to the debtor's home court and listed as at present.

Reference should be made to *Civil Court Service* (LexisNexis).

Procedure

Availability	Leave is required if it is sought to enforce arrears more than 12 months old under a financial provision or similar order The application for leave is made to the district judge on notice to the debtor Otherwise, the creditor may apply at any time. However, the court has a discretion whether to make the charging order or not; if the circumstances would require the creditor to obtain leave before issuing execution against goods, similar considerations apply as on an application for such leave; only in exceptional circumstances will an order be made if the debtor is not in default. The remedy will also not be granted if it would be oppressive, e g by reason of the small amount of the debt	MCA 1973, s 32; CPA 2004, Sch 5, para 63 FPR 2010, rr 18.1–18.5, 18.7, 18.8
Which court	Application is made to the Family Court or the High Court	COA 1979, s 1(2)(b),(ba),(c); FPR 2010, r 40.4(2) and notes thereunder
Which particular court	*High Court* The High Court or the district registry in which the judgment was entered or to which the proceedings have been transferred	FPR 2010, r 40.4(2) and notes thereunder

	Family Court The Family Court for the Designated Family Judge area within which the judgment or order was made The debtor may request in writing that the hearing of the application is transferred to a more convenient court	FPR PD40A, para 3.1
Application	The application is made by filing an application notice (in Form FE6 if the application relates to land, or Form FE7 if it relates to securities), verified by a statement of truth. The application notice must contain the following information: (a) The name and address of the judgment debtor; (b) Details of the judgment or order sought to be enforced; (c) The amount of money remaining due; (d) If the judgment is payable by instalments, the amount of money remaining due; (e) The names and (if known) the addresses of any other creditors of the debtor of whom the judgment creditor is aware; (f) The asset or assets that it is sought to charge; (g) Details of the judgment debtor's interest in each asset; (h) The names and addresses of the persons on whom an interim order must be served under FPR 2010, r 40.6	FPR 2010, r 40.4; PD40A, paras 1.2, 1.3 FPR PD40A, para 1.3(8)
	While the Practice Direction does not explicitly require this, it is good practice to set out how the amount remaining due is arrived at, by analogy with FPR 2010, r 33.3(1)(a) If a charging order is sought over the judgment debtor's interest in registered land, an official copy of the entries on the Land Register should be filed with the application notice If satisfied that the application notice contains the required information and that it is proper to make the order, the master or District Judge may make an interim charging order and fixes a date to consider whether a final order should be made	FPR 2010, r 40.5(1),(2)(b)
Fee	£100 in respect of each charging order applied for	FPFO 2008, fee 12.3
Debtor's address	It is for the creditor to provide the address of the debtor. In case of difficulty, assistance may sometimes be obtained from certain Government departments However, it may be necessary to obtain a High Court order authorising the disclosure	FPR PD6C *President's Office Guidance of November 2003*; FPR 2010, r 29.17(3)(b); PD29C
Service	A copy of the interim order, the application notice and the documents filed in support shall be served by the creditor not less than 21 (clear) days before the day fixed for the hearing If the judgment creditor serves, he must either file a certificate of service not less than 2 days before the hearing or produce the certificate at the hearing	FPR 2010, rr 2.9(2), 40.6(1) FPR 2010, r 40.6(2)

PART I

	Persons to be served: (a) the debtor; (b) any co-owner of an interest in land; (c) the debtor's spouse or civil partner; (d) such creditors as are identified in the application or as the court directs; (e) where the order relates to an interest under a trust, such of the trustees as the court may direct; (f) where the order relates to securities, the keeper of the stock register	FPR 2010, r 40.6(3)(a) FPR 2010, r 40.6(3)(b) FPR 2010, r 40.6(3)(c) FPR 2010, r 40.6(3)(d) FPR 2010, r 40.6(3)(e) FPR 2010, r 40.6(3)(f)
Objections to the order	Any person who wishes to object to the making of a final charging order must file and serve on the judgment creditor written evidence stating the grounds of his objection not less than 7 days before the hearing At the hearing the judge may make a final charging order confirming that the charge should remain in force with or without modifications. The order may be made subject to conditions, for example restricting enforcement A charging order affecting an interest in land can and should be protected by registration at HM Land Registry or HM Land Charges Registry as appropriate as soon as an interim order is made. If it is discharged on the hearing, the registration must be removed by the creditor	FPR 2010, r 40.8(1) COA 1979, s 3(1); FPR 2010, r 40.8(2)(a)
Composition of court	Any judge of the Family Court (except lay justices) may grant a charging order	FC(CDB)R 2014, Sch 2
Order for sale	The judgment creditor holding a charging order may apply for an order for sale of the property charged. Although the charging order may have been made in family proceedings, an order for sale is applied for by fresh proceedings which are not themselves family proceedings. If the debt secured does not exceed £350,000, the application may be made to the County Court; in any case, the application may be made to the Chancery Division of the High Court If the interest charged is merely a beneficial interest under a trust (e g if the property is in the joint names of the debtor and another), the creditor may apply (see Guide A4) for an order for sale of the trust property; in this case, the County Court has jurisdiction irrespective of the amount of the debt or the value of the property The court will have regard to the relative values of the debt and the property charged, and will be reluctant to make an order where either is small See the relevant Guide in *Civil Court Service* (LexisNexis)	CCA 1984, s 23(c), as amended; CPR 1998, r 73.10C; PD73, paras 4.1–4.5 TLATA 1996, s 14; HCCCJO 1991, art 2(1)(a)
Appeals	See Guide E2	

C6: Writ or Warrant of Delivery

Legal background

In the High Court, a writ of delivery is issued to an enforcement officer (formerly the sheriff) and in the Family Court, a warrant of delivery is issued to the bailiff, requiring him physically to take the goods from the person against whom the order was made. If the order provides the alternative of payment of the value of the goods, the writ or warrant will require the enforcement officer or bailiff to levy execution for the value if the goods cannot be uplifted, unless the court has ordered otherwise. See as to the High Court practice, CPR 1998, r 83.14, and as to the Family Court, rr 83.23–83.25, applied to the Family Court by FPR 2010, r 33.1(2).

Procedure

Availability	Permission is required to issue the writ or warrant if more than 6 years have elapsed since the order, if there has been a change of parties, if the judgment is against the assets of a deceased person, if the goods to be seized are in the hands of a receiver or sequestrator or if the order was conditional; otherwise, the person in whose favour the order is made may issue the writ or warrant as soon as it is made or, if it allows a time for compliance, as soon as that time has expired	CPR 1998, r 83.2(3)
	Permission is required if the judgment was obtained in default against one of several defendants and judgment has not been obtained against all the defendants	CPR 1998, r 12.8(3)
	The writ or warrant is valid for 12 months but can be renewed for 12 months at any one time	CPR 1998, r 83.3
Issue	*High Court* The applicant files a request together with the form of writ for sealing, the judgment or order on which the writ is to issue, and the order granting permission (if required). After issue, he sends the writ to the sheriffs' lodgement centre or other enforcement office of his choice	CPR 1998, r 83.9(5)
	Family Court The applicant files a form of request for the issue of the warrant	FPR 2010, r 33.1(2); CPR 1998, r 83.15
Fee	*High Court* £60 (NB a further fee is payable to the enforcement officer)	FPFO 2008, fee 14.1
	Family Court £110	FPFO 2008, fee 13.3
	No further court fee is payable if the writ or warrant is issued also to recover money	
Composition of court	Lay justices in the Family Court may not grant a warrant of delivery	FC(CDB)R 2014, Sch 2
Form	*High Court* Request in Request in Form PF90A, Form PF90B or Form PF90C, as appropriate; writ in Form 64 or Form 65 *Family Court* County Court: Form N324 should be adapted	
Appeals	See Guide E2	

C7: Execution against Goods

Legal background

In the High Court, a writ of control is issued, addressed to an 'enforcement officer' (formerly the sheriff) and, in the Family Court, a warrant of control is issued to the bailiff, requiring him to seize and sell the debtor's goods to produce the amount due under the order. The court may stay or suspend the execution if there are special circumstances or if the debtor is unable to pay.

Procedure

Availability	Permission is required if it is sought to enforce arrears more than 12 months old under a financial provision or similar order or where a variation application is pending	MCA 1973, s 32; CPA 2004, Sch 5, para 63; FPR 2010, r 33.20
	The application for permission is made to a district judge	FPR 2010, rr 18.1–18.5, 18.7, 18.8
	Permission is also required to issue the writ or warrant if more than 6 years have elapsed since the order, if there has been a change of parties, if the order was conditional, in certain circumstances if the order was against the estate of a deceased person or if a receiver or sequestrator has been appointed. In these cases the application may be made either with or without notice according to circumstance	
	Otherwise, the person in whose favour the order is made may issue the writ or warrant as soon as it is made or, if it allows a time for compliance, then as soon as that time has expired	CPR 1998, r 83.9(5)(b)
	In the case of an instalment order, the creditor issuing the warrant must certify that the whole or part of an instalment is due and unpaid	CPR 1998, r 83.15(6)(b)(i)
	If the payments are in arrears, a warrant can be issued for all or part of the debt then unpaid	CPR 1998, r 83.15(9)
	A writ or warrant of control may be stayed if the debtor is for any reason unable to pay the money, or there are special circumstances rendering it inexpedient to enforce the judgment or order	CCA 1984, ss 38, 71(2), 76; CPR 1998, r 83.7
	A Family Court order other than for periodical payments or arrears thereof may be transferred to the High Court and enforced as a High Court order. The application is made to the Family Court without notice, accompanied by a statement, verified by a statement of truth, of the amount due under the order and showing how that amount is arrived at. The transfer has immediate effect	FPR 2010, r 33.4
	However, it appears that there is no upper limit to the sum for which the Family Court may issue a warrant of control, so some cases that in the County Court would have been transferred to the High Court for enforcement will be enforceable by bailiffs in the Family Court	MFPA 1984, s 31E(2)
Issue	*High Court* The applicant files a statement, verified by a statement of truth, showing the amount due and how it is calculated and a request together with the form of writ for sealing; he then sends the writ to the sheriffs' lodgement centre	FPR 2010, r 33.3; CPR 1998, r 83.9

	Family Court The applicant files a statement, verified by a statement of truth, showing how the amount due and any interest claimed are calculated, together with a further copy of the interest calculation and a form of request for the issue of the warrant	FPR 2010, rr 33.1(2), 33.3; CPR 1998, r 83.15
Fee	*High Court* £60 (NB a further fee is payable to the enforcement officer) *Family Court* £100	FPFO 2008, fee 14.1 FPFO 2008, fee 13.1
Debtor's address	It is for the creditor to provide the address of the debtor. In case of difficulty, assistance may sometimes be obtained from certain Government departments However, it may be necessary to obtain a High Court order authorising the disclosure	FPR PD6C *President's Office Guidance of November 2003*
Composition of court	Lay justices in the Family Court may not grant a warrant of control	FC(CDB)R 2014, Sch 2
Form	*High Court* Request in Form PF86; Writ in Form Nos 53 to 63 *Family Court* Request in Form N323	
Appeals	Application for leave or for stay, see Guide E2	

C8: Application for a Third Party Debt Order

Procedure

Availability	The judgment creditor must have a money judgment against the judgment debtor and money must be owed to the judgment debtor by a third party who is or carries on business within England and Wales. The money judgment must be immediately enforceable, i e one that has not been stayed; where the date for payment has passed; or at least one instalment has not been paid under any instalment order There is no longer a requirement that the amount due to the applicant must exceed £50, but the order is discretionary and may be refused, for example if the administrative costs to which the third party is entitled in complying with the order are out of proportion with the judgment debt. A third-party debt order may not be made against the Crown	CPR 1998, r 72.1(1)

PART I

Which court	The application is made to the court in which the judgment was given or to which the case has since been transferred, or to the Family Court in the Designated Family Judge area within which the judgment or order was made, except that if the proceedings have since been transferred to a different Designated Family Judge area, it must be made to the Family Court in that area	CPR 1998, r 72.3(1)(b), as amended by FPR 2010, r 33.24(1A)
Application	By filing in the court office, an application notice in Form N349, verified by a statement of truth and containing the following information: (1) the name and address of the judgment debtor; (2) details of the judgment or order sought to be enforced; (3) the amount of money remaining due under the judgment or order; (4) if the judgment debt is payable by instalments, the amount of any instalments that have fallen due and remain unpaid; (5) the name and address of the third party; (6) if the third party is a bank or building society – (a) its name and the address of the branch at which the judgment debtor's account is believed to be held; and (b) the account number; (7) confirmation that to the best of the judgment creditor's knowledge or belief the third party – (a) is within the jurisdiction; and (b) owes money to or holds money to the credit of the judgment debtor (8) if the judgment creditor knows or believes that any person other than the judgment debtor has any claim to the money owed by the third party – (a) his name and (if known) his address; and (b) such information as is known to the judgment creditor about his claim (9) details of any other applications for third party debt orders issued by the judgment creditor in respect of the same judgment debt; and (10) the source or grounds of the judgment creditor's knowledge or belief of the matters referred to in (7), (8) and (9) While the Practice Direction does not explicitly require this, it is good practice to set out how the amount remaining due is arrived at, by analogy with FPR 2010, r 33.3(1)(a) The application is not normally served on the judgment debtor	CPR 1998, r 72.3 CPR PD72, para 1.2
Composition of court	Lay justices in the Family Court may not grant a third party debt order	FC(CDB)R 2014, Sch 2
Interim third party debt order	The master or district judge may make an interim third party debt order: (a) fixing a hearing date, not less than 28 days ahead, to consider whether to make a final third party debt order ('the final hearing'); and (b) directing that until the hearing the third party must not make any payment that reduces the amount that he owes to the judgment debtor to less than the figure specified in the order	CPR 1998, r 72.4(2)(a),(5) CPR 1998, r 72.4(2)(b)

	The amount specified will be the amount remaining due under the judgment, together with the fixed costs allowable to the judgment creditor for making the application	CPR PD72, para 2
	The order becomes binding on the third party when it is served on him	CPR 1998, r 72.4(4)
Service of the order	*On the third party* The order may be served by the court or by the judgment creditor (who might wish to deliver it immediately, rather than wait for the court to post it). It must be served not less than 21 (clear) days before the date of the hearing	CPR 1998, rr 2.8(2), 72.5(1)(a)
	On the judgment debtor The order may be served by the court or by the judgment creditor. It must be served not less than 7 (clear) days after service on the third party and not less than 7 (clear) days before the date of the hearing	CPR 1998, rr 2.8(2), 72.5(1)(b)
	The order must be served in accordance with CPR 1998, Pt 6 If served by the judgment creditor, he must file a certificate of service not less than 2 days before the hearing or produce the certificate at the hearing	CPR 1998, r 72.5(2)
	If the third party is a company, it may be served by posting it to the registered office	Companies Act 2006, ss 1139–1143
	Banks or building societies If the third party is a bank or building society, it must carry out a search immediately to identify any accounts held with it by the judgment debtor	CPR 1998, r 72.6(1)
	Unless otherwise ordered, this will not include accounts where the judgment debtor is not the sole account holder	CPR PD72, paras 3.1, 3.2
	In respect of each account identified, the bank or building society must within 7 days of service inform the court and the judgment creditor: (a) of the number of each account; (b) whether it is in credit; (c) if it is in credit, whether the balance is sufficient to cover the amount specified in the order; or, if the amount is insufficient, the credit balance at the date of service; and (d) if the bank or building society claims to be entitled to retain the money, details of that claim	CPR 1998, r 72.6(2)
	Alternatively, the bank or building society must inform the court and the judgment creditor within 7 days of service: (a) that the judgment debtor does not hold an account with the bank or building society; or (b) that it is unable to comply with the order for any other reason, for example that the information given is insufficient positively to identify the judgment debtor as the holder of a particular account	CPR 1998, r 72.6(3)
	The rules do not require banks or building societies to give the information in writing	
	Other third parties Third parties who are not banks or building societies must inform the court and the judgment creditor in writing if they claim – (a) not to owe money to the judgment debtor; or (b) to owe less than the amount specified in the order	CPR 1998, r 72.6(4)

Hardship order	Pending the final hearing, a judgment debtor may apply for a hardship payment order if the following conditions are satisfied: (a) he is an individual; (b) he is prevented from withdrawing money from his bank or building society as a result of an interim third party debt order; and (c) as a result he or his family is suffering hardship in meeting ordinary living expenses	CPR 1998, r 72.7(1)
	A judgment debtor may only apply to one court for a hardship payment order	CPR 1998, r 72.7(3)
	If the interim order was made in the High Court, the application may be made at either the Royal Courts of Justice, the Principal Registry or any district registry	FPR 2010, r 33.24(3)(a); CPR 1998, r 72.7(2)(a)
	If the interim order was made in the Family Court, the application may be made to the Family Court in *any* Designated Family Judge centre	FPR 2010, r 33.24(3)(b); CPR 1998, r 72.7(2)(b)
	Application is made by filing an application notice, quoting the case number and the court that made the interim order, verified by a statement of truth and setting out detailed evidence explaining why a hardship payment is needed. Documentary evidence, such as bank statements, wage slips, or mortgage statements should be included	CPR 1998, r 72.7(4)(a),(b); PD72, paras 5.1, 5.6
	The application will be dealt with at the court to which it is made	CPR PD72, paras 5.2, 5.3(1)
	The court in which the interim order has been made will send copies of the original application notice for the third party debt order and the interim order to the court dealing with the hardship application	CPR PD72, para 5.3(2)
	Unless the court otherwise orders, the judgment creditor must be given 2 days' notice of the hearing but the application need not be served on the third party	CPR 1998, r 72.7(5)
	In case of exceptional urgency the court may deal with the application without notice. If so, then wherever possible the judgment creditor will be informed of the application and given an opportunity to make representations by telephone, fax or other means of communication	CPR PD72, para 5.5
	A hardship payment order is directed to the third party and will permit one or more payments out of the account and may specify to whom those payments are to be made (for example by honouring standing order mandates)	CPR 1998, r 72.7(6)
Composition of court	While lay justices may not grant a third party debt order, it is suggested that if necessary they may hear an application for a hardship order	FC(CDB)R 2014, r 14
Transfer at the debtor's request	If the judgment debtor wishes to oppose the application for a final order, he may apply for the application to be transferred to the court for the district in which he resides or carries on business, or another court	CPR PD72, para 4
Notice of objection etc	If either the third party or the judgment debtor wishes to object to the final order, he must file and serve written evidence setting out the grounds of his objection not less than 3 days before the hearing	CPR 1998, r 72.8(1),(4)

	If either the third party or the judgment debtor knows or believes that any other person has a claim to the money specified in the interim order, he must file and serve written evidence stating his knowledge of that matter not less than 3 days before the hearing	CPR 1998, r 72.8(4)
	If the judgment creditor wishes to dispute a claim by a third party other than a bank or building society, either that it does not owe money to the judgment debtor or that the amount owing is less than the amount specified in the order, he must file and serve written evidence setting out his grounds for disputing the third party's claim not less than 3 days before the hearing	CPR 1998, r 72.8(3),(4)
	If the court is notified that some other person may have a claim to the money specified in the interim order it will serve notice on that person of the application and the date of hearing	CPR 1998, r 72.8(5)
Hearing	The court may, if the third party does not attend or dispute his indebtedness to the debtor, make a final third party debt order	CPR 1998, r 72.8(6)(a)
	The court may discharge the interim third party debt order and dismiss the application	CPR 1998, r 72.8(6)(b)
	The court may dispose summarily of issues in dispute between the parties and any other person claiming the money specified in the order and either make a final third party debt order or discharge the interim third party debt order and dismiss the application	CPR 1998, r 72.8(6)(c)
	If it is unable to dispose of the issues summarily, the court may direct the trial of an issue and give further directions	CPR 1998, r 72.8(6)(d)
Effect of final order	The final third party debt order requires the third party to pay to the creditor the lesser of: (a) the amount of the debt due from the third party to the debtor (except the last £1 in an account with a Building Society or Credit Union), less any costs allowed to the third party and expenses of £55 if it is a deposit-taking institution; or	CPR 1998, r 72.2(1); SCA 1981, s 40A
	(b) the amount of the debt due from the debtor to the creditor together with any costs allowed to the creditor	CCA 1984, s 109
	The order is enforceable against the third party as any other order for payment of money may be enforced	CPR 1998, r 72.9(1)
	To the extent of the payment made or enforced against him (but not enforcement costs) under the terms of the final third party debt order, the third party is discharged from his liability to the debtor	CPR 1998, r 72.9(2)
Fee	On application: £100 for each third party against whom the order is sought	FPFO 2008, fee 12.2
Forms	Application for third party debt order – Form N349 Application for hardship payment order – Form N244	

C9: Committal by way of Judgment Summons

Legal background

The court's usual powers to commit for contempt of court a person who disobeys an order do not apply in the case of an order to pay money. Instead, the court may imprison for up to 6 weeks (and no longer: *Zuk v Zuk* [2013] 2 FLR 1466, CA) a person who has been ordered to pay maintenance (including a lump sum), who has or has had the means to pay it and who neglects or refuses or has neglected or refused to do so. However, this special procedure does not change the character of the disobedience as contempt of court. The contemnor may be subjected to appropriate conditions in relation to other proceedings between the parties (*Mubarak v Mubarik* [2007] 1 FLR 722, FD).

FPR 2010 require the creditor to file and serve in advance his evidence to prove the debtor's means and neglect or refusal. Other procedural requirements reflect the view of judgment summons proceedings expressed in *Mubarak v Mubarak* [2001] 1 FLR 698, CA that they are penal in character.

Procedure

Availability	The remedy is only available in the case of a maintenance order (including a lump sum order)	AJA 1970, s 11, Sch 8
	Permission is required if it is sought to enforce arrears more than 12 months old under a financial provision or similar order. The application for permission may be combined with the summons, the prescribed forms including such an application for use if required	MCA 1973, s 32; CPA 2004, Sch 5, para 63
	Permission of the court is required before the summons is issued if the debtor is in default under a committal order made on an earlier judgment summons	FPR 2010, r 33.11
	A committal order will not be made unless refusal or neglect to pay, notwithstanding the means to pay, is proved	DA 1869, s 5; *Mubarak v Mubarik* [2007] 1 FLR 722, FD, at [71]
Which court	The High Court may hear a judgment summons to enforce a High Court maintenance order; the Family Court may hear a judgment summons to enforce a High Court or a Family Court maintenance order	
	The specific court may be chosen by the judgment creditor having regard to the place where the debtor resides or carries on business and irrespective of the court in which the original order was made	FPR 2010, r 33.10(1)
	Unlike under the former practice, a judgment summons may now be heard by any level of judge in the Family Court, including lay justices	FC(CDB)R 2014, r 14
	However, an order for committal for breach of an order may only be made by a judge of at least the same level as the judge who made the original order	FC(CDB)R 2014, r 17(5)
Application	The application must be filed in the appropriate court together with a statement, verified by a statement of truth, which states the amount due under the order, shows how that amount is arrived at, and contains all the evidence on which the judgment creditor intends to rely If interest is claimed, the statement should set out how it is calculated	FPR 2010, r 33.10(2)
Fee	£100	FPFO 2008, fee 12.4

Service	The judgment summons is issued by the court and must be served, together with the statement referred to in r 33.10(2), not less than 14 (clear) days before the hearing	FPR 2010, rr 2.9(2), 33.11(5)
	It may be served by post	FPR 2010, r 33.11(3)(b)
	It is for the creditor to provide the address of the debtor and if postal service is to be used, a certificate for postal service must be filed. In case of difficulty, assistance may sometimes be obtained from certain Government departments	FPR PD6C; FPR 2010, r 33.11(4)
	However, it may be necessary to obtain a High Court order authorising the disclosure	*President's Office Guidance of November 2003*; FPR 2010, r 29.17(3)(b); PD29C
Evidence	The evidence adduced by the creditor must prove beyond reasonable doubt that the debtor has or has had the means to pay and that he has neglected or refused or is neglecting or refusing to pay	FPR 2010, r 33.14(1),(c3)
Debtor's attendance	If the debtor fails to attend, the court may order him to attend an adjourned hearing and, if he disobeys, commit him for up to 14 days provided that travelling expenses have been tendered to him and the order to attend the adjourned hearing has been personally served	CCA 1984, s 110; FPR 2010, rr 33.13(2), 33.14(3)(a), 33.14A(1)
	However, as the proceedings are penal in character, the debtor cannot be compelled to give evidence	FPR 2010, r 33.14(4)
	If the court is satisfied that the judgment summons and evidence have been duly served, it may be prepared to proceed in the debtor's absence	
Order	If satisfied of his neglect or refusal to pay, the court may commit the debtor to prison for up to 6 weeks, but may and usually will suspend the order on condition that he makes payment (by instalments or otherwise)	DA 1869, s 5; FPR 2010, rr 33.14(1), 33.14(3), 33.16(2)
	Alternatively, the court may make a new order for payment	FPR 2010, r 33.16(1)
Form	Request in Form D62	
Appeals	See Guide E5	

C10: Means of Payment Order

Legal background

The court may order the debtor to make the required payments by standing order or by direct debit, and to open an account for the purpose.

Procedure

Availability	The order to be enforced must be a 'qualifying periodical maintenance order', i e one made when the debtor was ordinarily resident in England and Wales; it includes a lump sum order if the sum is payable by instalments	MEA 1991, s 1(2),(10)

	Any interested party may apply. If the order is sought to enforce arrears more than 12 months old, permission must be obtained (but may be requested in the same application)	MCA 1973, s 32
	An order may be made when the maintenance order is made or at any time thereafter, on application or (in the course of any proceedings concerning the maintenance order) of the court's own initiative; similarly, the court may revoke, suspend, revive or vary such an order	MEA 1991, s 1(1),(3),(7)
	An order to open an account cannot be made until the debtor has been given an opportunity to do so voluntarily	MEA 1991, s 1(6)
Application	In the course of proceedings concerning the maintenance order, the court will generally consider an oral invitation to exercise its powers, but it must (if practicable) give every interested party the opportunity to make representations; if a party is absent, this may necessitate an adjournment so that notice can be given	MEA 1991, s 1(8)
	Otherwise, the application is made to the court on notice and, if some other application is pending, may conveniently be made so as to be returnable on the same occasion	FPR 2010, rr 18.1–18.5, 18.7, 18.8
	The creditor must file a statement, verified by a statement of truth, of the amount due under the order and showing how that amount is arrived at	FPR 2010, r 33.3
Fee	£155 (NB it appears that no fee is payable if the order is made of the court's own initiative)	FPFO 2008, fee 5.3
Debtor's address	It is for the creditor to provide the address of the debtor. In case of difficulty, assistance may sometimes be obtained from certain Government departments	FPR PD6C
	However, it may be necessary to obtain a High Court order authorising the disclosure	*President's Office Guidance of November 2003*
Appeals	See Guides E2, E4 and E5	

C11: Seeking 'Such Method of Enforcement as the Court Considers Appropriate'

Legal background

Under FPR 2010, r 33.3(2)(b), application may be made for 'an order for such means of enforcement as the court may consider appropriate'. If an application is made under that paragraph, an order to attend court will be issued and CPR 1998, r 71.2(6),(7) will apply.

Procedure

Availability	The person who obtained the order may apply for an order for such means of enforcement as the court may consider appropriate	FPR 2010, r 33.3(2)(b)
	The application is made to the court that made the order that it is sought to enforce, unless the proceedings have been transferred to another court, in which case the application is made to that court	

Application	The application is made by filing an application notice, which must: – state the name and address of the judgment debtor; – identify the order that it is sought to enforce; – be accompanied by a statement, verified by a statement of truth, of the amount due under the order and showing how that amount is arrived at; The questioning should take place before a judge or lay justices, and not a court officer	FPR 2010, r 33.3(1) *Corbett v Corbett* [2003] 2 FLR 385, CA
Form	Form D50K	
Fee	£50	FPFO 2008, fee 12.1
Order	The order requires the debtor to attend at a court office on a specified appointment and to submit to cross-examination. Normally, the debtor will be directed to attend a court for the district in which he resides or carries on business	
Failure to attend	If the judgment debtor fails to attend, it appears that a bench warrant may be issued. The provisions for a suspended committal order to be made on paper contained in CPR 1998 r 71.8 do not appear to apply	
Further proceedings	The judge who has conducted the questioning may proceed to make an appropriate order	*Kaur v Randhawa* [2015] EWHC 1592 (Fam)
	Committal – in effect, treating a judgment summons as an appropriate means of enforcement and proceeding accordingly – will not be appropriate given that a debtor facing a judgment summons cannot be compelled to give evidence (as the debtor will have been). Note, however, that documents produced by the debtor could be the basis for a subsequent judgment summons, obviously before a different judge	FPR 2010, r 33.14(2)
Appeals	See Guide E2	

C12: Obtaining Information from the Debtor

Legal background

The court may order the debtor to attend and be cross-examined as to his means to pay the amount ordered or otherwise to comply with the order if it is not for payment of money. This procedure, while not itself an enforcement measure, is sometimes a valuable aid to enforcement.

CPR 1998, Pt 71 applies to family proceedings, with slight modification.

Under FPR 2010, r 33.3(2)(b), application may be made for 'an order for such means of enforcement as the court may consider appropriate' (see Guide C11) and in family proceedings that will generally be the more useful approach. This Guide considers solely the Pt 71 procedure.

Procedure

Availability	The person who obtained the order may apply for an order for the debtor to attend for questioning at any time after the judgment or order has become enforceable	CPR 1998, r 71.1

	The application is made to the court that made the order that it is sought to enforce, unless the proceedings have been transferred to another court, in which case the application is made to that court. In family proceedings, application must be made to: (i) the High Court if the High Court made the judgment or order that it is sought to enforce; or (ii) the Designated Family Court for the Designated Family Judge area within which the judgment or order was made, except that if the proceedings have since been transferred to a different Designated Family Judge area, it must be made to that area	CPR 1998, r 71.2(2)(b)(i)
Application	The application is made by filing an application notice without notice to the judgment debtor The notice must: – state the name and address of the judgment debtor; – identify the order that it is sought to enforce; – be accompanied by a statement, verified by a statement of truth, of the amount due under the order and showing how that amount is arrived at; – identify particular matters about which questions are to be asked; – if the judgment creditor wishes particular documents to be produced, identify them; – if the judgment creditor wishes the questioning to be before a judge, specify that request and the reasons for it. Those reasons must be 'compelling'; – where the questioning is to be conducted by a court officer and the judgment creditor wishes specific questions to be asked, a list of them should be attached to the application notice	CPR 1998, r 71.2(2)(a) FPR 2010, r 33.3(1) CPR PD71, para 1.2 CPR 1998, r 71.6(2); PD71, para 2.2 CPR PD71, para 4.2(2)
Fee	£50	FPFO 2008, fee 10.1
Order	The order requires the debtor to attend at a court office on a specified appointment and to submit to cross-examination. Unless otherwise ordered by a judge, the debtor will be directed to attend a court for the district in which he resides or carries on business	CPR PD71, para 2.1
Service	The order must be served personally on the debtor not less than 14 (clear) days before the hearing Service may be effected by the creditor, by a High Court enforcement officer (at the creditor's expense) or by a County Court bailiff (if the debtor is an individual litigant) The court may order service by an alternative method but as failure to attend may render the debtor liable to imprisonment, convincing evidence will be required both that personal service is impracticable and that the debtor will become aware of the order in time to comply	CPR 1998, rr 2.8(2), 71.3 CPR 1998, rr 6.15, 6.27
Affidavits	Where the judgment creditor has been responsible for service an affidavit must be sworn and filed evidencing how and when the order was served In any event, affidavits must be sworn and filed:	CPR 1998, r 71.5(1)(a)

	– evidencing that no request for travelling expenses has been received, or that if such a request has been received it has been complied with;	CPR 1998, r 71.5(1)(b)
	– stating how much of the judgment debt remains unpaid	CPR 1998, r 71.5(1)(c)
	NB affidavits, rather than witness statements, are required. Specifically, the amount unpaid must here be verified by affidavit	
Examination	Normally conducted by a senior member of the court staff, who will put standard questions to the debtor. This may not be appropriate in family proceedings; if the questioning is conducted by the district judge, the creditor or his representative must attend to question the debtor	CPR 1998 r 71.6(3)(b), PD71, para 4.1
Failure to attend, etc	If the judgment debtor fails to attend, refuses to take the oath; refuses to answer any questions or otherwise fails to comply with the order (e g by failing to produce documents he has been ordered to produce), the judge or court officer conducting the hearing will certify the manner in which the order has not been complied with	CPR 1998 r 71.8(1), PD71, para 6
	The matter will then be referred to a High Court or circuit judge	CPR 1998 r 71.8(2)
	The judge may make a suspended committal order against the debtor, but this should not be regarded as routine	*Broomleigh HA v Okonkwo* [2010] EWCA Civ 1113
	Any committal order made under this procedure will be suspended on terms that the person named in the order: (a) attends court for a further appointment at the time and place specified;	CPR 1998, r 71.8(4)
	(b) complies with the terms of the order and of the original order	
	If the suspended committal order has been duly served and the judgment debtor fails to attend on the further appointment, the judge or court officer conducting the hearing will certify in writing his failure to attend	CPR PD71, para 8.1
	Similarly, if the judgment debtor attends but fails to comply (e g by refusing to be sworn or answer questions), the judge or court officer will so certify in writing	CPR PD71, para 8.2
	In either case, on the basis of that certificate, the court will then issue a warrant for the arrest of the judgment debtor to be brought before a judge, who may be a master or district judge, and who will consider whether the committal order should be discharged or put into effect	CPR 1998, r 71.8(4); PD71, paras 8.3, 8.4
	In practice, the person arrested will be offered the opportunity to purge his contempt by complying with the original order to provide information. If he complies, the suspended committal order will be discharged	
	If he declines the opportunity, the court must proceed immediately to consider whether or not the committal order should be discharged or put into effect	

	At this point, to comply with HRA 1998 the person arrested must be given details in writing of his alleged contempt and be offered the opportunity both to have legal representation and to challenge the evidence against him. An adjournment may be essential, for example if the person arrested wishes to challenge the evidence of service either of the original order or the suspended committal order or the contents of a certificate of non-attendance	*Newman v Modern Bookbinders* [2000] 1 WLR 2559, CA; *Hammerton v Hammerton* [2007] 2 FLR 1133, CA
Failure to comply with the order	In the case of a breach of the order that cannot appropriately be dealt with under the summary procedure set out above, eg: – failure to produce required documents; – failure to answer specific questions; an application for committal may be made under CPR 1998, Pt 81, as to which see Guide C14	CPR 1998, r 81.4(1)(a); *Deutsche Bank AG v Sebastian Holdings Inc* [2016] EWHC 3222 (Comm)
Appeals	See Guide E2	

C13: Writ or Warrant of Possession of Land

Legal background

In the High Court, a writ of possession is issued to an enforcement officer (formerly the sheriff) and, in the Family Court, a possession warrant is issued to the bailiff, requiring him physically to take possession of the land (and buildings) and give it to the person in whose favour the order was made.

Procedure

Availability	In the High Court, permission is generally required In the Family Court, leave is required if more than 6 years have elapsed since the order or if there has been a change of parties Otherwise, the person in whose favour the order is made may issue the writ or warrant as soon as it is made or, if it allows a time for compliance, as soon as that time has expired	CPR 1998, r 83.13(2), but cf paras (3),(5),(6) CPR 1998, r 83.2(3)
Application for leave	In the High Court, the application for permission is made in accordance with CPR 1998, Pt 23 and may be made without notice unless the court directs otherwise	CPR 1998, r 83.2(4)
Issue	*High Court* The applicant files a request together with the form of writ for sealing, and then sends the writ to a High Court Enforcement Officer *Family Court* The applicant files a form of request for the issue of the warrant Lay justices in the Family Court may not issue a warrant of possession	CPR 1998, r 83.9 CPR 1998, r 83.26 FC(CDB)R 2014, Sch 2, para 16
Fee	*High Court* £60 (NB a further fee is payable to the enforcement officer) *Family Court* £110	FPFO 2008, fee 14.1 FPFO 2008, fee 13.3

	No further court fee is payable if the writ or warrant is issued also to recover money
Forms	*High Court* Request in Form PF88 or Form PF89; writ in Form No 66 *Family Court* Request in Form N325
Appeals	Application for leave or for stay, see Guide E2

C14: Committal and Arrest for Disobedience of an Injunctive Order or Breach of an Undertaking in the Family Court, the High Court and the County Court

Legal background

An injunctive order (including a non-molestation order or occupation order under FLA 1996, Pt IV; a CA 1989, s 8 order to which a penal notice has been attached; and an order under PHA 1997) directing a person to do an act at or within a specified time, or to abstain from doing an act, or an undertaking to like effect which incorporates a penal warning notice, may be enforced by committal proceedings initiated by the person entitled to the benefit of the direction or undertaking. Any undertaking for the payment of money that has effect as if it was an order made under Matrimonial Causes Act 1973, Pt II may be enforced as if it was an order and FPR 2010, Pt 33 applies (FPR PD33A). Some money orders may be enforceable by judgment summons under the Debtors Acts 1869 and 1878 (see Guide C9). Personal service of an injunctive order is required by CPR 1998, r 81.5 and FPR 2010, r 37.5. The court can dispense with service or provide for some other form of service, but an injunction cannot be enforced unless it can be proved that the person to whom it was directed knew about the order and, where an act is directed to be done, the order must have been served before the time set for the act to be done. 'Any procedural defect in the commencement or conduct by the applicant of a committal application may be waived by the court if satisfied that no injustice has been caused to the respondent by the defect' (*Nicholls v Nicholls* [1997] 1 FLR 649, CA; CPR PD81, para 16.2; FPR PD37A, para 13.2). However, grave procedural errors will result in the committal application being dismissed (see *Re L (A Child); Re Oddin* [2017] 1 FLR 1135, CA – failure to prominently display a penal notice) or, on appeal, findings being quashed (*Inplayer Ltd v Thorogood* [2014] EWCA Civ 1511).

The Lord Chief Justice issued *Practice Direction: Committal/Contempt of Court – Open Court* on 26 March 2015. It is reproduced in Part V and supersedes the President's 'Guidance' of 3 May 2013. The *Practice Direction* emphasises, for example, the need for the correct wording of the notice of hearing, which is to be in public save in rare exceptions, the service of the notice on the Press Association and provision of the judgment to both the Association and BAILII. No one can be committed without details of their name, the contempt and the reasons for committal being made public.

Which rules of court?

Applications for committal in respect of injunctive orders are interlocutory in nature (*Savings and Investment Bank v Gasco Investments (Netherlands) BV (No 2)* [1988] Ch 422, CA). Consequently, if the injunctive order was made in family proceedings an application for committal is made in family proceedings and is governed by FPR 2010, Pt 37. In civil proceedings, committal proceedings are governed by CPR 1998, Pt 81. However, Pt 81 does not apply to family proceedings. If the injunctive order was made in non-family civil proceedings, eg under PHA 1997, then CPR 1998 apply. In family cases, see generally FPR PD37A.

Committal proceedings begun by application

FPR 2010, r 37.10 provides that a committal application is made by an application notice using the Pt 18 procedure. PD5A provides that the application notice under Pt 18 is Form FP2. In civil proceedings, CPR 1998, r 81.10 provides that a committal application is made by an application notice under Pt 23. The relevant form is Form N244.

In all cases, the application must be supported by one or more affidavits containing all the evidence relied upon.

Committal proceedings begun by arrest under a power of arrest

The power to arrest for breach of an occupation order granted under FLA 1996, s 47(3) provides the police with authority to intervene and stop a breach while it is happening or where they have reason to believe that such a breach has occurred. A power of arrest can also be exercised after the disobedience has ended and after an arrest for a criminal offence (*Wheeldon v Wheeldon* [1998] 1 FLR 463, CA). Where the police use the civil power of arrest the arrested person must be brought before the civil court within 24 hours (FLA 1996, s 47(7)). Breach of a non-molestation order in Form FL404A made after 30 June 2007 is a criminal offence in respect of which the police may use their criminal powers of arrest.

There is no power to attach a power of arrest to an injunction under the PHA 1997 or at common law. Further, as from 1 July 2007, the power of arrest is abolished for non-molestation orders (see FLA 1996, s 42A).

Committal proceedings begun by arrest under a warrant of arrest

FLA 1996, s 47(8),(9) extended to the High Court and County Court a power to issue a warrant of arrest. This power is available where no power of arrest was attached to the breached direction (s 47(8)). The court can issue a warrant for the arrest of a person where the court has reasonable grounds, substantiated on oath (s 47(9)), to believe that he has failed to comply with a non-molestation or occupation order made under FLA 1996, Pt IV.

PHA 1997, s 3(3)–(5) provides the High Court and County Court with the power to issue a warrant of arrest where the court has reasonable grounds, substantiated on oath (s 3(5)), to believe that the respondent has failed to comply with an injunction which forbids harassment.

Since 16 June 2014, forced marriage is a criminal offence and the power of arrest on a FMPO is abolished. However, the courts' power to issue a warrant of arrest is retained (see FLA 1996, s 63J). Application is in Form FL407A accompanied by a sworn statement.

Remand following arrest

Once an arrested respondent is before the court, the court can immediately deal with the breach for which he has been arrested or adjourn (whether or not upon enlarged injunctive provisions). If adjourning, the court may remand. In FLA 1996 cases the power to remand is given to the High Court and County Court by s 47(11) and Sch 5, and exists in a magistrates' court by virtue of MCA 1980, ss 128 and 129. The remand can be in custody or on bail. Under FLA 1996, s 48, the power to remand can be exercised to enable a medical report to be made on the respondent.

There is no power to remand under PHA 1997.

Conduct of committal proceedings where the respondent is before the court following an arrest – preliminaries

Where a respondent is before the court for an alleged breach of an injunction, in order to ensure a fair trial there are essential preliminaries which the judge will consider. Is the respondent before the court within 24 hours of the arrest and is a lawful arrest admitted or proved? Is there proof of service of the injunction? Have the alleged breaches been reduced to writing and is Form N78 required? Is the respondent legally represented and, if not, is an adjournment sought to obtain it or to prepare? Is it appreciated that legal aid may be available? Is the applicant present or represented and, if not, is an adjournment required? If adjourning, what directions are required and should the respondent be remanded? If remanded, should it be on bail or in custody?

An arrest is effected on the basis of a particular alleged breach. Earlier breaches cannot be dealt with unless Form N78 is also served (see FPR 2010, r 10.11 and, in the case of PHA 1997, CPR 1998, r 65.29).

Conduct of committal proceedings when the respondent is before the court, whether on notice or following an arrest

Whether the respondent appears on notice in answer to a notice to show good reason, or following an arrest, the procedure to be followed for the determination of whether the respondent has disobeyed an order or breached an undertaking, and the disposal powers of the court, are the same. The breach must be proved to the criminal standard of proof. Thus, if not admitted, the applicant's evidence is heard first.

Absence of respondent

Provided that the court is satisfied that the respondent has been duly served, and has had the opportunity to obtain legal advice, the court can proceed in his absence. In *Begum v Anam* [2004] EWCA Civ 578 a committal order was set aside as the respondent had not had the opportunity to obtain legal representation nor to arrange a production warrant to secure his attendance from prison.

Penalties

The court can order imprisonment (immediate or suspended) and/or a fine, or adjourn consideration of penalty for a fixed period and/or extend or enlarge the injunction. (The common disposal orders are set out in County Court Form N79.) For the differing powers of judges of the Family Court, see the Family Court (Contempt of Court) (Powers) Regulations 2014 and commentary thereon.

PART I

Procedure

Preliminary matters	An injunctive order must be served personally on the person to whom it is directed, unless there has been an order for substituted service or dispensing with service	CPR 1998, r 81.5 (civil); FPR 2010, r 37.5 (family)
	However, pending service, if the respondent disobeys an injunctive order which requires him to abstain from doing an act, the court can impose a penalty if it is satisfied that he knew about the terms of the order	CPR 1998, r 81.8 (civil); FPR 2010, r 37.8 (family)
	Proof of service of the order is required. In all courts this is usually by Form FL415. Service should be effected in accordance with the Protocol	Family Justice Council *Protocol for Process Servers*, November 2011
	A mandatory injunctive order directing a person to do an act cannot be enforced unless it was served before the time at or by which the act was directed to be done	CPR 1998, r 81.5 (civil); FPR 2010, r 37.5 (family)
	An undertaking becomes enforceable on being given to and accepted by the court; however, the court can require the giver to sign a statement to the effect that he understands the terms of his undertaking and the consequences of failure to comply with it	*Hussain v Hussain* [1986] 2 FLR 271, CA; CPR PD81, para 2.2
	A copy of the undertaking is required to be delivered to the giver of the undertaking, but the giver is bound even if it is not	CPR 1998, r 81.7 (civil); FPR 2010, r 37.7 (family)
Who may apply for committal or enforcement?	Person in whose favour the injunctive order was granted or the undertaking was given	CPR 1998, r 81.3 (civil); FPR 2010, r 37.3 (family)
Which court?	The court which granted the injunctive order or accepted the undertaking	CPR PD81, para 10 (civil); FPR 2010, r 37.10 (family)
	The powers of the County Court to deal with disobedience or breach are the same as the High Court	CCA 1981; CCA 1984, s 38
	Lay justices' statutory powers to deal with disobedience or breach are limited to imposing immediate or suspended committal, fine or adjourning consideration of penalty	Family Court (Contempt of Court) (Powers) Regulations 2014
Application (family proceedings)	Application is made using the Pt 18 procedure	FPR 2010, r 37.10
	In every case, the summons or notice must 'identify, separately and numerically, each alleged act of contempt'	FPR 2010, r 37.10(3)
Committal applications (civil proceedings)	Application under CPR 1998, Pt 23, supported by affidavit	CPR 1998, r 81.10
Committal applications (general)	The affidavit or statement in support should narrate the facts relied on, but the list of alleged breaches *must* be given in the application notice; it is insufficient for the notice to say 'see affidavit'	CPR 1998, r 81.10 (civil); FPR 2010, r 37.10 (family); *Harmsworth v Harmsworth* [1988] 1 FLR 349, CA, at [354D]–[355B]
Fee	Fee on application in the Family Court: £155	FPFO 2008, fee 5.3
Application for warrant of arrest under FLA 1996, s 47(8) or s 63J	Application is made, without notice to the respondent, in Form FL407 (or Form FL407A for FMPO), to 'the relevant judicial authority', i e the convenient hearing centre in whichever tier of court the injunctive order was granted	FLA 1996, ss 47(8), 63(1) and 63J

	The application must be substantiated on oath and the court must have reasonable grounds for believing that the respondent has failed to comply with an order, or part of an order to which no power of arrest had been attached	FLA 1996, ss 47(9), 63J
	Breach of a non-molestation order is a criminal offence. However, the respondent cannot be both punished for a criminal offence and a contempt of court for the same breach. An application for a warrant of arrest to a civil court should confirm that there is no conviction	FLA 1996, s 42A(3),(4)
	The warrant is executed in the High Court by the Tipstaff, in the County Court by the bailiffs (or, in each case, by the police on request), and in the magistrates' court by the police	Form FL408
	In the magistrates' court the justices' clerk is responsible for delivering the warrant to the police	
Application for warrant of arrest under PHA 1997, s 3(3)	Application must be made in accordance with CPR Pt 23 and may be made without notice	PHA 1997, s 3(4); CPR 1998, r 65.29
	The application must be supported by affidavit evidence setting out the grounds for the application and state whether the claimant has informed the police and whether criminal proceedings are being pursued	PHA 1997, s 3(5); CPR 1998, r 65.29
Production in court following arrest under FLA 1996, s 47	A person arrested under a power of arrest must be brought before the relevant judicial authority within 24 hours not including Sunday, Christmas Day or Good Friday	FLA 1996, s 47(7)
	Neither FLA 1996 nor the rules prescribe how soon a person arrested under a warrant of arrest must be brought before the court. Nevertheless it must be as soon as practicable	FLA 1996, s 47(8)–(10)
Procedures open to court under FLA 1996, ss 47, 48 when arrested person produced in court	The court may hear the facts upon which the arrest was based, and decide penalty or adjourn, in which case the respondent must be given not less than 2 days' notice of the adjourned hearing, or	FLA 1996, s 47(7)(b), (10); FPR 2010, r 10.11(3)
	remand in custody for a period not exceeding 8 days or	FLA 1996, s 47(11), Sch 5 para 2(5)
	remand on bail on conditions and/or recognisances	FLA 1996, s 47(11),(12), Sch 5 para 2(5)
	where the court has reason to suspect mental illness or severe mental impairment, the court may remand, to enable a medical examination and report, for not more than 3 weeks if in custody or 4 weeks if on bail	FLA 1996, s 48
Powers of court under PHA 1997, s 3(5) when arrested person produced in court	The court may hear the facts upon which the arrest was based, and decide penalty, or adjourn for not more than 28 days, in which case the defendant must be given not less than 2 days' notice of the adjourned hearing	CPR 1998, r 65.30
Hearing without notice to the respondent	In exceptional circumstances, the court may, without notice having been given to the respondent, deal with an application begun by notice to show good reason, by dispensing with service of the summons or notice	CPR 1998, rr 39.3, 81.28 (civil); FPR 2010, r 37.27 (family)

	It is not appropriate for a court to proceed without notice where arrest under a power or warrant can be achieved under FLA 1996, s 47, or under PHA 1997, s 3(5). However, where a power or warrant of arrest is not available, proceeding without notice may exceptionally be appropriate. When the court takes this exceptional step and imposes imprisonment, the court should fix a date and time for the contemnor to be brought before the court	CPR 1998, r 81.28 (civil), FPR 2010, r 37.27 (family)
Service of application to commit	Personal service of the application is required In both family and civil proceedings, a period of 14 clear days after service is required unless the court directs otherwise by using its powers to abridge time for service In exceptional cases, the court can dispense with service	FPR 2010, r 37.27 CPR PD81, para 15.2 (civil); FPR PD37A, para 12.2 (family) see Hearing without notice to the respondent (above)
Service of notice of adjourned hearing	Where a hearing is adjourned, personal service of notice of the adjourned hearing is required, unless the respondent was present in court and was told when and where the adjourned hearing would resume and/or was remanded under FLA 1996, s 47(7),(10), Sch 5	*Chiltern DC v Keane* [1985] 1 WLR 619, at [622H]–[623C]
Case management	The court can make directions at any time as to service of evidence and conduct of the proceedings, or strike out an inappropriate application	CPR PD81, paras 15, 16 (civil); FPR PD37A, para 12.3 (family)
The hearing	District Judges as well as High Court and Circuit Judges have power to hear committal proceedings under FLA 1996, Parts 4 and 4A However District Judges do not have power to hear committal proceedings under PHA 1997 Normally held in open court If it is just to do so, the court can proceed if the respondent, having been duly served, fails to attend Procedure is akin to criminal trial. The criminal standard of proof ('beyond reasonable doubt') applies An application notice can be amended with the permission of the court but not otherwise An alleged contemnor cannot be directed or compelled to give information A deliberate act or failure to act (actus reus) with knowledge of the terms of the order (mens rea) must be proved An unmeritorious application to commit can result in an adverse costs order against the applicant	FLA 1996, ss 58, 63(1), 63O, 63S; Family Court (Contempt of Court) (Powers) Regulations 2014 PHA 1997, s 3(3), (4) only gives power to issue a warrant; CPR PD81, para 10.2(2) CPR 1998, rr 39.2, 81.28 (civil); Practice Direction of 26 March 2015 (family) *Begum v Anam* [2004] EWCA Civ 578; CPR 1998, r 39.3 *Re J (Children)* [2016] 2 FLR 1207, CA CPR PD81, paras 12(2), 13.2(2) (civil); FPR 2010, r 37.27 (family) CPR 1998, r 81.28 (civil); FPR 2010, r 37.27(3) *DG of Fair Trading v Smiths Concrete* [1992] QB 213, CA *PJSC Vseukrainskyi v Aktsionernyi Bank* [2014] EWHC 3771 (Comm)

Legal aid	Committal proceedings, although technically civil proceedings, are treated as criminal proceedings for the purposes of ECHR, Art 6. Consequently, persons in danger of losing their liberty are, subject to means, eligible for legal aid. (Contempt in the face of the court is separately dealt with in LASPOA 2012, s 14(g))	LASPOA 2012, Schs 1 and 3; Lord Chancellor's Guidance under s 4; *Chelmsford County Court v Ramet* [2014] 2 FLR 1081, FD
	The Court of Appeal has given detailed guidance on how legal aid is obtained in committal proceedings	*Brown v London Borough of Haringey* [2015] EWCA Civ 483
Powers of court	The disposal must be proportionate to the seriousness of the contempt, reflect the court's disapproval and be designed to secure compliance in future. The principles of sentencing in the CJA 2003 apply. The judge cannot sentence again for matters already dealt with by the criminal court. The court should briefly explain its reasons for the choice of disposal	*Murray v Robinson* [2006] 1 FLR 365, CA; *Hale v Tanner* [2000] 2 FLR 879, CA; *Lomas v Parle* [2004] 1 FLR 812, CA; *Slade v Slade* [2010] 1 FLR 160, CA
	Committal to prison is appropriate only where no reasonable alternative exists	*Hale v Tanner* (above)
	Imprisonment is restricted to total of 2 years in the High Court and the County Court, 2 months in a magistrates' court, and must be for a fixed term	CCA 1981, s 14; MCA 1980, s 63(3); Family Court (Contempt of Court) (Powers) Regulations 2014
	Sentence can be suspended or adjourned on terms	CPR 1998, r 81.29 (civil); FPR 2010, r 37.28 (family)
	Any time spent on remand in custody must be taken into account in the sentence	*Kerai v Patel* [2008] 2 FLR 2137, CA
	Person under the age of 21 can be detained under Powers of Criminal Courts (Sentencing) Act 2000, s 96	*R v Selby Justices ex parte Frame* [1992] QB 72, QBD
	Person under the age of 18 cannot be committed to any form of detention for contempt of court (but could be prosecuted for breach of a non-molestation order)	*R v Selby Justices* (above); FLA 1996, s 42A
	MHA powers are available	CCA 1981, s 14; MHA 1983, ss 35, 37, 38
	Fine can be imposed	*Hale v Tanner* [2000] 2 FLR 879, CA
	Sequestration is available only in the High Court	CPR 1998, rr 81.19–81.27, CPR PD81, paras 6, 7 (civil); FPR 2010, r 37.25 (family)
Form of order	The order must specify 'exact details' of each contempt found proved and specify the disposal ordered	*Nguyen v Phung* [1984] FLR 773, CA, at [778C]; *Re C (A Minor) (Contempt)* [1986] 1 FLR 578, CA, at [585A]
	Where sentence is suspended or adjourned, the period of suspension or adjournment and the precise terms for activation must be specified	*Pidduck v Molloy* [1992] 2 FLR 202, CA; CPR 1998, r 81.29 (civil), FPR 2010, r 37.28 (family)
	In the High Court, the order is issued in Form A85 and warrant in Form PF303. In the County Court, Form N79 and warrant in Form N80. In a magistrates' court, Form FL419 and warrant in Form FL420	

Service of order	Where immediate imprisonment or detention is imposed, the court serves the order	CPR 1998, rr 6.21(2), 81.30 (civil); FPR 2010, r 37.29 (family); *Clarke v Clarke* [1990] 2 FLR 115, CA
	Where sentence is suspended, the applicant must serve the order, unless the court directs otherwise	CPR 1998, r 81.29(2) (civil); FPR 2010, r 37.28 (family)
Review by Official Solicitor	The court sends a copy of every committal order and relevant details to the Official Solicitor, who reviews the case and may apply or appeal of his own motion or at the contemnor's request	*Lord Chancellor's Direction of 29 May 1963*; *Secretary's Circular of 28 September 1981*
Discharge of contemnor	A contemnor is entitled to apply to purge his contempt and be discharged from prison	CPR 1998, r 81.31 (civil); FPR 2010, r 37.30 (family)
	The application should be made in accordance with CPR 1998, Pt 23 or FPR 2010, Pt 18 but in practice a letter from the contemnor usually suffices	*CJ v Flintshire Borough Council* [2010] 2 FLR 1224, CA
	If the committal was made in civil proceedings, the application notice must be served as soon as practicable after it is filed and at least 3 days before the hearing. If made in family proceedings, the application must be served at least 7 days before the hearing	CPR 1998, r 23.7(1) (civil); FPR 2010, r 18.8
	The contemnor should be in court	*PD of 25 July 1983*
	On an application to purge, the court can say 'yes', 'no' or 'not yet' but may not suspend the remainder of the sentence	*Harris v Harris* [2002] 1 FLR 248, CA
Appeals	See Guide E5	

D1: Consent to Marriage of a Minor

Legal background

MA 1949, s 3(1) and CPA 2004, Sch 2, paras 3, 4 and 10 set out a general rule that those under the age of 18, who are not widows or widowers, may not marry under a superintendent registrar's certificate or a common licence without the consent of the persons mentioned in MA 1949, s 3(1A) or CPA 2004, Sch 2, para 1 (usually the parents but with variations according to circumstances, e g where a child arrangements order is in force or the child is in care). The child can apply to the court if no-one is available to give consent or to give consent instead of any person whose consent is required and who refuses that consent. Application is made under the Pt 19 procedure under FPR 2010, Pt 8, Ch 9.

Procedure

Who may apply	The child who needs the consent to marry	MA 1949, s 3; CPA 2004, Sch 2
Which court	High Court or Family Court	MA 1949, s 3(1)(b),(5); CPA 2004, Sch 2, paras 3.3(3), 4(3), 10(1)
Application	By Pt 19 application Application may be made without litigation friend	FPR 2010, rr 8.1, 19.3 FPR 2010, r 8.42
Fee	£245	FPFO 2008, fee 1.1
Respondents	Those refusing consent in the case of an application under MA 1949, s 3(1)(b); CPA 2004, Sch 2, para 4(3)	FPR 2010, r 8.43

Service	Effected 7 days before the hearing (unless otherwise ordered) in the County Court or the High Court	FPR 2010, Pt 6
Hearing	High Court and County Court: district judge Magistrates Hearing in private	FPR 2010, r 27.10(1)

D2: Emergency Protection Order

Legal background

An emergency protection order (EPO) may be sought under CA 1989, s 44, to ensure the short-term safety of a child where it appears that the child may be at risk. It can authorise the applicant to remove a child from where he is (e g from his home) to a safe place or to keep him in a safe place (e g a hospital). The maximum duration of an order is generally 8 days in the first instance but there can be one extension for a maximum of 7 days (see CA 1989, s 45). The grounds for making an order differ according to the status of the applicant. All applicants may rely on the ground that there is reasonable cause to believe that the child is likely to suffer significant harm if he is not removed to accommodation provided by or on behalf of the applicant, or does not remain where he is.

Where the applicant is a local authority which is making enquiries under CA 1989, s 47(1)(b), about a child in its area, it can obtain an order on the alternative ground that the enquiries are being frustrated by access to the child being unreasonably refused to a person authorised to seek access to the child and that it has reasonable cause to believe that access to the child is urgently required. Where the applicant is an authorised person, an order can be made on the ground that the applicant is making enquiries into the welfare of a child whom he has reasonable cause to suspect is suffering or is likely to suffer significant harm, that the enquiries are being frustrated by access being unreasonably refused to a person authorised to seek access and that the applicant has reasonable cause to believe that access to the child is urgently required.

Various directions may be given at the same time as an EPO is made (for example, as to medical, psychiatric or other assessment of the child and as to contact with him) and, under CA 1989, s 48, supplementary provisions can also be included in the order requiring another person to disclose information as to the child's whereabouts, authorising the applicant to enter specified premises to search for the child or for another child and authorising a constable to assist in the execution of the EPO.

Section 44A enables the court to include an exclusion requirement in an EPO and to attach a power of arrest to that provision. The purpose of an exclusion requirement is to safeguard a child by removing from the scene (whether from the child's home or from part of it or from the area in which it is situated) a person who poses a threat to the child.

There is no right of appeal against the grant of, or the refusal to grant, an emergency protection order. Accordingly, it is wrong for the court to refuse to list an application for an interim care order following a refusal to grant an emergency protection order. The local authority may wish to apply for an interim care order, in respect of which there is an avenue of appeal. A refusal to list, hear and determine an interim care application will deny the local authority a right of appeal (*Re B-C (A Child)* [2016] EWCA Civ 970).

An emergency protection order is a draconian measure and reference should be made to the guidance on the use of EPOs given in *X Council v B (Emergency Protection Orders)* [2005] 1 FLR 341, FD and *Re X (Emergency Protection Orders)* [2006] 2 FLR 701, FD. There is no appeal against the grant of or refusal to grant an EPO, but, if an order is made, an application to discharge it may be possible.

The PLO in FPR PD12A applies only to proceedings brought under Pt IV of CA 1989, which proceedings do not include an application for an emergency protection order. In the circumstances, the PLO in PD12A will not apply to emergency protection order proceedings (PD12A). However, pursuant to FPR 2010, r 12.22, the court remains under an obligation to draw up a timetable or revise that timetable with a view to disposing of the application without delay and in any event within 26 weeks beginning with the date on which the application is issued. Where the application for an EPO is granted and is then followed immediately by the commencement of Pt IV proceedings, the PLO in FPR PD12A will apply to the Pt IV proceedings.

Procedure

Who may apply	Any person including a local authority or an authorised person such as the NSPCC or a designated police officer	CA 1989, ss 44(1), 46(7)

Which court	The Family Court. The application will be allocated to the first available judge of the Family Court who is authorised to conduct emergency applications	FC(CDB)R 2014, r 16(2),(3)(a)(iii); FPR 2010, r 12.2(c)
	Where the application has been allocated without a hearing, a party may request the court to reconsider allocation at a hearing. The court may also reconsider allocation of its own initiative	FPR 2010, r 29.19
	A Family Court may transfer a case to another Family Court either of its own initiative or on the application of one of the parties	FPR 2010, r 29.17
	An application may be made for existing proceedings to be heard in a different Designated Family Judge area	FPR 2010, r 29.18
	The case may not be transferred to the High Court unless by order of a judge sitting in the Family Court who is either the President of the Family Division, a judge of the Court of Appeal or a High Court Judge or where the circumstances in PD29C apply	FPR 2010, r 29.17(3), (4); PD29C
Which proceedings	Freestanding application	CA 1989, ss 44(1), 46(7)
	EPO can be made on application for child assessment order	CA 1989, s 43(3),(4)
Application	On Form C110A with copies for each respondent; see below for without notice applications	FPR PD5A
	Fee: £215	FPFO 2008, fee 2.1(o)
Respondents	Every person whom applicant believes has parental responsibility Every person whom applicant believes had parental responsibility before care order The child	FPR 2010, r 12.3
Additional persons to whom notice in Form C6A is to be given	Local authority providing accommodation for child Persons caring for child at commencement of proceedings Person providing a CA 1989, s 51 refuge for child Every person whom applicant believes is a parent	FPR PD12C, para 3.1
Service	Copy of application to be served on respondents at least 1 day before date of hearing or directions appointment	FPR PD12C
	Form C6A to be served on additional persons at same time as application etc served on respondents	FPR PD12C, para 3.1
	At or before first directions appointment or hearing, applicant must file statement in Form C9 to prove that requirements for service have been complied with	FPR PD5A; PD12A
Without notice	Permitted. Where the application is made by telephone, file Form C110A the next business day after application or, in any other case, at time application is made	FPR 2010, r 12.16; PD12E
	The applicant must serve a copy of the application on each respondent within 48 hours after the order is made together with a copy of the order	FPR 2010, r 12.16; PD12E

Joinder or removal of parties	By court order, of its own initiative or on written request	FPR 2010, rr 4.3, 12.3(3)
Directions	Powers of the Family Court	FPR 2010, rr 12.12, 12.23, 12.24
Children's guardian	Must normally be appointed	CA 1989, s 41(1)
Who has power to make the order	Any judge of the Family Court	FC(CDB)R 2014, r 16(1), (3)(a)(iii)
	A single lay justice may grant an EPO without notice	CA 1989, s 93(2)(i); FPR 2010, r 2.6(1)(a)
	A justices' clerk has no such power	JCAR 2014
Order	The order must, wherever reasonably practicable, name the child or describe him as clearly as possible)	CA 1989, s 44(14)
	If without notice, applicant to serve copy within 48 hours after making of order on: – each party – any person with actual care of child or who had actual care immediately before order – local authority in whose area child lives or is found	FPR 2010, r 12.16(5)
Additional or alternative orders	No order	CA 1989, s 1(5)
Procedure for exclusion requirements	Applicant for EPO prepares separate statement of evidence in support re: exclusion requirement Applicant serves statement and copy of order containing exclusion requirement (and of any power of arrest attached) personally on relevant person (ie person who is excluded) and informs relevant person of right to apply to vary/discharge exclusion requirement. It is important when effecting service that the process server complies with the Family Justice Council *Protocol for Process Servers*	CA 1989, s 44A; FPR 2010, r 12.28(2); FJC Protocol of November 2011: *Process Servers: Non-Molestation Orders*
	If power of arrest attached, once relevant person served with order/informed of terms, copy of order shall be delivered to police together with statement showing relevant person served/informed of terms	FPR 2010, r 12.28(3); FJC Protocol of November 2011: *Process Servers: Non-Molestation Orders*
	Unless relevant person given notice and attended hearing, if power of arrest attached to exclusion order, court must announce in open court at earliest opportunity the name of person and fact that such order made	FPR PD12K
	Consent of person who is assuming care of child is required	CA 1989, s 44A(2); FPR 2010, r 12.29
Appeals	None possible	CA 1989, s 45(10)
Transitional arrangements	Implementation of CFA 2014	Children and Families Act 2014 (Transitional Proceedings) Order 2014

D3: Discharge of an Emergency Protection Order

Legal background

CA 1989, s 45(8) enables an application to be made for the discharge of an emergency protection order (EPO). However, there are two exceptions where: (a) the person who wishes to apply for the discharge was given due notice of the hearing at which the original order was made and was present at the hearing, and (b) the period of the EPO has been extended (CA 1989, s 45(11)). The CYPA 2008 repealed CA 1989, s 45(9), thereby removing the prohibition on applying to discharge the EPO before the expiry of 72 hours from the making of the original order.

Section 45(8A), (8B) deals with applications to vary or discharge an EPO insofar as it imposes an exclusion requirement, or to vary or discharge the attendant power of arrest. The PLO in FPR PD12A applies only to proceedings brought under Pt IV of the CA 1989, which proceedings do not include an application for an emergency protection order. In the circumstances, the PLO in PD12A will not apply to emergency protection order proceedings (PD12A). However, pursuant to FPR 2010, r 12.22, the court remains under an obligation to draw up a timetable or revise that timetable with a view to disposing of the application without delay and in any event within 26 weeks beginning with the date on which the application is issued.

Procedure

Who may apply	The child A parent Any person with parental responsibility Any person with whom the child was living immediately before the emergency protection order was made	CA 1989, s 45(8)
Which court	The Family Court. An application made within existing proceedings in the Family Court will be allocated to the level of judge who is dealing with the existing proceedings to which the application relates Where the application has been allocated without a hearing, a party may request the court to reconsider allocation at a hearing. The court may also reconsider allocation of its own initiative A Family Court may transfer a case to another Family Court either of its own initiative or on the application of one of the parties An application may be made for existing proceedings to be heard in a different Designated Family Judge area The application may not be transferred to the High Court unless by order of a judge sitting in the Family Court who is either the President of the Family Division, a judge of the Court of Appeal or a High Court Judge or where the circumstances in FPR PD29C apply	FC(CDB)R 2014, r 17(1); FPR 2010, r 12.2(f) FPR 2010, r 29.19 FPR 2010, r 29.17 FPR 2010, r 29.18 FPR 2010, r 29.17(3),(4); PD29C
Which proceedings	Freestanding application	CA 1989, s 45(8)
Application	On Form C2, with copies for each respondent	FPR PD5A
Fee	£215	FPFO 2008, fee 2.1(o)
Respondents	Every person whom applicant believes has parental responsibility Every person whom applicant believes had parental responsibility before care order The child The parties to the original proceedings	FPR 2010, r 12.3
Additional persons to whom notice in Form C6A is to be given	Local authority providing accommodation for child Persons caring for child at commencement of proceedings Person providing a CA 1989, s 51 refuge for child	FPR PD12C, para 3.1

Service	Copy of application, together with Form C6A, to be served on respondents at least 1 day before date of hearing or directions appointment	FPR PD12C
	Form C6A to be served on additional persons at same time as application etc served on respondents	FPR PD12C, para 3.1
	At or before first directions appointment or hearing, applicant must file statement in Form C9 to prove that requirements for service have been complied with	FPR PD5A; PD12A
Without notice	Permitted. Where the application is made by telephone, file Form C110A the next business day after application or, in any other case, at time application is made	FPR 2010, r 12.16; PD12E
	The applicant must serve a copy of the application on each respondent within 48 hours after the order is made, together with a copy of the order	FPR 2010, r 12.16; PD12E
Joinder or removal of parties	By court order, of its own initiative or on written request	FPR 2010, r 4.3, 12.3(3)
Answer to application	Respondent may file an answer; serve on other parties	FPR PD12A
Directions	Powers of the Family Court	FPR 2010, rr 12.12, 12.23, 12.24
Children's guardian	Must normally be appointed	CA 1989, s 41(1)
Special requirements	No application allowed where applicant had proper notice of original application and was present at the hearing or where EPO has already been extended	CA 1989, s 45(11)
Who has power to make the order	Any judge of the Family Court	FC(CDB)R 2014, r 16(1), (3)(a)(vi)
	A justices' clerk or single lay justice has no such power	JCAR 2014; CA 1989, s 93(2)(i); FPR 2010, r 2.6
Procedure for variation/ discharge of exclusion requirements and attendant power of arrest	Application for variation/discharge re: exclusion requirement or re: power of arrest by person to whom it applies, Form C2 suggested	CA 1989, s 45(8A),(8B)
	Applicant serves parties to the proceedings with application for variation/discharge	FPR 2010, r 12.28(5)
	Consider giving notice to person caring for child	FPR 2010, r 12.28(5)
	Steps to be taken on variation/discharge affecting exclusion requirement/power of arrest	FPR 2010, r 12.28(4),(6)
Appeals	None possible	CA 1989, s 45(10)
Transitional arrangements	Implementation of CFA 2014	Children and Families Act 2014 (Transitional Proceedings) Order 2014

D4: Extension of an Emergency Protection Order, Warrant under Children Act 1989, s 48(9) or Variation of Directions as to Contact or Assessment under Children Act 1989, s 44(9)(b)

Legal background

An emergency protection order (EPO) can be extended once for a period not exceeding 7 days if the court has reasonable cause to believe that the child concerned is likely to suffer significant harm if the order is not extended (CA 1989, s 45(4)–(6)). Where a person is attempting to exercise powers under an EPO and has been prevented from doing so by being refused entry to the premises concerned or access to the child concerned or is likely to be so prevented, the court may issue a warrant authorising a constable to give assistance, using reasonable force if necessary (CA 1989, s 48(9)).

When making an EPO or at any time while such an order is in force, the court may give directions under CA 1989, s 44(6) with respect to contact with the child concerned and as to medical or psychiatric examination or other assessment of him. Application may be made at any time under CA 1989, s 44(9) for such directions to be varied.

The PLO in FPR PD12A applies only to proceedings brought under Pt IV of the CA 1989, which proceedings do not include an application for an emergency protection order. In the circumstances, the PLO in PD12A will not apply to emergency protection order proceedings (PD12A). However, pursuant to FPR 2010, r 12.22, the court remains under an obligation to draw up a timetable or revise that timetable with a view to disposing of the application without delay and in any event within 26 weeks beginning with the date on which the application is issued.

Procedure

Who may apply	*Extension of EPO* Any person who has parental responsibility as a result of an EPO and is entitled to apply for a care order	CA 1989, s 45(4)
	CA 1989, s 48(9) warrant Any person	CA 1989, s 48(9)
	CA 1989, s 44(9)(b) variation Parties to original application Children's guardian Local authority in whose area child is ordinarily resident Anyone named in the directions	CA 1989, s 44(9); FPR 2010, r 12.3
Which court	The Family Court. The application will be allocated to the first available judge of the Family Court who is authorised to conduct emergency applications. An application made within existing proceedings in the Family Court will be allocated to the level of judge who is dealing with the existing proceedings to which the application relates	FC(CDB)R 2014, rr 16(3)(a)(ix), 17(1); FPR 2010, r 12.2(d), (e),(i)
	Where the application has been allocated without a hearing, a party may request the court to reconsider allocation at a hearing. The court may also reconsider allocation of its own initiative	FPR 2010, r 29.19
	A Family Court may transfer a case to another Family Court either of its own initiative or on the application of one of the parties	FPR 2010, r 29.17
	An application may be made for existing proceedings to be heard in a different Designated Family Judge area	FPR 2010, r 29.18

	The application may not be transferred to the High Court unless by order of a judge sitting in the Family Court who is either the President of the Family Division, a judge of the Court of Appeal or a High Court Judge or where the circumstances in PD29C apply	FPR 2010, r 29.17(3),(4); PD29C
Which proceedings	Freestanding application	CA 1989, ss 44(9), 45(4), 48(9)
Application	*Extension of EPO* On Form C2, with copies for each respondent Fee: £215 *CA 1989, s 48(9) warrant* On Form C2 and Supplement Form C12 (naming child wherever reasonably practicable or describing him as clearly as possible), with copies for each respondent Fee: £215 *CA 1989, s 44(9)(b) variation* On Form C2, with copies for each respondent Fee: £215	FPR PD5A FPFO 2008, fee 2.1(o) CA 1989, s 48(13); FPR PD5A FPFO 2008, fee 2.1(p) FPR PD5A FPFO 2008, fee 2.1(o)
Respondents	*In all cases* Every person whom applicant believes has parental responsibility Every person whom applicant believes had parental responsibility before care order The child AND *Extension of EPO or CA 1989, s 44(9)(b) variation* The parties to the original EPO proceedings *CA 1989, s 44(9)(b) variation* Any person who was caring for child before making of the order Any person whose contact with child is affected by the direction which is to be varied	FPR 2010, r 12.3
Additional persons to whom notice is to be given	*In all cases* Local authority providing accommodation for child Persons caring for child at commencement of proceedings Person providing a CA 1989, s 51 refuge for child AND *CA 1989, s 44(9)(b) variation* Local authority in whose area child is living Any person whom applicant believes is affected by the direction which is to be varied	FPR PD12C, para 3.1
Service	Copy of application, together with Form C6A, to be served on respondents at least 1 day before date of hearing or directions appointment Form C6A to be served on additional persons at same time as application etc served on respondents At or before first directions appointment or hearing, applicant must file statement in Form C9 to prove that requirements for service have been complied with	FPR PD12C, para 2.1 FPR PD12C FPR PD5A; PD12A

Without notice	*Extension of EPO or CA 1989, s 44(9)(b) variation* Permitted (see definition of 'emergency proceedings' in FPR 2010, r 12.2). Where the application is made by telephone, file Form C110A the next business day after application or, in any other case, at time application is made The applicant must serve a copy of the application on each respondent within 48 hours after the order is made, together with a copy of the order	FPR 2010, r 12.16; PD12E
	CA 1989, s 48(9) warrant Permitted. Where the application is made by telephone, file Form C110A the next business day after application or, in any other case, at time application is made The applicant must serve a copy of the application on each respondent within 48 hours after the order is made, together with a copy of the order	FPR 2010, r 12.16; PD5A
Joinder or removal of parties	By court order, of its own initiative or on written request	FPR 2010, rr 4.3, 12.13(3)
Answer to application	Respondent may file an answer; serve on other parties	FPR PD12A
Directions	Powers of the Family Court	FPR 2010, rr 12.12, 12.23, 12.24
Children's guardian	Must normally be appointed	CA 1989, s 41(1)
Who has power to make the order	Any judge of the Family Court	FC(CDB)R 2014, rr 16(1), (3)(a)(iv), (ix)
	A single lay justice may grant a without notice warrant under CA 1989, s 48(9) and variation under s 44(9)(b), but may not extend an EPO	CA 1989, s 93(2)(i); FPR 2010, r 2.6(1)(c)
	A justices' clerk has no such power	JCAR 2014
Order	*Extension of EPO* *CA 1989, s 48(9) warrant* Order naming child wherever reasonably practicable or describing him as clearly as possible. If without notice, applicant must serve copy, within 48 hours of making of order, on each party, on any person with actual care of child or who had actual care immediately before order and on the local authority in whose area the child lives or is found	CA 1989, s 48(13)
	CA 1989, s 44(9)(b) variation	FPR PD12A
Appeals	*Extension of EPO or CA 1989, s 44(9)(b) variation* None permitted	CA 1989, s 45(10)
	CA 1989, s 48(9) warrant See Guides E2, E4 and E5	
Transitional arrangements	Implementation of CFA 2014	Children and Families Act 2014 (Transitional Proceedings) Order 2014

D5: Recovery Order

Legal background

Where it appears to the court that there is reason to believe that a child who is in care or is the subject of an emergency protection order or is in police protection, is missing or has been unlawfully taken or kept away or has run away or is staying away from the person who has care of him under the care order etc, it may make a recovery order under CA 1989, s 50. The order has the following effects: (a) it operates as a direction to any person who is in a position to do so to produce the child to any authorised person on request; (b) it authorises any authorised person to remove the child; (c) it requires any person who has information as to the child's whereabouts to disclose that information, if asked to do so, to a constable or an officer of the court; and (d) it authorises a constable to enter any premises specified in the order and search for the child, using reasonable force if necessary. A recovery order is open-ended, remaining in force until it is discharged or until the child is recovered. The PLO in FPR PD12A applies only to proceedings brought under Pt IV of CA 1989, which proceedings do not include an application for a recovery order. In the circumstances, the PLO in PD12A will not apply to recovery order proceedings (PD12A).However, pursuant to FPR 2010 r 12.22, the court remains under an obligation to draw up a timetable or revise that timetable with a view to disposing of the application without delay and in any event within 26 weeks beginning with the date on which the application is issued.

Procedure

Who may apply	Any person with parental responsibility for child by virtue of care order or emergency protection order Where child is in police protection, designated officer	CA 1989, s 50(4)
Which court	The Family Court. The application will be allocated to the first available judge of the Family Court who is authorised to conduct emergency applications	FC(CDB)R 2014, rr 16(2), (3)(a)(x)
	Where the application has been allocated without a hearing, a party may request the court to reconsider allocation at a hearing. The court may also reconsider allocation of its own initiative	FPR 2010, r 29.19
	A Family Court may transfer a case to another Family Court either of its own initiative or on the application of one of the parties	FPR 2010, r 29.17
	An application may be made for existing proceedings to be heard in a different Designated Family Judge area	FPR 2010, r 29.18
	The application may not be transferred to the High Court unless by order of a judge sitting in the Family Court who is either the President of the Family Division, a judge of the Court of Appeal or a High Court Judge or where the circumstances in PD29C apply	FPR 2010, r 29.17(3); PD29C
Which proceedings	Freestanding application	CA 1989, s 50(4)
Application	On Form C1 and Supplement Form C18, with sufficient copies for each respondent; see below for without notice applications	FPR PD5A
	Fee: £215	FPFO 2008, fee 2.1(q)
Respondents	Every person whom applicant believes has parental responsibility Every person whom applicant believes had parental responsibility before care order The child Person whom applicant alleges to have effected, or to have been or to be responsible for, taking or keeping of child	FPR 2010, r 12.3

Additional persons to whom notice is to be given	Local authority providing accommodation for child Persons caring for child at commencement of proceedings Person providing a CA 1989, s 51 refuge for child	FPR PD12C, para 3.1
Service	Copy of application, together with Form C6A, to be served on respondents at least 1 day before date of hearing or directions appointment	FPR PD12C
	Form C6A to be served on additional persons at same time as application etc served on respondents	FPR PD12C, para 3.1
	At or before first directions appointment or hearing, applicant must file statement in Form C9 to prove that requirements for service have been complied with	FPR PD5A
Without notice	Permitted (see definition of 'emergency proceedings' in FPR 2010, r 12.2). Where the application is made by telephone, file Form C110A the next business day after application or, in any other case, at time application is made The applicant must serve a copy of the application on each respondent within 48 hours after the order is made, together with a copy of the order	FPR 2010, r 12.16; PD12E
Joinder or removal of parties	By court order, of its own initiative or on written request	FPR 2010, rr 4.3, 12.3(3)
Directions	Powers of the Family Court	FPR 2010, rr 12.12, 12.23, 12.24
Children's guardian	Must normally be appointed	CA 1989, s 41(1)
Who has power to make the order	Any judge of the Family Court	FC(CDB)R 2014, rr 16(1), (3)(a)(x)
	A single lay justice may grant a without notice order	CA 1989, s 93(2)(i); FPR 2010, r 2.6(1)(a)
	A justices' clerk has no such power	JCAR 2014
Order	Order naming child and any person with parental responsibility by virtue of care order or emergency protection order or designated officer where child in police protection	CA 1989, s 50(5)
	If without notice, applicant to serve copy within 48 hours after making of order on: – every party – any person with actual care of child or who had actual care immediately before order – local authority in whose area child lives or is found	FPR 2010, r 12.16
Appeals	See Guides E2, E4 and E5	
Transitional arrangements	Implementation of CFA 2014	Children and Families Act 2014 (Transitional Proceedings) Order 2014

D6: Parental Responsibility Order or Agreement (or Discharge of the Same)

Legal background

Parental responsibility (PR) comprises all the rights, duties, powers, responsibilities and authority which, by law, a parent has in relation to a child and his property, or which a guardian of a child's estate has in relation to his property (CA 1989, s 3).

A child's mother always has PR for the child; however, if she was not married to the child's father at the time of the birth, the father will only acquire PR by marrying the mother, by making a formal PR agreement with her (using Form C(PRA1)) or by obtaining an order from the court (CA 1989, s 4, to be read in conjunction with FLRA 1987, s 1(2)) or if his name is placed on the birth certificate at registration or re-registration of the birth under the Births and Deaths Registration Act 1953 (see CA 1989, s 4(1)(a)). A step-parent may acquire PR for a child of his spouse or civil partner by agreement (using Form C(PRA2)), or by order of the court (CA 1989, s 4A). A second female parent may acquire responsibility for a child by agreement (using Form C(PRA3)) or by order of the court (CA 1989, s 4ZA).The court must make a PR order in favour of the father (or second female parent) with whom the child is to live under a CAO; it has a discretion as to whether or not to make a PR order where the child has contact with the father (or second female parent) under a CAO (CA 1989, s 12(1)) and care should therefore be taken to consider this requirement when making or opposing an interim CAO application; otherwise, it is in the court's discretion whether to grant a specific application under CA 1989, s 4.

Children and Families Act 2014 (CFA 2014)

The amendments made by CFA 2014 to CA 1989 have removed residence and contact orders and replaced them with child arrangements orders. There are consequential changes to the provisions in s 12 that deal with PR. See further under Guide D7 for details.

The CAP came into force on 22 April 2014 and replaced the Private Law Programme in FPR PD12B. It sets out the process that applies where a dispute arises between separated parents and/or families about the arrangements concerning children. On making an application to the court, the applicant should file a completed Form C1 and Form FM1 confirming attendance at a mediation information and assessment meeting or giving reasons for not attending where the circumstances fall within the exceptions set out in FPR 2010, r 3.8 and FPR PD3A, paras 17–21.

The court may subsequently discharge a PR order or a PR agreement (which may not be revoked merely by agreement).

Note that the 1996 Hague Convention came into force in the UK on 1 November 2012. Art 1 defines the meaning of 'parental responsibility' in cases to which the Convention applies. The definition is purposively broad and should be given an autonomous Convention meaning rather than its purely domestic law meaning. Arts 16–18 cover the attribution, extinction and exercise of parental responsibility in such cases. See commentary under the Convention.

Procedure

Who may apply	Father without parental responsibility	CA 1989, s 4(1)(a)
	The spouse or civil partner of a parent with parental responsibility	CA 1989, s 4A
	The second female parent of a child	CA 1989, s 4ZA; HFEA 2008, s 43
	Discharge of parental responsibility order or agreement:	
	Any person with parental responsibility	
	The child (with permission)	CA 1989, ss 4(3), 4A
Which court	The Family Court (lay justices) if none of criteria in Schedule to the *Guidance* apply	CA 1989, ss 10(1); FC(CDB)R 2014; President's Guidance *Allocation and Gatekeeping*
	Proceedings can be transferred sideways, upwards or downwards, using order in Form C49	FC(CDB)R 2014

Which proceedings	Freestanding application Court must make a parental responsibility (PR) order on making CAO naming father, or second female parent, as a person with whom the child is to live, in favour of father or second female parent without PR, even if no specific application is made; it has a discretion as to whether or not to make a PR order where the child has contact with the father or second female parent	CA 1989, ss 4(1), 4ZA(1) CA 1989, s 12(1)
Application	On Form C1 (or Form C(PRA1), Form C(PRA2) or Form C(PRA3)) as appropriate, together with Form FM1, with sufficient copies for each respondent. Where it is alleged that the child who is the subject of the application has suffered, or is at risk of suffering, any harm from (a) any form of domestic abuse; (b) violence within the household; (c) child abduction; or (d) other conduct or behaviour, supplemental Form C1A must also be completed Fee: £215 Where child applies for permission to apply for discharge, use Form C2	FPR PD3A; PD5A FPFO 2008, fee 2.1(a),(b) FPR 2010, rr 18.1–18.13
Respondents	Notice to be served in Form C6 on every person with parental responsibility and on every person with parental responsibility before care order In specified proceedings, the child *Variation or discharge of parental responsibility order or agreement:* As above, and service on other parties to original proceedings	FPR 2010, r 12.3 FPR 2010, r 12.3
Additional persons to be served with notice of the proceedings	Notice to be served in Form C6A on local authority, if providing accommodation, and on person caring for child or providing refuge	FPR PD12C, para 3.1
Service	Applicant must serve a copy of the application, together with Form C6 (endorsed with date fixed for hearing), on each respondent at least 14 days before the hearing; notice of the proceedings must be served in Form C6A (endorsed with date fixed for hearing) on other persons to be served at least 14 days before the hearing At or before first directions appointment or hearing, applicant must file statement in Form C9 to prove that requirements for service have been complied with	FPR PD12B, para 8.8; PD12C, Annex B FPR PD5A
Answer to application	Respondent to an application must file a written answer and serve it on the other parties to the proceedings within 14 days of the date on which the application is served	FPR 2010, r 12.32
Joinder or removal of parties	By court order, of its own initiative or on written request on Form C2 together with Form C1A if necessary (see under 'Application' above)	FPR 2010, rr 4.3, 12.3(3)
Directions	As to applications for directions, see – NB A written request for directions must be made on Form C2 and Form C1A if necessary (see under 'Application' above)	FPR 2010, r 12.12

	Directions which may be given (e g timetable for the proceedings, submission of evidence or transfer of proceedings to another court) Timing of proceedings Attendance at the directions hearing	FPR 2010, r 12.12 FPR 2010, r 12.13 FPR 2010, r 12.14
Order	Conferring parental responsibility on the father, spouse, civil partner or second female parent, in Form C45 Terminating parental responsibility order or agreement, in Form C45	CA 1989, ss 4(1)(a), 4ZA(1), 4A(1), 12(1); FPR PD12B FPR PD12B
Appeals	See Guides E2, E4 and E5	
Transitional arrangements	Implementation of CFA 2014	Children and Families Act 2014 (Transitional Proceedings) Order 2014

D7: Child Arrangements Orders (or Discharge or Variation of the Same)

Legal background

When the CFA 2014 came into force on 22 April 2014, it removed residence and contact orders from CA 1989, s 8 and replaced them with a child arrangements order (CAO), which regulates the arrangements relating to (a) with whom a child is to live, spend time or otherwise have contact, and (b) when a child is to live, spend time or otherwise have contact with any person. Furthermore, as from the autumn of 2014, CA 1989, s 1(2A) now requires the court, when considering whether to make, vary or discharge a s 8 order that is opposed, to presume, unless the contrary is shown, that the involvement of that parent in the life of the child concerned will further the child's welfare. Section 1(2B) defines 'involvement' to mean involvement of some kind, either direct or indirect, but not any particular division of a child's time.

CA 1989, s 12(1) states that when making a CAO the court is required to give parental responsibility (PR) to the father of the child concerned, or to the child's second female parent (by virtue of HFEA 2008, s 43), in cases where he or she is named in the order as a person with whom the child is to live. This will only apply in cases in which the father or second female parent would not otherwise have PR.

CA 1989, s 12(1A) provides that the court may give PR to the child's father or second female parent in cases where he or she is named in the order as a person with whom the child is to spend time or otherwise have contact. However, it is for the court to determine whether it is appropriate for him or her to be given PR in the light of the specific provisions of the order; if the court considers it appropriate it must give PR to him or her. In cases where a court gives PR in either of these circumstances, it does so by means of an order under s 4 or 4ZA.

CA 1989, s 12(2) provides that where a CAO makes provision for a child to live with a person who is not his parent or guardian, that person will be given PR.

CA 1989, s 12(2A) enables the court to give PR to a person who is not a child's parent or guardian in cases where a CAO provides for the child to spend time with or otherwise have contact (but not live) with that person (although it is envisaged that this power will be exercised rarely).

In relation to both ss 12(2) and 12(2A), respectively, PR is given for the duration of the relevant provision.

The CAP came into force on 22 April 2014 and replaced the Private Law Programme in FPR PD12B. It sets out the process that applies where a dispute arises between separated parents and/or families about the arrangements concerning children. On making an application to the court, the applicant will be required when completing Form C100 to confirm their attendance at a mediation information and assessment meeting or to give reasons for not attending where the circumstances fall within the exceptions set out in FPR 2010, r 3.8 (PD12B; PD3A, paras 17–21).

The 1996 Hague Convention, in force from 1 November 2012, lays down rules in respect of measures directed to the protection of the person or property of the child in cases to which the Convention applies (Art 1). 'Measures of protection' include the attribution, exercise, termination, restriction and delegation of parental responsibility, and of custody and access (Art 3). 'Rights of custody' essentially include all measures relating to the care and upbringing of, and access, contact or visitation rights concerning the child (Art 3(b)). See further under the commentary to the Convention.

Activity directions and activity conditions

CA 1989, ss 11A–11P give the court power to enforce child arrangements orders (CAO). When there is some dispute about the arrangements for a child and the court is considering whether or not to make, vary or discharge a CAO it may make an 'activity direction' (s 11A), directing a party to the proceedings to undertake activities promoting contact, for example information meetings about mediation, parenting information programmes and domestic violence prevention programmes.

Whenever a court makes or varies a CAO it may make an 'activity condition' requiring the person named to take part in a specified activity (s 11C). Those who may be subject to an activity condition are the person with whom the child lives, the person in whose favour the child arrangements order is made, or a person subject to a s 11(7) condition.

Furthermore, the activities directed or imposed may relate to more than just promoting the contact provided for in the CAO. Instead, the activities will be about helping to establish, maintain or improve the involvement of a person in a child's life (s 11A(3)).

A court may ask a Cafcass officer to monitor compliance with an activity direction or condition and to report to the court if there is a failure to comply (s 11G). Activity providers may also be asked to provide a report to the court about the attendance and participation of those required to undertake an activity.

Monitoring compliance with child arrangements orders

A court may ask a Cafcass officer to monitor compliance with a child arrangements order for a period of up to 1 year after the making of the order (s 11H). Those who can be subject to monitoring are: a person who is required to allow contact with a child; a person whose contact with the child is provided for; a person subject to s 11(7) condition. However, the general assumption is that this provision should not be used in 'consent order' cases where proceedings have ended, but should be limited to those cases where the issue of contact has remained in dispute and where a trial and judicial determination of the contact issue has taken place.

Warning notices

Whenever a court makes or varies a child arrangements order (CAO), it is to attach a notice warning of the consequences of failing to comply with the CAO (s 11I) ie an enforcement order (for unpaid work) (ss 11J–11N), an order for financial compensation (ss 11O, 11P), and sanctions for contempt of court. The warning notice must also make clear the person to whom it is addressed, and the exact provisions of the order to which it relates.

The wording of s 11I looks as though it is mandatory for a court to attach a warning notice when it makes or varies any CAO. It follows that judges will have to decide whether the CAO that they propose to make is to be made in terms that comply with s 8(1), in which case a warning notice will be added automatically, or simply in declaratory terms, in which case there is no need for a warning notice to be attached. Equally, it may be more appropriate for consent orders to set out the agreed regime as a recital or schedule to the order on the basis of which the court then applies the 'no order' principle. Judges will need to make sure that orders set out in Form C45 accurately reflect what has actually been ordered.

See further the introduction to Guide D8.

Procedure

Who may apply	Parent, guardian, special guardian Child arrangements order holder Either party to marriage or civil partnership (in relation to whom child is a child of the family) Person with whom child has lived for 3 of the past 5 years and within the preceding 3 months Person with consent of those with parental responsibility LA foster parent, or relative of child, with whom child has lived for a period of 1 year immediately preceding application Any person with permission, except a local authority; special requirements apply to some foster-parents Application to discharge or vary: may be made by previous applicant, or person named in a child arrangements order	CA 1989, ss 9(2),(3), 10 CA 1989, ss 8(2), 10(6)
Fee	Application to discharge or vary: £215 Application for permission: £215	FPFO 2008, fee 2.1(d) FPFO 2008, fee 2.1(d)

Which court	The Family Court (lay justices) if none of criteria in Schedule to the Guidance apply	CA 1989, ss 10(1), 92(7); President's Guidance *Allocation and Gatekeeping*
	Proceedings can be transferred sideways, upwards or downwards, using order in Form C49	FC(CDB)R 2014; President's Guidance *Allocation and Gatekeeping*
Which proceedings	Freestanding application	CA 1989, s 10(2)
	Application made in family proceedings	CA 1989, s 10(1)(a)
	On court's own initiative in family proceedings	CA 1989, s 10(1)(b)
Application	On Form C100, with sufficient copies for each respondent. Where it is alleged that the child who is the subject of the application has suffered, or is at risk of suffering, any harm from (a) any form of domestic abuse; (b) violence within the household; (c) child abduction; or (d) other conduct or behaviour supplemental Form C1A must also be completed	FPR 2010, r 5.1; PD3A; PD5A; PD12B
Respondents	Court will serve notice in Form C6 on every person with parental responsibility, every person with parental responsibility before care order, and (on application to discharge or vary) parties to proceedings where order was made	FPR 2010, r 12.3; PD12B, para 8.8
Additional persons to whom notice in Form C6A is to be given	Local authority, if providing accommodation for child Person caring for child or providing refuge Person named in a court order (unless not relevant) Party to pending proceedings Person with whom the child has lived for 3 years	FPR PD12C, para 3.1
Service	The court will serve a copy of the application, together with Form C6 (endorsed with date fixed for hearing), on each respondent at least 14 days before the hearing, unless emergency (see Without notice procedure below)	FPR 2010, r 12.8(2); PD12C, Annex B
	The court will serve notice of the proceedings in Form C6A (endorsed with date fixed for hearing) on other persons to be served	FPR 2010, r 12.8(2); PD12C
Power to abridge time-limits	In appropriate cases, court has power to abridge time-limits set by rules	FPR 2010, rr 4.1(3)(a), 12.12
	Court has power to abridge time for service	FPR 2010, rr 4.1(3)(a), 12.12
Without notice procedure	If without notice order obtained by telephone, file application by the next business day; otherwise, file at time application is made (NB without notice child arrangements orders will be made only in exceptional circumstances)	*Re G* [1993] 1 FLR 910, CA; *Re P* [1993] 1 FLR 915, CA; FPR PD20A, paras 4.3–4.5; PD12B, para 12.2
	If an order is made, it must be served on respondents within 48 hours	FPR 2010, r 12.16
Joinder or removal of parties	By court order, of its own initiative or on written request on Form C2 together with Form C1A if necessary (see under 'Application' above)	FPR 2010, rr 4.3, 12.3(3)

Acknowledgement of application	Respondent must file acknowledgement of application in Form C7 and serve it on the parties within 14 days of service of the application together with Form C1A if necessary (see under 'Application' above). There is no requirement to file a written answer	FPR 2010, r 12.32; PD5A; PD12B, para 14.3
Withdrawal of application	Permitted only with permission; application may be made orally if parties and welfare officer present; otherwise, by written request on Form C2 giving reasons, served on parties	FPR 2010, rr 18.1–18.13, 29.4
	If by consent, court may grant request without a hearing; otherwise, hearing on 7 days' notice	FPR 2010, rr 18.8, 29.4
Directions	Court may give directions of own initiative or on written (or oral, if urgent) request, subject to certain procedural requirements	FPR 2010, r 12.12
	NB A written request for directions must be made on Form C2 together with Form C1A if necessary (see under 'Application' above)	
	Directions which may be given (e g as to timetable for the proceedings, submission of evidence or transfer of proceedings to another court)	FPR 2010, r 12.12
	Timing of proceedings	FPR 2010, r 12.13
	Attendance at the directions hearing	FPR 2010, r 12.14
	Activity direction	CA 1989, s 11A
Order	On Form CAP01, Form CAP02, Form CAP03 or Form CAP04, as appropriate, making, discharging or varying a child arrangements order; order may contain directions and conditions	CA 1989, ss 8, 11(7); FPR PD12B
	Activity condition	CA 1989, s 11C
	A warning notice *must* be added whenever court makes or varies a child arrangements order	CA 1989, s 11I
Additional or alternative orders	Parental responsibility order (Form C45)	CA 1989, s 4(1)(a)
	Appointment of guardian (Form C46)	CA 1989, s 5(2)
	Cafcass monitoring	CA 1989, s 11H
	Family assistance order (but only with the consent of persons named) (Form C42)	CA 1989, s 16
	Financial provision order (Form C21)	CA 1989, Sch 1, para 1
	Supervision order (Form C35)	CA 1989, ss 31(1)(b), 35, 38
	Education supervision order (provided the application is made by a local education authority) (Form C37)	CA 1989, s 36(1)
Restrictions on court's powers	A child arrangements order may not be made in respect of a child in care, unless s 9(6B) applies	CA 1989, s 9(1),(6B)
Appeals	See Guides E2, E4 and E5	
Transitional arrangements	Implementation of CFA 2014	Children and Families Act 2014 (Transitional Proceedings) Order 2014

D8: Enforcement of Child Arrangements Orders

Legal background

CA 1989, ss 11I–11P make extra provision for the enforcement of child arrangements orders.

CFA 2014 came into force on 22 April 2014 and removed residence and contact orders and replaced them with child arrangements orders (CAO). CA 1989, ss 11A–11E provide that when a CAO is breached the court may direct parties to undertake activities designed to help them understand the importance of complying with the order and making it work; these are known as 'activity directions' and 'activity conditions'. Furthermore, the activities directed or imposed will be able to relate to more than just promoting the contact provided for in the CAO. Instead, the activities will be about helping to establish, maintain or improve the involvement of a person in a child's life. See further Guide D7.

The CAP came into force on 22 April 2014 and replaced the Private Law Programme in FPR PD12B. It sets out the process that applies where a dispute arises between separated parents and/or families about the arrangements concerning children. Specific provisions relating to the enforcement of CAOs are set out at para 21 of the CAP at FPR PD12B.

Warning notices

Whenever a court makes or varies a child arrangements order, it is to attach a notice warning of the consequences of failing to comply (s 11I) i e an enforcement order (for unpaid work) (ss 11J–N), an order for financial compensation (ss 11O, 11P), and sanctions for contempt of court. The warning notice must also make clear the person to whom it is addressed, and the exact provisions of the order to which it relates. The procedure for applying for warning notices is set out in FPR 2010, r 12.33. The application is made using Form C78. Warning notices can be addressed to a much wider range of individuals than was the case previously, because applications for enforcement orders and financial compensation orders can be made not only by the person in whose favour the order is made, but also by the person with whom the child lives, or the child, or any other person subject to a s 11(7) condition or an activity condition. Judges need to make sure that orders set out in Form C45 accurately reflect what has actually been ordered.

FPR 2010, r 12.33 provides for the application to be made without notice, but there is no provision in Form C78 for the applicant to specify the provisions of the order to which he wishes the warning notice attached, or any space for him to say why the application is being made. The without notice order has potential quasi-criminal consequences for the respondent, but does not give him a right to apply to set it aside. In these circumstances, it is respectfully submitted that the safer course would be for the judge to direct a hearing inviting the applicant to file a brief statement setting out the provisions of the order to which he wishes the warning notice to be attached and explaining why he is asking for a warning notice.

If the relevant order does not comply with s 8(1), then the application should be dismissed as misconceived. The applicant would have to apply using Form C100 to vary the existing order to a mandatory order to which a warning notice can be added (see Guide D7).

Enforcement Orders (for unpaid work)

Where the court is satisfied beyond reasonable doubt that a person has failed to comply with a child arrangements order made under s 8 of CA 1989, it may make an enforcement order, or a suspended enforcement order, imposing on that person an 'unpaid work requirement' (community service): s 11J(2). The application is made using Form C79. The court may not make an enforcement order if satisfied that the person in breach had a 'reasonable excuse' for breaching the order: s 11J(3). The burden of proving a reasonable excuse is on the person in breach and the standard of proof is the balance of probabilities: s 11(4). The court may not make an enforcement order unless the person concerned has received a 'warning notice' or has been otherwise informed of its terms: s 11K. The factors to be considered by the court before making an enforcement order are set out in s 11L and in Sch A1, Pt I. The maximum number of hours of unpaid work that may be required is 200, and the minimum is 40. The court has power to amend or revoke an enforcement order: Sch A1, Pt II. The court may ask a Cafcass officer to monitor, or arrange for the monitoring of, a person's compliance with an enforcement order, and to report to the court on failure to comply and on any unsuitability to undertake the unpaid work: s 11M. Where an enforcement order is made, the court must attach a warning notice setting out the consequences of breaching the order i e imposition of a further enforcement order; enhancement of the existing enforcement order; use of existing sanctions for contempt. If the terms of an enforcement order are breached, the court may (in certain circumstances) amend the original order to make it more onerous, or impose another enforcement order: Sch A1, Pt II. See also FPR 2010, PD12N.

Financial compensation orders

The court may require a person who has caused financial loss to another person as a result of breaching a child arrangements order (including breaching a condition attached to the order), to pay compensation up to the amount of the loss: s 11O. Before making a compensation order the court must take into account the welfare of any child concerned, and the financial circumstances of the person in breach. The people who can apply for compensation are: the person with whom the child lives; the person whose contact with the child is provided for in the order; any individual subject to an activity condition or direction; the child concerned (with permission of the court). The court may not make an order for financial compensation where the person in breach did not receive a warning notice under s 11I and was not otherwise informed of its terms: s 11P.

Procedure

Note: The following procedure applies to cases where a warning notice has been attached properly to a child arrangements order and it is alleged that the order has been breached so that enforcement of the order is required.

Who may apply	The person with whom the child lives or is to live; the person in whose favour the order is made; a person subject to a s 11(7) condition or an activity condition; the child concerned (with permission)	CA 1989, s 11J(5), s 11O(6)
Fee	£215	FPFO 2008, fee 2.1(e)
Which court	The Family Court (lay justices) if none of criteria in the Schedule to the Guidance apply Proceedings can be transferred sideways, upwards or downwards, using order in Form C49	CA 1989, ss 10(1), 92(7); FC(CDB)R 2014; President's Guidance *Allocation and Gatekeeping* FC(CDB)R 2014
Which proceedings	Freestanding application Application made in family proceedings	CA 198 9, s 10(2) CA 1989, s 10(1)(a)
Application	On Form C79	FPR PD5A; PD12B
Respondents	Notice to be served in Form C6 on person the applicant alleges has failed to comply with the child arrangements order	FPR 2010, r 12.3
Additional persons on whom notice is to be served in Form C6A	Any Cafcass officer monitoring compliance with child arrangements order; where child was a party to contact proceedings, the children's guardian, guardian ad litem or child's next friend or child's legal representative	FPR PD12C, para 3.1
Service	Applicant must serve a copy of the application, together with Form C6 (endorsed with date fixed for hearing), on each respondent, at least 14 days before hearing date Notice of the proceedings must be served in Form C6A (endorsed with date fixed for hearing) on other persons to be served, at least 14 days before hearing date	FPR PD12C, para 2.1 FPR PD12C
Power to abridge time limits	In appropriate cases, court has power to abridge time limits Court has power to abridge time for service	FPR 2010, rr 4.1(3)(a), 12.12
Joinder or removal of parties	By court order, of its own initiative or on written request in Form C2	FPR 2010, r 12.3
Acknowledgement of application	Respondent must file acknowledgement of application in Form C7 and serve it on parties within 14 days of service of application	FPR 2010, r 12.32; PD12B, para 14.3
Withdrawal of application	Permitted only with permission; application may be made orally if parties and Cafcass officer present; otherwise by written request on Form C2 giving reasons, served on parties	FPR 2010, rr 18.1–18.13, 29.4

Directions	Court may give directions of own initiative or on written request in Form C2 (or oral request if urgent), subject to certain procedural requirements Directions as to timetable, evidence, transfer Directions as to timing of proceedings Directions as to attendance at directions hearing	FPR 2010, rr 4.3, 12.12 FPR 2010, r 12.12 FPR 2010, r 12.13 FPR 2010, r 12.14
Order	Enforcement order: Form C80 Revocation or amendment of enforcement order: Form C81 Financial compensation order: Form C82 Committal for breach of order or undertaking Attendance at activity, e g SPIP	FPR PD12B CA 1989, Sch A1, Pt II, para 4; FPR PD12B CA 1989, ss 11O, 11P; FPR PD12B FPR 2010, r 37.4 FPR PD12B, para 21
Service of enforcement order	Copy to be served as soon as practicable by proper officer on parties (except person against whom order is made), and Cafcass officer, and responsible officer Applicant to serve copy personally on person against whom order is made	FPR 2010, r 12.35; for meaning of 'responsible officer' see CA 1989, Sch A1, para 8(8) FPR 2010, r 12.35
Appeals	See Guides E2, E4 and E5	
Transitional arrangements	Implementation of CFA 2014	Children and Families Act 2014 (Transitional Proceedings) Order 2014

D9: Specific Issue Order or Prohibited Steps Order (or Discharge or Variation of the Same)

Legal background

A specific issue order under CA 1989, s 8(1) gives directions for the purpose of determining a specific question which has arisen, or which may arise, in connection with any aspect of parental responsibility for a child. In effect it is used to settle ad hoc disputes where those who share parental responsibility cannot agree over the issue in question.

A prohibited steps order under CA 1989, s 8(1), specifies that no step that could be taken by a parent in meeting his or her parental responsibility for a child, and which is of a kind specified in the order, can be taken by any person without the consent of the court. This is a negative version of a specific issue order.

The CAP came into force on 22 April 2014 and replaced the Private Law Programme in FPR PD12B. It sets out the process that applies where a dispute arises between separated parents and/or families about the arrangements concerning children. On making an application to the court, the applicant must file a completed Form C100 that includes confirmation of attendance at a mediation information and assessment meeting or giving reasons for not attending where the circumstances fall within the exceptions set out in FPR 2010, r 3.8 (FPR PD12B, PD3A, paras 17–21).

Note that the 1996 Hague Convention came into force in the UK on 1 November 2012. See introductions to Guides D6 and D7 and the commentary to the Convention.

Procedure

Who may apply	Parent, guardian or special guardian Child arrangements order holder Any step-parent with parental responsibility pursuant to s 4A Any person with permission *Application to discharge or vary*: may be made by previous applicant	CA 1989, ss 8(2), 10

Which court	The Family Court (lay justices) if none of the criteria in Schedule to the Guidance apply	CA 1989, ss 10(1), 92(7); FC(CDB)R 2014; President's Guidance *Allocation and Gatekeeping*
	Proceedings can be transferred sideways, upwards or downwards, using order in Form C49	FC(CDB)R 2014
Which proceedings	Freestanding application	CA 1989, s 10(2)
	Application made in family proceedings	CA 1989, s 10(1)(a)
	On court's own initiative in family proceedings	CA 1989, s 10(1)(b)
Application	On Form C100, with sufficient copies for service on each respondent. Where it is alleged that the child who is the subject of the application has suffered, or is at risk of suffering, any harm from (a) any form of domestic abuse; (b) violence within the household; (c) child abduction; or (d) other conduct or behaviour, supplemental Form C1A must also be completed	FPR PD3A; PD5A; PD12B
	Fee payable on application: £215	FPFO 2008, fee 2.1(d)
	Fee payable on application to discharge or vary order: £215	FPFO 2008, fee 2.1(d)
Respondents	Court will serve notice in Form C6 on every person with parental responsibility, every person with parental responsibility before care order, and (on application to discharge or vary) parties to proceedings where order was made	FPR 2010, r 12.3; PD12B, para 8.8
Additional persons to whom notice in Form C6A is to be given	Local authority, if providing accommodation for child	
	Person caring for child or providing refuge Person named in a court order (unless not relevant) Party to pending proceedings Person with whom the child has lived for 3 years	FPR PD12C, para 3.1
Service	At least 14 days, unless emergency (see Without notice procedure below) Court will serve copy of application, together with Form C6 (endorsed with date fixed for hearing) on each respondent Notice of the proceedings must be served in Form C6A (endorsed with date fixed for hearing) on other persons to be served	FPR PD12C
Power to abridge time-limits	In appropriate cases, court has power to abridge time-limits set by rules Court has power to abridge time for service	FPR 2010, rr 4.1(3)(a), 12.12
Without notice procedure	If without notice order obtained by telephone, file application the next business day; otherwise, file at time application is made	FPR PD20A, paras 4.3–4.5; PD12B, para 9
	If an order is made, it must be served on respondents within 48 hours	FPR 2010, r 12.16
Joinder or removal of parties	By court order, of its own initiative or on written request on Form C2 together with Form C1A if necessary (see under 'Application' above)	FPR 2010, rr 4.3, 12.3(3)

Acknowledgement of application	Respondent must file acknowledgement of application in Form C7 and serve it on the parties within 14 days of service of the application together with Form C1A if necessary (see under 'Application' above)	FPR 2010, r 12.32; PD5A; PD12B, para 14.3
Directions	Applications for directions NB A written request for directions must be made on Form C2 together with Form C1A if necessary (see under 'Application' above) Directions which may be given (e g as to timetable for the proceedings, submission of evidence or transfer of proceedings to another court) Timing of proceedings Attendance at the directions hearing	FPR 2010, rr 5.1, 12.12; PD5A FPR 2010, r 12.12 FPR 2010, r 12.13 FPR 2010, r 12.14
Order	On Form CAP01, Form CAP02, Form CAP03 or Form CAP04 as appropriate, making, discharging or varying a specific issue order or prohibited steps order; order may contain directions and conditions Penal notice may be attached on specific application	CA 1989, ss 8, 11(7); FPR PD12B FPR 2010, r 37.9
Appeals	See Guides E2, E4 and E5	
Transitional arrangements	Implementation of CFA 2014	Children and Families Act 2014 (Transitional Proceedings) Order 2014

D10: Special Guardianship Order (or Discharge or Variation of the Same)

Legal background

Special guardianship orders are private law orders which give the special guardian parental responsibility for the child concerned (CA 1989, ss 14A–14F). They provide permanence and security for those children for whom adoption is not suitable but who cannot live with their birth parents. The basic legal links between the child and his birth family are preserved. However, subject to any other existing CA 1989 order, a special guardian is entitled to exercise parental responsibility to the exclusion of any other person with parental responsibility (save for another special guardian) (CA 1989, s 14C(1)). It allows the special guardian to remove the child from the jurisdiction for up to 3 months without the consent of others with parental responsibility (however, he would need the consent of another special guardian) (CA 1989, s 14C(4)). The order can be varied or discharged (unlike an adoption order) (CA 1989, s 14D). Where the child himself applies for permission, the court may only grant permission if it is satisfied that the child has sufficient understanding to make the proposed application for a special guardianship order (CA 1989, ss 14A(12) and 10(8)). The court may not make a special guardianship order unless it has first received a report from the local authority (CA 1989, s 14A(11)) or has received the required information about the case in some other acceptable form, for example in a parental assessment. The report must deal with the matters prescribed by the Schedule to the Special Guardianship Regulations 2005 (SGR 2005) (as amended by the Special Guardianship (Amendment) Regulations 2016) and the matters required by CA 1989, s 10(9) (CA 1989, s 14A(12)). Once a special guardianship order has been made, the local authority is under a duty to make arrangements for the provision of a package of special guardian support services, including counselling, advice, information and financial support (CA 1989, s 14F; SGR 2005 (above)).

The CAP came into force on 22 April 2014 and replaced the Private Law Programme in FPR PD12B. It sets out the process that applies where a dispute arises between separated parents and/or families about the arrangements concerning children. On making an application to the court, the applicant must file a completed Form C100, and Form FM1 confirming attendance at a mediation information and assessment meeting or giving reasons for not attending where the circumstances fall within the exceptions set out in FPR 2010, r 3.8 and PD12B, paras 17–21.

Procedure

Who may apply	Applicant must be 18 or over and *not* the parent of the child in question, Guardian, Child arrangements order holder, Either party to marriage, Any civil partner in a civil partnership in relation to whom child is a child of the family Person with whom child has lived for 3 of the last 5 years and within the preceding 3 months Person with consent of those with parental responsibility Any person with permission, except a local authority, including the child (if sufficient understanding); Foster parents with whom child has lived for 1 year before application A relative with whom child has lived for 1 year before application If placement order in force, special requirements apply	CA 1989, s 14A(2); FPR 2010, r 12.3 CA 1989, ss 14A(3)–(7), 14D(4), 10(5), (8)–(10) CA 1989, s 14A(5)(d) CA 1989, s 14A(5)(e) CA 1989, s 14A(13)
Fee	Application for permission: £215 Application to discharge or vary: £215	FPFO 2008, fee 2.1(h) FPFO 2008, fee 2.1(h)
Which court	The Family Court (lay justices) if none of the criteria in Schedule to the Guidance apply	CA 1989, s 92(7); FC(CDB)R 2014; President's Guidance *Allocation and Gatekeeping*
	Proceedings can be transferred sideways, upwards or downwards using order in Form C49	FC(CDB)R 2014
	Where SGO in force and application is for permission to change name or remove from UK, commence in court which made SGO	CA 1989, s 14C(3), FC(CDB)R 2014
	Application which would vary or discharge SGO made by the Family Court of its own initiative must be made to a family hearing centre	FC(CDB)R 2014
	Application for permission to apply for a child arrangements order or SGO under CA 1989, ss 29(4)(b) or 29(5)(b) and any subsequent application for an order to be made to court in which adoption proceedings are pending	FC(CDB)R 2014
Which proceedings	Freestanding application Application made in family proceedings On court's own initiative in family proceedings (eg in care or adoption proceedings)	CA 1989, s 14A(3) CA 1989, s 14A(3) CA 1989, s 14A(6)(b)
Application	On Form C1, Form C13A and Form FM1 confirming attendance at a MIAM, with sufficient copies for each respondent	FPR PD3A; PD5A; PD12B
Respondents	The applicant must give the local authority 3 months' notice of the application in Form C6, so that the authority can prepare a report addressing the matters prescribed by regulations	SGR 2005, Sch; CA 1989, s 10(9)
	NB *Exception*: the requirement for 3 months' notice is waived where a placement order is in force and an application has been made for an adoption order and the applicant has obtained permission to apply for a SGO	ACA 2002, s 29(6); CA 1989, s 14A(13)

	Notice to be served in Form C6 on every person with parental responsibility, every person with parental responsibility before care order and (on application to vary or discharge) parties to proceedings where order was made	FPR 2010, r 12.3; PD12C
Additional persons to whom notice in Form C6A is to be given	If child not being accommodated, the authority in whose area applicant is ordinarily resident Person named in a court order which remains in force Person to be a party in pending proceedings in respect of child Person with whom child has lived for at least 3 years before application For application under s 14D, see below under 'Variation or discharge'	FPR PD12C, para 3.1
Service	Applicant must serve a copy of application, together with Form C6 (endorsed with date fixed for hearing), on each respondent at least 14 days before the hearing Notice of the proceedings must be served in Form C6A (endorsed with date of hearing) on other persons to be served At or before first directions hearing applicant must file statement in Form C9 to prove that requirements for service have been complied with	FPR PD12C FPR PD5A, PD12B
Power to abridge time-limits	In appropriate cases, court has power to abridge time-limits set by rules Court has power to abridge time for service	FPR 2010, rr 4.1(3)(a), 12.12 FPR 2010, rr 4.1(3)(a), 12.12
Joinder or removal of parties	By court order, of its own initiative or on written request on Form C2	FPR 2010, rr 4.3, 12.3
Acknowledgement of application	Respondent must file acknowledgement of application in Form C7 and serve it on the parties within 14 days of service of the application	FPR 2010, r 12.32; PD12B; r 14.3
Withdrawal of application	Permitted only with permission; application may be made orally if parties are present; otherwise, by written request on Form C2 giving reasons, served on the parties If by consent, the court may grant request without a hearing; otherwise, hearing on 7 days' notice	FPR 2010, rr 18.1–18.13, 29.4; PD5A
Directions	Court may give directions of own initiative or on written (or oral, if urgent) request, subject to certain procedural requirements NB A written request for directions must be made on Form C2 Directions which may be given e g as to timetable, submission of evidence or transfer to another court Timing of proceedings Attendance at the directions hearing	CA 1989, s 14E(1); FPR 2010, rr 4.3, 12.12 CA 1989, s 14E(1)–(3); FPR 2010, r 12.12 FPR 2010, r 12.13 FPR 2010, r 12.14
Children's guardian	The child will not automatically be represented in the proceedings. The court may appoint a children's guardian if it considers it to be in the child's best interests to do so	FPR 2010, rr 16.2, 16.4

Order	On Form C43A making, discharging or varying a special guardianship order; order may contain directions or conditions	CA 1989, ss 14E(5), 11(7)
	SGO (or order varying one) may contain provisions which are to have effect for a specified period	CA 1989, s 14E(4)
	Before making a SGO court must consider whether a child arrangements order should also be made with respect to the child, and whether any s 8 order in force with respect to the child should be varied or discharged	CA 1989, s 14B(1)
	On making a SGO the court may also give permission for the child to be known by a new surname; and grant permission to remove him from the UK	CA 1989, s 14B(2)–(4)
Variation or discharge	The court may vary or discharge a SGO on the application of: – the special guardian (or any of them if more than one) – any parent or guardian of the child – any child arrangements order holder – anyone else who has, or immediately before the making of the SGO, had parental responsibility – the child himself – a local authority designated in a care order with respect to the child	CA 1989, s 14D(1)
	The following must obtain permission before making an application to vary or discharge an SGO: – the child – any parent or guardian of the child – any step-parent of the child with parental responsibility under s 4A – anyone else who had parental responsibility for the child immediately before the making of the SGO	CA 1989, s 14D(3)–(5)
Appeals	See Guides E2, E4 and E5	
Transitional arrangements	Implementation of CFA 2014	Children and Families Act 2014 (Transitional Proceedings) Order 2014

D11: Private Law Proceedings for the Disclosure of Information as to the Whereabouts of a Child

Legal background

FLA 1986, s 33, provides a power for any court, in any proceedings in relation to a child within Pt I of that Act brought in that court, to order 'any person' to disclose information to the court as to the whereabouts of the child if his whereabouts are not sufficiently known. In the High Court, this adds nothing to the court's inherent powers, but the Family Court can proceed in this way only under s 33. The order directs that the information be given to the court, not to a party (*Chief Constable of West Yorkshire Police v S* [1998] 2 FLR 973, CA). Proceedings under FLA 1986, s 33 are classed as 'emergency proceedings' (FPR 2010, r 12.2).

The CAP came into force on 22 April 2014 and replaced the Private Law Programme in FPR PD12B. It sets out the process that applies where a dispute arises between separated parents and/or families about the arrangements concerning children.

Application without notice or with notice?

Where it is likely that the person who has the child may remove the child to frustrate the proceedings or order, an application may be made without notice; where the risk of the child being removed is negligible, it will usually be appropriate to apply with notice.

Procedure

Pre-condition	Missing child who is subject of proceedings or order within FLA 1986, Pt I 'Part I order' includes proceedings for or in relation to a CA 1989, s 8 order, or previous custody order, and similar orders made in Scotland, Northern Ireland and specified dependent territories; it does not include an order in proceedings for adoption or under CA 1989, Pt IV or V (public law) Where application is made in relation to an order made in Scotland, Northern Ireland or a specified dependent territory, the order must have been registered in the High Court, and proceedings for enforcement must have been begun in that court Recovery order in public law proceedings under CA 1989	FLA 1986, s 33 FLA 1986, s 25 FLA 1986, ss 25(3), 27(1), 29(1), 32(1) CA 1989, s 50
Who may apply	Any party with a legitimate interest in CA 1989, s 8 proceedings A person who has registered an order made elsewhere in the UK or a specified dependent territory, being a person on whom rights are conferred by the order	FLA 1986, s 27(1)
Who may be directed to provide information	Any person can be so directed; see also 'Duty of person to whom order is directed', below Where a mother has taken a child to stay at a women's refuge, the police should not be directed to disclose the address other than to the Court manager	FLA 1986, s 33(1) *Chief Constable of West Yorkshire Police v S* [1998] 2 FLR 973, CA
Which court	Where made in pending proceedings or in relation to a subsisting s 8 order, the application should be made in the same court Where made in relation to an order registered in the High Court, the application must be made in the High Court	FLA 1986, s 33(1) FLA 1986, ss 25(3), 29(1), 32(1)
Form of application	On Form C4, which should be supported by evidence. Where the application is made in proceedings in the Family Court under, or in relation to an order under, CA 1989, s 8, a statement that complies with FPR 2010, r 22.4 and PD22A should be ready for use at the hearing Where the application is made in the High Court otherwise than in relation to proceedings under CA 1989, s 8 (or previous custody order), an affidavit should be made in support	FPR 2010, rr 16.4, 22.4; PD5A; PD12B; PD22A FPR 2010, rr 22.12, 22.13; PD22A
Fee	In existing proceedings: £50	FPFO 2008, fee 5.1
Without notice procedure	Application may be made without notice; in an emergency, it may be made by telephone, in which case Form C4 must be (i) filed the next business day and (ii) served within 48 hours after the making of the order	FPR 2010, r 12.16

Service of application where made on notice	One day's notice in emergency proceedings An application for an order under FLA 1986, s 33 comes within the definition of 'emergency proceedings'	FPR 2010, r 12.16; PD12C
With notice response by respondent	The respondent should appear, and may prepare a statement that complies with FPR 2010, r 22.4 and PD22A, or affidavit, as appropriate	FPR 2010, r 22.4; PD22A
Hearing	The Family Court	FC(CDB)R 2014; President's Guidance *Allocation and Gatekeeping*; FPR 2010, r 27.10
	Permission needed to rely on statement of evidence in pending s 8 proceedings	FPR 2010, r 12.19
	Applicant should submit draft order, including formulation of the way in which the order should require information to be provided to the court; see –	Form C30
Form of order	C30 (note that Form C30 incorporates a penal notice)	FPR PD12B
Service of order	Personal service is advisable if penal enforcement may be needed	FPR 2010, r 37.9; MCA 1980, s 63(3)
Duty of person to whom order is directed	Person to whom order is directed must, forthwith after service, disclose to the court, in the way specified in the order, 'all the information' he has about the whereabouts of the child; the court will decide what to do with the information	FLA 1986, s 33(1); see also *Re B (A Minor) (Disclosure of Evidence)* [1993] 1 FLR 191, CA
	Refusal to comply cannot be excused on the basis that giving the information may tend to incriminate the giver (NB the statement or admission cannot be used in criminal proceedings other than for perjury)	FLA 1986, s 33(2)
	Legal professional privilege is no answer to the order; see under –	FLA 1986, s 33
Transitional arrangements	Implementation of CFA 2014	Children and Families Act 2014 (Transitional Proceedings) Order 2014

D12: Private Law Proceedings for an Order Authorising the Taking Charge of, and Delivery of, a Child

Legal background

Under FLA 1986, s 34 any court may authorise 'an officer of the court or a constable to take charge of [a] child and deliver him to' a person entitled, under an order within Pt I of that Act, to have the child given up to him. The authority under a s 34 order includes the power to 'enter and search any premises where ... the child may be found, and to use such force as may be necessary'. In the High Court, this power adds nothing to its inherent powers, but the Family Court can proceed in this way only under s 34. The powers under s 34 become available to the court only after 'the child has not been given up in accordance with the order' which entitles a person to have the child given up to him: thus, unlike the inherent power of the High Court, this power cannot be used if there has been no disobedience of a previous order. Proceedings under FLA 1986, s 34 are classed as 'emergency proceedings' (FPR 2010, r 12.2).

The CAP came into force on 22 April 2014 and replaced the Private Law Programme in FPR PD12B. It sets out the process that applies where a dispute arises between separated parents and/or families about the arrangements concerning children.

Suitability of order under s 34

An order which authorises the use of force to take charge of a child should not be granted, nor should the powers under a s 34 order be exercised, unless this is in the interests of the welfare of the child.

Without notice or with notice?

Where it is likely that the party who has the child may remove the child to frustrate the order, an application without notice is appropriate. Where the risk is negligible, it will usually be appropriate to apply with notice.

Exercise of the power under a s 34 order

Only 'an officer of the court or a constable' can exercise the power under a s 34 order. County Court bailiffs are not trained for this work and do not undertake it. The police cannot be compelled to act: *R v Chief Constable of Cheshire* [1990] 1 FLR 70, QBD. Although a solicitor is an officer of the Senior Courts (Solicitors Act 1974, s 50), he is not an officer of the County Court or the Family Court (CCA 1984, s 147).

An order under s 34 authorises taking charge of the child, but it is not directive. Anyone seeking to exercise the authority should exercise discretion, having regard to the welfare of the child.

Procedure

Pre-condition	Failure to comply with an order (within FLA 1986, Pt I) to give up a child	FLA 1986, s 34
	'Part I order' includes a CA 1989, s 8 order, or previous custody order, and similar orders made in Scotland and Northern Ireland; it does not include an order in proceedings for adoption or under CA 1989, Pt IV or V (public law)	FLA 1986, s 25
	In the Family Court, failure to comply with a child arrangements order that has been served, or a specific order to give up the child must have been ignored	CA 1989, ss 11J–11L; FLA 1986, s 34; FPR 2010, r 37.4
	The order to give up the child may be in the form of a condition or direction under CA 1989, s 11(7) attached to a s 8 order, and may be attached when the s 8 order is first made, or later	CA 1989, ss 11J–11L
	Where the order was made elsewhere in the UK or in a specified dependent territory, it must have been registered in the High Court, and proceedings for enforcement must have been begun in that court	FLA 1986, ss 25(3), 27(1), 29(1), 32(1)
	Recovery order in public law proceedings under CA 1989	CA 1989, s 50
Who may apply	Any party with a legitimate interest in s 8 proceedings	FLA 1986, s 34
	A person who has registered an order made elsewhere in the UK or a specified dependent territory, being a person on whom rights have been conferred by the order	FLA 1986, s 27(1)
Which court	In respect of an order made in England and Wales, the court which made the order not complied with	FLA 1986, s 34(1); FC(CDB)R 2014; President's Guidance *Allocation and Gatekeeping*
	Where made in relation to an order registered in the High Court, the application must be made in the High Court	FLA 1986, ss 25(3), 29(1), 32(1)
Form of application	On Form C3, which should be supported by evidence. Where the application is made in relation to an order under CA 1989, s 8 (or previous custody order), a statement that complies with FPR 2010, r 22.4 and PD22A should be ready for use at the hearing	FPR 2010, r 22.4; PD5A; PD12B; PD22A

	Where the application is made in the High Court or otherwise than in relation to proceedings under CA 1989, s 8 (or previous custody order), an affidavit should be made in support	FPR 2010, rr 22.12, 22.13; PD22A
Fee	If new application required: £245	FPFO 2008, fee 1.1
	In existing proceedings: £50	FPFO 2008, fee 5.1
Without notice procedure	Application may be made without notice; in an emergency, it may be made by telephone, in which case Form C3 must be (i) filed the next business day and (ii) served within 48 hours after the making of the order	FPR 2010, r 12.16
Service of application where made on notice	One day's notice in emergency proceedings An application for an order under FLA 1986, s 33 comes within the definition of 'emergency proceedings' Personal service is advisable so that the court may be satisfied that the respondent is aware of the hearing	FPR 2010, r 12.2; PD12C, Annex B
With notice response by respondent	The respondent should appear, and may prepare a statement which complies with FPR 2010, r 22.4 and PD22A or affidavit, as appropriate	
Hearing	The Family Court Permission needed to rely on statement of evidence in pending s 8 proceedings Applicant should submit draft order	FC(CDB)R 2014 FPR 2010, r 12.19 Form C31
Form of order	Form C31	FPR PD12B
'Unless' order	Form C31 may be adapted to state that, unless the respondent hands over the child at a specified time and place, the power may be exercised thereafter. This allows the respondent to save face by delivering the child	
Transitional arrangements	Implementation of CFA 2014	Children and Families Act 2014 (Transitional Proceedings) Order 2014

D13: Care or Supervision Order

Legal background

By virtue of CA 1989, s 31, the court may only make an order placing a child in the care of a local authority or putting him under the supervision of a local authority or a probation officer if it is satisfied that the child is suffering or is likely to suffer significant harm under the threshold criteria and that the harm or likelihood of harm is attributable to the care given to him (or likely to be given to him if an order were not made) falling below a reasonable standard or his being beyond parental control. If the court finds the threshold criteria proved, it must then decide whether or not to make an order and, if so, which sort of order would be appropriate. In deciding whether to make an order and, if so, which order, the court must give an adequately reasoned judgment that grapples with the competing options and gives them proper, focused attention. In so doing, it must take into account the CA 1989, s 1(1) welfare principle and the checklist of factors set out in CA 1989, s 1(3), bearing in mind the general principle that delay is likely to prejudice the welfare of the child (CA 1989, s 1(2)). It must not make an order unless it considers that to do so would be better for the child than to make no order at all (CA 1989, s 1(5)). Before making a care order, the court must consider the arrangements that the local authority have made, or propose to make, for affording any person contact with the child and invite the parties to comment on those arrangements (CA 1989, s 34(11)). When evaluating whether to grant a care order with a care plan of adoption, the court must also bear in mind that adoption can only occur if parents are unwilling, or are deemed by the court to be unable, to discharge their responsibilities towards the child and that, accordingly, the granting of a care order with a care plan of adoption is an option of last resort requiring a high degree of justification to be made only in exceptional circumstances where nothing else will do. The care proceedings should proceed concurrently with the application for a placement order. Where the application for a placement order falls to be considered at a later date, the court should carry out its balancing exercise in respect of the application for a care order by reference to both CA 1989, s 1(3) and ACA 2002, s 1(4).

While a care order is in force, the designated local authority has a duty to receive the child into its care and to keep him in its care for the duration of the order (see CA 1989, s 33(1)). Subject to certain restrictions set out in CA 1989, s 33, the local authority has parental responsibility for the child and has the power to decide what role his parents or guardian may play in the child's life. The order can be discharged or a supervision order substituted on an application under CA 1989, s 39, or it may be discharged by the making of a child arrangements order with respect to living arrangements in respect of the child (CA 1989, s 91(1)).

A supervision order lasts for 1 year in the first instance (though it can subsequently be extended so as to run for a period of up to 3 years from the date on which it was originally made) and imposes a general duty on the supervisor to advise, assist and befriend the child (see CA 1989, s 35 and Sch 3, Pts I and II). The supervisor must take such steps as are reasonably necessary to give effect to the order and, where the order is not wholly complied with or where he considers that it may no longer be necessary, he must consider whether he should apply to the court for it to be varied or discharged. The order can be discharged or varied on an application under CA 1989, s 39. A subsequent care order also discharges a supervision order (CA 1989, s 91(3)).

Where the main care or supervision proceedings are adjourned or the court gives a direction to the local authority under CA 1989, s 37(1) to investigate the child's circumstances, CA 1989, s 38(1) permits the making of an interim care or supervision order, provided that the court is satisfied that there are reasonable grounds for believing that the grounds for a full order exist (CA 1989, s 38(2)). There are stringent restrictions on the duration of interim orders (see CA 1989, s 38(4)). Directions with regard to the medical or psychiatric examination or other assessment of the child can be given either at the time of making an interim care or supervision order or at any time while it is in force (CA 1989, s 38(6)–(8)) and can be varied on application. Section 38A enables the court to include an exclusion requirement in an interim care order and to attach a power of arrest to that provision. The purpose of an exclusion requirement is to safeguard a child by removing from the scene (whether from the child's home or from part of it or from the area in which it is situated) a person who poses a threat to the child. Application can be made to vary or discharge the exclusion requirement and attendant power of arrest (CA 1989, s 39).

All applications made under CA 1989, Pt IV (care and supervision orders) are subject to FPR PD12A and the PLO contained therein. See Case management hearing, Further case management hearing and Issues resolution hearing within FPR PD12A. Pursuant to CA 1989, s 32(1)(a), applications for care and supervision orders must be disposed of without delay and in any event within 26 weeks of the day on which the application is issued. An extension beyond 26 weeks will be permitted only if it is 'necessary to enable the court to resolve the proceedings justly' for the purposes of s 32(5).

Under the FC(CDB)R 2014, r 20(2), when deciding to which level of judge of the Family Court an application for a care or supervision order is to be allocated, the decision must be taken based on consideration of the relative significance of the need to make most effective and efficient use of judicial resources, the need to avoid delay, the need for judicial continuity, the location of the parties and the child and the complexity of the case. The FC(CDB)R 2014 should be read with guidance that has been provided in respect of allocation and listing of care, supervision and other Pt IV proceedings. The President issued *Allocation and Gatekeeping* (see Part V) in order to ensure that all new care, supervision and other Pt IV proceedings proceeding under the PLO are allocated to the appropriate level of judge and, where appropriate, to a named case management judge. The allocated judge(s) must provide continuity for the proceedings in accordance with the President's Guidance entitled *Continuity and Deployment* (see Part V).

Procedure

Who may apply	Any local authority or authorised person (i e officer of NSPCC or anyone authorised by the Secretary of State)	CA 1989, s 31(1),(9)
Which court	The Family Court. The application will be allocated to the appropriate level of judge in the Family Court having regard to the allocation criteria	FC(CDB)R 2014, rr 3, 20
	Where the application has been allocated without a hearing, a party may request the court to reconsider allocation at a hearing. The court may also reconsider allocation of its own initiative	FPR 2010, r 29.19
	A Family Court may transfer a case to another Family Court either of its own initiative or on the application of one of the parties	FPR 2010, r 29.17

	An application may be made for existing proceedings to be heard in a different Designated Family Judge area	FPR 2010, r 29.18
	The application may not be transferred to the High Court unless by order of a judge sitting in the Family Court who is either the President of the Family Division, a judge of the Court of Appeal or a High Court Judge or where the circumstances in PD29C apply	FPR 2010, r 29.17(3),(4); PD29C
Which proceedings	Freestanding application or application in other family proceedings	CA 1989, s 31(4)
	Court may make supervision order on application for care order or vice versa, but otherwise has no power to make full care or supervision order of its own initiative	CA 1989, s 31(1),(5)
Pre-proceedings checklist	Local authority must carry out specified work set out in checklist before filing an application	FPR PD12A
Application	On Form C110A, with copies for each respondent. The local authority must send a copy of the application form and Annex Documents to Cafcass/CAFCASS Cymru	FPR PD12A; PD5A
	On filing Form C110A the timetable under the PLO starts at Day 1 (day of issue) and must be strictly adhered to until the conclusion of the case	FPR PD12A (PLO, stage 1)
	Within a day of issue (Day 2), the court must consider and decide allocation and set out the reasons for its allocation decision	FC(CDB)R 2014, r 20; FPR PD12A; President's Guidance *Allocation and Gatekeeping*
Fees	On application: £2055	FPFO 2008, fee 2.2
	Where IRH or PHR listed, at least 14 days before hearing: £795	SI 2013/1407
	Where final hearing listed, at least 14 days before hearing: £2155	FPFO 2008, fee 2.2(b)
	In certain circumstances part or all of the fee may be refunded	FPFO 2008, notes to fee 2.2
Respondents	Every person whom applicant believes has parental responsibility	
	The child	FPR 2010, r 12.3
Additional persons to whom notice in Form C6A is to be given	Local authority providing accommodation for child Persons caring for child at commencement of proceedings Person providing a CA 1989, s 51 refuge for child Every person whom applicant believes is a party to pending relevant proceedings re same child Every person whom applicant believes is a parent without parental responsibility for child	FPR PD12A
Service	Copy of application, together with the Annex Documents, evidential Checklist Documents and Form C6A, to be served on respondents together with notice of the date and time of the Case Management Hearing within a day of issue (Day 2 of PLO) and 7 days prior to the Case Management Hearing (except proceedings for an interim order)	FPR PD12A (PLO, stage 1); PD12C
	The court has discretion to shorten the time for service of the application	FPR 2010, r 4.1(3)(a)

	Form C6A to be served on additional persons at same time as application etc served on respondents	FPR PD12C
	At or before the Case Management Hearing (not before day 12 and no later than day 18), applicant must file statement in Form C9 to prove that requirements for service have been complied with	FPR PD12A (PLO, stage 1)
Without notice	May not be available (but see below as to interim orders)	FPR 2010, r 12.16
Joinder or removal of parties	By court order, of its own initiative or on written request	FPR 2010, rr 4.3, 12.3(3)
Answer to application	Upon Issue and Allocation, the court will give standard directions concerning the filing and serving of the parents' response	FPR PD12A
Directions	Upon Issue and Allocation, the court will give standard directions and will give further directions at the Case Management Hearing	FPR 2010, rr 12.12, 12.24; PD12A (PLO, stages 1 and 2)
Children's guardian	Must normally be appointed	CA 1989, s 41(1); FPR PD12A (PLO, stage 1)
Interim orders	Unless permission given, interim application must be in writing on notice (can be included on Form C110A) With permission, interim order can be sought without formal written application or notice	FPR 2010, r 12.5(2)(b)
Who has power to make the order	Any judge of the Family Court	FC(CDB)R 2014, rr 3, 20
	A justices' clerk or single lay justice has limited power to make interim orders by consent, but no power to make full care or supervision orders	JCAR 2014; CA 1989, s 93(2)(i); FPR 2010, r 2.6(2)
Order	Interim care order Care order Supervision order (interim or full) No order	FPR PD12A
Additional or alternative orders available without prior application	Interim care/supervision order with or without directions as to assessment	CA 1989, s 38(1),(6)
	Care order/supervision order	CA 1989, s 31(1),(5)
	A child arrangements order with respect to living arrangements (but not in favour of local authority and not with a care order)	CA 1989, ss 9(2), 10(1), 91(1)
	Prohibited steps order (but subject to s 9(5) and not with a care order)	CA 1989, ss 9(1), 10(1)
	Specific issue order (but subject to s 9(5) and not with a care order)	CA 1989, ss 9(1), 10(1)
	A child arrangements order with respect to with whom the child is to spend time (but not in favour of local authority and not with a care order)	CA 1989, ss 9(1),(2), 10(1)
	Section 34 child arrangements (in conjunction with care order)	CA 1989, s 34(5)
	Family assistance order	CA 1989, s 16(1)
	Order appointing children's guardian	CA 1989, s 5(2)
	Order terminating appointment of guardian	CA 1989, s 6(7)(c)
	Order for financial relief (in certain limited circumstances only)	CA 1989, s 15, Sch 1
	No order	CA 1989, s 1(5)

	There is no reason why other orders (eg a parental responsibility order under s 4) should not be sought at the same time as a care or supervision order in an appropriate case, but a prior application would need to be made in accordance with the rules (FPR 2010)	
Procedure for exclusion requirements	Applicant for interim care order prepares separate statement of evidence in support re: exclusion requirement Applicant serves statement and copy of order containing exclusion requirement (and of any power of arrest attached) personally on relevant person (i e person who is excluded) and informs relevant person of right to apply to vary/discharge exclusion requirement. It is important when effecting service that the process server complies with the Family Justice Council *Protocol for Process Servers* If power of arrest attached, once relevant person served with order/informed of terms, copy of order must be delivered to police together with statement showing relevant person served/informed of terms Unless relevant person given notice and attended hearing, if power of arrest attached to exclusion order, court must announce in open court at earliest opportunity the name of person and fact that such order made Consent of person who is assuming care of child is required	CA 1989, s 38A; FPR 2010, r 12.28(2); FJC Protocol of November 2011: *Process Servers: Non-Molestation Orders* FPR 2010, r 12.28(3); FJC Protocol of November 2011: *Process Servers: Non-Molestation Orders* FPR PD12K CA 1989, s 38A(2); FPR 2010, r 12.29
Variation/ discharge of exclusion requirement and attendant power of arrest	Application for variation/discharge re: exclusion requirement or re: power of arrest by person to whom it applies, Form C2 suggested Applicant serves parties to the proceedings with application for variation/discharge Consider giving notice to person caring for child Steps to be taken on variation/discharge affecting exclusion requirement/power of arrest	CA 1989, s 39(3A),(3B) FPR 2010, r 12.28(5) FPR PD12C FPR 2010, r 12.18(4),(6)
Appeals	See Guides E2, E4 and E5	
Transitional arrangements	Implementation of CFA 2014	Children and Families Act 2014 (Transitional Proceedings) Order 2014

D14: Discharge etc of a Care or Supervision Order, Substitution of a Supervision Order for a Care Order or Variation or Extension of a Supervision Order

Legal background

Under CA 1989, s 39, application may be made for the discharge of a care or supervision order or the variation of a supervision order. CA 1989, s 39(4) also empowers the court, on application, to substitute a supervision order for a care order, regardless of whether the threshold provisions set out in CA 1989, s 31(2) are satisfied at the time. In considering all s 39 applications, the court must apply the principle that the child's welfare is paramount (CA 1989, s 1(1)) and have regard to the checklist of factors in CA 1989, s 1(3) as well as to its duty not to make an order unless to do so would be more beneficial for the child than not to do so (CA 1989, s 1(5)).

Since the making of a child arrangements order with respect to living arrangements in relation to a child who is the subject of a care order discharges the care order (CA 1989, s 91(1)), an application for such an order can, in an appropriate case, be an alternative to an application under s 39(1) for discharge.

In every case where a parent decides to apply to discharge a care order in circumstances where the local authority has given notice of intention to remove a child placed at home under a care order, the parent should consider whether to apply in addition for an injunction under HRA 1998, s 8 to prevent the local authority from removing the child pending the determination of the discharge application. When a local authority, having given notice of its intention to remove a child placed at home under a care order, is given notice of an application for discharge of the care, the local authority must consider whether the child's welfare requires his immediate removal. Any removal of a child in circumstances where the child's welfare does not require immediate removal, or without proper consideration and consultation, is likely to be an unlawful interference with the Art 8 rights of the parent and child.

An application to extend the length of a supervision order should be made by the supervisor under CA 1989, Sch 3, para 6(3) rather than in reliance on the more general power in s 39(2) to vary a supervision order.

Applications made under CA 1989, Pt IV for the discharge of a care or supervision order, substitution of a supervision order for a care order or variation or extension of a supervision order are subject to FPR PD12A and the PLO contained therein. See Case management hearing, Further case management hearing and Issues resolution hearing within PD12A.

Procedure

Who may apply	*Discharge of care order* The child Any person with parental responsibility for the child Local authority designated in order *Discharge of supervision order* Supervisor and, where application is to vary a requirement affecting a person with whom child is living, that person	CA 1989, s 39(1)–(3)
	Extension of supervision order Supervisor only	CA 1989, Sch 3, para 6(3)
Which court	The Family Court. An application made within existing proceedings in the Family Court will be allocated to the level of judge who is dealing with the existing proceedings to which the application relates. An application made in connection with proceedings in the Family Court that have concluded will be allocated to the level of judge who last dealt with those proceedings	FC(CDB)R 2014, r 17(1),(2)
	Where the application has been allocated without a hearing, a party may request the court to reconsider allocation at a hearing. The court may also reconsider allocation of its own initiative	FPR 2010, r 29.19
	A Family Court may transfer a case to another Family Court either of its own initiative or on the application of one of the parties	FPR 2010, r 29.17
	An application may be made for existing proceedings to be heard in a different Designated Family Judge area	FPR 2010, r 29.18
	The application may not be transferred to the High Court unless by order of a judge sitting in the Family Court who is either the President of the Family Division, a judge of the Court of Appeal or a High Court Judge or where the circumstances in PD29C apply	FPR 2010, r 29.17(3),(4); PD29C
Which proceedings	Freestanding application	
Pre-proceedings checklist	Local authority must carry out specified work set out in checklist before filing an application	FPR PD12A

Application	On Form C110A, with sufficient copies for each respondent. The local authority must send a copy of the application form and Annex Documents to Cafcass/CAFCASS On filing Form C110A the timetable under the PLO starts at Day 1 and must be strictly adhered to until the conclusion of the case Within a day of issue (Day 2), the court must consider and decide allocation and set out the reasons for its allocation decision Fee: £215	FPR PD5A; PD12A; President's Guidance *The Use of Prescribed Documents* FPR PD12A (PLO, stage 1) FC(CDB)R 2014, r 20; President's Guidance *Allocation and Gatekeeping* FPFO 2008, fee 2.1(m)
Respondents	Every person whom applicant believes has parental responsibility Every person whom applicant believes had parental responsibility under a child arrangements order before care order was granted The child The parties to the original proceedings The supervisor (supervision order only)	FPR 2010, r 12.3
Additional persons to whom notice in Form C6A is to be given	Local authority providing accommodation for child Persons caring for child at commencement of proceedings Person providing a CA 1989, s 51 refuge for child	FPR PD12C
Service	Copy of application, together with Form C6, to be served on respondent by Day 2 Form C6A to be served on additional persons at same time as application etc served on respondents At or before the Case Management Hearing (not before day 12 but no later than day 18), applicant must file statement in Form C9 to prove that requirements for service have been complied with	FPR PD5A; PD12A (PLO, stage 1) FPR PD12C, para 3.1 PD12A (PLO, stage 1)
Without notice	Not available	FPR 2010, r 12.16
Joinder or removal of parties	By court order, of its own initiative or on written request	FPR 2010, rr 4.3, 12.3(3); PD12A (PLO, stage 2)
Answer to application	Upon Issue and Allocation, the court will give standard directions concerning the filing and serving of the responses of the respondents to the application	FPR PD12A
Directions	Upon Issue and Allocation, the court will give standard directions and will give further directions at the Case Management Hearing	FPR 2010, rr 12.12, 12.24; PD12A (PLO, stages 1 and 2)
Children's guardian	Must normally be appointed	CA 1989, s 41(1); FPR PD12A (PLO, stage 1)
Special requirements	Following application for discharge of care order, supervision order, education supervision order, or for substitution of supervision order for care order or for child assessment order, bar on further application within 6 months from disposal of application, unless permission given	CA 1989, s 91(15)

Who has power to make the order	Any judge of the Family Court A justices' clerk or single justice has no such power	FC(CDB)R 2014, rr 3, 20 JCAR 2014; CA 1989, s 93(2)(i); FPR 2010, r 2.6
Order	Discharge of care order Other applications	FPR PD12A
Additional or alternative orders available on applications under CA 1989, s 39 without prior application	Section 8 order but subject to certain restrictions	CA 1989, ss 9(1), (2), 10(1), 91(1)
	Section 34 child arrangements (if care order is to continue)	CA 1989, s 34(5)
	Family assistance order	CA 1989, s 16(1)
	Order appointing children's guardian	CA 1989, s 5(2)
	Order terminating appointment of guardian	CA 1989, s 6(7)(c)
	Order for financial relief (in certain limited circumstances only)	CA 1989, s 15, Sch 1
	No order	CA 1989, s 1(5)
	There is no reason why other orders (e g a parental responsibility order under s 4) should not be sought in an appropriate case at the same time as an application for discharge or variation is made, but a prior application would need to be made in accordance with the rules (FPR 2010)	
Appeals	See Guides E2, E4 and E5	
Transitional arrangements	Implementation of CFA 2014	Children and Families Act 2014 (Transitional Proceedings) Order 2014

D15: Regulating Contact with Children in Care

Legal background

The local authority has a duty to allow reasonable contact between a child in care and the child's parents, guardian, any person who had a child arrangements order with respect to living arrangements immediately before the care order was made and any person who had care of the child immediately before the care order by virtue of an order made under the High Court's inherent jurisdiction (CA 1989, s 34(1)). As a matter of urgency, the local authority may withhold contact for a period of up to 7 days if it is satisfied that it is necessary to do so to safeguard or promote the child's welfare (CA 1989, s 34(6)). If this is not sufficient to cover the situation, an order authorising the local authority to refuse contact to a named person can be obtained from the court under CA 1989, s 34(4) and is not limited in time.

The court also has a general power to make such an order (with or without conditions, CA 1989, s 34(7)) as it considers appropriate with respect to the contact that is to be allowed between the child and a named person (CA 1989, s 34(2), (3)), and this can be used to define contact where there is dissatisfaction with the level of contact the local authority has decided upon, to resolve a dispute with the local authority as to whether contact needs to be supervised etc. CA 1989, s 8 child arrangements orders cannot co-exist with a care order and the position is therefore regulated exclusively by CA 1989, s 34. If a CA 1989, s 8 child arrangements order existed before the making of the care order, the care order will automatically discharge it (CA 1989, s 91(2)), and no s 8 child arrangements order can be made in relation to a child in care (CA 1989, s 9(1)).

Applications made under CA 1989, Pt IV regulating contact with children in care are subject to FPR PD12A and the PLO contained therein. See Case management hearing, Further case management hearing and Issues resolution hearing within PD12A.

Procedure

Who may apply	Local authority Child AND (unless application is for refusal of contact) Parent Children's guardian Person who had child arrangements order with respect to living arrangements immediately before care order Person who had care of child immediately before care order by virtue of High Court order under inherent jurisdiction Any other person with permission	CA 1989, s 34(2)–(4)
Which court	The Family Court. The application will be allocated to the appropriate level of judge in the Family Court having regard to the allocation criteria. An application made within existing proceedings in the Family Court will be allocated to the level of judge who is dealing with the existing proceedings to which the application relates	FC(CDB)R 2014, rr 3, 17(1), 20
	Where the application has been allocated without a hearing, a party may request the court to reconsider allocation at a hearing. The court may also reconsider allocation of its own initiative	FPR 2010, r 29.19
	A Family Court may transfer a case to another Family Court either of its own initiative or on the application of one of the parties	FPR 2010, r 29.17
	An application may be made for existing proceedings to be heard in a different Designated Family Judge area	FPR 2010, r 29.18
	The application may not be transferred to the High Court unless by order of a judge sitting in the Family Court who is either the President of the Family Division, a judge of the Court of Appeal or a High Court Judge or where the circumstances in PD29C apply	FPR 2010, r 29.17(3),(4); PD29C
Which proceedings	Freestanding application	CA 1989, s 34(2)–(4)
	When making care order or in any family proceedings in connection with child in care, even though no application has been made	CA 1989, s 34(5)
Pre-proceedings checklist	Local authority must carry out specified work set out in checklist before filing an application	FPR PD12A
Application	*Contact* Form C110A and Supplement Form C15, with sufficient copies for each respondent. The local authority must send a copy of the application form and Annex Documents to Cafcass/CAFCASS *Refusal of contact* Form C110A and Supplement Form C14, with sufficient copies for each respondent	FPR PD5A, FPR PD12A; President's Guidance *The Use of Prescribed Documents*
	Within a day of issue (Day 2) the court must consider and decide allocation and set out the reasons for its allocation decision	FPR PD12A; President's Guidance *Allocation and Gatekeeping*
	On filing Forms C110A and C15/C14 the Timetable under the PLO starts at Day 1 and must be strictly adhered to until the conclusion of the case	FPR PD12A (PLO, stage 1)

	Fee: £215	FPFO 2008, fee 2.1(k)
Respondents	Every person whom applicant believes has parental responsibility Every person whom applicant believes had parental responsibility before care order The child The person whose contact with the child is the subject of the application	FPR 2010, r 12.3
Additional persons to whom notice in Form C6A is to be given	Local authority providing accommodation for child Persons caring for child at commencement of proceedings	
	Person providing a s 51 refuge for child	FPR PD12C, para 3.1
Service	Copy of application, together with the Annex Documents, evidential Checklist Documents and Form C6A, to be served on respondents together with notice of the date and time of the Case Management Hearing within a day of issue (Day 2 of PLO)	FPR PD12A (PLO, stage 1); PD12C
	Form C6A to be served on additional persons at same time as application etc served on respondents	FPR PD12C
	At or before the Case Management Hearing (not before day 12 and no later than day 18), applicant must file statement in Form C9 to prove that requirements for service have been complied with	FPR PD5A; PD12A (PLO, stage 1)
Without notice	Not available	FPR 2010, r 12.16
Joinder or removal of parties	By court order, of its own initiative or on written request	FPR 2010, rr 4.3, 12.3(3); PD12A (PLO, stage 2)
Answer to application	Upon Issue and Allocation, the court will give standard directions concerning the filing and serving of the parents' response	FPR PD12A
Directions	Upon Issue and Allocation, the court will give standard directions and will give further directions at the Case Management Hearing	FPR 2010, rr 12.12, 12.24; PD12A (PLO, stages 1 and 2)
Children's guardian	Must normally be appointed	CA 1989, s 41(1); FPR PD12A (PLO, stage 1)
Special requirements	Bar on further application within 6 months from refusal of application unless permission given	CA 1989, s 91(17)
Who has power to make the order	Any judge of the Family Court	FC(CDB)R 2014, rr 3, 20
	A justices' clerk or single justice has no such power, although a single lay justice may grant permission to make the application	JCAR 2014; FPR 2010, r 2.6(1)(c)
Additional or alternative orders	Child arrangements order with respect to living arrangements in favour of someone other than local authority (but subject to CA 1989, s 9 restrictions, and note that effect would be to discharge care order)	CA 1989, ss 9(1),(2), 10(1), 91(1)
	No order	CA 1989, s 1(5)
	Other orders which are theoretically possible but very unlikely to be appropriate: – family assistance order	CA 1989, s 16(1)
	– order appointing children's guardian/terminating appointment	CA 1989, ss 5(2), 6(7)(c)

Appeals	See Guides E2, E4 and E5	
Transitional arrangements	Implementation of CFA 2014	Children and Families Act 2014 (Transitional Proceedings) Order 2014

D16: Discharge or Variation of an Order Regulating Contact with Children in Care

Legal background

An order under CA 1989, s 34 may be varied or discharged by the court on an application under CA 1989, s 34(9); alternatively, the local authority and the person entitled to contact can agree a variation in accordance with the Contact with Children Regulations 1991.

Applications made under CA 1989, Pt IV for the variation or discharge of an order regulating contact with children in care are subject to FPR PD12A and the PLO contained therein. See Case management hearing, Further case management hearing and Issues resolution hearing within FPR PD12A.

Procedure

Who may apply	Local authority The child The person named in the order	CA 1989, s 34(9)
Which court	The Family Court. An application made within existing proceedings in the Family Court will be allocated to the level of judge who is dealing with the existing proceedings to which the application relates. An application made in connection with proceedings in the Family Court that have concluded will be allocated to the level of judge who last dealt with those proceedings	FC(CDB)R 2014, r 17(1),(2)
	Where the application has been allocated without a hearing, a party may request the court to reconsider allocation at a hearing. The court may also reconsider allocation of its own initiative	FPR 2010, r 29.19
	A Family Court may transfer a case to another Family Court either of its own initiative or on the application of one of the parties	FPR 2010, r 29.17
	An application may be made for existing proceedings to be heard in a different Designated Family Judge area	FPR 2010, r 29.18
	The application may not be transferred to the High Court unless by order of a judge sitting in the Family Court who is either the President of the Family Division, a judge of the Court of Appeal or a High Court Judge or where the circumstances in PD29C apply	FPR 2010, r 29.17(3),(4); PD29C
Which proceedings	Freestanding application	CA 1989, s 34(9)
	In any family proceedings in connection with child in care, even though no application has been made	CA 1989, s 34(5)
Pre-proceedings checklist	Local authority must carry out specified work set out in checklist before filing an application	FPR PD12A

Application	On Form C110A, with copies for each respondent. The local authority must send a copy of the application form and Annex Documents to Cafcass/CAFCASS Within a day of issue (Day 2), the court must consider and decide allocation and set out the reasons for its allocation decision On filing Form C110A the timetable under the PLO starts at Day 1 and must be strictly adhered to until the conclusion of the case Fee: £215	FPR PD5A; PD12A; President's Guidance *The Use of Prescribed Documents* FPR PD12A; President's Guidance *Allocation and Gatekeeping* FPR PD5A; PD12A (PLO, stage 1) FPFO 2008, fee 2.1(k)
Respondents	As for initial application, *plus* the parties to the original proceedings	FPR 2010, r 12.3
Additional persons to whom notice in Form C6A is to be given	Local authority providing accommodation for child Persons caring for child at commencement of proceedings Person providing a s 51 refuge for child	FPR PD12C, para 3.1
Service	Copy of application, together with the Annex Documents, evidential Checklist Documents and Form C6A, to be served on respondents together with notice of the date and time of the Case Management Hearing within a day of issue (Day 2 of PLO) Form C6A to be served on additional persons at same time as application etc served on respondents At or before the Case Management Hearing (not before day 12 and no later than day 18), applicant must file statement in Form C9 to prove that requirements for service have been complied with	FPR PD36C, Annex (PLO, stage 1); PD12C FPR PD12C FPR PD5A; PD12A
Without notice	Not available	FPR 2010, r 12.16
Joinder or removal of parties	By court order, of its own initiative or on written request	FPR 2010, rr 4.3, 12.3(3); PD12A (PLO, stage 1)
Answer to application	Upon Issue and Allocation, the court will give standard directions concerning the filing and serving of the parents' response	FPR PD36C, Annex
Directions	Upon Issue and Allocation, the court will give standard directions and will give further directions at the Case Management Hearing	FPR 2010, rr 12.12, 12.24; PD12A (PLO, stages 1 and 2)
Children's guardian	Must normally be appointed	CA 1989, s 41(1); FPR PD12A (PLO, stage 1)
Special requirements	Bar on further application within 6 months from refusal of application unless permission given	CA 1989, s 91(17)
Who has power to make the order	Any judge of the Family Court A justices' clerk or single lay justice has no such power	FC(CDB)R 2014, rr 3, 20 JCAR 2014; CA 1989, s 93(2)(i); FPR 2010, r 2.6
Additional or alternative orders	Child arrangements order with respect to living arrangements in favour of someone other than local authority (but subject to CA 1989, s 9 restrictions, and note that effect would be to discharge care order) No order	CA 1989, ss 9(1), (2), 10(1), 91(1) CA 1989, s 1(5)

	Other orders which are theoretically possible but very unlikely to be appropriate: – family assistance order – order appointing children's guardian/terminating appointment	CA 1989, s 16(1) CA 1989, ss 5(2), 6(7)(c)
Appeals	See Guides E2, E4 and E5	
Transitional arrangements	Implementation of CFA 2014	Children and Families Act 2014 (Transitional Proceedings) Order 2014

D17: Secure Accommodation Order

Legal background

Restricting the liberty of a child is a serious step and is therefore strictly regulated by CA 1989, s 25 and by the Children (Secure Accommodation) Regulations 1991 and the Children (Secure Accommodation) (No 2) Regulations 1991. With certain exceptions, a child may not be placed or kept in secure accommodation unless either he has a history of absconding and is likely to abscond if kept in any other type of accommodation and, if he absconds, to suffer significant harm or he is likely to injure himself or others if kept in any other type of accommodation. Where either of these criteria is satisfied, a child may be kept in secure accommodation for a maximum of 72 hours without court authority but, if there is a need to detain him for longer, an application must be made to the court. If the court is satisfied that the relevant criteria are met, it will make an order authorising the child to be kept in secure accommodation for a specified maximum period of time (up to 3 months for a first application and up to 6 months on any further application).

A freestanding application for an *interim* secure accommodation order cannot be made. Where the court is satisfied it has all the information needed to determine the issues raised by the application and that it would be procedurally fair to proceed, it is unlikely there would be grounds upon which the court could properly adjourn the application. Prolonging secure accommodation proceedings, simply in order to keep a children's guardian involved for the purposes of assisting the child or overseeing the performance of the local authority's statutory duties is not a proper use of the court's power (*Birmingham City Council v M* [2008] 2 FLR 542, FD).

The consent of the subject child is not required to him being accommodated pursuant to CA 1989, s 20(3) nor to a secure accommodation order being made in respect of him: *Re W (A Child) (Secure Accommodation)* [2016] EWCA Civ 804.

Where a child is detained under PACE 1984, s 38(6), the Youth Court has power to make a secure accommodation order even if the s 25 criteria are not met, provided that the criteria in reg 6(2) are met. The age range for the making of such an order is increased from under 17 to under 18: see SI 2015/1883.

Procedure

Who may apply	Where local authority looking after child, only the local authority Where health authority, National Health Service trust or local education authority providing accommodation for child, only the health authority etc, unless local authority looking after child Where child provided with accommodation in residential care home, nursing home or mental nursing home, only the person providing such accommodation, unless local authority looking after child	C(SA)R 1991, reg 8 C(SA)(No 2)R 1991, reg 2(1) C(SA)(No 2)R 1991, reg 2(2)
Which court	The Family Court	FC(CDB)R 2014, rr 14, 20; FPR 2010, rr 12.2, 12.3
Which proceedings	Freestanding application for a final order but may not apply for an interim order	

Which court for variation, extension	Court by which original order made (There is no provision to apply to discharge a SAO. It is suggested that the same may be effected by the issue of a writ of habeas corpus)	
Application	On Form C1 and Supplement Form C20, with sufficient copies for each respondent Fee: £215	FPR 2010, rr 12.5, 12.7, 12.8 and 12.16; PD12C, para 2.1(1) FPFO 2008, fee 2.1(i)
Respondents	Every person whom applicant believes has parental responsibility Every person whom applicant believes had parental responsibility before care order The child Where application is to vary etc, parties to original proceedings	FPR 2010, r 12.3
Additional persons to whom notice in Form C6A is to be given	Local authority providing accommodation for child Person caring for child at commencement of proceedings Person providing a CA 1989, s 51 refuge for child	FPR 2010, rr 12.3, 12.5, 12.7, 12.8 and 12.16; PD12C, para 3.1(1)
Additional persons to be notified of intention to apply	Where application relates to child already kept in secure accommodation in a community home: – child's independent visitor, if appointed – any other person whom local authority considers should be informed	C(SA)R 1991, reg 14
Service	Copy of application, together with Form C6, to be served on respondent at least 1 day before date of hearing or directions appointment Form C6A to be served on additional persons at same time as application etc served on respondents	FPR 2010, r 12.8; PD12C, para 2.1(6) FPR 2010, r 12.8; PD12C, paras 1.1, 3.1
Ex parte	May not be available	FPR 2010, r 12.16
Joinder or removal of parties	By court order, of its own motion or on written request	FPR 2010, rr 12.3(3), 16.2
Answer to application	Respondent may file answer; serve on other parties	
Directions	Powers of the justices' clerk or the court	FPR 2010, rr 2.5, 2.6, 12.12 and Pt 4
Children's guardian	Must normally be appointed	CA 1989, s 41(1)
Special requirements	Order may not be made unless child is legally represented or has been told of the right to apply for CLS funding and given opportunity to do so and has refused or failed to apply	CA 1989, s 25(6)
Who has power to make the order Order	Any judge of the Family Court, save for a single lay justice Form C26	FC(CDB)R 2014, rr 14, 20; FPR 2010, rr 2.5, 2.6, 12.12 and Pt 4; PD2A FPR 2010, Pt 5

Additional or alternative orders	No order Wide range of alternative orders may be available, eg s 8 orders, since CA 1989, s 25 proceedings are 'family proceedings' by virtue of s 92(2)	CA 1989, s 1(5)
Appeals	See Guides E2 and E5	

D18: Applications for Recognition, Non-Recognition and Enforcement of Court Orders under the 1996 Convention

Legal background

The Hague Convention on Jurisdiction, Applicable Law, Recognition and Enforcement and Co-operation in Respect of Parental Responsibility and Measures for Protection of Children (the 1996 Convention; see Part VI) was signed on 19 October 1996. It was ratified by the UK on 27 July 2012 and came into force on 1 November 2012. Its aim is to improve the protection of children and their property in cross-border cases. Its objects are (a) to determine which country's authorities have jurisdiction to take protective measures; (b) to determine which country's laws are to be applied in exercising the jurisdiction; (c) to determine the applicable law in relation to parental responsibility; (d) to provide for recognition and enforcement of measures taken in one Contracting State to apply in all other Contracting States; and (e) to establish co-operation and to provide a framework for the exchange of information and collaboration between the authorities in the Contracting States. It sets out a non-exhaustive list of protective measures that are within its scope and a list of issues to which it does not apply. Articles 23 and 25 deal with recognition and non-recognition by operation of Art 24 and set out the grounds on which recognition may be refused. Article 24 allows any interested party to ask for a declaration confirming whether or not a measure will be recognised in another state. The enforcement provisions are set out in Arts 26–28. The PRMPC(IO)(EWNI)R 2010 (see Part IV) facilitate the operation of the Convention.

FPR 2010, Pt 31 and PD31A apply to proceedings for recognition etc of applications under the Convention. Note that although the USA has signed the Convention, it has not ratified it.

Procedure

Who may apply	Any interested party	FPR 2010, r 31.4(1)
Which court	To a district judge of the Principal Registry	FPR 2010, r 31.3(1), 31.4(2)(a)
Form of application	Pt 19. If recognition of an order only is sought, the application must indicate that it does not extend to registration and enforcement	FPR PD31A, paras 1.1, 1.2
Fee	£245	FPFO 2008, fee 1.1
Evidence	All applications for recognition, registration and non-recognition must be supported by a sworn statement or an affidavit exhibiting the judgment or a verified or certified or otherwise authenticated copy of the judgment and a translation thereof Grounds for refusing recognition are set out in Art 23(2) of the Convention	FPR PD31A, para 2.2

Documents and information to be provided in relation to an application for registration etc	(a) All documents necessary to show that the judgment is enforceable according to the law of the Contracting State;	FPR PD31A, para 4.2(a)
	(b) Description of the opportunities provided to the child by the authorities that gave the judgment, to be heard except where the judgment was given in an emergency;	FPR PD31A, para 4.2(b)
	(c) Where the judgment was given in a case of urgency, a statement as to the circumstances of the urgency that led to the child not being heard;	FPR PD31A, para 4.2(c)
	(d) Details of any measures taken in a non-Contracting State of the child's habitual residence, if applicable, specifying the nature and effect of the measure and the date on which it was taken;	FPR PD31A, para 4.2(d)
	(e) In so far as it is not apparent from the copy judgment provided, a statement of the grounds on which the judgment was based together with any documentary evidence to support that statement;	FPR PD31A, para 4.2(e)
	(f) Where appropriate, a statement regarding whether Art 33 of the 1996 Convention (where it is contemplated placing a child in a foster placement or institutional care or an analogous institution) had been complied with, and the identity and address of the authority or authorities from which consent has been obtained together with any evidence of that consent;	FPR PD31A, para 4.2(f) and Art 33
	(g) The information set out in FPR PD31A, para 3.2(c)–(e)	
Service of application for registration	Subject to any directions given by the court, the court officer should serve the application on the person against whom registration is sought	FPR 2010, r 31.8(2)(a)
Grounds for refusing recognition	Limited to those set out in Art 23(2) (see Part VI)	
Evidence and documents in support of applications for an order that a judgment should not be recognised	(a) A statement of the ground(s) under Art 23 of the 1996 Convention on which it is requested that the judgment be not recognised, the reasons why the applicant asserts that such ground(s) is/are made out and any documentary evidence on which the applicant relies;	FPR PD31A, para 4.3
	(b) An address within the jurisdiction for service on the applicant and stating in so far as is known to the applicant, the name and usual or last known address or place of business of the person in whose favour judgment was given	FPR PD31A, para 4.3(b)
Service of application or an order that judgment should not be recognised	Subject to any directions given by the court, the court officer should serve the application on the person in whose favour judgment was given	FPR 2010 r 31.8(3)(a)
Documents in support of an application for recognition only	All the documents referred to above under applications for registration with the exception of documents to show that the judgment is enforceable according to the law the of the Contracting State in which it was given	FPR PD31A, para 4.4

Directions	As soon as practicable after an application is made, the court may give such directions as it considers appropriate, inter alia dealing with dispensation of service and other issues of service and filing of evidence and expedition of proceedings	FPR 2010, r 31.6
Answer to an application for an order that the judgment should not be recognised	Upon receipt of an application for an order that the judgment should not be recognised, the person in whose favour the judgment was given must file an answer and serve it on the applicant within 1 month of service or within 2 months if that person is habitually resident in another Member State, unless the court has extended the time on account of distance. The answer may request recognition or registration of the judgment and in this event must be accompanied by the documents, information and evidence set out in FPR 2010, r 31.4(2) (above) insofar as these are not included in the application	FPR 2010, r 31.8(3)(b),(4),(5)
If no answer is filed	In a case where the 1996 Convention applies and the Service Regulation does not, if an answer is not filed the Court will apply Art 15 of the 1965 Hague Convention if applicable and if it does not, in all other cases the court will not consider the application unless – (a) it is proved to the satisfaction of the court that the person in whose favour judgment was given was served with the application within a reasonable period of time to arrange his or her response; or (b) the court is satisfied that the circumstances of the case justify proceeding with the application	FPR 2010, r 31.8(7)
Directions if an application for non-recognition is refused	The court may direct that the judgment be recognised or alternatively that it should be treated as an application for enforcement and order that the judgment be registered for enforcement provided that the requirement for the filing of the relevant documents and information has been satisfied	FPR 2010, r 31.10
Action taken by the court upon an order being made	(1) Where the judgment is ordered to be registered, the court officer will serve a copy of the order on each party as soon as practicable (2) Where the court orders that the judgment should be registered for enforcement the court officer will: (a) register the judgment in the central index of judgments kept by the Principal Registry; (b) confirm on the order that the judgment has been registered; (c) serve on the parties the court's order endorsed with confirmation that the judgment has been registered (3) Where the court refuses an application for registration for enforcement, the court officer must serve the order on the applicant and the person against whom the judgment was given in the state of origin	FPR 2010, r 31.14(2) FPR 2010, r 31.11(3) FPR 2010, r 31.11(2)

Contents of the notice of registration or a sealed copy of the order	Full particulars of the judgment registered and the order for registration or the full particulars of the judgment recognised;	FPR 2010, rr 31.11(5)(a), 31.14(4)(a)
	the name of the party making the application and his address for service within the jurisdiction;	FPR 2010, rr 31.11(5)(b), 31.14(4)(b)
	the right of the person against whom the judgment was given to appeal against the order for registration or recognition as the case may be;	FPR 2010, rr 31.11(5)(c), 31.14(4)(c)
	the period within which an appeal against the order for registration or recognition as the case may be made.	FPR 2010, rr 31.11(5)(d), 31.14(4)(d)
Appeal	Must be made to a judge of the High Court within 1 month or in the case of an appellant habitually resident in another Contracting State within 2 months of the date of service or notice of registration refusal to recognise or to register for enforcement	FPR 2010, r 31.15(1),(2)
	Time cannot be extended Appeals from the High Court lie to the Court of Appeal and then to the Supreme Court, but permission to appeal is required	SCR 2009
Stay of proceedings	Stay of proceedings for recognition or non-recognition or enforcement of a registered order may be granted if an appeal is pending in the state of origin or the time for appeal has not yet expired	FPR 2010, rr 31.9, 31.16

D19: Application in Respect of an Abducted Child under the Hague Convention 1980 or European Convention 1980

Legal background

CACA 1985 ratifies the Hague Convention of 25 October 1980 and the European Convention of 20 May 1980. Applications under the Hague Convention are made: (a) to secure the prompt return of children wrongfully removed to or retained in any Contracting State; or (b) to ensure that rights of custody and of access under the law of the Contracting State are effectively respected in the other Contracting State. Also note the application of Brussels IIA, which regulates which Contracting State should be seised of the matter in the event of competing applications and the 1996 Hague Convention.

Applications under the European Convention are made for: (a) recognition and enforcement of a custody order, including enforcement by means of returning the child to the person in whose favour the custody order was made; (b) recognition of a custody or contact order; or (c) recognition and enforcement of an order for contact.

In relation to the Republic of Pakistan, see *Protocol of January 2003 (Child Abduction Cases Between the UK and Pakistan)* (see Part V) and *Re H (Child Abduction: Mother's Asylum)* [2003] 2 FLR 1105, FD where the principles of the Protocol were considered.

In relation to Egypt, see the *Cairo Declaration Resulting from Anglo-Egyptian Meetings on Judicial Co-operation in International Child Abduction Matters between Egypt and the United Kingdom* (see Part V) signed on 17 January 2005.

Procedure

Who may apply	*Hague Convention* Any person, institution or body who claims that a child has been removed or retained in breach of custody rights	CACA 1985, Sch 1, Art 8
	European Convention Any person who has a court order giving them rights of custody and contact	CACA 1985, Sch 2, Art 4
Which court	The High Court in England and Wales or Northern Ireland The Court of Session in Scotland	CACA 1985, s 4 (see also Schedule to the President's Guidance on *Allocation and Gatekeeping*)
	In England and Wales the application must be issued in the Principal Registry and heard by a judge of the High Court, unless the application is to join a party or dispense with service	FPR 2010, r 12.45
Fee	£245	FPFO 2008, fee 1.1
Conditions to be met	*Hague Convention* The child must be under 16	CACA 1985, Sch 1, Art 4
	If the child is aged 16–18 the application for the return of the child should be made under the inherent jurisdiction of the High Court	FPR PD12F, para 1.5
	The child must have been habitually resident in a Contracting State immediately before his removal or breach of contact rights	CACA 1985, Sch 1, Art 4; FPR PD12F, para 1.4
	The child must have been wrongfully taken or retained in breach of rights of custody (child arrangements order) after the date on which the Convention came into force between the two countries	CACA 1985, Sch 1, Art 3; FPR PD12F, Pt 2
	European Convention The child must be under 16	CACA 1985, Sch 2, Art 1
	At the time of removal the applicant must have a custody or contact order (child arrangements order) made in his favour	CACA 1985, Sch 2, Art 4
	The child must have been removed in breach of those custody or contact (child arrangements) rights to another Contracting State	CACA 1985, Sch 1, Art 3
	If, at the time of removal, there is no custody (child arrangements) order in force, the Convention may apply to an order made after the removal if it also contains a declaration that the removal was wrongful	CACA 1985, Sch 2, Art 12
Application procedure in England and Wales	In Form C67 it must be headed 'in the matter of the CACA 1985' and 'in the matter of Council Regulation (EC) No 2201/2003' and must contain the information set out in PD12F, para 2.11 failing which the court may fix a time within which the document must be produced, accept equivalent documents or dispense with their production	FPR 2010, r 12.46
Documents	*Hague Convention* Authenticated copy of any relevant decision or agreement Certificate or affidavit concerning the relevant law of the Contracting State	CACA 1985, Sch 1, Art 8
	A statement in support made by the applicant or on his behalf by the applicant's solicitor which must contain a statement of truth	FPR PD12F, paras 2.12–2.13; PD17A

	Any other relevant document *European Convention* Document of authorization Copy court order Evidence of service Document establishing that the order is enforceable in the Contracting State Statement indicating the whereabouts of the child Proposals on how the custody of the child should be restored	CACA 1985, Sch 2, Art 13
Respondents	The abductor The harbourer The parent or guardian within the UK Any person in whose favour a custody (child arrangements) order has been made Any other person who has an interest in the welfare of the child The child if directed by the court	FPR 2010, r 12.3 FPR PD12F, para 2.24
Service of answer	The answer must be filed and served within 7 days of service of the application unless extended by the court	FPR 2010, r 12.49
Statement in support	A statement verified by a statement of truth together with any further evidence may be filed and served with the answer within 7 days of service of the application. The statement must disclose where the child is and particulars of any defence to the application. For defences that may be raised see Arts 12 and 13	FPR 2010, r 12.50(1); CACA 1985, Sch 1; FPR PD12F, paras 2.22, 2.23
Affidavit in reply	May be filed and served within 7 days of service of the affidavit in answer	FPR 2010, r 12.50(2)
Without notice applications	May be made for: – interim directions under ss 5 or 19 of CACA 1985; – disclosure of information about the child; his or her whereabouts; or – for a collection, location or passport order (FPR 2010, r 12.47)	
Directions hearing	May be listed to deal with, among others, the matters set out in FPR 2010, r 12.48(1). It is essential that the issue of how best the child's wishes and feelings can be placed before the court and whether he/she should be represented, especially where the child's objection or settlement are relied on, is dealt with at the first hearing to avoid delay and subsequent serial applications being made The court has a duty to set a timetable to complete the case within 6 weeks	FPR PD12F, para 2.14
Orders	All the orders under the inherent jurisdiction, including: – collection and location orders in the prescribed form – see *Emergency Remedies in the Family Courts* (Family Law) – disclosure of whereabouts – disclosure of information from the Home Office – attendance order – surrender of passport	CACA 1985, s 24A FPR PD12F, para 4.14 FPR PD12F, para 4.10

	– port alert	FPR PD12F, paras 4.2–4.8 for 24 hours service available from the police for assistance without a court order
	– flight information – publicity	FPR PD12F, para 4.15
	– injunction prohibiting further removal and removal from UK	FPR PD12F, para 4.9
	– injunction freezing assets – GPS tagging orders in exceptional cases (for a precedent of tagging and GPS tagging order see *Emergency Remedies in the Family Courts* (Family Law) at B[4.13])	*Re X (Children) and Y (Children) (No 2)* [2015] 2 FLR 1515, FD
	– return of the child – dispensing with service	FPR 2010, r 12.48
	– stay of proceedings	FPR 2010, r 12.58
	– transfer of proceedings to Scotland or Northern Ireland	FPR 2010, r 12.54
	– interim direction	FPR 2010, r 12.47; CACA 1985, s 5;
	– any other direction, including ADR	*AI v MT (Alternative Dispute Resolution)* [2013] 2 FLR 371, FD
	– child arrangements order – where there is a breach a writ of sequestration may be issued under CPR 1998, r 81.19	CACA 1985, s 5
Appeals	See Guide E5	
Applications in non-Convention cases		
Who may apply	Any person who claims that a child has been removed or retained in breach of custody (child arrangements) rights	FPR PD12F, para 3.1
Which court	High Court under its inherent jurisdiction The application must be issued in the Principal Registry and heard by a Judge of the High Court	FPR PD12F, paras 3.1 and 3.2
Application	Must be in Form C66 and must include the information set out in PD12F, para 2.11	FPR PD12F, para 3.3
Documents	Statement in support verified by a statement of truth. The Statement must exhibit any relevant documents	FPR PD12F, para 3.4; PD17A
Timetable	Directions will be given to complete the case within 6 weeks except where exceptional circumstances make this impossible See further above under application under the Hague Convention and the Inherent Jurisdiction	FPR PD12F, paras 3.5 and 2.14

D20: Application for Registration of an Order under the Family Law Act 1986 in Respect of an Abducted Child

Legal background

Application for the registration of a Pt I order may be made by any person in whose favour rights have been conferred by the order, in another part of the UK under FLA 1986, s 27, or in the Isle of Man under a corresponding provision. The procedure for the registration of an order made in the High Court or the Family Court is set out in FPR 2010, r 32.25. In relation to registration of orders made in Scotland, Northern Ireland or a specified dependant territory, FPR 2010, r 32.26 applies.

Procedure

Who may apply	Any person on whom rights are conferred by a Pt I order	FLA 1986, s 27
Which court	(a) Application in respect of High Court orders must be made to the court which made the order, that is: (i) High Court in England and Wales and Northern Ireland (ii) The Court of Session in Scotland (iii) High Court of Justice of the Isle of Man (b) Applications in respect of an order made in the Family Court must be made to the court which made the order	FLA 1986, s 27 FPR 2010, r 32.25(1) FLA 1986 (DT)O 1991 FLA 1986 (DT)O 1991 FLA 1986, s 27; FPR 2010, r 32.25(1)
Which department	In respect of High Court orders the application should be made as follows: – in the Principal Registry, to the family proceedings department manager – in the district registry, to the court manager – in Northern Ireland, to the master (care and protection) of the High Court – in Scotland, to the deputy principal clerk of session or the sheriff clerk, as the case may be – in the Isle of Man, the corresponding officer of the High Court of Justice of the Isle of Man – in respect of an order made by the Family Court, to the court manager	FPR 2010, r 32.23 FPR 2010, r 32.23 FPR 2010, r 32.23
Application	Request in Form C2 signed by or on behalf of the applicant	FPR 2010, r 32.25; PD5A; Ord 90 (NI); CSR 260R (Scotland)
Documents	Copy of the letter of application Statement by the applicant, with a copy, stating the matters set out in FPR 2010, r 32.25(1)(c) exhibiting the following: • a certified copy of the order • a certified copy of any order which has varied the original order	FPR 2010, r 32.25(1); Ord 90 (NI); CSR 260R; RRCOSC 1988, r 3(2)
In the event of refusal to send documents	The applicant may apply to a judge for an order	FPR 2010, r 32.25(4),(5)

D21: Application to Enforce a Registered Order in Respect of an Abducted Child under the Family Law Act 1986

Procedure

Which court	As under Guide D20, the court at which the order is registered	FLA 1986, s 27
Application	On Form FP1, supported by statement In Scotland, by petition	FPR PD5A CSR 260V
Defendant	The abductor	
Service	No specific rules, but the court will give directions In Scotland, usually 21 days unless the court otherwise directs	FLA 1986, s 27; FPR 2010, r 32.29 CSR 260V(4)
Orders	All the orders under the inherent jurisdiction, including: – collection and location orders – disclosure of whereabouts – attendance order – surrender of passport – port alert – flight information – publicity – injunction prohibiting further removal and removal from UK – injunction freezing assets – any other direction – child arrangements order	 For prescribed forms see *Emergency Remedies in the Family Courts* (Family Law) CACA 1985, s 24A; FLA 1986, s 33 FLA 1986, s 37 CA 1989, s 8

D22: Applications under the Inherent Jurisdiction of the High Court, including Wardship

Legal background

The inherent jurisdiction of the High Court is generally unrestricted and unlimited, except insofar as restrictions have been imposed by statutes or by judicial decisions of the court itself. Statutory restriction on the court's jurisdiction is imposed on local authorities by CA 1989, s 100. A child who is the subject of a care order cannot be the subject of a wardship application. Wardship is just one of the ways in which the court exercises its inherent jurisdiction in relation to children; in such cases (save for the restrictions imposed) the court has powers to make such orders as are deemed necessary for the protection of the child. The High Court's inherent jurisdiction may also be invoked to protect the interest of a vulnerable adult. The procedure about inherent jurisdiction proceedings is set out in FPR 2010, rr 12.36–12.42 and PD12D but other rules in Pt 12 are also applicable. In urgent cases, where possible, the application should be made within court hours and liaison should be made with the Clerk of the Rules who will attempt to accommodate such application in the Family Division applications court. For out of office hours applications, contact should be made with the security officer at the RCJ: 020 7947 6000/6260. CAFCASS Cymru and members of the Official Solicitor's legal team should be given advance notice during office hours of urgent and out-of-hours applications and be provided with details of the circumstances (FPR PD12E, para 4.1) Note: all applications in relation to an adult who lacks capacity are dealt with in the Court of Protection (see PD12E, para 4.4).

Procedure

Who may apply	Local authority (subject to the restrictions imposed by CA 1989, s 100 and only with permission)	FPR 2010, r 12.3
	Any person with a genuine interest in the person who is the subject of the proceedings	FPR 2010, r 16.6(1)(c); see also *Re CT (A Minor)* [1993] 2 FLR 278, CA
	The ward (wardship only)	
In medical treatment and press injunction cases where an interim declaration or order is required	Either the NHS Trust or A local authority; An interested adult (where necessary with permission of the court) or By the child with sufficient understanding	FPR PD12E, para 3.2
Respondents	Parent or guardian of the child; Any other person who has an interest in or relationship to the child;	FPR 2010, r 12.3
	the child (wardship proceedings only) with the court's permission as described in r 12.37	FPR 2010, r 12.37 and Pt 16
	In medical treatment and press injunction cases it may be desirable for a child who is the subject of the proceedings to be made a party and represented by a children's guardian. A child of sufficient understanding to instruct his own solicitor should be made a party and given notice of the application	FPR PD12E, para 3.1
	Where the child has formed an undesirable relationship the other party should not be made a party to the substantive proceedings- only a respondent to the application and must not be allowed to see the documents other than those directly relating to the application for injunction or committal	FPR PD12D, para 3.1
Which court	Family Division of the High Court (Principal Registry or district registry)	FPR 2010, r 12.36(1); SCA 1981, Sch 1
	Proceedings may be transferred to an appropriate Family Court	MFPA 1984, s 38(2); FPR 2010, r 12.36(2); PD12D, para 2.1
Application	On Form C66 (including any supplementary forms) with written evidence in support, which must set out: – the question that the applicant wants the court to decide or the order that is sought and the legal basis for the same; – if the application is made under an enactment it must identify the enactment; – if the applicant or the respondent is applying in a representative capacity what that capacity is	
	The statement of case must be verified by a statement of truth	FPR 2010, rr 5, 17.2; PD5A
Fee	On substantive application that includes permission to apply: £170	FPFO 2008, fee 3.3
	On notice application: £155	FPFO 2008, fee 5.3
	Without notice application: £50	FPFO 2008, fee 5.1
Documents	Application on Form C66 and supplementary documents with copy for service Statement in support Notice of proceedings	

	Certified copy of the child's birth certificate or copy of entry in the Adopted Children Register Copies of any orders made relating to the child, e g parental order, care arrangement order, where appropriate	
Other applications in existing proceedings or proceedings that have been concluded, including without notice applications	By Pt 18 application, in Form C2. The procedure set out in Pt 18 and PD18A should be followed The application notice verified by a statement of truth must state: – what order is sought and – the reasons for seeking the order(s) A statement in support (if the evidence relied on is not set out in the application notice) must be verified by a statement of truth A draft order	FPR PD5A; FPR 2010, rr 18.1(1), 18.2, 18.7
Service/ Acknowledgement of service	The general provisions for service under FPR 2010, Pt 6 apply. Notice of wardship must be served with the application	
Documents to be served	Copy of without notice order; Copy of application Copy of statement in support Notice of wardship Notice of return date/directions hearing	FPR 2010, r 18.8(3)
Time for service	If served in Scotland, Northern Ireland, a Member State or Hague Convention country, within 21 days of service If served outside Europe, within 31 days of service	FPR 2010, r 6.42(1)–(3)
Respondent's evidence in answer	The respondent must file: – the acknowledgement of service within 14 days if served within the jurisdiction unless the court otherwise directs; and – a notice setting out the information required under r 12.39 If respondent wishes to rely on written evidence the statement verified by a statement of truth must be filed with the acknowledgement of service	FPR 2010, r 19.7(4)
Applicant's reply	Written evidence must be filed and served within 14 days of service of the respondent's evidence	FPR 2010, r 19.7(5),(6)
Further evidence	No written evidence may be relied on unless it has been served in accordance with r 19.7 or with the court's permission	FPR 2010, r 19.8 and see r 22.1
Case management	When the court receives the acknowledgment of service it will give directions as to case management of the case, but an appointment should be sought within 21 days in any event to confirm the wardship or the wardship will lapse In the case of a without notice application, the time for the directions appointment will usually be abridged on the applicant's application On the hearing for directions, if the case appears complex and uncertain in its outcome, the judge may give further directions, including directions for trial	SCA 1981, s 41(2); FPR 2010, r 12.5, see also r 12.13 and PD12B *Re C* [1990] 2 FLR 527, FD

Urgent out-of-hours telephone hearing	Should be by tape-recorded conference call arranged and paid for in the first instance by the applicant's solicitors. All parties, especially the judge, should be informed that the call is being recorded by the service provider The applicant's solicitors should order a transcript of the hearing from the service provider otherwise the applicant's legal representatives should prepare a note for approval by the judge	FPR PD12E, paras 1.4, 1.5
Orders in urgent applications	In suitable cases applications may be made for directions for: – anonymity of the parties and others in any order or listing of the case; – exceptionally for a reporting restriction order	FPR PD12E, para 2.2
Orders	Any order, directions or declaration sought and consequential orders that may be necessary Where appropriate, any of the following orders: – collection and location orders in the prescribed form – see *Emergency Remedies in the Family Courts* (Family Law)	
	– disclosure of whereabouts	CACA 1985, s 24A; FLA 1986, s 33
	– attendance order – surrender of passport	FLA 1986, s 37
	– port alert – flight information – orders to restrict publicity; prevent undesirable association – orders relating to medical treatment – orders for the return of children to and from another state	FPR PD12D, para 1.2
	– injunction prohibiting further removal and removal from UK – injunction freezing assets – GPS tagging orders in exceptional cases	*Re X (Children) and Y (Children) (No 2)* [2015] 2 FLR 1515, FD
	– any other direction – child arrangements order – where appropriate, any order under CA 1989, s 8	CA 1989, s 8
Appeals	See Guide E5	

D23: Placement Order

Legal background

Under ACA 2002, s 18 an adoption agency may only place a child for adoption if either each parent or guardian consents (s 19), or a court has made a placement order authorising a local authority to place the child for adoption (s 21). On the making of a placement order, parental responsibility for the child is given to the local authority and to the prospective adopters (while the child is placed with them) (s 25). Any parent or guardian retains parental responsibility, but the local authority may determine the extent of its use. Any previous care order is suspended during the placement order and any previous s 8 or supervision order ceases to have effect. Contact may be regulated by court order under s 26. Unless there has been a change of circumstances after a placement order, and the court gives leave to do so, a parent cannot oppose a subsequent application for adoption (s 47). A placement order may be revoked (s 24).

Placement order applications are conducted under FPR 2010, Pt 14.

Proceedings under ACA 2002 are 'family proceedings' under CA 1989, s 8 and FLA 1996, Pt IV; therefore the court may make orders under CA 1989, Pt II or non-molestation orders within ACA 2002 proceedings.

Procedure

Who may apply	A local authority	ACA 2002, s 22
Who may be the subject of a placement order	A child (being a person under the age of 18 years)	ACA 2002, ss 21(1) and 144(1)
Application	Originating application in Form A50 A fee of £455 is normally payable	FPR 2010, Pt 5; PD5A FPFO 2008, fee 3.2
Respondents	Each parent with PR or guardian of the child A person in whose favour there is a CA 1989 order in force relating to the child Any adoption agency that has parental responsibility for, is looking after, or is caring for the child The child; and The parties or any persons who are or have been parties to proceedings for a care order in respect to the child where those proceedings have led to the application for the placement order The court may direct that any other person be made (or removed as) a respondent	FPR 2010, r 14.3(1) FPR 2010, r 14.3(2),(3)
Documents	The applicant must file: – three copies of the completed application form; – a certified copy of the full entry in the Register of Live Births that relates to the child or, where the child has been adopted, a certified copy of the entry in the Adopted Children Register; – any written consent of the parent or guardian to the child being placed for adoption, and any notice of withdrawal of such consent; – if the applicant is asking the court to dispense with the consent of any parent or guardian to the child being placed for adoption, a brief statement of the facts relied on in support of the request, and two copies of the statement; – a copy of any final care order relating to the child; – if available, a copy of any parental responsibility order or parental responsibility agreement relating to the child; – if the authority was a party to the proceedings, a copy of any other final order relating to the child that is in force and, if available, a copy of any maintenance agreement or maintenance award relating to the child; – if the authority was a party to the proceedings, a copy of any final order relating to a full, half or step brother or sister of the child that is in force The applicant local authority (if directed to do so) must file a report on the child and birth family containing matters in PD14C, Annex B	Form A50 FPR 2010, r 14.11
Parental consent	Court must be satisfied in the case of each parent with PR or guardian of the child that *either* he has consented to the child being placed for adoption and has not withdrawn consent *or* that his consent should be dispensed with under ACA 2002, s 52(1) Consent of mother is ineffective if given within 6 weeks of birth	ACA 2002, ss 21(3) and 52 ACA 2002, s 52(3)

Reporting officer	Appointed if parent appears willing to consent to placement for adoption and is in England and Wales	FPR 2010, r 16.30
Children's guardian	Appointed in every case, unless it is not necessary to do so to safeguard child's interests Children's guardian must appoint a solicitor for the child	CA 1989, s 41(6)(hh); FPR 2010, r 16.3 FPR PD16A, para 6.2
Children and Family Reporter	Court may ask a C and FR to report on welfare issue(s)	FPR 2010, r 16.33
Reports	Local authority may be ordered to report on reasons for placing for adoption	FPR 2010, r 14.6(3)
Hearing	Notice to be served on all parties, any reporting officer, children's guardian or children and family reporter Proceedings under ACA 2002 are 'family proceedings' First directions hearing must be within 4 weeks of application (unless court directs otherwise) At first directions hearing court will consider matters listed at FPR 2010, r 14.8 No placement order can be made without the personal attendance of the child (unless court permits non-attendance) and attendance by a legal representative of the applicant	FPR 2010, r 14.6(1)(b) CA 1989, s 8(4); FLA 1996, s 63(2) FPR 2010, r 14.7 FPR 2010, r 14.16(6),(7),(9)
Order	A placement order authorises local authority to place the child for adoption and gives parental responsibility to the local authority and to any prospective adopters with whom child is placed. Parents with PR retain it, but local authority may restrict their exercise of PR	ACA 2002, ss 21 and 25
Appeals	See relevant Guide in Appeals section	

D24: Adoption Order

Legal background

An adoption order is an order giving parental responsibility for a child to the adopters made on their application (ACA 2002, s 46(1)). At the same time, the making of an adoption order operates to extinguish permanently the parental responsibility which any person had for the child immediately before the making of the order (s 46(2) – save in a single step-parent adoption, see s 46(3)(b)). Application may be by a single person, or by a couple (married, civil partners or partners (whether different or same sex) living in an enduring family relationship (s 144(4)–(6)). An adoption order is irrevocable, save in the very restricted circumstances of ACA 2002, s 55 (revocation on subsequent legitimation). The adopted child is deemed to be the adopter's legitimate child and, if adopted by a couple, is treated as the child of their relationship (s 67). Adoption is therefore the legal process by which a child becomes a permanent and full member of a new family. Adoption order applications are conducted under FPR 2010, Pt 14. Proceedings under ACA 2002 are 'family proceedings' under CA 1989, s 8 and FLA 1996, Pt IV; therefore the court may make orders under CA 1989, Pt II or non-molestation orders within ACA 2002 proceedings.

Intercountry adoptions

Adoption of a child who is habitually resident abroad in a state that is a signatory to the Hague Convention on Intercountry Adoption will be under a Convention adoption order – see notes to ACA 2002, s 67. If the state is not a signatory, and if the adoption is not otherwise recognised in the UK as a valid 'overseas adoption' (see notes to ACA 2002, s 87), an adoption application must be made in England and Wales. Strict limitations are imposed upon making arrangements for such an adoption, bringing the child into the country, preparing reports and making any payments (ACA 2002, ss 83, 92–96).

Procedure

Who may apply	*Joint applicants* Each applicant must be over 21 (save for the child's parent who must be over 18) Each applicant must be married, in a civil partnership or in an enduring family relationship One of the following conditions is met: (1) At least one of the applicants must be domiciled in the British Isles, or (2) Both have been habitually resident in a part of the British Isles for at least 1 year before application *Sole applicant* Must be over 21 Either: Must not be married or a civil partner or must satisfy court that spouse or civil partner cannot be found, or is permanently separated, or is mentally/physically incapable of applying Or: Is the partner of a parent of the person to be adopted May be the parent of the child provided that the other parent is dead or cannot be found or there is none or there is other good reason One of the following conditions is met: (1) Applicant must be domiciled in the British Isles; or (2) Applicant must have been habitually resident in a part of the British isles for at least 1 year before application In all 'non-agency' cases (joint or sole applications) proper notice of intention to apply to adopt must have been given to local authority	ACA 2002, ss 50, 144 ACA 2002, s 49 ACA 2002, s 51 ACA 2002, s 51(1); ACA 2002, s 51(3),(3A) ACA 2002, s 51(2) ACA 2002, s 51(4) ACA 2002, s 49(2),(3) ACA 2002, s 44(2)
Who may be adopted	Adoption order may be made only in respect of a child (a person under the age of 18) on date of application and still under 19, who has never been married or in a civil partnership at date of order Child must live with adopters for the relevant probationary period or court gives leave to apply to adopt The court must not be denied jurisdiction by ACA 2002, s 48	ACA 2002, ss 49(4), 47(8),(9) ACA 2002, s 42 ACA 2002, s 42(6) ACA 2002, s 48
Application	Form A58 A serial number must be assigned to keep the applicant's identity confidential Application for leave to apply to adopt A fee of £170 is normally payable	FPR 2010, Pt 5; PD5A FPR 2010, r 14.2 FPR 2010, Pt 18 FPFO 2008, fee 3.1
Respondents	Each parent with PR or guardian of the child (unless he has given notice of not wishing to be informed under ACA 2002, s 20(4)(a)) A person in whose favour there is provision for contact Any adoption agency that has parental responsibility under a placement order Any adoption agency involved in the adoption arrangements Any local authority to whom notice has been given under ACA 2002, s 44	

	Any local authority or voluntary organisation which has parental responsibility for, or is looking after or caring for, the child The child in specific circumstances The court may direct that the child or any other person be made (or removed as) a respondent	FPR 2010, r 14.3(1) FPR 2010, r 14.3(2),(3)
Documents	The applicant must file three copies of the application form together with the documents listed on Form A58, in particular: – a copy birth certificate – a statement of facts (if applying for dispensation of consent) and two copies – a copy of relevant order(s) – a copy of relevant certificates or marriage, civil partnership, divorce, dissolution of civil partnership, death – a medical report on each applicant and the child (not required in agency cases) The relevant adoption agency or local authority (not the applicant) must file: (a) a report on applicant's suitability; (b) a report on child's placement for adoption, that comply with FPR PD14C, Annex A	Form A58 FPR 2010, r 14.12 FPR 2010, r 14.11
Parental Consent or Placement Order	One of three conditions must be met: (1) In the case of each parent with PR or guardian of the child ('parent') that either he, with full understanding, agrees unconditionally to the making of an adoption order or that his consent should be dispensed with under ACA 2002, s 52(1); or (2) An adoption agency placed child for adoption and either the placement was with consent of each parent, or it was under a placement order and no parent has leave to oppose the adoption (if leave is granted, condition (1) must be used); or (3) Child is subject of Scottish permanence order with authority to adopt, or a Northern Ireland freeing for adoption order Consent must be proved in compliance with rules Consent of mother to adoption is ineffective if given within 6 weeks of birth	ACA 2002, s 4 Forms A100–106 ACA 2002, s 52(3)
Reporting officer	Appointed if parent appears willing to consent to adoption and is in England and Wales	FPR 2010, r 16.30
Children's guardian	Appointed if child is a party, unless it is not necessary to do so to safeguard child's interests Children's guardian must appoint a solicitor for the child	FPR 2010, r 16.3 FPR PD16A, para 6.2
Children and Family Reporter	Court may ask a C and FR to report on welfare issue(s)	FPR 2010, r 16.33
Hearing	Notice to be served on all parties, any reporting officer, children's guardian or children and family reporter Proceedings under ACA 2002 are 'family proceedings' First directions hearing must be within 4 weeks of application (unless court directs otherwise) At first directions hearing the court will consider matters listed at FPR 2010, r 14.8	FPR 2010, r 14.6(1)(b) CA 1989, s 8(4); FLA 1996, s 63(2) FPR 2010, r 14.8

	No order can be made without the personal attendance of the applicant(s) and the child (unless the court permits non-attendance)	FPR 2010, r 14.16(6)–(8)
Order	An adoption order gives parental responsibility to the adopters and extinguishes any previous parental responsibility and any earlier court orders. The child is treated as if he was born to the adopter(s) in marriage	ACA 2002, s 46
Appeals	See relevant Guide in Appeals section	

E1: Application for Judicial Review

Legal background

Judicial review is the process whereby the High Court exercises its supervisory jurisdiction to review the legality and validity of the actions and decisions of persons or bodies exercising administrative powers, whether of a legislative, executive, judicial or adjudicatory character. The jurisdiction is over the proceedings and decisions of inferior courts (such as magistrates' courts and County Court), tribunals and other bodies performing public acts and duties. It is not a system of appeal. The procedure must be used where the claimant is seeking a mandatory order (formerly known as an order of mandamus), a prohibiting order (formerly known as an order of prohibition) or a quashing order (formerly known as an order of certiorari). The procedure for an application for judicial review is prescribed by CPR 1998, Pt 54 and PD54A and SCA 1981, ss 29–31 (and CCA 1984, ss 83 and 84). Judicial review claims are dealt with in the Administrative Court (see further annotation under CPR 1998, r 54.1).

A *Pre-Action Protocol for Judicial Review* came into force on 4 March 2002. There is also a helpful booklet available from the Administrative Court Office entitled *Notes for Guidance on Applying for Judicial Review*.

For the interplay between judicial review and applications under HRA 1998, see notes to CPR 1998, Pt 54 and to the 1998 Act.

In exceptional cases, it is permissible to bring a judicial review challenge to a local authority decision when there are extant care proceedings (and an interim care order is in force) where the actual decision sought to be impugned cannot effectively be made the subject of review in family proceedings and there is no other appropriate remedy: *R (H) v Kingston Upon Hull City Council* [2014] 1 FLR 1094, QBD.

All applications for judicial review must be made to the Administrative Court, either at The Royal Courts of Justice, The Strand, London WC2A 2LL, or at one of the regional centres, namely: Cardiff Civil Justice Centre, 2 Park Street, Cardiff, CF10 1ET; Birmingham Civil Justice Centre Priory Courts, 5th Floor, 33 Bull Street, Birmingham B4 6DS; Leeds Combined Court, 1 Oxford Row, Leeds LS1 3BG; or Manchester Civil Justice Centre, 12th Floor, 1 Bridge Street West, Manchester M3 3FX.

Procedure

Who may apply	Any person with sufficient interest in the matter subject to the proposed review	SCA 1981, s 31(3)
Application for permission	Made by filing a claim form (Form N461) promptly, and in any event within 3 months of the decision, in the Administrative Court in London or in one of the regional centres, namely Cardiff, Birmingham, Leeds or Manchester	CPR 1998, rr 54.1, 54.5
	The prospective claimant should write a detailed letter before action allowing 14 days for the prospective defendant to respond (unless the nature of the claim precludes this)	*Judicial Review Protocol*, paras 8–17, Annexes A and B
	Note the additional provisions where an application is made following the refusal by the Upper Tribunal for permission to appeal against a decision of the First-Tier Tribunal	CPR 1998, r 54.7A; PD54A, para 19
The claim form must include or be accompanied by	(i) a detailed statement of the claimant's grounds for bringing the claim for judicial review (ii) a statement of facts relied on	CPR PD54A, para 5.6

	(iii) any application to extend the time limit for filing the claim form (iv) any application for directions (v) a time estimate for the hearing	
Additional documents to accompany the claim form	(i) written evidence in support of the claim (verified by a statement of truth) (ii) a copy of the order complained of (iii) where the decision complained of relates to a decision of a court or tribunal, an approved copy of the reasons for the decision (iv) copies of any documents on which the claimant proposes to rely (v) copies of any statutory material (vi) a list of essential documents for advance reading by the court (with page references to passages); and if necessary, reasons why the documents cannot be filed and details of any person considered to be an interested party	CPR PD54A, paras 5.7, 5.10
HRA 1998	Where the applicant seeks to raise any issue under HRA 1998, or seeks a remedy under that Act, the claim form must: (a) state that there is a claim in respect of a HRA issue; and (b) give details of the alleged convention right infringed (c) specify the relief sought (d) state if the relief sought includes a declaration of incompatibility or damages in respect of a judicial act (e) where there is a claim for a declaration of incompatibility, provide details of the legislative provision (f) where the claim relates to unlawfulness by another court or tribunal, give details of the finding (g) where the claim relates to a judicial act, give details of the act complained of and the court or tribunal concerned	CPR PD16, para 15.1
Acknowledgment of service	Must be filed within 21 days of service of the claim form and served within 7 days of filing It should state whether the defendant contests the claim and, if so, summarise his grounds for doing so (see under 'Response')	CPR 1998, r 54.8(2)(a) CPR 1998, r 54.8(2)(b) CPR 1998, r 54.8(4)
Determination of permission application	Usually determined without a hearing Reasons being provided (on Form JRJ) If refused without a hearing (or granted on terms), a request for reconsideration (at an oral hearing) must be filed within 7 days of the reasons given for refusal If refused after a hearing, an application for permission may be made to the Court of Appeal within 7 days of the refusal Fee: For permission to apply for judicial review: £154. On a request to reconsider permission at a hearing: £385. If permission is granted and the judicial review procedure has been started: £770 (but £385 if the reconsider permission fee has been paid). If the claim was started other than by using the judicial review procedure: £154	CPR PD54A, para 8.4 CPR PD54A, para 9.1 CPR 1998, r 54.12 CPR 1998, r 52.15 CPFO 2008, fee 1.9(a)–(d)

Application	The application must proceed on the claim form (see above) used to seek leave	CPR 1998, r 54.15
	Where the claimant seeks to rely on additional grounds he must give notice no later than 7 days before the hearing	CPFO 2008, fee 1.9(b)
Defendants	Where the claim relates to proceedings in a court or tribunal all parties to those proceedings must be named in the claim form as an interested party	CPR PD54A, para 5.1
	The claimant must serve all the parties within 7 days of the issue of the claim form	CPR 1998, r 54.7; PD54A, para 6.1
	The claimant must lodge a certificate of service in the Administrative Court within 7 days of service	
Additional persons to be served	The claim form must be served by the claimant upon any person the claimant considers to be an interested party within 7 days of the date of issue	CPR 1998, r 54.7
	Any person may apply for permission to file evidence or make representations at the hearing	CPR 1998, r 54.17
Intervener	The High Court or Court of Appeal may not order a relevant party to pay the costs of an intervener unless there are exceptional circumstances that make it appropriate to do so	Criminal Justice and Courts Act 2015, s 87; CPR 1998, r 46.15
Response	A defendant or any other person served with the claim form who wishes to contest or support the claim must: (a) file an acknowledgment of service (Form N462) within 21 days setting out a summary of the grounds for contesting the claim and the name and address of any person claiming to be an interested party; (b) serve the acknowledgment of service on the claimant and interested persons within 7 days of filing (the court will do this if requested)	CPR 1998, r 54.8
	(c) file and serve detailed grounds and any written evidence within 35 days after service of the order giving permission	CPR 1998, r 54.14
Case management directions	Directions may be given as to service or evidence The court may direct that the proceedings be heard by a Divisional Court	CPR 1998, r 54.10
	A court officer of the Administrative Court who is a barrister or solicitor may, with the consent of the President of the QBD, give incidental or non-contentious directions	CPR 1998, r 54.1A
	Where a claim is under HRA 1998 a direction may be made for giving notice to the Crown or joining the Crown as a party	CPR 1998, r 19.4A
	Case management directions may be sought	CPR 1998, Pt 23
	List of those to be served, see –	CPR PD66, Annex 1
Cost capping orders	An applicant may apply to the court for a costs capping order limiting or removing the applicant's liability to pay another party's costs where the proceedings are 'public interest proceedings'	Criminal Justice and Courts Act 2015, s 88–90; CPR 1998, rr 46.16–46.19
Interim remedy	A range of interim orders may be sought (including an interim injunction or declaration)	CPR 1998, Pt 25

Documents	The claimant must file two copies of a paginated and indexed bundle which must include the documents of the other parties	CPR PD54A, para 5.9
	The claimant should also provide a paginated indexed bundle of statutory material	CPR PD54A, para 5.9
	Skeleton argument must be filed by the claimant not less than 21 working days before the hearing (or the warned date for hearing) and by the defendant or any other person wishing to make representations not less than 14 days before the hearing	CPR PD54A, para 15.1
	The skeleton argument must contain: (a) a time estimate; (b) a list of issues; (c) a list of legal points with justification for citing more than one authority on any proposition of law (d) a chronology; (e) a list of essential reading (where only part of a page needs to be read, that part should be marked (not highlighted)) and; (f) a list of persons referred to	CPR PD54A, para 15.3
Hearing	When an application is ready to be heard it will be entered in the Administrative Court Warned List and all involved will be notified. The case will usually be heard by a single judge in open court but may be heard by two or more judges sitting as the Divisional Court	
Order	The court may: – make a mandatory order, a prohibiting order or a quashing order	CPR 1998, rr 54.2, 54.3
	– grant an injunction or declaration	SCA 1981, s 30
	– award damages, order restitution or the recovery of a sum due	SCA 1981, s 31(4); CPR 1998, r 54.3
Appeals	If permission to apply for judicial review has been refused, an application for permission to appeal must be made to the Court of Appeal within 7 days of the decision (the Court of Appeal may either grant permission to appeal or grant permission to apply for judicial review). In all other cases permission to appeal is required, which must be sought either from the Administrative Court or from the Court of Appeal within 21 days of the decision or within such other period as the Administrative Court may direct	CPR 1998, rr 52.8 and 52.12

E2: Family Court – Appeal from Lay Justice or a Judge of District Judge Level to a Judge of Circuit Judge Level or from a District Judge of the High Court to a Judge of High Court Level

Introductory note

With effect from 6 April 2011, all appeals from magistrates' courts and from district judges are governed by FPR 2010, Pt 30 and PD30A.

All appeals are dealt with as a review (unless an enactment or practice direction provides otherwise or the court considers it in the interests of justice to hold a re-hearing: FPR 2010, r 30.12(1)). In *Piglowska v Piglowski*

[1999] 2 FLR 763, HL, guidance was given to the profession in respect of the conduct of appeals. The parties do not begin the appeal with a 'clean sheet'. Lord Hoffmann, at [783H]–[784H], stated that the appellate court must always bear in mind: (i) the advantage that the trial judge has of seeing and hearing the witnesses; (ii) that there is a discretion vested in the trial court and the appellate court should resist the temptation to substitute their own discretion for that of the trial judge on a narrow textual analysis of the judgment below; and (iii) that there must be a consideration of proportionality between the amount at stake and the legal resources to be expended. The Court of Appeal has observed that it is more helpful to refer to the case of *Piglowska* rather than the classic authority of *G v G (Minors: Custody Appeal)* [1985] FLR 894, HL: *Re C (Adoption Proceedings: Change of Circumstances)* [2013] 2 FLR 1393, CA. In *Re J (Child Returned Abroad: Convention Rights)* [2005] 2 FLR 802, HL, at [12], Baroness Hale observed '[t]oo ready an interference by the appellate court, particularly if it always seems to be in the direction of one result rather than the other, risks robbing the trial judge of the discretion entrusted to him by law'.

The test on appeal is whether the decision of the court below was wrong. For a detailed consideration of the role of an appellate court in family cases and the issue of proportionality, see *Re B (Care Proceedings: Appeal)* [2013] 2 FLR 1075, SC, *Re G (A Child)* [2014] 1 FLR 670, CA, and the notes to Guide E5.

Legal background

The Family Court came into being on 22 April 2014. From that date, appeals from lay justices are made without permission to appeal to a judge of Circuit Judge level. An appeal from a District Judge (magistrates' court) now requires permission to appeal. Appeals from a judge of District Judge level (including a DJ(MC)) are to a judge of Circuit Judge level. Such appeals may be heard, however, by a judge of High Court level if the designated family judge or a judge of High Court level consider the appeal would raise an important point of principle or practice. Appeals from the Senior District Judge of the Family Division or from District Judges of the PRFD in financial remedy matters are made to a judge of High Court level. Appeals from the Senior District Judge of the Family Division or District Judges of the High Court are made to High Court judges: FC(CDB)R 2014, rr 2-7 and FPR PD30A, paras 1.2, 2.1, 2.2.

In relation to the power for a judge to change his mind after delivering a judgment at the conclusion of a fact-finding hearing, see the notes to Guide E5.

On an application for permission to appeal, the appeal court has five options: (1) dismiss the application; (2) order a further without notice hearing; (3) order a hearing of the application on notice to the other parties; (4) order a hearing of the application on notice with the appeal to follow; (5) grant the application: *NLW v ARC* [2012] 2 FLR 129, FD.

For listing of case management appeals, see the notes to Guide E5.

For the limits of robust case management, see the notes to Guide E5.

Mostyn J observed in *NLW v ARC* that 'real prospect of success' means it is more likely than not that the appeal would be allowed at the substantive hearing; 'anything less than a 50:50 threshold could only mean there was a real prospect of failure'. Moor J, however, has held that a 'real prospect of success' is one that is realistic rather than fanciful and does not mean a greater than 50:50 chance of success. He commented that a practice direction was required to clarify the procedure for applications for permission to appeal: *AV v RM (Appeal)* [2012] 2 FLR 709, FD. The weight of current first instance authority follows the approach of Moor J: see Jackson J in *H v G (Adoption: Appeal)* [2014] 1 FLR 691, FD and Moylan J in *CR v SR (Financial Remedies: Permission to Appeal)* [2014] 1 FLR 186, FD in a judgment that compares the two approaches.

It is suggested that an appellate court should exercise caution before directing at a without notice permission to appeal hearing that a matter should be remitted for rehearing by the lower court when (a) the respondent to the application has not been heard by the court and (b) the court has not determined the full appeal: *Livock v Livock* [2012] 1 FLR 776, FD.

A notice of appeal does not operate as a stay. The existence of an arguable appeal with reasonable prospects of success was the minimum requirement before a court could even consider granting a stay: *NB v Haringey LBC* [2012] 2 FLR 125, FD.

Where the court makes an ICO on a plan of immediate removal of the child into care then, absent a case that has the characters of a '999 emergency', the court should consider granting a short stay to enable an application to be made to the appeal court for a stay and permission to appeal: *Re T (Interim Care Order: Removal of Children Where No Immediate Emergency)* [2016] 1 FLR 347, CA.

Regarding transcripts of the hearing or of the evidence, where a party is considering obtaining transcripts for the purposes of an appeal, see the notes to Guide E5.

The Court of Appeal has observed that it would be 'enormously helpful' if a chronology was provided in all family appeals as they are for most first instance hearings: *Re H (Interim Contact: Domestic Violence Allegations)* [2014] 1 FLR 41, CA.

Where events change or develop after the making of an interim order, the appropriate course is to seek a variation of the order from the judge, rather than seek to appeal against the order: *Re H (A Child)* [2011] EWCA Civ 762.

The Court of Appeal has set out the mandatory requirements that must be followed in appeals against placement orders: see *Re C (Adoption Proceedings: Change of Circumstances)* [2013] 2 FLR 1393, CA and the notes to Guide E5.

The unlawful removal of a child from his usual place of residence called for a peremptory order to be sought for his return, rather than to seek to challenge the dismissal of an appeal for an interim child arrangements order by way of a second appeal to the Court of Appeal: *Re R (Children: Peremptory Return)* [2011] 2 FLR 863, CA.

Permission is required from the appeal court to instruct fresh experts for the purposes of an appeal: see the notes to Guide E5.

For the grounds on which an appeal against findings of fact may be allowed, see the notes to Guide E5.

For the procedure to follow when seeking to challenge findings of fact after the order is sealed, see the notes to Guide E5.

For the approach that an appellate court should adopt to (a) appeals where the adequacy of a trial judge's reasoning is in issue and (b) appeals against the exercise of a discretion by a trial judge, see the notes to Guide E5.

For the issues to be considered on the question of whether the appeal court should re-make the decision or remit the same, see the notes to Guide E5.

Where the party seeking to appeal an order in the Court of Appeal in public law proceedings is a litigant in person, the local authority has the responsibility to ensure the appeal court is properly provided with appeal bundles: *Re R (A Child)* [2014] EWCA Civ 597.

For the practice direction on citation of authorities, see the notes to Guide E5.

Note: it is proposed to amend the rules to provide for appeals in private law children's cases, from circuit judges or recorders, to be made to the High Court and to be heard by judges of the Family Division and not to the Court of Appeal. The dates on which the draft SI will come into force and the commencement date are not yet known.

Procedure

Who may appeal	Any party to the hearing against an order or refusal to make an order	FPR 2010, rr 30.1, 30.3
Which level of judge	From lay justices to a judge of Circuit Judge level From a judge of District Judge level (including DJ(MC)) to a judge of Circuit Judge level From a District Judge of the High Court to a judge of High Court level	FC(CDB)R 2014, rr 5-7; FPR PD30A, paras 2.1, 2.2
Permission to appeal	Permission to appeal is required in any appeal against a decision of a district judge or a costs judge but permission to appeal is not required in an appeal against a committal order or a secure accommodation order or against an order or decision made by a lay justice or a bench of two or three lay justices	FPR 2010, r 30.3(1),(2); PD30A, paras 2.1, 2.2, 4.1–4.24
Material omission	Where a party's advocate considers that there is a material omission from a judgment or written reasons of the lower court, the advocate should give the lower court the opportunity to consider whether there is an omission and should not immediately use the omission as a grounds for an application to appeal	FPR PD30A, para 4.6
	The court must consider whether there is a material omission and, if so, to provide additions to the judgment	PD30A, paras 4.7–4.9
Filing of appeal	To be filed within: (i) such period as may be directed by the lower court; or (ii) if no such direction is made, 21 days after the date of the decision to be appealed; except that in the case of an appeal against an order under CA 1989, s 38(1) or a case management decision, within 7 days	FPR 2010, r 30.4(2),(3)
	The notice of appeal must be served on each respondent (and those specified in r 30.4(5)) as soon as practicable and in any event no later than 7 days after filing	FPR 2010, r 30.4(4)

Amendment of notice	An appeal notice cannot be amended without the permission of the appeal court Fee: £215, where FPFO 2008, fees 2.3 and 2.4 apply. The fee for an appeal from a district judge, lay justice(s), justices' clerk is £125. The fee for an appeal under CSA 1991, s 20 is £165	FPR 2010, r 30.9 FPFO 2008, fees 2.3, 2.4, 6
Respondents	Any party to the proceedings in the lower court who is affected by the appeal and any person who is permitted by the appeal court to be a party to the appeal The appellant's notice must be served on: (i) any children's guardian, welfare officer or children and family reporter; (ii) a local authority that prepared a report under CA 1989, s 14A(8) or (9); (iii) an adoption agency or local authority that prepared a suitability report on the applicant to adopt; (iv) a local authority that prepared a report on the placement of the child for adoption;	FPR 2010, r 30.1(3) FPR 2010, r 30.4(5)
Respondent's notice	A respondent's notice may be filed within (i) such period as directed by the lower court or (ii) where no direction is made,14 days of (a) the date on which served with the appellant's notice (where no permission to appeal required or permission granted by lower court), or (b) the date of notification that the appeal court has granted permission to appeal or (c) the date of notification that the application for permission and the appeal itself are to be heard together. But note, where the appeal is under s 38(1), no respondent's notice may be filed and a respondent may not seek to appeal the order or invite the appeal court to uphold the order of the lower court for different or additional reasons to those given	FPR 2010, r 30.5; PD30A, paras 7.1–7.4
Documents	The appellant must file the following documents, together with an appeal bundle, with the appellant's notice: (i) two additional copies of the appellant's notice for the appeal court; (ii) one copy of the appellant's notice for each of the respondents; (iii) one copy of the appellant's skeleton argument for each copy of the appellant's notice that is filed; (iv) a sealed or stamped copy of the order being appealed or a copy of the notice of the making of an order; (v) a copy of any order giving or refusing permission to appeal together with a copy of the court's reasons for allowing or refusing the same; (vi) any witness statements or affidavits in support of any application included in the appellant's notice. Items (ii)–(vi) should be filed with the appellant's notice of appeal or as soon as practicable after filing of the appellant's notice	FPR PD30A, paras 5.8, 5.12
Appeal bundle	An appellant must include the following documents in the appeal bundle: (i) a sealed or stamped copy of the appellant's notice;	

	(ii) a sealed or stamped copy of the order being appealed or a copy of the notice of the making of an order; (iii) a copy of any order giving or refusing permission to appeal together with a copy of the court's reasons for allowing or refusing the same; (iv) any witness statements or affidavits in support of any application included in the appellant's notice; (v) where the appeal is against a consent order, a statement setting out the change in circumstances since the order was agreed or other circumstances justifying a review or re-hearing; (vi) a copy of the appellant's skeleton argument; (vii) a transcript or note of judgment or, in a magistrates' court, written reasons for the court's decision, and in cases where permission to appeal was given by the lower court or is not required those parts of any transcript of evidence that are directly relevant to any question or issue on the appeal; (viii) the application form; (ix) any application notice (or case management documentation) relevant to the subject of the appeal; (x) any other documents that the appellant reasonably considers necessary to enable the appeal court to reach its decision on the hearing of the application or appeal; and (xi) such other documents as the court may direct.	FPR PD30A, paras 5.9–5.12
	If a respondent considers that additional documents should be included in the appeal bundle, any amendments should be agreed with the appellant if possible If the parties are unable to reach an agreement, the respondent may prepare a supplemental bundle	FPR PD30A, paras 7.16, 7.17
Skeleton arguments	The skeleton argument may be included in the appellant's notice or filed and served with the notice Where it is impracticable to do so, the skeleton argument must be filed and served within 14 days of the filing of the notice A skeleton argument must contain 'a numbered list of the points which the party wishes to make. These should both define and confine the areas of controversy. Each point should be stated as concisely as the nature of the case allows' The skeleton argument must set out, in respect of each authority cited, the proposition of law that it demonstrates and identify the relevant page or paragraph. Where more than one authority is cited in support of a proposition, brief reasons must be given for doing so A party who files a respondent's notice but does not include a skeleton argument must file one within 14 days of filing the notice A party who does not file a respondent's notice but who proposes to file a skeleton argument must do so at least 7 days before the appeal hearing	FPR PD30A, paras 5.13–5.22

	The respondent's skeleton argument should, where appropriate, answer the arguments set out in the appellant's skeleton argument	FPR PD30A, paras 7.7–7.12, 7.14, 7.15
Directions	Applications to: – dismiss the appeal for want of prosecution – dismiss the appeal by consent or – seek leave to withdraw the appeal – may be made to the district judge Unless the court otherwise directs any interlocutory application may be made to a district judge	FPR PD30A, para 9.8
Stay	Unless the court otherwise directs, an appeal does not operate as a stay of the order or decision appealed against	FPR 2010, r 30.8
Hearing of appeal	The appeal is limited to a review of the decision of the court below unless statute provides otherwise or the appeal court considers that in the particular case it would be in the interests of justice to hold a re-hearing Unless the appeal court orders otherwise the court will not receive oral evidence or evidence which was not before the court below	FPR 2010, r 30.12(1),(2)
Grounds of appeal	The appeal court will allow the appeal where the decision of the court below was: (i) wrong; or (ii) unjust because of a serious procedural or other irregularity	FPR 2010, r 30.12(3)
Powers of the court	The appeal court may: – make such orders as may be necessary to give effect to the determination of the appeal – make such incidental or consequential orders as appear just The appeal court has all the powers of the court below and has the power to: (i) affirm, set aside or vary any order or judgment made; (ii) refer any application or issue for determination by the court below; (iii) order a new hearing (iv) make order for the payment of interest; (v) make a costs order; (vi) exercise its powers in relation to the whole of part of an order of the lower court	FPR 2010, r 30.11
Assignment to Court of Appeal	Where the lower court or appeal court considers the appeal raises an important point of principle or practice or there is some other compelling reason, it may direct the appeal be transferred to the Court of Appeal (Note: does not apply to proceedings in FPC)	FPR 2010, r 30.13
Re-opening final appeals	The High Court will not reopen a final determination of any appeal unless: (i) it is necessary to do so to avoid real injustice; (ii) the circumstances are exceptional; and (iii) there is no alternative effective remedy	FPR 2010, r 30.14
Appeals	To the Court of Appeal (with permission) and note the restrictions in respect of second appeals; or to the Supreme Court, if a certificate has been issued by the judge under AJA 1969, s 12	SCA 1981, s 16; CPR 1998, r 52.13; AJA 1999, s 55 AJA 1969, s 12; SCPD 1.2.17, 3.6.1 to 3.6.16

E3: Appeal from Magistrates under Child Support Act 1991

Legal background

MCA 1980, s 111A provides for appeals from the magistrates' courts (civil) to the Family Court. Procedure is governed by parts of FPR 2010, Pt 30 and PD30A, paras 9.2–9.12. Paragraph 9.4 applies r 30.1, r 30.2 (compliance with PD30A), r 30.4 (appellant's notice), r 30.6 (grounds of appeal), r 30.8 (stay) and r 30.9 (amendment of appeal notice).

Procedure

Who may appeal	Any party to the hearing	
Which court	Family Court	MCA 1980, s 111A(2)
Procedure on appeal	Filing of appellant's notice Appeal on question of law or procedural irregularity only	FPR 2010, r 30.4; PD30A, para 9.2
Permission	Not required	MCA 1980, s 111A(2)
Time for issue	21 days 'after the day on which the decision of the magistrates' court was given	MCA 1980, s 111A(4)
Respondents	The parties to the original hearing directly affected by the appeal	
Service	By appellant at time of issue	FPR 2010, r 30.4(3)
Appeal notice	As for Pt 30 appeals: Form N161	FPR PD5A
Fee	£125	FPFO 2008, fee 6.1
Powers of the court	(a) Affirm set aside or vary (b) Refer back for re-determination or rehearing (c) Orders for costs and interest	FPR 2010, r 30.11(2)
Stay of order	Filing appeal notice does not stay order Apply to magistrates at time of hearing; or to circuit judge (application included in appeal notice (Form N161))	FPR 2010, r 30.8
Appeals	To the Court of Appeal subject to AJA 1999, s 55 limitations ('second appeals')	

E4: Appeal from a Judge of the High Court or from the Court of Appeal to the Supreme Court

Legal background

On 1 October 2009, the Supreme Court replaced the House of Lords as the final court of appeal in the UK.

An appeal from a decision of a judge of the High Court lies to the Court of Appeal, unless a certificate has been issued by that judge stating that the case merits a 'leapfrog' appeal direct to the Supreme Court. Where such a certificate is granted, a prospective appellant must seek leave of the Supreme Court to appeal direct and, if such leave is refused, he may then appeal to the Court of Appeal (see AJA 1969, s 13). Note, Criminal Justice and Courts Act 2015, s 63(3) amends AJA 1969, s 12 to introduce new grounds for a 'leapfrog' appeal:

> (3A) The alternative conditions, in relation to a decision of the judge in any proceedings, are that a point of law of general public importance is involved in the decision and that –

(a) the proceedings entail a decision relating to a matter of national importance or consideration of such a matter,
(b) the result of the proceedings is so significant (whether considered on its own or together with other proceedings or likely proceedings) that, in the opinion of the judge, a hearing by the Supreme Court is justified, or
(c) the judge is satisfied that the benefits of earlier consideration by the Supreme Court outweigh the benefits of consideration by the Court of Appeal.

An appeal from a decision of the Court of Appeal must be made to the Supreme Court, but only with leave of the Court of Appeal or, if refused, from the Supreme Court. The procedure for all appeals to the Supreme Court is prescribed by the SCR 2009 and the 14 PDs (available at *www.supremecourt.uk/procedures/practice-directions.html*).

The Supreme Court has decided that there must be compelling reasons for withdrawing public funding from a party who had been publicly funded in the court below, had been successful in that court and wished to resist an appeal to a higher court by the unsuccessful party: *R (E) v Governing Body of JFS and the Admissions Appeal Panel of JFS and others* [2009] UKSC 1.

In a landmark decision (*Re B (Care Proceedings: Appeal)* [2013] 2 FLR 1075, SC), the Supreme Court decided that:

(i) the decision whether the threshold criteria of CA 1989, s 31(2) is satisfied and whether or not to make a care or supervision order is an evaluative exercise rather than the exercise of a judicial discretion;
(ii) the decision to adopt a child is one of last resort – only in a case of necessity will an adoption order removing a child from his or her parents be proportionate;
(iii) the test to be applied on appeal is whether the decision of the lower court is 'wrong' as opposed to 'plainly wrong'; and
(iv) an appeal court does not have to undertake afresh its own evaluation of the issue of the proportionality of the decision made by the lower court.

The general rule is that, absent reprehensible behaviour or the taking of an unreasonable stance, costs in public law proceedings are not awarded against any party, including local authorities, whether at first instance or on appeal: *Re T (Costs: Care Proceedings: Serious Allegation Not Proved)* [2013] 1 FLR 133, SC; *Re S (A Child) (Costs: Care Proceedings)* [2015] 2 FLR 208, SC.

The Supreme Court does not have jurisdiction to entertain appeals from the Court of Appeal (in respect of a decision of the High Court) in applications made pursuant to Brussels IIA: *Re D (A Child) (Supreme Court: Jurisdiction)* [2016] 2 FLR 379, SC.

Procedure

Who may appeal	If permission has been granted: – any party to a decision of the Court of Appeal – any party to a decision of the High Court where a certificate under AJA 1969, s 12 has been granted	CRA 2005, s 40(2) AJA 1969, s 12
Application for permission	*Appeal from Court of Appeal* Permission must be sought from the Court of Appeal or, if refused, from the Supreme Court: 28 days from the order or decision of the court below *Appeal from High Court* Permission must be sought from the Supreme Court: within 1 month of the grant of a certificate under AJA 1969, s 12 (unless extended by the Supreme Court) or The application for permission will be heard by the Appeal Panel of the Supreme Court	SCR 2009, r 10 SCR 2009, r 11(1) SCPD 1.2.17, 3.6.1–3.6.16
Documents for permission application	The appellant must file four copies of the following documents: (i) an application for permission to appeal (ii) a copy of the order appealed from (iii) a copy of the order refusing permission to appeal	SCR 2009, rr 11, 14; SCPD 3.2.1 and PD 7 Form 1

	and within 7 days after the filing of the application (iv) a transcript of the judgment appealed (v) all other orders made by the courts below (vi) all other judgments given by the courts below (vii) transcripts of any unreported authorities cited in the court below (viii) a document setting out the history of the matter	
Notice of objection	A respondent who wishes to object to an application for permission must file a notice of objection within 14 days after service of the application for permission	SCR 2009, r 13; SCPD 3.1.8–3.1.10 and PD 7 Form 3
Intervention in application for permission	Any person may make written submissions to the Supreme Court in support of an application for permission to appeal and request the court takes them into account The submissions must be served on the appellant, every respondent and every intervenor in the court below before four copies are filed with the court	SCR 2009, r 15; SCPD 3.3.17
Procedure on permission application	The application for permission will be considered on paper without a hearing by a panel of Justices who may: (i) grant or refuse permission (ii) invite the parties to file written submissions within 14 days as to the grant of permission on terms; or (iii) direct an oral hearing Fee payable on filing an application for permission to appeal: £1000 Fee payable on filing notice of objection: £160	SCR 2009, r 16; SCPD 3.3.1–3.4.8 SCFO 2009, fee 1.1 SCFO 2009, fee 1.2
Procedure on appeal	Where permission to appeal is granted (i) the application for permission shall stand as the notice of appeal; (ii) the grounds of appeal shall be limited to those on which permission has been granted; and (iii) the appellant must within 14 days after the grant of permission file a notice of intention to proceed Fee payable on filing a notice of intention to proceed: £800 Where permission is not required: (i) a notice of appeal in the appropriate form must be filed within 42 days of the date of the order or decision; (ii) a copy of the order appealed from; (iii) a copy of the order granting permission to appeal Fee payable on filing a notice of appeal: £1600	SCR 2009, r 18 SCFO 2009, fee 2.1 SCR 2009, r 19; SCPD 4 and PD 7 SCFO 2009, fee 2.2
Respondents	The parties to the hearing in the court below Each respondent who intends to participate in the appeal must within 14 days after service of a notice of intention to proceed or a rule 20 notice file a notice in the appropriate form Fee: £320	SCR 2009, r 21; SCPD 7 Form 3 SCFO 2009, fee 2.4

	A respondent who wishes to argue that the decision of the court below should be upheld on different grounds from those relied on by the court below, must state that clearly in the written case but need not cross-appeal	SCR 2009, r 25(1)
Cross-appeals	A respondent who wishes to argue that the order appealed from should be varied must obtain permission to cross-appeal from the court and SCR, Pt 2 applies	SCR 2009, rr 25(2) and 10–17; SCPD 8.3.1–8.3.8
Lodgement of documents	The appellant must lodge within 112 days after the filing of the notice to proceed or the notice of appeal: (i) the original and seven copies of statement of facts and issues; and (ii) eight copies of the appendix of the essential documents that were before or record the proceedings of the court below both of which must be agreed with by every respondent before filing Documents must be included in the appendix in the following order: (a) the order appealed against; (b) if separate from the order at (a) above, the order refusing permission to appeal to the Supreme Court; (c) the official transcript of the judgment of the court below; (d) the final order(s) of all other courts below; (e) the official transcript of the final judgment(s) of all other courts below; (f) (where they are necessary for understanding the legal issues and the argument) the relevant documents filed in the courts below; (g) (where they are necessary for understanding the legal issues and the argument) the relevant documents and correspondence relating to the appeal All documents must be numbered, and each part of the Appendix must include a list of its contents Fee payable on filing a statement of relevant facts and issues and an appendix of relevant documents: £4820	SCR 2009, r 22; SCPD 5.1.2–5.1.5 SCFO 2009, fee 2.5
Intervenors to appeal	Any person who wishes to intervene in the appeal may apply for permission, which will be considered on paper by a panel of justices No permission is required for intervention by the Crown under HRA 1998, s 5, or by the relevant officer when the court is exercising its devolution jurisdiction	SCR 2009, r 26
Appellants' and respondents' cases	The appellant and every respondent and every intervenor or advocate to the court must sequentially exchange and file their respective written cases	SCR 2009, r 22(4); SCPD 6.3.1–6.3.13
Core volumes	As soon as the parties' cases have been exchanged and in any event no later than 14 days after the date fixed for the hearing, the appellant must file 10 core volumes and 10 volumes of authorities The core volume must contain in the following order:	SCR 2009, rr 23 and 24; SCPD 6.4.1–6.4.4 and 6.5.1

	(a) Form 1 – a copy of the notice of appeal or the re-sealed application for permission to appeal; (b) notice of cross-appeal (if any); (c) statement of facts and issues; (d) appellants' and respondents' cases, with cross-references to the Appendix and authorities volume(s); (e) case of the advocate to the court or intervener, if any; (f) Pt 1 of the Appendix; and (g) index to the authorities volume(s) *Form of core volumes* The core volumes: (a) should be bound, preferably with plastic comb binding and with blue (or, for criminal appeals, red) card covers; (b) should include tabs for each of the documents set out in paragraph 6.4.3, preferably with the name of the document on the tab; (c) should show on the front cover a list of the contents and the names and addresses of the solicitors for all parties; (d) must indicate (by e.g. a label (printed in landscape) attached to the plastic spine) the volume number (in roman numerals) and the short title of the appeal	
Hearing of the appeal	Every contested appeal shall be heard in open court unless it is necessary in the interests of justice or in the public interest to sit in private for part of the appeal hearing	SCR 2009, r 27
Judgment	A judgment may be given in open court or, if the court so directs, promulgated by the Registrar	SCR 2009, r 28
Powers of the court	The Supreme Court has all the powers of the court below and may: (i) affirm, set aside or vary the order or judgment; (ii) remit any issue for determination by the court below; (iii) order a new trial or hearing; (iv) make an order for the payment of interest; and (v) make a costs order	

E5: Family Court – Appeal from Judge of Circuit Judge Level or a Judge of High Court Level to the Court of Appeal

Legal background

The Family Court came into being on 22 April 2014. Appeals from a judge of Circuit Judge level or from a judge of High Court level are to the Court of Appeal.

Note, an appeal from a judge of Circuit Judge level in all private law children's matters is now made to a judge of the High Court and not to the Court of Appeal: see Access to Justice Act 1999 (Destination of Appeals) (Family Proceedings) (Amendment) Order 2016 and Guide E6, below.

The Court of Appeal is a superior court of record, and has all the authority and jurisdiction of the court from which the appeal is brought (SCA 1981, s 15). The procedure for all appeals to the Court of Appeal is prescribed by CPR 1998, Pt 52 as supplemented by PDs 52A, 52C and 52D. Most decisions of the lower court require leave from that court or, if refused, from the Court of Appeal before an appeal may be made.

An appeal is against the order and not the judgment (*Vaughan v Vaughan* [2008] 1 FLR 1108, CA). It is not sufficient for a party to draw attention to an alleged deficiency in a judgment by way of an application for permission to appeal. It is incumbent on the party to point out the deficiency and to request clarification or a supplemental judgment on the issue (*Re S (Children) (Contact: Fact-finding Hearing)* [2007] EWCA Civ 694), but practitioners should proceed with caution: this practice should only be adopted as a prelude to an application for permission to appeal and should not be routinely used to invite the judge to reconsider a point of substance (*Egan v Motor Services (Bath) Ltd* [2008] 1 FLR 1346, CA). 'Before launching an application for permission to appeal, it is incumbent on the applicant to seek clarification of the judgment or amplification of the findings from the trial judge.' *Re A (Child Abuse)* [2008] 1 FLR 1423, CA. Where an alleged lack of reasons in the judgment had not been drawn to the attention of the trial judge or the judge had subsequently failed to elaborate his reasons, the normal procedure was remittal to the judge at first instance with a list of specific questions: *Re A & L (Appeal: Fact-Finding)* [2012] 1 FLR 134, CA.

Findings of fact made by a judge cannot be challenged on appeal by relying on material which had not been properly admitted in evidence and subjected to cross examination: *Re R (A Child)* [2014] EWCA Civ 270.

In care proceedings, a judge is entitled to change his mind – and thus his findings of fact – after delivering judgment, written or oral, at a fact-finding hearing even in the absence of an intervening change of circumstances. In *Re L-B (Reversal of Judgment)* [2013] 2 FLR 859, SC, the Supreme Court has held that a court should not be required to make welfare decisions concerning a child on a false factual basis. It declined to offer even a provisional view on whether the power was available after the order made at the conclusion of the fact-finding hearing had been perfected (ie sealed by the court): it was said the arguments either way were finely balanced. The power must be exercised 'judicially and not capriciously'. 'The best safeguard against having to do so is a fully and properly reasoned judgment in the first place.'

In *Re W, Re A, Re B (Change of Name)* [1999] 2 FLR 930, CA, the Court of Appeal held that the test to be applied by the appellate court in children cases, whether that be the High Court, County Court or Court of Appeal, should be the same – ie in accordance with the principles established by *G v G (Minors: Custody Appeal)* [1985] FLR 894, HL. More recently, however, the Court of Appeal has observed that it is more helpful to refer to the case of *Piglowska v Piglowski* [1999] 2 FLR 763, HL rather than the classic authority of *G v G (Minors: Custody Appeal)* [1985] FLR 894, HL: *Re C (Adoption Proceedings: Change of Circumstances)* [2013] 2 FLR 1393, CA. In *Piglowska*, the House of Lord gave guidance to the profession in respect of the conduct of appeals. The parties do not begin the appeal with a 'clean sheet'. Lord Hoffmann, at [783H]–[784H], stated the appellate court must always bear in mind: (i) the advantage that the trial judge has of seeing and hearing the witnesses; (ii) that there is a discretion vested in the trial court and the appellate court should resist the temptation to substitute their own discretion for that of the trial judge on a narrow textual analysis of the judgment below; and (iii) that there must be a consideration of proportionality between the amount at stake and the legal resources to be expended. In *Re J (Child Returned Abroad: Convention Rights)* [2005] 2 FLR 802, HL, at [12], Baroness Hale observed '[t]oo ready an interference by the appellate court, particularly if it always seems to be in the direction of one result rather than the other, risks robbing the trial judge of the discretion entrusted to him by law'.

In a landmark decision (*Re B (Care Proceedings: Appeal)* [2013] 2 FLR 1075, SC), the Supreme Court decided that:

(i) the decision whether the threshold criteria of CA 1989, s 31(2) is satisfied and whether or not to make a care or supervision order is an evaluative exercise rather than the exercise of a judicial discretion;
(ii) the decision to adopt a child is one of last resort – only in a case of necessity will an adoption order removing a child from his or her parents be proportionate;
(iii) the test to be applied on appeal is whether the decision of the lower court is 'wrong' as opposed to 'plainly wrong'; and
(iv) an appeal court does not have to undertake afresh its own evaluation of the issue of the proportionality of the decision made by the lower court (see also *Re G (A Child)* [2014] 1 FLR 670, CA).

The President has reiterated that appellate courts should respect brave discretionary decisions made at first instance and must be on 'secure ground' if they are to reverse the exercise of a discretion: *Re W (Relocation: Removal Outside Jurisdiction)* [2011] 2 FLR 409, CA.

The Court of Appeal has given guidance on the limited grounds on which the court may grant an application for permission to appeal and to allow an appeal (particularly for the benefit of litigants in person) (*Re W (Permission to Appeal)* [2008] 1 FLR 406, CA).

For further guidance on the approach that an appellate court should adopt to (a) appeals where the adequacy of a trial judge's reasoning is in issue and (b) appeals against the exercise of a discretion by a trial judge, see the notes to CPR 1998, Pt 52.

The Court of Appeal has set out the mandatory requirements that must be followed in appeals against placement orders: see *Re C (Adoption Proceedings: Change of Circumstances)* [2013] 2 FLR 1393, CA, namely:

(i) The appellant's notice must be filed as soon as possible.
(ii) Those advising the appellant must give careful thought to including in the appellant's notice any appropriate application for a stay or other interim relief.
(iii) If a transcript of the judgment being appealed against is not then available:

  - (a) the appellant's notice must be accompanied by whatever note of the judgment (even if unapproved) is available; and
  - (b) the transcript must be ordered immediately.
- (iv) When an application for a transcript is received, the court from which the appeal is being brought must deal with the application immediately.
- (v) Respondents who are parties to any application consequential upon the placement order (eg an application for an adoption order) must immediately inform both the appellant and the Court of Appeal of:
  - (a) the fact of the making of the application; and
  - (b) the date(s) of any hearing of the application.

Applications for permission to appeal in children's cases, especially those with an international element, have to be brought on for hearing swiftly. The filing of the notice of appeal should not be delayed until the applicant has received a copy of the approved judgment under appeal (*Re A (Children: Split Hearing)* [2007] 1 FLR 905, CA; *Re EC (Child Abduction: Stayed Proceedings)* [2007] 1 FLR 57, CA).

Appeals against case management orders should be dealt with in such a way as to avoid the adjournment of any substantive hearing already listed in the court below. It would be advisable for the Court of Appeal office to be alerted by any party who becomes aware of the possibility of delay and, in default of any other party, the children's guardian has an independent duty to keep the court informed: *Re L (Case Management: Child's Evidence)* [2014] 2 FLR 972, CA.

It is suggested that an appellate court should exercise caution before directing at a without notice permission to appeal hearing that a matter should be remitted for rehearing by the first instance court when (a) the respondent to the application has not been heard by the court and (b) the court has not determined the full appeal: *Livock v Livock* [2012] 1 FLR 776, FD.

In urgent cases where the judge has refused a stay of the order pending the application for permission to appeal, the prospective appellant may telephone the Court of Appeal to apply for a stay (during office hours the telephone number is 0207 947 6000 and out of hours contact is made to the security office at the RCJ on 0207 947 6260 who will refer the matter to the duty deputy master): PD52C, para 26. A deputy master will refer the matter to a Lord Justice who may grant the stay or list the matter urgently for consideration of the application for a stay (*Re S (Child Proceedings: Urgent Appeals)* [2007] 2 FLR 1044, CA; *Re A (A Child) (Residence Order)* [2007] EWCA Civ 899).

The Court of Appeal has emphasised that there is an obligation on an applicant seeking permission to appeal, or on an appellant who had obtained permission, to seek the Court of Appeal's leave before instructing a fresh expert and releasing court papers to him: see the notes to CPR 1998, r 52.11 (*Re McC (Care Proceedings: Fresh Evidence of Foreign Expert)* [2012] 2 FLR 121, CA and the Family Justice Council Guidelines of December 2011, *Instruction of Medical Experts from Overseas in Family Cases* (see Part V)).

Where an appeal is against findings of fact, Mostyn J has observed that 'an appellate court would only be able to say that a fact-finder has plainly got the wrong answer if:

- (i) His conclusion was demonstrably contrary to the weight of the evidence, or
- (ii) The decision-making process can be identified as being plainly defective so that it can be said that the findings in question are unsafe.

I would include in the second category errors of principle as to, say, the burden or standard of proof, or a failure to take into account well-established principles as to the weight to be given to proven lies or litigation misconduct in reaching the factual findings.' (*NG v SG (Appeal: Non-Disclosure)* [2012] 1 FLR 1211, FD).

The Court of Appeal does not have jurisdiction to entertain an appeal against a lower court's refusal to make findings of fact unless they concern the issue upon which the determination of the whole case ultimately turns or are otherwise subject of a declaration within the order: *Re M (Children)* [2013] EWCA Civ 1170. An appellate court should exercise caution when considering an invitation to interfere with the fact-finding determination of a trial judge. The trial judge's appraisal of the main witnesses attracted a very wide margin of appreciation: *Ray v Sekhri* [2014] 2 FLR 1168, CA.

Where findings of fact are challenged, the first instance court has no jurisdiction to re-open the findings of fact once an order is sealed and the court has no jurisdiction to permit expert evidence on the point since FPR 2010, r 25.4(3) provides that the Court may only give permission to adduce expert evidence if 'the court is of the opinion that the expert evidence is necessary to assist the court to resolve proceedings': *Re G (A Child)* [2014] EWCA Civ 1365.

In a fact-finding judgment, a judge made serious findings against two professional witnesses that were not sought by any party and of which the witnesses had not been given any advance warning either during the hearing or subsequently. Because the witnesses' right to a fair trial had been breached and the findings against them were capable of being held to be unlawful under HRA 1998, s 7(1), the findings could be the proper subject of an appeal without having to consider whether it was a decision, determination, order or judgment and/or whether the professional witnesses were intervenors or parties: *Re W (A Child)* [2016] EWCA Civ 1140, at [93], [95], [118].

There are limits to robust case management and the judicial voicing of pre-determined views is a step too far: *Re P (A Child)* [2014] EWCA Civ 888.

Where a single Lord Justice makes observations on Form 269C1, when granting permission to appeal or directing an oral hearing on notice with the appeal to follow immediately if permission was granted, they are to be obeyed. Primary responsibility for a failure to comply will usually lie with the party who brings the appeal/application: *Re M-W (Care Proceedings: Expert Evidence)* [2010] 2 FLR 46, CA.

When considering ordering a transcript of the whole, or a part, of the evidence or hearing in the court below, practitioners should bear in mind the following:

(i) The preparation of and authorisation of the payment for a transcript might take time, therefore practitioners should consider whether a transcript is an essential prerequisite before filing of a notice of appeal or before an application for permission to appeal is sought.
(ii) Practitioners should consider filing a notice of appeal even though a transcript might not be available.
(iii) The judge of the lower court could be contacted if necessary to speed up the process.
(iv) Pursuit of a transcript, which might be peripheral, should not affect the consideration of an application for permission to appeal: *Re GB (Children)* [2013] EWCA Civ 164; *Re C (Transcripts: Permission to Appeal)* [2014] 2 FLR 147, CA.

The President has made observations *B v B* [2014] EWHC 1804 (Fam) on the degree to which it is necessary to translate documents in the trial or appeal bundles for the benefit of parties who do not speak English: *Re L (Procedure: Bundles: Translation)* [2015] 1 FLR 1417, FD.

The Court of Appeal has observed that it would be 'enormously helpful' if a chronology was provided in all family appeals as they are for most first instance hearings: *Re H (Interim Contact: Domestic Violence Allegations)* [2014] 1 FLR 41, CA.

While the period in which the notice of appeal has to be lodged in the Court of Appeal has been increased from 14 to 21 days, such an extension might not generally be appropriate for family cases involving children where time is of the essence. CPR 1998, r 52.12(2)(a) permits the judge in the lower court to have regard to what time limit should be imposed for the issue of a notice of appeal (*Re M & H* [2006] EWCA Civ 499).

The Court of Appeal will only permit fresh evidence to be adduced in an appeal if the three *Ladd v Marshall* (1954) FLR Rep 422, CA conditions are satisfied, namely:

(i) first, it must be shown that the evidence could not have been obtained with reasonable diligence for use at the trial;
(ii) the evidence must be such that, if given, it would probably have an important influence on the result of the case, although it need not be decisive;
(iii) the evidence must be such as was presumably to be believed, or in other words, it must be apparently credible, although it need not be incontrovertible.

When a single Lord Justice wholly exceptionally orders an addendum to an expert report, it is not for the parties to alter the terms of the instruction by agreement between them and without recourse to the court: *Re R (Children)* [2014] EWCA Civ 1110.

Where events changed or developed after the making of an interim order, the appropriate course was to seek a variation of the order from the judge, rather than seek to appeal against the order: *Re H (A Child)* [2011] Fam Law 941, CA.

The unlawful removal of a child from his usual place of residence called for a peremptory order to be sought for his return, rather than to seek to challenge the dismissal of an appeal for an interim child arrangements order by way of a second appeal to the Court of Appeal: *Re R (Children: Peremptory Return)* [2011] 2 FLR 863, CA.

In those cases where it is plain that whatever the professionals' assessment of the prospects of success, the litigants cannot rest until they have exhausted their legal remedies, the court should consider imposing tight time limits on the filing of an application for permission to appeal and contact the Civil Appeals office to seek an early listing, so that finality may be achieved as soon as ever possible (*Re P (Residence: Appeal)* [2008] 1 FLR 198, CA).

The Supreme Court has criticised the imposition by the Court of Appeal of conditions to the grant of a stay pending determination of an application for permission to appeal by the Supreme Court. 'As a general rule, conditions such as were imposed by the Court of Appeal in this case should not be made where a party seeks permission to appeal, not least because these might be seen as an unwarranted disincentive to the pursuit of what proved in this case to be a fully merited application,' per Lord Kerr: *Re B (A Child)* [2010] 1 FLR 551, SC. The Court of Appeal had approved the decision of the court below to transfer residence from the maternal grandmother to the father: in granting a stay of the transfer of residence the court imposed a provision for extensive overnight staying contact to the father.

Where the court makes an ICO on a plan of immediate removal of the child into care then, absent a case that has the characters of a '999 emergency', the court should consider granting a short stay to enable an application to be made to the appeal court for a stay and permission to appeal: *Re T (Interim Care Order: Removal of Children Where No Immediate Emergency)* [2016] 1 FLR 347, CA. A judge erred in making an ICO and removing a child from his parents where, although there was a risk to the child of significant harm in their care, there was no imminent or immediate risk so as to justify his removal: *Re L (Children)* [2016] EWCA Civ 1110. A judge had been wrong to refuse to list an application for an ICO for hearing even though he had already refused an EPO 6 days earlier. There was no appeal against the grant or refusal of an EPO, as there is against an ICO, so in refusing to list the application he had denied the local authority a right of appeal: *Re B-C (A Child)* [2016] EWCA Civ 970.

The Court of Appeal may impose conditions on the grant of permission if compelling reasons were found to exist (unlike r 52.18, rr 52.5(4) and 52.6(2) do not specify the need for compelling reasons, but the court has held that the latter should be read as if those words were included in those rules). Thus, where a party had attempted to evade enforcement and was in gross breach of court orders, it was appropriate that conditions were attached to the grant of permission to appeal, including the transfer of a lump sum into this jurisdiction in a secure environment and a requirement to comply with existing court orders: *Radmacher v Granatino* [2009] 1 FLR 1566, CA.

The Court of Appeal has held that litigants in person as much as a represented party are required to comply with the procedural rules on appeals. McFarlane LJ said: 'The fact that an applicant for permission to appeal is a litigant in person may cause a judge to spend more time explaining the process and the requirements, but that fact is not, and should not be, a reason for relaxing or ignoring the ordinary procedural structure of an appeal or the requirements of the rules. Indeed, as I have suggested, adherence to the rules should be seen as a benefit to all parties, including litigants in person, rather than an impediment' (*Re D (Appeal: Procedure: Evidence)* [2016] 1 FLR 249, CA, at [40]).

Where, in public law proceedings, the party seeking permission to appeal is a litigant in person, the local authority should file a short position statement setting out the reasons, if that be its case, why permission to appeal should be refused: see CPR PD52C, para 19 and *Re B (A Child)* [2015] EWCA Civ 1053.

When considering an application for permission to appeal out of time, the appellate court may have regard to the underlying merits of the proposed appeal, especially where the grounds of appeal are either very strong or very weak: *Re H (Children) (Application to Extend Time: Merits of Proposed Appeal)* [2016] 1 FLR 952, CA.

All judgments, particularly ex tempore judgments, are to be read as a whole and on the assumption that the judge knew what matters had to be taken into account: *Re F (Children)* [2016] EWCA Civ 546. Nevertheless, the appellate court had to be satisfied that the judge had considered all realistic options before reaching a decision: *Re Y (Children)* [2016] EWCA Civ 1091.

A refusal of permission to appeal at an oral hearing cannot be renewed: *McHugh v McHugh* [2014] EWCA Civ 1671.

An appeal should proceed by way of a review of the decision of the lower court and only very exceptionally and rarely should an appeal proceed by way of a re-hearing: *Re C (Children)* [2016] EWCA Civ 356.

Once an appeal is allowed, the decision whether to re-make the decision or to remit to the lower court is fact-specific but the following are relevant considerations:

(i) an appeal court can fill in gaps in the reasoning of the lower court;
(ii) if the error of the lower court is sufficiently discrete, the appeal court can rectify the error;
(iii) if there is a lack of reasoning in the judgment, save for seeking further reasons from the judge in the court below, it is unlikely the same can be rectified on appeal;
(iv) if the key question on which the decision rests has not been answered, it is likely the appeal court will remit the matter for re-hearing: *Re B (A Child)* [2015] 1 FLR 884, CA.

The Master of the Rolls has emphasised 'in the strongest possible terms that it is only where it is clear that there is an unavoidable conflict of interest, as a matter of law, between two parties in the same interest that they should have separate legal representation, especially where public money is involved. The fact that the parties may have different factual points, or that one party's case may be seen as stronger than the other's, or that the parties' legal advisers may see the legal arguments or the prospects somewhat differently, are not good reasons for their incurring the expense and the court time of separate representation': *Oxfordshire County Council v X, Y and J* [2011] 1 FLR 272, CA.

There are detailed provisions in PDs 52A and 52C for the preparation of case bundles and appeal bundles and the revised provisions governing the content of skeleton arguments and the citing of authorities – PD52A, paras 5.1–5.3 and PD52C, paras 9, 13, 14, 16, 17, 21–24, 27, 29, 31 and 32.

On 24 March 2012, the Lord Chief Justice issued a practice direction entitled *Citation of Authorities*. In summary, the principal requirements are that:

(a) where a judgment is reported in the Official Law Reports, that report must be cited;
(b) if a judgment is not reported in the Official Law Reports but is reported in the WLR or All ER, that report should be cited;
(c) if a judgment is not reported in any of the above, but is reported in one of the authoritative specialist series of reports, that report should be cited if it contains a headnote and is made by an individual holding a Senior Courts qualification;
(d) if a judgment is not reported in any of the above but is reported in other reports, they may be cited; and
(e) if a judgment is not reported, reference may be made to the official transcript if that is available.

The bundle of authorities should comply with the requirements of Practice Direction of 24 March 2012: *Citation of Authorities* (PD52C, paras 29(2),(4)) and in general:

(a) have the relevant passages of the authorities marked;
(b) not include authorities for propositions not in dispute; and
(c) not contain more than 10 authorities unless the scale of the appeal warrants more extensive citation.

For appeals against case management decisions and discretionary decisions by first instance trial judges, see *Re W (Relocation: Removal Outside Jurisdiction)* [2011] 2 FLR 409, CA, at [7]–[12].

Litigants in Person – provided a litigant in person had been provided with copies of all of the documents in the trial bundle and with a copy of the index to the bundle, the failure to provide the litigant with a complete paginated trial bundle could not found a ground of appeal: *Re J (Appeal from Care Order)* [2014] 2 FLR 1351, CA.

Where the party seeking to appeal an order in the Court of Appeal in public law proceedings is a litigant in person, the local authority has the responsibility to ensure the appeal court is properly provided with appeal bundles: *Re R (A Child)* [2014] EWCA Civ 597.

Appeal notices may be filed by email (*www.justice.gov.uk/courts*). The guidelines on the use of email are as follows: there is 'a ceiling of 2Mb on attachments to e-mails, and the Civil Appeals Office cannot accept documents which exceed this limit. The Civil Appeals Office will not take responsibility for printing documents which exceed twenty pages or contain colour content. These should be provided in hard copy. Only documents in Word or PDF/Adobe Acrobat format will be acceptable. E-mail submissions will be checked twice daily at 9.30am and 2.00pm. For the purpose of adherence to time limits prescribed by the rules of procedure, e-mails received later than 4.30pm will be treated as having been received on the following working day.'

Note: when a draft judgment is provided to the parties pursuant to CPR 1998, PD40E it must remain confidential. Solicitors ought not to disclose a draft judgment to other members of their firms or organisations, save to the extent necessary for the taking of instructions in respect of the immediate conduct of the case and allowing for a junior solicitor to consult with a senior supervising solicitor. If any solicitor is in doubt as to the propriety of a particular disclosure, he should request permission from the judge concerned by emailing the judge's clerk (*Director of Public Prosecutions v P* [2007] EWHC 1144 (Admin)).

Note: CPR PDs 52A–52E have been substantially redrafted and re-ordered.

Procedure

Who may appeal	With permission, any party aggrieved by the decision	SCA 1981, s 16; CCA 1984, s 77
Permission to appeal	Required for all cases apart from where the appeal is against: (a) a committal order (b) a refusal to grant habeas corpus (c) a secure accommodation order; or (d) otherwise as provided by PD	CPR 1998, r 52.3
	Application should be made to the judge if possible (if not to the Court of Appeal) or, if refused, to the Court of Appeal	CPR 1998, r 52.3(2),(3); PD52A, para 4.1 and PD52C, paras 15 and 16
	Consideration of permission by the appeal judge is on the papers. An oral hearing will only be ordered if the appeal judge is of the opinion that the application cannot be fairly determined on paper without an oral hearing. The proposed appellant does not now have the right to request an oral hearing if permission is refused on the papers	CPR PD52C, para 15
	Respondents will be notified, but do not attend, unless requested by the Court of Appeal	CPR PD52C, paras 16, 19, 20
	For the permission hearing, the proposed appellant should lodge a Notice and an appeal bundle with as many documents as are available (see below)	
	Permission may be subject to conditions or may limit the issues	CPR 1998, rr 52.5(4), 52.6(2)
	Fee: £235	CPFO 2008, fee 13.1(a)
	But if permission to appeal is not required or permission was granted by the court below, fee: £465	CPFO 2008, fee 13.1(b)
Procedure on appeal	The Notice of Appeal (Form N161) must be filed within such period as directed by the lower court (which should not exceed 35 days) and where the lower court makes no direction, then within 21 days of the date of the order and it must be served not later than 7 days after filing	CPR 1998, r 52.4; PD52C, paras 3, 4
	A skeleton argument should be served with it	CPR PD52C, paras 3, 31

	The appellant must serve the Notice and any skeleton argument upon the respondents within 7 days of filing the Notice of Appeal. Once permission is granted by the lower court or the Court of Appeal or the permission hearing will be listed with the appeal to follow, the appellant must serve on each respondent an index of the proposed bundle of documents 7 days after the date of the listing window notification and file and serve a bundle of documents no later than 42 days before the appeal hearing	CPR 1998, r 52.12(3); PD52C, paras 21 and 27
	The appellant must complete the appeal questionnaire sent by the Court of Appeal 14 days after the listing window notification	CPR PD52C, para 23
	Fee: £465 (unless the appellant paid the fee required by 13.1(b))	CPFO 2008, fee 13.1(c)
Respondents	All parties to the proceedings who are affected by the appeal and anyone allowed to become a party	CPR 1998, r 52.1(3)
Lodgement of documents	The appellant must file (at the Civil Appeals Registry: RCJ Room E307) with his notice: (a) a copy of his notice for each respondent and three additional copies for the court; (b) one copy of his skeleton argument for each notice filed; (c) a sealed copy of the order being appealed and any order giving or refusing permission to appeal together with any reasons; (d) witness statements and affidavits; (e) a transcript or note of the judgment	CPR PD52C, para 3
	A bundle of authorities must be filed 7 days before the hearing which must comply with PD	CPR PD52C, paras 21 and 29
Respondent's notice	May be filed but *must* be filed where the respondent seeks to appeal or seeks to uphold the decision for different reasons Unless otherwise directed, must be filed within 14 days of (i) service of the notice of appeal if permission has been given by the lower court or is not needed, (ii) notification that permission has been granted by the CoA or (iii) notification that the permission application will be listed with the appeal to follow The respondent must file two additional copies of the notice for the court and one for each party A skeleton argument must be filed within 14 days of filing the notice and a copy served on each party	CPR 1998, r 52.13; PD52C, paras 8–10 and 21
	Fee: £235	CPFO 2008, fee 13.2
Appeal bundle	No later than 42 days before the appeal hearing the appellant must file and serve a bundle of documents. The bundle must be paginated and in chronological order and contain an index at the front. Subject to the order of the court, the bundle must contain: (a) a copy of the appellant's notice; (b) a copy of any respondent's notice; (c) a copy of the skeleton arguments; (d) a copy of the order under appeal; (e) a copy of the order granting or refusing permission to appeal, with reasons given, if any; (f) the approved transcript	

	The bundle may contain, where relevant to the appeal, statements of case, application notices, other orders, a chronology, witness statements and other documents but no original documents should be included	CPR PD52C, paras 21 and 27
Powers of the Court of Appeal	To receive fresh evidence To give any judgment and make any order that could have been made by the lower court To order a new trial or hearing	CPR 1998, rr 52.20(1), 52.21(2) CPR 1998, r 52.20(2)
Appeals	To the Supreme Court with leave of either the Court of Appeal or, if refused, the Supreme Court	CRA 2005, s 40(2); SCR 2009, r 11(1)

E6: Family Court – Appeal from Judge of Circuit Judge Level in Private Law Cases to a Judge of the High Court

Legal background

From October 2016, all appeals in private law children's cases from a judge of Circuit Judge level are to a High Court judge and are not to the Court of Appeal.

Most decisions of the lower court require leave from that court or, if refused, from the High Court before an appeal may proceed.

For commentary on procedural issues, see Guide E5, above.

Procedure

Who may appeal	With permission, any party aggrieved by the decision	SCA 1981, s 16; CCA 1984, s 77
Permission to appeal	Required for all cases apart from where the appeal is against: (a) a committal order (b) a refusal to grant habeas corpus (c) a secure accommodation order; or (d) otherwise as provided by PD	FPR 2010, r 30.3(1B),(2)
	Application may be made to the judge if possible (if not to a High Court Judge of the Family Division) or, if refused, to a High Court Judge of the Family Division	FPR 2010, r 30.3(4),(5)
	Consideration of permission is without a hearing unless a hearing is requested	FPR 2010, r 30.3(5); PD30A, para 4.10
	Respondents will be notified, but do not attend, unless requested by the appeal judge	FPR PD30A, para 4.15
	For the permission hearing, the proposed appellant should lodge a Notice and an appeal bundle with as many documents as are available (see below)	FPR PD30A, para 5.10A
	Permission may be subject to conditions or may limit the issues	FPR 2010, r 30.3(8); PD30A, para 4.18
	Permission to appeal may only be given where (a) the court considers that the appeal would have a real prospect of success or (b) there is some other compelling reason why the appeal should be heard	FPR 2010, r 30.3(7)
	An order giving permission may (a) limit the issues to be heard and (b) be made subject to conditions	FPR 2010, r 30.3(8)

Procedure on appeal	The Notice of Appeal must be filed within such period as directed by the lower court (which should not exceed 35 days) and where the lower court makes no direction, then within 21 days of the date of the order and it must be served not later than 7 days after filing	FPR 2010, r 30.4(2),(4)
	Where the appeal is against a case management decision or an order under CA 1989, s 38(1), the time for filing the notice of appeal is 7 days	FPR 2010, r 30.4(3)
	A skeleton argument should be served with it	FPR PD30A, para 5.13
	The appellant must serve the Notice and any skeleton argument upon the respondents within 7 days of filing the Notice of Appeal. Once permission is granted by the lower court or the High Court, the appellant must serve on each respondent a copy of the appeal bundle within 7 days of receiving the order giving permission to appeal	FPR 2010, r 30.4(4); PD30A, para 6.2
Respondents	All parties to the proceedings who are affected by the appeal and anyone allowed to become a party	FPR 2010, r 30.1
Appeal bundle	The appellant must file (at the Family Division of the High Court at the Royal Courts of Justice, Strand, London WC2A 2LL) with his notice: (a) a sealed or stamped copy of the appellant's notice (including the grounds of appeal); (b) a sealed or stamped copy of the order being appealed [or a copy of the notice of the making of an order]; (c) a transcript or note of the judgment; (d) copies of any documents specifically referred to in the judgment; (e) a copy of the appellant's skeleton argument Subject to filing a certificate signed by the appellant's solicitor and where permission is granted, adding to the appeal bundle the following (a) the respondent's notice and skeleton argument, if any; (b) the relevant parts of the transcripts of evidence; (c) the order granting permission to appeal and transcript or note of any judgment given; and (d) relevant additional documents sought to be included in the bundle by the respondent and agreed by the appellant; no further documents may be added to the bundle without the order of a High Court judge In addition to the appeal bundle, the appellant must file duplicate copies of the appellant's notice and skeleton argument for each of the respondents	FPR PD30A, paras 5.10A, 5.10B, 5.10C, 5.11 and 6.4(a)–(d)
Respondent's notice	May be filed but *must* be filed where the respondent seeks to appeal or seeks to uphold the decision for different reasons Unless otherwise directed, must be filed within 14 days of (i) service of the notice of appeal if permission has been given by the lower court or is not needed, (ii) notification that permission has been granted by the High Court or (iii) notification that the permission application will be listed with the appeal to follow	

	The respondent must file two additional copies of the notice for the court and one for each party A skeleton argument must be filed with the notice or within 14 days of filing the notice and a copy served on each party	FPR 2010, r 30.5(4),(5); PD30A, paras 7.1, 7.2, 7.14 and 7.15
Totally without merit	If the appeal court (a) refuses an application for permission to appeal, (b) strikes out an appellant's notice or (c) dismisses an appeal and it considers the application is totally without merit, the same must be recorded in the court order	FPR 2010, r 30.11(4),(5)
	Where a High Court judge refuses permission to appeal without a hearing and considers the application to be totally without merit, the judge may order that the person seeking permission may not request the decision to be reconsidered at an oral hearing	FPR 2010, r 30.3(5A)
The appeal hearing	Every appeal will be limited to a review of the decision of the lower court unless (a) different provision is made for a particular category of appeal or (b) the court considers it would be in the interests of justice to hold a re-hearing Unless the court otherwise orders, the court will not receive oral evidence or evidence that was not before the lower court The court will allow the appeal where the decision of the lower court was (a) wrong or (b) unjust because of a serious or other irregularity in the proceedings	FPR 2010, r 30.12
Appeal court powers	To affirm, set aside or vary any order or judgment of the lower court To refer any application or issue for determination by the lower court To order a new hearing To make orders for the payment of interest To make a costs order	FPR 2010, r 30.11
Appeals	To the Court of Appeal No appeal may be made to the Court of Appeal from that decision unless the Court of Appeal considers that (a) the appeal would raise an important point of principle or practice, or (b) there is some other compelling reason for the Court of Appeal to hear it	CPR 1998, r 52.7 AJA 1999, s 55

E7: Applications to Re-open or Set Aside Final Court Orders

Legal background

The law seeks finality in its orders (eg in *Ampthill Peerage* [1977] 1 AC 547, HL, at [569]). Exceptional circumstances may occur later that justify reconsideration of the original order. Circumstances may come to light of which the court was not aware at the time of a final hearing (eg non-disclosure of material financial information by one of the parties (*Sharland v Sharland* [2015] 2 FLR 1367, SC; *Gohil v Gohil* [2015] 2 FLR 1289, SC) or background information in relation to a child or a couple's matrimonial circumstances in relation to their divorce). Alternatively, an assumption on which the original order was based may change fundamentally (*Barder v Barder* [1987] 2 FLR 480, HL) such that it may be appropriate to seek permission out of time to appeal against the order.

Setting aside or seeking rescission of an order

If circumstances arise that existed at the time of the final hearing, it may be open to a party to apply to the court for the original order to be set aside and to seek a re-hearing; whether by interim application (FPR 2010, Pt 18), appeal (SCA 1981, s 16) or originating application (*Sharland* (above)). It may be possible for a party to apply to revoke or vary an order (FPR 2010, r 4.1(6); *Tibbles v SIG plc* [2012] EWCA Civ 518) or to apply to rescind an order (MFPA 1984, s 31F(6); *Norman v Norman* [2017] EWCA Civ 120).

With effect from 3 October 2016, a procedure for applications to set aside financial relief orders only has been introduced into FPR 2010 (r 9.9A), which rule is supported by a PD of 3 October 2016 that confirms that in pre-Family Court cases application is made in the Family Court (PD9A, para 13.2).

The result of an application to set aside in each tier of court is as follows:

Supreme Court The Supreme Court has power 'in appropriate cases to rescind or vary an earlier order' that it made (*R v Bow Street Metropolitan Stipendiary Magistrate, ex p Pinochet Ugarte (No 2)* [2000] 1 AC 119, HL).

Court of Appeal The Court of Appeal can review its own orders under the jurisdiction now available to it under CPR 1998, r 52.17, that is 'to avoid real injustice' (CPR 1998, r 52.17; FPR 2010, r 30.14; and see *Taylor v Lawrence* [2003] QB 528, CA; *Jaffray v Society of Lloyd's* [2008] 1 WLR 75, CA).

High Court The High Court has power to set aside its own order by fresh action upon an appeal (but see SCA 1981, s 17, which prevents application for a new trial) or application in the original proceedings (*Sharland*, at [38] and [42]), save in the case of divorce (FPR 2010, r 7.28: rescission, but only in the case of reconciliation) and financial relief (FPR 2010, r 9.9A).

Family Court In family proceedings, the Family Court can make the same orders as can the High Court (MFPA 1984, s 31E(1)(a)) and has an originating set aside jurisdiction under MFPA 1984, s 31F(6) (*Sharland*, at [41]; and see *CS v ACS (Consent Order: Non-Disclosure: Correct Procedure)* [2016] 1 FLR 131, FD, Sir James Munby P, at [10]).

FPR 2010, r 9.9A (in force since 3 October 2016) enables a party to a financial relief order (only) to apply to the court to set aside a judgment and order. The sole ground for so doing is that 'no error of the court is alleged' by the applicant. That is to say the applicant alleges that the court was not in error since information was withheld from it by the respondent (*Peek v Peek* [1948] P 46). If it is said that the court is in error, then the applicant seeks permission (probably out of time) to appeal. It appears that an application for permission to appeal out of time (*Barder v Barder* [1987] 2 FLR 480, HL) is intended to be issued under r 9.9A (see PD9A, para 13.5).

Rescission of divorce decrees and applications for a re-hearing of any order in the County Court were formerly possible on grounds that no error of the court is alleged. Other than in the High Court (because of SCA 1981, s 17(1)), application on this ground is available in all family proceedings (eg for divorce as in *Peek v Peek* (above)).

Application to set aside an arbitral award in family proceedings, before a final order has been made, is part of the show cause procedure for such awards and should be to a High Court judge (*DB v DLJ (Challenge to Arbitral Award)* [2016] 2 FLR 1308, at [90]).

(The term 'set aside' is defined in the Glossary (in FPR 2010 and CPR 1998) as 'Cancelling a judgment or order or a step taken by a party in proceedings' and it is applied by FPR 2010, r 9.9A(1)(b) to financial remedy proceedings in the High Court and Family Court. To set aside an order is one of the powers of an appellate court (CPR 1998, r 52.10(2)(a); FPR 2010, r 30.11(2)(a)). Applications to set aside an order arise in four main categories of circumstance:

(a) Where an order is vitiated by, for example, non-disclosure, fraud, mistake (see list in PD9A, para 13.5) or other such factors; or, for example, where judicial bias is successfully alleged (*Locabail (UK) Ltd v Bayfield Properties Ltd & Anor* [2000] QB 451
(b) Where the court is willing to assume jurisdiction to review case management decisions (CPR 1998, r 3.1(7); FPR 2010, r 4.1(6); and see *CS v ACS & BH* (above), at [36]);
(c) Where the court has powers internal to a particular rule: eg CPR 1998, r 3.3(5), FPR 2010, r 4.3(5) (set aside court's own initiative orders; CPR 1998, r 23.10), FPR 2010, r 18.11 (application notice orders made without a hearing); and
(d) Where an appellate court is willing to re-open an appeal court order (CPR 1998, r 52.17; FPR 2010, r 30.14 (see (3), below)).

This Guide does not deal with the 'slip rule' (CPR 1998, r 40.12; FPR 2010, r 29.16) or the power of the court to correct its own decision before the order is drawn (*Re Barrell Enterprises* [1973] 1 WLR 19, CA; *Re L-B (Reversal of Judgment)* [2013] 2 FLR 859, SC).

Procedure in summary

Procedure for set aside and re-opening of appeals is as follows:

- Re-opening of appeals (CPR 1998, r 52.17): Guide E7(1).
- Set aside by fresh application in the family proceedings (High Court or Family Court): Guide E7(2).

E7(1): Application to Re-Open a Final Appeal

Procedure

Who may apply	Any party to the appeal that led to the original order	
Application	For permission to a judge of the court that made the original order	CPR 1998, r 52.17(4); FPR 2010, r 30.14(4); CPR PD52A, para 7.1; FPR PD30A, para 18.3; *Taylor v Lawrence* [2003] QB 528, CA
	Application in the first instance is not on notice to any parties: it must be considered by a judge on a preliminary basis first	CPR PD52A, para 7.2; FPR PD30A, para 18.5
Grounds	The rules state the grounds as follows: (1) It is necessary to avoid real injustice (eg material non-disclosure, mistake, fraud, bias); (2) Exceptional circumstances and it is appropriate to re-open; and (3) There is no alternative effective remedy	CPR 1998, r 52.17(1); FPR 2010, r 30.14(1)
Procedure	Application is made by 'application notice'(ie CPR 1998, Pt 23 or FPR 2010, Pt 18 procedure), supported by written evidence verified by a statement of truth	CPR PD52A, para 7.2; FPR PD30A, para 18.4
Service of application	Only if directed by the court	CPR PD52A, para 7.2; FPR PD30A, para 18.5
Response	If the application is directed to be served 'on another party' and thereby is able to proceed, that party may file and serve a written reply Time for reply: 14 days	CPR 1998, r 52.17(6); FPR 2010, r 30.14(6); CPR PD52A, para 7.3; FPR PD30A, para 18.6
Consideration by single judge of appellate court	The application and documents in support and in reply will be considered on paper	CPR PD52A, para 7.4; FPR PD30A, para 18.7
	The application only proceeds to a hearing if 'exceptionally the judge so directs'	CPR 1998, r 52.17(5); FPR 2010, r 30.14(5)
Hearing of application	No right to an oral hearing, unless the judge directs	CPR 1998, r 52.17(5); FPR 2010, r 30.14(5)

E7(2): Setting Aside a Financial Relief Order

Procedure

Who may apply	Either party to financial relief order	FPR 2010, r 9.9A
Application	To set aside a court order or judgment so that – as far as possible, given the passage of time – the position reverts to that which it was prior to the order being made. No error of the court is alleged	FPR 2010, r 9.9A(2); FPR 2010, r 9.9A(2); *Peek v Peek* [1948] P 46; *Harris v Manahan* [1997] 1 FLR 205, CA

Form of application	Application notice: (1) in existing financial relief proceedings (2) by the FPR 2010, Pt 18 procedure	FPR 2010, r 9.9A(3),(4); PD9A, para 13.9; Form D11
Fee	£155	FPFO 2008, Fee 5.3
When to apply	As soon as possible after the grounds for application (see below) come to light *Delay* Delay is not fatal, but may be of concern to the court	The greater or more sure is the materiality (see Grounds) the greater is likely to be the court's tolerance of delay
Grounds	In summary, the main grounds are: (1) Non-disclosure that is material and that is (i) accidental or negligent (applicant to prove materiality) or (ii) fraudulent (materiality presumed) (2) Mutual mistake by the parties as to facts material to the order (3) Unlawfulness (eg the order was made without jurisdiction) (4) Procedural irregularity or alleged bias (5) *Barder* event	*Jenkins v Livesey (formerly Jenkins)* [1985] FLR 813, HL; *Gohil* (above), esp at [44]; *Sharland* (above) Note: (3) and (4) may as likely found an appeal out of time, or even re-opening of an appeal (CPR 1998, r 52.17 or FPR 2010, r 30.14) FPR 2010, r 9.9A
Pleading the Pt 8 application; particulars of claim	(a) Plead: one or more of the grounds (or other grounds) (above); (b) As ever, plead facts; evidence will follow; (c) If non-disclosure state: (i) whether accidental etc, in which case say why it is material; or (ii) if fraud is alleged, bear in mind rules about pleading fraud: i e that evidence thereof must be available to the pleader; (d) If other, plead accordingly. Note: follow Pt 18 assuming an early directions/case management appointment before the level of judge who will try the application	Modern rules of pleading: see CPR PD16, especially para 15.1 Bar Standards Board rules arising from *Medcalf v Mardell* [2002] UKHL 27
Case management	Particular matters: (1) Disclosure and production: pleading may need to be amended in the event of (non-)disclosure(s) (2) Transcript of original hearing: is this needed? (3) Marshalling of evidence: what evidence to be heard live and what on paper or on submissions only (4) Bundle from court below: how much needed? (5) Expert evidence: corrective valuation; medical	Courts powers to control evidence: FPR 2010 r 22.1 Apply in particulars of claim or in separate application: CPR 1998, r 25.4

[L]egal services [or]der	(1) If periodical payments still live, seek legal services order; (2) If periodical payments disposed of on the order under review, seek *A v A* order interim to the issue before the court Note: the court may refuse to deal with this until the set aside issue is resolved	MCA 1973, s 22ZA(1) *A v A (Maintenance Pending Suit: Provision for Legal Fees)* [2001] 1 FLR 377, FD and powers to make interim orders MFPA 1984, s 31F(2)(b)
[H]earing of set [a]side application	(1) If alleged, fraud is likely to have to be the subject of a full viva voce hearing (2) Most other hearings can be based on documents and submissions only	
[C]osts	Set aside application proceedings per r 9.9A are not 'financial remedy proceedings' and therefore application can be made for costs without constraint of FPR 2010, r 28.3(5)	FPR 2010, r 28.3(9)
[D]irections	If an order is set aside, the court that makes that order 'shall give directions' for the rehearing or other disposal of the original application	FPR 2010, r 9.9A(5)

F1: Proceedings involving a Protected Party

Legal background

Court rules have in the past defined the circumstances in which a person was to be treated as being 'under a disability' in relation to proceedings and the procedure then to be adopted. A person under disability was a person under the age of 18 years (variously described as a 'minor' or an 'infant') or a 'patient' (as defined). The terms 'child' and 'protected party' are now used and the expression 'under a disability' is no longer appropriate.

It has long been the case that a person under disability may not:

(i) bring or make a claim in any proceedings;
(ii) acknowledge service, defend, make a counterclaim or intervene in any proceedings; or
(iii) appear in any proceedings under a judgment or order, notice of which has been served on him;

other than by an appointed representative. This has traditionally been a next friend for the person bringing proceedings or a guardian ad litem for the person defending or responding but the term 'litigation friend' was introduced for both categories in civil proceedings by CPR 1998 and in family proceedings by FPR 2010.

Proceedings commenced or conducted in breach of these requirements will be of no effect unless the court orders otherwise and a solicitor who purports to act on the record for such a party might become personally liable for the costs of opposing parties.

F1(1): Family Proceedings involving a Protected Party

Procedure

Who is a protected party	A party, or an intended party, who lacks capacity (within the meaning of MCA 2005) to conduct the proceedings	FPR 2010, r 2.3

Who 'lacks capacity'	A person lacks capacity in relation to a matter if at the material time he is unable to make a decision for himself in relation to the matter because of an impairment of, or a disturbance in the functioning of, the mind or brain	MCA 2005, s 2(1)
When is a person unable to make a decision for himself	If unable to: – understand the information relevant to the decision; – retain that information; – use or weigh that information as part of the process of making the decision; or – communicate his decision (whether by talking, using sign language or any other means)	MCA 2005, s 3(1)
Requirement for litigation friend	A protected party must have a litigation friend to conduct proceedings on his behalf	FPR 2010, r 15.2; PD15A para 1.1
Title to proceedings	'A.B. (by C.D. his/her litigation friend)'	FPR PD15A, para 1.2
When must a litigation friend be appointed	Before taking any step in proceedings (unless court grants permission) except: – filing an application form; – applying for the appointment of a litigation friend Also if party becomes incapable of continuing proceedings	FPR 2010, r 15.3
What if litigation friend not appointed	Any step taken before a protected party has a litigation friend has no effect unless the court orders otherwise	FPR 2010, r 15.3(3)
Who is appointed	Person authorised by the Court of Protection as a deputy to conduct the proceedings in the name of protected party or on his behalf, or – suitable person; or – Official Solicitor	FPR 2010, r 15.4(2) FPR 2010, r 15.4(3) FPR 2010, r 15.4(4)
Who is a suitable person?	Person who: – can fairly and competently conduct proceedings on behalf of protected party; – has no adverse interest; and – undertakes to pay any costs awarded	FPR 2010, r 15.4(3)
Duties of litigation friend	Fairly and competently to conduct proceedings on behalf of protected party	FPR PD15A, para 2.1
Is a solicitor required to act	Failure to instruct may cause suitability to be questioned in a significant case	
Appointment without a court order	May be made on filing: – authority of deputy; or – a certificate of suitability Not by the Official Solicitor	FPR PD15A, para 3.1 FPR 2010, r 15.5
Certificate of suitability	States that the proposed litigation friend: – consents to act; – believes the party to be a protected party (with reasons/medical evidence); – can fairly and competently conduct proceedings on behalf of the party; – has no adverse interest; – undertakes to pay any costs which party may be ordered to pay (applicant or respondent)	FPR PD15A, para 3.1(b) Form FP9 Certificate of suitability of litigation friend

Appointment by court order	On court's own initiative or on the application of: – person wishing to be litigation friend; or – a party Any application must be supported by evidence Person appointed must be a suitable person (as above) or Official Solicitor	FPR PD15A, para 4 FPR 2010, r 15.6
Change of litigation friend	Court may: – direct that person may not act; – terminate an appointment; or – appoint a substitute Any application must be supported by evidence Person appointed must be (as above)	 FPR PD15A, para 5 FPR 2010, r 15.7
Ceasing to be protected party	Appointment continues until brought to end by court order Application made by: – former protected party; – litigation friend; or – a party	FPR PD15A, para 6 FPR 2010, r 15.9
Service before appointment of litigation friend	Service upon a protected party is effected on: – attorney (EPA or LPA); – deputy; or – adult with whom the protected party resides or in whose care he is	 FPR 2010, rr 6.28, 6.14(2)
Service of application	Application under r 15.6 or 15.7 must be sent by court to protected party (unless otherwise orders) Application under r 15.7 must be sent by court to former and proposed litigation friend	FPR 2010, r 15.8(1) FPR 2010, r 15.8(2)
Service after appointment of litigation friend	Service is upon the litigation friend	FPR 2010, r 6.29
Withdrawal of application	Permission of court required	FPR 2010, r 29.4
Compromise or settlement	No specific provision	
Control of money recovered	Court of Protection may need to be involved in absence of attorney or deputy In financial remedy (ancillary relief) proceedings court may order transfer of property or payments (including lump sum) to another person where party lacks capacity	MCA 2005 MCA 1973, s 40

F1(2): Family Proceedings involving a Child

Procedure

Who is a child	A person who is under the age of 18	FLRA 1969, ss 1, 12; FPR 2010, r 2.3
Requirement for litigation friend	A child must have a litigation friend to conduct proceedings on his behalf A child who is a party but is not the subject of the proceedings can bring or defend certain proceedings without a representative	FPR 2010, r 16.5 FPR 2010, r 16.6(1),(2)

Title to proceedings	'A.B. (a child by C.D. his/her litigation friend)'	FPR PD16A, para 1.1
When must a litigation friend be appointed	Before taking any step in proceedings (unless court grants permission) except: – filing an application form; – applying for the appointment of a litigation friend	FPR 2010, r 16.8
What if litigation friend not appointed	Any step taken before a child has a litigation friend has no effect unless the court orders otherwise	FPR 2010, r 16.8(3)
Who is appointed	– suitable person; or – Official Solicitor; or – officer as defined	FPR 2010, r 16.9(2),(3)
Who is a suitable person?	Person who: – can fairly and competently conduct proceedings on behalf of child; – has no adverse interest; and – undertakes to pay any costs awarded	FPR 2010, r 16.9(2)
Duties of litigation friend	Fairly and competently to conduct proceedings on behalf of protected party	FPR PD16A, para 2.1
Is a solicitor required to act	Failure to instruct may cause suitability to be questioned in a significant case	
Appointment without a court order	May be made on filing a certificate of suitability This rule does not apply to Official Solicitor	FPR 2010, r 16.10(1),(4); PD16A, para 3
Certificate of suitability	States that the proposed litigation friend: – consents to act – believes the party to be a child – can fairly and competently conduct proceedings on behalf of the party – has no adverse interest – undertakes to pay any costs which child may be ordered to pay (applicant and respondent)	FPR PD16A, para 3.1 Form FP9 Certificate of suitability of litigation friend
Appointment by court order	On court's own initiative or on the application of: – person wishing to be litigation friend; or – a party Any application must be supported by evidence Person appointed must be a suitable person (as above) or (with consent): – Official Solicitor; or – Officer as defined	FPR PD16A, para 4 FPR 2010, r 16.11
Change of litigation friend	Court may: – direct that person may not act; – terminate an appointment; or – appoint a substitute Any application must be supported by evidence Person appointed must be (as above)	FPR PD16A, para 5 FPR 2010, r 16.12
Ceasing to be a child	When a child who is not a protected party attains 18 the appointment ends Court gives notice to the other parties	FPR 2010, r 16.15

Service before appointment of litigation friend	Service upon a child is effected on: – a parent or guardian, or, if none – adult with whom child resides or in whose care he is	FPR 2010, rr 6.14(1), 6.28
Service of application	Application under r 16.11 or 16.12 must be sent by court to person to be served (as above) Application under r 16.12 must be sent by court to former and proposed litigation friend	FPR 2010, r 16.13(1) FPR 2010, r 16.13(2)
Service after appointment of litigation friend	Service is upon the litigation friend	FPR 2010, r 6.29
Withdrawal of application	Permission of court required	FPR 2010, r 29.4
Compromise or settlement	No specific provision	
Control of money recovered	No specific provision	

F1(3): Non-family Proceedings involving a Child or a Protected Party

Issue

When dealing with proceedings that are *not* family proceedings it is necessary to comply with CPR 1998. Pt 21 contains special provisions that apply in proceedings involving children and protected parties. These are supplemented by CPR PD21 (Children and Protected Parties). Unless the court orders otherwise (in the case of a child) it is necessary for the child or protected party to be represented by a litigation friend. The term 'under disability' is no longer used and under the Civil Procedure (Amendment) Rules 2007 the old term 'patient' was replaced by 'protected party' and a new definition applies. This became necessary because of the implementation on 1 October 2007 of MCA 2005.

The following is an abbreviated version of Guide D4 in *Civil Court Service* (LexisNexis).

Procedure

Who is a child	A person under 18	CPR 1998, r 21.1(2)(b)
Who is a protected party	A party, or an intended party, who lacks capacity (within the meaning of MCA 2005) to conduct the proceedings	CPR 1998, r 21.1(2)(d)
Who 'lacks capacity'	A person lacks capacity in relation to a matter if at the material time he is unable to make a decision for himself in relation to the matter because of an impairment of, or a disturbance in the functioning of, the mind or brain	MCA 2005, s 2(1)
When is a person unable to make a decision for himself	if unable to: – understand the information relevant to the decision; – retain that information; – use or weigh that information as part of the process of making the decision; or – communicate his decision (whether by talking, using sign language or any other means)	MCA 2005, s 3(1)

Requirement for a litigation friend (protected party)	A protected party must have a litigation friend to conduct proceedings on his behalf	CPR 1998, r 21.2(1)
Requirement for a litigation friend (child)	A child must have a litigation friend to conduct proceedings on his behalf unless the court orders otherwise the court may permit child to conduct proceedings without a litigation friend (for procedure see r 21.2(4)) if it subsequently appears desirable for there to be a litigation friend court may so appoint	CPR 1998, r 21.2(2) CPR 1998, rr 21.2(3),(4) CPR 1998, r 21.2(5)
When must a litigation friend be appointed	A person may not, without permission of the court: (a) make an application against a child or protected party before proceedings have started; or (b) take any step in proceedings except – (i) issuing/serving a claim form; or (ii) applying for the appointment of a litigation friend under r 21.6, until the child or protected party has a litigation friend If a party becomes a protected party during proceedings, no party may take any step in the proceedings without the permission of the court until the protected party has a litigation friend Any step taken before a child or protected party has a litigation friend is of no effect, unless the court otherwise orders	CPR 1998, r 21.3(2) CPR 1998, r 21.3(3) CPR 1998, r 21.3(4)
Title to proceedings	'A. B. (a child by . . . his litigation friend)' or, if a litigation friend is dispensed with, 'C. D. (a child)' 'A.B. (a protected party by . . . his litigation friend)'	CPR PD21, para 1.2 CPR PD21, para 1.1
Who is appointed (without court order)	A deputy appointed by the Court of Protection under MCA 2005, with power to conduct proceedings on the protected party's behalf, is entitled to be the litigation friend of the protected party in any proceedings to which his power extends If nobody has been appointed by the court (or appointed as a deputy), a person may act as a litigation friend if he: can fairly and competently conduct proceedings on behalf of the child or protected party; and has no interest adverse to that of the child or protected party; and (claim or counterclaim) undertakes to pay any costs that the child or protected party may be ordered to pay	CPR 1998, r 21.4(2) CPR 1998, r 21.4(3)
Appointment (without court order)	A person wishing to act as a litigation friend must: (if empowered by the Court of Protection) file an official copy of the order conferring the power; (otherwise) file a certificate of suitability – (claimant) when making the claim; (defendant) when first taking a step in the proceedings	CPR 1998, r 21.5
Certificate of suitability	States that proposed litigation friend: – consents to act;	

	– believes the person to be a child or protected party (with reasons/medical evidence); – can fairly and competently conduct proceedings on behalf of the person; – has no adverse interest; – (claimant) undertakes to pay any costs which claimant may be ordered to pay in the proceedings	Form N235; CPR 1998, r 21.4(3); PD21, para 2.2
	A counterclaim is treated like a claim for the purpose of the costs undertaking	CPR 1998, r 20.3(1)
Service of certificate	The litigation friend must: – serve the certificate of suitability on every person on whom the claim form should be served (it is good practice to serve the patient unless obviously unable to respond); and – file a certificate of service when filing the certificate of suitability	CPR 1998, rr 21.5(4)(a) CPR 1998, rr 6.13, 21.5(4)(b)
Certificate of service	Must set out required details of method of service	CPR 1998, r 6.17
Application for appointment by court	Application for an order appointing a litigation friend is made by person wishing to be appointed or a party Claimant must apply where claim against child or protected party with no litigation friend and either (i) someone who is not entitled files a defence or (ii) claimant wishes to take some step in the proceedings	CPR 1998, r 21.6; PD21, paras 3.1–3.4
	Application must be supported by evidence; court to be satisfied that the person appointed is 'suitable'	CPR 1998, rr 21.6(4),(5), 21.4(3)
Change of litigation friend	The court may: – direct that a person may not act as a litigation friend; – terminate the appointment; or appoint a substitute Application to be supported by evidence; court may not appoint a litigation friend unless satisfied that the person is suitable	CPR 1998, rr 21.4(3), 21.7
Who is appointed (by court)	On an application, court may appoint: – person proposed, or – any other person who complies with the conditions in r 21.4(3)	CPR 1998, r 21.8(4)
Official Solicitor	May be appointed provided he consents and provision is made for payment of his costs	CPR PD21, para 3.4
Appointment ceasing (child/protected party)	When a child who is not a protected party reaches 18 a litigation friend's appointment ceases	CPR 1998, r 21.9(1); PD21, paras 4.2–4.4
	When a protected party acquires capacity, appointment continues until ended by a court order	CPR 1998, r 21.9(2); PD21, paras 4.5, 4.6
Service of claim form (child)	Service of claim form is upon a parent or guardian or (if none) an adult with whom the child resides or in whose care he is	CPR 1998, r 6.13(1)
Service of claim form (protected party)	Service of the claim form is upon: (i) the attorney under a registered enduring power of attorney, (ii) the donee of a lasting power of attorney,	

	(iii) the deputy appointed by the Court of Protection; or (if none) an adult with whom the protected party resides or in whose care he is	CPR 1998, r 6.13(2)
Service of claim form – general	The court may by order: – permit the claim form to be served on the child or protected party, or on a person other than as specified; – treat a document as if it had been properly served although it has been served on someone other than as specified	CPR 1998, r 6.13(4) CPR 1998, r 6.13(6)
Service generally	On litigation friend once appointed (or child allowed to conduct proceedings) The court may by order: – permit service on child or protected party, or on a specified person; or – treat a document as if it had been properly served	CPR 1998, r 6.25(2),(6) CPR 1998, r 6.25(3) CPR 1998, r 6.25(5)
Service of application	Application for order appointing or changing litigation friend must be served on: – every person on whom claim form should be served; and – (if appointing) the protected party, unless court otherwise orders; or – (if changing) the existing and proposed litigation friend	CPR 1998, r 21.8(1) CPR 1998, r 21.8(2) CPR 1998, r 21.8(3)
Compromise or settlement	On a claim or counterclaim by or on behalf of, or against, a child or protected party, no settlement, compromise or payment and no acceptance of money paid into court is valid without court approval Procedures are available where the sole purpose of proceedings is to obtain the approval of the court	CPR 1998, r 21.10(1) CPR 1998, r 21.10(2); PD21, paras 5.1–5.6; Form N292
Who is a protected beneficiary	A protected party who lacks capacity to manage and control any money recovered by him or on his behalf or for his benefit in the proceedings	CPR 1998, r 21.1(2)(e)
Control of money recovered	Money recovered on behalf of or for the benefit of a child or protected beneficiary is dealt with under directions of the court These may provide that the money shall be wholly or partly paid into court and invested; or otherwise dealt with Applications may be made relating to payment out or investment	CPR 1998, r 21.11(1); PD21, paras 8.1–8.4 CPR 1998, r 21.11(2); PD21, paras 9.1–9.8, 10.1–10.7 CPR PD21, para 13.1
Guardian of child's estate	The court may appoint the Official Solicitor as a guardian of a child's estate	CPR 1998, r 21.13; PD21, para 12
Deputy for a protected beneficiary	For funds of £50,000 or more, it will usually be necessary for the Court of Protection to appoint a deputy to administer the property and affairs of a protected beneficiary money of a protected beneficiary will be transferred applications for payment out of funds are to the Court of Protection	CPR PD21, paras 10.1–10.7 Form CFO 200 CPR PD21, para 13.4
Costs	Costs of solicitor for child or protected party must be approved by court Liability of litigation friend continues until: – appointment ceases; and	CPR 1998, r 46.4

	– former child or protected party (or litigation friend) serves notice on other parties	CPR 1998, r 21.9(6)
Forms	Certificate of Suitability of Litigation Friend Order approving terms of a settlement or compromise	Form N235 Form N292

F1(4): Resolving Doubt about Capacity

Issue

When there is a significant doubt as to whether a party lacks capacity, the proceedings should not continue until this doubt has been resolved. The Rules assume that it is known whether a party lacks capacity so any doubt must be addressed as an issue in the proceedings and a finding of fact made. There is no simple solution but this Guide sets out some of the options available to the parties and the court in both family and civil proceedings.

Procedure

The procedural problem		
The relevance of capacity	Special provisions apply to parties who lack capacity – see generally Guides F1(1) and F1(3)	FPR 2010, Pt 15 and PD15A; CPR 1998, Pt 21 and PD21; MCA 2005, Pt 1
What aspects of capacity are relevant	Capacity to: – conduct the proceedings; – manage any monies recovered; – obey court orders; – make personal welfare decisions	 See generally MCA 2005
What are the implications	*Family and civil*: A party who lacks capacity to conduct the proceedings is a protected party *Civil only*: A party who lacks capacity to manage and control any monies recovered is a protected beneficiary	FPR 2010, r 2.3; CPR 1998, r 21.1(2)(d) CPR 1998, r 21.1(2)(e)
What are the consequences	*Family and civil*: A protected party will normally require a *litigation friend* to be appointed *Civil only*: A protected beneficiary will not be permitted to receive money	FPR 2010, r 15.2; CPR 1998, r 21.2(1) CPR 1998, r 21.11(3)
Who may raise doubts as to the capacity of a party	The solicitors for the party, another party or the court The court should investigate question of capacity whenever there is reason to suppose it may be absent	 *Masterman-Lister* [2003] 1 WLR 1511
What should be done when doubts are raised	The doubts should be resolved and any proceedings stayed until this has been done	FPR 2010, r 15.3(1); CPR 1998, r 21.3
What discretion does the court have	Steps may not be taken without the permission of the court The court can thus allow steps to be taken that are needed at that stage and may do so if these will not prejudice the party who may lack capacity	 FPR 2010, r 15.3(1); CPR 1998, r 21.3(2),(3)

What if a party is found to lack capacity during proceedings	Any step taken before a protected party has a litigation friend has no effect *unless the court orders otherwise* The court may thus waive the procedural irregularity and give consequential directions if this will not prejudice the party who lacked capacity and there has been no abuse of process	FPR 2010, r 15.3(3); CPR 1998, r 21.3(4)
How will the court know if there has been prejudice	A litigation friend will have been appointed and can make submissions as to the future conduct of the proceedings	
Resolving doubt as to capacity		
What is required	– Expert evidence – Factual evidence	
The expert evidence	Medical evidence as to an impairment of, or a disturbance in the functioning of, the mind or brain (the diagnostic threshold)	MCA 2005, s 2(1)
The factual evidence	Evidence of expert and lay witnesses as to whether the party is unable to make a decision in the matter for himself according to the statutory criteria	MCA 2005, s 3(1)
Are both types of evidence required	In practice the medical evidence may extend to ability to make and communicate decisions – unless challenged it will be all that is required	
What is the standard of proof	There is a presumption of capacity but lack of capacity may be proved on the balance of probability	MCA 2005, ss 1(2), 2(4)
Petitioner/ Applicant *or* Claimant	Where significant doubt arises, the court will expect this party to produce evidence to dispel that doubt Proceedings may be stayed until the party submits to a medical examination	
Respondent *or* Defendant	The court will expect the party bringing the proceedings to produce evidence if the Defendant/Respondent does not respond Not appropriate to make a default order that a defendant/respondent who fails to submit to an examination be treated as capable	*Carmarthenshire County Council v Lewis* [2010] EWCA Civ 1567
What if a respondent *or* defendant will not cooperate *The following options may be available to the claimant*		
Certificate of suitability	A suitable adult may be prepared to complete the required *Certificate of suitability* which states a belief that the person is a protected party and includes evidence in support	FPR 2010, r 15.5(3); Form FP9; CPR 1998, rr 21.4(3), 21.5; Form N235
Evidence	Medical evidence may already exist that establishes the diagnostic threshold Evidence of conduct may be available (e g as to how the party has responded to the claim) – this may in itself create doubts as to capacity	
Lack of medical evidence	The court has no power to force the party to submit to an examination A default order would not be appropriate because an actual finding of lack of capacity is required	

	In the absence of medical evidence, a court should be cautious before concluding that capacity is lacking	*Baker Tilly (A Firm) v Makar* [2013] COPLR 245, QBD
	Although expert evidence is likely to be of very considerable importance, the court may reach a different conclusion by weighing such evidence against findings on other evidence	*WBC (Local Authority) v Z and others* [2016] EWCOP 4
Involve social services	A recital in a court order that there is an appearance of needs for care and support coupled with a request for an indication as to whether such assessment has been or will be carried out may produce information. A social worker may be invited to attend the next directions hearing	Care Act 2014, s 9
Official Solicitor	Cannot act for party in the absence of a finding of lack of capacity The court can direct the Official Solicitor to make inquiries and report: The Official Solicitor, Victory House, 30–34 Kingsway, London WC2B 6EX, DX 141423 Bloomsbury 7; tel 020 3681 2751 (healthcare and welfare) or 020 3681 2758 (property and affairs); fax 020 3681 2762	*Harbin v Masterman* [1896] 1 Ch 351, CA
Court of Protection	See below	
Who will be the representative *The following options may be available, although in proceedings pursuant to CA 1989, Pt IV the only realistic option is likely to be the Official Solicitor*		
Person already involved	*Attorney* (under registered enduring or lasting power) *Deputy* appointed by Court of Protection *Appointee* for social security benefits	FPR 2010, r 15.4(2) CPR 1998, r 21.4(2) MCA 2005
Concerned person	Relative, partner, friend, carer or personal advocate	FPR 2010, r 15.4(3); CPR 1998, r 21.4(3)
Solicitor for party	Not usually appropriate – conflict of roles	
Official Solicitor	Litigation friend of last resort if consents May also act as solicitor Requires provision for costs	
Involving the Court of Protection		
What can this Court do	– Make declaration as to capacity – Make decisions on behalf of a person who lacks capacity – Appoint a deputy to do so – Nominate a person to conduct proceedings	MCA 2005, ss 15, 16
Why involve this Court	– Resolve capacity issues – Find someone to be litigation friend – Clarify whether the Court of Protection needs to be involved	MCA 2005
Advantages	– Expertise in this area – Power to give directions even before finding of incapacity – Additional powers to obtain reports	MCA 2005, ss 48, 49

What reports can be obtained	– Local authority (e g social services) – NHS body (clinical commissioning group or trust) – Court of Protection general visitor – Court of Protection special visitor – Public Guardian	MCA 2005, s 49
Disadvantages	– Cost and delay – Someone must apply to this Court (but that may become necessary anyway)	

F2: Scientific Test Direction

Legal background

In any civil proceedings in which an issue as to parentage arises, a party may apply to the court for a direction for the use of scientific tests or bodily samples to determine the issue, or the court may, on its own initiative, issue such a direction (FLRA 1969, s 20(1)). An application cannot be made on a freestanding basis but only in existing proceedings (e g FLA 1986, s 55A, CA 1989, s 9 or CSA 1991, s 27, TLATA 1996, s 14 or under I(PFD)A 1975). In a narrow range of cases, funding may be available through Cafcass/CAFCASS Cymru (see the commentary to FLRA 1969, s 20). The court issues a direction (see also *Re H (Paternity: Blood Test)* [1996] 2 FLR 65, CA). No sample can be taken without consent (FLRA 1969, s 21(1)) or by direction of the court where a person having care and control of a child refuses consent (FLRA 1969, s 21(3)): failure to comply with a direction enables the court to draw such inferences as appear proper in the circumstances of the particular case (FLRA 1969, s 23(1)). Application is by the FPR 2010, Pt 18 procedure.

A child under 16 or who lacks capacity acts by a 'responsible adult' as defined in CPR PD23B, para 1.1(3).

Procedure

Who may apply	Any party to the proceedings; or the court on own initiative	FLRA 1969, s 20(1)
The proceedings	Any civil (including family) proceedings in which parentage is in issue	FLRA 1969, s 20(1)
The application	By FPR 2010, Pt 18 procedure application notice (Form D11) The application must specify who is to carry out the tests If application is regarding (1) a person under 16 or (2) who is a protected party (per FPR 2010, Pt 15), the name and address of the responsible adult must be given	FPR 2010, r 18.1(2)(a) FLRA 1969, s 20(1A) CPR PD23B, para 1.2
Respondent/ Other parties	(1) All other parties to the existing proceedings (2) Anyone else from whom samples may be required	See, for example, FPR 2010, r 8.20 for declarations under r 8.18
Notice	(1) FPR 2010 proceedings: 7 days before hearing (2) CPR 1998 proceedings: 3 days before hearing	FPR 2010, r 18.8(1)(b)(ii) CPR 1998, r 23.7(1)(b)
Direction	Court gives a direction in form proposed in *Re H* The name of the tester must be included in the direction	*Re H (Paternity: Blood Test)* [1996] 2 FLR 65, CA, at [83]

Service of direction	By the court (1) on parties to proceedings (2) anyone from whom sample is to be taken	 CPR PD23B, para 1.4(1) CPR PD23B, para 1.4(2)
Report	Made to the court by the tester Report in form prescribed by Blood Tests (Evidence of Paternity) Regs 1971 Served by the court on (1) parties to proceedings, (2) responsible adult (as applicable) and (3) anyone from whom sample to be taken	FLRA 1969, s 20(2) FLRA 1969, ss 20(3), 22 CPR PD23B, para 1.5
Fees and costs	Fee for report payable by applicant for direction	FLRA 1969, s 20(6)

F3: Withdrawal of Treatment in Persistent Vegetative State etc Cases where the Patient is an Adult

See MCA 2005. All cases dealt with by the Court of Protection. See *Court of Protection Practice* and *Urgent Applications in the Court of Protection* (LexisNexis). See also the guidance *Decisions relating to cardiopulmonary resuscitation* (see *www.familylaw.co.uk*).

F4: Costs in Family Proceedings (High Court and Family Court)

Legal background

Costs may only be obtained by court order (SCA 1981, s 51(3)), save by consent of the parties. The factors that affect the award of costs, and the procedure to be followed, are governed by FPR 2010, rr 28.2 and 28.3, which apply CPR 1998, Pts 44 (except rr 44.2(2),(3) and 44.10(2),(3)), 46 and 47 and r 45.8 to all family proceedings.

Orders for costs are entirely in the discretion of the court (SCA 1981, s 51(1), which covers the Court of Appeal, the High Court and Family Court), subject to 'any other enactment and to rules of court'. However, there are factors which the court is required to take into account when exercising its discretion whether to award costs (CPR 1998, r 44.2(4),(5)).

Costs awarded to the 'successful party'

CPR 1998, r 44.2(2) provides that where the court decides to make an order as to costs, the general rule is that the 'unsuccessful party' should pay the costs of the 'successful party', but the court may make a different order (r 44.2(2)(b)). This rule does not apply in family proceedings (FPR 2010, r 28.2(1)). However, in the Family Court the judge must have some starting-point (e g that costs should be awarded to the 'successful party': *Gojkovic v Gojkovic (No 2)* [1991] 2 FLR 233, CA; and see for example *Baker v Rowe* (below)). See further Guide F4(1).

Costs against a third party

Costs may be awarded against a third party (i e who was not a party to the proceedings: *Symphony Group plc v Hodgson* [1994] QB 179, CA; (*Re OB (Private Law Proceedings: Costs)* [2016] 1 FLR 92, FD) or as between intervenors (*Baker v Rowe* [2010] 1 FLR 761, CA). These are not 'wasted costs' orders (see error in *X Local Authority v Trimega Laboratories* [2014] 2 FLR 232, FD).

Costs and children cases

Costs orders will be rare in children cases (*Keller v Keller and Legal Aid Board* [1995] 1 FLR 259, CA; *K v K* [2016] EWHC 2002 (Fam)), although costs orders are always entirely in the discretion of the court. *R v R (Costs: Child Case)* [1997] 2 FLR 95, CA suggested that a criterion for an order for costs in children cases might be whether or not a party has been guilty of unreasonable conduct in connection with a case. See further Guide F4(1).

In care proceedings, where the local authority is the applicant, they should not be inhibited from carrying out their statutory duties by the threat of costs orders 'in the absence of reprehensible behaviour or an unreasonable stance' on their part (*Re T (Children)* [2013] 1 FLR 133, SC, or where they are an unsuccessful appellate party in the Court of Appeal (e g *MW and Hertfordshire County Council v A & V and Mr & Mrs J* [2014] EWCA Civ 405).

In proceedings involving the Official Solicitor the 'general rule' is that the Official Solicitor should have half his costs in the absence of special features that override this 'rule' (*Re D (Costs)* [2012] COPLR 499, COP).

Costs in financial remedy proceedings

Under FPR 2010, r 28.3, costs orders may not be made in 'financial remedy proceedings' (as defined by r 28.3(4)(b): i e the majority of matrimonial and civil partnership proceedings), save in cases of litigation misconduct. The remaining proceedings for a financial remedy (e g interim hearings, preliminary issue hearings, enforcement of orders, appeals, set aside applications etc) will be dealt with on the basis of a 'clean sheet' principle (see commentary to r 28.3 and in *Judge v Judge* [2009] 1 FLR 1287, CA).

Costs awarded to person acting in a fiduciary capacity

CPR 1998, r 46.3 provides the court with power to award costs to a trustee, personal representative or other person acting in a fiduciary capacity, from the fund held by him. Where there is any doubt whatsoever in the mind of the trustee or his adviser as to whether the action should be continued on behalf of the beneficiaries of the fund, an application should be made to the court for a *Beddoe* order (*Re Beddoe* [1893] 1 Ch 547, CA).

Wasted costs

Where a legal representative behaves in a manner which is held to be 'improper, unreasonable or negligent' (SCA 1981, s 51(7)), a wasted costs order may be made against him or her. These words bear their ordinary meaning, as explained in *Ridehalgh v Horsefield and ors* [1994] 2 FLR 194, CA: (i) 'improper' means behaviour which amounts to a significant breach of professional conduct; (ii) 'unreasonable' means conduct which does not permit of a reasonable explanation; and (iii) 'negligent' means failure to act with the competence to be expected of ordinary members of the profession. Conduct of a hopeless or difficult case does not, of itself, justify a finding under s 51(7). See further Guide F4(2).

Funded (legal aid) cases

An order for costs may be made against a funded (legally aided) client as against any other party to proceedings; but the amount he can be ordered to pay cannot exceed the amount which it is reasonable for him to pay (LASPOA 2012, s 29).

Assessment of costs

The court must consider whether to order summary assessment (i e assessment on the day of hearing the costs application) or detailed assessment (formerly taxation of costs), in which case assessment will be delayed. Detailed assessment will always occur in a CLS funded case. When assessing the amount of any possible award of costs (either on the indemnity or standard basis) the court should have regard to the various factors set out in CPR 1998, rr 44.3, 44.4. See further Guides F4(3)–F4(4).

F4(1): Order for Costs Against Another Party to the Proceedings

Procedure

Who may apply	Any party to the proceedings. In appropriate circumstances application may be against a third party	SCA 1981, s 51(3)
Time for application	At any stage in the case; and in particular when the court is dealing with an application or makes an order	CPR PD44, para 4.1
Principles on which orders made	Costs are in the discretion of the court (i e whether, when and how much is to be paid), subject to 'any other enactment and to rules of court'	SCA 1981, s 51(1); CPR 1998, r 44.2(1)

Orders for costs	Costs orders may include: (a) a proportion of another party's costs; (b) a stated amount of those costs; (c) costs from or until a certain date; (d) costs incurred before issue of proceedings; (e) costs relating to particular steps; (f) costs relating only to one part of the proceedings; and (g) interest on costs from or until a certain date	CPR 1998, r 44.2(6)
	Types of order include: – costs in any event – costs in the case/application – costs reserved (NB means that if no later order is made, costs are in the application) – applicant's/respondent's costs in the application – no order as to costs	CPR PD44, para 4.2
	If a party is not present when an order is made his solicitor must notify him of the order made within 7 days	CPR 1998, r 44.8
	Note: (1) 'Clean sheet': separate rules apply in the case of certain financial remedy proceedings (see commentary to FPR 2010, r 28.3)	Eg *Judge v Judge* [2009] 1 FLR 1287, CA
	(2) Special provision is made for costs application in set aside applications	FPR 2010, r 28.3(3)
When to comply with order for costs	Within 14 days of: (a) date of judgment or order (if amount of costs fixed thereby); or (b) date of certificate following detailed assessment (see Guide F4(2))	CPR 1998, r 44.7
Factors in deciding the order for costs: general	All the circumstances of the case, including: (a) the conduct of all the parties; (b) whether a party has succeeded in only part of his case; and (c) any admissible (e g *Calderbank*) offer to settle made by a party which is drawn to the court's attention	CPR 1998, r 44.2(4)
'The conduct of the parties'	Conduct under CPR 1998, r 44.2(4) includes (non-exhaustive list): (a) conduct before, as well as during, the proceedings, and in particular the extent to which the parties followed any relevant pre-action protocol; (b) whether it was reasonable for a party to raise, pursue or contest a particular allegation or issue; (c) the manner in which a party has pursued or defended his case or a particular allegation or issue; and (d) whether a claimant who has succeeded in his claim, in whole or in part, exaggerated his claim	CPR 1998, r 44.2(5)
Factors in deciding the order for costs: 'financial remedy proceedings' (as defined by FPR 2010, r 28.3(4)(b))	The 'general rule' is that there is no order for costs, save where there has been 'conduct' relating to the proceedings and before or after they were commenced	FPR 2010, r 28.3(5),(6)
	Note (1) No *Calderbank* letter is admissible on the issue of costs	FPR 2010, r 28.3(8)

	(2) If the court chooses to ignore the 'general rule' for financial order proceedings, then SCA 1981, s 51 applies; in no circumstances can r 44.3(1)–(5) apply	FPR 2010, r 28.3(2)
'Conduct'	'Conduct' in relation to financial remedy proceedings is the following exhaustive list: (a) failure by a party to comply with FPR 2010, a court order or a relevant PD; (b) any open offer to settle made by a party; (c) whether it was reasonable for a party to raise, pursue or contest a particular allegation or issue; (d) the manner of response to the application or a particular issue (e) any other relevant aspect of a party's conduct in relation to the proceedings; and (f) the financial effect on the parties of any costs order	FPR 2010, r 28.3(7)
Payment on account	The court must make an order for payment of costs on account pending detailed assessment	CPR 1998, r 44.2(8)
Assessment of costs	Summary assessment (see Guide F4(3)) Detailed assessment (see Guide F4(4))	
Basis of assessment	*Standard* (i) Costs assessed on a standard basis are only costs which are proportionate to the matters in issue (ii) Any doubt which the court may have as to whether costs were reasonably incurred or reasonable and proportionate in amount are resolved in favour of the paying party (iii) If no basis for assessment is stated, costs are assessed on the standard basis	CPR 1998, rr 44.3(1)(a), (2),(4), 44.4(1)(a)
	Indemnity Any doubt as to whether costs were reasonably incurred is resolved in favour of the receiving party	CPR 1998, rr 44.3(1)(b), (3), 44.4(1)(b)
Factors in defining amount of costs on assessment	(a) the conduct of all parties, including in particular: (i) conduct before, and during, the proceedings; and (ii) attempts at mediation (if any) made before and during the proceedings; (b) the monetary value of the claim; (c) the importance of the case to all parties; (d) the complexity of the case or difficulty or novelty of the issues raised; (e) the skill, effort, specialised knowledge and responsibility involved; (f) the time spent on the case; and (g) the place where and circumstances in which work (or part of it) was done	CPR 1998, r 44.4(3)

F4(2): Order for Wasted Costs

Procedure

Who may apply	Any party to the proceedings The court on its own initiative	SCA 1981, s 51(6); CPR PD46, para 5.3
Time for application	At any stage in proceedings where an order for costs can be made but normally at the end of 'the trial' or final hearing of an application	CPR PD46, para 5.2
Application	(i) By notice of application. The application should be accompanied by evidence of what the legal representative is alleged to have done and specify the costs sought (ii) By making application in the course of hearing (as with any other application for costs)	CPR PD46, paras 5.4, 5.9; application: by FPR 2010, Pt 18 procedure CPR PD46, para 5.4
Order	Against legal or other representative, that they pay costs incurred and wasted by another party to the proceedings	SCA 1981, s 51(6), (7); CPR 1998, r 46.8
Factors in making the order	Has the legal representative behaved in a way which is 'improper, unreasonable or negligent'; or is there expenditure caused by the legal representative that the court considers the other party should not have to pay?	SCA 1981, s 51(6); cf *Ridehalgh v Horsefield* [1994] 2 FLR 194, CA SCA 1981, s 51(6)
Procedure	No order can be made unless the legal representative has had a reasonable opportunity to show cause why an order should not be made	CPR 1998, r 46.8; *Ridehalgh v Horsefield* (above)
Court's directions	The court gives directions as it sees fit for disposal of the application. Directions may include the following: (i) Court may direct that privileged documents be disclosed to both itself and to the applicant for wasted costs (ii) Before making an order the court can seek an enquiry from a costs judge or district judge (iii) The court can refer the decision on the issue of an order to a costs judge or district judge	CPR PD46, para 5.6; *Ridehalgh v Horsefield* (above) CPR 1998, r 46.8 CPR 1998, r 46.8 CPR 1998, r 46.8
Court's considerations	(i) Has the lawyer acted improperly, unreasonably or negligently? (ii) If so, has the applicant incurred unnecessary costs as a result? (iii) If so, is it just to require the lawyer to pay the applicant's relevant costs? If the court makes an order: it must specify the amount to be paid; or it may ask a costs judge/district judge to report on the amount to be paid	*Re A Barrister (Wasted Costs Order)* [1993] QB 293, CA (approved in *Ridehalgh v Horsefield* at [203H]) CPR 1998, r 46.8 CPR 1998, r 46.8

F4(3): Summary Assessment of Costs

Procedure

Stage in proceedings	When a party is ordered to pay costs (for detailed assessment see Guide F4(4))	CPR 1998, r 44.6

Application	Form N260 should be followed 'as closely as possible'	CPR PD44, paras 1.2, 9.5
Time for summary assessment	Whenever an order for costs is made the court should consider whether to make a summary assessment NB no summary assessment can be made for a receiving party who is: (i) a legally assisted party or LSC funded party (ii) a child or patient, unless the child's solicitor waives the right to further costs	CPR PD44, para 9.1 CPR PD44, para 9.8 CPR PD44, para 9.9
Factors in deciding on summary assessment	The court should make a summary assessment at the conclusion of a hearing: (i) of less than one day (ii) certain hearings in the Court of Appeal unless there is good reason not to do so, e g a substantial dispute as to amount due from the paying party which cannot be resolved immediately; or there is insufficient time	 CPR PD44, para 9.2 CPR PD44, para 9.2
Duty of legal representatives	Legal representatives who intend to seek an order for costs must prepare a statement of costs following Form N260 and setting out the detail required by CPR PD44 para 9.5	CPR PD44, para 9.5
Time for filing	The statement of costs should be filed and served not later than '24 hours before the date fixed for the hearing'	CPR PD44, para 9.5
Failure to comply	Failure ('without reasonable excuse') to comply with PD44, para 9.5 may be taken into account by the court in considering what order to make, e g no order for costs, costs in claim etc	CPR PD44, para 9.6; and see *Macdonald v Taree Hldgs Ltd* [2001] CPLR 439, CA
Factors in deciding basis of award and amount of assessment	See Guide F4(1)	CPR 1998, rr 44.2, 44.3

F4(4): Detailed Assessment of Costs

Procedure

Order for detailed assessment	On ordering a party to pay costs the court may order detailed assessment of costs, instead of making a summary assessment (see Guide F4(3))	CPR 1998, r 44.6
Time for order	(i) At the conclusion of proceedings (ii) At any other time when the court makes an order for detailed assessment; or (iii) When the parties agree NB An order for detailed assessment is not stayed pending appeal, save where so ordered by the court appealed from, or to which appeal is made	 CPR 1998, r 47.1; PD47, paras 1.1–1.4 CPR PD47, paras 1.1–1.4 CPR 1998, r 47.2; PD47, para 2
Parties	(i) receiving party (ii) paying party (iii) other parties ('relevant persons')	CPR 1998, r 44.1 CPR 1998, r 44.1 CPR 1998, r 47.6(2); PD47, para 5.5

Notice of commencement of proceedings	Commencement of detailed assessment proceedings occurs upon service by receiving party of the following: (i) notice of commencement (Form N252) (ii) a copy of the bill of costs (iii) fee notes of counsel, experts etc (iv) evidence of disbursements over £500 (v) addresses of persons to be served	CPR PD47, para 5.2
Service of notice of commencement and other documents	Notice of commencement etc served on: (i) paying party (ii) other parties ('relevant persons')	CPR 1998, r 47.6(1) CPR 1998, r 47.6(2)
Time for commencement of detailed assessment proceedings	(i) 3 months from date of judgment, direction or order (ii) If order stayed pending appeal, 3 months from lifting of stay (iii) Other period: as agreed by parties or ordered by the court NB There is no need for permission to commence out of time (but see CPR 1998, r 47.8 for sanctions for delay in commencement)	CPR 1998, r 47.7 CPR PD47, para 6.1 CPR PD47, para 5.2
Costs agreed	Where costs are agreed, the parties may apply (under CPR 1998, r 40.6) for a consent order setting out the amount to be paid and any terms for such payment	CPR 1998, r 47.10
Points of dispute	Served by paying party and any other party on receiving party and any other party Points of dispute should be succinct and should follow Precedent G Service: 21 days after receipt of notice of commencement Upon receipt, receiving party can: (i) apply for detailed assessment hearing (ii) serve reply to points of dispute	CPR 1998, r 47.9(1) CPR PD47, para 8.2 CPR 1998, r 47.9(2) CPR 1998, r 47.14(1) CPR 1998, r 47.13
Default costs certificate	Receiving party can request if no points of dispute are served within 21 days	CPR 1998, r 47.9(4)
Setting aside a default costs certificate	Where receiving party is not entitled to certificate, court must set aside The court has a discretion to set aside if there is some good reason for detailed assessment proceedings to continue If the notice of commencement is not received by the paying party within 21 days and a default costs certificate is issued, the receiving party must apply to set it aside or seek court directions	CPR 1998, r 47.12(1) CPR 1998, r 47.12(2) CPR 1998, r 47.12(3)
Detailed assessment hearing: application	Upon service of points of dispute the receiving party files a request for a detailed assessment hearing *Time for application* (i) by receiving party: within 3 months of the expiry of the period for commencement of detailed assessment (see above) or as directed (ii) by paying party: on application to the court to request receiving party to request a hearing	CPR 1998, r 47.14(1) CPR 1998, r 47.14(2) CPR 1998, r 47.14(3),(4)
Procedure for detailed assessment	Request for a detailed assessment must be in Form N258 and must be accompanied by the documents listed in PD47, para 13.2	CPR PD47, para 13.2

Parties to detailed assessment	The receiving party, the paying party and any party who has served points of dispute	CPR 1998, r 47.14(6)
Notice of hearing	Notice of hearing is given by the court	CPR PD47, paras 13.4, 13.6
Interim costs certificate	After the receiving party has applied for a detailed assessment hearing the court may, on a Pt 23 application, issue an interim costs certificate (Form N257): (i) for costs to be paid; or (ii) for costs to be paid into court	CPR 1998, r 47.16; PD47, para 15
	NB Where a party is ordered to pay costs he may be required to pay an amount on account before costs are assessed	CPR 1998, r 44.2
Detailed assessment hearing	Only items raised in points of dispute can be raised at the detailed assessment hearing	CPR 1998, r 47.14(7)
Final costs certificate	14 days from the end of the detailed assessment hearing a completed bill of costs must be filed	CPR 1998, r 47.17; PD47, paras 16.3–16.8
	The court then: (i) issues a final costs certificate (Form N256); and (ii) serves it on all parties to the detailed assessment hearing	CPR 1998, r 47.17
Time for payment of costs	Costs are payable 14 days from the date of the costs certificate	CPR 1998, r 44.7
Offers to settle	'Without prejudice offers' to settle the detailed assessment proceedings may be taken into account in ordering costs of assessment	
Costs of detailed assessment	Receiving party is entitled to the costs of the detailed assessment in the absence of any order, rule, PD etc which provides otherwise	CPR 1998, r 47.20
Appeals		CPR 1998, rr 47.21–47.24

F5: Application in Respect of the Human Rights Act 1998

Legal background

From 2 October 2000 by virtue of HRA 1998, s 3, all primary and subordinate legislation must be read and given effect in a way which is compatible with the European Convention of Human Rights (as prescribed in HRA 1998, s 1). The provisions of HRA 1998 are not retrospective (*R (Wright) v Secretary of State of the Home Department* [2006] EWCA Civ 67). Where it is not possible to read legislation in this way, an application may be made for a declaration of incompatibility (under s 4). Otherwise, a complaint that there has been a decision by a public authority (court, tribunal, local authority or any person whose functions are of a public nature) which is incompatible with a convention right (under s 6) may be the subject of separate proceedings (pursuant to s 7(1)(a)) or brought within existing proceedings (pursuant to s 7(1)(b)). For consideration of the definitions of 'a public authority' and 'functions of a public nature' see *YL v Birmingham City Council* [2008] 1 AC 95, HL. A claim pursuant to HRA 1998, s 7(1)(a) should be made to the Administrative Court as an application for judicial review (see Guide E1). Where there are extant public law proceedings, claims of a breach of Convention rights should be raised in those proceedings: s 7(1)(b); *Re V (Care Proceedings: Human Rights Claims)* [2004] 1 FLR 944, CA. However, in exceptional cases, it is permissible to bring a judicial review challenge to a local authority decision even when there are extant care proceedings (and an interim care order is in force) where the actual decision sought to be impugned cannot effectively be made the subject of review in family proceedings and there is no other appropriate remedy: *R (H) v Kingston upon Hull City Council* [2013] EWHC 388 (Admin): see also *Re W (Care Proceedings: Functions of Court and Local Authority)* [2014] 2 FLR 431, CA, at [87]–[89].

Although the ECtHR generally favours an award of damages in cases in which local authorities have infringed the rights of parents under Art 8 as a result of shortcomings in the procedures by which they have taken or kept children in care, there is a spectrum of ECHR 1950 violations. Where the breach has been purely procedural and not significant, an award of damages may be inappropriate: in such cases the declaration of a violation of Art 8 may afford the parent just satisfaction (*Re C (Breach of Human Rights: Damages)* [2007] 1 FLR 1957, CA per Wilson LJ at [64]-[71]). However, contrast the decision in *Re V (Care: Pre Birth Actions)* [2005] 1 FLR 627, CA, where the Court of Appeal took a much more restrictive approach to the concept of awarding damages for breach of ECHR 1950 rights in public law proceedings but see *Northamptonshire County Council v AS & others* [2015] EWHC 199 (Fam) where the local authority agreed the quantum of substantial damages for breaches of the child's Art 8 rights.

Procedure

Who may apply	Any person who is a victim of the action which is the subject of the complaint	HRA 1998, s 7(1)
	A claim under HRA 1998, s 7(1)(a) may only be brought within 12 months of the act complained of or such longer period as the court considers equitable	HRA 1998, s 7(5)
Which court	A claim under HRA 1998, s 7(1) (other than in respect of a judicial act) may be brought in any court in existing or ongoing proceedings	HRA 1998, s 9(1)
	A claim under HRA 1998, s 7(1)(a) in respect of a judicial act may only be brought in the High Court (in relation to the actions of an inferior court or tribunal)	CPR 1998, r 7.11; HRA 1998, s 9(1)
	A claim under HRA 1998, s 4 for a declaration of incompatibility must be brought in or transferred to the High Court	HRA 1998, s 4
Application	A claim made in existing or continuing proceedings should specify the details in the originating documentation or amend the documentation accordingly setting out:	FPR 2010, r 29.5
	(a) the precise details of the Convention right claimed to have been infringed and details; (b) specify the relief sought; and (c) state whether a declaration of incompatibility is claimed	
	Any application to amend documentation to make a claim should be made as soon as possible any in any event within 28 days, unless otherwise ordered	
	A separate claim (not one made in existing or ongoing proceedings) should be made by issuing proceedings under CPR 1998, Pt 8. Such a claim may be brought in the High Court or County Court	CPR 1998, r 7.11
	Where the claim is for damages in respect of a judicial act, the claim must be set out in the statement of case	
Defendants	The parties to the existing or ongoing proceedings, if the claim is made within those proceedings	
Additional persons to be served	Where a claim is in respect of damages for a judicial act notice must be given to the Crown	CPR 1998, r 19.4A; FPR 2010, r 29.5(5); PD29A

	Where a claim for a declaration of incompatibility is made pursuant to HRA 1998, s 4 notice must be given to the Crown, and the Crown or a Minister shall be joined as a party	HRA 1998, s 5; CPR 1998, r 19.4A; FPR 2010, r 29.5(3),(4) (Family Proceedings); CPR PD19A, para 6.1 (Non-Family Proceedings including judicial review and appeals to the Court of Appeal); Annex 1 to CPR PD66
Procedure	The claim form (Form N208) must state that Pt 8 applies; the question which the claimant wants the court to decide, or remedy sought and legal basis The court will then give directions as to the filing of an acknowledgment of service, date for hearing and filing of evidence	CPR 1998, r 8.2 CPR 1998, r 8.9
Order	The court may make such order as is within its power. Damages or compensation may be awarded only by a court that has power to make such an award On an application pursuant to HRA 1998, s 4 the court may make a declaration of incompatibility	HRA 1998, s 8

F6: Alternative Procedure for Applications in Family Proceedings (FPR 2010, Pt 19)

Legal background

FPR 2010, Pt 19 is derived from CPR 1998, Pt 8, which was introduced into civil proceedings to replace the former originating summons procedure. Its purpose is to provide an originating procedure where no 'alternative' exists to provide for the remedy a party seeks. Rule 19.1(2) provides that it is appropriate where:

- no form or other procedure is prescribed;
- 'the applicant seeks the court's decision on a question which is unlikely to involve a substantial dispute of fact' (r 19.1(2)(b), derived almost exactly from CPR 1998, r 8.1(2)(a));
- the Pt 19 procedure is prescribed by a rule or practice direction (r 19.2); or
- the Pt 19 procedure is permitted by a rule or practice direction (r 19.1).

It is prescribed by a number of the applications in FPR 2010, Pt 8 (declarations) and has been used, e g to obtain a bodily sample from a dead person: *CM v The Executor of the Estate of EJ (Deceased) and Her Majesty's Coroner* [2013] 2 FLR 1410, FD). It may be the appropriate procedure for such applications as:

- To obtain a freestanding unopposed order without the issue of proceedings (FPR PD19A, para 1.5)
- The making of a pre-decree nisi consent order (*JP v NP* [2015] 1 FLR 659, FD) or after arbitration (*S v S (Financial Remedies: Arbitral Award)* [2014] 1 FLR 1257, FD, Sir James Munby P)
- A consent order under CA 1989, Sch 1 where, at present, there is no prescribed procedure equivalent (say) to FPR 2010, r 9.26 where no CA 1989 proceedings have been issued.

Procedure

Who may apply	Anyone with a family proceedings claim that: • is permitted by FPR 2010, r 19.1 • is prescribed by a rule or PD (see e g FPR 2010, Pt 8 and r 19.2) • is not covered by an existing rule or PD (see examples in 'Legal background' above) • requires the court's decision, which is unlikely to involve a dispute of fact	FPR 2010, r 19.1(5) FPR 2010, r 19.1(2)(a) FPR 2010, r 19.1(2)(b)
Court applied to	Family Court (or High Court where prescribed)	

Pt 19 inappropriate	The court can direct that an application proceed as if not issued under the Pt 19 procedure	FPR 2010, r 19.1(3)
Application	Must comply with r 19.3, stating: • The question to be considered by the court or • The order sought by the applicant • Grounds in law for the order, including its statutory basis (if any) • Whether any party is involved in a representative capacity Note: application can be made without naming a respondent	FPR 2010, r 19.3 FPR 2010, r 19.4; PD19A, para 2.2
Application: evidence	Written evidence to be relied on by the applicant must be filed at the time of filing the application and served on the respondent If a respondent files evidence (see below) the applicant can file evidence in reply *14 days from service of the respondent's evidence* At a hearing, the applicant cannot rely on evidence not served per r 19.7 without permission of the court	FPR 2010, r 19.7(1),(2) FPR 2010, r 19.7(5) FPR 2010, r 19.8(1)
Response	A respondent replies by acknowledgement of service *14 days from service* The acknowledgement of service must state • whether the respondent intends to defend • if so, whether the respondent seeks an alternative order (and if so what) If a respondent fails to acknowledge service s/he can attend a hearing but not take part save with permission from the court	FPR 2010, r 19.5(1)(a) FPR 2010, r 19.5(3) FPR 2010, r 19.6(2)
Respondent: evidence	A respondent must file and serve written evidence when the acknowledgement of service is filed At a hearing a respondent cannot rely on evidence not served per r 19.7 without permission of the court	FPR 2010, r 19.7(3),(4) FPR 2010, r 19.8(1)
Respondent's objection to Pt 19 procedure	If the respondent objects to use of Pt 19, s/he must say so in the acknowledgement of service because a dispute of fact is involved or (the rule says 'and', but probably means 'or') the Pt 19 procedure is not permitted	FPR 2010, r 19.9(1); and see r 19.1(2),(4)
Case management	Once evidence is filed, the court 'will give' case management directions, for example: • r 19.1(3) (above) may be considered • scientific tests under FLRA 1969 in relation to a FLA 1986, s 55 declaration application (FPR 2010, r 8.18)	FPR 2010, r 19.9(2)
Application for a consent order	If the application is consensual – e g for a consent order – then both parties can jointly agree the evidence to be filed and to dispense with the respondent's acknowledgement of service	

PART II

Statutes

PART II: Statutes

Contents

All relevant provisions in the following legislation, as amended and fully annotated, and the principal core substantive provisions:

Access to Justice Act 1999 243
Administration of Justice Act 1960 244
Administration of Justice Act 1970 250
Adoption and Children Act 2002 252
Adoption (Intercountry Aspects) Act 1999 328
Anti-Social Behaviour, Crime and Policing Act 2014 337
Attachment of Earnings Act 1971 338
Charging Orders Act 1979 358
Child Abduction and Custody Act 1985 362
Child Support Act 1991 399
Children Act 1989 416
Children and Families Act 2014 685
Civil Jurisdiction and Judgments Act 1982 687
Civil Partnership Act 2004 699
Civil Procedure Act 1997 789
Contempt of Court Act 1981 790
County Courts Act 1984 794
Criminal Justice and Court Services Act 2000 806
Domestic and Appellate Proceedings (Restriction of Publicity) Act 1968 808
Domestic Proceedings and Magistrates' Courts Act 1978 810
Domicile and Matrimonial Proceedings Act 1973 826
Family Law Act 1986 835
Family Law Act 1996 872
Family Law Reform Act 1969 917
Family Law Reform Act 1987 924
Female Genital Mutilation Act 2003 927
Gender Recognition Act 2004 943
Human Fertilisation and Embryology Act 1990 959
Human Fertilisation and Embryology Act 2008 977

Human Rights Act 1998 992
Inheritance (Provision for Family and Dependants) Act 1975 1012
Judicial Proceedings (Regulation of Reports) Act 1926 1039
Law Reform (Miscellaneous Provisions) Act 1970 1041
Legal Aid, Sentencing and Punishment of Offenders Act 2012 1041
Legal Services Act 2007 1045
Legitimacy Act 1976 1055
Magistrates' Courts Act 1980 1059
Maintenance Enforcement Act 1991 1060
Maintenance Orders Act 1950 1062
Maintenance Orders Act 1958 1074
Maintenance Orders (Facilities for Enforcement) Act 1920 1079
Maintenance Orders (Reciprocal Enforcement) Act 1972 1085
Marriage (Same Sex Couples) Act 2013 1119
Married Women's Property Act 1882 1122
Married Women's Property Act 1964 1123
Matrimonial and Family Proceedings Act 1984 1123
Matrimonial Causes Act 1973 1145
Matrimonial Proceedings and Property Act 1970 1215
Mental Capacity Act 2005 1216
Presumption of Death Act 2013 1222
Protection from Harassment Act 1997 1229
Senior Courts Act 1981 1232
Social Security Administration Act 1992 1251
Solicitors Act 1974 1255
Surrogacy Arrangements Act 1985 1256
Trusts of Land and Appointment of Trustees Act 1996 1260
Welfare Reform and Pensions Act 1999 1264

Note—By virtue of CCA 2013, s 17, Sch 9, para 11, in relevant legislation: (i) any reference that is or is deemed to be a reference to a county court is to be read as a reference to the County Court; and (ii) any reference that is or is deemed to be a reference to a judge of a county court is, if the context permits, to be read as a reference to the County Court and otherwise is to be read as a reference to a judge of the County Court. Note that (ii) does not apply to a reference to a holder of a particular office (for example, a reference to a Circuit Judge).

Access to Justice Act 1999

****

PART IV
APPEALS, COURTS, JUDGES AND COURT PROCEEDINGS

Appeals

54 Permission to appeal

(1) Rules of court may provide that any right of appeal to –

- (a) the county court,
- (aa) the family court,
- (b) the High Court, or
- (c) the Court of Appeal,

may be exercised only with permission.

(2) This section does not apply to a right of appeal in a criminal cause or matter.

(3) For the purposes of subsection (1) rules of court may make provision as to –

- (a) the classes of case in which a right of appeal may be exercised only with permission,
- (b) the court or courts which may give permission for the purposes of this section,
- (c) any considerations to be taken into account in deciding whether permission should be given, and
- (d) any requirements to be satisfied before permission may be given,

and may make different provision for different circumstances.

(4) No appeal may be made against a decision of a court under this section to give or refuse permission (but this subsection does not affect any right under rules of court to make a further application for permission to the same or another court).

(5) For the purposes of this section a right to make an application to have a case stated for the opinion of the High Court constitutes a right of appeal.

(6) For the purposes of this section a right of appeal to the Court of Appeal includes –

- (a) the right to make an application for a new trial, and
- (b) the right to make an application to set aside a verdict, finding or judgment in any cause or matter in the High Court which has been tried, or in which any issue has been tried, by a jury.

Amendments—CCA 2013, s 17, Schs 9, 10.

Scope—This section provides the rule making power in relation to the requirement of permission to appeal to the Court of Appeal. CPR 1998, r 52.3 provides that permission to appeal is required in all cases (save for the limited exceptions set out there). While there can be no appeal against the refusal of permission to appeal, r 52.3(3) provides that where the lower court (the court which made the order which is the subject of the proposed appeal) refuses permission to appeal, a further application for permission to appeal may be made to the appeal court. This does not mean that permission to appeal is sought in relation to the refusal to grant permission to appeal, but in relation to the substantive order (*Bulled v Khayat and Another* [2002] EWCA Civ 804). Procedure for the application for permission to appeal is contained within CPR PDs 52A–52E (see Part III).

Permission to appeal—Permission to appeal from the Family Court is required from all levels of judges sitting in that court save for appeals from decisions made by a single lay justice or a bench of two or three lay justices: FPR PD30A, para 2.1.

PART II

Appeal against a refusal of permission to appeal—This is not a second appeal but is an impermissible application to challenge a permission to appeal. There is an unacceptable delay in obtaining transcripts of judgments that are the subject of an application for permission to appeal: *Re C (Transcripts: Permission to Appeal)* [2014] 2 FLR 147, CA.

55 Second appeals

(1) Where an appeal is made to the county court, the family court or the High Court in relation to any matter, and on hearing the appeal the court makes a decision in relation to that matter, no appeal may be made to the Court of Appeal from that decision unless the Court of Appeal considers that –

(a) the appeal would raise an important point of principle or practice, or
(b) there is some other compelling reason for the Court of Appeal to hear it.

(2) This section does not apply in relation to an appeal in a criminal cause or matter.

Amendments—CCA 2013, s 17, Schs 9, 10.

Scope—This section imposes a further hurdle in relation to a proposed appeal where the appeal to the Court of Appeal would be a second tier appeal. This further hurdle is in addition to the requirement of permission to appeal (CPR 1998, r 52.13); *McFarlane v McFarlane* [2004] 2 FLR 893, CA. An application for permission to adduce fresh evidence is an application preliminary to the appellate process and does not constitute the appellate process itself. Accordingly, it is not caught by s 1: *Kaur v Matharu* [2011] 1 FLR 698, CA.

****

57 Assignment of appeals to Court of Appeal

(1) Where in any proceedings in the county court, the family court or the High Court a person appeals, or seeks permission to appeal, to a court other than the Court of Appeal or the Supreme Court –

(a) the Master of the Rolls, or
(b) the court from which or to which the appeal is made, or from which permission to appeal is sought, or
(c) the President of the Family Division where it is the family court from which or to which the appeal is made, or from which permission to appeal is sought,

may direct that the appeal shall be heard instead by the Court of Appeal.

(2) The power conferred by subsection (1)(b) shall be subject to rules of court.

Amendments—CRA 2005, Sch 9, para 68(2); CCA 2013, s 17, Schs 9, 10.

Scope—Where the County Court or High Court is to hear an appeal which would raise an important point of principle or practice or there is some other compelling reason for it to be transferred, that court, the Master of the Rolls or the President of the Family Division may direct that the appeal be heard by the Court of Appeal. If transferred up in accordance with this provision, the Court of Appeal, the Master of the Rolls or the President of the Family Division may transfer it back for hearing by the original court (CPR 1998, r 52.14(2)).

****

Administration of Justice Act 1960

****

12 Publication of information relating to proceedings in private

(1) The publication of information relating to proceedings before any court sitting in private shall not of itself be contempt of court except in the following cases, that is to say –

(a) where the proceedings –
 (i) relate to the exercise of the inherent jurisdiction of the High Court with respect to minors;
 (ii) are brought under the Children Act 1989 or the Adoption and Children Act 2002; or
 (iii) otherwise relate wholly or mainly to the maintenance or upbringing of a minor;
(b) where the proceedings are brought under the Mental Capacity Act 2005, or under any

provision of the Mental Health Act 1983 authorising an application or reference to be made to the First-tier Tribunal, the Mental Health Review Tribunal for Wales or the county court;

(c), (d) …

(e) where the court (having power to do so) expressly prohibits the publication of all information relating to the proceedings or of information of the description which is published.

(2) Without prejudice to the foregoing subsection, the publication of the text or a summary of the whole or part of an order made by a court sitting in private shall not of itself be contempt of court except where the court (having power to do so) expressly prohibits the publication.

(3) In this section references to a court include references to a judge and to a tribunal and to any person exercising the functions of a court, a judge or a tribunal; and references to a court sitting in private include references to a court sitting in camera or in chambers.

(4) Nothing in this section shall be construed as implying that any publication is punishable as contempt of court which would not be so punishable apart from this section (and in particular where the publication is not so punishable by reason of being authorised by rules of court).

Amendments—CA 1989, s 108, Sch 13, para 14; CA 2004, s 62(2); MCA 2005, s 67(1), Sch 6, para 10; SI 2005/2213; SI 2008/2833; CCA 2013, s 17, Sch 9.

Scope—See also under CA 1989, s 97 and CYPA 1933, s 39 (set out under **Use of the inherent jurisdiction to prohibit publication**, below). A useful review of the use of these sections was carried out by the CA in *Clayton v Clayton* [2007] 1 FLR 11, CA and it should be noted that although the prohibition on identification under CA 1989, s 97 comes to an end once the proceedings are concluded, the limitation upon reporting information relating to the proceedings themselves under s 12 will remain. This section has the effect of abrogating the strict liability rule of contempt of court, except in certain types of proceedings (i e those mentioned in s 12(1)(a), which relate to most types of family proceedings in which children are the focal point). For an exposition of the strict liability rule, reference should be made to specialist works on contempt of court. Section 12 is designed to prevent the publication of information in respect of child law cases which are heard in private. Section 12 does not apply solely to wardship proceedings but includes proceedings under CA 1989 and ACA 2002 (*Her Majesty's Attorney-General v Pelling* [2006] 1 FLR 93, QBD). In *Re B (A Child) (Disclosure)* [2004] 2 FLR 142, FD, Munby J reviewed many of the authorities and made the following observations on the ambit of s 12:

'(i) Section 12(1)(a) of the Administration of Justice Act 1960 has the effect of prohibiting the publication of: 'information relating to proceedings before any court sitting in private … where the proceedings (i) relate to the exercise of the inherent jurisdiction of the High Court with respect to minors; (ii) are brought under Children Act 1989; or (iii) otherwise relate wholly or mainly to the … upbringing of a minor.'

(ii) Subject only to proof of knowledge that the proceedings in question are of the type referred to in s 12(1)(a), the publication of such information is a contempt of court.

(iii) There is a 'publication' for this purpose whenever the law of defamation would treat there as being a publication. This means that most forms of dissemination, whether oral or written, will constitute a publication. The only exception is where there is a communication of information by someone to a professional, each acting in furtherance of the protection of children.

…

(v) Section 12 does not of itself prohibit the publication of:

(a) the fact, if it be the case, that a child is a ward of court and is the subject of wardship proceedings or that a child is the subject of residence or other proceedings under the Children Act 1989 or of proceedings relating wholly or mainly to his maintenance or upbringing;

(b) the name, address or photograph of such a child;

(c) the name, address or photograph of the parties (or, if the child is a party, the other parties) to such proceedings;

(d) the date, time or place of a past or future hearing of such proceedings;

(e) the nature of the dispute in such proceedings;

(f) anything which has been seen or heard by a person conducting himself lawfully in the public corridor or other public precincts outside the court in which the hearing in private is taking place;

(g) the name, address or photograph of the witnesses who have given evidence in such proceedings;

(h) the party on whose behalf such a witness has given evidence; and

(i) the text or summary of the whole or part of any order made in such proceedings.

(vi) Section 12 prohibits the publication of:

(a) accounts of what has gone on in front of the judge sitting in private;

(b) documents such as affidavits, witness statements, reports, position statements, skeleton arguments or other documents filed in the proceedings, transcripts or notes of the evidence or submissions, and transcripts or notes of the judgment (this list is not necessarily exhaustive);

(c) extracts or quotations from such documents;

(d) summaries of such documents.

These prohibitions apply whether or not the information or the document being published has been anonymised.' at [82].

This section does not prevent the identification of witnesses (*British Broadcasting Corporation v Rochdale Metropolitan Borough Council & X & Y* [2007] 1 FLR 101, FD). However, in the cases of *Norfolk County Council v Webster & ors* [2007] 2 FLR 415, FD and *British Broadcasting Corporation v CAFCASS Legal & Ors* [2007] 2 FLR 765, FD, the court granted anonymity to both domestic and foreign experts.

Disclosure and restraint jurisdiction—*A v Ward* [2010] 1 FLR 1497, FD concerns two fundamental questions, first the meaning and effect of s 12(1)(a) and second the anonymity of professional witnesses in care proceedings under CA 1989, Pt IV. In relation to the first question, 'What brings a document within the scope of s 12 depends not on whether it is otherwise or already confidential but whether it is "information relating to [the] proceedings."' at [110]. What is and what is not included within the statutory prohibition? Further to his observations in *Re B (A Child) (Disclosure)* (see above):

'(i) "information relating to [the] proceedings" includes:

(a) documents prepared for the purpose of the proceedings; and

(b) information, even if not reduced to writing, which has emerged during the course of information gathering for the purpose of proceedings already on foot.

(ii) In contrast, "information relating to [the] proceedings" does *not* include:

(a) documents (or the information contained in documents) not prepared for the purpose of the proceedings, even if the documents are lodged with the court or referred to in or annexed to a witness statement or report; or

(b) information (even if contained in documents falling within paragraph (i)(a)) which does not fall within paragraph (i)(b);

unless the document or information is published in such a way as to link it with the proceedings so that it can sensibly be said that what is published is "information relating to [the] proceedings".' at [112].

In the instant case the care proceedings, in which the local authority had failed to prove the threshold criteria of s 31(2), had come to an end and the child had been restored to his parents' care. They wished to 'go public' about the case, which the judge found was a decision solely and entirely for the parents to take.

In relation to the second question, some of the medical expert witnesses involved in the care proceedings, the treating clinicians and the social workers (by their employer local authority) each sought contra mundum injunctions to prevent the parents disclosing their identities. The judge considered the applications by each group of witnesses but concluded that none of them were entitled to the orders sought.

The starting point is the same, namely that witnesses (experts, treating clinicians or social workers) are not afforded anonymity either by the general law or by section 12, and accordingly they need to be able to demonstrate that the balancing exercise tips in their favour (at [179]). The judge found that the applications for anonymity did not counter-balance the arguments in favour of openness and did not establish a 'pressing need' for the protection sought. Nevertheless the judge recognised that there may be cases where there was clear and specific evidence in respect of a particular witness that did justify the need for the protection of his/her identity and the granting of a contra mundum injunction.

In relation to the treating clinicians, the parents had earlier entered into a contractual agreement with the NHS Trust, one term of which was that the parents agreed not to disclose the identities of the treating clinicians. The judge held that the parents were bound by the terms of that agreement.

Routine disclosure of experts' reports—The President has observed that he would like to see a practice develop in which expert reports would be routinely disclosed: the practice would aid the need for the family justice system to be as transparent as possible and encourage informed debate about the quality and content of expert evidence: *Re X, Y and Z (Expert Witness)* [2011] 2 FLR 1437, FD.

Publication—In *Re B* above, Munby J held that, subject to the exception where there is communication of information by someone to a professional, each acting in furtherance of the protection of children, there is a 'publication' for the purposes of s 12 whenever the law of defamation would treat such communication as amounting to publication. This must be read in conjunction with CA 1989, s 97(2) which prevents publication of material 'to the public at large or any section of the public'. Furthermore reference should be made to FPR 2010, rr 12.72–12.75 and PD12G, which permits parties and other specified people to disclose certain information from family proceedings heard in private involving children, to other specified people for specific purposes without needing permission of the court and without being in contempt of court. In relation to further and wider onward disclosure, see *Commissioner of Police of the Metropolis v A Local Authority and Ors* [2016] EWHC 2400 (Fam). These rules are not applicable to disclosure in adoption proceedings where different rules apply. For guidance, see *http://formfinder.hmctsformfinder.justice.gov.uk/ex710-eng.pdf*.

Use of the inherent jurisdiction to prohibit publication—The High Court can use its inherent jurisdiction both to relax and increase the restrictions imposed by s 12. However, in *Harris v Harris; Attorney-General v Harris* [2001] 2 FLR 895, FD, Munby J stated that the court should only exercise its powers to restrain publicity under the inherent jurisdiction if the automatic restraints under s 12 of the 1960 Act, CCA 1981, s 2 and CA 1989, s 97(2) were inadequate to protect the child from harm and if the interests of the child could not be adequately protected under CYPA 1933, s 39 which provides as follows:

'(1) In relation to any proceedings in any court, the court may direct that –

(a) no newspaper report of the proceedings shall reveal the name, address, or school, or include particulars calculated to lead to the identification, of any child or young person concerned with the proceedings, either as being the person by or against whom or in respect of whom the proceedings are taken, or as being a witness therein;

(b) no picture shall be published in any newspaper as being or including a picture of any child or young person so concerned in the proceedings as aforesaid;

except in so far (if at all) as may be permitted by the direction of the court.

(2) Any person who publishes any matter in contravention of any such direction shall on summary conviction be liable in respect of each offence to a fine not exceeding level 5 on the standard scale.'

In *Re S (Identification: Restrictions on Publication)* [2005] 1 FLR 591, HL, the House of Lords was of the view that the foundation of the jurisdiction to restrain publicity was derived from rights under ECHR 1950 and that since HRA 1998 came into force, the earlier case-law concerning the existence and scope of the inherent jurisdiction need not be considered. The court needs to balance the Art 8 rights of the child and the Art 10 rights of the proposed publisher and to consider the proportionality of the potential interference with each right. In *British Broadcasting Corporation v Rochdale Metropolitan Borough Council and X and Y* [2007] 1 FLR 101, FD, Ryder J conducted an extensive analysis of the relevant domestic and ECHR 1950 case-law and an illustration of the balancing exercise required. See also *Practice Note (Official Solicitor: Deputy Director of Legal Services: Cafcass; Applications for Reporting Restriction Orders)* [2005] 2 FLR 111 (see Part V).

Matters to be considered when prohibiting the publication of information relating to proceedings in private—The proper approach is for the court to identify the various rights that are engaged and then to conduct the necessary balancing exercise between the competing rights, considering the proportionality of the potential interference with each right considered independently – see *Re B* above; *A Local Authority v W, L, W, T and R (by the Children's Guardian)* [2006] 1 FLR 1, FD. In *Re S* above, the House of Lords indicated that it was not helpful to provide a court with detailed analysis of past case-law. In *Norfolk County Council v Webster, BBC, Associated Newspapers Ltd and Archant Group; Re Webster* [2007] 1 FLR 1146, FD, four factors, namely (i) that the case was alleged to involve a miscarriage of justice; (ii) that the parents themselves wished for publicity; (iii) that the case had already been extensively publicised; and (iv) that, very importantly, there was a need for the full facts to emerge in a way which would command public confidence in the judicial system, led to Munby J finding that an order restricting access by the media to an interim hearing within care proceedings would be too wide and would interfere disproportionately with the freedom of expression of the parents whose child was the subject of proceedings. See also the *Practice Note* at [2005] 2 FLR 111 above. In *Norfolk County Council v Webster & ors* [2007] 2 FLR 415, FD, Munby J allowed publication of counsel's position statement in view of the current practice of significant advocacy being in written form, which is pre-read by the judge and not dealt with orally in court; such written material should be disclosed to allow the media to report in a fully informed way. However, Munby J declined to approve a draft press release prepared on behalf of the parents: it is not the function of the judge to give advice. In *Re LM (Reporting Restrictions: Coroner's Inquest)* [2008] 1 FLR 1360, FD the court was not satisfied that there would be lasting harm to a child arising from the reporting of a coroner's inquest relating to the death of a sibling. However, the court placed an embargo on publication of the name or existence of the surviving child or any information that was likely to lead to her identification. In relation to an application for a contra mundum injunction to prevent the identification of a child in respect of defendants based abroad and the publication of information on social media sites, see the decision of the President in *Re J (Reporting Restriction: Internet: Video)* [2014] 1 FLR 523, FD.

Proceedings restraining freedom of press to be heard in the High Court—Where an injunction is sought to impose a restraint on the freedom of the press and the media generally, the case should be transferred to a judge of High Court judge level– see *Practice Note* at [2005] 2 FLR 111 and *President's PD* at [2005] 2 FLR 120 (above).

Reporting Restrictions Orders—For guidance on the approach to applications for RROs, see *Re J (Reporting Restriction: Internet: Video)* [2014] 1 FLR 523, FD, *Re Al Hilli (Children Reporting Restrictions)* [2014] 1 FLR 403, FD, and *City and County of Swansea v XZ and YZ* [2014] 2 FLR 1091, FD.

Power of court to allow disclosure—See also FPR 2010, rr 12.73–12.75 and PD12G. The court has power to allow disclosure of information that would otherwise be subject to a prohibition on publication. However, now that FPR 2010, rr 12.73–12.75 and PD12G allow parties and other specified people to disclose certain information from family proceedings heard in private to other specified people for specific purposes without needing the permission of the court, it remains to be seen how often the additional power of the court to order disclosure will be called upon. These rules do not permit wider disclosure to the public at large but the court may permit such disclosure under the inherent jurisdiction. As Lord Dyson MR said in *Re C (A Child)* [2016] EWCA Civ 798, 'I am in no doubt that the court does have the power to order the disclosure of part or all of what takes place in private proceedings (including any judgment made by the court during the course of or at end of the proceedings). In my view the court has that power under its inherent jurisdiction. It had that power before the incorporation of the Convention by the Human Rights Act 1998: see *Kent County Council v The Mother, The Father, B* [2004] EWHC 411 (Fam) at paras 83 to 86 where Munby J summarised the relevant jurisprudence. The court continues to have that jurisdiction following the incorporation of the Convention. The domestic and Strasbourg jurisprudence is reflected in the Practice Guidance (*Family Courts: Transparency*) [2014] 1 WLR 230 ("the Practice Guidance") issued by Sir James Munby P in relation to the publication of judgments in family courts and the Court of Protection. See also per McFarlane LJ in *Re W (Children) (Care Proceedings: Publicity)* [2016] 4 WLR 39 at paras 32 to 40', at [12].

Experts—Two medical experts, who had been unsuccessfully reported to the GMC by an aggrieved parent after care proceedings, sought suitably redacted extracts of their reports and of the parent's medical records to be made public in order to defend their, alleged, damaged reputations. The President refused the same on the basis that it would result in an indefensible breach of the Art 8 rights of the parent: *Re C (A Child) (Application by Dr X and Y)* [2017] 1 FLR 82, FD.

Power of court to restrict publicity relating to the identity of a ward in criminal proceedings—A judge in wardship proceedings may have power to restrict publicity relating to the identity of a ward in criminal proceedings but, even if he does have such a power, he should not exercise it; any decision as to restraining the publicity relating to the identity of persons concerned in criminal proceedings should be a matter for the discretion of the criminal trial judge (*Re R (Wardship: Restrictions on Publication)* [1994] 2 FLR 637, CA; *R v Central Criminal Court ex parte Godwin and Crook* [1995] 1 FLR 132, CA – power of criminal court under CYPA 1933, s 39 to restrict the reporting of information relating to the identification of a child involved in criminal proceedings). However, Munby J, in care proceedings concerning unusually and exceptionally

PART II

vulnerable children, made injunctive orders preventing the media reporting details about the children and their family which might lead to the identification of the children. The injunction did not prevent the media from reporting the criminal proceedings against the father but importantly, he did prohibit the media from reporting the father's home address where the children lived, even if the same was referred to in the course of the criminal proceedings (*Re X (Children)* [2008] 1 FLR 589, FD): see also *Surrey County Council v ME and Others* [2014] 2 FLR 1267, FD.

Duration of prohibition on publication (s 12(1)(a)(i))—The prohibition on publication is not limited in time, and it thus remains a contempt to publish such information even if wardship proceedings are discharged (*Re E (A Minor) (Child Abuse: Evidence)* [1991] 1 FLR 420, FD). Presumably, the same principle applies to the prohibition in s 12(1)(a)(ii) and (iii).

Publication of court order and judgment (s 12(2))—In *Re G (Celebrities: Publicity)* [1999] 1 FLR 409, CA, the Court of Appeal indicated that it was hard to conceive of circumstances which would justify preventing the media from publishing the bare outcome of a hearing; the court should issue a terse statement approved by the judge and agreed between the parties. In *Pelling v Bruce-Williams (Secretary of State for Constitutional Affairs Intervening)* [2004] 2 FLR 823, CA, Dame Elizabeth Butler-Sloss P stated that it may be worth giving consideration to increasing the frequency in which anonymised family court judgments in general are made public, not just in cases where there are principles of law involved. In view of the current climate, and increasing complaints of 'secrecy' in the family justice system, a broader approach to making judgments public may be desirable. In *Re H (Freeing Orders: Publicity)* [2006] 1 FLR 815, CA, the Court of Appeal stated that there was a strong argument for judges in controversial cases, or cases that attracted media attention, to accompany delivery of their judgements with a short written summary of their conclusions and reasons, which could be made publicly available. The publication of a judgment, which in the interests of the child the court had determined should be kept private, is an interference with the interests of justice and is punishable as criminal contempt (*Her Majesty's Attorney-General v Pelling* [2006] 1 FLR 93, QBD).

When publicity involving the mother of children who had been the subject of care proceedings, gave an inaccurate and/or misleading account of those proceedings, and the reasons why the children were removed from the mother (including criticisms of the secrecy of the family courts), the president authorized the release of an agreed summary of the facts of the case to the media (*Medway Council v G and ors* [2008] 2 FLR 1687, FD).

Where most unusually, the court had granted permission for care proceedings to be heard in public subject to a schedule of anonymisations, and the family had been the subject of a documentary, Hedley J. refused to the mother's later application, to relax some of the anonymisations provisions, because to do so would have been highly likely to lead to the identification of the child who lived in a rural community and was therefore more likely to be identifiable than if he lived in a massive conurbation (*Z County Council v TS, DES, ES and A* [2008] 2 FLR 1800, FD.

Attendance of media—Accredited representatives of the media may attend family hearings held in private (but not hearings held for the purpose of judicially assisted conciliation or negotiation). The framework is set out in:

(a) FPR 2010, r 27.11;
(b) *President's Guidance in Relation to Applications Consequent Upon the Attendance of the Media in Family Proceedings* (22 April 2009) (see Part V); and
(c) FPR PD27B.

The provisions give accredited media representatives the right to attend private hearings in family proceedings but at any stage of the proceedings the court may direct that the media may not attend all or any part of the proceedings. The court may make such a direction of its own motion or at the request of a party, a witness in the proceedings, a children's guardian, a Cafcass officer or the child (if of sufficient age and understanding). The media representatives present must be given an opportunity to make representations.

A decision to exclude the media is not discretionary and may only be made if one of the four grounds set out in r 10.28(4) is satisfied: the burden of proof rests on the party seeking to exclude the media. The President considered the court's approach to an application to exclude in *Re Child X (Residence and Contact: Rights of Media Attendance – FPR r 10.28(4))* [2009] 2 FLR 1467, FD: see the notes to FPR 2010, r 27.11.

Court of Protection and the media—The general rule in the Court of Protection is that hearings are held in private, The court may, however, direct part or all of a hearing to be held in public or may direct that representatives of the media may attend all or part of the hearing if there is good reason to do so: COPR 2007, rr 90–93. The burden of establishing good reason rests on the party applying for a public hearing or for the media to attend. A finding of good reason does not automatically trigger a public hearing but does engage Art 10 and requires the court to conduct a balancing exercise between the respective Art 8 and Art 10 rights engaged: *Independent News Media Ltd & Ors v A (by the Official Solicitor)* [2009] COPLR Con Vol 702, FD.

Waiver of anonymity—Long after the conclusion of the care proceedings and at a time when there was no state involvement with the family, the mother and the children (10 and 15 respectively), sought permission to waive their anonymity and thus identify themselves to the media, as the subjects of the anonymised judgment. Munby J gave permission while observing that the wisdom of the decision to waive anonymity was not a matter for the court (*Re B; X Council v B (No 2)* [2008] 1 FLR 1460, FD).

Release of information—In exceptional cases, the court may permit the disclosure of information into the public domain about the proceedings to correct inaccurate or false versions of events given by a party to the proceedings: *Doncaster MBC v Haigh, Tune and X (by the Children's Guardian)* [2012] 1 FLR 577, FD.

Consular advice and attendance at hearings—The provisions of this section must not be interpreted as preventing a party seeking the assistance of consular officials or as inhibiting the latter's attendance at court hearings: *Re E (Brussels II Revised: Vienna Convention: Reporting Restrictions)* [2014] 2 FLR 151, FD.

Concurrent care and criminal proceedings—Baron J gave guidance on the duties of experts instructed in both care and concurrent criminal proceedings. It was preferable for different experts to be instructed in each set of proceedings, but where this was not practicable, it was important that the experts were clear about the boundaries and limits of their role in each set of proceedings, to avoid a breach of s 12. The judge urged the relevant medical colleges to issue very clear guidelines as a matter of urgency: the colleges have yet to respond or to issue any formal guidance (*Re M (Care Disclosure to Police)* [2008] 2 FLR 390, FD).

13 Appeal in cases of contempt of court

(1) Subject to the provisions of this section, an appeal shall lie under this section from any order or decision of a court in the exercise of jurisdiction to punish for contempt of court (including criminal contempt); and in relation to any such order or decision the provisions of this section shall have effect in substitution for any other enactment relating to appeals in civil or criminal proceedings.

(2) An appeal under this section shall lie in any case at the instance of the defendant and, in the case of an application for committal or attachment, at the instance of the applicant; and the appeal shall lie –

- (a) from an order or decision of any inferior court not referred to in the next following paragraph, to the High Court;
- (b) from an order or decision of the county court or any other inferior court from which appeals generally lie to the Court of Appeal, and from an order or decision (other than a decision on an appeal under this section) of a single judge of the High Court, or of any court having the powers of the High Court or of a judge of that court, to the Court of Appeal;
- (bb) from an order or decision of the Crown Court to the Court of Appeal;
- (c) from a decision of a single judge of the High Court on an appeal under this section, from an order or decision of a Divisional Court or the Court of Appeal (including a decision of either of those courts on an appeal under this section), and from an order or decision of the Court of Criminal Appeal or the Courts-Martial Appeal Court, to the Supreme Court.

(2A) Paragraphs (a) to (c) of subsection (2) of this section do not apply in relation to appeals under this section from an order or decision of the family court, but (subject to any provision made under section 56 of the Access of Justice Act 1999 or by or under any other enactment) such an appeal shall lie to the Court of Appeal.

(3) The court to which an appeal is brought under this section may reverse or vary the order or decision of the court below, and make such other orders as may be just; and without prejudice to the inherent powers of any court referred to in subsection (2) of this section, provision may be made by rules of court for authorising the release on bail of an appellant under this section.

(4) Subsections (2) to (4) of section one and section two of this Act shall apply to an appeal to the Supreme Court under this section as they apply to an appeal to the Supreme Court under the said section one, except that so much of the said subsection (2) as restricts the grant of leave to appeal shall apply only where the decision of the court below is a decision on appeal to that court under this section.

(5) In this section 'court' includes any tribunal or person having power to punish for contempt; and references in this section to an order or decision of a court in the exercise of jurisdiction to punish for contempt of court include references –

- (a) to an order or decision of the High Court, the family court, the Crown Court or the county court under any enactment enabling that court to deal with an offence as if it were contempt of court;
- (b) to an order or decision of the county court, or of any court having the powers of the county court, under section 14, 92 or 118 of the County Courts Act 1984;
- (c) to an order or decision of a magistrates' court under subsection (3) of section 63 of the Magistrates' Courts Act 1980,

but do not include references to orders under section five of the Debtors Act 1869, or under any provision of the Magistrates' Courts Act 1980 or the County Courts Act 1984, except those referred to in paragraphs (b) and (c) of this subsection and except sections 38 and 142 of the last-mentioned Act so far as those sections confer jurisdiction in respect of contempt of court.

(6) This section does not apply to a conviction or sentence in respect of which an appeal lies under Part I of the Criminal Appeal Act 1968, or to a decision of the criminal division of the Court of Appeal under that Part of that Act.

Amendments—Criminal Appeal Act 1968, s 52(1), Sch 5, Pt I; Courts Act 1971, s 56(1),(4), Sch 8, para 40(1),(2), Sch 11, Pt II; MCA 1980, s 154, Sch 7, para 37; SCA 1981, s 152(4), Sch 7; CCA 1984, s 148(1), Sch 2, para 25; AJA 1999, ss 64, 106, Sch 15; CRA 2005, Sch 9, para 13(7); CCA 2013, s 17, Schs 9, 10.

Scope—Proceedings on appeal under this section from an order or decision under MCA 1980, s 63(3) (the power to punish for breach of a court order) are assigned to the Family Division of the High Court by SCA 1981, s 61(1),(3), Sch 1, para 3(d), and the procedure on such appeal is prescribed by FPR 2010, Pt 30 and PD30A. The court has power to punish for an assault on an officer of the court (CCA 1984, s 14), for the rescue of goods seized in execution of process of the County Court (CCA 1984, s 92) and for contempt (CCA 1984, s 118).

Procedure—For the mandatory procedure to be followed at a committal hearing, see *Practice Direction: Committal for Contempt of Court – Open Court* (26 March 2015), issued by the Lord Chief Justice (see Part V). All committal hearings must be heard in open court. If in exceptional circumstances a court decides to depart from the general rule and to hear the application in private, the court must, before the hearing, (i) notify the national print and broadcast media of the fact of the committal hearing and (ii) sit in public to give a reasoned judgment as to why the application is being heard in private. In all cases, at the conclusion of the hearing the court must sit in public and (i) state the name of the contemnor, (ii) state in general terms the nature of the contempt, (iii) state the punishment being imposed and (iv) provide those details to the national print and broadcast media, via the CopyDirect service, and to the Judicial Office at judicialwebupdates@judiciary.gsi.gov.uk: see also *Re L (A Child); Re Oddin* [2017] 1 FLR 1135, CA.

****

Administration of Justice Act 1970

****

SCHEDULE 8
MAINTENANCE ORDERS FOR PURPOSES OF 1958 ACT AND PART II OF THIS ACT

1 An order for alimony, maintenance or other payments made, or having effect as if made, under Part II of the Matrimonial Causes Act 1965 (ancillary relief in actions for divorce etc).

2 An order for payments to or in respect of a child being an order made, or having effect as if made, under Part III of the said Act of 1965 (maintenance of children following divorce, etc).

2A An order for periodical or other payments made, or having effect as if made, under Part II of the Matrimonial Causes Act 1973.

3 An order for maintenance or other payments to or in respect of a spouse or child being an order made under Part I of the Domestic Proceedings and Magistrates' Courts Act 1978.

4 An order for periodical or other payments made or having effect as if made under Schedule 1 to the Children Act 1989.

5 (*repealed*)

6 An order –

(a) made or having effect as if made under paragraph 23 of Schedule 2 to the Children Act 1989 or under paragraph 3 of Schedule 1 to the Social Services and Well-being (Wales) Act 2014; or

(b) made under section 23 of the Ministry of Social Security Act 1966, section 18 of the Supplementary Benefits Act 1976, section 24 of the Social Security Act 1986 or section 106 of the Social Security Administration Act 1992 (various provisions for obtaining contributions from a person whose dependants are assisted or maintained out of public funds).

7 (*repealed*)

8 An order to which section 16 of the Maintenance Orders Act 1950 applies by virtue of subsection (2)(b) or (c) of that section (that is to say an order made by a court in Scotland or Northern Ireland and corresponding to one of those specified in the foregoing paragraphs) and which has been registered in a court in England and Wales under Part II of that Act.

9 A maintenance order within the meaning of the Maintenance Orders (Facilities for Enforcement) Act 1920 (Commonwealth orders enforceable in the United Kingdom) registered in, or confirmed by, a court in England and Wales under that Act.

10 An order for periodical or other payments made under Part I of the Matrimonial Proceedings and Property Act 1970.

11 A maintenance order within the meaning of Part I of the Maintenance Orders (Reciprocal Enforcement) Act 1972 registered in the family court under the said Part I.

12 (*repealed*)

13 A maintenance order within the meaning of Part I of the Civil Jurisdiction and Judgments Act 1982, which is registered in the family court under that Part.

13A A maintenance judgment within the meaning of Council Regulation (EC) No 44/2001 of 22 December 2000 on jurisdiction and the recognition and enforcement of judgments in civil and commercial matters, as amended from time to time and as applied by the Agreement made on 19 October 2005 between the European Community and the Kingdom of Denmark on jurisdiction and the recognition and enforcement of judgments in civil and commercial matters (OJ No. L 299 16.11.2005 at p 62), which is registered in a court in England and Wales' under that Regulation.

13B (1) A decision, court settlement or authentic instrument which falls to be enforced by the family court by virtue of the Maintenance Regulation and the Civil Jurisdiction and Judgments (Maintenance) Regulations 2011.

(2) In this paragraph –

'the Maintenance Regulation' means Council Regulation (EC) No 4/2009 including as applied in relation to Denmark by virtue of the Agreement made on 19 October 2005 between the European Community and the Kingdom of Denmark;

'decision', 'court settlement' and 'authentic instrument' have the meanings given by Article 2 of the Maintenance Regulation.

13C A decision or maintenance arrangement which is registered in the family court under the Convention on the International Recovery of Child Support and other forms of Family Maintenance done at The Hague on 23 November 2007.

14 An order for periodical or other payments made under Part III of the Matrimonial and Family Proceedings Act 1984.

15 An order for periodical or other payments made under Schedule 5, 6 or 7 to the Civil Partnership Act 2004.

Amendments—MPPA 1970, s 42(1), Sch 2, para 5; MO(RE)A 1972, s 22(1), Sch, para 6; MCA 1973, s 54(1), Sch 2, para 10(2); Supplementary Benefits Act 1976, s 35(2), Sch 7, para 17; DPMCA 1978, s 89, Sch 2, para 26; CJJA 1982, s 15(4), Sch 12, para 5; MFPA 1984, s 46(1), Sch 1, para 8; Social Security Act 1986, s 86, Sch 10, para 42; FLRA 1987, s 33(1), Sch 2, para 27, Sch 4; CLSA 1990, s 116, Sch 16, paras 6, 37; Social Security (Consequential Provisions) Act 1992, s 4, Sch 2, para 7; SI 2001/3929; CPA 2004, s 261(1), Sch 27, para 34, SI 2007/1655; Health and Social Care Act 2008, Sch 15; SI 2011/1484; SI 2012/2814; SI 2014/605; SI 2016/413.

Adoption and Children Act 2002

ARRANGEMENT OF SECTIONS

PART 1
ADOPTION

Chapter 1

Section		Page
	Introductory	
1	Considerations applying to the exercise of powers	255
	Chapter 3	
	Placement for Adoption and Adoption Orders	
	Placement of children by adoption agency for adoption	
18	Placement for adoption by agencies	257
19	Placing children with parental consent	258
20	Advance consent to adoption	259
21	Placement orders	260
22	Applications for placement orders	261
23	Varying placement orders	264
24	Revoking placement orders	264
25	Parental responsibility	265
26	Contact	266
27	Contact: supplementary	267
28	Further consequences of placement	268
29	Further consequences of placement orders	269
	Removal of children who are or may be placed by adoption agencies	
30	General prohibitions on removal	270
31	Recovery by parent etc where child not placed or is a baby	270
32	Recovery by parent etc where child placed and consent withdrawn	271
33	Recovery by parent etc where child placed and placement order refused	272
34	Placement orders: prohibition on removal	272
35	Return of child in other cases	273
	Removal of children in non-agency cases	
36	Restrictions on removal	274
37	Applicants for adoption	274
38	Local authority foster parents	274
39	Partners of parents	275
40	Other non-agency cases	275
	Breach of restrictions on removal	
41	Recovery orders	276
	Preliminaries to adoption	
42	Child to live with adopters before application	277
43	Reports where child placed by agency	278
44	Notice of intention to adopt	278
45	Suitability of adopters	279
	The making of adoption orders	
46	Adoption orders	279
47	Conditions for making adoption orders	280
48	Restrictions on making adoption orders	284

49	Applications for adoption	284
50	Adoption by couple	284
51	Adoption by one person	285

Post-adoption contact

51A	Post-adoption contact	286
51B	Orders under section 51A: supplementary	287

Placement and adoption: general

52	Parental etc consent	288
53	Modification of 1989 Act and 2014 Act in relation to adoption	290
54	Disclosing information during adoption process	291
55	Revocation of adoptions on legitimation	291

Chapter 4
Status of Adopted Children

66	Meaning of adoption in Chapter 4	291
67	Status conferred by adoption	292
68	Adoptive relatives	293
69	Rules of interpretation for instruments concerning property	294
70	Dispositions depending on date of birth	294
71	Property devolving with peerages etc	295
72	Protection of trustees and personal representatives	295
73	Meaning of disposition	295
74	Miscellaneous enactments	295
75	Pensions	296
76	Insurance	296

Chapter 5
The Registers
Adopted Children Register etc

77	Adopted Children Register	296
78	Searches and copies	297
79	Connections between the register and birth records	297

Adoption Contact Register

80	Adoption Contact Register	298
81	Adoption Contact Register: supplementary	299

General

82	Interpretation	299

Chapter 6
Adoptions with a Foreign Element

Bringing children into and out of the United Kingdom

83	Restriction on bringing children in	299
84	Giving parental responsibility prior to adoption abroad	301
85	Restriction on taking children out	302
86	Power to modify sections 83 and 85	303

Overseas adoptions

87	Overseas adoptions	303

Miscellaneous

88	Modification of section 67 for Hague Convention adoptions	304
89	Annulment etc of overseas or Hague Convention adoptions	304
90	Section 89: supplementary	304
91	Overseas determinations and orders	305

PART II

91A Power to charge 305

Chapter 7
Miscellaneous

Restrictions

92 Restriction on arranging adoptions etc 306
93 Offence of breaching restrictions under section 92 307
94 Restriction on reports 307
95 Prohibition of certain payments 307
96 Excepted payments 308
97 Sections 92 to 96: interpretation 308

Information

98 Pre-commencement adoptions: information 309

Proceedings

99 Proceedings for offences 309
101 Privacy 310

The Children and Family Court Advisory and Support Service

102 Officers of the Service 310
103 Right of officers of the Service to have access to adoption agency records 311

Evidence

104 Evidence of consent 311

Scotland, Northern Ireland and the Islands

105 Effect of certain Scottish orders and provisions 311
106 Effect of certain Northern Irish orders and provisions 312
107 Use of adoption records from other parts of the British Islands 312

General

109 Avoiding delay 312
110 Service of notices etc 313

PART 3
MISCELLANEOUS AND FINAL PROVISIONS

Chapter 1
Miscellaneous

Advertisements in the United Kingdom

123 Restriction on advertisements etc 313
124 Offence of breaching restriction under section 123 314

Chapter 2
Final provisions

140 Orders, rules and regulations 314
141 Rules of procedure 315
142 Supplementary and consequential provision 316
143 Offences by bodies corporate and unincorporated bodies 316
144 General interpretation etc 317
145 Devolution: Wales 319
146 Expenses 319
147 Glossary 319
148 Commencement 319
149 Extent 320
150 Short title 320

Schedule 1 – Registration of Adoptions 320
Schedule 2 – Disclosure of Birth Records by Registrar General 323
Schedule 4 – Transitional and Transitory Provisions and Savings 325
Schedule 6 – Glossary 327

PART 1
ADOPTION

Chapter 1
Introductory

1 Considerations applying to the exercise of powers

(1) Subsections (2) to (4) apply whenever a court or adoption agency is coming to a decision relating to the adoption of a child.

(2) The paramount consideration of the court or adoption agency must be the child's welfare, throughout his life.

(3) The court or adoption agency must at all times bear in mind that, in general, any delay in coming to the decision is likely to prejudice the child's welfare.

(4) The court or adoption agency must have regard to the following matters (among others) –

(a) the child's ascertainable wishes and feelings regarding the decision (considered in the light of the child's age and understanding),

(b) the child's particular needs,

(c) the likely effect on the child (throughout his life) of having ceased to be a member of the original family and become an adopted person,

(d) the child's age, sex, background and any of the child's characteristics which the court or agency considers relevant,

(e) any harm (within the meaning of the Children Act 1989) which the child has suffered or is at risk of suffering,

(f) the relationship which the child has with relatives, and with any other person in relation to whom the court or agency considers the relationship to be relevant, including –

(i) the likelihood of any such relationship continuing and the value to the child of its doing so,

(ii) the ability and willingness of any of the child's relatives, or of any such person, to provide the child with a secure environment in which the child can develop, and otherwise to meet the child's needs,

(iii) the wishes and feelings of any of the child's relatives, or of any such person, regarding the child.

(5) In placing a child for adoption, an adoption agency in Wales must give due consideration to the child's religious persuasion, racial origin and cultural and linguistic background.

(6) In coming to a decision relating to the adoption of a child, a court or adoption agency must always consider the whole range of powers available to it in the child's case (whether under this Act or the Children Act 1989); and the court must not make any order under this Act unless it considers that making the order would be better for the child than not doing so.

(7) In this section, 'coming to a decision relating to the adoption of a child', in relation to a court, includes –

(a) coming to a decision in any proceedings where the orders that might be made by the court include an adoption order (or the revocation of such an order), a placement order (or the revocation of such an order) or an order under section 26 or 51A (or the revocation or variation of such an order),

(b) coming to a decision about granting leave in respect of any action (other than the initiation of proceedings in any court) which may be taken by an adoption agency or individual under this Act,

but does not include coming to a decision about granting leave in any other circumstances.

(8) For the purposes of this section –

(a) references to relationships are not confined to legal relationships,
(b) references to a relative, in relation to a child, include the child's mother and father.

(9) In this section 'adoption agency in Wales' means an adoption agency that is –

(a) a local authority in Wales, or
(b) a registered adoption society whose principal office is in Wales.

Amendments—CFA 2014, ss 3, 9.

Defined terms—'adoption agency': s 2(1); 'child': ss 49(5), 144; 'harm': CA 1989, s 31(9); 'relative': ss 1(8), 144; 'adoption (in relation to Chapter 4 of Part 1)': s 66; 'adoption order': s 46(1); 'court': s 144; 'placement order': s 21; 'placing, or placed, for adoption': s 18(5), 19(4).

'welfare throughout his life' (s 1(2))—Paramount consideration must be given to the child's welfare 'throughout his life' when coming to a decision relating to adoption. Welfare interests are to be given a wide interpretation and include matters (such as achieving British citizenship) that may affect adulthood (*FAS v Secretary of State for the Home Department and Another* [2016] 2 FLR 1035, CA). The ECtHR has held that in identifying where a child's best interests lie, two considerations must be borne in mind: first, it is in the child's best interests that his ties with his family be maintained except in cases where the family has proved particularly unfit; and second, it is in the child's best interests to ensure his development in a safe and secure environment (*YC v United Kingdom* (Application No 4547/10) [2012] 2 FLR 332, ECHR).

'delay ... is likely to prejudice child's welfare' (s 1(3))—See notes to CA 1989, s 1.

Ceasing to be a member of the original family and becoming an adopted person (s 1(4)(c))—This element of the checklist has a twofold focus: (a) ceasing to be a member of the original family; and (b) becoming an adopted person.

On adoption the cessation of membership of the original family is total and intended to be so for all time. The original parents' parental responsibility is extinguished and there is a complete severing of all legal ties with the family. The cut off from his family of origin may have a potentially damaging impact on the child's sense of identity and emotional wellbeing. 'Becoming an adopted person' provides for the child a permanent substitute family, where the adopters are legally responsible and therefore fully committed to fulfilling their parental responsibilities.

In focusing upon the likely effect on the child of these changes, the court or adoption agency will be focusing upon the degree of interference with the child's ECHR 1950, Art 8 rights to family life that would be consequent upon an adoption. This will have to be balanced against the family life that the child is, or will be, enjoying with the adoptive family.

Relationship which the child has with relatives (s 1(4)(f))—A court or adoption agency is required to consider the child's existing family relationships to a degree and in a manner which is not expressly required by CA 1989, s 1(3).

A 'relative' in relation to a child means a grandparent, brother, sister, uncle or aunt, whether of the full blood or half-blood or by marriage or civil partnership and includes the child's mother and father (ss 1(8) and 144). The pool of relationships is not confined to relatives, but will include any de facto relationships considered to be of importance; on the facts of a particular case this might include foster parents.

Consideration must be given to: (i) the value to the child of a continuing relationship with his relatives (and any other person who is important to the child); and (ii) the wishes and feelings of those relatives. Particular importance is likely to be given to relationships between siblings. Any 'skewing' of family relationships must be considered (*Re S (Adoption Order or Special Guardianship Order)* [2007] 1 FLR 819, CA).

Choice between adoption and special guardianship—In *Re AJ (Adoption Order or Special Guardianship Order)* [2007] 1 FLR 507, CA, the Court of Appeal expressly endorsed a detailed schedule of the main differences between special guardianship orders and adoption orders.

Religious persuasion etc (s 1(5))—A parent's religious beliefs can never be determinative when considering the totality of a child's welfare; a parent's rights under ECHR 1950, Art 9 are qualified by the child's right to family life under Art 8 (*Re S; Newcastle City Council v Z* [2007] 1 FLR 861, FD). From 13 May 2014, s 1(5) only applies to an adoption agency in Wales. Irrespective of whether s 1(5) applies, in the case of a foreign national child these factors need most careful consideration (*Re N (Adoption: Jurisdiction)* [2016] 1 FLR 621, CA).

Dispensing with parental consent—The circumstances in which the paramountcy principle applies include those where the issue is whether or not to dispense with parental consent to placement and/or adoption (s 1(7)).

****

Chapter 3

Placement for Adoption and Adoption Orders

Placement of children by adoption agency for adoption

18 Placement for adoption by agencies

(1) An adoption agency may –

(a) place a child for adoption with prospective adopters, or

(b) where it has placed a child with any persons (whether under this Part or not), leave the child with them as prospective adopters,

but, except in the case of a child who is less than six weeks old, may only do so under section 19 or a placement order.

(2) An adoption agency may only place a child for adoption with prospective adopters if the agency is satisfied that the child ought to be placed for adoption.

(3) A child who is placed or authorised to be placed for adoption with prospective adopters by a local authority is looked after by the authority.

(4) If an application for an adoption order has been made by any persons in respect of a child and has not been disposed of –

(a) an adoption agency which placed the child with those persons may leave the child with them until the application is disposed of, but

(b) apart from that, the child may not be placed for adoption with any prospective adopters.

'Adoption order' includes a Scottish or Northern Irish adoption order.

(5) References in this Act (apart from this section) to an adoption agency placing a child for adoption –

(a) are to its placing a child for adoption with prospective adopters, and

(b) include, where it has placed a child with any persons (whether under this Act or not), leaving the child with them as prospective adopters;

and references in this Act (apart from this section) to a child who is placed for adoption by an adoption agency are to be interpreted accordingly.

(6) References in this Chapter to an adoption agency being, or not being, authorised to place a child for adoption are to the agency being or (as the case may be) not being authorised to do so under section 19 or a placement order.

(7) This section is subject to sections 30 to 35 (removal of children placed by adoption agencies).

Defined terms—'adoption agency': s 2(1); 'child': ss 49(5), 144; 'adoption (in relation to Chapter 4 of Part 1)': s 66; 'adoption agency placing a child for adoption': s 18(5); 'adoption order': s 46(1); 'local authority': s 144; 'Northern Irish adoption order': s 144; 'placement order': s 21; 'placing, or placed, for adoption': s 18(5), 19(4).

Placement—Before ACA 2002, the placing of a child for adoption was largely an administrative process conducted by a local authority or adoption agency either with the agreement of the parent(s) or under the authority provided by a care order (interim or full) or an order freeing a child for adoption. ACA 2002, ss 18–41 establish a statutory code regulating the circumstances in which a child can be placed for adoption and the consequences once such a placement is made. There is provision for substantial court involvement in the process.

The general effect of the placement provisions in ACA 2002, Ch 3 is twofold. First, before a placement for adoption can be made, a parent must be fully engaged in the decision making process, either by giving express consent or by having the opportunity to contest the issue in court proceedings. Secondly, if either a parent consents to placement for adoption, or the court makes a 'placement order', and an adoptive placement is then made the parent's options for later overturning the move towards adoption or challenging any eventual adoption application are significantly restricted.

A central aim of ACA 2002, Chapter 3 provisions is to bring the parent's opportunity to challenge the crucial adoption decision forward to a stage before any adoptive placement is made. A feature of the earlier law was that in many cases the first opportunity a parent had to challenge a placement in court might be months or years after the placement had been made.

In contrast to the repealed provisions 'freeing' a child for adoption, where a child is placed for adoption (by agreement or order) the birth parents remain the child's parents until any final adoption order but they will be required to share parental responsibility with the prospective adopters and the adoption agency. There is also some (albeit limited) ability to reverse a placement order or withdraw consent whereas a freeing order could only be reversed on appeal or revoked in very circumscribed circumstances.

'Placement for adoption'—'Placing a child for adoption' by an adoption agency is defined as 'placing a child for adoption with prospective adopters' and includes 'where it has placed a child with any persons (whether under ACA 2002 or not), leaving the child with them as prospective adopters' (s 18(5)).

A child who is placed or authorised to be placed for adoption by a local authority is a '*looked after*' child under the provisions of CA 1989, Pt III (s 18(3)). All adoption agencies, whether a local authority or voluntary agency, must comply with the requirements imposed by Adoption Agency Regulations 2005, Pt 6 regarding placement for adoption and conducting statutory reviews.

Two routes to placement for adoption—The ACA 2002 establishes two routes by which an adoption agency may be authorised to place a child for adoption:

(i) Placement with parental consent (s 19); or
(ii) Placement under a placement order (s 21).

19 Placing children with parental consent

(1) Where an adoption agency is satisfied that each parent or guardian of a child has consented to the child –

(a) being placed for adoption with prospective adopters identified in the consent, or
(b) being placed for adoption with any prospective adopters who may be chosen by the agency,

and has not withdrawn the consent, the agency is authorised to place the child for adoption accordingly.

(2) Consent to a child being placed for adoption with prospective adopters identified in the consent may be combined with consent to the child subsequently being placed for adoption with any prospective adopters who may be chosen by the agency in circumstances where the child is removed from or returned by the identified prospective adopters.

(3) Subsection (1) does not apply where –

(a) an application has been made on which a care order might be made and the application has not been disposed of, or
(b) a care order or placement order has been made after the consent was given.

(4) References in this Act to a child placed for adoption under this section include a child who was placed under this section with prospective adopters and continues to be placed with them, whether or not consent to the placement has been withdrawn.

(5) This section is subject to section 52 (parental etc consent).

Defined terms—'adoption agency': s 2(1); 'care order': Sch 6 and CA 1989, s 105(1); 'child': ss 49(5), 144; 'consent': s 52; 'parent': s 52(6); 'adoption (in relation to Chapter 4 of Part 1)': s 66; 'guardian': s 144; 'placement order': s 21; 'placing, or placed, for adoption': ss 18(5), 19(4).

Placement with parental consent (s 19(1))—An adoption agency may place a child for adoption where it is satisfied that each parent or guardian of the child has consented (and has not withdrawn the consent) to the child either: (a) being placed for adoption with prospective adopters identified in the consent; or (b) being placed for adoption with any prospective adopters who may be chosen by the agency. Where the question of parental consent is in doubt, a local authority may apply to the court for a declaration to clarify the issue (*A Local Authority v GC* [2009] 1 FLR 299, FD).

Once a child has been placed for adoption pursuant to a consent given under ACA 2002, s 19, he will continue to be regarded as placed there under that provision notwithstanding that a parent may have withdrawn their consent at a later stage (s 19(4)).

Consequences of parental consent to placement for adoption—The following important and potentially irrevocable consequences flow from a parent giving consent to the placement of a child for adoption:

- The parent may only oppose any adoption application with the leave of the court (s 47);
- The parent's ability to apply for a child arrangements order is restricted (s 28(1));
- The parent's ability to have contact with the child will be determined by the adoption agency or subject to a court order under ACA 2002, s 26;
- Parental responsibility is given to the adoption agency (and in due course to prospective adopters with whom the child is placed) (s 25);
- There are restrictions on a parent's ability to require removal/return of the child (ss 30–35).

'Consent' (s 19(1))—This means consent given unconditionally and with full understanding of what is involved (s 52(5)). Consent to a child being placed for adoption with prospective adopters identified in the consent (under s 19(1)(a)) may be combined with consent to the child subsequently being placed for adoption with any prospective adopters chosen by the agency (under s 19(1)(b)) if the child were to be removed from or returned by the identified adopters (s 19(2)). A child may be placed for adoption with maternal consent at under 6 weeks old, but that consent is not valid for any subsequent adoption (see s 47(4)(b)(i)).

Consent to placement for adoption may be withdrawn; however any purported withdrawal will be ineffective if it occurs after an adoption application has been made (s 52(4)).

Form of consent—Consent to placement for adoption and advance consent to adoption must be given using the relevant statutory form, or a form to like effect (ACA 2002, s 52(7); FPR 2010, r 14.10(1)(a))). The appropriate forms are:

- Consent to placement for adoption with any prospective adopters (Form A100);
- Consent to placement for adoption with identified prospective adopters (Form A101);
- Consent to placement for adoption with identified prospective adopters and, if the placement breaks down, with any prospective adopters (Form A102);
- Advance consent to adoption (Form A103);
- Form A106 for withdrawal of consent.

In England and Wales, any consent form must be witnessed by a Cafcass officer or by a Welsh family proceedings officer (Adoption Agency Regulations 2005, reg 20). In Scotland it should be witnessed by a Justice of the Peace or a Sheriff, and in Northern Ireland by a Justice of the Peace (see notes on relevant form). Outside the UK, the form should be witnessed by a person who is authorised by law in the place where the document is signed to administer an oath for any judicial or legal purpose, a British Consular Officer, a notary public, or, if the person executing the document is serving in the regular armed forces of the Crown, an officer holding a commission in any of those forces.

'Parent' (s 19(1))—This refers to a parent who has parental responsibility for the child (s 52(6)). Each such parent or guardian must consent before an agency is authorised to make an adoption placement under s 19.

Consensual route not available in care proceedings—The consensual route cannot be used where an application for a care or supervision order has been made under CA 1989, s 31 and that application has not been disposed of (s 19(3)). Also, where a care order has been made after parental consent to placement has been given, the consent does not give the agency authority to place the child for adoption. In such circumstances, if the appropriate local authority is satisfied that the child ought to be placed for adoption, it must apply for a placement order (s 22(2); see annotation to s 22 **Local authority required to apply for placement order** below).

Once a placement order has been made, it is that order, and not any earlier s 19 parental consent, that provides authority for an agency to place the child for adoption (s 19(3)).

Placing a child under 6 weeks old—Any consent 'to the making of an adoption order' given by a mother is ineffective if given less than 6 weeks after the child's birth (s 52(3); *A Local Authority v GC and Others* [2009] 1 FLR 299, FD). An adoption agency may not place a child who is less than 6 weeks old for adoption unless the parent or guardian of the child has agreed in writing with the agency that the child may be placed for adoption (Adoption Agencies Regulations 2005, reg 35(4)).

Limit on change of surname or removal from UK—Where a child is placed for adoption pursuant to parental consent under ACA 2002, s 19, or a placement order has been made, no person may:

- cause the child to be known by a new surname, or
- remove the child from the UK

unless the court gives leave to do so or each parent or guardian of the child gives written consent (s 28(2),(3)). A person who provides the child's home may however remove the child from the UK for a period of less than 1 month without the need to obtain parental consent or court leave (s 28(4)).

Discharge of CA 1989 child arrangements orders—On an agency being authorised to place a child for adoption pursuant to parental consent given under ACA 2002, s 19, any existing child arrangements orders under CA 1989 (s 8 or s 34) will cease to have effect and no application may be made for a child arrangements order (save where a s 8 contact application is to be heard together with the application to adopt) (s 26). However, an application for contact may be made during the currency of an agency's authorisation to place for adoption under ACA 2002, s 26.

20 Advance consent to adoption

(1) A parent or guardian of a child who consents to the child being placed for adoption by an adoption agency under section 19 may, at the same or any subsequent time, consent to the making of a future adoption order.

(2) Consent under this section –

(a) where the parent or guardian has consented to the child being placed for adoption with prospective adopters identified in the consent, may be consent to adoption by them, or

(b) may be consent to adoption by any prospective adopters who may be chosen by the agency.

(3) A person may withdraw any consent given under this section.

(4) A person who gives consent under this section may, at the same or any subsequent time, by notice given to the adoption agency –

(a) state that he does not wish to be informed of any application for an adoption order, or

(b) withdraw such a statement.

(5) A notice under subsection (4) has effect from the time when it is received by the adoption agency but has no effect if the person concerned has withdrawn his consent.

(6) This section is subject to section 52 (parental etc consent).

Defined terms—'adoption agency': s 2(1); 'child': ss 49(5), 144; 'consent': s 52; 'parent': s 52(6); 'adoption (in relation to Chapter 4 of Part 1)': s 66; 'adoption order': s 46(1); 'guardian', 'notice': s 144; 'placing, or placed, for adoption': ss 18(5) and 19(4).

Advance consent to adoption—A parent or guardian of a child who consents to the child being placed for adoption under ACA 2002, s 19 may, at the same time or any subsequent time, consent to the making of a future adoption order. In this context, where the placement consent is for placement with identified prospective adopters the additional consent may be advance consent to adoption by them, or it may be consent to adoption by any prospective adopters who may be chosen by the adoption agency (s 20(2)). Advance consent to adoption may be withdrawn (s 20(3)), but any such withdrawal is ineffective if it takes place after an application for an adoption order has been made (s 52(4)).

A parent who gives advance consent to adoption may, at the same time or any subsequent time, give notice to the adoption agency stating that he does not wish to be informed of any application for an adoption order. Such a notice, once given, may subsequently be withdrawn (s 20(4)).

'Consent' and form of consent (s 20(1))—See note to s 19.

21 Placement orders

(1) A placement order is an order made by the court authorising a local authority to place a child for adoption with any prospective adopters who may be chosen by the authority.

(2) The court may not make a placement order in respect of a child unless –

(a) the child is subject to a care order,

(b) the court is satisfied that the conditions in section 31(2) of the 1989 Act (conditions for making a care order) are met, or

(c) the child has no parent or guardian.

(3) The court may only make a placement order if, in the case of each parent or guardian of the child, the court is satisfied –

(a) that the parent or guardian has consented to the child being placed for adoption with any prospective adopters who may be chosen by the local authority and has not withdrawn the consent, or

(b) that the parent's or guardian's consent should be dispensed with.

This subsection is subject to section 52 (parental etc consent).

(4) A placement order continues in force until –

(a) it is revoked under section 24,

(b) an adoption order is made in respect of the child, or

(c) the child marries, forms a civil partnership or attains the age of 18 years.

'Adoption order' includes a Scottish or Northern Irish adoption order.

Amendments—CPA 2004, s 79(1),(2).

Defined terms—'child': ss 49(5), 144; 'care order': Sch 6 and CA 1989, s 105(1); 'civil partnership': CPA 2004, s 1; 'consent': s 52; 'parent': s 52(6); 'the 1989 Act': s 2(5); 'adoption (in relation to Chapter 4 of Part 1)': s 66; 'adoption order': s 46(1); 'court', 'guardian', 'local authority', 'Northern Irish adoption order': s 144; 'placement order': s 21; 'placing, or placed, for adoption': ss 18(5), 19(4).

Placement orders—A 'placement order' is 'an order made by the court authorising a local authority to place a child for adoption with any prospective adopters who may be chosen by the authority' (s 21(1)). While a placement order is in force, parental responsibility for the child is given to the local authority and, while the child is with prospective adopters, also to them (s 25). Unlike proceedings under CA 1989, Pt IV, jurisdiction relating to placement orders is not governed by Brussels IIA (*Re N (Adoption: Jurisdiction)* [2016] 1 FLR 621, CA).

Conditions for making a placement order (s 21(2),(3))—The court may not make a placement order unless:

- the child is subject to a care order, or
- the court is satisfied that the threshold conditions in CA 1989, s 31(2) are met, or
- the child has no parent or guardian

and

- each parent or guardian has consented to the child being placed for adoption with any prospective adopters who may be chosen by the local authority and has not withdrawn consent, or the parent's consent should be dispensed with under ACA 2002, s 52.

In addition to these conditions, a court will only make a placement order if that is justified having given paramount consideration to the child's welfare throughout his life and having regard to the other matters set out in ACA 2002, s 1. The drastic step of making a placement order should only be sanctioned when all avenues to rehabilitation have been reasonably explored, but, whereas the court must avoid infringement of ECHR, Art 8, there is no requirement for express analysis of Art 8 in every judgment (*D McG v Neath Talbot County Borough Council* [2010] 2 FLR 1827, CA). It is an insufficient foundation for a placement order that the long-term aim of the court is that the child should be adopted. The necessary foundation is that – broadly speaking – the child is presently in a condition to be adopted and is ready to be adopted (*Re T (Placement Order)* [2008] 1 FLR 1721, CA; *NS-H v Kingston upon Hull City Council and MC* [2008] 2 FLR 918, CA). Conversely, where the aim is for an adoptive placement, but the local authority realistically takes the view that such a placement may be impossible to find, the court is nevertheless justified in endorsing a dual (adoption/fostering) plan by making a placement order (*Re P (Placement Orders: Parental Consent)* [2008] 2 FLR 625, CA).

The statutory definition of the phrase 'care order' includes an interim care order (Sch 6 and CA 1989, ss 31(11) and 105(1)); whether proof of the lower CA 1989, s 38 threshold conditions is sufficient to support the making of a placement order must await judicial clarification.

PART II

Consequences of a placement order—Where a placement order has been made to a local authority and is in force the following consequences flow:

- The regime for the regulation of contact under s 26 applies;
- A parent or guardian may not apply for a child arrangements order (and no guardian may apply for a special guardianship order) unless an application for an adoption order has been made and the parent or guardian has obtained the court's leave to oppose the adoption application (s 28(1));
- Unless the court gives leave or each parent or guardian gives written consent, no person may:
  (i) cause the child to be known by a new surname;
  (ii) remove the child from the UK (save for a period of less than one month by a person who provides the child's home) (s 28(2),(3));
- Any existing care order on the child does not have effect at any time when the placement order is in force (s 29(1));
- Any pre-existing CA 1989, s 8 order or supervision order will cease to have effect on the making of a placement order (s 29(2));
- No prohibited steps, specific issue or child arrangements order and no supervision or child assessment orders may be made in respect of the child (s 29(3));
- No special guardianship order may be made (unless an adoption application has been made and the court has given leave to a person to apply for a special guardianship order or a guardian has been given leave to oppose the adoption) (s 29(5)).

Advertising child for adoption—Publications that advertise children as available for adoption are unlikely to advertise a child unless the adoption agency is authorised to place for adoption or a court has given leave for such advertising; *Re K (Adoption: Permission to Advertise)* [2007] 2 FLR 326, FD describes the court's approach when asked to give leave to advertise. An adoption agency must place the child's details on the National Adoption Register as soon as possible and in any event within 3 months of deciding to place for adoption (Adoption Agencies Regulations 2005, reg 19A).

22 Applications for placement orders

(1) A local authority must apply to the court for a placement order in respect of a child if –

(a) the child is placed for adoption by them or is being provided with accommodation by them,

(b) no adoption agency is authorised to place the child for adoption,

(c) the child has no parent or guardian or the authority consider that the conditions in section 31(2) of the 1989 Act are met, and

(d) the authority are satisfied that the child ought to be placed for adoption.

(2) If –

(a) an application has been made (and has not been disposed of) on which a care order might be made in respect of a child, or

(b) a child is subject to a care order and the appropriate local authority are not authorised to place the child for adoption,

the appropriate local authority must apply to the court for a placement order if they are satisfied that the child ought to be placed for adoption.

(3) If –

(a) a child is subject to a care order, and

(b) the appropriate local authority are authorised to place the child for adoption under section 19, the authority may apply to the court for a placement order.

(4) If a local authority –

(a) are under a duty to apply to the court for a placement order in respect of a child, or

(b) have applied for a placement order in respect of a child and the application has not been disposed of,

the child is looked after by the authority.

(5) Subsections (1) to (3) do not apply in respect of a child –

(a) if any persons have given notice of intention to adopt, unless the period of four months beginning with the giving of the notice has expired without them applying for an adoption order or their application for such an order has been withdrawn or refused, or

(b) if an application for an adoption order has been made and has not been disposed of.

'Adoption order' includes a Scottish or Northern Irish adoption order.

(6) Where –

(a) an application for a placement order in respect of a child has been made and has not been disposed of, and

(b) no interim care order is in force,

the court may give any directions it considers appropriate for the medical or psychiatric examination or other assessment of the child; but a child who is of sufficient understanding to make an informed decision may refuse to submit to the examination or other assessment.

(7) The appropriate local authority –

(a) in relation to a care order, is the local authority in whose care the child is placed by the order, and

(b) in relation to an application on which a care order might be made, is the local authority which makes the application.

Defined terms—'the 1989 Act': s 2(5); 'adoption (in relation to Chapter 4 of Part 1)': s 66; 'adoption agency': s 2(1); 'adoption order': s 46(1); 'care order': s 105(1) of the 1989 Act; 'child': ss 49(5), 144; 'court', 'guardian': s 144; 'interim care order': s 38 of the 1989 Act; 'local authority': s 144; 'Northern Irish adoption order', 'notice': s 144; 'notice of intention to adopt': s 44(2); 'placement order': s 21; 'placing, or placed, for adoption': ss 18(5), 19(4).

Local authority required to apply for a placement order—Section 22 places a mandatory requirement upon a local authority to apply for a placement order in the following circumstances:

(1) Where a child is placed for adoption by them or is being provided with accommodation by them, and
- no adoption agency is authorised to place the child for adoption, and
- they consider that the threshold conditions in CA 1989, s 31(2) are met (or that the child has no parent or guardian); and
- they are satisfied that the child ought to be placed for adoption.

(2) Where
- there is a pending application for a care or supervision order (which has not been disposed of) or
- the child is the subject of a care order and the appropriate local authority are not authorised to place, and
- they are satisfied that the child ought to be placed for adoption.

A local authority cannot be 'satisfied that the child ought to be placed for adoption' (s 22(1),(2)) until it has made a decision to that effect under Adoption Agencies Regulations 2005, reg 19; such a decision is not to be referred to an adoption panel but is to be taken by a decision maker within the local authority, who must consider the child's 'permanence report' and medical reports on the child and his parents (AAR 2005, reg 19, as amended).

In addition, a local authority has discretion whether to apply for a placement order where a child is subject to a care order and they are the appropriate authority authorised to place the child for adoption with parental consent under ACA 2002, s 19.

While it is not permissible for a local authority formally to place a child for adoption with prospective adopters without either parental consent or a placement order, there is no impediment to placing a child in foster care with a carer who is approved both as a local authority foster parent and as a prospective adopter (this includes an approved adopter who is given temporary approval as a foster carer) (Care Planning, Placement and Case Review (England) Regulations 2010, reg 25A).

The provisions of ACA 2002, s 22(1)–(3) do not apply in respect of a child if any person has given notice of intention to adopt the child, unless more than four months have gone by since the notice and no adoption application has been made (or it has been withdrawn or dismissed), or if an adoption application has been made and not disposed of.

Procedure—An application for a placement order is governed by FPR 2010, Pt 14. The application must be in Form A50 or a form to like effect (FPR 2010, r 5.1). There is no restriction upon the level of court in which an application relating to a placement order may be made.

The respondents to an application for a placement order will be (FPR 2010, r 14.3):

- Each parent who has parental responsibility for the child or guardian of the child;
- Any person in whose favour a CA 1989 order is in force with respect to the child;
- Any adoption agency or voluntary organisation which has parental responsibility for, or is looking after, or is caring for, the child;
- The child; and
- The parties, or any persons who are or have been parties to proceedings for a care order with respect to the child where those proceedings have led to the application for the placement order.

The court may at any time direct that a child, who is not already a respondent to proceedings, be made a respondent where the child wishes to make an application or has evidence to give to the court, or a legal submission to make, which has not been given or made by any other party, or there are other special circumstances. The court may at any time direct that a person or body be made a respondent or be removed as a respondent.

In addition to any respondents, a copy of the application form for a placement order must be sent to any appointed children's guardian, children and family reporter or reporting officer and to any other person directed by the court to receive a copy (PD, Pt 5).

The application must be accompanied by the documents referred to in Form A50, namely:

- Three copies of the completed application form;
- A certified copy of the full entry in the Register of Live Births that relates to the child or, where the child has been adopted, a certified copy of the entry in the Adopted Children Register;
- Any written consent of the parent or guardian to the child being placed for adoption, and any notice of withdrawal of such consent;
- If the applicant is asking the court to dispense with the consent of any parent or guardian to the child being placed for adoption, a brief statement of the facts relied on in support of the request, and two copies of the statement;
- A copy of any final care order relating to the child;
- If available, a copy of any parental responsibility order or parental responsibility agreement relating to the child;
- If the authority was a party to the proceedings, a copy of any other final order relating to the child that has effect and, if available, a copy of any maintenance agreement;
- If the authority was a party to the proceedings, a copy of any final order relating to a full, half or step brother or sister of the child that has effect.

Preliminary steps to be taken by court—As soon as practicable after an application for a placement order has been issued, the court must take the steps set out in FPR 2010, r 14.6(1),(3). If the court considers it appropriate to do so, instead of setting a date for a first directions hearing, the court may simply give the directions that would otherwise be considered at such a hearing (FPR 2010, r 14.6(4)).

Children's guardian—An application for the making or revocation of a placement order constitutes 'specified proceedings' under CA 1989, s 41 and there is a presumption that a children's guardian will be appointed for the child. The child is automatically a respondent to any application for a placement order and a children's guardian will be appointed unless it is not necessary to do so to safeguard the interests of the child (FPR 2010, rr 14.3, 16.3). The children's guardian must appoint a solicitor for the child unless a solicitor has already been appointed (FPR PD16A).

The first directions hearing—The parties or their legal representatives must attend the first directions hearing unless the court directs otherwise (FPR 2010, r 14.8(4)). The hearing must be held within 4 weeks of the application being issued, unless the court otherwise directs (FPR 2010, r 14.7). At the first directions hearing the matters listed at FPR 2010, r 14.8(1) must be considered.

Request to dispense with parental consent—For dispensing with parental consent, see notes to ACA 2002, s 52. Where the applicant applies for the court to dispense with the consent of a parent or guardian to the child being placed for adoption, the applicant must (FPR 2010, r 14.9):

- give notice of the request in the application form (or at a later stage by filing a written request);
- file a statement of facts setting out a summary of the history of the case and any other facts to satisfy the court of the ground(s) relied upon to dispense with consent.

The final hearing (FPR 2010, r 14.16)—Any person who has been given notice of the final hearing may attend the hearing and be heard on the question of whether a placement order should be made. The court may direct any other person to attend the final hearing. Any member or employee of a party which is a local authority, adoption agency or other body may address the court if he is authorised to do so.

The court cannot make a placement order unless a legal representative of the applicant and also the child personally attend the final hearing. The court may, however, direct that the child need not attend the hearing.

An application for permission to appeal a placement order should be filed as soon as possible and include any application for a stay or other interim relief. A note of the judgment must be supplied to the appeal court and a transcript of the judgment commissioned immediately (*Re C (Adoption Proceedings: Change of Circumstances)* [2013] 2 FLR 1393, CA).

Placement order application consolidated with care proceedings—A placement order application may be made during the currency of ongoing proceedings under CA 1989, Pt IV for a care or supervision order. The placement application will be allocated to the level of judiciary dealing with the care proceedings (FC(CDB)R 2014, Sch 1, para 5).

PART II

The implication is that the provisions of FPR 2010, both Pts 12 and 14 will apply. In particular, care must be taken to ensure that, when a placement order application is issued during the currency of CA 1989 proceedings, the additional requirements of FPR 2010, Pt 14 as to parties, documentation and reports are adhered to. Where the issue of adoption is already before the court in care proceedings, it is not necessarily unfair for a placement application to be issued and heard after the start of the final hearing (*Re P-B (Placement Order)* [2007] 1 FLR 1106, CA).

Where CA 1989 proceedings are pending in, or transferred to, the County Court any related placement order application must be heard by a County Court hearing centre that is an adoption centre (C(AP)O 1991, art 17).

Form of order—FPR 2010 do not establish a standard form of order for a placement order. It is not open to the court to place conditions upon a placement for adoption order or to seek to exert influence upon the choice adopters; such matters are for the local authority and not the court (*Re A (Placement Order: Imposition of Conditions on Adoption)* [2014] 2 FLR 351, CA).

Duration of a placement order (s 21(4))—A placement order remains in force until the first of the following takes place:

- the placement order is revoked by a court order made under ACA 2002, s 24; or
- an adoption order is made; or
- the child marries or forms a civil partnership; or
- the child attains 18.

Directions for assessment of child (s 22(6))—See notes to CA 1989, s 38(6).

23 Varying placement orders

(1) The court may vary a placement order so as to substitute another local authority for the local authority authorised by the order to place the child for adoption.

(2) The variation may only be made on the joint application of both authorities.

Defined terms—'adoption (in relation to Chapter 4 of Part 1)': s 66; 'child': ss 49(5), 144; 'court', 'local authority': s 144; 'placement order': s 21.

Application for change of local authority—Another local authority may be substituted for the local authority named in a placement order on a joint application made by both authorities.

24 Revoking placement orders

(1) The court may revoke a placement order on the application of any person.

(2) But an application may not be made by a person other than the child or the local authority authorised by the order to place the child for adoption unless –

(a) the court has given leave to apply, and
(b) the child is not placed for adoption by the authority.

(3) The court cannot give leave under subsection (2)(a) unless satisfied that there has been a change in circumstances since the order was made.

(4) If the court determines, on an application for an adoption order, not to make the order, it may revoke any placement order in respect of the child.

(5) Where –

(a) an application for the revocation of a placement order has been made and has not been disposed of, and
(b) the child is not placed for adoption by the authority,

the child may not without the court's leave be placed for adoption under the order.

Defined terms—'adoption (in relation to Chapter 4 of Part 1)': s 66; 'adoption order': s 46(1); 'child': ss 49(5), 144; 'court', 'local authority': s 144; 'placement order': s 21; 'placing, or placed, for adoption': ss 18(5), 19(4).

Revocation of a placement order—The child or local authority may apply to revoke a placement order at any time; however other persons (including the parents) may not apply to revoke the order unless they meet each of the following pre-conditions:

- the court gives leave, which it cannot do unless it is satisfied that there has been a change of circumstances since the order was made, and
- the child is not yet placed for adoption by the authority.

Where an application for revocation is pending and the child is not placed for adoption, the child may not be placed for adoption by the authority without the court's leave.

At the final adoption hearing, if the court decides not to make an adoption order and further considers that the child should not even be placed for adoption, it has the discretion to revoke the placement order. If, however, the court decides that the child should still be placed for a future adoption, then it may order the placement order to continue.

'Placed for adoption' (s 24(2)(b))—A child is not 'placed for adoption' merely because the current foster carer may be interested in adopting him. There are three stages that are required before a child can be said to be 'placed for adoption' with a prospective adopter, namely:

(a) adoption panel recommend child suitable for adoption;
(b) obtaining a placement order; and
(c) adoption panel recommend that the child is adopted by identified prospective adopters (who have been approved as adopters) (*Re S (Placement Order: Revocation)* [2009] 1 FLR 503, CA).

A child is not 'placed' for adoption until he has begun to live with the proposed adopter or, if already living there in foster care, once the adoption agency formally change the placement to a prospective adoptive home (*Coventry CC v O (Adoption)* [2011] 2 FLR 936, CA).

'Change in circumstances' (s 24(3))—The phrase 'change of circumstances' appears throughout ACA 2002 as the threshold justifying reopening an issue that has previously been determined by consent or court order. While the statute does not require that the change is 'significant', the Court of Appeal in *Re P (Adoption: Leave Provisions)* [2007] 2 FLR 1069, CA held that any such change must be of a nature and degree sufficient to reopen consideration of the issue. In the absence of a decision on appeal or by the first instance court that reopens previously determined factual issues, the production of 'fresh evidence' is not capable of amounting to a 'change in circumstances' within the meaning of s 47 (*Re M (Adoption: Leave to Oppose)* [2010] 1 FLR 238, FD). A change of circumstances can include a change, or clarification, of law (*The Prospective Adopters v IA and Croydon LBC* [2014] 2 FLR 1158, FD).

Grant of leave to apply to revoke placement order (s 24(2)(a))—The grant of leave is a two-stage process:

(a) has there been a change in circumstances?
(b) if so, should leave to apply be granted?

When exercising discretion at the second stage under s 24(3), the child's welfare is not the paramount consideration (in contrast to where a parent seeks leave to oppose an adoption – see **Leave to oppose adoption** under s 47(5)), and the court must consider whether the proposed application has 'a real prospect of success'. In considering the prospects of success the court will almost always include an analysis of the child's welfare (*M v Warwickshire County Council* [2008] 1 FLR 1093, CA). The question that the court should ask is 'whether in all the circumstances, including the parent's prospects of success in securing revocation of the placement order and the child's interests, leave should be given' (*NS-H v Kingston upon Hull City Council and MC* [2008] 2 FLR 918, CA). The prospects of success relate to achieving revocation of the placement order and not necessarily the return of the child to the parent's care (*NS-H v Kingston*, above).

The test at the second stage, described above, differs from the similarly worded test applicable to the second stage of an application under ACA 2002, s 47 for leave to oppose adoption, under which the child's welfare is the paramount consideration. The difference arises because an application for leave to apply to revoke a placement order is an application to initiate proceedings and therefore falls outside ACA 2002, s 1(7), which defines the matters to which the paramountcy principle in s 1(2) applies, whereas an application for leave to oppose adoption arises within existing proceedings and is a 'decision relating to adoption' to which s 1(2) does apply.

Procedure—The respondents to an application to revoke a placement order will be the parties to the proceedings leading to the placement order which it is sought to have revoked and any person in whose favour there is provision for contact (FPR 2010, r 14.3). The application will be governed by FPR 2010, Pt 14. The application should be made to the court which made the placement order (C(AP)O 1991, art 3C(2)).

Embargo on placement where revocation application pending (s 24(5))—The embargo upon placement only applies where a substantive revocation application is pending, and does not apply to a preliminary application for leave to apply (*Re F (Placement Order)* [2008] 2 FLR 550, CA). In *Re F* (above) the Court of Appeal stressed that it is the court (not the local authority) that should control arrangements and held that good practice required that:

(1) the parent should request that the local authority undertake not to take any steps to place the child with prospective adopters, pending the hearing of his ACA 2002, s 24 leave application; and
(2) the local authority should explain if its plans are at an advanced stage and about to be implemented. The LA could then apply to the Court, on short notice, for leave to place the child for adoption under s 24(5).

25 Parental responsibility

(1) This section applies while –

(a) a child is placed for adoption under section 19 or an adoption agency is authorised to place a child for adoption under that section, or
(b) a placement order is in force in respect of a child.

(2) Parental responsibility for the child is given to the agency concerned.

(3) While the child is placed with prospective adopters, parental responsibility is given to them.

(4) The agency may determine that the parental responsibility of any parent or guardian, or of prospective adopters, is to be restricted to the extent specified in the determination.

Defined terms—'adoption (in relation to Chapter 4 of Part 1)': s 66; 'adoption agency': s 2(1); 'child': ss 49(5), 144; 'guardian': s 144; 'parental responsibility': s 3 of the 1989 Act; 'placement order': s 21; 'placing, or placed, for adoption': ss 18(5), 19(4).

PART II

26 Contact

(1) On an adoption agency being authorised to place a child for adoption, or placing a child for adoption who is less than six weeks old –

(a) any contact provision in a child arrangements order under section 8 of the 1989 Act ceases to have effect,

(b) any order under section 34 of that Act (parental etc contact with children in care) ceases to have effect, and

(c) any activity direction made in proceedings for the making, variation or discharge of a child arrangements order with respect to the child, or made in other proceedings that relate to such an order, is discharged.

(2) While an adoption agency is so authorised or a child is placed for adoption –

(a) no application may be made for –

(i) a child arrangements order under section 8 of the 1989 Act containing contact provision, or

(ii) an order under section 34 of that Act, but

(b) the court may make an order under this section requiring the person with whom the child lives, or is to live, to allow the child to visit or stay with the person named in the order, or for the person named in the order and the child otherwise to have contact with each other.

(3) An application for an order under this section may be made by –

(a) the child or the agency,

(b) any parent, guardian or relative,

(c) any person in whose favour there was provision which ceased to have effect by virtue of subsection (1)(a) or an order which ceased to have effect by virtue of subsection (1)(b),

(d) if a child arrangements order was in force immediately before the adoption agency was authorised to place the child for adoption or (as the case may be) placed the child for adoption at a time when he was less than six weeks old, any person named in the order as a person with whom the child was to live,

(e) if a person had care of the child immediately before that time by virtue of an order made in the exercise of the High Court's inherent jurisdiction with respect to children, that person,

(f) any person who has obtained the court's leave to make the application.

(4) When making a placement order, the court may on its own initiative make an order under this section.

(5) This section does not prevent an application for a contact order under section 8 of the 1989 Act being made where the application is to be heard together with an application for an adoption order in respect of the child.

(5A) In this section 'contact provision' means provision which regulates arrangements relating to –

(a) with whom a child is to spend time or otherwise have contact, or

(b) when a child is to spend time or otherwise have contact with any person;

but in paragraphs (a) and (b) a reference to spending time or otherwise having contact with a person is to doing that otherwise than as a result of living with the person.

(6) In this section 'activity direction' has the meaning given by section 11A of the 1989 Act.

Amendments—CAA 2006, s 15(1), Sch 2, paras 13, 14; CFA 2014, s 12, Sch 2.

Defined terms—'the 1989 Act': s 2(5); 'adoption (in relation to Chapter 4 of Part 1)': s 66; 'adoption agency': s 2(1); 'adoption order': s 46(1); 'by virtue of': s 144; 'child': ss 49(5), 144; 'child arrangements order': s 8(1) of the 1989 Act; 'court', 'guardian': s 144; 'placement order': s 21; 'placing, or placed, for adoption': ss 18(5), 19(4); 'relative': s 144, read with s 1(8).

Contact where an adoption agency is authorised to place a child for adoption—Upon an adoption agency being authorised to place a child for adoption, any child arrangements order under CA 1989, s 8 or child arrangements order under s 34 ceases to have effect (s 26(1)). Further, no application for a child arrangements order under CA 1989 can be made while an agency is authorised to place for adoption (save where the contact application is to be heard with an application for adoption) (s 26(2),(5)). These provisions apply whether the placement is authorised as a result of parental consent or under a placement order.

Before making a placement order, the court is under a duty to consider the arrangements made or proposed by the agency for allowing contact with the child and to invite the parties to the proceedings to comment on those arrangements (s 27(4)). The agency must take into account the wishes and feelings of the parent (and, if appropriate, a father without parental responsibility), the advice of the adoption panel and the adoption welfare check list in ACA 2002, s 1 before making a decision on contact (Adoption Agency Regulations 2005, reg 46).

While an agency is authorised to place for adoption, or a child is so placed, the court may make an order under ACA 2002, s 26, requiring the person with whom the child lives, or is to live, to allow the child to visit or stay with the person named in the order, or for the person named in the order and the child otherwise to have contact with each other. When making the placement order, the court may of its own initiative make an order for contact (s 26(4)).

When considering whether to make a s 26 order the court must afford paramount consideration to the child's welfare in accordance with ACA 2002, s 1. A s 26 child arrangements order has effect while the adoption agency is authorised to place the child for adoption but may be varied or revoked by the court on an application by the child, the agency or the person named in the order (s 27(1)).

In *Re P (Placement Orders: Parental Consent)* [2008] 2 FLR 625, CA, the Court of Appeal held that the previous case-law relating to post-adoption contact needs to be revisited in the context of the court's jurisdiction to control contact under ACA 2002, s 26; issues of contact will be a matter for the court, rather than for the local authority with or without the prospective adopters.

The terms of any s 26 order may be departed from by agreement between the agency and any person for whose contact with the child the order provides, provided that the child (if of sufficient age and understanding) agrees, the prospective adopters agree and relevant persons have been informed of the change (Adoption Agency Regulations 2005, reg 47(2)).

Where the court is satisfied that the local authority is committed to the level of contact endorsed by the court, an order for contact is unnecessary (*Re C (Contact)* [2008] 1 FLR 1151, FD).

Adoption agency power to refuse to allow contact—Unlike the position that applies under a care order, there is no requirement upon an adoption agency to allow contact between the child and any person unless such contact is stipulated in an order under ACA 2002, s 26. Consequently, unless to do so would be in conflict with provision in a s 26 order, the agency may refuse contact without having to seek the court's approval.

In addition, an adoption agency is permitted to refuse to allow contact that would otherwise be required by virtue of a s 26 order, without first obtaining a court order, if it is satisfied that it is necessary to do so in order to safeguard or promote the child's welfare and the refusal is decided upon as a matter of urgency and does not last for more than seven days (s 27(2)). The agency is under a duty to inform relevant individuals as soon as any decision to refuse contact is made (Adoption Agency Regulations 2005, reg 47).

Application for contact when placement for adoption authorised (s 26(3))—An application for a s 26 child arrangements order may be made by (FPR 2010, r 14.3):

- the child;
- the agency;
- any parent or guardian or relative;
- any person in whose favour there was a CA child arrangements order (which ceased to have effect under s 26(1));
- the person with a child arrangements order in force immediately before the adoption agency was authorised to place;
- the person who had care of the child by an order under the High Court's inherent jurisdiction before the agency was authorised to place;
- any person with the court's permission.

The procedure is governed by FPR 2010, Pt 14. An application for contact should be made to the court which made the placement order (C(AP)O 1991, art 3C(2)).

The respondents to an application for a s 26 child arrangements order will be (FPR 2010, r 14.3):

- The adoption agency authorised to place the child (or which has placed the child) for adoption;
- The person with whom the child lives or is to live;
- Each parent with parental responsibility for the child or guardian of the child;
- The child where:
  - (i) the agency or a parent with parental responsibility order opposes the making of the child arrangements order;
  - (ii) he opposes the making of the child arrangements order;
  - (iii) existing provision for contact is to be revoked;
  - (iv) relatives of the child do not agree to the arrangements for contact;
  - (v) he is suffering or is at risk of suffering 'harm' within the meaning of CA 1989, s 31(9).

The court may at any time direct that a child, who is not already a respondent to proceedings be made a respondent where the child wishes to make an application or has evidence to give to the court, or a legal submission to make, which has not been given or made by any other party, or there are other special circumstances. The court may at any time direct that a person or body be made a respondent or be removed as a respondent (FPR 2010, r 14.3(2),(3)).

27 Contact: supplementary

(1) An order under section 26 –

PART II

(a) has effect while the adoption agency is authorised to place the child for adoption or the child is placed for adoption, but

(b) may be varied or revoked by the court on an application by the child, the agency or a person named in the order.

(2) The agency may refuse to allow the contact that would otherwise be required by virtue of an order under that section if –

(a) it is satisfied that it is necessary to do so in order to safeguard or promote the child's welfare, and

(b) the refusal is decided upon as a matter of urgency and does not last for more than seven days.

(3) Regulations may make provision as to –

(a) the steps to be taken by an agency which has exercised its power under subsection (2),

(b) the circumstances in which, and conditions subject to which, the terms of any order under section 26 may be departed from by agreement between the agency and any person for whose contact with the child the order provides,

(c) notification by an agency of any variation or suspension of arrangements made (otherwise than under an order under that section) with a view to allowing any person contact with the child.

(4) Before making a placement order the court must –

(a) consider the arrangements which the adoption agency has made, or proposes to make, for allowing any person contact with the child, and

(b) invite the parties to the proceedings to comment on those arrangements.

(5) An order under section 26 may provide for contact on any conditions the court considers appropriate.

Defined terms—'adoption (in relation to Chapter 4 of Part 1)': s 66; 'adoption agency': s 2(1); 'by virtue of': s 144; 'child': ss 49(5), 144; 'court': s 144; 'placement order': s 21; 'placing, or placed, for adoption': ss 18(5), 19(4); 'regulations': s 144.

28 Further consequences of placement

(1) Where a child is placed for adoption under section 19 or an adoption agency is authorised to place a child for adoption under that section –

(a) a parent or guardian of the child may not apply for a child arrangements order regulating the child's living arrangements unless an application for an adoption order has been made and the parent or guardian has obtained the court's leave under subsection (3) or (5) of section 47,

(b) if an application has been made for an adoption order, a guardian of the child may not apply for a special guardianship order unless he has obtained the court's leave under subsection (3) or (5) of that section.

(2) Where –

(a) a child is placed for adoption under section 19 or an adoption agency is authorised to place a child for adoption under that section, or

(b) a placement order is in force in respect of a child,

then (whether or not the child is in England and Wales) a person may not do either of the following things, unless the court gives leave or each parent or guardian of the child gives written consent.

(3) Those things are –

(a) causing the child to be known by a new surname, or

(b) removing the child from the United Kingdom.

(4) Subsection (3) does not prevent the removal of a child from the United Kingdom for a period of less than one month by a person who provides the child's home.

(5) For the purposes of subsection (1)(a), a child arrangements order regulates a child's living arrangements if the arrangements regulated by the order consist of, or include, arrangements which relate to either or both of the following –

(a) with whom the child is to live, and
(b) when the child is to live with any person.

Amendments—CFA 2014, s 12, Sch 2.

Defined terms—'adoption (in relation to Chapter 4 of Part 1)': s 66; 'adoption agency': s 2(1); 'adoption order': s 46(1); 'child': ss 49(5), 144; 'child arrangements order': s 8(1) of the 1989 Act; 'consent (in relation to making adoption orders or placing for adoption)': s 52; 'court', 'guardian': s 144; 'placement order': s 21; 'placing, or placed, for adoption': ss 18(5) and 19(4).

Application to court that made placement order (C(AP)O 1991, art 3C(2))—An application to change a child's surname or remove him from the UK should be made to the court which made the placement order.

29 Further consequences of placement orders

(1) Where a placement order is made in respect of a child and either –

(a) the child is subject to a care order, or
(b) the court at the same time makes a care order in respect of the child,

the care order does not have effect at any time when the placement order is in force.

(2) On the making of a placement order in respect of a child, any order mentioned in section 8(1) of the 1989 Act, and any supervision order in respect of the child, ceases to have effect.

(3) Where a placement order is in force –

(a) no prohibited steps order or specific issue order, and
(b) no supervision order or child assessment order,

may be made in respect of the child.

(4) Where a placement order is in force, a child arrangements order may be made with respect to the child's living arrangements only if –

(a) an application for an adoption order has been made in respect of the child, and
(b) the child arrangements order is applied for by a parent or guardian who has obtained the court's leave under subsection (3) or (5) of section 47 or by any other person who has obtained the court's leave under this subsection.

(4A) For the purposes of subsection (4), a child arrangements order is one made with respect to a child's living arrangements if the arrangements regulated by the order consist of, or include, arrangements which relate to either or both of the following –

(a) with whom the child is to live, and
(b) when the child is to live with any person.

(5) Where a placement order is in force, no special guardianship order may be made in respect of the child unless –

(a) an application has been made for an adoption order, and
(b) the person applying for the special guardianship order has obtained the court's leave under this subsection or, if he is a guardian of the child, has obtained the court's leave under section 47(5).

(6) Section 14A(7) of the 1989 Act applies in respect of an application for a special guardianship order for which leave has been given as mentioned in subsection (5)(b) with the omission of the words 'the beginning of the period of three months ending with'.

(7) Where a placement order is in force –

(a) section 14C(1)(b) of the 1989 Act (special guardianship: parental responsibility) has effect subject to any determination under section 25(4) of this Act,
(b) section 14C(3) and (4) of the 1989 Act (special guardianship: removal of child from UK etc) does not apply.

Amendments—CFA 2014, s 12, Sch 2.

Defined terms—'the 1989 Act': s 2(5); 'adoption (in relation to Chapter 4 of Part 1)': s 66; 'adoption order': s 46(1); 'care order': s 105(1) of the 1989 Act; 'child': ss 49(5) and 144; 'child arrangements order': s 8(1) of the 1989 Act; 'child assessment order': s 43(2) of the 1989 Act; 'court', 'guardian': s 144; 'parental responsibility': s 3 of the 1989 Act; 'placement order': s 21; 'prohibited steps order': s 8(1) of the 1989 Act; 'specific issue order': s 8(1) of the 1989 Act; 'supervision order': s 31(11) of the 1989 Act.

Removal of children who are or may be placed by adoption agencies

30 General prohibitions on removal

(1) Where –

(a) a child is placed for adoption by an adoption agency under section 19, or

(b) a child is placed for adoption by an adoption agency and either the child is less than six weeks old or the agency has at no time been authorised to place the child for adoption,

a person (other than the agency) must not remove the child from the prospective adopters.

(2) Where –

(a) a child who is not for the time being placed for adoption is being provided with accommodation by a local authority, and

(b) the authority have applied to the court for a placement order and the application has not been disposed of,

only a person who has the court's leave (or the authority) may remove the child from the accommodation.

(3) Where subsection (2) does not apply, but –

(a) a child who is not for the time being placed for adoption is being provided with accommodation by an adoption agency, and

(b) the agency is authorised to place the child for adoption under section 19 or would be so authorised if any consent to placement under that section had not been withdrawn,

a person (other than the agency) must not remove the child from the accommodation.

(4) This section is subject to sections 31 to 33 but those sections do not apply if the child is subject to a care order.

(5) This group of sections (that is, this section and those sections) apply whether or not the child in question is in England and Wales.

(6) This group of sections does not affect the exercise by any local authority or other person of any power conferred by any enactment, other than section 20(8) of the 1989 Act or section 76(5) of the 2014 Act (removal of children from local authority accommodation).

(7) This group of sections does not prevent the removal of a child who is arrested.

(8) A person who removes a child in contravention of this section is guilty of an offence and liable on summary conviction to imprisonment for a term not exceeding three months, or a fine not exceeding level 5 on the standard scale, or both.

Amendments—SI 2016/413.

Defined terms—'the 1989 Act': s 2(5); 'adoption (in relation to Chapter 4 of Part 1)': s 66; 'adoption agency': s 2(1); 'care order': s 105(1) of the 1989 Act; 'child': ss 49(5), 144; 'consent (in relation to making adoption orders or placing for adoption)': s 52; 'court', 'enactment', 'local authority': s 144; 'placement order': s 21; 'placing, or placed, for adoption': ss 18(5), 19(4).

Application in pending placement proceedings—Where an application for a placement order is pending, proceedings for leave to remove a child under ACA 2002, s 30(2)(b) will be allocated to the level of judge who is dealing with the existing proceedings (FC(CDB)R 2014, r 17(1)).

31 Recovery by parent etc where child not placed or is a baby

(1) Subsection (2) applies where –

(a) a child who is not for the time being placed for adoption is being provided with accommodation by an adoption agency, and

(b) the agency would be authorised to place the child for adoption under section 19 if consent to placement under that section had not been withdrawn.

(2) If any parent or guardian of the child informs the agency that he wishes the child to be returned to him, the agency must return the child to him within the period of seven days beginning with the request unless an application is, or has been, made for a placement order and the application has not been disposed of.

(3) Subsection (4) applies where –

(a) a child is placed for adoption by an adoption agency and either the child is less than six weeks old or the agency has at no time been authorised to place the child for adoption, and

(b) any parent or guardian of the child informs the agency that he wishes the child to be returned to him,

unless an application is, or has been, made for a placement order and the application has not been disposed of.

(4) The agency must give notice of the parent's or guardian's wish to the prospective adopters who must return the child to the agency within the period of seven days beginning with the day on which the notice is given.

(5) A prospective adopter who fails to comply with subsection (4) is guilty of an offence and liable on summary conviction to imprisonment for a term not exceeding three months, or a fine not exceeding level 5 on the standard scale, or both.

(6) As soon as a child is returned to an adoption agency under subsection (4), the agency must return the child to the parent or guardian in question.

Defined terms—'adoption (in relation to Chapter 4 of Part 1)': s 66; 'adoption agency': s 2(1); 'child': ss 49(5), 144; 'consent (in relation to making adoption orders or placing for adoption)': s 52; 'guardian', 'notice': s 144; 'placement order': s 21; 'placing, or placed, for adoption': ss 18(5), 19(4).

32 Recovery by parent etc where child placed and consent withdrawn

(1) This section applies where –

(a) a child is placed for adoption by an adoption agency under section 19, and
(b) consent to placement under that section has been withdrawn,

unless an application is, or has been, made for a placement order and the application has not been disposed of.

(2) If a parent or guardian of the child informs the agency that he wishes the child to be returned to him –

(a) the agency must give notice of the parent's or guardian's wish to the prospective adopters, and

(b) the prospective adopters must return the child to the agency within the period of 14 days beginning with the day on which the notice is given.

(3) A prospective adopter who fails to comply with subsection (2)(b) is guilty of an offence and liable on summary conviction to imprisonment for a term not exceeding three months, or a fine not exceeding level 5 on the standard scale, or both.

(4) As soon as a child is returned to an adoption agency under this section, the agency must return the child to the parent or guardian in question.

(5) Where a notice under subsection (2) is given, but –

(a) before the notice was given, an application –
(i) for an adoption order (including a Scottish or Northern Irish adoption order),
(ii) for a special guardianship order,
(iii) for a child arrangements order to which subsection (6) applies, or
(iv) for permission to apply for an order within subparagraph (ii) or (iii),
was made in respect of the child, and

(b) the application (and, in a case where permission is given on an application to apply for an order within paragraph (a)(ii) or (iii), the application for the order) has not been disposed of, the prospective adopters are not required by virtue of the notice to return the child to the agency unless the court so orders.

(6) A child arrangements order is one to which this subsection applies if it is an order regulating arrangements that consist of, or include, arrangements which relate to either or both of the following –

(a) with whom a child is to live, and
(b) when the child is to live with any person.

Amendments—CFA 2014, s 12, Sch 2.

Defined terms—'adoption (in relation to Chapter 4 of Part 1)': s 66; 'adoption agency': s 2(1); 'adoption order': s 46(1); 'by virtue of': s 144; 'child': ss 49(5), 144; 'child arrangements order': s 8(1) of the 1989 Act; 'consent (in relation to making adoption orders or placing for adoption)': s 52; 'court', 'guardian', 'Northern Irish adoption order', 'notice': s 144; 'placement order': s 21; 'placing, or placed, for adoption': ss 18(5), 19(4).

33 Recovery by parent etc where child placed and placement order refused

(1) This section applies where –

(a) a child is placed for adoption by a local authority under section 19,
(b) the authority have applied for a placement order and the application has been refused, and
(c) any parent or guardian of the child informs the authority that he wishes the child to be returned to him.

(2) The prospective adopters must return the child to the authority on a date determined by the court.

(3) A prospective adopter who fails to comply with subsection (2) is guilty of an offence and liable on summary conviction to imprisonment for a term not exceeding three months, or a fine not exceeding level 5 on the standard scale, or both.

(4) As soon as a child is returned to the authority, they must return the child to the parent or guardian in question.

Defined terms—'adoption (in relation to Chapter 4 of Part 1)': s 66; 'child': ss 49(5), 144; 'court', 'guardian', 'local authority': s 144; 'placement order': s 21; 'placing, or placed, for adoption': ss 18(5), 19(4).

34 Placement orders: prohibition on removal

(1) Where a placement order in respect of a child –

(a) is in force, or
(b) has been revoked, but the child has not been returned by the prospective adopters or remains in any accommodation provided by the local authority,

a person (other than the local authority) may not remove the child from the prospective adopters or from accommodation provided by the authority.

(2) A person who removes a child in contravention of subsection (1) is guilty of an offence.

(3) Where a court revoking a placement order in respect of a child determines that the child is not to remain with any former prospective adopters with whom the child is placed, they must return the child to the local authority within the period determined by the court for the purpose; and a person who fails to do so is guilty of an offence.

(4) Where a court revoking a placement order in respect of a child determines that the child is to be returned to a parent or guardian, the local authority must return the child to the parent or guardian as soon as the child is returned to the authority or, where the child is in accommodation provided by the authority, at once.

(5) A person guilty of an offence under this section is liable on summary conviction to imprisonment for a term not exceeding three months, or a fine not exceeding level 5 on the standard scale, or both.

(6) This section does not affect the exercise by any local authority or other person of a power conferred by any enactment, other than section 20(8) of the 1989 Act or section 76(5) of the 2014 Act (removal of children from local authority accommodation).

(7) This section does not prevent the removal of a child who is arrested.

(8) This section applies whether or not the child in question is in England and Wales.

Amendments—SI 2016/413.

Defined terms—'the 1989 Act': s 2(5); 'child': ss 49(5), 144; 'court', 'enactment', 'guardian', 'local authority': s 144; 'placement order': s 21; 'placing, or placed, for adoption': ss 18(5), 19(4).

35 Return of child in other cases

(1) Where a child is placed for adoption by an adoption agency and the prospective adopters give notice to the agency of their wish to return the child, the agency must –

- (a) receive the child from the prospective adopters before the end of the period of seven days beginning with the giving of the notice, and
- (b) give notice to any parent or guardian of the child of the prospective adopters' wish to return the child.

(2) Where a child is placed for adoption by an adoption agency, and the agency –

- (a) is of the opinion that the child should not remain with the prospective adopters, and
- (b) gives notice to them of its opinion,

the prospective adopters must, not later than the end of the period of seven days beginning with the giving of the notice, return the child to the agency.

(3) If the agency gives notice under subsection (2)(b), it must give notice to any parent or guardian of the child of the obligation to return the child to the agency.

(4) A prospective adopter who fails to comply with subsection (2) is guilty of an offence and liable on summary conviction to imprisonment for a term not exceeding three months, or a fine not exceeding level 5 on the standard scale, or both.

(5) Where –

- (a) an adoption agency gives notice under subsection (2) in respect of a child,
- (b) before the notice was given, an application –
  - (i) for an adoption order (including a Scottish or Northern Irish adoption order),
  - (ii) for a special guardianship order,
  - (iii) for a child arrangements order to which subsection (5A) applies, or
  - (iv) for permission to apply for an order within subparagraph (ii) or (iii), was made in respect of the child, and
- (c) the application (and, in a case where permission is given on an application to apply for an order within paragraph (b)(ii) or (iii), the application for the order) has not been disposed of,

prospective adopters are not required by virtue of the notice to return the child to the agency unless the court so orders.

(5A) A child arrangements order is one to which this subsection applies if it is an order regulating arrangements that consist of, or include, arrangements which relate to either or both of the following –

- (a) with whom a child is to live, and
- (b) when a child is to live with any person.

(6) This section applies whether or not the child in question is in England and Wales.

Amendments—CFA 2014, s 12, Sch 2.

Defined terms—'adoption (in relation to Chapter 4 of Part 1)': s 66; 'adoption agency': s 2(1); 'adoption order': s 46(1); 'by virtue of': s 144; 'child': ss 49(5), 144; 'child arrangements order': s 8(1) of the 1989 Act; 'court', 'guardian', 'Northern Irish adoption order', 'notice': s 144; 'placing, or placed, for adoption': ss 18(5), 19(4).

Return of child in emergency—Where a local authority seek the urgent return of the child (in a period shorter than the 7-day notice required by s 35(1)) or a return without any notice, the proper course is for the matter to come before the Family Court via an application for an emergency protection order or an interim care order (*DL and ML v Newham London Borough Council and Secretary of State for Education* [2011] 2 FLR 1033, QBD).

Removal of children in non-agency cases

36 Restrictions on removal

(1) At any time when a child's home is with any persons ('the people concerned') with whom the child is not placed by an adoption agency, but the people concerned –

(a) have applied for an adoption order in respect of the child and the application has not been disposed of,

(b) have given notice of intention to adopt, or

(c) have applied for leave to apply for an adoption order under section 42(6) and the application has not been disposed of,

a person may remove the child only in accordance with the provisions of this group of sections (that is, this section and sections 37 to 40).

The reference to a child placed by an adoption agency includes a child placed by a Scottish or Northern Irish adoption agency.

(2) For the purposes of this group of sections, a notice of intention to adopt is to be disregarded if –

(a) the period of four months beginning with the giving of the notice has expired without the people concerned applying for an adoption order, or

(b) the notice is a second or subsequent notice of intention to adopt and was given during the period of five months beginning with the giving of the preceding notice.

(3) For the purposes of this group of sections, if the people concerned apply for leave to apply for an adoption order under section 42(6) and the leave is granted, the application for leave is not to be treated as disposed of until the period of three days beginning with the granting of the leave has expired.

(4) This section does not prevent the removal of a child who is arrested.

(5) Where a parent or guardian may remove a child from the people concerned in accordance with the provisions of this group of sections, the people concerned must at the request of the parent or guardian return the child to the parent or guardian at once.

(6) A person who –

(a) fails to comply with subsection (5), or

(b) removes a child in contravention of this section,

is guilty of an offence and liable on summary conviction to imprisonment for a term not exceeding three months, or a fine not exceeding level 5 on the standard scale, or both.

(7) This group of sections applies whether or not the child in question is in England and Wales.

Defined terms—'adoption agency': s 2(1); 'adoption order': s 46(1); 'child': ss 49(5), 144; 'guardian', 'Northern Irish adoption agency', 'notice': s 144; 'notice of intention to adopt': s 44(2); 'placing, or placed, for adoption': ss 18(5), 19(4).

37 Applicants for adoption

If section 36(1)(a) applies, the following persons may remove the child –

(a) a person who has the court's leave,

(b) a local authority or other person in the exercise of a power conferred by any enactment, other than section 20(8) of the 1989 Act or section 76(5) of the 2014 Act.

Amendments—SI 2016/413.

Defined terms—'the 1989 Act': s 2(5); 'adoption (in relation to Chapter 4 of Part 1)': s 66; 'child': ss 49(5), 144; 'court', 'enactment', 'local authority': s 144.

38 Local authority foster parents

(1) This section applies if the child's home is with local authority foster parents.

(2) If –

(a) the child has had his home with the foster parents at all times during the period of five years ending with the removal and the foster parents have given notice of intention to adopt, or

(b) an application has been made for leave under section 42(6) and has not been disposed of,

the following persons may remove the child.

(3) They are –

(a) a person who has the court's leave,

(b) a local authority or other person in the exercise of a power conferred by any enactment, other than section 20(8) of the 1989 Act or section 76(5) of the 2014 Act.

(4) If subsection (2) does not apply but –

(a) the child has had his home with the foster parents at all times during the period of one year ending with the removal, and

(b) the foster parents have given notice of intention to adopt,

the following persons may remove the child.

(5) They are –

(a) a person with parental responsibility for the child who is exercising the power in section 20(8) of the 1989 Act or section 76(5) of 2014 Act,

(b) a person who has the court's leave,

(c) a local authority or other person in the exercise of a power conferred by any enactment, other than section 20(8) of the 1989 Act or section 76(5) of 2014 Act.

Amendments—SI 2016/413.

Defined terms—'the 1989 Act': s 2(5); 'child': ss 49(5), 144; 'court', 'enactment', 'local authority': s 144; 'local authority foster parent': s 23(3) of the 1989 Act; 'notice of intention to adopt': s 44(2); 'parental responsibility': s 3 of the 1989 Act.

39 Partners of parents

(1) This section applies if a child's home is with a partner of a parent and the partner has given notice of intention to adopt.

(2) If the child's home has been with the partner for not less than three years (whether continuous or not) during the period of five years ending with the removal, the following persons may remove the child –

(a) a person who has the court's leave,

(b) a local authority or other person in the exercise of a power conferred by any enactment, other than section 20(8) of the 1989 Act or section 76(5) of 2014 Act.

(3) If subsection (2) does not apply, the following persons may remove the child –

(a) a parent or guardian,

(b) a person who has the court's leave,

(c) a local authority or other person in the exercise of a power conferred by any enactment, other than section 20(8) of the 1989 Act or section 76(5) of 2014 Act.

Amendments—SI 2016/413.

Defined terms—'the 1989 Act': s 2(5); 'child': ss 49(5), 144; 'court', 'enactment', 'guardian', 'local authority': s 144; 'notice of intention to adopt': s 44(2); 'partner, in relation to a parent of a child': s 144(7).

40 Other non-agency cases

(1) In any case where sections 37 to 39 do not apply but –

(a) the people concerned have given notice of intention to adopt, or

(b) the people concerned have applied for leave under section 42(6) and the application has not been disposed of,

the following persons may remove the child.

(2) They are –

(a) a person who has the court's leave,
(b) a local authority or other person in the exercise of a power conferred by any enactment, other than section 20(8) of the 1989 Act or section 76(5) of 2014 Act.

Amendments—SI 2016/413.

Defined terms—'the 1989 Act': s 2(5); 'child': ss 49(5), 144; 'court', 'enactment', 'local authority': s 144; 'notice of intention to adopt': s 44(2).

Breach of restrictions on removal

41 Recovery orders

(1) This section applies where it appears to the court –

(a) that a child has been removed in contravention of any of the preceding provisions of this Chapter or that there are reasonable grounds for believing that a person intends to remove a child in contravention of those provisions, or
(b) that a person has failed to comply with section 31(4), 32(2), 33(2), 34(3) or 35(2).

(2) The court may, on the application of any person, by an order –

(a) direct any person who is in a position to do so to produce the child on request to any person mentioned in subsection (4),
(b) authorise the removal of the child by any person mentioned in that subsection,
(c) require any person who has information as to the child's whereabouts to disclose that information on request to any constable or officer of the court,
(d) authorise a constable to enter any premises specified in the order and search for the child, using reasonable force if necessary.

(3) Premises may only be specified under subsection (2)(d) if it appears to the court that there are reasonable grounds for believing the child to be on them.

(4) The persons referred to in subsection (2) are –

(a) any person named by the court,
(b) any constable,
(c) any person who, after the order is made under that subsection, is authorised to exercise any power under the order by an adoption agency which is authorised to place the child for adoption.

(5) A person who intentionally obstructs a person exercising a power of removal conferred by the order is guilty of an offence and liable on summary conviction to a fine not exceeding level 3 on the standard scale.

(6) A person must comply with a request to disclose information as required by the order even if the information sought might constitute evidence that he had committed an offence.

(7) But in criminal proceedings in which the person is charged with an offence (other than one mentioned in subsection (8)) –

(a) no evidence relating to the information provided may be adduced, and
(b) no question relating to the information may be asked,

by or on behalf of the prosecution, unless evidence relating to it is adduced, or a question relating to it is asked, in the proceedings by or on behalf of the person.

(8) The offences excluded from subsection (7) are –

(a) an offence under section 2 or 5 of the Perjury Act 1911 (false statements made on oath otherwise than in judicial proceedings or made otherwise than on oath),
(b) an offence under section 44(1) or (2) of the Criminal Law (Consolidation) (Scotland) Act 1995 (false statements made on oath or otherwise than on oath).

(9) An order under this section has effect in relation to Scotland as if it were an order made by the Court of Session which that court had jurisdiction to make.

Defined terms—'adoption (in relation to Chapter 4 of Part 1)': s 66; 'adoption agency': s 2(1); 'child': ss 49(5), 144; 'court', 'information': s 144.

Scope—Sections 30–40 make provision with regard to the ability of those connected with a child to remove him from an adoption placement in various circumstances. By s 41 the court may make a recovery order in the event that a child has been removed in contravention of those provisions, or there are reasonable grounds for believing that a person intends to do so or a person has failed to comply with a request to return the child. A recovery order may direct that a person produce the child, or authorise a person to remove the child, or require information about the child's whereabouts or authorise a constable to enter premises to search for the child. It is a criminal offence to obstruct a person acting under a recovery order.

Preliminaries to adoption

42 Child to live with adopters before application

(1) An application for an adoption order may not be made unless –

(a) if subsection (2) applies, the condition in that subsection is met,

(b) if that subsection does not apply, the condition in whichever is applicable of subsections (3) to (5) applies.

(2) If –

(a) the child was placed for adoption with the applicant or applicants by an adoption agency or in pursuance of an order of the High Court, or

(b) the applicant is a parent of the child,

the condition is that the child must have had his home with the applicant or, in the case of an application by a couple, with one or both of them at all times during the period of ten weeks preceding the application.

(3) If the applicant or one of the applicants is the partner of a parent of the child, the condition is that the child must have had his home with the applicant or, as the case may be, applicants at all times during the period of six months preceding the application.

(4) If the applicants are local authority foster parents, the condition is that the child must have had his home with the applicants at all times during the period of one year preceding the application.

(5) In any other case, the condition is that the child must have had his home with the applicant or, in the case of an application by a couple, with one or both of them for not less than three years (whether continuous or not) during the period of five years preceding the application.

(6) But subsections (4) and (5) do not prevent an application being made if the court gives leave to make it.

(7) An adoption order may not be made unless the court is satisfied that sufficient opportunities to see the child with the applicant or, in the case of an application by a couple, both of them together in the home environment have been given –

(a) where the child was placed for adoption with the applicant or applicants by an adoption agency, to that agency,

(b) in any other case, to the local authority within whose area the home is.

(8) In this section and sections 43 and 44(1) –

(a) references to an adoption agency include a Scottish or Northern Irish adoption agency,

(b) references to a child placed for adoption by an adoption agency are to be read accordingly.

Defined terms—'adoption (in relation to Chapter 4 of Part 1)': s 66; 'adoption agency': s 2(1); 'adoption order': s 46(1); 'child': ss 49(5), 144; 'child placed for adoption by an adoption agency': s 18(5); 'couple': s 144(4); 'court', 'local authority': s 144; 'local authority foster parent': s 23(3) of the 1989 Act; 'Northern Irish adoption agency': s 144; 'partner, in relation to a parent of a child': s 144(7); 'placing, or placed, for adoption': ss 18(5), 19(4).

'had his home with the applicant' (s 42(2)–(5))—The question of where a child has had his home is one of fact. (*ECC v M* [2008] EWHC 332 (Fam)). For whether the 'home' should be in England or Wales, see s 42(7). Even if the child is physically absent, he may still be held to have his home with the applicant(s) if they remain in effective parental control of him (*Re CSC* (*An Infant*) [1960] 1 WLR 304, ChD; *Re KT* (*Adoption Application*) (1993) Fam Law 567, FD). Time spent in boarding school is to be disregarded, but at least some significant time must be spent in a home with the applicant (*Re X (Adoption Application: Gateway Requirements)* [2014]

1 FLR 1281, FD). Where s 42(7)(b) applies the 'home' must be within a local authority area in England and Wales. Where, however, s 42(7)(a) applies (either to an adoption or an order under ACA 2002, s 84) there is no territorial restriction and the 'home environment' may be outside England and Wales (*Re A (A Child)* [2009] 2 FLR 597, CA – on appeal from *Haringey London Borough Council v MA, JN, IA* [2008] 2 FLR 1857, FD).

'application … if court gives leave' (s 42(6))—When determining a leave application under ACA 2002, s 42(6) the child's welfare is not the paramount consideration and the court must consider whether the proposed application has 'a real prospect of success'; this test applies to all categories of applicant. In considering the prospects of success, the court will almost always include an analysis of the child's welfare (*Re A; Coventry City Council v CC and A* [2008] 1 FLR 959, CA, applying *M v Warwickshire County Council* [2008] 1 FLR 1093, CA).

'sufficient opportunities to see the child … in the home environment' (s 42(7))—This requirement, coupled with s 44, means that, where the child has not been placed for adoption by an adoption agency, the applicant must have a 'home' within England and Wales (i e within the area of a local authority (as defined by s 144(1); *Re SL (Adoption: Home in Jurisdiction)* [2005] 1 FLR 118, FD). In intercountry adoptions the court requires the child to have been resident in the UK for 12 months before it will entertain an application – see **Intercountry adoptions** under s 47 below.

43 Reports where child placed by agency

Where an application for an adoption order relates to a child placed for adoption by an adoption agency, the agency must –

(a) submit to the court a report on the suitability of the applicants and on any other matters relevant to the operation of section 1, and

(b) assist the court in any manner the court directs.

Defined terms—'adoption (in relation to Chapter 4 of Part 1)': s 66; 'adoption agency': s 2(1); 'child': ss 49(5), 144; 'child placed for adoption by an adoption agency': s 18(5); 'court': s 144; 'placing, or placed, for adoption': ss 18(5), 19(4).

Adoption reports—The adoption agency or local authority must file a report on the suitability of the applicant to adopt a child within the timetable fixed by the court (FPR 2010, r 14.11(1),(2)). The reports must contain the matters set out in FPR PD14C. Any such report will be confidential (r 14.11(6)). The court may at any stage request a further report (r 14.11(4)).

44 Notice of intention to adopt

(1) This section applies where persons (referred to in this section as 'proposed adopters') wish to adopt a child who is not placed for adoption with them by an adoption agency.

(2) An adoption order may not be made in respect of the child unless the proposed adopters have given notice to the appropriate local authority of their intention to apply for the adoption order (referred to in this Act as a 'notice of intention to adopt').

(3) The notice must be given not more than two years, or less than three months, before the date on which the application for the adoption order is made.

(4) Where –

(a) if a person were seeking to apply for an adoption order, subsection (4) or (5) of section 42 would apply, but

(b) the condition in the subsection in question is not met,

the person may not give notice of intention to adopt unless he has the court's leave to apply for an adoption order.

(5) On receipt of a notice of intention to adopt, the local authority must arrange for the investigation of the matter and submit to the court a report of the investigation.

(6) In particular, the investigation must, so far as practicable, include the suitability of the proposed adopters and any other matters relevant to the operation of section 1 in relation to the application.

(7) If a local authority receive a notice of intention to adopt in respect of a child whom they know was (immediately before the notice was given) looked after by another local authority, they must, not more than seven days after the receipt of the notice, inform the other local authority in writing that they have received the notice.

(8) Where –

(a) a local authority have placed a child with any persons otherwise than as prospective adopters, and

(b) the persons give notice of intention to adopt,

the authority are not to be treated as leaving the child with them as prospective adopters for the purposes of section 18(1)(b).

(9) In this section, references to the appropriate local authority, in relation to any proposed adopters, are –

(a) in prescribed cases, references to the prescribed local authority,

(b) in any other case, references to the local authority for the area in which, at the time of giving the notice of intention to adopt, they have their home,

and 'prescribed' means prescribed by regulations.

Defined terms—'adoption (in relation to Chapter 4 of Part 1)': s 66; 'adoption agency': s 2(1); 'adoption order': s 46(1); 'child': ss 49(5), 144; 'court', 'local authority', 'notice': s 144; 'notice of intention to adopt': s 44(2); 'placing, or placed, for adoption': ss 18(5), 19(4); 'regulations': s 144.

'notice to the … local authority' (s 44(2))—The relevant local authority is the one in whose area the applicant has his home at the time of giving notice. The applicant must therefore have a home within England and Wales at the time of giving notice (*Re SL (Adoption: Home in Jurisdiction)* [2005] 1 FLR 118, FD). Notice, which must be in writing (s 144(1)), may be given by post (s 110). When notice has been given, the ability to remove the child from the home is governed by ss 36–40. Upon receipt of a s 44 notice in relation to a child from abroad living with non-agency prospective adopters, the local authority should immediately inform the DfE and clarify whether the intention to adopt was disclosed to an immigration officer. If it was not, or if the applicants are not able to produce written evidence of parental consent, or the applicants have not previously obtained a home study report, then any adoption application should be transferred to the High Court and listed for urgent directions before a judge (*Re R (Inter-Country Adoptions: Practice)* [1999] 1 FLR 1042, FD).

'appropriate local authority' (s 44(2))—The 'appropriate local authority' for the purpose of a s 44 notice either, where the applicant(s) no longer have a home in England or Wales, the authority where they last had such a home, or (in any other case) the authority for the area in which the applicants are living at the time that the notice is given (The Local Authority (Adoption) (Miscellaneous Provisions) Regulations 2005, reg 3 and The Local Authority (Non-agency Adoptions) (Wales) Regulations 2005, reg 3).

45 Suitability of adopters

(1) Regulations under section 9 may make provision as to the matters to be taken into account by an adoption agency in determining, or making any report in respect of, the suitability of any persons to adopt a child.

(2) In particular, the regulations may make provision for the purpose of securing that, in determining the suitability of a couple to adopt a child, proper regard is had to the need for stability and permanence in their relationship.

Defined terms—'adoption agency': s 2(1); 'child': ss 49(5), 144; 'couple': s 144(4); 'regulations': s 144.
Adoption reports—See note to s 43.

The making of adoption orders

46 Adoption orders

(1) An adoption order is an order made by the court on an application under section 50 or 51 giving parental responsibility for a child to the adopters or adopter.

(2) The making of an adoption order operates to extinguish –

(a) the parental responsibility which any person other than the adopters or adopter has for the adopted child immediately before the making of the order,

(b) any order under the 1989 Act or the Children (Northern Ireland) Order 1995 (SI 1995/755 (NI 2)),

(c) any order under the Children (Scotland) Act 1995 other than an excepted order, and

(d) any duty arising by virtue of an agreement or an order of a court to make payments, so far as the payments are in respect of the adopted child's maintenance or upbringing for any period after the making of the adoption order.

PART II

'Excepted order' means an order under section 9, 11(1)(d) or 13 of the Children (Scotland) Act 1995 or an exclusion order within the meaning of section 76(1) of that Act.

(3) An adoption order –

(a) does not affect parental responsibility so far as it relates to any period before the making of the order, and

(b) in the case of an order made on an application under section 51(2) by the partner of a parent of the adopted child, does not affect the parental responsibility of that parent or any duties of that parent within subsection (2)(d).

(4) Subsection (2)(d) does not apply to a duty arising by virtue of an agreement –

(a) which constitutes a trust, or

(b) which expressly provides that the duty is not to be extinguished by the making of an adoption order.

(5) An adoption order may be made even if the child to be adopted is already an adopted child.

(6) Before making an adoption order, the court must consider whether there should be arrangements for allowing any person contact with the child; and for that purpose the court must consider any existing or proposed arrangements and obtain any views of the parties to the proceedings.

Modifications—Section 46(2) is modified for certain purposes by SI 2013/1465, art 17, Sch 1, para 9.

Defined terms—'the 1989 Act': s 2(5); 'adoption order': s 46(1); 'by virtue of': s 144; 'child': ss 49(5), 144; 'child to be adopted, adopted child': s 49(5); 'court': s 144; 'parental responsibility': s 3 of the 1989 Act; 'partner, in relation to a parent of a child': s 144(7).

Scope—This section describes the legal consequences of the making of an adoption order and makes it clear that a child may be adopted more than once. Once made, an adoption order is irrevocable save in wholly exceptional circumstances (*Re M (Minors) (Adoption)* [1991] 1 FLR 458, CA) or on the child's subsequent legitimation (s 55). In *Re V (Long-Term Fostering or Adoption)* [2014] 1 FLR 1009, CA, Black LJ set out a list of the material differences between long-term fostering and adoption to demonstrate that the two forms of placement cannot be equated in terms of the security that they offer.

Procedure for making an adoption application—The relevant procedure is contained in FPR 2010, Pt 14. Unlike proceedings under CA 1989, Pt IV, jurisdiction in decisions relating to adoption is not governed by Brussel IIA (*Re N (Adoption: Jurisdiction)* [2016] 1 FLR 621, CA) and turns on the establishment of one of the two conditions relating to the applicant(s) in ACA 2002, s 49. Where a child is habitually resident in another state, jurisdiction is determined in accord with Adoption (Inter-Country Aspects) Act 1999 and the AFER 2005.

'extinguish' (s 46(2))—One effect of this provision is that a natural parent ceases to be regarded as a parent under CA 1989, and can only apply for subsequent s 8 orders with the leave of the court (see CA 1989, ss 9, 10; *M v C and Calderdale Metropolitan Borough Council* [1993] 1 FLR 505, CA). A natural parent will require leave to apply for a child arrangements order post-adoption (see **Meaning of 'parent'** under CA 1989, s 10).

'any order under the 1989 Act' (s 46(2)(b))—If it is intended that a pre-adoption CA 1989 order (eg a s 8 child arrangements order) is to continue after adoption, a fresh order will have to be made after the adoption order.

Arrangements for contact (s 46(6))—From 22 April 2014, where a court is making or has made an adoption order for a child who has been placed for adoption by an adoption agency, or an agency was authorised to place the child for adoption, any contact arrangements will be governed by ACA 2002, s 51 (inserted by CFA 2014, s 9). In all other (non-agency) adoptions, contact arrangements will proceed either by agreement or may be regulated by a child arrangements order under CA 1989, s 8, but in such a case the case-law commentary noted under s 51A may still have relevance.

Effect of adoption—See ss 66–76. The court does not have an inherent power to set aside an adoption order, but an appeal may be allowed in an exceptional case where there has been a breach of natural justice against a natural parent (*Re K (Adoption and Wardship)* [1997] 2 FLR 221, CA; *Re B (Adoption: Jurisdiction to Set Aside)* [1995] 2 FLR 1, CA). The effect of setting aside an adoption order is that the legal position in respect of parental responsibility reverts to the status immediately preceding the adoption order (*Re W (Adoption Order: Set Aside and Leave to Oppose)* [2011] 1 FLR 2153, CA).

47 Conditions for making adoption orders

(1) An adoption order may not be made if the child has a parent or guardian unless one of the following three conditions is met; but this section is subject to section 52 (parental etc consent).

(2) The first condition is that, in the case of each parent or guardian of the child, the court is satisfied –

(a) that the parent or guardian consents to the making of the adoption order,

(b) that the parent or guardian has consented under section 20 (and has not withdrawn the consent) and does not oppose the making of the adoption order, or

(c) that the parent's or guardian's consent should be dispensed with.

(3) A parent or guardian may not oppose the making of an adoption order under subsection (2)(b) without the court's leave.

(4) The second condition is that –

(a) the child has been placed for adoption by an adoption agency with the prospective adopters in whose favour the order is proposed to be made,

(b) either –

(i) the child was placed for adoption with the consent of each parent or guardian and the consent of the mother was given when the child was at least six weeks old, or

(ii) the child was placed for adoption under a placement order, and

(c) no parent or guardian opposes the making of the adoption order.

(5) A parent or guardian may not oppose the making of an adoption order under the second condition without the court's leave.

(6) The third condition is that the child –

(a) is the subject of a Scottish permanence order which includes provision granting authority for the child to be adopted, or

(b) is free for adoption by virtue of an order made under Article 17(1) or 18(1) of the Adoption (Northern Ireland) Order 1987 (SI 1987/2203).

(7) The court cannot give leave under subsection (3) or (5) unless satisfied that there has been a change in circumstances since the consent of the parent or guardian was given or, as the case may be, the placement order was made.

(8) An adoption order may not be made in relation to a person who is or has been married.

(8A) An adoption order may not be made in relation to a person who is or has been a civil partner.

(9) An adoption order may not be made in relation to a person who has attained the age of 19 years.

(10) In this section, 'Scottish permanence order' means a permanence order under section 80 of the Adoption and Children (Scotland) Act 2007 (including a deemed permanence order having effect by virtue of article 13(1), 14(2), 17(1) or 19(2) of the Adoption and Children (Scotland) Act 2007 (Commencement No 4, Transitional and Savings Provisions) Order 2009 (SSI 2009/267)).

Amendments—CPA 2004, s 79(1),(3); SI 2011/1740.

Modifications—Section 47(6) modified for certain purposes (SI 2010/2469).

Defined terms—'adoption (in relation to Chapter 4 of Part 1)': s 66; 'adoption agency': s 2(1); 'adoption order': s 46(1); 'by virtue of': s 144; 'child': ss 49(5), 144; 'consent (in relation to making adoption orders or placing for adoption)': s 52; 'court', 'guardian': s 144; 'placement order': s 21; 'placing, or placed, for adoption': ss 18(5), 19(4).

Scope—If the child has a parent or guardian, an adoption order may only be made if one of three conditions is met. The first condition is based upon parental consent to adoption being either given or dispensed with. The second condition is based upon the fact that the child has been placed for adoption. The third condition relates to the child being free for adoption in Scotland or N Ireland or under an AA 1976 freezing order (ACA 2002, Sch 4). Where a parent has given an earlier consent to placement or to adoption (which has not been validly withdrawn), or there has been a placement order, the parent may only oppose the making of an adoption order if there has been a subsequent change of circumstances and the court gives leave to oppose (s 47(7)).

First condition: parental consent (s 47(2))—The court has jurisdiction to make an adoption order if it is satisfied in the case of each parent or guardian of the child:

(a) that the parent or guardian consents to the making of the adoption order:
- unconditionally; and
- with full understanding of what is involved; or

(b) that the parent or guardian has given advance consent to adoption under ACA 2002, s 20 (and has not withdrawn that consent) and does not oppose the making of the adoption order; or

(c) that the parent or guardian's consent should be dispensed with under one of the two statutory grounds in s 52.

A parent who has given advance consent to adoption may only oppose the adoption order if a court is satisfied that there has been a change of circumstances and has given leave to oppose (s 47(3),(7)).

PART II

It should be noted that, in the case of an application for an adoption order, the consent of the parent or guardian is required to the particular adoption order which the court is being asked to make (even if the identity of the applicants is not known to the parent).

The provisions of ACA 2002, s 1, which require the court to give paramount consideration to the welfare of the child throughout his life, apply to a decision upon whether consent should be dispensed with (s 1(7)).

Second condition: placed for adoption (s 47(4))—The court has jurisdiction to make an adoption order if it is satisfied that the child has been placed for adoption by an adoption agency and either:

(a) the child was placed for adoption with the consent of each parent or guardian and the consent of the mother was given when the child was at least 6 weeks old; or
(b) the child was placed for adoption under a placement order;

and no parent or guardian opposes the making of the adoption order.

Third Condition: Scotland and Northern Ireland (s 47(6))—A Scottish permanence order authorising adoption, or a Northern Ireland freeing for adoption order, are recognised in England and Wales and, if so, an adoption order may be made without re-determining the issue of parental consent (see ACA 2002, ss 105(2) and 106(2) and *Re A (Children: Scottish Adoptions)* [2017] EWHC 35 (Fam)).

Leave to oppose adoption (s 47(5))—Where the second condition applies, a parent may only oppose the adoption order if a court is satisfied that there has been a change of circumstances and has granted leave to oppose (s 47(5),(7)). This provision only applies to 'a parent or guardian'; any other person seeking to oppose adoption should issue a freestanding application seeking leave to apply for a child arrangement order or a special guardianship order (CA 1989, ss 8 or 14 and s 10(9)). For **'change in circumstances'** see note to s 24(3). Where a change of circumstances is established, the child's welfare must be the paramount consideration when deciding whether to grant leave under s 47(5) (*Re P (Adoption: Leave Provisions)* [2007] 2 FLR 1069, CA; as clarified in *M v Warwickshire County Council* [2008] 1 FLR 1093, CA). In *Re B-S (Adoption: Application of s 47(5))* [2014] 1 FLR 1035, CA, the Court of Appeal disapproved *Re W (Adoption Order: Set Aside and Leave to Oppose)* [2011] 1 FLR 2153, CA, which had required a 'stringent approach' with leave only being granted in 'exceptionally rare circumstances'. The common factors that the child is already placed with prospective adopters, or that much time has elapsed since placement, cannot of themselves act as a bar to an application for leave to oppose. The test should not be set too high, because parents should not be discouraged either from bettering themselves or from seeking to prevent the adoption of their child by the imposition of a test that is unachievable. At the second stage, assuming that the court has found that there has been a change of circumstances, the evaluation of the child's welfare must be carried out in the light of the Supreme Court's guidance in *Re B (Care Proceedings: Appeal)* [2013] 2 FLR 1075, SC. The court must take an appropriately long-term view and should not be deterred by the prospect of short-term disruption from making an order that would be in the child's best interests throughout his life; *Re B-S* (at [74]) held that in a s 47(5) application 10 factors must be considered. The key issue is whether the parent's ultimate prospects of success have solidity. The judge should bear in mind the past, the current state of affairs and what will or may happen in future (*Re W (Adoption Order: Leave to Oppose); Re H (Adoption Order: Application for Permission for Leave to Oppose)* [2014] 1 FLR 1266, CA).

Due process must be observed and documents relevant to the leave to oppose issue must be disclosed to the applicant parent (*Re T (Adoption Order)* [2013] 1 FLR 360, CA). If leave to oppose is given, the case can only be proved using the first condition. If leave to oppose is refused, the making of an adoption order and any 'celebration' hearing should be postponed until time to appeal the refusal has expired (*Re W; Re H* (above); *Re W (Adoption: Procedure: Conditions)* [2016] 1 FLR 454, CA).

Parent—Section 52(6) defines the term 'parent' as meaning, in relation to a child, 'a parent having parental responsibility for the child under the CA 1989'. The following people are therefore included within the meaning of 'parent' for the purposes of the Act:

- the child's natural mother (unless parental responsibility has been removed by order of a foreign court or a previous adoption order);
- the child's natural father:
  - (i) if he was married to the child's mother at the time of the child's birth;
  - (ii) if he subsequently married the child's mother (Legitimacy Act 1976, s 2; FLRA 1987);
  - (iii) if after 1 December 2003 he is registered as the child's father on the birth certificate (CA 1989, s 4);
  - (iv) if he has obtained an order granting him parental responsibility with respect to the child (CA 1989, ss 4(1), 11(1));
  - (v) if, before the commencement of CA 1989, he has obtained an order granting him parental rights and duties in respect of the child as that order will be deemed to be an order under CA 1989, s 4 granting him parental responsibility for the child;
  - (vi) if he has acquired parental responsibility for the child under a parental responsibility agreement made with the mother (CA 1989, s 4);
- the child's adoptive parent if he has been the subject of a previous adoption. (In those circumstances, the child's natural parents' consent would not be relevant).

Firm evidence is required to prove that a parent has died (*Re K (Adoption and Wardship)* [1997] 2 FLR 221, CA).

Where an order made in a foreign jurisdiction purports to remove the parental rights of a parent (including a mother), it will be for the court in England and Wales to determine whether the consequence of the order is that the parent no longer has parental responsibility for the child (the court will require expert evidence relating to the foreign jurisdiction) (*Re AMR (Adoption: Procedure)* [1999] 2 FLR 807, FD. See also *Re AGN (Adoption: Foreign Adoption)* [2000] 2 FLR 431, FD).

An application for leave to oppose adoption under s 47 is only available to 'a parent or guardian'. Any other person may seek to apply for a child arrangements order (concerning living arrangements) within adoption proceedings but must first apply for leave to do so under CA 1989, s 10(9) or ACA 2002, s 29(4) (*Re G (Adoption: Leave to Oppose)* [2014] 2 FLR 525, CA).

Father without parental responsibility—The consent of the father of a child, who was not married to the child's mother, or deemed to be so married, at the time of the child's birth is not required within adoption proceedings, unless he has obtained parental responsibility for the child. The term 'parent' within ACA 2002 means, in relation to a child, 'a parent having parental responsibility' for the child under CA 1989 (ACA 2002, s 52(6)).

A father without parental responsibility may be made a respondent to the adoption application (FPR 2010, r 14.3(3). See also *Re L (A Minor) (Adoption: Procedure)* [1991] 1 FLR 171, CA).

Where the father of the child does not have parental responsibility for the child and the father's identity is known to the adoption agency and the agency is satisfied it is appropriate to do so, the agency must (Adoption Agency Regulations 2005, reg 14) –

(a) carry out in respect of the father the requirements of Adoption Agency Regulations 2005, reg 14(1)(a),(b)(i) and (iii) and (c) as if they applied to him, unless the agency is satisfied that the requirements have been carried out in respect of the father by another agency; and
(b) ascertain so far as possible whether the father –
    (i) wishes to acquire parental responsibility for the child under CA 1989, s 4; or
    (ii) intends to apply for a child arrangements order with respect to the child under CA 1989, s 8 or, where the child is subject to a care order, an order under CA 1989, s 34.

Where there is doubt about the appropriateness of contacting the father, a direction from the court may be sought. In any event the court may direct that the father be given notice of any court proceedings; such a direction may be sought before issuing any proceedings (*Re C (Adoption: Disclosure to Father)* [2006] 2 FLR 589, FD; FPR 2010, r 14.21); such an application can be made under FPR 2010, Pt 19 rather than issuing care proceedings (*Re C (A Child) v XYZ County Council* [2008] 1 FLR 1294, CA). Where a mother, who alone knows his identity, continues to refuse to identify the father then there is in reality nothing more that can or should be done (*Re C (A Child) v XYZ County Council*, above).

As a matter of practice, where the father has established 'family life' with respect to the child (ECHR 1950, Art 8), the court is likely to give him notice of the proceedings unless there are strong reasons to the contrary (*Re H; Re G (Adoption: Consultation of Unmarried Fathers)* [2001] 1 FLR 646, FD; *Keegan v Ireland* (No 16969/90) (1994) 18 EHRR 342, ECHR).

Guardian—A child's 'guardian', for the purpose of adoption proceedings, has the same meaning as in CA 1989, and includes a special guardian (s 144(1)). The definition of 'guardian' does not automatically include the father without parental responsibility.

Where a person, or institution, has been appointed to be the child's guardian by an order made in a foreign jurisdiction, it is for the court in England and Wales to determine whether the 'guardian' is a guardian within the meaning of the adoption legislation and the court will require expert evidence relating to the foreign jurisdiction (*Re AMR (Adoption: Procedure)* [1999] 2 FLR 807, FD; *Re AGN (Adoption: Foreign Adoption)* [2000] 2 FLR 431, FD).

When considering whether a person or authority in another jurisdiction is or is not to be treated as a guardian under ACA 2002, ss 47 and 52, the court should consider (per *Re J (Adoption: Consent of Foreign Public Authority)* [2002] 2 FLR 618, FD):

- the extent to which that person's duties, rights and responsibilities equated to those of a person (a) who had parental responsibility in English Law; and (b) whose consent to an adoption order had to be given or dispensed with;
- having particular regard to the purposes of ss 47 and 52, whether in all the circumstances that person's consent to an adoption order should be given or dispensed with before an adoption order was made.

Form and proof of consent—The relevant consent of a parent or guardian must be given in the relevant form required by FPR PD5A (Forms A100–A106) or a form to like effect (FPR 2010, r 14.10(1)). A document signifying consent that is witnessed in accordance with the rules is admissible as proof of the signature of the person giving consent without further proof (ACA 2002, s 104(1)).

Intercountry adoptions—For detailed guidance on intercountry adoptions, go to *www.gov.uk/government/uploads/system/uploads/attachment_data/file/270102/annex_c_adoptions_with_a_foreign_element.pdf*. On being notified of a foreign child's presence a local authority should immediately attempt to contact the natural parents to ascertain their views; if it appears that natural parents do not consent, the local authority should immediately inform the DfE and the Home Office; where the applicants cannot produce written parental consent to adoption (and a certified English translation), the application should be transferred to the High Court for urgent directions; there should be personal service on the natural parents (if necessary via the relevant British Embassy); the children's guardian should make early contact with the natural parents; where it appears that the natural parents oppose the adoption the court should consider dismissing the application summarily at an early directions hearing.

Dispensing with consent (s 47(2)(c))—See notes to s 52.

Adoption order not available over the age of 19 years (s 47(9))—An adoption application must be made before the person to be adopted's 18th birthday (s 49(4)) but the order may be made after that date but before the 19th birthday. See **'attained the age of'** under s 50.

Child under 6 weeks (s 47(4)(b)(i))—It is possible validly to place a child for adoption with maternal consent at under 6 weeks old, but s 47(4)(b)(i) expressly provides that such consent is not sufficient to satisfy the second ('placed for adoption') condition; consequently the adoption application will be under the first condition (with parental consent being determined at the time of that hearing) (*Local Authority v GC* [2009] 1 FLR 299, FD).

PART II

48 Restrictions on making adoption orders

(1) The court may not hear an application for an adoption order in relation to a child, where a previous application to which subsection (2) applies made in relation to the child by the same persons was refused by any court, unless it appears to the court that, because of a change in circumstances or for any other reason, it is proper to hear the application.

(2) This subsection applies to any application –

(a) for an adoption order or a Scottish or Northern Irish adoption order, or

(b) for an order for adoption made in the Isle of Man or any of the Channel Islands.

Defined terms—'adoption (in relation to Chapter 4 of Part 1)': s 66; 'adoption order': s 46(1); 'child': ss 49(5), 144; 'court', 'Northern Irish adoption order': s 144.

Procedure in respect of ACA 2002, s 48—If s 48 applies, as soon as practicable after an adoption application has been issued, the court must consider whether it is proper to hear the application (FPR 2010, r 14.6(1)(a)(i)).

49 Applications for adoption

(1) An application for an adoption order may be made by –

(a) a couple, or

(b) one person,

but only if it is made under section 50 or 51 and one of the following conditions is met.

(2) The first condition is that at least one of the couple (in the case of an application under section 50) or the applicant (in the case of an application under section 51) is domiciled in a part of the British Islands.

(3) The second condition is that both of the couple (in the case of an application under section 50) or the applicant (in the case of an application under section 51) have been habitually resident in a part of the British Islands for a period of not less than one year ending with the date of the application.

(4) An application for an adoption order may only be made if the person to be adopted has not attained the age of 18 years on the date of the application.

(5) References in this Act to a child, in connection with any proceedings (whether or not concluded) for adoption, (such as 'child to be adopted' or 'adopted child') include a person who has attained the age of 18 years before the proceedings are concluded.

Defined terms—'British Islands': Interpretation Act 1978, Sch 1; 'adoption (in relation to Chapter 4 of Part 1)': s 66; 'adoption order': s 46(1); 'child': ss 49(5), 144; 'child to be adopted, adopted child': s 49(5); 'couple': s 144(4).

Conditions precedent to making an adoption application (s 49)—An adoption order may only be made if the circumstances comply with either s 50 (adoption by couple) or s 51 (adoption by one person) and one of the two conditions in this section relating to domicile or habitual residence is met. For discussion of 'domicile', see under DMPA 1973, s 5 below.

First condition: domicile (s 49(2))—At least one of the couple, or the single applicant, must be domiciled in a part of the British Islands.

Second condition: habitual residence (s 49(3))—As an alternative to the first condition, both of the couple, or the single applicant, must have been habitually resident in a part of the British Islands for a period of not less than 1 year before making the application. See also **Habitual residence** under CACA 1985, Sch 1, Art 4, below.

Adoption of a person aged over 18 years (s 49(4) and (5))—An adoption application must be made before the person to be adopted's 18th birthday (s 49(4)) but the order may be made after that date but before the 19th birthday. See **'attained the age of'** under s 50.

50 Adoption by couple

(1) An adoption order may be made on the application of a couple where both of them have attained the age of 21 years.

(2) An adoption order may be made on the application of a couple where –

(a) one of the couple is the mother or the father of the person to be adopted and has attained the age of 18 years, and

(b) the other has attained the age of 21 years.

Defined terms—'adoption (in relation to Chapter 4 of Part 1)': s 66; 'adoption order': s 46(1); 'couple': s 144(4).

'a couple' (s 50)—In ACA 2002 'a couple' means a married couple, or civil partners or two people (whether of differing sexes or the same sex) living as partners in an enduring family relationship (s 144(4)). Two people, one of whom is the other's parent, grandparent, sister, brother, aunt or uncle, are not 'a couple' for these purposes (s 144(5),(6)). Potential adopters require assessment in accordance with the Suitability of Adopters Regulations 2005.

'attained the age of' (s 50(1),(2))—Age is attained at the commencement of the relevant anniversary of the person's date of birth (FLRA 1969, s 9(1)).

'father' (s 50(2)(a))—The term 'parent' is restricted to a parent with parental responsibility for the limited purpose of the consent provisions (s 52(3),(6)); it therefore seems that the term 'father' in s 50 includes a father without parental responsibility.

Validity of the marriage or civil partnership—The validity of the applicant's marriage is a factor which the court will consider. Documentary evidence of their marriage must be filed with the application (FPR PD5A, Form A58). The adoption agency is required to report on the applicant's marital status and the stability of their relationship, together with details of any previous marriages (FPR PD14C). The court may make an adoption order in favour of married applicants even where the couple have separated after the adoption application has been issued (*Re WM (Adoption: Non-patrial)* [1997] 1 FLR 132, FD). If an adoption order is made in favour of a couple whose marriage is later found to be bigamous, the adoption order will be regarded as valid until the court makes an order setting it aside (*Re F (Infants) (Adoption Order: Validity)* [1977] Fam 165, CA).

Step-parents—Although the statutory provisions relating to welfare (ACA 2002, s 1) and parental consent (s 52) apply in equal measure to all categories of adoption application, the manner in which they are applied will, in part, differ depending upon the impact that the proposed adoption will have on the ECHR, Art 8 rights of the children and their parents. Proportionality is the key to the approach to evaluating the needs of a child's welfare throughout his life; the degree of intervention that non-consensual stranger adoption represents may differ from a step-parent adoption within a well-established family unit in terms of evaluating proportionality (*Re P (Step-Parent Adoption)* [2015] 1 FLR 1327, CA).

Where an adoption application is made by a step-parent, the approach of the ECHR in *Söderbäck v Sweden* [1999] 1 FLR 250, ECHR should be applied according to the facts of each case (*Re P*, above). In doing so, the following central points are likely to be important:

(a) there is a distinction to be drawn between adoption in the context of compulsory, permanent placement outside the family against the wishes of parents and a step-parent adoption where, by definition, the child is remaining in the care of one or other of his parents;
(b) factors that are likely to reduce the degree of interference with the Art 8 rights of the child and the non-consenting parent ('Parent B'), and thereby make it more likely that adoption is a proportionate measure, are:
   (i) where Parent B has not had the care of the child or otherwise asserted his or her responsibility for the child;
   (ii) where Parent B has had only infrequent or no contact with the child;
   (iii) where there is a particularly well-established family unit in the home of the parent and step-parent in which 'de facto' family ties have existed for a significant period.

51 Adoption by one person

(1) An adoption order may be made on the application of one person who has attained the age of 21 years and is not married or a civil partner.

(2) An adoption order may be made on the application of one person who has attained the age of 21 years if the court is satisfied that the person is the partner of a parent of the person to be adopted.

(3) An adoption order may be made on the application of one person who has attained the age of 21 years and is married if the court is satisfied that –

(a) the person's spouse cannot be found,
(b) the spouses have separated and are living apart, and the separation is likely to be permanent, or
(c) the person's spouse is by reason of ill-health, whether physical or mental, incapable of making an application for an adoption order.

(3A) An adoption order may be made on the application of one person who has attained the age of 21 years and is a civil partner if the court is satisfied that –

(a) the person's civil partner cannot be found,
(b) the civil partners have separated and are living apart, and the separation is likely to be permanent, or
(c) the person's civil partner is by reason of ill-health, whether physical or mental, incapable of making an application for an adoption order.

(4) An adoption order may not be made on an application under this section by the mother or the father of the person to be adopted unless the court is satisfied that –

(a) the other natural parent is dead or cannot be found,
(b) by virtue of the provisions specified in subsection (5), there is no other parent, or
(c) there is some other reason justifying the child's being adopted by the applicant alone,

and, where the court makes an adoption order on such an application, the court must record that it is satisfied as to the fact mentioned in paragraph (a) or (b) or, in the case of paragraph (c), record the reason.

(5) The provisions referred to in subsection (4)(b) are –

(a) section 28 of the Human Fertilisation and Embryology Act 1990 (disregarding subsections (5A) to (5I) of that section), or
(b) sections 34 to 47 of the Human Fertilisation and Embryology Act 2008 (disregarding sections 39, 40 and 46 of that Act).

Amendments—CPA 2004, s 79(1),(4),(5); Human Fertilisation and Embryology (Deceased Fathers) Act 2003, s 2(1), Sch, para 18; HFEA 2008, Sch 6, para 39.

Defined terms: 'partner', s 144(7); 'adoption (in relation to Chapter 4 of Part 1)': s 66; 'adoption order': s 46(1); 'by virtue of': s 144; 'child': ss 49(5), 144; 'court': s 144.

Adoption by one person (s 51)—A sole applicant may obtain an adoption order if he is over 21 years old and if:

(a) he is neither married nor a civil partner; or
(b) he is the partner of a parent of one of the child's parent (in which case he is the sole adopter, but that parent's status and parental responsibility is not affected by the adoption (ss 46(3)(b), 67(2)); or
(c) he is married or a civil partner but the spouse or partner cannot be found or is for health reasons incapable of applying, or the couple are permanently separated.

'attained the age of' (s 51)—See note to s 50. The age limit of 21 years applies to all sole applicants, even if they are the child's mother or father.

Adoption by parent (s 51(4))—Where the applicant relies upon 'some other reason justifying the child's being adopted by the applicant alone', that reason must be sufficient to outweigh the adverse consequences an adoption order may have by reason of the exclusion of the other parent from the child's life. The other reason, which is likely to be exceptional, and which will depend on the circumstances of each case, does not have to be comparable with the death or disappearance of the other parent. Before making an order, the court must consider alternative orders under CA 1989; an adoption order is not to be used simply to prevent inappropriate intervention by the other parent (*Re B (Adoption: Natural Parent)* [2002] 1 FLR 196, HL). For entitlement to property on such an adoption, see s 67(4).

Post-adoption contact

51A Post-adoption contact

(1) This section applies where –

(a) an adoption agency has placed or was authorised to place a child for adoption, and
(b) the court is making or has made an adoption order in respect of the child.

(2) When making the adoption order or at any time afterwards, the court may make an order under this section –

(a) requiring the person in whose favour the adoption order is or has been made to allow the child to visit or stay with the person named in the order under this section, or for the person named in that order and the child otherwise to have contact with each other, or
(b) prohibiting the person named in the order under this section from having contact with the child.

(3) The following people may be named in an order under this section –

(a) any person who (but for the child's adoption) would be related to the child by blood (including half-blood), marriage or civil partnership;
(b) any former guardian of the child;
(c) any person who had parental responsibility for the child immediately before the making of the adoption order;
(d) any person who was entitled to make an application for an order under section 26 in

respect of the child (contact with children placed or to be placed for adoption) by virtue of subsection (3)(c), (d) or (e) of that section;

(e) any person with whom the child has lived for a period of at least one year.

(4) An application for an order under this section may be made by –

(a) a person who has applied for the adoption order or in whose favour the adoption order is or has been made,

(b) the child, or

(c) any person who has obtained the court's leave to make the application.

(5) In deciding whether to grant leave under subsection (4)(c), the court must consider –

(a) any risk there might be of the proposed application disrupting the child's life to such an extent that he or she would be harmed by it (within the meaning of the 1989 Act),

(b) the applicant's connection with the child, and

(c) any representations made to the court by –

(i) the child, or

(ii) a person who has applied for the adoption order or in whose favour the adoption order is or has been made.

(6) When making an adoption order, the court may on its own initiative make an order of the type mentioned in subsection (2)(b).

(7) The period of one year mentioned in subsection (3)(e) need not be continuous but must not have begun more than five years before the making of the application.

(8) Where this section applies, an order under section 8 of the 1989 Act may not make provision about contact between the child and any person who may be named in an order under this section.

Amendments—Inserted by CFA 2014, s 9.

Post-adoption contact—Before making an adoption order the court must consider whether there should be arrangements for allowing any person contact with the child (ACA 2002, s 46(6)). ACA 2002, s 51A only applies where a court is making, or has made, an adoption order following placement for adoption by an adoption agency; in all other cases, provision for post-adoption contact will be made under a CA 1989, s 8 child arrangements order. In addition to the statutory requirements contained in s 51A, the existing case-law will continue to be relevant. Where adopters are willing to agree to contact, it is unnecessary to make an order that binds the adopters to their agreement (*Re T (Adoption: Contact)* [1995] 2 FLR 251, CA). A child arrangements order made in relation to an adopted child is made under CA 1989, s 8 and is governed by the welfare checklist in CA 1989, s 1(3). In consequence, *Re P (Placement Orders: Parental Consent)* [2008] 2 FLR 625, CA relating to contact under a placement order does not affect the application and the approach described in *Re R (Adoption: Contact)* [2006] 1 FLR 373, CA should be followed to the effect that it is 'extremely unusual' to impose on adoptive parents some obligation that they are unwilling, voluntarily, to assume (*Oxfordshire County Council v X, Y and J* [2011] 1 FLR 272, CA).

Adoption orders and any arrangements for contact are intended to be permanent and final; it is therefore incompatible with that intention for known potential issues for contact to be left unresolved when making an adoption order (*X and Y v A Local Authority (Adoption: Procedure)* [2009] 2 FLR 984, FD).

In *Re G (Adoption: Contact)* [2003] 1 FLR 270, CA, Ward LJ summarised the modern approach to contact and adoption:

> 'the benefit [of contact] ... comes from the children simply knowing who the natural parental figures are. It is to remove the sense of ogre, as they reach adolescence and begin to search for their own identity, with the double crisis not only of adolescence itself but of coming to grips with the fact that they are adopted. That is why current research is in favour of some contact in adoption.'

In *Down Lisburn Health and Social Services Trust v H* [2007] 1 FLR 121, HL, the House of Lords reviewed the approach to post-adoption contact.

Once an adoption order has been made, a fundamental question such as contact, even if confined to indirect contact, should only be subsequently reopened if there is some fundamental change in circumstances (*Re C (A Minor) (Adopted Child: Contact)* [1993] 2 FLR 431, FD). In some cases, it may be necessary to transfer the case to the High Court, but that should not be the general rule; an application for leave to apply for contact should be served on the adoption agency (*Re T (Adopted Children: Contact)* [1995] 2 FLR 792, CA). A natural family member, in order to obtain leave to apply for contact, must satisfy the court that any decision of the adopters to oppose contact is sufficiently contrary to the best interests of the child, or sufficiently unreasonable, to warrant the court overriding the discretion concerning contact conferred on the adopters by the adoption order (*Re T (Adoption: Contact)* [2011] 1 FLR 1805, CA). Leave to apply is likely to be granted where adopters totally resile from an earlier agreement on contact (*Re R (Adoption: Contact)* [2006] 1 FLR 373, CA).

51B Orders under section 51A: supplementary

(1) An order under section 51A –

(a) may contain directions about how it is to be carried into effect,
(b) may be made subject to any conditions the court thinks appropriate,
(c) may be varied or revoked by the court on an application by the child, a person in whose favour the adoption order was made or a person named in the order, and
(d) has effect until the child's 18th birthday, unless revoked.

(2) Subsection (3) applies to proceedings –

(a) on an application for an adoption order in which –
   (i) an application is made for an order under section 51A, or
   (ii) the court indicates that it is considering making such an order on its own initiative;
(b) on an application for an order under section 51A;
(c) on an application for such an order to be varied or revoked.

(3) The court must (in the light of any rules made by virtue of subsection (4)) –

(a) draw up a timetable with a view to determining without delay whether to make, (or as the case may be) vary or revoke an order under section 51A, and
(b) give directions for the purpose of ensuring, so far as is reasonably practicable, that that timetable is adhered to.

(4) Rules of court may –

(a) specify periods within which specified steps must be taken in relation to proceedings to which subsection (3) applies, and
(b) make other provision with respect to such proceedings for the purpose of ensuring, so far as is reasonably practicable, that the court makes determinations about orders under section 51A without delay.

Amendments—Inserted by CFA 2014, s 9.

Placement and adoption: general

52 Parental etc consent

(1) The court cannot dispense with the consent of any parent or guardian of a child to the child being placed for adoption or to the making of an adoption order in respect of the child unless the court is satisfied that –

(a) the parent or guardian cannot be found or lacks capacity (within the meaning of the Mental Capacity Act 2005) to give consent, or
(b) the welfare of the child requires the consent to be dispensed with.

(2) The following provisions apply to references in this Chapter to any parent or guardian of a child giving or withdrawing –

(a) consent to the placement of a child for adoption, or
(b) consent to the making of an adoption order (including a future adoption order).

(3) Any consent given by the mother to the making of an adoption order is ineffective if it is given less than six weeks after the child's birth.

(4) The withdrawal of any consent to the placement of a child for adoption, or of any consent given under section 20, is ineffective if it is given after an application for an adoption order is made.

(5) 'Consent' means consent given unconditionally and with full understanding of what is involved; but a person may consent to adoption without knowing the identity of the persons in whose favour the order will be made.

(6) 'Parent' (except in subsections (9) and (10) below) means a parent having parental responsibility.

(7) Consent under section 19 or 20 must be given in the form prescribed by rules, and the rules may prescribe forms in which a person giving consent under any other provision of this Part may do so (if he wishes).

(8) Consent given under section 19 or 20 must be withdrawn –

(a) in the form prescribed by rules, or
(b) by notice given to the agency.

(9) Subsection (10) applies if –

(a) an agency has placed a child for adoption under section 19 in pursuance of consent given by a parent of the child, and
(b) at a later time, the other parent of the child acquires parental responsibility for the child.

(10) The other parent is to be treated as having at that time given consent in accordance with this section in the same terms as those in which the first parent gave consent.

Amendments—MCA 2005, s 67(1), Sch 6, para 45.

Defined terms—'adoption (in relation to Chapter 4 of Part 1)': s 66; 'adoption order': s 46(1); 'child': ss 49(5), 144; 'consent (in relation to making adoption orders or placing for adoption)': s 52; 'court', 'guardian', 'notice': s 144; 'parental responsibility': s 3 of the 1989 Act; 'placing, or placed, for adoption': ss 18(5), 19(4); 'rules': s 144; 'lacks capacity': MCA 2005, s 2.

Dispensing with consent (s 52(1))—Dispensing with agreement involves the court in a two-stage process:

(a) is adoption in the best interests of the child?
(b) If so, is a ground for dispensing with agreement established?

The English law permitting non-consensual adoption is not incompatible with the ECHR (*Re CB (A Child) (No 2) (Adoption Proceedings: Vienna Convention)* [2016] 1 FLR 1286, CA).

Parent—See note to s 47.

Father without parental responsibility—See note to s 47.

Guardian—See note to s 47.

'cannot be found' (s 52(1)(a))—To satisfy this ground, every reasonable effort should be made to contact the parent, for example via the extended family, last known address, the Post Office, DWP, housing authority, advertising or use of social media (*Re T (A Child)* [2017] EWFC 19). Where an adoption order is made on this ground, it may be set aside if the parent later comes forward (*Re T (Adoption Order: Leave to Appeal)* [1995] 3 FCR 299). Where to make contact with a mother in another jurisdiction might expose her, or the applicants, to adverse consequences, this ground may be established (*Re A (Adoption of a Russian Child)* [2000] 1 FLR 539).

'welfare of the child requires the consent to be dispensed with' (s 52(1)(b))—The question for the court on this point is not 'is adoption in the child's best interests?', but 'does the child's welfare require consent to adoption to be dispensed with?'. In *Re P (Placement Orders: Parental Consent)* [2008] 2 FLR 625, CA, the Court of Appeal held that the word 'requires' has a connotation of the imperative (i e what is demanded rather than what is merely optional or reasonable or desirable). What has to be shown is that the child's welfare throughout his life 'requires' adoption as opposed to something short of adoption. A child's circumstances may 'require' statutory intervention, perhaps may even 'require' the indefinite or long-term removal of the child from the family and his or her placement with strangers, but that is not to say that the same circumstances will necessarily 'require' that the child be adopted. The question, at the end of the day, is whether what is 'required' is adoption. But this does not mean that there is some enhanced welfare test to be applied in cases of adoption. The vital difference is simply that between s 1 of the 1989 Act and s 1 of the 2002 Act. In *Re B (Care Proceedings: Appeal)* [2013] 2 FLR 1075, SC, the Supreme Court emphasised the need for proportionality when the court examines whether or not to sanction the placement of a child for adoption. Such a course should only be approved 'as a last resort – when all else fails'; 'the court must be satisfied that there is no practical way of the authorities (or others) providing the requisite assistance and support' [per Lord Neuberger at [104] and [105] and where the child's welfare dictates that 'nothing else will do' [per Baroness Hale at [145], [198] and [214].

In *Re B-S (Adoption: Application of s 47(5))* [2014] 1 FLR 1035, CA, the Court of Appeal stressed the following three points drawn from the Supreme Court decision in *Re B (Care Proceedings: Appeal)* [2013] 2 FLR 1075, SC:

- although the child's interests are paramount, a court must never lose sight of the fact that those interests include being brought up by the natural family, unless the overriding requirements of the child's welfare make that not possible;
- the court must consider all of the realistic options before coming to a decision; and
- the court's assessment of a parent's ability to provide good enough care for a child must take into account the assistance and support that the authorities would offer.

The court in *Re B-S* held that the following two elements are 'essential' when a court is being asked to approve a care plan for adoption and to make a non-consensual placement order or adoption order:

(i) there must be proper evidence from the local authority and from the children's guardian that addresses all the realistic options that are realistically possible and that contains an analysis of the arguments for and against each option; and
(ii) there must be an adequately reasoned judgment by the judge.

In *Re R* [2015] 1 FLR 715, CA, the Court of Appeal gave guidance on the interpretation of *Re B-S* and stressed that the key principle for a local authority and for the court is that the child's welfare is the paramount consideration following evaluation in the context of the welfare checklist in ACA 2002, s 1(4). An option is not 'realistic' if it is plainly not one that would have any real prospect of being chosen if a full welfare evaluation of all the pros and cons were undertaken (*Re S (Care Proceedings: Evaluation of Grandmother)* [2016] 1 FLR 109, CA).

Judges should avoid a 'linear' analysis (as described by McFarlane LJ in *Re G (A Child)* [2014] 1 FLR 670, CA) in favour of a 'global, holistic evaluation' of the options available for the child (i e 'an old fashioned welfare balancing exercise' (*Re F (A Child) (International Relocation Cases)* [2017] 1 FLR 979, CA)). The phrase 'nothing else will do' is not to be used as a substitute for undertaking a full welfare analysis (*Re W (A Child)* [2016] EWCA Civ 793). Where, despite focused case management directions, the court does not have the kind of evidence described as 'essential' in *Re B-S*, it will not be properly equipped to decide the important adoption issue and the case must be adjourned, even where this will cause the timetable to exceed 26 weeks.

Where a court considers that adoption will only benefit a child if a number of strict requirements are satisfied, it is unlikely that the court will be able to hold that parental consent to the making of a placement order can be dispensed with on the basis that the child's welfare 'requires' adoption (*Re A (Placement Order: Imposition of Conditions on Adoption)* [2014] 2 FLR 351, CA).

Form and proof of consent—See note to s 47.

Intercountry adoption—See note to s 47.

Procedure for dispensing with consent (FPR 2010, r 14.9)—Where the applicant is asking the court to dispense with the consent of any parent or guardian of a child to:

- the child being placed for adoption;
- the making of an adoption order (except a Convention adoption order); or
- the making of an order facilitating the adoption of the child abroad (ACA 2002, s 84)

the applicant must:

(a) give notice of the request in the application form or at any later stage by filing a written request setting out the reasons for the request; and

(b) file a statement of facts file setting out a summary of the history of the case and any other facts to satisfy the court of the ground(s) relied upon to dispense with consent.

On receipt of the notice a court officer will inform the parent or guardian of the request and send a copy of the statement of facts to them and to any children's guardian, reporting officer or children and family reporter.

If the application relates to the parent being incapable of giving consent, the court must consider whether to appoint a litigation friend for the parent or guardian under FPR 2010, Pt 15.

53 Modification of 1989 Act and 2014 Act in relation to adoption

(1) Where –

(a) a local authority are authorised to place a child for adoption, or

(b) a child who has been placed for adoption by a local authority is less than six weeks old,

regulations may provide for the following provisions to apply with modifications, or not to apply, in relation to the child.

(2) The provisions are –

(a) section 22(4)(b), (c) and (d) and (5)(b) of the 1989 Act (duty to ascertain wishes and feelings of certain persons);

(b) sections 6(4)(b) and 78(3)(a) of the 2014 Act (duty to ascertain wishes and feelings of certain persons);

(c) paragraphs 15 and 21 of Schedule 2 to the 1989 Act (promoting contact with parents and parents' obligations to contribute towards maintenance);

(d) section 95 of and paragraph 1 of Schedule 1 to the 2014 Act (promoting contact with parents and parents' obligations to contribute towards maintenance).

(3) Where a registered adoption society is authorised to place a child for adoption or a child who has been placed for adoption by a registered adoption society is less than six weeks old, regulations may provide –

(a) for section 61 of the 1989 Act to have effect in relation to the child whether or not he is accommodated by or on behalf of the society,

(b) for subsections (2)(b) to (d) and (3)(b) of that section (duty to ascertain wishes and feelings of certain persons) to apply with modifications, or not to apply, in relation to the child.

(4) Where a child's home is with persons who have given notice of intention to adopt, no contribution is payable (whether under a contribution order or otherwise) under Part 3 of Schedule 2 to the 1989 Act (contributions towards maintenance of children looked after by local

authorities) or under Schedule 1 to the 2014 Act (contributions towards maintenance of looked after children) in respect of the period referred to in subsection (5).

(5) That period begins when the notice of intention to adopt is given and ends if –

(a) the period of four months beginning with the giving of the notice expires without the prospective adopters applying for an adoption order, or

(b) an application for such an order is withdrawn or refused.

(6) In this section, 'notice of intention to adopt' includes notice of intention to apply for a Scottish or Northern Irish adoption order.

Amendments—SI 2016/413.

Defined terms—'the 1989 Act': s 2(5); 'adoption (in relation to Chapter 4 of Part 1)': s 66; 'adoption order': s 46(1); 'adoption society': s 2(5); 'child': ss 49(5), 144; 'local authority', 'Northern Irish adoption order', 'notice': s 144; 'notice of intention to adopt': s 44(2); 'placing, or placed, for adoption': ss 18(5), 19(4); 'registered adoption society': s 2(2); 'regulations': s 144.

PART II

54 Disclosing information during adoption process

Regulations under section 9 may require adoption agencies in prescribed circumstances to disclose in accordance with the regulations prescribed information to prospective adopters.

Defined terms—'adoption (in relation to Chapter 4 of Part 1)': s 66; 'information', 'regulations': s 144.

55 Revocation of adoptions on legitimation

(1) Where any child adopted by one natural parent as sole adoptive parent subsequently becomes a legitimated person on the marriage of the natural parents, the court by which the adoption order was made may, on the application of any of the parties concerned, revoke the order.

(2) *(repealed)*

Amendments—Courts Act 2003, s 109(1), Sch 8, para 412; CCA 2013, s 17, Sch 11.

Defined terms—'adoption (in relation to Chapter 4 of Part 1)': s 66; 'adoption order': s 46(1); 'child': ss 49(5), 144; 'court': s 144.

Procedure—An application to revoke an adoption order under s 55 is governed by FPR 2010, Pt 18.

****

Chapter 4

Status of Adopted Children

66 Meaning of adoption in Chapter 4

(1) In this Chapter 'adoption' means –

(a) adoption by an adoption order or a Scottish or Northern Irish adoption order,

(b) adoption by an order made in the Isle of Man or any of the Channel Islands,

(c) an adoption effected under the law of a Convention country outside the British Islands, and certified in pursuance of Article 23(1) of the Convention (referred to in this Act as a 'Convention adoption'),

(d) an overseas adoption, or

(e) an adoption recognised by the law of England and Wales and effected under the law of any other country;

and related expressions are to be interpreted accordingly.

(2) But references in this Chapter to adoption do not include an adoption effected before the day on which this Chapter comes into force (referred to in this Chapter as 'the appointed day').

(3) Any reference in an enactment to an adopted person within the meaning of this Chapter includes a reference to an adopted child within the meaning of Part 4 of the Adoption Act 1976.

Defined terms—'adoption (in relation to Chapter 4 of Part 1)': s 66; 'adoption order': s 46(1); 'appointed day (in relation to Chapter 4 of Part 1)': s 66(2); 'child': ss 49(5), 144; 'child to be adopted, adopted child': s 49(5); 'the Convention': s 144; 'Convention adoption': s 66(1)(c); 'Convention country', 'enactment', 'Northern Irish adoption order': s 144; 'overseas adoption': s 87.

Pre-30 December 2005 adoptions—For adoptions effected before 30 December 2005, AA 1976, Pt IV remains in force (ACA 2002, Sch 5).

'Convention adoption' (s 66(1)(c))—A Convention adoption is an adoption within the terms of the 1993 Hague Convention on Protection of Children and Co-operation with respect to Intercountry Adoption (see Adoption (Intercountry Aspects) Act 1999, Sch 1). The Convention is essentially a framework setting out minimum standards for the control and regulation of the flow of children between states for adoption. It has been signed, ratified or acceded to by 69 Member States (for an up-to-date list of Convention States, see *www.hcch.net/index_en.php?act=conventions.status&cid=69*). The Hague Convention aims to ensure that intercountry adoption takes place in the best interests of the child, puts in place a system of co-operation between those states that have implemented the Convention, and ensures that adoption orders made under the Convention are recognised in all Hague Convention countries. Anyone wishing to adopt under the Hague Convention in the UK must comply with AFER 2005, Pt 3, Ch 1.

The UK Government has issued advisory guidance on Convention adoptions (available at *www.gov.uk/government/uploads/system/uploads/attachment_data/file/270102/annex_c_adoptions_with_a_foreign_element.pdf*).

'overseas adoption' (s 66(1)(d))—An 'overseas adoption' (as defined in ACA 2002, s 87(1)) ranks automatically as an adoption order, without the need to institute court proceedings. Specification of overseas adoptions has been made by the Adoption (Recognition of Overseas Adoptions) Regulations 2013. The Regulations cover adoptions made by statute law (and not customary or common law) in any of 87 countries named in the Schedule (not set out here).

'an adoption recognised by the law of England and Wales' (s 66(1)(e))—The relevant procedure is based on FLA 1986, s 57 (*Re G (Recognition of Brazilian Adoption)* [2015] 1 FLR 1402, FD). The effect of recognition is that the foreign adoption will rank as an adoption, so far as it relates to the status of the child, as if it had been made by an adoption order in England and Wales. Certain adoptions made in a jurisdiction outside England and Wales are recognised automatically as being adoption orders, without the need to initiate court proceedings either to obtain an adoption order or to establish the status of the adoption order made abroad.

The following are automatically recognised adoption orders:

(a) adoption orders made in Scotland, Northern Ireland, Isle of Man or the Channel Islands;
(b) 'overseas adoptions' (see note above);
(c) Convention adoption orders.

Any other adoption order made abroad will only be recognised as valid in England and Wales if it satisfies the criteria for recognition at common law. The key questions when considering whether or not to recognise a foreign adoption under common law are:

(a) Was/were the adoptive parent(s) domiciled in the foreign country at the time of the foreign adoption?
(b) Was the adoption obtained wholly lawfully in the foreign jurisdiction?
(c) If so, did the concept of adoption in that jurisdiction substantially conform with the English concept? and
(d) If so, was there any public policy consideration that should mitigate against recognition?

The child's welfare is not a relevant factor in determining recognition.
(*Re N (A Child)* [2016] EWHC 3085 (Fam).)

'Overseas adoptions' or Convention adoptions may be registered as adoptions by application to the Registrar General under Adopted Children and Adoption Contact Registers Regulations 2005 (ACA 2002, Sch 1, para 3(5)).

A foreign adoption which is neither automatically recognised, nor recognised at common law, will not be treated as a valid adoption. In those circumstances, it will be necessary for an application for an adoption order to be made in England and Wales.

Application to court for declaration as to status of adopted child—Any person whose status as an adopted child of any person depends on whether he has been validly adopted by that person by either a Convention adoption, an overseas adoption or an adoption recognised at common law may apply to the court for a declaration that the applicant either is or is not, for the purposes of ACA 2002, s 66, the adopted child of that person (FLA 1986, s 57(1),(2)). The application is made under the FPR 2010, Pt 19 procedure in the High Court or the County Court (FPR 2010, rr 8.18–8.21) (see also under those rules)). The fact that the 'child' has been adopted and is now an adult, does not prevent a court making a declaration of parentage with regard to the adopted person's natural father; indeed, the modern approach to adoption would support an adopted person having full and sound information about their background (*M v W (Declaration of Parentage)* [2007] 2 FLR 270, FD).

67 Status conferred by adoption

(1) An adopted person is to be treated in law as if born as the child of the adopters or adopter.

(2) An adopted person is the legitimate child of the adopters or adopter and, if adopted by –

(a) a couple, or
(b) one of a couple under section 51(2),

is to be treated as the child of the relationship of the couple in question.

(3) An adopted person –

(a) if adopted by one of a couple under section 51(2), is to be treated in law as not being the child of any person other than the adopter and the other one of the couple, and

(b) in any other case, is to be treated in law, subject to subsection (4), as not being the child of any person other than the adopters or adopter;

but this subsection does not affect any reference in this Act to a person's natural parent or to any other natural relationship.

(4) In the case of a person adopted by one of the person's natural parents as sole adoptive parent, subsection (3)(b) has no effect as respects entitlement to property depending on relationship to that parent, or as respects anything else depending on that relationship.

(5) This section has effect from the date of the adoption.

(6) Subject to the provisions of this Chapter and Schedule 4, this section –

(a) applies for the interpretation of enactments or instruments passed or made before as well as after the adoption, and so applies subject to any contrary indication, and

(b) has effect as respects things done, or events occurring, on or after the adoption.

Defined terms—'adoption (in relation to Chapter 4 of Part 1)': s 66; 'child': ss 49(5), 144; 'couple': s 144(4); 'enactment': s 144.

Status conferred by adoption—The effect of this section combined with s 46 is that upon the making of an adoption order, the adopters are given parental responsibility for the child, with the order effectively extinguishing the parental responsibility of any other person (together with any existing orders regarding the child) and the child is treated in law as if born as the child of the adopter(s) and of no other person.

The only exception to this effect is where the partner of one of the child's parents adopts as a sole applicant under s 51(2) (or an equivalent foreign adoption – *Re N (Recognition of Foreign Adoption Order)* [2010] 1 FLR 1102, FD). In such circumstances the said parent retains parental responsibility and the status of parent (ss 46(3)(b), 67(2),(3)), while the other parent loses parental responsibility and parental status as in a normal adoption. References to a child's 'natural parent' are unaffected (s 67(3)).

Convention adoptions that are not 'full' adoptions—Section 88 modifies the effect of s 67(3) (eradication of parental status) in relation to certain Convention adoptions. A UK adoption order achieves total severance of the legal tie between a child and his natural family and is a 'full' adoption. Adoption orders made in some Convention states do not necessarily achieve a complete severance of all ties with the natural family; such adoptions are referred to as 'simple' adoptions.

In order to be able to reflect the differences between a full or simple adoption in a Convention case the High Court may direct that ACA 2002, s 67(3), which provides that the child shall be treated in law as if he were not the child of any person other than the adopter(s), shall not apply, or shall not apply to such extent as may be specified by the court. Under ACA 2002, s 88 such a direction may be given where the court is satisfied:

- that under the law of the country in which the adoption was effected the adoption was not a full adoption;
- that the consents of the child and other persons or institutions whose consent is necessary for adoption referred to in Arts 4(c) and (d) of the Hague Convention have not been given for a full adoption, or that the UK is not the receiving state (within the meaning of Art 2 of the Convention); and
- that it would be more favourable to the adopted child for such a direction to be given.

An application for a s 88 direction may be made by the adopted child, the adopters, any parent or any other parent and is governed by FPR 2010, Pt 14. Form A62 (or one to like effect) must be used and the respondents will be the adopters, the parents, the adoption agency, local authority and the Attorney-General (FPR 2010, r 14.3).

68 Adoptive relatives

(1) A relationship existing by virtue of section 67 may be referred to as an adoptive relationship, and –

(a) an adopter may be referred to as an adoptive parent or (as the case may be) as an adoptive father or adoptive mother,

(b) any other relative of any degree under an adoptive relationship may be referred to as an adoptive relative of that degree.

(2) Subsection (1) does not affect the interpretation of any reference, not qualified by the word 'adoptive', to a relationship.

(3) A reference (however expressed) to the adoptive mother and father of a child adopted by –

(a) a couple of the same sex, or

(b) a partner of the child's parent, where the couple are of the same sex,

is to be read as a reference to the child's adoptive parents.

Defined terms—'by virtue of': s 144; 'child': ss 49(5), 144; 'couple': s 144(4); 'partner, in relation to a parent of a child': s 144(7); 'relative': s 144, read with s 1(8).

69 Rules of interpretation for instruments concerning property

(1) The rules of interpretation contained in this section apply (subject to any contrary indication and to Schedule 4) to any instrument so far as it contains a disposition of property.

(2) In applying section 67(1) and (2) to a disposition which depends on the date of birth of a child or children of the adoptive parent or parents, the disposition is to be interpreted as if –

(a) the adopted person had been born on the date of adoption,
(b) two or more people adopted on the same date had been born on that date in the order of their actual births;

but this does not affect any reference to a person's age.

(3) Examples of phrases in wills on which subsection (2) can operate are –

1. Children of A 'living at my death or born afterwards'.
2. Children of A 'living at my death or born afterwards before any one of such children for the time being in existence attains a vested interest and who attain the age of 21 years'.
3. As in example 1 or 2, but referring to grandchildren of A instead of children of A.
4. A for life 'until he has a child', and then to his child or children.

Note. Subsection (2) will not affect the reference to the age of 21 years in example 2.

(4) Section 67(3) does not prejudice –

(a) any qualifying interest,
(b) any interest expectant (whether immediately or not) upon a qualifying interest, or
(c) any contingent interest (other than a contingent interest in remainder) which the adopted person has immediately before the adoption in the estate of a deceased parent, whether testate or intestate.

'Qualifying interest' means an interest vested in possession in the adopted person before the adoption.

(5) Where it is necessary to determine for the purposes of a disposition of property effected by an instrument whether a woman can have a child –

(a) it must be presumed that once a woman has attained the age of 55 years she will not adopt a person after execution of the instrument, and
(b) if she does so, then (in spite of section 67) that person is not to be treated as her child or (if she does so as one of a couple) as the child of the other one of the couple for the purposes of the instrument.

(6) In this section, 'instrument' includes a private Act settling property, but not any other enactment.

Amendments—Inheritance and Trustees' Powers Act 2014, s 4.

Defined terms—'adoption (in relation to Chapter 4 of Part 1)': s 66; 'child': ss 49(5), 144; 'couple': s 144(4); 'disposition (in relation to Chapter 4 of Part 1)': s 73; 'enactment', 'rules': s 144.

70 Dispositions depending on date of birth

(1) Where a disposition depends on the date of birth of a person who was born illegitimate and who is adopted by one of the natural parents as sole adoptive parent, section 69(2) does not affect entitlement by virtue of Part 3 of the Family Law Reform Act 1987 (dispositions of property).

(2) Subsection (1) applies for example where –

(a) a testator dies in 2001 bequeathing a legacy to his eldest grandchild living at a specified time,
(b) his unmarried daughter has a child in 2002 who is the first grandchild,
(c) his married son has a child in 2003,
(d) subsequently his unmarried daughter adopts her child as sole adoptive parent.

In that example the status of the daughter's child as the eldest grandchild of the testator is not affected by the events described in paragraphs (c) and (d).

Defined terms—'by virtue of': s 144; 'child': ss 49(5), 144; 'disposition (in relation to Chapter 4 of Part 1)': s 73.

71 Property devolving with peerages etc

(1) An adoption does not affect the descent of any peerage or dignity or title of honour.

(2) An adoption does not affect the devolution of any property limited (expressly or not) to devolve (as nearly as the law permits) along with any peerage or dignity or title of honour.

(3) Subsection (2) applies only if and so far as a contrary intention is not expressed in the instrument, and has effect subject to the terms of the instrument.

Defined terms—'adoption (in relation to Chapter 4 of Part 1)': s 66.

72 Protection of trustees and personal representatives

(1) A trustee or personal representative is not under a duty, by virtue of the law relating to trusts or the administration of estates, to enquire, before conveying or distributing any property, whether any adoption has been effected or revoked if that fact could affect entitlement to the property.

(2) A trustee or personal representative is not liable to any person by reason of a conveyance or distribution of the property made without regard to any such fact if he has not received notice of the fact before the conveyance or distribution.

(3) This section does not prejudice the right of a person to follow the property, or any property representing it, into the hands of another person, other than a purchaser, who has received it.

Defined terms—'adoption (in relation to Chapter 4 of Part 1)': s 66; 'by virtue of', 'notice': s 144.

73 Meaning of disposition

(1) This section applies for the purposes of this Chapter.

(2) A disposition includes the conferring of a power of appointment and any other disposition of an interest in or right over property; and in this subsection a power of appointment includes any discretionary power to transfer a beneficial interest in property without the furnishing of valuable consideration.

(3) This Chapter applies to an oral disposition as if contained in an instrument made when the disposition was made.

(4) The date of death of a testator is the date at which a will or codicil is to be regarded as made.

(5) The provisions of the law of intestate succession applicable to the estate of a deceased person are to be treated as if contained in an instrument executed by him (while of full capacity) immediately before his death.

Defined terms—'disposition (in relation to Chapter 4 of Part 1)': s 73.

74 Miscellaneous enactments

(1) Section 67 does not apply for the purposes of –

(a) section 1 of and Schedule 1 to the Marriage Act 1949 or Schedule 1 to the Civil Partnership Act 2004 (prohibited degrees of kindred and affinity),

(b) sections 64 and 65 of the Sexual Offences Act 2003 (sex with an adult relative).

(2) Section 67 does not apply for the purposes of any provision of –

(a) the British Nationality Act 1981,

(b) the Immigration Act 1971,

(c) any instrument having effect under an enactment within paragraph (a) or (b), or

(d) any other provision of the law for the time being in force which determines British citizenship, British overseas territories citizenship, the status of a British National (Overseas) or British Overseas citizenship.

Amendments—CPA 2004, s 79(1),(7); Sexual Offences Act 2003, s 139, Sch 6, para 47.

Defined terms—'enactment': s 144.

75 Pensions

Section 67(3) does not affect entitlement to a pension which is payable to or for the benefit of a person and is in payment at the time of the person's adoption.

Defined terms—'adoption (in relation to Chapter 4 of Part 1)': s 66.

76 Insurance

(1) Where a child is adopted whose natural parent has effected an insurance with a friendly society or a collecting society or an industrial insurance company for the payment on the death of the child of money for funeral expenses, then –

(a) the rights and liabilities under the policy are by virtue of the adoption transferred to the adoptive parents, and

(b) for the purposes of the enactments relating to such societies and companies, the adoptive parents are to be treated as the person who took out the policy.

(2) Where the adoption is effected by an order made by virtue of section 51(2), the references in subsection (1) to the adoptive parents are to be read as references to the adopter and the other one of the couple.

Defined terms—'by virtue of': s 144; 'child': ss 49(5), 144; 'couple', 'enactment': s 144.

Chapter 5
The Registers

Adopted Children Register etc

77 Adopted Children Register

(1) The Registrar General must continue to maintain in the General Register Office a register, to be called the Adopted Children Register.

(2) The Adopted Children Register is not to be open to public inspection or search.

(3) No entries may be made in the Adopted Children Register other than entries –

(a) directed to be made in it by adoption orders, or

(b) required to be made under Schedule 1.

(4) A certified copy of an entry in the Adopted Children Register, if purporting to be sealed or stamped with the seal of the General Register Office, is to be received as evidence of the adoption to which it relates without further or other proof.

(5) Where an entry in the Adopted Children Register contains a record –

(a) of the date of birth of the adopted person, or

(b) of the country, or the district and sub-district, of the birth of the adopted person,

a certified copy of the entry is also to be received, without further or other proof, as evidence of that date, or country or district and sub-district, (as the case may be) in all respects as if the copy were a certified copy of an entry in the registers of live-births.

(6) Schedule 1 (registration of adoptions and the amendment of adoption orders) is to have effect.

Defined terms—'Adopted Children Register': s 77; 'adoption (in relation to Chapter 4 of Part 1)': s 66; 'adoption order': s 46(1); 'registers of live-births (in relation to Chapter 5 of Part 1)': s 82.

Scope—Every domestic adoption must be registered in the Adopted Children Register by the Registrar General in the prescribed form (see ACA 2002, Sch 1 and The Adopted Children and Adoption Contact Registers Regulations 2005). The child's entry in the Register of Births must also be marked 'adopted'. Where a foreign adoption satisfies the requirements for registration it must also be entered in the Register. A certified copy of an entry in the Adopted Children Register, if sealed and stamped with the Registrar General's seal, is, without further proof, to be received as evidence of the adoption as if it were a birth certificate. Adoption records in Scotland, Northern Ireland, Isle of Man or Channel Islands are admissible as evidence of adoption in England and Wales (ACA 2002, s 107).

General Register Office—Smedley Hydro, Trafalgar Road, Birkdale, Southport PR8 2HH.

Foreign adoptions (s 77(3)(b) and Sch 1, para 3)—A foreign adoption which is either a Convention adoption or an 'overseas adoption' (see note to s 66), and which satisfies the requirement of the Adopted Children and Adoption Contact Registers Regulations 2005, must be entered in the Adopted Children Register (ACA 2002,

Sch 1, para 3). Such adoptions are automatically recognised in English law as a valid adoption; the effect of registration is to provide domestic documentary proof of adopted status.

78 Searches and copies

(1) The Registrar General must continue to maintain at the General Register Office an index of the Adopted Children Register.

(2) Any person may –

(a) search the index,
(b) have a certified copy of any entry in the Adopted Children Register.

(3) But a person is not entitled to have a certified copy of an entry in the Adopted Children Register relating to an adopted person who has not attained the age of 18 years unless the applicant has provided the Registrar General with the prescribed particulars.

'Prescribed' means prescribed by regulations made by the Registrar General with the approval of the Secretary of State.

(4) The terms, conditions and regulations as to payment of fees, and otherwise, applicable under the Births and Deaths Registration Act 1953, and the Registration Service Act 1953, in respect of –

(a) searches in the index kept in the General Register Office of certified copies of entries in the registers of live-births,
(b) the supply from that office of certified copies of entries in those certified copies,

also apply in respect of searches, and supplies of certified copies, under subsection (2).

Amendments—SI 2008/678.

Defined terms—'Adopted Children Register': s 77; 'fee': s 144; 'registers of live-births (in relation to Chapter 5 of Part 1)': s 82; 'regulations': s 144.

High Court power to restrict disclosure from records—The Registrar General can refuse to allow access to the birth records on grounds of public policy (see *R v Registrar General ex parte Smith* [1990] 2 FLR 79, QBD). The High Court may, under its inherent jurisdiction, attach to an adoption order an order that the Registrar General should not reveal details of an adoption which are recorded in the Adopted Children Register without the leave of the court (*Re X (A Minor) (Adoption Details: Disclosure)* [1994] 2 FLR 450, CA; *Re W (Adoption Details: Disclosure)* [1998] 2 FLR 625, FD). A local authority is required to obtain leave to make such an application (under CA 1989, s 100(3)) and any application for an order restricting disclosure must be made in, or transferred to, the High Court (*President's Direction of 17 December 1998*).

79 Connections between the register and birth records

(1) The Registrar General must make traceable the connection between any entry in the registers of live-births or other records which has been marked 'Adopted' and any corresponding entry in the Adopted Children Register.

(2) Information kept by the Registrar General for the purposes of subsection (1) is not to be open to public inspection or search.

(3) Any such information, and any other information which would enable an adopted person to obtain a certified copy of the record of his birth, may only be disclosed by the Registrar General in accordance with this section.

(4) In relation to a person adopted before the appointed day the court may, in exceptional circumstances, order the Registrar General to give any information mentioned in subsection (3) to a person.

(5) On an application made in the prescribed manner by the appropriate adoption agency in respect of an adopted person a record of whose birth is kept by the Registrar General, the Registrar General must give the agency any information relating to the adopted person which is mentioned in subsection (3).

'Appropriate adoption agency' has the same meaning as in section 65.

(6) In relation to a person adopted before the appointed day, Schedule 2 applies instead of subsection (5).

(7) On an application made in the prescribed manner by an adopted person a record of whose birth is kept by the Registrar General and who –

(a) is under the age of 18 years, and
(b) intends to be married or form a civil partnership,

the Registrar General must inform the applicant whether or not it appears from information contained in the registers of live-births or other records that the applicant and the intended spouse or civil partner may be within the prohibited degrees of relationship for the purposes of the Marriage Act 1949 or for the purposes of the Civil Partnership Act 2004.

(8) Before the Registrar General gives any information by virtue of this section, any prescribed fee which he has demanded must be paid.

(9) In this section –

'appointed day' means the day appointed for the commencement of sections 56 to 65,

'prescribed' means prescribed by regulations made by the Registrar General with the approval of the Secretary of State.

Amendments—CPA 2004, s 79(1),(8); SI 2005/3542; SI 2008/678.

Defined terms—'Adopted Children Register': s 77; 'adoption agency': s 2(1); 'appointed day (in relation to Chapter 4 of Part 1)': s 66(2); 'by virtue of', 'court', 'fee', 'information': s 144; 'records (in relation to Chapter 5 of Part 1)': s 82; 'registers of live-births (in relation to Chapter 5 of Part 1)': s 82; 'regulations': s 144.

Adoption Contact Register

80 Adoption Contact Register

(1) The Registrar General must continue to maintain at the General Register Office in accordance with regulations a register in two Parts to be called the Adoption Contact Register.

(2) Part 1 of the register is to contain the prescribed information about adopted persons who have given the prescribed notice expressing their wishes as to making contact with their relatives.

(3) The Registrar General may only make an entry in Part 1 of the register for an adopted person –

(a) a record of whose birth is kept by the Registrar General,
(b) who has attained the age of 18 years, and
(c) who the Registrar General is satisfied has such information as is necessary to enable him to obtain a certified copy of the record of his birth.

(4) Part 2 of the register is to contain the prescribed information about persons who have given the prescribed notice expressing their wishes, as relatives of adopted persons, as to making contact with those persons.

(5) The Registrar General may only make an entry in Part 2 of the register for a person –

(a) who has attained the age of 18 years, and
(b) who the Registrar General is satisfied is a relative of an adopted person and has such information as is necessary to enable him to obtain a certified copy of the record of the adopted person's birth.

(6) Regulations may provide for –

(a) the disclosure of information contained in one Part of the register to persons for whom there is an entry in the other Part,
(b) the payment of prescribed fees in respect of the making or alteration of entries in the register and the disclosure of information contained in the register.

Defined terms—'Adoption Contact Register': s 80; 'fee', 'information', 'notice', 'regulations', 'relative': s 144, read with s 1(8).

Adoption Contact Register—The Adoption Contact Register is divided into two parts: in Pt I are details relating to the adopted person; in Pt II are details of any relative of the adoptee, by blood, half-blood or marriage (but not adoption), who wishes to make contact with the adoptee. The system operates by the Registrar General transmitting, to the adopted person whose name appears in Pt I, the name and address of any relative entered in Pt II. A fee is payable for entry on the register (Adopted Children and Adoption Contact Registers Regulations 2005, reg 9). The Register is held at OPCS, Smedley Hydro, Trafalgar Road, Birkdale, Southport PR8 2HH.

81 Adoption Contact Register: supplementary

(1) The Adoption Contact Register is not to be open to public inspection or search.

(2) In section 80, 'relative', in relation to an adopted person, means any person who (but for his adoption) would be related to him by blood (including half-blood), marriage or civil partnership.

(3) The Registrar General must not give any information entered in the register to any person except in accordance with subsection (6)(a) of that section or regulations made by virtue of section 64(4)(b).

(4) In section 80, 'regulations' means regulations made by the Registrar General with the approval of the Secretary of State, and 'prescribed' means prescribed by such regulations.

Amendments—CPA 2004, s 79(1),(9); SI 2008/678.

Defined terms—'adoption (in relation to Chapter 4 of Part 1)': s 66; 'adoption agency placing a child for adoption': s 80; 'by virtue of', 'information', 'regulations', 'relative': s 144, read with s 1(8).

General

82 Interpretation

(1) In this Chapter –

'records' includes certified copies kept by the Registrar General of entries in any register of births,

'registers of live-births' means the registers of live-births made under the Births and Deaths Registration Act 1953.

(2) Any register, record or index maintained under this Chapter may be maintained in any form the Registrar General considers appropriate; and references (however expressed) to entries in such a register, or to their amendment, marking or cancellation, are to be read accordingly.

Defined terms—'records (in relation to Chapter 5 of Part 1)', 'registers of live-births (in relation to Chapter 5 of Part 1)': s 82.

Chapter 6
Adoptions with a Foreign Element

Bringing children into and out of the United Kingdom

83 Restriction on bringing children in

(1) This section applies where a person who is habitually resident in the British Islands (the 'British resident') –

(a) brings, or causes another to bring, a child who is habitually resident outside the British Islands into the United Kingdom for the purpose of adoption by the British resident, or

(b) at any time brings, or causes another to bring, into the United Kingdom a child adopted by the British resident under an external adoption effected within the period of twelve months ending with that time.

The references to adoption, or to a child adopted, by the British resident include a reference to adoption, or to a child adopted, by the British resident and another person.

(2) But this section does not apply if the child is intended to be adopted under a Convention adoption order.

(3) An external adoption means an adoption, other than a Convention adoption, of a child effected under the law of any country or territory outside the British Islands, whether or not the adoption is –

(a) an adoption within the meaning of Chapter 4, or

(b) a full adoption (within the meaning of section 88(3)).

(4) Regulations may require a person intending to bring, or to cause another to bring, a child into the United Kingdom in circumstances where this section applies –

(a) to apply to an adoption agency (including a Scottish or Northern Irish adoption agency) in the prescribed manner for an assessment of his suitability to adopt the child, and
(b) to give the agency any information it may require for the purpose of the assessment.

(5) Regulations may require prescribed conditions to be met in respect of a child brought into the United Kingdom in circumstances where this section applies.

(6) In relation to a child brought into the United Kingdom for adoption in circumstances where this section applies, regulations may –

(a) provide for any provision of Chapter 3 to apply with modifications or not to apply,
(b) if notice of intention to adopt has been given, impose functions in respect of the child on the local authority to which the notice was given.

(7) If a person brings, or causes another to bring, a child into the United Kingdom at any time in circumstances where this section applies, he is guilty of an offence if –

(a) he has not complied with any requirement imposed by virtue of subsection (4), or
(b) any condition required to be met by virtue of subsection (5) is not met,

before that time, or before any later time which may be prescribed.

(8) A person guilty of an offence under this section is liable –

(a) on summary conviction to imprisonment for a term not exceeding six months, or a fine not exceeding the statutory maximum, or both,
(b) on conviction on indictment, to imprisonment for a term not exceeding twelve months, or a fine, or both.

(9) In this section, 'prescribed' means prescribed by regulations and 'regulations' means regulations made by the Secretary of State, after consultation with the Assembly.

Amendments—CAA 2006, s 14(1).

Defined terms—'adoption (in relation to Chapter 4 of Part 1)': s 66; 'adoption agency': s 2(1); 'adoption order': s 46(1); 'Assembly', 'by virtue of': s 144; 'child': ss 49(5) and 144; 'Convention adoption': s 66(1)(c); 'Convention adoption order', 'information', 'local authority', 'Northern Irish adoption agency', 'notice': s 144; 'notice of intention to adopt': s 44(2); 'regulations': s 144.

Bringing in a child from a 'restricted country'—Under CAA 2006, s 9 the Secretary of State may, by order, declare that special restrictions set out in CAA 2006, Pt 2 are to apply to bringing a child into the UK from certain named states (currently Cambodia and Guatemala are named as 'restricted countries'.

Bringing in a child for adoption (s 83(1)(a))—It is a criminal offence, punishable with up to 12 months' imprisonment and/or a fine, for a person who is habitually resident in the British Isles to bring a child, who is habitually resident outside the British Isles, into the UK for the purpose of adoption, unless the requirements of the AFER 2005 have been satisfied (ACA 2002, s 83(7),(8)).

Before the child enters the UK it will be necessary to obtain permission for him to enter. Permission is available on two general bases:

– where there has been a formal legal or de facto (customary) adoption before entry, by adoptive parents who have a right to enter the UK (see **Bringing in an adopted child** below);
– in any event, the Home Secretary has a discretion to permit entry or extend a temporary visa so that adoption proceedings may be heard.

To avoid uncertainty, practitioners are recommended to advise prospective adopters to apply for prior entry clearance. The procedure is fully described in the comprehensive government guidance: *Adoption Guidance: Adoption and Children Act 2002* (DfES 2005), Annex C (available at *www.gov.uk/government/uploads/system/uploads/attachment_data/file/270102/annex_c_adoptions_with_a_foreign_element.pdf*).

'twelve months' (s 83(1)(b))—The period of 12 months applies only in relation to a child adopted under an external adoption effected after 1 October 2007; in all other cases the period is 6 months (CAA 2006, s 14(2)).

Statutory requirements—AFER 2005, reg 3, provides that a prospective adopter must satisfy the following requirements before bringing a child into the UK for adoption:

– apply in writing to an adoption agency for an assessment of his suitability to adopt; and
– give the adoption agency any information it may require for the purposes of the assessment.

Before the child's entry into the UK, in order to comply with AFER 2005, reg 5, the person bringing the child into the UK must receive written notification from the Secretary of State that he has issued a certificate confirming to the relevant foreign authority (which performs the functions of an adoption agency or of the Government with respect to foreign adoptions) the following:

– that the person has been assessed and approved as eligible and suitable to be an adoptive parent; and
– if entry clearance and leave to enter and remain, as may be necessary, is granted and not revoked or curtailed, and an adoption order is made or an overseas adoption is effected, that the child will be authorised to enter and reside permanently in the UK.

Before bringing a child into the UK, each prospective adopter must visit the child in the state of origin (and before doing so have given required information to the relevant local authority). On return to the UK, the adopter must confirm that the visit has taken place and inform the local authority of the expected date of the child's arrival in the UK. Unless there has been prior agreement that only one adopter will accompany the child, each adopter must travel into the UK with the child.

A prospective adopter must also, within a period of 14 days beginning with the date on which he brings the child into the UK, give notice to the local authority within whose area he has his home of his intention to apply for an adoption order in accordance with ACA 2002, s 44 or his intention not to give the child a home.

Bringing in an adopted child—If a child who has been adopted abroad is brought into the UK, and that adoption is recognised in England and Wales, there will normally be no need for a subsequent adoption order.

A child who has been genuinely adopted abroad has a right of entry into the UK if one of the adoptive parents has such a right. Reference should be made to paragraphs 310–313 of the Immigration Rules (see *www.gov.uk/government/publications/immigration-rules-part-8*). The immigration authorities will need to be satisfied that (i) the child's adoption has been due to the inability of the original parents or current carers to care for the child, and (ii) there has been a genuine transfer of parental responsibility.

Where natural parents lack neither the skill, ability nor opportunity to care for their child, but simply have chosen not to do so, there is no 'inability' sufficient to satisfy the immigration requirements (*RS v Entry Clearance Officer (New Delhi)* [2005] 2 FLR 219, CA).

Where there is doubt about the validity of a foreign adoption order, the local authority should at once seek information from the relevant embassy or consulate; any delay may affect the quality of a later court decision (*Re An Adoption Application* [1992] 1 FLR 341, FD).

PART II

84 Giving parental responsibility prior to adoption abroad

(1) The High Court may, on an application by persons who the court is satisfied intend to adopt a child under the law of a country or territory outside the British Islands, make an order giving parental responsibility for the child to them.

(2) An order under this section may not give parental responsibility to persons who the court is satisfied meet those requirements as to domicile, or habitual residence, in England and Wales which have to be met if an adoption order is to be made in favour of those persons.

(3) An order under this section may not be made unless any requirements prescribed by regulations are satisfied.

(4) An application for an order under this section may not be made unless at all times during the preceding ten weeks the child's home was with the applicant or, in the case of an application by two people, both of them.

(5) Section 46(2) to (4) has effect in relation to an order under this section as it has effect in relation to adoption orders.

(6) Regulations may provide for any provision of this Act which refers to adoption orders to apply, with or without modifications, to orders under this section.

(7) In this section, 'regulations' means regulations made by the Secretary of State, after consultation with the Assembly.

Defined terms—'adoption (in relation to Chapter 4 of Part 1)': s 66; 'adoption order': s 46(1); 'Assembly': s 144; 'child': ss 49(5), 144; 'court': s 144; 'parental responsibility': s 3 of the 1989 Act; 'regulations': s 144.

Section 84 application treated as adoption application—A s 84 application is treated in relation to key parts of ACA 2002 exactly as if it were an application for an adoption order (AFER 2005, reg 11(1)). The paramount consideration when determining whether an order should be made will be the welfare of the child throughout his life (reg 11(1)(a)). A s 84 order may only be made if either the first or second condition required before an adoption order can be made (i e parental consent or placed for adoption by an agency) is satisfied (ACA 2002, s 47). It follows that a s 84 order may only be made if the consent of each parent or guardian with parental responsibility has either been given or dispensed with.

'the preceding ten weeks the child's home was with the applicant' (s 84(4))—This statutory requirement (which, coupled with ss 42(7) and 44) seeks to enable the local adoption agency to see the child with the applicant in a home environment, to ensure that a relationship between the adopters and the child has begun, to assess the applicants and to assess the relationship. The word 'home' in s 84(4) is not geographically defined; where prospective adopters live abroad, the phrase in s 84(4) 'the child's home was with the applicants' is applicable to the child being in the applicants' home abroad and there is no requirement that the 10-week period is to be spent somewhere in England and Wales (*Re A (Adoption: Removal)* [2009] 2 FLR 597, CA (on appeal from *Haringey London Borough Council v MA, JN, IA* [2008] 2 FLR 1857, FD)). Where s 42(7)(b) applies the 'home' must be within a local authority area in England and Wales. Where, however, s 42(7)(a) applies there is no territorial restriction and the 'home environment' may be outside England and Wales (*Re A (Adoption: Removal)* above). CA 1989, Sch 2, para 19, which permits a local authority in certain circumstances to make arrangements for a child to live abroad, does not apply 'to a local authority placing a child for adoption with prospective adopters' (CA 1989, Sch 2, para 19(9)). Arrangements that fall short of actually 'placing the child for adoption' (eg for assessment) are permissible under Sch 2, para 19 (*Re A (Adoption: Removal)* above).

'regulations' (s 84(7))—See AFER 2005 in Part IV. Regulation 10(b) requires that 'the relevant foreign authority' has counselled the prospective adopter, prepared a report, confirmed his eligibility to adopt and confirmed that the child will be allowed entry and permanent residence. The 'authority' is to be taken as the foreign equivalent of the English adoption agency; a government body is not required and the confirmation does not have to be in absolute terms (*Re G* above).

85 Restriction on taking children out

(1) A child who –

(a) is a Commonwealth citizen, or

(b) is habitually resident in the United Kingdom,

must not be removed from the United Kingdom to a place outside the British Islands for the purpose of adoption unless the condition in subsection (2) is met.

(2) The condition is that –

(a) the prospective adopters have parental responsibility for the child by virtue of an order under section 84, or

(b) the child is removed under the authority of an order under section 59 of the Adoption and Children (Scotland) Act 2007 or Article 57 of the Adoption (Northern Ireland) Order 1987 (SI 1987/2203).

(3) Removing a child from the United Kingdom includes arranging to do so; and the circumstances in which a person arranges to remove a child from the United Kingdom include those where he –

(a) enters into an arrangement for the purpose of facilitating such a removal of the child,

(b) initiates or takes part in any negotiations of which the purpose is the conclusion of an arrangement within paragraph (a), or

(c) causes another person to take any step mentioned in paragraph (a) or (b).

An arrangement includes an agreement (whether or not enforceable).

(4) A person who removes a child from the United Kingdom in contravention of subsection (1) is guilty of an offence.

(5) A person is not guilty of an offence under subsection (4) of causing a person to take any step mentioned in paragraph (a) or (b) of subsection (3) unless it is proved that he knew or had reason to suspect that the step taken would contravene subsection (1).

But this subsection only applies if sufficient evidence is adduced to raise an issue as to whether the person had the knowledge or reason mentioned.

(6) A person guilty of an offence under this section is liable –

(a) on summary conviction to imprisonment for a term not exceeding six months, or a fine not exceeding the statutory maximum, or both,

(b) on conviction on indictment, to imprisonment for a term not exceeding twelve months, or a fine, or both.

(7) In any proceedings under this section –

(a) a report by a British consular officer or a deposition made before a British consular officer and authenticated under the signature of that officer is admissible, upon proof that the officer or the deponent cannot be found in the United Kingdom, as evidence of the matters stated in it, and

(b) it is not necessary to prove the signature or official character of the person who appears to have signed any such report or deposition.

Amendments—SI 2011/1740.

Defined terms—'adoption (in relation to Chapter 4 of Part 1)': s 66; 'by virtue of': s 144; 'child': ss 49(5), 144; 'parental responsibility': s 3 of the 1989 Act.

Scope—This section creates a blanket ban upon the removal of any child out of the UK for the purpose of adoption unless (in the case of England and Wales) the prospective adopters have parental responsibility for the child under ACA 2002, s 84 (in order to facilitate adoption abroad). A local authority must comply with ss 84 and 85 if contemplating placing a child abroad for adoption (CA 1989, Sch 2, Para 19 does not apply to arrangements for adoption). There may be no breach of s 85 where removal abroad is for the purpose of assessment of a prospective placement with a view to an adoption order subsequently being made here (*ECC (The Local Authority) v SM* [2011] 1 FLR 234, FD).

86 Power to modify sections 83 and 85

(1) Regulations may provide for section 83 not to apply if –

(a) the adopters or (as the case may be) prospective adopters are natural parents, natural relatives or guardians of the child in question (or one of them is), or

(b) the British resident in question is a partner of a parent of the child,

and any prescribed conditions are met.

(2) Regulations may provide for section 85(1) to apply with modifications, or not to apply, if –

(a) the prospective adopters are parents, relatives or guardians of the child in question (or one of them is), or

(b) the prospective adopter is a partner of a parent of the child,

and any prescribed conditions are met.

(3) On the occasion of the first exercise of the power to make regulations under this section –

(a) the statutory instrument containing the regulations is not to be made unless a draft of the instrument has been laid before, and approved by a resolution of, each House of Parliament, and

(b) accordingly section 140(2) does not apply to the instrument.

(4) In this section, 'prescribed' means prescribed by regulations and 'regulations' means regulations made by the Secretary of State after consultation with the Assembly.

Defined terms—'Assembly': s 144; 'child': ss 49(5), 144; 'guardian': s 144; 'partner, in relation to a parent of a child': s 144(7); 'regulations': s 144; 'relative': s 144, read with s 1(8).

Overseas adoptions

87 Overseas adoptions

(1) In this Act, 'overseas adoption' –

(a) means an adoption of a description specified in an order made by the Secretary of State, being a description of adoptions effected under the law of any country or territory outside the British Islands, but

(b) does not include a Convention adoption.

(2) Regulations may prescribe the requirements that ought to be met by an adoption of any description effected after the commencement of the regulations for it to be an overseas adoption for the purposes of this Act.

(3) At any time when such regulations have effect, the Secretary of State must exercise his powers under this section so as to secure that subsequently effected adoptions of any description are not overseas adoptions for the purposes of this Act if he considers that they are not likely within a reasonable time to meet the prescribed requirements.

(4) In this section references to this Act include the Adoption Act 1976.

(5) An order under this section may contain provision as to the manner in which evidence of any overseas adoption may be given.

(6) In this section –

'adoption' means an adoption of a child or of a person who was a child at the time the adoption was applied for,

'regulations' means regulations made by the Secretary of State after consultation with the Assembly.

Defined terms—'adoption (in relation to Chapter 4 of Part 1)': s 66; 'Assembly': s 144; 'child': ss 49(5), 144; 'Convention adoption': s 66(1)(c); 'overseas adoption': s 87; 'regulations': s 144.

Miscellaneous

88 Modification of section 67 for Hague Convention adoptions

(1) If the High Court is satisfied, on an application under this section, that each of the following conditions is met in the case of a Convention adoption, it may direct that section 67(3) does not apply, or does not apply to any extent specified in the direction.

(2) The conditions are –

- (a) that under the law of the country in which the adoption was effected, the adoption is not a full adoption,
- (b) that the consents referred to in Article 4(c) and (d) of the Convention have not been given for a full adoption or that the United Kingdom is not the receiving State (within the meaning of Article 2 of the Convention),
- (c) that it would be more favourable to the adopted child for a direction to be given under subsection (1).

(3) A full adoption is an adoption by virtue of which the child is to be treated in law as not being the child of any person other than the adopters or adopter.

(4) In relation to a direction under this section and an application for it, sections 59 and 60 of the Family Law Act 1986 (declarations under Part 3 of that Act as to marital status) apply as they apply in relation to a direction under that Part and an application for such a direction.

Defined terms—'adoption (in relation to Chapter 4 of Part 1)': s 66; 'by virtue of': s 144; 'child': ss 49(5), 144; 'child to be adopted, adopted child': s 49(5); 'consent (in relation to making adoption orders or placing for adoption)': s 52; 'the Convention': s 144; 'Convention adoption': s 66(1)(c).

89 Annulment etc of overseas or Hague Convention adoptions

(1) The High Court may, on an application under this subsection, by order annul a Convention adoption or Convention adoption order on the ground that the adoption is contrary to public policy.

(2) The High Court may, on an application under this subsection –

- (a) by order provide for an overseas adoption or a determination under section 91 to cease to be valid on the ground that the adoption or determination is contrary to public policy or that the authority which purported to authorise the adoption or make the determination was not competent to entertain the case, or
- (b) decide the extent, if any, to which a determination under section 91 has been affected by a subsequent determination under that section.

(3) The High Court may, in any proceedings in that court, decide that an overseas adoption or a determination under section 91 is to be treated, for the purposes of those proceedings, as invalid on either of the grounds mentioned in subsection (2)(a).

(4) Subject to the preceding provisions, the validity of a Convention adoption, Convention adoption order or overseas adoption or a determination under section 91 cannot be called in question in proceedings in any court in England and Wales.

Defined terms—'adoption (in relation to Chapter 4 of Part 1)': s 66; 'adoption order': s 46(1); 'Convention adoption': s 66(1)(c); 'Convention adoption order', 'court': s 144; 'overseas adoption': s 87.

Procedure—An application under s 89 is governed by FPR 2010, Pt 14 and must be made in Form A63 (or a form to like effect).

90 Section 89: supplementary

(1) Any application for an order under section 89 or a decision under subsection (2)(b) or (3) of that section must be made in the prescribed manner and within any prescribed period.

'Prescribed' means prescribed by rules.

(2) No application may be made under section 89(1) in respect of an adoption unless immediately before the application is made –

- (a) the person adopted, or

(b) the adopters or adopter,

habitually reside in England and Wales.

(3) In deciding in pursuance of section 89 whether such an authority as is mentioned in section 91 was competent to entertain a particular case, a court is bound by any finding of fact made by the authority and stated by the authority to be so made for the purpose of determining whether the authority was competent to entertain the case.

Defined terms—'adoption (in relation to Chapter 4 of Part 1)': s 66; 'court', 'rules': s 144.

91 Overseas determinations and orders

(1) Subsection (2) applies where any authority of a Convention country (other than the United Kingdom) or of the Channel Islands, the Isle of Man or any British overseas territory has power under the law of that country or territory –

(a) to authorise, or review the authorisation of, an adoption order made in that country or territory, or
(b) to give or review a decision revoking or annulling such an order or a Convention adoption.

(2) If the authority makes a determination in the exercise of that power, the determination is to have effect for the purpose of effecting, confirming or terminating the adoption in question or, as the case may be, confirming its termination.

(3) Subsection (2) is subject to section 89 and to any subsequent determination having effect under that subsection.

Defined terms—'adoption (in relation to Chapter 4 of Part 1)': s 66; 'adoption order': s 46(1); 'Convention adoption': s 66(1)(c); 'Convention country': s 144.

91A Power to charge

(1) This section applies to adoptions to which –

(a) section 83 applies, or
(b) regulations made under section 1 of the Adoption (Intercountry Aspects) Act 1999 apply.

(2) The Secretary of State may charge a fee to adopters for services provided or to be provided by him in relation to adoptions to which this section applies.

(3) The Assembly may charge a fee to adopters for services provided or to be provided by it as the Central Authority in relation to adoptions to which this section applies by virtue of subsection (1)(b).

(4) The Secretary of State and the Assembly may determine the level of fee as he or it sees fit, and may in particular –

(a) charge a flat fee or charge different fees in different cases or descriptions of case, and
(b) in any case or description of case, waive a fee.

(5) But the Secretary of State and the Assembly must each secure that, taking one financial year with another, the income from fees under this section does not exceed the total cost to him or, as the case may be, to it of providing the services in relation to which the fees are imposed.

(6) In this section –

references to adoptions and adopters include prospective adoptions and prospective adopters,

'Central Authority' is to be construed in accordance with section 2 of the Adoption (Intercountry Aspects) Act 1999,

'financial year' means a period of twelve months ending with 31 March.

Amendments—Inserted by CAA 2006, s 13.

Chapter 7
Miscellaneous

Restrictions

92 Restriction on arranging adoptions etc

(1) A person who is neither an adoption agency nor acting in pursuance of an order of the High Court or the family court must not take any of the steps mentioned in subsection (2).

(2) The steps are –

(a) asking a person other than an adoption agency to provide a child for adoption,
(b) asking a person other than an adoption agency to provide prospective adopters for a child,
(c) offering to find a child for adoption,
(d) offering a child for adoption to a person other than an adoption agency,
(e) handing over a child to any person other than an adoption agency with a view to the child's adoption by that or another person,
(f) receiving a child handed over to him in contravention of paragraph (e),
(g) entering into an agreement with any person for the adoption of a child, or for the purpose of facilitating the adoption of a child, where no adoption agency is acting on behalf of the child in the adoption,
(h) initiating or taking part in negotiations of which the purpose is the conclusion of an agreement within paragraph (g),
(i) causing another person to take any of the steps mentioned in paragraphs (a) to (h).

(3) Subsection (1) does not apply to a person taking any of the steps mentioned in paragraphs (d), (e), (g), (h) and (i) of subsection (2) if the following condition is met.

(4) The condition is that –

(a) the prospective adopters are parents, relatives or guardians of the child (or one of them is), or
(b) the prospective adopter is the partner of a parent of the child.

(5) References to an adoption agency in subsection (2) include a prescribed person outside the United Kingdom exercising functions corresponding to those of an adoption agency, if the functions are being exercised in prescribed circumstances in respect of the child in question.

(6) The Secretary of State may, after consultation with the Assembly, by order make any amendments of subsections (1) to (4), and any consequential amendments of this Act, which he considers necessary or expedient.

(7) In this section –

(a) 'agreement' includes an arrangement (whether or not enforceable),
(b) 'prescribed' means prescribed by regulations made by the Secretary of State after consultation with the Assembly.

Amendments—CCA 2013, s 17, Sch 11.

Defined terms—'adoption (in relation to Chapter 4 of Part 1)': s 66; 'adoption agency': s 2(1); 'Assembly': s 144; 'child': ss 49(5), 144; 'guardian': s 144; 'partner, in relation to a parent of a child': s 144(7); 'regulations': s 144; 'relative': s 144, read with s 1(8).

Restrictions upon arranging adoptions—Section 92(2) sets out a list of steps relating to adoption that are illegal, unless taken by an adoption agency or a person acting in pursuance of a High Court order. While the prohibited steps apply to domestic as much as to intercountry adoptions, s 92 extends to the adoption of persons wherever they may be habitually resident, effected under the law of any country or territory, within or outside the British Isles (s 97(c)). The steps itemised in s 92(3) are permitted if the prospective adopters are parents, relatives, or guardians of the child (or the sole adopter is a parent's partner). Breach of s 92(1) is a criminal offence under s 93.

Restrictions on advertisements—Specific restrictions upon advertising in relation to adoption are made by s 123.

93 Offence of breaching restrictions under section 92

(1) If a person contravenes section 92(1), he is guilty of an offence; and, if that person is an adoption society, the person who manages the society is also guilty of the offence.

(2) A person is not guilty of an offence under subsection (1) of taking the step mentioned in paragraph (f) of section 92(2) unless it is proved that he knew or had reason to suspect that the child was handed over to him in contravention of paragraph (e) of that subsection.

(3) A person is not guilty of an offence under subsection (1) of causing a person to take any of the steps mentioned in paragraphs (a) to (h) of section 92(2) unless it is proved that he knew or had reason to suspect that the step taken would contravene the paragraph in question.

(4) But subsections (2) and (3) only apply if sufficient evidence is adduced to raise an issue as to whether the person had the knowledge or reason mentioned.

(5) A person guilty of an offence under this section is liable on summary conviction to imprisonment for a term not exceeding six months, or a fine not exceeding £10,000, or both.

Defined terms—'adoption society': s 2(5); 'child': ss 49(5), 144.

94 Restriction on reports

(1) A person who is not within a prescribed description may not, in any prescribed circumstances, prepare a report for any person about the suitability of a child for adoption or of a person to adopt a child or about the adoption, or placement for adoption, of a child.

'Prescribed' means prescribed by regulations made by the Secretary of State after consultation with the Assembly.

(2) If a person –

(a) contravenes subsection (1), or

(b) causes a person to prepare a report, or submits to any person a report which has been prepared, in contravention of that subsection,

he is guilty of an offence.

(3) If a person who works for an adoption society –

(a) contravenes subsection (1), or

(b) causes a person to prepare a report, or submits to any person a report which has been prepared, in contravention of that subsection,

the person who manages the society is also guilty of the offence.

(4) A person is not guilty of an offence under subsection (2)(b) unless it is proved that he knew or had reason to suspect that the report would be, or had been, prepared in contravention of subsection (1).

But this subsection only applies if sufficient evidence is adduced to raise an issue as to whether the person had the knowledge or reason mentioned.

(5) A person guilty of an offence under this section is liable on summary conviction to imprisonment for a term not exceeding six months, or a fine not exceeding level 5 on the standard scale, or both.

Defined terms—'adoption (in relation to Chapter 4 of Part 1)': s 66; 'adoption society': s 2(5); 'Assembly': s 144; 'child': ss 49(5), 144; 'regulations': s 144.

Restriction on reports—Section 94 and the Preparation of Adoption Reports Regulations 2005 establish tight parameters, outside which it is illegal for a person to prepare a report in connection with a proposed adoption or adoptive placement. The prohibition extends to the adoption of persons wherever they may be habitually resident, effected under the law of any country or territory, within or outside the British Isles (s 97(c)). Contravention of these provisions constitutes a criminal offence (s 94(2)).

95 Prohibition of certain payments

(1) This section applies to any payment (other than an excepted payment) which is made for or in consideration of –

(a) the adoption of a child,

(b) giving any consent required in connection with the adoption of a child,
(c) removing from the United Kingdom a child who is a Commonwealth citizen, or is habitually resident in the United Kingdom, to a place outside the British Islands for the purpose of adoption,
(d) a person (who is neither an adoption agency nor acting in pursuance of an order of the High Court or family court) taking any step mentioned in section 92(2),
(e) preparing, causing to be prepared or submitting a report the preparation of which contravenes section 94(1).

(2) In this section and section 96, removing a child from the United Kingdom has the same meaning as in section 85.

(3) Any person who –

(a) makes any payment to which this section applies,
(b) agrees or offers to make any such payment, or
(c) receives or agrees to receive or attempts to obtain any such payment,

is guilty of an offence.

(4) A person guilty of an offence under this section is liable on summary conviction to imprisonment for a term not exceeding six months, or a fine not exceeding £10,000, or both.

Amendments—CCA 2013, s 17, Sch 11.

Defined terms—'adoption (in relation to Chapter 4 of Part 1)': s 66; 'adoption agency': s 2(1); 'child': ss 49(5), 144; 'consent (in relation to making adoption orders or placing for adoption)': s 52.

Prohibition on certain payments—Section 95 renders any payment which is made for, or in consideration of, the adoption of a child or any of the other steps listed in s 95(1) unless the payment is an 'excepted payment' within s 96. 'Payment' includes reward (s 97(b)). The prohibition extends to the adoption of persons wherever they may be habitually resident, effected under the law of any country or territory, within or outside the British Isles (s 97(c)). Breach of these provisions constitutes a criminal offence (s 95(3)).

96 Excepted payments

(1) A payment is an excepted payment if it is made by virtue of, or in accordance with provision made by or under, this Act, the Adoption (Scotland) Act 1978, the Adoption and Children (Scotland) Act 2007 or the Adoption (Northern Ireland) Order 1987 (SI 1987/2203 (NI 22)).

(2) A payment is an excepted payment if it is made to a registered adoption society by –

(a) a parent or guardian of a child, or
(b) a person who adopts or proposes to adopt a child,

in respect of expenses reasonably incurred by the society in connection with the adoption or proposed adoption of the child.

(3) A payment is an excepted payment if it is made in respect of any legal or medical expenses incurred or to be incurred by any person in connection with an application to a court which he has made or proposes to make for an adoption order, a placement order, or an order under section 26, 51A or 84.

(4) A payment made as mentioned in section 95(1)(c) is an excepted payment if –

(a) the condition in section 85(2) is met, and
(b) the payment is made in respect of the travel and accommodation expenses reasonably incurred in removing the child from the United Kingdom for the purpose of adoption.

Amendments—SI 2011/1740; CFA 2014, s 9.

Defined terms—'adoption (in relation to Chapter 4 of Part 1)': s 66; 'adoption order': s 46(1); 'adoption society': s 2(5); 'by virtue of': s 144; 'child': ss 49(5), 144; 'court', 'guardian': s 144; 'placement order': s 21; 'registered adoption society': s 2(2).

97 Sections 92 to 96: interpretation

In sections 92 to 96 –

(a) 'adoption agency' includes a Scottish or Northern Irish adoption agency,
(b) 'payment' includes reward,

(c) references to adoption are to the adoption of persons, wherever they may be habitually resident, effected under the law of any country or territory, whether within or outside the British Islands.

Defined terms—'adoption (in relation to Chapter 4 of Part 1)': s 66; 'adoption agency': s 2(1); 'Northern Irish adoption agency': s 144.

Information

98 Pre-commencement adoptions: information

(1) Regulations under section 9 may make provision for the purpose of –

(a) assisting persons adopted before the appointed day who have attained the age of 18 to obtain information in relation to their adoption, and

(b) facilitating contact between such persons and their relatives.

(1A) Regulations under section 9 may make provision for the purpose of facilitating contact between persons with a prescribed relationship to a person adopted before the appointed day and that person's relatives.

(2) For a purpose within subsection (1) or (1A) the regulations may confer functions on –

(a) registered adoption support agencies,

(b) the Registrar General,

(c) adoption agencies.

(3) For a purpose within subsection (1) or (1A) the regulations may –

(a) authorise or require any person mentioned in subsection (2) to disclose information,

(b) authorise or require the disclosure of information contained in records kept under section 8 of the Public Records Act 1958 (court records),

and may impose conditions on the disclosure of information, including conditions restricting its further disclosure.

(4) The regulations may authorise the charging of prescribed fees by any person mentioned in subsection (2) or in respect of the disclosure of information under subsection (3)(b).

(5) An authorisation or requirement to disclose information by virtue of subsection (3)(a) has effect in spite of any restriction on the disclosure of information in Chapter 5.

(6) The making of regulations by virtue of subsections (2) to (4) which relate to the Registrar General requires the approval of the Secretary of State.

(7) In this section –

'appointed day' means the day appointed for the commencement of sections 56 to 65,

'prescribed' means prescribed by regulations under section 9;

'registered adoption support agency' means an adoption support agency in respect of which a person is registered under Part 2 of the Care Standards Act 2000,

'relative', in relation to an adopted person, means any person who (but for his adoption) would be related to him by blood (including half-blood), marriage or civil partnership.

Amendments—CPA 2004, s 79(1),(10); SI 2008/678; CFA 2014, s 1.

Defined terms—'adoption (in relation to Chapter 4 of Part 1)': s 66; 'adoption support agency': s 8; 'appointed day (in relation to Chapter 4 of Part 1)': s 66(2); 'by virtue of', 'court', 'fee', 'information': s 144; 'records (in relation to Chapter 5 of Part 1)': s 82; 'regulations': s 144; 'relative': s 144, read with s 1(8).

Proceedings

99 Proceedings for offences

Proceedings for an offence by virtue of section 9 or 59 may not, without the written consent of the Attorney General, be taken by any person other than Her Majesty's Chief Inspector of Education, Children's Services and Skills or the Assembly.

Amendments—Health and Social Care (Community Health and Standards) Act 2003, s 147, Sch 9, para 32; Education and Inspections Act 2006, Sch 14, para 76.
Defined terms—'Assembly', 'by virtue of': s 144.

****

101 Privacy

(1) Proceedings under this Act in the High Court or the family court may be heard and determined in private.

(2)–(3) …

Amendments—CCA 2013, s 17, Sch 11.

The Children and Family Court Advisory and Support Service

102 Officers of the Service

(1) For the purposes of –

(a) any relevant application,
(b) the signification by any person of any consent to placement or adoption,

rules must provide for the appointment in prescribed cases of an officer of the Children and Family Court Advisory and Support Service ('the Service') or a Welsh Family proceedings officer.

(2) The rules may provide for the appointment of such an officer in other circumstances in which it appears to the Lord Chancellor to be necessary or expedient to do so.

(3) The rules may provide for the officer –

(a) to act on behalf of the child upon the hearing of any relevant application, with the duty of safeguarding the interests of the child in the prescribed manner,
(b) where the court so requests, to prepare a report on matters relating to the welfare of the child in question,
(c) to witness documents which signify consent to placement or adoption,
(d) to perform prescribed functions.

(4) A report prepared in pursuance of the rules on matters relating to the welfare of a child must –

(a) deal with prescribed matters (unless the court orders otherwise), and
(b) be made in the manner required by the court.

(5) A person who –

(a) in the case of an application for the making, varying or revocation of a placement order, is employed by the local authority which made the application,
(b) in the case of an application for an adoption order in respect of a child who was placed for adoption, is employed by the adoption agency which placed him, or
(c) is within a prescribed description,

is not to be appointed under subsection (1) or (2).

(6) In this section, 'relevant application' means an application for –

(a) the making, varying or revocation of a placement order,
(b) the making of an order under section 26, or the varying or revocation of such an order,
(c) the making of an adoption order, or
(d) the making of an order under section 84.

(7) Rules may make provision as to the assistance which the court may require an officer of the Service to give to it.

(8) In this section and section 103 'Welsh family proceedings officer' has the meaning given to it by section 35 of the Children Act 2004.

Amendments—CA 2004, s 40, Sch 3, paras 15, 16.

Defined terms—'adoption (in relation to Chapter 4 of Part 1)': s 66; 'adoption agency': s 2(1); 'adoption order': s 46(1); 'child': ss 49(5), 144; 'consent (in relation to making adoption orders or placing for adoption)': s 52; 'court', 'local authority': s 144; 'placement order': s 21; 'placing, or placed, for adoption': ss 18(5), 19(4); 'rules': s 144.

103 Right of officers of the Service to have access to adoption agency records

(1) Where an officer of the Service or a Welsh family proceedings officer has been appointed to act under section 102(1), he has the right at all reasonable times to examine and take copies of any records of, or held by, an adoption agency which were compiled in connection with the making, or proposed making, by any person of any application under this Part in respect of the child concerned.

(2) Where an officer of the Service or a Welsh family proceedings officer takes a copy of any record which he is entitled to examine under this section, that copy or any part of it is admissible as evidence of any matter referred to in any –

(a) report which he makes to the court in the proceedings in question, or
(b) evidence which he gives in those proceedings.

(3) Subsection (2) has effect regardless of any enactment or rule of law which would otherwise prevent the record in question being admissible in evidence.

Amendments—CA 2004, s 40, Sch 3, paras 15, 17.

Defined terms—'adoption agency': s 2(1); 'child': ss 49(5), 144; 'court', 'enactment': s 144; 'records (in relation to Chapter 5 of Part 1)': s 82.

Evidence

104 Evidence of consent

(1) If a document signifying any consent which is required by this Part to be given is witnessed in accordance with rules, it is to be admissible in evidence without further proof of the signature of the person by whom it was executed.

(2) A document signifying any such consent which purports to be witnessed in accordance with rules is to be presumed to be so witnessed, and to have been executed and witnessed on the date and at the place specified in the document, unless the contrary is proved.

Defined terms—'consent (in relation to making adoption orders or placing for adoption)': s 52; 'rules': s 144.

Scotland, Northern Ireland and the Islands

105 Effect of certain Scottish orders and provisions

(1) A Scottish adoption order or an order under section 25 of the Adoption (Scotland) Act 1978 (interim adoption orders) has effect in England and Wales as it has in Scotland, but as if references to the parental responsibilities and the parental rights in relation to a child were to parental responsibility for the child.

(2) A Scottish permanence order which includes provision granting authority for the child to be adopted has the same effect in England and Wales as it has in Scotland, but as if references to the parental responsibilities and the parental rights in relation to a child were to parental responsibility for the child.

(3) Any person who contravenes any of the provisions of the Adoption and Children (Scotland) Act 2007 mentioned in subsection (3A) is guilty of an offence and is liable on summary conviction to imprisonment for a term not exceeding 3 months, or a fine not exceeding level 5 on the standard scale or both.

(3A) The provisions are –

(a) section 20 (restrictions on removal: child placed for adoption);
(b) section 21 (restrictions on removal: notice of intention to adopt given);
(c) section 22 (restrictions on removal: application for adoption order pending).]

(4) Orders made under section 24 of the Adoption and Children (Scotland) Act 2007 (return of child removed in breach of certain provisions) are to have effect in England and Wales as if they were orders of the High Court under section 41 of this Act.

(5) In this section, "Scottish permanence order" means a permanence order under section 80 of the Adoption and Children (Scotland) Act 2007 (including a deemed permanence order having effect by virtue of article 13(1), 14(2), 17(1) or 19(2) of the Adoption and Children (Scotland) Act 2007 (Commencement No 4, Transitional and Savings Provisions Order 2009 (SSI 2009/267)).

Amendments—SI 2011/1740.

106 Effect of certain Northern Irish orders and provisions

(1) A Northern Irish adoption order or an order under Article 26 of the Adoption (Northern Ireland) Order 1987 (SI 1987/2203) (interim orders) has effect in England and Wales as it has in Northern Ireland.

(2) An order made under Article 17 or 18 of the Adoption (Northern Ireland) Order 1987 (freeing orders), or the variation or revocation of such an order under Article 20 or 21 of that Order, have effect in England and Wales as they have in Northern Ireland.

(3) Any person who –

(a) contravenes Article 28(1) or (2) of the Adoption (Northern Ireland) Order 1987 (removal where adoption agreed etc), or

(b) contravenes Article 29(1) or (2) of that Order (removal where applicant provided home),

is guilty of an offence and liable on summary conviction to imprisonment for a term not exceeding three months, or a fine not exceeding level 5 on the standard scale, or both.

(4) Orders made under Article 30 of that Order (order to return or not to remove child) are to have effect in England and Wales as if they were orders of the High Court under section 41 of this Act.

107 Use of adoption records from other parts of the British Islands

Any document which is receivable as evidence of any matter –

(a) in Scotland under section 56(1) or (2) of the Adoption and Children (Scotland) Act 2007 (admissibility of extracts as evidence),

(b) in Northern Ireland under Article 63(1) of the Adoption (Northern Ireland) Order 1987, or

(c) in the Isle of Man or any of the Channel Islands under an enactment corresponding to section 77(3) of this Act,

is also receivable as evidence of that matter in England and Wales.

Amendments—SI 2011/1740.

****

General

109 Avoiding delay

(1) In proceedings in which a question may arise as to whether an adoption order or placement order should be made, or any other question with respect to such an order, the court must (in the light of any provision in rules of court that is of the kind mentioned in subsection (2)(a) or (b)) –

(a) draw up a timetable with a view to determining such a question without delay, and

(b) give such directions as it considers appropriate for the purpose of ensuring that the timetable is adhered to.

(2) Rules may –

(a) prescribe periods within which prescribed steps must be taken in relation to such proceedings, and

(b) make other provision with respect to such proceedings for the purpose of ensuring that such questions are determined without delay.

Amendments—CFA 2014, s 14.

Defined terms—'adoption order': s 46(1); 'by virtue of', 'court': s 144; 'placement order': s 21.

110 Service of notices etc

Any notice or information required to be given by virtue of this Act may be given by post.

Defined terms—'by virtue of', 'information', 'notice': s 144.

****

PART 3
MISCELLANEOUS AND FINAL PROVISIONS

Chapter 1
Miscellaneous

Advertisements in the United Kingdom

123 Restriction on advertisements etc

(1) A person must not –

(a) publish or distribute an advertisement or information to which this section applies, or

(b) cause such an advertisement or information to be published or distributed.

(2) This section applies to an advertisement indicating that –

(a) the parent or guardian of a child wants the child to be adopted,

(b) a person wants to adopt a child,

(c) a person other than an adoption agency is willing to take any step mentioned in paragraphs (a) to (e), (g) and (h) and (so far as relating to those paragraphs) (i) of section 92(2),

(d) a person other than an adoption agency is willing to receive a child handed over to him with a view to the child's adoption by him or another, or

(e) a person is willing to remove a child from the United Kingdom for the purposes of adoption.

(3) This section applies to –

(a) information about how to do anything which, if done, would constitute an offence under section 85 or 93, Article 11 or 58 of the Adoption (Northern Ireland) Order 1987 (SI 1987/2203 (NI 22)) or section 60 or 75 of the Adoption and Children (Scotland) Act 2007 (whether or not the information includes a warning that doing the thing in question may constitute an offence),

(b) information about a particular child as a child available for adoption.

(4) For the purposes of this section and section 124 –

(a) publishing or distributing an advertisement or information means publishing it or distributing it to the public and includes doing so by electronic means (for example, by means of the internet),

(b) the public includes selected members of the public as well as the public generally or any section of the public.

(5) Subsection (1) does not apply to publication or distribution by or on behalf of an adoption agency.

(6) The Secretary of State may by order make any amendments of this section which he considers necessary or expedient in consequence of any developments in technology relating to publishing or distributing advertisements or other information by electronic or electro-magnetic means.

(7) References to an adoption agency in this section include a prescribed person outside the United Kingdom exercising functions corresponding to those of an adoption agency, if the functions are being exercised in prescribed circumstances.

'Prescribed' means prescribed by regulations made by the Secretary of State.

(8) Before exercising the power conferred by subsection (6) or (7), the Secretary of State must consult the Scottish Ministers, the Department of Health, Social Services and Public Safety and the Assembly.

(9) In this section –

(a) 'adoption agency' includes a Scottish or Northern Irish adoption agency,
(b) references to adoption are to the adoption of persons, wherever they may be habitually resident, effected under the law of any country or territory, whether within or outside the British Islands.

Amendments—SI 2011/1740.

Defined terms—'adoption (in relation to Chapter 4 of Part 1)': s 66; 'adoption agency': s 2(1); 'Assembly': s 144; 'child': ss 49(5), 144; 'child to be adopted, adopted child': s 49(5); 'guardian', 'information', 'Northern Irish adoption agency', 'regulations': s 144.

124 Offence of breaching restriction under section 123

(1) A person who contravenes section 123(1) is guilty of an offence.

(2) A person is not guilty of an offence under this section unless it is proved that he knew or had reason to suspect that section 123 applied to the advertisement or information.

But this subsection only applies if sufficient evidence is adduced to raise an issue as to whether the person had the knowledge or reason mentioned.

(3) A person guilty of an offence under this section is liable on summary conviction to imprisonment for a term not exceeding three months, or a fine not exceeding level 5 on the standard scale, or both.

Defined terms—'information': s 144.

****

Chapter 2
Final provisions

140 Orders, rules and regulations

(1) Any power to make subordinate legislation conferred by this Act on the Lord Chancellor, the Secretary of State, the Scottish Ministers, the Assembly or the Registrar General is exercisable by statutory instrument.

(2) A statutory instrument containing subordinate legislation made under any provision of this Act (other than section 14 or 148 or an instrument to which subsection (3) applies) is to be subject to annulment in pursuance of a resolution of either House of Parliament.

(3) A statutory instrument containing subordinate legislation –

(za) under section 3A(2)
(a) under section 9 which includes provision made by virtue of section 45(2),
(b) under section 92(6), 94 or 123(6), or
(c) which adds to, replaces or omits any part of the text of an Act,

is not to be made unless a draft of the instrument has been laid before, and approved by resolution of, each House of Parliament.

(4) Subsections (2) and (3) do not apply to an Order in Council or to subordinate legislation made –

(a) by the Scottish Ministers, or
(b) by the Assembly, unless made jointly by the Secretary of State and the Assembly.

(5) A statutory instrument containing regulations under section 63(2) made by the Scottish Ministers is to be subject to annulment in pursuance of a resolution of the Scottish Parliament.

(6) The power of the Department of Health, Social Services and Public Safety to make regulations under section 63(2) is to be exercisable by statutory rule for the purposes of the Statutory Rules (Northern Ireland) Order 1979 (SI 1979/1573 (NI 12)); and any such regulations are to be subject to negative resolution within the meaning of section 41(6) of the Interpretation Act (Northern Ireland) 1954 as if they were statutory instruments within the meaning of that Act.

(7) Subordinate legislation made under this Act may make different provision for different purposes or areas.

(8) A power to make subordinate legislation under this Act (as well as being exercisable in relation to all cases to which it extends) may be exercised in relation to –

- (a) those cases subject to specified exceptions, or
- (b) a particular case or class of case.

(9) In this section, 'subordinate legislation' does not include a direction.

Amendments—CFA 2014, ss 4, 7.

Defined terms—'Assembly', 'by virtue of', 'regulations', 'rules', 'subordinate legislation': s 144.

141 Rules of procedure

(1) Family Procedure Rules may make provision in respect of any matter to be prescribed by rules made by virtue of this Act and dealing generally with all matters of procedure.

(2) *(repealed)*

(3) In the case of an application for a placement order, for the variation or revocation of such an order, or for an adoption order, the rules must require any person mentioned in subsection (4) to be notified –

- (a) of the date and place where the application will be heard, and
- (b) of the fact that, unless the person wishes or the court requires, the person need not attend.

(4) The persons referred to in subsection (3) are –

- (a) in the case of a placement order, every person who can be found whose consent to the making of the order is required under subsection (3)(a) of section 21 (or would be required but for subsection (3)(b) of that section) or, if no such person can be found, any relative prescribed by rules who can be found,
- (b) in the case of a variation or revocation of a placement order, every person who can be found whose consent to the making of the placement order was required under subsection (3)(a) of section 21 (or would have been required but for subsection (3)(b) of that section),
- (c) in the case of an adoption order –
  - (i) every person who can be found whose consent to the making of the order is required under subsection (2)(a) of section 47 (or would be required but for subsection (2)(c) of that section) or, if no such person can be found, any relative prescribed by rules who can be found,
  - (ii) every person who has consented to the making of the order under section 20 (and has not withdrawn the consent) unless he has given a notice under subsection (4)(a) of that section which has effect,
  - (iii) every person who, if leave were given under section 47(5), would be entitled to oppose the making of the order.

(5) *(repealed)*

(6) Rules may, for the purposes of the law relating to contempt of court, authorise the publication in such circumstances as may be specified of information relating to proceedings held in private involving children.

Amendments—Courts Act 2003, s 109(1), Sch 8, para 413, Sch 10; CA 2004, s 62(6); CCA 2013, s 17, Sch 11.

Defined terms—'adoption order': s 46(1); 'by virtue of': s 144; 'child': ss 49(5), 144; 'consent (in relation to making adoption orders or placing for adoption)': s 52; 'court', 'information', 'notice': s 144; 'placement order': s 21; 'relative': s 144, read with s 1(8); 'rules': s 144.

142 Supplementary and consequential provision

(1) The appropriate Minister may by order make –

(a) any supplementary, incidental or consequential provision,
(b) any transitory, transitional or saving provision,

which he considers necessary or expedient for the purposes of, in consequence of or for giving full effect to any provision of this Act.

(2) For the purposes of subsection (1), where any provision of an order extends to England and Wales, and Scotland or Northern Ireland, the appropriate Minister in relation to the order is the Secretary of State.

(3) Before making an order under subsection (1) containing provision which would, if included in an Act of the Scottish Parliament, be within the legislative competence of that Parliament, the appropriate Minister must consult the Scottish Ministers.

(4) Subsection (5) applies to any power of the Lord Chancellor, the Secretary of State or the Assembly to make regulations, rules or an order by virtue of any other provision of this Act.

(5) The power may be exercised so as to make –

(a) any supplementary, incidental or consequential provision,
(b) any transitory, transitional or saving provision,

which the person exercising the power considers necessary or expedient.

(6) The provision which may be made under subsection (1) or (5) includes provision modifying Schedule 4 or amending or repealing any enactment or instrument.

In relation to an Order in Council, 'enactment' in this subsection includes an enactment comprised in, or in an instrument made under, an Act of the Scottish Parliament.

(7) The power of the Registrar General to make regulations under Chapter 5 of Part 1 may, with the approval of the Secretary of State, be exercised so as to make –

(a) any supplementary, incidental or consequential provision,
(b) any transitory, transitional or saving provision,

which the Registrar General considers necessary or expedient.

Amendments—SI 2008/678; CFA 2014, s 7, Sch 1.
Defined terms—'appropriate Minister', 'Assembly', 'by virtue of', 'enactment', 'regulations', 'rules': s 144.

143 Offences by bodies corporate and unincorporated bodies

(1) Where an offence under this Act committed by a body corporate is proved to have been committed with the consent or connivance of, or to be attributable to any neglect on the part of, any director, manager, secretary or other similar officer of the body, or a person purporting to act in any such capacity, that person as well as the body is guilty of the offence and liable to be proceeded against and punished accordingly.

(2) Where the affairs of a body corporate are managed by its members, subsection (1) applies in relation to the acts and defaults of a member in connection with his functions of management as it applies to a director of a body corporate.

(3) Proceedings for an offence alleged to have been committed under this Act by an unincorporated body are to be brought in the name of that body (and not in that of any of its members) and, for the purposes of any such proceedings in England and Wales or Northern Ireland, any rules of court relating to the service of documents have effect as if that body were a corporation.

(4) A fine imposed on an unincorporated body on its conviction of an offence under this Act is to be paid out of the funds of that body.

(5) If an unincorporated body is charged with an offence under this Act –

(a) in England and Wales, section 33 of the Criminal Justice Act 1925 and Schedule 3 to the Magistrates' Courts Act 1980 (procedure on charge of an offence against a corporation),

(b) in Northern Ireland, section 18 of the Criminal Justice Act (Northern Ireland) 1945 and Schedule 4 to the Magistrates' Courts (Northern Ireland) Order 1981 (SI 1981/1675 (NI 26)) (procedure on charge of an offence against a corporation),

have effect in like manner as in the case of a corporation so charged.

(6) Where an offence under this Act committed by an unincorporated body (other than a partnership) is proved to have been committed with the consent or connivance of, or to be attributable to any neglect on the part of, any officer of the body or any member of its governing body, he as well as the body is guilty of the offence and liable to be proceeded against and punished accordingly.

(7) Where an offence under this Act committed by a partnership is proved to have been committed with the consent or connivance of, or to be attributable to any neglect on the part of, a partner, he as well as the partnership is guilty of the offence and liable to be proceeded against and punished accordingly.

Defined terms—'body', 'court', 'rules': s 144.

144 General interpretation etc

(1) In this Act –

'appropriate Minister' means –

(a) in relation to England, Scotland or Northern Ireland, the Secretary of State,

(b) in relation to Wales, the Assembly,

and in relation to England and Wales means the Secretary of State and the Assembly acting jointly,

'the Assembly' means the National Assembly for Wales,

'body' includes an unincorporated body,

'by virtue of' includes 'by' and 'under',

'child', except where used to express a relationship, means a person who has not attained the age of 18 years,

'the Convention' means the Convention on Protection of Children and Co-operation in respect of Intercountry Adoption, concluded at the Hague on 29th May 1993,

'Convention adoption order' means an adoption order which, by virtue of regulations under section 1 of the Adoption (Intercountry Aspects) Act 1999 (regulations giving effect to the Convention), is made as a Convention adoption order,

'Convention country' means a country or territory in which the Convention is in force,

'court' means the High Court or the family court,

'enactment' includes an enactment comprised in subordinate legislation,

'fee' includes expenses,

'guardian' has the same meaning as in the 1989 Act and includes a special guardian within the meaning of that Act,

'information' means information recorded in any form,

'local authority' means any unitary authority, or any county council so far as they are not a unitary authority,

'Northern Irish adoption agency' means an adoption agency within the meaning of Article 3 of the Adoption (Northern Ireland) Order 1987 (SI 1987/2203 (NI 22)),

'Northern Irish adoption order' means an order made, or having effect as if made, under Article 12 of the Adoption (Northern Ireland) Order 1987,

'notice' means a notice in writing,

'registration authority' (in Part 1) has the same meaning as in the Care Standards Act 2000,

'regulations' means regulations made by the appropriate Minister, unless they are required to be made by the Lord Chancellor, the Secretary of State or the Registrar General,

'relative', in relation to a child, means a grandparent, brother, sister, uncle or aunt, whether of the full blood or half-blood or by marriage or civil partnership,

'rules' means Family Procedure Rules made by virtue of section 141(1),

...

'subordinate legislation' has the same meaning as in the Interpretation Act 1978,

'unitary authority' means –

(a) the council of any county so far as they are the council for an area for which there are no district councils,

(b) the council of any district comprised in an area for which there is no county council,

(c) the council of a county borough,

(d) the council of a London borough,

(e) the Common Council of the City of London.

(2) Any power conferred by this Act to prescribe a fee by regulations includes power to prescribe –

(a) a fee not exceeding a prescribed amount,

(b) a fee calculated in accordance with the regulations,

(c) a fee determined by the person to whom it is payable, being a fee of a reasonable amount.

(3) In this Act, 'Scottish adoption agency' means –

(a) a local authority, or

(b) a voluntary organisation providing a registered adoption service;

but in relation to the provision of any particular service, references to a Scottish adoption agency do not include a voluntary organisation unless it is registered in respect of that service or a service which, in Scotland, corresponds to that service.

Expressions used in this subsection have the same meaning as in the Regulation of Care (Scotland) Act 2001 and 'registered' means registered under Part 1 of that Act.

(4) In this Act, a couple means –

(a) a married couple, or

(aa) two people who are civil partners of each other, or

(b) two people (whether of different sexes or the same sex) living as partners in an enduring family relationship.

(5) Subsection (4)(b) does not include two people one of whom is the other's parent, grandparent, sister, brother, aunt or uncle.

(6) References to relationships in subsection (5) –

(a) are to relationships of the full blood or half blood or, in the case of an adopted person, such of those relationships as would exist but for adoption, and

(b) include the relationship of a child with his adoptive, or former adoptive, parents,

but do not include any other adoptive relationships.

(7) For the purposes of this Act, a person is the partner of a child's parent if the person and the parent are a couple but the person is not the child's parent.

Amendments—Courts Act 2003, s 109(1), Sch 8, para 414; CPA 2004, s 79(1),(11),(12); CCA 2013, s 17, Sch 11; CFA 2014, s 7, Sch 1.

Defined terms—'the 1989 Act': s 2(5); 'adoption (in relation to Chapter 4 of Part 1)': s 66; 'adoption agency': s 2(1); 'adoption order': s 46(1); 'Adoption Service': s 2(1); 'appropriate Minister', 'Assembly', 'body', 'by virtue of': s 144; 'child': ss 49(5), 144; 'the Convention', 'Convention adoption order', 'Convention country': s 144; 'couple': s 144(4); 'court', 'enactment', 'fee', 'guardian', 'information', 'local authority', 'Northern Irish adoption agency', 'Northern Irish adoption order', 'notice': s 144; 'partner, in relation to a parent of a child': s 144(7); 'registration authority (in Part 1)', 'regulations' and 'relative': s 144, read with s 1(8); 'rules': s 144; 'Scottish adoption agency': s 144(3); 'Scottish adoption order', 'subordinate legislation', 'unitary authority': s 144; 'voluntary organisation': s 2(5).

'relative' (s 144(1))—The definition is in precise terms – a great-uncle does not come within the definition (*Re C (Minors) (Wardship: Adoption)* [1989] 1 FLR 222, CA); however, a step-grandparent *is* within the definition (for example, see *Re U (Application to Free for Adoption)* [1993] 2 FLR 992, CA).

'couple' (s 144(4))—To establish that a couple are 'living as partners in an enduring family relationship', there must first be an unambiguous intention to create and maintain family life and, second, a factual matrix consistent with that intention. Both matters are a question of fact and degree in each case. There is no requirement that both partners should reside in the same property (*Re T and M (Adoption)* [2011] 1 FLR 1487, FD).

145 Devolution: Wales

(1) The references to the Adoption Act 1976 and to the 1989 Act in Schedule 1 to the National Assembly for Wales (Transfer of Functions) Order 1999 (SI 1999/672) are to be treated as referring to those Acts as amended by virtue of this Act.

(2) This section does not affect the power to make further Orders varying or omitting those references.

(3) In Schedule 1 to that Order, in the entry for the Adoption Act 1976, '9' is omitted.

(4) The functions exercisable by the Assembly under sections 9 and 9A of the Adoption Act 1976 (by virtue of paragraphs 4 and 5 of Schedule 4 to this Act) are to be treated for the purposes of section 44 of the Government of Wales Act 1998 (parliamentary procedures for subordinate legislation) as if made exercisable by the Assembly by an Order in Council under section 22 of that Act.

Defined terms—'the 1989 Act': s 2(5); 'Assembly', 'by virtue of', 'subordinate legislation': s 144.

146 Expenses

There shall be paid out of money provided by Parliament –

(a) any expenditure incurred by a Minister of the Crown by virtue of this Act,
(b) any increase attributable to this Act in the sums payable out of money so provided under any other enactment.

Defined terms—'by virtue of', 'enactment': s 144.

147 Glossary

Schedule 6 (glossary) is to have effect.

148 Commencement

(1) This Act (except sections 116 and 136, this Chapter and the provisions mentioned in subsections (5) and (6)) is to come into force on such day as the Secretary of State may by order appoint.

(2) Before making an order under subsection (1) (other than an order bringing paragraph 53 of Schedule 3 into force) the Secretary of State must consult the Assembly.

(3) Before making an order under subsection (1) bringing sections 123 and 124 into force, the Secretary of State must also consult the Scottish Ministers and the Department of Health, Social Services and Public Safety.

(4) Before making an order under subsection (1) bringing sections 125 to 131 into force, the Secretary of State must also consult the Scottish Ministers.

(5) The following are to come into force on such day as the Scottish Ministers may by order appoint –

(a) section 41(5) to (9), so far as relating to Scotland,
(b) sections 132 to 134,
(c) paragraphs 21 to 35 and 82 to 84 of Schedule 3,
(d) paragraphs 15 and 23 of Schedule 4,
(e) the entries in Schedule 5, so far as relating to the provisions mentioned in paragraphs (c) and (d),
(f) section 139, so far as relating to the provisions mentioned in the preceding paragraphs.

(6) Sections 2(6), 3(3) and (4), 4 to 17, 27(3), 53(1) to (3), 54, 56 to 65 and 98, paragraphs 13, 65, 66 and 111 to 113 of Schedule 3 and paragraphs 3 and 5 of Schedule 4 are to come into force on such day as the appropriate Minister may by order appoint.

Defined terms—'appropriate Minister', 'Assembly': s 144.

PART II

149 Extent

(1) The amendment or repeal of an enactment has the same extent as the enactment to which it relates.

(2) Subject to that and to the following provisions, this Act except section 137 extends to England and Wales only.

(3) The following extend also to Scotland and Northern Ireland –

(a) sections 63(2) to (5), 65(2)(a) and (b) and (3), 123 and 124,
(b) this Chapter, except sections 141 and 145.

(4) The following extend also to Scotland –

(a) section 41(5) to (9),
(b) *(repealed)*
(c) section 138,
(d) section 139, so far as relating to provisions extending to Scotland.

(5) In Schedule 4, paragraph 23 extends only to Scotland.

Amendments—CFA 2014, s 7, Sch 1

Defined terms—'enactment': s 144.

150 Short title

This Act may be cited as the Adoption and Children Act 2002.

SCHEDULE 1
REGISTRATION OF ADOPTIONS

1 Registration of adoption orders

(1) Every adoption order must contain a direction to the Registrar General to make in the Adopted Children Register an entry in the form prescribed by regulations made by the Registrar General with the approval of the Secretary of State.

(2) Where, on an application to a court for an adoption order in respect of a child, the identity of the child with a child to whom an entry in the registers of live-births or other records relates is proved to the satisfaction of the court, any adoption order made in pursuance of the application must contain a direction to the Registrar General to secure that the entry in the register or, as the case may be, record in question is marked with the word 'Adopted'.

(3) Where an adoption order is made in respect of a child who has previously been the subject of an adoption order made by a court in England or Wales under Part 1 of this Act or any other enactment –

(a) sub-paragraph (2) does not apply, and
(b) the order must contain a direction to the Registrar General to mark the previous entry in the Adopted Children Register with the word 'Re-adopted'.

(4) Where an adoption order is made, the prescribed officer of the court which made the order must communicate the order to the Registrar General in the prescribed manner; and the Registrar General must then comply with the directions contained in the order.

'Prescribed' means prescribed by rules.

Amendments—SI 2008/678.

Defined terms—'Adopted Children Register': s 77; 'adoption order': s 46(1); 'child': ss 49(5), 144; 'court', 'enactment': s 144; 'records (in relation to Chapter 5 of Part 1)': s 82; 'registers of live-births (in relation to Chapter 5 of Part 1)': s 82; 'regulations', 'rules': s 144.

2 Registration of adoptions in Scotland, Northern Ireland, the Isle of Man and the Channel Islands

(1) Sub-paragraphs (2) and (3) apply where the Registrar General is notified by the authority maintaining a register of adoptions in a part of the British Islands outside England and Wales that an order has been made in that part authorising the adoption of a child.

(2) If an entry in the registers of live-births or other records (and no entry in the Adopted Children Register) relates to the child, the Registrar General must secure that the entry is marked with –

(a) the word 'Adopted', followed by
(b) the name, in brackets, of the part in which the order was made.

(3) If an entry in the Adopted Children Register relates to the child, the Registrar General must mark the entry with –

(a) the word 'Re-adopted', followed by
(b) the name, in brackets, of the part in which the order was made.

(4) Where, after an entry in either of the registers or other records mentioned in sub-paragraphs (2) and (3) has been so marked, the Registrar General is notified by the authority concerned that –

(a) the order has been quashed,
(b) an appeal against the order has been allowed, or
(c) the order has been revoked,

the Registrar General must secure that the marking is cancelled.

(5) A copy or extract of an entry in any register or other record, being an entry the marking of which is cancelled under sub-paragraph (4), is not to be treated as an accurate copy unless both the marking and the cancellation are omitted from it.

Defined terms—'Adopted Children Register': s 77; 'adoption (in relation to Chapter 4 of Part 1)': s 66; 'child': ss 49(5), 144; 'records (in relation to Chapter 5 of Part 1)': s 82; 'registers of live-births (in relation to Chapter 5 of Part 1)': s 82.

3 Registration of other adoptions

(1) If the Registrar General is satisfied, on an application under this paragraph, that he has sufficient particulars relating to a child adopted under a registrable foreign adoption to enable an entry to be made in the Adopted Children Register for the child he must make the entry accordingly.

(2) If he is also satisfied that an entry in the registers of live-births or other records relates to the child, he must –

(a) secure that the entry is marked 'Adopted', followed by the name, in brackets, of the country in which the adoption was effected, or
(b) where appropriate, secure that the overseas registers of births are so marked.

(3) An application under this paragraph must be made, in the prescribed manner, by a prescribed person and the applicant must provide the prescribed documents and other information.

(4) An entry made in the Adopted Children Register by virtue of this paragraph must be made in the prescribed form.

(5) In this Schedule 'registrable foreign adoption' means an adoption which satisfies prescribed requirements and is either –

(a) adoption under a Convention adoption, or
(b) adoption under an overseas adoption.

(6) In this paragraph –

(a) 'prescribed' means prescribed by regulations made by the Registrar General with the approval of the Secretary of State,
(b) 'overseas register of births' includes –

(i) a register made under regulations made by the Secretary of State under section 41(1)(g), (h) or (i) of the British Nationality Act 1981,

(ii) a record kept under an Order in Council made under section 1 of the Registration of Births, Deaths and Marriages (Special Provisions) Act 1957 (other than a certified copy kept by the Registrar General).

Amendments—SI 2008/678.

Defined terms—'Adopted Children Register': s 77; 'adoption (in relation to Chapter 4 of Part 1)': s 66; 'by virtue of': s 144; 'child': ss 49(5), 144; 'Convention adoption': s 66(1)(c); 'information': s 144; 'overseas adoption': s 87; 'records (in relation to Chapter 5 of Part 1)': s 82; 'registers of live-births (in relation to Chapter 5 of Part 1)': s 82; 'regulations': s 144.

4 Amendment of orders and rectification of Registers and other records

(1) The court by which an adoption order has been made may, on the application of the adopter or the adopted person, amend the order by the correction of any error in the particulars contained in it.

(2) The court by which an adoption order has been made may, if satisfied on the application of the adopter or the adopted person that within the period of one year beginning with the date of the order any new name –

(a) has been given to the adopted person (whether in baptism or otherwise), or

(b) has been taken by the adopted person,

either in place of or in addition to a name specified in the particulars required to be entered in the Adopted Children Register in pursuance of the order, amend the order by substituting or, as the case may be, adding that name in those particulars.

(3) The court by which an adoption order has been made may, if satisfied on the application of any person concerned that a direction for the marking of an entry in the registers of live-births, the Adopted Children Register or other records included in the order in pursuance of paragraph 1(2) or (3) was wrongly so included, revoke that direction.

(4) Where an adoption order is amended or a direction revoked under sub-paragraphs (1) to (3), the prescribed officer of the court must communicate the amendment in the prescribed manner to the Registrar General.

'Prescribed' means prescribed by rules.

(5) The Registrar General must then –

(a) amend the entry in the Adopted Children Register accordingly, or

(b) secure that the marking of the entry in the registers of live-births, the Adopted Children Register or other records is cancelled,

as the case may be.

(6) Where an adoption order is quashed or an appeal against an adoption order allowed by any court, the court must give directions to the Registrar General to secure that –

(a) any entry in the Adopted Children Register, and

(b) any marking of an entry in that Register, the registers of live-births or other records as the case may be, which was effected in pursuance of the order,

is cancelled.

(7) Where an adoption order has been amended, any certified copy of the relevant entry in the Adopted Children Register which may be issued pursuant to section 78(2)(b) must be a copy of the entry as amended, without the reproduction of –

(a) any note or marking relating to the amendment, or

(b) any matter cancelled in pursuance of it.

(8) A copy or extract of an entry in any register or other record, being an entry the marking of which has been cancelled, is not to be treated as an accurate copy unless both the marking and the cancellation are omitted from it.

(9) If the Registrar General is satisfied –

- (a) that a registrable foreign adoption has ceased to have effect, whether on annulment or otherwise, or
- (b) that any entry or mark was erroneously made in pursuance of paragraph 3 in the Adopted Children Register, the registers of live-births, the overseas registers of births or other records,

he may secure that such alterations are made in those registers or other records as he considers are required in consequence of the adoption ceasing to have effect or to correct the error.
'Overseas register of births' has the same meaning as in paragraph 3.

(10) Where an entry in such a register is amended in pursuance of sub-paragraph (9), any copy or extract of the entry is not to be treated as accurate unless it shows the entry as amended but without indicating that it has been amended.

Defined terms—'Adopted Children Register': s 77; 'adoption (in relation to Chapter 4 of Part 1)': s 66; 'adoption order': s 46(1); 'court': s 144; 'records (in relation to Chapter 5 of Part 1)': s 82; 'registers of live-births (in relation to Chapter 5 of Part 1)': s 82; 'rules': s 144.

5 Marking of entries on re-registration of birth on legitimation

(1) Without prejudice to paragraphs 2(4) and 4(5), where, after an entry in the registers of live-births or other records has been marked in accordance with paragraph 1 or 2, the birth is re-registered under section 14 of the Births and Deaths Registration Act 1953 (re-registration of births of legitimated persons), the entry made on the re-registration must be marked in the like manner.

(2) Without prejudice to paragraph 4(9), where an entry in the registers of live-births or other records is marked in pursuance of paragraph 3 and the birth in question is subsequently re-registered under section 14 of that Act, the entry made on re-registration must be marked in the like manner.

Defined terms—'records (in relation to Chapter 5 of Part 1)', 'registers of live-births (in relation to Chapter 5 of Part 1)': s 82.

6 Cancellations in registers on legitimation

(1) This paragraph applies where an adoption order is revoked under section 55(1).

(2) The prescribed officer of the court must communicate the revocation in the prescribed manner to the Registrar General who must then cancel or secure the cancellation of –

- (a) the entry in the Adopted Children Register relating to the adopted person, and
- (b) the marking with the word 'Adopted' of any entry relating to the adopted person in the registers of live-births or other records.

'Prescribed' means prescribed by rules.

(3) A copy or extract of an entry in any register or other record, being an entry the marking of which is cancelled under this paragraph, is not to be treated as an accurate copy unless both the marking and the cancellation are omitted from it.

Defined terms—'Adopted Children Register': s 77; 'court': s 144; 'records (in relation to Chapter 5 of Part 1)' and 'registers of live-births (in relation to Chapter 5 of Part 1)': s 82; 'rules': s 144.

SCHEDULE 2
DISCLOSURE OF BIRTH RECORDS BY REGISTRAR GENERAL

1 On an application made in the prescribed manner by an adopted person –

- (a) a record of whose birth is kept by the Registrar General, and
- (b) who has attained the age of 18 years,

the Registrar General must give the applicant any information necessary to enable the applicant to obtain a certified copy of the record of his birth.

'Prescribed' means prescribed by regulations made by the Registrar General with the approval of the Secretary of State.

Amendments—SI 2008/678.

Defined terms—'information', 'regulations': s 144.

2 (1) Before giving any information to an applicant under paragraph 1, the Registrar General must inform the applicant that counselling services are available to the applicant –

(a) from a registered adoption society, an organisation within section 144(3)(b) or an adoption society which is registered under Article 4 of the Adoption (Northern Ireland) Order 1987 (SI 1987/2203 (NI 22)),
(b) if the applicant is in England and Wales, at the General Register Office or from any local authority or registered adoption support agency,
(c) if the applicant is in Scotland, from any council constituted under section 2 of the Local Government etc (Scotland) Act 1994,
(d) if the applicant is in Northern Ireland, from any Board.

(2) In sub-paragraph (1)(b), 'registered adoption support agency' means an adoption support agency in respect of which a person is registered under Part 2 of the Care Standards Act 2000.

(3) In sub-paragraph (1)(d), 'Board' means a Health and Social Services Board established under Article 16 of the Health and Personal Social Services (Northern Ireland) Order 1972 (SI 1972/1265 (NI 14)); but where the functions of a Board are exercisable by a Health and Social Services Trust, references in that sub-paragraph to a Board are to be read as references to the Health and Social Services Trust.

(4) If the applicant chooses to receive counselling from a person or body within sub-paragraph (1), the Registrar General must send to the person or body the information to which the applicant is entitled under paragraph 1.

Defined terms—'adoption society': s 2(5); 'adoption support agency': s 8; 'body', 'information', 'local authority': s 144; 'registered adoption society': s 2(2).

3 (1) Where an adopted person who is in England and Wales –

(a) applies for information under paragraph 1 or Article 54 of the Adoption (Northern Ireland) Order 1987, or
(b) is supplied with information under section 55(4)(b) of the Adoption and Children (Scotland) Act 2007,

the persons and bodies mentioned in sub-paragraph (2) must, if asked by the applicant to do so, provide counselling for the applicant.

(2) Those persons and bodies are –

(a) the Registrar General,
(b) any local authority,
(c) a registered adoption society, an organisation within section 144(3)(b) or an adoption society which is registered under Article 4 of the Adoption (Northern Ireland) Order 1987.

Amendments—SI 2011/1740.

Defined terms—'adoption society': s 2(5); 'information', 'local authority': s 144; 'registered adoption society': s 2(2).

4 (1) Where a person –

(a) was adopted before 12th November 1975, and
(b) applies for information under paragraph 1,

the Registrar General must not give the information to the applicant unless the applicant has attended an interview with a counsellor arranged by a person or body from whom counselling services are available as mentioned in paragraph 2.

(2) Where the Registrar General is prevented by sub-paragraph (1) from giving information to a person who is not living in the United Kingdom, the Registrar General may give the information to any body which –

(a) the Registrar General is satisfied is suitable to provide counselling to that person, and
(b) has notified the Registrar General that it is prepared to provide such counselling.

Defined terms—'body', 'information': s 144.

****

SCHEDULE 4
TRANSITIONAL AND TRANSITORY PROVISIONS AND SAVINGS

1 General rules for continuity

(1) Any reference (express or implied) in Part 1 or any other enactment, instrument or document to –

(a) any provision of Part 1, or
(b) things done or falling to be done under or for the purposes of any provision of Part 1,

must, so far as the nature of the reference permits, be construed as including, in relation to the times, circumstances or purposes in relation to which the corresponding provision repealed by this Act had effect, a reference to that corresponding provision or (as the case may be) to things done or falling to be done under or for the purposes of that corresponding provision.

(2) Any reference (express or implied) in any enactment, instrument or document to –

(a) a provision repealed by this Act, or
(b) things done or falling to be done under or for the purposes of such a provision,

must, so far as the nature of the reference permits, be construed as including, in relation to the times, circumstances or purposes in relation to which the corresponding provision of Part 1 has effect, a reference to that corresponding provision or (as the case may be) to things done or falling to be done under or for the purposes of that corresponding provision.

2 General rule for old savings

(1) The repeal by this Act of an enactment previously repealed subject to savings does not affect the continued operation of those savings.

(2) The repeal by this Act of a saving made on the previous repeal of an enactment does not affect the operation of the saving in so far as it is not specifically reproduced in this Act but remains capable of having effect.

3–5 *(repealed)*

6 Pending applications for freeing orders

Nothing in this Act affects any application for an order under section 18 of the Adoption Act 1976 (freeing for adoption) where –

(a) the application has been made and has not been disposed of immediately before the repeal of that section, and
(b) the child in relation to whom the application is made has his home immediately before that repeal with a person with whom he has been placed for adoption by an adoption agency.

7 Freeing orders

(1) Nothing in this Act affects any order made under section 18 of the Adoption Act 1976 and –

(a) sections 19 to 21 of that Act are to continue to have effect in relation to such an order, and

(b) Part 1 of Schedule 6 to the Magistrates' Courts Act 1980 is to continue to have effect for the purposes of an application under section 21 of the Adoption Act 1976 in relation to such an order.

(2) Section 20 of that Act, as it has effect by virtue of this paragraph, is to apply as if, in subsection (3)(c) after '1989' there were inserted –

'(iia) any care order, within the meaning of that Act'.

(3) Where a child is free for adoption by virtue of an order made under section 18 of that Act, the third condition in section 47(6) is to be treated as satisfied.

8 Pending applications for adoption orders

Nothing in this Act affects any application for an adoption order under section 12 of the Adoption Act 1976 where –

(a) the application has been made and has not been disposed of immediately before the repeal of that section, and

(b) the child in relation to whom the application is made has his home immediately before that repeal with a person with whom he has been placed for adoption by an adoption agency.

9 Notification of adoption applications

Where a notice given in respect of a child by the prospective adopters under section 22(1) of the Adoption Act 1976 is treated by virtue of paragraph 1(1) as having been given for the purposes of section 44(2) in respect of an application to adopt the child, section 42(3) has effect in relation to their application for an adoption order as if for 'six months' there were substituted 'twelve months'.

10–16 (*repealed*)

17 Status

(1) Section 67 –

(a) does not apply to a pre-1976 instrument or enactment in so far as it contains a disposition of property, and

(b) does not apply to any public general Act in its application to any disposition of property in a pre-1976 instrument or enactment.

(2) Section 73 applies in relation to this paragraph as if this paragraph were contained in Chapter 4 of Part 1; and an instrument or enactment is a pre-1976 instrument or enactment for the purposes of this Schedule if it was passed or made at any time before 1 January 1976.

18 Section 69 does not apply to a pre-1976 instrument.

19 In section 70(1), the reference to Part 3 of the Family Law Reform Act 1987 includes Part 2 of the Family Law Reform Act 1969.

20 Registration of adoptions

(1) The power of the court under paragraph 4(1) of Schedule 1 to amend an order on the application of the adopter or adopted person includes, in relation to an order made before 1 April 1959, power to make any amendment of the particulars contained in the order which appears to be required to bring the order into the form in which it would have been made if paragraph 1 of that Schedule had applied to the order.

(2) In relation to an adoption order made before the commencement of the Adoption Act 1976, the reference in paragraph 4(3) of that Schedule to paragraph 1(2) or (3) is to be read –

(a) in the case of an order under the Adoption of Children Act 1926, as a reference to section 12(3) and (4) of the Adoption of Children Act 1949,

(b) in the case of an order under the Adoption Act 1950, as a reference to section 18(3) and (4) of that Act,

(c) in the case of an order under the Adoption Act 1958, as a reference to section 21(4) and (5) of that Act.

21 The Child Abduction Act 1984

Paragraph 43 of Schedule 3 does not affect the Schedule to the Child Abduction Act 1984 in its application to a child who is the subject of –

(a) an order under section 18 of the Adoption Act 1976 freeing the child for adoption,
(b) a pending application for such an order, or
(c) a pending application for an order under section 12 of that Act.

22 The Courts and Legal Services Act 1990

Paragraph 80 of Schedule 3 does not affect section 58A(2)(b) of the Courts and Legal Services Act 1990 in its application to proceedings under the Adoption Act 1976.

****

SCHEDULE 6
GLOSSARY

In this Act, the expressions listed in the left-hand column below have the meaning given by, or are to be interpreted in accordance with, the provisions of this Act or (where stated) of the 1989 Act or the 2014 Act listed in the right-hand column.

Expression	*Provision*
the 1989 Act	section 2(5)
the 2014 Act	section 2(5)
Adopted Children Register	section 77
Adoption and Children Act Register	section 125
adoption (in relation to Chapter 4 of Part 1)	section 66
adoption agency	section 2(1)
adoption agency placing a child for adoption	section 18(5)
Adoption Contact Register	section 80
adoption order	section 46(1)
Adoption Service	section 2(1)
adoption society	section 2(5)
adoption support agency	section 8
adoption support services	section 2(6)
appointed day (in relation to Chapter 4 of Part 1)	section 66(2)
appropriate Minister	section 144
Assembly	section 144
Body	section 144
by virtue of	section 144
care order	section 105(1) of the 1989 Act
Child	sections 49(5) and 144
child arrangements order	section 8(1) of the 1989 Act
child assessment order	section 43(2) of the 1989 Act
child in the care of a local authority	section 105(1) of the 1989 Act
child looked after by a local authority (in relation to a local authority in England)	section 22 of the 1989 Act
child looked after by a local authority (in relation to a local authority in Wales)	section 74 of the 2014 Act
child placed for adoption by an adoption agency	section 18(5)
child to be adopted, adopted child	section 49(5)
consent (in relation to making adoption orders or placing for adoption)	section 52

Expression	*Provision*
the Convention	section 144
Convention adoption	section 66(1)(c)
Convention adoption order	section 144
Convention country	section 144
Couple	section 144(4)
Court	section 144
disposition (in relation to Chapter 4 of Part 1)	section 73
Enactment	section 144
Fee	section 144
Guardian	section 144
Information	section 144
interim care order	section 38 of the 1989 Act
local authority	section 144
local authority foster parent	section 105(1) of the 1989 Act
Northern Irish adoption agency	section 144
Northern Irish adoption order	section 144
Notice	section 144
notice of intention to adopt	section 44(2)
overseas adoption	section 87
parental responsibility	section 3 of the 1989 Act
partner, in relation to a parent of a child	section 144(7)
placement order	section 21
placing, or placed, for adoption	sections 18(5) and 19(4)
prohibited steps order	section 8(1) of the 1989 Act
records (in relation to Chapter 5 of Part 1)	section 82
registered adoption society	section 2(2)
registers of live-births (in relation to Chapter 5 of Part 1)	section 82
registration authority (in Part 1)	section 144
Regulations	section 144
Relative	section 144, read with section 1(8)
Rules	section 144
Scottish adoption agency	section 144(3)
Scottish adoption order	section 144
specific issue order	section 8(1) of the 1989 Act
subordinate legislation	section 144
supervision order	section 31(11) of the 1989 Act
unitary authority	section 144
voluntary organisation	section 2(5)

Amendments—CYPA 2008, s 8(3), Sch 1, para 14; CFA 2014, s 12, Sch 2; SI 2016/413.

Adoption (Intercountry Aspects) Act 1999

Guidance—Comprehensive government guidance on intercountry adoption is available at *www.gov.uk* and search on 'intercountry adoption'. For an up-to-date list of Convention States go to *www.hcch.net/index_en.php?act=conventions.status&cid=69*.

Liaison judge—In February [2008] Fam Law at [105] Lord Justice Thorpe offered the following information as to his role:

> 'In trans-national cases there is a high chance of contemporaneous proceedings in both the involved jurisdictions. Unless the two responsible judges communicate, there is an obvious risk of conflict, legal complexity, delay and wasted costs. Each jurisdiction needs a co-ordinator, a liaison judge available to facilitate the essential communication. In this jurisdiction I am responsible for that service. My office is well equipped to initiate the process that results in judge communicating with judge.'

The preferred route for contact for the Office of the Head of International Family Justice is tel: 020 7947 7197; email: IFJOffice@hmcts.gsi.gov.uk.

Implementation of Convention

1 Regulations giving effect to Convention

(1) Subject to the provisions of this Act, regulations made by the Secretary of State may make provision for giving effect to the Convention on Protection of Children and Co-operation in respect of Intercountry Adoption, concluded at the Hague on 29th May 1993 ('the Convention').

(2) The text of the Convention (so far as material) is set out in Schedule 1 to this Act.

(3) Regulations under this section may –

- (a) apply, with or without modifications, any provision of the enactments relating to adoption;
- (b) provide that any person who contravenes or fails to comply with any provision of the regulations is to be guilty of an offence and liable on summary conviction to imprisonment for a term not exceeding three months, or a fine not exceeding level 5 on the standard scale, or both;
- (c) make different provision for different purposes or areas; and
- (d) make such incidental, supplementary, consequential or transitional provision as appears to the Secretary of State to be expedient.

(4) Regulations under this section shall be made by statutory instrument which shall be subject to annulment in pursuance of a resolution of either House of Parliament.

(5) Subject to subsection (6), any power to make subordinate legislation under or for the purposes of the enactments relating to adoption includes power to do so with a view to giving effect to the provisions of the Convention.

(6) Subsection (5) does not apply in relation to any power which is exercisable by the National Assembly for Wales.

(7) References in this section to enactments include references to Acts of the Scottish Parliament.

Amendments—SI 2011/1740.

Regulations giving effect to the Convention—For procedure see the Intercountry Adoption (Hague Convention) Regulations 2003.

2 Central Authorities and accredited bodies

(1) The functions under the Convention of the Central Authority are to be discharged –

- (a) separately in relation to England and Scotland by the Secretary of State; and
- (b) in relation to Wales by the National Assembly for Wales.

(2) A communication may be sent to the Central Authority in relation to any part of Great Britain by sending it (for forwarding if necessary) to the Central Authority in relation to England.

(2A) A registered adoption society is an accredited body for the purposes of the Convention if, in accordance with the conditions of the registration, the society may provide facilities in respect of Convention adoptions and adoptions effected by Convention adoption orders.

(2B) (*applies to Scotland only*)

(3) An approved adoption society is an accredited body for the purposes of the Convention if the approval extends to the provision of facilities in respect of Convention adoptions and adoptions effected by Convention adoption orders.

(4) The functions under Article 9(a) to (c) of the Convention are to be discharged by local authorities and accredited bodies on behalf of the Central Authority.

(5) In this section, 'registered adoption society' has the same meaning as in section 2 of the Adoption and Children Act 2002 (basic definitions); and expressions used in this section in its application to England and Wales which are also used in that Act have the same meanings as in that Act.

(6) (*applies to Scotland only*)

Amendments—Care Standards Act 2000, s 116, Sch 4, para 27; ACA 2002, s 139(1), Sch 3, paras 96, 97(a).

★★★★

SCHEDULE 1
CONVENTION ON PROTECTION OF CHILDREN AND CO-OPERATION IN RESPECT OF INTERCOUNTRY ADOPTION

The States signatory to the present Convention.

Recognizing that the child, for the full and harmonious development of his or her personality, should grow up in a family environment, in an atmosphere of happiness, love and understanding,

Recalling that each State should take, as a matter of priority, appropriate measures to enable the child to remain in the care of his or her family of origin,

Recognizing that intercountry adoption may offer the advantage of a permanent family to a child for whom a suitable family cannot be found in his or her State of origin,

Convinced of the necessity to take measures to ensure that intercountry adoptions are made in the best interests of the child and with respect for his or her fundamental rights, and to prevent the abduction, the sale of, or traffic in children,

Desiring to establish common provisions to this effect, taking into account the principles set forth in international instruments, in particular the United Nations Convention on the Rights of the Child, of 20 November 1989, and the United Nations Declaration on Social and Legal Principles relating to the Protection and Welfare of Children, with Special Reference to Foster Placement and Adoption Nationally and Internationally (General Assembly Resolution 41/85, of 3 December 1986),

Have agreed upon the following provisions –

CHAPTER I
SCOPE OF THE CONVENTION

Article 1

The objects of the present Convention are –

(a) to establish safeguards to ensure that intercountry adoptions take place in the best interests of the child and with respect for his or her fundamental rights as recognised in international law;

(b) to establish a system of co-operation amongst Contracting States to ensure that those safeguards are respected and thereby prevent the abduction, the sale of, or traffic in children;

(c) to secure the recognition in Contracting States of adoptions made in accordance with the Convention.

Article 2

1 The Convention shall apply where a child habitually resident in one Contracting State ('the State of origin') has been, is being, or is to be moved to another Contracting State ('the receiving State') either after his or her adoption in the State of origin by spouses or a person habitually resident in the receiving State, or for the purposes of such an adoption in the receiving State or in the State of origin.

2 The Convention covers only adoptions which create a permanent parent-child relationship.

Article 3

The Convention ceases to apply if the agreements mentioned in Article 17, sub-paragraph (c), have not been given before the child attains the age of eighteen years.

CHAPTER II
REQUIREMENTS FOR INTERCOUNTRY ADOPTIONS

Article 4

An adoption within the scope of the Convention shall take place only if the competent authorities of the State of origin –

(a) have established that the child is adoptable;
(b) have determined, after possibilities for placement of the child within the State of origin have been given due consideration, that an intercountry adoption is in the child's best interests;
(c) have ensured that –
  (i) the persons, institutions and authorities whose consent is necessary for adoption, have been counselled as may be necessary and duly informed of the effects of their consent, in particular whether or not an adoption will result in the termination of the legal relationship between the child and his or her family of origin,
  (ii) such persons, institutions and authorities have given their consent freely, in the required legal form, and expressed or evidenced in writing,
  (iii) the consents have not been induced by payment or compensation of any kind and have not been withdrawn, and
  (iv) the consent of the mother, where required, has been given only after the birth of the child; and
(d) have ensured, having regard to the age and degree of maturity of the child, that –
  (i) he or she has been counselled and duly informed of the effects of the adoption and of his or her consent to the adoption, where such consent is required,
  (ii) consideration has been given to the child's wishes and opinions,
  (iii) the child's consent to the adoption, where such consent is required, has been given freely, in the required legal form, and expressed or evidenced in writing, and
  (iv) such consent has not been induced by payment or compensation of any kind.

Article 5

An adoption within the scope of the Convention shall take place only if the competent authorities of the receiving State –

(a) have determined that the prospective adoptive parents are eligible and suited to adopt;
(b) have ensured that the prospective adoptive parents have been counselled as may be necessary; and
(c) have determined that the child is or will be authorised to enter and reside permanently in that State.

CHAPTER III
CENTRAL AUTHORITIES AND ACCREDITED BODIES

Article 6

(1) A Contracting State shall designate a Central Authority to discharge the duties which are imposed by the Convention upon such authorities.

(2) Federal States, States with more than one system of law or States having autonomous territorial units shall be free to appoint more than one Central Authority and to specify the territorial or personal extent of their functions. Where a State has appointed more than one Central Authority, it shall designate the Central Authority to which any communication may be addressed for transmission to the appropriate Central Authority within that State.

Article 7

(1) Central Authorities shall co-operate with each other and promote co-operation amongst the competent authorities in their States to protect children and to achieve the other objects of the Convention.

(2) They shall take directly all appropriate measures to –

(a) provide information as to the laws of their States concerning adoption and other general information, such as statistics and standard forms;

(b) keep one another informed about the operation of the Convention and, as far as possible, eliminate any obstacles to its application.

Article 8

Central Authorities shall take, directly or through public authorities, all appropriate measures to prevent improper financial or other gain in connection with an adoption and to deter all practices contrary to the objects of the Convention.

Article 9

Central Authorities shall take, directly or through public authorities or other bodies duly accredited in their State, all appropriate measures, in particular to –

(a) collect, preserve and exchange information about the situation of the child and the prospective adoptive parents, so far as is necessary to complete the adoption;

(b) facilitate, follow and expedite proceedings with a view to obtaining the adoption;

(c) promote the development of adoption counselling and post-adoption services in their States;

(d) provide each other with general evaluation reports about experience with intercountry adoption;

(e) reply, in so far as is permitted by the law of their State, to justified requests from other Central Authorities or public authorities for information about a particular adoption situation.

Article 10

Accreditation shall only be granted to and maintained by bodies demonstrating their competence to carry out properly the tasks with which they may be entrusted.

Article 11

An accredited body shall –

(a) pursue only non-profit objectives according to such conditions and within such limits as may be established by the competent authorities of the State of accreditation;

(b) be directed and staffed by persons qualified by their ethical standards and by training or experience to work in the field of intercountry adoption; and

(c) be subject to supervision by competent authorities of that State as to its composition, operation and financial situation.

Article 12

A body accredited in one Contracting State may act in another Contracting State only if the competent authorities of both States have authorised it to do so.

Article 13

The designation of the Central Authorities and, where appropriate, the extent of their functions, as well as the names and addresses of the accredited bodies shall be communicated by each Contracting State to the Permanent Bureau of the Hague Conference on Private International Law.

CHAPTER IV
PROCEDURAL REQUIREMENTS IN INTERCOUNTRY ADOPTION

Article 14

Persons habitually resident in a Contracting State, who wish to adopt a child habitually resident in another Contracting State, shall apply to the Central Authority in the State of their habitual residence.

Article 15

(1) If the Central Authority of the receiving State is satisfied that the applicants are eligible and suited to adopt, it shall prepare a report including information about their identity, eligibility and suitability to adopt, background, family and medical history, social environment, reasons for adoption, ability to undertake an intercountry adoption, as well as the characteristics of the children for whom they would be qualified to care.

(2) It shall transmit the report to the Central Authority of the State of origin.

Article 16

(1) If the Central Authority of the State of origin is satisfied that the child is adoptable, it shall –

(a) prepare a report including information about his or her identity, adoptability, background, social environment, family history, medical history including that of the child's family, and any special needs of the child;

(b) give due consideration to the child's upbringing and to his or her ethnic, religious and cultural background;

(c) ensure that consents have been obtained in accordance with Article 4; and

(d) determine, on the basis in particular of the reports relating to the child and the prospective adoptive parents, whether the envisaged placement is in the best interests of the child.

(2) It shall transmit to the Central Authority of the receiving State its report on the child, proof that the necessary consents have been obtained and the reasons for its determination on the placement, taking care not to reveal the identity of the mother and the father if, in the State of origin, these identities may not be disclosed.

Article 17

Any decision in the State of origin that a child should be entrusted to prospective adoptive parents may only be made if –

(a) the Central Authority of that State has ensured that the prospective adoptive parents agree;

(b) the Central Authority of the receiving State has approved such decision, where such approval is required by the law of that State or by the Central Authority of the State of origin;

(c) the Central Authorities of both States have agreed that the adoption may proceed; and

(d) it has been determined, in accordance with Article 5, that the prospective adoptive parents are eligible and suited to adopt and that the child is or will be authorised to enter and reside permanently in the receiving State.

Article 18

The Central Authorities of both States shall take all necessary steps to obtain permission for the child to leave the State of origin and to enter and reside permanently in the receiving State.

Article 19

(1) The transfer of the child to the receiving State may only be carried out if the requirements of Article 17 have been satisfied.

(2) The Central Authorities of both States shall ensure that this transfer takes place in secure and appropriate circumstances and, if possible, in the company of the adoptive or prospective adoptive parents.

(3) If the transfer of the child does not take place, the reports referred to in Articles 15 and 16 are to be sent back to the authorities who forwarded them.

Article 20

The Central Authorities shall keep each other informed about the adoption process and the measures taken to complete it, as well as about the progress of the placement if a probationary period is required.

Article 21

(1) Where the adoption is to take place after the transfer of the child to the receiving State and it appears to the Central Authority of that State that the continued placement of the child with the prospective adoptive parents is not in the child's best interests, such Central Authority shall take the measures necessary to protect the child, in particular –

(a) to cause the child to be withdrawn from the prospective adoptive parents and to arrange temporary care;

(b) in consultation with the Central Authority of the State of origin, to arrange without delay a new placement of the child with a view to adoption or, if this is not appropriate, to arrange alternative long-term care; an adoption shall not take place until the Central Authority of the State of origin has been duly informed concerning the new prospective adoptive parents;

(c) as a last resort, to arrange the return of the child, if his or her interests so require.

(2) Having regard in particular to the age and degree of maturity of the child, he or she shall be consulted and, where appropriate, his or her consent obtained in relation to measures to be taken under this Article.

Article 22

(1) The functions of a Central Authority under this Chapter may be performed by public authorities or by bodies accredited under Chapter III, to the extent permitted by the law of its State.

(2) Any Contracting State may declare to the depositary of the Convention that the functions of the Central Authority under Articles 15 to 21 may be performed in that State, to the extent permitted by the law and subject to the supervision of the competent authorities of that State, also by bodies or persons who –

(a) meet the requirements of integrity, professional competence, experience and accountability of that State; and

(b) are qualified by their ethical standards and by training or experience to work in the field of intercountry adoption.

(3) A Contracting State which makes the declaration provided for in paragraph 2 shall keep the Permanent Bureau of the Hague Conference on Private International Law informed of the names and addresses of these bodies and persons.

(4) Any Contracting State may declare to the depositary of the Convention that adoptions of children habitually resident in its territory may only take place if the functions of the Central Authorities are performed in accordance with paragraph 1.

(5) Notwithstanding any declaration made under paragraph 2, the reports provided for in Articles 15 and 16 shall, in every case, be prepared under the responsibility of the Central Authority or other authorities or bodies in accordance with paragraph 1.

CHAPTER V
RECOGNITION AND EFFECTS OF THE ADOPTION

Article 23

(1) An adoption certified by the competent authority of the State of the adoption as having been made in accordance with the Convention shall be recognised by operation of law in the other Contracting States. The certificate shall specify when and by whom the agreements under Article 17, sub-paragraph (c), were given.

(2) Each Contracting State shall, at the time of signature, ratification, acceptance, approval or accession, notify the depositary of the Convention of the identity and the functions of the authority or the authorities which, in that State, are competent to make the certification. It shall also notify the depositary of any modification in the designation of these authorities.

Article 24

The recognition of an adoption may be refused in a contracting State only if the adoption is manifestly contrary to its public policy, taking into account the best interests of the child.

Article 25

Any Contracting State may declare to the depositary of the convention that it will not be bound under this Convention to recognise adoptions made in accordance with an agreement concluded by application of Article 39, paragraph 2.

Article 26

(1) The recognition of an adoption includes recognition of –

- (a) the legal parent-child relationship between the child and his or her adoptive parents;
- (b) parental responsibility of the adoptive parents for the child;
- (c) the termination of a pre-existing legal relationship between the child and his or her mother and father, if the adoption has this effect in the Contracting State where it was made.

(2) In the case of an adoption having the effect of terminating a pre-existing legal parent-child relationship, the child shall enjoy in the receiving State, and in any other Contracting State where the adoption is recognised, rights equivalent to those resulting from adoptions having this effect in each such State.

(3) The preceding paragraphs shall not prejudice the application of any provision more favourable for the child, in force in the Contracting State which recognises the adoption.

Article 27

(1) Where an adoption granted in the State of origin does not have the effect of terminating a pre-existing legal parent-child relationship, it may, in the receiving State which recognises the adoption under the Convention, be converted into an adoption having such an effect –

- (a) if the law of the receiving State so permits; and
- (b) if the consents referred to in Article 4, sub-paragraphs (c) and (d), have been or are given for the purpose of such an adoption.

(2) Article 23 applies to the decision converting the adoption.

CHAPTER VI
GENERAL PROVISIONS

Article 28

The Convention does not affect any law of a State of origin which requires that the adoption of a child habitually resident within that State take place in that State or which prohibits the child's placement in, or transfer to, the receiving State prior to adoption.

Article 29

There shall be no contact between the prospective adoptive parents and the child's parents or any other person who has care of the child until the requirements of Article 4, sub-paragraphs (a) to (c), and Article 5, sub-paragraph (a), have been met, unless the adoption takes place within a family or unless the contact is in compliance with the conditions established by the competent authority of the State of origin.

Article 30

(1) The competent authorities of a Contracting State shall ensure that information held by them concerning the child's origin, in particular information concerning the identity of his or her parents, as well as the medical history, is preserved.

(2) They shall ensure that the child or his or her representative has access to such information, under appropriate guidance, in so far as is permitted by the law of that State.

Article 31

Without prejudice to Article 30, personal data gathered or transmitted under the Convention, especially data referred to in Articles 15 and 16, shall be used only for the purposes for which they were gathered or transmitted.

Article 32

(1) No one shall derive improper financial or other gain from an activity related to an intercountry adoption.

(2) Only costs and expenses, including reasonable professional fees of persons involved in the adoption, may be charged or paid.

(3) The directors, administrators and employees of bodies involved in an adoption shall not receive remuneration which is unreasonably high in relation to services rendered.

Article 33

A competent authority which finds that any provision of the Convention has not been respected or that there is a serious risk that it may not be respected, shall immediately inform the Central Authority of its State. This Central Authority shall be responsible for ensuring that appropriate measures are taken.

Article 34

If the competent authority of the State of destination of a document so requests, a translation certified as being in conformity with the original must be furnished. Unless otherwise provided, the costs of such translation are to be borne by the prospective adoptive parents.

Article 35

The competent authorities of the contracting States shall act expeditiously in the process of adoption.

Article 36

In relation to a State which has two or more systems of law with regard to adoption applicable in different territorial units –

(a) any reference to habitual residence in that State shall be construed as referring to habitual residence in a territorial unit of that State;

(b) any reference to the law of that State shall be construed as referring to the law in force in the relevant territorial unit;

(c) any reference to the competent authorities or to the public authorities of that State shall be construed as referring to those authorised to act in the relevant territorial unit;

(d) any reference to the accredited bodies of that State shall be construed as referring to bodies accredited in the relevant territorial unit.

Article 37

In relation to a State which with regard to adoption has two or more systems of law applicable to different categories of persons, any reference to the law of that State shall be construed as referring to the legal system specified by the law of that State.

Article 38

A State within which different territorial units have their own rules of law in respect of adoption shall not be bound to apply the Convention where a State with a unified system of law would not be bound to do so.

Article 39

(1) The convention does not affect any international instrument to which Contracting States are Parties and which contains provisions on matters governed by the Convention, unless a contrary declaration is made by the States parties to such instrument.

(2) Any Contracting State may enter into agreements with one or more other Contracting States, with a view to improving the application of the Convention in their mutual relations. These agreements may derogate only from the provisions of Articles 14 to 16 and 18 to 21. The States which have concluded such an agreement shall transmit a copy to the depositary of the Convention.

Article 40

No reservation to the Convention shall be permitted.

Article 41

The Convention shall apply in every case where an application pursuant to Article 14 has been received after the Convention has entered into force in the receiving State and the State of origin.

Article 42

The Secretary General of the Hague Conference on Private International Law shall at regular intervals convene a Special Commission in order to review the practical operation of the Convention.

****

Anti-Social Behaviour, Crime and Policing Act 2014

****

121 Offence of forced marriage: England and Wales

(1) A person commits an offence under the law of England and Wales if he or she –

- (a) uses violence, threats or any other form of coercion for the purpose of causing another person to enter into a marriage, and
- (b) believes, or ought reasonably to believe, that the conduct may cause the other person to enter into the marriage without free and full consent.

(2) In relation to a victim who lacks capacity to consent to marriage, the offence under subsection (1) is capable of being committed by any conduct carried out for the purpose of causing the victim to enter into a marriage (whether or not the conduct amounts to violence, threats or any other form coercion).

(3) A person commits an offence under the law of England and Wales if he or she –

- (a) practises any form of deception with the intention of causing another person to leave the United Kingdom, and
- (b) intends the other person to be subjected to conduct outside the United Kingdom that is an offence under subsection (1) or would be an offence under that subsection if the victim were in England or Wales.

(4) 'Marriage' means any religious or civil ceremony of marriage (whether or not legally binding).

(5) 'Lacks capacity' means lacks capacity within the meaning of the Mental Capacity Act 2005.

(6) It is irrelevant whether the conduct mentioned in paragraph (a) of subsection (1) is directed at the victim of the offence under that subsection or another person.

(7) A person commits an offence under subsection (1) or (3) only if, at the time of the conduct or deception –

(a) the person or the victim or both of them are in England or Wales,
(b) neither the person nor the victim is in England or Wales but at least one of them is habitually resident in England and Wales, or
(c) neither the person nor the victim is in the United Kingdom but at least one of them is a UK national.

(8) 'UK national' means an individual who is –

(a) a British citizen, a British overseas territories citizen, a British National (Overseas) or a British Overseas citizen;
(b) a person who under the British Nationality Act 1981 is a British subject; or
(c) a British protected person within the meaning of that Act.

(9) A person guilty of an offence under this section is liable –

(a) on summary conviction, to imprisonment for a term not exceeding 12 months or to a fine or both;
(b) on conviction on indictment, to imprisonment for a term not exceeding 7 years.

(10) In relation to an offence committed before the commencement of section 154(1) of the Criminal Justice Act 2003, the reference to 12 months in subsection (9)(a) is to be read as a reference to six months.

Offence of forced marriage—There are two distinct offences created by s 121 as set out in subsections (1) and (3). In relation to those who lack capacity, a separate criteria is applied (see below). Sections 173 and 174 of the Act, which provided for anonymity to victims of forced marriage offences, have now been amended to make provision for anonymity for victims of forced marriages in England and Wales and Northern Ireland within a new s 122A and Sch 6A. This gives effect to the Government's commitment to introduce lifelong anonymity for victims of forced marriages and the Government's and cross-government's 'Ending violence against women and girls strategy' published on 8 March 2016. Sch 6A, para 1 makes provision for lifelong non-disclosure of any matter, in any publication that may lead to identification of a victim against whom an offence of forced marriage has been committed. Publication includes speech, writing, a relevant programme or other communication (in whatever form) that is addressed to or is accessible by the public at large or any section of the public. The court is empowered to direct that the restrictions imposed by the section and the Schedule are not to apply if the two conditions set out in Sch 6A, para 1(4),(5) are met. Those within an organisation who are considered 'responsible persons' are defined in Sch 6A, para 2. Breach of this prohibition is made a criminal offence liable on summary conviction of a fine. The defences that are available to a person charged with the offence are limited to those set out in para 3.

'Lacks capacity to consent to marriage'—Since lack of capacity is defined as that within MCA 2005, it will necessarily involve consideration of the principles set out in ss 1–3 of that Act and case-law under the Act. There is no clear test identified in any of the first instance decisions. It has been referred to as a 'legal fog' (*A Local Authority v H* [2012] COPLR 305, COP). For a commentary on the complex issues involved, see *Urgent Applications in the Court of Protection* (LexisNexis).

★★★★

Attachment of Earnings Act 1971

ARRANGEMENT OF SECTIONS

Section Page

Cases in which attachment is available

Section		Page
1	Courts with power to attach earnings	339
1A	Orders to which this Act applies	340
2	Principal definitions	340

3 Application for order and conditions of court's power to make it 341

Consequences of attachment order

6 Effect and contents of order 342
7 Compliance with order by employer 343
8 Interrelation with alternative remedies open to creditor 344

Subsequent proceedings

9 Variation, lapse and discharge of orders 344
10 Normal deduction rate to be reduced in certain cases 345
11 Attachment order in respect of maintenance payments to cease to have effect on the occurrence of certain events 346
12 Termination of employer's liability to make deductions 346

Administrative provisions

13 Application of sums received by collecting officer 347
14 Power of court to obtain statement of earnings etc 347
15 Obligation of debtor and his employers to notify changes of employment and earnings 348
16 Power of court to determine whether particular payments are earnings 348

Special provisions with respect to magistrates' courts

18 Certain action not to be taken by collecting officer except on request 349
20 Jurisdiction in respect of persons residing outside England and Wales 349

Miscellaneous provisions

22 Persons employed under the Crown 350
23 Enforcement provisions 350
24 Meaning of 'earnings' 352
25 General interpretation 353

Schedule 1 – Maintenance Orders to which this Act Applies 354
Schedule 3 – Deductions by Employer under Attachment of Earnings Order 356
Part I – Scheme of Deductions 356
Part II – Priority as between Orders 357

Cases in which attachment is available

1 Courts with power to attach earnings

(1) The High Court may make an attachment of earnings order to secure payments under a High Court maintenance order.

(1A) The family court may make an attachment of earnings order to secure payments under a High Court or family court maintenance order.

(2) The county court may make an attachment of earnings order to secure –

- (a) *(repealed)*
- (b) the payment of a judgment debt, other than a debt of less than £5 or such other sum as may be prescribed by rules of court; or
- (c) payments under an administration order.

(3) A magistrates' court may make an attachment of earnings order to secure –

- (a), (b) *(repealed)*
- (c) the payment of any sum required to be paid under regulations under section 23 or 24 of the Legal Aid, Sentencing and Punishment of Offenders Act 2012.

(4) *(repealed)*

PART II

(5) Any power conferred by this Act to make an attachment of earnings order includes a power to make such an order to secure the discharge of liabilities arising before the coming into force of this Act.

Amendments—AJA 1999, s 24, Sch 4, para 8; Criminal Defence Service Act 2006, s 4(1); SI 2006/1737; LASPOA 2012, s 39, Sch 5, para 6; CCA 2013, s 17, Schs 9, 10.

Defined terms—'administration order': s 25(1); 'judgment debt': s 2(c); 'maintenance order': s 2(a).

Rules—Note that the rules governing attachment of earnings orders in the County Court, now contained in CPR 1998, Pt 89, differ appreciably from those governing attachment of earnings orders in the Family Court (or the enforcement of High Court maintenance orders) in FPR 2010, Pt 39.

'maintenance order'—The Act contains many provisions special to maintenance orders (including, for example, lump sum orders – see **'maintenance order'** under s 2 below). It is always necessary to bear in mind whether a particular attachment of earnings application or order secures a maintenance order.

'£5 or such other sum' (s 1(2)(b))—The minimum (in the case of a County Court judgment debt) is £50 (CPR 1998, r 89.7(14)). There is no corresponding provision in the family jurisdiction because an attachment of earnings order can explicitly be made whether or not arrears have accrued (FPR 2010, r 39.1).

1A Orders to which this Act applies

The following provisions of this Act apply, except where otherwise stated, to attachment of earnings orders made, or to be made, by any court under this Act or under Schedule 5 to the Courts Act 2003, or by a fines officer under that Schedule.

Amendments—Inserted by SI 2006/1737.

2 Principal definitions

In this Act –

(a) 'maintenance order' means any order, decision, settlement, arrangement or instrument specified in Schedule 1 to this Act and includes one which has been discharged or has otherwise ceased to operate if any arrears are recoverable thereunder;

(b) 'High Court maintenance order' and 'family court maintenance order' mean respectively a maintenance order enforceable by the High Court and the family court;

(c) 'judgment debt' means a sum payable under –

(i) a judgment or order enforceable by a court in England and Wales (not being a magistrates' court);

(ii) an order of a magistrates' court for the payment of money recoverable summarily as a civil debt; or

(iii) an order of any court which is enforceable as if it were for the payment of money so recoverable;

but does not include any sum payable under a maintenance order or an administration order;

(d) 'the relevant adjudication', in relation to any payment secured or to be secured by an attachment of earnings order, means the conviction, judgment, order or other adjudication from which there arises the liability to make the payment; and

(e) 'the debtor', in relation to an attachment of earnings order, or to proceedings in which a court has power to make an attachment of earnings order, or to proceedings arising out of such an order, means the person by whom payment is required by the relevant adjudication to be made.

Amendments—SI 2011/1484; SI 2012/2814; CCA 2013, s 17, Schs 9, 10.

Defined terms—'administration order': s 25(1).

Scope—This section contains the definitions of the expressions which are fundamental to the Act. Other definitions are set out in ss 24 and 25.

'maintenance order' (s 2(a))—In addition to periodical payments, the definitions in Sch 1 include 'other payments made or having effect as if made under' the provisions referred to, including, for example, MCA 1973, Pt II, which makes provision for lump sum orders and other orders for payment of money which would not normally be thought of as maintenance orders. See the discussion in *TJB v RJB* [2016] EWHC 1171 (Fam).

'judgment debt' (s 2(c))—In family proceedings, the most common judgment debt is an order for costs.

3 Application for order and conditions of court's power to make it

(A1) This section shall not apply to an attachment of earnings order to be made under Schedule 5 to the Courts Act 2003.

(1) The following persons may apply for an attachment of earnings order –

(a) the person to whom payment under the relevant adjudication is required to be made (whether directly or through any court or an officer of any court);

(b) where the relevant adjudication is an administration order, any one of the creditors scheduled to the order;

(c) without prejudice to paragraph (a) above, an officer of the family court if the application is to the family court for an order to secure maintenance payments and there is in force an order that those payments be made to the court or an officer of the court;

(ca) without prejudice to paragraphs (a) and (c) above, an officer of the family court if the application is to the family court to secure payments under a maintenance order described in paragraphs 13, 14, 14A or 14B of Schedule 1 and those payments are to be made to the court;

(d) in the following cases the debtor –

(i) where the application is to a magistrates' court; or

(ii) where the application is to the High Court or the family court for an order to secure maintenance payments.

(2) *(repealed)*

(3) Subject to subsection (3A) below for an attachment of earnings order to be made on the application of any person other than the debtor it must appear to the court that the debtor has failed to make one or more payments required by the relevant adjudication.

(3A) Subsection (3) above shall not apply when the relevant adjudication is a maintenance order.

(3B), (3C) *(repealed)*

(4) Where proceedings are brought –

(a) in the High Court or the family court for the enforcement of a maintenance order by committal under section 5 of the Debtors Act 1869;

(b) *(repealed)*

then the court may make an attachment of earnings order to secure payments under the maintenance order, instead of dealing with the case under section 5 of the said Act of 1869.

(5) *(repealed)*

(6) …

(7) The county court shall not make an attachment of earnings order to secure the payment of a judgment debt if there is in force an order or warrant for the debtor's committal, under section 5 of the Debtors Act 1869, in respect of that debt; but in any such case the court may discharge the order or warrant with a view to making an attachment of earnings order instead.

Amendments—MCA 1980, s 154, Sch 7, para 97; MEA 1991, s 11(1), Sch 2, para 1; Criminal Procedure and Investigations Act 1996, s 53; AJA 1999, s 90, Sch 13, para 65; Powers of Criminal Courts (Sentencing) Act 2000, s 165, Sch 9, para 44; Courts Act 2003, s 109(1), Sch 8, para 141; SI 2006/1737; TCEA 2007, s 62(3), Sch 13, para 36; SI 2012/2814; CCA 2013, s 17, Schs 9, 10.

Defined terms—'administration order': s 25(1); 'debtor': s 2(e); 'maintenance order': s 2(a); 'maintenance payments': s 25(1); 'relevant adjudication': s 2(d).

'Schedule 5 to the Courts Act 2003' (s 3(A1))—The Schedule only applies to collection of fines and other sums imposed upon conviction.

Restriction on order (s 3(3))—No attachment of earnings order may be made (unless it is applied for by the debtor) if the debtor has not defaulted under the judgment or order. This restriction does not apply in the case of a maintenance order (s 3(3A)).

'subsection (3) above shall not apply' (s 3(3A))—Section 3(3) is disapplied from all maintenance orders as defined by s 2(e). Where the relevant adjudication is a 'qualifying periodical maintenance order' within the meaning of MEA 1991, s 1 (one where money is to be paid periodically (including a lump sum order payable by instalments) and where the payer at the time the order is made is ordinarily resident in England and Wales), wider powers to make an attachment of earnings order exist. In such a case, the High Court and the Family

PART II

Court may make an attachment of earnings order on making the relevant maintenance order and, subsequently, on application or of the court's own motion in the course of any proceedings concerning the order (MEA 1991, s 1).

Own motion powers (s 3(4))—The court can make an attachment of earnings order, without an application, in lieu of committal or when hearing applications for that remedy, even where the extended powers under MEA 1991, s 1 do not apply.

****

Consequences of attachment order

6 Effect and contents of order

(1) An attachment of earnings order shall be an order directed to a person who appears to the court, or as the case may be the fines officer, making the order to have the debtor in his employment and shall operate as an instruction to that person –

- (a) to make periodical deductions from the debtor's earnings in accordance with Part I of Schedule 3 to this Act; and
- (b) at such times as the order may require, or as the court, or where the order is made under Schedule 5 to the Courts Act 2003, as the court or the fines officer as the case may be, may allow, to pay the amounts deducted to the collecting officer of the court, as specified in the order.

(2) For the purposes of this Act, the relationship of employer and employee shall be treated as subsisting between two persons if one of them, as a principal and not as a servant or agent, pays to the other any sums defined as earnings by section 24 of this Act.

(3) An attachment of earnings order shall contain prescribed particulars enabling the debtor to be identified by the employer.

(4) Except where it is made to secure maintenance payments, the order shall specify the whole amount payable under the relevant adjudication (or so much of that amount as remains unpaid), including any relevant costs.

(5) Subject to subsection (5A) below, the order shall specify –

- (a) the normal deduction rate, that is to say, the rate (expressed as a sum of money per week, month or other period) at which the court thinks it reasonable for the debtor's earnings to be applied to meeting his liability under the relevant adjudication; and
- (b) the protected earnings rate, that is to say the rate (so expressed) below which, having regard to the debtor's resources and needs, the court thinks it reasonable that the earnings actually paid to him should not be reduced.

(5A) If the order is made under Schedule 5 to the Courts Act 2003 then it shall specify the percentage deduction rate in accordance with fines collection regulations made under that Schedule.

(6) In the case of an order made to secure payments under a maintenance order (not being an order for the payment of a lump sum), the normal deduction rate –

- (a) shall be determined after taking account of any right or liability of the debtor to deduct income tax when making the payments; and
- (b) shall not exceed the rate which appears to the court necessary for the purpose of –
  - (i) securing payment of the sums falling due from time to time under the maintenance order, and
  - (ii) securing payment within a reasonable period of any sums already due and unpaid under the maintenance order.

(7) For the purposes of an attachment of earnings order, the collecting officer of the court shall be (subject to later variation of the order under section 9 of this Act) –

- (a) in the case of an order made by the High Court, either –
  - (i) the proper officer of the High Court, or

(ii) the appropriate officer of the family court or the county court if the order so specifies;

(aa) in the case of an order made by the family court, the appropriate officer of that court;

(b) in the case of an order made by the county court, the appropriate officer of that court; and

(c) in the case of an order made by a magistrates' court, the designated officer for that court or for another magistrates' court specified in the order.

(8) In subsection (7) above 'appropriate officer' means an officer designated by the Lord Chancellor.

(9)–(12) …

Amendments—AJA 1977, s 19(5); AJA 1999, s 90, Sch 13, para 66; SI 2006/1737; Courts Act 2003, s 109(1), Sch 8, para 142; CCA 2013, s 17, Schs 9, 10.

Defined terms—'the debtor': s 2(e); 'earnings': s 24; 'maintenance order': s 2(a); 'maintenance payments': s 25(1); 'the relevant adjudication': s 2(d); 'relevant costs': s 25(2).

Employer (s 6(2))—The relationship of employer/employee, for the purposes of this Act, is determined solely by the nature of the payments made by one to the other. If they fall within the definition in s 24 (and the payer is not merely a servant or agent of another) then the payer is the employer notwithstanding that no other attribute of employment exists.

'prescribed particulars' (s 6(3))—For the prescribed particulars see FPR 2010, r 39.7(2).

'normal deduction rate' (s 6(5)(a),(6))—In establishing the normal deduction rate, regard may be had only to the debtor's actual earnings, not to his earning potential, even though this may result in the normal deduction rate being less than the rate of the relevant periodical payments order, on the making of which unrealised earning capacity may have been taken into account (*Pepper v Pepper* [1960] 1 WLR 131, PDAD).

'protected earnings rate' (s 6(5)(b))—The rate set will not normally be below the income support threshold; although this is not impossible in an appropriate case, in most cases it would be unreasonable so to do (*Billington v Billington* [1974] Fam 24, FD). In practice it will usually be set a little above that threshold so that the debtor is not discouraged from continuing in employment. The debtor's needs include those of his dependants (s 25(3)).

'right or liability of the debtor to deduct income tax' (s 6(6)(a))—Maintenance orders are paid gross of tax.

Insolvency—The fact that the debtor may become bankrupt does not (if he retains his employment) stay an attachment of earnings application or prevent an attachment of earnings order from being made or continuing to have effect to enforce a judgment or order made in family proceedings. There may be a hiatus in the payments received under an existing attachment of earnings order, since it was held in *Re Green; Official Receiver v Cutting* [1979] 1 WLR 1211, ChD, that deductions made by the employer which have not reached the court when the bankruptcy commences fall into the bankrupt's estate. However, that case was decided under the Bankruptcy Act 1914 and the changed status of periodical payments orders in relation to bankruptcy by virtue of the Insolvency Act 1986 and Insolvency Rules 1986, r 12.3 might lead a court to reach a different conclusion today.

Forms—Family Court Form FE15 has now been prescribed for this purpose.

7 Compliance with order by employer

(1) Where an attachment of earnings order has been made, the employer shall, if he has been served with the order, comply with it; but he shall be under no liability for non-compliance before seven days have elapsed since the service.

(2) Where a person is served with an attachment of earnings order directed to him and he has not the debtor in his employment, or the debtor subsequently ceases to be in his employment, he shall (in either case), within ten days from the date of service or, as the case may be, the cesser, give notice of that fact to the court.

(3) Part II of Schedule 3 to this Act shall have effect with respect to the priority to be accorded as between two or more attachment of earnings orders directed to a person in respect of the same debtor.

(4) On any occasion when the employer makes, in compliance with the order, a deduction from the debtor's earnings –

(a) he shall be entitled to deduct, in addition, five new pence, or such other sum as may be prescribed by order made by the Lord Chancellor, towards his clerical and administrative costs; and

(b) he shall give to the debtor a statement in writing of the total amount of the deduction.

(5) An order of the Lord Chancellor under subsection (4)(a) above –

PART II

(a) may prescribe different sums in relation to different classes of cases;
(b) may be varied or revoked by a subsequent order made under that paragraph; and
(c) shall be made by statutory instrument subject to annulment by resolution of either House of Parliament.

Defined terms—'the debtor': s 2(e); 'the employer': s 25(2).

'seven days' (s 7(1))—The employer is given a period of grace to give effect to the order.

Priority of orders (s 7(3))—There are two categories of attachment of earnings order – those which secure judgment debts and administration orders and those which secure other liabilities (including maintenance orders). The latter are usually termed 'priority orders' and must be applied to the debtor's earnings first. Within each category, priority follows the dates the orders were made – see AEA 1971, Sch 3, para 7.

Prescribed deduction (s 7(4)(a))—The current figure is £1 (prescribed by Attachment of Earnings (Employer's Deduction) Order 1991, SI 1991/356).

8 Interrelation with alternative remedies open to creditor

(1) Where an attachment of earnings order has been made to secure maintenance payments, no order or warrant of commitment shall be issued in consequence of any proceedings for the enforcement of the related maintenance order begun before the making of the attachment of earnings order.

(2) Where the county court has made an attachment of earnings order to secure the payment of a judgment debt –

(a) no order or warrant of commitment shall be issued in consequence of any proceedings for the enforcement of the debt begun before the making of the attachment of earnings order; and
(b) so long as the order is in force, no execution for the recovery of the debt shall issue against any property of the debtor without the leave of the county court.

(3) An attachment of earnings order made to secure maintenance payments shall cease to have effect upon the making of an order of commitment or the issue of a warrant of commitment for the enforcement of the related maintenance order.

(4) An attachment of earnings order made to secure the payment of a judgment debt shall cease to have effect on the making of an order of commitment or the issue of a warrant of commitment for the enforcement of the debt.

(5) An attachment of earnings order made to secure –

(a) any payment mentioned in section 1(3)(c) of this Act; or
(b) the payment of any sum mentioned in paragraph 1 of Schedule 5 to the Courts Act 2003,

shall cease to have effect on the issue of a warrant committing the debtor to prison for default in making that payment.

Amendments—MCA 1980, s 154, Sch 7, para 98; SI 2006/1737; CCA 2013, s 17, Schs 9, 10.

Defined terms—'judgment debt': s 2(c); 'maintenance order': s 2(a); 'maintenance payments': s 25(2).

Subsequent proceedings

9 Variation, lapse and discharge of orders

(1) The court, or where an attachment of earnings order is made under Schedule 5 to the Courts Act 2003, the court or the fines officer as the case may be, may make an order discharging or varying an attachment of earnings order.

(2) Where an order is varied, the employer shall, if he has been served with notice of the variation, comply with the order as varied; but he shall be under no liability for non-compliance before seven days have elapsed since the service.

(3) Rules of court may make provision –

(a) as to the circumstances in which an attachment of earnings order made under this Act may be varied or discharged by the court of its own motion:

(aa) as to the circumstances in which an attachment of earnings order made under Schedule 5 to the Courts Act 2003 may be varied or discharged by the court or the fines officer of its or his own motion;

(b) in the case of an attachment of earnings order made by a magistrates' court, for enabling a single justice, on an application made by the debtor on the ground of a material change in his resources and needs since the order was made or last varied, to vary the order for a period of not more than four weeks by an increase of the protected earnings rate.

(4) Where an attachment of earnings order has been made and the person to whom it is directed ceases to have the debtor in his employment, the order shall lapse (except as respects deduction from earnings paid after the cesser and payment to the collecting officer of amounts deducted at any time) and be of no effect unless and until the court, or where the order was made under Schedule 5 to the Courts Act 2003, unless and until the court or the fines officer as the case may be, again directs it to a person (whether the same as before or another) who appears to the court or the fines officer (as the case may be) to have the debtor in his employment.

(5) The lapse of an order under subsection (4) above shall not prevent its being treated as remaining in force for other purposes.

Amendments—SI 2006/1737.

Defined terms—'the debtor': s 2(e); 'the employer': s 25(1); 'protected earnings rate': s 6(5)(b).

'seven days' (s 9(2))—The employer is given a period of grace to give effect to the variation.

'Rules of court' (s 9(3))—For the relevant rules, see CPR 1998, Pt 89 (for County Court proceedings) and FPR 2010, Pt 39 (for family proceedings).

'resources and needs' (s 9(3)(b))—See **'normal deduction rate'** and **'protected earnings rate'** under s 6.

Lapse of order (s 9(4),(5))—If the debtor loses or changes his employment, this creates a temporary hiatus. As soon as the court learns of a new employer, the order will be redirected, and varied as appropriate (CPR 1998, r 89.14(3) (County Court) and FPR 2010, r 39.16(3) (for family proceedings)).

10 Normal deduction rate to be reduced in certain cases

(1) The following provisions shall have effect, in the case of an attachment of earnings order made to secure maintenance payments, where it appears to the collecting officer of the court that –

(a) the aggregate of the payments made for the purposes of the related maintenance order by the debtor (whether under the attachment of earnings order or otherwise) exceeds the aggregate of the payments required up to that time by the maintenance order; and

(b) the normal deduction rate specified by the attachment of earnings order (or, where two or more such orders are in force in relation to the maintenance order, the aggregate of the normal deduction rates specified by those orders) exceeds the rate of payments required by the maintenance order; and

(c) no proceedings for the variation or discharge of the attachment of earnings order are pending.

(2) In the case of an order made by the High Court or the family court, the collecting officer shall give the prescribed notice to the person to whom he is required to pay sums received under the attachment of earnings order, and to the debtor; and the court shall make the appropriate variation order, unless the debtor requests it to discharge the attachment of earnings order, or to vary it in some other way, and the court thinks fit to comply with the request.

(3) *(repealed)*

(4) In this section, 'the appropriate variation order' means an order varying the attachment of earnings order in question by reducing the normal deduction rate specified thereby so as to secure that that rate (or, in the case mentioned in subsection (1)(b) above, the aggregate of the rates therein mentioned) –

(a) is the same as the rate of payments required by the maintenance order; or

(b) is such lower rate as the court thinks fit having regard to the amount of the excess mentioned in subsection (1)(a).

Amendments—CCA 2013, s 17, Schs 9, 10.

PART II

Defined terms—'collecting officer': s 6(7); 'the debtor': s 2(e); 'maintenance order': s 2(a); 'maintenance payments': s 25(1); 'normal deduction rate': s 6(5)(a).

Restriction (s 10(1)(c))—This section does not apply if an application to vary or discharge the maintenance order is pending.

Variation—Arrears having been cleared, the court is likely to vary the normal deduction rate to the level of the maintenance order, but the debtor may apply for another variation or for the attachment of earnings order to be discharged.

11 Attachment order in respect of maintenance payments to cease to have effect on the occurrence of certain events

(1) An attachment of earnings order made to secure maintenance payments shall cease to have effect –

(a) upon the grant of an application for registration of the related maintenance order under section 2 of the Maintenance Orders Act 1958 (which provides for the registration in the family court of a High Court maintenance order);

(b) where the related maintenance order is registered under Part I of the said Act of 1958, upon the giving of notice with respect thereto under section 5 of that Act (notice with view to cancellation of registration);

(c) subject to subsection (3) below, upon the discharge of the related maintenance order while it is not registered under Part I of the said Act of 1958;

(d) upon the related maintenance order ceasing to be registered in a court in England or Wales, or becoming registered in a court in Scotland or Northern Ireland, under Part II of the Maintenance Orders Act 1950.

(2) Subsection (1)(a) above shall have effect, in the case of an application for registration under section 2(1) of the said Act of 1958, notwithstanding that the grant of the application may subsequently become void under subsection (2) of that section.

(3) Where the related maintenance order is discharged as mentioned in subsection (1)(c) above and it appears to the court discharging the order that arrears thereunder will remain to be recovered after the discharge, that court may, if it thinks fit, direct that subsection (1) shall not apply.

Amendments—CCA 2013, s 17, Sch 10.

Defined terms—'maintenance order': s 2(a); 'maintenance payments': s 25(1).

Registration and cancellation of registration—If the function of enforcement of the order later passes to another English or Welsh court, a fresh application for an attachment of earnings order may be made.

12 Termination of employer's liability to make deductions

(1) Where an attachment of earnings order ceases to have effect under section 8 or 11 of this Act, the proper officer of the prescribed court shall give notice of the cesser to the person to whom the order was directed.

(2) Where, in the case of an attachment of earnings order made otherwise than to secure maintenance payments, the whole amount payable under the relevant adjudication has been paid, and also any relevant costs, the court shall give notice to the employer that no further compliance with the order is required.

(3) Where an attachment of earnings order –

(a) ceases to have effect under section 8 or 11 of this Act; or

(b) is discharged under section 9,

the person to whom the order has been directed shall be under no liability in consequence of his treating the order as still in force at any time before the expiration of seven days from the date on which the notice required by subsection (1) above or, as the case may be, a copy of the discharging order is served on him.

Defined terms—'employer', 'maintenance payments': s 25(1); 'relevant adjudication': s 2(d); 'relevant costs': s 25(2).

'seven days' (s 12(3))—The employer is under no liability for a period of grace if he continues to treat the order as in force after service of the relevant notice or copy order.

Administrative provisions

13 Application of sums received by collecting officer

(1) Subject to subsection (3) below, the collecting officer to whom a person makes payments in compliance with an attachment of earnings order shall, after deducting such court fees, if any, in respect of proceedings for or arising out of the order, as are deductible from those payments, deal with the sums paid in the same way as he would if they had been paid by the debtor to satisfy the relevant adjudication.

(2) Any sums paid to the collecting officer under an attachment of earnings order made to secure maintenance payments shall, when paid to the person entitled to receive those payments, be deemed to be payments made by the debtor (with such deductions, if any, in respect of income tax as the debtor is entitled or required to make) so as to discharge –

- (a) first, any sums for the time being due and unpaid under the related maintenance order (a sum due at an earlier date being discharged before a sum due at a later date); and
- (b) secondly, any costs incurred in proceedings relating to the related maintenance order which were payable by the debtor when the attachment of earnings order was made or last varied.

(3) When the county court makes an attachment of earnings order to secure the payment of a judgment debt and also, under section 4(1) of this Act, orders the debtor to furnish to the court a list of his creditors, sums paid to the collecting officer in compliance with the attachment of earnings order shall not be dealt with by him as mentioned in subsection (1) above, but shall be retained by him pending the decision of the court whether or not to make an administration order and shall then be dealt with by him as the court may direct.

Amendments—CCA 2013, s 17, Sch 9.

Defined terms—'administration order': s 25(1); 'collecting officer': s 6(7); 'the debtor': s 2(e); 'maintenance order': s 2(a); 'maintenance payments' s 25(1); 'relevant adjudication': s 2(d).

Income tax (s 13(2))—Maintenance is no longer taxable in the hands of the recipient and hence no tax is deductible from payments.

14 Power of court to obtain statement of earnings etc

(1) Where in any proceedings a court has the power under this Act or under Schedule 5 to the Courts Act 2003, or a fines officer has power under that Schedule, to make an attachment of earnings order, the court or the fines officer, as the case may be, may –

- (a) order the debtor to give to the court or the fines officer, as the case may be, within a specified period, a statement signed by him of –
  - (i) the name and address of any person by whom earnings are paid to him;
  - (ii) specified particulars as to his earnings and anticipated earnings, and as to his resources and needs; and
  - (iii) specified particulars for the purpose of enabling the debtor to be identified by any employer of his;
- (b) order any person appearing to the court or the fines officer, as the case may be, to have the debtor in his employment to give to the court or the fines officer, as the case may be, within a specified period, a statement signed by him or on his behalf of specified particulars of the debtor's earnings and anticipated earnings.

(2) Where an attachment of earnings has been made, the court or the fines officer, as the case may be, may at any time thereafter while the order is in force –

- (a) make such an order as is described in subsection (1)(a) or (b) above; and
- (b) order the debtor to attend before the court on a day and at a time specified in the order to give the information described in subsection (1)(a) above.

(3) In the case of an application to a magistrates' court for an attachment of earnings order, or for the variation or discharge of such an order, the power to make an order under subsection (1) or (2) above shall be exercisable also, before the hearing of the application, by a single justice.

(4) Without prejudice to subsections (1) to (3) above, rules of court may provide that where notice of application for an attachment of earnings order is served on the debtor it shall include a requirement that he shall give to the court, within such period and in such manner as may be prescribed, a statement in writing of the matters specified in subsection (1)(a) above and of any other prescribed matters which are, or may be, relevant under section 6 of this Act to the determination of the normal deduction rate and the protected earnings rate to be specified in any order made on the application.

This subsection does not apply to an attachment of earnings order to be made under Schedule 5 to the Courts Act 2003.

(5) In any proceedings in which a court has the power under this Act or under Schedule 5 to the Courts Act 2003, or a fines officer has power under that Schedule, to make an attachment of earnings order, and in any proceedings for the making, variation or discharge of such an order, a document purporting to be a statement given to the court or the fines officer, as the case may be, in compliance with an order under subsection (1)(a) or (b) above, or with any such requirement of a notice of application for an attachment of earnings order as is mentioned in subsection (4) above, shall, in the absence of proof to the contrary, be deemed to be a statement so given and shall be evidence of the facts stated therein.

Amendments—AJA 1982, s 53(1); SI 2006/1737.

Defined terms—'the debtor': s 2(e); 'earnings': s 24; 'employer': s 25(1); 'normal deduction rate': s 6(5)(a); 'protected earnings rate': s 6(5)(b).

'in any proceedings' (s 14(1))—The power to order the apparent employer to provide information may be exercised, for example, in judgment summons proceedings or in any High Court or Family Court proceedings concerning a qualifying periodical maintenance order within the meaning of MEA 1991, s 1.

'resources and needs' (s 14(1)(a)(ii))—The debtor's needs include those of his dependants (s 25(3)).

'order the debtor to attend' (s 14(2)(b))—Unlike a failure to comply with an order to provide information by signed statement made under s 14(1), failure to attend pursuant to an order is not an offence under s 23 and the consequence of non-compliance is *not* committal but a further order to attend under s 23(1), breach of which may lead to arrest or committal.

15 Obligation of debtor and his employers to notify changes of employment and earnings

(1) While an attachment of earnings order is in force –

(a) the debtor shall from time to time notify the court in writing of every occasion on which he leaves any employment, or becomes employed or re-employed, not later (in each case) than seven days from the date on which he did so;

(b) the debtor shall, on any occasion when he becomes employed or re-employed, include in his notification under paragraph (a) above particulars of his earnings and anticipated earnings from the relevant employment; and

(c) any person who becomes the debtor's employer and knows that the order is in force and by, or (if the order was made by a fines officer) for, which court it was made shall, within seven days of his becoming the debtor's employer or of acquiring that knowledge (whichever is the later) notify that court in writing that he is the debtor's employer, and include in his notification a statement of the debtor's earnings and anticipated earnings.

(2) In the case of an attachment of earnings order made by a fines officer, the reference to 'the court' in subsection (1)(a) above shall mean the court for which that order was made.

Amendments—SI 2006/1737.

Defined terms—'the debtor': s 2(e); 'earnings': s 24; 'employer': s 25(1).

16 Power of court to determine whether particular payments are earnings

(1) Where an attachment of earnings order is in force, the court shall, on application of a person specified in subsection (2) below, determine whether payments to the debtor of a particular class or description specified by the application are earnings for the purposes of the order; and the employer shall be entitled to give effect to any determination for the time being in force under this section.

(2) The persons referred to in subsection (1) above are –

(a) the employer;
(b) the debtor;
(c) the person to whom payment under the relevant adjudication is required to be made (whether directly or through the officer of any court); and
(d) without prejudice to paragraph (c) above, where the application is in respect of an attachment of earnings order made to secure payments under a family court maintenance order, the collecting officer.

(3) Where an application under this section is made by the employer, he shall not incur any liability for non-compliance with the order as respects any payments of the class or description specified by the application which are made by him to the debtor while the application, or any appeal in consequence thereof, is pending; but this subsection shall not, unless the court otherwise orders, apply as respects such payments if the employer subsequently withdraws the application or, as the case may be, abandons the appeal.

Amendments—CCA 2013, s 17, Sch 10.

Defined terms—'collecting officer': s 6(7); 'the debtor': s 2(e); 'earnings': s 24; 'the employer': s 25(1); 'the relevant adjudication': s 2(d).

****

Special provisions with respect to magistrates' courts

18 Certain action not to be taken by collecting officer except on request

(1) Where payments under a maintenance order are payable to the family court or an officer of the family court for transmission to a person, no officer of the family court is to –

(a) apply for an attachment of earnings order to secure payments under the maintenance order; or
(b) except as provided by section 10(3) of this Act, apply for an order discharging or varying such an attachment of earnings order; or
(c) apply for a determination under section 16 of this Act,

unless he is requested in writing to do so by a person entitled to receive the payments through the family court or an officer of that court.

(2) Where an officer of the family court is so requested –

(a) he shall comply with the request unless it appears to him unreasonable in the circumstances to do so; and
(b) the person by whom the request was made shall have the same liabilities for all the costs properly incurred in or about any proceedings taken in pursuance of the request as if the proceedings had been taken by that person.

(3) (*repealed*)

Amendments—AJA 1999, s 90, Sch 13, para 68; Courts Act 2003, s 109(1), Sch 8, para 143; CCA 2013, s 17, Sch 10.

****

20 Jurisdiction in respect of persons residing outside England and Wales

(1) It is hereby declared that the family court has jurisdiction to hear an application by or against a person residing outside England and Wales for the discharge or variation of an attachment of earnings order made by the family court to secure maintenance payments; and where such an application is made, the following provisions shall have effect.

(2) If the person resides in Scotland or Northern Ireland, section 15 of the Maintenance Orders Act 1950 (which relates to the service of process on persons residing in those countries) shall have effect in relation to the application as it has effect in relation to the proceedings therein mentioned.

(3) Subject to the following subsection, if the person resides outside the United Kingdom and does not appear at the time and place appointed for the hearing of the application, the court may, if it

thinks it reasonable in all the circumstances to do so, proceed to hear and determine the application at the time and place appointed for the hearing, or for any adjourned hearing, in like manner as if the person had then appeared.

(4) Subsection (3) above shall apply only if it is proved to the satisfaction of the court, on oath or in such other manner as may be prescribed, that the applicant has taken such steps as may be prescribed to give to the said person notice of the application and of the time and place appointed for the hearing of it.

Amendments—CCA 2013, s 17, Sch 10.

Defined terms—'maintenance payments': s 25(1).

'such steps as may be prescribed' (s 20(4))—The relevant steps were formerly prescribed by MC(AE)R 1971, rr 10, 11. These rules no longer apply to family proceedings but similar steps should be taken such as service of notice to the last known address or place of business.

★★★★

Miscellaneous provisions

22 Persons employed under the Crown

(1) The fact that an attachment of earnings order is made at the suit of the Crown shall not prevent its operation at any time when the debtor is in the employment of the Crown.

(2) Where a debtor is in the employment of the Crown and an attachment of earnings order is made in respect of him, then for the purposes of this Act –

(a) the chief officer for the time being of the department, office or other body in which the debtor is employed shall be treated as having the debtor in his employment (any transfer of the debtor from one department, office or body to another being treated as a change of employment); and

(b) any earnings paid by the Crown or a Minister of the Crown, or out of the public revenue of the United Kingdom, shall be treated as paid by the said chief officer.

(3) If any question arises, in the proceedings for or arising out of an attachment of earnings order, as to what department, office or other body is concerned for the purposes of this section, or as to who for those purposes is the chief officer thereof, the question shall be referred to and determined by the Minister for the Civil Service; but that Minister shall not be under any obligation to consider a reference under this subsection unless it is made by the court.

(4) A document purporting to set out a determination of the said Minister under subsection (3) above and to be signed by an official of the Office of Public Service shall, in any such proceedings as are mentioned in that subsection, be admissible in evidence and be deemed to contain an accurate statement of such a determination unless the contrary is shown.

(5) This Act shall have effect notwithstanding any enactment passed before 29 May 1970 and preventing or avoiding the attachment or diversion of sums due to a person in respect of service under the Crown, whether by way of remuneration, pension or otherwise.

Amendments—SI 1992/1296; SI 1995/2985.

Defined terms—'the debtor': s 2(e).

'notwithstanding any enactment' (s 22(5))—The protection formerly given to, for example, the pensions of ex-servicemen is removed; as to servicemen's pay, see s 24(2)(b).

23 Enforcement provisions

(1) If, after being served with notice of an application to the county court for an attachment of earnings order or for the variation of such an order or with an order made under section 14(2)(b) above, the debtor fails to attend on the day and at the time specified for any hearing of the application or specified in the order, the court may adjourn the hearing and order him to attend at a specified time on another day; and if the debtor –

(a) fails to attend at that time on that day; or

(b) attends, but refuses to be sworn or give evidence,

he may be ordered by the court to be imprisoned for not more than fourteen days.

(1A) In any case where the court has the power to make an order of imprisonment under subsection (1) for failure to attend, the court may, in lieu of or in addition to making that order, order the debtor to be arrested and brought to the court either forthwith or at such time as the court may direct.

(2) Subject to this section, a person commits an offence if –

(a) being required by section 7(1) or 9(2) of this Act to comply with an attachment of earnings order, he fails to do so; or

(b) being required by section 7(2) of this Act to give a notice for the purposes of that subsection, he fails to give it, or fails to give it within the time required by that subsection; or

(c) he fails to comply with an order under section 14(1) of this Act or with any such requirement of a notice of application for an attachment of earnings order as is mentioned in section 14(4), or fails (in either case) to comply within the time required by the order or notice; or

(d) he fails to comply with section 15 of this Act; or

(e) he gives notice for the purposes of section 7(2) of this Act, or a notification for the purposes of section 15, which he knows to be false in a material particular, or recklessly gives such a notice or notification which is false in a material particular, or

(f) in purported compliance with section 7(2) or 15 of this Act, or with an order under section 14(1), or with any such requirement of a notice of application for an attachment of earnings order as is mentioned in section 14(4), he makes any statement which he knows to be false in a material particular, or recklessly makes any statement which is false in a material particular.

(3) Where a person commits an offence under subsection (2) above in relation to proceedings in, or to an attachment of earnings order made by, the High Court or the county court, he shall be liable on summary conviction to a fine of not more than level 2 on the standard scale or he may be ordered by a judge of the High Court or by the county court (as to the case may be) to pay a fine of not more than £250 or, in the case of an offence specified in subsection (4) below, to be imprisoned for not more than fourteen days; and where a person commits an offence under subsection (2) otherwise than as mentioned above in this subsection, he shall be liable on summary conviction to a fine of not more than level 2 on the standard scale.

(4) The offences referred to above in the case of which a judge or court may impose imprisonment are –

(a) an offence under subsection (2)(c) or (d), if committed by the debtor; and

(b) an offence under subsection (2)(e) or (f), whether committed by the debtor or any other person.

(5) It shall be a defence –

(a) for a person charged with an offence under subsection (2)(a) above to prove that he took all reasonable steps to comply with the attachment of earnings order in question;

(b) for a person charged with an offence under subsection (2)(b) to prove that he did not know, and could not reasonably be expected to know, that the debtor was not in his employment, or (as the case may be) had ceased to be so, and that he gave the required notice as soon as reasonably practicable after the fact came to his knowledge.

(6) Where a person is convicted or dealt with for an offence under subsection (2)(a), the court may order him to pay, to whoever is the collecting officer of the court for the purposes of the attachment of earnings order in question, any sums deducted by that person from the debtor's earnings and not already paid to the collecting officer.

(7) Where under this section a person is ordered by a judge of the High Court or by the county court to be imprisoned, the judge or court may at any time revoke the order and, if the person is already in custody, order his discharge.

(8) Any fine imposed by a judge of the High Court under subsection (3) above and any sums ordered by the High Court to be paid under subsection (6) above shall be recoverable in the same

way as a fine imposed by that court in the exercise of its jurisdiction to punish for contempt of court; section 129 of the County Courts Act 1984 (enforcement of fines) shall apply to payment of a fine imposed by the county court under subsection (3) and of any sums ordered by the county court to be paid under subsection (6); and any sum ordered by a magistrates' court to be paid under subsection (6) shall be recoverable as a sum adjudged to be paid on a conviction by that court.

(9) For the purposes of section 13 of the Administration of Justice Act 1960 (appeal in cases of contempt of court), subsection (3) above shall be treated as an enactment enabling the High Court or the county court to deal with an offence under subsection (2) above as if it were contempt of court.

(10) In this section references to proceedings in a court are to proceedings in which that court has power to make an attachment of earnings order or has made such an order.

(10A) This section applies in relation to the family court as it applies in relation to the county court, but as if the reference in subsection (8) to section 129 of the County Courts Act 1984 were a reference to section 31L(1) of the Matrimonial and Family Proceedings Act 1984.

(11) *(repealed)*

Amendments—CCA 1981, s 41(5), Sch 2; AJA 1982, s 53(2); Criminal Justice Act 1982, ss 37, 38, 46; CCA 1984, s 148(1), Sch 2, para 41; CLSA 1990, s 125(2), Sch 17; Criminal Justice Act 1991, s 17, Sch 4, Pt I; CCA 2013, s 17, Schs 9, 10.

Defined terms—'the debtor': s 2(e).

Offences and penalties—Section 23(2) creates a number of offences which are punishable on summary conviction by a fine. Section 23(1) and (1A) empowers the County Court to order the attendance of a debtor who has failed to attend the hearing of an application or pursuant to an order under s 14(2)(b); and if he again fails to attend or refuses to be sworn or give evidence then to order either his imprisonment for up to 14 days or his arrest and production to the court or both. Further, s 23(3) empowers the High Court or the County Court, in proceedings before it, when one of the offences has been committed, directly to order payment of a fine or, in the cases identified in s 23(4), to order that the offender be imprisoned for up to 14 days. It has been said in relation to orders for questioning that the threat of imprisonment should not be regarded as routine (*Broomleigh HA v Okonkwo* [2010] EWCA Civ 1113) and directing the debtor's arrest may avoid difficulties.

'level 2 on the standard scale' (s 23(3))—Currently £500 (Criminal Justice Act 1982, s 37(2), as substituted).

Appeal (s 23(9))—An appeal from 'any order or decision of a court in the exercise of jurisdiction to punish for contempt of court' lies under AJA 1960, s 13 to the Court of Appeal; orders under s 23(1) or (1A) clearly fall within this description. Section 23(9) applies the same provision to orders dealing with the offences created by s 23(2).

'as if it were contempt' (s 23(9))—Punishment for an offence under this section is not punishment for contempt of court and so, for example, it is not necessary for a judgment to be placed in the public domain.

District judge (s 23(11))—The district judge has the same powers in the County Court under this section as the circuit judge. Although an appeal from his order will lie direct to the Court of Appeal under AJA 1960, s 13, this does not remove the right of appeal to the circuit judge under FPR 2010, r 30.3 and that procedure is to be preferred (*King v Read & Slack* [1999] 1 FLR 425, CA).

24 Meaning of 'earnings'

(1) For the purposes of this Act, but subject to the following subsection, 'earnings' are any sums payable to a person –

(a) by way of wages or salary (including any fees, bonus, commission, overtime pay or other emoluments payable in addition to wages or salary or payable under a contract of service);

(b) by way of pension (including an annuity in respect of past services, whether or not rendered to the person paying the annuity, and including periodical payments by way of compensation for the loss, abolition or relinquishment, or diminution in emoluments, of any office or employment);

(c) by way of statutory sick pay.

(2) The following shall not be treated as earnings –

(a) sums payable by any department of the Government of Northern Ireland or of a territory outside the United Kingdom;

(b) pay or allowances payable to the debtor as a member of Her Majesty's forces other than pay or allowances payable by his employer to him as a special member of a reserve force (within the meaning of the Reserve Forces Act 1996);

(ba) a tax credit (within the meaning of the Tax Credits Act 2002);

(c) pension, allowances or benefit payable under any enactment relating to social security;

(d) pension or allowances payable in respect of disablement or disability;

(e) except in relation to a maintenance order wages payable to a person as a seaman, other than wages payable to him as a seaman of a fishing boat;

(f) guaranteed minimum pension within the meaning of the Pension Schemes Act 1993.

(3) In subsection (2)(e) above –

'fishing boat' means a vessel of whatever size, and in whatever way propelled, which is for the time being employed in sea fishing or in the sea-fishing service;

'seaman' includes every person (except masters and pilots) employed or engaged in any capacity on board any ship; and

'wages' includes emoluments.

Amendments—Social Security Pensions Act 1975, s 65(1), Sch 4, para 15; Merchant Shipping Act 1979, s 39(1); Social Security Act 1985, s 21, Sch 4, para 1; Social Security Act 1986, s 86(1), Sch 10, Pt VI, para 102; Pension Schemes Act 1993, s 190, Sch 8, para 4; Merchant Shipping Act 1995, s 314(2), Sch 13, para 46; SI 1998/3086; Tax Credits Act 2002, s 47, Sch 3, para 1.

Defined terms—'maintenance order': s 2(a).

Scope—This section defines earnings to include pensions and sick pay but subject to significant exceptions.

Holiday pay (s 24(1)(a))—Although holiday pay is not 'wages' (*London County Council v Henry Boot & Sons Ltd* [1959] 1 WLR 1609, HL), it would seem to be caught by 'other emoluments payable in addition to wages … or payable under a contract of service'.

Pension (s 24(1)(b))—A pension may be attachable under the Act, but the making of the order may breach a prohibition against diversion of the pension contained in the relevant trust deed and so terminate entitlement to pension (see e g *Edmonds v Edmonds* [1965] 1 WLR 58, PDAD).

Her Majesty's forces (s 24(2)(b))—This exception protects the pay or allowances of a serviceman (but not the pension of an ex-serviceman, as to which see **'notwithstanding any enactment'** under s 22). However, arrangements exist (see Armed Forces (Forfeitures and Deductions) Regulations 2009) under which relevant authorities may order deductions from the serviceman's pay to meet maintenance orders (and judgment debts) if the serviceman will not comply voluntarily with the judgment or order. The amount of such a deduction is in the discretion of the relevant authority, which is not bound to follow the rate indicated in any order of the court. Any request for such an order should set out the efforts made to secure voluntary compliance, enclose a copy of the judgment or order and set out the state of account under it. The appropriate authorities are:

(a) *Navy* All ranks: The Director of Naval Pay and Pensions (Accounts), Ministry of Defence, Room 1045, HMS Centurion, Grange Road, Gosport, Hants. PO13 9AX.

(b) *Army Officers*: Ministry of Defence, PF 2d (Army), Lansdowne House, Berkeley Square, London W1X 6AA; other ranks: the appropriate regimental pay office.

(c) *RAF Officers*: Ministry of Defence, DPS2 (RAF), Adastral House, Theobalds Road, London WC1X 8RU; other ranks: Ministry of Defence, DGPM (RAF), Eastern Avenue, Barnwood, Gloucester.

'pension or allowances payable in respect of disablement or disability' (s 24(2)(d))—This exception does not extend to a pension taken on early retirement due to ill-health (*Miles v Miles* [1979] 1 WLR 371, CA).

25 General interpretation

(1) In this Act, except where the context otherwise requires –

'administration order' means an order made under, and so referred to in, Part VI of the County Courts Act 1984;

'the court', in relation to an attachment of earnings order, means the court which made the order, subject to rules of court as to the venue for, and the transfer of, proceedings in the county court and magistrates' courts;

'debtor' and 'relevant adjudication' have the meanings given by section 2 of this Act;

'the employer', in relation to the attachment of earnings order, means the person who is required by the order to make deductions from earnings paid by him to the debtor;

'the fines officer', in relation to a debtor who is subject to a collection order made under Schedule 5 to the Courts Act 2003, means any fines officer working at the fines office specified in that order;

'judgment debt' has the meaning given by section 2 of this Act;

'maintenance order' has the meaning given by section 2 of this Act;

'maintenance payments' means payments required under a maintenance order;
'prescribed' means prescribed by rules of court.

(2) Any reference in this Act to sums payable under a judgment or order, or to the payment of such sums, includes a reference to costs and the payment of them; and the references in sections 6(4) and 12(2) to relevant costs are to any costs of the proceedings in which the attachment of earnings order in question was made, being costs which the debtor is liable to pay.

(3) References in sections 6(5)(b), 9(3)(b) and 14(1)(a) of this Act to the debtor's needs include references to the needs of any person for whom he must, or reasonably may, provide.

(4) *(repealed)*

(5) Any power to make rules which is conferred by this Act is without prejudice to any other power to make rules of court.

(6) This Act, so far as it relates to magistrates' courts, and Part III of the Magistrates' Courts Act 1980 shall be construed as if this Act were contained in that Part.

(7) References in this Act to any enactment include references to that enactment amended by or under any other enactment, including this Act.

Amendments—MCA 1980, s 154, Sch 7, para 101; CCA 1984, s 148(1), Sch 2, para 42; Legal Aid Act 1988, Sch 5, para 3; Dock Work Act 1989, Sch 1, Pt I; AJA 1999, s 106, Sch 15; Courts Act 2003, s 109(1), Sch 8, para 145; SI 2006/1737; CCA 2013, s 17, Sch 9.

★★★★

SCHEDULE 1
MAINTENANCE ORDERS TO WHICH THIS ACT APPLIES

1 An order for alimony, maintenance or other payments made, or having effect as if made, under Part II of the Matrimonial Causes Act 1965 (ancillary relief in actions for divorce etc).

2 An order for payments to or in respect of a child, being an order made, or having effect as if made, under Part III of the said Act of 1965 (maintenance of children following divorce etc).

3 An order for periodical or other payments made or having effect as if made under Part II of the Matrimonial Causes Act 1973.

4 An order for maintenance or other payments to or in respect of a spouse or child, being an order made under Part I of the Domestic Proceedings and Magistrates' Courts Act 1978.

5 An order for periodical or other payments made or having effect as if made under Schedule 1 to the Children Act 1989.

6 *(repealed)*

7 An order under paragraph 23 of Schedule 2 to the Children Act 1989, paragraph 3 of Schedule 1 to the Social Services and Well-being (Wales) Act 2014, section 23 of the Ministry of Social Security Act 1966, section 18 of the Supplementary Benefits Act 1976, section 24 of the Social Security Act 1986, or section 106 of the Social Security Administration Act 1992 (various provisions for obtaining contributions from a person whose dependants are assisted or maintained out of public funds).

8 *(repealed)*

9 An order to which section 16 of the Maintenance Orders Act 1950 applies by virtue of subsection (2)(b) or (c) of that section (that is to say an order made by a court in Scotland or Northern Ireland and corresponding to one of those specified in the foregoing paragraphs) and which has been registered in a court in England and Wales under Part II of that Act.

10 A maintenance order within the meaning of the Maintenance Orders (Facilities for Enforcement) Act 1920 (Commonwealth orders enforceable in the United Kingdom) registered in, or confirmed in England and Wales under that Act.

11 A maintenance order within the meaning of Part I of the Maintenance Orders (Reciprocal Enforcement) Act 1972 registered in the family court under the said Part I.

12 An order under section 34(1)(b) of the Children Act 1975 (payments of maintenance in respect of a child to his custodian).

13 A maintenance order within the meaning of Part I of the Civil Jurisdiction and Judgments Act 1982 which is registered in the family court under that Part.

14 A maintenance judgment within the meaning of Council Regulation (EC) No 44/2001 of 22 December 2000 on jurisdiction and the recognition and enforcement of judgments in civil and commercial matters, as amended from time to time and as applied by the Agreement made on 19th October 2005 between the European Community and the Kingdom of Denmark on jurisdiction and the recognition and enforcement of judgments in civil and commercial matters (OJ No. L 299 16.11.2005 at p 62), which is registered in a court in England and Wales under that Regulation.

14A (1) A decision, court settlement or authentic instrument which falls to be enforced by the family court by virtue of the Maintenance Regulation and the Civil Jurisdiction and Judgments (Maintenance) Regulations 2011.

(2) In this paragraph –

'the Maintenance Regulation' means Council Regulation (EC) No 4/2009 including as applied in relation to Denmark by virtue of the Agreement made on 19 October 2005 between the European Community and the Kingdom of Denmark;

'decision', 'court settlement' and 'authentic instrument' have the meanings given by Article 2 of that Regulation.

14B A decision or maintenance arrangement which is registered in the family court under the Convention on the International Recovery of Child Support and other forms of Family Maintenance done at The Hague on 23 November 2007.

15 An order made under Schedule 5 to the Civil Partnership Act 2004 (financial relief: provision corresponding to provision made by Part 2 of the Matrimonial Causes Act 1973), for periodical or other payments.

16 An order made under Schedule 6 to the 2004 Act (financial relief: provision corresponding to provision made by the Domestic Proceedings and Magistrates' Courts Act 1978), for maintenance or other payments to or in respect of a civil partner or child.

Amendments—MO(RE)A 1972, s 22(1), Sch, para 7; Guardianship Act 1973, s 9; MCA 1973, s 53, Sch 2, para 13; Children Act 1975, Sch 3, para 76; Supplementary Benefits Act 1976, s 35(2), Sch 7, para 20; DPMCA 1978, Sch 2, para 32; CJJA 1982, s 15(4), Sch 12, para 6; Social Security Act 1986, s 86(1), Sch 10, para 43; FLRA 1987, Schs 2, 3; CA 1989, s 108(5), Sch 13, para 29; CLSA 1990, s 116, Sch 16, para 38; Social Security (Consequential Provisions) Act 1992, s 4, Sch 2, para 7; SI 2001/3929; CPA 2004, s 261(1), Sch 27, para 35; SI 2007/1655; Health and Social Care Act 2008, Sch 15; SI 2011/1484; SI 2012/2814; SI 2014/605; SI 2016/413.

Scope—Schedule 1 provides the specific definition of maintenance orders for the purposes of the Act; the definition is not confined to orders for periodical maintenance payments.

****

SCHEDULE 3
DEDUCTIONS BY EMPLOYER UNDER ATTACHMENT OF EARNINGS ORDER

PART I
SCHEME OF DEDUCTIONS

Preliminary definitions

1 The following three paragraphs have effect for defining and explaining, for purposes of this Schedule, expressions used therein.

2 'Pay-day', in relation to earnings paid to a debtor, means an occasion on which they are paid.

3 'Attachable earnings', in relation to a pay-day, are the earnings which remain payable to the debtor on that day after deduction by the employer of –

(a) income tax;

(b) (*repealed*)

(bb) Primary Class I contributions under Part I of the Social Security Act 1975;

(c) amounts deductible under any enactment, or in pursuance of a request in writing by the debtor, for the purposes of a superannuation scheme, namely any enactment, rules, deed or other instrument providing for the payment of annuities or lump sums –

(i) to the persons with respect to whom the instrument has effect on their retirement at a specified age or on becoming incapacitated at some earlier age, or

(ii) to the personal representatives or the widows, relatives or dependants of such persons on their death or otherwise,

whether with or without any further or other benefits.

4 (1) On any pay-day –

(a) 'the normal deduction' is arrived at by applying the normal deduction rate (as specified in the relevant attachment of earnings order) with respect to the relevant period; and

(b) 'the protected earnings' are arrived at by applying the protected earnings rate (as so specified) with respect to the relevant period.

(2) For the purposes of this paragraph the relevant period in relation to any pay-day is the period beginning –

(a) if it is the first pay-day of the debtor's employment with the employer, with the first day of employment; or

(b) if on the last pay-day earnings were paid in respect of a period falling wholly or partly after that pay-day, with the first day after the end of that period; or

(c) in any other case, with the first day after the last pay-day, and ending –

(i) where earnings are paid in respect of a period falling wholly or partly after the pay-day, with the last day of that period; or

(ii) in any other case, with the pay-day.

5 Employer's deduction (judgment debts and administration orders)

In the case of an attachment of earnings order made to secure the payment of a judgment debt or payments under an administration order, the employer shall on any pay-day –

(a) if the attachable earnings exceed the protected earnings, deduct from the attachable earnings the amount of the excess or the normal deduction, whichever is the less;

(b) make no deduction if the attachable earnings are equal to, or less than, the protected earnings.

6 Employer's deduction (other cases)

(1) The following provision shall have effect in the case of an attachment of earnings order to which paragraph 5 above and paragraph 6A below do not apply.

(2) If on a pay-day the attachable earnings exceed the sum of –

(a) the protected earnings; and

(b) so much of any amount by which the attachable earnings on any previous pay-day fell short of the protected earnings as has not been made good by virtue of this sub-paragraph on another previous pay-day,

then, in so far as the excess allows, the employer shall deduct from the attachable earnings the amount specified in the following sub-paragraph.

(3) The said amount is the sum of –

(a) the normal deduction; and

(b) so much of the normal deduction on any previous pay-day as was not deducted on that day and has not been paid by virtue of this sub-paragraph on any other previous pay-day.

(4) No deduction shall be made on any pay-day when the attachable earnings are equal to, or less than, the protected earnings.

Amendments—SI 2006/1737.

6A In the case of an attachment of earnings order made under Schedule 5 to the Courts Act 2003, the employer shall make deductions from the debtor's earnings in accordance with fines collection regulations made under that Schedule.

Amendments—SI 2006/1737.

PART II
PRIORITY AS BETWEEN ORDERS

7 Where the employer is required to comply with two or more attachment of earnings orders in respect of the same debtor, all or none of which orders are made to secure either the payment of judgment debts or payments under an administration order, then on any pay-day the employer shall, for the purpose of complying with Part I of this Schedule, –

(a) deal with the orders according to the respective dates on which they were made, disregarding any later order until an earlier one has been dealt with;

(b) deal with any later order as if the earnings to which it relates were the residue of the debtor's earnings after the making of deduction to comply with any earlier order.

8 Where the employer is required to comply with two or more attachment of earnings orders, and one or more (but not all) of those orders are made to secure either the payment of judgment debts or payments under an administration order, then on any pay-day the employer shall, for the purpose of complying with Part I of this Schedule –

(a) deal first with any order which is not made to secure the payment of a judgment debt or payments under an administration order (complying with paragraph 7 above if there are two or more such orders); and

(b) deal thereafter with any order which is made to secure the payment of a judgment debt or payments under an administration order as if the earnings to which it relates were the residue of the debtor's earnings after the making of any deduction to comply with an order having priority by virtue of sub-paragraph (a) above; and

(c) if there are two or more orders to which sub-paragraph (b) above applies, comply with paragraph 7 above in respect of those orders.

Amendments—Social Security Pensions Act 1975, s 65(3), Sch 5; Social Security (Consequential Provisions) Act 1975, s 1(3), Sch 2, para 43; AJA 1982, s 54; Wages Act 1986, s 32(1), Sch 4, para 4; Employment Rights Act 1996, s 240, Sch 1, para 3; SI 2006/1737.

Priority orders—These are the orders which the employer must deal with first (para 8). If the net pay does not exceed the protected earnings rate sufficiently to allow the entire normal deduction to be made, the shortfall is carried forward and added to the normal deduction on the next pay-day. The shortfall may thus accumulate

PART II

from pay-day to pay-day (para 6(3)). If in any pay period the net pay is less than the protected earnings rate, the unused protected earnings are similarly carried forward and 'rolled up' (para 6(2)).

Other orders—The net pay is the amount left after any deductions have been made for priority orders (para 8(b)). The 'roll-up' provisions do not apply. Deductions are made whenever the debtor's net pay exceeds the protected earnings rate and are limited to the normal deduction rate without regard to any shortfall (para 5). The result can be surprising: for example, if a debtor, having a priority order and another order against him, through absence has little or no pay for a time, on his return no deductions will be made under the priority order until his accumulated protected earnings have been used up; thereafter, all of the excess of his pay over the protected earnings rate will be deducted under the priority order until his accumulated normal deductions have been used up. In the meantime, deductions under the other order will recommence as soon as his pay exceeds the protected earnings rate but are likely to cease once the priority order takes effect and resume only after it has been caught up.

****

Charging Orders Act 1979

1 Charging orders

(1) Where, under a judgment or order of the High Court or the family court or the county court, a person (the 'debtor') is required to pay a sum of money to another person (the 'creditor') then, for the purpose of enforcing that judgment or order, the appropriate court may make an order in accordance with the provisions of this Act imposing on any such property of the debtor as may be specified in the order a charge for securing the payment of any money due or to become due under the judgment or order.

(2) The appropriate court is –

(a) in a case where the property to be charged is a fund in court, the court in which that fund is lodged;

(b) in a case where paragraph (a) above does not apply and the order to be enforced is a maintenance order of the High Court or an order for costs made in family proceedings in the High Court, the High Court or the family court;

(ba) in a case where paragraph (a) does not apply and the order to be enforced is an order of the family court, the family court;

(c) in a case where none of paragraphs (a), (b) and (ba) above applies and the judgment or order to be enforced is a judgment or order of the High Court for a sum exceeding the county court limit, the High Court or the county court; and

(d) in any other case, the county court.

In this section 'county court limit' means the county court limit for the time being specified in an Order in Council under section 145 of the County Courts Act 1984 as the county court limit for the purposes of this section and 'maintenance order' has the same meaning as in section 2(a) of the Attachment of Earnings Act 1971.

(3) An order under subsection (1) above is referred to in this Act as a 'charging order'.

(4) Where a person applies to the High Court for a charging order to enforce more than one judgment or order, that court shall be the appropriate court in relation to the application if it would be the appropriate court, apart from this subsection, on an application relating to one or more of the judgments or orders concerned.

(5) In deciding whether to make a charging order the court shall consider all the circumstances of the case and, in particular, any evidence before it as to –

(a) the personal circumstances of the debtor, and

(b) whether any other creditor of the debtor would be likely to be unduly prejudiced by the making of the order.

(6) Subsections (7) and (8) apply where, under a judgment or order of the High Court or the family court or the county court, a debtor is required to pay a sum of money by instalments.

(7) The fact that there has been no default in payment of the instalments does not prevent a charging order from being made in respect of that sum.

(8) But if there has been no default, the court must take that into account when considering the circumstances of the case under subsection (5).

(9) In this section 'family proceedings' means proceedings in the Family Division of the High Court which are business assigned, by or under section 61 of (and Schedule 1 to) the Senior Courts Act 1981, to that Division of the High Court and no other.

Amendments—AJA 1982, s 34(3); TCEA 2007, s 93(2); CCA 2013, s 17, Schs 9, 10; SI 2014/605.

'required to pay a sum of money' (s 1(1))—There is no power to make a charging order until the sum is ascertained. Thus, an order for costs to be determined by detailed assessment will not found a charging order until after assessment (*Magiera v Magiera* [2016] EWCA Civ 1292, approving *Monte Developments Ltd v Court Management Consultants Ltd and others* [2010] EWHC 3071 (Ch)).

'to another person' (s 1(1))—A charging order cannot be made to secure an order to pay into court (*Ward v Shakeshaft* [1860] 1 Dr & Sm 269) or an order to settle a sum of money for the benefit of a child (*Re N (a child) (payments for the benefit of child)* [2009] 1 FLR 1442, FD – although in that case the court achieved virtually the same result by granting an injunction.

'due or to become due' (s 1(1))—A charging order may secure amounts which have not yet fallen due for payment under the judgment, but the court may exercise its discretion not to include such payments in an order (see **'consider all the circumstances'** below). A charging order may be made to secure *arrears* under a periodical payments order; in view of the specific provision in MCA 1973, s 23(1)(b),(e), it is doubtful that a charging order may secure future payments under such an order.

'maintenance order' (s 1(2)(b))—As to the extended meaning of this expression, see AEA 1971, Sch 1 above and **'expressions used'** under FPR 2010, r 39.2.

County court limit (s 1(2))—The relevant limit remains at £5000 (County Court Jurisdiction Order 2014).

'consider all the circumstances' (s 1(5))—The court has a general discretion. A charging order will not lightly be made where the costs of and consequent on doing so (including the costs of discharging the charge in due course) would be disproportionate in comparison with the judgment debt. A charging order will not be made where the creditor would gain security in the face of a pending liquidation (*Roberts Petroleum Ltd v Bernard Kenny Ltd* [1983] AC 192, CA). In the absence of a pending bankruptcy of which the court is aware, the fact that the debtor may actually be insolvent is immaterial (*Nationwide Building Society v Wright* [2009] BPIR 1047, CA).

The position of the debtor's spouse must be considered. In the absence of divorce proceedings, her interests will not prevent the order being made as her beneficial interest is not affected and the creditor will be in no better position than the debtor would be (on, for example, an application under TLATA 1996, s 14); however, the interests of the debtor's resident family must be taken into account (*Lloyds Bank plc v Byrne* [1993] 1 FLR 369, CA). Where a divorce petition has been issued, the spouse's expectation of financial provision and of security of accommodation must be balanced against the creditor's expectation of payment so that it may be appropriate to hear the applications for ancillary relief and for the charging order together (*Harman v Glencross* [1986] 2 FLR 241, CA; *Austin-Fell v Austin-Fell and Midland Bank* [1989] 2 FLR 497, FD).

If the judgment debt is subject to an instalment order, a charging order may be made even though the payments are up to date when the application is made (reversing *Mercantile Credit Co Ltd v Ellis* (1987) *The Times*, 1 April, CA), but the fact that the instalments are up to date is a factor for the court to take into account in deciding whether to make the order final (cf *Ropaigealach v Allied Irish Bank plc* [2001] EWCA Civ 1790, CA). Similar considerations would no doubt apply to an instalment agreement.

2 Property which may be charged

(1) Subject to subsection (3) below, a charge may be imposed by a charging order only on –

- (a) any interest held by the debtor beneficially –
  - (i) in any asset of a kind mentioned in subsection (2) below, or
  - (ii) under any trust; or
- (b) any interest held by a person as trustee of a trust ('the trust'), if the interest is in such an asset or is an interest under another trust and –
  - (i) the judgment or order in respect of which a charge is to be imposed was made against that person as trustee of the trust, or
  - (ii) the whole beneficial interest under the trust is held by the debtor unencumbered and for his own benefit, or
  - (iii) in a case where there are two or more debtors all of whom are liable to the creditor for the same debt, they together hold the whole beneficial interest under the trust unencumbered and for their own benefit.

(2) The assets referred to in subsection (1) above are –

- (a) land,
- (b) securities of any of the following kinds –
  - (i) government stock,

(ii) stock of any body (other than a building society) incorporated within England and Wales,

(iii) stock of any body incorporated outside England and Wales or of any state or territory outside the United Kingdom, being stock registered in a register kept at any place within England and Wales,

(iv) units of any unit trust in respect of which a register of the unit holders is kept at any place within England and Wales, or

(c) funds in court.

(3) In any case where a charge is imposed by a charging order on any interest in an asset of a kind mentioned in paragraph (b) or (c) of subsection (2) above, the court making the order may provide for the charge to extend to any interest or dividend payable in respect of the asset.

Defined terms—'building society': s 6(1); 'charging order', 'debtor': s 1; 'dividend', 'stock': s 6(1).

Partnerships—A debtor's share in a partnership may also be made the subject of a charging order by virtue of Partnership Act 1890, s 23.

3 Provisions supplementing sections 1 and 2

(1) A charging order may be made absolutely or subject to conditions as to notifying the debtor or as to the time when the charge is to become enforceable, or as to other matters.

(2) The Land Charges Act 1972 and the Land Registration Act 2002 shall apply in relation to charging orders as they apply in relation to other orders or writs issued or made for the purpose of enforcing judgments.

(3) *(repealed)*

(4) Subject to the provisions of this Act, a charge imposed by a charging order shall have the like effect and shall be enforceable in the same courts and in the same manner as an equitable charge created by the debtor by writing under his hand.

(4A) Subsections (4C) to (4E) apply where –

(a) a debtor is required to pay a sum of money in instalments under a judgment or order of the High Court or the family court or the county court (an 'instalments order'), and

(b) a charge has been imposed by a charging order in respect of that sum.

(4B) In subsections (4C) to (4E) references to the enforcement of a charge are to the making of an order for the enforcement of the charge.

(4C) The charge may not be enforced unless there has been default in payment of an instalment under the instalments order.

(4D) Rules of court may –

(a) provide that, if there has been default in payment of an instalment, the charge may be enforced only in prescribed cases, and

(b) limit the amounts for which, and the times at which, the charge may be enforced.

(4E) Except so far as otherwise provided by rules of court under subsection (4D) –

(a) the charge may be enforced, if there has been default in payment of an instalment, for the whole of the sum of money secured by the charge and the costs then remaining unpaid, or for such part as the court may order, but

(b) the charge may not be enforced unless, at the time of enforcement, the whole or part of an instalment which has become due under the instalments order remains unpaid.

(5) The court by which a charging order was made may at any time, on the application of the debtor or of any person interested in any property to which the order relates, make an order discharging or varying the charging order.

(6) Where a charging order has been protected by an entry registered under the Land Charges Act 1972 or the Land Registration Act 2002, an order under subsection (5) above discharging the charging order may direct that the entry be cancelled.

(7) The Lord Chancellor may by order made by statutory instrument amend section 2(2) of this Act by adding to, or removing from, the kinds of asset for the time being referred to there, any asset of a kind which in his opinion ought to be so added or removed.

(8) Any order under subsection (7) above shall be subject to annulment in pursuance of a resolution of either House of Parliament.

Amendments—LRA 2002, s 133, Schs 11, 13; TCEA 2007, s 93(3); CCA 2013, s 17, Schs 9, 10.

Defined terms—'charging order', 'debtor': s 1.

'enforceable' (s 3(4))—An application for an order for sale to enforce the charge must be brought by separate proceedings. See CPR 1998, r 73.10.

'person interested' (s 3(5))—The interest need not be a beneficial interest in the property charged (*Harman v Glencross* [1986] 2 FLR 241, CA.

3A Power to set financial thresholds

(1) The Lord Chancellor may by regulations provide that a charge may not be imposed by a charging order for securing the payment of money of an amount below that determined in accordance with the regulations.

(2) The Lord Chancellor may by regulations provide that a charge imposed by a charging order may not be enforced by way of order for sale to recover money of an amount below that determined in accordance with the regulations.

(3) Regulations under this section may –

(a) make different provision for different cases;

(b) include such transitional provision as the Lord Chancellor thinks fit.

(4)–(6) …

Amendments—Inserted by TCEA 2007, s 94.

'may not be enforced by way of order for sale' (s 3A(2))—The minimum figure stipulated is £1000 and that only in relation to consumer credit debts: Charging Orders (Orders for Sale: Financial Thresholds) Regulations 2013. Courts are likely to remain ready to enforce debts arising in family proceedings or from failure to pay child support.

****

5 Stop orders and notices

(1) In this section –

'stop order' means an order of the court prohibiting the taking, in respect of any of the securities specified in the order, of any of the steps mentioned in subsection (5) below;

'stop notice' means a notice requiring any person or body on whom it is duly served to refrain from taking, in respect of any of the securities specified in the notice, any of those steps without first notifying the person by whom, or on whose behalf, the notice was served; and

'prescribed securities' means securities (including funds in court) of a kind prescribed by rules of court made under this section.

(2) The power to make rules of court under section 1 of, and Schedule 1 to, the Civil Procedure Act 1997 shall include power by any such rules to make provision –

(a) for the High Court to make a stop order on the application of any person claiming to be entitled to an interest in prescribed securities; and

(b) for the service of a stop notice by any person claiming to be entitled to an interest in prescribed securities.

(3) (*repealed*)

(4) Rules of court made by virtue of subsection (2) above shall prescribe the person or body on whom a copy of any stop order or a stop notice is to be served.

(5) The steps mentioned in subsection (1) above are –

(a) the registration of any transfer of the securities;

(b) in the case of funds in court, the transfer, sale, delivery out, payment or other dealing with the funds, or of the income thereon;

(c) the making of any payment by way of dividend, interest or otherwise in respect of the securities; and

(d) in the case of a unit trust, any acquisition of or other dealing with the units by any person or body exercising functions under the trust.

(6) Any rules of court made by virtue of this section may include such incidental, supplemental and consequential provisions as the authority making them consider necessary or expedient, and may make different provision in relation to different cases or classes of case.

Amendments—SCA 1981, s 152(1), Sch 5; CCA 1984, s 148(1), Sch 2, para 72; SI 2002/439.

6 Interpretation

(1) In this Act –

'building society' has the same meaning as in the Building Societies Act 1986;

'charging order' means an order made under section 1(1) of this Act;

'debtor' and 'creditor' have the meanings given by section 1(1) of this Act;

'dividend' includes any distribution in respect of any unit of a unit trust;

'government stock' means any stock issued by Her Majesty's government in the United Kingdom or any funds of, or annuity granted by, that government;

'stock' includes shares, debentures and any securities of the body concerned, whether or not constituting a charge on the assets of that body;

'unit trust' means any trust established for the purpose, or having the effect, of providing, for persons having funds available for investment, facilities for the participation by them, as beneficiaries under the trust, in any profits or income arising from the acquisition, holding, management or disposal of any property whatsoever.

(2) For the purposes of sections 1 and 3 of this Act references to a judgment or order of the High Court or the family court or the county court shall be taken to include references to a judgment, order, decree or award (however called) of any court or arbitrator (including any foreign court or arbitrator) which is or has become enforceable (whether wholly or to a limited extent) as if it were a judgment or order of the High Court or the family court or the county court.

(3) References in section 2 of this Act to any securities include references to any such securities standing in the name of the Accountant General.

Amendments—Building Societies Act 1986, s 120(1), Sch 18, Pt I, para 14; TCEA 2007, s 93(4); CCA 2013, s 17, Schs 9, 10.

★★★★

Child Abduction and Custody Act 1985

ARRANGEMENT OF SECTIONS

PART I
INTERNATIONAL CHILD ABDUCTION

Section		Page
1	The Hague Convention	363
2	Contracting States	364
3	Central Authorities	364
4	Judicial authorities	365
5	Interim powers	365
6	Reports	366
7	Proof of documents and evidence	366
8	Declarations by United Kingdom courts	367
9	Suspension of court's powers in cases of wrongful removal	367

10 Rules of court 367
11 Cost of applications 368

PART II
RECOGNITION AND ENFORCEMENT OF CUSTODY DECISIONS

12 The European Convention 368
13 Contracting States 369
14 Central Authorities 369
15 Recognition of decisions 369
16 Registration of decisions 370
17 Variation and revocation of registered decisions 370
18 Enforcement of decisions 371
19 Interim powers 371
20 Suspension of court's powers 371
21 Reports 372
22 Proof of documents and evidence 372
23 Decisions of United Kingdom courts 372
24 Rules of court 373

PART III
SUPPLEMENTARY

24A Power to order disclosure of child's whereabouts 373
25 Termination of existing custody orders etc 374
26 Expenses 374
27 Interpretation 374
28 Application as respects British Islands and colonies 374
29 Short title, commencement and extent 375
Schedule 1 – Convention on the Civil Aspects of International Child Abduction 375
Schedule 2 – European Convention on Recognition and Enforcement of Decisions Concerning Custody of Children 393
Schedule 3 – Custody Orders 397
Part I – England and Wales 397
Part II – Scotland 398
Part III – Northern Ireland 399

PART I
INTERNATIONAL CHILD ABDUCTION

1 The Hague Convention

(1) In this Part of this Act 'the Convention' means the Convention on the Civil Aspects of International Child Abduction which was signed at The Hague on 25 October 1980.

(2) Subject to the provisions of this Part of this Act, the provisions of that Convention set out in Schedule 1 to this Act shall have the force of law in the United Kingdom.

(3) But –

(a) those provisions of the Convention,
(b) this Part of this Act, and
(c) rules of court under section 10 of this Act,

are subject to Article 60 of the Council Regulation (by virtue of which the Regulation takes precedence over the Hague Convention, in so far as it concerns matters governed by the Regulation).

(4) 'The Council Regulation' means Council Regulation (EC) No 2201/2003 of 27 November 2003 concerning jurisdiction and the recognition and enforcement of judgments in matrimonial matters and matters of parental responsibility.

Amendments—SI 2005/265.

Scope—The 1980 Hague Convention provides a mechanism for the return of a child who has been wrongfully removed or retained, but its provisions are superseded by Brussels IIA, as between Member States, insofar as its provisions deal with matters that are also governed by the Convention. Since 1 November 2012, the impact of the 1996 Hague Convention (see Part VI) must also be considered where appropriate in child abduction cases. Brussels IIA strengthens the application of the Hague Convention: *Re D (Abduction: Rights of Custody)* [2007] 1 FLR 961, HL and in many respects so will the 1996 Convention.

Object of the Convention—The Hague Convention seeks to protect rights of custody and access and to provide through legal process the expeditious return of any child who is under the age of 16 who has been wrongfully removed or retained in another Contracting State (Sch 1, Arts 3, 4) to the country of his habitual residence. Its first objective is to provide an effective mechanism for the prompt return of children through administrative and judicial procedures so that parents do not resort to self-help and secondary abduction. The second is to ensure that rights of custody and access under the law of one contracting state are effectively respected in the other contracting states. Since this is an international convention to be applied under a variety of systems of law, it must be given a 'purposive construction in order to make as effective as possible the machinery set up under it' (see *Re H (Abduction: Rights of Custody)* [2000] 1 FLR 374, HL). Where the child is between 16 and 18 years of age, the 1996 Convention may be relied on to obtain the appropriate relief, provided the respective states are Contracting States under that Convention.

Subject to Article 60 of the Council Regulation—The provisions of the Hague Convention 1980 do not automatically apply as Brussels IIA, Art 60 specifically provides that Brussels IIA takes precedence over the 1980 Convention. The 1996 Convention, Art 50 also provides that nothing precludes its provisions from being invoked for the purposes of obtaining the return of an abducted child. Thus, the 'applicable law' provisions in Art 15 and the parental responsibility provisions in Arts 16–18 are relevant. There will also be other instances when the inter-relationship between the two Conventions will need to be considered (see Part VI).

2 Contracting States

(1) For the purposes of the Convention as it has effect under this Part of this Act the Contracting States other than the United Kingdom shall be those for the time being specified by an Order in Council under this section.

(2) An Order in Council under this section shall specify the date of the coming into force of the Convention as between the United Kingdom and any State specified in the Order; and except where the Order otherwise provides, the Convention shall apply as between the United Kingdom and that State only in relation to wrongful removals or retentions occurring on or after that date.

(3) Where the Convention applies, or applies only, to a particular territory or particular territories specified in a declaration made by a Contracting State under Article 39 or 40 of the Convention references to that State in subsections (1) and (2) above shall be construed as references to that territory or those territories.

Defined terms—'the Convention': s 1(1).

'specified by an Order in Council under this section'—See the Child Abduction and Custody (Parties to Conventions) Order 1986 in Part IV for the Contracting States and the website of the permanent Bureau of the Hague Conference on Private International Law at *www.hcch.net*. To facilitate the goal of uniform interpretation the Bureau has set up a database (INCADAT) of decisions taken under the Convention, which can be accessed at *www.incadat.com*.

3 Central Authorities

(1) Subject to subsection (2) below, the functions under the Convention of a Central Authority shall be discharged –

- (a) in England and Wales by the Lord Chancellor; and
- (b) in Scotland by the Secretary of State; and
- (c) in Northern Ireland by the Department of Justice in Northern Ireland.

(2) Any application made under the Convention by or on behalf of a person outside the United Kingdom may be addressed to the Lord Chancellor as the Central Authority in the United Kingdom.

(3) Where any such application relates to a function to be discharged under subsection (1) above by an authority ('the responsible authority') other than the authority to which the application is addressed, the authority to which the application is addressed shall transmit it to the responsible authority.

Amendments—SI 2010/976.

Defined terms—'the Convention': s 1(1); 'Central Authority in relation to England and Wales': FPR 2010, r 12.44.

Central Authority for England and Wales—The authority is the Lord Chancellor. Application should be made to the International Child Abduction Unit, Official Solicitor & Public Trustee, Victory House, 30–34 Kingsway, London WC2B 6EX; Tel: 020 3681 2608; Fax: 020 3681 2762; Email: enquiries@offsol.gsi.gov.uk; new applications only: ICACU@offsol.gsi.gov.uk. An application form, which can be downloaded, will need to be completed within which authority is given to ICACU to act as agents for the applicant to take all necessary steps.

Scottish Central Authority—The Authority should be contacted at: Scottish Executive Justice Department, EU and International Law Branch, St Andrew's House, Regent Road, Edinburgh EH1 3DG. Contacts: Dawn Livingstone, Tel: +44 (0)131 244 4827, Email: dawn.livingstone@scotland.gsi.gov.uk; Bill Galbraith, Tel: +44 (0)131 244 4832, Email: bill.galbraith@scotland.gsi.gov.uk. Fax: 0131 244 4848. Web: *www.scotland.gov.uk/Topics/Justice/law/17867/fm-children-root/18533/13589*.

NI Central Authority—NI Courts and Tribunals Service, Civil Policy and Tribunal Reform Division, 4th Floor Laganside House, 23–27 Oxford Street, Belfast BT1 3LA. Tel: +44 (0)28 9072 8808/8819; Fax: 02890 728 945; DX: 478 NR Belfast 1; Email: businessdevelopmentgroup@courtsni.gov.uk; Web: *www.northernireland.gov.uk* or *www.courtsni.gov.uk/en-GB/Services/ChildAbduction* (cf the appropriate Central Authority under the 1996 Convention in Part VI and the PRMPC(IO)(EWNI)R 2010 in Part IV).

Isle of Man—The Attorney General has the responsibility for the Administration of the Manx Central Authority. Contact: Ms Michelle Norman, Attorney General's Chamber, 3rd floor, St Mary's Court, Hill Street, Douglas, Isle of Man IM1 1EU; tel: 01624 685452; fax: 01624 629162; email: childabduction@attgen.gov.im; *www.gov.im/about-the-government/offices/attorney-generals-chambers/*

'functions … of a Central Authority'—These are specified by Arts 7–11, 15, 21, 26–28 of the Convention.

The ICACU—The President's Guidance of 10 November 2014 on the International Child Abduction and Contact Unit (ICACU) in Part V should also be referred to.

4 Judicial authorities

The courts having jurisdiction to entertain applications under this Convention shall be –

(a) in England and Wales or in Northern Ireland the High Court; and

(b) in Scotland the Court of Session.

Defined terms—'the Convention': s 1(1); 'courts': FPR 2010, rr 12.45 and 12.54(4).

'applications under this Convention'—For procedure, see FPR 2010, r 12.43. On receiving the application, the ICACU may apply on behalf of the applicant to the Central Authority in the Contracting State. Where a child has been brought to England and Wales, the Central Authority in the Contracting State which is the country of the child's habitual residence should apply to the ICACU for assistance in securing the return of the child. The ICACU may then apply to the High Court as the judicial and administrative authority for the purposes of the Convention for assistance in ascertaining the whereabouts of the child and securing its return. It is also open to the applicant to apply directly to the High Court under Art 29. For contact details, see under s 3. In an emergency, including out of normal working hours, contact the RCJ on 020 7947 6000/6260. See further FPR PD12F.

5 Interim powers

Where an application has been made to a court in the United Kingdom under the Convention, the court may, at any time before the application is determined, give such interim directions as it thinks fit for the purpose of securing the welfare of the child concerned or of preventing changes in the circumstances relevant to the determination of the application.

Defined terms—'the Convention': s 1(1).

Application for interim directions—See FPR 2010, r 12.47.

Extent of court's power on interim direction—The court has very wide powers to deal with all interlocutory matters, including taking all appropriate steps to ascertain the whereabouts of the child, to safeguard his interests, to order disclosure of information under s 24A and to ensure his return (Sch 1, Arts 7 and 10; FPR 2010, r 12.47). The court can exercise jurisdiction even before a child's arrival within England and Wales (*A v A (Abduction: Jurisdiction)* [1995] 1 FLR 341, FD). It may make a collection and location order and passport order (FPR 2010 r 12.47; for the prescribed forms see *Emergency Remedies in the Family Courts* (Family Law)). A solicitor representing the abductor may be ordered to disclose the whereabouts of the abductor and all documents in his possession relating to the abductor's whereabouts until the order is served or comes to the knowledge of the abductor; but thereafter it would be inappropriate to adopt such a course as it is unlikely to assist in the recovery of the child (*Re H (Abduction: Whereabouts Order to Solicitors)* [2000] 1 FLR 766, FD). The court may grant injunctions, order a Cafcass reporter to prepare a report (s 9), give specific directions for trial (see FPR PD12F), order publicity (FPR PD12F, para 4.15), dispense with service (FPR 2010, r 12.48), adjourn the hearing for up to 21 days (FPR 2010, r 12.51) and stay the proceedings (FPR 2010, r 12.52). The court has power to give directions concerning the manner in which a child's welfare and whereabouts are to be managed, if removal from an abducting parent to temporary placement is necessary. In exceptional circumstances, to protect and safeguard the child's welfare, particularly if the child has special needs, or to prevent further harm to the child or prejudice to an interested party (Art 7(b)), the court may direct a local authority to accommodate the child and the abducting parent. If such an order is contemplated, the appropriate authority should be given notice, supported by evidence. In the event that it is not clear which local authority should bear the burden of accommodation, the court has a discretion to identify the local authority having regard to the welfare of the child. 'Domestic statutory provisions designed to deal with transition from one local authority to another are not engaged' (*Re A (Abduction: Interim Directions: Accommodation by Local Authority)* [2011] 1 FLR 1, CA). Electronic tagging of the abducting parent may be directed as part of the package of protective measures to secure the welfare of the child and/or to prevent changes in the circumstances. Where tagging is under consideration, the representatives of the parties should contact the service providers. See the April 2015 Guidance on *Tagging or Electronic Monitoring in Family Cases* issued by HM Courts and Tribunals Service. It is debatable whether GPS tagging is within the scope of the family courts but in exceptional circumstances where GPS tagging is considered the National Offender Management Service (NOMS) should be contacted and provided with details of who will be responsible for the monitoring costs (see *Re X (Children) and Y (Children) (No 2)* [2015] 2 FLR 1515, FD for guidance and procedure, which is also set out in Part V). Where Brussels IIA applies, Art 20 enables courts of Member States in urgent cases to take all necessary interim protective measures (see further Council Regulation (EC) No 2201/2003 and Hague Convention 1996, Arts 11 and 12 in Part VI). Although Art 12 of the 1996 Convention also empowers the authorities of a Contracting State to take provisional (non-urgent) measures for the protection of the person and property of a child, provided such measures are not incompatible with those taken by authorities within the jurisdiction of the child's habitual residence, Art 7(3) excludes the exercise of such powers in cases where the child has been wrongfully removed or retained. Pursuant to art 23 of the 1996 Convention, undertakings given by a parent to facilitate the return of an abducted child, where a defence under Art 13(b) of the Hague Convention 1980 is raised, amounts to 'protective measures' within Art 11(4) of BIIR as they are capable of recognition and enforcement by other Contracting States under the 1996 Convention. It is not necessary for the protective measures to be in the form of a court order (*Re Y (Abduction: Undertakings Given for Return of Child)* [2013] 2 FLR 649, CA). Nevertheless, in *B v B* [2014] EWHC 1804 (Fam) interim orders were made pursuant to Art 11 and in *RB v DB* [2015] EWHC 1817 (Fam) orders were made under both the 1996 Convention and Brussels IIA to ensure the measures were 'doubly enforceable'.

The court may adjourn the application for parties to take part in mediation where appropriate. Where there are very exceptional circumstances, the court may endorse the parties' agreement to a non-binding arbitration (including religious ADR) process to resolve all their matrimonial disputes but if it includes decisions relating to a child, this will be only be approved if it is in line with English legal principles and the welfare of the child (ie the paramountcy principle: *AI v MT (Alternative Dispute Resolution)* [2013] 2 FLR 371, FD).

6 Reports

Where the Lord Chancellor, the Department of Justice in Northern Ireland or the Secretary of State is requested to provide information relating to a child under Article 7(d) of the Convention he may –

(a) request a local authority or an officer of the Service or a Welsh family proceedings officer to make a report to him in writing with respect to any matter which appears to him to be relevant;

(b) request the Department of Health and Social Services for Northern Ireland to arrange for a suitably qualified person to make such a report to him;

(c) request any court to which a written report relating to the child has been made to send him a copy of the report;

and such a request shall be duly complied with.

Amendments—CJCSA 2000, s 74, Sch 7, para 80; CA 2004, Sch 3, para 3; SI 2010/976.

Defined terms—'the Convention': s 1(1); 'local authority': s 27(3).

Additional powers—Reference should also be made to Arts 55 and 56 of Brussels IIA and Arts 30–37 of the 1996 Convention (see Part VI).

7 Proof of documents and evidence

(1) For the purposes of Article 14 of the Convention a decision or determination of a judicial or administrative authority outside the United Kingdom may be proved by a duly authenticated copy of the decision or determination; and any document purporting to be such a copy shall be deemed to be a true copy unless the contrary is shown.

(2) For the purposes of subsection (1) above a copy is duly authenticated if it bears the seal, or is signed by a judge or officer, of the authority in question.

(3) For the purposes of Articles 14 and 30 of the Convention any such document as is mentioned in Article 8 of the Convention, or a certified copy of any such document, shall be sufficient evidence of anything stated in it.

Defined terms—'the Convention': s 1(1).

8 Declarations by United Kingdom courts

The High Court or Court of Session may, on an application made for the purposes of Article 15 of the Convention by any person appearing to the court to have an interest in the matter, make a declaration or declarator that the removal of any child from, or his retention outside, the United Kingdom was wrongful within the meaning of Article 3 of the Convention.

Defined terms—'the Convention': s 1(1).

Scope—The declaration is often necessary to enable the applicant in proceedings outside the UK to obtain an order for the return of a child who has been wrongly removed or retained. Applications for such a declaration should be made to the High Court (FPR PD12F, para 2.15). Applications may be made for the purposes of Art 15 by *any person* appearing to the court to have an interest in the matter and is not limited to the applicant or to the circumstances within the narrow definition of Art 15. See *Re G (Abduction: Rights of Custody)* [2002] 2 FLR 703, CA, where an unmarried father and his mother were regarded as having an interest in the child within the terms of Art 8. Relevant considerations include, inter alia, whether the applicant parent had rights of custody according to English law at the time of removal and possible issues of habitual residence and any breach (*A v B (Abduction: Declaration)* [2009] 1 FLR 1253, FD).

'wrongful'—See **Wrongful removal or retention** under Sch 1, Art 3.

9 Suspension of court's powers in cases of wrongful removal

The reference in Article 16 of the Convention to deciding on the merits of rights of custody shall be construed as a reference to –

(a) making, varying or revoking a custody order, or a supervision order under section 31 of the Children Act 1989 or Article 50 of the Children (Northern Ireland) Order 1995;

(aa) enforcing under section 29 of the Family Law Act 1986 a custody order within the meaning of Chapter V of Part I of that Act;

(b) registering or enforcing a decision under Part II of this Act;

(ba) registering or enforcing a decision under the Convention on Jurisdiction, Applicable Law, Recognition, Enforcement and Co-Operation in respect of Parental Responsibility and Measures for the Protection of Children that was signed at The Hague on 19 October 1996 ('the 1996 Convention'), except where provisions of the 1996 Convention are invoked in accordance with Article 50 of the 1996 Convention;

(c)–(e) …

Amendments—FLA 1986, s 68(1), Sch 1, para 28; CA 1989, s 108(5), Sch 13, para 57(1), Sch 15; Children (Scotland) Act 1995, s 105(4), Sch 4, para 37; SI 1995/756; SI 2010/1898.

Defined terms—'the Convention': s 1(1); 'custody order': s 27(1), Sch 3; 'rights of custody': Sch 1, Art 5.

Scope—This section supports Art 16 of the Hague Convention (see Sch 1, Art 16) which prevents the court from deciding on the merits of rights of custody until it has determined that a child is not to be returned or unless an application under the Convention is not lodged within a reasonable time after notice of wrongful removal or retention of the child. FPR 2010, rr 12.52 and 12.53 provide a procedure that inter alia guards against any court proceeding to determine rights of custody in ignorance of an application under the Convention and to stay all proceedings before it until the proceedings under the 1980 Hague Convention have been disposed of.

10 Rules of court

(1) An authority having power to make rules of court may make such provision for giving effect to this Part of this Act as appears to that authority to be necessary or expedient.

(2) Without prejudice to the generality of subsection (1) above, rules of court may make provision –

(a) with respect to the procedure on applications for the return of a child and with respect to the documents and information to be furnished and the notices to be given in connection with any such application;

(b) for the transfer of any such application between the appropriate courts in the different parts of the United Kingdom;

(c) for the giving of notices by or to a court for the purposes of the provisions of Article 16 of the Convention and section 9 above and generally as respects proceedings to which those provisions apply;

(d) for enabling a person who wishes to make an application under the Convention in a

Contracting State other than the United Kingdom to obtain from any court in the United Kingdom an authenticated copy of any decision of that court relating to the child to whom the application is to relate.

Defined terms—'appropriate court': s 27(2); 'the Convention': s 1(1); 'part of the United Kingdom': s 27(2).

Rules of court—FPR 2010, Pt 12 (in particular Ch 6, rr 12.51–12.57 and PDs 12D, 12E and 12F) applies to this Part.

11 Cost of applications

The United Kingdom having made such a reservation as is mentioned in the third paragraph of Article 26 of the Convention, the costs mentioned in that paragraph shall not be borne by any Minister or other authority in the United Kingdom except so far as they fall to be so borne by virtue of –

(a) the provision of any civil legal services (within the meaning of Part 1 of the Legal Aid, Sentencing and Punishment of Offenders Act 2012) under arrangements made for the purposes of that Part of that Act, or

(aa) the provision of civil legal services by the Northern Ireland Legal Services Commission, or

(b) the grant of legal aid or legal advice and assistance under the Legal Aid (Scotland) Act 1967 or Part I of the Legal Advice and Assistance Act 1972.

Amendments—Legal Aid Act 1988, s 45(1),(3), Sch 5, para 16; AJA 1999, s 24, Sch 4, para 31; SI 2003/435; LASPOA 2012, s 39, Sch 5, para 26.

Defined terms—'the Convention': s 1(1).

Reservation on costs—The UK is not bound to meet any costs other than those that may be covered by the Legal Aid Agency. Article 26 (see Sch 1, Art 26) permits a Contracting State to require the payment of expenses incurred in the return of the child (e g air fare).

Power to order payment of costs and expenses—Art 26 in its relevant parts provides that 'upon ordering the return of a child … the judicial authorities may … [d]irect the person who has removed or retained the child … to pay the necessary expenses incurred by or on behalf of the applicant, including travel expenses, any costs incurred or payments made for locating the child, the costs of legal representation of the applicant, and those of returning the child'. Similar provisions apply under the 1996 Convention (see Art 38). Jurisdiction is thus conferred upon the court that made the return order under the Convention but not under the freestanding domestic proceedings (e g s 8 orders). 'Any other interpretation in cases where the courts of two jurisdictions were working to achieve the return of a child would result in a potential proliferation of costs applications, possible double-counting and wasted costs' (*B v B (Foreign Hague Convention Proceedings: Costs)* [2016] 2 FLR 1019, CA, at [14]). Where a child is retained in another jurisdiction and an order is made by the High Court in England for the return of the child and then an order is applied for in the State where the child is retained, the application for costs including travel expenses under the scheme of the Convention should be made to the requested court (in *B v B* the German court; the English court therefore had no jurisdiction to order payment of the father's travel costs). Where an application for costs is made, the court should be supplied with a schedule justifying the claim that is made to enable a proper assessment of costs to be undertaken. Where a party's legal representatives fail to comply with the principles and procedures relating to without notice applications and have acted negligently, the court may exercise its discretion to make a wasted costs order: *B v A (Wasted Costs Order)* [2013] 2 FLR 958, FD.

PART II
RECOGNITION AND ENFORCEMENT OF CUSTODY DECISIONS

12 The European Convention

(1) In this Part of this Act 'the Convention' means the European Convention on Recognition and Enforcement of Decisions concerning Custody of Children and on the Restoration of Custody of Children which was signed in Luxembourg on 20 May 1980.

(2) Subject to the provisions of this Part of this Act, the provisions of that Convention set out in Schedule 2 to this Act (which include Articles 9 and 10 as they have effect in consequence of a reservation made by the United Kingdom under Article 17) shall have the force of law in the United Kingdom.

(3) But –

(a) those provisions of the Convention,
(b) this Part of this Act, and
(c) rules of court under section 24 of this Act,

are subject to Article 60 of the Council Regulation (by virtue of which the Regulation takes precedence over the European Convention, in so far as it concerns matters governed by the Regulation).

(4) 'The Council Regulation' means Council Regulation (EC) No 2201/2003 of 27 November 2003 concerning jurisdiction and the recognition and enforcement of judgments in matrimonial matters and matters of parental responsibility.

Amendments—SI 2001/310; SI 2005/265.

Object of the Convention—The European Convention provides for the registration, recognition and enforcement of decisions relating to custody where there has been an improper removal of a child in breach of such a decision. Note, however, that where Brussels IIA applies, its provisions take precedence over both the Hague Convention 1980 and the European Convention 1980 (see Procedural Guide D18 and FPR 2010, Pt 31 for procedure for registration etc where Brussels IIA and the 1996 Convention apply). Where the matter is not governed by Brussels IIA, the Convention will continue to apply in relations between states (*Purrucker v Vallés Pérez (No 1)* (Case C-256/09) [2012] 1 FLR 903, CJEU).

13 Contracting States

(1) For the purposes of the Convention as it has effect under this Part of this Act the Contracting States other than the United Kingdom shall be those for the time being specified by an Order in Council under this section.

(2) An Order in Council under this section shall specify the date of the coming into force of the Convention as between the United Kingdom and any State specified in the Order.

(3) Where the Convention applies, or applies only, to a particular territory or particular territories specified by a Contracting State under Article 24 or 25 of the Convention references to that State in subsections (1) and (2) above shall be construed as references to that territory or those territories.

Amendments—SI 2010/976.

Defined terms—'the Convention': s 12(1).

'specified by an Order in Council under this section'—See the Child Abduction and Custody (Parties to Conventions) Order 1986, which specifies the Contracting States for this purpose.

14 Central Authorities

(1) Subject to subsection (2) below, the functions under the Convention of a Central Authority shall be discharged –

(a) in England and Wales by the Lord Chancellor; and

(b) in Scotland by the Secretary of State; and

(c) in Northern Ireland by the Department of Justice in Northern Ireland.

(2) Any application made under the Convention by or on behalf of a person outside the United Kingdom may be addressed to the Lord Chancellor as the Central Authority in the United Kingdom.

(3) Where any such application relates to a function to be discharged under subsection (1) above by an authority ('the responsible authority') other than the authority to which the application is addressed, the authority to which the application is addressed shall transmit it to the responsible authority.

Amendments—SI 2010/976.

Defined terms—'the Convention': s 12(1).

'functions of a Central Authority'—These are specified in Arts 7–11, 15, 21, 26–28 of the Convention.

15 Recognition of decisions

(1) Articles 7 and 12 of the Convention shall have effect in accordance with this section.

(2) A decision to which either of those Articles applies which was made in a Contracting State other than the United Kingdom shall be recognised in each part of the United Kingdom as if made by a court having jurisdiction to make it in that part but –

(a) the appropriate court in any part of the United Kingdom may, on the application of any person appearing to it to have an interest in the matter, declare on any of the grounds specified in Article 9 or 10 of the Convention that the decision is not to be recognised in any part of the United Kingdom; and

(b) the decision shall be enforceable in any part of the United Kingdom unless registered in the appropriate court under section 16 below.

(3) The references in Article 9(1)(c) of the Convention to the removal of the child are to his improper removal within the meaning of the Convention.

Defined terms—'appropriate court': s 27(2); 'child': Sch 2, Art 1(a); 'the Convention': s 12(1); 'improper removal': Sch 2, Art 1(d); 'part of the United Kingdom': s 27(2).

16 Registration of decisions

(1) A person on whom any rights are conferred by a decision relating to custody made by an authority in a Contracting State other than the United Kingdom may make an application for the registration of the decision in an appropriate court in the United Kingdom.

(2) The Central Authority in the United Kingdom shall assist a person in making such an application if a request for such assistance is made by him or on his behalf by the Central Authority of the Contracting State in question.

(3) An application under subsection (1) above or a request under subsection (2) above shall be treated as a request for enforcement for the purposes of Articles 10 and 13 of the Convention.

(4) The High Court or Court of Session shall refuse to register a decision if –

(a) the court is of the opinion that on any of the grounds specified in Article 9 or 10 of the Convention the decision should not be recognised in any part of the United Kingdom;

(b) the court is of the opinion that the decision is not enforceable in the Contracting State where it was made and is not a decision to which Article 12 of the Convention applies;

(c) an application in respect of the child under Part I of this Act is pending.

(5) Where an authority mentioned in subsection (1) of section 14 above is requested to assist in making an application under this section to the appropriate court in a part of the United Kingdom ('the relevant part of the United Kingdom') other than the part in relation to which the authority has functions under that subsection, the authority shall transmit the request to the authority which has functions under that subsection in relation to the relevant part of the United Kingdom.

(6) In this section 'decision relating to custody' has the same meaning as in the Convention.

Amendments—SI 2010/976.

Defined terms—'appropriate court': s 27(2); 'authority': Sch 2, Art 1(b); 'Central Authority in the United Kingdom': s 14; 'child': Sch 2, Art 1(a); 'the Convention': s 12(1); 'Contracting State': s 13(1); 'decision relating to custody': Sch 2, Art 1(c).

Procedure on application—The procedure is set out in Sch 2, Arts 4 and 13 and FPR 2010, Pt 12, Ch 6 and PD12F. In the majority of cases the matters are dealt with under the provisions of Brussels IIA (see Part VI), under which there has been a proliferation of case-law on practice and decisions of the ECtHR (FPR PD12F, paras 2.20, 5.1–5.6). See also the commentary under FPR 2010, rr 12.58–12.71.

Shall refuse to register—Although the language of s 16(4) is mandatory, see Art 10 of the European Convention (Sch 2) which is permissive and thus gives the court a discretion.

17 Variation and revocation of registered decisions

(1) Where a decision which has been registered under section 16 above is varied or revoked by an authority in the Contracting State in which it was made, the person on whose behalf the application for registration of the decision was made shall notify the court in which the decision is registered of the variation or revocation.

(2) Where a court is notified under subsection (1) above of the revocation of a decision, it shall –

(a) cancel the registration, and

(b) notify such persons as may be prescribed by rules of court of the cancellation.

(3) Where a court is notified under subsection (1) above of the variation of a decision, it shall –

(a) notify such persons as may be prescribed by rules of court of the variation; and

(b) subject to any conditions which may be so prescribed, vary the registration.

(4) The court in which a decision is registered under section 16 above may also, on the application of any person appearing to the court to have an interest in the matter, cancel or vary the registration if it is satisfied that the decision has been revoked or, as the case may be, varied by an authority in the Contracting State in which it was made.

Defined terms—'authority': Sch 2, Art 1(b); 'Contracting State': s 13(1).
Procedure—See under FPR 2010, r 12.55.

18 Enforcement of decisions

Where a decision relating to custody has been registered under section 16 above, the court in which it is registered shall have the same powers for the purpose of enforcing the decision as if it had been made by that court; and proceedings for or with respect to enforcement may be taken accordingly.

19 Interim powers

Where an application has been made to a court for the registration of a decision under section 16 above or for the enforcement of such a decision, the court may, at any time before the application is determined, give such interim directions as it thinks fit for the purpose of securing the welfare of the child concerned or of preventing changes in the circumstances relevant to the determination of the application or, in the case of an application for registration, to the determination of any subsequent application for the enforcement of the decision.

Defined terms—'child': Sch 2, Art 1(a).
Application for interim directions—For procedure see FPR 2010, r 12.47.
Extent of court's power on interim directions—The court has broadly similar powers to those described under s 5. See also *T v R* [2002] 2 FLR 544, FD.

20 Suspension of court's powers

(1) Where it appears to any court in which such proceedings as are mentioned in subsection (2) below are pending in respect of a child that –

(a) an application has been made for the registration of a decision in respect of the child under section 16 above (other than a decision mentioned in subsection (3) below) or that such a decision is registered; and

(b) the decision was made in proceedings commenced before the proceedings which are pending,

the powers of the court with respect to the child in those proceedings shall be restricted as mentioned in subsection (2) below unless, in the case of an application for registration, the application is refused.

(2) Where subsection (1) above applies the court shall not –

(a) in the case of custody proceedings, make, vary or revoke any custody order, or a supervision order under section 31 of the Children Act 1989 or Article 50 of the Children (Northern Ireland) Order 1995;

(aa) in the case of proceedings under section 29 of the Family Law Act 1986 for the enforcement of a custody order within the meaning of Chapter V or Part I of that Act, enforce that order; or

(b)–(e) …

(2A) Where it appears to the Secretary of State –

(a) that an application has been made for the registration of a decision in respect of a child under section 16 above (other than a decision mentioned in subsection (3) below); or

(b) that such a decision is registered;

the Secretary of State shall not make, vary or revoke any custody order in respect of the child unless, in the case of an application for registration, the application is refused.

(3) The decision referred to in subsection (1) or (2A) above is a decision which is only a decision relating to custody within the meaning of section 16 of this Act by virtue of being a decision relating to rights of access.

(4) Paragraph (b) of Article 10(2) of the Convention shall be construed as referring to custody proceedings within the meaning of this Act.

(5) This section shall apply to a children's hearing (as defined in section 93(1) of the Children (Scotland) Act 1995) as it does to a court.

Amendments—FLA 1986, ss 67(2),(3), 68(1), Sch 1, para 29; CA 1989, s 108(5), Sch 13, para 57(1), Sch 15; Children (Scotland) Act 1995, s 105(4), Sch 4, para 37; SI 1995/756.

Modifications—Section 20 is modified for certain purposes by SI 2013/1465, art 17, Sch 1, para 1, Pt 3.

Defined terms—'child': Sch 2, Art 1(a); 'the Convention': s 12(1); 'custody order', 'custody proceedings': s 27(1), Sch 3.

Scope—See annotation under s 9.

21 Reports

Where the Lord Chancellor, the Department of Justice in Northern Ireland or the Secretary of State is requested to make enquiries about a child under Article 15(1)(b) of the Convention he may –

(a) request a local authority or an officer of the Service to make a report to him in writing with respect to any matter relating to the child concerned which appears to him to be relevant;

(b) request the Department of Health and Social Services for Northern Ireland to arrange for a suitably qualified person to make such a report to him;

(c) request any court to which a written report relating to the child has been made to send him a copy of the report;

and any such request shall be duly complied with.

Amendments—CJCSA 2000 s 74, Sch 7, para 80; SI 2010/976.

Defined terms—'child': Sch 2, Art 1(a); 'the Convention': s 12(1); 'local authority': s 27(3).

22 Proof of documents and evidence

(1) In any proceedings under this Part of this Act a decision of an authority outside the United Kingdom may be proved by a duly authenticated copy of the decision; and any document purporting to be such a copy shall be deemed to be a true copy unless the contrary is shown.

(2) For the purpose of subsection (1) above a copy is duly authenticated if it bears the seal, or is signed by a judge or officer, of the authority in question.

(3) In any proceedings under this Part of this Act any such document as is mentioned in Article 13 of the Convention, or a certified copy of any such document, shall be sufficient evidence of anything stated in it.

Defined terms—'authority': Sch 2, Art 1(b); 'the Convention': s 12(1).

23 Decisions of United Kingdom courts

(1) Where a person on whom any rights are conferred by a decision relating to custody made by a court in the United Kingdom makes an application to the Lord Chancellor, the Department of Justice in Northern Ireland or the Secretary of State under Article 4 of the Convention with a view to securing its recognition or enforcement in another Contracting State, the Lord Chancellor, the Department of Justice in Northern Ireland or the Secretary of State may require the court which made the decision to furnish him with all or any of the documents referred to in Article 13(1)(b), (c) and (d) of the Convention.

(2) Where in any custody proceedings a court in the United Kingdom makes a decision relating to a child who has been removed from the United Kingdom, the court may also, on an application made by any person for the purposes of Article 12 of the Convention, declare the removal to have been unlawful if it is satisfied that the applicant has an interest in the matter and that the child has been taken from or sent or kept out of the United Kingdom without the consent of the person (or, if more than one, all the persons) having the right to determine the child's place of residence under the law of the part of the United Kingdom in which the child was habitually resident.

(3) In this section 'decision relating to custody' has the same meaning as in the Convention.

Amendments—SI 2010/976.

Defined terms—'child': Sch 2, Art 1(a); 'Contracting State': s 13(1); 'the Convention': s 12(1); 'decision relating to custody': Sch 2, Art 1(c); 'part of the United Kingdom': s 27(2).

Decision of UK court relating to custody—Where a court makes a without notice order in proceedings under CA 1989, s 8 of which the abducting parent has notice, the order is both recognised and enforceable for the purposes of Art 9, and the court has jurisdiction to declare the removal unlawful even though the applicant did not possess the appropriate 'rights' when the child was removed (*Re S (Abduction: Hague and European Convention)* [1996] 1 FLR 660, FD).

'Article 12 of the Convention'—In cases where the provisions of both Conventions may apply, if a custody order existed, for example to a mother whose child has been abducted to France, it would be advisable to obtain a declaration under s 23(2) so that both Conventions may be relied on.

'unlawful'—Where a removal is declared unlawful then the removal is an improper removal (Sch 2, Art 1(d)).

24 Rules of court

(1) An authority having power to make rules of court may make such provision for giving effect to this Part of this Act as appears to that authority to be necessary or expedient.

(2) Without prejudice to the generality of subsection (1) above, rules of court may make provision –

(a) with respect to the procedure on application to a court under any provision of this Part of this Act and with respect to the documents and information to be furnished and the notices to be given in connection with any such application;

(b) for the transfer of any such application between the appropriate courts in the different parts of the United Kingdom;

(c) for the giving of directions requiring the disclosure of information about any child who is the subject of proceedings under this Part of this Act and for safeguarding its welfare.

Defined terms—'appropriate court': s 27(2); 'authority': Sch 2, Art 1(b); 'child': Sch 2, Art 1(a); 'part of the United Kingdom': s 27(2).

Rules of court—FPR 2010, rr 12.44–12.57 apply to this Part, along with PD12F.

PART III
SUPPLEMENTARY

24A Power to order disclosure of child's whereabouts

(1) Where –

(a) in proceedings for the return of a child under Part I of this Act; or

(b) on an application for the recognition, registration or enforcement of a decision in respect of a child under Part II of this Act,

there is not available to the court adequate information as to where the child is, the court may order any person who it has reason to believe may have relevant information to disclose it to the court.

(2) A person shall not be excused from complying with an order under subsection (1) above by reason that to do so may incriminate him or his spouse or civil partner of an offence; but a statement or admission made in compliance with such an order shall not be admissible in evidence against either of them in proceedings for any offence other than perjury.

Amendments—Inserted by FLA 1986, s 67(4). Amended by CPA 2004, s 261(1), Sch 27, para 110.

Defined terms—'child': Sch 2, Art 1(a).

Scope—This section supplements the court's wide powers under its inherent jurisdiction. Where disclosure is sought from a person under 18 years of age, before making the order consideration should be given to: (a) the fact that imprisonment or other forms of detention or contempt is not available to enforce the order; (b) the impact, especially upon a family member, of giving evidence and being cross-examined; (c) the extent of the disclosure sought; (d) whether it is proportionate; and (e) the young person's Art 8 rights (see *Re B (A Child)* [2015] 1 FLR 871, CA).

Self-incrimination—See under CA 1989, s 98.

Rules—FPR 2010, r 12.57 makes further provision as to orders for disclosure of information on applications under the European Convention.

25 Termination of existing custody orders etc

(1) Where –

(a) an order is made for the return of a child under Part I of this Act; or

(b) a decision with respect to a child (other than a decision mentioned in subsection (2) below) is registered under section 16 of this Act,

any custody order relating to him shall cease to have effect.

(2) The decision referred to in subsection (1)(b) above is a decision which is only a decision relating to custody within the meaning of section 16 of this Act by virtue of being a decision relating to rights of access.

(3)–(7) *(repealed)*

Amendments—CA 1989, s 108(7), Sch 15; Children (Scotland) Act 1995, s 105(4), Sch 4, para 37(1),(4); SI 1995/756.

Defined terms—'child': Sch 2, Art 1(a).

26 Expenses

There shall be paid out of money provided by Parliament –

(a) any expenses incurred by the Lord Chancellor or the Secretary of State by virtue of this Act; and

(b) any increase attributable to this Act in the sums so payable under any other Act.

27 Interpretation

(1) In this Act 'custody order' means (unless contrary intention appears) any such order as is mentioned in Schedule 3 to this Act and 'custody proceedings' means proceedings in which an order within paragraphs 1, 2, 5, 6, 8 or 9 of that Schedule may be made, varied or revoked.

(2) For the purposes of this Act 'part of the United Kingdom' means England and Wales, Scotland or Northern Ireland and 'the appropriate court', in relation to England and Wales or Northern Ireland means the High Court and, in relation to Scotland, the Court of Session.

(3) In this Act 'local authority' means –

(a) in relation to England and Wales, the council of a non-metropolitan county, a metropolitan district, a London borough or the Common Council of the City of London; and

(b) in relation to Scotland, a council constituted under section 2 of the Local Government etc (Scotland) Act 1994.

(4) In this Act a decision relating to rights of access in England and Wales or Scotland or Northern Ireland means a decision as to the contact which a child may, or may not, have with any person.

(5) In this Act 'officer of the Service' has the same meaning as in the Criminal Justice and Court Services Act 2000.

(5A) In this Act 'Welsh family proceedings officer' has the meaning given by section 35 of the Children Act 2004.

Amendments—FLA 1986, ss 67(5), 68(1), Sch 1, para 30; CA 1989, s 108(5), Sch 13, para 57(2); Local Government etc (Scotland) Act 1994, s 180(1), Sch 13, para 139; Children (Scotland) Act 1995, s 105(4), Sch 4, para 37(5); SI 1995/756; CJCSA 2000 s 74, Sch 7, para 81; CA 2004, Sch 3, para 4.

28 Application as respects British Islands and colonies

(1) Her Majesty may by Order in Council direct that any of the provisions of this Act specified in the Order shall extend, subject to such modifications as may be specified in the Order, to –

(a) the Isle of Man,

(b) any of the Channel Islands, and

(c) any colony.

(2) Her Majesty may by Order in Council direct that this Act shall have effect in the United Kingdom as if any reference in this Act, or in any amendment made by this Act, to any order

which may be made, or any proceedings which may be brought or any other thing which may be done in, or in any part of, the United Kingdom included a reference to any corresponding order which may be made or, as the case may be, proceedings which may be brought or other thing which may be done in any of the territories mentioned in subsection (1) above.

(3) An Order in Council under this section may make such consequential, incidental and supplementary provision as Her Majesty considers appropriate.

(4) An Order in Council under this section shall be subject to annulment in pursuance of a resolution of either House of Parliament.

Orders under this section—With effect from 6 December 1994, the Child Abduction and Custody Act 1985 (Isle of Man) Order 1994 extends the provisions of this Act to the Isle of Man.

With effect from 2 December 1997, the Child Abduction and Custody (Cayman Islands) Order 1997 extends ss 1–24A, 25(1),(2), 27 and Schs 1–3 of this Act (as modified in the Schedule thereto) to the Cayman Islands.

29 Short title, commencement and extent

(1) This Act may be cited as the Child Abduction and Custody Act 1985.

(2) This Act shall come into force on such day as may be appointed by an order made by statutory instrument by the Lord Chancellor and the Lord Advocate; and different days may be so appointed for different provisions.

(3) This Act extends to Northern Ireland.

SCHEDULE 1
CONVENTION ON THE CIVIL ASPECTS OF INTERNATIONAL CHILD ABDUCTION

Liaison judge—Black LJ is the Liaison Judge for England and Wales. Her role is to communicate and liaise with the appropriate judge in the Requested State. See further February [2008] Fam Law at p 105. (See also Brussels IIA, Art 8 in Part VI.)

The preferred route for contact for the Office of the Head of International Family Justice is tel: 020 7947 7197; email: IFJOffice@hmcts.gsi.gov.uk.

Article 3

The removal or the retention of a child is to be considered wrongful where –

(a) it is in breach of rights of custody attributed to a person, an institution or any other body, either jointly or alone, under the law of the State in which the child was habitually resident immediately before the removal or retention; and

(b) at the time of removal or retention those rights were actually exercised, either jointly or alone, or would have been so exercised but for the removal or retention.

The rights of custody mentioned in sub-paragraph (a) above, may arise in particular by operation of law or by reason of a judicial or administrative decision, or by reason of an agreement having legal effect under the law of that State.

Defined terms—'rights of custody': Art 5; see also FPR PD12F, paras 2.16–2.19. Similar definitions are given under Brussels IIA, Art 2(9) and the 1996 Convention, Art 3(b) (see Part VI).

Custody rights—Disputed rights of custody should not be determined by the English court unless it is unavoidable (see *A v B (Abduction: Declaration)* [2009] 1 FLR 1253, FD, where a declaration was granted to correct an inaccurate and incomplete opinion of English law on which the French court had made its decision). It should be adjudicated upon by the foreign court at the highest level, but for expediency may be dealt with by a court at a lower level (*Re T (Abduction: Rights of Custody)* [2008] 2 FLR 1794, FD; *Re D (Abduction: Rights of Custody)* [2007] 1 FLR 961, HL). Reliance on experts rather than the decision of the foreign court was criticised by the House of Lords in *Re D*, but in *Re F (Abduction: Rights of Custody)* [2008] 2 FLR 1239, FD, despite the lack of evidence on Polish law, with the consent of the parties, the court reached a decision as to rights of custody. Art 1(2) and Ch III of the 1996 Convention relating to parental responsibility are relevant when determining whether the applicant has 'custody rights' (see further the narrative in Part VI and the Supreme Court's decision in *Re J (Jurisdiction: Abduction)* [2016] 1 FLR 170, SC, referred to under Art 7 of the 1996 Convention).

A person with whom a child is placed on a long-term placement with the authority to make decisions may acquire 'custody rights', as will an unmarried father with no parental responsibility if he lives in the same household and exercises parental rights for a period of time (see *Re K (Abduction: Inchoate Rights)* [2014] 2 FLR 629, SC, in which the court identified the limited category of persons who may acquire inchoate custody rights) or where his rights have been confirmed (*Re E (Abduction: Rights of Custody)* [2005] 2 FLR 759, FD) (see ACA 2002, s 111). Where a mother has custody rights and then agrees that the child should reside with the father, the agreement is simply a continuing exercise of the mother's custody rights; the agreement does not revoke her rights nor does it enable the father to acquire custody rights (*Re W (Abduction: Procedure)* [1995] 1 FLR 878, FD; *Re J (Abduction: Acquiring Custody Rights by Caring For Child)* [2005] 2 FLR 791, FD). See also *Re J (Jurisdiction: Abduction)* [2016] 1 FLR 170, SC, which deals with the court's jurisdiction under Arts 7 and 11 of the 1996 Convention (referred to in Part VI) where custody rights have been given to a parent under an order made by a Contracting State of the 1996 Convention that is not a party to the 1980 Convention or Brussels IIA.

The issue of whether the removal of a child was in contravention of custody rights should be resolved by reference to the Convention law as applied by the English courts, so that where the father had been awarded the right to 'decide vital problems' with the mother (*Re F (Abduction: Rights of Custody)* [2008] 2 FLR 1239, FD) and where a father had enjoyed equal and separate rights the removal of the child by the mother was found to be in breach of those rights (*Re F (Child Abduction: Risk if Returned)* [1995] 2 FLR 31, CA, applied in *S v H (Abduction: Access Rights)* [1997] 1 FLR 971, FD and see *Re P (Abduction: Declaration)* [1995] 1 FLR 831, CA). See also **'rights of custody'** under Art 5 and *Practice Note of 14 October 1997* (see *The Family Court Practice 2011*).

Wrongful removal or retention—Removal is usually wrongful when it is in breach of someone else's rights (*C v S (A Minor) (Abduction)* [1990] 2 FLR 442, HL). Removal can be wrongful where it is in breach of the defendant's own rights of custody (*Re H (A Minor) (Abduction)* [1990] 2 FLR 439, FD) or where it is in breach of an express court order (*Re E (Abduction: Rights of Custody)* [2005] 2 FLR 759, FD). Removal is also wrongful within the terms of the Convention where it is in breach of an implied prohibition established on case-law, but not by reason of a court order (*C v C (Minors) (Child Abduction)* [1992] 1 FLR 163, FD). See also *Re H (Minors) (Abduction: Custody Rights), Re S (Minors) (Abduction: Custody Rights)* [1991] 2 FLR 262, HL and **Scope** under Art 8. See the identical definition in Art 7(2) of the 1996 Convention but also the provisions of Art 7(1) under which the state of the child's habitual residence immediately before the child's removal or retention retains jurisdiction and also the wider definition set out in Brussels IIA, Art 2(11) (see Part VI).

Retention—'Retention' for the purposes of the Convention is 'an event which occurs on a specific occasion rather than enjoying its usual and wider connotation of a continuous state of affairs. It occurs when a child who has been outside the state of habitual residence for a limited period is not returned to that state on the expiry of that period' (*RS v Poland (Application No 63777/09)* [2015] 2 FLR 848, ECHR and *GS v Georgia (Application No 2361/13)* [2015] 2 FLR 647, ECHR (failure to return after a holiday) but see *De L v H* [2010] 1 FLR 1229, FD, where although the initial non-return was held not to be wrongful the father's later conduct was found to constitute retention. Removal and retention has to be mutually exclusive (*Re H (Abduction: Custody Rights)* [1991] 2 FLR 262, HL) but in *RS v KS (Abduction: Wrongful Retention)* [2009] 2 FLR 1231, FD, the court departed from the decision in *Re H*, in holding that wrongful retention could subsume a wrongful removal, applied Lord Slynn's view in *Re S (A Minor) (Custody: Habitual Residence)* [1998] 1 FLR 122, HL that although the two are mutually exclusive both can occur on the facts in relation to the same child at different times. A lawful removal can become a wrongful retention if a return order is made by the court of the child's habitual residence (*Mercredi v Chaffe* [2011] 1 FLR 1293, CJEU).Where the evidence is confused or uncertain as to the agreement between the parties the court will determine the date of retention after a proper analysis of the evidence (*Re G (Abduction: Withdrawal of Proceedings)* [2008] 2 FLR 351, FD). 'Retention' includes not only acts of physical restraint but also court orders obtained on the initiative of the offending parent 'which have the effect of frustrating the child's return to the jurisdiction of its habitual residence' (*Re G* and *RS v Poland* (above)).

A unilateral decision by one parent not to return a child to the country of the child's habitual residence may constitute wrongful retention (*Re S (Minors) (Abduction: Wrongful Retention)* [1994] 1 FLR 82, FD; *H v H (Child Abduction: Stay of Domestic Proceedings)* [1994] 1 FLR 530, FD where, on the basis that there were exceptional circumstances, the court decided to deal with the merits of the application). Where the retention by one parent has been equivocal pending a determination by the court of the place from where the child has been abducted, a clear finding in that court requiring the return of the child would be sufficient to convert an equivocal retention into an unlawful one (*Re R (Minors) (Abduction)* [1994] 1 FLR 190, FD). A removal which is not in breach of domestic law may nevertheless be wrongful for the purposes of the Convention (*Re F (Child Abduction: Risk if Returned)* [1995] 2 FLR 31, CA and *Practice Note of 14 October 1997* in *The Family Court Practice 2011*). See also *Re S (Custody: Habitual Residence)* [1998] 1 FLR 122, HL where, although the initial removal and retention of the child was not wrongful because the unmarried father had no rights of custody capable of being breached, once he had acquired such rights by virtue of an order giving him care and control, the retention of the child thereafter, contrary to the order and his wishes, became wrongful (notwithstanding the fact that the abductors had obtained an order from the foreign court).

Article 4

The Convention shall apply to any child who was habitually resident in a Contracting State immediately before any breach of custody or access rights. The Convention shall cease to apply when the child attains the age of sixteen years.

Age of the child—Age is relevant when the application is heard. If the child is over 16, the court may consider dealing with the application for the return of the child under its inherent jurisdiction (*Re H (Abduction: Child of 16)* [2000] 2 FLR 51, FD). An alternative is to apply for recognition, registration and enforcement of measures taken in a Contracting State under the 1996 Convention, under which the age limit is 18. The Convention does not apply to an unborn child (*Re F (Abduction: Unborn Child)* [2007] 1 FLR 627, FD).

Habitual residence—The concept of habitual residence is central to the Hague Convention 1980, Brussels IIA and the 1996 Convention. Therefore, the court will avoid reaching any definitive conclusion on habitual residence and order the summary return of a child on an application made without notice and before all parties have had an opportunity to adduce evidence and make submissions, save in very exceptional circumstances where an order is necessary to protect the welfare of a child who is a British national (see *Re K and D (Wardship Without Notice Return Order)* [2017] EWHC 153 (Fam)). The term is not defined in the Act or the Conventions, but this may be because it is an issue dependant on the particular facts of the case. The CJEU test has centred on some degree of integration by a child in a social family environment. To that end, the factors that will be relevant are: duration, which reflects an adequate degree of permanence; regularity; conditions; reasons for the stay in the territory of that Member State and for the parent's move to that state; the child's nationality; place and conditions of attendance at school; linguistic knowledge; and the family and social relationships of the child in that state; and whether the person has (i) brought possessions, (ii) a right of abode and (iii) 'durable ties' with the country of residence or intended residence (objective factors) (*Mercredi v Chaffe* [2011] 2 FLR 515, CA; *Re A (Area of Freedom, Security and Justice)* [2009] 2 FLR 1, ECJ). Brussels IIA does not lay down any minimum period of duration. This test has now been adopted by the English courts following the decision of the UKSC in *Re A (Jurisdiction: Return of Child)* [2014] 1 FLR 111, SC in which Baroness Hale specifically said that the 'essentially factual and individual nature of the inquiry should not be glossed with legal concepts which would produce a different result from that which the factual inquiry would produce' (at [54], and applied in *Re J (A Child) (Finland) (Habitual Residence)* [2017] EWCA Civ 80, at [27]–[28], and *Re K and D*, above). This approach was applied in *Re LC (Reunite: International Child Abduction Centre Intervening)* [2014] 1 FLR 1486, SC but an additional factor that the court considered to be relevant in determining habitual residence was a child's assertion as to her state of mind during her stay in the requested state (at [57]). See also Lord Wilson's difference of emphasis in relation to a young child (at [37]). However, the court warned that this decision is not to be taken as opening the floodgates for those who have unlawfully abducted their child to raise the issue that the child was not habitually resident in the requesting state. A child can thus autonomously acquire habitual residence that is different to that of the parent with whom the child is living. Whether habitual residence in fact has been acquired will therefore depend on objective factors as well as subjective factors such as the reason for the child being in the state in question and the child's perceptions of the circumstances and the child's state of mind. See also *Re B (A Child) (Habitual Residence: Inherent Jurisdiction)* [2016] 1 FLR 561, SC, at [49]–[50], where a see-saw analogy and balance sheet approach (taking account of the circumstances of the child's life in the country he has left as well as the circumstances in his new country) was adopted to feed into the question of whether the child has achieved a degree of integration with the social and family environment in the country. In the substantive application (see [2017] EWHC 488 (Fam)), a care arrangement order was made for the child to live in Pakistan with her mother, with defined contact and limited parental responsibility to the applicant. Russell J also stated that in future, where there is a dispute as to habitual residence, early consideration should be given to join the children in the proceedings so that the court maintains a fluid picture of the children's circumstances, wishes and feelings to avoid the focus being on the dispute between the parents and/or care givers and their rights. The scope of the enquiry depends entirely on the particular facts of the case. The court's review of all the evidence about habitual residence should not become an unworkable obstacle course through which a judge is required to adopt a prescribed route. In some cases, a detailed analysis of the situation that the child has left may be necessary; in other cases, it can be explained shortly (see *Re J (A Child)*, at [62], [66]–[70]). Overall, therefore, it is the stability of the living conditions that matters in establishing habitual residence and the evaluation and assessment of all the factual evidence before arriving at a final determination is important (*AR v RN (Habitual Residence)* [2015] 2 FLR 503, SC; *Re R (Habitual Residence)* [2015] 2 FLR 124, CA; *Re S (Habitual Residence and Child's Objections: Brazil)* [2015] 2 FLR 1338, CA). In this regard, practitioners' attention is drawn to the observations made by Hayden J in *Re B (A Minor) (Habitual Residence)* [2016] EWHC 2174 (Fam). Owing to the need to deal with abduction cases expeditiously, the court should be provided with a properly focused written statement directed to the question of the child's habitual residence to be dealt with as a preliminary issue and may be dealt with on submissions without oral evidence (see *Re J (A Child)*, at [64]; see further under FPR 2010, r 12.46). See *London Borough of Barking and Dagenham v SS* [2015] 2 FLR 181, FD, where the 15-year-old girl who had lived on the fringes of society was held to have acquired habitual residence in England. See also *Re D (A Child: Habitual Residence: Consent and Acquiescence)* [2016] 1 FLR 937, FD in relation to the habitual residence of a child born to a surrogate mother. Where there are a number of children and they form a family unit, the result may be that the habitual residence of one or more of the older children in that unit might impact on the habitual residence of the younger children. In this respect, depending on the circumstances, the court may need to consider and determine whether or not it is necessary to grant party status to a child. However, even where the facts establish that the child has acquired habitual residence in the UK, the court may make a return order if on applying the best interest test and striking the balance between whether it is in the child's best interests to remain in the UK so that the dispute between the parents can be dealt with in this jurisdiction or whether, given the child's connection with the country of his birth and his extended family, the length of time he had lived with his parents in the foreign county and the effect of his relationship with the left-behind parent, it is in the child's interest to return him to the country with which he has the strongest and closest connection (*Re KL (A Child)* [2014] 1 FLR 772, SC). The basis of the court's jurisdiction in abduction cases based on the child's habitual residence under Brussels IIA, Art 10 applies when the child is removed from an EU country to another EU Member State, even though the jurisdictional scheme in Brussels IIA is not geographically limited to the EU (*Re H (Jurisdiction)* [2015] 1 FLR 1132, CA). A short period of time spent in another country with a view to effecting a reconciliation that fails would be insufficient (*Re B (Child Abduction: Habitual Residence)* [1994] 2 FLR 915, FD); *Re W (Abduction: Acquiescence: Children's Objections)* [2010] 2 FLR 1150, FD). The mere fact of taking a child out of the country is not enough to establish habitual residence (*Re M (Abduction: Habitual Residence)* [1996] 1 FLR 887, CA). A stay in a country for a holiday or children sent abroad for education does not lead to a change of the child's habitual residence (*B v D (Abduction: Inherent Jurisdiction)* [2009] 1 FLR 1015, FD). For an impact of an agreement reached following an abduction, see *Re H (Abduction: Habitual Residence: Agreement)* [2013] 2 FLR 1426; *ZA and PA v NA (Abduction: Habitual Residence)* [2013] 1 FLR 1041, CA. A move in connection with the father's employment on a short and temporary basis, notwithstanding the fact that the family maintained a constant principal home in another country, has been held to be the family's residence for settled purposes (*Re S (Habitual Residence)* [2010] 1 FLR 1146, CA). A mother who moved to the US, with a clear intention of settling there with the father and the child, can acquire residence in the US, though she was not entitled to remain in the US for longer than 90 days: *Re A (Abduction: Habitual Residence: Consent)* [2006] 2 FLR 1, FD. In *Re H-K (Habitual Residence)* [2012] 1 FLR 436, CA, an intended stay for only a year was held to be sufficient (see also *Leicester City Council v Chhatbar* [2014] 2 FLR 1365, FD and *MB v GK* [2014] EWHC 963 (Fam), where a temporary placement of a child with his grandparents in Singapore while the mother completed her education was held not to result in a change of the child's habitual residence because the child's integration into the social and family environment in Singapore was temporary in nature both factually and intentionally (*Re A (Area of Freedom, Security and Justice)* above applied).

Habitual residence cannot be acquired by a child who is not present in the country concerned (*Re A (Abduction: Habitual Residence: Consent)* and *ZA and PA v NA (Abduction: Habitual Residence)* (above)), nor can an unborn child acquire habitual residence during his/her mother's pregnancy and before his/her birth (*Re F (Abduction: Unborn Child)* [2007] 1 FLR 627, FD). However, it seems that this rule if universally applied may lead to injustice where a parent is forced to give birth in another country. Although the issue of physical presence was raised in *Re A*, the court did not make a decision on it as it relied on its inherent jurisdiction and the British nationality of the child to achieve the desired result. In *FM & KAH v SU & SA (by their guardian)* [2017] EWHC 441 (Fam), the referral to the court was made by the Passport Office, which had received applications for the renewal of British passports for three children who had been warded over a decade ago following their abduction by their father. Since then, there had been several proceedings both in England and Australia, including a refusal of a return order under the Hague Convention by the Australian Family Court. The mother, among other orders, asked the court to refuse the application for renewal of their passport. The issues before the court related to whether the court had jurisdiction when the children were clearly habitually resident in Australia and issues relating to their future, therefore, should be decided in Australia. The mother expressed concerns about the father's intention regarding the girls' future. Baker J made an order on the basis of the children's British nationality but limited in time to enable the mother to make the appropriate application in Australia because, as he stated: 'In view of the history of this case, and in particular the circumstances of the children's removal from England, I am persuaded that it would be in the children's interests for this court to exercise its protective jurisdiction in a limited way, namely by permitting the mother an opportunity to apply to the Australian court before the British passports are renewed and released to the father and the children. By ordering a short further pause before the renewal of the passports, this court will allow the mother to apply to the Australian court. I consider this to be consistent with the duty of this court to take measures necessary for the protection of children. In making such an order, this court is not intruding into the jurisdiction of the Australian court. On the contrary, I consider such an order to be consistent with the principles of comity to which the Supreme Court referred in *Re B*' (see also *Lachaux v Lachaux* [2017] EWHC 385 (Fam), where Mostyn J indicated that in exceptional circumstances the court could and would rely on the child's British nationality to make an appropriate order should the father fail to adhere to the assurances he gave to the court on the child's contact with the mother). The court indicated that were it to arise in another case it should be the subject of a referral to the CJEU. Where a family has two homes, and part of the year is spent in one country and part in another, there is continuity of residence for habitual residence to arise in both countries, but in Convention cases there cannot be habitual residence in more than one place at the same time. In such cases, the child's habitual residence will be where the child was living at the moment when the wrongful retention or removal occurred applying the 'centre of interests' tests (*Re V (Abduction: Habitual Residence)* [1995] 2 FLR 992, FD).

Fraud or mistake may prevent the acquisition or retention of habitual residence. Whether a move agreed to be of limited period prevents the acquisition of habitual residence will depend on the facts of the case (see *Re Z (Abduction)* [2009] 2 FLR 298, FD in which the court rejected the mother's argument that it does not). Going to a country for a trial period does not establish habitual residence nor is it established from the mere fact of ownership of property; it will be a question of fact and degree in each case (*High Tech International AG & Ors v Deripaska* [2006] EWHC 3276 (QB)).

FLA 1986, s 41 does not apply to conflicts on the issue of habitual residence under the Hague Convention (*Re S (A Child: Abduction)* [2003] 1 FLR 1008, CA). It is for the applicant initially to satisfy the court that it has jurisdiction (*Re R (Wardship: Child Abduction) (No 2)* [1993] 1 FLR 249, FD). In deciding the issue of habitual residence the court does not need to make a searching and microscopic inquiry. Generally it will suffice for the court to stand back and take a general panoramic view of the evidence (*Re B (Minors) (Abduction) (No 1)* [1993] 1 FLR 988, FD). Once habitual residence is established, the burden shifts on to the defendant to show otherwise or that a change has occurred (*Re R (Wardship: Child Abduction)* [1992] 2 FLR 481, CA). As to the residence of a child, a child aged four who is in the sole custody of the mother will necessarily have the same habitual residence as the mother (*Re J* (above)). Where parents separate, the child's habitual residence follows that of the parent who has the day-to-day care of the child and with whom the child lives. Similarly, where the mother alone has parental responsibility for her child, the child will take on the habitual residence of its mother (*Re G (Abduction: Withdrawal of Proceedings, Acquiescence)* [2008] 2 FLR 351, FD; she alone can determine where they should live and change the habitual residence of her child. However, see the see-saw analogy engaged in *Re B (A Child) (Habitual Residence: Inherent Jurisdiction)* [2016] 1 FLR 561, SC (not a case under the Hague Convention) to determine whether the child had acquired habitual residence in the state where she moved with her mother. By a majority, the Court concluded that the requisite disengagement of the child's roots from her former resident state had not been reached. When parents separate, the general view has been that the child's habitual residence will follow that of its principal carer, but in some circumstances the child may acquire habitual residence autonomously (see *Re LC (Reunite: International Child Abduction Centre Intervening)* [2014] 1 FLR 1486, SC and the commentary in the paragraph below). Where the parents are habitually resident in different places at the time of the child's birth the issue will depend on the circumstances of the individual case (see *Re G* above). In the case of a married couple or where both parents have parental responsibility, it was generally considered that one parent could not unilaterally change the habitual residence of the child without the consent or acquiescence of the other by removing the child from one jurisdiction to another wrongfully and in breach of the other parent's rights. However, in *Re A (Children)* (above) Baroness Hale stated that this is not necessarily the case and disapproved of this concept (applied in *Re H (Jurisdiction)* [2015] 1 FLR 1132, CA, at [34]). Passage of time such as acknowledged by the provisions of Brussels IIA, Art 10, may lead to a change of habitual residence even where a child may have been abducted. For a change to take effect, the child must be actually transferred into the care of the parent who seeks to establish habitual residence (*Re O (A Minor) (Abduction: Habitual Residence)* [1993] 2 FLR 594, FD). Where the mother has been the sole carer of the child, her death will not immediately strip the child of the habitual residence acquired from her. Nor will the clandestine removal of the child, without a court order or the consent of any interested party, immediately clothe the child with the habitual residence of the person removing him. The longer the child lives in the new jurisdiction without challenge, the more likely it is that the child will be said to acquire the habitual residence of those who continue to care for him without opposition. There is no need to identify a specific point in time at which the children ceased to be habitually resident in England, because the loss of one habitual residence and the acquisition of another is gradual (*Re B (A Minor) (Habitual Residence)* (above); *Re A (Removal Outside Jurisdiction: Habitual Residence)* [2011] 1 FLR 2025, CA). See also *Re G (Abduction: Rights of Custody)* [2002] 2 FLR 703, CA; *Re S (Custody: Habitual Residence)* [1998] 1 FLR 122, HL. On the issue of jurisdiction under Brussels IIA and habitual residence, see *Mercredi v Chaffe* [2011] 1 FLR 1293, CJEU and *H v H (Jurisdiction to Grant Wardship)* [2012] 1 FLR 23, CA.

Where a parent abducts a baby, fails to comply with any court order for the child's return and successfully goes to ground for many years, there is a powerful argument that it would be an affront to common sense to hold, perhaps 10–12 years later, that the habitual residence of the child was other than the country in which he had spent virtually the whole of his life (*Re B (Abduction: Children's Objection)* [1998] 1 FLR 667, FD; cf *Re H (Abduction: Habitual Residence: Agreement)*, above, where the mother had gone to ground in Mexico for almost 3 years). On the issue of the habitual residence of a child born to a surrogate mother with whom she has no biological connection see *W and B v H (Child Abduction: Surrogacy)* [2002] 1 FLR 1008, FD and *W and W v H (Child Abduction: Surrogacy) No 2* [2002] 2 FLR 252, FD. It is clear from these two decisions that, in appropriate cases, where there is any doubt about proving the habitual residence of a child it would be advisable to seek relief under the Convention and, alternatively under the inherent jurisdiction, to enable the court to exercise the full range of powers available to it.

The habitual residence of a child in England before the abduction will give the High Court inherent jurisdiction to entertain an application in respect of the child. The issue of wardship proceedings, and any orders made by the English court giving interim care and control, will stand, and give both the court and the parent in whose favour the order is made 'custody rights' within Art 3 of the Convention, even though an order may have been obtained by the abductors from the foreign court (*Re S* above). The habitual residence of a child of a US serviceman who is posted to a non-Convention country is that country and not the US (*Re A (Abduction: Habitual Residence)* [1996] 1 FLR 1, FD).

It should be noted that Art 4 does not require that, at the time of the application, the child should be habitually resident in the state under which the rights of custody or access arose; it does require, however, that the child should be habitually resident in 'a Contracting State' (*Re G (A Minor) (Hague Convention: Access)* [1993] 1 FLR 669, CA; see also *A v A (Child Abduction)* [1993] 2 FLR 225, FD).

Habitual residence and the impact of Brussels IIA, Arts 8–10 on jurisdiction—See *Re J (A Child) (Finland) (Habitual Residence)* [2017] EWCA Civ 80 and *Re K and D (Wardship Without Notice Return Order)* [2017] EWHC 153 (Fam).

Article 5

For the purposes of this Convention –

(a) 'rights of custody' shall include rights relating to the care of the person of the child and, in particular, the right to determine the child's place of residence;

(b) 'rights of access' shall include the right to take a child for a limited period of time to a place other than the child's habitual residence.

'rights of custody'—See also the notes under Art 3. The right of custody may arise by operation of law or by reason of a judicial or administrative decision or by reason of an agreement having legal effect under the law of that state. A parent of a child who is serving a sentence retains 'custody rights'. Such rights are not suspended but are merely curtailed (*Re A (Abduction: Rights of Custody: Imprisonment)* [2004] 1 FLR 1, FD and *Re L (A Child)* [2006] 1 FLR 843, FD). The following confers or amounts to 'custody rights': a provision in an order that a child is not to be removed from the jurisdiction of a state without the prior approval of the court or the written agreement of the parties (*Re P (Abduction: Consent)* [2004] 2 FLR 1057, CA; an implied prohibition on such removal (*C v C (Child Abduction)* [1992] 1 FLR 163, FD); rights relating to the care of the child and, in particular, the right to determine the child's place of residence but not the right to be informed about a decision to change the residence of the child (*Re V-B (Abduction: Custody Rights)* [1999] 2 FLR 192, CA) or his education; and a 'right to veto' removal (*Re D (Abduction: Rights of Custody)* [2007] 1 FLR 961, HL). See also *S v H (Abduction: Access Rights)* [1997] 1 FLR 971, FD; *Re B (A Minor) (Abduction)* [1994] 2 FLR 249, CA and the dissenting judgment of Peter Gibson LJ. A court may have a right of custody at the relevant time in the sense that it has a right to determine the child's place of residence when its jurisdiction is invoked in respect of matters within the meaning of the Convention. The date on which the court's jurisdiction is invoked is at the latest when the proceedings are served, or in special cases where an order is made or direction given on a without notice application and before the application or order is served (*A v B (Abduction:*

Declaration) [2009] 1 FLR 1253, FD; *X County Council v B (Abduction: Rights of Custody in the Court)* [2010] 1 FLR 1197, FD; *Re H (Abduction: Rights of Custody)* [2000] 1 FLR 374, HL) and in any event once it has made an interim order (*Re W; Re B (Child Abduction: Unmarried Father)* [1998] 2 FLR 146, FD); where the court has adjourned the hearing for the issue to be resolved by agreement (*Re C (Abduction: Wrongful Removal)* [1999] 2 FLR 859, FD); where wardship proceedings have been issued (*Re S (Custody: Habitual Residence)* [1998] 1 FLR 122, HL). Where Brussels IIA, Art 16 applies, the court is deemed to be seised only where a document instituting proceedings or an equivalent document is lodged with the court. Hence an application made by telephone does not operate to confer those rights in the court until the formal application is made: *Mercredi v Chaffe* [2011] 1 FLR 1293, CJEU.

Where an issue is raised regarding whether the foreign law gives the applicant custody rights or not, the court will normally be bound by the decision of the court of the Requesting State as to the applicant's rights and the legality of the child's removal from that state (*Re D (Abduction: Rights of Custody)* (above)). The court may determine the issue on expert evidence adduced before it (see *Re JB (Child Abduction) (Rights of Custody: Spain)* [2004] 1 FLR 796, FD) but where a foreign court has made a decision, that should be relied on (*Re D (Abduction: Rights of Custody)*, above). (See also under Art 3.) The court should resist the temptation to make its own findings as to the foreign laws applicable and should be reluctant to allow rights of access to a child to metamorphose into rights of custody (*Re F (Abduction: Rights of Custody)* [2008] 2 FLR 1239, FD). Where the court is faced with conflicting expert evidence, it is for the applicant to prove his rights under the relevant foreign law.

Custody rights and unmarried fathers—The parental responsibility and applicable law provisions of the 1996 Convention affect how an unmarried father's custody rights are viewed under the Hague Convention 1980. An unmarried father has parental responsibility if he is registered as the child's father (ACA 2002, s 111) but for such registration to be valid and effective to confer parental responsibility, s 10 of the Births and Deaths Registration Act 1953 must be strictly complied with (*AAA v ASH, Registrar-General for England and Wales and The Secretary for Justice Intervening* [2010] 1 FLR 1, FD). Where the issue relates to an unmarried father's rights under a foreign law the usual procedure is to make a referral pursuant to Art 15 for the foreign court to determine the issue, but see: *Re K (Rights of Custody: Spain)* [2010] 1 FLR 57, FD; *Kennedy v Kennedy* [2010] 1 FLR 782, CA. The rights within Art 3 may extend to 'inchoate rights of those who are carrying out duties and enjoying privileges of a custodial or parental character which, though not yet formally recognised or granted by law, a court would nevertheless be likely to uphold in the interests of the child' (*Re B (A Minor) (Abduction)* [1994] 2 FLR 249, CA). In *Re F (Abduction: Unmarried Father: Sole Carer)* [2003] 1 FLR 839, FD this principle was extended to a father to whom the primary care of his children and a child of whom he was not the father had been delegated by the mother; but cf *Re C (Child Abduction) (Unmarried Father: Rights of Custody)* [2003] 1 FLR 252, FD. Confirmation in solicitors' correspondence, in which the offending party confirms that there is no intention to remove the child from the jurisdiction and in consequence thereof immediate steps are not taken to issue proceedings to prevent removal, has been held to attribute 'custody rights' (*Re H (Child Abduction) (Unmarried Father: Rights of Custody)* [2003] 2 FLR 153, FD). See also *Re C (Abduction: Wrongful Removal)* [1999] 2 FLR 859, FD and *Re S (Custody: Habitual Residence)* [1998] 1 FLR 122, HL. In *JMcB v Le* (Case C-400/10) [2011] 1 FLR 518, ECJ, the court held that the concept of rights of custody in the Regulation is an autonomous one. It follows that its content is not to be determined by reference to the laws of the individual Member States even if the question of who enjoys such rights is left to that State. A Member State is not precluded from requiring by its law that the father of a child who is not married to the mother shall have obtained an order of a court of competent jurisdiction granting him custody in order to qualify as having 'custody rights' that render the removal of that child from its country of habitual residence wrongful for the purposes of Art 2(1) of Brussels IIA. Brussels IIA must therefore be interpreted to mean that whether a child's removal is wrongful is entirely dependent on the existence of custody rights conferred by the national law in breach of which the child was removed. How those who possess that strictly limited category of rights are to be defined consistently with the principles and purposes of the Convention and the Regulation was considered by the UKSC in *Re K (Abduction: Inchoate Rights)* [2014] 2 FLR 629, SC. Lady Hale defined people with this strictly limited category of rights as follows: '(a) They must be undertaking the responsibilities, and thus enjoying the concomitant rights and powers, entailed in the primary care of the child. Thus, for example, our law recognises the obvious truth that people who are actually looking after a child, even if they do not have parental responsibility, may "do what is reasonable in all the circumstances of the case for the purpose of safeguarding and promoting the child's welfare" (Children Act 1989, s 3(5)). (b) They must not be sharing those responsibilities with the person or persons having a legally recognised right to determine where the child shall live and how he shall be brought up. They would not then have the rights normally associated with looking after the child. (c) That person or persons must have either abandoned the child or delegated his primary care to them. (d) There must be some form of legal or official recognition of their position in the country of habitual residence. This is to distinguish those whose care of the child is lawful from those whose care is not lawful. Examples might be the payment of state child-related benefits or parental maintenance for the child. And (e) there must be every reason to believe that, were they to seek the protection of the courts of that country, the status quo would be preserved for the time being, so that the long term future of the child could be determined in those courts in accordance with his best interests, and not by the pre-emptive strike of abduction.', at [59] (see, however, Lord Wilson's dissenting judgment). The court, however, stayed its order to give the mother the opportunity to apply to the High Court in Northern Ireland for an order that the child not be returned pursuant to Art 13 of the Convention.

The fact that the national law provides for the mother to have parental responsibility alone would not be contrary to Art 8 of the ECHR, provided that it permitted the child's father to apply to the national court to grant him parental responsibility. (See further FPR PD12F, para 2.17 in Part III and *Practice Note of 14 October 1997*, which is set out in *The Family Court Practice 2011*.)

Custody rights of same-sex female partners where a child is born as result of assisted reproduction—See HFEA 2008.

Orders made after removal—The view expressed in *Practice Note of 14 October 1997* that an application for parental responsibility does not involve an exercise by the court of 'rights of custody' was challenged in *Re C* (above).

'rights of access'—The definition in the 1996 Convention, Art 3(b) and Brussels IIA, Art 2(10) are in similar terms. Under Art 21, an application to make arrangements for organising or securing the effective exercise of rights of access may be presented to the Central Authority of a Contracting State in the same way as an application for the return of a child. Article 21 also provides that Central Authorities are bound by the obligations of co-operation in Art 7 to promote the peaceful enjoyment of access rights and the fulfilment of any conditions to which the exercise of those rights may be subject.

****

Article 8

Any person, institution or other body claiming that a child has been removed or retained in breach of custody rights may apply either to the Central Authority of the child's habitual residence or to the Central Authority of any other Contracting State for assistance in securing the return of the child. The application shall contain –

(a) information concerning the identity of the applicant, of the child and of the person alleged to have removed or retained the child;

(b) where available, the date of birth of the child;

(c) the grounds on which the applicant's claim for return of the child is based;

(d) all available information relating to the whereabouts of the child and the identity of the person with whom the child is presumed to be.

The application may be accompanied or supplemented by –

(e) an authenticated copy of any relevant decision or agreement;

(f) a certificate or an affidavit emanating from a Central Authority or other competent authority of the State of the child's habitual residence, or from a qualified person, concerning the relevant law of that State:

(g) any other relevant document.

Scope—See **'rights of custody'** under Art 5.

Procedure on application—See FPR 2010, rr 12.44–12.57 and PD12F.

****

Article 11

The judicial or administrative authorities of Contracting States shall act expeditiously in proceedings for the return of children.

If the judicial or administrative authority concerned has not reached a decision within six weeks from the date of commencement of the proceedings, the applicant or the Central Authority of the requested State, on its own initiative or if asked by the Central Authority of the requested State, shall have the right to request a statement of the reasons for the delay. If a reply is received by the Central Authority of the requested State, that Authority shall transmit the reply to the Central Authority of the requesting State, or to the applicant, as the case may be.

'act expeditiously'—In Convention proceedings and under Brussels IIA, there is 6-week time-limit. FPR PD12F, para 2.14 specifically refers to the need for expedition and confirms the procedure set out in *Vigreux v Michel* [2006] 2 FLR 1180, CA. The state has an obligation to take positive and effective measures to enforce the right of a parent to be re-united with his/her child and to deal swiftly with the abduction proceedings, including imposing sanctions against the offending parent (ECHR 1950, Art 8; in *Ferrari v Romania (Application No 1714/10)* [2015] 2 FLR 303, ECHR a delay of 13 months and failure to enforce the order was held to be a breach of the father's Art 8 rights for which damages were awarded; in *RS v Poland (Application No 63777/09)* [2015] 2 FLR 848, ECHR and *KJ v Poland (Application No 30813/14)* [2017] 1 FLR 1006, ECHR a delay of more than 6 months and 12 months respectively without any satisfactory explanation for the delay and procedural inadequacies were held to contravene Art 11 and also Art 8 of the European Convention; *Caras (Iosub) v Romania* (Application No 7198/04) [2007] 1 FLR 661, ECHR; *Maire v Portugal* (Application No 48206/99) [2004] 2 FLR 653, ECHR; *Re C (Abduction: Interim Directions: Accommodation by Local Authority)* [2004] 1 FLR 653, FD; and *Karadzic v Croatia* [2006] 1 FCR 36, ECHR). For unjustified delay caused by use of experts, see *Deak v Romania and UK* (Application No 19055/05) ECHR. The obligation to act expeditiously does not exonerate judicial authorities from the duty to undertake an effective examination of allegations made by one of the parties on the basis of one of the exceptions in Art 13: *X v Latvia (Application No 27853/09)* [2014] 1 FLR 1135, ECHR. Delay may be justified where the court is seeking to ensure there is an equality of arms between the two parents in relation to legal representation where legal aid is denied

PART II

(*Kinderis v Kineriene* [2013] EWHC 4139 (Fam)). The observations made by Holman J in *Kinderis* on the need that public funding be made available and the option he suggested for the LAA to grant immediate legal aid subject to review if necessary after a Cafcass report is filed should be brought to the attention of the LAA when applying for legal aid. For the procedure to be followed when an appeal is contemplated, see *Klentzeris v Klentzeris* [2007] 2 FLR 996, CA and *Re F (Abduction: Child's Wishes)* [2007] 2 FLR 697, CA. In *Re K (Rights of Custody: Spain)* [2010] 1 FLR 57, FD, the court dealt with the issues without reference to the foreign court pursuant to Art 15 to avoid delay (see also **Brussels IIA** under Art 12). Also note that, in contrast, the 1996 Hague Convention does not make any reference to time limits.

Article 12

Where a child has been wrongfully removed or retained in terms of Article 3 and, at the date of the commencement of the proceedings before the judicial or administrative authority of the Contracting State where the child is, a period of less than one year has elapsed from the date of the wrongful removal or retention, the authority concerned shall order the return of the child forthwith.

The judicial or administrative authority, even where the proceedings have been commenced after the expiration of the period of one year referred to in the preceding paragraph, shall also order the return of the child, unless it is demonstrated that the child is now settled in its new environment.

Where the judicial or administrative authority in the requested state has reason to believe that the child has been taken to another State, it may stay the proceedings or dismiss the application for the return of the child.

'a period of less than one year'—Under similar provisions in Brussels IIA and the 1996 Convention, the relevant date when time begins to run is not 'from the date of the wrongful removal or retention', but the date when the holder of the rights of custody has or should have had knowledge of the whereabouts of the child. For the purposes of establishing the 1-year period, where the parties have agreed the date of the child's return, in the absence of any communication of the change of intention or decision not to return the child, the relevant date at which a wrongful retention takes place is the date on which the child should have been returned. An uncommunicated decision to retain the child does not constitute retention (*RS v KS (Abduction: Wrongful Retention)* [2009] 2 FLR 1231, FD.

'shall order the return of the child'—This is a mandatory provision where less than 1 year has elapsed and discretionary when the period is in excess of 1 year. For examples of the inter-relationship between these provisions and the jurisdiction of the home court or where the court's involvement preceded the non-return order by a Contracting State on a Convention application under Brussels IIA, see *Re AJ (Brussels II Revised)* [2012] 2 FLR 689, FD and the final determination as *Re AJ (Contact: Brussels II Revised)* [2012] 2 FLR 1065, FD. See also the provisions of Hague Convention 1996, Art 7 in Part VI, which set out the jurisdiction of the Contracting State under the Convention to take such urgent measures under Art 11 as are necessary for the protection of a child in cases of urgency and the decision of the Supreme Court on the issue of jurisdiction in *Re J (Jurisdiction: Abduction)* [2016] 1 FLR 170, SC.

'now settled in its new environment'—Contrast with the additional conditions required under Brussels IIA, Art 10(b). For meaning of and what constitutes settlement, see *Re H and L (Abduction: Acquiescence)* [2010] 2 FLR 1277, FD. Delay is an issue that should be taken into account in the analysis of whether, as a result of the delay, the children have become settled but it is inappropriate to raise it as an abuse of the process of the court and a ground for striking out the application (*Re W (Children: Abducton: Striking Out* [2015] EWHC 4002 (Fam)) but not where the applicant has actively pursued the application and the delay is not due to his/her conduct: *RS v KS (Abduction: Wrongful Retention)* [2009] 2 FLR 1231, FD; cf *SP v EB and KP* [2016] 1 FLR 228, FD, where account was taken of the father's inaction in taking proceedings in the home country and the length of time it would take for the matter to be dealt with there. See also *Re B (Hague Convention Proceedings)* [2015] 1 FLR 389, CA, where a child's placement with an uncle and presence in the UK for a period in excess of 12 months was not considered to be sufficient to amount to settlement). A party's conduct, immoderate and underhand activities are relevant factors (*Re O (Abduction: Settlement)* [2011] 2 FLR 1307, CA), as is applicant's unexplained delay in the court exercising its discretion not to return the children (*Re C (Child Abduction: Settlement)* [2006] 2 FLR 797, FD; *Re F (Abduction: Rights of Custody)* [2008] 2 FLR 1239, FD) but in *F v M and N (Abduction: Acquiescence: Settlement)* [2008] 2 FLR 1270, FD, although almost 2 years had elapsed, the court held that the father had not acquiesced in her retention as he had actively pursued proceedings in Poland and the Polish court had been seised of the matter before the mother abducted the child and had gone a long way into its determination of what arrangements should be in her best interests. A return order was made but suspended to enable the mother to pursue an application before the Polish court and also to apply for permission to remove the child to England. Whereas a return order may be delayed in order for travel arrangements to be made and for the parent who has abducted the child to wind down his/her genuine affairs, an application for a delayed return will be refused if it is clearly made to frustrate the order especially where there has been a finding against that parent in relation to the abduction of a child and attempts made to frustrate the court process of the requesting state: *AT v SS (No 2)* [2016] 2 FLR 1122, FD. Settlement includes physical, psychological and emotional elements and a return order is likely to be refused where there is a grave risk that the child would be exposed to psychological harm if returned (see *SP v EB and KP*, above, where although the Art 12 defence was not available the fact that the child had been in the UK for 18 months was held to be relevant when considering the defence under Art 13; *Re E (Abduction: Intolerable Situation)* [2009] 2 FLR 485, FD). The impact of separation of the child from its half-sibling is also relevant (see *RS v KS (Abduction: Wrongful Retention)* above. Settlement is used as a defence to avoid return when more than 12 months has elapsed since the abduction (see below).

'now settled'—This refers to the date when the proceedings were commenced (*SP v EB and KP* [2016] 1 FLR 228, FD) as otherwise any delay in hearing the case might affect the outcome.

The word 'settlement' has two constituents: (i) it involves a physical element of relating to, being established in, a community and an environment; (ii) it has physical, emotional and psychological constituents denoting security and stability in the sense of permanence. The word 'new' encompasses place, home, school, people, friends, activities and opportunities, but not, per se, the relationship with the mother (see *Re H and L* and *Re N* [1991] 1 FLR 413, FD, applied in *Kent County Council v C, G and A* [2015] 1 FLR 115, FD).

Duty to order the return of the child and protection of human rights and fundamental freedoms—When exercising the court's discretion whether or not to order the return of a child, the principles and approach set out in *Re E (Children) (Abduction: Custody Appeal)* [2011] 2 FLR 758, SC and *Re M (Abduction: Zimbabwe)* [2008] 1 FLR 251, HL should be followed (see *Re M (Children)* [2016] EWCA Civ 942). Hague policy considerations, while relevant in exercising discretion in settlement cases, should be weighed with other welfare considerations. In assessing the adaptability of a child to a return order, particularly to the impact of the disruption in the living arrangement of a young child, the court should consider the individual circumstances of each child and examine and weigh this in the balance when exercising its discretion under the Hague Convention (the approach adopted in *RS v KS (Abduction: Wrongful Retention)* [2009] 2 FLR 1231, FD, was approved). Protection of rights under the European Convention is also relevant, especially since Article 20 of the Hague Convention provides that the return of the child under the provisions of Art 12 may be refused if this would not be permitted by the fundamental principles of the requested state relating to the protection of human rights and fundamental freedoms. This Article has not been included in Sch 1 to the Act and does not therefore have the force of law in England and Wales. However, it was successfully raised and the competing right of the father and that of the child was struck in favour of the child to make a non-return order in *SP v EB and KP* [2016] 1 FLR 228, FD, because of the exceptional circumstances; in *Re K (Abduction: Psychological Harm)* [1995] 2 FLR 550, CA, it was raised as an aid to establish that, in considering the issue of whether the return of the child should be ordered under Art 12 and the provisions of Art 13(b), the court can and should have regard to the provisions of Art 20 relating to the 'protection of human rights', which includes the respondent being given adequate notice of the hearing and of the case which that parent has to meet and an opportunity to participate in the proceedings. In *Re J (Abduction: Wrongful Removal)* [2000] 1 FLR 78, CA, breach of ECHR 1950, Art 6 was raised where orders had been made without notice, but in *Caras v Romania* (Application No 7198/04) [2007] 1 FLR 661, ECHR and *Sylvester v Austria* (Application Nos 36812/97 and 40114/98) [2003] 2 FLR 210, ECHR, the Court held that, if there is a risk that contact between a child and his parent may be threatened, there is an obligation on the national authority, under ECHR 1950, Art 8, to take immediate and all necessary steps to facilitate an abducted child's return to the jurisdiction of its habitual residence in order to avoid the effect of delay adversely affecting the future relationship between the child and his parent and the determination of that issue by the passage of time (see *RS v Poland* (Application No 63777/09) [2015] 2 FLR 848, ECHR and *KJ v Poland (Application No 30813/14)* [2017] 1 FLR 1006, ECHR, where Art 8 was raised to establish breach of a father's rights to family life).

It may be appropriate for the court to delay the return for a limited period to enable the offending parent to settle his/her affairs before the return: *R v K (Abduction: Return Order)* [2010] 1 FLR 1456, FD. See also *Gill and Aui v Spain* [2005] 1 FLR 190, ECHR. However, where appeal proceedings are withdrawn, it would be wholly inappropriate for the appeal court to interfere with or add provision to the trial judge's order especially in relation to the timescale for the return of the child, save to add undertakings offered by one of the parties: *Re G (A Child)* [2016] EWCA Civ 297. In *Re H (Child Abduction: Mother's Asylum)* [2003] 2 FLR 1105, FD, the principles of the *Protocol of January 2003 (Child Abduction Cases Between the UK and Pakistan)* (see Part V) were considered, as was the mother's asylum status, but the court did not regard itself as inhibited by her status in ordering the return of the child. For the application of ECHR 1950 in non-Convention abduction cases, see *Re J (Child Returned Abroad: Human Rights)* [2004] 2 FLR 85, CA and *Re R (Abduction: Immigration Concerns)* [2005] 1 FLR 33, FD and *Re E* above where there is a conflict between immigration and welfare concerns. The principle that the court of the state of the child's habitual residence is best placed to deal with issues relating to the child is reinforced by Art 7.1 of the 1996 Convention, which confirms that in abduction cases the state of the child's habitual residence before the wrongful removal or retention retains jurisdiction until the child has acquired habitual residence in another state and the person/s having rights of custody has acquiesced in the removal or retention or the child has resided in that other state for a period of at least 1 year after the person with rights of custody has or should have had knowledge of the child's whereabouts, and no request for a return lodged within that period is pending and the child is settled in his or her new environment. Owing to the differences in the provisions relating to when time begins to run, in some cases reliance on this provision may be a better option.

Court's power to stay, dismiss, strike out or permit the withdrawal of proceedings and set aside orders—Art 12 provides that the court may stay the proceedings or dismiss the application for the return of the child where it has reason to believe that the child has been taken to another state. Although in *Re D (Children) (Child Abduction: Practice)* [2016] EWHC 504 (Fam) it was acknowledged that the court has this power, it was confirmed that it is unlikely to be used save in exceptional circumstances. It is inappropriate to apply for an application to be struck out on the ground of significant delay in issuing proceedings or where proceedings have not been conducted expeditiously (*Re W (Children) (Abduction: Striking Out)* [2015] EWHC 4002 (Fam). It is likely to do so where circumstances leading to the proceedings being issued have been overtaken by subsequent events such as changes in family circumstances or, as in *Re D* (above), where developments in the foreign court resulted in proceedings before it being restored and orders made, which make it unnecessary or inappropriate for the Hague Convention proceedings to continue. The circumstances in which the court is likely to adopt an 'ultra-summary' approach in Hague Convention cases are limited and the cases in which it could ever be appropriate to do so are likely to be rare (see *Re D*, at [26]). In *Re D* the father applied for and was granted permission to withdraw the proceedings but the court indicated that if he had not the court would have summarily dismissed the proceedings. The court's permission will be required to withdraw an application under the 1980 Hague Convention (see also *Ciccone v Ritchie (No 2)* [2017] 1 FLR 812, FD). As regards the court's power to set aside its order, see *Re H (A Child)* [2016] EWCA Civ 988.

Court's power to set aside vary, rescind, suspend or revoke a return order—Although setting aside will rarely be granted, it is arguable that in Hague Convention cases the first instance court does have the power to vary its order in very limited and exceptional circumstances: *Re C (Abduction: Setting Aside Return Order: Remission)* [2013] 1 FLR 403, CA. The issue, if raised, should be dealt with expeditiously to avoid the child becoming settled in England with the result that a return order cannot be made (*DL v EL (Hague Abduction Convention: Effect of Reversal of Return Order on Appeal)* [2013] 2 FLR 163, FD) but even in such a situation the Supreme Court on appeal ruled that the court retained a common law power to make the necessary order and that the court's approach should be what is in the best interests of the child: *Re KL (Abduction: Habitual Residence: Inherent Jurisdiction)* [2014] 1 FLR 772, SC. The issue of the court's power to set aside a return order and the procedure to be followed has been raised in three recent cases, two of which were Convention cases: *TF v PJ* [2015] 1 FLR 861, FD; *Re F (Children)* [2016] EWCA Civ 1253; and in a non-Convention case *Re H (A Child)* [2016] EWCA Civ 988. The issue in relation to the appropriate procedure related to whether any such application should be to the judge at first instance or did SCA 1981, s 17 require the application to be by way of appeal. In *Re F*, although it was conceded at first instance that in an appropriate case the High Court had the power to set aside a return order made under the 1980 Hague Convention, the Court was requested to give guidance on this issue in relation to Convention cases. In the absence of comprehensive submissions, the court was reluctant to make a definitive pronouncement on the existence and (if it exists) the nature of the High Court's powers. It was, however, acknowledged that it was 'desirable that there *should* be such a power in the High Court, albeit that it can be anticipated that it would rarely be used'. The Court also pointed out that the Court of Appeal is not well suited to hearings of this type and any application to the Court would have to take its turn in an already very over-loaded list. In *TF v PH*, after reviewing relevant civil and family law cases, Mostyn J concluded that pursuant to FPR 2010, r 4.1(6) the High Court has a power to vary or revoke its order where there has been material non-disclosure or significant change in circumstances. The provision of s 17 were not considered. This decision followed the decision in *Arif v Zar* [2012] EWCA Civ 986 relating to an identical CPR 1998, r 3.1(7), where Patten LJ ruled that there is a long line of authority beginning with the decision in *Lloyds Investment (Scandinavia) Ltd v Ager Handerssen* [2003] EWHC 1740 (Ch) and culminating in the decision in *Tibbles v SIG plc* [2012] EWCA Civ 518, which confirms that the power of the court to vary or revoke one of its own orders is ordinarily limited to cases where there has been a material change of circumstances since the order was made or the original order can be shown to have been based on mis-stated facts or material non-disclosure. In most other cases, the finality of the court's orders has to be respected and the proper way of challenging the order is by way of appeal. Before the rule change in relation to financial orders under MCA 1973, in *Gohil v Gohil* [2015] 2 FLR 1289, SC and *Sharland v Sharland* [2015] 2 FLR 1367, SC, the Supreme Court considered the implication of SCA 1981, s 17: while acknowledging there was a need for definitive confirmation, nevertheless having considered all the case-law including civil cases, Lady Hale in setting out three options that were available – (a) a fresh action, (b) an appeal and (c) application to the judge at first instance – concluded that (a) and (c) were the preferred options and stated that the CA is not the most suitable vehicle for hearing evidence and resolving factual issues involved in such cases (*Sharland*, at [38], [40]; the sentiments now expressed by Black LJ in *Re F* and see the concerns she raised at [28]). In particular, referring to the President's judgment in *CS v ACS (Consent Order: Non-Disclosure: Correct Procedure)* [2016] 1 FLR 131, FD, she concluded that FPR 2010, r 4.1(6) did give the court power to entertain an application to set aside a final order in financial remedy proceedings. In *Re H* (above), a non-Convention case in which the child had been warded, the court varied a previous return order on the basis that proceedings under the inherent jurisdiction were family proceedings in which welfare considerations applied and the court was entitled to act in the ward's best interests. The appropriate procedure to follow seems unresolved. It is arguable that the earlier cases of *Re C*, *DL v EL*, *Re KL* and *CS v ACS* indicate that the court is concerned with the best interests of a child and the High Court exercises its inherent jurisdiction in relation to many of the orders it makes and in determining the issues it has to take account of the best interests of the child, including the risk of a return order causing physical or psychological harm or otherwise placing the child in an intolerable situation. In Convention cases, there is a duty to deal with cases expeditiously. The court's common law duties under its inherent jurisdiction are therefore engaged and continue to apply if the child is present in England and Wales. The Supreme Court in *Re KL* (above) applied this approach. Additionally, insofar as the provisions of SCA 1981, s 17 are concerned, an application seeking a new trial or review of the court's original decision and/or to have it set aside on the ground of material and significant change of circumstances will be based upon new circumstances that have occurred since the order was made and that were not foreseeable when the original order was made, and not upon the facts already rehearsed and tried. Before granting the application, the court will of course still need to consider all options and in particular liaise with the authorities in the home country to ensure the safety and security of the family and that the child's needs are met. It may be prudent in the first instance to suspend the order while enquiries are being made rather than set aside the order. The Pt 18 procedure should be followed when making the application to the judge at first instance.

Brussels IIA—For the application of Brussels IIA in child abduction cases see: *Re J (A Child) (Finland) (Habitual Residence)* [2017] EWCA Civ 80 and *Re K and D (Wardship Without Notice Return Order)* [2017] EWHC 153 (Fam); (for the impact of Brussels IIA, Arts 9 and 10 on the continuing jurisdiction of the child's former habitual residence in certain circumstances), *Povse v Alpago* [2010] 2 FLR 1343, ECJ, and earlier cases of *F v M (Abduction: Grave Risk of Harm)* [2008] 2 FLR 1263, FD; *Vigreux v Michel* [2006] 2 FLR 1180, CA and *Re A (Custody Decision After Maltese Non-Return Order)* [2007] 1 FLR 1923, FD. For the issue of 'rights of custody' of an unmarried father without parental responsibility under Brussels IIA, Art 2(9), see *JMcB v Le* (Case C-400/10) [2011] 1 FLR 518, ECJ. For the inter-relationship between Brussels IIA, the Hague Convention and domestic law see *Re RC and BC (Child Abduction: Brussels II Revised: Article 11(7))* [2009] 1 FLR 574, FD; *Re RD (Child Abduction: Brussels II Revised: Articles 11(7) and 19)* [2009] 1 FLR 586, FD; *Re H (Abduction)* [2009] 2 FLR 1513, FD; and *Re S (Habitual Residence)* [2010] 1 FLR 1146, CA and see *Re F (Abduction: Refusal to Return)* [2009] 2 FLR 1023, CA, which recommends that the procedure under Art 11 of the Regulation should be followed when the court refuses to make a return order instead of pursuing the matter by way of appeal. Where an application under Brussels IIA, Art 11(7) is issued the following procedure is recommended: (a) a directions appointment should be sought for the court to consider whether the case should be determined on a summary basis and/or whether there should be a welfare inquiry and if so, the extent of such an inquiry; (b) Cafcass Legal and its High Court Team should be notified as soon as such an application is made and at the first directions hearing the court should be asked to consider whether or not to join the child as a party and whether Cafcass Legal or its High Court Team should be invited to make representations; (c) if the child is joined and Cafcass is directed to take an active role directions must be given on the nature and extent of their role; (d) at an early stage issues relating to interim contact should be considered; and (e) the court should set a timetable for the final hearing with a timescale that complies with the provisions of Art 11 and the need for urgency (*M v T (Abduction: Brussels IIR Art (7))* [2010] 2 FLR 1685, FD. Where an application is governed by Art 13 of the Hague Convention it should be headed under both CACA 1985 and Brussels IIA. On issue, the outside of the court file should be clearly marked to draw attention to the nature of the application and should state the date on which the 6-week period will expire; this will draw to the court administration's attention the 'hear-by' date which stringent compliance with Brussels IIA would require (FPR PD12F, para 2.14). The following steps should be taken by a parent who has not secured the return of a child under the Hague Convention: (1) where a non-return order is made before the commencement of proceedings in England the application should be commenced by Pt 18 application issued out of the High Court in London (or if issued in a District Registry transferred to London forthwith) and should be headed 'in the Matter of an application pursuant to the Brussels Revised Regulation Article 11(7) for the return of the child from [The Member State in question]'; (2) where English proceedings have already been issued, a Hague Convention non-return order is made and the home parent wishes to pursue an application for a return of a child, an application should be made in the existing proceedings; the terms of the application should be for 'Directions in light of the Order made in the [Member State] on [date] declining in reliance of Art 13 of the Hague Convention on Child Abduction to order the return of the child[ren] to England and Wales' and the proceedings should be transferred to the Family Division in London, if not already proceeding there (*Re A, HA v MB (Brussels II Revised: Article 11(7) Application)* [2008] 1 FLR 289, FD). The case also raises other issues, which should be considered by practitioners, where a non-return order is made. Attention is also drawn to the provisions set out in FPR 2010, rr 12.58–12.71 and the commentary provided, which deals with procedural issues when a non-return order is made and to the Council Regulations set out in Part VI of this work. See also *Re F (Abduction: Child Wishes)* [2007] 2 FLR 697, CA for the procedure to be followed in other cases where Brussels IIA applies.

The following guidance on the operation of Brussels IIA, Art 11(7) and the effect of a non-return order by a Member State was given in *D v N and D (by her Guardian ad Litem)* [2011] 2 FLR 464, FD: (a) proceedings under Art 11(7) should be determined as soon as possible; (b) in determining a return order, the court is exercising a welfare jurisdiction and it has the whole range of orders that would normally be available to a judge if the child had not been abducted; but (c) the issue of an Art 42(2) certificate should be considered only where the conditions set out in Art 42(2) are satisfied. In *AF v T and Another (Brussels II Revised: Art 11(7) Application)* [2011] 2 FLR 891, FD, following a non-return order, notwithstanding the lapse of time since that order was made, the court dealt with the father's application and made orders for residence and contact on the ground that the maintenance of the child's relationship with the parent left behind formed an intrinsic purpose of both the Hague Convention and Brussels IIA (see further under Art 13). For the operation of Brussels IIA, Art 20, see *Detiček v Sgueglia* (Case C–403/09) [2010] 1 FLR 1381, ECJ.

Duty to return in non-Convention cases—The principles that apply to non-Convention countries are set out in *Re J (Child Returned Abroad: Convention Rights)* [2005] 2 FLR 802, HL. In all such cases, the court must act in accordance with the welfare of the child. Within those principles, the court has jurisdiction to order the return of the child without a full investigation of the merits (*Re J* applied in *Re U (Abduction: Nigeria)* [2011] 1 FLR 354, FD and see FPR PD12F, para 3.1). Relevant factors are the child's connection with the country, including nationality, residence, language, race, ethnicity; religion, culture and education. The effect of such an order on the primary carer, although not decisive, is relevant, as is the sincerity of the refusal to return the child and its effect on the child (see *AR v AS (Abduction: Non-Convention Country)* [2016] 2 FLR 1280, FD, where an order for return of the child to Saudi Arabia was refused, the court being satisfied that under Sharia law the mother would not be able to remove the child from the jurisdiction of Saudi Arabia if she was unmarried and it was therefore not in the best interest of the child to make a return order). In *Re H (A Child)* [2016] EWCA Civ 988, a decision in wardship proceedings to set aside a return order, the CA considered the following issues: (i) the duty of the court presented with a consent order should consider whether the order is in the child's best interests; (ii) whether the child should be separately represented; (iii) the court's powers to set aside its order; (iv) the effect on the court's power of a 'return order' where the child has been granted asylum by the country of return; (v) whether the grant of asylum can be set aside where it was granted based on untested and disputed allegations against the other party and if so by whom. The relevance and extent of the difference between the legal system in England and the foreign country will depend upon the particular facts of each case and not on any concept of child welfare which exactly corresponds to that in England and Wales. These principles were applied and summarised in *Re S (Wardship: Summary Return: Non-Convention Country)* [2015] EWHC 176 (Fam), where a summary return order was made, but see *Re H (Abduction: Non-Convention Application)* [2006] 2 FLR 314, FD where the child was not returned by reason of the local court's unwillingness to apply international standards. The provision of Art 20 of the Hague Convention, which provides that the return of a child under Art 12 may be refused if this would not be permitted by reason of human rights principles in the requesting state, is also relevant. However, the decision in *Re H (Abduction: Dominica:*

Corporal Punishment) [2007] 1 FLR 72, CA seems to suggest that in non-Hague Convention cases a full investigation on the merits and a welfare inquiry should be undertaken unless the children's return could be safeguarded by appropriate undertakings and a full inquiry in the country of the children's habitual residence. Although welfare of the child should be the paramount consideration, in *Re S* (above) it was held that this issue should be determined not on the basis that the English system is to be preferred but what is in the best interests of the child. Where it is evident that the father's wishes have primacy, the court would have to determine whether it would be in the best interests of the child for the issues to be determined in the country of the child's habitual residence.

Duty to order the return of the child after the expiration of 12 months—While the expiration of this period is often used as a defence, the court has a discretion to return the child notwithstanding that settlement has been established. In exercising its discretion, the court should have regard to the overriding objectives of the Convention and the welfare of the child and its rights. However, there is no principle which requires that the Convention policies should always outweigh other considerations save in exceptional cases. It would be 'wrong to import any test of exceptionality into the exercise of discretion under the Hague Convention. The circumstances in which return may be refused are themselves exceptions to the general rule. That in itself is sufficient exceptionality. It is neither necessary nor desirable to import an additional gloss into the Convention' (*Re M (Abduction: Zimbabwe)* [2008] 1 FLR 251, HL). In settlement cases, the major objective of the Convention (swift return) cannot be achieved and therefore it can no longer be assumed that the country of origin is the best forum for the resolution of the dispute. Other considerations, such as the child's objections and its integration into the community, are relevant factors to be taken into account. The policy of the Convention has to be weighed together with the circumstances which produced the exception and such pointers as there are towards the welfare of the particular child (applied in *F v M and N (Abduction: Acquiescence: Settlement)* [2008] 2 FLR 1270, FD, *Re S (Abduction: Children's Representation)* [2008] 2 FLR 1918, FD and *Re H and L (Abduction: Acquiescence)* [2010] 2 FLR 1277, FD. The approach to be adopted in non-Convention cases remains as set out by the House of Lords in *Re J (A Child) (Custody Rights: Jurisdiction)* [2005] 2 FLR 802, HL. For interpretation of 'settlement' and return orders, see *M v M* [2008] 2 FLR 1884, FD and *Cannon v Cannon* [2005] 1 FLR 169, CA. Delay is a relevant factor when weighing up the child's objections against the whole policy of the Convention (*Re C (Abduction: Residence and Contact)* [2006] 2 FLR 277, FD; *Re S (Child Abduction: Delay)* [1998] 1 FLR 651, FD). The reason for the delay in bringing the proceedings and the parties' conduct (*SP v EB and KP* [2016] 1 FLR 228, FD), particularly that of the abducting parent in concealing the child's whereabouts are relevant factors in determining the issue of settlement and the exercise of the discretion (*Re C (Abduction: Settlement)* [2005] 1 FLR 127, FD and *Re C (Child Abduction: Settlement)* [2006] 2 FLR 797, FD – for an exceptional and extreme case of concealment). See *D v S (Abduction: Acquiescence)* [2008] 2 FLR 293, FD where delay was considered but where on balance the court ruled that a return was justified on welfare grounds and the fact that the issues between the parties were likely to be easier to manage in Mexico (see also under **Court's power to stay etc**, above).

Separate representation for the child—Brussels IIA, Art 11 provides that when applying Hague Convention, Arts 12 and 13, the court should ensure that the child is given the opportunity to be heard during the proceedings unless this appears to be inappropriate having regard to the child's age or maturity. The need to hear the child is reinforced by the provision in the 1996 Convention, Art 23.2, under which the failure of the child being given the opportunity to be heard is one of the grounds for refusing to recognise measures taken in a Contracting State. Account must also be taken of the child's right enshrined in Art 12 of the UN Convention on the Rights of the Child to express his/her views freely in all matters affecting the child and for those views to be given weight in accordance with the age and maturity of the child. This issue was discussed by the President in *Re F (Children)* [2016] EWCA Civ 546, who referred to the 'sea change' that had occurred in the approach to the issue and the fact that the judges and practitioners had been too slow in keeping up with the changes. Where there are unusual circumstances, the court should of its own initiative consider whether the child should be separately represented, especially where the facts suggest that the factors set out in FPR PD16A are met (*Re H (A Child)* [2016] EWCA Civ 988). (See also *Re E (A Child)* [2016] EWCA Civ 473.) For this purpose, the child should be provided with the opportunity to be heard in 'any judicial or administrative proceedings affecting the child, either directly, or through a representative or an appropriate body, in a manner consistent with the procedural rules of national law'. In *Re M (Abduction: Zimbabwe)* [2008] 1 FLR 251, HL, Lady Hale stated that where settlement is argued there are powerful arguments to suggest that separate representation should be ordered for the children. Similar sentiments are expressed in *Re LC (Reunite: International Child Abduction Centre Intervening)* [2014] 1 FLR 1486, SC, where the Supreme Court also pointed out that the court determining the issue has a wide discretion to determine the extent of the role that the child should play in the proceedings. More recently, in *Re B (A child by her Guardian)* [2017] EWHC 488 (Fam), Russell J expressed the view that in future, where there is a dispute as to habitual residence, early consideration should be given to join the children in the proceedings so that the court maintains a fluid picture of the children's circumstances, wishes and feelings to avoid the focus being on the dispute between the parents and/or care-givers and their rights. The child's participation may be confined to (i) the submission of a witness statement by her or of a report by her guardian that is focused on the child's account including her state of mind and/or (ii) her advocate's cross-examination and the advancement of submissions on her behalf. See also guidance given in *SP v EB and KP* [2016] 1 FLR 228, FD, at [53]. The starting point thus may be to consider whether it would be in the best interests of the child to be made a party (FPR 2010, r 16.2 and the guidance set out in PD16A, paras 7.2 and 7.3. See also the observation of Thorpe LJ in *Re G (Abduction: Children's Objections)* [2011] 1 FLR 1645, CA. In *WF v FJ, BF and RF (Abduction: Child's Objections)* [2011] 1 FLR 1153, FD, Baker J said: (i) that 'in view of the recent developments in the law, it is now even more important that the voice of the child is heard in proceedings under the Hague Convention' and that without laying down any rigid rules, it is clearly preferable where time and resources permitted for the child to be seen by the Cafcass High Court Team before the decision is taken to give the child party status; and (ii) that FPR 1991, r 9.2A, which had made provisions for a child to conduct proceedings without a litigation friend in proceedings under CA 1989 and FLA 1996, Pt 4A, does not apply to proceedings under the Hague Convention and that in 'the light of the great emphasis now being given to children's objections under Art 13' it is hoped that the FPR Committee would find time to review this lacuna (which in that case was overcome by the appointment of a child's solicitor to act as litigation friend with the agreement of all parties). In *Re M (Abduction: Child's Objections: Appeal)* [2016] 1 FLR 296, CA, Black LJ emphasised the need for consideration to be given at the earliest possible stage in Hague Convention proceedings to the participation of the children who are the subject of the application and any older child who is no longer within the scope of the Convention in the proceedings. (On this issue and the evidence required, see *Re S (Child Abduction: Joinder of Sibling: Child Objections)* [2016] EWHC 1227 (Fam).) She pointed out the general power that the court has under FPR 2010, r 12.3(3) to make any person a party at the first instance stage and referred to r 16.2, which empowers the court to make a child a party if it considers it in his or her best interests. In relation to a child becoming a party to any appeal, Black LJ referred to the provisions set out in CPR 1998, rr 19.1 and 19.2. See the principles applied in *Ciccone v Ritchie (No 1)* [2017] 1 FLR 795, FD, where the child expressed his wish to participate in the decision-making process as opposed to passively through a medium of a Cafcass report and MacDonald J joined the child as a party to the proceedings and, although it is a decision within public law proceedings, see also *Re W (A Child: Separate representation)* [2016] EWCA Civ 1051. There is thus a presumption that the child will be heard during Hague Convention proceedings unless this appears inappropriate (*Re D (Abduction: Rights of Custody)* [2007] 1 FLR 961, HL. Sir James Munby P has referred to participation of a child in all proceedings and to rule change in a lecture at Swansea University on 25 June 2015 ([2015] Fam Law 895). To this end, draft rules (*https://consult.justice.gov.uk/digital-communications/draft-amendments-to-family-procedure-rules*) have been published for consultation, the period for which expired on 25 September 2015. The draft rules give a flavour of how the issue of a child's participation in proceedings should be explored. (See also commentary under FPR 2010, r 31.6.)

In summary, therefore, currently a child's views and the strength of his or her objections will be adequately represented by one of the parties assisted by the appointment of a Cafcass officer to report on the child's degree of maturity and wishes; secondly, by a face-to-face meeting with the judge; and thirdly by the child being afforded full party status with legal representation. Where a judge meets the child, the purpose of the meeting is for the judge to hear what the child may wish to say and for the child to hear the judge explain the nature of the process and, in particular, why despite hearing what the child may say, the courts order may direct a different outcome (see *Re KP (Abduction: Child's Objections)* [2014] 2 FLR 660, CA).

Practice Note of April 2010: *Guidelines for Judges Meeting Children who are Subject to Family Proceedings* and the Family Justice Council's Guidelines of December 2011 in relation to children giving evidence in family proceedings gives guidance on how the meeting should be conducted. Both guidelines are currently under review. It is expected that the revised Guidelines will be published alongside the new rules and practice directions to supplement the rules. Until new guidelines are issued, it should be noted that the current guidance clearly states that a meeting with the child is not to be used for evidence-gathering but for the child to be heard, understood and to be reassured. In any meeting between a young person and a judge, the judge's role should be that of a passive recipient of whatever communication the young person wishes to transmit. The purpose is not to obtain evidence and the judge should not probe or seek to test whatever it is that the child wishes to say. The meeting is primarily for the benefit of the child rather than for the benefit of the forensic process by providing additional evidence to the judge. If the meeting takes place prior to the judge deciding the central issues, it should be for the dual purpose of allowing the judge to hear what the young person may wish to volunteer and for the young person to hear the judge explain the nature of the court process. Although such a meeting will proceed at the pace of the child, without being prescriptive in most cases it should not last for more than 20 minutes or so. If the child volunteers evidence that would or might be relevant to the outcome of the proceedings, the judge should report back to the parties and determine whether, and if so how, the evidence should be adduced: *Re KP (A Child)* (above) at [56] and in which the principle authorities on judges meeting children are analysed (see also the commentary to FPR 2010, r 12.21).

In most cases, it will not be necessary to join the child as a party to the proceedings but the court should consider the issue of the child's participation at the earliest opportunity and preferably when the first directions are given: *Re S (Abduction: Hearing the Child)* [2015] 2 FLR 588, CA, where Ryder J (as he then was) said that it could not 'seriously be argued that where a child is of an age and understanding to be heard that the child's voice is itself irrelevant to welfare or that it can be assumed that the child's parents will be an effective vehicle to articulate the child's voice or to provide effective access to justice for the child', at [27]. See also *M and M v Croatia (Application No 10161/13)* [2016] 2 FLR 18, ECHR where the failure of the state to make provision to give the child an opportunity to express her view to the court in protracted custody proceedings was held to be a breach of fundamental rights. In *Cambra v Jones (Contempt Proceedings: Child Joined as Party)* [2015] 1 FLR 263, FD, party status was given to a 14-year-old child where reliance was also placed on Arts 31 and 12 of the UN Convention on the Rights of the Child 1989 to justify the child's application for party status. Where the child is removed or retained in Wales, the matter should be referred to the Cafcass High Court Team and not CAFCASS Cymru, as Hague Convention cases do not come within CA 1989, s 35. The Practice Note *Cafcass and the National Assembly for Wales Practice Note 2006* (para 9) is incorrect (*Cambra v Jones* [2014] 1 FLR 5, FD).

If the child is made a party, the appointment of a guardian and/or representation for the child and attendance of the child should be dealt with (*D v N and D (by her Guardian ad Litem)* [2011] 2 FLR 464, FD). If the child is not made a party, the court should consider the manner in which the child's wishes and feelings are to be ascertained (FPR 2010, r 12.48).

Although the exceptional circumstances gloss has been removed, the circumstances where party status is given to a child are likely to be where: there has been state intervention in the affairs of the family; the facts disclose that it would be inappropriate for Cafcass to be invited to report (*Re D (Abduction: Rights of Custody)* [2007] 1 FLR 961, HL; *Re F (Abduction: Joinder of Child as Party)* [2007] 2 FLR 313, CA; and *Re H (Abduction)*

[2007] 1 FLR 242, CA). There must also be an arguable case that the discretion under Art 13 should be exercised (*Re S (Abduction: Children: Separate Representation)* [1997] 1 FLR 486, FD).

Where settlement is argued under Art 12 the separate point of view of the children is particularly important and should not be lost in the competing claims of the adults (see *Re M (Abduction: Zimbabwe)* [2008] 1 FLR 251, HL). If this were routine in such cases there would be no additional delay. In *Re C (Abduction: Separate Representation of Children)* [2008] 2 FLR 6, FD the five children's application to be separately represented was allowed because of their ages, understanding and experiences and because it was felt that it was more likely to cause them harm if they were not allowed to voice their views. The court was also dealing with the issue of returning the oldest child, who was over 16 and not subject to the Convention, under its inherent jurisdiction, where different welfare issues apply to those under the Convention. This case also confirms that in non-Convention cases the test of best interests should be applied on the issue of whether a child should be made a party to proceedings.

Enforcement of order to return—Article 12 places a duty on the court to order the return of the child forthwith. In exercising that duty, the court has jurisdiction to enforce the order for return by issuing a writ of sequestration against the property of a third party, provided it is satisfied so that it is sure that the third party knew of the order requiring the return of the child and that he nevertheless deliberately frustrated the order or aided and abetted the abducting parent in avoiding compliance with the order (*Re S (Abduction: Sequestration)* [1995] 1 FLR 858, FD). Committal and successive orders may be appropriate where there has been repeated failure to comply with court orders (*Button v Salama* [2014] 2 FLR 471, FD). For other means adopted by the court, see *Cambra v Jones* [2014] 1 FLR 5, FD, *Re C (Abduction: Setting Aside Return Order: Remission)* [2013] 1 FLR 403, CA and *Re KL (A Child)* [2014] 1 FLR 772, SC.

Article 13

Notwithstanding the provisions of the preceding Article, the judicial or administrative authority of the requested State is not bound to order the return of the child if the person, institution or other body which opposes its return establishes that –

(a) the person, institution or other body having the care of the person of the child was not actually exercising the custody rights at the time of removal or retention, or had consented to or subsequently acquiesced in the removal or retention; or

(b) there is a grave risk that his or her return would expose the child to physical or psychological harm or otherwise place the child in an intolerable situation.

The judicial or administrative authority may also refuse to order the return of the child if it finds that the child objects to being returned and has attained an age and degree of maturity at which it is appropriate to take account of its views.

In considering the circumstances referred to in this Article, the judicial and administrative authorities shall take into account the information relating to the social background of the child provided by the Central Authority or other competent authority of the child's habitual residence.

Consent or acquiescence—The leading case on the meaning of consent or acquiescence is *Re H (Abduction: Acquiescence)* [1997] 1 FLR 872, HL, in which the House of Lords laid down the following principles to be adopted when considering the meaning of 'acquiescence' within Art 13 of the Convention:

(a) The English law concept of acquiescence, which was normally viewed objectively, had no direct application to the proper construction of Art 13. Under the Convention, it must have the same meaning and effect throughout the laws of all the Contracting States. Acquiescence in Art 13 means looking to the subjective state of mind of the wronged parent and asking has he in fact consented to the continued presence of the children in the jurisdiction to which they have been abducted. It is a question of the actual subjective intention of the wronged parent, not the outside world's perception of his intention.

(b) Acquiescence is a pure question of fact to be determined by the trial judge on the material before him. In the process of the fact-finding operation to ascertain the subjective intention, the court is more likely to attach weight to the contemporaneous express words and actions of the wronged party than to his subsequent bare assertions in evidence of his intention.

(c) The burden of proving that the wronged party has consented to, or acquiesced in, the abduction is on the abducting parent (See *Re P (Abduction: Consent)* [2004] 2 FLR 1057, CA).

(d) Judges should be slow to infer an intention to acquiesce from attempts by the wronged parent to effect a reconciliation, or agree a voluntary return of the abducted child.

(e) There is only one exception to this general principle. Where the words or actions of the wronged parent clearly and unequivocally lead the other parent to believe that the wronged parent is not asserting or going to assert his right to the summary return of the child and are inconsistent with such return, justice requires that the wronged parent be held to have acquiesced (for a recent example see *D v S* [2008] 2 FLR 293, FD).

For cases on the application of this guidance and the issue of 'subjective' and 'non-subjective' acquiescence see *Re H, R and E (Abduction: Consent: Acquiescence)* [2014] 2 FLR 385, FD; *F v Y (Abduction: Acquiescence)* [2014] 2 FLR 875, FD; *Re G (Abduction: Withdrawal of Proceedings, Acquiescence and Habitual Residence)* [2008] 2 FLR 351, FD; *B-G v B-G* [2008] 2 FLR 965, FD; *Re E (Abduction: Intolerable*

Situation) [2009] 2 FLR 485, FD; and *Re H and L (Abduction: Acquiescence)* [2010] 2 FLR 1277, FD. For consent to removal in surrogacy cases, see *Re D (A Child: Habitual Residence: Consent and Acquiescence)* [2016] 1 FLR 937, FD.

The evidence to establish consent must be clear, compelling and unequivocal (*D v S (Abduction: Acquiescence)* [2008] 2 FLR 293, FD; *Re R (Child Abduction: Acquiescence)* [1995] 1 FLR 716, CA). Evidence of consent may be in writing or in documentary form. It can be deduced from the words and conduct of the wronged parent; (*Re M (Abduction) (Consent: Acquiescence)* [1999] 1 FLR 171, FD). It cannot be passive, but must be positive consent to the removal of the child (*Re D, above*). A third party cannot give consent on behalf of the parent even if under the law of the foreign state such consent is permissible (*C v H (Abduction: Consent)* [2010] 1 FLR 225, FD). In *Re P-J (Abduction: Habitual Residence)* [2009] 2 FLR 1051, CA and *K v K (Abduction) (No 1)* [2010] 1 FLR 1295, FD the suggestion that 'consent' could be given after removal was rejected. An effective consent to removal can be given in advance provided it subsisted at the time of removal (*Re L (Abduction: Future Consent)* [2008] 1 FLR 914, FD). A refusal by a custodial parent to assist the non-custodial parent in returning the child is unlikely to amount to acquiescence (*De L v H* [2010] 1 FLR 1229, FD). The means of proof will vary according to the circumstances of the case, and may include the court receiving oral evidence from the parties (*Re C (Abduction: Consent)* [1996] 1 FLR 414, FD).

PART II

Whether a purported consent to the child's removal is a valid consent will depend on the circumstances of the case (*R v R (Jurisdiction and Acquiescence)* [2016] EWHC 1339 (Fam), where MacDonald J also gave guidance to courts dealing with private law cases involving an international element; *Re S (A Child: Abduction)* [2003] 1 FLR 1008, CA). Consent to the removal of a child may be valid even if it is dependent on a future event provided it is not too vague, uncertain or subjective and the facts at the time are not wholly or manifestly different to those prevailing at the time of removal (*Re L (Abduction: Future Consent)* [2008] 1 FLR 914, FD) and may be conditional (*BT v JRT (Abduction: Conditional Acquiescence and Consent)* [2008] 2 FLR 972, FD). Consent to a removal in the future may be withdrawn but circumstances may result in it being too late to withdraw (eg where the parent who was given permission had begun to depart: *VK v JV (Abduction: Consent)* [2013] 2 FLR 237, FD). A consent obtained by fraud or deception is unlikely to be regarded as valid (see *Re F (Abduction: Consent)* [2014] EWHC 484 (Fam); *M v T (Abduction)* [2009] 1 FLR 1309, FD; *Re B (Abduction: Art 13 Defence)* [1997] 2 FLR 573, FD; *Re B (A Minor) (Abduction)* [1994] 2 FLR 249, CA; and *BT v JRT* (above)). The court should be slow to infer an intention to acquiesce where the father was doing his best to keep on good terms with the mother for the sake of his contact with his child (*Re F*, above) or from attempts by the wronged parent to effect a reconciliation or to reach an agreed voluntary return of the child (Arts 7(c), 10; and *Re G (Abduction: Withdrawal of Proceedings, Acquiescence, Habitual Residence)* [2008] 2 FLR 351, FD). A similar approach applies to discussions between the parents after separation with a view to possible reconciliation (*M v M* [2007] 2 FLR 1010, FD). The defence of acquiescence is fact-specific. The factors that the court has consistently taken into account are those set out in *Re H* (above). Following *Re S (Abduction: Acquiescence)* [1998] 2 FLR 115, CA, it was considered that reliance by the wronged parent on incorrect advice could not be regarded as acquiescence to a child's removal, but acting on 'adequate and realistic advice' could. However, this issue has become confused as *D v S* (above) appears to suggest that it is not necessary to have received correct advice nor does the advice need to be 'adequate or realistic'. It is difficult to understand how 'incorrect' advice can be adequate. In *B-G v B-G* (above), Coleridge J appears to have taken the view that full legal advice or knowledge is not necessary to conclude that the wronged parent has acquiesced. The only common factor which emerges from these cases is the fact that once a person becomes aware of the Convention and the process for the return of the child but fails to act expeditiously, he may be considered to have acquiesced.

Once acquiescence has been established, it is not necessary for the court to consider grave harm. The court can go on to consider what is in the child's best interest and how it should exercise its discretion on whether the child's return should be ordered (see *Re A (Minors) (Abduction: Acquiescence) (No 2)* [1993] 1 FLR 396, CA) but in *D v S* (above) the court entered into a full inquiry on the evidence and made findings and expressed its views on the issue of welfare.

'grave risk'—For the meaning of 'grave risk', see *Re A (A Minor) (Abduction)* [1988] 1 FLR 365, CA: there must be a weighty risk of substantial harm (*C v B (Abduction: Grave Risk)* [2006] 1 FLR 1095, FD). The Art 13(b) defence 'is likely to apply in the most extreme cases, where evidence of the exposure to physical or psychological harm or otherwise place the child in an intolerable situation' (*Re D (A Minor) (Child Abduction) Note* [1989] 1 FLR 97, FD). Domestic violence will not be considered as sufficient: *Re W (Abduction: Domestic Violence)* [2005] 1 FLR 727, CA. Where an exceptional degree of violence on the mother is established, the effect of this on the child and his/her needs and welfare and the need to be reunited with his/her parent will be one of the factors to be taken into account to determine whether the threshold of harm is crossed (*DT v LBT* [2011] 1 FLR 1215, FD and confirmed in *Re E (Children) (Abduction: Custody Appeal)* [2011] 2 FLR 758, SC, in which the issue of one parent gaining an unfair advantage over another through passage of time and the child's need to be brought up in a secure environment were considered as relevant factors to strike a balance between the interests of the child and those of the parents and thus avoid any issues concerning a breach of Art 8). *Re E* (above) has also confirmed that the provision of Art 13(b) needed no gloss or elaboration and that the decision in *Neulinger and Shuruk v Switzerland* [2011] 1 FLR 122, ECHR has not changed the principle of a summary process provided that the decision was not arbitrary or mechanical. The Court of Appeal and Supreme Court judgments in *Re E (Children)* [2011] 2 FLR 724, CA, [2011] 2 FLR 758, SC should be read in full because they assess fully the effect of the decision in *Neulinger* and a number of other cases.

Where allegations and counter-allegations are made, the court is required to consider what protective measures could be put in place in the Requesting State for the protection of the children (see *Re Y (Abduction: Undertakings Given for Return of Child)* [2013] 2 FLR 649, CA. Undertakings are considered to come within 'protective measures' under Brussels IIA and the 1996 Convention). Undertakings offered may be incorporated within a court order where appropriate to render them 'doubly enforceable': *RB v DB* [2015] EWHC 1817 (Fam)). Permission to instruct an expert to support the defence of psychological harm and to determine that a return order would adversely affect the mental health of the mother will not be justified unless it meets the threshold set out in FPR 2010, r 25.1, i e that expert evidence should be restricted to that which in the opinion of the court is necessary to assist the court to resolve the proceedings: *Re F (Abduction: Art 13(b): Psychiatric Assessment)* [2014] 2 FLR 1115, CA. In *KS v MK* [2015] EWHC 3276 (Fam), psychological risk to the mother of a return order was established by expert evidence but the father applied for and was granted a care arrangement order for regular contact. See also *F v M (Abduction: Grave Risk of Harm)* [2008] 2 FLR 1263, FD, *R v K (Abduction: Return Order)* [2010] 1 FLR 1456, FD and the article of Professor Bates 'The Child Abduction Convention: Troubles in Australia' [2007] *International Family Law* 24. It may be helpful to utilise the arrangements for international co-operation between the liaison judges (*www.judiciary.gov.uk/about-the-judiciary/international/international-family-justice*; tel: 020 7947 7197; email: ifjoffice@hmcts.gsi.gov.uk). The court will require clear, compelling and substantial evidence of the grave risk or other intolerable situation, that is 'a situation which this particular child in these particular circumstances should not be expected to tolerate', but contrast with *Re S (A Child) (Abduction: Rights of Custody)* [2012] 2 FLR 442, SC where the Supreme Court, while confirming its earlier decision, nevertheless concluded that if it is established that the mother would suffer such anxiety as to affect her mental health such that it would create an intolerable situation for the child, a return should not be ordered irrespective of whether on an objective basis her anxieties were reasonable or not. Subjective perceptions could found the defence under Art 13 and if there was a grave risk to the child, the source of the mother's anxieties are irrelevant. Although the court reaffirmed its decision in *Re E* (above), the non-return order in this case may have been fact-specific. Such risks were confirmed in *Re E* and *RS v KS (Abduction: Wrongful Retention)* above. See also *X v Y and Z Police Force, A, B and C (By Their Children's Guardian)* [2013] 1 FLR 1277, FD (where a return order was refused as it would place the children at grave risk of harm due to the father's previous employment as an undercover police officer), *Klentzeris v Klentzeris* [2007] 2 FLR 996, CA (where despite the provision of Brussels IIA, Art 11(4) the court did not consider it appropriate to return the children because of the strength of the evidence of the Cafcass officer) and *SP v EB and KP* [2016] 1 FLR 228, FD (where the exceptional welfare and human rights considerations were said to outweigh Convention considerations). As to risk of harm posed by reason of terrorist attacks, the issue is whether there is a risk of specific harm to the particular child and not whether there was a general risk of harm (*Re S (Abduction: Custody Rights)* [2002] 2 FLR 815, CA; cf *Re D (Article 13(B): Non-Return)* [2006] 2 FLR 305, CA where the risk was specific and targeted and involved extreme violence and danger). It will rarely be appropriate to hear oral evidence (*Re E*, above). Such exceptional circumstances may include the risk in the jurisdiction of the habitual residence of persecution, discrimination or some other overt harm, being subjected to criminal process or otherwise denied justice, or real fear for the safety of the mother and children: *Re D (Article 13(B): Non-Return)* [2006] 2 FLR 305, CA. Exceptional circumstances may be established by expert evidence on the law and practice in the state of habitual residence, provided it does not lead to undue delay (*B v El-B (Abduction: Sharia Law: Welfare of Child)* [2003] 1 FLR 811, FD). Where it is alleged that the applicant has breached conditions attached to an order made by a court in the requesting state, the proper course should be to return the children for that court to consider the issues raised on a renewed application: *C v B (Abduction: Grave Risk)* [2006] 1 FLR 1095, FD. The evidence will be considered objectively. The approach taken will be that adopted when considering the hostility of a mother to contact (*Re M (Abduction: Intolerable Situation)* [2000] 1 FLR 930, FD). See also *Re J (A Minor) (Abduction: Ward of Court)* [1990] 1 FLR 276, FD; *Re N (Minors) (Abduction)* [1991] 1 FLR 413, FD; *Re L (Child Abduction: Psychological Harm)* [1993] 2 FLR 401, FD. In *Re M (Abduction: Acquiescence)* [1996] 1 FLR 315, FD, the court found that a fuller investigation of the issue of risk, and the consequent need for protection, needed to be established. In *C v D (Abduction: Grave Risk of Harm)* [2014] 2 FLR 724, FD, the mother's claim that she would be prosecuted if returned failed because there was no reason to suggest that the approach in *Re L (Abduction: Pending Criminal Proceeding)* [1999] 1 FLR 433, FD would not be applied and that the prosecutors would not take account of the interests of the child. Additionally, undertakings or other protective measures can be made, which would subsist until orders were obtained from the requesting state.

The burden of proof on the defendant to establish that the exception should apply is a very heavy one (*Re E (A Minor) (Abduction)* [1989] 1 FLR 135, CA). The court will require clear and compelling evidence (see *Re M (Child Abduction: Existence of Undertakings)* [2000] 3 FCR 693, FD and the cases cited therein). The court should not make findings on the basis of contested and untested allegations (*Re H (Abduction: Grave Risk)* [2003] 2 FLR 141, CA). For the degree of intolerability that must be established, see *B v B (Abduction: Custody Rights)* [1993] 1 FLR 238, CA; see also *C v C (Abduction: Jurisdiction)* [1994] 1 FCR 6, FD, where a delay of 12 months for the proceedings to be heard in the foreign jurisdiction was held to fall within Art 13(b). Problems that arise from the fact of abduction and that are self-induced will not generally suffice (*M v T (Abduction)* [2009] 1 FLR 1309, FD). Evidence of a grave risk to the children of psychological harm if they are returned is likely to be more significant than the importance of the court marking its disapproval of the abducting parent's behaviour because the child's welfare will be the primary concern in Hague Convention proceedings (*Re S (A Child) (Abduction: Rights of Custody)* [2012] 2 FLR 442, SC).

The defence of grave risk of exposing the child to physical or psychological harm must be weighed both in the light of the immediate past and in comparative terms. As to the latter, the court is entitled to weigh the risk of psychological harm of return against the psychological consequences of refusing to order the return of the child (see *SP v EB and KP*, above). Where both risks are substantial, the court must, in exercising its discretion, give due weight to the primary purpose of the Convention, i e to ensure the swift return of abducted children (*N v N (Abduction: Article 13 Defence)* [1995] 1 FLR 107, FD). See *DT v LBT* [2011] 1 FLR 1215, FD, where the impact on one of the children who suffered from an autistic-spectrum disorder and the lack of any protective measures from the father's abusive behaviour led the court to conclude that the children would be at risk of psychological harm if returned (see also *B v B (Abduction: Child with Learning Difficulties)* [2012] 1 FLR 881, FD, where the child suffered from Asperger's syndrome).

The child's objections—When this defence is raised, distinction needs to be made between a child's wishes and feelings and the 'child's objection' expressed with conviction, rationality and with his own perspective rather than merely expressing preference or the views of others (*Re K (Abduction: Case Management)* [2011] 1 FLR 1268, CA considered and applied in *B v B (Abduction: Child with Learning Difficulties)* [2012] 1 FLR 881, FD). The term 'objects' does not mean a wholesale objection to returning to the country of habitual residence. The approach to be applied was set out by Black LJ in *Re M (Republic of Ireland) (Child's Objections) (Joinder of Children as Parties to Appeal)* [2015] 2 FLR 1074, CA – she discouraged 'an over-prescriptive or over-intellectualised approach to what, if it is to work with proper dispatch, has got to be a straightforward and robust process' (at [77]) and in *Re F (Child's Objections)* [2015] EWCA Civ 1022. The judge must ask him or herself simply, "Does the child object to being returned to his or her country of habitual residence?"', at [33].

The traditional approach has been to carry out three discrete inquiries: (i) whether the objections are made out; (ii) whether the child is of sufficient age and maturity for the court to take account of its objections and whether in the circumstances it is appropriate to take account of his views (referred to as the 'gateway stage'); and (iii) whether the court should exercise its discretion ('the discretionary stage'). See *Re M (Republic of Ireland) (Child's Objections) (Joinder of Children as Parties to Appeal)* [2015] 2 FLR 1074, CA; *Re M (Abduction: Child's Objections)* [2007] 2 FLR 72, CA. Black LJ in *Re M (Republic of Ireland)* disapproved of the 'highly technical structured approach' adopted in *Re T (Abduction: Child's Objection to Return)* [2000] 2 FLR 192, CA, which required the court to explore in detail the circumstances in which a child objects and the nature of the objections. She said that in determining the 'gateway state of establishing the child's objections the preference was for the "straightforward and robust" approach' and that the line taken in *Re T* should be abandoned. In relation to the discretion stage, she said that there must not be 'over-engineering of the basis for the exercise of that discretion' (see *Re S (Habitual Residence and Child's Objections: Brazil)* [2015] 2 FLR 1338, CA) and that there is to be no gloss on the terms of the Convention. In the majority of cases, the decision not to return the child is very much a fact-specific issue.

PART II

For further guidance and the relevance of the impact of splitting siblings, see *WF v FJ* [2011] 1 FLR 1153, FD. See *M v T (Abduction)* above in which the children's views were influenced by the mother; and *Re E (Abduction: Intolerable Situation)* [2009] 2 FLR 485, FD, where the child's objections were weighed against other relevant specific facts in the case when refusing a summary return; *Re M (Abduction: Child's Objections)* [2007] 2 FLR 72, CA and *Re C (Abduction: Separate Representation of Children)* [2008] 2 FLR 6, FD. Where Brussels IIA, Art 11(2) applies the procedure to be followed has been set out in *Re F (Abduction: Child's Wishes)* [2007] 2 FLR 697, CA. In exercising the discretion, the conduct of both parties will be relevant, particularly where such conduct has led to delay (*Re L (Abduction: Child's Objections to Return)* [2002] 2 FLR 1042, FD; *Re R (A Minor) (Abduction)* [1992] 1 FLR 105, FD). For recent cases where these principles were applied, see *Re A (Abduction: Children's Objections: Domestic Violence)* [2014] 1 FLR 1433, CA and the cases referred in the judgment, including *Re W* (below).

Expressed views of the children must be carefully and cautiously assessed, bearing in mind that the wishes and feelings which children express may vary according to mood, adult influence and/or their reaction to the person carrying out the assessment. The court may have to consider the extent of inconsistencies in the child's evidence, how far the views are genuinely held and to what extent they are influenced by those of others (*FK v ML & A* [2016] EWHC 517 (Fam)). There is no absolute threshold below which a child is not considered sufficiently mature to voice his objection. It is for the court to determine the attributes of the child and the nature of his objections to the return (*Re W (Abduction: Acquiescence: Children's Objections)* [2010] 2 FLR 1150, FD and upheld on appeal: *Re W (Abduction: Child's Objections)* [2010] 2 FLR 1165, CA). In *De L v H* [2010] 1 FLR 1229, FD, the judge saw the child who was 13 in the presence of a Cafcass officer and was satisfied of the child's maturity and his strong, rational and sound objections and strong feelings about not wishing to return to the state of his habitual residence and exercised his discretion to refuse the child's return on the grounds that it would cause disruption, distress and feelings of disillusion. Similar sentiments were expressed by a 15½ year old in *K v B (Abduction: Child's Objection to Return)* [2014] EWHC B7 (Fam), cf *AVH v SI & Anr (Abduction: Child's Objection)* [2015] 2 FLR 269, FD, where on the facts despite a 15 year old's objections a return order was made. See above under separate representation for child and also *Re G (Abduction: Children's Objections)* [2011] 1 FLR 1645, CA, *DT v LBT* [2011] 1 FLR 1215, FD, *Re E (Children)* [2011] 2 FLR 724, CA and *B v B (Abduction: Child with Learning Difficulties)* [2012] 1 FLR 881, FD.

Separate representation of children—See under Art 12, above.

Intolerable situation—In relation to a child, 'intolerable' must mean 'a situation which this particular child in these particular circumstances should not be expected to tolerate' (*Re S (A Child) (Abduction: Rights of Custody)* [2012] 2 FLR 442, SC). It will be necessary to establish a high degree of intolerability (*E v E (Child Abduction: Intolerable Situation)* [1998] 2 FLR 980, FD) – hardship or discomfort or the application of the religious laws or dual system of justice to a parent is insufficient (*Re S (Abduction: Intolerable Situation: Beth Din)* [2000] 1 FLR 454, FD; *B v B (Abduction: Custody Rights)* [1993] 1 FLR 238, CA). The intolerability complained of must relate to the child. Litigation in a country and language foreign to both parents, resulting in financial chaos could render an order to return intolerable: *Re J (Abduction: Acquiring Custody Rights by Caring for Child)* [2005] 2 FLR 791, FD. Problems created by the offending party's conduct (*Re C (Abduction: Grave Risk of Psychological Harm)* [1999] 1 FLR 1145, CA) and dependence on welfare benefits (*Re M (Abduction: Undertakings)* [1995] 1 FLR 1021, CA; *Re A (Minors) (Abduction: Acquiescence)* [1992] 2 FLR 14, CA) are insufficient. Delay in the determination of the issues in the country of habitual residence may be considered as placing the child in an intolerable position (*SP v EB and KP* [2016] 1 FLR 228, FD, where it was anticipated that proceedings in the home country would take more than a year to be determined). For the effect of Art 20 on the provisions of Art 13 and, in particular, Art 13(b) and the use of undertakings see **Duty to order the return of the child and protection of human rights and fundamental freedoms** under Art 12. Note also the provisions of Brussels IIA, Art 11(4), which states that a court cannot refuse to return a child on the basis of the Hague Convention, Art 13(b) if it is 'established that adequate arrangements have been made to secure the protection of the child after his return'.

Abduction and the claim for asylum—The court's jurisdiction to order the return of an abducted child is not restricted by the provisions of the Immigration and Asylum Act 1999 and, in particular, the prohibition on removal under s 15 of the 1999 Act is directed at the immigration authorities. It is not intended to circumscribe the duty and discretion of a judge exercising the wardship, Convention or family jurisdiction (*Re S (Child Abduction: Asylum Appeal)* [2002] 2 FLR 465, CA). See also *Re H (A Child)* [2016] EWCA Civ 988 – a decision in wardship proceedings to set aside a return order.

Art 13 and the welfare test—The welfare of the child in CACA 1985 cases is not the paramount consideration but a primary consideration (see **'grave risk'**, above). The court will apply a two-stage process when considering the application of Art 13, namely: (i) establish whether a prima facie case under the Article is made out; and (ii) consider whether or not to order the return of the children. The Art 13 threshold is strictly applied and it is only in exceptional circumstances that the court will consider not returning the children. See *Re S (A Child) (Abduction: Rights of Custody)* [2012] 2 FLR 442, SC, *Re M (Abduction: Child's Objections)* [2007] 2 FLR 72, CA and *Klentzeris v Klentzeris* [2007] 2 FLR 996, CA where due to the exceptional circumstances welfare considerations outweighed Hague Convention considerations, and applied in *SP v EB and KP* [2016] 1 FLR 228, FD.

Article 14

In ascertaining whether there has been a wrongful removal or retention within the meaning of Article 3, the judicial or administrative authorities of the requested State may take notice directly of the law of, and of judicial or administrative decisions, formally recognised or not in the State of the habitual residence of the child, without recourse to the specific procedures for the proof of that law or for the recognition of foreign decisions which would otherwise be applicable.

Article 15

The judicial or administrative authorities of a Contracting State may, prior to the making of an order for the return of the child, request that the applicant obtain from the authorities of the State of the habitual residence of the child a decision or other determination that the removal or retention was wrongful within the meaning of Article 3 of the Convention, where such a decision or determination may be obtained in that State. The Central Authorities of the Contracting States shall so far as practicable assist applicants to obtain such a decision or determination.

Request by the judicial or administrative authorities of a Contracting State—This Article should be read with s 8, which contemplates applications for the purposes of Art 15 to be made by any person who appears to have an interest in the matter. Its terms are broader than the limited ones set out in this Article. See *Re P (Abduction: Declaration)* [1995] 1 FLR 831, CA for an example where s 8 was applied, and a declaration made, although it involved making a preliminary decision on the issues of habitual residence and breach which were to be decided by the court in the requested state. It is, however, not appropriate to seek a declaration on a matter of interpretation of the Convention from the foreign court. This task falls to be determined by the Court seised of the application. Whether it would be right to seek an Article 15 determination would depend on the nature of the dispute, whether the parties intended to adduce expert evidence and the delay that would be caused (*Hunter v Murrow (Abduction: Rights of Custody)* [2005] 2 FLR 1119, CA). In any event, an Article 15 determination made in another country is not binding on the English court (*Re J (A Minor)* [1990] 2 FLR 442, HL).

Article 16

After receiving notice of a wrongful removal or retention of a child in the sense of Article 3, the judicial or administrative authorities of the Contracting State to which the child has been removed or in which it has been retained shall not decide on the merits of rights of custody until it has been determined that the child is not to be returned under this Convention or unless an application under this Convention is not lodged within a reasonable time following receipt of the notice.

'notice'—This reference is not restricted to notice from any particular source or in any particular form (*R v R (Residence Order: Child Abduction)* [1995] 2 FLR 625, FD). As soon as the court learns that it is concerned with a child who has formerly lived abroad in a Convention country and one parent wishes, or may wish, to return to that country, a possible case under the Hague Convention may arise. If there is any doubt, the matter should be transferred to the High Court. It is the duty of the practitioners involved to draw the attention of the court to the possibility that the Hague Convention may apply (*Re H (Abduction: Habitual Residence: Consent)* [2000] 2 FLR 294, FD). Similarly, in care proceedings where it appears that the child is habitually resident in a Convention country and where one or both parents lives abroad, every effort should be made to locate the parent living abroad and steps taken to secure legal representation for such parties (see *Kent County Council v C, G and A* [2015] 1 FLR 115, FD at [12] for full guidance). See also *R v R (Jurisdiction and Acquiescence)* [2016] EWHC 1339 (Fam), where MacDonald J also gave guidance to courts dealing with private law cases involving an international element.

Application—The machinery of the Convention contemplates a summary procedure, to be operated only once. There cannot be second or subsequent applications under the Convention. This principle also applies where the application has been made and the summary procedure has taken place in another Contracting State (*Re O (Child Abduction: Re-Abduction)* [1997] 2 FLR 712, FD).

Lodging of application within a reasonable time—The question of what is reasonable time must be considered objectively but, unless the court makes a finding that no application has been lodged within a reasonable time, it should refrain from deciding the merits of right of custody and making a child arrangements order, including one which is interim (*R v R* (above)).

Procedural steps to be taken by the court—Where the court becomes seised of a matter relating to a child, and it becomes apparent that there has been wrongful removal or retention within the meaning of the Convention, the court has a duty to take steps to secure that the parent in the other state is informed of his rights under the Convention. The English central authority should be requested to inform the central authority of the state from which the child has been removed of the circumstances of the case. The court should also communicate with the parent in that state by means of directions to the effect that he should seek legal advice expeditiously as to his rights, and communicate with the central authority of his state, of which he should be given the name and address.

★★★★

SCHEDULE 2
EUROPEAN CONVENTION ON RECOGNITION AND ENFORCEMENT OF DECISIONS CONCERNING CUSTODY OF CHILDREN

Liaison judge—See under Sch 1.

Article 1

For the purposes of this Convention:

(a) 'child' means a person of any nationality, so long as he is under 16 years of age and has not the right to decide on his own place of residence under the law of his habitual residence, the law of his nationality or the internal law of the State addressed;

(b) 'authority' means a judicial or administrative authority;

(c) 'decision relating to custody' means a decision of an authority in so far as it relates to the care of the person of the child, including the right to decide on the place of his residence, or to the right of access to him;

(d) 'improper removal' means the removal of a child across an international frontier in breach of a decision relating to his custody which has been given in a Contracting State and which is enforceable in such a State; 'improper removal' also includes:

   (i) the failure to return a child across an international frontier at the end of a period of the exercise of the right of access to this child or at the end of any other temporary stay in a territory other than that where the custody is exercised;

   (ii) a removal which is subsequently declared unlawful within the meaning of Article 12.

Scope—Although this Convention provides for the recognition and enforcement of custody orders of Contracting Member States, it has been superseded by Brussels IIA and as from 1 November 2012 by the 1996 Hague Convention, as both these instruments take precedence over the European Convention. Thus, its provisions, save insofar as they relate to Denmark, are almost redundant.

★★★★

Article 4

(1) Any person who has obtained in a Contracting State a decision relating to the custody of a child and who wishes to have that decision recognised or enforced in another Contracting State may submit an application for this purpose to the central authority in any Contracting State.

(2) The application shall be accompanied by the documents mentioned in Article 13.

(3) The central authority receiving the application, if it is not the central authority in the State addressed, shall send the documents directly and without delay to that central authority.

(4) The central authority receiving the application may refuse to intervene where it is manifestly clear that the conditions laid down by this Convention are not satisfied.

(5) The central authority receiving the application shall keep the applicant informed without delay of the progress of his application.

Procedure on application—See FPR 2010, rr 12.44–12.57 and FPR PD12F, para 20, but see the note under Art 3.

Determination of application—Determination of the application under the European Convention should not be made while Hague Convention proceedings are pending (*Re R (Abduction: Hague and European Conventions)* [1997] 1 FLR 663, CA).

'decision relating to the custody of a child'—This term refers to a decision of an authority insofar as it relates to the care of the person of the child, including the right to decide on the place of his residence, or to the right of access to him (Art 1(c)). Where there is a subsisting order, it is irrelevant that the order was made before the ratification of the European Convention between England and the other Contracting party and, by virtue of Art 7, it is required to be recognised and enforced (*Re L (Child Abduction: European Convention)* [1992] 2 FLR 178, FD). Where a final order has been made in matrimonial proceedings, permitting the mother to remove the children to England where they remain habitually resident, enforcement of any order for contact should be sought under Brussels IIA and not under the Convention: *Re G (Foreign Contact Order: Enforcement)* [2004] 1 FLR 378, CA; *Re S (Brussels II Revised: Enforcement of Contact Order)* [2008] 2 FLR 1358, FD.

****

Article 7

A decision relating to custody given in a Contracting State shall be recognised and, where it is enforceable in the State of origin, made enforceable in every other Contracting State.

'decision relating to custody'—Where the abducting parent had notice of the proceedings for a care arrangement order and parental responsibility order, an ex parte care arrangement order and an order requiring the abductor to return the child to England, the order is enforceable in other Contracting States, because the recognition and enforcement of such an order could not be refused under the provisions of Art 9 (*Re S (Custody: Habitual Residence)* [1998] 1 FLR 122, HL).

****

Article 9

(1) Recognition and enforcement may be refused if:

- (a) in the case of a decision given in the absence of the defendant or his legal representative, the defendant was not duly served with the document which instituted the proceedings or an equivalent document in sufficient time to enable him to arrange his defence; but such a failure to effect service cannot constitute a ground for refusing recognition or enforcement where service was not effected because the defendant had concealed his whereabouts from the person who instituted the proceedings in the State of origin;
- (b) in the case of a decision given in the absence of the defendant or his legal representative, the competence of the authority giving the decision was not founded:
  - (i) on the habitual residence of the defendant; or
  - (ii) on the last common habitual residence of the child's parents, at least one parent being still habitually resident there, or
  - (iii) on the habitual residence of the child;
- (c) the decision is incompatible with a decision relating to custody which became enforceable in the State addressed before the removal of the child, unless the child has had his habitual residence in the territory of the requesting State for one year before his removal.

(3) In no circumstances may the foreign decision be reviewed as to its substance.

Scope—This Article provides for the court to refuse recognition and enforcement on procedural grounds; see *Re G (A Minor) (Child Abduction: Enforcement)* [1990] 2 FLR 325, FD.

Recognition and enforcement—This should be construed disjunctively; thus, a court is entitled to refuse an order which has been registered, eg where it is found that, by reason of changes in the circumstances including the passage of time, the effects of the original decision are manifestly no longer in the interests of the child (*Re H (A Minor) (Foreign Custody Order: Enforcement)* [1994] 1 FLR 512, CA). The court's powers to refuse or recognise and enforce an order are discretionary (*Re G (A Minor) (Child Abduction: Enforcement)* [1990] 2 FLR 325, FD).

'decision is incompatible with a decision ... enforceable in the State addressed' (Art 9(1)(c))—Recognition and enforcement was refused in *Re M (Child Abduction) (European Convention)* [1994] 1 FLR 551, FD.

Review of foreign decision—Under no circumstances may the foreign decision be reviewed as to its substance; see also *Re A (Foreign Access Order: Enforcement)* [1996] 1 FLR 561, CA and *Re G (Foreign Contact Order: Enforcement)* [2004] 1 FLR 378, CA.

Article 10

(1) Recognition and enforcement may also be refused on any of the following grounds –

(a) if it is found that the effects of the decision are manifestly incompatible with the fundamental principles of the law relating to the family and children in the State addressed;

(b) if it is found that by reason of a change in the circumstances including the passage of time but not including a mere change in the residence of the child after an improper removal, the effects of the original decision are manifestly no longer in accordance with the welfare of the child;

(c) if at the time when the proceedings were instituted in the State of origin:

(i) the child was a national of the State addressed or was habitually resident there and no such connection existed with the State of origin;

(ii) the child was a national both of the State of origin and of the State addressed and was habitually resident in the State addressed;

(d) if the decision is incompatible with a decision in the State addressed or enforceable in that State after being given in a third State, pursuant to proceedings begun before the submission of the request for recognition or enforcement, and if the refusal is in accordance with the welfare of the child.

(2) Proceedings for recognition or enforcement may be adjourned on any of the following grounds:

(a) if an ordinary form of review of the original decision has been commenced;

(b) if proceedings relating to the custody of the child, commenced before the proceedings in the State of origin were instituted, are pending in the State addressed;

(c) if another decision concerning the custody of the child is the subject of proceedings for enforcement or of any other proceedings concerning the recognition of the decision.

Scope—This Article sets out the substantive ground for refusal of recognition and enforcement. See *Re G (A Minor) (Abduction: Enforcement)* [1990] 2 FLR 325, FD; *Re F (Minors) (Custody: Foreign Order: Enforcement)* [1989] 1 FLR 335, FD; *Re K (A Minor) (Abduction)* [1990] 1 FLR 387, FD. Notwithstanding the mandatory terms of s 16(4), the use of the word 'may' in the Article gives the court a discretion, but in *Re A (Foreign Contact Order: Jurisdiction)* [2004] 1 FLR 641, FD it was held that the Article should be construed and applied stringently. When Brussels IIA (Council Regulation (EC) No 2201/2003) applies, it takes precedence over the European Convention. However, if the court permits registration, in view of the provisions of Art 9(3) which prohibit a review of the foreign order, enforcement of that order must follow. Therefore, in exercising its discretion on whether to allow registration, the court will also necessarily have to consider the effect on the child of enforcing the order.

'effects of the original decision'—This refers to the effects of the enforcement of the decision, in particular in relation to the welfare of the child, at the date of the determination of the application by the requested state without delay, review or alteration. It does not refer to the effects of taking steps towards its enforcement or the return of the child to the state of origin to enable the original order to be enforced. This flows from:

'(a) the language of the phrase;

(b) the underlying purpose of the European Convention which is concerned with the enforcement of existing orders made in the State of origin by the courts of the State addresses;

(c) the terms of Art 7;

(d) the terms of Art 5(1)(d);

(e) Art 9(3) which precludes the State addressed from reviewing the substance of the original order; and

(f) Art 10(2)(a) which provides for the possibility of adjournment if an ordinary review has been commenced'. (*T v R* [2002] 2 FLR 544, FD.)

Change in the circumstances and the child's views are relevant in respect of any dispute under Art 10(1)(b), unless this is impracticable having regard to the child's age and understanding (Art 15(1)(a)). A report by a Cafcass reporter may be ordered to ascertain the child's feelings and views (see also *Re T (Abduction: Appointment of Guardian ad Litem)* below).

'Incompatible with the fundamental principles of family law'—Foreign law relating to the importance of contact and its conclusion that the residence of a child should be changed when a custodial parent opposes and refuses contact with the other parent (which does not reasonably warrant such opposition), is not incompatible with the approach to residence and contact in England having regard to the welfare principle and the application of the welfare check list (see *T v R* (above) and *Re M (Child Abduction) (European Convention)* [1994] 1 FLR 551, FD).

'improper removal'—For definition see Art 1(c) and note that the phrase 'decisions relating to custody' includes access. Any action which thwarts such access by the removal of the child to another jurisdiction amounts to improper removal (see *T v R* (above)).

Issues to be determined—The essential tasks of the court under this Article are: to establish what the circumstances were at the time of the original decision; to ascertain whether any or all of the grounds set out in the Article have been proved; and whether the original decision can no longer be sustained because it does not accord with the welfare of the child (*Re R (Abduction: Hague and European Conventions)* [1997] 1 FLR 663, CA).

'manifestly no longer in accordance with the welfare of the child'—It is only in circumstances where it is clear that a return of the child would be manifestly against the interest of the child, and that the original decision is manifestly no longer in accordance with the welfare of the child, that the court should exercise its discretion not to comply with the spirit and terms of the Act and Convention. The party who seeks to persuade the court as to this bears a very high burden of proof (*Re L (Child Abduction: European Convention)* [1992] 2 FLR 178, FD). See also *Re A (Foreign Access Order: Enforcement)* [1996] 1 FLR 561, CA, where the decision was found not to come within the exceptions provided by Art 10(2). In appropriate cases a child may be joined as a party to the proceedings and represented by a children's guardian (*Re T (Abduction: Appointment of Guardian Ad Litem)* [1999] 2 FLR 796, FD). Although recognition and enforcement may be refused, the court under its inherent jurisdiction may go on to consider what is the appropriate forum for determining the welfare of the child and any dispute relating to the child's residence and contact and whether, in the circumstances, it would be in the interests of the child to order his/her return while the dispute is resolved in the appropriate forum.

Article 11

(1) Decisions on rights of access and provisions of decisions relating to custody which deal with the rights of access shall be recognised and enforced subject to the same conditions as other decisions relating to custody.

(2) However, the competent authority of the State addressed may fix the conditions for the implementation and exercise of the right of access taking into account, in particular, undertakings given by the parties on this matter.

(3) Where no decision on the right of access has been taken or where recognition or enforcement of the decision relating to custody is refused, the central authority of the State addressed may apply to its competent authorities for a decision on the right of access if the person claiming a right of access so requests.

Discretion to fix condition—Conditions may be imposed to implement and to exercise right of access. This discretion must be exercised in the light of Art 9(3), which provides that under no circumstances may a foreign decision be reviewed as to its substance (*Re A (Foreign Access Order: Enforcement)* [1996] 1 FLR 561, CA). See *Re G (Foreign Contact Order: Enforcement)* [2004] 1 FLR 378, CA, where the court directed that the father should have preliminary visiting contact as a condition of implementation of the original order.

Article 12

Where, at the time of the removal of a child across an international frontier, there is no enforceable decision given in a Contracting State relating to his custody, the provisions of this Convention shall apply to any subsequent decision, relating to the custody of that child and declaring the removal to be unlawful, given in a Contracting State at the request of any interested person.

Declaration of unlawful removal—Art 12 prohibits the continued retention of a child when an enforceable decision relating to his custody has been made in a Contracting State. Once the court has found that the child has been wrongfully removed or retained under Art 3 of the Hague Convention, it can give a declaration that he has been unlawfully removed from the jurisdiction contrary to Art 12 (*Re S (Custody: Habitual Residence)* [1998] 1 FLR 122, HL).

'any subsequent decision'—Where the father of an illegitimate child did not have any care arrangement order or parental responsibility order in his favour relating to his child who had been unlawfully removed to Denmark, but obtained a without notice care arrangement order providing for the child to live with him and an order requiring the mother to return the child to the father in England, it was held that the removal of the child was covered by the provisions of s 23(2) and thereby entitled the court to make a declaration under Art 12 that the removal of the child was unlawful (*Re S (Custody: Habitual Residence)* [1998] 1 FLR 122, HL).

Article 13

(1) A request for recognition or enforcement in another Contracting State of a decision relating to custody shall be accompanied by:

(a) a document authorising the central authority of the State addressed to act on behalf of the applicant or to designate another representative for that purpose;

(b) a copy of the decision which satisfies the necessary conditions of authenticity;

(c) in the case of a decision given in the absence of the defendant or his legal representative, a document which establishes that the defendant was duly served with the document which instituted the proceedings or an equivalent document;

(d) if applicable, any document which establishes that, in accordance with the law of the State of origin, the decision is enforceable;

(e) if possible, a statement indicating the whereabouts or likely whereabouts of the child in the State addressed;
(f) proposals as to how the custody of the child should be restored.

****

Article 15

(1) Before reaching a decision under paragraph (1)(b) of Article 10, the authority concerned in the State addressed:

(a) shall ascertain the child's views unless this is impracticable having regard in particular to his age and understanding; and
(b) may request that any appropriate enquiries be carried out.

(2) The cost of enquiries in any Contracting State shall be met by the authorities of the State where they are carried out.

Requests for enquiries and the results of enquiries may be sent to the authority concerned through the central authorities.

****

Article 26

(1) In relation to a State which has in matters of custody two or more systems of law of territorial application:

(a) reference of the law of a person's habitual residence or to the law of a person's nationality shall be construed as referring to the system of law determined by the rules in force in that State or, if there are no such rules, to the system of law with which the person concerned is most closely connected;
(b) reference to the State of origin or to the State addressed shall be construed as referring, as the case may be, to the territorial unit where the decision was given or to the territorial unit where recognition or enforcement of the decision or restoration of custody is requested.

(2) Paragraph (1)(a) of this Article also applies mutatis mutandis to States which have in matters of custody two or more systems of law of personal application.

SCHEDULE 3
CUSTODY ORDERS

PART I
ENGLAND AND WALES

1 The following are the orders referred to in section 27(1) of this Act –

(a) a care order under the Children Act 1989 (as defined by section 31(11) of that Act, read with section 105(1) and Schedule 14);
(b) a child arrangements order (as defined by section 8 of the Act of 1989) if the arrangements regulated by the order consist of, or include, arrangements relating to either or both of the following –
  (i) with whom a child is to live, or
  (ii) when a child is to live with any person;
(bb) a special guardianship order (within the meaning of the Act of 1989); and
(c) any order made by a court in England and Wales under any of the following enactments –
  (i) section 9(1), 10(1)(a) of the Guardianship of Minors Act 1971;
  (ii) section 42(1) or (2) or 43(1) of the Matrimonial Causes Act 1973;
  (iii) section 2(2)(b), (4)(b) or (5) of the Guardianship Act 1973 as applied by section 34(5) of the Children Act 1975;

PART II

(iv) section 8(2)(a), 10(1) or 19(1)(ii) of the Domestic Proceedings and Magistrates' Courts Act 1978.

Amendments—CA 1989, s 108(5), Sch 13, para 57(3); ACA 2002, Sch 3, para 45; CFA 2014, s 12, Sch 2.

2 An order made by the High Court in the exercise of its jurisdiction relating to wardship so far as it gives the care and control of a child to any person.

3 (*repealed*)

4 An authorisation given by the Secretary of State under section 26(2) of the Children and Young Persons Act 1969 (except where the relevant order, within the meaning of that section, was made by virtue of the court which made it being satisfied that the child was guilty of an offence).

PART II
SCOTLAND

5 An order made by a court of civil jurisdiction in Scotland under any enactment or rule of law with respect to the residence, custody, care or control of a child or contact with or access to a child, excluding –

(i) an order placing a child under the supervision of a local authority;

(ii), (iia) (*repealed*)

(iii) an order relating to the guardianship of a child;

(iv) an order made under section 86 of the Children (Scotland) Act 1995;

(v) an order made, or warrant or authorisation granted, under or by virtue of Chapter 2 or 3 of Part II of the Children (Scotland) Act 1995 to remove the child to a place of safety or to secure accommodation, to keep him at such a place or in such accommodation, or to prevent his removal from a place where he is being accommodated (or an order varying or discharging any order, warrant or authorisation so made or granted);

(vi) an order made in proceedings under this Act;

(vii) an adoption order (as defined in section 28(1) of the Adoption and Children (Scotland) Act 2007);

(viii) a permanence order (as defined in subsection (2) of section 80 of that Act) which includes provision such as is mentioned in paragraph (c) of that subsection.

Amendments—FLA 1986, s 68(1), Sch 1, para 31; Children (Scotland) Act 1995, s 105(4), Sch 4, para 37(6)(a); SI 2011/1740.

Modifications—Schedule 3, para 5 is modified for certain purposes by SI 2013/1465, art 17, Sch 1, para 1, Pt 3.

5A The reference in paragraph 5(viii) to a permanence order includes a deemed permanence order having effect by virtue of article 13(1), 14(2), 17(1) or 19(2) of the Adoption and Children (Scotland) Act 2007 (Commencement No 4, Transitional and Savings Provisions) Order 2009.

Amendments—Inserted by SI 2011/1740.

6 A supervision requirement made by a children's hearing under section 70 of the Children (Scotland) Act 1995 (whether or not continued under section 73 of that Act) or made by the sheriff under section 51(5)(c)(iii) of that Act and any order made by a court in England and Wales or in Northern Ireland if it is an order which, by virtue of section 33(1) of that Act, has effect as if it were such a supervision requirement.

Amendments—Substituted by Children (Scotland) Act 1995, s 105(4), Sch 4, para 37(6)(b).

Modifications—Schedule 3, para 6 is modified for certain purposes by SI 2013/1465, art 17, Sch 1, para 1.

7 (*repealed*)

PART III

NORTHERN IRELAND

8 The following orders –

(a) a care order under the Children (Northern Ireland) Order 1995 (as defined by Article 49(1) of that Order read with Article 2(2) and Schedule 8);

(b) a residence order (as defined by Article 8 of that Order);

(c) any order made by a court in Northern Ireland under any of the following enactments –

(i) section 5 of the Guardianship of Infants Act 1886 (except so far as it relates to costs);

(ii) section 49 of the Mental Health Act (Northern Ireland) 1961;

(iii) Article 45(1) or (2) or 46 of the Matrimonial Causes (Northern Ireland) Order 1978;

(iv) Article 10(2)(a), 12(1) or 20(1)(ii) of the Domestic Proceedings (Northern Ireland) Order 1980;

(v) Article 27(1)(b) of the Adoption (Northern Ireland) Order 1987.

Amendments—Substituted by SI 1995/756.

9 An order made by the High Court in the exercise of its jurisdiction relating to wardship so far as it gives the care and control of a child to any person.

10 (*repealed*)

Child Support Act 1991

ARRANGEMENT OF SECTIONS

Section		Page
	The basic principles	
1	The duty to maintain	400
2	Welfare of children: the general principle	401
3	Meaning of certain terms used in this Act	401
4	Child support maintenance	402
8	Role of the courts with respect to maintenance for children	404
9	Agreements about maintenance	407
10	Relationship between maintenance calculations and certain court orders and related matters	408
	Reviews and appeals	
26	Disputes about parentage	410
27	Applications for declaration of parentage under Family Law Act 1986	410
	Collection and enforcement	
33	Liability orders	411
36	Enforcement in county courts	412
39A	Commitment to prison and disqualification from driving	413
	Jurisdiction	
44	Jurisdiction	414
	Miscellaneous and supplemental	
54	Interpretation	415
55	Meaning of 'child'	416

The basic principles

General note—CSA 1991 has been extensively amended by four later substantial sets of legislation: by the Child Support Act 1995, the Social Security Act 1998, the Child Support, Pensions and Social Security Act 2000 and by the CMOPA 2008. The Secretary of State for Work and Pensions has resumed responsibility for the scheme, now in the guise of the Child Maintenance Service. CSA 1991 remains the lead legislation, but is extensively amended. Three schemes are in operation under CSA 1991: that under the 1991 Act based on a formula; then the scheme under the 2000 Act based on a percentage of the non-resident parent's net income (in operation from 3 March 2003); and a gross income scheme under the 2008 Act.

Procedural and practice rules—Court action under the scheme can proceed in seven different courts and tribunals (see below). The appeals structure was amended by the Tribunals Courts and Enforcement Act 2007 (TCEA 2007): appeals under CSA 1991, s 20 lie to the First-tier Tribunal (formerly an appeal tribunal) and then ('on a question of law, and with permission': TCEA 2007, s 11) to the Upper Tribunal (operation of the tribunals is outside the scope of *The Family Court Practice*) (except in the case of parentage appeals: see Procedural Guide E3).

The Child Support Act 1991 – procedural overview

The seven judicial systems with jurisdiction

Court	*Types of application covered*	*CSA 1991 reference*	*Procedure*
1 Magistrates' courts	(1) Liability order	s 33	MCR 1981
	(2) Committal/ disqualification	ss 39A, 40	MCR 1981
	(3) Deduction from earnings order appeal	C&E Regs, reg 22	MCR 1981
2 County courts	(1) Declaration of parentage (FLA 1986, s 55A)	s 27	FPR 2010, r 8.18(b)
	(2) Charging order	s 36	FPR 2010, Pt 33, Ch 8
	(3) Third party debt order	s 36	FPR 2010, Pt 33, Ch 7
	(4) Declaration of parentage (FLA 1986, s 55A)	s 27	FPR 2010, rr 8.18(b), 8.19
	(5) Parentage appeals from Secretary of State decisions	CSA 1991, s 20	FPC(CSA 1991)R 1993
	(6) Appeals from magistrates at (1) above	Magistrates' Courts Act 1980 s 111A	FPR 2010, Pt 30
	(7) Appeals from deduction orders	CSA 1991, ss 32A, 32E and 32G	CS(CE)R 1992 (SI 1992/1989), reg 25B
3A High Court – Family Division	Declaration of parentage (FLA 1986, s 55A)	s 27	FPR 2010, r 8.18(b)
3B High Court	Judicial Review	SCA 1981, s 29	CPR 1998, Pt 54
4 First-tier Tribunal	Appeals from CSA ss 11, 16 and 17	s 20	*(Beyond the scope of The Family Court Practice)*
5 Upper Tribunal	Appeals on a point of law from appeal tribunal	s 24, TCEA 2007, s 11	*(Beyond the scope of The Family Court Practice)*
6 Court of Appeal	Appeals on a point of law from the Commissioners	TCEA 2007, s 13	CPR 1998, Pt 52
7 Supreme Court	Appeal from Court of Appeal	N/a	SCPD

1 The duty to maintain

(1) For the purposes of this Act, each parent of a qualifying child is responsible for maintaining him.

(2) For the purposes of this Act, a non-resident parent shall be taken to have met his responsibility to maintain any qualifying child of his by making periodical payments of maintenance with respect to the child of such amount, and at such intervals, as may be determined in accordance with the provisions of this Act.

(3) Where a maintenance calculation made under this Act requires the making of periodical payments, it shall be the duty of the non-resident parent with respect to whom the calculation was made to make those payments.

Amendments—CSPSSA 2000, ss 1(2), 26, Sch 3, para 11(1),(2).

Defined terms—'non-resident parent': s 3(2); 'child': s 55(1); 'maintenance calculation', 'parent': s 54; 'periodical payments': s 3(6); 'qualifying child': s 3(1).

'parent' (s 1(1))—The term is defined narrowly at s 54 to comprise only those 'in law the mother or father of the child'. Adoptive parents are included, but step-parents are not.

'child' (s 1(2))—The term is defined at s 55 in different terms from, for example, 'child of the family' in MCA 1973, s 52(1) and CA 1989, s 105(1) and 'child' in CA 1989, s 105(1).

'periodical payments' and 'maintenance' (s 1(2),(3))—The scheme uses these terms more or less interchangeably; but the term most used is 'child support maintenance' (s 3(6)).

PART II

2 Welfare of children: the general principle

Where, in any case which falls to be dealt with under this Act, the Secretary of State is considering the exercise of any discretionary power conferred by this Act, the Secretary of State shall have regard to the welfare of any child likely to be affected by the decision.

Amendments—Social Security Act 1998, s 86, Sch 7, para 18, Sch 8; CMOPA 2008, s 13(4), Sch 3, paras 1, 2; SI 2012/2007.

Defined terms—'child': s 55(1).

Judicial review: discretion—Only decisions under CSA 1991 (mostly as to calculation under s 11 or revision or supersession) can be appealed against under CSA 1991, s 20. Where a decision-maker exercises a discretion (e g as to whether to enforce arrears of child support maintenance or quantification of arrears) there is no statutory appeal under the 1991 Act. Such a decision can only be challenged by means of judicial review (see e g *R v Secretary of State for Social Security ex parte Biggin* [1995] 1 FLR 851, QBD). To succeed in an application for judicial review, the applicant must show that the grounds summarised by Lord Diplock in *Council of Civil Service Unions v Minister for the Civil Service* [1985] AC 374, HL at [408] apply, namely unlawfulness, unreasonableness and/or procedural impropriety.

'he shall have regard'—That is to say, the welfare of the child is only one of the factors, not the paramount consideration, for the Secretary of State, but it is a factor for which the Secretary of State has a statutory duty to have regard (*Brookes v Secretary of State for Work and Pensions* [2010] 2 FLR 1038, CA).

'any child'—The reference to '*any* child likely to be affected' (emphasis supplied) makes it clear that it is not only qualifying children who are entitled to be considered; though in practice their welfare may weigh more heavily with the decision-maker than that of other children. The definition would include children living with the person with care in her household, but it could also include children in the non-resident parent's household who might, for example, be affected by his committal to prison (*Brookes*, above, provides an example of this: none of the children in the case were qualifying children).

3 Meaning of certain terms used in this Act

(1) A child is a 'qualifying child' if –

(a) one of his parents is, in relation to him, a non-resident parent; or
(b) both of his parents are, in relation to him, non-resident parents.

(2) The parent of any child is a 'non-resident parent', in relation to him, if –

(a) that parent is not living in the same household with the child; and
(b) the child has his home with a person who is, in relation to him, a person with care.

(3) A person is a 'person with care', in relation to any child, if he is a person –

(a) with whom the child has his home;
(b) who usually provides a day to day care for the child (whether exclusively or in conjunction with any other person); and
(c) who does not fall within a prescribed category of person.

(4) The Secretary of State shall not, under subsection (3)(c), prescribe as a category –

(a) parents;
(b) guardians;

(c) persons named, in a child arrangements order under section 8 of the Children Act 1989, as persons with whom a child is to live;
(d) in Scotland, persons with whom a child is to live by virtue of a residence order under section 11 of the Children (Scotland) Act 1995.

(5) For the purposes of this Act there may be more than one person with care in relation to the same qualifying child.

(6) Periodical payments which are required to be paid in accordance with a maintenance calculation are referred to in this Act as 'child support maintenance'.

(7) Expressions are defined in this section only for the purposes of this Act.

Amendments—Children (Scotland) Act 1995, s 105(4), Sch 4, para 52; CSPSSA 2000, ss 1(2)(a), 26, Sch 3, para 11(1),(2); CFA 2014, s 12, Sch 2.

Defined terms—'child': s 55(1); 'guardian': CA 1989, s 5.

'person with care' (s 3(3))—The person who has care of the child and is therefore entitled to seek a maintenance calculation against the non-resident parent(s). The person with care need not be a parent of the child, nor need they have parental responsibility (per CA 1989, s 3) for the child. There may be more than one person with care (s 3(5); and see *C v Secretary of State for Work and Pensions and B* [2003] 1 FLR 829, CA).

'prescribed category of person' (s 3(3)(c))—Child Support (Maintenance Calculation Procedure) Regulations 2001, reg 21 prescribes, for the purposes of s 3(3)(c), local authorities and foster parents with whom a child is placed when looked after by the local authority under CA 1989, s 22, who cannot therefore be a person with care.

4 Child support maintenance

(1) A person who is, in relation to any qualifying child or any qualifying children, either the person with care or the non-resident parent may apply to the Secretary of State for a maintenance calculation to be made under this Act with respect to that child, or any of those children.

(2) Where a maintenance calculation has been made in response to an application under this section the Secretary of State may, if the person with care applies to the Secretary of State under this subsection, arrange for –

(a) the collection of the child support maintenance payable in accordance with the calculation;
(b) the enforcement of the obligation to pay child support maintenance in accordance with the calculation.

(2A) The Secretary of State may only make arrangements under subsection (2)(a) if –

(a) the non-resident parent agrees to the arrangements, or
(b) the Secretary of State is satisfied that without the arrangements child support maintenance is unlikely to be paid in accordance with the calculation.

(3) Where an application under subsection (2) for the enforcement of the obligation mentioned in subsection (2)(a) authorises the Secretary of State to take steps to enforce that obligation whenever the Secretary of State considers it necessary to do so, the Secretary of State may act accordingly.

(4) A person who applies to the Secretary of State under this section shall, so far as that person reasonably can, comply with such regulations as may be made by the Secretary of State with a view to the Secretary of State being provided with the information which is required to enable –

(a) the non-resident parent to be identified or traced (where that is necessary);
(b) the amount of child support maintenance payable by the non-resident parent to be calculated; and
(c) that amount to be recovered from the non-resident parent.

(5) Any person who has applied to the Secretary of State under this section may at any time request the Secretary of State to cease acting under this section.

(6) It shall be the duty of the Secretary of State to comply with any request made under subsection (5) (but subject to any regulations made under subsection (8)).

(7) The obligation to provide information which is imposed by subsection (4) –

(a) shall not apply in such circumstances as may be prescribed; and
(b) may, in such circumstances as may be prescribed, be waived by the Secretary of State.

(8) The Secretary of State may by regulations make such incidental, supplemental or transitional provision as he thinks appropriate with respect to cases in which he is requested to cease to act under this under this section.

(9) *(repealed)*

(10) No application may be made at any time under this section with respect to a qualifying child or any qualifying children if –

(a) there is in force a written maintenance agreement made before 5 April 1993, or a maintenance order made before a prescribed date, in respect of that child or those children and the person who is, at that time, the non-resident parent; or

(aa) a maintenance order made on or after the date prescribed for the purposes of paragraph (a) is in force in respect of them, but has been so for less than the period of one year beginning with the date on which it was made; or

(ab) a maintenance agreement –

(i) made on or after the date prescribed for the purposes of paragraph (a); and

(ii) registered for execution in the Books of Council and Session or the sheriff court books,

is in force in respect of them, but has been so for less than the period of one year beginning with the date on which it was made.

(11) *(repealed)*

Amendments—Child Support Act 1995, s 18; Social Security Act 1998, s 86, Sch 7, para 19, Sch 8; CSPSSA 2000, s 2(1),(2); CMOPA 2008, ss 1(2), s 2(1),(3), ss 13(4), 26, 35(1), s 58, Sch 3, paras 1, 3, 11(1)–(3)(a), Sch 8; SI 2012/2007; Welfare Reform Act 2012, s 137.

Defined terms—'non-resident parent': s 3(2); 'child': s 55(1); 'child support maintenance': s 3(6); 'maintenance calculation', 'parent': s 54; 'periodical payments': s 3(6); 'qualifying child': s 3(1).

Outline of child support calculation—There are three schemes running in parallel:

- Original scheme under CSA 1991 (April 1993 – 2 March 2003) (**CS1**)
- Scheme under CSPSSA 2000 from 3 March 2003 (**CS2**)
- Gross income scheme under CMOPA 2008 (**CS3**) starting 12 December 2012.

Calculation and effective date

Under CS2 and CS3, the calculation goes through up to four stages: (1) calculation based on earned income and number of qualifying children; adjustment for (2) 'relevant other children' and (3) 'shared care'; and (4) revision/supersession to take account of any variation direction. Figures below are weekly amounts. For CS3, the sources for the new gross income calculations are:

- CSA 1991, s 11 and Sch 1 (inserted by CMOPA 2008)
- Child Support Maintenance Calculation Regulations 2012 (CSMCR 2012).

Stage 1

The first stage is to assess whether the payer is a 'basic', 'reduced', 'flat' or 'nil' rate payer, as follows.

Basic rate

CS2 – net earned income of £200–£2,000 a week

- 15% for one qualifying child
- 20% for two qualifying children
- 25% for three or more qualifying children

CS3 – (1) Gross income of £200–£800 a week

- 12% for one qualifying child
- 16% for two qualifying children
- 19% for three or more qualifying children

(2) Gross income of £800–£3,000 a week

- 9% for one qualifying child
- 12% for two qualifying children
- 15% for three qualifying children and more

Reduced rate—Takes the calculation on a straight-line graph from £7 where payments are required at the flat rate to payments at the basic rate on an income of £200 or more, achieved by reference to a formula in CSA 1991, Sch 1.

Flat rate—Income less than £100 a week and certain prescribed benefits: £7 a week is the fixed amount of child support maintenance.

Stage 2

Relevant other children—Where the non-resident parent is living in a household where there are other dependent children, his income is reduced proportionately before the Stage 1 calculation is carried out, as follows:

For CS2

- 12% where the non-resident parent has one relevant other child;
- 16% where the non-resident parent has two relevant other children;
- 19% where the non-resident parent has three or more relevant other children

For CS3

- 12% where the non-resident parent has one relevant other child;
- 16% where the non-resident parent has two relevant other children;
- 19% where the non-resident parent has three or more relevant other children

Stage 3 – shared care

If the non-resident parent has 'shared care' for an average of one night a week or more, there is a proportionate reduction to the calculation: 1/7 for 52 days and more a year, 2/7 for 104, etc (CSA 1991, Sch 1 para 7).

Stage 4 – variation directions

CSA 1991 (as amended), ss 28A–28F, Schs 4A and 4B and Child Support (Variations) Regulations 2000 (CS3 variation regulations are in CSMCR 2012).

'either the person with care or the non-resident parent may apply' (s 4(1))—Either the person with care or the non-resident parent of the qualifying children may apply. There may be circumstances where the payment under the pre-March 2003 scheme would have been less than under the new. Broadly, the non-resident parent whose gross income exceeds £75,000 will pay more under the new scheme than the old.

Request to Secretary of State to 'cease acting' (s 4(5),(6))—In respect of a current assessment (old scheme), or a maintenance calculation, the parent with care may request the Secretary of State to 'cease acting' (s 4(5)) in collection and recovery of child support maintenance (eg where private arrangements are made between the parties concerning payments and repayment of any arrears). The assessment or calculation then terminates. There may then remain a live issue as to whether arrears due to the Secretary of State will be pursued by him (and this must be borne in mind in connection with any case settled under this provision).

'a maintenance order made on or after the date prescribed' (s 4(10)(aa))—As a result of s 4(10(aa) no application for child support maintenance under s 4 can be made within 1 year of a court-ordered child periodical payments order, where that original order post-dates the 'prescribed' date (i e 3 March 2003 (see SI 2003/194)). The order ceases to have effect on the effective date of the application (see below). Either parent may apply to the Secretary of State under s 4 after the s 4(10(aa) 1-year period. This provision does not apply to pre-March 2003 orders, which are immune from application under s 4 (and also under s 6, which is repealed with effect from 14 July 2008 (SI 2008/1476)).

Effective date—In the case of a new calculation made where there is an existing court order, the order 'ceases to have effect on the effective date of the maintenance calculation' (CS(MAJ)R 1992, reg 3(2)). That effective date – when the new maintenance arrangements start to run – is 'two months and two days after the application [for a calculation] is made'. Until that date payments under the order will continue to run.

Variation of periodical payments orders—So long as the order remains effective either parent may apply to the originating court for a variation of child periodical payments (CSA 1991, s 8(3A); MCA 1973, s 31(1)).

****

8 Role of the courts with respect to maintenance for children

(1) This subsection applies in any case where the Secretary of State would have jurisdiction to make a maintenance calculation with respect to a qualifying child and a non-resident parent of his on an application duly made by a person entitled to apply for such a calculation with respect to that child.

(2) Subsection (1) applies even though the circumstances of the case are such that the Secretary of State would not make a calculation if it were applied for.

(3) Except as provided in subsection (3A), in any case where subsection (1) applies, no court shall exercise any power which it would otherwise have to make, vary or revive any maintenance order in relation to the child and non-resident parent concerned.

(3A) In any case in which section 4(10) or 7(10) prevents the making of an application for a maintenance calculation, and –

(a) no application has been made for a maintenance calculation under section 6, or

(b) such an application has been made but no maintenance calculation has been made in response to it, subsection (3) shall have effect with the omission of the word 'vary'.

(3A) Unless a maintenance calculation has been made with respect to the child concerned, subsection (3) does not prevent a court from varying a maintenance order in relation to that child and the non-resident parent concerned –

(a) if the maintenance order was made on or after the date prescribed for the purposes of section 4(10)(a) or 7(10)(a); or

(b) where the order was made before then, in any case in which section 4(10) or 7(10) prevents the making of an application for a maintenance calculation with respect to or by that child.

(4) Subsection (3) does not prevent a court from revoking a maintenance order.

(5) The Lord Chancellor or in relation to Scotland the Lord Advocate may by order provide that, in such circumstances as may be specified by the order, this section shall not prevent a court from exercising any power which it has to make a maintenance order in relation to a child if –

(a) a written agreement (whether or not enforceable) provides for the making, or securing, by a non-resident parent of the child of periodical payments to or for the benefit of the child; and

(b) the maintenance order which the court makes is, in all material respects, in the same terms as that agreement.

(5A) The Lord Chancellor may make an order under subsection (5) only with the concurrence of the Lord Chief Justice.

(6) This section shall not prevent a court from exercising any power which it has to make a maintenance order in relation to a child if –

(a) a maintenance calculation is in force with respect to the child;

(b) the non-resident parent's gross weekly income exceeds the figure referred to in paragraph 10(3) of Schedule 1 (as it has effect from time to time pursuant to regulations made under paragraph 10A(1)(b)); and

(c) the court is satisfied that the circumstances of the case make it appropriate for the non-resident parent to make or secure the making of periodical payments under a maintenance order in addition to the child support maintenance payable by him in accordance with the maintenance calculation.

(7) This section shall not prevent a court from exercising any power which it has to make a maintenance order in relation to a child if –

(a) the child is, will be or (if the order were to be made) would be receiving instruction at an educational establishment or undergoing training for a trade, profession or vocation (whether or not while in gainful employment); and

(b) the order is made solely for the purposes of requiring the person making or securing the making of periodical payments fixed by the order to meet some or all of the expenses incurred in connection with the provision of the instruction or training.

(8) This section shall not prevent a court from exercising any power which it has to make a maintenance order in relation to a child if –

(a) an allowance under Part 4 of the Welfare Reform Act 2012 (personal independence payment) or a disability living allowance is paid to or in respect of him; or

(b) no such allowance is paid but he is disabled,

and the order is made solely for the purpose of requiring the person making or securing the making of periodical payments fixed by the order to meet some or all of any expenses attributable to the child's disability.

(9) For the purposes of subsection (8), a child is disabled if he is blind, deaf or dumb or is substantially and permanently handicapped by illness, injury, mental disorder or congenital deformity or such other disability as may be prescribed.

(10) This section shall not prevent a court from exercising any power which it has to make a maintenance order in relation to a child if the order is made against a person with care of the child.

(11) In this Act 'maintenance order', in relation to any child, means an order which requires the making or securing of periodical payments to or for the benefit of the child and which is made under –

(a) Part II of the Matrimonial Causes Act 1973;
(b) the Domestic Proceedings and Magistrates' Courts Act 1978;
(c) Part III of the Matrimonial and Family Proceedings Act 1984;
(d) the Family Law (Scotland) Act 1985;
(e) Schedule 1 to the Children Act 1989;
(ea) Schedule 5, 6 or 7 to the Civil Partnership Act 2004; or
(f) any other prescribed enactment,

and includes any order varying or reviving such an order.

(12) The Lord Chief Justice may nominate a judicial office holder (as defined in section 109(4) of the Constitutional Reform Act 2005) to exercise his functions under this section.

Amendments—Child Support Act 1995, s 18; Social Security Act 1998, s 86(1), Sch 7, para 22; CSPSSA 2000, s 1(2), s 26, Sch 3, para 11(1),(2); CPA 2004, ss 254(1), 261(4), Sch 24, para 1, Sch 30; CRA 2005, s 15(1), Sch 4, paras 218, 219; CMOPA 2008, ss 13(4), 57(1), 58, Sch 3, paras 1, 6, Sch 7, para 1(2) (subject to savings), Sch 8; SI 2012/2007; WRA 2012, s 91, Sch 9, para 2.

Defined terms—'non-resident parent': s 3(2); 'child': s 55(1); 'child support maintenance': s 3(6); 'maintenance calculation', 'parent': s 54; 'periodical payments': s 3(6); 'person with care': s 3(3); 'qualifying child': s 3(1).

'jurisdiction to make a maintenance calculation' (s 8(1))—The jurisdiction of the Secretary of State to make a calculation depends upon:

(a) one or both of a child's parents not being resident with the child (s 3);
(b) the child coming within the definition of 'child' (s 55 as amended by CMOPA 2008); and
(c) each of the non-resident parent, the person with care and the qualifying child being habitually resident in the UK (s 44).

Cohabitation—A child support calculation terminates after cohabitation for more than 6 months (CSA 1991, Sch 1, para 16(1)(d); *Brough v Law* [2012] 1 FLR 375, CA; cf payments under CA 1989, Sch 1, para 3(4), where an order ceases upon the parents living together for more than 6 months). During the period of resumption of cohabitation for less than 3 months, the surviving duty to pay child support maintenance is 'suspended ... and cease at the expiry of six months' (*Brough v Law* (above) at [58]).

'no court shall exercise any power' (s 8(3))—Provided that the Secretary of State has jurisdiction, and even though no application is made to him, the court has no jurisdiction to hear a contested application for child periodical payments. This is subject to the following exceptions where the court has power to make an order:

(i) *Applications for top up orders* Where s 8(5)–(10) applies, application can be made to the court for one or more of the top-up orders therein referred to (see *Re P (Child: Financial Provision)* [2003] 2 FLR 865, CA).
(ii) *Variations of existing periodical payments orders* (s 8(3A)) *V v V (Child Maintenance)* [2001] 2 FLR 799, FD, at [804], clarifies that it remains possible for the court to vary existing orders, whether made before or after April 1993, subject to (where the parent with care is on benefit) there being no application for a child support calculation.
(iii) *'Segal' orders* The court can make an order for periodical payments for a parent which will later absorb any subsequent child support maintenance calculation (a 'Segal' order); but only where the order contains a substantial amount of spousal maintenance (*Dorney-Kingdom v Dorney-Kingdom* [2000] 2 FLR 855, CA).
(iv) *Lump sums for children* The court has power in proceedings under MCA 1973, s 23(1)(f) and CA 1989, Sch 1, para 1(2)(c) to make lump sum orders (in the narrow circumstances where this may be appropriate) including interim orders for expenses reasonably incurred (MCA 1973, s 23(3)(b); CA 1989, Sch 1, para 5(1); and see *Askew-Page v Page* [2001] Fam Law 794, Cty Ct, HH Judge Meston QC). A lump sum order can be made for children where the husband withdraws his consent to varying an agreed order (*V v V (Child Maintenance)* [2001] 2 FLR 799, FD).
(v) *Costs allowances* It may be possible to obtain a costs allowance for the financially disadvantaged parent in top-up child maintenance proceedings (*MT v OT (Financial provision: costs)* [2008] 2 FLR 1311, FD; and see CA 1989, Sch 1, para 5(1) (MCA 1973, ss 22ZA and 22ZB and CPA 2004, ss 38A and 38B (LASPOA 2012, ss 49, 50) for matrimonial and civil partnership (only) financial proceedings).
(vi) *Consent orders* See under **Written Agreements and consent orders**, below.

Maintenance Regulation: Council Regulation (EC) No 4/2009—For purposes of enforcement of child support maintenance in Europe, an enforceable 'decision' includes all 'matters relating to maintenance obligations given in a third state' (Council Regulation (EC) No 4/2009, Art 2(1)(1)). Art 64(1) provides that enforcement of decisions applies in respect of public bodies acting in place of individuals to whom maintenance is owed. These provisions may enable a parent with care to enforce maintenance obligations abroad (if the non-resident parent leaves the jurisdiction) where she cannot do so in the UK (*R (Kehoe) v Secretary of State for Work and Pensions* [2005] 2 FLR 1249, HL).

Application for a top-up order—Application is made for a top-up order in FPR 2010 financial remedies proceedings under MCA 1973, CPA 2004 proceedings by Form A, alongside existing proceedings (eg, for a school fees order: s 8(7)(a)); or as a freestanding application in proceedings under CA 1989, Sch 1, where there are (or have been) no MCA 1973/CPA 2004 proceedings or the couple were not married. In all cases, procedure is governed by FPR 2010, Pt 9. Applications for a top-up order where the maximum calculation has been reached (s 8(6)) should generally be transferred to be heard before a judge of the Family Division (*Re P (Child: Financial Provision)* (above)).

Interim applications—Interim application for orders and a costs allowance can be made (*CF v KM* [2011] 1 FLR 208, FD) and such applications will still be necessary (e g under CA 1989, Sch 1). It will be important to define the applicant's budget and her costs requirements before any interim hearing:

(i) *MCA 1973/CPA 2004* The court has its general powers to award interim financial provision on Pt 18 procedure application being made in existing proceedings in accordance with FPR 2010, r 9.7;
(ii) *CA 1989, Sch 1* Provision for interim provision is set out in Sch 1, para 9. The applicant proceeds by Pt 18 procedure in accordance with FPR 2010, r 9.7; and see *CF v KM*, above.

PART II

Backdating of orders—Backdating of any final top-up order will depend upon when the application for the top-up order (the application) is made and the date (the effective date) from which the child support maintenance calculation is effective (MCA 1973, s 29(5) and (6); CA 1989, Sch 1, para 3(5) and (6); and as explained in *Re P (Child: Financial Provision)* (above): the provisions of s 29 and CA 1989, Sch 1, para 3 are identical). The order, and thus any provision for arrears, runs from the 'earliest permitted date' (s 29(6); para 3(5)), namely the later of 6 months before the application (s 29(6)(a); para 3(5)(a)) or the 'effective date' of the original calculation that led to the maximum assessment calculation that enables the top-up application to be made (s 29(6)(b); para 3(5)(b)).

Date for application for a top-up order—There is no reason why application cannot be made (including for interim financial provision) where a maximum assessment has not yet been made (*CF v KM* [2011] 1 FLR 208, FD) and, because of the effects of CA 1989, Sch 1, para 3(5) (see above) in unmarried couples' cases, every reason why an application should be made. (For an example of this and of back-dating arrears see e g *H v C* [2009] 2 FLR 1540, FD, where the appeals process to reach a maximum assessment took more than 3 years: but for an early application the children's arrears would have been back-dated to any later application as the 'later' of the two 'earliest dates'.)

Effective date—The effective date of a maintenance calculation is:

(1) New calculation – the date on which the application is made, including any revision of that calculation (Child Support (Maintenance Calculation Procedure) Regulations 2001, Pt VII);
(2) Supersession (CSA 1991, s 17) – the date on which any application for a decision to supersede is made (CSA 1991, s 17(4)).

Effect of calculation and ceasing of a maintenance order—See under s 10 below.

Termination of child periodical payments order—See annotation to s 4(10)(aa) above.

FPR 2010—To ensure that applications in respect of qualifying children are not wrongly pursued in the courts, there are procedures in FPR 2010, r 29.8, which requires the court to give notice to the applicant concerning possible rejection of such applications.

Written agreements and consent orders (s 8(5))—Child Maintenance (Written Agreements) Order 1993, art 2 gives effect to s 8(5) and provides:

> 'Section 8 shall not prevent a court from exercising any power which it has to make a maintenance order in relation to a child in any circumstances in which paragraphs (a) and (b) of section 8(5) apply.'

Thus the court retains its powers, subject to the provisions of s 4(10)(aa), to make orders by consent of the parties, even though the Secretary of State would have had jurisdiction were application to be made to the Agency.

'mental disorder' (s 8(9))—By virtue of MHA 1983, s 1(2), this means 'mental illness, arrested or incomplete development of mind, psychopathic disorder and any other disorder or disability of mind and 'mentally disordered' shall be construed accordingly'.

'any other prescribed enactment' (s 8(11)(f))—Child Support (Maintenance Arrangements and Jurisdiction) Regulations 1992, reg 2 adds a number of further enactments under which maintenance orders are covered for the purposes of s 8.

Voluntary payments—The treatment of voluntary payments is dealt with in CSA 1991, s 28J. The Secretary of State has a discretion to allow payments and for them to be set against child support maintenance arrears (and see CSA 1991, s 41C: power to treat liability as satisfied). In *R (Green) v Secretary of State for Work and Pensions* [2010] EWHC 1278 (Admin) Black J found that a decision-maker had a discretion to permit school fees to be offset against child support. The decision-maker must consider its internal guidance and document the exercise. Where school fees have been dealt with by court order (by consent or otherwise under s 8(7)), this is not 'voluntary payments' in terms of s 28J nor a component in agreement to a variation direction under s 28D (*DB v CMEC* [2010] UKUT 356).

9 Agreements about maintenance

(1) In this section 'maintenance agreement' means any agreement for the making, or for securing the making, of periodical payments by way of maintenance, or in Scotland aliment, to or for the benefit of any child.

(2) Nothing in this Act shall be taken to prevent any person from entering into a maintenance agreement.

(2A) The Secretary of State may, with a view to reducing the need for applications under sections 4 and 7 –

(a) take such steps as the Secretary of State considers appropriate to encourage the making and keeping of maintenance agreements, and .

(b) in particular, before accepting an application under those sections, invite the applicant to consider with the Secretary of State whether it is possible to make such an agreement.

(3) Subject to section 4(10)(a) and (ab) and section 7(10), the existence of a maintenance agreement shall not prevent any party to the agreement, or any other person, from applying for a maintenance calculation with respect to any child to or for whose benefit periodical payments are to be made or secured under the agreement.

(4) Where any agreement contains a provision which purports to restrict the right of any person to apply for a maintenance calculation, that provision shall be void.

(5) Where section 8 would prevent any court from making a maintenance order in relation to a child and a non-resident parent of his, no court shall exercise any power that it has to vary any agreement so as –

(a) to insert a provision requiring that non-resident parent to make or secure the making of periodical payments by way of maintenance, or in Scotland aliment, to or for the benefit of that child; or

(b) to increase the amount payable under such a provision.

(6) In any case in which section 4(10) or 7(10) prevents the making of an application for a maintenance calculation, subsection (5) shall have effect with the omission of paragraph (b).

Amendments—Child Support Act 1995, s 18; CSPSSA 2000, s 1(2), 26, Sch 3, para 11(2),(6), CMOPA 2008, ss 35(3), 58, Sch 8; WRA 2009, s 136; SI 2012/2007.

Defined terms—'non-resident parent': s 3(2); 'child': s 55(1); 'maintenance calculation', 'parent': s 54; 'periodical payments': s 3(6).

'maintenance agreement' (s 9(1))—This definition can be contrasted with that in MCA 1973, s 34(2) and CSA 1991, s 8(5)(a), which state that the agreement must be in writing; however, s 9(1) contemplates the existence of agreements other than in writing (which must raise questions, beyond the scope of this note, as to their enforceability). In any event, whatever the nature of the agreement and the extent of its enforceability, s 9(3) ensures that its existence cannot prevent application being made for a maintenance calculation in respect of the child concerned.

'any child' (s 9(1),(3))—Although the section uses the term 'any child', the context – applications for a maintenance calculation, which can only be for qualifying children (ss 4(1) and 6(1)) – makes it clear that it can only apply to qualifying children.

Restriction on the right to apply for maintenance calculation (s 9(4))—Any restriction on the right to apply for a maintenance calculation recorded in a consent order would also fail under s 9(4) within the terms of the definition in s 9(1): it may be assumed that the term 'maintenance agreement' includes the consent application which would have led to the order.

Alteration of maintenance agreements (s 9(5))—MCA 1973, s 35 and CA 1989, Sch 1, para 10 enable a party to a maintenance agreement to apply to the court for its variation. Section 9(5) prevents this where application is in respect of a qualifying child, save for the following: (i) existing agreements to which s 9(6) applies; and (ii) where the variation is by agreement, in which case it could be made the subject of a consent application to the court, either where matrimonial proceedings are contemplated or are under way (MCA 1973, s 7) or under DPMCA 1978, s 6. The difference between this arrangement and MCA 1973, s 35 is that the new 'agreement' becomes a court order totally separate from the original agreement; whereas under s 35 and CA 1989, Sch 1, para 10 the whole agreement stands subject only as varied by the court order. See *Morgan v Hill* [2007] 1 FLR 1480, CA on the court's powers to vary agreements between parents not married to one another.

Written agreements and consent orders—The Child Maintenance (Written Agreements) Order 1993 gives effect to s 8(5), whereby the court retains its powers to make orders in accordance with a written agreement. This is so even though the Secretary of State would have had jurisdiction and whether or not the written agreement on which the order is to be based postdates the coming into operation of the Act.

10 Relationship between maintenance calculations and certain court orders and related matters

(1) Where an order of a kind prescribed for the purposes of this subsection is in force with respect to any qualifying child with respect to whom a maintenance calculation is made, the order –

(a) shall, so far as it relates to the making or securing of periodical payments, cease to have effect to such extent as may be determined in accordance with regulations made by the Secretary of State; or

(b) where the regulations so provide, shall, so far as it so relates, have effect subject to such modifications as may be so determined.

(2) Where an agreement of a kind prescribed for the purposes of this subsection is in force with respect to any qualifying child with respect to whom a maintenance calculation is made, the agreement –

(a) shall, so far as it relates to the making or securing of periodical payments, be unenforceable to such extent as may be determined in accordance with regulations made by the Secretary of State; or

(b) where the regulations so provide, shall, so far as it so relates, have effect subject to such modifications as may be so determined.

(3) Any regulations under this section may, in particular, make such provision with respect to –

(a) any case where any person with respect to whom an order or agreement of a kind prescribed for the purposes of subsection (1) or (2) has effect applies to the prescribed court, before the end of the prescribed period, for the order or agreement to be varied in the light of the maintenance calculation and of the provisions of this Act;

(b) the recovery of any arrears under the order or agreement which fell due before the coming into force of the maintenance calculation,

as the Secretary of State considers appropriate and may provide that, in prescribed circumstances, an application to any court which is made with respect to an order of a prescribed kind relating to the making or securing of periodical payments to or for the benefit of a child shall be treated by the court as an application for the order to be revoked.

(4) The Secretary of State may by regulations make provision for –

(a) notification to be given by the Secretary of State concerned to the prescribed person in any case where the Secretary of State considers that the making of a maintenance calculation has affected, or is likely to affect, any order of a kind prescribed for the purposes of this subsection;

(b) notification to be given by the prescribed person to the Secretary of State in any case where a court makes an order which it considers has affected, or is likely to affect, a maintenance calculation.

(5) Rules of court may require any person who, in prescribed circumstances, makes an application to the family court for a maintenance order to furnish the court with a statement in a prescribed form, and signed by an officer of the Secretary of State, as to whether or not, at the time when the statement is made, there is a maintenance calculation in force with respect to that person or the child concerned.

In this subsection –

'maintenance order' means an order of a prescribed kind for the making or securing of periodical payments to or for the benefit of a child; and

'prescribed' means prescribed by the rules.

Amendments—Social Security Act 1998, s 86(1), Sch 7, para 23; CSPSSA 2000, s 1(2); CMOPA 2008, s 13(4), Sch 3, paras 1, 7; SI 2012/2007; CCA 2013, s 17, Sch 11.

Defined terms—'child': s 55(1); 'child support maintenance': s 3(6); 'maintenance calculation', 'parent': s 54; 'periodical payments': s 3(6); 'qualifying child': s 3(1).

'an agreement of a kind prescribed' (s 10(2),(3)(a))—Maintenance agreements as defined in s 9(1) are those which are prescribed for this subsection (Child Support (Maintenance Arrangements and Jurisdiction) Regulations 1992, reg 4(1)).

Child Support (Maintenance Arrangements and Jurisdiction) Regulations 1992—CSA 1991, s 10 and these Regulations deal with the relationship between child support maintenance calculations and court orders for periodical payments, namely any court order ceases to have effect except to the extent that CSA 1991, s 8(7),(8) apply (top-up orders and for education and disability expenses).

Effective date—The effective date of a calculation is the date from which child support maintenance payments are due. CSA 1991, s 10(1)(a) provides powers to the Secretary of State to deal with the 'ceasing to

PART II

have effect' of a child maintenance order where a calculation is made. Any child periodical payments order (other than under s 8(7),(8)) ceases to have effect on the effective date of the new maintenance calculation (Child Support (Maintenance Arrangements and Jurisdiction) Regulations 1992, reg 3(2). The 'effective date of the maintenance calculation' is defined by Child Support (Maintenance Calculation Procedure) Regulations 2000, regs 26 and 28 (CS2: for reference see under CSA 1991, s 4) and Child Support Maintenance Calculation Regulations 2012, reg 12 (CS3), which provide for court orders to cease to have effect (i e can be taken to mean that the order is discharged and that it cannot be revived (*Askew-Page v Page* [2001] Fam Law 794, Cty Ct)).

****

Reviews and appeals

****

26 Disputes about parentage

(1) Where a person who is alleged to be a parent of the child with respect to whom an application for a maintenance assessment has been made ('the alleged parent') denies that he is one of the child's parents, the Secretary of State shall not make a maintenance assessment on the assumption that the alleged parent is one of the child's parents unless the case falls within one of those set out in subsection (2).

****

Amendments—SI 1995/756; Social Security Act 1998, s 86(1), Sch 7, para 31(1); CMOPA 2008, ss 13(4), 58, Sch 3, paras 1, 18, Sch 8; SI 2012/2007.

Defined terms—'child': s 55(1); 'maintenance calculation', 'parent': s 54.

Denial of parentage (s 26(1))—This section provides for an alleged parent's entitlement to deny parentage which brings the application for a calculation to an end, unless one of the presumptions called 'Cases' set out in s 26(2) apply, when the onus shifts to the putative male parent to prove that he is not the parent. The cases set out in s 26(2) include:

- where the person was married to the mother at some time in the period 'beginning with conception' and ending with the birth of the child (Case A1);
- registration of the father on the birth certificate (Case A2);
- the alleged parent refuses to take a 'scientific test' (a paternity test, normally by DNA samples); or a test shows that he is the parent (Case A3);
- a parent has adopted the child (Case A);
- where there is a previous parentage declaration under FLA 1986, s 55A (Case C);
- the parent has already been adjudged to be the father in other relevant court proceedings (Case F).

Inference of parentage—Where a married woman gives birth to a child, the husband is presumed to be the father (Case A1). However, where a man who has been clearly identified by the mother as the father refuses to undergo scientific tests, the magistrates may draw appropriate inferences from such a refusal (FLRA 1969, s 23; *Secretary of State for Work and Pensions v Jones* [2004] 1 FLR 282, FD, Dame Elizabeth Butler-Sloss P; and see *Re A (A Minor) (Paternity: Refusal of Blood Test)* [1994] 2 FLR 463, CA).

27 Applications for declaration of parentage under Family Law Act 1986

(1) This section applies where –

(a) an application for a maintenance calculation has been made or a maintenance calculation is in force, with respect to a person ('the alleged parent') who denies that he is a parent of a child with respect to whom the application or calculation was made,

(b) the Secretary of State is not satisfied that the case falls within one of those set out in section 26(2); and

(c) the Secretary of State or the person with care makes an application for a declaration under section 55A of the Family Law Act 1986 as to whether or not the alleged parent is one of the child's parents.

(2) Where this section applies –

(a) if it is the person with care who makes the application, she shall be treated as having a sufficient personal interest for the purposes of subsection (3) of that section; and

(b) if it is the Secretary of State who makes the application, that subsection shall not apply.

(3) This section does not apply to Scotland.

Amendments—Substituted by CSPSSA 2000, s 83(5), Sch 8, para 13; CMOPA 2008, ss 13(4), 58, Sch 3, paras 1, 19, Sch 8; SI 2012/2007.

Defined terms—'alleged parent': s 26(1); 'child': s 55(1); 'maintenance calculation', 'parent': s 54; 'person with care': s 3(3).

Parentage applications—Parentage applications may come before the Family Court in the context of CSA 1991 in one of two ways:

(1) *Under FLA 1986, s 55A* On application to the courts as a freestanding declaration application (FPR 2010, Pt 8, Ch 5, and see FLA 1986, s 55A procedure, below).
(2) *On appeal by a parent to first-tier tribunal* Under CSA 1991, s 20 (see below).

'sufficient personal interest' (s 27(2)(a))—Where the applicant is a person with care she does not have to go through the s 55A(3) filter of establishing whether she has a sufficient personal interest in the application. As a parent she will automatically have sufficient personal interest (s 55A(4)), so this section can apply only to persons with care who are not also parents.

Scientific tests—The issue of parentage is likely to turn on the outcome of scientific testing (under FLRA 1969, s 20, see below), which, if the court does not direct of its own initiative, one of the parties will require the court to direct (see Procedural Guide F2). Where scientific tests have been carried out, any fee paid by the Secretary of State for such test 'may be recovered by the Secretary of State from the alleged parent as a debt due to the Crown' (CSA 1991, s 27A(3)).

Appeals under CSA 1991, s 20 to first-tier tribunal on parentage—An appeal under CSA 1991, s 20 on a parentage issue is heard by the Family Court, rather than in the First-tier Tribunal (Child Support Appeals (Jurisdiction of Courts) Order 2002).

****

Collection and enforcement

Enforcement of arrears of child support maintenance under CSA 1991—The scheme of enforcement under CSA 1991 currently contains two categories of means of enforcement. Both involve the Family Court at different levels:

(1) *Administrative direction (ss 31–32K)* Known as 'orders', these provisions enable the Secretary of State to impose a direction upon the liable parent. Of the orders available under CSA 1991 and CMOPA 2008, only a limited number have been introduced: the deduction from earnings orders (CSA 1991, s 31) and (for payments from 'deposit-takers' and other creditors of the liable parent) the regular deduction orders (CMOPA 2008; CSA 1991, s 32A) and lump sum deduction orders (s 32E).
(2) *Enforcement following a liability order* A liability order under s 33 provides the Secretary of State with the means of enforcement set out in s 34 (distress: bailiffs), s 36 (enforcement in the County Court by charging order or third-party debt order) and s 39A (committal and disqualification from driving). Court involvement is built into the enforcement procedures (CS(CE)R 1992, Pt IV) under ss 33 and 39A.

Involvement of the Family Court

(1) Appeals from a deductions from earnings order lie to the magistrates' courts (civil) in the restricted circumstances of CS(CE)R 1992, reg 22.
(2) Appeal is direct to the Family Court (circuit or High Court judge level: FC(CDB)R 2014, r 6(3)) in respect of orders made by the Secretary of State under CSA 1991, ss 32A and 32E.
(3) Appeal lies to the County Court (MCA 1980, s 111A; FPR 2010, Pt 30) against liability (s 33) and commitment (ss 39–40B) orders.
(4) There is an appeal direct to the magistrates' court (civil) in connection with distress (which requires no court involvement beyond the liability order) under CS(CE)R 1992, reg 31.

'welfare of any child affected' (s 2)—Each means of enforcement involves an exercise of a decision-maker's discretion, thus engaging CSA 1991, s 2, and an assessment of whether 'any' child is likely to be affected by his/her decision (*Brookes v Secretary of State for Work and Pensions* [2010] 2 FLR 1038, CA). This decision must be taken in accordance with the principles summarised by Wyn Wilson J in *R (Equality & Human Rights Commission) v Secretary of State for Justice and anor* [2010] EWHC 147 (Admin), at [45]–[46]: has the decision-maker had regard to the relevant statutory duty, the 'relevant statutory need' demanded by that duty and discharged his/her duty with an open mind. The judgment at [46] contains a helpful decision analysis of recent case-law on decision-making duties.

Judicial review—Where there is no statutory means under CSA 1991, s 20 to challenge the decision of the Secretary of State, the route for challenge of the decision-maker may be by judicial review.

****

33 Liability orders

(1) This section applies where –

(a) a person who is liable to make payments of child support maintenance ('the liable person') fails to make one or more of those payments; and

(b) it appears to the Secretary of State that –

(i) it is inappropriate to make a deduction from earnings order against him (because, for example, he is not employed); or

(ii) although such an order has been made against him, it has proved ineffective as a means of securing that payments are made in accordance with the maintenance calculation in question.

(2) The Secretary of State may apply to a magistrates' court or, in Scotland, to the sheriff for an order ('a liability order') against the liable person.

(3) Where the Secretary of State applies for a liability order, the magistrates' court or (as the case may be) sheriff shall make the order if satisfied that the payments in question have become payable by the liable person and have not been paid.

(4) On an application under subsection (2), the court or (as the case may be) the sheriff shall not question the maintenance calculation under which the payments of child support maintenance fell to be made.

(5) If the Secretary of State designates a liability order for the purposes of this subsection it shall be treated as a judgment entered in a county court for the purposes of section 98 of the Courts Act 2003 (register of judgments and orders etc).

(6) Where regulations have been made under section 29(3)(a) –

(a) the liable person fails to make a payment (for the purposes of subsection (1)(a) of this section); and

(b) a payment is not paid (for the purposes of subsection (3)),

unless the payment is made to, or through, the person specified in or by virtue of those regulations for the case of the liable person in question.

Amendments—Child Support Act 1995, s 30, Sch 3, para 10; CSPSSA 2000, s 26, Sch 3, para 11(1), (17); SI 2006/1001; CMOPA 2008, s 13(4), Sch 3, paras 1, 36; SI 2012/2007.

Defined terms—'child support maintenance': s 3(6); 'deduction from earnings order': s 31(2); 'maintenance calculation': s 54.

Discretion of the Secretary of State—All decisions to enforce are discretionary and must therefore be exercised subject to considerations under s 2 (welfare of any child affected: eg what would the effect be of any enforcement of arrears on 'any' child concerned and affected by the decision?). The discretion must be exercised fairly and without irrationality. If it is not so exercised, the only challenge to the Secretary of State is by judicial review (see CPR 1998, Pt 54).

Magistrates 'shall not question the maintenance calculation' (s 33(4))—The magistrates are not able to question the underlying calculation on which the calculation decision is based. (If there is an appeal pending that goes to the question of the amount of the calculation or the Secretary of State's jurisdiction, the magistrates may wish to consider adjourning the application for an order (*Farley v Secretary of State for Department of Work and Pensions and Another* [2006] 2 FLR 1243, HL).)

Function of the magistrates: 'payments in question' (s 33(3))—The magistrates must be satisfied that payments in question remain payable: for example if paid by the liable person, although not specifically by a method dictated by the Secretary of State (eg direct on a voluntary basis to the other parent) (*Bird v Secretary of State for Work and Pensions* [2009] 2 FLR 660, QBD).

Appeals—An appeal against a liability order is by MCA 1980, s 111A.

****

36 Enforcement in county courts

(1) Where a liability order has been made against a person, the amount in respect of which the order was made, to the extent that it remains unpaid, shall, if a county court so orders, be recoverable by means of a third party debt order or a charging order, as if it were payable under a county court order.

(2) *(repealed)*

Amendments—CMOPA 2008, Sch 7, para 1(10), Sch 8.

Defined terms—'liability order': s 33(2).

'if a county court so orders' (s 36(1))—While the magistrates' court has little discretion but to make a liability order (see s 33(1)), the wording of s 36(1) reflects the wording of COA 1979, s 1(1) which give the County Court a discretion as to whether or not the orders should be made.

Application in the County Court—Whereas application for the other means of enforcement (distress or commitment) is by the Secretary of State, s 36 is silent as to who should make the application in the County Court. It may therefore be open to the person with care to make her own application. (This point does not appear to have been considered in *R (Kehoe) v Secretary of State for Work and Pensions* [2005] 2 FLR 1249, HL which stated that only the Secretary of State can enforce arrears.)

Jurisdiction of the County Court—Applications under s 36(1) are to the County Court. Application is by CPR 1998, Pt 73.

****

39A Commitment to prison and disqualification from driving

(1) Where the Secretary of State has sought –

(a) in England and Wales to recover an amount by virtue of section 35(1); or
(b) to recover an amount by virtue of section 36 or 38,

and that amount, or any portion of it, remains unpaid the Secretary of State may apply to the court under this section.

(2) An application under this section is for whichever the court considers appropriate in all the circumstances of –

(a) the issue of a warrant committing the liable person to prison; or
(b) an order for him to be disqualified from holding or obtaining a driving licence.

(3) On any such application the court shall (in the presence of the liable person) inquire as to –

(a) whether he needs a driving licence to earn his living;
(b) his means; and
(c) whether there has been wilful refusal or culpable neglect on his part.

(4) The Secretary of State may make representations to the court as to whether the Secretary of State thinks it more appropriate to commit the liable person to prison or to disqualify him from holding or obtaining a driving licence; and the liable person may reply to those representations.

(5) In this section and section 40B, 'driving licence' means a licence to drive a motor vehicle granted under Part III of the Road Traffic Act 1988.

(6) In this section 'the court' means –

(a) in England and Wales, a magistrates' court;
(b) in Scotland, the sheriff.

Amendments—Inserted by CSPSSA 2000, s 16(1). Amended by TCEA 2007, s 62(3), Sch 13, para 95; CMOPA 2008, s 13(4), Sch 3, paras 1, 41; SI 2012/2007.

Defined terms—'the court': s 39A(6); 'driving licence': s 39A(5); 'liable person': s 33(1).

'wilful refusal or culpable neglect' (s 39A(3)(c))—In *R v Luton Magistrates' Courts* [1992] 2 FLR 196, FD, Waite J defined the meaning of this term as: 'blameworthiness … at a very high level. It is not just a matter of improvidence or dilatoriness. Something in the nature of a deliberate defiance or reckless disregard of the court's order is required'.

Evidence and onus of proof—The evidence required and procedure for committal (equivalent to the judgment summons under Debtors Act 1869, s 5 and FPR 2010, rr 33.9–33.17) was explained in *Prest v Prest (Judgment Summons: Appeal)* [2016] 1 FLR 773, CA, at [55] (and see *Iqbal v Iqbal* [2017] EWCA Civ 19). It is a process that may result in the respondent serving a term of imprisonment. The application amounts to a criminal trial (*Engel and Others v The Netherlands (No 1)* (1979) 1 EHRR 647, at [80] and [81]) and European Convention 1950, Art 6(3)(c) applies. A court must therefore be clear as to the following:

- *Standard of proof* That the respondent has or has had, since the date of the order or judgment, the means to pay the sum due must be proved to the criminal standard of proof.
- *Proof of refusal or neglect* That the respondent has refused or neglected, or refuses or neglects, to pay the sum due must also be proved to the criminal standard.
- *Burden of proof* The burden of proof is at all times on the applicant.
- *Self-incrimination privilege* The respondent cannot be compelled to give evidence.

Disposal of the application—If wilful refusal or culpable neglect is proved under s 39A(3), the court has four discretionary disposals: to issue a warrant of commitment (CSA 1991, s 40(3)(a)); to postpone commitment on terms (s 40(3)(b)); to disqualify from driving (s 40B(1)(a)); or to make a disqualification order but suspend its operation (s 40B(1)(b)):

CSA 1991, s 40(3)(a)

'(3) If, but only if, the court is of the opinion that there has been wilful refusal or culpable neglect on the part of the liable person it may –
(a) issue a warrant of commitment against him; or
(b) fix a term of imprisonment and postpone the issue of the warrant until such time and on such conditions (if any) as it thinks just.'

PART II

CSA 1991, s 40B(1)

'(1) If, but only if, the court is of the opinion that there has been wilful refusal or culpable neglect on the part of the liable person, it may –

(a) order him to be disqualified, for such period specified in the order but not exceeding two years as it thinks fit, from holding or obtaining a driving licence (a 'disqualification order'); or

(b) make a disqualification order but suspend its operation until such time and on such conditions (if any) as it thinks just.

(2) The court may not take action under both section 40 and this section.'

Warrant of commitment or imprisonment (s 40(3))—The powers of the magistrates' courts to commit for breach of their own order are provided for by MCA 1980, s 76, and their power to postpone issue of a warrant by MCA 1980, s 77 (the terminology of which resembles s 40(3)). The justices must make a judgment concerning the conduct of the liable person over his failure to pay and whether that failure constitutes wilful refusal or culpable neglect. If they do so find, and having had regard to his means, they have a discretion as to whether or not to commit to prison immediately. Alternatively they can fix a term of imprisonment but suspend issue of the warrant of commitment to prison on 'such conditions as [the court] thinks just'.

'such conditions (if any) as [the court] thinks just' (s 40(3)(b))—This provision will enable the magistrates, for example, to suspend the warrant on terms that the liable person maintains payments due and pays off the arrears and costs (the amount stated on the warrant: s 40(4)) by fixed periodic instalments (*Fowler v Fowler* (1981) 2 FLR 141, FD).

Delay in enforcement of liability order—All enforcement process must comply with ECHR 1950, Art 6(1), that application to the court must be within a 'reasonable' time (and see *Lloyd v Bow Street Magistrates' Court* [2003] EWHC 2294 (Admin)). Applications under s 39A are not proceedings to recover money and therefore cannot be caught by any limitation periods under Limitation Act 1980, s 9 (*Child Maintenance and Enforcement Commission v Mitchell* [2010] 2 FLR 622, CA).

Execution of the warrant (s 40(9),(11)(f))—CS(CE)R 1992, reg 34(3),(4) deals with execution of the warrant by the person to whom it is addressed or by the police constable within his area.

Appeals—An appeal against a committal application is by MCA 1980, s 111A.

****

Jurisdiction

44 Jurisdiction

(1) The Secretary of State shall have jurisdiction to make a maintenance calculation with respect to a person who is –

(a) a person with care;

(b) a non-resident parent; or

(c) a qualifying child,

only if that person is habitually resident in the United Kingdom, except in the case of a non-resident parent who falls within subsection (2A).

(2) Where the person with care is not an individual, subsection (1) shall have effect as if paragraph (a) were omitted.

(2A) A non-resident parent falls within this subsection if he is not habitually resident in the United Kingdom, but is –

(a) employed in the civil service of the Crown, including Her Majesty's Diplomatic Service and Her Majesty's Overseas Civil Service;

(b) a member of the naval, military or air forces of the Crown, including any person employed by an association established for the purposes of Part XI of the Reserve Forces Act 1996;

(c) employed by a company of a prescribed description registered under the Companies Act 2006; or

(d) employed by a body of a prescribed description.

(3) *(repealed)*

(4) The Secretary of State does not have jurisdiction under this section if the exercise of jurisdiction would be contrary to the jurisdictional requirements of the Maintenance Regulation.

(5) In subsection (4) 'the Maintenance Regulation' means Council Regulation (EC) No 4/2009 including as applied in relation to Denmark by virtue of the Agreement made on 19 October 2005 between the European Community and the Kingdom of Denmark.

Amendments—Social Security Act 1998, s 86(1), Sch 7, para 41; CSPSSA 2000, ss 1(2), 22, 26, 85, Sch 3, para 11, Sch 9, Pt I; CMOPA 2008, s 13(4), Sch 3, paras 1, 46; SI 2009/1941; SI 2011/1484; SI 2012/2007.

Defined terms—'child': s 55(1); 'maintenance calculation': s 54; 'maintenance order': s 8(11); 'Maintenance Regulation': s 44(5); 'parent': s 54; 'qualifying child': s 3(1).

Habitual residence (s 44(1))—The term 'habitual residence' is not defined in the Act, nor has it been authoritatively considered under the Act. Reference may be made to authorities where the applicant seeks to invoke the jurisdiction of the English courts (eg DMPA, s 5(2)(b) or **Habitual residence** under CACA 1985, Sch 1, Art 4), where the term was authoritatively considered by Lord Brandon of Oakbrook in *C v S (A Minor) (Abduction: Illegitimate Child)* [1990] 2 FLR 442, HL, at [454] (affirmed by Baker J in the child maintenance context in *O v P (Jurisdiction under Children Act 1989 Sch 1)* [2012] 1 FLR 329, FD).

Want of residential jurisdiction

(i) If any of: (a) the person with care, (b) the qualifying children or (c) the non-resident parent are not habitually resident, or treated as habitually resident, no calculation can be made under CSA 1991.

(ii) If any of: (a) the person with care; (b) non-resident parent; or (c) qualifying child cease to be habitually resident while a calculation is in force, then an application is made to the Secretary of State for the calculation to be superseded (CSA 1991, s 17) and terminated with effect from the date habitual residence ceased.

If the Secretary of State does not have jurisdiction or a calculation otherwise comes to an end, application for child periodical payments is to the court under MCA 1973 or CPA 2004 (if parents were married) or under CA 1989, Sch 1.

****

Miscellaneous and supplemental

****

54 Interpretation

(1) In this Act –

'non-resident parent', has the meaning given in section 3(2);

'application for a variation' means an application under section 28A or 28G;

'benefit Acts' means the Social Security Contributions and Benefits Act 1992 and the Social Security Administration Act 1992;

'charging order' has the same meaning as in section 1 of the Charging Orders Act 1979;

'Chief Adjudication Officer' has the same meaning as in the benefit Acts;

'child benefit' has the same meaning as in the Child Benefit Act 1975;

'child support maintenance' has the meaning given in section 3(6);

…

'deduction from earnings order' has the meaning given in section 31(2);

'default maintenance decision' has the meaning given in section 12;

'deposit-taker' means a person who, in the course of a business, may lawfully accept deposits in the United Kingdom;

'disability living allowance' has the same meaning as in the benefit Acts;

…

'income support' has the same meaning as in the benefit Acts;

'income-based jobseeker's allowance' has the same meaning as in the Jobseekers Act 1995;

'income-related employment and support allowance' means an income-related allowance under Part 1 of the Welfare Reform Act 2007 (employment and support allowance);

'interim maintenance decision' has the meaning given in section 12;

'liability order' has the meaning given in section 33(2);

'maintenance agreement' has the meaning given in section 9(1);

'maintenance calculation' means a calculation of maintenance made under this Act and, except in prescribed circumstances, includes a default maintenance decision and an interim maintenance decision;

'maintenance order' has the meaning given in section 8(11);

'parent', in relation to any child, means any person who is in law the mother or father of the child;

'parent with care' means a person who is, in relation to a child, both a parent and a person with care;

'parental responsibility', in the application of this Act –

(a) to England and Wales, has the same meaning as in the Children Act 1989; and

(b) to Scotland, shall be construed as a reference to 'parental responsibilities' within the meaning given by section 1(3) of the Children (Scotland) Act 1995;

...

'person with care' has the meaning given in section 3(3);

'prescribed' means prescribed by regulations made by the Secretary of State;

'qualifying child' has the meaning given in section 3(1);

'voluntary payment' has the meaning given in section 28J;

(2) The definition of 'deposit-taker' in subsection (1) is to be read with –

(a) section 22 of the Financial Services and Markets Act 2000;

(b) any relevant order under that section; and

(c) Schedule 2 to that Act.

Amendments—Social Security (Consequential Provisions) Act 1992, s 4, Sch 2, para 114; Child Support Act 1995, s 30, Sch 3, para 16; Children (Scotland) Act 1995, s 105(4), Sch 4, para 52, Sch 5; Jobseekers Act 1995, s 41, Sch 2, para 20; Social Security Act 1998, s 86(1),(2) Sch 7, para 47, Sch 8; Tax Credits Act 1999, s 1(2), Sch 1, paras 1, 6(f)(ii); CSPSSA 2000, ss 1(2), 26, 85, Sch 3, para 11(1),(2),(20), Sch 9, Pt I; Tax Credits Act 2002, s 60, Sch 6; Tribunals, Courts and Enforcement Act 2007, s 146, Sch 23, Pt 2; Welfare Reform Act 2007, s 28(1), Sch 3, para 7(1),(7); CMOPA 2008, s 57, Sch 7, para 1(1),(25),(26); SI 2008/2833; WRA 2009, ss 9(3)(b), 58(1), Sch 7; SI 2012/2007.

55 Meaning of 'child'

(1) In this Act, 'child' means (subject to subsection (2)) a person who –

(a) has not attained the age of 16, or

(b) has not attained the age of 20 and satisfies such conditions as may be prescribed.

(2) A person who is or has been party to a marriage or civil partnership is not a child for the purposes of this Act.

(3) For the purposes of subsection (2), 'marriage' and 'civil partnership' include a void marriage and a void civil partnership respectively.

Amendments—CPA 2004, s 254(1), Sch 24, para 3; CMOPA 2008, s 42.

'not attained the age of 20'—This gives effect to the reforms outlined in CMOPA 2008, s 42, so that the upper age for child support increases.

****

Children Act 1989

ARRANGEMENT OF SECTIONS

PART I
INTRODUCTORY

Section		Page
1	Welfare of the child	422
2	Parental responsibility for children	424
3	Meaning of 'parental responsibility'	425
4	Acquisition of parental responsibility by father	426
4ZA	Acquisition of parental responsibility by second female parent	429
4A	Acquisition of parental responsibility by step-parent	430
5	Appointment of guardians	431
6	Guardians: revocation and disclaimer	433
7	Welfare reports	434

PART II
ORDERS WITH RESPECT TO CHILDREN IN FAMILY PROCEEDINGS

General

8	Child arrangements orders and other orders with respect to children	438
9	Restrictions on making section 8 orders	450
10	Power of court to make section 8 orders	451
11	General principles and supplementary provisions	456
11A	Activity directions	458
11B	Activity directions: further provision	459
11C	Activity conditions	460
11D	Activity conditions: further provision	461
11E	Activity directions and conditions: making	461
11F	Activity directions and conditions: financial assistance	461
11G	Activity directions and conditions: monitoring	462
11H	Monitoring contact and shared residence	463
11I	Child arrangements orders: warning notices	464
11J	Enforcement orders	465
11K	Enforcement orders: further provision	466
11L	Enforcement orders: making	466
11M	Enforcement orders: monitoring	467
11N	Enforcement orders: warning notices	468
11O	Compensation for financial loss	468
11P	Orders under section 11O(2): further provision	469
12	Child arrangements orders and parental responsibility	469
13	Change of child's name or removal from jurisdiction	470

Special guardianship

14A	Special guardianship orders	473
14B	Special guardianship orders: making	476
14C	Special guardianship orders: effect	477
14D	Special guardianship orders: variation and discharge	477
14E	Special guardianship orders: supplementary	478
14F	Special guardianship support services	479

Financial relief

15	Orders for financial relief with respect to children	480

Family assistance orders

16	Family assistance orders	481
16A	Risk assessments	483

PART III
SUPPORT FOR CHILDREN AND FAMILIES PROVIDED BY LOCAL AUTHORITIES IN ENGLAND

Application to local authorities in England

16B	Application to local authorities in England	484

Provision of services for children and their families

17	Provision of services for children in need, their families and others	484
17ZA	Young carers' needs assessments	487
17ZB	Young carers' needs assessments: supplementary	488
17ZC	Consideration of young carers' needs assessments	488
17ZD	Parent carers' needs assessments	489
17ZE	Parent carers' needs assessments: supplementary	490
17ZF	Consideration of parent carers' needs assessments	490
17ZG	Section 17 services: continued provision where EHC plan maintained	490
17ZH	Section 17 services: transition for children to adult care and support.	491

17ZI Section 17 services: provision after EHC plan no longer maintained 492

Provision of accommodation for children

20 Provision of accommodation for children: general 492
21 Provision of accommodation for children in police protection or detention or on remand etc 495

Duties of local authorities in relation to children looked after by them

22 General duty of local authority in relation to children looked after by them 496
22A Provision of accommodation for children in care 498
22B Maintenance of looked after children 498
22C Ways in which looked after children are to be accommodated and maintained 498
22D Review of child's case before making alternative arrangements for accommodation 500
22E Children's homes provided by Secretary of State or Welsh Ministers 500
22F Regulations as to children looked after by local authorities 500
22G General duty of local authority to secure sufficient accommodation for looked after children 500

Visiting

23ZA Duty of local authority to ensure visits to, and contact with, looked after children and others 501
23ZB Independent visitors for children looked after by a local authority 501

Advice and assistance for certain children and young persons

23A The responsible authority and relevant children 502
23B Additional functions of the responsible authority in respect of relevant children 503
23C Continuing functions in respect of former relevant children 504
23CZA Arrangements for certain former relevant children to continue to live with former foster parents 505
23CA Further assistance to pursue education or training 505

Personal advisers and pathway plans

23D Personal advisers 506
23E Pathway plans 506
24 Persons qualifying for advice and assistance 507
24A Advice and assistance 508
24B Employment, education and training 509
24C Information 509
24D Representations: sections 23A to 24B 510

Secure accommodation

25 Use of accommodation for restricting liberty 510

Independent reviewing officers

25A Appointment of independent reviewing officer 513
25B Functions of the independent reviewing officer 513
25C Referred cases 514

Supplemental

26 Review of cases and inquiries into representations 514
26A Advocacy services 517
27 Co-operation between authorities 518
29 Recoupment of cost of providing services etc 518
30 Miscellaneous 520

PART IV
CARE AND SUPERVISION

General

31	Care and supervision orders	520
31A	Care orders: care plans	544
32	Period within which application for order under this Part must be disposed of	546

Care orders

33	Effect of care order	548
34	Parental contact etc with children in care	549

Supervision orders

35	Supervision orders	553
36	Education supervision orders	553

Powers of court

37	Powers of court in certain family proceedings	554
38	Interim orders	557
38A	Power to include exclusion requirement in interim care order	562
38B	Undertakings relating to interim care orders	563
39	Discharge and variation etc of care orders and supervision orders	563
40	Orders pending appeals in cases about care or supervision orders	565

Representation of child

41	Representation of child and of his interests in certain proceedings	567
42	Right of officer of the Service to have access to local authority records	570

PART V
PROTECTION OF CHILDREN

43	Child assessment orders	571
44	Orders for emergency protection of children	572
44A	Power to include exclusion requirement in emergency protection order	575
44B	Undertakings relating to emergency protection orders	576
45	Duration of emergency protection orders and other supplemental provisions	576
46	Removal and accommodation of children by police in cases of emergency	578
47	Local authority's duty to investigate	580
48	Powers to assist in discovery of children who may be in need of emergency protection	582
49	Abduction of children in care etc	583
50	Recovery of abducted children etc	583
51	Refuges for children at risk	585
52	Rules and regulations	586

PART VI
COMMUNITY HOMES

53	Provision of community homes by local authorities	586
55	Determination of disputes relating to controlled and assisted community homes	587
56	Discontinuance by voluntary organisation of controlled or assisted community home	588
57	Closure by local authority of controlled or assisted community home	588
58	Financial provisions applicable on cessation of controlled or assisted community home or disposal etc of premises	589

PART VII
VOLUNTARY HOMES AND VOLUNTARY ORGANISATIONS

59	Provision of accommodation by voluntary organisations	590

PART II

60	Voluntary homes	591
61	Duties of voluntary organisations	591
62	Duties of local authorities	592

PART VIII

REGISTERED CHILDREN'S HOMES

63	Private children's homes etc	593
64	Welfare of children in children's homes	593
65	Persons disqualified from carrying on, or being employed in, children's homes	594
65A	Appeal against refusal of authority to give consent under section 65	595

PART IX

PRIVATE ARRANGEMENTS FOR FOSTERING CHILDREN

66	Privately fostered children	595
67	Welfare of privately fostered children	595
68	Persons disqualified from being private foster parents	596
69	Power to prohibit private fostering	597
70	Offences	598

PART XA

CHILD MINDING AND DAY CARE FOR CHILDREN IN WALES

Introductory

79A	Child minders and day care providers	598
79B	Other definitions, etc	599

Regulations

79C	Regulations etc governing child minders and day care providers	600

Registration

79D	Requirement to register	601
79E	Applications for registration	601
79F	Grant or refusal of registration	602
79G	Cancellation of registration	602
79H	Suspension of registration	603
79J	Resignation of registration	603
79K	Protection of children in an emergency	603
79L	Notice of intention to take steps	604
79M	Appeals	604

Supplementary

79U	Rights of entry etc	605
79V	Function of local authorities	606

Checks on suitability of persons working with children over the age of seven

79W	Requirement for certificate of suitability	606

Time limit for proceedings

79X	Time limit for proceedings	607

PART XI

SECRETARY OF STATE'S SUPERVISORY FUNCTIONS AND RESPONSIBILITIES

80	Inspection of children's homes etc by persons authorised by Secretary of State	607
82	Financial support by Secretary of State	609
83	Research and returns of information	610
84	Local authority failure to comply with statutory duty: default power of Secretary of State	611

PART XII
MISCELLANEOUS AND GENERAL

Notification of children accommodated in certain establishments

85	Children accommodated by health authorities and local education authorities	611
86	Children accommodated in care homes or independent hospitals	612
86A	Visitors for children notified to local authority	613
87	Welfare of children in boarding schools and colleges	613
87A	Suspension of duty under section 87(3)	615
87B	Duties of inspectors under section 87A	616
87BA	Quality assurance of inspectors under section 87A.	616
87C	Boarding schools: national minimum standards	617
87D	Annual fee for boarding school inspections	617

Criminal care and supervision orders

90	Care and supervision orders in criminal proceedings	617

Effect and duration of orders etc

91	Effect and duration of orders etc	617

Jurisdiction and procedure etc

92	Jurisdiction of courts	621
93	Rules of court	621
95	Attendance of child at hearing under Part IV or V	622
96	Evidence given by, or with respect to, children	623
97	Privacy for children involved in certain proceedings	626
98	Self-incrimination	629
100	Restrictions on use of wardship jurisdiction	630
101	Effect of orders as between England and Wales and Northern Ireland, the Channel Islands or the Isle of Man	632

Search warrants

102	Power of constable to assist in exercise of certain powers to search for children or inspect premises	633

General

103	Offences by bodies corporate	633
104	Regulations and orders	634
104A	Regulations made by the Welsh Ministers under section 31A or Part 7	634
105	Interpretation	634
106	Financial provisions	638
107	Application to Channel Islands	638
108	Short title, commencement, extent etc	638
	Schedule A1 – Enforcement orders	640
	Part I – Unpaid work requirement	640
	Part II – Revocation, amendment or breach of enforcement order	641
	Schedule 1 – Financial Provision for Children	644
	Schedule 2 – Support for Children and Families Provided by Local Authorities in England	657
	Part I – Provision of Services for Families	657
	Part II – Children Looked After by Local Authorities in England	660
	Part III – Contributions Towards Maintenance of Children Looked After by Local Authorities in England	666
	Schedule 3 – Supervision Orders	670
	Part I – General	670
	Part II – Miscellaneous	672
	Part III – Education Supervision Orders	673
	Schedule 7 – Foster Parents: Limits on Number of Foster Children	676

PART II

Schedule 8 – Privately Fostered Children 678
Schedule 9A – Child Minding and Day Care for Young Children in Wales 681

PART I
INTRODUCTORY

1 Welfare of the child

(1) When a court determines any question with respect to –

(a) the upbringing of a child; or
(b) the administration of a child's property or the application of any income arising from it,

the child's welfare shall be the court's paramount consideration.

(2) In any proceedings in which any question with respect to the upbringing of a child arises, the court shall have regard to the general principle that any delay in determining the question is likely to prejudice the welfare of the child.

(2A) A court, in the circumstances mentioned in subsection (4)(a) or (7), is as respects each parent within subsection (6)(a) to presume, unless the contrary is shown, that involvement of that parent in the life of the child concerned will further the child's welfare.

(2B) In subsection (2A) 'involvement' means involvement of some kind, either direct or indirect, but not any particular division of a child's time.

(3) In the circumstances mentioned in subsection (4), a court shall have regard in particular to –

(a) the ascertainable wishes and feelings of the child concerned (considered in the light of his age and understanding);
(b) his physical, emotional and educational needs;
(c) the likely effect on him of any change in his circumstances;
(d) his age, sex, background and any characteristics of his which the court considers relevant;
(e) any harm which he has suffered or is at risk of suffering;
(f) how capable each of his parents, and any other person in relation to whom the court considers the question to be relevant, is of meeting his needs;
(g) the range of powers available to the court under this Act in the proceedings in question.

(4) The circumstances are that –

(a) the court is considering whether to make, vary or discharge a section 8 order, and the making, variation or discharge of the order is opposed by any party to the proceedings; or
(b) the court is considering whether to make, vary or discharge a special guardianship order or an order under Part IV.

(5) Where a court is considering whether or not to make one or more orders under this Act with respect to a child, it shall not make the order or any of the orders unless it considers that doing so would be better for the child than making no order at all.

(6) In subsection (2A) 'parent' means parent of the child concerned; and, for the purposes of that subsection, a parent of the child concerned –

(a) is within this paragraph if that parent can be involved in the child's life in a way that does not put the child at risk of suffering harm; and
(b) is to be treated as being within paragraph (a) unless there is some evidence before the court in the particular proceedings to suggest that involvement of that parent in the child's life would put the child at risk of suffering harm whatever the form of the involvement.

(7) The circumstances referred to are that the court is considering whether to make an order under section 4(1)(c) or (2A) or 4ZA(1)(c) or (5) (parental responsibility of parent other than mother).

Amendments—ACA 2002, s 115; CFA 2014, s 11.

Defined terms—'child', 'upbringing': s 105(1).

Delay generally (s 1(2))—The general principle that delay is harmful applies to any proceedings concerning 'the upbringing' of a child, but does not apply where the question at issue is the child's maintenance. Both practitioners and courts have a duty to avoid delay in children cases. A children's guardian has a duty to review the file regularly and, if the case is not making satisfactory progress, should apply for directions (*B v B (Minors) (Interviews and Listing Arrangements)* [1994] 2 FLR 489, CA, *Re A and B (Minors) (No 2)* [1995] 1 FLR 351, FD, and *B v B (Child Abuse: Contact)* [1994] 2 FLR 713, FD). The possibility of avoiding delay by arranging for a split hearing should be borne in mind (*Re S (Care Proceedings: Split Hearing)* [1996] 2 FLR 773, FD, considered further under s 31), but a split hearing should not be ordered unless the case cannot properly be decided without one. See further **Split hearings** under s 31 and FPR 2010, r 12.12. See *London Borough of Redbridge v A, B and E (Failure to Comply with Directions)* [2016] EWHC 2627 (Fam), where the court adjourned a final hearing in care proceedings concerning a 2-year old child where the local authority had failed comprehensively to comply with case management directions. The court reiterated the importance of compliance with case management directions to the fair administration of justice, stating that such directions were the key tool by which the court maintained fidelity to the statutory principle in s 1(2).

However, it is the welfare of the child that is the court's paramount consideration (s 1(1)) and there are bound to be cases in which delay will improve the chances of meeting the child's needs satisfactorily (for example, where a parent needs time to resolve housing difficulties, or where it is felt that the court would benefit from a full investigation and report from a psychiatrist, or where, as in *C v Solihull MBC* [1993] 1 FLR 290, FD and *Hounslow LBC v A* [1993] 1 FLR 702, FD, an investigation by the local authority is not yet complete, or where, as in *Re W (Welfare Reports)* [1995] 2 FLR 142, CA, the need to ensure that the court is as fully informed and advised as possible outweighs the disadvantage of delay caused by ordering a court welfare report). See, for example, *Re T (A Child)* [2016] EWCA Civ 1210, where it was held that in a father's application for contact, the court had been wrong to decide not to hold a fact-finding hearing to investigate the mother's allegations that when she herself was a teenager the father had abused her. Despite the long delays in the case, it was necessary, proportionate and fair to have a fact-finding hearing before deciding the welfare issues.

See also **Delay occasioned by obtaining a welfare report** and **Court differing with recommendations in welfare report** under s 7. For consideration of the difficult problem of when the court should cease to be involved in the case and should hand over to the local authority by making a full care order, see under s 38.

Public Law Outline (PLO)—The PLO is contained in PD12A and applies to all courts hearing applications issued by local authorities under CA 1989, Pt IV (care and supervision orders). See further **Public Law Outline (PLO)** under FPR 2010, r 12.22 and **Case management hearing** and **Issues resolution hearing** under FPR 2010, Pt 12.

Child Arrangements Programme (CAP)—The framework for private law cases is contained in the CAP in FPR PD12B; replaces the Private Law Programme.

Delay and pending criminal proceedings—The fact that criminal proceedings are pending does not prevent the court exercising its discretion to proceed to hear a related children's case in order to avoid undesirable delay. The court must balance all the factors involved, taking into account any risk of prejudice to the accused and any risk so far as the child is concerned (*Re TB (Care Proceedings: Criminal Trial)* [1995] 2 FLR 801, CA). Each case must be decided on its merits. The welfare of the child has to take precedence over the detriment to the family facing criminal proceedings. In October 2013, a Protocol and Good Practice Model (see Part V) was published to provide guidance on disclosure of information in cases of alleged child abuse and linked criminal and care directions hearings. The protocol came into force on 1 January 2014 and applies to cases involving criminal investigations into alleged child abuse (child victims who were aged 17 and under at the time of the alleged offending) and/or Family Court proceedings concerning a child (aged 17 and under).

Related provisions—The provision as to delay is related to other provisions of the Act, namely s 11 (duty of the court in s 8 proceedings to draw up a timetable and to give appropriate directions) and s 32(1) (corresponding duty in proceedings under s 31 for a care or supervision order). See also the provisions as to timing contained in FPR 2010, rr 12.12 (Directions) and 12.13 (Timetables).

Presumption of involvement of both parents (ss 1(2A) and 1(2B))—From October 2014, s 1 has been amended (by CFA 2014) so that the court is now required, when considering whether to make, vary or discharge a s 8 order that is opposed, to presume, unless the contrary is shown, that the involvement of that parent in the life of the child concerned will further the child's welfare, provided that the parent concerned can be involved in a way that does not put the child at risk of suffering harm. Section 1(2B) defines 'involvement' as meaning involvement of some kind, either direct or indirect, but not any particular division of a child's time.

Welfare checklist factors—The s 1(3) checklist sets out a range of factors to be taken into account and the weight of each factor will vary from case to case. The court does not need expressly to highlight each matter in the checklist when giving reasons because any experienced family judge will be assumed to be well aware of the contents of the statutory checklist and can be assumed to have had regard to it whether or not this is spelled out in a judgment (*H v H (Residence Order: Leave to Remove from Jurisdiction)* [1995] 1 FLR 529, CA; *Re G (Children)* [2006] 2 FLR 629, HL). However, it is important is for the judge to demonstrate that he or she has the relevant factors in mind and to indicate that the analysis itself has relied on an approach compatible with the law (*Re E (Adoption Order: Proportionality of Outcome to Circumstances)* [2014] 2 FLR 514, CA; *Re T (A Child) (Suspension of Contact: Section 91(14) CA 1989)* [2016] 1 FLR 916, CA). In a case where a child has complex needs, it is particularly important for the judge to engage adequately in the welfare exercise and to highlight the parts that are relevant to the issues in the case so the parties can understand the reasons for the judge's decision (*Re H (A Child)* 29 June 2016, CA, McFarlane, Lindblom LJJ, unreported). The checklist can ensure that all relevant matters in a case are considered and balanced (*B v B (Residence Order: Reasons for Decision)* [1997] 2 FLR 602, CA; *Re F (Children)* [2015] EWCA Civ 1315). However, it is always open to the court to specify other matters that are relevant. It has also been cautioned that the checklist cannot be

PART II

construed so as to read into it some hierarchy of weight or presumptions (*Re P-S* [2014] 2 FLR 27, CA; *Re D (Withdrawal of Parental Responsibility)* [2015] 1 FLR 166, CA).

Children's wishes and feelings—Section 1(3)(a) is a statement of fundamental principle and in every case the court is required to ensure that the child is given the opportunity to be heard; that means asking whether and, if so, how the child is to be heard (*Re D (A Child) (International Recognition)* [2016] 2 FLR 347, CA). However, children's wishes and feelings are not determinative – it is their welfare that takes priority (*Re H (A Child)* [2014] EWCA Civ 271; *Re M (Children)* [2015] EWCA Civ 994). The wishes and feelings of a mature child do not carry any precedence over any other factors *Re P-S* [2014] 2 FLR 27, CA), although see for example *Re X (A Child)* [2014] EWHC 1871 (Fam), where a 13-year-old girl's wishes were a determinative factor in the court's decision that it would be in her best interests to have the pregnancy terminated, and *Re JS (Disposal of Body)* [2016] EWHC 2859 (Fam), where a terminally ill 14-year-old girl's wishes were a key factor in the court's decision to make a specific issue order granting the mother to make arrangements during the child's lifetime for the preservation of her body after death. However, it is not always possible to find out reliably, or at all, what the root cause of a child's wishes and feelings is and there are very often a number of factors in play (*Re W (Children) (Contact Dispute) (No 2)* [2014] EWCA Civ 401). In *Re A and B (Contact) (No 4)* [2016] 2 FLR 429, FD, it was held that a child's wishes and feelings about contact may be overridden by the court's assessment of his or her best interests. In relocation cases, the welfare checklist should be applied and the child's wishes and feelings are a factor in that process, although they will not necessarily be determinative (*Re M (Republic of Ireland) (Child's Objections) (Joinder of Children as Parties to Appeal)* [2015] 2 FLR 1074, CA). In the majority of cases, it is usual to obtain an independent Cafcass report on the child's wishes and feelings, and that will be the case if the child is having contact that would be disrupted by relocation. The court should discourage any over-prescriptive or over-intellectualised approach, and instead require a 'straightforward' analysis of the simple question: 'does the child object to being returned to his or her country of habitual residence?' (*Re M (Republic of Ireland) (Child's Objections) (Joinder of Children as Parties to Appeal)* [2015] 2 FLR 1074, CA). Whether a child objects will be a question of fact to be analysed on the evidence (*Re F (Child's Objections)* [2015] EWCA Civ 1022). However, in some cases no report will be necessary and to order it would be a misuse of resources: *Re T (A Child)* (19 November 2015, Elias LJ , Beatson LJ, Baker J, unreported).

No order (s 1(5))—Section 1(5) does not create a presumption one way or the other. All it demands is that before the court makes any order it must ask the question: 'Will it be better for the child to make the order than making no order at all?' (*Re G (Children)* [2006] 1 FLR 771, CA). For an example of the approach being adopted by the courts in relation to the 'no order' principle see *Re J (Refusal of Contact)* [2013] 2 FLR 1042, CA and *Re L & B (Children) (Specific Issues: Temporary Leave to Remove from the Jurisdiction; Circumcision)* [2016] EWHC 849 (Fam). Where the court makes no order, there should still be a written order to that effect (*S v R (Parental Responsibility)* [1993] 1 FCR 331, FD). If appropriate, it is possible for the order to recite the intention of the parties at the time of the order, as a preliminary to stating that the court considered an order unnecessary (*M v M (Defined Contact Application)* [1998] 2 FLR 244, FD in which there was an order of 'no order as to defined contact' but with the parents' joint wishes and expectations set out in the preamble). The all-encompassing nature of the concept of parental responsibility underpins the no-order principle in s 1(5): the expectation that, all other things being equal, parents will exercise their responsibility so as to contribute to the welfare of their child without the need for a court order defining or restricting that exercise (*Re D (Withdrawal of Parental Responsibility)* [2015] 1 FLR 166, CA).

2 Parental responsibility for children

(1) Where a child's father and mother were married to each other at the time of his birth, they shall each have parental responsibility for the child.

(1A) Where a child –

(a) has a parent by virtue of section 42 of the Human Fertilisation and Embryology Act 2008; or

(b) has a parent by virtue of section 43 of that Act and is a person to whom section 1(3) of the Family Law Reform Act 1987 applies,

the child's mother and the other parent shall each have parental responsibility for the child.

(2) Where a child's father and mother were not married to each other at the time of his birth –

(a) the mother shall have parental responsibility for the child;

(b) the father shall have parental responsibility for the child if he has acquired it (and has not ceased to have it) in accordance with the provisions of this Act.

(2A) Where a child has a parent by virtue of section 43 of the Human Fertilisation and Embryology Act 2008 and is not a person to whom section 1(3) of the Family Law Reform Act 1987 applies –

(a) the mother shall have parental responsibility for the child;

(b) the other parent shall have parental responsibility for the child if she has acquired it (and has not ceased to have it) in accordance with the provisions of this Act.

(3) References in this Act to a child whose father and mother were, or (as the case may be) were not, married to each other at the time of his birth must be read with section 1 of the Family Law Reform Act 1987 (which extends their meaning).

(4) The rule of law that a father is the natural guardian of his legitimate child is abolished.

(5) More than one person may have parental responsibility for the same child at the same time.

(6) A person who has parental responsibility for a child at any time shall not cease to have that responsibility solely because some other person subsequently acquires parental responsibility for the child.

(7) Where more than one person has parental responsibility for a child, each of them may act alone and without the other (or others) in meeting that responsibility; but nothing in this Part shall be taken to affect the operation of any enactment which requires the consent of more than one person in a matter affecting the child.

(8) The fact that a person has parental responsibility for a child shall not entitle him to act in any way which would be incompatible with any order made with respect to the child under this Act.

(9) A person who has parental responsibility for a child may not surrender or transfer any part of that responsibility to another but may arrange for some or all of it to be met by one or more persons acting on his behalf.

(10) The person with whom any such arrangement is made may himself be a person who already has parental responsibility for the child concerned.

(11) The making of any such arrangement shall not affect any liability of the person making it which may arise from any failure to meet any part of his parental responsibility for the child concerned.

Amendments—ACA 2002, s 111; HFEA 2008, s 56, Sch 6, Pt 1, para 26(1)–(3).

3 Meaning of 'parental responsibility'

(1) In this Act 'parental responsibility' means all the rights, duties, powers, responsibilities and authority which by law a parent of a child has in relation to the child and his property.

(2) It also includes the rights, powers and duties which a guardian of the child's estate (appointed, before the commencement of section 5, to act generally) would have had in relation to the child and his property.

(3) The rights referred to in subsection (2) include, in particular, the right of the guardian to receive or recover in his own name, for the benefit of the child, property of whatever description and wherever situated which the child is entitled to receive or recover.

(4) The fact that a person has, or does not have, parental responsibility for a child shall not affect –

- (a) any obligation which he may have in relation to the child (such as a statutory duty to maintain the child); or
- (b) any rights which, in the event of the child's death, he (or any other person) may have in relation to the child's property.

(5) A person who –

- (a) does not have parental responsibility for a particular child; but
- (b) has care of the child,

may (subject to the provisions of this Act) do what is reasonable in all the circumstances of the case for the purpose of safeguarding or promoting the child's welfare.

Meaning of parental responsibility—The concept of parental responsibility describes an adult's responsibility to secure the welfare of their child, which is to be exercised for the benefit of the child, not the adult. It is clear that the status relates to welfare, not the mere existence of paternity or parenthood (*Re D (Withdrawal of Parental Responsibility)* [2015] 1 FLR 166, CA). See also *Re A and B (Children: Restrictions on Parental Responsibility: Radicalisation and Extremism)* [2016] 2 FLR 977, FD as an example where the court granted prohibited steps and specific issue orders permitting the mother to change the children's names and preventing the father from accessing their health and education information, thus effectively terminating his parental responsibility. Parental responsibility is an important part of family life – 'Whether or not a parent has parental responsibility is not simply a matter that achieves the ticking of a box on a form. It is a significant matter of status as between parent and child and, just as important, as between each of the parents' (*Re W*

(Direct Contact) [2013] 1 FLR 494, CA). See also *Re H-B (Contact)* [2015] EWCA Civ 389, where the court examined the true meaning of parental responsibility and outlined the conduct it expected of parents separating in hostile circumstances – parents too often focus on their 'rights' at the expense of their 'duties' and 'responsibilities'; each parent has to take full responsibility for ensuring that their children, no matter what age, have a good relationship with the other parent.

Hague Convention 1996—The Hague Convention 1996 came into force in the UK on 1 November 2012. Art 1 defines the meaning of 'parental responsibility' in cases to which the Convention applies. The definition is purposively broad and should be given an autonomous Convention meaning rather than its purely domestic law meaning. Arts 16-18 cover the attribution, extinction and exercise of parental responsibility in such cases. See commentary under the Convention in Part VI.

4 Acquisition of parental responsibility by father

(1) Where a child's father and mother were not married to each other at the time of his birth, the father shall acquire parental responsibility for the child if –

(a) he becomes registered as the child's father under any of the enactments specified in subsection (1A);

(b) he and the child's mother make an agreement (a 'parental responsibility agreement') providing for him to have parental responsibility for the child; or

(c) the court, on his application, orders that he shall have parental responsibility for the child.

(1A) The enactments referred to in subsection (1)(a) are –

(a) paragraphs (a), (b) and (c) of section 10(1) and of section 10A(1) of the Births and Deaths Registration Act 1953;

(b) paragraphs (a), (b)(i) and (c) of section 18(1), and sections 18(2)(b) and 20(1)(a) of the Registration of Births, Deaths and Marriages (Scotland) Act 1965; and

(c) sub-paragraphs (a), (b) and (c) of Article 14(3) of the Births and Deaths Registration (Northern Ireland) Order 1976.

(1B) The Secretary of State may by order amend subsection (1A) so as to add further enactments to the list in that subsection.

(2) No parental responsibility agreement shall have effect for the purposes of this Act unless –

(a) it is made in the form prescribed by regulations made by the Lord Chancellor; and

(b) where regulations are made by the Lord Chancellor prescribing the manner in which such agreements must be recorded, it is recorded in the prescribed manner.

(2A) A person who has acquired parental responsibility under subsection (1) shall cease to have that responsibility only if the court so orders.

(3) The court may make an order under subsection (2A) on the application –

(a) of any person who has parental responsibility for the child; or

(b) with leave of the court, of the child himself,

subject, in the case of parental responsibility acquired under subsection (1)(c), to section 12(4).

(4) The court may only grant leave under subsection (3)(b) if it is satisfied that the child has sufficient understanding to make the proposed application.

Amendments—ACA 2002, s 111; SI 2003/3191.

Defined terms—'child': s 105(1); 'parental responsibility': s 3.

Duty on parents to work to put aside differences—It is an integral aspect of parental responsibility that parents should work to put aside differences and ensure that their children have relationships with both parents (*Re W (Direct Contact)* [2013] 1 FLR 494, CA). See *T v S* [2013] EWHC 2521 (Fam), where Hedley J confirmed the general principle that the court cannot 'micro-manage' parenting (in this case the parents appeared unable even to agree where on the platform at Clapham Junction station they were to effect a handover of care – 'if the parties have other ideas and want to hand over on some empty platform or disused siding, that is a matter for them'.

Disputed paternity cases—From November 2015, Cafcass is able, in defined circumstances, to facilitate and fund the provision of DNA tests directed under FLRA 1969, s 20. See **Funding in disputed paternity cases** under CA 1989, s 8.

Father and mother not married to each other at time of child's birth (s 4(1))—Section 2(3) provides that references in the Act to a child whose father and mother were not married to each other at the time of his birth must be read with FLRA 1987, s 1. Consequently, where the child in question is treated as legitimate by virtue of the Legitimacy Act 1976, s 1 (legitimacy of children of certain void marriages), is a legitimated person under s 10 of that Act (legitimation in various circumstances such as by subsequent marriage of the child's parents), has been adopted by the parents within the meaning of AA 1976, Pt IV, or is otherwise treated in law as legitimate, the case does not fall within the provisions of s 4(1) (FLRA 1987, s 1(2), (3)). The time of a person's birth must be taken to include any time during the period beginning with the insemination resulting in his birth or, where there was no such insemination, his conception, and ending with his actual birth (FLRA 1987, s 1(4)). As to the parents of a child born of in vitro fertilisation, artificial insemination etc see HFEA 1990, ss 33–48.

Unmarried father acquires parental responsibility on registration or re-registration of birth—Since 1 December 2003 (under changes introduced by ACA 2002, s 111), a father who was not married to the mother at the time of the child's birth has parental responsibility if his name is placed on the birth certificate at registration or re-registration of the birth under the Births and Deaths Registration Act 1953, ss 10, 10A. Parental responsibility will run from the date of the registration rather than the birth. However, in reality, the unmarried father will not be able to register his name without the consent of the mother. Once the unmarried father acquires parental responsibility by such registration then parental responsibility can only be removed by order of court, on application by any person with parental responsibility for the child or, with permission, on the application of the child himself (provided he has sufficient understanding).

Parental responsibility order on application of father (s 4(1)(c))—Where the parents agree that the father should have parental responsibility, they may enter into a parental responsibility agreement. Where the mother is not prepared to do this or cannot be found, the father will have to apply to the court for a parental responsibility order (see Procedural Guide D6). The mother cannot apply under s 4 for an order against the father but, if she felt the father was not pulling his weight with regard to the child's upbringing, she would have other remedies open to her, for example a s 8 application or an application under Sch 1 for financial relief for the child. A father is entitled to ask the court to recognise his position as the father of the child irrespective of any question of residence or contact. The order confers on the committed father the status of parenthood for which nature has already ordained he must bear responsibility (*Re S (Parental Responsibility)* [1995] 2 FLR 648, CA, which contains a helpful review of the authorities; see also *Re D (Withdrawal of Parental Responsibility)* [2015] 1 FLR 166, CA, which encouraged the exercise of parental responsibility by fathers and confirmed that children have a right to that benefit). The court considers the degree of commitment the father has shown towards the child, the degree of attachment between him and the child and the reasons why he is applying for the order but these three requirements, though a starting point, are not intended to be exhaustive and the court must take into account all the relevant circumstances, bearing in mind that CA 1989, s 1 applies and the welfare of the child is therefore paramount (*Re H (Parental Responsibility)* [1998] 1 FLR 855, CA; *Re D (A Child)*, above). The leading case on the proper approach to determine parental responsibility is *Re C and V (Minors) (Contact: Parental Responsibility Order)* [1998] 1 FLR 392, CA and this indicates that such applications are to be considered wholly separately. In *Re W (Parental Responsibility Order: Inter-Relationship with Direct Contact)* [2013] 2 FLR 1337, CA, although a court had been entitled to refuse a father's application for direct contact with his son on the basis that the mother's fears from his playing any role in the child's life put his future stability and well-being at risk, it was wrong to refuse to grant the father parental responsibility based on that same reason; the PR application should have been considered separately and not refused because of the mother's speculative anxiety about contact. Where a father is unable to exercise such responsibility his application will be refused (*M v M (Parental Responsibility)* [1999] 2 FLR 737, FD). However, see *JB v KS and E (Contact: Parental Responsibility)* [2015] 2 FLR 1180, FD, where notwithstanding the court's order that the birth register should be amended so that the name of a committed biological father could appear on the child's birth certificate, he did not automatically obtain parental responsibility for the child as a result and protracted litigation ensued before the situation could be resolved.

Parental responsibility and same-sex families—In *A v B and C (Lesbian Co-Parents: Role of Father)* [2012] 2 FLR 607, CA, the Court of Appeal declined to give generalised guidance on parental responsibility and same-sex families and stressed that the only principle is the paramountcy of child welfare. See *Re G (Shared Residence Order: Biological Mother of Donor Egg)* [2014] 2 FLR 897, CA, for Black LJ's thorough review of the development of the case-law in relation to the court's approach to this issue – 'there is no universal solution and each case depends on its individual facts'. Each case must be looked at on its own facts in the absence of any guidance from the High Court or the Court of Appeal as to how to approach welfare issues such as parental responsibility and contact in families where children were conceived by adult arrangement outside sexual intercourse. See *JB v KS and E (Contact: Parental Responsibility)* [2015] 2 FLR 1180, FD, where Hayden J considered in detail the correct approach to determining whether a parental responsibility order should be made for a 4-year-old boy whose birth father and single lesbian mother had met on a co-parenting website and developed a relationship with the shared intention of parenting a child. Hayden J confirmed that it would be entirely wrong to approach the case as if the child had been born in the context of a loving heterosexual relationship and determine any of the issues on that premise. In that case, the court held that moral imperative was clear. The legal framework was predicated not on empowering anybody but ultimately in signalling responsibility for the child, the parents took their responsibilities to the child seriously and the legal framework should merely reflect that achievement. In that case, Hayden J identified a number of key features that pointed compellingly to the making of a parental responsibility order:

- the parents had a relationship spanning many years in which they had shown a real capacity to work co-operatively towards a shared objective, both prior to and after the child's birth;
- both had agreed at the outset that the father would be known to the child and play a part in his life;
- they had common aspirations for the child's future, both agreeing that the mother, as primary carer, was likely to take the key decisions in the child's life;
- it was highly unlikely that the father would use a parental responsibility order in any way to undermine the mother;
- the father provided financial support for the child;

PART II

- the order merely reflected the proper legal status of the father in the child's life and properly equipped him to exercise it; and
- the guardian supported the making of a parental responsibility order.

Known sperm donors—Where a man donates his sperm to a lesbian woman or couple, his application for parental responsibility must be considered in terms of the paramountcy of the child's welfare (*A v B and C (Lesbian Co-Parents: Role of Father)* [2012] 2 FLR 607, CA). See, for example, *Re D (Contact and PR: Lesbian Mothers and Known Father) (No 2)* [2006] EWHC 2 (Fam), where the sperm donor father was granted a parental responsibility order. By contrast, in *Re B (Role of Biological Father)* [2008] 1 FLR 1015, FD, *R v E and F (Female Parents: Known Father)* [2010] 2 FLR 383, FD, and *Re R (Parental Responsibility)* [2011] 2 FLR 1132, FD, the court dismissed the sperm donor fathers' applications for parental responsibility orders on a welfare basis. See *JB v KS and E (Contact: Parental Responsibility)* [2015] 2 FLR 1180, FD (see also **Same-sex parenting** under s 8).

Parental responsibility subject to conditions—When a parental responsibility order has been granted but it is necessary to limit the practical impact of the order so as to protect the integrity of the child's family, the court may impose certain conditions when making the accompanying child arrangements order (*Re D (Contact and PR: Lesbian Mothers and Known Father) (No 2)* [2006] EWHC 2 (Fam)).

Parental responsibility order not susceptible to suspension—Where the court decides to make a parental responsibility order it has no power under s 4 to suspend its operation, but it can adjourn the application with liberty to restore it if circumstances change (*Re G (Parental Responsibility Order)* [2006] 2 FLR 1092, CA).

Where natural unmarried father has not signed Birth Register but wishes to be acknowledged as the parent—In these circumstances, the father may make an application, either himself or jointly with the mother, to have the birth re-registered so as to show him as the father (Births and Deaths Registration Act 1953, s 10A). This may be done in one of several ways, by presenting the court with the appropriate declaration, statutory declaration of parentage (as to which see **Statutory declaration of parentage**, below), parental responsibility agreement or parental responsibility order in the prescribed form. Where he does so, he will acquire parental responsibility for the child (CA 1989, s 4(1)).

Statutory declaration of parentage—FLA 1986, s 55A provides for declarations of parentage and enables a person to apply to the High Court, the County Court or a magistrates' court for a declaration of parentage to confirm whether or not a person named in the application is or was the parent of another person so named (s 55A(1)). This remedies defects in the pre-existing law whereby, for example, a person could seek a declaration that someone else was his parent, but he could not seek confirmation of his own claim that he was a parent. Furthermore, previously it was not possible to obtain a declaration that a named person was *not* the parent of a particular child. There are various restrictions on applications made under s 55A (s 55A(2)), but the general rule is that the applicant must have a sufficient personal interest in the determination of the application (s 55A(3); see further s 55A). The procedure to be followed is set out in FPR 2010, rr 8.18–8.22. It would seem that, strictly speaking, a district judge (DJ) does not have jurisdiction to make a s 55A declaration, since the Family Proceedings (Allocation to Judiciary Directions) 2009, Sch D, provides that a nominated district judge can only deal with interlocutory matters on such an application. However, in *Re H (Contact with Biological Father)* [2012] 2 FLR 627, CA, the DJ had conducted a 3-day final hearing in such a case and, although the CA were critical of much of what the DJ did, they seemed to be untroubled about his making a s 55A declaration and that declaration being submitted to the Registrar General to have the birth certificate altered.

Parental responsibility where a care order is in force—As to the granting of a parental responsibility order where a care order is in force, see *Re G (A Minor) (Parental Responsibility Order)* [1994] 1 FLR 504, CA and *Re CB (A Minor) (Parental Responsibility Order)* [1993] 1 FLR 920, FD). Where a care order and a parental responsibility order co-exist, the local authority will also have parental responsibility for the child (s 33(3)(a)) and will have the power, subject to the provisions of s 33, to determine the extent to which the father may meet his parental responsibility (s 33(3)(b)). A local authority responsible for a child under a care order has no power to prevent the child's mother from entering into a parental responsibility agreement with the child's unmarried father (*Re X (Parental Responsibility Agreement: Children in Care)* [2000] 1 FLR 517, FD – where the court held that the facility under s 4(1)(b) for parents of a non-marital child to enter into a parental responsibility agreement is self-contained and does not depend on the exercise of such responsibility. The local authority's argument, that where a care order is in force it shares parental responsibility by virtue of s 33 and therefore has power to determine the extent to which a parent of a child might meet that responsibility, was rejected because the entry into the agreement by the mother did not amount to an exercise by her of parental responsibility).

Parental responsibility where child is accommodated by local authority—Where a child is simply accommodated by a local authority parental responsibility remains vested in the child's parents (i e is not shared by the local authority, as would be the case if a care order or interim care order were in force) and the local authority has no right to move the child from residential care to the home of foster parents without the consent of the child's parents, since parental responsibility includes the right to decide where the child lives (*R v Tameside Metropolitan Borough Council ex parte J* [2000] 1 FLR 942, QBD).

Jurisdiction—The jurisdiction of the court to make a parental responsibility order is not limited by the FLA 1986 and can be exercised in relation to a child who is permanently out of the jurisdiction, even if that child was also born out of the jurisdiction (*Re S (Parental Responsibility: Jurisdiction)* [1998] 2 FLR 921, CA).

Parental responsibility – ECHR 1950—The fact that English law treats unmarried fathers differently from married fathers in relation to the automatic acquisition of parental rights in relation to their children does not amount to a breach of Article 8 of the Convention (*B v UK* [2000] 1 FLR 1, ECHR). It is clear that the status of parental responsibility relates to welfare, not the mere existence of paternity or parenthood (*Smallwood v UK (29779/96)* (1999) 27 EHRR CD 155).

Automatic parental responsibility order for unmarried father—Where the court makes a child arrangements order in favour of an unmarried father naming him as a person with whom the child is to live, it must also, if he would not otherwise have parental responsibility for the child, make a parental responsibility order (s 12(1)). In *Re A (Joint Residence: Parental Responsibility)* [2008] 2 FLR 1593, CA the mother's former partner was not the biological parent of her child, but he brought up the child while they cohabited. The court made a joint residence order (under the old law) to ensure that the ex-partner would acquire parental responsibility and so prevent the mother from marginalising him in the future upbringing of the child. If, however, the father is only named as a person with whom the child is to spend time or otherwise have contact, (rather than being named in the order as a person with whom the child is to live), the court has a discretion as to whether also to make a parental responsibility order (s 12(1A)).

Parental responsibility agreement to be in prescribed form (s 4(2)(a))—The form of agreement is prescribed by Parental Responsibility Agreement Regulations 1991, reg 2 and is set out in the Schedule thereto. It must be signed by both parents and witnessed.

Agreement to be recorded in the prescribed manner (s 4(2)(b))—Parental Responsibility Agreement Regulations 1991, reg 3 prescribes the manner in which such agreements must be recorded.

Application for a parental responsibility order—On making an application to the court for parental responsibility, the applicant must also file a completed Form FM1 confirming attendance at a mediation information and assessment meeting (MIAM) or giving reasons for not attending (FPR PD3A, Annex A). See Guide D6 for procedure.

Application to terminate parental responsibility order or agreement (s 4(3))—Anyone with parental responsibility may apply as of right (see Procedural Guide D6). A child who wishes to apply must first seek permission (in accordance with FPR 2010, rr 8.1–8.13.

Section 1(1) applies when the court is considering whether to terminate parental responsibility (*Re A (Termination of Parental Responsibility)* [2014] 1 FLR 1305, FD; *Re D (Withdrawal of Parental Responsibility)* [2015] 1 FLR 166, CA). An unmarried father who has acquired parental responsibility pursuant to any of the routes in s 4(1) may have it terminated by the court; an unmarried father whose name was registered on the child's birth certificate is therefore placed in the same category as other unmarried fathers, rather than in the same category as married fathers (*CW v SG (Parental Responsibility: Consequential Orders)* [2013] 2 FLR 655, FD). Section 12(4) prevents the court bringing to an end a parental responsibility order made as a consequence of s 12(1) (see **Automatic parental responsibility order for unmarried father** above) at any time while the child arrangements order to which it is linked remains in force.

Leave under s 4(3)(b) not to be given unless child of sufficient understanding (s 4(4))—Although there are no reported authorities considering the question of the child's understanding in the context of an application for permission to seek the discharge of a parental responsibility order, assistance may be gained from authorities in relation to the child's understanding in other contexts within CA 1989. These are gathered together in the annotation **'able … to give such instructions on his own behalf'** under FPR 2010, r 16.29. The understanding of the child is the factor to which the court's attention is specifically directed, but it is unlikely to be the only relevant factor. Although the checklist of factors in s 1(3) does not apply specifically (see s 1(4)), it indicates the sort of matters that the court might want to consider in an appropriate case. By analogy with permission and other similar applications under other provisions of the Act and rules, the court will no doubt take into account the likelihood of success of the proposed application (see further under s 10). Whether the welfare of the child is paramount on the permission application seems to be a moot point and one which has not yet been considered in the context of s 4(3). See further under **Application for leave by child** under s 10.

Procedure where leave is given—If permission is given, the application proceeds in the normal way save that there is no need for an application form to be filed because the court will already have received a draft with the appropriate number of copies as part of the permission application (FPR 2010, rr 18.1–18.13).

Family proceedings—Any application under this section is classified as 'family proceedings' (s 8(3),(4)).

Hague Convention 1996—See under s 3.

4ZA Acquisition of parental responsibility by second female parent

(1) Where a child has a parent by virtue of section 43 of the Human Fertilisation and Embryology Act 2008 and is not a person to whom section 1(3) of the Family Law Reform Act 1987 applies, that parent shall acquire parental responsibility for the child if –

(a) she becomes registered as a parent of the child under any of the enactments specified in subsection (2);

(b) she and the child's mother make an agreement providing for her to have parental responsibility for the child; or

(c) the court, on her application, orders that she shall have parental responsibility for the child.

(2) The enactments referred to in subsection (1)(a) are –

(a) paragraphs (a), (b) and (c) of section 10(1B) and of section 10A(1B) of the Births and Deaths Registration Act 1953;

(b) paragraphs (a), (b) and (d) of section 18B(1) and sections 18B(3)(a) and 20(1)(a) of the Registration of Births, Deaths and Marriages (Scotland) Act 1965; and

(c) sub-paragraphs (a), (b) and (c) of Article 14ZA(3) of the Births and Deaths Registration (Northern Ireland) Order 1976.

(3) The Secretary of State may by order amend subsection (2) so as to add further enactments to the list in that subsection.

(4) An agreement under subsection (1)(b) is also a 'parental responsibility agreement', and section 4(2) applies in relation to such an agreement as it applies in relation to parental responsibility agreements under section 4.

(5) A person who has acquired parental responsibility under subsection (1) shall cease to have that responsibility only if the court so orders.

(6) The court may make an order under subsection (5) on the application –

(a) of any person who has parental responsibility for the child; or

(b) with the leave of the court, of the child himself,

subject, in the case of parental responsibility acquired under subsection (1)(c), to section 12(4).

(7) The court may only grant leave under subsection (6)(b) if it is satisfied that the child has sufficient understanding to make the proposed application.

Amendments—Inserted by HFEA 2008, s 56, Sch 6, Pt 1, para 27.

Scope—This provision enables a second female parent to acquire parental responsibility for a child where she becomes registered as a parent of the child under the statutory provisions set out in subsection (2), or enters into an agreement with the child's mother or by order of the court. An agreement will be a 'parental responsibility agreement' within the definition of CA 1989, s 4(2) and will only be terminated by the court on application by anyone with parental responsibility for the child or, with permission, on application by the child himself.

Procedure—The procedure for applying for a parental responsibility order under s 4ZA, and for applying to discharge a parental responsibility or agreement, is the same as for s 4: see Procedural Guide D6.

Automatic parental responsibility order for second female parent—Where the court makes a child arrangements order in favour of a woman who is a parent of the child by virtue of HFEA 2008, s 43 naming her as a person with whom the child is to live, it must also, if she would not otherwise have parental responsibility for the child, make a parental responsibility order (s 12(1)). If, however, the woman is only named as a person with whom the child is to spend time or otherwise have contact, (rather than being named in the order as a person with whom the child is to live), the court has a discretion as to whether also to make a parental responsibility order (s 12(1A)).

Principles—See *Re G (Shared Residence Order: Biological Mother of Donor Egg)* [2014] 2 FLR 897, CA for a comprehensive review of the legal framework governing parental responsibility in the context of the expanded boundaries of legal parenthood, including confirmation that in the context of same-sex relationships, while the only governing principle remains the paramountcy of the child's welfare, particular consideration must be given to the part that each adult can play in the child's life. See also *L v C* [2015] 1 FLR 674, FD, where the court confirmed that there is no precise definition of 'family life'; it is a question of fact, and one of substance not form. There is no pre-determined model of what constitutes a family. With less conventional family structures, the court must take a broad, purposive approach and family life must be interpreted in the light of modern trends.

Prescribed form for parental responsibility agreement—See under s 4.

Application to terminate parental responsibility order or agreement—See under s 4.

Leave under s 4ZA(7) not to be given unless child of sufficient understanding—See under s 4.

Procedure where leave is given—See under s 4.

Hague Convention 1996—See under s 3.

4A Acquisition of parental responsibility by step-parent

(1) Where a child's parent ('parent A') who has parental responsibility for the child is married to, or a civil partner of, a person who is not the child's parent ('the step-parent') –

(a) parent A or, if the other parent of the child also has parental responsibility for the child, both parents may by agreement with the step-parent provide for the step-parent to have parental responsibility for the child; or

(b) the court may, on the application of the step-parent, order that the step-parent shall have parental responsibility for the child.

(2) An agreement under subsection (1)(a) is also a 'parental responsibility agreement', and section 4(2) applies in relation to such agreements as it applies in relation to parental responsibility agreements under section 4.

(3) A parental responsibility agreement under subsection (1)(a), or an order under subsection (1)(b), may only be brought to an end by an order of the court made on the application –

(a) of any person who has parental responsibility for the child; or
(b) with the leave of the court, of the child himself.

(4) The court may only grant leave under subsection (3)(b) if it is satisfied that the child has sufficient understanding to make the proposed application.

Amendments—Inserted by ACA 2002, s 112. Amended by CPA 2004, s 75(1),(2).

Scope—This provision enables a step-parent to acquire parental responsibility for a child of his spouse by agreement between the step-parent and the parents who have parental responsibility for the child, or by order of the court. This will be a 'parental responsibility agreement' within the definition of CA 1989, s 4(2) and will only be terminated by the court on application by any person with parental responsibility for the child, or, with permission, on application by the child himself.

Procedure—The procedure for applying for a parental responsibility order under s 4A, and for applying to discharge a parental responsibility order or agreement, is the same as that for s 4: see Procedural Guide D6.

Extent of court's power under s 4A—Where the husband is married to the mother of the child but is not the biological parent, s 4A is the only available route by which he can seek parental responsibility. The fact that he has become the psychological parent of the child is significant but will not necessarily be sufficient to invest him with an ongoing major role in the child's life (*Re R (Parental Responsibility)* [2011] 2 FLR 1132, FD).

Automatic parental responsibility for a step-parent or other non-parent—Where the court makes a child arrangements order (CAO) for a person who is not a parent or guardian of the child, naming them as a person with whom the child is to live, that person must also be given parental responsibility for the child while the order remains in force in those terms (s 12(2)). However, where a court makes a CAO for that person but they are only named in the order as a person with whom the child is to spend time or otherwise have contact (but not to live) then the court has a discretion as to whether also to make a parental responsibility order (s 12(2A)).

Parental responsibility agreement to be in prescribed form—See under s 4.

Agreement to be recorded in the prescribed manner—See under s 4.

Application to terminate parental responsibility order or agreement—See under s 4.

Leave under s 4A(3)(b) not to be given unless child of sufficient understanding (s 4A(4))—See under s 4.

Procedure where leave is given—See under s 4.

Hague Convention 1996—See under s 3.

5 Appointment of guardians

(1) Where an application with respect to a child is made to the court by any individual, the court may by order appoint that individual to be the child's guardian or special guardian if –

(a) the child has no parent with parental responsibility for him; or
(b) a parent, guardian or special guardian of the child's was named in a child arrangements order as a person with whom the child was to live and has died while the order was in force; or
(c) paragraph (b) does not apply, and the child's only or last surviving special guardian dies.

(2) The power conferred by subsection (1) may also be exercised in any family proceedings if the court considers that the order should be made even though no application has been made for it.

(3) A parent who has parental responsibility for his child may appoint another individual to be the child's guardian in the event of his death.

(4) A guardian of a child may appoint another individual to take his place as the child's guardian in the event of his death; and a special guardian of a child may appoint another individual to be the child's guardian in the event of his death.

(5) An appointment under subsection (3) or (4) shall not have effect unless it is made in writing, is dated and is signed by the person making the appointment or –

(a) in the case of an appointment made by a will which is not signed by the testator, is signed at the direction of the testator in accordance with the requirements of section 9 of the Wills Act 1837; or

(b) in any other case, is signed at the direction of the person making the appointment, in his presence and in the presence of two witnesses who each attest the signature.

(6) A person appointed as a child's guardian under this section shall have parental responsibility for the child concerned.

(7) Where –

(a) on the death of any person making an appointment under subsection (3) or (4), the child concerned has no parent with parental responsibility for him; or

(b) immediately before the death of any person making such an appointment, a child arrangements order was in force in which the person was named as a person with whom the child was to live or the person was the child's only (or last surviving) special guardian,

the appointment shall take effect on the death of that person.

(8) Where, on the death of any person making an appointment under subsection (3) or (4) –

(a) the child concerned has a parent with parental responsibility for him; and

(b) subsection (7)(b) does not apply,

the appointment shall take effect when the child no longer has a parent who has parental responsibility for him.

(9) Subsections (1) and (7) do not apply if the child arrangements order referred to in paragraph (b) of those subsections also named a surviving parent of the child as a person with whom the child was to live.

(10) Nothing in this section shall be taken to prevent an appointment under subsection (3) or (4) being made by two or more persons acting jointly.

(11) Subject to any provision made by rules of court, no court shall exercise the High Court's inherent jurisdiction to appoint a guardian of the estate of any child.

(12) Where the rules of court are made under subsection (11) they may prescribe the circumstances in which, and conditions subject to which, an appointment of such a guardian may be made.

(13) A guardian of a child may only be appointed in accordance with the provisions of this section.

Amendments—ACA 2002, s 115; CFA 2014, s 12, Sch 2.

Defined terms—'child': s 105(1); 'child arrangements order': s 8(1); 'family proceedings': s 8(3); 'parental responsibility': s 3.

Scope—A guardian appointed under this section will generally take over parental responsibility for the child after the death of a parent and must, of course, be distinguished from a guardian ad litem appointed for the purposes of legal proceedings.

Application by any individual (s 5(1))—Application must be made by the person who wishes to be appointed as guardian. 'Individual' is not defined in the Act; it clearly does not include a company or a local authority, or even an 'artificial individual' within the local authority such as the director of social services (*Re SH (Care Order: Orphan)* [1995] 1 FLR 746, FD). However, there is nothing to prevent a number of individuals each launching separate applications and this could lead to the appointment of a couple, for example, an aunt and uncle. Although there does not seem to be any bar on an application by a minor, good sense suggests that the court would be unlikely to grant an application by one child to be appointed to act as guardian for another.

'power ... may also be exercised in any family proceedings' (s 5(2))—If it thinks fit, the court may, in any family proceedings, make an order appointing a guardian of its own initiative without any formal application having been filed. No doubt such an order will most frequently be prompted at the suggestion of a party to the proceedings or of an interested friend or relative who has been allowed to address the court, or even of the child himself, but there is nothing to prevent the court itself taking the lead in appropriate circumstances.

Date from which the appointment is effective—There may be a delay between a guardian being named (eg in a will or in a court order) and the time when he actually acquires parental responsibility for the child concerned. Although the Act makes no specific provision, it is apparent that the guardian is not regarded as having been appointed in accordance with the provisions of this section until the later stage.

Family proceedings—Any application under this section is classified as 'family proceedings' (s 8(3),(4)).

Procedure—A guardian may be appointed in writing by a parent with parental responsibility, the appointment to take effect when he dies (if he has in his favour a child arrangements order naming him as a person with whom the child is to live) or when the last surviving parent with parental responsibility dies. In default (or in addition), the court has a concurrent right of appointment. The court may also terminate the appointment of a guardian, whether he had been appointed by the court or a parent (CA 1989, s 6(7)). On making an application to the court, the applicant must also file a completed Form FM1 confirming attendance at a mediation information and assessment meeting or giving reasons for not attending (FPR PD3A, para 12(c)).

Hague Convention 1996—The Hague Convention 1996 came into force in the UK on 1 November 2012. It lays down rules in respect of measures directed to the protection of the person or property of the child in cases to which the Convention applies (Art 1). 'Measures of protection' include guardianship, curatorship or analogous institutions (Art 3). They are intended to include systems of protection, representation or assistance that are established in favour of a child when his parents are deceased or are no longer authorised to represent him (*Handbook*, para 3.23; *Lagarde Report*, para 21). See further under the Convention in Part VI.

6 Guardians: revocation and disclaimer

(1) An appointment under section 5(3) or (4) revokes an earlier such appointment (including one made in an unrevoked will or codicil) made by the same person in respect of the same child, unless it is clear (whether as the result of an express provision in the later appointment or by any necessary implication) that the purpose of the later appointment is to appoint an additional guardian.

(2) An appointment under section 5(3) or (4) (including one made in an unrevoked will or codicil) is revoked if the person who made the appointment revokes it by a written and dated instrument which is signed –

- (a) by him; or
- (b) at his direction, in his presence and in the presence of two witnesses who each attest the signature.

(3) An appointment under section 5(3) or (4) (other than one made in a will or codicil) is revoked if, with the intention of revoking the appointment, the person who made it –

- (a) destroys the instrument by which it was made; or
- (b) has some other person destroy that instrument in his presence.

(3A) An appointment under section 5(3) or (4) (including one made in an unrevoked will or codicil) is revoked if the person appointed is the spouse of the person who made the appointment and either –

- (a) a decree of a court of civil jurisdiction in England and Wales dissolves or annuls the marriage, or
- (b) the marriage is dissolved or annulled and the divorce or annulment is entitled to recognition in England and Wales by virtue of Part II of the Family Law Act 1986,

unless a contrary intention appears by the appointment.

(3B) An appointment under section 5(3) or (4) (including one made in an unrevoked will or codicil) is revoked if the person appointed is the civil partner of the person who made the appointment and either –

- (a) an order of a court of civil jurisdiction in England and Wales dissolves or annuls the civil partnership, or
- (b) the civil partnership is dissolved or annulled and the dissolution or annulment is entitled to recognition in England and Wales by virtue of Chapter 3 of Part 5 of the Civil Partnership Act 2004,

unless a contrary intention appears by the appointment.

(4) For the avoidance of doubt, an appointment under section 5(3) or (4) made in a will or codicil is revoked if the will or codicil is revoked.

(5) A person who is appointed as a guardian under section 5(3) or (4) may disclaim his appointment by an instrument in writing signed by him and made within a reasonable time of his first knowing that the appointment has taken effect.

(6) Where regulations are made by the Lord Chancellor prescribing the manner in which such disclaimers must be recorded, no such disclaimer shall have effect unless it is recorded in the prescribed manner.

(7) Any appointment of a guardian under section 5 may be brought to an end at any time by order of the court –

(a) on the application of any person who has parental responsibility for the child;
(b) on the application of the child concerned, with leave of the court; or
(c) in any family proceedings, if the court considers that it should be brought to an end even though no application has been made.

Amendments—Law Reform (Succession) Act 1995, s 4; CPA 2004, s 76.

Defined terms—'child': s 105(1); 'family proceedings': s 8(3); 'parental responsibility': s 3.

Scope—This section deals with the ways in which the appointment of a guardian may be brought to an end (i e by revocation, disclaimer or court order). It has been extended to provide for the revocation of appointment of a guardian, in the absence of any express contrary intention, in the case of an appointment of a former spouse or civil partner as guardian in the will of a testator dying after 1 January 1996 by dissolution or annulment of the marriage or civil partnership. In practical terms, this will affect appointments made by a testator in favour of his or her former spouse or civil partner in respect of a child who is not the child of the former spouse or civil partner. Where the child is the child of both parties, the revocation will not have any practical effect since the former spouse or civil partner will continue to have parental responsibility for the child.

'Where regulations are made' (s 6(6))—No such regulations have yet been made.

'on the application of any person who has parental responsibility for the child' (s 6(7)(a))—As the guardian himself will have acquired parental responsibility for the child under s 5(6), he could apply for an order terminating his own appointment if the circumstances made it inappropriate for him to disclaim under s 6(5).

'on the application of the child concerned, with leave' (s 6(7)(b))—Permission must be sought in accordance with FPR 2010, rr 18.1–18.13. As to the circumstances in which leave should be given, see **Leave under s 4(3)(b) not to be given unless child of sufficient understanding** under s 4. As is the case with s 4, the checklist of factors in s 1(3) does not apply specifically but gives examples of factors that may be relevant. The position is also likely to be the same under ss 4 and 6 with regard to the relevance of the chances of success of the proposed application, and there is similar uncertainty with regard to the applicability of s 1(1). One difference between the two provisions is that the court is not, under s 6(7), expressly directed to consider whether the child is of sufficient understanding to make the proposed application, but it will no doubt bear this factor in mind.

Once permission has been given, the application proceeds in the normal way save that there is no need for an application form to be filed because the court will already have received a draft with the appropriate number of copies as part of the permission application (FPR 2010, rr 18.1–18.13).

'in any family proceedings ... even though no application has been made' (s 6(7)(c))—If it thinks fit, the court may, in any family proceedings, make an order terminating the appointment of a guardian even though no formal application has been filed. No doubt such an order will most frequently be prompted at the suggestion of a party to the proceedings or of an interested friend or relative who has been allowed to address the court, or even of the child himself, but there is nothing to prevent the court itself taking the lead in appropriate circumstances. Section 6(7)(c) could be used by an individual who seeks to replace an existing guardian but who does not have parental responsibility and therefore cannot apply directly for the termination of the existing guardian's appointment. Where such an individual launches an application under s 5(1) for his own appointment (which application is classified as family proceedings), he could then invite the court in the course of that application not only to appoint him as guardian for the child but also to terminate the appointment of the existing guardian.

Hague Convention 1996—See notes to s 5.

7 Welfare reports

(1) A court considering any question with respect to a child under this Act may –

(a) ask an officer of the Service or a Welsh family proceedings officer; or
(b) ask a local authority to arrange for –
  (i) an officer of the authority; or
  (ii) such other person (other than an officer of the Service or a Welsh family proceedings officer) as the authority considers appropriate,

to report to the court on such matters relating to the welfare of that child as are required to be dealt with in the report.

(2) The Lord Chancellor may, after consulting the Lord Chief Justice, make regulations specifying matters which, unless the court orders otherwise, must be dealt with in any report under this section.

(3) The report may be made in writing, or orally, as the court requires.

(4) Regardless of any enactment or rule of law which would otherwise prevent it from doing so, the court may take account of –

(a) any statement contained in the report; and
(b) any evidence given in respect of the matters referred to in the report,

in so far as the statement or evidence is, in the opinion of the court, relevant to the question which it is considering.

(5) It shall be the duty of the authority or officer of the Service or a Welsh family proceedings officer to comply with any request for a report under this section.

(6) The Lord Chief Justice may nominate a judicial office holder (as defined in section 109(4) of the Constitutional Reform Act 2005) to exercise his functions under subsection (2).

Amendments—CJCSA 2000 s 74, Sch 7, para 88; CA 2004, s 40, Sch 3, paras 5, 6; CRA 2005, s 15(1), Sch 4, paras 203, 204.

Defined terms—'child', 'local authority': s 105(1); 'officer of the Service': CJCSA 2000, s 11(3).

Cafcass (Children and Family Court Advisory and Support Service)—Cafcass combines the Family Court welfare function previously provided by the Guardian ad litem and Reporting Officer Service, the Family Court Welfare Service and the Children's Branch of the Official Solicitor's Office within one unified service under the responsibility of the Ministry of Justice. The central functions of Cafcass are (i) to safeguard and promote the welfare of children; (ii) to give advice to any court about any application made to it in such proceedings; (iii) to make provision for children to be represented in such proceedings; and (iv) to provide information, advice and other support for children and their families. The Operating Framework for Cafcass is available at *www.cafcass.gov.uk*. It sets out Cafcass policy in line with changes to legislation and guidance, in particular as to child protection, domestic violence and information-sharing with other agencies. It sets out the minimum standards that are expected in working with families where domestic violence may have been an issue.

References to guardians ad litem, reporting officers and probation officers are subsumed within CJCSA 2000 as 'officers of the service'. For details of the terminology see annotations to CJCSA 2000, s 11.

FPR 2010, rr 16.33, 16.38 and PD16A, respectively, set out the principal functions of officers of the service in relation to court proceedings. The rules include section 7 reporting by officers of Cafcass and certain children cases formerly handled by the Official Solicitor. The rules do not generally extend to cover local authority officers reporting under section 7. However, the one exception is that the power of courts to request reports under CA 1989, s 7(1)(b) from the local authority is unaffected by the Cafcass provisions and officers so instructed will still be referred to as 'welfare officers'.

A protocol has been agreed between Cafcass and the National Youth Advocacy Service (NYAS) with respect to children made parties in private law proceedings under FPR 2010, 16.4 (*Protocol of December 2005 Between the National Youth Advocacy Service and the Children and Family Court Advisory and Support Service* (see Part V)). The protocol states that Cafcass should be approached first and will usually provide a guardian. However, in certain cases NYAS may be asked by the court to provide a guardian, for example, where despite the best efforts of Cafcass, one or more members of the family can no longer work with the organisation.

Role of National Youth Advocacy Service (NYAS)—Where there is an intractable contact dispute, the court may give permission for NYAS to be approached and shown the court papers in order that they might provide advice and a voice for the children (*Re A-H (Contact Order)* [2008] 2 FLR 1188, CA). For examples of such cases see *Re S (Unco-operative Mother)* [2004] 2 FLR 710, CA, *Re H (National Youth Advocacy Service)* [2007] 1 FLR 1028, CA, *Re C (A Child)* [2005] EWCA Civ 300 and *Re B (A Child)* [2006] EWCA Civ 716. In *Re C (Contact: Moratorium: Change of Gender)* [2007] 1 FLR 1642, CA, NYAS were invited to represent two children who had not seen their father since he began to live as a woman and had no idea that he had undergone gender reassignment surgery. On the recommendation of the expert instructed in the case NYAS were also to be involved in informing the children of the truth about their father's gender.

International social services—Where the assistance of international social services, now called Children and Families Across Borders (CFAB) is required contact may be made on their UK advice and information hotline on 0207 735 8941. The line is open to all statutory and voluntary agencies as well as to private individuals in the UK. Their website is at *www.cfab.org.uk* and they also provide a secure online enquiry system which may be accessed from the website. Common subjects for inquiry include: children who are taken abroad where there are child protection concerns; assessing the capacity of relatives overseas to care for a child in an out of home placement; tracing and re-establishing contacts with family members abroad when a child presents unaccompanied; living and contact arrangements of children whose parents' have separated and live in different countries; and information about adoption.

President's Interim Guidance to address backlog of work for Cafcass—On 1 October 2010, the President of the Family Division issued *Agreement to Assist Cafcass Pending Implementation of the Family Justice Review*, which was to be read alongside the PLO in FPR PD12A. It urged full and effective implementation of the PLO and aimed to enhance interagency working, reduce backlogs in the allocation of public law guardians, assist guardians to make the best use of their time and minimise the use of Cafcass 'duty advisers'. Particular emphasis was given to the need for judicial continuity and active case management (para 2). Although the Agreement expired on 30 September 2011, it was felt that the good practice generated by it is now so well established that it would continue without the need for any formal agreement. A joint message to this effect was published by the President of the Family Division and the Chief Executive of Cafcass on 29 July 2011 (see Part V).

Rules as to children and family reporter's duties—See FPR 2010, r 16.33 and PD16A.

'A court considering any question with respect to a child under this Act' (s 7(1))—The court's power is a very wide one and can be used not only in the traditional way in proceedings for child arrangements orders under s 8 but also, for example, in connection with parental responsibility applications, applications for specific issue or prohibited steps orders, applications by children for permission to commence proceedings under the Act, and emergency protection order applications.

Where children's guardian acting—Although there is power both at first instance (CA 1989, s 7) and on appeal to the High Court from the Family Court (lay justices) (CA 1989, ss 7 and 94(5)) to appoint a children and family reporter in public law proceedings, only in exceptional circumstances will a welfare report be sought when a children's guardian is already involved (*Re S (A Minor) (Guardian ad litem/Welfare Officer)* [1993] 1 FLR 110, CA). The roles of the children and family reporter and the children's guardian are not identical, in that a children's guardian has an extra duty to represent the child in court and to instruct legal representation for him if necessary, but they are similar in many respects. Therefore, it will usually be a duplication of effort and expense to appoint both in the same proceedings. The general principle in *Re S* was confirmed by the Court of Appeal in *L v L (Minors) (Separate Representation)* [1994] 1 FLR 156, CA (s 8 case), but the court expressed the hope that the welfare officer (children and family reporter) who had already begun investigations would report despite the subsequent appointment of a guardian ad litem (children's guardian) in that particular difficult case.

Conciliation as an alternative—At the First Hearing Dispute Resolution Appointment (see FPR 2010, r 12.31, and PD12B) the district judge is attended by a children and family reporter, and it is essential that both parties and their legal advisers attend. There is an opportunity for the parties to attempt to reach agreement with the assistance of the children and family reporter. If they are able to do so, the district judge will make the appropriate orders; if not, he will give directions for hearing. Under the CAP, the FHDRA is not privileged (PD12B, para 14.9), so that what is said there may be referred to at a later court hearing. Outside the Principal Registry, before ordering an inquiry and report by a children and family reporter, a judge or district judge should, where local conciliation facilities exist, consider whether the case is suitable for conciliation; if so, a direction should be given to that effect (PD12B, para 14.11). If conciliation fails, any report which is ordered must be by a children and family reporter who did not act as a conciliator (see also *Re H (Conciliation: Welfare Reports)* [1986] 1 FLR 476, FD).

When a children and family reporter is reporting as opposed to acting as conciliator, he must investigate and report on the situation, but it is not his role to attempt conciliation although he may encourage the parties to settle their differences if the likelihood of a settlement arises during the course of his enquiries.

Statements made by parties in conciliation meetings are not admissible in evidence, except where the statement clearly indicates that the maker has in the past caused, or is likely in the future to cause, serious harm to the well-being of a child. Even in such a case, the judge has a discretion whether to admit the evidence and should do so only if the public interest in protecting the child outweighs the public interest in the confidentiality of attempted conciliation (*Re D (Minors) (Conciliation: Privilege)* [1993] 1 FLR 932, CA).

Officer of the Service—Historically, children and family reporters have usually been officers of the Service; however, the court has power to invite a report from the local authority. In this context, the old terminology 'welfare officer' remains, since the welfare officer is appointed to report under CA 1989, s 7(1)(b) (see under **Cafcass (Children and Family Court Advisory and Support Service)** (above) and under FPR 2010, r 16.33 and PD16A). *Re W (Welfare Reports)* [1995] 2 FLR 142, CA, highlights the different expertise that can be expected from the two classes of reporter. Welfare officers are accustomed to the court process, to interviewing the child and relevant adults, to attending court, to making recommendations orally or in writing and to submitting to questioning by the parties. Social workers are familiar with the reporting routine in the context of preparing reports for use at case conferences and for placing on file for the assistance of other social workers etc. Their knowledge of the court process may be much more limited, and their role will frequently be confined to fact-finding reports and will not involve the making of any recommendations at all.

Despite the fact that paras (a) and (b) of s 7(1) are expressed as alternatives, it appears that it can be right to order a report from the children and family reporter as well as a report from a social worker (see *Re W (Welfare Reports)* (above) and *Re A and B (Minors) (No 2)* [1995] 1 FLR 351, FD). When there has been a referral to or involvement by Social Services, it is sensible that the local authority be directed to provide a s 7 report rather than Cafcass to ease the burden placed on Cafcass. Once the report is received, the court will consider the conduct of the case further in the light of it at a directions hearing. The local authority will be expected to make the social worker who writes the s 7 report available to give evidence (which will be at the invitation of the court rather than as a witness for any party) and to be cross-examined at the substantive hearing or at any interim hearing where oral evidence is required and to agree to discovery of relevant documentation underlying the report (as to this, see also *W v Wakefield City Council* [1995] 1 FLR 170, FD). Wall J clearly contemplates that, having received the local authority's report, the court might direct that a further report be prepared, this time by a children and family reporter.

In deciding whether to direct a local authority report under s 7, the alternative of s 37 must, of course, be kept in mind. This entitles the court to direct the local authority to investigate the child's circumstances, provided that it appears that it may be appropriate for a care or supervision order to be made in respect of him. However, Wall J points out in *Re A and B (Minors) (No 2)* (above) that, in most cases, s 37 does not apply and that, in any event, it does not appear appropriate in circumstances where the court is requesting the local authority to provide information about an investigation that has already been undertaken rather than requiring it to embark on an investigation.

For further guidance as to whether a children and family reporter or a local authority should be used, see **Best practice guidance on s 37(1) directions** under CA 1989, s 37, which also provides guidance on the communication to a local authority of a s 7(1) referral and draws attention to the need to fix a hearing at the time of referral. See **Public Law Outline (PLO)** under FPR 2010, r 12.22, and PD12A.

'such other person ... as the authority considers appropriate' (s 7(1)(b)(ii))—It is not appropriate to use s 7(1)(b)(ii) to make an order requiring the local authority to appoint an officer to obtain a report from a child psychiatrist (*Re K (Contact: Psychiatric Report)* [1995] 2 FLR 432, CA). Section 7(1)(b)(ii) confers on the local authority discretion as to the other person appointed, and the court has no power to control that appointment or to require the local authority to pay for expert advice. In specified proceedings, a psychiatric report can be obtained independently through a s 41 children's guardian but there can be no such guardian appointed in private law proceedings. Section 41(6A) includes within the category of proceedings which may be 'specified for the time being ... by rules of court' any proceedings for the making, varying or discharging of an order under CA 1989, s 8 (i e child arrangements, specific issue and prohibited steps orders). This potential to widen the definition of 'specified proceedings' reflects the growing pressure for the appointment of children's guardians in certain private law children cases, for example bitterly contested child disputes, where children frequently have particular needs and interests that do not coincide with or cannot be adequately represented by the parents (*Re H (Contact Order) (No 2)* [2002] 1 FLR 22, FD; *Re M (Intractable Contact Dispute: Interim Care Order)* [2003] 2 FLR 636, FD). The use of expert evidence and the instruction of experts in family proceedings is governed by FPR Pt 25 and PD25A–PD25F.

Delay occasioned by obtaining a welfare report—Obtaining a welfare report will normally take some weeks or months and will not infrequently cause delay in achieving a final resolution of the issues between the parties. In deciding whether to order a report, the court will therefore have to have in mind s 1(2) (the delay principle) and balance any prejudice that there is likely to be to the child through delay against the desirability of obtaining a report, the child's welfare being the paramount consideration (see *Re H (Minors) (Welfare Reports)* [1990] 2 FLR 172, CA). For the position where delay may be occasioned through the need to adjourn proceedings for the children and family reporter to attend to give oral evidence, see **Court differing with recommendations in welfare report** below.

PART II

'such matters relating to the welfare of that child as are required' (s 7(1))—Although there is nothing to prevent the court issuing a general request for a report on the child's welfare (in which case, the children and family reporter must simply comply with any regulations in force under s 7(2) and be guided by the Operating Framework for Cafcass), it is usually more efficient to indicate which matters should be addressed. If the children and family reporter becomes concerned about other matters in the course of preparing his report, it would, of course, be entirely proper for him to bring these (and any other relevant factors) to the attention of the court. See *Re D (Safeguarding Checks)* [2015] 1 FLR 991, FD.

By virtue of FPR PD12J *Residence and Contact Orders: Domestic Violence and Harm*, and the Cafcass Safeguarding Framework, copies of all applications for child arrangements orders are sent to Cafcass to enable them to undertake initial screening of the parties, including seeking information from the police about any previous convictions and information from the local authority about any previous referrals concerning them. Before the first hearing, Cafcass notifies the court of the results of their searches (see the CAP in FPR PD12B). There are circulars governing the obtaining of details of previous convictions of parties, spouses etc from the police: Home Office Circulars 88/1982, 105/1982, 47/1993. As to the desirability of the court knowing of previous convictions of a party, see *Re R (Minors) (Custody)* [1986] 1 FLR 6, CA. See also the *Police/Family Disclosure Protocol* of July 2007 in Part V. (Note that the London Request Form (LRF) was introduced on 5 August 2013 to replace the Protocol within the London area.)

'regulations specifying matters which ... must be dealt with' (s 7(2))—No regulations have yet been made in this respect. The reporter must therefore pay careful attention to any specific directions given by the commissioning court about the scope of the report and derive guidance from authorities and from the Operating Framework for Cafcass (see note above). Subject to any limitations expressly imposed by the court it will generally be appropriate to visit the child's home (and, where a change of accommodation is proposed, any proposed new home), to interview the protagonists (mother, father and grandparents if closely involved), local authority social workers with knowledge of the family and anyone else whose view might be of assistance (for example, playgroup leader, teacher or health visitor) and to meet the child (alone and/or in company with parents or carers as appropriate to the application before the court) so as to ascertain, where possible, his wishes and feelings. In *Re R (A Minor) (Court Welfare Report)* [1993] Fam Law 722, CA the court emphasised the duty to see all relevant parties and, whenever possible, the child with each of the protagonists.

Duty of local authority or officer of the Service to comply (s 7(5))—In theory, there is no room for argument once the court has made its request for a report; the officer of the Service or local authority chosen has a duty to report as requested. The time for representations about who should be responsible for the report and what it is feasible for it to cover is therefore before the report is commissioned. The problem is that this depends upon a representative of Cafcass or the local authority being on hand at the relevant time which will not always be the case. In the event that the court's request does cause difficulties, contact should be made with the court explaining the nature of the obstacle and asking for directions to be given under FPR 2010, r 12.12. If the difficulty is an inability to meet the time-limits set down by the court or, in default of any time-limit set by the court, by the rules (see FPR 2010, r 16.33 and PD16A), the court will have to balance the prejudice that there is likely to be to the welfare of the child (see s 1(2)) against the desirability of obtaining a relevant report, the child's welfare being the paramount consideration (*Re H (Minors) (Welfare Reports)* [1990] 2 FLR 172, CA). The power to vary time-limits derives from FPR 2010, rr 4.1(3), 12.12(2) and 12.13. Normally, the appropriate course is to find out from Cafcass how long is required for the report and to fix a date in the light of that information so that the report will be available for the fixed hearing (*B v B (Minors) (Interviews and Listing Arrangements)* [1994] 2 FLR 489, CA; *Re A and B (Minors) (No 2)* [1995] 1 FLR 351, FD). In a case which is clearly going to be contested, it is desirable that the direction for a welfare report should, as was pointed out in *Re A and B (Minors) (No 2)*, be given in the context of overall directions for the filing of evidence and a fixed date for final determination.

Statements and evidence otherwise inadmissible (s 7(4))—The welfare report and the children and family reporter's evidence will often contain reports of conversations that he has had with third parties (e g relatives, neighbours and teachers) and with the child, and may also contain other statements traditionally viewed as inadmissible. Section 7(4) is a very broad provision enabling the court to disregard all rules of evidence and to take into account any statement or evidence which is relevant to the question in issue. Plainly certain statements or evidence will be more influential than others and the court must decide what weight is appropriate to attach to each (*R v B County Council ex parte P* [1991] 1 FLR 470, CA; see also the Children (Admissibility of Hearsay Evidence) Order 1993 in Part IV). Where the children and family reporter includes hearsay in his report, he should identify it as such, give the source of it and give any reasons he has for agreeing with any opinions he passes on (*Thompson v Thompson* [1986] 1 FLR 212, CA). Although it is always difficult for a party to deal with hearsay evidence that is prejudicial to him, this practice will at least alert the court to the deficiencies of the evidence and enable the party who feels himself prejudiced to interview the original author of the statement or opinion with a view to calling him to give evidence if he has been inaccurately reported. It appears that, in accordance with s 7(4)(b), once a particular matter has found its way into the welfare report, the court may entertain any relevant evidence with regard to it from any witness (not just the parties and the children and family reporter) with no restrictions as to hearsay.

Guarantees of confidentiality not appropriate—A children and family reporter cannot guarantee confidentiality to a person who makes allegations to him while he is investigating the circumstances of the case. It is for the judge to decide whether or not evidence must be disclosed to the parties (*Re G (Minors) (Welfare Report: Disclosure)* [1993] 2 FLR 293, CA). The principles applicable are set out in **Submission of evidence** under FPR 2010, r 12.12.

Court differing with recommendation in welfare report—The final decision as to any question in issue rests with the court, but the welfare report and any recommendations that the children and family reporter makes must be taken into account (*Re P (Custody of Children: Split Custody Order)* [1991] 1 FLR 337, CA). If the court decides not to follow the recommendation of the children and family reporter, it should give its reasons (*Re J (Children) (Residence: Expert Evidence)* [2001] 2 FCR 44, CA). In *Re R (Residence Order)* [2010] 1 FLR 509, CA, the Court of Appeal held that the judge had erred in setting on one side the firm evidence of the child's own wishes (a boy aged 9) and in rejecting the Cafcass officer's clear recommendation, together with the reasons for both, without any new evidence or any reasoned challenge to either, and without having heard the officer's oral evidence. There should have been a short adjournment to allow for the attendance of the officer.

Clearly, it will usually be desirable to set out *in terms* the reasons for differing from the children and family reporter's recommendations, but *Re V (Residence: Review)* [1995] 2 FLR 1010, CA, shows that failure to do so will not necessarily vitiate the decision, provided that the reasons for the decision were sound and either explained or constituted a sound basis for dissenting from the children and family reporter. In *Re CB (Access: Attendance of Court Welfare Officer)* [1995] 1 FLR 622, CA (a case concerning the risk of sexual abuse of a child by a Sch 1 offender), it was said to be a defective exercise of discretion for a judge to reject clear-cut recommendations and warnings in a children and family reporter's report without availing himself of the opportunity of receiving further assistance from the officer by way of oral evidence. The court suggested that where, as in *Re CB*, the children and family reporter is not available in person for some reason, it is open to the judge to adjourn the case and demand his or her presence. He can then put to the children and family reporter the reasons why he, the judge, does not agree with him and obtain from the officer an explanation of the officer's views. However, in *Re C (Section 8 Order: Court Welfare Officer)* [1995] 1 FLR 617, CA, the Court of Appeal pointed out that *Re CB* is not a hard and fast rule of law. Whether to adjourn a case so that the children and family reporter can attend is a matter for the judge's discretion and he must carry out the balancing act which is required by the paramount consideration of the child's welfare and the provisions as to delay in s 1(2). Many factors will have to be taken into account, including how much further assistance the children and family reporter can give, what his attendance is likely to change and the extent to which it would be safe and proper to depart from any recommendations made. Whereas in *Re CB*, the children and family reporter had made clear recommendations and warnings of the most serious kind and it was not proper to reject these in his absence, in *Re C* the report was in reality an account of the interviews that the children and family reporter had had with both parents and with the child and reached conclusions which set out the arguments and considerations very fairly and did not make firm recommendations in any particular directions, although the tenor of the considerations was in favour of the status quo (residence with the mother). In these circumstances, the judge had been entitled to exercise his discretion by refusing the father's application for an adjournment for the children and family reporter to attend.

Position of children and family reporter in court—See under CJCSA 2000, s 16.

Independent welfare reports—The *Family Justice Review Final Report* recommends that independent social workers should only be used exceptionally (paras 3.131, 3.132).

PART II
ORDERS WITH RESPECT TO CHILDREN IN FAMILY PROCEEDINGS

General

8 Child arrangements orders and other orders with respect to children

(1) In this Act –

'child arrangements order' means an order regulating arrangements relating to any of the following –

(a) with whom a child is to live, spend time or otherwise have contact, and

(b) when a child is to live, spend time or otherwise have contact with any person;

…

'a prohibited steps order' means an order that no step which could be taken by a parent in meeting his parental responsibility for a child, and which is of a kind specified in the order, shall be taken by any person without the consent of the court;

… and

'a specific issue order' means an order giving directions for the purpose of determining a specific question which has arisen, or which may arise, in connection with any aspect of parental responsibility for a child.

(2) In this Act 'a section 8 order' means any of the orders mentioned in subsection (1) and any order varying or discharging such an order.

(3) For the purposes of this Act 'family proceedings' means any proceedings –

(a) under the inherent jurisdiction of the High Court in relation to children; and
(b) under the enactments mentioned in subsection (4),

but does not include proceedings on an application for leave under section 100(3).

(4) The enactments are –

(a) Parts I, II and IV of this Act;
(b) the Matrimonial Causes Act 1973;
(ba) Schedule 5 to the Civil Partnership Act 2004;
(c) *(repealed)*
(d) the Adoption Act and Children Act 2002;
(e) the Domestic Proceedings and Magistrates' Courts Act 1978;
(ea) Schedule 6 to the Civil Partnership Act 2004;
(f) *(repealed)*
(g) Part III of the Matrimonial and Family Proceedings Act 1984;
(h) the Family Law Act 1996.
(i) sections 11 and 12 of the Crime and Disorder Act 1998.

Amendments—FLA 1996, s 66(1), (3), Sch 8, para 60(1), Sch 10; Crime and Disorder Act 1998, s 119, Sch 8, para 68; ACA 2002, Sch 3, para 55; CPA 2004, s 261(1), Sch 27, para 129(1)–(3); CFA 2014, ss 9, 12, Sch 2.

Defined terms—'child': s 105(1); 'parental responsibility': s 3.

Scope—The Act seeks to set up a flexible system which enables the court to have as wide a choice of orders as possible so that any question which arises with regard to the welfare of a child can be resolved, whatever the nature of the proceedings before the court. The wide definition of 'family proceedings' that is contained in the section facilitates this.

Jurisdiction—See FLA 1986, Pt I.

Funding issues—Now that public funding is in general no longer available for private law children cases, it might be appropriate in certain circumstances for the court to direct that the cost of certain activities, such as bringing an expert to court and providing advice to parents accused of sexual offending within the family, should be borne by the Courts and Tribunals Service. Such issues may not be ones that the judge can determine without the benefit of legal argument on both sides. If the judge is deprived of adversarial argument, and if a parent is denied access to legal advice both before and during the hearing, there must be a very real risk of his or her rights under Arts 6 and 8 being breached. However, an order directing that the cost of certain activities should be borne by the Courts and Tribunals Service is an order of last resort (the provision of interpreters and translators apart) and no such order should be made except by a High Court judge or a designated family judge (*Q v Q (Funding of Representation and Expert Attendance)* [2015] 1 FLR 318, FD). However, see *Re K and H (Private Law: Public Funding)* [2016] 1 FLR 754, CA, where the Court of Appeal did not follow *Q v Q* and held that the Family Court did not have the power to order that the Court Service provide funding for legal representation outside the legal aid scheme for an unrepresented party to cross-examine a child in family proceedings. The court suggested possible case management orders to deal with cross-examination and suggested that consideration be given to a statutory provision enabling payment out of central funds.

In *Re J and K (Children: Private Law)* [2015] 1 FLR 86, FD, the court emphasised how the involvement of skilled and insightful advocates has immeasurable advantages in achieving a better understanding of the case and in assisting parents to an infinitely more constructive way of working together for the benefit of their children. *D v K and B (By Her Guardian)* [2014] EWHC 700 (Fam) was exceptional private law litigation where there were very serious allegations involved, including rape, but the father had been refused public funding. The court highlighted the difficulties for the proper administration of justice where one party is unrepresented. Given the child's age, the factual analysis would be relevant for many years to come and the father's lack of representation posed very serious challenges to the court.

See also *R (Teresa Gudanaviciene & 5 Ors) (Claimants/ Respondents) v (1) Director of Legal Aid Casework (2) Lord Chancellor (Defendants/ Appellants) & British Red Cross Society (Intervener)* [2014] EWCA Civ 1622 where the Lord Chancellor's guidance on exceptional funding in civil legal aid was held to be incompatible with ECHR, Art 6(1) and Charter of Fundamental Rights of the European Union, Art 47 in that it had impermissibly signalled that the refusal of legal aid would amount to a breach of such rights only in rare and extreme cases. In *R (Rights of Women) v Secretary of State for Justice* [2017] 1 FLR 615, CA, the Civil Legal Aid (Procedure) Regulations 2012, reg 33, which specified the supporting evidence to be provided by a legal aid applicant who claimed to be the victim of domestic violence, was not ultra vires LASPOA 2012. However, the Regulations frustrated the purposes of the Act and were invalid insofar as they required that the verification of domestic violence had to be dated within a period of 24 months before a legal aid application and insofar as they made no provision for victims of financial abuse. The Court of Appeal held that once it was accepted that part of the statutory purpose of LASPOA 2012 was to ensure that legal aid was available to the great majority of domestic violence victims, it was necessary to ask why so many of them were excluded by the 24-month rule; it was held that the rule operated in a completely arbitrary manner and there was no safety valve that enabled the victims of domestic violence to explain why they were unable to obtain verification of that violence less than 24 months before proceedings began. See also *Director of Legal Aid Casework and Another v IS* [2016] 2 FLR 392, CA, where the Court of Appeal held that the exceptional case-funding scheme for the administration of legal aid under LASPOA 2012, s 10 was lawful (albeit Briggs LJ dissenting and noting that the fact that many solicitors worked pro bono to assist people in obtaining the funding did not rescue the scheme from inherent unlawfulness); there had clearly been difficulties with the scheme and there was room for improvement, particularly concerning lay applicants and those with disabilities, but its operation was a learning curve and there had been improvements since its inception.

Other recent cases dealing with funding difficulties include *JG v The Lord Chancellor and Others* [2014] 2 FLR 1218, CA, where the claimant father successfully obtained a declaration in judicial review proceedings that the LSC's decision not to meet the cost of an expert psychotherapist's report in private law proceedings had been unlawful. In *BC v DE* [2016] EWHC 1806 (Fam), Cobb J took the unusual step of ordering the father to fund the mother's legal costs in pursuit of the private law aspects of her case where she had no resources or income of her own, could not reasonably obtain legal costs funding elsewhere and where the father was extraordinarily wealthy. The court was concerned to ensure that the parties had equality of arms and equal access to justice, and strove to exercise its discretionary power with a view to promoting fairness between them.

In *Re D (Children)* [2016] EWCA Civ 89, the court had previously ordered that the father should bear the costs of contact with his children being supervised by a social worker, but had failed to give precise and comprehensive terms about the payment of costs, which were now disputed. The Court of Appeal held that the Family Court did not have jurisdiction to resolve the dispute about those costs where the social worker had been acting on a contractual basis rather than as a court-appointed expert, and confirmed that the Family Court's jurisdiction was confined only to the family proceedings and not to resolving a contractual dispute involving a third party.

Funding in disputed paternity cases—From November 2015, Cafcass is able, in defined circumstances, to facilitate and fund the provision of DNA tests directed under FLRA 1969, s 20. The service is limited to the following circumstances: (a) an application has been made for a Child Arrangements Order under CA 1989, s 8; (b) the application cannot be determined unless a dispute about the child's paternity is resolved; and (c) the parents or persons with care of the child are prepared to cooperate with the direction made by the court. The court's order must contain a reference to Cafcass meeting the costs of the DNA test facilitated by them and that the direction is made of the court's own volition.

Arbitration—In July 2016, the Institute of Family Law Arbitrators (IFLA) launched the Family Law Arbitration Scheme, which aims to increase the use of arbitration relating to family disputes. The scheme, originally dealing with financial matters, now offers the opportunity to resolve disputes concerning the exercise of parental responsibility and the welfare of children by arbitration. It provides a choice of arbitrator, continuity of tribunal, confidentiality and speed of decision-making for children disputes.

Children and Families Act 2014—Section 8 has been amended by the Children and Families Act 2014 so that residence and contact orders have been removed and replaced with child arrangements orders (CAO), which regulates the arrangements relating to (a) with whom a child is to live, spend time or otherwise have contact, and (b) when a child is to live, spend time or otherwise have contact with any person (s 8(1)). There is also a requirement that when the court is considering whether to make, vary or discharge a s 8 order that is opposed, the court is to presume that the involvement of that parent in the life of the child will further the child's welfare, provided that the parent concerned can be involved in a way that does not put the child at risk of suffering harm (s 1(2a),(2B)). Specific issue orders and prohibited steps orders continue as before.

Child Arrangements Programme (CAP)—The CAP came into force on 22 April 2014. FPR PD12B sets out the process that applies where a dispute arises between separated parents and/or families about the arrangements concerning children.

Duty on parents to work to put aside differences—It is an integral aspect of parental responsibility that parents should work to put aside differences and ensure that their children have relationships with both parents (*Re W (Direct Contact)* [2013] 1 FLR 494, CA; *Re W (Contact: Permission to Appeal)* [2013] 1 FLR 609, CA; *Re J and K (Children: Private Law)* [2015] 1 FLR 86, FD); *Re H-B (Contact)* [2015] EWCA Civ 389.

Child arrangements order for adult 'child'—Where the local authority felt that an adult child of 17 with a mental age of between 5 and 8 years was at risk of significant harm if she lived at home with her mother, but was too old to be made the subject of a care order, the court held that it had inherent declaratory jurisdiction to keep the 'child' in local authority accommodation and to restrict and supervise the child's contact with her family (*Re F (Adult: Court's Jurisdiction)* [2000] 2 FLR 512, CA). The doctrine of necessity could be invoked in such circumstances and the inherent jurisdiction was not excluded by the statutory framework. There is no presumption of a right to contact between a parent and an adult child. Where the adult child is under a disability and is not in a position to consent to contact, the question is whether it is in the adult child's best interests to spend time with her parents (*Re D-R (Adult: Contact)* [1999] 1 FLR 1161, CA). The jurisdictional basis for such an application is unclear, but would not appear to fall within s 8, where the definition of 'child' for the purposes of an application for a child arrangements order refers to a child under the age of 18 (s 105(1)). Furthermore, the court is required by CA 1989, s 9(6) not to make any s 8 order which is to have effect for a period that will end after the child has reached the age of 16, unless the circumstances of the case are exceptional. The MCA 2005 contains remedies in respect of welfare, finance and health issues for those persons over 16 years of age who lack capacity.

Same-sex parenting—In same-sex cases where parental responsibility does not automatically exist in law or where it cannot be agreed (for example, the mother does not agree that the child's other female parent should acquire parental responsibility (see s 4ZA)), the court may consider making a parental responsibility order (see s 4) or a child arrangements order in favour of both same-sex parents after the breakdown of the relationship in order to confer parental responsibility on the child's other parent. In *Re G (Children)* [2006] 2 FLR 629, HL, a lesbian couple brought up their child (conceived via an unknown sperm donor) jointly until the relationship ended. The House of Lords confirmed that the issues and legal principles arising in the dispute about the child's living arrangements were just the same as those arising between heterosexual couples. In particular, the court considered the weight to be attached to the fact that one party is both the natural and legal parent of the child and the other is not. The court also considered the concept of 'natural parenthood' and its significance both for the adults and for the child. The court identified at least three ways in which a person may become the natural parent of a child, each of which may be a very significant factor in the child's welfare, depending upon the circumstances of the particular case: genetic parenthood (provision of the gametes), gestational motherhood (conceiving and bearing of the child) and social and psychological parenthood (the relationship that develops through the child demanding and the parent providing for the child's needs). The HL cautioned that courts should not allow the unusual context of a case 'to distract them from principles which are of universal application'. However, see *T v B* [2010] 2 FLR 1966, FD, where the court considered the definition of 'parent' (in the context of CA 1989, Sch 1) and held that, as a matter of statutory interpretation, those against whom orders could be made under Sch 1 were confined to those who were parents in the legal meaning of that word; the court distinguished the analysis in *Re G (Children)* (above) and held that the determination of who was a parent for the purposes of Sch 1 was not a discretionary, welfare-informed decision, but was a matter of status (see s 10). This objectively surprising decision was justified by the court's view that it is for the legislature to determine who should be financially responsible for children if it is to extend beyond those who are legal parents (see s 10). Note also that in *Re G (Shared Residence Order: Biological Mother of Donor Egg)* [2014] 2 FLR 897, CA, Black LJ cautioned against devoting too much time to trying to work out whether a parent could properly be called a 'psychological parent', when what matters is the parent's involvement in fact – both past and future.

In *Re B (A Child)* [2010] 1 FLR 551, SC, the Supreme Court held that the importance of parenthood is only as a contributor to the child's welfare and that to talk in terms of a child's rights – as opposed to his or her best interests – diverts from the child's welfare as the focus when making decisions as to where the child should live. Furthermore, when considering such decisions there is no place for the question whether the proposed placement would be 'good enough' or a supposedly adequate alternative. See also *Re E-R (Child Arrangements Order)* [2016] 1 FLR 521, CA, where the Court of Appeal confirmed that there is no presumption of a parental right or 'broad natural parent presumption' that might override the welfare of the child as the court's paramount consideration; the fact that a person was a natural parent was a factor of significance to be given appropriate weight when determining the child's best interests.

Known sperm donors—Where a father donates his sperm to a lesbian couple so that they can have a child but then wishes to have a relationship with the child, it is wrong to class him as a 'secondary' parent because it has the danger of demeaning him and his potential future role in the child's life; his application to spend time with the child must be considered in terms of the paramountcy of the child's welfare (*A v B and C (Lesbian Co-Parents: Role of Father)* [2012] 2 FLR 607, CA). In both *T v T* [2010] EWCA Civ 1366 and *A v B and C* (above) the court emphasised that whatever the original intentions of the parties when children are conceived, the court's focus should be on dealing with the position as it actually is, rather than the position that the adults had wanted or originally planned (see also s 4). See, for example, *Re X (No 2) (Application for contact by the biological father)* [2015] EWFC 84.

Child arrangements orders for shared living arrangements—Note that the following cases were decided before the amendment of CA 1989, s 8 by CFA 2014 to remove residence and contact orders and replace them with child arrangements orders specifying with whom the child is to live, spend time or otherwise have contact (see **Children and Families Act 2014**, above). It is not necessary to show that exceptional circumstances exist before orders for shared living arrangements may be granted (*D v D (Shared Residence Order)* [2001] 1 FLR 495, CA; *Re F (Shared Residence Order)* [2003] 2 FLR 397, CA). Nor is it strictly necessary to show a positive benefit to the child. What is required is a demonstration that the order is in the interests of the child in accordance with the requirements of s 1(1) (*D v D* (above)). It is not open to a judge to make an order for shared living arrangements as a means of ensuring that there is no resistance to an order for contact (*Re W (Children)* [2003] EWCA Civ 116, CA). In *A v A (Shared Residence)* [2004] 1 FLR 1195, FD, there was a history of acrimony and failed contact between the father and children. Eventually, the children were separately represented by the National Youth Advocacy Service and Wall J made an order for shared living arrangements based on the time spent in each home and the need for the importance of each parent to be recognised. The failure of the parents to co-operate is not a bar to the making of an order for shared living arrangements where this would in all other respects be the right order: *Re R (Residence: Shared Care: Children's Views)* [2006] 1 FLR 491, CA; *Re W (Shared Residence Order)* [2009] 2 FLR 436, CA. Because an order for shared living arrangements might serve the interests of the child even where the division of time between the two homes was not equal, the two aspects of the application, (1) an equal division of time and (2) an order for shared living arrangements, do not stand or fall together. They had to be considered separately, with the court considering the issues together but ruling first on the optimum division of the child's time and then considering how that division of time should best be expressed in an order (*Re K (Shared Residence Order)* [2008] 2 FLR 380, CA; *Re W (Shared Residence Order)* (above)). Where the facts dictated

PART II

that an order for shared living arrangements was in the interests of the child, equality of time with each parent was the starting point (*Re M (Residence Order)* [2008] 1 FLR 1087, CA). However, in *Re P (Shared Residence Order)* [2006] 2 FLR 347, CA, the children spent 55% of their time with the mother and 45% of their time with the father and the court held that this was a plain case for an order for shared living arrangements that would reflect the reality that the parents had established for the child. Where a mother's former partner was not the biological parent of her child, but the child was brought up by him while they cohabited, an order for shared living arrangements could be made so that he acquires parental responsibility (*Re A (A Child: Joint Residence: Parental Responsibility)* [2008] 2 FLR 1593, CA – where such an order was made so as to prevent the mother from marginalising the role of her ex-partner in the upbringing of her child).

Practical difficulties may arise where parents with shared care both claim that they are 'in priority need' of council accommodation. In such cases, the Housing Act 1996, s 189(1)(b) requires the authority to consider whether the applicant is a person with whom dependent children reside or might reasonably be expected to reside. In *Holmes-Moorhouse v Richmond-upon-Thames London Borough Council* [2009] 1 FLR 904, HL, the House of Lords gave guidance on the approach to be followed by local authorities in determining whether an applicant for council housing who has been granted an order for shared residence was a person with whom dependent children 'might reasonably be expected to reside', pursuant to Housing Act 1996, s 189(1)(b). Their Lordships warned that family courts should not use residence orders to try to exert pressure on housing authorities to allocate their resources in a particular way. Only in exceptional circumstances would it be reasonable to expect children who had a home with one parent to be provided by the housing authority with another so that they could also reside with the other parent. Housing is a scarce resource and the procedures for deciding how it is to be allocated should not be entangled with the procedures for deciding children's welfare.

Shared living arrangements – domestic relocation—Note that the following cases were decided before the amendments to CA 1989, ss 1 and 8 that were made by the CFA 2014 (see **Child arrangements orders for shared living arrangements**, above). The approach for the court where the question of relocation arises in the context of orders for shared living arrangements is to look at the underlying factual substratum in welfare terms, bearing in mind the tension that may well exist between a parent's freedom to relocate and the welfare of the child, which may militate against relocation. The balance is critical and, as a matter of law, the danger of distinguishing the case from the authorities because it involves shared living arrangements as opposed to a living arrangements order is that the court might either lose sight of, or give insufficient weight to, the former consideration (*Re L (Shared Residence: Relocation)* [2009] 1 FLR 1157, CA – where the judge refused the mother's application for internal relocation from London to Somerset as he reached the conclusion that she sought to undermine the shared living arrangements). An order for shared living arrangements should not be seen as an automatic bar to relocation. It may well be in the child's best interests to relocate, notwithstanding the existence of such an order. In *Re M (A Child)* [2014] EWCA Civ 1755, the Court of Appeal confirmed that it was wrong to order a 5-year-old boy to be returned from Newcastle where he lived with his mother to live with his father in London, with the mother having equal shared time with the child should she return to London. That amounted to the imposition of a condition in a way that would clearly have been impermissible had it been overt. It was held that although the court's power to impose a condition under s 11(7) remained in force, it would be exceptional for a court to do so where both parents lived in the UK, especially England; that would amount to an unwarranted imposition on where, and with whom, a parent might live.

Shared living arrangements – relocation abroad—See **Removal from jurisdiction** under s 13. See *Re F (A Child) (International Relocation Cases)* [2017] 1 FLR 979, CA, where the Court of Appeal reviewed the guidelines in *Payne v Payne* [2001] 1 FLR 1052, CA and restated useful guidelines for cases in which permission is sought to remove a child permanently from the jurisdiction. See the following cases (but note that all were decided before the decision in *Re F*). The question of relocation abroad was considered in *Re D (Leave to Remove: Shared Residence)* [2006] Fam Law 1006, FD, where the court allowed the mother to remove the children permanently from the UK to the USA, but made an order for shared living arrangements with the father because the children would spend significant time with each parent in each jurisdiction. In *Re F (Relocation)* [2013] 1 FLR 645, CA, the court granted an order for shared living arrangements but granted the mother permission permanently to remove the child from the jurisdiction, allowing for certain holidays to be spent with the father in the UK. In *Re AR (A Child: Relocation)* [2010] 2 FLR 1577, FD, Mostyn J held that orders for shared residence should be normative for they avoid the psychological baggage of right, power and control that attends an order for sole residence; they were not inapt even where permission to relocate was granted (see further under CA 1989, s 13).

Child arrangements orders for contact cannot be made without first determining with whom a child lives—CA 1989 does not require that in every case there should be an order specifying where the child should live as a prerequisite for a contact application; all that is necessary is that there should be a person defined or capable of definition with whom the child lives. If one parent is the primary carer but does not trouble to obtain an order enshrining her role, an order for contact can still be made against her as the person with whom the child lives (*Re H (Contact: Adverse Findings of Fact)* [2011] 2 FLR 1201, CA).

Enforcement of child arrangements orders—The court has specific powers to impose directions and conditions on child arrangements orders (ss 11A, 11B). The court can impose contact activities (ss 11D–11G) and require Cafcass officers to monitor a person's compliance (s 11G). When the court makes a child arrangements order it may order a Cafcass officer to facilitate and monitor compliance for up to 12 months and report to the court (s 11H). Courts have additional tools for enforcement where such orders are breached, including curfews, tagging and unpaid work: ss 11J–11N. Financial compensation may be ordered for losses sustained by failure, without reasonable excuse, to comply with an order (ss 11O–11P). However, none of these provisions apply to children who are subject to an application for an adoption order (s 11B(4)). See also FPR PD12N *Enforcement of Children Act 1989 Contact orders: Disclosure of Information to Officers of the National Probation Service*.

Warning notices on child arrangements orders—All child arrangements orders made or varied after 8 December 2008 must have a warning notice on them, setting out the consequences of not complying with the order. It is no longer necessary to make a separate application for a penal notice to be attached. Transitional provisions allow parties to apply to have a warning notice attached to an existing order for contact (CAA 2006, s 8). The application must be made on Form C78 by a person who falls within the criteria set down by CA 1989, s 11J(5)(a)–(d). See further s 11I.

Care required when drafting child arrangements orders to which warning notices are to be attached—It is *mandatory* for a court to attach a warning notice when it makes or varies *any* child arrangements order. It follows that a child arrangements order must be made in terms that comply with s 8(1), whereas a recital in declaratory terms does not require a warning notice to be attached. Thus, it may be more appropriate for consent orders to set out the agreed regime as a recital or schedule to the order on the basis of which the court then applies the 'no order' principle. See further under s 11I. See also **Orders generally** under FPR 2010, r 12.21.

Revised protocol for referrals of families to Supported Child Contact Centres by Judges and Magistrates—See Protocol on the NACC website at *www.naccc.org.uk* (tel 0845 4500 280).

Contact - ECHR 1950—The ECHR 1950 was implemented in this jurisdiction on the coming into force of HRA 1998. There are a number of cases in which unmarried fathers have complained that the refusal of the court to grant them contact with their children constitutes a breach of their right to family life, which right is protected by ECHR 1950, Art 8. The ECtHR upheld such complaints by unmarried fathers in *Elsholz v Germany* [2000] 2 FLR 486, ECHR; *Ciliz v The Netherlands* [2000] 2 FLR 469, ECHR; *Elsholz v Italy* [2000] Fam Law 680, ECHR, but rejected the father's complaint in *Glaser v UK* (Case No 32346/96) [2001] 1 FLR 153, ECHR. In *S and G v Italy* [2000] 2 FLR 771, ECHR, a mother's complaint that the authorities had prevented her having contact with her children was upheld and found to constitute a breach of Art 8. In three cases the ECtHR considered the approach of the German courts to contact applications by unmarried fathers and held that consideration of what lies in the best interests of the child is of crucial importance in every case of this kind. A fair balance has to be struck between the interests of each parent and those of the child and in doing so particular importance must be attached to the best interests of the child which, depending on their nature and seriousness, may override those of the parent. A parent's rights are secondary to the child's health and development (*Sahin v Germany; Sommerfeld v Germany; Hoffmann v Germany* [2002] 1 FLR 119, ECHR). However, it is going too far to say that domestic courts should always hear evidence from a child in court on the issue of access or that a psychological expert should be involved (see Grand Chamber decision, *Sahin v Germany; Sommerfeld v Germany* [2003] 2 FLR 671, ECHR). There will be no violation of Art 8 where a reduction in contact is justified in the child's interests (*Hoppe v Germany* [2003] 1 FLR 384, ECHR). Where the court makes a private law order there is a positive obligation on public authorities under Art 8 to take measures to enforce a parent's right to be reunited with his child, although the obligation is not absolute and the interests and freedoms of all parties must be taken into account (*Sylvester v Austria* [2003] 2 FLR 210, ECHR; *Hansen v Turkey* (Application No 36141/97) [2004] 1 FLR 142, ECHR; *Kosmopoulou v Greece* [2004] 1 FLR 800, ECHR). In *Bove v Italy* [2005] Fam Law 752, ECHR, the failure of the court to enforce the father's access rights had infringed his Art 8 rights to respect for his family life. The key question to be asked is whether the national authority has taken all steps that are reasonable in the circumstances (*Zawadka v Poland* [2005] 2 FLR 897, ECHR). These include ensuring that the parent concerned can exercise effective contact at a time compatible with his work and on suitable premises (*Gluhakovic v Croatia* [2011] 2 FLR 294, ECHR). For a succinct recital of the principles to be derived from case-law both from the ECtHR and the domestic courts, see the judgment of Munby LJ in *Re C (Direct Contact: Suspension)* [2011] 2 FLR 912, CA, at [47].

For the procedure to be followed in making a claim under HRA 1998, see annotation thereto and FPR 2010, r 29.5.

Implacable hostility to contact - Guidance—Where one parent is implacably hostile to the prospect of the child spending time with the other parent, Munby LJ has set out guidance that requires that in all such cases there must be judicial continuity, judicial case management (including effective timetabling), a judicial set strategy and consistency of judicial approach (*Re L-W (Enforcement and Committal: Contact); CPL v CH-W and Others* [2011] 1 FLR 1095, CA, at [97]). If, as part of that strategy, the court makes an order requiring the parent with care to comply with a child arrangements order (CAO) and that order is breached, the judge must, in the absence of good reasons, support the order by considering enforcement under CA 1989, ss 11J–11N. The first time a judge should give serious consideration to whether they would be prepared to enforce a CAO is before the order is made, not only after a breach has occurred; such forward thinking should be part of the judge's overall strategy for the case. (*Re A (Intractable Contact Dispute: Human Rights Violations)* [2014] 1 FLR 1185, CA).

Intractable opposition by children to contact—In cases of intractable opposition by children to having contact with a parent, their welfare rather than their wishes and feelings should be determinative of the court's decisions in balancing harm to the children of not seeing a relative against the harm in forcing direct contact upon them against their wishes (*Re H (A Child)* [2014] EWCA Civ 271). See *Re D (A Child)* [2014] EWCA Civ 1057, where it was proportionate for the court to order no contact between child (aged 11) and his father because the child had such entrenched negative views of his father and was maintaining his opposition to direct contact. However, see *Re A and B (Contact) (No 4)* [2016] 2 FLR 429, FD, where although a daughter was opposed to any form of contact with her father, the court made a child arrangements order for indirect contact as it would be in her best interests.

In high-conflict cases involving older children, it is important that, before the court makes an order, it considers the child and family dynamics, whether there is a real possibility that the order is practical and workable and whether, in the event of non-compliance, there is a realistic possibility of it being successfully enforced (*Re G (Intractable Contact Dispute)* [2014] 1 FLR 1185, FD). In *Re W (Children) (Contact Dispute) (No 2)* [2014] EWCA Civ 401, the Court of Appeal confirmed that there are limits to the attempts that can be

PART II

undertaken to establish contact with unwilling children, particularly in cases where it is contrary to the child's welfare to continue with attempts to establish direct contact. If all possible avenues have been explored appropriately, then the court is entitled to order that such efforts should no longer be pursued. See *Re Q (Implacable Contact Dispute)* [2016] 2 FLR 287, CA, where a child had been influenced by his mother's hostility towards his father and had suffered emotional harm as a result of court proceedings concerning contact; the judge was realistic in concluding that any further attempt to enforce contact was almost bound to fail and would be harmful to the child, and was entitled to make no further order regarding child arrangements and instead to direct the parents to cooperate in the child's referral for therapy.

Transfer of living arrangements—There have been a number of reported cases in which the court has ordered that a child who was living with one parent should move to live with the other parent with whom contact has been frustrated or sabotaged. However, this is a judicial weapon of last resort (*Re A (Residence Order)* [2010] 1 FLR 1083, CA – where the judge had been wrong to make an order transferring the living arrangements of three children to their father, following the mother's refusal to allow contact, as no clear order for contact had been made by the court). Nevertheless, in *Re C (Residence Order)* [2008] 1 FLR 211, CA, the court did transfer the children's living arrangements from the mother to the father as a result of the mother's implacable hostility to him having contact with the children. The draconian step of an immediate order for transfer without giving time for a relationship to develop between the child and father had been necessary because of the mother's intractability. In *Re Y (Private Law: Interim Change of Residence)* [2014] EWHC 1068 (Fam), the court took the highly unusual step of transferring residence at an interim stage due to mounting concerns about the mother's delusional beliefs that the father had sexually abused the child, which were entirely without foundation. Where the court has no confidence that any scheme of prohibitory orders to accompany an order for shared living arrangements will alter the attitude or conduct of the intractable parent in the future then a transfer of living arrangements while the child is relatively young may be the appropriate option (*TB v DB (Change of Residence)* [2013] EWHC 2275 (Fam)). In *Re V (A Child)* [2013] EWCA Civ 1649, the court was entitled to transfer the residence of a 6-year-old child from mother to father where the mother had allegedly inculcated false memories in the child that the child had been physically and sexually assaulted by her father. There is no consensus in the research as to the approach that should be taken in a case involving an alienated child. In *Re S (Transfer of Residence)* [2011] 1 FLR 1789, FD, the court considered three approaches to effecting the transfer of residence: (a) a stepping-stone process involving a period in foster care before transfer; (b) a therapeutic approach; and (c) use of the tipstaff. In *Re S* (above) the judge said, per curiam, that when determining any high-conflict case involving an alienated child, it is essential that the court has the benefit of professional evidence from an expert. See also *Re M (Contact)* [2013] 1 FLR 1403, FD in note **Section 11(7)** under s 11. In *Re E-R (Child Arrangements)* [2016] EWHC 805 (Fam), the court made a child arrangements order in respect of a 6-year old girl following the death of her mother where the parents had previously separated. The court held that a change in residence was likely to cause psychological harm to her and that she should remain living with family friends. However, the court also noted that it was fundamental to her psychological well-being that her father should play a full part in her life and therefore made provision for contact with him.

Suspended transfer of living arrangements—Where a parent persists in disobeying an order for the other parent to have contact with the children, the court may order the transfer of the living arrangements of the children, but suspend the operation of the transfer upon the obdurate parent complying with the order (*Re D (Children)* [2009] EWCA Civ 1467).

Contact – domestic violence—The definition of domestic violence applies to any incidents of controlling, coercive or threatening behaviour, violence or abuse between those aged 16 or over who are or have been intimate partners or family members regardless of gender, sexuality or ethnic group. This definition, which is not a legal definition, includes, but is not limited to, psychological, physical, sexual, financial and emotional abuse, so-called 'honour'-based violence, female genital mutilation and forced marriage. The Court of Appeal in *Re L (Contact: Domestic Violence)*, *Re V (Contact: Domestic Violence)*. *Re M (Contact: Domestic Violence)* and *Re H (Contact: Domestic Violence)* [2000] 2 FLR 334, CA laid down useful guidelines as to the way in which courts should approach the hearing of contact applications in which allegations of domestic violence are raised. Their lordships referred to the joint report of Drs Sturge and Glaser ([2000] Fam Law 615) and it is recommended that practitioners read it in full. FPR PD12J *Child Arrangements and Contact Order: Domestic Violence and Harm* places a duty on the court at all stages of the proceedings to consider whether domestic violence is an issue and, if so, to identify the factual and welfare issues involved. The PD represents good practice and judges are not entitled to take short-cuts that either run the risk of compromising the welfare of the children or that fail to follow accepted practice (*Re Z (Unsupervised Contact: Allegations of Domestic Violence)* [2009] EWCA Civ 430). See *Re A (Supervised Contact Order: Assessment of Impact of Domestic Violence)* [2016] 1 FLR 689, CA, where the Court of Appeal confirmed that any court dealing with a case where domestic violence or abuse was established is required to afford appropriate weight to such findings in accordance with *Re L* (above) and to conduct a risk assessment in accordance with FPR PD12J. However, FPR PD12J does not prevent a judge from making an order for contact without making findings of fact in relation to disputed allegations of domestic violence. See *Re V (A Child) (Inadequate Reasons for Findings of Fact)* [2015] 2 FLR 1472, CA, which demonstrates the dangers of a 'knee-jerk' reaction to allegations of domestic violence. Allegations, even if proved, must be relevant to the issue of contact; although domestic violence can be an important factor in the issue of contact, what has to be considered is a relevant risk of harm. See *Re K (Contact)* [2017] 1 FLR 530, CA as an example of a case where if the judge who was determining a father's application for direct contact had been referred to FPR PD12J, paras 33 and 34 and had been informed of the available options of direct work with the father and the children, he might not have fallen into the trap of reaching a 'premature decision' that the father was to have no direct contact.

Para 13 does not dictate that there must be a fact-finding hearing; it simply requires the court to determine as soon as possible whether it is necessary to conduct such a hearing before it can proceed to consider any final child arrangements order (*Re H (Interim Contact: Domestic Violence Allegations)* [2014] 1 FLR 41, CA, at [54]). Once findings of fact of domestic violence have been made, the judge must ensure that he considers all the evidence necessary to determine the children's best interests (*Re W (Children: Domestic Violence)* [2014] 1 FLR 260, CA). See further under **Fact-finding hearings** (below).

The Domestic Violence, Crime and Victims Act 2004 makes breach of a non-molestation order a criminal offence as from 1 July 2007. Consequently, it is no longer possible to attach a power of arrest to a non-molestation order. However, breach of a non-molestation order automatically becomes an arrestable offence under PACE 1984, s 24(1). See further under Procedural Guide A8.

Where there is a conflict between the rights and interests of a child and those of a parent, the interests of the child must prevail under ECHR 1950, Art 8(2) (*Re L* etc (above)). See further **Contact – ECHR 1950** (above).

Fact-finding hearings—FPR PD12J *Child Arrangements and Contact Order: Domestic Violence and Harm*, which supersedes the *President's Guidance in Relation to Split Hearings*, May 2010, makes it clear that a split hearing should not be ordered unless the case cannot properly be decided without one (para 17). Allegations of violence do not automatically justify a preliminary fact-finding hearing. FPR PD12J, para 19 contemplates a two-stage process of fact-finding and welfare hearing, but it does not require two separate hearings. PD12J should be read as imposing an obligation on the court to determine whether findings need to be made about factual issues at all and whether, if so, that should be done in a separate fact-finding hearing or as part of a composite fact-finding and welfare hearing. If the court decides that a separate fact-finding hearing is necessary then it must give directions for it and fix a date for the welfare hearing there and then (*Re H (Interim Contact: Domestic Violence Allegations)* [2014] 1 FLR 41, CA and see annotation **Contact – Domestic Violence** (above)). The court must consider the nature of the allegations and the extent to which, if admitted or proved, they would be relevant in making its decision. If they are unlikely to have any impact on the court's order, there is no need for a separate fact-finding hearing. Where there is a multiplicity of allegations and counter-allegations the court must be careful to establish whether or not a fact-finding hearing has a true purpose and whether the scale of the inquiry is proportionate to the nature of the allegations made: see the guidance given in *AA v NA and KAB* [2010] 2 FLR 1173, FD. However, a judge must be very cautious before reversing the decision of another judge that a fact-finding hearing is necessary (*Re F-H (Dispensing With Fact-Finding Hearing)* [2009] 1 FLR 349, CA). Only when he has heard all the evidence and made findings of fact can he determine where the best interests of the child really lie (*Re Z (Unsupervised Contact: Allegations of Domestic Violence)* [2009] 2 FLR 877, CA). The simple balance of probabilities test is to be applied to the fact-finding exercise (*Re B (Children) (Care Proceedings: Standard of Proof)* [2008] 2 FLR 141, HL). It is not appropriate for the judge to accept a submission of no case to answer because of the quasi-inquisitorial nature of his enquiry and the objective of identifying and resolving issues of fact relevant to the best interests of the child (*Re R (Fact-Finding Hearing)* [2009] 2 FLR 83, CA). The judicial task is to lay the foundation for subsequent hearings and in the interim to inform professionals who have to make assessments and report to the court. Where a fact-finding hearing is adjourned part-heard it is unusual for the court to order interim contact. However, in *S v S (Interim Contact)* [2009] 2 FLR 1586, FD, the district judge ordered 1 hour of interim supervised contact a fortnight when he was forced to adjourn the hearing part-heard for several months. In upholding his decision on appeal, Hedley J observed that an order for interim contact raises the very question at issue in the proceedings, namely whether there should be contact at all. On the other hand, the longer the delay, if it be that contact should be ordered, the more inimical for the child. The burden of proof lies on the party making the allegations. Even if allegations made are of a very serious nature, that does not alter the standard of proof, which is the balance of probabilities (per Baroness Hale in *Re B (Children) (Care Proceedings: Standard of Proof)* [2008] 2 FLR 141, HL). See *Re A (Supervised Contact Order: Assessment of Impact of Domestic Violence)* [2016] 1 FLR 689, CA, where the Court of Appeal held that the fact-finding process requires a judge to identify those facts that have been proved to his or her satisfaction on the balance of probabilities; any allegations found to be so proved will become established facts in the proceedings and any not so proved are not established facts and therefore cannot be relied upon in forming any other conclusions in relation, for example, to a child's welfare. In *JEG v IS and Another (Sexual Abuse Allegations)* [2014] EWHC 287 (Fam), Russell J confirmed (obiter) that the need for judicial determination of the facts in private law cases is as necessary as it is in public law cases, because the court has a duty to protect children and ensure that decisions and orders are made that are consistent with their best interests and welfare: 'An early determination of the facts followed swiftly by a welfare hearing at which the medium and long term pattern for time spent with each [parent] can be put in place is the just and proportionate way to deal with private law cases'.

Honour-based violence—In *Re S (Findings of Fact: Honour Based Violence)* [2013] EWHC 15 (Fam), the court heard evidence from a specialist witness experienced in honour-based family systems that emphasised the lengths to which some traditional families will go when a member is considered to have brought dishonour upon them.

Risk assessments—The CA 1989, s 16A requires a Cafcass officer carrying out any function in private law CA 1989 proceedings to carry out a risk assessment if he has cause to suspect that the child concerned is at risk of harm, and to provide that assessment to the court. See further under s 16A and FPR 2010, rr 16.33 and 12.34, and see PD16A, paras 11.1–11.7 and the amended Form 42. See also FPR PD12L *Risk Assessments under Section 16A*.

Interim contact – pending assessments—Judges must be very cautious before adjusting any interim order for contact while an important assessment, which they have commissioned, is pending (*Re A (A Child)* [2013] EWCA Civ 543).

Refusal of contact—Complete refusals of direct contact and resultant orders for only very limited indirect contact lie at the very extremities of the court's powers; there should almost always be some contact between child and parent – see *Re Q (Implacable Contact Dispute)* [2016] 2 FLR 287, CA. It will only be in a rare and exceptional case that the court should agree there should be no contact – see for example *Q v Q (Contact:*

PART II

Undertakings) (No 3) [2017] 1 FLR 438, FD. *Re W (Children) (Contact Dispute) (No 2)* [2014] EWCA Civ 401 contains a useful review of the case-law on refusing parental contact (see also *Re P (Contact: Supervision)* [1996] 2 FLR 314, CA and *Re C (Direct Contact: Suspension)* [2011] 2 FLR 912, CA). See, for example, *Re A (A Child: Application for leave to apply for a child arrangements order)* [2015] EWCA Civ 910, where it was not wrong to order direct contact between a 12-year-old boy and his father where there had been no contact for several years, where the boy was adamantly opposed to any contact and where contact would worsen his mother's already poor mental health, despite the evidence that when the boy was younger he had had an extremely strong attachment to his father. See also *Re S (A Child) (Child Arrangements Order: Effect of Long-Term Supervised Contact on Welfare)* [2016] 2 FLR 217, CA, where the fact that there would have to be long-term supervision of contact was not in itself a reason to refuse direct contact. Before the reintroduction of direct contact could be refused on grounds of disturbance to the child or caring parent, it would have to be shown that the disturbance went well beyond mere inconvenience. See also *Re M (Children)* [2015] EWCA Civ 280, where a judge was entitled to impose as a condition of direct contact between a mother and her children a requirement for her to undergo a risk assessment, including a psychiatric referral. In *Re J-M (A Child)* [2015] 1 FLR 838, CA, the Court of Appeal outlined the propositions underpinning the correct judicial approach to the refusal or termination of contact as follows:

(i) the welfare of the child is paramount;
(ii) it is almost always in the interests of a child whose parents are separated that he or she should have contact with the parent with whom he or she is not living;
(iii) there is a positive obligation on the state and therefore on the judge to take measures to promote contact, grappling with all available options and taking all necessary steps that can reasonably be demanded, before abandoning hope of achieving contact;
(iv) excessive weight should not be accorded to short-term problems and the court should take a medium- and long-term view; and
(v) contact should be terminated only in exceptional circumstances where there are cogent reasons for doing so, as a last resort, when there is no alternative, and only if contact will be detrimental to the child's welfare.

See *Re F (Children)* [2015] EWCA Civ 1315, where the judge failed to follow the established guidelines. Very clear reasons are required to deny contact. In particular, the judge had not given reasons for departing from the recommendations of the Cafcass officer, the issue of contact had not been properly ventilated at the hearing and the judge's analysis was inadequate.

Contact disputes – separate representation of children—As a matter of principle where the court is faced with difficult contact issues, consideration may be given to the children being separately represented (*Re H (Contact Order) (No 2)* [2002] 1 FLR 22, FD; *Re W (Contact: Joining Child as Party)* [2003] 1 FLR 681, CA; *Re M (Intractable Contact Dispute: Interim Care Order)* [2003] 2 FLR 636, FD). In difficult private law cases where the child does need separate representation, the appropriate course will be to invite Cafcass Legal to provide a guardian to represent the child and take over the child's case (*Re W (A Child)* [2001] All ER (D) 348 (Nov), CA; and see further under FPR 2010, r 16.4 and PD16A). General guidance in relation to the appointment of a children's guardian is to be found under CA 1989, s 7 **Cafcass Practice Note**.

See annotation **Role of National Youth Advocacy Service (NYAS)** under CA 1989, s 7 for details of the increased importance of NYAS in the separate representation of children, particularly in acrimonious contact disputes.

Electronic tagging in family proceedings—The availability of electronic tagging arrangements in family proceedings was established in *Re C (Abduction: Interim Directions: Accommodation by Local Authority)* [2004] 1 FLR 653, FD. The President confirmed this and devised a process whereby tagging could be arranged through the Tagging Team of the National Office for the Management of Offenders. The decision in *Re A (Family Proceedings: Electronic Tagging)* [2009] 2 FLR 891, FD sets out the procedure to be adopted, including a Specimen Electronic Tagging Order.

'shall be taken by any person' (s 8(1))—In the definition of a prohibited steps order, 'any person' includes someone who is not a party to the proceedings (*Re H (Prohibited Steps Order)* [1995] 1 FLR 638, CA – prohibited steps order requiring mother's former cohabitee, who was not a party, not to have or to seek contact with the children, liberty being given to him to apply on notice to vary or discharge the order under s 11(7)(d)).

Change of surname—At birth, a child must be registered in accordance with the Births and Deaths Registration Act 1953. Where the parents are married, the duty to register lies on both the mother and father; where they are not married at the time of the birth, the duty is the mother's alone. The surname entered is to be the one by which at the date of the registration it is intended that the child shall be known. However, it is possible either for the parents jointly or for the mother alone to apply for the name of the father to be entered into the Register of Births, on the production of Statutory Declarations (see Births and Deaths Registration Act 1953, s 10A). See further **Where natural unmarried father has not signed Birth Register but wishes to be acknowledged as the parent** under s 4. Once the surname has been registered, there is nothing in BDRA 1953 to permit it to be changed in the register (see the consideration of BDRA 1953 in *Dawson v Wearmouth* [1997] 2 FLR 629, CA and [1999] 1 FLR 1167, HL; *Re C (Change of Surname)* [1998] 2 FLR 656, CA and *Re W, Re A, Re B (Change of Name)* [1999] 2 FLR 930, CA). Accordingly, the courts' powers are limited to regulating the name by which a child should be known. However, there is a requirement that the parents of a child who is legitimated by their subsequent marriage must re-register the child's birth within 3 months of the date of the marriage by virtue of which he was legitimated (Legitimacy Act 1976, s 9).

A change of the name by which a child is known can be evidenced by deed poll or, in practice, can be achieved more informally, by a parent simply arranging for a child to be known on a day-to-day basis by a new surname (for example at school). In each case, there are important pre-conditions for the change of name. The general principle that must be observed is that 'the registration or change of a child's surname is a profound and not a merely formal issue, whatever the age of the child. Any dispute on such an issue must be referred to the court for determination whether or not there is a child arrangements order in force and whoever has or has not parental responsibility. No disputed registration or change should be made unilaterally' (*Dawson v Wearmouth* (above); *Re T (Change of Surname)* [1998] 2 FLR 620, CA). Note the reconsideration by the House of Lords (reported at [1999] 1 FLR 1167, HL) of some aspects of the Court of Appeal's decision in *Dawson v Wearmouth*. The House of Lords reviewed the principles to be applied to a change of name application (including the question of what weight is to be given to the name in which the child has been duly registered) but the procedural aspects of such an application were not the subject of an appeal and were not considered.

It appears that the proper course in all cases in which a change of name is contemplated will be as follows:

(1) There should first be consultation with anyone who has parental responsibility. This should happen whether or not there is a child arrangements order in force (*Re PC (Change of Surname)* [1997] 2 FLR 730, FD).

(2) There remains uncertainty about the extent to which consent of a father who does not have parental responsibility is material to a change of name. Thorpe LJ in *Re T* (above) remarked at p 623B when speaking of the decision in *Re PC* that it was 'persuasively indicative of the clear principle that children's names are important and in any situation of dispute, either the consent of the other parent or the permission of the court is an essential pre-requisite, *certainly where both parents have parental responsibility*' (author's emphasis) thus begging the question. Holman J in *Re PC* had, in fact, held (p 739) that where a child is born of parents who are not married to each other and there is no order or agreement for parental responsibility, the mother can lawfully change the child's surname without any other permission or consent. Furthermore, it will be noted that CA 1989, s 13 (which applies where there is a child arrangements order specifying with whom the child should live) only refers to the consent of those with parental responsibility and it may be reasonable to infer from this a more general view that a father without parental responsibility should not be entitled to prior consultation about name changes. On the other hand, if a father without parental responsibility learns of, and disagrees with, plans to change his child's name (or wishes to contest a fait accompli), he is entitled to bring the matter before the court under s 8 (*Dawson v Wearmouth*, see further below), despite the absence of a right to prior consultation. The Court of Appeal in *Re C (Change of Surname)* (above), considering the action of a mother who effected a change of name by deed poll at a time when the father did not have parental responsibility but had made his opposition to the name change known, commented that at the first signs of dispute about a child's name the court should be involved, but expressly left to one side whether that arose as a matter of wisdom, common decency or binding obligation.

(3) If consent is forthcoming, it would be prudent in all cases to have it put in writing. Written consent of everyone with parental responsibility is, in any event, a statutory requirement by virtue of CA 1989, s 13(1) where there is a child arrangements order specifying with whom the child should live. Written consent will also generally be required if a deed poll is to be enrolled (see below).

(4) If the change of name is disputed, the matter must be referred to the court for determination.

   (a) Where there is in force a child arrangements order, specifying with whom the child should live, a freestanding application for permission should be made under CA 1989, s 13. An application under s 8 is not appropriate (*Re B (Change of Surname)* (above) as explained in *Dawson v Wearmouth* [1997] 2 FLR 629, CA, undisturbed by the House of Lords decision at [1999] 1 FLR 1167).

   (b) Where there is no child arrangements order specifying with whom the child should live, the application should be made under CA 1989, s 8. An application under s 13 is not appropriate (*Dawson v Wearmouth* (above)). Whether the application will be for a specific issue order or for a prohibited steps order may depend upon the circumstances. In both *Dawson v Wearmouth* and *Re T (Change of Surname)* (above), the order sought was a specific issue order; in *Re PC* both specific issue and prohibited steps orders were made.

There looks, technically, to be a difference in the way in which a court should approach s 8 and s 13 applications. Section 1(1) applies in both cases to make the child's welfare the court's paramount consideration but s 1(3) (welfare check list), while applicable to s 8 applications, is not applicable to s 13 applications (see s 1(4)). However, as the Court of Appeal pointed out in *Dawson v Wearmouth*, the distinction is more theoretical than real because the judge entertaining an application under s 13 will invariably have regard, in fact, to the considerations identified in s 1(3) in his search for welfare as the paramount consideration even if under no specific statutory duty so to do. It is anticipated that the review by the House of Lords in *Dawson v Wearmouth* of the approach that should be taken with a s 8 application will accordingly be influential also in s 13 applications. The present position in cases which deal with changing the name of a child is helpfully summarised by Butler-Sloss LJ in *Re W, Re A, Re B (Change of Name)* [1999] 2 FLR 930, CA, with the caveat that the summary only lays down guidelines and does not purport to be exhaustive. Each case must be decided on its own facts, with the welfare of the child the paramount consideration and all the relevant factors weighed in the balance by the court at the time of the hearing. The factors are set out at page 933F of the judgment.

A deed poll evidences a change of name in a formal way. It is first executed then enrolled with the Central Office of the High Court. Enrolment will not be permitted unless certain conditions are complied with. Reference should be made to the Enrolment of Deeds (Change of Name) Regulations 1994 and CPR PD5A, para 6.1 and its Appendix.

Re PC (above) raises (but does not rule upon) the possibility that the position as to name change may be different for an older child, in particular a child of over 16, where the consent of the child *may* be necessary and sufficient. See also *Re S (Change of Surname)* [1999] 1 FLR 672, CA (annotated under CA 1989, s 33).

It may be appropriate in certain cases for a child to use the surnames of both his mother and father (*Re R (Surname: Using Both Parents')* [2001] 2 FLR 1358, CA – where the child was to move to Spain with his mother and the parents were urged to follow the Spanish practice of using both parents' surnames in order to ease the child's adjustment to a life in that culture and to encourage transparency as to his parentage).

Although a change of surname should not be permitted without evidence that it would improve the children's welfare, in certain circumstances the court may find that it is justified and give permission accordingly (*Re F (Contact)* [2008] 1 FLR 1163, FD – where a change of surname for the children gave them some extra protection against the possibility of abduction by their father; *AA v BB and Children (Through their Children's Guardian)* [2014] 1 FLR 178, FD – where a change of surname was granted as it would be very detrimental to the children if their father tracked them down).

Statutory declaration of parentage—See **Statutory declaration of parentage** under CA 1989, s 4.

Revealing the identity of the child's father; revealing the fact of the existence of the child—There have been a number of cases concerning the circumstances in which it may be in the child's interests to be informed of the identity of his father, and whether the child's family have a right to know of his existence. It is difficult to draw any consistent principles from these cases as each appears to turn upon its own facts (*Re L (Adoption: Contacting Natural Father)* [2008] 1 FLR 1079, FD; *Re C v X Y Z County Council* [2008 1 FLR 1294, CA; *Birmingham City Council v S, R and A* [2007] 1 FLR 1223, FD; *Re F (Paternity Jurisdiction)* [2008] 1 FLR 225, CA; *Re J (Paternity: Welfare of Child)* [2007] 1 FLR 1064, FD; *Re D (Paternity)* [2007] 2 FLR 26, FD). However, what is clear is that the courts will not sanction the withholding of information about the existence of a child from his parent, or dispense with service on that parent of proceedings relating to the child, in anything other than exceptional circumstances (*Re A (Father: Knowledge of Child's Birth)* [2011] 2 FLR 123, CA).

Where there is an unduly long delay in proceedings relating to the establishment of a child's paternity this may amount to a violation of ECHR 1950, Arts 6, 8, 10 and 13 because of the resulting uncertainty for the child as to his or her personal identity (*Jevremović v Serbia* (Application No 3150/05) [2008] 1 FLR 550, ECHR).

Change of forenames—The choosing of a name for a child and the parents' compliance with their duty under Births and Deaths Registration Act 1953, s 2 to give the registrar the information required to register the child's birth are acts of parental responsibility (*Re D, L and LA (Care: Change of Forename)* [2003] 1 FLR 339, FD). However, the forename(s) given to a child at the registration of his birth are less concrete than the surname, since it is commonplace for a child to receive a statutory registered name and also to receive different given names during the course of family life (see *Re H (Child's Name: First Name)* [2002] 1 FLR 973, CA – where the father and mother, who were separated, had each registered the child with different forenames; although the father's registration was first in time the mother should be permitted to use the forename she had chosen for the child both at home and when dealing with external authorities). The High Court can invoke its inherent jurisdiction to prevent a parent with parental responsibility from registering their child with the forename of their choice, but such power is to be exercised only in the most extreme cases where the parent's choice of forename gives rise to reasonable cause to believe that the child would suffer significant harm: see *Re C (Children: Power to Choose Forenames)* [2017] 1 FLR 487, CA. See also **Meaning of parental responsibility** under s 3.

Birth registration in transgender cases—The UK's birth registration scheme does not breach ECHR, Arts 8 or 14 by requiring a man who has changed gender from male to female to be listed as the 'father' on the birth certificates of his biological children: *R (on the application of JK) v Registrar General for England & Wales & Ors* [2015] EWHC 990 (Admin).

Prohibited Steps Orders (PSO)—A PSO may be made against 'any person', but the prohibition may only relate to steps that could be taken by 'a parent in meeting his parental responsibility'. The order does not prohibit the child from taking steps for himself. Thus, while an order may prohibit any person allowing a particular individual to have contact with the child, the child will not breach the order if he seeks that individual out and contacts him himself. The older the child becomes, the less likely it is that a PSO will be made against the child's wishes (*Gillick v West Norfolk and Wisbech Area Health Authority and Another* [1986] 1 FLR 224, HL).

A PSO cannot be granted to forbid a child's parents from having any contact with each other (*Croydon London Borough Council v A (No 1)* [1992] 2 FLR 341, FD). Neither may a PSO be used to restrain assault or molestation, although the High Court and County Court may have jurisdiction to grant injunctive relief as an ancillary order when making s 8 orders, even where no formal application for such relief has been filed (*M v M (Residence Order: Ancillary Injunction)* [1994] Fam Law 440, FD, but see *Re M (Minors) (Disclosure of Evidence)* [1994] 1 FLR 760, CA).

A PSO may be made against a person who is neither a party to proceedings nor present in court (*Re H (Prohibited Steps Order)* [1995] 1 FLR 638, CA); for example, an order may be made prohibiting a named person from having contact with a child (*Re H* (above)). Examples of possible PSOs are:

(a) an order preventing the removal of the child from the UK (when there is no child arrangements order and consequently no automatic ban on removal (CA 1989, s 13(1); *Croydon London Borough Council v A (No 1)* [1992] 2 FLR 341, FD; *Re D (A Minor) (Child: Removal from Jurisdiction)* [1992] 1 FLR 637, CA);
(b) an order preventing the child undergoing certain surgery, or receiving a blood transfusion (*Re S (A Minor) (Medical Treatment)* [1993] 1 FLR 376, FD);
(c) an order preventing the changing of a child's religion (*M v H (Education Welfare)* [2008] 1 FLR 1400, FD)
(d) an order preventing a change in the child's schooling (*Re N (A Child: Religion: Jehovah's Witness)* [2012] 2 FLR 917, FD, at [31])
(e) an order that the child's name should not be changed (*Re PC (Change of Surname)* [1997] 2 FLR 730, FD; *Re C (Change of Surname)* [1998] 1 FLR 549, CA; and *Re T (Change of Surname)* [1998] 2 FLR 620, CA);
(f) an order preventing a parent from accessing a child's health and education information (*Re A and B (Children: Restrictions on Parental Responsibility: Radicalisation and Extremism)* [2016] 2 FLR 977, FD);

(g) an order preventing a parent from exercising his right to see the child's school record under the Education (School Records) Regulations 1989 (*R v Leicestershire Education Authority ex parte C* [1991] Fam Law 302, QBD);
(h) an order prohibiting a non-parent from allowing the child to have contact with a named individual;
(i) an order restraining a party with parental responsibility from involving the social services or police in investigating the child's circumstances (if the court is satisfied that such an involvement would be detrimental to the child) (*D v D (County Court: Jurisdiction: Injunctions)* [1993] 2 FLR 802, CA).

It is wrong to make a PSO for the purpose of regulating contact even if the regulation is for no contact other than supervised contact (CA 1989, s 9(5)(a); *Nottinghamshire County Council v P* [1993] 2 FLR 134, CA). Where an order prohibiting contact is directed to a person with whom the child does not live, a PSO may be appropriate (*Re H (Prohibited Steps Order)* [1995] 1 FLR 638, CA). A PSO may not be used to prevent a father from contacting a mother or child, or from entering school premises (*Re H (Prohibited Steps Order)*, above). As an alternative, some conduct may properly be restrained by means of a condition attached to a s 8 order (*F v R (Contact: Justices' Reasons)* [1995] 1 FLR 227, FD).

Other restrictions on the making of a PSO include the following:

(a) No court may make a PSO with a view to achieving a result that could be achieved by making a child arrangements order (CA 1989, s 9(5)(a); see also *Re B (A Minor) (Residence Order: Ex Parte)* [1992] 2 FLR 1, CA);
(b) An order prohibiting contact between a child and another person cannot be made by a PSO against the person with whom the child lives, but may be made by a PSO against the person who is not to have contact (*Re H (Prohibited Steps Order)* [1995] 1 FLR 638, CA).
(c) A PSO cannot be granted for the purpose of excluding a parent from the family home (*Nottinghamshire County Council v P* [1993] 2 FLR 134, CA; *Re D (Residence: Imposition of Conditions)* [1996] 2 FLR 281, CA; *Re K (Contact Order: Condition Ousting Parent from Family Home)* [2012] 2 FLR 635, CA).
(d) No court may make a PSO in any way that is denied to the High Court (CA 1989, s 100(2)) in the exercise of its inherent jurisdiction with respect to children (CA 1989, s 9(5));
(e) The court cannot make a PSO with respect to a child who is in care under a care order (CA 1989, s 9(1)).

In *Re C (Due Process)* [2014] 1 FLR 1239, CA, Ryder LJ emphasised that a prohibited steps order (PSO) is a statutory restriction on a parent's exercise of their parental responsibility for a child and can have profound consequences. It is not a reflection of any power in one parent to restrict the other (which power does not exist), it is a court order that must be based on objective evidence. It can only be relaxed by the court and not by agreement between the parties. Accordingly, there is a high responsibility on the court not to impose such a restriction without good cause and the reason must be given. Furthermore, where a PSO is appropriate, consideration should also be given to the duration of that prohibition and the finite nature of the order must be expressed on the face of the order (*R (Casey) v Restormel Borough Council* [2007] EWHC 2554 (Admin), at [38]).

Specific Issue Orders (SIO) (s 8(1))—A SIO is appropriate where there is only one specific issue between the parties, for example:

(a) to determine where the child should be educated (*R v Leicestershire Education Authority ex parte C* [1991] Fam Law 302, QBD; *Re A (Specific Issue Order: Parental Dispute)* [2001] 1 FLR 121, CA; *Re W (Children) (Education: Choice of School)* [2002] EWCA Civ 1411);
(b) to determine issues of religion or medical treatment, for example: blood transfusions (*Re R (A Minor) (Blood Transfusion)* [1993] 2 FLR 757, FD); circumcision (*Re J (Specific Issue Orders: Child's Religious Upbringing and Circumcision)* [2000] 1 FLR 571, CA and *Re L & B (Children) (Specific Issues: Temporary Leave to Remove from the Jurisdiction; Circumcision)* [2016] EWHC 849 (Fam)); sterilisation (see (f), below);
(c) to determine whether or not a child should be told the truth about his or her origins (*Re F (Paternity: Jurisdiction)* [2008] 1 FLR 225, CA);
(d) to order that a child be returned to the jurisdiction (*Re D (A Minor) (Child: Removal from Jurisdiction)* [1992] 1 FLR 637, CA);
(e) where there is no child arrangements order in force specifying with whom the child is to live, a SIO may be made to determine a child's surname (*Dawson v Wearmouth* [1997] 2 FLR 629, CA; *Re PC (Change of Surname)* [1997] 2 FLR 730, FD; *Re W* [1997] Fam Law 766, CA; *Re C (Change of Surname)* [1998] 2 FLR 656, CA; *Re T (Change of Surname)* [1998] 2 FLR 620, CA);
(f) an application for a SIO may be used to seek authorisation for the sterilisation of a girl of 17 years (*Re HG (Specific Issue Order: Sterilisation)* [1993] 1 FLR 587, FD). However, such an application should only be brought in the High Court, with the involvement of the Official Solicitor (*Re HG*, above). In such cases, there will be a need for the child to be granted party status and to be legally represented. The representation of children in family proceedings is governed by FPR 2010, Pt 16 and PD16A.
(g) when determining whether a SIO should be made permitting the police to interview a child, the child's welfare is not the paramount consideration, but is one factor in the balance of rights and interests that must be struck (*Chief Constable of Greater Manchester v KI and KW (by their guardian) and PN* [2008] 1 FLR 504, FD);
(h) where the court's authorisation is sought for the use of blood products on a child, against the parent's wishes, a local authority applicant should apply for a SIO rather than proceed under the inherent jurisdiction (*Re R (A Minor) (Blood Transfusion)* [1993] 2 FLR 757, FD (the ratio in this case expressly disapproves the obiter dicta in *Re O (A Minor) (Medical Treatment)* [1993] 2 FLR 149, FD). Such applications should be made to the High Court (*Re R*, above).

A SIO cannot be made so as to determine an issue of where the child should live or to require that the children be returned to the care of one parent (*M v C (Children Orders: Reasons)* [1993] 2 FLR 584, FD).

PART II

The court gives directions for the purpose of determining the issue. Thus, it may determine the issue itself by making a direction that will, as a matter of law, determine the issues between the parties (*Re B (A Minor) (Residence Order: Ex Parte)* [1992] 2 FLR 1, CA, at [8]). The court may also give ancillary directions as to the carrying out of its decision.

The court must not abdicate its primary obligation to decide issues relating to parental responsibility by directing that one or other parent should determine issues of a particular type (for example education) (*Re P (Parental Dispute: Judicial Determination)* [2003] 1 FLR 286, CA).

A SIO may be made alone or alongside other s 8 orders.

The restrictions on making SIOs are the same as those in relation to prohibited steps orders (see above).

'the inherent jurisdiction of the High Court' (s 8(3)(a))—The inherent jurisdiction of the High Court was, before CA 1989, most commonly exercised in wardship proceedings. The Act has put an end to the majority of wardship applications, but applications are still made under the inherent jurisdiction of the court; see, in particular, under s 100.

'application for leave under section 100(3)' (s 8(3))—This is a reference to an application by a local authority for permission to apply for the exercise of the court's inherent jurisdiction with respect to children.

'Parts I, II and IV of this Act' (s 8(4))—Broadly speaking, this means that most proceedings under the Act are classed as family proceedings but those relating to the protection of children (under Pt V), such as applications for emergency protection orders etc, are not so classified.

Enforcement of s 8 orders—For the implementation of orders, see s 11(7) directions and conditions and ss 11A–11P for enforcement of orders for contact; for enforcement under MCA 1980, s 63(3), see s 14; for orders for recovery of a child, see FLA 1986, s 34. See Procedural Guide D8 for enforcement of orders for contact.

Costs orders in children cases—FPR 2010 disapply that part of CPR 1998 that provides a starting point that the unsuccessful party pays the costs of the successful party so that in family cases the court has a broad discretion to make such order as it thinks just. However, on an application for permission to appeal, the court may take the view that although the appeal has a real prospect of success it must be refused because it lacks any proportionality to the amount at stake (*HH v BLW (Appeal: Costs: Proportionality)* [2013] 1 FLR 420, FD). See further under FPR 2010, Pt 28 and r 30.11.

Hague Convention 1996—The Hague Convention 1996 came into force in the UK on 1 November 2012. It lays down rules in respect of measures directed to the protection of the person or property of the child in cases to which the Convention applies (Art 1). 'Measures of protection' include the attribution, exercise, termination, restriction and delegation of parental responsibility, and of custody and access (Art 3). 'Rights of custody' essentially include all measures relating to the care and upbringing of, and access, contact or visitation rights concerning the child (Art 3(b)). See also the commentary to the Convention in Part VI.

9 Restrictions on making section 8 orders

(1) No court shall make any section 8 order, other than a child arrangements order to which subsection (6B) applies, with respect to a child who is in the care of a local authority.

(2) No application may be made by a local authority for a child arrangements order and no court shall make such an order in favour of a local authority.

(3) A person who is, or was at any time within the last six months, a local authority foster parent of a child may not apply for leave to apply for a section 8 order with respect to the child unless –

(a) he has the consent of the authority;
(b) he is a relative of the child; or
(c) the child has lived with him for at least one year preceding the application.

(4) *(repealed)*

(5) No court shall exercise its powers to make a specific issue order or prohibited steps order –

(a) with a view to achieving a result which could be achieved by making a child arrangements order or an order under section 51A of the Adoption and Children Act 2002 (post-adoption contact); or
(b) in any way which is denied to the High Court (by section 100(2)) in the exercise of its inherent jurisdiction with respect to children.

(6) No court shall make a section 8 order which is to have effect for a period which will end after the child has reached the age of sixteen unless it is satisfied that the circumstances of the case are exceptional.

(6A) Subsection (6) does not apply to a child arrangements order to which subsection (6B) applies.

(6B) This subsection applies to a child arrangements order if the arrangements regulated by the order relate only to either or both of the following –

(a) with whom the child concerned is to live, and

(b) when the child is to live with any person.

(7) No court shall make any section 8 order, other than one varying or discharging such an order, with respect to a child who has reached the age of sixteen unless it is satisfied that the circumstances of the case are exceptional.

Amendments—ACA 2002, ss 113, 114(2); CYPA 2008, s 37(1); CFA 2014, ss 9, 12, Sch 2.

Defined terms—'child': s 105(1); 'child arrangements order': s 8(1); 'local authority': s 105(1); 'local authority foster parent': s 23(3); 'relative': s 105(1); 'section 8 order': s 8(2).

'child who is in the care of a local authority' (s 9(1))—A child who is the subject of a care order as defined in ss 31(11) and 105(1). There is power to make an order under s 34 (parental contact with child in care) as this is not a child arrangements order within the meaning of s 8(1). An order made under s 8 on the application of a child in care for him to have contact with his siblings would be an order in respect of the siblings rather than in respect of the child in care and would not therefore fall foul of s 9(1) (*Re F (Contact: Child in Care)* [1995] 1 FLR 510, FD).

No application by a local authority for a child arrangements order (s 9(2))—See, for example, *Re C (Contact: Jurisdiction)* [1995] 1 FLR 777, CA (local authority could not apply for contact or variation of contact in relation to children who had been freed for adoption).

'local authority foster parent of a child' (s 9(3))—The mere fact that a person is a local authority foster parent does not bring him within the section. His right to seek permission will be restricted only if he is or has been the foster parent of the particular child who would be the subject of the s 8 application. A person with whom a local authority places a child for adoption is a 'local authority foster parent' and therefore precluded by s 9(3) from applying for permission (*Re C (Adoption: Notice)* [1999] 1 FLR 384, FD). For applications by local authority foster parents, see *JR v Merton London Borough* [1992] 2 FCR 174, FD & CA reversed on appeal as *Re A and W (Minors) (Residence Order: Leave to Apply)* [1992] 2 FLR 154, CA and *C v Salford City Council and Others* [1994] 2 FLR 926, FD. The court cannot make a s 8 order in favour of a local authority foster parent of its own initiative if s 9(3) would debar that foster parent from applying for permission to apply for such an order. The power to make orders of the court's own initiative is subject to the restrictions in s 9 (see CA 1989, s 10(3), but note the exception in *Gloucestershire County Council v P* [1999] 2 FLR 61, CA, which is referred to in **When the court may make a s 8 order** under s 10).

Leave to apply (s 9(3))—Certain people may apply as of right for a s 8 order (see s 10(4),(5),(7)) and a foster parent is not prevented by s 9(3) from making such an application should he fall into any of these categories. For example, he may apply for a child arrangements order for the child to live with him where the child is in care and the local authority for whom he fosters gives its consent (s 10(5)(c)(ii)) or where the child has been living with him for at least 1 year (s 10(5A)(b)). In all other situations, permission must be obtained before an application is launched (see s 10(1)–(3)) and s 9(3) restricts the foster parents who may seek permission, as s 10 is expressed to be subject to the restrictions imposed by s 9.

'consent of the authority' (s 9(3)(a))—It is the consent of the social services authority accommodating the child that is required where the child is simply accommodated rather than being the subject of a care order (*C v Salford City Council and Others* [1994] 2 FLR 926, FD), just as it appears that it will be the authority that is responsible for the placement of the child with the foster parents that will have to consent where a care order is in force. It is ambiguous whether it is enough for the authority to consent to the foster parent making a permission application or whether the consent must be to the making of the full s 8 application or indeed to the granting of the s 8 order that the foster parent wishes to seek. There is no requirement as to the form of the consent but it would be prudent for it to be given in writing.

Restrictions on specific issue and prohibited steps orders (s 9(5))—*Nottinghamshire County Council v P* [1993] 2 FLR 134, CA, is an example of an attempt by a local authority to obtain a prohibited steps order (instead of proceeding by way of the public law provisions of CA 1989, Pt IV) which failed because it contravened s 9(5). Supervision orders with an order restraining the mother from removing the children from their foster homes are also contrary to ss 9(5) and 100(2)(b) (*Re S and D (Children: Powers of Court)* [1995] 2 FLR 456, CA). For further examples of contravention of s 9(5), see *M v C (Children Orders: Reasons)* [1993] 2 FLR 584, FD (without notice specific issue order for the return of children to their mother from their father) and *Re H (Prohibited Steps Order)* [1995] 1 FLR 638, CA (prohibited steps order requiring mother to prevent contact between children and former cohabitee contravened s 9(5), but prohibited steps order against former cohabitee requiring him not to have contact was acceptable). *Re M (Care: Leave to Interview Child)* [1995] 1 FLR 825, FD, also illustrates the limitations imposed by s 9(5) (not possible to use specific issue order to deal with question of whether father's solicitor could interview his two sons who were in care for purposes of preparing his defence to criminal charges; inherent jurisdiction of court used instead).

10 Power of court to make section 8 orders

(1) In any family proceedings in which a question arises with respect to the welfare of any child, the court may make a section 8 order with respect to the child if –

(a) an application for the order has been made by a person who –
  (i) is entitled to apply for a section 8 order with respect to the child; or
  (ii) has obtained the leave of the court to make the application; or

(b) the court considers that the order should be made even though no such application has been made.

PART II

(2) The court may also make a section 8 order with respect to any child on the application of a person who –

(a) is entitled to apply for a section 8 order with respect to the child; or
(b) has obtained the leave of the court to make the application.

(3) This section is subject to the restrictions imposed by section 9.

(4) The following persons are entitled to apply to the court for any section 8 order with respect to a child –

(a) any parent, guardian or special guardian of the child;
(aa) any person who by virtue of section 4A has parental responsibility for the child;
(b) any person who is named, in a child arrangements order that is in force with respect to the child, as a person with whom the child is to live.

(5) The following persons are entitled to apply for a child arrangements order with respect to a child –

(a) any party to a marriage (whether or not subsisting) in relation to whom the child is a child of the family;
(aa) any civil partner in a civil partnership (whether or not subsisting) in relation to whom the child is a child of the family;
(b) any person with whom the child has lived for a period of at least three years;
(c) any person who –
 (i) in any case where a child arrangements order in force with respect to the child regulates arrangements relating to with whom the child is to live or when the child is to live with any person, has the consent of each of the persons named in the order as a person with whom the child is to live;
 (ii) in any case where the child is in the care of a local authority, has the consent of that authority; or
 (iii) in any other case, has the consent of each of those (if any) who have parental responsibility for the child.
(d) any person who has parental responsibility for the child by virtue of provision made under section 12(2A).

(5A) A local authority foster parent is entitled to apply for a child arrangements order to which subsection (5C) applies with respect to a child if the child has lived with him for a period of at least one year immediately preceding the application.

(5B) A relative of a child is entitled to apply for a child arrangements order to which subsection (5C) applies with respect to the child if the child has lived with the relative for a period of at least one year immediately preceding the application.

(5C) This subsection applies to a child arrangements order if the arrangements regulated by the order relate only to either or both of the following –

(a) with whom the child concerned is to live, and
(b) when the child is to live with any person.

(6) A person who would not otherwise be entitled (under the previous provisions of this section) to apply for the variation or discharge of a section 8 order shall be entitled to do so if –

(a) the order was made on his application; or
(b) in the case of a child arrangements order, he is named in provisions of the order regulating arrangements relating to –
 (i) with whom the child concerned is to spend time or otherwise have contact, or
 (ii) when the child is to spend time or otherwise have contact with any person..

(7) Any person who falls within a category of person prescribed by rules of court is entitled to apply for any such section 8 order as may be prescribed in relation to that category of person.

(7A) If a special guardianship order is in force with respect to a child, an application for a child arrangements order to which subsection (7B) applies may only be made with respect to him, if apart from this subsection the leave of the court is not required, with such leave.

(7B) This subsection applies to a child arrangements order if the arrangements regulated by the order consist of, or include, arrangements which relate to either or both of the following –

(a) with whom the child concerned is to live, and

(b) when the child is to live with any person.

(8) Where the person applying for leave to make an application for a section 8 order is the child concerned, the court may only grant leave if it is satisfied that he has sufficient understanding to make the proposed application for the section 8 order.

(9) Where the person applying for leave to make an application for a section 8 order is not the child concerned, the court shall, in deciding whether or not to grant leave, have particular regard to –

(a) the nature of the proposed application for the section 8 order;

(b) the applicant's connection with the child;

(c) any risk there might be of that proposed application disrupting the child's life to such an extent that he would be harmed by it; and

(d) where the child is being looked after by a local authority –

(i) the authority's plans for the child's future; and

(ii) the wishes and feelings of the child's parents.

(10) The period of three years mentioned in subsection (5)(b) need not be continuous but must not have begun more than five years before, or ended more than three months before, the making of the application.

Amendments—ACA 2002, s 139(1), Sch 3, paras 54, 56; CPA 2004, s 77; CYPA 2008, s 36; CFA 2014, s 12, Sch 2.

Defined terms—'child', 'child of the family': s 105(1); 'child arrangements order': s 8(1); 'family proceedings': s 8(3); 'guardian', 'local authority': s 105(1); 'parental responsibility': s 3; 'section 8 order': s 8(2).

When the court may make a s 8 order—The net effect of s 10(1)–(4) is that (subject to the restrictions set out in s 9) the court may make a s 8 order either:

(a) on the application of a person who is entitled to apply as of right, or on the application of a person who can apply with permission and has obtained permission; any such application may be an independent application (s 10(2)) or may be made in the course of existing family proceedings in which a question arises with respect to the welfare of the child (s 10(1)(a)); or

(b) in any family proceedings in which a question arises with respect to the welfare of a child, where it considers that a s 8 order should be made in respect of the child despite the fact that no application has actually been made (s 10(1)(b)).

No doubt the court will normally be prompted to make an order under s 10(1)(b) at the suggestion of one of the parties to the proceedings or of an interested friend or relative who has been allowed to address the court, or even at the suggestion of the child himself, but there is nothing to prevent the court itself taking the lead in appropriate circumstances (see eg *Re H (A Minor) (Contact)* [1994] 2 FLR 969, CA). The power to make orders of the court's own initiative is subject to the restrictions in s 9 (see s 10(3)). However, in *Gloucestershire County Council v P* [1999] 2 FLR 61, CA, the Court of Appeal (Thorpe LJ dissenting) held that although s 10(3) stated that s 10 is subject to the restrictions in s 9, it did not clearly refer to the restriction in s 9(3) which is purely procedural in nature. Therefore, the court did have power under s 10(1)(b), on the exceptional facts of the case, to make an order of its own initiative, in the interests of the child, unlimited by s 9(3); this meant that the court could grant a child arrangements order to foster-parents specifying that the child live with them even where they were not entitled themselves to seek leave to apply for residence. As to the court's power to make a s 8 order even though it is not in a position to dispose finally of the proceedings before it, see s 11(3).

Application for a s 8 order—For the procedure on an application for a s 8 order, see FPR 2010, r 5.1, PD5A, PD12B and Procedural Guide D7. Where an application for permission has already been made, there is no need for an application form to be filed because the court will already have received a draft with the appropriate number of copies as part of the permission application (FPR 2010, rr 18.1–18.13), but the procedure is otherwise the same as for applications without permission.

Jurisdiction and international issues—In *R v R (Jurisdiction and Acquiescence)* [2016] EWHC 1339 (Fam), the court highlighted the need for legal practitioners to pay proper regard to the question of jurisdiction when issuing private law proceedings under CA 1989 in any case that has, or appears to have, an international element, particularly where a parent has recently arrived in the jurisdiction with the children.

'In any family proceedings' (s 10(1))—Where orders of a 'final' nature have already been made, care must be taken to ensure that there are extant family proceedings for the purposes of s 10(1); see, for example, *Re C (Contact: Jurisdiction)* [1995] 1 FLR 777, CA.

'a person who … is entitled to apply for a section 8 order' (s 10(1)(a))—Those persons who are entitled to apply for a s 8 order without permission are specified in s 10(4) (those entitled to apply for any s 8 order), s 10(5) (those entitled to apply for a child arrangements order) and s 10(7) (those entitled to apply by virtue of

PART II

rules of court). Where the child is in care or the proposed applicant is a local authority or a local authority foster parent, the restrictions imposed by s 9 apply (s 10(3)).

Meaning of 'parent' (s 10(4))—This term is not defined in the Act. A child's natural mother and father (including, by virtue of FLRA 1987, s 1, an unmarried father whether or not he has parental responsibility) are his parents unless he has been adopted, in which case his adoptive mother and father are his parents (ACA 2002, s 67). A child's natural parents are not parents within the meaning of s 10 once an adoption order has been made in respect of the child (*Re C (A Minor) (Adopted Child: Contact)* [1993] 2 FLR 431, FD). A step parent is not a parent but may nevertheless be entitled to apply as of right for a s 8 order by virtue of s 10(5)(a). Where a child's mother cohabits with but does not marry a man who is not the child's natural father, that man cannot be classed as a parent of the child (*J v J (A Minor: Property Transfer)* [1993] 2 FLR 56, FD). As to the parents of children born of in vitro fertilisation, artificial insemination etc, see HFEA 2008, ss 33–48. See also **Same-sex parenting** under s 8.

Guardians (s 10(4)(a))—There may be a delay between a guardian being named (for example, in a will or in a court order) and the time when he actually acquires parental responsibility for the child concerned (see **Date from which the appointment is effective** under s 5). See also s 6 as to the circumstances in which an appointment can be disclaimed or revoked.

'a child arrangements order is in force with respect to the child, as a person with whom the child is to live' (s 10(4)(b))—Although most child arrangements orders specifying with whom the child is to live are open-ended, such an order can be made for a specified period of time (s 11(7)), in which case it will cease to be in force at the end of that period. Such an order will also cease to have effect where the court makes a further order to that effect, in certain circumstances where the parents resume cohabitation (see s 11(5)).

'person with whom the child has lived' (s 10(5)(b))—It is usually obvious where a child has been living, but it is less clear to whom the provision applies in cases where he has had more than one base, for example where he has spent weekdays with his aunt and stayed with his grandmother from Friday teatime to Monday morning. In such circumstances, it is submitted that both parties may qualify under s 10(5)(b).

'child is in the care of a local authority' (s 10(5)(c)(ii))—This refers to a child who is the subject of a care order as defined in ss 31(11) and 105(1).

Form of consent (s 10(5)(c)(iii))—Although neither the Act nor any rules stipulate the form in which consent must be expressed, it would be prudent for written consent to be obtained wherever possible and for this to be filed with the application. This will prevent difficulties arising if consent is subsequently withdrawn or the person concerned denies that it was ever given.

Persons not otherwise entitled to apply for variation or discharge (s 10(6))—An order varying or discharging a s 8 order is itself a s 8 order (s 8(2)). Consequently, anyone who may apply for a s 8 order may apply for a variation or discharge as well, with permission where appropriate. Section 10(6) adds two extra categories of person who can apply for variation or discharge, namely the original applicant for the order and, where the application concerns an order for contact, any person named in that order. A person who has obtained an order for indirect contact with a child is entitled, by virtue of s 10(6), subsequently to apply for face-to-face contact without permission (*Re W (Application for Leave)* [1996] Fam Law 665, FD).

Procedure on application for variation or discharge— The procedure for variation or discharge of a s 8 order is the same as for the original application. See FPR 2010, Pt 12 and Procedural Guides D7 and D9.

Rules of court entitling persons to apply for a s 8 order (s 10(7))—No rules specifically list additional persons who may apply for a s 8 order; however, *Re HG (Specific Issue Order: Sterilisation)* [1993] 1 FLR 587, FD held that FPR 1991, r 9.2 (see FPR 2010, r 16.14 and PD16A, para 2.1) does make such a prescription in relation to a child's next friend.

Application by a person requiring leave—If a proposed applicant is not one of those specifically listed in s 10, he will require permission of the court before he can apply. Such applicants could include the child himself, a local authority wishing to apply for a specific issue or prohibited steps order (though note the restrictions on local authority applications imposed by s 9), past carers and relatives other than parents who cannot establish the requisite period of residence.

Application for leave by child (s 10(8))—Where the child is seeking permission, the only factor to which the court is specifically directed is that in s 10(8). However, the fact that the child has sufficient understanding does not mean that the court is bound to grant permission; it has a discretion, and his welfare is not paramount (*M v Warwickshire County Council* [2008] 1 FLR 1093, CA. Nor is it paramount where the permission application is by anyone other than the child concerned (*Re A and W (Minors) (Residence Order: Leave to Apply)* [1992] 2 FLR 154, CA). Such applications should be approached cautiously; once a child is a party to proceedings between warring parents, he will be exposed to hearing evidence of the parents which it might be better for him not to hear and may have to be cross-examined (*Re N (Contact: Minor Seeking Leave to Defend and Removal of Guardian)* [2003] 1 FLR 652, FD – where the 11-year-old child did not have sufficient understanding to participate as a party in contact proceedings or give instructions that would be fully considered in their implications). For guidance as to the role that a child applicant is likely to play in the proceedings, see the notes to FPR 2010, r 12.12.

The court should also have regard to the likelihood of success of the proposed application (*Re C (Residence: Child's Application for Leave)* [1995] 1 FLR 927, FD and *Re SC (A Minor) (Leave to Seek Residence Order)* [1994] 1 FLR 96, FD). *Re M (Care: Contact: Grandmother's Application for Leave)* [1995] 2 FLR 86, CA, although a case where permission was sought under CA 1989, s 34, has been taken to provide the most authoritative guidance as to the appropriate test with regard to the prospects of success, see further under **Application for leave by person other than child concerned**, below. *Re M (Care: Contact: Grandmother's Application)* is fully annotated at CA 1989, s 34 and is helpful also in demonstrating the correct approach to permission applications.

While the checklist in s 1(3) probably does not strictly apply, the matters listed there may be relevant to the court's consideration of whether to grant permission. The court will also consider why the child is seeking to apply for an order to be made in favour of someone else rather than the application being made by that person directly (*Re SC (A Minor) (Leave to Seek Residence Order)* (above) – girl of 14 sought permission to apply for residence order in favour of family friend). As to assessing the understanding of a child, see the annotation **'able ... to give such instructions on his own behalf'** to FPR 2010, r 16.29. As to the possibility of a s 8 application by a child through his next friend when the child does not have sufficient understanding to satisfy s 10(8), see *Re HG (Specific Issue Order: Sterilisation)* [1993] 1 FLR 587, FD and the comment thereon at [1993] Fam Law 403.

Applications for permission by children should be made in the High Court using the procedure in FPR 2010, rr 18.1–18.13.

Section 10(8) does not make provision for children to be joined as additional respondents to applications; application for that purpose is properly made under FPR 2010, rr 12.3 and 16.2 (*Re N (A Minor)* (unreported) 25 September 1997, CA).

Application for leave by person other than child concerned (s 10(9))—Section 10(9) applies to any case in which the applicant for permission is not the child who would be the subject of the substantive application, notwithstanding that the permission applicant is himself a child (*Re S (Contact: Application by Sibling)* [1998] 2 FLR 897, FD. An order granting leave to apply for orders under s 8 of the Children Act is a case management order. It is not a 'final' order in the sense of an order that determines the substantive outcome of the proceedings. The court is obliged under the rules to exercise its case management powers in accordance with the overriding objective (*Re G; Re Z (Children: Sperm Donors: Leave to Apply for Children Act Orders)* [2013] 1 FLR 1334, FD, at [58]).

Section 10(9) lists the factors to which the court should have particular regard in deciding an application for permission by someone other than the child himself, but other factors may also be relevant. The case-law relating to these factors was re-examined thoroughly by Black LJ in *Re B (Paternal Grandmother: Joinder as Party)* [2012] 2 FLR 1358, CA, at [63]–[65]. The s 1(3) checklist does not apply here, nor does s 1(1) (*Re S (Contact: Application by Sibling)* (above)). The same test should be applied to applications for party status in public and private law proceedings; the test is also the same where an applicant seeks party status without making, or intending to make, any application for a specific order (*Re W (Care Proceedings: Leave to Apply)* [2005] 2 FLR 468, FD).

It is well accepted that the court must have regard to the merits of the proposed application (see *Re S (Contact: Application by Sibling)* and the *Warwickshire* case (above)). *Re M (Care: Contact: Grandmother's Application)* [1995] 2 FLR 86, CA, although a case where permission was sought under CA 1989, s 34, has been taken to provide the most authoritative guidance as to the appropriate test with regard to the prospects of success. It is essential, however, that the court gives proper weight to the statutory criterion and does not place too great an emphasis on the factors in *Re M* (above) (*Re J (Leave to Issue Application for Residence Order)* [2003] 1 FLR 114, CA – where the judge erred in dismissing an application by the maternal grandmother to join contested care proceedings and apply for a residence order in relation to her granddaughter). See *KS v Neath Port Talbot Borough Council* [2014] EWCA Civ 941, where the paternal grandmother successfully appealed refusal of her application for joinder to care proceedings; the Court of Appeal held that her case was arguable, the assessment of her having contained both positive and negative judgments about her and went to the critical proportionality evaluation of whether 'nothing else would do' than adoption. The grandmother's application accordingly demanded rigorous scrutiny of the factors in s 10(9). See also *Re N (Children)* [2016] EWCA Civ 656, where an adult brother was granted leave on appeal to apply for contact with his sister where he was her only relative, was likely to be the most important person in her life and had a view on what was best for her. The Court of Appeal held that the issue of contact was of the utmost importance and that no judge could properly have dismissed his application.

In considering the risk of disruption (s 10(9)(c)), it is not only the risk of disruption from the making of the substantive application that is relevant but also the disruption that there may be to the child's life if the application succeeds (*Re M (Care: Contact: Grandmother's Application)* (above), at [95H]). In *Re M* it was emphasised that the risk of disruption which is primarily contemplated in the subsection is the risk of disruption to the extent that the child would be harmed. By virtue of s 105(1), harm is defined in s 31(9). Ward LJ identified disruption as a factor of crucial significance, a fortiori for a child in care. *Re M (Prohibited Steps Order: Application for Leave)* [1993] 1 FLR 275, FD exemplifies the application of s 10(9)(d)(ii) which specifically requires the court to have regard to the local authority's plans for the child's future (former guardian ad litem of child in emergency protection order proceedings sought permission to apply for a s 8 order). *Re S (Contact: Application by Sibling)* (above) deals with disruption in the context of an adopted child.

The difficulty that natural parents will experience in obtaining permission to seek a s 8 order where their child has been adopted or freed for adoption is illustrated by *Re E (Adopted Child: Contact: Leave)* [1995] 1 FLR 57, FD. See also the *Warwickshire* case (above), which concerned an application under ACA 2002, s 24(3) for permission to apply to revoke a placement order and in which the Court of Appeal suggested that when deciding whether or not to grant permission the court might usefully borrow the language of the test set out in CPR 1998, r 52.3(6) and ask whether the applicant would have a real prospect of success. Applications in relation to siblings who have been adopted will also be subject to special considerations (*Re S (Contact: Application by Sibling)*, above).

The fact that permission has been granted does not create a presumption in favour of a substantive order (*Re A (Section 8 Order: Grandparent Application)* [1995] 2 FLR 153, CA; *G v F (Contact and Shared Residence: Applications for Leave)* (above)) or elevate a person who is not a natural parent to the position of a natural parent (*Re W (Contact: Application by Grandparent)* [1997] 1 FLR 793, FD). Decisions in disputes between two female parents and a biological father are so fact-specific that 'this is an area of law in which generalised guidance is not possible' (per Black LJ in *A v B and C (Lesbian Co-Parents: Role of Father)* [2012] 2 FLR 607, CA. As part of the analysis, the court will consider the rights of legal parents to family life, including the right to make decisions about their children. Those rights are widely recognised both as a long-standing principle of English law and under ECHR 1950, Art 8. In this regard, the position of a lesbian couple who have been granted the status of legal parents by the HFEA 2008 is exactly the same as any other legal parent. Having taken those rights into account, however, it is still open to the court, after considering all relevant factors, to grant leave to other persons to apply for s 8 orders. In this regard, the position of biological fathers who have been deprived of the status of legal parent by the 2008 Act is the same as any other person (*Re G; Re Z (Children: Sperm Donors: Leave to Apply for Children Act Orders)* (above), at [115]). However, where the lesbian couple, who are vested with legal parenthood, encourage and enable the biological father to become a psychological parent by involving him in the child's life and where the facts establish that the relationship that has developed between him and the child amounts to, or is capable of amounting to, 'family life' within Art 8, those are also important facts to be taken into consideration. (See further under HFEA 2008, ss 42, 45 and 48.)

'the applicant's connection with the child' (s 10(9)(b))—It is right for half siblings to be brought up together wherever possible. In *Re H (Leave to Apply for Residence Order)* [2008] 2 FLR 848, CA the applicants applied for permission to apply for a residence order. Their connection with the child was an 'indirect' one as they were the adopters of his older half-brother. However, the court considered their connection to be of crucial importance in this case since the applicants were the older child's legal parents and the two boys were half-brothers and aware of each other's existence.

'child ... being looked after by a local authority' (s 10(9)(d))—See s 22(1),(2).

Procedure on application for leave—Permission must be sought in accordance with FPR 2010, rr 18.1–18.13.

11 General principles and supplementary provisions

(1) In proceedings in which any question of making a section 8 order, or any other question with respect to such an order, arises, the court shall (in the light of any provision in rules of court that is of the kind mentioned in subsection (2)(a) or (b)) –

(a) draw up a timetable with a view to determining the question without delay; and

(b) give such directions as it considers appropriate for the purpose of ensuring, so far as is reasonably practicable, that that timetable is adhered to.

(2) Rules of court may –

(a) specify periods within which specified steps must be taken in relation to proceedings in which such questions arise; and

(b) make other provision with respect to such proceedings for the purpose of ensuring, so far as is reasonably practicable, that such questions are determined without delay.

(3) Where a court has power to make a section 8 order, it may do so at any time during the course of the proceedings in question even though it is not in a position to dispose finally of those proceedings.

(4) *(repealed)*

(5) Where –

(a) a child arrangements order has been made with respect to a child; and

(b) the child has two parents who each have parental responsibility for him,

the order, so far as it has the result that there are times when the child lives or is to live with one of the parents, shall cease to have effect if the parents live together for a continuous period of more than six months.

(6) A child arrangements order made with respect to a child, so far as it provides for the child to spend time or otherwise have contact with one of the child's parents at times when the child is living with the child's other parent, shall cease to have effect if the parents live together for a continuous period of more than six months.

(7) A section 8 order may –

(a) contain directions about how it is to be carried into effect;

(b) impose conditions which must be complied with by any person –

(i) who is named in the order as a person with whom the child concerned is to live, spend time or otherwise have contact;

(ii) who is a parent of the child;

(iii) who is not a parent of his but who has parental responsibility for him; or

(iv) with whom the child is living,

and to whom the conditions are expressed to apply;

(c) be made to have effect for a specified period, or contain provisions which are to have effect for a specified period;

(d) make such incidental, supplemental or consequential provision as the court thinks fit.

Amendments—CFA 2014, ss 12, 13, Sch 2.

Defined terms—'section 8 order': s 8(2).

Scope—This section contains provisions designed to ensure that any question that arises with regard to a s 8 order is determined without delay (s 11(1) and (2)) and enabling the court to make a s 8 order at any stage during proceedings even where it is not yet ready finally to dispose of the proceedings (s 11(3)). It also contains miscellaneous provisions as to the content and duration of s 8 orders.

Avoidance of delay—Section 11(1) forces the court to take a firm hold of the reins and to lay down a procedural timetable and give appropriate directions (under FPR 2010, rr 12.12 and 12.13) to ensure that any material question is determined without delay. Both practitioners and courts have a duty to avoid delay in children cases. The PLO in PD12A applies to all applications issued by local authorities under CA 1989, Pt IV in any court (see annotations **Public Law Outline (PLO)** under FPR 2010, r 12.22 and **First hearing**, **Case management conference** and **Issues resolution hearing** under FPR 2010, r 12.25). In private law cases, the CAP (which replaces the Private Law Programme) in PD12B applies to any application issued under CA 1989, Pt II.

The non-adversarial approach to children's litigation means that the solicitors for the parties have a duty, irrespective of whether delay might be tactically advantageous to their client, to ensure that a case does not drift and is resolved with the minimum of delay. Courts have a duty to be proactive in ensuring (through the giving of precise directions) that applications, once launched, are not allowed to moulder but are brought into court in a fully prepared state at the earliest opportunity. A children's guardian, be he the Official Solicitor or an officer of Cafcass, has a duty to review the file regularly and, if the case is not making satisfactory progress, should apply to the court for further directions (see *B v B (Minors) (Interviews and Listing Arrangements)* [1994] 2 FLR 489, CA). It is good practice to avoid the delay that might otherwise be occasioned by awaiting a court welfare report by finding out in advance from Cafcass how long is required for the report and fixing a date in the light of that information. Where an assessment is in progress, it may be right to timetable the proceedings to enable them to be concluded as soon as possible once the assessment is completed; the fact that the timetable might need to be revised is not of itself a reason not to timetable (*E v Humberside County Council and S* [1996] Fam Law 444, FD). Although the general principle stated in s 1(2) is that delay is likely to be prejudicial, speed should not be the only consideration in making arrangements for the determination of an issue. The welfare of the child is the paramount consideration when a court determines any question with respect to the upbringing of a child (s 1(1)) and certain cases benefit from the passage of time which can allow tempers to cool, housing arrangements to be sorted out, medical investigations to take place etc. For cases approving planned and purposeful delay in the public law sphere, see *C v Solihull MBC* [1993] 1 FLR 290, FD and *Hounslow LBC v A* [1993] 1 FLR 702, FD, and see also *Re W (Welfare Reports)* [1995] 2 FLR 142, CA, a private law case in which it was proper to call for a welfare report despite the delay that would thereby be occasioned. For the position where there are criminal proceedings pending, see **Delay generally** under s 1. As Wall J pointed out in *Re A and B (Minors) (No 2)*, above, in such a case the Family Court will need to be made aware of the current state of the criminal investigation and criminal process (if there is a prosecution) at every stage so that it can make a fully informed decision about the extent to which the duty under s 11 can be fulfilled.

'proceedings in which any question of making a section 8 order … arises' (s 11(1))—The court's duty with regard to timetabling and the giving of directions applies whenever any question of making a s 8 order or any other question with respect to such an order arises. It is not therefore confined to applications specifically for a s 8 order.

Making a s 8 order before final disposal of proceedings (s 11(3))—Section 11(3) is equivalent to the power to make interim orders. It applies whenever the court has power to make a s 8 order (see s 10 and, as to the restrictions on that power, s 9). It can, of course, be used in the traditional way, for example to grant one parent a temporary child arrangements order pending the final determination of an issue as to where the child lives or to regulate with whom the child spends time or otherwise has contact pending determination of such an issue. However, given that the court has power to make a s 8 order of its own initiative in any family proceedings in which a question arises as to the welfare of a child (see FPR 2010, r 4.3), and given the wide definition of family proceedings in s 8(3), it could be used in a much wider variety of circumstances as well, for example where an issue arises over the children in the course of pending proceedings under FLA 1996 or financial proceedings under MCA 1973. For a case in which the father's residence order was left in force to run alongside an interim order placing the children with their mother pending a fuller hearing of the question of residence, see *Re M (Minors) (Interim Residence Order)* [1997] 2 FCR 28, CA.

The object of an interim order should normally be to hold the balance so as to cause the least possible harm to the child; see e g *B v B (Interim Contact with Grandparents)* [1993] Fam Law 393, FD. By analogy with *Re L (Interim Care Order: Power of Court)* [1996] 2 FLR 742, CA, it should not be treated as an indication of how the matter will finally be disposed of; it is not an irreversible decision. Some useful guidance as to the approach to be taken to interim hearings can be found in *RE v North Yorkshire County Council, LO and A (A Child)* [2015] EWCA Civ 1169, albeit a public law case (see further under FPR 2010, r 12.21: interim hearings). When a court hears an application for an interim order for residence it is not necessary for it to give elaborate consideration to the welfare check list under CA 1989, s 1(3) (*Re C (A Child)* [2001] EWCA Civ 718). As to the difficulties that may be encountered in persuading the court to make without notice interim orders, particularly in cases concerned with children's living arrangements, see **Power to make without notice orders** under FPR 2010, r 12.16 and PD12E (*Urgent Business*). As to the situation in which it may be appropriate to make a child arrangements order on an interim application in pending care proceedings, see *Re RJ (Fostering: Person Disqualified)* [1999] 1 FLR 605, CA (noted under s 38).

When events develop following the making of an interim child arrangements order concerning living arrangements—The appropriate course is to seek a variation from the judge, rather than apply to the Court of Appeal (*Re H (A Child)* [2011] EWCA Civ 762).

Section 11(7)—Section 11(7)(d) can be used to afford liberty to a non-party to apply to vary or discharge a s 8 order (*Re H (Prohibited Steps Order)* [1995] 1 FLR 638, CA – prohibited steps order against mother's former cohabitee, J, requiring him not to have or to seek contact with the children, with liberty to J to apply on notice to vary or discharge the order). However, the section must not be used to regulate occupation of the former family home for the purpose of facilitating contact (*Re K (Contact Order: Condition Ousting Parent from Family Home)* [2012] 2 FLR 635, CA).

Section 11(7) should not be used to restrict a parent to an area of residence within the UK save in exceptional circumstances. See further **Relocation within the UK** under CA 1989, s 13. The court has jurisdiction under s 11(7) to impose any condition that secures the paramountcy of the welfare of the child, but the greater the restriction on the freedom of the parent subject to the condition, the more exceptional the case must be to justify it (*Re H (A Child)* [2002] EWCA Civ 2005; *Re M (A Child)* [2014] EWCA Civ 1755 – discussed further in **Orders for shared living arrangements** under CA 1989, s 8). For example, in *Re M (Contact)* [2013] 1 FLR 1403, FD, the court made a conditional residence order, ordering that staying contact take place and that if it did not there would be a transfer of residence from the mother to the father. The court has no power in private law proceedings concerning the residence of a child to use s 11(7) to order a residential assessment of one parent with the child against the wishes of the other parent (*R v R (Private Law Proceedings: Residential Assessment)* [2002] 2 FLR 953, FD; *Birmingham City Council v H* [1992] 2 FLR 323, FD).

Enforcement of s 11(7) directions and conditions—For enforcement under MCA 1980, s 63(3), see s 14; for penal notices, see FPR 2010, r 33.7; and for orders for recovery of a child, see FLA 1986, s 34.

Enforcement of child arrangements orders—CA 1989, ss 11A–11P give the court specific powers to impose directions and conditions on child arrangements orders and to improve enforcement. See further annotation **Enforcement of child arrangements orders** under s 8, and ss 11A–11P below, and see Procedural Guide D8.

11A Activity directions

(1) Subsection (2) applies in proceedings in which the court is considering whether to make provision about one or more of the matters mentioned in subsection (1A) by making –

- (a) a child arrangements order with respect to the child concerned, or
- (b) an order varying or discharging a child arrangements order with respect to the child concerned.

(1A) The matters mentioned in this subsection are –

- (a) with whom a child is to live,
- (b) when a child is to live with any person,
- (c) with whom a child is to spend time or otherwise have contact, and
- (d) when a child is to spend time or otherwise have contact with any person.

(2) The court may make an activity direction in connection with the provision that the court is considering whether to make.

(2A) Subsection (2B) applies in proceedings in which subsection (2) does not apply and in which the court is considering –

- (a) whether a person has failed to comply with a provision of a child arrangements order, or
- (b) what steps to take in consequence of a person's failure to comply with a provision of a child arrangements order.

(2B) The court may make an activity direction in connection with that provision of the child arrangements order.

(3) An activity direction is a direction requiring an individual who is a party to the proceedings concerned to take part in an activity that would, in the court's opinion, help to establish, maintain or improve the involvement in the life of the child concerned of –

- (a) that individual, or
- (b) another individual who is a party to the proceedings.

(4) The direction is to specify the activity and the person providing the activity.

(5) The activities that may be so required include, in particular –

- (a) programmes, classes and counselling or guidance sessions of a kind that –

(i) may assist a person as regards establishing, maintaining or improving contact with a child;

(ii) may, by addressing a person's violent behaviour, enable or facilitate involvement in a child's life;

(b) sessions in which information or advice is given as regards making or operating arrangements for involvement in a child's life, including making arrangements by means of mediation.

(6) No individual may be required by an activity direction –

(a) to undergo medical or psychiatric examination, assessment or treatment;

(b) to take part in mediation.

(7) A court may not on the same occasion –

(a) make an activity direction under subsection (2), and

(b) dispose finally of the proceedings as they relate to the matters mentioned in subsection (1A) in connection with which the activity direction is made.

(7A) A court may not on the same occasion –

(a) make an activity direction under subsection (2B), and

(b) dispose finally of the proceedings as they relate to failure to comply with the provision in connection with which the activity direction is made.

(8) Each of subsections (2) and (2B) has effect subject to the restrictions in sections 11B and 11E.

(9) In considering whether to make an activity direction, the welfare of the child concerned is to be the court's paramount consideration.

Amendments—Inserted by CAA 2006, s 1. Amended by CFA 2014, s 12, Sch 2.

Activity directions—CA 1989, ss 11A–11E have been amended by CFA 2014 so that when there is some dispute (s 11B(1)) about child arrangements and the court is considering whether or not to make, vary or discharge a child arrangements order (CAO) it may make an 'activity direction': s 11A. This allows the court to direct a *party* to undertake activities designed to help them understand the importance of complying with the order and making it work. The activities directed or imposed can relate to more than just promoting the contact provided for in the CAO. Instead, the activities will be about helping to establish, maintain or improve the involvement of a person in a child's life (s 11A(3),(5)).

Cafcass Guidance—The provisions place a number of specific new duties on Cafcass officers and the President of the Family Division endorsed *Guidance to Cafcass practitioners on their roles in supporting the courts in their use of the s 11A–P provisions* ('Cafcass Guidance'). The Cafcass Guidance (para 2.2) refers to three types of 'activity': (1) Information meetings about mediation – provided by LSC-approved providers on a one-off basis, free of charge to both parties if either party is publicly funded. Both parties will be required to participate, but can initially be seen separately; (2) Separated parents information programmes – provided by Cafcass-commissioned providers, typically involving group sessions lasting for a total of 4 hours, free of charge to all. Generally, both parties are required to participate, though the programmes will be delivered to them separately; (3) Domestic violence prevention programmes – run by Cafcass-commissioned providers, involving an intensive programme of 60 hours' intervention. The Cafcass Guidance (paras 2.4, 2.5) observes that in practice the Cafcass officer is likely to have suggested to the court that participation in an activity might be beneficial. Much will depend on the attitude of the parties towards the activity. This will be an important factor to be addressed in any oral or written report to the court.

11B Activity directions: further provision

(1) A court may not make an activity direction under section 11A(2) in connection with any matter mentioned in section 11A(1A) unless there is a dispute as regards the provision about that matter that the court is considering whether to make in the proceedings.

(2) A court may not make an activity direction requiring an individual who is a child to take part in an activity unless the individual is a parent of the child in relation to whom the court is considering provision about a matter mentioned in section 11A(1A).

(3) A court may not make an activity direction in connection with the making, variation or discharge of a child arrangements order, if the child arrangements order is, or would if made be, an excepted order.

(4) A child arrangements order with respect to a child is an excepted order if –

(a) it is made in proceedings that include proceedings on an application for a relevant adoption order in respect of the child; or

(b) it makes provision as regards contact between the child and a person who would be a parent or relative of the child but for the child's adoption by an order falling within subsection (5).

(5) An order falls within this subsection if it is –

(a) a relevant adoption order;

(b) an adoption order, within the meaning of section 72(1) of the Adoption Act 1976, other than an order made by virtue of section 14 of that Act on the application of a married couple one of whom is the mother or the father of the child;

(c) a Scottish adoption order, within the meaning of the Adoption and Children Act 2002, other than an order made –

(i) by virtue of section 14 of the Adoption (Scotland) Act 1978 on the application of a married couple one of whom is the mother or the father of the child, or

(ii) by virtue of section 15(1)(aa) of that Act; or

(iii) by virtue of an application under section 30 of the Adoption and Children (Scotland) Act 2007 where subsection (3) of that section applies; or

(d) a Northern Irish adoption order, within the meaning of the Adoption and Children Act 2002, other than an order made by virtue of Article 14 of the Adoption (Northern Ireland) Order 1987 on the application of a married couple one of whom is the mother or the father of the child.

(6) A relevant adoption order is an adoption order, within the meaning of section 46(1) of the Adoption and Children Act 2002, other than an order made –

(a) on an application under section 50 of that Act by a couple (within the meaning of that Act) one of whom is the mother or the father of the person to be adopted, or

(b) on an application under section 51(2) of that Act.

(7) A court may not make an activity direction in relation to an individual unless the individual is habitually resident in England and Wales; and a direction ceases to have effect if the individual subject to the direction ceases to be habitually resident in England and Wales.

Amendments—Inserted by CAA 2006, s 1. Amended by SI 2011/1740; CFA 2014, s 12, Sch 2.

11C Activity conditions

(1) This section applies if in any family proceedings the court makes –

(a) a child arrangements order containing –

(i) provision for a child to live with different persons at different times,

(ii) provision regulating arrangements relating to with whom a child is to spend time or otherwise have contact, or

(iii) provision regulating arrangements relating to when a child is to spend time or otherwise have contact with any person; or

(b) an order varying a child arrangements order so as to add, vary or omit provision of a kind mentioned in paragraph (a)(i), (ii) or (iii).

(2) The child arrangements order, may impose, or the child arrangements order may be varied so as to impose, a condition (an 'activity condition') requiring an individual falling within subsection (3) to take part in an activity that would, in the court's opinion, help to establish, maintain or improve the involvement in the life of the child concerned of –

(a) that individual, or

(b) another individual who is a party to the proceedings.

(3) An individual falls within this subsection if he is –

(a) for the purposes of the child arrangements order so made or varied, a person with whom the child concerned lives or is to live;

(b) a person whose contact with the child concerned is provided for in that order; or

(c) a person upon whom that order imposes a condition under section 11(7)(b).

(4) The condition is to specify the activity and the person providing the activity.

(5) Subsections (5) and (6) of section 11A have effect as regards the activities that may be required by an activity condition as they have effect as regards the activities that may be required by an activity direction.

(6) Subsection (2) has effect subject to the restrictions in sections 11D and 11E.

Amendments—Inserted by CAA 2006, s 1. Amended by CFA 2014, s 12, Sch 2.

Activity condition—Whenever the court makes or varies a child arrangements order it may make an 'activity condition' requiring the person named to take part in an activity; the activities are the same as those for a 'activity direction' – see annotation **Cafcass Guidance** under s 11A, above.

11D Activity conditions: further provision

(1) A child arrangements order may not impose an activity condition on an individual who is a child unless the individual is a parent of the child concerned.

(2) If a child arrangements order is an excepted order (within the meaning given by section 11B(4)), it may not impose (and it may not be varied so as to impose) an activity condition.

(3) A child arrangements order may not impose an activity condition on an individual unless the individual is habitually resident in England and Wales; and a condition ceases to have effect if the individual subject to the condition ceases to be habitually resident in England and Wales.

Amendments—Inserted by CAA 2006, s 1. Amended by CFA 2014, s 12, Sch 2.

11E Activity directions and conditions: making

(1) Before making an activity direction (or imposing an activity condition by means of a child arrangements order), the court must satisfy itself as to the matters falling within subsections (2) to (4).

(2) The first matter is that the activity proposed to be specified is appropriate in the circumstances of the case.

(3) The second matter is that the person proposed to be specified as the provider of the activity is suitable to provide the activity.

(4) The third matter is that the activity proposed to be specified is provided in a place to which the individual who would be subject to the direction (or the condition) can reasonably be expected to travel.

(5) Before making such a direction (or such an order), the court must obtain and consider information about the individual who would be subject to the direction (or the condition) and the likely effect of the direction (or the condition) on him.

(6) Information about the likely effect of the direction (or the condition) may, in particular, include information as to –

- (a) any conflict with the individual's religious beliefs;
- (b) any interference with the times (if any) at which he normally works or attends an educational establishment.

(7) The court may ask an officer of the Service or a Welsh family proceedings officer to provide the court with information as to the matters in subsections (2) to (5); and it shall be the duty of the officer of the Service or Welsh family proceedings officer to comply with any such request.

(8) In this section 'specified' means specified in an activity direction (or in an activity condition).

Amendments—Inserted by CAA 2006, s 1. Amended by CFA 2014, s 12, Sch 2.

Factors to be taken into account when making activity directions or activity conditions—Before the court makes an activity direction or condition, it must first be satisfied that the activity is appropriate in the circumstances of the case, that the provider of the activity is suitable to provide it, and that the activity is available in a place to which it is reasonable to expect the person in question to travel. The court must also consider the likely *effect* of the activity on the person required to undertake it, e g any conflict with the person's religious beliefs, the times when he works, and the times when he attends an educational establishment. The court may ask a Cafcass officer to provide information about these matters (s 11E(7)).

11F Activity directions and conditions: financial assistance

(1) The Secretary of State may by regulations make provision authorising him to make payments to assist individuals falling within subsection (2) in paying relevant charges or fees.

(2) An individual falls within this subsection if he is required by an activity direction or condition to take part in an activity that is expected to help to establish, maintain or improve the involvement of that or another individual in the life of a child, not being a child ordinarily resident in Wales.

(3) The National Assembly for Wales may by regulations make provision authorising it to make payments to assist individuals falling within subsection (4) in paying relevant charges or fees.

(4) An individual falls within this subsection if he is required by an activity direction or condition to take part in an activity that is expected to help to establish, maintain or improve the involvement of that or another individual in the life of a child who is ordinarily resident in Wales.

(5) A relevant charge or fee, in relation to an activity required by an activity direction or condition, is a charge or fee in respect of the activity payable to the person providing the activity.

(6) Regulations under this section may provide that no assistance is available to an individual unless –

- (a) the individual satisfies such conditions as regards his financial resources as may be set out in the regulations;
- (b) the activity in which the individual is required by an activity direction or condition to take part is provided to him in England or Wales;
- (c) where the activity in which the individual is required to take part is provided to him in England, it is provided by a person who is for the time being approved by the Secretary of State as a provider of activities required by a contact activity direction or condition;
- (d) where the activity in which the individual is required to take part is provided to him in Wales, it is provided by a person who is for the time being approved by the National Assembly for Wales as a provider of activities required by an activity direction or condition.

(7) Regulations under this section may make provision –

- (a) as to the maximum amount of assistance that may be paid to or in respect of an individual as regards an activity in which he is required by an activity direction or condition to take part;
- (b) where the amount may vary according to an individual's financial resources, as to the method by which the amount is to be determined;
- (c) authorising payments by way of assistance to be made directly to persons providing activities required by an activity direction or condition.

Amendments—Inserted by CAA 2006, s 1. Amended by CFA 2014, s 12, Sch 2.

11G Activity directions and conditions: monitoring

(1) This section applies if in any family proceedings the court –

- (a) makes an activity direction in relation to an individual, or
- (b) makes a child arrangements order that imposes, or varies a contact order so as to impose, an activity condition on an individual.

(2) The court may on making the direction (or imposing the condition by means of a child arrangements order) ask an officer of the Service or a Welsh family proceedings officer –

- (a) to monitor, or arrange for the monitoring of, the individual's compliance with the direction (or the condition);
- (b) to report to the court on any failure by the individual to comply with the direction (or the condition).

(3) It shall be the duty of the officer of the Service or Welsh family proceedings officer to comply with any request under subsection (2).

Amendments—Inserted by CAA 2006, s 1. Amended by CFA 2014, s 12, Sch 2.

Monitoring compliance with a activity direction or activity condition—A court may ask a Cafcass officer to monitor compliance with an activity direction or condition and to report to the court if there is a failure to comply. The Cafcass Guidance (para 2.6) (see further under s 11A, above) observes that the court may also ask Cafcass to provide information about the impact, beneficial or otherwise, of attendance, in terms of helping to address the issues in the case. Both elements require there to be liaison with the provider, information from which should be reported to the court, together with any additional Cafcass analysis and recommendations. In some cases, the Cafcass officer will have been asked by the court to have other forms of involvement with the parties and/or child during the period of participation in the activities, the outcome of which should also be reported to the court. Activity providers may also be asked to provide a report to the court, not just to Cafcass, about the attendance, participation etc of parties.

11H Monitoring contact and shared residence

(1) This section applies if in any family proceedings the court makes –

(a) a child arrangements order containing provision of a kind mentioned in section 11C(1)(a)(i), (ii) or (iii), or

(b) an order varying a child arrangements order so as to add, vary or omit provision of any of those kinds.

(2) The court may ask an officer of the Service or a Welsh family proceedings officer –

(a) to monitor whether an individual falling within subsection (3) complies with each provision of any of those kinds that is contained in the child arrangements order (or in the child arrangements order as varied);

(b) to report to the court on such matters relating to the individual's compliance as the court may specify in the request.

(3) An individual falls within this subsection if the child arrangements order so made (or the child arrangements order as so varied) –

(za) provides for the child concerned to live with different persons at different times and names the individual as one of those persons;

(a) imposes requirements on the individual with regard to the child concerned spending time or otherwise having contact with some other person;

(b) names the individual as a person with whom the child concerned is to spend time or otherwise have contact; or

(c) imposes a condition under section 11(7)(b) on the individual.

(4) If the child arrangements order (or the child arrangements order as varied) includes an activity condition, a request under subsection (2) is to be treated as relating to the provisions of the order other than the activity condition.

(5) The court may make a request under subsection (2) –

(a) on making the child arrangements order (or the order varying the child arrangements order), or

(b) at any time during the subsequent course of the proceedings as they relate to contact with or to the child's living arrangements.

(6) In making a request under subsection (2), the court is to specify the period for which the officer of the Service or Welsh family proceedings officer is to monitor compliance with the order; and the period specified may not exceed twelve months.

(7) It shall be the duty of the officer of the Service or Welsh family proceedings officer to comply with any request under subsection (2).

(8) The court may order any individual falling within subsection (3) to take such steps as may be specified in the order with a view to enabling the officer of the Service or Welsh family proceedings officer to comply with the court's request under subsection (2).

(9) But the court may not make an order under subsection (8) with respect to an individual who is a child unless he is a parent of the child with respect to whom the order falling within subsection (1) was made.

(10) A court may not make a request under subsection (subsection (2) in relation to a child arrangements order that is an excepted order (within the meaning given by section 11B(4)).

Amendments—Inserted by CAA 2006, s 1. Amended by CFA 2014, s 12, Sch 2.

Monitoring compliance with child arrangements orders for contact and shared residence—A court may ask a Cafcass officer to monitor compliance with a child arrangements order, and to report to the court on such matters relating to compliance as the court may specify. The court may ask the Cafcass officer to carry out this role for up to 1 year. The people who can be subject to monitoring are: a person who is required to allow contact with a child; a person whose contact with the child is provided for; and, a person who is subject to a condition under s 11(7)(b). The Cafcass Guidance (paras 3.2, 3.3) (see further under s 11A, above) observes that with nearly 40,000 contact orders having been made in 2007, this provision has major resource implications for Cafcass. It has been agreed with the President of the Family Division that the general assumption is that the provision should not be used in 'consent order' cases where proceedings have ended. Instead, consideration of its use should be limited to those cases where the issue of contact has remained in dispute during the proceedings and where a trial and judicial determination of the contact issue has taken place. Eg, where there is a strong feeling of dissatisfaction on the part of one or both parties, the court may consider that the imposition of a monitoring requirement is appropriate. The consent of the parties is *not* required (unlike Family Assistance Orders).

The court may end the proceedings, having made a child arrangements order for contact with a monitoring requirement, or it may set a further date for a review hearing (usually before the same judge). In either event, it is essential that timely monitoring takes place in the immediate aftermath of the order being made. This is likely primarily to take the form of telephone contact with both parties and, where the children are of sufficient age and understanding, also with the children.

The court may request that it be notified in writing about the outcome of the monitoring, either at the end of the monitoring period if compliance has been adequate, or at an earlier stage if the Cafcass officer deems it to have been inadequate. Non-compliance can range from outright refusal to allow contact, to a chronic series of more minor failures to observe the terms of the order. Chronic cases should not be allowed to 'drag on' and the Cafcass officer should notify the court and ask for guidance as to how to proceed (para 3.4).

On receipt of such notification from Cafcass, the court may, if a review date has been set, choose to bring forward the hearing. Alternatively, if proceedings have ended, the court will have to await the making of an application for enforcement by a party. Once non-compliance has been notified to the court, the parties and, in the most appropriate way, the children, monitoring should continue while guidance of the court is awaited (para 3.5).

11I Child arrangements orders: warning notices

Where the court makes (or varies) a child arrangements order, it is to attach to the child arrangements order (or the order varying the child arrangements order) a notice warning of the consequences of failing to comply with the child arrangements order.

Amendments—Inserted by CAA 2006, s 1. Amended by CFA 2014, s 12, Sch 2.

Consequences of failing to comply with child arrangements order—The consequences of failure to comply with a child arrangements order may be an enforcement order, an order for financial compensation, or the use of the courts' sanctions for contempt.

Care required when drafting child arrangements orders to which warning notices are to be attached—Whenever a court makes or varies a child arrangements order, it is to attach a notice warning of the consequences of failing to comply with the order (s 11I) ie an enforcement order (for unpaid work) (ss 11J–N), an order for financial compensation (ss 11 O–P), and sanctions for contempt of court. The wording of s 11I looks as though it is *mandatory* for a court to attach a warning notice when it makes or varies *any* child arrangements order. It follows that judges have to decide whether the order which they propose to make is to be made in terms that comply with s 8(1), in which case a warning notice will be added automatically, or whether it would be more appropriate for consent orders to set out the agreed regime as a recital or schedule to the order on the basis of which the court then applies the 'no order' principle. Judges will need to make sure that orders that go out in Form C45 accurately reflect what has actually been ordered.

Procedure for applying for a warning notice to be attached—The procedure for applying for warning notices is set out in FPR 2010, r 12.33. The application is made using Form C78. Warning notices can be addressed to a much wider range of individuals than was the case previously, because applications for enforcement orders and financial compensation orders can be made not only by the person in whose favour the order is made, but also by the person with whom the child lives, or the child, or any other person subject to a s 11(7) condition or activity condition.

FPR 2010, r 12.33 requires that an application for a warning notice to be attached to a child arrangements order should be made to the Family Court without notice, but there is no provision in Form C78 for the applicant to specify the provisions of the order to which he wishes the warning notice attached, or any space for him to say why the application is being made. The without notice order has potential quasi-criminal consequences for the respondent, but does not give him a right to apply to set it aside. In these circumstances, it is respectfully submitted that the safer course would be for the judge to direct a hearing inviting the applicant to file a brief statement setting out the provisions of the order to which he wishes the warning notice to be attached and explaining why he is asking for a warning notice.

If the relevant order does not comply with s 8(1), then the application should be dismissed as misconceived. The applicant would have to apply using Form C100 to vary the existing order to a mandatory order to which a warning notice can be added (see Procedural Guide D7).

Transitional orders—Applications to attach a warning notice to an existing order must be made on Form C78. The application can be made to any court with family jurisdiction. When faced with a C78 application the judge should first obtain a copy of the original order, but in itself that may not be enough. Without the existing court file it may be impossible to discover whether the order is still in force. Furthermore, the relevant provisions may be contained in more than one order. The proper course may be to ask the court in which the order was made either to transfer the existing proceedings or to order transfer of the C78 application back to the court that made the existing order.

11J Enforcement orders

(1) This section applies if a child arrangements order with respect to a child has been made.

(2) If the court is satisfied beyond reasonable doubt that a person has failed to comply with a provision of the child arrangements order, it may make an order (an 'enforcement order') imposing on the person an unpaid work requirement.

(3) But the court may not make an enforcement order if it is satisfied that the person had a reasonable excuse for failing to comply with the provision.

(4) The burden of proof as to the matter mentioned in subsection (3) lies on the person claiming to have had a reasonable excuse, and the standard of proof is the balance of probabilities.

(5) The court may make an enforcement order in relation to the child arrangements order only on the application of –

- (a) a person who is, for the purposes of the child arrangements order, a person with whom the child concerned lives or is to live;
- (b) a person whose contact with the child concerned is provided for in the child arrangements order;
- (c) any individual subject to a condition under section 11(7)(b) or an activity condition imposed by the child arrangements order; or
- (d) the child concerned.

(6) Where the person proposing to apply for an enforcement order in relation to a child arrangements order is the child concerned, the child must obtain the leave of the court before making such an application.

(7) The court may grant leave to the child concerned only if it is satisfied that he has sufficient understanding to make the proposed application.

(8) Subsection (2) has effect subject to the restrictions in sections 11K and 11L.

(9) The court may suspend an enforcement order for such period as it thinks fit.

(10) Nothing in this section prevents a court from making more than one enforcement order in relation to the same person on the same occasion.

(11) Proceedings in which any question of making an enforcement order, or any other question with respect to such an order, arises are to be regarded for the purposes of section 11(1) and (2) as proceedings in which a question arises with respect to a section 8 order.

(12) In Schedule A1 –

- (a) Part 1 makes provision as regards an unpaid work requirement;
- (b) Part 2 makes provision in relation to the revocation and amendment of enforcement orders and failure to comply with such orders.

(13) (*repealed*)

Amendments—Inserted by CAA 2006, s 1. Amended by CCA 2013, s 17, Sch 11; CFA 2014, s 12, Sch 2.

Enforcement orders—Where the court is satisfied beyond reasonable doubt that a person has failed to comply with a child arrangements order made under CA 1989, s 8, it may make an enforcement order, imposing on that person an 'unpaid work requirement' (community service): s 11J(2). The court may not make an enforcement order if satisfied that the person in breach had a 'reasonable excuse' for breaching the order: s 11J(3). The burden of proving a reasonable excuse is on the person in breach and the standard of proof is the balance of probabilities: s 11(4). The court may not make an enforcement order unless the person concerned has received a 'warning notice' or has been otherwise informed of its terms: s 11K. The court has a discretion as to whether to join the child as a party and may ask the Cafcass officer to consider this and report to the court with his opinion (FPR 2010, r 16.39). The factors to be considered by the court before making an enforcement order are set out in s 11L and in Sch A1, Pt I. The maximum number of hours of unpaid work that may be required is 200, and the minimum is 40. The court has power to amend or revoke an enforcement order: Sch A1, Pt II. The court may ask a Cafcass officer to monitor, or arrange for the monitoring of, a person's compliance with an enforcement order, and to report to the court on failure to comply and on any unsuitability to undertake the unpaid work: s 11M. Where an enforcement order is made, the court must attach a warning notice setting out the consequences of breaching the order i e imposition of a further enforcement order; enhancement of the existing enforcement order; use of existing sanctions for contempt. If the terms of an enforcement order are breached, the court may (in certain circumstances) amend the original order to make it more onerous, or impose another enforcement order: Sch A1, Pt II.

Committal to prison for contempt—The court will take a robust approach to the question of committal to prison for contempt in family proceedings (*Re W (Family Proceedings: Applications)* [2011] 1 FLR 2163, FD; *Doncaster MBC v Watson and Haigh* [2012] 1 FLR 599, FD). In committal proceedings it is vital to ensure that the evidential and procedural rules are obeyed, and extra vigilance is required when the respondent to such proceedings is a litigant in person (*Hammerton v Hammerton* [2007] 2 FLR 1133, CA). Where the respondent's breach is an active breach that directly strikes at the heart of what the court ordered, it may be appropriate to impose a custodial sentence (*Re X (A Child by His Litigation Friend)* [2011] 2 FLR 793, CA) and an appellate court is unlikely to interfere unless the sentence passed is manifestly disproportionate or excessive (*Slade v Slade* [2010] 1 FLR 160, CA). The length of any sentence for committal for contempt must bear some reasonable relationship to the statutory maximum of 2 years (*Hale v Tanner* [2000] 2 FLR 879, CA). A sentence for contempt in civil proceedings can be the subject of an application for early discharge (*CJ v Flintshire Borough Council* [2010] 2 FLR 1224, CA; *Doncaster Metropolitan District Council v Watson* [2012] 1 FLR 613, FD). However, where the court allows an application to purge contempt it cannot then suspend the relevant term of imprisonment. The court has three choices when dealing with an application to purge contempt: (1) grant the application and order the immediate release of the contemnor; (2) defer the contemnor's release until a stated future date; or (3) refuse the application (*Doncaster Metropolitan Borough Council v Watson (No 2)* [2012] 1 FLR 619, FD). See further under CCA 1981, s 14.

Enforcement of child arrangements orders when child does not wish to go—Where the parent's obligation is to 'allow' contact and to 'make [the child] available' for contact, that wording does not place him in breach of the order if the child refuses to co-operate (*Re L-W (Enforcement and Committal: Contact); CPL v CH-W and Others* [2011] 1 FLR 1095, CA). Neither is the father under a legally enforceable obligation to take such steps in the exercise of his parental discipline, guidance and encouragement as are reasonable in all of the circumstances to ensure that contact takes place. Before deciding that a parent is the author of a child's resistance to contact so that he can be made the subject of a coercive order, the court must be sure that the parent can still reverse the child's attitude. Even then, a court (despite the affront to its dignity) might have to be prepared, if it comes to the point of committal, to accept that the predictive premise on which it initially acted has turned out to be wrong: for example, where the child has internalised the residential parent's hostility so that punishing that parent could no longer produce the intended outcome and might produce the opposite. See also **Transfer of living arrangements** and **Suspended transfer of living arrangements** under s 8.

Procedure for applying for an enforcement order—An application for an enforcement order must be made on Form C79 by a person who falls within the criteria set out in s 11J (5)(a)–(d). See Procedural Guide D8.

11K Enforcement orders: further provision

(1) A court may not make an enforcement order against a person in respect of a failure to comply with a provision of a child arrangements order unless it is satisfied that before the failure occurred the person had been given (in accordance with rules of court) a copy of, or otherwise informed of the terms of –

- (a) in the case of a failure to comply with a provision of a child arrangements order where the order was varied before the failure occurred, a notice under section 11I relating to the order varying the child arrangements order or, where more than one such order has been made, the last order preceding the failure in question;
- (b) in any other case, a notice under section 11I relating to the child arrangements order.

(2) A court may not make an enforcement order against a person in respect of any failure to comply with a provision of a child arrangements order occurring before the person attained the age of 18.

(3) A court may not make an enforcement order against a person in respect of a failure to comply with a provision of a child arrangements order where the child arrangements order is an excepted order (within the meaning given by section 11B(4)).

(4) A court may not make an enforcement order against a person unless the person is habitually resident in England and Wales; and an enforcement order ceases to have effect if the person subject to the order ceases to be habitually resident in England and Wales.

Amendments—Inserted by CAA 2006, s 1. Amended by CFA 2014, s 12, Sch 2.

11L Enforcement orders: making

(1) Before making an enforcement order as regards a person in breach of a provision of a child arrangements order, the court must be satisfied that –

- (a) making the enforcement order proposed is necessary to secure the person's compliance with the child arrangements order or any child arrangements order that has effect in its place;

(b) the likely effect on the person of the enforcement order proposed to be made is proportionate to the seriousness of the breach.

(2) Before making an enforcement order, the court must satisfy itself that provision for the person to work under an unpaid work requirement imposed by an enforcement order can be made in the local justice area in which the person in breach resides or will reside.

(3) Before making an enforcement order as regards a person in breach of a provision of a child arrangements order, the court must obtain and consider information about the person and the likely effect of the enforcement order on him.

(4) Information about the likely effect of the enforcement order may, in particular, include information as to –

(a) any conflict with the person's religious beliefs;

(b) any interference with the times (if any) at which he normally works or attends an educational establishment.

(5) A court that proposes to make an enforcement order may ask an officer of the Service or a Welsh family proceedings officer to provide the court with information as to the matters in subsections (2) and (3).

(6) It shall be the duty of the officer of the Service or Welsh family proceedings officer to comply with any request under this section.

(7) In making an enforcement order in relation to a child arrangements order, a court must take into account the welfare of the child who is the subject of the child arrangements order.

Amendments—Inserted by CAA 2006, s 1. Amended by CFA 2014, s 12, Sch 2.

Factors to be considered by the court before making an enforcement order—In deciding whether to make an enforcement order, the court must be satisfied that doing so is necessary to secure compliance with the child arrangements order, and that the order is proportionate to the seriousness of the breach. Before making an enforcement order the court must obtain and consider information about the person on whom the order would be imposed, and the likely effect of the order on him e g any conflict with the person's religious beliefs, the times when he works, and the times when he attends an educational establishment. The court may ask a Cafcass officer to provide information about these matters. The Cafcass Guidance (para 4.1) (see further under s 11A, above) observes that where an enforcement order imposing an unpaid work requirement (of between 40 and 200 hours) is made, Cafcass will be sent a copy of each Form C79 enforcement application, to enable it to undertake updating screening checks with the relevant local authority and the police. The outcome of these checks must be promptly notified to the court, together with any other requested information. The court has a discretion to join the child as a party to enforcement proceedings. The child is not automatically a party even where he was a party to the original proceedings. In practice, it will rarely be necessary, and Cafcass Legal will advise in cases of difficulty. The court must also take into account the welfare of the child concerned, but this is *not* its paramount consideration (see Cafcass Guidance, para 4.2). The Cafcass Guidance (para 4.2) observes that in order to inform the court about the local availability of unpaid work, it will be necessary to liaise with the local National Probation Service (NPS), which stands ready to provide unpaid work to those ordered by the court to undertake it. When making the order, the court should give leave to the officer to disclose to NPS such information in relation to the proceedings as necessary (see FPR PD12N *Enforcement of Children Act 1989 Child Arrangements Orders: Disclosure of Information to Officers of the National Probation Service*).

11M Enforcement orders: monitoring

(1) On making an enforcement order in relation to a person, the court is to ask an officer of the Service or a Welsh family proceedings officer –

(a) to monitor, or arrange for the monitoring of, the person's compliance with the unpaid work requirement imposed by the order;

(b) to report to the court if a report under paragraph 8 of Schedule A1 is made in relation to the person;

(c) to report to the court on such other matters relating to the person's compliance as may be specified in the request;

(d) to report to the court if the person is, or becomes, unsuitable to perform work under the requirement.

(2) It shall be the duty of the officer of the Service or Welsh family proceedings officer to comply with any request under this section.

Amendments—Inserted by CAA 2006, s 1.

PART II

Monitoring enforcement orders—The court may ask a Cafcass officer to monitor, or arrange for the monitoring of, a person's compliance with an enforcement order, and to report to the court on failure to comply and on any unsuitability to undertake the unpaid work. The Cafcass Guidance (para 4.3) (see further under s 11A, above) observes that the monitoring of individuals' compliance with unpaid work requirements will be undertaken by the National Probation Service (NPS), which in turn will report to Cafcass. When making the order, the court should give leave to the officer to disclose to NPS such information in relation to the proceedings as necessary (see FPR PD12N *Enforcement of Children Act 1989 Child Arrangements Orders: Disclosure of Information to Officers of the National Probation Service*). Where NPS determines there has been non-compliance without reasonable excuse, this will be reported to Cafcass. Similarly, if an individual is or becomes unsuitable to perform unpaid work, NPS will notify Cafcass of this. In both instances, Cafcass must report such matters to the court. There may be other matters that should be reported to the court eg where someone moves from their address without providing a new address.

11N Enforcement orders: warning notices

Where the court makes an enforcement order, it is to attach to the order a notice warning of the consequences of failing to comply with the order.

Amendments—Inserted by CAA 2006, s 1.

Attaching a warning notice to an enforcement order—Where an enforcement order is made, the court must attach a warning notice setting out the consequences of breaching the order ie the imposition of a further enforcement order, the enhancement of the existing enforcement order, and the use of existing sanctions for contempt. Schedule A1 makes further provision about enforcement orders: the maximum number of hours of unpaid work that may be required is 200 and the minimum is 40; the court has power to amend or revoke an enforcement order; if terms of an enforcement order are breached, the court may (in certain circumstances) amend the original order to make it more onerous, or impose another enforcement order.

11O Compensation for financial loss

(1) This section applies if a child arrangements order with respect to a child has been made.

(2) If the court is satisfied that –

(a) an individual has failed to comply with a provision of the child arrangements order, and

(b) a person falling within subsection (6) has suffered financial loss by reason of the breach,

it may make an order requiring the individual in breach to pay the person compensation in respect of his financial loss.

(3) But the court may not make an order under subsection (2) if it is satisfied that the individual in breach had a reasonable excuse for failing to comply with the particular provision of the child arrangements order.

(4) The burden of proof as to the matter mentioned in subsection (3) lies on the individual claiming to have had a reasonable excuse.

(5) An order under subsection (2) may be made only on an application by the person who claims to have suffered financial loss.

(6) A person falls within this subsection if he is –

(a) a person who is, for the purposes of the child arrangements order, a person with whom the child concerned lives or is to live;

(b) a person whose contact with the child concerned is provided for in the child arrangements order;

(c) an individual subject to a condition under section 11(7)(b) or an activity condition imposed by the child arrangements order; or

(d) the child concerned.

(7) Where the person proposing to apply for an order under subsection (2) is the child concerned, the child must obtain the leave of the court before making such an application.

(8) The court may grant leave to the child concerned only if it is satisfied that he has sufficient understanding to make the proposed application.

(9) The amount of compensation is to be determined by the court, but may not exceed the amount of the applicant's financial loss.

(10) In determining the amount of compensation payable by the individual in breach, the court must take into account the individual's financial circumstances.

(11) An amount ordered to be paid as compensation may be recovered by the applicant as a civil debt due to him.

(12) Subsection (2) has effect subject to the restrictions in section 11P.

(13) Proceedings in which any question of making an order under subsection (2) arises are to be regarded for the purposes of section 11(1) and (2) as proceedings in which a question arises with respect to a section 8 order.

(14) In exercising its powers under this section, a court is to take into account the welfare of the child concerned.

Amendments—Inserted by CAA 2006, s 1. Amended by CFA 2014, s 12, Sch 2.

Financial compensation orders—The court may require a person who has caused financial loss to another person as a result of breaching a child arrangements order (including breaching a condition attached to an order for contact), to pay compensation up to the amount of the loss: s 11O. Before making a compensation order the court must take into account the welfare of any child concerned, and the financial circumstances of the person in breach. The applicant must fall within the criteria set down by s 11O(6)(a)–(d). The court may not make an order for financial compensation where the person in breach did not receive a warning notice under s 11I and was not otherwise informed of its terms: s 11P. The Cafcass Guidance (para 5.1) (see further under s 11A, above) observes that while Cafcass is unlikely to be aware of applications being made for compensation, it is possible that the court may seek information from Cafcass about the welfare of the child. Cafcass should respond in accordance with the specific request made by the court. The court has a discretion as to whether to join the child as a party (see para 4.1) and may ask the Cafcass officer to consider this and report to the court with his opinion (FPR 2010, r 16.39 and PD16A). Section 11P provides for circumstances in which a court may not make an order for financial compensation; these include: where a person did not receive a warning notice under s 11I; where he was not otherwise informed of the terms; or where the order is a excepted order (see s 11B(4) for meaning of 'excepted' orders).

Procedure for applying for a financial compensation order—See Procedural Guide D8.
Draft Legislation on Family Justice—See under ss 11A and 11H.

11P Orders under section 11O(2): further provision

(1) A court may not make an order under section 11O(2) requiring an individual to pay compensation in respect of a failure by him to comply with a provision of a child arrangements order unless it is satisfied that before the failure occurred the individual had been given (in accordance with rules of court) a copy of, or otherwise informed of the terms of –

(a) in the case of a failure to comply with a provision of a child arrangements order where the order that was varied before the failure occurred, a notice under section 11I relating to the order varying the child arrangements order or, where more than one such order has been made, the last order preceding the failure in question;

(b) in any other case, a notice under section 11I relating to the child arrangements order.

(2) A court may not make an order under section 11O(2) requiring an individual to pay compensation in respect of a failure by him to comply with a provision of a child arrangements order where the failure occurred before the individual attained the age of 18.

(3) A court may not make an order under section 11O(2) requiring an individual to pay compensation in respect of a failure by him to comply with a provision of a child arrangements order where the child arrangements order is an excepted order (within the meaning given by section 11B(4)).

Amendments—Inserted by CAA 2006, s 1. Amended by CFA 2014, s 12, Sch 2.

12 Child arrangements orders and parental responsibility

(1) Where –

(a) the court makes a child arrangements order with respect to a child,

(b) the father of the child, or a woman who is a parent of the child by virtue of section 43 of the Human Fertilisation and Embryology Act 2008, is named in the order as a person with whom the child is to live, and

(c) the father, or the woman, would not otherwise have parental responsibility for the child, the court must also make an order under section 4 giving the father, or under section 4ZA giving the woman, that responsibility.

(1A) Where –

PART II

(a) the court makes a child arrangements order with respect to a child,

(b) the father of the child, or a woman who is a parent of the child by virtue of section 43 of the Human Fertilisation and Embryology Act 2008, is named in the order as a person with whom the child is to spend time or otherwise have contact but is not named in the order as a person with whom the child is to live, and

(c) the father, or the woman, would not otherwise have parental responsibility for the child,

the court must decide whether it would be appropriate, in view of the provision made in the order with respect to the father or the woman, for him or her to have parental responsibility for the child and, if it decides that it would be appropriate for the father or the woman to have that responsibility, must also make an order under section 4 giving him, or under section 4ZA giving her, that responsibility.

(2) Where the court makes a child arrangements order and a person who is not a parent or guardian of the child concerned is named in the order as a person with whom the child is to live, that person shall have parental responsibility for the child while the order remains in force so far as providing for the child to live with that person.

(2A) Where the court makes a child arrangements order and –

(a) a person who is not the parent or guardian of the child concerned is named in the order as a person with whom the child is to spend time or otherwise have contact, but

(b) the person is not named in the order as a person with whom the child is to live, the court may provide in the order for the person to have parental responsibility for the child while paragraphs (a) and (b) continue to be met in the person's case.

(3) Where a person has parental responsibility for a child as a result of subsection (2) or (2A), he shall not have the right –

(a) *(repealed)*

(b) to agree, or refuse to agree, to the making of an adoption order, or an order under section 84 of the Adoption and Children Act 2002, with respect to the child; or

(c) to appoint a guardian for the child.

(4) Where subsection (1) requires the court to make an order under section 4 or 4ZA in respect of a parent of a child, the court shall not bring that order to an end at any time while the child arrangements order concerned remains in force so far as providing for the child to live with that parent.

(5), (6) *(repealed)*

Amendments—ACA 2002, ss 114, 139, Sch 3, paras 54, 57; CYPA 2008, s 37(2); HFEA 2008, s 56, Sch 6, Pt 1, para 28(1),(2); CFA 2014, s 12, Sch 2.

Children and Families Act 2014—CA 1989, s 12 has been amended by CFA 2014 so as to remove residence and contact orders and replace them with child arrangements orders (CAO). The provisions in s 12(1) provide that when making a CAO the court is required to give parental responsibility to the father of the child concerned, or to the child's second female parent (by virtue of HFEA 2008, s 43), in cases where he or she is named in the order as a person with whom the child is to live. This would only apply in cases in which the father or second female parent would not otherwise have parental responsibility. Section 12(1A) gives the court the power to give parental responsibility to the child's father or second female parent in cases where he or she is named in the order as a person with whom the child is to spend time or otherwise have contact. It would be for the court to determine whether it is appropriate for him or her to be given parental responsibility in the light of the specific provisions of the order and, if the court considers it appropriate, it must give parental responsibility to him or her. In cases where a court gives parental responsibility in either of these circumstances, it does so by means of an order under s 4 or 4ZA. Section 12(2) provides that where a CAO makes provision for a child to live with a person who is not his parent or guardian, that person would be given parental responsibility. Section 12(2A) enables the court to give parental responsibility to a person who is not a child's parent or guardian in cases where a CAO provides for the child to spend time with or otherwise have contact (but not live) with that person (although it is envisaged that this power would be exercised rarely). In relation to both ss 12(2) and 12(2A), respectively, parental responsibility is given for the duration of the relevant provision.

13 Change of child's name or removal from jurisdiction

(1) Where a child arrangements order to which subsection (4) applies is in force with respect to a child, no person may –

(a) cause the child to be known by a new surname; or

(b) remove him from the United Kingdom;

without either the written consent of every person who has parental responsibility for the child or the leave of the court.

(2) Subsection (1)(b) does not prevent the removal of a child, for a period of less than one month, by a person named in the child arrangements order as a person with whom the child is to live.

(3) In making a child arrangements order to which subsection (4) applies, the court may grant the leave required by subsection (1)(b), either generally or for specified purposes.

(4) This subsection applies to a child arrangements order if the arrangements regulated by the order consist of, or include, arrangements which relate to either or both of the following –

(a) with whom the child concerned is to live, and

(b) when the child is to live with any person.

Amendments—CFA 2014, s 12, Sch 2.

Defined terms—'child': s 105(1); 'child arrangements order': s 8(1); 'parental responsibility': s 3.

Change of surname (s 13(1)(a))—See annotations to s 8.

Method of application for leave (s 13(1)(a),(b))—The permission application is a freestanding application and not a species of s 8 application (*Re B (Change of Surname)* [1996] 1 FLR 791, CA). It is made in accordance with FPR 2010, rr 18.1–18.13, which deal only with applications for permission to commence proceedings. Although the application can be made in the Family Court, where it is for permission to remove a child permanently from the jurisdiction, it should not be heard by lay justices but should be transferred upwards for determination by a District Judge, Circuit Judge or High Court judge, depending on the complexity and difficulty of the decision (FC(CDB)R 2014, *President's Guidance on Allocation and Gatekeeping (Private Law)*). There is a lack of clarity about how relocation applications are to be classified – the debate is whether such applications should be made under s 13 or by way of an application for a specific issue order under s 8. Under s 13, where a shared residence order or child arrangements order was in force, the child could not be removed from the jurisdiction without consent of all those with parental responsibility or the leave of the court. Under s 9(7), the court could not make a s 8 order, other than one varying or discharging such an order, in respect of a child who had reached 16 unless there were exceptional circumstances. That bar would not apply if the application fell to be considered under s 13. In *Re C (Older Children: Relocation)* [2016] 2 FLR 1159, CA; sub nom *H v C & E (A Child by his solicitor, Anne-Marie Hutchinson)*, the Court of Appeal confirmed that the general intention of CA 1989 was to prevent the imposition of inappropriate requirements on older children and that it was inappropriate to have left a shared residence order in place in relation to a mature and intelligent older child.

External relocation and removal from jurisdiction (s 13(1)(b))—The only principle to be applied when determining an application to remove a child permanently from the UK is that the welfare of the child is paramount: *K v K (Relocation: Shared Care Arrangement)* [2012] 2 FLR 880, CA; *Re F (A Child) (International Relocation Cases)* [2017] 1 FLR 979, CA and *Re C (Internal Relocation)* [2017] 1 FLR 103, CA. A welfare analysis is always required in any decision about a child's upbringing but the level of sophistication required in doing so depends on the facts of the case. In *Re F (A Child)*, the Court of Appeal reiterated that earlier guidance in *Payne v Payne* [2001] 1 FLR 1052, CA should not be seen as directing judges and parties to all the relevant considerations in any relocation case because: (i) the 'gender-based assumptions as to the role and relationships of parents with a child', which underpin *Payne* and which can now be seen as outdated and reflecting only one of many ways in which parents exercise the responsibility for raising their children in modern times; and (ii) 'The absence of any emphasis on the child's wishes and feelings or, to take the question one step back, the child's participation in the decision-making process' when looking at the *Payne* judgments. The following principles were also highlighted –

- Selective or partial legal citation from *Payne* without any wider legal analysis is likely to be regarded as an error of law.
- In particular, a judgment that not only focuses solely on *Payne*, but also compounds that error by only referring to the four-point 'discipline' set out by Thorpe LJ in *Payne*, is likely to be 'wholly wrong'.
- A step as significant as the relocation of a child to a foreign jurisdiction where the fundamental interference between one parent and a child is envisaged requires that the parents' plans be scrutinised and evaluated by reference to the proportionality of the same.

It is not essential to have a Cafcass investigation into the circumstances; ordering a report may not always be helpful to the court in reaching its decision, and it is a matter for the judge's discretion (*Re R (Leave to Remove: Contact)* [2011] 1 FLR 1336, CA). In relocation cases, the welfare checklist should be applied and the child's wishes and feelings are a factor in that process. In the majority of cases, it is normal to obtain an independent Cafcass report on the child's wishes and feelings, and that will be the case if the child is having contact that would be disrupted by relocation. However, in some cases no report will be necessary and to order it would be a misuse of resources: *Re T (A Child)* (19 November 2015, Elias LJ , Beatson LJ, Baker J, unreported). The judge is entitled to depart from the recommendations of the Cafcass officer where the report is not balanced and the judge has to look at the case in the round (*Re E (Relocation: Removal from Jurisdiction)* [2013] 2 FLR 290, CA). In *Re R* Wilson LJ stated his firm view that orders for contact should not be made when granting leave to relocate, as they are contrary to principle and the court must recognize that it is relinquishing jurisdiction to the courts of the state to which the parent is moving. In *S v T (Permission to Relocate to Russia)* [2013] 2 FLR 457, FD, Hedley J said of the increasing phenomenon of transnational parenting that while the impact upon breaking up can be devastating, parents enter it with their eyes open and fully alert to the consequences of it 'going wrong'. *Re N (Leave to Remove from the Jurisdiction) (No 2)* [2014] EWHC B16 (Fam) demonstrates that relocation outside the jurisdiction almost always involves a decision to bring up a child in a different culture and social milieu.

There are a number of cases in which non-residential parents have argued that the permanent removal of their child from the jurisdiction by the residential parent constitutes a breach of Art 8, which guarantees the right to family life. The task for the court under ECHR 1950, Art 8(2) is to balance the right of the non-residential parent to family life (guaranteed by Art 8(1)) against the right of the residential parent to their own right to private life when the two rights are in conflict – see the commentary on *Re F (A Child) (International Relocation Cases)*, above. In *K v K (Relocation: Shared Care Arrangement)* [2012] 2 FLR 880, CA, the Court of Appeal held that, in a shared care arrangement, the only principle to be extracted from *Payne* is that the child's welfare is the court's paramount consideration. In *Re O (Residence)* [2014] 1 FLR 89, CA, the Court of Appeal reiterated that the welfare principle and the s 1(3) checklist determine the outcome. In *Re K (A Child)* [2016] EWCA Civ 931, the Court of Appeal confirmed that the analysis of a child's best interests would necessarily involve a careful examination of the parents' wishes and their interests, and their Art 8 rights, given the potential for the impact of the decision on the parents to affect the child as well. The balancing exercise to be carried out in relocation exercises was one in which each and every factor relating to a child's welfare was weighed to determine which of a range of options best met the requirement to afford paramount consideration to the child's welfare.

Where there is more than one child involved, the court must consider separately the interests of each child in the light of their ages, stages of development and the nature of their needs (*Re S (Relocation: Interests of Siblings)* [2011] 2 FLR 678, CA). See also *DH v CL and Others* [2014] EWHC 1836 (Fam), which provides a useful summary of the legal principles governing, and the holistic balancing exercise required in, the determination of an application permanently to remove a child from the jurisdiction, namely that in determining the application: (i) the court is required by s 1(1) to consider the child's welfare as the paramount consideration; (ii) in applying that test, the court must consider the welfare checklist in s 1(3); (iii) the welfare principles govern applications for international relocation just as they govern other welfare-based determinations regarding children and there is no presumption in favour of such an application; (iv) the court must consider the positives and negatives, the benefits and the detriments, of the proposed placement options by reference to the evidence and the welfare checklist, guarding against a linear approach and instead adopting a global, holistic evaluation; (v) in the overall evaluation of competing outcomes, particular importance is to be attached to the relationship that the child enjoys with each parent following the guidance of the House of Lords in *Re G (Residence: Same-Sex Partner) (sub nom CG v CW)* [2006] 2 FLR 629, HL and the Supreme Court in *Re B (A Child)* [2010] 1 FLR 551, SC; (vi) the child's Art 8 rights are engaged and these rights are not merely theoretical, but real and dynamic, deserving of the closest consideration; (vii) regard must be given to the extent or absence of any meaningful reciprocal enforcement regime in the foreign country, and the court must assess carefully the risk of breach of any contact arrangements and the magnitude of any breach – it is for the court to achieve what security it can for the child by building in all practical safeguards to its order (*Re T (Staying Contact in Non-Convention Country)* [1999] 1 FLR 262, FD, *Re A (Security for Return to the Jurisdiction) (Note)* [1999] 2 FLR 1, FD, *Re K (Removal From Jurisdiction: Practice)* [1999] 2 FLR 1084, CA). The more finely balanced any decision may be regarding the future welfare of a child, the less likely it is that any consequent appeal will succeed against the judge's decision to choose one viable option against another: *Re C (Permission to Relocate*) [2014] EWCA Civ 705.

In *Re B (Removal from Jurisdiction); Re S (Removal from Jurisdiction)* [2003] 2 FLR 1043, CA, the Court of Appeal emphasised that where a mother cared for the children within a new family, the impact of refusal on the new family and the stepfather must also be carefully evaluated. However, where removal from the jurisdiction will cause a significant loss to the child in relation to emotional and educational issues permission may be refused (*Re Y (Leave to Remove from Jurisdiction)* [2004] 2 FLR 330, FD). For examples of the court refusing permission to relocate, see *Re AR (A Child: Relocation)* [2010] 2 FLR 1577, FD; *Re A (Removal from Jurisdiction)* [2014] 1 FLR 1, CA; *C v C* (above).

Note that where there is a child arrangements order for residence in place, the removal of a child from England and Wales to Scotland does not require an application for permission to remove the child from the jurisdiction, since Scotland is part of the UK (*Re T (A Child)* [2001] EWCA Civ 1067).

For specific guidance in radicalisation cases, see the President's Guidance of 8 October 2015: *Radicalisation Cases in the Family Courts* (set out in Part V) and the commentary thereto.

Internal relocation within the UK—Relocation within the UK can present problems because while the primary carer might not have an obligation to apply under s 13(1)(b), he or she may still have to defeat the challenge of an application for a prohibited steps order under s 8 or for the imposition of a condition to the child arrangements order under s 11(7). However, because welfare is the governing principle in any internal relocation case, there is no reason to differentiate between those cases and external relocation cases. The approach set out in *K v K (Relocation: Shared Care Arrangement)* [2012] 2 FLR 880, CA and *Re F (A Child) (International Relocation Cases)* [2017] 1 FLR 979, CA should apply equally to internal relocation cases. Clearly, however, the outcome of that approach will depend entirely on the facts of the individual case. In *Re R (Internal Relocation: Appeal)* [2016] EWCA Civ 1016, the Court of Appeal considered the proper approach to applications for the return of children who had unilaterally been removed from their home by one parent and taken to another place in England and Wales, and confirmed that there is no general principle in favour of summary return to the place where the child was formerly resident. Such proceedings are normally brought under CA 1989 and must be decided by applying the welfare principle and the welfare checklist.

In making such decisions, the welfare of the child is always paramount (*Re H (Children) (Residence Order: Condition)* [2001] 2 FLR 1277, CA. In *Re C (Internal Relocation)* [2017] 1 FLR 103, CA, the Court of Appeal confirmed the proper approach to the whole issue of relocation, which can be summarised as follows:

- There was no difference in basic approach as between external relocation and internal relocation; the decision in either type of case hinged ultimately on the welfare of the child.
- The wishes, feelings and interests of the parents and the likely impact of the decision on each of them were of great importance, but in the context of evaluating and determining the welfare of the child.
- In either type of relocation case, external or internal, a judge was likely to find helpful some or all of the considerations referred to in *Payne*, but not as a prescriptive blueprint, rather and merely as a checklist of the sort of factors that would or might need to be weighed in the balance when determining which decision would better serve the welfare of the child.

It is wrong in principle to apply different criteria if an order for shared living arrangements is in place as opposed to an order for sole care; the correct approach is to examine the underlying facts and decide in all of the circumstances whether it is in the child's interests to relocate with the parent who wishes to move (*Re L (Shared Residence Order)* [2009] 1 FLR 1157, CA). See, for example, *Re H (Children) (Residence Order: Condition)* [2001] 2 FLR 1277, CA, the medical evidence showed that the effect of the father moving the children away from the area where the mother lived would be devastating and therefore a condition attached to the residence order was justified; *Re S (A Child) (Residence Order: Condition) (No 2)* [2002] EWCA Civ 1795, where the court imposed a condition on a living arrangements order to prevent the mother from moving her 9-year-old Down's Syndrome child to Cornwall; and *B v B (Residence: Condition Limiting Geographical Area)* [2004] 2 FLR 979, FD, where the court attached to the mother's residence order a condition that she reside in a defined area of Southern England as she had no good reasons for her proposed move to Newcastle other than to be distanced further from the father.

Temporary removal from jurisdiction—Where it is intended that the removal of a child from the jurisdiction is only temporary, different considerations will apply to those relating to permanent removal (*Re A (Temporary Removal from Jurisdiction)* [2005] 1 FLR 639, CA). However, in *Re R (Prohibited Steps Order)* [2014] 1 FLR 643, CA, the Court of Appeal confirmed that the overriding consideration of the court in deciding whether to allow a parent to take a child to a non-Hague Convention country remains whether the making of that order would be in the best interests of the child. Where there is some risk of abduction and an obvious risk to the child if that risk were to materialise, the court must be positively satisfied that the advantages to the child of visiting that country outweigh the risks to their welfare that the visit would entail. The court should routinely be involved in investigating what safeguards could be put in place to minimise the risk of retention and to secure the child's return. Safeguards should be capable of having a real and tangible effect in the jurisdiction in which they are to operate and be capable of being easily accessed by the UK-based parent. For a suggested menu of undertakings and declarations in holiday applications to a non-Convention country, see *Re DS (Removal from Jurisdiction)* [2010] 1 FLR 576, FD. For examples of cases where permission for temporary removal was granted, see *Re S and O (Temporary Removal from Jurisdiction)* [2009] Fam Law 114, FD, *Re C-W (A Child) (Contact Overseas)* [2017] 1 FLR 131, CA, *C v K (Children: Application for Temporary Removal to Algeria)* [2015] 2 FLR 791, FD and *Re L & B (Children) (Specific Issues: Temporary Leave to Remove from the Jurisdiction; Circumcision)* [2016] EWHC 849 (Fam). In most cases, there is a need for the effectiveness of any suggested safeguard to be established by competent expert evidence that deals specifically, and in detail, with the issue.

****

Special guardianship

14A Special guardianship orders

(1) A 'special guardianship order' is an order appointing one or more individuals to be a child's 'special guardian' (or special guardians).

(2) A special guardian –

(a) must be aged eighteen or over; and

(b) must not be a parent of the child in question,

and subsections (3) to (6) are to be read in that light.

(3) The court may make a special guardianship order with respect to any child on the application of an individual who –

(a) is entitled to make such an application with respect to the child; or

(b) has obtained the leave of the court to make the application,

or on the joint application of more than one such individual.

(4) Section 9(3) applies in relation to an application for leave to apply for a special guardianship order as it applies in relation to an application for leave to apply for a section 8 order.

(5) The individuals who are entitled to apply for a special guardianship order with respect to a child are –

(a) any guardian of the child;

(b) any individual who is named in a child arrangements order as a person with whom the child is to live;

(c) any individual listed in subsection (5)(b) or (c) of section 10 (as read with subsection (10) of that section);

(d) a local authority foster parent with whom the child has lived for a period of at least one year immediately preceding the application;

(e) a relative with whom the child has lived for a period of at least one year immediately preceding the application.

(6) The court may also make a special guardianship order with respect to a child in any family proceedings in which a question arises with respect to the welfare of the child if –

(a) an application for the order has been made by an individual who falls within subsection (3)(a) or (b) (or more than one such individual jointly); or

(b) the court considers that a special guardianship order should be made even though no such application has been made.

(7) No individual may make an application under subsection (3) or (6)(a) unless, before the beginning of the period of three months ending with the date of the application, he has given written notice of his intention to make the application –

(a) if the child in question is being looked after by a local authority, to that local authority, or

(b) otherwise, to the local authority in whose area the individual is ordinarily resident.

(8) On receipt of such a notice, the local authority must investigate the matter and prepare a report for the court dealing with –

(a) the suitability of the applicant to be a special guardian;

(b) such matters (if any) as may be prescribed by the Secretary of State; and

(c) any other matter which the local authority consider to be relevant.

(9) The court may itself ask a local authority to conduct such an investigation and prepare such a report, and the local authority must do so.

(10) The local authority may make such arrangements as they see fit for any person to act on their behalf in connection with conducting an investigation or preparing a report referred to in subsection (8) or (9).

(11) The court may not make a special guardianship order unless it has received a report dealing with the matters referred to in subsection (8).

(12) Subsections (8) and (9) of section 10 apply in relation to special guardianship orders as they apply in relation to section 8 orders.

(13) This section is subject to section 29(5) and (6) of the Adoption and Children Act 2002.

Amendments—Inserted by ACA 2002, s 115. Amended by CYPA 2008, s 38; CFA 2014, s 12, Sch 2.

Scope—Special guardianship orders (SGOs) are private law orders that enable the special guardian to exercise parental responsibility to the exclusion of others with parental responsibility. They provide permanence and security for those children for whom adoption is not suitable but who cannot live with their birth parents. The basic legal links between the child and his birth family are preserved. Where the child himself applies for permission, the court may only grant permission if it is satisfied that the child has sufficient understanding to make the proposed application for a SGO: ss 14A(12) and 10(8). The court may not make a SGO unless it has received a report from the local authority: s 14A(11). The report must deal with the matters prescribed by the Schedule to the Special Guardianship Regulations 2005 (as amended by the Special Guardianship (Amendment) Regulations 2016 (see below)) and the matters required by s 10(9): s 14A(12).

Procedure—The procedure for applying for a special guardianship order (SGO) is set out in Procedural Guide D10. The court cannot make a SGO unless it has received a report from the local authority.

Guidance on making special guardianship orders—In *Re S (Adoption Order or Special Guardianship Order)* [2007] 1 FLR 819, CA, the Court of Appeal gave detailed guidance at [40]–[77] as to the statutory framework, the making of special guardianship orders (SGOs) within pre-existing family relationships and the need under a SGO for permission for a parent to apply for a s 8 order. This guidance has been endorsed by the President of the Family Division. See also *Re M-J (Adoption Order or Special Guardianship Order)* [2007] 1 FLR 691, CA and *Re AJ (Adoption Order or Special Guardianship Order)* [2007] 1 FLR 507, CA, which should be read together with *Re S* (above). In *A Local Authority v Y, Z and Others* [2006] 2 FLR 41, FD, the court approved SGOs in respect of three older children who had been in settled wider family placements for around 2 years. The court also made an order for defined contact to the mother. In *Re L (Special Guardianship: Surname)*

[2007] 2 FLR 50, CA, the court refused to allow the child's surname to be changed as it was important that as she grew up she knew that she was being raised by her grandparents rather than her parents. In *Re F (Special Guardianship Order: Contact with Birth Family)* [2016] 1 FLR 593, FD, an SGO was made, rather than an adoption order, to enable a very young child with special needs to remain with long-term foster carers so that he could maintain a connection with his cultural and ethnic background, which was essential for his development and sense of identity. In *Surrey County Council v Al-Hilli and Others* [2014] 2 FLR 217, FD, an SGO was appropriate where the parents had been shot dead in traumatic circumstances and the children needed both to retain a link with their family and a greater degree of stability and permanence than that provided by a residence order. In *Re H (A Child) (Analysis of Realistic Options and SGOs)* [2016] 1 FLR 286, CA, where an appeal was allowed against an SGO that had been made in proceedings in which poor case management had led to an assumption that the special guardian was a realistic option for the care of the child and that the father was not.

Special Guardianship Regulations 2005—The Special Guardianship Regulations 2005 form part of the legislative framework for special guardianship orders. They relate mainly to the special guardianship support services (SGSS), which local authorities are required to provide by virtue of section 14F. They prescribe the services which are SGSS and state which bodies other than local authorities can provide services on the local authority's behalf and which local authority should be responsible for providing SGSS in cross-border arrangements (regs 3–5). The Regulations set out the circumstances in which financial support is payable and the considerations to which an authority must have regard when deciding on the amount of that financial support (regs 6–10). They set out the procedure for an assessment of special guardianship support needs, identifying those entitled to an assessment and how those assessments should be carried out (regs 11–16). They specify the steps an authority must take following an assessment to notify the relevant persons of the outcome and they require the authority to plan and review their service provision where appropriate (regs 17–18). The Regulations prescribe the matters that local authorities are required to include in the report that the court must receive before it can make a SGO (reg 21 and Schedule). They also specify which local authority is to be the relevant local authority where the child becomes entitled to advice and assistance under the provisions relating to care leavers (reg 22).

Special Guardianship (Amendment) Regulations 2016—These amend the Schedule to the Special Guardianship Regulations 2005 by prescribing additional matters that must be dealt with by a local authority in their report to the court about prospective special guardians in certain circumstances (see **Need for a local authority report before order can be made**, below).

Special Guardianship Guidance—The Special Guardianship Guidance issued under the Local Authority Social Services Act 1970, s 7, by the Department for Education and Skills, was amended on 29 February 2016. While the Guidance does not have the full force of statute, it should be complied with unless exceptional circumstances justify departure from it (*B v Lewisham Borough Council* [2008] 2 FLR 523, QBD).

Guidance where more than one local authority is involved—In *Suffolk CC v Nottinghamshire CC* [2013] 2 FLR 106, CA, the court held that where more than one local authority is involved in an out-of-area placement in special guardianship proceedings, the key question in determining which authority is responsible is whether a child is 'looked after' by one of them within the meaning of s 22(1); if so, then that authority is responsible. If the child is not a 'looked after' child, the responsible authority is the one in whose area the child is living. A child ceases to be 'looked after' as soon as parental responsibility becomes vested in another by, for example, the making of a child arrangements order for residence or a special guardianship order. In such a situation, local authorities are bound by Special Guardianship Regulations 2005, reg 5 to co-operate with one another in the discharge of functions. Every authority will be both a sender and a receiver over time and there ought to be self-regulation in respect of who would fund the statutory duties.

Special guardianship not confined to kinship cases—In *Re I (Adoption: Appeal: Special Guardianship)* [2012] Fam Law 1461, CA, McFarlane LJ emphasised that where the issue is whether to dispense with parental consent for the purposes of an adoption or placement order, the test in s 52(1)(b) is that the court must be satisfied that 'the welfare of the child requires the consent to be dispensed with' and it will be difficult – or indeed impossible – for the judge to be satisfied of this, unless relevant alternatives have been considered. Here, where the foster carers would continue to be the carers of the child and where the paternal family would continue to have contact with the child, special guardianship should have been properly considered. The judgment is therefore also a helpful reminder that special guardianship is by no means intended to be confined to cases of kinship care.

Leave to apply (s 14A(4))—The factors governing an application for permission to apply for a SGO are the same as those for s 8 orders: see under CA 1989, s 9(3). Where the person applying for permission is the child concerned, the court may only grant permission if it is satisfied that the child has sufficient understanding to make the proposed application for the SGO (see s 14A(12) and **Application for leave by child** under s 10(8)). Where the person applying for permission is not the child concerned, the court must have regard to the factors in s 10(9) in just the same way as it does when considering an application for permission to apply for a s 8 order (see s 14A(12) and **Application for leave by person other than child concerned** under s 10(9)).

Orders can be made of court's own motion (s 14A(6))—The court can make a SGO in an appropriate case, even where no application has been made. However, see *Re H (A Child) (Analysis of Realistic Options and SGOs)* [2016] 1 FLR 286, CA, where neither the special guardian nor the local authority on her behalf made an application for an SGO and the Court of Appeal noted that this meant the important procedural hurdle of the satisfaction of the test in CA 1989, s 10(9) was not addressed. It was further noted that it is only where parties agree that an application for an SGO should be dispensed with that the court's power under s 14A(6)(b) to make an SGO of its own motion power can be exercised without good reason; in any other case, the use by the court of this power must be reasoned.

Need for a local authority report before order can be made (s 14A(7),(8),(11))—Anyone wishing to apply for a SGO must give 3 months' notice to the relevant local authority so that a report can be prepared as to his suitability and any other relevant matters (but see below for those cases in which the requirement for 3 months' notice will be waived: ACA 2002, s 29(5), (6)). The court may not make a SGO unless it has received the prescribed report (s 14A (11); *Re S (Adoption Order or Special Guardianship Order) (No 2)*) [2007] 1 FLR 855, CA)). In *Birmingham City Council v R* [2007] 1 FLR 564, CA, the Court of Appeal held that a person who requires the permission of the court to make an application for a SGO cannot either make an application for such an order or give notice of an intention to do so unless and until he has obtained the court's permission to make an application. Section 14A(8), which requires the authority to investigate and prepare a report, is not triggered when a person who requires the court's permission to make an application but has not obtained it, purports to give notice of an intention to make an application for a SGO. The matters that the local authority must include in their report to the court are set out in the Special Guardianship Regulations, reg 21, and in the Schedule thereto (as amended by SG(A)R 2016). The amendments to the requirements (in force in cases where an individual has given written notice after 29 February 2016) extend the scope of the local authority's assessment of the suitability of prospective special guardians by including:

(a) a consideration of any harm that the child has suffered,
(b) any risk of future harm to the child posed by the child's parents, relatives or any other person the local authority considers relevant,
(c) an assessment of the nature of the prospective special guardian's current and past relationship with the child,
(d) an assessment of the prospective special guardian's parenting capacity, including their understanding of and ability to meet the child's current and likely future needs, particularly any needs the child may have arising from harm that the child has suffered, their understanding of and ability to protect the child from any current or future risk of harm posed by the child's parents, relatives or any other person the local authority considers relevant, particularly in relation to contact, and their ability and suitability to bring up the child until the child reaches the age of 18.

However, these additional requirements do not apply in circumstances where the court has asked a local authority to conduct an investigation and prepare a report in accordance with CA 1989, s 14A(9). In *Re E-R (Child Arrangements Order)* [2016] 1 FLR 521, CA, the Court of Appeal confirmed the need for a detailed investigation and analysis of the child's circumstances, whether produced by a child's guardian, Cafcass or the local authority.

'subject to section 29(5) and (6) of the Adoption and Children Act 2002' (s 14A(13))—ACA 2002, s 29(5) states that where a placement order is in force, no SGO may be made in respect of the child unless: (a) an application has been made for an adoption order; and (b) the person applying for the SGO has obtained the court's permission, or if he is a guardian of the child, has obtained the court's permission under s 47(5). Where permission has been given in these circumstances, the applicant must still give written notice of his application to the relevant local authority but the requirement for 3 months' notice is waived (ACA 2002, s 29(6)).

Hague Convention 1996—The Hague Convention 1996 came into force in the UK on 1 November 2012. It lays down rules in respect of measures directed to the protection of the person or property of the child in cases to which the Convention applies (Art 1). 'Measures of protection' include guardianship, curatorship or analogous institutions (Art 3). They are intended to include systems of protection, representation or assistance that are established in favour of a child when his parents are deceased or are no longer authorised to represent him (*Handbook*, para 3.23; *Lagarde Report*, para 21). See further under the Convention in Part VI.

14B Special guardianship orders: making

(1) Before making a special guardianship order, the court must consider whether, if the order were made –

(a) a child arrangements order containing contact provision should also be made with respect to the child,
(b) any section 8 order in force with respect to the child should be varied or discharged,
(c) where provision contained in a child arrangements order made with respect to the child is not discharged, any enforcement order relating to that provision should be revoked, and
(d) where an activity direction has been made –
   (i) in proceedings for the making, variation or discharge of a child arrangements order with respect to the child, or
   (ii) in other proceedings that relate to such an order,

   that direction should be discharged.

(1A) In subsection (1) 'contact provision' means provision which regulates arrangements relating to –

(a) with whom a child is to spend time or otherwise have contact, or
(b) when a child is to spend time or otherwise have contact with any person;

but in paragraphs (a) and (b) a reference to spending time or otherwise having contact with a person is to doing that otherwise than as a result of living with the person.

(2) On making a special guardianship order, the court may also –

(a) give leave for the child to be known by a new surname;
(b) grant the leave required by section 14C(3)(b), either generally or for specified purposes.

Amendments—Inserted by ACA 2002, s 115. Amended by CAA 2006, s 15, Sch 2, paras 7, 8, Sch 3; CFA 2014, s 12, Sch 2.

14C Special guardianship orders: effect

(1) The effect of a special guardianship order is that while the order remains in force –

(a) a special guardian appointed by the order has parental responsibility for the child in respect of whom it is made; and
(b) subject to any other order in force with respect to the child under this Act, a special guardian is entitled to exercise parental responsibility to the exclusion of any other person with parental responsibility for the child (apart from another special guardian).

(2) Subsection (1) does not affect –

(a) the operation of any enactment or rule of law which requires the consent of more than one person with parental responsibility in a matter affecting the child; or
(b) any rights which a parent of the child has in relation to the child's adoption or placement for adoption.

(3) While a special guardianship order is in force with respect to a child, no person may –

(a) cause the child to be known by a new surname; or
(b) remove him from the United Kingdom,

without either the written consent of every person who has parental responsibility for the child or the leave of the court.

(4) Subsection (3)(b) does not prevent the removal of a child, for a period of less than three months, by a special guardian of his.

(5) If the child with respect to whom a special guardianship order is in force dies, his special guardian must take reasonable steps to give notice of that fact to –

(a) each parent of the child with parental responsibility; and
(b) each guardian of the child,

but if the child has more than one special guardian, and one of them has taken such steps in relation to a particular parent or guardian, any other special guardian need not do so as respects that parent or guardian.

(6) This section is subject to section 29(7) of the Adoption and Children Act 2002.

Amendments—Inserted by ACA 2002, s 115.

Scope—Subject to any other existing CA 1989 order, a special guardian is entitled to exercise parental responsibility to the exclusion of any other person with parental responsibility (save for another special guardian): s 14C(1). It allows the special guardian to remove the child from the jurisdiction for up to 3 months without the consent of others with parental responsibility (but he would need the consent of another special guardian): s 14C(4).

'subject to section 29(7) of the Adoption and Children Act 2002' (s 14C(6))—ACA 2002, s 29(7) states that, where a placement order is in force, s 14C(1)(b) has effect subject to any determination made by the adoption agency under ACA 2002, s 25(4), to restrict the exercise of parental responsibility. CA 1989, s 14C(3) and (4) do not apply.

14D Special guardianship orders: variation and discharge

(1) The court may vary or discharge a special guardianship order on the application of –

(a) the special guardian (or any of them, if there are more than one);
(b) any parent or guardian of the child concerned;
(c) any individual who is named in a child arrangements order as a person with whom the child is to live;

(d) any individual not falling within any of paragraphs (a) to (c) who has, or immediately before the making of the special guardianship order had, parental responsibility for the child;
(e) the child himself; or
(f) a local authority designated in a care order with respect to the child.

(2) In any family proceedings in which a question arises with respect to the welfare of a child with respect to whom a special guardianship order is in force, the court may also vary or discharge the special guardianship order if it considers that the order should be varied or discharged, even though no application has been made under subsection (1).

(3) The following must obtain the leave of the court before making an application under subsection (1) –

(a) the child;
(b) any parent or guardian of his;
(c) any step-parent of his who has acquired, and has not lost, parental responsibility for him by virtue of section 4A;
(d) any individual falling within subsection (1)(d) who immediately before the making of the special guardianship order had, but no longer has, parental responsibility for him.

(4) Where the person applying for leave to make an application under subsection (1) is the child, the court may only grant leave if it is satisfied that he has sufficient understanding to make the proposed application under subsection (1).

(5) The court may not grant leave to a person falling within subsection (3)(b),(c) or (d) unless it is satisfied that there has been a significant change in circumstances since the making of the special guardianship order.

Amendments—Inserted by ACA 2002, s 115. Amended by CFA 2014, s 12, Sch 2.

Scope—A special guardianship order can be varied or discharged (unlike an adoption order).

Application for leave by child (s 14D(4))—See **Application for leave by child** under s 10(9).

Leave to apply to discharge special guardianship order (s 14D(5))—In *Re G (A Child) (Special Guardianship Order)* [2010] 2 FLR 696, CA, the court gave guidance as to the construction of s 14D(5) and the correct approach to applications for permission to apply to discharge special guardianship orders (SGOs). The judge observed that whereas permission to apply for revocation of a placement order under ACA 2002, s 24 required 'a change in circumstances', permission to apply for the discharge of an SGO under CA 1989, s 14D(5) required 'a significant change in circumstances'. For the time being, the Court of Appeal takes the view that there is no relevant difference between the two. Until the emergence of further guidance, the proper approach should be that commended in *M v Warwickshire County Council* [2008] 1 FLR 1093, CA, i e that the approach to permission to apply for revocation of a placement order should also apply to permission to apply for the discharge of an SGO. CA 1989, s 10(9), is not the right approach because that section applies to those who need to apply for permission to apply for a s 8 order and there appears to be no ground for considering that the matters specified there should be formally weighed upon an application to discharge a SGO.

14E Special guardianship orders: supplementary

(1) In proceedings in which any question of making, varying or discharging a special guardianship order arises, the court shall (in the light of any provision in rules of court that is of the kind mentioned in section 11(2)(a) or (b)) –

(a) draw up a timetable with a view to determining the question without delay; and
(b) give such directions as it considers appropriate for the purpose of ensuring, so far as is reasonably practicable, that the timetable is adhered to.

(2) Subsection (1) applies also in relation to proceedings in which any other question with respect to a special guardianship order arises.

(3) The power to make rules in subsection (2) of section 11 applies for the purposes of this section as it applies for the purposes of that.

(4) A special guardianship order, or an order varying one, may contain provisions which are to have effect for a specified period.

(5) Section 11(7) (apart from paragraph (c)) applies in relation to special guardianship orders and orders varying them as it applies in relation to section 8 orders.

Amendments—Inserted by ACA 2002, s 115. Amended by CFA 2014, s 13.

'Section 11(7)' (s 14E(5))—Section 11(7) permits the court to attach to the special guardianship order directions as to how it is to be carried into effect and to impose conditions which must be complied with.

14F Special guardianship support services

(1) Each local authority must make arrangements for the provision within their area of special guardianship support services, which means –

- (a) counselling, advice and information; and
- (b) such other services as are prescribed,

in relation to special guardianship.

(2) The power to make regulations under subsection (1)(b) is to be exercised so as to secure that local authorities provide financial support.

(3) At the request of any of the following persons –

- (a) a child with respect to whom a special guardianship order is in force;
- (b) a special guardian;
- (c) a parent;
- (d) any other person who falls within a prescribed description,

a local authority may carry out an assessment of that person's needs for special guardianship support services (but, if the Secretary of State so provides in regulations, they must do so if he is a person of a prescribed description, or if his case falls within a prescribed description, or if both he and his case fall within prescribed descriptions).

(4) A local authority may, at the request of any other person, carry out an assessment of that person's needs for special guardianship support services.

(5) Where, as a result of an assessment, a local authority decide that a person has needs for special guardianship support services, they must then decide whether to provide any such services to that person.

(6) If –

- (a) a local authority decide to provide any special guardianship support services to a person, and
- (b) the circumstances fall within a prescribed description,

the local authority must prepare a plan in accordance with which special guardianship support services are to be provided to him, and keep the plan under review.

(7) The Secretary of State may by regulations make provision about assessments, preparing and reviewing plans, the provision of special guardianship support services in accordance with plans and reviewing the provision of special guardianship support services.

(8) The regulations may in particular make provision –

- (a) about the type of assessment which is to be carried out, or the way in which an assessment is to be carried out;
- (b) about the way in which a plan is to be prepared;
- (c) about the way in which, and the time at which, a plan or the provision of special guardianship support services is to be reviewed;
- (d) about the considerations to which a local authority are to have regard in carrying out an assessment or review or preparing a plan;
- (e) as to the circumstances in which a local authority may provide special guardianship support services subject to conditions (including conditions as to payment for the support or the repayment of financial support);
- (f) as to the consequences of conditions imposed by virtue of paragraph (e) not being met (including the recovery of any financial support provided);
- (g) as to the circumstances in which this section may apply to a local authority in respect of persons who are outside that local authority's area;
- (h) as to the circumstances in which a local authority may recover from another local authority the expenses of providing special guardianship support services to any person.

(9) A local authority may provide special guardianship support services (or any part of them) by securing their provision by –

(a) another local authority; or

(b) a person within a description prescribed in regulations of persons who may provide special guardianship support services,

and may also arrange with any such authority or person for that other authority or that person to carry out the local authority's functions in relation to assessments under this section.

(10) A local authority may carry out an assessment of the needs of any person for the purposes of this section at the same time as an assessment of his needs is made under any other provision of this Act or under any other enactment.

(11) Section 27 (co-operation between authorities) applies in relation to the exercise of functions of a local authority in England under this section as it applies in relation to the exercise of functions of a local authority under Part 3 and see sections 164 and 164A of the Social Services and Well-being (Wales) Act 2014 for provision about co-operation between local authorities in Wales and other bodies.

Amendments—Inserted by ACA 2002, s 115. Amended by SI 2016/413.

Scope—Once a special guardianship order has been made, the local authority is under a duty to make arrangements for the provision of a package of special guardian support services, including counselling, advice, information and financial support. The Special Guardianship Regulations 2005 set out the details of those support services.

Financial support for special guardians—Under the Special Guardianship Regulations 2005, the local authority must make appropriate financial support available to special guardians (regs 6–10) and must make an assessment of their relevant needs (regs 12–13). In doing so it must comply with the Special Guardianship Guidance issued under the Local Authority Social Services Act 1970, s 7, by the Department for Education and Skills. While the Guidance does not have the full force of statute, it should be complied with by local authorities unless exceptional circumstances justify departure from it (*B v Lewisham Borough Council* [2008] 2 FLR 523, QBD – it was unlawful for the authority to make a rigid link with adoption allowances rather than focusing on fostering allowances). In *B v Kirklees Metropolitan Council* [2010] 2 FLR 405, QBD, the authority's decision that the SGO allowance should be two-thirds of the core fostering allowance was unlawful. It had deviated substantially from the Ministerial Guidance without justification. The authority is expected to consider the fostering allowance as a starting point and then to make appropriate adjustments to it (*R (TT) v London Borough of Merton* [2012] EWHC 2055 (Admin)).

Guidance where more than one local authority is involved—In *Suffolk CC v Nottinghamshire CC* [2013] 2 FLR 106, CA, the court held that where more than one local authority is involved in an out-of-area placement in special guardianship proceedings, the key question in determining which authority is responsible is whether a child is 'looked after' by one of them within the meaning of s 22(1); if so, then that authority is responsible. If the child is not a 'looked after' child, the responsible authority is the one in whose area the child is living. A child ceases to be 'looked after' as soon as parental responsibility becomes vested in another by, for example, the making of a child arrangements order for residence or a SGO. In such a situation, local authorities are bound by the Special Guardianship Regulations 2005, reg 5 to cooperate with one another in the discharge of functions. Every authority will be both a sender and a receiver over time and there ought to be self-regulation in respect of who would fund the statutory duties. It is therefore of critical importance when a child is placed out of area to have regard as to whether a child should or will remain looked after (i e under an interim care order or accommodated) or not (i e under a child arrangements order for residence). At the same time, the local authorities involved should cooperate from the earliest stage in deciding who will in fact execute the statutory duties that arise and who will fund that work. Local authorities have powers to make sensible arrangements between themselves wherever primary legal responsibility may in fact lie. The role of the court should also be carefully considered. Section 14F imposes duties on a local authority but it does not empower the Family Court to direct how or (in some aspects) even whether such duties are to be performed. Moreover, the statute gives the court no power to make directions as to payment of money or provision of services. Of course, judges may properly express views to local authorities and are entitled no doubt to expect that they will receive serious consideration (just as judges can and do express views about adoption and care plans) and of course it is only the judge who in the end can make the SGO.

14G *(repealed)*

Financial relief

15 Orders for financial relief with respect to children

(1) Schedule 1 (which consists primarily of the re-enactment, with consequential amendments and minor modifications, of provisions of section 6 of the Family Law Reform Act 1969, the

Guardianship of Minors Acts 1971 and 1973, the Children Act 1975 and of sections 15 and 16 of the Family Law Reform Act 1987) makes provision in relation to financial relief for children.

(2) *(repealed)*

Amendments—CLSA 1990, s 116, Sch 16, para 10(1); MEA 1991, s 11(1), Sch 2, para 10; CCA 2013, s 17, Sch 11.

Scope—This section introduces Sch 1 which contains the court's powers to make financial orders for children. Subject to CSA 1991, which restricts the court's power to order child maintenance (see Procedural Guide A2), Sch 1 covers three situations, namely:

(a) orders that a parent pay maintenance or a lump sum or transfer property to children when the first application for such an order is made while the child is under the age of 18 (although an order for periodical payments can subsequently be extended if the child is continuing in education or there are special circumstances);
(b) orders for periodical payments or a lump sum where the first time an application is made is when the child is aged over 18;
(c) alteration, either during the joint lives of the parents or after the death of one of them, of maintenance agreements containing financial provision for a child.

Orders for financial relief against parents—An order under para 1 is made either on application or without application at the time a child arrangements order is made, varied or discharged. If the child's parents are married, an alternative application for financial relief for the child is MCA 1973, ss 23 and 24, if there are divorce proceedings, or if there are no such proceedings, under s 27. By applying for relief for the child under those sections, the practitioner is able to take advantage of the power under MCA 1973, s 37 to restrain anticipated disposals of assets and to set aside past disposals where the intention is to defeat the claim.

Orders for financial relief for persons aged over 18—Schedule 1, para 2 enables a child who has reached 18 and who is continuing in education or to whom special circumstances apply to obtain from his parents an order for periodical payments or a lump sum where his parents are not living with each other in the same household and there was no periodical payments order in force in respect of him before he reached the age of 16. This is the only provision in the Act which permits an original application for relief by a child aged over 18. Paragraph 16(1) of Sch 1 provides that, for this purpose, a person who has reached the age of 18 falls within the meaning of 'child'. If there was a periodical payments order in force before the child reached the age of 16, the child's remedy is to apply in the proceedings in which that order was made to extend that order. If, however, there was no such order and the applicant's parents are living with each other in the same household, then the applicant has no remedy against his parents. Thus, for instance, the adult child whose parents are living together and for no valid reason are refusing to support him or her through university is in a markedly worse situation than an adult child whose parents have separated.

Alteration of maintenance agreements containing financial provision for a child—Schedule 1, paras 10 and 11 re-enact the powers contained in FLRA 1987, ss 15 and 16 to alter agreements made between parents for the maintenance of a child. The jurisdiction is similar to that contained in MCA 1973, ss 35 (lifetime variations) and 36 (variation after death), except that ss 35 and 36 apply only where the parents are married. Where the parents are married, the more sophisticated procedural provisions of ss 35 and 36 (including the power to restrain dealings under s 37) make it sensible to bring the application under those sections; where the parents are not married, there is no alternative but to bring the application under Sch 1.

Procedure—An application under s 15 for financial relief with respect to children follows the shorter procedure as set out in FPR 2010, rr 9.19, 9.20, PD9A, para 1.2(a)(ii), and see Procedural Guide A2. Where a father's resources are subject to a criminal restraint order under the Proceeds of Crime Act 2002, a mother seeking relief including the disclosure of the father's means should apply to the Crown Court that made the order, on notice: *T v B and Revenue and Customs Prosecutions Office* [2009] 1 FLR 1231, FD.

Costs—Applications under CA 1989, s 15 and Sch 1 are financial remedy proceedings under FPR 2010, r 2.3. However, they are not included within the application provided for in r 28.3(4)(b), so the costs rule in r 28.3 does not apply to s 15 and Sch 1 applications. The court may exercise its discretion as to costs in the light of CPR 1998, r 44.2. See FPR PD28A.

Family assistance orders

16 Family assistance orders

(1) Where, in any family proceedings, the court has power to make an order under this Part with respect to any child, it may (whether or not it makes such an order) make an order requiring –

(a) an officer of the Service or a Welsh family proceedings officer to be made available; or
(b) a local authority to make an officer of the authority available,

to advise, assist and (where appropriate) befriend any person named in the order.

(2) The persons who may be named in an order under this section ('a family assistance order') are –

(a) any parent, guardian or special guardian of the child;

(b) any person with whom the child is living or who is named in a child arrangements order as a person with whom the child is to live, spend time or otherwise have contact;
(c) the child himself.

(3) No court may make a family assistance order unless –

(a) *(repealed)*
(b) it has obtained the consent of every person to be named in the order other than the child.

(4) A family assistance order may direct –

(a) the person named in the order; or
(b) such of the persons named in the order as may be specified in the order,

to take such steps as may be so specified with a view to enabling the officer concerned to be kept informed of the address of any person named in the order and to be allowed to visit any such person.

(4A) If the court makes a family assistance order with respect to a child and the order is to be in force at the same time as a contact provision contained in a child arrangements order made with respect to the child, the family assistance order may direct the officer concerned to give advice and assistance as regards establishing, improving and maintaining contact to such of the persons named in the order as may be specified in the order.

(4B) In subsection (4A) 'contact provision' means provision which regulates arrangements relating to –

(a) with whom a child is to spend time or otherwise have contact, or
(b) when a child is to spend time or otherwise have contact with any person.

(5) Unless it specifies a shorter period, a family assistance order shall have effect for a period of twelve months beginning with the day on which it is made.

(6) If the court makes a family assistance order with respect to a child and the order is to be in force at the same time as a section 8 order made with respect to the child, the family assistance order may direct the officer concerned to report to the court on such matters relating to the section 8 order as the court may require (including the question whether the section 8 order ought to be varied or discharged).

(7) A family assistance order shall not be made so as to require a local authority to make an officer of theirs available unless –

(a) the authority agree; or
(b) the child concerned lives or will live within their area.

(8), (9) *(repealed)*

Amendments—CJCSA 2000 ss 74, 75, Sch 7, paras 87, 89, Sch 8; CA 2004, s 40, Sch 3, paras 5, 7; ACA 2002, Sch 3, para 58; CAA 2006, s 6(1)–(5); CFA 2014, s 12, Sch 2.

Defined terms—'child': s 105(1); 'family proceedings': s 8(3); 'local authority': s 105(1); 'officer of the Service': CJCSA 2000, s 11(3).

Scope—A family assistance order (FAO) is a short-term order lasting for no more than 12 months that obliges an officer of the Service or local authority officer to advise, assist and (where appropriate) befriend a named person or persons. See, for example, *Re L and M (Children: Private Law)* [2014] EWHC 939 (Fam) as an example of a 12-month FAO requiring Cafcass to provide help to the father with writing child-appropriate letters to children. Any of the following may be named in the order: a parent, guardian or special guardian of the child, anyone with whom the child is living or who has an order for contact with respect to the child and the child himself (s 16(2)). An order is to be made only where every person who is to be named in the order (other than the child) has given consent (s 16(3)). Normally the court will make a FAO of its own initiative, but although the rules and the Act do not specifically prescribe any procedure for applying for a s 16 order neither do they prohibit such an application and therefore presumably one can be made.

Where a FAO is to be in force at the same time as a child arrangements order for contact, the officer may give advice and assistance to establish, improve and maintain contact to the persons named in that order (s 16(4A)). Where a FAO is in force at the same time as a s 8 order in relation to the child, the officer may be directed to report to the court on such matters relating to the s 8 order as the court may require, including variation and discharge (s 16(6)).

Practice Direction—FPR PD12M *Family Assistance Orders: Consultation* requires that, before making a Family Assistance Order (FAO) the court must have obtained the opinion (verbally or in writing) of the appropriate officer about whether it would be in the best interests of the child for a FAO to be made and, if so, how the order could operate and for what period. Furthermore, before making a FAO, the court must give any person whom it proposes be named in the order an opportunity to comment upon any opinion given by the officer.

Risk assessments—CA 1989, s 16A requires a Cafcass officer carrying out any function in private law CA 1989 proceedings to carry out a risk assessment if he has cause to suspect that the child concerned is at risk of harm and to provide that assessment to the court. See further under s 16A below and **Contact – Domestic Violence** under CA 1989, s 8.

'order under this Part' (s 16(1))—The orders available under Pt II are: a child arrangements order, a prohibited steps order and a specific issue order (all under s 8). It would also seem that an order for financial relief under Sch 1 may be classified as an order under Pt II as Sch 1 derives from s 15. The power to make a family assistance order (FAO) is not limited to applications for s 8 orders; it may be exercised in any family proceedings where there is power to make an order under Pt II and 'family proceedings' is widely defined by s 8(3). It follows that a FAO could, for example, be made on an application for a care or supervision order.

Enforcement of family assistance order—In *Re C (Family Assistance Order)* [1996] 1 FLR 424, FD, a family assistance order (FAO) had been made directed to a local authority. The local authority did not have the resources to implement it and restored the matter before the court. There being no remedy provided in CA 1989 for such a circumstance, the judge supposed that one might make an order directed to the director of social services, endorsed with a penal notice, so that enforcement proceedings could ensue, but commented that that would be totally contrary to the best interests of the child concerned and the child care system as a whole. See *H v Dent and Others* [2016] 2 FLR 566, FD, where a costs order was made against the father who unsuccessfully sought to bring committal proceedings for an alleged failure by Cafcass to implement a family assistance order. See also *Re E (Family Assistance Order)* [1999] 2 FLR 512, FD, in which an FAO was made against a local authority in spite of the authority's reluctance to submit to it; on the exceptional facts of the case supervised contact between the child and his mother could not have taken place without such an order.

Children and Adoption Act 2006—CAA 2006, s 6(2), removed the requirement for family assistance orders (FAOs) to be made only in exceptional circumstances. It inserted s 16(4A) to provide that where a FAO is to be in force at the same time as a child arrangements order for contact, the officer may give advice and assistance to establish, improve and maintain contact to the persons named in the order (CAA 2006, s 6(3)). It increased the maximum duration of a FAO from 6 to 12 months (CAA 2006, s 6(4)). It substituted s 16(6) to provide that if the FAO is in force at the same time as a s 8 order in relation to the child, the officer may be directed to report to the court on such matters relating to the s 8 order as the court may require (including variation or discharge) (CAA 2006, s 6(5)).

16A Risk assessments

(1) This section applies to the following functions of officers of the Service or Welsh family proceedings officers –

(a) any function in connection with family proceedings in which the court has power to make an order under this Part with respect to a child or in which a question with respect to such an order arises;

(b) any function in connection with an order made by the court in such proceedings.

(2) If, in carrying out any function to which this section applies, an officer of the Service or a Welsh family proceedings officer is given cause to suspect that the child concerned is at risk of harm, he must –

(a) make a risk assessment in relation to the child, and

(b) provide the risk assessment to the court.

(3) A risk assessment, in relation to a child who is at risk of suffering harm of a particular sort, is an assessment of the risk of that harm being suffered by the child.

Amendments—Inserted by CAA 2006, s 7.

Scope—CA 1989, s 16A requires a Cafcass officer carrying out any function in private law CA 1989 proceedings to carry out a risk assessment if he has cause to suspect that the child concerned is at risk of harm and to provide that assessment to the court.

Practice direction—FPR PD12L *Risk Assessments under Section 16A* applies to any family proceedings in the Family Court in which a risk assessment is made under s 16A. Where an officer of the service makes a risk assessment he must provide it to the court irrespective of the outcome of the assessment and even if he reaches the conclusion that there is no risk of harm to the child. In reporting the outcome, the officer should make clear the factors that triggered the decision to carry out the assessment.

Duty arising even where there are no pending proceedings—It is possible that the duty to make a risk assessment could arise even where there are no pending proceedings. For example, if the court makes a final s 8 order and an associated family assistance order (FAO) the proceedings would be concluded but the officer would still be exercising his functions for the life of the FAO. If the officer perceives a risk to the child he must make a risk assessment and provide it to the court (s 16A(2)). See FPR 2010, r 16.38 and PD16A, paras 11.1–11.7 and the amended Form 42.

Protocol for information-sharing in the family justice system—In October 2013, a Protocol and Good Practice Model came into force governing the *Disclosure of Information in Cases of Alleged Child Abuse and Linked Criminal and Care Directions Hearings* (see Part V).

PART III
SUPPORT FOR CHILDREN AND FAMILIES PROVIDED BY LOCAL AUTHORITIES IN ENGLAND

Amendments—SI 2016/413.

Wales—On 6 April 2016, the Social Services and Wellbeing (Wales) Act 2014 made major changes to social services functions in Wales. These changes included the repeal of CA 1989, Pt III, meaning that s 17 (Children in need) and s 20 (Looked-after children) are now covered by separate legal frameworks in England and Wales. The 2014 Act attaches a duty to local authorities' social services to promote a person's wellbeing, which applies to adults and their carers (including young carers), children, and carers of disabled children. To take account of the divergence of Welsh and English children law, *The Family Court Practice Autumn Supplement* contains a new Part VII, reproducing essential materials relating to children law in Wales. In addition, these appear in *The Family Court Practice Online*, where you will also find the relevant codes of practice.

Application to local authorities in England

16B Application to local authorities in England

(1) This Part applies in relation to local authorities in England.

(2) Accordingly, unless the contrary intention appears, a reference in this Part to a local authority means a local authority in England.

Amendments—Provision and heading inserted by SI 2016/413.

Provision of services for children and their families

17 Provision of services for children in need, their families and others

(1) It shall be the general duty of every local authority (in addition to the other duties imposed on them by this Part) –

(a) to safeguard and promote the welfare of children within their area who are in need; and
(b) so far as is consistent with that duty, to promote the upbringing of such children by their families,

by providing a range and level of services appropriate to those children's needs.

(2) For the purpose principally of facilitating the discharge of their general duty under this section, every local authority shall have the specific duties and powers set out in Part I of Schedule 2.

(3) Any service provided by an authority in the exercise of functions conferred on them by this section may be provided for the family of a particular child in need or for any member of his family, if it is provided with a view to safeguarding or promoting the child's welfare.

(4) The Secretary of State may by order amend any provision of Part I of Schedule 2 or add any further duty or power to those for the time being mentioned there.

(4A) Before determining what (if any) services to provide for a particular child in need in the exercise of functions conferred on them by this section, a local authority shall, so far as is reasonably practicable and consistent with the child's welfare –

(a) ascertain the child's wishes and feelings regarding the provision of those services; and
(b) give due consideration (having regard to his age and understanding) to such wishes and feelings of the child as they have been able to ascertain.

(5) Every local authority –

(a) shall facilitate the provision by others (including in particular voluntary organisations) of services which it is a function of the authority to provide by virtue of this section, or section 18, 20, 22A to 22C, 23B to 23D, 24A or 24B; and
(b) may make such arrangements as they see fit for any person to act on their behalf in the provision of any such service.

(6) The services provided by a local authority in the exercise of functions conferred on them by this section may include providing accommodation and giving assistance in kind or in cash.

(7) Assistance may be unconditional or subject to conditions as to the repayment of the assistance or of its value (in whole or in part).

(8) Before giving any assistance or imposing any conditions, a local authority shall have regard to the means of the child concerned and of each of his parents.

(9) No person shall be liable to make any repayment of assistance or of its value at any time when he is in receipt of universal credit (except in such circumstances as may be prescribed), of income support under Part VII of the Social Security Contributions and Benefits Act 1992, of any element of child tax credit other than the family element, of working tax credit, of an income-based jobseeker's allowance or of an income-related employment and support allowance.

(10) For the purposes of this Part a child shall be taken to be in need if –

(a) he is unlikely to achieve or maintain, or to have the opportunity of achieving or maintaining, a reasonable standard of health or development without the provision for him of services by a local authority under this Part;

(b) his health or development is likely to be significantly impaired, or further impaired, without the provision for him of such services; or

(c) he is disabled,

and 'family,' in relation to such a child, includes any person who has parental responsibility for the child and any other person with whom he has been living.

(11) For the purposes of this Part, a child is disabled if he is blind, deaf or dumb or suffers from mental disorder of any kind or is substantially and permanently handicapped by illness, injury or congenital deformity or such other disability as may be prescribed; and in this Part –

'development' means physical, intellectual, emotional, social or behavioural development; and

'health' means physical or mental health.

(12) The Treasury may by regulations prescribe circumstances in which a person is to be treated for the purposes of this Part (or for such of those purposes as are prescribed) as in receipt of any element of child tax credit other than the family element or of working tax credit.

(13) The duties imposed on a local authority by virtue of this section do not apply in relation to a child in the authority's area who is being looked after by a local authority in Wales in accordance with Part 6 of the Social Services and Well-being (Wales) Act 2014.

Amendments—Disability Living Allowance and Disability Working Allowance Act 1991, s 7(2), Sch 3, para 13; Social Security (Consequential Provisions) Act 1992, s 4, Sch 2, para 108; Jobseekers Act 1995, s 41, Sch 2, para 19; Children (Leaving Care) Act 2000, s 7(2); ACA 2002, s 116(1); Tax Credits Act 2002, s 47, Sch 3, paras 15, 16; CA 2004, s 53; Welfare Reform Act 2007, s 28(1), Sch 3, para 6(1),(2); CYPA 2008, ss 8(3), 24, 39, Sch 1, para 1, Sch 3, paras 1, 2; Welfare Reform Act 2012, s 31, Sch 2, para 1; SI 2016/413.

Extent of local authorities' duties (s 17(1))—Section 17(1) imposes a general and overriding duty on local authorities to maintain a level and range of services in their area sufficient to enable them to discharge their functions under CA 1989, Pt III for the benefit of children in need. The other specific duties which follow must be performed in each individual case by reference to the general duty in s 17(1). However, s 17(1) does not itself impose a duty to meet the assessed needs of a particular child (*R (G) v Barnet London Borough Council; R (W) v Lambeth London Borough Council; R (A) v Lambeth London Borough Council* [2004] 1 FLR 454, HL. The principle that there is no duty under s 17(1) to meet the assessed needs of a particular child applies even where it can be demonstrated that the delivery of the assessed services is feasible having regard to the local authority's available resources (*R (VC) v Newcastle City Council and Secretary of State for the Home Department* [2012] 1 FLR 944, QBD). Whereas the failure of a local authority to discharge its duties under CA 1989, Pt III may lead to an infringement of a person's rights under ECHR, Art 3, the consequences of such a failure are likely to be far too nebulous, speculative or slight to lead to the conclusion that there has been a breach of ECHR, Art 8 (*R (TG) v Lambeth Borough Council* [2011] 2 FLR 1007, CA).

'who are in need' (s 17(1)(a))—Unless and until a local authority has determined that a child within its area is 'in need', the powers under s 17 to provide accommodation or any other assistance are not engaged (*MN and KN v Hackney Borough Council* [2013] EWHC 1205 (Admin)). The s 17 scheme involves an exercise of social work judgment based on the analysis of information derived from an assessment that is applicable to a heterogeneous group of those in need. The question of whether a child is in need will involve a number of different value judgements, such as what would be a reasonable standard of health or development for a particular child. In other words, there can be a range of reasonable conclusions about the matter, which are therefore subjective. The phrase 'child in need' in s 17 is a composite phrase and is not a limiting condition stated in wholly objective terms. The evaluative process is neither limited nor constrained by a comparison

PART II

with the support that may be available to any other defined group, no matter how similar they may be to the s 17 child in need. There are no categories or sub-divisions of 'children in need' in the statutory scheme (*R (on the application of (1) C (2) T (3) M (4) U) (Appellant) v Southwark London Borough Council (Respondent) & Coram Children's Legal Centre (Intervener)* [2016] EWCA Civ 707). The Secretary of State has issued guidance to local authorities in accordance with Local Authority and Social Services Act 1970, s 7 about assessments of need for the purposes of s 17. That guidance is to be followed save in exceptional circumstances (see *R v London Borough of Islington ex parte Rixon* [1997] ELR 66, QBD, in which it was decided that a local authority has liberty to deviate from the Secretary of State's guidance only on admissible grounds for good reason but without the freedom to take a substantially different course). For an assessment to be lawful, it must be compliant with the guidance having regard to the *Rixon* principle (*R (AB and SB) v Nottingham City Council* [2001] EWHC Admin 235). Where the local authority provides accommodation and financial support under CA 1989, s 17 and not as a consequence of any other statutory scheme, the local authority is not required to have regard to guidance issued under another statutory scheme when making its assessment (*R (on the application of (1) C (2) T (3) M (4) U) (Appellant)*, above). CA 2004, s 11 imposes an overarching obligation on local authorities in England (and their specified partner agencies) to 'make arrangements for ensuring that (a) their functions are discharged having regard to the need to safeguard and promote the welfare of children and (b) any services provided by another person pursuant to arrangements made by the person or body in the discharge of their functions are provided having regard to that need'. In *R (on the application of (1) C (2) T (3) M (4) U) (Appellant),* the Court of Appeal held this to mean that a decision based on an assessment undertaken for the purposes of CA 1989, s 17 should identify how the local authority has had regard to the need to safeguard and promote the welfare of children both individually (i e the subject children as regards the claim) and collectively (see also *Nzolameso v Westminster City Council* [2015] UKSC 22, at [24]–[27]). The evaluative judgement under s 17 is for the local authority to make, subject to the control of the courts on the ordinary principles of judicial review (*R (A) v London Borough of Croydon*; *R (M) v London Borough of Lambeth* [2010] 1 FLR 959, SC). The adequacy of an assessment under CA 1989, s 17 may also be the subject of judicial review. However, the ambit of the judicial review process, and any subsequent appeal, is limited to determining whether the assessment can stand. Where the assessment cannot stand and a fresh assessment is thus required, the Administrative Court cannot dictate how the local authority should go about that further assessment (*ET, BT, CT v Islington London Borough Council* [2013] EWCA Civ 323).

Assessing the age of a 'child' (s 17(1))—A local authority has a duty to safeguard and promote the welfare of children within their area who are in need. The definition of 'child' means a person under the age of 18. Where there is difficulty in assessing the exact age of the claimant, the test to be applied is described in *R (B) v Merton London Borough Council* [2003] 2 FLR 888, QBD. Where social workers dispute a person's claim to be under the age of 18 for the purposes of s 20(1), the question of age is an objective fact that has a right and a wrong answer and is subject, in the event of challenge, to determination by the court rather than by other kinds of decision-makers (*R (A) v London Borough of Croydon*; *R (M) v London Borough of Lambeth* [2010] 1 FLR 959, SC).

R (F) v Lewisham London Borough Council; R (D) v Manchester City Council; Secretary of State (Interested Party) and Others [2010] 1 FLR 1463, QBD contains useful guidance to assist courts in managing proceedings where the issue of age is to be determined for the purposes of CA 1989 and to indicate to those representing the parties what steps can and cannot be taken in preparing for the hearing.

Where the local authority receives an expert's report about the age of a child it is not entitled to disregard the report unless there is evidence to show that the report is unreliable; it must give such reports proper consideration (*R (A) v London Borough of Croydon* [2009] 2 FLR 173, QBD).

Children of failed asylum seekers (s 17(1))—Where Immigration and Asylum Act 1999, s 4 (asylum support for failed asylum seekers) and CA 1989, s 17 are both engaged, the more advantageous regime under s 17 will apply. A local authority will not be able to justify the non-provision of assessed services under s 17 on the ground that s 4 support is available unless it can be shown that the Secretary of State is able and willing (or if not willing, can be compelled) to provide such services and that those services are sufficient to meet the child's needs. Given the residual nature of the Secretary of State's functions under s 4 and the likely very significant difference between the services available under s 4 and the services assessed as required under s 17, in the general run of cases a local authority is very unlikely to be able to justify non-intervention under CA 1989, s 17 by reliance on Immigration and Asylum Act 1999, s 4 (*R (VC) v Newcastle City Council and Secretary of State for the Home Department* [2012] 1 FLR 944, QBD).

'within their area' (s 17(2) and Sch 2, para 1(1))—Sch 2, para 1(1) requires that 'every local authority shall take reasonable steps to identify the extent to which there are children in need within their area'. The definition of 'within their area' requires physical presence within the relevant area (*R v Wandsworth London Borough Council, Hammersmith & Fulham London Borough Council and Lambeth London Borough Council ex parte Stewart* [2002] 1 FLR 469, QBD; *R v London Borough of Barking & Dagenham ex parte Bilkisu Mohammed* [2002] EWHC 2663 (Admin)). The duty to assess a child's needs thus will not be dependent on the child being 'ordinarily resident' in the area of a local authority but rather simply on the child's physical presence in the area of a local authority (*N and N v Newham London Borough Council and Essex Borough Council* [2013] EWHC 2475 (Admin)). The power under s 17(1) can be exercised by a local authority in respect of a child in need who has moved outside the area of that local authority, regardless of the circumstances that have led to the child being no longer physically present in the local authority's area. In considering what services should be provided for such a child, legitimate considerations will include the child's connection with the area, how long it is intended that the child will be away, whether the child would be staying for short periods in many different locations and whether the child is likely ever to return (*J, R (on Application of) v Worcestershire County Council* [2015] 2 FLR 1053, CA). Since there are no formal guidelines to assist local authorities in cases where more than one authority may be involved, it is vital, particularly in cases involving children, that the needs of the children are considered and that, as far as possible, arguments about who considers and meets those needs do not hold up the provision of services to those children; the needs should be met first and the redistribution of resources should, if necessary, take place afterwards (*R v London Borough of Barking & Dagenham ex parte Bilkisu Mohammed*).

'mental disorder' (s 17(11))—The definition of 'mental disorder' in MHA 1983, s 1(2) has been amended by MHA 2007, s 1(2) to 'any disorder or disability of the mind' (for details of the representation of children suffering from a disability see FPR 2010, r 16.2 and PD16A).

Deprivation of liberty—For guidance concerning the principles applicable in respect of children in need who might be subject to a deprivation of liberty, see *A Local Authority v D and Others* [2016] 2 FLR 601, FD and **Deprivation of liberty** under s 20.

17ZA Young carers' needs assessments

(1) A local authority must assess whether a young carer within their area has needs for support and, if so, what those needs are, if –

(a) it appears to the authority that the young carer may have needs for support, or
(b) the authority receive a request from the young carer or a parent of the young carer to assess the young carer's needs for support.

(2) An assessment under subsection (1) is referred to in this Part as a 'young carer's needs assessment'.

(3) In this Part 'young carer' means a person under 18 who provides or intends to provide care for another person (but this is qualified by section 17ZB(3)).

(4) Subsection (1) does not apply in relation to a young carer if the local authority have previously carried out a care-related assessment of the young carer in relation to the same person cared for.

(5) But subsection (1) does apply (and so a young carer's needs assessment must be carried out) if it appears to the authority that the needs or circumstances of the young carer or the person cared for have changed since the last care-related assessment.

(6) 'Care-related assessment' means –

(a) a young carer's needs assessment;
(b) an assessment under any of the following –
  (i) section 1 of the Carers (Recognition and Services) Act 1995;
  (ii) section 1 of the Carers and Disabled Children Act 2000;
  (iii) section 4(3) of the Community Care (Delayed Discharges) Act 2003;
  (iv) Part 1 of the Care Act 2014.

(7) A young carer's needs assessment must include an assessment of whether it is appropriate for the young carer to provide, or continue to provide, care for the person in question, in the light of the young carer's needs for support, other needs and wishes.

(8) A local authority, in carrying out a young carer's needs assessment, must have regard to –

(a) the extent to which the young carer is participating in or wishes to participate in education, training or recreation, and
(b) the extent to which the young carer works or wishes to work.

(9) A local authority, in carrying out a young carer's needs assessment, must involve –

(a) the young carer,
(b) the young carer's parents, and
(c) any person who the young carer or a parent of the young carer requests the authority to involve.

(10) A local authority that have carried out a young carer's needs assessment must give a written record of the assessment to –

(a) the young carer,
(b) the young carer's parents, and
(c) any person to whom the young carer or a parent of the young carer requests the authority to give a copy.

(11) Where the person cared for is under 18, the written record must state whether the local authority consider him or her to be a child in need.

(12) A local authority must take reasonable steps to identify the extent to which there are young carers within their area who have needs for support.

Amendments—Inserted by CFA 2014, s 96. Amended by SI 2015/914; SI 2016/413.

17ZB Young carers' needs assessments: supplementary

(1) This section applies for the purposes of section 17ZA.

(2) 'Parent', in relation to a young carer, includes –

- (a) a parent of the young carer who does not have parental responsibility for the young carer, and
- (b) a person who is not a parent of the young carer but who has parental responsibility for the young carer.

(3) A person is not a young carer if the person provides or intends to provide care –

- (a) under or by virtue of a contract, or
- (b) as voluntary work.

(4) But in a case where the local authority consider that the relationship between the person cared for and the person under 18 providing or intending to provide care is such that it would be appropriate for the person under 18 to be regarded as a young carer, that person is to be regarded as such (and subsection (3) is therefore to be ignored in that case).

(5) The references in section 17ZA and this section to providing care include a reference to providing practical or emotional support.

(6) Where a local authority –

- (a) are required to carry out a young carer's needs assessment, and
- (b) are required or have decided to carry out some other assessment of the young carer or of the person cared for;

the local authority may, subject to subsection (7), combine the assessments.

(7) A young carer's needs assessment may be combined with an assessment of the person cared for only if the young carer and the person cared for agree.

(8) The Secretary of State may by regulations make further provision about carrying out a young carer's needs assessment; the regulations may, in particular –

- (a) specify matters to which a local authority is to have regard in carrying out a young carer's needs assessment;
- (b) specify matters which a local authority is to determine in carrying out a young carer's needs assessment;
- (c) make provision about the manner in which a young carer's needs assessment is to be carried out;
- (d) make provision about the form a young carer's needs assessment is to take.

(9) The Secretary of State may by regulations amend the list in section 17ZA(6)(b) so as to –

- (a) add an entry,
- (b) remove an entry, or
- (c) vary an entry.

Amendments—Inserted by CFA 2014, s 96.

17ZC Consideration of young carers' needs assessments

A local authority that carry out a young carer's needs assessment must consider the assessment and decide –

- (a) whether the young carer has needs for support in relation to the care which he or she provides or intends to provide;
- (b) if so, whether those needs could be satisfied (wholly or partly) by services which the authority may provide under section 17; and

(c) if they could be so satisfied, whether or not to provide any such services in relation to the young carer.

Amendments—Inserted by CFA 2014, s 96.

17ZD Parent carers' needs assessments

(1) A local authority must, if the conditions in subsections (3) and (4) are met, assess whether a parent carer within their area has needs for support and, if so, what those needs are.

(2) In this Part 'parent carer' means a person aged 18 or over who provides or intends to provide care for a disabled child for whom the person has parental responsibility.

(3) The first condition is that –

- (a) it appears to the authority that the parent carer may have needs for support, or
- (b) the authority receive a request from the parent carer to assess the parent carer's needs for support.

(4) The second condition is that the local authority are satisfied that the disabled child cared for and the disabled child's family are persons for whom they may provide or arrange for the provision of services under section 17.

(5) An assessment under subsection (1) is referred to in this Part as a 'parent carer's needs assessment'.

(6) Subsection (1) does not apply in relation to a parent carer if the local authority have previously carried out a care-related assessment of the parent carer in relation to the same disabled child cared for.

(7) But subsection (1) does apply (and so a parent carer's needs assessment must be carried out) if it appears to the authority that the needs or circumstances of the parent carer or the disabled child cared for have changed since the last care-related assessment.

(8) 'Care-related assessment' means –

- (a) a parent carer's needs assessment;
- (b) an assessment under any of the following –
  - (i) section 1 of the Carers (Recognition and Services) Act 1995;
  - (ii) section 6 of the Carers and Disabled Children Act 2000;
  - (iii) section 4(3) of the Community Care (Delayed Discharges) Act 2003;
  - (iv) Part 1 of the Care Act 2014.

(9) A parent carer's needs assessment must include an assessment of whether it is appropriate for the parent carer to provide, or continue to provide, care for the disabled child, in the light of the parent carer's needs for support, other needs and wishes.

(10) A local authority in carrying out a parent carer's needs assessment must have regard to –

- (a) the well-being of the parent carer, and
- (b) the need to safeguard and promote the welfare of the disabled child cared for and any other child for whom the parent carer has parental responsibility.

(11) In subsection (10) 'well-being' has the same meaning as in Part 1 of the Care Act 2014.

(12) A local authority, in carrying out a parent carer's needs assessment, must involve –

- (a) the parent carer,
- (b) any child for whom the parent carer has parental responsibility, and
- (c) any person who the parent carer requests the authority to involve.

(13) A local authority that have carried out a parent carer's needs assessment must give a written record of the assessment to –

- (a) the parent carer, and
- (b) any person to whom the parent carer requests the authority to give a copy.

(14) A local authority must take reasonable steps to identify the extent to which there are parent carers within their area who have needs for support.

Amendments—Inserted by CFA 2014, s 97. Amended by SI 2015/914; SI 2016/413.

17ZE Parent carers' needs assessments: supplementary

(1) This section applies for the purposes of section 17ZD.

(2) The references in section 17ZD to providing care include a reference to providing practical or emotional support.

(3) Where a local authority –

(a) are required to carry out a parent carer's needs assessment, and
(b) are required or have decided to carry out some other assessment of the parent carer or of the disabled child cared for,

the local authority may combine the assessments.

(4) The Secretary of State may by regulations make further provision about carrying out a parent carer's needs assessment; the regulations may, in particular –

(a) specify matters to which a local authority is to have regard in carrying out a parent carer's needs assessment;
(b) specify matters which a local authority is to determine in carrying out a parent carer's needs assessment;
(c) make provision about the manner in which a parent carer's needs assessment is to be carried out;
(d) make provision about the form a parent carer's needs assessment is to take.

(5) The Secretary of State may by regulations amend the list in section 17ZD(8)(b) so as to –

(a) add an entry,
(b) remove an entry, or
(c) vary an entry.

Amendments—Inserted by CFA 2014, s 97.

17ZF Consideration of parent carers' needs assessments

A local authority that carry out a parent carer's needs assessment must consider the assessment and decide –

(a) whether the parent carer has needs for support in relation to the care which he or she provides or intends to provide;
(b) whether the disabled child cared for has needs for support;
(c) if paragraph (a) or (b) applies, whether those needs could be satisfied (wholly or partly) by services which the authority may provide under section 17; and
(d) if they could be so satisfied, whether or not to provide any such services in relation to the parent carer or the disabled child cared for.

Amendments—Inserted by CFA 2014, s 97.

17ZG Section 17 services: continued provision where EHC plan maintained

(1) This section applies where, immediately before a child in need reaches the age of 18 –

(a) a local authority is providing services for the child in the exercise of functions conferred by section 17, and
(b) an EHC plan is maintained for the child.

(2) The local authority may continue to provide services for the child in the exercise of those functions after the child reaches the age of 18, but may not continue to do so after the EHC plan has ceased to be maintained.

(3) In this section 'EHC plan' means a plan within section 37(2) of the Children and Families Act 2014.

Amendments—Inserted by CFA 2014, s 50. Amended by SI 2016/413.

EHC plan (s 17ZG)—An ECH plan is an 'Education, health and care plan'. An EHC plan must be prepared where an EHC needs assessment has shown that it is necessary for special educational provision to be made for the child or young person in accordance with an EHC plan. The EHC plan will specify, inter alia, the child or young person's special educational needs, the special education provision required by him or her, any healthcare provision reasonably required arising out of his or her special educational needs, any social care provision that must be made for him or her and any social care provision reasonably required that is not already specified in the ECH plan (CFA 2014, s 37).

17ZH Section 17 services: transition for children to adult care and support.

(1) Subsections (2) to (4) apply where a local authority providing services for a child in need in the exercise of functions conferred by section 17 –

(a) are required by section 58(1) or 63(1) of the Care Act 2014 to carry out a child's needs assessment or young carer's assessment in relation to the child, or

(b) are required by section 60(1) of that Act to carry out a child's carer's assessment in relation to a carer of the child.

(2) If the local authority carry out the assessment before the child reaches the age of 18 and decide to treat it as a needs or carer's assessment in accordance with section 59(6), 61(6) or 64(7) of the Care Act 2014 (with Part 1 of that Act applying to the assessment as a result), the authority must continue to comply with section 17 after the child reaches the age of 18 until they reach a conclusion in his case.

(3) If the local authority carry out the assessment before the child reaches the age of 18 but decide not to treat it as a needs or carer's assessment in accordance with section 59(6), 61(6) or 64(7) of the Care Act 2014 –

(a) they must carry out a needs or carer's assessment (as the case may be) after the child reaches the age of 18, and

(b) they must continue to comply with section 17 after he reaches that age until they reach a conclusion in his case.

(4) If the local authority do not carry out the assessment before the child reaches the age of 18, they must continue to comply with section 17 after he reaches that age until –

(a) they decide that the duty under section 9 or 10 of the Care Act 2014 (needs or carer's assessment) does not apply, or

(b) having decided that the duty applies and having discharged it, they reach a conclusion in his case.

(5) Subsection (6) applies where a local authority providing services for a child in need in the exercise of functions conferred by section 17 –

(a) receive a request for a child's needs assessment or young carer's assessment to be carried out in relation to the child or for a child's carer's assessment to be carried out in relation to a carer of the child, but

(b) have yet to be required by section 58(1), 60(1) or 63(1) of the Care Act 2014 to carry out the assessment.

(6) If the local authority do not decide, before the child reaches the age of 18, whether or not to comply with the request, they must continue to comply with section 17 after he reaches that age until –

(a) they decide that the duty under section 9 or 10 of the Care Act 2014 does not apply, or

(b) having decided that the duty applies and having discharged it, they reach a conclusion in his case.

(7) A local authority reach a conclusion in a person's case when –

(a) they conclude that he does not have needs for care and support or for support (as the case may be), or

(b) having concluded that he has such needs and that they are going to meet some or all of them, they begin to do so, or

PART II

(c) having concluded that he has such needs, they conclude that they are not going to meet any of those needs (whether because those needs do not meet the eligibility criteria or for some other reason).

(8) In this section, 'child's needs assessment', 'child's carer's assessment', 'young carer's assessment', 'needs assessment', 'carer's assessment' and 'eligibility criteria' each have the same meaning as in Part 1 of the Care Act 2014.

Amendments—Inserted by Care Act 2014, s 66. Amended by SI 2016/413.

17ZI Section 17 services: provision after EHC plan no longer maintained

(1) This section applies where a local authority providing services for a person in the exercise, by virtue of section 17ZG, of functions conferred by section 17 are required to carry out a needs assessment in that person's case.

(2) If the EHC plan for the person ceases to be maintained before the local authority reach a conclusion in the person's case, they must continue to comply with section 17 until they do reach a conclusion in his case.

(3) The references to the local authority reaching a conclusion in a person's case are to be read with section 17ZH(7).

(4) In this section, 'needs assessment' has the same meaning as in Part 1 of the Care Act 2014.

Amendments—Inserted by Care Act 2014, s 66. Amended by SI 2016/413.

****

Provision of accommodation for children

20 Provision of accommodation for children: general

(1) Every local authority shall provide accommodation for any child in need within their area who appears to them to require accommodation as a result of –

(a) there being no person who has parental responsibility for him;
(b) his being lost or having been abandoned; or
(c) the person who has been caring for him being prevented (whether or not permanently, and for whatever reason) from providing him with suitable accommodation or care.

(2) Where a local authority provide accommodation under subsection (1) for a child who is ordinarily resident in the area of another local authority, that other local authority may take over the provision of accommodation for the child within –

(a) three months of being notified in writing that the child is being provided with accommodation; or
(b) such other longer period as may be prescribed in regulations made by the Secretary of State.

(2A) Where a local authority in Wales provide accommodation under section 76(1) of the Social Services and Well-being (Wales) Act 2014 (accommodation for children without parents or who are lost or abandoned etc) for a child who is ordinarily resident in the area of a local authority in England, that local authority in England may take over the provision of accommodation for the child within –

(a) three months of being notified in writing that the child is being provided with accommodation; or
(b) such other longer period as may be prescribed in regulations made by the Secretary of State.

(3) Every local authority shall provide accommodation for any child in need within their area who has reached the age of sixteen and whose welfare the authority consider is likely to be seriously prejudiced if they do not provide him with accommodation.

(4) A local authority may provide accommodation for any child within their area (even though a person who has parental responsibility for him is able to provide him with accommodation) if they consider that to do so would safeguard or promote the child's welfare.

(5) A local authority may provide accommodation for any person who has reached the age of sixteen but is under twenty-one in any community home which takes children who have reached the age of sixteen if they consider that to do so would safeguard or promote his welfare.

(6) Before providing accommodation under this section, a local authority shall, so far as is reasonably practicable and consistent with the child's welfare –

(a) ascertain the child's wishes and feelings regarding the provision of accommodation; and
(b) give due consideration (having regard to his age and understanding) to such wishes and feelings of the child as they have been able to ascertain.

(7) A local authority may not provide accommodation under this section for any child if any person who –

(a) has parental responsibility for him; and
(b) is willing and able to –
   (i) provide accommodation for him; or
   (ii) arrange for accommodation to be provided for him,

objects.

(8) Any person who has parental responsibility for a child may at any time remove the child from accommodation provided by or on behalf of the local authority under this section.

(9) Subsections (7) and (8) do not apply while any person –

(a) who is named in a child arrangements order as a person with whom the child is to live;
(aa) who is a special guardian of the child; or
(b) who has care of the child by virtue of an order made in the exercise of the High Court's inherent jurisdiction with respect to children,

agrees to the child being looked after in accommodation provided by or on behalf of the local authority.

(10) Where there is more than one such person as is mentioned in subsection (9), all of them must agree.

(11) Subsections (7) and (8) do not apply where a child who has reached the age of sixteen agrees to being provided with accommodation under this section.

Amendments—ACA 2002, s 139(1),(3), Sch 3, paras 54, 59, Sch 5; CA 2004, s 53; CFA 2014, s 12, Sch 2; SI 2016/413.

Local authority has no power to transfer accommodated child out of residential care and into foster care without permission of natural parents—Where a child is being accommodated by a local authority under a voluntary arrangement with her natural parents the local authority has no power to arrange a transfer of the child from a residential institution to foster care without the permission of her natural parents; parental responsibility includes the right to decide where a child lives (*R v Tameside Metropolitan Borough Council ex parte J* [2000] 1 FLR 942, QBD).

Definition of children who are eligible for accommodation—For the definitions of 'looked after' child see CA 1989, s 22(1); for 'relevant child' see CA 1989, s 23A(2); for 'eligible child' see CA 1989, s 23A(2) and Sch 2, para 19B. If a child meets the criteria in s 20 then he is entitled to support under that section. The discharge of the s 20 duty may be assisted by a housing authority but it cannot simply be passed over to the housing authority (*R (G) v Southwark London Borough Council* [2009] 2 FLR 380, HL). The accommodation of a child pursuant to CA 1989, s 20 does not act as a bar to that child being made a ward of court in an appropriate case (*Re E (Wardship Order: Child in Voluntary Accommodation)* [2013] 2 FLR 63, CA).

A local authority cannot determine or specify that they provided accommodation under s 17 when, on the facts of the case, they were also under a duty to do so under s 20(1). A local authority cannot 'finesse away' their specific duty under s 20(1), claiming merely to act under their general s 17 duty (*H, Barhanu & B v London Borough of Wandsworth, London Borough of Hackney, London Borough of Islington & Secretary of State for Education & Skills (Interested Party)* [2007] 2 FLR 822, QBD; *R (W) v North Lincolnshire Council* [2008] 2 FLR 2150, QBD). For examples of cases where the local authority has been held to owe a duty under s 20 on the facts of the case, see *R (C) v Knowsley Metropolitan Borough Council* [2009] 1 FLR 493, QBD, *R (A) v Coventry City Council* [2009] 1 FLR 1202, QBD and *O (A Child) v Doncaster Metropolitan Borough Council* [2014] EWHC 2309 (Admin).

Where a residential placement is provided wholly or mainly to meet the child's special educational needs, it might be reasonable for that placement to be provided solely by exercising the local authority's powers under

Pt IV of the 1996 Act, although even in those circumstances the child may still require accommodation within CA 1989, s 20(1) or be provided with accommodation under CA 1989, s 20(4). Where, however, the placement was not provided wholly or mainly to meet the child's special educational needs and the child was within CA 1989, s 20(1), or s 20(4) applied, then the local authority could not side-step its duties under CA 1989, s 20 and the placement should be provided under either CA 1989 alone or under both Acts (see *R (O) v East Riding of Yorkshire County Council (Secretary of State for Education Intervening)* [2011] 2 FLR 207, CA).

Meaning of 'prevented' (s 20(1)(c))—Under s 20(1)(c) 'prevention' involves an objective test. It is not satisfied if the facts are only that the child does not want to live with someone who is willing to provide suitable accommodation (*R (M) v London Borough of Barnet* [2009] 2 FLR 725, QBD); circumstances can arise where people are so incompatible that they simply cannot live together (*R (S) v Sutton London Borough Council* [2007] 2 FLR 849, QBD).

Deprivation of liberty—For guidance concerning the principles applicable in respect of looked-after children who might be subject to a deprivation of liberty, see *A Local Authority v D & Ors* [2016] 1 WLR 1160, FD. Local authorities are under a duty to consider whether children who are looked after are subject to restrictions amounting to a deprivation of liberty. The *Cheshire West* criteria (see *P (By His Litigation Friend the Official Solicitor) v Cheshire West and Chester Council and Another; P and Q (By Their Litigation Friend the Official Solicitor) v Surrey County Council* [2014] COPLR 313, SC) must be rigorously applied to the circumstances of each case. The comparison to be made is with another child of the same age. A deprivation of liberty will be lawful if warranted under CA 1989, s 25, MHA 1983 or if the child has received a custodial sentence. Where the child is not looked after, the exercise of parental responsibility might amount to valid consent, meaning that the second limb of the test in *Cheshire West* is not met. However, where the child is looked after, different considerations will apply regardless of whether the parents consent to the deprivation of liberty. If the child is subject to an interim care order, it is extremely unlikely that a parent could consent to deprivation of liberty and a local authority cannot consent to deprivation of liberty in those circumstances. The local authority will need to consider whether CA 1989, s 25 is applicable. If not, then the permission criteria in CA 1989, s 100(4) for invoking the inherent jurisdiction are likely to be met. The deprivation of liberty should cease as soon as the CA 1989, s 25 criteria are not met or the reasons justifying the deprivation of liberty no longer subsist.

Need for care when using CA 1989, s 20 (s 20(7))—There is no express statutory requirement on a local authority to obtain a positive expression of consent from a parent before accommodating a child under s 20: see *Hackney Borough Council v John Williams and Adineke Williams* [2017] EWCA Civ 26. However, in this case, the Court of Appeal emphasised that its decision does not operate to change the good practice guidance contained in previous decisions concerning consent in the context of s 20. The Court made clear that that guidance should continue to be followed, albeit a failure to follow it will not of itself give rise to an actionable wrong. The following guidance can be extracted from those earlier decisions. In *Re N (Adoption: Jurisdiction)* [2016] 1 FLR 621, CA, the President reiterated that local authorities should exercise great care to ensure that the powers under s 20 are not used improperly. In particular, the local authority should take care to obtain the informed consent from the parent or parents at the outset when concluding voluntary arrangements under s 20 so as to ensure that consent has been validly given by the parent to the accommodation of the child. When combined with the observations of Hedley J in *Coventry City Council v C, B, CA and CH* [2012] COPLR 658, FD, the following guidance results:

(a) Every parent has a right, if he or she is capacitous, to exercise his or her parental responsibility to consent under s 20 to have their child accommodated by the local authority;
(b) Every local authority has the power under s 20(4) so to accommodate, provided it is consistent with the child's welfare;
(c) Every social worker obtaining consent from a parent is under a personal duty to be satisfied that the person giving consent does not lack the required capacity;
(d) The social worker must actively address the issue of capacity, take into account all the prevailing circumstances and must consider the questions raised by MCA 2005, s 3 and in particular the mother's capacity to use and weigh all the relevant information;
(e) If the social worker has doubts about capacity, no further attempt should be made to obtain consent on that occasion. Advice should be sought from the social work team leader or management;
(f) If the social worker is satisfied that the person does not lack capacity, they then have to be satisfied that the consent is fully informed. Being satisfied that the consent is fully informed involves (i) questioning whether the parent understands fully the consequences of giving such a consent, (ii) whether they appreciate fully the range of choices available and the consequences of refusal and (iii) whether the parent is in possession of all the facts and issues material to the giving of consent;
(g) If not satisfied that the answers to the questions at (f) are all 'yes', once again, no further attempt should be made to obtain consent on that occasion. Advice should be sought and the social work team should further consider taking legal advice if thought necessary;
(h) If satisfied that the consent is fully informed, the social worker must then be satisfied that the giving of such consent and the subsequent removal is both fair and proportionate;
(i) In considering whether the giving of consent is both fair and proportionate, it might be necessary to ask (i) what the current physical and psychological state of the parent is, (ii) whether they have a solicitor, (iii) whether they have been encouraged to seek legal advice and/or advice from family or friends, (iv) whether it is necessary for the safety of the child for the child to be removed at that time and (v) whether it would be fairer for the matter to be the subject of a court order rather than an agreement;
(j) If, having taken all of these steps and, if necessary, having taken further advice, including where necessary legal advice, the social worker considers that a fully informed consent had been received from a capacitous mother in circumstances where removal was necessary and proportionate, that fully informed consent may be acted upon by the social worker;
(k) In the context of newborn children, local authorities may wish to approach with great care the obtaining of

s 20 consent from mothers in the aftermath of birth, especially where there is no immediate danger to the child and where it is probable that no order would be made by the court.

(m) The documentation prepared in respect of an agreement to the accommodation of a child under s 20 should adhere to the following principles:
  (i) Wherever possible, the agreement of a parent to the accommodation of their child under s 20 should be properly recorded in writing and evidenced by the parent's signature;
  (ii) The written document should be clear and precise as to its terms, drafted in simple and straightforward language that the particular parent can readily understand;
  (iii) The written document should spell out, following the language of s 20(8), that the parent can 'remove the child' from the local authority accommodation 'at any time';
  (iv) The written document should not seek to impose any fetters on the exercise of the parent's right under s 20(8);
  (v) Where the parent is not fluent in English, the written document should be translated into the parent's own language and the parent should sign the foreign language text, adding, in the parent's language, words to the effect that 'I have read this document and I agree to its terms'.

For an example of damages being awarded against a local authority for breaching the Art 6 and Art 8 rights of a parent as a result of the local authority misusing s 20, see *Kent County Council v M and K* [2016] EWFC 28.

21 Provision of accommodation for children in police protection or detention or on remand etc

(1) Every local authority shall make provision for the reception and accommodation of children who are removed or kept away from home under Part V.

(2) Every local authority shall receive, and provide accommodation for, children –
  (a) in police protection whom they are requested to receive under section 46(3)(f);
  (b) whom they are requested to receive under section 38(6) of the Police and Criminal Evidence Act 1984;
  (c) who are –
    (i) …
    (ia) remanded to accommodation provided by or on behalf of a local authority by virtue of paragraph 4 of Schedule 1 or paragraph 6 of Schedule 8 to the Powers of Criminal Courts (Sentencing) Act 2000 (breach etc. of referral orders and reparation orders);
    (ii) remanded to accommodation provided by or on behalf of a local authority by virtue of paragraph 21 of Schedule 2 to the Criminal Justice and Immigration Act 2008 (breach etc. of youth rehabilitation orders);
    (iia) remanded to accommodation provided by or on behalf of a local authority by virtue of paragraph 10 of the Schedule to the Street Offences Act 1959 (breach of orders under section 1(2A) of that Act);
    (iii) the subject of a youth rehabilitation order imposing a local authority residence requirement or a youth rehabilitation order with fostering,

  and with respect to whom they are the designated authority.

(2A) In subsection (2)(c)(iii), the following terms have the same meanings as in Part 1 of the Criminal Justice and Immigration Act 2008 (see section 7 of that Act) –
  'local authority residence requirement';
  'youth rehabilitation order';
  'youth rehabilitation order with fostering'.

(3) Where a child has been –
  (a) removed under Part V; or
  (b) detained under section 38 of the Police and Criminal Evidence Act 1984,

and he is not being provided with accommodation by a local authority or by a local authority in Wales or in a hospital vested in the Secretary of State or the Welsh Ministers or otherwise made available pursuant to arrangements made by the Secretary of State, the National Health Service Commissioning Board or a clinical commissioning group under the National Health Service Act 2006 or a Local Health Board, any reasonable expenses of accommodating him shall be recoverable from the local authority, or local authority in Wales, in whose area he is ordinarily resident.

Amendments—CLSA 1990, s 116, Sch 16, para 11; National Health Service and Community Care Act 1990, s 66(1), Sch 9, para 36; Health Authorities Act 1995, s 2, Sch 1, para 118; SI 2000/90; Powers of Criminal Courts (Sentencing) Act 2000, s 165, Sch 9, para 126; Anti-social Behaviour Act 2003, s 88, Sch 2, para 5; SI 2007/961; CYPA 2008, s 39, Sch 3, paras 1, 5; Criminal Justice and Immigration Act 2008, ss 6(2), 6(3), 149, Sch 4, paras 34 and 105, Sch 28, Pt 1; Policing and Crime Act 2009, s 112, Sch 7, para 21; LASPOA 2012, s 105, Sch 12, para 24 (subject to savings in certain cases); Health and Social Care Act 2012, s 55(2), Sch 5, para 48; SI 2016/413.

Geographic extent of local authorities' duties (s 21(2)(a),(b))—The duty on every local authority under CA 1989, s 22(2)(a),(b) to receive, and provide accommodation for, children in police protection whom they are requested to receive under s 46(3)(f) or whom they are requested to receive under PACE 1984, s 38(6) falls on the authority receiving the request, irrespective of the area from which the child comes (*R (M) v Gateshead Council* [2006] 2 FLR 379, CA).

Secure accommodation—Although s 21(2)(b) imposes a duty on the local authority to receive and accommodate children when requested to do so under PACE 1984, s 38(6), it does not impose a duty to provide secure accommodation where such is requested (*R (M) v Gateshead Council* [2006] 2 FLR 379, CA). The local authority has a discretionary power to provide secure accommodation when requested to do so, in so far as it is practicable in order to further the policy objective of preventing children from being detained in police cells.

Police Protection Guidance—Government circular *The Duties and Powers of the Police under the Children Act 1989* (number 017/2008) explains when and how police protection powers should be used under CA 1989. It can be found at *http://safeguarding.publishpath.com/the-duties-and-powers-of-the-police*. Paragraph 25 sets out the meaning of 'suitable accommodation'; this would normally be local authority accommodation, a registered children's home or foster care. If appropriate, the child may be placed with relatives provided that the relevant police checks as to their suitability are carried out beforehand (para 30). A police station is not deemed suitable accommodation and the child should not be taken there unless the circumstances are exceptional (para 28).

Duties of local authorities in relation to children looked after by them

22 General duty of local authority in relation to children looked after by them

(1) In this section, any reference to a child who is looked after by a local authority is a reference to a child who is –

- (a) in their care; or
- (b) provided with accommodation by the authority in the exercise of any functions (in particular those under this Act) which are social services functions within the meaning of the Local Authority Social Services Act 1970, apart from functions under sections 17, 23B and 24B.

(2) In subsection (1) 'accommodation' means accommodation which is provided for a continuous period of more than 24 hours.

(3) It shall be the duty of a local authority looking after any child –

- (a) to safeguard and promote his welfare; and
- (b) to make such use of services available for children cared for by their own parents as appears to the authority reasonable in his case.

(3A) The duty of a local authority under subsection (3)(a) to safeguard and promote the welfare of a child looked after by them includes in particular a duty to promote the child's educational achievement.

(3B) A local authority must appoint at least one person for the purpose of discharging the duty imposed by virtue of subsection (3A).

(3C) A person appointed by a local authority under subsection (3B) must be an officer employed by that authority or another local authority.

(4) Before making any decision with respect to a child whom they are looking after, or proposing to look after, a local authority shall, so far as is reasonably practicable, ascertain the wishes and feelings of –

- (a) the child;
- (b) his parents;
- (c) any person who is not a parent of his but who has parental responsibility for him; and
- (d) any other person whose wishes and feelings the authority consider to be relevant,

regarding the matter to be decided.

(5) In making any such decision a local authority shall give due consideration –

(a) having regard to his age and understanding, to such wishes and feelings of the child as they have been able to ascertain;

(b) to such wishes and feelings of any person mentioned in subsection (4)(b) to (d) as they have been able to ascertain; and

(c) to the child's religious persuasion, racial origin and cultural and linguistic background.

(6) If it appears to a local authority that it is necessary, for the purposes of protecting members of the public from serious injury, to exercise their powers with respect to a child whom they are looking after in a manner which may not be consistent with their duties under this section, they may do so.

(7) If the Secretary of State considers it necessary, for the purpose of protecting members of the public from serious injury, to give directions to a local authority with respect to the exercise of their powers with respect to a child whom they are looking after, the Secretary of State may give such directions to the authority.

(8) Where any such directions are given to an authority they shall comply with them even though doing so is inconsistent with their duties under this section.

Amendments—Children (Leaving Care) Act 2000, s 2(1), (2); Local Government Act 2000, s 107(1), Sch 5, para 19; ACA 2002, s 116(2); CA 2004, s 52; CYPA 2008, s 39, Sch 3, paras 1, 6; CFA 2014, s 99; SI 2016/413.

Meaning of 'a child who is looked after by a local authority' (s 22(1))—The local authority have a duty when assessing the needs of homeless 16 and 17 year olds to consider whether the criteria of CA 1989, s 20, are met. If they are met, then social services (and not the housing department) should take long-term responsibility for the child, including the additional responsibilities involved in helping and supporting their transition to independent adult life. Social services are not able to avoid those responsibilities by looking to the housing authority to accommodate the child *(R (M) v Hammersmith and Fulham London Borough Council* [2008] 1 FLR 1384, HL).

Care Planning, Placement and Case Review (England) Regulations 2010—These Regulations, set out in Part IV, make provision, inter alia, for care planning for looked-after children. A revised edition of Vol 2 of the *Children Act 1989 Guidance and Regulations* entitled *Care Planning, Placement and Case Review* accompanies the Regulations. Part 2 of the Regulations requires that in respect of a child who is to become looked after (but who is not the subject of a care order) the local authority must assess the child's need for services to achieve or maintain a reasonable standard of health or development, and prepare a care plan if one has not been prepared already. The assessment of the child's needs for the purposes of preparing the plan must include an assessment of whether the child's placement meets the requirements under CA 1989, Pt III. The plan must be prepared before the child is accommodated or, if this is not practicable, within 10 working days of the start of the first placement. As far as is reasonably practicable, the plan should be agreed by the local authority with the child's parent, any person holding parental responsibility for the child and, if there is no such person, the person who was caring for the child immediately before the placement being arranged. Where the child is aged 16 or over and agrees to be provided with accommodation under CA 1989, s 20, the care plan should be agreed with the child. The care plan must be kept under review by the local authority in accordance with Pt 6 of the Regulations.

The Children Act 1989 Guidance and Regulation Volume 4: Fostering Services—This guidance sets out the functions and responsibilities of local authorities and their partner agencies in relation to fostering services under CA 1989, Pts 3, 7 and 8. It also sets out the responsibilities arising from the Children Act 2004 and the Children and Young Persons Act 2008 in relation to fostering services. It is issued as guidance under Local Authority Social Services Act 1970, s 7, which requires local authorities in exercising their social services functions, to act under the general guidance of the Secretary of State.

Fostering Services (England) Regulations 2011—These regulations provide a regulatory framework for fostering agencies and local authority fostering services by placing duties on the 'fostering service provider'. Pt 2 requires each fostering service provider to have, and keep under review, a statement of purpose setting out the aims, objectives, services and facilities provided by the fostering service, and a children's guide to the service. Pt 3 makes provision about the management of fostering services: the fitness of the provider and the appointment and fitness of the manager. Pt 4 concerns the conduct of the fostering service, including safeguarding duties, the promotion of contact between foster children and their families, promoting the health and development of foster children, providing support and information for foster parents, and ensuring that there is an effective complaints procedure. Pt 5 concerns the approval of foster parents by the fostering service provider, and reviews of approval. Pt 6 relates only to fostering agencies; it makes provision about fostering agencies that cease to carry out the functions of fostering agencies. Pt 7 provides for the regulations to apply to 'short breaks' with certain modifications.

Arrangements for Placement of Children by Voluntary Organisations and others (England) Regulations 2011—These regulations make provision for children who are not looked after by a local authority but are provided with accommodation by voluntary organisations or in private children's homes. Pt 2 contains general provisions about placements, including the placement plan to be prepared by the voluntary organisation or the private children's home, the assessment of the child's health, the persons who must be notified of the arrangements and the arrangements for contact. Pt 3 makes provisions about the placement of children by voluntary organisations with foster parents and imposes general requirements on responsible authorities as to the making and supervision of placements. Pt 4 makes prelates to other duties, including the circumstances in which responsible authorities or local authorities must terminate placements, and prohibiting the placement of a child by a voluntary organisation outside the British Islands. It also places a duty on local authorities to visit children who are placed by voluntary organisations or in children's homes and requires the authority to report concerns to the Chief Inspector Pt 5 prescribes the manner in which children's cases must be reviewed. Pt 6 makes provision in respect of short-term placements.

Duty to ascertain wishes and feelings of the parents (s 22(4)(b))—The duty of the local authority to ascertain the wishes and feelings of the parents before making any decision with respect to a looked-after child is directory and not mandatory; the result of any non-compliance with the provisions should be treated as an irregularity (*Re P (Children Act 1989, ss 22 and 26: Local Authority Compliance)* [2000] 2 FLR 910, FD). In exceptional circumstances the court has power to make a declaration that the local authority be absolved from the duty to provide information to a parent and from the duty to consult them in any way about the child (*Re C (Care: Consultation with Parents Not in Child's Best Interests)* [2006] 2 FLR 787, FD).

Duty to ascertain wishes and feelings of any other person (s 22(4)(d))—There is no general duty on a local authority to consult foster parents in every case where it is proposed to move a child (*R v Hereford and Worcester County Council ex p D* [1992] 1 FLR 448, QBD). However, the local authority should consult the foster carer with whom the children is placed before deciding to terminate the placement of the children, although each matter will be fact-specific (*R (Bewry) v Norfolk County Council* [2011] 1 FLR 945, QBD).

Adoption Agencies Regulations 2005—These Regulations state that where: (a) a local authority is authorised to place a child for adoption; or (b) a child who has been placed for adoption by a local authority is less than 6 weeks old, s 22(4)(b) does not apply (reg 45(2)(a)). Section 22(4)(c) will apply as if there were instead inserted '(c) any prospective adopter with whom the local authority has placed the child for adoption' (reg 45(2)(b)). Section 22(5)(b) applies as if for the words '(4)(b) to (d)' there were inserted '(4)(c) and (d)' (reg 45(2)(c)). Schedule 2, paras 15 and 21 do not apply (reg 45(2)(d)).

22A Provision of accommodation for children in care

When a child is in the care of a local authority, it is their duty to provide the child with accommodation.

Amendments—Inserted by CYPA 2008, s 8(1).

22B Maintenance of looked after children

It is the duty of a local authority to maintain a child they are looking after in other respects apart from the provision of accommodation.

Amendments—Inserted by CYPA 2008, s 8(1).

Payment of foster allowances—It is unlawful and in breach of ECHR 1950, Arts 8 and 14 for a local authority to have a policy whereby it pays its short-term foster carers who are friends or relatives of the child concerned at a different and significantly lower rate than it pays other such foster carers (*The Queen OTA L and Others v Manchester City Council; The Queen OTA of R and another v Manchester City Council* [2002] 1 FLR 43, QBD and see *London Borough of Tower Hamlets v R (X)* [2014] 1 FLR 1076, CA).

Recovery of contributions towards child's maintenance—The parents of a child who is looked after by the local authority or, where the child has reached the age of 16, the child himself, can be required to contribute towards the child's maintenance (CA 1989, s 29(6) and Sch 2, Pt III).

22C Ways in which looked after children are to be accommodated and maintained

(1) This section applies where a local authority are looking after a child ('C').

(2) The local authority must make arrangements for C to live with a person who falls within subsection (3) (but subject to subsection (4)).

(3) A person ('P') falls within this subsection if –

- (a) P is a parent of C;
- (b) P is not a parent of C but has parental responsibility for C; or
- (c) in a case where C is in the care of the local authority and there was a child arrangements order in force with respect to C immediately before the care order was made, P was a person named in the child arrangements order as a person with whom C was to live.

(4) Subsection (2) does not require the local authority to make arrangements of the kind mentioned in that subsection if doing so –

- (a) would not be consistent with C's welfare; or
- (b) would not be reasonably practicable.

(5) If the local authority are unable to make arrangements under subsection (2), they must place C in the placement which is, in their opinion, the most appropriate placement available.

(6) In subsection (5) 'placement' means –

(a) placement with an individual who is a relative, friend or other person connected with C and who is also a local authority foster parent;
(b) placement with a local authority foster parent who does not fall within paragraph (a);
(c) placement in a children's home in respect of which a person is registered under Part 2 of the Care Standards Act 2000; or
(d) subject to section 22D, placement in accordance with other arrangements which comply with any regulations made for the purposes of this section.

(7) In determining the most appropriate placement for C, the local authority must, subject to [subsection (9B) and]the other provisions of this Part (in particular, to their duties under section 22) –

(a) give preference to a placement falling within paragraph (a) of subsection (6) over placements falling within the other paragraphs of that subsection;
(b) comply, so far as is reasonably practicable in all the circumstances of C's case, with the requirements of subsection (8); and
(c) comply with subsection (9) unless that is not reasonably practicable.

(8) The local authority must ensure that the placement is such that –

(a) it allows C to live near C's home;
(b) it does not disrupt C's education or training;
(c) if C has a sibling for whom the local authority are also providing accommodation, it enables C and the sibling to live together;
(d) if C is disabled, the accommodation provided is suitable to C's particular needs.

(9) The placement must be such that C is provided with accommodation within the local authority's area.

(9A) Subsection (9B) applies (subject to subsection (9C)) where the local authority –

(a) are considering adoption for C, or
(b) are satisfied that C ought to be placed for adoption but are not authorised under section 9 of the Adoption and Children Act 2002 (placement with parental consent) or by virtue of section 21 of that Act (placement orders) to place C for adoption.

(9B) Where this subsection applies –

(a) subsections (7) to (9) do not apply to the local authority,
(b) the local authority must consider placing C with an individual within subsection (6)(a), and
(c) where the local authority decide that a placement with such an individual is not the most appropriate placement for C, the local authority must consider placing C with a local authority foster parent who has been approved as a prospective adopter.

(9C) Subsection (9B) does not apply where the local authority have applied for a placement order under section 21 of the Adoption and Children Act 2002 in respect of C and the application has been refused.

(10) The local authority may determine –

(a) the terms of any arrangements they make under subsection (2) in relation to C (including terms as to payment); and
(b) the terms on which they place C with a local authority foster parent (including terms as to payment but subject to any order made under section 49 of the Children Act 2004).

(11) The Secretary of State may make regulations for, and in connection with, the purposes of this section.

(12) For the meaning of 'local authority foster parent' see section 105(1).

Amendments—Inserted by CYPA 2008, s 8(1). Amended by CFA 2014, ss 2, 12, Sch 2; SI 2016/413.

22D Review of child's case before making alternative arrangements for accommodation

(1) Where a local authority are providing accommodation for a child ('C') other than by arrangements under section 22C(6)(d), they must not make such arrangements for C unless they have decided to do so in consequence of a review of C's case carried out in accordance with regulations made under section 26.

(2) But subsection (1) does not prevent a local authority making arrangements for C under section 22C(6)(d) if they are satisfied that in order to safeguard C's welfare it is necessary –

(a) to make such arrangements; and
(b) to do so as a matter of urgency.

Amendments—Inserted by CYPA 2008, s 8(1).

Regulations—Care Planning, Placement and Case Review (England) Regulations 2010, Pt 6 governs the review of a looked-after child's case.

22E Children's homes provided by Secretary of State or Welsh Ministers

Where a local authority place a child they are looking after in a children's home provided, equipped and maintained by the Secretary of State or the Welsh Ministers under section 82(5), they must do so on such terms as the Secretary of State or the Welsh Ministers (as the case may be) may from time to time determine.

Amendments—Inserted by CYPA 2008, s 8(1). Substituted by SI 2016/413.

22F Regulations as to children looked after by local authorities

Part 2 of Schedule 2 has effect for the purposes of making further provision as to children looked after by local authorities and in particular as to the regulations which may be made under section 22C(11).

Amendments—Inserted by CYPA 2008, s 8(1).

22G General duty of local authority to secure sufficient accommodation for looked after children

(1) It is the general duty of a local authority to take steps that secure, so far as reasonably practicable, the outcome in subsection (2).

(2) The outcome is that the local authority are able to provide the children mentioned in subsection (3) with accommodation that –

(a) is within the authority's area; and
(b) meets the needs of those children.

(3) The children referred to in subsection (2) are those –

(a) that the local authority are looking after,
(b) in respect of whom the authority are unable to make arrangements under section 22C(2), and
(c) whose circumstances are such that it would be consistent with their welfare for them to be provided with accommodation that is in the authority's area.

(4) In taking steps to secure the outcome in subsection (2), the local authority must have regard to the benefit of having –

(a) a number of accommodation providers in their area that is, in their opinion, sufficient to secure that outcome; and
(b) a range of accommodation in their area capable of meeting different needs that is, in their opinion, sufficient to secure that outcome.

(5) In this section 'accommodation providers' means –

local authority foster parents; and
children's homes in respect of which a person is registered under Part 2 of the Care Standards Act 2000.

Amendments—Inserted by CYPA 2008, s 9.

Care Planning, Placement and Case Review (England) Regulations 2010 (s 23(4),(5))—These regulations are set out in Part IV. Where the local authority plans to place a child in care with his parents, regs 14–20 will apply. See further under CA 1989, s 33. A revised edition of Vol 2 of the *Children Act 1989 Guidance and Regulations* entitled *Care Planning, Placement and Case Review* accompanies the Regulations, replacing some existing volumes and integrating guidance issued since 1991. It covers each of the elements of care planning required throughout the child's journey in the care system. Further guidance, *Sufficiency: statutory guidance securing sufficient accommodation* (see *www.gov.uk/government/publications/children-act-1989-care-planning-placement-and-case-review*) seeks to improve outcomes for looked after children and young people by providing guidance on the implementation of section 22G. This section requires local authorities to take steps that secure, so far as reasonably practicable, sufficient accommodation within the authority's area that meets the needs of children that the local authority are looking after, and whose circumstances are such that it would be consistent with their welfare for them to be provided with accommodation that is in the local authority's area ('the sufficiency duty').

****

Visiting

23ZA Duty of local authority to ensure visits to, and contact with, looked after children and others

(1) This section applies to –

(a) a child looked after by a local authority;
(b) a child who was looked after by a local authority but who has ceased to be looked after by them as a result of prescribed circumstances.

(2) It is the duty of the local authority –

(a) to ensure that a person to whom this section applies is visited by a representative of the authority ('a representative');
(b) to arrange for appropriate advice, support and assistance to be available to a person to whom this section applies who seeks it from them.

(3) The duties imposed by subsection (2) –

(a) are to be discharged in accordance with any regulations made for the purposes of this section by the Secretary of State;
(b) are subject to any requirement imposed by or under an enactment applicable to the place in which the person to whom this section applies is accommodated.

(4) Regulations under this section for the purposes of subsection (3)(a) may make provision about –

(a) the frequency of visits;
(b) circumstances in which a person to whom this section applies must be visited by a representative; and
(c) the functions of a representative.

(5) In choosing a representative a local authority must satisfy themselves that the person chosen has the necessary skills and experience to perform the functions of a representative.

Amendments—Inserted by CYPA 2008, s 15. Amended by SI 2016/413.

Regulations—Care Planning, Placement and Case Review (England) Regulations 2010, Pt 5 governs visits to and contact with a looked-after child.

23ZB Independent visitors for children looked after by a local authority

(1) A local authority looking after a child must appoint an independent person to be the child's visitor if –

(a) the child falls within a description prescribed in regulations made by the Secretary of State; or
(b) in any other case, it appears to them that it would be in the child's interests to do so.

(2) A person appointed under this section must visit, befriend and advise the child.

(3) A person appointed under this section is entitled to recover from the appointing authority any reasonable expenses incurred by that person for the purposes of that person's functions under this section.

(4) A person's appointment as a visitor in pursuance of this section comes to an end if –

(a) the child ceases to be looked after by the local authority;
(b) the person resigns the appointment by giving notice in writing to the appointing authority; or
(c) the authority give him notice in writing that they have terminated it.

(5) The ending of such an appointment does not affect any duty under this section to make a further appointment.

(6) Where a local authority propose to appoint a visitor for a child under this section, the appointment shall not be made if –

(a) the child objects to it; and
(b) the authority are satisfied that the child has sufficient understanding to make an informed decision.

(7) Where a visitor has been appointed for a child under this section, the local authority shall terminate the appointment if –

(a) the child objects to its continuing; and
(b) the authority are satisfied that the child has sufficient understanding to make an informed decision.

(8) If the local authority give effect to a child's objection under subsection (6) or (7) and the objection is to having anyone as the child's visitor, the authority does not have to propose to appoint another person under subsection (1) until the objection is withdrawn.

(9) The Secretary of State may make regulations as to the circumstances in which a person is to be regarded for the purposes of this section as independent of the appointing authority.

Amendments—Inserted by CYPA 2008, s 16. Amended by SI 2016/413.

Regulations—Care Planning, Placement and Case Review (England) Regulations 2010, Pt 8 governs the provision of independent visitors for children looked after by a local authority.

Advice and assistance for certain children and young persons

23A The responsible authority and relevant children

(1) The responsible local authority shall have the functions set out in section 23B in respect of a relevant child.

(2) In subsection (1) 'relevant child' means (subject to subsection (3)) a child who –

(a) is not being looked after by any local authority in England or by any local authority in Wales;
(b) was, before last ceasing to be looked after, an eligible child for the purposes of paragraph 19B of Schedule 2; and
(c) is aged sixteen or seventeen.

(3) The Secretary of State may prescribe –

(a) additional categories of relevant children; and
(b) categories of children who are not to be relevant children despite falling within subsection (2).

(4) In subsection (1) the 'responsible local authority' is the one which last looked after the child.

(5) If under subsection (3)(a) the Secretary of State prescribes a category of relevant children which includes children who do not fall within subsection (2)(b) (for example, because they were being looked after by a local authority in Scotland), the Secretary of State may in the regulations also provide for which local authority is to be the responsible local authority for those children.

Amendments—Inserted by Children (Leaving Care) Act 2000, s 2(1),(4). Amended by CYPA 2008, s 39, Sch 3, paras 1, 8; SI 2016/413.

Care Leavers (England) Regulations 2010—These Regulations revoke, and in part replace, the Children (Leaving Care) (England) Regulations 2001. They make provision about support to be provided to 'relevant children' (as defined in CA 1989, s 23A(2) and reg 3) and to 'former relevant children' (as defined in CA 1989, s 23C; the position of 'eligible' children as defined by CA 1989, Sch 2, para 19B is dealt with under the Care Planning, Placement and Case Review (England) Regulations 2010). The Care Leavers (England) Regulations 2010 make provision about the way in which the local authority must carry out an assessment of the needs of relevant and former relevant children, about the preparation and review of pathway plans for such children, about the functions of personal advisers appointed for relevant and former relevant children and also about other support, the suitability of accommodation and the provision of vacation accommodation.

Meaning of 'relevant child' (s 23A(2))—In determining whether a child is a 'relevant child' for the purposes of s 23A(2), reference must also be made to Care Leavers (England) Regulations 2010, reg 3, which prescribes additional categories of relevant children to whom local authorities will or, as the case may be, will not, owe additional duties as provided for CA 1989, Pt III.

23B Additional functions of the responsible authority in respect of relevant children

(1) It is the duty of each local authority to take reasonable steps to keep in touch with a relevant child for whom they are the responsible authority, whether he is within their area or not.

(2) It is the duty of each local authority to appoint a personal adviser for each relevant child (if they have not already done so under paragraph 19C of Schedule 2).

(3) It is the duty of each local authority, in relation to any relevant child who does not already have a pathway plan prepared for the purposes of paragraph 19B of Schedule 2 –

(a) to carry out an assessment of his needs with a view to determining what advice, assistance and support it would be appropriate for them to provide him under this Part; and

(b) to prepare a pathway plan for him.

(4)–(7) *(repealed)*

(8) The responsible local authority shall safeguard and promote the child's welfare and, unless they are satisfied that his welfare does not require it, support him by –

(a) maintaining him;
(b) providing him with or maintaining him in suitable accommodation; and
(c) providing support of such other descriptions as may be prescribed.

(9) Support under subsection (8) may be in cash.

(10) The Secretary of State may by regulations make provision about the meaning of 'suitable accommodation' and in particular about the suitability of landlords or other providers of accommodation.

(11) If the local authority have lost touch with a relevant child, despite taking reasonable steps to keep in touch, they must without delay –

(a) consider how to re-establish contact; and
(b) take reasonable steps to do so,

and while the child is still a relevant child must continue to take such steps until they succeed.

(12) Subsections (7) to (9) of section 17 apply in relation to support given under this section as they apply in relation to assistance given under that section.

(13) Subsections (4) and (5) of section 22 apply in relation to any decision by a local authority for the purposes of this section as they apply in relation to the decisions referred to in that section.

Amendments—Inserted by Children (Leaving Care) Act 2000, s 2(1),(4). Amended by CYPA 2008, ss 22, 39, Sch 3, paras 1, 9; SI 2016/413.

Functions of personal advisers (s 23B(2))—The functions of a personal adviser are set out in Care Leavers (England) Regulations 2010, reg 8.

Duty to carry out an assessment (s 23B(3)(a))—Pursuant to Care Leavers (England) Regulations 2010, reg 4, in carrying out an assessment of the relevant child's, or former relevant child's, needs the local authority must, unless it is not reasonably practicable, seek and have regard to the views of the child and take all reasonable steps to enable the child to attend and participate in any meetings at which their case is to be considered. The assessment itself must take account of the matters set out in Care Leavers (England) Regulations 2010, reg 5.

Meaning of 'suitable accommodation' (s 23B(8)(b),(10))—Reg 9(2) and Sch 2 of the Care Leavers (England) Regulations 2010 prescribe the meaning of 'suitable accommodation' for the purposes of CA 1989, s 23B.

23C Continuing functions in respect of former relevant children

(1) Each local authority shall have the duties provided for in this section towards –

(a) a person who has been a relevant child for the purposes of section 23A (and would be one if he were under eighteen), and in relation to whom they were the last responsible authority; and

(b) a person who was being looked after by them when he attained the age of eighteen, and immediately before ceasing to be looked after was an eligible child,

and in this section such a person is referred to as a 'former relevant child'.

(2) It is the duty of the local authority to take reasonable steps –

(a) to keep in touch with a former relevant child whether he is within their area or not; and

(b) if they lose touch with him, to re-establish contact.

(3) It is the duty of the local authority –

(a) to continue the appointment of a personal adviser for a former relevant child; and

(b) to continue to keep his pathway plan under regular review.

(4) It is the duty of the local authority to give a former relevant child –

(a) assistance of the kind referred to in section 24B(1), to the extent that his welfare requires it;

(b) assistance of the kind referred to in section 24B(2), to the extent that his welfare and his educational or training needs require it;

(c) other assistance, to the extent that his welfare requires it.

(5) The assistance given under subsection (4)(c) may be in kind or, in exceptional circumstances, in cash.

(5A) It is the duty of the local authority to pay the relevant amount to a former relevant child who pursues higher education in accordance with a pathway plan prepared for that person.

(5B) The Secretary of State may by regulations –

(a) prescribe the relevant amount for the purposes of subsection (5A);

(b) prescribe the meaning of 'higher education' for those purposes;

(c) make provision as to the payment of the relevant amount;

(d) make provision as to the circumstances in which the relevant amount (or any part of it) may be recovered by the local authority from a former relevant child to whom a payment has been made.

(5C) The duty set out in subsection (5A) is without prejudice to that set out in subsection (4)(b).

(6) Subject to subsection (7), the duties set out in subsections (2), (3) and (4) subsist until the former relevant child reaches the age of twenty-one.

(7) If the former relevant child's pathway plan sets out a programme of education or training which extends beyond his twenty-first birthday –

(a) the duty set out in subsection (4)(b) continues to subsist for so long as the former relevant child continues to pursue that programme; and

(b) the duties set out in subsections (2) and (3) continue to subsist concurrently with that duty.

(8) For the purposes of subsection (7)(a) there shall be disregarded any interruption in a former relevant child's pursuance of a programme of education or training if the local authority are satisfied that he will resume it as soon as is reasonably practicable.

(9) Section 24B(5) applies in relation to a person being given assistance under subsection (4)(b) or who is in receipt of a payment under subsection (5A) as it applies in relation to a person to whom section 24B(3) applies.

(10) Subsections (7) to (9) of section 17 apply in relation to assistance given under this section as they apply in relation to assistance given under that section.

Amendments—Inserted by Children (Leaving Care) Act 2000, s 2(1),(4). Amended by CYPA 2008, s 21; SI 2016/413.

Meaning of 'other assistance' (s 23C(4)(c))—The words 'other assistance' can include the provision of accommodation for the former relevant child (*R (O) v London Borough of Barking and Dagenham (SSHD and the Children's Society Intervening)* [2011] 1 FLR 734, CA).

23CZA Arrangements for certain former relevant children to continue to live with former foster parents

(1) Each local authority have the duties provided for in subsection (3) in relation to a staying put arrangement.

(2) A 'staying put arrangement' is an arrangement under which –

(a) a person who is a former relevant child by virtue of section 23C(1)(b), and

(b) a person (a 'former foster parent') who was the former relevant child's local authority foster parent immediately before the former relevant child ceased to be looked after by the local authority, continue to live together after the former relevant child has ceased to be looked after.

(3) It is the duty of the local authority (in discharging the duties in section 23C(3) and by other means) –

(a) to monitor the staying put arrangement, and

(b) to provide advice, assistance and support to the former relevant child and the former foster parent with a view to maintaining the staying put arrangement.

(4) Support provided to the former foster parent under subsection (3)(b) must include financial support.

(5) Subsection (3)(b) does not apply if the local authority consider that the staying put arrangement is not consistent with the welfare of the former relevant child.

(6) The duties set out in subsection (3) subsist until the former relevant child reaches the age of 21.

Amendments—Inserted by CFA 2014, s 98. Amended by SI 2016/413.

23CA Further assistance to pursue education or training

(1) This section applies to a person if –

(a) he is under the age of twenty-five or of such lesser age as may be prescribed by the Secretary of State;

(b) he is a former relevant child (within the meaning of section 23C) towards whom the duties imposed by subsections (2), (3) and (4) of that section no longer subsist; and

(c) he has informed the responsible local authority that he is pursuing, or wishes to pursue, a programme of education or training.

(2) It is the duty of the responsible local authority to appoint a personal adviser for a person to whom this section applies.

(3) It is the duty of the responsible local authority –

(a) to carry out an assessment of the needs of a person to whom this section applies with a view to determining what assistance (if any) it would be appropriate for them to provide to him under this section; and

(b) to prepare a pathway plan for him.

(4) It is the duty of the responsible local authority to give assistance of a kind referred to subsection (5) to a person to whom this section applies to the extent that his educational or training needs require it.

(5) The kinds of assistance are –

(a) contributing to expenses incurred by him in living near the place where he is, or will be, receiving education or training; or

(b) making a grant to enable him to meet expenses connected with his education and training.

(6) If a person to whom this section applies pursues a programme of education or training in accordance with the pathway plan prepared for him, the duties of the local authority under this section (and under any provision applicable to the pathway plan prepared under this section for that person) subsist for as long as he continues to pursue that programme.

(7) For the purposes of subsection (6), the local authority may disregard any interruption in the person's pursuance of a programme of education or training if they are satisfied that he will resume it as soon as is reasonably practicable.

(8) Subsections (7) to (9) of section 17 apply to assistance given to a person under this section as they apply to assistance given to or in respect of a child under that section, but with the omission in subsection (8) of the words 'and of each of his parents'.

(9) Subsection (5) of section 24B applies to a person to whom this section applies as it applies to a person to whom subsection (3) of that section applies.

(10) Nothing in this section affects the duty imposed by subsection (5A) of section 23C to the extent that it subsists in relation to a person to whom this section applies; but the duty to make a payment under that subsection may be taken into account in the assessment of the person's needs under subsection (3)(a).

(11) In this section 'the responsible local authority' means, in relation to a person to whom this section applies, the local authority which had the duties provided for in section 23C towards him.

Amendments—Inserted by CYPA 2008, s 22. Amended by SI 2016/413.

Personal advisers and pathway plans

23D Personal advisers

(1) The Secretary of State may by regulations require local authorities to appoint a personal adviser for children or young persons of a prescribed description who have reached the age of sixteen but not the age of twenty-five who are not –

(a) children who are relevant children for the purposes of section 23A;
(b) the young persons referred to in section 23C;
(c) the children referred to in paragraph 19C of Schedule 2; or
(d) persons to whom section 23CA applies.

(2) Personal advisers appointed under or by virtue of this Part shall (in addition to any other functions) have such functions as the Secretary of State prescribes.

Amendments—Inserted by Children (Leaving Care) Act 2000, s 3. Amended by CYPA 2008, ss 23(1), 39, Sch 3, paras 1, 10; SI 2016/413.

Functions of personal adviser—These are set out in Care Planning, Placement and Case Review (England) Regulations 2010, reg 44 (see Part IV) and Care Leavers (England) Regulations 2010, reg 8(1).

23E Pathway plans

(1) In this Part, a reference to a 'pathway plan' is to a plan setting out –

(a) in the case of a plan prepared under paragraph 19B of Schedule 2 –
  (i) the advice, assistance and support which the local authority intend to provide a child under this Part, both while they are looking after him and later; and
  (ii) when they might cease to look after him; and
(b) in the case of a plan prepared under section 23Bor 23CA, the advice, assistance and support which the local authority intend to provide under this Part,

and dealing with such other matters (if any) as may be prescribed in regulations made by the Secretary of State.

(1A) A local authority may carry out an assessment under section 23B(3) or 23CA(3) of a person's needs at the same time as any assessment of his needs is made under –

(a) the Chronically Sick and Disabled Persons Act 1970;
(b) Part 4 of the Education Act 1996 or Part 3 of the Children and Families Act 2014 (in the case of an assessment under section 23B(3));

(c) the Disabled Persons (Services, Consultation and Representation) Act 1986; or
(d) any other enactment.

(1B) The Secretary of State may by regulations make provision as to assessments for the purposes of section 23B(3) or 23CA.

(1C) Regulations under subsection (1B) may in particular make provision about –

(a) who is to be consulted in relation to an assessment;
(b) the way in which an assessment is to be carried out, by whom and when;
(c) the recording of the results of an assessment;
(d) the considerations to which a local authority are to have regard in carrying out an assessment.

(1D) A local authority shall keep each pathway plan prepared by them under section 23B or 23CA under review.

(2) The Secretary of State may by regulations make provision about pathway plans and their review.

Amendments—Inserted by Children (Leaving Care) Act 2000, s 3. Amended by CYPA 2008, ss 22, 39, Sch 3, paras 1, 11; CFA 2014, s 82, Sch 3; SI 2016/413.

Care Planning, Placement and Case Review (England) Regulations 2010—These regulations came into force on 1 April 2011 (see Part IV). Pt 7 sets out arrangements to be made by the local authority for ceasing to look after a child. It is a re-enactment of provisions in the Children (Leaving Care) (England) Regulations 2001 (above) relating to 'eligible' children, as defined in CA 1989, Sch 2, para 19B. It provides for the assessment of needs, the preparation and review of pathway plans, the keeping of records, assistance with education and training, and accommodation. Regulation 44 prescribes the functions of a personal adviser. In *R (G) v Nottingham City Council and Nottingham University Hospital* [2008] 1 FLR 1668, QBD the authority acted unlawfully by failing to conduct a lawful assessment or produce a lawful pathway plan. The statutory scheme in CA 1989, ss 23A–23C and Sch 2, and the Regulations envisage two separate stages:

(1) the assessment, culminating in the preparation of a written record, and
(2) the preparation of a pathway plan. There was a serious failure by the authority to comply with its statutory duties and to heed judicial authority. The plan lacked specificity and the mother's personal adviser had been involved in its preparation, which was impermissible (*R (J) v Caerphilly County Borough Council* [2005] 2 FLR 860, QBD).

Care Leavers (England) Regulations 2010—Reg 6 governs the preparation and contents of pathway plans for relevant children and former relevant children. Reg 7 prescribes the duties on the local authority concerning review of the pathway plans of relevant and former relevant children.

24 Persons qualifying for advice and assistance

(1) In this Part 'a person qualifying for advice and assistance' means a person to whom subsection (1A) or (1B) applies.

(1A) This subsection applies to a person –

(a) who has reached the age of sixteen but not the age of twenty-one;
(b) with respect to whom a special guardianship order is in force (or, if he has reached the age of eighteen, was in force when he reached that age); and
(c) who was, immediately before the making of that order, looked after by a local authority.

(1B) This subsection applies to a person to whom subsection (1A) does not apply, and who –

(a) is under twenty-one; and
(b) at any time after reaching the age of sixteen but while still a child was, but is no longer, looked after, accommodated or fostered.

(2) In subsection (1B)(b), 'looked after, accommodated or fostered' means –

(a) looked after by a local authority (without subsequently being looked after by a local authority in Wales);
(b) accommodated by or on behalf of a voluntary organisation;
(c) accommodated in a registered children's home;
(d) accommodated for a consecutive period of at least three months –
    (i) by any Local Health Board, Special Health Authority or by a local authority in the exercise of education functions, or
    (ii) in any residential care home, nursing home or mental nursing home or in any

accommodation provided pursuant to arrangements made by the Secretary of State, the National Health Service Commissioning Board or a clinical commissioning group under the National Health Service Act 2006 or by a National Health Service trust or an NHS foundation trust, or by a local authority in Wales in the exercise of education functions; or

(e) privately fostered.

(3) Subsection (2)(d) applies even if the period of three months mentioned there began before the child reached the age of sixteen.

(4) In the case of a person qualifying for advice and assistance by virtue of subsection (2)(a), it is the duty of the local authority which last looked after him to take such steps as they think appropriate to contact him at such times as they think appropriate with a view to discharging their functions under sections 24A and 24B.

(5) In each of sections 24A and 24B, the local authority under the duty or having the power mentioned there ('the relevant authority') is –

(za) in the case of a person to whom subsection (1A) applies, a local authority determined in accordance with regulations made by the Secretary of State;

(a) in the case of a person qualifying for advice and assistance by virtue of subsection (2)(a), the local authority which last looked after him; or

(b) in the case of any other person qualifying for advice and assistance, the local authority within whose area the person is (if he has asked for help of a kind which can be given under section 24A or 24B).

Amendments—Substituted by Children (Leaving Care) Act 2000, s 4(1). Amended by Health and Social Care (Community Health and Standards) Act 2003, s 34, Sch 4, paras 75, 76; ACA 2002, s 139(1), Sch 3, paras 54, 60; SI 2007/961; CYPA 2008, s 39, Sch 3, paras 1, 12, SI 2010/1158; Health and Social Care Act 2012, s 55(2), Sch 5, para 49; SI 2016/413.

24A Advice and assistance

(1) The relevant authority shall consider whether the conditions in subsection (2) are satisfied in relation to a person qualifying for advice and assistance.

(2) The conditions are that –

(a) he needs help of a kind which they can give under this section or section 24B; and

(b) in the case of a person to whom section 24(1A) applies, or to whom section 24(1B) applies and who was not being looked after by any local authority or local authority in Wales, they are satisfied that the person by whom he was being looked after does not have the necessary facilities for advising or befriending him.

(3) If the conditions are satisfied –

(a) they shall advise and befriend him if he is a person to whom section 24(1A) applies, or he is a person to whom section 24(1B) applies and he was being looked after by a local authority (without subsequently being looked after by a local authority in Wales), or was accommodated by or on behalf of a voluntary organisation; and

(b) in any other case they may do so.

(4) Where as a result of this section a local authority are under a duty, or are empowered, to advise and befriend a person, they may also give him assistance.

(5) The assistance may be in kind and, in exceptional circumstances, assistance may be given –

(a) by providing accommodation, if in the circumstances assistance may not be given in respect of the accommodation under section 24B, or

(b) in cash.

(6) Subsections (7) to (9) of section 17 apply in relation to assistance given under this section or section 24B as they apply in relation to assistance given under that section.

Amendments—Inserted by Children (Leaving Care) Act 2000, s 4(1). Amended by ACA 2002, ss 116(3), 139(1), Sch 3, paras 54, 61; SI 2016/413.

Care Planning, Placement and Case Review (England) Regulations 2010—These regulations are set out in Part IV. Regulations 28–31 set out the arrangements that a local authority should make to visit the child and to provide him with advice, support and assistance.

24B Employment, education and training

(1) The relevant local authority may give assistance to any person who qualifies for advice and assistance by virtue of section 24(1A) or section 24(2)(a) by contributing to expenses incurred by him in living near the place where he is, or will be, employed or seeking employment.

(2) The relevant local authority may give assistance to a person to whom subsection (3) applies by –

(a) contributing to expenses incurred by the person in question in living near the place where he is, or will be, receiving education or training; or
(b) making a grant to enable him to meet expenses connected with his education or training.

(3) This subsection applies to any person who –

(a) is under twenty-five; and
(b) qualifies for advice and assistance by virtue of section 24(1A) or section 24(2)(a), or would have done so if he were under twenty-one.

(4) Where a local authority are assisting a person under subsection (2) they may disregard any interruption in his attendance on the course if he resumes it as soon as is reasonably practicable.

(5) Where the local authority are satisfied that a person to whom subsection (3) applies who is in full-time further or higher education needs accommodation during a vacation because his term-time accommodation is not available to him then, they shall give him assistance by –

(a) providing him with suitable accommodation during the vacation; or
(b) paying him enough to enable him to secure such accommodation himself.

(6) The Secretary of State may prescribe the meaning of 'full-time', 'further education', 'higher education' and 'vacation' for the purposes of subsection (5).

Amendments—Inserted by Children (Leaving Care) Act 2000, s 4(1). Amended by ACA 2002, s 139(1), Sch 3, paras 54, 62; CYPA 2008, ss 22, 39, Sch 3, paras 1, 13; SI 2016/413.

24C Information

(1) Where it appears to a local authority that a person –

(a) with whom they are under a duty to keep in touch under section 23B, 23C or 24; or
(b) whom they have been advising and befriending under section 24A; or
(c) to whom they have been giving assistance under section 24B,

proposes to live, or is living, in the area of another local authority, or in the area of a local authority in Wales, they must inform that other authority.

(2) Where a child who is accommodated in England –

(a) by a voluntary organisation or in a private children's home;
(b) by or on behalf of any Local Health Board or Special Health Authority;
(c) by or on behalf of a clinical commissioning group or the National Health Service Commissioning Board;
(d) by or on behalf of a local authority in the exercise of education functions;
(e) by or on behalf of a local authority in Wales in the exercise of education functions;
(f) in any care home or independent hospital; or
(g) in any accommodation provided by or on behalf of a National Health Service trust or by or on behalf of an NHS Foundation Trust,

ceases to be so accommodated after reaching the age of 16, the person by whom or on whose behalf the child was accommodated or who carries on or manages the home or hospital (as the case may be) must inform the local authority or local authority in Wales within whose area the child proposes to live.

(3) Subsection (2) only applies, by virtue of any of paragraphs (b) to (g), if the accommodation has been provided for a consecutive period of at least three months.

(4) In a case where a child was accommodated by or on behalf of a local authority, or a local authority in Wales, in the exercise of education functions, subsection (2) applies only if the authority who accommodated the child is different from the authority within whose area the child proposes to live.

Amendments—Inserted by Children (Leaving Care) Act 2000, s 4(1). Amended by Health and Social Care (Community Health and Standards) Act 2003, s 34, Sch 4, paras 75, 77; SI 2007/961; SI 2010/1158; Health and Social Care Act 2012, s 55(2), Sch 5, para 50; SI 2016/413.

24D Representations: sections 23A to 24B

(1) Every local authority shall establish a procedure for considering representations (including complaints) made to them by –

(a) a relevant child for the purposes of section 23A or a young person falling within section 23C;
(b) a person qualifying for advice and assistance; or
(c) a person falling within section 24B(2),

about the discharge of their functions under this Part in relation to him.

(1A) Regulations may be made by the Secretary of State imposing time limits on the making of representations under subsection (1).

(2) In considering representations under subsection (1), a local authority shall comply with regulations (if any) made by the Secretary of State for the purposes of this subsection.

Amendments—Inserted by Children (Leaving Care) Act 2000, s 5. Amended by ACA 2002, s 117; CYPA 2008, s 39, Sch 3, paras 1, 14; SI 2016/413.

Secure accommodation

25 Use of accommodation for restricting liberty

(1) Subject to the following provisions of this section, a child who is being looked after by a local authority or local authority in Wales may not be placed, and, if placed, may not be kept, in accommodation in England provided for the purpose of restricting liberty ('secure accommodation') unless it appears –

(a) that –
  (i) he has a history of absconding and is likely to abscond from any other description of accommodation; and
  (ii) if he absconds, he is likely to suffer significant harm, or
(b) that if he is kept in any other description of accommodation he is likely to injure himself or other persons.

(2) The Secretary of State may by regulations –

(a) specify a maximum period –
  (i) beyond which a child may not be kept in secure accommodation in England without the authority of the court; and
  (ii) for which the court may authorise a child to be kept in secure accommodation in England;
(b) empower the court from time to time to authorise a child to be kept in secure accommodation in England for such further period as the regulations may specify; and
(c) provide that applications to the court under this section shall be made only by local authorities or local authorities in Wales.

(3) It shall be the duty of a court hearing an application under this section to determine whether any relevant criteria for keeping a child in secure accommodation are satisfied in his case.

(4) If a court determines that any such criteria are satisfied, it shall make an order authorising the child to be kept in secure accommodation and specifying the maximum period for which he may be so kept.

(5) On any adjournment of the hearing of an application under this section, a court may make an interim order permitting the child to be kept during the period of the adjournment in secure accommodation.

(6) No court shall exercise the powers conferred by this section in respect of a child who is not legally represented in that court unless, having been informed of his right to apply for the provision of representation under Part 1 of the Legal Aid, Sentencing and Punishment of Offenders Act 2012 and having had the opportunity to do so, he refused or failed to apply.

(7) The Secretary of State may by regulations provide that –

(a) this section shall or shall not apply to any description of children specified in the regulations;

(b) this section shall have effect in relation to children of a description specified in the regulations subject to such modifications as may be so specified;

(c) such other provisions as may be so specified shall have effect for the purpose of determining whether a child of a description specified in the regulations may be placed or kept in secure accommodation in England.

(8) The giving of an authorisation under this section shall not prejudice any power of any court in England and Wales or Scotland to give directions relating to the child to whom the authorisation relates.

(9) This section is subject to section 20(8).

Amendments—AJA 1999, s 24, Sch 4, para 45; CYPA 2008, s 39, Sch 3, paras 1, 15; LASPOA 2012, s 39, Sch 5, para 38; SI 2016/413.

Defined terms—'child': s 105(1).

Scope—The C(SA)R 1991 and the C(SA)(No 2)R 1991 have been made under this section and reference should also be made to these.

'secure accommodation'—To constitute 'secure accommodation' a place does not have to be so designated; each case will depend on its own facts. It is the restriction of liberty which is the essential factor in determining what is secure accommodation, see *A Metropolitan Borough Council v DB* [1997] 1 FLR 767, FD, in which Cazalet J held that a maternity ward was secure accommodation where entrance was only by way of a key or pass. The 17-year-old mother had not been given a key or pass and staff were instructed not to let her leave. However, contrast *Re C (Detention: Medical Treatment)* [1997] 2 FLR 180, FD, where Wall J, while agreeing that premises which are not designed as secure accommodation may become such by virtue of the use to which they are put in the particular circumstances of individual cases, held that the more natural meaning of the words 'provided for the purpose of restricting liberty' in s 25(1) is 'designed for, or having as its primary purpose the restriction of liberty'. In *Re C* a clinic for the treatment of anorexia nervosa was held not to be secure accommodation because the primary purpose of the clinic was to achieve treatment, and the restriction of liberty was only incidental to that end. However, a similar result was achieved by invoking the inherent jurisdiction under CA 1989, s 100 to direct that the minor remain an in-patient at the clinic. A secure accommodation order is a deprivation of liberty within the meaning of Art 5 of the ECHR, but is not incompatible with the Convention where it is justified under one of the exceptions in Art 5(1), for example where the order is for the purposes of educational supervision (*Re K (Secure Accommodation Order: Right to Liberty)* [2001] 1 FLR 526, CA).

Maximum periods—The maximum period that a child may be held in secure accommodation without a court order is 72 hours per 28 days: C(SA)R 1991, reg 10. The initial maximum period for which a court may authorise a child to be held in secure accommodation is 3 months and thereafter for periods of up to 6 months: C(SA)R 1991, regs 11, 12.

'being looked after by a local authority' (s 25(1))—See CA 1989, s 22(1) and, as to a child who is bailed with a condition of residence to the local authority, see *Re C (Secure Accommodation: Bail)* [1994] 2 FLR 922, FD.

'may not be placed, and, if placed, may not be kept' (s 25(1))—The legislation does not specify that a child should already have been placed in secure accommodation before an order is sought. The court's authority is not required for the first 72 hours that a child is placed in secure accommodation. While in ordinary cases a child ought to be in secure accommodation at the time of the application, having satisfied either the absconding or injury criterion, exceptional circumstances can justify the making of an application where a child is not already so placed. Neither knowing that the child is absconding nor the lack of suitable accommodation amount to exceptional circumstances (*Re AK (Secure Accommodation Order)* [2000] 1 FLR 317, FD (NI)).

Criteria for order (s 25(1)(a),(b))—The two limbs of s 25(1) should be read disjunctively and not conjunctively. Therefore, the court does not have to find both s 25(1)(a) and (b) satisfied before making an order, since either is sufficient (*Re D (Secure Accommodation Order) (No 1)* [1997] 1 FLR 197, FD). It is essential that there should be a clear record of facts as found by the court and for which sworn evidence was necessary (*Re AS (Secure Accommodation Order)* [1999] 1 FLR 103, FD). The phrase 'likely to abscond' in s 25(1)(a)(i) should be construed in the same way as the threshold criteria in s 31. 'Likely' is used in the sense of a real possibility, a possibility that cannot be sensibly ignored having regard to the nature and gravity of the feared harm in the particular case (*S v Knowsley Borough Council* [2004] 2 FLR 716, FD). The consent of a young person to the making of a SAO is not required nor is the consent of a child under the age of 16 necessary to be accommodated by a local authority pursuant to s 20: *Re W (A Child)* [2016] EWCA Civ 804.

'child who is not legally represented' (s 25(6))—A child who is instructing a solicitor himself (in accordance with FPR 2010, r 16.29(2)) is obviously legally represented within the meaning of this section. From the wording of the Act and the rules, it is clear that a child is also legally represented where it is his children's guardian who is actually giving instructions to the solicitor (the more normal case since a children's guardian *will* normally be appointed by virtue of s 41(1)). It is implicit that in order for legal representation to be effective it must involve the taking of instructions (*Re AS (Secure Accommodation Order)* [1999] 1 FLR 103, FD – where an application for a s 25 order was held to be procedurally flawed because the child was not informed of the hearing and a guardian was not appointed). However, where the local authority have complied with the service requirements by serving the application on the parents and the solicitor appointed on behalf of the guardian it may still be fair to allow the application to proceed where the child and her own solicitor have only a short time to consult; although in such circumstances it may be preferable to make an interim order and adjourn for a few days to allow the child to respond to the application (*Re C (Secure Accommodation Order: Representation)* [2001] 2 FLR 169, CA).

Attendance of child at hearing—While the court can allow the child who is the subject of the application to attend court, it must always bear in mind that attendance is likely to be harmful to the child and should only permit it if satisfied that it is in the interests of the child (*Re W (Secure Accommodation Order: Attendance at Court)* [1994] 2 FLR 1092, FD, and see further **Use of the power to exclude** under FPR 2010, rr 12.14 and see also r 27.4(1),(3). However, the ordinary practice in relation to children attending court hearings has evolved since the decision in *Re W* (see *A City Council v T, J and K* [2011] 2 FLR 803, FD). There is no in-built presumption against a child attending a hearing. The starting point should be an open evaluation of the consequences of attendance or non-attendance in terms of the child's welfare and the court's ability to manage its proceedings fairly. The following factors were relevant: (a) the age and level of understanding of the child; (b) the nature and strength of the child's wishes; (c) the child's emotional and psychological state; (d) the effect of influence from others; (e) the matters to be discussed; (f) the evidence to be given; (g) the child's behaviour; (h) practical and logistical considerations; and (i) the integrity of the proceedings.

The fact that the child would need to be physically restrained during the hearing in order to control him (as in *Re W* above) would, in itself, be sufficient ground for refusing to allow the child to be in court. Further examples given in *Re W* of situations in which the court would not allow a child to be present are where there is a prospect of disturbance or unruliness in court or the possibility of the child being educationally subnormal or where the child is much younger than the 10-year-old boy in that case. But see *J v Merthyr Tydfil County Borough Council* [1997] Fam Law 522, FD, where a 15-year-old girl successfully appealed the magistrates' decision to exclude her from a hearing, on the grounds that: (i) they failed to balance her interests against the risk of her behaving in an unruly manner; (ii) reached the decision to exclude her without hearing from her guardian or solicitor; and (iii) refused to allow her solicitor an opportunity of seeing her before the hearing.

Role of children's guardian in secure accommodation proceedings—The welfare of the child is not the paramount consideration, and although it remains relevant, CA 1989, s 1 does not apply. The guardian has to adapt his general duties to the specific requirements of the application before the court and recommend what he believes to be in the best interests of the child (*Re M (Secure Accommodation Order)* [1995] 1 FLR 418, CA).

Specified placement—Although it is desirable that a specified placement is identified in the order, it is not a prerequisite for an order to be made under the section: *Re A (A Child)* [2015] EWHC 1709 (Fam).

Duration of order—A s 25 order runs from the date of the court order and not from the date when the child is actually placed in secure accommodation (*Re B (A Minor) (Secure Accommodation)* [1994] 2 FLR 707, CA). The power to make an interim order is confined to circumstances when the application is adjourned. That power is commonly used where the court lacks sufficient information to justify a finding on the s 25(1) criteria (*Re A (Secure Accommodation Order)* [2001] Fam Law 806, FD). A free-standing application for an *interim* secure accommodation order cannot be made. Where the court is satisfied it has all the information needed to determine the issues raised by the application, and that it would be procedurally fair to proceed, it is unlikely there would be grounds upon which the court could properly adjourn the application. Prolonging secure accommodation proceedings simply in order to keep a children's guardian involved for the purposes of assisting the child or overseeing the performance of the local authority's statutory duties, was not a proper use of the court's power (*Birmingham City Council v M* [2008] 2 FLR 542, FD).

Where an interim order is made, the court, at the adjourned hearing, is still seised of the original application and must take into account the interim period as part of the maximum period of secure accommodation permitted by the regulations (*C v Humberside County Council* [1994] 2 FLR 759, FD). A local authority cannot lawfully keep a child in secure accommodation within the maximum period specified in an order under s 25(4), or the maximum period permitted without the authority of the court, at a time when the local authority itself does not consider the criteria in s 25(1) continue to be met (*LM v Essex County Council* [1999] 1 FLR 988, FD). It is unclear whether the authority can lawfully keep the child in secure accommodation for some further period (provided it is within the maximum period specified in the order) while suitable alternative arrangements are made. There is no provision for discharge of secure accommodation orders within s 25. Once a s 25 order has been made, the Family Court cannot discharge or set the order aside if the facts subsequently change, nor can a higher court do so under CA 1989, s 94, unless the order has been incorrectly made. Where the local authority themselves no longer considered that the criteria were satisfied, the proper remedy was a writ of habeas corpus under CPR 1998, Pt 50, Sch 1 and PDRSC54 (*LM v Essex County Council* (above)). Where there is disagreement as to whether the criteria are still satisfied, the role of the local authority is susceptible to judicial review and that is likely to be the most appropriate remedy (see *S v Knowsley Borough Council* [2004] 2 FLR 716, FD). The court does not have power to make an order under s 25 in respect of someone who is already 16 and is being accommodated under s 20(5), but does have power to make an order in respect of a child who is not yet 16, and therefore not yet accommodated under s 20(5), even if the period of the order extends beyond the child's 16th birthday and thereafter the child's accommodation will fall under s 20(5) (*Re G (Secure Accommodation)* [2000] 2 FLR 259, CA). (Note the court does have the power to make an order under s 25 in respect of a young person who is 16 or older and is accommodated under s 20(3) or is the subject of a care order.)

Appropriate court—Where a child has been remanded to local authority accommodation by a youth court pursuant to Criminal Justice Act 1991, s 60(3), any application by the local authority under CA 1989, s 25 should be made to the appropriate youth court rather than the Family Court (*Liverpool City Council v B* [1995] 2 FLR 84, FD; *Re G (Secure Accommodation Order)* [2001] 1 FLR 884, FD; and see C(SA)R 1991, reg 6 in Part IV).

Placement out of England—Where it is proposed to place a child or young person in a secure unit outside of England and which, therefore, has not been approved by the Secretary of State, the placement can be authorised by the High Court under the inherent jurisdiction: *Re X (A Child), Re Y (A Child)* [2016] EWHC 2271 (Fam). Where such a placement is authorised, the local authority must apply to the Court of Session in Scotland for a mirror order under the nobile officium: *Cumbria County Council, Petitioner* [2016] CSIH 92.

Relationship between secure accommodation orders and refusal of bail—Where magistrates decide that bail is inappropriate in relation to children charged with criminal offences, it does not follow that the court is bound in principle to make a secure accommodation order; it is open to the court to consider other methods of disposal, such as remanding the children to local authority accommodation and imposing conditions on them (*Re W and D (Secure Accommodation)* [1995] 2 FLR 807, FD; and see C(SA)R 1991, reg 6 in Part IV). Note that in respect of children aged 12 or over but under the age of 18 who are detained under PACE 1984, s 38(6), the criteria set out in s 1 are modified by C(SA)R 1991, reg 6(1)(a): see SI 2015/1883. The modified criteria are set out in C(SA)R 1991, reg 6(2)(a),(b).

PART II

Independent reviewing officers

25A Appointment of independent reviewing officer

(1) If a local authority are looking after a child, they must appoint an individual as the independent reviewing officer for that child's case.

(2) The initial appointment under subsection (1) must be made before the child's case is first reviewed in accordance with regulations made under section 26.

(3) If a vacancy arises in respect of a child's case, the local authority must make another appointment under subsection (1) as soon as is practicable.

(4) An appointee must be of a description prescribed in regulations made by the Secretary of State.

Amendments—Inserted by CYPA 2008, s 10. Amended by SI 2016/413.

25B Functions of the independent reviewing officer

(1) The independent reviewing officer must –

- (a) monitor the performance by the local authority of their functions in relation to the child's case;
- (b) participate, in accordance with regulations made by the Secretary of State, in any review of the child's case;
- (c) ensure that any ascertained wishes and feelings of the child concerning the case are given due consideration by the local authority;
- (d) perform any other function which is prescribed in regulations made by the Secretary of State.

(2) An independent reviewing officer's functions must be performed –

- (a) in such manner (if any) as may be prescribed in regulations made by the Secretary of State; and
- (b) having regard to such guidance as that authority may issue in relation to the discharge of those functions.

(3) If the independent reviewing officer considers it appropriate to do so, the child's case may be referred by that officer to –

- (a) an officer of the Children and Family Court Advisory and Support Service.
- (b) *(repealed)*

(4) If the independent reviewing officer is not an officer of the local authority, it is the duty of the authority –

(a) to co-operate with that individual; and

(b) to take all such reasonable steps as that individual may require of them to enable that individual's functions under this section to be performed satisfactorily.

Amendments—Inserted by CYPA 2008, s 10. Amended by SI 2016/413.

Functions of Independent Reviewing Officers (IROs)—The functions of IROs are to participate in the review process, chair the review meeting, monitor the local authority's functions in respect of the review and refer the case to Cafcass if the IRO considers it appropriate to do so. The Care Planning, Placement and Case Review (England) Regulations 2010, which came into force on 1 April 2011 (see Part IV), set out the requirements for the qualifications and experience of IROs (reg 46). Reg 45 sets out their additional functions, including the duty to: ensure that the child has been informed of his right to apply, with leave, for a CA 1989, s 8 order and, where he is in the care of the local authority, to apply for the discharge of the care order; ensure that the child has been informed about the procedure for making representations and complaints to the authority; and ensure that if the child wishes to take legal proceedings under CA 1989 he has access to legal advice. Where appropriate, the IRO must ensure that the authority has given due consideration to the child's wishes and feelings, and must consider whether to request a review of his case (reg 45(4)). Concerns have been expressed about the independence of IROs. They may be wholly independent of, or employed by, the local authority. If the latter, then they should not be subject to the same line management that is responsible for the decision-making in relation to the care plan. The *IRO Handbook* (see *www.gov.uk/government/publications/independent-reviewing-officers-handbook*) provides guidance to IROs about how they should discharge their distinct responsibilities to looked-after children. It also provides guidance to local authorities on their strategic and managerial responsibilities in establishing an effective IRO service and replaces the 2004 *Independent Reviewing Officers Guidance*. For further detailed guidance on the proper role of the IRO and the steps required to ensure the IRO's effectiveness, see *A and S v Lancashire County Council* [2013] 2 FLR 803, FD and *S (A Child Acting by the Official Solicitor) v Rochdale Metropolitan Borough Council and the Independent Reviewing Officer* [2009] 1 FLR 1090, FD.

Referral to Cafcass (s 25B(3))—In the circumstances defined in Care Planning, Placement and Case Review (England) Regulations 2010, reg 45(3), the IRO must consider whether it would be appropriate to refer the child's case to a Cafcass officer. Cafcass Legal will only be able to accept referrals from IROs and their options would be to: reject the referral; attempt to resolve the matter by mediation; refer the matter to another agency; or bring civil proceedings against the local authority. If further proceedings under CA 1989 are required, Cafcass Legal will refer the case back to the children's guardian from the care proceedings: see the Children and Family Court Advisory and Support Service (Reviewed Case Referral) Regulations 2004, which empower officers of Cafcass Legal to bring civil actions against local authorities. If a civil action is brought against the local authority, one of the social work practitioners in Cafcass Legal will act as the child's litigation friend. The options for civil action are: judicial review proceedings; a compensation claim; or a freestanding HRA 1998 application (for the latter, see *A and S v Lancashire County Council* [2013] 2 FLR 803, FD). For detailed guidance on the functions and duties of Cafcass in relation to referrals made to it in accordance with s 25B(3)(a), see the Cafcass Practice Note of April 2011 in Part V. See further **Procedure for raising issues under the Human Rights Act 1998** under CA 1989, s 31, and annotation to HRA 1998.

25C Referred cases

(1) In relation to children whose cases are referred to officers under section 25B(3), the Lord Chancellor may by regulations –

(a) extend any functions of the officers in respect of family proceedings (within the meaning of section 12 of the Criminal Justice and Court Services Act 2000) to other proceedings;

(b) require any functions of the officers to be performed in the manner prescribed by the regulations.

(2) *(repealed)*

Amendments—Inserted by CYPA 2008, s 10. Amended by SI 2016/413.

Supplemental

26 Review of cases and inquiries into representations

(1) The Secretary of State may make regulations requiring the case of each child who is being looked after by a local authority to be reviewed in accordance with the provisions of the regulations.

(2) The regulations may, in particular, make provision –

(a) as to the manner in which each case is to be reviewed;

(b) as to the considerations to which the local authority are to have regard in reviewing each case;

(c) as to the time when each case is first to be reviewed and the frequency of subsequent reviews;

(d) requiring the authority, before conducting any review, to seek the views of –

(i) the child;

(ii) his parents;

(iii) any person who is not a parent of his but who has parental responsibility for him; and

(iv) any other person whose views the authority consider to be relevant, including, in particular, the views of those persons in relation to any particular matter which is to be considered in the course of the review;

(e) requiring the authority, in the case of a child who is in their care –

(i) to keep the section 31A plan for the child under review and, if they are of the opinion that some change is required, to revise the plan, or make a new plan, accordingly,

(ii) to consider whether an application should be made to discharge the care order;

(f) requiring the authority, in the case of a child in accommodation provided by the authority –

(i) if there is no plan for the future care of the child, to prepare one,

(ii) if there is such a plan for the child, to keep it under review and, if they are of the opinion that some change is required, to revise the plan or make a new plan, accordingly,

(iii) to consider whether the accommodation accords with the requirements of this Part;

(g) requiring the authority to inform the child, so far as is reasonably practicable, of any steps he may take under this Act;

(h) requiring the authority to make arrangements, including arrangements with such other bodies providing services as it considers appropriate, to implement any decision which they propose to make in the course, or as a result, of the review;

(i) requiring the authority to notify details of the result of the review and of any decision taken by them in consequence of the review to –

(i) the child;

(ii) his parents;

(iii) any person who is not a parent of his but who has had parental responsibility for him; and

(iv) any other person whom they consider ought to be notified;

(j) requiring the authority to monitor the arrangements which they have made with a view to ensuring that they comply with the regulations;

(k) for the authority to appoint a person in respect of each case to carry out in the prescribed manner the functions mentioned in subsection (2A) and any prescribed function.

(2A) The functions referred to in subsection (2)(k) are –

(a) participating in the review of the case in question,

(b) monitoring the performance of the authority's functions in respect of the review,

(c) referring the case to an officer of the Children and Family Court Advisory and Support Service or a Welsh family proceedings officer, if the person appointed under subsection (2)(k) considers it appropriate to do so.

(2B) A person appointed under subsection (2)(k) must be a person of a prescribed description.

(2C) In relation to children whose cases are referred to officers under subsection (2A)(c), the Lord Chancellor may by regulations –

(a) extend any functions of the officers in respect of family proceedings (within the meaning of section 12 of the Criminal Justice and Court Services Act 2000) to other proceedings,
(b) require any functions of the officers to be performed in the manner prescribed by the regulations.

(2D) The power to make regulations in subsection (2C) is exercisable in relation to functions of Welsh family proceedings officers only with the consent of the Welsh Ministers.

(3) Every local authority shall establish a procedure for considering any representations (including any complaint) made to them by –

(a) any child who is being looked after by them or who is not being looked after by them but is in need;
(b) a parent of his;
(c) any person who is not a parent of his but who has parental responsibility for him;
(d) any local authority foster parent;
(e) such other person as the authority consider has a sufficient interest in the child's welfare to warrant his representations being considered by them,

about the discharge of the authority of any of their qualifying functions in relation to the child.

(3A) The following are qualifying functions for the purposes of subsection (3) –

(a) functions under this Part,
(b) such functions under Part 4 or 5 as are specified by the Secretary of State in regulations.

(3B) The duty under subsection (3) extends to representations (including complaints) made to the authority by –

(a) any person mentioned in section 3(1) of the Adoption and Children Act 2002 (persons for whose needs provision is made by the Adoption Service) and any other person to whom arrangements for the provision of adoption support services (within the meaning of that Act) extend,
(b) such other person as the authority consider has sufficient interest in a child who is or may be adopted to warrant his representations being considered by them,

about the discharge by the authority of such functions under the Adoption and Children Act 2002 as are specified by the Secretary of State in regulations.

(3C) The duty under subsection (3) extends to any representations (including complaints) which are made to the authority by –

(a) a child with respect to whom a special guardianship order is in force,
(b) a special guardian or a parent of such a child,
(c) any other person the authority consider has a sufficient interest in the welfare of such a child to warrant his representations being considered by them, or
(d) any person who has applied for an assessment under section 14F(3) or (4), about the discharge by the authority of such functions under section 14F as may be specified by the Secretary of State in regulations.

(4) The procedure shall ensure that at least one person who is not a member or officer of the authority takes part in –

(a) the consideration; and
(b) any discussions which are held by the authority about the action (if any) to be taken in relation to the child in the light of the consideration

but this subsection is subject to subsection (5A).

(4A) Regulations may be made by the Secretary of State imposing time limits on the making of representations under this section.

(5) In carrying out any consideration of representations under this section a local authority shall comply with any regulations made by the Secretary of State for the purpose of regulating the procedure to be followed.

(5A) Regulations under subsection (5) may provide that subsection (4) does not apply in relation to any consideration or discussion which takes place as part of a procedure for which provision is made by the regulations for the purpose of resolving informally the matters raised in the representations.

(6) The Secretary of State may make regulations requiring local authorities to monitor the arrangements that they have made with a view to ensuring that they comply with any regulations made for the purposes of subsection (5).

(7) Where any representation has been considered under the procedure established by a local authority under this section, the authority shall –

(a) have due regard to the findings of those considering the representation; and

(b) take such steps as are reasonably practicable to notify (in writing) –

(i) the person making the representation;

(ii) the child (if the authority consider that he has sufficient understanding); and

(iii) such other persons (if any) as appear to the authority to be likely to be affected,

of the authority's decision in the matter and their reasons for taking that decision and of any action which they have taken, or propose to take.

(8) Every local authority shall give such publicity to their procedure for considering representations under this section as they consider appropriate.

Amendments—ACA 2002, ss 117, 118, 139; Health and Social Care (Community Health and Standards) Act 2003, s 117; CA 2004, s 40, Sch 3, paras 5, 8(1)–(3); CYPA 2008, s 39, Sch 3, paras 1, 16; SI 2016/413, subject to saving provisions.

Section 26 and judicial review—For the potential relevance of the s 26 representation procedure in judicial review proceedings, see under CA 1989, s 84 and see Children Act 1989 Representations Procedure (England) Regulations 2006, reg 8(1).

Scope of complaints procedure—In deciding not to apply for a care order, the local authority is exercising a function under CA 1989, Pt III and the complaints procedure is applicable to such a decision (*R v East Sussex CC ex parte W* [1998] 2 FLR 1082, QBD).

Duty to consider representations made by a parent – (s 26(3)(b))—The duty of the local authority to establish a procedure to consider any representations made to them by the persons named in s 26(3) is directory and not mandatory; the result of any non-compliance with the provisions should be treated as an irregularity (*Re P (Children Act 1989, ss 22 and 26: Local Authority Compliance)* [2000] 2 FLR 910, FD). In exceptional circumstances the court has power to make a declaration that the local authority be absolved from the duty to provide information to a parent and from the duty to consult them in any way about the child (*Re C (Care: Consultation with Parents Not in Child's Best Interests)* [2006] 2 FLR 787, FD).

Review of cases of looked-after children—ACA 2002, s 118 created the role of independent reviewing officer (IRO) and amended CA 1989, s 26(2)(e) (requirement to consider the discharge of a care order) to encompass a review of the care plan and revision of it as necessary. Once a care order has been made, the responsibility for the child is transferred to the local authority, removing it from the control of the court even in cases where a judge feels that it is necessary for the court to monitor the progress of the child in care. See **Functions of Independent Reviewing Officers (IROs)** under CA 1989, s 25B.

26ZB *(repealed)*

26A Advocacy services

(1) Every local authority shall make arrangements for the provision of assistance to –

(a) persons who make or intend to make representations under section 24D; and

(b) children who make or intend to make representations under section 26.

(2) The assistance provided under the arrangements shall include assistance by way of representation.

…

(3) The arrangements –

(a) shall secure that a person may not provide assistance if he is a person who is prevented from doing so by regulations made by the Secretary of State; and

(b) shall comply with any other provision made by the regulations in relation to the arrangements.

(4) The Secretary of State may make regulations requiring local authorities to monitor the steps that they have taken with a view to ensuring that they comply with regulations made for the purposes of subsection (3).

(5) Every local authority shall give such publicity to their arrangements for the provision of assistance under this section as they consider appropriate.

Amendments—Inserted by ACA 2002, s 119. Amended by CYPA 2008, s 39, Sch 3, paras 1, 18; SI 2016/413.

27 Co-operation between authorities

(1) Where it appears to a local authority that any authority mentioned in subsection (3) could, by taking any specified action, help in the exercise of any of their functions under this Part, they may request the help of that other authority, specifying the action in question.

(2) An authority whose help is so requested shall comply with the request if it is compatible with their own statutory or other duties and obligations and does not unduly prejudice the discharge of any of their functions.

(3) The authorities are –

- (a) any local authority;
- (b) *(repealed)*
- (c) any local housing authority;
- (ca) the National Health Service Commissioning Board;
- (d) any clinical commissioning group, Local Health Board, Special Health Authority, National Health Service trust or NHS foundation trust;
- (da) any local authority in Wales; and
- (e) any person authorised by the Secretary of State for the purposes of this section.

(3A) The Secretary of State must not authorise the Welsh Ministers under subsection (3)(e) without their consent.

(4) *(repealed)*

Amendments—CLSA 1990, ss 116, 125(7), Sch 16, para 14, Sch 20; Education Act 1993, s 307, Sch 19, para 147, Sch 21, Pt II; Health Authorities Act 1995, s 2, Sch 1, para 118; SI 2000/90; Health and Social Care (Community Health and Standards) Act 2003, s 34, Sch 4, para 78; SI 2007/961; CYPA 2008, s 39, Sch 3, paras 1, 19; SI 2010/1158; Health and Social Care Act 2012, s 55(2), Sch 5, para 51; SI 2016/413.

28 *(repealed)*

29 Recoupment of cost of providing services etc

(1) Where a local authority provide any service under section 17 or 18, other than advice, guidance or counselling, they may recover from a person specified in subsection (4) such charge for the service as they consider reasonable.

(2) Where the authority are satisfied that that person's means are insufficient for it to be reasonably practicable for him to pay the charge, they shall not require him to pay more than he can reasonably be expected to pay.

(3) No person shall be liable to pay any charge under subsection (1) for a service provided under section 17 or section 18(1) or (5) at any time when he is in receipt of universal credit (except in such circumstances as may be prescribed), of income support under Part VII of the Social Security Contributions and Benefits Act 1992, of any element of child tax credit other than the family element, of working tax credit, of an income-based jobseeker's allowance or of an income-related employment and support allowance.

(3A) No person shall be liable to pay any charge under subsection (1) for a service provided under section 18(2) or (6) at any time when he is in receipt of universal credit (except in such circumstances as may be prescribed), of income support under Part VII of the Social Security and Benefits Act 1992, of an income-based jobseeker's allowance or of an income-related employment and support allowance.

(3B) No person shall be liable to pay any charge under subsection (1) for a service provided under section 18(2) or (6) at any time when –

(a) he is in receipt of guarantee state pension credit under section 1(3)(a) of the State Pension Credit Act 2002, or

(b) he is a member of a couple (within the meaning of that Act) the other member of which is in receipt of guarantee state pension credit.

(4) The persons are –

(a) where the service is provided for a child under sixteen, each of his parents;

(b) where it is provided for a child who has reached the age of sixteen, the child himself; and

(c) where it is provided for a member of the child's family, that member.

(5) Any charge under subsection (1) may, without prejudice to any other method of recovery, be recovered summarily as a civil debt.

(6) Part III of Schedule 2 makes provision in connection with contributions towards the maintenance of children who are being looked after by local authorities and consists of the re-enactment with modifications of provisions in Part V of the Child Care Act 1980.

(7) Where a local authority provide any accommodation under section 20(1) for a child who was (immediately before they began to look after him) ordinarily resident within the area of another local authority or the area of a local authority in Wales, they may recover from that other authority any reasonable expenses incurred by them in providing the accommodation and maintaining him.

(8) Where a local authority provide accommodation under section 21(1) or (2)(a) or (b) for a child who is ordinarily resident within the area of another local authority or the area of a local authority in Wales and they are not maintaining him in –

(a) a community home provided by them;

(b) a controlled community home; or

(c) a hospital vested in the Secretary of State or the Welsh Ministers, or any other hospital made available pursuant to arrangements made by the Secretary of State, the National Health Service Commissioning Board or a clinical commissioning group under the National Health Service Act 2006 or by Local Health Board,

they may recover from that other authority any reasonable expenses incurred by them in providing the accommodation and maintaining him.

(9) Except where subsection (10) or subsection (11) applies, where a local authority comply with any request under section 27(2) or section 164A(2) of the Social Services and Wellbeing (Wales) Act 2014 (duty of other persons to co-operate and provide information) in relation to a child or other person who is not ordinarily resident within their area, they may recover from the local authority or a local authority in Wales in whose area the child or person is ordinarily resident any reasonable expenses incurred by them in respect of that person.

(10) Where a local authority ('authority A') comply with any request under section 27(2) from another local authority ('authority B') in relation to a child or other person –

(a) whose responsible authority is authority B for the purposes of section 23B or 23C; or

(b) whom authority B are advising or befriending or to whom they are giving assistance by virtue of section 24(5)(a),

authority A may recover from authority B any reasonable expenses incurred by them in respect of that person.

(11) Where a local authority ('authority A') comply with any request under section 164A(2) of the Social Services and Well-being (Wales) Act 2014 (duty of other persons to co-operate and provide information) from a local authority in Wales ('authority B') in relation to a person, and authority B are the responsible local authority for that person (within the meaning of section 104(5)(b) (except for category 4 young persons) or (d) of that Act), then authority A may recover from authority B any reasonable expenses incurred by them in respect of that person.

Amendments—CLSA 1990, s 116, Sch 16, para 15; National Health Service and Community Care Act 1990, s 66(1), Sch 9, para 36(3); Disability Living Allowance and Disability Working Allowance Act 1991, s 7(2), Sch 3, para 14; Social Security (Consequential Provisions) Act 1992, s 4, Sch 2, para 108; Health Authorities Act 1995, s 2, Sch 1, para 118; Jobseekers Act 1995, s 41, Sch 2, para 19; Tax Credits Act 1999, s 1(2), Sch 1,

PART II

paras 1, 6(d)(ii); Children (Leaving Care) Act 2000, s 7; Local Government Act 2000, s 103; SI 2000/90; Tax Credits Act 2002, s 47, Sch 3, paras 15, 18; SI 2002/2469; State Pension Credit Act 2002, s 14, Sch 2, para 30; SI 2005/3129; SI 2007/961; Welfare Reform Act 2007, s 28(1), Sch 3, para 6; CYPA 2008, s 39, Sch 3, paras 1, 20; Health and Social Care Act 2012, s 55(2), Sch 5, para 52; Welfare Reform Act 2012, s 31, Sch 2, para 1; SI 2016/413.

30 Miscellaneous

(1) Nothing in this Part shall affect any duty imposed on a local authority by or under any other enactment.

(2) Any question arising under section 20(2), 21(3) or 29(7) to (9) as to the ordinary residence of a child shall be determined by agreement between the local authorities concerned or, in default of agreement, by the Secretary of State but see subsection (2C).

(2A), (2B) *(repealed)*

(2C) Any question arising as to whether a child is ordinarily resident –

(a) in the area of a local authority under section 20(2), 21(3) or 29(7) to (9), or
(b) in the area of a local authority in Wales under section 76(2), 77(4) or (5), or 193(3) to (6) of the Social Services and Well-being (Wales) Act 2014,

shall be determined by the local authority and local authority in Wales concerned, or in default of agreement, by the Secretary of State.

(2D) The Secretary of State must consult the Welsh Ministers before making a determination under subsection (2C).

(3) *(repealed)*

(4) The Secretary of State may make regulations for determining, as respects any education functions specified in the regulations, whether a child who is being looked after by a local authority is to be treated, for purposes so specified, as a child of parents of sufficient resources or as a child of parents without resources.

Amendments—CYPA 2008, s 39, Sch 3, paras 1, 21; SI 2010/1158; SI 2016/413.

30A *(repealed)*

PART IV
CARE AND SUPERVISION

General

31 Care and supervision orders

(1) On the application of any local authority or authorised person, the court may make an order –

(a) placing the child with respect to whom the application is made in the care of a designated local authority; or
(b) putting him under the supervision of a designated local authority.

(2) A court may only make a care order or supervision order if it is satisfied –

(a) that the child concerned is suffering, or is likely to suffer, significant harm; and
(b) that the harm, or likelihood of harm, is attributable to –
    (i) the care given to the child, or likely to be given to him if the order were not made, not being what it would be reasonable to expect a parent to give to him; or
    (ii) the child's being beyond parental control.

(3) No care order or supervision order may be made with respect to a child who has reached the age of seventeen (or sixteen, in the case of a child who is married).

(3A) A court deciding whether to make a care order –

(a) is required to consider the permanence provisions of the section 31A plan for the child concerned, but

(b) is not required to consider the remainder of the section 31A plan, subject to section 34(11).

(3B) For the purposes of subsection (3A), the permanence provisions of a section 31A plan are such of the plan's provisions setting out the longterm plan for the upbringing of the child concerned as provide for any of the following –

(a) the child to live with any parent of the child's or with any other member of, or any friend of, the child's family;
(b) adoption;
(c) long-term care not within paragraph (a) or (b).

(3C) The Secretary of State may by regulations amend this section for the purpose of altering what for the purposes of subsection (3A) are the permanence provisions of a section 31A plan.

(4) An application under this section may be made on its own or in any other family proceedings.

(5) The court may –

(a) on an application for a care order, make a supervision order;
(b) on an application for a supervision order, make a care order.

(6) Where an authorised person proposes to make an application under this section he shall –

(a) if it is reasonably practicable to do so; and
(b) before making the application,

consult the local authority appearing to him to be the authority in whose area the child concerned is ordinarily resident.

(7) An application made by an authorised person shall not be entertained by the court if, at the time when it is made, the child concerned is –

(a) the subject of an earlier application for a care order, or supervision order, which has not been disposed of; or
(b) subject to –
  (i) a care order or supervision order;
  (ii) a youth rehabilitation order within the meaning of Part 1 of the Criminal Justice and Immigration Act 2008; or
  (iii) a supervision requirement within the meaning of Part II of the Children (Scotland) Act 1995.

(8) The local authority designated in a care order must be –

(a) the authority within whose area the child is ordinarily resident; or
(b) where the child does not reside in the area of a local authority, the authority within whose area any circumstances arose in consequence of which the order is being made.

(9) In this section –

'authorised person' means –
  (a) the National Society for the Prevention of Cruelty to Children and any of its officers; and
  (b) any person authorised by order of the Secretary of State to bring proceedings under this section and any officer of a body which is so authorised;

'harm' means ill-treatment or the impairment of health or development including, for example, impairment suffered from seeing or hearing the ill-treatment of another;

'development' means physical, intellectual, emotional, social or behavioural development;

'health' means physical or mental health; and

'ill-treatment' includes sexual abuse and forms of ill-treatment which are not physical.

(10) Where the question of whether harm suffered by a child is significant turns on the child's health or development, his health or development shall be compared with that which could reasonably be expected of a similar child.

(11) In this Act –

'a care order' means (subject to section 105(1)) an order under subsection (1)(a) and (except where express provision to the contrary is made) includes an interim care order made under section 38; and

'a supervision order' means an order under subsection (1)(b) and (except where express provision to the contrary is made) includes an interim supervision order made under section 38.

Amendments—Children (Scotland) Act 1995, s 105(4), Sch 4, para 48(1),(2); CJCSA 2000 ss 74, 75, Sch 7, paras 87, 90; Powers of Criminal Courts (Sentencing) Act 2000, s 165, Sch 9, para 127; ACA 2002, ss 120, 121; Criminal Justice and Immigration Act 2008, ss 6(2), 149, Sch 4, para 35; CFA 2014, s 15.

Modifications—Section 31 is modified for certain purposes by SI 2010/1898, reg 5(3) and by SI 2013/1465, art 17, Sch 1, para 2.

Defined terms—'authorised person': s 31(9); 'care order': ss 31(11), 105(1); 'child'; s 105(1); 'family proceedings': s 8(3); 'local authority': s 105(1); 'supervision order': s 31(11).

Allocation of applications for care or supervision orders—Under FC(CDB)R 2014, r 20(2), when deciding to which level of judge of the Family Court an application for a care or supervision order is to be allocated, the decision must be taken based on consideration of the relative significance of the need to make most effective and efficient use of judicial resources, the need to avoid delay, the need for judicial continuity, the location of the parties and the child and the complexity of the case. FC(CDB)R 2014 should be read with the President's guidance of 22 April 2014 on *Allocation and Gatekeeping* and *Continuity and Deployment* (both set out in Part V).

Jurisdiction—European Council Regulation (EC) No 2201/2003 concerning Jurisdiction and the Recognition and Enforcement in Judgments in Matrimonial Matters and Matters of Parental Responsibility (Brussels IIA) (see Part VI) applies to care proceedings under CA 1989, Pt IV (*Re A (Area of Freedom, Security and Justice)* [2009] 2 FLR 1, ECJ and *Re C* [2008] 1 FLR 490, ECJ). Note that care proceedings where the care plan is for adoption are not a 'measure preparatory' to adoption for the purposes of Art 1(3)(b) (*Re N (Adoption: Jurisdiction)* [2016] 1 FLR 621, CA).

The question of habitual residence must be addressed by the court at the outset of proceedings whether raised by the parties or not (*Re N*, above, and *Re F (A Child)* [2014] EWCA Civ 789). The starting point in considering the question of jurisdiction under Brussels IIA is the examination of habitual residence pursuant to Art 8 of that Regulation (*Re B (Care Order: Jurisdiction)* [2014] 1 FLR 900, CA). Where the child is habitually resident in England and Wales for the purposes of Art 8, the domestic court will have jurisdiction. Where the domestic court considers that it does not have jurisdiction and that the court of another Member State does have jurisdiction, the domestic court must declare that it has no jurisdiction whether or not there are proceedings in another Member State (Re B, above, and *Re E (Brussels II Revised: Vienna Convention: Reporting Restrictions)* [2014] 2 FLR 151, FD).

As to the meaning of 'habitual residence' in this context, see **'Habitually resident'** under Art 8 of Council Regulation (EC) No 2201/2003 in Part VI and *Re A (Jurisdiction: Return of Child)* [2014] 1 FLR 111, SC and see further under CA 1989, s 105(6) and CACA 1985, Sch 1, Art 4. The widest permissible approach should be adopted for the jurisdictional basis for an application under CA 1989, Pt IV. Habitual residence is a child-centred concept and not one focused on the parent. If possible, it should be established where the child considers him or herself to be integrated. Where the court is unable to determine the habitual residence of the child by reference to the test in *Re A* (above), the court can proceed on the basis of jurisdiction under Art 13 of Brussels IIA (presence in the jurisdiction (*Lambeth LBC v JO* [2014] EWHC 3597 (Fam)). Where a child living in England at the time of the application is habitually resident in Scotland, the child's presence at the time of the application will give the English court jurisdiction throughout the currency of the proceedings (*Re M (Care Orders: Jurisdiction)* [1997] 1 FLR 456, FD). A parent or child's diplomatic immunity does not act to oust jurisdiction under CA 1989, s 31 (*Re B (Care Proceedings: Diplomatic Immunity)* [2003] 1 FLR 241, FD).

Where the child is habitually resident in a state that is not a Member State of the European Union but is a Contracting State of the Hague Convention on Jurisdiction, Applicable Law, Recognition, Enforcement and Co-Operation in Respect of Parental Responsibility and Measures for the Protection of Children 1996, the latter Convention will apply (see Part IV). Thus, in what will be the vast majority of cases, where the child who is subject to proceedings under CA 1989, Pt IV is habitually resident in the European Union, in respect of matters falling within its scope, Brussels IIA must be applied. In a smaller number of cases where the child is habitually resident in a state that is not subject to Brussels IIA but is a party to the 1996 Convention, the 1996 Convention will apply.

Where there are both care proceedings and proceedings under the Hague Convention on the Civil Aspects of International Child Abduction 1980 on foot at the same time, it is likely that input from the local authority into the proceedings under the Hague Convention will be extremely valuable in many cases and indispensable in some cases (*Re B (Hague Convention Proceedings)* [2015] 1 FLR 389, CA). The Government has issued departmental guidance for local authorities on Council Regulation (EC) No 2201/2003 and the 1996 Hague Convention (see *Cross-border child protection cases: the 1996 Hague Convention* (October 2012, Department of Education) and *Working with foreign authorities: child protection and court orders* (September 2014, Department of Education). In Wales, see *Handling cross-border child protection cases*, published by the Welsh Government).

Note that an appeal against a decision of the High Court declining to recognise and enforce an order of another Member State concerning the parental responsibility for a child may be made to the Court of Appeal, but there is no further right of appeal to the Supreme Court (*Re D (A Child) (Supreme Court: Jurisdiction)* [2016] 2 FLR 379, SC).

Jurisdiction and case management—In every care case with a foreign dimension, jurisdiction should be identified as an issue: when the application for a care or supervision order is made, during the process of issue and allocation; and at the Case Management Hearing to ensure timely directions are given for determination of the question of jurisdiction (*S v Slough Borough Council and others* [2009] All ER (D) 182 (Apr), FD; *Re S (Care: Jurisdiction)* [2009] 2 FLR 550, FD; *Tower Hamlets LBC v MK and others* [2012] 2 FLR 762, FD; *Re E (A Child)* above; *Re M (Brussels II Revised: Art 15)* [2014] 2 FLR 1372, CA; *Kent County Council v C, G and A* [2015] 1 FLR 115, FD; *Re B (Hague Convention Proceedings)*, above; and *Re F (A Child)* [2014] EWCA Civ 789). The latter authorities make clear that in care cases with a foreign dimension the following procedure should be adopted from the outset:

(a) The local authority should make a prompt assessment of the needs and risks to the child to determine an action plan;
(b) The local authority should immediately notify both parents (including a parent who lives abroad) and any adult involved with the child to tell them what has happened, to inform them of their rights (including under the Hague Conventions where appropriate) and obtain their views about the placement sought for the child;
(c) Once contacted, the parties and, if necessary, the court should take active steps to assist the parents to secure legal representation;
(d) The local authority should give notice to the consulate of the relevant country to inform them of the situation and, where they have not been located, seek assistance in finding the parents, with care being taken to recognise the relevant jurisdictional points and thus the roles of the respective national authorities (see the commentary below regarding *Re E (Brussels II Revised: Vienna Convention: Reporting Restrictions)* [2014] 2 FLR 151, FD);
(e) The local authority should apply for a prompt hearing, on notice if possible, at which hearing should be considered:
    (i) the circumstances of the case and the local authority's proposals for the child;
    (ii) the possibility of transfer to a judge of High Court level;
    (iii) the interim arrangements;
    (iv) the international obligations and any relevant Convention rights; and
    (v) the issues requiring resolution;
(f) The court should thereafter timetable for determination any jurisdictional issues identified so as to avoid delay;
(g) The court cannot come to any final determination as to habitual residence until a proper opportunity has been given to all relevant parties to adduce evidence and make submissions. If a party chooses not to avail themselves of the opportunity then that is a matter for that party, although it is important that the court bears in mind that a declaration cannot be made by default, concession or agreement, but only if the court is satisfied by evidence;
(h) In determining questions of habitual residence at the case management stage, the court must apply the principles explained in *Re A (Jurisdiction: Return of Child)* [2014] 1 FLR 111, SC. The key principles are that the test of habitual residence is 'the place which reflects some degree of integration by the child in a social and family environment' in the country concerned and that, as the social and family environment of an infant or young child is shared with those (whether parents or others) upon whom he is dependent, it is necessary to assess the integration of that person or persons in the social and family environment of the country concerned;
(i) Having determined the question of habitual residence, the court must set out explicitly, both in its judgment and in its order, the basis upon which it has either accepted or rejected jurisdiction;
(j) A declaration as to habitual residence made on a 'without notice' application is valueless, potentially misleading and should never be granted. If it is necessary to address the issue of jurisdiction before there has been time for proper investigation and determination, the order should contain a recital along the lines of 'Upon it provisionally appearing that the child is habitually resident …'
(k) Once the matter has been finally determined, the order can contain either a declaration ('It is declared that …') or a recital ('Upon the court being satisfied that …') as to the child's habitual residence.

In *Re E (A Child)*, above, the President of the Family Division made clear that, having regard to the provisions of the Vienna Convention on Consular Relations Arts 36 and 37, as a matter of good practice the court should not in general impose or permit any obstacle to free communication and access between a party who is a foreign national and the consular authorities of the relevant foreign state. In particular, no injunctive or other order should be made that might interfere with such communication and access, nor should AJA 1960, s 12 be permitted to have that effect. Whenever the court is sitting in private, it should normally accede to any request, whether from the foreign national or from the consular authorities of the relevant foreign state, for permission for an accredited consular official to be present at the hearing as an observer in a non-participatory capacity and/or permission for an accredited consular official to obtain a transcript of the hearing, a copy of the order and copies of other relevant documents. Wherever a party, whether an adult or a child, who is a foreign national is represented by a Children's Guardian, guardian ad litem or litigation friend and/or is detained, the court should ascertain whether that fact has been brought to the attention of the relevant consular officials and, if it has not, the court should normally do so itself without delay.

Interim protective measures pending determination of jurisdiction—Pursuant to Art 20(1) of BIIA, the courts of a Member State may in an urgent case take provisional, including protective, measures

PART II

notwithstanding that another Member State has jurisdiction as to the substance of the proceedings (*Detiček v Sgueglia* (Case C–403/09) [2010] 1 FLR 1381, ECJ). Art 20 contemplates short-term holding arrangements (*Re B (Care Order: Jurisdiction)* [2014] 1 FLR 900, CA and *Re E (Brussels II Revised: Vienna Convention: Reporting Restrictions)* [2014] 2 FLR 151, FD). Such measures include the power to make interim orders, including interim care orders, in public law proceedings in respect of a child who is habitually resident in another Member State where the child is present in the Member State making the order (*Re A (Area of Freedom, Security and Justice)*, above; *Re S (Care: Jurisdiction)* (above)).

Where the 1996 Convention applies, a local authority that wishes to make an application under s 31 concerning a child in respect of whom the authorities of another Contracting State have jurisdiction under the 1996 Convention, must make an application to the High Court requesting that the court exercise its power under Art 9 of the Convention to request from the competent authority of that Contracting State authorisation to exercise jurisdiction (PRMPC(IO)(EWNI)R 2010, reg 4 (see Part IV)).

Request for another Member State to assume jurisdiction—Under Art 15(1) of Brussels IIA, the courts of a Member State having jurisdiction as to the substance of the matter under Art 8 may introduce a request before the court of that other Member State to assume jurisdiction or itself request the court of that other Member State to assume jurisdiction. In *Child and Family Agency v JD* (Case C-428/15), CJEU, the Court held that Art 15 will be applicable in public law proceedings commenced in one Member State even where a necessary consequence of transfer to the jurisdiction of another Member State would be the commencement of proceedings in that second Member State pursuant to its own domestic law and possibly relating to different factual circumstances, and that are separate from the proceedings commenced in the first Member State.

Article 15 provides an exceptional mechanism to transfer a (specific part of a) case to another Member State with which the child has a particular connection if that court is better placed to hear the case and it is in the best interests of the child. As to the exceptional nature of this mechanism, see *Re EC (Child Abduction: Stayed Proceedings)* [2007] 1 FLR 57, CA, *Mercredi v Chaffe* [2011] 2 FLR 515, CA, *A v B (Jurisdiction)* [2012] 1 FLR 768, FD and *J v J (Relinquishment of Jurisdiction)* [2012] 1 FLR 1259, FD. Article 15 applies only to questions of parental responsibility dealt with in Brussels IIA, Section 2. Note that care proceedings where the care plan is for adoption are not a 'measure preparatory' to adoption for the purposes of Art 1(3)(b) (*Re N (Adoption: Jurisdiction)* [2016] 1 FLR 621, CA). An application for a transfer under Art 15 creates a preliminary issue that must be tried before there can be any determination of the substantive issues (*Re K (A Child); sub nom Re T (A Child: Article 15 of Brussels II Revised)* [2014] 1 FLR 749, CA). Note, however, that in every case with a European dimension the court needs to consider whether to exercise its powers under Art 15 (*Re E (Brussels II Revised: Vienna Convention: Reporting Restrictions)* [2014] 2 FLR 151, FD). A collaborative approach and cooperation between judges is required as to the tier of judiciary to which contested Art 15 cases should go. District judges might consider that the work should go to circuit judges in their own court or to a High Court judge. Individual judges should discuss allocation with the Designated Family Judge and/or the Family Division Liaison Judge (*Re J (A Child: Brussels II Revised: Art 15 – Practice and Procedure)* [2014] EWFC 41). The procedure for transfer of proceedings under Art 15 is set out in FPR 2010, rr 12.61–12.66.

Art 15 contemplates a simple and straightforward process and does not require a full investigation of the merits of the case (*Re M (Brussels II Revised: Art 15)* [2014] 2 FLR 1372, CA and *Re I (A Child) (Contact Application: Jurisdiction)* [2010] 1 FLR 361, SC). The essential exercise under Art 15 is one of judicial evaluation (*Re N (Adoption: Jurisdiction)* [2016] 1 FLR 621, CA). It may be appropriate for the judge at the initial without notice stage to give directions for a hearing on notice at which the parents or local authority can argue that the court should not accept jurisdiction. However, this should not be automatic and, where the case appears clear cut, the court can, and ordinarily should, make an order nisi, i e an order that will take effect without further hearing unless the parents (or local authority) give notice of their wish to make further representations as to why the order should not be made.

The only court able to make the decision under Art 15 is the court having jurisdiction as to the substance of the matter, although a court not having such jurisdiction can make an application to the court with jurisdiction seeking a transfer under Art 15.2(c) (*Re H (Abduction)* [2009] 2 FLR 1513, FD). More than one such application may be made, but to justify a request for a reconsideration of an earlier decision it is not enough to demonstrate changed circumstances. It has to be shown that it is highly probable that the court seised would now come to a different decision because of a decisive change in circumstances (*AB v JLB (Brussels II Revised: Article 15)* [2009] 1 FLR 517, FD and see *Re MP (Fact Finding: Care Proceedings: Art 15)* [2014] 1 FLR 702, FD and *Re J and S (Children)* [2015] 1 FLR 850, FD). It is unnecessary for the English court to request a foreign court to transfer jurisdiction under Art 15 in relation to family proceedings involving a child, where it can properly assume jurisdiction under Art 8 where the child is habitually resident in England and where the foreign court's jurisdiction under Art 12.3 (prorogation of jurisdiction) has ceased (*Re S (Jurisdiction: Prorogation); sub nom PB v SE* [2013] 2 FLR 1584, FD).

An Art 15 transfer request should be made promptly through the International Judicial Network and should be accompanied by a request pursuant to Brussels IIA, Art 56 that the relevant competent authority consent to the placement of the child in the requested jurisdiction. Note that Brussels IIA, Art 56(1),(2) requires only (i) that a court that is considering authorising the placement of a child in institutional or foster care in another Member State consults the competent authority responsible for child placement in that Member State and (ii) that a court that is considering authorising the placement of a child in institutional or foster care in another Member State does not decide on any such placement without first obtaining that competent authority's consent (*Re AB (BIIR: Care Proceedings)* [2013] 1 FLR 168, CA; *Health Service Executive v SC and AC* [2012] 2 FLR 1040, CJEU). Art 56(1),(2) does not give a Member State an entitlement to call for the placement of the child within its jurisdiction (*Re AB (BIIR: Care Proceedings)*, above).

Where a transfer request under Brussels IIA, Art 15(1) has been made, a court in a Member State may only decline jurisdiction or declare that it does not have jurisdiction under Art 17 following a proper judicial process conducted within ongoing proceedings in that state. It is wholly inappropriate to use the European Judicial Network to seek an authoritative determination as to jurisdiction from the court of the requested European

Judicial Network judge where, either, there are no proceedings relating to the child before that court or, if there are proceedings before that court, the determination as to jurisdiction sought is one that will be made outside those proceedings (*Re B (Care Order: Jurisdiction)* [2014] 1 FLR 900, CA). For a full explanation of the appropriate scope and mechanics of international judicial liaison, see *N v K (Jurisdiction: International Liaison) (No 2)* [2014] 2 FLR 1147, FD and the guidance set out in *Direct Judicial Communications* (*https://assets.hcch.net/docs/62d073ca-eda0-494e-af66-2ddd368b7379.pdf*).

Under Art 8 of the 1996 Convention, the court may request an authority of another Contracting State to assume jurisdiction in relation to an application and stay the proceedings on the application. The PRMPC(IO)(EWNI)R 2010, reg 4 (see Part IV) permits the court to remove the stay if the other Contracting State does not assume jurisdiction within the period for which the court granted the stay or the parties do not, within the period specified by the court, request the authority in the other Contracting State to assume jurisdiction. See also the President's Guidance of April 2016 on *Transfer of proceedings under Article 15 of Brussels IIa and Articles 8 and/or 9 of the 1996 Hague Convention* (see Part V).

PART II

The test under Art 15—The essential exercise under Art 15 is one of judicial evaluation. Three questions fall to be determined when the court is considering whether to exercise its powers under Art 15. First, as a question of simple fact, does the child have, within the meaning of Art 15(3), a particular connection with the relevant other Member State. Secondly, in light of all the circumstances of the case, is the court of that other Member State better placed to hear the case or a specific part thereof. Thirdly, in light of all the circumstances of the case, is transfer to the other court in the best interests of the child (*AB v JLB (Brussels II Revised: Article 15)* [2009] 1 FLR 517, FD). See also the President's Guidance of April 2016 on *Transfer of proceedings under Article 15 of Brussels IIa and Articles 8 and/or 9 of the 1996 Hague Convention* (see Part V).

In evaluating whether a court of another Member State would be better placed to hear the case, the principles of comity and cooperation between Member States of the EU require that the judicial and social care arrangements in other Member States are to be treated by the courts in England and Wales as equally competent (*Re K (A Child); sub nom Re T (A Child: Article 15 of Brussels II Revised)* [2014] 1 FLR 749, CA and *Re M (Brussels II Revised: Art 15)*, above). In *Child and Family Agency v JD* (Case C-428/15) CJEU, the Court held that in order to determine that a court of another Member State with which the child had a particular connection was better placed, Art 15(1) requires the court having jurisdiction in a Member State to be satisfied that the transfer of the case to that other court will provide genuine and specific added value to the examination of that case, taking into account the rules of procedure applicable in that other Member State and that such a transfer was in the best interests of the child. In particular, the court having jurisdiction in a Member State must be satisfied that transfer is not liable to be detrimental to the situation of the child. It will be rare for a case to be transferred at a point where the judge has heard and read all the evidence that the parties wish to put before the court and is in a position to decide the outcome (*Re N (Adoption: Jurisdiction)* [2016] 1 FLR 1082, SC).

With respect to the question of whether transfer would be in the best interests of the child, Art 15 must be given a uniform construction throughout the courts of Member States and cannot be dominated by a domestic law approach in cases brought under the domestic jurisdiction, whether it be statutory or inherent (*Re K (A Child)*, above). Thus, in considering whether transfer to the other court is in the child's best interest, the autonomous meaning of best interests in Art 15(1) should not be enlarged by reference to the domestic principle of 'paramountcy' (*Re M (Brussels II Revised: Art 15)*, above). When considering an application under Art 15, the court is required to take into account views expressed by the subject child having regard to their age and maturity even if such views were not expressed strictly in terms of the questions posed by Art 15 (*Medway Council v JB and Others* [2016] 2 FLR 1360, FD).

Under Art 15, the issue of whether the court is better place to hear proceedings and the issue of whether transfer is in the best interests of the child are questions that must be addressed separately. A conclusion that a foreign court is better placed to hear the proceedings will not necessarily lead to the conclusion that transfer is in the child's best interests. The best interests test in Art 15 is not truncated as such. Rather, the question to which the best interests test is to be applied is limited in its scope. The question to which the best interests test is applied is whether it is in the child's best interests for the proceedings to be transferred. This is a different question to that of what final welfare outcome will be in the child's best interests. When considering whether to transfer proceedings, it is also necessary to consider the impact of that transfer on the options available to the court with respect to the eventual outcome for the child (*Re N (Adoption: Jurisdiction)* [2016] 1 FLR 1082, SC).

Note that in *Child and Family Agency v JD* (Case C-428/15), CJEU, the Court held that when applying that provision in a given case relating to parental responsibility, the court having jurisdiction in a Member State must not take into account either the effect of a possible transfer on the right of freedom of movement of persons concerned other than the child in question, or the reason why the parent of that child exercised that right prior to that court being seised, unless those considerations were such that there may be adverse repercussions on the situation of that child. See also the Advocate General's Opinion entitled 'Case C-428/15 *Child and Family Agency v JD* Advocate General Opinion' (*http://eur-lex.europa.eu/legal-content/EN/TXT/?uri=CELEX%3A62015CC0428*).

Request from another Member State for the court in England and Wales to assume jurisdiction—Under Brussels IIA, Art 15(1)(b), the court of another jurisdiction may make a request that the English court accept jurisdiction over care proceedings begun in that foreign jurisdiction. Note, however, that a stated willingness on the part of a judge in another Member State to transfer child protection proceedings to the English court will not amount to a formal request for the purposes of Art 15 for the English court to assume substantive jurisdiction in the proceedings. Without a request under Art 15, there is no basis upon which the English judge can assume substantive jurisdiction over the child and the court will be entitled to do no more than continue to take provisional, including protective, measures in respect of that child under Art 20 and decline jurisdiction insofar as the proceedings relate to longer term welfare issues (*Re L (A Child)* [2016] EWCA Civ 821).

Where a domestic court is considering whether or not to accept a request for transfer from another jurisdiction under Art 15, it should not do so unless it is satisfied that transfer is in the child's best interests. As set out above, consideration of the child's best interests under Art 15 does not require a full hearing concerning the child's welfare in general but rather consideration of the child's best interests as a preliminary issue within the context of the question of transfer to a more convenient jurisdiction. Where the English or Welsh court receives a transfer request from the court of another jurisdiction, the English or Welsh court should determine whether to accept that request by reference to the child's best interests rather than a wider review of all of the criteria for transfer set out in Art 15. Where the English or Welsh court accepts that it is in the child's best interests for proceedings to be transferred, FPR 2010, r 12.66(2) permits the English or Welsh court to take preparatory steps to give effect to the imminent receipt of the proceedings. The provisions of Pt V of CA 1989 will apply in their entirety to the future management of the proceedings once the jurisdiction of the English or Welsh court has been engaged. In such cases, the applicant local authority will be the authority that is likely to become the designated authority under CA 1989, s 31(8) if a care or supervision order is granted (*Re L-M (Transfer of Irish Proceedings)* [2013] 2 FLR 708, FD).

Note that Brussels IIA does not apply to jurisdictional disputes or issues arising between the different jurisdictions of the UK. Accordingly, Art 15 cannot be used, for example, to transfer care proceedings from England to Scotland (*Re W-B (Family Proceedings: Appropriate Jurisdiction Within the UK)* [2013] 1 FLR 394, CA), although the issue may merit more extensive argument (*Re PC, YC and KM (Children); sub nom Camden LBC v PC, GM, YC, PC and KM* [2014] 1 FLR 605, FD). However, in an appropriate case and where the English court is satisfied that an issue arising in care proceedings could and should be litigated in another part of the UK, it has the power as part of its general case management powers to stay the proceedings (*Re PC, YC and KM (Children)*).

Cases in which assistance is sought from authorities abroad—In *Re V-Z (Children)* [2016] EWCA Civ 475, the Court of Appeal made clear that when the English court seeks the assistance of foreign authorities in public law proceedings in this jurisdiction, the court should ensure that:

(i) the foreign authorities are informed clearly and comprehensively what questions they are requested to answer as part of their assessment;
(ii) the foreign authorities are provided with all the information they need to carry out the enquiry/assessment asked of them;
(iii) the material sent to the foreign authorities is documented carefully and comprehensively;
(iv) any queries posed by the foreign authorities during the course of their assessment are answered;
(v) any matters that require further exploration by them, or in respect of which they may be able to provide material information, such as details of local resources to assist in or supervise the care of the children are followed up assiduously;
(vi) the manner in which progress might be made in the event that obstacles are encountered is considered creatively, bearing in mind that it may be possible to communicate directly with those who are responsible for carrying out the assessment in the foreign state, although it would be prudent first to consult our Central Authority for advice as to whether that would be acceptable to the foreign state in question.

In international cases in which a court is seeking to invoke diplomatic assistance, see the President's Guidance of April 2016: *Liaison between Courts in England and Wales and British Embassies and High Commissions Abroad* (see Part V).

Case management and the Public Law Outline—Applications for care and supervision orders under s 31 are subject to the provisions of FPR 2010, Pt 12 and PD12A and the PLO contained therein. See in particular Case management hearing, Further case management hearing and Issues resolution hearing in FPR PD12A. Important guidance as to the preparation of public law cases by local authorities and other parties is contained in *Re R (Care: Disclosure: Nature of Proceedings)* [2002] 1 FLR 755, FD and *Re L (Care: Assessment: Fair Trial)* [2002] 2 FLR 730, FD.

Case management orders are to be obeyed, to be complied with on time and to the letter and any party finding themselves unable to comply must apply for an extension of time before the time for compliance has expired. The burden of other work is not an excuse for non-compliance with the directions of the court. Whatever the difficulties presented by reforms to public funding, the court will not tolerate a failure to comply timeously with orders (*Bexley LBC v V, W and D* [2014] EWHC 2187 (Fam)). It is essential that rules and practice directions are applied. Casual non-compliance is not an option precisely because further harm will likely be caused to the child (*Re H (A Child) (Analysis of Realistic Options and SGOs)* [2016] 1 FLR 286, CA and see *London Borough of Redbridge v A, B and E (Failure to Comply with Directions)* [2016] EWHC 2627 (Fam)). Failure by a local authority to comply with court orders causing unnecessary and harmful delay may result in a breach of Arts 6 and 8 and in an award of damages being made against a local authority (*Northamptonshire County Council v AS, KS and DS* [2015] EWHC 199 (Fam)).

Agreements between the parties to amend the timetable set by the Family Court are forbidden by FPR 2010, r 4.5(3). The parties are categorically not permitted to end the timetable fixed by the court without the court's prior approval and every party is under a duty to inform the court of non-compliance with the timetable set (*Re W (Children) (Strict Compliance with Court Orders)* [2015] 1 FLR 1092, FD). The court is entitled to refuse to permit applications by consent to adduce evidence in family proceedings where the rules have not been complied with (see *Cooper-Hohn v Hohn* [2014] EWCA Civ 896).

The court should adopt a robust but fair approach to case management in public law cases (*Re G (A Child)* [2015] EWCA Civ 834). Under the PLO, the court will place great emphasis on ensuring that the first hearing, the Case Management Hearing (CMH), is effective and will expect full case management to take place. The task of the case management judge is to arrange a trial that is fair by reference to domestic standards and Arts 6 and 8 of the ECHR. In case managing the proceedings, the court should aim to achieve the overriding objective set out in FPR 2010, r 1.1 (*Re TG (Care Proceedings: Case Management: Expert Evidence)* [2013] 1 FLR 1250, CA; *Re H-L (Expert Evidence: Test for Permission)* [2013] 2 FLR 1434, CA; *Re S-W (Children)* [2015] 2 FLR 136, CA).

In *Re TG*, the President emphasised that the circumstances in which the Court of Appeal will interfere with a case management decision are limited. The Court of Appeal will only interfere if it is satisfied that the case management judge erred in principle, took account of irrelevant matters, failed to take account of relevant matters or came to a decision that is so plainly wrong that it must be regarded as outside the generous ambit of the discretion entrusted to the judge. This approach was reiterated by McFarlane LJ in *Re H-L*, above, and in *Re B (A Child)* [2015] EWCA Civ 974 the Court of Appeal again reiterated that the longstanding guidance as to the willingness of the court to entertain appeals against short-term interim decisions in private law cases remains as sound today as it was when it was first enunciated.

There are however limits to robust case management (see for example *Re B (Case Management)* [2013] 1 FLR 963, CA, where the judge's decision to refuse to permit certain witnesses to be called deprived him of the evidence necessary to make safe findings of fact). Notwithstanding the pressures in family proceedings for speed and efficient use of resources, judges must also be careful as to how they express themselves at the case management stage. If giving a provisional view, the judge must emphasise and underscore to the parties that the view is provisional (*Re P (A Child)* [2014] EWCA Civ 888).

Although there will be care cases where a final care order is made at the case management stage, unless the application is conceded or the order made by consent, only exceptionally, in unusual circumstances and on rare occasions can this ever be appropriate. Such a course would not be appropriate, for example, where there remain significant issues as to threshold or where the children's guardian has not at least had an opportunity of seeing the child or children and to prepare a case analysis considering the s 31A care plan (*Re S-W (Children)* [2015] 2 FLR 136, CA). That said, the court must always give consideration to making final orders at the issues resolution hearing. It is the professional duty of the advocates in every case to direct their attention to the obligation to achieve finality at the issues resolution hearing wherever possible. The lay parties are always required to attend the issues resolution hearing (*RE v North Yorkshire County Council, LO and A (A Child)* [2015] EWCA Civ 1169).

In discharging its difficult role in cases involving litigants in person, the court must ensure that all reasonable assistance is afforded to the non-represented party in putting their case, it being unrealistic to require advocates representing other parties who oppose the non-represented litigant's application to assist in promoting it (*MW and Hertfordshire County Council v A & V and Mr & Mrs J* [2014] EWCA Civ 405 and see *Re B (Litigants In Person: Timely Service of Documents)* [2016] EWHC 2365 (Fam)).

Statutory 26-week time limit—See **Avoidance of delay** under CA 1989, s 32.

Disclosure—For a comprehensive summary of the legal principles pertaining to disclosure, see the **Introductory note** to FPR 2010, Pt 21.The principles underpinning the duty of disclosure on local authorities in public law cases are also clearly and comprehensively summarised by Baker J in *Kent County Council v A Mother, F and X, X and Z (IR Intervener)* [2011] EWHC 402 (Fam), at [153]–[158]. For a public law case in which issues arose concerning disclosure to the Security Service, see *Commissioner of Police of the Metropolis v A Local Authority and Ors* [2016] EWHC 2400 (Fam). Where a child has revealed sensitive information about him or herself to professionals and the question arises as to whether it would be appropriate to allow the local authority to disclose that information to the parents or others, the court must consider (a) the relevance of the information, (b) whether the child's overall interests would benefit from non-disclosure, (c) the interests of the child having the material in question properly tested and the magnitude of the risk that harm will occur and the gravity of that harm if it does occur and (d) the interests of the respondents in having the opportunity to see and respond to the material, having regard to a rigorous consideration of the engagement of their Art 6 and Art 8 rights (*Local Authority X v HI and Ors* [2016] EWHC 1123 (Fam) and see *Re D (Adoption Reports: Confidentiality)* [1995] 2 FLR 687, HL).

Translation of documentary evidence—Where an issue arises as to the extent to which documents in the proceedings should be translated into the language spoken by a particular party, the test to be adopted is whether it is 'necessary' to direct the translation of a given document in order to assist the court to resolve the proceedings justly. In considering whether translation is necessary, it is essential to focus on the forensic context (*Re L (Procedure: Bundles: Translation)* [2015] 1 FLR 1417, FD). In *Re L*, the President of the Family Division considered that it was necessary to direct the translation of only those documents or parts of documents that enable a father to understand the central essence of the local authority's case or that relate or refer specifically to him, with the remaining documents being summarised for him in his own language.

Hearing bundles—FPR PD27A mandates a hearing bundle of no more than 350 pages unless the court has directed otherwise on the grounds that such a direction is necessary to enable the proceedings to be disposed of justly. In *Re L (Procedure: Bundles: Translation)* [2015] 1 FLR 1417, FD, the President of the Family Division made clear that the word 'necessary' is used in the sense in which it is used in CA 1989, s 38(7A) and CFA 2014, s 13(6), namely that which is demanded rather than that which is merely optional or reasonable or desirable (cf *Re TG (Care Proceedings: Case Management: Expert Evidence)* [2013] 1 FLR 1250, CA and *Re H-L (Expert Evidence: Test for Permission)* [2013] 2 FLR 1434, CA). The President further made clear in *Re L (A Child)* that the requirements of PD27A must be complied with. These requirements include: the need for only those documents that are relevant for the hearing and necessary for the court to read or that will actually be referred to during the hearing (FPR PD27A, para 4.1); for all statements, affidavits, care plans, expert reports and other reports to be copies of the originals that have been signed and dated (para 4.2); for those documents included in the bundle to be as short and succinct as possible (para 4.4); for the bundle to be contained in an A4-size ring binder (para 5.1); and for documents to be copied on one side of paper only (para 5.2). The President reiterated that preliminary documents in the bundle (case summary, statement of issues, position statements, chronology, skeleton arguments, list of essential reading and time estimate) must be lodged by no later than 11 am on the day before the hearing, and by email to the judge's clerk where the case is before a judge of the High Court (para 6.4). A witness bundle should not be lodged with the court but rather brought to court by the party responsible for lodging the bundle if oral evidence may be called (para 7.4). The court office will refuse to accept witness bundles unless the judge has specifically directed that they are to be lodged. A so called 'core bundle' accompanied by other bundles does not satisfy PD27A unless the court has directed accordingly. In *Re L (A Child)* the President made clear that those who are in default of the requirements of PD27A can expect to be exposed to public condemnation in judgments in which they are named, to financial penalties and to adjournments while the default is remedied. A revised Practice Direction dealing with hearing bundles is currently out for consultation.

Care proceedings and ECHR 1950—Under HRA 1998, a parent may complain that his right to respect for his family life, protected by ECHR 1950, Art 8(1), has been violated by the making of a care order. In dealing with such a claim the court must consider whether, if there has been such an interference with the right, that interference was justified under Art 8(2) as being necessary in a democratic society for the protection of the health and morals and of the rights and freedoms of others. If such interference is justified the court must also consider whether it is proportionate to the aim of protecting the rights of the child concerned (*Re B (Care: Interference with Family Life)* [2003] 2 FLR 813, CA and *Re B (Care Proceedings: Appeal)* [2013] 2 FLR 1075, SC). The task of the domestic court when faced with such a complaint under Art 8(1) is to review under ECHR 1950 decisions taken by other public authorities in the exercise of their similar powers and to compare them with the case currently before the court. The width of the discretion allowed to a public authority in each case will vary according to the issues and the interests at stake. While the public authority will have a wide discretion in relation to the actual decision to take a child into care, a stricter scrutiny will be applied to any further steps proposed by the authority which might have the effect of restricting even more tightly the family relations between parents and a young child, for example limits on the amount and/or frequency of contact between the parents and the child in care (*Scott v UK* [2000] 1 FLR 958, ECHR and *HK v Finland* (Application No 36065/97) [2007] 1 FLR 633, ECHR).

In judicial decisions where the Art 8 rights of parents and those of a child are at stake, the domestic courts, relying on the decision of the ECtHR in *Yousef v The Netherlands* [2003] 1 FLR 210, ECHR, have held that the child's interests remain the paramount consideration, so that if any balancing of interests is necessary as between the parents and the child, the child's interests must prevail (*Dawson v Wearmouth* [1997] 2 FLR 629, CA and [1999] 1 FLR 1167, HL; *Payne v Payne* [2001] 1 FLR 1052, CA; *CF v Secretary of State for the Home Department* [2004] 2 FLR 517, FD and *Re S (Contact: Promoting Relationship with Absent Parent)* [2004] 1 FLR 1279, CA). The ECtHR has confirmed that where the Art 8 rights of the parents and those of the children are at stake, the child's best interests will remain the paramount consideration. (*R and H v United Kingdom* (Application No 35348/06) [2011] 2 FLR 1236, ECHR and *YC v United Kingdom* (Application No 4547/10) [2012] 2 FLR 332, ECHR).

It is unclear how these decisions of the ECtHR fit with a long line of European authority, beginning with *Johansen v Norway* [1996] ECHR 31, which stipulates that the correct approach under Art 8 is to strike a fair balance between the interests of the child and those of the parent, attaching particular importance to the best interest of the child, which interests, depending on their nature and seriousness, may override those of the parents (see, for example, *C v Finland* [2006] 2 FLR 597, ECHR; *HK v Finland*, above; *Dolhamre v Sweden* [2010] 2 FLR 912, ECHR and *Neulinger and Shuruk v Switzerland* [2011] 1 FLR 122, ECHR).

The Draconian step of removing a baby from its mother shortly after birth must be supported by relevant and sufficient reasons and must be regarded as necessary in a democratic society (*R (G) v Nottingham City Council and Nottingham University Hospital* [2008] 1 FLR 1668, QBD and see *CF v Secretary of State for the Home Department* (above). See further under **Removal of babies at birth** (below). In *Re B (Care Proceedings: Appeal)* [2013] 2 FLR 1075, SC, the Supreme Court reiterated that a judge cannot properly decide that a care order with a care plan of adoption should be made unless the order is proportionate, bearing in mind the requirements of Art 8 and the UN Convention on the Rights of the Child, emphasising that the granting of a care order with a care plan of adoption is an option of last resort requiring a high degree of justification to be made only in exceptional circumstances where nothing else will do. Note, however, that the Court of Appeal has made clear that where adoption can be shown to be in the child's best interests, the child's welfare is not to be compromised by keeping the child within their family at all costs. The evaluation of realistic options for permanency must be undertaken with the factors set out in CA 1989, s 1 in full focus (*Re R* [2015] 1 FLR 715, CA).

Article 6 of the Convention guarantees the right to a fair hearing and in *L v Finland* [2000] 2 FLR 118, ECHR, it was successfully argued that there was a violation of Art 6 because no oral hearing had been held before the decision to take the children concerned into care. The need to take emergency action and to limit the notice given to the parents must be balanced with the circumstances of the case (*KA v Finland* [2003] 1 FLR 696, ECHR – where the social services had not made any serious effort to reunite the family). A refusal to grant an adjournment during the final hearing so that a parent can obtain alternative representation does not constitute a breach of Art 6 where the Court has given a prior indication that there would be no such adjournment and has thereafter conducted the trial so as to ensure that the party who has dispensed with her legal representation is on an equal footing in accordance with FPR 2010, r 1.1(2)(c) (*Re GB (Children)* [2013] EWCA Civ 164). Emergency measures to take children into care must be justified and there will be a breach of Arts 6 and 8 if parents are not given sufficient opportunity to participate in proceedings which will potentially disrupt their family life (*Venema v The Netherlands* [2003] 1 FLR 552, ECHR and *Haase v Germany* [2004] 2 FLR 39, ECHR). In *G v N County Council* [2009] 1 FLR 774, FD the court made a declaration that the local authority acted unlawfully by removing children from the mother without first involving or consulting with the parents, and without giving them due notice of their intention to remove the children; their actions were not proportionate to the level of concern in the case.

The local authority, when seeking to take a child into care, is under a heavy obligation to ensure that the procedure at all stages is transparent and fair, both in and out of court. Article 8 requires the local authority to involve parents fully in the decision-making process, at all stages of the child protection procedure, whether before, during or after the making of a care order (*Re G (Care: Challenge to Local Authority's Decision)* [2003] 2 FLR 42, FD; *Haase v Germany* (above); and *Moser v Austria* (Application No 12643/02) [2007] 1 FLR 702, ECHR). In *Jucius and Juciuvienė v Lithuania* [2009] 1 FLR 403, ECHR, the court had determined the appeal of the children's uncle and his wife by way of written procedure. The ECHR held that questions of fact could not be resolved adequately in this way and there should have been a hearing to ensure that the best interests of the children were considered. In particular, it is vital that a litigant has a proper opportunity in care proceedings to examine and comment on experts' reports and other documents being considered by the court and to cross-examine witnesses interviewed and relied on therein (*Re L (Care: Assessment: Fair Trial)* [2002] 2 FLR 730, FD). PD25A–PD25F regulate the use of expert evidence and the instruction of experts in family proceedings.

Procedure for raising issues under the Human Rights Act 1998—For the procedure to be followed when raising an issue under HRA 1998, see the annotation thereto and FPR 2010, r 29.5 and PD29B. Where care proceedings have come to an end the appropriate remedy may well be a freestanding application under HRA 1998, s 7(1)(a). Where the proceedings are still ongoing s 7(1)(b) provides an appropriate remedy within the care proceedings themselves. Therefore, where a HRA 1998 complaint arises before the making of a final care order, it should normally be dealt with within the context of the care proceedings and by the court dealing with those proceedings (*Re L (Care Proceedings: Human Rights Claims)* [2003] 2 FLR 160, FD; *Re L (Care: Assessment: Fair Trial)* [2002] 2 FLR 730, FD and see *Re V (Care Proceedings: Human Rights Claim)* [2004] 1 FLR 944, CA). Note, however, that if a parent or child seeks a remedy under HRA 1998, s 8 within ongoing care proceedings, care must be taken in considering the implications of the statutory charge for any damages awarded as in such circumstances the statutory charge will likely comprise the entirety of the parent or child's costs of the care proceedings and not just the costs of the claim under s 7(1)(b).

PART II

Scrutiny of care plan (s 31(3A))—Pursuant to s 31A, where an application is made on which a care order might be made, the local authority must prepare a care plan. When considering whether to make an order under s 31, the court is now required by s 31(3A) to scrutinise the care plan only to the extent of considering the permanence provisions within that plan, those being those provisions of the care plan that concern the long-term upbringing of the child in his or her family, in an adoptive placement or in long-term foster care. There is no longer a requirement for the court to scrutinise the remainder of the plan subject to the requirements of s 34(11) (duty to consider the arrangements for contact). Note that the court can require the local authority to specify the services that are practicable under each of the range of orders that the court is considering and can direct the local authority to file a care plan that meets a particular formulation or assessment of risk even though that plan does not reflect the position of the local authority (*Re W (Care Proceedings: Functions of Court and Local Authority)* [2014] 2 FLR 431, CA).

Requirement to keep parents properly involved in the planning process—It is essential that the local authority keeps the parents properly involved in the planning process when care proceedings are initiated and the care plan is being formulated (*Re S (Minors) (Care Order: Implementation of Care Plan)*; *Re W (Minors) (Care Order: Adequacy of Care Plan)* [2002] 1 FLR 815, HL). Likewise, it is essential to ensure that children are given the appropriate opportunity to participate in the decisions being made. A failure to do so may leave it open for the parents of the child concerned, or the child himself, to bring an application under HRA 1998, ss 6, 7 and 8 for breaches of ECHR 1950, Art 6 (right to a fair trial) and Art 8 (right to respect for private and family life) (*Re C (Care Plan: Human Rights Challenge)* [2002] Fam Law 790, FD; *Re G (Care: Challenge to Local Authority's Decision)* [2003] 2 FLR 42, FD; *Venema v The Netherlands* [2003] 1 FLR 552, ECHR). See further **Procedure for raising issues under the Human Rights Act 1998** above and annotation to HRA 1998. *Re L (Care: Assessment: Fair Trial)* [2002] 2 FLR 730, ECHR sets out useful guidelines for local authorities and all professionals concerned in care proceedings as to the proper conduct and recording of meetings and the provision of documents. In January 2013, the Children Act Sub-Committee of the Law Society has published guidance entitled *Attendance of Solicitors at Local Authority Children Act Meetings*, which provides guidance on the role and professional conduct of solicitors representing all parties at such meetings.

Removal of babies at birth—The separation of a newborn baby from his mother is unlawful where there is no prior judicial sanction, no suggestion that the mother poses a risk of exposing him to immediate physical attack or physical harm and no medical justification for the intervention (*R (G) v Nottingham City Council and Nottingham University Hospital* [2008] 1 FLR 1668, QBD). However, in an appropriate case the court may, in the public interest and for the proper protection of a public authority, grant anticipatory relief that a proposed course of conduct is lawful or unlawful. In *Re D (Unborn Baby)* [2009] 2 FLR 313, FD, the court granted a declaration that the authority was acting lawfully and in accordance with ECHR 1950 in not engaging the parents in the planning process in the way that Art 8 would normally require. The circumstances of the case were exceptional in that the experts considered that the mother posed a severe risk to the child, herself and others and was likely to react adversely and harm both herself and the baby immediately after birth. The authority therefore sought a declaration that it was lawful to conceal the nature of their birth plan from the mother before the point at which, immediately following the birth, the child was removed. The court has jurisdiction to injunct a local authority from separating mother and child under HRA 1998, s 8(1) (*Re H (Care Plan: Human Rights)* [2012] 1 FLR 191, FD). In *Nottingham City Council v LM and Others* [2016] 2 FLR 1221, FD, Keehan J made clear that where the local authority is dealing with a newborn baby the following principles of good practice should always be followed to avoid unnecessary delay and procedural unfairness:

(a) a risk assessment of the parents should be commenced immediately upon the social workers being made aware of the pregnancy, and completed at least 4 weeks before the expected delivery date. The assessment should be updated to take account of relevant events immediately pre- and post-delivery that could potentially affect the initial conclusions on risk and care planning for the unborn child;

(b) the assessment should be disclosed to the parents and, if instructed, to their solicitors, to enable them to challenge it and the proposed care plan;

(c) the social work team should provide all relevant documentation necessary for the legal department to issue care proceedings and the application for an interim care order no less than 7 days before the mother's expected due date;
(d) the birth plan should have been rigorously adhered to by all social work practitioners and managers, and by the local authority's legal department;
(e) immediately on issue, if not before, the local authority's solicitors should serve the applications and supporting documents on the parents and their solicitors; and
(f) immediately on issue, the local authority should seek from the court an initial hearing date, on the best time estimate that its solicitors can provide.

Intervention by court after making of care order—Once a care order has been made the responsibility for the child is transferred to the local authority, removing it from the control of the court even in cases where, for example, a judge feels that it is necessary for the court to monitor the progress of the child in care, or where a care plan goes wrong at an early stage (see *A Local Authority v K and Others* [2012] 1 FLR 765, FD and *Re W (Care Proceedings: Functions of Court and Local Authority)* [2014] 2 FLR 431, CA). ACA 2002, s 118, has amended CA 1989, s 26(2)(e) (requirement to consider the discharge of a care order) to encompass a requirement for the authority to review the care plan and revise it as necessary, together with a route for returning it to the court through the intervention of a Cafcass officer where appropriate. See further **Review of cases of looked-after children** under CA 1989, s 26. A remedy also exists under HRA 1998, ss 6, 7 and 8 on the basis that the process adopted by the authority is incompatible with ECHR 1950, Art 8 (the right to respect for family life), and Art 6 (right to a fair trial) (*Re S (Minors) (Care Order: Implementation of Care Plan)*; *Re W (Minors) (Care Order: Adequacy of Care Plan)* [2002] 1 FLR 815, HL; *Re C (Care Plan: Human Rights Challenge)* [2002] Fam Law 790, FD). See further **Procedure for raising issues under the Human Rights Act 1998** above, annotation to HRA 1998 and FPR 2010, r 29.5.

Local authority good practice where adoption is the preferred option—Where adoption is, or is likely to be, the preferred option, the court will need to be advised at an early stage of the likely steps and timescales required to implement that plan. Local authorities must follow the Local Authority Circular of 28 August 1998 (LAC(98)20) *Adoption – Achieving the Right Balance*, paras 28–33 of which were reissued in an amended form in *Chief Inspector Letter* of June 1999 (CI(99)6). Paragraph 29 of the amended Circular provides that where the choice of placement depends significantly on findings of fact then, even though it may be difficult to effect much preparatory work concerning possible adoptive placement before the final hearing, it should still be possible to explain within the care plan the key steps that would need to be taken before an adoptive placement could be made and give estimated time-scales for each of these steps. Even where the facts of the care application are not disputed and the preferred option is adoption, paragraph 30 makes it clear that local authorities must have satisfied themselves that sufficient assessment has taken place in order to rule out rehabilitation or placement with relatives, for example, under a s 8 child arrangements order with respect to living arrangements. In *Re B (Care Proceedings: Appeal)* [2013] 2 FLR 1075, SC, the Supreme Court emphasised that the granting of a care order with a care plan of adoption is an option of last resort requiring a high degree of justification to be made only in exceptional circumstances where nothing else will do. However, see *Re R* under **Care orders – ECHR 1950**, above. See further **Welfare and proportionality** below for the strict analytical and evidential requirements when the local authority seeks to advance a care plan of adoption as its preferred option for the child. In those cases in which the local authority has ruled out rehabilitation or placement with relatives and has confirmed adoption as the preferred option, paragraph 31 sets out the steps which should always have been addressed before the final care hearing, including:

(a) the co-ordination of information between the team responsible for the care proceedings application and those responsible for family finding;
(b) the completion, as far as possible, of the BAAF Form E giving details about the child;
(c) consideration of the case by the adoption panel with a view to making a recommendation on whether adoption is in the child's best interests;
(d) the identification by the local authority of the key steps and timetable which would lead to an adoptive placement if the court made a care order;
(e) a contingency plan to be used if the preferred option for adoption cannot be achieved.

In care proceedings in which the local authority is proposing a care plan of adoption, the care proceedings should proceed concurrently with the application for a placement order. In the circumstances, the Agency Decision Maker's decision should also be timetabled so that both applications can be before the court. If the applications for care and placement orders are considered separately, the court is likely to be missing important evidence and analysis relevant to evaluating the local authority's care plan of adoption. Without the ADM's decision, any care plan for adoption cannot be carried into effect and is likely to be inchoate, or at least conditional (*Surrey County Council v S* [2014] EWCA Civ 601). Note also that where the applications are considered separately, the parents' public funding certificates will have been discharged before the application for a placement order is heard. See also the Safeguarding Committee of the Family Justice Council guidance: *Linked Care and Placement Order Applications* (*www.judiciary.gov.uk/about-the-judiciary/advisory-bodies/fjc*).

Cases in which the care plan is adoption—The ACA 2002 governs the legal process for placing a child for adoption. A placement order authorises the local authority to place a child with prospective adopters (ACA 2002, ss 18–29). The ACA 2002, s 1(2) makes the child's welfare the court's paramount concern in all decisions relating to adoption, bringing the law into line with the guiding principle in CA 1989, s 1(1). Thus a court hearing applications for care and placement orders at the same time is able to hear all the evidence needed for both orders in the course of one hearing, adopting the paramountcy principle for both issues.

Where the court is asked on an application for a care order to approve a care plan of placement for adoption, the court should carry out its balancing exercise by reference to both CA 1989, s 1(3) and ACA 2002, s 1(4), even where the application for a placement order falls to be decided at a later date (*Re C (Appeal from Care and Placement Orders)* [2014] 2 FLR 131, CA). Note, however, that care proceedings in which the local authority is proposing a care plan of adoption, the care proceedings should proceed concurrently with the application for a placement order (*Surrey County Council v S* [2014] EWCA Civ 601). Note that the Court of Appeal has made it clear that *Re B-S (Adoption: Application of s 47(5))* [2014] 1 FLR 1035, CA has not changed the statutory test for dispensing with parental consent to adoption (*CM v Blackburn with Darwen Borough Council* [2015] 2 FLR 290, CA).

Concurrent planning—'Concurrent planning' (now more commonly known as 'fostering to adopt') describes a scheme whereby the local authority choose foster parents who are trained and willing to foster children on the basis that they work with the natural family towards rehabilitation, but who in the event that rehabilitation is ruled out wish to adopt the children. The aim is to reduce the number of moves a child experiences while in care and to reduce temporary placements so that children can achieve permanence, whether rehabilitated with their family or with the foster family, with minimum disruption. Bracewell J explained in *Re D and K (Care Plan: Twin Track Planning)* [1999] 2 FLR 872, FD, at [875C], that 'contact between carers and birth children is encouraged and there is openness between the parties, about the primary aim of rehabilitation with the alternative secondary plan of permanent placement'. Therefore, in cases in which concurrent planning takes place it is vital that the two options are clearly explained to the natural family from the outset and that they are reassured that it in no way pre-empts the outcome of the care proceedings. Her Ladyship emphasised (at [875D]): 'Not every case will be suitable for such placement. Generally it is likely to apply to babies or young children where there are some but by no means optimistic prospects in relation to rehabilitation to the natural family.' There have been concerns among those who are resistant to concurrent planning that unless it is implemented very carefully, and appropriately resourced, the very fact of being within the process runs the risk of having a negative impact on the prospects of the child returning to the birth family. For an example of the application of concurrent planning in relation to a 15-year-old mother and her baby see *B Metropolitan Borough Council v H (Goodman Project: Concurrent Planning)* [2000] Fam Law 237, Cty Ct.

See also **Local authority good practice where adoption is the preferred option** and **Procedure for adoption** (above).

Teenage mothers and their children—The case of *Re R (Child of a Teenage Mother)* [2000] 2 FLR 660, FD sets out guidelines to be followed by local authorities in the very difficult cases dealing with teenage mothers and their babies.

Social work practice—In *Re E (Care Proceedings: Social Work Practice)* [2000] 2 FLR 254, FD, Bracewell J set out guidance in relation to social work practice in the light of lessons learned in the case, which covered a 20-year period of social work intervention with a highly dysfunctional family. It is vital that social workers making child protection decisions check and analyse the sources of information upon which they rely to make those decisions and assess its reliability. Social workers must appreciate that the mere repetition of a piece of information out of context from one professional to another does not enhance the reliability of that piece of information (*Surrey County Council v M, F and E* [2013] EWHC 2400 (Fam)).

Working Together to Safeguard Children (2015) (*www.gov.uk/government/publications/working-together-to-safeguard-children–2*) sets out how individuals and organisations should work together to safeguard and promote the welfare of children. See also *Information sharing: Advice for practitioners providing safeguarding services to children, young people, parents and carers* (*www.gov.uk/government/publications/safeguarding-practitioners-information-sharing-advice*). *Working Together 2015* is issued as statutory guidance and although it does not have the force of statute, generally speaking it must be followed (*R v London Borough of Islington ex parte Rixon* [1997] ELR 66, QBD; *R v Cornwall County Council ex parte LH* [2000] 1 FLR 236, QBD). However, whereas a local authority is bound by the guidance in *Working Together*, a judge may proceed without a core assessment or similar social work document where there is other evidence available to the court that makes it clear that no matter how favourable the social work assessment may be there are obstacles in the way that prevent the parent caring for his or her child. Where there are gaps in the material provided by a core assessment, the judge is entitled to disregard them in the light of the entirety of the evidence that is available (*Re D O'H (Parenting Assessment)* [2012] 2 FLR 713, CA). Where assessments are incomplete at the date of the final hearing, the court will have to look again at the evidence available and determine afresh whether further assessment is required having regard, inter alia, to developments since the assessment was ordered, the impact of delay and the totality of the evidence available. It may transpire that other evidence is available that covers the ground intended to be covered by the assessment (*Re K (Special Guardianship Order)* [2012] 1 FLR 1265, CA).

Whereas it is inevitable and quite proper for there to be discussions between the members of the local authority and officers of Cafcass during the currency of a case, such discussions should be (i) rare, (ii) strictly necessary for the progress of the case, (iii) minuted and (iv) disclosed to all other parties to the proceedings and available, if necessary, to the court (*A County Council v K, T and C* [2011] 2 FLR 817, FD). The evidence of the children's guardian does not carry additional weight by reason of his or her 'special' status in the proceedings. The children's guardian starts with no special advantage in the proceedings as compared with other witnesses (*MW and Hertfordshire County Council v A & V and Mr & Mrs J* [2014] EWCA Civ 405).

Basic Guidance to Good Practice in Care Proceedings across London—This guidance highlights the basic requirements of good practice during the currency of care proceedings in London. It was issued by DJ Richard Harper and HHJ John Altman and came into effect in October 2010.

Care Monitoring System—The Care Monitoring System (CMS) is a judicially led management information programme intended to provide accurate ongoing information about case volumes, case progress and allocation. The programme is intended to assist judges of the Family Court to focus on avoiding delay for children and to help identify the real causes of delay. The system has been piloted nationwide since 2 April 2012, from which date all new care and supervision cases are entered onto the system and orders are required to contain information that is monitored by the system, in particular the timetable for the child expressed as the expected number of weeks necessary to conclude the proceedings. All cases are given a standard 26-week timetable on issue (CA 1989, s 32(1)(a)).

Objective nature of threshold test—The nature of the test prescribed by s 31(2) to determine whether a court has jurisdiction to make a care or supervision order is, and has to be, objective (*Re D (Care Order: Evidence)* [2011] 1 FLR 447, CA).

'suffering' and 'is likely to suffer' (s 31(2)(a))—The first limb of s 31(2)(a) (suffering significant harm) predicates an existing state of affairs: that the child is suffering significant harm. The relevant time for this purpose is the date of the care order application or, if temporary protective arrangements have been continuously in place from an earlier date, the date when those arrangements were initiated (*Re M (A Minor) (Care Order: Threshold Conditions)* [1994] 2 FLR 577, HL). However, the local authority does not have to be in possession of all the information it wishes to rely upon at the date of the application. Evidence-gathering continues after proceedings have begun and later acquired information as to the state of affairs at the relevant date can be taken into account (*Re G (Care Proceedings: Threshold Conditions)* [2001] 2 FLR 1111, CA). In *Re G*, Hale LJ identified three different sets of circumstances where this issue might arise: (i) where information is discovered after the relevant date that throws light on what the facts were at the relevant date; (ii) entirely new events may indicate a completely different risk that did not exist at the relevant date; and (iii) where there are new events that may or may not be capable of proving that there was a risk of significant harm at the relevant time.

The relevant time for the second limb (likely to suffer significant harm) is the same (*Southwark LBC v B* [1998] 2 FLR 1095, FD). The Supreme Court in *Re B (Care Proceedings: Appeal)* [2013] 2 FLR 1075, SC re-examined the meaning of 'is likely to suffer' and concluded that the threshold of likelihood, namely 'a real possibility, a possibility that cannot sensibly be ignored having regard to the gravity of the feared harm in the particular case' (*Re H and R (Minors) (Child Sexual Abuse: Standard of Proof)* [1996] 1 FLR 80, HL) is comparatively low (see also *Re L-K (Children)* [2015] EWCA Civ 830). The Supreme Court in *Re B (Care Proceedings: Appeal)* reiterated the principle articulated in *Re S-B (Children)* [2010] 1 FLR 1161, SC that the more significant the harm the less the required level of likelihood and vice versa. Risk of significant harm must be established on the basis of evidence and not assumptions or speculation about future behaviour. The local authority must not only prove on the balance of probabilities the facts on which it relies by calling witnesses who can speak to matters first-hand but must link the facts upon which it relies with the assertion that the child is at risk by demonstrating exactly why, on the given set of facts, the child is at risk of significant harm. In undertaking its analysis, the local authority must bear in mind society's willingness to tolerate very diverse standards of parenting (*Re A (Application for Care and Placement Orders: Local Authority Failings); sub nom Darlington Borough Council v M, F, GM and GF* [2016] 1 FLR 1, FD).

Degree of 'significant harm' to be proved (s 31(2),(9))—CA 1989, s 31 defines the nature of the harm that may be suffered, but does not indicate the necessary degree of that harm. In the original guidance to CA 1989 issued by the Department of Health *The Children Act 1989: Guidance and Regulations (Volume 1, Court Orders*) (HMSO 1991) at para 3.21 it was stated that: 'Minor shortcomings in health care or minor deficits in physical, psychological or social development should not require compulsory intervention unless cumulatively they are having, or are likely to have, serious and lasting effects on the child'. All types of female genital mutilation (FGM) will amount to significant harm (*Re B and G (Children) (No 2); sub nom Leeds City Council v M, F, B, G (B and G by their Children's Guardian)* [2015] 1 FLR 905, FD). Male circumcision also amounts to significant harm, but see **Requirement of attribution of harm to care that is not reasonable**, below. A male child may be caused significant harm by reason of being made to live as a girl (*Re J (A Minor)* [2016] EWHC 2430 (Fam)).

The Court of Appeal in *Re MA (Care Threshold)* [2010] 1 FLR 431, CA considered the dividing line between 'harm' and 'significant harm' and held that the harm must be significant enough to justify the intervention of the state and disturb the autonomy of the parents to bring up their children by themselves in the way they choose. It must be significant enough to enable the court to make a care or supervision order if the welfare of the child so demands. The Supreme Court in *Re B (Care Proceedings: Appeal)* [2013] 2 FLR 1075, SC made clear that while the court should avoid attempting to explain the meaning of the word 'significant' (the concept of 'significant harm' being fact-specific) consistency of application is important and, as already established, 'significant' means something more than commonplace failure or human inadequacy and something considerable, noteworthy or important. To be 'significant' conduct does not have to be intentional or deliberate. A deficiency in parental care rather than parental character is required, although character will remain relevant to the extent that it affects the quality of parental care (*Re B (Care Proceedings: Appeal)*). See also the speech of Baroness Hale in *Re B (Children) (Care Proceedings: Standard of Proof)* [2008] 2 FLR 141, HL where she referred to the 'unacceptable risk of harm'. It is not open to the local authority to decline to accept the court's evaluation of risk (*Re W (Care Proceedings: Functions of Court and Local Authority)* [2014] 2 FLR 431, CA).

Requirement of attribution of harm to care that is not reasonable (s 31(2)(b))—The 'threshold' test in s 31(2) is a two-stage test. Not only must the court be satisfied that the child is suffering or is likely to suffer significant harm under s 31(2)(a), the court must also be satisfied pursuant to s 31(2)(b) that the significant harm or risk of significant harm is attributable to care given or likely to be given to the child, that care not being what it would be reasonable to expect a parent to give the child. In *Re B and G (Children) (No 2); sub nom Leeds City Council v M, F, B, G (B and G by their Children's Guardian)* [2015] 1 FLR 905, FD, the President of the Family Division considered whether female genital mutilation amounted to significant harm. Reiterating that FGM is a criminal offence under FGMA 2003, an abuse of human rights and with no basis in any religion, the President concluded that FGM constitutes significant harm within the meaning of CA 1989, ss 31 and 100. The President further concluded that if, as it is, Type IV FGM amounts to significant harm for the purposes of s 31(2)(a), the same must be so of the practice of male circumcision. Turning to the second limb of the threshold test in s 31(2)(b), however, the President made clear that while the infliction of FGM can never be an aspect of reasonable parenting for the purposes of s 31(2)(b), the position is quite different with male circumcision. Noting that male circumcision is tolerated by society and the law for religious or even purely cultural or conventional reasons while FGM is not tolerated in any of its forms, it having no religious, medical or health justification, the President concluded that FGM in any form will be sufficient to establish the threshold under CA 1989, s 31(2) but male circumcision without more will not, as 'reasonable' parenting is treated as permitting male circumcision.

Extended definition of 'harm' (s 31(9))—The definition has been extended by ACA 2002, s 120 to include 'impairment suffered from seeing or hearing the ill-treatment of another'. As a consequence, the court forms for applications in respect of a child have been amended to include questions relating to harm.

Cases of relinquished babies—The fact that the baby has been given up for adoption will not by itself satisfy the threshold criteria in s 31(2). In cases where the baby has been simply abandoned on a doorstep, it is likely that the threshold criteria will be satisfied. However, in cases where the mother has reached the decision that she cannot keep the baby, has notified the local authority accordingly in advance and has made responsible plans for the relinquishment of the baby in a way that minimises the risk of harm, it is unlikely that the threshold criteria under s 31(2) will be satisfied (*Re AO (Care Proceedings)* [2016] EWFC 36). See also *Re RA (Baby Relinquished for Adoption: Case Management)* [2016] EWFC 25 in respect of the steps that local authorities should take to avoid delay in the resolution of proceedings relating to a foreign national baby relinquished by parents at birth where the family abroad seeks to care for the child.

Cases of alleged radicalisation—Exposure to material propounding an extremist ideology can amount to emotional harm and a risk of emotional harm (*London Borough of Tower Hamlets v B* [2016] 2 FLR 877, FD; *Re X (Children) and Y (Children) (No 1)* [2015] 2 FLR 1487, FD). The ordinary legal principles governing the making of findings of fact apply in cases of alleged radicalisation (see *Re X* [2015] EWHC 3651 (Fam)). Note that the President's Practice Guidance entitled *Tagging or Electronic Monitoring in Family Cases* is set out in Part V.

There is no rule that in cases of alleged radicalisation the local authority should use wardship proceedings in preference to care proceedings. Each case will depend on its own facts. Where the issue is limited to the threatened removal from the jurisdiction of older children to a dangerous conflict zone, then wardship and related orders made under the court's inherent jurisdiction are likely to be appropriate, at least initially. Where, however, the welfare issues extend beyond the risk of removal to issues such as exposure to extremist material in the family home or the impact of a parent's extremist ideology, care proceedings are likely to be preferable once any risk of removal has been addressed using the court's powers under the inherent jurisdiction. In the latter situation, there will be considerable advantages to using care proceedings and such a course may in any event be mandated by the terms of CA 1989, s 100(4) (*HB v A Local Authority & Anor (Wardship – Costs Funding Order)* [2017] EWHC 524 (Fam)).

For procedural guidance on the proper approach to care proceedings in which issues of alleged radicalisation are raised, see the President's Guidance of 8 October 2015: *Radicalisation Cases in the Family Courts* (see Part V) and the cases listed at the conclusion of that guidance. The key points set out by the guidance are as follows:

(a) All cases where there are allegations that children, with their parents or on their own, are planning or attempting or being groomed with a view to travel to areas controlled by the so-called Islamic State; that children have been or are at risk of being radicalised; or that children have been or at are at risk of being involved in terrorist activities either in this country or abroad should be heard by a High Court judge of the Family Division save in exceptional circumstances where they may be heard by a Designated Family judge or judge authorised to sit as a High Court judge under SCA 1981, s 9;

(b) Judges hearing cases of this nature will be alert to: (i) the need to protect the Art 6 rights of all the parties; (ii) the fact that much of the information gathered by the police and other agencies will not be relevant to the issues before the court; (iii) the fact that some of the information gathered by the police and other agencies is highly sensitive and such that its disclosure may damage the public interest or even put lives at risk; (iv) the need to avoid inappropriately wide or inadequately defined requests for disclosure of information or documents by the police or other agencies; (v) the need to avoid seeking disclosure from the police or other agencies of information or material that may be subject to PII, or the disclosure of which might compromise ongoing investigations, damage the public interest or put lives at risk, unless the judge is satisfied that such disclosure is 'necessary to enable the court to resolve the proceedings justly' within the meaning given to those words when used in, for example, CA 1989, ss 32(5) and 38(7A) and CFA 2014, s 13(6); (vi) the need to safeguard the custody of, and in appropriate cases limit access to, any sensitive materials provided to the court by the police or other agencies; (vii) the need to consider any PII issues and whether there is a need for a closed hearing or use of a special advocate; (viii) the need to safeguard the custody of, and in appropriate cases limit access to the tape or digital recordings of the proceedings or any transcripts; (ix) the need to ensure that the operational requirements of the police and other agencies are not inadvertently compromised or inhibited either because a child is a ward of court or because of any order made by the court; and (x) the assistance that may be gained if the police or other agencies are represented in court, including, in appropriate cases, by suitably expert counsel.

(c) Consideration will need to be given to whether there is a need to exclude the media or make a reporting restriction or anti-tipping off order.

(d) Regard must be had to the importance of coordinated strategy, predicated on open and respectful cooperation between all the safeguarding agencies involved and the need for open dialogue, appropriate sharing of information, mutual respect for the differing roles involved and inter-agency cooperation.

Cases of alleged child sexual exploitation—In cases of alleged child exploitation, practitioners should have regard the guidance set out by Keehan J in *Birmingham CC v SK* [2016] EWHC 310 (Fam), which details the proper approach to be adopted by the police, local authorities and other relevant agencies.

Cases of alleged fabricated or induced illness (FII) in care proceedings—In *Coventry City Council v X, Y and Z (Care Proceedings: Costs)* [2011] 1 FLR 1045, FD, HHJ Bellamy, sitting as a deputy judge of the High Court, drawing upon *London Borough of Southwark v B* [1993] 2 FLR 559, CA, *Re X (Emergency Protection*

Orders) [2006] 2 FLR 701, FD, *Re N (Leave to Withdraw Care Proceedings)* [2000] 1 FLR 134, FD, *Re M (Local Authority's Costs)* [1995] 1 FLR 533, FD and *Re R (Care: Disclosure: Nature of Proceedings)* [2002] 1 FLR 755, FD alongside *Fabricated or induced illness by carers* (2002; the report of a working party of the Royal College of Paediatrics and Child Health), listed points that he considered to be of particular importance where allegations of FII were concerned. These included: (a) before making an allegation of FII, a local authority had to be rigorous in satisfying itself that the evidence was capable of establishing the fact of the FII to the requisite standard; (b) in a case of suspected FII, the letter of instruction to the expert should make it clear that he or she should have regard to *Fabricated or Induced Illness by Carers (FII): A Practical Guide for Paediatricians* (Royal College of Paediatricians and Child Health 2009); (c) in reaching the decision to allege FII, the authority should normally seek the views of the health professionals involved in the children's care rather than relying on the report of one independent expert; and (d) all of those involved should consider and review the expert's report and raise any relevant points with the expert.

Cases of alleged female genital mutilation—In *Re B and G (Children) (No 2); sub nom Leeds City Council v M, F, B, G (B and G by their Children's Guardian)* [2015] 1 FLR 905, FD, the President of the Family Division gave guidance regarding the use of the World Health Organization classification for FGM and on the proper process, conduct and recording of intimate examinations in respect of alleged FGM. See **Requirement of attribution of harm to care that is not reasonable**, above.

Cases in which one parent has been killed by the other—Cases where one parent has been killed by the other are relatively rare but raise particularly difficult issues. Comprehensive guidance on the proper conduct of such cases is set out in *Re A and B (One Parent Killed by the Other: Guidance)* [2011] 1 FLR 783, FD.

Split hearings—In May 2010 the President of the Family Division issued *Guidance in Relation to Split Hearings* (see Part V). This applies to both private and public law proceedings and warns that split hearings are taking place when they need not do so. The Guidance reminds judges that a fact-finding hearing should only be ordered if the court takes the view that the case cannot properly be decided without one (para 7). Even in cases where delay will not be occasioned, the use of split hearings should be confined to cases in which there is a discrete issue the early determination of which will enable the substantive determination to be made more expeditiously. Where delay will result, unless a decision to sever off discrete facts from their welfare context is reasoned so that the inevitable delay involved is justified, it is wrong in principle to adopt such a course of action in care proceedings (*Re S (Split Hearing)* [2014] 1 FLR 1421, CA). A decision at a case management hearing to direct a split hearing must be reasoned in court and those reasons recorded on the face of the order (*Re S (A Child)*). Practitioners will also find it useful to refer to *Re S (Care Proceedings: Split Hearing)* [1996] 2 FLR 773, FD, *Re P (Care Proceedings: Split Hearings)* [2007] EWCA Civ 1265, *Re C (Domestic Violence: Fact-finding Hearing)* [2010] 1 FLR 1728, CA and *A Local Authority v K and N* [2011] 2 FLR 1165, FD. All public law applications issued by local authorities under CA 1989, Pt IV (care and supervision orders) are subject to the time limits contained in CA 1989, s 32(1)(a); see **Case management conference** and **Issues resolution hearing** under FPR 2010, r 12.25. The outcome of a fact-finding hearing provides an essential foundation for resolving welfare issues and determining the future care of the children (*Re B and H (Children)* [2012] EWCA Civ 1359).

Opinions are only as sound as the facts upon which they are based. If the facts that are material to the opinion are in dispute then factual findings should be made (*Re H-C (Children)* [2014] EWCA Civ 536). In preparing for a split hearing it is essential that the local authority defines precisely what facts it is inviting the court to find (*CL v East Riding Yorkshire Council, MB and BL (A Child)* [2006] 2 FLR 24, CA). The document should set out the nature of the local authority's case, what the essential factual basis of the case is, what the evidence is upon which the local authority wishes to rely to establish its case and what the local authority is asking the court to do, and why (*Re J (A Child)* [2015] EWCA Civ 222). The document setting out those facts should avoid using terminology that confuses the distinction between an assertion of fact and the evidence required to prove that assertion, thus 'X lied' rather than 'it is reported that X lied' (*Re A (Application for Care and Placement Orders: Local Authority Failings); sub nom Darlington Borough Council v M, F, GM and GF* [2016] 1 FLR 1, FD).

In *Re W (Care Proceedings: Functions of Court and Local Authority)* [2014] 2 FLR 431, CA, Ryder LJ (citing the view of Pitchford LJ in *R (CJ) v Cardiff City Council* [2011] EWCA Civ 1590 that in care proceedings it is not appropriate to speak of the burden of proving precedent or jurisdictional facts as resting with a particular party but rather that the court, in its inquisitorial role, is required to ask itself whether the precedent or jurisdictional facts in issue exist on the balance of probability) held that, given the quasi-inquisitorial nature of care proceedings, the factual basis on which the threshold is satisfied is a matter for the judge and not the parties and that the court is not confined to those matters which the local authority seeks to prove. Where the judge wishes to make findings of fact not contained within the schedule or sought by the authority, he must ensure that those findings are securely founded in evidence and that the fairness of the fact-finding process is not compromised (*Re G and B (Fact-Finding Hearing)* [2009] 1 FLR 1145, CA and see *Re J-L (Findings of Fact: Schedule of Allegations)* [2013] 1 FLR 1240, CA). A judge should not introduce a new finding after all the evidence and submissions have been heard, this will constitute a serious procedural irregularity (*Re S (Children)* [2016] EWCA Civ 1020). Nonetheless, a judge is not required to adhere slavishly to the local authority's proposed findings, provided there is a very good reason to depart from them (*Re S (Children)*). Further, a judge is not limited to expert evidence; he or she can, for example, include their own assessment of credibility. Furthermore, issues that have not been known to exist can emerge during oral evidence and in these cases it would be absurd if such matters had to be ignored.

Judges need to apply a rigorous intellectual discipline to fact-finding hearings to ensure that they do not overstep the mark and address questions more fitted to the welfare stage of the proceedings, when the judge considers the best, or least worst, outcome for the child in the light of the findings made and the assessments undertaken by others consequent upon them (*Re L (Care Proceedings: Risk Assessment)* [2010] 1 FLR 790, CA). The difficulties created by the fact that a parent has learning difficulties is not a valid reason for abandoning a fact-finding hearing (*Re B and H (Children)* [2012] EWCA Civ 1359). However, where a parent has learning difficulties or limited cognitive abilities, the court should consider the use of special measures during the fact-finding hearing in order to facilitate that parent giving evidence. A failure to follow recommendations for such measures may breach the parent's right to a fair trial under Art 6 (*Re M (A Child)* [2012] EWCA Civ 1905). The court should make the appropriate findings without regard to the gravity of the consequences of doing so (*Re D (Children)* [2012] EWCA Civ 1584).

Where there is a split hearing there is nothing wrong in the court determining at the preliminary hearing, in advance of the local authority's final care plan, that a particular individual will not be in a position to care for a child safely within the timescale that the child needs, provided, of course, that the evidence substantiates this conclusion. The split hearing and the subsequent disposal hearing is a single process (*North Yorkshire County Council v B* [2008] 1 FLR 1645, FD). However, the judge should not prejudge the outcome of the care proceedings, however clear that outcome might appear to be (see *Re L*, above), and there will be some cases where the true abilities of an individual to care for a child can only be assessed reliably by a process carried out by relevant professionals outside the court room (*Re S-L* [2011] EWCA Civ 1022).

PART II

In *Re A (A Child)* [2010] EWCA Civ 1413 it was held that the Court of Appeal has jurisdiction to hear an appeal from a fact-finding hearing even if there is no order, following the decision in *Re B (Split Hearings: Jurisdiction)* [2000] 1 FLR 334, CA. However, in *Re M (Children)* [2013] EWCA Civ 1170, the Court of Appeal held that findings of fact do not comprise a determination, order or judgment for the purposes of CCA 1984, s 77 and CPR 1998, r 52.10(2) unless they concern the issue on which the determination of the whole case ultimately turns or are the subject of a declaration in the order of the type envisaged in *Compagnie Noga d'Importation et d'Exportation SA v Abacha (No 3)* [2003] 1 WLR 307, CA. Findings that do not concern the issue on which the determination of the whole case ultimately turns or are the subject of a declaration in the order may not be the subject of an appeal to the Court of Appeal.

The court must make clear and sufficiently reasoned findings of fact with respect to any disputed issues, to identify whether, and if so how, any of the facts found, either alone or in combination with each other, establish that the child is likely to suffer significant harm in the care of either or both parents and to identify (at least in broad terms) the category of significant harm that the judge concludes is likely to suffered by the child (*Re J (A Child)* [2015] EWCA Civ 222). Where findings are made at a preliminary hearing but subsequent evidence casts doubts upon them, the judge is entitled to reconsider his findings at the disposal hearing in the light of that new evidence (*Re B and H (Children)* [2003] EWCA Civ 1818). The judge must be astute to express at the preliminary hearing such views as he is able to, in order to assist social workers and psychiatrists in making their assessments and drafting the care plan. To that end, transcripts of judgments given at the preliminary hearing should always be made available when required so that reliance does not have to be placed on summaries or even bare statements of conclusions (*Re O and N: Re B* [2003] 1 FLR 1169, HL, at [35]). After a judge has given judgment, counsel have a positive duty to raise with the judge not just any alleged deficiency in the judge's reasoning process but also any genuine query or ambiguity that arises in relation to the judgment (*Re M (Fact-Finding Hearing: Burden of Proof)* [2009] 1 FLR 1177, CA).

The requirement for judicial continuity in all care cases is a core element of the PLO (FPR PD12A). However, there may be exceptions to judicial continuity, for example, where a judge has died or is ill and it is unlikely to be proportionate or in the interests of the child or in conformity with the overriding objective for the court to start again from scratch. Similar considerations apply where a litigant has legitimately lost confidence in the judge or where there could be an appearance of bias (*Re G and B (Fact-Finding Hearing)* [2009] 1 FLR 1145, CA). Furthermore, where an expert is asked to express an opinion, he must have all the relevant information, including a copy of any judgment given in the case; the summary of a judgment is not sufficient (*Re G (Care Proceedings: Split Trials)* [2001] 1 FLR 872, CA).

Application for reconsideration or review of findings of fact—In deciding whether to accede to an application for a re-hearing in respect of findings made, the court should adopt the three-stage process set out in *Birmingham City Council v H and ors* [2005] EWHC 2885 (Fam), as endorsed in *Re Z (Children) (Care Proceedings: Review of Findings)* [2015] 1 WLR 95, FD. First, the court must decide whether to permit a reconsideration, review or challenge to the findings. In the case of *Re AD and AM (Fact-Finding Hearing) (Application for Re-Hearing)* [2016] 2 FLR 1247, FD, Cobb J made clear that on an application for a re-hearing with respect to findings of fact in determining whether to permit a review or re-hearing, the court is required to consider only the first stage of the three-stage process set out in *Re Z (Children) (Care Proceedings: Review of Findings)*. As confirmed in *Re Z*, to move beyond the first stage the court must be satisfied that there is a real reason to believe that the findings require revisiting. At this stage speculation is not enough; there must be solid grounds for challenge. All new evidence requires careful evaluation at the first stage. Against this, however, the court cannot undertake a detailed critique of the newly obtained evidence as it has yet to be tested. In *Re AD & AM*, Cobb J gave detailed guidance at [71] as to how the difficult task of evaluating new medical evidence should be accomplished within this context. If the first stage is satisfied, the court must then go on to consider the second stage, which involves determining the proper ambit of the review or re-hearing. The ambit will depend on the forensic context and the circumstances of the particular case. The third stage is the hearing of the review. At this stage, the evidential burden is on the party who seeks to displace the earlier evidential finding. When considering an application for a re-hearing of findings of fact, two powerful public interests operate, namely the public interest in there being finality to litigation and the public interest in identifying the perpetrators of serious abuse to children (see *Birmingham City Council v H and ors* (above) and *Re K (Non-Accidental Injuries: Perpetrator: New Evidence)* [2005] 1 FLR 285, CA).

Burden of proof—The legal burden of establishing the existence of the threshold conditions in s 31(2) rests on the applicant for a care order. In cases of alleged injury, the court should be careful not inadvertently to reverse the burden of proof by requiring a parent to prove that the injuries in question have an innocent explanation as opposed to requiring the local authority to prove that they do not (see *Re M (Fact-Finding Hearing: Burden of Proof)* [2013] 2 FLR 874, CA). The fact that the local authority relies on the lack of a satisfactory explanation for the injuries does not amount to a reversal of the burden of proof (*Re M-B (Children)* [2015] EWCA Civ 1027, considering *Re M (Fact Finding: Burden of Proof)* (above), at [881]). It is important to remember that family proceedings are subject to the same rigorous evidential and forensic principles that govern all civil proceedings. In *Re A (Application for Care and Placement Orders: Local Authority Failings); sub nom Darlington Borough Council v M, F, GM and GF* [2016] 1 FLR 1, FD, *Re J (A Child)* [2015] EWCA Civ 222 and *Re R (Children)* [2015] EWCA Civ 167, the following principles were reiterated:

(a) The general rule, often neglected by advocates in the Family Court, is that where a party witness provides an appropriately verified written statement of her evidence, and is willing to attend for cross-examination, the court cannot be invited by other parties to disbelieve that evidence on a matter within her personal knowledge, unless it has been tested in cross-examination. This is a basic and deep-rooted aspect of the fair conduct of a trial, and reflects the central role that cross-examination plays in the ascertainment of the truth;

(b) If the local authority's case on a factual issue is challenged, the local authority must adduce proper evidence to establish the fact it seeks to prove. If a local authority asserts that a parent 'does not admit, recognise or acknowledge' that a matter of concern to the authority is the case, then if that matter of concern is put in issue, it is for the local authority to prove it is the case and, furthermore, that the matter of concern 'has the significance attributed to it by the local authority'. Note that where a respondent fails to prove on a balance of probabilities an affirmative case that he or she has chosen to set up by way of defence, this does not of itself establish the local authority's case (see *Re X* [2015] EWHC 3651 (Fam));

(c) Hearsay evidence about issues that appear in reports produced on behalf of the local authority, although admissible, has strict limitations if a parent challenges that hearsay evidence by giving contrary oral evidence at a hearing. If the local authority is unwilling or unable to produce a witness who can speak to the relevant matter by first-hand evidence, it may find itself in 'great, or indeed insuperable' difficulties in proving the fact or matter alleged by the local authority but which is challenged;

(d) The formulation of 'Threshold' issues and proposed findings of fact must be done with the utmost care and precision. The distinction between a fact and evidence alleged to prove a fact is fundamental and must be recognised. The document must identify the relevant facts that are sought to be proved. It can be cross-referenced to evidence relied on to prove the facts asserted but should not contain mere allegations ('he appears to have lied' etc);

(e) It is for the local authority to prove that there is the necessary link between the facts upon which it relies and its case on Threshold. The local authority must demonstrate why certain facts, if proved, 'justify the conclusion that the child has suffered or is at the risk of suffering significant harm' of the type asserted by the local authority. 'The local authority's evidence and submissions must set out the arguments and explain explicitly why it is said that, in the particular case, the conclusion [that the child has suffered or is at the risk of suffering significant harm] indeed follows from the facts [proved]';

(f) It is vital that local authorities, and, even more importantly, judges, bear in mind that nearly all parents will be imperfect in some way or other. The State will not take away the children of 'those who commit crimes, abuse alcohol or drugs or suffer from physical or mental illness or disability, or who espouse antisocial, political or religious beliefs' simply because those facts are established. It must be demonstrated by the local authority, in the first place, that by reason of one or more of those facts, the child has suffered or is at risk of suffering significant harm. Even if that is demonstrated, adoption will not be ordered unless it is demonstrated by the local authority that 'nothing else will do' when having regard to the overriding requirements of the child's welfare. The court must guard against 'social engineering';

(g) When a judge considers the evidence, he must take all of it into account and consider each piece of evidence in the context of all the other evidence, and, to use a metaphor, examine the canvas overall.

Standard of proof—The standard of proof is the ordinary civil standard of balance of probabilities (*Re B (Care Proceedings: Standard of Proof)* [2008] 2 FLR 141, HL; *Re H and R (Minors) (Child Sexual Abuse: Standard of Proof)* [1996] 1 FLR 80, HL; *Re M and R (Child Abuse: Evidence)* [1996] 2 FLR 195, CA). If a judge finds it more likely than not that something has taken place, then it is treated as having taken place; if he finds it more likely than not that it has not taken place, then it is treated as not having taken place.

In *Re B (Care Proceedings: Standard of Proof)* [2008] 2 FLR 141, HL, the House of Lords noted that neither the seriousness of the allegation nor the seriousness of the consequences should make any difference to the standard of proof to be applied in determining the facts. There is no 'heightened standard' and no legal rule that 'the more serious the allegation, the more cogent the evidence needed to prove it' (for a reiteration of this point see most recently *F v Cumbria County Council* [2016] EWHC 14 (Fam)). Baroness Hale emphasised that there is no logical or necessary connection between seriousness and probability. Inherent probability remains simply something to be taken into account, where relevant, in deciding where the truth lies (*Re B (Care Proceedings: Standard of Proof)*). In this context, it remains an essential part of the judge's fact-finding exercise to test the conclusion seemingly suggested by the evidence against its inherent improbability (*Re R (A Child)* [2013] EWCA Civ 899). In the context of care proceedings the lack of any logical or necessary connection between seriousness and probability applies with particular force to the identification of the perpetrator. It may be unlikely that any person looking after a baby would take him by the wrist and swing him against a wall, causing multiple fractures and other injuries. But once the evidence is clear that that is indeed what happened, it ceases to be improbable. Someone looking after the child at the relevant time must have done it. The inherent improbability of the event has no relevance to deciding who that was. The simple balance of probabilities test should be applied (*Re S-B (Children)* [2010] 1 FLR 1161, SC).

It is in the public interest that those who cause non-accidental injuries be identified (*Re K (Non-accidental Injuries: Perpetrator: New Evidence)* [2005] 1 FLR 285, CA). The court should not, however, 'strain' the evidence before it to identify on the simple balance of probabilities the individual who inflicted the injuries. If it is clear that identification of the perpetrator is not possible and the judge remains genuinely uncertain, then the judge should reach that conclusion (*Re D (Care Proceedings: Preliminary Hearing)* [2009] 2 FLR 668, CA). A judge considering non-accidental injuries always has to consider the whole picture before determining causation. For example, an injury that might be accepted as accidental if it stood alone might take on a wholly different aspect if it is only one of a number of injuries (*Re L-K (Children)* [2015] EWCA Civ 830). In assessing alternative possible explanations for a medical finding, the court will consider each possibility on its merits. There is no hierarchy of possibilities to be taken in sequence as part of a process of elimination. The court will not conclude that an injury has been inflicted merely because known or unknown medical conditions are improbable: that conclusion will only be reached if the entire evidence shows that inflicted injury is more likely than not to be the explanation for the medical findings (*Re BR (Proof of Facts)* [2015] EWFC 41). The absence of any history of a memorable event where such a history might be expected in the individual case may be very significant. Medical and other professionals are entitled to rely upon such knowledge and experience in forming an opinion about the likely response of the individual child to the particular injury, and the court should not deter them from doing so. The weight that is then given to any such opinion is a matter for the judge (*Re BR*, above).

The Supreme Court in *Re S-B (Children)* [2010] 1 FLR 1161, SC emphasised that if the judge cannot identify a perpetrator or perpetrators, it is still important to identify the pool of possible perpetrators (para 40) by asking whether the evidence establishes that there is a 'likelihood or real possibility' that a given person perpetrated the injuries in question (*North Yorkshire CC v SA* [2003] 2 FLR 849, CA). In such circumstances, it is all the more important to scrutinise the evidence carefully and consider whether anyone, and if so who, should be included in the pool of possible perpetrators (*Re S (A Child)* [2014] 1 FLR 739, CA). However, it is not helpful for the judge to give an indication of percentages as to the likelihood that one or other of the pool of possible perpetrators was responsible and judges should be cautious about amplifying in this way a judgment in which they have been unable to identify a specific perpetrator (*Re S-B (Children)* [2010] 1 FLR 1161, SC). It is important to note that the court remains under a duty to consider the welfare of the child under CA 1989, s 1(3) where that child has suffered injury and thereby significant harm, even where it is not possible to say who the perpetrator of harm is (*Re S (A Child)*). Note that the Court of Appeal has held that, in the context of the requirements of the Children Act 1989, s 31(2), the terms 'non-accidental' and 'accidental' injury are, in addition to being tautologous and oxymoronic, unhelpful, the threshold criteria not being concerned with intent or blame but rather with an objective standard of care (*Re S (Split Hearing)* [2014] 1 FLR 1421, CA).

PART II

Where the court is satisfied that the child has suffered significant harm, the threshold conditions under CA 1989, s 31(2)(b)(i) will be met in relation to that child even though the court is unable to identify who within the pool of possible perpetrators inflicted the harm: *Lancashire County Council v B* [2000] 1 FLR 583, HL, in which helpful guidance is given as to how evidence needs to be tested to establish the threshold criteria for the purposes of s 31 where the perpetrator is uncertain. In determining whether a person is properly included in the pool of potential perpetrators, it is essential that the court weighs any lies told by that person against any evidence that points away from them having been responsible for the injuries (*H v City and Council of Swansea and Others* [2011] EWCA Civ 195). In these 'uncertain perpetrator' cases, the correct approach is for the case to proceed at the welfare stage on the basis that each of the possible perpetrators is treated as such (*Re O and N: Re B* [2003] 1 FLR 1169, HL). The House of Lords held in that case that it would be grotesque if, because neither parent had been proved to be the perpetrator, the court had to proceed at the welfare stage as though the child were not at risk from either parent, even though one or other of them was the perpetrator of significant harm. The judge conducting the welfare hearing should have regard to the facts found at the preliminary hearing when they leave open the possibility that a parent or carer was a perpetrator of proved harm and that conclusion should not be excluded from consideration.

Whether either limb of s 31(2)(a) is satisfied is an issue to be decided by the court on the basis of the facts admitted or proved on the balance of probability before it; suspicion is not sufficient (*Re M and R (Child Abuse: Evidence)* [1996] 2 FLR 195, CA; *Re B and W (Threshold Criteria)* [1999] 2 FLR 833, CA). The range of facts that may properly be taken into account is infinite (see *Re H and R (Minors) (Child Sexual Abuse: Standard of Proof)* [1996] 1 FLR 80, HL, at [101B] for examples) and facts that are minor or even trivial if considered in isolation, when taken together may suffice to satisfy the court of harm or the likelihood of future harm. The role of the court is to consider the evidence in its totality and to make findings on the balance of probabilities accordingly. There is no principle that a certain type of evidence is incapable of establishing that an inflicted injury has occurred (*Re P (Findings of Fact)* [2014] EWCA Civ 89). In *Re S-B (Children)* [2010] 1 FLR 1161, SC, the first instance judge had found that the threshold had been crossed in relation to the younger of the two children on the basis that there was a real possibility that the mother had injured the older child. Lady Hale said that this was not a permissible approach to a finding of likelihood of future harm. A prediction of future harm has to be based on findings of actual fact made on the balance of probabilities, since it is only once those facts have been found that the degree of likelihood of future events becomes the 'real possibility' required by the test adopted in *Re H* (above). Lady Hale noted that it might have been open to the judge to find the threshold crossed in relation to child B on a different basis, but she did not do so.

The Supreme Court reiterated these principles in *Re J (Care Proceedings: Possible Perpetrators)* [2013] 1 FLR 1373, SC, holding that because a previous finding that a person was within the 'pool' of possible perpetrators of established injuries occurring in a prior family unit is a finding made on the basis of a 'real possibility' (as opposed to the balance of probabilities), such a finding is not capable by itself of supporting a finding of likelihood of future harm in subsequent proceedings concerning a new family unit. Lady Hale made clear that there must be a clearly established objective basis for interference by the state in family life and, accordingly, that while reasonable suspicion is a sufficient basis for the local authority to investigate and to take interim protective measures, it cannot be a sufficient basis for long-term intervention. Within this context, Lady Hale reiterated that only a finding of fact made on the balance of probabilities is sufficient to ground a finding of likelihood of future harm. The requirement of proven factual foundations on which to base a finding of likelihood of future harm has been described as a precious bulwark against the removal by the state of a child from his or her family (*Re F (Interim Care Order)* [2011] 2 FLR 856, CA and *Re J*). Lady Hale pointed out in *Re J* that the inability to identify a past perpetrator on the balance of probabilities does not preclude a finding of likelihood of future harm where there are other facts established on the balance of probabilities from which such likelihood could itself be established. In this regard, when the case was before the Court of

Appeal, McFarlane LJ stated that in determining whether the threshold criteria are satisfied in relation to children in the new family unit, a judge is under a duty to become acquainted with all of the available evidence and then bring it to bear on the ultimate question of whether, in the context of the particular case, each or any of the children can be said to be 'likely to suffer significant harm' attributable to failures in parental care likely to be given to him as at that date. The court is also under a duty to ensure that it has before it not only evidence of what may have happened in one of the parent's lives years before, but also some account of the events in that parent's life during the following years and the current circumstances in the family unit that is now before the court (*Re J (Care Proceedings: Past Possible Perpetrators in a New Family Unit)* [2012] 2 FLR 842, CA). Note in this context that Lady Hale, Lord Hope and Lord Reed suggest that, whereas a person's consignment to the 'pool' of possible perpetrators on the basis of a real possibility cannot on its own constitute a factual foundation for the prediction of likelihood of future harm, in combination with other established facts and circumstances it may figure as part of the requisite factual foundation. In partly dissenting judgments in *Re J*, Lord Wilson and Lord Sumption rejected this approach as illogical, holding that if, for the purpose of establishing the factual foundation of likelihood of future harm, a person's consignment to the 'pool' of possible perpetrators on the basis of a real possibility has a value of zero on its own, it can for that purpose have no greater value in the company of facts established on the balance of probabilities.

It is important for the court to hear proper evidence before making a finding of sexual abuse in the face of a complete and consistent denial by the alleged perpetrator (see *Re D (Sexual Abuse Allegations: Evidence of Adult Victim)* [2002] 1 FLR 723, FD, where the findings of the magistrates were not supported by direct evidence and were overturned on appeal). There will be cases in which a failure to follow the Achieving Best Evidence (ABE) guidance when interviewing children will undermine that evidence such that no reliance can safely be placed upon it. However, even where the court identifies a failure to follow best practice, it is entitled in an appropriate case to conclude that there is a core of truth in what has been described in the ABE interview unless the whole process is so flawed that nothing reliable emerges (*Re H (A Child)* [2014] EWCA Civ 232).

Welfare and proportionality—Where the court is satisfied that the threshold criteria in s 31(2) are made out, the court has jurisdiction to make a care or supervision order and must decide whether or not to do so by reference to the child's best interests under s 1(1) evaluated in accordance with the welfare checklist in s 1(3). In *Re B (Care Proceedings: Appeal)* [2013] 2 FLR 1075, SC, the Supreme Court reiterated that adoption can only occur if parents are unwilling, or are deemed by judicial process to be unable, to discharge their responsibilities towards the child and that, accordingly, the granting of a care order with a care plan of adoption is an option of last resort requiring a high degree of justification to be made only in exceptional circumstances where nothing else will do (see also *Re P (A Child)* [2014] 1 FLR 824, CA). It is, however, important to note that the phrase 'nothing else will do' must not be applied as some freestanding, short-cut test divorced from, or even in place of, an overall evaluation of the child's welfare. The phrase must be applied so that it is tied to the welfare of the child. Used properly, the phrase is a useful distillation, but no more than that, of the proportionality and necessity test embodied in Art 8 and reflects the need to afford paramount consideration to the welfare of the child throughout his or her lifetime. The phrase must not be used to bypass the need to undertake a full, comprehensive welfare evaluation of all the relevant competing advantages and disadvantages of each option. Only once this evaluation has been done will the overall proportionality of any adoption plan fall to be evaluated and the phrase 'nothing else will do' can properly be deployed. If the outcome of the comprehensive welfare evaluation favours placement for adoption or an adoption order, it is that outcome that falls to be evaluated against the yardstick of necessity and proportionality and the phrase that embodies those principles (*Re W (A Child)* [2016] EWCA Civ 793). The key point is that the Supreme Court emphasised in *Re B* that a judge cannot properly decide that a care order with a care plan of adoption should be made unless the order is proportionate, bearing in mind the requirements of Art 8 and the relevant provisions of the UN Convention on the Rights of the Child. The principles articulated in *Re B* are relevant wherever the court is required to police by rigorous judicial scrutiny the proportionate response of involuntary state intervention into family life (*MW and Hertfordshire County Council v A & V and Mr & Mrs J* [2014] EWCA Civ 405).

In light of the decision of the Supreme Court in *Re B*, the Court of Appeal has emphasised in a series of subsequent decisions the need for a rigorous approach to the evaluation of the child's best interests by reference to the principle of proportionality when the court is deciding whether to make an order and, if so, which order to make. This approach comprises two stages. The court must first undertake a global, holistic evaluation and analysis of the child's welfare needs. The court must then evaluate proportionality by conducting a balancing exercise in which each of the realistically available options for meeting the child's identified welfare needs is evaluated in the degree of detail necessary to analyse its own internal positives and negatives in order, having regard to the duty to afford paramount consideration to the welfare of the child, to reach a decision as to which of the realistically available options is the most proportionate means of meeting those needs and avoiding a linear analysis whereby the available options are rejected one by one with the final option left standing (*Re G (A Child)* [2014] 1 FLR 670, CA). The welfare analysis is not a proportionality evaluation. The proportionality evaluation requires a comparison of the welfare analysis for each placement/welfare option and a consideration of whether, having regard to the benefits and detriments of each realistic option, the proportionality of interference proposed by the local authority is justified (*Surrey County Council v S* [2014] EWCA Civ 601). The court is required to measure the proportionality of the proposed outcome against the evidence. The examination of proportionality will thus include an examination of the conduct of the local authority and the steps it has taken to assist parents in addressing the concerns identified by the local authority (*Re E (A Child)* [2013] EWCA Civ 1592).

In reaching its decision on proportionality, full weight must be given to the importance of a family placement unless it has been established that it would be so contrary to the child's welfare that a long-term placement in public care or adoption is necessary (*Re M'P-P (Children)* [2015] EWCA Civ 584). However, there is no presumption that a child will be brought up by his or her natural family. The arrangements for the child fall to be determined by affording paramount consideration to her welfare throughout her life in a manner that is proportionate and compatible with the need to respect any Art 8 rights engaged (*Re W (A Child)* [2016] EWCA Civ 793). In circumstances where the evaluation of realistic options for permanency has been undertaken with the factors set out in CA 1989, s 1 in full focus, if adoption is shown to be in the child's best interests, the child's welfare is not to be compromised by keeping the child within their family at all costs (*Re R* [2015] 1 FLR 715, CA). The principle that adoption should be sanctioned only if nothing else would do has to be interpreted with a careful eye to the realities of a child's life (*Re M (A Child: Long Term Foster Care)* [2015] 2 FLR 197, CA).

While the list of factors in ACA 2002, s 1(4) is a vital starting point, it is not an exhaustive set of criteria. The fact that speedy action will improve the prospects of a successful adoption for a child of a particular age has to take its place in the overall appraisal of a case. In some cases, the fact that speedy action will improve the prospects of a successful adoption will dictate approval of a plan for adoption, even when full weight is given to the principle in *Re B* that adoption is to be contemplated only if it is necessary. What is 'necessary' for the purposes of the evaluation mandated by *Re B* is a complex question requiring an evaluation of all the circumstances. The question is not simply whether any other course is realistic, but whether there is another course that is possible and in the child's interests (*Re M (A Child: Long Term Foster Care)*, above).

PART II

For the impact of a finding of significant harm due to female genital mutilation on the overall welfare evaluation, see *Re B and G (Children) (No 2); sub nom Leeds City Council v M, F, B, G (B and G by their Children's Guardian)* [2015] 1 FLR 905, FD.

Where within the context of care proceedings any 'status quo' argument falls to be considered, the factors relevant to the weight to be attached to the child's status quo will be wide ranging and many of them will be practically based. However, within this wide range, the significance for the child of any particular relationship is likely to be a highly salient factor. Full weight must be given to the importance of a family placement, unless it had been established that it would be so contrary to a child's welfare that a long-term placement in public care or adoption is necessary (*Re M'P-P (Children)* [2015] EWCA Civ 584).

The approach mandated by *Re B* requires that there must be proper evidence from the local authority and the Children's Guardian addressing all the realistically possible options for the child and containing an analysis of the arguments for and against each option (*Re V (Long-Term Fostering or Adoption)* [2014] 1 FLR 1009, CA, *K v London Borough of Brent and others* [2013] EWCA Civ 926 and *Re B-S*, above). The evidence from the local authority should not be restricted to the local authority's preferred outcome (*Re Y (A Child)* [2013] EWCA Civ 1337) and must also set out the range of services that are available in respect of each option and under each of the orders that the court can impose (*Re W (Care Proceedings: Functions of Court and Local Authority)* [2014] 2 FLR 431, CA). The court can require the local authority to specify the services that are practicable under each of the range of orders that the court is considering and can direct the local authority to file a care plan that meets a particular formulation or assessment of risk, even though that plan does not reflect the position of the local authority (*Re W*, above).

In deciding whether to make an order and, if so, which order, the court must give an adequately reasoned judgment that grapples with the competing options and gives them proper, focused attention (*Re B-S (Children)* and see *Re P (Care Proceedings: Appeal)* [2017] 1 FLR 417, CA). When constructing a judgment concerning the required evaluative welfare exercise in accordance with *Re B-S*, the judge is entitled to construct the strategic welfare analysis required by s 1(3) of the 1989 Act and s 1(4) of the 2002 Act from the evidence in the case including his or her own reasons for the conclusions he or she reaches. That analysis does not require expert evidence, the welfare analysis undertaken by the judge being distinct from the professional advice on an issue that is outside the expertise of the court (*Surrey County Council v S* [2014] EWCA Civ 601). Where there is an error of form in that the judge does not undertake the neat balancing of welfare factors described in *Re B-S* by comparing one option with another, the decision will not be amenable to appeal where the judge has clearly engaged with the core, long-term welfare decisions and addressed them in a holistic way (*M, GP and AK v Suffolk County Council* [2014] EWCA Civ 942 and *Re R* [2015] 1 FLR 715, CA).

Care order or supervision order (s 31(5))—Whereas the court has no jurisdiction to compel a local authority to issue an application for an order under s 31 (s 31(1); *Nottinghamshire County Council v P* [1993] 2 FLR 134, CA), once the local authority has issued its application and satisfied the court that the threshold criteria under s 31(2) are met, it is for the court to decide which out of a supervision order or a care order is the more appropriate order to make, if satisfied that an order is in the child's best interests. Thus, if the threshold criteria are satisfied, the court may make a care order where such an order is in the child's best interests even if the applicant local authority does not seek the same (*Re K (Care Order or Residence Order)* [1995] 1 FLR 675, FD; *Re C (Care or Supervision Order)* [1999] 2 FLR 621, FD). It is for the court to decide which order is the more appropriate, but the court should nonetheless satisfy itself that very cogent reasons exist before it imposes on a local authority an order that the local authority does not seek (*Oxfordshire County Council v L* [1998] 1 FLR 70, FD; *Re T (Care Order)* [2009] 2 FLR 574, CA).

The protection of the child is the decisive factor when the court is deciding whether to make a care order or a supervision order (*Re D (A Minor) (Care or Supervision Order)* [1993] 2 FLR 423, FD; *Re K (Care Order or Residence Order)* [1995] 1 FLR 675, FD). When determining which of a care order or a supervision order is appropriate, the court should first make a careful assessment of the likelihood of future harm to the child and then weigh that harm against the harm that would follow the child being removed from his parents under a care order (*Re S (Care or Supervision Order)* [1996] 1 FLR 753, CA; *Re V (Care or Supervision Order)* [1996] 1 FLR 776, CA). A care order rather than a supervision order should be made only if the stronger order is necessary for the protection of the child (*Re B (Care or Supervision Order)* [1996] 2 FLR 693, FD). In deciding whether to make a care order or a supervision order in a particular case where the balance between the two is equal, the court should adopt the least interventionist approach (*Re D (Care or Supervision Order)* [2000] Fam Law 600, FD).

The choice between a care order and a supervision order has also to be considered in the light of HRA 1998 and ECHR 1950. The key in each case is to decide whether a supervision order is a proportionate response to the risk presented (*Re O (Supervision Order)* [2001] 1 FLR 923, CA; *Re C (Care Order or Supervision Order)* [2001] 2 FLR 466, FD). There must be strong and cogent reasons to force upon a local authority a more draconian order than that for which they had asked, particularly when the guardian supported a less draconian order as appropriate to the child's needs (*Re T (Care Order)*, above – in which no such strong and cogent reasons were demonstrated). See further under **Care Orders – ECHR 1950**, above.

There is no authority to support the proposition that the court, exercising its inherent jurisdiction, can authorise a local authority to provide care for a child where it would not otherwise have power to do so under the statutory scheme. The most the court can do is to support arrangements that are otherwise legitimately in place by making orders that are not excluded from the court's jurisdiction by s 100 (*Re M (Children)* [2016] EWCA Civ 937).

Agreed orders—The agreement of the parties cannot deprive the court of its duty to satisfy itself by evidence that the strict criteria for a care order have been fulfilled, but the degree of investigation required of the court will vary from case to case, and the factors relevant to the exercise of that discretion are set out in *A County Council v DP, RS, BS by his Children's Guardian* [2005] 2 FLR 1031, FD. Where the parties are agreed on a care order and also as to the factual substratum underlying the fulfilment of the threshold criteria, the court's duty may be discharged by perusing the documents and approving the agreed order (*Devon County Council v S* [1992] 2 FLR 244, FD).

In some cases parents are prepared to make concessions in relation to the threshold criteria and do not seek to argue as to the disposal of the case, but other parties do not agree that the concessions reflect the nature of the case appropriately. It is a matter for the discretion of the judge as to whether the concessions are sufficient to meet the justice of the matter and the best interests of the children (*Re B (Agreed Findings of Fact)* [1998] 2 FLR 968, CA; *Re M (Threshold Criteria: Parental Concessions)* [1999] 2 FLR 728, CA; and *Re W (Children) (Threshold Criteria: Parental Concessions)* [2001] 1 FCR 139, CA). Where parents agree with the local authority to make concessions, this in no way ties the hands of the judge and arguments by the parents of 'issue estoppel' are wholly inappropriate (*Re D (Child: Threshold Criteria)* [2001] 1 FLR 274, CA). No such strong and cogent reasons were demonstrated in this case. That said, the power to make a care order where the application had been for a supervision order was not 'neutered by an agreement reached between the parties outside the court'. What is important is that the court examines the background facts and reasons underlying the agreement and justifies the order made, particularly where this involves departing from professional assessment and guidance.

In determining whether further investigation is appropriate and deciding upon the extent of that investigation, the court will take into account the circumstances of the case including the interests of the children, whether there is likely to be future litigation in which the disputed facts would be relevant, the relevance of the disputed allegations to the local authority's care plan and management of the case, the time likely to be spent investigating any given issue and the cost to public funds of the investigation, the likely evidential result of the investigation and the emotional toll of the court hearing. See also *Re K (Supervision Orders)* [1999] 2 FLR 303, FD.

It is unhelpful to have no findings as to the facts underlying the s 31 conditions. Where the parties agree that the threshold criteria are met, they should at the very least be invited by the court to agree the factual basis for this and to acknowledge it by the signature of the parties or of the legal representatives (*Re C (A Minor) (Care Order: Appeal)* [1996] 1 FCR 332, FD). Even where the s 31 threshold is conceded, it is the court's duty to be satisfied that the circumstances under s 31(2) are met and it is therefore generally appropriate for the court to record the basis upon which this is so (*Oxfordshire County Council v L* [1998] 1 FLR 70, FD). Sometimes it may do so by making its own findings of fact upon the agreed evidence. Sometimes it may do so by reference to an agreed statement of facts. Without such a statement, it is difficult to know what the basis for making an order has been. Where orders are made without judicial investigation on oral evidence, it is inappropriate for the court to make findings of fact; the court may deal with the matter by simply accepting the formal admissions made by the parents and pronouncing the orders sought (*Stockport MBC v D* [1995] 1 FLR 873, FD).

Summary disposal by judge may not be appropriate—In care proceedings where there are issues that require a full investigation and are likely to have a direct impact on the case it is inappropriate for the judge to summarily dismiss them (*Re H (Children)* [2002] EWCA Civ 1692).

'designated local authority' (s 31(8))—Sections 31(8) and 105(6) should be construed so as to provide a simple mechanism for designation (*Northamptonshire County Council v Islington County Council* [1999] 2 FLR 881, CA). To ensure that s 31(8) provides a test applicable in all cases, it is legitimate to construe s 31(8)(b) as though it reads 'where the child does not ordinarily reside' in a local authority area, inserting the word 'ordinarily'. The preferred approach to periods that have to be disregarded under s 105(6) is notionally to extend the child's residence in the authority area where he or she has been ordinarily resident immediately before the commencement of the disregard period. By virtue of ss 31(8)(a) and 105(6), this simple test will identify the local authority to be designated in the care order. If there are exceptional circumstances, such as developments affecting the family during the period to be disregarded (eg the movement of the entire family into a different authority area) then these can be considered. If the child has no ordinary residence, the designated local authority will be the one for the principal area in which the primary circumstances that led to the care order being made occurred. In *Northamptonshire County Council v Islington County Council*, Thorpe LJ emphasised that the function of the judge was limited to carrying out a rapid and not over-sophisticated review of the history in order to make a purely factual determination of the child's place of ordinary residence or, if there was no place of ordinary residence, of the place where the case was carried over the s 31 threshold, and to designate a local authority accordingly. It is open to the court to hold that a newborn baby is incapable of ordinary residence apart from the mother, so that the baby's ordinary residence is the same as that of the mother (*C (A Child) v Plymouth County Council* [2000] 1 FLR 875, CA). For the purpose of designation, the time to consider a child's ordinary residence is at the time the matter is being considered by the court and not, for example, at the time of commencement of proceedings (*London Borough of*

Redbridge v Newport City Council [2004] 2 FLR 226, FD). A designation of a local authority at an interim hearing is subject to reconsideration and possible variation at a later date. In *Sheffield CC v Bradford CC* [2013] 1 FLR 1027, FD, Bodey J held that the repeal of CA 1989, s 23 meant that the decision of the Court of Appeal in *Re H (Care Order: Appropriate Local Authority)* [2004] 1 FLR 534, CA that a child placed with relatives ceases to be 'provided with accommodation by or on behalf of a local authority' within the meaning of CA 1989, s 105(6) could no longer be considered correct. Under CA 1989, s 22C, a child placed with a relative is 'provided with accommodation by the local authority' for the purposes of s 105(6) and the disregard period has to be applied. For the principles governing the designation of local authorities in the context of special guardianship support services, see CA 1989, s 14F and *Re D (Local Authority Responsibility)* [2013] 2 FLR 673, CA and *Suffolk CC v Nottinghamshire CC* [2013] 2 FLR 106, CA.

Where it is clear that a care order, if made, would designate a local authority other than the applicant authority, full and early liaison needs to take place between the authorities and the care plan must be prepared in co-operation between them. Even if the second authority is not present or represented throughout the hearing, proper arrangements should be made in advance for a representative of the authority to attend court to deal with any issues that might arise and to assure the court and the parents of the authority's commitment to the care plan and its capacity to implement it (*L v London Borough of Bexley* [1996] 2 FLR 595, FD and see *Suffolk CC v Nottinghamshire CC* (above) on the need for local authorities to cooperate in respect of special guardianship support services under the CA 1989). The arrangements for contact which the court has to consider under s 34(11) before making a care order are the arrangements proposed by the authority into whose care the child would be placed. *Re C (Care Order: Appropriate Local Authority)* [1997] 1 FLR 544, FD endorsed *L v London Borough of Bexley*. See further under s 105 and **Habitual residence** under CACA 1985, Sch 1, Art 4.

'ordinarily resident' (s 31(6),(8))—See under s 105(6) and **Habitual residence** under CACA 1985, Sch 1, Art 4.

'any person authorised by order of the Secretary of State' (s 31(9))—No person has yet been so authorised.

Assessment of capacity to litigate—The issue of litigation capacity is a critical one in care proceedings (*Re D (Children)* [2015] EWCA Civ 749). Where there is concern that a party to care proceedings may lack capacity to litigate, the court should address this issue at the case management hearing and, if necessary, direct an expert report to consider the issue (FPR PD12A). If a party takes issue with an assessment of litigation capacity, that party can apply to instruct an expert to provide a second opinion on the question. If, following written questions to the experts, there remains disagreement between those experts, the court will hear evidence and make a determination as to litigation capacity. In securing expert evidence as to capacity to litigate, the statutory code for the provision of expert evidence created by CFA 2014, s 13 and supplemented by FPR 2010, Pt 25 must be followed strictly (*Re D (Children)*, above).

Parents can be compelled to give evidence in care proceedings—Parents can be compelled to give evidence in any care proceedings. They have no right to refuse to do so, nor to refuse to answer questions that may incriminate them (*per curiam* in *Re Y and K (Split Hearing: Evidence)* [2003] 2 FLR 273, CA; *R v B County Council ex parte P* [1991] 1 FLR 470, CA) and if they decline to answer questions or to give evidence, the court should usually draw the inference that the allegations made against them are true (*Re O (Care Proceedings: Evidence)* [2004] 1 FLR 161, FD). A refusal by a parent to answer questions having been warned that they are compellable may lead to their committal to prison for contempt of court (see for example *Re L-R (Children)* [2013] EWCA Civ 1129, in which the Court of Appeal upheld an 18-month custodial sentence for contempt in respect of a parent who refused to give evidence in a case involving the death of a child). Such committal proceedings must be conducted in accordance with the *Practice Direction: Committal for Contempt of Court – Open Court* issued by the Lord Chief Justice on 26 March 2015. See also the Family Court (Contempt of Court) (Powers) Regulations 2014 and further under CA 1989, s 98.

Where a case is actively contested, it is very important that parents should give evidence. Family courts can make allowances for the impact of stress and emotion on the way in which the parents give their evidence. The process of giving evidence is the parents' opportunity to put their points to the court, to explain their actions and to set out their version of disputed facts and is vital in order that the court can make reliable findings of fact, gauge the soundness of professional opinions that have been offered to it and make decisions about the future welfare of the children (*Re H-C (Children)* [2014] EWCA Civ 536).

Parents with disabilities—The court, Cafcass and the local authority must each carry out their functions within the terms of the Equality Act 2010. Where a parent's disability may affect their ability to participate in the proceedings, this should be identified as a feature of the case at the earliest opportunity and be made known to the court at the time the proceedings are issued. Thereafter, care must be taken to ensure that the court has available to it at the very earliest stage expert analysis and support from a suitably qualified professional to advise on how best to address the issue. To this end, a properly constituted application for leave to instruct an expert pursuant to FPR 2010, Pt 25 should be made at the case management hearing. The issue of funding must likewise be addressed at the earliest opportunity. It is vital to recognise that parents with disabilities may require assistance not only during the course of the proceedings but also during the pre-proceedings stages, for example when being asked to consent to the accommodation of the child pursuant to CA 1989, s 20 (*Re C (Care Proceedings: Parents with Disabilities)* [2015] 1 FLR 521, CA, in which the Court of Appeal considered the provision of assistance to a mother who had a low level of cognitive functioning and a degree of speech and hearing impediment and a father who was profoundly deaf, and see *Re A (Care Proceedings: Learning Disabled Parent)* [2014] 2 FLR 591, FD). Where parents who are parties to care proceedings have a learning disability, the court must take steps to ensure that the parents can participate effectively in the decisions that affect their lives and that there are no barriers to justice within the process itself (see the guidance set out in the decision of the Family Division of the High Court of Justice in Northern Ireland in *Re G and A (Care Order: Freeing Order: Parents with a Learning Disability)* [2006] NIFam 8, at [5] cited by the President in *Re D (Adoption) (No 3)* [2017] 1 FLR 237, FD). Parents with learning disabilities must be supported and provided with the assistance that, because of their particular deficits, they need in order to be able to care for their child. The positive obligation on the State under Art 8 imposes a broad obligation on the local authority to provide such support as will enable the child to remain with his parents. However, it is also important to recognise that there will be some cases where, even if a sustainable package of support and assistance can be devised, that package will not promote the child's best interests in circumstances where (by reason of the gap between what the parents can offer the child and what the child needs being too large to be capable of being bridged by even the most extensive support package) it would constitute parenting by professional and other carers, rather than by his parents, with all the adverse consequences for the child's emotional development and future welfare (*Re D (A Child) (No 3)*).

Litigants in person—In a jurisdiction where the best interests of the children are paramount, judges must be alive to issues and points that should, and would, have been put forward on behalf of the parents had they been legally represented. This includes realistic options for the long-term care of the children. Similarly, the applicant local authority has an absolute obligation to ensure that the court considers all matters relevant to the child's welfare even if, in doing so, it might be seen to be undermining its own case (*Re Y (Children)* [2016] EWCA Civ 1091).

In family proceedings, the documents produced for the court pursuant to FPR PD27A should be served on litigants in person at least 3 days before the final hearing and the court should consider directing the translation of key documents where the litigant does not speak English. The court should also consider adjourning the case where late service causes genuine unfairness (*Re B (Litigants In Person: Timely Service of Documents)* [2016] EWHC 2365 (Fam)).

Children giving evidence—The Supreme Court made clear in *Re W (Children) (Abuse: Oral Evidence)* [2010] 1 FLR 1485, SC that the presumption against children giving evidence in family proceedings was unjustified and must be replaced by an evaluation in each case. The judge must evaluate the question by reference to the available evidence and it is likely that the judge will have to view the ABE interview under challenge before making the decision whether the child is called to be cross-examined on the contents of the ABE interview (*Re E (A Child)* [2016] EWCA Civ 473). Proper adherence to the principles laid down in *Re W (Children)* will likely mean that there will be more cases in future where a child either gives evidence without being joined as a party or is joined as a party (*Re F (Children)* [2016] EWCA Civ 546).

The test for whether a child should give oral evidence in family proceedings is set out in *Re W (Children)*. In *Re R (Children)* [2015] EWCA Civ 167, the Court of Appeal summarised the steps to be taken by the court when applying the test in *Re W* as follows:

(a) The fair balance between Art 6 rights and the Art 8 rights of the perceived victim may mean that in care proceedings a child should not be called to give evidence but that outcome (i e that a child should not give evidence) is a result of the balancing exercise and not a presumption or even a starting point;
(b) The essential test is whether justice can be done without further questioning of the child;
(c) The court weighs two considerations:
  (i) The advantages that the child giving evidence will bring to the determination of the truth, in which the following (non-exhaustive) set of factors will be relevant:
    - The issues it is necessary for the court to decide;
    - The quality of the evidence already available, including whether there is enough evidence to make the findings without the child being cross examined;
    - Whether there is anything useful to be gained by oral evidence in circumstances where the child has not made concrete allegations;
    - The quality of any ABE interview and the nature of the challenge (noting that the court will not be helped by generalised accusations of lying or a fishing expedition but that focused questions putting forward an alternative explanation for certain events may help the court to do justice);
    - Age and maturity of the child and the length of time since the events.
  (ii) The damage giving evidence may do to the welfare of this or any other child, in which the following (non-exhaustive) set of factors will be relevant:
    - Age and maturity of the child and the length of time since the events;
    - The child's wishes and feelings about giving evidence. An unwilling child should rarely if ever be obliged to give evidence and, where there are parallel criminal proceedings, the child having to give evidence twice may increase the risk of harm;
    - The level of support the child has and the views of the Guardian and those with parental responsibility;
    - The fact that the Family Court has to give less weight to the evidence of a child who is not called may be damaging to the child.

In considering whether the child should give evidence, the court is entitled to have regard to the general understanding of the harm that giving evidence may do to a child as well as features peculiar to the child and case under consideration. The risk, and therefore weight, will vary from case to case. The essential test, and hence the yardstick against which both limbs of the test in *Re W* must be considered is that justice must be done to all the parties when deciding whether permission should be given for a child or young person to give evidence. The court must also consider what steps can be taken to improve the quality of the child's evidence while minimising the risk of harm to the child, whether by special measures or other means (*Re R (Children)*, above). Those instructed on behalf of a vulnerable young person facing serious charges must be utterly clear as to their professional responsibilities and astute to ensure that their client's rights are properly protected with respect to the issue of legal professional privilege (*Re E (A Child)* [2016] EWCA Civ 473).

Legal professional privilege—Where a parent has, when viewed objectively, waived legal professional privilege, then the application of the principle of fairness may demand further disclosure to meet the risk that the parties might otherwise have only a partial and potentially misleading understanding of the material disclosed as a result of the waiver (*Re D (Care Proceedings: Legal Privilege)* [2011] 2 FLR 1183, CA). The undesirability of breaching confidentiality between the parent and his or her legal representatives has to be balanced against the unfairness to the other parties if it is not. Counsel and solicitors ought to be aware of the fact that advice might have been given to prompt a change of attitude by their client and they should be on guard to protect their client from revealing that advice either in written or oral evidence. Judges need to be astute to anticipate an unintentional observation that might result in privilege being waived and should be ready to warn witnesses of any such danger.

'Lucas direction'—In determining the facts in a family case, the court should have regard to the guidance given in *R v Lucas* [1981] QB 720, CA to the effect that a conclusion that a person is lying or telling the truth about point A does not mean that he is lying or telling the truth about point B (known in criminal proceedings as a *Lucas* direction). Where the local authority seeks to rely on the dishonesty of a parent as proving a risk of significant harm, the local authority must demonstrate why the parent's particular lies create the likelihood of significant harm to the children and what weight should reasonable be afforded to the fact of the parent's deceit in the overall balance (*Re Y (A Child)* [2013] EWCA Civ 1337; *Re A (Application for Care and Placement Orders: Local Authority Failings); sub nom Darlington Borough Council v M, F, GM and GF* [2016] 1 FLR 1, FD).

Multi-agency risk assessment conferences (MARACs)—MARAC meetings collate information about high-risk cases of domestic abuse with a view to creating a coordinated safety plan for the victim and children (if any). The work is case-specific and all relevant agencies will attend or contribute to the conference. MARACs may be a valuable source of information in public law proceedings where domestic abuse towards an adult or a child may be an issue. However, it should be noted that the information shared at MARACs is confidential and will invariably be sensitive in nature. Accordingly, any disclosure of such information should be dealt with by way of an application for disclosure within the proceedings. For the principles governing the disclosure of documents or other information generated by MARACs, see **Multi-agency risk assessment conferences (MARACs) – disclosure in public law and private law proceedings** under FPR 2010, r 12.12.

Concurrent care and criminal proceedings—Where there are criminal proceedings ongoing at the same time as care proceedings, linked directions hearings in the two sets of proceedings should be held where practicable. A pending criminal trial is not, by itself, sufficient reason to delay the care proceedings. The court must balance all the factors involved, taking into account any risk of prejudice to the accused and any risk as far as the child is concerned. The welfare of the child has to take precedence over the detriment to the family facing criminal proceedings (*Re TB (Care Proceedings: Criminal Trial)* [1995] 2 FLR 801, CA). There are some cases where the care proceedings may need to be the subject of an adjournment pending the outcome of the criminal proceedings (see *Re S (Care Order: Criminal Proceedings)* [1995] 1 FLR 151, CA and *Re A and B (Minors) (No 2)* [1995] 1 FLR 351, FD). A party to care proceedings is not excused from complying with case management directions in those care proceedings, including directions to file a response to threshold and/or a narrative statement simply because he or she is also the subject of criminal proceedings. It is wholly inappropriate and potentially a contempt of court for a legal practitioner to advise a client in criminal proceedings not to comply with an order made in concurrent care proceedings (*A Local Authority v DG and Others* [2014] 2 FLR 713, FD).There is no contradiction between a positive finding in care proceedings and an acquittal on the same facts in criminal proceedings (*Re W (Care Order: Sexual Abuse)* [2009] 2 FLR 1106, CA). The Association of Chief Police Officers, the Crown Prosecution Service and HMCTS have agreed a protocol designed to expedite criminal cases involving child witnesses under the age of 10 years (*A Protocol Between the Association of Chief Police Officers, the Crown Prosecution Service and Her Majesty's Courts & Tribunals Service to Expedite Cases Involving Witnesses under 10 Years* (19 January 2015)).

Concurrent care and immigration proceedings—Where there are immigration proceedings ongoing at the same time as care proceedings, the Family Court can ascertain the issues arising in the immigration proceedings, the procedure in those proceedings, the timescales for their determination and any information disclosed in them using the *Protocol on Communications between Judges of the Family Court and Immigration and Asylum Chambers of the First-tier Tribunal and Upper Tribunal*. In accordance with the *Protocol*, regard should also be had to *Re M and N (Parallel Family and Immigration Proceedings)* [2008] 2 FLR 2030, FD.

Children's guardian has no continuing role after making of care order—Following the repeal of CJCSA 2000, s 12(5)(b) by ACA 2002, there is no longer jurisdiction for a court to provide for a continuing role for a children's guardian following the making of a care order. Therefore, *Re MH (A Child); Re SB and MB (Children)* [2001] 2 FLR 1334, FD, which was based on s 12(5)(b), is no longer a correct statement of the law.

Undertakings and injunctions—Prior to the inception of the Family Court, it was held that the County Court had no jurisdiction to grant injunctions in relation to the exercise by local authorities of their statutory powers in public law proceedings (*D v D (County Court: Jurisdiction: Injunctions)* [1993] 2 FLR 802, CA (no jurisdiction to grant order restraining local authority and police from investigating alleged abuse), *Re S and D (Children: Powers of Court)* [1995] 2 FLR 456, CA (no power to add to a supervision order a provision prohibiting the mother from removing the children from foster parents) and *Devon County Council v B* [1997] 1 FLR 591, CA (no jurisdiction to grant an injunction restraining the mother from entering the town where her child who was in care was living)). The position would appear to be the same in the Family Court under the Matrimonial and Family Proceedings Act 1984 as amended.

Prior to the inception of the Family Court, the County Court has a statutory jurisdiction under CCA 1984, s 38 to grant injunctions in care proceedings where a care order is made to protect local authority employees from violence and intimidation by the parents (*Tameside Metropolitan Borough Council v M (Injunctive Relief: County Courts: Jurisdiction)* [2001] Fam Law 873, Cty Ct; see also *D v D (County Court Jurisdiction: Injunctions)* [1993] 2 FLR 802, CA). It is unclear whether this jurisdiction subsists in the Family Court. The County Court did not have inherent jurisdiction to accept undertakings in care proceedings. Where appropriate, the agreement or acknowledgements of a party to do or refrain from doing any act may be recorded in a preamble to the order made (*Re B (Supervision Order: Parental Undertaking)* [1996] 1 FLR 676, CA). The position would appear to be the same in the Family Court under the Matrimonial and Family Proceedings Act 1984, as amended.

The powers conferred on the High Court by SCA 1981, s 37 are available in support of the rights conferred by CA 1989, s 33, and in particular s 33(3) (the right of the local authority to determine the extent to which a parent may meet his parental responsibility for a child in care) after a care order has been made. Section 100 does not apply to the general statutory power to make injunctions and therefore it is not necessary for the local authority to have permission to apply for such injunctive relief (*Re P (Care Orders: Injunctive Relief)* [2000] 2 FLR 385, FD – where the local authority sought injunctions ancillary to a care order requiring the parents to allow the child to attend college without interference, and permitting the local authority to monitor the family). However, care proceedings may only be transferred to the High Court by order of a judge sitting in the Family Court who is either the President of the Family Division, a judge of the Court of Appeal or a High Court Judge or where the circumstances in FPR PD29C apply (FPR 2010, r 29.17).

The High Court's inherent jurisdiction can only be invoked once permission of that court has been obtained under s 100. However, once again, care proceedings may now only be transferred to the High Court by order of a judge sitting in the Family Court who is either the President of the Family Division, a judge of the Court of Appeal or a High Court Judge or where the circumstances in PD29C apply (FPR 2010, r 29.17). For further discussion, see the notes to s 100.

As to the partial change that FLA 1996 introduces with regard to undertakings, see under CA 1989, s 38B.

Orders for anonymity of social workers only made in exceptional cases—It has to be recognized that social workers receive threats and actual violence from adults engaged in bitterly contested public law cases at the end of which they face a forced and permanent separation from their children. This is part of their job and it will not generally be possible to obtain an order for anonymity of a social worker involved in such proceedings unless the circumstances are exceptional (*Re W (Care Proceedings: Witness Anonymity)* [2003] 1 FLR 329, CA and see *Re J (Reporting Restriction: Internet: Video)* [2014] 1 FLR 523, FD). A comprehensive review of the law in this respect was undertaken by Keehan J in *Surrey County Council v ME and Others* [2014] 2 FLR 1267, FD.

Withdrawal of care proceedings—Care proceedings may only be withdrawn with the permission of the court (FPR 2010, r 29.4). The applicant must file a written request for permission setting out his reasons (FPR 2010, r 29.4(3)). The court may deal with the written request without a hearing if the other parties have had an opportunity to make written representations to the court about it (FPR 2010, r 29.4(6)). The request may be made orally to the court if the parties are present (FPR 2010, r 29.4(4)). Where the local authority is unable to satisfy the threshold criteria under CA 1989, s 31(2) the application for permission to withdraw will succeed. However, where the threshold could be established, the granting of permission to withdraw depends on the court concluding under CA 1989, s 1(5) that no order is required because withdrawal is consistent with the child's welfare (*Redbridge LBC v B and C and A (Through his Children's Guardian)* [2011] 2 FLR 117, FD). In such circumstances, CA 1989, s 1(1) is engaged in the giving of permission, the use of the welfare checklist in s 1(3) is not mandatory; the application to withdraw care proceedings falls outside s 1(4) and therefore s 1(3) is not engaged. On such an application the court should take into account the principles set out in CPR 1998, Pt 1 as to the 'overriding objective' (which has been included in the FPR 2010, r 1.1) (*WSCC v M, F, W, X, Y and Z* [2011] 1 FLR 188, FD and see *Ciccone v Ritchie (No 2)* [2017] 1 FLR 812, FD). A refusal of permission to withdraw in this case would commit the parties to the listed 15-day hearing and, while proportionality could not be allowed to trump welfare, it nonetheless remained a factor to which the court should give proper consideration. Where an application is made to withdraw public law child care proceedings on the basis that to continue them would amount to an interference with the right of the parents of the child concerned under Art 8(1) of the Convention to respect for their private and family life, the court must assess whether such interference is necessary to protect one of the interests set out in Art 8(2) (*Re N (Leave to Withdraw Care Proceedings)* [2000] 1 FLR 134, FD). Where there is a serious conflict between the interests of the child and one of its parents which can only be resolved to the disadvantage of one of them, the interests of the child must prevail under Art 8(2) (*Hendriks v The Netherlands* (1982) 5 EHRR 223, ECHR).

An application for permission to withdraw care proceedings is made in the course of existing proceedings and therefore should be made using the procedure in FPR 2010, rr 18.1–18.13.

Costs—The principle that costs orders should only be made in children's cases in unusual circumstances applies with equal force in care proceedings (*Re S (A Child) (Costs: Care Proceedings)* [2015] 2 FLR 208, SC). Further, local authorities should not be in any better or worse position than private parties when it comes to paying the other parties' costs. Thus, if the best outcome for the child is to be brought up by her own family, there may be cases where real hardship would be caused if the family has to bear its own costs of achieving that outcome. If a child's welfare will be put at risk, it may be appropriate to order the local authority to pay the parent's costs. In *Re S (A Child)*, the local authority was not condemned in costs, having properly exercised its statutory duty to institute proceedings notwithstanding that the ultimate conclusion of the court was not to make a care order.

31A Care orders: care plans

(1) Where an application is made on which a care order might be made with respect to a child, the appropriate local authority must, within such time as the court may direct, prepare a plan ('a care plan') for the future care of the child.

(2) While the application is pending, the authority must keep any care plan prepared by them under review and, if they are of the opinion some change is required, revise the plan, or make a new plan, accordingly.

(3) A care plan must give any prescribed information and do so in the prescribed manner.

(4) For the purposes of this section, the appropriate local authority, in relation to a child in respect of whom a care order might be made, is the local authority proposed to be designated in the order.

(5) In section 31(3A) and this section, references to a care order do not include an interim care order.

(6) A plan prepared, or treated as prepared, under this section is referred to in this Act as a 'section 31A plan'.

Amendments—Inserted by ACA 2002, s 121.

Modifications—Section 31A is modified for certain purposes by SI 2010/1898, reg 5(3).

Need to file a care plan—Section 31A places a statutory duty on the local authority to prepare a care plan (known as a 's 31A care plan') in every case in which it seeks a care order. However, the statutory duty does not apply where the authority seeks only an interim care order. The local authority is required by statute to keep the care plan under review and to make changes as and when necessary. The amendment of the care plan during the course of proceedings does not need the consent or permission of the judge; once the amendment has been made the revised plan should be presented to the judge (*Re A (Care Plan)* [2008] 2 FLR 1183, CA). The court can require the local authority to specify the services that are practicable under each of the range of orders that the court is considering and can direct the local authority to file a care plan that meets a particular formulation or assessment of risk, even though that plan does not reflect the position of the local authority (*Re W (Care Proceedings: Functions of Court and Local Authority)* [2014] 2 FLR 431, CA).

The care plan must accord with the Care Planning, Placement and Case Review (England) Regulations 2010 (see Part IV), which came into force on 1 April 2011. Part 2 of the Regulations prescribes the contents of the care plan. The care plan must include the long-term plans for the child, must state the arrangements made to meet the child's needs in respect of health, education, emotional and behavioural development, identity, family and social relationships, social presentation and self-care skills and must set out the wishes and feelings of those persons specified in CA 1989, s 22(4). The care plan should contain the name of the Independent Reviewing Officer (IRO) and the IRO should be given a copy of the care plan. The Regulations are accompanied by four sets of statutory guidance, as follows: (1) a revised edition of Vol 2 of the *Children Act 1989 Guidance and Regulations* entitled *Care Planning, Placement and Case Review*, which is statutory guidance in relation to the relevant provisions in the 1989 Act and the 2010 Regulations. It covers each of the elements of care planning required throughout the child's journey in the care system; (2) *IRO Handbook: Statutory Guidance For Local Authorities and Independent Reviewing Officers on Reviewing Arrangements for Looked After Children*, which provides statutory guidance for independent reviewing officers about their distinct responsibilities in relation to looked after children under CA 1989 and the 2010 Regulations, and replaces the 2004 *Independent Reviewing Officers Guidance*; (3) *Statutory Guidance: Securing Sufficient Accommodation for Looked After Children*, which provides guidance for local authorities and their partners about the local authority's duty under CA 1989, s 22G to take steps that secure, so far as reasonably practicable, sufficient accommodation for looked after children within the local authority area; (4) *Short Breaks Statutory Guidance: How to Safeguard and Promote the Welfare of Disabled Children Using Short Breaks,* which sets out how the legal requirements on short break services and support for children in need apply for different settings and arrangements. See also the PLO in PD12A and **First appointment**, **Case Management Hearing** and **Issues resolution hearing** under FPR 2010, r 12.25. Wherever possible, evidence in support of material parts of the care plan should be available and form part of it. For example, where the plan involves a particular foster placement for the child, it should contain a description of the placement and of the foster carers by a worker who has interviewed them and knows them sufficiently to satisfy the court that the placement is suitable (*Re J (Minors) (Care: Care Plan)* [1994] 1 FLR 253, FD, in which much further guidance as to the making of a care plan is also to be found). Note that the Care Planning, Placement and Case Review (England) Regulations 2010 do not apply in Wales. Instead, the National Assembly for Wales Circular 1/2000 applies.

When considering whether to make an order under s 31, subject to the requirements of s 34(11) (duty to consider the arrangements for contact), the court is now required by s 31(3A) to scrutinise the care plan only to the extent of considering the permanence provisions within that plan, they being those provisions of the care plan that concern the long-term upbringing of the child in his or her family, in an adoptive placement or in long-term foster care. However, this does not mean the court is prohibited from considering certain other aspects of the plan. There will be situations where a particular child's individual identified needs will mean that the court forms the view that the child's welfare necessitates the court satisfying itself in relation to aspects of the care plan not found within the permanence provisions themselves. In particular, where a care plan anticipates that a child will live permanently with a family or friend, the identity and sufficient information about that family member or friend must be before the court (*Re S-W (Children)* [2015] 2 FLR 136, CA). The court will scrutinise the relevant parts of the plan rigorously and if it is not satisfied that it is in the best interests of the child it can refuse to make a care order (*Re J (Minors) (Care: Care Plan)*, above, *Re T (A Minor) (Care Order: Conditions)* [1994] 2 FLR 423, CA, *Re C (Care Order: Appropriate Local Authority)* [1997] 1 FLR 544, FD). In *Re X; Barnet London Borough Council v Y and X* [2006] 2 FLR 998, Cty Ct, Munby J sets out important recommendations concerning the operation of placement panels and the reasoning behind care plans.

The issue of when the court relinquishes control of the case to the local authority by making a full care order as opposed to an interim order is dealt with further under s 38 **Interim care order or full care order?**. Where the care order will designate a local authority other than the applicant local authority, the care plan must be prepared in co-operation between the two authorities (*L v London Borough of Bexley* [1996] 2 FLR 595, FD).

Reference should be made to the *Handbook of Best Practice in Children Act cases* produced by the Children Act Advisory Committee (see Part V, *Best Practice Guidance of June 1997*) for advice as to the care plan (see paras 7–12).

32 Period within which application for order under this Part must be disposed of

(1) A court in which an application for an order under this Part is proceeding shall (in the light of any provision in rules of court that is of the kind mentioned in subsection (2)(a) or (b)) –

- (a) draw up a timetable with a view to disposing of the application –
  - (i) without delay, and
  - (ii) in any event within twenty-six weeks beginning with the day on which the application was issued; and
- (b) give such directions as it considers appropriate for the purpose of ensuring, so far as is reasonably practicable, that that timetable is adhered to.

(2) Rules of court may –

- (a) specify periods within which specified steps must be taken in relation to such proceedings; and
- (b) make other provision with respect to such proceedings for the purpose of ensuring, so far as is reasonably practicable, that they are disposed of without delay.

(3) A court, when drawing up a timetable under subsection (1)(a), must in particular have regard to –

- (a) the impact which the timetable would have on the welfare of the child to whom the application relates; and
- (b) the impact which the timetable would have on the conduct of the proceedings.

(4) A court, when revising a timetable drawn up under subsection (1)(a) or when making any decision which may give rise to a need to revise such a timetable (which does not include a decision under subsection (5)), must in particular have regard to –

- (a) the impact which any revision would have on the welfare of the child to whom the application relates; and
- (b) the impact which any revision would have on the duration and conduct of the proceedings.

(5) A court in which an application under this Part is proceeding may extend the period that is for the time being allowed under subsection (1)(a)(ii) in the case of the application, but may do so only if the court considers that the extension is necessary to enable the court to resolve the proceedings justly.

(6) When deciding whether to grant an extension under subsection (5), a court must in particular have regard to –

- (a) the impact which any ensuing timetable revision would have on the welfare of the child to whom the application relates, and
- (b) the impact which any ensuing timetable revision would have on the duration and conduct of the proceedings;

and here 'ensuing timetable revision' means any revision, of the timetable under subsection (1)(a) for the proceedings, which the court considers may ensue from the extension.

(7) When deciding whether to grant an extension under subsection (5), a court is to take account of the following guidance: extensions are not to be granted routinely and are to be seen as requiring specific justification.

(8) Each separate extension under subsection (5) is to end no more than eight weeks after the later of –

- (a) the end of the period being extended; and
- (b) the end of the day on which the extension is granted.

(9) The Lord Chancellor may by regulations amend subsection (1)(a)(ii), or the opening words of subsection (8), for the purpose of varying the period for the time being specified in that provision.

(10) Rules of court may provide that a court –

(a) when deciding whether to exercise the power under subsection (5), or

(b) when deciding how to exercise that power,

must, or may or may not, have regard to matters specified in the rules, or must take account of any guidance set out in the rules.

Amendments—CFA 2014, s 14.

Avoidance of delay—This section forces the court to take a firm hold of the case, to lay down a procedural timetable and give appropriate directions (under FPR 2010, r 12.12) to ensure that the application in question is determined without delay. Pursuant to amendments brought about by CFA 2014, applications for care and supervision orders must now be disposed of without delay and on a default timetable of 26 weeks. Note that within these time constraints the court is required (a) to ensure that there is proper evidence from the local authority and the Children's Guardian addressing all the realistically possible options for the child and containing an analysis of the arguments for and against each option and (b) to give an adequately reasoned judgment that grapples with the competing options and gives them proper, focused attention. Where the care plan is for non-consensual adoption, the case should not be determined by rigorous adherence to an inflexible timetable (*Re B-S (Adoption: Application of s 47(5))* [2014] 1 FLR 1035, CA).

PART II

The length by which and the circumstances in which the applicable time limits may be extended are strictly circumscribed by reference to the child's welfare and the impact on the duration and conduct of the proceedings.

Pursuant to CA 1989, s 32(1)(a), applications for care and supervision orders must be disposed of without delay and in any event within 26 weeks of the day on which the application is issued. The statutory time limit of 26 weeks is not some mere aspiration or target and nor does it prescribe an average. The statutory time limit defines, subject only to the qualification in s 32(5) and compliance with the requirements of ss 32(6),(7), a mandatory limit that applies to all cases. The term 'planned and purposeful delay' used in *C v Solihull MBC* [1993] 1 FLR 290, FD is no longer the applicable test in light of the coming into force of CA 1989, s 32(5) (*Re M-F (Children)* [2014] EWCA Civ 991). However, Pauffley J stated in *Re NL (Appeal: Interim Care Order: Facts and Reasons)* [2014] 1 FLR 1384, FD that 'Justice must never be sacrificed upon the altar of speed' and there can be exceptions to the 26-week time limit. Nonetheless, an extension beyond 26 weeks will be permitted only if it is 'necessary to enable the court to resolve the proceedings justly' for the purposes of s 32(5). As this is precisely the same language as appears in s 38(7A) of the 1989 Act and s 13(6) of the 2014 Act, the principles in *Re TG (Care Proceedings: Case Management: Expert Evidence)* [2013] 1 FLR 1250, CA and *Re H-L (Expert Evidence: Test for Permission)* [2013] 2 FLR 1434, CA will apply as much to s 32(5) of the 1989 Act as they do to s 38(7A) of the 1989 Act and s 13(6) of the 2014 Act. As such, extensions to the statutory time limit are 'not to be granted routinely' and require 'specific justification'. In *Re S (A Child)* [2014] EWCC B44 (Fam), the President identified three particular forensic contexts in which an extension to the 26-week limit in accordance with s 32(5) may be 'necessary', namely:

(a) Cases that can be identified from the outset, or at least very early on, as ones that it may not be possible to resolve justly within 26 weeks. Four examples were given by the President, namely (i) very heavy cases involving the most complex medical evidence where a separate fact-finding hearing is directed in accordance with *Re S (Split Hearing)* [2014] 1 FLR 1421, CA, at [29], (ii) Family Drug and Alcohol Court (FDAC) type cases, (iii) cases with an international element where investigations or assessments have to be carried out abroad and (iv) cases where the parent's disabilities require recourse to special assessments or measures;

(b) Cases where, despite appropriately robust and vigorous judicial case management, something unexpectedly emerges to change the nature of the proceedings too late in the day to enable the case to be concluded justly within 26 weeks. Three examples were given by the President, namely (i) cases proceeding on allegations of neglect or emotional harm where allegations of sexual abuse subsequently surface, (ii) cases that are unexpectedly 'derailed' because of the death, serious illness or imprisonment of the proposed carer, and (iii) cases where a realistic alternative family carer emerges late in the day;

(c) Cases where litigation failure on the part of one or more of the parties makes it impossible to complete the case justly within 26 weeks.

However, in *Re M-F (Children)* (above), the President further stated that the examples given in *Re S* should not be read as if they are the text of the statute. The President reiterated that the imperative language of s 32(5),(7) required that an extension beyond 26 weeks is to be permitted only if it is 'necessary to enable the court to resolve the proceedings justly'. The President further reiterated that only the imperative demands of justice, namely fair process, or of the child's welfare will suffice. For circumstances in which an adjournment of care proceedings was considered appropriate, see *Re G (Children)* [2015] EWCA Civ 1091 (proceeding to a hearing would have an adverse effect on the health of a father acting in person in circumstances where his blood pressure was dangerously high and a court-directed cardiologist's report had not yet been received).

Both practitioners and courts have a duty to avoid delay in children cases and the court will direct the parties to monitor compliance with the court's directions and tell the court about any failure to comply with a direction by the court and any other delay in the proceedings (FPR 2010, r 12.24). For details, see 'Pre-proceedings checklist', 'Case management hearing', 'Further case management hearing' and 'Issues resolution hearing' within FPR PD12A.

See further the notes on continuity of judge and legal representatives and on the timetable for proceedings under FPR 2010, r 12.12. A children's guardian has a duty to review the file regularly and, if the case is not making satisfactory progress, should apply for further directions (*Re A and B (Minors) (No 2)* [1995] 1 FLR 351, FD; *Re O (Care: Delay)* [2001] Fam Law 339, Cty Ct). The fact that the timetable might need to be revised is not of itself a reason not to timetable (*E v Humberside County Council and S* [1996] Fam Law 444, FD). Those who wish to participate in caring for a child need to make their position clear as soon as possible; otherwise, delay can result, for example because the local authority has not been able to assess the suitability of potential carers (*Re JC (Care Proceedings: Procedure)* [1995] 2 FLR 77, FD). The question of whether a split hearing will reduce delay must be considered, see **Split hearings** under s 31. Where there are criminal proceedings pending the Family Court will need to be made aware of the current state of the criminal investigation and criminal process (if there is a prosecution) at every stage so that it can make a fully informed decision about the extent to which the duty with regard to timetabling can be fulfilled (see *Re A and B (Minors) (No 2)*, above, **Concurrent care and criminal proceedings** under s 31 and the annotation on delay, under s 1). See **Concurrent planning** for discussion of twin track planning as a strategy for reducing delay and **Care monitoring system** (both under CA 1989, s 31) for discussion of the judicially led CMS management information programme intended to provide accurate ongoing information about case volumes, case progress and allocation.

Timetable must be expressly extended where judgment delayed—Where the time required by the court to prepare and deliver judgment will take the case over the statutory 26-week time limit for disposing of the proceedings, the court must make express provision for that purpose by means of an extension of up to 8 weeks in the timetable. Pursuant to FPR 2010, r 12.26B, in determining whether to grant an extension, the court must follow the formal process mandated by FPR 2010, r 12.26A and must have regard to the need for any extension to be limited to what 'is necessary to enable the court to resolve the proceedings justly' and to the need to have regard to the impact of any extension on the welfare of the child. Pursuant to CA 1989, s 32(7), the judge must identify the specific justification for an extension of time to prepare the judgment. Pursuant to FPR 2010, r 12.26C, the court must announce its decision to extend the timetable and give reasons, including a short explanation of the impact on the welfare of the child of the decision to extend the timetable. Moreover, if the date fixed for the conclusion of proceedings pursuant to s 32 passes by reason of delay in the handing down of judgment without the court extending the timetable, it is incumbent upon the parties to raise the matter with the court pursuant to FPR 2010, r 12.24. Where there is a substantial delay between the conclusion of the evidence and the delivery of judgment, the court should consider whether short updating evidence should be filed (*Re T (Children)* [2016] 1 WLR 14, CA).

Care orders

33 Effect of care order

(1) Where a care order is made with respect to a child it shall be the duty of the local authority designated by the order to receive the child into their care and to keep him in their care while the order remains in force.

(2) Where –

- (a) a care order has been made with respect to a child on the application of an authorised person; but
- (b) the local authority designated by the order was not informed that that person proposed to make the application,

the child may be kept in the care of that person until received into the care of the authority.

(3) While a care order is in force with respect to a child, the local authority designated by the order shall –

- (a) have parental responsibility for the child; and
- (b) have the power (subject to the following provisions of this section) to determine the extent to which
  - (i) a parent, guardian or special guardian of the child; or
  - (ii) a person who by virtue of section 4A has parental responsibility for the child

may meet his parental responsibility for him.

(4) The authority may not exercise the power in subsection (3)(b) unless they are satisfied that it is necessary to do so in order to safeguard or promote the child's welfare.

(5) Nothing in subsection (3)(b) shall prevent a person mentioned in that provision who has care of the child from doing what is reasonable in all the circumstances of the case for the purpose of safeguarding or promoting his welfare.

(6) While a care order is in force with respect to a child, the local authority designated by the order shall not –

- (a) cause the child to be brought up in any religious persuasion other than that in which he would have been brought up if the order had not been made; or

(b) have the right –
  (i) *(repealed)*
  (ii) to agree or refuse to agree to the making of an adoption order, or an order under section 84 of the Adoption and Children Act 2002, with respect to the child; or
  (iii) to appoint a guardian for the child.

(7) While a care order is in force with respect to a child, no person may –
  (a) cause the child to be known by a new surname; or
  (b) remove him from the United Kingdom,

without either the written consent of every person who has parental responsibility for the child or the leave of the court.

(8) Subsection (7)(b) does not –
  (a) prevent the removal of such a child, for a period of less than one month, by the authority in whose care he is; or
  (b) apply to arrangements for such a child to live outside England and Wales (which are governed by paragraph 19 of Schedule 2 in England, and section 124 of the Social Services and Well-being (Wales) Act 2014 in Wales).

(9) The power in subsection (3)(b) is subject (in addition to being subject to the provisions of this section) to any right, duty, power, responsibility or authority which a person mentioned in that provision has in relation to the child and his property by virtue of any other enactment.

Amendments—ACA 2002, s 139(1), Sch 3, paras 54, 63, Sch 5; SI 2016/413.

Defined terms—'authorised person': s 31(9); 'care order': ss 31(11), 105(1); 'child', 'guardian', 'local authority': s 105(1); 'parental responsibility': ss 3, 105(1).

Effect of s 33(3)—The effect of s 33(3) is to prevent the exercise of parental responsibility adverse to the views of the local authority, subject to the provisions of s 33(4)–(9) (see *A Local Authority v A, B and E* [2012] 2 FLR 601, FD). A local authority does not have the power to prevent a mother entering into a parental responsibility agreement with the father under CA 1989, s 4(1)(b) because that facility to enter an agreement is self-contained and does not depend on the exercise of parental responsibility (*Re X (Parental Responsibility Agreement: Children in Care)* [2000] 1 FLR 517, FD).

Care Planning, Placement and Case Review (England) Regulations 2010 (see Part IV)—These Regulations came into force on 1 April 2011 and they revoke, inter alia, the Placement of Children with Parents etc Regulations 1991. They make provision about care planning for looked-after children, whether or not they are in the care of the local authority by virtue of care order, and associated matters. Pt 4 concerns particular types of placement, with parents, with local authority foster parents and other arrangements.

Religious upbringing (s 33(6)(a))—Section 33(6)(a) must be construed in a subtle and careful way. The local authority is bound to ensure that the child is brought up in the religious persuasion of the parents, but it is also bound to have regard to any change of religion, even if only one parent changes (*Re A and D (Local Authority: Religious Upbringing)* [2011] 1 FLR 615, FD).

New surname (s 33(7))—In *Re J (A Minor) (Change of Name)* [1993] 1 FLR 699, FD, an application under s 33(7)(a) was dealt with without notice and without the appointment of a children's guardian, as would normally be required in accordance with s 41.

In *Re M, T, P, K and B (Care: Change of Name)* [2000] 2 FLR 645, FD, the court held that a similar approach should be adopted for public law and private law cases and the principles established in private law change of name cases should not be ignored. On any application to change a child's surname the welfare of the children concerned was paramount. In addition to the welfare check list factors the court should give very careful consideration to: (i) the wishes, feelings, needs and objectives of the applicant; (ii) the motives and stated objections of the respondents; and (iii) the opinion of the children's guardian. If a foster carer wishes to change a child's name (forename or surname) he should consult the local authority and the parents' views should be sought. If necessary, an application should be made to the court (*Re D, L and LA (Care: Change of Forename)* [2003] 1 FLR 339, FD). See **Change of surname** under s 8, for details of the private law approach to a change of name.

Allocation of application for permission under s 33(7)—Upon an application for permission to cause a child to be known by a new surname or to remove him from the UK being issued in the Family Court, the case will be allocated to the appropriate level of judge by reference to the criteria in the FC(CDB)R 2014. The application for permission should be commenced in accordance with FPR 2010, rr 18.1–18.13.

34 Parental contact etc with children in care

(1) Where a child is in the care of a local authority, the authority shall (subject to the provisions of this section and their duty under section 22(3)(a) or, where the local authority is in Wales, under section 78(1)(a) of the Social Services and Well-being (Wales) Act 2014) allow the child reasonable contact with –

(a) his parents;
(b) any guardian or special guardian of his;
(ba) any person who by virtue of section 4A has parental responsibility for him;
(c) where there was a child arrangements order in force with respect to the child immediately before the care order was made, any person named in the child arrangements order as a person with whom the child was to live; and
(d) where, immediately before the care order was made, a person had care of the child by virtue of an order made in the exercise of the High Court's inherent jurisdiction with respect to children, that person.

(2) On an application made by the authority or the child, the court may make such order as it considers appropriate with respect to the contact which is to be allowed between the child and any named person.

(3) On an application made by –

(a) any person mentioned in paragraph (a) to (d) of subsection (1); or
(b) any person who has obtained the leave of the court to make the application,

the court may make such order as it considers appropriate with respect to the contact which is to be allowed between the child and that person.

(4) On an application made by the authority or the child, the court may make an order authorising the authority to refuse to allow contact between the child and any person who is mentioned in paragraphs (a) to (d) of subsection (1) and named in the order.

(5) When making a care order with respect to a child, or in any family proceedings in connection with a child who is in the care of a local authority, the court may make an order under this section, even though no application for such an order has been made with respect to the child, if it considers that the order should be made.

(6) An authority may refuse to allow the contact that would otherwise be required by virtue of subsection (1) or an order under this section if –

(a) they are satisfied that it is necessary to do so in order to safeguard or promote the child's welfare; and
(b) the refusal –
  (i) is decided upon as a matter of urgency; and
  (ii) does not last for more than seven days.

(6A) Where (by virtue of an order under this section, or because subsection (6) applies) a local authority in England are authorised to refuse to allow contact between the child and a person mentioned in any of paragraphs (a) to (c) of paragraph 15(1) of Schedule 2, paragraph 15(1) of that Schedule does not require the authority to endeavour to promote contact between the child and that person.

(6B) Where (by virtue of an order under this section, or because subsection (6) applies) a local authority in Wales is authorised to refuse contact between the child and a person mentioned in any of paragraphs (a) to (c) of section 95(1) of the Social Services and Wellbeing (Wales) Act 2014, section 95(1) of that Act does not require the authority to promote contact between the child and that person.

(7) An order under this section may impose such conditions as the court considers appropriate.

(8) The Secretary of State may by regulations make provision as to –

(za) what a local authority in England must have regard to in considering whether contact between a child and a person mentioned in any of paragraphs (a) to (d) of subsection (1) is consistent with safeguarding and promoting the child's welfare;
(a) the steps to be taken by a local authority who have exercised their power under subsection (6);
(b) the circumstances in which, and conditions subject to which, the terms of any order under this section may be departed from by agreement between the local authority and the person in relation to whom the order is made;

(c) notification by a local authority of any variation or suspension of arrangements made (otherwise than under an order under this section) with a view to affording any person contact with a child to whom this section applies.

(9) The court may vary or discharge any order made under this section on the application of the authority, the child concerned or the person named in the order.

(10) An order under this section may be made either at the same time as the care order itself or later.

(11) Before making, varying or discharging an order under this section or making a care order with respect to any child the court shall –

(a) consider the arrangements which the authority have made, or propose to make, for affording any person contact with a child to whom this section applies; and

(b) invite the parties to the proceedings to comment on those arrangements.

Amendments—ACA 2002, s 139(1), Sch 3, paras 54, 64; CFA 2014, ss 8, 12, Sch 2; SI 2016/413.

Defined terms—'care order': ss 31(11), 105(1); 'child': s 105(1); 'child arrangements order': s 8(1); 'family proceedings': s 8(3); 'guardian', 'local authority': s 105(1).

'parents' (s 34(1)(a))—See **Meaning of 'parent'** under s 10. See the Care Planning, Placement and Case Review (England) Regulations 2010 in Part IV, which are referred to under s 33.

High Court's inherent jurisdiction (s 34(1)(d))—The inherent jurisdiction of the High Court was, before CA 1989, most commonly exercised in wardship proceedings. The Act has put an end to the majority of wardship applications, but applications may still be made under the inherent jurisdiction of the court; see, in particular, under s 100.

Leave to make an application (s 34(3))—An application for permission to make an application should be made using the procedure in FPR 2010, rr 18.1–18.13. In determining the application for permission under s 34 the court should consider the criteria set out in s 10(9) of the Act. It must have regard to all of the circumstances of the case and have particular regard to the following factors: (a) the nature of the contact sought; (b) the applicant's connection to the child; (c) the risk of the child's life being disrupted by the proposed application to such an extent that the child would be harmed by it; and (d) the wishes of the parents and local authority. In weighing up these factors, the following approach should be adopted: (a) if the application is frivolous, vexatious or an abuse of process, it will fail; (b) if the permission application fails to disclose any real prospect of eventual success (or the prospect is remote so that the application is obviously unsustainable), it must be dismissed; and (c) the applicant must satisfy the court that there is a serious issue to try and must present a good arguable case – is there a real issue that the applicant may reasonably ask the court to try and has he a case that is better than merely arguable yet not necessarily one that is shown to have a better-than-even chance, a fair chance, of success? Over-analysis of these 'tests' should be avoided and the matter approached 'in the loosest way possible, looking at the matter in the round', because it is important that the exercise of discretion by the court is unfettered. The court should also consider whether the person seeking to be made a party has an independent or separate point of view, or is putting forward an interest identical to that of another party. If there is no independent or separate point of view or different interest, then it is unlikely that the court will permit that person to become a party (*Re W (Care Proceedings: Leave to Apply)* [2005] 2 FLR 468, FD).

Because contact between a child and his family will be assumed to be beneficial by virtue of CA 1989, Sch 2, para 15, a local authority which considers that it is not reasonably practicable or consistent with the child's welfare to promote that contact will need to file evidence to justify its stance (*Re M (Care: Contact: Grandmother's Application for Leave)* [1995] 2 FLR 86, CA).

Interim contact hearing—See *West Glamorgan County Council v P (No 1)* [1992] 2 FLR 369, FD. For the approach to be adopted by the court see *Hampshire County Council v S* [1993] 1 FLR 559, FD and *Re W (A Minor) (Interim Care Order)* [1994] 2 FLR 892, CA (discussed under FPR 2010, r 12.21); and in relation to a final order under s 34 during interim care see *A v M and Walsall MBC* [1993] 2 FLR 244, FD. In cases of emergency, where the court is not satisfied that adequate safeguards can be put in place to ensure the safety of the child, the court may make a short order under s 34(4) authorising the local authority to refuse contact prior to the court having time to fully consider the matter (*Re W (A Child)* [2013] EWCA Civ 314. Care should be taken before altering interim contact arrangements where there is a pending assessment that will address the risks to which such a course of action may give rise (*Re A (A Child)* [2013] EWCA Civ 543, decided in the context of a private law application). See also **No order as to contact/no contact order** below.

Review of contact by the court—It is not open to the court to retain control over the issue of contact with a child in care by providing for a general review of the progress of the care plan and of contact arrangements at some date after the making of a care order (*Re B (A Minor) (Care Order: Review)* [1993] 1 FLR 421, FD). See also *Kent County Council v C* [1993] 1 FLR 308, FD, in which Ewbank J held that the court cannot fetter the local authority's plans by adding a direction to a care order that the guardian ad litem (children's guardian) remain involved with the child. What the court *can* do, according to *Re B* (above), is to make what is in effect an interim contact order with a specific provision for a further hearing with a view to making more enduring provision for contact at the subsequent hearing. It may be, however, that *Re S (A Minor) (Care: Contact Order)* [1994] 2 FLR 222, CA casts doubt on this approach: the Court of Appeal there held that, where the nature and extent of the contact was an integral part of the local authority's care plan, it was not for the court to decide precisely what contact was reasonable. The judge had made a care order, but adjourned the issue of contact for further directions and this was, in effect, providing for a review of the implementation of the care plan which would lead the judge into the forbidden territory of supervising the administration of the local authority's arrangements for rehabilitation. The court has no jurisdiction under s 34 to prohibit a local authority, into whose care a child has been placed, from permitting parental contact with the child; if the court did make such an order it would be unenforceable because, by virtue of the Care Planning, Placement and Case Review (England) Regulations 2010, reg 8 (see Part IV), a local authority can, with the parents' agreement, depart from the terms of any order made under s 34 (*Re W (Section 34(2) Orders)* [2000] 1 FLR 502, CA). The whole question of the court relinquishing control of a child's case to the local authority is considered further under s 38 **Interim care order or full care order?**. See also **Review of cases of looked-after children** under CA 1989, s 26, for a summary of the role of the independent reviewing officer in relation to the review of care orders under the amendments made to s 26(2)(e) by ACA 2002, s 118.

Contact at the discretion of the local authority—Orders for contact at the discretion of the local authority must be interpreted in accordance with CA 1989, s 34(1) and Sch 2, para 15(1). It is inappropriate for the court to indicate the frequency of such contact. Notwithstanding the no order principle in s 1(5), in many cases it is beneficial that when contact with a child is to be within the discretion of the local authority the court should spell it out (*L v London Borough of Bromley* [1998] 1 FLR 709, FD; *Re P (Minors) (Contact with Children in Care)* [1993] 2 FLR 156, FD, where the judge distinguished between an order for contact with a parent at the discretion of the local authority and an order for reasonable contact).

Contact – ECHR 1950—Where care orders have been made together with orders under s 34(4) authorising the local authority to terminate contact with the parents of the child concerned, the Convention should not be used routinely as a make-weight ground of appeal, nor should there be extensive citation of authorities from the ECtHR, particularly where such authorities pre-dated CA 1989 (see *Re F (Care Proceedings: Contact)* [2000] Fam Law 708, FD, where the mother's argument that the decision to terminate contact was an essentially administrative rather than judicial decision failed, and her reliance on *W v UK* (1988) 10 EHHR 29, ECHR was found to be misplaced).

Contact with father is just as important as contact with mother—Where a care order was made in relation to children who had suffered serious injuries caused by one of the parents, although the court was unable to say which, and the mother was to continue to have contact, there was no reason to terminate the father's contact. The benefit of keeping the family link alive by way of contact operates just as much for the father as for the mother (*Re G (Adoption: Contact)* [2003] 1 FLR 270, CA). In *A Local Authority v A, B and E* [2012] 2 FLR 601, FD, the court considered the merits of indirect contact between the child and his violent father, who was serving a prison sentence. Hedley J determined that contact was in the best interests of the child unless the risk posed made any form of contact unacceptably unsafe, observing that while the preeminent concern was one of risk, there were other important issues to take into account, including the identity of parenthood, which, if at all feasible, should not be a closed book to the child.

Contact – domestic violence—See the guidance given in *Re L (Contact: Domestic Violence); Re V (Contact: Domestic Violence); Re M (Contact: Domestic Violence); Re H (Contact: Domestic Violence)* [2000] 2 FLR 334, CA and the principles embodied in FPR PD12J *Residence and Contact Orders: Domestic Violence and Harm*, which apply to any application for child arrangements orders and in which domestic violence or risk of it is alleged. The principles are equally applicable to public law cases (*Re G (Domestic Violence: Direct Contact)* [2000] 2 FLR 865, FD). The outcome of any Multi-agency risk assessment conferences (MARACs), which collate information about high-risk cases of domestic abuse with a view to creating a coordinated safety plan for the victim and any children, may be relevant in determining applications for contact under s 34 where alleged domestic violence is an issue. For the principles governing the disclosure of documents or other information generated by MARACs, see **Multi-agency risk assessment conferences (MARACs) – disclosure in public law and private law proceedings** under FPR 2010, r 12.12. See also **Contact – Domestic violence** under s 8.

No order as to contact/no contact order—The court has power to make an order for no contact between a parent and child (*Kent County Council v C* [1993] 1 FLR 308, FD) but in the light of the provisions of the Care Planning, Placement and Case Review (England) Regulations 2010 (see Part IV), where the court thinks there should be no contact, it should make such an order and care must be taken in drafting it to avoid any misunderstanding in relation to the local authority's duty to allow contact (*Re SW (A Minor)* [1993] 2 FLR 609, FD). Although *Re S (A Minor) (Care: Contact Order)* [1994] 2 FLR 222, CA suggests that such an order, or an order providing for reasonable contact, is not necessary, *L v London Borough of Bromley)* [1998] 1 FLR 709, FD recognises that there can be a benefit in spelling things out in certain circumstances; see **Contact at the discretion of the local authority** (above). A s 34(4) order should not be made merely against the possibility that circumstances might change to justify the termination of contact (*Re S (Care: Parental Contact)* [2005] 1 FLR 469, CA). In the early stages of care proceedings extraordinarily compelling reasons must be shown to justify a s 34(4) order (*Re K (Contact)* [2008] 2 FLR 581, FD – where the baby's safety demanded such an order, although it would be too drastic for it to last until the final hearing; at the case management conference it would be for the mother to show that carefully supervised contact should resume). Note that in Wales Care Planning, Placement and Case Review (Wales) Regulations 2015, regs 8 and 9 apply (see Part 7 of *The Family Court Practice Autumn Supplement* and *The Family Court Practice Online*).

Discharge of a s 34(4) 'no contact' order—There must be some material change of circumstances between the making of the order and the application to discharge it (*Re T (Termination of Contact: Discharge of Order)* [1997] 1 FLR 517, CA). In determining such an application the court should consider (i) the extent to which circumstances have changed since the original order, and (ii) bearing those changes in mind, the extent to which it is appropriate to reinvestigate the central question and apply the paramountcy principle. The greater the change in circumstances, the more intensively the court would be prepared to reconsider the desirability of leaving the s 34(4) order in place. As to the power of local authorities to override no contact orders without having further recourse to the court, see Care Planning, Placement and Case Review (England) Regulations 2010, reg 8 (in Part IV).

Disclosure of information concerning prospective adopters—For disclosure to parents where a s 34(4) application is running concurrently with an adoption application, see *Re S (A Minor) (Adoption)* [1993] 2 FLR 204, CA.

Contact arrangements (s 34(11))—This applies to the arrangements proposed in the care plan. Where the arrangements will be made by a local authority other than the applicant authority, directions should be given for that authority to be represented to deal with any issues that might arise and to assure the court and the parents of the authority's commitment to the care plan and its capacity to implement it (*L v London Borough of Bexley* [1996] 2 FLR 595, FD).

Supervision of contact—The fact that ongoing direct contact will require long-term supervision is not, in itself, a reason to refuse to direct that such contact takes place (*Re S (A Child) (Child Arrangements Order: Effect of Long-Term Supervised Contact on Welfare)* [2016] 2 FLR 217, CA and see *NA (Applicant) v ZA and ors* [2015] EWHC 2188 (Fam)). Before the reintroduction of direct contact can be refused on grounds of disturbance to the child or caring parent, it must be shown that the disturbance goes well beyond mere inconvenience (*Re S*).

Enforcement of public law child arrangements orders—A public law child arrangements order made under CA 1989 can be enforced by committal. Pursuant to FPR 2010, r 33.1(2), as far as they are relevant the CCR and RSC continue to apply to family proceedings, subject to FPR 2010.

Supervision orders

35 Supervision orders

(1) While a supervision order is in force it shall be the duty of the supervisor –

(a) to advise, assist and befriend the supervised child;
(b) to take such steps as are reasonably necessary to give effect to the order; and
(c) where –
  (i) the order is not wholly complied with; or
  (ii) the supervisor considers that the order may no longer be necessary,
  to consider whether or not to apply to the court for its variation or discharge.

(2) Parts I and II of Schedule 3 make further provision with respect to supervision orders.

36 Education supervision orders

(1) On the application of any local authority, the court may make an order putting the child with respect to whom the application is made under the supervision of a designated local authority.

(2) In this Act 'an education supervision order' means an order under subsection (1).

(3) A court may only make an education supervision order if it is satisfied that the child concerned is of compulsory school age and is not being properly educated.

(4) For the purposes of this section, a child is being properly educated only if he is receiving efficient full-time education suitable to his age, ability and aptitude and any special educational needs he may have.

(5) Where a child is –

(a) the subject of a school attendance order which is in force under section 437 of the Education Act 1996 and which has not been complied with; or
(b) is not attending regularly within the meaning of section 444 of that Act –
  (i) a school at which he is a registered pupil,
  (ii) any place at which education is provided for him in the circumstances mentioned in subsection (1) of section 444ZA of that Act, or
  (iii) any place which he is required to attend in the circumstances mentioned in subsection (2) of that section,

then, unless it is proved that he is being properly educated, it shall be assumed that he is not.

(6) An education supervision order may not be made with respect to a child who is in the care of a local authority.

(7) The local authority designated in an education supervision order must be –

(a) the authority within whose area the child concerned is living or will live; or

(b) where –
   (i) the child is a registered pupil at a school; and
   (ii) the authority mentioned in paragraph (a) and the authority within whose area the school is situated agree,

the latter authority.

(8) Where a local authority propose to make an application for an education supervision order they shall, before making the application, consult the appropriate local authority if different.

(9) The appropriate local authority is –

(a) in the case of a child who is being provided with accommodation by, or on behalf of, a local authority, that authority; and
(b) in any other case, the local authority within whose area the child concerned lives, or will live.

(10) Part III of Schedule 3 makes further provision with respect to education supervision orders.

Amendments—Education Act 1993, s 307(1),(3), Sch 19, para 149, Sch 21, Pt II; Education Act 1996, s 582(1), Sch 37, Pt I, para 85; Education Act 2005, s 117, Sch 18, para 1; SI 2010/1158.

Defined terms—'appropriate local authority': s 36(9); 'child': s 105(1); 'education supervision order': s 36(2); 'local authority': s 105(1).

'local authority'—Section 36(7) specifies which authority must be designated.

'in the care of the local authority' (s 36(6))—This refers to a child who is in the care of a local authority by virtue of a care order (see ss 31(11) and 105(1)).

Powers of court

37 Powers of court in certain family proceedings

(1) Where, in any family proceedings in which a question arises with respect to the welfare of any child, it appears to the court that it may be appropriate for a care or supervision order to be made with respect to him, the court may direct the appropriate authority to undertake an investigation of the child's circumstances.

(2) Where the court gives a direction under this section the local authority concerned shall, when undertaking the investigation, consider whether they should –

(a) apply for a care order or for a supervision order with respect to the child;
(b) provide services or assistance for the child or his family; or
(c) take any other action with respect to the child.

(3) Where a local authority undertake an investigation under this section, and decide not to apply for a care order or supervision order with respect to the child concerned, they shall inform the court of –

(a) their reasons for so deciding;
(b) any service or assistance which they have provided, or to intend to provide, for the child and his family; and
(c) any other action which they have taken, or propose to take, with respect to the child.

(4) The information shall be given to the court before the end of the period of eight weeks beginning with the date of the direction, unless the court otherwise directs.

(5) The local authority named in a direction under subsection (1) must be –

(a) the authority in whose area the child is ordinarily resident; or
(b) where the child is not ordinarily resident in the area of a local authority, the authority within whose area any circumstances arose in consequence of which the direction is being given.

(6) If, on the conclusion of any investigation or review under this section, the authority decide not to apply for a care order or supervision order with respect to the child –

(a) they shall consider whether it would be appropriate to review the case at a later date; and

(b) if they decide that it would be, they shall determine the date on which that review is to begin.

Amendments—CLSA 1990, s 116, Sch 16, para 16.

Defined terms—'care order': ss 31(11), 105(1); 'child': s 105(1); 'family proceedings': s 8(3); 'local authority': s 105(1); 'supervision order': s 31(11).

Scope—This section empowers the court, of its own initiative, to direct the local authority to look into the circumstances of a child with a view to the possibility of taking action with respect to the child and to report to the court about what, if any, action it intends to take, including the matters referred to in s 37(4)–(6). The court is not limited to one s 37 direction for each set of proceedings. Where a judge is satisfied that the local authority has either not complied with a direction under s 37 or failed to conduct an investigation that met the court's concerns, the court may extend or renew its direction under s 37 (*Re K (Children)* [2012] EWCA Civ 1549). An interim order may be made pending the results of the investigation (s 38(1)). If the local authority decides not to issue proceedings the court has no power to make a care or supervision order of its own initiative (see eg *Nottinghamshire County Council v P* [1993] 2 FLR 134, CA). In *Re L (Interim Care Order: Extended Family)* [2013] 2 FLR 302, CA, the Court of Appeal declined, in the particular circumstances of the case, to criticise the judge's use of s 37 to direct the local authority to undertake an investigation of the child's situation and to grant an interim care order in circumstances where the local authority had already provided a report under CA 1989, s 7 and made the decision to issue an application for a care order.

'appropriate authority' (s 37(1))—See **'designated local authority'** under s 31.

'ordinarily resident' (s 37(5))—See under s 31.

Procedure—For the procedure where a direction is given under s 37 by the Family Court, see FPR 2010, r 12.17. Applications for care and supervision orders under s 31 are subject to the provisions of FPR 2010, Pt 12 and PD12A and the PLO contained therein. See in particular Case management hearing, Further case management hearing and Issues resolution hearing within FPR PD12A. Note that there may be a new protocol for s 37(1) applications in due course. It is a requirement of the CAP (FPR PD12B) that the need for a s 37 investigation be considered at the first hearing dispute resolution appointment in private law proceedings.

Best Practice Guidance on s 37(1) directions—This Guidance was issued by the Children Act Advisory Committee (before its abolition) in its *Annual Report 1992/93* to deal with the unjustified and overuse of s 37(1) provisions. The text that remains relevant is as follows:

(1) A direction under s 37(1) is appropriate where the court desires an investigation because 'it appears to the court that it may be appropriate for a care or supervision order to be made' (s 37(1)).

(2) A direction under s 37(1) is not lawful unless it appears to the court that a care or supervision order may be appropriate. Thus, in private law proceedings, a direction under s 37(1) should not be used as a device for the purpose of enabling the court to appoint a guardian ad litem. Unless 'it appears to the court that it may be appropriate for a care or supervision order to be made', any referral for a welfare investigation should be made under s 7.

(3) The purpose of a s 37(1) direction is to enable the court to cause the local authority to assess whether a care or supervision order is needed. It is not to obtain a general welfare report. However, the making of a s 37(1) direction will also cause the local authority to consider whether and which child welfare support services should be provided by the local authority, or other action taken, as well as or instead of a care or supervision order: s 37(2), and note the details of the duty of the local authority to report to the court under s 37(3).

(4) Upon a direction under s 37, the local authority must report back within 8 weeks unless the court otherwise directs: s 37(4). The date for the next hearing must be fixed: FPR 2010, r 12.13(1). The date for the report should also be specified under FPR 2010, r 12.12(2).

Appointment of a panel guardian ad litem

(5) When a court has made a direction under s 37(1), and 'has made, or is considering whether to make, an interim care order' (s 41(6)(b)), 'the court shall appoint an officer of the Service or a Welsh family proceedings officer for the child concerned unless satisfied that it is not necessary to do so in order to safeguard his interests': s 41(1).

(6) The court cannot appoint a panel guardian unless the proceedings are 'specified' within s 41(6). Section 41 does not authorise the court to appoint a guardian ad litem, upon making a s 37(1) direction, if the court has not made and is not considering whether to make an interim care order: s 41(6)(b).

Section 7(1) referrals

(7) Section 7(1) is for cases where the court desires a welfare investigation and report. This might include a child protection issue, for example, abusive interference with a child by a parent or other person who does not have care of the child: in such a case an injunction may be the appropriate remedy.

(8) The reporter under a s 7(1) order is the eyes and ears of the court and is required to investigate and to report to the court on the welfare of the child. The reporter is an independent agent of the court, is not a party to the proceedings and is not legally represented.

(9) Whether an order under s 7(1) should be directed to the court welfare service or the local authority may be affected by:

(i) previous involvement with and knowledge of the family by the local authority, in which case the local authority is likely to be appropriate, particularly if the involvement is recent or continuing;

(ii) local arrangements between the court welfare service and the local authority for distribution or sharing of investigation work.

(10) When considering whether to make a s 7(1) referral or a s 37(1) direction, the court should as far as

practicable obtain the available relevant information from any social worker or court welfare officer who is currently involved with the child, or a duty court welfare officer.

(11) Upon making a s 7(1) referral, the date for the next hearing must be fixed: FPR 2010, r 12.13(1). The date for the report should also be specified under FPR 2010, r 12.12(2).

Communication to local authority of s 37(1) direction or s 7(1) referral

(12) It is important that whenever a court makes a s 37(1) direction or a s 7(1) referral to a local authority, the authority should be informed as quickly as possible. An immediate telephone notification should be confirmed in writing. FPR 2010, r 12.17(4)(a) require that a copy of a s 37(1) direction shall be served on the local authority as soon as practicable. FPR 2010, r 12.17(4)(b) provides for the court to direct which parts of the documentary evidence should be served on the local authority where a s 37(1) direction has been made.

Practical considerations—The court must spell out the reasons for making the s 37 order very carefully and a transcript (or very full note) of the judgment should be made available to the local authority at the earliest opportunity (*Re M (Intractable Contact Dispute: Interim Care Order)* [2003] 2 FLR 636, FD). It is not sufficient for the local authority simply to be told that the judge has ordered a s 37 report. The court should be clear about how, and by whom, the order is going to be communicated to the local authority (*Re M* (above), at [14], for example, by facsimile to an identified officer of the authority). See *Re H (A Minor) (Section 37 Direction)* [1993] 2 FLR 541, FD ('child's circumstances' under s 37(1) to be widely construed and should include any situation which might have a bearing on the child being likely to suffer significant harm in the future; judge's s 37 order went into detail with regard to investigations to be carried out, and included a time-scale for the investigation). The judge must not, however, seek to fetter the local authority in the execution of its statutory function under s 37 (*Re M (Official Solicitor's Role)* [1998] 2 FLR 815, CA in which the judge wrongly sought to use the Official Solicitor to regulate the s 37 enquiry). In *Re A and B (Minors) (No 2)* [1995] 1 FLR 351, FD, Wall J questioned whether s 37 was appropriate where the local authority had already carried out an investigation and what the court wanted was information about this; he saw s 7 as the better choice (see **Officer of the Service** under s 7). In *Re D (Residence: Imposition of Conditions)* [1996] 2 FLR 281, CA, a children and family reporter was ordered to investigate the issue of residence, and the local authority (which had recently been involved in the matter) was also invited to report pursuant to s 37. A s 37 investigation is not to be ordered in private law proceedings unless it appears that a public law order might be appropriate (*Re F (Family Proceedings: Section 37 Investigation)* [2006] 1 FLR 1122, FD; *Re L (Section 37 Direction)* [1999] 1 FLR 984, CA).

Section 37 can be utilised in intractable contact disputes to remove children who are being denied all contact with the parent with whom they are not living and are suffering significant harm because of the false and distorted belief system of the parent with whom the child is living about the other parent (*Re M (Intractable Contact Dispute: Interim Care Order)* (above) – where the children were removed from their mother under an interim care order and residence orders were subsequently made in favour of the father, with 2-year supervision orders to the local authority – and see *Re W (A Child)* [2014] EWCA Civ 772). However, in *Re M* (above) Wall J was careful to point out that this procedure is not a panacea and must only be used when the circumstances truly justify it.

Duty of local authority—Where the court makes an unopposed direction to a local authority under s 37(1) there can be no appeal against that direction by the authority. Section 37 sets out three threshold requirements for the exercise of the court's power, namely that: (1) there is a child; (2) there are family proceedings; and (3) that a question has arisen with respect to the child's welfare. It is for the court to determine whether those criteria are satisfied or not, e.g. the age of the child. Where an issue arises, a fact-finding hearing should be directed to determine it (*Lambeth London Borough Council v TK and KK* [2008] 1 FLR 1229, CA). A local authority's hard-pressed financial position will not release it from its clear statutory responsibility under s 37. Where an order under s 37 is made, the local authority will be sufficiently closely connected to the litigation to justify a non-party costs order against it in circumstances where any failings on the part of the local authority reach the threshold of exceptionality for making such an order (*Re OB (Private Law Proceedings: Costs)* [2016] 1 FLR 92, FD).

Position of children's guardian—Proceedings which become specified by virtue of s 41(6)(b) following the making of a s 37 order cease to be specified if the local authority, as a result of its investigation (albeit as yet incomplete), decides not to apply for a care order or supervision order and so informs the court (*Re CE (Section 37 Direction)* [1995] 1 FLR 26, FD). In that case, however, it was in the child's interests for the children's guardian, who had been appointed on the proceedings originally becoming specified, to remain involved until the local authority's final assessment was in place and a final resolution could be ordered or sanctioned by the court. The guardian had consented to her continuing involvement and could be funded as an expert on the child's legal aid certificate, so the court invoked its jurisdiction under FPR 1991, r 9.5 (FPR 2010, r 16.4) to appoint a guardian in private law proceedings.

When considering whether to make an interim care order and appoint a guardian on the making of a direction under s 37, regard should be had to the considerations set out in *Re CE (Section 37 Direction)*, above, and in s 41. Where all contact has ceased and the issue of contact has become intractable the child should be separately represented (*Re M (Intractable Contact Dispute: Interim Care Order)* [2003] 2 FLR 636, FD, where the court made a s 37 direction as a result of the mother's denial of all contact to the father because of her false and distorted belief system about him and ordered that the children be separately represented).

Local authority as party—In *F v Cambridgeshire County Council* [1995] 1 FLR 516, FD, it was held that it had been an error to permit a local authority which had carried out a s 37 investigation and decided not to seek a care or supervision order to become a party in private law proceedings by a father against a mother for contact, given the restrictions on local authorities seeking private law orders.

38 Interim orders

(1) Where –

(a) in any proceedings on an application for a care order or supervision order, the proceedings are adjourned; or

(b) the court gives a direction under section 37(1).

the court may make an interim care order or an interim supervision order with respect to the child concerned.

(2) A court shall not make an interim care order or interim supervision order under this section unless it is satisfied that there are reasonable grounds for believing that circumstances with respect to the child are as mentioned in section 31(2).

(3) Where, in any proceedings on an application for a care order or supervision order, a court makes a child arrangements order with respect to the living arrangements of the child concerned, it shall also make an interim supervision order with respect to him unless satisfied that his welfare will be satisfactorily safeguarded without an interim order being made.

(3A) For the purposes of subsection (3), a child arrangements order is one made with respect to the living arrangements of the child concerned if the arrangements regulated by the order consist of, or include, arrangements which relate to either or both of the following –

(a) with whom the child is to live, and

(b) when the child is to live with any person.

(4) An interim order made under or by virtue of this section shall have effect for such period as may be specified in the order, but shall in any event cease to have effect on whichever of the following events first occurs –

(a), (b) *(repealed)*

(c) in a case which falls within subsection (1)(a), the disposal of the application;

(d) in a case which falls within subsection (1)(b), the disposal of an application for a care order or a supervision order made by the authority with respect to the child;

(da) in a case which falls within subsection (1)(b) and in which –

(i) no direction has been given under section 37(4), and

(ii) no application for a care order or supervision order has been made with respect to the child, the expiry of the period of eight weeks beginning with the date on which the order is made;

(e) in a case which falls within subsection (1)(b) and in which –

(i) the court has given a direction under section 37(4), but

(ii) no application for a care order or supervision order has been made with respect to the child,

the expiry of the period fixed by that direction.

(5) *(repealed)*

(6) Where the court makes an interim care order, or interim supervision order, it may give such directions (if any) as it considers appropriate with regard to the medical or psychiatric examination or other assessment of the child; but if the child is of sufficient understanding to make an informed decision he may refuse to submit to the examination or other assessment.

(7) A direction under subsection (6) may be to the effect that there is to be –

(a) no such examination or assessment; or

(b) no such examination or assessment unless the court directs otherwise.

(7A) A direction under subsection (6) to the effect that there is to be a medical or psychiatric examination or other assessment of the child may be given only if the court is of the opinion that the examination or other assessment is necessary to assist the court to resolve the proceedings justly.

(7B) When deciding whether to give a direction under subsection (6) to that effect the court is to have regard in particular to –

(a) any impact which any examination or other assessment would be likely to have on the welfare of the child, and any other impact which giving the direction would be likely to have on the welfare of the child,
(b) the issues with which the examination or other assessment would assist the court,
(c) the questions which the examination or other assessment would enable the court to answer,
(d) the evidence otherwise available,
(e) the impact which the direction would be likely to have on the timetable, duration and conduct of the proceedings,
(f) the cost of the examination or other assessment, and
(g) any matters prescribed by Family Procedure Rules.

(8) A direction under subsection (6) may be –

(a) given when the interim order is made or at any time while it is in force; and
(b) varied at any time on the application of any person falling within any class of person prescribed by rules of court for the purposes of this subsection.

(9) Paragraphs 4 and 5 of Schedule 3 shall not apply in relation to an interim supervision order.

(10) Where a court makes an order under or by virtue of this section it shall, in determining the period for which the order is to be in force, consider whether any party who was, or might have been, opposed to the making of the order was in a position to argue his case against the order in full.

Amendments—CFA 2014, ss 12, 13, Sch 2.

Modifications—Section 38 is modified for certain purposes by SI 2010/1898, reg 5(2).

Defined terms—'care order': ss 31(11), 105(1); 'child arrangements order': s 8(1); 'child': s 105(1); 'relevant period': s 38(5); 'supervision order': s 31(11).

Public Law Outline (PLO)—Applications for interim care and supervision orders under s 38 are subject to the provisions of FPR 2010, Pt 12 and PD12A and the PLO contained therein. See in particular Case management hearing, Further case management hearing and Issues resolution hearing within FPR PD36C. The demands of the PLO should not be permitted to allow the need for expedition to threaten the fairness of the proceedings (*Re NL (Appeal: Interim Care Order: Facts and Reasons)* [2014] 1 FLR 1384, FD).

Abolition of requirement to renew interim orders—The requirement to renew an interim care order initially after 8 weeks and thereafter every 4 weeks has been abolished by CFA 2014. An interim care order will now have effect for such period as may be specified in the interim care order or until the disposal of the application for a care or supervision order (or, where a direction under s 37 has been made by the court, for 8 weeks after the date on which the direction was given or such other period specified in the direction).

Nature of interim orders—The object of an interim order should normally be to hold the balance so as to cause the least possible harm to the child; see eg *B v B (Interim Contact with Grandparents)* [1993] Fam Law 393, FD (s 8 case), *Hampshire County Council v S* [1993] 1 FLR 559, FD (interim order re contact with child in care). An interim care order is not a step involving any advance judgment of the final issue on the part of the court (see *Re H (A Child)* [2002] EWCA Civ 1932). In circumstances where the court should refrain from making findings of fact at an interim stage in the proceedings, it is open to the court to refuse to hear oral evidence at an interim hearing (*Re W (Interim Care Order)* [2012] 2 FLR 240, CA). However, while there is a spectrum of procedure for interim hearings there is also a line beyond which it is impermissible for the court to go in abbreviating that procedure. The court should be careful not to truncate procedure to a point where the hearing becomes unfair (see *Re N (Care Proceedings: Adoption)* [2013] 1 FLR 1244, CA). An interim care order can be a neutral and effective way of preserving the status quo, an essentially impartial step favouring neither one side nor the other and affording to no-one, least of all the local authority in whose favour it is made, an opportunity for tactical or adventitious advantage. An interim care order may be used as a temporary measure to safeguard the child's welfare while sufficient information is gathered to inform a final decision by the court as to whether or not a care order should be made; the information gathering process is intended to be completed speedily (*Re G (Interim Care Order: Residential Assessment)* [2006] 1 FLR 601, HL). Where the children have been removed from the jurisdiction, the court should not automatically equate the need for a recovery order with the need to make an interim care order. The merits of each order should be considered separately and there is no presumption that the making of a recovery order also requires the making of an interim care order (*Re O-C (Children)* [2013] EWCA Civ 162). An interim care order may be made solely to vest the local authority with the power to transmit sensitive information to a child (*Re M (Child Abuse: Disclosure)* [2012] 1 FLR 205, CA). For guidance concerning the principles applicable in respect of children who are the subject of an interim care order who might also be subject to a deprivation of liberty, see *A Local Authority v D & Ors* [2016] 1 WLR 1160, FD and **Deprivation of liberty** under s 20.

Removal under an interim order—The court should not equate satisfaction of the interim threshold criteria with satisfaction of the case for removing the child from a parent. The test to be applied in considering the question of removal is set out in no less than eight Court of Appeal authorities. *Re H (A Child) (Interim Care Order)* [2002] EWCA Civ 1932, at [38] and [39] states two propositions: (1) that the decision taken by the court on an interim care order application must necessarily be limited to issues that cannot await the final hearing and must not extend to issues that are being prepared for determination at that hearing; and (2) that separation is only to be ordered if the child's safety demands immediate separation. In *Re M (Interim Care Order: Removal)* [2006] 1 FLR 1043, CA, at [27], Thorpe LJ stated that a local authority in seeking to justify the continuing removal of a child from home necessarily must meet a very high standard. In *Re K and H* [2007] 1 FLR 2043, CA, at [16], the court held that 'at an interim stage the removal of children from their parents is not to be sanctioned unless the child's safety requires interim protection'. In *Re L-A (Care: Chronic Neglect)* [2010] 1 FLR 80, CA, the Court of Appeal reviewed these authorities and made it clear that the words of Ryder J in *Re L (Care Proceedings: Removal of Child)* [2008] 1 FLR 575, FD requiring 'an imminent risk of really serious harm' were not intended to 'raise the bar' for a new standard to be reached before the making of an interim care order, but were simply intended to restate the test defined in the appellate cases. In *Re B (Care Proceedings: Interim Care Order)* [2010] 1 FLR 1211, CA, Wall LJ asked whether the child's safety, using that word in a broad sense to include psychological welfare, required interim protection (see also *Re GR (Care Order)* [2011] 1 FLR 669, CA). In *Re B (Interim Care Order)* [2010] 2 FLR 283, CA, Wall LJ reviewed the jurisprudence and held that the continued removal of a child must be proportionate to the risk of harm to which she would be exposed if she were allowed to return to the parent's care, cited with approval in *Re S (Care Proceedings: Human Rights)* [2012] 2 FLR 209, CA). In *Re G (Interim Care Order)* [2011] 2 FLR 955, CA, the President summarised the authorities on removal as requiring the court to ask itself (i) whether the children's safety (using that term to include both psychological and physical elements) requires removal and (ii) whether removal is proportionate in the light of the risks posed by leaving the children where they are. See also *Dolhamre v Sweden* [2010] 2 FLR 912, ECHR, in which the European Court of Human Rights held that a fair balance had to be struck between the interests of the child remaining in care and those of the parent in being reunited with the child, attaching particular importance to the best interests of the child, which, depending on their nature and seriousness, might override those of the parent. For a case in which the Family Proceedings Court failed to have regard to these principles see *Re NL (Appeal: Interim Care Order: Facts and Reasons)* [2014] 1 FLR 1384, FD. In *Re F (Care Proceedings: Interim Care Order)* [2010] 2 FLR 1455, CA, Thorpe LJ held that the judge's elevation of emotional harm to satisfy the making of an interim care order for separation of parents and children did not begin to meet the high threshold set by the authorities on removal at an interim stage.

In *R (G) v Nottingham City Council* [2008] 1 FLR 1660, QBD, Munby J emphasised that no local authority and no social worker has any power to remove a child from its parent, or, without the agreement of the parent, to take a child into care, unless they have first obtained a court order authorizing that step, whether that be an emergency protection order, an interim care order, or, in an exceptional case, a wardship order. For useful guidance as to the nature of interim care orders see *Re S (Minors) (Care Order: Implementation of Care Plan); Re W (Minors) (Care Order: Adequacy of Care Plan)* [2002] 1 FLR 815, HL, at [89]–[102]. When making an interim care order in relation to a young child, where it is impossible to fix the final hearing for several months, the court must balance the effect of long-term removal on the child with the risk of short-term harm if left with the parents (*Re M (Interim Care Order: Removal)* (above)). An interim care order is not irreversible either in law or in fact (*Re L (Interim Care Order: Power of Court)* [1996] 2 FLR 742, CA). It does not follow that an interim care order will be made automatically upon the threshold criteria having been met in a particular case (*Re A (Children) (Interim Care Order)* [2001] 3 FCR 402, FD – although in that case interim care orders were made). Where an application for an interim care order has been made, in anything other than wholly exceptional circumstances, the rule must be that it is for the court to make the decision to remove the child (*Re S (Care Proceedings: Human Rights)* [2012] 2 FLR 209, CA, in which the local authority had decided to arrange for the baby to be separated from the mother under police protection despite an application for an interim care order having been made and being listed before the court the next day). The circumstances that demand removal without notice to the parents will be rare. Where this is necessary, the matter must be listed as a matter of extreme urgency to allow the parent(s) to challenge the removal (*Re S (Authorising Children's Immediate Removal)* [2010] 2 FLR 873, CA).

Vaccination of children subject to an interim care order—Where a child is in the care of the local authority, by virtue of CA 1989, s 9(1) the local authority cannot apply for a specific issue order where it seeks to facilitate the vaccination of the child in the face of objection by a parent. Given the gravity of the issue in dispute, it is not appropriate for the local authority simply to give its consent to immunisation pursuant to the provisions of CA 1989, s 33(3) based on its shared parental responsibility for the child under the interim care order (see *A Local Authority v SB, AB & MB* [2010] 2 FLR 1203, FD and *Re Jake (Withholding of Medical Treatment*) [2015] EWHC 2442 (Fam)). In the circumstances, the local authority must apply for relief under the inherent jurisdiction of the High Court. The local authority requires leave to make such an application, which application for leave is to be considered against the criteria set out in CA 1989, s 100(4). The test for whether permission should be given to vaccinate the child is whether vaccination is in the child's best interests, having regard to those interests as the court's paramount consideration (see *Re SL (Permission to Vaccinate)* [2017] EWHC 125 (Fam), *Re C (Welfare of Child: Immunisation)* [2003] 2 FLR 1054 (upheld on appeal in *Re C (Welfare of Child: Immunisation)* [2003] 2 FLR 1095, CA), *LCC v A & Ors* [2011] EWHC 4033 (Fam) and *F v F (MMR Vaccine)* [2014] 1 FLR 1328, FD).

Interim care order or full care order?—In *Re S (Minors) (Care Order: Implementation of Care Plan); Re W (Minors) (Care Order: Adequacy of Care Plan)* [2002] 1 FLR 815, HL, at [89]–[102], Lord Nicholls gives useful guidance as to the nature of interim care orders and sets out examples of cases that fall either side of the line. See also *Re G (Interim Care Order: Residential Assessment)* [2006] 1 FLR 601, HL, at [55]. This guidance must now be read subject to the abolition of the requirement to renew interim care orders initially after 8 weeks and thereafter every 4 weeks.

The court must go through a two-stage process before making a care order, namely: (i) it must be satisfied that the threshold criteria have been met; and (ii) it must consider whether the making of a care order is better than no order. The court must carefully scrutinise the care plan and satisfy itself that it is in the child's best interests. If the court is not satisfied of this or is not satisfied by any material aspect of the care plan it may refuse to make the care order. The court should only pass responsibility to the local authority by a final care order when all of the facts are as clearly known as can be hoped. On the other hand, the court should be alert to the danger of (wrongly) using an interim care order as a means of exercising the defunct supervisory role of the court (*Re J (Minors) (Care: Care Plan)* [1994] 1 FLR 253, FD, approved by the Court of Appeal in *Re CH (Care or Interim Care Order)* [1998] 1 FLR 402, CA; *Re L (Sexual Abuse: Standard of Proof)* [1996] 1 FLR 116, CA). When current issues regarding care have been determined, it can seldom, if ever, be right for the court to continue to adjourn a case on an interim order (*Re P (Minors) (Interim Order)* [1993] 2 FLR 742, CA). On the other hand, the fact that a care order is the inevitable eventual outcome should not deflect the judge from using the litigation process to its maximum effect (*Re CH*). In deciding whether to grant or continue an interim or grant a final care orders the essential question is whether the court has a sufficiently clear picture of the way forward. The child's well-being demands that the court be satisfied by the local authority's proposals and it is primarily for the trial judge to decide when a sufficiently clear position has been reached (*Re H (Children)* [2011] EWCA Civ 1218). It is open to the court to use an interim care order, rather than a full care order, at the disposal or second stage of care proceedings where the circumstances are exceptional (*Re F (Interim Care Order)* [2007] 2 FLR 891, CA – where the court considered that the mother deserved a further chance to prove her parenting abilities). The court may, in appropriate cases, use a combination of other orders under CA 1989 to allow a parent the chance to further prove his or her parenting abilities (see *Re H (Care Proceedings: Foster Care Placement for Mother and Baby)* [2013] 1 FLR 1445, CA). It is not, however, permissible for the court to treat the hearing as final while only making an interim care order (*Re G (Interim Care Order)* [2011] 2 FLR 955, CA).

The point at which the court withdraws from further control over the child and passes responsibility to the local authority is a matter of the exercise of discretion by the court and will vary with each set of circumstances (*Re L (Sexual Abuse: Standard of Proof)* above). Where the care plan does not contain any proposals for direct post-adoption contact when it is appropriate the court should approve the care plan, save in relation to contact; it should make a care order and then proceed to deal with the question of contact there and then or by giving directions for future determination of the issue, or by leaving the mother or the guardian to make an appropriate application (*Re K (Care Proceedings: Care Plan)* [2008] 1 FLR 1, FD).

Subject to s 38(6), the court cannot on the making of an interim care order impose conditions on the local authority as to the manner in which a child is cared for. Where the care plan is unacceptable, the judge has to decide whether to make a child arrangements order with respect to living arrangements in the interim and subject to supervision instead (*Re L (Interim Care Order: Power of Court)* [1996] 2 FLR 742, CA). Where a care order is made a case may be returned to court in certain circumstances (e g where the care plan has not been properly implemented) under s 26(2)(e), which encompasses a requirement for the authority to review the care plan and revise it as necessary, together with a route for returning it to the court through the intervention of a Cafcass officer where appropriate. See further **Review of cases of looked-after children** under CA 1989, s 26.

Child arrangements order on interim application in pending care proceedings—There is jurisdiction to make a child arrangements order with respect to living arrangements on an interim application in pending care proceedings (see s 38(3)) but the view was expressed in *Re RJ (Fostering: Disqualified Person)* [1999] 1 FLR 605, CA that where the effect of the interim order would be to alter the status quo, the jurisdiction should only be used in those exceptional cases in which, at the time of the interim application, the court can be confident that, following a substantive hearing, a long-term child arrangements order with respect to living arrangements will be made in favour of the same persons. It is wrong for the court to make child arrangements orders with respect to living arrangements rather than an interim care order pending the final hearing (*Re B (Children)* [2002] 3 FCR 562, CA, but see also *Re H (Care Proceedings: Foster Care Placement for Mother and Baby)* [2013] 1 FLR 1445, CA).

Interim orders and split hearings—Where the court conducts a split hearing, it appears to be assumed, in practice, that the period between the preliminary or fact-finding hearing and the final hearing can appropriately be regulated by an interim order.

Directions under s 38(6)—CFA 2014 amends CA 1989, s 38 to provide a statutory test in s 38(7A) for determining whether to direct a medical or psychiatric examination or other assessment of the child, namely that such an assessment must be necessary to assist the court to resolve the proceedings justly. The phrase 'necessary to resolve the proceedings' has the same meaning in both the context of expert evidence and the context of further assessment, namely that set out in *Re TG (Care Proceedings: Case Management: Expert Evidence)* [2013] 1 FLR 1250, CA, at [30], and *Re H-L (Expert Evidence: Test for Permission)* [2013] 2 FLR 1434, CA, at [3] (*Re S (A Child)* [2014] EWCC B44 (Fam)).

In determining whether this test is met, the court must have regard to any impact that any examination or other assessment would be likely to have on the welfare of the child, and any other impact that giving the direction would be likely to have on the welfare of the child, the issues with which the examination or other assessment would assist the court, the questions that the examination or other assessment would enable the court to answer, the evidence otherwise available, the impact that the direction would be likely to have on the timetable, duration and conduct of the proceedings, the cost of the examination or other assessment, and any matters prescribed by FPR 2010. The latter requirement will encompass consideration of the Overriding Objective. The case-law set out below must now be read subject to the statutory test in s 38(6), as amended.

In *Re C (Interim Care Order: Residential Assessment)* [1997] 1 FLR 1, HL, a direction under s 38(6) for a residential assessment of the child and his parents was upheld, the House of Lords holding that s 38(6) and (7) enables the court to order or prohibit any assessment (whether of a type similar to a medical or psychiatric assessment or not) which involves the participation of the child and is directed to providing the court with material which, in the view of the court, is required to enable it to reach a proper decision at the final hearing of the application for a full care order (*Re B (Interim Care Order: Directions)* [2002] 1 FLR 545, CA). The local authority assumes control of the child once an interim care order has been made, save in specified cases where the court has power to intervene under s 38(6) (*Re B* (above) – it was within the court's jurisdiction to make a direction for residency at a mother and baby unit under s 38(6) even though the local authority objected, since the residential placement was important for assessment purposes). The giving of directions for therapeutic treatment for a parent is not within the court's s 38(6) powers. What is directed under s 38(6) must clearly be an examination or assessment of the child, including where appropriate, his relationship with his parents, the risk that his parents may present to him and the ways in which those risks may be avoided or managed, all with a view to enabling the court to make the decisions which it has to make under the Act with the minimum of delay. Any services which are provided for the child and his family must be ancillary to that end. They must not be an end in themselves (*Re G (Interim Care Order: Residential Assessment)* [2006] 1 FLR 601, HL – where the House of Lords held that the court had no power to make an order for a s 38(6) 'assessment' if the main purpose of the order was to provide a continuing course of psychotherapy to the mother with a view to giving her the opportunity to change sufficiently so as to become a safe and acceptable carer for her child).

Before taking the step of removing children permanently from their natural families and placing them for adoption with strangers, the court must be satisfied that the threshold criteria for a care order are met and that care orders with care plans for adoption are in the best interests of the children concerned. This requires the court to be astute to ensure that the case has been fully investigated and that all the relevant evidence necessary for the decision is in place (*Re L and H (Residential Assessment)* [2007] 1 FLR 1370, CA – where the court held that any final hearing which followed a denial to these parents of the opportunity to take part in a residential assessment of the child would be unfair; *Re M (Assessment: Official Solicitor)* [2009] 2 FLR 950, CA – where the Court of Appeal held that a judge should be slow to refuse an independent psychiatric assessment on the mother when the immediate and foreseeable consequence would be to deprive an incapacitated litigant of any prospect of averting the care and placement orders sought by the local authority).

PART II

However, in *Re T (Residential Parenting Assessment)* [2012] 2 FLR 308, CA, Black LJ made clear, having comprehensively reviewed the authorities, that insofar as earlier Court of Appeal decisions might be taken to suggest that a parent facing the permanent removal of their child has a right in all cases to an assessment of their choice rather than one carried out or commissioned by the local authority, this is not what the court intended. Still less do those authorities establish a principle that parents must be given the chance to put forward a positive case to the judge determining the issue of whether a care order should be made. Referring to the case of *Re G*, Black LJ reiterated that further or other assessments should only be commissioned if they can bring something important to the case that neither the local authority nor the guardian is able to bring. Care proceedings must be fair, but it is not necessary for the purposes of ECHR, Art 6 to continue to assess parents if the process is not going to contribute anything to the information that is needed for the ultimate decision.

In *Re W (Assessment of Child)* [1998] 2 FLR 130, CA, it was held that the court had jurisdiction to direct a particular social worker, as a named employee of the local authority, to carry out a s 38(6) assessment but that applications naming social workers were not to be encouraged. An individual could not be directed to carry out the assessment if unwilling or unable to do so and it should be ascertained in advance that the person concerned was willing and able to act. Account ought to be taken of the resources of the local authority employing the social worker and any difficulties with regard to the authority's responsibility for and duty to supervise him. The court commented that a better direction might be that given in *Berkshire CC v C and Others* [1993] 1 FLR 569, FD (i e that assessment should be carried out by a 'suitably qualified social worker').

Pursuant to s 38(7B)(f), the court has to take into account the cost of the proposed assessment. In exercising its discretion whether to order any particular examination or assessment, the court should also take account of the limits on local authority resources. It is important in determining whether to order a local authority to provide residential assessment to give proper weight to the benefits to the children from such an assessment, compared with the wider responsibility of the authority generally (*Re C (Children) (Residential Assessment)* [2001] EWCA Civ 1305 – where the authority was ordered to provide a residential assessment in spite of the fact that the cost was so high that it would allegedly absorb most of the authority's remaining budget; *B County Council v L and Others* [2002] EWHC 2327 (Fam) – where the local authority was criticised for terminating an assessment early because of staff commitments and funding problems and a further assessment was ordered before a full care order could be considered). There are useful guidelines in *Sheffield City Council v V (Legal Services Commission Intervening)* [2007] 1 FLR 279, FD: (i) s 38(6) directions should not be made until the court has had an opportunity to examine the details of the proposed assessment; (ii) the assessment provider should be told in advance what it is proposed that the assessment should cover; (iii) the parties should obtain from the assessment provider clear information as to the nature, timing and cost of the work it expects to undertake; (iv) if the work includes elements of therapy, training or treatment then that element of the work should be separately stated by the provider; (v) upon receipt of this information all parties should endeavour to agree whether and how the costs are to be apportioned; (vi) if the court does have to rule on a contested funding issue it should take a common-sense view; (vii) when an assessment is genuinely of a mixed nature the court should identify the work that is outside s 38(6) and which therefore cannot be ordered or paid for; and (viii) the issue of funding should be determined at the same hearing as the application for permission to commission the assessment. Since 1 October 2007 the Legal Services Commission Funding Code has been amended so that where a party is publicly funded the court can no longer direct the LSC to make a contribution to the costs, thus leaving the local authority to bear the entire bill. In *A Local Authority v M (Funding of Residential Assessments)* [2008] 1 FLR 1579, FD, the already financially over-stretched local authority was ordered to pay for the mother to participate in a shortened residential assessment period of 7 weeks (rather than the recommended 12 weeks) with a report and prognosis at the end; if things went well then a further period of assessment may be ordered.

In *Re T (Residential Parenting Assessment)* [2012] 2 FLR 308, CA, Black LJ (recognising that a hearing for the purposes of determining whether to make a direction under s 38(6) is inevitably shorter and more focused than a full hearing at which the threshold criteria are considered and/or a final welfare decision is taken) made clear that it is a matter for the individual judge to regulate the nature and extent of the material upon which the s 38(6) decision is taken and the format of the s 38(6) hearing, and that this aspect of the judge's case management will, like most case management, be highly dependent on the facts of the individual case.

For guidance on new rates of payment for most types of experts involved in family proceedings, see **Legal aid remuneration for expert evidence** under CFA 2014, s 13.

'class of person prescribed by rules of court' (s 38(8))—See FPR 2010, r 12.27(2), which refers the practitioner to the table in r 12.3, for a list of the appropriate applicants and respondents.

38A Power to include exclusion requirement in interim care order

(1) Where –

(a) on being satisfied that there are reasonable grounds for believing that the circumstances with respect to a child are as mentioned in section 31(2)(a) and (b)(i), the court makes an interim care order with respect to a child, and

(b) the conditions mentioned in subsection (2) are satisfied,

the court may include an exclusion requirement in the interim care order.

(2) The conditions are –

(a) that there is reasonable cause to believe that, if a person ('the relevant person') is excluded from a dwelling-house in which the child lives, the child will cease to suffer, or cease to be likely to suffer, significant harm, and

(b) that another person living in the dwelling-house (whether a parent of the child or some other person) –

(i) is able and willing to give to the child the care which it would be reasonable to expect a parent to give him, and

(ii) consents to the inclusion of the exclusion requirement.

(3) For the purposes of this section an exclusion requirement is any one or more of the following –

(a) a provision requiring the relevant person to leave a dwelling-house in which he is living with the child,

(b) a provision prohibiting the relevant person from entering a dwelling-house in which the child lives, and

(c) a provision excluding the relevant person from a defined area in which a dwelling-house in which the child lives is situated.

(4) The court may provide that the exclusion requirement is to have effect for a shorter period than the other provisions of the interim care order.

(5) Where the court makes an interim care order containing an exclusion requirement, the court may attach a power of arrest to the exclusion requirement.

(6) Where the court attaches a power of arrest to an exclusion requirement of an interim care order, it may provide that the power of arrest is to have effect for a shorter period than the exclusion requirement.

(7) Any period specified for the purposes of subsection (4) or (6) may be extended by the court (on one or more occasions) on an application to vary or discharge the interim care order.

(8) Where a power of arrest is attached to an exclusion requirement of an interim care order by virtue of subsection (5), a constable may arrest without warrant any person whom he has reasonable cause to believe to be in breach of the requirement.

(9) Sections 47(7), (11) and (12) and 48 of, and Schedule 5 to, the Family Law Act 1996 shall have effect in relation to a person arrested under subsection (8) of this section as they have effect in relation to a person arrested under section 47(6) of that Act.

(10) If, while an interim care order containing an exclusion requirement is in force, the local authority have removed the child from the dwelling-house from which the relevant person is excluded to other accommodation for a continuous period of more than 24 hours, the interim care order shall cease to have effect in so far as it imposes the exclusion requirement.

Amendments—Inserted by FLA 1996, s 52, Sch 6, para 1.

Defined terms—'child': s 105(1); 'relevant person': s 38A(2)(a).

Scope—Providing the conditions in s 38A(2) are satisfied, the court can safeguard a child by granting an interim care order including a provision excluding from the home the person ('the relevant person') who is putting the child at risk. A power of arrest can be attached to the exclusion requirement. Note the requirement under s 38A(2)(b)(ii) that another person living in the house, whether a parent of the child or some other person, must consent to the exclusion requirement.

Interim care order—See s 38.

Power of arrest (s 38A(5))—Under s 38A(5) and s 44A(5) the court may attach a power of arrest to an exclusion requirement included in an interim care order or an emergency protection order. Where a power of arrest is attached, once the relevant person has been served with the order/informed of its terms, a copy of the order must be delivered to police together with a statement showing that the relevant person has been served with the order/informed of its terms. In serving the relevant person and delivering a copy of the order to the police, it is important to comply with the guidance set out in the Family Justice Council *Protocol for Process Servers* of November 2011 (see Part V). In cases where an order is made which includes an exclusion requirement, FPR PD12K *Children Act 1989: Exclusion Requirement*, sets out requirements to ensure that unless the person to whom the exclusion requirement refers was given notice of the hearing and attended, the name of that person and that an order has been made must be announced in open court at the earliest opportunity (PD12K, para 1). Paragraph 2 sets out the arrangements for bringing the person arrested before the relevant judicial authority, and para 3 requires that any order of committal made otherwise than in public must be announced in open court at the earliest opportunity.

Family Court (Contempt of Court) (Powers) Regulations 2014—These Regulations, set out in Part IV of this work, prescribe the powers of the different levels of judiciary of the Family Court to punish for contempt of court.

Procedure—See FPR 2010, r 12.28.

38B Undertakings relating to interim care orders

(1) In any case where the court has power to include an exclusion requirement in an interim care order, the court may accept an undertaking from the relevant person.

(2) No power of arrest may be attached to any undertaking given under subsection (1).

(3) An undertaking given to a court under subsection (1) –

(a) shall be enforceable as if it were an order of the court, and

(b) shall cease to have effect if, while it is in force, the local authority have removed the child from the dwelling-house from which the relevant person is excluded to other accommodation for a continuous period of more than 24 hours.

(4) This section has effect without prejudice to the powers of the High Court and family court apart from this section.

(5) In this section 'exclusion requirement' and 'relevant person' have the same meaning as in section 38A.

Amendments—Inserted by FLA 1996, s 52, Sch 6, para 1; CCA 2013, s 17, Sch 11.

Defined terms—'child': s 105(1); 'exclusion requirement': s 38A(3); 'relevant person': s 38A(2)(a).

Procedure—See under FLA 1996, s 46 for assistance as to procedure which will be the same, albeit that the context is different.

Powers of Family Court apart from s 38B (s 38B(4))—As to the question of the Family Court accepting undertakings in public law proceedings, see **Undertakings and injunctions** under CA 1989, s 31. As to the inherent jurisdiction of the High Court, see CA 1989, s 100.

39 Discharge and variation etc of care orders and supervision orders

(1) A care order may be discharged by the court on the application of –

(a) any person who has parental responsibility for the child;
(b) the child himself; or
(c) the local authority designated by the order.

(2) A supervision order may be varied or discharged by the court on the application of –

(a) any person who has parental responsibility for the child;
(b) the child himself; or
(c) the supervisor.

(3) On the application of a person who is not entitled to apply for the order to be discharged, but who is a person with whom the child is living, a supervision order may be varied by the court in so far as it imposes a requirement which affects that person.

PART II

(3A) On the application of a person who is not entitled to apply for the order to be discharged, but who is a person to whom an exclusion requirement contained in the order applies, an interim care order may be varied or discharged by the court in so far as it imposes the exclusion requirement.

(3B) Where a power of arrest has been attached to an exclusion requirement of an interim care order, the court may, on the application of any person entitled to apply for the discharge of the order so far as it imposes the exclusion requirement, vary or discharge the order in so far as it confers a power of arrest (whether or not any application has been made to vary or discharge any other provision of the order).

(4) Where a care order is in force with respect to a child the court may, on the application of any person entitled to apply for the order to be discharged, substitute a supervision order for the care order.

(5) When a court is considering whether to substitute one order for another under subsection (4) any provision of this Act which would otherwise require section 31(2) to be satisfied at the time when the proposed order is substituted or made shall be disregarded.

Amendments—FLA 1996, s 52, Sch 6, para 2.

Defined terms—'care order': ss 31(11), 105(1); 'child', 'exclusion requirement': s 38A(3); 'local authority': s 105(1); 'parental responsibility': s 3; 'relevant person': s 38A(2)(a); 'supervision order': s 31(11); 'supervisor': s 105(1).

'any person who has parental responsibility' (s 39(1),(2))—Parental responsibility may be acquired (and lost) in a number of ways, for example by virtue of being the child's mother or married father (s 2(1)), by a parental responsibility agreement or order under s 4, or by being appointed a child's guardian under s 5(6).

'the child himself' (s 39(1)(b))—The child does not require permission to make his application (*Re A (Care: Discharge Application by Child)* [1995] 1 FLR 599, FD). For guidance as to the role that a child applicant should play in the proceedings, see *Re A* (above) and the notes to FPR 2010, r 12.14.

Supervision orders imposing a requirement (s 39(3))—The requirements that may be imposed under a supervision order are set out in Sch 3, which applies by virtue of s 35(2).

Application to discharge where local authority seeks to remove child placed at home under a care order—In *Re DE (A Child)* [2015] 1 FLR 1001, FD, Baker J gave further guidance, approved by the President of the Family Division, as to the proper approach in circumstances where the local authority seeks to remove a child who is in the care of his or her parents at home under a care order:

(a) In every case where a care order is made on the basis of a care plan providing that a child should live at home with his or her parents, it should be a term of the care plan, and a recital in the care order, that the local authority agrees to give not less than 14 days' notice of a removal of the child, save in an emergency. 14 days is an appropriate period, on the one hand to avoid unnecessary delay but, on the other hand, to allow the parents an opportunity to obtain legal advice.

(b) Where a care order has been granted on the basis of a care plan providing that the child should remain at home, a local authority considering changing the plan and removing the child permanently from the family must have regard to the fact that permanent placement outside the family is to be preferred only as a last resort where nothing else will do and must rigorously analyse all the realistic options, considering the arguments for and against each option. Furthermore, it must involve the parents properly in the decision-making process.

(c) In every case where a parent decides to apply to discharge a care order in circumstances where the local authority has given notice of intention to remove a child placed at home under a care order, the parent should consider whether to apply in addition for an injunction under HRA 1998, s 8 to prevent the local authority from removing the child pending the determination of the discharge application. If the parent decides to apply for an injunction, that application should be issued at the same time as the discharge application.

(d) When a local authority, having given notice of its intention to remove a child placed at home under a care order, is given notice of an application for discharge of the care order, the local authority must consider whether the child's welfare requires his immediate removal. Furthermore, the authority must keep a written record demonstrating that it has considered this question, recording the reasons for its decision. In reaching its decision on this point, the local authority must again inter alia consult with the parents. Any removal of a child in circumstances where the child's welfare does not require immediate removal, or without proper consideration and consultation, is likely to be an unlawful interference with the Art 8 rights of the parent and child.

(e) On receipt of an application to discharge a care order, where the child has been living at home, the allocation gatekeeper at the designated family centre should check whether it is accompanied by an application under HRA 1998, s 8 and, if not, whether the circumstances might give rise to such an application. This check is needed because automatic legal aid is not at present available for such applications to discharge a care order and it is therefore likely that such applications may be made by parents acting in person. In cases where the discharge application is accompanied by an application for an order under HRA 1998, s 8, or the allocation gatekeeper considers that the circumstances might give rise to such an application, he or she should allocate the case as soon as possible to a circuit judge for case management. Any application for an injunction in these circumstances must be listed for an early hearing.

(f) On hearing an application for an injunction under HRA 1998, s 8 to restrain a local authority removing a child living at home under a care order pending determination of an application to discharge the care order, the court should normally grant the injunction unless the child's welfare requires his immediate removal from the family home.

Note that in *Re DE (A Child)* [2015] 1 FLR 1001, FD, Baker J highlights the need for any application to be allocated as soon as possible to a circuit judge for case management. In the circumstances, the appropriate tier of allocation in the first instance will be to a judge of circuit judge level.

Applicants for variation/discharge of an exclusion requirement—Section 39(1) establishes three categories of applicant for the discharge of a care order. Section 39(3A) speaks of the discharge of a care order in so far as it imposes an exclusion requirement. It is therefore submitted that s 39(1) entitles a person with parental responsibility, the child himself or the local authority designated in the interim care order to apply for an exclusion requirement to be discharged. Whether an application can be made under s 39(1) for the variation of an exclusion requirement, however, is a moot point. Section 39(3A) appears to draw a distinction between discharge of that part of the interim order which imposes the exclusion requirement and variation of it. A similar distinction between discharge and variation can be found in s 39(2) concerning supervision orders. No doubt the reason that the Act, as originally drafted, was silent as to variation of care orders was that care orders were a bald transfer of responsibility to a local authority and could not, under the statutory scheme, stipulate any particular requirements whereas, in accordance with CA 1989, Sch 3, supervision orders could impose specified obligations. This has, of course, changed with the introduction of the concept of exclusion requirements and it may be that, in the amendment process, the need to extend s 39(1) to provide a right to local authorities etc to apply for a variation of an exclusion requirement, as well as for its discharge, was overlooked. The only person who is secure in his right to apply for a variation of the exclusion requirement is the person to whom it applies (s 39(3A)). This must mean the 'relevant person' who has been excluded in accordance with s 38A(1) and (2). Certainly the s 39(3A) right cannot extend to local authorities, the child or those with parental responsibility because they are all entitled to apply for discharge of the order, and therefore expressly excluded by the opening words of the subsection. To what extent the limitation on the categories of applicant really matters in practice remains to be seen. How each case develops will naturally depend on its own particular circumstances. Where the local authority fear for the welfare of the child who is the subject of the interim care order, they can remove him forthwith without further recourse to the court and, if the removal persists for more than 24 hours, s 38A(10) provides that the exclusion requirement ceases to be effective automatically. At the other end of the scale, if time is not of the essence and an application to the court is the most appropriate way forward, the matter can be raised at the next renewal of the interim care order when the court can reconsider the whole picture. Should an earlier application about the exclusion requirement be needed, it seems extremely likely that, whatever the strict technicalities of s 39, an application could legitimately be launched by an interested party (whether for variation or discharge) and that the court would proceed to review the matter broadly.

Applicants for variation or discharge of power of arrest (s 39(3B))—This provision is slightly less unhappily drafted than s 39(3A) and may entitle all those listed in s 39(1), plus the person excluded by the exclusion requirement, to apply for an attendant power of arrest to be varied or discharged.

Burden of proving application—The criterion for deciding on discharge of a care order is the welfare test in CA 1989, s 1(1) and it is the person applying for the care order to be discharged who has the burden of showing that the child's welfare requires the revocation of the order (*Re MD and TD (Minors) (No 2)* [1994] Fam Law 489, FD, and see *Re S (Discharge of Care Order)* [1995] 2 FLR 639, CA).

40 Orders pending appeals in cases about care or supervision orders

(1) Where –

(a) a court dismisses an application for a care order; and

(b) at the time when the court dismisses the application, the child concerned is the subject of an interim care order,

the court may make a care order with respect to the child to have effect subject to such directions (if any) as the court may see fit to include in the order.

(2) Where –

(a) a court dismisses an application for a care order, or an application for a supervision order; and

(b) at the time when the court dismisses the application, the child concerned is the subject of an interim supervision order,

the court may make a supervision order with respect to the child to have effect subject to such directions (if any) as the court sees fit to include in the order.

(3) Where a court grants an application to discharge a care order or supervision order, it may order that –

(a) its decision is not to have effect; or

(b) the care order, or supervision order, is to continue to have effect but subject to such directions as the court sees fit to include in the order.

(4) An order made under this section shall only have effect for such a period, not exceeding the appeal period, as may be specified in the order.

(5) Where –

(a) an appeal is made against any decision of a court under this section; or

(b) any application is made to the appellate court in connection with a proposed appeal against that decision,

the appellate court may extend the period for which the order in question is to have effect, but not so as to extend it beyond the end of the appeal period.

(6) In this section 'the appeal period' means –

(a) where an appeal is made against the decision in question, the period between the making of that decision and the determination of the appeal; and

(b) otherwise, the period during which an appeal may be made against the decision.

Defined terms—'care order': s 31(11); 'child': s 105(1); 'the court': s 92(7).

Scope—This section provides the court with power to make a care or supervision order pending an appeal. The power may be exercised when dismissing an application for such an order or granting an application to discharge such an order (if there was an interim order in force beforehand) or on an application to discharge such an order. If the original court refused to make a care order pending appeal, the appeal court has no power to make such an order. The appeal court can only make an interim order pending appeal (*Croydon London Borough Council v A (No 2)* [1992] 2 FLR 348, FD).

Appeal period—Where the appeal relates to an order (or refusal to make an order) made by lay justices or a judge of District Judge level, the appeal must be lodged within 21 days, or 7 days if appealing the making of an interim care order or an interim supervision order or a case management decision (FPR 2010, r 30.4(2),(3)). Where the appeal lies to the Court of Appeal, the appeal should be lodged within the time directed by the lower court and within 21 days in the absence of a direction by the lower court (CPR 1998, r 52.4). As a general rule in children's cases, courts should direct a period of less than 21 days within which to lodge a notice of appeal and the appeal should be brought on swiftly (*Re M-H (Children)* [2006] EWCA Civ 499; *Re A (Children: Split Hearing)* [2007] 1 FLR 905, CA). To extend the time in which to lodge the appeal an application must be made to the appeal court (FPR 2010, r 30.7(1)).

In those cases where it is plain that whatever the professionals' assessment of the prospects of success the litigants cannot rest until they have exhausted their legal remedies, the court should consider imposing tight time limits on the filing of an application for permission to appeal, and contact the Civil Appeals office to seek an early listing so that finality may be achieved as soon as ever possible (*Re P (Residence: Appeal)* [2008] 1 FLR 198, CA).

Directions—When making an order under this section pending appeal, the court has wide powers to make the order subject to such directions 'as the court sees fit'. An order under this section is governed by the principles contained in CA 1989, s 1.

Stay—This section does not give the court power to grant a stay of the operation of a care or supervision order pending appeal. Once an appeal has been filed, the appeal court has the power to grant a stay (FPR 2010, r 30.8). The lower court has the power to grant a stay and any application should first be made to that court and thereafter to the appeal court (FPR 2010, r 30.8; CPR 1998, r 52.7). If the appeal is against the making of an adoption order, an application should be made immediately for a stay of the order (together with an application for an expedited hearing). The existence of an arguable appeal with reasonable prospects of success is the minimum requirement before a court can even consider granting a stay: *NB v Haringey LBC* [2012] 2 FLR 125, FD. Where a party challenges the making of an ICO that would lead to the removal of the child from his carers and where there is no immediate emergency, the court making the order should permit a short and reasonable stay to enable an application to be made for permission to appeal: *Re T (Interim Care Order: Removal of Children Where No Immediate Emergency)* [2016] 1 FLR 347, CA.

Imposition of conditions to grant of stay—The Supreme Court has criticised the imposition by the Court of Appeal of conditions to the grant of a stay pending determination of an application for permission to appeal by the Supreme Court. 'As a general rule, conditions such as were imposed by the Court of Appeal in this case should not be made where a party seeks permission to appeal, not least because these might be seen as an unwarranted disincentive to the pursuit of what proved in this case to be a fully merited application,' per Lord Kerr: *Re B (A Child)* [2010] 1 FLR 551, SC. The Court of Appeal had approved the decision of the court below to transfer residence from the maternal grandmother to the father: in granting a stay of the transfer of residence the court imposed a provision for extensive overnight staying contact to the father.

Urgent appeals—In urgent cases where the judge has refused a stay of the order pending the application for permission to appeal, the prospective appellant may telephone the Court of Appeal to apply for a stay (during office hours the telephone number is 0207 947 6000 and out of hours contact is made to the security office at the RCJ on 0207 947 6260 who will refer the matter to the duty deputy master): see CPR PD52C, para 26. A deputy master will refer the matter to a Lord Justice who may grant the stay or list the matter urgently for consideration of the application for a stay (*Re S (Child Proceedings: Urgent Appeals)* [2007] 2 FLR 1044, CA).

'appellate court may extend the period' (s 40(5))—In *Re M (A Minor) (Appeal: Interim Order)* [1994] 1 FLR 54, CA, the Court of Appeal held that, where there was an appeal against the refusal to make a care order, an order under this section should be extended by the Court of Appeal unless the appeal is utterly hopeless, so as to preserve the position of the child pending appeal.

Representation of child

41 Representation of child and of his interests in certain proceedings

(1) For the purpose of any specified proceedings, the court shall appoint an officer of the Service or a Welsh family proceedings officer for the child concerned unless satisfied that it is not necessary to do so in order to safeguard his interests.

(2) The officer of the Service or a Welsh family proceedings officer shall –

- (a) be appointed in accordance with rules of court; and
- (b) be under a duty to safeguard the interests of the child in the manner prescribed by such rules.

(3) Where –

- (a) the child concerned is not represented by a solicitor; and
- (b) any of the conditions mentioned in subsection (4) is satisfied,

the court may appoint a solicitor to represent him.

(4) The conditions are that –

- (a) no officer of the Service or Welsh family proceedings officer has been appointed for the child;
- (b) the child has sufficient understanding to instruct a solicitor and wishes to do so;
- (c) it appears to the court that it would be in the child's best interests for him to be represented by a solicitor.

(5) Any solicitor appointed under or by virtue of this section shall be appointed, and shall represent the child, in accordance with rules of court.

(6) In this section 'specified proceedings' means any proceedings –

- (a) on an application for a care order or supervision order;
- (b) in which the court has given a direction under section 37(1) and has made, or is considering whether to make, an interim care order;
- (c) on an application for the discharge of a care order or the variation or discharge of a supervision order;
- (d) on an application under section 39(4);
- (e) in which the court is considering whether to make a child arrangements order with respect to the living arrangements of a child who is the subject of a care order;
- (f) with respect to contact between a child who is the subject of a care order and any other person;
- (g) under Part V;
- (h) on an appeal against –
  - (i) the making of, or refusal to make, a care order, supervision order or any order under section 34;
  - (ii) the making of, or refusal to make, a child arrangements order with respect to the living arrangements of a child who is the subject of a care order; or
  - (iii) the variation or discharge of, or refusal of an application to vary or discharge, an order of a kind mentioned in sub-paragraph (i) or (ii);
  - (iv) the refusal of an application under section 39(4);
  - (v) the making of, or refusal to make, an order under Part V;
- (hh) on an application for the making or revocation of a placement order (within the meaning of section 21 of the Adoption and Children Act 2002); or
- (i) which are specified for the time being, for the purposes of this section, by rules of court.

(6A) The proceedings which may be specified under subsection (6)(i) include (for example) proceedings for the making, varying or discharging of a section 8 order.

(6B) For the purposes of subsection (6), a child arrangements order is one made with respect to the living arrangements of a child if the arrangements regulated by the order consist of, or include, arrangements which relate to either or both of the following –

(a) with whom the child is to live, and
(b) when the child is to live with any person.

(7)–(9) *(repealed)*

(10) Rules of court may make this provision as to –

(a) the assistance which any officer of the Service or Welsh family proceedings officer may be required by the court to give to it;
(b) the consideration to be given by any officer of the Service or Welsh family proceedings officer, where an order of a specified kind has been made in the proceedings in question, as to whether to apply for the variation or discharge of the order;
(c) the participation of officers of the Service or Welsh family proceedings officers in reviews, of a kind specified in the rules, which are conducted by the court.

(11) Regardless of any enactment or rule of law which would otherwise prevent it from doing so, the court may take account of –

(a) any statement contained in a report made by an officer of the Service or a Welsh family proceedings officer who is appointed under this section for the purpose of the proceedings in question; and
(b) any evidence given in respect of the matters referred to in the report,

in so far as the statement or evidence is, in the opinion of the court, relevant to the question which the court is considering.

(12) *(repealed)*

Amendments—CLSA 1990, s 116, Sch 16, para 17; CJCSA 2000, ss 74, 75, Sch 7, paras 87, 91, Sch 8; ACA 2002, s 122(1); CA 2004, s 40, Sch 3, paras 5, 9; CFA 2014, s 12, Sch 2.

Modifications—Section 41(3)–(5) is modified for certain purposes by SI 2011/2866, Art 8(1), Sch 2. Section 41(6) is modified for certain purposes by SI 2010/1898, reg 5(3).

Defined terms—'care order': ss 31(11), 105(1); 'child': s 105(1); 'supervision order': s 31(11).

'the child concerned' (s 41(1))—This would appear to mean the child who is the subject of the proceedings and not any other children who may happen to be parties to them (for example, if the mother of a baby in respect of whom a care order was being sought was herself a minor, a children's guardian could not be appointed under s 41 although in the Family Court a children's guardian with different powers and duties may be constituted for her under FPR 2010, Pt 16).

'unless satisfied that it is not necessary to do so' (s 41(1))—In *Re J (A Minor) (Change of Name)* [1993] 1 FLR 699, FD, an ex parte application was made by the local authority for leave to change the name of a child in its care. Booth J was satisfied that, although the application fell within CA 1989, s 41, it was not necessary to appoint a guardian ad litem (children's guardian) in order to safeguard the interests of the child. In this particular case, the guardian could not have said any more than counsel for the local authority, and there was no conflict of interest. See also under **'direction under s 37(1)'** below.

Appointment of Official Solicitor—The Official Solicitor no longer represents children who are the subject of family proceedings (other than in very exceptional circumstances and after liaison with Cafcass) see further PD16A, which governs the representation of children in family proceedings.

Appointment of Official Solicitor as amicus curiae (advocate to the court)—There may arise cases in which the Official Solicitor has initially been appointed to act as guardian ad litem to the child who is subject to the proceedings, but is then removed from his position as guardian ad litem as a result of an application made by the child under FPR 2010, r 16.6(5). In such circumstances, it is likely that the Official Solicitor will be invited to remain involved in the case as amicus curiae (advocate to the court) – see *Re H (A Minor) (Role of Official Solicitor)* [1993] 2 FLR 552, FD; see also PD16A, which governs the representation of children in family proceedings. For further discussion of recent case-law, see under FPR 2010, r 16.6(5).

'appointed in accordance with rules of court' (s 41(2)(a))—The relevant rules are FPR 2010, rr 12.6, 12.7, 14.6 and 16.3.

Duration of appointment—See under See FPR 2010, r 16.19.

'safeguard the interests of the child in the manner prescribed by such rules' (s 41(2)(b))—The relevant rules are set out in PD16A, Pts 3 and 4.

'court may appoint a solicitor to represent him' (s 41(3))—The power to appoint a solicitor under this section relates only to 'specified proceedings' as defined in s 41(6); it does not apply, for example, to proceedings brought under CA 1989, s 8 (*Re W (A Minor) (Contact)* [1994] 1 FLR 843, FD). The conditions in s 41(4) relating to the appointment of a solicitor are not confined to a situation where the court has decided that the appointment of a guardian is not necessary to safeguard the interests of the child, but include the situation where there are practical difficulties leading to delay in appointing a guardian (*R v Children and Family Court Advisory and Support Service* [2003] 1 FLR 953, QBD). The Law Society has produced the guidance *Appointing a Solicitor for the Child in Specified Proceedings: Guidelines for Courts* (see Part V) intended for use nationally throughout England and Wales from April 2007 and a practice note *Acting in the Absence of a Children's Guardian* 25 August 2009.

'child has sufficient understanding' (s 41(4)(b))—See **'able ... to give such instructions on his own behalf'** under FPR 2010, r 16.29.

Appointment of solicitor (s 41(5))—The appointment, removal and role of a solicitor under this section is regulated by FPR 2010, r 16.29.

'specified proceedings' (s 41(6))—ACA 2002, s 122 inserts in CA 1989, s 41(6A) so as to include within the category of proceedings which may be 'specified for the time being ... by rules of court' (s 41(6)(i)) any proceedings for the making, varying or discharging of an order under CA 1989, s 8. This extension of the definition of 'specified proceedings' reflects the growing pressure for the appointment of children's guardians in certain private law children cases, for example bitterly contested child arrangements disputes, where children frequently have particular needs and interests which do not coincide with or cannot be adequately represented by the parents (*Re M (Intractable Contact Dispute: Interim Care Order)* [2003] 2 FLR 636, FD). Proceedings for an education supervision order are *not* specified proceedings within the meaning of s 41(6) and so the court in such proceedings cannot appoint a guardian for the child under that section (*Essex County Council v B* [1993] 1 FLR 866, FD). However, in a case where applications were made by the police for disclosure of documents, and by parents for the variation of injunctions restricting publicity in respect of care proceedings which had terminated the day before those applications were made, the court allowed the guardian to continue to represent the child's interests despite the fact that, strictly speaking, the proceedings were no longer specified under s 41(6) (*Oxfordshire County Council v L and F* [1997] 1 FLR 235, FD). Following the repeal of CJCSA 2000, s 12(5)(b) by ACA 2002, as from 28 November 2003 there is no longer jurisdiction for a court to provide for a continuing role for a children's guardian following the making of a supervision order, and therefore *Re MH (A Child) and Re SB and MB (Children)* [2001] 2 FLR 1334, FD is no longer a correct statement of the law. Provision is made in FPR 2010, rr 16.2, 16.4, 16.24 and 16.27 for the appointment in the High Court or the County Court of the Official Solicitor or some other person where it appears to the court that the child should be separately represented. See FPR 2010, Pt 16 and PD16A, which govern the representation of children in family proceedings.

Hybrid proceedings—In hybrid proceedings, or in any straightforward adoption proceedings, where the wishes and feelings of the child are in conflict with the guardian's assessment of welfare and disposal, it may be necessary to give the child an independent voice through his own legal representation (*Re O (Transracial Adoption: Contact)* [1995] 2 FLR 597, FD – where the court considered an application for adoption of a child in the care of the local authority together with applications by the mother for discharge of the care order and the making of a child arrangements order in her favour). The modern approach to hearing the voice of the child was expressed by the Court of Appeal in *Re D (A Child) (International Recognition)* [2016] 2 FLR 347, CA, namely 'the rule of law in England and Wales includes the right of the child to participate in the process that is about him or her. That is the fundamental principle that is reflected in our legislation, our rules and practice directions and jurisprudence. At its most basic level it involves asking at an early stage in family proceedings whether and how that child is going to be given the opportunity to be heard. The qualification in section 1(3)(a) [of the Children Act 1989] like that in article 12(1) [of the United Nations Convention on the Rights of the Child 1989] relates to the weight to be put upon a child's wishes and feelings, not their participation', at [44].

'direction under section 37(1)' (s 41(6)(b))—See also annotations under s 37. In *Re CE (Section 37 Direction)* [1995] 1 FLR 26, FD, Wall J gave guidance as to the approach that should be taken by the court when considering the appointment of a guardian in such cases. A guardian should not be appointed automatically when a s 37 direction is made; the purpose for which a s 37 report is required should be carefully considered. The following matters should be borne in mind although the list was not said to be definitive:

(a) Is the court actually making an interim care order, or merely considering whether to do so? If so, the circumstances are likely to be serious and it may well be appropriate to appoint a guardian immediately.
(b) If an interim order is only being considered, what factors require an appointment to be made?
(c) Will there be sufficient time for the guardian to be informed of the issues and play a useful role?
(d) Is there any specific role to be played by the guardian in the s 37 investigation itself?
(e) If there is no appointment, will the child's interests be properly safeguarded in the interim and during the course of the investigation?
(f) Does the child have a solicitor?

Sections 37 and 41 should not be used to avoid the restrictions on appointing a guardian in private law proceedings.

The proceedings cease to be 'specified proceedings' if the local authority, having investigated, decides not to apply for an order. Once a guardian has been appointed, the appointment subsists until terminated by the court (unless the terms of the appointment specify when it otherwise comes to an end). This remains so even where the proceedings cease to be 'specified'. It is good practice for the order making the appointment to contain a direction that the guardian's continuing involvement be reviewed on completion of the s 37 report. The appointment has to be terminated by order of the court following the procedure set out in FPR 2010, r 16.19 (*Re CE* above).

Discharge of a care order and discharge or variation of a supervision order (s 41(6)(c))—Discharge and variation of such orders are dealt with in s 39.

PART II

'application under section 39(4)' (s 41(6)(d),(h)(iv))—Section 39(4) provides for an application to substitute a supervision order for a care order which is in force.

'proceedings in which the court is considering whether to make a child arrangements order with respect to the living arrangements' (s 41(6)(e))—The court may consider making such an order on a specific application for a child arrangements order or in any family proceedings (see s 10(1),(2)).

Contact with a child in care (s 41(6)(f))—Applications for contact with a child who is the subject of a care order are made under s 34.

Part V (s 41(6)(g),(h)(v))—Pt V (ss 43–52) provides for proceedings for the protection of children, such as emergency protection orders, child assessment orders and recovery orders.

'specified ... by rules of court' (s 41(6)(i))—See FPR 2010, rr 2.3, 12.27.

'regardless of any enactment or rule of law which would otherwise prevent it from doing so' (s 41(11))—Section 41(11) is aimed at the hearsay rule, which would otherwise render a report inadmissible save where the cumbersome procedures laid down under the Civil Evidence Acts are followed. It makes it clear that the court may take account of the contents of a guardian's written report regardless of whether it is otherwise technically admissible as evidence.

Art 12, UNCRC—The appointment of a children's guardian under this provision and the appointment of a solicitor meet this jurisdiction's state obligations under Art 12 to provide the child with the opportunity to be heard in any judicial and administrative proceedings affecting the child: *Re P-S* [2014] 2 FLR 27, CA.

42 Right of officer of the Service to have access to local authority records

(1) Where an officer of the Service or Welsh family proceedings officer has been appointed under section 41 he shall have the right at all reasonable times to examine and take copies of –

(a) any records of, or held by, a local authority or an authorised person which were compiled in connection with the making, or proposed making, by any person of any application under this Act with respect to the child concerned;

(b) any records of, or held by, a local authority which were compiled in connection with any functions which are social services functions within the meaning of the Local Authority Social Services Act 1970 or for the purposes of the Social Services and Well-being (Wales) Act 2014, so far as those records relate to that child; or

(c) any records of, or held by, an authorised person which were compiled in connection with the activities of that person, so far as those records relate to that child.

(2) Where an officer of the Service or Welsh family proceedings officer takes a copy of any record which he is entitled to examine under this section, that copy or any part of it shall be admissible as evidence of any matter referred to in any –

(a) report which he makes to the court in the proceedings in question; or

(b) evidence which he gives in those proceedings.

(3) Subsection (2) has effect regardless of any enactment or rule of law which would otherwise prevent the record in question being admissible in evidence.

(4) In this section 'authorised person' has the same meaning as in section 31.

Amendments—CLSA 1990, ss 116, 125(7), Sch 16, para 18, Sch 20; CJCSA 2000 s 74, Sch 7, paras 87, 92; Local Government Act 2000, s 107(1), Sch 5, para 20; CA 2004, s 40, Sch 3, paras 5, 10; SI 2016/413.

Defined terms—'authorised person': s 31(9); 'child', 'local authority': s 105(1).

Public interest immunity—Where an issue arises as to whether, because of public interest immunity, certain material (often material in the possession of the local authority) should or should not be disclosed, guidance as to the procedure to be followed can be derived from *Re C (Expert Evidence: Disclosure: Practice)* [1995] 1 FLR 204, FD and *Re R (Care: Disclosure: Nature of Proceedings)* [2002] 1 FLR 755, FD.

'officer of the Service ... appointed under section 41' (s 42(1))—The rights granted by this section are available only to guardians appointed under s 41 and not those appointed under FPR 2010, Pt 16 in non-specified proceedings or for minors who are parties to specified proceedings other than as the subject of those proceedings. For example, the guardian ad litem of a minor mother of a child in respect of whom a care order is being sought will not have a right to inspect the records covered by this section, but the guardian ad litem for her child will have that right.

Local Authority Social Services Act 1970 (s 42(1)(b))—Section 2(1) of that Act requires every local authority to establish a social services committee and provides for certain things to stand referred to it. These include all the local authority's functions under the enactments mentioned in Sch 1 to the Act and such other functions as may be designated by the Secretary of State by order. A report of an area child protection committee into a half-brother's death is a document held by the local authority and is compiled in connection with its functions under the Local Authority Social Services Act 1970. The guardian therefore has a right to see such a report in order to ascertain if there is any material relevant to a child (who is the subject of subsequent proceedings) which may help him to give the appropriate advice and provide the appropriate report to the court. Once the guardian has seen the report, he ought to be very careful as to how the information is further disseminated and, if there are particular concerns, the agency can alert the guardian to its sensitivity or request that the information should not be further disseminated (*Re R (Care Proceedings: Disclosure)* [2000] 2 FLR 751, FD). The same applies to the report of an independent inquiry by a senior member of a neighbouring local authority (*Re J (Care Proceedings: Disclosure)* [2003] 2 FLR 522, FD).

Adoption records—In care proceedings, s 42(1)(b) entitles a guardian ad litem of the child to see Form F (a case record prepared by the local authority giving detailed information concerning the prospective adopters with whom it is intended to place the child if a care order is granted), and s 42(2)(a) entitles him to include the relevant information derived from it in his report in the care proceedings (*Re T (A Minor) (Guardian ad Litem: Case Record)* [1994] 1 FLR 632, CA).

'any enactment or rule of law which would otherwise prevent' (s 42(3))—Section 42(3) is aimed at the hearsay rule, which would otherwise often make a copy of a record inadmissible save where the cumbersome procedures laid down under the Civil Evidence Acts are followed. It has also been held to override the Adoption Agencies Regulations 1983, reg 14 which makes a local authority's Form F concerning prospective adopters a confidential record (see *Re T*, above).

Limitations of s 42—Section 42 does not entitle a guardian ad litem to see witness statements and similar documents disclosed by the Crown Prosecution Service or the police to the local authority, although their existence is likely to be reflected in the social work records so that, if the guardian feels they are likely to be of particular importance to the parents' case, steps would be taken to determine whether they should be disclosed to the parents (*Nottinghamshire County Council v H* [1995] 1 FLR 115, FD).

Furthermore, s 42 does not entitle a guardian to disclose documents which are covered by public interest immunity – see **Public interest immunity** above.

Access to materials held by the prosecution authorities in Scotland—See *Cheshire County Council v C* [1995] 2 FLR 862, FD.

PART V
PROTECTION OF CHILDREN

43 Child assessment orders

(1) On the application of a local authority or authorised person for an order to be made under this section with respect to a child, the court may make the order if, but only if, it is satisfied that –

- (a) the applicant has reasonable cause to suspect that the child is suffering, or is likely to suffer, significant harm;
- (b) an assessment of the state of the child's health or development, or of the way in which he has been treated, is required to enable the applicant to determine whether or not the child is suffering, or is likely to suffer, significant harm; and
- (c) it is unlikely that such an assessment will be made, or be satisfactory, in the absence of an order under this section.

(2) In this Act 'a child assessment order' means an order under this section.

(3) A court may treat an application under this section as an application for an emergency protection order.

(4) No court shall make a child assessment order if it is satisfied –

- (a) that there are grounds for making an emergency protection order with respect to the child; and
- (b) that it ought to make such an order rather than a child assessment order.

(5) A child assessment order shall –

- (a) specify a date by which the assessment is to begin; and
- (b) have effect for such period, not exceeding 7 days beginning with that date, as may be specified in the order.

(6) Where a child assessment order is in force with respect to a child it shall be the duty of any person who is in a position to produce the child –

- (a) to produce him to such person as may be named in the order; and
- (b) to comply with such directions relating to the assessment of the child as the court thinks fit to specify in the order.

(7) A child assessment order authorises any person carrying out the assessment, or any part of the assessment, to do so in accordance with the terms of the order.

(8) Regardless of subsection (7), if the child is of sufficient understanding to make an informed decision he may refuse to submit to a medical or psychiatric examination or other assessment.

(9) The child may only be kept away from home –

(a) in accordance with directions specified in the order;
(b) if it is necessary for the purposes of the assessment; and
(c) for such period or periods as may be specified in the order.

(10) Where the child is to be kept away from home, the order shall contain such directions as the court thinks fit with regard to the contact that he must be allowed to have with other persons while away from home.

(11) Any person making an application for a child assessment order shall take such steps as are reasonably practicable to ensure that notice of the application is given to –

(a) the child's parents;
(b) any person who is not a parent of his but who has parental responsibility for him;
(c) any other person caring for the child;
(d) any person named in a child arrangements order as a person with whom the child is to spend time or otherwise have contact;
(e) any person who is allowed to have contact with the child by virtue of an order under section 34; and
(f) the child,

before the hearing of the application.

(12) Rules of court may make provision as to the circumstances in which –

(a) any of the persons mentioned in subsection (11); or
(b) such other person as may be specified in the rules,

may apply to the court for a child assessment order to be varied or discharged.

(13) In this section 'authorised person' means a person who is an authorised person for the purposes of section 31.

Amendments—CFA 2014, s 12, Sch 2.

Defined terms—'authorised person': s 43(13); 'child': s 105(1); 'child arrangements order': s 8(1); 'child assessment order': s 43(2); 'emergency protection order': s 44(4); 'local authority': s 105(1); 'parental responsibility': s 3; 'significant harm': s 31(10).

'authorised person' (s 43(1))—An authorised person is, according to s 43(13), a person who is authorised for the purposes of s 31, i e the National Society for the Prevention of Cruelty to Children and any of its officers. Any person authorised by order of the Secretary of State to bring proceedings under s 31 would also be an 'authorised person' (s 31(9)), but no such order has yet been made.

Persons who are to be given notice of application (s 43(11))—The table set out in FPR 2010, r 12.3(2) sets out the persons who should be made respondents to a s 43 application or should be given notice of it.

'the child's parents' (s 43(11)(a))—The term 'parent' is not defined in the Act (see **Meaning of 'parent'** under s 10).

'any person ... who has parental responsibility' (s 43(11)(b))—Parental responsibility may be acquired in a variety of ways, for example automatically (see s 2), by order or agreement under s 4, or by virtue of being appointed a guardian of the child under s 5(6).

'order under section 34' (s 43(11)(e))—An order under s 34 is an order for contact with a child in care.

44 Orders for emergency protection of children

(1) Where any person ('the applicant') applies to the court for an order to be made under this section with respect to a child, the court may make the order if, but only if, it is satisfied that –

(a) there is reasonable cause to believe that the child is likely to suffer significant harm if –
    (i) he is not removed to accommodation provided by or on behalf of the applicant; or
    (ii) he does not remain in the place in which he is then being accommodated;
(b) in the case of an application made by the local authority –
    (i) enquiries are being made with respect to the child under section 47(1)(b); and
    (ii) those enquiries are being frustrated by access to the child being unreasonably refused to a person authorised to seek access and that the applicant has reasonable cause to believe that access to the child is required as a matter of urgency; or

(c) in the case of an application made by an authorised person –
  (i) the applicant has reasonable cause to suspect that a child is suffering, or is likely to suffer, significant harm;
  (ii) the applicant is making enquiries with respect to the child's welfare; and
  (iii) those enquiries are being frustrated by access to the child being unreasonably refused to a person authorised to seek access and the applicant has reasonable cause to believe that access to the child is required as a matter of urgency.

(2) In this section –

(a) 'authorised person' means a person who is an authorised person for the purposes of section 31; and
(b) 'a person authorised to seek access' means –
  (i) in the case of an application by a local authority, an officer of the local authority or a person authorised by the local authority to act on their behalf in connection with the enquiries; or
  (ii) in the case of an application by an authorised person, that person.

(3) Any person –

(a) seeking access to a child in connection with enquiries of a kind mentioned in subsection (1); and
(b) purporting to be a person authorised to do so,

shall, on being asked to do so, produce some duly authenticated document as evidence that he is such a person.

(4) While an order under this section ('an emergency protection order') is in force it –

(a) operates as a direction to any person who is in a position to do so to comply with any request to produce the child to the applicant;
(b) authorises –
  (i) the removal of the child at any time to accommodation provided by or on behalf of the applicant and his being kept there; or
  (ii) the prevention of the child's removal from any hospital, or other place, in which he was being accommodated immediately before the making of the order; and
(c) gives the applicant parental responsibility for the child.

(5) Where an emergency protection order is in force with respect to a child, the applicant –

(a) shall only exercise the power given by virtue of subsection (4)(b) in order to safeguard the welfare of the child;
(b) shall take, and shall only take, such action in meeting his parental responsibility for the child as is reasonably required to safeguard or promote the welfare of the child (having regard in particular to the duration of the order); and
(c) shall comply with the requirements of any regulations made by the Secretary of State for the purposes of this subsection.

(6) Where the court makes an emergency protection order, it may give such directions (if any) as it considers appropriate with respect to –

(a) the contact which is, or is not, to be allowed between the child and any named person;
(b) the medical or psychiatric examination or other assessment of the child.

(7) Where any direction is given under subsection (6)(b), the child may, if he is of sufficient understanding to make an informed decision, refuse to submit to the examination or other assessment.

(8) A direction under subsection (6)(a) may impose conditions and one under subsection (6)(b) may be to the effect that there is to be –

(a) no such examination or assessment; or
(b) no such examination or assessment unless the court directs otherwise.

(9) A direction under subsection (6) may be –

(a) given when the emergency protection order is made or at any time while it is in force; and

(b) varied at any time on the application of any person falling within any class of person prescribed by rules of court for the purposes of this subsection.

(10) Where an emergency protection order is in force with respect to a child and –

(a) the applicant has exercised the power given by subsection (4)(b)(i) but it appears to him that it is safe for the child to be returned; or

(b) the applicant has exercised the power given by subsection (4)(b)(ii) but it appears to him that it is safe for the child to be allowed to be removed from the place in question,

he shall return the child or (as the case may be) allow him to be removed.

(11) Where he is required by subsection (10) to return the child the applicant shall –

(a) return him to the care of the person from whose care he was removed; or

(b) if that is not reasonably practicable, return him to the care of –

(i) a parent of his;

(ii) any person who is not a parent of his but who has parental responsibility for him; or

(iii) such other person as the applicant (with the agreement of the court) considers appropriate.

(12) Where the applicant has been required by subsection (10) to return the child, or to allow him to be removed, he may again exercise his powers with respect to the child (at any time while the emergency protection order remains in force) if it appears to him that a change in the circumstances of the case makes it necessary for him to do so.

(13) Where an emergency protection order has been made with respect to a child, the applicant shall, subject to any direction given under subsection (6), allow the child reasonable contact with –

(a) his parents;

(b) any person who is not a parent of his but who has parental responsibility for him;

(c) any person with whom he was living immediately before the making of the order;

(d) any person named in a child arrangements order as a person with whom the child is to spend time or otherwise have contact;

(e) any person who is allowed to have contact with the child by virtue of an order under section 34; and

(f) any person acting on behalf of any of those persons.

(14) Wherever it is reasonably practicable to do so, an emergency protection order shall name the child; and where it does not name him it shall describe him as clearly as possible.

(15) A person shall be guilty of an offence if he intentionally obstructs any person exercising the power under subsection (4)(b) to remove, or prevent the removal of, a child.

(16) A person guilty of an offence under subsection (15) shall be liable on summary conviction to a fine not exceeding level 3 on the standard scale.

Amendments—CFA 2014, s 12, Sch 2.

Defined terms—'authorised person': s 44(2)(a); 'child', 'child arrangements order', 'harm', 'local authority': s 105(1); 'parental responsibility': s 3; 'person authorised to seek access': s 44(2)(b).

'any person falling within any class of person prescribed by rules of court' (s 44(9))—See FPR 2010, r 12.27(3).

Procedure for application for an emergency protection order—An emergency protection order is a draconian measure and in *X Council v B (Emergency Protection Orders)* [2005] 1 FLR 341, FD, Munby J gave guidance as to the way in which such applications should be approached. A guardian must be appointed immediately on issue of the proceedings. There are unusual and exceptional cases (of which this was an example) in which a without notice application is appropriate, but adequate evidence must be presented and a proper note of the hearing prepared by the local authority and made available to the parents. In this case, it was not clear that the removal of the children had been justified in view of both of the requirements of CA 1989, s 44(5),(10) and Art 8. Even in emergency situations, it is desirable that, where possible, the local authority works in partnership with parents and that the least interventionist approach is taken (*A v East*

Sussex County Council and Chief Constable of Sussex [2010] 2 FLR 1596, CA). Further detailed guidance on the use of EPOs can be found in *Re X (Emergency Protection Orders)* [2006] 2 FLR 701, FD.

Public Law Outline (PLO)—The PLO in FPR PD12A applies only to proceedings brought under CA 1989, Pt IV, which proceedings do not include an application for an emergency protection order. In the circumstances, the PLO will not apply to emergency protection order proceedings (PD12A). However, pursuant to FPR 2010, r 12.22 the court remains under an obligation to draw up a timetable or revise that timetable with a view to disposing of the application without delay and on a default timetable of 26 weeks. Where the application for an EPO is granted and is then followed immediately by the commencement of Pt IV proceedings, the PLO will apply to the Pt IV proceedings.

Listing a subsequent application for an interim care order—There is no right of appeal against the grant of, or the refusal to grant, an emergency protection order. Accordingly, it is wrong for the court to refuse to list an application for an interim care order following a refusal to grant an emergency protection order. The local authority may wish to apply for an interim care order, in respect of which there is an avenue of appeal. A refusal to list, hear and determine an interim care application will deny the local authority a right of appeal (*Re B-C (A Child)* [2016] EWCA Civ 970).

44A Power to include exclusion requirement in emergency protection order

(1) Where –

(a) on being satisfied as mentioned in section 44(1)(a), (b) or (c), the court makes an emergency protection order with respect to a child, and

(b) the conditions mentioned in subsection (2) are satisfied,

the court may include an exclusion requirement in the emergency protection order.

(2) The conditions are –

(a) that there is reasonable cause to believe that, if a person ('the relevant person') is excluded from a dwelling-house in which the child lives, then –

(i) in the case of an order made on the ground mentioned in section 44(1)(a), the child will not be likely to suffer significant harm, even though the child is not removed as mentioned in section 44(1)(a)(i) or does not remain as mentioned in section 44(1)(a)(ii), or

(ii) in the case of an order made on the ground mentioned in paragraph (b) or (c) of section 44(1), the enquiries referred to in that paragraph will cease to be frustrated, and

(b) that another person living in the dwelling-house (whether a parent of the child or some other person) –

(i) is able and willing to give to the child the care which it would be reasonable to expect a parent to give him, and

(ii) consents to the inclusion of the exclusion requirement.

(3) For the purposes of this section an exclusion requirement is any one or more of the following –

(a) a provision requiring the relevant person to leave a dwelling-house in which he is living with the child,

(b) a provision prohibiting the relevant person from entering a dwelling-house in which the child lives, and

(c) a provision excluding the relevant person from a defined area in which a dwelling-house in which the child lives is situated.

(4) The court may provide that the exclusion requirement is to have effect for a shorter period than the other provisions of the order.

(5) Where the court makes an emergency protection order containing an exclusion requirement, the court may attach a power of arrest to the exclusion requirement.

(6) Where the court attaches a power of arrest to an exclusion requirement of an emergency protection order, it may provide that the power of arrest is to have effect for a shorter period than the exclusion requirement.

(7) Any period specified for the purposes of subsection (4) or (6) may be extended by the court (on one or more occasions) on an application to vary or discharge the emergency protection order.

(8) Where a power of arrest is attached to an exclusion requirement of an emergency protection order by virtue of subsection (5), a constable may arrest without warrant any person whom he has reasonable cause to believe to be in breach of the requirement.

(9) Sections 47(7), (11) and (12) and 48 of, and Schedule 5 to, the Family Law Act 1996 shall have effect in relation to a person arrested under subsection (8) of this section as they have effect in relation to a person arrested under section 47(6) of that Act.

(10) If, while an emergency protection order containing an exclusion requirement is in force, the applicant has removed the child from the dwelling-house from which the relevant person is excluded to other accommodation for a continuous period of more than 24 hours, the order shall cease to have effect in so far as it imposes the exclusion requirement.

Amendments—Inserted by FLA 1996, s 52, Sch 6, para 3.

Defined terms—'child': s 105(1); 'emergency protection order': s 44(4); 'relevant person': s 44A(2)(a).

Procedure—See FPR 2010, r 12.28.

Power of arrest (s 44A(5))—See under s 38A(5).

44B Undertakings relating to emergency protection orders

(1) In any case where the court has power to include an exclusion requirement in an emergency protection order, the court may accept an undertaking from the relevant person.

(2) No power of arrest may be attached to any undertaking given under subsection (1).

(3) An undertaking given to a court under subsection (1) –

(a) shall be enforceable as if it were an order of the court, and

(b) shall cease to have effect if, while it is in force, the applicant has removed the child from the dwelling-house from which the relevant person is excluded to other accommodation for a continuous period of more than 24 hours.

(4) This section has effect without prejudice to the powers of the High Court and family court apart from this section.

(5) In this section 'exclusion requirement' and 'relevant person' have the same meaning as in section 44A.

Amendments—Inserted by FLA 1996, s 52, Sch 6, para 3; CCA 2013, s 17, Sch 11.

Defined terms—'child': s 105(1); 'emergency protection order': s 44(4); 'exclusion requirement': s 44A(3); 'relevant person': s 44A(2)(a).

Procedure—See under FLA 1996, s 46 for assistance as to procedure which will be the same, albeit that the context is different.

Powers of the Family Court apart from s 44B (s 44B(4))—As to the question of the Family Court accepting undertakings in public law proceedings, see **Undertakings and injunctions** under CA 1989, s 31. As to the inherent jurisdiction of the High Court, see CA 1989, s 100.

45 Duration of emergency protection orders and other supplemental provisions

(1) An emergency protection order shall have effect for such period, not exceeding eight days, as may be specified in the order.

(2) Where –

(a) the court making an emergency protection order would, but for this subsection, specify a period of eight days as the period for which the order is to have effect; but

(b) the last of those eight days is a public holiday (that is to say, Christmas Day, Good Friday, a bank holiday or a Sunday),

the court may specify a period which ends at noon on the first later day which is not such a holiday.

(3) Where an emergency protection order is made on an application under section 46(7), the period of eight days mentioned in subsection (1) shall begin with the first day on which the child was taken into police protection under section 46.

(4) Any person who –

(a) has parental responsibility for a child as the result of an emergency protection order; and

(b) is entitled to apply for a care order with respect to the child, may apply to the court for the period during which the emergency protection order is to have effect to be extended.

(5) On an application under subsection (4) the court may extend the period during which the order is to have effect by such period, not exceeding seven days, as it thinks fit, but may do so only if it has reasonable cause to believe that the child concerned is likely to suffer significant harm if the order is not extended.

(6) An emergency protection order may only be extended once.

(7) Regardless of any enactment or rule of law which would otherwise prevent it from doing so, a court hearing an application for, or with respect to, an emergency protection order may take account of –

(a) any statement contained in any report made to the court in the course of, or in connection with, the hearing; or

(b) any evidence given during the hearing,

which is, in the opinion of the court, relevant to the application.

(8) Any of the following may apply to the court for an emergency protection order to be discharged –

(a) the child;

(b) a parent of his;

(c) any person who is not a parent of his but who has parental responsibility for him; or

(d) any person with whom he was living immediately before the making of the order.

(8A) On the application of a person who is not entitled to apply for the order to be discharged, but who is a person to whom an exclusion requirement contained in the order applies, an emergency protection order may be varied or discharged by the court in so far as it imposes the exclusion requirement.

(8B) Where a power of arrest has been attached to an exclusion requirement of an emergency protection order, the court may, on the application of any person entitled to apply for the discharge of the order so far as it imposes the exclusion requirement, vary or discharge the order in so far as it confers a power of arrest (whether or not any application has been made to vary or discharge any other provision of the order).

(9) (*repealed*)

(10) No appeal may be made against –

(a) the making of, or refusal to make, an emergency protection order;

(b) the extension of, or refusal to extend, the period during which such an order is to have effect;

(c) the discharge of, or refusal to discharge, such an order; or

(d) the giving of, or refusal to give, any direction in connection with such an order.

(11) Subsection (8) does not apply –

(a) where the person who would otherwise be entitled to apply for the emergency protection order to be discharged –

  (i) was given notice (in accordance with rules of court) of the hearing at which the order was made; and

  (ii) was present at that hearing; or

(b) to any emergency protection order the effective period of which has been extended under subsection (5).

(12) A court making an emergency protection order may direct that the applicant may, in exercising any powers which he has by virtue of the order, be accompanied by a registered medical practitioner, registered nurse or registered midwife, if he so chooses.

(13) The reference in subsection (12) to a registered midwife is to such a midwife who is also registered in the Specialist Community Public Health Nurses' Part of the register maintained under article 5 of the Nursing and Midwifery Order 2001.

PART II

Amendments—CLSA 1990, s 116, Sch 16, para 19; FLA 1996, s 52, Sch 6, para 4; SI 2002/253; SI 2004/1771; CYPA 2008, s 30.

Defined terms—'care order': s 31(11); 'child': s 105(1); 'emergency protection order': s 44(4); 'parental responsibility': s 3.

Police Protection Guidance—Government circular *The Duties and Powers of the Police under the Children Act 1989* (number 017/2008) explains when and how police protection powers should be used under CA 1989. It can be found at *http://safeguarding.publishpath.com/the-duties-and-powers-of-the-police*.

'Person with parental responsibility' (s 45(4),(8))—Parental responsibility may be acquired in a variety of ways, for example automatically (see s 2), by order or agreement under s 4, or by virtue of being appointed a guardian under s 5(6). Section s 45(8) encompasses anyone who has parental responsibility whereas s 45(4)(a) is restricted to anyone who has parental responsibility as a result of an emergency protection order (i e by virtue of s 44(4)(c)). See also Emergency Protection Order (Transfer of Responsibilities) Regulations 1991, which apply where the original applicant for the emergency protection order was not the local authority in whose area the child is ordinarily resident.

'any person who … is entitled to apply for a care order' (s 45(4)(b))—As to who is entitled to apply for a care order, see s 31(1).

'parent' (s 45(8)(b))—This term is not defined in the Act (see **Meaning of 'parent'** under s 10).

Variation/discharge of exclusion requirement and power of arrest (s 45(8A),(8B))—Section 45(8) lists those who may apply for an emergency protection order to be discharged. Discharge of the order itself would discharge any exclusion requirement or power of arrest attached to it. In addition, by virtue of s 45(8A), discharge/variation of the exclusion requirement element of the order can be sought by the person to whom it applies. That person is also entitled to apply, under s 45(8B), for any attendant power of arrest to be varied or discharged. It is far from clear whether the combined effect of s 45(8) and ss 45(8A),(8B) permits anyone other than the person to whom the exclusion requirement applies to seek a limited order from the court discharging/varying the exclusion requirement or power of arrest, or whether the only application open to these other interested parties (local authority, parent etc) is one for complete discharge (see also **Applicants for variation/discharge of an exclusion requirement** under CA 1989, s 39).

Restrictions on appeal generally (s 45(10))—Where the court adjourned an emergency protection order application on the basis that the mother had not had one clear day's notice of the proceedings and refused to grant an without notice emergency protection order, the court had refused to make an order within the meaning of s 45(10) and there was no appeal from the court's decision (*Essex County Council v F* [1993] 1 FLR 847, FD). If the court has acted unreasonably, the only remedy is judicial review proceedings. *Re P (Emergency Protection Order)* [1996] 1 FLR 482, FD, illustrates the dangers of the lack of any appeal procedure, and various devices were there suggested in order to get round the problem (see at [484G]).

Prohibition on appeal relating to direction (s 45(10)(d))—It is assumed that s 45(10)(d) also prohibits an appeal against the outcome of an application under s 44(9)(b) for the variation of a s 44(6) direction as to contact with or assessment of the child.

'notice (in accordance with rules of court) of the hearing' (s 45(11)(a))—As to the rules concerning notice, see FPR 2010, r 12.3(1).

'was present at the hearing' (s 45(11)(a))—A person who attends through his legal representative but not in person may nevertheless have been present (see, for example, MCA 1980, s 122). However, the position in this context is far from clear. See, for example, *Re AS (Secure Accommodation Order)* [1999] 1 FLR 103, FD (annotated under FPR 2010, r 12.14).

46 Removal and accommodation of children by police in cases of emergency

(1) Where a constable has reasonable cause to believe that a child would otherwise be likely to suffer significant harm, he may –

(a) remove the child to suitable accommodation and keep him there; or

(b) take such steps as are reasonable to ensure that the child's removal from any hospital, or other place, in which he is then being accommodated is prevented.

(2) For the purposes of this Act, a child with respect to whom a constable has exercised his powers under this section is referred to as having been taken into police protection.

(3) As soon as is reasonably practicable after taking a child into police protection, the constable concerned shall –

(a) inform the local authority within whose area the child was found of the steps that have been, and are proposed to be, taken with respect to the child under this section and the reasons for taking them;

(b) give details to the authority within whose area the child is ordinarily resident ('the appropriate authority') of the place at which the child is being accommodated;

(c) inform the child (if he appears capable of understanding) –

(i) of the steps that have been taken with respect to him under this section and of the reasons for taking them; and;

(ii) of the further steps that may be taken with respect to him under this section;

(d) take such steps as are reasonably practicable to discover the wishes and feelings of the child;

(e) secure that the case is inquired into by an officer designated for the purposes of this section by the chief officer of the police area concerned; and

(f) where the child was taken into police protection by being removed to accommodation which is not provided –

(i) by or on behalf of a local authority; or

(ii) as a refuge, in compliance with the requirements of section 51,

secure that he is moved to accommodation which is so provided.

(4) As soon as is reasonably practicable after taking a child into police protection, the constable concerned shall take such steps as are reasonably practicable to inform –

(a) the child's parents;

(b) every person who is not a parent of his but who has parental responsibility for him; and

(c) any other person with whom the child was living immediately before being taken into police protection,

of the steps that he has taken under this section with respect to the child, the reasons for taking them and the further steps that may be taken with respect to him under this section.

(5) On completing any inquiry under subsection (3)(e), the officer conducting it shall release the child from police protection unless he considers that there is still reasonable cause for believing that the child would be likely to suffer significant harm if released.

(6) No child may be kept in police protection for more than 72 hours.

(7) While a child is being kept in police protection, the designated officer may apply on behalf of the appropriate authority for an emergency protection order to be made under section 44 with respect to the child.

(8) An application may be made under subsection (7) whether or not the authority know of it or agree to its being made.

(9) While a child is being kept in police protection –

(a) neither the constable concerned nor the designated officer shall have parental responsibility for him; but

(b) the designated officer shall do what is reasonable in all the circumstances of the case for the purpose of safeguarding or promoting the child's welfare (having regard in particular to the length of the period during which the child will be so protected).

(10) Where a child has been taken into police protection, the designated officer shall allow –

(a) the child's parents;

(b) any person who is not a parent of the child but who has parental responsibility for him;

(c) any person with whom the child was living immediately before he was taken into police protection;

(d) any person named in a child arrangements order as a person with whom the child is to spend time or otherwise have contact;

(e) any person who is allowed to have contact with the child by virtue of an order under section 34; and

(f) any person acting on behalf of any of those persons,

to have such contact (if any) with the child as, in the opinion of the designated officer, is both reasonable and in the child's best interests.

(11) Where a child who has been taken into police protection is in accommodation provided by, or on behalf of, the appropriate authority, subsection (10) shall have effect as if it referred to the authority rather than to the designated officer.

Amendments—CFA 2014, s 12, Sch 2.

Defined terms—'appropriate authority': s 46(3)(b); 'child', 'child arrangements order': s 105(1); 'designated officer': s 46(3)(e); 'emergency protection order': s 44(4); 'police protection': s 46(2).

Removal where an emergency protection order is in force—The s 46 power to remove a child can be exercised even where an emergency protection order (EPO) is in force in respect of the child. However, where a police officer knows that an EPO is in force, he should not exercise the s 46 power unless there are compelling reasons to do so (*Langley v Liverpool City Council* [2006] 1 FLR 342, CA and see *Lumba (Congo) v SSHD; Mighty (Jamaica) v SSHD* [2012] AC 245, SC, per Lord Dyson SCJ, at [80]–[82]).

Court of Appeal guidance as to the use of s 46—Even in an emergency it is desirable, where possible, to work in partnership with a parent. Where parents have access to a solicitor, the solicitor should be apprised of the local authority's concerns and proposals and then be invited, if the solicitor thinks it proper to do so, to advise the parent. Even where emergency powers are obtained under s 44 or exercised under s 46, the least amount of intervention is best. Removal of a child to a known destination is to be preferred to removal to a stranger. However, if there is to be removal to a stranger, the parent should, in the absence of a good reason, be informed of the fact and allowed to pass relevant information to the carer and speedy arrangements should be made for contact. If a court order has not been obtained, or has been obtained without notice, a with-notice hearing should be arranged as soon as possible. A hearing in 2 days should be normal. Where practicable, a court order should be sought in preference to the use of the s 46 powers (*A v East Sussex County Council and Chief Constable of Sussex* [2010] 2 FLR 1596, CA).

Designated officer—It is the responsibility of the chief officer of each police area to designate an officer for the purposes of this section (s 46(3)(e)).

'on behalf of the appropriate authority' (s 46(7))—The appropriate authority is the local authority within whose area the child is ordinarily resident (s 46(3)(b)). For assistance in identifying which local authority this is, see the annotations to s 31. Although only the designated police officer may make an application on behalf of the local authority, any police officer is entitled to apply for an emergency protection order in his own right by virtue of the wide terms of s 44(1).

47 Local authority's duty to investigate

(1) Where a local authority –

(a) are informed that a child who lives, or is found, in their area –

(i) is the subject of an emergency protection order; or

(ii) is in police protection; or

(iii) has contravened a ban imposed by a curfew notice within the meaning of Chapter I of Part I of the Crime and Disorder Act 1998; or

(b) have reasonable cause to suspect that a child who lives, or is found, in their area is suffering, or is likely to suffer, significant harm,

the authority shall make, or cause to be made, such enquiries as they consider necessary to enable them to decide whether they should take any action to safeguard or promote the child's welfare.

In the case of a child falling within paragraph (a)(iii) above, the enquiries shall be commenced as soon as practicable and, in any event, within 48 hours of the authority receiving the information.

(2) Where a local authority have obtained an emergency protection order with respect to a child, they shall make, or cause to be made, such enquiries as they consider necessary to enable them to decide what action they should take to safeguard or promote the child's welfare.

(3) The enquiries shall, in particular, be directed towards establishing –

(a) whether the authority should –

(i) make any application to court under this Act;

(ii) exercise any of their other powers under this Act;

(iii) exercise any of their powers under section 11 of the Crime and Disorder Act 1998 (child safety orders); or

(iv) (where the authority is a local authority in Wales) exercise any of their powers under the Social Services and Well-being (Wales) Act 2014;

with respect to the child;

(b) whether, in the case of a child –

(i) with respect to whom an emergency protection order has been made; and

(ii) who is not in accommodation provided by or on behalf of the authority,

it would be in the child's best interests (while an emergency protection order remains in force) for him to be in such accommodation; and

(c) whether, in the case of a child who has been taken into police protection, it would be in the child's best interests for the authority to ask for an application to be made under section 46(7).

(4) Where enquiries are being made under subsection (1) with respect to a child, the local authority concerned shall (with a view to enabling them to determine what action, if any, to take with respect to him) take such steps as are reasonably practicable –

(a) to obtain access to him; or
(b) to ensure that access to him is obtained, on their behalf, by a person authorised by them for the purpose,

unless they are satisfied that they already have sufficient information with respect to him.

(5) Where, as a result of any such enquiries, it appears to the authority that there are matters connected with the child's education which should be investigated, they shall consult the local authority (as defined in section 579(1) of the Education 1996), if different, specified in subsection (5ZA).

(5ZA) The local authority referred to in subsection (5) is –

(a) the local authority who –
   (i) maintain any school at which the child is a pupil, or
   (ii) make arrangements for the provision of education for the child otherwise than at school pursuant to section 19 of the Education Act 1996, or
(b) in a case where the child is a pupil at a school which is not maintained by a local authority, the local authority in whose area the school is situated.

(5A) For the purposes of making a determination under this section as to the action to be taken with respect to a child, a local authority shall, so far as is reasonably practicable and consistent with the child's welfare –

(a) ascertain the child's wishes and feelings regarding the action to be taken with respect to him; and
(b) give due consideration (having regard to his age and understanding) to such wishes and feelings of the child as they have been able to ascertain.

(6) Where, in the course of enquiries made under this section –

(a) any officer of the local authority concerned; or
(b) any person authorised by the authority to act on their behalf in connection with those enquiries –
   (i) is refused access to the child concerned; or
   (ii) is denied information as to his whereabouts,

the authority shall apply for an emergency protection order, a child assessment order, a care order or a supervision order with respect to the child unless they are satisfied that his welfare can be satisfactorily safeguarded without their doing so.

(7) If, on the conclusion of any enquiries or review made under this section, the authority decide not to apply for an emergency protection order, a care order, a child assessment order or a supervision order they shall –

(a) consider whether it would be appropriate to review the case at a later date; and
(b) if they decide that it would be, determine the date on which that review is to begin.

(8) Where, as a result of complying with this section, a local authority conclude that they should take action to safeguard or promote the child's welfare they shall take that action (so far as it is both within their power and reasonably practicable for them to do so).

(9) Where a local authority are conducting enquiries under this section, it shall be the duty of any person mentioned in subsection (11) to assist them with those enquiries (in particular by providing relevant information and advice) if called upon by the authority to do so.

(10) Subsection (9) does not oblige any person to assist a local authority where doing so would be unreasonable in all the circumstances of the case.

(11) The persons are –

(a) any local authority;
(b) (*repealed*)

(c) any local housing authority;
(ca) the National Health Service Commissioning Board;
(d) any clinical commissioning group, Local Health Board, Special Health Authority, National Health Service trust or NHS foundation trust; and
(e) any person authorised by the Secretary of State for the purposes of this section.

(12) Where a local authority are making enquiries under this section with respect to a child who appears to them to be ordinarily resident within the area of another authority, they shall consult that other authority, who may undertake the necessary enquiries in their place.

Amendments—CLSA 1990, s 116, Sch 16, para 20; Health Authorities Act 1995, s 2, Sch 1, para 118; Crime and Disorder Act 1998, ss 15(4), 119, Sch 8, para 69; SI 2000/90; Health and Social Care (Community Health and Standards) Act 2003, s 34, Sch 4, para 79; CA 2004, s 53; SI 2007/961; SI 2010/1158; Health and Social Care Act 2012, s 55(2), Sch 5, para 53; SI 2016/413.

'reasonable cause to suspect' (s 47(1)(b))—The threshold contained in s 47 is clearly and deliberately lower than that of 'reasonable cause to believe' contained in ss 38, 44 and 46, which all involve a compulsory intervention in the lives of both the child and the family and constitute an interference with family life under ECHR 1950, Art 6, incorporated into domestic law by HRA 1998. By contrast, a s 47 investigation does not generally infringe rights, but merely imposes a duty to conduct investigations necessary for decisions about the child's welfare (*G v Hertfordshire County Council* [2000] Fam Law 883, CA). The adequacy of a risk assessment under CA 1989, s 47 may be the subject of judicial review. However, the ambit of the judicial review process, and any subsequent appeal, is limited to determining whether the assessment can stand. Where the assessment cannot stand and a fresh assessment is thus required, the Administrative court cannot dictate how the local authority should go about that further assessment (*ET, BT, CT v Islington London Borough Council* [2013] EWCA Civ 323).

48 Powers to assist in discovery of children who may be in need of emergency protection

(1) Where it appears to a court making an emergency protection order that adequate information as to the child's whereabouts –

(a) is not available to the applicant for the order; but
(b) is available to another person,

it may include in the order a provision requiring that other person to disclose, if asked to do so by the applicant, any information that he may have as to the child's whereabouts.

(2) No person shall be excused from complying with such a requirement on the ground that complying might incriminate him or his spouse or civil partner of an offence; but a statement of admission made in complying shall not be admissible in evidence against either of them in proceedings for any offence other than perjury.

(3) An emergency protection order may authorise the applicant to enter premises specified by the order and search for the child with respect to whom the order is made.

(4) Where the court is satisfied that there is reasonable cause to believe that there may be another child on those premises with respect to whom an emergency protection order ought to be made, it may make an order authorising the applicant to search for that other child on those premises.

(5) Where –

(a) an order has been made under subsection (4);
(b) the child concerned has been found on the premises; and
(c) the applicant is satisfied that the grounds for making an emergency protection order exist with respect to him,

the order shall have effect as if it were an emergency protection order.

(6) Where an order has been made under subsection (4), the applicant shall notify the court of its effect.

(7) A person shall be guilty of an offence if he intentionally obstructs any person exercising the power of entry and search under subsection (3) or (4).

(8) A person guilty of an offence under subsection (7) shall be liable on summary conviction to a fine not exceeding level 3 on the standard scale.

(9) Where, on an application made by any person for a warrant under this section, it appears to the court –

(a) that a person attempting to exercise powers under an emergency protection order has been prevented from doing so by being refused entry to the premises concerned or access to the child concerned; or

(b) that any such person is likely to be so prevented from exercising any such powers,

it may issue a warrant authorising any constable to assist the person mentioned in paragraph (a) or (b) in the exercise of those powers, using reasonable force if necessary.

(10) Every warrant issued under this section shall be addressed to, and executed by, a constable who shall be accompanied by the person applying for the warrant if –

(a) that person so desires; and

(b) the court by whom the warrant is issued does not direct otherwise.

(11) A court granting an application for a warrant under this section may direct that the constable concerned may, in executing the warrant, be accompanied by a registered medical practitioner, registered nurse or registered midwife if he so chooses.

(11A) The reference in subsection (11) to a registered midwife is to such a midwife who is also registered in the Specialist Community Public Health Nurses' Part of the register maintained under article 5 of the Nursing and Midwifery Order 2001.

(12) An application for a warrant under this section shall be made in the manner and form prescribed by rules of court.

(13) Wherever it is reasonably practicable to do so, an order under subsection (4), an application for a warrant under this section and any such warrant shall name the child; and where it does not name him it shall describe him as clearly as possible.

Amendments—SI 2002/253; CPA 2004, s 261(1), Sch 27, para 130; SI 2004/1771.

Defined terms—'child': s 105(1); 'emergency protection order': s 44(4).

Authority to search for another child (s 48(4))—The order giving authority should be in Form C27.

Issue of warrants—A warrant may be issued under s 48(9) to authorise a constable to assist in the enforcement of an emergency protection order.

'prescribed by rules of court' (s 48(12))—See FPR 2010, Pt 5 and PD5A. The application for a warrant should be made on Form C1 with the prescribed supplement Form C12.

49 Abduction of children in care etc

(1) A person shall be guilty of an offence if, knowingly and without lawful authority or reasonable excuse, he –

(a) takes a child to whom this section applies away from the responsible person;

(b) keeps such a child away from the responsible person; or

(c) induces, assists or incites such a child to run away or stay away from the responsible person.

(2) This section applies in relation to a child who is –

(a) in care;

(b) the subject of an emergency protection order; or

(c) in police protection,

and in this section 'the responsible person' means any person who for the time being has care of him by virtue of the care order, the emergency protection order, or section 46, as the case may be.

(3) A person guilty of an offence under this section shall be liable on summary conviction to imprisonment for a term not exceeding six months, or to a fine not exceeding level 5 on the standard scale, or to both.

50 Recovery of abducted children etc

(1) Where it appears to the court that there is reason to believe that a child to whom this section applies –

(a) has been unlawfully taken away or is being unlawfully kept away from the responsible person;

(b) has run away or is staying away from the responsible person; or

(c) is missing,

the court may make an order under this section ('a recovery order').

(2) This section applies to the same children to whom section 49 applies and in this section 'the responsible person' has the same meaning as in section 49.

(3) A recovery order –

(a) operates as a direction to any person who is in a position to do so to produce the child on request to any authorised person;

(b) authorises the removal of the child by any authorised person;

(c) requires any person who has information as to the child's whereabouts to disclose that information, if asked to do so, to a constable or an officer of the court;

(d) authorises a constable to enter any premises specified in the order and search for the child, using reasonable force if necessary.

(4) The court may make a recovery order on the application of –

(a) any person who has parental responsibility for the child by virtue of a care order or emergency protection order; or

(b) where the child is in police protection, the designated officer.

(5) A recovery order shall name the child and –

(a) any person who has parental responsibility for the child by virtue of a care order or emergency protection order; or

(b) where the child is in police protection, the designated officer.

(6) Premises may only be specified under subsection (3)(d) if it appears to the court that there are reasonable grounds for believing the child to be on them.

(7) In this section –

'an authorised person' means –

(a) any person specified by the court;

(b) any constable;

(c) any person who is authorised –

(i) after the recovery order is made; and

(ii) by a person who has parental responsibility for the child by virtue of a care order or an emergency protection order,

to exercise any power under a recovery order; and

'the designated officer' means the officer designated for the purposes of section 46.

(8) Where a person is authorised as mentioned in subsection (7)(c) –

(a) the authorisation shall identify the recovery order; and

(b) any person claiming to be so authorised shall, if asked to do so, produce some duly authenticated document showing that he is so authorised.

(9) A person shall be guilty of an offence if he intentionally obstructs an authorised person exercising the power under subsection (3)(b) to remove a child.

(10) A person guilty of an offence under this section shall be liable on summary conviction to a fine not exceeding level 3 on the standard scale.

(11) No person shall be excused from complying with any request made under subsection (3)(c) on the ground that complying with it might incriminate him or his spouse or civil partner of an offence; but a statement or admission made in complying shall not be admissible in evidence against either of them in proceedings for an offence other than perjury.

(12)–(14) …

Amendments—CPA 2004, s 261(1), Sch 27, para 131.

Defined terms—'care order': ss 31(11), 105(1); 'child': s 105(1); 'designated officer': s 50(7); 'emergency protection order': s 44(4); 'parental responsibility': s 3; 'police protection': s 46(2); 'recovery order': s 50(1).

'child to whom this section applies' (s 50(1))—See ss 50(2) and 49(2).

'responsible person' (s 50(1))—See ss 50(2) and 49(2). See also *Re R (Recovery Orders)* [1998] 2 FLR 401, FD.

'any person who has parental responsibility' (s 50(4),(5))—In the case of a care order, the local authority designated by the order (see s 33(3)) will have parental responsibility and, in the case of an emergency protection order, the applicant for the emergency protection order (see s 44(4)(c)) will have parental responsibility. Where either the applicant was a designated police officer applying by virtue of s 46(7) on behalf of the local authority or the local authority has taken over the emergency protection order from the original applicant in accordance with the Emergency Protection Order (Transfer of Responsibilities) Regulations 1991, the local authority has parental responsibility.

'designated officer' (s 50(4)(b),(5)(b))—It is the responsibility of the chief officer for each police area to designate an officer for the purpose of the police protection provisions contained in s 46 (s 46(3)(e)).

Procedure—For consideration of the proper procedure where a local authority has replaced a parent or carer as a 'responsible person' shortly before seeking a recovery order, see *Re R (Recovery Orders)* [1998] 2 FLR 401, FD which also deals with the role the child should play in the proceedings (13-year-old boy's wishes and feelings as to his schooling were properly taken into account even though he was not separately represented at the recovery order hearing). The PLO in FPR PD12A applies only to proceedings brought under CA 1989, Pt IV, which proceedings do not include an application for a recovery order. In the circumstances, the PLO will not apply to recovery order proceedings (PD12A). However, pursuant to FPR 2010, r 12.22 the court remains under an obligation to draw up a timetable or revise that timetable with a view to disposing of the application without delay and in any event within 26 weeks beginning with the date on which the application is issued.

51 Refuges for children at risk

(1) Where it is proposed to use a voluntary home or private children's home to provide a refuge for children who appear to be at risk of harm, the Secretary of State may issue a certificate under this section with respect to that home.

(2) Where a local authority or voluntary organisation arrange for a foster parent to provide such a refuge, the Secretary of State may issue a certificate under this section with respect to that foster parent.

(3) In subsection (2) 'foster parent' means a person who is, or who from time to time is, a local authority foster parent or a foster parent with whom children are placed by a voluntary organisation.

(4) The Secretary of State may by regulations –

- (a) make provision as to the manner in which certificates may be issued;
- (b) impose requirements which must be complied with while any certificate is in force; and
- (c) provide for the withdrawal of certificates in prescribed circumstances.

(5) Where a certificate is in force with respect to a home, none of the provisions mentioned in subsection (7) shall apply in relation to any person providing a refuge for any child in that home.

(6) Where a certificate is in force with respect to a foster parent, none of those provisions shall apply in relation to the provision by him of a refuge for any child in accordance with arrangements made by the local authority or voluntary organisation.

(7) The provisions are –

- (a) section 49;
- (b) sections 82 (recovery of certain fugitive children) and 83 (harbouring) of the Children (Scotland) Act 1995, so far as they apply in relation to anything done in England and Wales;
- (c) section 32(3) of the Children and Young Persons Act 1969 (compelling, persuading, inciting or assisting any person to be absent from detention etc), so far as it applies in relation to anything done in England and Wales;
- (d) section 2 of the Child Abduction Act 1984.

Amendments—Children (Scotland) Act 1995, s 105(4), Sch 4, para 48(1),(3); Care Standards Act 2000, s 116, Sch 4, para 14(1),(7).

Modifications—Section 51(7) is modified for certain purposes by SI 2013/1465, art 17, Sch 1, para 2.

PART II

52 Rules and regulations

(1) Without prejudice to section 93 or any other power to make such rules, rules of court may be made with respect to the procedure to be followed in connection with proceedings under this Part.

(2) The rules may in particular make provision –

(a) as to the form in which any application is to be made or direction is to be given;
(b) prescribing the persons who are to be notified of –
  (i) the making, or extension, of an emergency protection order; or
  (ii) the making of an application under section 45(4) or (8) or 46(7); and
(c) as to the content of any such notification and the manner in which, and person by whom, it is to be given.

(3) The Secretary of State may by regulations provide that, where –

(a) an emergency protection order has been made with respect to a child;
(b) the applicant for the order was not the local authority within whose area the child is ordinarily resident; and
(c) that local authority are of the opinion that it would be in the child's best interests for the applicant's responsibilities under the order to be transferred to them,

that authority shall (subject to their having complied with any requirements imposed by the regulations) be treated, for the purposes of this Act, as though they and not the original applicant had applied for, and been granted, the order.

(4) Regulations made under subsection (3) may, in particular, make provision as to –

(a) the considerations to which the local authority shall have regard in forming an opinion as mentioned in subsection (3)(c); and
(b) the time at which responsibility under any emergency protection order is to be treated as having been transferred to a local authority.

PART VI
COMMUNITY HOMES

53 Provision of community homes by local authorities

(1) Every local authority shall make such arrangements as they consider appropriate for securing that homes ('community homes') are available –

(a) for the care and accommodation of children looked after by them; and
(b) for purposes connected with the welfare of children (whether or not looked after by them),

and may do so jointly with one or more other local authorities.

(2) In making such arrangements, a local authority shall have regard to the need for ensuring the availability of accommodation –

(a) of different descriptions; and
(b) which is suitable for different purposes and the requirements of different descriptions of children.

(3) A community home may be a home –

(a) provided, equipped, maintained and (subject to subsection (3A)) managed by a local authority; or
(b) provided by a voluntary organisation but in respect of which a local authority and the organisation –
  (i) propose that, in accordance with an instrument of management, the equipment, maintenance and (subject to subsection (3B)) management of the home shall be the responsibility of the local authority; or
  (ii) so propose that the management, equipment and maintenance of the home shall be the responsibility of the voluntary organisation.

(3A) A local authority may make arrangements for the management by another person of accommodation provided by the local authority for the purpose of restricting the liberty of children.

(3B) Where a local authority are to be responsible for the management of a community home provided by a voluntary organisation, the local authority may, with the consent of the body of managers constituted by the instrument of management for the home, make arrangements for the management by another person of accommodation provided for the purpose of restricting the liberty of children.

(4) Where a local authority are to be responsible for the management of a community home provided by a voluntary organisation, the authority shall designate the home as a controlled community home.

(5) Where a voluntary organisation are to be responsible for the management of a community home provided by the organisation, the local authority shall designate the home as an assisted community home.

(6) Schedule 4 shall have effect for the purpose of supplementing the provisions of this Part.

Amendments—Criminal Justice and Public Order Act 1994, s 22.

54 (*repealed*)

55 Determination of disputes relating to controlled and assisted community homes

(1) Where any dispute relating to a controlled community home arises between the local authority specified in the home's instrument of management and –

- (a) the voluntary organisation by which the home is provided; or
- (b) any other local authority who have placed, or desire or are required to place, in the home a child who is looked after by them,

the dispute may be referred by either party to the Secretary of State for his determination.

(2) Where any dispute relating to an assisted community home arises between the voluntary organisation by which the home is provided and any local authority who have placed, or desire to place, in the home a child who is looked after by them, the dispute may be referred by either party to the Secretary of State for his determination.

(3) Where a dispute is referred to the Secretary of State under this section he may, in order to give effect to his determination of the dispute, give such directions as he thinks fit to the local authority or voluntary organisation concerned.

(4) This section applies even though the matter in dispute may be one which, under or by virtue of Part II of Schedule 4, is reserved for the decision, or is the responsibility, of –

- (a) the local authority specified in the home's instrument of management; or
- (b) (as the case may be) the voluntary organisation by which the home is provided.

(5) Where any trust deed relating to a controlled or assisted community home contains provision whereby a bishop or any other ecclesiastical or denominational authority has power to decide questions relating to religious instruction given in the home, no dispute which is capable of being dealt with in accordance with that provision shall be referred to the Secretary of State under this section.

(6) In this Part 'trust deed', in relation to a voluntary home, means any instrument (other than an instrument of management) regulating –

- (a) the maintenance, management or conduct of the home; or
- (b) the constitution of a body of managers or trustees of the home.

PART II

56 Discontinuance by voluntary organisation of controlled or assisted community home

(1) The voluntary organisation by which a controlled or assisted community home is provided shall not cease to provide the home except after giving to the Secretary of State and the local authority specified in the home's instrument of management not less than two years' notice in writing of their intention to do so.

(2) A notice under subsection (1) shall specify the date from which the voluntary organisation intend to cease to provide the home as a community home.

(3) Where such a notice is given and is not withdrawn before the date specified in it, the home's instrument of management shall cease to have effect on that date and the home shall then cease to be a controlled or assisted community home.

(4) Where a notice is given under subsection (1) and the home's managers give notice in writing to the Secretary of State that they are unable or unwilling to continue as its managers until the date specified in the subsection (1) notice, the Secretary of State may by order –

- (a) revoke the home's instrument of management; and
- (b) require the local authority who were specified in that instrument to conduct the home until –
  - (i) the date specified in the subsection (1) notice; or
  - (ii) such earlier date (if any) as may be specified for the purposes of this paragraph in the order,

as if it were a community home provided by the local authority.

(5) Where the Secretary of State imposes a requirement under subsection (4)(b) –

- (a) nothing in the trust deed for the home shall affect the conduct of the home by the local authority;
- (b) the Secretary of State may by order direct that for the purposes of any provision specified in the direction and made by or under any enactment relating to community homes (other than this section) the home shall, until the date or earlier date specified as mentioned in subsection (4)(b), be treated as a controlled or assisted community home;
- (c) except in so far as the Secretary of State so directs, the home shall until that date be treated for the purposes of any such enactment as a community home provided by the local authority; and
- (d) on the date or earlier date specified as mentioned in subsection (4)(b) the home shall cease to a community home.

57 Closure by local authority of controlled or assisted community home

(1) The local authority specified in the instrument of management for a controlled or assisted community home may give –

- (a) the Secretary of State; and
- (b) the voluntary organisation by which the home is provided,

not less than two years' notice in writing of their intention to withdraw their designation of the home as a controlled or assisted community home.

(2) A notice under subsection (1) shall specify the date ('the specified date') on which the designation is to be withdrawn.

(3) Where –

- (a) a notice is given under subsection (1) in respect of a controlled or assisted community home;
- (b) the home's managers give notice in writing to the Secretary of State that they are unable or unwilling to continue as managers until the specified date; and
- (c) the managers' notice is not withdrawn,

the Secretary of State may by order revoke the home's instrument of management from such date earlier than the specified date as may be specified in the order.

(4) Before making an order under subsection (3), the Secretary of State shall consult the local authority and the voluntary organisation.

(5) Where a notice has been given under subsection (1) and is not withdrawn, the home's instrument of management shall cease to have effect on –

(a) the specified date; or

(b) where an earlier date has been specified under subsection (3), that earlier date,

and the home shall then cease to be a community home.

58 Financial provisions applicable on cessation of controlled or assisted community home or disposal etc of premises

(1) Where –

(a) the instrument of management for a controlled or assisted community home is revoked or otherwise ceases to have effect under section 56(3) or (4)(a) or 57(3) or (5); or

(b) any premises used for the purposes of such a home are (at any time after 13 January 1987) disposed of, or put to use otherwise than for those purposes,

the proprietor shall become liable to pay compensation ('the appropriate compensation') in accordance with this section.

(2) Where the instrument of management in force at the relevant time relates –

(a) to a controlled community home; or

(b) to an assisted community home which, at any time before the instrument came into force, was a controlled community home,

the appropriate compensation is a sum equal to that part of the value of any premises which is attributable to expenditure incurred in relation to the premises, while the home was a controlled community home, by the authority who were then the responsible authority.

(3) Where the instrument of management in force at the relevant time relates –

(a) to an assisted community home; or

(b) to a controlled community home which, at any time before the instrument came into force, was an assisted community home,

the appropriate compensation is a sum equal to that part of the value of the premises which is attributable to the expenditure of money provided by way of grant under section 82, section 65 of the Children and Young Persons Act 1969 or section 82 of the Child Care Act 1980.

(4) Where the home is, at the relevant time, conducted in premises which formerly were used as an approved school or were an approved probation hostel or home, the appropriate compensation is a sum equal to that part of the value of the premises which is attributable to the expenditure –

(a) of sums paid towards the expenses of the managers of an approved school under section 104 of the Children and Young Persons Act 1933;

(b) of sums paid under section 51(3)(c) of the Powers of Criminal Courts Act 1973 or section 20(1)(c) of the Probation Service Act 1993 in relation to expenditure on approved probation hostels or homes; or

(c) of sums paid under section 3, 5 or 9 of the Criminal Justice and Court Services Act 2000 in relation to expenditure on approved premises (within the meaning of Part I of that Act).

(5) The appropriate compensation shall be paid –

(a) in the case of compensation payable under subsection (2), to the authority who were the responsible authority at the relevant time; and

(b) in any other case, to the Secretary of State.

(6) In this section –

'disposal' includes the grant of a tenancy and any other conveyance, assignment, transfer, grant, variation or extinguishment of an interest in or right over land, whether made by instrument or otherwise;

'premises' means any premises or part of premises (including land) used for the purposes of the home and belonging to the proprietor;

'the proprietor' means –

(a) the voluntary organisation by which the home is, at the relevant time, provided; or

(b) if the premises are not, at the relevant time, vested in that organisation, the persons in whom they are vested;

'the relevant time' means the time immediately before the liability to pay arises under subsection (1); and

'the responsible authority' means the local authority specified in the instrument of management in question.

(7) For the purposes of this section an event of a kind mentioned in subsection (1)(b) shall be taken to have occurred –

(a) in the case of a disposal, on the date on which the disposal was completed or, in the case of a disposal which is effected by a series of transactions, the date on which the last of those transactions was completed;

(b) in the case of premises which are put to different use, on the date on which they first begin to be put to their new use.

(8) The amount of any sum payable under this section shall be determined in accordance with such arrangements –

(a) as may be agreed between the voluntary organisation by which the home is, at the relevant time, provided and the responsible authority or (as the case may be) the Secretary of State; or

(b) in default of agreement, as may be determined by the Secretary of State.

(9) With the agreement of the responsible authority or (as the case may be) the Secretary of State, the liability to pay any sum under this section may be discharged, in whole or in part, by the transfer of any premises.

(10) This section has effect regardless of –

(a) anything in any trust deed for a controlled or assisted community home;

(b) the provisions of any enactment or instrument governing the disposition of the property of a voluntary organisation.

Amendments—Probation Service Act 1993, s 32, Sch 3, para 9; CJCSA 2000, ss 74, 75, Sch 7, paras 87, 93, Sch 8; Care Standards Act 2000, s 117, Sch 6.

PART VII
VOLUNTARY HOMES AND VOLUNTARY ORGANISATIONS

59 Provision of accommodation by voluntary organisations

(1) Where a voluntary organisation provide accommodation for a child, they shall do so by –

(a) placing him (subject to subsection (2)) with –

(i) a family;

(ii) a relative of his; or

(iii) any other suitable person,

on such terms as to payment by the organisation and otherwise as the organisation may determine (subject to section 49 of the Children Act 2004);

(aa) maintaining him in a children's home in respect of which a person is registered under Part 2 of the Care Standards Act 2000;

(b)–(e) *(repealed)*

(f) making such other arrangements (subject to subsection (3)) as seem appropriate to them.

(1A) Where under subsection (1)(aa) a voluntary organisation maintains a child in a home provided, equipped and maintained by an appropriate national authority under section 82(5), it shall do so on such terms as the that national authority may from time to time determine.

(2) The appropriate national authority may make regulations as to the placing of children with foster parents by voluntary organisations.

(3) The appropriate national authority may make regulations as to the arrangements which may be made under subsection (1)(f).

(3A) Regulations made in relation to England under subsection (2) or (3) may in particular make provision which (with any necessary modifications) is similar to that which may be made under section 22C by virtue of any of paragraphs 12B, 12E and 12F of Schedule 2.

(3B) Regulations made in relation to Wales under subsection (2) or (3) may in particular make provision which (with any necessary modifications) is similar to that which may be made under sections 81 or 87 of the Social Services and Well-being (Wales) Act 2014, including provision which may be made under section 87 in accordance with the examples given in sections 89, 92 and 93 of that Act.

(4) The appropriate national authority may make regulations requiring any voluntary organisation who are providing accommodation for a child –

(a) to review his case; and
(b) to consider any representations (including any complaint) made to them by any person falling within a prescribed class of person,

in accordance with the provisions of the regulations.

(5A) Regulations made in relation to England under subsection (4) may, in particular –

(a) apply with modifications any provision of section 25A or 25B;
(b) make provision which (with any necessary modifications) is similar to any provision which may be made under section 25A, 25B or 26.

(5B) Regulations made in relation to Wales under subsection (4) may in particular make provision which (with any necessary modifications) is similar to that which may be made under section 99, 100 or 102 of the Social Services and Well-being (Wales) Act 2014.

(6) Regulations under subsections (2) to (4) may provide that any person who, without reasonable excuse, contravenes or fails to comply with a regulation shall be guilty of an offence and liable on summary conviction to a fine not exceeding level 4 on the standard scale.

(7) In this Part 'appropriate national authority' means –

(a) in relation to England, the Secretary of State; and
(b) in relation to Wales, the Welsh Ministers.

Amendments—Care Standards Act 2000, s 116, Sch 4, para 14(1), (8); CA 2004, s 49(4); CYPA 2008, ss 8, 39, Sch 1, para 2, Sch 3, paras 1, 23; SI 2016/413.

60 Voluntary homes

(1), (2) *(repealed)*

(3) In this Act 'voluntary home' means a children's home which is carried on by a voluntary organisation but does not include a community home.

(4) Schedule 5 shall have effect for the purpose of supplementing the provisions of this Part.

Amendments—Registered Homes (Amendment) Act 1991, s 2(6); Care Standards Act 2000, s 116, Sch 4, para 14(1), (9), Sch 6.

61 Duties of voluntary organisations

(1) Where a child is accommodated by or on behalf of a voluntary organisation, it shall be the duty of the organisation –

(a) to safeguard and promote his welfare;
(b) to make such use of the services and facilities available for children cared for by their own parents as appears to the organisation reasonable in his case; and
(c) to advise, assist and befriend him with a view to promoting his welfare when he ceases to be so accommodated.

(2) Before making any decision with respect to any such child the organisation shall, so far as is reasonably practicable, ascertain the wishes and feelings of –

(a) the child;
(b) his parents;
(c) any person who is not a parent of his but who has parental responsibility for him; and
(d) any other person whose wishes and feelings the organisation consider to be relevant,

regarding the matter to be decided.

(3) In making any such decision the organisation shall give due consideration –

(a) having regard to the child's age and understanding, to such wishes and feelings of his as they have been able to ascertain;
(b) to such other wishes and feelings mentioned in subsection (2) as they have been able to ascertain; and
(c) to the child's religious persuasion, racial origin and cultural and linguistic background.

Adoption Agencies Regulations 2005—The Adoption Agencies Regulations 2005, came into force on 30 December 2005. They state that where a registered adoption society is authorised to place a child for adoption, or a child who has been so placed for adoption is less than 6 weeks old, s 61(2)(a) has effect in relation to the child whether or not he is accommodated by or on behalf of the society (reg 45(4)(a)). Furthermore, s 61(2)(b) does not apply, and s 61(2)(c) applies as if there were instead inserted '(c) any prospective adopter with whom the registered adoption society has placed the child for adoption' (reg 45(4)(b) and (c)).

62 Duties of local authorities

(1) Every local authority shall satisfy themselves that any voluntary organisation providing accommodation –

(a) within the authority's area for any child; or
(b) outside that area for any child on behalf of the authority,

are satisfactorily safeguarding and promoting the welfare of the children so provided with accommodation.

(2) Every local authority shall arrange for children who are accommodated within their area by or on behalf of voluntary organisations to be visited, from time to time, in the interests of their welfare.

(3) The appropriate national authority may make regulations –

(a) requiring every child who is accommodated within a local authority's area, by or on behalf of a voluntary organisation, to be visited by an officer of the authority –
  (i) in prescribed circumstances; and
  (ii) on specified occasions or within specified periods; and
(b) imposing requirements which must be met by any local authority, or officer of a local authority, carrying out functions under this section.

(4) Subsection (2) does not apply in relation to community homes.

(5) Where a local authority are not satisfied that the welfare of any child who is accommodated by or on behalf of a voluntary organisation is being satisfactorily safeguarded or promoted they shall –

(a) unless they consider that it would not be in the best interests of the child, take such steps as are reasonably practicable to secure that the care and accommodation of the child is undertaken by –
  (i) a parent of his;
  (ii) any person who is not a parent of his but who has parental responsibility for him; or
  (iii) a relative of his; and
(b) consider the extent to which (if at all) they should exercise any of their functions with respect to the child.

(6) Any person authorised by a local authority may, for the purpose of enabling the authority to discharge their duties under this section –

- (a) enter, at any reasonable time, and inspect any premises in which children are being accommodated as mentioned in subsection (1) or (2);
- (b) inspect any children there;
- (c) require any person to furnish him with such records of a kind required to be kept by regulations made under section 22 of the Care Standards Act 2000 (in whatever form they are held), or allow him to inspect such records, as he may at any time direct.

(7) Any person exercising the power conferred by subsection (6) shall, if asked to do so, produce some duly authenticated document showing his authority to do so.

(8) Any person authorised to exercise the power to inspect records conferred by subsection (6) –

- (a) shall be entitled at any reasonable time to have access to, and inspect and check the operation of, any computer and any associated apparatus or material which is or has been in use in connection with the records in question; and
- (b) may require –
  - (i) the person by whom or on whose behalf the computer is or has been so used; or
  - (ii) any person having charge of, or otherwise concerned with the operation of, the computer, apparatus or material,

  to afford him such assistance as he may reasonably require.

(9) Any person who intentionally obstructs another in the exercise of any power conferred by subsection (6) or (8) shall be guilty of an offence and liable on summary conviction to a fine not exceeding level 3 on the standard scale.

(10) This section does not apply in relation to any voluntary organisation which is an institution within the further education sector, as defined in section 91 of the Further and Higher Education Act 1992, a 16 to 19 Academy or a school.

Amendments—Care Standards Act 2000, ss 105(5), 116, Sch 4, para 14(1), (10); CYPA 2008, s 39, Sch 3, paras 1, 24; Education Act 2011, s 54, Sch 13, para 6.

PART VIII
REGISTERED CHILDREN'S HOMES

63 Private children's homes etc

(1)–(10) *(repealed)*

(11) Schedule 6 shall have effect with respect to private children's homes.

(12) Schedule 7 shall have effect for the purpose of setting out the circumstances in which a person may foster more than three children without being treated, for the purposes of this Act and the Care Standards Act 2000, as carrying on a children's home.

Amendments—Registered Homes (Amendment) Act 1991, s 2(6); Education Act 1996, s 582(1), Sch 37, Pt I, para 86; Care Standards Act 2000, ss 116, 117, Sch 4, para 14(1),(11), Sch 6.

64 Welfare of children in children's homes

(1) Where a child is accommodated in a private children's home, it shall be the duty of the person carrying on the home to –

- (a) safeguard and promote the child's welfare;
- (b) make such use of the services and facilities available for children cared for by their own parents as appears to that person reasonable in the case of the child; and
- (c) advise, assist and befriend him with a view to promoting his welfare when he ceases to be so accommodated.

(2) Before making any decision with respect to any such child the person carrying on the home shall, so far as is reasonably practicable, ascertain the wishes and feelings of –

- (a) the child;
- (b) his parents;

PART II

(c) any other person who is not a parent of his but who has parental responsibility for him; and

(d) any person whose wishes and feelings the person carrying on the home considers to be relevant,

regarding the matter to be decided.

(3) In making any such decision the person concerned shall give due consideration –

(a) having regard to the child's age and understanding, to such wishes and feelings of his as he has been able to ascertain;

(b) to such other wishes and feelings mentioned in subsection (2) as he has been able to ascertain; and

(c) to the child's religious persuasion, racial origin and cultural and linguistic background.

(4) Section 62, except subsection (4), shall apply in relation to any person who is carrying on a private children's home as it applies in relation to any voluntary organisation.

Amendments—Care Standards Act 2000, s 116, Sch 4, para 14(1), (12).

65 Persons disqualified from carrying on, or being employed in, children's homes

(A1) A person ('P') who is disqualified (under section 68) from fostering a child privately must not carry on, or be otherwise concerned in the management of, or have any financial interest in, a children's home in England unless –

(a) P has, within the period of 28 days beginning with the day on which P became aware of P's disqualification, disclosed to the appropriate authority the fact that P is so disqualified, and

(b) P has obtained the appropriate authority's written consent.

(A2) A person ('E') must not employ a person ('P') who is so disqualified in a children's home in England unless –

(a) E has, within the period of 28 days beginning with the day on which E became aware of P's disqualification, disclosed to the appropriate authority the fact that P is so disqualified, and

(b) E has obtained the appropriate authority's written consent.

(1) A person who is disqualified (under section 68) from fostering a child privately shall not carry on, or be otherwise concerned in the management of, or have any financial interest in, a children's home in Wales unless he has –

(a) disclosed to the appropriate authority the fact that he is so disqualified; and

(b) obtained its written consent.

(2) No person shall employ a person who is so disqualified in a children's home in Wales unless he has –

(a) disclosed to the appropriate authority the fact that that person is so disqualified; and

(b) obtained its written consent.

(3) Where the appropriate authority refuses to give its consent under this section, it shall inform the applicant by a written notice which states –

(a) the reason for the refusal;

(b) the applicant's right to appeal under section 65A against the refusal to the First-tier Tribunal; and

(c) the time within which he may do so.

(4) Any person who contravenes subsection (A1), (A2), (1) or (2) shall be guilty of an offence and liable on summary conviction to imprisonment for a term not exceeding six months or to a fine not exceeding level 5 on the standard scale or to both.

(5) Where a person contravenes subsection (A2) or (2) he shall not be guilty of an offence if he proves that he did not know, and had no reasonable grounds for believing, that the person whom he was employing was disqualified under section 68.

(6) In this section and section 65A 'appropriate authority' means –

(a) in relation to England, Her Majesty's Chief Inspector of Education, Children's Services and Skills; and
(b) in relation to Wales, the National Assembly for Wales.

Amendments—Care Standards Act 2000, s 116, Sch 4, para 14(1), (13); Health and Social Care (Community Health and Standards) Act 2003, s 147, Sch 9, para 10; Education and Inspections Act 2006, Sch 14, para 12; SI 2008/2833; CFA 2014, s 105.

65A Appeal against refusal of authority to give consent under section 65

(1) An appeal against a decision of an appropriate authority under section 65 shall lie to the First-tier Tribunal.

(2) On an appeal the Tribunal may confirm the authority's decision or direct it to give the consent in question.

Amendments—Inserted by Care Standards Act 2000, s 116, Sch 4, para 14(1),(14). Amended by SI 2008/2833.

PART IX
PRIVATE ARRANGEMENTS FOR FOSTERING CHILDREN

66 Privately fostered children

(1) In this Part –

(a) 'a privately fostered child' means a child who is under the age of sixteen and who is cared for, and provided with accommodation in their own home by, someone other than –
  (i) a parent of his;
  (ii) a person who is not a parent of his but who has parental responsibility for him; or
  (iii) a relative of his; and
(b) 'to foster a child privately' means to look after the child in circumstances in which he is a privately fostered child as defined by this section.

(2) A child is not a privately fostered child if the person caring for and accommodating him –

(a) has done so for a period of less than 28 days; and
(b) does not intend to do so for any longer period.

(3) Subsection (1) is subject to –

(a) the provisions of section 63; and
(b) the exceptions made by paragraphs 1 to 5 of Schedule 8.

(4) In the case of a child who is disabled, subsection (1)(a) shall have effect as if for 'sixteen' there were substituted 'eighteen'.

(4A) The Secretary of State may by regulations make provision as to the circumstances in which a person who provides accommodation to a child is, or is not, to be treated as providing him with accommodation in the person's own home.

(5) Schedule 8 shall have effect for the purposes of supplementing the provision made by this Part.

Amendments—Care Standards Act 2000, s 116, Sch 4, para 14(1),(15).

67 Welfare of privately fostered children

(1) It shall be the duty of every local authority to satisfy themselves that the welfare of children who are or are proposed to be privately fostered within their area is being or will be satisfactorily safeguarded and promoted and to secure that such advice is given to those concerned with them as appears to the authority to be needed.

(2) The Secretary of State may make regulations –

(a) requiring every child who is privately fostered within a local authority's area to be visited by an officer of the authority –
  (i) in prescribed circumstances; and

(ii) on specified occasions or within specified periods; and

(b) imposing requirements which are to be met by any local authority, or officer of a local authority, in carrying out functions under this section.

(2A) Regulations under subsection (2)(b) may impose requirements as to the action to be taken by a local authority for the purposes of discharging their duty under subsection (1) where they have received notification of a proposal that a child be privately fostered.

(3) Where any person who is authorised by a local authority for the purpose has reasonable cause to believe that –

(a) any privately fostered child is being accommodated in premises within the authority's area; or

(b) it is proposed to accommodate any such child in any such premises,

he may at any reasonable time inspect those premises and any children there.

(4) Any person exercising the power under subsection (3) shall, if so required, produce some duly authenticated document showing his authority to do so.

(5) Where a local authority are not satisfied that the welfare of any child who is or is proposed to be privately fostered within their area is being or will be satisfactorily safeguarded or promoted they shall –

(a) unless they consider that it would not be in the best interests of the child, take such steps as are reasonably practicable to secure that the care and accommodation of the child is undertaken by –

(i) a parent of his;

(ii) any person who is not a parent of his but who has parental responsibility for him; or

(iii) a relative of his; and

(b) consider the extent to which (if at all) they should exercise any of their functions under this Act with respect to the child.

(6) The Secretary of State may make regulations requiring a local authority to monitor the way in which the authority discharge their functions under this Part (and the regulations may in particular require the authority to appoint an officer for that purpose).

Amendments—CA 2004, s 44.

68 Persons disqualified from being private foster parents

(1) Unless he has disclosed the fact to the appropriate local authority and obtained their written consent, a person shall not foster a child privately if he is disqualified from doing so by regulations made by the Secretary of State for the purposes of this section.

(2) The regulations may, in particular, provide for a person to be so disqualified where –

(a) an order of a kind specified in the regulations has been made at any time with respect to him;

(b) an order of a kind so specified has been made at any time with respect to any child who has been in his care;

(c) a requirement of a kind so specified has been imposed at any time with respect to any such child, under or by virtue of any enactment;

(d) he has been convicted of any offence of a kind so specified, or discharged absolutely or conditionally for any such offence;

(e) a prohibition has been imposed on him at any time under section 69 or under any other specified enactment;

(f) his rights and powers with respect to a child have at any time been vested in a specified authority under a specified enactment.

(2A) A conviction in respect of which a probation order was made before 1 October 1992 (which would not otherwise be treated as a conviction) is to be treated as a conviction for the purposes of subsection (2)(d).

(3) Unless he has disclosed the fact to the appropriate local authority and obtained their written consent, a person shall not foster a child privately if –

(a) he lives in the same household as a person who is himself prevented from fostering a child by subsection (1); or
(b) he lives in a household at which any such person is employed.

(4) Where an authority refuse to give their consent under this section, they shall inform the applicant by a written notice which states –

(a) the reason for the refusal;
(b) the applicant's right under paragraph 8 of Schedule 8 to appeal against the refusal; and
(c) the time within which he may do so.

(5) In this section –

'the appropriate authority' means the local authority within whose area it is proposed to foster the child in question; and

'enactment' means any enactment having effect, at any time, in any part of the United Kingdom.

Amendments—CJCSA 2000 s 74, Sch 7, para 94; CJA 2003, ss 304, 332, Sch 32, Pt 1, paras 59, 60, Sch 37, Pt 7.

69 Power to prohibit private fostering

(1) This section applies where a person –

(a) proposes to foster a child privately; or
(b) is fostering a child privately.

(2) Where the local authority for the area within which the child is proposed to be, or is being, fostered are of the opinion that –

(a) he is not a suitable person to foster a child;
(b) the premises in which the child will be, or is being, accommodated are not suitable; or
(c) it would be prejudicial to the welfare of the child for him to be, or continue to be, accommodated by that person in those premises,

the authority may impose a prohibition on him under subsection (3).

(3) A prohibition imposed on any person under this subsection may prohibit him from fostering privately –

(a) any child in any premises within the area of the local authority; or
(b) any child in premises specified in the prohibition;
(c) a child identified in the prohibition, in premises specified in the prohibition.

(4) A local authority who have imposed a prohibition on any person under subsection (3) may, if they think fit, cancel the prohibition –

(a) of their own motion; or
(b) on an application made by that person,

if they are satisfied that the prohibition is no longer justified.

(5) Where a local authority impose a requirement on any person under paragraph 6 of Schedule 8, they may also impose a prohibition on him under subsection (3).

(6) Any prohibition imposed by virtue of subsection (5) shall not have effect unless –

(a) the time specified for compliance with the requirement has expired; and
(b) the requirement has not been complied with.

(7) A prohibition imposed under this section shall be imposed by notice in writing addressed to the person on whom it is imposed and informing him of –

(a) the reason for imposing the prohibition;
(b) his right under paragraph 8 of Schedule 8 to appeal against the prohibition; and
(c) the time within which he may do so.

PART II

70 Offences

(1) A person shall be guilty of an offence if –

- (a) being required, under any provision made by or under this Part, to give any notice or information –
  - (i) he fails without reasonable excuse to give the notice within the time specified in that provision; or
  - (ii) he fails without reasonable excuse to give the information within a reasonable time; or
  - (iii) he makes, or causes or procures another person to make, any statement in the notice or information which he knows to be false or misleading in a material particular;
- (b) he refuses to allow a privately fostered child to be visited by a duly authorised officer of a local authority;
- (c) he intentionally obstructs another in the exercise of the power conferred by section 67(3);
- (d) he contravenes section 68;
- (e) he fails without reasonable excuse to comply with any requirement imposed by a local authority under this Part;
- (f) he accommodates a privately fostered child in any premises in contravention of a prohibition imposed by a local authority under this Part;
- (g) he knowingly causes to be published, or publishes, an advertisement which he knows contravenes paragraph 10 of Schedule 8.

(2) Where a person contravenes section 68(3), he shall not be guilty of an offence under this section if he proves that he did not know, and had no reasonable ground for believing, that any person to whom section 68(1) applied was living or employed in the premises in question.

(3) A person guilty of an offence under subsection (1)(a) shall be liable on summary conviction to a fine not exceeding level 5 on the standard scale.

(4) A person guilty of an offence under subsection (1)(b), (c) or (g) shall be liable on summary conviction to a fine not exceeding level 3 on the standard scale.

(5) A person guilty of an offence under subsection (1)(d) or (f) shall be liable on summary conviction to imprisonment for a term not exceeding six months, or to a fine not exceeding level 5 on the standard scale, or to both.

(6) A person guilty of an offence under subsection (1)(e) shall be liable on summary conviction to a fine not exceeding level 4 on the standard scale.

(7) If any person who is required, under any provision of this Part, to give a notice fails to give the notice within the time specified in that provision, proceedings for the offence may be brought at any time within six months from the date when evidence of the offence came to the knowledge of the local authority.

(8) Subsection (7) is not affected by anything in section 127(1) of the Magistrates' Courts Act 1980 (time limit for proceedings).

****

PART XA
CHILD MINDING AND DAY CARE FOR CHILDREN IN WALES

Introductory

79A Child minders and day care providers

(1) This section and section 79B apply for the purposes of this Part.

(2) 'Act as a child minder' means (subject to the following subsections) look after one or more children under the age of eight on domestic premises for reward; and 'child minding' shall be interpreted accordingly.

(3) A person who –

(a) is the parent, or a relative, of a child;
(b) has parental responsibility for a child;
(c) is a local authority foster parent in relation to a child;
(d) is a foster parent with whom a child has been placed by a voluntary organisation; or
(e) fosters a child privately,

does not act as a child minder when looking after that child.

(4) Where a person –

(a) looks after a child for the parents ('P1'), or
(b) in addition to that work, looks after another child for different parents ('P2'),

and the work consists (in a case within paragraph (a)) of looking after the child wholly or mainly in P1's home or (in a case within paragraph (b)) of looking after the children wholly or mainly in P1's home or P2's home or both, the work is not to be treated as child minding.

(5) In subsection (4), 'parent', in relation to a child, includes –

(a) a person who is not a parent of the child but who has parental responsibility for the child;
(b) a person who is a relative of the child.

(6) 'Day care' means care provided at any time for children under the age of eight on premises other than domestic premises.

(7) This Part does not apply in relation to a person who acts as a child minder, or provides day care on any premises, unless the period, or the total of the periods, in any day which he spends looking after children or (as the case may be) during which the children are looked after on the premises exceeds two hours.

(8) In determining whether a person is required to register under this Part for child minding, any day on which he does not act as a child minder at any time between 2 am and 6 pm is to be disregarded.

Amendments—Inserted by Care Standards Act 2000, s 79(1). Part heading amended by Childcare Act 2006, s 103, Sch 2, para 5, Sch 3, Pt 2.

79B Other definitions, etc

(1) *(repealed)*

(2) In this Act 'the Assembly' means the National Assembly for Wales.

(3) A person is qualified for registration for child minding if –

(a) he, and every other person looking after children on any premises on which he is or is likely to be child minding, is suitable to look after children under the age of eight;
(b) every person living or employed on the premises in question is suitable to be in regular contact with children under the age of eight;
(c) the premises in question are suitable to be used for looking after children under the age of eight, having regard to their condition and the condition and appropriateness of any equipment on the premises and to any other factor connected with the situation, construction or size of the premises; and
(d) he is complying with regulations under section 79C and with any conditions imposed under this Part.

(4) A person is qualified for registration for providing day care on particular premises if –

(a) he has made adequate arrangements to ensure that –
   (i) every person (other than himself and the responsible individual) looking after children on the premises is suitable to look after children under the age of eight; and
   (ii) every person (other than himself and the responsible individual) living or working on the premises is suitable to be in regular contact with children under the age of eight;

(b) the responsible individual –
   (i) is suitable to look after children under the age of eight, or
   (ii) if he is not looking after such children, is suitable to be in regular contact with them;

(c) the premises are suitable to be used for looking after children under the age of eight, having regard to their condition and the condition and appropriateness of any equipment on the premises and to any other factor connected with the situation, construction or size of the premises; and

(d) he is complying with regulations under section 79C and with any conditions imposed under this Part.

(5) For the purposes of subsection (4)(a) a person is not treated as working on the premises in question if –

(a) none of his work is done in the part of the premises in which children are looked after; or

(b) he does not work on the premises at times when children are looked after there.

(5ZA) For the purposes of subsection (4), 'the responsible individual' means –

(a) in a case of one individual working on the premises in the provision of day care, that person;

(b) in a case of two or more individuals so working, the individual so working who is in charge.

(5A) Where, for the purposes of determining a person's qualification for registration under this Part –

(a) the Assembly requests any person ('A') to consent to the disclosure to the authority by another person ('B') of any information relating to A which is held by B and is of a prescribed description, and

(b) A does not give his consent (or withdraws it after having given it),

the Assembly may, if regulations so provide and it thinks it appropriate to do so, regard A as not suitable to look after children under the age of eight, or not suitable to be in regular contact with such children.

(6) 'Domestic premises' means any premises which are wholly or mainly used as a private dwelling and 'premises' includes any area and any vehicle.

(7) 'Regulations' means regulations made by the Assembly.

(8) *(repealed)*

(9) Schedule 9A (which supplements the provisions of this Part) shall have effect.

Amendments—Inserted by Care Standards Act 2000, s 79(1). Amended by Education Act 2002, s 152, Sch 13, para 1; CA 2004, s 48, Sch 4, paras 1, 2, 6; Education and Inspections Act 2006, Sch 14, para 13; Childcare Act 2006, s 103, Sch 2, paras 6, 7, Sch 3, Pt 2; SI 2008/2833.

Regulations

79C Regulations etc governing child minders and day care providers

(1) *(repealed)*

(2) The Assembly may make regulations governing the activities of registered persons who act as child minders, or provide day care, on premises in Wales.

(3) The regulations under this section may deal with the following matters (among others) –

(a) the welfare and development of the children concerned;

(b) suitability to look after, or be in regular contact with, children under the age of eight;

(c) qualifications and training;

(d) the maximum number of children who may be looked after and the number of persons required to assist in looking after them;

(e) the maintenance, safety and suitability of premises and equipment;

(f) the keeping of records;
(g) the provision of information.

(4), (5) *(repealed)*

(6) If the regulations require any person (other than the Assembly) to have regard to or meet factors, standards and other matters prescribed by or referred to in the regulations, they may also provide for any allegation that the person has failed to do so to be taken into account –

(a) by the registration authority in the exercise of its functions under this Part, or
(b) in any proceedings under this Part.

(7) Regulations may provide –

(a) that a registered person who without reasonable excuse contravenes, or otherwise fails to comply with, any requirement of the regulations shall be guilty of an offence; and
(b) that a person guilty of the offence shall be liable on summary conviction to a fine not exceeding level 5 on the standard scale.

Amendments—Inserted by Care Standards Act 2000, s 79(1). Amended by Childcare Act 2006, s 103, Sch 2, paras 6, 8, Sch 3, Pt 2.

Registration

79D Requirement to register

(1) No person shall act as a child minder in Wales unless he is registered under this Part for child minding by the Assembly.

(2) Where it appears to the Assembly that a person has contravened subsection (1), the authority may serve a notice ('an enforcement notice') on him.

(3) An enforcement notice shall have effect for a period of one year beginning with the date on which it is served.

(4) If a person in respect of whom an enforcement notice has effect contravenes subsection (1) without reasonable excuse, he shall be guilty of an offence.

(5) No person shall provide day care on any premises in Wales unless he is registered under this Part for providing day care on those premises by the Assembly.

(6) If any person contravenes subsection (5) without reasonable excuse, he shall be guilty of an offence.

(7) A person guilty of an offence under this section shall be liable on summary conviction to a fine not exceeding level 5 on the standard scale.

Amendments—Inserted by Care Standards Act 2000, s 79(1). Amended by Childcare Act 2006, s 103, Sch 2, paras 6, 9, Sch 3, Pt 2.

79E Applications for registration

(1) A person who wishes to be registered under this Part shall make an application to the Assembly.

(2) The application shall –

(a) give prescribed information about prescribed matters;
(b) give any other information which the Assembly reasonably requires the applicant to give;
(c) be accompanied by the prescribed fee.

(3) Where a person provides, or proposes to provide, day care on different premises, he shall make a separate application in respect of each of them.

(4) Where the Assembly has sent the applicant notice under section 79L(1) of its intention to refuse an application under this section, the application may not be withdrawn without the consent of the authority.

PART II

(5) A person who, in an application under this section, knowingly makes a statement which is false or misleading in a material particular shall be guilty of an offence and liable, on summary conviction, to a fine not exceeding level 5 on the standard scale.

Amendments—Inserted by Care Standards Act 2000, s 79(1). Amended by CA 2004, s 48, Sch 4, paras 1, 3(1); Childcare Act 2006, s 103, Sch 2, para 6.

79F Grant or refusal of registration

(1) If, on an application under section 79E by a person for registration for child minding –

(a) the Assembly is of the opinion that the applicant is, and will continue to be, qualified for registration for child minding (so far as the conditions of section 79B(3) are applicable);

(b) (*repealed*)

the Assembly shall grant the application; otherwise, it shall refuse it.

(2) If, on an application under section 79E by any person for registration for providing day care on any premises –

(a) the Assembly is of the opinion that the applicant is, and will continue to be, qualified for registration for providing day care on those premises (so far as the conditions of section 79B(4) are applicable);

(b) (*repealed*)

the Assembly shall grant the application; otherwise, it shall refuse it.

(3) An application may, as well as being granted subject to any conditions the Assembly thinks necessary or expedient for the purpose of giving effect to regulations under section 79C, be granted subject to any other conditions the authority thinks fit to impose.

(4) The Assembly may as it thinks fit vary or remove any condition to which the registration is subject or impose a new condition.

(5) Any register kept by the Assembly of persons who act as child minders or provide day care shall be open to inspection by any person at all reasonable times.

(6) A registered person who without reasonable excuse contravenes, or otherwise fails to comply with, any condition imposed on his registration shall be guilty of an offence.

(7) A person guilty of an offence under subsection (6) shall be liable on summary conviction to a fine not exceeding level 5 on the standard scale.

Amendments—Inserted by Care Standards Act 2000, s 79(1). Amended by CA 2004, ss 48, 64, Sch 4, paras 1, 3(2), Sch 5; Childcare Act 2006, s 103, Sch 2, para 6.

79G Cancellation of registration

(1) The Assembly may cancel the registration of any person if –

(a) in the case of a person registered for child minding, the Assembly is of the opinion that the person has ceased or will cease to be qualified for registration for child minding;

(b) in the case of a person registered for providing day care on any premises, the Assembly is of the opinion that the person has ceased or will cease to be qualified for registration for providing day care on those premises,

or if a fee which is due from the person has not been paid.

(2) Where a requirement to make any changes or additions to any services, equipment or premises has been imposed on a registered person, his registration shall not be cancelled on the ground of any defect or insufficiency in the services, equipment or premises if –

(a) the time set for complying with the requirements has not expired; and

(b) it is shown that the defect or insufficiency is due to the changes or additions not having been made.

(3) Any cancellation under this section must be in writing.

Amendments—Inserted by Care Standards Act 2000, s 79(1). Amended by CA 2004, ss 48, 64, Sch 4, paras 1, 2(2), 4, Sch 5; Childcare Act 2006, s 103, Sch 2, para 6.

79H Suspension of registration

(1) Regulations may provide for the registration of any person for acting as a child minder or providing day care to be suspended for a prescribed period by the Assembly in prescribed circumstances.

(2) Any regulations made under this section shall include provision conferring on the person concerned a right of appeal to the First-tier Tribunal against suspension.

(3)–(6) …

Amendments—Inserted by Care Standards Act 2000, s 79(1). Amended by Childcare Act 2006, s 103, Sch 2, para 6; SI 2008/2833.

79J Resignation of registration

(1) A person who is registered for acting as a child minder or providing day care may by notice in writing to the Assembly resign his registration.

(2) But a person may not give a notice under subsection (1) –

(a) if the Assembly has sent him a notice under section 79L(1) of its intention to cancel the registration, unless the authority has decided not to take that step; or

(b) if the Assembly has sent him a notice under section 79L(5) of its decision to cancel the registration and the time within which an appeal may be brought has not expired or, if an appeal has been brought, it has not been determined.

Amendments—Inserted by Care Standards Act 2000, s 79(1). Amended by Childcare Act 2006, s 103, Sch 2, para 6.

79K Protection of children in an emergency

(1) If, in the case of any person registered under this Part for acting as a child minder or providing day care –

(a) the Assembly applies to a justice of the peace for an order –

(i) cancelling the registration;

(ii) varying or removing any condition to which the registration is subject; or

(iii) imposing a new condition; and

(b) it appears to the justice that a child who is being, or may be, looked after by that person, or (as the case may be) in accordance with the provision for day care made by that person, is suffering, or is likely to suffer, significant harm,

the justice may make the order.

(2) The cancellation, variation, removal or imposition shall have effect from the time when the order is made.

(3) An application under subsection (1) may be made without notice.

(4) An order under subsection (1) shall be made in writing.

(5) Where an order is made under this section, the Assembly shall serve on the registered person, as soon as is reasonably practicable after the making of the order –

(a) a copy of the order;

(b) a copy of any written statement of the Assembly's reasons for making the application for the order which supported that application; and

(c) notice of any right of appeal conferred by section 79M.

(6) Where an order has been so made, the Assembly shall, as soon as is reasonably practicable after the making of the order, notify the local authority in whose area the person concerned acts or acted as a child minder, or provides or provided day care, of the making of the order.

Amendments—Inserted by Care Standards Act 2000, s 79(1). Amended by Childcare Act 2006, s 103, Sch 2, para 6.

Procedure – applications without notice—Section 79K authorises without notice applications and where the justice of the peace accedes to such an application they must make the order in writing. The with notice procedure in s 79L (below) obviously does not apply to such applications, but it should be used when circumstances permit. It is suggested that it would nevertheless be sensible for the authority, in without notice applications to the court, to follow the procedure in FPR 2010, rr 12.5, 5.1–5.3 and PD5A and to use Form C5 so as to give a written statement of their reasons, indicating at para 2 'About the Respondent' that the application will be made without notice. The order should be on Form C41.

There appears, however, to be no requirement for an order made without notice to be served on the person registered; it only has to be served on the registration authority who, in turn, notify the local authority in whose area the person concerned acts as child minder or as a provider of day care. Section 79M provides a right of appeal to the Tribunal against any order made under s 79K.

Under the repealed s 75 there was provision for notice of the order, and a copy of the authority's reasons supporting the application, to be served on the person registered as soon as possible after the making of the order. However, it is suggested that it would constitute good practice for the authority to continue to serve a copy of the order and a copy of the authority's reasons supporting the application for the order on the person registered, as previously required by s 75(4), since the person registered will need this information in order to decide whether to appeal to the Tribunal or, alternatively, whether it is appropriate to pursue redress through judicial review (see *R v St Albans Magistrates' Court ex parte J* [1993] Fam Law 518, QBD for the principles applied under the pre-existing law).

79L Notice of intention to take steps

(1) Not less than 14 days before –

(a) refusing an application for registration;
(b) cancelling a registration;
(c) removing or varying any condition to which a registration is subject or imposing a new condition; or
(d) refusing to grant an application for the removal or variation of any condition to which a registration is subject,

the Assembly shall send to the applicant, or (as the case may be) registered person, notice in writing of its intention to take the step in question.

(2) Every such notice shall –

(a) give the Assembly's reasons for proposing to take the step; and
(b) inform the person concerned of his rights under this section.

(3) Where the recipient of such a notice informs the Assembly in writing of his desire to object to the step being taken, the Assembly shall afford him an opportunity to do so.

(4) Any objection made under subsection (3) may be made orally or in writing, by the recipient of the notice or a representative.

(5) If the Assembly, after giving the person concerned an opportunity to object to the step being taken, decides nevertheless to take it, it shall send him written notice of its decision.

(6) A step of a kind mentioned in subsection (1)(b) or (c) shall not take effect until the expiry of the time within which an appeal may be brought under section 79M or, where such an appeal is brought, before its determination.

(7) Subsection (6) does not prevent a step from taking effect before the expiry of the time within which an appeal may be brought under section 79M if the person concerned notifies the Assembly in writing that he does not intend to appeal.

Amendments—Inserted by Care Standards Act 2000, s 79(1). Amended by Childcare Act 2006, s 103, Sch 2, para 6.

Procedure – applications with notice—Although s 79K(3) (above) permits an application to be made without notice to the person registered, the with notice procedure in this section should be used when circumstances permit. It would appear that the registration authority alone has the power to grant or refuse the application. Section 79M provides a right of appeal to the Tribunal against any step mentioned in s 79L(1). On an appeal, the Tribunal will be able to (a) confirm the taking of the step or the making of the order or direct that it shall not have, or shall cease to have, effect; and (b) impose, vary or cancel any condition.

79M Appeals

(1) An appeal against –

(a) the taking of any step mentioned in section 79L(1);
(b) an order under section 79K; or

(c) a determination made by the Assembly under this Part (other than one falling within paragraph (a) or (b)) which is of a prescribed description

shall lie to the First-tier Tribunal.

(2) On an appeal, the First-tier Tribunal may –

(a) confirm the taking of the step or the making of the order or determination or direct that it shall not have, or shall cease to have, effect; and
(b) impose, vary or cancel any condition.

Amendments—Inserted by Care Standards Act 2000, s 79(1). Amended by Education Act 2002, ss 148, 155, 215, Sch 13, para 3, Sch 14, para 3, Sch 22, Pt 3; Childcare Act 2006, s 103, Sch 2, para 6; SI 2008/2833.

Procedure—It is likely that the procedure to be followed by the Care Standards Tribunal will be a rehearing rather than a review of the decision which is the subject of appeal (*Tameside Metropolitan Borough Council v Grant* [2002] 1 FLR 318, FD: a decision on the repealed CA 1989, s 71). Where there is a right of appeal to the Care Standards Tribunal, judicial review is not appropriate (*R (M) v London Borough of Bromley* [2002] 2 FLR 802, CA).

79N–79R *(repealed)*

★★★★

Supplementary

79U Rights of entry etc

(1) Any person authorised for the purposes of this subsection by the Assembly may at any reasonable time enter any premises in Wales on which child minding or day care is at any time provided.

(2) Where a person who is authorised for the purposes of this subsection by the Assembly has reasonable cause to believe that a child is being looked after on any premises in contravention of this Part, he may enter those premises at any reasonable time.

(2A) Authorisation under subsection (1) or (2) –

(a) may be given for a particular occasion or period;
(b) may be given subject to conditions.

(3) A person entering premises under this section may (subject to any conditions imposed under subsection (2A)(b)) –

(a) inspect the premises;
(b) inspect, and take copies of –
  (i) any records kept by the person providing the child minding or day care; and
  (ii) any other documents containing information relating to its provision;
(c) seize and remove any document or other material or thing found there which he has reasonable grounds to believe may be evidence of a failure to comply with any condition or requirement imposed by or under this Part;
(d) require any person to afford him such facilities and assistance with respect to matters within the person's control as are necessary to enable him to exercise his powers under this section;
(e) take measurements and photographs or make recordings;
(f) inspect any children being looked after there, and the arrangements made for their welfare;
(g) interview in private the person providing the child minding or day care; and
(h) interview in private any person looking after children, or living or working, there who consents to be interviewed.

(4) Section 58 of the Education Act 2005 (inspection of computer records for purposes of Part I of that Act) shall apply for the purposes of subsection (3) as it applies for the purposes of Part I of that Act.

(5) *(repealed)*

PART II

(6) A person exercising any power conferred by this section shall, if so required, produce some duly authenticated document showing his authority to do so.

(7) It shall be an offence wilfully to obstruct a person exercising any such power.

(8) Any person guilty of an offence under subsection (7) shall be liable on summary conviction to a fine not exceeding level 4 on the standard scale.

(9) In this section –

'documents' and 'records' each include information recorded in any form.

Amendments—Inserted by Care Standards Act 2000, s 79(1). Amended by Education Act 2002, ss 152, 215(2), Sch 13, para 5, Sch 22, Pt 3; Education Act 2005, s 53, Sch 7, para 6; Childcare Act 2006, s 103, Sch 2, paras 6, 14, Sch 3, Pt 2.

79V Function of local authorities

Each local authority in Wales shall, in accordance with regulations, secure the provision –

(a) of information and advice about child minding and day care; and
(b) of training for persons who provide or assist in providing child minding or day care.

Amendments—Inserted by Care Standards Act 2000, s 79(1), amended by Childcare Act 2006, s 103, Sch 2, para 15.

Checks on suitability of persons working with children over the age of seven

79W Requirement for certificate of suitability

(1) This section applies to any person not required to register under this Part who looks after, or provides care for, children in Wales and meets the following conditions.

References in this section to children are to those under the age of 15 or (in the case of disabled children) 17.

(2) The first condition is that the period, or the total of the periods, in any week which he spends looking after children or (as the case may be) during which the children are looked after exceeds five hours.

(3) The second condition is that he would be required to register under this Part (or, as the case may be, this Part if it were subject to prescribed modifications) if the children were under the age of eight.

(4) Regulations may require a person to whom this section applies to hold a certificate issued by the Assembly as to his suitability, and the suitability of each prescribed person, to look after children.

(5) The regulations may make provision about –

(a) applications for certificates;
(b) the matters to be taken into account by the Assembly in determining whether to issue certificates;
(c) the information to be contained in certificates;
(d) the period of their validity.

(6) The regulations may provide that a person to whom this section applies shall be guilty of an offence –

(a) if he does not hold a certificate as required by the regulations; or
(b) if, being a person who holds such a certificate, he fails to produce it when reasonably required to do so by a prescribed person.

(7) The regulations may provide that a person who, for the purpose of obtaining such a certificate, knowingly makes a statement which is false or misleading in a material particular shall be guilty of an offence.

(8) The regulations may provide that a person guilty of an offence under the regulations shall be liable on summary conviction to a fine not exceeding level 5 on the standard scale.

Amendments—Inserted by Care Standards Act 2000, s 79(1). Amended by Childcare Act 2006, s 103, Sch 2, paras 6, 16.

Time limit for proceedings

79X Time limit for proceedings

Proceedings for an offence under this Part or regulations made under it may be brought within a period of six months from the date on which evidence sufficient in the opinion of the prosecutor to warrant the proceedings came to his knowledge; but no such proceedings shall be brought by virtue of this section more than three years after the commission of the offence.

Amendments—Inserted by Care Standards Act 2000, s 79(1).

PART XI
SECRETARY OF STATE'S SUPERVISORY FUNCTIONS AND RESPONSIBILITIES

80 Inspection of children's homes etc by persons authorised by Secretary of State

(1) The Secretary of State may cause to be inspected from time to time any –

- (a) private children's home;
- (b) premises in which a child who is being looked after by a local authority is living;
- (c) premises in which a child who is being accommodated by or on behalf of a local authority in the exercise of education functions or a or voluntary organisation is living;
- (d) premises in which a child who is being accommodated by or on behalf of a Local Health Board, Special Health Authority, National Health Service trust or NHS foundation trust or pursuant to arrangements made by the Secretary of State, the National Health Service Commissioning Board or a clinical commissioning group under the National Health Service Act 2006 is living;
- (e)–(f) *(repealed)*
- (g) premises in which a privately fostered child, or child who is treated as a foster child by virtue of paragraph 9 of Schedule 8, is living or in which it is proposed that he will live;
- (h) premises on which any person is acting as a child minder;
- (i) premises with respect to which a person is registered under section 71(1)(b) or with respect to which a person is registered for providing day care under Part XA;
- (j) care home or independent hospital used to accommodate children;
- (k) premises which are provided by a local authority and in which any service is provided by that authority under Part III;
- (l) school or college providing accommodation for any child.

(2) An inspection under this section shall be conducted by a person authorised to do so by the Secretary of State.

(3) An officer of a local authority shall not be authorised except with the consent of that authority.

(4) The Secretary of State may require any person of a kind mentioned in subsection (5) to furnish him with such information, or allow him to inspect such records (in whatever form they are held), relating to –

- (a) any premises to which subsection (1) or, in relation to Scotland, subsection (1)(h) or (i) applies;
- (b) any child who is living in any such premises;
- (c) the discharge by the Secretary of State of any of his functions under this Act;
- (d) the discharge by any local authority of any of their functions under this Act,

as the Secretary of State may at any time direct.

(5) The persons are any –

- (a) local authority;
- (b) voluntary organisation;
- (c) person carrying on a private children's home;
- (d) proprietor of an independent school or governing body of any other school;

(da) governing body of an institution designated under section 28 of the Further and Higher Education Act 1992;
(db) further education corporation;
(dc) sixth form college corporation;
(dd) proprietor of a 16 to 19 Academy;
(e) person fostering any privately fostered child or providing accommodation for a child on behalf of a local authority, Health Authority, Special Local Health Board, National Health Service trust, NHS foundation trust or voluntary organisation;
(ea) person providing accommodation for a child pursuant to arrangements made by the Secretary of State, the National Health Service Commissioning Board or a clinical commissioning group under the National Health Service Act 2006;
(f) (*repealed*)
(g) person employed in a teaching or administrative capacity at any educational establishment (whether or not maintained by a local authority) at which a child is accommodated on behalf of a local authority;
(h) person who is the occupier of any premises in which any person acts as a child minder (within the meaning of Part X) or provides day care for young children (within the meaning of that Part);
(hh) person who is the occupier of any premises –
  (i) in which any person required to be registered for child minding under Part XA acts as a child minder (within the meaning of that Part); or
  (ii) with respect to which a person is required to be registered under that Part for providing day care;
(i) person carrying on any home of a kind mentioned in subsection (1)(j);
(j) person carrying on a fostering agency.

(6) Any person inspecting any home or other premises under this section may –

(a) inspect the children there; and
(b) make such examination into the state and management of the home or premises and the treatment of the children there as he thinks fit.

(7) Any person authorised by the Secretary of State to exercise the power to inspect records conferred by subsection (4) –

(a) shall be entitled at any reasonable time to have access to, and inspect and check the operation of, any computer and any associated apparatus or material which is or has been in use in connection with the records in question; and
(b) may require –
  (i) the person by whom or on whose behalf the computer is or has been so used; or
  (ii) any person having charge of, or otherwise concerned with the operation of, the computer, apparatus or material,

to afford him such reasonable assistance as he may require.

(8) A person authorised to inspect any premises under this section shall have a right to enter the premises for that purpose, and for any purpose specified in subsection (4), at any reasonable time.

(9) Any person exercising that power shall, if so required, produce some duly authenticated document showing his authority to do so.

(10) Any person who intentionally obstructs another in the exercise of that power shall be guilty of an offence and liable on summary conviction to a fine not exceeding level 3 on the standard scale.

(11) The Secretary of State may by order provide for subsections (1), (4) and (6) not to apply in relation to such homes, or other premises, as may be specified in the order.

(12) Without prejudice to section 104, any such order may make different provision with respect to each of those subsections.

(13) In this section –

'college' means an institution within the further education sector as defined in section 91 of the Further and Higher Education Act 1992 or a 16 to 19 Academy;

'fostering agency' has the same meaning as in the Care Standards Act 2000;

'further education corporation' has the same meaning as in the Further and Higher Education Act 1992;

'sixth form college corporation' has the same meaning as in that Act;

'proprietor' has the same meaning as in the Education Act 1996.

Amendments—National Health Service and Community Care Act 1990, s 66(1), Sch 9, para 36(4); Health Authorities Act 1995, s 2, Sch 1, para 118; Care Standards Act 2000, ss 109, 116, 117, Sch 4, para 14(1),(16), Sch 6; SI 2000/90; Health and Social Care (Community Health and Standards) Act 2003, s 34, Sch 4, paras 75, 80; ACA 2002, Sch 3, para 65; SI 2007/961; SI 2010/1080, SI 2010/1185; Education Act 2011, s 54, Sch 13, para 6; Health and Social Care Act 2012, s 55(2), Sch 5, para 54.

81 *(repealed)*

82 Financial support by Secretary of State

(1) The Secretary of State may (with the consent of the Treasury) defray or contribute towards –

- (a) any fees or expenses incurred by any person undergoing approved child care training;
- (b) any fees charged, or expenses incurred, by any person providing approved child care training or preparing material for use in connection with such training; or
- (c) the cost of maintaining any person undergoing such training.

(2) The Secretary of State may make grants to local authorities in respect of expenditure incurred by them in providing secure accommodation in community homes other than assisted community homes.

(3) Where –

- (a) a grant has been made under subsection (2) with respect to any secure accommodation; but
- (b) the grant is not used for the purpose for which it was made or the accommodation is not used as, or ceases to be used as, secure accommodation,

the Secretary of State may (with the consent of the Treasury) require the authority concerned to repay the grant, in whole or in part.

(4) The Secretary of State may make grants to voluntary organisations towards –

- (a) expenditure incurred by them in connection with the establishment, maintenance or improvement of voluntary homes which, at the time when the expenditure was incurred –
  - (i) were assisted community homes; or
  - (ii) were designated as such; or
- (b) expenses incurred in respect of the borrowing of money to defray any such expenditure.

(5) The Secretary of State may arrange for the provision, equipment and maintenance of homes for the accommodation of children who are in need of particular facilities and services which –

- (a) are or will be provided in those homes; and
- (b) in the opinion of the Secretary of State, are unlikely to be readily available in community homes.

(6) In this Part –

'child care training' means training undergone by any person with a view to, or in the course of –

- (a) his employment for the purposes of any of the functions mentioned in section 83(9) or in connection with the adoption of children or with the accommodation of children in a care home or independent hospital; or
- (b) his employment by a voluntary organisation for similar purposes;

'approved child care training' means child care training which is approved by the Secretary of State; and 'secure accommodation' means accommodation provided for the purpose of restricting the liberty of children.

(7) Any grant made under this section shall be of such amount, and shall be subject to such conditions, as the Secretary of State may (with the consent of the Treasury) determine.

Amendments—Care Standards Act 2000, s 116, Sch 4, para 14(1),(18).

83 Research and returns of information

(1) The Secretary of State may conduct, or assist other persons in conducting, research into any matter connected with –

- (a) his functions, or the functions of local authorities, under the enactments mentioned in subsection (9);
- (aa) the functions of Local Safeguarding Children Boards;
- (b) the adoption of children; or
- (c) the accommodation of children in a care home or independent hospital.

(2) Any local authority may conduct, or assist other persons in conducting, research into any matter connected with –

- (a) their functions under the enactments mentioned in subsection (9);
- (aa) the functions of Local Safeguarding Children Boards;
- (b) the adoption of children; or
- (c) the accommodation of children in a care home or independent hospital.

(3) Every local authority shall, at such times and in such form as the Secretary of State may direct, transmit to him such particulars as he may require with respect to –

- (a) the performance by the local authority of all or any of their functions –
  - (i) under the enactments mentioned in subsection (9); or
  - (ii) in connection with the accommodation of children in a care home or independent hospital; and
- (b) the children in relation to whom the authority have exercised those functions; and
- (c) the performance by the Local Safeguarding Children Board established by them under the Children Act 2004 of all or any of its functions.

(4) Every voluntary organisation shall, at such times and in such form as the Secretary of State may direct, transmit to him such particulars as he may require with respect to children accommodated by them or on their behalf.

(4A) Particulars required to be transmitted under subsection (3) or (4) may include particulars relating to and identifying individual children.

(5) The Secretary of State may direct an officer of the family court to transmit –

- (a) to such person as may be specified in the direction; and
- (b) at such times and in such form as he may direct,

such particulars as he may require with respect to proceedings of the court which relate to children.

(6) The Secretary of State shall in each year lay before Parliament a consolidated and classified abstract of the information transmitted to him under subsections (3) to (5).

(7) The Secretary of State may institute research designed to provide information on which requests for information under this section may be based.

(8) The Secretary of State shall keep under review the adequacy of the provision of child care training and for that purpose shall receive and consider any information from or representations made by –

- (a) the Central Council for Education and Training in Social Work;
- (b) such representatives of local authorities as appear to him to be appropriate; or
- (c) such other persons or organisations as appear to him to be appropriate,

concerning the provision of such training.

(9) The enactments are –

(a) this Act;
(b) the Children and Young Persons Acts 1933 to 1969;
(c) section 116 of the Mental Health Act 1983 (so far as it relates to children looked after by local authorities);
(ca) Part 1 of the Adoption and Children Act 2002;
(cb) the Children Act 2004;
(cc) the Children and Young Persons Act 2008.
(d) *(repealed)*

Amendments—AJA 1999, s 90, Sch 13, para 160; Care Standards Act 2000, s 116, Sch 4, para 14(1),(19); Courts Act 2003, s 109(1), Sch 8, para 336; CA 2004, s 54; SI 2005/2078; CYPA 2008, s 33; CCA 2013, s 17, Sch 11.

84 Local authority failure to comply with statutory duty: default power of Secretary of State

(1) If the Secretary of State is satisfied that any local authority has failed, without reasonable excuse, to comply with any of the duties imposed on them by or under this Act he may make an order declaring that authority to be in default with respect to that duty.

(2) An order under subsection (1) shall give the Secretary of State's reasons for making it.

(3) An order under subsection (1) may contain such directions for the purpose of ensuring that the duty is complied with, within such period as may be specified in the order, as appear to the Secretary of State to be necessary.

(4) Any such direction shall, on the application of the Secretary of State, be enforceable by mandamus.

Defined terms—'local authority': s 105(1).

Scope—This section does not confer either an express or an implied right on any individual to appeal from a decision by a local authority by which he is aggrieved and, although the existence of a default power such as s 84 can be taken into consideration by the court as an avenue of redress alternative to judicial review, it can be wrong, in view of the particular features of s 84, to treat it as a more suitable remedy for an individual than judicial review (*R v London Borough of Brent ex parte S* [1994] 1 FLR 203, CA).

There exists under s 26(3) a representation procedure which can be used by a person aggrieved by the way in which a local authority has exercised its functions, and this may have relevance as to whether relief will be granted in judicial review proceedings (*R v East Sussex CC ex parte W* [1998] 2 FLR 1082, QBD).

In *R v Hampshire CC ex parte H* [1999] 2 FLR 359, CA, judicial review was held to be appropriate in relation to a decision of a local authority case conference.

Declaration absolving local authority from duty to consult and provide information—In exceptional circumstances the court has power to make a declaration that the local authority be absolved from the duty to provide information to a parent and from the duty to consult him or her in any way about the child (*Re C (Care: Consultation with Parents not in Child's Best Interests)* [2006] 2 FLR 787, FD).

PART XII
MISCELLANEOUS AND GENERAL

Notification of children accommodated in certain establishments

85 Children accommodated by health authorities and local education authorities

(1) Where a child is provided with accommodation in England by any Special Health Authority, National Health Service trust or NHS foundation trust or by a local authority in England in the exercise of education functions ('the accommodating authority') –

(a) for a consecutive period of at least three months; or
(b) with the intention, on the part of that authority, of accommodating him for such a period,

the accommodating authority shall notify the appropriate officer of the responsible authority.

(2) Where subsection (1) applies with respect to a child, the accommodating authority shall also notify the appropriate officer of the responsible authority when they cease to accommodate the child.

(2ZA) Where a child is provided with accommodation –

(a) by a body which is not mentioned in subsection (1), and
(b) pursuant to arrangements made by the Secretary of State, the National Health Service Commissioning Board or a clinical commissioning group under the National Health Service Act 2006,

subsections (1) and (2) apply in relation to the Secretary of State, the Board or (as the case may be) the clinical commissioning group as if it were the accommodating authority.

(2A) In a case where the child is provided with accommodation in England by a local authority in England in the exercise of education functions, subsections (1) and (2) apply only if the local authority providing the accommodation is different from the responsible authority.

(3) In this section 'the responsible authority' means –

(a) the local authority appearing to the accommodating authority to be the authority within whose area the child was ordinarily resident immediately before being accommodated; or
(b) where it appears to the accommodating authority that a child was not ordinarily resident within the area of any local authority, the local authority within whose area the accommodation is situated.

(3A) In this section and sections 86 and 86A 'the appropriate officer' means –

(a) in relation to a local authority in England, their director of children's services; and.
(b) in relation to a local authority in Wales, their director of social services.

(4) Where the appropriate officer of a local authority in England has been notified under this section, or under section 120 of the Social Services and Well-being (Wales) Act 2014 (assessment of children accommodated by health authorities and education authorities), the local authority shall –

(a) take such steps as are reasonably practicable to enable them to determine whether the child's welfare is adequately safeguarded and promoted while he is accommodated by the accommodating authority; and
(b) consider the extent to which (if at all) they should exercise any of their functions under this Act with respect to the child.

(5) For the purposes of subsection 4)(b), if the child is not in the area of the local authority, they must treat him as if he were in that area.

Amendments—National Health Service and Community Care Act 1990, s 66(1), Sch 9, para 36; Health Authorities Act 1995, s 2, Sch 1, para 118; SI 2000/90; Health and Social Care (Community Health and Standards) Act 2003, s 34, Sch 4, paras 75, 81; SI 2007/961; SI 2010/1185; CYPA 2008, s 17; Health and Social Care Act 2012, s 55(2), Sch 5, para 55; SI 2016/413.

86 Children accommodated in care homes or independent hospitals

(1) Where a child is provided with accommodation in any care home or independent hospital –

(a) for a consecutive period of at least three months; or
(b) with the intention, on the part of the person taking the decision to accommodate him, of accommodating him for such period,

the person carrying on the establishment in question shall notify the appropriate officer of the local authority in England within whose area the establishment is carried on.

(2) Where subsection (1) applies with respect to a child, the person carrying on the establishment shall also notify the appropriate officer of that authority when he ceases to accommodate the child in the establishment.

(3) Where the appropriate officer of a local authority has been notified under this section, the local authority shall –

(a) take such steps as are reasonably practicable to enable them to determine whether the child's welfare is adequately safeguarded and promoted while he is accommodated in the establishment in question; and

(b) consider the extent to which (if at all) they should exercise any of their functions under this Act with respect to the child.

(4) If the person carrying on any care home or independent hospital fails, without reasonable excuse, to comply with this section he shall be guilty of an offence.

(5) A person authorised by a local authority in England may enter any care home or independent hospital within the authority's area for the purpose of establishing whether the requirements of this section have been complied with.

(6) Any person who intentionally obstructs another in the exercise of the power of entry shall be guilty of an offence.

(7) Any person exercising the power of entry shall, if so required, produce some duly authenticated document showing his authority to do so.

(8) Any person committing an offence under this section shall be liable on summary conviction to a fine not exceeding level 3 on the standard scale.

Amendments—Care Standards Act 2000, s 116, Sch 4, para 14(1),(20); CYPA 2008, s 17; SI 2016/413.

86A Visitors for children notified to local authority

(1) This section applies if the appropriate officer of a local authority in England –

(a) has been notified with respect to a child under section 85(1) or 86(1), or under section 120(2)(a) of the Social Services and Well-being (Wales) Act 2014; and

(b) has not been notified with respect to that child under section 85(2), 86(2), or under section 120(2)(b) of the Social Services and Wellbeing (Wales) Act 2014, as the case may be.

(2) The local authority must, in accordance with regulations made under this section, make arrangements for the child to be visited by a representative of the authority ('a representative').

(3) It is the function of a representative to provide advice and assistance to the local authority on the performance of their duties under section 85(4) or, as the case may be, 86(3).

(4) Regulations under this section may make provision about –

(a) the frequency of visits under visiting arrangements;
(b) circumstances in which visiting arrangements must require a child to be visited; and
(c) additional functions of a representative.

(5) Regulations under this section are to be made by the Secretary of State.

(6) In choosing a representative a local authority must satisfy themselves that the person chosen has the necessary skills and experience to perform the functions of a representative.

(7) In this section 'visiting arrangements' means arrangements made under subsection (2).

Amendments—Inserted by CYPA 2008, s 18. Amended by SI 2016/413.

87 Welfare of children in boarding schools and colleges

(1) Where a school or college provides accommodation for any child, it shall be the duty of the relevant person to safeguard and promote the child's welfare.

(1A) For the purposes of this section and sections 87A to 87D, a school or college provides accommodation for a child if –

(a) it provides accommodation for the child on its own premises, or
(b) it arranges for accommodation for the child to be provided elsewhere (other than in connection with a residential trip away from the school).

(2) Subsection (1) does not apply in relation to a school or college which is a children's home or care home.

(3) Where accommodation is provided for a child by any school or college the appropriate authority shall take such steps as are reasonably practicable to enable them to determine whether the child's welfare is adequately safeguarded and promoted while accommodation for the child is provided by the school or college.

(3A) Where accommodation is provided for a child by a school or college in England, the Secretary of State may at any time (including a time when the duty under subsection (3) is suspended by virtue of section 87A) direct the Chief Inspector for England to take the steps referred to in subsection (3).

(3B) Where accommodation is provided for a child by a school or college in Wales, the Welsh Ministers may, at any time when the duty under subsection (3) is suspended by virtue of section 87A, take the steps referred to in subsection (3).

(4) Where the Chief Inspector for England is of the opinion that there has been a failure to comply with subsection (1) in relation to a child provided with accommodation by a school or college in England, he shall –

- (a) in the case of a school other than an independent school or a special school, notify the local authority for the area in which the school is situated;
- (b) in the case of a special school which is maintained by a local authority, notify that authority;
- (c) in any other case, notify the Secretary of State.

(4A) Where the National Assembly for Wales are of the opinion that there has been a failure to comply with subsection (1) in relation to a child provided with accommodation by a school or college in Wales, they shall –

- (a) in the case of a school other than an independent school or a special school, notify the local authority for the area in which the school is situated;
- (b) in the case of a special school which is maintained by a local authority, notify that authority;

(5) Where accommodation is, or is to be, provided for a child by any school or college, a person authorised by the appropriate authority may, for the purpose of enabling that authority to discharge any of its functions under this section, enter at any time premises which are, or are to be, premises of the school or college.

(6) Any person exercising the power conferred by subsection (5) may carry out such inspection of premises, children and records as is prescribed by regulations made by the Secretary of State for the purposes of this section.

(7) Any person exercising that power shall, if asked to do so, produce some duly authenticated document showing his authority to do so.

(8) Any person authorised by the regulations to inspect records –

- (a) shall be entitled at any reasonable time to have access to, and inspect and check the operation of, any computer and any associated apparatus or material which is or has been in use in connection with the records in question; and
- (b) may require –
  - (i) the person by whom or on whose behalf the computer is or has been so used; or
  - (ii) any person having charge of, or otherwise concerned with the operation of, the computer, apparatus or material,

  to afford him such assistance as he may reasonably require.

(9) Any person who intentionally obstructs another in the exercise of any power conferred by this section or the regulations shall be guilty of an offence and liable on summary conviction to a fine not exceeding level 3 on the standard scale.

(9A)–(9C) …

(10) In this section and sections 87A to 87D –

'the 1992 Act' means the Further and Higher Education Act 1992;

'appropriate authority' means –

- (a) in relation to England, the Chief Inspector for England;
- (b) in relation to Wales, the National Assembly for Wales;

'the Chief Inspector for England' means Her Majesty's Chief Inspector of Education, Children's Services and Skills;

'college' means an institution within the further education sector as defined in section 91 of the 1992 Act or a 16 to 19 Academy;
'further education corporation' has the same meaning as in the 1992 Act;
'local authority' and 'proprietor' have the same meanings as in the Education Act 1996;
'sixth form college corporation' has the same meaning as in the 1992 Act.

(11) In this section and sections 87A and 87D 'relevant person' means –

(a) in relation to an independent school, the proprietor of the school;
(b) in relation to any other school, or an institution designated under section 28 of the 1992 Act, the governing body of the school or institution;
(c) in relation to an institution conducted by a further education corporation or sixth form college corporation, the corporation;
(d) in relation to a 16 to 19 Academy, the proprietor of the Academy.

(12) Where a person other than the proprietor of an independent school is responsible for conducting the school, references in this section to the relevant person include references to the person so responsible.

Amendments—Registered Homes (Amendment) Act 1991, s 2(6); Education Act 1996, s 582(1), Sch 37, Pt I, para 87; Care Standards Act 2000, s 105; Health and Social Care (Community Health and Standards) Act 2003, s 147, Sch 9, para 10; Education and Inspections Act 2006, s 184, Sch 14, para 16, Sch 18, Pt 5; SI 2010/1080; SI 2010/1185; Education Act 2011, ss 43, 54, Sch 13, para 6.

87A Suspension of duty under section 87(3)

(1) The Secretary of State may appoint a person to be an inspector for the purposes of this section if –

(a) that person already acts as an inspector for other purposes in relation to schools or colleges to which section 87(1) applies, and
(b) the Secretary of State is satisfied that the person is an appropriate person to determine whether the welfare of children provided with accommodation by such schools or colleges is adequately safeguarded and promoted while accommodation for the children is provided by them.

(2) Where –

(a) the relevant person enters into an agreement in writing with a person appointed under subsection (1),
(b) the agreement provides for the person so appointed to have in relation to the school or college the function of determining whether section 87(1) is being complied with, and
(c) the appropriate authority receive from the person mentioned in paragraph (b) ('the inspector') notice in writing that the agreement has come into effect,

the authority's duty under section 87(3) in relation to the school or college shall be suspended.

(3) Where the appropriate authority's duty under section 87(3) in relation to any school or college is suspended under this section, it shall cease to be so suspended if the appropriate authority receive –

(a) a notice under subsection (4) relating to the inspector, or
(b) a notice under subsection (5) relating to the relevant agreement.

(4) The Secretary of State shall terminate a person's appointment under subsection (1) if –

(a) that person so requests, or
(b) the Secretary of State ceases, in relation to that person, to be satisfied that he is such a person as is mentioned in paragraph (b) of that subsection,

and shall give notice of the termination of that person's appointment to the appropriate authority.

(4A) The Secretary of State may by regulations specify matters that must be taken into account in deciding whether to appoint a person to be an inspector for the purposes of this section in relation to schools or colleges in England, or to terminate the appointment of such a person under subsection (4)(b).

PART II

(5) Where –

(a) the appropriate authority's duty under section 87(3) in relation to any school or college is suspended under this section, and

(b) the relevant agreement ceases to have effect,

the inspector shall give to the appropriate authority notice in writing of the fact that it has ceased to have effect.

(6) In this section references to the relevant agreement, in relation to the suspension of the appropriate authority's duty under section 87(3) as regards any school or college, are to the agreement by virtue of which the appropriate authority's duty under that provision as regards that school or college is suspended.

Amendments—Substituted by Care Standards Act 2000, s 106(1). Amended by Education Act 2011, s 43.

87B Duties of inspectors under section 87A

(1) The Secretary of State may impose on a person appointed under section 87A(1) ('an authorised inspector') such requirements relating to, or in connection with, the carrying out under substitution agreements of the function mentioned in section 87A(2)(b) as the Secretary of State thinks fit.

(2) Where, in the course of carrying out under a substitution agreement the function mentioned in section 87A(2)(b), it appears to an authorised inspector that there has been a failure to comply with section 87(1) in the case of a child provided with accommodation by the school or college to which the agreement relates, the inspector shall give notice of that fact –

(a) in the case of a school other than an independent school or a special school, to the local authority for the area in which the school is situated;

(b) in the case of a special school which is maintained by a local authority, to that authority;

(c) in any other case, to the Secretary of State.

(3) Where, in the course of carrying out under a substitution agreement the function mentioned in section 87A(2)(b), it appears to an authorised inspector that a child provided with accommodation by the school or college to which the agreement relates is suffering, or is likely to suffer, significant harm, the inspector shall –

(a) give notice of the fact to the local authority in whose area the school or college is situated, and

(b) where the inspector is required to make inspection reports to the Secretary of State, supply that local authority with a copy of the latest inspection report to have been made by the inspector to the Secretary of State in relation to the school or college.

(4) In this section 'substitution agreement' means an agreement by virtue of which the duty of the appropriate authority under section 87(3) in relation to a school or college is suspended.

Amendments—Inserted by Deregulation and Contracting Out Act 1994, s 38. Amended by Education Act 1996, s 582(1), Sch 37, Pt I, para 89; Care Standards Act 2000, s 106(2); SI 2010/1185.

87BA Quality assurance of inspectors under section 87A.

(1) The Chief Inspector for England must, at intervals of no more than a year, prepare and send to the Secretary of State a report about inspectors who are appointed under section 87A in relation to schools or colleges in England.

(2) In preparing a report under this section the Chief Inspector for England must have regard to such matters as the Secretary of State may direct.

(3) The Secretary of State may in particular give directions about –

(a) matters to be taken into account in preparing a report, and

(b) the form and contents of a report.

Amendments—Inserted by Education Act 2011, s 43.

87C Boarding schools: national minimum standards

(1) The Secretary of State may prepare and publish statements of national minimum standards for safeguarding and promoting the welfare of children for whom accommodation is provided by a school or college.

(2) The Secretary of State shall keep the standards set out in the statements under review and may publish amended statements whenever he considers it appropriate to do so.

(3) Before issuing a statement, or an amended statement which in the opinion of the Secretary of State effects a substantial change in the standards, the Secretary of State shall consult any persons he considers appropriate.

(4) The standards shall be taken into account –

- (a) in the making by the appropriate authority of any determination under section 87(4) or (4A);
- (b) in the making by a person appointed under section 87A(1) of any determination under section 87B(2); and
- (c) in any proceedings under any other enactment in which it is alleged that the person has failed to comply with section 87(1).

Amendments—Inserted by Care Standards Act 2000, s 107. Amended by Education Act 2011, s 43.

87D Annual fee for boarding school inspections

(1) Regulations under subsection (2) may be made in relation to any school or college in respect of which the appropriate authority is required to take steps under section 87(3).

(2) The Secretary of State may by regulations require the relevant person to pay the appropriate authority an annual fee of such amount, and within such time, as the regulations may specify.

(3) A fee payable by virtue of this section may, without prejudice to any other method of recovery, be recovered summarily as a civil debt.

Amendments—Inserted by Care Standards Act 2000, s 108.

****

Criminal care and supervision orders

90 Care and supervision orders in criminal proceedings

(1) The power of a court to make an order under subsection (2) of section 1 of the Children and Young Persons Act 1969 (care proceedings in youth courts) where it is of the opinion that the condition mentioned in paragraph (f) of that subsection ('the offence condition') is satisfied is hereby abolished.

(2) The powers of the court to make care orders –

- (a) under section 7(7)(a) of the Children and Young Persons Act 1969 (alteration in treatment of young offenders etc); and
- (b) under section 15(1) of that Act, on discharging a supervision order made under section 7(7)(b) of that Act,

are hereby abolished.

(3) The powers given by that Act to include requirements in supervision orders shall have effect subject to amendments made by Schedule 12.

Amendments—Criminal Justice Act 1991, s 100, Sch 11, para 40.

Effect and duration of orders etc

91 Effect and duration of orders etc

(1) The making of a child arrangements order with respect to the living arrangements of a child who is the subject of a care order discharges the care order.

PART II

(1A) For the purposes of subsection (1), a child arrangements order is one made with respect to the living arrangements of a child if the arrangements regulated by the order consist of, or include, arrangements which relate to either or both of the following –

(a) with whom the child is to live, and
(b) when the child is to live with any person.

(2) The making of a care order with respect to a child who is the subject of any section 8 order discharges that order.

(2A) Where an activity direction has been made with respect to a child, the making of a care order with respect to the child discharges the direction.

(3) The making of a care order with respect to a child who is the subject of a supervision order discharges that other order.

(4) The making of a care order with respect to a child who is a ward of court brings that wardship to an end.

(5) The making of a care order with respect to a child who is the subject of a school attendance order made under section 437 of the Education Act 1996 discharges the school attendance order.

(5A) The making of a special guardianship order with respect to a child who is the subject of –

(a) a care order; or
(b) an order under section 34,

discharges that order.

(6) Where an emergency protection order is made with respect to a child who is in care, the care order shall have effect subject to the emergency protection order.

(7) Any order made under section 4(1), 4ZA(1), 4A(1) or 5(1) shall continue in force until the child reaches the age of eighteen, unless it is brought to an end earlier.

(8) Any –

(a) agreement under section 4, 4ZA or 4A; or
(b) appointment under section 5(3) or (4),

shall continue in force until the child reaches the age of eighteen, unless it is brought to an end earlier.

(9) An order under Schedule 1 has effect as specified in that Schedule.

(10) A section 8 order shall, if it would otherwise still be in force, cease to have effect when the child reaches the age of sixteen, unless it is to have effect beyond that age by virtue of section 9(6).

(10A) Subsection (10) does not apply to provision in a child arrangements order which regulates arrangements relating to –

(a) with whom a child is to live, or
(b) when a child is to live with any person.

(11) Where a section 8 order has effect with respect to a child who has reached the age of sixteen, it shall, if it would otherwise still be in force, cease to have effect when he reaches the age of eighteen.

(12) Any care order, other than an interim care order, shall continue in force until the child reaches the age of eighteen, unless it is brought to an end earlier.

(13) Any order made under any other provision of this Act in relation to a child shall, if it would otherwise still be in force, cease to have effect when he reaches the age of eighteen.

(14) On disposing of any application for an order under this Act, the court may (whether or not it makes any other order in response to the application) order that no application for an order under this Act of any specified kind may be made with respect to the child concerned by any person named in the order without leave of the court.

(15) Where an application ('the previous application') has been made for –

(a) the discharge of a care order;

(b) the discharge of a supervision order;
(c) the discharge of an education supervision order;
(d) the substitution of a supervision order for a care order; or
(e) a child assessment order,

no further application of a kind mentioned in paragraphs (a) to (e) may be made with respect to the child concerned, without leave of the court, unless the period between the disposal of the previous application and the making of the further application exceeds six months.

(16) Subsection (15) does not apply to applications made in relation to interim orders.

(17) Where –

(a) a person has made an application for an order under section 34;
(b) the application has been refused; and
(c) a period of less than six months has elapsed since the refusal,

that person may not make a further application for such an order with respect to the same child, unless he has obtained the leave of the court.

Amendments—Education Act 1996, s 582(1), Sch 37, Pt I, para 90; ACA 2002, ss 114(5), 139(1), Sch 3, paras 54 and 68; CAA 2006, s 15(1), Sch 2, paras 7, 9; CYPA 2008, s 37(3); HFEA 2008, s 56, Sch 6, para 31; CFA 2014, s 12, Sch 2.

Defined terms—'care order': ss 31(11), 105(1); 'child': s 105(1); 'child assessment order': s 43(2); 'education supervision order': s 36(2); 'supervision order': s 31(11).

Care order discharges s 8 order (s 91(2))—Where an English court made a care order it had the effect of discharging a Dutch custody order, just as it would discharge a s 8 order (*Oxfordshire County Council v S* [2000] Fam Law 20, FD). The making of a care order also discharges any current activity direction (s 91(2A)).

'The making of a care order ... brings that wardship to an end' (s 91(4))—Although an injunction made within wardship proceedings would ordinarily end on the discharge of the wardship, the court has power to order that such an injunction is to continue after the discharge of those proceedings (*Re E (A Minor) (Child Abuse: Evidence)* [1991] 1 FLR 420, FD, at [455F]). It is probable that the injunction does not subsist beyond the date when the minor achieves majority (*Re D (A Minor) (Adoption Order: Validity)* [1991] 2 FLR 66, CA, at [76E]) or the death of the minor during his minority.

'no application ... without leave of the court' (s 91(14))—This subsection has produced many reported decisions concerning the circumstances in which an order restricting future applications should be made. In *Re P (Section 91(14) Guidelines) (Residence and Religious Heritage)* [1999] 2 FLR 573, CA, Butler-Sloss LJ drew up a number of guidelines from the reported cases, while indicating that the court always has to carry out a balancing exercise between the welfare of the child and the right of unrestricted access of the litigant to the court. The guidelines are as follows:

1 Section 91(14) should be read in conjunction with s 1(1) which makes the welfare of the child the paramount consideration.
2 The power to restrict applications to the court is discretionary and in the exercise of its discretion the court must weigh in the balance all the relevant circumstances.
3 An important consideration is that to impose a restriction is a statutory intrusion into the right of a party to bring proceedings before the court and to be heard in matters affecting his/her child.
4 The power is therefore to be used with great care and sparingly, the exception and not the rule.
5 It is generally to be seen as a weapon of last resort in cases of repeated and unreasonable applications.
6 In suitable circumstances (and on clear evidence), a court may impose the leave restriction in cases where the welfare of the child requires it, although there is no past history of making unreasonable applications (see also *Re P (Children Act 1989, ss 22 and 26: Local Authority Compliance)* [2000] 2 FLR 910, FD).
7 In cases under para 6 above, the court will need to be satisfied first that the facts go beyond the commonly encountered need for a time to settle to a regime ordered by the court and the all too common situation where there is animosity between the adults in dispute or between the local authority and the family; and secondly that there is a serious risk that, without the imposition of the restriction, the child or the primary carers will be subject to unacceptable strain (see also *Re S (Contact: Promoting Relationship with Absent Parent)* [2004] 1 FLR 1279, CA). The Court of Appeal has reiterated the principle that a need for time to settle to the regime ordered is not sufficient to justify a s 91(14) order: the purpose of the order could and should have been achieved by giving the order time to work itself out: *Re G (Residence: Restrictions on Further Applications)* [2009] 1 FLR 894, CA.
8 A court may impose the restriction on making applications in the absence of a request from any of the parties, subject, of course, to the rules of natural justice such as an opportunity for the parties to be heard on the point. In particular it is wrong in principle, except in exceptional circumstances, to put a litigant in person in the position, at short notice, of having to contest a s 91(14) order (*Re C (Prohibition on Further Applications)* [2002] 1 FLR 1136, CA).
9 A restriction may be imposed with or without limitation of time. In *Re B (Section 91(14) Order: Duration)* [2004] 1 FLR 871, CA, it was said that where the mother was determined to excise the father from a child's life the court should never abandon endeavours to right the wrongs within the family dynamics. A s 91(14) order which was to last during the child's minority and was without limitation to specific

applications gave the wrong message in a case in which the father had not abused the family justice system nor undermined the mother's primary care. An order which is indeterminate or is to last until a child is 16 should be an exceptional step because it is, in effect, an acknowledgement that nothing more can be done. If such an order is made the court must spell out why and what needs to be done to make a successful application in the future (*Re S (Permission to Seek Relief)* [2007] 1 FLR 482, CA). In *S v B & Newport City Council: Re K* [2007] 1 FLR 1116, FD, a special guardianship order and a s 91(14) order were made preventing the natural parents making any application for contact without limitation of time because the child's needs required that order to be made and failure to do so, in the light of the parents volatile behaviour, would impose an unacceptable strain on the carers.

10 The degree of restriction should be proportionate to the harm it is intended to avoid. Therefore the court imposing the restriction should carefully consider the extent of the restriction to be imposed and specify, where appropriate, the type of application to be restrained and the duration of order (see also *Re G (Contempt: Committal)* [2003] 2 FLR 58, CA).

11 It would be undesirable in other than the most exceptional cases to make the order ex parte.

Furthermore, Butler-Sloss LJ stated that in her view an absolute prohibition on making any application to the court could not be made under s 91(14). Additionally, a s 91(14) order did not infringe the HRA 1998 or ECHR 1950, Art 6(1) because it did not deny access to the court, only access to an immediate inter partes hearing. An order imposing an absolute prohibition would have to be made under the inherent jurisdiction of the court (see *Re R (Residence: Contact: Restricting Applications)* [1998] 1 FLR 749, CA); where an order is made under the principles of *Grepe v Loam* (1887) 37 Ch D 168 preventing applications by any party without leave, and ordering that any application is to be filed with the court only and dealt with on paper, the guidelines in *Re P* above should apply (*Harris v Harris; Attorney-General v Harris* [2001] 2 FLR 895, FD). It is not appropriate to make a s 91(14) order in contempt proceedings unless there is an application for a child arrangements order before the court (*Heathcote v Crackles* [2002] EWCA Civ 222).

General principles:

(i) Orders without limit of time should only be made in outstandingly bad cases, which merit the strongest degree of forensic protection for the child from ill-founded conflict (*Re J (A Child) (Restriction on Applications)* [2008] 1 FLR 369, CA and *Re G (Residence: Restrictions on Further Applications)* [2009] 1 FLR 894, CA). Wilson LJ has repeated that s 91(14) orders are to be used with great care, sparingly and as a weapon of last resort in cases of repeated and unreasonable applications. A court was not entitled to take the view that there was no undue hardship in requiring a parent to show an arguable case in support of a proposed application. The Court of Appeal spent a surprising and unfortunate amount of its time in reversing orders made on an inappropriately summary basis: *Re A (Contact: Section 91(14))* [2010] 2 FLR 151, CA.

(ii) It is not permissible to impose conditions on a s 91(14) order (*Re S (Permission to Seek Relief)* [2007] 1 FLR 482, CA). However, it is permissible for a judge imposing a s 91(14) order to identify a particular issue and to suggest to the litigant that unless he could show that that particular issue had been addressed any future application for permission to apply to the court for further relief was unlikely to be successful (*Stringer v Stringer* [2007] 1 FLR 1532, CA).

(iii) Once a prohibition under s 91(14) has been made, any further applications for leave to bring proceedings should generally be heard inter partes rather than ex parte; this enables the court to investigate fully whether or not there is a genuine need for further proceedings (*Re N (Section 91(14) Order)* [1996] 1 FLR 356, CA, but cf *Re S (Permission to Seek Relief)*, above). It is open to a judge making a s 91(14) order to direct that any permission to apply during its operation shall not in the first instance be served on the respondent, but should be considered by the judge on paper. However, an applicant should not be denied an oral hearing if that is sought (*Re Bradford; Re O'Connell* [2007] 1 FLR 530, CA). The test for granting such leave once a s 91(14) order has been made is whether there is an arguable case with some chance of success (*Re P (Section 91(14) Guidelines) (Residence and Religious Heritage)* [1999] 2 FLR 573, CA, at [54]). The application should demonstrate there is a need for renewed judicial investigation (*Re A (Application for Leave)* [1998] 1 FLR 1, CA, at [53]). These two tests complement each other (*Re S (Permission to Seek Relief)* [2007] 1 FLR 482, CA, at [78]).

Imperative requirements—Before making a s 91(14) order, the court must be satisfied that the parties affected:

(i) are fully aware that the court is seised of an application and is considering making such an order;
(ii) understand the meaning and effect of such an order;
(iii) have full knowledge of the evidential basis on which such an order is sought; and
(iv) have had a proper opportunity to make representations in relation to the making of such an order; this may of course mean adjourning the application for it to be made in writing and on notice: *Re T (A Child) (Suspension of Contact) (s 91(14) CA 1989)* [2016] 1 FLR 916, CA.

Loss of self-control—Where a party loses their temper in court and/or walks out of the hearing it is wrong, on this ground alone, to make a s 91(14) order against that party. The appropriate course is to allow the party time to repent and come to his/her senses by adjourning the matter for a minimum of 24 hours to 'draw the party back into the proceedings and not to put a further barrier on his further engagement with the system': *Re M (Section 91(14) Order)* [2012] 2 FLR 758, CA.

Litigants in person—The Court of Appeal has handed down guidance on the approach to be taken when considering making an order under s 91(14). It is of utmost importance that the party, parties or other persons affected by the order, particularly if they are in person: (a) understand that such an application is being made, or that consideration is being given to making a s 91(14) order; (b) understand the meaning and effect of such an order; and (c) have a proper opportunity to make submissions to the court. A request for a short adjournment to consider the position should normally be granted: *Re C (Litigant in Person: s 91(14) Order)* [2009] 2 FLR 1461, CA, at [13].

'order under section 34' (s 91(17)(a))—Section 34 provides for various types of order regulating the contact of children in care with their parents and others.

Leave of the court—Where any of the provisions of s 91(14)–(17) requires the leave of the court to be obtained before a particular application under the Act may be made, leave should be sought in accordance with FPR 2010, Pt 18. The application for leave should be made in Form C2 (see FPR 2010, r 5 and PD5A, Table 1). If leave is granted, the applicant will proceed to issue an application for an order in Form C1.

Jurisdiction and procedure etc

92 Jurisdiction of courts

(1)–(6) *(repealed)*

(7) For the purposes of this Act 'the court' means the High Court or the family court.

(8) Subsection (7) is subject to any express provision as to the jurisdiction of any court made by any other provision of this Act.

(9)–(10A) *(repealed)*

(11) Part II of Schedule 11 makes amendments consequential on this section.

Amendments—CRA 2005, s 15(1), Sch 4, paras 203, 205; CCA 2013, s 17, Sch 11.

Defined terms—'child': s 105(1).

Jurisdiction under the Act generally—The general scheme of the Act is to give courts as much flexibility as possible so, broadly speaking, most orders may be made by any court. Section 92(4) prevents lay justices in the Family Court from dealing with the administration or application of any property belonging to or held in trust for a child or the income of any such property. They are also limited in the financial orders which they may make by the provisions of Sch 1, paras 1 and 5. The distribution of business of the Family Court and the allocation among the judges is now governed by FC(CDB)R 2014. The High Court has full jurisdiction to hear all cases regarding children.

93 Rules of court

(1) An authority having power to make rules of court may make such provision for giving effect to –

(a) this Act;
(b) the provisions of any statutory instrument made under this Act; or
(c) any amendment made by this Act in any other enactment,

as appears to that authority to be necessary or expedient.

(2) The rules may, in particular, make provision –

(a) with respect to the procedure to be followed in any relevant proceedings (including the manner in which any application is to be made or other proceedings commenced);
(b) as to the persons entitled to participate in any relevant proceedings, whether as parties to the proceedings or by being given the opportunity to make representations to the court;
(bb) for children to be separately represented in relevant proceedings,
(c) with respect to the documents and information to be furnished, and notices to be given, in connection with any relevant proceedings;
(d) *(repealed)*
(e) with respect to preliminary hearings;
(f), (g) *(repealed)*
(h) enabling the court, in such circumstances as may be prescribed, to proceed on any application even though the respondent has not been given notice of the proceedings;
(i), (j) *(repealed)*

(3) In subsection (2) –

'notice of proceedings' means a summons or such other notice of proceedings as is required; and 'given', in relation to a summons, means 'served',

'prescribed' means prescribed by the rules; and

'relevant proceedings' means any application made, or proceedings brought, under any of the provisions mentioned in paragraphs (a) to (c) of subsection (1) and any part of such proceedings.

(4) This section and any other power in this Act to make rules of court are not to be taken as in any way limiting any other power of the authority in question to make rules of court.

(5) When making any rules under this section an authority shall be subject to the same requirements as to consultation (if any) as apply when the authority makes rules under its general rule making power.

Amendments—CLSA 1990, s 116, Sch 16, para 22; ACA 2002, s 122(2); CCA 2013, s 17, Sch 11.

94 *(repealed)*

95 Attendance of child at hearing under Part IV or V

(1) In any proceedings in which a court is hearing an application for an order under Part IV or V, or is considering whether to make any such order, the court may order the child concerned to attend such stage or stages of the proceedings as may be specified in the order.

(2) The power conferred by subsection (1) shall be exercised in accordance with rules of court.

(3) Subsections (4) to (6) apply where –

(a) an order under subsection (1) has not been complied with; or
(b) the court has reasonable cause to believe that it will not be complied with.

(4) The court may make an order authorising a constable, or such person as may be specified in the order –

(a) to take charge of the child and to bring him to the court; and
(b) to enter and search any premises specified in the order if he has reasonable cause to believe that the child may be found on the premises.

(5) The court may order any person who is in a position to do so to bring the child to the court.

(6) Where the court has reason to believe that a person has information about the whereabouts of the child it may order him to disclose it to the court.

Defined terms—'child': s 105(1).

'Part IV or V' (s 95(1))—Parts IV and V concern public law orders, such as care and supervision orders, emergency protection orders and child assessment orders.

Court hearing an application or considering making an order (s 95(1))—The court's power to require the attendance of the child is not confined to cases in which there has been an original application for an order under Pt IV or V but may also be exercised where the court is considering making an order of its own initiative (for example, where it is entertaining family proceedings and considering making a s 34 child arrangements order of its own initiative under s 34(5)).

Use of s 95(1) to compel attendance of child as witness—It is suggested that it may be inappropriate to use the power in s 95(1) to compel the attendance of a child to give evidence and that it would be more appropriate, in the very few instances in which the child's attendance for this reason should be compelled, to use those provisions expressly designed for the purpose (see **Children as witnesses in family proceedings** under s 96).

Rules of court (s 95(2))—The relevant rules of court are FPR 2010, r 12.14. The provisions as to the representations of the children's guardian, the child's solicitor and, in certain circumstances, the child where the court is considering who should be present or absent are contained in FPR 2010, rr 16.20, 16.29 and PD16A, para 6.6.

General position as to attendance of child—The application of CA 1989, s 95 and FPR 2010, r 12.14 was comprehensively considered by Jackson J in *A City Council v T, J and K* [2011] 2 FLR 803, FD and guidance provided. See **Child at court** under FPR 2010, r 12.14.

'reasonable cause to believe' (s 95(3)(b),(4)(b))—This phrase appears twice in this section and contrasts with the phrase 'reason to believe' used in s 95(6). In s 95(3), it is the court which has to have reasonable cause to believe that its s 95(1) order will not be complied with whereas, in s 95(4), it is the constable or other specified person who has to have reasonable cause to believe that the child may be found on any premises before he enters and searches them.

'enter and search any premises specified in the order' (s 95(4))—The court will have to be given some idea of where the child may be because it is not empowered to grant a general authority to enter premises and look for him, only an authority in relation to specified premises. Furthermore, even when authorised to enter and search, the constable or other authorised person will not be able to do so unless *he* has reasonable cause to believe that the child may be found on the premises. He cannot therefore simply rely on the court's order but must give the matter independent thought and satisfy himself, presumably at the time when he is about to enter, that he is entitled to do so.

'reason to believe' (s 95(6))—It is submitted that the phrase 'reason to believe' used in s 95(6) denotes a rather lower standard than the phrase 'reasonable cause to believe' which is used elsewhere in this section; the s 95(6) terminology mirrors that used in FLA 1986, s 33, which provides for the court to order disclosure of information about the whereabouts of a child in various private law proceedings.

Application for an order under s 95—Although the general tenor of this section suggests that orders will normally be made of the court's own initiative, there does not appear to be anything preventing a party applying for such an order in an appropriate case.

96 Evidence given by, or with respect to, children

(1) Subsection (2) applies in any civil proceedings where a child who is called as a witness in any civil proceedings does not, in the opinion of the court, understand the nature of an oath.

(2) The child's evidence may be heard by the court if, in its opinion –

(a) he understands that it is his duty to speak the truth; and

(b) he has sufficient understanding to justify his evidence being heard.

(3) The Lord Chancellor may, with the concurrence of the Lord Chief Justice, by order make provision for the admissibility of evidence which would otherwise be inadmissible under any rule of law relating to hearsay.

(4) An order under subsection (3) may only be made with respect to –

(a) civil proceedings in general or such civil proceedings, or class of civil proceedings, as may be prescribed; and

(b) evidence in connection with the upbringing, maintenance or welfare of a child.

(5) An order under subsection (3) –

(a) may, in particular, provide for the admissibility of statements which are made orally or in a prescribed form or which are recorded by any prescribed method of recording;

(b) may make different provision for different purposes and in relation to different descriptions of court; and

(c) may make such amendments and repeals in any enactment relating to evidence (other than in this Act) as the Lord Chancellor considers necessary or expedient in consequence of the provision made by the order.

(6) Subsection (5)(b) is without prejudice to section 104(4):

(7) In this section –

'civil proceedings' means civil proceedings, before any tribunal, in relation to which the strict rules of evidence apply, whether as a matter of law or by agreement of the parties, and references to 'the court' shall be construed accordingly;

'prescribed' means prescribed by an order under subsection (3).

Amendments—Civil Evidence Act 1995, s 15(1), Sch 1, para 16; CRA 2005, s 15(1), Sch 4, paras 203, 207.

Defined terms—'child': s 105(1).

Scope—Section 96(1) and (2) allows a child who does not understand the oath to give unsworn evidence providing he understands his duty to speak the truth and has sufficient understanding to justify his evidence being heard; s 96(3)–(6) are enabling provisions facilitating the making of orders by the Lord Chancellor as to the admissibility of hearsay evidence (see Children (Admissibility of Hearsay Evidence) Order 1993 in Part IV.

Judge meeting the child—There is a very clear distinction to be made between a meeting between the child and the judge with a view to evidence-gathering and a meeting for the purposes of communicating generally; these two different processes should be distinguished with care. In *Re F (Children)* [2016] EWCA Civ 546, the President emphasised that a meeting between the child and the judge was an opportunity for the judge to hear what the child might wish to say and for the child to hear the judge explain the nature of the process; its purpose was not to obtain evidence. In that case, the President also confirmed that practitioners and the courts had been too slow to recognise the need for change or to acknowledge the pace of change, and confirmed that proper adherence to the *Re W (Children)* [2010] 1 FLR 1485, SC principles would mean that there were likely to be more cases in future where a child either gave evidence without being joined as a party, or was joined as a party. (See **Judge seeing child** under FPR 2010, r 12.21.) Note also the guidance in *Re S (Abduction: Hearing the Child)* [2015] 2 FLR 588, CA, where the Court of Appeal cautioned that the policies relevant to Hague Convention and European abduction cases should not be imported into the inherent jurisdiction to the exclusion of the obligation to hear the child, which is both an integral part of the welfare evaluation and the guarantee of the child's effective access to justice. In those cases, as a matter of principile,

PART II

there is an obligation on the High Court sitting in its inherent jurisdiction in relation to an abduction application to consider whether and how to hear the child concerned.

Children as witnesses in family proceedings—A child can give sworn evidence or, if he does not understand the nature of the oath but comes within s 96(2), unsworn evidence. There is no longer a presumption against children giving evidence in family proceedings because such a preumption cannot be reconciled with the approach of the ECtHR, which always aims to strike a fair balance between competing convention rights under ECHR 1950: *Re W (Children)* [2010] 1 FLR 1485, SC. Following the Supreme Court's decision in *Re W*, the Working Party of the Family Justice Council issued *Guidelines in Relation to Children Giving Evidence in Family Proceedings* (see Part V) to be used when the court is considering the possible advantages that the child being called will bring to the determination of truth, as balanced against the possible damage to the child's welfare from giving evidence (paras 8–11). It lists the practical matters that should be considered before a hearing at which a child is to give evidence (paras 13–17) and the practical steps to be taken at the hearing itself (para 18). Paragraph 19 sets out the ground rules for the examination of the child, taking into account the matters set out in *R v Barker* [2010] EWCA Crim 4 (at [42]), which called for advocacy to be adapted 'to enable the child to give the best evidence of which her or she is capable'. The *Family Advocates' Gateway to Best Practice for Vulnerable Witnesses* is a useful source of guidance for such cases: see *www.theadvocatesgateway.org*. In *Re B (Private Law Proceedings: Child's Evidence)* [2015] 1 FLR 1381, CA, the Court of Appeal reiterated the message from *Re W* (above) that it was not expected to become routine for children to give evidence in family cases.

Article 6 of the EHCR requires that the proceedings be fair, and this normally entails an opportunity to challenge evidence presented by the other side. However, account must be taken of the Article 8 rights of the perceived victim. Striking that balance in care proceedings may mean that the child is not called in the great majority of cases, but this will be the result of the balancing exercise and not a presumption. The Supreme Court in *Re W* held that the approach in private family proceedings between parents is the same in principle, although there are specific risks. In such cases the allegations of abuse are made by a parent seeking to gain advantage, not by a neutral local authority. This does not mean that the allegations are false, but it does increase the risk of fabrication or exaggeration. Furthermore, the child would not routinely have the protection of a Cafcass guardian, and there are many more litigants in person in private law proceedings, meaning that the court would have to take very careful precautions to ensure that the child was not harmed. However, in *Re M (Sexual Abuse: Evidence)* [2010] EWCA Civ 1030, Hughes LJ, sitting as a single judge in the Court of Appeal, held that there should not, even now, be any question of young children giving oral evidence, at least in the Family Court. The child's welfare is very important, albeit not the paramount consideration. In cases where the court is being requested to permit a child to be called to answer questions arising from an ABE interview (see **ABE evidence**, below), it is crucial that such requests are determined at the earliest possible stage, well before the final hearing but after the judge has taken the time to view the interviews and to evaluate them – see *Re E (A Child)* [2016] EWCA Civ 473.

Covert evidence—It is almost always wrong for a recording device to be placed on a child for the purpose of gathering evidence in family proceedings, whether or not the child was aware of its presence; in such circumstances, anyone who was considering taking such action should think carefully about the consequences. In *M v F & C (A Child by her Children's Guardian); sub nom Re M & F (Covert Recording of Children)* [2016] EWFC 29, the court observed that experience suggested that the covert recording of others normally said more about the recorder than the recorded.

ABE evidence—Video-recorded interviews with children are hearsay evidence but may be admitted as evidence of truth of the statement in family proceedings. Such interviews should be conducted in accordance with the detailed guidance in *Achieving Best Evidence in Criminal Proceedings* (ABE) (March 2011) although this guidance is non-statutory. The court can make findings based on ABE evidence so long as it is alive to the hearsay nature of the evidence and the age of the children at the time of interview (*Re M (Sexual Abuse: Evidence)* [2010] EWCA Civ 1030). In *TW v A City Council* [2011] 1 FLR 1597, CA, the Court of Appeal found that the inadequacies of the ABE interview were so manifest, even allowing for a broad margin of latitude to anyone conducting such an interview, that no evidential weight could be placed on it. In particular, it was not sufficient for a judge to rely primarily on the fact that a child might be able to stand up to and overcome a thoroughly unsatisfactory interview; rather, a clear analysis of all the evidence was required and the child's interview had to be assessed in that context. In *Re W; Re F (Children)* [2015] EWCA Civ 1300, the forensic value of the ABE interviews was found to be minimal such that the trial judge had been wrong to attach any weight to them. Whether the flaws in ABE evidence are so fundamental as to render the interviews wholly unreliable is a matter for the trial judge who must analyse the process thoroughly to evaluate whether any of the allegations made in such interviews can be relied upon (see *Re E (A Child)* [2016] EWCA Civ 473).

Veracity of children's evidence—Veracity or validity assessments by experts of children's evidence have a limited role to play in family proceedings – see *A London Borough Council v K and Others* [2009] EWHC 850 (Fam). The ultimate judge of veracity, namely where the truth lies, is the judge and the judge alone; the judge cannot delegate that decision to any expert because only the judge sees and hears all the evidence. See also *Wigan Borough Council v M and Others (Veracity Assessments)* [2016] 1 FLR 126, FD.

Compelling children to give evidence—Section 95(1) enables the court to require the attendance of the child concerned in a Pt IV or Pt V application. There is some support for the suggestion from comments in *R v B County Council ex parte P* [1991] 1 FLR 470, CA, at [475], [479] that this procedure may not, however, be appropriate where the attendance of the child as a witness is required and that, in such cases, recourse should be had to provisions expressly designed for the purpose. The rules setting out the power of the court to control evidence are in FPR 2010, rr 22.1–22.17 and PD22A. Where a parent wishes to call a willing child to give evidence, he may be prevented from doing so in an appropriate case by means of a specific issue order. However, it will be rare for an unwilling child to be compelled to give evidence, although unwillingness is not of itself determinative (*SMBC v PR (SR Intervening) (Care Proceedings: Children's Evidence) (No 1)* [2012] 1 FLR

842, FD). In *SMBC v PR (SR Intervening) (Care Proceedings: Children's Evidence) (No 2)* [2012] 1 FLR 852, FD, the court pointed out that there is little authority on the compellability of an alleged perpetrator who is also a minor (in this case, SR, aged 17) and who is not a party to the care proceedings, but is merely an intervener, and did not wish to give evidence. *R v B County Council ex parte P*, above (which has not subsequently been overruled) indicated that such a minor was compellable. However, there was no direct authority as to whether SR should, in the circumstances of that case, be so compelled. Balancing the relevant considerations, the court decided that it would not be appropriate to force him to give evidence. See also *Re R (Children)* [2015] EWCA Civ 167, where the objections of the local authority and the children's guardian to a 14-year-old child giving evidence were overruled by the Court of Appeal; it was considered that the need to form a view as to the child's credibility was a key issue. See also *Re S (Children)* [2016] EWCA Civ 83, where the Court of Appeal upheld the decision of the judge in care proceedings not to require a girl who had made, but then retracted, allegations of sexual abuse to give oral evidence at the fact-finding hearing (albeit Gloster LJ robustly dissenting).

Children as perpetrators—In cases where vulnerable children or young people face serious charges, it is essential that those instructed on their behalf are utterly clear as to their professional responsibilities and astute to ensure that their client's rights are properly protected (if necessary, by asserting legal professional privilege) – see *R v Derby Magistrates' Court (ex parte B)* [1996] 1 FLR 513, HL (followed most recently in *Re E (A Child)* [2016] EWCA Civ 473). In *Re E*, a 15-year-old party in care proceedings was alleged to be a perpetrator as well as a victim and had borderline-to-low ability. The Court of Appeal expressed concern that despite the child being entitled to the same legal professional privilege as any other party, the judge had made an order (apparently without opposition) requiring his representative to file a statement setting out what transpired at a meeting that had been arranged for him to provide instructions to his lawyers about serious allegations of sexual abuse.

Child understanding the nature of the oath—See *R v Hayes* [1977] 1 WLR 234, CA, where it was held that a child could give evidence on oath if he has a sufficient appreciation of the solemnity of the occasion and the added responsibility to tell the truth which is involved in taking the oath, over and above the duty to tell the truth which is an ordinary duty of normal social conduct. The court in *R v Hayes* thought that the dividing line between children who are competent to give sworn evidence and those who are not is normally between the ages of eight and ten. However, under Criminal Justice Act 1988, s 33A, which governs the competence of children to give evidence in criminal proceedings, the general rule is that under-14s give unsworn evidence and children of 14 and over give sworn evidence.

Intermediaries—It is important that questions that challenge the child's account are fairly put to the child so that the child may answer them. This could be done through an early videoed cross-examination or through cross-examination via video-link. However, another way might be through use of an intermediary – the intermediary could be the court itself, as would be common in continental Europe (*Re W (Children)* [2010] 1 FLR 1485, SC, at [28]). The Family Justice Council Guidelines of December 2011 in relation to children giving evidence in family proceedings (see Part V) require specifically that if 'live' cross-examination is appropriate, there should be early consideration of the need for and use of a registered intermediary or other communication specialist to facilitate the communication of others with the child or relay questions directly, if indicated by the needs of the child (para 14). Intermediaries are a 'special measure', but a relatively new one. The use of intermediaries in England and Wales came about as a result of the Youth Justice and Criminal Evidence Act 1999, s 29. They operate in the criminal courts and are recruited and regulated by the MoJ. They are known as Registered Intermediaries (RIs) and their remit is to facilitate communication with vulnerable witnesses in the criminal justice system. The MoJ's Better Trials Unit (BTU) current policy is that it will agree to assist in the provision of a RI for Family Court proceedings only where there is a direct link with a criminal case in which the witness is involved and where a RI has already been used and provided for that witness. In addition, assistance will only be provided where the RI used in the criminal trial is available and doing so does not affect the provision of RIs under the 1999 Act. In *Re A (Care Proceedings: Learning Disabled Parent)* [2014] 2 FLR 591, FD, an intermediary was described as 'a type of interpretation service' and the services of an intermediary were used to assist a father with learning disabilities to participate in a fact-finding hearing. In *Re K and H (Children: unrepresented father: cross-examination of child)* [2015] 2 FLR 802, FD, the court confirmed that an intermediary is properly to be regarded as an 'expert', as is the case with interpreters, lip-readers and signers. See the two articles by Penny Cooper 'Child Witnesses in Family Proceedings: Should Intermediaries be Showing Us the Way?' [2011] Fam Law 397 and 'Intermediaries and vulnerable witnesses: what do we do now?' [2012] Fam Law 868. The Final Report of the Family Justice Review, chaired by Sir David Norgrove, recommended (at para 4.151) that the government and judiciary should actively consider how children and young witnesses may be protected when giving evidence in family proceedings. In *Re A (Vulnerable Witness)* [2013] 2 FLR 1473, FD, Pauffley J sanctioned the instruction and involvement of an intermediary (Communicourt) to work with a 17-year-old witness in protracted contact proceedings, and in *Re A (Vulnerable Witness: Fact Finding)* [2014] 1 FLR 146, FD, that witness gave oral evidence via video link with the assistance of the experienced intermediary. Useful guidance for advocates in such cases can be found in the Advocacy Training Council's toolkit: *Vulnerable Witnesses and Parties in the Family Courts* (October 2014) at *www.theadvocatesgateway.org*. In relation to the factors to be considered when deciding whether or not to use an intermediary for a person who lacks capacity and is a vulnerable person, see the implications of *Re X (A Child)* [2012] 2 FLR 456, FD under FPR 2010, rr 11.4 and 15.1.

'sufficient understanding' (s 96(2)(b))—See **'able ... to give such instructions on his own behalf'** under FPR 2010, r 16.29.

Child giving unsworn evidence under s 96(2)—A child who gives unsworn evidence is still liable to be cross-examined.

Compelling attendance of a party to give evidence—A subpoena or witness summons can be issued to compel the attendance of a party to the proceedings to give evidence, irrespective of whether that party is a child or an adult (*R v B County Council ex parte P* [1991] 1 FLR 470, CA).

97 Privacy for children involved in certain proceedings

(1) (*repealed*)

(2) No person shall publish to the public at large or any section of the public any material which is intended, or likely, to identify –

- (a) any child as being involved in any proceedings before the High Court or the family court in which any power under this Act or the Adoption and Children Act 2002 may be exercised by the court with respect to that or any other child; or
- (b) an address or school as being that of a child involved in any such proceedings.

(3) In any proceedings for an offence under this section it shall be a defence for the accused to prove that he did not know, and had no reason to suspect, that the published material was intended, or likely, to identify the child.

(4) The court or the Lord Chancellor may, if satisfied that the welfare of the child requires it and, in the case of the Lord Chancellor, if the Lord Chief Justice agrees, by order dispense with the requirements of subsection (2) to such extent as may be specified in the order.

(5) For the purposes of this section –

'publish' includes –

- (a) include in a programme service (within the meaning of the Broadcasting Act 1990); or
- (b) cause to be published; and

'material' includes any picture or representation.

(6) Any person who contravenes this section shall be guilty of an offence and liable, on summary conviction, to a fine not exceeding level 4 on the standard scale.

(6A) It is not a contravention of this section to -

- (a) enter material in the Adoption and Children Act Register (established under section 125 of the Adoption and Children Act 2002), or
- (b) permit persons to search and inspect that register pursuant to regulations made under section 128A of that Act.

(7), (8) (*repealed*)

(9) The Lord Chief Justice may nominate a judicial office holder (as defined in section 109(4) of the Constitutional Reform Act 2005) to exercise his functions under subsection (4).

Amendments—Broadcasting Act 1990, s 203(1), Sch 20, para 53; CLSA 1990, s 116, Sch 16, para 24; SI 1992/709; AJA 1999, s 72; ACA 2002, s 101(2),(3); Courts Act 2003, s 109(1), Sch 8, para 337; CA 2004, s 62(1); CRA 2005, s 15(1), Sch 4, paras 203, 208; CCA 2013, s 17, Sch 10; CFA 2014, s 7.

Defined terms—'child', 'school'; s 105(1).

Scope—This section makes provision to ensure that court proceedings in which powers under the Act may be exercised remain confidential. See also AJA 1960 (contempt by way of publishing information relating to children proceedings) and the Practice Guidance of 16 Jan 2014: *Transparency in the Family Courts*.

Privacy (s 97(1))—FPR 2010, r 27.10 provides for proceedings to which FPR 2010 apply to be held in private, except where the rules provide otherwise or, subject to any enactment, where the court directs otherwise. 'In private' means that the general public have no right to be present (r 27.10(2)). Attendance at private hearings is regulated by FPR 2010, r 27.11.

'publish' (s 97(2),(5))—The word 'publish' in s 97 should be given its ordinary meaning. AJA 1960, s 12 does not apply to the contents of a judgment handed down in public and there is no need for a judge's permission to publish or report a judgment given in public unless there has been some specific injunctive or other order preventing publication (see *Re X (A Child)* [2016] EWHC 1668 (Fam)). Neither does the prohibition extend to the situation where a children and family reporter communicates concerns to the relevant statutory authority charged with the collection and investigation of material suggestive of child abuse (*Re M (Disclosure: Children and Family Reporter)* [2002] 2 FLR 893, CA – where the children and family reporter in the course of his enquiries encounters suspicion of child abuse he has an unfettered independent discretion as to whether to make an immediate report to social services or the police; he must, however, inform the judge of any such steps he has taken at the earliest convenient opportunity). In *London Borough of Sutton v MH, RH and NH (No 2)* [2016] EWHC 1371 (Fam), the court confirmed that it is in the public interest for any account of court proceedings to be balanced to fully inform any public debate arising out of them; therefore, as much of the court record as possible should be made available. See for example *Doncaster Metropolitan Borough Council v Haigh & Ors* [2011] EWHC 2412 (Fam), where a judge released into the public domain two judgments delivered in the course of care proceedings so that the public might know that harmful allegations that the mother had made, and continued to make, about the father had been found by the courts to be false. See also *H v A (No 2)* [2016] 2 FLR 723, FD, where it was held that it was in the public interest for a Family Court judgment to be published that proscribed completely the operation of a father's parental responsibility for the remainder of the children's minority; however, in that case the court retained a discretion not to publish such a judgment or to make an order restricting its use, balancing the competing human rights involved.

Material which is intended or likely to identify a child (s 97(2))—The prohibition is not an absolute prohibition against publishing material about a child. In *Clayton v Clayton* [2007] 1 FLR 11, CA the court held that although the s 97(2) prohibition ends once the proceedings have been concluded, the provisions of AJA 1960, s 12 remain. Furthermore, in the course of the proceedings the judge may make an injunction or order prohibiting identification for a period beyond the proceedings in the welfare interests of the child, or in order to protect privacy under ECHR 1950, Art 8. However, in deciding to make a long-term injunction aimed at restricting the reporting and publication of proceedings, the court is obliged to conduct a balancing exercise between the Art 8 rights of the child and the Art 10 (freedom of expression) rights of a parent asserting such a right. In *Re R (Secure Editing of Documents)* [2007] 2 FLR 759, FD, the court made an order permitting omission of the mother's address and contact details from any evidence and documents filed and served in the course of the proceedings in order to protect her and the children from the father. Owing to inadequate editing of the documents by the various solicitors involved, the father discovered the mother's new name and he contacted her. The court held that this amounted to a gross breach of the mother's rights under ECHR 1950, Art 8. In order to avoid repetition of such instances, the court issued detailed guidelines with the approval of the President of the Family Division and these are set out in the judgment. In *Clayton* the court held that the father was free to discuss or communicate matters about the case, but the making of a film and the taking of the child back to Portugal for that purpose related to her upbringing and thus engaged her welfare interests and infringed her Art 8 rights. See *Re J (A Minor)* [2016] EWHC 2595 (Fam), where the court made an order preventing the mother from speaking about any aspect of gender dysphoria or gender identification insofar as those matters related to her child, and was furthermore prevented from broadcasting or publishing any detail of J's life that might identify him as the child subject to the proceedings.

See *JC and RT v Central Criminal Court, CPS, BBC & Just For Kids Law* [2014] EWHC 1041 (QB), which confirmed that orders made in criminal proceedings under CYPA 1933, s 39 do not cease when proceedings are over, but cover any report of the proceedings whenever published if the child is still under 18.

Reporting restrictions—Any presumption or principle in favour of open justice that applies generally to court proceedings does not apply to proceedings held in private and that relate to children (*Re W (Children)* [2016] EWCA Civ 113). However, the court has the power to order the disclosure of all or part of what took place in private proceedings, including any judgment at the end of proceedings, under its inherent jurisdiction as reflected in the *Practice Guidance of 16 January 2014: Transparency in the Family Courts: Publication of Judgments* (set out in Part V). The Practice Guidance makes it clear that the judge should have regard to all the circumstances and it will be a question of fact and degree how serious a risk publication would be in any particular case to the fairness of potential future criminal proceedings. The more uncertain the prospect of future criminal proceedings, the less weight should be given to the Art 6 rights of an individual who might be affected by the publication; the converse also applies (see *Re C (A Child)* [2016] EWCA Civ 798).

Courts have moved towards the lifting of reporting restrictions in certain circumstances, see *Re Webster; Norfolk County Council v Webster and Ors* [2007] 1 FLR 1146, FD, where Munby J analysed publicity issues both in principle and in relation to detailed statutory provisions and rights under ECHR 1950; *Re LM (Reporting Restrictions: Coroner's Inquest)* [2008] 1 FLR 1360, FD, where the press was permitted to report certain details at an inquest into the death of the child's sister; *Re B; X Council v B* [2008] 1 FLR 482, FD, where an order was made enabling the local authority to be named; *Re B; X Council v B (No 2)* [2008] 1 FLR 1460, FD, where an order was made allowing the mother and two of the children to waive their anonymity should they so wish; *Re H (Care Plan)* [2008] 2 FLR 21, FD, where an order was made allowing a short summary of the judicial criticism of the social workers involved and of the local authority's response; *Z County Council v TS, DS, ES and A* [2008] 2 FLR 1800, FD, where the judge allowed the care proceedings to be held in public, subject to a schedule of anonymisation covering all parties and witnesses; *Medway Council v G and Others* [2008] 2 FLR 1687, FD, where, in the course of care proceedings, the court gave permission for a newspaper to interview the stepfather about related criminal proceedings on the basis of an agreed statement of facts prepared by the parties, provided that the child was not identified; *Birmingham City Council v Riaz and Others* [2015] 2 FLR 763, FD, where the court was satisfied that while the evidence of risk to the respondents of publicity was, at best, speculative, there was a powerful public interest in favour of the public knowing the details of cases of child sexual exploitation. See also *S v H and another* [2015] EWHC 3313 (Fam), where the court amended an existing reporting restriction order – made by consent – to allow the mother to a limited, defined extent to communicate with the press and provide photographs of herself and the child, so long as they were sufficiently obscured. See *Natasha Armes v Notts County Council* [2016] EWHC 2864 (QB), where the court held that, after making findings of fact supporting a claimant's allegations of abuse by her former foster carers, there was no justification for continuing an anonymity order to protect the foster carers' identities. In lifting the anonymity order, the court had regard to the consequences of identification and the fact that a standard of proof had applied that took account of the need for strong evidence; the allegations related to a matter of legitimate public concern and the claimant ought to be free to tell her story as she wished.

However, in *Re R (Identification: Restrictions on Publication)* [2008] 1 FLR 1252, FD, the court made injunctions restraining the parents from seeking to identify the prospective adopters and stopping them from contacting the children, and restraining publication of any details identifying the children. In *S (A Child Acting by the Official Solicitor) v Rochdale Metropolitan Borough Council and the Independent Reviewing Officer* [2009] 1 FLR 1090, FD, the court approved a confidentiality clause reached by agreement between the child and the authority as part of a compromise approved by the court. In *H v A (No 2)* [2016] 2 FLR 723, FD, it was held that it was in the public interest for a Family Court judgment to be published that proscribed completely the operation of a father's parental responsibility for the remainder of his children's minority; however, the court retained a discretion not to publish such a judgment, or to make an order restricting its use, balancing the competing human rights involved. In *Re C (Publication of Judgment)* [2016] 1 FLR 495, CA, the Court of Appeal confirmed that the move within the family justice system away from it being unusual or exceptional to publish a judgment in private law proceedings was an ongoing process and discouraged judges from giving full judgments on the question of publication: they should be short decisions with only basic reasons for permitting or refusing publication.

In cases where the media wish to publish information about a public law family case, it is important for there to be a sensible, collaborative and responsible dialogue between the local authority and the media as soon as they realise there is an issue about how much of a case is reportable; the aim should be to find a common-sense outcome, steering a path between the need for greater transparency in the public interest and the need to respect the privacy and sensitivities of those whose lives were involved, thereby avoiding the need for a court application: *Tickle v Council of the Borough of North Tyneside and others* [2015] EWHC 2991 (Fam).

Courts should take great care when imposing orders restricting the reporting of criminal proceedings, and before doing so should carry out a balancing exercise with regard to the public interest under ECHR 1950, Arts 8 and 10 (*LB of Waltham Forest v AD* [2014] EWHC 1985 (Fam)). See *Re C (A Child)* [2016] EWCA Civ 798, where the Court of Appeal held that a judge was wrong to restrict publication of a judgment in care proceedings that concerned a father convicted of murdering his daughter because although the father intended to appeal against his conviction, the risk of prejudice from publication of the judgment was so negligible that it should have been given little or no weight in the balancing exercise. In *Re W (Children)* [2016] EWCA Civ 113, the court permitted the introduction of daily reporting of an ongoing fact-finding hearing in a child protection case, which, although a highly unusual step, was plainly within the judge's discretion. However, a proportionate approach required that an additional sub-paragraph was attached to the order stating that such reporting (whether by live reporting, Twitter or otherwise) could not take place until after the court proceedings had concluded on any given day, in order to ensure that the court had had an opportunity to consider whether any additional directions were required. Such a measure allowed the court to take stock of any evidence that should be embargoed before any reporting could take place. In *Re J (A Minor)* [2016] EWHC 2595 (Fam), the court refused the local authority's application for a reporting restriction order following care proceedings in which it was found that a mother had caused her son emotional harm by her unjustified conviction that he was gender dysphoric or identified as a girl. The court ordered that the experts instructed in the case and the social workers and Cafcass officers should be named because it was right that their conclusions and analyses were likely to be held up to public scrutiny.

Members of the press should be asked whether they wished to make submissions. See *Surrey County Council v ME and Others* [2014] 2 FLR 1267, FD for a useful review of the case-law and see *Re X (A Child)* [2016] EWHC 1668 (Fam), where the President gives important guidance on the need to give proper notification to the media of applications for reporting restriction orders and the responsibility of judges to decide whether BAILII should be invited to take down a judgment. There are very few cases where orders have been made restricting the reporting of a criminal trial (*A Local Authority v W, L, W, T and R (by the Children's Guardian)* [2006] 1 FLR 1, FD; *A Council v M and Others (No 3) (Reporting Restriction Order; Adoption; Artificial Insemination)* [2013] 2 FLR 1270, FD; *City and County of Swansea v XZ and YZ* [2014] 2 FLR 1091, FD; *Cumbria CC v M & Ors* [2014] EWHC 2596 (Fam)).

Power to dispense with restrictions on publicity (s 97(4))—This power might be used by the court where, for example, a child is missing and press publicity may help in tracing him. It would appear that an order may be made of the court's own initiative or on application. If an application is to be made, it may be appropriate to use the directions procedure under FPR 2010, r 12.12. The Government's recent decision to allow attendance of the media at hearings in family proceedings has been implemented by a change to FPR 2010, r 27.11(2). See further under FPR 2010, r 27.11. In *Re K (Adoption: Permission to Advertise)* [2007] 2 FLR 326, FD, the local authority applied under s 97(4) for permission to advertise a child for adoption by placing potentially identifying details about him in national and local publications. The Family Proceedings Court (FPC) gave permission to advertise in relevant publications, provided that it was anonymous. These restrictions were upheld on appeal. It was not open to a local authority to place a full identifying advertisement for the adoption of a particular child until they had obtained the necessary recommendation from the adoption panel and had decided that the child ought to be placed for adoption. When such an application is made before a final care hearing and where the care plan for adoption has yet to be endorsed, the court is unlikely to give permission to advertise unless the adoption plan is unopposed or there is some exceptional feature to the case justifying advertising. In *Re P (Enforced Caesarean: Reporting Restrictions)* [2014] 2 FLR 410, FD, the President ruled that a mother who had undergone an involuntary Caesarean section and then had the child removed and placed for adoption would not be prevented by a reporting restriction from identifying herself using her maiden name if she wished to tell her story to the media. Held that the mother's case was 'compelling' and the court had to conduct a balancing exercise, focusing on the comparative importance of the specific rights in play in the individual case and treating the interests of the child, although not paramount, as a primary consideration. In *Re K (Wardship: Publicity) (No 2)* [2014] 2 FLR 310, FD, the court granted parents leave to publish, in anonymised form, their experiences of post-adoption breakdown of placement on the basis that there was already sufficient material in the public domain to enable them to have a meaningful discussion in the media. In *London Borough of Sutton v MH, RH and NH (No 2)* [2016] EWHC 1371 (Fam), a variation was made to a reporting restriction order in the case of a 16-year old child who had been removed from the jurisdiction while on a temporary stay in the UK. The court held that the removal was necessary in view of the strong public interest in maintaining the principle of open justice in public law proceedings, and varied the order to permit the reporting of the facts of the case while maintaining the anonymity of the child. In *Re Alcott* [2016] EWHC 2414 (Fam), reporting restrictions were lifted to allow the publication of a judgment in an abduction case where that judgment identified the parents, who were well-known figures. Even though that publication led indirectly to the identification of the child, the likelihood of harm was low in view of the content of the judgment and was outweighed by the public interest in publication. However, the court refused to lift reporting restrictions on the evidence at the private hearing, which contained full details of the parents' private lives.

98 Self-incrimination

(1) In any proceedings in which a court is hearing an application for an order under Part IV or V, no person shall be excused from –

(a) giving evidence on any matter; or

(b) answering any question put to him in the course of his giving evidence,

on the ground that doing so might incriminate him or his spouse or civil partner of an offence.

(2) A statement or admission made in such proceedings shall not be admissible in evidence against the person making it or his spouse or civil partner in proceedings for an offence other than perjury.

Amendments—CPA 2004, s 261(1), Sch 27, para 132.

Self-incrimination—The general rule, to which this section creates an exception, is that a person is not bound to answer any question if his answer would, in the opinion of the court, tend to expose him to any criminal charge or penalty which the court regards as reasonably likely to be preferred or sued for (*Blunt v Park Lane Hotels* [1942] 2 KB 253, CA).

'Part IV or V' (s 98(1))—Parts IV and V concern public law orders, such as care and supervision orders, emergency protection orders, and child assessment orders.

Ambit of s 98—Ultimately, it will be the criminal court which decides the degree of protection afforded by s 98(2) in any given case. However, there have been a number of views expressed, in the context of family proceedings, about its extent.

(a) *Meaning of 'statement or admission made in such proceedings'* (s 98(2)) In *Oxfordshire County Council v P* [1995] 1 FLR 552, FD, Ward J considered that s 98(2) provided protection with regard to oral admissions made in advance of care proceedings to a children's guardian. In *Cleveland County Council v F* [1995] 1 FLR 797, FD, Hale J agreed with him and added her view that it extends also to statements made to social workers investigating in a child protection case, at least once the proceedings have begun. *Oxfordshire County Council v P* was referred to without demur in *Oxfordshire County Council v L and F* [1997] 1 FLR 235, FD. In *Re K and Others (Minors) (Disclosure)* [1994] 1 FLR 377, FD, Booth J (albeit in a different context) may have been expressing a narrower view when she said that it provided 'protection to a witness who is required to give evidence in relation to a child when such evidence could incriminate him or his spouse'. In *Re G (Social Worker: Disclosure)* [1996] 1 FLR 276, CA, Butler-Sloss LJ, obiter, doubted that s 98(2) could be extended as far as Ward and Hale JJ had suggested.

(b) *Meaning of 'admissible in evidence'* (s 98(2)) In *Re EC (Disclosure of Material)* [1996] 2 FLR 725, CA, the Court of Appeal decided inter alia that transcripts of an admission made by the father when giving evidence should be disclosed to the police, who would then be free to use it when questioning him. The content of any further interview may, of course, be the subject of submissions as to admissibility in criminal proceedings by virtue of PACE 1984, and that would be a matter for the discretion of the trial judge in those proceedings. According to *Re EC* (above), s 98(2) gives protection only against statements being admissible in evidence in criminal proceedings except for an offence of perjury, and does not protect against their use in a police inquiry into the commission of an offence (see also *Re X (Children)* [2008] 1 FLR 589, FD; *Re X (Disclosure for Purposes of Criminal Proceedings)* [2008] 2 FLR 944, FD); *Re M (Care Disclosure to Police)* [2008] 2 FLR 390, FD). A judge cannot give a witness in family proceedings any absolute guarantee as to confidentiality, since there is power to order disclosure even of material falling within s 98(2). In *Re EC*, before they gave evidence, the judge had told all members of the child's family who were suspected of causing her injuries that anything they said from the witness-box could not be used in any criminal trial against them relating to the death of the child. The Court of Appeal said that judges may well like to point out to witnesses to whom such a statement is made that guarantees of confidentiality cannot be given; almost certainly legal advisers should do so. As to applications for disclosure of Children Act material for the purposes of criminal proceedings/investigation, by virtue of the Criminal Justice Act 2003, s 119, a previous inconsistent statement by a witness that is put to him in criminal proceedings is admissible as evidence of any matter stated of which oral evidence by him would be admissible (subject to the discretion of the court to exclude it under PACE 1984). Note that this statutory provision supersedes the decision in *Re L (Care: Confidentiality)* [1999] 1 FLR 165, FD. In *Re O (Care Proceedings: Evidence)* [2004] 1 FLR 161, FD, Johnson J held that where a parent declines to answer questions or to give oral evidence, the court should usually draw the inference that the allegations made against him or her are true. The provisions of s 98(2) do apply to any statement or admission which a parent gives to an expert witness (*Re AB (Care Proceedings: Disclosure of Medical Evidence to Police)* [2003] 1 FLR 579, FD – where Wall J held (at [134]) that the position of expert witnesses is analogous for these purposes with that of the guardian and therefore a statement made to an expert witness is a statement made in the proceedings and thus entitled to the protection of s 98(2)). Before being interviewed by an expert witness, parents should have the terms and purpose of s 98(2) explained to them by their lawyers (*Re AB* (above) at [134]).

Legal professional privilege—See notes under s 31, above.

★★★★

100 Restrictions on use of wardship jurisdiction

(1) Section 7 of the Family Law Reform Act 1969 (which gives the High Court power to place a ward of court in the care, or under the supervision, of a local authority) shall cease to have effect.

(2) No court shall exercise the High Court's inherent jurisdiction with respect to children –

(a) so as to require a child to be placed in the care, or put under the supervision, of a local authority;
(b) so as to require a child to be accommodated by or on behalf of a local authority;
(c) so as to make a child who is the subject of a care order a ward of court; or
(d) for the purpose of conferring on any local authority power to determine any question which has arisen, or which may arise, in connection with any aspect of parental responsibility for a child.

(3) No application for any exercise of the court's inherent jurisdiction with respect to children may be made by a local authority unless the authority have obtained the leave of the court.

(4) The court may only grant leave if it is satisfied that –

(a) the result which the authority wish to achieve could not be achieved through the making of any order of a kind to which subsection (5) applies; and
(b) there is reasonable cause to believe that if the court's inherent jurisdiction is not exercised with respect to the child he is likely to suffer significant harm.

(5) This subsection applies to any order –

(a) made otherwise than in the exercise of the court's inherent jurisdiction; and
(b) which the local authority is entitled to apply for (assuming, in the case of any application which may only be made with leave, that leave is granted).

Scope—This section prevents a child from being both in care and a ward of court, and restricts any application by the local authority for the exercise of the court's inherent jurisdiction without leave; see further s 91(4), Sch 14, para 16A and FPR 2010, rr 12.36–12.42 and FPR PD12D; FPR 2010, Pt 18 appears to be the appropriate procedure for applying for permission. While the effect of s 100(2) is to prevent orders in wardship being used to require a child to be placed in the care or under the supervision of the local authority, the provisions of this section do not (either explicitly or implicitly) preclude the court from making a child a ward of court where the child has been accommodated voluntarily by the local authority under CA 1989, s 20 with the consent of the parent(s) and that consent has not been withdrawn (*Re E (Wardship Order: Child in Voluntary Accommodation)* [2013] 2 FLR 63, CA) but the court cannot exercise its inherent jurisdiction to authorise the local authority to provide care for a child where it could not otherwise have power to do so under the statutory scheme of CA 1989, eg to provide care for a 17-year-old person who could not be made a subject of a care order: *Re M (Children)* [2016] EWCA Civ 937. It may also be relied on when the Fostering Services Regulations 2002 prevent the placement of children with their grandparents by making the children wards of court and placing them with the grandparents in conjunction with a supervision order (*W and X (Wardship: Relatives Rejected as Foster Carers)* [2004] 1 FLR 415, FD). In *Re F (Mental Health Act: Guardianship)* [2000] 1 FLR 192, CA, wardship was considered to be the preferred option to an application for guardianship under MHA 1983. Where the circumstances are unusual and require a 'unique solution to a unique case', the court will on the application of the local authority or the police ward children where there are reasonable grounds or suspicion that they are likely to travel to join ISIS in Syria or where there are grounds for suspecting that they will be taken there by their families (see *Re M (Wardship: Jurisdiction and Powers)* [2016] 1 FLR 1055, FD; *London Borough of Tower Hamlets v M and Others* [2015] 2 FLR 1431, FD. The court will also consider warding a child within care proceedings to maintain control over decisions relating to a child and to remind the parties that they remain accountable to the court (*Re K (Children with Disabilities: Wardship)* [2012] 2 FLR 745, FD). Leave to invoke the inherent jurisdiction will be granted only if there are exceptional circumstances and the remedy sought is in the best interests of the child (*Re W Inherent Jurisdiction: Permission Application)* [2013] EWHC 1957 (Fam): the local authority's application to invoke the inherent jurisdiction to revoke an adoption order was refused but in *London Borough of Tower Hamlets v Ali* [2015] 1 FLR 205, FD the local authority was permitted to invoke the inherent jurisdiction to obtain a location order). In *North Somerset Council v LW & Others (Care & RRO)* [2014] EWHC 1670 (Fam), because of the 'extraordinarily compelling reasons', the local authority's application for permission under the inherent jurisdiction not to disclose a plan of immediate removal at birth to the mother on the basis of the risk to the mother and for a restriction order was granted for a limited period (see also *X CC v M & Others* [2014] EWHC 2262 (Fam)). In *Re B (Secure Accommodation: Inherent Jurisdiction) (No 1)* [2013] EWHC 4654 (Fam) and *Re B (Secure Accommodation) (No 2)* [2013] EWHC 4655 (Fam), the inherent jurisdiction was invoked to obtain a secure accommodation order in respect of a 17 year old who was considered to be at significant risk of self-harm. Where the local authority has been involved in the care of a child because of concerns, and child protection plans are in place, when a child is removed from the jurisdiction the local authority may apply without notice for intervention by the court under its inherent jurisdiction for the summary return of the child from an EU or non-EU State to the jurisdiction of the Court on the basis of the child's British nationality. The circumstances must be exceptional and there must be clear evidence that the child is or would be at risk, especially where the evidence establishes that there is no one to exercise parental responsibility and that any steps taken by the court for the protection of the child would be frustrated by the abducting parent and steps taken by him/her to manipulate the child and encourage him/her to abscond from its current location (*Re K and D (Wardship Without Notice Return Order)* [2017] EWHC 153 (Fam)).

There have, however, been conflicting decisions on the correct procedure to be followed when the need arises for the court to authorise the administration or withdrawal of medical treatment. In *Re T (Wardship: Medical Treatment)* [1997] 1 FLR 502, CA the local authority was granted leave under s 100(3) to commence proceedings where the issue before the court was whether it was in the best interests of a baby to undergo liver transplant surgery. In *Re S (A Minor) (Medical Treatment)* [1993] 1 FLR 376, FD, *Re O (A Minor) (Medical Treatment)* [1993] 2 FLR 149, FD and *South Glamorgan County Council v W and B* [1993] 1 FLR 574, FD, the court considered that the appropriate procedure was to invoke the inherent jurisdiction of the court. In *A Local Authority v SB, AB & MB* [2010] 2 FLR 1203, FD the specific issue route was rejected as an appropriate procedure where the medical treatment initially proposed was for surgery for a child who suffered from a rare and progressive brain disease (see further under FPR 2010, r 12.36).

The inherent jurisdiction is available to exclude a parent from his property indefinitely if there is reasonable cause to believe that the child otherwise would suffer significant harm. Wall J laid down the following propositions in *C v K (Inherent Powers: Exclusion Order)* [1996] 2 FLR 506, FD:

'(1) Where judicial interference with the rights of occupation of property, as between spouses, cohabitees or former cohabitees, is specifically governed by statute, the relevant statutory provisions apply.

(2) Leaving on one side the parens patriae jurisdiction of the High Court over children who are specifically its wards, there exists an inherent jurisdiction in both the High Court and the county court to protect children from harm which is exercisable irrespective of the proceedings in which the issue of the need to protect the children arises.

(3) There is a co-existing jurisdiction given in the High Court by s 37 of the Senior Courts Act and in the county court by s 38 of the County Courts Act to grant injunctive relief in support of legal and equitable rights.

(4) The powers exercisable under ss 37 and 38 of the respective statutes may be invoked in support of the rights and duties conferred on a person by a child arrangements order. Thus, in cases where neither the Matrimonial Homes Act 1983 nor the Domestic Violence and Matrimonial Proceedings Act 1976 applies, a non-residential parent may be restrained from interfering with the residential parent's exercise of parental responsibility. The powers of the court in this context extend to orders against molestation and to ouster injunctions.

(5) The powers exercisable by the court under ss 37 and 38 extend to the grant of injunctions against third parties. Thus, a person who is not a parent of the child may be restrained from interfering with the exercise of parental responsibility by a person who has a child arrangements order in relation to the child. The powers of the court to grant injunctive relief include the power to exclude the stranger from property in which he has a beneficial interest.

(6) There is no reported case in which the inherent jurisdiction, unaffected by ss 37 and 38, has been used to exclude anybody who is not a parent from the occupation of property in which he has a proprietary interest. While the power to make such an order may exist, the better course, in my judgment, is to invoke the jurisdiction under ss 37 and 38, since the need to protect the child is then bolstered by the need to protect the rights of the party with parental responsibility to exercise that parental responsibility appropriately.

(7) The powers of the court to exclude a person from property in which he has a proprietary interest should be exercised with extreme caution. By analogy with s 100(4) of the Children Act the jurisdiction is likely only to be exercised where the court is satisfied that if the jurisdiction is not exercised the child is likely to suffer significant harm. In reaching any conclusion the court must look at all the circumstances of the case, including of course the circumstances of each of the parties and the conduct of the parties towards each other and the child. The court must make findings of fact upon which the assessment of likely future harm can be made.

(8) While the jurisdiction exists to make a final order excluding a person from occupation of property in which he has a proprietary interest, without limitation of time, the court cannot by these means vary proprietary interests and must in every such case consider whether an indefinite order is required in order to protect the child from the likelihood of significant harm, and to achieve a result which is just.'

In relation to (4) above, the issue of whether the court had jurisdiction to make injunctive orders against the father of three girls who were at risk of FGM being committed against them, to not only protect them but also their mother, was considered in *Re E (Children) (Female Genital Mutilation Protection Orders)* [2015] 2 FLR 997, FD. On the facts, the order was granted but Holman J observed that although the provisions of FGMA 2003, Sch 2, para 1(3) were wide enough for such relief to be granted, it was important not to allow these powers to become stretched to provide protection for somebody else, e g the mother in the case. If the mother needed protection she should apply for protection under FLA 1996. It is submitted that where the safety and protection of the children depends also on the safety and protection of their primary carer the Act is wide enough to make the appropriate orders but in any event the powers under SCA 1981, s 37 can be used, as suggested in *C v K*, above

Where a care order is made in favour of a local authority, the authority has parental responsibility for the child, and it can be argued that the jurisdiction under SCA 1981, s 37 and CCA 1984, s 38 may be invoked to protect its rights to exercise that parental responsibility appropriately and, in particular, to protect the child. Therefore, in an appropriate case, application may be made for injunctive relief by the local authority against a parent or a third party, pursuant to the power conferred by SCA 1981, s 37 or CCA 1984, s 38 instead of invoking the court's inherent jurisdiction, provided that it can be shown that, if the jurisdiction is not exercised, the child is likely to suffer significant harm. The court's inherent jurisdiction may be relied on where injunctive relief under any other provision proves impossible, provided it is necessary to protect the child from significant harm, and it is needed to enable the party with parental responsibility to exercise that legal right appropriately and effectively (*Re P (Care Orders: Injunctive Relief)* [2000] 2 FLR 385, FD). This is best illustrated in relation to the court's powers to make an exclusion order and accept undertakings under CA 1989, ss 38 and 44, respectively. However, the remedy available under ss 38A and 38B, and ss 44A and 44B, is limited in its nature and extent and is subject to the conditions set out in those sections. It is therefore submitted that the decision in *C v K* will continue to be of importance to cover both private and public law cases, which do not come within any statutory provisions, to provide relief where it is required to enable a person or body with parental responsibility to exercise those rights and duties.

Inherent jurisdiction and forced marriages—The Forced Marriage (Civil Protection) Act 2007 is in force (see FLA 1996, s 63B).

101 Effect of orders as between England and Wales and Northern Ireland, the Channel Islands or the Isle of Man

(1) The Secretary of State may make regulations providing –

(a) for prescribed orders which –

(i) are made by a court in Northern Ireland; and

(ii) appear to the Secretary of State to correspond in their effect to orders which may be made under any provision of this Act,

to have effect in prescribed circumstances, for prescribed purposes of this Act, as if they were orders of a prescribed kind made under this Act;

(b) for prescribed orders which –

(i) are made by a court in England and Wales; and

(ii) appear to the Secretary of State to correspond in their effect to orders which may be made under any provision in force in Northern Ireland,

to have effect in prescribed circumstances, for prescribed purposes of the law of Northern Ireland, as if they were orders of a prescribed kind made in Northern Ireland.

(2) Regulations under subsection (1) may provide for the order concerned to cease to have effect for the purposes of the law of Northern Ireland, or (as the case may be) the law of England and Wales, if prescribed conditions are satisfied.

(3) The Secretary of State may make regulations providing for prescribed orders which –

(a) are made by a court in the Isle of Man or in any of the Channel Islands; and

(b) appear to the Secretary of State to correspond in their effect to orders which may be made under this Act,

to have effect in prescribed circumstances for prescribed purposes of this Act, as if they were orders of a prescribed kind made under this Act.

(4) Where a child who is in the care of a local authority is lawfully taken to live in Northern Ireland, the Isle of Man or in any of the Channel Islands, the care order in question shall cease to have effect if the conditions prescribed in regulations by the Secretary of State are satisfied.

(5) Any regulations made under this section may –

(a) make such consequential amendments (including repeals) in –

(i) section 25 of the Children and Young Persons Act 1969 (transfers between England and Wales and Northern Ireland); or

(ii) section 26 (transfers between England and Wales and Channel Islands or Isle of Man) of that Act,

as the Secretary of State considers necessary or expedient; and

(b) modify any provision of this Act, in its application (by virtue of the regulations) in relation to an order made otherwise than in England and Wales.

Defined terms—'prescribed': s 105(1).

Scope—This section gives reciprocal effect to orders as between England, Northern Ireland, the Channel Islands and the Isle of Man. It complements the provisions under Sch 2, para 19(2),(3)(d), which permit the local authority to arrange for a child in its care to live outside England and Wales. If a child who is the subject of a care order is moved to live in Northern Ireland, the Channel Islands or the Isle of Man, the care order may be transferred in accordance with regulations to the public authority there (see s 101(4) and Children

(Prescribed Orders – Northern Ireland, Guernsey and Isle of Man) Regulations 1991). Where a child is lawfully moved, the care order ceases to have effect if the conditions prescribed in the regulations are satisfied.

Search warrants

102 Power of constable to assist in exercise of certain powers to search for children or inspect premises

(1) Where, on an application made by any person for a warrant under this section, it appears to the court –

(a) that a person attempting to exercise powers under any enactment mentioned in subsection (6) has been prevented from doing so by being refused entry to the premises concerned or refused access to the child concerned; or

(b) that any such person is likely to be so prevented from exercising any such powers,

it may issue a warrant authorising any constable to assist that person in the exercise of those powers, using reasonable force if necessary.

(2) Every warrant issued under this section shall be addressed to, and executed by, a constable who shall be accompanied by the person applying for the warrant if –

(a) that person so desires; and

(b) the court by whom the warrant is issued does not direct otherwise.

(3) A court granting an application for a warrant under this section may direct that the constable concerned may, in executing the warrant, be accompanied by a registered medical practitioner, registered nurse or registered midwife if he so chooses.

(3A) The reference in subsection (3) to a registered midwife is to such a midwife who is also registered in the Specialist Community Public Health Nurses' Part of the register maintained under article 5 of the Nursing and Midwifery Order 2001.

(4) An application for a warrant under this section shall be made in the manner and form prescribed by rules of court.

(5) Where –

(a) an application for a warrant under this section relates to a particular child; and

(b) it is reasonably practicable to do so,

the application and any warrant granted on the application shall name the child; and where it does not name him it shall describe him as clearly as possible.

(6) The enactments are –

(a) sections 62, 64, 67, 76, 80, 86 and 87;

(b) paragraph 8(1)(b) and (2)(b) of Schedule 3;

(c) *(repealed)*

Amendments—ACA 2002, s 139(1),(3), Sch 3, paras 54, 69; SI 2002/253; SI 2004/1771.

Defined terms—'child': s 105(1).

'manner and form prescribed by rules of court' (s 102(4))—FPR 2010, r 12.16 allows an application under this section to be made without notice, in which case r 2.6(1)(a) empowers a single justice to determine it. The proceedings are not 'specified proceedings' for the purposes of s 41(6). Form C19 in FPR 2010, r 5 and PD5A is the form prescribed (under the 2010 Rules the format of orders and warrants is no longer prescribed – for an example of the format of the warrant see the former FPC(CA 1989)R 1991, Sch 1, Form 28).

General

103 Offences by bodies corporate

(1) This section applies where any offence under this Act is committed by a body corporate.

(2) If the offence is proved to have been committed with the consent or connivance of or to be attributable to any neglect on the part of any director, manager, secretary or other similar officer

of the body corporate, or any person who was purporting to act in any such capacity, he (as well as the body corporate) shall be guilty of the offence and shall be liable to be proceeded against and punished accordingly.

104 Regulations and orders

(1) Any power of the Lord Chancellor, the Treasury, the Secretary of State or the National Assembly for Wales under this Act to make an order, regulations, or rules, except an order under section 56(4)(a), 57(3), 84 or 97(4) or paragraph 1(1) of Schedule 4, shall be exercisable by statutory instrument.

(2) Any such statutory instrument, except one made under section 4(1B), 4ZA(3), 17(4), 107 or 108(2) or one containing regulations which fall within subsection (3AA), (3AB), (3B), (3BA) or (3C), shall be subject to annulment in pursuance of a resolution of either House of Parliament.

(2A) *(repealed)*

(3A) An order under section 4(1B), 4ZA(3) or 17(4) or regulations which fall within subsection (3AA), (3AB), (3B), (3BA) or (3C) shall not be made by the Secretary of State unless a draft of the statutory instrument containing the order or regulations has been laid before, and approved by a resolution of, each House of Parliament.

(3AA) Regulations fall within this subsection if they are regulations made in the exercise of the power conferred by section 17ZB(9).

(3AB) Regulations fall within this subsection if they are regulations made in the exercise of the power conferred by section 17ZE(5).

(3B) Regulations fall within this subsection if they are the first regulations to be made by the Secretary of State in the exercise of the power conferred by section 23C(5B)(b).

(3BA) Regulations fall within this subsection if they are regulations made in the exercise of the power conferred by section 31(3C) or 32(9).

(3C) Regulations fall within this subsection if they are the first regulations to be made by the Secretary of State in the exercise of the power conferred by paragraph 6(2) of Schedule 2.

(4) Any statutory instrument made under this Act may –

(a) make different provision for different cases;
(b) provide for exemptions from any of its provisions; and
(c) contain incidental, supplemental and transitional provisions.

Amendments—Care Standards Act 2000, s 117, Sch 6; ACA 2002, s 111; Tax Credits Act 2002, s 47, Sch 3; CAA 2006, s 15(1), Sch 2, paras 7, 10; HFEA 2008, s 56, Sch 6, para 30; CYPA 2008, ss 39, 42, Sch 3, paras 1, 25, Sch 4, SI 2009/1892; CFA 2014, ss 16, 96, 97.

104A Regulations made by the Welsh Ministers under section 31A or Part 7

(1) Any power of the Welsh Ministers under section 31A or Part 7 to make regulations shall be exercisable by statutory instrument.

(2) Any such statutory instrument shall be subject to annulment in pursuance of a resolution of the National Assembly for Wales.

Amendments—Inserted by CYPA 2008, s 39, Sch 3, paras 1, 26. Substituted by SI 2016/413.

105 Interpretation

(1) In this Act –

'activity condition' has the meaning given by section 11C;
'activity direction' has the meaning given by section 11A;
'adoption agency' means a body which may be referred to as an adoption agency by virtue of section 2 of the Adoption and Children Act 2002;
'bank holiday' means a day which is a bank holiday under the Banking and Financial Dealings Act 1971;
'care home' has the same meaning as in the Care Standards Act 2000;

'care order' has the meaning given by section 31(11) and also includes any order which by or under any enactment has the effect of, or is deemed to be, a care order for the purposes of this Act; and any reference to a child who is in the care of an authority is a reference to a child who is in their care by virtue of a care order;

'child' means, subject to paragraph 16 of Schedule 1, a person under the age of eighteen;

'child arrangements order' has the meaning given by section 8(1);

'child assessment order' has the meaning given by section 43(2);

'child minder' has the meaning given by section 71;

'child of the family', in relation to parties to a marriage, or to two people who are civil partners of each other, means –

(a) a child of both of them, and

(b) any other child, other than a child placed with them as foster parents by a local authority or voluntary organisation, who has been treated by both of them as a child of their family;

'children's home' has the same meaning as it has for the purposes of the Care Standards Act 2000 (see section 1 of that Act);

'clinical commissioning group' means a body established under section 14D of the National Health Service Act 2006;

'community home' has the meaning given by section 53;

...

'day care' (except in Part XA) has the same meaning as in section 18;

'disabled', in relation to a child, has the same meaning as in section 17(11);

'domestic premises' has the meaning given by section 71(12);

'dwelling-house' includes –

(a) any building or part of a building which is occupied as a dwelling;

(b) any caravan, house-boat or structure which is occupied as a dwelling;

and any yard, garden, garage or outhouse belonging to it and occupied with it;

'education functions' has the meaning given by section 579(1) of the Education Act 1996;

'education supervision order' has the meaning given in section 36;

'emergency protection order' means an order under section 44;

'enforcement order' has the meaning given by section 11J;

'family assistance order' has the meaning given in section 16(2);

'family proceedings' has the meaning given by section 8(3);

'functions' includes powers and duties;

'guardian of a child' means a guardian (other than a guardian of the estate of a child) appointed in accordance with the provisions of section 5;

'harm' has the same meaning as in section 31(9) and the question of whether harm is significant shall be determined in accordance with section 31(10);

'Health Authority' means a Health Authority established under section 8 of the National Health Service Act 1977;

'health service hospital' has the same meaning as in the National Health Service Act 1977;

'hospital' (except in Schedule 9A) has the same meaning as in the Mental Health Act 1983, except that it does not include a hospital at which high security psychiatric services within the meaning of that Act are provided;

'ill-treatment' has the same meaning as in section 31(9);

'income-based jobseeker's allowance' has the same meaning as in the Jobseekers Act 1995;

'income-related employment and support allowance' means an income-related allowance under Part 1 of the Welfare Reform Act 2007 (employment and support allowance);

'independent hospital' has the same meaning as in the Care Standards Act 2000;

'independent school' has the same meaning as in the Education Act 1996;

'local authority' means, in relation to England, the council of a county, a metropolitan district, a London Borough or the Common Council of the City of London, in relation to Wales, the council of a county or a county borough and, in relation to Scotland, a local authority within the meaning of section 1(2) of the Social Work (Scotland) Act 1968;

'local authority foster parent' means a person authorised as such in accordance with regulations made by virtue of –
(a) paragraph 12F of Schedule 2; or
(b) sections 87 and 93 of the Social Services and Well-being (Wales) Act 2014 (regulations providing for approval of local authority foster parents);

'Local Health Board' means a Local Health Board established under section 11 of the National Health Service (Wales) Act 2006;

'local housing authority' has the same meaning as in the Housing Act 1985;

'officer of the Service' has the same meaning as in the Criminal Justice and Court Services Act 2000;

'parental responsibility' has the meaning given in section 3;

'parental responsibility agreement' has the meaning given in sections 4(1), 4ZA(4) and 4A(2);

'prescribed' means prescribed by regulations made under this Act;

…

'private children's home' means a children's home in respect of which a person is registered under Part II of the Care Standards Act 2000 which is not a community home or a voluntary home;

'privately fostered child' and 'to foster a child privately' have the same meaning as in section 66;

'prohibited steps order' has the meaning given by section 8(1);

'registered pupil' has the same meaning as in the Education Act 1996;

'relative', in relation to a child, means a grandparent, brother, sister, uncle or aunt (whether of the full blood or half blood or by marriage or civil partnership) or step-parent;

…

'responsible person', in relation to a child who is the subject of a supervision order, has the meaning given in paragraph 1 of Schedule 3;

'school' has the same meaning as in the Education Act 1996 or, in relation to Scotland, in the Education (Scotland) Act 1980;

'section 31A plan' has the meaning given by section 31A(6);

'service', in relation to any provision made under Part III, includes any facility;

'signed', in relation to any person, includes the making by that person of his mark;

'special educational needs' has the same meaning as in the Education Act 1996;

'special guardian' and 'special guardianship order' have the meaning given by section 14A;

'Special Health Authority' means a Special Health Authority established under section 11 of the National Health Service Act 1977;

'specific issue order' has the meaning given by section 8(1);

…

'supervision order' has the meaning given by section 31(11);

'supervised child' and 'supervisor', in relation to a supervision order or an education supervision order, mean respectively the child who is (or is to be) under supervision and the person under whose supervision he is (or is to be) by virtue of the order;

'upbringing', in relation to any child, includes the care of the child but not his maintenance;

'voluntary home' has the meaning given by section 60;

'voluntary organisation' means a body (other than a public or local authority) whose activities are not carried on for profit;

'Welsh family proceedings officer' has the meaning given by section 35 of the Children Act 2004.

(2) References in this Act to a child whose father and mother were, or (as the case may be) were not, married to each other at the time of his birth must be read with section 1 of the Family Law Reform Act 1987 (which extends the meaning of such references).

(3) *(repealed)*

(4) References in this Act to a child who is looked after –

(a) in relation to a child who is looked after by a local authority in England, has the meaning given in section 22; and

(b) in relation to a child who is looked after by a local authority in Wales, has the meaning given in section 74 of the Social Services and Well-being (Wales) Act 2014 (child or young person looked after by a local authority).

(5) References in this Act to accommodation provided by or on behalf of a local authority are references to accommodation so provided in the exercise of functions of that or any other local authority which are social services functions.

(5A) References in this Act to a child minder shall be construed –

(a) *(repealed)*

(b) in relation to Wales, in accordance with section 79A.

(5B) In subsection (5) 'social services functions' means –

(a) in England, social services functions within the meaning of the Local Authority Social Services Act 1970, and

(b) in Wales, social services functions within the meaning of the Social Services and Well-being (Wales) Act 2014.

(6) In determining the 'ordinary residence' of a child for any purpose of this Act, there shall be disregarded any period in which he lives in any place –

(a) which is a school or other institution;

(b) in accordance with the requirements of a supervision order under this Act;

(ba) in accordance with the requirements of a youth rehabilitation order under Part 1 of the Criminal Justice and Immigration Act 2008; or

(c) while he is being provided with accommodation by or on behalf of a local authority.

(7) References in this Act to children who are in need shall be construed in accordance with section 17.

(7A) References in this Act to a hospital or accommodation made available or provided pursuant to arrangements made by the Secretary of State under the National Health Service Act 2006 are references to a hospital or accommodation made available or provided pursuant to arrangements so made in the exercise of the public health functions of the Secretary of State (within the meaning of that Act).

(7B) References in this Act to arrangements made by the National Health Service Commissioning Board or a clinical commissioning group under the National Health Service Act 2006 include references to arrangements so made by virtue of section 7A of that Act.

(8) Any notice or other document required under this Act to be served on any person may be served on him by being delivered personally to him, or being sent by post to him in a registered letter or by the recorded delivery service at his proper address.

(9) Any such notice or other document required to be served on a body corporate or a firm shall be duly served if it is served on the secretary or clerk of that body or a partner of that firm.

(10) For the purposes of this section, and of section 7 of the Interpretation Act 1978 in its application to this section, the proper address of a person –

(a) in the case of a secretary or clerk of a body corporate, shall be that of the registered or principal office of that body;

(b) in the case of a partner of a firm, shall be that of the principal office of the firm; and

(c) in any other case, shall be the last known address of the person to be served.

Amendments—Registered Homes (Amendment) Act 1991, s 2(6); Local Government (Wales) Act 1994, ss 22, 66, Sch 10, para 13, Sch 18; Health Authorities Act 1995, ss 2, 5 Sch 1, para 118, Sch 3; Jobseekers Act 1995, s 41, Sch 2, para 19; Education Act 1996, s 582(1), Sch 37, Pt I, para 91; FLA 1996, s 52, Sch 6, para 5; Care Standards Act 2000, s 116, Sch 4, para 14(23); CJCSA 2000 s 74, Sch 7, para 95; Local Government Act 2000, s 107(1), Sch 5, para 22; Powers of Criminal Courts (Sentencing) Act 2000, s 165, Sch 9, para 129; SI 2000/90; SI 2002/2469; CA 2004, s 40, Sch 3, paras 5, 11; ACA 2002, Sch 3, para 70; CPA 2004, s 75(1),(3),(4); Childcare Act 2006, s 103, Sch 2, para 17, Sch 3, Pt 2; CAA 2006, s 15(1), Sch 2, paras 7, 11; SI 2007/961; Welfare Reform Act 2007, s 28(1), Sch 3, para 6(1),(5); CYPA 2008, s 8(3), Sch 1,para 3; HFEA 2008, s 56, Sch 6, para 31; Criminal Justice and Immigration Act 2008, ss 6(2), 149, Sch 4, para 36; SI 2010/1185; Health and Social Care Act 2012, s 55(2), Sch 5, para 56; CFA 2014, s 12, Sch 2; SI 2016/413.

'ordinary residence' (s 105(6))—A young child who cannot decide for himself where to live is ordinarily resident in his parents' matrimonial home, and this ordinary residence cannot be changed by one parent without the consent of the other (*Re P (GE) (An Infant)* [1965] Ch 568, CA). If a child's parents are living apart and they have agreed that the child is to live with one of them, he is ordinarily resident in the home of that one and his ordinary residence is not changed just because the other parent removes the child from that home (*Re P* (above)). In *London Borough of Southwark v B* [1993] 2 FLR 559, CA, a young child, in respect of whom the local authority was about to issue care proceedings, was removed from England to Algeria by her mother. It was held that the local authority still had locus standi to apply for a return order. The precipitate way in which she was removed, and the very limited information available as to the nature or permanence of the arrangements for her accommodation in Algeria, gave the judge ample justification for treating the child as being 'ordinarily resident' in the area of the authority at the date of the application for the return order.

Subsection 105(6) is closely allied to s 31(8) and the interrelationship between the provisions was considered by the Court of Appeal in *Northamptonshire County Council v Islington County Council* [1999] 2 FLR 881, CA, where Thorpe LJ held that s 31(8) and s 105(6) are to be construed in a way which provides a simple mechanism to determine the question of administration. The subsections are not about child protection or the promotion of child welfare. They are to be read as a simple test to determine which local authority is to be responsible for the care plan and its implementation. It is not appropriate to apply the s 1(3) checklist to this determination. In *C (A Child) v Plymouth County Council* [2000] 1 FLR 875, CA, the Court of Appeal reiterated that the *Northamptonshire* case was not meant to give judges a discretionary exit from the plain application of the statutory mechanisms of ss 31 and 105, but only to indicate that the simple rules of construction should be sufficient to determine all but the most exceptional cases. Where the child is not accommodated by the local authority, because the local authority permits the child to reside with (i) a parent, (ii) a person with parental responsibility or (iii) a person who was the holder of a child arrangements order before the care proceedings commenced under an interim care order, s 105(6)(c) does not apply and the court is free to apply conventional principles to the definition of 'ordinary residence', see *Re C (Care Order: Appropriate Local Authority)* [1997] 1 FLR 544, FD. The decision in *Re H (Care Order: Appropriate Local Authority)* [2004] 1 FLR 534, CA, where the Court of Appeal applied the same principle to a placement with grandparents, does not survive amendments to the 1989 Act and the provisions of s 22. Accordingly, placement with a relative who does not satisfy condition (i), (ii) or (iii) above is caught by the provisions of s 105(6) and the 'disregard' has to be applied: *Sheffield CC v Bradford CC* [2013] 1 FLR 1027, FD. See also *Kirklees MBC v London Borough of Brent* [2004] 2 FLR 800, FD. A useful list of the principles to be applied when considering the application of ss 31(8) and 105(6) is set out at [24] of *London Borough of Redbridge v Newport City Council* [2004] 2 FLR 226, FD. See also **'designated local authority'** under s 31. Where the mother is herself a child in the care of a local authority but resides with her child in the area of another local authority, the provisions of s 105(6) do not apply for the purpose of determining the child's ordinary residence. It is a question of fact: *Re D (Local Authority Responsibility)* [2013] 2 FLR 673, CA.

106 Financial provisions

(1) Any –

(a) grants made by the Secretary of State under this Act; and

(b) any other expenses incurred by the Secretary of State under this Act,

shall be payable out of money provided by Parliament.

(2) Any sums received by the Secretary of State under section 58, or by way of the repayment of any grant made under section 82(2) or (4) shall be paid into the Consolidated Fund.

107 Application to Channel Islands

Her Majesty may by Order in Council direct that any of the provisions of this Act shall extend to any of the Channel Islands with such exceptions and modifications as may be specified in the Order.

108 Short title, commencement, extent etc

(1) This Act may be cited as the Children Act 1989.

(2) Sections 89 and 96(3) to (7), and paragraph 35 of Schedule 12, shall come into force on the passing of this Act and paragraph 36 of Schedule 12 shall come into force at the end of the period of two months beginning with the day on which this Act is passed but otherwise this Act shall come into force on such date as may be appointed by order made by the Lord Chancellor or the Secretary of State, or by both acting jointly.

(3) Different dates may be appointed for different provisions of this Act in relation to different cases.

(4) The minor amendments set out in Schedule 12 shall have effect.

(5) The consequential amendments set out in Schedule 13 shall have effect.

(6) The transitional provisions and savings set out in Schedule 14 shall have effect.

(7) The repeals set out in Schedule 15 shall have effect.

(8) An order under subsection (2) may make such transitional provisions or savings as appear to the person making the order to be necessary or expedient in connection with the provisions brought into force by the order, including –

(a) provisions adding to or modifying the provisions of Schedule 14; and
(b) such adaptations –
(i) of the provisions brought into force by the order; and
(ii) of any provisions of this Act then in force,
as appear to him necessary or expedient in consequence of the partial operation of this Act.

(9) The Lord Chancellor may by order make such amendments or repeals, in such enactments as may be specified in the order, as appear to him to be necessary or expedient in consequence of any provision of this Act.

(10) This Act shall, in its application to the Isles of Scilly, have effect subject to such exceptions, adaptations and modifications as the Secretary of State may by order prescribe.

(11) The following provisions of this Act extend to Scotland –

section 19;
section 25(8);
section 50(13);
Part X;
section 80(1)(h) and (i), (2) to (4), (5)(a), (b) and (h) and (6) to (12);
section 88;
section 104 (so far as necessary);
section 105 (so far as necessary);
subsections (1) to (3), (8) and (9) and this subsection;
in Schedule 2, paragraph 24;
in Schedule 12, paragraphs 1, 7 to 10, 18, 27, 30(a) and 41 to 44;
in Schedule 13, paragraphs 18 to 23, 32, 46, 47, 50, 57, 62, 63, 68(a), (b) and 71;
in Schedule 14, paragraphs 1, 33 and 34;
in Schedule 15, the entries relating to –
(a) the Custody of Children Act 1891;
(b) the Nurseries and Child Minders Regulation Act 1948;
(c) section 53(3) of the Children and Young Persons Act 1963;
(d) section 60 of the Health Services and Public Health Act 1968;
(e) the Social Work (Scotland) Act 1968;
(f) the Adoption (Scotland) Act 1978;
(g) the Child Care Act 1980;
(h) the Foster Children (Scotland) Act 1984;
(i) the Child Abduction and Custody Act 1985; and
(j) the Family Law Act 1986.

(12) The following provisions of this Act extend to Northern Ireland –

section 101(1)(b), (2) and (5)(a)(i);
subsections (1) to (3), (8) and (9) and this subsection;
in Schedule 2, paragraph 24;
in Schedule 12, paragraphs 7 to 10, 18 and 27;
in Schedule 13, paragraphs 21, 22, 46, 47, 57, 62, 63, 68(c) to (e) and 69 to 71;
in Schedule 14, paragraphs 28 to 30 and 38(a); and
in Schedule 15, the entries relating to the Guardianship of Minors Act 1971, the Children Act 1975, the Child Care Act 1980, and the Family Law Act 1986.

Amendments—CLSA 1990, ss 116, 125(7), Sch 16, para 25, Sch 20.

SCHEDULE A1
ENFORCEMENT ORDERS

PART I
UNPAID WORK REQUIREMENT

1 General

Subject to the modifications in paragraphs 2 and 3, Chapter 4 of Part 12 of the Criminal Justice Act 2003 has effect in relation to an enforcement order as it has effect in relation to a community order (within the meaning of Part 12 of that Act).

2 References to an offender

Subject to paragraph 3, references in Chapter 4 of Part 12 of the Criminal Justice Act 2003 to an offender are to be treated as including references to a person subject to an enforcement order.

3 Specific modifications

(1) *(repealed)*

(2) In section 198 (duties of responsible officer) –

(a) *(repealed)*
(b) after subsection (1) insert –

'(1A) Subsection (1B) applies where –

(a) an enforcement order is in force, and
(b) an officer of the Children and Family Court Advisory and Support Service or a Welsh family proceedings officer (as defined in section 35 of the Children Act 2004) is required under section 11M of the Children Act 1989 to report on matters relating to the order.

(1B) The officer of the Service or the Welsh family proceedings officer may request the responsible officer to report to him on such matters relating to the order as he may require for the purpose of making a report under section 11M(1)(c) or (d); and it shall be the duty of the responsible officer to comply with such a request.'

(3) In section 199 (unpaid work requirement) –

(a) in subsection (2) (minimum and maximum hours of unpaid work) for paragraph (b) substitute –
'(b) not more than 200.',
(b) omit subsections (3) and (4), and
(c) in subsection (5) for the words from the beginning to 'of them' substitute 'Where on the same occasion and in relation to the same person the court makes more than one enforcement order imposing an unpaid work requirement'.

(4) In section 200 (obligations of person subject to unpaid work requirement), for subsection (2) substitute –

'(2) Subject to paragraphs 7 and 9 of Schedule A1 to the Children Act 1989, the work required to be performed under an unpaid work requirement imposed by an enforcement order must be performed during a period of twelve months.

(2A) But the period of twelve months is not to run while the enforcement order is suspended under section 11J(9) of the Children Act 1989.'

(5) Section 217 (requirement to avoid conflict with religious beliefs, etc) is omitted.

(6) In section 218 (availability of arrangements in local area), subsection (1) (condition for imposition of unpaid work requirement) is omitted.

(7) Section 219 (provision of copies of relevant order) is omitted.

(8) The power of the Secretary of State to make rules under section 222 in relation to persons subject to relevant orders may also be exercised in relation to persons subject to enforcement orders.

(9) The power of the Secretary of State by order under section 223(1) to amend the provision mentioned in section 223(1)(a) includes power to amend this Part so as to make such modifications of Chapter 4 of Part 12 of the Criminal Justice Act 2003 as appear to the Secretary of State to be necessary or expedient in consequence of any amendment of the provision mentioned in section 223(1)(a).

Amendments—Offender Rehabilitation Act 2014, s 14, Sch 4, para 9.

PART II
REVOCATION, AMENDMENT OR BREACH OF ENFORCEMENT ORDER

4 Power to revoke

(1) This paragraph applies where a court has made an enforcement order in respect of a person's failure to comply with a provision of a child arrangements order and the enforcement order is in force.

(2) The court may revoke the enforcement order if it appears to the court that –

- (a) in all the circumstances no enforcement order should have been made,
- (b) having regard to circumstances which have arisen since the enforcement order was made, it would be appropriate for the enforcement order to be revoked, or
- (c) having regard to the person's satisfactory compliance with the contact order or any child arrangements order that has effect in its place, it would be appropriate for the enforcement order to be revoked.

(3) The enforcement order may be revoked by the court under sub-paragraph (2) of its own motion or on an application by the person subject to the enforcement order.

(4) In deciding whether to revoke the enforcement order under sub-paragraph (paragraph (2)(b), the court is to take into account –

- (a) the extent to which the person subject to the enforcement order has complied with it, and
- (b) the likelihood that the person will comply with the child arrangements order or any contact order that has effect in its place in the absence of an enforcement order.

(5) In deciding whether to revoke the enforcement order under sub-paragraph (2)(c), the court is to take into account the likelihood that the person will comply with the child arrangements order or any contact order that has effect in its place in the absence of an enforcement order.

Amendments—CFA 2014, s 12, Sch 2.

5 Amendment by reason of change of residence

(1) This paragraph applies where a court has made an enforcement order in respect of a person's failure to comply with a provision of a child arrangements order and the enforcement order is in force.

(2) If the court is satisfied that the person has changed, or proposes to change, his residence from the local justice area specified in the order to another local justice area, the court may amend the order by substituting the other area for the area specified.

(3) The enforcement order may be amended by the court under sub-paragraph (2) of its own motion or on an application by the person subject to the enforcement order.

Amendments—CFA 2014, s 12, Sch 2.

6 Amendment of hours specified under unpaid work requirement

(1) This paragraph applies where a court has made an enforcement order in respect of a person's failure to comply with a provision of a child arrangements order and the enforcement order is in force.

(2) If it appears to the court that, having regard to circumstances that have arisen since the enforcement order was made, it would be appropriate to do so, the court may reduce the number of hours specified in the order (but not below the minimum specified in section 199(2)(a) of the Criminal Justice Act 2003).

(3) In amending the enforcement order under sub-paragraph (2), the court must be satisfied that the effect on the person of the enforcement order as proposed to be amended is no more than is required to secure his compliance with the contact order or any child arrangements order that has effect in its place.

(4) The enforcement order may be amended by the court under sub-paragraph (2) of its own motion or on an application by the person subject to the enforcement order.

Amendments—CFA 2014, s 12, Sch 2.

7 Amendment to extend unpaid work requirement

(1) This paragraph applies where a court has made an enforcement order in respect of a person's failure to comply with a provision of a child arrangements order and the enforcement order is in force.

(2) If it appears to the court that, having regard to circumstances that have arisen since the enforcement order was made, it would be appropriate to do so, the court may, in relation to the order, extend the period of twelve months specified in section 200(2) of the Criminal Justice Act 2003 (as substituted by paragraph 3).

(3) The period may be extended by the court under sub-paragraph (2) of its own motion or on an application by the person subject to the enforcement order.

Amendments—CFA 2014, s 12, Sch 2.

8 Warning and report following breach

(1) This paragraph applies where a court has made an enforcement order in respect of a person's failure to comply with a provision of a child arrangements order.

(2) If the responsible officer is of the opinion that the person has failed without reasonable excuse to comply with the unpaid work requirement imposed by the enforcement order, the officer must give the person a warning under this paragraph unless –

(a) the person has within the previous twelve months been given a warning under this paragraph in relation to a failure to comply with the unpaid work requirement, or

(b) the responsible officer reports the failure to the appropriate person.

(3) A warning under this paragraph must –

(a) describe the circumstances of the failure,

(b) state that the failure is unacceptable, and

(c) inform the person that, if within the next twelve months he again fails to comply with the unpaid work requirement, the warning and the subsequent failure will be reported to the appropriate person.

(4) The responsible officer must, as soon as practicable after the warning has been given, record that fact.

(5) If –

(a) the responsible officer has given a warning under this paragraph to a person subject to an enforcement order, and

(b) at any time within the twelve months beginning with the date on which the warning was given, the responsible officer is of the opinion that the person has since that date failed without reasonable excuse to comply with the unpaid work requirement imposed by the enforcement order,

the officer must report the failure to the appropriate person.

(6) A report under sub-paragraph (5) must include a report of the warning given to the person subject to the enforcement order.

(7) The appropriate person, in relation to an enforcement order, is the officer of the Service or the Welsh family proceedings officer who is required under section 11M to report on matters relating to the enforcement order.

(8) 'Responsible officer', in relation to a person subject to an enforcement order, has the same meaning as in section 197 of the Criminal Justice Act 2003 (as modified by paragraph 2).

Amendments—CFA 2014, s 12, Sch 2.

9 Breach of an enforcement order

(1) This paragraph applies where a court has made an enforcement order ('the first order') in respect of a person's failure to comply with a provision of a child arrangements order.

(2) If the court is satisfied beyond reasonable doubt that the person has failed to comply with the unpaid work requirement imposed by the first order, the court may –

- (a) amend the first order so as to make the requirement more onerous, or
- (b) make an enforcement order ('the second order') in relation to the person and (if the first order is still in force) provide for the second order to have effect either in addition to or in substitution for the first order.

(3) But the court may not exercise its powers under sub-paragraph (2) if it is satisfied that the person had a reasonable excuse for failing to comply with the unpaid work requirement imposed by the first order.

(4) The burden of proof as to the matter mentioned in sub-paragraph (3) lies on the person claiming to have had a reasonable excuse, and the standard of proof is the balance of probabilities.

(5) The court may exercise its powers under sub-paragraph (2) in relation to the first order only on the application of a person who would be able to apply under section 11J for an enforcement order if the failure to comply with the first order were a failure to comply with a provision of the child arrangements order to which the first order relates.

(6) Where the person proposing to apply to the court is the child with respect to whom the child arrangements order was made, subsections (6) and (7) of section 11J have effect in relation to the application as they have effect in relation to an application for an enforcement order.

(7) An application to the court to exercise its powers under sub-paragraph (2) may only be made while the first order is in force.

(8) The court may not exercise its powers under sub-paragraph (2) in respect of a failure by the person to comply with the unpaid work requirement imposed by the first order unless it is satisfied that before the failure occurred the person had been given (in accordance with rules of court) a copy of, or otherwise informed of the terms of, a notice under section 11N relating to the first order.

(9) In dealing with the person under sub-paragraph (2)(a), the court may –

- (a) increase the number of hours specified in the first order (but not above the maximum specified in section 199(2)(b) of the Criminal Justice Act 2003, as substituted by paragraph 3);
- (b) in relation to the order, extend the period of twelve months specified in section 200(2) of the Criminal Justice Act 2003 (as substituted by paragraph 3).

(10) In exercising its powers under sub-paragraph (2), the court must be satisfied that, taking into account the extent to which the person has complied with the unpaid work requirement imposed by the first order, the effect on the person of the proposed exercise of those powers –

- (a) is no more than is required to secure his compliance with the contact order or any child arrangements order that has effect in its place, and
- (b) is no more than is proportionate to the seriousness of his failures to comply with the provisions of the child arrangements order and with the first order.

(11) Where the court exercises its powers under sub-paragraph (2) by making an enforcement order in relation to a person who has failed to comply with another enforcement order –

- (a) sections 11K(4), 11L(2) to (7), 11M and 11N have effect as regards the making of the order in relation to the person as they have effect as regards the making of an enforcement order in relation to a person who has failed to comply with a provision of a child arrangements order;

(b) this Part of this Schedule has effect in relation to the order so made as if it were an enforcement order made in respect of the failure for which the other order was made.

(12) Sub-paragraph (2) is without prejudice to section 63(3) of the Magistrates' Courts Act 1980 as it applies in relation to enforcement orders.

Amendments—CFA 2014, s 12, Sch 2.

10 Provision relating to amendment of enforcement orders

Sections 11L(2) to (7) and 11M have effect in relation to the making of an order under paragraph 6(2), 7(2) or 9(2)(a) amending an enforcement order as they have effect in relation to the making of an enforcement order; and references in sections 11L(2) to (7) and 11M to an enforcement order are to be read accordingly.

Amendments—Schedule inserted by CAA 2006, s 4(2), Sch 1.

SCHEDULE 1
FINANCIAL PROVISION FOR CHILDREN

1 Orders for financial relief against parents

(1) On an application made by a parent, guardian or special guardian of a child, or by any person who is named in a child arrangements order as a person with whom a child is to live, the court may make one or more of the orders mentioned in sub-paragraph (2).

(2) The orders referred to in sub-paragraph (1) are –

(a) an order requiring either or both parents of a child –
   (i) to make to the applicant for the benefit of the child; or
   (ii) to make to the child himself,
   such periodical payments, for such term, as may be specified in the order;

(b) an order requiring either or both parents of a child –
   (i) to secure to the applicant for the benefit of the child; or
   (ii) to secure to the child himself,
   such periodical payments, for such term, as may be so specified;

(c) an order requiring either or both parents of a child –
   (i) to pay to the applicant for the benefit of the child; or
   (ii) to pay to the child himself,
   such lump sum as may be so specified;

(d) an order requiring a settlement to be made for the benefit of the child, and to the satisfaction of the court, of property –
   (i) to which either parent is entitled (either in possession or in reversion); and
   (ii) which is specified in the order;

(e) an order requiring either or both parents of a child –
   (i) to transfer to the applicant, for the benefit of the child; or
   (ii) to transfer to the child himself,
   such property to which the parent is, or the parents are, entitled (either in possession or in reversion) as may be specified in the order.

(3) The powers conferred by this paragraph may be exercised at any time.

(4) An order under sub-paragraph (2)(a) or (b) may be varied or discharged by a subsequent order made on the application of any person by or to whom payments were required to be made under the previous order.

(5) Where a court makes an order under this paragraph –

(a) it may at any time make a further such order under sub-paragraph (2)(a), (b) or (c) with respect to the child concerned if he has not reached the age of eighteen;

(b) it may not make more than one order under sub-paragraph (2)(d) or (e) against the same person in respect of the same child.

(6) On making, varying or discharging a special guardianship order, or on making, varying or discharging provision in a child arrangements order with respect to the living arrangements of a child, the court may exercise any of its powers under this Schedule even though no application has been made to it under this Schedule.

(6A) For the purposes of sub-paragraph (6) provision in a child arrangements order is with respect to the living arrangements of a child if it regulates arrangements relating to –

(a) with whom the child is to live, or

(b) when the child is to live with any person.

(7) Where a child is a ward of court, the court may exercise any of its powers under this Schedule even though no application has been made to it.

Amendments—CLSA 1990, s 116, Sch 16, para 10(2); ACA 2002, Sch 3, para 71; CCA 2013, s 17, Sch 11; CFA 2014, s 12, Sch 2.

Scope—Subject to CSA 1991, which restricts the court's power to order child maintenance (see Procedural Guide A2), this provision enables the High Court and the Family Court to make orders for periodical payments, secured periodical payments, lump sum(s), settlement of property or transfer of property. Magistrates' courts may make periodical payments, secured periodical payments or a lump sum order. The power is irrespective of whether the parents are married. The court may make an order without an application being made where a child arrangements order is made, varied or discharged, or on application by a parent, guardian or holder of a child arrangements order. The child must be aged under 18, but para 3 allows a periodical payments order to be extended for a child over 18 in tertiary education or where special circumstances apply. There is no jurisdiction to make an order against a father for the benefit of the mother's children by a different partner: *Morgan v Hill* [2007] 1 FLR 1480, CA. The applicant party is required to hold a child arrangements order for the child: where a mother had become the non-resident parent, her claim for the provision of a home for herself was dismissed and her claim for periodical payments was found to be in contravention of CSA 1991, s 8(1),(3) and also dismissed: *N v C (Financial Provision; Schedule 1 Claims Dismissed)* [2013] EWHC 399 (Fam)). A 'top up' periodical payments order for the benefit of a child is not permissible unless the Child Maintenance Service has made a maximum assessment in relation to the respondent's income, i e an assessment based on a gross weekly income in excess of £3,000 (*Dickson v Rennie* [2015] 2 FLR 978, FD).

The words 'for the benefit of the child' in para 1(2) include financial and welfare benefit. The power of the court is construed widely, where a benefit to the mother also benefits the child. In *Re S (Child: Financial Provision)* [2005] 2 FLR 94, CA, the court made a financial order to include the costs of the mother's travel to the Sudan to see the child and to pursue contact: the court has the power to make an order against a parent who is out of the jurisdiction with the child. A parent bringing a Sch 1 application is acting in a quasi-representative capacity for the benefit of the child and may be entitled to an interim costs order to pursue the application: see *M-T v T* [2007] 2 FLR 925, FD, disapproving *W v J (Child: variation of financial provision)* [2004] 2 FLR 300, FD, where the court had declined to make a costs order because it was held to benefit the mother, not the child. The width of the court's jurisdiction is shown in *MB v KB* [2007] 2 FLR 586, FD, where a mother who had secured periodical payments and the right to reside in a house owned by the husband's family under MCA 1973 was permitted to apply for a settlement of property and a lump sum under Sch 1: the application of estoppel was disapproved in cases involving children and a change of circumstances and the child's needs entitled the mother to make her Sch 1 application. The mother may have concluded her own claims for housing, but not the right to claim on behalf of her child. See *PK v BC (Financial Remedies: Schedule 1)* [2012] 2 FLR 1426, FD: jurisdiction to consider a further lump sum existed after a clean break in divorce proceedings, but circumstances had to be exceptional. There was a very high hurdle to be overcome to achieve a further award as to housing, and no jurisdiction to award a car, where there had been a consent order for financial provision in divorce. The wide discretion of the court in respect of capital payments is apparent in *Re M-M (Schedule 1 Provision)* 2 FLR 1391, CA: payment of applicant's credit cards debts, and repairs to her own property, approved in principle. Where a maintenance order is permissible, the starting point is the level of maintenance payable in accordance with the statutory child support formula, as in *GW v RW (Financial Provision: Departure from Equality)* [2003] 2 FLR 108, FD; *SW v RC* [2008] 1 FLR 1703, FD. An income order may take account of bonus payments, but overall should be at CSA levels: *Re M–M* above. The concept of a carer's allowance, used historically to enhance an award, was deemed inappropriate in *PG v TW (No 2) (Child: Financial Provision)* [2014] 1 FLR 923, FD; the court instead should provide the resources for back-up childcare and housekeeping to allow the mother to go out to work without anxiety. It is not permitted for the primary carer to 'profit' from a periodical payments order for the benefit of a child pursuant to Sch 1.

Power to order lump sum—There is jurisdiction to order a lump sum, which may be used for the applicant's costs. A lump sum is not precluded by CSA 1991, s 8, which prohibits maintenance awards by the court for a child: however, care must be taken to ensure that any lump sum ordered is not, in effect, a payment to make up a shortfall between a CMS maintenance award and a parent's expenditure, see *Dickson v Rennie* [2015] 2 FLR 978, FD, at [38].

Power to transfer/settle property—There is power to transfer property to the applicant for the benefit of the child, or directly to the child, or to settle property upon a child. Property is usually a house for the mother and child to live in; it may include a joint tenancy: *K v K (Minors: Property Transfer)* [1992] 2 FLR 220, CA. Property settled or transferred for the benefit of a child reverts to the settlor/transferor upon the child reaching majority (or some other date agreed by the parents or ordered by the court).

Power to enforce lump sum and transfer of property orders—Where a reluctant father had not complied with orders for the payment of a lump sum to enable the purchase of a property for a child for more than 5 years, the court had the power to order a binding obligation to pay by a fixed date, and in default to consider orders under TLATA 1996 or the inherent jurisdiction to direct the performance of the trust. There was no need for a separate trust deed in straightforward cases where the court order served to set out the terms of the trust arising out of capital provision: *G v A (Financial Remedy: Enforcement) (No 1)* [2012] 1 FLR 389, FD. There was power to order the disclosure of the father's assets to assist the mother in enforcing the order: *G v A (Financial Remedy: Enforcement) (No 2)* [2012] 1 FLR 402, FD. Where there is conflict over the operation of the trust, the court may override or supersede the trust deed and a transfer to the Chancery division is not required: *G v A (Financial Remedy: Enforcement) (No 3)* [2012] 1 FLR 415, FD. Such powers may include the discharge of one party's trustee: *G v A (Financial Remedy: Enforcement) (No 4)* [2012] 1 FLR 427, FD.

Interim orders—Paragraph 1 gives the court the jurisdiction to make more than one order for a lump sum and to order a lump sum 'at any time', although there is no specific reference to interim lump sum payments: *CF v KM* [2011] 1 FLR 208, FD. There is also jurisdiction to award interim maintenance by way of periodical payments, which may be used for legal costs: *G v G (Child Maintenance: Interim Costs Provision)* [2010] 2 FLR 1264, FD and interim lump sums, which may be used to fund relevant proceedings, for example, an appeal to the CMS First Tier Tribunal against a maintenance assessment: *Dickson v Rennie* [2015] 2 FLR 978, FD).

Power to order a review—The court may order a review of payments, expressed as 'subject to further order of the court', where the father's capital and income is in transition: *FG v MBW (Financial Remedy for Child)* [2012] 1 FLR 152, FD.

Costs allowances in Sch 1 applications—The court retains the discretion to make costs allowances to assist a party with litigation: LASPOA 2012 has restricted judicial discretion in relation to costs orders only in the matrimonial and civil partnership jurisdiction. The approach to costs orders set out in the matrimonial jurisdiction in *Currey v Currey (No 2)* [2007] 1 FLR 946, CA remains good law in relation to Sch 1 applications. There is a risk of unfairness to the payer who funds both sides and may then not be able to recoup his costs. The applicant must demonstrate that she could not reasonably procure legal advice and representation at the appropriate level of expertise by any other means. The court must then have regard to all other relevant circumstances, including the reasonableness of the mother's stance in the proceedings, and the merits of her claim: *G v G (Child Maintenance: Interim Costs Provision)* [2010] 2 FLR 1264, FD. There are advantages flowing from competent representation and equality of arms, which would be of benefit ultimately to the child: see *CF v KM* [2011] 1 FLR 208, FD, following *M-T v T* [2007] 2 FLR 925, FD. The court should conduct a broad-brush approach in relation to costs to avoid a full-blown contested financial hearing, which would not be proportionate. An application for costs allowance in Sch 1 proceedings should be issued without delay: *R v F (Schedule One: Child Maintenance: Mother's Costs of Contact Proceedings)* [2011] 2 FLR 991, FD. The court may take the father's costs as a benchmark, allowing for the extra costs for the mother in making the application: *PG v TW (No 1) (Child: Financial Provision: Legal Funding)* [2014] 1 FLR 508, FD.

Costs orders in Sch 1 applications—The principle of no order for costs is now found in FPR 2010, r 28.3, but Sch 1 proceedings have been excepted from the general rule. Costs may therefore follow the event, although this has been doubted where the mother in Sch 1 proceedings is in effect acting in a representative capacity for the child. However, in appeals under Sch 1, costs should follow the event: *KS v ND (Schedule 1: Appeal: Costs)* [2013] 2 FLR 698, FD.

2 Orders for financial relief for persons over eighteen

(1) If, on an application by a person who has reached the age of eighteen, it appears to the court –

(a) that the applicant is, will be or (if an order were made under this paragraph) would be receiving instruction at an educational establishment or undergoing training for a trade, profession or vocation, whether or not while in gainful employment; or

(b) that there are special circumstances which justify the making of an order under this paragraph,

the court may make one or both of the orders mentioned in sub-paragraph (2).

(2) The orders are –

(a) an order requiring either or both of the applicant's parents to pay to the applicant such periodical payments, for such term, as may be specified in the order;

(b) an order requiring either or both of the applicant's parents to pay to the applicant such lump sum as may be so specified.

(3) An application may not be made under this paragraph by any person if, immediately before he reached the age of sixteen, a periodical payments order was in force with respect to him.

(4) No order shall be made under this paragraph at a time when the parents of the applicant are living with each other in the same household.

(5) An order under sub-paragraph (2)(a) may be varied or discharged by a subsequent order made on the application of any person by or to whom payments were required to be made under the previous order.

(6) In sub-paragraph (3) 'periodical payments order' means an order made under –

(a) this Schedule;
(b) *(repealed)*
(c) section 23 or 27 of the Matrimonial Causes Act 1973;
(d) Part I of the Domestic Proceedings and Magistrates' Courts Act 1978, for the making or securing of periodical payments;
(e) Part 1 or 9 of Schedule 5 to the Civil Partnership Act 2004 (financial relief in the High Court or a county court etc);
(f) Schedule 6 to the 2004 Act (financial relief in the magistrates' courts etc).

(7) The powers conferred by this paragraph shall be exercisable at any time.

(8) Where the court makes an order under this paragraph it may from time to time while that order remains in force make a further such order.

Amendments—CSA 1991, s 58(14); CPA 2004, s 78(1),(2).

Scope—Subject to CSA 1991 (see Procedural Guide A2), this paragraph enables an adult child, whose parents are not living with each other in the same household and in respect of whom there was no periodical payments order in force before he reached the age of 16, to apply for periodical payments or a lump sum if either he is receiving further education or training or there are special circumstances.

'periodical payments order' (para 2(3),(6))—The term 'periodical payments order' as defined by para 2(6) means an order under (i) this Schedule, (ii) MCA 1973, s 23, which provides maintenance in divorce, nullity or judicial separation proceedings, (iii) s 27 of that Act, which provides maintenance on an application for wilful neglect to maintain in the High Court or County Court, or (iv) DPMCA 1978, Pt I in the magistrates' court, on the same ground as in (iii).

3 Duration of orders for financial relief

(1) The term to be specified in an order for periodical payments made under paragraph 1(2)(a) or (b) in favour of a child may begin with the date of the making of an application for the order in question or any later date or a date ascertained in accordance with sub-paragraph (5) or (6) but –

(a) shall not in the first instance extend beyond the child's seventeenth birthday unless the court thinks it right in the circumstances of the case to specify a later date; and
(b) shall not in any event extend beyond the child's eighteenth birthday.

(2) Paragraph (b) of sub-paragraph (1) shall not apply in the case of a child if it appears to the court that –

(a) the child is, or will be or (if an order were made without complying with that paragraph) would be receiving instruction at an educational establishment or undergoing training for a trade, profession or vocation, whether or not while in gainful employment; or
(b) there are special circumstances which justify the making of an order without complying with that paragraph.

(3) An order for periodical payments made under paragraph 1(2)(a) or 2(2)(a) shall, notwithstanding anything in the order, cease to have effect on the death of the person liable to make payments under the order.

(4) Where an order is made under paragraph 1(2)(a) or (b) requiring periodical payments to be made or secured to the parent of a child, the order shall cease to have effect if –

(a) any parent making or securing the payments; and
(b) any parent to whom the payments are made or secured,

live together for a period of more than six months.

(5) Where –

(a) a maintenance calculation ('the current calculation') is in force with respect to a child; and

(b) an application is made for an order under paragraph 1(2)(a) or (b) of this Schedule for periodical payments in favour of that child –
   (i) in accordance with section 8 of the Child Support Act 1991; and
   (ii) before the end of the period of 6 months beginning with the making of the current calculation,

the term to be specified in any such order made on that application may be expressed to begin on, or at any time after, the earliest permitted date.

(6) For the purposes of subsection (5) above, 'the earliest permitted date' is whichever is the later of –

(a) the date 6 months before the application is made; or
(b) the date on which the current calculation took effect or, where successive maintenance calculations have been continuously in force with respect to a child, on which the first of those calculations took effect.

(7) Where –

(a) a maintenance calculation ceases to have effect by or under any provision of the Child Support Act 1991, and
(b) an application is made, before the end of the period of 6 months beginning with the relevant date, for an order for periodical payments under paragraph 1(2)(a) or (b) in favour of a child with respect to whom that maintenance calculation was in force immediately before it ceases to have effect,

the term to be specified in any such order, or in any interim order under paragraph 9, made on that application may begin with the date on which that maintenance calculation ceased to have effect, or any later date.

(8) In sub-paragraph (7)(b) –

(a) where the maintenance calculation ceased to have effect, the relevant date is the date on which it so ceased; and
(b) *(repealed)*

Amendments—SI 1993/623; CSPSSA 2000, ss 26, 85, Sch 3, para 10, Sch 9.

Scope—This paragraph is equivalent to MCA 1973, s 29(2)–(4) and provides the upper limit for the duration of a periodical payments order. It also provides that any order ceases to have effect if the child's parents live together for more than 6 months.

'special circumstances' (para 3(2)(b))—Compare MCA 1973, s 29(3)(b). Where there are special circumstances the order can continue beyond 18 years despite CSA 1991, ss 8 and 55. Special circumstances may include physical or other disability, and the expenses attributed to the child's disability should be interpreted the broadest sense (*C v F (Disabled Child: Maintenance Orders)* [1998] 2 FLR 1, CA). Special circumstances have been held not to include the extreme wealth of the father or the possibility that the child might not inherit upon his death: *MT v OT (Financial Provision: Costs)* [2008] 2 FLR 1311, FD. The tendency of adult children to remain living at home with a parent is not a special circumstance: however, payment for a gap year before or after tertiary education may be permissible: see *Re N (Payments for Benefit of Child)* [2009] 1 FLR 1442, FD, following *A v A (A Minor: Financial Provision)* [1994] 1 FLR 657, FD; *Phillips v Peace* [1996] 2 FLR 230, FD. In the absence of 'special circumstances', any capital settlement under Sch 1 should be expressed as terminating when the child attains 18 or completes tertiary education.

Orders for financial relief shall not in any event extend beyond the child's 18th birthday, unless the child is receiving tertiary education or training or where 'special circumstances' apply; the exception is despite CSA 1991, ss 8 and 55.

4 Matters to which court is to have regard in making orders for financial relief

(1) In deciding whether to exercise its powers under paragraph 1 or 2, and if so in what manner, the court shall have regard to all the circumstances including –

(a) the income, earning capacity, property and other financial resources which each person mentioned in sub-paragraph (4) has or is likely to have in the foreseeable future;
(b) the financial needs, obligations and responsibilities which each person mentioned in sub-paragraph (4) has or is likely to have in the foreseeable future;
(c) the financial needs of the child;
(d) the income, earning capacity (if any), property and other financial resources of the child;

(e) any physical or mental disability of the child;
(f) the manner in which the child was being, or was expected to be, educated or trained.

(2) In deciding whether to exercise its powers under paragraph 1 against a person who is not the mother or father of the child, and if so in what manner, the court shall in addition have regard to –

(a) whether that person had assumed responsibility for the maintenance of the child, and, if so, the extent to which and basis on which he assumed that responsibility and the length of the period during which he met that responsibility;
(b) whether he did so knowing that the child was not his child;
(c) the liability of any other person to maintain the child.

(3) Where the court makes an order under paragraph 1 against a person who is not the father of the child, it shall record in the order that the order is made on the basis that the person against whom the order is made is not the child's father.

(4) The persons mentioned in sub-paragraph (1) are –

(a) in relation to a decision whether to exercise its powers under paragraph 1, any parent of the child;
(b) in relation to a decision whether to exercise its powers under paragraph 2, the mother and father of the child;
(c) the applicant for the order;
(d) any other person in whose favour the court proposes to make the order.

(5) In the case of a child who has a parent by virtue of section 42 or 43 of the Human Fertilisation and Embryology Act 2008, any reference in sub-paragraph (2), (3) or (4) to the child's father is a reference to the woman who is a parent of the child by virtue of that section.

Amendments—HFEA 2008, s 56, Sch 6, para 32(1),(2).

Scope—An award under Sch 1 is discretionary; it involves striking a balance between the statutory factors set out in para 4 above. These factors do not replicate those in MCA 1973, s 25. The parties' conduct and the duration of their relationship are not, for example, explicit statutory considerations. However, the court must consider 'all the circumstances', which can include (a) the fact that a long relationship has accustomed a child to a particular standard of living (*N v D* [2008] 1 FLR 1629, PRFD) or (b) particularly egregious conduct, such as convictions for inciting a partner's murder (*O v P (No 2) (Sch 1 Application: Stay: Forum Conveniens)* [2015] 2 FLR 77, FD). *Re P (Child: Financial Provision)* [2003] 2 FLR 865, CA remains the leading authority as to the proper approach to an application pursuant to Sch 1 (for those families on the spectrum from affluent to fabulously rich). The court is guided to approach a claim using the following analytical framework set out at [45]–[47], per Thorpe LJ):

(i) The starting point is the decision, at least generically, on the home to be provided by the respondent in value, size and location;
(ii) That choice bears upon and frames the reasonable capital cost of furnishing and equipping the house as well as future income needs both directly in the case of outgoings and indirectly in the case of external expenditure such as travel, education and holidays;
(iii) A lump sum appropriate within that determination will provide for the cost of furnishing, equipping the home and a car;
(iv) The next step is to determine the budget the mother reasonably requires to fund her expenditure on maintaining the home, content and meeting other expenditure external to the home including school fees, holidays, routine travel expenses, entertainments, presents etc.
(v) The assessment is broad but will include the mother's allowance, which is checked but not diminished by the absence of any entitlement in her own right. While there is to be no slack or margin for saving, the court must recognise the sacrifice of the unmarried parents, generally the mother as primary and usually exclusive carer, with a budget that reflects both her position and the position of the father, both social and financial. She is to be free from anxiety or resort to parsimony where the other parent chooses to live lavishly.
(vi) The Court is required to navigate between rival budgets produced by specialist family lawyers on a broad commonsense assessment, at [47]. In addition, on both sides this is a calculation of a household not formed and election between an aspirational budget and a critique of proposed alleged extravagance quite different from the factual task performed by a court under s 25 forming an evidential view as to the standard of living actually enjoyed and the accuracy of its recollection by the parties.
(vii) Bodey J in a helpful and succinct supporting judgment proposed that in big-money cases the mother's budget should be painted with a broad brush without being bogged down in detailed analyses and categorisations of specific items making up opposing budgetary presentations. The better approach is to seek to achieve a fair and realistic outcome by the application of broad commonsense to the overall circumstances of the particular case.

The court will consider the welfare of the child. Strictly, welfare is not the court's paramount consideration, as questions about the upbringing of a child, which trigger considerations of paramountcy, specifically exclude maintenance (CA 1989, ss 1(1)(a) and 105(1)). However, the Court of Appeal in *Re P (Child: Financial Provision)* [2003] 2 FLR 865, CA confirmed that the child's welfare is 'in most cases a constant influence on the discretionary outcome', an approach followed in *N v D*. *Re P* established that the exercise of the jurisdiction was highly discretionary and involved 'an essentially broad brush assessment to be taken by Family judges with much expertise and experience in the specialist field of ancillary relief': *Re M-M (A Child)* [2014] 2 FLR 1391, CA. For example, a clause seeking to prevent a parent from using a housing fund to purchase a property abroad (against that parent's wishes) may not be compatible with the best interests of the child: (*G v S* [2017] EWHC 365 (Fam)).

Large awards have been secured in cases with wealthy fathers. In *Re P* (above) £1m was awarded for a home in central London, plus £70,000 in periodical payments. The child may be entitled to be brought up in circumstances which bear some relation to the father's resources and standard of living (*J v C (Child: Financial Provision)* [1999] 1 FLR 152, FD; *F v G (Child: Financial Provision)* [2005] 1 FLR 261, FD; *MT v OT (Financial Provision: Costs)* [2008] 2 FLR 1311, FD; *H v C* [2009] 2 FLR 1540, FD). The court will consider as a starting point what home must be provided and how this is to be settled/transferred for the child's benefit until the child's majority and thereafter the size of any lump sum required, for example, to equip the home and to provide a car. Secondly, the mother may be entitled to a carer's allowance for looking after the child if she has to give up work, a principle developed in *Haroutunian v Jennings* (1980) 1 FLR 62, FD. Thirdly, the court will consider periodical payments for the maintenance of the child, in line with the mother's budget, on the basis of a 'broad common-sense assessment' (*Re P*).

A wealthy father may claim the 'millionaire's defence', avoiding detailed financial disclosure on the basis he is wealthy enough to meet any financial order a court may reasonably make (*Re A (A Child)* [2015] 2 FLR 625, CA, approving *AH v PH (Scandinavian Marriage Settlement)* [2014] 2 FLR 251, FD). A broad indication of a father's wealth may suffice as essential information. Despite the wealth of a father, the court must still decide on what is reasonable provision for the child, starting from the obvious baseline of the child's home environment: *Re P* approved. This is not matrimonial litigation, and principles of sharing and compensation have no place in Sch 1 applications.

In *Re P*, it was suggested that although the mother has control of the budget, the father may receive an account of what is spent and deduct state benefits. In *Re C (Financial Provision)* [2007] 2 FLR 13, FD, the notion of the mother producing detailed accounts for the father's scrutiny would 'almost always be unhelpful and counterproductive'. However, in *Re N (Payments for Benefit of Child)* [2009] 1 FLR 1442, FD, where there had been difficulties about the setting up of the trust, the court suggested ground rules to be followed: the mother was to account to the father for moneys not used for the intended purpose, including receipts for items over £10, and the mother in turn was entitled to interest from the father on unpaid sums. The case deals with the procedure for the appointment of trustees and the entitlement of the mother to buy out the father's interest. Where a father failed to settle a sum upon the mother for the benefit of the child, no judgment debt arose and therefore no charging order could be made; however, the mother could be protected by an injunction preventing the father from dealing with the property.

The needs of the individual child in the light of the available resource are likely to be the determining factor. Equally, the economic circumstances and means of the payer will be scrutinised: where a father could not pay maintenance out of income but used capital and borrowing to provide himself with a good lifestyle, maintenance could be paid from capital resources: *SW v RC* [2008] 1 FLR 1703, FD. The focus must be on the real needs of the child, not the aspirations of the mother for an enhanced lifestyle. The future needs of the carer after the child reaches its majority should play no part in the calculation of a Sch 1 award: *Re A (A Child)* [2015] 2 FLR 625, CA. It has been suggested that in some cases the child should have separate representation (*Re S (Unmarried Parents: Financial Provision)* [2006] 2 FLR 950, CA).

5 Provisions relating to lump sums

(1) Without prejudice to the generality of paragraph 1, an order under that paragraph for the payment of a lump sum may be made for the purpose of enabling any liabilities or expenses –

(a) incurred in connection with the birth of the child or in maintaining the child; and

(b) reasonably incurred before the making of the order,

to be met.

(2) *(repealed)*

(3) The power of the court under paragraph 1 or 2 to vary or discharge an order for the making or securing of periodical payments by a parent shall include power to make an order under that provision for the payment of a lump sum by that parent.

(4) *(repealed)*

(5) An order made under paragraph 1 or 2 for the payment of a lump sum may provide for the payment of that sum by instalments.

(6) Where the court provides for the payment of a lump sum by instalments the court, on an application made either by the person liable to pay or the person entitled to receive that sum, shall have power to vary that order by varying –

(a) the number of instalments payable;

(b) the amount of any instalment payable;

(c) the date on which any instalment becomes payable.

(7) The Lord Chief Justice may nominate a judicial office holder (as defined in section 109(4) of the Constitutional Reform Act 2005) to exercise his functions under this paragraph.

Amendments—SI 1992/709; CRA 2005, s 15(1), Sch 4, paras 203, 209; CCA 2013, s 17, Sch 11.

6 Variation etc of orders for periodical payments

(1) In exercising its powers under paragraph 1 or 2 to vary or discharge an order for the making or securing of periodical payments the court shall have regard to all the circumstances of the case, including any change in any of the matters to which the court was required to have regard when making the order.

(2) The power of the court under paragraph 1 or 2 to vary an order for the making or securing of periodical payments shall include power to suspend any provision of the order temporarily and to revive any provision so suspended.

(3) Where on an application under paragraph 1 or 2 for the variation or discharge of an order for the making or securing of periodical payments the court varies the payments required to be made under that order, the court may provide that the payments as so varied shall be made from such date as the court may specify except that, subject to sub-paragraph (9), the date shall not be earlier than the date of the making of the application.

(4) An application for the variation of an order made under paragraph 1 for the making or securing of periodical payments to or for the benefit of a child may, if the child has reached the age of sixteen, be made by the child himself.

(5) Where an order for the making or securing of periodical payments made under paragraph 1 ceases to have effect on the date on which the child reaches the age of sixteen, or at any time after that date but before or on the date on which he reaches the age of eighteen, the child may apply to the court which made the order for an order for its revival.

(6) If on such an application it appears to the court that –

(a) the child is, will be or (if an order were made under this sub-paragraph) would be receiving instruction at an educational establishment or undergoing training for a trade, profession or vocation, whether or not while in gainful employment; or

(b) there are special circumstances which justify the making of an order under this paragraph,

the court shall have power by order to revive the order from such date as the court may specify, not being earlier than the date of the making of the application.

(7) Any order which is revived by an order under sub-paragraph (5) may be varied or discharged under that provision, on the application of any person by whom or to whom payments are required to be made under the revived order.

(8) An order for the making or securing of periodical payments made under paragraph 1 may be varied or discharged, after the death of either parent, on the application of a guardian or special guardian of the child concerned.

(9) Where –

(a) an order under paragraph 1(2)(a) or (b) for the making or securing of periodical payments in favour of more than one child ('the order') is in force;

(b) the order requires payments specified in it to be made to or for the benefit of more than one child without apportioning those payments between them;

(c) a maintenance calculation ('the calculation') is made with respect to one or more, but not all, of the children with respect to whom those payments are to be made; and

(d) an application is made, before the end of the period of 6 months beginning with the date on which the calculation was made, for the variation or discharge of the order, the court may, in exercise of its powers under paragraph 1 to vary or discharge the order, direct that the variation or discharge shall take effect from the date on which the calculation took effect or any later date.

Amendments—SI 1993/623; CSPSSA 2000, s 26, Sch 3, para 10; ACA 2002, Sch 3, para 71.

Scope—Subject to CSA 1991 (see **Outline of child support calculation** under CSA 1991, s 4), this paragraph contains the court's powers to vary orders made either under para 1 (order for financial relief for a child against parents) or para 2 (order for financial relief against parents where the child is applying for the first time when the child is over 18).

6A Variation of orders for periodical payments etc made by magistrates' courts

(1) Subject to sub-paragraph (7), the power of the family court –

- (a) under paragraph 1 or 2 to vary an order for the making of periodical payments, or
- (b) under paragraph 5(6) to vary an order for the payment of a lump sum by instalments,

shall include power, if the court is satisfied that payment has not been made in accordance with the order, to exercise one of its powers under section 1(4) and (4A) of the Maintenance Enforcement Act 1991.

(2)–(5) *(repealed)*

(6) Subsection (6) of section 1 of the Maintenance Enforcement Act 1991 (power of court to order that account be opened) shall apply for the purposes of sub-paragraph (1) as it applies for the purposes of that section.

(7) Before varying the order by exercising one of its powers under section 1(4) and (4A) of the Maintenance Enforcement Act 1991, the court shall have regard to any representations made by the parties to the application.

(8) *(repealed)*

(9) None of the powers of the court conferred by this paragraph shall be exercisable in relation to an order under this Schedule for the making of periodical payments, or for the payment of a lump sum by instalments, unless at the time when the order was made the person required to make the payments was ordinarily resident in England and Wales.

(10) *(repealed)*

Amendments—Inserted by MEA 1991, s 6. Amended by SI 1994/731; AJA 1999, s 90, Sch 13, para 161; Courts Act 2003, s 109(1), Sch 8, para 338(1)–(4); CCA 2013, s 17, Sch 11.

Scope—This paragraph gives to the court the same power to determine method of payment on an application to vary as it has on the making of a new order.

7 Variation of orders for secured periodical payments after death of parent

(1) Where the parent liable to make payments under a secured periodical payments order has died, the persons who may apply for the variation or discharge of the order shall include the personal representatives of the deceased parent.

(2) No application for the variation of the order shall, except with the permission of the court, be made after the end of the period of six months from the date on which representation in regard to the estate of that parent is first taken out.

(3) The personal representatives of a deceased person against whom a secured periodical payments order was made shall not be liable for having distributed any part of the estate of the deceased after the end of the period of six months referred to in sub-paragraph (2) on the ground that they ought to have taken into account the possibility that the court might permit an application for variation to be made after that period by the person entitled to payments under the order.

(4) Sub-paragraph (3) shall not prejudice any power to recover any part of the estate so distributed arising by virtue of the variation of an order in accordance with this paragraph.

(5) Where an application to vary a secured periodical payments order is made after the death of the parent liable to make payments under the order, the circumstances to which the court is required to have regard under paragraph 6(1) shall include the changed circumstances resulting from the death of the parent.

(6) The following are to be left out of account when considering for the purposes of sub-paragraph (2) when representation was first taken out –

(a) a grant limited to settled land or to trust property,
(b) any other grant that does not permit any of the estate to be distributed,
(c) a grant limited to real estate or to personal estate, unless a grant limited to the remainder of the estate has previously been made or is made at the same time,
(d) a grant, or its equivalent, made outside the United Kingdom (but see sub-paragraph (6A)).

(6A) A grant sealed under section 2 of the Colonial Probates Act 1892 counts as a grant made in the United Kingdom for the purposes of sub-paragraph (6), but is to be taken as dated on the date of sealing.

(7) In this paragraph 'secured periodical payments order' means an order for secured periodical payments under paragraph 1(2)(b).

Amendments—Inheritance and Trustees' Powers Act 2014, s 6, Sch 2.

8 Financial relief under other enactments

(1) This paragraph applies where a child arrangements order to which sub-paragraph (1A) applies or a special guardianship order is made with respect to a child at a time when there is in force an order ('the financial relief order') made under any enactment other than this Act and requiring a person to contribute to the child's maintenance.

(1A) This sub-paragraph applies to a child arrangements order if the arrangements regulated by the order consist of, or include, arrangements which relate to either or both of the following –

(a) with whom the child concerned is to live, and
(b) when the child is to live with any person.

(2) Where this paragraph applies, the court may, on the application of –

(a) any person required by the financial relief order to contribute to the child's maintenance; or
(b) any person who is named in a child arrangements order as a person with whom the child is to live or in whose favour a special guardianship order with respect to the child is in force,

make an order revoking the financial relief order, or varying it by altering the amount of any sum payable under that order or by substituting the applicant for the person to whom any such sum is otherwise payable under that order.

Amendments—ACA 2002, s 139(1), Sch 3, para 71; CFA 2014, s 12, Sch 2.

Defined terms—'child': s 105(1), Sch 1, para 16(1); 'child arrangements order': s 8(1).

Scope—Where an order for periodical payments or secured periodical payments for the support of a child made outside Sch 1 (for instance in financial remedy proceedings) already exists and a child arrangements order is then made, this paragraph enables the court to vary that original order by varying the sum payable or the person to whom payment is to be made.

9 Interim orders

(1) Where an application is made under paragraph 1 or 2 the court may, at any time before it disposes of the application, make an interim order –

(a) requiring either or both parents to make such periodical payments, at such times and for such term as the court thinks fit; and
(b) giving any direction which the court thinks fit.

(2) An interim order made under this paragraph may provide for payments to be made from such date as the court may specify except that, subject to paragraph 3(5) and (6), the date shall not be earlier than the date of the making of the application under paragraph 1 or 2.

(3) An interim order made under this paragraph shall cease to have effect when the application is disposed of or, if earlier, on the date specified for the purposes of this paragraph in the interim order.

(4) An interim order in which a date has been specified for the purposes of sub-paragraph (3) may be varied by substituting a later date.

Amendments—SI 1993/623.

Scope—This paragraph enables the court to make interim orders.

10 Alteration of maintenance agreements

(1) In this paragraph and in paragraph 11 'maintenance agreement' means any agreement in writing made with respect to a child, whether before or after the commencement of this paragraph, which –

- (a) is or was made between the father and mother of the child; and
- (b) contains provision with respect to the making or securing of payments, or the disposition or use of any property, for the maintenance or education of the child,

and any such provisions are in this paragraph, and paragraph 11, referred to as 'financial arrangements'.

(2) Subject to sub-paragraph (2A), where a maintenance agreement is for the time being subsisting and each of the parties to the agreement is for the time being either domiciled or resident in England and Wales, then, either party may apply for an order under this paragraph.

(2A) If an application or part of an application relates to a matter where jurisdiction falls to be determined by reference to the jurisdictional requirements of the Maintenance Regulation and Schedule 6 to the Civil Jurisdiction and Judgments (Maintenance) Regulations 2011 –

- (a) the requirement as to domicile or residence in sub-paragraph (2) does not apply to the application or that part of it, but
- (b) the court may not entertain the application or that part of it unless it has jurisdiction to do so by virtue of that Regulation and that Schedule.

(2B) In sub-paragraph (2A), 'the Maintenance Regulation' means Council Regulation (EC) No 4/2009 including as applied in relation to Denmark by virtue of the Agreement made on 19 October 2005 between the European Community and the Kingdom of Denmark.

(3) If the court to which the application is made is satisfied either –

- (a) that, by reason of a change in the circumstances in the light of which any financial arrangements contained in the agreement were made (including a change foreseen by the parties when making the agreement), the agreement should be altered so as to make different financial arrangements; or
- (b) that the agreement does not contain proper financial arrangements with respect to the child,

then that court may by order make such alterations in the agreement by varying or revoking any financial arrangements contained in it as may appear to it to be just having regard to all the circumstances.

(4) If the maintenance agreement is altered by an order under this paragraph, the agreement shall have effect thereafter as if the alteration had been made by agreement between the parties and for valuable consideration.

(5) Where a court decides to make an order under this paragraph altering the maintenance agreement –

- (a) by inserting provision for the making or securing by one of the parties to the agreement of periodical payments for the maintenance of the child; or
- (b) by increasing the rate of periodical payments required to be made or secured by one of the parties for the maintenance of the child,

then, in deciding the term for which under the agreement as altered by the order the payments or (as the case may be) the additional payments attributable to the increase are to be made or secured for the benefit of the child, the court shall apply the provisions of sub-paragraphs (1) and (2) of paragraph 3 as if the order were an order under paragraph 1(2)(a) or (b).

(6) *(repealed)*

(7) For the avoidance of doubt it is hereby declared that nothing in this paragraph affects any power of a court before which any proceedings between the parties to a maintenance agreement are brought under any other enactment to make an order containing financial arrangements or any right of either party to apply for such an order in such proceedings.

(8) In the case of a child who has a parent by virtue of section 42 or 43 of the Human Fertilisation and Embryology Act 2008, the reference in sub-paragraph (1)(a) to the child's father is a reference to the woman who is a parent of the child by virtue of that section.

Amendments—Justices of the Peace Act 1997, s 73(2), Sch 5, para 27; AJA 1999, s 106, Sch 15; Courts Act 2003, s 109(1), Sch 8, para 339; HFEA 2008, s 56, Sch 6, para 32(1),(3); SI 2011/1484; CCA 2013, s 17, Sch 11.

Defined terms—'child': s 105(1), Sch 1, para 16(1).

Scope—Subject to CSA 1991 (see Procedural Guides A2 and A5), this paragraph is equivalent to MCA 1973, s 35 and sets out the code for altering maintenance agreements during the lives of the parents. The major difference between this paragraph and MCA 1973, s 35 is that jurisdiction under s 35 depends on the parents being married. By para 10(6), the power of magistrates' courts is limited to inserting provision for periodical payments where none has been made in the maintenance agreement, or, where the agreement does include provision for periodical payments, increasing, reducing or terminating those payments. Previous agreements between parents for financial provision for their child cannot oust the duty of the court under s 15 and Sch 1. The court is free to depart from an agreement unless satisfied that the agreement makes appropriate financial provision for the child: see *Morgan v Hill* [2007] 1 FLR 1480, CA, where the court set aside the agreement and made more substantial financial provision for the child. Such agreements are given less weight than in MCA 1973 applications.

11 (1) Where a maintenance agreement provides for the continuation, after the death of one of the parties, of payments for the maintenance of a child and that party dies domiciled in England and Wales, the surviving party or the personal representatives of the deceased party may apply to the High Court or the family court for an order under paragraph 10.

(2) If a maintenance agreement is altered by a court on an application under this paragraph, the agreement shall have effect thereafter as if the alteration had been made, immediately before the death, by agreement between the parties and for valuable consideration.

(3) An application under this paragraph shall not, except with leave of the High Court or the family court, be made after the end of the period of six months beginning with the day on which representation in regard to the estate of the deceased is first taken out.

(4) The following are to be left out of account when considering for the purposes of sub-paragraph (3) when representation was first taken out –

(a) a grant limited to settled land or to trust property,
(b) any other grant that does not permit any of the estate to be distributed,
(c) a grant limited to real estate or to personal estate, unless a grant limited to the remainder of the estate has previously been made or is made at the same time,
(d) a grant, or its equivalent, made outside the United Kingdom (but see sub-paragraph (4A)).

(4A) A grant sealed under section 2 of the Colonial Probates Act 1892 counts as a grant made in the United Kingdom for the purposes of sub-paragraph (4), but is to be taken as dated on the date of sealing.

(5) (*repealed*)

(6) The provisions of this paragraph shall not render the personal representatives of the deceased liable for having distributed any part of the estate of the deceased after the expiry of the period of six months referred to in sub-paragraph (3) on the ground that they ought to have taken into account the possibility that a court might grant leave for an application by virtue of this paragraph to be made by the surviving party after that period.

(7) Sub-paragraph (6) shall not prejudice any power to recover any part of the estate so distributed arising by virtue of the making of an order in pursuance of this paragraph.

Amendments—CCA 2013, s 17, Sch 11; Inheritance and Trustees' Powers Act 2014, s 6, Sch 2.

Defined terms—'child': s 105(1), Sch 1, para 16(1); 'financial arrangements', 'maintenance agreement': para 10(1).

PART II

Scope—This paragraph is equivalent to MCA 1973, s 36 and enables a maintenance agreement containing provision for a child to be varied on the death of one of the parties to that agreement. MCA 1973, s 36 confers jurisdiction only if the parents are married; this paragraph applies irrespective of whether the parents have been married. The application must be made to the High Court or the Family Court: FPR 2010, r 9.5(2).

12 Enforcement of orders for maintenance

(1) Any person for the time being under an obligation to make payments in pursuance of any order for the payment of money made by the family court under this Act shall give notice of any change of address to such person (if any) as may be specified in the order.

(2) Any person failing without reasonable excuse to give such a notice shall be guilty of an offence and liable on summary conviction to a fine not exceeding level 2 on the standard scale.

(3) *(repealed)*

Amendments—CCA 2013, s 17, Sch 11.

13 Direction for settlement of instrument by conveyancing counsel

Where the High Court or the family court decides to make an order under this Act for the securing of periodical payments or for the transfer or settlement of property, it may direct that the matter be referred to one of the conveyancing counsel of the court to settle a proper instrument to be executed by all necessary parties.

Amendments—CCA 2013, s 17, Sch 11.

14 Jurisdiction in relation to matters relating to maintenance

(1) If an application under paragraph 1 or 2, or part of such an application, relates to a matter where jurisdiction falls to be determined by reference to the jurisdictional requirements of the Maintenance Regulation and Schedule 6 to the Civil Jurisdiction and Judgments (Maintenance) Regulations 2011, the court may not entertain the application or that part of it unless it has jurisdiction to do so by virtue of that Regulation and that Schedule.

(2) In sub-paragraph (1), 'the Maintenance Regulation' means Council Regulation (EC) No 4/2009 including as applied in relation to Denmark by virtue of the Agreement made on 19 October 2005 between the European Community and the Kingdom of Denmark.

Amendments—Substituted by SI 2011/1484. Amended by SI 2012/2814.

Scope—The restriction on the power to make financial provision against a parent in England and Wales where a child resides outside the jurisdiction (previously limited to periodical payments and secured periodical payments) is abolished. By the operation of the Maintenance Regulation and CJJ(M)R 2011, where an application relates to a matter where jurisdiction falls to be determined by reference to the Maintenance Regulation, then those jurisdictional provisions apply. The types of financial relief sought under this paragraph are no longer restricted to periodical payments and secured periodical payments.

15 Local authority contribution to child's maintenance

(1) Where a child lives, or is to live, with a person as the result of a child arrangements order, a local authority may make contributions to that person towards the cost of the accommodation and maintenance of the child.

(2) Sub-paragraph (1) does not apply where the person with whom the child lives, or is to live, is a parent of the child or the husband or wife or civil partner of a parent of the child.

Amendments—CPA 2004, s 78(1), (3); CFA 2014, s 12, Sch 2.

Defined terms—'child': s 105(1), Sch 1, para 16(1); 'child arrangements order': s 8(1); 'local authority': s 105(1).

'may make contributions'—A local authority's contribution to a child's maintenance under this provision is discretionary, and will not apply where the child lives with a parent, or the parent's spouse or civil partner: *R (M) v Birmingham City Council* [2009] 1 FLR 1068, QBD.

16 Interpretation

(1) In this Schedule 'child' includes, in any case where an application is made under paragraph 2 or 6 in relation to a person who has reached the age of eighteen, that person.

(2) In this Schedule except paragraphs 2 and 15, 'parent' includes –

(a) any party to a marriage (whether or not subsisting) in relation to whom the child concerned is a child of the family, and
(b) any civil partner in a civil partnership (whether or not subsisting) in relation to whom the child concerned is a child of the family;

and for this purpose any reference to either parent or both parents shall be read as a reference to any parent of his and to all of his parents.

(3) In this Schedule, 'maintenance calculation' has the same meaning as it has in the Child Support Act 1991 by virtue of section 54 of that Act as read with any regulations in force under that section.

Amendments—SI 1993/623; CSPSSA 2000, s 26, Sch 3, para 10; CPA 2004, s 78(1),(4).

Defined terms—'child of the family': s 105(1); 'parent' means (in the strict legal sense) any party to a marriage or civil partnership. An order cannot be made against a same-sex former partner where there is no biological relationship or civil partnership: *T v B* [2010] 2 FLR 1966, FD. See also **Same-sex parenting** under s 8.

SCHEDULE 2
SUPPORT FOR CHILDREN AND FAMILIES PROVIDED BY LOCAL AUTHORITIES IN ENGLAND

Amendments—SI 2016/413.

Application to local authorities in England

A1 (1) This Schedule applies only in relation to local authorities in England.

(2) Accordingly, unless the contrary intention appears, a reference in this Schedule to a local authority means a local authority in England.

Amendments—Provision (and heading) inserted by SI 2016/413.

PART I
PROVISION OF SERVICES FOR FAMILIES

1 Identification of children in need and provision of information

(1) Every local authority shall take reasonable steps to identify the extent to which there are children in need within their area.

(2) Every local authority shall –

(a) publish information –
  (i) about services provided by them under sections 17, 18, 20, 23B to 23D, 24A and 24B; and
  (ii) where they consider it appropriate, about the provision by others (including, in particular, voluntary organisations) of services which the authority have power to provide under those sections; and
(b) take such steps as are reasonably practicable to ensure that those who might benefit from the services receive the information relevant to them.

Amendments—Children (Leaving Care) Act 2000, s 7(4).

1A *(repealed)*

2 Maintenance of a register of disabled children

(1) Every local authority shall open and maintain a register of disabled children within their area.

(2) The register may be kept by means of a computer.

3 Assessment of children's needs

Where it appears to a local authority that a child within their area is in need, the authority may assess his needs for the purposes of this Act at the same time as any assessment of his needs is made under –

(a) the Chronically Sick and Disabled Persons Act 1970;
(b) Part IV of the Education Act 1996;
(ba) Part 3 of the Children and Families Act 2014;
(c) the Disabled Persons (Services, Consultation and Representation) Act 1986; or
(d) any other enactment.

Amendments—Education Act 1996, s 582(1), Sch 37, Pt I, para 92; CFA 2014, s 82, Sch 3.

Court's function—In *R (LH and MH) v London Borough of Lambeth* [2006] 2 FLR 1275, QBD the claimants sought judicial review of a core assessment relating to a 10-year-old child with moderate learning disabilities, autism and certain physical conditions. It was not the function of the court to decide what was best for a child; its function was one of review and to decide whether there had been a failure to fulfil the legal obligations of the local authority.

Age of child—Where it is in dispute whether an individual who is said to be in need is a child or not, the resolution of that issue is for the court to determine and not for the local authority to decide subject only to challenge by judicial review: *R (A) (FC) v London Borough of Croydon & Others* [2010] 1 FLR 959, SC. A local authority undertaking age assessments for the purposes of CA 1989 is not bound by age assessments undertaken by the Secretary of State for the Home Department in discharging her immigration functions, nor is it bound by age assessments made by the First Tier Tribunal (Immigration and Asylum Chamber) on appeal: *R (Kadri) v Birmingham City Council & Othrs* [2013] 1 WLR 1755, CA.

4 Prevention of neglect and abuse

(1) Every local authority shall take reasonable steps, through the provision of services under Part III of this Act, to prevent children within their area suffering ill-treatment or neglect.

(2) Where a local authority believe that a child who is at any time within their area –

(a) is likely to suffer harm; but
(b) lives or proposes to live in the area of another local authority or in the area of a local authority in Wales

they shall inform that other local authority or the local authority in Wales, as the case may be.

(3) When informing that other local authority or the local authority in Wales they shall specify –

(a) the harm that they believe he is likely to suffer; and
(b) (if they can) where the child lives or proposes to live.

Amendments—SI 2016/413.

5 Provision of accommodation in order to protect child

(1) Where –

(a) it appears to a local authority that a child who is living on particular premises is suffering, or is likely to suffer, ill treatment at the hands of another person who is living on those premises; and
(b) that other person proposes to move from the premises,

the authority may assist that other person to obtain alternative accommodation.

(2) Assistance given under this paragraph may be in cash.

(3) Subsections (7) to (9) of section 17 shall apply in relation to assistance given under this paragraph as they apply in relation to assistance given under that section.

6 Provision for disabled children

(1) Every local authority shall provide services designed –

(a) to minimise the effect on disabled children within their area of their disabilities;
(b) to give such children the opportunity to lead lives which are as normal as possible; and
(c) to assist individuals who provide care for such children to continue to do so, or to do so more effectively, by giving them breaks from caring.

(2) The duty imposed by sub-paragraph (1)(c) shall be performed in accordance with regulations made by the Secretary of State.

Amendments—CYPA 2008, s 25; SI 2016/413.

7 Provision to reduce need for care proceedings etc

Every local authority shall take reasonable steps designed –

(a) to reduce the need to bring –

(i) proceedings for care or supervision orders with respect to children within their area;

(ii) criminal proceedings against such children;

(iii) any family or other proceedings with respect to such children which might lead to them being placed in the authority's care; or

(iv) proceedings under the inherent jurisdiction of the High Court with respect to children;

(b) to encourage children within their area not to commit criminal offences; and

(c) to avoid the need for children within their area to be placed in secure accommodation within the meaning given in section 25 and in section 119 of the Social Services and Well-being (Wales) Act 2014.

Amendments—SI 2016/413.

'reasonable steps' (para 7)—The duty to take 'reasonable steps' in relation to the housing needs of an autistic child accommodated by the local authority meant that the council must do its best within the bounds of what is reasonably practicable to secure 'not unsuitable' accommodation for the child; the accommodation to be secured was not required to be suitable to the particular needs of the child, only to be 'not unsuitable' (*R v London Borough of Brent ex parte S* [1994] 1 FLR 203, CA).

8 Provision for children living with their families

Every local authority shall make such provision as they consider appropriate for the following services to be available with respect to children in need within their area while they are living with their families –

(a) advice, guidance and counselling;

(b) occupational, social, cultural or recreational activities;

(c) home help (which may include laundry facilities);

(d) facilities for, or assistance with, travelling to and from home for the purpose of taking advantage of any other service provided under this Act or of any similar service;

(e) assistance to enable the child concerned and his family to have a holiday.

8A Provision for accommodated children

(1) Every local authority shall make provision for such services as they consider appropriate to be available with respect to accommodated children.

(2) 'Accommodated children' are those children in respect of whose accommodation the local authority have been notified under section 85 or 86 or under section 120 of the Social Services and Well-being (Wales) Act 2014 (assessment of children accommodated by health authorities and education authorities).

(3) The services shall be provided with a view to promoting contact between each accommodated child and that child's family.

(4) The services may, in particular, include –

(a) advice, guidance and counselling;

(b) services necessary to enable the child to visit, or to be visited by, members of the family;

(c) assistance to enable the child and members of the family to have a holiday together.

(5) Nothing in this paragraph affects the duty imposed by paragraph 10.

Amendments—Inserted by CYPA 2008, s 19. Amended by SI 2016/413.

9 Family centres

(1) Every local authority shall provide such family centres as they consider appropriate in relation to children within their area.

(2) 'Family centre' means a centre at which any of the persons mentioned in sub-paragraph (3) may –

PART II

(a) attend for occupational, social, cultural or recreational activities;
(b) attend for advice, guidance or counselling; or
(c) be provided with accommodation while he is receiving advice, guidance or counselling.

(3) The persons are –

(a) a child;
(b) his parents;
(c) any person who is not a parent of his but who has parental responsibility for him;
(d) any other person who is looking after him.

10 Maintenance of the family home

Every local authority shall take such steps as are reasonably practicable, where any child within their area who is in need and whom they are not looking after is living apart from his family –

(a) to enable him to live with his family; or
(b) to promote contact between him and his family,

if, in their opinion, it is necessary to do so in order to safeguard or promote his welfare.

'such steps as are reasonably practicable'—A local authority is not required to contact extended family where a mother wants a child adopted without them being so informed (*Z County Council v R* [2001] 1 FLR 365, FD and *Re C (A Child) v XYZ County Council* [2008] 1 FLR 1294, CA).

11 Duty to consider racial groups to which children in need belong

Every local authority shall, in making any arrangements –

(a) for the provision of day care within their area; or
(b) designed to encourage persons to act as local authority foster parents,

have regard to the different racial groups to which children within their area who are in need belong.

PART II
CHILDREN LOOKED AFTER BY LOCAL AUTHORITIES IN ENGLAND
Amendments—SI 2016/413.

12A Regulations as to conditions under which child in care is allowed to live with parent, etc

Regulations under section 22C may, in particular, impose requirements on a local authority as to –

(a) the making of any decision by a local authority to allow a child in their care to live with any person falling within section 22C(3) (including requirements as to those who must be consulted before the decision is made and those who must be notified when it has been made);
(b) the supervision or medical examination of the child concerned;
(c) the removal of the child, in such circumstances as may be prescribed, from the care of the person with whom the child has been allowed to live;
(d) the records to be kept by local authorities.

12B Regulations as to placements of a kind specified in section 22C(6)(d)

Regulations under section 22C as to placements of the kind specified in section 22C(6)(d) may, in particular, make provision as to –

(a) the persons to be notified of any proposed arrangements;
(b) the opportunities such persons are to have to make representations in relation to the arrangements proposed;
(c) the persons to be notified of any proposed changes in arrangements;
(d) the records to be kept by local authorities;
(e) the supervision by local authorities of any arrangements made.

12C Placements out of area

Regulations under section 22C may, in particular, impose requirements which a local authority must comply with –

- (a) before a child looked after by them is provided with accommodation at a place outside the area of the authority; or
- (b) if the child's welfare requires the immediate provision of such accommodation, within such period of the accommodation being provided as may be prescribed.

12D Avoidance of disruption in education

(1) Regulations under section 22C may, in particular, impose requirements which a local authority must comply with before making any decision concerning a child's placement if he is in the fourth key stage.

(2) A child is 'in the fourth key stage' if he is a pupil in the fourth key stage for the purposes of Part 6 or 7 of the Education 2002 (see section 82 and 103 of that Act).

12E Regulations as to placing of children with local authority foster parents

Regulations under section 22C may, in particular, make provision –

- (a) with regard to the welfare of children placed with local authority foster parents;
- (b) as to the arrangements to be made by local authorities in connection with the health and education of such children;
- (c) as to the records to be kept by local authorities;
- (d) for securing that where possible the local authority foster parent with whom a child is to be placed is –
  - (i) of the same religious persuasion as the child; or
  - (ii) gives an undertaking that the child will be brought up in that religious persuasion;
- (e) for securing the children placed with local authority foster parents, and the premises in which they are accommodated, will be supervised and inspected by a local authority and that the children will be removed from those premises if their welfare appears to require it.

12F (1) Regulations under section 22C may, in particular, also make provision –

- (a) for securing that a child is not placed with a local authority foster parent unless that person is for the time being approved as a local authority foster parent by such local authority as may be prescribed in regulations made by the Secretary of State;
- (b) establishing a procedure under which any person in respect of whom a qualifying determination has been made may apply to the Secretary of State for a review of that determination by a panel constituted by the Secretary of State.

(2) A determination is a qualifying determination if –

- (a) it relates to the issue of whether a person should be approved, or should continue to be approved, as a local authority foster parent; and
- (b) it is of a prescribed description.

(3) Regulations made by virtue of sub-paragraph (1)(b) may include provision as to –

- (a) the duties and powers of a panel;
- (b) the administration and procedures of a panel;
- (c) the appointment of members of a panel (including the number, or any limit on the number, of members who may be appointed and any conditions for appointment);
- (d) the payment of fees to members of a panel;
- (e) the duties of any person in connection with a review conducted under the regulations;
- (f) the monitoring of any such reviews.

(4) Regulations made by virtue of sub-paragraph (3)(e) may impose a duty to pay to the Secretary of State such sum as that national authority may determine; but such a duty may not be imposed upon a person who has applied for a review of a qualifying determination.

(5) The Secretary of State must secure that, taking one financial year with another, the aggregate of the sums which become payable to it under regulations made by virtue of subparagraph (4) does not exceed the cost to it of performing its independent review functions.

(6) The Secretary of State may make an arrangement with an organisation under which independent review functions are performed by the organisation on the national authority's behalf.

(7) If the Secretary of State makes such an arrangement with an organisation, the organisation is to perform its functions under the arrangement in accordance with any general or special directions given by that national authority.

(8) The arrangement may include provision for payments to be made to the organisation by the Secretary of State.

(9) Payments made by the Secretary of State in accordance with such provision shall be taken into account in determining (for the purpose of sub-paragraph (5)) the cost to that national authority of performing its independent review functions.

(10) Where the Welsh Ministers are the Secretary of State, sub-paragraphs (6) and (8) also apply as if references to an organisation included references to the Secretary of State.

(11) In this paragraph –

'financial year' means a period of twelve months ending with 31 March;

'independent review function' means a function conferred or imposed on a national authority by regulations made by virtue of sub-paragraph (1)(b);

'organisation' includes the Welsh Ministers, a public body and a private or voluntary organisation.

Amendments—SI 2016/413.

12G Regulations under section 22C may, in particular, also make provision as to the circumstances in which local authorities may make arrangements for duties imposed on them by the regulations to be discharged on their behalf.

Amendments—CLSA 1990, s 116, Sch 16, para 26; CYPA 2008, s 8(2), Sch 1, para 4.

15 Promotion and maintenance of contact between child and family

(1) Where a child is being looked after by a local authority, the authority shall, unless it is not reasonably practicable or consistent with his welfare, endeavour to promote contact between the child and –

(a) his parents;
(b) any person who is not a parent of his but who has parental responsibility for him; and
(c) any relative, friend or other person connected with him.

(2) Where a child is being looked after by a local authority –

(a) the authority shall take such steps as are reasonably practicable to secure that
  (i) his parents; and
  (ii) any person who is not a parent of his but who has parental responsibility for him,
  are kept informed of where he is being accommodated; and
(b) every such person shall secure that the authority are kept informed of his or her address.

(3) Where a local authority ('the receiving authority') take over the provision of accommodation for a child from another local authority or a local authority in Wales ('the transferring authority') under section 20(2) –

(a) the receiving authority shall (where reasonably practicable) inform
  (i) the child's parents; and
  (ii) any person who is not a parent of his but who has parental responsibility for him;
(b) sub-paragraph (2)(a) shall apply to the transferring authority, as well as the receiving authority, until at least one such person has been informed of the change; and
(c) sub-paragraph (2)(b) shall not require any person to inform the receiving authority of his address until he has been so informed.

(4) Nothing in this paragraph requires a local authority to inform any person of the whereabouts of a child if –

(a) the child is in the care of the authority; and

(b) the authority has reasonable cause to believe that informing the person would prejudice the child's welfare.

(5) Any person who fails (without reasonable excuse) to comply with sub-paragraph (2)(b) shall be guilty of an offence and liable on summary conviction to a fine not exceeding level 2 on the standard scale.

(6) It shall be a defence in any proceedings under sub-paragraph (5) to prove that the defendant was residing at the same address as another person who was the child's parent or had parental responsibility for the child and had reasonable cause to believe that the other person had informed the appropriate authority that both of them were residing at that address.

Amendments—SI 2016/413.

'local authority shall … endeavour to promote contact' (para 15(1))—In *Re P (Minors) (Contact with Children in Care)* [1993] 2 FLR 156, FD, it was observed that: 'The previous practice of access at the discretion of the local authority should not be the regular practice as s 34 provides that reasonable contact should be the norm, not contact at the local authority's discretion which is not the same'. Bearing in mind that, even in cases of urgent necessity, s 34(6) only permits refusal of contact for up to 7 days, reasonable contact should not be unduly restricted, unless by agreement or pursuant to a court order applied for by the local authority itself under s 34(2) (*Re T (Termination of Contact)* [1997] 1 FLR 517, CA).

'any relative, friend or other person connected with him' (para 15(1)(c))—A person who for a period of time occupies the status of stepfather falls within the ambit of this paragraph, as do half-siblings (*L v London Borough of Bromley)* [1998] 1 FLR 709, FD).

16 Visits to or by children: expenses

(1) This paragraph applies where –

(a) a child is being looked after by a local authority; and

(b) the conditions mentioned in sub-paragraph (3) are satisfied.

(2) The authority may –

(a) make payments to –

(i) a parent of the child;

(ii) any person who is not a parent of his but who has parental responsibility for him; or

(iii) any relative, friend or other person connected with him,

in respect of travelling, subsistence or other expenses incurred by that person in visiting the child; or

(b) make payments to the child, or to any person on his behalf, in respect of travelling, subsistence or other expenses incurred by or on behalf of the child in his visiting –

(i) a parent of his;

(ii) any person who has parental responsibility for him; or

(iii) any relative, friend or other person connected with him.

(3) The conditions are that –

(a) it appears to the authority that the visit in question could not otherwise be made without undue financial hardship; and

(b) the circumstances warrant the making of the payments.

17 *(repealed)*

18 Power to guarantee apprenticeship deeds etc

(1) While a child is being looked after by a local authority, or is a person qualifying for advice and assistance, the authority may undertake any obligation by way of guarantee under any deed of apprenticeship or articles of clerkship which he enters into.

(2) Where a local authority have undertaken any such obligation under any deed or articles they may at any time (whether or not they are still looking after the person concerned) undertake the like obligation under any supplemental deed or articles.

19 Arrangements to assist children to live abroad

(1) A local authority may only arrange for, or assist in arranging for, any child in their care to live outside England and Wales with the approval of the court.

(2) A local authority may, with the approval of every person who has parental responsibility for the child arrange for, or assist in arranging for, any other child looked after by them to live outside England and Wales.

(3) The court shall not give its approval under sub-paragraph (1) unless it is satisfied that –

- (a) living outside England and Wales would be in the child's best interests;
- (b) suitable arrangements have been, or will be, made for his reception and welfare in the country in which he will live;
- (c) the child has consented to living in that country; and
- (d) every person who has parental responsibility for the child has consented to his living in that country.

(4) Where the court is satisfied that the child does not have sufficient understanding to give or withhold his consent, it may disregard sub-paragraph (3)(c) and give its approval if the child is to live in the country concerned with a parent, guardian, special guardian or other suitable person.

(5) Where a person whose consent is required by sub-paragraph (3)(d) fails to give his consent, the court may disregard that provision and give its approval if it is satisfied that that person –

- (a) cannot be found;
- (b) is incapable of consenting; or
- (c) is withholding his consent unreasonably.

(6) Section 85 of the Adoption and Children Act 2002 (which imposes restrictions on taking children out of the United Kingdom) shall not apply in the case of any child who is to live outside England and Wales with the approval of the court given under this paragraph.

(7) Where a court decides to give its approval under this paragraph it may order that its decision is not to have effect during the appeal period.

(8) In sub-paragraph (7) 'the appeal period' means –

- (a) where an appeal is made against the decision, the period between the making of the decision and the determination of the appeal; and
- (b) otherwise, the period during which an appeal may be made against the decision.

(9) This paragraph does not apply to a local authority placing a child for adoption with prospective adopters.

Amendments—ACA 2002, s 139(1), Sch 3, paras 54, 72.

'with the approval of the court' (para 19(1))—An application by a local authority to move children in its care to Northern Ireland was considered in *Re P (Minors) (Interim Order)* [1993] 2 FLR 742, CA. In *Re G (Leave to Appeal: Jurisdiction)* [1999] 1 FLR 771, CA, approval was not necessary because, on an application under Sch 2, para 19, the judge had decided that the best interests of the child were met by making an interim child arrangements order in favour of her father in Scotland. The Court of Appeal held that the court was entitled to dispense with unnecessary procedural difficulties in order to achieve what was in the best interests of the child. In the circumstances of *Flintshire County Council v K* [2001] 2 FLR 476, FD it was found to be appropriate to order the return of children to the USA under a care order rather than the inherent jurisdiction as it enabled the local authority to manage the arrangements. The court approved a placement of a child abroad with the father pursuant to this provision rather than adopt the artificial exercise of permitting the local authority to withdraw the care proceedings, make the child a ward of court and place the child with the father in Turkey: *Islington LBC v EV & Othrs* [2011] 1 FLR 1681, FD.

Paragraph 19 and adoption abroad—An assessment of potential carers for a child who lives abroad, and who may be approved as prospective adopters, may be undertaken in their country of residence and does not have to take place in the UK. A local authority was entitled to use this provision to place a child out of the country with the potential carers for an assessment which may lead to adoption, but may not do so: *Re A (Adoption: Removal)* [2009] 2 FLR 597, CA. The court may also grant an adoption agency permission to remove a child from the jurisdiction for placement with prospective adopters: *Kent County Council v PA-K and IA (A Child)* [2013] 2 FLR 541, FD.

'in the child's best interests' (para 19(3)(a))—The child's best interests are not paramount in this context; they are merely one of the four specific factors which the court must consider (*Re G (Minors) (Care: Leave to Place Outside Jurisdiction)* [1994] 2 FLR 301, FD).

'is withholding his consent unreasonably' (para 19(5)(c))—In determining whether the parent's refusal is within the broad band of reasonable decisions which a responsible parent might take, the court should apply the test set out in *Re G* (above). It is surprising that this provision was not amended to reflect the 'welfare' test contained in s 52 of ACA 2002 when considering the issue of the dispensation of parental consent.

Preparation for ceasing to be looked after

19A It is the duty of the local authority looking after a child to advise, assist and befriend him with a view to promoting his welfare when they have ceased to look after him.

Amendments—Inserted by Children (Leaving Care) Act 2000, s 1.

19B (1) A local authority shall have the following additional functions in relation to an eligible child whom they are looking after.

(2) In sub-paragraph (1) 'eligible child' means, subject to sub-paragraph (3), a child who –

(a) is aged sixteen or seventeen; and
(b) has been looked after by a local authority or by a local authority in Wales for a prescribed period, or periods amounting in all to a prescribed period, which began after he reached a prescribed age and ended after he reached the age of sixteen.

(3) The Secretary of State may prescribe –

(a) additional categories of eligible children; and
(b) categories of children who are not to be eligible children despite falling within sub-paragraph (2).

(4) For each eligible child, the local authority shall carry out an assessment of his needs with a view to determining what advice, assistance and support it would be appropriate for them to provide him under this Act –

(a) while they are still looking after him; and
(b) after they cease to look after him,

and shall then prepare a pathway plan for him.

(5) The local authority shall keep the pathway plan under regular review.

(6) Any such review may be carried out at the same time as a review of the child's case carried out by virtue of section 26.

(7) The Secretary of State may by regulations make provision as to assessments for the purposes of sub-paragraph (4).

(8) The regulations may in particular provide for the matters set out in section 23B(6).

Amendments—Inserted by Children (Leaving Care) Act 2000, s 1. Amended by CYPA 2008, s 39, Sch 3, paras 1, 27; SI 2016/413.

Pathway plans (para 19B(4),(5))—The statutory scheme envisages two quite separate stages: the assessment, culminating in the preparation of a written record; and the preparation of a pathway plan. The assessment of needs is to go beyond mere identification of needs: it involves analysis and evaluation of the nature, extent and severity of the child's needs, a process that has to go far enough to enable a pathway plan to be prepared, setting out in sufficiently precise detail the 'manner in which' those needs are to be met (*R (G) v Nottingham City Council & Nottingham University Hospital* [2008] 1 FLR 1668, QBD; see also *R (S) v Sutton London Borough Council* [2007] 2 FLR 849, QBD).

19BA Preparation for ceasing to be looked after: staying put arrangements

(1) This paragraph applies in relation to an eligible child (within the meaning of paragraph 19B) who has been placed by a local authority with a local authority foster parent.

(2) When carrying out the assessment of the child's needs in accordance with paragraph 19B(4), the local authority must determine whether it would be appropriate to provide advice, assistance and support under this Act in order to facilitate a staying put arrangement, and with a view to maintaining such an arrangement, after the local authority cease to look after him or her.

(3) The local authority must provide advice, assistance and support under this Act in order to facilitate a staying put arrangement if –

(a) the local authority determine under sub-paragraph (2) that it would be appropriate to do so, and

PART II

(b) the eligible child and the local authority foster parent wish to make a staying put arrangement.

(4) In this paragraph, 'staying put arrangement' has the meaning given by section 23CZA.

Amendments—Inserted by CFA 2014, s 98. Amended by SI 2016/413.

19C Personal advisers

A local authority shall arrange for each child whom they are looking after who is an eligible child for the purposes of paragraph 19B to have a personal adviser.

Amendments—Inserted by Children (Leaving Care) Act 2000, s 1.

'Personal advisers'—See *R (J)* (above) for guidance as to who should be a personal adviser and what their role should be as between the local authority and the child.

20 Death of children being looked after by local authorities

(1) If a child who is being looked after by a local authority dies, the authority –

(a) shall notify the Secretary of State and Her Majesty's Chief Inspector of Education, Children's Services and Skills;

(b) shall, so far as is reasonably practicable, notify the child's parents and every person who is not a parent of his but who has parental responsibility for him;

(c) may, with the consent (so far as it is reasonably practicable to obtain it) of every person who has parental responsibility for the child, arrange for the child's body to be buried or cremated; and

(d) may, if the conditions mentioned in sub-paragraph (2) are satisfied, make payments to any person who has parental responsibility for the child, or any relative, friend or other person connected with the child, in respect of travelling, subsistence or other expenses incurred by that person in attending the child's funeral.

(2) The conditions are that –

(a) it appears to the authority that the person concerned could not otherwise attend the child's funeral without undue financial hardship; and

(b) that the circumstances warrant the making of the payments.

(3) Sub-paragraph (1) does not authorise cremation where it does not accord with the practice of the child's religious persuasion.

(4) Where a local authority have exercised their power under sub-paragraph (1)(c) with respect to a child who was under sixteen when he died, they may recover from any parent of the child any expenses incurred by them.

(5) Any sums so recoverable shall, without prejudice to any other method of recovery, be recoverable summarily as a civil debt.

(6) Nothing in this paragraph affects any enactment regulating or authorising the burial, cremation or anatomical examination of the body of a deceased person.

Amendments—Health and Social Care (Community Health and Standards) Act 2003, s 147, Sch 9, para 10; Education and Inspection Act 2006, Sch 14, para 17; CYPA 2008, s 39, Sch 3, paras 1, 27; SI 2016/413.

PART III
CONTRIBUTIONS TOWARDS MAINTENANCE OF CHILDREN LOOKED AFTER BY LOCAL AUTHORITIES IN ENGLAND

Amendments—SI 2016/413.

21 Liability to contribute

(1) Where a local authority are looking after a child (other than in the cases mentioned in sub-paragraph (7)) they shall consider whether they should recover contributions towards the child's maintenance from any person liable to contribute ('a contributor').

(2) An authority may only recover contributions from a contributor if they consider it reasonable to do so.

(3) The persons liable to contribute are –

(a) where the child is under sixteen, each of his parents;
(b) where he has reached the age of sixteen, the child himself.

(4) A parent is not liable to contribute during any period when he is in receipt of universal credit (except in such circumstances as may be prescribed), income support under Part VII of the Social Security Contributions and Benefits Act 1992, of any element of child tax credit other than the family element, of working tax credit of an income-based jobseeker's allowance or of an income-related employment and support allowance.

(5) A person is not liable to contribute towards the maintenance of a child in the care of a local authority in respect of any period during which the child is living with, under arrangements made by the authority in accordance with section 22C, a parent of his.

(6) A contributor is not obliged to make any contribution towards a child's maintenance except as agreed or determined in accordance with this Part of this Schedule.

(7) The cases are where the child is looked after by a local authority under –

(a) section 21;
(b) an interim care order;
(c) section 92 of the Powers of Criminal Courts (Sentencing) Act 2000.

Amendments—Disability Living Allowance and Disability Working Allowance Act 1991, s 7(2), Sch 3, para 15; Social Security (Consequential Provisions) Act 1992, s 4, Sch 2, para 108; Jobseekers Act 1995, s 41, Sch 2, para 19; Tax Credits Act 1999, s 1(2), Sch 1, paras 1, 6(d)(iii); Powers of Criminal Courts (Sentencing) Act 2000, s 165, Sch 9, para 130; Tax Credits Act 2002, s 47, Sch 3, paras 15, 20; Welfare Reform Act 2007, s 28(1), Sch 3, para 6(1),(6); CYPA 2008, s 8(3), Sch 1, para 5; Welfare Reform Act 2012, s 31, Sch 2, para 1.

22 Agreed contributions

(1) Contributions towards a child's maintenance may only be recovered if the local authority have served a notice ('a contribution notice') on the contributor specifying –

(a) the weekly sum which they consider that he should contribute; and
(b) arrangements for payment.

(2) The contribution notice must be in writing and dated.

(3) Arrangements for payment shall, in particular, include –

(a) the date on which liability to contribute begins (which must not be earlier than the date of the notice);
(b) the date on which liability under the notice will end (if the child has not before that date ceased to be looked after by the authority); and
(c) the date on which the first payment is to be made.

(4) The authority may specify in a contribution notice a weekly sum which is a standard contribution determined by them for all children looked after by them.

(5) The authority may not specify in a contribution notice a weekly sum greater than that which they consider –

(a) they would normally be prepared to pay if they had placed a similar child with local authority foster parents; and
(b) it is reasonably practicable for the contributor to pay (having regard to his means).

(6) An authority may at any time withdraw a contribution notice (without prejudice to their power to serve another).

(7) Where the authority and the contributor agree –

(a) the sum which the contributor is to contribute; and
(b) arrangements for payment,

(whether as specified in the contribution notice or otherwise) and the contributor notifies the authority in writing that he so agrees, the authority may recover summarily as a civil debt any contribution which is overdue and unpaid.

PART II

(8) A contributor may, by serving a notice in writing on the authority, withdraw his agreement in relation to any period of liability falling after the date of service of the notice.

(9) Sub-paragraph (7) is without prejudice to any other method of recovery.

'reasonably practicable for the contributor to pay (having regard to his means)' (para 22(5)(a))—See **'A contribution order ... shall be made with due regard to the contributor's means'** under para 23.

23 Contribution orders

(1) Where a contributor has been served with a contribution notice and has –

- (a) failed to reach any agreement with the local authority as mentioned in paragraph 22(7) within the period of one month beginning with the day on which the contribution notice was served; or
- (b) served a notice under paragraph 22(8) withdrawing his agreement,

the authority may apply to the court for an order under this paragraph.

(2) On such an application the court may make an order ('a contribution order') requiring the contributor to contribute a weekly sum towards the child's maintenance in accordance with arrangements for payment specified by the court.

(3) A contribution order –

- (a) shall not specify a weekly sum greater than that specified in the contribution notice; and
- (b) shall be made with due regard to the contributor's means.

(4) A contribution order shall not –

- (a) take effect before the date specified in the contribution notice; or
- (b) have effect while the contributor is not liable to contribute (by virtue of paragraph 21); or
- (c) remain in force after the child has ceased to be looked after by the authority who obtained the order.

(5) An authority may not apply to the court under sub-paragraph (1) in relation to a contribution notice which they have withdrawn.

(6) Where –

- (a) a contribution order is in force;
- (b) the authority serve another contribution notice; and
- (c) the contributor and the authority reach an agreement under paragraph 22(7) in respect of that other contribution notice,

the effect of the agreement shall be to discharge the order from the date on which it is agreed that the agreement shall take effect.

(7) Where an agreement is reached under sub-paragraph (6) the authority shall notify the court –

- (a) of the agreement; and
- (b) of the date on which it took effect.

(8) A contribution order may be varied or revoked on the application of the contributor or the authority.

(9) In proceedings for the variation of a contribution order, the authority shall specify –

- (a) the weekly sum which, having regard to paragraph 22, they propose that the contributor should contribute under the order as varied; and
- (b) the proposed arrangements for payment.

(10) Where a contribution order is varied, the order –

- (a) shall not specify a weekly sum greater than that specified by the authority in the proceedings for variation; and
- (b) shall be made with due regard to the contributor's means.

(11) An appeal shall lie in accordance with rules of court from any order made under this paragraph.

Defined terms—'contribution notice': para 22(1); 'contributor': para 21(1).

Jurisdiction—C(AP)O 1991, art 3 requires proceedings under this paragraph to be commenced in a magistrates' court. Articles 5 and 7(2) have the effect of preventing proceedings so commenced from being transferred to the County Court; jurisdiction is therefore restricted, in effect, to magistrates' courts.

'A contribution order … shall be made with due regard to the contributor's means' (para 23(3)(b))—The criteria to be applied in assessing the contribution to be made by a parent in respect of a child who is being accommodated by a local authority are different to those applied when assessing maintenance for a child. The court must assess the contributor's means by reference to the sources of income available to him and to the manner in which he has expended that income; so long as the money was reasonably expended, the court cannot superimpose a value judgment as to priorities for family spending (*Re C (A Minor) (Contribution Notice)* [1994] 1 FLR 111, FD).

24 Enforcement of contribution orders etc

(1) *(repealed)*

(2) Where a contributor has agreed, or has been ordered, to make contributions to a local authority, any other local authority within whose area the contributor is for the time being living may –

- (a) at the request of the local authority who served the contribution notice; and
- (b) subject to agreement as to any sum to be deducted in respect of services rendered,

collect from the contributor any contributions due on behalf of the authority who served the notice.

(3) In sub-paragraph (2) the reference to any other local authority includes a reference to –

- (aa) a local authority in Wales;
- (a) a local authority within the meaning of section 1(2) of the Social Work (Scotland) Act 1968; and
- (b) a Health and Social Services Board established under Article 16 of the Health and Personal Social Services (Northern Ireland) Order 1972.

(4) The power to collect sums under sub-paragraph (2) includes the power to –

- (a) receive and give a discharge for any contributions due; and
- (b) (if necessary) enforce payment of any contributions,

even though those contributions may have fallen due at a time when the contributor was living elsewhere.

(5) Any contributions collected under sub-paragraph (2) shall be paid (subject to any agreed deduction) to the local authority who served the contribution notice.

(6) In any proceedings under this paragraph, a document which purports to be –

- (a) a copy of an order made by a court under or by virtue of paragraph 23; and
- (b) certified as a true copy by the designated officer for the court,

shall be evidence of the order.

(7) In any proceedings under this paragraph, a certificate which –

- (a) purports to be signed by the clerk or some other duly authorised officer of the local authority who obtained the contribution order; and
- (b) states that any sum due to the authority under the order is overdue and unpaid,

shall be evidence that the sum is overdue and unpaid.

Amendments—AJA 1999, s 90, Sch 13, para 162; Courts Act 2003, s 109(1), Sch 8, para 340; CCA 2013, s 17, Sch 11; SI 2016/413.

Defined terms—'contribution notice': para 22(1); 'contribution order': para 23(2); 'contributor': para 21(1); 'local authority': s 105(1).

25 Regulations

The Secretary of State may make regulations –

- (a) as to the considerations which a local authority must take into account in deciding –
  - (i) whether it is reasonable to recover contributions; and
  - (ii) what the arrangements for payment should be;

(b) as to the procedures they must follow in reaching agreements with –
   (i) contributors (under paragraphs 22 and 23); and
   (ii) any other local authority under paragraph 24(2).

Amendments—CYPA 2008, s 39, Sch 3, paras 1, 27; SI 2016/413.

SCHEDULE 3
SUPERVISION ORDERS

PART I
GENERAL

1 Meaning of 'responsible person'

In this Schedule, 'the responsible person', in relation to a supervised child, means –

(a) any person who has parental responsibility for the child; and
(b) any other person with whom the child is living.

2 Power of supervisor to give directions to supervised child

(1) A supervision order may require the supervised child to comply with any directions given from time to time by the supervisor which require him to do all or any of the following things –

(a) to live at a place or places specified in the directions for a period or periods so specified;
(b) to present himself to a person or persons specified in the directions at a place or places and on a day or days so specified;
(c) to participate in activities specified in the directions on a day or days so specified.

(2) It shall be for the supervisor to decide whether, and to what extent, he exercises his power to give directions and to decide the form of any directions which he gives.

(3) Sub-paragraph (1) does not confer on a supervisor power to give directions in respect of any medical or psychiatric examination or treatment (which are matters dealt with in paragraphs 4 and 5).

Court specifying directions for supervisor to give—See under para 3 below.

3 Imposition of obligations on responsible person

(1) With the consent of any responsible person, a supervision order may include a requirement –

(a) that he take all reasonable steps to ensure that the supervised child complies with any direction given by the supervisor under paragraph 2;
(b) that he take all reasonable steps to ensure that the supervised child complies with any requirement included in the order under paragraph 4 or 5;
(c) that he comply with any directions given by the supervisor requiring him to attend at a place specified in the directions for the purpose of taking part in activities so specified.

(2) A direction given under sub-paragraph (1)(c) may specify the time at which the responsible person is to attend and whether or not the supervised child is required to attend with him.

(3) A supervision order may require any person who is a responsible person in relation to the supervised child to keep the supervisor informed of his address, if it differs from the child's.

Court cannot specify directions to be given—In *Re V (Care or Supervision Order)* [1996] 1 FLR 776, CA, a supervision order cannot have conditions attached (in that case, the judge had wrongly made a supervision order subject to a condition that the child continue as a weekly boarder at a particular school). Sch 3 deals only with:

(a) directions given by the supervisor (see Sch 3, para 2);
(b) requirements which the court can impose with the consent of any responsible person (see Sch 3, para 3); and
(c) a detailed regime for psychiatric and medical examination of the child (see Sch 3, paras 4 and 5).

The only sanction for infringement of the terms of a supervision order, or of any directions given under it, is for the supervisor to return to court for the order to be varied or discharged; the ultimate sanction would be the substitution of a care order.

Re V was followed in *Re S (Care or Supervision Order)* [1996] 1 FLR 753, CA; *Re H (Supervision Order)* [1994] 2 FLR 979, FD (no power in court under para 3 to specify that supervisor should impose a particular direction on a responsible person); *Re H (Prohibited Steps Order)* [1995] 1 FLR 638, CA (court cannot impose on supervision order a condition of no contact with mother's former cohabitee); and *Re B (Supervision Order: Parental Undertaking)* [1996] 1 FLR 676, CA. The cases of *Croydon London Borough Council v A (No 3)* [1992] 2 FLR 350, FD, and *Re T (A Minor) (Care Order: Conditions)* [1994] 2 FLR 423, CA, which appear to suggest that conditions (e g of residence in a particular place) *can* be attached to a supervision order by the court, would seem to be wrong. Even though the Family Court appears to have no inherent jurisdiction to accept undertakings in care proceedings or as part of a supervision order, a parent's agreement to behave in a particular way (in that case, to undergo medical treatment) could be recorded in a preamble to the order, and any failure to honour this agreement could be brought to the attention of the court in due course *Re B (Supervision Order: Parental Undertaking)*.

4 Psychiatric and medical examinations

(1) A supervision order may require the supervised child –

(a) to submit to a medical or psychiatric examination; or
(b) to submit to any such examination from time to time as directed by the supervisor.

(2) Any such examination shall be required to be conducted –

(a) by, or under the direction of, such registered medical practitioner as may be specified in the order;
(b) at a place specified in the order and at which the supervised child is to attend as a non-resident patient; or
(c) at –
  (i) a health service hospital; or
  (ii) in the case of a psychiatric examination, a hospital, independent hospital or care home,

at which the supervised child is, or is to attend as, a resident patient.

(3) A requirement of a kind mentioned in sub-paragraph (2)(c) shall not be included unless the court is satisfied, on the evidence of a registered medical practitioner, that –

(a) the child may be suffering from a physical or mental condition that requires, and may be susceptible to, treatment; and
(b) a period as a resident patient is necessary if the examination is to be carried out properly.

(4) No court shall include a requirement under this paragraph in a supervision order unless it is satisfied that –

(a) where the child has sufficient understanding to make an informed decision, he consents to its inclusion; and
(b) satisfactory arrangements have been, or can be, made for the examination.

Amendments—Care Standards Act 2000, s 116, Sch 4, para 14(24).

5 Psychiatric and medical treatment

(1) Where a court which proposes to make or vary a supervision order is satisfied, on the evidence of a registered medical practitioner approved for the purposes of section 12 of the Mental Health Act 1983, that the mental condition of the supervised child –

(a) is such as requires, and may be susceptible to, treatment; but
(b) is not such as to warrant his detention in pursuance of a hospital order under Part III of that Act,

the court may include in the order a requirement that the supervised child shall, for a period specified in the order, submit to such treatment as is so specified.

(2) The treatment specified in accordance with sub-paragraph (1) must be –

(a) by, or under the direction of, such registered medical practitioner as may be specified in the order;
(b) as a non-resident patient at such a place as may be so specified; or
(c) as a resident patient in a hospital, independent hospital or care home.

(3) Where a court which proposes to make or vary a supervision order is satisfied, on the evidence of a registered medical practitioner, that the physical condition of the supervised child is such as requires, and may be susceptible to, treatment, the court may include in the order a requirement that the supervised child shall, for a period specified in the order, submit to such treatment as is so specified.

(4) The treatment specified in accordance with sub-paragraph (3) must be –

(a) by, or under the direction of, such registered medical practitioner as may be specified in the order;

(b) as a non-resident patient at such place as may be so specified; or

(c) as a resident patient in a health service hospital.

(5) No court shall include a requirement under this paragraph in a supervision order unless it is satisfied –

(a) where the child has sufficient understanding to make an informed decision, that he consents to its inclusion; and

(b) that satisfactory arrangements have been, or can be, made for the treatment.

(6) If a medical practitioner by whom or under whose direction a supervised person is being treated in pursuance of a requirement included in a supervision order by virtue of this paragraph is unwilling to continue to treat or direct the treatment of the supervised child or is of the opinion that –

(a) the treatment should be continued beyond the period specified in the order;

(b) the supervised child needs different treatment;

(c) he is not susceptible to treatment; or

(d) he does not require further treatment,

the practitioner shall make a report in writing to that effect to the supervisor.

(7) On receiving a report under this paragraph the supervisor shall refer it to the court, and on such a reference the court may make an order cancelling or varying the requirement.

Amendments—Care Standards Act 2000, s 116, Sch 4, para 14(24).

PART II
MISCELLANEOUS

6 Life of supervision order

(1) Subject to sub-paragraph (2) and section 91, a supervision order shall cease to have effect at the end of the period of one year beginning with the date on which it was made.

(2) A supervision order shall also cease to have effect if an event mentioned in section 25(1)(a) or (b) of the Child Abduction and Custody Act 1985 (termination of existing orders) occurs with respect to the child.

(3) Where the supervisor applies to the court to extend, or further extend, a supervision order the court may extend the order for such period as it may specify.

(4) A supervision order may not be extended so as to run beyond the end of the period of three years beginning with the date on which it was made.

Defined terms—'supervision order': s 31(11); 'supervisor': s 105(1).

Duration of supervision orders—Normally (subject to s 91 and to Sch 3, para 6(2)), a supervision order lasts for a maximum of 1 year in the first instance (para 6(1)) and there is no jurisdiction in the court to allow the making of an extended supervision order for 3 years from the outset (*Wakefield Metropolitan District Council v T* [2008] 1 FLR 1569, CA); there is nothing to preclude an order for less than 1 year (*M v Warwickshire County Council* [1994] 2 FLR 593, FD). Although para 6(3) facilitates the extension of this period, on more than one occasion if necessary, it nonetheless appears that the effect of para 6(4) is that the longest that the extended order can run is 3 years from the date of the original order (*Re A (Supervision Order: Extension)* [1995] 1 FLR 335, CA). Thereafter, there would have to be a fresh application under CA 1989, s 31, and the threshold criteria would have to be satisfied.

Test on extension application—To obtain an extension, the applicant must satisfy the court that the welfare of the child requires the supervision order to continue; the s 31 threshold test need not be satisfied again (*Re A (Supervision Order: Extension)* [1995] 1 FLR 335, CA).

CA 1989, s 38 not applicable—CA 1989, s 38 has no application to extension orders. If an application for an extension is made within time and is opposed, and the hearing date will be after the expiry of the original order, the court can make one or more short extension orders pending final determination (*Re A (Supervision Order: Extension)*, above). The court cannot make either a care order or an interim care order on an extension application (ibid).

Procedure—The supervisor must apply for an extension to the court which made the original order (C(AP)O 1991, art 4(1)) though by virtue of art 4(2) the court has power subsequently to transfer the proceedings in accordance with arts 5–13. See FPR 2010, rr 5.1–5.3 and PD5A, PD12A. For respondents to the application and other persons who must be given written notice, see the table set out in FPR 2010, r 12.3. As proceedings relating to an extension are 'specified proceedings' within the meaning of s 41(6) (s 41(6)(i), and FPR 2010, r 12.27(1)(d)), a children's guardian will normally be appointed. In *Wakefield Metropolitan District Council v T* [2008] 1 FLR 1569, CA, the Court of Appeal gave general guidance as to the procedure for applying for the extension of a supervision order.

Alternative applications—The court has a general power under s 39(2) and (3) to vary or discharge a supervision order.

7 *(repealed)*

8 Information to be given to supervisor etc

(1) A supervision order may require the supervised child –

(a) to keep the supervisor informed of any change in his address; and
(b) to allow the supervisor to visit him at the place where he is living.

(2) The responsible person in relation to any child with respect to whom a supervision order is made shall –

(a) if asked by the supervisor, inform him of the child's address (if it is known to him); and
(b) if he is living with the child, allow the supervisor reasonable contact with the child.

9 Selection of supervisor

(1) A supervision order shall not designate a local authority as the supervisor unless –

(a) the authority agree; or
(b) the supervised child lives or will live within their area.

(2)–(5) *(repealed)*

Amendments—Probation Service Act 1993, s 32, Sch 3, para 9; CJCSA 2000, ss 74, 75, Sch 7, paras 87, 96, Sch 8.

10 Effect of supervision order on earlier orders

The making of a supervision order with respect to any child brings to an end any earlier care or supervision order which –

(a) was made with respect to that child; and
(b) would otherwise continue in force.

11 Local authority functions and expenditure

(1) The Secretary of State may make regulations with respect to the exercise by a local authority of their functions where a child has been placed under their supervision by a supervision order.

(2) Where a supervision order requires compliance with directions given by virtue of this section, any expenditure incurred by the supervisor for the purposes of the directions shall be defrayed by the local authority designated in the order.

PART III
EDUCATION SUPERVISION ORDERS

Effect of orders

12 (1) Where an education supervision order is in force with respect to a child, it shall be the duty of the supervisor –

(a) to advise, assist and befriend, and give directions to –
 (i) the supervised child; and

(ii) his parents;

in such a way as will, in the opinion of the supervisor, secure that he is properly educated;

(b) where any such directions given to

(i) the supervised child; or

(ii) a parent of his,

have not been complied with, to consider what further steps to take in the exercise of the supervisor's powers under this Act.

(2) Before giving any directions under sub-paragraph (1) the supervisor shall, so far as is reasonably practicable, ascertain the wishes and feelings of –

(a) the child; and

(b) his parents;

including, in particular, their wishes as to the place at which the child should be educated.

(3) When settling the terms of any such directions, the supervisor shall give due consideration –

(a) having regard to the child's age and understanding, to such wishes and feelings of his as the supervisor has been able to ascertain; and

(b) to such wishes and feelings of the child's parents as he has been able to ascertain.

(4) Directions may be given under this paragraph at any time while the education supervision order is in force.

13 (1) Where an education supervision order is in force with respect to a child, the duties of the child's parents under sections 7 and 444 of the Education Act 1996 (duties to secure education of children and to secure regular attendance of registered pupils) shall be superseded by their duty to comply with any directions in force under the education supervision order.

(2) Where an education supervision order is made with respect to a child –

(a) any school attendance order –

(i) made under section 437 of the Education Act 1996 with respect to the child; and

(ii) in force immediately before the making of the education supervision order,

shall cease to have effect; and

(b) while the education supervision order remains in force, the following provisions shall not apply with respect to the child –

(i) section 437 of that Act (school attendance orders);

(ii) section 9 of that Act (pupils to be educated in accordance with wishes of their parents);

(iii) sections 411 and 423 of that Act (parental preference and appeals against admission decisions);

(c) a youth rehabilitation order made under Part 1 of the Criminal Justice and Immigration Act 2008 with respect to the child, while the education supervision order is in force, may not include an education requirement (within the meaning of that Part);

(d) any education requirement of a kind mentioned in paragraph (c), which was in force with respect to the child immediately before the making of the education supervision order, shall cease to have effect.

Amendments—Education Act 1996, s 582(1), Sch 37, Pt I, para 93; Powers of Criminal Courts (Sentencing) Act 2000, s 165, Sch 9, para 131; Criminal Justice and Immigration Act 2008, ss 6(2), 149, Sch 4, para 37.

14 Effect where child also subject to supervision order

(1) This paragraph applies where an education supervision order and a supervision order, or youth rehabilitation order (within the meaning of Part 1 of the Criminal Justice and Immigration Act 2008), are in force at the same time with respect to the same child.

(2) Any failure to comply with a direction given by the supervisor under the education supervision order shall be disregarded if it would not have been reasonably practicable to comply with it without failing to comply with a direction or instruction given under the other order.

Amendments—Powers of Criminal Courts (Sentencing) Act 2000, s 165, Sch 9, para 131; Criminal Justice and Immigration Act 2008, ss 6(2), 149, Sch 4, para 37.

15 Duration of orders

(1) An education supervision order shall have effect for a period of one year, beginning with the date on which it is made.

(2) An education supervision order shall not expire if, before it would otherwise have expired, the court has (on the application of the authority in whose favour the order was made) extended the period during which it is in force.

(3) Such an application may not be made earlier than three months before the date on which the order would otherwise expire.

(4) The period during which an education supervision order is in force may be extended under sub-paragraph (2) on more than one occasion.

(5) No one extension may be for a period of more than three years.

(6) An education supervision order shall cease to have effect on –

(a) the child's ceasing to be of compulsory school age; or
(b) the making of a care order with respect to the child;

and sub-paragraphs (1) to (4) are subject to this sub-paragraph.

Defined terms—'education supervision order': s 36(2).

Duration of education supervision orders—Normally (subject to para 15(6)) an education supervision order lasts for a maximum of 1 year in the first instance (para 15(1)). In contrast with para 6(2) and (3), which allow an ordinary supervision order to be extended for no more than 3 years from the original order, an ESO may be extended for any number of 3-year periods until the child ceases to be of compulsory school age or a care order is made and the order expires in accordance with para 15(6). For cases on duration and extension of ordinary supervision orders which may assist with education supervision orders by analogy, see **Duration of supervision orders** under para 6.

'authority in whose favour the order was made' (para 15(2))—Under s 36(1), the designated local education authority is the authority in whose favour the order was made.

16 Information to be given to supervisor etc

(1) An education supervision order may require the child –

(a) to keep the supervisor informed of any change in his address; and
(b) to allow the supervisor to visit him at the place where he is living.

(2) A person who is the parent of a child with respect to whom an education supervision order has been made shall –

(a) if asked by the supervisor, inform him of the child's address (if it is known to him); and
(b) if he is living with the child, allow the supervisor reasonable contact with the child.

17 Discharge of orders

(1) The court may discharge any education supervision order on the application of –

(a) the child concerned;
(b) a parent of his; or
(c) the local authority designated in the order.

(2) On discharging an education supervision order, the court may direct the local authority within whose area the child lives, or will live, to investigate the circumstances of the child.

Defined terms—'child': s 105(1); 'education supervision order': s 36(2); 'local authority': s 105(1).

Scope—This paragraph gives the court the option, if it does discharge the order, to require the local authority to investigate the circumstances of the child, no doubt with a view to the local authority seeking a care or supervision order if it considers such action appropriate.

'parent' (para 17(1)(a))—By virtue of para 21, for the purposes of Sch 3, Pt III (which includes para 17), 'parent' has the same meaning as in the Education Act 1996, i e it includes any person who is not a parent of a child but who has parental responsibility for him or care of him (see Education Act 1996, s 576).

'local authority' (para 17(1)(c))—This refers to the local authority designated in the order under s 36(1).

Directing local authority investigation (para 17(2))—The wording of para 17(2) contrasts with that of s 37, which is of wider application and empowers the court to direct an investigation in family proceedings.

However, a direction under s 37 can only be given where it appears to the court that it may be appropriate for a care or supervision order to be made in respect of the child whereas there is no such restriction under para 17(2). For further detail as to s 37 directions see that section and the annotation **Best Practice Guidance on s 37(1) directions** thereunder.

18 Offences

(1) If a parent of a child with respect to whom an education supervision order is in force persistently fails to comply with a direction given under the order he shall be guilty of an offence.

(2) It shall be a defence for any person charged with such an offence to prove that –

- (a) he took all reasonable steps to ensure that the direction was complied with;
- (b) the direction was unreasonable; or
- (c) he had complied with –
  - (i) a requirement included in a supervision order made with respect to the child; or
  - (ii) directions given under such a requirement,

and that it was not reasonably practicable to comply both with the direction and with the requirement or directions mentioned in this paragraph.

(3) A person guilty of an offence under this paragraph shall be liable on summary conviction to a fine not exceeding level 3 on the standard scale.

19 Persistent failure of child to comply with directions

(1) Where a child with respect to whom an education supervision order is in force persistently fails to comply with any direction given under the order, the local authority designated in the order shall notify the appropriate local authority, if different.

(2) Where a local authority have been notified under sub-paragraph (1) they shall investigate the circumstances of the child.

(3) In this paragraph 'the appropriate local authority' has the same meaning as in section 36.

20 Miscellaneous

The Secretary of State may by regulations make provision modifying, or displacing, the provisions of any enactment about education in relation to any child with respect to whom an education supervision order is in force to such extent as appears to the Secretary of State to be necessary or expedient in consequence of the provision made by this Act with respect to such orders.

21 Interpretation

In this part of this Schedule 'parent' has the same meaning as in the Education Act 1996.

Amendments—Education Act 1996, s 582(1), Sch 37, para 93; SI 2010/1185.

****

SCHEDULE 7
FOSTER PARENTS: LIMITS ON NUMBER OF FOSTER CHILDREN

1 Interpretation

For the purposes of this Schedule, a person fosters a child if –

- (a) he is a local authority foster parent in relation to the child;
- (b) he is a foster parent with whom the child has been placed by a voluntary organisation; or
- (c) he fosters the child privately.

2 The usual fostering limit

Subject to what follows, a person may not foster more than three children ('the usual fostering limit').

3 Siblings

A person may exceed the usual fostering limit if the children concerned are all siblings with respect to each other.

4 Exemption by local authority

(1) A person may exceed the usual fostering limit if he is exempted from it by the local authority within whose area he lives.

(2) In considering whether to exempt a person, a local authority shall have regard, in particular, to –

- (a) the number of children whom the person proposes to foster;
- (b) the arrangements which the person proposes for the care and accommodation of the fostered children;
- (c) the intended and likely relationship between the person and the fostered children;
- (d) the period of time for which he proposes to foster the children; and
- (e) whether the welfare of the fostered children (and of any other children who are or will be living in the accommodation) will be safeguarded and promoted.

(3) Where a local authority exempt a person, they shall inform him by notice in writing –

- (a) that he is so exempted;
- (b) of the children, described by name, whom he may foster; and
- (c) of any condition to which the exemption is subject.

(4) A local authority may at any time by notice in writing –

- (a) vary or cancel an exemption; or
- (b) impose, vary or cancel a condition to which the exemption is subject,

and, in considering whether to do so, they shall have regard in particular to the considerations mentioned in sub-paragraph (2).

(5) The Secretary of State may make regulations amplifying or modifying the provisions of this paragraph in order to provide for cases where children need to be placed with foster parents as a matter of urgency.

5 Effect of exceeding fostering limit

(1) A person shall cease to be treated, for the purposes of this Act and the Care Standards Act 2000 as fostering and shall be treated as carrying on a children's home if –

- (a) he exceeds the usual fostering limit; or
- (b) where he is exempted under paragraph 4, –
  - (i) he fosters any child not named in the exemption; and
  - (ii) in so doing, he exceeds the usual fostering limit.

(2) Sub-paragraph (1) does not apply if the children concerned are all siblings in respect of each other.

Amendments—Care Standards Act 2000, s 116, Sch 4, para 14(25).

6 Complaints etc

(1) Every local authority shall establish a procedure for considering any representations (including any complaint) made to them about the discharge of their functions under paragraph 4 by a person exempted or seeking to be exempted under that paragraph.

(2) In carrying out any consideration of representations under subparagraph (1), a local authority shall comply with any regulations made by the Secretary of State for the purposes of this paragraph.

PART II

SCHEDULE 8
PRIVATELY FOSTERED CHILDREN

Exemptions

1 A child is not a privately fostered child while he is being looked after by a local authority.

2 (1) A child is not a privately fostered child while he is in the care of any person –

(a) in premises in which any –

(i) parent of his;

(ii) person who is not a parent of his but who has parental responsibility for him; or

(iii) person who is a relative of his and who has assumed responsibility for his care,

is for the time being living;

(b) (*repealed*)

(c) in accommodation provided by or on behalf of any voluntary organisation;

(d) in any school in which he is receiving full-time education;

(e) in any health service hospital;

(f) in any care home or independent hospital;

(g) in any home or institution not specified in this paragraph but provided, equipped and maintained by the Secretary of State.

(2) Sub-paragraph (1)(c) to (g) does not apply where the person caring for the child is doing so in his personal capacity and not in the course of carrying out his duties in relation to the establishment mentioned in the paragraph in question.

Amendments—Registered Homes (Amendment) Act 1991, s 2(6); Care Standards Act 2000, s 116, Sch 4, para 14(27),(28).

3 A child is not a privately fostered child while he is in the care of any person in compliance with –

(a) a youth rehabilitation order made under section 1 of the Criminal Justice and Immigration Act 2008; or

(b) a supervision requirement within the meaning of Part II of the Children (Scotland) Act 1995.

Amendments—Children (Scotland) Act 1995, s 105(4), Sch 4, para 48(1),(5); Powers of Criminal Courts (Sentencing) Act 2000, s 165, Sch 9, para 132; Criminal Justice and Immigration Act 2008, ss 6(2), 149, Sch 4, para 38.

Modifications—Schedule 8, para 3(b) is modified for certain purposes by SI 2013/1465, art 17, Sch 1, para 2.

4 A child is not a privately fostered child while he is liable to be detained, or subject to guardianship, under the Mental Health Act 1983.

5 A child is not a privately fostered child while he is placed in the care of a person who proposes to adopt him under arrangements made by an adoption agency within the meaning of –

(a) section 2 of the Adoption and Children Act 2002;

(b), (c) …

or while he is a child in respect of whom a local authority have functions by virtue of regulations under section 83(6)(b) of the Adoption and Children Act 2002 (which relates to children brought into the United Kingdom for adoption), or corresponding functions by virtue of regulations under section 1 of the Adoption (Intercountry Aspects) Act 1999 (regulations to give effect to Hague Convention on Protection of Children and Co-operation in respect of Intercountry Adoption).

Amendments—ACA 2002, Sch 3, para 73; CAA 2006, s 14(3).

6 Power of local authority to impose requirements

(1) Where a person is fostering any child privately, or proposes to foster any child privately, the appropriate local authority may impose on him requirements as to –

(a) the number, age and sex of the children who may be privately fostered by him;

(b) the standard of the accommodation and equipment to be provided for them;
(c) the arrangements to be made with respect to their health and safety; and
(d) particular arrangements which must be made with respect to the provision of care for them,

and it shall be his duty to comply with any such requirement before the end of such period as the authority may specify unless, in the case of a proposal, the proposal is not carried out.

(2) A requirement may be limited to a particular child, or class of child.

(3) A requirement (other than one imposed under sub-paragraph (1)(a)) may be limited by the authority so as to apply only when the number of children fostered by the person exceeds a specified number.

(4) A requirement shall be imposed by notice in writing addressed to the person on whom it is imposed and informing him of –

(a) the reason for imposing the requirement;
(b) his right under paragraph 8 to appeal against it; and
(c) the time within which he may do so.

(5) A local authority may at any time vary any requirement, impose any additional requirement or remove any requirement.

(6) In this Schedule –

(a) 'the appropriate local authority' means –
   (i) the local authority within whose area the child is being fostered; or
   (ii) in the case of a proposal to foster a child, the local authority within whose area it is proposed that he will be fostered; and
(b) 'requirement', in relation to any person, means a requirement imposed on him under this paragraph.

7 Regulations requiring notification of fostering etc

(1) The Secretary of State may by regulations make provision as to –

(a) the circumstances in which notification is required to be given in connection with children who are, have been or are proposed to be fostered privately; and
(b) the manner and form in which such notification is to be given.

(2) The regulations may, in particular –

(a) require any person who is, or proposes to be, involved (whether or not directly) in arranging for a child to be fostered privately to notify the appropriate authority;
(b) require any person who is –
   (i) a parent of a child; or
   (ii) a person who is not a parent of his but who has parental responsibility for a child,

   and who knows that it is proposed that the child should be fostered privately, to notify the appropriate authority;
(c) require any parent of a privately fostered child, or person who is not a parent of such a child but who has parental responsibility for him, to notify the appropriate authority of any change in his address;
(d) require any person who proposes to foster a child privately, to notify the appropriate authority of his proposal;
(e) require any person who is fostering a child privately, or proposes to do so, to notify the appropriate authority of –
   (i) any offence of which he has been convicted;
   (ii) any disqualification imposed on him under section 68; or
   (iii) any prohibition imposed on him under section 69;
(f) require any person who is fostering a child privately, to notify the appropriate authority of any change in his address;
(g) require any person who is fostering a child privately to notify the appropriate authority in writing of any person who begins, or ceases, to be part of his household;

PART II

(h) require any person who has been fostering a child privately, but has ceased to do so, to notify the appropriate authority (indicating, where the child has died, that that is the reason).

7A Every local authority must promote public awareness in their area of requirements as to notification for which provision is made under paragraph 7.

Amendments—CA 2004, s 44.

8 Appeals

(1) A person aggrieved by –

(a) a requirement imposed under paragraph 6;
(b) a refusal of consent under section 68;
(c) a prohibition imposed under section 69;
(d) a refusal to cancel such a prohibition;
(e) a refusal to make an exemption under paragraph 4 of Schedule 7;
(f) a condition imposed in such an exemption; or
(g) a variation or cancellation of such an exemption,

may appeal to the court.

(2) The appeal must be made within fourteen days from the date on which the person appealing is notified of the requirement, refusal, prohibition, condition, variation or cancellation.

(3) Where the appeal is against –

(a) a requirement imposed under paragraph 6;
(b) a condition of an exemption imposed under paragraph 4 of Schedule 7; or
(c) a variation or cancellation of such an exemption,

the requirement, condition, variation or cancellation shall not have effect while the appeal is pending.

(4) Where it allows an appeal against a requirement or prohibition, the court may, instead of cancelling the requirement or prohibition –

(a) vary the requirement, or allow more time for compliance with it; or
(b) if an absolute prohibition has been imposed, substitute for it a prohibition on using the premises after such time as the court may specify unless such specified requirements as the local authority had power to impose under paragraph 6 are complied with.

(5) Any requirement or prohibition specified or substituted by a court under this paragraph shall be deemed for the purposes of Part IX (other than this paragraph) to have been imposed by the local authority under paragraph 6 or (as the case may be) section 69.

(6) Where it allows an appeal against a refusal to make an exemption, a condition imposed in such an exemption or a variation or cancellation of such an exemption, the court may –

(a) make an exemption;
(b) impose a condition; or
(c) vary the exemption.

(7) Any exemption made or varied under sub-paragraph (6), or any condition imposed under that sub-paragraph, shall be deemed for the purposes of Schedule 7 (but not for the purpose of this paragraph) to have been made, varied or imposed under that Schedule.

(8) Nothing in sub-paragraph (1)(e) to (g) confers any right of appeal on –

(a) a person who is, or would be if exempted under Schedule 7, a local authority foster parent; or
(b) a person who is, or would be if so exempted, a person with whom a child is placed by a voluntary organisation.

Jurisdiction—Proceedings under Sch 8, para 8 are to be commenced in the Family Court.

'person aggrieved' (para 8(1))—Despite the apparently wide category of potential appellants, the restrictions contained in para 8(8) apply.

'section 68' (para 8(1)(b))—Section 68 relates to the need to obtain the consent of the local authority to foster a child privately.

'section 69' (para 8(1)(c))—Section 69 empowers a local authority to prohibit private fostering.

'paragraph 4 of Schedule 7' (para 8(1)(e))—Schedule 7, para 4 allows a local authority to provide an exemption from the usual fostering limit.

9 Extension of Part IX to certain school children during holidays

(1) Where a child under sixteen who is a pupil at a school lives at the school during school holidays for a period of more than two weeks, Part IX shall apply in relation to the child as if –

- (a) while living at the school, he were a privately fostered child; and
- (b) paragraphs 2(1)(c) and (d) and 6 were omitted.

But this sub-paragraph does not apply to a school which is a children's home in respect of which a person is registered under Part 2 of the Care Standards Act 2000.

(2) Sub-paragraph (3) applies to any person who proposes to care for and accommodate one or more children at a school in circumstances in which some or all of them will be treated as private foster children by virtue of this paragraph.

(3) That person shall, not less than two weeks before the first of those children is treated as a private foster child by virtue of this paragraph during the holiday in question, give written notice of his proposal to the local authority within whose area the child is ordinarily resident ('the appropriate authority'), stating the estimated number of the children.

(4) A local authority may exempt any person from the duty of giving notice under sub-paragraph (3).

(5) Any such exemption may be granted for a special period or indefinitely and may be revoked at any time by notice in writing given to the person exempted.

(6) Where a child who is treated as a private foster child by virtue of this paragraph dies, the person caring for him at the school shall, not later than 48 hours after the death, give written notice of it –

- (a) to the appropriate local authority; and
- (b) where reasonably practicable, to each parent of the child and to every person who is not a parent of his but who has parental responsibility for him.

(7) Where a child who is treated as a foster child by virtue of this paragraph ceases for any other reason to be such a child, the person caring for him at the school shall give written notice of the fact to the appropriate local authority.

Amendments—Care Standards Act 2000, ss 110, 116, Sch 4, para 14(27); CYAP 2008, s 8(3), Sch 1, para 6.

10 Prohibition of advertisements relating to fostering

No advertisement indicating that a person will undertake, or will arrange for, a child to be privately fostered shall be published, unless it states that person's name and address.

11 Avoidance of insurances on lives of privately fostered children

A person who fosters a child privately and for reward shall be deemed for the purposes of the Life Assurance Act 1774 to have no interest in the life of the child.

****

SCHEDULE 9A
CHILD MINDING AND DAY CARE FOR YOUNG CHILDREN IN WALES

1 Exemption of certain schools

(1) Except in prescribed circumstances, Part XA does not apply to provision of day care within sub-paragraph (2) for any child looked after in –

- (a) a maintained school;
- (b) a school assisted by a local authority;

(c) a school in respect of which payments are made by the Assembly under section 485 of the Education Act 1996;

(d) an independent school.

(2) The provision mentioned in sub-paragraph (1) is provision of day care made by –

(a) the person carrying on the establishment in question as part of the establishment's activities; or

(b) a person employed to work at that establishment and authorised to make that provision as part of the establishment's activities.

(3) In sub-paragraph (1) –

'assisted' has the same meaning as in the Education Act 1996;

'maintained school' has the meaning given by section 20(7) of the School Standards and Framework Act 1998.

Amendments—Childcare Act 2006, s 103, Sch 2, paras 6, 18, Sch 3, Pt 2; SI 2010/1185.

2 Exemption for other establishments

(1) Part XA does not apply to provision of day care within sub-paragraph (2) for any child looked after –

(a) in a children's home in respect of which a person is registered under Part 2 of the Care Standards Act 2000;

(b) in a care home;

(c) as a patient in a hospital (within the meaning of the Care Standards Act 2000);

(d) in a residential family centre.

(2) The provision mentioned in sub-paragraph (1) is provision of day care made by –

(a) the department, authority or other person carrying on the establishment in question as part of the establishment's activities; or

(b) a person employed to work at that establishment and authorised to make that provision as part of the establishment's activities.

Amendments—CYAP 2008, s 8(3), Sch 1, para 7.

2A (1) Part XA does not apply to provision of day care in a hotel, guest house or other similar establishment for children staying in that establishment where –

(a) the provision takes place only between 6pm and 2am; and

(b) the person providing the care is doing so for no more than two different clients at the same time.

(2) For the purposes of sub-paragraph (1)(b), a 'client' is a person at whose request (or persons at whose joint request) day care is provided for a child.

Amendments—CA 2004, s 48, Sch 4, paras 1, 7.

3 Exemption for occasional facilities

(1) Where day care is provided on particular premises on less than six days in any year, that provision shall be disregarded for the purposes of Part XA if the person making it has notified the Assembly in writing before the first occasion on which the premises concerned are so used in that year.

(2) In sub-paragraph (1) 'year' means the year beginning with the day (after the commencement of paragraph 5 of Schedule 9) on which the day care in question was or is first provided on the premises concerned and any subsequent year.

Amendments—Childcare Act 2006, s 103, Sch 2, para 6.

4 Disqualification for registration

(1) Regulations may provide for a person to be disqualified for registration for child minding or providing day care in Wales.

(2) The regulations may, in particular, provide for a person to be disqualified where –

(a) he is included in the list kept under section 1 of the Protection of Children Act 1999;
(b) he is subject to a direction under section 142 of the Education Act 2002, given on the grounds that he is unsuitable to work with children or on grounds relating to his health;
(c) an order of a prescribed kind has been made at any time with respect to him;
(d) an order of a prescribed kind has been made at any time with respect to any child who has been in his care;
(e) a requirement of a prescribed kind has been imposed at any time with respect to such a child, under or by virtue of any enactment;
(f) he has at any time been refused registration under Part X or Part XA, or Part 3 of the Childcare Act 2006, or any prescribed enactment or had any such registration cancelled;
(g) he has been convicted of any offence of a prescribed kind, or has been discharged absolutely or conditionally for any such offence;
(ga) he has been given a caution in respect of any offence of a prescribed kind;
(h) he has at any time been disqualified from fostering a child privately;
(j) a prohibition has been imposed on him at any time under section 69, section 10 of the Foster Children (Scotland) Act 1984 or any prescribed enactment;
(k) his rights and powers with respect to a child have at any time been vested in a prescribed authority under a prescribed enactment.

(3) Regulations may provide for a person who lives –

(a) in the same household as a person who is himself disqualified for registration for child minding or providing day care in Wales; or
(b) in a household at which any such person is employed,

to be disqualified for registration for child minding or providing day care in Wales.

(3A) …

(4) A person who is disqualified for registration for providing day care in Wales shall not provide day care in Wales, or be directly concerned in the management of any provision of day care in Wales.

(5) No person shall employ, in connection with the provision of day care in Wales, a person who is disqualified for registration for providing day care in Wales.

(6) In this paragraph –

'caution' includes a reprimand or warning within the meaning of section 65 of the Crime and Disorder Act 1998;

'enactment' means any enactment having effect, at any time, in any part of the United Kingdom.

(7) A conviction in respect of which a probation order was made before 1 October 1992 (which would not otherwise be treated as a conviction) is to be treated as a conviction for the purposes of this paragraph.

Amendments—Criminal Justice Act 2003, Sch 32, para 61; CA 2004, s 48, Sch 4, paras 1, 8; Childcare Act 2006, ss 102(1),(2)(a),(b), 103, Sch 2, paras 6, 18.

5 (1) If any person –

(a) acts as a child minder in Wales at any time when he is disqualified for registration for child minding in Wales; or
(b) contravenes any of sub-paragraphs (3) to (5) of paragraph 4,

he shall be guilty of an offence.

(2) Where a person contravenes sub-paragraph (3) of paragraph 4, he shall not be guilty of an offence under this paragraph if he proves that he did not know, and had no reasonable grounds for believing, that the person in question was living or employed in the household.

(3) Where a person contravenes sub-paragraph (5) of paragraph 4, he shall not be guilty of an offence under this paragraph if he proves that he did not know, and had no reasonable grounds for believing, that the person whom he was employing was disqualified.

(4) A person guilty of an offence under this paragraph shall be liable on summary conviction to imprisonment for a term not exceeding six months, or to a fine not exceeding level 5 on the standard scale, or to both.

5A (1) References in Part XA to a person, so far as relating to the provision of day care, include an unincorporated association.

(2) Proceedings for an offence under Part XA which is alleged to have been committed by an unincorporated association must be brought in the name of the association (and not in that of any of its members).

(3) For the purpose of any such proceedings, rules of court relating to the service of documents are to have effect as if the association were a body corporate.

(4) In proceedings for an offence under Part XA brought against an unincorporated association, section 33 of the Criminal Justice Act 1925 and Schedule 3 to the Magistrates' Courts Act 1980 (procedure) apply as they do in relation to a body corporate.

(5) A fine imposed on an unincorporated association on its conviction of an offence under Part XA is to be paid out of the funds of the association.

(6) If an offence under Part XA committed by an unincorporated association is shown–

(a) to have been committed with the consent or connivance of an officer of the association or a member of its governing body, or
(b) to be attributable to any neglect on the part of such an officer or member,

the officer or member as well as the association is guilty of the offence and liable to proceeded against and punished accordingly.

Amendments—Inserted by CA 2004, s 48, Sch 4, paras 1, 9.

6 Certificates of registration

(1) If an application for registration is granted, the Assembly shall give the applicant a certificate of registration.

(2) A certificate of registration shall give prescribed information about prescribed matters.

(3) Where, due to a change of circumstances, any part of the certificate requires to be amended, the Assembly shall issue an amended certificate.

(4) Where the Assembly is satisfied that the certificate has been lost or destroyed, the Assembly shall issue a copy, on payment by the registered person of any prescribed fee.

(5) For the purposes of Part XA, a person is –

(a) registered for providing child minding in Wales; or
(b) registered for providing day care on any premises in Wales,

if a certificate of registration to that effect is in force in respect of him.

Amendments—Childcare Act 2006, s 103, Sch 2, paras 6, 18.

7 Fees

Regulations may require registered persons to pay to the Assembly, at or by the prescribed times, fees of the prescribed amounts in respect of the discharge by the Assembly of its functions under Part XA.

Amendments—CA 2004, ss 48, 64, Sch 4, paras 1, 4(2)(b), Sch 5, Pt 2; Childcare Act 2006, s 103, Sch 2, para 6.

8 Co-operation between authorities

(1) *(repealed)*

(2) Where it appears to the Assembly that any local authority in Wales could, by taking any specified action, help in the exercise of any of its functions under Part XA, the Assembly may request the help of that authority specifying the action in question.

(3) An authority whose help is so requested shall comply with the request if it is compatible with their own statutory or other duties and obligations and does not unduly prejudice the discharge of any of their functions.

Amendments—Schedule inserted by Care Standards Act 2000, s 79(2), Sch 3. Amended by Education Act 2002, s 215(1), Sch 21; Childcare Act 2006, s 103, Sch 2, para 18, Sch 3, Pt 2.

****

Children and Families Act 2014

****

13 Control of expert evidence, and of assessments, in children proceedings

(1) A person may not without the permission of the court instruct a person to provide expert evidence for use in children proceedings.

(2) Where in contravention of subsection (1) a person is instructed to provide expert evidence, evidence resulting from the instructions is inadmissible in children proceedings unless the court rules that it is admissible.

(3) A person may not without the permission of the court cause a child to be medically or psychiatrically examined or otherwise assessed for the purposes of the provision of expert evidence in children proceedings.

(4) Where in contravention of subsection (3) a child is medically or psychiatrically examined or otherwise assessed, evidence resulting from the examination or other assessment is inadmissible in children proceedings unless the court rules that it is admissible.

(5) In children proceedings, a person may not without the permission of the court put expert evidence (in any form) before the court.

(6) The court may give permission as mentioned in subsection (1), (3) or (5) only if the court is of the opinion that the expert evidence is necessary to assist the court to resolve the proceedings justly.

(7) When deciding whether to give permission as mentioned in subsection (1), (3) or (5) the court is to have regard in particular to –

- (a) any impact which giving permission would be likely to have on the welfare of the children concerned, including in the case of permission as mentioned in subsection (3) any impact which any examination or other assessment would be likely to have on the welfare of the child who would be examined or otherwise assessed,
- (b) the issues to which the expert evidence would relate,
- (c) the questions which the court would require the expert to answer,
- (d) what other expert evidence is available (whether obtained before or after the start of proceedings),
- (e) whether evidence could be given by another person on the matters on which the expert would give evidence,
- (f) the impact which giving permission would be likely to have on the timetable for, and duration and conduct of, the proceedings,
- (g) the cost of the expert evidence, and
- (h) any matters prescribed by Family Procedure Rules.

(8) References in this section to providing expert evidence, or to putting expert evidence before a court, do not include references to –

- (a) the provision or giving of evidence –
  - (i) by a person who is a member of the staff of a local authority or of an authorised applicant,
  - (ii) in proceedings to which the authority or authorised applicant is a party, and
  - (iii) in the course of the person's work for the authority or authorised applicant,

(b) the provision or giving of evidence –
 (i) by a person within a description prescribed for the purposes of subsection (1) of section 94 of the Adoption and Children Act 2002 (suitability for adoption etc.), and
 (ii) about the matters mentioned in that subsection,
(c) the provision or giving of evidence by an officer of the Children and Family Court Advisory and Support Service when acting in that capacity, or
(d) the provision or giving of evidence by a Welsh family proceedings officer (as defined by section 35(4) of the Children Act 2004) when acting in that capacity.

(9) In this section –

'authorised applicant' means –
 (a) the National Society for the Prevention of Cruelty to Children, or
 (b) a person authorised by an order under section 31 of the Children Act 1989 to bring proceedings under that section;

'child' means a person under the age of 18;

'children proceedings' has such meaning as may be prescribed by Family Procedure Rules;

'the court', in relation to any children proceedings, means the court in which the proceedings are taking place;

'local authority' –
 (a) in relation to England means –
  (i) a county council,
  (ii) a district council for an area for which there is no county council,
  (iii) a London borough council,
  (iv) the Common Council of the City of London, or
  (v) the Council of the Isles of Scilly, and
 (b) in relation to Wales means a county council or a county borough council.

(10) The preceding provisions of this section are without prejudice to sections 75 and 76 of the Courts Act 2003 (power to make Family Procedure Rules).

FPR 2010, Pt 25 and s 13—Much of what is to be found in s 13 has been extracted from FPR 2010, Pt 25 and the section should be read alongside that Part. Section 13 applies only to children proceedings, whereas Pt 25 and its accompanying practice directions apply to all family proceedings under FPR 2010.

For the scheme under CFA 2014, s 13(1),(3),(5) and FPR 2010, rr 25.4(2), 25.5 and 25.6 for procedure for permission to call expert evidence in children and all family proceedings, see under FPR 2010, r 25.5.

'expert evidence for use in children proceedings' (s 13(1))—Section 13(1) prevents a party from seeking expert evidence by any means other than with permission of, and by direction of, the court. It is counter to the common law, which is that a party to proceedings may always commission expert evidence. (Such evidence will be covered by litigation privilege (save in care proceedings: *Re L (Police Investigation: Privilege)* [1996] 1 FLR 731, HL): see notes to FPR 2010, Pt 21. Any such evidence may only be adduced with permission from the court (see, for example, FPR 2010, r 25.4).)

'evidence resulting from the instructions is inadmissible ... unless the court rules that it is admissible' (s 13(2))—Although Parliament has outlawed the obtaining of expert evidence in any form in children proceedings, it plainly anticipates that parties will continue to do so. If they do, they may then take a chance that, after all, the court will relent and permit the evidence to be adduced.

'necessary to assist the court' (s 13(6))—The epithet 'necessary' is used for other family proceedings by FPR 2010, r 25.4(3). In all other civil proceedings, the rule is that permission for opinion evidence depends on its being 'reasonably required' (CPR 1998, r 35.1) by the court. The term 'necessary' was explained by Sir James Munby P in *Re H-L (Expert Evidence: Test for Permission)* [2013] 2 FLR 1434, CA. The intention is that the test for the adducing of opinion evidence in family proceedings should be more exacting, although in *Kennedy v Cordia (Services) LLP* [2016] UKSC 6 the Supreme Court said – whether the report is treated as 'necessary' or 'reasonably required – the court must ask whether the report was such that it would assist the court, and if so it should be admitted. The more serious the allegation the more 'necessary' may be the need for assistance to the court from an expert: what is regarded as 'necessary' as against 'reasonably required' will therefore vary in inverse proportion to the seriousness of the issue.

Legal aid remuneration for expert evidence—The Civil Legal Aid (Remuneration) Regulations 2013 (as amended) introduced new rates for payment for most types of expert involved in family proceedings. These rates apply to all work undertaken by experts from 2 December 2013 as explained by the Legal Aid Agency remuneration guidance. That guidance has been extended (with effect from 1 April 2015) to deal with instruction of experts in the context of when application can be made for prior legal aid authority in specific areas, including transcripts of judgments, translation work, communicating with clients at court, and instructions of experts on foreign law.

'whether to give permission' (s 13(7))—This inclusive list is reproduced in slightly abbreviated form in CA 1989, s 38(7B). If an issue arises over adducing expert evidence, this will be resolved under Convention for the Protection of Human Rights and Fundamental Freedoms 1950, Arts 6(1) and 8. For example, will interference with the justice of the case as the parents see it (Art 6(1)) justify the interference with the child's Art 8 rights (see test of proportionality in *Re S (Identification: Restrictions on Publication)* [2005] 1 FLR 591, HL per Lord Steyn and the preponderance of the welfare of the child in, for example, *HH & PH v Italy; FK v Poland* [2013] 1 AC 338, SC)?

Expert evidence from social workers etc (s 13(8))—This section must be read as meaning not that local authority social workers cannot give opinion evidence, but that restrictions on 'providing' (s 13(1)) or 'putting' (s 13(5)) their evidence before the court do not apply to their evidence. Such witnesses give evidence, even though of opinion, in the capacity of working for the applicant local authority or because directed by the court, and they do not therefore need to seek permission etc (by definition) (but see *Field v Leeds City Council* [2001] CPLR 129, CA (**Introductory Note** to FPR 2010, Pt 25) in connection with the evidence of an employed opinion witness).

****

Civil Jurisdiction and Judgments Act 1982

ARRANGEMENT OF SECTIONS

PART I
IMPLEMENTATION OF THE CONVENTIONS

Section		Page
	Main implementing provisions	
1	Interpretation of references to the Conventions and Contracting States	688
2	The Brussels Conventions to have the force of law	689
	Supplementary provisions as to recognition and enforcement of judgments	
4B	Registration and enforcement of judgments under the 2005 Hague Convention	689
5	Recognition and enforcement of maintenance orders	689
5A	Recognition and enforcement of maintenance orders under the Lugano Convention	690
6	Appeals under Article 37, second paragraph and Article 41	691
6A	Appeals under Article 44 and Annex IV of the Lugano Convention	692
6B	Appeals in relation to registration of judgments under the 2005 Hague Convention	692
7	Interest on registered judgments	692
8	Currency of payment under registered maintenance orders	693
	Other supplementary provisions	
11	Proof of admissibility of certain judgments and related documents	693
11A	Proof and admissibility of certain judgments and related documents for the purposes of the Lugano Convention	694
11B	Proof and admissibility of certain judgments and related documents for the purposes of the 2005 Hague Convention	694
12	Provision for issue of copies of, and certificates in connection with, UK judgments	694
15	Interpretation of Part I and consequential amendments	695

PART IV
MISCELLANEOUS PROVISIONS

Section		Page
	Provisions relating to jurisdiction	
25	Interim relief in England and Wales and Northern Ireland in the absence of substantive proceedings	695
	Provisions relating to recognition and enforcement of judgments	
36	Registration of maintenance orders in Northern Ireland	696

PART I
IMPLEMENTATION OF THE CONVENTIONS

Main implementing provisions

1 Interpretation of references to the Conventions and Contracting States

(1) In this Act –

'the 1968 Convention' means the Convention on jurisdiction and the enforcement of judgments in civil and commercial matters (including the Protocol annexed to that Convention), signed at Brussels on 27 September 1968;

...

'the 2005 Hague Convention' means the Convention on Choice of Court Agreements concluded on 30 June 2005 at the Hague;

'the 2007 Hague Convention' means the Convention on the International Recovery of Child Support and other forms of Family Maintenance done at The Hague on 23 November 2007;

'the Brussels Conventions' means the 1968 Convention, the 1971 Protocol, the Accession Convention, the 1982 Accession Convention, the 1989 Accession Convention and the 1996 Accession Convention;

'the Lugano Convention' means the Convention on jurisdiction and the recognition and enforcement of judgments in civil and commercial matters, between the European Community and the Republic of Iceland, the Kingdom of Norway, the Swiss Confederation and the Kingdom of Denmark signed on behalf of the European Community on 30 October 2007;

'the Maintenance Regulation' means Council Regulation (EC) No 4/2009 including as applied in relation to Denmark by virtue of the Agreement made on 19 October 2005 between the European Community and the Kingdom of Denmark;

'the Regulation' means Regulation (EU) No 1215/2012 of the European Parliament and of the Council of 12 December 2012 on jurisdiction and the recognition and enforcement of judgments in civil and commercial matters (recast) as amended from time to time and as applied by virtue of the Agreement made on 19 October 2005 between the European Community and the Kingdom of Denmark on jurisdiction and the recognition and enforcement of judgments in civil and commercial matters (OJ No L 299, 16.11.2005, p62; OJ No L79, 21.3.2013, p4);

(2) ...

(3) In this Act –

'2005 Hague Convention State', in any provision, in the application of that provision in relation to the 2005 Hague Convention, means a State bound by that Convention;

'2007 Hague Convention State', in any provision, in the application of that provision in relation to the 2007 Hague Convention, means a State bound by that Convention;

'Contracting State', without more, in any provision means –

(a) in the application of the provision in relation to the Brussels Convention, a Brussels Contracting State;

(b) in the application of the provision in relation to the Lugano Convention, a State bound by the Lugano Convention; and

(c) in the application of the provision in relation to the 2005 Hague Convention, a 2005 Hague Convention State;

'Brussels Contracting State' means a state which is one of the original parties to the 1968 Convention or one of the parties acceding to that Convention under the Accession Convention, or under the 1982 Accession Convention, or under the 1989 Accession Convention, but only with respect to any territory –

(a) to which the Brussels Conventions apply; and

(b) which is excluded from the scope of the Regulation pursuant to Articles 349 and 355 of the Treaty on the Functioning of the European Union;

'Maintenance Regulation State', in any provision, in the application of that provision in relation to the Maintenance Regulation means a Member State;

'State bound by the Lugano Convention' in any provision, in the application of that provision in relation to the Lugano Convention has the same meaning as in Article 1(3) of that Convention;

'Regulation State' in any provision, in the application of that provision in relation to the Regulation, means a Member State.

(4) …

Amendments—SI 1989/1346; SI 1990/2591; CJJA 1991, s 2; SI 2000/1824; SI 2001/3929; SI 2007/1655; SI 2009/3131; SI 2011/1215; SI 2012/1770; SI 2012/1809; SI 2014/2947; SI 2015/1644.

2 The Brussels Conventions to have the force of law

(1) The Brussels Conventions shall have the force of law in the United Kingdom, and judicial notice shall be taken of them.

(2) …

Defined terms—'The Brussels Conventions': s 1(1).

****

Supplementary provisions as to recognition and enforcement of judgments

****

4B Registration and enforcement of judgments under the 2005 Hague Convention

(1) A judgment which is required to be recognised and enforced under the 2005 Hague Convention in any part of the United Kingdom must be registered in the prescribed manner in the appropriate court, on the application of any interested party.

(2) In subsection (1) 'the appropriate court' means –

- (a) in England and Wales or Northern Ireland, the High Court;
- (b) in Scotland, the Court of Session.

(3) A judgment which is required to be recognised and enforced under the 2005 Hague Convention must be registered without delay on completion of the formalities in Article 13 of the 2005 Hague Convention if the registering court considers that it meets the condition for recognition in Article 8(3) of the 2005 Hague Convention, without any review of whether a ground for refusal under Article 9 applies.

(4) The party against whom enforcement is sought shall not be entitled to make any submission on the application for registration.

(5) Where a judgment which is required to be recognised and enforced under the 2005 Hague Convention has been registered, the reasonable costs or expenses of and incidental to its registration shall be recoverable as if they were sums recoverable under the judgment.

(6) A judgment which is required to be recognised and enforced under the 2005 Hague Convention shall, for the purposes of its enforcement, be of the same force and effect, the registering court shall have in relation to its enforcement the same powers, and proceedings for or with respect to its enforcement may be taken, as if the judgment had been originally given by the registering court and had (where relevant) been entered.

(7) Subsection (6) is subject to section 7 (interest on registered judgments) and to any provision made by rules of court as to the manner in which and conditions subject to which a judgment registered under the 2005 Hague Convention may be enforced.

Amendments—Inserted by SI 2015/1644.

5 Recognition and enforcement of maintenance orders

(1) The function of transmitting to the appropriate court an application under Article 31 of the 1968 Convention for the recognition or enforcement in the United Kingdom of a maintenance order shall be discharged –

(a) as respects England and Wales, by the Lord Chancellor;
(b) as respects Scotland, by the Secretary of State; and
(c) as respects Northern Ireland, by the Department of Justice in Northern Ireland.

In this subsection 'the appropriate court' means the magistrates' court or sheriff court having jurisdiction in the matter in accordance with the second paragraph of Article 32 but, if the appropriate court is a magistrates' court in England and Wales, the Lord Chancellor is to transmit the application to the family court.

(2) Such an application shall be determined in the first instance by the prescribed officer –

(a) of the family court if the application is transmitted to that court, or
(b) in any other case, of the court having jurisdiction in the matter.

(3) Where on such an application the enforcement of the order is authorised to any extent, the order shall to that extent be registered in the prescribed manner in that court.

(4) A maintenance order registered under this section shall, for the purposes of its enforcement, be of the same force and effect, the registering court shall have in relation to its enforcement the same powers, and proceedings for or with respect to its enforcement may be taken, as if the order had been originally made by the registering court.

(5) Subsection (4) is subject to Article 39 (restriction on enforcement where appeal pending or time for appeal unexpired), to section 7 and to any provision made by rules of court as to the manner in which and conditions subject to which an order registered under this section may be enforced.

(5A)–(5C) *(repealed)*

(6) A maintenance order which by virtue of this section is enforceable by a magistrates' court in Northern Ireland shall, subject to the modifications of Article 98 of the Magistrates' Courts (Northern Ireland) Order 1981 specified in subsection (6A) below, be enforceable as an order made by that court to which that Article applies.

(6A) …

(7) The payer under a maintenance order registered under this section in a magistrates' court in Northern Ireland shall give notice of any change of address to the clerk of that court.

A person who without reasonable excuse fails to comply with this subsection shall be guilty of an offence and liable on summary conviction to a fine not exceeding level 2 on the standard scale.

(8) In subsection (7) 'proper officer' means –

(a) in relation to a magistrates' court in England and Wales the designated officer for the court.
(b) *(repealed)*

Amendments—Criminal Justice Act 1982, s 46; FLRA 1987, s 33(1), Sch 2, para 89; CJJA 1991, s 3, Sch 2, para 2; MEA 1991, s 10, Sch 1, para 21; SI 1992/709; SI 1993/1576; SI 1995/755; Courts Act 2003, Sch 8, para 268; SI 2009/3131; SI 2010/976; CCA 2013, s 17, Sch 11.

Defined terms—'maintenance order': s 15(1).

'level 2 on the standard scale' (s 5(7))—Currently £500 (Criminal Justice Act 1982, s 37(2), as substituted).

5A Recognition and enforcement of maintenance orders under the Lugano Convention

(1) The Secretary of State's function (under Article 39 and Annex II of the Lugano Convention) of transmitting to the appropriate court an application for the recognition or enforcement in the United Kingdom of a maintenance order (made under Article 38 of the Lugano Convention) shall be discharged –

(a) as respects England and Wales by the Lord Chancellor; and
(b) as respects Scotland, by the Scottish Ministers; and
(c) as respects Northern Ireland, by the Department of Justice in Northern Ireland.

In this subsection 'the appropriate court' means the magistrates' court or sheriff court having jurisdiction in the matter in accordance with the second paragraph of Article 39 but, if the appropriate court is a magistrates' court in England and Wales, the Lord Chancellor is to transmit the application to the family court.

(2) Such an application shall be determined in the first instance by the prescribed officer –

(a) of the family court if the application is transmitted to that court, or

(b) in any other case, of the court having jurisdiction in the matter.

(3) A maintenance order registered under the Lugano Convention shall, for the purposes of its enforcement, be of the same force and effect, the registering court shall have in relation to its enforcement the same powers, and proceedings for or with respect to its enforcement may be taken, as if the order had been made by the registering court.

(4) Subsection (3) is subject to Article 47 of the Lugano Convention (restriction on enforcement where appeal pending or time for appeal unexpired), to subsection (6) and to any provision made by rules of court as to the manner in which and conditions subject to which an order registered under the Lugano Convention may be enforced.

(5) *(repealed)*

(6) A maintenance order which by virtue of the Lugano Convention is enforceable by a magistrates' court in Northern Ireland shall, subject to the modifications of Article 98 of the Magistrates' Courts (Northern Ireland) Order 1981 specified in section 5(6A) of this Act, be enforceable as an order made by that court to which that Article applies.

(7) The payer under a maintenance order registered under the Lugano Convention in a magistrates' court in Northern Ireland shall give notice of any change of address to the proper officer of that court.

(8) A person who without reasonable excuse fails to comply with subsection (7) shall be guilty of an offence and liable on summary conviction to a fine not exceeding level 2 on the standard scale.

(9) In subsection (7) 'proper officer' means –

(a) *(repealed)*

(b) in relation to a magistrates' court in Northern Ireland, the clerk of the court.

Amendments—Inserted by SI 2009/3131. Amended by SI 2010/976; CCA 2013, s 17, Sch 11.

6 Appeals under Article 37, second paragraph and Article 41

(1) The single further appeal on a point of law referred to in the 1968 Convention in Article 37, second paragraph and Article 41 in relation to the recognition or enforcement of a judgment other than a maintenance order lies –

(a) in England and Wales or Northern Ireland, to the Court of Appeal or to the Supreme Court in accordance with Part II of the Administration of Justice Act 1969 (appeals direct from the High Court to the Supreme Court);

(b) in Scotland, to the Inner House of the Court of Session

(2) Paragraph (a) of subsection (1) has effect notwithstanding section 15(2) of the Administration of Justice Act 1969 (exclusion of direct appeal to the Supreme Court in cases where no appeal to the Supreme Court lies from a decision of the Court of Appeal).

(3) The single further appeal on a point of law referred to in the 1968 Convention in Article 37, second paragraph and Article 41 in relation to the recognition or enforcement of a maintenance order lies –

(a) *(repealed)*

(b) in Scotland, to the Inner House of the Court of Session;

(c) in Northern Ireland, to the Court of Appeal.

Amendments—CJJA 1991, s 3, Sch 2, para 3; SI 2009/871; CRA 2005, Sch 9, para 39; SI 2009/3131; CCA 2013, s 17, Sch 11.

Defined terms—'1968 Convention', 'the Lugano Convention': s 1(1); 'maintenance order': s 15(1).

6A Appeals under Article 44 and Annex IV of the Lugano Convention

(1) The single further appeal on a point of law referred to in Article 44 and Annex IV of the Lugano Convention in relation to the recognition or enforcement of a judgment other than a maintenance order lies –

(a) in England and Wales or Northern Ireland, to the Court of Appeal or to the Supreme Court in accordance with Part II of the Administration of Justice Act 1969 (appeals direct from the High Court to the Supreme Court);
(b) in Scotland, to the Inner House of the Court of Session.

(2) Paragraph (a) of subsection (1) has effect notwithstanding section 15(2) of the Administration of Justice Act 1969 (exclusion of direct appeal to the Supreme Court in cases where no appeal to that House lies from a decision of the Court of Appeal).

(3) The single further appeal on a point of law referred to in Article 44 and Annex IV of the Lugano Convention in relation to the recognition or enforcement of a maintenance order lies –

(a) *(repealed)*
(b) in Scotland, to the Inner House of the Court of Session;
(c) in Northern Ireland, to the Court of Appeal.

Amendments—Inserted by SI 2009/3131; CCA 2013, s 17, Sch 11.

6B Appeals in relation to registration of judgments under the 2005 Hague Convention

(1) A decision on the application for registration of a judgment required to be recognised and enforced under the 2005 Hague Convention may be appealed against by either party.

(2) The appeal referred to in subsection (1) lies –

(a) in England and Wales or Northern Ireland, to the High Court;
(b) in Scotland, to the Court of Session.

(3) The court to which an appeal referred to in subsection (1) is brought must refuse or revoke registration only if –

(a) the condition for recognition in Article 8(3) of the 2005 Hague Convention is not met;
(b) the ground for postponement or refusal of recognition in Article 8(4) of the 2005 Hague Convention applies; or
(c) one or more of the grounds specified in Article 9 of the 2005 Hague Convention apply.

(4) A single further appeal on a point of law against the judgment given on the appeal referred to in subsection (1) lies –

(a) in England and Wales or Northern Ireland, to the Court of Appeal or to the Supreme Court in accordance with Part II of the Administration of Justice Act 1969 (appeals direct from the High Court to the Supreme Court);
(b) in Scotland, to the Inner House of the Court of Session.

(5) Paragraph (a) of subsection (4) has effect notwithstanding section 15(2) of the Administration of Justice Act 1969 (exclusion of direct appeal to the Supreme Court in cases where no appeal to that Court lies from a decision of the Court of Appeal).

Amendments—Inserted by SI 2015/1644.

7 Interest on registered judgments

(1) Subject to subsection (4), where in connection with an application for registration of a judgment under section 4, 4A, 4B, 5 or 5A the applicant shows –

(a) that the judgment provides for the payment of a sum of money; and
(b) that in accordance with the law of the Contracting State in which the judgment was given interest on that sum is recoverable under the judgment from a particular date or time,

the rate of interest and the date or time from which it is so recoverable shall be registered with the judgment and, subject to any provision made under subsection (2), the debt resulting, apart from section 4(2), from the registration of the judgment shall carry interest in accordance with the registered particulars.

(2) Provision may be made by rules of court as to the manner in which and the periods by reference to which any interest payable by virtue of subsection (1) is to be calculated and paid, including provision for such interest to cease to accrue as from a prescribed date.

(3) Costs or expenses recoverable by virtue of section 4(2) shall carry interest as if they were the subject of an order for the payment of costs or expenses made by the registering court on the date of registration.

(4) Interest on arrears of sums payable under a maintenance order registered under section 5 in a magistrates' court in Northern Ireland shall not be recoverable in that court, but without prejudice to the operation in relation to any such order of section 11A of the Maintenance and Affiliation Orders Act (Northern Ireland) 1966 (which enables interest to be recovered if the order is re-registered for enforcement in the High Court).

(5) Except as mentioned in subsection (4), debts under judgments registered under section 4, 4A, 4B, 5 or 5A shall carry interest only as provided by this section.

Amendments—SI 2009/3131; CCA 2013, s 17, Sch 11; SI 2015/1644.

Defined terms—'Contracting State': s 1(3); 'judgment', 'maintenance order': s 15(1).

Scope—This section makes limited provision for the enforcement of interest on registered orders. Interest may only be enforced if the original judgment provided for the payment of interest (no more than 6 years' interest may be recovered (*Lowsley and another v Forbes* [1998] 1 AC 329, HL)).

8 Currency of payment under registered maintenance orders

(1) Sums payable in the United Kingdom under a maintenance order by virtue of its registration under section 5 or 5A, including any arrears so payable, shall be paid in the currency of the United Kingdom.

(2) Where the order is expressed in any other currency, the amounts shall be converted on the basis of the exchange rate prevailing on the date of registration of the order.

(3) For the purposes of this section, a written certificate purporting to be signed by an officer of any bank in the United Kingdom and stating the exchange rate prevailing on a specified date shall be evidence, and in Scotland sufficient evidence, of the facts stated.

Amendments—SI 2009/3131.

Defined terms—'maintenance order': s 15(1).

****

Other supplementary provisions

****

11 Proof of admissibility of certain judgments and related documents

(1) For the purposes of the 1968 Convention –

- (a) a document, duly authenticated, which purports to be a copy of a judgment given by a court of a Contracting State other than the United Kingdom shall without further proof be deemed to be a true copy, unless the contrary is shown; and
- (b) the original or a copy of any such document as is mentioned in Article 46(2) or 47 (supporting documents to be produced by a party seeking recognition or enforcement of a judgment) shall be evidence, and in Scotland sufficient evidence, of any matter to which it relates.

(2) A document purporting to be a copy of a judgment given by any such court as is mentioned in subsection (1)(a) is duly authenticated for the purposes of this section if it purports –

- (a) to bear the seal of that court; or

(b) to be certified by any person in his capacity as a judge or officer of that court to be a true copy of a judgement given by that court.

(3) Nothing in this section shall prejudice the admission in evidence of any document which is admissible apart from this section.

Amendments—CJJA 1991, s 3, Sch 2, para 6; SI 2009/3131.

Defined terms—'Contracting State': s 1(3); 'judgment': s 15(1); 'the 1968 Convention', 'the Lugano Convention': s 1(1).

11A Proof and admissibility of certain judgments and related documents for the purposes of the Lugano Convention

(1) For the purposes of the Lugano Convention –

(a) a document, duly authenticated, which purports to be a copy of a judgment given by a court of a State bound by the Lugano Convention other than the United Kingdom shall without further proof be deemed to be a true copy, unless the contrary is shown; and

(b) a certificate obtained in accordance with Article 54 and Annex V shall be evidence, and in Scotland sufficient evidence, that the judgment is enforceable in the State of origin which is bound by the Lugano Convention.

(2) A document purporting to be a copy of a judgment given by any such court as is mentioned in subsection (1)(a) is duly authenticated for the purposes of this section if it purports –

(a) to bear the seal of that court; or

(b) to be certified by any person in his capacity as a judge or officer of that court to be a true copy of a judgment given by that court.

(3) Nothing in this section shall prejudice the admission in evidence of any document which is admissible apart from this section.

Amendments—Inserted by SI 2009/3131.

11B Proof and admissibility of certain judgments and related documents for the purposes of the 2005 Hague Convention

(1) For the purposes of the 2005 Hague Convention –

(a) a document, duly authenticated, which purports to be a copy of a judgment given by a court of a 2005 Hague Convention State other than the United Kingdom shall without further proof be deemed to be a true copy, unless the contrary is shown; and

(b) a certificate issued by the court of the 2005 Hague Convention State of origin, in the form recommended for use under the 2005 Hague Convention and published by the Hague Conference on Private International Law, as referred to in Article 13(3) of the 2005 Hague Convention, shall be evidence, and in Scotland sufficient evidence, as to whether the judgment has effect or is enforceable in the 2005 Hague Convention State of origin.

(2) A document purporting to be a copy of a judgment given by any such court as is mentioned in subsection (1)(a) is duly authenticated for the purposes of this section if it purports –

(a) to bear the seal of that court; or

(b) to be certified by any person in their capacity as judge or officer of that court to be a true copy of a judgment given by that court.

(3) Nothing in this section shall prejudice the admission in evidence of any document which is admissible apart from this section.

Amendments—Inserted by SI 2015/1644.

12 Provision for issue of copies of, and certificates in connection with, UK judgments

Rules of court may make provision for enabling any interested party wishing to secure under the 1968 Convention, the Lugano Convention or the 2005 Hague Convention the recognition or enforcement in another Contracting State of a judgment given by a court in the United Kingdom to obtain, subject to any conditions specified in the rules –

(a) a copy of the judgment; and

(b) a certificate giving particulars relating to the judgment and the proceedings in which it was given.

Amendments—CJJA 1991, s 3, Sch 2, para 7; SI 2015/1644.

Defined terms—'Contracting State': s 1(3); 'judgment': s 15(1), 'the 1968 Convention', 'the Lugano Convention': s 1(1).

Scope—This section provides for rules to be made concerning the issue of copies of, and certificates in connection with, maintenance orders: see FPR 2010, r 34.39.

****

15 Interpretation of Part I and consequential amendments

(1) In this Part, unless the context otherwise requires –

'judgment' has the meaning given by Article 25 of the 1968 Convention or, as the case may be, Article 32 of the Lugano Convention or Article 4(1) of the 2005 Hague Convention;

'maintenance order' means a maintenance judgment within the meaning of the 1968 Convention or, as the case may be, the Lugano Convention;

'payer', in relation to a maintenance order, means the person liable to make the payments for which the order provides;

'prescribed' means prescribed by rules of court.

(2) References in this Part to a judgment registered under section 4, 4A, 4B, 5 or 5A include, to the extent of its registration, references to a judgment so registered to a limited extent only.

(3) Anything authorised or required by the 1968 Convention, the Lugano Convention or this Part to be done by, to or before a particular magistrates' court in Northern Ireland may be done by, to or before any magistrates' court acting for the same petty sessions district as that court.

(4) The enactments specified in Part I of Schedule 12 shall have effect with the amendments specified there, being amendments consequential on this Part.

Amendments—CJJA 1991, s 3, Sch 2, para 10; Courts Act 2003, Sch 8, para 269; SI 2009/3131; CCA 2013, s 17, Sch 11; SI 2015/1644.

****

PART IV
MISCELLANEOUS PROVISIONS

Provisions relating to jurisdiction

****

25 Interim relief in England and Wales and Northern Ireland in the absence of substantive proceedings

(1) The High Court in England and Wales or Northern Ireland shall have power to grant interim relief where –

(a) proceedings have been or are to be commenced in a Brussels Contracting State or a State bound by the Lugano Convention or a 2005 Hague Convention State or a Regulation State or a Maintenance Regulation State other than the United Kingdom or in a part of the United Kingdom other than that in which the High Court in question exercises jurisdiction; and

(b) they are or will be proceedings whose subject-matter is either within the scope of the Regulation, as determined by Article 1 of the Regulation, within the scope of the Maintenance Regulation as determined by Article 1 of that Regulation, within scope of the Lugano Convention as determined by Article 1 of the Lugano Convention or within scope of the 2005 Hague Convention as determined by Articles 1 and 2 of the 2005

Hague Convention (whether or not the Regulation, the Maintenance Regulation, the Lugano Convention or the 2005 Hague Convention has effect in relation to the proceedings).

(2) On an application for any interim relief under subsection (1) the court may refuse to grant that relief if, in the opinion of the court, the fact that the court has no jurisdiction apart from this section in relation to the subject-matter of the proceedings in question makes it inexpedient for the court to grant it.

(3) Her Majesty may by Order in Council extend the power to grant interim relief conferred by subsection (1) so as to make it exercisable in relation to proceedings of any of the following descriptions, namely –

- (a) proceedings commenced or to be commenced otherwise than in a Brussels Contracting State or a State bound by the Lugano Convention or a 2005 Hague Convention State or Regulation State or a Maintenance Regulation State;
- (b) proceedings whose subject-matter is not within the scope of the Regulation as determined by Article 1 of the Regulation, the Maintenance Regulation as determined by Article 1 of that Regulation, the Lugano Convention as determined by Article 1 of the Lugano Convention or the 2005 Hague Convention as determined by Articles 1 and 2 of the 2005 Hague Convention.
- (c) *(repealed)*

(4) An Order in Council under subsection (3) –

- (a) may confer power to grant only specified descriptions of interim relief;
- (b) may make different provision for different classes of proceedings, for proceedings pending in different countries or courts outside the United Kingdom or in different parts of the United Kingdom, and for other different circumstances; and
- (c) may impose conditions or restrictions on the exercise of any power conferred by the Order.

(5) *(repealed)*

(6) Any Order in Council under subsection (3) shall be subject to annulment in pursuance of a resolution of either House of Parliament.

(7) In this section 'interim relief', in relation to the High Court in England and Wales or Northern Ireland, means interim relief of any kind which that court has power to grant in proceedings relating to matters within its jurisdiction, other than –

- (a) a warrant for the arrest of property; or
- (b) provision for obtaining evidence.

Amendments—CJJA 1991, s 3, Sch 2, para 12; Arbitration Act 1996, s 107(2), Sch 4; SI 2001/3929; SI 2009/3131; SI 2011/1484; SI 2015/1644.

Scope—Where there are proceedings for financial relief outside the UK, this section enables the court, by injunction or other interim orders, to preserve the assets which are the subject of that overseas litigation. *Credit Suisse Fides Trust SA v Cuoghi* [1998] QB 818, CA and *Ryan v Friction Dynamics* [2001] CP Rep 75, ChD set out the principles governing the court's jurisdiction to grant interim relief.

****

Provisions relating to recognition and enforcement of judgments

****

36 Registration of maintenance orders in Northern Ireland

(1) Where –

- (a) a High Court order or a Court of Session order has been registered in the High Court of Justice in Northern Ireland ('the Northern Ireland High Court') under Part II of the Maintenance Orders Act 1950; or
- (b) a family court order or a sheriff court order has been registered in a court of summary jurisdiction in Northern Ireland under that Part,

an application may be made to the original court for the registration of the order in, respectively, a court of summary jurisdiction in Northern Ireland or the Northern Ireland High Court.

(2) In subsection (1) 'the original court', in relation to an order, means the court by which the order was made.

(3) Section 2 (except subsection (6A)) and section 2A of the Maintenance Orders Act 1958 shall have effect for the purposes of an application under subsection (1), and subsections (2), (3), (4) and (4A) of section 5 of that Act shall have effect for the purposes of the cancellation of a registration made on such an application, as if –

(a) 'registration' in those provisions included registration in the appropriate Northern Ireland court ('registered' being construed accordingly);

(b) any reference in those provisions to a High Court order or a magistrates' court order included, respectively, a Court of Session order or a sheriff court order; and

(c) any other reference in those provisions to the High Court or a magistrates' court included the Northern Ireland High Court or a court of summary jurisdiction in Northern Ireland.

(d) for section 2(6), there were substituted the following subsections –

'(6) Where a magistrates' court order is registered under this Part of this Act in the High Court, then –

(a) if payments under the magistrates' court order are required to be made (otherwise than to a collecting officer) by any method of payment falling within Article 85(7) of the Magistrates' Courts (Northern Ireland) Order 1981 (standing order, etc), any order requiring payment by that method shall continue to have effect after registration;

(b) any order by virtue of which sums payable under the magistrates' court order are required to be paid to the collecting officer (whether or not by any method of payment falling within Article 85(7) of that Order) on behalf of the person entitled thereto shall cease to have effect.

(6ZA) Where a High Court or county court order is registered under this Part of this Act in a magistrates' court, then –

(a) if a means of payment order (within the meaning of Article 96A(7) of the Judgments Enforcement (Northern Ireland) Order 1981) has effect in relation to the order in question, it shall continue to have effect after registration; and

(b) in any other case, the magistrates' court shall order that all payments to be made under the order in question (including any arrears accrued before registration) shall be made to the collecting officer.

(6ZB) Any such order as to payment –

(a) as is referred to in paragraph (a) of subsection (6) of this section may be revoked, suspended, revived or varied by an exercise of the powers conferred by section 13A of the Maintenance and Affiliation Orders Act (Northern Ireland) 1966; and

(b) as is referred to in paragraph (a) or (b) of subsection (6ZA) of this section may be varied or revoked by an exercise of the powers conferred by section 12(2) or 13(2A) or (5A) of that Act of 1966.

(6ZC) Where by virtue of the provisions of this section or any order under subsection (6ZA)(b) of this section payments under an order cease to be or become payable to the collecting officer, the person liable to make the payments shall, until he is given the prescribed notice to that effect, be deemed to comply with the order if he makes payments in accordance with the order and any order under subsection (6ZA)(b) of this section of which he has received such notice.

(6ZD) In subsections (6), (6ZA) and (6ZC) of this section "collecting officer" means the officer mentioned in Article 85(4) of the Magistrates' Courts (Northern Ireland) Order 1981.'

PART II

(4) Where an order is registered in Northern Ireland under this section, Part II of the Maintenance and Affiliation Orders Act (Northern Ireland) 1966, except sections 11, 11A and 14(2) and (3), shall apply as if the order had been registered in accordance with the provisions of that Part, as if –

(a) in section 12(2), for modifications of Article 98(8B) to (8D) of the Magistrates' Court (Northern Ireland) Order 1981 specified in that subsection there were substituted the modifications specified in section 18(3ZA) of the Maintenance Orders Act 1950 (enforcement of registered orders); and

(b) for section 13(5A), there were substituted the following subsection –

'(5A) Subject to the following provisions of this section, paragraphs (4) to (11) of Article 86 of the Magistrates' Courts (Northern Ireland) Order 1981 (power of clerk and court to vary maintenance orders) shall apply in relation to a registered order as they apply in relation to a maintenance order made by a court of summary jurisdiction (disregarding Article 25(2) of the Domestic Proceedings (Northern Ireland) Order 1980) but –

(a) as if for paragraph (4)(b) there were substituted –

"(b) payments under the order are required to be made to the collecting officer, by any method of payment falling within Article 85(7) (standing order, etc)";

and as if after the words "petty sessions" there were inserted "for the petty sessions district for which the court which made the order acts";

(b) as if in paragraph (5) for the words "to the collecting officer" there were substituted "in accordance with sub-paragraph (a) of paragraph (9)";

(c) as if in paragraph (7), sub-paragraph (c) and the word "and" immediately preceding it were omitted;

(d) as if in paragraph (8) for the words "sub-paragraphs (a) to (d) of Article 85(3)" there were substituted "paragraph (9)";

(e) as if for paragraphs (9) and (10) there were substituted the following paragraphs –

"(9) The powers of the court are –

(a) the power to order that payments under the order be made directly to the collecting officer;

(b) the power to order that payments under the order be made to the collecting officer, by such method of payment falling within Article 85(7) (standing order, etc) as may be specified;

(c) the power to make an attachment of earnings order under Part IX to secure payments under the order.

(10) In deciding which of the powers under paragraph (9) above it is to exercise, the court shall have regard to any representations made by the debtor.

(10A) Paragraph (5) of Article 85 (power of court to require debtor to open account) shall apply for the purposes of paragraph (9) as it applies for the purposes of that Article but as if for sub-paragraph (a) there were substituted –

'(a) the court proposes to exercise its power under sub-paragraph (b) of Article 86(9)'.".'.

(5) A court of summary jurisdiction in Northern Ireland shall have jurisdiction to hear an application by or against a person residing outside Northern Ireland for the discharge or variation of an order registered in Northern Ireland under this section; and where such an application is made against a person residing outside Northern Ireland, then, if he resides in England and Wales or Scotland, section 15 of the Maintenance Orders Act 1950 (which relates to the service of process on persons residing in those countries) shall have effect in relation to the application as it has effect in relation to the proceedings therein mentioned.

(5A) Article 165 of the Children (Northern Ireland) Order 1995 (provision which may be made by magistrates' courts rules, etc) shall apply for the purpose of giving effect to subsection (5) above as it applies for the purpose of giving effect to that Order, except that in the application of that Article by virtue of this subsection 'relevant proceedings' means any application made, or proceedings brought, by virtue of that subsection and any part of such proceedings.

(6) The enactments specified in Part III of Schedule 12 shall have effect with the amendments specified there, being amendments consequential on this section.

Amendments—SI 1993/1576; SI 1995/755; CCA 2013, s 17, Sch 11.

★★★★

Civil Partnership Act 2004

ARRANGEMENT OF SECTIONS

PART 1
INTRODUCTION

Section		Page
1	Civil partnership	703

PART 2
CIVIL PARTNERSHIP: ENGLAND AND WALES

Introduction

37	Powers to make orders and effect of orders	703
38	The period before conditional orders may be made final	704
39	Intervention of the Queen's Proctor	704
40	Proceedings before order has been made final	705
41	Time bar on applications for dissolution orders	705
42	Attempts at reconciliation of civil partners	705
43	Consideration by the court of certain agreements or arrangements	706

Dissolution of civil partnership

44	Dissolution of civil partnership which has broken down irretrievably	706
45	Supplemental provisions as to facts raising presumption of breakdown	707
46	Dissolution order not precluded by previous separation order etc	708
47	Refusal of dissolution in 5 year separation cases on ground of grave hardship	708
48	Proceedings before order made final: protection for respondent in separation cases	709

Nullity

49	Grounds on which civil partnership is void	710
50	Grounds on which civil partnership is voidable	710
51	Bars to relief where civil partnership is voidable	710
52	Proof of certain matters not necessary to validity of civil partnership	711
53	Power to validate civil partnership	711
54	Validity of civil partnerships registered outside England and Wales	712

Presumption of death orders

55	Presumption of death orders	713

Separation orders

56	Separation orders	713
57	Effect of separation order	713

Declarations

58	Declarations	714
59	General provisions as to making and effect of declarations	714
60	The Attorney General and proceedings for declarations	714
61	Supplementary provisions as to declarations	715

PART II

General provisions

62	Relief for respondent in dissolution proceedings	715
64	Parties to proceedings under this Chapter	715
65	Contribution by civil partner to property improvement	715
66	Disputes between civil partners about property	716
67	Applications under section 66 where property not in possession etc	716
68	Applications under section 66 by former civil partners	717
69	Actions in tort between civil partners	717
70	Assurance policy by civil partner for benefit of other civil partner etc	717
72	Financial relief for civil partners and children of family	718
73	Civil partnership agreements unenforceable	718
74	Property where civil partnership agreement is terminated	718
84	Evidence	719

PART 5

CIVIL PARTNERSHIP FORMED OR DISSOLVED ABROAD ETC

212	Meaning of 'overseas relationship'	719
213	Specified relationships	720
214	The general conditions	720
215	Overseas relationships treated as civil partnerships: the general rule	721
216	The same-sex requirement	721
217	Person domiciled in a part of the United Kingdom	722
218	The public policy exception	722

Introduction

219	Power to make provision corresponding to EC Regulation 2201/2003	722

Jurisdiction of courts in England and Wales

220	Meaning of 'the court'	723
221	Proceedings for dissolution, separation or nullity order	724
222	Proceedings for presumption of death order	724
223	Proceedings for dissolution, nullity or separation order: supplementary	725
224	Applications for declarations as to validity etc	725

Recognition of dissolution, annulment and separation

233	Effect of dissolution, annulment or separation obtained in the UK	725
234	Recognition in the UK of overseas dissolution, annulment or separation	726
235	Grounds for recognition	726
236	Refusal of recognition	727
237	Supplementary provisions relating to recognition of dissolution etc	728
238	Non-recognition elsewhere of dissolution or annulment	729

Schedule 5 – Financial relief: provision corresponding to provision made by Part 2 of the Matrimonial Causes Act 1973 729
- Part 1 – Financial Provision in Connection with Dissolution, Nullity or Separation 730
- Part 2 – Property Adjustment on or after Dissolution, Nullity or Separation 732
- Part 3 – Sale of Property Orders 733
- Part 4 – Pension Sharing Orders on or after Dissolution or Nullity Order 734
- Part 4A – Pension compensation sharing orders on or after dissolution or nullity order 736
- Part 5 – Matters to which Court is to have Regard under Parts 1 to 4A 738
- Part 6 – Making of Part 1 Orders Having Regard to Pension Benefits 740
- Part 7 – Pension Protection Fund Compensation etc 742
- Part 8 – Maintenance and Other Payments Pending Outcome of Dissolution, Nullity or Separation Proceedings 745
- Part 9 – Failure to Maintain: Financial Provision (and Interim Orders) 747

Part 10 – Commencement of Certain Proceedings and Duration of Certain Orders 749
Part 11 – Variation, Discharge etc of Certain Orders for Financial Relief 751
Part 12 – Arrears and Repayments 756
Part 13 – Consent Orders and Maintenance Agreements 758
Part 14 – Miscellaneous and Supplementary 761
Schedule 6 – Financial relief: provision corresponding to provision made by the Domestic Proceedings and Magistrates' Courts Act 1978 764
Part 1 – Failure to Maintain etc: Financial Provision 764
Part 2 – Orders for Agreed Financial Provision 766
Part 3 – Orders of Court Where Civil Partners Living Apart by Agreement 768
Part 4 – Interim Orders 769
Part 5 – Commencement and Duration of Orders under Parts 1, 2 and 3 770
Part 6 – Variation etc of Orders 773
Part 7 – Arrears and Repayments 776
Part 8 – Supplementary 777
Schedule 7 – Financial Relief in England and Wales after Overseas Dissolution etc of a Civil Partnership 778
Part 1 – Financial Relief 778
Part 2 – Steps to Prevent Avoidance Prior to Application for Leave under Paragraph 4 786
Part 3 – Supplementary 787
Schedule 20 – Meaning of Overseas Relationship: Specified Relationships 787

Scope of Act—The Act came into force on 5 December 2005. There are 8 Parts, 264 sections and 30 Schedules. The purpose of the Act is to enable same-sex couples to obtain legal recognition of their relationship by registration of a civil partnership. The Marriage (Same Sex Couples) Act 2013 extends marriage to same-sex couples. The 2013 Act came into force (mostly) on 13 March 2014. Section 9 of the 2013 Act enables a civil partnership to be converted into marriage from 10 December 2014.

Under a civil partnership, civil partners assume legal rights and responsibilities with regard to each other and to third parties including the state. Same-sex couples acquire many of the legal rights and benefits currently enjoyed by married couples. The Act does not, however, purport to create same-sex marriage; civil partnership is a distinct institution with specific statutory rights and responsibilities. Nevertheless, in terms of the conditions of entering into and dissolving a civil partnership, and the legal consequences flowing from it, the Act adopts a model based closely on marriage which is closer to that of marriage than the registered partnership models in other EU Member States, while falling short of same-sex marriage as permitted in, e g the Netherlands and Belgium. Civil partnership is not available to heterosexual couples (*Steinfeld v Secretary of State for Education* [2017] EWCA Civ 81). However, heterosexual couples may enter into a civil partnership on the Isle of Man from 22 July 2016 (Marriage and Civil Partnership (Amendment) Act 2016). A Private Member's Bill (the Civil Partnership Act 2004 (Amendment) Bill 2016/17) is currently before Parliament to allow heterosexual civil partnerships in England, Wales, Scotland or Northern Ireland.

The commentary below summarises the provisions not reproduced in this work.

Registration of civil partnerships—This is provided for by Ch 1 of Pt 2 of the Act and the Civil Partnership (Registration Provisions) Regulations 2005, as amended. In much the same way as for marriage, each party to the partnership must under the standard procedure give notice to their relevant registration authority of their intention to form the partnership and also must have resided in the same registration authority in England and Wales for 7 days immediately before the notice is given (s 8). There is then a waiting period of 28 days (s 11), which may be shortened (s 12), before which the registration authority may issue a civil partnership schedule (s 14). Specified relevant information must be publicised during the waiting period (s 10). The couple then have 12 months from the date the notice is registered in which to form and register their civil partnership (s 17).

To form a civil partnership, a civil partnership document (s 7) must be signed by both parties in the presence of each other and in the presence of a civil partnership registrar and two witnesses (s 2). No religious service is to be used while a civil partnership registrar is officiating (s 2(5)). However, a ceremony may take place on religious premises in certain circumstances (ss 6 and 6A; Marriages and Civil Partnerships (Approved Premises) (Amendment) Regulations 2011).

In the same way as for married couples, there are prohibited degrees of relationship. Other prohibitions include parties who are not of the same sex, parties who are already married or in a civil partnership and if either party is under the age of 16 (s 3). Parental consent will be required for any party under the age of 18 in normal circumstances (s 4).

Modified procedures apply to partners who are housebound (s 18), detained (s 19) and non-resident (s 20). There is also a special procedure for those who are seriously ill and not expected to recover (ss 21–27).

Children (Chapter 5 of Pt 2)—Chapter 5 makes various amendments to CA 1989 and ACA 2002 to reflect the creation of the status of civil partnership. The Act enables a civil partner to acquire parental responsibility for their civil partner's child (in the same way as a step-parent) by agreement between the parent (and any other parent who also has parental responsibility) and the civil partner, or by court order on the application of the civil partner (CA 1989, s 4A, as amended by s 75(1),(2)). As to the acquisition of parental responsibility by civil partners in cases of assisted conception, see CA 1989, ss 2(1A),(2A) and 4ZA and HFEA 2008, ss 42–45. As to disputes over parental responsibility and contact involving lesbian mothers and a known father, see: *Re D (Contact and Parental Responsibility: Lesbian Mothers and Known Father) (No 2) (sub nom B v A)* [2006] EWHC 2 (Fam); *Re B (Role of Biological Father)* [2008] 1 FLR 1015, FD; *R v E and F (Female Parents: Known Father)* [2010] 2 FLR 383, FD; *T v T* [2010] EWCA Civ 1366; A *v B and C (Lesbian Co-Parents: Role of Father)* [2012] 2 FLR 607, CA, which rejected the concept of primary and secondary parenting roles developed in *MA v RS (Contact: Parenting Roles)* [2012] 1 FLR 1056, FD and *Re P and L (Contact)* [2012] 1 FLR 1068, FD; *AB v CD and the Z Fertility Clinic* [2013] 2 FLR 1357, FD; and *DB v AB and CB* [2014] 2 FLR 1197, FD). While there is no presumption in favour of a biological parent when determining a dispute between same-sex partners, the fact of parentage is still an important and significant factor in determining the child's best interests (*Re G (Residence: Same-Sex Partner) (sub nom CG v CW)* [2006] 2 FLR 629, HL and, post, *Re G (Shared Residence)* [2013] 1 FLR 1323, CA). The definition of 'child of the family' in CA 1989 is amended to include civil partners as well as parties to a marriage (s 75(3)). A civil partner is also entitled to make an application for a child arrangements order (s 77). The right to apply for financial provision for children under CA 1989, Sch 1 is extended to civil partners (s 78). ACA 2002 is amended to ensure that civil partners are recognised for the purposes of adoption (s 79), eg by restricting adoption of a person who is or has been a civil partner, generally, by substituting 'marriage or civil partnership' for 'marriage', and by adding 'two people who are civil partners of each other' to the definition of 'couple' in s 144(4) of the 2002 Act.

Miscellaneous (Chapter 6 of Pt 2 and Pt 7)—Section 81 and Sch 8 amend certain enactments relating to housing and tenancies. Section 82 and Sch 9 amend FLA 1996, Pt IV to allow civil partners the same rights to occupy the civil partnership home as married persons have to occupy the matrimonial home and to apply for non-molestation and occupation orders. Section 83 amends the Fatal Accidents Act 1976 to include a civil partner as a dependant.

Pt 7 includes other miscellaneous amendments, including immigration control (s 249) and gender recognition (s 250). The Sex Discrimination Act 1975 is amended so that civil partners have the right not to be discriminated against in the employment field on the grounds of their civil partnership just as married persons have the right not to be discriminated against on the grounds of their marriage (s 251). Civil partners have an unlimited insurable interest in each other (s 253).

Amendments are made to social security, child support and tax credits legislation with the intention that, in general, civil partners are treated in the same way as married persons and that same-sex couples who are living together are treated in the same way as opposite sex unmarried couples who are living together as husband and wife (s 254 and Sch 24). Civil partners are treated in the same way as married couples for tax purposes (Finance Act 2005, s 103) (*cf* the inheritance tax position of unmarried sisters living together: *Burden v UK* [2008] 2 FLR 787, ECHR).

Pensions—Section 255 gives Ministers power to amend the Act and other enactments in relation to pensions by order to make provision with respect to pensions, allowances or gratuities for the surviving civil partners or dependants of deceased civil partners. Reference should be made to the Civil Partnership (Contracted-out Occupational and Appropriate Personal Pension Schemes) (Surviving Civil Partners) Order 2005, the Civil Partnership (Pensions and Benefit Payments) (Consequential, etc Provisions) Order 2005, the Civil Partnership (Miscellaneous and Consequential Provisions) Order 2005 and the Tax and Civil Partnership Regulations 2007.

Amendments to the Social Security Contributions and Benefits Act 1992 ensure that state pension rights are extended to civil partners (s 254 and Sch 24, Pt 3) (see Civil Partnership (Pensions and Benefit Payments) (Consequential, etc Provisions) Order 2005; Civil Partnership (Pensions, Social Security and Child Support) (Consequential, etc Provisions) Order 2005; Civil Partnership Act 2004 (Tax Credits, etc) (Consequential Amendments) Order 2005). Sch 24, paras 23–33 and 51 extend state pension rights to civil partners. A civil partner may also, in the same circumstances as surviving spouses, become entitled to widowed parents' allowance, bereavement allowance and bereavement payment. The formation of a new civil partnership or same-sex cohabitation has the same effect as remarriage (Sch 41, paras 16–22). As to the changes to the state retirement scheme from April 2016, see annotations to MCA 1973, s 21A.

Surviving civil partners of members of contracted-out schemes are eligible for survivors' benefits based on contracted-out rights earned by service from 6 April 1988. Additionally, they are eligible for survivors' benefits non-contracted-out schemes based upon pensionable service from 5 December 2005. In summary, civil partners do not enjoy full equality in relation to survivors' benefits: survivors' benefits in respect of pre-5 December 2005 non-contracted-out service depend upon an amendment to the relevant scheme rules (Equality Act 2010, Sch 9, para 18(1); *O'Brien v Ministry of Justice; Walker v Innospec* [2015] EWCA Civ 1000).

Widows'/widowers' rights are extended to certain surviving civil partners by ss 256 and 257 and Schs 25 and 26 (statutory pensions).

Wills, administration of estates and family provision (Sch 4)—Section 71 and Sch 4 amend the Wills Act 1837, Public Trustee Act 1906, Administration of Estates Act 1925, Intestates' Estates Act 1952, Family Provision Act 1966 and I(PFD)A 1975 so that civil partners are given the same rights as those that exist for married couples.

A will is revoked, as upon marriage, when a testator forms a civil partnership, unless it is expressed to be made in expectation of registration (Wills Act 1837, s 18B(1) (as inserted); *Court v Despallieres; Re Ikin (Deceased)* [2010] 1 FLR 1734, ChD) and once a civil partnership is dissolved, annulled or there is a presumption of death order, former civil partners, where named as executors and beneficiaries, are prevented from becoming such unless the will provides otherwise (Wills Act 1837, s 18C (as inserted)).

Civil partners are entitled to inherit the estate of their deceased civil partners under the intestacy rules in the same way as surviving spouses and to acquire the home that they have shared with the deceased civil partners.

Civil partners are among the class of person entitled to make an application for reasonable financial provision from the estate of their deceased civil partner (I(PFD)A 1975, s 1(1)(a),(b) as amended by s 71 and Sch 4, para 15(1)–(6); see also, *Baynes v Hedger* [2008] 2 FLR 1805, ChD, at [122]).

Guidance for litigants in person—The Family Justice Council guide 'Sorting out Finances on Divorce' provides information about financial settlements for unrepresented couples who are getting divorced or ending a civil partnership; see *www.judiciary.gov.uk/wp-content/uploads/2016/04/fjc-financial-needs-april-16-final.pdf*

PART 1
INTRODUCTION

1 Civil partnership

(1) A civil partnership is a relationship between two people of the same sex ('civil partners') –

- (a) which is formed when they register as civil partners of each other –
  - (i) in England or Wales (under Part 2),
  - (ii) in Scotland (under Part 3),
  - (iii) in Northern Ireland (under Part 4), or
  - (iv) outside the United Kingdom under an Order in Council made under Chapter 1 of Part 5 (registration at British consulates etc or by armed forces personnel), or
- (b) which they are treated under Chapter 2 of Part 5 as having formed (at the time determined under that Chapter) by virtue of having registered an overseas relationship.

(2) Subsection (1) is subject to the provisions of this Act under or by virtue of which a civil partnership is void.

(3) A civil partnership ends only –

- (a) on death, dissolution or annulment, or
- (b) in the case of a civil partnership formed as mentioned in subsection (1)(a)(i) or (iv), on the conversion of the civil partnership into a marriage under section 9 of the Marriage (Same Sex Couples) Act 2013.

(4) The references in subsection (3) to dissolution and annulment are to dissolution and annulment having effect under or recognised in accordance with this Act.

(5) References in this Act to an overseas relationship are to be read in accordance with Chapter 2 of Part 5.

Amendments—Marriage (Same Sex Couples) Act 2013, s 17, Sch 7, para 34.

PART 2
CIVIL PARTNERSHIP: ENGLAND AND WALES

****

Introduction

37 Powers to make orders and effect of orders

(1) The court may, in accordance with this Chapter –

- (a) make an order (a 'dissolution order') which dissolves a civil partnership on the ground that it has broken down irretrievably;
- (b) make an order (a 'nullity order') which annuls a civil partnership which is void or voidable;
- (c) make an order (a 'presumption of death order') which dissolves a civil partnership on the ground that one of the civil partners is presumed to be dead;
- (d) make an order (a 'separation order') which provides for the separation of the civil partners.

(2) Every dissolution, nullity or presumption of death order –

- (a) is, in the first instance, a conditional order, and
- (b) may not be made final before the end of the prescribed period (see section 38);

and any reference in this Chapter to a conditional order is to be read accordingly.

PART II

(3) A nullity order made where a civil partnership is voidable annuls the civil partnership only as respects any time after the order has been made final, and the civil partnership is to be treated (despite the order) as if it had existed up to that time.

(4) In this Chapter, other than in sections 58 to 61, 'the court' means –

(a) the High Court, or
(b) the family court.

(5) This Chapter is subject to sections 219 to 224 (jurisdiction of the court).

Amendments—CCA 2013, s 17, Sch 11.

Defined term—'civil partners': s 1(1).

Scope—This section provides for four types of orders which may be made in relation to a civil partnership: a dissolution order (s 44), a nullity order (ss 49–50), a presumption of death order (s 55) and a separation order (s 56). Irretrievable breakdown is the sole ground for the court to grant a dissolution order (ss 37(1)(a) and 44). Dissolution, nullity and presumption of death orders are granted in two stages and are initially conditional for a period of 6 weeks (ss 37(2) and 38). Jurisdiction to entertain proceedings is provided for by s 221 and the Civil Partnership (Jurisdiction and Recognition of Judgments) Regulations 2005 (dissolution, separation or nullity) and s 222 (presumption of death). The circumstances in which a presumption of death order may be made under the Act are now limited: see annotations to s 222.

38 The period before conditional orders may be made final

(1) Subject to subsections (2) to (4), the prescribed period for the purposes of section 37(2)(b) is –

(a) 6 weeks from the making of the conditional order, or
(b) if the 6 week period would end on a day on which the office or registry of the court dealing with the case is closed, the period of 6 weeks extended to the end of the first day on which the office or registry is next open.

(2) The Lord Chancellor may by order amend this section so as to substitute a different definition of the prescribed period for the purposes of section 37(2)(b).

(3) But the Lord Chancellor may not under subsection (2) provide for a period longer than 6 months to be the prescribed period.

(4) In a particular case the court dealing with the case may by order shorten the prescribed period.

(5) The power to make an order under subsection (2) is exercisable by statutory instrument.

(6) An instrument containing such an order is subject to annulment in pursuance of a resolution of either House of Parliament.

Defined terms—'conditional order': s 37(2); 'the court' s 37(4).

39 Intervention of the Queen's Proctor

(1) This section applies if an application has been made for a dissolution, nullity or presumption of death order.

(2) The court may, if it thinks fit, direct that all necessary papers in the matter are to be sent to the Queen's Proctor who must under the directions of the Attorney General instruct counsel to argue before the court any question in relation to the matter which the court considers it necessary or expedient to have fully argued.

(3) If any person at any time –

(a) during the progress of the proceedings, or
(b) before the conditional order is made final,

gives information to the Queen's Proctor on any matter material to the due decision of the case, the Queen's Proctor may take such steps as the Attorney General considers necessary or expedient.

(4) If the Queen's Proctor intervenes or shows cause against the making of the conditional order in any proceedings relating to its making, the court may make such order as may be just as to –

(a) the payment by other parties to the proceedings of the costs incurred by him in doing so, or

(b) the payment by the Queen's Proctor of any costs incurred by any of those parties because of his doing so.

(5) The Queen's Proctor is entitled to charge as part of the expenses of his office –

(a) the costs of any proceedings under subsection (2);
(b) if his reasonable costs of intervening or showing cause as mentioned in subsection (4) are not fully satisfied by an order under subsection (4)(a), the amount of the difference;
(c) if the Treasury so directs, any costs which he pays to any parties under an order made under subsection (4)(b).

Defined terms—'conditional order': s 37(2); 'the court': s 37(4); 'dissolution order': s 37(1)(a); 'nullity order': s 37(1)(b); 'presumption of death order': s 37(1)(c).

Procedure—The rules relating to an application by the Queen's Proctor are found in FPR 2010, r 7.31(6).

40 Proceedings before order has been made final

(1) This section applies if –

(a) a conditional order has been made, and
(b) the Queen's Proctor, or any person who has not been a party to proceedings in which the order was made, shows cause why the order should not be made final on the ground that material facts have not been brought before the court.

(2) This section also applies if –

(a) a conditional order has been made,
(b) 3 months have elapsed since the earliest date on which an application could have been made for the order to be made final,
(c) no such application has been made by the civil partner who applied for the conditional order, and
(d) the other civil partner makes an application to the court under this subsection.

(3) The court may –

(a) make the order final,
(b) rescind the order,
(c) require further inquiry, or
(d) otherwise deal with the case as it thinks fit.

(4) Subsection (3)(a) –

(a) applies despite section 37(2) (period before conditional orders may be made final), but
(b) is subject to section 48(4) (protection for respondent in separation cases).

Amendments—CFA 2014, s 17.

Defined terms—'civil partner': s 1(1); 'conditional order': s 37(2); 'the court': s 37(4).

Procedure—The procedure for showing cause why a conditional order should not be made final is set out in FPR 2010, r 7.31.

41 Time bar on applications for dissolution orders

(1) No application for a dissolution order may be made to the court before the end of the period of 1 year from the date of the formation of the civil partnership.

(2) Nothing in this section prevents the making of an application based on matters which occurred before the end of the 1 year period.

Defined terms—'the court': s 37(4); 'dissolution order': s 37(1)(a).

42 Attempts at reconciliation of civil partners

(1) This section applies in relation to cases where an application is made for a dissolution or separation order.

(2) Rules of court must make provision for requiring the legal representative acting for the applicant to certify whether he has –

(a) discussed with the applicant the possibility of a reconciliation with the other civil partner, and

(b) given the applicant the names and addresses of persons qualified to help effect a reconciliation between civil partners who have become estranged.

(3) If at any stage of proceedings for the order it appears to the court that there is a reasonable possibility of a reconciliation between the civil partners, the court may adjourn the proceedings for such period as it thinks fit to enable attempts to be made to effect a reconciliation between them.

(4) The power to adjourn under subsection (3) is additional to any other power of adjournment.

Amendments—Legal Services Act 2007, s 208(1), Sch 21, para 150.

Defined terms—'civil partners': s 1(1); 'the court': s 37(4); 'dissolution order': s 37(1)(a); 'separation order': s 37(1)(d).

Scope—This section provides for any solicitor for a petitioner to certify that reconciliation has been discussed with his client and enables the court to adjourn the proceedings if reconciliation appears to be a possibility.

'Rules of court must make provision' (s 42(2))—Such provision is made by FPR 2010, r 7.6 and PD5A, which require the solicitor acting for the petitioner in dissolution or separation proceedings to file a certificate concerning reconciliation.

43 Consideration by the court of certain agreements or arrangements

(1) This section applies in relation to cases where –

(a) proceedings for a dissolution or separation order are contemplated or have begun, and

(b) an agreement or arrangement is made or proposed to be made between the civil partners which relates to, arises out of, or is connected with, the proceedings.

(2) Rules of court may make provision for enabling –

(a) the civil partners, or either of them, to refer the agreement or arrangement to the court, and

(b) the court –

(i) to express an opinion, if it thinks it desirable to do so, as to the reasonableness of the agreement or arrangement, and

(ii) to give such directions, if any, in the matter as it thinks fit.

Defined terms—'civil partners': s 1(1); 'the court': s 37(4); 'dissolution order': s 37(1)(a); 'separation order': s 37(1)(d).

Scope—This section is a curious perpetuation of MCA 1973, s 7 described in *Brockwell v Brockwell* (1975) 6 Fam Law 46, CA as 'an almost vestigial provision, not unlike the human appendix'. At the time of writing, no rules have been made under s 43(2).

Dissolution of civil partnership

44 Dissolution of civil partnership which has broken down irretrievably

(1) Subject to section 41, an application for a dissolution order may be made to the court by either civil partner on the ground that the civil partnership has broken down irretrievably.

(2) On an application for a dissolution order the court must inquire, so far as it reasonably can, into –

(a) the facts alleged by the applicant, and

(b) any facts alleged by the respondent.

(3) The court hearing an application for a dissolution order must not hold that the civil partnership has broken down irretrievably unless the applicant satisfies the court of one or more of the facts described in subsection (5)(a), (b), (c) or (d).

(4) But if the court is satisfied of any of those facts, it must make a dissolution order unless it is satisfied on all the evidence that the civil partnership has not broken down irretrievably.

(5) The facts referred to in subsections (3) and (4) are –

(a) that the respondent has behaved in such a way that the applicant cannot reasonably be expected to live with the respondent;

(b) that –
  (i) the applicant and the respondent have lived apart for a continuous period of at least 2 years immediately preceding the making of the application ('2 years' separation'), and
  (ii) the respondent consents to a dissolution order being made;
(c) that the applicant and the respondent have lived apart for a continuous period of at least 5 years immediately preceding the making of the application ('5 years' separation');
(d) that the respondent has deserted the applicant for a continuous period of at least 2 years immediately preceding the making of the application.

Defined terms—'civil partner': s 1(1); 'the court': s 37(4); 'dissolution order': s 37(1)(a).

Scope—Subject to the 1-year time bar (s 41), the sole ground for the dissolution of a civil partnership is that it has irretrievably broken down, as evidenced by one of the four facts in s 44(5). Adultery is not included as a separate fact (cf same-sex marriage). Infidelity which leads to an irretrievable breakdown of a civil partnership may be regarded as unreasonable behaviour within s 44(5)(a).

45 Supplemental provisions as to facts raising presumption of breakdown

(1) Subsection (2) applies if –
(a) in any proceedings for a dissolution order the applicant alleges, in reliance on section 44(5)(a), that the respondent has behaved in such a way that the applicant cannot reasonably be expected to live with the respondent, but
(b) after the date of the occurrence of the final incident relied on by the applicant and held by the court to support his allegation, the applicant and the respondent have lived together for a period (or periods) which does not, or which taken together do not, exceed 6 months.

(2) The fact that the applicant and respondent have lived together as mentioned in subsection (1)(b) must be disregarded in determining, for the purposes of section 44(5)(a), whether the applicant cannot reasonably be expected to live with the respondent.

(3) Subsection (4) applies in relation to cases where the applicant alleges, in reliance on section 44(5)(b), that the respondent consents to a dissolution order being made.

(4) Rules of court must make provision for the purpose of ensuring that the respondent has been given such information as will enable him to understand –
(a) the consequences to him of consenting to the making of the order, and
(b) the steps which he must take to indicate his consent.

(5) For the purposes of section 44(5)(d) the court may treat a period of desertion as having continued at a time when the deserting civil partner was incapable of continuing the necessary intention, if the evidence before the court is such that, had he not been so incapable, the court would have inferred that the desertion continued at that time.

(6) In considering for the purposes of section 44(5) whether the period for which the civil partners have lived apart or the period for which the respondent has deserted the applicant has been continuous, no account is to be taken of –
(a) any one period not exceeding 6 months, or
(b) any two or more periods not exceeding 6 months in all,

during which the civil partners resumed living with each other.

(7) But no period during which the civil partners have lived with each other counts as part of the period during which the civil partners have lived apart or as part of the period of desertion.

(8) For the purposes of section 44(5)(b) and (c) and this section civil partners are to be treated as living apart unless they are living with each other in the same household, and references in this section to civil partners living with each other are to be read as references to their living with each other in the same household.

Defined terms—'civil partners': s 1(1); 'the court': s 37(4); 'dissolution order': s 37(1)(a).

Rules of court to ensure respondent's consent under s 44(5)(b) (s 45(4))—See FPR 2010, r 7.12(4),(6) and (12).

46 Dissolution order not precluded by previous separation order etc

(1) Subsections (2) and (3) apply if any of the following orders has been made in relation to a civil partnership –

(a) a separation order;
(b) an order under Schedule 6 (financial relief in magistrates' courts etc);
(c) an order under section 33 of the Family Law Act 1996 (occupation orders);
(d) an order under section 37 of the 1996 Act (orders where neither civil partner entitled to occupy the home).

(2) Nothing prevents –

(a) either civil partner from applying for a dissolution order, or
(b) the court from making a dissolution order,

on the same facts, or substantially the same facts, as those proved in support of the making of the order referred to in subsection (1).

(3) On the application for the dissolution order, the court –

(a) may treat the order referred to in subsection (1) as sufficient proof of any desertion or other fact by reference to which it was made, but
(b) must not make the dissolution order without receiving evidence from the applicant.

(4) If –

(a) the application for the dissolution order follows a separation order or any order requiring the civil partners to live apart,
(b) there was a period of desertion immediately preceding the institution of the proceedings for the separation order, and
(c) the civil partners have not resumed living together and the separation order has been continuously in force since it was made,

the period of desertion is to be treated for the purposes of the application for the dissolution order as if it had immediately preceded the making of the application.

(5) For the purposes of section 44(5)(d) the court may treat as a period during which the respondent has deserted the applicant any period during which there is in force –

(a) an injunction granted by the High Court, the family court or the county court which excludes the respondent from the civil partnership home, or
(b) an order under section 33 or 37 of the 1996 Act which prohibits the respondent from occupying a dwelling-house in which the applicant and the respondent have, or at any time have had, a civil partnership home.

Amendments—CCA 2013, s 17, Sch 11.

Defined terms—'civil partners': s 1(1); 'the court': s 37(4); 'dissolution order': s 37(1)(a); 'separation order': s 37(1)(d).

Scope—This section replicates the provisions of MCA 1973, s 4, the commentary to which reference should be made.

47 Refusal of dissolution in 5 year separation cases on ground of grave hardship

(1) The respondent to an application for a dissolution order in which the applicant alleges 5 years' separation may oppose the making of an order on the ground that –

(a) the dissolution of the civil partnership will result in grave financial or other hardship to him, and
(b) it would in all the circumstances be wrong to dissolve the civil partnership.

(2) Subsection (3) applies if –

(a) the making of a dissolution order is opposed under this section,
(b) the court finds that the applicant is entitled to rely in support of his application on the fact of 5 years' separation and makes no such finding as to any other fact mentioned in section 44(5), and
(c) apart from this section, the court would make a dissolution order.

(3) The court must –

(a) consider all the circumstances, including the conduct of the civil partners and the interests of the civil partners and of any children or other persons concerned, and

(b) if it is of the opinion that the ground mentioned in subsection (1) is made out, dismiss the application for the dissolution order.

(4) 'Hardship' includes the loss of the chance of acquiring any benefit which the respondent might acquire if the civil partnership were not dissolved.

Defined terms—'civil partners': s 1(1); 'the court': s 37(4); 'dissolution order': s 37(1)(a).

Scope—This section replicates the provisions of MCA 1973, s 5, the commentary to which reference should be made.

48 Proceedings before order made final: protection for respondent in separation cases

(1) The court may, on an application made by the respondent, rescind a conditional dissolution order if –

(a) it made the order on the basis of a finding that the applicant was entitled to rely on the fact of 2 years' separation coupled with the respondent's consent to a dissolution order being made,

(b) it made no such finding as to any other fact mentioned in section 44(5), and

(c) it is satisfied that the applicant misled the respondent (whether intentionally or unintentionally) about any matter which the respondent took into account in deciding to give his consent.

(2) Subsections (3) to (5) apply if –

(a) the respondent to an application for a dissolution order in which the applicant alleged –

(i) 2 years' separation coupled with the respondent's consent to a dissolution order being made, or

(ii) 5 years' separation,

has applied to the court for consideration under subsection (3) of his financial position after the dissolution of the civil partnership, and

(b) the court –

(i) has made a conditional dissolution order on the basis of a finding that the applicant was entitled to rely in support of his application on the fact of 2 years' or 5 years' separation, and

(ii) has made no such finding as to any other fact mentioned in section 44(5).

(3) The court hearing an application by the respondent under subsection (2) must consider all the circumstances, including –

(a) the age, health, conduct, earning capacity, financial resources and financial obligations of each of the parties, and

(b) the financial position of the respondent as, having regard to the dissolution, it is likely to be after the death of the applicant should the applicant die first.

(4) Subject to subsection (5), the court must not make the order final unless it is satisfied that –

(a) the applicant should not be required to make any financial provision for the respondent, or

(b) the financial provision made by the applicant for the respondent is –

(i) reasonable and fair, or

(ii) the best that can be made in the circumstances.

(5) The court may if it thinks fit make the order final if –

(a) it appears that there are circumstances making it desirable that the order should be made final without delay, and

(b) it has obtained a satisfactory undertaking from the applicant that he will make such financial provision for the respondent as it may approve.

Defined terms—'the court': s 37(4); 'conditional order': s 37(2); 'dissolution order': s 37(1)(a).

Scope—This section replicates the provisions of MCA 1973, s 10, the commentary to which reference should be made.

Nullity

49 Grounds on which civil partnership is void

Where two people register as civil partners of each other in England and Wales, the civil partnership is void if –

(a) at the time when they do so, they are not eligible to register as civil partners of each other under Chapter 1 (see section 3),

(b) at the time when they do so they both know –

(i) that due notice of proposed civil partnership has not been given,

(ii) that the civil partnership document has not been duly issued,

(iii) that the civil partnership document is void under section 17(3) or 27(2) (registration after end of time allowed for registering),

(iv) that the place of registration is a place other than that specified in the notices (or notice) of proposed civil partnership and the civil partnership document,

(v) that a civil partnership registrar is not present, or

(vi) that the place of registration is on premises that are not approved premises although the registration is purportedly in accordance with section 6(3A)(a), or

(c) the civil partnership document is void under paragraph 6(5) of Schedule 2 (civil partnership between child and another person forbidden).

Amendments—SI 2005/2000.

Defined terms—'civil partners': s 1(1); 'civil partnership document': s 7; 'civil partnership registrar': s 29.

Scope—A nullity order annuls a civil partnership which is either void or voidable (s 37(1)(b)). This section sets out the circumstances in which a civil partnership is void, i e invalid from the outset.

50 Grounds on which civil partnership is voidable

(1) Where two people register as civil partners of each other in England and Wales, the civil partnership is voidable if –

(a) either of them did not validly consent to its formation (whether as a result of duress, mistake, unsoundness of mind or otherwise);

(b) at the time of its formation either of them, though capable of giving a valid consent, was suffering (whether continuously or intermittently) from mental disorder of such a kind or to such an extent as to be unfitted for civil partnership;

(c) at the time of its formation, the respondent was pregnant by some person other than the applicant;

(d) an interim gender recognition certificate under the GRA 2004 has, after the time of its formation, been issued to either civil partner;

(e) the respondent is a person whose gender at the time of its formation had become the acquired gender under the 2004 Act.

(2) In this section and section 51 'mental disorder' has the same meaning as in the Mental Health Act 1983.

Defined terms—'civil partners': s 1(1); 'the acquired gender': GRA 2004, ss 1(2), 25.

Scope—A nullity order annuls a civil partnership which is either void or voidable (s 37(1)(b)). This section sets out the grounds for obtaining a nullity order where the civil partnership is voidable, i e invalid from the date of the final order (s 37(3)). The bars to relief where a civil partnership is voidable are contained in s 51. In particular, the application for a nullity order must be made within 3 years of registration, unless the court gives leave for the institution of proceedings after that period (s 51(2)). There is no requirement for a civil partnership to be consummated. The provisions of s 50(1)(c) appear to be a replication of MCA 1973, s 12(f). There is, however, no corresponding provision to MCA 1973, s 12(e) that 'the respondent was suffering from venereal disease in a communicable form'.

51 Bars to relief where civil partnership is voidable

(1) The court must not make a nullity order on the ground that a civil partnership is voidable if the respondent satisfies the court –

(a) that the applicant, with knowledge that it was open to him to obtain a nullity order, conducted himself in relation to the respondent in such a way as to lead the respondent reasonably to believe that he would not seek to do so, and
(b) that it would be unjust to the respondent to make the order.

(2) Without prejudice to subsection (1), the court must not make a nullity order by virtue of section 50(1)(a), (b), (c) or (e) unless –

(a) it is satisfied that proceedings were instituted within 3 years from the date of the formation of the civil partnership, or
(b) leave for the institution of proceedings after the end of that 3 year period has been granted under subsection (3).

(3) A judge of the court may, on an application made to him, grant leave for the institution of proceedings if he –

(a) is satisfied that the applicant has at some time during the 3 year period suffered from mental disorder, and
(b) considers that in all the circumstances of the case it would be just to grant leave for the institution of proceedings.

(4) An application for leave under subsection (3) may be made after the end of the 3 year period.

(5) Without prejudice to subsection (1), the court must not make a nullity order by virtue of section 50(1)(d) unless it is satisfied that proceedings were instituted within the period of 6 months from the date of issue of the interim gender recognition certificate.

(6) Without prejudice to subsections (1) and (2), the court must not make a nullity order by virtue of section 50(1)(c) or (e) unless it is satisfied that the applicant was at the time of the formation of the civil partnership ignorant of the facts alleged.

Defined terms—'the court': s 37(4); 'nullity order': s 37(1)(b); 'mental disorder': s 50(2).

52 Proof of certain matters not necessary to validity of civil partnership

(1) Where two people have registered as civil partners of each other in England and Wales, it is not necessary in support of the civil partnership to give any proof –

(a) that any person whose consent to the civil partnership was required by section 4 (parental etc consent) had given his consent, or
(aa) that before the registration either of the civil partners resided, or resided for any period, in the area stated in the notices of proposed civil partnership to be the area of that person's place of residence;
(b) *(repealed)*

and no evidence is to be given to prove the contrary in any proceedings touching the validity of the civil partnership.

(2) Subsection (1)(a) is subject to section 49(c) (civil partnership void if forbidden).

Amendments—SI 2005/2000.

Defined terms—'civil partners': s 1(1); 'civil partnership registrar': s 29; 'registration authority': s 28.

53 Power to validate civil partnership

(1) Where two people have registered as civil partners of each other in England and Wales, the Lord Chancellor may by order validate the civil partnership if it appears to him that it is or may be void under section 49(b).

(2) An order under subsection (1) may include provisions for relieving a person from any liability under section 31(2), 32(2) or 33(5) or (7).

(3) The draft of an order under subsection (1) must be advertised, in such manner as the Lord Chancellor thinks fit, not less than one month before the order is made.

(4) The Lord Chancellor must –

(a) consider all objections to the order sent to him in writing during that month, and

(b) if it appears to him necessary, direct a local inquiry into the validity of any such objections.

(5) An order under subsection (1) is subject to special parliamentary procedure.

Defined terms—'civil partners': s 1(1).

54 Validity of civil partnerships registered outside England and Wales

(1) Where two people register as civil partners of each other in Scotland, the civil partnership is –

(a) void, if it would be void in Scotland under section 123, and
(b) voidable, if the circumstances fall within section 50(1)(d).

(2) Where two people register as civil partners of each other in Northern Ireland, the civil partnership is –

(a) void, if it would be void in Northern Ireland under section 173, and
(b) voidable, if the circumstances fall within any paragraph of section 50(1).

(3) Subsection (4) applies where two people register as civil partners of each other under an Order in Council under –

(a) section 210 (registration at British consulates etc), or
(b) section 211 (registration by armed forces personnel),

('the relevant section').

(4) The civil partnership is –

(a) void, if –
(i) the condition in subsection (2)(a) or (b) of the relevant section is not met, or
(ii) a requirement prescribed for the purposes of this paragraph by an Order in Council under the relevant section is not complied with, and
(b) voidable, if –
(i) the appropriate part of the United Kingdom is England and Wales or Northern Ireland and the circumstances fall within any paragraph of section 50(1), or
(ii) the appropriate part of the United Kingdom is Scotland and the circumstances fall within section 50(1)(d).

(5) The appropriate part of the United Kingdom is the part by reference to which the condition in subsection (2)(b) of the relevant section is met.

(6) Subsections (7) and (8) apply where two people have registered an apparent or alleged overseas relationship.

(7) The civil partnership is void if –

(a) the relationship is not an overseas relationship, or
(b) (even though the relationship is an overseas relationship) the parties are not treated under Chapter 2 of Part 5 as having formed a civil partnership.

(8) The civil partnership is voidable if –

(a) the overseas relationship is voidable under the relevant law,
(b) the circumstances fall within section 50(1)(d), or
(c) where either of the parties was domiciled in England and Wales or Northern Ireland at the time when the overseas relationship was registered, the circumstances fall within section 50(1)(a), (b), (c) or (e).

(9) Section 51 applies for the purposes of –

(a) subsections (1)(b), (2)(b) and (4)(b),
(b) subsection (8)(a), in so far as applicable in accordance with the relevant law, and
(c) subsection (8)(b) and (c).

(10) In subsections (8)(a) and (9)(b) 'the relevant law' means the law of the country or territory where the overseas relationship was registered (including its rules of private international law).

(11) For the purposes of subsections (8) and (9)(b) and (c), references in sections 50 and 51 to the formation of the civil partnership are to be read as references to the registration of the overseas relationship.

Defined terms—'civil partners': s 1(1); 'overseas relationship': s 212(1).

Presumption of death orders

55 Presumption of death orders

(1) The court may, on an application made by a civil partner, make a presumption of death order if it is satisfied that reasonable grounds exist for supposing that the other civil partner is dead.

(2) In any proceedings under this section the fact that –

(a) for a period of 7 years or more the other civil partner has been continually absent from the applicant, and

(b) the applicant has no reason to believe that the other civil partner has been living within that time,

is evidence that the other civil partner is dead until the contrary is proved.

Defined terms—'civil partner': s 1(1); 'the court': s 37(4); 'presumption of death order': s 37(1)(c).

Scope—The fact that a civil partner has been continually absent for 7 years and the applicant has no reason to believe him to be alive during that time creates a rebuttable presumption of the death of that civil partner. A presumption of death order is granted in two stages and is initially conditional for a period of 6 weeks (ss 37(2) and 38). While MCA 1973, s 19 (which had been the counterpart to this section) has been repealed by the Presumption of Death Act 2013, Sch 2, para 1, no amendments have been made to s 55: see annotations to s 222.

Separation orders

56 Separation orders

(1) An application for a separation order may be made to the court by either civil partner on the ground that any such fact as is mentioned in section 44(5)(a), (b), (c) or (d) exists.

(2) On an application for a separation order the court must inquire, so far as it reasonably can, into –

(a) the facts alleged by the applicant, and

(b) any facts alleged by the respondent,

but whether the civil partnership has broken down irretrievably is irrelevant.

(3) If the court is satisfied on the evidence of any such fact as is mentioned in section 44(5)(a), (b), (c) or (d) it must make a separation order.

(4) Section 45 (supplemental provisions as to facts raising presumption of breakdown) applies for the purposes of an application for a separation order alleging any such fact as it applies in relation to an application for a dissolution order alleging that fact.

Amendments—CFA 2014, s 17.

Defined terms—'civil partner': s 1(1); 'the court': s 37(4); 'separation order': s 37(1)(d).

Scope—A separation order provides for the separation of the civil partners. The grounds are as for dissolution (s 56(1)). If either party dies intestate, while a separation order is in effect, his or her property would devolve as though the other civil partner were dead (s 57).

57 Effect of separation order

If either civil partner dies intestate as respects all or any of his or her real or personal property while –

(a) a separation order is in force, and

(b) the separation is continuing,

the property as respects which he or she died intestate devolves as if the other civil partner had then been dead.

Defined terms —'civil partner': s 1(1); 'separation order': s 37(1)(d).

Declarations

58 Declarations

(1) Any person may apply to the High Court or the family court for one or more of the following declarations in relation to a civil partnership specified in the application –

(a) a declaration that the civil partnership was at its inception a valid civil partnership;
(b) a declaration that the civil partnership subsisted on a date specified in the application;
(c) a declaration that the civil partnership did not subsist on a date so specified;
(d) a declaration that the validity of a dissolution, annulment or legal separation obtained outside England and Wales in respect of the civil partnership is entitled to recognition in England and Wales;
(e) a declaration that the validity of a dissolution, annulment or legal separation so obtained in respect of the civil partnership is not entitled to recognition in England and Wales.

(2) Where an application under subsection (1) is made to a court by a person other than a civil partner in the civil partnership to which the application relates, the court must refuse to hear the application if it considers that the applicant does not have a sufficient interest in the determination of that application.

Amendments—CCA 2013, s 17, Sch 11.

Defined term —'civil partner': s 1(1).

Scope—Sections 58–61 contain provisions enabling the court to make declarations in relation to a civil partnership, eg that a civil partnership was at its inception a valid civil partnership or that a civil partnership subsisted or did not subsist on a specified date, which are akin to the provisions relating to declarations as to marital status in FLA 1986, s 55. The procedure is to be found in FPR 2010, Pt 8, Ch 5. Jurisdiction to entertain an application under this section is provided for by s 224. Applications under this section are assigned to the Family Division of the High Court (SCA 1981, s 61(1)(iii), Sch 1, para 3).

59 General provisions as to making and effect of declarations

(1) Where on an application for a declaration under section 58 the truth of the proposition to be declared is proved to the satisfaction of the court, the court must make the declaration unless to do so would be manifestly contrary to public policy.

(2) Any declaration under section 58 binds Her Majesty and all other persons.

(3) The court, on the dismissal of an application for a declaration under section 58, may not make any declaration for which an application has not been made.

(4) No declaration which may be applied for under section 58 may be made otherwise than under section 58 by any court.

(5) No declaration may be made by any court, whether under section 58 or otherwise, that a civil partnership was at its inception void.

(6) Nothing in this section affects the powers of any court to make a nullity order in respect of a civil partnership.

Defined term—'nullity order': s 37(1)(b).

60 The Attorney General and proceedings for declarations

(1) On an application for a declaration under section 58 the court may at any stage of the proceedings, of its own motion or on the application of any party to the proceedings, direct that all necessary papers in the matter be sent to the Attorney General.

(2) The Attorney General, whether or not he is sent papers in relation to an application for a declaration under section 58, may –

(a) intervene in the proceedings on that application in such manner as he thinks necessary or expedient, and
(b) argue before the court dealing with the application any question in relation to the application which the court considers it necessary to have fully argued.

(3) Where any costs are incurred by the Attorney General in connection with any application for a declaration under section 58, the court may make such order as it considers just as to the payment of those costs by parties to the proceedings.

61 Supplementary provisions as to declarations

(1) Any declaration made under section 58, and any application for such a declaration, must be in the form prescribed by rules of court.

(2) Rules of court may make provision –

(a) as to the information required to be given by any applicant for a declaration under section 58;
(b) requiring notice of an application under section 58 to be served on the Attorney General and on persons who may be affected by any declaration applied for.

(3) No proceedings under section 58 affect any final judgment or order already pronounced or made by any court of competent jurisdiction.

(4) The court hearing an application under section 58 may direct that the whole or any part of the proceedings must be heard in private.

(5) An application for a direction under subsection (4) must be heard in private unless the court otherwise directs.

General provisions

62 Relief for respondent in dissolution proceedings

(1) If in any proceedings for a dissolution order the respondent alleges and proves any such fact as is mentioned in section 44(5)(a), (b), (c) or (d) the court may give to the respondent the relief to which he would have been entitled if he had made an application seeking that relief.

(2) When applying subsection (1), treat –

(a) the respondent as the applicant, and
(b) the applicant as the respondent,

for the purposes of section 44(5).

Defined terms—'the court': s 37(4); 'dissolution order': s 37(1)(a).

Scope—This section is the counterpart of MCA 1973, s 20, the commentary to which reference should be made.

63 *(repealed)*

64 Parties to proceedings under this Chapter

(1) Rules of court may make provision with respect to –

(a) the joinder as parties to proceedings under sections 37 to 56 of persons involved in allegations of improper conduct made in those proceedings,
(b) the dismissal from such proceedings of any parties so joined, and
(c) the persons who are to be parties to proceedings on an application under section 58.

(2) Rules of court made under this section may make different provision for different cases.

(3) In every case in which the court considers, in the interest of a person not already a party to the proceedings, that the person should be made a party, the court may if it thinks fit allow the person to intervene upon such terms, if any, as the court thinks just.

Defined terms—'the court': s 37(4).

Scope—This section is the counterpart to MCA 1973, s 49.

65 Contribution by civil partner to property improvement

(1) This section applies if –

(a) a civil partner contributes in money or money's worth to the improvement of real or personal property in which or in the proceeds of sale of which either or both of the civil partners has or have a beneficial interest, and

(b) the contribution is of a substantial nature.

(2) The contributing partner is to be treated as having acquired by virtue of the contribution a share or an enlarged share (as the case may be) in the beneficial interest of such an extent –

(a) as may have been then agreed, or

(b) in default of such agreement, as may seem in all the circumstances just to any court before which the question of the existence or extent of the beneficial interest of either of the civil partners arises (whether in proceedings between them or in any other proceedings).

(3) Subsection (2) is subject to any agreement (express or implied) between the civil partners to the contrary.

Defined terms—'civil partners': s 1(1).

Scope—This section provides that substantial contributions in money or money's worth to the improvement of property in which either or both civil partners have an interest entitles that contributing civil partner to a share or enlarged share in the property as may have been agreed or, in default of agreement, as may seem in all the circumstances just (subject to any agreement, express or implied, to the contrary) (s 65). This mirrors MPPA 1970, s 37. This section also applies where a civil partnership agreement is terminated (s 74(2)).

66 Disputes between civil partners about property

(1) In any question between the civil partners in a civil partnership as to title to or possession of property, either civil partner may apply to –

(a) the High Court, or

(b) the family court.

(2) On such an application, the court may make such order with respect to the property as it thinks fit (including an order for the sale of the property).

(3) *(repealed)*

Amendments—CCA 2013, s 17, Sch 11.

Defined term—'civil partners': s 1(1).

Scope—Civil partners may apply to the court where there is a dispute as to the title or possession of property and the court may make an order as it sees fit including an order for sale (s 66) (corresponding to MWPA 1882, s 17) subject to a limitation period of 3 years from the date of dissolution or annulment (s 68). This section also applies where a civil partnership agreement is terminated (s 74(3)). The procedure is found in FPR 2010, Pt 8, Ch 4.

67 Applications under section 66 where property not in possession etc

(1) The right of a civil partner ('A') to make an application under section 66 includes the right to make such an application where A claims that the other civil partner ('B') has had in his possession or under his control –

(a) money to which, or to a share of which, A was beneficially entitled, or

(b) property (other than money) to which, or to an interest in which, A was beneficially entitled,

and that either the money or other property has ceased to be in B's possession or under B's control or that A does not know whether it is still in B's possession or under B's control.

(2) For the purposes of subsection (1)(a) it does not matter whether A is beneficially entitled to the money or share –

(a) because it represents the proceeds of property to which, or to an interest in which, A was beneficially entitled, or

(b) for any other reason.

(3) Subsections (4) and (5) apply if, on such an application being made, the court is satisfied that B –

(a) has had in his possession or under his control money or other property as mentioned in subsection (1)(a) or (b), and

(b) has not made to A, in respect of that money or other property, such payment or disposition as would have been appropriate in the circumstances.

(4) The power of the court to make orders under section 66 includes power to order B to pay to A –

(a) in a case falling within subsection (1)(a), such sum in respect of the money to which the application relates, or A's s share of it, as the court considers appropriate, or
(b) in a case falling within subsection (1)(b), such sum in respect of the value of the property to which the application relates, or A's interest in it, as the court considers appropriate.

(5) If it appears to the court that there is any property which –

(a) represents the whole or part of the money or property, and
(b) is property in respect of which an order could (apart from this section) have been made under section 66,

the court may (either instead of or as well as making an order in accordance with subsection (4)) make any order which it could (apart from this section) have made under section 66.

(6) Any power of the court which is exercisable on an application under section 66 is exercisable in relation to an application made under that section as extended by this section.

Defined term—'civil partner': s 1(1).

Scope—This section replicates the provisions of the Matrimonial Causes (Property and Maintenance) Act 1958, s 7 and extends s 66 to enable the court to make orders where money or property has ceased to be in the possession or under the control of one of the civil partners. This section also applies where a civil partnership agreement is terminated (s 74(3)).

68 Applications under section 66 by former civil partners

(1) This section applies where a civil partnership has been dissolved or annulled.

(2) Subject to subsection (3), an application may be made under section 66 (including that section as extended by section 67) by either former civil partner despite the dissolution or annulment (and references in those sections to a civil partner are to be read accordingly).

(3) The application must be made within the period of 3 years beginning with the date of the dissolution or annulment.

69 Actions in tort between civil partners

(1) This section applies if an action in tort is brought by one civil partner against the other during the subsistence of the civil partnership.

(2) The court may stay the proceedings if it appears –

(a) that no substantial benefit would accrue to either civil partner from the continuation of the proceedings, or
(b) that the question or questions in issue could more conveniently be disposed of on an application under section 66.

(3) Without prejudice to subsection (2)(b), the court may in such an action –

(a) exercise any power which could be exercised on an application under section 66, or
(b) give such directions as it thinks fit for the disposal under that section of any question arising in the proceedings.

Defined term—'civil partner': s 1(1).

70 Assurance policy by civil partner for benefit of other civil partner etc

Section 11 of the Married Women's Property Act 1882 (money payable under policy of assurance not to form part of the estate of the insured) applies in relation to a policy of assurance –

(a) effected by a civil partner on his own life, and
(b) expressed to be for the benefit of his civil partner, or of his children, or of his civil partner and children, or any of them,

PART II

as it applies in relation to a policy of assurance effected by a husband and expressed to be for the benefit of his wife, or of his children, or of his wife and children, or of any of them.

Defined term—'civil partner': s 1(1).

Scope—If a civil partner takes out a life insurance policy to provide for his or her civil partner or children, the application of MWPA 1882, s 11 is extended so that the money payable under the policy is not to form part of the estate of the insured. While this section deals with assurance policies effected by a civil partner on his own life, a civil partner is presumed for the purposes of the Life Assurance Act 1774, s 1 to have an unlimited insurable interest in the life of his civil partner (s 253).

****

72 Financial relief for civil partners and children of family

(1) Schedule 5 makes provision for financial relief in connection with civil partnerships that corresponds to provision made for financial relief in connection with marriages by Part 2 of the Matrimonial Causes Act 1973.

(2) Any rule of law under which any provision of Part 2 of the 1973 Act is interpreted as applying to dissolution of a marriage on the ground of presumed death is to be treated as applying (with any necessary modifications) in relation to the corresponding provision of Schedule 5.

(3) Schedule 6 makes provision for financial relief in connection with civil partnerships that corresponds to provision made for financial relief in connection with marriages by the Domestic Proceedings and Magistrates' Courts Act 1978.

(4) Schedule 7 makes provision for financial relief in England and Wales after a civil partnership has been dissolved or annulled, or civil partners have been legally separated, in a country outside the British Islands.

Defined term—'civil partners': s 1(1).

Scope—This section makes provision for financial relief for civil partners corresponding to Pt II of MCA 1973 (Sch 5), corresponding with DPMCA 1978 (Sch 6) and corresponding to MFPA 1984, Pt III after a civil partnership has been dissolved or annulled, or civil partners have been legally separated, in a country outside the British Isles (Sch 7). Reference should be made to the commentary in Schs 5–7.

73 Civil partnership agreements unenforceable

(1) A civil partnership agreement does not under the law of England and Wales have effect as a contract giving rise to legal rights.

(2) No action lies in England and Wales for breach of a civil partnership agreement, whatever the law applicable to the agreement.

(3) In this section and section 74 'civil partnership agreement' means an agreement between two people –

- (a) to register as civil partners of each other –
  - (i) in England and Wales (under this Part),
  - (ii) in Scotland (under Part 3),
  - (iii) in Northern Ireland (under Part 4), or
  - (iv) outside the United Kingdom under an Order in Council made under Chapter 1 of Part 5 (registration at British consulates etc or by armed forces personnel), or
- (b) to enter into an overseas relationship.

(4) This section applies in relation to civil partnership agreements whether entered into before or after this section comes into force, but does not affect any action commenced before it comes into force.

Defined terms—'civil partners': s 1(1); 'overseas relationship': s 212.

Scope—A civil partnership agreement is an agreement between two people to register as the civil partners of each other (ie the counterpart of an engagement) (s 73(3)). Such an agreement does not give rise to legal rights (s 73(1),(2)). A person is associated with another person if they have entered into a civil partnership agreement (FLA 1996, s 62(3)(eza)) and may thus be entitled to apply for an occupation order or a non-molestation order under ss 33 and 42 respectively of the 1996 Act. Further, certain rights are conferred by s 74.

74 Property where civil partnership agreement is terminated

(1) This section applies if a civil partnership agreement is terminated.

(2) Section 65 (contributions by civil partner to property improvement) applies, in relation to any property in which either or both of the parties to the agreement had a beneficial interest while the agreement was in force, as it applies in relation to property in which a civil partner has a beneficial interest.

(3) Sections 66 and 67 (disputes between civil partners about property) apply to any dispute between or claim by one of the parties in relation to property in which either or both had a beneficial interest while the agreement was in force, as if the parties were civil partners of each other.

(4) An application made under section 66 or 67 by virtue of subsection (3) must be made within 3 years of the termination of the agreement.

(5) A party to a civil partnership agreement who makes a gift of property to the other party on the condition (express or implied) that it is to be returned if the agreement is terminated is not prevented from recovering the property merely because of his having terminated the agreement.

Defined terms—'civil partners': s 1(1); 'civil partnership agreement': s 73(3).

Scope—Although a civil partnership agreement does not give rise to legal rights (s 73(1),(2)), the provisions of the Act in respect of contributions to property (s 65) and disputes as to title or possession (ss 66 and 67) apply when a civil partnership agreement is terminated provided an application under ss 66 and 67 is made within 3 years of the termination of the agreement (s 74(4)).

****

84 Evidence

(1) Any enactment or rule of law relating to the giving of evidence by a spouse applies in relation to a civil partner as it applies in relation to the spouse.

(2) Subsection (1) is subject to any specific amendment made by or under this Act which relates to the giving of evidence by a civil partner.

(3) For the avoidance of doubt, in any such amendment, references to a person's civil partner do not include a former civil partner.

(4) References in subsections (1) and (2) to giving evidence are to giving evidence in any way (whether by supplying information, making discovery, producing documents or otherwise).

(5) Any rule of law –

- (a) which is preserved by section 7(3) of the Civil Evidence Act 1995 or section 118(1) of the Criminal Justice Act 2003, and
- (b) under which in any proceedings evidence of reputation or family tradition is admissible for the purpose of proving or disproving the existence of a marriage,

is to be treated as applying in an equivalent way for the purpose of proving or disproving the existence of a civil partnership.

Defined term—'civil partner': s 1(1).

****

PART 5
CIVIL PARTNERSHIP FORMED OR DISSOLVED ABROAD ETC

****

212 Meaning of 'overseas relationship'

(1) For the purposes of this Act an overseas relationship is a relationship which –

- (a) is either a specified relationship or a relationship which meets the general conditions, and
- (b) is registered (whether before or after the passing of this Act) with a responsible authority in a country or territory outside the United Kingdom, by two people –
  - (i) who under the relevant law are of the same sex at the time when they do so, and
  - (ii) neither of whom is already a civil partner or lawfully married.

PART II

(1A) But, for the purposes of the application of this Act to England and Wales, marriage is not an overseas relationship.

(2) In this Chapter, 'the relevant law' means the law of the country or territory where the relationship is registered (including its rules of private international law).

Amendments—SI 2014/560.

Defined terms—'civil partner': s 1(1); 'specified relationship': s 213 and Sch 20; 'general conditions': s 214.

Scope—It is possible for overseas relationships to be treated as civil partnerships (even though entered into before the Act came into force) providing the requirements of Pt 5 are met (ss 212–218 and Sch 20). Pt 5 of the Act also permits registration abroad at a British Consulate (s 210) or by armed forces personnel (s 211). An overseas relationship, which is either a specified relationship (s 213) or a relationship meeting the general conditions (s 214) will be treated as a civil partnership providing the requirements of s 215 are met. The same-sex requirement (s 216) is relaxed where a full gender recognition certificate has been issued under GRA 2004. These provisions may give rise to applications in England and Wales where jurisdiction permits, as some forms of foreign civil partnership give fewer rights and responsibilities than a civil partnership in England and Wales. Formerly, marriage between same-sex couples in eg, Belgium, The Netherlands or British Columbia was only afforded civil partnership status under the Act (*Wilkinson v Kitzinger and Her Majesty's Attorney-General (the Lord Chancellor Intervening)* [2006] 2 FLR 397, FD (preliminary costs issue) and *Wilkinson v Kitzinger* [2007] 1 FLR 295, FD (substantive hearing)). However, the Marriage (Same Sex Couples) Act 2013, s 13 and Sch 6 makes provision for same-sex marriage overseas (Pt 1: consular marriage under UK law; Pt 2: marriage under foreign law; and Pt 3: marriage of forces personnel under UK law). The Marriage (Same Sex Couples) Act 2013, s 10, Sch 2, Pts 1 and 2 make provision for the treatment of English and Welsh marriages of same-sex couples in Scotland and Northern Ireland.

213 Specified relationships

(1) A specified relationship is a relationship which is specified for the purposes of section 212 by Schedule 20.

(1A) But, for the purposes of the application of this Act to England and Wales, marriage is not an overseas relationship.

(2) The Secretary of State may by order amend Schedule 20 by –

(a) adding a relationship,
(b) amending the description of a relationship, or
(c) omitting a relationship.

(3) No order may be made under this section without the consent of the Scottish Ministers and the Department of Finance and Personnel.

(4) The power to make an order under this section is exercisable by statutory instrument.

(5) An order which contains any provision (whether alone or with other provisions) amending Schedule 20 by –

(a) amending the description of a relationship, or
(b) omitting a relationship,

may not be made unless a draft of the statutory instrument containing the order is laid before, and approved by a resolution of, each House of Parliament.

(6) A statutory instrument containing any other order under this section is subject to annulment in pursuance of a resolution of either House of Parliament.

Amendments—SI 2007/2914; SI 2010/1839; Marriage (Same Sex Couples) Act 2013, s 17, Sch 7, para 34.

Subordinate legislation—The orders made under this section are the Civil Partnership Act 2004 (Overseas Relationships and Consequential, etc Amendments) Order 2005, the Civil Partnership Act 2004 (Overseas Relationships) Order 2005 and Civil Partnership Act 2004 (Overseas Relationships) Order 2012.

214 The general conditions

The general conditions are that, under the relevant law –

(a) the relationship may not be entered into if either of the parties is already a party to a relationship of that kind or lawfully married,
(b) the relationship is of indeterminate duration, and

(c) the effect of entering into it is that the parties are –
  (i) treated as a couple either generally or for specified purposes, or
  (ii) treated as married.

Defined terms—'relevant law': s 212(2).

215 Overseas relationships treated as civil partnerships: the general rule

(1) Two people are to be treated as having formed a civil partnership as a result of having registered an overseas relationship if, under the relevant law, they –

(a) had capacity to enter into the relationship, and
(b) met all requirements necessary to ensure the formal validity of the relationship.

(2) Subject to subsection (3), the time when they are to be treated as having formed the civil partnership is the time when the overseas relationship is registered (under the relevant law) as having been entered into.

(3) If the overseas relationship is registered (under the relevant law) as having been entered into before this section comes into force, the time when they are to be treated as having formed a civil partnership is the time when this section comes into force.

(4) But if –

(a) before this section comes into force, a dissolution or annulment of the overseas relationship was obtained outside the United Kingdom, and
(b) the dissolution or annulment would be recognised under Chapter 3 if the overseas relationship had been treated as a civil partnership at the time of the dissolution or annulment,

subsection (3) does not apply and subsections (1) and (2) have effect subject to subsection (5).

(5) The overseas relationship is not to be treated as having been a civil partnership for the purposes of any provisions except –

(a) Schedules 7, 11 and 17 (financial relief in United Kingdom after dissolution or annulment obtained outside the United Kingdom);
(b) such provisions as are specified (with or without modifications) in an order under section 259;
(c) Chapter 3 (so far as necessary for the purposes of paragraphs (a) and (b)).

(6) This section is subject to sections 216, 217 and 218.

Defined terms—'overseas relationship': s 212(1); 'relevant law': s 212(2).

'such provisions as are specified' (s 215(5)(b))—The relevant provisions are Civil Partnership (Treatment of Overseas Relationships) Order 2005 and Civil Partnership (Treatment of Overseas Relationships) (No 2) Order 2005.

216 The same-sex requirement

(1) Two people are not to be treated as having formed a civil partnership as a result of having registered an overseas relationship if, at the critical time, they were not of the same sex under United Kingdom law.

(2) But if a full gender recognition certificate is issued under the 2004 Act to a person who has registered an overseas relationship which is within subsection (4), after the issue of the certificate the relationship is no longer prevented from being treated as a civil partnership on the ground that, at the critical time, the parties were not of the same sex.

(3) However, subsection (2) does not apply to an overseas relationship which is within subsection (4) if either of the parties has formed a subsequent civil partnership or lawful marriage.

(4) An overseas relationship is within this subsection if (and only if), at the time mentioned in section 215(2) –

(a) one of the parties ('A') was regarded under the relevant law as having changed gender (but was not regarded under United Kingdom law as having done so), and
(b) the other party was (under United Kingdom law) of the gender to which A had changed under the relevant law.

(5) In this section –

'the critical time' means the time determined in accordance with section 215(2) or (as the case may be) (3);

'the 2004 Act' means the GRA 2004;

'United Kingdom law' means any enactment or rule of law applying in England and Wales, Scotland and Northern Ireland.

(6) Nothing in this section prevents the exercise of any enforceable Community right.

Defined terms—'overseas relationship': s 212(1).

217 Person domiciled in a part of the United Kingdom

(1) Subsection (2) applies if an overseas relationship has been registered by a person who was at the time mentioned in section 215(2) domiciled in England and Wales.

(2) The two people concerned are not to be treated as having formed a civil partnership if, at the time mentioned in section 215(2) –

(a) either of them was under 16, or

(b) they would have been within prohibited degrees of relationship under Part 1 of Schedule 1 if they had been registering as civil partners of each other in England and Wales.

(3) Subsection (4) applies if an overseas relationship has been registered by a person who at the time mentioned in section 215(2) was domiciled in Scotland.

(4) The two people concerned are not to be treated as having formed a civil partnership if, at the time mentioned in section 215(2), they were not eligible by virtue of paragraph (b), (c) or (e) of section 86(1) to register in Scotland as civil partners of each other.

(5) Subsection (6) applies if an overseas relationship has been registered by a person who at the time mentioned in section 215(2) was domiciled in Northern Ireland.

(6) The two people concerned are not to be treated as having formed a civil partnership if, at the time mentioned in section 215(2) –

(a) either of them was under 16, or

(b) they would have been within prohibited degrees of relationship under Schedule 12 if they had been registering as civil partners of each other in Northern Ireland.

Defined terms—'civil partners': s 1(1); 'overseas relationship': s 212(1).

Scope—Where one of the parties was domiciled in England and Wales when the overseas relationship was registered, it will not be recognised as a civil partnership if either of the parties was under 16 or they would have been within the prohibited degrees of relationship if they had been registering in England and Wales (s 217(1),(2)).

218 The public policy exception

Two people are not to be treated as having formed a civil partnership as a result of having entered into an overseas relationship if it would be manifestly contrary to public policy to recognise the capacity, under the relevant law, of one or both of them to enter into the relationship.

Defined terms—'overseas relationship': s 212(1); 'relevant law': s 212(2).

Introduction

219 Power to make provision corresponding to EC Regulation 2201/2003

(1) The Lord Chancellor may by regulations make provision –

(a) as to the jurisdiction of courts in England and Wales in proceedings for the dissolution or annulment of a civil partnership or for legal separation of the civil partners in cases where a civil partner –

(i) is or has been habitually resident in a member State,

(ii) is a national of a member State, or

(iii) is domiciled in a part of the United Kingdom or the Republic of Ireland, and

(b) as to the recognition in England and Wales of any judgment of a court of another member State which orders the dissolution or annulment of a civil partnership or the legal separation of the civil partners.

(1A) The Department of Justice in Northern Ireland may by regulations make provision –

(a) as to the jurisdiction of courts in Northern Ireland in proceedings for the dissolution or annulment of a civil partnership or for legal separation of the civil partners in such cases as are mentioned in subsection (1)(a), and

(b) as to the recognition in Northern Ireland of any such judgment as is mentioned in subsection (1)(b).

(2) The Scottish Ministers may by regulations make provision –

(a) as to the jurisdiction of courts in Scotland in proceedings for the dissolution or annulment of a civil partnership or for legal separation of the civil partners in such cases as are mentioned in subsection (1)(a), and

(b) as to the recognition in Scotland of any such judgment as is mentioned in subsection (1)(b).

(3) The regulations may in particular make provision corresponding to that made by Council Regulation (EC) No 2201/2003 of 27 November 2003 in relation to jurisdiction and the recognition and enforcement of judgments in matrimonial matters.

(4) The regulations may provide that for the purposes of this Part and the regulations 'member State' means –

(a) all member States with the exception of such member States as are specified in the regulations, or

(b) such member States as are specified in the regulations.

(5) The regulations may make provision under subsections (1)(b), (1A)(b) and (2)(b) which applies even if the date of the dissolution, annulment or legal separation is earlier than the date on which this section comes into force.

(6) Regulations under subsection (1) are to be made by statutory instrument and may only be made if a draft has been laid before and approved by resolution of each House of Parliament.

(6A) Regulations under subsection (1A) are to be made by statutory rule for the purposes of the Statutory Rules (Northern Ireland) Order 1979.

(6B) No regulations shall be made under subsection (1A) unless a draft has been laid before and approved by resolution of the Northern Ireland Assembly.

(6C) Section 41(3) of the Interpretation Act (Northern Ireland) 1954 applies for the purposes of subsection (6B) in relation to the laying of a draft as it applies in relation to the laying of a statutory document under an enactment.

(7) Regulations under subsection (2) are to be made by statutory instrument and may only be made if a draft has been laid before and approved by resolution of the Scottish Parliament.

(8) In this Part 'section 219 regulations' means regulations made under this section.

Amendments—SI 2010/976.

Defined term—'civil partners': s 1(1).

Scope—This section provides the basis of jurisdiction in England and Wales for proceedings for dissolution, separation or annulment of a civil partnership, or the recognition of the termination of a civil partnership by another EU Member State. Jurisdiction for the termination of a civil partnership is as on divorce adopting Brussels IIA criteria. Reference should also be made to Civil Partnership (Jurisdiction and Recognition of Judgments) Regulations 2005.

Jurisdiction of courts in England and Wales

220 Meaning of 'the court'

In sections 221 to 224 'the court' means –

(a) the High Court, or

(b) the family court.

Amendments—CCA 2013, s 17, Sch 11.

221 Proceedings for dissolution, separation or nullity order

(1) The court has jurisdiction to entertain proceedings for a dissolution order or a separation order if (and only if) –

(a) the court has jurisdiction under section 219 regulations,

(b) no court has, or is recognised as having, jurisdiction under section 219 regulations and either civil partner is domiciled in England and Wales on the date when the proceedings are begun, or

(c) the following conditions are met –

(i) the two people concerned registered as civil partners of each other in England or Wales,

(ii) no court has, or is recognised as having, jurisdiction under section 219 regulations, and

(iii) it appears to the court to be in the interests of justice to assume jurisdiction in the case.

(2) The court has jurisdiction to entertain proceedings for a nullity order if (and only if) –

(a) the court has jurisdiction under section 219 regulations,

(b) no court has, or is recognised as having, jurisdiction under section 219 regulations and either civil partner –

(i) is domiciled in England and Wales on the date when the proceedings are begun, or

(ii) died before that date and either was at death domiciled in England and Wales or had been habitually resident in England and Wales throughout the period of 1 year ending with the date of death, or

(c) the following conditions are met –

(i) the two people concerned registered as civil partners of each other in England or Wales,

(ii) no court has, or is recognised as having, jurisdiction under section 219 regulations, and

(iii) it appears to the court to be in the interests of justice to assume jurisdiction in the case.

(3) At any time when proceedings are pending in respect of which the court has jurisdiction by virtue of subsection (1) or (2) (or this subsection), the court also has jurisdiction to entertain other proceedings, in respect of the same civil partnership, for a dissolution, separation or nullity order, even though that jurisdiction would not be exercisable under subsection (1) or (2).

Defined terms—'civil partners': s 1(1); 'the court': s 220; 'dissolution order': s 37(1)(a); 'nullity order': s 37(1)(b); 'section 219 regulations': s 219(8); 'separation order': s 37(1)(d).

Scope—This section sets out the basis of jurisdiction in England and Wales for dissolution, nullity and separation orders on the basis of Brussels IIA criteria as set out in the s 219 Regulations and, where no court has jurisdiction under the s 219 regulations, on the ground that either party is domiciled in England and Wales. The provisions of s 221(1)(c) and (2)(c) are intended to meet the situation where a civil partnership has been registered in England or Wales, but the civil partners are unable to obtain a termination of the partnership in the jurisdiction in which they are resident as a result of which one or both of them would have otherwise to return to England or Wales in order to establish jurisdiction.

222 Proceedings for presumption of death order

The court has jurisdiction to entertain proceedings for a presumption of death order if (and only if) –

(a), (b) *(repealed)*

(ba) at the time the application is made, the High Court does not have jurisdiction to entertain an application by that civil partner under section 1 of the Presumption of Death Act 2013 for a declaration that the other civil partner is presumed to be dead, and

(c) the two people concerned registered as civil partners of each other in England and Wales and it appears to the court to be in the interests of justice to assume jurisdiction in the case.

Amendments—Presumption of Death Act 2013, s 16, Sch 2, para 3.

Defined terms—'civil partners': s 1(1); 'the court': s 220; 'presumption of death order': s 37(1)(c).

Scope—This section provides a residual jurisdictional basis for proceedings for a presumption of death order under s 55 on an application made by a civil partner. The primary jurisdictional basis for declarations of presumed death is contained in the Presumption of Death Act 2013, s 1(3),(4), which came into force on 1 October 2014. Section 222 provides only a residual basis for jurisdiction where s 1 of the 2013 Act does not apply, ie in summary, where the civil partnership was registered in England and Wales, but the partners subsequently moved abroad.

223 Proceedings for dissolution, nullity or separation order: supplementary

(1) Rules of court may make provision in relation to civil partnerships corresponding to the provision made in relation to marriages by Schedule 1 to the Domicile and Matrimonial Proceedings Act 1973.

(2) The rules may in particular make provision –

(a) for the provision of information by applicants and respondents in proceedings for dissolution, nullity or separation orders where proceedings relating to the same civil partnership are continuing in another jurisdiction, and

(b) for proceedings before the court to be stayed by the court where there are concurrent proceedings elsewhere in respect of the same civil partnership.

Defined terms—'the court': s 220; 'dissolution order': s 37(1)(a); 'nullity order': s 37(1)(b); 'separation order': s 37(1)(d).

'Rules of court' (s 223(1))—The relevant rules are Family Procedure (Civil Partnership: Staying of Proceedings) Rules 2010, which make provision in relation to civil partnerships corresponding to the DMPA 1973, Sch 1. The procedure is contained in FPR 2010, r 7.27.

224 Applications for declarations as to validity etc

The court has jurisdiction to entertain an application under section 58 if (and only if) –

(a) either of the civil partners in the civil partnership to which the application relates –

(i) is domiciled in England and Wales on the date of the application,

(ii) has been habitually resident in England and Wales throughout the period of 1 year ending with that date, or

(iii) died before that date and either was at death domiciled in England and Wales or had been habitually resident in England and Wales throughout the period of 1 year ending with the date of death, or

(b) the two people concerned registered as civil partners of each other in England and Wales and it appears to the court to be in the interests of justice to assume jurisdiction in the case.

Defined terms—'civil partners': s 1(1); 'the court': s 220.

★★★★

Recognition of dissolution, annulment and separation

233 Effect of dissolution, annulment or separation obtained in the UK

(1) No dissolution or annulment of a civil partnership obtained in one part of the United Kingdom is effective in any part of the United Kingdom unless obtained from a court of civil jurisdiction.

(2) Subject to subsections (3) and (4), the validity of a dissolution or annulment of a civil partnership or a legal separation of civil partners which has been obtained from a court of civil jurisdiction in one part of the United Kingdom is to be recognised throughout the United Kingdom.

(3) Recognition of the validity of a dissolution, annulment or legal separation obtained from a court of civil jurisdiction in one part of the United Kingdom may be refused in any other part if

the dissolution, annulment or separation was obtained at a time when it was irreconcilable with a decision determining the question of the subsistence or validity of the civil partnership –

(a) previously given by a court of civil jurisdiction in the other part, or
(b) previously given by a court elsewhere and recognised or entitled to be recognised in the other part.

(4) Recognition of the validity of a dissolution or legal separation obtained from a court of civil jurisdiction in one part of the United Kingdom may be refused in any other part if the dissolution or separation was obtained at a time when, according to the law of the other part, there was no subsisting civil partnership.

Defined terms—'annulment': s 237(5); 'civil partners': s 1(1); 'part of the United Kingdom': s 237(5).

Scope—This section provides for the recognition of dissolution, annulment and legal separation in one part of the UK in another part of the UK.

234 Recognition in the UK of overseas dissolution, annulment or separation

(1) Subject to subsection (2), the validity of an overseas dissolution, annulment or legal separation is to be recognised in the United Kingdom if, and only if, it is entitled to recognition by virtue of sections 235 to 237.

(2) This section and sections 235 to 237 do not apply to an overseas dissolution, annulment or legal separation as regards which provision as to recognition is made by section 219 regulations.

(3) For the purposes of subsections (1) and (2) and sections 235 to 237, an overseas dissolution, annulment or legal separation is a dissolution or annulment of a civil partnership or a legal separation of civil partners which has been obtained outside the United Kingdom (whether before or after this section comes into force).

Defined terms—'annulment': s 237(5); 'civil partners': s 1(1); 'section 219 regulations': s 219(8).

Scope—This section, along with ss 235–7, provides for the recognition in the UK of overseas dissolution, annulment or legal separation other than those granted in another EU Member State (apart from Denmark) (s 219). Reference should also be made to Civil Partnership (Supplementary Provisions relating to the Recognition of Overseas Dissolutions, Annulments or Legal Separations) (England and Wales and Northern Ireland) Regulations 2005.

235 Grounds for recognition

(1) The validity of an overseas dissolution, annulment or legal separation obtained by means of proceedings is to be recognised if –

(a) the dissolution, annulment or legal separation is effective under the law of the territory in which it was obtained, and at the relevant date either civil partner was habitually resident or domiciled in that territory, or
(b) the dissolution, annulment or legal separation is effective throughout the country in which it was obtained and at the relevant date either civil partner was a national of that country.

(1A) The validity of an overseas dissolution, annulment or legal separation obtained by means of proceedings is also to be recognised if –

(a) the dissolution, annulment or legal separation is effective under the law of the country in which it was obtained, and
(b) at the relevant date neither civil partner –
    (i) was habitually resident in the country in which the dissolution, annulment or legal separation was obtained,
    (ii) was domiciled in that country, or
    (iii) was a national of that country.
(c) at the relevant date the party seeking the dissolution, annulment or legal separation was either habitually resident or domiciled in a country whose law does not recognise legal relationships between people of the same sex and does not provide for dissolution, annulment or legal separation as regards such relationships.

(1B) References in paragraph (1A) to 'country' shall, where appropriate, include a territory which comprises part of a country in which different systems of law are in force in matters relating to the dissolution or annulment of a civil partnership or the legal separation of civil partners.

(2) The validity of an overseas dissolution, annulment or legal separation obtained otherwise than by means of proceedings is to be recognised if –

(a) the dissolution, annulment or legal separation is effective under the law of the territory in which it was obtained,

(b) at the relevant date –

(i) each civil partner was domiciled in that territory, or

(ii) either civil partner was domiciled in that territory and the other was domiciled in a country or territory under whose law the dissolution, annulment or legal separation is recognised as valid, and

(c) neither civil partner was habitually resident in the United Kingdom throughout the period of 1 year immediately preceding that date.

(2A) The validity of an overseas dissolution, annulment or legal separation obtained otherwise than by means of proceedings is also to be recognised if –

(a) the dissolution, annulment or legal separation is effective under the law of the country in which it was obtained,

(b) at the relevant date one civil partner was domiciled in that country and the other was domiciled in a country whose law does not recognise legal relationships between people of the same sex and does not provide for recognition of the validity of dissolutions, annulments or legal separations as regards such relationships, and

(c) neither civil partner was habitually resident in the United Kingdom throughout the period of 1 year immediately preceding that date.

(2B) References in paragraph (2A) to 'country' shall include a territory which comprises part of a country in which different systems of law are in force in matters relating to the dissolution or annulment of a civil partnership or the legal separation of civil partners.

(3) In this section 'the relevant date' means –

(a) in the case of an overseas dissolution, annulment or legal separation obtained by means of proceedings, the date of the commencement of the proceedings;

(b) in the case of an overseas dissolution, annulment or legal separation obtained otherwise than by means of proceedings, the date on which it was obtained.

(4) Where in the case of an overseas annulment the relevant date fell after the death of either civil partner, any reference in subsection (1) or (2) to that date is to be read in relation to that civil partner as a reference to the date of death.

Amendments—SI 2005/3104.

Defined terms—'annulment': s 237(5); 'civil partner': s 1(1); 'proceedings': s 237(5).

Scope—This section provides, under s 234, the grounds for recognition in the UK of an overseas dissolution, annulment or legal separation other than one granted in another EU Member State (apart from Denmark).

236 Refusal of recognition

(1) Recognition of the validity of an overseas dissolution, annulment or legal separation may be refused in any part of the United Kingdom if the dissolution, annulment or separation was obtained at a time when it was irreconcilable with a decision determining the question of the subsistence or validity of the civil partnership –

(a) previously given by a court of civil jurisdiction in that part of the United Kingdom, or

(b) previously given by a court elsewhere and recognised or entitled to be recognised in that part of the United Kingdom.

(2) Recognition of the validity of an overseas dissolution or legal separation may be refused in any part of the United Kingdom if the dissolution or separation was obtained at a time when, according to the law of that part of the United Kingdom, there was no subsisting civil partnership.

(3) Recognition of the validity of an overseas dissolution, annulment or legal separation may be refused if –

(a) in the case of a dissolution, annulment or legal separation obtained by means of proceedings, it was obtained –
   (i) without such steps having been taken for giving notice of the proceedings to a civil partner as, having regard to the nature of the proceedings and all the circumstances, should reasonably have been taken, or
   (ii) without a civil partner having been given (for any reason other than lack of notice) such opportunity to take part in the proceedings as, having regard to those matters, he should reasonably have been given, or

(b) in the case of a dissolution, annulment or legal separation obtained otherwise than by means of proceedings –
   (i) there is no official document certifying that the dissolution, annulment or legal separation is effective under the law of the territory in which it was obtained, or
   (ii) where either civil partner was domiciled in another country or territory at the relevant date, there is no official document certifying that the dissolution, annulment or legal separation is recognised as valid under the law of that other country or territory, or

(c) in either case, recognition of the dissolution, annulment or legal separation would be manifestly contrary to public policy.

(4) In this section –

'official', in relation to a document certifying that a dissolution, annulment or legal separation is effective, or is recognised as valid, under the law of any country or territory, means issued by a person or body appointed or recognised for the purpose under that law;

'the relevant date' has the same meaning as in section 235.

Amendments—SI 2005/3104.

Defined terms—'annulment': s 237(5); 'civil partner': s 1(1); 'part of the United Kingdom', 'proceedings': s 237(5).

Scope—This section provides for the grounds upon which recognition of the validity of an overseas dissolution, annulment or legal separation may be refused under s 234, where granted in jurisdiction other than another EU Member State (apart from Denmark).

237 Supplementary provisions relating to recognition of dissolution etc

(1) For the purposes of sections 235 and 236,

(a) where a civil partner has obtained an overseas dissolution, annulment or legal separation in a territory, he is to be treated as domiciled in that territory if he was domiciled there –
   (i) according to the law of that territory in family matters, or
   (ii) the law of the part of the United Kingdom in which the question of recognition arises,

(b) in all other cases a civil partner is to be treated as domiciled in a country or territory if he was domiciled in that country or territory –
   (i) according to the law of that country or territory in family matters, or
   (ii) according to the law of the part of the United Kingdom in which the question of recognition arises.

(2) The Lord Chancellor or the Scottish Ministers may by regulations make provision –

(a) applying sections 235 and 236 and subsection (1) with modifications in relation to any country whose territories have different systems of law in force in matters of dissolution, annulment or legal separation;

(b) applying sections 235 and 236 with modifications in relation to –
   (i) an overseas dissolution, annulment or legal separation in the case of an overseas relationship (or an apparent or alleged overseas relationship);
   (ii) any case where a civil partner is domiciled in a country or territory whose law does not recognise legal relationships between two people of the same sex;

(c) with respect to recognition of the validity of an overseas dissolution, annulment or legal separation in cases where there are cross-proceedings;

(d) with respect to cases where a legal separation is converted under the law of the country or territory in which it is obtained into a dissolution which is effective under the law of that country or territory;

(e) with respect to proof of findings of fact made in proceedings in any country or territory outside the United Kingdom.

(3) The power to make regulations under subsection (2) is exercisable by statutory instrument.

(4) A statutory instrument containing such regulations –

(a) if made by the Lord Chancellor, is subject to annulment in pursuance of a resolution of either House of Parliament;

(b) if made by the Scottish Ministers, is subject to annulment in pursuance of a resolution of the Scottish Parliament.

(5) In this section (except subsection (4)) and sections 233 to 236 and 238 –

'annulment' includes any order annulling a civil partnership, however expressed;

'part of the United Kingdom' means England and Wales, Scotland or Northern Ireland;

'proceedings' means judicial or other proceedings.

(6) Nothing in this Chapter is to be read as requiring the recognition of any finding of fault made in proceedings for dissolution, annulment or legal separation or of any maintenance, custody or other ancillary order made in any such proceedings.

Amendments—SI 2005/3104.

Defined term—'civil partner': s 1(1).

Regulations—The regulations made under this section are the Civil Partnership (Supplementary Provisions relating to the Recognition of Overseas Dissolutions, Annulments or Legal Separations) (England and Wales and Northern Ireland) Regulations 2005.

Scope—This section provides supplementary provisions relating to the recognition in the UK under s 234 of an overseas dissolution, annulment or legal separation granted other than in another EU Member State (apart from Denmark).

238 Non-recognition elsewhere of dissolution or annulment

(1) This section applies where, in any part of the United Kingdom –

(a) a dissolution or annulment of a civil partnership has been granted by a court of civil jurisdiction, or

(b) the validity of a dissolution or annulment of a civil partnership is recognised by virtue of this Chapter.

(2) The fact that the dissolution or annulment would not be recognised outside the United Kingdom does not –

(a) preclude either party from forming a subsequent civil partnership or marriage in that part of the United Kingdom, or

(b) cause the subsequent civil partnership or marriage of either party (wherever it takes place) to be treated as invalid in that part.

Defined terms—'annulment', 'part of the United Kingdom': s 237(5).

Scope—Where an overseas dissolution, annulment or legal separation is recognised under Pt 5 (s 219: other EU Member States apart from Denmark; s 233: other parts of the UK; s 234: other jurisdictions), a party is not precluded from forming a subsequent civil partnership or divorce in the UK because the dissolution or annulment would not be recognised outside the UK nor will the subsequent civil partnership or divorce be treated as invalid.

****

SCHEDULE 5
FINANCIAL RELIEF: PROVISION CORRESPONDING TO PROVISION MADE BY PART 2 OF THE MATRIMONIAL CAUSES ACT 1973

Amendments—CCA 2013, s 17, Sch 11.

Scope—Section 72(1) and Sch 5 make provision for financial relief for civil partners on dissolution, nullity or separation. It should be noted that the provision corresponds to the provision made for financial relief in connection with marriages by Pt II of MCA 1973, thus indicating that the purpose of the civil partnership regime is to extend, so far as financial remedies are concerned, all the rights and responsibilities of married couples to civil partners (*Lawrence v Gallagher* [2012] 2 FLR 643, CA). Pt 1 of Sch 5 relates to financial provision; Pt 2 to property adjustment; Pt 3 to sale of property orders; Pt 4 to pension sharing; and Pt 4A to pension compensation sharing. The matters to which the court is to have regard under Pts 1–4A are provided for by Pt 5. The court must take into account all the circumstances of the case, giving first consideration to the welfare of any child of the family who is under 18 (para 20). More specifically, when exercising its powers under Parts 1–4A in relation to civil partners, the court must take into account the factors contained in para 21(2) which mirror the checklist in MCA 1973, s 25(2). Where the court is asked to exercise its powers under Parts 1–3 in relation to a child of the family, it must have particular regard to the factors contained in para 22(2), which mirror MCA 1973, s 25(3). Further, unless an adoption order has been made in favour of the non-biological parent, a child of the family will not be a child of those civil partners and therefore the additional factors in para 22(3), which mirror MCA 1973, s 25(4), will come into operation where the court is asked to exercise its powers in relation to a child of the family who is not that civil partner's child. Paragraph 23 provides for the termination of financial obligations and translates the principle of the clean break from MCA 1973, s 25A into civil partnerships. Pt 6 makes provision for pension attachment orders made under Pt 1. Pt 7 makes provision for the Pension Protection Fund in a manner comparable to MCA 1973, s 25E (see annotations), including pension compensation attachment (paras 34A and 34B) (cf MCA 1973, ss 21C, 25F and 25G). Pt 8 (para 38) makes provision for maintenance pending outcome in dissolution, nullity or separation proceedings, which is the counterpart of maintenance pending suit under MCA 1973, s 22. Pt 8 (paras 38A–39B) make provision for orders in respect of legal services, the counterpart of MCA 1973, ss 22ZA–22ZB. Pt 9 makes provision for financial provision on failure to maintain in a manner comparable to MCA 1973, s 27. Pt 10 provides for the commencement of proceedings and duration of orders mirror-imaging MCA 1973, ss 26, 28 and 29. It should be noted that para 48 replicates the lacuna in MCA 1973, s 28(3) in that a subsequent civil partnership or marriage does not bar an application for a pension sharing order. Pt 11 provides for the variation, discharge, suspension or revival of certain orders for financial relief comparable to MCA 1973, s 31. Pt 12 provides for arrears and repayments in a manner comparable to MCA 1973, ss 32, 33. Pt 14 makes provision for consent orders and maintenance agreements in a manner comparable to MCA 1973, ss 33A–36. Pt 13 contains miscellaneous and supplementary provisions dealing with avoidance of transactions intended to prevent or reduce financial relief (para 74: the counterpart of MCA 1973, s 37), the direction for a settlement of an instrument (para 76: the counterpart of the MCA 1973, s 30), bankruptcy (para 77: the counterpart of MCA 1973, s 39), payments in favour of persons suffering from mental disorder (para 78: the counterpart of MCA 1973, s 40), appeals relating to pension sharing orders (para 79: the counterpart of MCA 1973, s 40A) and appeals relating to pension compensation sharing orders (para 79A: the counterpart of MCA 1937, s 40B).

PART 1
FINANCIAL PROVISION IN CONNECTION WITH DISSOLUTION, NULLITY OR SEPARATION

1 Circumstances in which orders under this Part may be made

(1) The court may make any one or more of the orders set out in paragraph 2(1) –

(a) on making a dissolution, nullity or separation order, or
(b) at any time afterwards.

(2) The court may make any one or more of the orders set out in paragraph 2(1)(d), (e) and (f) –

(a) in proceedings for a dissolution, nullity or separation order, before making the order;
(b) if proceedings for a dissolution, nullity or separation order are dismissed after the beginning of the trial, either straightaway or within a reasonable period after the dismissal.

(3) The power of the court to make an order under sub-paragraph (1) or (2)(a) in favour of a child of the family is exercisable from time to time.

(4) If the court makes an order in favour of a child under sub-paragraph (2)(b), it may from time to time make a further order in the child's favour of any of the kinds set out in paragraph 2(1)(d), (e) or (f).

2 The orders: periodical and secured periodical payments and lump sums

(1) The orders are –

(a) an order that either civil partner must make to the other such periodical payments for such term as may be specified;

(b) an order that either civil partner must secure to the other, to the satisfaction of the court, such periodical payments for such term as may be specified;
(c) an order that either civil partner must pay to the other such lump sum or sums as may be specified;
(d) an order that one of the civil partners must make –
   (i) to such person as may be specified for the benefit of a child of the family, or
   (ii) to a child of the family,

   such periodical payments for such term as may be specified;
(e) an order that one of the civil partners must secure –
   (i) to such person as may be specified for the benefit of a child of the family, or
   (ii) to a child of the family,

   to the satisfaction of the court, such periodical payments for such term as may be specified;
(f) an order that one of the civil partners must pay such lump sum as may be specified –
   (i) to such person as may be specified for the benefit of a child of the family, or
   (ii) to a child of the family.

(2) 'Specified' means specified in the order.

3 Particular provision that may be made by lump sum orders

(1) An order under this Part requiring one civil partner to pay the other a lump sum may be made for the purpose of enabling the other civil partner to meet any liabilities or expenses reasonably incurred by the other in maintaining –

(a) himself or herself, or
(b) a child of the family,

before making an application for an order under this Part in his or her favour.

(2) An order under this Part requiring a lump sum to be paid to or for the benefit of a child of the family may be made for the purpose of enabling any liabilities or expenses reasonably incurred by or for the benefit of the child before making an application for an order under this Part to be met.

(3) An order under this Part for the payment of a lump sum may –

(a) provide for its payment by instalments of such amount as may be specified, and
(b) require the payment of the instalments to be secured to the satisfaction of the court.

(4) Sub-paragraphs (1) to (3) do not restrict the powers to make the orders set out in paragraph 2(1)(c) and (f).

(5) If the court –

(a) makes an order under this Part for the payment of a lump sum, and
(b) directs that –
   (i) payment of the sum or any part of it is to be deferred, or
   (ii) the sum or any part of it is to be paid by instalments,

it may provide for the deferred amount or the instalments to carry interest at such rate as may be specified from such date as may be specified until the date when payment of it is due.

(6) A date specified under sub-paragraph (5) must not be earlier than the date of the order.

(7) 'Specified' means specified in the order.

4 When orders under this Part may take effect

(1) If an order is made under paragraph 2(1)(a), (b) or (c) on or after making a dissolution or nullity order, neither the order nor any settlement made in pursuance of it takes effect unless the dissolution or nullity order has been made final.

(2) This paragraph does not affect the power of the court to give a direction under paragraph 76 (settlement of instrument by conveyancing counsel).

5 Restrictions on making of orders under this Part

The power to make an order under paragraph 2(1)(d), (e) or (f) is subject to paragraph 49(1) and (5) (restrictions on orders in favour of children who have reached 18).

PART 2
PROPERTY ADJUSTMENT ON OR AFTER DISSOLUTION, NULLITY OR SEPARATION

6 Circumstances in which property adjustment orders may be made

(1) The court may make one or more property adjustment orders –

- (a) on making a dissolution, nullity or separation order, or
- (b) at any time afterwards.

(2) In this Schedule 'property adjustment order' means a property adjustment order under this Part.

7 Property adjustment orders

(1) The property adjustment orders are –

- (a) an order that one of the civil partners must transfer such property as may be specified, being property to which he is entitled –
  - (i) to the other civil partner,
  - (ii) to a child of the family, or
  - (iii) to such person as may be specified for the benefit of a child of the family;
- (b) an order that a settlement of such property as may be specified, being property to which one of the civil partners is entitled, be made to the satisfaction of the court for the benefit of –
  - (i) the other civil partner and the children of the family, or
  - (ii) either or any of them;
- (c) an order varying for the benefit of –
  - (i) the civil partners and the children of the family, or
  - (ii) either or any of them,

  a relevant settlement;
- (d) an order extinguishing or reducing the interest of either of the civil partners under a relevant settlement.

(2) The court may make a property adjustment order under sub-paragraph (1)(c) even though there are no children of the family.

(3) In this paragraph –

'entitled' means entitled in possession or reversion,

'relevant settlement' means, in relation to a civil partnership, a settlement made, during its subsistence or in anticipation of its formation, on the civil partners including one made by will or codicil, but not including one in the form of a pension arrangement (within the meaning of Part 4), and

'specified' means specified in the order.

8 When property adjustment orders may take effect

(1) If a property adjustment order is made on or after making a dissolution or nullity order, neither the property adjustment order nor any settlement made under it takes effect unless the dissolution or nullity order has been made final.

(2) This paragraph does not affect the power to give a direction under paragraph 76 (settlement of instrument by conveyancing counsel).

9 Restrictions on making property adjustment orders

The power to make a property adjustment order under paragraph 7(1)(a) is subject to paragraph 49(1) and (5) (restrictions on making orders in favour of children who have reached 18).

PART 3
SALE OF PROPERTY ORDERS

10 Circumstances in which sale of property orders may be made

(1) The court may make a sale of property order –

- (a) on making –
  - (i) under Part 1, a secured periodical payments order or an order for the payment of a lump sum,
  - (ii) a property adjustment order, or
  - (iii) an order under paragraph 38A for a payment in respect of legal services, or
- (b) at any time afterwards.

(2) In this Schedule 'sale of property order' means a sale of property order under this Part.

Amendments—LASPOA 2012, s 54.

11 Sale of property orders

(1) A sale of property order is an order for the sale of such property as may be specified, being property in which, or in the proceeds of sale of which, either or both of the civil partners has or have a beneficial interest, either in possession or reversion.

(2) A sale of property order may contain such consequential or supplementary provisions as the court thinks fit.

(3) A sale of property order may in particular include –

- (a) provision requiring the making of a payment out of the proceeds of sale of the property to which the order relates, and
- (b) provision requiring any property to which the order relates to be offered for sale to a specified person, or class of persons.

(4) 'Specified' means specified in the order.

12 When sale of property orders may take effect

(1) If a sale of property order is made on or after the making of a dissolution or nullity order, it does not take effect unless the dissolution or nullity order has been made final.

(2) Where a sale of property order is made, the court may direct that –

- (a) the order, or
- (b) such provision of it as the court may specify,

is not to take effect until the occurrence of an event specified by the court or the end of a period so specified.

13 When sale of property orders cease to have effect

If a sale of property order contains a provision requiring the proceeds of sale of the property to which the order relates to be used to secure periodical payments to a civil partner, the order ceases to have effect –

- (a) on the death of the civil partner, or
- (b) on the formation of a subsequent civil partnership or marriage by the civil partner.

14 Protection of third parties

(1) Sub-paragraphs (2) and (3) apply if –

- (a) a civil partner has a beneficial interest in any property, or in the proceeds of sale of any property, and
- (b) another person ('A') who is not the other civil partner also has a beneficial interest in the property or the proceeds.

(2) Before deciding whether to make a sale of property order in relation to the property, the court must give A an opportunity to make representations with respect to the order.

(3) Any representations made by A are included among the circumstances to which the court is required to have regard under paragraph 20.

PART 4
PENSION SHARING ORDERS ON OR AFTER DISSOLUTION OR NULLITY ORDER

Scope—The Parts of Sch 5 that make provision for pensions are explained in the table below.

Pensions on making of dissolution, nullity or separation orders in relation to civil partnerships

Remedy	CPA 2004, Sch 5	MCA 1973 counterpart (see annotations)	Relevant SIs	Availability
Pension sharing order	Part 4	Sections 21A, 24B–24D	Dissolution etc (Pensions) Regulations 2005, SI 2005/2920	Dissolution or nullity
Pension compensation sharing orders	Part 4A	Sections 21B, 21C, 24E–24G and 25G	Pension Protection Fund (Pension Compensation Sharing and Attachment on Divorce etc) Regulations 2011, SI 2011/731; Divorce and Dissolution etc (Pension Protection Fund) Regulations 2011, SI 2011/780	Dissolution or nullity
Pension attachment orders	Part 6	Sections 25B–25D	Dissolution etc (Pensions Regulations) 2005, SI 2005/2920	Dissolution, nullity or separation
Pension compensation attachment orders	Part 7, paras 34A and 34B	Sections 21C, 25F and 25G	Pension Protection Fund (Pension Compensation Sharing and Attachment on Divorce etc) Regulations 2011, SI 2011/731; Divorce and Dissolution etc (Pension Protection Fund) Regulations 2011, SI 2011/780	Dissolution, nullity or separation
Pension sharing orders: subsequent assumption of responsibility by Pension Protection Fund	Pensions Act 2004, s 220, Sch 7	Sections 25E(1), 25E(7) and 25E(9); Pensions Act 2004, s 220, Sch 7	Pension Protection Fund (Pension Sharing) Regulations 2006, SI 2006/1690	Dissolution or nullity
Pension attachment orders: subsequent assumption of responsibility by Pension Protection Fund	Part 7, paras 31–34 and 35–37	Section 25E	Dissolution etc (Pension Protection Fund) Regulations 2006, SI 2006/1934	Dissolution, nullity or separation

15 Circumstances in which pension sharing orders may be made

(1) The court may make a pension sharing order –

(a) on making a dissolution or nullity order, or
(b) at any time afterwards.

(2) In this Schedule 'pension sharing order' means a pension sharing order under this Part.

16 Pension sharing orders

(1) A pension sharing order is an order which –

(a) provides that one civil partner's –
(i) shareable rights under a specified pension arrangement, or
(ii) shareable state scheme rights,
are to be subject to pension sharing for the benefit of the other civil partner, and
(b) specifies the percentage value to be transferred.

(2) Shareable rights under a pension arrangement are rights in relation to which pension sharing is available under –

(a) Chapter 1 of Part 4 of the Welfare Reform and Pensions Act 1999, or
(b) corresponding Northern Ireland legislation.

(3) Shareable state scheme rights are rights in relation to which pension sharing is available under –

(a) Chapter 2 of Part 4 of the 1999 Act, or
(b) corresponding Northern Ireland legislation.

(4) In this Part 'pension arrangement' means –

(a) an occupational pension scheme,
(b) a personal pension scheme,
(c) a retirement annuity contract,
(d) an annuity or insurance policy purchased, or transferred, for the purpose of giving effect to rights under –
(i) an occupational pension scheme, or
(ii) a personal pension scheme, and
(e) an annuity purchased, or entered into, for the purpose of discharging liability in respect of a pension credit under –
(i) section 29(1)(b) of the 1999 Act, or
(ii) corresponding Northern Ireland legislation.

(5) In sub-paragraph (4) –

'occupational pension scheme' has the same meaning as in the Pension Schemes Act 1993;
'personal pension scheme' has the same meaning as in the 1993 Act;
'retirement annuity contract' means a contract or scheme approved under Chapter 3 of Part 14 of the Income and Corporation Taxes Act 1988.

17 Pension sharing orders: apportionment of charges

If a pension sharing order relates to rights under a pension arrangement, the court may include in the order provision about the apportionment between the civil partners of any charge under –

(a) section 41 of the 1999 Act (charges in respect of pension sharing costs), or
(b) corresponding Northern Ireland legislation.

18 Restrictions on making of pension sharing orders

(1) A pension sharing order may not be made in relation to a pension arrangement which –

(a) is the subject of a pension sharing order in relation to the civil partnership, or
(b) has been the subject of pension sharing between the civil partners.

(2) A pension sharing order may not be made in relation to shareable state scheme rights if –

(a) such rights are the subject of a pension sharing order in relation to the civil partnership, or
(b) such rights have been the subject of pension sharing between the civil partners.

(3) A pension sharing order may not be made in relation to the rights of a person under a pension arrangement if there is in force a requirement imposed by virtue of Part 6 which relates to benefits or future benefits to which that person is entitled under the pension arrangement.

19 When pension sharing orders may take effect

(1) A pension sharing order is not to take effect unless the dissolution or nullity order on or after which it is made has been made final.

(2) No pension sharing order may be made so as to take effect before the end of such period after the making of the order as may be prescribed by regulations made by the Lord Chancellor.

(3) The power to make regulations under sub-paragraph (2) is exercisable by statutory instrument which is subject to annulment in pursuance of a resolution of either House of Parliament.

PART 4A
PENSION COMPENSATION SHARING ORDERS ON OR AFTER DISSOLUTION OR NULLITY ORDER

Scope—See annotations to Pt 4.

19A Circumstances in which pension compensation sharing orders may be made

(1) The court may make a pension compensation sharing order –

(a) on making a dissolution or nullity order, or
(b) at any time afterwards.

(2) In this Schedule 'pension compensation sharing order' means a pension compensation sharing order under this Part.

Amendments—Inserted by Pensions Act 2008, Sch 6, Pt 3.

19B Pension compensation sharing orders

(1) A pension compensation sharing order is an order which –

(a) provides that one civil partner's shareable rights to PPF compensation that derive from rights under a specified pension scheme are to be subject to pension compensation sharing for the benefit of the other civil partner, and
(b) specifies the percentage value to be transferred.

(2) Shareable rights to PPF compensation are rights in relation to which pension compensation sharing is available under –

(a) Chapter 1 of Part 3 of the Pensions Act 2008, or
(b) corresponding Northern Ireland legislation.

(3) In sub-paragraph (1) 'specified' means specified in the order.

Amendments—Inserted by Pensions Act 2008, Sch 6, Pt 3.

19C Pension compensation sharing orders: apportionment of charges

The court may include in a pension compensation sharing order provision about the apportionment between the civil partners of any charge under –

(a) section 117 of the Pensions Act 2008 (charges in respect of pension compensation sharing costs), or
(b) corresponding Northern Ireland legislation.

Amendments—Inserted by Pensions Act 2008, Sch 6, Pt 3.

19D Restrictions on making pension compensation sharing orders

(1) A pension compensation sharing order may not be made in relation to rights to PPF compensation that –

(a) are the subject of pension attachment,
(b) derive from rights under a pension scheme that were the subject of pension sharing between the civil partners,
(c) are the subject of pension compensation attachment, or
(d) are or have been the subject of pension compensation sharing between the civil partners.

(2) For the purposes of sub-paragraph (1)(a), rights to PPF compensation 'are the subject of pension attachment' if any of the following three conditions is met.

(3) The first condition is that –
(a) the rights derive from rights under a pension scheme in relation to which an order was made under Part 1 imposing a requirement by virtue of paragraph 25(2), and
(b) that order, as modified under paragraph 31, remains in force.

(4) The second condition is that –
(a) the rights derive from rights under a pension scheme in relation to which an order was made under Part 1 imposing a requirement by virtue of paragraph 25(5), and
(b) that order –
(i) has been complied with, or
(ii) has not been complied with and, as modified under paragraph 32, remains in force.

(5) The third condition is that –
(a) the rights derive from rights under a pension scheme in relation to which an order was made under Part 1 imposing a requirement by virtue of paragraph 26, and
(b) that order remains in force.

(6) For the purposes of sub-paragraph (1)(b), rights under a pension scheme 'were the subject of pension sharing between the civil partners' if the rights were at any time the subject of a pension sharing order in relation to the civil partnership or a previous civil partnership between the same parties.

(7) For the purposes of sub-paragraph (1)(c), rights to PPF compensation 'are the subject of pension compensation attachment' if there is in force a requirement imposed by virtue of Part 6 relating to them.

(8) For the purposes of sub-paragraph (1)(d), rights to PPF compensation 'are or have been the subject of pension compensation sharing between the civil partners' if they are or have ever been the subject of a pension compensation sharing order in relation to the civil partnership or a previous civil partnership between the same parties.

Amendments—Inserted by Pensions Act 2008, Sch 6, Pt 3.

19E When pension compensation sharing orders may take effect

(1) A pension compensation sharing order is not to take effect unless the dissolution or nullity order on or after which it is made has been made final.

(2) No pension compensation sharing order may be made so as to take effect before the end of such period after the making of the order as may be prescribed by regulations made by the Lord Chancellor.

(3) The power to make regulations under sub-paragraph (2) is exercisable by statutory instrument which is subject to annulment in pursuance of a resolution of either House of Parliament.

Amendments—Inserted by Pensions Act 2008, Sch 6, Pt 3.

19F Interpretation

In this Schedule –

'PPF compensation' means compensation payable under the pension compensation provisions;

'the pension compensation provisions' means –

(a) Chapter 3 of Part 2 of the Pensions Act 2004 (pension protection) and any regulations or order made under it,

(b) Chapter 1 of Part 3 of the Pensions Act 2008 (pension compensation sharing) and any regulations or order made under it, and

(c) any provision corresponding to the provisions mentioned in paragraph (a) or (b) in force in Northern Ireland.

Amendments—Inserted by Pensions Act 2008, Sch 6, Pt 3.

PART 5
MATTERS TO WHICH COURT IS TO HAVE REGARD UNDER PARTS 1 TO 4A

20 General

The court in deciding –

(a) whether to exercise its powers under –

(i) Part 1 (financial provision on dissolution etc),

(ii) Part 2 (property adjustment orders),

(iii) Part 3 (sale of property orders),

(iv) any provision of Part 4 (pension sharing orders) other than paragraph 17 (apportionment of charges), or

(v) any provision of Part 4A (pension compensation sharing orders) other than paragraph 19C (apportionment of charges), and

(b) if so, in what way,

must have regard to all the circumstances of the case, giving first consideration to the welfare, while under 18, of any child of the family who has not reached 18.

Amendments—Pensions Act 2008, Sch 6, Pt 3.

21 Particular matters to be taken into account when exercising powers in relation to civil partners

(1) This paragraph applies to the exercise by the court in relation to a civil partner of its powers under –

(a) Part 1 (financial provision on dissolution etc) by virtue of paragraph 2(1)(a), (b) or (c),

(b) Part 2 (property adjustment orders),

(c) Part 3 (sale of property orders),

(d) Part 4 (pension sharing orders), or

(e) Part 4A (pension compensation sharing orders).

(2) The court must in particular have regard to –

(a) the income, earning capacity, property and other financial resources which each civil partner –

(i) has, or

(ii) is likely to have in the foreseeable future,

including, in the case of earning capacity, any increase in that capacity which it would in the opinion of the court be reasonable to expect a civil partner in the civil partnership to take steps to acquire;

(b) the financial needs, obligations and responsibilities which each civil partner has or is likely to have in the foreseeable future;

(c) the standard of living enjoyed by the family before the breakdown of the civil partnership;

(d) the age of each civil partner and the duration of the civil partnership;

(e) any physical or mental disability of either of the civil partners;

(f) the contributions which each civil partner has made or is likely in the foreseeable future to make to the welfare of the family, including any contribution by looking after the home or caring for the family;

(g) the conduct of each civil partner, if that conduct is such that it would in the opinion of the court be inequitable to disregard it;

(h) in the case of proceedings for a dissolution or nullity order, the value to each civil partner of any benefit which, because of the dissolution or annulment of the civil partnership, that civil partner will lose the chance of acquiring.

Amendments—Pensions Act 2008, Sch 6, Pt 3.

22 Particular matters to be taken into account when exercising powers in relation to children

(1) This paragraph applies to the exercise by the court in relation to a child of the family of its powers under –

(a) Part 1 (financial provision on dissolution etc) by virtue of paragraph 2(1)(d), (e) or (f)),

(b) Part 2 (property adjustment orders), or

(c) Part 3 (sale of property orders).

(2) The court must in particular have regard to –

(a) the financial needs of the child;

(b) the income, earning capacity (if any), property and other financial resources of the child;

(c) any physical or mental disability of the child;

(d) the way in which the child was being and in which the civil partners expected the child to be educated or trained;

(e) the considerations mentioned in relation to the civil partners in paragraph 21(2)(a), (b), (c) and (e).

(3) In relation to the exercise of any of those powers against a civil partner ('A') in favour of a child of the family who is not A's child, the court must also have regard to –

(a) whether A has assumed any responsibility for the child's maintenance;

(b) if so, the extent to which, and the basis upon which, A assumed such responsibility and the length of time for which A discharged such responsibility;

(c) whether in assuming and discharging such responsibility A did so knowing that the child was not A's child;

(d) the liability of any other person to maintain the child.

23 Terminating financial obligations

(1) Sub-paragraphs (2) and (3) apply if, on or after the making of a dissolution or nullity order, the court decides to exercise its powers under –

(a) Part 1 (financial provision on dissolution etc) by virtue of paragraph 2(1)(a), (b) or (c),

(b) Part 2 (property adjustment orders),

(c) Part 3 (sale of property orders),

(d) Part 4 (pension sharing orders), or

(e) Part 4A (pension compensation sharing orders),

in favour of one of the civil partners.

(2) The court must consider whether it would be appropriate to exercise those powers in such a way that the financial obligations of each civil partner towards the other will be terminated as soon after the making of the dissolution or nullity order as the court considers just and reasonable.

(3) If the court decides to make –

(a) a periodical payments order, or

(b) a secured periodical payments order,

in favour of one of the civil partners ('A'), it must in particular consider whether it would be appropriate to require the payments to be made or secured only for such term as would in its opinion be sufficient to enable A to adjust without undue hardship to the termination of A's financial dependence on the other civil partner.

(4) If –

(a) on or after the making of a dissolution or nullity order, an application is made by one of the civil partners for a periodical payments or secured periodical payments order in that civil partner's favour, but

(b) the court considers that no continuing obligation should be imposed on either civil partner to make or secure periodical payments in favour of the other,

the court may dismiss the application with a direction that the applicant is not entitled to make any future application in relation to that civil partnership for an order under Part 1 by virtue of paragraph 2(1)(a) or (b).

Amendments—Pensions Act 2008, Sch 6, Pt 3.

PART 6
MAKING OF PART 1 ORDERS HAVING REGARD TO PENSION BENEFITS

Scope—See annotations to Pt 4.

24 Pension benefits to be included in matters to which court is to have regard

(1) The matters to which the court is to have regard under paragraph 21(2)(a) include any pension benefits under a pension arrangement or by way of pension which a civil partner has or is likely to have; and, accordingly, in relation to any pension benefits paragraph 21(2)(a)(ii) has effect as if 'in the foreseeable future' were omitted.

(2) The matters to which the court is to have regard under paragraph 21(2)(h) include any pension benefits which, because of the making of a dissolution or nullity order, a civil partner will lose the chance of acquiring.

(3) 'Pension benefits' means –

(a) benefits under a pension arrangement, or

(b) benefits by way of pension (whether under a pension arrangement or not).

25 Provisions applying where pension benefits taken into account in decision to make Part 1 order

(1) This paragraph applies if, having regard to any benefits under a pension arrangement, the court decides to make an order under Part 1.

(2) To the extent to which the Part 1 order is made having regard to any benefits under a pension arrangement, it may require the person responsible for the pension arrangement, if at any time any payment in respect of any benefits under the arrangement becomes due to the civil partner with pension rights, to make a payment for the benefit of the other civil partner.

(3) The Part 1 order must express the amount of any payment required to be made by virtue of sub-paragraph (2) as a percentage of the payment which becomes due to the civil partner with pension rights.

(4) Any such payment by the person responsible for the arrangement –

(a) discharges so much of his liability to the civil partner with pension rights as corresponds to the amount of the payment, and

(b) is to be treated for all purposes as a payment made by the civil partner with pension rights in or towards the discharge of that civil partner's liability under the order.

(5) If the civil partner with pension rights has a right of commutation under the arrangement, the Part 1 order may require that civil partner to exercise it to any extent.

(6) This paragraph applies to any payment due in consequence of commutation in pursuance of the Part 1 order as it applies to other payments in respect of benefits under the arrangement.

(7) The power conferred by sub-paragraph (5) may not be exercised for the purpose of commuting a benefit payable to the civil partner with pension rights to a benefit payable to the other civil partner.

(8) The powers conferred by sub-paragraphs (2) and (5) may not be exercised in relation to a pension arrangement which –

(a) is the subject of a pension sharing order in relation to the civil partnership, or
(b) has been the subject of pension sharing between the civil partners.

Pension Protection Fund—Paragraph 25 is modified for certain purposes when the Pension Protection Fund has assumed responsibility for the pension arrangement in question by Pt 7, paras 31 and 32 and the Divorce etc (Pension Protection Fund) Regulations 2006.

26 Pensions: lump sums

(1) This paragraph applies if the benefits which the civil partner with pension rights has or is likely to have under a pension arrangement include any lump sum payable in respect of that civil partner's death.

(2) The court's power under Part 1 to order a civil partner to pay a lump sum to the other civil partner includes the power to make by the order any provision in sub-paragraph (3) to (5).

(3) If the person responsible for the pension arrangement has power to determine the person to whom the sum, or any part of it, is to be paid, the court may require him to pay the whole or part of that sum, when it becomes due, to the other civil partner.

(4) If the civil partner with pension rights has power to nominate the person to whom the sum, or any part of it, is to be paid, the court may require the civil partner with pension rights to nominate the other civil partner in respect of the whole or part of that sum.

(5) In any other case, the court may require the person responsible for the pension arrangement in question to pay the whole or part of that sum, when it becomes due, for the benefit of the other civil partner instead of to the person to whom, apart from the order, it would be paid.

(6) Any payment by the person responsible for the arrangement under an order made under Part 1 made by virtue of this paragraph discharges so much of his liability in respect of the civil partner with pension rights as corresponds to the amount of the payment.

(7) The powers conferred by this paragraph may not be exercised in relation to a pension arrangement which –

(a) is the subject of a pension sharing order in relation to the civil partnership, or
(b) has been the subject of pension sharing between the civil partners.

27 Pensions: supplementary

If – (a) a Part 1 order made by virtue of paragraph 25 or 26 imposes any requirement on the person responsible for a pension arrangement ('the first arrangement'),
(b) the civil partner with pension rights acquires rights under another pension arrangement ('the new arrangement') which are derived (directly or indirectly) from the whole of that civil partner's rights under the first arrangement, and
(c) the person responsible for the new arrangement has been given notice in accordance with regulations made by the Lord Chancellor,

the Part 1 order has effect as if it had been made instead in respect of the person responsible for the new arrangement.

28 Regulations

(1) The Lord Chancellor may by regulations –

(a) make provision, in relation to any provision of paragraph 25 or 26 which authorises the court making a Part 1 order to require the person responsible for a pension arrangement to make a payment for the benefit of the other civil partner, as to –
   (i) the person to whom, and
   (ii) the terms on which,
   the payment is to be made;
(b) make provision, in relation to payment under a mistaken belief as to the continuation in force of a provision included by virtue of paragraph 25 or 26 in a Part 1 order, about the rights or liabilities of the payer, the payee or the person to whom the payment was due;

PART II

(c) require notices to be given in respect of changes of circumstances relevant to Part 1 orders which include provision made by virtue of paragraphs 25 and 26;

(d) make provision for the person responsible for a pension arrangement to be discharged in prescribed circumstances from a requirement imposed by virtue of paragraph 25 or 26;

(e) make provision about calculation and verification in relation to the valuation of –

(i) benefits under a pension arrangement, or

(ii) shareable state scheme rights (within the meaning of paragraph 16(3)),

for the purposes of the court's functions in connection with the exercise of any of its powers under this Schedule.

(2) Regulations under sub-paragraph (1)(e) may include –

(a) provision for calculation or verification in accordance with guidance from time to time prepared by a prescribed person, and

(b) provision by reference to regulations under section 30 or 49(4) of the 1999 Act.

(3) The power to make regulations under paragraph 27 or this paragraph is exercisable by statutory instrument which is subject to annulment in pursuance of a resolution of either House of Parliament.

(4) 'Prescribed' means prescribed by regulations.

Subordinate legislation—Dissolution etc (Pensions) Regulations 2005.

29 Interpretation of provisions relating to pensions

(1) In this Part 'the civil partner with pension rights' means the civil partner who has or is likely to have benefits under a pension arrangement.

(2) In this Part 'pension arrangement' has the same meaning as in Part 4.

(3) In this Part, references to the person responsible for a pension arrangement are to be read in accordance with section 26 of the Welfare Reform and Pensions Act 1999.

PART 7
PENSION PROTECTION FUND COMPENSATION ETC

Scope—See annotations to Pt 4.

30 PPF compensation to be included in matters to which court is to have regard

(1) The matters to which a court is to have regard under paragraph 21(2)(a) include any PPF compensation to which a civil partner is or is likely to be entitled; and, accordingly, in relation to any PPF compensation paragraph 21(2)(a)(ii) has effect as if 'in the foreseeable future' were omitted.

(2) The matters to which a court is to have regard under paragraph 21(2)(h) include any PPF compensation which, because of the making of a dissolution or nullity order, a civil partner will lose the chance of acquiring entitlement to.

Amendments—Pensions Act 2008, Sch 6, Pt 3.

31 Assumption of responsibility by PPF Board in paragraph 25(2) cases

(1) This paragraph applies to an order under Part 1 so far as it includes provision made by virtue of paragraph 25(2) which –

(a) imposed requirements on the trustees or managers of an occupational pension scheme for which the Board has assumed responsibility, and

(b) was made before the trustees or managers received the transfer notice.

(2) From the time the trustees or managers of the scheme receive the transfer notice, the order has effect –

(a) except in descriptions of case prescribed by regulations, with the modifications set out in sub-paragraph (3), and

(b) with such other modifications as may be prescribed by regulations.

(3) The modifications are that –

(a) references in the order to the trustees or managers of the scheme have effect as references to the Board, and

(b) references in the order to any pension or lump sum to which the civil partner with pension rights is or may become entitled under the scheme have effect as references to any PPF compensation to which that person is or may become entitled in respect of the pension or lump sum.

32 Assumption of responsibility by PPF Board in paragraph 25(5) cases

(1) This paragraph applies to an order under Part 1 if –

(a) it includes provision made by virtue of paragraph 25(5) which requires the civil partner with pension rights to exercise his right of commutation under an occupational pension scheme to any extent, and

(b) before the requirement is complied with the Board has assumed responsibility for the scheme.

(2) From the time the trustees or managers of the scheme receive the transfer notice, the order has effect with such modifications as may be prescribed by regulations.

33 Lump sums: power to modify paragraph 26 in respect of assessment period

Regulations may modify paragraph 26 in its application to an occupational pension scheme during an assessment period in relation to the scheme.

34 Assumption of responsibility by the Board not to affect power of court to vary order etc

(1) This paragraph applies where the court makes, in relation to an occupational pension scheme –

(a) a pension sharing order, or

(b) an order including provision made by virtue of paragraph 25(2) or (5).

(2) If the Board subsequently assumes responsibility for the scheme, that does not affect –

(a) the powers of the court under paragraph 51 to vary or discharge the order or to suspend or revive any provision of it;

(b) on an appeal, the powers of the appeal court to affirm, reinstate, set aside or vary the order.

34A Attachment of PPF compensation

(1) This paragraph applies if, having regard to any PPF compensation to which a civil partner is or is likely to be entitled, the court decides to make an order under Part 1.

(2) To the extent to which the Part 1 order is made having regard to such compensation, it may require the Board, if at any time any payment in respect of PPF compensation becomes due to the civil partner with compensation rights, to make a payment for the benefit of the other civil partner.

(3) The Part 1 order must express the amount of any payment required to be made by virtue of sub-paragraph (2) as a percentage of the payment which becomes due to the civil partner with compensation rights.

(4) Any such payment by the Board –

(a) discharges so much of its liability to the civil partner with compensation rights as corresponds to the amount of the payment, and

(b) is to be treated for all purposes as a payment made by the civil partner with compensation rights in or towards the discharge of that civil partner's liability under the order.

(5) If the civil partner with compensation rights has a right to commute any PPF compensation, the Part 1 order may require that civil partner to exercise it to any extent.

PART II

(6) This paragraph applies to any payment due in consequence of commutation in pursuance of the Part 1 order as it applies to other payments in respect of PPF compensation.

(7) The power conferred by sub-paragraph (5) may not be exercised for the purpose of commuting a benefit payable to the civil partner with compensation rights to a benefit payable to the other civil partner.

(8) The powers conferred by sub-paragraphs (2) and (5) may not be exercised in relation to rights to PPF compensation that –

(a) derive from rights under a pension scheme that were at any time the subject of a pension sharing order in relation to the civil partnership or a previous civil partnership between the same parties, or.

(b) are or have ever been the subject of a pension compensation sharing order in relation to the civil partnership or a previous civil partnership between the same parties.

Amendments—Pensions Act 2008, Sch 6, Pt 3.

34B (1) Regulations may –

(a) make provision, in relation to any provision of paragraph 34A which authorises the court making a Part 1 order to require the Board to make a payment for the benefit of the other civil partner, as to the person to whom, and the terms on which, the payment is to be made;

(b) make provision, in relation to payment under a mistaken belief as to the continuation in force of a provision included by virtue of paragraph 34A in a Part 1 order, about the rights or liabilities of the payer, the payee or the person to whom the payment was due;

(c) require notices to be given in respect of changes of circumstances relevant to Part 1 orders which include provision made by virtue of paragraph 34A;

(d) make provision for the Board to be discharged in prescribed circumstances from a requirement imposed by virtue of paragraph 34A;

(e) make provision about calculation and verification in relation to the valuation of PPF compensation for the purposes of the court's functions in connection with the exercise of any of its powers under this Schedule.

(2) Regulations under sub-paragraph (1)(e) may include –

(a) provision for calculation or verification in accordance with guidance from time to time prepared by a prescribed person;

(b) provision by reference to regulations under section 112 of the Pensions Act 2008.

Amendments—Pensions Act 2008, Sch 6, Pt 3.

35 Regulations

Regulations may make such consequential modifications of any provision of, or made by virtue of, this Schedule as appear to the Lord Chancellor necessary or expedient to give effect to the provisions of this Part.

36 (1) In this Part 'regulations' means regulations made by the Lord Chancellor.

(2) A power to make regulations under this Part is exercisable by statutory instrument which is subject to annulment in pursuance of a resolution of either House of Parliament.

37 Interpretation

(1) In this Part –

'assessment period' means –

(a) an assessment period within the meaning of Part 2 of the Pensions Act 2004 (pension protection), or

(b) an equivalent period under corresponding Northern Ireland legislation;

'the Board' means the Board of the Pension Protection Fund;

'the civil partner with compensation rights' means the civil partner who is or is likely to be entitled to PPF compensation;

'the civil partner with pension rights' has the meaning given by paragraph 29(1);
'occupational pension scheme' has the same meaning as in the Pension Schemes Act 1993;
'prescribed' means prescribed by regulations;
'transfer notice' has the same meaning as in –
(a) Chapter 3 of Part 2 of the 2004 Act, or
(b) corresponding Northern Ireland legislation.

(2) References in this Part to the Board assuming responsibility for a scheme are to the Board assuming responsibility for the scheme in accordance with –

(a) Chapter 3 of Part 2 of the 2004 Act (pension protection), or
(b) corresponding Northern Ireland legislation.

Amendments—Pensions Act 2008, Sch 6, Pt 3.

PART 8
MAINTENANCE AND OTHER PAYMENTS PENDING OUTCOME OF DISSOLUTION, NULLITY OR SEPARATION PROCEEDINGS

Amendments—LASPOA 2012, s 52.

38 Maintenance orders

(1) On an application for a dissolution, nullity or separation order, the court may make an order requiring either civil partner to make to the other for the other's maintenance such periodical payments for such term –

(a) beginning no earlier than the date on which the application was made, and
(b) ending with the date on which the proceedings are determined,

as the court thinks reasonable.

(2) An order under this paragraph may not require one civil partner to pay to the other any amount in respect of legal services for the purposes of the proceedings.

(3) In sub-paragraph (2) 'legal services' has the same meaning as in paragraph 38A.

Amendments—LASPOA 2012, s 52.

38A Orders in respect of legal services

(1) In proceedings for a dissolution, nullity or separation order, the court may make an order or orders requiring one civil partner to pay to the other ('the applicant') an amount for the purpose of enabling the applicant to obtain legal services for the purposes of the proceedings.

(2) The court may also make such an order or orders in proceedings under this Schedule for financial relief in connection with proceedings for a dissolution, nullity or separation order.

(3) The court must not make an order under this paragraph unless it is satisfied that, without the amount, the applicant would not reasonably be able to obtain appropriate legal services for the purposes of the proceedings or any part of the proceedings.

(4) For the purposes of sub-paragraph (3), the court must be satisfied, in particular, that –

(a) the applicant is not reasonably able to secure a loan to pay for the services, and
(b) the applicant is unlikely to be able to obtain the services by granting a charge over any assets recovered in the proceedings.

(5) An order under this paragraph may be made for the purpose of enabling the applicant to obtain legal services of a specified description, including legal services provided in a specified period or for the purposes of a specified part of the proceedings.

(6) An order under this paragraph may –

(a) provide for the payment of all or part of the amount by instalments of specified amounts, and
(b) require the instalments to be secured to the satisfaction of the court.

(7) An order under this paragraph may direct that payment of all or part of the amount is to be deferred.

(8) The court may at any time in the proceedings vary an order made under this paragraph if it considers that there has been a material change of circumstances since the order was made.

(9) For the purposes of the assessment of costs in the proceedings, the applicant's costs are to be treated as reduced by any amount paid to the applicant pursuant to an order under this section for the purposes of those proceedings.

(10) In this paragraph 'legal services', in relation to proceedings, means the following types of services –

(a) providing advice as to how the law applies in the particular circumstances,
(b) providing advice and assistance in relation to the proceedings,
(c) providing other advice and assistance in relation to the settlement or other resolution of the dispute that is the subject of the proceedings, and
(d) providing advice and assistance in relation to the enforcement of decisions in the proceedings or as part of the settlement or resolution of the dispute,

and they include, in particular, advice and assistance in the form of representation and any form of dispute resolution, including mediation.

(11) In sub-paragraphs (5) and (6) 'specified' means specified in the order concerned.

Amendments—Inserted by LASPOA 2012, s 52.

38B (1) When considering whether to make or vary an order under paragraph 38A, the court must have regard to –

(a) the income, earning capacity, property and other financial resources which each of the applicant and the paying party has or is likely to have in the foreseeable future,
(b) the financial needs, obligations and responsibilities which each of the applicant and the paying party has or is likely to have in the foreseeable future,
(c) the subject matter of the proceedings, including the matters in issue in them,
(d) whether the paying party is legally represented in the proceedings,
(e) any steps taken by the applicant to avoid all or part of the proceedings, whether by proposing or considering mediation or otherwise,
(f) the applicant's conduct in relation to the proceedings,
(g) any amount owed by the applicant to the paying party in respect of costs in the proceedings or other proceedings to which both the applicant and the paying party are or were party, and
(h) the effect of the order or variation on the paying party.

(2) In sub-paragraph (1)(a) 'earning capacity', in relation to the applicant or the paying party, includes any increase in earning capacity which, in the opinion of the court, it would be reasonable to expect the applicant or the paying party to take steps to acquire.

(3) For the purposes of sub-paragraph (1)(h), the court must have regard, in particular, to whether the making or variation of the order is likely to –

(a) cause undue hardship to the paying party, or
(b) prevent the paying party from obtaining legal services for the purposes of the proceedings.

(4) The Lord Chancellor may by order amend this paragraph by adding to, omitting or varying the matters mentioned in sub-paragraphs (1) to (3).

(5) An order under sub-paragraph (4) must be made by statutory instrument.

(6) A statutory instrument containing an order under sub-paragraph (4) may not be made unless a draft of the instrument has been laid before, and approved by a resolution of, each House of Parliament.

(7) In this paragraph 'legal services' has the same meaning as in paragraph B38A.

Amendments—Inserted by LASPOA 2012, s 53.

PART 9
FAILURE TO MAINTAIN: FINANCIAL PROVISION (AND INTERIM ORDERS)

39 Circumstances in which orders under this Part may be made

(1) Either civil partner in a subsisting civil partnership may apply to the court for an order under this Part on the ground that the other civil partner ('the respondent') –

(a) has failed to provide reasonable maintenance for the applicant, or
(b) has failed to provide, or to make a proper contribution towards, reasonable maintenance for any child of the family.

(2) The court must not entertain an application under this paragraph unless it has jurisdiction to do so by virtue of the Maintenance Regulation and Schedule 6 to the Civil Jurisdiction and Judgments (Maintenance) Regulations 2011.

(3) If, on an application under this paragraph, it appears to the court that –

(a) the applicant or any child of the family to whom the application relates is in immediate need of financial assistance, but
(b) it is not yet possible to determine what order, if any, should be made on the application,

the court may make an interim order.

(4) If, on an application under this paragraph, the applicant satisfies the court of a ground mentioned in sub-paragraph (1), the court may make one or more of the orders set out in paragraph 41.

(5) In this paragraph, 'the Maintenance Regulation' means Council Regulation (EC) No 4/2009 including as applied in relation to Denmark by virtue of the Agreement made on 19 October 2005 between the European Community and the Kingdom of Denmark.

Amendments—SI 2011/1484.

40 Interim orders

An interim order is an order requiring the respondent to make to the applicant, until the determination of the application, such periodical payments as the court thinks reasonable.

41 Orders that may be made where failure to maintain established

(1) The orders are –

(a) an order that the respondent must make to the applicant such periodical payments for such term as may be specified;
(b) an order that the respondent must secure to the applicant, to the satisfaction of the court, such periodical payments for such term as may be specified;
(c) an order that the respondent must pay to the applicant such lump sum as may be specified;
(d) an order that the respondent must make such periodical payments for such term as may be specified –
  (i) to such person as may be specified, for the benefit of the child to whom the application relates, or
  (ii) to the child to whom the application relates;
(e) an order that the respondent must secure –
  (i) to such person as may be specified for the benefit of the child to whom the application relates, or
  (ii) to the child to whom the application relates,

  to the satisfaction of the court, such periodical payments for such term as may be specified;
(f) an order that the respondent must pay such lump sum as may be specified –
  (i) to such person as may be specified for the benefit of the child to whom the application relates, or
  (ii) to the child to whom the application relates.

(2) In this Part 'specified' means specified in the order.

42 Particular provision that may be made by lump sum orders

(1) An order under this Part for the payment of a lump sum may be made for the purpose of enabling any liabilities or expenses reasonably incurred in maintaining the applicant or any child of the family to whom the application relates before the making of the application to be met.

(2) An order under this Part for the payment of a lump sum may –

(a) provide for its payment by instalments of such amount as may be specified, and
(b) require the payment of the instalments to be secured to the satisfaction of the court.

(3) Sub-paragraphs (1) and (2) do not restrict the power to make an order by virtue of paragraph 41(1)(c) or (f).

43 Matters to which the court is to have regard on application under paragraph 39(1)(a)

(1) This paragraph applies if an application under paragraph 39 is made on the ground mentioned in paragraph 39(1)(a).

(2) In deciding –

(a) whether the respondent has failed to provide reasonable maintenance for the applicant, and
(b) what order, if any, to make under this Part in favour of the applicant,

the court must have regard to all the circumstances of the case including the matters mentioned in paragraph 21(2).

(3) If an application is also made under paragraph 39 in respect of a child of the family who has not reached 18, the court must give first consideration to the welfare of the child while under 18.

(4) Paragraph 21(2)(c) has effect as if for the reference in it to the breakdown of the civil partnership there were substituted a reference to the failure to provide reasonable maintenance for the applicant.

44 Matters to which the court is to have regard on application under paragraph 39(1)(b)

(1) This paragraph applies if an application under paragraph 39 is made on the ground mentioned in paragraph 39(1)(b).

(2) In deciding –

(a) whether the respondent has failed to provide, or to make a proper contribution towards, reasonable maintenance for the child of the family to whom the application relates, and
(b) what order, if any, to make under this Part in favour of the child,

the court must have regard to all the circumstances of the case.

(3) Those circumstances include –

(a) the matters mentioned in paragraph 22(2)(a) to (e), and
(b) if the child of the family to whom the application relates is not the child of the respondent, the matters mentioned in paragraph 22(3).

(4) Paragraph 21(2)(c) (as it applies by virtue of paragraph 22(2)(e)) has effect as if for the reference in it to the breakdown of the civil partnership there were substituted a reference to –

(a) the failure to provide, or
(b) the failure to make a proper contribution towards,

reasonable maintenance for the child of the family to whom the application relates.

45 Restrictions on making orders under this Part

The power to make an order under paragraph 41(1)(d), (e) or (f) is subject to paragraph 49(1) and (5) (restrictions on orders in favour of children who have reached 18).

PART 10
COMMENCEMENT OF CERTAIN PROCEEDINGS AND DURATION OF CERTAIN ORDERS

46 Commencement of proceedings for ancillary relief, etc

(1) Sub-paragraph (2) applies if an application for a dissolution, nullity or separation order has been made.

(2) Subject to sub-paragraph (3), proceedings for –

- (a) an order under Part 1 (financial provision on dissolution etc),
- (b) a property adjustment order, or
- (c) an order under Part 8 (maintenance pending outcome of dissolution, nullity or separation proceedings),

may be begun (subject to and in accordance with rules of court) at any time after the presentation of the application.

(3) Rules of court may provide, in such cases as may be prescribed by the rules, that –

- (a) an application for any such relief as is mentioned in sub-paragraph (2) must be made in the application or response, and
- (b) an application for any such relief which –
  - (i) is not so made, or
  - (ii) is not made until after the end of such period following the presentation of the application or filing of the response as may be so prescribed,

may be made only with the leave of the court.

47 Duration of periodical and secured periodical payments orders for a civil partner

(1) The court may specify in a periodical payments or secured periodical payments order in favour of a civil partner such term as it thinks fit, except that the term must not –

- (a) begin before the date of the making of an application for the order, or
- (b) extend beyond the limits given in sub-paragraphs (2) and (3).

(2) The limits in the case of a periodical payments order are –

- (a) the death of either civil partner;
- (b) where the order is made on or after the making of a dissolution or nullity order, the formation of a subsequent civil partnership or marriage by the civil partner in whose favour the order is made.

(3) The limits in the case of a secured periodical payments order are –

- (a) the death of the civil partner in whose favour the order is made;
- (b) where the order is made on or after the making of a dissolution or nullity order, the formation of a subsequent civil partnership or marriage by the civil partner in whose favour the order is made.

(4) In the case of an order made on or after the making of a dissolution or nullity order, sub-paragraphs (1) to (3) are subject to paragraphs 23(3) and 59(4).

(5) If a periodical payments or secured periodical payments order in favour of a civil partner is made on or after the making of a dissolution or nullity order, the court may direct that that civil partner is not entitled to apply under paragraph 51 for the extension of the term specified in the order.

(6) If –

- (a) a periodical payments or secured periodical payments order in favour of a civil partner is made otherwise than on or after the making of a dissolution or nullity order, and
- (b) the civil partnership is subsequently dissolved or annulled but the order continues in force,

the order ceases to have effect (regardless of anything in it) on the formation of a subsequent civil partnership or marriage by that civil partner, except in relation to any arrears due under it on the date of its formation.

48 Subsequent civil partnership or marriage

If after the making of a dissolution or nullity order one of the civil partners forms a subsequent civil partnership or marriage, that civil partner is not entitled to apply, by reference to the dissolution or nullity order, for –

(a) an order under Part 1 in that civil partner's favour, or
(b) a property adjustment order,

against the other civil partner in the dissolved or annulled civil partnership.

49 Duration of continuing orders in favour of children, and age limit on making certain orders in their favour

(1) Subject to sub-paragraph (5) –

(a) no order under Part 1,
(b) no property adjustment order made by virtue of paragraph 7(1)(a) (transfer of property), and
(c) no order made under Part 9 (failure to maintain) by virtue of paragraph 41,

is to be made in favour of a child who has reached 18.

(2) The term to be specified in a periodical payments or secured periodical payments order in favour of a child may begin with –

(a) the date of the making of an application for the order or a later date, or
(b) a date ascertained in accordance with sub-paragraph (7) or (8).

(3) The term to be specified in such an order –

(a) must not in the first instance extend beyond the date of the birthday of the child next following the child's reaching the upper limit of the compulsory school age unless the court considers that in the circumstances of the case the welfare of the child requires that it should extend to a later date, and
(b) must not in any event, subject to sub-paragraph (5), extend beyond the date of the child's 18th birthday.

(4) Sub-paragraph (3)(a) must be read with section 8 of the Education Act 1996 (which applies to determine for the purposes of any enactment whether a person is of compulsory school age).

(5) Sub-paragraphs (1) and (3)(b) do not apply in the case of a child if it appears to the court that –

(a) the child is, or will be, or, if an order were made without complying with either or both of those provisions, would be –
(i) receiving instruction at an educational establishment, or
(ii) undergoing training for a trade, profession or vocation,

whether or not the child also is, will be or would be in gainful employment, or

(b) there are special circumstances which justify the making of an order without complying with either or both of sub-paragraphs (1) and (3)(b).

(6) A periodical payments order in favour of a child, regardless of anything in the order, ceases to have effect on the death of the person liable to make payments under the order, except in relation to any arrears due under the order on the date of the death.

(7) If –

(a) a maintenance calculation ('the current calculation') is in force with respect to a child, and
(b) an application is made under this Schedule for a periodical payments or secured periodical payments order in favour of that child –
(i) in accordance with section 8 of the Child Support Act 1991, and

(ii) before the end of 6 months beginning with the making of the current calculation,

the term to be specified in any such order made on that application may be expressed to begin on, or at any time after, the earliest permitted date.

(8) 'The earliest permitted date' is whichever is the later of –

(a) the date 6 months before the application is made, or
(b) the date on which the current calculation took effect or, where successive maintenance calculations have been continuously in force with respect to a child, on which the first of those calculations took effect.

(9) If –

(a) a maintenance calculation ceases to have effect by or under any provision of the 1991 Act, and
(b) an application is made, before the end of 6 months beginning with the relevant date, for a periodical payments or secured periodical payments order in favour of a child with respect to whom that maintenance calculation was in force immediately before it ceased to have effect,

the term to be specified in any such order made on that application may begin with the date on which that maintenance calculation ceased to have effect or any later date.

(10) 'The relevant date' means the date on which the maintenance calculation ceased to have effect.

(11) In this paragraph 'maintenance calculation' has the same meaning as it has in the 1991 Act by virtue of section 54 of the 1991 Act as read with any regulations in force under that section.

Child support—Civil Partnership (Pensions, Social Security and Child Support) (Consequential, etc Provisions) Order 2005, art 2(5), Sch 5, paras 1, 2(1),(2) provide that, in relation to old scheme cases, para 49 is to apply with certain prescribed amendments.

PART 11
VARIATION, DISCHARGE ETC OF CERTAIN ORDERS FOR FINANCIAL RELIEF

50 Orders etc to which this Part applies

(1) This Part applies to the following orders –

(a) a periodical payments order under Part 1 (financial provision on dissolution etc) or Part 9 (failure to maintain);
(b) a secured periodical payments order under Part 1 or 9;
(c) an order under Part 8 (maintenance pending outcome of dissolution proceedings etc);
(d) an interim order under Part 9;
(e) an order made under Part 1 by virtue of paragraph 3(3) or under Part 9 by virtue of paragraph 42(2) (lump sum by instalments);
(f) a deferred order made under Part 1 by virtue of paragraph 2(1)(c) (lump sum for civil partner) which includes provision made by virtue of –
  (i) paragraph 25(2),
  (ii) paragraph 26, or
  (iii) paragraph 34A(2),
  (provision in respect of pension rights or pension compensation rights);
(g) a property adjustment order made on or after the making of a separation order by virtue of paragraph 7(1)(b), (c) or (d) (order for settlement or variation of settlement);
(h) a sale of property order;
(i) a pension sharing order, or a pension compensation sharing order, made before the dissolution or nullity order has been made final.

(2) If the court has made an order referred to in sub-paragraph (1)(f)(ii), this Part ceases to apply to the order on the death of either of the civil partners.

(3) The powers exercisable by the court under this Part in relation to an order are also exercisable in relation to any instrument executed in pursuance of the order.

Amendments—Pensions Act 2008, Sch 6, Pt 3.

51 Powers to vary, discharge, suspend or revive order

(1) If the court has made an order to which this Part applies, it may –

(a) vary or discharge the order,
(b) suspend any provision of it temporarily, or
(c) revive the operation of any provision so suspended.

(2) Sub-paragraph (1) is subject to the provisions of this Part and paragraph 47(5).

52 Power to remit arrears

(1) If the court has made an order referred to in paragraph 50(1)(a), (b), (c) or (d), it may remit the payment of any arrears due under the order or under any part of the order.

(2) Sub-paragraph (1) is subject to the provisions of this Part.

53 Additional powers on discharging or varying a periodical or secured periodical payments order after dissolution of civil partnership

(1) Sub-paragraph (2) applies if, after the dissolution of a civil partnership, the court –

(a) discharges a periodical payments order or secured periodical payments order made in favour of a civil partner, or
(b) varies such an order so that payments under the order are required to be made or secured only for such further period as is determined by the court.

(2) The court may make supplemental provision consisting of any of the following –

(a) an order for the payment of a lump sum in favour of one of the civil partners;
(b) one or more property adjustment orders in favour of one of the civil partners;
(c) one or more pension sharing orders;
(ca) a pension compensation sharing order;
(d) a direction that the civil partner in whose favour the original order discharged or varied was made is not entitled to make any further application for –
 (i) a periodical payments or secured periodical payments order, or
 (ii) an extension of the period to which the original order is limited by any variation made by the court.

(3) The power under sub-paragraph (2) is in addition to any power the court has apart from that sub-paragraph.

Amendments—Pensions Act 2008, Sch 6, Pt 3.

54 (1) An order for the payment of a lump sum under paragraph 53 may –

(a) provide for the payment of it by instalments of such amount as may be specified, and
(b) require the payment of the instalments to be secured to the satisfaction of the court.

(2) Sub-paragraphs (5) and (6) of paragraph 3 (interest on deferred instalments) apply where the court makes an order for the payment of a lump sum under paragraph 53 as they apply where it makes such an order under Part 1.

(3) If under paragraph 53 the court makes more than one property adjustment order in favour of the same civil partner, each of those orders must fall within a different paragraph of paragraph 7(1) (types of property adjustment orders).

(4) Part 3 (orders for the sale of property) and paragraph 76 (direction for settlement of instrument) apply where the court makes a property adjustment order under paragraph 53 as they apply where it makes any other property adjustment order.

(5) Paragraph 18 (restrictions on making of pension sharing order) applies in relation to a pension sharing order under paragraph 53 as it applies in relation to any other pension sharing order.

(6) Paragraph 19D (restrictions on making pension compensation sharing orders) applies in relation to a pension compensation sharing order under paragraph 53 as it applies in relation to any other pension compensation sharing order.

Amendments—Pensions Act 2008, Sch 6, Pt 3.

55 Variation etc of periodical or secured periodical payments orders made in cases of failure to maintain

(1) An application for the variation under paragraph 51 of a periodical payments order or secured periodical payments order made under Part 9 in favour of a child may, if the child has reached 16, be made by the child himself.

(2) Sub-paragraph (3) applies if a periodical payments order made in favour of a child under Part 9 ceases to have effect –

- (a) on the date on which the child reaches 16, or
- (b) at any time after that date but before or on the date on which the child reaches 18.

(3) If, on an application made to the court for an order under this sub-paragraph, it appears to the court that –

- (a) the child is, will be or, if an order were made under this sub-paragraph, would be –
  - (i) receiving instruction at an educational establishment, or
  - (ii) undergoing training for a trade, profession or vocation,

whether or not the child also is, will be or would be in gainful employment, or

- (b) there are special circumstances which justify the making of an order under this sub-paragraph,

the court may by order revive the order mentioned in sub-paragraph (2) from such date as it may specify.

(4) A date specified under sub-paragraph (3) must not be earlier than the date of the application under that sub-paragraph.

(5) If under sub-paragraph (3) the court revives an order it may exercise its power under paragraph 51 in relation to the revived order.

56 Variation etc of property adjustment, pension sharing and pension compensation sharing orders

The court must not exercise the powers conferred by this Part in relation to a property adjustment order falling within paragraph 7(1)(b), (c) or (d) (order for settlement or for variation of settlement) except on an application made in proceedings –

- (a) for the rescission of the separation order by reference to which the property adjustment order was made, or
- (b) for a dissolution order in relation to the civil partnership.

Amendments—Pensions Act 2008, Sch 6, Pt 3.

57 (1) In relation to a pension sharing order or pension compensation sharing order which is made at a time before the dissolution or nullity order has been made final –

- (a) the powers conferred by this Part (by virtue of paragraph 50(1)(i)) may be exercised –
  - (i) only on an application made before the pension sharing order or pension compensation sharing order has or, but for paragraph (b), would have taken effect, and
  - (ii) only if, at the time when the application is made, the dissolution or nullity order has not been made final, and
- (b) an application made in accordance with paragraph (a) prevents the pension sharing order or pension compensation sharing order from taking effect before the application has been dealt with.

(2) No variation of a pension sharing order or pension compensation sharing order is to be made so as to take effect before the order is made final.

(3) The variation of a pension sharing order or pension compensation sharing order prevents the order taking effect before the end of such period after the making of the variation as may be prescribed by regulations made by the Lord Chancellor.

(4) The power to make regulations under sub-paragraph (3) is exercisable by statutory instrument which is subject to annulment in pursuance of a resolution of either House of Parliament.

Amendments—Pensions Act 2008, Sch 6, Pt 3.

58 (1) Sub-paragraphs (2) and (3) –

(a) are subject to paragraphs 53 and 54, and
(b) do not affect any power exercisable by virtue of paragraph 50(e), (f), (g) or (i) or otherwise than by virtue of this Part.

(2) No property adjustment order, pension sharing order or pension compensation sharing order may be made on an application for the variation of a periodical payments or secured periodical payments order made (whether in favour of a civil partner or in favour of a child of the family) under Part 1.

(3) No order for the payment of a lump sum may be made on an application for the variation of a periodical payments or secured periodical payments order in favour of a civil partner (whether made under Part 1 or 9).

Amendments—Pensions Act 2008, Sch 6, Pt 3.

59 Matters to which court is to have regard in exercising powers under this Part

(1) In exercising the powers conferred by this Part the court must have regard to all the circumstances of the case, giving first consideration to the welfare, while under 18, of any child of the family who has not reached 18.

(2) The circumstances of the case include, in particular, any change in any of the matters to which the court was required to have regard when making the order to which the application relates.

(3) Sub-paragraph (4) applies in the case of –

(a) a periodical payments order, or
(b) a secured periodical payments order,

made on or after the making of a dissolution or nullity order.

(4) The court must consider whether in all the circumstances, and after having regard to any such change, it would be appropriate to vary the order so that payments under the order are required –

(a) to be made, or
(b) to be secured,

only for such further period as will in the opinion of the court be sufficient to enable the civil partner in whose favour the order was made to adjust without undue hardship to the termination of those payments.

(5) In considering what further period will be sufficient, the court must, if the civil partnership has been dissolved, take into account any proposed exercise by it of its powers under paragraph 53.

(6) If the civil partner against whom the order was made has died, the circumstances of the case also include the changed circumstances resulting from that civil partner's death.

60 Variation of secured periodical payments order where person liable has died

(1) This paragraph applies if the person liable to make payments under a secured periodical payments order has died.

(2) Subject to sub-paragraph (3), an application under this Part relating to the order (and to any sale of property order which requires the proceeds of sale of property to be used for securing those payments) may be made by –

(a) the person entitled to payments under the periodical payments order, or
(b) the personal representatives of the deceased person.

(3) No such application may be made without the leave of the court after the end of 6 months from the date on which representation in regard to the estate of that person is first taken out.

(4) The personal representatives of the person who has died are not liable for having distributed any part of the estate of the deceased after the end of the 6 month period on the ground that they ought to have taken into account the possibility that the court might allow an application under this paragraph to be made after that period by the person entitled to payments under the order.

(5) Sub-paragraph (4) does not affect any power to recover any part of the estate so distributed arising by virtue of the making of an order in pursuance of this paragraph.

(6) The following are to be left out of account when considering for the purposes of sub-paragraph (3) when representation was first taken out –

- (a) a grant limited to settled land or to trust property,
- (b) any other grant that does not permit any of the estate to be distributed,
- (c) a grant limited to real estate or to personal estate, unless a grant limited to the remainder of the estate has previously been made or is made at the same time,
- (d) a grant, or its equivalent, made outside the United Kingdom (but see sub-paragraph (7)).

(7) A grant sealed under section 2 of the Colonial Probates Act 1892 counts as a grant made in the United Kingdom for the purposes of sub-paragraph (6), but is to be taken as dated on the date of sealing.

Amendments—Inheritance and Trustees' Powers Act 2014, s 6, Sch 2.

61 Power to direct when variation etc is to take effect

(1) If the court, in exercise of its powers under this Part, decides –

- (a) to vary, or
- (b) to discharge,

a periodical payments or secured periodical payments order, it may direct that the variation or discharge is not to take effect until the end of such period as may be specified in the order.

(2) Sub-paragraph (1) is subject to paragraph 47(1) and (6).

62 (1) If –

- (a) a periodical payments or secured periodical payments order in favour of more than one child ('the order') is in force,
- (b) the order requires payments specified in it to be made to or for the benefit of more than one child without apportioning those payments between them,
- (c) a maintenance calculation ('the calculation') is made with respect to one or more, but not all, of the children with respect to whom those payments are to be made, and
- (d) an application is made, before the end of the period of 6 months beginning with the date on which the calculation was made, for the variation or discharge of the order,

the court may, in exercise of its powers under this Part to vary or discharge the order, direct that the variation or discharge is to take effect from the date on which the calculation took effect or any later date.

(2) If –

- (a) an order ('the child order') of a kind prescribed for the purposes of section 10(1) of the Child Support Act 1991 is affected by a maintenance calculation,
- (b) on the date on which the child order became so affected there was in force a periodical payments or secured periodical payments order ('the civil partner's order') in favour of a civil partner having the care of the child in whose favour the child order was made, and
- (c) an application is made, before the end of the period of 6 months beginning with the date on which the maintenance calculation was made, for the civil partner's order to be varied or discharged,

the court may, in exercise of its powers under this Part to vary or discharge the civil partner's order, direct that the variation or discharge is to take effect from the date on which the child order became so affected or any later date.

(3) For the purposes of sub-paragraph (2), an order is affected if it ceases to have effect or is modified by or under section 10 of the 1991 Act.

(4) Sub-paragraphs (1) and (2) do not affect any other power of the court to direct that the variation of discharge of an order under this Part is to take effect from a date earlier than that on which the order for variation or discharge was made.

(5) In this paragraph 'maintenance calculation' has the same meaning as it has in the 1991 Act by virtue of section 54 of the 1991 Act as read with any regulations in force under that section.

Child support—Civil Partnership (Pensions, Social Security and Child Support) (Consequential, etc Provisions) Order 2005, art 2(5), Sch 5, paras 1, 2(1), (3) provide that, in relation to old scheme cases, para 62 is to apply with certain prescribed amendments.

PART 12
ARREARS AND REPAYMENTS

63 Payment of certain arrears unenforceable without the leave of the court

(1) This paragraph applies if any arrears are due under –

- (a) an order under Part 1 (financial provision on dissolution etc),
- (b) an order under Part 8 (maintenance pending outcome of dissolution, nullity or separation proceedings), or
- (c) an order under Part 9 (failure to maintain),

and the arrears became due more than 12 months before proceedings to enforce the payment of them are begun.

(2) A person is not entitled to enforce through the High Court or the family court the payment of the arrears without the leave of that court.

(3) The court hearing an application for the grant of leave under this paragraph may –

- (a) refuse leave,
- (b) grant leave subject to such restrictions and conditions (including conditions as to the allowing of time for payment or the making of payment by instalments) as that court thinks proper, or
- (c) remit the payment of the arrears or of any part of them.

(4) An application for the grant of leave under this paragraph must be made in such manner as may be prescribed by rules of court.

Amendments—CCA 2013, s 17, Sch 11.

64 Orders for repayment in certain cases of sums paid under certain orders

(1) This paragraph applies if –

- (a) a person ('R') is entitled to receive payments under an order listed in sub-paragraph (2), and
- (b) R's circumstances or the circumstances of the person ('P') liable to make payments under the order have changed since the order was made, or the circumstances have changed as a result of P's death.

(2) The orders are –

- (a) any order under Part 8 (maintenance pending outcome of dissolution, nullity or separation proceedings);
- (b) any interim order under Part 9;
- (c) any periodical payments order;
- (d) any secured periodical payments order.

(3) P or P's personal representatives may (subject to sub-paragraph (7)) apply for an order under this paragraph against R or R's personal representatives.

(4) If it appears to the court that, because of the changed circumstances or P's death, the amount received by R in respect of a relevant period exceeds the amount which P or P's personal representatives should have been required to pay, it may order the respondent to the application to pay to the applicant such sum, not exceeding the amount of the excess, as it thinks just.

(5) 'Relevant period' means a period after the circumstances changed or (as the case may be) after P's death.

(6) An order under this paragraph for the payment of any sum may provide for the payment of that sum by instalments of such amount as may be specified in the order.

(7) An application under this paragraph –

(a) may be made in proceedings in the High Court or the family court for –
  (i) the variation or discharge of the order listed in sub-paragraph (2), or
  (ii) leave to enforce, or the enforcement of, the payment of arrears under that order, but

(b) if not made in such proceedings, must be made to the family court;

and accordingly references in this paragraph to the court are references to the High Court or the family court, as the circumstances require.

(8) *(repealed)*

65 Orders for repayment after cessation of order because of subsequent civil partnership etc

(1) Sub-paragraphs (3) and (4) apply if –

(a) a periodical payments or secured periodical payments order in favour of a civil partner ('R') has ceased to have effect because of the formation of a subsequent civil partnership or marriage by R, and

(b) the person liable to make payments under the order ('P') (or P's personal representatives) has made payments in accordance with it in respect of a relevant period in the mistaken belief that the order was still subsisting.

(2) 'Relevant period' means a period after the date of the formation of the subsequent civil partnership or marriage.

(3) P (or P's personal representatives) is not entitled to bring proceedings in respect of a cause of action arising out of the circumstances mentioned in sub-paragraph (1)(a) and (b) against R (or R's personal representatives).

(4) But, on an application under this paragraph by P (or P's personal representatives) against R (or R's personal representatives), the court –

(a) may order the respondent to pay to the applicant a sum equal to the amount of the payments made in respect of the relevant period, or

(b) if it appears to the court that it would be unjust to make that order, may –
  (i) order the respondent to pay to the applicant such lesser sum as it thinks fit, or
  (ii) dismiss the application.

(5) An order under this paragraph for the payment of any sum may provide for the payment of that sum by instalments of such amount as may be specified in the order.

(6) An application under this paragraph –

(a) may be made in proceedings in the High Court or the family court for leave to enforce, or the enforcement of, payment of arrears under the order in question, but

(b) if not made in such proceedings, must be made to the family court;

and accordingly references in this paragraph to the court are references to the High Court or the family court, as the circumstances require.

(7) *(repealed)*

(8) Subject to sub-paragraph (9) –

(a) an officer of the family court is not liable for any act done by him, in pursuance of a payments order requiring payments to be made to the court or an officer of the court, after the date on which that order ceased to have effect because of the formation of a subsequent civil partnership or marriage by the person entitled to payments under it, and

(b) the collecting officer under an attachment of earnings order made to secure payments under a payments order is not liable for any act done by him after that date in accordance with any enactment or rule of court specifying how payments made to him in compliance with the attachment of earnings order are to be dealt with.

(9) Sub-paragraph (8) applies if (and only if) the act –

(a) was one which the officer would have been under a duty to do had the payments order not ceased to have effect, and

(b) was done before notice in writing of the formation of the subsequent civil partnership or marriage was given to him by or on behalf of –

(i) the person entitled to payments under the payments order,

(ii) the person liable to make payments under it, or

(iii) the personal representatives of either of them.

(10) In sub-paragraphs (8) and (9) 'payments order' means a periodical payments order or secured periodical payments order and 'collecting officer', in relation to an attachment of earnings order, means –

(a) the officer of the High Court, or

(aa) the officer of the family court,

(b), (c) *(repealed)*

to whom a person makes payments in compliance with the order.

Amendments—CCA 2013, s 17, Sch 11.

PART 13
CONSENT ORDERS AND MAINTENANCE AGREEMENTS

66 Consent orders for financial relief

(1) Regardless of anything in the preceding provisions of this Schedule, on an application for a consent order for financial relief, the court may, unless it has reason to think that there are other circumstances into which it ought to inquire, make an order in the terms agreed on the basis only of such information supplied with the application as is required by rules of court.

(2) Sub-paragraph (1) applies to an application for a consent order varying or discharging an order for financial relief as it applies to an application for an order for financial relief.

(3) In this paragraph –

'consent order', in relation to an application for an order, means an order in the terms applied for to which the respondent agrees;

'order for financial relief' means an order under any of Parts 1, 2, 3, 4 and 9.

67 Meaning of 'maintenance agreement' and 'financial arrangements'

(1) In this Part 'maintenance agreement' means any agreement in writing between the civil partners in a civil partnership which –

(a) is made during the continuance or after the dissolution or annulment of the civil partnership and contains financial arrangements, or

(b) is a separation agreement which contains no financial arrangements but is made in a case where no other agreement in writing between the civil partners contains financial arrangements.

(2) In this Part 'financial arrangements' means provisions governing the rights and liabilities towards one another when living separately of the civil partners in a civil partnership (including a civil partnership which has been dissolved or annulled) in respect of –

(a) the making or securing of payments, or
(b) the disposition or use of any property,

including such rights and liabilities with respect to the maintenance or education of a child (whether or not a child of the family).

(3) 'Education' includes training.

68 Validity of maintenance agreements

If a maintenance agreement includes a provision purporting to restrict any right to apply to a court for an order containing financial arrangements –

(a) that provision is void, but
(b) any other financial arrangements contained in the agreement –
  (i) are not void or unenforceable as a result, and
  (ii) unless void or unenforceable for any other reason, are (subject to paragraphs 69 and 73) binding on the parties to the agreement.

69 Alteration of agreements by court during lives of parties

(1) Subject to sub-paragraph (1A), either party to a maintenance agreement may apply to the court for an order under this paragraph if –

(a) the maintenance agreement is for the time being subsisting, and
(b) each of the parties to the agreement is for the time being domiciled or resident in England and Wales.

(1A) If an application or part of an application relates to a matter where jurisdiction falls to be determined by reference to the jurisdictional requirements of the Maintenance Regulation and Schedule 6 to the Civil Jurisdiction and Judgments (Maintenance) Regulations 2011 –

(a) the requirement as to domicile or residence in sub-paragraph (1)(b) does not apply to the application or that part of it, but
(b) the court may not entertain the application or that part of it unless it has jurisdiction to do so by virtue of that Regulation and that Schedule.

(2) The court may make an order under this paragraph if it is satisfied that –

(a) because of a change in the circumstances in the light of which –
  (i) any financial arrangements contained in the agreement were made, or
  (ii) financial arrangements were omitted from it,

  the agreement should be altered so as to make different financial arrangements or so as to contain financial arrangements, or
(b) that the agreement does not contain proper financial arrangements with respect to any child of the family.

(3) In sub-paragraph (2)(a) the reference to a change in the circumstances includes a change foreseen by the parties when making the agreement.

(4) An order under this paragraph may make such alterations in the agreement –

(a) by varying or revoking any financial arrangements contained in it, or
(b) by inserting in it financial arrangements for the benefit of one of the parties to the agreement or of a child of the family,

as appear to the court to be just having regard to all the circumstances, including, if relevant, the matters mentioned in paragraph 22(3).

(5) The effect of the order is that the agreement is to be treated as if any alteration made by the order had been made by agreement between the partners and for valuable consideration.

(6) The power to make an order under this paragraph is subject to paragraph 71.

PART II

(7) In this paragraph, 'the Maintenance Regulation' means Council Regulation (EC) No 4/2009 including as applied in relation to Denmark by virtue of the Agreement made on 19 October 2005 between the European Community and the Kingdom of Denmark.

Amendments—SI 2011/1484; CCA 2013, s 17, Sch 1.

70 *(repealed)*

71 Provisions relating to periodical and secured periodical payments: duration

(1) If a court decides to make an order under paragraph 69 altering an agreement –

(a) by inserting provision for the making or securing by one of the parties to the agreement of periodical payments for the maintenance of the other party, or

(b) by increasing the rate of the periodical payments which the agreement provides shall be made by one of the parties for the maintenance of the other,

it may specify such term as it thinks fit as the term for which the payments or, as the case may be, the additional payments attributable to the increase are to be made under the altered agreement, except that the term must not extend beyond the limits in sub-paragraphs (2) and (3).

(2) The limits if the payments are not to be secured are –

(a) the death of either of the parties to the agreement, or

(b) the formation of a subsequent civil partnership or marriage by the party to whom the payments are to be made.

(3) The limits if the payments are to be secured are –

(a) the death of the party to whom the payments are to be made, or

(b) the formation of a subsequent civil partnership or marriage by that party.

(4) Sub-paragraph (5) applies if a court decides to make an order under paragraph 69 altering an agreement by –

(a) inserting provision for the making or securing by one of the parties to the agreement of periodical payments for the maintenance of a child of the family, or

(b) increasing the rate of the periodical payments which the agreement provides shall be made or secured by one of the parties for the maintenance of such a child.

(5) The court, in deciding the term for which under the agreement as altered by the order –

(a) the payments are to be made or secured for the benefit of the child, or

(b) the additional payments attributable to the increase are to be made or secured for the benefit of the child,

must apply paragraph 49(2) to (5) (age limits) as if the order in question were a periodical payments or secured periodical payments order in favour of the child.

72 Saving

Nothing in paragraphs 68 to 71 affects –

(a) any power of a court before which any proceedings between the parties to a maintenance agreement are brought under any other enactment (including a provision of this Schedule) to make an order containing financial arrangements, or

(b) any right of either party to apply for such an order in such proceedings.

73 Alteration of agreements by court after death of one party

(1) This paragraph applies if –

(a) a maintenance agreement provides for the continuation of payments under the agreement after the death of one of the parties, and

(b) that party ('A') dies domiciled in England and Wales.

(2) Subject to sub-paragraph (4), the surviving party or A's personal representatives may apply to the court for an order under paragraph 69.

(3) If a maintenance agreement is altered by a court on an application made under sub-paragraph (2), the same consequences follow as if the alteration had been made immediately before the death by agreement between the parties and for valuable consideration.

(4) An application under this paragraph may not, without the leave of the court, be made after the end of 6 months from the date on which representation in regard to A's estate is first taken out.

(5) A's personal representatives are not liable for having distributed any part of A's estate after the end of the 6 month period on the ground that they ought to have taken into account the possibility that a court might allow an application by virtue of this paragraph to be made by the surviving party after that period.

(6) Sub-paragraph (5) does not affect any power to recover any part of the estate so distributed arising by virtue of the making of an order in pursuance of this paragraph.

(7) Paragraph 60(6) applies for the purposes of sub-paragraph (4) as it applies for the purposes of paragraph 60(3).

Amendments—CCA 2013, s 17, Sch 11.

PART 14
MISCELLANEOUS AND SUPPLEMENTARY

74 Avoidance of transactions intended to prevent or reduce financial relief

(1) This paragraph applies if proceedings for relief ('financial relief') are brought by one person ('A') against another ('B') under Part 1, 2, 4, 8, 9, or 11 (other than paragraph 60(2)), or paragraph 69.

(2) If the court is satisfied, on an application by A, that B is, with the intention of defeating A's claim for financial relief, about to –

- (a) make any disposition, or
- (b) transfer out of the jurisdiction or otherwise deal with any property,

it may make such order as it thinks fit for restraining B from doing so or otherwise for protecting the claim.

(3) If the court is satisfied, on an application by A, that –

- (a) B has, with the intention of defeating A's claim for financial relief, made a reviewable disposition, and
- (b) if the disposition were set aside, financial relief or different financial relief would be granted to A,

it make an order setting aside the disposition.

(4) If the court is satisfied, on an application by A in a case where an order has been obtained by A against B under any of the provisions mentioned in sub-paragraph (1), that B has, with the intention of defeating A's claim for financial relief, made a reviewable disposition, it may make an order setting aside the disposition.

(5) An application for the purposes of sub-paragraph (3) must be made in the proceedings for the financial relief in question.

(6) If the court makes an order under sub-paragraph (3) or (4) setting aside a disposition it must give such consequential directions as it thinks fit for giving effect to the order (including directions requiring the making of any payments or the disposal of any property).

75 (1) Any reference in paragraph 74 to defeating A's claim for financial relief is to –

- (a) preventing financial relief from being granted to A, or to A for the benefit of a child of the family,
- (b) reducing the amount of any financial relief which might be so granted, or
- (c) frustrating or impeding the enforcement of any order which might be or has been made at A's instance under any of those provisions.

(2) In paragraph 74 and this paragraph 'disposition' –

(a) does not include any provision contained in a will or codicil, but
(b) subject to paragraph (a), includes any conveyance, assurance or gift of property of any description (whether made by an instrument or otherwise).

(3) Any disposition made by B (whether before or after the commencement of the proceedings for financial relief) is a reviewable disposition for the purposes of paragraphs 74(3) and (4) unless it was made –

(a) for valuable consideration (other than formation of a civil partnership), and
(b) to a person who, at the time of the disposition, acted in relation to it in good faith and without notice of any intention on B's part to defeat A's claim for financial relief.

(4) If an application is made under paragraph 74 with respect to a disposition which took place less than 3 years before the date of the application or with respect to a disposition or other dealing with property which is about to take place and the court is satisfied –

(a) in a case falling within paragraph 74(2) or (3), that the disposition or other dealing would (apart from paragraph 74) have the consequence of defeating A's claim for financial relief, or
(b) in a case falling within paragraph 74(4), that the disposition has had the consequence of defeating A's claim for financial relief,

it is presumed, unless the contrary is shown, that the person who disposed of or is about to dispose of or deal with the property did so or, as the case may be, is about to do so, with the intention of defeating A's claim for financial relief.

76 Direction for settlement of instrument for securing payments or effecting property adjustment

(1) This paragraph applies if the court decides to make –

(a) an order under Part 1 or 9 requiring any payments to be secured, or
(b) a property adjustment order.

(2) The court may direct that the matter be referred to one of the conveyancing counsel of the court for him to settle a proper instrument to be executed by all necessary parties.

(3) If the order referred to in sub-paragraph (1) is to be made in proceedings for a dissolution, nullity or separation order, the court may, if it thinks fit, defer the making of the dissolution, nullity or separation order until the instrument has been duly executed.

77 Settlement, etc, made in compliance with a property adjustment order may be avoided on bankruptcy of settlor

The fact that –

(a) a settlement, or
(b) a transfer of property,

had to be made in order to comply with a property adjustment order does not prevent the settlement or transfer from being a transaction in respect of which an order may be made under section 339 or 340 of the Insolvency Act 1986 (transfers at an undervalue and preferences).

78 Payments, etc, under order made in favour of person suffering from mental disorder

(1) This paragraph applies if –

(a) the court makes an order under this Schedule requiring –
  (i) payments (including a lump sum payment) to be made, or
  (ii) property to be transferred,

to a civil partner, and

(b) the court is satisfied that the person in whose favour the order is made is incapable, because of mental disorder, of managing and administering his or her property and affairs.

(2) 'Mental disorder' has the same meaning as in the Mental Health Act 1983.

(3) Subject to any order, direction or authority made or given in relation to that person under Part 8 of the 1983 Act, the court may order the payments to be made or, as the case may be, the property to be transferred to such persons having charge of that person as the court may direct.

79 Appeals relating to pension sharing orders which have taken effect

(1) Sub-paragraphs (2) and (3) apply if an appeal against a pension sharing order is begun on or after the day on which the order takes effect.

(2) If the pension sharing order relates to a person's rights under a pension arrangement, the appeal court may not set aside or vary the order if the person responsible for the pension arrangement has acted to his detriment in reliance on the order taking effect.

(3) If the pension sharing order relates to a person's shareable state scheme rights, the appeal court may not set aside or vary the order if the Secretary of State has acted to his detriment in reliance on the taking effect of the order.

(4) In determining for the purposes of sub-paragraph (2) or (3) whether a person has acted to his detriment in reliance on the taking effect of the order, the appeal court may disregard any detriment which in its opinion is insignificant.

(5) Where sub-paragraph (2) or (3) applies, the appeal court may make such further orders (including one or more pension sharing orders) as it thinks fit for the purpose of putting the parties in the position it considers appropriate.

(6) Paragraph 19 only applies to a pension sharing order under this paragraph if the decision of the appeal court can itself be the subject of an appeal.

(7) In sub-paragraph (2), the reference to the person responsible for the pension arrangement is to be read in accordance with paragraph 29(3).

79A Appeals relating to pension compensation sharing orders which have taken effect

(1) This paragraph applies where an appeal against a pension compensation sharing order is begun on or after the day on which the order takes effect.

(2) If the Board of the Pension Protection Fund has acted to its detriment in reliance on the taking effect of the order the appeal court –

(a) may not set aside or vary the order;
(b) may make such further orders (including a pension compensation sharing order) as it thinks fit for the purpose of putting the parties in the position it considers appropriate.

(3) In determining for the purposes of sub-paragraph (2) whether the Board has acted to its detriment the appeal court may disregard any detriment which in the court's opinion is insignificant.

(4) Paragraph 19E only applies to a pension compensation sharing order under this paragraph if the decision of the appeal court can itself be the subject of an appeal.

Amendments—Inserted by Pensions Act 2008, Sch 6, Pt 3.

80 Interpretation

(1) References in this Schedule to –

(a) periodical payments orders,
(b) secured periodical payments orders, and
(c) orders for the payment of a lump sum,

are references to such of the orders that may be made under Parts 1 and 9 (other than interim orders) as are relevant in the context of the reference in question.

(2) In this Schedule 'child of the family', in relation to two people who are civil partners of each other, means –

(a) a child of both of them, and
(b) any other child, other than a child placed with them as foster parents by a local authority or voluntary organisation, who has been treated by both the civil partners as a child of their family.

(3) In this Schedule 'the court' (except where the context otherwise requires) means –

(a) the High Court, or
(b) the family court.

(4) References in this Schedule to a subsequent civil partnership include a civil partnership which is by law void or voidable.

(5) References in this Schedule to a subsequent marriage include a marriage which is by law void or voidable.

Amendments—CCA 2013, s 17, Sch 11.

SCHEDULE 6
FINANCIAL RELIEF: PROVISION CORRESPONDING TO PROVISION MADE BY THE DOMESTIC PROCEEDINGS AND MAGISTRATES' COURTS ACT 1978

Amendments—CCA 2013, s 17, Sch 11.

Scope—Schedule 6 defines the powers of lay justices in the Family Court to order periodical payments and lump sums to either party or to a child of the family.

PART 1
FAILURE TO MAINTAIN ETC: FINANCIAL PROVISION

1 Circumstances in which orders under this Part may be made

(1) On an application to it by one of the civil partners, the family court may make any one or more of the orders set out in paragraph 2 if it is satisfied that the other civil partner –

(a) has failed to provide reasonable maintenance for the applicant,
(b) has failed to provide, or to make a proper contribution towards, reasonable maintenance for any child of the family,
(c) has behaved in such a way that the applicant cannot reasonably be expected to live with the respondent, or
(d) has deserted the applicant.

(2) The power of the court under sub-paragraph (1) is subject to the following provisions of this Schedule.

Amendments—CCA 2013, s 17, Sch 11.

2 The orders: periodical and secured periodical payments and lump sums

(1) The orders are –

(a) an order that the respondent must make to the applicant such periodical payments for such term as may be specified;
(b) an order that the respondent must pay to the applicant such lump sum as may be specified;
(c) an order that the respondent must make –
  (i) to the applicant for the benefit of a child of the family to whom the application relates, or
  (ii) to a child of the family to whom the application relates;
  such periodical payments for such term as may be specified;
(d) an order that the respondent must pay such lump sum as may be specified –
  (i) to the applicant for the benefit of a child of the family to whom the application relates, or

(ii) to such a child of the family to whom the application relates.

(2) The amount of a lump sum required to be paid under sub-paragraph (1)(b) or (d) must not exceed –

(a) £1,000, or
(b) such larger amount as the Lord Chancellor may from time to time by order fix for the purposes of this sub-paragraph.

(3) The power to make an order under sub-paragraph (2) is exercisable by statutory instrument which is subject to annulment in pursuance of a resolution of either House of Parliament.

(4) 'Specified' means specified in the order.

3 Particular provision that may be made by lump sum orders

(1) An order under this Part for the payment of a lump sum may be made for the purpose of enabling any liability or expenses reasonably incurred in maintaining the applicant or any child of the family to whom the application relates before the making of the order to be met.

(2) Sub-paragraph (1) does not restrict the power to make the orders set out in paragraph 2(1)(b) and (d).

4 Matters to which court is to have regard in exercising its powers under this Part – general

If an application is made for an order under this Part, the court, in deciding –

(a) whether to exercise its powers under this Part, and
(b) if so, in what way,

must have regard to all the circumstances of the case, giving first consideration to the welfare while under 18 of any child of the family who has not reached 18.

5 Particular matters to be taken into account when exercising powers in relation to civil partners

(1) This paragraph applies in relation to the exercise by the court of its power to make an order by virtue of paragraph 2(1)(a) or (b).

(2) The court must in particular have regard to –

(a) the income, earning capacity, property and other financial resources which each civil partner –
  (i) has, or
  (ii) is likely to have in the foreseeable future,

  including, in the case of earning capacity, any increase in that capacity which it would in the opinion of the court be reasonable to expect a civil partner in the civil partnership to take steps to acquire;
(b) the financial needs, obligations and responsibilities which each civil partner has or is likely to have in the foreseeable future;
(c) the standard of living enjoyed by the civil partners before the occurrence of the conduct which is alleged as the ground of the application;
(d) the age of each civil partner and the duration of the civil partnership;
(e) any physical or mental disability of either civil partner;
(f) the contributions which each civil partner has made or is likely in the foreseeable future to make to the welfare of the family, including any contribution by looking after the home or caring for the family;
(g) the conduct of each civil partner, if that conduct is such that it would in the opinion of the court be inequitable to disregard it.

6 Particular matters to be taken into account when exercising powers in relation to children

(1) This paragraph applies in relation to the exercise by the court of its power to make an order by virtue of paragraph 2(1)(c) or (d).

(2) The court must in particular have regard to –

(a) the financial needs of the child;
(b) the income, earning capacity (if any), property and other financial resources of the child;
(c) any physical or mental disability of the child;
(d) the standard of living enjoyed by the family before the occurrence of the conduct which is alleged as the ground of the application;
(e) the way in which the child was being and in which the civil partners expected the child to be educated or trained;
(f) the considerations mentioned in relation to the civil partners in paragraph 5(2)(a) and (b).

(3) In relation to the exercise of its power to make an order in favour of a child of the family who is not the respondent's child, the court must also have regard to –

(a) whether the respondent has assumed any responsibility for the child's maintenance;
(b) if so, the extent to which, and the basis on which, the respondent assumed that responsibility and the length of time during which the respondent discharged that responsibility;
(c) whether in assuming and discharging that responsibility the respondent did so knowing that the child was not the respondent's child;
(d) the liability of any other person to maintain the child.

7 Reconciliation

(1) If an application is made for an order under this Part –

(a) the court, before deciding whether to exercise its powers under this Part, must consider whether there is any possibility of reconciliation between the civil partners, and
(b) if at any stage of the proceedings on that application it appears to the court that there is a reasonable possibility of such a reconciliation, the court may adjourn the proceedings for such period as it thinks fit to enable attempts to be made to effect a reconciliation.

(2) If the court adjourns any proceedings under sub-paragraph (1), it may request –

(a) an officer of the Children and Family Court Advisory and Support Service, or
(b) any other person,

to attempt to effect a reconciliation between the civil partners.

(3) If any such request is made, the officer or other person –

(a) must report in writing to the court whether the attempt has been successful, but
(b) must not include in the report any other information.

8 *(repealed)*

PART 2
ORDERS FOR AGREED FINANCIAL PROVISION

9 Orders for payments which have been agreed by the parties

(1) Either civil partner may apply to the family court for an order under this Part on the ground that that civil partner or the other civil partner has agreed to make such financial provision as may be specified in the application.

(2) On such an application, the court may order that the applicant or the respondent (as the case may be) is to make the financial provision specified in the application, if –

(a) it is satisfied that the applicant or the respondent (as the case may be) has agreed to make that provision, and

(b) it has no reason to think that it would be contrary to the interests of justice to do so.

(3) Sub-paragraph (2) is subject to paragraph 12.

Amendments—CCA 2013, s 17, Sch 11.

10 Meaning of 'financial provision' and of references to specified financial provision

(1) In this Part 'financial provision' means any one or more of the following –

(a) the making of periodical payments by one civil partner to the other;

(b) the payment of a lump sum by one civil partner to the other;

(c) the making of periodical payments by one civil partner to a child of the family or to the other civil partner for the benefit of such a child;

(d) the payment by one party of a lump sum to a child of the family or to the other civil partner for the benefit of such a child.

(2) Any reference in this Part to the financial provision specified in an application or specified by the court is a reference –

(a) to the type of provision specified in the application or by the court,

(b) to the amount so specified as the amount of any payment to be made under the application or order, and

(c) in the case of periodical payments, to the term so specified as the term for which the payments are to be made.

11 Evidence to be produced where respondent not present etc

(1) This paragraph applies if –

(a) the respondent is not present, or

(b) is not represented by counsel or a solicitor,

at the hearing of an application for an order under this Part.

(2) The court must not make an order under this Part unless there is produced to it such evidence as may be prescribed by rules of court of –

(a) the consent of the respondent to the making of the order,

(b) the financial resources of the respondent, and

(c) if the financial provision specified in the application includes or consists of provision in respect of a child of the family to be made by the applicant to the respondent for the benefit of the child or to the child, the financial resources of the child.

12 Exercise of powers in relation to children

(1) This paragraph applies if the financial provision specified in an application under this Part –

(a) includes, or

(b) consists of,

provision in respect of a child of the family.

(2) The court must not make an order under this Part unless it considers that the provision which the applicant or the respondent (as the case may be) has agreed to make in respect of the child provides for, or makes a proper contribution towards, the financial needs of the child.

13 Power to make alternative orders

(1) This paragraph applies if on an application under this Part the court decides –

(a) that it would be contrary to the interests of justice to make an order for the making of the financial provision specified in the application, or

(b) that any financial provision which the applicant or the respondent (as the case may be) has agreed to make in respect of a child of the family does not provide for, or make a proper contribution towards, the financial needs of that child.

(2) If the court is of the opinion –

(a) that it would not be contrary to the interests of justice to make an order for the making of some other financial provision specified by the court, and

(b) that, in so far as that other financial provision contains any provision for a child of the family, it provides for, or makes a proper contribution towards, the financial needs of that child,

then, if both the civil partners agree, the court may order that the applicant or the respondent (as the case may be) is to make that other financial provision.

14 Relationship between this Part and Part 1

(1) A civil partner who has applied for an order under Part 1 is not precluded at any time before the determination of the application from applying for an order under this Part.

(2) If –

(a) an order is made under this Part on the application of either civil partner, and

(b) either of them has also made an application for a Part 1 order,

the application for the Part 1 order is to be treated as if it had been withdrawn.

PART 3
ORDERS OF COURT WHERE CIVIL PARTNERS LIVING APART BY AGREEMENT

15 Powers of court where civil partners are living apart by agreement

(1) If –

(a) the civil partners have been living apart for a continuous period exceeding 3 months, neither civil partner having deserted the other, and

(b) one of the civil partners has been making periodical payments for the benefit of the other civil partner or of a child of the family,

the other civil partner may apply to the family court for an order under this Part.

(2) An application made under sub-paragraph (1) must specify the total amount of the payments made by the respondent during the period of 3 months immediately preceding the date of the making of the application.

(3) If on an application for an order under this Part the court is satisfied that the respondent has made the payments specified in the application, the court may make one or both of the orders set out in paragraph 16.

(4) Sub-paragraph (3) is subject to the provisions of this Schedule.

Amendments—CCA 2013, s 17, Sch 11.

16 The orders that may be made under this Part

(1) The orders are –

(a) an order that the respondent is to make to the applicant such periodical payments for such term as may be specified;

(b) an order that the respondent is to make –

(i) to the applicant for the benefit of a child of the family to whom the application relates, or

(ii) to a child of the family to whom the application relates.

such periodical payments for such term as may be specified.

(2) 'Specified' means specified in the order.

17 Restrictions on orders under this Part

The court in the exercise of its powers under this Part must not require –

(a) the respondent to make payments whose total amount during any period of 3 months exceeds the total amount paid by him for the benefit of –
  (i) the applicant, or
  (ii) a child of the family,
  during the period of 3 months immediately preceding the date of the making of the application;
(b) the respondent to make payments to or for the benefit of any person which exceed in amount the payments which the court considers that it would have required the respondent to make to or for the benefit of that person on an application under Part 1;
(c) payments to be made to or for the benefit of a child of the family who is not the respondent's child, unless the court considers that it would have made an order in favour of that child on an application under Part 1.

18 Relationship with powers under Part 1

(1) Sub-paragraph (2) applies if on an application under this Part the court considers that the orders which it has the power to make under this Part –

(a) would not provide reasonable maintenance for the applicant, or
(b) if the application relates to a child of the family, would not provide, or make a proper contribution towards, reasonable maintenance for that child.

(2) The court –

(a) must refuse to make an order under this Part, but
(b) may treat the application as if it were an application for an order under Part 1.

19 Matters to be taken into consideration

Paragraphs 4 to 6 apply in relation to an application for an order under this Part as they apply in relation to an application for an order under Part 1, subject to the modification that for the reference in paragraph 5(2)(c) to the occurrence of the conduct which is alleged as the ground of the application substitute a reference to the living apart of the civil partners.

PART 4
INTERIM ORDERS

20 Circumstances in which interim orders may be made

(1) This paragraph applies if an application has been made for an order under Part 1, 2 or 3.

(2) The family court may make an interim order –

(a) at any time before making a final order on, or dismissing, the application.
(b) *(repealed)*

(3) *(repealed)*

(4) Not more than one interim order may be made with respect to an application for an order under Part 1, 2 or 3.

(5) Sub-paragraph (4) does not affect the power of a court to make an interim order on a further application under Part 1, 2 or 3.

Amendments—CCA 2013, s 17, Sch 11.

21 Meaning of interim order

(1) An interim order is an order requiring the respondent to make such periodical payments as the court thinks reasonable –

(a) to the applicant,
(b) to any child of the family who is under 18, or
(c) to the applicant for the benefit of such a child.

(2) In relation to an interim order in respect of an application for an order under Part 2 by the civil partner who has agreed to make the financial provision specified in the application, sub-paragraph (1) applies as if –

(a) the reference to the respondent were a reference to the applicant, and
(b) the references to the applicant were references to the respondent.

22 When interim order may start

(1) An interim order may provide for payments to be made from such date as the court may specify, except that the date must not be earlier than the date of the making of the application for an order under Part 1, 2 or 3.

(2) Sub-paragraph (1) is subject to paragraph 27(7) and (8).

23 *(repealed)*

24 When interim order ceases to have effect

(1) Subject to sub-paragraphs (2) and (3), an interim order made on an application for an order under Part 1, 2 or 3 ceases to have effect on the earliest of the following dates –

(a) the date, if any, specified for the purpose in the interim order;
(b) the date on which the period of 3 months beginning with the date of the making of the interim order ends;
(c) the date on which the family court either makes a final order on, or dismisses, the application.

(2) If an interim order made under this Part would, but for this sub-paragraph, cease to have effect under sub-paragraph (1)(a) or (b) –

(a) the family court,
(b) *(repealed)*

may by order provide that the interim order is to continue in force for a further period.

(3) An order continued in force under sub-paragraph (2) ceases to have effect on the earliest of the following dates –

(a) the date, if any, specified for the purpose in the order continuing it;
(b) the date on which ends the period of 3 months beginning with –
 (i) the date of the making of the order continuing it, or
 (ii) if more than one such order has been made with respect to the application, the date of the making of the first such order;
(c) the date on which the court either makes a final order on, or dismisses, the application.

Amendments—CCA 2013, s 17, Sch 11.

25 Supplementary

(1) *(repealed)*

(2) No appeal lies from the making of or refusal to make, the variation of or refusal to vary, or the revocation of or refusal to revoke, an interim order.

Amendments—CCA 2013, s 17, Sch 11.

PART 5
COMMENCEMENT AND DURATION OF ORDERS UNDER PARTS 1, 2 AND 3

26 Duration of periodical payments order for a civil partner

(1) The court may specify in a periodical payments order made under paragraph 2(1)(a) or Part 3 in favour of a civil partner such term as it thinks fit, except that the term must not –

(a) begin before the date of the making of the application for the order, or
(b) extend beyond the death of either of the civil partners.

(2) If –

(a) a periodical payments order is made under paragraph 2(1)(a) or Part 3 in favour of one of the civil partners, and

(b) the civil partnership is subsequently dissolved or annulled but the order continues in force,

the periodical payments order ceases to have effect (regardless of anything in it) on the formation of a subsequent civil partnership or marriage by that civil partner, except in relation to any arrears due under the order on the date of that event.

27 Age limit on making orders for financial provision for children and duration of such orders

(1) Subject to sub-paragraph (5), no order is to be made under paragraph 2(1)(c) or (d) or Part 3 in favour of a child who has reached 18.

(2) The term to be specified in a periodical payments order made under paragraph 2(1)(c) or Part 3 in favour of a child may begin with –

(a) the date of the making of an application for the order or a later date, or

(b) a date ascertained in accordance with sub-paragraph (7) or (8).

(3) The term to be specified in such an order –

(a) must not in the first instance extend beyond the date of the birthday of the child next following his reaching the upper limit of the compulsory school age unless the court considers that in the circumstances of the case the welfare of the child requires that it should extend to a later date, and

(b) must not in any event, subject to sub-paragraph (5), extend beyond the date of the child's 18th birthday.

(4) Sub-paragraph (3)(a) must be read with section 8 of the Education Act 1996 (which applies to determine for the purposes of any enactment whether a person is of compulsory school age).

(5) Sub-paragraphs (1) and (3)(b) do not apply in the case of a child if it appears to the court that –

(a) the child is, or will be, or, if such an order were made without complying with either or both of those provisions, would be –

(i) receiving instruction at an educational establishment, or

(ii) undergoing training for a trade, profession or vocation,

whether or not also the child is, will be or would be, in gainful employment, or

(b) there are special circumstances which justify the making of the order without complying with either or both of sub-paragraphs (1) and (3)(b).

(6) Any order made under paragraph 2(1)(c) or Part 3 in favour of a child, regardless of anything in the order, ceases to have effect on the death of the person liable to make payments under the order.

(7) If –

(a) a maintenance calculation ('current calculation') is in force with respect to a child, and

(b) an application is made for an order under paragraph 2(1)(c) or Part 3 –

(i) in accordance with section 8 of the Child Support Act 1991, and

(ii) before the end of 6 months beginning with the making of the current calculation,

the term to be specified in any such order made on that application may be expressed to begin on, or at any time after, the earliest permitted date.

(8) 'The earliest permitted date' is whichever is the later of –

(a) the date 6 months before the application is made, or

(b) the date on which the current calculation took effect or, where successive maintenance calculations have been continuously in force with respect to a child, on which the first of those calculations took effect.

(9) If –

- (a) a maintenance calculation ceases to have effect by or under any provision of the 1991 Act, and
- (b) an application is made, before the end of 6 months beginning with the relevant date, for a periodical payments order under paragraph 2(1)(c) or Part 3 in favour of a child with respect to whom that maintenance calculation was in force immediately before it ceased to have effect,

the term to be specified in any such order, or in any interim order under Part 4, made on that application, may begin with the date on which that maintenance calculation ceased to have effect or any later date.

(10) 'The relevant date' means the date on which the maintenance calculation ceased to have effect.

(11) In this Schedule 'maintenance calculation' has the same meaning as it has in the 1991 Act by virtue of section 54 of the 1991 Act as read with any regulations in force under that section.

28 Application of paragraphs 26 and 27 to Part 2 orders

(1) Subject to sub-paragraph (3), paragraph 26 applies in relation to an order under Part 2 which requires periodical payments to be made to a civil partner for his own benefit as it applies in relation to an order under paragraph 2(1)(a).

(2) Subject to sub-paragraph (3), paragraph 27 applies in relation to an order under Part 2 for the making of financial provision in respect of a child of the family as it applies in relation to an order under paragraph 2(1)(c) or (d).

(3) If –

- (a) the court makes an order under Part 2 which contains provision for the making of periodical payments, and
- (b) by virtue of paragraph 14, an application for an order under Part 1 is treated as if it had been withdrawn,

the term which may be specified under Part 2 as the term for which the payments are to be made may begin with the date of the making of the application for the order under Part 1 or any later date.

29 Effect on certain orders of parties living together

(1) Sub-paragraph (2) applies if periodical payments are required to be made to a civil partner (whether for the civil partner's own benefit or for the benefit of a child of the family) –

- (a) by an order made under Part 1 or 2, or
- (b) by an interim order made under Part 4 (otherwise than on an application under Part 3).

(2) The order is enforceable even though –

- (a) the civil partners are living with each other at the date of the making of the order, or
- (b) if they are not living with each other at that date, they subsequently resume living with each other;

but the order ceases to have effect if after that date the parties continue to live with each other, or resume living with each other, for a continuous period exceeding 6 months.

(3) Sub-paragraph (4) applies if –

- (a) an order is made under Part 1 or 2 which requires periodical payments to be made to a child of the family, or
- (b) an interim order is made under Part 4 (otherwise than on an application under Part 3) which requires periodical payments to be made to a child of the family.

(4) Unless the court otherwise directs, the order continues to have effect and is enforceable even if –

- (a) the civil partners are living with each other at the date of the making of the order, or

(b) if they are not living with each other at that date, they subsequently resume living with each other.

(5) An order made under Part 3, and any interim order made on an application for an order under that Part, ceases to have effect if the civil partners resume living with each other.

(6) If an order made under this Schedule ceases to have effect under –

(a) sub-paragraph (2) or (5), or
(b) a direction given under sub-paragraph (4),

the family court may, on an application made by either civil partner, make an order declaring that the order ceased to have effect from such date as the court may specify.

Amendments—CCA 2013, s 17, Sch 11.

PART 6
VARIATION ETC OF ORDERS

30 Power to vary, revoke, suspend or revive order

(1) If the family court has made an order for the making of periodical payments under Part 1, 2 or 3, the court may, on an application made under this Part –

(a) vary or revoke the order,
(b) suspend any provision of it temporarily, or
(c) revive any provision so suspended.

(2) If the family court has made an interim order under Part 4, the court may, on an application made under this Part –

(a) vary or revoke the order,
(b) suspend any provision of it temporarily, or
(c) revive any provision so suspended,

except that it may not by virtue of this sub-paragraph extend the period for which the order is in force.

Amendments—CCA 2013, s 17, Sch 11.

31 Powers to order lump sum on variation

(1) If the family court has made an order under paragraph 2(1)(a) or (c) for the making of periodical payments, the court may, on an application made under this Part, make an order for the payment of a lump sum under paragraph 2(1)(b) or (d).

(2) If the family court has made an order under Part 2 for the making of periodical payments by a civil partner the court may, on an application made under this Part, make an order for the payment of a lump sum by that civil partner –

(a) to the other civil partner, or
(b) to a child of the family or to that other civil partner for the benefit of that child.

(3) Where the court has power by virtue of this paragraph to make an order for the payment of a lump sum –

(a) the amount of the lump sum must not exceed the maximum amount that may at that time be required to be paid under Part 1, but
(b) the court may make an order for the payment of a lump sum not exceeding that amount even if the person required to pay it was required to pay a lump sum by a previous order under this Schedule.

(4) Where –

(a) the court has power by virtue of this paragraph to make an order for the payment of a lump sum, and

(b) the respondent or the applicant (as the case may be) has agreed to pay a lump sum of an amount exceeding the maximum amount that may at that time be required to be paid under Part 1,

the court may, regardless of sub-paragraph (3), make an order for the payment of a lump sum of that amount.

Amendments—CCA 2013, s 17, Sch 11.

32 Power to specify when order as varied is to take effect

An order made under this Part which varies an order for the making of periodical payments may provide that the payments as so varied are to be made from such date as the court may specify, except that, subject to paragraph 33, the date must not be earlier than the date of the making of the application under this Part.

33 (1) If –

(a) there is in force an order ('the order') –
  (i) under paragraph 2(1)(c),
  (ii) under Part 2 making provision of a kind set out in paragraph 10(1)(c) (regardless of whether it makes provision of any other kind mentioned in paragraph 10(1)(c)),
  (iii) under paragraph 16(1)(b), or
  (iv) which is an interim order under Part 4 under which the payments are to be made to a child or to the applicant for the benefit of a child,
(b) the order requires payments specified in it to be made to or for the benefit of more than one child without apportioning those payments between them,
(c) a maintenance calculation ('the calculation') is made with respect to one or more, but not all, of the children with respect to whom those payments are to be made, and
(d) an application is made, before the end of 6 months beginning with the date on which the calculation was made, for the variation or revocation of the order,

the court may, in exercise of its powers under this Part to vary or revoke the order, direct that the variation or revocation is to take effect from the date on which the calculation took effect or any later date.

(2) If –

(a) an order ('the child order') of a kind prescribed for the purposes of section 10(1) of the Child Support Act 1991 is affected by a maintenance calculation,
(b) on the date on which the child order became so affected there was in force an order ('the civil partner's order') –
  (i) under paragraph 2(1)(a),
  (ii) under Part 2 making provision of a kind set out in paragraph 10(1)(a) (regardless of whether it makes provision of any other kind mentioned in paragraph 10(1)(a)),
  (iii) under paragraph 16(1)(a), or
  (iv) which is an interim order under Part 4 under which the payments are to be made to the applicant (otherwise than for the benefit of a child), and
(c) an application is made, before the end of 6 months beginning with the date on which the maintenance calculation was made, for the civil partner's order to be varied or revoked,

the court may, in exercise of its powers under this Part to vary or revoke the civil partner's order, direct that the variation or revocation is to take effect from the date on which the child order became so affected or any later date.

(3) For the purposes of sub-paragraph (2), an order is affected if it ceases to have effect or is modified by or under section 10 of the 1991 Act.

34 Matters to which court is to have regard in exercising powers under this Part

(1) In exercising the powers conferred by this Part the court must, so far as it appears to the court just to do so, give effect to any agreement which has been reached between the civil partners in relation to the application.

(2) If –

(a) there is no such agreement, or

(b) if the court decides not to give effect to the agreement,

the court must have regard to all the circumstances of the case, giving first consideration to the welfare while under 18 of any child of the family who has not reached 18.

(3) Those circumstances include any change in any of the matters –

(a) to which the court was required to have regard when making the order to which the application relates, or

(b) in the case of an application for the variation or revocation of an order made under Part 2 or on an appeal made by virtue of paragraph 46, to which the court would have been required to have regard if that order had been made under Part 1.

35 Variation of orders for periodical payments: further provisions

(1) The power of the court under paragraphs 30 to 34 to vary an order for the making of periodical payments includes power, if the court is satisfied that payment has not been made in accordance with the order, to exercise one of its powers under section 1(4) and (4A) of the Maintenance Enforcement Act 1991.

(2) Sub-paragraph (1) is subject to paragraph 37.

Amendments—CCA 2013, s 17, Sch 11.

36 *(repealed)*

37 (1) Before varying the order by exercising one of its powers under section 1(4) and (4A) of the 1991 Act, the court must have regard to any representations made by the parties to the application.

(2) *(repealed)*

Amendments—CCA 2013, s 17, Sch 11.

38 (1) Section 1(6) of the 1991 Act (power of court to order that account be opened) applies for the purposes of paragraph 35 as it applies for the purposes of section 1 of the 1991 Act.

(2) None of the powers of the court conferred by paragraphs 35 to 37 and sub-paragraph (1) is exercisable in relation to an order under this Schedule for the making of periodical payments unless, at the time when the order was made, the person required to make the payments was ordinarily resident in England and Wales.

Amendments—CCA 2013, s 17, Sch 11.

39 Persons who may apply under this Part

An application under paragraph 30 or 31 may be made –

(a) if it is for the variation or revocation of an order under Part 1, 2, 3 or 4 for periodical payments, by either civil partner, and

(b) if it is for the variation of an order under paragraph 2(1)(c) or Part 2 or 3 for periodical payments to or in respect of a child, also by the child himself, if he has reached 16.

Amendments—CCA 2013, s 17, Sch 11.

40 Revival of orders for periodical payments

(1) If an order made by the family court under this Schedule for the making of periodical payments to or in respect of a child (other than an interim order) ceases to have effect –

(a) on the date on which the child reaches 16, or

(b) at any time after that date but before or on the date on which he reaches 18, the child may apply to the court which made the order for an order for its revival.

(2) If on such an application it appears to the court that –

(a) the child is, will be or (if an order were made under this sub-paragraph) would be receiving instruction at an educational establishment or undergoing training for a trade, profession or vocation, whether or not while in gainful employment, or

(b) there are special circumstances which justify the making of an order under this sub-paragraph,

the court may by order revive the order from such date as the court may specify, not being earlier than the date of the making of the application.

(3) Any order revived under this paragraph may be varied or revoked under paragraphs 30 to 34 in the same way as it could have been varied or revoked had it continued in being.

Amendments—CCA 2013, s 17, Sch 11.

41–42 *(repealed)*

PART 7
ARREARS AND REPAYMENTS

43 Enforcement etc of orders for payment of money

Section 32 of the Domestic Proceedings and Magistrates' Courts Act 1978 applies in relation to orders under this Schedule as it applies in relation to orders under Part 1 of that Act.

44 Orders for repayment after cessation of order because of subsequent civil partnership etc

(1) Sub-paragraphs (3) and (4) apply if –

(a) an order made under paragraph 2(1)(a) or Part 2 or 3 has, under paragraph 26(2), ceased to have effect because of the formation of a subsequent civil partnership or marriage by the party ('R') in whose favour it was made, and

(b) the person liable to make payments under the order ('P') made payments in accordance with it in respect of a relevant period in the mistaken belief that the order was still subsisting.

(2) 'Relevant period' means a period after the date of the formation of the subsequent civil partnership or marriage.

(3) No proceedings in respect of a cause of action arising out of the circumstances mentioned in sub-paragraph (1)(a) and (b) is maintainable by P (or P's personal representatives) against R (or R's personal representatives).

(4) But on an application made under this paragraph by P (or P's personal representatives) against R (or R's personal representatives) the family court –

(a) may order the respondent to pay to the applicant a sum equal to the amount of the payments made in respect of the relevant period, or

(b) if it appears to the court that it would be unjust to make that order, may –

(i) order the respondent to pay to the applicant such lesser sum as it thinks fit, or

(ii) dismiss the application.

(5) An order under this paragraph for the payment of any sum may provide for the payment of that sum by instalments of such amount as may be specified in the order.

(6) An application under this paragraph –

(a) may (but need not) be made in proceedings for leave to enforce, or the enforcement of, the payment of arrears under an order made under paragraph 2(1)(a) or Part 2 or 3.

(b) *(repealed)*

(7) *(repealed)*

(8) Subject to sub-paragraph (9) –

(a) an officer of the family court is not liable for any act done by him, in pursuance of an order under paragraph 2(1)(a), or Part 2 or 3, requiring payments to be made to the court or an officer of the court, after the date on which that order ceased to have effect because of the formation of a subsequent civil partnership or marriage by the person entitled to payments under it, and

(b) the collecting officer under an attachment of earnings order made to secure payments under an order under paragraph 2(1)(a), or Part 2 or 3, is not liable for any act done by him, after the date on which that order ceased to have effect because of the formation of a subsequent civil partnership or marriage by the person entitled to payments under it, in accordance with any enactment or rule of court specifying how payments made to him in compliance with the attachment of earnings order are to be dealt with.

(9) Sub-paragraph (8) applies if (but only if) the act –

(a) was one which he would have been under a duty to do had the order under paragraph 2(1)(a) or Part 2 or 3 not ceased to have effect, and

(b) was done before notice in writing of the formation of the subsequent civil partnership or marriage was given to him by or on behalf of –

(i) the person entitled to payments under the order,

(ii) the person liable to make payments under it, or

(iii) the personal representatives of either of them.

(10) In this paragraph 'collecting officer', in relation to an attachment of earnings order, means –

(a) the officer of the High Court, or

(b) the officer designated by the Lord Chancellor,

to whom a person makes payments in compliance with the order.

Amendments—CCA 2013, s 17, Sch 11.

PART 8
SUPPLEMENTARY

45 Restrictions on making of orders under this Schedule: welfare of children

If – (a) an application is made by a civil partner for an order under Part 1, 2 or 3, and

(b) there is a child of the family who is under 18,

the court must not dismiss or make a final order on the application until it has decided whether to exercise any of its powers under the Children Act 1989 with respect to the child.

46 Constitution of courts, powers of High Court and county court in relation to orders and appeals

The following provisions of the Domestic Proceedings and Magistrates' Courts Act 1978 apply in relation to an order under this Schedule relating to a civil partnership as they apply in relation to an order under Part 1 of that Act relating to a marriage –

(a) section 28 (powers of the High Court and the family court in relation to certain orders).

(b), (c) *(repealed)*

Amendments—CCA 2013, s 17, Sch 11.

47 Provisions as to jurisdiction and procedure

(1) *(repealed)*

(1A) If an application or part of an application for an order under this Schedule relates to a matter where jurisdiction falls to be determined by reference to the jurisdictional requirements of the Maintenance Regulation and Schedule 6 to the Civil Jurisdiction and Judgments (Maintenance) Regulations 2011, the family court may not entertain that application or that part of it unless it has jurisdiction to do so by virtue of that Regulation and that Schedule.

(2) Any jurisdiction conferred on the family court by this Schedule is exercisable even if any party to the proceedings is not domiciled in England and Wales.

(3) The Lord Chancellor may make a determination for the purposes of sub-paragraph (1) only with the concurrence of the Lord Chief Justice.

(4) The Lord Chief Justice may nominate a judicial office holder (as defined in section 109(4) of the Constitutional Reform Act 2005) to exercise his functions under this paragraph.

(5) In this paragraph 'the Maintenance Regulation' means Council Regulation (EC) No 4/2009 including as applied in relation to Denmark by virtue of the Agreement made on 19 October 2005 between the European Community and the Kingdom of Denmark.

Amendments—SI 2006/1016; SI 2011/1484; CCA 2013, s 17, Sch 11.

48 Meaning of 'child of the family'

In this Schedule 'child of the family', in relation to two people who are civil partners of each other, means –

(a) a child of both of them, and

(b) any other child, other than a child placed with them as foster parents by a local authority or voluntary organisation, who has been treated by both the civil partners as a child of their family.

SCHEDULE 7
FINANCIAL RELIEF IN ENGLAND AND WALES AFTER OVERSEAS DISSOLUTION ETC OF A CIVIL PARTNERSHIP

Scope—When a civil partnership has been dissolved or annulled or there has been a legal separation by means of judicial or other proceedings outside the British Isles, and the dissolution, annulment or legal separation is entitled to be recognised as valid in England and Wales (ss 219 and 234), such recognition confers on either of the civil partners the right to make an application to the court in England and Wales for financial relief (para 2) including financial provision, property adjustment, pension sharing and pension compensation sharing (para 9) and transfers of tenancies (para 13). However, any such application will be barred if either of the civil partners has formed a subsequent civil partnership or marriage (para 3). Further, the leave of the court is required in order to make an application (para 4). Where leave is granted, the court may make an interim order for maintenance (para 5). The jurisdictional requirements are set out in para 7. Before deciding an application for financial relief, the court must consider whether England and Wales is the appropriate venue (para 8). Sch 7 is the counterpart to Pt III in MFPA 1984 which provides for financial relief in England and Wales after an overseas divorce, annulment or legal separation. Reference should be made to the commentary on the comparable provisions in the 1984 Act. The relevant procedure is found in FPR 2010, Pt 8, Ch 6.

PART 1
FINANCIAL RELIEF

1 Part applies where civil partnership has been dissolved etc overseas

(1) This Part of this Schedule applies where –

(a) a civil partnership has been dissolved or annulled, or the civil partners have been legally separated, by means of judicial or other proceedings in an overseas country, and

(b) the dissolution, annulment or legal separation is entitled to be recognised as valid in England and Wales.

(2) This Part of this Schedule applies even if the date of the dissolution, annulment or legal separation is earlier than the date on which the Part comes into force.

(3) In this Schedule 'overseas country' means a country or territory outside the British Islands.

(4) In this Part of this Schedule 'child of the family' means –

(a) a child of both of the civil partners, and

(b) any other child, other than a child placed with them as foster parents or by a local authority or voluntary organisation, who has been treated by both the civil partners as a child of their family.

2 Either civil partner may make application for financial relief

(1) Either of the civil partners may make an application to the court for an order under paragraph 9 or 13.

(2) The rights conferred by sub-paragraph (1) are subject to –

(a) paragraph 3 (civil partner may not apply after forming subsequent civil partnership etc), and

(b) paragraph 4 (application may not be made until leave to make it has been granted).

(3) An application for an order under paragraph 9 or 13 must be made in a manner prescribed by rules of court.

3 No application after formation of subsequent civil partnership or marriage

(1) If –

(a) the civil partnership has been dissolved or annulled, and

(b) after the dissolution or annulment, one of the civil partners forms a subsequent civil partnership or marriage,

that civil partner shall not be entitled to make, in relation to the civil partnership, an application for an order under paragraph 9 or 13.

(2) The reference in sub-paragraph (1) to the forming of a subsequent civil partnership or marriage includes a reference to the forming of a civil partnership or marriage which is by law void or voidable.

4 Leave of court required for making of application

(1) No application for an order under paragraph 9 or 13 shall be made unless the leave of the court has been obtained in accordance with rules of court.

(2) The court shall not grant leave under this paragraph unless it considers that there is substantial ground for the making of an application for such an order.

(3) The court may grant leave under this paragraph notwithstanding that an order has been made by a court in a country outside England and Wales requiring the other civil partner to make any payment, or transfer any property, to the applicant or to a child of the family.

(4) Leave under this paragraph may be granted subject to such conditions as the court thinks fit.

5 Interim orders for maintenance

(1) Where –

(a) leave is granted under paragraph 4, and

(b) it appears to the court that the civil partner who applied for leave, or any child of the family, is in immediate need of financial assistance,

the court may, subject to sub-paragraph (4), make an interim order for maintenance.

(2) An interim order for maintenance is one requiring the other civil partner to make –

(a) to the applicant, or

(b) to the child,

such periodical payments as the court thinks reasonable for such term as the court thinks reasonable.

(3) The term must be one –

(a) beginning not earlier than the date of the grant of leave, and

(b) ending with the date of the determination of the application made under the leave.

(4) If it appears to the court that the court will, in the event of an application being made under the leave, have jurisdiction to entertain the application only under paragraph 7(4), the court shall not make an interim order under this paragraph.

(5) An interim order under this paragraph may be made subject to such conditions as the court thinks fit.

6 Paragraphs 7 and 8 apply where application made for relief under paragraph 9 or 13

Paragraphs 7 and 8 apply where –

(a) one of the civil partners has been granted leave under paragraph 4, and
(b) acting under the leave, that civil partner makes an application for an order under paragraph 9 or 13.

7 Jurisdiction of the court

(1) Subject to sub-paragraph (6), the court shall have jurisdiction to entertain the application only if one or more of the following jurisdictional requirements is satisfied.

(2) The first requirement is that either of the civil partners –

(a) was domiciled in England and Wales on the date when the leave was applied for, or
(b) was domiciled in England and Wales on the date when the dissolution, annulment or legal separation took effect in the overseas country in which it was obtained.

(3) The second is that either of the civil partners –

(a) was habitually resident in England and Wales throughout the period of one year ending with the date when the leave was applied for, or
(b) was habitually resident in England and Wales throughout the period of one year ending with the date on which the dissolution, annulment or legal separation took effect in the overseas country in which it was obtained.

(4) The third is that either or both of the civil partners had, at the date when the leave was applied for, a beneficial interest in possession in a dwelling-house situated in England or Wales which was at some time during the civil partnership a civil partnership home of the civil partners.

(5) In sub-paragraph (4) 'possession' includes receipt of, or the right to receive, rents and profits, but here 'rent' does not include mortgage interest.

(6) If an application or part of an application relates to a matter where jurisdiction falls to be determined by the jurisdictional requirements of the Maintenance Regulation and Schedule 6 to the Civil Jurisdiction and Judgments (Maintenance) Regulations 2011, those requirements are to determine whether the court has jurisdiction to entertain the application or that part of it.

(7) In sub-paragraph (6) 'the Maintenance Regulation' means Council Regulation (EC) No 4/2009 including as applied in relation to Denmark by virtue of the Agreement made on 19 October 2005 between the European Community and the Kingdom of Denmark.

Amendments—SI 2011/1484.

8 Duty of the court to consider whether England and Wales is appropriate venue for application

(1) Before deciding the application, the court must consider whether in all the circumstances of the case it would be appropriate for an order of the kind applied for to be made by a court in England and Wales.

(2) Subject to sub-paragraph (4), if the court is not satisfied that it would be appropriate, the court shall dismiss the application.

(3) The court must, in particular, have regard to the following matters –

(a) the connection which the civil partners have with England and Wales;
(b) the connection which the civil partners have with the country in which the civil partnership was dissolved or annulled or in which they were legally separated;
(c) the connection which the civil partners have with any other country outside England and Wales;

(d) any financial benefit which, in consequence of the dissolution, annulment or legal separation –
   (i) the applicant, or
   (ii) a child of the family,

   has received, or is likely to receive, by virtue of any agreement or the operation of the law of a country outside England and Wales;

(e) in a case where an order has been made by a court in a country outside England and Wales requiring the other civil partner –
   (i) to make any payment, or
   (ii) to transfer any property,

   for the benefit of the applicant or a child of the family, the financial relief given by the order and the extent to which the order has been complied with or is likely to be complied with;

(f) any right which the applicant has, or has had, to apply for financial relief from the other civil partner under the law of any country outside England and Wales and, if the applicant has omitted to exercise that right, the reason for that omission;

(g) the availability in England and Wales of any property in respect of which an order under this Schedule in favour of the applicant could be made;

(h) the extent to which any order made under this Schedule is likely to be enforceable;

(i) the length of time which has elapsed since the date of the dissolution, annulment or legal separation.

(4) If the court has jurisdiction in relation to the application or part of it by virtue of the Maintenance Regulation and Schedule 6 to the Civil Jurisdiction and Judgments (Maintenance) Regulations 2011, the court may not dismiss the application or that part of it on the ground mentioned in sub-paragraph (2) if to do so would be inconsistent with the jurisdictional requirements of that Regulation and that Schedule.

(5) In sub-paragraph (4) 'the Maintenance Regulation' means Council Regulation (EC) No 4/2009 including as applied in relation to Denmark by virtue of the Agreement made on 19 October 2005 between the European Community and the Kingdom of Denmark.

Amendments—SI 2011/1484.

PART II

9 Orders for financial provision, property adjustment, pension sharing and pension compensation sharing

(1) Sub-paragraphs (2) and (3) apply where one of the civil partners has made an application for an order under this paragraph.

(2) If the civil partnership has been dissolved or annulled, the court may on the application make any one or more of the orders which it could make under Part 1, 2, 4 or 4A of Schedule 5 (financial provision, property adjustment, pension sharing and pension compensation sharing) if a dissolution order or nullity order had been made in respect of the civil partnership under Chapter 2 of Part 2 of this Act.

(3) If the civil partners have been legally separated, the court may on the application make any one or more of the orders which it could make under Part 1 or 2 of Schedule 5 (financial provision and property adjustment) if a separation order had been made in respect of the civil partners under Chapter 2 of Part 2 of this Act.

(4) Where under sub-paragraph (2) or (3) the court makes –

(a) an order which, if made under Schedule 5, would be a secured periodical payments order,

(b) an order for the payment of a lump sum, or

(c) an order which, if made under that Schedule, would be a property adjustment order,

then, on making that order or at any time afterwards, the court may make any order which it could make under Part 3 of Schedule 5 (sale of property) if the order under sub-paragraph (2) or (3) had been made under that Schedule.

(5) The powers under sub-paragraphs (2) to (4) are subject to paragraph 11.

Amendments—Pensions Act 2008, Sch 6, Pt 3.

10 Matters to which court is to have regard in exercising its powers under paragraph 9

(1) The court, in deciding –

(a) whether to exercise its powers under paragraph 9, and
(b) if so, in what way,

must act in accordance with this paragraph.

(2) The court must have regard to all the circumstances of the case, giving first consideration to the welfare, while under 18, of any child of the family who has not reached 18.

(3) The court, in exercising its powers under paragraph 9 in relation to one of the civil partners –

(a) must in particular have regard to the matters mentioned in paragraph 21(2) of Schedule 5, and
(b) shall be under duties corresponding to those imposed by sub-paragraphs (2) and (3) of paragraph 23 of that Schedule (duties to consider termination of financial obligations) where it decides to exercise under paragraph 9 powers corresponding to the powers referred to in those sub-paragraphs.

(4) The matters to which the court is to have regard under sub-paragraph (3)(a), so far as relating to paragraph 21(2)(a) of Schedule 5 (regard to be had to financial resources), include –

(a) any benefits under a pension arrangement which either of the civil partners has or is likely to have, and
(b) any PPF compensation to which a civil partner is or is likely to be entitled,

(whether or not in the foreseeable future).

(5) The matters to which the court is to have regard under sub-paragraph (3)(a), so far as relating to paragraph 21(2)(h) of Schedule 5 (regard to be had to benefits that cease to be acquirable), include –

(a) any benefits under a pension arrangement which, because of the dissolution or annulment of the civil partnership, one of the civil partners will lose the chance of acquiring, and
(b) any PPF compensation which, because of the making of the dissolution or nullity order, a civil partner will lose the chance of acquiring entitlement to.

(6) The court, in exercising its powers under paragraph 9 in relation to a child of the family, must in particular have regard to the matters mentioned in paragraph 22(2) of Schedule 5.

(7) The court, in exercising its powers under paragraph 9 against a civil partner ('A') in favour of a child of the family who is not A's child, must also have regard to the matters mentioned in paragraph 22(3) of Schedule 5.

(8) Where an order has been made by a court outside England and Wales for –

(a) the making of payments, or
(b) the transfer of property,

by one of the civil partners, the court in considering in accordance with this paragraph the financial resources of the other civil partner, or of a child of the family, shall have regard to the extent to which that order has been complied with or is likely to be complied with.

(9) In this paragraph –

(a) 'pension arrangement' has the same meaning as in Part 4 of Schedule 5,
(b) references to benefits under a pension arrangement include any benefits by way of pension, whether under a pension arrangement or not, and
(c) 'PPF compensation' has the same meaning as in Schedule 5.

Amendments—Pensions Act 2008, Sch 6, Pt 3.

11 Restriction of powers under paragraph 9 where jurisdiction depends on civil partnership home in England or Wales

(1) Sub-paragraphs (2) to (4) apply where the court has jurisdiction to entertain an application for an order under paragraph 9 only because a dwelling-house which was a civil partnership home of the civil partners is situated in England or Wales.

(2) The court may make under paragraph 9 any one or more of the following orders (but no other) –

(a) an order that one of the civil partners shall pay to the other a specified lump sum;
(b) an order that one of the civil partners shall pay to a child of the family, or to a specified person for the benefit of a child of the family, a specified lump sum;
(c) an order that one of the civil partners shall transfer that civil partner's interest in the dwelling-house, or a specified part of that interest –
  (i) to the other,
  (ii) to a child of the family, or
  (iii) to a specified person for the benefit of a child of the family;
(d) an order that a settlement of the interest of one of the civil partners in the dwelling-house, or a specified part of that interest, be made to the satisfaction of the court for the benefit of any one or more of –
  (i) the other civil partner and the children of the family, or
  (ii) either or any of them;
(e) an order varying for the benefit of any one or more of –
  (i) the civil partners and the children of the family, or
  (ii) either or any of them,
  a relevant settlement so far as that settlement relates to an interest in the dwelling-house;
(f) an order extinguishing or reducing the interest of either of the civil partners under a relevant settlement so far as that interest is an interest in the dwelling-house;
(g) an order for the sale of the interest of one of the civil partners in the dwelling-house.

(3) Where under paragraph 9 the court makes just one order for the payment of a lump sum by one of the civil partners, the amount of the lump sum must not exceed the amount specified in sub-paragraph (5).

(4) Where under paragraph 9 the court makes two or more orders each of which is an order for the payment of a lump sum by the same civil partner, the total of the amounts of the lump sums must not exceed the amount specified in sub-paragraph (5).

(5) That amount is –

(a) if the interest of the paying civil partner in the dwelling-house is sold in pursuance of an order made under sub-paragraph (2)(g), the amount of the proceeds of sale of that interest after deducting from those proceeds any costs incurred in the sale of that interest;
(b) if that interest is not so sold, the amount which in the opinion of the court represents the value of that interest.

(6) Where the interest of one of the civil partners in the dwelling-house is held jointly or in common with any other person or persons –

(a) the reference in sub-paragraph (2)(g) to the interest of one of the civil partners shall be construed as including a reference to the interest of that other person, or the interest of those other persons, in the dwelling-house, and
(b) the reference in sub-paragraph (5)(a) to the amount of the proceeds of a sale ordered under sub-paragraph (2)(g) shall be construed as a reference to that part of those proceeds which is attributable to the interest of that civil partner in the dwelling-house.

(7) In sub-paragraph (2) –

'relevant settlement' means a settlement made, during the subsistence of the civil partnership or in anticipation of its formation, on the civil partners, including one made by will or codicil;

PART II

'specified' means specified in the order.

12 Consent orders under paragraph 9

(1) On an application for a consent order under paragraph 9, the court may make an order in the terms agreed on the basis only of the prescribed information furnished with the application.

(2) Sub-paragraph (1) does not apply if the court has reason to think that there are other circumstances into which it ought to inquire.

(3) Sub-paragraph (1) applies to an application for a consent order varying or discharging an order under paragraph 9 as it applies to an application for such an order.

(4) Sub-paragraph (1) applies despite paragraph 10.

(5) In this paragraph –

'consent order', in relation to an application for an order, means an order in the terms applied for to which the respondent agrees;

'prescribed' means prescribed by rules of court.

13 Orders for transfers of tenancies of dwelling-houses

(1) This paragraph applies if –

(a) an application is made by one of the civil partners for an order under this paragraph, and
(b) one of the civil partners is entitled, either in his own right or jointly with the other civil partner, to occupy a dwelling-house in England or Wales by virtue of a tenancy which is a relevant tenancy within the meaning of Schedule 7 to the Family Law Act 1996.

(2) The court may make in relation to that dwelling-house any order which it could make under Part 2 of that Schedule (order transferring tenancy or switching statutory tenants) if it had power to make a property adjustment order under Part 2 of Schedule 5 to this Act with respect to the civil partnership.

(3) The provisions of paragraphs 10, 11 and 14(1) of Schedule 7 to the Family Law Act 1996 (payments by transferee, pre-transfer liabilities and right of landlord to be heard) apply in relation to any order under this paragraph as they apply to any order under Part 2 of that Schedule.

14 Application to orders under paragraphs 5 and 9 of provisions of Schedule 5

(1) The following provisions of Schedule 5 apply in relation to an order made under paragraph 5 or 9 of this Schedule as they apply in relation to a like order made under that Schedule –

(a) paragraph 3(1) to (3) and (7) (lump sums);
(b) paragraph 11(2) to (4), 12(2), 13 and 14 (orders for sale);
(c) paragraphs 17, 18 and 19(2) and (3) (pension sharing);
(ca) paragraphs 19C, 19D and 19E(2) and (3) (pension compensation sharing);
(d) paragraphs 25 and 26 (orders under Part 1 relating to pensions);
(e) paragraphs 31 to 34 and 35 to 37 (orders under Part 1 relating to pensions where Board has assumed responsibility for scheme);
(ea) paragraph 34A (orders under Part 1 relating to pension compensation attachment);
(f) paragraphs 47(1) to (4) and (6) and 49 (duration of orders);
(g) paragraphs 50 to 54 and 57 to 62, except paragraph 50(1)(g) (variation etc of orders);
(h) paragraphs 63 to 65 (arrears and repayments);
(i) paragraphs 76 to 79A (drafting of instruments, bankruptcy, mental disorder, pension-sharing appeals and pension compensation-sharing appeals).

(2) Sub-paragraph (1)(d) and (ea) does not apply where the court has jurisdiction to entertain an application for an order under paragraph 9 only because a dwelling-house which was a civil partnership home of the civil partners is situated in England or Wales.

(3) Paragraph 27 of Schedule 5 (change of pension arrangement under which rights are shared) applies in relation to an order made under paragraph 9 of this Schedule by virtue of sub-paragraph (1)(d) above as it applies to an order made under Part 1 of Schedule 5 by virtue of paragraph 25 or 26 of that Schedule.

(4) The Lord Chancellor may by regulations make for the purposes of this Schedule provision corresponding to any provision which may be made by him under paragraph 28(1) to (3) of Schedule 5 (supplementary provision about orders relating to pensions under Part 1 of that Schedule) or under paragraphs 34B to 36 of that Schedule (supplementary provision about orders relating to pension compensation).

(5) The power to make regulations under this paragraph is exercisable by statutory instrument which is subject to annulment in pursuance of a resolution of either House of Parliament.

Amendments—Pensions Act 2008, Sch 6, Pt 3.
Subordinate legislation—See annotations to Pt 4.

15 Avoidance of transactions designed to defeat claims under paragraphs 5 and 9

(1) Sub-paragraphs (2) and (3) apply where one of the civil partners ('A') is granted leave under paragraph 4 to make an application for an order under paragraph 9.

(2) If the court is satisfied, on application by A, that the other civil partner ('B') is, with the intention of defeating a claim by A, about to –

- (a) make any disposition, or
- (b) transfer out of the jurisdiction, or otherwise deal with, any property,

it may make such order as it thinks fit for restraining B from doing so or otherwise for protecting the claim.

(3) If the court is satisfied, on application by A –

- (a) that the other civil partner ('B') has, with the intention of defeating a claim by A, made a reviewable disposition, and
- (b) that, if the disposition were set aside –
  - (i) financial relief under paragraph 5 or 9, or
  - (ii) different financial relief under paragraph 5 or 9,

  would be granted to A,

it may make an order setting aside the disposition.

(4) If –

- (a) an order under paragraph 5 or 9 has been made by the court at the instance of one of the civil partners ('A'), and
- (b) the court is satisfied, on application by A, that the other civil partner ('B') has, with the intention of defeating a claim by A, made a reviewable disposition,

the court may make an order setting aside the disposition.

(5) Where the court has jurisdiction to entertain an application for an order under paragraph 9 only under paragraph 7(4), it shall not make any order under sub-paragraph (2), (3) or (4) in respect of any property other than the dwelling-house concerned.

(6) Where the court makes an order under sub-paragraph (3) or (4) setting aside a disposition, it shall give such consequential directions as it thinks fit for giving effect to the order (including directions requiring the making of any payments or the disposal of any property).

(7) For the purposes of sub-paragraphs (3) and (4), but subject to sub-paragraph (8), any disposition made by B is a 'reviewable disposition' (whether made before or after the commencement of A's application under that sub-paragraph).

(8) A disposition made by B is not a reviewable disposition for those purposes if made for valuable consideration (other than formation of a civil partnership) to a person who, at the time of the disposition, acted in relation to it in good faith and without notice of any intention on the part of B to defeat A's claim.

(9) A reference in this paragraph to defeating a claim by one of the civil partners is a reference to –

- (a) preventing financial relief being granted, or reducing the amount of financial relief which might be granted, under paragraph 5 or 9 at the instance of that civil partner, or

(b) frustrating or impeding the enforcement of any order which might be, or has been, made under paragraph 5 or 9 at the instance of that civil partner.

16 Presumptions for the purposes of paragraph 15

(1) Sub-paragraph (3) applies where –

(a) an application is made under paragraph 15(2) or (3) by one of the civil partners with respect to –

(i) a disposition which took place less than 3 years before the date of the application, or

(ii) a disposition or other dealing with property which is about to take place, and

(b) the court is satisfied that the disposition or other dealing would (apart from paragraph 15 and this paragraph of this Schedule) have the consequence of defeating a claim by the applicant.

(2) Sub-paragraph (3) also applies where –

(a) an application is made under paragraph 15(4) by one of the civil partners with respect to a disposition which took place less than 3 years before the date of the application, and

(b) the court is satisfied that the disposition has had the consequence of defeating a claim by the applicant.

(3) It shall be presumed, unless the contrary is shown, that the person who –

(a) disposed of, or

(b) is about to dispose of or deal with the property,

did so, or (as the case may be) is about to do so, with the intention of defeating the applicant's claim.

(4) A reference in this paragraph to defeating a claim by one of the civil partners has the meaning given by paragraph 15(9).

PART 2
STEPS TO PREVENT AVOIDANCE PRIOR TO APPLICATION FOR LEAVE UNDER PARAGRAPH 4

17 Prevention of transactions intended to defeat prospective claims under paragraphs 5 and 9

(1) If it appears to the court, on application by one of the persons ('A') who formed a civil partnership –

(a) that the civil partnership has been dissolved or annulled, or that the civil partners have been legally separated, by means of judicial or other proceedings in an overseas country,

(b) that A intends to apply for leave to make an application for an order under paragraph 9 as soon as he or she has been habitually resident in England and Wales for the period of one year, and

(c) that the other civil partner ('B') is, with the intention of defeating A's claim, about to –

(i) make any disposition, or

(ii) transfer out of the jurisdiction, or otherwise deal with, any property,

the court may make such order as it thinks fit for restraining B from taking such action as is mentioned in paragraph (c).

(2) Sub-paragraph (1) applies even if the date of the dissolution, annulment or legal separation is earlier than the date on which that sub-paragraph comes into force.

(3) Sub-paragraph (4) applies where –

(a) an application is made under sub-paragraph (1) with respect to –

(i) a disposition which took place less than 3 years before the date of the application, or

(ii) a disposition or other dealing with property which is about to take place, and

(b) the court is satisfied that the disposition or other dealing would (apart from this paragraph of this Schedule) have the consequence of defeating a claim by the applicant.

(4) It shall be presumed, unless the contrary is shown, that the person who –

(a) disposed of, or
(b) is about to dispose of or deal with the property,

did so, or (as the case may be) is about to do so, with the intention of defeating the applicant's claim.

(5) A reference in this paragraph to defeating a person's claim is a reference to preventing financial relief being granted, or reducing the amount of financial relief which might be granted, under paragraph 5 or 9 at the instance of that person.

PART 3
SUPPLEMENTARY

18 Paragraphs 15 to 17: meaning of 'disposition' and saving

(1) In paragraphs 15 to 17 'disposition' does not include any provision contained in a will or codicil but, with that exception, includes any conveyance, assurance or gift of property of any description, whether made by an instrument or otherwise.

(2) The provisions of paragraphs 15 to 17 are without prejudice to any power of the High Court to grant injunctions under section 37 of the Senior Courts Act 1981.

Amendments—CRA 2005, Sch 11, para 1(2).

19 Interpretation of Schedule

In this Schedule –

'the court' means the High Court or the family court;

'dwelling-house' includes –

(a) any building, or part of a building, which is occupied as a dwelling, and
(b) any yard, garden, garage or outhouse belonging to, and occupied with, the dwelling-house;

'overseas country' has the meaning given by paragraph 1(3).

Amendments—CCA 2013, s 17, Sch 11.

****

SCHEDULE 20
MEANING OF OVERSEAS RELATIONSHIP: SPECIFIED RELATIONSHIPS

A relationship is specified for the purposes of section 213 (meaning of 'overseas relationship') if it is registered in a country or territory given in the first column of the table and fits the description given in relation to that country or territory in the second column –

Country or territory	*Description*
Andorra	unio estable de parella
Argentina	marriage
Argentina: Autonomous City of Buenos Aires	unión civil
Australia: Australian Capital Territory	civil partnership
Australia: New South Wales	a relationship registered under the Relationships Register Act 2010
Australia: Queensland	civil partnership
Australia: Tasmania	significant relationship
Australia: Victoria	registered domestic relationship
Austria	eingetragene Partnerschaft

Country or territory	*Description*
Belgium	the relationship referred to as cohabitation légale, wettelijke samenwoning or gesetzliches zusammenwohnen
Belgium	marriage
Brazil	marriage
Brazil	união estável
Canada	marriage
Canada: Manitoba	the relationship referred to as common-law relationship or as union de fait
Canada: Nova Scotia	domestic partnership
Canada: Quebec	the relationship referred to as union civile or as civil union
Colombia	unión de hecho
Czech Republic	registrované partnertsví
Denmark	marriage
Denmark	registreret partnerskab
Ecuador	unión civil
Finland	the relationship referred to as rekisteröity parisuhde or as registrerad partnerskap
France	pacte civil de solidarité
Germany	Lebenspartnerschaft
Greenland	the relationship referred to as nalunaarsukkamik inooqatigiinneq or as registreret partnerskab
Hungary	bejegyzett élettársi kapcsolat
Iceland	marriage
Iceland	staðfesta samvist
Ireland	civil partnership
Isle of Man	civil partnership
Jersey	civil partnership
Liechtenstein	eingetragene Partnerschaft
Luxembourg	the relationship referred to as partenariat enregistré or eingetragene partnerschaft
Mexico: Coahuila	pacto civil de solidaridad
Mexico: Mexico City Federal District	marriage
Mexico: Mexico City Federal District	sociedad de convivencia
Netherlands	geregistreerd partnerschap
Netherlands	marriage
New Zealand	civil union
Norway	marriage
Norway	registrert partnerskap
Portugal	marriage
Slovenia	zakon o registraciji istospolne partnerske skupnosti
South Africa	civil partnership
South Africa	marriage
Spain	marriage
Sweden	registrerat partnerskap
Switzerland	the relationship referred to as eingetragene Partnerschaft, as partnenariat enregistré or as unione domestica registrata
United States of America: California	domestic partnership
United States of America: California	marriage
United States of America: Colorado	the relationship between designated beneficiaries
United States of America: Connecticut	civil union
United States of America: Connecticut	marriage

Country or territory	Description
United States of America: Delaware	civil union
United States of America: District of Columbia	marriage
United States of America: Hawaii	civil union
United States of America: Hawaii	reciprocal beneficiary relationship
United States of America: Illinois	civil union
United States of America: Iowa	marriage
United States of America: Maine	domestic partnership
United States of America: Massachusetts	marriage
United States of America: Nevada	domestic partnership
United States of America: New Hampshire	marriage
United States of America: New Jersey	civil union
United States of America: New Jersey	domestic partnership
United States of America: New York	marriage
United States of America: Oregon	domestic partnership
United States of America: Rhode Island	civil union
United States of America: Vermont	civil union
United States of America: Vermont	marriage
United States of America: Washington	state registered domestic partnership
United States of America: Wisconsin	domestic partnership
Uruguay	unión concubinaria

Amendments—SI 2005/3129; SI 2005/3135; SI 2012/2976.

****

Civil Procedure Act 1997

****

7 Power of courts to make orders for preserving evidence, etc

(1) The court may make an order under this section for the purpose of securing, in the case of any existing or proposed proceedings in the court –

(a) the preservation of evidence which is or may be relevant, or
(b) the preservation of property which is or may be the subject-matter of the proceedings or as to which any question arises or may arise in the proceedings.

(2) A person who is, or appears to the court likely to be, a party to proceedings in the court may make an application for such an order.

(3) Such an order may direct any person to permit any person described in the order, or secure that any person so described is permitted –

(a) to enter premises in England and Wales, and
(b) while on the premises, to take in accordance with the terms of the order any of the following steps.

(4) Those steps are –

(a) to carry out a search for or inspection of anything described in the order, and
(b) to make or obtain a copy, photograph, sample or other record of anything so described.

(5) The order may also direct the person concerned –

(a) to provide any person described in the order, or secure that any person so described is provided, with any information or article described in the order, and
(b) to allow any person described in the order, or secure that any person so described is allowed, to retain for safe keeping anything described in the order.

(6) An order under this section is to have effect subject to such conditions as are specified in the order.

(7) This section does not affect any right of a person to refuse to do anything on the ground that to do so might tend to expose him or his spouse or civil partner to proceedings for an offence or for the recovery of a penalty.

(8) In this section –

'court' means the High Court, and
'premises' includes any vehicle;

and an order under this section may describe anything generally, whether by reference to a class or otherwise.

Amendments—CPA 2004, s 261(1), Sch 27, para 154.

Preservation of 'evidence' and of 'property'—Section 7(1) confirms the powers of the court to make specific forms of orders (see also SCA 1981, s 37 for the court's general powers), namely 'search orders' (formerly *Anton Piller*) and 'freezing orders' (formerly *Mareva* injunctions). The procedure is dealt with under FPR 2010, Pt 20.

'A person who ... appears to the court likely to be, a party to proceedings' (s 7(2))—FPR 2010, r 20.3(1)(a) specifically provides for application 'before proceedings are started' in line with s 7(2) and, if such order is made, the court must give directions as to how the proceedings are to be started (r 20.3(3)).

Without notice application—Application can be made without notice for orders under s 7 and on an interim basis (MFPA 1984, s 31F(2)(b)). In family proceedings, the procedure is governed by FPR 2010, rr 20.3 and 20.4.

Preservation of electronic information—There appears to be no reason why s 7 cannot be used to preserve electronic documents and other information (eg *Rybak v Langbar International Ltd* [2010] EWHC 2015 (Ch): e-disclosure was unsatisfactory – order that the computers in which the information had been stored should be handed over).

****

Contempt of Court Act 1981

****

11 Publication of matters exempted from disclosure in court

In any case where a court (having power to do so) allows a name or other matter to be withheld from the public in proceedings before the court, the court may give such directions prohibiting the publication of that name or matter in connection with the proceedings as appear to the court to be necessary for the purpose for which it was so withheld.

Directions by the court to protect the position of witnesses and parties in public hearings—The general rule is that hearings are in public (ECHR 1950, Art 6) and that evidence put before the court should be put in public (*Attorney-General v Leveller Magazine* [1979] AC 440, HL). In exceptional cases, which are necessarily rare, s 11 allows the court to give directions which are designed to protect the position of witnesses and parties who are involved in hearings conducted in open court (*Re G (Adult Patient: Publicity)* [1995] 2 FLR 528, FD – where the court decided that, although the application by the hospital for permission to discontinue life-sustaining treatment for a patient who was in a persistent vegetative state should take place in open court, the very greatest of care should be taken to protect the positions and anonymity of the wife and mother of the patient and the doctors and nurses caring for him). However, the power must be carefully exercised and cannot be used simply to protect privacy or avoid embarrassment (*Attorney-General v Leveller Magazine*, above). The applicant must be able to establish that the failure to grant anonymity would render the attainment of justice really doubtful or impracticable (*Scott v Scott* (1913) FLR Rep 657, HL; *R v Westminster City Council ex parte Castelli; R v Same ex parte Tristran-Garcia* [1996] 1 FLR 534, QBD – where the identity of applicants who were HIV positive had already been revealed at an earlier stage of the proceedings, the court refused to allow their subsequent application that identifying information need not be revealed in the hearing of their later substantive applications for judicial review). The court has power to consider at any stage of the hearing whether any particular evidence ought to be given in private (see *Re G (Adult Patient: Publicity)*, at [533A]). Ideally, applications for anonymity and orders under s 11 should be made at the same time as the application for leave. These applications can be heard ex parte and, where appropriate, in camera (*R v Westminster City Council ex parte Castelli; R v Same ex parte Tristran-Garcia* (above)). Any order needs to be precisely worded (*Briffett v DPP* [2001] EWHC Admin 841). In *X v Dartford and Gravesham NHS Trust (Personal Injury Bar Association and another intervening)* [2015] 1 WLR 3647, CA, the Court of Appeal restated the constitutional importance of the principle of open justice and the need to justify any derogation from it on grounds of necessity. This is not a matter of discretion: either it is necessary in the interest of justice or it is not.

Section 11 applies whether the proceedings are heard in public or in private. As to the court sitting in private, see generally FPR 2010, Pt 27 and PD27A, and CPR 1998, r 39.2 and PD39B.

****

14 Proceedings in England and Wales

(1) In any case where a court has power to commit a person to prison for contempt of court and (apart from this provision) no limitation applies to the period of committal, the committal shall (without prejudice to the power of the court to order his earlier discharge) be for a fixed term, and that term shall not on any occasion exceed two years in the case of committal by a superior court, or one month in the case of committal by an inferior court.

(2) In any case where an inferior court has power to fine a person for contempt of court and (apart from this provision) no limit applies to the amount of the fine, the fine shall not on any occasion exceed £2,500.

(2A) In the exercise of jurisdiction to commit for contempt of court or any kindred offence the court shall not deal with the offender by making an order under section 60 of the Powers of Criminal Courts (Sentencing) Act 2000 (an attendance centre order) if it appears to the court after considering any available evidence, that he is under 17 years of age.

(2A) A fine imposed under subsection (2) above shall be deemed, for the purposes of any enactment, to be a sum adjudged to be paid by a conviction.

(3) *(repealed)*

(4) Each of the superior courts shall have the like power to make a hospital order or guardianship order under section 37 of the Mental Health Act 1983 or an interim hospital order under section 38 of that Act in the case of a person suffering from mental disorder within the meaning of that Act who could otherwise be committed to prison for contempt of court as the Crown Court has under that section in the case of a person convicted of an offence.

(4A) Each of the superior courts shall have the like power to make an order under section 35 of the said Act of 1983 (remand for report on accused's mental condition) where there is reason to suspect that a person who could be committed to prison for contempt of court is suffering from mental disorder within the meaning of that Act as the Crown Court has under that section in the case of an accused person within the meaning of that section.

(4A) For the purposes of the preceding provisions of this section a county court shall be treated as a superior court and not as an inferior court.

(4B) The preceding provisions of this section do not apply to the family court, but –

- (a) this is without prejudice to the operation of section 31E(1)(a) of the Matrimonial and Family Proceedings Act 1984 (family court has High Court's powers) in relation to the powers of the High Court that are limited or conferred by those provisions of this section, and .
- (b) section 31E(1)(b) of that Act (family court has county court's powers) does not apply in relation to the powers of the county court that are limited or conferred by those provisions of this section.

(5) The enactments specified in Part III of Schedule 2 shall have effect subject to the amendments set out in that Part, being amendments relating to the penalties and procedure in respect of certain offences of contempt in coroners' courts, county courts and magistrates' courts.

Amendments—Criminal Justice Act 1982, ss 77, 78, Sch 14, para 60, Sch 16; Mental Health (Amendment) Act 1982, s 65(1), Sch 3, paras 59, 60; MHA 1983, s 148, Sch 4, para 57; County Courts (Penalties for Contempt) Act 1983, s 1; SI 1984/447; Criminal Justice Act 1991, s 17, Sch 4, Pt I, Pt V, para 4; Criminal Justice Act 1993, s 65(3), Sch 3, para 6(5); Powers of Criminal Courts (Sentencing) Act 2000, s 165, Sch 9, para 84. Due to an error in drafting, two subsections have been numbered (2A) and (4A) respectively, MHA 2007, s 1(4), Sch 1, para 19; CCA 2013, s 17, Schs 9, 10.

Defined terms—'court', 'superior court': s 19.

Standard of proof—A contempt has to be proved beyond reasonable doubt. But where a contemnor is absent, the judge has to be satisfied on the balance of probabilities that they had had proper notice of the committal hearing (*Otkritie International Investment Management Ltd v Olessia Jemai* [2016] EWCA Civ 1316).

Sentencing—The guideline case on sentencing is *Hale v Tanner* [2000] 2 FLR 879, CA, as supplemented by *Lomas v Parle* [2004] 1 FLR 812, CA and *Murray v Robinson* [2006] 1 FLR 365, CA. On a committal application the court has to direct itself whether committal to prison is appropriate. The full range of sentencing options available to the criminal courts is not available but there is still a range of options. If prison is appropriate, the length of sentence and whether it should be suspended are separate questions. The length of sentence depends on the court's objectives: one objective is to mark disapproval of disobedience of its order; another is to secure future compliance. The length needs to bear some reasonable relationship to the 2 years' maximum. The power to suspend is wider than in criminal cases and its length requires separate consideration. The context of the breach may be aggravating or mitigating. The court should explain the choices it has made in a particular case. On the facts of *Hale v Tanner*, a sentence of 6 months for abusive and threatening telephone calls was reduced to 28 days. See also *Lomas v Parle* (4 months increased to 8 months). If there are parallel criminal proceedings there is no need to adjourn or anticipate the outcome: it is for the second court to reflect the prior sentence in its judgment but a civil judge can sentence only for conduct that was not the subject of criminal proceedings and cannot 'top up' a sentence thought to be too lenient (see *Chelmsford County Court v Ramet* [2014] 2 FLR 1081, FD, per Munby P). In cases involving a second breach, it is necessary to impose a sentence no longer than is required to mark the gravity of the breach (*Bartley (t/a Lundy) v Wilson* [2004] EWCA Civ 1338). Generally the civil court should follow the criminal court guidelines (see *Murray v Robinson* [2006] 1 FLR 365, CA). In *Wood v Collins* [2006] EWCA Civ 743 an 'unduly lenient' suspended sentence of 28 days was increased to 3 months (though still suspended). Where there is a continuing breach, a fresh order and a further committal order can be made (*Re W (Abduction: Committal)* [2012] 2 FLR 133, CA). In *Re C (Children)* [2011] EWCA Civ 1230, breaches of an injunction restraining a mother from approaching within 200 metres of her children's foster home were serious enough to justify an immediate sentence of imprisonment. In *W v W* [2011] 2 FLR 1268, FD, Baron J imposed a 1-year sentence for breach of an undertaking suspended on terms including the immediate payment of a lump sum.

Sentence must be for a fixed term—Once a contemnor has been found guilty of having breached an undertaking or an order, the court has no power to detain in custody pending consideration of the appropriate sentence to be imposed (*Delaney v Delaney* [1996] 1 FLR 458, CA).

Non-payment—Failure to comply with an order to pay money (eg a lump sum) can be a contempt of court. However, the maximum sentence is the 6 weeks prescribed by DA 1869, s 5, not the 2 years under the 1981 Act (*Zuk v Zuk* [2012] EWCA Civ 1871). See further Procedural Guide C11.

Contempt in the face of the court—A High Court judge has power to order overnight detention of the alleged contemnor to allow both for a period of reflection and for arrangements to be made for legal representation. If the case cannot be dealt with the next day, detention until the next working day is 'the very limit of what could be either lawful or acceptable' (see *Wilkinson v S & anor* [2003] 1 WLR 1254, CA). In the County Court, see CCA 1984, s 118. No breach of ECHR 1950, Art 6 is involved if the judge invokes the summary procedure and deals with the case (see *Wilkinson* (above)). The procedure to be followed by a judge faced with such a contempt is set out in CPR 1998, r 81.16 and PD81, para 4 (civil) and FPR 2010, r 37.12 and PD37A, para 3 (family).

'shall not on any occasion exceed two years in the case of committal by a superior court' (s 14(1))—A court may not, on any single occasion, impose on a contemnor a sentence of imprisonment which exceeds 2 years, even where it activates a sentence which was previously suspended (*Villiers v Villiers* [1994] 1 FLR 647, CA). Where a contemnor acknowledges breach of the relevant order, apologises to the court and thus avoids the need for witnesses to give oral evidence substantiating the breach, he is entitled to some credit to reduce the length of the total sentence to a period below the maximum of 2 years' imprisonment (*Re R (A Minor) (Contempt)* [1994] 2 FLR 185, CA).

Early release—A person sentenced to imprisonment for contempt of court does not serve the full sentence imposed by the court. As soon as he has served one-half 'it shall be the duty of the Secretary of State to release him unconditionally' (see CJA 2003, s 258). As release is unconditional, he is not on licence ('parole') and not subject to re-call. The early release provisions of CJA 2003 impose an obligation on the Secretary of State which cannot be overreached by a sentencing judge. It is therefore not lawful to sentence until a specified date (*Thomson v Mitchell* [2004] EWCA Civ 1271, CA). The sentence must be for a fixed term.

Further, a contemnor may apply at any time to purge his contempt. Any such application is best heard by the sentencing judge. See **Purging of contempt**, below.

County court to be treated as superior court (s 14(4A))—County courts may equally impose prison sentences and fines and make hospital orders and guardianship orders.

Powers of inferior courts (s 14(1),(2))—This section imposes a general limit on the powers of inferior courts to punish for contempt, namely one month's imprisonment or a fine of £2500 or both.

Breach of non-molestation order—See commentary on FLA 1996 and FPR 2010, Pt 10.

Power of court to order earlier discharge—A court may release a contemnor before the end of the term of imprisonment whether or not the contempt is purged (*Enfield London Borough Council v Mahoney* [1983] 1 WLR 749, CA). However, the court does not have power to suspend the remainder of a part-served sentence (*Harris v Harris* [2002] 1 FLR 248, CA).

Purging of contempt—As part of the admission to prison process it is explained to a contemnor that he can apply to purge his contempt. Unfortunately, this results in applications that are premature and without genuine remorse. In *CJ v Flintshire Borough Council* [2010] 2 FLR 1224, CA, when dismissing an appeal against refusal to release, the Court of Appeal asked eight non-exhaustive questions to be considered on an application to purge: (i) Could the court conclude that the contemnor had suffered punishment proportionate to his contempt? (ii) Would the interest of the state significantly be prejudiced by early discharge? (iii) How genuine was any expression of contrition? (iv) Had the contemnor demonstrated a resolve and ability not to commit a further breach? (v) Had he done all that he reasonably could to minimise the risk of committing a further breach if discharged? (vi) Had any specific proposal been made to augment the protection of those that the order was designed to protect against a further breach? (vii) How long had been served, taking account of the full term imposed and the early release provision of CJA 2003, s 258(2)? (viii) Were there any special factors impinging on the exercise of discretion either way? A successful application does not depend on affirmative answers to all eight questions.

Age (s 14(2A))—A person attains a particular age expressed in years at the commencement of the relevant anniversary of the date of birth (FLRA 1969, s 9). Where a contemnor is aged under 18, there is no power at all to commit to any form of detention (*R v Selby Justices ex parte Frame* [1992] QB 72, QBD). A person under the age of 21 cannot be sent to prison for contempt but, if aged 18 years or more, can be detained under Powers of Criminal Courts (Sentencing) Act 2000, s 96 (see *R v Selby Justices ex parte Frame* (above); see also *Mason v Lawton* [1991] 2 FLR 50, CA). Now that breach of a non-molestation order is a criminal offence arguably any minor who has attained the age of criminal responsibility can (through a litigation friend) be made subject to such an order as it would be possible to prosecute for a breach even though not for a civil contempt.

Treatment of contempt prisoners—A person sentenced to imprisonment for contempt of court is not a 'convicted prisoner' within the meaning of the Prison Rules 1999. Accordingly, they have the same rights and privileges as an 'unconvicted prisoner'.

Time on remand—If a contemnor has been remanded in custody (eg under FLA 1996, Sch 5) before sentence, time spent in custody is not automatically taken into account as part of the sentence. The sentencing judge must take this into consideration when passing sentence and should make it clear in sentencing remarks that he has done so. *Kerai v Patel* [2008] 2 FLR 2137, CA explains how this should be done bearing in mind the early release provisions (see above). If a judge say activates a 3-month suspended sentence and imposes a further sentence of 12 months but the contemnor has served 3 months on remand, then the sentence to be imposed is one of 9 months (of which four and a half will be served), the 3 months on remand in custody being the equivalent of a 6-month sentence.

Power of court to order contemnor to attend at attendance centre (s 14(2A))—This section, by implication, contemplates that a contemnor aged at least 17, but less than 21, may be ordered to attend at an attendance centre. However, see arguments to the contrary in *R v Selby Justices ex parte Frame* [1992] QB 72, QBD, where the Divisional Court upheld a submission by counsel as amicus curiae that, since a person found guilty of contempt had not been 'convicted of an offence', it followed that no other means of disposal provided by criminal justice legislation, such as an attendance centre order, was available.

Mentally disordered contemnors (s 14(4),(4A))—Under MHA 1983, the court has power to remand a person to a hospital for a report on his mental condition (s 35), to authorise his admission to and detention in hospital, or to place him under the guardianship of a local social services authority or other approved person (s 37), and, where two registered medical practitioners certify that he is suffering from mental illness and that there is reason to suppose that it may be appropriate to make a hospital order, to make an *interim* hospital order (s 38). However, these powers cannot be exercised until the person has been found guilty of contempt. This is clear from the use in s 14(4) and (4A) of the words 'a person who could be committed to prison for contempt of court'.

Once a person has been found guilty of contempt of court, the High Court or County Court has power:

(a) if there is reason to suspect that he is suffering from mental illness or severe mental impairment, to remand him in custody for reports under s 35 for not more than 28 days at a time or 12 weeks in all; and
(b) if satisfied that he is suffering from mental illness or severe mental impairment, to make either (i) an interim hospital order under s 38 for not more than 12 weeks initially or six months in all, or (ii) a hospital order under s 37.

However, none of these powers can be exercised unless the court has before it the required evidence of the relevant medical practitioner(s) as to the matters set out in MHA 1983, ss 35, 37 and 38. There is no general power to remand a contemnor before sentence, so the court may have to adjourn until the medical evidence is available. In FLA 1996, Pt IV cases, there is specific power to remand for a medical examination and report (see FLA 1996, s 48).

Pending Appeal—In *Devon County Council v Kirk* [2016] EWCA Civ 1221, a litigant in person had applied for permission to appeal but not for a stay of the order. The court erred in proceeding to commit the 71-year-old woman of good character for 6 months where it was 'almost certain' that a stay would have been granted. The President criticised not only the court below for proceeding in a case that was not urgent but also the 5-month delay in obtaining a transcript of the judgment and the prison authorities for obstructing access between the litigant and her pro bono counsel; see the President's judgment especially at [44]–[52].

Appeal—Either the applicant or respondent can appeal to the Court of Appeal any order made in exercise of jurisdiction to punish for contempt of court. The contemnor does not need permission to appeal a committal order (CPR 1998, r 52.3) but the applicant does (*Poole BC v Hambridge* [2007] EWCA Civ 990). A fine is not a 'committal order', so a respondent appealing a fine does require permission to appeal and is not within the exception in CPR 1998, r 52.3(1)(a): *Masri v Consolidated Contractors* [2012] 1 WLR 223, CA.

****

16 Enforcement of fines imposed by certain superior courts

(1) Payment of a fine for contempt of court imposed by a superior court, other than the Crown Court or one of the courts specified in subsection (4) below, may be enforced upon the order of the court –

(a) in like manner as a judgment of the High Court for the payment of money; or
(b) in like manner as a fine imposed by the Crown Court.

(2) Where payment of a fine imposed by any court falls to be enforced as mentioned in paragraph (a) of subsection (1) –

(a) the court shall, if the fine is not paid in full forthwith or within such time as the court may allow, certify to Her Majesty's Remembrancer the sum payable;
(b) Her Majesty's Remembrancer shall thereupon proceed to enforce payment of that sum as if it were due to him as a judgment debt;
(c) *(repealed)*

(3) Where payment of a fine imposed by any court falls to be enforced as mentioned in paragraph (b) of subsection (1), the provisions of sections 139 and 140 of the Powers of Criminal Courts (Sentencing) Act 2000 shall apply as they apply to a fine imposed by the Crown Court.

(4) Subsection (1) of this section does not apply to fines imposed by the criminal division of the Court of Appeal or by the Supreme Court on appeal from that division.

(5) The Fines Act 1833 shall not apply to a fine to which subsection (1) of this section applies.

(6) *(repealed)*

Amendments—SCA 1981, s 152(4), Sch 7; Industrial Tribunals Act 1996, s 45, Sch 3, Pt I; Powers of Criminal Courts (Sentencing) Act 2000, s 165, Sch 9, para 85; CRA 2005, Sch 9, para 35(2).

Defined terms—'court', 'superior court': s 19.

'Her Majesty's Remembrancer' (s 16(2))—The Senior Master of the Queen's Bench Division is traditionally also the Queen's Remembrancer.

****

County Courts Act 1984

ARRANGEMENT OF SECTIONS

PART I
CONSTITUTION AND ADMINISTRATION

Section		Page
14	Penalty for assaulting officers	795

PART II
JURISDICTION AND TRANSFER OF PROCEEDINGS

25	Jurisdiction under Inheritance (Provision for Family and Dependants) Act 1975	796
38	Remedies available in county courts	796
70	Finality of judgments and orders	798

PART IV
APPEALS ETC

Appeals

77	Appeals: general provisions	798
79	Agreement not to appeal	799
80	Judge's note on appeal	799
81	Powers of Court of Appeal on appeal from county court	799

Certiorari and prohibition

83	Stay of proceedings in case of certiorari or prohibition	800
84	Prohibition	800

PART V
ENFORCEMENT OF JUDGMENTS AND ORDERS
Execution against goods

85	Execution of judgments or orders for payment of money	801
86	Execution of orders for payment by instalments	801
87	Indorsement of amount on warrant	801
88	Power to stay execution	802

Receivers and attachment of debts

107	Receivers	802
108	Attachment of debts	802
109	Administrative and clerical expenses of garnishees	803

Miscellaneous provisions as to enforcement of judgments and orders

110	Penalty for non-attendance on judgment summons	803

PART VII
COMMITTALS

118	Power to commit for contempt	804
119	Issue and execution of orders of committal	805
121	Power of judge to order discharge	805

PART IX
MISCELLANEOUS AND GENERAL

147	Interpretation	805

PART I
CONSTITUTION AND ADMINISTRATION

****

14 Penalty for assaulting officers

(1) If any person assaults an officer of the county court while in the execution of his duty, he shall be liable –

(a) on summary conviction, to imprisonment for a term not exceeding 3 months or to a fine of an amount not exceeding level 5 on the standard scale, or both; or

(b) on an order made by the court in that behalf, to be committed for a specified period not exceeding 3 months to prison or to such a fine as aforesaid, or to be so committed and to such a fine,

and an officer of the court may take the offender into custody, with or without warrant, and bring him before the court.

(2) The court may at any time revoke an order committing a person to prison under this section and, if he is already in custody, order his discharge.

(3) *(repealed)*

Amendments—Statute Law (Repeals) Act 1986; CLSA 1990, s 74(4); CCA 2013, s 17, Sch 9.

'in the execution of his duty' (s 14(1))—An honest mistake as to whether the person assaulted was 'an officer of the court' and/or was 'in the execution of his duty' may be a defence (*Blackburn v Bowering* [1994] 1 WLR 1324, CA).

'fine of an amount not exceeding level 5' (s 14(1)(a))—The current figure is £5000.

Procedure—See CPR 1998, Pt 81, S 9 (civil) and FPR 2010, Pt 37 (family).

Standard of proof—Contempt proceedings are 'criminal proceedings' for the purposes of ECHR 1950, Art 6. Thus proof to the criminal standard ('beyond reasonable doubt') is required: the judge must be sure that the case is proved. (See *Re J (Children)* [2016] 2 FLR 1207, CA; *Asia Islamic Trade Finance Fund Ltd v Drum Risk Management Ltd & Ors* [2015] EWHC 3748 (Comm).)

Legal aid—Persons in danger of losing their liberty (as is possible under s 14) are, subject to means, eligible for legal aid under LASPOA 2012.

Family Court—See also Family Court (Contempt of Court) (Powers) Regulations 2014.

Appeal—See AJA 1960, s 13.

Sentence—If the contemnor has already been prosecuted and sentenced in a criminal court, the County Court cannot impose a further penalty: *Chelmsford County Court v Ramet* [2014] EWHC 56 (Fam), per Munby P.

****

PART II
JURISDICTION AND TRANSFER OF PROCEEDINGS

****

25 Jurisdiction under Inheritance (Provision for Family and Dependants) Act 1975

The county court shall have jurisdiction to hear and determine any application for an order under section 2 of the Inheritance (Provision for Family and Dependants) Act 1975 (including any application for permission to apply for such an order and any application made, in the proceedings on an application for such an order, for an order under any other provision of that Act).

Amendments—SI 1991/724; CCA 2013, s 17, Sch 9.

Transfer of proceedings—CPR 1998, r 30.6 empowers the court to specify the particular court where the trial or some other hearing in the proceedings will take place, without an order for such transfer.

****

38 Remedies available in county courts

(1) Subject to what follows, in any proceedings in the county court the court may make any order which could be made by the High Court if the proceedings were in the High Court.

(2) Any order made by the county court may be –

(a) absolute or conditional;
(b) final or interlocutory.

(3) Neither the county court nor the family court has power –

(a) to order mandamus, certiorari or prohibition; or
(b) to make any order of a prescribed kind.

(4) Regulations under subsection (3) –

(a) may provide for any of their provisions not to apply in such circumstances or descriptions of case as may be specified in the regulations;
(b) may provide for the transfer of the proceedings to the High Court for the purpose of enabling an order of a kind prescribed under subsection (3) to be made;
(c) *(repealed)*
(d) may make provision amending or repealing any provision made by or under any enactment, so far as may be necessary or expedient in consequence of the regulations.
(e) may make different provision for different purposes.

(4A) If regulations are made under subsection (3), rules may be made in accordance with Part 1 of Schedule 1 to the Constitutional Reform Act 2005 about procedure relevant to the matters prescribed in the regulations.

(5) In this section 'prescribed' means prescribed by regulations made under this section by the Lord Chancellor after consulting the Lord Chief Justice.

(6) The power to make regulations under this section shall be exercised by statutory instrument.

(7) No such statutory instrument shall be made unless a draft of the instrument has been approved by both Houses of Parliament.

Amendments—CLSA 1990, s 3; CRA 2005, ss 12(2), 15(1), 146, Sch 1, para 17, Sch 4, paras 160, 167, Sch 18, Pt 1; CCA 2013, s 17, Schs 9, 10.

Scope—This section provides the County Court with the same powers as the High Court, subject to certain exceptions. Thus the County Court may grant an injunction in support of a legal right, even though no other remedy is claimed in the proceedings. The power to commit for disobedience of an injunction, or breach of an undertaking, is a power of the High Court which is devolved on the County Court by virtue of CCA 1984, s 38. The County Court has no inherent jurisdiction to grant injunctions to restrain either a local authority from exercising its statutory powers in relation to children or the police from exercising their statutory or common law powers (*D v D (County Court Jurisdiction: Injunctions)* [1993] 2 FLR 802, CA).

Regulations restricting powers of the County Court—The current regulations under s 38(3)(b),(4) are the CCRR 2014, which restrict its power to make search orders.

Personal protection injunctions—At common law, 'harassment' or 'molestation' can be prohibited in proceedings founded in the law of tort, if the conduct complained of amounts to a tort (*Burris v Azadani* [1996] 1 FLR 266, CA). This usually involves proceedings for trespass to the person or trespass to land. However, PHA 1997, s 3 (below) has, in effect, created a statutory tort of harassment, and proceedings based on that Act will invariably be a better way of restraining a course of conduct amounting to harassment (see notes to that Act). See also FLA 1996, Pt IV and notes thereon.

Form of non-molestation injunction—It is vital, when submitting a draft injunction or undertaking, to use precise and explicit wording. It must be clear to the respondent what he must do or not do, as the case may be. Only an order requiring a person to do an act within a specified time, or to abstain from doing an act, can be enforced by committal proceedings (CPR 1998, r 81.4; *Parsons v Nasar* [1990] 2 FLR 103, CA).

Power of arrest—There is no power at common law to attach a 'power of arrest' to an injunction. A power of arrest can be attached only where authorised by statute, eg FLA 1996, s 47; Housing Act 1996, s 153C. There is no 'power of arrest' available under the Protection from Harassment Act 1997, but see s 3(3) of that Act which provides for a 'warrant of arrest'.

Penal notice—Before an order can be enforced by committal proceedings, it must be endorsed with a 'penal notice': CPR 1998, r 81.9, CPR PD81, para 1 and Form N77 (civil) and FPR 2010, r 37.9 and PD37A (family). (Different wording is prescribed for orders under FLA 1996.)

Enforcement of injunctions and undertakings—Injunctions and undertakings cannot be enforced by committal proceedings unless the direction or promise is to do or refrain from doing a specific act or acts. An undertaking to pay money is not enforceable by committal, save as permitted by Debtors Act 1869, s 5 (*Symmons v Symmons* [1993] 1 FLR 317, FD). See also *Mubarak v Mubarak* [2007] 1 FLR 722, FD, where Bodey J held that non-payment of a matrimonial order was itself contempt of court and the husband was placed under strict terms. In most cases where an order to pay money is made, or an undertaking to pay money is given, the appropriate remedy is by way of judgment summons. For the procedure to be adopted for breach of injunctions and undertakings, see Procedural Guide C14.

Undertakings—A formal undertaking given by the parties and recorded in court is equivalent to an injunction (*Gandolfo v Gandolfo (Standard Chartered Bank, Garnishee)* [1981] QB 359, CA), save that an undertaking to pay money can only be enforced by committal in very limited circumstances (see **Enforcement of injunctions and undertakings**, above). A power of arrest cannot be attached to an undertaking (*Carpenter v Carpenter* [1988] 1 FLR 121, CA; FLA 1996, s 46(2)). An undertaking in FLA cases is enforceable by a warrant of arrest (FLA 1996, s 46(4)).

Injunction under MWPA 1882—In order to restrain a sale or disposal of property which is the subject matter of a dispute under MWPA 1882, s 17, an injunction may be sought. The injunction must be ancillary or incidental to any relief sought in the s 17 proceedings, which are governed by FPR 2010, Pt 8, Ch 4.

Injunction under MCA 1973, s 37—When proceedings for financial relief have been brought by one person against another under MCA 1973, the court may, pursuant to s 37(2)(a), grant an injunction to restrain disposal of property. The injunction may be granted by a district judge (FPR 2010, r 2.5). 'Property' includes real and personal property and that situated outside the jurisdiction (*Hamlin v Hamlin* [1986] 1 FLR 61, CA). However a court will not exercise its discretion so as to make an order under s 37 concerning foreign property if such an order cannot be enforced.

Freezing injunctions—CCRR 2014 govern the power of the County Court to grant a freezing injunction. The freezing injunction may be useful in two situations in which an injunction under MCA 1973, s 37 is not available:

(a) Where a party is not involved in a disposition to a third party, but is just putting obstacles in the way of the other party from recovering any sum awarded, or is making it difficult for the court to deal with the case, or where there is no evidence of intent to defeat a claim for ancillary relief (see *Shipman v Shipman* [1991] 1 FLR 250, FD, where an injunction was used to restrain the husband from transferring his assets abroad notwithstanding the absence of any intention to avoid his obligations).

(b) Where the property is not yet in existence (eg award of damages in a civil action; redundancy payment; maturing insurance policy) but is to be paid at some future date. In the case of *Ghoth v Ghoth* [1992] 2 FLR 300, CA, the Court of Appeal held that there is jurisdiction to grant freezing injunctions in matrimonial cases, but that the court should be cautious about granting such an injunction in respect of property outside the jurisdiction. The court can only act because it has personal jurisdiction over the respondent. Therefore the order should be limited to restraining the respondent from disposing of those foreign assets, or at least be limited to the extent in which an injunction would be enforced in that foreign court (*Babanaft International Co SA v Bassatne and Another* [1990] Ch 13, CA). The injunction should not extend beyond the size of the fund necessary to achieve the maximum which the applicant is likely to be awarded in divorce proceedings.

For further detail as to the procedures to be followed and the law and practice involved, see *Emergency Remedies in the Family Courts* (Family Law). As to the forms and procedures, see **Freezing injunctions** et seq under SCA 1981, s 37.

LRA 2002, section 46—This section enables the court to make an order requiring a restriction to be entered in the register for the purpose of protecting a right or claim in relation to a registered estate or charge. The order may include a direction that the entry is to have overriding priority. The order may be made, for example, ancillary to a freezing order.

****

70 Finality of judgments and orders

Every judgment and order of the county court shall, except as provided by this or any other Act or as may be prescribed, be final and conclusive between the parties.

Amendments—CCA 2013, s 17, Sch 9.

Scope—A judgment or order of the County Court is final and cannot be altered by the court, except by consent (*Irving v Askew* (1870) LR 5 QB 208), although the court is entitled to amend the judgment to explain the sense of an ambiguous phrase which might be misunderstood (*Lowery v Walker* [1911] AC 10, HL), and accidental slips and errors may be corrected (*Chessum & Sons v Gordon* [1901] 1 KB 694, CA). A judgment or order may be set aside on appeal to the Court of Appeal (see s 77). If an error of the court is alleged, an appeal must be pursued to the Court of Appeal (see **Scope** under s 77).

****

PART IV
APPEALS ETC

Appeals

77 Appeals: general provisions

(1) Subject to the provisions of this section and the following provisions of this Part of this Act and to any order made by the Lord Chancellor under section 56(1) of the Access to Justice Act 1999, if any party to any proceedings in the county court is dissatisfied with the determination of a judge or jury, he may appeal from it to the Court of Appeal in such manner and subject to such conditions as may be provided by Civil Procedure Rules.

(1A) Without prejudice to the generality of the power to make rules of court, such rules may make provision for any appeal from the exercise by a judge of the county court of any power given to him by virtue of any enactment to be to another judge of the county court.

(2)–(4) *(repealed)*

(5) Subject to the provisions of this section and the following provisions of this Part of this Act, where an appeal is brought under subsection (1) in any action, an appeal may be brought under that subsection in respect of any claim or counterclaim in the action notwithstanding that there could have been no such appeal if that claim had been the subject of a separate action.

(6) In proceedings in which either the plaintiff or the defendant is claiming possession of any premises this section shall not confer any right of appeal on any question of fact if by virtue of –

(a) section 13(4) of the Landlord and Tenant Act 1954; or
(b) Cases III to IX in Schedule 4 to the Rent (Agriculture) Act 1976; or
(c) section 98 of the Rent Act 1977, as it applies to Cases 1 to 6 and 8 and 9 in Schedule 15 to that Act, or that section as extended or applied by any other enactment; or
(d) section 99 of the Rent Act 1977, as it applies to Cases 1 to 6 and 9 in Schedule 15 to that Act; or
(e) section 84(2)(a) of the Housing Act 1985; or
(ee) section 7 of the Housing Act 1988, as it applies to the grounds in Part II of Schedule 2 to that Act; or
(f) any other enactment,

the court can only grant possession on being satisfied that it is reasonable to do so.

(7) This section shall not –

(a) confer any right of appeal from any judgment or order where a right of appeal is conferred by some other enactment; or

(b) take away any right of appeal from any judgment or order where a right of appeal is so conferred,

and shall have effect subject to any enactment other than this Act.

(8) In this section –

'enactment' means an enactment whenever passed.

Amendments—Housing (Consequential Provisions) Act 1985, s 4, Sch 2, para 57(3); Housing Act 1988, s 140(1), Sch 17, para 35(2); CLSA 1990, s 125(2), Sch 17, para 15; Civil Procedure Act 1997, s 10, Sch 2, para 2(1),(2),(7); AJA 1999, s 106, Sch 15; SI 2000/1071; CCA 2013, s 17, Sch 9; SI 2016/917.

Scope—Appeals from the decision of a judge of Circuit Judge level in the Family Court lie to the Court of Appeal, in accordance with CPR 1998, Pt 52. Appeals from the decision of a judge of District Judge level in the Family Court lie to a judge of Circuit Judge level in accordance with FPR 2010, Pt 30 and PD30A: see Procedural Guide E2.

Permission to appeal—Permission to appeal to the Court of Appeal is required in all cases save for a few limited exceptions as prescribed by CPR 1998, r 52.3 and FPR 2010, r 30.3(2).

****

79 Agreement not to appeal

(1) No appeal shall lie from any judgment, direction, decision or order of a judge of the county court if, before the judgment, direction, decision or order is given or made, the parties agree, in writing signed by themselves or their legal representatives or agents, that it shall be final.

(2) *(repealed)*

Amendments—Statute Law (Repeals) Act 1986; CLSA 1990, s 125(3), Sch 18, para 49(3); CCA 2013, s 17, Sch 9.

80 Judge's note on appeal

(1) At the hearing of any proceedings in the county court in which there is a right of appeal or from which an appeal may be brought with leave, the judge shall, at the request of any party, make a note –

(a) of any question of law raised at the hearing; and

(b) of the facts in evidence in relation to any such question; and

(c) of the decision on any such question and of his determination of the proceedings.

(2) Where such a note has been taken, the judge shall (whether notice of appeal has been served or not), on the application of any party to the proceedings, and on payment by that party of such fee as may be prescribed by the fees orders, furnish him with a copy of the note, and shall sign the copy, and the copy so signed shall be used at the hearing of the appeal.

Amendments—CCA 2013, s 17, Sch 9.

Scope—If the judge refuses to supply a note he may be ordered to do so (*R v Sheffield County Court Judge* (1889) 5 TLR 303, QBD). In practice the parties may submit to the judge a note agreed by them for his approval. If an appeal alleges misconduct of the judge the notes should be submitted to the judge with any appeal notes and the judge may comment and communicate those comments to the Court of Appeal and to the parties (*Re R (A Minor) (Adoption: Parental Agreement)* [1987] 1 FLR 391, CA).

'at the request of any party' (s 80(1))—Strictly this means that the request should be made direct to the judge (*Re Lock ex parte Poppleton (No 1)* (1891) 8 Morr 44, DC), but in practice the application is made to the court clerk.

Approved transcripts for appeal—It is the duty of the appellant to include in his bundle of documents for the Court of Appeal the approved transcript of the judgment (CPR PD52C, para 3.3(h)).

81 Powers of Court of Appeal on appeal from county court

(1) On the hearing of an appeal, the Court of Appeal may draw any inference of fact and either –

(a) order a new trial on such terms as the court thinks just; or

(b) order judgment to be entered for any party; or

(c) make a final or other order on such terms as the court thinks proper to ensure the determination on the merits of the real question in controversy between the parties.

PART II

(2) Subject to Civil Procedure Rules, on any appeal from the county court the Court of Appeal may reverse or vary, in favour of a party seeking to support the judgment or order of the county court in whole or in part, any determinations made in the county court on questions of fact, notwithstanding that the appeal is an appeal on a point of law only, or any such determinations on points of law, notwithstanding that the appeal is an appeal on a question of fact only.

(3) Subsection (2) shall not enable the Court of Appeal to reverse or vary any determination, unless the party dissatisfied with the determination would have been entitled to appeal in respect of it if aggrieved by the judgment or order.

Amendments—Civil Procedure Act 1997, s 10, Sch 2, para 2(1),(8); CCA 2013, s 17, Sch 9.

Scope—The Court of Appeal has power to order a new trial (see CPR 1998, r 52.10(2)). It also has power to make or substitute a final order, and, under CPR 1998, r 52.11(2), to admit fresh evidence, where special grounds exist, as to matters that have arisen since the hearing in the court below.

****

Certiorari and prohibition

83 Stay of proceedings in case of certiorari or prohibition

(1) The grant by the High Court of leave to make an application for an order of certiorari or prohibition to the county court shall, if the High Court so directs, operate as a stay of the proceedings in question until the determination of the application, or until the High Court otherwise orders.

(2) Where any proceedings are so stayed, the county court shall from time to time adjourn the hearing of the proceedings to such day as the court thinks fit.

Amendments—CCA 2013, s 17, Sch 9.

Scope—Where an application is made either to quash a decision of the County Court by a quashing order (formerly 'certiorari') or to require the County Court to make a certain order, by a mandatory order (formerly 'mandamus'), the High Court may stay the proceedings which are the subject of judicial review (or relevant to them) until the application for judicial review is determined. This provision is to avoid the effects of an order taking place, possibly undermining the judicial review proceedings, until such an application is determined. An application to quash a decision of the County Court is likely to be rare. Where the complaint is against the decision or order, the usual course is to appeal under CCA 1984, s 77. Where it is desired to move the proceedings to the High Court, the application will usually be under CCA 1984, ss 41, 42.

84 Prohibition

(1) Where an application is made to the High Court for an order of prohibition addressed to the county court, the matter shall be finally disposed of by order.

(2) Upon any such application, no judge of the county court is to be served with notice of it or, except by the order of a judge of the High Court –

(a) be required to appear or be heard; or

(b) be liable to any order for the payment of the costs of the application;

but the application shall be proceeded with and heard in the same manner in all respects as an appeal duly brought from a decision of a judge of the county court, and notice of the application shall be given to or served upon the same parties as in the case of an order made or refused by a judge of the county court in a matter within his jurisdiction.

Amendments—CCA 2013, s 17, Sch 9.

Scope—Applications for mandatory orders (formerly 'mandamus'), quashing orders (formerly 'certiorari') and prohibiting orders (formerly 'prohibition') are made by way of application for judicial review under CPR 1998, Pt 54. Permission to make such application is required (CPR 1998, r 54.4). A mandatory order is appropriate where a judge, district judge or officer of the County Court has improperly refused or declined to perform his ordinary duty under CCA 1984, but not where he has erred in performing it. Where the complaint is against the decision, the usual course will be an appeal under CCA 1984, s 77 (see *R v Sir Donald Hurst, ex parte Smith* [1960] 2 QB 133, QBD). A prohibiting or quashing order may be granted if the County Court acts without jurisdiction or in excess of it. Such orders are rare, and an appeal is more usual; see also CCA 1984, s 83.

PART V
ENFORCEMENT OF JUDGMENTS AND ORDERS
Execution against goods

85 Execution of judgments or orders for payment of money

(1) Subject to article 8 of the High Court and County Courts Jurisdiction Order 1991, any sum of money payable under a judgment or order of the county court may be recovered, in case of default or failure of payment, forthwith or at the time or times and in the manner thereby directed, under a warrant under subsection (2).

(2) A judge of the county court, on the application of the party prosecuting any such judgment or order, shall issue a warrant of control whereby any person authorised by or on behalf of the Lord Chancellor is empowered to use the procedure in Schedule 12 to the Tribunals, Courts and Enforcement Act 2007 (taking control of goods) to recover the money payable under the judgment or order.

(2A) The person to whom a warrant under subsection (2) must be directed is to be determined in accordance with arrangements made by a person authorised by or on behalf of the Lord Chancellor.

(3) *(repealed)*

(4) It shall be the duty of every constable within his jurisdiction to assist in the execution of every such warrant.

Amendments—CLSA 1990, s 74(3); SI 1991/724; TCEA 2007, ss 62(3), 67, Sch 13, para 69; CCA 2013, s 17, Sch 9.

'Subject to article 8' (s 85(1))—HCCCJO 1991 does not apply to family proceedings (art 12(a)).

'application of the party' (s 85(2))—The procedure is contained in CPR 1998, Pts 83 and 84.

86 Execution of orders for payment by instalments

(1) Where the court has made an order for payment of any sum of money by instalments, a warrant of control to recover any of that sum shall not be issued until after default in payment of some instalment according to the order.

(2) Rules of court may prescribe the cases in which a warrant of control is to be issued if there is any such default and limit the amounts for which and the times at which a warrant of control may be issued.

(3) Except so far as may be otherwise provided by rules of court made for those purposes, a warrant or successive warrants of control may be issued if there is any such default for the whole of the said sum of money and costs then remaining unpaid or for such part as the court may order either at the time of the original order or at any subsequent time; but except so far as may be otherwise provided by such rules, warrant of control may be issued unless when it is issued the whole or some part of an instalment which has already become due remains unpaid.

Amendments—Civil Procedure Act 1997, s 10, Sch 2, para 2(1),(2); TCEA 2007, s 62(3), Sch 13, para 70.

'rules of court' (s 86(2),(3))—See CPR 1998, r 83.2(3).

87 Indorsement of amount on warrant

(1) In or upon every warrant of control issued from the county court against the goods of any person, the court shall cause to be inserted or indorsed the total amount to be recovered, inclusive of the fee for issuing the warrant but exclusive of the fees for its execution.

(2) *(repealed)*

Amendments—TCEA 2007, s 62(3), Sch 13, para 71; CCA 2013, s 17, Sch 9.

'the total amount to be levied' (s 87(1))—Where the creditor is represented by a solicitor and the warrant is issued for more than £25, a fixed sum of costs (currently £2.25 – CPR 1998, r 45.8) is endorsed on the warrant in addition to the issue fee.

88 Power to stay execution

If at any time it appears to the satisfaction of the court that any party to any proceedings is unable from any cause to pay any sum recovered against him (whether by way of satisfaction of the claim or counterclaim in the proceedings or by way of costs or otherwise), or any instalment of such a sum, the court may, in its discretion, stay any execution issued in the proceedings for such time and on such terms as the court thinks fit, and so from time to time until it appears that the cause of inability has ceased.

Similar powers—The court may for similar reasons stay the judgment or order itself, s 71(2). Enforcement of a judgment or order may be stayed pending an appeal (CPR 1998, r 52.7; FPR 2010, r 30.8) or application to set aside an order (FPR 2010, r 18.11). The High Court's power under CPR 1998, r 83.7 to stay execution against goods on the ground that there are special circumstances which render it inexpedient to enforce the judgment or order may be exercised by the County Court by virtue of ss 38 and 76, but generally the matter will be transferred to a District Registry for the application to be considered.

****

Receivers and attachment of debts

107 Receivers

(1) The power of the county court to appoint a receiver by way of equitable execution shall operate in relation to all legal estates and interests in land.

(2) The said power may be exercised in relation to an estate or interest in land whether or not a charge has been imposed on that land under section 1 of the Charging Orders Act 1979 for the purpose of enforcing the judgment, decree, order or award in question, and the said power shall be in addition to and not in derogation of any power of any court to appoint a receiver in proceedings for enforcing such a charge.

(3) Where an order under section 1 of the Charging Orders Act 1979 imposing a charge for the purpose of enforcing a judgment, decree, order or award has been registered under section 6 of the Land Charges Act 1972, subsection (4) of that section (which provides that, amongst other things, an order appointing a receiver and any proceedings pursuant to the order or in obedience to it, shall be void against a purchaser unless the order is for the time being registered under that section) shall not apply to an order appointing a receiver made either in proceedings for enforcing the charge or by way of equitable execution of the judgment, decree, order or award or, as the case may be, of so much of it as requires payment of moneys secured by the charge.

Procedure—As to the appointment of receivers, both under this section and generally, see CPR 1998, Pt 69 in *Civil Court Service* (LexisNexis).

108 Attachment of debts

(1) Subject to any order for the time being in force under subsection (4), this section applies to any deposit account, and any withdrawable share account, with a deposit-taker.

(2) In determining whether, for the purposes of the jurisdiction of the county court to attach debts for the purpose of satisfying judgments or orders for the payment of money, a sum standing to the credit of a person in an account to which this section applies is a sum due or accruing to that person and, as such, attachable in accordance with rules of court, any condition mentioned in subsection (3) which applies to the account shall be disregarded.

(3) Those conditions are –

- (a) any condition that notice is required before any money or share is withdrawn;
- (b) any condition that a personal application must be made before any money or share is withdrawn;
- (c) any condition that a deposit book or share-account book must be produced before any money or share is withdrawn; or
- (d) any other prescribed condition.

(4) The Lord Chancellor may by order make such provision as he thinks fit, by way of amendment of this section or otherwise, for all or any of the following purposes, namely –

(a) including in, or excluding from, the accounts to which this section applies accounts of any description specified in the order;

(b) excluding from the accounts to which this section applies all accounts with any particular deposit-taker so specified or with any deposit-taker of a description so specified.

(5) An order under subsection (4) shall be made by statutory instrument subject to annulment in pursuance of a resolution of either House of Parliament.

Amendments—Civil Procedure Act 1997, s 10, Sch 2, para 2(1),(2); SI 2001/3649.

'order' (s 108(1),(4),(5))—No such order has been made.

'rules of court' (s 108(2))—As to third party debt orders, see CPR Pt 72 as modified for family proceedings by FPR 2010, r 33.24.

109 Administrative and clerical expenses of garnishees

(1) Where an interim third party debt order made in the exercise of the jurisdiction mentioned in subsection (2) of the preceding section is served on a deposit-taker, it may, subject to the provisions of this section, deduct from the relevant debt or debts an amount not exceeding the prescribed sum towards its administrative and clerical expenses in complying with the order; and the right to make a deduction under this subsection shall be exercisable as from the time the interim third party debt order is served on it.

(1A) In subsection (1) 'the relevant debt or debts', in relation to an interim third party debt order served on a deposit-taker, means the amount, as at the time the order is served on it, of the debt or debts of which the whole or a part is expressed to be attached by the order.

(1B) A deduction may be made under subsection (1) in a case where the amount referred to in subsection (1A) is insufficient to cover both the amount of the deduction and the amount of the judgment debt and costs in respect of which the attachment was made, notwithstanding that the benefit of the attachment to the creditor is reduced as a result of the deduction.

(2) An amount may not in pursuance of subsection (1) be deducted or, as the case may be, retained in a case where by virtue of section 346 of the Insolvency Act 1986 or section 325 of the Companies Act 1948 or otherwise, the creditor is not entitled to retain the benefit of the attachment.

(3) In this section 'prescribed' means prescribed by an order made by the Lord Chancellor.

(4) An order under this section –

(a) may make different provision for different cases;

(b) without prejudice to the generality of paragraph (a) may prescribe sums differing according to the amount due under the judgment or order to be satisfied.

(c) may provide for this section not to apply to deposit-takers of any prescribed description.

(5) Any such order shall be made by statutory instrument subject to annulment in pursuance of a resolution of either House of Parliament.

Amendments—AJA 1985, ss 52, 67(2), Sch 8, Pt II; Insolvency Act 1986, s 439(2), Sch 14; SI 2001/3649; SI 2002/439.

'prescribed sum' (s 109(1))—The current sum is £55: SI 1996/3098.

Miscellaneous provisions as to enforcement of judgments and orders

110 Penalty for non-attendance on judgment summons

(1) If a debtor summoned to attend the county court by a judgment summons fails to attend on the day and at the time fixed for any hearing of the summons, the court may adjourn or further adjourn the summons to a specified time on a specified day and order the debtor to attend at that time on that day.

(2) If –

(a) a debtor, having been ordered under subsection (1) to attend at a specified time on a specified day, fails to do so;

(b) *(repealed)*

the court may make an order committing him to prison for a period not exceeding 14 days in respect of the failure or refusal.

(3) In any case where the court has power to make an order of committal under subsection (2) for failure to attend, he may in lieu of or in addition to making that order, order the debtor to be arrested and brought before the court either forthwith or at such time as the court may direct.

(4) A debtor shall not be committed to prison under subsection (2) for having failed to attend as required by an order under subsection (1) unless there was paid to him at the time of the service of the judgment summons, or paid or tendered to him at the time of the service of the order, such sum in respect of his expenses as may be prescribed for the purposes of this section.

(5) The court may at any time revoke an order committing a person to prison under this section and, if he is already in custody, order his discharge.

Amendments—SI 2002/439; CCA 2013, s 17, Sch 9.

Defined terms—'judgment summons': s 147.

'prescribed sum' (s 110(4))—This is 'a sum reasonably sufficient to cover his expenses in travelling to and from the court': FPR 2010, r 33.14A.

****

PART VII
COMMITTALS

118 Power to commit for contempt

(1) If any person –

(a) wilfully insults a judge of the county court, or any juror or witness, or any officer of the court during his sitting or attendance in court, or in going to or returning from the court; or

(b) wilfully interrupts the proceedings of the county court or otherwise misbehaves in court;

any officer of the court, with or without the assistance of any other person, may, by order of the judge, take the offender into custody and detain him until the rising of the court, and the judge may, if he thinks fit, –

(i) make an order committing the offender for a specified period not exceeding one month to prison; or

(ii) impose upon the offender, for every offence, a fine of an amount not exceeding £2,500,

or may both make such an order and impose such a fine.

(2) A judge of the county court may at any time revoke an order committing a person to prison under this section and, if he is already in custody, order his discharge.

(3) *(repealed)*

Amendments—Statute Law (Repeals) Act 1986; CLSA 1990, s 74(6); Criminal Justice Act 1991, s 17(3)(a), Sch 4; CCA 2013, s 17, Sch 9.

Procedure by judge upon a contempt in the face of the court—The procedure to be followed upon a contempt in the face of the court is set out in CPR 1998, r 81.16 and PD81, para 4 (civil) and FPR 2010, r 37.12 and PD37A, para 3 (family). The procedure in the PDs is distilled from a series of cases, including *King v Read and Slack* [1999] 1 FLR 425, CA and *Newman (t/a Mantella Publishing) v Modern Bookbinders Ltd* [2000] 1 WLR 2559, CA.

There are two important principles: first the need to protect the administration of justice and preserve the authority of the court (*Chapman v Honig* [1963] 2 QB 502, CA); and second the need to preserve the alleged contemnor's right to a fair trial. Contempt proceedings are criminal proceedings within the meaning of ECHR 1950, Art 6. Adopting a summary procedure to deal with a contempt in the face of the court is not, of itself, unfair or a breach of Art 6 (*Wilkinson v S* [2003] 1 WLR 1254, CA).

Invariably, it is better for the judge to deal with any disruption/contempt immediately following the procedure in CPR PD81 or FPR PD37A, as appropriate. The judge does have the option of referring the incident to another judge (in which case a witness statement will be required). However, if the judge can restore order and continue (if necessary after an adjournment) it is usually better to do so. It is crucial that the right to a fair trial is preserved (*Amberley Construction Ltd v Beamish* [2003] EWCA Civ 1267).

Contempt of Court Act 1981—See commentary to that Act.

Summons procedure—See CPR 1998, r 81.34 (civil) and FPR 2010, r 37.33 (family), which permits the issue of a summons for an alleged breach of s 118 in line with the procedure under CCA 1984, ss 14 and 92.

Sentence—The maximum sentence is limited by s 118(1)(b) to 1 month and/or a fine of £2500. In contrast, the High Court deals with contempt in the face of the court under its inherent jurisdiction and its maximum sentence, formerly unlimited, is that prescribed by CCA 1981 (2 years).

Family Court—See also Family Court (Contempt of Court) (Powers) Regulations 2014.

119 Issue and execution of orders of committal

(1) Whenever any order or warrant for the committal of any person to prison is made or issued by the county court (whether in pursuance of this or any other Act or of rules of court), the order or warrant shall be directed to the officers of the court, who shall thereby be empowered to take the body of the person against whom the order is made or warrant issued.

(2) It shall be the duty of every constable within his jurisdiction to assist in the execution of every such order or warrant.

(3) The governor of the prison mentioned in any such order or warrant shall be bound to receive and keep the person mentioned in it until he is lawfully discharged.

Amendments—Civil Procedure Act 1997, s 10, Sch 2, para 2(1),(2); CCA 2013, s 17, Sch 9.

****

121 Power of judge to order discharge

If at any time it appears to the satisfaction of the county court that any debtor arrested or confined in prison by order of the court is unable from any cause to pay any sum recovered against him (whether by way of satisfaction of a claim or counterclaim or by way of costs or otherwise), or any instalment thereof, and ought to be discharged, the court may order his discharge upon such terms (including liability to re-arrest if the terms are not complied with) as the court thinks fit.

Amendments—CCA 2013, s 17, Sch 9.

'unable from any cause to pay'—A debtor will not have been committed unless it was proved that he had the means but neglected or refused to pay (Debtors Act 1869, s 5). Any inability to pay apparent at the time of hearing the judgment summons will have been taken into account in the order made. This section allows the judge to deal with the case where further information comes to light subsequently, for example, where the debtor failed to attend the hearing and the judge proceeded in his absence.

****

PART IX
MISCELLANEOUS AND GENERAL

****

147 Interpretation

(1) In this Act, unless the context otherwise requires –

'action' means any proceedings in the county court which may be commenced as prescribed by plaint;

…

'Admiralty proceedings' means proceedings which, if commenced in the High Court, would involve the exercise of the High Court's Admiralty jurisdiction;

…

'the county court limit' means –

(a) in relation to any enactment contained in this Act for which a limit is for the time being specified by an Order under section 145, that limit,

(b) *(repealed)*

(c) in relation to any enactment contained in this Act and not within paragraph (a), the county court limit for the time being specified by any other Order in Council or order defining the limit of county court jurisdiction for the purposes of that enactment;

'court' means the county court;

'deposit-taking institution' means a person who may, in the course of his business, lawfully accept deposits in the United Kingdom;

…

'hearing' includes trial, and 'hear' and 'heard' shall be construed accordingly;

'hereditament' includes both a corporeal and an incorporeal hereditament;

…

'judgment summons' means a summons issued on the application of a person entitled to enforce a judgment or order under section 5 of the Debtors Act 1869 requiring a person, or, where two or more persons are liable under the judgment or order, requiring any one or more of them, to attend court;

'landlord', in relation to any land, means the person entitled to the immediate reversion or, if the property therein is held in joint tenancy, any of the persons entitled to the immediate reversion;

'legal representative' means a person who, for the purposes of the Legal Services Act 2007, is an authorised person in relation to an activity which constitutes the exercise of a right of audience or the conduct of litigation (within the meaning of that Act);

'matter' means every proceeding in the county court which may be commenced as prescribed otherwise than by plaint;

'officer', in relation to the county court, means any clerk, bailiff, usher or messenger in the service of that court;

…

'party' includes every person served with notice of, or attending, any proceeding, whether named as a party to that proceeding or not;

'prescribed' means prescribed by rules of court;

…

'proceedings' includes both actions and matters;

'return day' means the day appointed in any summons or proceeding for the appearance of the defendant or any other day fixed for the hearing of any proceedings;

'rules of court' means rules made under section 75;

'ship' includes any description of vessel used in navigation;

'solicitor' means solicitor of the Senior Courts.

(1A) The definition of 'deposit-taking institution' in subsection (1) must be read with –

(a) section 22 of the Financial Services and Markets Act 2000;

(b) any relevant order under that section; and

(c) Schedule 2 to that Act.

(2), (3) *(repealed)*

Amendments—MFPA 1984, s 46(3), Sch 3; Banking Act 1987, s 108(1), Sch 6, para 15; CLSA 1990, s 125(3), Sch 18, para 49(1); SI 1990/776; SI 1991/724; Statute Law (Repeals) Act 1993; Civil Procedure Act 1997, s 10, Sch 2, para 2(1),(2),(9); SI 2001/3649; SI 2002/439; Courts Act 2003, s 109, Sch 10; CRA 2005, Sch 11, para 4(1); Legal Services Act 2007, s 208(1), Sch 21, para 61; TCEA 2007, s 62(3), Sch 13, para 82; CCA 2013, s 17, Sch 9.

****

Criminal Justice and Court Services Act 2000

****

Chapter II

Children and Family Court Advisory and Support Service

11 Establishment of the Service

(1) There shall be a body corporate to be known as the Children and Family Court Advisory and Support Service (referred to in this Part as the Service) which is to exercise the functions conferred on it by virtue of this Act and any other enactment.

(2) Schedule 2 (which makes provision about the constitution of the Service, its powers and other matters relating to it) is to have effect.

(3) References in this Act or any other enactment to an officer of the Service are references to –

(a) any member of the staff of the Service appointed under paragraph 5(1)(a) of that Schedule, and

(b) any other individual exercising functions of an officer of the Service by virtue of section 13(2) or (4).

Status of Cafcass—Cafcass vested as a non-departmental public body, answerable to Parliament through the Department for Constitutional Affairs, on 1 April 2001.

'officer of the Service'—An officer of the Service is a person appointed by the Service under CJCSA 2000, Sch 2, para 5(1)(a) or authorised by the Service under s 13(2) or (4) to undertake one or more of the following functions:

(i) As a 'children and family reporter', to investigate and provide a welfare report under CA 1989, s 7(1)(a);
(ii) As an 'officer of the Service' or as a 'local authority officer', to implement a family assistance order made under CA 1989, s 16(1)(a);
(iii) As a 'children's guardian' under CA 1989, s 41(1),(2), to take appropriate steps to safeguard the interests of a child in specified proceedings;
(iv) As a 'children's guardian' under Adoption Act 1976, s 65(1) and Adoption Rules 1984, r 6(1) or (2) or r 18(1) or (2), to investigate and report in relation to safeguarding the interests of a child who is the subject of freeing or adoption proceedings;
(v) As a 'reporting officer' under AA 1976, s 65(2) and AR 1984, r 5(1) or r 17(1), to investigate and report on the attitude of a parent or guardian of a child who is the subject of freeing or adoption proceedings;
(vi) As a 'parental order reporter' under FPR 2010, rr 13.1 and 13.9 to investigate and report on the circumstances relevant under HFEA 1990 and to carry out duties under FPR 2010, r 16.35 and PD16A.

12 Principal functions of the Service

(1) In respect of family proceedings in which the welfare of children other than children ordinarily resident in Wales is or may be in question, it is a function of the Service to –

(a) safeguard and promote the welfare of the children,

(b) give advice to any court about any application made to it in such proceedings,

(c) make provision for the children to be represented in such proceedings,

(d) provide information, advice and other support for the children and their families.

(2) The Service must also make provision for the performance of any functions conferred on officers of the Service by virtue of this Act or any other enactment (whether or not they are exercisable for the purposes of the functions conferred on the Service by subsection (1)).

(3) Regulations may provide for grants to be paid by the Service to any person for the purpose of furthering the performance of any of the Service's functions.

(4) The regulations may provide for the grants to be paid on conditions, including conditions –

(a) regulating the purposes for which the grant or any part of it may be used,

(b) requiring repayment to the Service in specified circumstances.

(5) In this section, 'family proceedings' has the same meaning as in the Matrimonial and Family Proceedings Act 1984 and also includes any other proceedings which are family proceedings for the purposes of the Children Act 1989, but –

(a) references to family proceedings include (where the context allows) family proceedings which are proposed or have been concluded,

(b) *(repealed)*

Amendments—ACA 2002, s 139(1), Sch 3, para 118; CA 2004, s 40, Sch 3, paras 5, 12, 13.

'functions of the Service'—The Service is responsible for fulfilling the requirements of courts in respect of investigations and reporting, and implementing family assistance orders – see annotation to s 11 above.

The Service inherited the functions of the Official Solicitor where he was appointed to act in wardship or other proceedings under the inherent jurisdiction of the High Court; also where he accepted an invitation to investigate and report in the County Court. The representation of children in family proceedings is governed by FPR 2010, Pt 16 and PD16A.

The Service also inherited involvement of local Probation Services in additional services such as mediation or pre-court advice for families. The Service is seeking to sustain these for the time being, subject to constraints of budget and to assessment of future viability of such services. Budgetary constraints inhibit significant development of additional services.

PART II

Duty to provide guardian as soon as practicable—Section 12 does not impose on Cafcass a specific duty to individual children to allocate a guardian and does not spell out any specific timescale within which to do so. The duty is to appoint a guardian as soon as reasonably practicable, having regard to the resources of Cafcass (*R and Others v Cafcass* [2012] 2 FLR 1432, CA). See further under FPR 2010, rr 16.3 and 16.18.

****

15 Right to conduct litigation and right of audience

(1) The Service may authorise an officer of the Service of a prescribed description –

(a) to conduct litigation in relation to any proceedings in any court,

(b) to exercise a right of audience in any proceedings before any court,

in the exercise of his functions.

(2) An officer of the Service exercising a right to conduct litigation by virtue of subsection (1)(a) who would otherwise have such a right by virtue of the fact that he is a person who, for the purposes of the Legal Services Act 2007, is an authorised person in relation to that activity is to be treated as having acquired that right solely by virtue of this section.

(3) An officer of the Service exercising a right of audience by virtue of subsection (1)(b) who would otherwise have such a right by virtue of the fact that he is a person who, for the purposes of the Legal Services Act 2007, is an authorised person in relation to that activity is to be treated as having acquired that right solely by virtue of this section.

(4) In this section and section 16, 'right to conduct litigation' and 'right of audience' have the same meanings as in section 119 of the Courts and Legal Services Act 1990.

Amendments—Legal Services Act 2007, s 208(1), Sch 21, para 133.

'conduct litigation' and 'exercise a right of audience'—The legal profession has expressed concern that the power to authorise an officer of the Service to conduct litigation or exercise a right of audience might be used to supplant lawyers by officers of the Service. The Government has disavowed this and stated that the intention was to allow functions previously undertaken by staff of the Official Solicitor to continue to be performed by appropriate officers of the Service.

16 Cross-examination of officers of the Service

(1) An officer of the Service may, subject to rules of court, be cross-examined in any proceedings to the same extent as any witness.

(2) But an officer of the Service may not be cross-examined merely because he is exercising a right to conduct litigation or a right of audience granted in accordance with section 15.

'officer of the Service – witness'—This provision settles the question raised by erroneous dicta in the Court of Appeal that a Family Court welfare officer was an officer of the court who could not be required to give sworn evidence. An officer of Cafcass is not an officer of the court. The officer prepares the report and gives evidence as an investigating expert, albeit with authority to perform statutory responsibilities bestowed by the court under the appointment to act in the individual case. Hence, an officer of Cafcass who exercises a right to conduct litigation or a right of audience under CJCSA 2000, s 15, but does not submit evidence as a reporter, under CJCSA 2000, s 16(2) cannot be cross-examined. This may happen when a representative of the Director of Legal Services of Cafcass exercises legal service functions which used to be exercised by the Official Solicitor's Office.

A children and family reporter appointed to report under CA 1989, s 16(1)(a) and FPR 2010, r 16.33 must attend court as directed by the court under PD16A, para 9.4(a). A children and family reporter who does attend should give evidence as soon as possible after the case has opened (and in any event on the first day) and be released after giving evidence.

****

Domestic and Appellate Proceedings (Restriction of Publicity) Act 1968

1 Power of court hearing certain appeals and applications to sit in private

(1) Where an appeal is brought against a decision of any of the courts mentioned in subsection (4) below, or an application is made for leave to appeal against a decision of any of those courts, and that court had power to sit in private during the whole or any part of the proceedings in which the

decision was given, then, subject to subsections (2) and (3) below, the court hearing the appeal or application shall have power to sit in private during the whole or any part of the proceedings on the appeal or application.

(2) Without prejudice to the next following subsection, the court hearing the appeal or application shall give its decision and the reason for its decision in public unless there are good and sufficient grounds for giving them in private and in that case the court shall state those grounds in public.

(3) Where the decision of any of the courts mentioned in subsection (4) below against which an appeal is brought –

- (a) is a conviction, or a sentence or other order made on conviction, or
- (b) was given in the exercise of jurisdiction to punish for contempt of court,

the court hearing the appeal or any further appeal arising out of the same proceedings shall, notwithstanding that it sat in private during the whole of any part of the proceedings on the appeal, state in open court the order made by it on the appeal.

(4) The courts referred to in subsections (1) and (3) above are the Court of Appeal, the High Court, the Crown Court, the family court, the county court and a magistrates' court.

(5) An application to a court to sit in private during the whole of any part of the proceedings on such an appeal or application as is mentioned in subsection (1) above shall be heard in private unless the court otherwise directs.

(6) The powers conferred on a court by this section shall be in addition to any other power of the court to sit in private.

(7) In this section references to a power to sit in private are references to a power to sit in camera or in chambers, but the power conferred by this section on a court which has no power to sit in chambers is a power to sit in camera only.

(8) In this section 'appeal' includes appeal by case stated, and references to a court include references to a judge exercising the powers of a court.

Amendments—Courts Act 1971, s 56, Sch 8, para 58, Sch 11, Pt IV; SI 2013/294; CCA 2013, s 17, Schs 9, 10.

PART II

2 Restriction of publicity for legitimacy proceedings etc and certain proceedings by a wife for maintenance

(1) The following provisions of this section shall have effect with a view to preventing or restricting publicity for –

- (a) *(repealed)*
- (b) proceedings under section 22 of that Act (which relates to proceedings by a wife against her husband for maintenance), including any proceedings begun before the said commencement and carried on under that section and any proceedings for the discharge or variation of an order made or deemed to have been made under that section or for the temporary suspension of any provision of any such order or the revival of the operation of any provision so suspended;
- (c) proceedings under section 27 of the Matrimonial Causes Act 1973 (which relates to proceedings by a wife against her husband, or by a husband against his wife, for financial provision) and any proceedings for the discharge or variation of an order made under that section or for the temporary suspension of any provision of any such order or the revival of the operation of any provision so suspended;
- (d) proceedings under Part III of the Family Law Act 1986;
- (da) proceedings under Part 9 of Schedule 5 to the Civil Partnership Act 2004 (provision corresponding to the provision referred to in paragraph (c) above);
- (db) proceedings under section 58 of the 2004 Act (declarations as to subsistence etc. of civil partnership).
- (e) *(repealed)*

(2) *(repealed)*

(3) Section 1(1)(b) of the Judicial Proceedings (Regulation of Reports) Act 1926 (which restricts the reporting of matrimonial causes) shall extend to any such proceedings as are mentioned in subsection (1) above subject, in the case of the proceedings mentioned in subsection (1)(d) or (db) to the modification that the matters allowed to be printed or published by virtue of sub-paragraph (ii) of the said section 1(1)(b) shall be particulars of the declaration sought by a petition (instead of a concise statement of the charges, defences and counter-charges in support of which evidence has been given).

Amendments—MPPA 1970, s 42(1), Sch 2, para 3; MCA 1973, ss 53, 54, Sch 1, Sch 2, para 7(1), Sch 3; FLA 1986, s 68, Sch 1, para 9, Sch 2; FLRA 1987, s 33, Sch 2, para 19, Sch 4; CSPSSA 2000, s 85, Sch 9; CPA 2004, s 261(1), Sch 27, para 29.

****

Domestic Proceedings and Magistrates' Courts Act 1978

ARRANGEMENT OF SECTIONS

PART I
MATRIMONIAL PROCEEDINGS IN MAGISTRATES' COURTS

Section		Page
	Powers of court to make orders for financial provision for parties to a marriage and children of the family	
1	Grounds of application for financial provision	811
2	Powers of court to make orders for financial provision	811
3	Matters to which the court is to have regard in exercising its powers under s 2	812
4	Duration of orders for financial provision for a party to a marriage	813
5	Age limit on making orders for financial provision for children and duration of such orders	813
6	Orders for payments which have been agreed by the parties	815
7	Powers of court where parties are living apart by agreement	816
	Powers of court as to the custody etc of children	
8	Restrictions on making of orders under this Act: welfare of children	817
	Interim orders	
19	Interim orders	818
	Variation, revocation and cessation of orders etc	
20	Variation, revival and revocation of orders for periodical payments	819
20ZA	Variation of orders for periodical payments: further provisions	821
20A	Revival of orders for periodical payments	821
25	Effect on certain orders of parties living together	822
	Reconciliation	
26	Reconciliation	822
	Provisions relating to the High Court and county court	
28	Powers of High Court and family court in relation to certain orders under Part I	823
	Provisions relating to procedure, jurisdiction and enforcement	
30	Provisions as to jurisdiction and procedure	823
32	Enforcement etc of orders for payment of money	823
35	Orders for repayment in certain cases of sums paid after cessation of order by reason of remarriage or formation of civil partnership	824

PART V
SUPPLEMENTARY PROVISIONS

88 Interpretation 825

PART I
MATRIMONIAL PROCEEDINGS IN MAGISTRATES' COURTS

Powers of court to make orders for financial provision for parties to a marriage and children of the family

1 Grounds of application for financial provision

Either party to a marriage may apply to the family court for an order under section 2 of this Act on the ground that the other party to the marriage –

(a) has failed to provide reasonable maintenance for the applicant; or

(b) has failed to provide, or to make a proper contribution towards, reasonable maintenance for any child of the family; or

(c) has behaved in such a way that the applicant cannot reasonably be expected to live with the respondent; or

(d) has deserted the applicant.

Amendments—MFPA 1984, s 46(1), Sch 1, para 21; CCA 2013, s 17, Sch 11.

Defined terms—'child', 'child of the family': s 88(1); 'live with': s 88(2).

Procedure on application—For the procedure to be followed, see FPR 2010, Pt 9 and PD9A in Part III. Unless an exemption applies, applicants are required to attend a mediation information assessment meeting (MIAM) before making an application (CFA 2014, s 10(1); FPR 2010, Pt 3, Ch 3; PD3A, para 13(1)(e)).

Fee payable—See FPFO 2008, fee 11.1.

2 Powers of court to make orders for financial provision

(1) Where on an application for an order under this section the applicant satisfies the court of any ground mentioned in section 1 of this Act, the court may, subject to the provisions of this Part of this Act, make any one or more of the following orders, that is to say –

(a) an order that the respondent shall make to the applicant such periodical payments, and for such term, as may be specified in the order;

(b) an order that the respondent shall pay to the applicant such lump sum as may be so specified;

(c) an order that the respondent shall make to the applicant for the benefit of a child of the family to whom the application relates, or to such a child, such periodical payments, and for such term, as may be so specified;

(d) an order that the respondent shall pay to the applicant for the benefit of a child of the family to whom the application relates, or to such a child, such lump sum as may be so specified.

(2) Without prejudice to the generality of subsection (1)(b) or (d) above, an order under this section for the payment of a lump sum may be made for the purpose of enabling any liability or expenses reasonably incurred in maintaining the applicant, or any child of the family to whom the application relates, before the making of the order to be met.

(3) The amount of any lump sum required to be paid by an order under this section shall not exceed £1,000 or such larger amount as the Lord Chancellor may from time to time by order fix for the purposes of this subsection.

(4) An order made by the Lord Chancellor under this section –

(a) shall be made only after consultation with the Lord Chief Justice;

(b) shall be made by statutory instrument and be subject to annulment in pursuance of a resolution of either House of Parliament.

(5) The Lord Chief Justice may nominate a judicial office holder (as defined in section 109(4) of the Constitutional Reform Act 2005) to exercise his functions under this section.

Amendments—SI 1988/1069; SI 1992/709; CRA 2005, ss 15(1), 146, Sch 4, para 96, Sch 18, Pt 2.

Defined terms—'child', 'child of the family': s 88(1).

Scope—This section defines the powers of lay justices to order periodical payments and lump sum payments to either party or to a child of the family. Separate but complementary provision for orders for financial provision for children is contained in CA 1989, Sch 1. The courts' powers in respect of child maintenance under this Act and under CA 1989 are subject to the radical restrictions imposed by CSA 1991. However, proceedings under CA 1989 are to be allocated to district judges (FC(CDB)R 2014, Sch 1, para 2(d)).

'the applicant satisfies the court' (s 2(1))—For the procedure where the respondent fails to appear see FPR 2010, r 27.4. The court is entitled to consider written details of the respondent's means where the respondent does not appear and the applicant agrees the details but, if the applicant does not agree with the information supplied in this way, the case should be adjourned and the respondent required to attend (*Whittingstall v Whittingstall* [1990] 2 FLR 368, FD). For power to change the application to an agreed application, see s 6(4).

'the court may … make any one or more of the following orders' (s 2(1))—Although an apparent discretion is given to the court, it has been held that there is a duty to exercise this power where the applicant has proved his case (*Hill v Hill* (1972) 116 Sol Jo 565, DC). Before making an order, the court is obliged under s 26 to consider the possibility of reconciliation.

Form of order—If an order is made, it should include a statement that the ground of the application is found to be true (*Wilcox v Wilcox* (1902) 66 JP 166, DC; *Dodd v Dodd* [1906] P 189, PDAD). If there is a finding of desertion, the date of commencement of desertion should be included in the order (*Fengl v Fengl* [1914] P 274, DC). Where the person against whom an order is to be made is a member of Her Majesty's forces, see the Army Act 1955, ss 144 and 150–152, the Air Force Act 1955, ss 144 and 150–152 and *Barnish v Barnish* (1976) Fam Law 174, FD. Further guidance is given in Home Office Circulars 251/1970, 12/1982 (Royal Navy and Royal Marines) and 25/1986.

Lump sums (s 2(1)(b))—The general power to order payments by instalments appears to apply equally to lump sums (MFPA 1984, s 31F(5); see s 22 for the power to vary the instalments). Even though a payer does not have capital resources, the court may order a lump sum payment provided it has had regard to the payer's ability to pay from income (or potential income).

'a child of the family to whom the application relates' (s 2(1)(c))—These words seem to indicate that financial provision for children under this Act is dependent upon an application being made in respect of them and may not be awarded where the application relates only to the applicant spouse.

Method of payment—See MEA 1991, s 1 for the requirement for payment to be ordered directly between the parties, through the designated officer, by standing order (or similar method) or by attachment of earnings.

3 Matters to which the court is to have regard in exercising its powers under s 2

(1) Where an application is made for an order under section 2 of this Act, it shall be the duty of the court, in deciding whether to exercise its powers under that section and, if so, in what manner, to have regard to all the circumstances of the case, first consideration being given to the welfare while a minor of any child of the family who has not attained the age of eighteen.

(2) As regards the exercise of its powers under subsection (1)(a) or (b) of section 2, the court shall in particular have regard to the following matters –

(a) the income, earning capacity, property and other financial resources which each of the parties to the marriage has or is likely to have in the foreseeable future, including in the case of earning capacity any increase in that capacity which it would in the opinion of the court be reasonable to expect a party to the marriage to take steps to acquire;

(b) the financial needs, obligations and responsibilities which each of the parties to the marriage has or is likely to have in the foreseeable future;

(c) the standard of living enjoyed by the parties to the marriage before the occurrence of the conduct which is alleged as the ground of the application;

(d) the age of each party to the marriage and the duration of the marriage;

(e) any physical or mental disability of either of the parties to the marriage;

(f) the contributions which each of the parties has made or is likely in the foreseeable future to make to the welfare of the family, including any contribution by looking after the home or caring for the family;

(g) the conduct of each of the parties, if that conduct is such that it would in the opinion of the court be inequitable to disregard it.

(3) As regards the exercise of its power under subsection (1)(c) or (d) of section 2, the court shall in particular have regard to the following matters –

(a) the financial needs of the child;

(b) the income, earning capacity (if any), property and other financial resources of the child;
(c) any physical or mental disability of the child;
(d) the standard of living enjoyed by the family before the occurrence of the conduct which is alleged as the ground of the application;
(e) the manner in which the child was being and in which the parties to the marriage expected him to be educated or trained;
(f) the matters mentioned in relation to the parties to the marriage in paragraphs (a) and (b) of subsection (2) above.

(4) As regards the exercise of its power under section 2 in favour of a child of the family who is not the child of the respondent, the court shall also have regard –

(a) to whether the respondent has assumed any responsibility for the child's maintenance and, if he did, to the extent to which, and the basis on which, he assumed that responsibility and to the length of time during which he discharged that responsibility;
(b) to whether in assuming and discharging that responsibility the respondent did so knowing that the child was not his own child;
(c) to the liability of any other person to maintain the child.

Amendments—MFPA 1984, s 9.

Defined terms—'child of the family': s 88(1).

Scope—This section outlines the matters to which the court is to have regard in making an order under s 2. It follows (with only minor modifications) the guidelines set out in MCA 1973 (particularly s 25) and so the principles followed by judges in divorce proceedings are of equal application to lay justices when making maintenance orders (*Macey v Macey* (1982) 3 FLR 7, FD).

For those cases where jurisdiction is retained by the courts, there is no express duty to apply Child Maintenance Service formula to establish a starting-point for maintenance but the likely amount of child support maintenance which would be payable may provide the court with useful and 'strongly persuasive' information (*E v C (Child Maintenance)* [1996] 1 FLR 472, FD). There are three 'ranging shots': the prescribed figures set out in the National Foster Care Allowance (see latest rates at *www.gov.uk/foster-carers/help-with-the-cost-of-fostering*), in the DWP allowances, and the child maintenance calculator (see *www.gov.uk/calculate-your-child-maintenance*). The court finds it helpful to know all three figures. Good reasons must exist for any substantial differences between maintenance calculations and maintenance orders.

'shall in particular have regard' (s 3(2))—The procedure to be adopted should be for the court to make a finding upon each of the factors contained in the section. Each of the factors should then be balanced in order to arrive at a just and reasonable order (*Vasey v Vasey* [1985] FLR 596, CA).

4 Duration of orders for financial provision for a party to a marriage

(1) The term to be specified in any order made under section 2(1)(a) of this Act shall be such term as the court thinks fit except that the term shall not begin earlier than the date of the making of the application for the order and shall not extend beyond the death of either of the parties to the marriage.

(2) Where the order is made under the said section 2(1)(a) and the marriage of the parties affected by the order is subsequently dissolved or annulled but the order continues in force, the order shall, notwithstanding anything in it, cease to have effect on the remarriage of, or formation of a civil partnership by, the party in whose favour it was made, except in relation to any arrears due under the order on the date of the remarriage or formation of the civil partnership.

Amendments—CPA 2004, s 261(1), Sch 27, para 57.

Revival of orders—The power to revive an order under s 20(6) is restricted to orders that have been temporarily suspended. An expired term order cannot be revived.

5 Age limit on making orders for financial provision for children and duration of such orders

(1) Subject to subsection (3) below, no order shall be made under section 2(1)(c) or (d) of this Act in favour of a child who has attained the age of eighteen.

(2) The term to be specified in an order made under section 2(1)(c) of this Act in favour of a child may begin with the date of the making of an application for the order in question or any later date or a date ascertained in accordance with subsection (5) or (6) below but –

(a) shall not in the first instance extend beyond the date of the birthday of the child next following his attaining the upper limit of the compulsory school age (construed in accordance with section 8 of the Education Act 1996) unless the court considers that in the circumstances of the case the welfare of the child requires that it should extend to a later date; and

(b) shall not in any event, subject to subsection (3) below, extend beyond the date of the child's eighteenth birthday.

(3) The court –

(a) may make an order under section 2(1)(c) or (d) of this Act in favour of a child who has attained the age of eighteen, and

(b) may include in an order made under section 2(1)(c) of this Act in relation to a child who has attained that age a provision for extending beyond the date when the child will attain that age the term for which by virtue of the order any payments are to be made to or for the benefit of that child,

if it appears to the court –

(i) that the child is, or will be, or if such an order or provision were made would be receiving instruction at an educational establishment or undergoing training for a trade, profession or vocation, whether or not he is also, or will also be, in gainful employment; or

(ii) that there are special circumstances which justify the making of the order or provision.

(4) Any order made under section 2(1)(c) of this Act in favour of a child shall, notwithstanding anything in the order, cease to have effect on the death of the person liable to make payments under the order.

(5) Where –

(a) a maintenance calculation ('the current calculation') is in force with respect to a child; and

(b) an application is made for an order under section 2(1)(c) of this Act –

(i) in accordance with section 8 of the Child Support Act 1991; and

(ii) before the end of the period of 6 months beginning with the making of the current calculation,

the term to be specified in any such order made on that application may be expressed to begin on, or at any time after, the earliest permitted date.

(6) For the purposes of subsection (5) above, 'the earliest permitted date' is whichever is the later of –

(a) the date 6 months before the application is made; or

(b) the date on which the current calculation took effect or, where successive maintenance calculations have been continuously in force with respect to a child, on which the first of those calculations took effect.

(7) Where –

(a) a maintenance calculation ceases to have effect by or under any provision of the Child Support Act 1991; and

(b) an application is made, before the end of the period of 6 months beginning with the relevant date, for an order under section 2(1)(c) of this Act in relation to a child with respect to whom that maintenance calculation was in force immediately before it ceased to have effect,

the term to be specified in any such order, or in any interim order under section 19 of this Act, made on that application, may begin with the date on which that maintenance calculation ceased to have effect, or any later date.

(8) In subsection (7)(b) above –

(a) where the maintenance calculation ceased to have effect, the relevant date is the date on which it so ceased

(b) *(repealed)*

Amendments—MFPA 1984, s 9(2); SI 1993/623; Education Act 1996, s 582(1), Sch 37, para 138; CSPSSA 2000, ss 26, 85, Sch 3, para 4, Sch 9.

Defined terms—'child': s 88(1).

Scope—This section sets out the permissible duration of an order for financial provision for a child. An existing maintenance calculation terminates when the child ceases to be a 'child' under CSA 1991, s 55. A calculation will be cancelled by the Secretary of State in the event that one or more of the person with care, the non-resident parent or the child leaves the jurisdiction (Child Support (Maintenance Arrangements and Jurisdiction) Regulations 1992, reg 7). For power to backdate to the termination or cancellation of the calculation, see DPMCA 1978, s 5(7). For power to backdate a 'top-up' order under CSA 1991, s 8(6), see DPMCA 1978, s 5(5).

Revival of orders—There are limited powers to revive an expired order (see s 20A).

6 Orders for payments which have been agreed by the parties

(1) Either party to a marriage may apply to the family court for an order under this section on the ground that either the party making the application or the other party to the marriage has agreed to make such financial provision as may be specified in the application and, subject to subsection (3) below, the court on such an application may, if –

(a) it is satisfied that the applicant or the respondent, as the case may be, has agreed to make that provision, and

(b) it has no reason to think that it would be contrary to the interests of justice to exercise its powers hereunder,

order that the applicant or the respondent, as the case may be, shall make the financial provisions specified in the application.

(2) In this section 'financial provision' means the provision mentioned in any one or more of the following paragraphs, that is to say –

(a) the making of periodical payments by one party to the other,

(b) the payment of a lump sum by one party to the other,

(c) the making of periodical payments by one party to a child of the family or to the other party for the benefit of such a child,

(d) the payment by one party of a lump sum to a child of the family or to the other party for the benefit of such a child,

and any reference in this section to the financial provision specified in an application made under subsection (1) above or specified by the court under subsection (5) below is a reference to the type of provision specified in the application or by the court, as the case may be, to the amount so specified as the amount of any payment to be made thereunder and, in the case of periodical payments, to the term so specified as the term for which the payments are to be made.

(3) Where the financial provision specified in an application under subsection (1) above includes or consists of provision in respect of a child of the family, the court shall not make an order under that subsection unless it considers that the provision which the applicant or the respondent, as the case may be, has agreed to make in respect of that child provides for, or makes a proper contribution towards, the financial needs of the child.

(4) A party to a marriage who has applied for an order under section 2 of this Act shall not be precluded at any time before the determination of that application from applying for an order under this section; but if an order is made under this section on the application of either party and either of them has also made an application for an order under section 2 of this Act, the application made for the order under section 2 shall be treated as if it had been withdrawn.

(5) Where on an application under subsection (1) above the court decides –

(a) that it would be contrary to the interests of justice to make an order for the making of the financial provision specified in the application, or

(b) that any financial provision which the applicant or the respondent, as the case may be, has agreed to make in respect of a child of the family does not provide for, or make a proper contribution towards, the financial needs of that child,

but it is of the opinion –

(i) that it would not be contrary to the interests of justice to make an order for the making of some other financial provision specified by the court, and

(ii) that, in so far as that other financial provision contains any provision for a child of the family, it provides for, or makes a proper contribution towards, the financial needs of that child,

then if both the parties agree, the court may order that the applicant or the respondent, as the case may be, shall make that other financial provision.

(6) Subject to subsection (8) below, the provisions of section 4 of this Act shall apply in relation to an order under this section which requires periodical payments to be made to a party to a marriage for his own benefit as they apply in relation to an order under section 2(1)(a) of this Act.

(7) Subject to subsection (8) below, the provisions of section 5 of this Act shall apply in relation to an order under this section for the making of financial provision in respect of a child of the family as they apply in relation to an order under section 2(1)(c) or (d) of this Act.

(8) Where the court makes an order under this section which contains provision for the making of periodical payments and, by virtue of subsection (4) above, an application for an order under section 2 of this Act is treated as if it had been withdrawn, then the term which may be specified as the term for which the payments are to be made may begin with the date of the making of the application for the order under section 2 or any later date.

(9) Where the respondent is not present or represented by counsel or solicitor at the hearing of an application for an order under subsection (1) above, the court shall not make an order under this section unless there is produced to the court such evidence as may be prescribed by rules of court of –

(a) the consent of the respondent to the making of the order,

(b) the financial resources of the respondent, and

(c) in a case where the financial provision specified in the application includes or consists of provision in respect of a child of the family to be made by the applicant to the respondent for the benefit of the child or to the child, the financial resources of the child.

Amendments—MFPA 1984, s 10; Courts Act 2003, Sch 8, para 191; CCA 2013, s 17, Sch 11.

Defined terms—'child', 'child of the family': s 88(1).

Form of application—The form of application and the procedure on application is prescribed by the FPR 2010.

Method of payment—See under s 2.

Lump sums (s 6(2)(b))—The amount of any agreed lump sum is not limited by this section. Contrast the limitation imposed under s 2. The general power to order payment by instalments appears to apply to payment of lump sums under this section (MFPA 1984, s 31F(5)); for the power to vary instalments see s 22.

Relationship with applications under s 2 (s 6(4))—It is possible to make an application under this section while an application under s 2 is outstanding; s 6(4) prescribes the procedure to be adopted in such circumstances.

'such evidence as may be prescribed' (s 6(9))—FPR 2010, r 9.26 prescribes the evidence that must be produced.

Fee payable—See FPFO 2008, fee 11.1.

7 Powers of court where parties are living apart by agreement

(1) Where the parties to a marriage have been living apart for a continuous period exceeding three months, neither party having deserted the other, and one of the parties has been making periodical payments for the benefit of the other party or of a child of the family, that other party may apply to the family court for an order under this section, and any application made under this subsection shall specify the aggregate amount of the payments so made during the period of three months immediately preceding the date of the making of the application.

(2) Where on an application for an order under this section the court is satisfied that the respondent has made the payments specified in the application, the court may, subject to the provisions of this Part of this Act, make one or both of the following orders, that is to say –

(a) an order that the respondent shall make to the applicant such periodical payments, and for such term, as may be specified in the order;

(b) an order that the respondent shall make to the applicant for the benefit of a child of the family to whom the application relates, or to such a child, such periodical payments, and for such term, as may be so specified.

(3) The court in the exercise of its powers under this section –

(a) shall not require the respondent to make payments which exceed in aggregate during any period of three months the aggregate amount paid by him for the benefit of the applicant or a child of the family during the period of three months immediately preceding the date of the making of the application;

(b) shall not require the respondent to make payments to or for the benefit of any person which exceed in amount the payments which the court considers that it would have required the respondent to make to or for the benefit of that person on an application under section 1 of this Act;

(c) shall not require payments to be made to or for the benefit of a child of the family who is not a child of the respondent unless the court considers that it would have made an order in favour of that child on an application under section 1 of this Act.

(4) Where on an application under this section the court considers that the orders which it has the power to make under this section –

(a) would not provide reasonable maintenance for the applicant, or

(b) if the application relates to a child of the family, would not provide, or make a proper contribution towards reasonable maintenance for that child,

the court shall refuse to make an order under this section, but the court may treat the application as if it were an application for an order under section 2 of this Act.

(5) The provisions of section 3 of this Act shall apply in relation to an application for an order under this section as they apply in relation to an application for an order under section 2 of this Act subject to the modification that for the reference in subsection (2)(c) of the said section 3 to the occurrence of the conduct which is alleged as the ground of the application there shall be substituted a reference to the living apart of the parties to the marriage.

(6) The provisions of section 4 of this Act shall apply in relation to an order under this section which requires periodical payments to be made to the applicant for his own benefit as they apply in relation to an order under section 2(1)(a) of this Act.

(7) The provisions of section 5 of this Act shall apply in relation to an order under this section for the making of periodical payments in respect of a child of the family as they apply in relation to an order under section 2(1)(c) of this Act.

Amendments—MFPA 1984, s 46(1), Sch 1, para 22; CCA 2013, s 17, Sch 11.

Defined terms—'child of the family': s 88(1); 'marriage': s 88(3).

Method of payment—See under s 2.

Fee payable—See FPFO 2008, fee 11.1.

Powers of court as to the custody etc of children

8 Restrictions on making of orders under this Act: welfare of children

Where an application is made by a party to a marriage for an order under section 2, 6 or 7 of this Act, then, if there is a child of the family who is under the age of eighteen, the court shall not dismiss or make a final order on the application until it has decided whether to exercise any of its powers under the Children Act 1989 with respect to the child.

Amendments—CA 1989, s 108(5), Sch 13, para 36.

Defined terms—'child', 'child of the family': s 88(1).

'dismiss or make a final order'—An interim order under s 19 is not prohibited.

****

Interim orders

19 Interim orders

(1) Where an application is made for an order under section 2, 6 or 7 of this Act –

(a) the family court at any time before making a final order on, or dismissing the application,

(b), (c) *(repealed)*

shall, subject to the provisions of this Part of this Act, have the

(i) power to make an order (in this Part of this Act referred to as an 'interim maintenance order') which requires the respondent to make to the applicant or to any child of the family who is under the age of eighteen, or to the applicant for the benefit of such a child, such periodical payments as the court thinks reasonable;

(ii) *(repealed)*

(2) *(repealed)*

(3) An interim maintenance order may provide for payments to be made from such date as the court may specify, except that, subject to section 5(5) and (6) of this Act, the date shall not be earlier than the date of the making of the application for an order under section 2, 6 or 7 of this Act.

(3A) Where an application is made for an order under section 6 of this Act by the party to the marriage who has agreed to make the financial provision specified in the application –

(a) subsection (1) shall apply as if the reference in paragraph (i) to the respondent were a reference to the applicant and the references to the applicant were references to the respondent; and

(b) subsection (3) shall apply accordingly.

(4) *(repealed)*

(5) Subject to subsection (6) below, an interim order made on an application for an order under section 2, 6 or 7 of this Act shall cease to have effect on whichever of the following dates occurs first, that is to say –

(a) the date, if any, specified for the purpose in the interim order;

(b) the date of the expiration of the period of three months beginning with the date of the making of the interim order;

(c) the date on which the family court either makes a final order on or dismisses the application.

(6) Where an interim order made under subsection (1) above would, but for this subsection, cease to have effect by virtue of subsection (5)(a) or (b) above, the family court shall have power by order to provide that the interim order shall continue in force for a further period, and any order continued in force under this subsection shall cease to have effect on whichever of the following dates occurs first, that is to say –

(a) the date, if any specified for the purpose in the order made under this subsection;

(b) the date of the expiration of the period of three months beginning with the date of the making of the order under this subsection or, if more than one order has been made under this subsection with respect to the application, beginning with the date of the making of the first of those orders;

(c) the date on which the court either makes a final order on, or dismisses, the application.

(7) Not more than one interim maintenance order may be made with respect to any application for an order under section 2, 6 or 7 of this Act, but without prejudice to the powers of the court under this section on any further such application.

(8) No appeal shall lie from the making of or refusal to make, the variation of or refusal to vary, or the revocation of or refusal to revoke, an interim maintenance order.

(9) *(repealed)*

Amendments—MFPA 1984, s 46(1), Sch 1, para 24; CA 1989, s 108(5),(7), Sch 13, para 37, Sch 15; SI 1993/623; SI 2009/871; CCA 2013, s 17, Sch 11.

Defined terms—'child', 'child of the family': s 88(1).

'an order' (s 19(1))—Only one interim order may be made with respect to an application (s 19(7)) but there is power under s 19(6) to extend the original interim order for up to a further 3 months.

'if more than one order has been made' (s 19(6)(b))—While only one interim order may be made, a number of extension orders is permissible provided that the aggregate period of extension orders does not exceed 3 months.

Variation, revocation and cessation of orders etc

20 Variation, revival and revocation of orders for periodical payments

(1) Where the family court has made an order under section 2(1)(a) or (c) of this Act for the making of periodical payments the court shall have power, on an application made under this section, to vary or revoke that order and also to make an order under section 2(1)(b) or (d) of this Act.

(2) Where the family court has made an order under section 6 of this Act for the making of periodical payments by a party to a marriage the court shall have power, on an application made under this section, to vary or revoke that order and also to make an order for the payment of a lump sum by that party either –

(a) to the other party to the marriage, or

(b) to a child of the family or to that other party for the benefit of that child.

(3) Where the family court has made an order under section 7 of this Act for the making of periodical payments, the court shall have power, on an application made under this section, to vary or revoke that order.

(4) *(repealed)*

(5) Where the family court has made an interim maintenance order under section 19 of this Act, the court, on an application made under this section, shall have power to vary or revoke that order, except that the court shall not by virtue of this subsection extend the period for which the order is in force.

(6) The power of the court under this section to vary an order for the making of periodical payments shall include power to suspend any provisions thereof temporarily and to revive any provision so suspended.

(7) Where the court has power by virtue of this section to make an order for the payment of a lump sum, the amount of the lump sum shall not exceed the maximum amount that may at that time be required to be paid under section 2(3) of this Act, but the court may make an order for the payment of a lump sum not exceeding that amount notwithstanding that the person required to pay the lump sum was required to pay a lump sum by a previous order under this Part of this Act.

(8) Where the court has power by virtue of subsection (2) above to make an order for the payment of a lump sum and the respondent or the applicant, as the case may be, has agreed to pay a lump sum of an amount exceeding the maximum amount that may at that time be required to be paid under section 2(3) of this Act, the court may, notwithstanding anything in subsection (7) above, make an order for the payment of a lump sum of that amount.

(9) An order made by virtue of this section which varies an order for the making of periodical payments may provide that the payments as so varied shall be made from such date as the court may specify, except that, subject to subsections (9A) and (9B) below, the date shall not be earlier than the date of the making of the application under this section.

(9A) Where –

(a) there is in force an order ('the order') –

(i) under section 2(1)(c) of this Act,

(ii) under section 6(1) of this Act making provision of a kind mentioned in paragraph (c) of section 6(2) of this Act (regardless of whether it makes provision of any other kind mentioned in that paragraph),

(iii) under section 7(2)(b) of this Act, or

(iv) which is an interim maintenance order under which the payments are to be made to a child or to the applicant for the benefit of a child;

(b) the order requires payments specified in it to be made to or for the benefit of more than one child without apportioning those payments between them;

(c) a maintenance calculation ('the calculation') is made with respect to one or more, but not all, of the children with respect to whom those payments are to be made; and

(d) an application is made, before the end of the period of 6 months beginning with the date on which the calculation was made, for the variation or revocation of the order,

the court may, in exercise of its powers under this section to vary or revoke the order, direct that the variation or revocation shall take effect from the date on which the calculation took effect or any later date.

(9B) Where –

(a) an order ('the child order') of a kind prescribed for the purposes of section 10(1) of the Child Support Act 1991 is affected by a maintenance calculation;

(b) on the date on which the child order became so affected there was in force an order ('the spousal order') –

(i) under section 2(1)(a) of this Act,

(ii) under section 6(1) of this Act making provision of a kind mentioned in section 6(2)(a) of this Act (regardless of whether it makes provision of any other kind mentioned in that paragraph),

(iii) under section 7(2)(a) of this Act, or

(iv) which is an interim maintenance order under which the payments are to be made to the applicant (otherwise than for the benefit of a child); and

(c) an application is made, before the end of the period of 6 months beginning with the date on which the maintenance calculation was made, for the spousal order to be varied or revoked,

the court may, in exercise of its powers under this section to vary or revoke the spousal order, direct that the variation or revocation shall take effect from the date on which the child order became so affected or any later date.

(9C) For the purposes of subsection (9B) above, an order is affected if it ceases to have effect or is modified by or under section 10 of the Child Support Act 1991.

(10) *(repealed)*

(11) In exercising the powers conferred by this section the court shall, so far as it appears to the court just to do so, give effect to an agreement which has been reached between the parties in relation to the application and, if there is no such agreement or if the court decides not to give effect to the agreement, the court shall have regard to all the circumstances of the case, first consideration being given to the welfare while a minor of any child of the family who has not attained the age of eighteen, and the circumstances of the case shall include any change in any of the matters to which the court was required to have regard when making the order to which the application relates or, in the case of an application for the variation or revocation of an order made under section 6 of this Act or on an appeal under section 29 of this Act, to which the court would have been required to have regard if that order had been made under section 2 of this Act.

(12) An application under this section may be made –

(a) where it is for the variation or revocation of an order under section 2, 6, 7 or 19 of this Act for periodical payments, by either party to the marriage in question; and

(b) where it is for the variation of an order under section 2(1)(c), 6 or 7 of this Act for periodical payments to or in respect of a child, also by the child himself, if he has attained the age of sixteen.

(13) *(repealed)*

Amendments—MFPA 1984, ss 9(3), 11, 46(1), Sch 1, para 25; FLRA 1987, s 33, Sch 4; CA 1989, s 108(5),(7), Sch 13, para 38, Sch 15; SI 1993/623; CSPSSA 2000, s 26, Sch 3, para 4; CCA 2013, s 17, Sch 11.

Defined terms—'child', 'child of the family': s 88(1).

Variation—The court is required to have regard to all relevant factors under s 3 on an application to vary an order (s 20(11)). The factors must be considered afresh (*Riley v Riley* [1986] 2 FLR 429, CA). The order may not be varied to include periodical payments or a lump sum payment unless the original order contained provision for periodical payments. Section 20(9B) permits an additional power to backdate an order for the variation of a spouse's payment following a child maintenance calculation under CSA 1991. As to the effect of CSA 1991 on existing orders for child maintenance, see further **Scope** under DPMCA 1978, s 2.

'give effect to any agreement' (s 20(11))—Consent may be given in writing by the party or through the party's solicitor. The court should interfere with an agreement only if a question of injustice to the parties arises (*Whitton v Devizes Justices* [1985] Fam Law 125, QBD). For procedure relating to applications for consent orders see FPR 2010, r 9.26.

Fee payable—See FPFO 2008, fees 5.1 and 5.3.

20ZA Variation of orders for periodical payments: further provisions

(1) Subject to subsections (7) and (8) below, the power of the court under section 20 of this Act to vary an order for the making of periodical payments shall include power, if the court is satisfied that payment has not been made in accordance with the order, to exercise one of its powers under section 1(4) and (4A) of the Maintenance Enforcement Act 1991.

(2)–(5) *(repealed)*

(6) Subsection (6) of section 1 of the Maintenance Enforcement Act 1991 (power of court to order that account be opened) shall apply for the purposes of subsection (1) above as it applies for the purposes of that section.

(7) Before varying the order by exercising one of its powers under section 1(4) and (4A) of the Maintenance Enforcement Act 1991, the court shall have regard to any representation made by the parties to the application.

(8), (9) *(repealed)*

(10) None of the powers of the court conferred by this section shall be exercisable in relation to an order under this Part of this Act for the making of periodical payments unless, at the time when the order was made, the person required to make the payments was ordinarily resident in England and Wales.

Amendments—Inserted by MEA 1991, s 5. Amended by SI 1994/731; AJA 1999, s 90, Sch 13, para 91; Courts Act 2003, Sch 8, para 192; CCA 2013, s 17, Sch 11.

'section 1(4) and 1(4A) of the Maintenance Enforcement Act 1991' (s 20ZA(1))—This subsection permits orders for payments direct between the parties, through the designated officer, by standing order (or similar method) or by attachment of earnings.

20A Revival of orders for periodical payments

(1) Where an order made by the family court under this Part of this Act for the making of periodical payments to or in respect of a child (other than an interim maintenance order) ceases to have effect –

- (a) on the date on which the child attains the age of sixteen, or
- (b) at any time after that date but before or on the date on which he attains the age of eighteen,

the child may apply to the court for an order for its revival.

(2) If on such an application it appears to the court that –

- (a) the child is, will be or (if an order were made under this subsection) would be receiving instruction at an educational establishment or undergoing training for a trade, profession or vocation, whether or not while in gainful employment, or
- (b) there are special circumstances which justify the making of an order under this subsection,

the court shall have power by order to revive the order from such date as the court may specify, not being earlier than the date of the making of the application.

(3) Any order revived under this section may be varied or revoked under section 20 in the same way as it could have been varied or revoked had it continued in being.

Amendments—Inserted by FLRA 1987, s 33(1), Sch 2, para 69. Amended by CA 1989, s 108(5), Sch 13, para 39; CCA 2013, s 17, Sch 11.

★★★★

25 Effect on certain orders of parties living together

(1) Where –

(a) periodical payments are required to be made to one of the parties to a marriage (whether for his own benefit or for the benefit of a child of the family) by an order made under section 2 or 6 of this Act or by an interim maintenance order made under section 19 of this Act (otherwise than on an application under section 7 of this Act),

(b) *(repealed)*

the order shall be enforceable notwithstanding that the parties to the marriage are living with each other at the date of the making of the order or that, although they are not living with each other at that date, they subsequently resume living with each other; but the order shall cease to have effect if after that date the parties continue to live with each other, or resume living with each other, for a continuous period exceeding 6 months.

(2) Where any of the following orders is made under this Part of this Act, that is to say –

(a) an order under section 2 or 6 of this Act which requires periodical payments to be made to a child of the family, or

(b) an interim maintenance order under section 19 of this Act (otherwise than on an application under section 7 of this Act) which requires periodical payments to be made to a child of the family,

(c)–(d) *(repealed)*

then, unless the court otherwise directs, the order shall continue to have effect and be enforceable notwithstanding that the parties to the marriage in question are living with each other at the date of the making of the order or that, although they are not living with each other at that date, they subsequently resume living with each other.

(3) Any order made under section 7 of this Act, and any interim maintenance order made on an application for an order under that section, shall cease to have effect if the parties to the marriage resume living with each other.

(4) Where an order made under this Part of this Act ceases to have effect by virtue of subsection (1) or (3) above or by virtue of a direction given under subsection (2) above, the family court may, on an application made by either party to the marriage, make an order declaring that the first mentioned order ceased to have effect from such date as the court may specify.

Amendments—CA 1989, s 108(5),(7), Sch 13, para 41, Sch 15; CCA 2013, s 17, Sch 11.
Defined terms—'child', 'child of the family': s 88(1); 'living with each other': s 88(2).

Reconciliation

26 Reconciliation

(1) Where an application is made for an order under section 2 of this Act the court, before deciding whether to exercise its powers under that section, shall consider whether there is any possibility of reconciliation between the parties to the marriage in question; and if at any stage of the proceedings on that application it appears to the court that there is a reasonable possibility of such a reconciliation, the court may adjourn the proceedings for such period as it thinks fit to enable attempts to be made to effect a reconciliation.

(2) Where the court adjourns any proceedings under subsection (1) above, it may request an officer of the Service (within the meaning of the Criminal Justice and Court Services Act 2000), a Welsh family proceedings officer (within the meaning given by section 35 of the Children Act 2004) or any other person to attempt to effect a reconciliation between the parties to the

marriage, and where any such request is made, that officer or other person shall report in writing to the court whether the attempt has been successful or not, but shall not include in that report any other information.

Amendments—CJCSA 2000, s 74, Sch 7, para 57; CA 2004, s 40, Sch 3, para 1.

'an officer of the Service' (s 26(2))—That is an officer of the Children and Family Court Advisory and Support Service (Cafcass).

'shall not include in that report any other information' (s 26(2))—The content of the report is restricted to the outcome of the attempt at reconciliation.

Provisions relating to the High Court and county court

27 *(repealed)*

28 Powers of High Court and family court in relation to certain orders under Part I

(1) Where after the making by the family court of an order under this Part of this Act proceedings between, and relating to the marriage of, the parties to the proceedings in which that order was made have been commenced in the High Court or the family court, then, except in the case of an order for the payment of a lump sum, the court in which the proceedings or any application made therein are or is pending may, if it thinks fit, direct that the order under this Part shall cease to have effect on such date as may be specified in the direction.

(2) *(repealed)*

(3) Nothing in this section shall be taken as prejudicing the effect of any order made by the High Court or the family court so far as it implicitly supersedes or revokes an order or part of an order made by the family court.

Amendments—FLA 1996, s 66(3), Sch 10; CCA 2013, s 17, Sch 11; SI 2014/605.

Scope—See FPR 2010, r 9.21A for duty of the court officer to note the particulars of the direction in the court's records.

29 *(repealed)*

Provisions relating to procedure, jurisdiction and enforcement

30 Provisions as to jurisdiction and procedure

(1)–(4) *(repealed)*

(5) It is hereby declared that any jurisdiction conferred on the family court by this Part of this Act is exercisable notwithstanding that any party to the proceedings is not domiciled in England.

(6) *(repealed)*

Amendments—MCA 1980, s 154, Sch 7, para 163; FLA 1986, s 68(1), Sch 1, para 24; CLSA 1990, s 125(7), Sch 20; Police and Magistrates' Courts Act 1994, s 91, Sch 8, para 29; Courts Act 2003, Sch 8, para 194; SI 2011/1484; CCA 2013, s 17, Sch 11.

31 *(repealed)*

32 Enforcement etc of orders for payment of money

(1) *(repealed)*

(2) The family court when making an order under this Part of this Act for the making of a periodical payment by one person to another may direct that it shall be made to some third party on that other person's behalf instead of directly to that other person.

(3) Any person for the time being under an obligation to make payments in pursuance of any order for the payment of money made under this Part of this Act shall give notice of any change of address to such person, if any, as may be specified in the order; and any person who without reasonable excuse fails to give such a notice shall be liable on summary conviction to a fine not exceeding level 2 on the standard scale.

(4) A person shall not be entitled to enforce through the family court the payment of any arrears due under an order made by virtue of this Part of this Act without the leave of that court if those arrears became due more than twelve months before proceedings to enforce the payment of them are begun.

(5) The court hearing an application for the grant of leave under subsection (4) above may refuse leave, or may grant leave subject to such restrictions and conditions (including conditions as to the allowing of time for payment or the making of payment by instalments) as that court thinks proper, or may remit the payment of such arrears or any part thereof.

(6) An application for the grant of leave under subsection (4) above shall be made in such manner as may be prescribed by rules of court.

Amendments—MCA 1980, s 154, Sch 7, para 164; Criminal Justice Act 1982, s 46; FLRA 1987, s 33(1), Sch 2, para 70; MEA 1991, s 11(1), Sch 2, para 3; AJA 1999, s 90, Sch 13, para 92; Courts Act 2003, Sch 8, para 195; CCA 2013, s 17, Sch 11.

'address' (s 32(3))—See FPR PD6C for disclosure of addresses by government departments.

'level 2 on the standard scale' (s 32(3))—Currently £500 (Criminal Justice Act 1982, s 37(2), as substituted).

****

35 Orders for repayment in certain cases of sums paid after cessation of order by reason of remarriage or formation of civil partnership

(1) Where –

(a) an order made under section 2(1)(a), 6 or 7 of this Act has, by virtue of section 4(2) of this Act, ceased to have effect by reason of the remarriage of, or formation of a civil partnership by, the party in whose favour it was made, and

(b) the person liable to make payments under the order made payments in accordance with it in respect of a period after the date of that remarriage or the formation of that civil partnership in the mistaken belief that the order was still subsisting,

no proceedings in respect of a cause of action arising out of the circumstances mentioned in paragraphs (a) and (b) above shall be maintainable by the person so liable or his personal representatives against the person so entitled or his personal representatives, but on an application made under this section the family court may exercise the powers conferred on it by subsection (2) below.

(2) The family court may order the respondent to an application made under this section to pay to the applicant a sum equal to the amount of the payments made in respect of the period mentioned in subsection (1)(b) above or, if it appears to the court that it would be unjust to make that order, it may either order the respondent to pay to the applicant such lesser sum as it thinks fit or dismiss the application.

(3) An application under this section may be made by the person liable to make payments under the order made under section 2(1)(a), 6 or 7 of this Act or his personal representatives and may be made against the person entitled to payments under that order or his personal representatives.

(4) An application under this section may (but need not) be made in proceedings for leave to enforce, or the enforcement of, the payment of arrears under an order made under section 2(1)(a), 6 or 7; and accordingly references in this section to the court are references to the High Court or a county court, as the circumstances require.

(5) An order under this section for the payment of any sum may provide for the payment of that sum by instalments of such amount as may be specified in the order.

(6) *(repealed)*

(7) An officer of the family court, and the collecting officer under an attachment of earnings order made to secure payments under an order made under section 2(1)(a), 6 or 7 of this Act, shall not be liable –

(a) in the case of an officer of the family court, for any act done by him, in pursuance of an order made under section 2(1)(a), 6 or 7 of this Act requiring payments to be made to the court or an officer of the court, after the date on which that order ceased to have effect by reason of the remarriage of, or formation of a civil partnership by, the person entitled to payments under it, and

(b) in the case of the collecting officer, for any act done by him after that date in accordance with any enactment or rule of court specifying how payments made to him in compliance with the attachment of earnings order are to be dealt with,

if, but only if, the act was one which he would have been under a duty to do had the order made under section 2(1)(a), 6 or 7 of this Act not ceased to have effect by reason of the remarriage or the formation of that civil partnership and the act was done before notice in writing of the fact that the person so entitled had remarried or formed a civil partnership was given to him by or on behalf of that person, the person liable to make payments under the order made under section 2(1)(a), 6 or 7 of this Act or the personal representatives of either of those persons.

(8) In this section 'collecting officer', in relation to an attachment of earnings order, means the officer of the High Court or the officer designated by the Lord Chancellor to whom a person makes payments in compliance with the order.

Amendments—AJA 1999, s 90, Sch 13, para 93; CPA 2004, s 261(1), Sch 27, para 58(1); Courts Act 2003, Sch 8, para 196; CCA 2013, s 17, Sch 11.

****

PART V
SUPPLEMENTARY PROVISIONS

****

88 Interpretation

(1) In this Act –

…

'child', in relation to one or both of the parties to a marriage, includes a child whose father and mother were not married to each other at the time of his birth;

'child of the family', in relation to the parties to a marriage, means –

(a) a child of both of those parties; and

(b) any other child, not being a child who is placed with those parties as foster parents by a local authority or voluntary organisation, who has been treated by both of those parties as a child of their family;

…

'local authority' means the council of a county (other than a metropolitan county), of a metropolitan district or of a London borough, or the Common Council of the City of London;

…

'maintenance calculation' has the same meaning as it has in the Child Support Act 1991 by virtue of section 54 of that Act as read with any regulations in force under that section.

(2) References in this Act to the parties to a marriage living with each other shall be construed as references to their living with each other in the same household.

(3) For the avoidance of doubt it is hereby declared that references in this Act to remarriage include references to a marriage which is by law void or voidable.

(4) *(repealed)*

(5) Any reference in this Act to an enactment shall be construed as a reference to that enactment as amended or extended by or under any subsequent enactment, including this Act.

Amendments—MCA 1980, s 154, Sch 7, para 167; Local Government Act 1985, s 12; FLRA 1987, Sch 2; CA 1989, ss 92, 108(5), (7), Sch 11, para 6, Sch 13, para 43, Sch 15; SI 1993/623; Justices of the Peace Act 1997, s 73(2), Sch 5, para 18; AJA 1999, s 106, Sch 15; CSPSSA 2000, s 26, Sch 3, para 4; Courts Act 2003, Sch 8, para 197; CCA 2013, s 17, Sch 11.

****

PART II

Domicile and Matrimonial Proceedings Act 1973

1 Abolition of wife's dependent domicile

(1) Subject to subsection (2) below, the domicile of a married woman as at any time after the coming into force of this section shall, instead of being the same as her husband's by virtue only of marriage, be ascertained by reference to the same factors as in the case of any other individual capable of having an independent domicile.

(2) Where immediately before this section came into force a woman was married and then had her husband's domicile by dependence, she is to be treated as retaining that domicile (as a domicile of choice, if it is not also her domicile of origin) unless and until it is changed by acquisition or revival of another domicile either on or after the coming into force of this section.

(3) This section extends to England and Wales, Scotland and Northern Ireland.

Scope—A court's matrimonial jurisdiction is founded on 'habitual residence' and 'domicile' (s 5(2)). Originally, a wife shared the domicile of her husband, and domicile alone (as distinct from habitual residence) determined jurisdiction. This position was eased in 1937 and 1949, and, with effect from 1 January 1974, this section ensures that a wife's domicile is decided independently of that of her husband. At the time of the coming into operation of the Act, a woman's domicile of dependence (on her husband) was retained as her domicile of choice (if not also her domicile of origin) until her domicile was changed (s 1(2); *IRC v Duchess of Portland* (1982) 3 FLR 293, ChD; *Plummer v IRC* [1988] 1 WLR 292, ChD; see also **Domicile** under s 5).

Domicile—This term is used in the UK and the Republic of Ireland. Elsewhere, jurisdiction depends, where applicable, on a person being a national of the Member State (Council Regulation (EC) No 2201/2003 (Brussels IIA) – see Part VI).

****

3 Age at which independent domicile can be acquired

(1) The time at which a person first becomes capable of having an independent domicile shall be when he attains the age of sixteen or marries under that age; and in the case of a person who immediately before 1 January 1974 was incapable of having an independent domicile, but had then attained the age of sixteen or been married, it shall be that date.

(2) This section extends to England and Wales and Northern Ireland (but not to Scotland).

Scope—A child is attributed a domicile of origin at birth. However, a child's domicile of origin may be replaced by a domicile of dependence until the child first becomes capable of having an independent domicile at the age of 16 or by marrying under that age. The domicile of a legitimate, legitimated or adopted dependent child follows any change in the domicile of his father (*Henderson v Henderson* [1967] P 77, PDAD; AA 1976, s 39; ACA 2002: s 67(1)). After the father's death, a child's domicile will generally follow any change in the mother's domicile (*Re Beaumont* [1893] 3 Ch 490, ChD). An illegitimate child is regarded as having a domicile of dependence being that of his mother (s 4(4)).

4 Dependent domicile of child not living with his father

(1) Subsection (2) of this section shall have effect with respect to the dependent domicile of a child as at any time after the coming into force of this section when his father and mother are alive but living apart.

(2) The child's domicile as at that time shall be that of his mother if –

(a) he then has his home with her and has no home with his father; or
(b) he has at any time had her domicile by virtue of paragraph (a) above and has not since had a home with his father.

(3) As at any time after the coming into force of this section, the domicile of a child whose mother is dead shall be that which she last had before she died if at her death he had her domicile by virtue of subsection (2) above and he has not since had a home with his father.

(4) Nothing in this section prejudices any existing rule of law as to the cases in which a child's domicile is regarded as being, by dependence, that of his mother.

(5) In this section, 'child' means a person incapable of having an independent domicile.

(6) This section extends to England and Wales, Scotland and Northern Ireland.

Amendments—Children Act 1975, s 108(1)(b), Sch 4, Pt I.

Scope—Where the parents of a legitimate, legitimated or adopted child are living apart, the child's domicile will be that of his mother if he has his home with his mother and has no home with his father or if, having once acquired his mother's domicile in this way, he has not since had his home with his father (s 4(1),(2)). Where a dependent child has his mother's domicile under s 4 and she then dies, he retains his last domicile until he has a home with his father (in which case he takes his father's domicile) or acquires an independent domicile of choice (s 4(3)). The provisions of s 4 do not affect the position of an illegitimate child who is regarded as having the domicile of his mother by dependence (s 4(4)).

5 Jurisdiction of High Court and county courts

(1) Subsections (2) to (5) below shall have effect, subject to section 6(3) and (4) of this Act, with respect to the jurisdiction of the court to entertain any of the following proceedings in relation to a marriage of a man and a woman –

(a) proceedings for divorce, judicial separation or nullity of marriage.

(b) *(repealed)*

(1A) In this Part of this Act –

'the Council Regulation' means Council Regulation (EC) No 2201/2003 of 27 November 2003 concerning jurisdiction and the recognition and enforcement of judgments in matrimonial matters and matters of parental responsibility;

'Contracting State' means –

(a) a party to the Council Regulation, that is to say, Belgium, Cyprus, Czech Republic, Germany, Greece, Spain, Estonia, France, Hungary, Ireland, Italy, Latvia, Lithuania, Luxembourg, Malta, Netherlands, Austria, Poland, Portugal, Slovakia, Slovenia, Finland, Sweden and the United Kingdom, and

(b) a party which has subsequently adopted the Council Regulation; and

'the court' means the High Court and the family court.

(2) The court shall have jurisdiction to entertain proceedings for divorce or judicial separation if (and only if) –

(a) the court has jurisdiction under the Council Regulation; or

(b) no court of a Contracting State has jurisdiction under the Council Regulation and either of the parties to the marriage is domiciled in England and Wales on the date when the proceedings are begun.

(3) The court shall have jurisdiction to entertain proceedings for nullity of marriage if (and only if) –

(a) the court has jurisdiction under the Council Regulation; or

(b) no court of a Contracting State has jurisdiction under the Council Regulation and either of the parties to the marriage –

(i) is domiciled in England and Wales on the date when the proceedings are begun; or

(ii) died before that date and either was at death domiciled in England and Wales or had been habitually resident in England and Wales throughout the period of one year ending with the date of death.

(3A)–(5) *(repealed)*

(5A) Schedule A1 (jurisdiction in relation to marriage of same sex couples) has effect.

(6) Schedule 1 to this Act shall have effect as to the cases in which matrimonial proceedings in England and Wales (whether the proceedings are in respect of the marriage of a man and a woman or the marriage of a same sex couple) are to be, or may be, stayed by the court where there are concurrent proceedings elsewhere in respect of the same marriage, and as to the other matters dealt with in that Schedule; but nothing in the Schedule –

(a) requires or authorises a stay of proceedings which are pending when this section comes into force; or

(b) prejudices any power to stay proceedings which is exercisable by the court apart from the Schedule.

(6A) Subsection (6) and Schedule 1, and any power as mentioned in subsection (6)(b), are subject to Article 19 of the Council Regulation.

Amendments—MFPA 1984, s 46(1), Sch 1, para 17; SI 2001/310; SI 2005/265; Marriage (Same Sex Couples) Act 2013, s 11, Sch 4, para 6; CCA 2013, s 17, Sch 11; Presumption of Death Act 2013, s 16, Sch 2, para 2.

Scope—This section provides the basis for jurisdiction in England and Wales for divorce, judicial separation and nullity. Jurisdiction for applying for a declaration of presumed death is governed by the Presumption of Death Act 2013, s 1(3),(4) from 1 October 2014. In the case of divorce, judicial separation or nullity, jurisdiction is based primarily on Brussels IIA, Art 3 (i e by reference to the parties' habitual residence or joint domicile in England and Wales). The sole domicile of either party is not available as a basis for jurisdiction, unless no other EU Member State has jurisdiction (s 5(2)). In the case of a divorce petition issued after 18 June 2011 on the basis of the sole domicile of one party, the English/Welsh court will not have jurisdiction to hear a claim for 'maintenance', unless the Maintenance Regulation, Art 3(a) or (b) can be relied upon (Maintenance Regulation, Art 3). The section also sets out the circumstances in which proceedings should be stayed where there are concurrent matrimonial proceedings in another jurisdiction (s 5(6),(6A)). For the corresponding jurisdictional provisions relating to civil partnerships, see CPA 2004, ss 219–223 and the Civil Partnership (Jurisdiction and Recognition of Judgments) Regulations 2005, SI 2005/3334. Same-sex marriages also have corresponding jurisdictional provisions: see s 5(5A) and Sch A1 and the Marriage (Same Sex Couples) (Jurisdiction and Recognition of Judgments) Regulations 2014.

Domicile—Domicile may be 'of origin', 'of choice' or 'of dependence'. Domicile of origin is acquired at birth and from parents. Domicile of dependence is considered under ss 3 and 4. Domicile of choice places a burden of proof on the applicant, and involves satisfying the court that a person's domicile has changed: 'The burden of establishing a change of domicile – from a domicile of origin to a domicile of choice – is ... a heavy one', per Stephen Brown LJ in *Cramer v Cramer* [1987] 1 FLR 116, CA at [120]. This heavy burden of proof to establish the loss of a domicile of origin goes beyond a mere balance of probabilities (*R v R (Divorce: Jurisdiction: Domicile)* [2006] 1 FLR 389, FD). However, the balance of probability test applies to the acquisition of a domicile of choice (*Holliday v Musa* [2010] 2 FLR 702, CA). In *Divall v Divall* [2014] 2 FLR 1104, FD, it was held that the evidential test for the abandonment of a domicile of choice is less stringent than the test applicable to an acquisition of such a domicile. See also, *Ray v Sekhri* [2014] 2 FLR 1168, CA following the principles relating to domicile summarised by Arden LJ in *Barlow Clowes International Limited v Henwood* [2008] BPIR 778, CA. For further discussion of the law relating to domicile, see *The International Family Law Practice (5th edn)* (Hodson; Family Law).

Habitual residence—This term is not defined by the Act. The leading decision in relation to the forum for divorce and finance is *Marinos v Marinos* [2007] 2 FLR 1018, FD, in which Munby J (as he then was) held that habitual residence must be defined in accordance with EC law rather than domestic law. Habitual residence is defined differently for the purposes of Brussels IIA, Arts 8 and 10. *Marinos* was followed in *V v V (Divorce: Jurisdiction)* [2011] 2 FLR 778, FD, *Tan v Choy* [2015] 1 FLR 492, CA and *Peng v Chai* [2017] 1 FLR 318, CA in preference to *Munro v Munro* [2008] 1 FLR 1613, FD. Habitual residence is more directed to a person's fixed centre of interest rather than length of residency. A person can have only one habitual residence at any one time, although a person can be resident in more than one country at any one time. Habitual residence can be lost and gained (akin to domicile) contemporaneously or virtually contemporaneously in the case of a planned, purposeful and permanent relocation from one country to another, especially where there is already existing simple residency (*Marinos*). The previous English case-law on residency and habitual residency still applies in non-EU cases. See, further, annotations to Brussels IIA, Art 3 (in Part VI) and *The International Family Law Practice (4th edn)* (Hodson; Family Law), 6.3.

Stay of proceedings (s 5(6),(6A) and Form D8N (Notes))—A petitioner is obliged to state in her petition if there are proceedings in another jurisdiction and whether they concern the marriage or are capable of affecting its validity or subsistence (Sch 1, para 7). In the event of reference being made to such proceedings, the court gives consideration to staying the proceedings as follows:

(a) *Obligatory (Sch 1, para 8) (another UK jurisdiction)* Where there are divorce/nullity proceedings within a 'related jurisdiction' (Sch 1, para 3(2)) and where certain residence conditions apply, the court in divorce proceedings *must* stay any further proceedings on application by either party to the marriage. Where an obligatory stay does not apply because the residence conditions are not met, a discretionary stay may still be possible (*A v A (forum conveniens)* [1999] 1 FLR 1, FD); or

(b) *Discretionary (Sch 1, para 9) (non-UK, non-EU proceedings)* Where there are matrimonial proceedings in another jurisdiction (other than another EU Member State), the question of a stay is discretionary. As to the balance of fairness test, see *Shemshadford v Shemshadford* [1980] Fam Law 189, FD; *Spiliada Maritime Corporation v Cansulex* [1997] AC 460, HL; *De Dampierre v De Dampierre* [1987] 2 FLR 300, HL; *Gadd v Gadd* [1985] FLR 220, CA; *Butler v Butler (Nos 1 and 2)* [1997] 2 FLR 311, CA; *Otobo v Otobo* [2003] 1 FLR 192, CA; *Wermuth v Wermuth (No 2)* [2003] 1 FLR 1029, CA; *R v R (Divorce: Hemain Injunction)* [2005] 1 FLR 386, FD; *Ella v Ella* [2007] 2 FLR 35, CA. See also *JKN v JCN (Divorce: Forum)* [2011] 1 FLR 826, FD (discretionary stays after Brussels IIA); *M v M (sub nom Mittal v Mittal)* [2014] 1 FLR 1514, CA; *T v P (Jurisdiction: Lugano Convention and Forum Conveniens)* [2013] 1 FLR 478, FD (interaction with Lugano Convention: Switzerland); *M v M* (above) (divorce petition stayed on grounds of *forum non conveniens* in favour of prior competing proceedings in non-Member State: not appropriate to extend reasoning in *Owusu v Jackson* [2005] QB 801, ECJ; *Chai v Peng* [2015] 2 FLR 424, FD and [2015] 2 FLR 412, FD, confirmed on appeal: *Peng v Chai* [2017] 1 FLR 318, CA; *Tan v Choy* [2015] 1 FLR 492, CA)).

(c) *Mandatory (Brussels IIA), Art 19(1)) (proceedings in another EU Member State)* Where there are proceedings relating to divorce, separation or nullity between the same parties in another EU Member State, the court second seised must of its own initiative stay proceedings until such time as the jurisdiction of the court first seised is established. See annotation to Brussels IIA, Arts 3 and 19.

While the stay subsists, the court still has powers to make certain financial relief orders and orders under CA 1989, s 8 (Sch 1, para 11). The stay may be discharged if it appears that the other proceedings are stayed or concluded or they have been unreasonably delayed by the party pursuing them (Sch 1, para 10).

See, generally, *The International Family Law Practice (5th edn)* (Hodson; Family Law).

Applications for stay: procedure—An application for an obligatory or discretionary stay may be made with or without notice adopting the FPR 2010, Pt 18 procedure (see FPR 2010, r 7.27 and annotations thereto). The application is made initially to a district judge who may either deal with it himself or transfer to the High Court. An application for a stay should be made at the outset and before other significant steps have been taken in the proceedings (*Mansour v Mansour* [1989] 1 FLR 418, CA). A delay carries a real risk that a stay will not be granted (*Krenge v Krenge* [1999] 1 FLR 969, FD). The court may also order a discretionary stay on its own initiative under its inherent jurisdiction where there are proceedings in a concurrent jurisdiction. This power has not been abrogated by DMPA 1973 (s 5(6)(b)). However, DMPA 1973, s 5(6A) expressly provides that s 5(6)(b) is subject to Brussels IIA, Art 19 (*Jefferson v O'Connor* [2014] 2 FLR 759, CA).

★★★★

SCHEDULE A1
JURISDICTION IN RELATION TO MARRIAGE OF SAME SEX COUPLES

1 Introduction

This Schedule shall have effect, subject to section 6(3) and (4), with respect to the jurisdiction of the court to entertain any of the following proceedings in relation to a marriage of a same sex couple –

(a) proceedings for divorce, judicial separation or nullity of marriage;
(b) proceedings for an order which ends a marriage on the ground that one of the couple is dead; and
(c) proceedings for a declaration of validity.

2 Divorce, judicial separation or annulment

(1) The court has jurisdiction to entertain proceedings for divorce or judicial separation if (and only if) –

(a) the court has jurisdiction under regulations under paragraph 5,
(b) no court has, or is recognised as having, jurisdiction under regulations under paragraph 5 and either of the married same sex couple is domiciled in England and Wales on the date when the proceedings are begun, or
(c) the following conditions are met –
  (i) the two people concerned married each other under the law of England and Wales,
  (ii) no court has, or is recognised as having, jurisdiction under regulations under paragraph 5, and
  (iii) it appears to the court to be in the interests of justice to assume jurisdiction in the case.

(2) The court has jurisdiction to entertain proceedings for nullity of marriage if (and only if) –

(a) the court has jurisdiction under regulations under paragraph 5,
(b) no court has, or is recognised as having, jurisdiction under regulations under paragraph 5 and either of the married same sex couple –
  (i) is domiciled in England and Wales on the date when the proceedings are begun, or
  (ii) died before that date and either was at death domiciled in England and Wales or had been habitually resident in England and Wales throughout the period of 1 year ending with the date of death, or
(c) the following conditions are met –
  (i) the two people concerned married each other under the law of England and Wales,
  (ii) no court has, or is recognised as having, jurisdiction under regulations under paragraph 5, and
  (iii) it appears to the court to be in the interests of justice to assume jurisdiction in the case.

(3) At any time when proceedings are pending in respect of which the court has jurisdiction by virtue of sub-paragraph (1) or (2) (or this sub-paragraph), the court also has jurisdiction to entertain other proceedings, in respect of the same marriage, for divorce, judicial separation or nullity of marriage, even though that jurisdiction would not be exercisable under subsection (1) or (2).

3 Presumption of death order

The court has jurisdiction to entertain proceedings for an order which ends a marriage on the ground that one of the couple is dead on an application made by the other of the couple ('the applicant') if (and only if) –

- (a) at the time the application is made, the High Court does not have jurisdiction to entertain an application by the applicant under section 1 of the Presumption of Death Act 2013 for a declaration that the applicant's spouse is presumed to be dead, and
- (b) the two people concerned married each other under the law of England and Wales and it appears to the court to be in the interests of justice to assume jurisdiction in the case.

4 Declaration of validity

The court has jurisdiction to entertain an application for a declaration of validity if (and only if) –

- (a) either of the parties to the marriage to which the application relates –
  - (i) is domiciled in England and Wales on the date of the application,
  - (ii) has been habitually resident in England and Wales throughout the period of 1 year ending with that date, or
  - (iii) died before that date and either was at death domiciled in England and Wales or had been habitually resident in England and Wales throughout the period of 1 year ending with the date of death, or
- (b) the two people concerned married each other under the law of England and Wales and it appears to the court to be in the interests of justice to assume jurisdiction in the case.

5 Power to make provision corresponding to EC Regulation 2201/2003

(1) The Lord Chancellor may by regulations make provision –

- (a) as to the jurisdiction of courts in England and Wales in proceedings for the divorce of, or annulment of the marriage of, a same sex couple or for judicial separation of a married same sex couple where one of the couple –
  - (i) is or has been habitually resident in a member State,
  - (ii) is a national of a member State, or
  - (iii) is domiciled in a part of the United Kingdom or the Republic of Ireland, and
- (b) as to the recognition in England and Wales of any judgment of a court of another member State which orders the divorce of, or annulment of a marriage of, a same sex couple or the judicial separation of a married same sex couple.

(2) The regulations may in particular make provision corresponding to that made by Council Regulation (EC) No 2201/2003 of 27 November 2003 in relation to jurisdiction and the recognition and enforcement of judgments in matrimonial matters.

(3) The regulations may provide that for the purposes of the regulations 'member State' means –

- (a) all member States with the exception of such member States as are specified in the regulations, or
- (b) such member States as are specified in the regulations.

(4) The regulations may make provision under sub-paragraph (1)(b) which applies even if the date of the divorce, annulment or judicial separation is earlier than the date on which this paragraph comes into force.

(5) Regulations under this paragraph are to be made by statutory instrument.

(6) A statutory instrument containing regulations under this paragraph may not be made unless a draft of the statutory instrument containing the order or regulations has been laid before, and approved by resolution of, each House of Parliament.

6 Interpretation

In this Schedule 'declaration of validity' means –

(a) a declaration as to the validity of a marriage,
(b) a declaration as to the subsistence of a marriage, or
(c) a declaration as to the validity of a divorce, annulment or judicial separation obtained outside England and Wales in respect of a marriage.

Amendments—Schedule inserted by Marriage (Same Sex Couples) Act 2013, s 11, Sch 4, para 8.

SCHEDULE 1
STAYING OF MATRIMONIAL PROCEEDINGS (ENGLAND AND WALES)

Interpretation

Corresponding stay provision for civil partnerships—The Family Procedure (Civil Partnership: Staying of Proceedings) Rules 2010 make corresponding provision for stay of civil partnership proceedings.

1 The following five paragraphs have effect for the interpretation of this Schedule.

2 'Matrimonial proceedings' means any proceedings so far as they are one or more of the five following kinds (whether relating to a marriage of a man and a woman or a marriage of a same sex couple), namely, proceedings for –

divorce,
judicial separation,
nullity of marriage,
a declaration as to the validity of a marriage of the petitioner, and
a declaration as to the subsistence of such a marriage.

Amendments—Marriage (Same Sex Couples) Act 2013, s 11, Sch 4, para 9.

3 (1) 'Another jurisdiction' means any country outside England and Wales.

(2) Related jurisdiction' means any of the following countries, namely, Scotland, Northern Ireland, Jersey, Guernsey and the Isle of Man (the reference to Guernsey being treated as including Alderney and Sark).

4 (1) References to the trial or first trial in any proceedings do not include references to the separate trial of an issue as to jurisdiction only.

(2) For purposes of this Schedule, proceedings in the court are continuing if they are pending and not stayed.

5 Any reference in this Schedule to proceedings in another jurisdiction is to proceedings in a court of that jurisdiction, and to any other proceedings in that jurisdiction, which are of a description prescribed for the purposes of this paragraph; and provision may be made by rules of court as to when proceedings of any description in another jurisdiction are continuing for the purposes of this Schedule.

6 'Prescribed' means prescribed by rules of court.

7 Duty to furnish particulars of concurrent proceedings in another jurisdiction

While matrimonial proceedings are pending in the court in respect of a marriage and the trial or first trial in those proceedings has not begun, it shall be the duty of any person who is a petitioner in the proceedings, or is a respondent and has in his answer included a prayer for relief to furnish, in such manner and to such persons and on such occasions as may be prescribed, such particulars as may be prescribed of any proceedings which –

(a) he knows to be continuing in another jurisdiction; and

(b) are in respect of that marriage or capable of affecting its validity or subsistence.

8 Obligatory stays

(1) Where before the beginning of the trial or first trial in any proceedings for divorce which are continuing in the court it appears to the court on the application of a party to the marriage –

(a) that in respect of the same marriage proceedings for divorce or nullity of marriage are continuing in a related jurisdiction; and

(b) that the parties to the marriage have resided together after they entered into it; and

(c) that the place where they resided together when the proceedings in the court were begun or, if they did not then reside together, where they last resided together before those proceedings were begun, is in that jurisdiction; and

(d) that either of the said parties was habitually resident in that jurisdiction throughout the year ending with the date on which they last resided together before the date on which the proceedings in the court were begun,

it shall be the duty of the court, subject to paragraph 10(2) below, to order that the proceedings in the court be stayed.

(2) References in sub-paragraph (1) above to the proceedings in the court are, in the case of proceedings which are not only proceedings for divorce, to the proceedings so far as they are proceedings for divorce.

Amendments—SI 2014/3168.
Defined term—'related jurisdiction': para 3(2).
Note—See annotation to s 5.

9 Discretionary stays

(1) Where before the beginning of the trial or first trial in any matrimonial proceedings, other than proceedings governed by the Council Regulation, which are continuing in the court it appears to the court –

(a) that any proceedings in respect of the marriage in question, or capable of affecting its validity or subsistence, are continuing in another jurisdiction; and

(b) that the balance of fairness (including convenience) as between the parties to the marriage is such that it is appropriate for the proceedings in that jurisdiction to be disposed of before further steps are taken in the proceedings in the court or in those proceedings so far as they consist of a particular kind of matrimonial proceedings,

the court may then, if it thinks fit, order that the proceedings in the court be stayed or, as the case may be, that those proceedings be stayed so far as they consist of proceedings of that kind.

(2) In considering the balance of fairness and convenience for the purposes of sub-paragraph (1)(b) above, the court shall have regard to all factors appearing to be relevant, including the convenience of witnesses and any delay or expense which may result from the proceedings being stayed, or not being stayed.

(3) In the case of any proceedings so far as they are proceeding for divorce, the court shall not exercise the power conferred on it by sub-paragraph (1) above while an application under paragraph 8 above in respect of the proceedings is pending.

(4) If, at any time after the beginning of the trial or first trial in any matrimonial proceedings which are pending in the court, the court declares by order that it is satisfied that a person has failed to perform the duty imposed on him in respect of the proceedings by paragraph 7 above, sub-paragraph (1) above shall have effect in relation to those proceedings and, to the other proceedings by reference to which the declaration is made, as if the words 'before the beginning of the trial or first trial' were omitted; but no action shall lie in respect of the failure of a person to perform such a duty.

Amendments—SI 2001/310.
Defined term—'another jurisdiction': para 3(1).
Note—See annotation to s 5.

10 Supplementary

(1) Where an order staying any proceedings is in force in pursuance of paragraph 8 or 9 above, the court may, if it thanks fit, on the application of a party to the proceedings, discharge the order if it appears to the court that the other proceedings by reference to which the order was made are stayed or concluded, or that a party to those other proceedings has delayed unreasonably in prosecuting them.

(2) If the court discharges an order staying any proceedings and made in pursuance of paragraph 8 above, the court shall not again stay those proceedings in pursuance of that paragraph.

11 (1) The provisions of sub-paragraphs (2) and (3) below shall apply (subject to sub-paragraph (4)) where proceedings for divorce, judicial separation or nullity of marriage are stayed by reference to proceedings in a related jurisdiction for divorce, judicial separation of nullity of marriage; and in this paragraph –

'lump sum order' means such an order as is mentioned in paragraph (f) of section 23(1) of the Matrimonial Causes Act 1973 (lump sum payment for children), being an order made under section 23(1) or (2)(a) or an order made in equivalent circumstances under Schedule 1 to the Children Act 1989 and of a kind mentioned in paragraph 1(2)(c) of that Schedule;

'the other proceedings', in relation to any stayed proceedings, means the proceedings in another jurisdiction by reference to which the stay was imposed;

'relevant order' means –

(a) an order under section 22 of the Matrimonial Causes Act 1973 (maintenance for spouse pending suit),

(b) such an order as is mentioned in paragraph (d) or (e) of section 23(1) of that Act (periodical payments for children) being an order made under section 23(1) or (2)(a) or an order in equivalent circumstances under Schedule 1 to the Children Act 1989 and of a kind mentioned in paragraph 1(2)(a) or (b) of that Schedule,

(c) an order under section 42(1)(a) of that Act (orders for the custody and education of children) or a section 8 order under the Children Act 1989, and

(d) except for the purposes of sub-paragraph (3) below, any order restraining a person removing a child out of England and Wales or out of the care of another person; and

'stayed' means stayed in pursuance of this Schedule.

(2) Where any proceedings are stayed, then, without prejudice to the effect of the stay apart from this paragraph –

(a) the court shall not have power to make a relevant order or a lump sum order in connection with the stayed proceedings except in pursuance of paragraph (c) below; and

(b) subject to paragraph (c) below, any relevant order made in connection with the stayed proceedings shall, unless the stay is previously removed or the order previously discharged, cease to have effect on the expiration of the period of three months beginning with the date on which the stay was imposed; but

(c) if the court considers that, for the purpose of dealing with circumstances needing to be dealt with urgently, it is necessary during or after that period to make a relevant order or a lump sum order in connection with the stayed proceedings or to extend or further extend the duration of a relevant order made in connection with the stayed proceedings, the court may do so and the order shall not cease to have effect by virtue of paragraph (b) above.

(3) Where any proceedings are stayed and at the time when the stay is imposed an order is in force, or at a subsequent time an order comes into force, which was made in connection with the other proceedings and provides for any of the following matters, namely, periodical payments for a spouse of the marriage in question, periodical payments for a child, or any provision which could

be made by a section 8 order under the Children Act 1989 then, on the imposition of the stay in a case where the order is in force when the stay is imposed and on the coming into force of the order in any other case –

- (a) any relevant order made in connection with the stayed proceedings shall cease to have effect in so far as it makes for a spouse or child any provision for any of those matters as respects which the same or different provision for that spouse or child is made by the other order;
- (b) the court shall not have power in connection with the stayed proceedings to make a relevant order containing for a spouse or child provision for any of those matters as respects which any provision for that spouse or child is made by the other order; and
- (c) if the other order contains provision for periodical payments for a child, the court shall not have power in connection with the stayed proceedings to make a lump sum order for that child.

(3A) Where any such order as is mentioned in paragraph (e) of section 23(1) of the Matrimonial Causes Act 1973, being an order made under section 23(1) or (2)(a) of that Act, ceases to have effect by virtue of sub-paragraph (2) or (3) above, any order made under section 24A(1) of the Act which requires the proceeds of sale of property to be used for securing periodical payments under the first mentioned order shall also cease to have effect.

(4) If any proceedings are stayed so far as they consist of matrimonial proceedings of a particular kind but are not stayed so far as they consist of matrimonial proceedings of a different kind, sub-paragraphs (2) and (3) above shall not apply to the proceedings but, without prejudice to the effect of the stay apart from this paragraph, the court shall not have power to make a relevant order or a lump sum order in connection with the proceedings so far as they are stayed; and in this sub-paragraph references to matrimonial proceedings do not include proceedings for a declaration.

(4A) Sub-paragraph (4B) applies where –

- (a) proceedings are stayed as described in sub-paragraph (1), and
- (b) at the time when the stay is imposed, a child arrangements order (within the meaning of the Children Act 1989) made in connection with the stayed proceedings is in force.

(4B) While the stay applies to the proceedings, the court may not –

- (a) make an enforcement order (within the meaning of the Children Act 1989) in relation to the child arrangements order, or
- (b) as regards an enforcement order already made in relation to the child arrangements order, exercise its powers under paragraph 9(2) of Schedule A1 to the Children Act 1989 in relation to the enforcement order.

(5) Except as provided in sub-paragraph (4B), nothing in this paragraph affects any power of the court –

- (a) to vary or discharge a relevant order so far as the order is for the time being in force; or
- (b) to enforce a relevant order as respects any period when it is or was in force; or
- (c) to make a relevant order or a lump sum order in connection with proceedings which were but are no longer stayed.

Amendments—Matrimonial Homes and Property Act 1981, s 8(3); CA 1989, s 108(5),(7), Sch 13, para 33, Sch 15; CAA 2006, s 15(1), Sch 2, paras 1, 12; CFA 2014, s 12, Sch 2.

Family Law Act 1986

ARRANGEMENT OF SECTIONS

PART I
CHILD CUSTODY

Chapter I

Section		Page
	Preliminary	
1	Orders to which Part I applies	836
	Chapter II	
	Jurisdiction of Courts in England and Wales	
2	Jurisdiction: general	838
2A	Jurisdiction in or in connection with matrimonial proceedings or civil partnership proceedings	839
3	Habitual residence or presence of child	840
5	Power of court to refuse application or stay proceedings	841
6	Duration and variation of custody orders	843
7	Interpretation of Chapter II	844
	Chapter III	
	Jurisdiction of Courts in Scotland	
8	Jurisdiction in independent proceedings	845
9	Habitual residence	845
10	Presence of child	845
11	Provisions supplementary to sections 9 and 10	845
12	Emergency jurisdiction	846
13	Jurisdiction ancillary to matrimonial proceedings	846
14	Power of court to refuse application or sist proceedings	847
15	Duration, variation and recall of orders	847
16	Tutory and curatory	847
17	Orders for delivery of child	848
18	Interpretation of Chapter III	848
	Chapter IV	
	Jurisdiction of Courts in Northern Ireland	
19	Northern Ireland: jurisdiction in cases other than divorce, dissolution of a civil partnership, etc	848
19A	Jurisdiction in or in connection with matrimonial proceedings or civil partnership proceedings	849
20	Habitual residence or presence of child	849
22	Power of court to refuse application or stay proceedings	850
23	Duration and variation of custody orders	851
24	Interpretation of Chapter IV	852
	Chapter V	
	Recognition and Enforcement	
25	Recognition of custody orders: general	852
27	Registration	853
28	Cancellation and variation of registration	853
29	Enforcement	854
30	Staying or sisting of enforcement proceedings	855
31	Dismissal of enforcement proceedings	855
32	Interpretation of Chapter V	856

Chapter VI
Miscellaneous and Supplemental

33	Power to order disclosure of child's whereabouts	856
34	Power to order recovery of child	857
36	Effect of orders restricting removal	858
37	Surrender of passports	859
38	Automatic restriction on removal of wards of court	859
39	Duty to furnish particulars of other proceedings	860
40	Interpretation of Chapter VI	860
41	Habitual residence after removal without consent etc	860
42	General interpretation of Part I	861

PART II
RECOGNITION OF DIVORCES, ANNULMENTS AND LEGAL SEPARATIONS

Divorces, annulments and judicial separations granted in the British Islands

44	Recognition in United Kingdom of divorces, annulments and judicial separations granted in the British Islands	863

Overseas divorces, annulments and legal separations

45	Recognition in the United Kingdom of overseas divorces, annulments and legal separations	863
46	Grounds for recognition	863
47	Cross-proceedings and divorces following legal separations	865
48	Proof of facts relevant to recognition	865

Supplemental

49	Modifications of Part II in relation to countries comprising territories having different systems of law	865
50	Non-recognition of divorce or annulment in another jurisdiction no bar to remarriage	866
51	Refusal of recognition	866
52	Provisions as to divorces, annulments etc obtained before commencement of Part II	867
54	Interpretation of Part II	868

PART III
DECLARATIONS OF STATUS

55	Declarations as to marital status	869
55A	Declarations of parentage	869
56	Declarations as to legitimacy or legitimation	870
57	Declarations as to adoptions effected overseas	871
58	General provisions as to the making and effect of declarations	871
59	Provisions relating to the Attorney-General	872

PART I
CHILD CUSTODY

Chapter I
Preliminary

1 Orders to which Part I applies

(1) Subject to the following provisions of this section, in this Part 'Part I order' means –

(a) a section 8 order made by a court in England and Wales under the Children Act 1989, other than an order varying or discharging such an order;

(aa) a special guardianship order made by a court in England and Wales under the Children Act 1989;

(ab) an order made under section 26 of the Adoption and Children Act 2002 (contact), other than an order varying or revoking such an order;

(ac) an order made under section 51A of the Adoption and Children Act 2002 (post-adoption contact), other than an order varying or revoking such an order;

(b) an order made by a court of civil jurisdiction in Scotland under any enactment or rule of law with respect to the residence, custody, care or control of a child, contact with or access to a child or the education or upbringing of a child, excluding –

(i) an order committing the care of a child to a local authority or placing a child under the supervision of a local authority;

(ii), (iii) (*repealed*)

(iv) an order giving parental responsibilities and parental rights in relation to a child made in the course of proceedings for the adoption of the child (other than an order made following the making of a direction under section 53(1) of the Children Act 1975);

(v) an order made under the Education (Scotland) Act 1980;

(vi) an order made under Part II and III of the Social Work (Scotland) Act 1968;

(vii) an order made under the Child Abduction and Custody Act 1985;

(viii) an order for the delivery of a child or other order for the enforcement of a Part I order;

(ix) an order relating to the guardianship of a child;

(x) an adoption order (as defined in section 28(1) of the Adoption and Children (Scotland) Act 2007);

(xi) a permanence order (as defined in subsection (2) of section 80 of that Act) which includes provision such as is mentioned in paragraph (c) of that subsection.

(c) an Article 8 order made by a court in Northern Ireland under the Children (Northern Ireland) Order 1995, other than an order varying or discharging such an order;

(d) an order made by a court in England and Wales in the exercise of the inherent jurisdiction of the High Court with respect to children –

(i) so far as it gives care of a child to any person or provides for contact with, or the education of, a child; but

(ii) excluding an order varying or revoking such an order;

(e) an order made by the High Court in Northern Ireland in the exercise of its inherent jurisdiction with respect to children –

(i) so far as it gives care of a child to any person or provides for contact with, or the education of, a child; but

(ii) excluding an order varying or discharging such an order;

(f) an order made by a court in a specified dependent territory corresponding to an order within paragraphs (a) to (e) above.

(2) In this Part 'Part I order' does not include –

(a)–(c) (*repealed*)

(3) In this Part, 'Part I order' –

(a) includes any order which would have been a custody order by virtue of this section in any form in which it was in force at any time before its amendment by the Children Act 1989 or the Children (Northern Ireland) Order 1995, as the case may be; and

(b) (subject to sections 32 and 40 of this Act) excludes any order which would have been excluded from being a custody order by virtue of this section in any such form, and

(c) excludes any order falling within subsection (1)(f) above made before the date specified opposite the name of the territory concerned in Column 2 of Schedule 1 to the Family Law Act 1986 (Dependent Territories) Order 1991, as from time to time in force.

PART II

(3A) In subsection (1)(b)(xi) 'permanence order' includes a deemed permanence order having effect by virtue of article 13(1), 14(2), 17(1) or 19(2) of the Adoption and Children (Scotland) Act 2007 (Commencement No 4, Transitional and Savings Provisions) Order 2009.

(6) Provision may be made by act of sederunt prescribing, in relation to orders within subsection (1)(b) above, what constitutes an application for the purposes of this Part.

Amendments—CA 1989, s 108, Sch 13, paras 62, 63, Sch 15; Age of Legal Capacity (Scotland) Act 1991, s 10(1), Sch 1, para 44; SI 1991/1723; Children (Scotland) Act 1995, s 105(4), Sch 4, para 41; SI 1995/756; ACA 2002, Sch 3, para 47; SI 2011/1740; CFA 2014, s 9.

'order made by a court in a specified dependent territory' (s 1(1)(f))—See FLA 1986(DT)O 1991, Sch 3. See also FPR 2010, r 32.23.

'date specified ... Family Law Act 1986 (Dependent Territories) Order 1991' (s 1(3)(c))—The territories named in Sch 1 to that Order are the Isle of Man (specified date: 14 October 1991) and Jersey (specified date: 10 July 2006).

Care orders and supervision orders under CA 1989, Pt IV—See under s 2.

Chapter II
Jurisdiction of Courts in England and Wales

2 Jurisdiction: general

(1) A court in England and Wales shall not make a section 1(1)(a) order with respect to a child unless –

(a) it has jurisdiction under the Council Regulation or the Hague Convention, or
(b) neither the Council Regulation nor the Hague Convention applies but –
  (i) the question of making the order arises in or in connection with matrimonial proceedings or civil partnership proceedings and the condition in section 2A of this Act is satisfied, or
  (ii) the condition in section 3 of this Act is satisfied.

(2) *(repealed)*

(2A) A court in England and Wales shall not have jurisdiction to make a special guardianship order under the Children Act 1989 unless the condition in section 3 of this Act is satisfied.

(2B) A court in England and Wales shall not have jurisdiction to make an order under section 26 of the Adoption and Children Act 2002 unless the condition in section 3 of this Act is satisfied.

(2C) A court in England and Wales shall not have jurisdiction to make an order under section 51A of the Adoption and Children Act 2002 unless –

(a) it has jurisdiction under the Council Regulation or the Hague Convention, or
(b) neither the Council Regulation nor the Hague Convention applies but the condition in section 3 of this Act is satisfied.

(3) A court in England and Wales shall not make a section 1(1)(d) order unless –

(a) it has jurisdiction under the Council Regulation or the Hague Convention, or
(b) neither the Council Regulation nor the Hague Convention applies but –
  (i) the condition in section 3 of this Act is satisfied, or
  (ii) the child concerned is present in England and Wales on the relevant date and the court considers that the immediate exercise of its powers is necessary for his protection.

Amendments—CA 1989, s 108(5), Sch 13, para 64; SI 2001/310; SI 2005/265; ACA 2002, Sch 3, para 47; SI 2005/3336; SI 2010/1898; CFA 2014, s 9.

Defined terms—'child': ss 7, 42(4); 'corresponding dependent territory order': s 42(1); 'the Council Regulation': s 42(1); 'matrimonial proceedings', 'relevant date': s 7; 'specified dependent territory': s 42(1).

Brussels IIA—Jurisdiction primarily depends on whether Brussels IIA applies and only if it does not does the court's jurisdiction depend on either habitual residence or physical presence: *Re A (Removal Outside Jurisdiction: Habitual Residence)* [2011] 1 FLR 2025, CA. Brussels IIA applies not only between Member States but also to cases involving the UK and non-Member States: *Re A (Jurisdiction: Return of Child)* [2014] 1 FLR 111, SC.

Supreme Court—The Supreme Court does not have jurisdiction to hear appeals from the Court of Appeal in applications made pursuant to Brussels IIA: *Re D (A Child) (Supreme Court: Jurisdiction)* [2016] 2 FLR 379, SC.

Child resident outside EU—In appropriate circumstances, the UK courts may have jurisdiction under Brussels IIA to determine the future of a child who is habitually resident outside the EU where the parties have unequivocally accepted the jurisdiction of the UK courts at the date the court is seised of the matter: *Re I (A Child) (Contact Application: Jurisdiction)*[2010] 1 FLR 361, SC; see the notes to Art 12 of the Convention. The UK courts may unusually have jurisdiction based on nationality: *Re A (Jurisdiction: Return of Child)* [2014] 1 FLR 111, SC.

Matrimonial proceedings (s 2(1))—In matrimonial proceedings, a court in England and Wales only has jurisdiction to make an order under CA 1989, s 8 (other than an order varying or discharging a s 8 order) where the conditions in FLA 1986, s 2A are satisfied. The mere fact that a court in England and Wales had jurisdiction in respect of the parents' divorce proceedings did not establish jurisdiction in relation to issues of parental responsibility, concerning children who were habitually resident in another EU country in the absence of the unequivocal consent of both parents to the same. The scheme of Brussels IIA, was to ensure that jurisdiction rested with the courts of the child's habitual residence (*Bush v Bush* [2008] 2 FLR 1437, CA). A parent may not rely on the residual jurisdiction provided for by this provision to found the court's jurisdiction for an application under CA 1989, s 8 in respect of the child or children of the family. An application under s 8 is not made 'in or in connection with' divorce proceedings: *Lachaux v Lachaux* [2017] EWHC 385 (Fam), at [146]–[149].

Care orders and supervision orders under CA 1989, Pt IV—See **Jurisdiction and case management** under CA 1989, s 31.

Proceedings under the inherent jurisdiction (s 2(3))—See also s 3 and *B v B (Scottish Contact Order: Jurisdiction to Vary)* [1996] 1 FLR 688, FD. The inclusion of the exercise of the inherent jurisdiction within the orders which can be made in s 1(1)(d) gives the English court the jurisdiction to make orders in respect of a child, provided he is habitually resident in England and Wales, even if he is an alien and not physically within the jurisdiction at the start of the proceedings (*Re S (Custody: Habitual Residence)* [1998] 1 FLR 122, HL). However, in *Re B; RB v FB and MA (Forced Marriage: Wardship: Jurisdiction)* [2008] 2 FLR 1624, FD, Hogg J made a 15 year old a ward of court and made orders for her to come to the UK, even though she was not present in the jurisdiction at the time of the order nor habitually resident in the UK. Her only connection to the UK was that her deceased father had been a British national. The judge held that the very dire circumstances in which the child found herself, namely the victim of a proposed forced marriage, justified the making of the order when the child wanted to leave Pakistan to join her half-brother in the UK and the FCO had indicated its willingness to assist provided there were court orders in place. Where the child is not present in the UK and jurisdiction is claimed solely on the basis of the child's British nationality, the Court of Appeal held that, although the limits of the jurisdiction are not definitely set down, if such jurisdiction exists, it is only in extreme circumstances: *Re N (Abduction: Appeal)* [2013] 1 FLR 457, CA. The Supreme Court has since held that there is no doubt the jurisdiction exists, insofar as it has not been taken away by the provisions of FLA 1986 (which it has been in relation to orders for care, contact and the education of a child (s 1(d)(i)) but not in respect of orders for return or recovery): *Re A (Jurisdiction: Return of Child)* [2014] 1 FLR 111, SC, at [63]. An order made under the inherent jurisdiction for a return of a child to this jurisdiction trumps a later order of a foreign court for the return of the child to that jurisdiction: *IS v DBS* [2015] EWHC 219 (Fam).

Section 2(3)(b) has been used to make mirror orders required for the implementation of orders made in a USA court, in respect of a child resident in the USA, allowing contact to take place in England – see *Re P (A Child: Mirror Orders)* [2000] 1 FLR 435, FD, where Singer J held that it was a very small step from the wording of s 2(3)(b) to make an order which expressly only had currency as far as the English courts were concerned while the child was present in the jurisdiction for the purposes of contact. In that context, assistance was to be derived from the general power of the court to make orders in anticipation of the institution of formal process. Singer J indicated that the jurisdiction should be invoked economically, and after appropriate investigation, and should be reserved to judges of the Family Division.

Loss of habitual residence—The Supreme Court has decided that the observation of Lord Brandon in *Re J (A Minor) (Abduction: Custody Rights)* 2 FLR 442, HL, that a child could lose habitual residence in a single day, is no longer applicable to the modern concept of habitual residence. Lord Wilson held that just as gaining a new habitual residence is a process of establishing the requisite degree of social integration, so losing habitual residence is a process of disengagement of the child's roots in the old state of habitual residence. Habitual residence is lost at the stage when the child achieves the requisite degree of disengagement from the old state: *Re B (A Child) (Habitual Residence: Inherent Jurisdiction)* [2016] 1 FLR 561, SC, at [45] and [54].

2A Jurisdiction in or in connection with matrimonial proceedings or civil partnership proceedings

(1) The condition referred to in section 2(1) of this Act is that the proceedings are proceedings in respect of the marriage or civil partnership of the parents of the child concerned and –

- (a) the proceedings –
  - (i) are proceedings for divorce or nullity of marriage or dissolution or annulment of a civil partnership, and
  - (ii) are continuing;
- (b) the proceedings –
  - (i) are proceedings for judicial separation or legal separation of civil partner,

PART II

(ii) are continuing,

and the jurisdiction of the court is not excluded by subsection (2) below; or

(c) the proceedings have been dismissed after the beginning of the trial but –

(i) the section 1(1)(a) order is being made forthwith, or

(ii) the application for the order was made on or before the dismissal.

(2) For the purposes of subsection (1)(b) above, the jurisdiction of the court is excluded if –

(a) after the grant of a decree of judicial separation, on the relevant date, proceedings for divorce or nullity in respect of the marriage, or

(b) after the making of a separation order, on the relevant date, proceedings for the dissolution or annulment in respect of the civil partnership,

are continuing in Scotland or Northern Ireland.

(3) Subsection (2) above shall not apply if the court in which the other proceedings there referred to are continuing has made –

(a) an order under section 13(6) or 19A(4) of this Act (not being an order made by virtue of section 13(6)(a)(i)), or a corresponding dependent territory order, or

(b) an order under section 14(2) or 22(2) of this Act, or a corresponding dependent territory order, which is recorded as being made for the purpose of enabling Part I proceedings to be taken in England and Wales with respect to the child concerned.

(4) Where a court –

(a) has jurisdiction to make a section 1(1)(a) order by virtue of section 2(1)(b)(i) of this Act, but

(b) considers that it would be more appropriate for Part I matters relating to the child to be determined outside England and Wales,

the court may by order direct that, while the order under this subsection is in force, no section 1(1)(a) order shall be made by any court by virtue of section 2(1)(b)(i) of this Act.

Amendments—Inserted by CA 1989, s 108(5), Sch 13, para 64. Amended by SI 1991/1723; SI 1995/756; SI 2005/265; SI 2005/3336.

Defined terms—'child': ss 7, 42(4); 'corresponding dependent territory order': s 42(1) (and see notes to s 42); 'matrimonial proceedings': s 7; 'Part I proceedings', 'Part I matters': s 42(7); 'relevant date': s 7; 'specified dependent territory': s 42(1) (and see notes to s 42).

General interpretation—See s 42 in the case of Pt I of the Act.

'proceedings … are continuing'—Although proceedings may be continuing and the decree absolute not yet pronounced, the court would decline jurisdiction if the continuance would not impinge on the children because the children's issues had already been decided. Where that was the case and international considerations arose, no encouragement should be given to reopening that issue within a comparatively short time. Nevertheless, the court would have jurisdiction if an urgent and serious issue arose over child protection (*Re L (Residence: Jurisdiction)* [2007] 1 FLR 1686, FD).

'dependent territory' (s 2A(3))—Within the meaning of the British Nationality Act 1981, this term is to be read as a reference to 'British overseas territory' (see British Overseas Territories Act 2002, s 1(2)).

Discretion to make order under s 2A(4)—Where the English court in principle has jurisdiction over the living arrangements for a child by reason of current divorce proceedings between the child's parents, which fact would normally deprive courts in Scotland of jurisdiction, the English court nevertheless has a discretion contained in s 2A(4) to order that it would be more appropriate for matters relating to that child to be decided in Scotland (*Re S (Jurisdiction to Stay Application)* [1995] 1 FLR 1093, FD – where in reality the child had been looked after in Scotland for many years by her maternal grandmother).

Residual jurisdiction—To fall within the 'residual jurisdiction' of ss 2 and 2A as a question connected with matrimonial or civil partnership proceedings, there must be a proximity between the divorce proceedings and the court being asked to determine a question of making an order in relation to children: *AP v TD (Relocation: Retention of Jurisdiction)* [2011] 1 FLR 1851, FD.

3 Habitual residence or presence of child

(1) The condition referred to in section 2(1)(b)(ii) of this Act is that on the relevant date the child concerned –

(a) is habitually resident in England and Wales, or

(b) is present in England and Wales and is not habitually resident in any part of the United Kingdom or a specified dependent territory, and, in either case, the jurisdiction of the court is not excluded by subsection (2) below.

(2) For the purposes of subsection (1) above, the jurisdiction of the court is excluded if, on the relevant date, matrimonial proceedings or civil partnership proceedings are continuing in a court in Scotland, Northern Ireland or a specified dependent territory in respect of the marriage or civil partnership of the parents of the child concerned.

(3) Subsection (2) above shall not apply if the court in which the other proceedings there referred to are continuing has made –

(a) an order under section 13(6) or 19A(4) of this Act (not being an order made by virtue of section 13(6)(a)(i)), or a corresponding dependent territory order, or

(b) an order under section 14(2) or 22(2) of this Act, or a corresponding dependent territory order, which is recorded as made for the purpose of enabling Part I proceedings with respect to the child concerned to be taken in England and Wales,

and that order is in force.

(4)–(6) *(repealed)*

Amendments—CA 1989, s 108(5),(7) Sch 13, paras 62, 65, Sch 15; SI 1991/1723; SI 1995/756; SI 2005/265; SI 2005/3336.

Defined terms—'child': ss 7, 42(4); 'corresponding dependent territory order': s 42(1); 'matrimonial proceedings': s 7; 'Part I proceedings', 'Part I matters': s 42(7); 'relevant date': s 7; 'specified dependent territory': s 42(1).

General interpretation—See s 42.

'proceedings are continuing'—Section 3(2) proceedings are not continuing if they have been stayed (*Re B (Court's Jurisdiction)* [2004] 2 FLR 741, CA).

'habitually resident' (s 3(1)(a))—There is no statutory definition of habitual residence, and its meaning is essentially a question of fact to be determined by reference to all the circumstances of a particular case. See **Habitual residence** under CACA 1985, Sch 1, Art 4. The Court of Appeal has clearly and helpfully summarised the firmly established principles in relation to the issue of habitual residence: *Re P-J (Abduction: Habitual Residence: Consent)* [2009] 2 FLR 1051, CA, at [26]. Habitual residence could not be founded, in respect of a child who had never been to England, on the grounds that her father was a British national and at the time of her birth her mother had a settled intention to live and become habitually resident in England: *H v H (Jurisdiction to Grant Wardship)* [2012] 1 FLR 23, CA. The issue of whether a child born abroad who had never been present in the jurisdiction, and who had been born to parents who were habitually resident in this jurisdiction, could acquire habitual residence in this jurisdiction was considered by the Supreme Court in *Re A (Jurisdiction: Return of Child)* [2014] 1 FLR 111, SC. Baroness Hale, giving the lead judgment, expressed the view 'that presence as a necessary pre-cursor to residence' was to be preferred to 'an approach which focuses on the relationship between the child and the primary carer'. The court held, however, it could not resolve that question without referring it to the European Court of Justice. The matter was remitted to the first instance judge. Parker J. determined the issue of jurisdiction on the basis of the child's British nationality and thus the need for a referral did not arise: *A v A (Return Order on the Basis of British Nationality)* [2014] 2 FLR 244, FD. Habitual residence is a question of fact that 'should not be glossed with legal concepts which would produce a different result from that which the factual enquiry would produce': see para 54 of *Re A (Children)* (above) and *Re KL (A Child)* [2014] 1 FLR 772, SC. In relation to an adolescent child, her state of mind is relevant to whether or not she has acquired habitual residence in the place where she is living. Query whether the state of mind of a younger child is also relevant in determining his habitual residence: *Re LC (Reunite: International Child Abduction Centre Intervening)* [2014] 1 FLR 1486, SC. See also *Re B (A Child) (Habitual Residence: Inherent Jurisdiction)* [2016] 1 FLR 561, SC.

Determination of jurisdiction—See the notes under s 2 above in respect of *Re F (A Child)* [2014] EWCA Civ 789.

Loss of habitual residence—See the commentary under s 2, above.

****

5 Power of court to refuse application or stay proceedings

(1) A court in England and Wales which has jurisdiction to make a Part I order may refuse an application for the order in any case where the matter in question has already been determined in proceedings outside England and Wales.

(2) Where, at any stage of the proceedings on an application made to a court in England and Wales for a Part I order, or for the variation of a Part I order, it appears to the court –

(a) that proceedings with respect to the matters to which the application relates are continuing outside England and Wales,

(b) that it would be more appropriate for those matters to be determined in proceedings to be taken outside England and Wales,

(c) that it should exercise its powers under Article 15 of the Council Regulation (transfer to a court better placed to hear the case), or

(d) that it should exercise its powers under Article 8 of the Hague Convention (request to authority in another Contracting State to assume jurisdiction),

the court may stay the proceedings on the application or (as the case may be) exercise its powers under Article 15 of the Council Regulation or Article 8 of the Hague Convention.

(2A) If the proceedings on the application are proceedings in which an activity direction has been made under section 11A of the Children Act 1989 (or an enforcement order has been made under section 11J of that Act), the court may when granting a stay under or by virtue of subsection (2) also suspend the activity direction (or the enforcement order).

(3) The court may remove a stay granted by virtue of subsection (2)(a) or (b) above if it appears to the court that there has been unreasonable delay in the taking or prosecution of the other proceedings referred to in that subsection, or that those proceedings are stayed, sisted or concluded.

(3A) The court may remove a stay granted under Article 15 of the Council Regulation only in accordance with that Article.

(3AA) The court may remove a stay granted in order for it to exercise its powers under Article 8 of the Hague Convention, and withdraw any request made by it to an authority in another Contracting State to assume jurisdiction, if –

(a) the authority in the other Contracting State does not assume jurisdiction within the period for which the court granted the stay, or

(b) the parties do not, within the period specified by the court, request the authority in the other Contracting State to assume jurisdiction.

(3B) If the stay removed under subsection (3), (3A) or (3AA) is a stay in relation to which the court suspended an activity direction made under section 11A of the Children Act 1989 (or an enforcement order made under section 11J of that Act), the court may when removing the stay under subsection (3) or (3A) also bring the suspension to an end.

(4) Nothing in this section so far as it relates to proceedings not governed by the Council Regulation shall affect any power exercisable apart from this section to refuse an application or to grant or remove a stay.

Amendments—CA 1989, s 108(5), Sch 13, para 62; SI 2001/310; SI 2005/265; CAA 2006, s 15(1), Sch 2, paras 2, 3; SI 2010/1898; CFA 2014, s 12, Sch 2.

Defined terms—'Part I order': ss 1(2),(3), 42(5),(6).

General interpretation—See s 42.

'the court may stay the proceedings' (s 5(2))—In *H v H (Minors) (Forum Conveniens) (Nos 1 and 2)* [1993] 1 FLR 958, FD, an application was made under s 5(2). In *Re V (Forum Conveniens)* [2005] 1 FLR 718, FD, the court reviewed many of the authorities and held that: (a) the principles to be applied were those set out in *Spiliada Maritime Corporation v Cansulex* [1997] AC 460; and (b) the child's interests were not paramount (but were nonetheless very important), because a choice between international jurisdictions was not 'a question with respect to the upbringing of a child' within the meaning of CA 1989 s 1(1)(a). Where an application for a stay coincided with an application to return to South Africa, in which interests of the child were paramount, the two applications stood or fell together and the correct approach was to apply the paramountcy principle and decide whether it was in the child's best interests to return to South Africa; and then, if so, to cross-check whether the criteria for a stay were satisfied: *M v M (Stay of Proceedings: Return of Children)* [2006] 1 FLR 138, FD.

In *Re S (A Minor) (Stay of Proceedings)* [1993] 2 FLR 912, CA, the Court of Appeal upheld a decision to grant a stay of English proceedings instituted by the father for a child arrangements order because similar proceedings were already in existence in Scotland. Furthermore, the Court of Appeal approved his decision to allow the father's application for a parental responsibility order to proceed in England. A parental responsibility order was not within the definition of 'Part I order' under FLA 1986 and the statutory provisions did not apply. However, the court still retained an inherent power to stay proceedings in appropriate cases. In *H v H (A Minor) (No 2) (Forum Conveniens)* [1997] 1 FCR 603, FD Bracewell J held that the court could act of its own volition, irrespective of whether or not a party had applied for a stay. A stay should not be granted unless it is demonstrated that a more appropriate forum is available elsewhere (*M v B (Residence)* [1994] 2 FLR 819, FD). Where the application for a Pt I order is in the context of matrimonial proceedings, see also DMPA 1973, Sch 1, paras 8 and 9, above. By virtue of FLA 1986, s 5(2) and DMPA 1973, Sch 1, para 9 the court *may* stay proceedings if either FLA 1986, s 5(2)(a) or (b) is satisfied. However, under DMPA 1973, Sch 1, para 8 the court is obliged to stay proceedings if the parties resided in a related jurisdiction and either of them was habitually resident there for 1 year before they separated. For further guidance, see *M v M (Abduction: England and Scotland)* [1997] 2 FLR 263, CA, where it was held that the same jurisdiction should deal both with the dissolution of the marriage and the consequential decisions regarding the welfare of the children. In relation to the applicability of Art 15, see *A v B (Jurisdiction)* [2012] 1 FLR 768, FD.

The Inner House of the Court of Session has held that the test for forum non conveniens was not the practical convenience of the witnesses, but whether the alternative forum contended for was one in which the case may be tried more suitably for the interests of all of the parties and the ends of justice. It concluded that the Scottish courts had jurisdiction as of right which jurisdiction could be abdicated only in exceptional circumstances (*RAB v MIB* [2009] 1 FLR 602, IH).

6 Duration and variation of custody orders

(1) If a Part I order made by a court in Scotland, Northern Ireland or a specified dependent territory (or a variation of such an order) comes into force with respect to child at a time when a Part I order made by a court in England and Wales has effect with respect to him, the latter order shall cease to have effect so far as it makes provision for any matter for which the same or different provision is made by (or by the variation of) the order made by the court in Scotland, Northern Ireland or the territory.

(2) Where by virtue of subsection (1) above a Part I order has ceased to have effect so far as it makes provision for any matter, a court in England or Wales shall not have jurisdiction to vary that order so as to make provision for that matter.

(3) A court in England and Wales shall not have jurisdiction to vary a Part I order if, on the relevant date, matrimonial proceedings or civil partnership proceedings are continuing in Scotland, Northern Ireland or a specified dependent territory in respect of the marriage or civil partnership of the parents of the child concerned.

(3A) Subsection (3) above shall not apply if –

- (a) the Part I order was made in or in connection with proceedings –
  - (i) for divorce or nullity in England and Wales in respect of the marriage of the parents of the child concerned; or
  - (ii) for dissolution or annulment in England and Wales in respect of the civil partnership of the parents of the child concerned; and
- (b) those proceedings are continuing.

(3B) Subsection (3) above shall not apply if –

- (a) the Part I order was made in or in connection with proceedings –
  - (i) for judicial separation in England and Wales; or
  - (ii) for a separation order in England and Wales; and
- (b) those proceedings are continuing; and
- (c) as the case may be, the decree of judicial separation has not yet been granted or the separation order has not yet been made.

(4) Subsection (3) above shall not apply if the court in which the proceedings there referred to are continuing has made –

- (a) an order under section 13(6) or 19A(4) of this Act (not being an order made by virtue of section 13(6)(a)(i)), or a corresponding dependent territory order, or
- (b) an order under section 14(2) or 22(2) of this Act, or a corresponding dependent territory order, which is recorded as made for the purpose of enabling Part I proceedings with respect to the child concerned to be taken in England and Wales,

and that order is in force.

(5) Subsection (3) above shall not apply in the case of a variation of section 1(1)(d) order if the child concerned is present in England and Wales on the relevant date and the court considers that the immediate exercise of its powers is necessary for his protection.

(5A) Subsection (7) below applies where a Part I order which is a child arrangements order (within the meaning of section 8(1) of the Children Act 1989) ceases by virtue of subsection (1) above to name a person as someone with whom a child is to live.

(6) Subsection (7) below also applies where a Part I order which is –

(a) *(repealed)*

(b) an order made in the exercise of the High Court's inherent jurisdiction with respect to children by virtue of which a person has care of a child, or

(c) an order –

(i) of a kind mentioned in section 1(3)(a) of this Act,

(ii) under which a person is entitled to the actual possession of a child,

ceases to have effect in relation to that person by virtue of subsection (1) above.

(7) Where this subsection applies, any family assistance order made under section 16 of the Children Act 1989 with respect to the child shall also cease to have effect.

(8) For the purposes of subsection (7) above the references to a family assistance order under section 16 of the Children Act 1989 shall be deemed to include a reference to an order for the supervision of a child made under –

(a) section 7(4) of the Family Law Reform Act 1969,

(b) section 44 of the Matrimonial Causes Act 1973,

(c) section 2(2)(a) of the Guardianship Act 1973,

(d) section 34(5) or 36(3)(b) of the Children Act 1975, or

(e) section 9 of the Domestic Proceedings and Magistrates' Courts Act 1978;

but this subsection shall cease to have effect once all such orders for the supervision of children have ceased to have effect in accordance with Schedule 14 to the Children Act 1989.

Amendments—CA 1989, s 108(5), Sch 13, paras 62, 66; SI 1991/1723; SI 1995/756; SI 2005/3336; CFA 2014, s 12, Sch 2.

Defined terms—'child': ss 7, 42(4); 'corresponding dependent territory order': s 42(1); 'matrimonial proceedings': s 7; 'Part I order': ss 1(2),(3), 42(5),(6); 'Part I proceedings', 'Part I matters': s 42(7); 'relevant date': s 7; 'specified dependent territory': s 42(1).

General interpretation—See s 42.

7 Interpretation of Chapter II

In this Chapter –

(a) 'child' means a person who has not attained the age of eighteen;

(aa) 'civil partnership proceedings' means proceedings for the dissolution or annulment of a civil partnership or for legal separation of the civil partners;

(b) 'matrimonial proceedings' means proceedings for divorce, nullity of marriage or judicial separation;

(c) 'the relevant date' means in relation to the making or variation of an order –

(i) where an application is made for an order to be made or varied, the date of the application (or first application, if two or more are determined together), and

(ii) where no such application is made, the date on which the court is considering whether to make or, as the case may be, vary the order; and

(d) 'section 1(1)(a) order' and 'section 1(1)(d) order' mean orders falling within section 1(1)(a) and (d) of this Act respectively.

Amendments—CA 1989, s 108(5), Sch 13, para 67; SI 2005/3336.

'the relevant date' (s 7(c))—Jurisdiction primarily depends on whether Brussels IIA applies and only if it does not does the court's jurisdiction depend on either habitual residence or physical presence: *Re A (Removal Outside Jurisdiction: Habitual Residence)* [2011] 1 FLR 2025, CA. Subject to the foregoing, presence in the jurisdiction on the 'relevant date', for any reason and brought about in any way, is sufficient to give jurisdiction to make a 'Part I order' under the Act (ie a s 8 order 'other than an order varying or discharging such an order') (*Re F (Residence Order: Jurisdiction)* [1995] 2 FLR 518, FD, but see *Re S (Residence Order: Forum Conveniens)* [1995] 1 FLR 314, FD, where Thorpe J expressed concern at the possibility of jurisdiction turning on 'what might be either chance or strategic manoeuvre' resulting in the child's presence on the date of issue of proceedings). In *Re H (Residence Order: Placement Out of Jurisdiction)* [2006] 1 FLR 1140, FD, it was agreed that the court had jurisdiction, where at the date of the hearing, the children were living in the UAE under an interim care order. The local authority were entitled at any time to recall them to England and thus they were still habitually resident in England and Wales and had not acquired habitual residence in the UAE. Where no application has been made, the relevant date under s 7(c)(ii) is that on which the court is considering whether to make or vary the order (*Re F (Residence Order: Jurisdiction)*, above – where the relevant date was the date of the directions hearing and not the date of the substantive hearing of the abduction issue). Similarly where an application has been made, the relevant date is when the court first addresses its mind to the application and makes directions, even if the order ultimately made is different in terms to that originally sought (*Re J (Abduction: Declaration of Wrongful Removal)* [1999] 2 FLR 653, FD).

Chapter III
Jurisdiction of Courts in Scotland

8 Jurisdiction in independent proceedings

A court in Scotland may entertain an application for a Part I order otherwise than in matrimonial proceedings only if it has jurisdiction under section 9, 10, 12 or 15(2) of this Act.

9 Habitual residence

Subject to section 11 of this Act, an application for a Part I order otherwise than in matrimonial proceedings may be entertained by –

(a) the Court of Session if, on the date of the application, the child concerned is habitually resident in Scotland;

(b) the sheriff if, on the date of the application, the child concerned is habitually resident in the sheriffdom.

Amendments—CA 1989, s 108, Sch 13, para 62.

10 Presence of child

Subject to section 11 of this Act, an application for a Part I order otherwise than in matrimonial proceedings may be entertained by –

(a) the Court of Session if, on the date of the application, the child concerned –
  (i) is present in Scotland; and
  (ii) is not habitually resident in any part of the United Kingdom or a specified dependent territory;

(b) the sheriff if, on the date of the application, –
  (i) the child is present in Scotland;
  (ii) the child is not habitually resident in any part of the United Kingdom or a specified dependent territory; and
  (iii) either the pursuer or the defender in the application is habitually resident in the sheriffdom.

Amendments—CA 1989, s 108, Sch 13, para 62; SI 1991/1723.

11 Provisions supplementary to sections 9 and 10

(1) Subject to subsection (2) below, the jurisdiction of the court to entertain an application for a Part I order with respect to a child by virtue of section 9, 10 or 15(2) of this Act is excluded if, on the date of the application, matrimonial proceedings are continuing in a court in any part of the United Kingdom or a specified dependent territory in respect of the marriage of the parents of the child.

(2) Subsection (1) above shall not apply in relation to an application for a Part I order if the court in which the matrimonial proceedings are continuing has made one of the following orders, that is to say –

(a) an order under section 2A(4), 13(6) or 19A(4) of the Act (not being an order made by virtue of section 13(6)(a)(ii) or a corresponding dependent territory order; or

(b) an order under section 5(2), 14(2) or 22(2) of this Act, or a corresponding dependent territory order, which is recorded as made for the purpose of enabling Part I proceedings with respect to the child concerned to be taken in Scotland or, as the case may be, in another court in Scotland,

and that order is in force.

Amendments—CA 1989, s 108, Sch 13, paras 62, 68; SI 1991/1723; SI 1995/756.

12 Emergency jurisdiction

Notwithstanding that any other court, whether within or outside Scotland, has jurisdiction to entertain an application for a Part I order, the Court of Session or the sheriff shall have jurisdiction to entertain such an application if –

(a) the child concerned is present in Scotland or, as the case may be, in the sheriffdom on the date of the application; and
(b) the Court of Session or sheriff considers that, for the protection of the child, it is necessary to make such order immediately.

Amendments—CA 1989, s 108, Sch 13, para 62.

13 Jurisdiction ancillary to matrimonial proceedings

(1) The jurisdiction of a court in Scotland to entertain an application for a Part I order in matrimonial proceedings shall be modified by the following provisions of this section.

(2) A court in Scotland shall not have jurisdiction, after the dismissal of matrimonial proceedings or after decree of absolvitor is granted therein, to entertain an application for a Part I order under section 9(1) of the Matrimonial Proceedings (Children) Act 1958 unless the application therefore was made on or before such dismissal or the granting of the decree of absolvitor.

(3) Where, after a decree of separation has been granted, an application is made in the separation process for a Part I order, the court in Scotland shall not have jurisdiction to entertain that application if, on the date of the application, proceedings for divorce or nullity of marriage in respect of the marriage concerned are continuing in another court in the United Kingdom or a specified dependent territory.

(4) A court in Scotland shall not have jurisdiction to entertain an application for the variation of a Part I order made under section 9(1) of the Matrimonial Proceedings (Children) Act 1958 if, on the date of the application, matrimonial proceedings in respect of the marriage concerned are continuing in another court in the United Kingdom or a specified dependent territory.

(5) Subsections (3) and (4) above shall not apply if the court in which the other proceedings there referred to are continuing has made –

(a) an order under section 2A(4) or 19A(4) of this Act or under subsection (6) below (not being an order made by virtue of paragraph (a)(ii) of that subsection), or a corresponding dependent territory order, or
(b) an order under section 5(2), 14(2) or 22(2) of this Act, or a corresponding dependent territory order, which is recorded as made for the purpose of enabling Part I proceedings with respect to the child concerned to be taken in Scotland or, as the case may be, in another court in Scotland, and that order is in force.

(6) A court in Scotland which has jurisdiction in matrimonial proceedings to entertain an application for a Part I order with respect to a child may make an order declining such jurisdiction if –

(a) it appears to the court with respect to that child that –
    (i) but for section 11(1) of this Act, another court in Scotland would have jurisdiction to entertain an application for a Part I order, or
    (ii) but for section 3(2), 6(3), 20(2) or 23(3) of this Act or a corresponding territory provision, a court in another part of the United Kingdom or a specified dependent territory would have jurisdiction to make a Part I order or an order varying a Part I order; and
(b) the court considers that it would be more appropriate for Part I matters relating to that child to be determined in that other court or part.

(7) The court may recall an order made under subsection (6) above.

Amendments—CA 1989, s 108, Sch 13, paras 62, 68; SI 1991/1723; SI 1995/756.

14 Power of court to refuse application or sist proceedings

(1) A court in Scotland which has jurisdiction to entertain an application for a Part I order may refuse the application in any case where the matter in question has already been determined in other proceedings.

(2) Where, at any stage of the proceedings on an application made to a court in Scotland for a Part I order, it appears to the court –

- (a) that proceedings with respect to the matter to which the application relates are continuing outside Scotland or in another court in Scotland; or
- (b) that it would be more appropriate for those matters to be determined in proceedings outside Scotland or in another court in Scotland and that such proceedings are likely to be taken there.

the court may sist the proceedings on that application.

Amendments—CA 1989, s 108, Sch 13, para 62.

15 Duration, variation and recall of orders

(1) Where, after the making by a court in Scotland of a Part I order ('the existing order') with respect to a child, –

- (a) a Part I order, or an order varying a Part I order, competently made by another court in any part of the United Kingdom or in a specified dependent territory with respect to that child; or
- (b) an order for the custody of that child which is made outside the United Kingdom and any specified dependent territory and recognised in Scotland by virtue of section 26 of this Act,

comes into force, the existing order shall cease to have effect so far as it makes provision for any matter for which the same or different provision is made by the order of the other court in the United Kingdom or in the specified dependent territory or, as the case be, the order so recognised.

(2) Subject to sections 11(1) and 13(3) and (4) of this Act, a court in Scotland which has made a Part I order ('the original order') may, notwithstanding that it would no longer have jurisdiction to make the original order, make an order varying or recalling the original order; but if the original order has by virtue of subsection (1) above ceased to have effect so far as it makes provision for any matter, the court shall not have power to vary that order under this subsection so as to make provision for that matter.

(3) In subsection (2) above, an order varying an original order means any Part I order made with respect to the same child as the original order was made.

(4) Where any person who is entitled to the custody of a child under a Part I order made by a court in Scotland ceases to be so entitled by virtue of subsection (1) above, then, if there is in force an order made by a court in Scotland providing for the supervision of that child by a local authority, that order shall cease to have effect.

Amendments—CA 1989, s 108, Sch 13, para 62; SI 1991/1723; Children (Scotland) Act 1995, s 105(5), Sch 5.

Effect in relation to 'interim' child arrangements orders (s 15(1))—An 'interim' CAO is no different in principle from a CAO, particularly since CA 1989 does not recognise that there is such an order as an interim CAO; instead, the court has power to make a CAO limited in time. Therefore, by the operation of s 15(1), the making of an 'interim' CAO by an English court has the consequence that any order previously made by a Scottish court as to the living arrangements for a child no longer has any effect in law, since it makes 'provision for any matter for which the same or different provision is made by the order of the other court in the United Kingdom' (*S v S (Custody: Jurisdiction)* [1995] 1 FLR 155, FD; *T v T (Custody: Jurisdiction)* [1992] 1 FLR 43, FD).

16 Tutory and curatory

(1) Subject to subsections (2) and (3) below, an application made after the commencement of this Part for an order relating to the guardianship of a child may be entertained by –

- (a) the Court of Session if, on the date of the application, the pupil or minor is habitually resident in Scotland;

(b) the sheriff if, on the date of the application, the pupil or minor is habitually resident in the sheriffdom.

(2) Subsection (1) above shall not apply to an application for the appointment or removal of a judicial factor or of a curator bonis or any application made by such factor or curator.

(3) Subsection (1) above is without prejudice to any other ground of jurisdiction on which the Court of Session or the sheriff may entertain an application mentioned therein.

(4) Provision may be made by act of sederunt prescribing, in relation to orders relating to the guardianship of a child, what constitutes an application for the purposes of this Chapter.

Amendments—Age of Legal Capacity (Scotland) Act 1991, s 10, Sch 1, para 45.

17 Orders for delivery of child

(1) An application by one parent of a child for an order for the delivery of the child from the other parent, where the order is not sought to implement a Part I order, may be entertained by the Court of Session or a sheriff if, but only if, the Court of Session or, as the case may be, the sheriff would have jurisdiction under this Chapter to make a Part I order with respect to the child concerned.

(2) *(repealed)*

(3) Subsection (1) above shall apply to an application by one party to a marriage for an order for the delivery of the child concerned from the other party where the child is the child of one of the parties and has been accepted as one of the family by the other party as it applies to an application by one parent of a child for an order for the delivery of the child from the other parent.

Amendments—CA 1989, s 108, Sch 13, para 62; Children (Scotland) Act 1995, s 105(5), Sch 5.

18 Interpretation of Chapter III

(1) In this Chapter –

'child' means a person who has not attained the age of sixteen;

'matrimonial proceedings' means proceedings for divorce, nullity of marriage or judicial separation.

(2) In this Chapter, 'the date of the application' means, where two or more applications are pending, the date of the first of those applications; and, for the purposes of this subsection, an application is pending until a Part I order or, in the case of an application mentioned in section 16(1) of this Act, an order relating to the guardianship of a child, has been granted in pursuance of the application or the court has refused to grant such an order.

Amendments—CA 1989, s 108, Sch 13, para 62; Age of Legal Capacity (Scotland) Act 1991, s 10, Sch 1, para 46.

Chapter IV
Jurisdiction of Courts in Northern Ireland

19 Northern Ireland: jurisdiction in cases other than divorce, dissolution of a civil partnership, etc

(1) A court in Northern Ireland shall not make a section 1(1)(c) order with respect to a child unless –

(a) it has jurisdiction under the Council Regulation or the Hague Convention, or

(b) neither the Council Regulation nor the Hague Convention applies but –

(i) the question of making the order arises in or in connection with matrimonial proceedings or civil partnership proceedings and the condition in section 19A of this Act is satisfied, or

(ii) the condition in section 20 of this Act is satisfied.

(2) *(repealed)*

(3) A court in Northern Ireland shall not make a section 1(1)(e) order unless –

(a) it has jurisdiction under the Council Regulation or the Hague Convention, or

(b) neither the Council Regulation nor the Hague Convention applies but –
 (i) the condition in section 20 of this Act is satisfied, or
 (ii) the child concerned is present in Northern Ireland on the relevant date and the court considers that the immediate exercise of its powers is necessary for his protection.

Amendments—Substituted by SI 1995/755. Amended by SI 2001/660; SI 2005/265; SI 2005/3336; SI 2010/1898.

19A Jurisdiction in or in connection with matrimonial proceedings or civil partnership proceedings

(1) The condition referred to in section 19(1) of this Act is that the proceedings are proceedings in respect of the marriage or civil partnership of the parents of the child concerned and –

(a) the proceedings –
 (i) are proceedings for divorce or nullity of marriage, or dissolution or annulment of a civil partnership, and
 (ii) are continuing;
(b) the proceedings –
 (i) are proceedings for judicial separation or legal separation of civil partners, and
 (ii) are continuing;

and the jurisdiction of the court is not excluded by subsection (2) below; or

(c) the proceedings have been dismissed after the beginning of the trial but –
 (i) the section 1(1)(c) order is being made forthwith, or
 (ii) the application for the order was made on or before the dismissal.

(2) For the purposes of subsection (1)(b) above, the jurisdiction of the court is excluded if –

(a) after the grant of a decree of judicial separation, on the relevant date, proceedings for divorce or nullity in respect of the marriage, or
(b) after the making of a separation order, on the relevant date, proceedings for dissolution or annulment in respect of the civil partnership,

are continuing in England and Wales or Scotland.

(3) Subsection (2) above shall not apply if the court in which the other proceedings there referred to are continuing has made –

(a) an order under section 2A(4) or 13(6) of this Act (not being an order made by virtue of section 13(6)(a)(i)), or
(b) an order under section 5(2) or 14(2) of this Act which is recorded as being made for the purpose of enabling Part I proceedings to be taken in Northern Ireland with respect to the child concerned.

(4) Where a court –

(a) has jurisdiction to make a section 1(1)(c) order by virtue of section 19(1)(b)(i) of this Act, but
(b) considers that it would be more appropriate for Part I matters relating to the child to be determined outside Northern Ireland,

the court may by order direct that, while the order under this subsection is in force, no section 1(1)(c) order shall be made by any court by virtue of section 19(1)(b)(i) of this Act.

Amendments—Inserted by SI 1995/755. Amended by SI 2005/265; SI 2005/3336.

20 Habitual residence or presence of child

(1) The condition referred to in section 19(1)(b)(ii) of this Act is that on the relevant date the child concerned –

(a) is habitually resident in Northern Ireland, or
(b) is present in Northern Ireland and is not habitually resident in any part of the United Kingdom or in a specified dependent territory

PART II

and, in either case, the jurisdiction of the court is not excluded by subsection (2) below.

(2) For the purposes of subsection (1) above, the jurisdiction of the court is excluded if, on the relevant date, matrimonial proceedings or civil partnership proceedings are continuing in a court in England and Wales, Scotland or a specified dependent territory in respect of the marriage or civil partnership of the parents of the child concerned.

(3) Subsection (2) above shall not apply if the court in which the other proceedings there referred to are continuing has made –

(a) an order under section 2A(4) or 13(6) of this Act (not being an order made by virtue of section 13(6)(a)(i)), or a corresponding dependent territory order, or

(b) an order under section 5(2) or 14(2) of this Act, or a corresponding dependent territory order, which is recorded as made for the purpose of enabling Part I proceedings with respect to the child concerned to be taken in Northern Ireland,

and that order is in force.

(4)–(6) *(repealed)*

Amendments—CA 1989, s 108, Sch 13, paras 62, 68, 69; SI 1991/1723; SI 1995/755; SI 2005/265; SI 2005/3443.

21 *(repealed)*

22 Power of court to refuse application or stay proceedings

(1) A court in Northern Ireland which has jurisdiction to make a Part I order may refuse an application for the order in any case where the matter in question has already been determined in proceedings outside Northern Ireland.

(2) Where, at any stage of the proceedings on an application made to a court in Northern Ireland for a Part I order, or for the variation of a Part I order, it appears to the court –

(a) that proceedings with respect to the matters to which the application relates are continuing outside Northern Ireland;

(b) that it would be more appropriate for those matters to be determined in proceedings to be taken outside Northern Ireland,

(c) that it should exercise its powers under Article 15 of the Council Regulation (transfer to a court better placed to hear the case), or

(d) that it should exercise its powers under Article 8 of the Hague Convention (request to authority in another Contracting State to assume jurisdiction),

the court may stay the proceedings on the application or (as the case may be) exercise its powers under Article 15 of the Council Regulation or Article 8 of the Hague Convention.

(3) The court may remove a stay granted by virtue of subsection (2)(a) or (b) above if it appears to the court that there has been unreasonable delay in the taking or prosecution of the other proceedings referred to in that subsection, or that those proceedings are stayed, sisted or concluded.

(3A) The court may remove a stay granted under Article 15 of the Council Regulation only in accordance with that Article.

(3B) The court may remove a stay granted in order for it to exercise its powers under Article 8 of the Hague Convention, and withdraw any request made by it to an authority in another Contracting State to assume jurisdiction, if –

(a) the authority in the other Contracting State does not assume jurisdiction within the period for which the court granted the stay, or

(b) the parties do not, within the period specified by the court, request the authority in the other Contracting State to assume jurisdiction.

(4) Nothing in this section so far as it relates to proceedings not governed by the Council Regulation shall affect any power exercisable apart from this section to refuse an application or to grant or remove a stay.

Amendments—CA 1989, s 108, Sch 13, para 62; SI 2001/660; SI 2005/265; SI 2010/1898.

23 Duration and variation of custody orders

(1) If a Part I order made by a court in England and Wales, Scotland or a specified dependent territory (or a variation of such an order) comes into force with respect to a child at a time when a Part I order made by a court in Northern Ireland has effect with respect to him, the latter order shall cease to have effect so far as it makes provision for any matter for which the same or different provision is made by (or by the variation of) the order made by the court in England and Wales, Scotland or the territory.

(2) Where by virtue of subsection (1) above a Part I order has ceased to have effect so far as it makes provision for any matter, a court in Northern Ireland shall not have jurisdiction to vary that order so as to make provision for that matter.

(3) A court in Northern Ireland shall not have jurisdiction to vary a Part I order if, on the relevant date, matrimonial proceedings or civil partnership proceedings are continuing in England and Wales or Scotland in respect of the marriage or civil partnership of the parents of the child concerned.

(3A) Subsection (3) above shall not apply if –

- (a) the Part I order was made in or in connection with proceedings –
  - (i) for divorce or nullity in Northern Ireland in respect of the marriage of the parents of the child concerned; or
  - (ii) for dissolution or annulment in Northern Ireland in respect of the civil partnership of the parents of the child concerned; and
- (b) those proceedings are continuing.

(3B) Subsection (3) above shall not apply if –

- (a) the Part I order was made in or in connection with proceedings –
  - (i) for judicial separation in Northern Ireland; or
  - (ii) for a separation order in Northern Ireland; and
- (b) those proceedings are continuing; and
- (c) as the case may be, the decree of judicial separation has not yet been granted or the separation order has not yet been made.

(4) Subsection (3) above shall not apply if the court in which the proceedings there referred to are continuing has made –

- (a) an order under section 2A(4) or 13(6) of this Act (not being an order made by virtue of section 13(6)(a)(i), or a corresponding dependent territory order, or
- (b) an order under section 5(2) or 14(2) of this Act, or a corresponding dependent territory order, which is recorded as made for the purpose of enabling Part I proceedings with respect to the child concerned to be taken in Northern Ireland,

and that order is in force.

(5) Subsection (3) above shall not apply in the case of a variation of a section 1(1)(e) order if the child concerned is present in Northern Ireland on the relevant date and the court considers that the immediate exercise of its powers is necessary for his protection.

(6) Subsection (7) below applies where a Part I order which is –

- (a) a residence order (within the meaning of the Children (Northern Ireland) Order 1995) in favour of a person with respect to a child,
- (b) an order made in the exercise of the High Court's inherent jurisdiction with respect to children by virtue of which a person has care of a child, or
- (c) an order –
  - (i) of a kind mentioned in section 1(3)(a) of this Act,
  - (ii) under which a person is entitled to the actual possession of a child,

ceases to have effect in relation to that person by virtue of subsection (1) above.

(7) Where this subsection applies, any family assistance order made under Article 16 of the Children (Northern Ireland) Order 1995 with respect to a child shall also cease to have effect.

PART II

(8) For the purposes of subsection (7) above the reference to a family assistance order under Article 16 of the Children (Northern Ireland) Order 1995 shall be deemed to include a reference to an order for the supervision of a child made under –

(a) Article 47 of the Matrimonial Causes (Northern Ireland) Order 1978, or
(b) Article 11 of the Domestic Proceedings (Northern Ireland) Order 1980;

but this subsection shall cease to have effect once all such orders for the supervision of children have ceased to have effect in accordance with Schedule 8 to the Children (Northern Ireland) Order 1995.

Amendments—CA 1989, s 108, Sch 13, paras 62, 68, 69; SI 1991/1723; SI 1995/755; SI 2005/3336.

24 Interpretation of Chapter IV

In this Chapter –

(a) 'child' means a person who has not attained the age of 18;
(aa) 'civil partnership proceedings' means proceedings for the dissolution or annulment of a civil partnership or for legal separation of the civil partners;
(b) 'matrimonial proceedings' means proceedings for divorce, nullity of marriage or judicial separation;
(c) 'the relevant date' means, in relation to the making or variation of an order –
  (i) where an application is made for an order to be made or varied, the date of the application (or first application, if two or more are determined together), and
  (ii) where no such application is made, the date on which the court is considering whether to make or, as the case may be, vary the order; and
(d) 'section 1(1)(c) order' and 'section 1(1)(e) order' mean orders falling within section 1(1)(c) and (e) of this Act respectively.

Amendments—Substituted by SI 1995/755. Amended by SI 2005/3336.

Chapter V
Recognition and Enforcement

25 Recognition of custody orders: general

(1) Where a Part I order made by a court in any part of the United Kingdom or in a specified dependent territory is in force with respect to a child who has not attained the age of sixteen, then, subject to subsection (2) below, the order shall be recognised in any other part or, in the case of a dependent territory order, any part of the United Kingdom as having the same effect in that part as if it had been made by the appropriate court in that part and as if that court had had jurisdiction to make it.

(2) Where a Part I order includes provision as to the means by which rights conferred by the order are to be enforced, subsection (1) above shall not apply to that provision.

(3) A court in a part of the United Kingdom in which a Part I order is recognised in accordance with subsection (1) above shall not enforce the order unless it has been registered in that part of the United Kingdom under section 27 of this Act and proceedings for enforcement are taken in accordance with section 29 of this Act.

Amendments—CA 1989, s 108(5), Sch 13, para 62; SI 1991/1723.

Defined terms—'appropriate court': s 32(1) (and see notes to s 32); 'part of the United Kingdom': s 42(1).

Scope—Recognition and enforcement are not automatic. The initiative and responsibility for pursuing enforcement proceedings lies with the aggrieved party, not with the court (*Glaser v United Kingdom* (Case No 32346/96) [2001] 1 FLR 153, ECHR). An order may be enforced only if it has been registered under s 27 and proceedings for enforcement are taken in accordance with s 29.

'Part I order'—By virtue of ss 1, 32 and 42(5), Pt I orders include those set out in s 1(a)–(f). FLA 1986 is not retrospective and it does not affect any orders made before the Act came into force, and orders which vary or revoke previous orders are excluded.

'specified dependent territory' (s 25(1))—See FLA 1986 (DT)O 1991, art 2 and FPR 2010, r 32.23.

****

27 Registration

(1) Any person on whom any rights are conferred by a Part I order may apply to the court which made it for the order to be registered in another part of the United Kingdom under this section, or in a specified dependent territory under a corresponding provision.

(2) An application under this section shall be made in the prescribed manner and shall contain the prescribed information and be accompanied by such documents as may be prescribed.

(3) On receiving an application under this section the court which made the Part I order shall, unless it appears to the court that the order is no longer in force, cause the following documents to be sent to the appropriate court in the part of the United Kingdom or dependent territory specified in the application, namely –

- (a) a certified copy of the order, and
- (b) where the order has been varied, prescribed particulars of any variation which is in force, and
- (c) a copy of the application and of any accompanying documents.

(4) Where the prescribed officer of the appropriate court in any part of the United Kingdom receives a certified copy of a Part I order under subsection (3) above or under a corresponding dependent territory provision, he shall forthwith cause the order, together with particulars of any variation, to be registered in that court in the prescribed manner.

(5) An order shall not be registered under this section in respect of a child who has attained the age of sixteen, and the registration of an order in respect of a child who has not attained the age of sixteen shall cease to have effect on the attainment by the child of that age.

Amendments—CA 1989, s 108(5), Sch 13, para 62; SI 1991/1723.

Defined terms—'appropriate court': s 32(1) (and see notes to s 32 and FPR 2010, r 32.23); 'certified copy', 'corresponding dependent territory provision', 'corresponding provision', 'part of the UK', 'prescribed': s 42(1).

General note—The mere act of registering is not sufficient to cause the enforcement of the order. A separate application must be made to the registering court to enforce the order.

'Part I order'—See under s 25.

'specified dependent territory' (s 27(1))—See FLA 1986(DT)O 1991, art 2 and FPR 2010, r 32.23.

Application (s 27(2))—Procedure for making applications is set out in FPR 2010, r 32.26. See *Re W-B (Family Proceedings: Appropriate Jurisdiction Within the UK)* [2013] 1 FLR 394, CA, which warns against an application to vary a final order being made in England after a period of 12 months has elapsed since the child's move to Scotland and acquiring habitual resident there. The appropriate procedure is to apply for registration and enforcement under ss 27–29 or to make applications in Scotland for fresh orders.

Documents (s 27(3))—A certified copy and a copy of the original order, any order which has varied any of the terms of the original order and any further orders obtained (e g an additional order under s 33 or 34), together with a statement in support and a copy must be filed (FPR 2010, r 32.25).

'appropriate court in the part of the United Kingdom specified' (s 27(3))—An order may be registered in any part of the UK to where the child has been or is likely to be abducted and where the order is sought to be enforced. A decision will need to be taken as to the jurisdiction in which the order is required to be registered. In most cases, registration in one jurisdiction will suffice; there may, however, be cases where it is desirable to have the order registered in more than one jurisdiction, particularly where there is a fear that the child may be moved about in order to avoid being traced.

'forthwith' (s 27(4))—The order must be registered as soon as practicable having regard to the circumstances and nature of the act to be done (see *Re Southam ex parte Lamb* (1881) 19 Ch D 169, CA; *Re Muscovitch ex parte M* [1939] Ch 694, CA).

'in the prescribed manner' (s 27(4))—Registration in the appropriate court is to be in the prescribed manner. The following rules apply: in England and Wales, FPR 2010, rr 32.23–32.32; in Northern Ireland, Rules of the Court of Judicature (NI) 1980, Ord 90, rr 26–35, CCR (Northern Ireland) 1991, Ord 51, rr 6–11, and the Magistrates' Courts (Family Law Act 1986) Rules (Northern Ireland) 1988; in Scotland, Court of Session Rules of Court, Act of Sederunt (Rules for the Registration of Custody Orders of the Sheriff Court) 1988.

28 Cancellation and variation of registration

(1) A court which revokes, recalls or varies an order registered under section 27 of this Act shall cause notice of the revocation, recall or variation to be given in the prescribed manner to the prescribed officer of the court in which it is registered and, on receiving the notice, the prescribed officer –

- (a) in the case of the revocation or recall of the order, shall cancel the registration, and

(b) in the case of the variation of the order, shall cause particulars of the variation to be registered in the prescribed manner.

(2) Where –

(a) an order registered under section 27 of this Act ceases (in whole or in part) to have effect in the part of the United Kingdom or in a specified dependent territory in which it was made, otherwise than because of its revocation, recall or variation, or

(b) an order registered under section 27 of this Act in Scotland ceases (in whole or in part) to have effect there as a result of the making of an order in proceedings outside the United Kingdom and any specified dependent territory,

the court in which the order is registered may, of its own motion or on the application of any person who appears to the court to have an interest in the matter, cancel the registration (or, if the order has ceased to have effect in part, cancel the registration so far as it relates to the provisions which have ceased to have effect).

Amendments—SI 1991/1723.

Defined terms—'part of the United Kingdom', 'prescribed': s 42(1).

Scope—FPR 2010, rr 32.27 and 32.28 set out the procedure for making such an application. The alteration in the register is made by the prescribed officer. Where however the order ceases to have effect otherwise than by revocation or variation, eg by lapse of time or by continued cohabitation or by resumption of cohabitation, or in the case of an order registered in Scotland, as a result of the making of an order in proceedings outside the UK, the cancellation may take place only where the court acts of its own motion or on an application of any person who has an interest in the matter.

'in the prescribed manner' (s 28(1)(b))—See under s 27 and FPR 2010, rr 32.23–32.32.

'specified dependent territory' (s 28(2))—See FLA 1986(DT)O 1991, art 2 and FPR 2010, r 32.23.

29 Enforcement

(1) Where a Part I order has been registered under section 27 of this Act, the court in which it is registered shall have the same powers for the purpose of enforcing the order (including, where an order with respect to contact is registered in England and Wales, the powers under section 11O of the Children Act 1989) as it would have if it had itself made the order and had jurisdiction to make it; and proceedings for or with respect to enforcement may be taken accordingly.

(2) Where an application has been made to any court for the enforcement of an order registered in that court under section 27 of this Act, the court may, at any time before the application is determined, give such interim directions as it thinks fit for the purpose of securing the welfare of the child concerned or of preventing changes in the circumstances relevant to the determination of the application.

(3) The references in subsection (1) above to a Part I order do not include references to any provision of the order as to the means by which rights conferred by the order are to be enforced.

Amendments—CA 1989, s 108(5), Sch 13, para 62; CAA 2006, s 15(1), Sch 2, paras 2, 4.

Court's powers to make orders (s 29(1))—Since the court has the same powers for the purposes of enforcement of a registered order as it would if it had itself made the order the court has the power:

(a) to order disclosure of the child's whereabouts under s 33 and the discovery of information held by Government departments;
(b) to order the recovery of the child under s 34;
(c) to order surrender of passports under s 37;
(d) to direct that wardship proceedings be commenced (subject to restrictions on jurisdiction);
(e) to grant injunctions and in particular restrain the further removal of the child from the country or from his present address;
(f) to order welfare reports and to give directions regarding evidence to be filed;
(g) to order the return of the child to the applicant and to his country of origin.

Interim directions (s 29(2))—FPR 2010, r 32.29 provides inter alia that all parties to the proceedings for enforcement, and the applicant for the Pt I order if he is not a party, must be made parties to the application for interim directions.

'Part I order'—See under s 25.

Matters to be considered—When considering an application to enforce a custody order made in another part of the UK, an English court is bound to have regard to the principle of comity and not, in effect, purport to act as a court of appeal from the court having jurisdiction in another part of the UK. The English judge should not question the correctness of the procedures and orders of the Scottish court (*Re M (Minors) (Custody: Jurisdiction)* [1992] 2 FLR 382, CA).

30 Staying or sisting of enforcement proceedings

(1) Where in accordance with section 29 of this Act proceedings are taken in any court for the enforcement of an order registered in that court, any person who appears to the court to have an interest in the matter may apply for the proceedings to be stayed or sisted on the ground that he has taken or intends to take other proceedings (in the United Kingdom or elsewhere) as a result of which the order may cease to have effect, or may have a different effect, in the part of the United Kingdom in which it is registered.

(1A) No application may be made under subsection (1) for proceedings to be stayed or sisted if the proceedings are proceedings on an application for an order under section 11O(2) of the Children Act 1989.

(2) If after considering an application under subsection (1) above the court considers that the proceedings for enforcement should be stayed or sisted in order that other proceedings may be taken or concluded, it shall stay or sist the proceedings for enforcement accordingly.

(3) The court may remove a stay or recall a sist granted in accordance with subsection (2) above if it appears to the court –

- (a) that there has been unreasonable delay in the taking or prosecution of the other proceedings referred to in that subsection, or
- (b) that those other proceedings are concluded and that the registered order, or a relevant part of it, is still in force.

(4) Nothing in this section shall affect any power exercisable apart from this section to grant, remove or recall a stay or sist.

Amendments—CAA 2006, s 15(1), Sch 2, paras 2, 5.

Defined terms—'part of the United Kingdom': s 42(1).

Procedure—FPR 2010, r 32.30 makes provision for the procedure on an application under this section.

Grounds of application—In addition to the grounds mentioned in this section, where the enforcement proceedings are in Scotland, application may also be made that the court should deal with the application on its merits under s 12.

Stay by reason of other proceedings—See *Re M (Minors) (Custody: Jurisdiction)* [1992] 2 FLR 382, CA and the effect of DMPA 1973, Sch 3, para 8. For an example of proceedings being sisted/stayed see *P v G* [2010] 2 FLR 1888, FD and *Emergency Remedies in the Family Courts* (Family Law).

31 Dismissal of enforcement proceedings

(1) Where in accordance with section 29 of this Act proceedings are taken in any court for the enforcement of an order registered in that court, any person who appears to the court to have an interest in the matter may apply for those proceedings to be dismissed on the ground that the order has (in whole or in part) ceased to have effect in the part of the United Kingdom or specified dependent territory in which it was made.

(1A) No application may be made under subsection (1) for proceedings to be dismissed if the proceedings are proceedings on an application for an order under section 11O(2) of the Children Act 1989.

(2) Where in accordance with section 29 of this Act proceedings are taken in the Court of Session for the enforcement of an order registered in that court, any person who appears to the court to have an interest in the matter may apply for those proceedings to be dismissed on the ground that the order has (in whole or in part) ceased to have effect in Scotland as a result of the making of an order in proceedings outside the United Kingdom and any specified dependent territory.

(3) If, after considering an application under subsection (1) or (2) above, the court is satisfied that the registered order has ceased to have effect, it shall dismiss the proceedings for enforcement (or, if it is satisfied that the order has ceased to have effect in part, it shall dismiss the proceedings so far as they relate to the enforcement of provisions which have ceased to have effect).

Amendments—SI 1991/1723; CAA 2006, s 15(1), Sch 2, paras 2, 6.

Defined terms—'part of the United Kingdom': s 42(1).

Procedure—FPR 2010, r 32.30 makes provision as to the procedure on an application under this section.

Grounds of application—See annotation under s 30.

32 Interpretation of Chapter V

(1) In this Chapter –

'the appropriate court', in relation to England and Wales or Northern Ireland, means the High Court and, in relation to Scotland, means the Court of Session and, in relation to a specified dependent territory, means the corresponding court in that territory;

'Part I order' includes (except where the context otherwise requires) any order within section 1(3) of this Act which, on the assumptions mentioned in subsection (3) below –

- (a) could have been made notwithstanding the provisions of this Part or the corresponding dependent territory provisions;
- (b) would have been a Part I order for the purpose of this Part; and
- (c) would not have ceased to have effect by virtue of section 6, 15 or 23 of this Act.

(2) In the application of this Chapter to Scotland, 'Part I order' also includes (except where the context otherwise requires) any order within section 1(3) of this Act which, on the assumptions mentioned in subsection (3) below –

- (a) would have been a Part I order for the purpose of this Part; and
- (b) would not have ceased to have effect by virtue of section 6 or 23 of this Act,

and which, but for the provisions of this Part, would be recognised in Scotland under any rule of law.

(3) The said assumptions are –

- (a) that this Part or the corresponding dependent territory provisions, as the case may be, had been in force at all material times; and
- (b) that any reference in section 1 of this Act to any enactment included a reference to any corresponding enactment previously in force.

Amendments—CA 1989, s 108(5), Sch 13, para 62; SI 1991/1723.

Defined terms—'corresponding dependent territory provisions', 'specified dependent territory': s 42(1) (and see notes to s 42 and FPR 2010, r 32.23).

'appropriate court', 'corresponding court' (s 32(1))—See FPR 2010, r 32.23.

'Part I order'—See under s 25.

Chapter VI

Miscellaneous and Supplemental

33 Power to order disclosure of child's whereabouts

(1) Where in proceedings for or relating to a Part I order in respect of a child there is not available to the court adequate information as to where the child is, the court may order any person who it has reason to believe may have relevant information to disclose it to the court.

(2) A person shall not be excused from complying with an order under subsection (1) above by reason that to do so may incriminate him or his spouse of an offence; but a statement or admission made in compliance with such an order shall not be admissible in evidence against either of them in proceedings for any offence other than perjury.

(3) A court in Scotland before which proceedings are pending for the enforcement of an order relating to parental responsibilities or parental rights in relation to a child made outside the United Kingdom and any specified dependent territory which is recognised in Scotland shall have the same powers as it would have under subsection (1) above if the order were its own.

Amendments—CA 1989, s 108(5), Sch 13, para 62; SI 1991/1723; Children (Scotland) Act 1995, s 105(4), Sch 4, para 41(1),(7).

Scope—This section provides a power to the Family Court in private law proceedings similar to an inherent power of the High Court in relation to children. This section also provides for an order for the purpose of giving effect to an order, akin to a CA 1989, s 8 order, made elsewhere in the UK or in a specified dependent territory, which has been registered in the High Court.

An order under this section may be directed to persons who are not parties to the proceedings, including a legal adviser, the manager of a women's refuge or the police, as well as relatives or friends of a person who may be keeping the child. However, where a mother has taken a child to stay at a women's refuge, the police should not be directed to disclose the address (*Chief Constable of West Yorkshire Police v S* [1998] 2 FLR

973, CA). An order under the inherent jurisdiction of the High Court must be obeyed by a legal adviser and 'privilege' is overridden (*Burton v Earl of Darnley* (1869) LR 8 Eq 576; *Ramsbotham v Senior* (1869) FLR Rep 591, CE). The power given by s 33(1) is unqualified and, it is suggested, also overrides privilege. In *HH v SH* [2016] EWHC 1252 (Fam), the High Court took the unusual step of ordering an Afghan national with British citizenship to provide information about the whereabouts of his 6-year-old son who, although he was a British national, was not known to have ever been present in the UK. The order was deemed necessary for the child's welfare and protection because his whereabouts and circumstances were unknown, even though there was a lack of actual evidence of serious harm.

'Part I order'—See under s 25.

Application for s 33 order—An application for an order under s 33 comes within the definition of 'emergency proceedings' (FPR 2010, r 12.2). The application may be made at any time during CA 1989, s 8 proceedings and will usually be made without notice using the procedure in FPR 2010, r 12.16. The application is made in Form C4 (FPR 2010, r 5.1 and PD5A). If made without notice by telephone, as permitted by the rules, the Form C4 must be filed the next business day after making the application (FPR 2010, r 12.16(2),(3)). Where the court makes an order without notice, the rules provide that a copy of the application must be served on each respondent within 48 hours after the making of the order (FPR 2010, r 12.16(4),(5)). It is impractical to make an application without notice by telephone to the Family Court (lay justices) as there is no provision for the application to be heard by a single justice (FPR 2010, r 2.6). PD12E (*Urgent Business*) provides further details of the procedure for out of hours applications. See also PD12D (*Inherent Jurisdiction (including Wardship) Proceedings*).

Evidence in support of application—The application should be supported by evidence. When the application is made in pending CA 1989, s 8 proceedings, the evidence should be by a statement which complies with FPR 2010, r 12.19. When the application is made without notice, permission under FPR 2010, r 12.12 for the statement to be adduced may be sought at the hearing. See also FPR 2010, r 22.1 and PD22A, which deal with the power of the court to control evidence.

Form of order and enforcement—The order is issued in Form C30 (FPR 2010, r 5.1 and PD5A). Note that the order directs the person to disclose the information to the court. The order should not purport to direct disclosure to a party to the proceedings (*Chief Constable of West Yorkshire Police v S* [1998] 2 FLR 973, CA). The court will decide what to do with the information. Form C30 incorporates a penal (warning) notice and may be enforced in the County Court by application under CPR 1998, r 81.4 (and PD81). See also FPR PD6C (power to seek addresses from Government departments to trace the whereabouts of a child).

34 Power to order recovery of child

(1) Where –

(a) a person is required by a Part I order, or an order for the enforcement of a Part I order, to give up a child to another person ('the person concerned'), and

(b) the court which made the order imposing the requirement is satisfied that the child has not been given up in accordance with the order,

the court may make an order authorising an officer of the court or a constable to take charge of the child and deliver him to the person concerned.

(2) The authority conferred by subsection (1) above includes authority –

(a) to enter and search any premises where the person acting in pursuance of the order has reason to believe the child may be found, and

(b) to use such force as may be necessary to give effect to the purpose of the order.

(3) Where by virtue of –

(a) section 14 of the Children Act 1989, or

(b) Article 14 (enforcement of residence orders) of the Children (Northern Ireland) Order 1995,

a Part I order (or a provision of a Part I order) may be enforced as if it were an order requiring a person to give up a child to another person, subsection (1) above shall apply as if the Part I order had included such a requirement.

(4) This section is without prejudice to any power conferred on a court by or under any other enactment or rule of law.

Amendments—CA 1989, s 108(5), Sch 13, paras 62, 70; SI 1995/755.

Scope—This section empowers the Family Court in private law proceedings to authorise the physical taking charge of a child, with the use of such force as may be necessary, and delivery of the child to the person entitled, when a child has not been given up in accordance with an order of the same court. This section also provides for such a power in the High Court in respect of an order, akin to a CA 1989, s 8 order, made elsewhere in the UK or in a specified dependent territory, which has been registered in the High Court. The power given to the Family Court is similar to, but more restricted than, an inherent power of the High Court in relation to children. Unlike the power of the High Court to direct the tipstaff to take charge of a child even

PART II

though no previous order has been disobeyed, the power under s 34 cannot be exercised unless the court is satisfied that an order requiring the giving up of the child has been disobeyed. Therefore, on an application for a s 34 order, proof is required that the order to give up the child has been served on, or effectively communicated to, the person bound by the order.

'officer of the court' (s 34(1))—The Family Court does not have any person who is trained to undertake the functions of the tipstaff of the High Court, and Family Court bailiffs do not undertake this function.

'Part I order'—See under s 25.

Procedure on application for s 34 order—An application for an order under s 34 comes within the definition of 'emergency proceedings' (FPR 2010, r 12.2). The application is made in Form C3 (FPR 2010, r 5.1 and PD5A). When the application is made to the Family Court that made a CA 1989, s 8 order that has not been complied with, or to the High Court in respect of an order made elsewhere but registered in the High Court, it is submitted that the application may be made within the proceedings in which the order was made or the registration proceedings; the court can make injunctive orders to give effect to a judgment after the trial has concluded, in matrimonial proceedings (*Webb v Webb* [1986] 1 FLR 541, CA, *Lucas v Lucas* [1992] 2 FLR 53, CA) and in civil actions (*Zeeland Navigation Company Ltd v Banque Worms* (1995) *The Times*, 26 December, QBD). Where the order was made by the Family Court and the proceedings are no longer in motion, a fresh application may be required.

An application should not be made in respect of a Family Court order unless the order explicitly requires the person bound to 'give up' the child, preferably specifying when or by when (cf CPR 1998,r 81.5(1)), and where, the child is to be given up. If a Family Court order does not so specify, an order to give up the child (which may be applied for without notice) should be obtained and served and have been disobeyed, before an application can be made for a s 34 order.

Without notice or with notice—Application should be made with notice unless there is reason to suppose that the child has been, or is likely to be, removed or hidden, or is likely to suffer significant harm. Proceedings under s 34 come within the definition of 'emergency proceedings' (FPR 2010, r 12.2). If made without notice by telephone, as permitted by the rules (FPR 2010, r 12.16(2)), the Form C3 must be filed the next business day within 24 hours after making the application. It is impractical to make an application without notice by telephone to the Family Court (lay justices) as there is no provision for the application to be heard by a single justice (FPR 2010, r 2.6). Where the court makes an order without notice, the rules provide that a copy of the application must be served on each respondent within 48 hours after the making of the order (FPR 2010, r 12.16(4),(5)). PD12E (*Urgent Business*) provides further details of the procedure for out of hours applications. See also PD12D (*Inherent Jurisdiction (including Wardship) Proceedings*).

Evidence in support of application—The application should be supported by evidence. When the application is made to the court which made a CA 1989, s 8 order, the statement should comply with FPR 2010, r 12.19. When an application is made in the High Court in relation to an order made elsewhere in the UK or in a specified dependent territory, which has been registered in the High Court, the application should be supported by affidavit. When the application is made without notice, permission under r 12.12 for the statement to be adduced may be sought at the hearing. See also FPR 2010, r 22.1 and PD22A, which deal with the power of the court to control evidence.

Form of order—The order is issued in Form C31 (FPR 2010, r 5.1 and PD5A).

Execution of order—An order under s 34(1) gives authority to an officer of the court or a constable, but it does not direct them to act. Execution of an order under s 34(1) needs to be conducted with discretion, in order to avoid harmful distress to the child. The police are not obliged to assist and may refuse (*R v Chief Constable of Cheshire ex parte K* [1990] 1 FLR 70, QBD). Although a solicitor is an officer of the Senior Courts (Solicitors Act 1974, s 50), he is not an officer of the Family Court or the County Court (CCA 1984, s 147).

****

36 Effect of orders restricting removal

(1) This section applies to any order made by a court in the United Kingdom or any specified dependent territory prohibiting the removal of a child from the United Kingdom or from any specified part of it or from any such territory.

(2) An order to which this section applies, made by a court in one part of the United Kingdom or in a specified dependent territory, shall have effect in each other part, or, in the case of an order made in a dependent territory, each part of the United Kingdom –

- (a) as if it had been made by the appropriate court in that part, and
- (b) in the case of an order which has the effect of prohibiting the child's removal to that part, as if it had included a prohibition on his further removal to any place except one to which he could be removed consistently with the order.

(3) The references in subsections (1) and (2) above to prohibitions on a child's removal include references to prohibitions subject to exceptions; and in a case where removal is prohibited except with the consent of the court, nothing in subsection (2) above shall be construed as affecting the identity of the court whose consent is required.

(4) In this section 'child' means a person who has not attained the age of sixteen; and this section shall cease to apply to an order relating to a child when he attains the age of sixteen.

Amendments—SI 1991/1723.

Defined terms—'appropriate court': ss 40, 32(1) (and see below); 'specified dependent territory': s 42(1).

'appropriate court' (s 36(2)(a))—In England and Wales, the High Court.

General interpretation—See s 42.

Radicalisation cases—For guidance on orders restricting the removal of children from this jurisdiction in radicalisation cases and the use of electronic tagging of parents to prevent the same, see the Practice Guidance of April 2015 set out in Part V and the decision of the President in *Re X (Children) and Y (Children) (No 1)* [2015] 2 FLR 1487, FD.

37 Surrender of passports

(1) Where there is in force an order prohibiting or otherwise restricting the removal of a child from the United Kingdom or from any specified part of it or from a specified dependent territory, the court by which the order was in fact made, or by which it is treated under section 36 of this Act as having been made, may require any person to surrender any United Kingdom passport which has been issued to, or contains particulars of, the child.

(2) In this section 'United Kingdom passport' means a current passport issued by the Government of the United Kingdom.

Amendments—SI 1991/1723.

Defined terms—'specified dependent territory': s 42(1).

General interpretation—See ss 42, 40, 32(1).

Power to order the surrender of passports—This provision can only be invoked if the court makes an order prohibiting or otherwise restricting the removal of a child from the UK. Its scope is further restricted in that the court can only require the surrender of *any UK passport* which has been issued *to a child* or contains particulars *of a child*. It does not apply to non-UK passports and passports that do not contain particulars of the child concerned. See *Re C-W (A Child) (Contact Overseas)* [2017] 1 FLR 131, CA for an unusual situation where the court ordered the child's UK passport to be retained by independent agents during periods of the child's contact with her mother in the US. The aim to compel relatives of the mother and child to persuade, influence or put pressure on the mother to return the child to the jurisdiction was not a permissible basis upon which to make passport orders – see *Re B (A Child)* [2015] 1 FLR 871, CA, where the Court of Appeal considered the circumstances in which the High Court, in the exercise of its inherent jurisdiction, can properly make a passport order requiring a person, including a non-party, to lodge their passport with the court or with some suitable custodian (eg the Tipstaff). See also *SC v BH (Passport Order)* [2014] EWHC 1584 (Fam). See *B v M; sub nom Re G (A Child)* [2015] EWHC 2941 (Fam), where a mother's fiancé was sentenced to 2 months' imprisonment (suspended for 12 months) for breach of a passport order. However, in *Re L (A Child)* [2016] EWCA Civ 146, a mother could not be held in contempt of court for breaching the stay of an order that required her to disclose orders to the Passport Office where there was no evidence to suggest the order had been disclosed after it was stayed and where the law prior to the stay permitted her to disclose the order to the Passport Office.

'the court ... by which [the order] is treated under section 36 as having been made'—Section 36 enables the appropriate court in each part of the UK to make an order under s 37 as though it had made the prohibitory order in fact made in another part of the UK or a specified dependent territory. Note that the 'appropriate court' in England and Wales which can exercise the power under s 37 is the High Court.

Other remedies for prevention of removal of a child from the jurisdiction—For arrangements for police to institute a port alert, and for giving notice to the Passport Office that passport facilities should not be provided without the permission of the court, see FPR PD12P. See the commentary for FPR 2010, r 12.39, PD12D and PD12F for detailed guidance as to the wording of orders relating to Port Alerts.

Application for s 37 order—The application may be made by making an application in the court which made, or under s 36 is treated as having made, the order. The application may be made without notice where removal is thought to be imminent. The parties to the proceedings are set out in the table in FPR 2010, r 12.3(1). There is no prescribed form of notice for an application.

38 Automatic restriction on removal of wards of court

(1) The rule of law which (without any order of the court) restricts the removal of a ward of court from the jurisdiction of the court shall, in a case to which this section applies, have effects subject to the modifications in subsection (3) below.

(2) This section applies in relation to a ward of court if –

(a) proceedings for divorce, nullity or judicial separation in respect of the marriage of his parents are continuing in a court in another part of the United Kingdom (that is to say, in a part of the United Kingdom outside the jurisdiction of the court of which he is a ward), or in a specified dependent territory, or (aa) proceedings for dissolution or annulment or legal separation in respect of the civil partnership of his parents are continuing in a court in another part of the United Kingdom (that is to say, in a part of the United Kingdom outside the jurisdiction of the court of which he is a ward), or

(b) he is habitually resident in another part of the United Kingdom or in a specified dependent territory,

except where that other part is Scotland and he has attained the age of sixteen.

(3) Where this section applies, the rule referred to in subsection (1) above shall not prevent –

(a) the removal of the ward of court, without the consent of any court, to the other part of the United Kingdom or the specified dependent territory mentioned in subsection (2) above, or

(b) his removal to any other place with the consent of either the appropriate court in that other part of the United Kingdom or the specified dependent territory or the court mentioned in subsection (2)(a) or (aa) above.

Amendments—SI 1991/1723; SI 2005/3336.

Defined terms—'appropriate court': ss 40, 32(1); 'specified dependent territory': s 42(1).

General interpretation—See s 42.

'habitually resident' (s 38(2)(b))—See under s 3 and **Habitual residence** under CSA 1991, s 44.

Radicalisation cases—See notes to s 36, above.

39 Duty to furnish particulars of other proceedings

Parties to proceedings for or relating to a Part I order shall, to such extent and in such manner as may be prescribed, give particulars of other proceedings known to them which relate to the child concerned (including proceedings instituted abroad and proceedings which are no longer continuing).

Amendments—CA 1989, s 108(5), Sch 13, para 62.

Defined terms—'Part I order': ss 1(2),(3), 42(5),(6); 'prescribed': s 42(1).

General interpretation—See s 42.

'Part I order'—See under s 25.

'to such extent and in such manner as may be prescribed'—Section 42(1) defines 'prescribed' in relation to England and Wales as meaning prescribed by rules of court.

40 Interpretation of Chapter VI

(1) In this Chapter –

'the appropriate court' has the same meaning as in Chapter V;

'Part I order' includes (except where the context otherwise requires) any such order as is mentioned in section 32(1) of this Act.

(2) In the application of this Chapter to Scotland, 'Part I order' also includes (except where the context otherwise requires) any such order as is mentioned in section 32(2) of this Act.

Amendments—CA 1989, s 108(5), Sch 13, para 62.

41 Habitual residence after removal without consent etc

(1) Where a child who –

(a) has not attained the age of sixteen, and

(b) is habitually resident in a part of the United Kingdom or in a specified dependent territory,

becomes habitually resident outside that part of the United Kingdom or that territory in consequence of circumstances of the kind specified in subsection (2) below, he shall be treated for the purposes of this Part as continuing to be habitually resident in that part of the United Kingdom or that territory for the period of one year beginning with the date on which those circumstances arise.

(2) The circumstances referred to in subsection (1) above exist where the child is removed from or retained outside, or himself leaves or remains outside, the part of the United Kingdom or the territory in which he was habitually resident before his change of residence –

(a) without the agreement of the person or all the persons having, under the law of that part of the United Kingdom or that territory, the right to determine where he is to reside, or

(b) in contravention of an order made by a court in any part of the United Kingdom or in a specified dependent territory.

(3) A child shall cease to be treated by virtue of subsection (1) above as habitually resident in a part of the United Kingdom or a specified dependent territory if, during the period there mentioned –

(a) he attains the age of sixteen, or

(b) he becomes habitually resident outside that part of the United Kingdom or that territory with the agreement of the person or persons mentioned in subsection (2)(a) above and not in contravention of an order made by a court in any part of the United Kingdom or in any specified dependent territory.

Amendments—SI 1991/1723.

Defined terms—'specified dependent territory': s 42(1).

Scope—Section 41 has no application to the determination of questions of habitual residence under Art 3 of the Hague Convention. Section 41(1) is a deeming provision that applies only to Pt I of the 1986 Act. It regulates any jurisdictional or enforcement conflict between the constituent jurisdictions of the UK, but has no application to conflicts between UK jurisdictions and any jurisdiction that is not a constituent part of the UK. Questions of habitual residence in relation to Art 3 of the Hague Convention are to be determined by reference to international jurisprudence (*Re S (A Child: Abduction)* [2003] 1 FLR 1008, CA).

General interpretation—See s 42.

'habitually resident' (s 41(1))—See under s 3 and **Habitual residence** under CSA 1991, s 44.

'one year period' (s 41(1))—When an order was made without jurisdiction in the 12-month period following a move from Scotland where the child had been habitually resident, the order remained in force until it was discharged. Where no application was made to discharge such an order in the 12-month period the English court had jurisdiction and it mattered not that the original order had been made unlawfully (*Re B (Court's Jurisdiction)* [2004] 2 FLR 741, CA).

'agreement of the person or persons mentioned in subsection (2)(a)' (s 41(3)(b))—A parent's preliminary or interim views expressed during the course of legal proceedings taken to determine the child's future residence cannot be taken as consent to a change of habitual residence; a parent's participation in such legal proceedings is a sensible course of action and should not be held against the parent (*D v D (Custody: Jurisdiction)* [1996] 1 FLR 574, FD).

42 General interpretation of Part I

(1) In this Part –

'certified copy', in relation to an order of any court, means a copy certified by the prescribed officer of the court to be a true copy of the order or of the official record of the order;

'corresponding dependent territory order', 'corresponding dependent territory provision' and similar expressions, in relation to a specified dependent territory, shall be construed in accordance with Schedule 3 to the Family Law Act 1986 (Dependent Territories) Order 1991 as from time to time in force: 'dependent territory' has the meaning given by section 43(2) of this Act;

'parental responsibilities' and 'parental rights' have the meanings respectively given by sections 1(3) and 2(4) of the Children (Scotland) Act 1995;

'part of the United Kingdom' means England and Wales, Scotland or Northern Ireland;

'prescribed' means prescribed by rules of court or act of sederunt;

'specified dependent territory' means a dependent territory for the time being specified in Schedule 1 to the said order of 1991.

'the Council Regulation' means Council Regulation (EC) No 2201/2003 of 27 November 2003 concerning jurisdiction and the recognition and enforcement of judgments in matrimonial matters and matters of parental responsibility.

'the Hague Convention' means the Convention on Jurisdiction, Applicable Law, Recognition, Enforcement and Co-Operation in respect of Parental Responsibility and Measures for the Protection of Children that was signed at The Hague on 19 October 1996.

(2) For the purposes of this Part proceedings in England and Wales, Northern Ireland or a specified dependent territory for divorce, nullity or judicial separation in respect of the marriage of the parents of a child shall, unless they have been dismissed, be treated as continuing until the child concerned attains the age of eighteen (whether or not a decree has been granted and whether or not, in the case of a decree of divorce or nullity of marriage, that decree has been made absolute).

(2A) For the purposes of this Part proceedings in England and Wales or in Northern Ireland for dissolution, annulment or legal separation in respect of the civil partnership of the parents of the child shall, unless they have been dismissed, be treated as continuing until the child concerned attains the age of eighteen (whether or not a dissolution, nullity or separation order has been made and whether or not, in the case of a dissolution or nullity order, that order has been made final).

(3) For the purposes of this Part, matrimonial proceedings or civil partnership proceedings in a court in Scotland which has jurisdiction in those proceedings to make a Part I order with respect to a child shall, unless they have been dismissed or decree of absolvitor has been granted therein, be treated as continuing until the child concerned attains the age of sixteen.

(4) Any reference in this Part to proceedings in respect of the marriage of the parents of a child shall, in relation to a child who, although not a child of both parties to the marriage, is a child of the family of those parties, be construed as a reference to proceedings in respect of that marriage; and for this purpose 'child of the family' –

(a) if the proceedings are in England and Wales, means any child who has been treated by both parties as a child of their family, except a child who is placed with those parties as foster parents by a local authority or a voluntary organisation;

(b) if the proceedings are in Scotland, means any child who has been treated by both parties as a child of their family, except a child who has been placed with those parties as foster parents by a local authority or a voluntary organisation;

(c) if the proceedings are in Northern Ireland, means any child who has been treated by both parties as a child of their family, except a child who is placed with those parties as foster parents by an authority within the meaning of the Children (Northern Ireland) Order 1995;

(d) if the proceedings are in a specified dependent territory, means any child who has been treated by both parties as a child of their family, except a child who has been placed with those parties as foster parents by a public authority in that territory.

(4A) Any reference in this Part to proceedings in respect of the civil partnership of the parents of a child shall, in relation to a child who, although not a child of the civil partners, is a child of the family of the civil partners, be construed as a reference to proceedings in respect of that civil partnership; and for this purpose 'child of the family' has the meaning given in paragraphs (a) to (c) of subsection (4) (but substituting references to the civil partners for references to the parties to the marriage).

(5) References in this Part to Part I orders include (except where the context otherwise requires) references to Part I orders as varied.

(6) For the purposes of this Part each of the following orders shall be treated as varying the Part I order to which it relates –

(a) an order which provides for a person to be allowed contact with or to be given access to a child who is the subject of a Part I order, or which makes provision for the education of such a child,

(b)–(e) *(repealed)*

(7) In this Part –

(a) references to Part I proceedings in respect of a child are references to any proceedings for a Part I order or an order corresponding to a Part I order and include, in relation to proceedings outside the United Kingdom and any specified dependent territory, references to proceedings before a tribunal or other authority having power under the law having effect there to determine Part I matters; and

(b) references to Part I matters are references to matters that might be determined by a Part I order or an order corresponding to a Part I order.

Amendments—CA 1989, s 108(5), (7), Sch 13, paras 62, 71, Sch 15; SI 1991/1723; Children (Scotland) Act 1995, s 105(4), Sch 4, para 41(1),(9); SI 1995/756; SI 2001/310; SI 2001/660; SI 2005/265; SI 2005/3336; SI 2010/1898.

'dependent territory'—Within the meaning of the British Nationality Act 1981, this term is to be read as a reference to 'British overseas territory' (see British Overseas Territories Act 2002, s 1(2)).

'corresponding dependent territory order' etc—In relation to the Isle of Man, see FLA 1986(DT)O 1991, Sch 3 for specific interpretation.

'specified dependent territory'—See also Family Law Act 1986 (Dependent Territories) (Amendment) Order 1994 and FPR 2010, r 32.23.

****

PART II
RECOGNITION OF DIVORCES, ANNULMENTS AND LEGAL SEPARATIONS

Divorces, annulments and judicial separations granted in the British Islands

44 Recognition in United Kingdom of divorces, annulments and judicial separations granted in the British Islands

(1) Subject to section 52(4) and (5)(a) of this Act, no divorce or annulment obtained in any part of the British Islands shall be regarded as effective in any part of the United Kingdom unless granted by a court of civil jurisdiction.

(2) Subject to section 51 of this Act, the validity of any divorce, annulment or judicial separation granted by a court of civil jurisdiction in any part of the British Islands shall be recognised throughout the United Kingdom.

Defined terms—'annulment', 'part of the United Kingdom': s 54(1).

Overseas divorces, annulments and legal separations

45 Recognition in the United Kingdom of overseas divorces, annulments and legal separations

(1) Subject to subsection (2) of this section and to sections 51 and 52 of this Act, the validity of a divorce, annulment or legal separation obtained in a country outside the British Islands (in this Part referred to as an overseas divorce, annulment or legal separation) shall be recognised in the United Kingdom if, and only if, it is entitled to recognition –

(a) by virtue of sections 46 to 49 of this Act, or

(b) by virtue of any enactment other than this Part.

(2) Subsection (1) and the following provisions of this Part do not apply to an overseas divorce, annulment or legal separation as regards which provision as to recognition is made by Articles 21 to 27, 41(1) and 42(1) of the Council Regulation.

Amendments—SI 2001/310; SI 2005/265.
Defined terms—'annulment': s 54(1); 'country': s 54(2).

46 Grounds for recognition

(1) The validity of an overseas divorce, annulment or legal separation obtained by means of proceedings shall be recognised if –

(a) the divorce, annulment or legal separation is effective under the law of the country in which it was obtained; and

(b) at the relevant date either party to the marriage –

(i) was habitually resident in the country in which the divorce, annulment or legal separation was obtained; or

(ii) was domiciled in that country; or

(iii) was a national of that country.

(2) The validity of an overseas divorce, annulment or legal separation obtained otherwise than by means of proceedings shall be recognised if –

(a) the divorce, annulment or legal separation is effective under the law of the country in which it was obtained;

(b) at the relevant date –

(i) each party to the marriage was domiciled in that country; or

(ii) either party to the marriage was domiciled in that country and the other party was domiciled in a country under whose law the divorce, annulment or legal separation is recognised as valid; and

(c) neither party to the marriage was habitually resident in the United Kingdom throughout the period of one year immediately preceding that date.

(3) In this section 'the relevant date' means –

(a) in the case of an overseas divorce, annulment or legal separation obtained by means of proceedings, the date of the commencement of the proceedings;

(b) in the case of an overseas divorce, annulment or legal separation obtained otherwise than by means of proceedings, the date on which it was obtained.

(4) Where in the case of an overseas annulment, the relevant date fell after the death of either party to the marriage, any reference in subsection (1) or (2) above to that date shall be construed in relation to that party as a reference to the date of death.

(5) For the purpose of this section, a party to a marriage shall be treated as domiciled in a country if he was domiciled in that country either according to the law of that country in family matters or according to the law of the part of the United Kingdom in which the question of recognition arises.

Defined terms—'annulment': s 54(1); 'country': s 54(2); 'part of the United Kingdom', 'proceedings' s 54(1).

'effective under the law of the country in which it was obtained' (s 46(1)(a))—Where a husband had applied for a divorce to a tribunal in Ghana and had made his wife's mother a defendant to the proceedings, but where his wife had no knowledge of the proceedings and there was no evidence that her mother had voluntarily submitted to the jurisdiction of the tribunal, or that the tribunal had made adequate efforts by adjourning the case to hear the wife's side of the case, Wall J held that the order dissolving the marriage was not effective since the High Court in Ghana would not have upheld the decree on a judicial review. Even if this were not the case, FLA 1986, s 51(3)(a)(i) gives the court a wide discretion to refuse what would otherwise be mandatory recognition afforded under s 46 by applying the English concept of what would constitute 'reasonable steps' to give notice of the proceedings to the wife (*D v D (Recognition of Foreign Divorce)* [1994] 1 FLR 38, FD). See further under s 51(3)(a)(i). For an example of a case under s 46(2)(a) see *Wicken v Wicken* [1999] 1 FLR 293, FD where expert evidence called by both parties established that a divorce letter was, as a matter of substantive law, effective under the law of The Gambia to dissolve the marriage. There was a requirement that in the event of a dispute in The Gambia the authenticity of the document be proved by the testimony of two righteous male witnesses. However, that requirement was a matter of evidence and not substantive law, and as the dispute as to authenticity arose in England, the rules of evidence of England and Wales applied. Applying those rules, the letter was held to be authentic and therefore valid under Gambian law.

Ordinarily, a talaq is not the product of judicial or other proceedings but is the product of a simple pronouncement. However, where Lebanese law required a talaq to be recorded with the Sharia court, that registration process was properly described as 'proceedings' for the purposes of s 46(1), even though no judicial decision was required (*El Fadl v El Fadl* [2000] 1 FLR 175, FD). In *H v H (Talaq Divorce)* [2008] 2 FLR 857, FD although a unilateral process that might offend English sensibilities, the talaq divorce (on the facts of this case) would be recognised; it was important that marriages and divorces recognised in one country be recognised in another. However, a bare talaq pronounced in England between nationals of Saudi Arabia did not dissolve a marriage, even if it was subsequently registered with the Sharia court in Saudi Arabia, because divorces obtained in the UK other than by proceedings in a court of civil jurisdiction are not recognised (s 44(1)). Furthermore, neither was it an overseas divorce within the meaning of s 45 (1)(a) as it was obtained in the UK not Saudi Arabia (*Sulaiman v Juffali* [2002] 1 FLR 479, FD). A Japanese kyogi rikon was held to be a divorce obtained by a means of proceedings; it is a divorce agreed between the parties and registered with the state. The registration by the state is fundamental and not merely probative (*H v H (The Queen's Proctor Intervening)* [2007] 1 FLR 1318, FD).

'Effective' connotes a less rigorous standard than 'valid'. 'Effective' can mean a decree which, although invalid per se in the granting state, is none the less to be treated as valid by virtue of some supervening legal decision or equitable principle such as estoppel (*Kellman v Kellman* [2000] 1 FLR 785, FD).

'habitually resident' (s 46(1)(b)(i),(2)(c))—See under s 3 and **Habitual residence** under CSA 1991, s 44.

Transnational divorces (s 46(3))—FLA 1986 contemplates that the proceedings by which the 'overseas divorce' has been obtained should have been commenced and concluded in the same place. The mere fact that a divorce was pronounced or finalised in one country does not entitle the court to overlook the fact that part of the proceedings has been conducted elsewhere. The word 'obtained' connotes a process rather than a single act. Where an important step in the proceedings leading to the divorce has taken place in England rather than in the jurisdiction in which the divorce was pronounced, that divorce is properly to be regarded not as an 'overseas divorce' but rather as a transnational divorce. If the divorce has not been terminated by means of 'overseas proceedings', it cannot be recognised in England and Wales under FLA 1986 (*Berkovits v Grinberg (Attorney-General Intervening)* [1995] 1 FLR 477, FD).

47 Cross-proceedings and divorces following legal separations

(1) Where there have been cross-proceedings, the validity of an overseas divorce, annulment or legal separation obtained either in the original proceedings or in the cross-proceedings shall be recognised if –

(a) the requirements of section 46(1)(b)(i), (ii) or (iii) of this Act are satisfied in relation to the date of the commencement either of the original proceedings or of the cross-proceedings, and

(b) the validity of the divorce, annulment or legal separation is otherwise entitled to recognition by virtue of the provisions of this Part.

(2) Where a legal separation, the validity of which is entitled to recognition by virtue of the provisions of section 46 of this Act or of subsection (1) above is converted, in the country in which it was obtained, into a divorce which is effective under the law of that country, the validity of the divorce shall be recognised whether or not it would itself be entitled to recognition by virtue of those provisions.

Defined terms—'annulment': s 54(1); 'country': s 54(2); 'proceedings': s 54(1).

48 Proof of facts relevant to recognition

(1) For the purpose of deciding whether an overseas divorce, annulment or legal separation obtained by means of proceedings is entitled to recognition by virtue of section 46 and 47 of this Act, any finding of fact made (whether expressly or by implication) in the proceedings and on the basis of which jurisdiction was assumed in the proceedings shall –

(a) if both parties to the marriage took part in the proceedings, be conclusive evidence of the fact found; and

(b) in any other case, be sufficient proof of that fact unless the contrary is shown.

(2) In this section 'finding of fact' includes a finding that either party to the marriage –

(a) was habitually resident in the country in which the divorce, annulment or legal separation was obtained; or

(b) was under the law of that country domiciled there; or

(c) was a national of that country.

(3) For the purposes of subsection (1)(a) above, a party to the marriage who has appeared in judicial proceedings shall be treated as having taken part in them.

Defined terms—'annulment': s 54(1); 'country': s 54(2); 'proceedings': s 54(1).
'habitually resident' (s 48(2)(a))—See under s 3 and **Habitual residence** under CSA 1991, s 44.

Supplemental

49 Modifications of Part II in relation to countries comprising territories having different systems of law

(1) In relation to a country comprising territories in which different systems of law are in force in matters of divorce, annulment or legal separation, the provisions of this Part mentioned in subsections (2) to (5) below shall have effect subject to the modifications there specified.

(2) In the case of a divorce, annulment or legal separation the recognition of the validity of which depends on whether the requirements of subsection (1)(b)(i) or (ii) of section 46 of this Act are satisfied, that section and, in the case of a legal separation, section 47(2) of this Act shall have effect as if each territory were a separate country.

(3) In the case of a divorce, annulment or legal separation the recognition of the validity of which depends on whether the requirements of subsection (1)(b)(iii) of section 46 of this Act are satisfied –

(a) that section shall have effect as if for paragraph (a) of subsection (1) there were substituted the following paragraph –

'(a) the divorce, annulment or legal separation is effective throughout the country in which it was obtained;'; and

(b) in the case of a legal separation, section 47(2) of this Act shall have effect as if for the words 'is effective under the law of that country' there were substituted the words 'is effective throughout that country'.

(4) In the case of a divorce, annulment or legal separation the recognition of the validity of which depends on whether the requirements of subsection (2)(b) of section 46 of this Act are satisfied, that section and section 52(3) and (4) of this Act and, in the case of a legal separation, section 47(2) of this Act shall have effect as if each territory were a separate country.

(5) Paragraphs (a) and (b) of section 48(2) of this Act shall each have effect as if each territory were a separate country.

Defined terms—'annulment': s 54(1); 'country': s 54(2).

50 Non-recognition of divorce or annulment in another jurisdiction no bar to remarriage

Where, in any part of the United Kingdom –

(a) a divorce or annulment has been granted by a court of civil jurisdiction, or

(b) the validity of a divorce or annulment is recognised by virtue of this Part,

the fact that the divorce or annulment would not be recognised elsewhere shall not preclude either party to the marriage from forming a subsequent marriage or civil partnership in that part of the United Kingdom or cause the subsequent marriage or civil partnership of either party (wherever it takes place) to be treated as invalid in that part.

Defined terms—'annulment', 'part of the United Kingdom': s 54(1); CPA 2004, s 261(1), Sch 27, para 125.

51 Refusal of recognition

(1) Subject to section 52 of this Act, recognition of the validity of –

(a) a divorce, annulment or judicial separation granted by a court of civil jurisdiction in any part of the British Islands, or

(b) an overseas divorce, annulment or legal separation,

may be refused in any part of the United Kingdom if the divorce, annulment or separation was granted or obtained at a time when it was irreconcilable with a decision determining the question of the subsistence or validity of the marriage of the parties previously given (whether before or after the commencement of this Part) by a court of civil jurisdiction in that part of the United Kingdom or by a court elsewhere and recognised or entitled to be recognised in that part of the United Kingdom.

(2) Subject to section 52 of this Act, recognition of the validity of –

(a) a divorce or judicial separation granted by a court of civil jurisdiction in any part of the British Islands, or

(b) an overseas divorce or legal separation,

may be refused in any part of the United Kingdom if the divorce or separation was granted or obtained at a time when, according to the law of that part of the United Kingdom (including its rules of private international law and the provisions of this Part), there was no subsisting marriage between the parties.

(3) Subject to section 52 of this Act, recognition by virtue of section 45 of this Act of the validity of an overseas divorce, annulment or legal separation may be refused if –

(a) in the case of a divorce, annulment or legal separation obtained by means of proceedings, it was obtained –
   (i) without such steps having been taken for giving notice of the proceedings to a party to the marriage as, having regard to the nature of the proceedings and all the circumstances, should reasonably have been taken; or
   (ii) without a party to the marriage having been given (for any reason other than lack of notice) such opportunity to take part in the proceedings as, having regard to those matters, he should reasonably have been given; or

(b) in the case of a divorce, annulment or legal separation obtained otherwise than by means of proceedings –
   (i) there is no official document certifying that the divorce, annulment or legal separation is effective under the law of the country in which it was obtained; or
   (ii) where either party to the marriage was domiciled in another country at the relevant date, there is no official document certifying that the divorce, annulment or legal separation is recognised as valid under the law of that other country; or

(c) in either case, recognition of the divorce, annulment or legal separation would be manifestly contrary to public policy.

(4) In this section –

'official', in relation to a document certifying that a divorce, annulment or legal separation is effective, or is recognised as valid, under the law of any country, means issued by a person or body appointed or recognised for the purpose under that law;

'the relevant date' has the same meaning as in section 46 of this Act;

and subsection (5) of that section shall apply for the purposes of this section as it applies for the purposes of that section.

(5) Nothing in this Part shall be construed as requiring the recognition of any finding of fault made in any proceedings for divorce, annulment or separation or of any maintenance, custody or other ancillary order made in any such proceedings.

Defined terms—'annulment': s 54(1); 'country': s 54(2); 'part of the United Kingdom', 'proceedings': s 54(1).

'without such steps having been taken for giving notice of the proceedings to a party to the marriage' (s 51(3)(a)(i))—A foreign divorce may be refused even where the requirements of FLA 1986, s 46 are satisfied if it was obtained 'without such steps being taken for giving notice of the proceedings to a party to the marriage as, having regard to the nature of the proceedings and all the circumstances, should reasonably have been taken' – see *Duhur-Johnson v Duhur-Johnson (Attorney-General intervening)* [2005] 2 FLR 1042, FD for an analysis of previous authorities and the approach that the court should take. See also **'effective under the law of the country in which it was obtained'** under s 46.

'manifestly contrary to public policy' (s 51(3)(c))—The discretion to refuse recognition on the grounds that it would be manifestly contrary to public policy is one to be exercised sparingly – see *El Fadl v El Fadl* [2000] 1 FLR 175, FD and *Kellman v Kellman* [2000] 1 FLR 785, FD. The motive for the divorce is generally irrelevant to the exercise of that discretion. While fraud is not a ground for refusal of recognition, there may be exceptional circumstances where one party may have deceived the other and the foreign court which may be relevant to the exercise of the discretion. In *Eroglu v Eroglu* [1994] 2 FLR 287, FD, where the petitioner participated with the respondent in a ruse to obtain a Turkish divorce which was designed to achieve material advantage for the respondent, and which material advantage was enjoyed and shared by the petitioner, the petitioner fell far short of persuading the court that the recognition of the Turkish divorce would be manifestly contrary to public policy. A divorce granted by a state that is not recognised by the UK Government can be recognised, provided that it was obtained in accordance with the relevant conditions applicable within the area and that the provisions under ss 46–54 have been complied with. However, such recognition must never be inconsistent with foreign policy or the diplomatic stance of the government and therefore when the court is asked to recognise the acts of an unrecognised state or its courts, it should, where possible, be assisted by representations on behalf of the Attorney-General (*Emin v Yeldag (Attorney-General and Secretary of State for Foreign and Commonwealth Affairs Intervening)* [2002] 1 FLR 956, FD).

52 Provisions as to divorces, annulments etc obtained before commencement of Part II

(1) The provisions of this Part shall apply –

(a) to a divorce, annulment or judicial separation granted by a court of civil jurisdiction in the British Islands before the date of the commencement of this Part, and

(b) to an overseas divorce, annulment or legal separation obtained before that date,

as well as to one granted or obtained on or after that date.

(2) In the case of such a divorce, annulment or separation as is mentioned in subsection (1)(a) or (b) above, the provisions of this Part shall require or, as the case may be, preclude the recognition of its validity in relation to any time before that date as well as in relation to any subsequent time, but those provisions shall not –

(a) affect any property to which any person became entitled before that date, or
(b) affect the recognition of the validity of the divorce, annulment or separation if that matter has been decided by any competent court in the British Islands before that date.

(3) Subsections (1) and (2) above shall apply in relation to any divorce or judicial separation granted by a court of civil jurisdiction in the British Islands before the date of the commencement of this Part whether granted before or after the commencement of section 1 of the Recognition of Divorces and Legal Separations Act 1971.

(4) The validity of any divorce, annulment or legal separation mentioned in subsection (5) below shall be recognised in the United Kingdom whether or not it is entitled to recognition by virtue of any of the foregoing provisions of this Part.

(5) The divorces, annulments and legal separations referred to in subsection (4) above are –

(a) a divorce which was obtained in the British Islands before 1 January 1974 and was recognised as valid under rules of law applicable before that date;
(b) an overseas divorce which was recognised as valid under the Recognition of Divorces and Legal Separations Act 1971 and was not affected by section 16(2) of the Domicile and Matrimonial Proceedings Act 1973 (proceedings otherwise than in a court of law where both parties resident in the United Kingdom);
(c) a divorce of which the decree was registered under section 1 of the Indian and Colonial Divorce Jurisdiction Act 1926;
(d) a divorce or annulment which was recognised as valid under section 4 of the Matrimonial Causes (War Marriages) Act 1944; and
(e) an overseas legal separation which was recognised as valid under the Recognition of Divorces and Legal Separations Act 1971.

Defined terms—'annulment': s 54(1).

★★★★

54 Interpretation of Part II

(1) In this Part –

'annulment' includes any decree or declarator of nullity of marriage, however expressed;

'the Council Regulation' means Council Regulation (EC) No 2201/2003 of 27 November 2003 concerning jurisdiction and the recognition and enforcement of judgments in matrimonial matters and matters of parental responsibility;

'part of the United Kingdom' means England and Wales, Scotland or Northern Ireland;

'proceedings' means judicial or other proceedings.

(2) In this Part 'country' includes a colony or other dependent territory of the United Kingdom but for the purposes of this Part a person shall be treated as a national of such a territory only if it has a law of citizenship or nationality separate from that of the United Kingdom and he is a citizen or national of that territory under that law.

Amendments—SI 2001/310; SI 2005/265.

'dependent territory' (s 54(2))—Within the meaning of the British Nationality Act 1981, this term is to be read as a reference to 'British overseas territory' (see British Overseas Territories Act 2002, s 1(2)).

PART III
DECLARATIONS OF STATUS

55 Declarations as to marital status

(1) Subject to the following provisions of this section, any person may apply to the High Court or the family court for one or more of the following declarations in relation to a marriage specified in the application, that is to say –

(a) a declaration that the marriage was at its inception a valid marriage;
(b) a declaration that the marriage subsisted on a date specified in the application;
(c) a declaration that the marriage did not subsist on a date so specified;
(d) a declaration that the validity of a divorce, annulment or legal separation obtained in any country outside England and Wales in respect of the marriage is entitled to recognition in England and Wales;
(e) a declaration that the validity of a divorce, annulment or legal separation so obtained in respect of the marriage is not entitled to recognition in England and Wales.

(2) A court shall have jurisdiction to entertain an application under subsection (1) above if, and only if, either of the parties to the marriage to which the application relates –

(a) is domiciled in England and Wales on the date of the application, or
(b) has been habitually resident in England and Wales throughout the period of one year ending with that date, or
(c) died before that date and either –
  (i) was at death domiciled in England and Wales, or
  (ii) had been habitually resident in England and Wales throughout the period of one year ending with the date of death.

(3) Where an application under subsection (1) above is made to a court by any person other than a party to the marriage to which the application relates, the court shall refuse to hear the application if it considers that the applicant does not have a sufficient interest in the determination of that application.

Amendments—CSPSSA 2000, s 83, Sch 8, para 4; CCA 2013, s 17, Sch 11.

'Deferral to court in another jurisdiction'—In *Abbassi v Abbassi and another* [2006] 2 FLR 415, CA, the Court of Appeal indicated that it was within the discretion of a judge to defer an issue of the validity of a marriage to a court in another jurisdiction. Each case turned on its own facts. In family proceedings with an international dimension it was becoming increasingly common to have regard to the sensible transfer by the court acting on its own motion. It would be appropriate to use a liaison judge to facilitate collaboration.

Overseas same-sex relationship—In *Wilkinson v Kitzinger* [2007] 1 FLR 295, FD, the President refused to declare a valid marriage between two women, domiciled in England and Wales who went through a ceremony of marriage in British Columbia which was a valid marriage there.

Marriage not subsisting—In the case of couples who have a second 'marriage' in the UK, they should no longer need to apply for a declaration of non-marriage (s 55(1)(c)), suggests Mostyn J, on production of his judgment in *Galloway v Goldstein* [2012] 1 FLR 1254, FD (at [15]).

'habitually resident' (s 55(2)(b),(c)(i))—See under s 3 and **Habitual residence** under CSA 1991, s 44.

Procedure—See Procedural Guide B1.

55A Declarations of parentage

(1) Subject to the following provisions of this section, any person may apply to the High Court or the family court for a declaration as to whether or not a person named in the application is or was the parent of another person so named.

(2) A court shall have jurisdiction to entertain an application under subsection (1) above if, and only if, either of the persons named in it for the purposes of that subsection –

(a) is domiciled in England and Wales on the date of the application, or
(b) has been habitually resident in England and Wales throughout the period of one year ending with that date, or
(c) died before that date and either –
  (i) was at death domiciled in England and Wales, or

(ii) had been habitually resident in England and Wales throughout the period of one year ending with the date of death.

(3) Except in a case falling within subsection (4) below, the court shall refuse to hear an application under subsection (1) above unless it considers that the applicant has a sufficient personal interest in the determination of the application (but this is subject to section 27 of the Child Support Act 1991).

(4) The excepted cases are where the declaration sought is as to whether or not –

(a) the applicant is the parent of a named person;
(b) a named person is the parent of the applicant; or
(c) a named person is the other parent of a named child of the applicant.

(5) Where an application under subsection (1) above is made and one of the persons named in it for the purposes of that subsection is a child, the court may refuse to hear the application if it considers that the determination of the application would not be in the best interests of the child.

(6) Where a court refuses to hear an application under subsection (1) above it may order that the applicant may not apply again for the same declaration without leave of the court.

(7) Where a declaration is made by a court on an application under subsection (1) above, the prescribed officer of the court shall notify the Registrar General, in such a manner and within such period as may be prescribed, of the making of that declaration.

Amendments—Inserted by CSPSSA 2000, s 83(1),(2). Amended by CCA 2013, s 17, Sch 11.

Procedure—Application is made by (1) FPR 2010, Pt 19 and rr 8.18–8.22 as a freestanding application or (2) alongside existing proceedings where an issue of parentage arises in those proceedings.

Child Support Act 1991, s 27—Application for a declaration by non-resident parent, parent with care or the Secretary of State for Work and Pensions (under CSA 1991, s 27, see above) where needed to prove parentage under the 1991 Act is under s 55A, that is where a parent or the Secretary of State disagree with a decision as to parentage.

Scientific tests direction—The court may direct scientific tests (FLRA 1969, s 20) to determine whether a person is the parent of the child. Application for a scientific tests direction can only be made in existing civil (including family) proceedings in which the issue of parentage arises, including in proceedings under FLA 1986, s 55A).

Appeal in the Family Court—Where the issue of parentage arises on an appeal under CSA 1991, s 20, the appeal is transferred for hearing from the first-tier tribunal to the family proceedings court. The Family Court hearing an appeal under CSA 1991, s 20 cannot make a declaration under s 55A where no application has been made for such a declaration and the child in question has not been made a party (*Re L (Family Proceedings Court) (Appeal: Jurisdiction)* [2005] 1 FLR 210, FD).

'parent' (s 55A(1))—Includes a person who is to be treated as a parent by virtue of HFEA 1990, s 27 or 28 (*Re R (IVF: Paternity of Child)* [2003] 1 FLR 1183, CA). See also the commentary under HFEA 2008, s 37.

'habitually resident' (s 55A(2))—See under s 3 and **Habitual residence** under CSA 1991, s 44.

Notification to the Registrar General (s 55A(7))—If a declaration is granted, the birth may be re-registered accordingly (Births and Deaths Registration Act 1953, s 14A). Registration of a declaration is prescribed by FPR 2010, r 8.22 as 21 days, although this period may be diverged from in exceptional circumstances (*Re F (Children)* [2013] 2 FLR 1036, CA: 4 months is permissible; 4 years was plainly too long).

56 Declarations as to legitimacy or legitimation

(1) Any person may apply to the High Court or the family court for a declaration –

(a) (*repealed*)
(b) that he is the legitimate child of his parents.

(2) Any person may apply to the High Court or the family court for one (or for one or, in the alternative, the other) of the following declarations, that is to say –

(a) a declaration that he has become a legitimated person;
(b) a declaration that he has not become a legitimated person.

(3) A court shall have jurisdiction to entertain an application under this section if, and only if, the applicant –

(a) is domiciled in England and Wales on the date of the application, or
(b) has been habitually resident in England and Wales throughout the period of one year ending with that date.

(4) Where a declaration is made by a court on an application under subsection (1) above, the prescribed officer of the court shall notify the Registrar General, in such a manner and within such period as may be prescribed, of the making of that declaration.

(5) In this section 'legitimated person' means a person legitimated or recognised as legitimated –

(a) under section 2, 2A or 3 of the Legitimacy Act 1976; or
(b) under section 1 or 8 of the Legitimacy Act 1926; or
(c) by a legitimation (whether or not by virtue of the subsequent marriage of his parents) recognised by the law of England and Wales and effected under the law of another country.

Amendments—Substituted by FLRA 1987, s 22; CSPSSA 2000, s 83, Sch 8, para 5, Sch 9; HFEA 2008, s 56, Sch 6, Pt 1, para 23; CCA 2013, s 17, Sch 11.

'habitually resident' (s 56(3)(b))—See under s 3 and **Habitual residence** under CSA 1991, s 44.

57 Declarations as to adoptions effected overseas

(1) Any person whose status as an adopted child of any person depends on whether he has been adopted by that person by either –

(a) a Convention adoption, or an overseas adoption, within the meaning of the Adoption and Children Act 2002, or
(b) an adoption recognised by the law of England and Wales and effected under the law of any country outside the British Islands,

may apply to the High Court or the family court for one (or for one or, in the alternative, the other) of the declarations mentioned in subsection (2) below.

(2) The said declarations are –

(a) a declaration that the applicant is for the purposes of section 39 of the Adoption Act 1976 or section 67 of the Adoption and Children Act 2002 the adopted child of that person;
(b) a declaration that the applicant is not for the purposes of that section the adopted child of that person.

(3) A court shall have jurisdiction to entertain an application under subsection (1) above if, and only if, the applicant –

(a) is domiciled in England and Wales on the date of the application, or
(b) has been habitually resident in England and Wales throughout the period of one year ending with that date.

(4) …

Amendments—Adoption (Intercountry Aspects) Act 1999, s 15(1), Sch 2, para 5; CSPSSA 2000, s 83, Sch 8, para 6; ACA 2002, Sch 3, para 49; CCA 2013, s 17, Sch 11.

58 General provisions as to the making and effect of declarations

(1) Where on an application to a court for a declaration under this Part the truth of the proposition to be declared is proved to the satisfaction of the court, the court shall make that declaration unless to do so would manifestly be contrary to public policy.

(2) Any declarations made under this Part shall be binding on Her Majesty and all other persons.

(3) A court, on the dismissal of an application for a declaration under this Part, shall not have power to make any declaration for which an application has not been made.

(4) No declaration which may be applied for under this Part may be made otherwise than under this Part by any court.

(5) No declaration may be made by any court, whether under this Part or otherwise –

(a) that a marriage was at its inception void;
(b) *(repealed)*

(6) Nothing in this section shall affect the powers of any court to grant a decree of nullity of marriage.

Amendments—CSPSSA 2000, s 83(3), Sch 8, para 7, Sch 9.

59 Provisions relating to the Attorney-General

(1) On an application to a court for a declaration under this Part the court may at any stage of the proceedings, of its own motion or on the application of any party to the proceedings, direct that all necessary papers in the matter be sent to the Attorney-General.

(2) The Attorney-General, whether or not he is sent papers in relation to an application to a court for a declaration under this Part, may –

- (a) intervene in the proceedings on that application in such manner as he thinks necessary or expedient, and
- (b) argue before the court any question in relation to the application which the court considers it necessary to have fully argued.

(3) Where any costs are incurred by the Attorney-General in connection with any application to a court for a declaration under this Part, the court may make such order as it considers just as to the payment of those costs by parties to the proceedings.

Amendments—CSPSSA 2000, s 83(3), Sch 8, para 8.

The Attorney-General's role—There are two main reasons for these provisions. First, to minimise the risk of success of unopposed, or collusive, proceedings which have been brought fraudulently to obtain a declaration. Section 58(2) provides that 'Any declaration made under this Part shall be binding on Her Majesty and all other persons'; this creates scope for collusive proceedings to be brought for the purpose of obtaining some collateral result in relation to the state or other third parties, such as British citizenship. The role of the Attorney-General is therefore not dissimilar to that which the Queen's Proctor may play in undefended divorce proceedings. Secondly, quite apart from this aspect, s 58(1) provides that 'Where on an application to a court for a declaration under this Part the truth of the proposition to be declared is proved to the satisfaction of the court, the court shall make that declaration unless to do so would manifestly be contrary to public policy'. The Attorney-General may wish to express a view on the requirements of public policy in a particular case.

****

Family Law Act 1996

ARRANGEMENT OF SECTIONS

PART IV
FAMILY HOMES AND DOMESTIC VIOLENCE

Section		Page
	Rights to occupy matrimonial home	
30	Rights concerning matrimonial home where one spouse has no estate etc	874
31	Effect of home rights as charge on dwelling-house	875
32	Further provisions relating to home rights	877
	Occupation orders	
33	Occupation orders where applicant has estate or interest etc or has home rights	877
34	Effect of order under s 33 where rights are charge on dwelling-house	879
35	One former spouse or former civil partner with no existing right to occupy	879
36	One cohabitant or former cohabitant with no existing right to occupy	881
37	Neither spouse or civil partner entitled to occupy	883
38	Neither cohabitant or former cohabitant entitled to occupy	884
39	Supplementary provisions	885
40	Additional provisions that may be included in certain occupation orders	885
	Non-molestation orders	
42	Non-molestation orders	886

42A	Offence of breaching non-molestation order	888
	Further provisions relating to occupation and non-molestation orders	
43	Leave of court required for applications by children under sixteen	888
44	Evidence of agreement to marry or form a civil partnership	889
45	Ex parte orders	889
46	Undertakings	890
47	Arrest for breach of order	891
48	Remand for medical examination and report	893
49	Variation and discharge of orders	893
	Transfer of tenancies	
53	Transfer of certain tenancies	894
	Dwelling-house subject to mortgage	
54	Dwelling-house subject to mortgage	894
55	Actions by mortgagees: joining connected persons as parties	895
56	Actions by mortgagees: service of notice on certain persons	895
	Jurisdiction and procedure etc	
57	Jurisdiction of courts	896
58	Contempt proceedings	896
	General	
62	Meaning of 'cohabitants', 'relevant child' and 'associated persons'	896
63	Interpretation of Part IV	897
	PART 4A	
	FORCED MARRIAGE	
	Forced marriage protection orders	
63A	Forced marriage protection orders	899
63B	Contents of orders	900
63C	Applications and other occasions for making orders	900
63CA	Offence of breaching order	902
	Further provision about orders	
63D	Ex parte orders: Part 4A	902
63E	Undertakings instead of orders	903
63F	Duration of orders	904
63G	Variation of orders and their discharge	904
	Arrest for breach of orders	
63J	Arrest under warrant	904
63K	Remand: general	905
63L	Remand: medical examination and report	905
	Jurisdiction and procedure	
63M	Jurisdiction of courts: Part 4A	906
63O	Contempt proceedings: Part 4A	906
	Supplementary	
63Q	Guidance	906
63R	Other protection or assistance against forced marriage	906
63S	Interpretation of Part 4A	906
	Schedule 4 – Provisions Supplementary to Sections 30 and 31	907
	Schedule 5 – Powers of High Court and County Court to Remand	909

Schedule 7 – Transfer of Certain Tenancies on Divorce etc or on Separation of Cohabitants 911
Part I – General 911
Part II – Orders that may be made 913
Part III – Supplementary Provisions 915

****

PART IV
FAMILY HOMES AND DOMESTIC VIOLENCE

Rights to occupy matrimonial home

30 Rights concerning matrimonial home where one spouse has no estate etc

(1) This section applies if –

(a) one spouse or civil partner ('A') is entitled to occupy a dwelling-house by virtue of –
 (i) a beneficial estate or interest or contract; or
 (ii) any enactment giving 'A' the right to remain in occupation; and
(b) the other spouse or civil partner ('B') is not so entitled.

(2) Subject to the provisions of this Part, 'B' has the following rights ('home rights') –

(a) if in occupation, a right not to be evicted or excluded from the dwelling-house or any part of it by 'A' except with the leave of the court given by an order under section 33;
(b) if not in occupation, a right with the leave of the court so given to enter into and occupy the dwelling-house.

(3) If 'B' is entitled under this section to occupy a dwelling-house or any part of a dwelling-house, any payment or tender made or other thing done by 'B' in or towards satisfaction of any liability of 'A' in respect of rent, mortgage payments or other outgoings affecting the dwelling-house shall, whether or not it is made or done in pursuance of an order under section 40, be as good as if made or done by 'A'.

(4) 'B's' occupation by virtue of this section –

(a) is to be treated, for the purposes of the Rent (Agriculture) Act 1976 and the Rent Act 1977 (other than Part V and sections 103 to 106 of that Act), as occupation by A as A's residence, and
(b) if B occupies the dwelling-house as B's only or principal home, is to be treated, for the purposes of the Housing Act 1985, Part I of the Housing Act 1988, Chapter 1 of Part 5 of the Housing Act 1996 and the Prevention of Social Housing Fraud Act 2013, as occupation by A as A's only or principal home.

(5) If B –

(a) is entitled under this section to occupy a dwelling-house or any part of a dwelling-house, and
(b) makes any payment in or towards satisfaction of any liability of A in respect of mortgage payments affecting the dwelling-house,

the person to whom the payment is made may treat it as having been made by A, but the fact that that person has treated any such payment as having been so made does not affect any claim of B against A to an interest in the dwelling-house by virtue of the payment.

(6) If B is entitled under this section to occupy a dwelling-house or part of a dwelling-house by reason of an interest of A under a trust, all the provisions of subsections (3) to (5) apply in relation to the trustees as they apply in relation to A.

(7) This section does not apply to a dwelling-house which –

(a) in the case of spouses, has at no time been, and was at no time intended by them to be, a matrimonial home of theirs; and

(b) in the case of civil partners, has at no time been, and was at no time intended by them to be, a civil partnership home of theirs.

(8) B's home rights continue –

(a) only so long as the marriage or civil partnership subsists, except to the extent that an order under section 33(5) otherwise provides; and

(b) only so long as A is entitled as mentioned in subsection (1) to occupy the dwelling-house, except where provision is made by section 31 for those rights to be a charge on an estate or interest in the dwelling-house.

(9) It is hereby declared that a person –

(a) who has an equitable interest in a dwelling-house or in its proceeds of sale, but

(b) is not a person in whom there is vested (whether solely or as joint tenant) a legal estate in fee simple or a legal term of years absolute in the dwelling-house,

is to be treated, only for the purpose of determining whether he has home rights, as not being entitled to occupy the dwelling-house by virtue of that interest.

Amendments—SI 1997/74; CPA 2004, s 82, Sch 9, para 1(1)–(11); Prevention of Social Housing Fraud Act 2013, s 10, Sch, para 6 (applies to England only).

Scope—This section provides that where one spouse or civil partner has the right to occupy a dwelling-house, either because he owns it or has a contractual tenancy or is a statutory tenant of it, the other party has home rights. Those rights are, if in occupation, not to be evicted without leave of the court or, if not in occupation, the right, with leave of the court, to return. The provision mirrors Matrimonial Homes Act 1983, s 1 but is different in three respects: first, the rights are known as 'home rights' instead of rights of occupation; secondly, by virtue of s 63(1), a 'dwelling-house' includes a caravan or houseboat; and thirdly, under ss 30(7) and 33(1)(b), a dwelling-house which has not yet been, but is intended to be, a home is included (*Gull v Gull* [2008] 1 FLR 232, CA). There are limitations to the right of a co-owner to go into property occupied by an estranged spouse. A husband, who is a co-owner with wife of a matrimonial property, in which he did not reside but had not been formally excluded and who used violence to gain entry, is not a protected occupier under Criminal Law Act 1977, s 12A and could be convicted of the use of violence to gain entry under s 6 of that Act: *Wakolo v DPP* [2012] EWHC 611 (Admin).

Duration of matrimonial home rights (s 30(8))—Matrimonial home rights subsist only for the duration of the marriage unless an order is made under s 33(5) before the marriage is ended by death or decree of divorce or nullity.

Treatment of one spouse's rights and obligations as those of the other spouse (s 30(3)–(5))—These subsections provide that payment of rent or mortgage by the spouse who does not have an interest or tenancy in the property is as good as payment by the other, and that the occupation of one spouse is to be treated as occupation by the other. Thus, if there is a statutory tenancy, even though the statutory tenant has left, the remaining spouse's occupation is as good as that of the statutory tenant. This protection lasts only so long as the status of the spouse is not ended by decree absolute. In s 30(4)(b) the references to the Housing Act 1985, the Housing Act 1988, Pt I and Housing Act 1996 are respectively to occupation by virtue of a secure tenancy, an assured tenancy/assured shorthold tenancy and an introductory tenancy (in effect a shorthold tenancy in the private sector).

Prevention of unilateral termination of tenancy—As set out in Procedural Guide A11, a tenancy in the other spouse's name or in joint names can be destroyed unilaterally by surrender or notice to quit. Consideration should therefore be given to applying for an injunction to prevent such action.

'matrimonial home' (s 30(7))—There is no definition of this term, although it includes a dwelling-house which has not yet been but is intended to be a matrimonial home, and a caravan or houseboat (see **Scope** above). However, for the purpose of certain sections, a caravan and a houseboat are *not* within the definition of dwelling-house (see s 63(4)). Whether a dwelling-house is or is intended to be a matrimonial home is a question of fact, having regard to any periods of time spent living there and any agreement between the parties as to whether a property is to be treated as their present or intended matrimonial home (*King v King* [1942] P 1, PDAD).

31 Effect of home rights as charge on dwelling-house

(1) Subsections (2) and (3) apply if, at any time during a marriage or civil partnership, A is entitled to occupy a dwelling-house by virtue of a beneficial estate or interest.

(2) B's home rights are a charge on the estate or interest.

(3) The charge created by subsection (2) has the same priority as if it were an equitable interest created at whichever is the latest of the following dates –

(a) the date on which A acquires the estate or interest;

(b) the date of the marriage or of the formation of the civil partnership; and

(c) 1 January 1968 (the commencement date of the Matrimonial Homes Act 1967).

(4) Subsections (5) and (6) apply if, at any time when B's home rights are a charge on an interest of A under a trust, there are, apart from A or B, no persons, living or unborn, who are or could become beneficiaries under the trust.

(5) The rights are a charge also on the estate or interest of the trustees for A.

(6) The charge created by subsection (5) has the same priority as if it were an equitable interest created (under powers overriding the trusts) on the date when it arises.

(7) In determining for the purposes of subsection (4) whether there are any persons who are not, but could become, beneficiaries under the trust, there is to be disregarded any potential exercise of a general power of appointment exercisable by either or both of A and B alone (whether or not the exercise of it requires the consent of another person).

(8) Even though B's home rights are a charge on an estate or interest in the dwelling-house, those rights are brought to an end by –

(a) the death of A, or
(b) the termination (otherwise than by death) of the marriage or civil partnership,

unless the court directs otherwise by an order made under section 33(5).

(9) If –

(a) B's home rights are a charge on an estate or interest in the dwelling-house, and
(b) that estate or interest is surrendered to merge in some other estate or interest expectant on it in such circumstances that, but for the merger, the person taking the estate or interest would be bound by the charge,

the surrender has effect subject to the charge and the persons thereafter entitled to the other estate or interest are, for so long as the estate or interest surrendered would have endured if not so surrendered, to be treated for all purposes of this Part as deriving title to the other estate or interest under A or, as the case may be, under the trustees for A, by virtue of the surrender.

(10) If the title to the legal estate by virtue of which A is entitled to occupy a dwelling-house (including any legal estate held by trustees for A) is registered under the Land Registration Act 2002 or any enactment replaced by that Act –

(a) registration of a land charge affecting the dwelling-house by virtue of this Part is to be effected by registering a notice under that Act; and
(b) B's home rights are not to be capable of falling within paragraph 2 of Schedule 1 or 3 to that Act.

(11) *(repealed)*

(12) If –

(a) B's home rights are a charge on the estate of A or of trustees of A, and
(b) that estate is the subject of a mortgage,

then if, after the date of the creation of the mortgage ('the first mortgage'), the charge is registered under section 2 of the Land Charges Act 1972, the charge is, for the purposes of section 94 of the Law of Property Act 1925 (which regulates the rights of mortgagees to make further advances ranking in priority to subsequent mortgages), to be deemed to be a mortgage subsequent in date to the first mortgage.

(13) It is hereby declared that a charge under subsection (2) or (5) is not registrable under subsection 10 or under section 2 of the Land Charges Act 1972 unless it is a charge on a legal estate.

Amendments—CPA 2004, s 82, Sch 9, para 2(1)–(12); LRA 2002, s 34(2)(a),(b), Sch 13.

Protecting the charge—No protection under FLA 1996 is required in cases where the home is held jointly, both legally and beneficially, by the spouse or civil partner and the other spouse or the other civil partner. To give protection against third parties such as mortgagees or purchasers, in cases of sole ownership, it is essential that the charge is registered under either LRA 2002 (agreed notice) or the Land Charges Act 1972 (Class F land charge), as appropriate. For the purpose of LRA 2002, home rights are not an overriding interest, but constitute a charge on the home that can be protected in the register by an agreed notice (Land Registration Rules 2003, r 82). If the spouse or civil partner has home rights in relation to the other spouse's or civil partner's interest under a trust, notice of the charge can only be registered if there are no persons, living or unborn, who are or could become beneficiaries under the trust (s 31(4),(6),(13)). The charge should be registered as soon as the legal adviser is informed that the marriage or civil partnership is in difficulty (*Miles v Bull* [1969] 1 QB 258, QBD). The Land Registration Rules 2003 provide that notice of the charge is automatically given to the owner. Protection ends with the termination of the marriage or civil partnership subject to the power of the court, during the subsistence of the marriage or civil partnership, to direct that the home rights shall continue even though the marriage or civil partnership may have come to an end (FLA 1996, s 33(5)). Therefore, where no order is made under FLA 1996, s 33(5), immediately before final decree, an application should be made for a financial order or remedy, including a claim for a property adjustment order. The Class F land charge (unregistered land)/agreed notice (registered land) must be replaced with a pending action land charge (unregistered land)/notice or restriction (registered land) in respect of the pending application for a property adjustment order (see *Perez-Adamson v Perez-Rivas* [1987] 2 FLR 472, CA for applications in relation to unregistered land). A spouse's or civil partner's rights of occupation may only be protected in respect of one home at any one time, whether the other spouse's or civil partner's estate or interest in the home is held under a registered or unregistered title (FLA 1996, Sch 4, para 2).

For further procedural information on applications under FLA 1996, see Land Registry Practice Guide 20. See also, Land Registry Practice Guide 19 – Notices, Restrictions and the Protection of Third Party Interests. Consideration should also be given to the procedures available under LRA 2002, ss 42 (power of registrar to enter a restriction) and 46 (power of court to enter a restriction).

Cessation of rights—A spouse's or civil partner's rights of occupation may be brought to an end in the following ways:

- by the death of either spouse or civil partner (s 31(8)(a));
- by the ending of the marriage or civil partnership otherwise than by death (s 31(8)(b), unless the court directs otherwise under s 33(5));
- by an order of the court under FLA 1996, s 33(3) (an occupation order) (including an interim order: *BR v VT (Financial Remedies: Interim)* [2016] 2 FLR 519, FD) (FLA 1996, Sch 4, para 4(1));
- by the spouse or civil partner voluntarily releasing the rights in writing (FLA 1996, Sch 4, para 5(1)).

If the charge under s 31 has been improperly registered, for example, where the applicant is not in occupation of home and does not wish to enter (*Barnett v Hassett* [1982] 1 WLR 1385, CA), the court can set aside the charge or injunct its removal. It is submitted, by analogy with *Poon v Poon* [1994] 2 FLR 857, FD (where it was held that a family court rather than a companies court should deal with the future of a company, by injunction if need be), that where a respondent is caused severe prejudice by registration of the charge, by for instance a bank refusing further borrowing, and the merits justify his application, the Family Court can set aside the charge.

Criminal liability—An individual who is freeholder of a matrimonial property, from which he is not formally excluded and which is occupied by his estranged wife, is not a protected intending occupier under the Criminal Law Act 1977, s 12A and thus cannot avail himself of the defence under s 6(1A) of that Act and can be convicted of the use of violence to gain entry to a property (*Wakolo v DPP* [2012] EWHC 611 (Admin)).

32 Further provisions relating to home rights

Schedule 4 (provisions supplementary to sections 30 and 31) has effect.

Amendments—Substituted by CPA 2004, s 82, Sch 9, para 3.

Occupation orders

33 Occupation orders where applicant has estate or interest etc or has home rights

(1) If –

(a) a person ('the person entitled') –

(i) is entitled to occupy a dwelling-house by virtue of a beneficial estate or interest or contract or by virtue of any enactment giving him the right to remain in occupation, or

(ii) has home rights in relation to a dwelling-house, and

(b) the dwelling-house –

(i) is or at any time has been the home of the person entitled and of another person with whom he is associated, or

(ii) was at any time intended by the person entitled and any such other person to be their home,

the person entitled may apply to the court for an order containing any of the provisions specified in subsections (3), (4) and (5).

(2) If an agreement to marry is terminated, no application under this section may be made by virtue of section 62(3)(e) by reference to that agreement after the end of the period of three years beginning with the date on which it is terminated.

(2A) If a civil partnership agreement (as defined by section 73 of the Civil Partnership Act 2004) is terminated, no application under this section may be made by virtue of section 62(3)(eza) by reference to that agreement after the end of the period of three years beginning with the day on which it is terminated.

(3) An order under this section may –

(a) enforce the applicant's entitlement to remain in occupation as against the other person ('the respondent');
(b) require the respondent to permit the applicant to enter and remain in the dwelling-house or part of the dwelling-house;
(c) regulate the occupation of the dwelling-house by either or both parties;
(d) if the respondent is entitled as mentioned in subsection (1)(a)(i), prohibit, suspend or restrict the exercise by him of his right to occupy the dwelling-house;
(e) if the respondent has home rights in relation to the dwelling-house and the applicant is the other spouse or civil partner, restrict or terminate those rights;
(f) require the respondent to leave the dwelling-house or part of the dwelling-house; or
(g) exclude the respondent from a defined area in which the dwelling-house is included.

(4) An order under this section may declare that the applicant is entitled as mentioned in subsection (1)(a)(i) or has home rights.

(5) If the applicant has home rights and the respondent is the other spouse or civil partner, an order under this section made during the marriage or civil partnership may provide that those rights are not brought to an end by –

(a) the death of the other spouse or civil partner; or
(b) the termination (otherwise than by death) of the marriage or civil partnership.

(6) In deciding whether to exercise its powers under subsection (3) and (if so) in what manner, the court shall have regard to all the circumstances including –

(a) the housing needs and housing resources of each of the parties and of any relevant child;
(b) the financial resources of each of the parties;
(c) the likely effect of any order, or of any decision by the court not to exercise its powers under subsection (3), on the health, safety or well-being of the parties and of any relevant child; and
(d) the conduct of the parties in relation to each other and otherwise.

(7) If it appears to the court that the applicant or any relevant child is likely to suffer significant harm attributable to conduct of the respondent if an order under this section containing one or more of the provisions mentioned in subsection (3) is not made, the court shall make the order unless it appears to the court that –

(a) the respondent or any relevant child is likely to suffer significant harm if the order is made; and
(b) the harm likely to be suffered by the respondent or child in that event is as great as, or greater than, the harm attributable to conduct of the respondent which is likely to be suffered by the applicant or child if the order is not made.

(8) The court may exercise its powers under subsection (5) in any case where it considers that in all the circumstances it is just and reasonable to do so.

(9) An order under this section –

(a) may not be made after the death of either of the parties mentioned in subsection (1); and
(b) except in the case of an order made by virtue of subsection (5)(a), ceases to have effect on the death of either party.

(10) An order under this section may, in so far as it has continuing effect, be made for a specified period, until the occurrence of a specified event or until further order.

Amendments—CPA 2004, s 82, Sch 9, para 4(1)–(7).

Defined terms—'associated': s 62(3); 'relevant child': s 62(2).

Occupation orders – general—Sections 33–41 deal with occupation orders. Occupation orders can be made under five different sections, namely ss 33, 35, 36, 37 and 38. Under each section the court can make orders to regulate occupation of the home, to exclude the respondent from the home and the vicinity of the home and to prohibit, terminate or restrict the exercise of the respondent's occupation rights, as appropriate. The court's powers, the factors to which regard is to be had in deciding what, if any, order to make, and the maximum duration of orders, differ from section to section, each representing a self-contained code. It is therefore important that the order is made under the correct section. (See also Sch 7 for transfer of tenancies.)

Scope—Section 33 is much wider in scope than the other sections dealing with occupation orders. Applications can be made under this section if the three conditions in s 33(1) are satisfied, namely that the applicant 'is entitled to occupy'; the respondent is 'associated'; and the house is, was, or was intended to be their home. Thus, most applications by spouses will be made under this section as the majority of spouses are entitled to occupy by virtue of their interest in the property or have home rights. Further, the section is wide enough to include an application by, for example, an owning parent seeking to exclude an adult child. Many cohabitants too will be 'entitled to occupy' and can apply under s 33 rather than under s 36.

'home rights'—See s 30.

Court's powers—These are set out in s 33(3) and include the power in s 33(3)(f) to require the respondent to leave the dwelling-house. There is no maximum duration for an order under s 33 (s 33(10)).

Criteria—The criteria to be applied by the court in deciding whether to exercise its powers are prescribed in s 33(6). In *Lake v Lake* [2007] 1 FLR 427, CA, the Court of Appeal included the conduct of the parties in the balancing exercise. The balance of harm test in s 33(7) must also be considered. In *Re K (A Child)* [2012] 2 FLR 635, CA, the judge had acted outside his jurisdiction in ordering a father to vacate his home so that the mother could remain there while having contact. However, in *Re L (Occupation Order)* [2012] 2 FLR 1417, CA, a father was excluded for 3 months after a finding that the children would suffer serious harm if the parents lived together.

The 'balance of harm' test—Making or not making an order under s 33(3) inevitably causes some harm, and s 33(7) requires the court to balance the harm caused by not making an order against the harm that would be caused by making one. The wording of the section is important: in summary, if it appears that the applicant or any relevant child is likely to suffer significant harm, attributable to conduct of the respondent, if an order is not made, then the court *shall* make the order unless it appears that the respondent or any relevant child is likely to suffer significant harm if the order is made and that harm is as great as, or greater than, the harm likely to be suffered by the applicant or child if the order is not made. The balance of harm test may well prove decisive in many cases and require the court to make the order in the applicant's favour. Even if the test is not decisive (because, for example, the harm would be equal) the court still could make the order having regard to the criteria in s 33(6). The court must consider s 33(7) before s 33(6) (*Chalmers v Johns* [1999] 1 FLR 392, CA).

Extension of home rights—The court has power to issue declarations under s 33(4) and to extend home rights beyond death or dissolution (s 33(5), subject to s 33(8)). Save where a declaration has been made under s 33(5)(a), an order ceases to have effect on the death of either party (s 33(9)).

34 Effect of order under s 33 where rights are charge on dwelling-house

(1) If B's home rights are a charge on the estate or interest of A or of trustees for the other spouse –

(a) any order under section 33 against the other spouse has, except so far as a contrary intention appears, the same effect against persons deriving title under the other spouse or under the trustees and affected by the charge, and

(b) subsections 33(1), (3), (4) and (10) and 30(3) to (6) apply in relation to any person deriving title under the other spouse or under the trustees and affected by the charge as they apply in relation to the other spouse.

(2) The court may make an order under section 33 by virtue of subsection (1)(b) if it considers that in all the circumstances it is just and reasonable to do so.

Amendments—CPA 2004, s 82, Sch 9, para 5.

35 One former spouse or former civil partner with no existing right to occupy

(1) This section applies if –

(a) one former spouse or former civil partner is entitled to occupy a dwelling-house by virtue of a beneficial estate or interest or contract, or by virtue of any enactment giving him the right to remain in occupation;

(b) the other former spouse or former civil partner is not so entitled; and

(c) the dwelling-house –

(i) in the case of former spouses, was at any time their matrimonial home or was at any time intended by them to be their matrimonial home, or

PART II

(ii) in the case of former civil partners, was at any time their civil partnership home or was at any time intended by them to be their civil partnership home.

(2) The former spouse or former civil partner not so entitled may apply to the court for an order under this section against the other former spouse or former civil partner ('the respondent').

(3) If the applicant is in occupation, an order under this section must contain provision –

(a) giving the applicant the right not to be evicted or excluded from the dwelling-house or any part of it by the respondent for the period specified in the order; and

(b) prohibiting the respondent from evicting or excluding the applicant during that period.

(4) If the applicant is not in occupation, an order under this section must contain provision –

(a) giving the applicant the right to enter into and occupy the dwelling-house for the period specified in the order; and

(b) requiring the respondent to permit the exercise of that right.

(5) An order under this section may also –

(a) regulate the occupation of the dwelling-house by either or both of the parties;

(b) prohibit, suspend or restrict the exercise by the respondent of his right to occupy the dwelling-house;

(c) require the respondent to leave the dwelling-house or part of the dwelling-house; or

(d) exclude the respondent from a defined area in which the dwelling-house is included.

(6) In deciding whether to make an order under this section containing provision of the kind mentioned in subsection (3) or (4) and (if so) in what manner, the court shall have regard to all the circumstances including –

(a) the housing needs and housing resources of each of the parties and of any relevant child;

(b) the financial resources of each of the parties;

(c) the likely effect of any order, or of any decision by the court not to exercise its powers under subsection (3) or (4), on the health, safety or well-being of the parties and of any relevant child;

(d) the conduct of the parties in relation to each other and otherwise;

(e) the length of time that has elapsed since the parties ceased to live together;

(f) the length of time that has elapsed since the marriage or civil partnership was dissolved or annulled; and

(g) the existence of any pending proceedings between the parties –

(i) for an order under section 23A or 24 of the Matrimonial Causes Act 1973 (property adjustment orders in connection with divorce proceedings etc);

(ia) for a property adjustment order under Part 2 of Schedule 5 to the Civil Partnership Act 2004;

(ii) for an order under paragraph 1(2)(d) or (e) of Schedule 1 to the Children Act 1989 (orders for financial relief against parents); or

(iii) relating to the legal or beneficial ownership of the dwelling-house.

(7) In deciding whether to exercise its power to include one or more of the provisions referred to in subsection (5) ('a subsection (5) provision') and (if so) in what manner, the court shall have regard to all the circumstances including the matters mentioned in subsection (6)(a) to (e).

(8) If the court decides to make an order under this section and it appears to it that, if the order does not include a subsection (5) provision, the applicant or any relevant child is likely to suffer significant harm attributable to conduct of the respondent, the court shall include the subsection (5) provision in the order unless it appears to the court that –

(a) the respondent or any relevant child is likely to suffer significant harm if the provision is included in the order; and

(b) the harm likely to be suffered by the respondent or child in that event is as great as or greater than the harm attributable to conduct of the respondent which is likely to be suffered by the applicant or child if the provision is not included.

(9) An order under this section –

(a) may not be made after the death of either of the former spouses or former civil partners; and

(b) ceases to have effect on the death of either of them.

(10) An order under this section must be limited so as to have effect for a specified period not exceeding six months, but may be extended on one or more occasions for a further specified period not exceeding six months.

(11) A former spouse or former civil partner who has an equitable interest in the dwelling-house or in the proceeds of sale of the dwelling-house but in whom there is not vested (whether solely or as joint tenant) a legal estate in fee simple or a legal term of years absolute in the dwelling-house is to be treated (but only for the purpose of determining whether he is eligible to apply under this section) as not being entitled to occupy the dwelling-house by virtue of that interest.

(12) Subsection (11) does not prejudice any right of such a former spouse or former civil partner to apply for an order under section 33.

(13) So long as an order under this section remains in force, subsections (3) to (6) of section 30 apply in relation to the applicant –

(a) as if he were B (the person entitled to occupy the dwelling-house by virtue of that section); and

(b) as if the respondent were A (the person entitled as mentioned in subsection (1)(a) of that section).

Amendments—CPA 2004, s 82, Sch 9, para 6(1)–(10).

Occupation orders - general—See under s 33.

Scope—Section 35 applies only to former spouses or former civil partners. There are three conditions (s 35(1),(2)): the applicant is not entitled to occupy; the respondent is entitled to occupy; and the dwelling-house in question was, or was intended to be, their home.

Declarations—An order under s 35 must contain a declaration pursuant to s 35(3) or s 35(4), as appropriate.

Subsection (5) provisions—In addition to the appropriate declaration, an order may also contain any of the provisions referred to in s 35(5). This includes a provision requiring the respondent to leave the dwelling-house.

Criteria—The criteria are prescribed in subsections (6),(7) and (8). Section 35(6)(a),(b),(c) and (d) are the same as s 33(6)(a),(b),(c) and (d) but s 35(6)(e),(f) and (g) are additional factors. Section 35(7) limits the factors to be considered in deciding whether or not to include a 'subsection (5) provision'.

The 'balance of harm' test—The 'balance of harm' test in s 35(8) differs from the 'balance of harm' test in s 33(7). For s 35(8) to apply, the court must first decide to make an order but is then required to 'include a subsection (5) provision' if (in summary) not doing so would cause greater harm attributable to conduct of the respondent than doing so.

Duration—Section 35 orders can only be for a specified period not exceeding 6 months (s 35(10)) but can be extended on one or more occasions for a maximum of 6 months each time.

36 One cohabitant or former cohabitant with no existing right to occupy

(1) This section applies if –

(a) one cohabitant or former cohabitant is entitled to occupy a dwelling-house by virtue of a beneficial estate or interest or contract or by virtue of any enactment giving him the right to remain in occupation;

(b) the other cohabitant or former cohabitant is not so entitled; and

(c) that dwelling-house is the home in which they cohabit or a home in which they at any time cohabited or intended to cohabit.

(2) The cohabitant or former cohabitant not so entitled may apply to the court for an order under this section against the other cohabitant or former cohabitant ('the respondent').

(3) If the applicant is in occupation, an order under this section must contain provision –

(a) giving the applicant the right not to be evicted or excluded from the dwelling-house or any part of it by the respondent for the period specified in the order, and

(b) prohibiting the respondent from evicting or excluding the applicant during that period.

(4) If the applicant is not in occupation, an order under this section must contain provision –

(a) giving the applicant the right to enter into and occupy the dwelling-house for the period specified in the order; and
(b) requiring the respondent to permit the exercise of that right.

(5) An order under this section may also –

(a) regulate the occupation of the dwelling-house by either or both of the parties;
(b) prohibit, suspend or restrict the exercise by the respondent of his right to occupy the dwelling-house;
(c) require the respondent to leave the dwelling-house or part of the dwelling-house; or
(d) exclude the respondent from a defined area in which the dwelling-house is included.

(6) In deciding whether to make an order under this section containing provision of the kind mentioned in subsection (3) or (4) and (if so) in what manner, the court shall have regard to all the circumstances including –

(a) the housing needs and housing resources of each of the parties and of any relevant child;
(b) the financial resources of each of the parties;
(c) the likely effect of any order, or of any decision by the court not to exercise its powers under subsection (3) or (4), on the health, safety or well-being of the parties and of any relevant child;
(d) the conduct of the parties in relation to each other and otherwise;
(e) the nature of the parties' relationship and in particular the level of commitment involved in it;
(f) the length of time during which they have cohabited;
(g) whether there are or have been any children who are children of both parties or for whom both parties have or have had parental responsibility;
(h) the length of time that has elapsed since the parties ceased to live together; and
(i) the existence of any pending proceedings between the parties –
   (i) for an order under paragraph 1(2)(d) or (e) of Schedule 1 to the Children Act 1989 (orders for financial relief against parents), or
   (ii) relating to the legal or beneficial ownership of the dwelling-house.

(7) In deciding whether to exercise its powers to include one or more of the provisions referred to in subsection (5) ('a subsection (5) provision') and (if so) in what manner, the court shall have regard to all the circumstances including –

(a) the matters mentioned in subsection (6)(a) to (d); and
(b) the questions mentioned in subsection (8).

(8) The questions are –

(a) whether the applicant or any relevant child is likely to suffer significant harm attributable to conduct of the respondent if the subsection (5) provision is not included in the order; and
(b) whether the harm likely to be suffered by the respondent or child if the provision is included is as great as or greater than the harm attributable to conduct of the respondent which is likely to be suffered by the applicant or child if the provision is not included.

(9) An order under this section –

(a) may not be made after the death of either of the parties; and
(b) ceases to have effect on the death of either of them.

(10) An order under this section must be limited so as to have effect for a specified period not exceeding six months, but may be extended on one occasion for a further specified period not exceeding six months.

(11) A person who has an equitable interest in the dwelling-house or in the proceeds of sale of the dwelling-house but in whom there is not vested (whether solely or as joint tenant) a legal estate in fee simple or a legal term of years absolute in the dwelling-house is to be treated (but only for the

purpose of determining whether he is eligible to apply under this section) as not being entitled to occupy the dwelling-house by virtue of that interest.

(12) Subsection (11) does not prejudice any right of such a person to apply for an order under section 33.

(13) So long as the order remains in force, subsections (3) to (6) of section 30 apply in relation to the applicant –

- (a) as if he were B (the person entitled to occupy the dwelling-house by virtue of that section); and
- (b) as if the respondent were A (the person entitled as mentioned in subsection (1)(a) of that section).

Amendments—CPA 2004, s 82, Sch 9, para 7; Domestic Violence, Crime and Victims Act 2004, s 2(2), Sch 10, para 34.

Occupation orders – general—See under s 33.

Scope—Section 36 applies only to cohabitants and former cohabitants. (Applicants should first consider if they are eligible to apply under s 33.) There are three conditions for an application under s 36: namely that the applicant cohabitant, or former cohabitant, is not entitled to occupy; the respondent cohabitant, or former cohabitant, is entitled to occupy; and the dwelling-house in question is the home in which they live, did live or intended to live (s 36(1)).

Mandatory provisions—If the court does make an order under s 36 it must contain a provision under s 36(3) or s 36(4), as appropriate.

Discretionary provisions—The order may also contain any of the provisions in s 36(5). This includes requiring the respondent to leave the dwelling-house.

Criteria—The criteria are prescribed in s 36(6)–(8).

The 'balance of harm' test—Note that the 'balance of harm' test in s 36(8) is quite different from that in s 33(7) and s 35(8) as it imposes no duty on the court to make the order but merely requires the court to consider the questions posed.

Duration—A s 36 order is limited in time to 6 months and can be extended once only for a further period not exceeding 6 months (s 36(10)).

37 Neither spouse or civil partner entitled to occupy

(1) This section applies if –

- (a) one spouse or former spouse and the other spouse or former spouse occupy a dwelling-house which is or was the matrimonial home; but
- (b) neither of them is entitled to remain in occupation –
  - (i) by virtue of a beneficial estate or interest or contract; or
  - (ii) by virtue of any enactment giving him the right to remain in occupation.

(1A) This section also applies if –

- (a) one civil partner or former civil partner and the other civil partner or former civil partner occupy a dwelling-house which is or was the civil partnership home; but
- (b) neither of them is entitled to remain in occupation –
  - (i) by virtue of a beneficial estate or interest or contract; or
  - (ii) by virtue of any enactment giving him the right to remain in occupation.

(2) Either of the parties may apply to the court for an order against the other under this section.

(3) An order under this section may –

- (a) require the respondent to permit the applicant to enter and remain in the dwelling-house or part of the dwelling-house;
- (b) regulate the occupation of the dwelling-house by either or both of the parties;
- (c) require the respondent to leave the dwelling-house or part of the dwelling-house; or
- (d) exclude the respondent from a defined area in which the dwelling-house is included.

(4) Subsections (6) and (7) of section 33 apply to the exercise by the court of its powers under this section as they apply to the exercise by the court of its powers under subsection (3) of that section.

(5) An order under this section must be limited so as to have effect for a specified period not exceeding six months, but may be extended on one or more occasions for a further specified period not exceeding six months.

PART II

Amendments—CPA 2004, s 82, Sch 9, para 8(1)–(4).

Occupation orders – general—See under s 33.

Scope—An application under s 37 can be made if three conditions are satisfied: namely that the applicant is a spouse, former spouse, civil partner or former civil partner; the respondent is the spouse, former spouse, civil partner or formal civil partner; and neither of them is entitled to occupy the dwelling-house which is or was their home. Applications under s 37 will be relatively rare but can be made, for example, where the parties occupy under a bare licence and the property is owned by trustees, or even where applicant and respondent are squatters.

Court's powers—The orders which the court can make are specified in s 37(3). This includes power to require the respondent to leave the dwelling-house.

Criteria—The criteria are the same as those set out in s 33(6).

The 'balance of harm' test—The balance of harm test in s 33(7) applies (s 37(4)).

Duration—Orders can be for a maximum period of 6 months but can be extended on one or more occasions each for 6 months (s 37(5)).

38 Neither cohabitant or former cohabitant entitled to occupy

(1) This section applies if –

- (a) one cohabitant or former cohabitant and the other cohabitant or former cohabitant occupy a dwelling-house which is the home in which they cohabit or cohabited; but
- (b) neither of them is entitled to remain in occupation –
  - (i) by virtue of a beneficial estate or interest or contract; or
  - (ii) by virtue of any enactment giving him the right to remain in occupation.

(2) Either of the parties may apply to the court for an order against the other under this section.

(3) An order under this section may –

- (a) require the respondent to permit the applicant to enter and remain in the dwelling-house or part of the dwelling-house;
- (b) regulate the occupation of the dwelling-house by either or both of the parties;
- (c) require the respondent to leave the dwelling-house or part of the dwelling-house; or
- (d) exclude the respondent from a defined area in which the dwelling-house is included.

(4) In deciding whether to exercise its powers to include one or more of the provisions referred to in subsection (3) ('a subsection (3) provision') and (if so) in what manner, the court shall have regard to all the circumstances including –

- (a) the housing needs and housing resources of each of the parties and of any relevant child;
- (b) the financial resources of each of the parties;
- (c) the likely effect of any order, or of any decision by the court not to exercise its powers under subsection (3), on the health, safety or well-being of the parties and of any relevant child;
- (d) the conduct of the parties in relation to each other and otherwise; and
- (e) the questions mentioned in subsection (5).

(5) The questions are –

- (a) whether the applicant or any relevant child is likely to suffer significant harm attributable to conduct of the respondent if the subsection (3) provision is not included in the order; and
- (b) whether the harm likely to be suffered by the respondent or child if the provision is included is as great as or greater than the harm attributable to conduct of the respondent which is likely to be suffered by the applicant or child if the provision is not included.

(6) An order under this section shall be limited so as to have effect for a specified period not exceeding six months, but may be extended on one occasion for a further specified period not exceeding six months.

Amendments—Domestic Violence, Crime and Victims Act 2004, s 58(1), Sch 10, para 35.

Occupation orders – general—See under s 33.

Scope—An application can be made under s 38 if the applicant is a cohabitant or former cohabitant, the respondent is the other cohabitant or former cohabitant and neither of them is entitled to occupy the dwelling-house which is the home in which they live or lived together.

Court's powers—The court's powers are in s 38(3). This includes power to require the respondent to leave the dwelling-house.

Criteria—The criteria to be applied are in s 38(4) and (5).

The 'balance of harm' test—The 'balance of harm' test in s 38(5) imposes no duty on the court to make the order (unlike s 33(7) and s 35(8)) and the balancing of the harm caused by making or not making the order is merely a factor to be considered.

Duration—Orders under s 38 can be for a maximum duration of 6 months and can be extended once (s 38(6)).

39 Supplementary provisions

(1) In this Part an 'occupation order' means an order under section 33, 35, 36, 37 or 38.

(2) An application for an occupation order may be made in other family proceedings or without any other family proceedings being instituted.

(3) If –

- (a) an application for an occupation order is made under section 33, 35, 36, 37 or 38, and
- (b) the court considers that it has no power to make the order under the section concerned, but that it has power to make an order under one of the other sections,

the court may make an order under that other section.

(4) The fact that a person has applied for an occupation order under sections 35 to 38, or that an occupation order has been made, does not affect the right of any person to claim a legal or equitable interest in any property in any subsequent proceedings (including subsequent proceedings under this Part).

Scope—Applications for occupation orders can be freestanding or ancillary to other family proceedings (s 39(2)). In either case the procedure is the same. Form FL401 is used to make the application (see Procedural Guide A8). Occupation orders often have to be sought at short notice where solicitors have to act on prima facie instructions, often given when the client is under emotional stress. It is inevitable therefore that despite every effort to proceed under the correct section, it may transpire at the hearing that the application has in fact been made under the wrong section. Section 39(3) prevents the court having to dismiss the application and gives it power to make the order as if the application had been made under the correct section.

Section 39(4) avoids an applicant being estopped from asserting an interest in the property. A misinformed applicant claiming a legal or beneficial interest will not be prejudiced by the fact that an application for an occupation order initially stated that the applicant had no interest in the property.

40 Additional provisions that may be included in certain occupation orders

(1) The court may on, or at any time after, making an occupation order under section 33, 35 or 36 –

- (a) impose on either party obligations as to –
  - (i) the repair and maintenance of the dwelling-house; or
  - (ii) the discharge of rent, mortgage payments or other outgoings affecting the dwelling-house;
- (b) order a party occupying the dwelling-house or any part of it (including a party who is entitled to do so by virtue of a beneficial estate or interest or contract or by virtue of any enactment giving him the right to remain in occupation) to make periodical payments to the other party in respect of the accommodation, if the other party would (but for the order) be entitled to occupy the dwelling-house by virtue of a beneficial estate or interest or contract or by virtue of any such enactment;
- (c) grant either party possession or use of furniture or other contents of the dwelling-house;
- (d) order either party to take reasonable care of any furniture or other contents of the dwelling-house;
- (e) order either party to take reasonable steps to keep the dwelling-house and any furniture or other contents secure.

(2) In deciding whether and, if so, how to exercise its powers under this section, the court shall have regard to all the circumstances of the case including –

(a) the financial needs and financial resources of the parties; and
(b) the financial obligations which they have, or are likely to have in the foreseeable future, including financial obligations to each other and to any relevant child.

(3) An order under this section ceases to have effect when the occupation order to which it relates ceases to have effect.

Scope—This section contains ancillary provisions which need to be considered in every case where an occupation order is sought under s 33, 35 or 36. Section 40(1)(a)(ii) enables the court, at the initial or a subsequent application, to order that rent or mortgage payments should be paid. It will sometimes be better, and certainly quicker, to obtain an order under this provision rather than, for example, making a separate application for maintenance pending suit. Under s 40(3) the additional provision cannot last longer than the occupation order itself. See **Duration** in the commentary to the relevant section. Unfortunately, s 40 is seriously defective in that there is no procedure for enforcing compliance: 'it was clear that orders under s 40 ... were unenforceable and of no value to the spouse or cohabitee remaining in occupation. That was a serious omission which required urgent alteration' (per Butler-Sloss P in (*Nwogbe v Nwogbe* [2000] 2 FLR 744, CA). Thus s 40 is only of value if the respondent is likely to comply without the need for enforcement.

41 (*repealed*)

Non-molestation orders

42 Non-molestation orders

(1) In this Part a 'non-molestation order' means an order containing either or both of the following provisions –

(a) provision prohibiting a person ('the respondent') from molesting another person who is associated with the respondent;
(b) provision prohibiting the respondent from molesting a relevant child.

(2) The court may make a non-molestation order –

(a) if an application for the order has been made (whether in other family proceedings or without any other family proceedings being instituted) by a person who is associated with the respondent; or
(b) if in any family proceedings to which the respondent is a party the court considers that the order should be made for the benefit of any other party to the proceedings or any relevant child even though no such application has been made.

(3) In subsection (2) 'family proceedings' includes proceedings in which the court has made an emergency protection order under section 44 of the Children Act 1989 which includes an exclusion requirement (as defined in section 44A(3) of that Act).

(4) Where an agreement to marry is terminated, no application under subsection (2)(a) may be made by virtue of section 62(3)(e) by reference to that agreement after the end of the period of three years beginning with the day on which it is terminated.

(4ZA) If a civil partnership agreement (as defined by section 73 of the Civil Partnership Act 2004) is terminated, no application under this section may be made by virtue of section 62(3)(eza) by reference to that agreement after the end of the period of three years beginning with the day on which it is terminated.

(4A) A court considering whether to make an occupation order shall also consider whether to exercise the power conferred by subsection (2)(b).

(4B) In this Part 'the applicant', in relation to a non-molestation order, includes (where the context permits) the person for whose benefit such an order would be or is made in exercise of the power conferred by subsection (2)(b).

(5) In deciding whether to exercise its powers under this section and, if so, in what manner, the court shall have regard to all the circumstances including the need to secure the health, safety and well-being –

(a) of the applicant; and
(b) of any relevant child.

(6) A non-molestation order may be expressed so as to refer to molestation in general, to particular acts of molestation, or to both.

(7) A non-molestation order may be made for a specified period or until further order.

(8) A non-molestation order which is made in other family proceedings ceases to have effect if those proceedings are withdrawn or dismissed.

Amendments—CPA 2004, s 82, Sch 9, para 9; Domestic Violence, Crime and Victims Act 2004, s 58(1),(2), Sch 10, para 36(1)–(3), Sch 11.

Defined terms—'associated': s 62(3); 'relevant child': s 62(2).

Scope—All non-molestation orders are made under s 42.This provides a civil remedy. Serious Crime Act 2015, s 76 creates a criminal offence of controlling or coercive behaviour if person A repeatedly or continuously engages in such behaviour towards person B at a time when they are in an intimate and family relationship and where A knows or ought to know that the behaviour would have a serious effect on B. The meaning of the term 'serious effect' is that it causes B to fear at least on two occasions that violence will be used against B or it causes alarm or distress that has a substantial adverse effect on B's usual day-to-day activities. See also the definition provided for 'members of the family'. These provisions may be relevant in relation to the court's exercise of its powers under FLA 1996, s 42(6). Provision is made for a limited defence in certain circumstances and also for circumstances when the defence would not be available (Serious Crime Act 2015, ss 76(8)–(10)). The maximum penalty on conviction on indictment is imprisonment for 5 years, fine or both and on summary conviction to a term not exceeding 12 months, fine or both (s 76(11)).

'Molesting'—The term 'molesting' is not defined in FLA 1996. 'Molest' has been considered synonymous with 'pester' (*Vaughan v Vaughan* [1973] 1 WLR 1159, CA) where the court considered the definition of molestation in the *Shorter Oxford Dictionary*, namely 'to cause trouble; to vex; to annoy; to put to inconvenience'. It includes conduct which does not amount to violent behaviour (*Davis v Johnson* [1979] AC 264, 334, HL) and applies to any conduct which can properly be regarded as constituting such a degree of harassment as to call for the intervention of the court (*C v C* [2001] EWCA Civ 1625). The Home Office definition of domestic violence and abuse is: 'Any incident or pattern of incidents of controlling, coercive or threatening behaviour, violence or abuse between those aged 16 or over who are or have been intimate partners or family members regardless of gender or sexuality. This can encompass, but is not limited to, the following types of abuse: psychological, physical, sexual, financial, emotional. Controlling behaviour is: a range of acts designed to make a person subordinate and/or dependent by isolating them from sources of support, exploiting their resources and capacities for personal gain, depriving them of the means needed for independence, resistance and escape and regulating their everyday behaviour. Coercive behaviour is: an act or a pattern of acts of assault, threats, humiliation and intimidation or other abuse that is used to harm, punish, or frighten their victim.' This definition, although not a legal or statutory definition, is used by all government departments. It is submitted that any applicant who comes within it qualifies for a non-molestation order. Particular care is required when one or both parties is a litigant in person (see *Mr R v Mrs R* [2014] EWFC 48).

Wording of non-molestation orders—In *R v Shane Tony P* [2004] EWCA Crim 287 and *Boness v R* [2005] EWCA Crim 2395 (both cases concerning ASBOs) the Court of Appeal emphasised that the terms of an order must be precise and capable of being understood; the findings of fact giving rise to the order must be recorded; the order must be explained and that the exact terms of the order must be pronounced in open court and the written order must accurately reflect the order as pronounced. It is suggested that these points, particularly the first, apply with equal force to non-molestation orders. Thus, for example, a respondent may be forbidden to:

1 use or threaten any violence towards [applicant];
2 come within [100] metres of [address];
3 communicate with [applicant] whether directly or indirectly, whether orally, by telephone, text message, email, social media or any other means except through her solicitors [name and address];
4 threaten [applicant];
5 post any derogatory, insulting, threatening or harassing posts regarding the applicant on any social media.

Although such an order will necessarily contain more paragraphs, each paragraph of itself is clear and meets modern standards.

A 'stay away' clause, such as in 2 above, could be expressed as part of an occupation order but it is not necessary to make an occupation order solely for that purpose and can be included in a non-molestation order. Such a provision should not be included as a matter of routine, must be proportionate and necessary and supported by evidence (*Mr R v Mrs R* [2014] EWFC 48). A 'get-out' order, i e an order requiring a party to leave, cannot form part of a non-molestation order and must be made as part of an occupation order. If the court makes both types of order each must be drawn up separately.

Criteria—The criteria for the making of a non-molestation order are in s 42(5), namely 'all the circumstances including the need to secure the health, safety and well-being of the applicant or of any relevant child'. The following three principles should be considered when deciding whether to grant a non-molestation injunction:

(a) there must be evidence of molestation (*C v C (Non-Molestation Order: Jurisdiction)* [1998] 1 FLR 554, FD);
(b) the applicant (or child) must need protection; and
(c) the judge must be satisfied on the balance of probabilities that judicial intervention is required to control the behaviour which is the subject of the complaint (see for example *C v C* [2001] EWCA Civ 1625).

Without notice (ex parte) applications—See notes to s 45.

Duration—By virtue of s 42(7) the order can be for a specified period or until further order. An injunction made 'until further order' will last until such time as either the applicant or respondent applies to discharge it (see s 49): such orders are made only in exceptional cases, e g where there is a history of expired injunctions. It is established practice to stipulate a time-limit in the majority of cases. Obsolete Practice Notes issued under the old law suggested that 'a period of up to 3 months is likely to suffice'. Three months should be regarded as a minimum but experience shows that an order as short as this is often insufficient (see e g *Research Findings No 46 – Home Office Research and Statistics Directorate*). Orders are frequently made for 6 months, a year or longer duration where the case so requires (see e g *Galan v Galan* [1985] FLR 905, CA; *Horgan v Horgan* [2002] EWCA Civ 1371). Application can be made to vary, extend, or discharge an order (see FPR 2010, Pt 10).

Forms—The form of application is Form FL401, and the order is in Form FL404.

Power of arrest—It is no longer possible to attach a power of arrest to a non-molestation order: see further ss 42A and 47.

Undertakings—See notes to s 46.

Service of application—Not less than 2 clear days before the hearing date unless otherwise ordered (FPR 2010, r 10.3).

Service of order—Both orders made without notice and at an inter partes hearing must be served on the respondent personally (FPR 2010, r 10.6).

Multi-agency risk assessment conferences—See the notes on MARACs under FPR 2010, r 12.12 and the FJC Guidance of December 2011: *MARACS and Disclosure into Court Proceedings* in Part V.

Legal Aid—The Legal Aid Agency has published a guide to assist parties and professionals with applications for legal aid where domestic abuse is alleged to have occurred and protection is sought (see *www.gov.uk/legal-aid/domestic-abuse-or-violence*).

42A Offence of breaching non-molestation order

(1) A person who without reasonable excuse does anything that he is prohibited from doing by a non-molestation order is guilty of an offence.

(2) In the case of a non-molestation order made by virtue of section 45(1), a person can be guilty of an offence under this section only in respect of conduct engaged in at a time when he was aware of the existence of the order.

(3) Where a person is convicted of an offence under this section in respect of any conduct, that conduct is not punishable as a contempt of court.

(4) A person cannot be convicted of an offence under this section in respect of any conduct which has been punished as a contempt of court.

(5) A person guilty of an offence under this section is liable –

(a) on conviction on indictment, to imprisonment for a term not exceeding five years, or a fine, or both;

(b) on summary conviction, to imprisonment for a term not exceeding 12 months, or a fine not exceeding the statutory maximum, or both.

(6) A reference in any enactment to proceedings under this Part, or to an order under this Part, does not include a reference to proceedings for an offence under this section or to an order made in such proceedings.

'Enactment' includes an enactment contained in subordinate legislation within the meaning of the Interpretation Act 1978.

Amendments—Inserted by Domestic Violence, Crime and Victims Act 2004, s 1.

Scope—The section makes breach of a non-molestation order a criminal offence if the defendant is aware of the existence of the order and, without reasonable excuse, does anything prohibited by the non-molestation order. A defendant cannot be both punished for a contempt of court and convicted under s 42A. Generally, it is the policy of the Crown Prosecution Service to prosecute all cases of domestic violence referred to it where it considers that there is a sufficient evidence to secure a conviction.

Section 42A came into force on 1 July 2007 and thus, the power to attach a 'power of arrest' to a non-molestation order is abolished (Domestic Violence, Crime and Victims Act 2004, Sch 10, para 38). The power to issue a warrant of arrest under s 47(8) remains (but note ss 42A(3) and (4) above) and a power of arrest can still be attached to an occupation order.

Further provisions relating to occupation and non-molestation orders

43 Leave of court required for applications by children under sixteen

(1) A child under the age of sixteen may not apply for an occupation order or a non-molestation order except with the leave of the court.

(2) The court may grant leave for the purposes of subsection (1) only if it is satisfied that the child has sufficient understanding to make the proposed application for the occupation order or non-molestation order.

Scope—Applications for leave under this section need no longer be made to a High Court Judge. By FC(CDB)R 2014, r 16(5), the application is allocated to 'the first available judge of the Family Court other than lay justices'. At the hearing of the application for leave, the court will also consider the need for a litigation friend (see FPR 2010, Pt 16).

44 Evidence of agreement to marry or form a civil partnership

(1) Subject to subsection (2) the court shall not make an order under section 33 or 42 by virtue of section 62(3)(e) unless there is produced to it evidence in writing of the existence of the agreement to marry.

(2) Subsection (1) does not apply if the court is satisfied that the agreement to marry was evidenced by –

- (a) the gift of an engagement ring by one party to the agreement to the other in contemplation of their marriage, or
- (b) a ceremony entered into by the parties in the presence of one or more other persons assembled for the purpose of witnessing the ceremony.

(3) Subject to subsection (4), the court shall not make an order under section 33 or 42 by virtue of section 62(3)(eza) unless there is produced to it evidence in writing of the existence of the civil partnership agreement (as defined by section 73 of the Civil Partnership Act 2004).

(4) Subsection (3) does not apply if the court is satisfied that the civil partnership agreement was evidenced by –

- (a) a gift by one party to the agreement to the other as a token of the agreement, or
- (b) a ceremony entered into by the parties in the presence of one or more other persons assembled for the purpose of witnessing the ceremony.

Amendments—CPA 2004, s 82, Sch 9, para 10(1)–(4).

45 Ex parte orders

(1) The court may, in any case where it considers that it is just and convenient to do so, make an occupation order or a non-molestation order even though the respondent has not been given such notice of the proceedings as would otherwise be required by rules of court.

(2) In determining whether to exercise its powers under subsection (1), the court shall have regard to all the circumstances including –

- (a) any risk of significant harm to the applicant or a relevant child, attributable to conduct of the respondent, if the order is not made immediately;
- (b) whether it is likely that the applicant will be deterred or prevented from pursuing the application if an order is not made immediately; and
- (c) whether there is reason to believe that the respondent is aware of the proceedings but is deliberately evading service and that the applicant or a relevant child will be seriously prejudiced by the delay involved in effecting substituted service.

(3) If the court makes an order by virtue of subsection (1) it must afford the respondent an opportunity to make representations relating to the order as soon as just and convenient at a full hearing.

(4) If, at a full hearing, the court makes an occupation order ('the full order'), then –

- (a) for the purposes of calculating the maximum period for which the full order may be made to have effect, the relevant section is to apply as if the period for which the full order will have effect began on the date on which the initial order first had effect; and
- (b) the provisions of section 36(10) or 38(6) as to the extension of orders are to apply as if the full order and the initial order were a single order.

(5) In this section –

'full hearing' means a hearing of which notice has been given to all the parties in accordance with rules of court;

'initial order' means an occupation order made by virtue of subsection (1); and

'relevant section' means section 33(10), 35(10), 36(10), 37(5) or 38(6).

Amendments—CCA 2013, s 17, Sch 11.

Without notice—FPR 2010 follow CPR 1998 in referring to applications being made 'without notice' rather than using 'ex parte'. However, the Act is unamended and still says 'ex parte'.

Scope—It has long been established practice to make orders on a without notice basis where the circumstances of the case so justify. Under s 45 the court can only make a without notice order where it is 'just and convenient' and, although s 45(1) enables the court to make either an occupation order or a non-molestation order even though the respondent has not been served, there is an important difference of approach between these two different types of order. It is recognised that victims of domestic violence often need immediate protection which can be effectively granted only on a without notice basis. As the respondent has no legal right to inflict or threaten violence, it follows that his legal rights are not infringed by a non-molestation order. This may be quite different in the case of an occupation order and it will be extremely unusual to deprive a respondent of his home on a without notice basis. Unlike non-molestation orders, occupation orders override proprietary rights (*Chalmers v Johns* [1999] 1 FLR 392, CA). In *G v G (Ouster: Ex parte application)* [1990] 1 FLR 395, CA and *Masich v Masich* (1977) Fam Law 245, CA it was stated that exclusion orders should seldom be granted without notice. This still applies to occupation orders, and although the court clearly has power under s 45(1) to make a without notice occupation order, this is reserved for exceptional cases only. An application on notice requires only 2 days' notice and the court has power to abridge time (FPR 2010, r 10.3). Even though the court may not feel able to grant a without notice occupation order, it will very often grant a without notice non-molestation order pending the hearing of the application for an occupation order on notice provided that the evidence justifies an order on a without notice basis. See *Mr R v Mrs R* [2014] EWFC 48, where an order was set aside as it should not have been applied for or granted without notice. Particular care is required where a party is a litigant in person.

Full hearing—Whenever an order has been made ex parte there must be a full hearing as soon as just and convenient thereafter. There are no circumstances in English law in which it is appropriate to make an ex parte order without provision for review once the order has been served. Any such order would be unlawful. It is the duty of the court to list for a full hearing as required by s 45. See *Horgan v Horgan* [2002] EWCA Civ 1371.

Duration—The Act does not require the ex parte order to be limited in time but in practice it always should be. An ex parte order should be for a defined period (say 12 months) with a clear expiry date. It must be reconsidered at a full hearing within 14 days. This practice has the advantage that, if no change is required to the terms of the order (as often proves to be the case), no further order need be made, drawn up and served thus saving time and costs. Further, if it is necessary for the court to give directions because the order is contested, the applicant remains protected while the case proceeds. An ex parte order should never be made to last only to the return day as this creates a risk that the applicant will be left without protection during the gap between the expiry of the ex parte order and service of an inter partes order. See further the revised Practice Guidance of 18 January 2017 in Part V.

46 Undertakings

(1) In any case where the court has power to make an occupation order or non-molestation order, the court may accept an undertaking from any party to the proceedings.

(2) No power of arrest may be attached to any undertaking given under subsection (1).

(3) The court shall not accept an undertaking under subsection (1) instead of making an occupation order in any case where apart from this section a power of arrest would be attached to the order.

(3A) The court shall not accept an undertaking under subsection (1) instead of making a non-molestation order in any case where it appears to the court that –

(a) the respondent has used or threatened violence against the applicant or a relevant child; and

(b) for the protection of the applicant or child it is necessary to make a non-molestation order so that any breach may be punishable under section 42A.

(4) An undertaking given to a court under subsection (1) is enforceable as if the court had made an occupation order or a non-molestation order in terms corresponding to those of the undertaking.

(5) This section has effect without prejudice to the powers of the High Court and the family court apart from this section.

Amendments—Domestic Violence, Crime and Victims Act 2004, s 58(1), Sch 10, para 37(1)–(4); CCA 2013, s 17, Sch 11.

Scope—Where an undertaking is given it may be enforced as if it were an injunction (s 46(4)), i e as a contempt of court punishable by committal proceedings. An undertaking is a promise by the respondent to the court, not to the other party. Powers of arrest cannot be attached to undertakings (s 46(2)).

Procedure—The following procedural points arise in connection with undertakings:

(a) *Recording of undertaking* The undertaking should be in Form N117. It should be explained to the respondent by the judge and the respondent asked to sign it.
(b) *Mutual undertakings* Where both parties give undertakings, two separate forms must be used.
(c) *Service of undertakings* The court must provide a copy of the undertaking to the person who has given it. This may be effected by handing a copy to him before he leaves the court building, by posting him a copy, through his solicitor or, if none of these is practical, by personal service (FPR 2010, r 37.7). The better practice is for a copy of the undertaking to be given to both parties before they leave the court building. In any event the court clerk must record the way in which delivery was effected in the relevant box on the back of Form N117.
(d) *Judge's responsibility* Where an undertaking is to be given, the judge has the following responsibilities:
  (i) to approve the terms of the proposed promises.
  (ii) to ensure that the giver of the undertaking understands what has been promised and the consequences of breach.
  (iii) to consider whether the signature of the giver should be included in the box on the back of Form N117 in order to avoid argument about what happened when the undertaking was given; and
  (iv) where an undertaking is given in the absence of the giver through his advocate, to ensure that the advocate has been given specific instructions to give the undertaking and that the giver understands the consequences of breach. (In practice it is rare for undertakings to be taken in the absence of the giver.)

Restriction on undertakings (s 46(3))—By virtue of s 46(3) the court is prohibited from accepting an undertaking in any case where a power of arrest would be attached to the order. In fact the requirement to impose a power of arrest is 'almost mandatory' (per Butler-Sloss LJ in *Chechi v Bashier* [1999] 2 FLR 489, CA, at [495], commenting on s 47). The power of arrest is confined to occupation orders, as a breach of a non-molestation order is a criminal offence. Breach of an undertaking is not a crime, but s 46(3A) prohibits the court from accepting an undertaking where the respondent has used or threatened violence and, for the protection of the applicant or relevant child, it is necessary to make a non-molestation order so that any breach is punishable under s 42A.

Warrant of arrest—The effect of the amendment to s 46(4), effected by the 2004 Act, is to enable a warrant of arrest (see s 47(8)) to be applied for to enforce an undertaking.

47 Arrest for breach of order

(1) *(repealed)*

(2) If –

  (a) the court makes an occupation order; and
  (b) it appears to the court that the respondent has used or threatened violence against the applicant or a relevant child,

it shall attach a power of arrest to one or more provisions of the order unless the court is satisfied that in all the circumstances of the case the applicant or child will be adequately protected without such a power of arrest.

(3) Subsection (2) does not apply in any case where the occupation order is made by virtue of section 45(1), but in such a case the court may attach a power of arrest to one or more provisions of the order if it appears to it –

  (a) that the respondent has used or threatened violence against the applicant or a relevant child; and
  (b) that there is a risk of significant harm to the applicant or child, attributable to conduct of the respondent, if the power of arrest is not attached to those provisions immediately.

(4) If, by virtue of subsection (3), the court attaches a power of arrest to any provisions of an occupation order, it may provide that the power of arrest is to have effect for a shorter period than the other provisions of the order.

(5) Any period specified for the purposes of subsection (4) may be extended by the court (on one or more occasions) on an application to vary or discharge the occupation order.

(6) If, by virtue of subsection (2) or (3), a power of arrest is attached to certain provisions of an order, a constable may arrest without warrant a person whom he has reasonable cause for suspecting to be in breach of any such provision.

PART II

(7) If a power of arrest is attached under subsection (2) or (3) to certain provisions of the order and the respondent is arrested under subsection (6) –

(a) he must be brought before the relevant judicial authority within the period of 24 hours beginning at the time of his arrest; and
(b) if the matter is not then disposed of forthwith, the relevant judicial authority before whom he is brought may remand him.

In reckoning for the purposes of this subsection any period of 24 hours, no account is to be taken of Christmas Day, Good Friday or any Sunday.

(8) If the court –

(a) has made a non-molestation order, or
(b) has made an occupation order but has not attached a power of arrest under subsection (2) or (3) to any provision of the order, or has attached that power only to certain provisions of the order,

then, if at any time the applicant considers that the respondent has failed to comply with the order, he may apply to the relevant judicial authority for the issue of a warrant for the arrest of the respondent.

(9) The relevant judicial authority shall not issue a warrant on an application under subsection (8) unless –

(a) the application is substantiated on oath; and
(b) the relevant judicial authority has reasonable grounds for believing that the respondent has failed to comply with the order.

(10) If a person is brought before a court by virtue of a warrant issued under subsection (9) and the court does not dispose of the matter forthwith, the court may remand him.

(11) Schedule 5 (which makes provision corresponding to that applying in magistrates' courts in civil cases under sections 128 and 129 of the Magistrates' Courts Act 1980) has effect in relation to the powers of the High Court and the family court to remand a person by virtue of this section.

(12) If a person remanded under this section is granted bail, he may be required by the relevant judicial authority to comply, before release on bail or later, with such requirements as appear to that authority to be necessary to secure that he does not interfere with witnesses or otherwise obstruct the course of justice.

Amendments—Domestic Violence, Crime and Victims Act 2004, s 58(1), Sch 10, para 38(1)–(5); CCA 2013, s 17, Sch 11.

Note—Section 42A (see above) made breach of a non-molestation order an arrestable offence.

Powers of arrest—There is no inherent power to attach a power of arrest. The power of arrest was initially introduced in a restrictive way by Domestic Violence and Matrimonial Proceedings Act 1976. In its original form s 47 was much wider; attaching a power of arrest was 'almost mandatory' (per Butler-Sloss LJ in *Chechi v Bashier* [1999] 2 FLR 489, CA, at [495]). However, the power of arrest is confined to occupation orders, having been abolished for non-molestation orders (see s 42A).

Without notice orders—A power of arrest can be attached to a without notice order. The criteria are set out in s 47(3). The court has to be satisfied that the respondent has used or threatened violence and that there is a risk of significant harm if a power of arrest is not attached. The power of arrest must be announced in open court.

Order—Non-molestation orders and occupation orders must be drawn up as separate orders (Form FL404a and Form FL404 respectively) and not as part of one order. If a power of arrest is attached to the occupation order the clauses to which the power is attached (and only those clauses) must be set out on Form FL406. An order requiring the respondent to 'keep away' from a stated address can be made either as part of an occupation order or a non-molestation order, whereas an order requiring the respondent to leave a stated address can be made only as part of an occupation order.

Penal notice—A penal notice, warning of the consequences of disobedience, must appear on the face of every order in the nature of an injunction. Although it is the court's task to endorse the order appropriately it is the solicitor's duty to ensure that this has been done. The penal notice on an occupation order is in the standard form but the penal notice on a non-molestation order reads: 'If, without reasonable excuse, you do anything which you are forbidden from doing, you will be committing a criminal offence and liable on conviction to a term of imprisonment not exceeding 5 years or to a fine or to both. Alternatively, if you do not obey this order you will be guilty of contempt of court and may be sent to prison'.

Duration—Section 47(4) expressly enables the court when attaching a power of arrest to a without notice order to provide that the power of arrest is to have effect for a shorter period than the other provisions of the order. This provision is rarely used although the Court of Appeal has held that s 47(2) permits a similar order in the case of final orders (see *Re B-J (Power of Arrest)* [2000] 2 FLR 443, CA).

Delivery to police station—By virtue of FPR 2010, Pt 10, a copy of Form FL406a (non-molestation order) and/or Form FL406 (the provisions of the occupation order to which a power of arrest is attached) must be delivered to the officer for the time being in charge of any police station for the applicant's address or of such other police station as the court may specify. The form must be accompanied by a statement showing that the respondent has been served with the order or informed of its terms (whether by being present when the order was made or by telephone or otherwise). Thus the police must only be notified of the non-molestation order and/or those provisions (only) of an occupation order to which the power of arrest is attached after the respondent has been notified. Where the relevant police authority has a Domestic Violence Unit which deals with all domestic violence cases within its area, it may be sensible to specify the address of the police station where the unit is located as the appropriate police station to be served, rather than the police station for the applicant's address. Service should be effected in compliance with the FJC Protocol of November 2011: *Process Servers: Non-Molestation Orders* (see Part V).

Arrest without warrant—The significance of a power of arrest is that, pursuant to s 47(6), a constable may arrest without warrant any person whom he has reasonable cause for suspecting to be in breach of the order to which the power has been attached. Any person arrested must then be brought before the relevant judicial authority within 24 hours. Where a person arrested under a power of arrest cannot conveniently be brought to a courtroom, he may be brought before the relevant judicial authority at any convenient place. If the person arrested is not dealt with immediately the court has power to remand. Remand can be on bail or in custody.

Warrant of arrest—Section 47(8) provides a procedure which involves the police even in cases where no power of arrest has been attached. As an alternative to applying for an order for committal under FPR 2010, Pt 37 the applicant can apply to the court for a warrant for arrest. The police will then arrest the respondent and bring him before the court. Section 46(4) has been amended to make it clear that a warrant can be applied for to enforce an undertaking.

Remand—FLA 1996, Sch 5 gives power to the High Court and the County Court to remand. Following the creation of the Family Court, see also Family Court (Contempt of Court) (Powers) Regulations 2014.

48 Remand for medical examination and report

(1) If the relevant judicial authority has reason to consider that a medical report will be required, any power to remand a person under section 47(7)(b) or (10) may be exercised for the purpose of enabling a medical examination and report to be made.

(2) If such a power is so exercised, the adjournment must not be for more than 4 weeks at a time unless the relevant judicial authority remands the accused in custody.

(3) If the relevant judicial authority so remands the accused, the adjournment must not be for more than 3 weeks at a time.

(4) If there is reason to suspect that a person who has been arrested –

(a) under section 47(6), or

(b) under a warrant issued on an application made under section 47(8),

is suffering from mental disorder within the meaning of the Mental Health Act 1983, the relevant judicial authority has the same power to make an order under section 35 of that Act (remand for report on accused's mental condition) as the Crown Court has under that section in the case of an accused person within the meaning of that section.

Amendments—MHA 2007, s 1(4), Sch 1, para 20.

Remand—Remands in custody are normally limited to 8 days (Sch 5, para 2(5)). Section 48 enables remands in custody to be for up to 3 weeks if the remand is for the purpose of a medical report. The section is silent on the question of who is to pay for the medical report. If the person to be medically examined is publicly funded, the Legal Aid Agency will pay pursuant to the order of the court. If he is not publicly funded, no doubt, in an appropriate case, a party can be ordered to pay but quaere whether the prison to which he is remanded can be required to obtain the medical report and/or HMCTS be required to fund it.

For the powers of the court to make a hospital order once the medical report has been obtained see CCA 1981, s 14 and the sections of MHA 1983 there referred to, and FPR 2010, r 10.15.

49 Variation and discharge of orders

(1) An occupation order or non-molestation order may be varied or discharged by the court on an application by –

(a) the respondent, or

(b) the person on whose application the order was made.

(2) In the case of a non-molestation order made by virtue of section 42(2)(b), the order may be varied or discharged by the court even though no such application has been made.

(3) If B's home rights are, under section 31, a charge on the estate or interest of the other spouse or of trustees for A, an order under section 33 against A may also be varied or discharged by the court on an application by any person deriving title under the other spouse or under the trustees and affected by the charge.

(4) If, by virtue of section 47(3), a power of arrest has been attached to certain provisions of an occupation order, the court may vary or discharge the order under subsection (1) in so far as it confers a power of arrest (whether or not any application has been made to vary or discharge any other provision of the order).

Amendments—CPA 2004, s 82, Sch 9, para 11; Domestic Violence, Crime and Victims Act 2004, s 58(1), Sch 10, para 39.

****

Transfer of tenancies

53 Transfer of certain tenancies

Schedule 7 makes provision in relation to the transfer of certain tenancies on divorce etc or on separation of cohabitants.

Procedure—Applications for a transfer of a tenancy under s 53 and Sch 7 are governed by FPR 2010, rr 8.29–8.34. See Procedural Guide A11.

Scope—This section and FLA 1996, Sch 7 (which re-enact Matrimonial Homes Act 1983, s 7 and Sch 1) provide the court with the power to transfer tenancies, including statutory tenancies. By virtue of MCA 1973, s 24, the court has jurisdiction to transfer a contractual tenancy where there is no covenant against assignment, but it has no power to transfer a statutory tenancy because that is not within the definition of property. Under Sch 7 the court has jurisdiction to transfer a contractual tenancy and may do so even where there is a covenant against assignment (although whether the court will, in its discretion, exercise its jurisdiction to transfer when there is such a covenant remains to be seen). It also has jurisdiction under Sch 7 to transfer a statutory tenancy. However, in contrast to the old provisions of MHA 1983, Sch 1, Sch 7 contains two new powers: first, tenancies of cohabitants can be transferred; and secondly, the party to whom the tenancy is being transferred can be ordered to make a payment to the other.

Prevention of unilateral termination of tenancy—As set out in Procedural Guide A11, a tenancy in the other spouse's or partner's name or in joint names can be destroyed unilaterally by surrender or notice to quit. Once the tenancy is surrendered it is lost and therefore a party should ask the other tenant for an undertaking not to surrender it. If the undertaking is given, it should be served on the landlord. If it is not given, application should be made for an injunction to prevent the tenancy being surrendered and, once made, the injunction order should be served on the landlord (*Bater v Greenwich London Borough Council* [1999] 2 FLR 993, CA).

Dwelling-house subject to mortgage

54 Dwelling-house subject to mortgage

(1) In determining for the purposes of this Part whether a person is entitled to occupy a dwelling-house by virtue of an estate or interest, any right to possession of the dwelling-house conferred on a mortgagee of the dwelling-house under or by virtue of his mortgage is to be disregarded.

(2) Subsection (1) applies whether or not the mortgagee is in possession.

(3) Where a person ('A') is entitled to occupy a dwelling-house by virtue of an estate or interest, a connected person does not by virtue of –

(a) any home rights conferred by section 30, or
(b) any rights conferred by an order under section 35 or 36,

have any larger right against the mortgagee to occupy the dwelling-house than A has by virtue of his estate or interest and of any contract with the mortgagee.

(4) Subsection (3) does not apply, in the case of home rights, if under section 31 those rights are a charge, affecting the mortgagee, on the estate or interest mortgaged.

(5) In this section 'connected person', in relation to any person, means that person's spouse, former spouse, civil partner, former civil partner, cohabitant or former cohabitant.

Amendments—CPA 2004, s 82, Sch 9, para 12.

55 Actions by mortgagees: joining connected persons as parties

(1) This section applies if a mortgagee of land which consists of or includes a dwelling-house brings an action in any court for the enforcement of his security.

(2) A connected person who is not already a party to the action is entitled to be made a party in the circumstances mentioned in subsection (3).

(3) The circumstances are that –

(a) the connected person is enabled by section 30(3) or (6) (or by section 30(3) or (6) as applied by section 35(13) or 36(13)), to meet the mortgagor's liabilities under the mortgage;

(b) he has applied to the court before the action is finally disposed of in that court; and

(c) the court sees no special reason against his being made a party to the action and is satisfied –

(i) that he may be expected to make such payments or do such other things in or towards satisfaction of the mortgagor's liabilities or obligations as might affect the outcome of the proceedings; or

(ii) that the expectation of it should be considered under section 36 of the Administration of Justice Act 1970.

(4) In this section 'connected person' has the same meaning as in section 54.

Scope—This section which is based on Matrimonial Homes Act 1983, s 8(2) entitles the spouse, civil partner, cohabitant, former spouse, former civil partner or former cohabitant to be made a party in mortgage possession proceedings.

56 Actions by mortgagees: service of notice on certain persons

(1) This section applies if a mortgagee of land which consists, or substantially consists, of a dwelling-house brings an action for the enforcement of his security, and at the relevant time there is –

(a) in the case of unregistered land, a land charge of Class F registered against the person who is the estate owner at the relevant time or any person who, where the estate owner is a trustee, preceded him as trustee during the subsistence of the mortgage; or

(b) in the case of registered land, a subsisting registration of –

(i) a notice under section 31(10);

(ii) a notice under section 2(8) of the Matrimonial Homes Act 1983; or

(iii) a notice or caution under section 2(7) of the Matrimonial Homes Act 1967.

(2) If the person on whose behalf –

(a) the land charge is registered, or

(b) the notice or caution is entered,

is not a party to the action, the mortgagee must serve notice of the action on him.

(3) If –

(a) an official search has been made on behalf of the mortgagee which would disclose any land charge of Class F, notice or caution within subsection (1)(a) or (b),

(b) a certificate of the result of the search has been issued, and

(c) the action is commenced within the priority period,

the relevant time is the date of the certificate.

(4) In any other case the relevant time is the time when the action is commenced.

(5) The priority period is, for both registered and unregistered land, the period for which, in accordance with section 11(5) and (6) of the Land Charges Act 1972, a certificate on an official search operates in favour of a purchaser.

Defined terms—'dwelling-house': s 63(1),(4); 'mortgage': s 63(1).

Jurisdiction and procedure etc

57 Jurisdiction of courts

(1) For the purposes of this Act 'the court' means the High Court or the family court.

(2)–(12) *(repealed)*

Amendments—CRA 2005, s 15(1), Sch 4, paras 252, 253; CCA 2013, s 17, Sch 11.

58 Contempt proceedings

The powers of the court in relation to contempt of court arising out of a person's failure to comply with an order under this Part may be exercised by the relevant judicial authority.

Family Court (Contempt of Court) (Powers) Regulations 2014—These regulations (see Part IV) came into force on 22 April 2014.

'contempt of court'—The term has been in use since at least the 13th century. The court's powers to punish for contempt of court are in the CCA 1981. Committal must be for a specified (not sine die) period not exceeding 2 years. Proceedings for committal for contempt of court in a civil action are civil proceedings. Nevertheless the appropriate standard of proof to be applied in committal proceedings is the criminal standard of proof (*Dean v Dean* [1987] 1 FLR 517, CA). An order of committal must be made in a courtroom open to the public or announced in open court at the earliest opportunity. See CCA 1981 and commentary thereon.

★★★★

General

62 Meaning of 'cohabitants', 'relevant child' and 'associated persons'

(1) For the purposes of this Part –

- (a) 'cohabitants' are two persons who are neither married to each other nor civil partners of each other but are living together as husband and wife or as if they were civil partners; and
- (b) 'cohabit' and 'former cohabitants' is to be read accordingly, but the latter expression does not include cohabitants who have subsequently married each other or become civil partners of each other.

(2) In this Part, 'relevant child', in relation to any proceedings under this Part, means –

- (a) any child who is living with or might reasonably be expected to live with either party to the proceedings;
- (b) any child in relation to whom an order under the Adoption Act 1976, the Adoption and Children Act 2002, or the Children Act 1989 is in question in the proceedings; and
- (c) any other child whose interests the court considers relevant.

(3) For the purposes of this Part, a person is associated with another person if –

- (a) they are or have been married to each other;
- (aa) they are or have been civil partners of each other;
- (b) they are cohabitants or former cohabitants;
- (c) they live or have lived in the same household, otherwise than merely by reason of one of them being the other's employee, tenant, lodger or boarder;
- (d) they are relatives;
- (e) they have agreed to marry one another (whether or not that agreement has been terminated);
- (eza) they have entered into a civil partnership agreement (as defined by section 73 of the Civil Partnership Act 2004) (whether or not that agreement has been terminated);
- (ea) they have or have had an intimate personal relationship with each other which is or was of significant duration;
- (f) in relation to any child, they are both persons falling within subsection (4); or
- (g) they are parties to the same family proceedings (other than proceedings under this Part).

(4) A person falls within this subsection in relation to a child if –

- (a) he is a parent of the child; or

(b) he has or has had parental responsibility for the child.

(5) If a child has been adopted or falls within subsection (7), two persons are also associated with each other for the purpose of this Part if –

(a) one is a natural parent of the child or a parent of such a natural parent, and

(b) the other is the child or any person –

(i) who had become a parent of the child by virtue of an adoption order or has applied for an adoption order, or

(ii) with whom the child has at any time been placed for adoption.

(6) A body corporate and another person are not, by virtue of subsection (3)(f) or (g), to be regarded for the purposes of this Part as associated with each other.

(7) A child falls within this subsection if –

(a) an adoption agency, within the meaning of section 2 of the Adoption and Children Act 2002, has power to place him for adoption under section 19 of that Act (placing children with parental consent) or he has become the subject of an order under section 21 of that Act (placement orders), or

(b) he is freed for adoption by virtue of an order made –

(i) in England and Wales, under section 18 of the Adoption Act 1976,

...

Amendments—ACA 2002, Sch 3, para 86, 87; Domestic Violence, Crime and Victims Act 2004, ss 3, 58(1), Sch 10, para 40; CPA 2004, s 82, Sch 9, para 13(1)–(4).

Defined terms—'relative': s 63.

Associated persons (s 62(3))—Only 'associated persons' and 'a relevant child' can apply for a non-molestation order under s 42. To obtain an occupation order under s 33, the respondent must be associated with the applicant. The policy of the 1996 Act is to extend protection from domestic violence to 'associated persons' (i e to virtually all family members). However, if the family relationship is merely incidental, e g to a dispute over land to be resolved by other civil proceedings, an order under FLA 1996 may be refused (*Chechi v Bashir* [1999] 2 FLR 489, CA). The definition of 'associated persons' was extended by Domestic Violence, Crime and Victims Act 2004, which inserts para (ea) in s 62(3). Section 62(3)(a) and (b) enables former spouses and cohabitants to seek the court's protection under FLA 1996 irrespective of when the relationship ended (*G v F (Non-molestation Order: Jurisdiction)* [2000] 2 FLR 533, FD). An omission from the definition is, as the equivalent US statute states, 'persons who are or have been dating'. Such persons, if they do not fall within s 62(3)(ea) (or any other paragraph), will need to sue under PHA 1997 (see Procedural Guide A10, the Act and the commentary) or in tort (e g for assault).

63 Interpretation of Part IV

(1) In this Part –

'adoption order' means an adoption order within the meaning of section 72(1) of the Adoption Act 1976 or section 46(1) of the Adoption and Children Act 2002;

'associated', in relation to a person, is to be read with section 62(3) to (6);

'child' means a person under the age of eighteen years;

'cohabit', 'cohabitant' and 'former cohabitant' have the meaning given by section 62(1);

'the court' is to be read with section 57;

'development' means physical, intellectual, emotional, social or behavioural development;

'dwelling-house' includes (subject to subsection (4)) –

(a) any building or part of a building which is occupied as a dwelling,

(b) any caravan, house-boat or structure which is occupied as a dwelling,

and any yard, garden, garage or outhouse belonging to it and occupied with it;

'family proceedings' means any proceedings –

(a) under the inherent jurisdiction of the High Court in relation to children; or

(b) under the enactments mentioned in subsection (2),

'harm' –

(a) in relation to a person who has reached the age of eighteen years, means ill-treatment or the impairment of health; and

(b) in relation to a child, means ill-treatment or the impairment of health or development;

'health' includes physical or mental health;

'home rights' has the meaning given by section 30;

'ill-treatment' includes forms of ill-treatment which are not physical and, in relation to a child, includes sexual abuse;

'mortgage', 'mortgagor' and 'mortgagee' have the same meaning as in the Law of Property Act 1925;

'mortgage payments' includes any payments which, under the terms of the mortgage, the mortgagor is required to make to any person;

'non-molestation order' has the meaning given by section 42(1);

'occupation order' has the meaning given by section 39;

'parental responsibility' has the same meaning as in the Children Act 1989;

'relative', in relation to a person, means –

(a) the father, mother, stepfather, stepmother, son, daughter, stepson, stepdaughter, grandmother, grandfather, grandson or granddaughter of that person or of that person's spouse, former spouse, civil partner or former civil partner, or

(b) the brother, sister, uncle, aunt, niece nephew or first cousin (whether of the full blood or of the half blood or by marriage or civil partnership) of that person or of that person's spouse or former spouse,

and includes, in relation to a person who is cohabiting or has cohabited with another person, any person who would fall within paragraph (a) or (b) if the parties were married to each other or were civil partners of each other;

'relevant child', in relation to any proceedings under this Part, has the meaning given by section 62(2);

'the relevant judicial authority', in relation to any order under this Part, means –

(a) where the order was made by the High Court, a judge of that court;

(aa) where the order was made by the family court, a judge of that court.

(b), (c) *(repealed)*

(2) The enactments referred to in the definition of 'family proceedings' are –

(a) Part II;
(b) this Part;
(ba) Part 4A;
(c) the Matrimonial Causes Act 1973;
(d) the Adoption Act 1976;
(e) the Domestic Proceedings and Magistrates' Court Act 1978;
(f) Part III of the Matrimonial and Family Proceedings Act 1984;
(g) Parts I, II and IV of the Children Act 1989;
(h) section 30 of the Human Fertilisation and Embryology Act 1990;
(i) the Adoption and Children Act 2002;
(ia) Part 1 of Schedule 2 to the Female Genital Mutilation Act 2003, other than paragraph 3 of that Schedule;
(j) Schedules 5 to 7 to the CPA 2004.

(3) Where the question of whether harm suffered by a child is significant turns on the child's health or development, his health or development shall be compared with that which could reasonably be expected of a similar child.

(4) For the purposes of sections 31, 32, 53 and 54 and such other provisions of this Part (if any) as may be prescribed, this Part is to have effect as if paragraph (b) of the definition of 'dwelling-house' were omitted.

(5) It is hereby declared that this Part applies as between the parties to a marriage even though either of them is, or has at any time during the marriage been, married to more than one person.

Amendments—ACA 2002, s 139(1), Sch 3, paras 85, 88; Domestic Violence, Crime and Victims Act 2004, s 58(1), Sch 10, para 41; CPA 2004, ss 82, 261(4), Sch 9, para 13(1)–(5), and Sch 30; Forced Marriage (Civil Protection) Act 2007, s 3(1), Sch 2, para 3; CCA 2013, s 17, Sch 11; Serious Crime Act 2015, s 85, Sch 4, para 17.

PART 4A
FORCED MARRIAGE

Amendments—Inserted by Forced Marriage (Civil Protection) Act 2007, s 1.

Forced marriage protection orders

63A Forced marriage protection orders

(1) The court may make an order for the purposes of protecting –

(a) a person from being forced into a marriage or from any attempt to be forced into a marriage; or

(b) a person who has been forced into a marriage.

(2) In deciding whether to exercise its powers under this section and, if so, in what manner, the court must have regard to all the circumstances including the need to secure the health, safety and well-being of the person to be protected.

(3) In ascertaining that person's well-being, the court must, in particular, have such regard to the person's wishes and feelings (so far as they are reasonably ascertainable) as the court considers appropriate in the light of the person's age and understanding.

(4) For the purposes of this Part a person ('A') is forced into a marriage if another person ('B') forces A to enter into a marriage (whether with B or another person) without A's free and full consent.

(5) For the purposes of subsection (4) it does not matter whether the conduct of B which forces A to enter into a marriage is directed against A, B or another person.

(6) In this Part –

'force' includes coerce by threats or other psychological means (and related expressions are to be read accordingly); and

'forced marriage protection order' means an order under this section.

Amendments—Inserted by Forced Marriage (Civil Protection) Act 2007, s 1.

Scope—This provision defines the term 'forced marriage', which must be distinguished from an 'arranged marriage'. It gives certain specified Family Courts (see below) the jurisdiction to make a forced marriage protection order (FMPO) with a view to protecting a person (the person to be protected)from being forced into marriage or one who has been forced into such a marriage. The force or threatened use of force may be directed at the potential victim or the perpetrator or another. Pursuant to the Anti-Social Behaviour Crime and Policing Act 2014, s 121, (1) it is a criminal offence for a person to (a) use violence, threats or any other form of coercion for the purpose of causing another person to enter into a marriage and (b) use conduct that they believe, or ought reasonably to believe, may cause the other person to enter into the marriage without free and full consent, and (2) if a person (a) practises any form of deception with the intention of causing another person to leave the UK and (b) intends the other person to be subjected to conduct outside the UK that is an offence under s 121(1) of that Act or would be an offence under that subsection if the victim were in England or Wales. Breach of a FMPO is also a criminal offence (see below). The penalties for the offences in England and Wales are a fine or a term of imprisonment not exceeding 6 months, or both on summary conviction, and imprisonment for a term not exceeding 7 years for a conviction on indictment. The penalties in Scotland are different. Note also that effect is now given to the Government's commitment to introduce lifelong anonymity for victims against whom an offence of forced marriage has been committed in England and Wales and Northern Ireland by the insertion in the Anti-Social Behaviour, Crime and Policing Act 2014 of s 122A and Sch 6A (see the annotation to the Act).

Defined terms—'court': s 63M. Where an emergency application without notice is made, the application should be allocated to the first available judge of the Family Court, other than lay justices who, where applicable, are authorised to deal with such an application (Family Court Composition and Distribution of Business) Rules 2014, r 16(4),(5)(b)).

Forced marriage—This is defined in s 1(4),(5),(6). Where a marriage has taken place, the remedy is a FMPO and the annulment of the marriage. Where annulment is not available (eg by reason of lapse of time), relief may be sought for a declaration under the inherent jurisdiction of the court and under FLA 1996, Pt 4A for a declaration of non-marriage as in *XCC v AA and Others* [2012] COPLR 730, or that the marriage entered into was invalid because no proper free and full consent was given by the party in respect of that ceremony and it is the duty of the court to protect the individual from abuse or potential abuse. In such cases, it will be necessary to establish that 'the threats, pressure, or whatever it is, is such as to destroy the reality of consent and overbears the will of the individual' (see *Re P (Forced Marriage)* [2011] 1 FLR 2060, FD and the earlier cases referred to and applied in that case).

Evidence and disclosure of all the circumstances of the case—The evidence relied upon by the applicant when seeking the order may include information that was shared in a multi-agency risk assessment conference (MARAC) and which is confidential. The perpetrator may either suspect that such a conference has taken place or wish to know whether it has and may wish to seek disclosure of the information by making an application under FPR 2010, r 21.2. When dealing with such an application, the FJC Guidance *MARACs and Disclosure into Court Proceedings* (see Part V) should be followed. The information shared at these risk-assessment conferences will invariably be sensitive and if disclosed is most likely to place the person to be protected (PTBP) and others (eg informants) in danger, particularly as many police authorities and local authorities use MARACs to handle forced marriage cases, to share information and to assess the risks to the PTBP, who may be a minor. It is therefore important where such disclosure is applied for that the application is heard on notice. If it is heard without notice, it is essential to include a statement in the order that the person to whom it is addressed has a right to object to the disclosure of all or part of it and to apply to the court to have the order varied or discharged; the person to whom the order is addressed should be directed to the Guidance. In any event, to protect the PTBP and others and safeguard their interests, the order should in the first instance direct that the disclosure of the information should be to the court and/or the local authority or, where appropriate, to Cafcass or a litigation friend only. The matter can then be determined under the court's powers under FPR 2010, r 21.3 and the cases cited under s 63D. See also the notes to FPR 2010, rr 12.12, 21.2 and 21.3.

63B Contents of orders

(1) A forced marriage protection order may contain –

(a) such prohibitions, restrictions or requirements; and
(b) such other terms;

as the court considers appropriate for the purposes of the order.

(2) The terms of such orders may, in particular, relate to –

(a) conduct outside England and Wales as well as (or instead of) conduct within England and Wales;
(b) respondents who are, or may become, involved in other respects as well as (or instead of) respondents who force or attempt to force, or may force or attempt to force, a person to enter into a marriage;
(c) other persons who are, or may become, involved in other respects as well as respondents of any kind.

(3) For the purposes of subsection (2) examples of involvement in other respects are –

(a) aiding, abetting, counselling, procuring, encouraging or assisting another person to force, or to attempt to force, a person to enter into a marriage; or
(b) conspiring to force, or to attempt to force, a person to enter into a marriage.

Amendments—Inserted by Forced Marriage (Civil Protection) Act 2007, s 1.

Contents of the order—The court is given a wide discretion in relation to the terms which it may include within an FMPO. (For precedent, see the proposed 'standard orders' currently under consultation (*www.familylaw.co.uk/news_and_comment/family-court-draft-standard-orders*), which may be adapted, and *Emergency Remedies in the Family Court* (Family Law.)) It gives the court the jurisdiction to make orders which relate to conduct within and outside the jurisdiction and any other orders which may be appropriate to protect the potential victim or a person who has been forced into a marriage. The order may be directed at a wide range of persons whose identity may not be known and thus reflects the High Court's power under its inherent jurisdiction and extends this jurisdiction to the judge of the Family Court (district and circuit judge level who are so authorised) in which the application is issued. It will also include the Central Family Court (formerly the PRFD) (see FC(CDB)R 2014,, rr 4, 20). There may still, however, be cases (particularly those that relate to and are to be enforced in a foreign jurisdiction with the involvement of the Foreign and Commonwealth Office and the International Family Justice Office) when it would be more appropriate to commence proceedings in the High Court or if proceedings have been commenced in the Family Court to apply for the case to be transferred to the High Court.

63C Applications and other occasions for making orders

(1) The court may make a forced marriage protection order –

(a) on an application being made to it; or
(b) without an application being made to it but in the circumstances mentioned in subsection (6).

(2) An application may be made by –

(a) the person who is to be protected by the order; or
(b) a relevant third party.

(3) An application may be made by any other person with the leave of the court.

(4) In deciding whether to grant leave, the court must have regard to all the circumstances including –

(a) the applicant's connection with the person to be protected;
(b) the applicant's knowledge of the circumstances of the person to be protected; and
(c) the wishes and feelings of the person to be protected so far as they are reasonably ascertainable and so far as the court considers it appropriate, in the light of the person's age and understanding, to have regard to them.

(5) An application under this section may be made in other family proceedings or without any other family proceedings being instituted.

(6) The circumstances in which the court may make an order without an application being made are where –

(a) any other family proceedings are before the court ('the current proceedings');
(b) the court considers that a forced marriage protection order should be made to protect a person (whether or not a party to the current proceedings); and
(c) a person who would be a respondent to any such proceedings for a forced marriage protection order is a party to the current proceedings.

(7) In this section –

'family proceedings' has the same meaning as in Part 4 (see section 63(1) and (2)) but also includes –

(a) proceedings under the inherent jurisdiction of the High Court in relation to adults;
(b) proceedings in which the court has made an emergency protection order under section 44 of the Children Act 1989 which includes an exclusion requirement (as defined in section 44A(3) of that Act); and
(c) proceedings in which the court has made an order under section 50 of the Act of 1989 (recovery of abducted children etc.); and

'relevant third party' means a person specified, or falling within a description of persons specified, by order of the Lord Chancellor.

(8) An order of the Lord Chancellor under subsection (7) may, in particular, specify the Secretary of State.

Amendments—Inserted by Forced Marriage (Civil Protection) Act 2007, s 1.

Defined terms—'family proceedings', 'relevant third party': s 63C(7).

Who may apply—'the person to be protected': there is no age restriction for applicants for an FMPO. A child applicant does not require the leave of the court but FPR 2010, rr 16.6(1),(3) apply to such applications. Thus a child may apply without a guardian or next friend if the court grants leave or a solicitor considers that the child has the capacity to give instructions. The court may provide that the child is separately represented. For representation of children see FPR 2010, r 16.

Relevant third party—Pursuant to FLA 1996(FM)(RTP)O 2009, as from 1 November 2009 the local authority is identified as a relevant third party in respect of both adults and children. See also the Guidance issued to the local authority by the MoJ.

It is essential to establish as soon as practicable whether the person to be protected has mental capacity within the meaning of MCA 2005 to enter into the marriage (see *Re E (An Alleged Patient); Sheffield City Council v E and S* [2005] 1 FLR 965, FD) and also to conduct the proceedings. It should be noted that in relation to a PTBP who lacks capacity to consent to marriage, pursuant to Anti-social Behaviour Crime and Policing Act 2014, s 121, it is an offence for any person by any conduct carried out for the purpose of causing the PTBP to enter into a marriage (whether the conduct amounts to violence, threats or any other form of coercion). FPR 2010, Pt 15 deals with representation of protected persons. Attention is also drawn to the Checklist 'Protected Parties in Family Proceedings: Check List For the Appointment of a Litigation Friend (including the Official Solicitor)' [2014] Fam Law 98. Also see *Forced Marriage and Learning Disabilities: Multi-Agency Practice Guidelines* at *www.fco.gov.uk*).

The relevant third party may apply without seeking leave of the court and without the consent or knowledge of the potential victim but in deciding whether to grant the order the court will apply the criteria set out in s 63A(2) and (3). In the case of an application by a third party, leave of the court must be obtained and the court must be satisfied that the criteria set out in s 63C(4) have been met.

Application/order—The application may be freestanding or an order may be made without an application within other family proceedings if considered necessary to protect a person. An order may also be made of the court's own motion under s 63C but it must set out in the order a summary of its reasons for making the order and the names of the persons who are to be served with the order. It may also give directions on who is to be served and how service should be effected (FPR 2010, r 11.8).

63CA Offence of breaching order

(1) A person who without reasonable excuse does anything that the person is prohibited from doing by a forced marriage protection order is guilty of an offence.

(2) In the case of a forced marriage protection order made by virtue of section 63D(1), a person can be guilty of an offence under this section only in respect of conduct engaged in at a time when the person was aware of the existence of the order.

(3) Where a person is convicted of an offence under this section in respect of any conduct, that conduct is not punishable as a contempt of court.

(4) A person cannot be convicted of an offence under this section in respect of any conduct which has been punished as a contempt of court.

(5) A person guilty of an offence under this section is liable –

(a) on conviction on indictment, to imprisonment for a term not exceeding five years, or a fine, or both;

(b) on summary conviction, to imprisonment for a term not exceeding 12 months, or a fine, or both.

(6) A reference in any enactment to proceedings under this Part, or to an order under this Part, does not include a reference to proceedings for an offence under this section or to an order made in proceedings for such an offence.

(7) 'Enactment' includes an enactment contained in subordinate legislation within the meaning of the Interpretation Act 1978.

Amendments—Inserted by Anti-Social Behaviour, Crime and Policing Act 2014, s 120.

Modifications—In relation to an offence committed before the commencement of Criminal Justice Act 2003, s 154(1), the reference to 12 months in s 63CA(5)(b) is to be read as a reference to 6 months.

Breach of FMPO—A power of arrest cannot be attached to a FMPO. Breach of a FMPO is a criminal offence if the defendant is aware of the existence of the order and without reasonable excuse does anything that is prohibited by the FMPO. If the contemnor is charged and convicted, he cannot then subsequently be punished for contempt of court. Whether the Crown Prosecution Service (CPS) will prosecute the contemnor when a complaint is made will depend on whether there is sufficient evidence to meet the criminal standard of proof, namely 'beyond reasonable doubt', to secure a conviction. The offence of breaching a FMPO will be triable either summarily or on indictment. The maximum penalty on summary conviction is 6 months' imprisonment or a fine or both and on indictment is 5 years' imprisonment. The PTBP will have a choice whether to pursue the breach in the criminal courts or to apply in the Family Court for committal for contempt of court. If the CPS does decide not to prosecute, it will still be open to enforce the breach by issuing proceedings for contempt of court. It is thus essential to ensure that the FMPO is endorsed with a penal notice that warns the defendant of the consequences of not complying with the order, ie he will be liable to prosecution or proceedings in the Family Court for contempt of court and if it is found that he has been in breach of the order he is liable to be sent to prison or fined or his assets may be seized (FPR PD37A, para 1.1). If a committal application is issued, it must contain a prominent notice stating the possible consequences of the court making a committal order and of the respondent not attending the hearing. A form of notice that should be annexed to the application is annexed to PD37A, para 10.4 (see PD37A for details of the evidence and procedure of committal proceedings). For the consequences of failure to ensure that the penal notice and warnings are endorsed prominently on the front of the order, see *Re Dad* [2015] EWHC 2655 (Fam)*; sub nom Application to commit Muhammed Nawaz Chaudry* where the original order failed to insert the warnings etc prominently on the front page as required by the rules and even when they appeared on page 5 of the order the text was in the same font as all the other text.

Further provision about orders

63D Ex parte orders: Part 4A

(1) The court may, in any case where it considers that it is just and convenient to do so, make a forced marriage protection order even though the respondent has not been given such notice of the proceedings as would otherwise be required by rules of court.

(2) In deciding whether to exercise its powers under subsection (1), the court must have regard to all the circumstances including –

(a) any risk of significant harm to the person to be protected or another person if the order is not made immediately;

(b) whether it is likely that an applicant will be deterred or prevented from pursuing an application if an order is not made immediately; and

(c) whether there is reason to believe that –

(i) the respondent is aware of the proceedings but is deliberately evading service; and

(ii) the delay involved in effecting substituted service will cause serious prejudice to the person to be protected or (if a different person) an applicant.

(3) The court must give the respondent an opportunity to make representations about any order made by virtue of subsection (1).

(4) The opportunity must be –

(a) as soon as just and convenient; and

(b) at a hearing of which notice has been given to all the parties in accordance with rules of court.

Amendments—Inserted by Forced Marriage (Civil Protection) Act 2007, s 1.

Without notice orders—The criteria set out in subsection (2) must be met before a without notice order is granted. The court has a discretion to withhold any submission made or any evidence adduced for or at any hearing in the proceedings to protect the person to be protected or any other person or for any good reason (FPR 2010, r 11.7(2)). The court may also withhold disclosure of any other information under FPR 2010, r 21.3 on the ground that disclosure would damage the public interest. If such an order is made, the applicant must as soon as reasonably practicable serve personally a copy of the order, a record of the hearing and a copy of the application with any statement in support on the respondent and the person to be protected with a notice that the person affected by the order has a right to make representations to the court (FPR 2010, r 11.7). Service of orders made with or without notice must be effected in accordance with the FJC Protocol of November 2011: *Process Servers: Non-Molestation Orders* (see Part V). The statement of service must be a sworn statement and contain the information set out in the Protocol. See also *A Chief Constable v YK and Others* [2011] 1 FLR 1493, FD and *A County Council v SB, MA and AA* [2011] 1 FLR 651, FD on the circumstances when the withholding of information may be justified and on the issue of the use of special advocates. See also *BCC v FZ, AZ, HZ and TVP* [2013] 1 FLR 974, FD and *A (A Child) v Chief Constable of Dorset Police* [2011] 1 FLR 11, QBD, which although not a forced marriage case deals with the way in which the issue of sensitive information should be dealt with and the circumstances when it would be appropriate to appoint a special advocate.

'full hearing'—Where a without notice order is made, the court must list the case on notice as soon as is 'just and convenient', to enable the parties against whom the order is made, to make representation. Hence, Art 6 rights are preserved. The order must contain a statement required by FPR 2010, r 18.11. Personal service must be effected not less than 2 clear days before the hearing but the court may abridge time for service (FPR 2010, r 11.4).

63E Undertakings instead of orders

(1) In any case where the court has power to make a forced marriage protection order, the court may accept an undertaking from the respondent instead of making the order.

(2) But a court may not accept an undertaking under subsection (1) if it appears to the court –

(a) that the respondent has used or threatened violence against the person to be protected, and

(b) that, for the person's protection, it is necessary to make a forced marriage protection order so that any breach of it by the respondent may be punishable under section 63CA.

(3) *(repealed)*

(4) An undertaking given to the court under subsection (1) is enforceable as if the court had made the order in terms corresponding to those of the undertaking.

(5) This section is without prejudice to the powers of the court apart from this section.

Amendments—Inserted by Forced Marriage (Civil Protection) Act 2007, s 1. Amended by Anti-Social Behaviour, Crime and Policing Act 2014, s 120.

Undertakings—Undertakings may not be accepted if the conditions under s 63E(2) above are met. It is submitted that in the majority of cases an undertaking would not be appropriate. A power of arrest may not be attached to an undertaking. If an undertaking is accepted, it must be endorsed with a notice setting out the consequences of disobedience in the terms set out in FPR PD37A, para 2.1. It must also contain a statement signed by the respondent to the effect that he understands the undertaking and that if he breaks any of his promises to the court he may be sent to prison or fined or his assets may be seized for contempt of court. Where an undertaking is given, it may be enforced as if it were an injunction by issuing proceedings for contempt of court. Breach of an undertaking is not a crime (PD37A, para 2.2 and see under s 46). For enforcement of undertakings, see FPR 2010, r 10.13 (for undertakings generally and the form of undertakings, see FPR 2010, r 33, Pt 37, Ch 2 and PD37A, paras 2.1–2.3).

63F Duration of orders

A forced marriage protection order may be made for a specified period or until varied or discharged.

Amendments—Inserted by Forced Marriage (Civil Protection) Act 2007, s 1.

Duration of orders—Where an order is made without notice, the order must be limited in time, give a return date and contain a provision that the respondent has the right to apply to the court to have the terms of the order varied or revoked.

63G Variation of orders and their discharge

(1) The court may vary or discharge a forced marriage protection order on an application by –

- (a) any party to the proceedings for the order;
- (b) the person being protected by the order (if not a party to the proceedings for the order); or
- (c) any person affected by the order.

(2) In addition, the court may vary or discharge a forced marriage protection order made by virtue of section 63C(1)(b) even though no application under subsection (1) above has been made to the court.

(3) Section 63D applies to a variation of a forced marriage protection order as it applies to the making of such an order.

(4) Section 63E applies to proceedings for a variation of a forced marriage protection order as it applies to proceedings for the making of such an order.

(5) Accordingly, references in sections 63D and 63E to making a forced marriage protection order are to be read for the purposes of subsections (3) and (4) above as references to varying such an order.

(6), (7) *(repealed)*

Amendments—Inserted by Forced Marriage (Civil Protection) Act 2007, s 1. Amended by Anti-Social Behaviour, Crime and Policing Act 2014, s 120.

Arrest for breach of orders

63H, 63I *(repealed)*

63J Arrest under warrant

(1) *(repealed)*

(2) An interested party may apply to the relevant judge for the issue of a warrant for the arrest of a person if the interested party considers that the person has failed to comply with a forced marriage protection order or is otherwise in contempt of court in relation to the order.

(3) The relevant judge must not issue a warrant on an application under subsection (2) unless –

- (a) the application is substantiated on oath; and
- (b) the relevant judge has reasonable grounds for believing that the person to be arrested has failed to comply with the order or is otherwise in contempt of court in relation to the order.

(4) In this section 'interested party', in relation to a forced marriage protection order, means –

- (a) the person being protected by the order;
- (b) (if a different person) the person who applied for the order; or
- (c) any other person;

but no application may be made under subsection (2) by a person falling within paragraph (c) without the leave of the relevant judge.

Amendments—Inserted by Forced Marriage (Civil Protection) Act 2007, s 1. Amended by Anti-Social Behaviour, Crime and Policing Act 2014, s 120.

Application for a warrant of arrest—The provisions of the Anti-Social Behaviour Crime and Policing Act 2014 retain the court's power to issue a warrant of arrest. This must be made in Form FL407A and must be accompanied by a sworn statement. If the application is made by a person other than the person to be protected or the person who applied for the order, the application will be treated as an application for permission to apply. In this case the court will either grant the application or list the application for a hearing. Notice of the court's decision will be given by the court to the person applying for the warrant, the person to be protected and any other person directed by the court (FPR 2010, r 11.13).

63K Remand: general

(1) The court before which an arrested person is brought by virtue of a warrant issued under section 63J may, if the matter is not then disposed of immediately, remand the person concerned.

(2) Schedule 5 has effect in relation to the powers of the court to remand a person by virtue of this section but as if the following modifications were made to the Schedule.

(3) The modifications are that –

(a) in paragraph 2(1) of Schedule 5, the reference to section 47 is to be read as a reference to this section; and

(b) in paragraph 2(5)(b) of the Schedule, the reference to section 48(1) is to be read as a reference to section 63L(1).

(4) Subsection (5) applies if a person remanded under this section is granted bail under Schedule 5 as modified above.

(5) The person may be required by the relevant judge to comply, before release on bail or later, with such requirements as appear to the relevant judge to be necessary to secure that the person does not interfere with witnesses or otherwise obstruct the course of justice.

Amendments—Inserted by Forced Marriage (Civil Protection) Act 2007, s 1. Amended by Anti-Social Behaviour, Crime and Policing Act 2014, s 120.

Remand—Schedule 5 of FLA 1996 applies to this provision as it does to 'occupation orders' under FLA 1996 (see further the notes under FLA 1996, Sch 5).

Release on bail—For application for bail, see FPR PD10A, para 6 for the information to support the application. The application may be made in writing or orally. If made in writing it must be served on the person who obtained the injunction. Where a person who is arrested cannot be brought before a relevant judicial authority sitting in a court room within 24 hours after his arrest, that person may be brought before the judicial authority at any convenient place. As the liberty of the subject is involved, the press and the public should be permitted to be present unless security needs makes this impracticable.

63L Remand: medical examination and report

(1) Any power to remand a person under section 63K(1) may be exercised for the purpose of enabling a medical examination and report to be made if the relevant judge has reason to consider that a medical report will be required.

(2) If such a power is so exercised, the adjournment must not be for more than 4 weeks at a time unless the relevant judge remands the accused in custody.

(3) If the relevant judge remands the accused in custody, the adjournment must not be for more than 3 weeks at a time.

(4) Subsection (5) applies if there is reason to suspect that a person who has been arrested –

(a) …

(b) under a warrant issued on an application made under section 63J(2);

is suffering from mental illness or severe mental impairment.

(5) The relevant judge has the same power to make an order under section 35 of the Mental Health Act 1983 (remand for report on accused's mental condition) as the Crown Court has under section 35 of that Act in the case of an accused person within the meaning of that section.

Amendments—Inserted by Forced Marriage (Civil Protection) Act 2007, s 1. Amended by Anti-Social Behaviour, Crime and Policing Act 2014, s 120.

Power under the Mental Health Act 1983—Attention is drawn to the provisions of FPR PD10A, para 7.1.

Jurisdiction and procedure

63M Jurisdiction of courts: Part 4A

(1) For the purposes of this Part 'the court' means the High Court or the family court.

(2)–(4) *(repealed)*

Amendments—Inserted by Forced Marriage (Civil Protection) Act 2007, s 1. Amended by CCA 2013, s 17, Sch 11.

63N *(repealed)*

63O Contempt proceedings: Part 4A

The powers of the court in relation to contempt of court arising out of a person's failure to comply with a forced marriage protection order or otherwise in connection with such an order may be exercised by the relevant judge.

Amendments—Inserted by Forced Marriage (Civil Protection) Act 2007, s 1.

Contempt of court—The court's powers to commit for contempt of court are set out in CCA 1981. For procedure, see FPR 2010, Pt 37 and PD37A.

63P *(repealed)*

Supplementary

63Q Guidance

(1) The Secretary of State may from time to time prepare and publish guidance to such descriptions of persons as the Secretary of State considers appropriate about –

(a) the effect of this Part or any provision of this Part; or
(b) other matters relating to forced marriages.

(2) A person exercising public functions to whom guidance is given under this section must have regard to it in the exercise of those functions.

(3) Nothing in this section permits the Secretary of State to give guidance to any court or tribunal.

Amendments—Inserted by Forced Marriage (Civil Protection) Act 2007, s 1.

63R Other protection or assistance against forced marriage

(1) This Part does not affect any other protection or assistance available to a person who –

(a) is being, or may be, forced into a marriage or subjected to an attempt to be forced into a marriage; or
(b) has been forced into a marriage.

(2) In particular, it does not affect –

(a) the inherent jurisdiction of the High Court;
(b) any criminal liability;
(c) any civil remedies under the Protection from Harassment Act 1997;
(d) any right to an occupation order or a non-molestation order under Part 4 of this Act;
(e) any protection or assistance under the Children Act 1989;
(f) any claim in tort; or
(g) the law of marriage.

Amendments—Inserted by Forced Marriage (Civil Protection) Act 2007, s 1.

63S Interpretation of Part 4A

In this Part –

'the court' is to be read with section 63M;

'force' (and related expressions), in relation to a marriage, are to be read in accordance with section 63A(4) to (6);

'forced marriage protection order' has the meaning given by section 63A(6);

'marriage' means any religious or civil ceremony of marriage (whether or not legally binding); and

'the relevant judge', in relation to any order under this Part, means –

(a) where the order was made by the High Court, a judge of that court; and

(b) where the order was made by the family court, a judge of that court.

Amendments—Inserted by Forced Marriage (Civil Protection) Act 2007, s 1. Amended by CCA 2013, s 17, Sch 11.

****

SCHEDULE 4
PROVISIONS SUPPLEMENTARY TO SECTIONS 30 AND 31

1 Interpretation

In this Schedule 'legal representative' means a person who, for the purposes of the Legal Services Act 2007, is an authorised person in relation to an activity which constitutes a reserved instrument activity (within the meaning of that Act).

Amendments—Substituted by Legal Services Act 2007, s 208(1), Sch 21, para 121.

2 Restriction on registration where spouse entitled to more than one charge

Where one spouse or civil partner is entitled by virtue of section 31 to a registrable charge in respect of each of two or more dwelling-houses, only one of the charges to which that spouse or civil partner is so entitled shall be registered under section 31(10) or under section 2 of the Land Charges Act 1972 at any one time, and if any of those charges is registered under either of those provisions the Chief Land Registrar, on being satisfied that any other of them is so registered, shall cancel the registration of the charge first registered.

Amendments—CPA 2004, s 82, Sch 9, para 15(1),(2).

3 Contract for sale of house affected by registered charge to include term requiring cancellation of registration before completion

(1) Where one spouse or civil partner is entitled by virtue of section 31 to a charge on an estate in a dwelling-house and the charge is registered under section 31(10) or section 2 of the Land Charges Act 1972, it shall be a term of any contract for the sale of that estate whereby the vendor agrees to give vacant possession of the dwelling-house on completion of the contract that the vendor will before such completion procure the cancellation of the registration of the charge at his expense.

(2) Sub-paragraph (1) shall not apply to any such contract made by a vendor who is entitled to sell the estate in the dwelling-house freed from any such charge.

(3) If, on the completion of such a contract as is referred to in sub-paragraph (1), there is delivered to the purchaser or his legal representative an application by the spouse or civil partner entitled to the charge for the cancellation of the registration of that charge, the term of the contract for which sub-paragraph (1) provides shall be deemed to have been performed.

(4) This paragraph applies only if and so far as a contrary intention is not expressed in the contract.

(5) This paragraph shall apply to a contract for exchange as it applies to a contract for sale.

(6) This paragraph shall, with the necessary modifications, apply to a contract for the grant of a lease or underlease of a dwelling-house as it applies to a contract for the sale of an estate in a dwelling-house.

Amendments—CPA 2004, s 82, Sch 9, para 15(1),(3); Legal Services Act 2007, s 208(1), Sch 21, para 121.

4 Cancellation of registration after termination of marriage or civil partnership etc

(1) Where a spouse's or civil partner's home rights are a charge on an estate in the dwelling-house and the charge is registered under section 31(10) or under section 2 of the Land Charges Act 1972, the Chief Land Registrar shall, subject to sub-paragraph (2), cancel the registration of the charge if he is satisfied –

(a) in the case of a marriage –

(i) by the production of a certificate or other sufficient evidence, that either spouse is dead,

(ii) by the production of an official copy of a decree or order of a court, that the marriage has been terminated otherwise than by death, or

(iii) by the production of an order of the court, that the spouse's home rights constituting the charge have been terminated by the order, and

(b) in the case of a civil partnership –

(i) by the production of a certificate or other sufficient evidence, that either civil partner is dead,

(ii) by the production of an official copy of an order or decree of a court, that the civil partnership has been terminated otherwise than by death, or

(iii) by the production of an order of the court, that the civil partner's home rights constituting the charge have been terminated by the order.

(2) Where –

(a) the marriage or civil partnership in question has been terminated by the death of the spouse or civil partner entitled to an estate in the dwelling-house or otherwise than by death, and

(b) an order affecting the charge of the spouse or civil partner not so entitled had been made under section 35(5),

then if, after the making of the order, registration of the charge was renewed or the charge registered in pursuance of sub-paragraph (3), the Chief Land Registrar shall not cancel the registration of the charge in accordance with sub-paragraph (1) unless he is also satisfied that the order has ceased to have effect.

(3) Where such an order has been made, then, for the purposes of sub-paragraph (2), the spouse or civil partner entitled to the charge affected by the order may –

(a) if before the date of the order the charge was registered under section 31(10) or under section 2 of the Land Charges Act 1972, renew the registration of the charge, and

(b) if before the said date the charge was not so registered, register the charge under section 31(10) or under section 2 of the Land Charges Act 1972.

(4) Renewal of the registration of a charge in pursuance of sub-paragraph (3) shall be effected in such manner as may be prescribed, and an application for such renewal or for registration of a charge in pursuance of that sub-paragraph shall contain such particulars of any order affecting the charge made under section 33(5) as may be prescribed.

(5) The renewal in pursuance of sub-paragraph (3) of the registration of a charge shall not affect the priority of the charge.

(6) In this paragraph 'prescribed' means prescribed by rules made under section 16 of the Land Charges Act 1972 or by land registration rules under the Land Registration Act 2002, as the circumstances of the case require.

Amendments—CPA 2004, s 82, Sch 9, para 15(1)–(8); LRA 2002, s 34(3).

5 Release of home rights

(1) A spouse or civil partner entitled to home rights may by a release in writing release those rights or release them as respects part only of the dwelling-house affected by them.

(2) Where a contract is made for the sale of an estate or interest in a dwelling-house, or for the grant of a lease or underlease of a dwelling-house, being (in either case) a dwelling-house affected by a charge registered under section 31(10) or under section 2 of the Land Charges Act 1972, then, without prejudice to sub-paragraph (1), the home rights constituting the charge shall be deemed to have been released on the happening of whichever of the following events first occurs –

(a) the delivery to the purchaser or lessee, as the case may be, or his legal representative on completion of the contract of an application by the spouse or civil partner entitled to the charge for the cancellation of the registration of the charge; or

(b) the lodging of such an application at Her Majesty's Land Registry.

Amendments—CPA 2004, s 82, Sch 9, para 15(1),(9)–(11); Legal Services Act 2007, s 208(1), Sch 21, para 121.

General note—Irrespective of this provision allowing voluntary release of matrimonial home rights, the court retains jurisdiction to set aside the registration of matrimonial home rights where they have been improperly registered or where the registration is causing severe prejudice to the other party (see **Cessation of rights** under s 31).

6 Postponement of priority of charge

A spouse or civil partner entitled by virtue of section 31 to a charge on an estate or interest may agree in writing that any other charge on, or interest in, that estate or interest shall rank in priority to the charge to which that spouse or civil partner is so entitled.

Amendments—CPA 2004, s 82, Sch 9, para 15(1),(12).

SCHEDULE 5

POWERS OF HIGH COURT AND COUNTY COURT TO REMAND

1 Interpretation

In this Schedule 'the court' means the High Court or the family court and includes –

(a) in relation to the High Court, a judge of that court, and
(b) in relation to the family court, a judge of that court.

Amendments—CCA 2013, s 17, Sch 11.

2 Remand in custody or on bail

(1) Where a court has power to remand a person under section 47, the court may –

(a) remand him in custody, that is to say, commit him to custody to be brought before the court at the end of the period of remand or at such earlier time as the court may require, or
(b) remand him on bail –
  (i) by taking from him a recognizance (with or without sureties) conditioned as provided in sub-paragraph (3), or
  (ii) by fixing the amount of the recognizances with a view to their being taken subsequently in accordance with paragraph 4 and in the meantime committing the person to custody in accordance with paragraph (a).

(2) Where a person is brought before the court after remand, the court may further remand him.

(3) Where a person is remanded on bail under sub-paragraph (1), the court may direct that his recognizance be conditioned for his appearance –

(a) before that court at the end of the period of remand, or
(b) at every time and place to which during the course of the proceedings the hearing may from time to time be adjourned.

(4) Where a recognizance is conditioned for a person's appearance in accordance with sub-paragraph (1)(b), the fixing of any time for him next to appear shall be deemed to be a remand; but nothing in this sub-paragraph or sub-paragraph (3) shall deprive the court of power at any subsequent hearing to remand him afresh.

(5) Subject to paragraph 3, the court shall not remand a person under this paragraph for a period exceeding 8 clear days, except that –

(a) if the court remands him on bail, it may remand him for a longer period if he and the other party consent, and
(b) if the court adjourns a case under section 48(1), the court may remand him for the period of the adjournment.

(6) Where the court has power under this paragraph to remand a person in custody it may, if the remand for a period not exceeding 3 clear days, commit him to the custody of a constable.

Scope—Schedule 5 introduced a remand scheme for the High Court and the County Court. Magistrates' courts already had power to remand in civil cases pursuant to MCA 1980, ss 128, 129.

Persons alleged to be in breach of injunctions will appear before the court in one of three ways:

(a) persons arrested pursuant to a power of arrest under s 47(6);
(b) persons arrested pursuant to a warrant of arrest issued under s 47(8);
(c) persons brought before the court under an application to show cause why they should not be committed (generally in Form N78) under FPR 2010, Pt 37.

In all cases the court would prefer to deal with the matter at the first hearing. However, before dealing with the person for contempt of court, the court must record findings of fact and therefore the facts have to be either admitted or proved by evidence. If the facts are not admitted and the evidence is not before the court, the court will not be able to deal with the matter. This may arise, for example, where the respondent has been arrested pursuant to a power of arrest but the person who has the benefit of the injunction is not before the court to give evidence (the arresting officer is not usually required to attend). In such circumstances, as an alternative to merely adjourning, the court can remand and has to decide whether the remand should be in custody or on bail. A remand in custody cannot be for a period exceeding 8 clear days (3 clear days, if in the custody of a constable).

Although Sch 5 clearly envisages conditional bail, it is submitted that this in practice is not necessary. The injunction will still be in force and therefore imposing similar terms as a condition of bail achieves no purpose. The injunction itself could still be enforced whereas there is no procedure for enforcing breach of bail conditions. It is respectfully submitted that the Schedule has overlooked the fundamental distinction between bail in criminal matters and bail in civil matters. Bail in a criminal case is primarily to ensure that the defendant is before the court when the case comes up for trial. The criminal trial may have to be adjourned, and a bench warrant issued, if the defendant does not answer to bail. The situation is different in a civil matter whereby, provided the court is satisfied that the respondent has notice of the hearing date, and that it is just to do so, the court can proceed in the absence of a party. Thus no practical purpose is served by conditional bail in the context of civil cases. Indeed, it is submitted that bail itself, conditional or not, serves no practical purpose in the context of injunction cases. If the court is unable to deal with the alleged breach of the injunction at the first hearing and has decided that a remand in custody is not necessary, how does a remand on bail differ from an adjournment, given that the injunction itself is still in force? An adjournment without a remand on bail is adequate, and if conditions are required to protect the applicant they could be in the form of an amended or expanded injunction, with a power of arrest. However, the term 'bail' is widely understood, and perhaps a remand on bail, following arrest, could have a psychological impact, given that the court's main purpose will be to secure future compliance with its order. If the court does remand a person on bail it is obliged to take a recognizance (para 2(1)(b)(i)).

Re-remand—The maximum period of any remand in custody is 8 days (see Sch 5, para 2(5)). The alleged contemnor has to be brought before the court again on expiry of the remand and the order in Form FL409 should expressly provide for this. However, Sch 5, para 2(2) gives express power to further remand and does not limit the maximum number of remands nor number of days in total for a remand in custody. In practice, contempt proceedings are to be treated as urgent and dealt with as quickly as possible. A remand in custody has to be taken into consideration in any subsequent sentence. See further *Kerai v Patel* [2008] 2 FLR 2137, CA and commentary to CCA 1981 and to FPR 2010, Pt 10.

Contempt of court—The court's powers to commit for contempt of court are in CCA 1981. See that Act and commentary thereon.

3 Further remand

(1) If the court is satisfied that any person who has been remanded under paragraph 2 is unable by reason of illness or accident to appear or be brought before the court at the expiration of the period for which he was remanded, the court may, in his absence, remand him for a further time; and paragraph 2(5) shall not apply.

(2) Notwithstanding anything in paragraph 2(1), the power of the court under sub-paragraph (1) to remand a person on bail for a further time may be exercised by enlarging his recognizance and those of any sureties for him to a later time.

(3) Where a person remanded on bail under paragraph 2 is bound to appear before the court at any time and the court has no power to remand him under sub-paragraph (1), the court may in his absence enlarge his recognizance and those of any sureties for him to a later time; and the enlargement of his recognizance shall be deemed to be a further remand.

4 Postponement of taking of recognizance

Where under paragraph 2(1)(b)(ii) the court fixes the amount in which the principal and his sureties, if any, are to be bound, the recognizance may thereafter be taken by such person as may be prescribed by rules of court, and the same consequences shall follow as if it had been entered into before the court.

'prescribed by rules of court'—The relevant rule is FPR 2010, r 10.17. The persons prescribed in the High Court or the County Court are a district judge, a police officer of at least the rank of inspector or in charge of a police station, and (where the person making the application is in his custody) the governor or keeper of a prison.

★★★★

SCHEDULE 7
TRANSFER OF CERTAIN TENANCIES ON DIVORCE ETC OR ON SEPARATION OF COHABITANTS

Scope—Taking into account the matters set out in para 5, including the suitability of the parties as tenants (the landlord has the right to be heard by virtue of para 14), the court can transfer a range of tenancies including statutory tenancies held by one or both spouses, civil partners or former spouses or former civil partners (subject to the pronouncement of an appropriate decree and the applicant has not remarried or entered into a new civil partnership), cohabitants or former cohabitants. The transferee can be ordered to pay compensation to the transferor (para 10). If immediate payment of the compensation causes the transferee greater financial hardship than the transferor, payment can be deferred or be by instalments. The court can direct that both be liable under the obligations of the tenancy and that one indemnify the other (para 11). If jurisdiction is founded on a decree of divorce or nullity, the order cannot take effect until the decree is absolute (para 12).

Procedure—Applications for a transfer of a tenancy under s 53 and Sch 7 are governed by FPR 2010, rr 8.29–8.34. See Procedural Guide A11.

PART II

PART I
GENERAL

Interpretation

1 In this Schedule –

'civil partner', except in paragraph 2, includes (where the context requires) former civil partner;

'cohabitant', except in paragraph 3, includes (where the context requires) former cohabitant,

'the court' means the High Court or the family court,

'landlord' includes –

(a) any person from time to time deriving title under the original landlord; and

(b) in relation to any dwelling-house, any person other than the tenant who is, or (but for Part VII of the Rent Act 1977 or Part II of the Rent (Agriculture) Act 1976) would be, entitled to possession of the dwelling-house;

'Part II order' means an order under Part II of this Schedule;

'a relevant tenancy' means –

(a) a protected tenancy or statutory tenancy within the meaning of the Rent Act 1977;

(b) a statutory tenancy within the meaning of the Rent (Agriculture) Act 1976;

(c) a secure tenancy within the meaning of section 79 of the Housing Act 1985;

(d) an assured tenancy or assured agricultural occupancy within the meaning of Part I of the Housing Act 1988; or

(e) an introductory tenancy within the meaning of Chapter I of Part V of the Housing Act 1996;

'spouse', except in paragraph 2, includes (where the context requires) former spouse; and

'tenancy' includes sub-tenancy.

Amendments—SI 1997/74; CPA 2004, s 82, Sch 9, para 16(1),(2); CCA 2013, s 17, Sch 11.

Costs—The costs rule in FPR 2010, r 28.3 does not apply to applications under FLA 1996, Sch 7. The court may exercise its discretion as to costs in the light of CPR 1998, r 44.2. See FPR PD28A.

Cases in which court may make order

2 (1) This paragraph applies if one spouse or civil partner is entitled, either in his own right or jointly with the other spouse or civil partner, to occupy a dwelling-house by virtue of a relevant tenancy.

(2) The court may make a Part II order –

(a) on granting a decree of divorce, a decree of nullity of marriage or a decree of judicial separation or at any time thereafter (whether, in the case of a decree of divorce or nullity of marriage, before or after the decree is made absolute), or

(b) at any time when it has power to make a property adjustment order under Part 2 of Schedule 5 to the Civil Partnership Act 2004 with respect to the civil partnership.

Amendments—SI 1997/1892; CPA 2004, s 82, Sch 9, para 16(1),(3),(4).

'dwelling-house'—In contrast to s 30, 33 et seq, this term is restricted so that it does not include a caravan or houseboat (see s 63(1),(4)). Additionally, by virtue of para 4 below, a court may only make an order in respect of a dwelling-house which is or was a matrimonial home, as opposed to one intended to be a matrimonial home.

3 (1) This paragraph applies if one cohabitant is entitled, either in his own right or jointly with the other cohabitant, to occupy a dwelling-house by virtue of a relevant tenancy.

(2) If the cohabitants cease to cohabit, the court may make a Part II order.

Amendments—By virtue of Domestic Violence, Crime and Victims Act 2004, s 58(1), Sch 10, para 42(1),(2).

Note—The court cannot transfer a tenancy to one cohabitant if that tenancy is held jointly by the other cohabitant with a third party. Nor can it do so if it is a statutory tenancy whose security has been lost by the tenant being out of occupation (*Gay v Sheeran* [1999] 2 FLR 519, CA).

4 The court shall not make a Part II order unless the dwelling-house is or was –

(a) in the case of spouses, a matrimonial home;

(aa) in the case of civil partners, a civil partnership home; or

(b) in the case of cohabitants, a home in which they cohabited.

Amendments—CPA 2004, s 82, Sch 9, para 16(1),(5); by virtue of Domestic Violence, Crime and Victims Act 2004, s 58(1), Sch 10, para 42(1), (3).

Matters to which the court must have regard

5 In determining whether to exercise its powers under Part II of this Schedule and, if so, in what manner, the court shall have regard to all the circumstances of the case including –

(a) the circumstances in which the tenancy was granted to either or both of the spouses, civil partners or cohabitants or, as the case requires, the circumstances in which either or both of them became tenant under the tenancy;

(b) the matters mentioned in section 33(6)(a), (b) and (c) and, where the parties are cohabitants and only one of them is entitled to occupy the dwelling-house by virtue of the relevant tenancy, the further matters mentioned in section 36(6)(e), (f), (g) and (h); and

(c) the suitability of the parties as tenants.

Amendments—By virtue of CPA 2004, s 82, Sch 9, para 16(1),(6).

Scope—The Court of Appeal has noted the absence of reference in Sch 7, para 5 to FLA 1996, s 33(6), which provides that the court in making an occupation order should have regard to 'all the circumstances' including s 33(6)(d): 'the conduct of the parties in relation to each other and otherwise'. In *Lake v Lake* [2007] 1 FLR 427, CA, the court had to take a balanced and fair decision as to which spouse should have the benefit of a joint tenancy following the dissolution of the marriage, having regard to all the circumstance of the case, including the conduct of the parties. It is good practice to seek to furnish the court with evidence of the private and local authority housing options for each party, particularly if one party's vulnerability by virtue of a disability may justify him/her being in priority need of housing pursuant to Housing Act 1996, Pt VII: *Guerroudj v Rymarczyk* [2016] 1 FLR 1349, CA.

PART II

ORDERS THAT MAY BE MADE

References to entitlement to occupy

6 References in this Part of this Schedule to a spouse, a civil partner or a cohabitant being entitled to occupy a dwelling-house by virtue of a relevant tenancy apply whether that entitlement is in his own right or jointly with the other spouse, civil partner or cohabitant.

Amendments—CPA 2004, s 82, Sch 9, para 16(1),(7).

Protected, secure or assured tenancy or assured agricultural occupancy

7 (1) If a spouse, civil partner or cohabitant is entitled to occupy the dwelling-house by virtue of a protected tenancy within the meaning of the Rent Act 1977, a secure tenancy within the meaning of the Housing Act 1985, an assured tenancy or assured agricultural occupancy within the meaning of Part I of the Housing Act 1988 or an introductory tenancy within the meaning of Chapter I of Part V of the Housing Act 1996, the court may by order direct that, as from such date as may be specified in the order, there shall, by virtue of the order and without further assurance, be transferred to, and vested in, the other spouse, civil partner or cohabitant –

(a) the estate or interest which the spouse or cohabitant so entitled had in the dwelling-house immediately before that date by virtue of the lease or agreement creating the tenancy and any assignment of that lease or agreement, with all rights, privileges and appurtenances attaching to that estate or interest but subject to all covenants, obligations, liabilities and incumbrances to which it is subject; and

(b) where the spouse or cohabitant so entitled is an assignee of such lease or agreement, the liability of that spouse or cohabitant under any covenant of indemnity by the assignee express or implied in the assignment of the lease or agreement to that spouse or cohabitant.

(2) If an order is made under this paragraph, any liability or obligation to which the spouse or cohabitant so entitled is subject under any covenant having reference to the dwelling-house in the lease or agreement, being a liability or obligation falling due to be discharged or performed on or after the date so specified, shall not be enforceable against that spouse or cohabitant.

(3) If the spouse, civil partner or cohabitant so entitled is a successor within the meaning of Part 4 of the Housing Act 1985 –

(a) his former spouse (or, in the case of judicial separation, his spouse),
(b) his former civil partner (or, if a separation order is in force, his civil partner), or
(c) his former cohabitant,

is to be deemed also to be a successor within the meaning of that Part.

(3A) If the spouse, civil partner or cohabitant so entitled is a successor within the meaning of section 132 of the Housing Act 1996 –

(a) his former spouse (or, in the case of judicial separation, his spouse),
(b) his former civil partner (or, if a separation order is in force, his civil partner), or
(c) his former cohabitant,

is to be deemed also to be a successor within the meaning of that section.

(4) If the spouse, civil partner or cohabitant so entitled is for the purposes of section 17 of the Housing Act 1988 a successor in relation to the tenancy or occupancy –

(a) his former spouse (or, in the case of judicial separation, his spouse),
(b) his former civil partner (or, if a separation order is in force, his civil partner), or
(c) his former cohabitant,

is to be deemed to be a successor in relation to the tenancy or occupancy for the purposes of that section.

(5) If the transfer under sub-paragraph (1) is of an assured agricultural occupancy, then, for the purposes of Chapter III of Part I of the Housing Act 1988 –

(a) the agricultural worker condition is fulfilled with respect to the dwelling-house while the spouse, civil partner or cohabitant to whom the assured agricultural occupancy is transferred continues to be the occupier under that occupancy, and
(b) that condition shall be treated as so fulfilled by virtue of the same paragraph of Schedule 3 to the Housing Act 1988 as was applicable before the transfer.

(6) …

Amendments—SI 1997/74; SI 1997/1892; CPA 2004, ss 82, 261(4), Sch 9, para 16(1),(8)–(11).

Interrelation with MCA 1973, s 24 where parties are married—By virtue of MCA 1973, s 24, the court can transfer a tenancy but not a statutory tenancy, as it is not property. The advantages of applying for a transfer of a tenancy under this Schedule as opposed to MCA 1973 are:

(a) the court order operates as the transfer 'without further assurance' so that, in the case of a reluctant transferor, there is no need to apply for the district judge to execute the transfer on his behalf;
(b) if there is a covenant against assignment, an order under MCA, s 24 is a breach of that covenant (except in the case of a secured tenancy under Housing Act 1985, s 91(3)). However, under Sch 7, para 7(1), the transfer operates to vest the interest as it existed immediately before the date of the transfer, so on the literal wording of this provision no assignment has taken place.

Statutory tenancy within the meaning of the Rent Act 1977

8 (1) This paragraph applies if the spouse, civil partner or cohabitant is entitled to occupy the dwelling-house by virtue of a statutory tenancy within the meaning of the Rent Act 1977.

(2) The court may by order direct that, as from the date specified in the order –

(a) that spouse or cohabitant is to cease to be entitled to occupy the dwelling-house; and
(b) the other spouse or cohabitant is to be deemed to be the tenant or, as the case may be, the sole tenant under that statutory tenancy.

(3) The question whether the provisions of paragraphs 1 to 3, or (as the case may be) paragraphs 5 to 7 of Schedule 1 to the Rent Act 1977, as to the succession by the surviving spouse or surviving civil partner of a deceased tenant, or by a member of the deceased tenant's family, to the right to retain possession are capable of having effect in the event of the death of the person deemed by an order under this paragraph to be the tenant or sole tenant under the statutory tenancy is to be determined according as those provisions have or have not already had effect in relation to the statutory tenancy.

Amendments—CPA 2004, s 82, Sch 9, para 16(1),(12),(13).

Statutory tenancy within the meaning of the Rent (Agriculture) Act 1976

9 (1) This paragraph applies if the spouse or cohabitant is entitled to occupy the dwelling-house by virtue of a statutory tenancy within the meaning of the Rent (Agriculture) Act 1976.

(2) The court may by order direct that, as from such date as may be specified in the order –

(a) that spouse or cohabitant is to cease to be entitled to occupy the dwelling-house; and
(b) the other spouse or cohabitant is to be deemed to be the tenant or, as the case may be, the sole tenant under that statutory tenancy.

(3) A spouse, civil partner or cohabitant who is deemed under this paragraph to be the tenant under a statutory tenancy is (within the meaning of that Act) a statutory tenant in his own right, or a statutory tenant by succession, according as the other spouse, civil partner or cohabitant was a statutory tenant in his own right or a statutory tenant by succession.

Amendments—CPA 2004, s 82, Sch 9, para 16(1),(14).

PART III
SUPPLEMENTARY PROVISIONS

Compensation

10 (1) If the court makes a Part II order, it may by the order direct the making of a payment by the spouse, civil partner or cohabitant to whom the tenancy is transferred ('the transferee') to the other spouse or cohabitant ('the transferor').

(2) Without prejudice to that, the court may, on making an order by virtue of sub-paragraph (1) for the payment of a sum –

(a) direct that payment of that sum or any part of it is to be deferred until a specified date or until the occurrence of a specified event, or

(b) direct that that sum or any part of it is to be paid by instalments.

(3) Where an order has been made by virtue of sub-paragraph (1), the court may, on the application of the transferee or the transferor –

(a) exercise its powers under sub-paragraph (2), or

(b) vary any direction previously given under that sub-paragraph,

at any time before the sum whose payment is required by the order is paid in full.

(4) In deciding whether to exercise its powers under this paragraph and, if so, in what manner, the court shall have regard to all the circumstances including –

(a) the financial loss that would otherwise be suffered by the transferor as a result of the order;

(b) the financial needs and financial resources of the parties; and

(c) the financial obligations which the parties have, or are likely to have in the foreseeable future, including financial obligations to each other and to any relevant child.

(5) The court shall not give any direction under sub-paragraph (2) unless it appears to it that immediate payment of the sum required by the order would cause the transferee financial hardship which is greater than any financial hardship that would be caused to the transferor if the direction were given.

Amendments—CPA 2004, s 82, Sch 9, para 16(1),(14).

Liabilities and obligations in respect of the dwelling-house

11 (1) If the court makes a Part II order, it may by the order direct that both spouses, civil partners or cohabitants are to be jointly and severally liable to discharge or perform any or all of the liabilities and obligations in respect of the dwelling-house (whether arising under the tenancy or otherwise) which –

(a) have at the date of the order fallen due to be discharged or performed by one only of them; or

(b) but for the direction, would before the date specified as the date on which the order is to take effect fall due to be discharged or performed by one only of them.

(2) If the court gives such a direction, it may further direct that either spouse, civil partner or cohabitant is to be liable to indemnify the other in whole or in part against any payment made or expenses incurred by the other in discharging or performing any such liability or obligation.

Amendments—CPA 2004, s 82, Sch 9, para 16(1),(15),(16).

Date when order made between spouses is to take effect

12 Date when order made between spouses or civil partners takes effect

The date specified in a Part II order as the date on which the order is to take effect must not be earlier than –

(a) in the case of a marriage in respect of which a decree of divorce or nullity has been granted, the date on which the decree is made absolute;
(b) in the case of a civil partnership in respect of which a dissolution or nullity order has been made, the date on which the order is made final.

Amendments—Substituted by CPA 2004, s 82, Sch 9, para 16(1),(17).

Remarriage of either spouse

13 Effect of remarriage or subsequent civil partnership

(1) If after the grant of a decree dissolving or annulling a marriage either spouse remarries or forms a civil partnership, that spouse is not entitled to apply, by reference to the grant of that decree, for a Part II order.

(2) If after the making of a dissolution or nullity order either civil partner forms a subsequent civil partnership or marries, that civil partner is not entitled to apply, by reference to the making of that order, for a Part II order.

(3) In sub-paragraphs (1) and (2) –

(a) the references to remarrying and marrying include references to cases where the marriage is by law void or voidable, and
(b) the references to forming a civil partnership include references to cases where the civil partnership is by law void or voidable.

Amendments—Substituted by CPA 2004, s 82, Sch 9, para 16(1),(18).

Rules of court

14 (1) Rules of court shall be made requiring the court, before it makes an order under this Schedule, to give the landlord of the dwelling-house to which the order will relate an opportunity of being heard.

(2) Rules of court may provide that an application for a Part II order by reference to an order or decree may not, without the leave of the court by which that order was made or decree was granted, be made after the expiration of such period from the order or grant as may be prescribed by the rules.

Scope—FPR 2010, rr 8.29–8.34 provides for applications under FLA 1996, Pt IV. No rules have been made under para 14(2) prohibiting the application if not made within a specific time, although para 13 provides that an application must be made before remarriage. The landlord must be served, unless the court directs otherwise, and may be a party to the proceedings: FPR 2010, rr 8.31, 8.32.

Saving for other provisions of Act

15 (1) If a spouse or civil partner is entitled to occupy a dwelling-house by virtue of a tenancy, this Schedule does not affect the operation of sections 30 and 31 in relation to the other spouse's or civil partner's home rights.

(2) If a spouse, civil partner or cohabitant is entitled to occupy a dwelling-house by virtue of a tenancy, the court's powers to make orders under this Schedule are additional to those conferred by sections 33, 35 and 36.

Amendments—CPA 2004, s 82, Sch 9, para 16(1),(19),(20).

****

Family Law Reform Act 1969

ARRANGEMENT OF SECTIONS

PART I

REDUCTION OF AGE OF MAJORITY AND RELATED PROVISIONS

Section		Page
1	Reduction of age of majority from 21 to 18	917
8	Consent by persons over 16 to surgical, medical and dental treatment	918
9	Time at which a person attains a particular age	919

PART III

PROVISIONS FOR USE OF SCIENTIFIC TESTS IN DETERMINING PATERNITY

20	Power of court to require use of scientific tests	919
21	Consents etc required for taking of bodily samples	921
22	Power to provide for manner of giving effect to direction for use of scientific tests	922
23	Failure to comply with direction for taking scientific tests	923
24	Penalty for personating another, etc, for purpose of providing bodily sample	923
25	Interpretation of Part III	923

PART IV

MISCELLANEOUS AND GENERAL

26	Rebuttal of presumption as to legitimacy and illegitimacy	924

PART I

REDUCTION OF AGE OF MAJORITY AND RELATED PROVISIONS

1 Reduction of age of majority from 21 to 18

(1) As from the date on which this section comes into force a person shall attain full age on attaining the age of eighteen instead of on attaining the age of twenty-one; and a person shall attain full age on that date if he has then already attained the age of eighteen but not the age of twenty-one.

(2) The foregoing subsection applies for the purposes of any rule of law, and, in the absence of a definition or of any indication of a contrary intention, for the construction of 'full age', 'infant', 'infancy', 'minor', 'minority' and similar expressions in –

- (a) any statutory provision, whether passed or made before, on or after the date on which this section comes into force; and
- (b) any deed, will or other instrument of whatever nature (not being a statutory provision) made on or after that date.

(3) In the statutory provisions specified in Schedule 1 to this Act for any reference to the age of twenty-one years there shall be substituted a reference to the age of eighteen years; but the amendment by this subsection of the provisions specified in Part II of that Schedule shall be without prejudice to any power of amending or revoking those provisions.

(4) This section does not affect the construction of any such expression as is referred to in subsection (2) of this section in any of the statutory provisions described in Schedule 2 to this Act, and the transitional provisions and savings contained in Schedule 3 to this Act shall have effect in relation to this section.

(5) The Lord Chancellor may by order made by statutory instrument amend any provision in any local enactment passed on or before the date on which this section comes into force (not being a provision described in paragraph 2 of Schedule 2 to this Act) by substituting a reference to the age

of eighteen years for any reference therein to the age of twenty-one years; and any statutory instrument containing an order under this subsection shall be subject to annulment in pursuance of a resolution of either House of Parliament.

(6) In this section 'statutory provision' means any enactment (including, except where the context otherwise requires, this Act) and any order, rule, regulation, byelaw or other instrument made in the exercise of a power conferred by any enactment.

(7) Notwithstanding any rule of law, a will or codicil executed before the date on which this section comes into force shall not be treated for the purposes of this section as made on or after that date by reason only that the will or codicil is confirmed by a codicil executed on or after that date.

****

8 Consent by persons over 16 to surgical, medical and dental treatment

(1) The consent of a minor who has attained the age of sixteen years to any surgical, medical or dental treatment which, in the absence of consent, would constitute a trespass to his person, shall be as effective as it would be if he were of full age; and where a minor has by virtue of this section given an effective consent to any treatment it shall not be necessary to obtain any consent for it from his parent or guardian.

(2) In this section 'surgical, medical or dental treatment' includes any procedure undertaken for the purposes of diagnosis, and this section applies to any procedure (including, in particular, the administration of an anaesthetic) which is ancillary to any treatment as it applies to that treatment.

(3) Nothing in this section shall be construed as making ineffective any consent which would have been effective if this section had not been enacted.

Scope—This section gives to minors who have attained the age of 16 a right to consent to surgical, medical or dental treatment. The effect of consent to treatment by the minor, or someone else with authority to give it, is limited to protecting the medical or dental practitioner from claims for damages for trespass to the person. Such consent cannot be overridden by those with parental responsibility for the minor, although it can be overridden by the court. This statutory right does not extend to the donation of blood or organs (*Re W (A Minor) (Consent to Medical Treatment)* [1993] 1 FLR 1, CA). This section is of no significance where the case concerns the effect of a *refusal* as distinct from a *consent* to treatment. The court or any person with parental responsibility can override the refusal of any minor who is under or over 16 years to consent to medical treatment, although the minor's wishes are a crucial consideration to be taken into account. In *Re W (A Minor) (Consent to Medical Treatment)* (above), a 16-year-old girl suffering from anorexia nervosa opposed the plans of the local authority to move her to a new treatment unit and to give her medical treatment without her consent. The local authority applied under CA 1989, s 100(3) for leave of the court to carry out its plans. The Court of Appeal held that the only purpose of FLRA 1969, s 8 was to enable a 16-year-old to consent to medical treatment which, in the absence of consent by the child or its parents, would constitute a trespass to the person; further, as the section was silent on the question whether a minor of 16 had an absolute right to refuse medical treatment, it could not be construed to confer such a right. There was no overriding limitation to preclude the exercise by the court of its inherent jurisdiction over minors to act in the minor's best interests. The court authorised the plans of the local authority.

Guidance where children are nearly 16 years of age—Useful guidance in this area is to be found in the conclusions set out by Lord Donaldson MR in *Re R (A Minor) (Wardship: Consent to Treatment)* [1992] 1 FLR 190, CA, where the court considered the case of a 15-year-old girl who refused medication for her psychotic state. The court found that, due to her mental state, she was not '*Gillick* competent' within the guidelines set out in *Gillick v West Norfolk and Wisbech Area Health Authority and Another* [1986] 1 FLR 224, HL. The court authorised the proposed treatment, holding as follows:

(a) No doctor could be required to treat a child since the decision to do so was a matter for his own professional judgement, subject only to obtaining, where necessary, the consent of someone with the authority to give that consent. In forming that judgement, the wishes of the child were a factor whose importance increases with the increase in the child's intelligence and understanding.

(b) There can be concurrent powers to consent. If more than one body or person has a power to consent, only a failure to, or refusal of, consent by all having that power will create a veto.

(c) A '*Gillick*-competent' child or a child over the age of 16 will have a power to consent, but that will be concurrent with that of a parent or guardian.

(d) '*Gillick* competence' is a developmental concept and will not be lost or acquired on a day-to-day or a week-by-week basis. In the case of mental disability, that disability must also be taken into account, particularly where it is fluctuating in its effect.

(e) The court, in the exercise of its wardship or statutory jurisdiction, has power to override the decisions of a '*Gillick*-competent' child as much as those of parents or guardians.

In the case of *R (Axon) v The Secretary of State for Health and the Family Planning Association* [2006] 2 FLR 206, QBD, Silber J reaffirmed the principles set out in *Gillick* and held that a medical professional is entitled to provide advice and treatment on sexual matters, including abortion, without a parent's knowledge provided that he or she is satisfied that:

(a) the young person, although under 16, understands all aspects of the advice and that this understanding includes all relevant matters and is not limited to family and moral aspects, as well as all adverse consequences which might follow from the advice;
(b) the medical professional cannot persuade the young person to inform the parents or to allow the medical professional to inform them that their child is seeking advice and/or treatment on sexual matters;
(c) the young person is very likely to begin or to continue having sexual intercourse with or without contraceptive treatment or treatment for a sexually transmissible disease;
(d) unless the young person receives advice and treatment on the relevant sexual matters, his or her physical or mental health or both are likely to suffer; and
(e) the best interests of the young person require him or her to receive advice and treatment on sexual matters without parental consent or notification.

Silber J also stated that the parent's right to respect for family life under ECHR 1950, Art 8 dwindles as his or her child gets older and is able to understand the consequence of different choices and then to make decisions relating to them. It remains to be seen whether these principles of autonomy, when an appropriate level of maturity is reached, will be applied to the refusal of treatment or whether the guidance in *Re R* (above) will continue to apply.

9 Time at which a person attains a particular age

(1) The time at which a person attains a particular age expressed in years shall be the commencement of the relevant anniversary of the date of his birth.

(2) This section applies only where the relevant anniversary falls on a date after that on which this section comes into force, and, in relation to any enactment, deed, will or other instrument, has effect subject to any provision therein.

****

PART III

PROVISIONS FOR USE OF SCIENTIFIC TESTS IN DETERMINING PATERNITY

20 Power of court to require use of scientific tests

(1) In any civil proceedings in which the parentage of any person falls to be determined, the court may, either of its own motion or on an application by any party to the proceedings, give a direction –

(a) for the use of scientific tests to ascertain whether such tests show that a party to the proceedings is or is not the father or mother of that person; and
(b) for the taking, within a period specified in the direction, of bodily samples from all or any of the following, namely, that person, any party who is alleged to be the father or mother of that person and any other party to the proceedings;

and the court may at any time revoke or vary a direction previously given by it under this subsection.

(1A) Tests required by a direction under this section may only be carried out by a body which has been accredited for the purposes of this section by –

(a) the Lord Chancellor, or
(b) a body appointed by him for the purpose.

(2) The individual carrying out scientific tests in pursuance of a direction under subsection (1) above ('the tester') shall make to the court a report in which he shall state –

(a) the results of the tests;
(b) whether the party to whom the report relates is or is not excluded by the results from being the father or mother of the person whose parentage is to be determined; and
(c) in relation to any party who is not so excluded, the value, if any, of the results in determining whether that party is the father or mother of that person;

and the report shall be received by the court as evidence in the proceedings of the matters stated in it.

PART II

(2A) Where the proceedings in which the parentage of any person falls to be determined are proceedings on an application under section 55A or 56 of the Family Law Act 1986, any reference in subsection (1) or (2) of this section to any party to the proceedings shall include a reference to any person named in the application.

(3) A report under subsection (2) of this section shall be in the form prescribed by regulations made under section 22 of this Act.

(4) Where a report has been made to a court under subsection (2) of this section, any party may, with the leave of the court, or shall, if the court so directs, obtain from 'the tester' a written statement explaining or amplifying any statement made in the report, and that statement shall be deemed for the purposes of this section (except subsection (3) thereof) to form part of the report made to the court.

(5) Where a direction is given under this section in any proceedings, a party to the proceedings, unless the court otherwise directs, shall not be entitled to call as a witness the tester, or any other person by whom any thing necessary for the purpose of enabling those tests to be carried out was done, unless within fourteen days after receiving a copy of the report he serves notice on the other parties to the proceedings, or on such of them as the court may direct, of his intention to call the tester, or that other person; and where the tester or any such person is called as a witness the party who called him shall be entitled to cross-examine him.

(6) Where a direction is given under this section the party on whose application the direction is given shall pay the cost of taking and testing bodily samples for the purpose of giving effect to the direction (including any expenses reasonably incurred by any person in taking any steps required of him for the purpose), and of making a report to the court under this section, but the amount paid shall be treated as costs incurred by him in the proceedings.

Amendments—FLRA 1987, ss 23(1), 33(1), Sch 2, para 21; CA 1989, s 89; CLSA 1990, s 116, Sch 16, para 3; CSPSSA 2000, s 82(1),(2), Sch 8, para 9.

Defined terms—'bodily samples', 'scientific tests', 'excluded': s 25.

'civil proceedings' (s 20(1))—This includes proceedings under FPR 2010.

'the parentage of any person falls to be determined' (s 20(1))—This section adopts terminology similar to that of FLA 1986, s 55A and enables the court to give a direction designed to show whether or not a person is the parent of the child ('the person') concerned. Section 55A enables a parent or other party 'with sufficient personal interest' (FLA 1986, s 55A(3)) to make a freestanding application for parentage. However, application for a scientific tests direction can only be made in existing civil (including family) proceedings in which the issue of parentage arises (eg under FLA 1986, s 55A). The direction can be made by the court of its own initiative or on application by a party to the proceedings.

'the party on whose application the direction is given shall pay the costs'—The cost of the tests falls on the applicant save that for a period of only 12 months from 23 November 2015 Cafcass and CAFCASS Cymru will facilitate and fund the provision of DNA tests in limited circumstances, namely: (a) where an application has been made for a child arrangements order under CA 1989, s 8; and (b) the application cannot be determined unless a dispute about the paternity of the child is resolved; and (c) the parents or person with care of the child are prepared to cooperate with the direction made by the court. See *www.cafcass.gov.uk/media/268569/information_for_courts_cafcass_cafcass_cymru_funding_for_dna_tests_in_child_arrangements_cases.pdf*.

Form of Directions for scientific tests where the above circumstances apply—The court must compete the template (Form BD1) contained in Sch 1 to the Blood Tests (Evidence of Paternity) Regulations 1971 and ensure that: (a) the Form CAP02 contains reference to the fact that the order for DNA tests has been made; (b) the order contains reference to Cafcass/CAFCASS Cymru meeting the costs of the DNA tests and that the direction is made of the court's own volition; (c) the order specifies who is the person with care and control who is to bring and take the sample from the child under supervision; and (d) the parents are provided with a copy of the service user leaflet that explains the process.

Service of the order—For cases involving children ordinarily resident in England, the order must be sent by secure email to inboundpost@cafcass.gsi.gov.uk copying in dnarequests@cafcass.gsi.gov.uk or by post to Cafcass PP, PO Box 222, Warrington WA3 9DA, DX: Cafcass, Fujitsu Digitisation Mail, DX 307201 Warrington 17 and to DNA Requests, Cafcass National Business Centre, Millburn Hill Road, University of Warwick Science Park, Coventry CV44 7JJ. In the case of children resident in Wales, the order must be sent to CAFCASS Cymru's Central Administrative Team (CAT) by secure email to CafcasscymruCAT@wales.gsi.gov.uk and or by post to DNA Requests, CAFCASS Cymru CAT Team, Welsh Government, Rhydycar Business Park, Merthyr Tydfil CF48 1UZ.

'body accredited to carry out tests'—Eurofins Medigenomix Forensik is a MoJ-accredited laboratory with whom Cafcass has a contract to undertake the tests and DNA Legal is their representative in England and Wales.

Timescale for the submission of the tests report—The laboratory have a timescale for filing the report with the court within 30 days from the receipt of the sealed order. This time limit is subject to review and may be reduced. The report will be filed by Eurofins directly with the court and the court is responsible for serving the report on the parties, if appropriate.

Procedure—Application for a test is by the FPR 2010, Pt 18 procedure.

Responsible adult—CPR PD23B, para 1.1(3) defines a responsible adult as (1) a person who has 'care and control' of a person under 16 and (2) where a person lacks capacity under MCA 2005 to give consent to tests, a person who has power to give consent or, lacking that, a person with whom he lives or in whose care he is (and see discussion under FPR 2010, r 15.1). Where application is made in respect of a person who is under 16 or who lacks capacity, the application notice must include the name and address of the responsible adult (para 1.2).

'party to the proceedings' (s 20(1),(2A))—In proceedings under FLA 1986, ss 55A and 56, individuals may be named in an application (see FPR 2010, r 8.20). If so named in the application, the individual may be joined as a party, or may apply to be joined for the purposes of a direction under s 20(1) (FPR 2010, r 8.20(4),(5)).

Interests of justice—The interests of justice in terms of exercise of the discretion whether to make a direction was explained in *Re H and A (Paternity: Blood Tests)* [2002] 1 FLR 1145, CA: that the truth about parentage was known and that the court should have access to the best available science.

Discretion to direct—The direction of a blood test is a discretionary remedy and should only be made if in the interests of the child concerned. In *Re H (Paternity: Blood Test)* [1996] 2 FLR 65, CA, Ward LJ explained fully the factors to be borne in mind when the court exercises its discretion:

(1) A parent's refusal to comply with a direction was not determinative of the issue of whether or not a direction should be made;
(2) The welfare of the child is a relevant but not paramount factor in deciding whether or not to make a direction; the interests of other persons may also be involved (and see *S v S, W v Official Solicitor* (above));
(3) The outcome of the proceedings in which the direction is sought is not a factor in deciding whether to make a direction: the paternity question was a freestanding application entitled to its own considerations; and
(4) A child's welfare generally demands that it know the truth about his or her parentage.

The tests direction—In *Re H (Paternity: Blood Test)* [1996] 2 FLR 65, CA, Ward LJ stressed the fact that the court is required to make a direction for tests, and not an order, since the court cannot order the taking of samples against a person's consent (s 21(1)). He proposed (at [83D]) a form of words for the direction as follows:

'It is directed pursuant to s 20(1) of the Family Law Reform Act 1969:
(a) that blood tests (including DNA tests) be used to ascertain whether such tests show that [Mr A] is or is not excluded from being the father of [child B] born on [ ]; and
(b) that for that purpose blood samples be taken on or before [ ] from the following persons: [Mr A], [Mrs X (mother of child B)] and [child B]; and
(c) that the person appearing to the court to have care and control of [child B], who is under the age of 16, is [Mrs X];
(d) that such tests be carried out by [Mr CD of].'

'any party' (s 20(1))—An intervener would be included in this definition as would, for example, a non-parent who had obtained permission to apply for a CA 1989, s 8 order. Where a person not already a party to the proceedings is made the subject of a direction the court may at any time direct that he be made a party to the proceedings (FPR 2010, r 8.20(4)).

Two or more putative fathers—In *Re A (A Minor) (Paternity: Refusal of Blood Test)* [1994] 2 FLR 463, CA, Waite LJ left open the issue of whether or not a mother could make successive claims, leading to further applications under s 20, against two or more putative fathers where a first or subsequent claim had failed, although he felt that to deny her the ability to do this would be illogical.

21 Consents etc required for taking of bodily samples

(1) Subject to the provisions of subsections (3) and (4) of this section, a bodily sample which is required to be taken from any person for the purpose of giving effect to a direction under section 20 of this Act shall not be taken from that person except with his consent.

(2) The consent of a minor who has attained the age of sixteen years to the taking from himself of a bodily sample shall be as effective as it would be if he were of full age; and where a minor has by virtue of this subsection given an effective consent to the taking of a bodily sample it shall not be necessary to obtain any consent for it from any other person.

(3) A bodily sample may be taken from a person under the age of sixteen years, not being such a person as is referred to in subsection (4) of this section –

(a) if the person who has the care and control of him consents; or
(b) where that person does not consent, if the court considers that it would be in his best interests for the sample to be taken.

(4) A bodily sample may be taken from a person who lacks capacity (within the meaning of the Mental Capacity Act 2005) to give his consent, if consent is given by the court giving the direction under section 20 or by –

(a) a donee of an enduring power of attorney or lasting power of attorney (within the meaning of that Act), or

(b) a deputy appointed, or any other person authorised, by the Court of Protection,

with power in that respect.

(5) The foregoing provisions of this section are without prejudice to the provisions of section 23 of this Act.

Amendments—MHA 1983, s 148, Sch 4, para 25; FLRA 1987, s 33(1), Sch 2, para 22; CSPSSA 2000, s 82(1),(3); MCA 2005, s 67(1), Sch 6, para 15.

Defined terms—'bodily sample': s 25.

'consent' (s 21(1))—The effect of failing to comply with a direction which, by virtue of s 23(3), is implicit in refusing to consent, is dealt with in s 23.

Direction where court considers that it is in a child's best interests for sample to be taken (s 21(3))—The amendment to s 21(3), by the addition of s 21(3)(b), enables the court to direct tests where a person having care and control of the child does *not* consent. This reverses the decision in *Re O and J (Paternity: Blood Tests)* [2000] 1 FLR 418, FD. In considering whether to make such a direction the court will, in appropriate cases, want to take account of *Gillick v West Norfolk and Wisbech Area Health Authority* [1986] 1 FLR 224, HL and CA 1989 (see in particular ss 38(6), 43(8), 44(7): children, if of sufficient understanding, may refuse to submit to medical examination or other assessment). Balanced against the interests of a child's mother and her husband it may, nevertheless, be in a child's interests to have a test against the wishes of the person with care and control (*Re T (Paternity: Ordering Blood Tests)* [2001] 2 FLR 1190, FD).

Lacks capacity (s 21(4))—On a properly constituted application, the Court of Protection can give consent to bodily sample tests in respect of a person who lacks capacity, depending on the evidence in the particular case (*LG v DK* [2012] COPLR 80, COP). In the first instance, application for a declaration of parentage (FLA 1986, s 55A) is in the Family Court (see under FPR 2010, r 8.20).

22 Power to provide for manner of giving effect to direction for use of scientific tests

(1) The Lord Chancellor may by regulations make provision as to the manner of giving effect to directions under section 20 of this Act and, in particular, any such regulations may –

(a) provide that bodily samples shall not be taken except by registered medical practitioners or members of such professional bodies as may be prescribed by the regulations;

(aa) prescribe the bodily samples to be taken;

(b) regulate the taking, identification and transport of bodily samples;

(c) require the production at the time when a bodily sample is to be taken of such evidence of the identity of the person from whom it is to be taken as may be prescribed by the regulations;

(d) require any person from whom a bodily sample is to be taken, or, in such cases as may be prescribed by the regulations, such other person as may be so prescribed, to state in writing whether he or the person from whom the sample is to be taken, as the case may be, has during such period as may be specified in the regulations suffered from any such illness or condition or undergone any such treatment as may be so specified or received a transfusion of blood;

(e) prescribe conditions which a body must meet in order to be eligible for accreditation for the purposes of section 20 of this Act;

(f) prescribe the scientific tests to be carried out and the manner in which they are to be carried out;

(g) regulate the charges that may be made for the taking and testing of bodily samples and for the making of a report to a court under section 20 of this Act;

(h) make provisions for securing that so far as practicable the bodily samples to be tested for the purpose of giving effect to a direction under section 20 of this Act are tested by the same person;

(i) prescribe the form of the report to be made to a court under section 20 of this Act;

(j) make different provision for different cases or for different descriptions of case.

(2) The power to make regulations under this section shall be exercisable by statutory instrument which shall be subject to annulment in pursuance of a resolution of either House of Parliament.

Amendments—FLRA 1987, s 33(1), Sch 2, para 23; SI 1992/709; CSPSSA 2000, s 82(1),(4).

Defined terms—'bodily sample', 'scientific test': s 25.

Regulations—The regulations are the Blood Tests (Evidence of Paternity) Regulations 1971.

23 Failure to comply with direction for taking scientific tests

(1) Where a court gives a direction under section 20 of this Act and any person fails to take any step required of him for the purpose of giving effect to the direction, the court may draw such inferences, if any, from that fact as appear proper in the circumstances.

(2) Where in any proceedings in which the parentage of any person falls to be determined by the court hearing the proceedings there is a presumption of law that that person is legitimate, then if –

(a) a direction is given under section 20 of this Act in those proceedings, and

(b) any party who is claiming any relief in the proceedings and who for the purpose of obtaining that relief is entitled to rely on the presumption fails to take any step required of him for the purpose of giving effect to the direction,

the court may adjourn the hearing for such period as it thinks fit to enable that party to take that step, and if at the end of that period he has failed without reasonable cause to take it the court may, without prejudice to subsection (1) of this section, dismiss his claim for relief notwithstanding the absence of evidence to rebut the presumption.

(3) Where any person named in a direction under section 20 of this Act fails to consent to the taking of a bodily sample from himself or from any person named in the direction of whom he has the care and control, he shall be deemed for the purposes of this section to have failed to take a step required of him for the purpose of giving effect to the direction.

Amendments—FLRA 1987, s 33(1), Sch 2, para 24.

Defined terms—'scientific test': s 25.

'the court may draw such inference' (s 23(1))—Where a sample is refused, the court is entitled to infer that this corroborates the applicant's case (see eg *McV v B* [1988] 2 FLR 67, FD). The fact that more than one man might also be the father of the child, and none of those men was being proceeded against, did not entitle a respondent father to avoid the consequences of refusing to consent to a test (*Re A (A Minor) (Paternity: Refusal of Blood Test)* [1994] 2 FLR 463, CA).

Refusal of tests—If an inference is to be drawn from the refusal of a test, such inference can be drawn, even though a direction has not been made, if a parent clearly indicates an intention not to comply with any direction made by the court (*Re H (Paternity: Blood Test)* [1996] 2 FLR 65, CA).

'presumption of law' (s 23(2))—There is a presumption that a child born in wedlock is legitimate. If, in reliance on this, application is made to the court and paternity is challenged, the applicant for the test must submit to any tests directed (*Secretary of State for Work and Pensions v Jones* [2004] 1 FLR 282, FD). If he does not, he risks having his application dismissed even though there is no evidence to rebut the presumption which would otherwise operate in his favour. For example, a person over 18 can apply for his parent to provide financial relief (CA 1989, s 15, Sch 1, para 2). If he applies against his mother's estranged husband, who then challenges his paternity, he will have to submit to a test if one is directed; and if he does not comply with the direction, the court has a discretion to dismiss his application.

'deemed ... to have failed to take a step required' (s 23(3))—This subsection refers back to consent under s 21(3) and involves children under 16.

24 Penalty for personating another, etc, for purpose of providing bodily sample

If for the purpose of providing a bodily sample for a test required to give effect to a direction under section 20 of this Act any person personates another, or proffers a child knowing that it is not the child named in the direction, he shall be liable –

(a) on conviction on indictment, to imprisonment for a term not exceeding two years, or

(b) on summary conviction, to a fine not exceeding the prescribed sum.

Amendments—MCA 1980, s 32(2); FLRA 1987, s 33(1), Sch 2, para 25.

Defined terms—'bodily sample': s 25.

25 Interpretation of Part III

In this Part of this Act the following expressions have the meanings hereby respectively assigned to them, that is to say –

PART II

'bodily sample' means a sample of bodily fluid or bodily tissue taken for the purpose of scientific tests;

'excluded' means excluded subject to the occurrence of mutation to section 27 of the Family Law Reform Act 1987, to sections 27 to 29 of the Human Fertilisation and Embryology Act 1990 and to sections 33 to 47 of the Human Fertilisation and Embryology Act 2008;

'scientific tests' means scientific tests carried out under this Part of this Act and made with the object of ascertaining the inheritable characteristics of bodily fluids or bodily tissue.

Amendments—FLRA 1987, s 23(2); HFEA 1990, s 49(5), Sch 4, para 1; HFEA 2008, s 56, Sch 6, para 13(a).

PART IV
MISCELLANEOUS AND GENERAL

26 Rebuttal of presumption as to legitimacy and illegitimacy

Any presumption of law as to the legitimacy or illegitimacy of any person may in any civil proceedings be rebutted by evidence which shows that it is more probable than not that that person is illegitimate or legitimate, as the case may be, and it shall not be necessary to prove that fact beyond reasonable doubt in order to rebut the presumption.

Standard of proof—For a discussion of the subject of 'standard of proof', see *Cross and Tapper on Evidence* (12th Edn; Oxford), at [154] et seq. The 'civil standard' is required here, as explained, for example, in *Re B (Children) (Care Proceedings: Standard of Proof)* [2008] 2 FLR 141, HL.

****

Family Law Reform Act 1987

1 General principle

(1) In this Act and enactments passed and instruments made after the coming into force of this section, references (however expressed) to any relationship between two persons shall, unless the contrary intention appears, be construed without regard to whether or not the father and mother of either of them, or the father and mother of any person through whom the relationship is deduced, have or had been married to each other at any time.

(2) In this Act and enactments passed after the coming into force of this section, unless the contrary intention appears –

(a) references to a person whose father and mother were married to each other at the time of his birth include; and

(b) references to a person whose father and mother were not married to each other at the time of his birth do not include,

references to any person to whom subsection (3) below applies, and cognate references shall be construed accordingly.

(3) This subsection applies to any person who –

(a) is treated as legitimate by virtue of section 1 of the Legitimacy Act 1976;

(b) is a legitimated person within the meaning of section 10 of that Act;

(ba) has a parent by virtue of section 42 of the Human Fertilisation and Embryology Act 2008 (which relates to treatment provided to a woman who is at the time of treatment married to a woman or a party to a civil partnership or, in certain circumstances, a void marriage or civil partnership);

(bb) has a parent by virtue of section 43 of that Act (which relates to treatment provided to woman who agrees that second woman to be parent) who –

(i) is married to or the civil partner of the child's mother at the time of the child's birth, or

(ii) was married to or the civil partner of the child's mother at any time during the period beginning with the time mentioned in section 43(b) of that Act and ending with the child's birth;

(c) is an adopted person within the meaning of Chapter 4 of Part 1 of the Adoption and Children Act 2002; or

(d) is otherwise treated in law as legitimate.

(4) For the purpose of construing references falling within subsection (2) above, the time of a person's birth shall be taken to include any time during the period beginning with –

(a) the insemination resulting in his birth; or

(b) where there was no such insemination, his conception,

and (in either case) ending with his birth.

(5) A child whose parents are parties to a void civil partnership shall, subject to subsection (6), be treated as falling within subsection (3)(bb) if at the time when the parties registered as civil partners of each other both or either of the parties reasonably believed that the civil partnership was valid.

(6) Subsection (5) applies only where the woman who is a parent by virtue of section 43 was domiciled in England and Wales at the time of the birth or, if she died before the birth, was so domiciled immediately before her death.

(7) Subsection (5) applies even though the belief that the civil partnership was valid was due to a mistake as to law.

(8) It shall be presumed for the purposes of subsection (5), unless the contrary is shown, that one of the parties to a void civil partnership reasonably believed at the time of the formation of the civil partnership that the civil partnership was valid.

Amendments—ACA 2002, Sch 3, para 51; HFEA 2008, s 56, Sch 6, Pt 1, paras 24(1)–(3); SI 2014/560.

****

18 Succession on intestacy

(1) In Part IV of the Administration of Estates Act 1925 (which deals with the distribution of the estate of an intestate), references (however expressed) to any relationship between two persons shall be construed in accordance with section 1 above.

(2) For the purposes of subsection (1) above and that Part of that Act, a person whose father and mother were not married to each other at the time of his birth shall be presumed not to have been survived by his father, or by any person related to him only through his father, unless the contrary is shown.

(2ZA) Subsection (2) does not apply if a person is recorded as the intestate's father, or as a parent (other than the mother) of the intestate –

(a) in a register of births kept (or having effect as if kept) under the Births and Deaths Registration Act 1953, or

(b) in a record of a birth included in an index kept under section 30(1) of that Act (indexes relating to certain other registers etc).

(2A) In the case of a person who has a parent by virtue of section 43 of the Human Fertilisation and Embryology Act 2008 (treatment provided to woman who agrees that second woman to be parent), the second and third references in subsection (2) to the person's father are to be read as references to the woman who is a parent of the person by virtue of that section.

(3) In section 50(1) of the Administration of Estates Act 1925 (which relates to the construction of documents), the reference to Part IV of that Act, or to the foregoing provisions of that Part, shall in relation to an instrument inter vivos made, or a will or codicil coming into operation, after the coming into force of this section (but not in relation to instruments inter vivos made or wills or codicils coming into operation earlier) be construed as including references to this section.

(4) This section does not affect any rights under the intestacy of a person dying before the coming into force of this section.

Amendments—HFEA 2008, s 56, Sch 6, Pt 1, para 25(1),(3); Inheritance and Trustees' Powers Act 2014, s 5.

Effect of subsection (2ZA)—The intestacy rule that disadvantage unmarried fathers when their child dies intestate has been rectified provided they are recorded as the father or as a parent (other than the mother) of the intestate in the named register of births.

19 Dispositions of property

(1) In the following dispositions, namely –

(a) dispositions inter vivos made on or after the date on which this section comes into force; and

(b) dispositions by will or codicil where the will or codicil is made on or after that date,

references (whether express or implied) to any relationship between two persons shall be construed in accordance with section 1 above.

(2) It is hereby declared that the use, without more, of the word 'heir' or 'heirs' or any expression purporting to create an entailed interest in real or personal property does not show a contrary intention for the purposes of section 1 as applied by subsection (1) above.

(3) In relation to the dispositions mentioned in subsection (1) above, section 33 of the Trustee Act 1925 (which specifies the trust implied by a direction that income is to be held on protective trusts for the benefit of any person) shall have effect as if any reference (however expressed) to any relationship between two persons were construed in accordance with section 1 above.

(4) Where under any disposition of real or personal property, any interest in such property is limited (whether subject to any preceding limitation or charge or not) in such a way that it would, apart from this section, devolve (as nearly as the law permits) along with a dignity or title of honour, then –

(a) whether or not the disposition contains an express reference to the dignity or title of honour; and

(b) whether or not the property or some interest in the property may in some event become severed from it,

nothing in this section shall operate to sever the property or any interest in it from the dignity or title, but the property or interest shall devolve in all respects as if this section had not been enacted.

(5) This section is without prejudice to section 42 of the Adoption Act 1976 or section 69 of the Adoption and Children Act 2002 (construction of dispositions in cases of adoption).

(6) In this section 'disposition' means a disposition, including an oral disposition, of real or personal property whether inter vivos or by will or codicil.

(7) Notwithstanding any rule of law, a disposition made by will or codicil executed before the date on which this section comes into force shall not be treated for the purposes of this section as made on or after that date by reason only that the will or codicil is confirmed by a codicil executed on or after that date.

Amendments—TLATA 1996, s 25(1), Sch 3, para 25; ACA 2002, Sch 3, para 52.

****

21 Entitlement to grant probate etc

(1) For the purpose of determining the person or persons who would in accordance with probate rules be entitled to a grant of probate or administration in respect of the estate of a deceased person, the deceased shall be presumed, unless the contrary is shown, not to have been survived –

(a) by any person related to him whose father and mother were not married to each other at the time of his birth; or

(b) by any person whose relationship with him is deduced through such a person as is mentioned in paragraph (a) above.

(2) In this section 'probate rules' means rules of court made under section 127 of the Senior Courts Act 1981.

(3) This section does not apply in relation to the estate of a person dying before the coming into force of this section.

Amendments—CRA 2005, Sch 11, para 1(2).

****

Female Genital Mutilation Act 2003

1 Offence of female genital mutilation

(1) A person is guilty of an offence if he excises, infibulates or otherwise mutilates the whole or any part of a girl's labia majora, labia minora or clitoris.

(2) But no offence is committed by an approved person who performs –

(a) a surgical operation on a girl which is necessary for her physical or mental health, or

(b) a surgical operation on a girl who is in any stage of labour, or has just given birth, for purposes connected with the labour or birth.

(3) The following are approved persons –

(a) in relation to an operation falling within subsection (2)(a), a registered medical practitioner,

(b) in relation to an operation falling within subsection (2)(b), a registered medical practitioner, a registered midwife or a person undergoing a course of training with a view to becoming such a practitioner or midwife.

(4) There is also no offence committed by a person who –

(a) performs a surgical operation falling within subsection (2)(a) or (b) outside the United Kingdom, and

(b) in relation to such an operation exercises functions corresponding to those of an approved person.

(5) For the purpose of determining whether an operation is necessary for the mental health of a girl it is immaterial whether she or any other person believes that the operation is required as a matter of custom or ritual.

'excises, infibulates or otherwise mutilates the whole or any part of a girl's labia majora, labia minora or clitoris'—This provision criminalises all forms of female genital mutilation (FGM). These have been classified into different types by the World Health Organization (WHO). In a statement published in 2003, WHO refers to four types, namely:

Type I Partial or total removal of the clitoris and/or the prepuce (clitoridectomy).This has two subdivisions, namely: Type Ia – removal of the clitoral hood or prepuce only; and Type Ib – removal of the clitoris with the prepuce.

Type II Partial or total removal of the clitoris and the labia minora, with or without excision of the labia majora (excision) with proposed subdivisions, namely: Type IIa – removal of the labia minora only; Type IIb – partial or total removal of the clitoris and the labia minora; and Type IIc – partial or total removal of the clitoris, the labia minora and the labia majora.

Type III Narrowing of the vaginal orifice with creation of a covering seal by cutting and appositioning the labia minora and/or the labia majora, with or without excision of the clitoris (infibulation) with proposed subdivisions, namely: Type IIIa – removal and apposition of the labia minors; and Type IIIb – removal and apposition of the labia majora.

Type IV Unclassified. All other harmful procedures to the female genitalia for non-medical purposes, e g pricking, piercing, incising, scraping and cauterisation.

These four types are also classified by WHO in an FGM factsheet published in February 2014 as: 1 Clitoridectomy; 2 Excision; 3 Infibulation; and 4 Other. Therefore, all forms of Type I,II and III come within the ingredients of the offence and Type IV only if it involves mutilation (see below). UNICEF uses a different classification that does not fully match the WHO typology. The WHO classification is the one that is widely used and in *Re B and G (Children) (No 2); sub nom Leeds City Council v M, F, B, G (B and G by their Children's Guardian)* [2015] 1 FLR 905, FD, Sir James Munby P recommended that for forensic purposes the WHO classification should be used in family cases (para 79(ii)). See also below under Sch 2, para 3 for the court's power to make an FGM protection order in criminal proceedings to protect a girl whether or not she is a victim of the offence.

'mutilation'—This term is not defined in the Act but was considered by the President in *Re B and G* (above) by turning to the dictionary: 'The Oxford English Dictionary defines "mutilation" as meaning "the action of mutilating a person or animal; the severing or maiming of a limb or bodily organ"; "mutilate" being defined as

PART II

meaning "to deprive a person or animal) of the use of a limb or bodily organ, by dismemberment or otherwise; to cut off or destroy (a limb or organ); to wound severely, inflict violent or disfiguring injury on' (at [12]).

2 Offence of assisting a girl to mutilate her own genitalia

A person is guilty of an offence if he aids, abets, counsels or procures a girl to excise, infibulate or otherwise mutilate the whole or any part of her own labia majora, labia minora or clitoris.

3 Offence of assisting a non-UK person to mutilate overseas a girl's genitalia

(1) A person is guilty of an offence if he aids, abets, counsels or procures a person who is not a United Kingdom national or United Kingdom resident to do a relevant act of female genital mutilation outside the United Kingdom.

(2) An act is a relevant act of female genital mutilation if –

(a) it is done in relation to a United Kingdom national or United Kingdom resident, and
(b) it would, if done by such a person, constitute an offence under section 1.

(3) But no offence is committed if the relevant act of female genital mutilation –

(a) is a surgical operation falling within section 1(2)(a) or (b), and
(b) is performed by a person who, in relation to such an operation, is an approved person or exercises functions corresponding to those of an approved person.

Amendments—Serious Crime Act 2015, s 70.

3A Offence of failing to protect girl from risk of genital mutilation

(1) If a genital mutilation offence is committed against a girl under the age of 16, each person who is responsible for the girl at the relevant time is guilty of an offence. This is subject to subsection (5).

(2) For the purposes of this section a person is 'responsible' for a girl in the following two cases.

(3) The first case is where the person –

(a) has parental responsibility for the girl, and
(b) has frequent contact with her.

(4) The second case is where the person –

(a) is aged 18 or over, and
(b) has assumed (and not relinquished) responsibility for caring for the girl in the manner of a parent.

(5) It is a defence for the defendant to show that –

(a) at the relevant time, the defendant did not think that there was a significant risk of a genital mutilation offence being committed against the girl, and could not reasonably have been expected to be aware that there was any such risk, or
(b) the defendant took such steps as he or she could reasonably have been expected to take to protect the girl from being the victim of a genital mutilation offence.

(6) A person is taken to have shown the fact mentioned in subsection (5)(a) or (b) if –

(a) sufficient evidence of the fact is adduced to raise an issue with respect to it, and
(b) the contrary is not proved beyond reasonable doubt.

(7) For the purposes of subsection (3)(b), where a person has frequent contact with a girl which is interrupted by her going to stay somewhere temporarily, that contact is treated as continuing during her stay there.

(8) In this section –

'genital mutilation offence' means an offence under section 1, 2 or 3 (and for the purposes of subsection (1) the prosecution does not have to prove which section it is);

'parental responsibility' –

(a) in England Wales, has the same meaning as in the Children Act 1989;
(b) in Northern Ireland, has the same meaning as in the Children (Northern Ireland) Order 1995 (SI 1995/755);

'the relevant time' means the time when the mutilation takes place.

Amendments—Inserted by Serious Crime Act 2015, s 72.

4 Extension of sections 1 to 3A to extra-territorial acts or omissions

(1) Sections 1 to 3 extend to any act done outside the United Kingdom by a United Kingdom national or United Kingdom resident.

(1A) An offence under section 3A can be committed wholly or partly outside the United Kingdom by a person who is a United Kingdom national or a United Kingdom resident.

(2) If an offence under this Act is committed outside the United Kingdom –

(a) proceedings may be taken, and

(b) the offence may for incidental purposes be treated as having been committed,

in any place in England and Wales or Northern Ireland.

Amendments—Serious Crime Act 2015, ss 70, 72.

4A Anonymity of victims

Schedule 1 provides for the anonymity of persons against whom a female genital mutilation offence (as defined in that Schedule) is alleged to have been committed.

Amendments—Inserted by Serious Crime Act 2015, s 71.

5 Penalties for offences

(1) A person guilty of an offence under section 1, 2 or 3 is liable –

(a) on conviction on indictment, to imprisonment for a term not exceeding 14 years or a fine (or both),

(b) on summary conviction, to imprisonment for a term not exceeding six months or a fine not exceeding the statutory maximum (or both).

(2) A person guilty of an offence under section 3A is liable –

(a) on conviction on indictment, to imprisonment for a term not exceeding seven years or a fine (or both),

(b) on summary conviction in England and Wales, to imprisonment for a term not exceeding 12 months or a fine (or both),

(c) on summary conviction in Northern Ireland, to imprisonment for a term not exceeding 6 months or a fine not exceeding the statutory maximum (or both).

Amendments—Serious Crime Act 2015, ss 70, 72.

****

5A Female genital mutilation protection orders

(1) Schedule 2 provides for the making of female genital mutilation protection orders.

(2) In that Schedule –

(a) Part 1 makes provision about powers of courts in England and Wales to make female genital mutilation protection orders;

(b) Part 2 makes provision about powers of courts in Northern Ireland to make such orders.

Amendments—Inserted by Serious Crime Act 2015, s 73.

5B Duty to notify police of female genital mutilation

(1) A person who works in a regulated profession in England and Wales must make a notification under this section (an 'FGM notification') if, in the course of his or her work in the profession, the person discovers that an act of female genital mutilation appears to have been carried out on a girl who is aged under 18.

(2) For the purposes of this section –

(a) a person works in a 'regulated profession' if the person is –

(i) a healthcare professional,

(ii) a teacher, or

(iii) a social care worker in Wales;

(b) a person 'discovers' that an act of female genital mutilation appears to have been carried out on a girl in either of the following two cases.

(3) The first case is where the girl informs the person that an act of female genital mutilation (however described) has been carried out on her.

(4) The second case is where –

(a) the person observes physical signs on the girl appearing to show that an act of female genital mutilation has been carried out on her, and

(b) the person has no reason to believe that the act was, or was part of, a surgical operation within section 1(2)(a) or (b).

(5) An FGM notification –

(a) is to be made to the chief officer of police for the area in which the girl resides;

(b) must identify the girl and explain why the notification is made;

(c) must be made before the end of one month from the time when the person making the notification first discovers that an act of female genital mutilation appears to have been carried out on the girl;

(d) may be made orally or in writing.

(6) The duty of a person working in a particular regulated profession to make an FGM notification does not apply if the person has reason to believe that another person working in that profession has previously made an FGM notification in connection with the same act of female genital mutilation. For this purpose, all persons falling within subsection (2)(a)(i) are to be treated as working in the same regulated profession.

(7) A disclosure made in an FGM notification does not breach –

(a) any obligation of confidence owed by the person making the disclosure, or

(b) any other restriction on the disclosure of information.

(8) The Secretary of State may by regulations amend this section for the purpose of adding, removing or otherwise altering the descriptions of persons regarded as working in a 'regulated profession' for the purposes of this section.

(9) The power to make regulations under this section –

(a) is exercisable by statutory instrument;

(b) includes power to make consequential, transitional, transitory or saving provision.

(10) A statutory instrument containing regulations under this section is not to be made unless a draft of the instrument has been laid before, and approved by a resolution of, each House of Parliament.

(11) In this section –

'act of female genital mutilation' means an act of a kind mentioned in section 1(1);

'healthcare professional' means a person registered with any of the regulatory bodies mentioned in section 25(3) of the National Health Service Reform and Health Care Professions Act 2002 (bodies within remit of the Professional Standards Authority for Health and Social Care);

'registered', in relation to a regulatory body, means registered in a register that the body maintains by virtue of any enactment;

'social care worker' means a person registered in a register maintained by the Care Council for Wales under section 56 of the Care Standards Act 2000;

'teacher' means –

(a) in relation to England, a person within section 141A(1) of the Education Act 2002 (persons employed or engaged to carry out teaching work at schools and other institutions in England);

(b) in relation to Wales, a person who falls within a category listed in the table in paragraph 1 of Schedule 2 to the Education (Wales) Act 2014 (anaw 5) (categories of registration for purposes of Part 2 of that Act) or any other person employed or engaged as a teacher at a school (within the meaning of the Education Act 1996) in Wales.

(12) For the purposes of the definition of 'healthcare professional', the following provisions of section 25 of the National Health Service Reform and Health Care Professions Act 2002 are to be ignored –

(a) paragraph (g) of subsection (3);
(b) subsection (3A).

Amendments—Inserted by Serious Crime Act 2015, s 74.

Scope—This section imposes a mandatory duty on a person who works in a 'regulated profession' (identified in s 5B(2) and further defined in s 5B(11),(12)) to give an FGM notification to the chief officer of police in the area in which the girl against whom FGM appears to have been carried out resides when that person discovers that FGM appears to have been carried out.

Defined terms—'regulated profession': s 5 B(2); 'health professional', social worker in Wales'; 'teacher': s 5B(11),(12) –note that this description of persons may be amended by the Secretary of State pursuant to powers contained in s 5B(8),(9); 'girl' means a girl under 18 years of age (s 5B(1)).

'"discovers" that an act of female genital mutilation appears to have been carried out'—This covers two circumstances, i e when disclosure is made by the girl and, on observation of physical signs with no reason to believe that the act was, or was part of, a surgical operation that is necessary for the girl's health or mental health; or a surgical operation on a girl who is in any stage of labour, or has just given birth, for purposes connected with the labour or birth (s 1(2)(a),(b)).

PART II

5C Guidance

(1) The Secretary of State may issue guidance to whatever persons in England and Wales the Secretary of State considers appropriate about –

(a) the effect of any provision of this Act, or
(b) other matters relating to female genital mutilation.

(2) A person exercising public functions to whom guidance is given under this section must have regard to it in the exercise of those functions.

(3) Nothing in this section permits the Secretary of State to give guidance to any court or tribunal.

(4) Before issuing guidance under this section the Secretary of State must consult –

(a) the Welsh Ministers so far as the guidance is to a body exercising devolved Welsh functions;
(b) any person whom the Secretary of State considers appropriate.

(5) A body is exercising 'devolved Welsh functions' if its functions are exercisable only in or as regards Wales and are wholly or mainly functions relating to –

(a) a matter in respect of which functions are exercisable by the Welsh Ministers, the First Minister for Wales or the Counsel General to the Welsh Government, or
(b) a matter within the legislative competence of the National Assembly for Wales.

(6) The Secretary of State may from time to time revise any guidance issued under this section.

(7) Subsections (2) and (3) have effect in relation to any revised guidance.

(8) Subsection (4) has effect in relation to any revised guidance unless the Secretary of State considers the proposed revisions of the guidance are insubstantial.

(9) The Secretary of State must publish the current version of any guidance issued under this section.

Amendments—Inserted by Serious Crime Act 2015, s 75.

Guidance—See *www.jordanpublishing.co.uk/practice-areas/family/news_and_comment/mandatory-fgm-reporting-in-healthcare-updated-guidance-and-resources.*

****

SCHEDULE 2
FEMALE GENITAL MUTILATION PROTECTION ORDERS

PART 1
ENGLAND AND WALES

1 Power to make FGM protection order

(1) The court in England and Wales may make an order (an 'FGM protection order') for the purposes of –

- (a) protecting a girl against the commission of a genital mutilation offence, or
- (b) protecting a girl against whom any such offence has been committed.

(2) In deciding whether to exercise its powers under this paragraph and, if so, in what manner, the court must have regard to all the circumstances, including the need to secure the health, safety and well-being of the girl to be protected.

(3) An FGM protection order may contain –

- (a) such prohibitions, restrictions or requirements, and
- (b) such other terms, as the court considers appropriate for the purposes of the order.

(4) The terms of an FGM protection order may, in particular, relate to –

- (a) conduct outside England and Wales as well as (or instead of) conduct within England and Wales;
- (b) respondents who are, or may become, involved in other respects as well as (or instead of) respondents who commit or attempt to commit, or may commit or attempt to commit, a genital mutilation offence against a girl;
- (c) other persons who are, or may become, involved in other respects as well as respondents of any kind.

(5) For the purposes of sub-paragraph (4) examples of involvement in other respects are –

- (a) aiding, abetting, counselling, procuring, encouraging or assisting another person to commit, or attempt to commit, a genital mutilation offence against a girl;
- (b) conspiring to commit, or to attempt to commit, such an offence.

(6) An FGM protection order may be made for a specified period or until varied or discharged (see paragraph 6).

Defined terms—'the court': the High Court or the Family Court; 'genital mutilation offence': an offence under ss 1–3 (see above); 'FGM protection order' (Sch 2, para 17); ' girl' is defined to include a woman (s 6(1)).

Purpose of making the order—Protection of a girl against the commission of an FGM offence or protecting a girl against whom any such offence has been committed. The latter situation may arise where the girl on whom FGM has been carried out makes a disclosure or resists or fears infibulations. See the commentary under s 1. Note that although the provision refers to a 'girl', there is no age limit because 'girl' includes a woman (s 6).

Criteria for deciding whether or not to make the order—The provisions set out in para 1(2) are identical to those for a forced marriage protection order (FMPO) under FLA 1996, s 63A – see *Re E (Children) (Female Genital Mutilation Protection Orders)* [2015] 2 FLR 997, FD, where the evidence of the mother of the girls was considered sufficient but in *Re E (Female Genital Mutilation and Permission to Remove)* [2016] EWHC 1052 (Fam), MacDonald J found insufficient evidence to support the mother's claim. He also heard evidence that the area in Nigeria from which the family originated were the first to campaign against FGM and statistical evidence as corroborative proof of the prevalence of the practice (statistics are available from the Home Office and UNICEF). See also **Evidence and disclosure of all the circumstances of the case**. Note also that (a) s 5B of the 2003 Act imposes a duty on 'regulated professions' to serve an FGM notification on the chief officer of police for the area in which the girl resides where the girl informs the person that an act of FGM has been carried out and also where the person observes physical signs on the girl that appear to show that such an act has been carried out on the girl and the person has no reason to believe that the act was, or was part of, a surgical operation within s 2(1)(a),(b) (see above); and (b) that disclosure made in an 'FGM notification' does not breach an obligation owed by the person making the disclosure or any other restriction on the disclosure of material (s 5B(7)). For the contents of the FGM notification, see s 5B(5)).

Contents of orders—The provisions in para 1(3)–(5) are the same as for FMPO (see under FLA 1996, s 63B). For the extensive orders that may be made to ensure the return of children taken to a country where FGM is practised, see *Re F and X (Female Genital Mutilation)* [2016] 2 FLR 1032, FD and against those who may claim diplomatic immunity see *Re FGMPO* (2016) *The Times,* 1 March. In *Re E* (above), it was held that although the court has very wide powers to make protective orders, they should not be stretched to provide protection for somebody else (the mother in this case). If she had been the victim of domestic violence, her remedy was to obtain an order under FLA 1996. The court, however, made an order in this case restricting the father from coming within 100 metres of the home or the children's school purely because it was necessary to protect the girls from FGM and not for purposes of protecting the mother.

Duration of the order—The order may be for a specified period or indefinitely until varied or discharged so as to ensure that the protection is available so long as it is necessary, especially where the girl is very young (see *Emergency Remedies in the Family Court* (Family Law), where this subject is dealt with in detail).

2 Applications and other occasions for making orders

(1) The court may make an FGM protection order –

(a) on an application being made to it, or
(b) without an application being made to it but in the circumstances mentioned in sub-paragraph (6).

(2) An application may be made by –

(a) the girl who is to be protected by the order, or
(b) a relevant third party.

(3) An application may be made by any other person with the leave of the court.

(4) In deciding whether to grant leave, the court must have regard to all the circumstances including –

(a) the applicant's connection with the girl to be protected;
(b) the applicant's knowledge of the circumstances of the girl.

(5) An application under this paragraph may be made in other family proceedings or without any other family proceedings being instituted.

(6) The circumstances in which the court may make an order without an application being made are where –

(a) any other family proceedings are before the court ('the current proceedings'),
(b) the court considers that an FGM protection order should be made to protect a girl (whether or not a party to the proceedings), and
(c) a person who would be a respondent to any proceedings for an FGM protection order is a party to the current proceedings.

(7) In this paragraph –

'family proceedings' has the same meaning as in Part 4 of the Family Law Act 1996 (see section 63(1) and (2) of that Act), but also includes –

(a) proceedings under the inherent jurisdiction of the High Court in relation to adults,
(b) proceedings in which the court has made an emergency protection order under section 44 of the Children Act 1989 which includes an exclusion requirement (as defined in section 44A(3) of that Act), and
(c) proceedings in which the court has made an order under section 50 of the Children Act 1989 (recovery of abducted children etc);

'relevant third party' means a person specified, or falling within a description of persons specified, by regulations made by the Lord Chancellor (and such regulations may, in particular, specify the Secretary of State).

(8) Regulations under sub-paragraph (7) are to be made by statutory instrument, and any such instrument is subject to annulment in pursuance of a resolution of either House of Parliament.

Defined terms—'family proceedings', 'relevant third party': Sch 2, para 1(7); 'girl': s 6(1) (see under para 1, above).

Who may apply without leave—A 'girl who is to be protected' – in view of the definition of 'girl' in s 6(1) there is no age limit for the applicant. A child applicant does not require the leave of the court to make the application. FPR 2010 have not yet been amended to deal with application for an FGM protection order. When they are, it will become clear if a child applicant may apply without a guardian or next friend. In view of the amendments made by the Family Proceedings Fees (Amendment) Order 2015, it is likely that no fee will be payable on an application for an FGM protection order.

Relevant third party—These have yet to be identified but it will be a person or someone within a class of persons specified by regulations made by the Lord Chancellor (and such regulations may specify the Secretary of State (Sch 2, para (7) but see para (8)).

Application with leave—This is by any person subject to the conditions set out in para 2(4). See *Re E (Children) (Female Genital Mutilation Protection Orders)* [2015] 2 FLR 997, FD, where permission was given to the mother to apply because of her connection with her daughters and her knowledge of the circumstances.

Making of an order without an application—An order may be made within other family proceedings if considered necessary to protect a girl, and a person who would be a respondent to any proceedings for an FGM protection order is a party to the current proceedings. An order may also be made on the court's own initiative provided the circumstances mentioned in sub-para (6) are met.

3 Power to make order in criminal proceedings

The court before which there are criminal proceedings in England and Wales for a genital mutilation offence may make an FGM protection order (without an application being made to it) if –

(a) the court considers that an FGM protection order should be made to protect a girl (whether or not the victim of the offence in relation to the criminal proceedings), and

(b) a person who would be a respondent to any proceedings for an FGM protection order is a defendant in the criminal proceedings.

Scope—This provision enables any court in which criminal proceedings are pending to make an FGM protection order without an application being made, pending trial and even where the defendant has not been convicted of the offence, if the court considers that there is a risk of the defendant carrying out the act of FGM or procuring, aiding or assisting FGM on a victim or potential victim of FGM irrespective of whether the girl is the subject of the alleged offence in the proceedings, eg to protect a younger sibling of a victim or another member of the family.

4 Offence of breaching order

(1) A person who without reasonable excuse does anything that the person is prohibited from doing by an FGM protection order is guilty of an offence.

(2) In the case of an FGM protection order made by virtue of paragraph 5(1), a person can be guilty of an offence under this paragraph only in respect of conduct engaged in at a time when the person was aware of the existence of the order.

(3) Where a person is convicted of an offence under this paragraph in respect of any conduct, the conduct is not punishable as a contempt of court.

(4) A person cannot be convicted of an offence under this paragraph in respect of any conduct which has been punished as a contempt of court.

(5) A person guilty of an offence under this paragraph is liable –

(a) on conviction on indictment, to imprisonment for a term not exceeding five years, or a fine, or both;

(b) on summary conviction, to imprisonment for a term not exceeding 12 months, or a fine, or both.

(6) A reference in any enactment to proceedings under this Part of this Schedule, or to an order under this Part of this Schedule, does not include a reference to proceedings for an offence under this paragraph or to an order made in proceedings for such an offence.

(7) 'Enactment' includes an enactment contained in subordinate legislation within the meaning of the Interpretation Act 1978.

Breach of FGM protection order—FPR 2010, Pt 11 has been amended to include applications under FGMA 2003 for a FGM protection order. Note, however, that alternatively a breach of the order may be dealt with as a contempt of court in the Family Court.

5 Ex parte orders

(1) The court may, in any case where it is just and convenient to do so, make an FGM protection order even though the respondent has not been given such notice of the proceedings as would otherwise be required by rules of court.

(2) In deciding whether to exercise its powers under sub-paragraph (1), the court must have regard to all the circumstances including –

(a) the risk to the girl, or to another person, of becoming a victim of a genital mutilation offence if the order is not made immediately,

(b) whether it is likely that an applicant will be deterred or prevented from pursuing an application if an order is not made immediately, and

(c) whether there is reason to believe that –

(i) the respondent is aware of the proceedings but is deliberately evading service, and

(ii) the delay involved in effecting substituted service will cause serious prejudice to the girl to be protected or (if different) an applicant.

(3) The court must give the respondent an opportunity to make representations about an order made by virtue of sub-paragraph (1).

(4) The opportunity must be –

(a) as soon as just and convenient, and

(b) at a hearing of which notice has been given to all the parties in accordance with rules of court.

Without notice orders—The criteria in sub-para (2) must be met before a without notice order is granted. Where the order is made without notice, the order must contain the statement required under FPR 2010, r 18.11 and any orders made must contain a penal notice and a warning of the consequences of breach of the order or any part of it, as required under FPR 2010, Pt 37, and of the respondent's right to apply to the court to vary or discharge the order. See also FPR 2010, r 21.3 and the notes under FLA 1996, s 63D.

6 Variation and discharge of orders

(1) The court may vary or discharge an FGM protection order on an application by –

(a) any party to the proceedings for the order,

(b) the girl being protected by the order (if not a party to the proceedings for the order), or

(c) any person affected by the order.

(2) In the case of an order made in criminal proceedings under paragraph 3, the reference in sub-paragraph (1)(a) to a party to the proceedings for the order is to be read as a reference to the prosecution and the defendant.

(3) In addition, the court may vary or discharge an FGM protection order made by virtue of paragraph 2(1)(b) or 3 even though no application under sub-paragraph (1) above has been made to the court.

(4) Paragraph 5 applies to a variation of an FGM protection order as it applies to the making of such an order (and references in that paragraph to the making of an FGM protection order are to be read accordingly).

7 Arrest under warrant

(1) An interested party may apply to the relevant judge for the issue of a warrant for the arrest of a person if the interested party considers that the person has failed to comply with an FGM protection order or is otherwise in contempt of court in relation to such an order.

(2) The relevant judge must not issue a warrant on an application under sub-paragraph (1) unless –

(a) the application is substantiated on oath, and

(b) the relevant judge has reasonable grounds for believing that the person to be arrested has failed to comply with the order or is otherwise in contempt of court in relation to the order.

(3) In this paragraph 'interested party', in relation to an FGM protection order, means –

(a) the girl being protected by the order,

(b) (if a different person) the person who applied for the order, or

(c) any other person; but no application may be made under sub-paragraph (1) by a person falling within paragraph (c) without leave of the relevant judge.

Defined terms—'relevant judge': Sch 2, para 17(1); 'interested party': Sch 2, para 7(3).

Form of application—in Form FL407A accompanied by a sworn statement by the applicant.

Who may apply—The girl being protected by the order, the person who applied for the order or any other person with leave of the court.

Rules—FPR 2010, Pt 11 has been extended to apply to FGM protection orders.

8 Remand: general

(1) The court before which an arrested person is brought by virtue of a warrant under paragraph 7 may, if the matter is not then disposed of immediately, remand the person concerned.

(2) Paragraphs 9 to 14 contain further provision about the powers of a court to remand under this paragraph.

(3) Sub-paragraph (4) applies if a person remanded under this paragraph is granted bail under paragraphs 10 to 14.

(4) The person may be required by the relevant judge to comply, before release on bail or later, with such requirements as appear to the judge to be necessary to secure that the person does not interfere with witnesses or otherwise obstruct the course of justice.

Defined terms—'relevant judge': Sch 2, para 17(1).

Application for bail—See the notes under FLA 1996, s 63K and Sch 5, which contain similar provisions.

9 Remand: medical examination and report

(1) Any power to remand a person under paragraph 8(1) may be exercised for the purpose of enabling a medical examination and report to be made if the relevant judge has reason to consider that a medical report will be required.

(2) If such a power is so exercised, the adjournment must not be for more than four weeks at a time unless the relevant judge remands the accused in custody.

(3) If the relevant judge remands the accused in custody, the adjournment must not be for more than three weeks at a time.

(4) Sub-paragraph (5) applies if there is reason to suspect that a person who has been arrested under a warrant issued on an application under paragraph 7(1) is suffering from mental disorder within the meaning of the Mental Health Act 1983.

(5) The relevant judge has the same power to make an order under section 35 of the Mental Health Act 1983 (remand for report on accused's mental condition) as the Crown Court has under section 35 of that Act in the case of an accused person within the meaning of that section.

Remand for medical reports—See notes under FLA 1996, s 63L.

10 Remand: further provision

(1) Where a court has power to remand a person under paragraph 8, the court may remand the person in custody or on bail.

(2) If remanded in custody, the person is to be committed to custody to be brought before the court –

- (a) at the end of the period of remand, or
- (b) at such earlier time as the court may require.

(3) The court may remand a person on bail –

- (a) by taking from the person a recognizance (with or without sureties) conditioned as provided in paragraph 11, or
- (b) by fixing the amount of the recognizances with a view to their being taken subsequently in accordance with paragraph 14 and, in the meantime, committing the person to custody as mentioned in sub-paragraph (2) above.

(4) Where a person is brought before the court after remand the court may further remand the person.

(5) In this paragraph and in paragraphs 11 to 14, references to 'the court' includes a reference to a judge of the court or, in the case of proceedings in a magistrates' court, a justice of the peace.

Remand in custody—See notes under FLA 1996, Sch 5, para 2(1),(2).

11 (1) Where a person is remanded on bail, the court may direct that the person's recognizance be conditioned for his or her appearance –

- (a) before the court at the end of the period of remand, or

(b) at every time and place to which during the course of the proceedings the hearing may from time to time be adjourned.

(2) Where a recognizance is conditioned for a person's appearance as mentioned in sub-paragraph (1), the fixing of any time for the person next to appear is to be treated as a remand.

(3) Nothing in this paragraph deprives the court of power at any subsequent hearing to remand a person afresh.

Remand on bail—See notes under FLA 1996, Sch 5, para 2(3).

12 (1) The court may not remand a person for a period exceeding 8 clear days unless –

(a) the court adjourns a case under paragraph 9(1), or

(b) the person is remanded on bail and both that person and the other party to the proceedings (or, in the case of criminal proceedings, the prosecution) consent.

(2) If sub-paragraph (1)(a) applies, the person may be remanded for the period of the adjournment.

(3) Where the court has power to remand a person in custody, the person may be committed to the custody of a constable if the remand is for a period not exceeding 3 clear days.

13 (1) If the court is satisfied that a person who has been remanded is unable by reason of illness or accident to appear before the court at the end of the period of remand, the court may further remand the person in his or her absence.

(2) The power in sub-paragraph (1) may, in the case of a person who was remanded on bail, be exercised by enlarging the person's recognizance and those of any sureties to a later time.

(3) Where a person remanded on bail is bound to appear before the court at any time and the court has no power to remand the person under sub-paragraph (1), the court may, in the person's absence, enlarge the person's recognizance and those of any sureties for the person to a later time.

(4) The enlargement of a person's recognizance is to be treated as a further remand.

(5) Paragraph 12(1) (limit of remand) does not apply to the exercise of the powers conferred by this paragraph.

14 (1) This paragraph applies where under paragraph 10(3)(b) the court fixes the amount in which the principal and the sureties (if any) are to be bound.

(2) The recognizance may afterwards be taken by a person prescribed by rules of court (with the same consequences as if it had been entered into before the court).

15 Contempt proceedings

The powers of the court in relation to contempt of court arising out of a person's failure to comply with an FGM protection order, or otherwise in connection with such an order, may be exercised by the relevant judge.

Defined terms—'relevant judge': Sch 2, para 17(1).

16 Other protection or assistance against female genital mutilation

(1) Nothing in this Part of this Schedule affects any other protection or assistance available to a girl who is or may become the victim of a genital mutilation offence.

(2) In particular, it does not affect –

(a) the inherent jurisdiction of the High Court;

(b) any criminal liability;

(c) any civil remedies under the Protection from Harassment Act 1997;

(d) any right to an occupation order or a non-molestation order under Part 4 of the Family Law Act 1996;

(e) any right to a forced marriage protection order under Part 4A of that Act;

(f) any protection or assistance under the Children Act 1989;

(g) any claim in tort.

Scope—This provision retains the right to apply for additional remedies that are available to support the FGM protection order or as a further means of securing protection for the girl as in the case of an FMPO (for other protection measure available, see Division E of *Emergency Remedies in the Family Court* (Family Law)).

Inherent jurisdiction—The court may exercise its inherent jurisdiction and make all ancillary orders necessary to protect 'the girl' who is at risk of FGM. Where an international element is involved, the President's Guidance issued in April 2016 (see Part V) should be followed in respect of liaison between courts in England and Wales and foreign governments and British Embassies etc. The FMU now has a FGM lead and although the cost is not funded by the Unit they should be contacted where repatriation is required and where emergency travel documents are needed and assistance is necessary with travel arrangements.

Any protection or assistance under CA 1989—This includes a prohibited steps order, police protection order, emergency protection order and a care order (see under CA 1989, s 31).

17 Interpretation

(1) In this Part of this Schedule –

'the court', except as provided in sub-paragraph (2), means the High Court, or the family court, in England and Wales;

'FGM protection order' means an order under paragraph 1;

'genital mutilation offence' means an offence under section 1, 2 or 3;

'the relevant judge', in relation to an FGM protection order, means –

- (a) where the order was made by the High Court, a judge of that court;
- (b) where the order was made by the family court, a judge of that court;
- (c) where the order was made by a court in criminal proceedings under paragraph 3 –
  - (i) a judge of that court, or
  - (ii) a judge of the High Court or of the family court.

(2) Where the power to make an FGM protection order is exercisable by a court in criminal proceedings under paragraph 3, references in this Part of this Schedule to 'the court' (other than in paragraph 2) are to be read as references to that court.

(3) In paragraph (c)(i) of the definition of 'relevant judge' in sub-paragraph (1), the reference to a judge of the court that made the order includes, in the case of criminal proceedings in a magistrates' court, a reference to a justice of the peace.

PART 2
NORTHERN IRELAND

18 Power to make FGM protection order

(1) The court in Northern Ireland may make an order (an 'FGM protection order') for the purposes of –

- (a) protecting a girl against the commission of a genital mutilation offence, or
- (b) protecting a girl against whom any such offence has been committed.

(2) In deciding whether to exercise its powers under this paragraph and, if so, in what manner, the court must have regard to all the circumstances, including the need to secure the health, safety and well-being of the girl to be protected.

(3) An FGM protection order may contain –

- (a) such prohibitions, restrictions or requirements, and
- (b) such other terms, as the court considers appropriate for the purposes of the order.

(4) The terms of an FGM protection order may, in particular, relate to –

- (a) conduct outside Northern Ireland as well as (or instead of) conduct within Northern Ireland;
- (b) respondents who are, or may become, involved in other respects as well as (or instead of) respondents who commit or attempt to commit, or may commit or attempt to commit, a genital mutilation offence against a girl;
- (c) other persons who are, or may become, involved in other respects as well as respondents of any kind.

(5) For the purposes of sub-paragraph (4) examples of involvement in other respects are –

(a) aiding, abetting, counselling, procuring, encouraging or assisting another person to commit, or attempt to commit, a genital mutilation offence against a girl;
(b) conspiring to commit, or to attempt to commit, such an offence.

(6) An FGM protection order may be made for a specified period or until varied or discharged (see paragraph 23).

19 Applications and other occasions for making orders

(1) The court may make an FGM protection order –

(a) on an application being made to it, or
(b) without an application being made to it but in the circumstances mentioned in sub-paragraph (6).

(2) An application may be made by –

(a) the girl who is to be protected by the order, or
(b) a relevant third party.

(3) An application may be made by any other person with the leave of the court.

(4) In deciding whether to grant leave, the court must have regard to all the circumstances including –

(a) the applicant's connection with the girl to be protected;
(b) the applicant's knowledge of the circumstances of the girl.

(5) An application under this paragraph may be made in family proceedings or without any family proceedings being instituted.

(6) The circumstances in which the court may make an order without an application being made are where –

(a) any family proceedings are before the court ('the current proceedings'),
(b) the court considers that an FGM protection order should be made to protect a girl (whether or not a party to the proceedings), and
(c) a person who would be a respondent to any proceedings for an FGM protection order is a party to the current proceedings.

(7) In this paragraph –

'family proceedings' has the same meaning as in the Family Homes and Domestic Violence (Northern Ireland) Order 1998 (SI 1998/1071) (see Article 2(2) and (3) of that Order), but also includes –

(a) proceedings under the inherent jurisdiction of the High Court in relation to adults,
(b) proceedings in which the court has made an emergency protection order under Article 63 of the Children (Northern Ireland) Order 1995 (SI 1995/755) which includes an exclusion requirement (as defined in Article 63A of that Order), and
(c) proceedings in which the court has made an order under Article 69 of that 1995 Order (recovery of abducted children etc);

'relevant third party' means a person specified, or falling within a description of persons specified, by order made by the Department of Finance and Personnel (and any such order may, in particular, specify that Department).

20 Power to make order in criminal proceedings

The court before which there are criminal proceedings in Northern Ireland for a genital mutilation offence may make an FGM protection order (without an application being made to it) if –

(a) the court considers that an FGM protection order should be made to protect a girl (whether or not the victim of the offence in relation to the criminal proceedings), and
(b) a person who would be a respondent to any proceedings for an FGM protection order is a defendant in the criminal proceedings.

21 Offence of breaching order

(1) A person who without reasonable excuse does anything that the person is prohibited from doing by an FGM protection order is guilty of an offence.

(2) A person guilty of an offence under this paragraph is liable –

(a) on conviction on indictment, to imprisonment for a term not exceeding five years, or a fine, or both;

(b) on summary conviction, to imprisonment for a term not exceeding six months, or a fine not exceeding the statutory maximum, or both.

22 Ex parte orders

(1) The court may, in any case where it is just and convenient to do so, make an FGM protection order even though the respondent has not been given such notice of the proceedings as would otherwise be required by rules of court.

(2) In deciding whether to exercise its powers under sub-paragraph (1), the court must have regard to all the circumstances including –

(a) the risk to the girl, or to another person, of becoming a victim of a genital mutilation offence if the order is not made immediately,

(b) whether it is likely that an applicant will be deterred or prevented from pursuing an application if an order is not made immediately, and

(c) whether there is reason to believe that –

(i) the respondent is aware of the proceedings but is deliberately evading service, and

(ii) the delay involved in effecting substituted service will cause serious prejudice to the girl to be protected or (if different) an applicant.

(3) If the court makes an order by virtue of sub-paragraph (1), it must specify a date for a full hearing.

(4) In sub-paragraph (3), 'full hearing' means a hearing of which notice has been given to all the parties in accordance with rules of court.

23 Variation and discharge of orders

(1) The court may vary or discharge an FGM protection order on an application by –

(a) any party to the proceedings for the order,

(b) the girl being protected by the order (if not a party to the proceedings for the order), or

(c) any person affected by the order.

(2) In the case of an order made in criminal proceedings under paragraph 20, the reference in sub-paragraph (1)(a) to a party to the proceedings for the order is to be read as a reference to the prosecution and the defendant.

(3) In addition, the court may vary or discharge an FGM protection order made by virtue of paragraph 19(1)(b) or 20 even though no application under sub-paragraph (1) above has been made to the court.

(4) Paragraph 22 applies to a variation of an FGM protection order as it applies to the making of such an order (and references in that paragraph to the making of an FGM protection order are to be read accordingly).

24 Jurisdiction of courts

(1) For the purposes of this Part of this Schedule, 'the court' means the High Court, or a county court, in Northern Ireland.

(2) Sub-paragraph (1) is subject to –

(a) sub-paragraph (3), and

(b) any provision made by virtue of sub-paragraph (4) or (5).

(3) Where the power to make an FGM protection order is exercisable by a court in criminal proceedings under paragraph 20, references in this Part of this Schedule to 'the court' (other than in paragraph 19) are to be read as references to that court.

(4) Article 34(3) to (10) of the Family Homes and Domestic Violence (Northern Ireland) Order 1998 (SI 1998/1071) (allocation of proceedings to courts etc) applies for the purposes of this Part of this Schedule as it applies for the purposes of that Order but as if the following modification were made.

(5) The modification is that Article 34(8) is to be read as if there were substituted for it –

'(8) For the purposes of paragraphs (3), (4) and (5), there are two levels of court –

(a) the High Court; and
(b) a county court.'

25 Power to extend jurisdiction to courts of summary jurisdiction

(1) The Department of Justice in Northern Ireland may, after consulting the Lord Chief Justice, by order provide for courts of summary jurisdiction to be included among the courts who may hear proceedings under this Part of this Schedule.

(2) An order under sub-paragraph (1) may, in particular, make any provision in relation to courts of summary jurisdiction which corresponds to provision made in relation to such courts by or under the Family Homes and Domestic Violence (Northern Ireland) Order 1998 (SI 1998/1071).

(3) Any power to make an order under this paragraph (including the power as extended by paragraph 29(1)) may, in particular, be exercised by amending, repealing, revoking or otherwise modifying any provision made by or under this Part of this Schedule or any other enactment.

(4) In sub-paragraph (3) 'enactment' includes Northern Ireland legislation.

(5) The Lord Chief Justice may nominate any of the following to exercise the Lord Chief Justice's functions under this Part of this Schedule –

(a) the holder of one of the offices listed in Schedule 1 to the Justice (Northern Ireland) Act 2002;
(b) a Lord Justice of Appeal (as defined by section 88 of that Act).

26 Contempt proceedings

The powers of the court in relation to contempt of court arising out of a person's failure to comply with an FGM protection order, or otherwise in connection with such an order, may be exercised by the relevant judge.

27 Appeals from county courts

(1) An appeal lies to the High Court against –

(a) the making by a county court of any order under this Part of this Schedule, or
(b) any refusal by a county court to make such an order, as if the decision had been made in the exercise of the jurisdiction conferred by Part 3 of the County Courts (Northern Ireland) Order 1980 (SI 1980/397) (original civil jurisdiction) and the appeal were brought under Article 60 of that Order (ordinary appeals in civil cases).

(2) But an appeal does not lie to the High Court under sub-paragraph (1) where the county court is a divorce county court exercising jurisdiction under the Matrimonial Causes (Northern Ireland) Order 1978 (SI 1978/1045) in the same proceedings.

(3) Provision must be made by rules of court for an appeal to lie (upon a point of law, a question of fact or the admission or rejection of any evidence) to the Court of Appeal against –

(a) the making of any order under this Part of this Schedule, or
(b) any refusal to make such an order, by a county court of the type referred to in sub-paragraph (2).

(4) Sub-paragraph (3) is without prejudice to Article 61 of the County Courts (Northern Ireland) Order 1980 (SI 1980/397) (cases stated).

(5) On an appeal under sub-paragraph (1), the High Court may make such orders as may be necessary to give effect to its determination of the appeal.

(6) Where an order is made under sub-paragraph (5), the High Court may also make such incidental or consequential orders as appear to it to be just.

(7) Any order of the High Court made on an appeal under sub-paragraph (1) (other than one directing that an application be re-heard by the county court) is to be treated, for the purposes of –

(a) the enforcement of the order, and
(b) any power to vary, revive or discharge orders, as if it were an order of the county court from which the appeal was brought and not an order of the High Court.

(8) This paragraph is subject to paragraph 28.

28 Appeals: transfers and proposed transfers

(1) The Department of Justice in Northern Ireland may, after consulting the Lord Chief Justice, by order make provision as to the circumstances in which appeals may be made against decisions taken by courts on questions arising in connection with the transfer, or proposed transfer, of proceedings by virtue of an order made under Article 34(5) of the Family Homes and Domestic Violence (Northern Ireland) Order 1998 (SI 1998/1071) as applied by paragraph 24(4) and (5) above.

(2) Except so far as provided for in any order made under sub-paragraph (1), no appeal may be made against any decision of a kind mentioned in that sub-paragraph.

(3) The Lord Chief Justice may nominate any of the following to exercise the Lord Chief Justice's functions under this paragraph –

(a) the holder of one of the offices listed in Schedule 1 to the Justice (Northern Ireland) Act 2002;
(b) a Lord Justice of Appeal (as defined in section 88 of that Act).

29 Orders

(1) An order made under or by virtue of paragraph 19(7), 24(4) and (5), 25(1) or 28(1) –

(a) may make different provision for different purposes;
(b) may contain incidental, supplemental, consequential, transitional, transitory or saving provision;
(c) is to be made by statutory rule for the purposes of the Statutory Rules (Northern Ireland) Order 1979 (SI 1979/1573).

(2) An order made under or by virtue of paragraph 19(7), 24(4) and (5) or 28(1) is subject to negative resolution (within the meaning of section 41(6) of the Interpretation Act (Northern Ireland) 1954).

(3) An order under paragraph 25(1) may not be made unless a draft of the order has been laid before, and approved by a resolution of, the Northern Ireland Assembly.

(4) Section 41(3) of the Interpretation Act (Northern Ireland) 1954 applies for the purposes of sub-paragraph (3) in relation to the laying of a draft as it applies in relation to the laying of a statutory document under an enactment.

30 Other protection or assistance against female genital mutilation

(1) Nothing in this Part of this Schedule affects any other protection or assistance available to a girl who is or may become the victim of a genital mutilation offence.

(2) In particular, it does not affect –

(a) the inherent jurisdiction of the High Court;
(b) any criminal liability;
(c) any right to an occupation order or a non-molestation order under the Family Homes and Domestic Violence (Northern Ireland) Order 1998 (SI 1998/1071);

(d) any civil remedies under the Protection from Harassment (Northern Ireland) Order 1997 (SI 1997/1180);
(e) any protection or assistance under the Children (Northern Ireland) Order 1995 (SI 1995/755);
(f) any right to a forced marriage protection order under Schedule 1 to the Forced Marriage (Civil Protection) Act 2007;
(g) any claim in tort.

31 Interpretation

In this Part of this Schedule –

'the court' is to be read in accordance with paragraph 24;

'FGM protection order' means an order under paragraph 18;

'genital mutilation offence' means an offence under section 1, 2 or 3;

'the relevant judge', in relation to an FGM protection order, means –

(a) where the order was made by the High Court, a judge of that court;
(b) where the order was made by a county court, a judge or district judge of that or any other county court;
(c) where the order was made by a court in criminal proceedings under paragraph 20 –
  (i) a judge of that court, or
  (ii) a judge of the High Court or a judge or district judge of a county court.

Amendments—Schedule inserted by Serious Crime Act 2015, s 73.

Gender Recognition Act 2004

ARRANGEMENT OF SECTIONS

Section		Page
	Applications for gender recognition certificate	
1	Applications	944
2	Determination of applications	945
3	Evidence	945
3A	Alternative grounds for granting applications	946
3B	Evidence for granting applications on alternative grounds	947
4	Successful applications	948
	Issue of full certificate after interim certificate: applicant married	
4A	Married person with interim certificate: issue of full certificate	949
4B	Application under section 4A: death of spouse	950
5	Issue of full certificates where applicant has been married	950
5A	Issue of full certificates where applicant has been a civil partner	951
	Other provision about applications and certificates	
5B	Applications by both civil partners	951
6	Errors	952
7	Applications: supplementary	952
8	Appeals etc	952
	Consequences of issue of gender recognition certificate etc.	
9	General	953
10	Registration	954
11A	Change in gender of party to marriage.	954
11B	Change in gender of civil partners	955
12	Parenthood	955

PART II

15	Succession etc	955
17	Trustees and personal representatives	955
18	Orders where expectations defeated	956
21	Foreign gender change and marriage	956
	Supplementary	
22	Prohibition on disclosure of information	957
25	Interpretation	958
26	Commencement	958

General note—The purpose of the Act, which came into force on 4 April 2005 (SI 2005/54, art 2), is to provide transsexual people with legal recognition in their acquired gender. It remedies breaches of the human rights of transsexuals revealed by decisions of the ECtHR and the House of Lords, e g *Goodwin v United Kingdom* [2002] 2 FLR 487, ECHR; *Bellinger v Bellinger* [2003] 1 FLR 1043, HL. See, however, *Carpenter v Secretary of State for Justice* [2015] EWHC 464 (Admin) (requirements of s 3(3) not incompatible with ECHR, Arts 8 and 143); *R (JK) v Registrar General for England & Wales & Ors* [2015] EWHC 990 (Admin) (requirement to disclose previous gender by not allowing a change to a biological child's birth certificate to show the acquired gender justified under ECHR, Arts 8 and 14). Legal recognition in the acquired gender follows from the issue of a full gender recognition certificate (see annotations to s 4). Sections 1–8 and Schs 1 and 2 establish the process for the issue of a gender recognition certificate to a transsexual person and create a Gender Recognition Panel (PO Box 9300, Leicester LE1 8DJ; *www.justice.gov.uk/tribunals/gender-recognition-panel*; tel: 0300 1234 503). Sections 9–21 and Schs 3–6 set out the consequences of the issue of a full gender recognition certificate.

There are three routes/tracks for obtaining a gender recognition certificate:

1 Standard route (Form T450).
2 Alternative route (protected marriages/civil partnerships) (Form T464).
3 Overseas route (acquired gender recognised under the law of another country) (Form T453).

It is an offence under s 22 of the Act for a person who has acquired protected information, being information concerning an application under ss 1(1), 5(2), 5A(2) or 6(1) or concerning the person's gender before it becomes an acquired gender, in an official capacity to disclose the information to any other person subject to certain exceptions (s 22(4),(5),(7)).

Section 13 and Sch 5 ensure that transsexual persons are treated according to their acquired gender in respect of certain gender specific benefits, e g widowed mother's allowance, widow's pension, widowed parent's allowance, long-term incapacity benefit and state retirement pension. (In relation to changes to state retirement pension, see annotations to MCA 1973, s 21A.) Certain social security policies retaining data as to previous gender do not contravene ECHR, Arts 8 and 14, as it is not disproportionate to retain such data given the legitimate objectives of fraud detection and pension calculation (*R (C) v Secretary of State for Work and Pensions* [2016] EWCA Civ 47).

Section 14 and Sch 6 provide that a person who is recognised under the Act as being of an acquired gender is to be treated as being of the acquired gender under the Sex Discrimination Act 1975. The relevant parts of FPR 2010 are r 7.11 (Nullity: Interim and full gender recognition certificate), Pt 8, Ch 2 (rr 8.2–8.5) (Application for corrected gender recognition certificate) and r 29.6 (Documents in proceedings).

See, also, the Gender Recognition Register (Marriage and Civil Partnership) Regulations 2015, which provide for the registration of marriages and civil partnerships in which one or both parties have obtained a full gender recognition certificate.

Marriage (Same Sex Couples) Act 2013—Significant changes are made to the Act by the 2013 Act (s 12 and Sch 5). Sch 5, Pt 1 amends the Act with effect from 10 December 2014 to enable couples in 'protected marriages' (see annotations to s 3A) to remain married following one or both parties obtaining gender recognition, if both parties to the marriage wish the marriage to continue, thus overcoming the issues raised by *MB v Secretary of State for Work and Pensions* [2016] UKSC 53. Sch 5, Pt 2 amends the Act (ss 3A and 3B) to enable applicants who were or who are currently in protected marriages and who started living in their acquired gender 6 years before the commencement of the 2013 Act to apply for gender recognition under a modified medical evidence procedure.

Applications for gender recognition certificate

1 Applications

(1) A person of either gender who is aged at least 18 may make an application for a gender recognition certificate on the basis of –

(a) living in the other gender, or
(b) having changed gender under the law of a country or territory outside the United Kingdom.

(2) In this Act 'the acquired gender', in relation to a person by whom an application under subsection (1) is or has been made, means –

(a) in the case of an application under paragraph (a) of that subsection, the gender in which the person is living, or

(b) in the case of an application under paragraph (b) of that subsection, the gender to which the person has changed under the law of the country or territory concerned.

(3) An application under subsection (1) is to be determined by a Gender Recognition Panel.

(4) Schedule 1 (Gender Recognition Panels) has effect.

Defined terms—'gender recognition certificate', 'the acquired gender': s 25; 'Gender Recognition Panel': s 25, Sch 1.

Scope—An application may be made for a gender recognition certificate by a person aged at least 18 living in another gender or by a person who has changed gender in another jurisdiction. The application is determined by a Gender Recognition Panel, the composition of which is prescribed in Sch 1.

'having changed gender under the law of a country or territory outside the United Kingdom' (s 1(1)(b))—See s 21.

2 Determination of applications

(1) In the case of an application under section 1(1)(a), the Panel must grant the application if satisfied that the applicant –

(a) has or has had gender dysphoria,

(b) has lived in the acquired gender throughout the period of two years ending with the date on which the application is made,

(c) intends to continue to live in the acquired gender until death, and

(d) complies with the requirements imposed by and under section 3.

(2) In the case of an application under section 1(1)(b), the Panel must grant the application if satisfied –

(a) that the country or territory under the law of which the applicant has changed gender is an approved country or territory, and

(b) that the applicant complies with the requirements imposed by and under section 3.

(3) The Panel must reject an application under section 1(1) if not required by subsection (1) or (2) to grant it.

(3A) This section does not apply to an application under section 1(1)(a) which states that it is an application for a certificate to be granted in accordance with section 3A.

(4) In this Act 'approved country or territory' means a country or territory prescribed by order made by the Secretary of State after consulting the Scottish Ministers and the Department of Finance and Personnel in Northern Ireland.

Amendments—Marriage (Same Sex Couples) Act 2013, s 12, Sch 5, para 16.

Defined terms—'gender dysphoria': s 25; 'the acquired gender': ss 1(2) and 25; 'Panel': s 25, Sch 1; 'approved country or territory': s 2(4) and Gender Recognition (Approved Countries and Territories) Order 2011.

Scope—This section contains the criteria to be met when determining an application for a gender recognition certificate.

'2 years' (s 2(1)(b))—See, for example, *M v Revenue and Customs Commissioners* [2010] UKFTT 356 (TC).

3 Evidence

(1) An application under section 1(1)(a) must include either –

(a) a report made by a registered medical practitioner practising in the field of gender dysphoria and a report made by another registered medical practitioner (who may, but need not, practise in that field), or

(b) a report made by a registered psychologist practising in that field and a report made by a registered medical practitioner (who may, but need not, practise in that field).

(2) But subsection (1) is not complied with unless a report required by that subsection and made by –

(a) a registered medical practitioner, or

(b) a registered psychologist,

practising in the field of gender dysphoria includes details of the diagnosis of the applicant's gender dysphoria.

(3) And subsection (1) is not complied with in a case where –

(a) the applicant has undergone or is undergoing treatment for the purpose of modifying sexual characteristics, or

(b) treatment for that purpose has been prescribed or planned for the applicant,

unless at least one of the reports required by that subsection includes details of it.

(4) An application under section 1(1)(a) must also include a statutory declaration by the applicant that the applicant meets the conditions in section 2(1)(b) and (c).

(5) An application under section 1(1)(b) must include evidence that the applicant has changed gender under the law of an approved country or territory.

(6) Any application under section 1(1) must include –

(a) a statutory declaration as to whether or not the applicant is married or a civil partner,

(b) any other information or evidence required by an order made by the Secretary of State, and

(c) any other information or evidence which the Panel which is to determine the application may require,

and may include any other information or evidence which the applicant wishes to include.

(6A) If the applicant is married, an application under section 1(1) must include a statutory declaration as to whether the marriage is a marriage under the law of England and Wales, of Scotland, of Northern Ireland, or of a country or territory outside the United Kingdom.

(6B) If the applicant is married, and the marriage is a protected marriage, an application under section 1(1) must also include –

(a) a statutory declaration by the applicant's spouse that the spouse consents to the marriage continuing after the issue of a full gender recognition certificate ('a statutory declaration of consent') (if the spouse has made such a declaration), or

(b) a statutory declaration by the applicant that the applicant's spouse has not made a statutory declaration of consent (if that is the case).

(6C) If an application includes a statutory declaration of consent by the applicant's spouse, the Gender Recognition Panel must give the spouse notice that the application has been made.

(7) The Secretary of State may not make an order under subsection (6)(b) without consulting the Scottish Ministers and the Department of Finance and Personnel in Northern Ireland.

(8) If the Panel which is to determine the application requires information or evidence under subsection (6)(c) it must give reasons for doing so.

(9) This section does not apply to an application under section 1(1)(a) which states that it is an application for a certificate to be granted in accordance with section 3A.

Amendments—CPA 2004, s 250(1),(2); SI 2009/1182; Marriage (Same Sex Couples) Act 2013, s 12, Sch 5, paras 2, 18.

Defined terms—'gender dysphoria', 'chartered psychologist': s 25; 'approved country or territory': ss 2(4), 25; 'Panel': s 25, Sch 1.

Scope—This section sets out the evidential requirements to support an application under s 1(1). The evidence required for an application under s 1(1)(a) is a report from a registered medical practitioner or chartered psychologist practising in the field of gender dysphoria and a second report from any registered medical practitioner. At least one report must include details of the diagnosis of the applicant's gender dysphoria and of any treatment undergone, prescribed or planned for the purpose of modifying sexual characteristics.

Section 3(3)—The provision of the information required by s 3(3) is necessary and proportionate to the legitimate aim of the Act, representing no incompatibility with the right to respect for privacy under ECHR, Art 8, nor does it discriminate against a post-operative transsexual person such that there was no incompatibility with ECHR, Art 14 (*Carpenter v Secretary of State for Justice* [2015] EWHC 464 (Admin)).

3A Alternative grounds for granting applications

(1) This section applies to an application under section 1(1)(a) which states that it is an application for a certificate to be granted in accordance with this section.

(2) The Panel must grant the application if satisfied that the applicant complies with the requirements imposed by and under section 3B and meets the conditions in subsections (3) to (6).

(3) The first condition is that the applicant was a party to a protected marriage or a protected civil partnership on or before the date the application was made.

(4) The second condition is that the applicant –

(a) was living in the acquired gender six years before the commencement of section 12 of the Marriage (Same Sex Couples) Act 2013,
(b) continued to live in the acquired gender until the date the application was made, and
(c) intends to continue to live in the acquired gender until death.

(5) The third condition is that the applicant –

(a) has or has had gender dysphoria, or
(b) has undergone surgical treatment for the purpose of modifying sexual characteristics.

(6) The fourth condition is that the applicant is ordinarily resident in England, Wales or Scotland.

(7) The Panel must reject the application if not required by subsection (2) to grant it.

Amendments—Inserted by Marriage (Same Sex Couples) Act 2013, s 12, Sch 5, para 17.

Defined terms—'Acquired gender', 'gender dysphoria', 'protected civil partnership', 'protected marriage': s 25.

Scope—This section permits those who are already married or in a civil partnership (a 'protected marriage'/a 'protected civil partnership') to obtain a full gender recognition certificate without first having to end their marriage/civil partnership providing the four conditions set out are met.

3B Evidence for granting applications on alternative grounds

(1) This section applies to an application under section 1(1)(a) which states that it is an application for a certificate to be granted in accordance with section 3A.

(2) The application must include either –

(a) a report made by a registered medical practitioner, or
(b) a report made by a registered psychologist practising in the field of gender dysphoria.

(3) If the application is based on the applicant having or having had gender dysphoria –

(a) the reference in subsection (2) to a registered medical practitioner is to one practising in the field of gender dysphoria, and
(b) that subsection is not complied with unless the report includes details of the diagnosis of the applicant's gender dysphoria.

(4) Subsection (2) is not complied with in a case where –

(a) the applicant has undergone or is undergoing treatment for the purpose of modifying sexual characteristics, or
(b) treatment for that purpose has been prescribed or planned for the applicant,

unless the report required by that subsection includes details of it.

(5) The application must also include a statutory declaration by the applicant that the applicant meets the conditions in section 3A(3) and (4).

(6) The application must include –

(a) a statutory declaration as to whether or not the applicant is married or a civil partner,
(b) any other information or evidence required by an order made by the Secretary of State, and
(c) any other information or evidence which the Panel which is to determine the application may require,

and may include any other information or evidence which the applicant wishes to include.

(7) If the applicant is married, the application must include a statutory declaration as to whether the marriage is a marriage under the law of England and Wales, of Scotland, of Northern Ireland, or of a country or territory outside the United Kingdom.

PART II

(8) If the applicant is married, and the marriage is a protected marriage, the application must also include –

(a) a statutory declaration of consent by the applicant's spouse (if the spouse has made such a declaration), or

(b) a statutory declaration by the applicant that the applicant's spouse has not made a statutory declaration of consent (if that is the case).

(9) If the application includes a statutory declaration of consent by the applicant's spouse, the Panel must give the spouse notice that the application has been made.

(10) If the Panel which is to determine the application requires information or evidence under subsection (6)(c) it must give reasons for doing so.

Amendments—Inserted by Marriage (Same Sex Couples) Act 2013, s 12, Sch 5, para 17.

Defined terms—'Gender dysphoria', 'registered psychologist', 'statutory declaration of consent': s 25.

****

4 Successful applications

(1) If a Gender Recognition Panel grants an application under section 1(1) it must issue a gender recognition certificate to the applicant.

(2) The certificate is to be a full gender recognition certificate if –

(a) the applicant is neither a civil partner nor married,

(b) the applicant is a party to a protected marriage and the applicant's spouse consents to the marriage continuing after the issue of a full gender recognition certificate, or

(c) the applicant is a party to a protected civil partnership and the Panel has decided to issue a full gender recognition certificate to the other party to the civil partnership.

(3) The certificate is to be an interim gender recognition certificate if –

(a) the applicant is a party to a protected marriage and the applicant's spouse does not consent to the marriage continuing after the issue of a full gender recognition certificate,

(b) the applicant is a party to a marriage that is not a protected marriage,

(c) the applicant is a party to a protected civil partnership and the other party to the civil partnership has not made an application under section 1(1),

(d) the applicant is a party to a protected civil partnership and the Panel has decided not to issue a full gender recognition certificate to the other party to the civil partnership, or

(e) the applicant is a party to a civil partnership that is not a protected civil partnership.

(3A) If a Gender Recognition Panel issues a full gender recognition certificate under this section to an applicant who is a party to a protected marriage, the Panel must give the applicant's spouse notice of the issue of the certificate.

(3B) Subsection (2)(c) is subject to section 5B.

(4) Schedule 2 (annulment or dissolution of marriage after issue of interim gender recognition certificate) has effect.

(5) The Secretary of State may, after consulting the Scottish Ministers and the Department of Finance and Personnel in Northern Ireland, specify the content and form of gender recognition certificates.

Amendments—CPA 2004, s 250(1),(2); Marriage (Same Sex Couples) Act 2013, s 12, Sch 5, para 3.

Defined terms—'Full gender recognition certificate', 'Gender Recognition Panel': s 25, Sch 1; 'gender recognition certificate': s 25; 'full gender recognition certificate': ss 5, 5A and 25; 'interim gender recognition certificate', 'protected civil partnership', 'protected marriage': s 25.

Scope—This section provides that the Gender Recognition Panel must issue a gender recognition certificate to a successful applicant. Where the applicant is single or in a protected marriage or (in the case of a protected civil partnership) the Gender Recognition Panel has decided to issue a full gender recognition certificate to the applicant's civil partner, a full gender recognition certificate is issued. Where the applicant is otherwise married or a civil partner, an interim gender recognition certificate is issued, subject to the transitional provisions of ss 4A and 4B. Section 4(4) and Sch 2 provide that the grant of an interim gender recognition certificate to *either* party to a marriage is in England and Wales a ground on which a marriage is voidable. The MCA 1973, s 12 (marriage celebrated *after* 31 July 1971) and Sch 1, para 11 (marriages celebrated *before* 1 August 1971) are amended accordingly. See, also, CPA 2004, s 50(1)(d). Nullity proceedings must be commenced within 6 months of the grant of the interim gender recognition certificate (MCA 1973, s 13(2A) and Sch 1, para 11(3A) and CPA 2004, s 51(5)).

Section 11 and Sch 4, para 5 provide a further ground upon which a marriage celebrated *after* 31 July 1971 is voidable (MCA 1973, s 12(h)), namely, that the respondent is a person whose gender at the time of the marriage had become the acquired gender under the Act. The petitioner must have been ignorant of the fact that the respondent was previously of another gender.

Section 6 provides for the correction of an error in a gender recognition certificate on the application of the person to whom it has been issued or the Secretary of State by the court or the Gender Recognition Panel which issued the certificate. Section 8 permits an appeal to the High Court by an applicant to a Gender Recognition Panel under ss 1(1), 5(2), 5A(2) or 6(1) on a point of law against a decision by the Panel to reject the application. Section 8(5) provides for the Secretary of State to refer cases to the High Court where he considers an application for a gender recognition certificate has been secured by fraud. Proceedings under ss 6 and 8 are assigned to the Family Division (High Court (Distribution of Business) Order 2004).

'full gender recognition certificate' (s 4(2))—On the issue of a full gender recognition certificate, s 10 and Sch 3 establish a procedure for the creation of a new entry in the UK birth registers which supersede the original entry, thereby reversing *Rees v United Kingdom* [1987] 2 FLR 111, ECHR and *Cossey v United Kingdom* [1991] 2 FLR 492, ECHR.

PART II

Issue of full certificate after interim certificate: applicant married

4A Married person with interim certificate: issue of full certificate

(1) A Gender Recognition Panel must issue a full gender recognition certificate to a person in either of the following cases.

(2) Case A is where, on an application by the person, the Panel is satisfied that –

- (a) an interim gender recognition certificate has been issued to the person;
- (b) the person was a party to a protected marriage at the time when the interim gender recognition certificate was issued;
- (c) the person is a party to a protected marriage; and
- (d) the person's spouse now consents to the marriage continuing after the issue of the full gender recognition certificate.

(3) Case B is where, on an application by the person, the Panel is satisfied that –

- (a) an interim gender recognition certificate has been issued to the person;
- (b) the person was a party to a civil partnership at the time when the interim gender recognition certificate was issued;
- (c) a conversion application has been made within the period of six months beginning with the day on which that certificate was issued;
- (d) the conversion application has resulted in the civil partnership being converted into a marriage;
- (e) the person is a party to that marriage; and
- (f) the person's spouse consents to the marriage continuing after the issue of the full gender recognition certificate.

(4) If, on an application under subsection (2) or (3), the Panel is not satisfied as mentioned in that subsection, the Panel must reject the application.

(5) An application under subsection (2) must be made within the period of six months beginning with the day on which the interim gender recognition certificate is issued.

(6) An application under subsection (3) must be made within the period of six months beginning with the day on which the civil partnership is converted into a marriage.

(7) An application under subsection (2) or (3) must include a statutory declaration of consent made by the person's spouse.

(8) An application under subsection (3) must also include –

- (a) evidence of the date on which the conversion application was made, and
- (b) evidence of the conversion of the civil partnership into a marriage.

(9) If an application is made under this section, the Gender Recognition Panel must give the applicant's spouse –

(a) notice of the application; and
(b) if the Panel grants the application, notice of the issue of the full gender recognition certificate.

(10) In this section 'conversion application' means an application for the conversion of a civil partnership into a marriage under regulations under section 9 of the Marriage (Same Sex Couples) Act 2013.

Amendments—Inserted by Marriage (Same Sex Couples) Act 2013, s 12, Sch 5, para 4.

Defined terms—'Full gender recognition certificate', 'Interim gender recognition certificate', 'protected marriage': s 25; 'Gender Recognition Panel': s 25, Sch 1.

Scope—This section enables those to whom an interim gender recognition certificate has been issued in certain circumstances to obtain a full gender recognition certificate without obtaining a decree of nullity.

4B Application under section 4A: death of spouse

(1) In a case where an application is made under section 4A(2) or (3) and the applicant's spouse dies before the application is determined –

(a) the application is to be treated as an application, made under section 5(2) in a case where a spouse has died, for a full gender recognition certificate to be issued; and
(b) that application is to be treated as having been made at the time when the application under section 4A was made.

(2) The Gender Recognition Panel determining the application must specify the period within which the applicant is to produce the required evidence in support of the new application.

(3) In this section –

'new application' means the application under section 5(2) which the person is, by virtue of subsection (1), treated as having made;

'required evidence' means the evidence required by section 5(4).

Amendments—Inserted by Marriage (Same Sex Couples) Act 2013, s 12, Sch 5, para 4.

Defined terms—'Full gender recognition certificate': s 25; 'Gender Recognition Panel': s 25, Sch 1.

5 Issue of full certificates where applicant has been married

(1) A court which –

(a) makes absolute a decree of nullity granted on the ground that an interim gender recognition certificate has been issued to a party to the marriage, or
(b) (in Scotland) grants a decree of divorce on that ground,

must, on doing so, issue a full gender recognition certificate to that party and send a copy to the Secretary of State.

(2) If an interim gender recognition certificate has been issued to a person and either –

(a) the person's marriage is dissolved or annulled (otherwise than on the ground mentioned in subsection (1)) in proceedings instituted during the period of six months beginning with the day on which it was issued, or
(b) the person's spouse dies within that period,

the person may make an application for a full gender recognition certificate at any time within the period specified in subsection (3) (unless the person is again married or is a civil partner).

(3) That period is the period of six months beginning with the day on which the marriage is dissolved or annulled or the death occurs.

(4) An application under subsection (2) must include evidence of the dissolution or annulment of the marriage and the date on which proceedings for it were instituted, or of the death of the spouse and the date on which it occurred.

(5) An application under subsection (2) is to be determined by a Gender Recognition Panel.

(6) The Panel –

(a) must grant the application if satisfied that the applicant is neither married nor a civil partner, and

(b) otherwise must reject it.

(7) If the Panel grants the application it must issue a full gender recognition certificate to the applicant.

Amendments—CPA 2004, s 250(1),(3).

Defined terms—'interim gender recognition certificate': ss 4(1) and 25; 'Gender Recognition Panel': s 25, Sch 1; 'full gender recognition certificate': ss 4(2) and 25.

Scope—This section provides for the issue of a full gender recognition certificate in two situations. First, where an interim gender recognition certificate has been issued to a party to a marriage and a decree of nullity is subsequently granted on the ground of the issue of such a certificate (s 4(3),(4)), a full gender recognition certificate must be issued. Secondly, if an interim gender recognition certificate has been issued to a person whose marriage is dissolved or annulled (otherwise than on the ground of the issue of an interim gender recognition certificate) in proceedings instituted during the 6-month period beginning with the issue of the interim gender recognition certificate, or the person's spouse dies within that period, the person may apply to the Gender Recognition Panel for a full gender recognition certificate within three months of the date of dissolution, annulment or death, unless the person is again married or is a civil partner.

PART II

5A Issue of full certificates where applicant has been a civil partner

(1) A court which –

(a) makes final a nullity order made on the ground that an interim gender recognition certificate has been issued to a civil partner, or

(b) (in Scotland) grants a decree of dissolution on that ground,

must, on doing so, issue a full gender recognition certificate to that civil partner and send a copy to the Secretary of State.

(2) If an interim gender recognition certificate has been issued to a person and either –

(a) the person's civil partnership is dissolved or annulled (otherwise than on the ground mentioned in subsection (1)) in proceedings instituted during the period of six months beginning with the day on which it was issued, or

(b) the person's civil partner dies within that period,

the person may make an application for a full gender recognition certificate at any time within the period specified in subsection (3) (unless the person is again a civil partner or is married).

(3) That period is the period of six months beginning with the day on which the civil partnership is dissolved or annulled or the death occurs.

(4) An application under subsection (2) must include evidence of the dissolution or annulment of the civil partnership and the date on which proceedings for it were instituted, or of the death of the civil partner and the date on which it occurred.

(5) An application under subsection (2) is to be determined by a Gender Recognition Panel.

(6) The Panel –

(a) must grant the application if satisfied that the applicant is neither a civil partner nor married, and

(b) otherwise must reject it.

(7) If the Panel grants the application it must issue a full gender recognition certificate to the applicant.

Amendments—Inserted by CPA 2004, s 250(1),(4).

Defined terms—'Gender Recognition Panel': s 25, Sch 1; 'interim gender recognition certificate': ss 4(1) and 25; 'full gender recognition certificate': ss 4(2) and 25.

Scope—This section makes provision where the applicant has been a civil partner comparable to that applicable to a married applicant found in s 5.

Other provision about applications and certificates

5B Applications by both civil partners

(1) This section applies where the Panel decides to issue a full gender recognition certificate to a party to a protected civil partnership.

(2) The Panel must not issue the full gender recognition certificate to that person unless the Panel issues a full gender recognition certificate to the other party to the protected civil partnership.

(3) In such a case, the Panel must issue both certificates on the same day.

(4) Those certificates take effect at the beginning of the day on which they are issued.

Amendments—Inserted by Marriage (Same Sex Couples) Act 2013, s 12, Sch 5, para 5.

Defined terms—'Full gender recognition certificate', 'protected civil partnership': s 25; 'Gender Recognition Panel': s 25, Sch 1.

6 Errors

(1) Where a gender recognition certificate has been issued to a person, the person or the Secretary of State may make an application for –

- (a) an interim gender recognition certificate, on the ground that a full gender recognition certificate has incorrectly been issued instead of an interim certificate;
- (b) a full gender recognition certificate, on the ground that an interim gender recognition certificate has incorrectly been issued instead of a full certificate; or
- (c) a corrected certificate, on the ground that the certificate which has been issued contains an error.

(2) If the certificate was issued by a court the application is to be determined by the court but in any other case it is to be determined by a Gender Recognition Panel.

(3) The court or Panel –

- (a) must grant the application if satisfied that the ground on which the application is made is correct, and
- (b) otherwise must reject it.

(4) If the court or Panel grants the application it must issue a correct, or a corrected, gender recognition certificate to the applicant.

Amendments—Marriage (Same Sex Couples) Act 2013, s 12, Sch 5, para 6.

Defined terms—'gender recognition certificate': s 25; 'Gender Recognition Panel': s 25, Sch 1.

'Determined by the court' (s 6(2))—The procedure is set out in FPR 2010, Pt 8, Ch 2 (rr 8.2–8.5).

Scope—This section enables a gender recognition certificate containing an error to be corrected on application to the court (where the certificate was issued by the court) or otherwise by a Gender Recognition Panel. Where the application is to a court, the procedure is governed by FPR 2010, Pt 8, Ch 2.

7 Applications: supplementary

(1) An application to a Gender Recognition Panel under section 1(1), 4A, 5(2), 5A(2) or 6(1) must be made in a form and manner specified by the Secretary of State after consulting the Scottish Ministers and the Department of Finance and Personnel in Northern Ireland.

(2) The applicant must pay to the Secretary of State a non-refundable fee of an amount prescribed by order made by the Secretary of State unless the application is made in circumstances in which, in accordance with provision made by the order, no fee is payable; and fees of different amounts may be prescribed for different circumstances.

Amendments—CPA 2004, s 250(1),(5); Marriage (Same Sex Couples) Act 2013, s 12, Sch 5, para 7.

Defined terms—'Gender Recognition Panel': s 25, Sch 1; 'fee': Gender Recognition (Application Fees) Order 2006, as amended.

8 Appeals etc

(1) An applicant to a Gender Recognition Panel under section 1(1), 4A, 5(2), 5(A)2 or 6(1) may appeal to the High Court, family court or Court of Session on a point of law against a decision by the Panel to reject the application.

(2) An appeal under subsection (1) must be heard in private if the applicant so requests.

(3) On such an appeal the court must –

- (a) allow the appeal and issue the certificate applied for,
- (b) allow the appeal and refer the matter to the same or another Panel for re-consideration, or

(c) dismiss the appeal.

(4) If an application under section 1(1) is rejected, the applicant may not make another application before the end of the period of six months beginning with the date on which it is rejected.

(5) If an application under section 1(1), 4A, 5(2), 5A(2) or 6(1) is granted but the Secretary of State considers that its grant was secured by fraud, the Secretary of State may refer the case to the High Court, family court or Court of Session.

(5A) If an application under section 1(1), 4A, 5(2), 5A(2) or 6(1) is granted, the applicant's spouse may apply to the High Court or Court of Session to quash the decision to grant the application on the grounds that its grant was secured by fraud.

(6) On a reference under subsection (5) or an application under subsection (5A) the court –

(a) must either quash or confirm the decision to grant the application, and

(b) if it quashes it, must revoke the gender recognition certificate issued on the grant of the application and may make any order which it considers appropriate in consequence of, or otherwise in connection with, doing so.

Amendments—CPA 2004, s 250(1),(5); CCA 2013, s 17, Sch 11; Marriage (Same Sex Couples) Act 2013, s 12, Sch 5, para 8.

Defined terms—'gender recognition certificate': s 25; 'Gender Recognition Panel': s 25, Sch 1.

Scope—This section provides the applicant with a right of appeal against a rejection decision on a point of law to the High Court, or Court of Session in Scotland. Where such an appeal is rejected, the applicant may not lodge a further appeal until 6 months have elapsed. The Secretary of State has a right to refer a case to the High Court (or Court of Session) if he considers that the grant of an application was secured by fraud. An appeal will only lie where there has been a decision to reject the application and not as a result of, for example, distress arising from the delayed progress of an application or loss of state pension rights (*Carpenter v Secretary of State for Justice* [2012] EWHC 4421 (Fam)).

Consequences of issue of gender recognition certificate etc.

9 General

(1) Where a full gender recognition certificate is issued to a person, the person's gender becomes for all purposes the acquired gender (so that, if the acquired gender is the male gender, the person's sex becomes that of a man and, if it is the female gender, the person's sex becomes that of a woman).

(2) Subsection (1) does not affect things done, or events occurring, before the certificate is issued; but it does operate for the interpretation of enactments passed, and instruments and other documents made, before the certificate is issued (as well as those passed or made afterwards).

(3) Subsection (1) is subject to provision made by this Act or any other enactment or any subordinate legislation.

Defined terms—'full gender recognition certificate': ss 4(2) and 25; 'acquired gender': ss 1(2) and 25; 'enactment', 'subordinate legislation': s 25.

Scope—The general principle of the Act is that, where a full gender recognition certificate is issued to a transsexual person, he/she will for all purposes be regarded as being of the acquired gender without any presumption that the person has physical characteristics other than those that he/she actually possesses (eg *R (AB) v Secretary of State for Justice and another* [2009] EWHC 2220 (Admin)). Recognition of the acquired gender is not retrospective (*J v C (Void Marriage: Status of Children)* [2006] 2 FLR 1098, CA; *Timbrell v Secretary of State for Work & Pensions* [2011] 1 FLR 332, CA). This general principle is subject to exceptions contained in the Act (eg parenthood (s 12), succession (s 15) peerages (s 16), sport (s 19) or gender-specific offences (s 20)) or in later primary or subordinate legislation.

Much of the case-law relating to the consequences of the issue of a gender recognition certificate has related to the statutory provisions about state pensionable age. Originally, before the Act, it had been held that a male at birth who had successfully undergone gender reassignment surgery had to be treated as a male (for the purposes of the MCA 1973) (*Bellinger v Bellinger* [2003] 1 FLR 1043, HL). In *Goodwin v UK* [2002] 2 FLR 487, ECHR, it was held that the UK's failure to provide a means to obtain legal recognition of gender reassignment had been a breach of that applicant's rights under ECHR, Art 8, which decision led to the enactment of the Act. Following *Goodwin,* the ECtHR held in *Grant v United Kingdom* (2007) 44 EHRR 1, ECHR that there was no justification for failing to recognise the change of gender of post-operative transsexuals. The applicant was entitled to claim to be the victim of the denial of legal recognition of gender reassignment from the date of the decision in *Goodwin* until the Act came into force as violating her rights under ECHR, Art 8. A different approach was adopted in *Richards v Secretary of State for Work & Pensions* [2006] 2 FLR 487, ECJ, where it was held on a preliminary ruling from the ECJ that the Pensions Act 1995 was discriminatory (under the directly effective right under art 4(1) of Council Directive 79/7 on the equal treatment for men and women in matters of social security) as it constituted unequal treatment for the claimant as a result of her inability to have her new gender recognised under the 1995 Act. This approach, under which it was found that UK legislation before the Act was discriminatory with regard to acquired gender and pension entitlement, was followed in *Timbrell v Secretary of State for Work & Pensions* [2011] 1 FLR 332, CA. The decision in *Timbrell* was, however, distinguished in *M v Revenue and Customs Commissioners* [2010] UKFTT 356 (TC), where the appellant's gender reassignment surgery had been performed after the Act came into force.

Section 11 and Sch 4 amend MA 1949 so that, for example, a male is able to contract a valid marriage with a transsexual whose acquired gender under the Act is female, thereby reversing decisions such as *Corbett v Corbett* [1971] P 83, PDAD and *Bellinger v Bellinger* [2003] 1 FLR 1043, HL.

10 Registration

(1) Where there is a UK birth register entry in relation to a person to whom a full gender recognition certificate is issued, the Secretary of State must send a copy of the certificate to the appropriate Registrar General.

(1A) Where a full gender recognition certificate is issued to a person who is a party to –

(a) a marriage under the law of England and Wales, or

(b) a civil partnership under that law,

the Secretary of State must send a copy of the certificate to the Registrar General for England and Wales.

(2) In this Act 'UK birth register entry', in relation to a person to whom a full gender recognition certificate is issued, means –

(a) an entry of which a certified copy is kept by a Registrar General, or

(b) an entry in a register so kept,

containing a record of the person's birth or adoption (or, if there would otherwise be more than one, the most recent).

(3) 'The appropriate Registrar General' means whichever of –

(a) the Registrar General for England and Wales,

(b) the Registrar General for Scotland, or

(c) the Registrar General for Northern Ireland,

keeps a certified copy of the person's UK birth register entry or the register containing that entry.

(4) Schedule 3 (provisions about registration) has effect.

Amendments—Marriage (Same Sex Couples) Act 2013, s 12, Sch 5, para 9.

Defined term—'full gender recognition certificate': s 25.

Scope—Sch 3 provides for the maintenance of a Gender Recognition Register, which is not open to public inspection and which is regulated by the Gender Recognition Register Regulations 2005, as amended.

****

11A Change in gender of party to marriage.

(1) This section applies in relation to a protected marriage if (by virtue of section 4(2)(b) or 4A) a full gender recognition certificate is issued to a party to the marriage.

(2) The continuity of the protected marriage is not affected by the relevant change in gender.

(3) If the protected marriage is a foreign marriage –

(a) the continuity of the marriage continues by virtue of subsection (2) notwithstanding any impediment under the proper law of the marriage;

(b) the proper law of the marriage is not affected by its continuation by virtue of subsection (2).

(4) In this section –

'foreign marriage' means a marriage under the law of a country or territory outside the United Kingdom;

'impediment' means anything which affects the continuation of a marriage merely by virtue of the relevant change in gender;

'proper law', in relation to a protected marriage, means the law of the country or territory under which the marriage was entered into;

'relevant change in gender' means the change or changes of gender occurring by virtue of the issue of the full gender recognition certificate or certificates.

Amendments—Inserted by Marriage (Same Sex Couples) Act 2013, s 12, Sch 5, para 10.

Defined terms—'Full gender recognition certificate', 'protected marriage': s 25.

11B Change in gender of civil partners

The continuity of a civil partnership is not affected by the issuing of full gender recognition certificates (by virtue of section 4(2)(c)) to both civil partners.

Amendments—Inserted by Marriage (Same Sex Couples) Act 2013, s 12, Sch 5, para 11.

Defined terms—'Full gender recognition certificate': s 25.

12 Parenthood

The fact that a person's gender has become the acquired gender under this Act does not affect the status of the person as the father or mother of a child.

Defined terms—'acquired gender': ss 1(2), 25.

Scope—This section aims to ensure continuity of parental rights and responsibilities given that, though a person is regarded as being of the acquired gender, that person will retain their original status either as father or mother of a child.

****

15 Succession etc

The fact that a person's gender has become the acquired gender under this Act does not affect the disposal or devolution of property under a will or other instrument made before the appointed day.

Defined terms—'acquired gender': ss 1(2), 25; 'the appointed day': ss 25, 26 (4 April 2005; SI 2005/54, art 2).

Scope—This section contains one of the exceptions to the general rule contained in s 9 that, following the issue of a full gender recognition certificate, a person's gender becomes for all purposes the acquired gender. Under s 17, trustees and personal representatives are not placed under a duty to enquire whether a full gender recognition certificate has been issued or revoked before conveying or distributing property if that fact could affect entitlement to the property (s 17(1)). Trustees/personal representatives are not liable to any person in the circumstances envisaged by s 17(1) where no notice of the issue or revocation had been received before the conveyance or distribution (s 17(2)). A person will still be able to trace to the property or its proceeds into the hands of another person, unless that person has purchased it for value in good faith and without notice (s 17(3)). This section deals with wills made before 4 April 2005; where the will is made on or after 5 April 2005, see s 18.

****

17 Trustees and personal representatives

(1) A trustee or personal representative is not under a duty, by virtue of the law relating to trusts or the administration of estates, to enquire, before conveying or distributing any property, whether a full gender recognition certificate has been issued to any person or revoked (if that fact could affect entitlement to the property).

(2) A trustee or personal representative is not liable to any person by reason of a conveyance or distribution of the property made without regard to whether a full gender recognition certificate has been issued to any person or revoked if the trustee or personal representative has not received notice of the fact before the conveyance or distribution.

(3) This section does not prejudice the right of a person to follow the property, or any property representing it, into the hands of another person who has received it unless that person has purchased it for value in good faith and without notice.

Defined term—'full gender recognition certificate': s 25.

Scope—This section relieves a trustee or personal representative from any fiduciary duty to inquire whether a gender recognition certificate has been issued to any person or revoked, even if that fact could affect entitlement to property which he/she is responsible for distributing. The beneficiary will nevertheless retain his/her claim to the property and may enforce this claim. See annotations to s 15.

PART II

18 Orders where expectations defeated

(1) This section applies where the disposition or devolution of any property under a will or other instrument (made on or after the appointed day) is different from what it would be but for the fact that a person's gender has become the acquired gender under this Act.

(2) A person may apply to the High Court or Court of Session for an order on the ground of being adversely affected by the different disposition or devolution of the property.

(3) The court may, if it is satisfied that it is just to do so, make in relation to any person benefiting from the different disposition or devolution of the property such order as it considers appropriate.

(4) An order may, in particular, make provision for –

- (a) the payment of a lump sum to the applicant,
- (b) the transfer of property to the applicant,
- (c) the settlement of property for the benefit of the applicant,
- (d) the acquisition of property and either its transfer to the applicant or its settlement for the benefit of the applicant.

(5) An order may contain consequential or supplementary provisions for giving effect to the order or for ensuring that it operates fairly as between the applicant and the other person or persons affected by it; and an order may, in particular, confer powers on trustees.

Defined terms—'the appointed day': ss 25, 26 (4 April 2005 (SI 2005/54, art 2)); 'acquired gender': ss 1(2), 25.

Scope—This section applies where disposition of property under a will made on or after 5 April 2005 is different from what it would be but for the fact that a person's gender has become the acquired gender under the Act. For the position in relation to wills made before 4 April 2005, see s 15. The section gives the High Court power to make orders of the type set out in s 18(4) and (5) on the sole ground of a person being adversely affected by the different disposition (s 18(2)). In considering such an application, the court must be satisfied that it is just to make an order (s 18(3)).

****

21 Foreign gender change and marriage

(1) A person's gender is not to be regarded as having changed by reason only that it has changed under the law of a country or territory outside the United Kingdom.

(1A) Subsections (2) to (5) apply only in Scotland and Northern Ireland.

(2) In accordance with subsection (1), a person is not to be regarded as being married by reason of having entered into a foreign post-recognition marriage.

(3) But if a full gender recognition certificate is issued to a person who has entered into a foreign post-recognition marriage, after the issue of the certificate the marriage is no longer to be regarded as being void on the ground that (at the time when it was entered into) the parties to it were not respectively male and female.

(4) However, subsection (3) does not apply to a foreign post-recognition marriage if a party to it has entered into a later (valid) marriage or civil partnership before the issue of the full gender recognition certificate.

(5) For the purposes of this section a person has entered into a foreign post-recognition marriage if (and only if) –

- (a) the person has entered into a marriage in accordance with the law of a country or territory outside the United Kingdom,
- (b) before the marriage was entered into the person had changed gender under the law of that or any other country or territory outside the United Kingdom,
- (c) the other party to the marriage was not of the gender to which the person had changed under the law of that country or territory, and
- (d) by virtue of subsection (1) the person's gender was not regarded as having changed under the law of any part of the United Kingdom.

(6) Nothing in this section prevents the exercise of any enforceable Community right.

Amendments—CPA 2004, s 250(1),(6); Marriage (Same Sex Couples) Act 2013, s 12, Sch 5, para 12.

Defined terms—'foreign post-recognition marriage': s 21(5); 'full gender recognition certificate': ss 4(2), 25.

Scope—This section provides that a person's gender is not to be regarded as having changed only by reason of a foreign gender change (s 21(1)). Accordingly, a person will not be regarded as being married by reason of having entered into a foreign post-recognition marriage as defined by s 21(5) (s 21(2)). Where, however, a full gender recognition certificate is issued to a person who has entered into a foreign post-recognition marriage, the marriage will no longer be regarded as being void (subject to the exceptions in s 21(4)) after the issue of the certificate on the ground that at the time it was entered into the parties were not respectively male and female (s 21(3)).

Supplementary

22 Prohibition on disclosure of information

(1) It is an offence for a person who has acquired protected information in an official capacity to disclose the information to any other person.

(2) 'Protected information' means information which relates to a person who has made an application under section 1(1) and which –

- (a) concerns that application or any application by the person under section 4A, 5(2), 5A(2) or 6(1), or
- (b) if the application under section 1(1) is granted, otherwise concerns the person's gender before it becomes the acquired gender.

(3) A person acquires protected information in an official capacity if the person acquires it –

- (a) in connection with the person's functions as a member of the civil service, a constable or the holder of any other public office or in connection with the functions of a local or public authority or of a voluntary organisation,
- (b) as an employer, or prospective employer, of the person to whom the information relates or as a person employed by such an employer or prospective employer, or
- (c) in the course of, or otherwise in connection with, the conduct of business or the supply of professional services.

(4) But it is not an offence under this section to disclose protected information relating to a person if –

- (a) the information does not enable that person to be identified,
- (b) that person has agreed to the disclosure of the information,
- (c) the information is protected information by virtue of subsection (2)(b) and the person by whom the disclosure is made does not know or believe that a full gender recognition certificate has been issued,
- (d) the disclosure is in accordance with an order of a court or tribunal,
- (e) the disclosure is for the purpose of instituting, or otherwise for the purposes of, proceedings before a court or tribunal,
- (f) the disclosure is for the purpose of preventing or investigating crime,
- (g) the disclosure is made to the Registrar General for England and Wales, the Registrar General for Scotland or the Registrar General for Northern Ireland,
- (h) the disclosure is made for the purposes of the social security system or a pension scheme,
- (i) the disclosure is in accordance with provision made by an order under subsection (5), or
- (j) the disclosure is in accordance with any provision of, or made by virtue of, an enactment other than this section.

(5) The Secretary of State may by order make provision prescribing circumstances in which the disclosure of protected information is not to constitute an offence under this section.

(6) The power conferred by subsection (5) is exercisable by the Scottish Ministers (rather than the Secretary of State) where the provision to be made is within the legislative competence of the Scottish Parliament.

(6A) The power conferred by subsection (5) is exercisable by the Department of Justice in Northern Ireland (rather than the Secretary of State) where the provision to be made could be made by an Act of the Northern Ireland Assembly without the consent of the Secretary of State (see sections 6 to 8 of the Northern Ireland Act 1998).

PART II

(7) An order under subsection (5) may make provision permitting –

(a) disclosure to specified persons or persons of a specified description,

(b) disclosure for specified purposes,

(c) disclosure of specified descriptions of information, or

(d) disclosure by specified persons or persons of a specified description.

(8) A person guilty of an offence under this section is liable on summary conviction to a fine not exceeding level 5 on the standard scale.

Amendments—CPA 2004, s 250(1),(5); SI 2010/976; Marriage (Same Sex Couples) Act 2013, s 12, Sch 5, para 13.

Defined terms—'the acquired gender': ss 1(2), 25; 'enactment', 'full gender recognition certificate': s 25.

Scope—This section makes it an offence for a person who has acquired protected information (s 22(2)) in an official capacity to disclose that information. Circumstances in which disclosure of protected information does not constitute an offence (s 22(5) and (7)) are contained in the Gender Recognition (Disclosure of Information) (England, Wales and Northern Ireland) (No 2) Order 2005, which concerns disclosure for the purpose of obtaining legal advice (art 3); for religious purposes (art 4); or medical purposes (art 5); by or on behalf of a credit reference agency (art 6); and in relation to insolvency (art 7).

'Protected information' (s 22(4))—Disclosure should not be permitted in those cases where it is unnecessary and irrelevant to the issues (Guidance issued by the President of the Family Division on Protected Information relating to a person who has a Gender Recognition Certificate, 11 March 2014).

****

25 Interpretation

In this Act –

'the acquired gender' is to be construed in accordance with section 1(2),

'approved country or territory' has the meaning given by section 2(4),

'the appointed day' means the day appointed by order under section 26,

'enactment' includes an enactment contained in an Act of the Scottish Parliament or in any Northern Ireland legislation,

'full gender recognition certificate' and 'interim gender recognition certificate' mean the certificates issued as such under section 4 or 5 or 5A and 'gender recognition certificate' means either of those sorts of certificate,

'gender dysphoria' means the disorder variously referred to as gender dysphoria, gender identity disorder and transsexualism,

'Gender Recognition Panel' (and 'Panel') is to be construed in accordance with Schedule 1,

'protected civil partnership' means a civil partnership under the law of England and Wales;

'protected marriage' means –

(a) a marriage under the law of England and Wales, or

(b) a marriage under the law of a country or territory outside the United Kingdom,

'registered psychologist' means a person registered in the part of the register maintained under the Health and Social Work Professions Order 2001 which relates to practitioner psychologists,

'statutory declaration of consent' has the meaning given by section 3(6B)(a),

'subordinate legislation' means an Order in Council, an order, rules, regulations, a scheme, a warrant, bye-laws or any other instrument made under an enactment, and

'UK birth register entry' has the meaning given by section 10(2).

Amendments—CPA 2004, s 250(1),(7); SI 2009/1182; Health and Social Care Act 2012, s 213(8); Marriage (Same Sex Couples) Act 2013, s 12, Sch 5, para 14.

26 Commencement

Apart from sections 23 to 25, this section and sections 28 and 29, this Act does not come into force until such day as the Secretary of State may appoint by order made after consulting the Scottish Ministers and the Department of Finance and Personnel in Northern Ireland.

Orders under this section—The Gender Recognition Act 2004 (Commencement) Order 2005 brought the Act into force, insofar as it was not already in force, on 4 April 2005.

****

Human Fertilisation and Embryology Act 1990

ARRANGEMENT OF SECTIONS

Section		Page
	Principal terms used	
1	Meaning of 'embryo', 'gamete' and associated expressions	959
1A	Reference to Directives	960
2	Other terms	960
2A	Third party agreements	962
	Activities governed by the Act	
3	Prohibitions in connection with embryos	962
3ZA	Permitted eggs, permitted sperm and permitted embryos	963
3A	Prohibition in connection with germ cells	963
4	Prohibitions in connection with gametes	964
4A	Prohibitions in connection with genetic material not of human origin	964
	The Human Fertilisation and Embryology Authority, its functions and procedure	
5	The Human Fertilisation and Embryology Authority	965
	Scope of licences	
11	Licences for treatment, storage and research	966
	Licence conditions	
12	General conditions	966
13	Conditions of licences for treatment	967
13A	Conditions of licences for non-medical fertility services	969
14	Conditions of storage licences	969
14A	Conditions of licences: human application	970
34	Disclosure in interests of justice	971
35	Disclosure in interests of justice: congenital disabilities etc	972
35A	Mitochondrial donation	972
35B	Fees	972
	Schedule 2 – Activities for which Licences may be Granted	973
	Schedule 3A – Supplementary Licence Conditions: Human Application	975

Principal terms used

1 Meaning of 'embryo', 'gamete' and associated expressions

(1) In this Act (except in section 4A or in the term 'human admixed embryo') –

- (a) embryo means a live human embryo and does not include a human admixed embryo (as defined by section 4A(6)), and
- (b) references to an embryo include an egg that is in the process of fertilisation or is undergoing any other process capable of resulting in an embryo.

(2) This Act, so far as it governs bringing about the creation of an embryo, applies only to bringing about the creation of an embryo outside the human body; and in this Act –

- (a) references to embryos the creation of which was brought about in vitro (in their application to those where fertilisation or any other process by which an embryo is created is complete) are to those where fertilisation or any other process by which the embryo was created began outside the human body whether or not it was completed there, and
- (b) references to embryos taken from a woman do not include embryos whose creation was brought about in vitro.

(3) This Act, so far as it governs the keeping or use of an embryo, applies only to keeping or using an embryo outside the human body.

(4) In this Act (except in section 4A) –

- (a) references to eggs are to live human eggs, including cells of the female germ line at any stage of maturity, but (except in subsection (1)(b)) not including eggs that are in the process of fertilisation or are undergoing any other process capable of resulting in an embryo,
- (b) references to sperm are to live human sperm, including cells of the male germ line at any stage of maturity, and
- (c) references to gametes are to be read accordingly.

(5) For the purposes of this Act, sperm is to be treated as partner-donated sperm if the donor of the sperm and the recipient of the sperm declare that they have an intimate physical relationship.

(6) If it appears to the Secretary of State necessary or desirable to do so in the light of developments in science or medicine, regulations may provide that in this Act (except in section 4A) 'embryo', 'eggs', 'sperm' or 'gametes' includes things specified in the regulations which would not otherwise fall within the definition.

(7) Regulations made by virtue of subsection (6) may not provide for anything containing any nuclear or mitochondrial DNA that is not human to be treated as an embryo or as eggs, sperm or gametes.

Amendments—SI 2007/1522; HFEA 2008, s 1.

Definition—The Act redefines 'embryo' and 'gametes', introduces and defines 'human admixed embryo' and is drafted widely enough to include any possible future scientific changes that may be developed. It gives the Secretary of State powers to make regulations in the light of any new scientific developments but excluding those set out in s 1(7).

'embryo'—Human embryos created by cell nuclear replacement fall within the definition of embryo in s 1(1) and are subject to regulation under the 1990 Act (*R (Quintavelle) v Secretary of State for Health* [2002] QB 628, CA).

'embryo and human rights'—An embryo cannot be considered to be a person or to have a 'qualified' right to life, and ECHR 1950, Art 2 does not apply to it (*Evans v Amicus Healthcare and others; Hadley v Midland Fertility Services Ltd and others* [2004] 1 FLR 67, FD. See also *Re F (In Utero) (Wardship)* [1988] 2 FLR 307, CA; *Re MB (Medical Treatment)* [1997] 2 FLR 426, CA and *Paton v United Kingdom* (1980) 3 EHRR 408, ECHR.

1A Reference to Directives

In this Act –

'the first Directive' means Directive 2004/23/EC of the European Parliament and of the Council of 31 March 2004 on setting standards of quality and safety for the donation, procurement, testing, processing, preservation, storage and distribution of human tissues and cells,

'the second Directive' means Commission Directive 2006/17/EC of 8 February 2006 implementing Directive 2004/23/EC of the European Parliament and of the Council as regards certain technical requirements for the donation, procurement and testing of human tissues and cells, as amended by Commission Directive 2012/39/EU, and

'the third Directive' means Commission Directive 2006/86/EC of 24 October 2006 implementing Directive 2004/23/EC of the European Parliament and of the Council as regards traceability requirements, notification of serious adverse reactions and events and certain technical requirements for the coding, processing, preservation, storage and distribution of human tissues and cells.

Amendments—Inserted by SI 2007/1522. Amended by SI 2014/2884.

'the First Directive'—For notes generally on consent see footnote to Sch 3 below.

2 Other terms

(1) In this Act –

'the Authority' means the Human Fertilisation and Embryology Authority established under section 5 of this Act,

'basic partner treatment services' means treatment services that are provided for a woman and a man together without using –
 (a) the gametes of any other person, or
 (b) embryos created outside the woman's body,

'competent authority', in relation to an EEA state other than the United Kingdom or in relation to Gibraltar, means an authority designated in accordance with the law of that state or territory as responsible for implementing the requirements of the first, second and third Directives,

'directions' means directions under section 23 of this Act,

'distribution', in relation to gametes or embryos intended for human application, means transportation or delivery, and related terms are to be interpreted accordingly,

'human application' means use in a human recipient,

'licence' means a licence under Schedule 2 to this Act and, in relation to a licence, 'the person responsible' has the meaning given by section 17 of this Act, and

'non-medical fertility services' means any services that are provided, in the course of a business, for the purpose of assisting women to carry children, but are not medical, surgical or obstetric services,

'nuclear DNA', in relation to an embryo, includes DNA in the pronucleus of the embryo,

'processing', in relation to gametes or embryos intended for human application, means any operation involved in their preparation, manipulation or packaging, and related terms are to be interpreted accordingly,

'procurement', in relation to gametes or embryos intended for human application, means any process by which they are made available, and related terms are to be interpreted accordingly,

'serious adverse event' means –
 (a) any untoward occurrence which may be associated with the procurement, testing, processing, storage or distribution of gametes or embryos intended for human application and which, in relation to a donor of gametes or a person who receives treatment services or non-medical fertility services –
  (i) might lead to the transmission of a communicable disease, to death, or life-threatening, disabling or incapacitating conditions, or
  (ii) might result in, or prolong, hospitalisation or illness, or
 (b) any type of gametes or embryo misidentification or mix-up,

'serious adverse reaction' means an unintended response, including a communicable disease, in a donor of gametes intended for human application or a person who receives treatment services or non-medical fertility services, which may be associated with the procurement or human application of gametes or embryos and which is fatal, life-threatening, disabling, incapacitating or which results in, or prolongs, hospitalisation or illness,

'store', in relation to gametes, embryos or human admixed embryos, means preserve, whether by cryopreservation or in any other way, and 'storage' and 'stored' are to be interpreted accordingly,

'traceability' means the ability –
 (a) to identify and locate gametes and embryos during any step from procurement to use for human application or disposal,
 (b) to identify the donor and recipient of particular gametes or embryos,
 (c) to identify any person who has carried out any activity in relation to particular gametes or embryos, and
 (d) to identify and locate all relevant data relating to products and materials coming into contact with particular gametes or embryos and which can affect their quality or safety,

'treatment services' means medical, surgical or obstetric services provided to the public or a section of the public for the purpose of assisting women to carry children.

(2) References in this Act to keeping, in relation to embryos, gametes or human admixed embryos, include keeping while preserved in storage.

PART II

(2A) For the purposes of this Act, a person who, from any premises, controls the provision of services for transporting gametes or embryos is to be taken to distribute gametes or embryos on those premises.

(2B) In this Act, any reference to a requirement of a provision of the first, second or third Directive is a reference to a requirement which that provision requires to be imposed.

(3) For the purposes of this Act, a woman is not to be treated as carrying a child until the embryo has become implanted.

Amendments—SI 2007/1522; HFEA 2008, s 2, Sch 7, para 2.

'treatment ... for the purpose of assisting women to carry children'—Treatment for producing a child free from genetic defects or producing a child with stem cells matching a sick or dying sibling (tissue typing) constitutes treatment for the purpose of assisting a woman to carry children (*Quintavelle v Human Fertilisation and Embryology Authority* [2005] 2 FLR 349, HL).

2A Third party agreements

(1) For the purposes of this Act, a 'third party agreement' is an agreement in writing between a person who holds a licence and another person which is made in accordance with any licence conditions imposed by the Authority for the purpose of securing compliance with the requirements of Article 24 of the first Directive (relations between tissue establishments and third parties) and under which the other person –

- (a) procures, tests or processes gametes or embryos (or both), on behalf of the holder of the licence, or
- (b) supplies to the holder of the licence any goods or services (including distribution services) which may affect the quality or safety of gametes or embryos.

(2) In this Act –

'relevant third party premises', in relation to a licence, means any premises (other than premises to which the licence relates) –

- (a) on which a third party procures, tests, processes or distributes gametes or embryos on behalf of any person in connection with activities carried out by that person under a licence, or
- (b) from which a third party provides any goods or services which may affect the quality or safety of gametes or embryos to any person in connection with activities carried out by that person under a licence;

'third party' means a person with whom a person who holds a licence has a third party agreement.

(3) References in this Act to the persons to whom a third party agreement applies are to –

- (a) the third party,
- (b) any person designated in the third party agreement as a person to whom the agreement applies, and
- (c) any person acting under the direction of a third party or of any person so designated.

Amendments—Inserted by SI 2007/1522.

Activities governed by the Act

3 Prohibitions in connection with embryos

(1) No person shall bring about the creation of an embryo except in pursuance of a licence.

(1A) No person shall keep or use an embryo except –

- (a) in pursuance of a licence, or
- (b) in the case of –
  - (i) the keeping, without storage, of an embryo intended for human application, or
  - (ii) the processing, without storage, of such an embryo,

in pursuance of a third party agreement.

(1B) No person shall procure or distribute an embryo intended for human application except in pursuance of a licence or a third party agreement.

(2) No person shall place in a woman –

(a) an embryo other than a permitted embryo (as defined by section 3ZA), or
(b) any gametes other than permitted eggs or permitted sperm (as so defined).

(3) A licence cannot authorise –

(a) keeping or using an embryo after the appearance of the primitive streak,
(b) placing an embryo in any animal, or
(c) keeping or using an embryo in any circumstances in which regulations prohibit its keeping or use.
(d) *(repealed)*

(4) For the purposes of subsection (3)(a) above, the primitive streak is to be taken to have appeared in an embryo not later than the end of the period of 14 days beginning with the day on which the process of creating the embryo began, not counting any time during which the embryo is stored.

Amendments—SI 2007/1522; HFEA 2008, s 3.

'Prohibition'—Contravention of s 3(1) is an offence (s 41(2)(a)) and see *R v HFEA ex parte Blood* [1997] 2 FLR 742, CA.

Use of an embryo—See *Quintavelle v Human Fertilisation and Embryology Authority* [2005] 2 FLR 349, HL; *Evans v Amicus Healthcare and others; Hadley v Midland Fertility Services Ltd and others* [2004] 1 FLR 67, FD.

'placing in a woman a human embryo'—The Human Reproductive Cloning Act 2001 makes it an offence to place in a woman a human embryo which has been created otherwise than by fertilisation (which on conviction on indictment carries a maximum sentence of 10 years or a fine or both).

3ZA Permitted eggs, permitted sperm and permitted embryos

(1) This section has effect for the interpretation of section 3(2).

(2) A permitted egg is one –

(a) which has been produced by or extracted from the ovaries of a woman, and
(b) whose nuclear or mitochondrial DNA has not been altered.

(3) Permitted sperm are sperm –

(a) which have been produced by or extracted from the testes of a man, and
(b) whose nuclear or mitochondrial DNA has not been altered.

(4) An embryo is a permitted embryo if –

(a) it has been created by the fertilisation of a permitted egg by permitted sperm,
(b) no nuclear or mitochondrial DNA of any cell of the embryo has been altered, and
(c) no cell has been added to it other than by division of the embryo's own cells.

(5) Regulations may provide that –

(a) an egg can be a permitted egg, or
(b) an embryo can be a permitted embryo, even though the egg or embryo has had applied to it in prescribed circumstances a prescribed process designed to prevent the transmission of serious mitochondrial disease.

(6) In this section –

(a) 'woman' and 'man' include respectively a girl and a boy (from birth), and
(b) 'prescribed' means prescribed by regulations.

Amendments—Inserted by HFEA 2008, s 3(5).

Scope—The amendments prohibit the placing into any woman of any embryo other than a 'permitted embryo' as defined in s 3ZA to ensure that embryos created by the use of artificial or genetically modified gametes or embryos created by cloning cannot be placed into a woman.

3A Prohibition in connection with germ cells

(1) No person shall, for the purpose of providing fertility services for any woman, use female germ cells taken or derived from an embryo or a foetus or use embryos created by using such cells.

(2) In this section –

'female germ cells' means cells of the female germ line and includes such cells at any stage of maturity and accordingly includes eggs; and

'fertility services' means medical, surgical or obstetric services provided for the purpose of assisting women to carry children.

Amendments—Inserted by Criminal Justice and Public Order Act 1994, s 156(1),(2).

4 Prohibitions in connection with gametes

(1) No person shall –

(a) store any gametes, or

(b) in the course of providing treatment services for any woman, use –

(i) any sperm, other than partner-donated sperm which has been neither processed nor stored,

(ii) the woman's eggs after processing or storage, or

(iii) the eggs of any other woman,

(c) *(repealed)*

except in pursuance of a licence.

(1A) No person shall procure, test, process or distribute any gametes intended for human application except in pursuance of a licence or a third party agreement.

(2) A licence cannot authorise storing or using gametes in any circumstances in which regulations prohibit their storage or use.

(3) No person shall place sperm and eggs in a woman in any circumstances specified in regulations except in pursuance of a licence.

(4) Regulations made by virtue of subsection (3) above may provide that, in relation to licences only to place sperm and eggs in a woman in such circumstances, sections 12 to 22 of this Act shall have effect with such modifications as may be specified in the regulations.

(5) Activities regulated by this section or section 3 or 4A of this Act are referred to in this Act as 'activities governed by this Act'.

Amendments—SI 2007/1522; HFEA 2008, s 4(1).
Defined terms—'treatment services': Sch 2, para 1.

4A Prohibitions in connection with genetic material not of human origin

(1) No person shall place in a woman –

(a) a human admixed embryo,

(b) any other embryo that is not a human embryo, or

(c) any gametes other than human gametes.

(2) No person shall –

(a) mix human gametes with animal gametes,

(b) bring about the creation of a human admixed embryo, or

(c) keep or use a human admixed embryo, except in pursuance of a licence.

(3) A licence cannot authorise keeping or using a human admixed embryo after the earliest of the following –

(a) the appearance of the primitive streak, or

(b) the end of the period of 14 days beginning with the day on which the process of creating the human admixed embryo began, but not counting any time during which the human admixed embryo is stored.

(4) A licence cannot authorise placing a human admixed embryo in an animal.

(5) A licence cannot authorise keeping or using a human admixed embryo in any circumstances in which regulations prohibit its keeping or use.

(6) For the purposes of this Act a human admixed embryo is –

(a) an embryo created by replacing the nucleus of an animal egg or of an animal cell, or two animal pronuclei, with –
 (i) two human pronuclei,
 (ii) one nucleus of a human gamete or of any other human cell, or
 (iii) one human gamete or other human cell,

(b) any other embryo created by using –
 (i) human gametes and animal gametes, or
 (ii) one human pronucleus and one animal pronucleus,

(c) a human embryo that has been altered by the introduction of any sequence of nuclear or mitochondrial DNA of an animal into one or more cells of the embryo,

(d) a human embryo that has been altered by the introduction of one or more animal cells, or

(e) any embryo not falling within paragraphs (a) to (d) which contains both nuclear or mitochondrial DNA of a human and nuclear or mitochondrial DNA of an animal ('animal DNA') but in which the animal DNA is not predominant.

(7) In subsection (6) –

(a) references to animal cells are to cells of an animal or of an animal embryo, and

(b) references to human cells are to cells of a human or of a human embryo.

(8) For the purposes of this section an 'animal' is an animal other than man.

(9) In this section 'embryo' means a live embryo, including an egg that is in the process of fertilisation or is undergoing any other process capable of resulting in an embryo.

(10) In this section –

(a) references to eggs are to live eggs, including cells of the female germ line at any stage of maturity, but (except in subsection (9)) not including eggs that are in the process of fertilisation or are undergoing any other process capable of resulting in an embryo, and

(b) references to gametes are to eggs (as so defined) or to live sperm, including cells of the male germ line at any stage of maturity.

(11) If it appears to the Secretary of State necessary or desirable to do so in the light of developments in science or medicine, regulations may –

(a) amend (but not repeal) paragraphs (a) to (e) of subsection (6);

(b) provide that in this section 'embryo', 'eggs' or 'gametes' includes things specified in the regulations which would not otherwise fall within the definition.

(12) Regulations made by virtue of subsection (11)(a) may make any amendment of subsection (7) that appears to the Secretary of State to be appropriate in consequence of any amendment of subsection (6).

Amendments—Inserted by HFEA 2008, s 4(2).

Scope—Section 4A provides for certain types of embryos to be subject to regulations. It prohibits the placing into a woman of a human admixed embryo or any other embryo or gametes that are not human. It also prohibits the placing of an admixed embryo in an animal.

The Human Fertilisation and Embryology Authority, its functions and procedure

5 The Human Fertilisation and Embryology Authority

(1) There shall be a body corporate called the Human Fertilisation and Embryology Authority.

(2) The Authority shall consist of –

(a) a chairman and deputy chairman, and

(b) such number of other members as the Secretary of State appoints.

(3) Schedule 1 to this Act (which deals with the membership of the Authority, etc.) shall have effect.

****

Scope of licences

11 Licences for treatment, storage and research

(1) The Authority may grant the following and no other licences –

(a) licences under paragraph 1 of Schedule 2 to this Act authorising activities in the course of providing treatment services,

(aa) licences under paragraph 1A of that Schedule authorising activities in the course of providing non-medical fertility services,

(b) licences under that Schedule authorising the storage of gametes, embryos or human admixed embryos, and

(c) licences under paragraph 3 of that Schedule authorising activities for the purposes of a project of research.

(2) Paragraph 4 of that Schedule has effect in the case of all licences.

Amendments—SI 2007/1522; HFEA 2008, s 11(1).
'providing treatment services'—See s 2 and Sch 2, paras 1–1ZC.

Licence conditions

12 General conditions

(1) The following shall be conditions of every licence granted under this Act –

(a) except to the extent that the activities authorised by the licence fall within paragraph (aa), that those activities shall be carried on only on the premises to which the licence relates and under the supervision of the person responsible,

(aa) that any activities to which section 3(1A)(b) or (1B) or 4(1A) applies shall be carried on only on the premises to which the licence relates or on relevant third party premises,

(b) that any member or employee of the Authority, on production, if so required, of a document identifying the person as such, shall at all reasonable times be permitted to enter those premises and inspect them (which includes inspecting any equipment or records and observing any activity),

(c) except in relation to the use of gametes in the course of providing basic partner treatment services, that the provisions of Schedule 3 to this Act shall be complied with,

(d) that proper records shall be maintained in such form as the Authority may specify in directions,

(e) that no money or other benefit shall be given or received in respect of any supply of gametes, embryos or human admixed embryos unless authorised by directions,

(f) that, where gametes, embryos or human admixed embryos are supplied to a person to whom another licence applies, that person shall also be provided with such information as the Authority may specify in directions, and

(g) that the Authority shall be provided, in such form and at such intervals as it may specify in directions, with such copies of or extracts from the records, or such other information, as the directions may specify.

(2) Subsection (3) applies to –

(a) every licence under paragraph 1 or 1A of Schedule 2,

(b) every licence under paragraph 2 of that Schedule, so far as authorising the storage of gametes or embryos intended for human application, and

(c) every licence under paragraph 3 of that Schedule, so far as authorising activities in connection with the derivation from embryos of stem cells that are intended for human application.

(3) It shall be a condition of every licence to which this subsection applies that –

(a) such information as is necessary to facilitate the traceability of gametes and embryos, and

(b) any information relating to the quality or safety of gametes or embryos,

shall be recorded and provided to the Authority upon request.

Amendments—SI 2007/1522; HFEA 2008, s 12.

Schedule 3 compliance (s 12(1)(c))—Schedule 3 compliance deals with the procedure for obtaining consents to the use or storage of gametes, embryos or human admixed embryos in the course of providing treatment and is therefore 'an important aspect of the HFE Authority's approach to the regulation of licenced premises', especially where there is any indication or suggestion of posthumous use of the eggs, gametes etc and export overseas where it is essential to ensure that the person understands the implications of any decision made and of the impact of foreign law on the decision. See *R (M and MM) v Human Fertilisation and Embryology Authority* [2016] 1 FLR 1211 (Admin) where the application of the deceased's parents to export their daughter's eggs for fertilisation and implantation in the mother was refused at first instance but allowed on appeal: *R (M) v Human Fertilisation and Embryology Authority* [2017] 1 FLR 452, CA. The relevant provision of Sch 3 that applied in this case are those set out in paras 1–3, 5–6 and 8. Paragraph 1 provides that the consent and any notice varying or withdrawing consent must be in writing and signed by the person giving it. The consent to the use of any embryo must also specify one or more of the purposes set out in para 2(1) and a consent to the storage of any gametes etc must specify the period of storage if less than the statutory period and what is to be done with the gametes etc if the person who gave the consent dies or is unable by reason of lack of capacity to do so to vary the terms of the consent (para 2(2). Consent must be fully informed, ie before consent is obtained the person must be given a suitable opportunity to receive proper counselling about the implications and the person must be provided with relevant information (para 3). The gametes may only be used for the purposes for which effective consent is given by that person and must not be received for use other than for those purposes for which there is effective consent (para 5). It is also forbidden to use the gametes or human cells to bring about the creation of an embryo in vitro or for the gametes to be kept in storage unless there is effective consent (para 6(1) and 8(1). (See the Legislation and Forms section of Family Law Online for the full text of Sch 3.)

13 Conditions of licences for treatment

(1) The following shall be conditions of every licence under paragraph 1 of Schedule 2 to this Act.

(2) Such information shall be recorded as the Authority may specify in directions about the following –

(a) the persons for whom services are provided in pursuance of the licence,
(b) the services provided for them,
(c) the persons whose gametes are kept or used for the purposes of services provided in pursuance of the licence or whose gametes have been used in bringing about the creation of embryos so kept or used,
(d) any child appearing to the person responsible to have been born as a result of treatment in pursuance of the licence,
(e) any mixing of egg and sperm and any taking of an embryo from a woman or other acquisition of an embryo, and
(f) such other matters as the Authority may specify in directions.

(3) The records maintained in pursuance of the licence shall include any information recorded in pursuance of subsection (2) above and any consent of a person whose consent is required under Schedule 3 to this Act.

(4) No information shall be removed from any records maintained in pursuance of the licence before the expiry of such period as may be specified in directions for records of the class in question.

(5) A woman shall not be provided with treatment services unless account has been taken of the welfare of any child who may be born as a result of the treatment (including the need of that child for supportive parenting), and of any other child who may be affected by the birth.

(6) A woman shall not be provided with treatment services of a kind specified in Part 1 of Schedule 3ZA unless she and any man or woman who is to be treated together with her have been given a suitable opportunity to receive proper counselling about the implications of her being provided with treatment services of that kind, and have been provided with such relevant information as is proper.

(6A) A woman shall not be provided with treatment services after the happening of any event falling within any paragraph of Part 2 of Schedule 3ZA unless (before or after the event) she and the intended second parent have been given a suitable opportunity to receive proper counselling

PART II

about the implications of the woman being provided with treatment services after the happening of that event, and have been provided with such relevant information as is proper.

(6B) The reference in subsection (6A) to the intended second parent is a reference to –

(a) any man as respects whom the agreed fatherhood conditions in section 37 of the Human Fertilisation and Embryology Act 2008 ('the 2008 Act') are for the time being satisfied in relation to treatment provided to the woman mentioned in subsection (6A), and
(b) any woman as respects whom the agreed female parenthood conditions in section 44 of the 2008 Act are for the time being satisfied in relation to treatment provided to the woman mentioned in subsection (6A).

(6C) In the case of treatment services falling within paragraph 1 of Schedule 3ZA (use of gametes of a person not receiving those services) or paragraph 3 of that Schedule (use of embryo taken from a woman not receiving those services), the information provided by virtue of subsection (6) or (6A) must include such information as is proper about –

(a) the importance of informing any resulting child at an early age that the child results from the gametes of a person who is not a parent of the child, and
(b) suitable methods of informing such a child of that fact.

(6D) Where the person responsible receives from a person ('X') notice under section 37(1)(c) or 44(1)(c) of the 2008 Act of X's withdrawal of consent to X being treated as the parent of any child resulting from the provision of treatment services to a woman ('W'), the person responsible –

(a) must notify W in writing of the receipt of the notice from X, and
(b) no person to whom the licence applies may place an embryo or sperm and eggs in W, or artificially inseminate W, until W has been so notified.

(6E) Where the person responsible receives from a woman ('W') who has previously given notice under section 37(1)(b) or 44(1)(b) of the 2008 Act that she consents to another person ('X') being treated as a parent of any child resulting from the provision of treatment services to W –

(a) notice under section 37(1)(c) or 44(1)(c) of the 2008 Act of the withdrawal of W's consent, or
(b) a notice under section 37(1)(b) or 44(1)(b) of the 2008 Act in respect of a person other than X,

the person responsible must take reasonable steps to notify X in writing of the receipt of the notice mentioned in paragraph (a) or (b).

(7) Suitable procedures shall be maintained –

(a) for determining the persons providing gametes or from whom embryos are taken for use in pursuance of the licence, and
(b) for the purpose of securing that consideration is given to the use of practices not requiring the authority of a licence as well as those requiring such authority.

(8) Subsections (9) and (10) apply in determining any of the following –

(a) the persons who are to provide gametes for use in pursuance of the licence in a case where consent is required under paragraph 5 of Schedule 3 for the use in question;
(b) the woman from whom an embryo is to be taken for use in pursuance of the licence, in a case where her consent is required under paragraph 7 of Schedule 3 for the use of the embryo;
(c) which of two or more embryos to place in a woman.

(9) Persons or embryos that are known to have a gene, chromosome or mitochondrion abnormality involving a significant risk that a person with the abnormality will have or develop –

(a) a serious physical or mental disability,
(b) a serious illness, or
(c) any other serious medical condition, must not be preferred to those that are not known to have such an abnormality.

(10) Embryos that are known to be of a particular sex and to carry a particular risk, compared with embryos of that sex in general, that any resulting child will have or develop –

- (a) a gender-related serious physical or mental disability,
- (b) a gender-related serious illness, or
- (c) any other gender-related serious medical condition, must not be preferred to those that are not known to carry such a risk.

(11) For the purposes of subsection (10), a physical or mental disability, illness or other medical condition is gender-related if –

- (a) it affects only one sex, or
- (b) it affects one sex significantly more than the other.

(12) No embryo appropriated for the purpose mentioned in paragraph 1(1)(ca) of Schedule 2 (training in embryological techniques) shall be kept or used for the provision of treatment services.

(13) The person responsible shall comply with any requirement imposed on that person by section 31ZD.

Amendments—SI 2007/1522; HFEA 2008, ss 14(2)–(4).

'unless account has been taken of the welfare of any child' (s 13(5))—Under both HFEA 1990 and HFEA 2008, the resulting child's welfare must be discussed before any treatment is provided whether or not the treatment is given before or after the death of the donor. Welfare includes the need of that child for supportive parenting rather than a father. See Code of Practice (8th Edn, 2009), laid down by the Human Fertilisation and Embryology Authority, which sets out every aspect of the 'welfare checklist' with which the licence holders must comply (*Evans v Amicus Healthcare and others; Hadley v Midland Fertility Services Ltd and others* [2004] 1 FLR 67, FD; *Centre for Reproductive Medicine v U* [2002] 1 FLR 927, FD; *Leeds Teaching Hospitals NHS Trust v A* [2003] 1 FLR 412, QBD). See also DHSS Circular (LAC(85)12), which draws attention to the need to be aware of possible risks to the child in such circumstances and the duty to investigate. For the impact of a failure to provide all the information necessary and the conditions and the period of storage and, where appropriate, an extension of the period of 10 years under s 14, see *Warren v CARE and the HFEA* [2014] 2 FLR 1284, FD. See also under s 14, below.

'opportunity to receive proper counselling' and 'provided with such relevant information as is proper'—Relevant information includes the strict time limits relating to storage and, where appropriate, an extension of the 10-year period. It is a condition of the granting of a treatment licence that a woman shall not be treated unless she and any partner who are being treated together have been given suitable opportunity to receive proper counselling and have been provided with relevant information. For the impact of the failure to provide all the relevant information and an opportunity to receive counselling, see *Warren v CARE and the HFEA* (above).

13A Conditions of licences for non-medical fertility services

(1) The following shall be conditions of every licence under paragraph 1A of Schedule 2.

(2) The requirements of section 13(2) to (4) and (7) shall be complied with.

(3) A woman shall not be provided with any non-medical fertility services involving the use of sperm other than partner-donated sperm unless the woman being provided with the services has been given a suitable opportunity to receive proper counselling about the implications of taking the proposed steps, and has been provided with such relevant information as is proper.

(4) *(repealed)*

Amendments—Inserted by SI 2007/1522. Amended by HFEA 2008, Sch 7, para 5.

14 Conditions of storage licences

(1) The following shall be conditions of every licence authorising the storage of gametes, embryos or human admixed embryos –

- (a) that gametes of a person shall be placed in storage only if –
  - (i) received from that person,
  - (ii) acquired in circumstances in which by virtue of paragraph 9 or 10 of Schedule 3 that person's consent to the storage is not required, or
  - (iii) acquired from a person to whom a licence or third party agreement applies,
- (aa) that an embryo taken from a woman shall be placed in storage only if –
  - (i) received from that woman, or

(ii) acquired from a person to whom a licence or third party agreement applies,

(ab) that an embryo the creation of which has been brought about in vitro otherwise than in pursuance of that licence shall be placed in storage only if acquired from a person to whom a licence or third party agreement applies,

(ac) that a human admixed embryo the creation of which has been brought about in vitro otherwise than in pursuance of that licence shall be placed in storage only if acquired from a person to whom a licence under paragraph 2 or 3 of Schedule 2 applies,

(b) that gametes or embryos which are or have been stored shall not be supplied to a person otherwise than in the course of providing treatment services unless that person is a person to whom a licence applies,

(ba) that human admixed embryos shall not be supplied to a person unless that person is a person to whom a licence applies,

(c) that no gametes, embryos or human admixed embryos shall be kept in storage for longer than the statutory storage period and, if stored at the end of the period, shall be allowed to perish, and

(d) that such information as the Authority may specify in directions as to the persons whose consent is required under Schedule 3 to this Act, the terms of their consent and the circumstances of the storage and as to such other matters as the Authority may specify in directions shall be included in the records maintained in pursuance of the licence.

(2) No information shall be removed from any records maintained in pursuance of such a licence before the expiry of such period as may be specified in directions for records of the class in question.

(3) The statutory storage period in respect of gametes is such period not exceeding ten years as the licence may specify.

(4) The statutory storage period in respect of embryos is such period not exceeding ten years as the licence may specify.

(4A) The statutory storage period in respect of human admixed embryos is such period not exceeding ten years as the licence may specify.

(5) Regulations may provide that subsection (3), (4) or (4A) above shall have effect as if for ten years there were substituted –

(a) such shorter period, or

(b) in such circumstances as may be specified in the regulations, such longer period,

as may be specified in the regulations.

Amendments—SI 2007/1522; HFEA 2008, ss 15(2)–(5).

Regulations—The Human Fertilisation and Embryology (Statutory Storage Period for Embryos and Gametes) Regulations 2009, which came into force on 1 October 2009, make provision for how the 'relevant period' is to be calculated. In relation to the storage in excess of 10 years, the regulations provide for the extension of the 10-year period where the person to be treated is prematurely infertile or is likely to become prematurely infertile or the gamete provider is prematurely infertile or is likely to become prematurely infertile. In either case, the person who provided the gamete in question must have consented in writing to the gamete being stored for a period in excess of 10 years for the provision of treatment services and on any day within the relevant period a registered medical practitioner must have given a written opinion that the person to be treated or the gamete provider is prematurely infertile or is likely to become prematurely infertile. However, despite the fact that the regulations use the present tense in relation to the provision of the medical certificate, Hogg J in *Warren v CARE and the HFEA* [2014] 2 FLR 1284, FD interpreted the words to include the words 'was, or may have been likely to become prematurely infertile on the basis that the statutory provisions should be interpreted in a purposive way and if possible in a way which is compatible with the parties' right under Art 8, particularly where the clinic had failed to provide all the relevant information and counselling to the parties concerned. Neither the State, through the HFE Authority nor the court should interfere with those rights' at [139] and [142]. The maximum period for storage is 55 years.

14A Conditions of licences: human application

(1) This section applies to –

(a) every licence under paragraph 1 or 1A of Schedule 2,

(b) every licence under paragraph 2 of that Schedule, so far as authorising storage of gametes or embryos intended for human application, and

(c) every licence under paragraph 3 of that Schedule, so far as authorising activities in connection with the derivation from embryos of stem cells that are intended for human application.

(2) A licence to which this section applies may not authorise the storage, procurement, testing, processing or distribution of gametes or embryos unless it contains the conditions required by Schedule 3A.

(3) In relation to any gametes or embryos imported into the United Kingdom from an EEA state other than the United Kingdom or from Gibraltar, compliance with the requirements of the laws or other measures adopted in the relevant state or territory for the purpose of implementing the first, second and third Directives shall be taken to be compliance with the conditions required by Schedule 3A.

(4) Subsection (3) shall not apply to any licence conditions imposed by the Authority which amount to more stringent protective measures for the purposes of Article 4(2) of the first Directive.

Amendments—Inserted by SI 2007/1522. Amended by HFEA 2008, Sch 7, para 6.

****

34 Disclosure in interests of justice

(1) Where in any proceedings before a court the question whether a person is or is not the parent of a child by virtue of sections 27 to 29 of this Act or sections 33 to 47 of the Human Fertilisation and Embryology Act 2008 falls to be determined, the court may on the application of any party to the proceedings make an order requiring the Authority –

(a) to disclose whether or not any information relevant to that question is contained in the register kept in pursuance of section 31 of this Act, and

(b) if it is, to disclose so much of it as is specified in the order,

but such an order may not require the Authority to disclose any information falling within section 31(2)(c) to (e) of this Act.

(2) The court must not make an order under subsection (1) above unless it is satisfied that the interests of justice require it to do so, taking into account –

(a) any representations made by any individual who may be affected by the disclosure, and

(b) the welfare of the child, if under 18 years old, and of any other person under that age who may be affected by the disclosure.

(3) If the proceedings before the court are civil proceedings, it –

(a) may direct that the whole or any part of the proceedings on the application for an order under subsection (2) above shall be heard in camera, and

(b) if it makes such an order, may then or later direct that the whole or any part of any later stage of the proceedings shall be heard in camera.

(4) An application for a direction under subsection (3) above shall be heard in camera unless the court otherwise directs.

Amendments—HFEA 2008, Sch 6, para 34, Sch 7, para 12.

Defined terms—'the Authority': s 2(1).

Sections 33–47—These sections contain the 'fatherhood conditions' and 'female parenthood conditions' that must be satisfied when a woman carries a child as a result of placing in her an embryo or sperm and eggs, or her artificial insemination, to determine who is to be treated as the other parent of the child.

'register' (s 34(1)(a))—A register is required to be maintained by the Authority under s 31 containing information relating to the provision of treatment services for any identifiable individual or the keeping or use of any gametes of any identifiable individual or of an embryo taken from any identifiable woman or information showing that any identifiable individual was, or may have been, born as a consequence of treatment services.

'information falling within section 31(2)(b)' (s 34(1))—This is information obtained by any member or employee of the Authority on terms or in circumstances requiring it to be held in confidence.

PART II

35 Disclosure in interests of justice: congenital disabilities etc

(1) Where for the purpose of instituting proceedings under section 1 of the Congenital Disabilities (Civil Liability) Act 1976 (civil liability to child born disabled) it is necessary to identify a person who would or might be the parent of a child but for the relevant statutory provisions, the court may, on the application of the child, make an order requiring the Authority to disclose any information contained in the register kept in pursuance of section 31 of this Act identifying that person.

(2) …

(2A) In subsections (1) and (2) 'the relevant statutory provisions' means –

- (a) sections 27 to 29 of this Act, and
- (b) sections 33 to 47 of the Human Fertilisation and Embryology Act 2008.

(3) Subsections (2) to (4) of section 34 of this Act apply for the purposes of this section as they apply for the purposes of that.

(4) …

Amendments—HFEA 2008, Sch 6, para 35.

35A Mitochondrial donation

(1) Regulations may provide for any of the relevant provisions to have effect subject to specified modifications in relation to cases where –

- (a) an egg which is a permitted egg for the purposes of section 3(2) by virtue of regulations made under section 3ZA(5), or
- (b) an embryo which is a permitted embryo for those purposes by virtue of such regulations, has been created from material provided by two women.

(2) In this section 'the relevant provisions' means –

- (a) the following provisions of this Act –
  - (i) section 13(6C) (information whose provision to prospective parents is required by licence condition),
  - (ii) section 31 (register of information),
  - (iii) sections 31ZA to 31ZE (provision of information), and
  - (iv) Schedule 3 (consents to use or storage of gametes, embryos or human admixed embryos etc.), and
- (b) section 54 of the Human Fertilisation and Embryology Act 2008 (parental orders).

Amendments—Inserted by HFEA 2008, s 26.

35B Fees

(1) The Authority may charge a fee in respect of any of the following –

- (a) an application for a licence,
- (b) the grant or renewal of a licence,
- (c) an application for the revocation or variation of a licence, or
- (d) the exercise by the Authority of any other function conferred on it by or under this Act or by or under any other enactment –
  - (i) in relation to a licence,
  - (ii) in relation to premises which are or have been premises to which a licence relates,
  - (iii) in relation to premises which are or have been relevant third party premises in relation to a licence, or
  - (iv) in relation to premises which, if an application is granted, will be premises to which a licence relates or relevant third party premises.

(2) The amount of any fee charged by virtue of subsection (1) is to be fixed in accordance with a scheme made by the Authority with the approval of the Secretary of State and the Treasury.

(3) In fixing the amount of any fee to be charged by virtue of that subsection, the Authority may have regard to the costs incurred by it –

(a) in exercising the functions conferred on it by or under this Act (apart from sections 31ZA to 31ZG and 33D), and

(b) in exercising any other function conferred on it by or under any other enactment.

(4) The Authority may also charge such fee as it thinks fit in respect of any of the following –

(a) the giving of notice under section 31ZA(1) or 31ZB(1), or

(b) the provision of information under section 31ZA, 31ZB or 31ZE.

(5) In fixing the amount of any fee to be charged by virtue of subsection (4) the Authority may have regard to the costs incurred by it in exercising the function to which the fee relates.

(6) When exercising its power to charge fees under section 8(2), 31ZF(2)(d) or this section, the Authority may fix different fees for different circumstances.

Amendments—Inserted by HFEA 2008, s 27.

****

SCHEDULE 2
ACTIVITIES FOR WHICH LICENCES MAY BE GRANTED

1 Licences for treatment

(1) A licence under this paragraph may authorise any of the following in the course of providing treatment services –

(a) bringing about the creation of embryos in vitro,

(b) procuring, keeping, testing, processing or distributing embryos,

(c) procuring, testing, processing, distributing or using gametes,

(ca) using embryos for the purpose of training persons in embryo biopsy, embryo storage or other embryological techniques,

(d) other practices designed to secure that embryos are in a suitable condition to be placed in a woman,

(e) placing any permitted embryo in a woman,

(f) mixing sperm with the egg of a hamster, or other animal specified in directions, for the purpose of testing the fertility or normality of the sperm, but only where anything which forms is destroyed when the test is complete and, in any event, not later than the two cell stage, and

(g) such other practices, apart from practices falling within section 4A(2), as may be specified in, or determined in accordance with, regulations.

(2) Subject to the provisions of this Act, a licence under this paragraph may be granted subject to such conditions as may be specified in the licence and may authorise the performance of any of the activities referred to in sub-paragraph (1) above in such manner as may be so specified.

(3) A licence under this paragraph cannot authorise any activity unless it appears to the Authority to be necessary or desirable for the purpose of providing treatment services.

(4) A licence under this paragraph cannot authorise altering the nuclear or mitochondrial DNA of a cell while it forms part of an embryo, except for the purpose of creating something that will by virtue of regulations under section 3ZA(5) be a permitted embryo.

(4A) A licence under this paragraph cannot authorise the use of embryos for the purpose mentioned in sub-paragraph (1)(ca) unless the Authority is satisfied that the proposed use of embryos is necessary for that purpose.

(5) A licence under this paragraph shall be granted for such period not exceeding five years as may be specified in the licence.

(6) In this paragraph, references to a permitted embryo are to be read in accordance with section 3ZA.

Amendments—HFEA 2008, Sch 2, para 2.

'treatment services'—See annotation under s 2 above.

'designed to secure that embryos are in a suitable condition to be placed in a woman'—The meaning of 'suitable' has to be determined having regard to its context. When the object of the treatment is to enable a woman to bear a child with a tissue type that will allow stem cells to be provided to a sick sibling, an embryo would only be suitable for the purpose of being placed within her if it will lead to the birth of a child with the tissue type in question. The HFEA therefore has the authority to grant a treatment licence for the purpose of tissue typing, subject to such conditions as it considers appropriate. The suitability of the embryo to be placed in a particular woman may be considered in the context of objectively established aims and perceived needs relating to the child-to-be-born's parents and to an affected sibling (*R (Quintavelle) v Human Fertilisation and Embryology Authority (Secretary of State for Health Intervening)* [2003] 2 FLR 335, CA).

1ZA Embryo testing

(1) A licence under paragraph 1 cannot authorise the testing of an embryo, except for one or more of the following purposes –

- (a) establishing whether the embryo has a gene, chromosome or mitochondrion abnormality that may affect its capacity to result in a live birth,
- (b) in a case where there is a particular risk that the embryo may have any gene, chromosome or mitochondrion abnormality, establishing whether it has that abnormality or any other gene, chromosome or mitochondrion abnormality,
- (c) in a case where there is a particular risk that any resulting child will have or develop –
  - (i) a gender-related serious physical or mental disability,
  - (ii) a gender-related serious illness, or
  - (iii) any other gender-related serious medical condition, establishing the sex of the embryo,
- (d) in a case where a person ('the sibling') who is the child of the persons whose gametes are used to bring about the creation of the embryo (or of either of those persons) suffers from a serious medical condition which could be treated by umbilical cord blood stem cells, bone marrow or other tissue of any resulting child, establishing whether the tissue of any resulting child would be compatible with that of the sibling, and
- (e) in a case where uncertainty has arisen as to whether the embryo is one of those whose creation was brought about by using the gametes of particular persons, establishing whether it is.

(2) A licence under paragraph 1 cannot authorise the testing of embryos for the purpose mentioned in sub-paragraph (1)(b) unless the Authority is satisfied –

- (a) in relation to the abnormality of which there is a particular risk, and
- (b) in relation to any other abnormality for which testing is to be authorised under sub-paragraph (1)(b), that there is a significant risk that a person with the abnormality will have or develop a serious physical or mental disability, a serious illness or any other serious medical condition.

(3) For the purposes of sub-paragraph (1)(c), a physical or mental disability, illness or other medical condition is gender-related if the Authority is satisfied that –

- (a) it affects only one sex, or
- (b) it affects one sex significantly more than the other.

(4) In sub-paragraph (1)(d) the reference to 'other tissue' of the resulting child does not include a reference to any whole organ of the child.

Amendments—Inserted by HFEA 2008, Sch 2, para 3.

1ZB Sex selection

(1) A licence under paragraph 1 cannot authorise any practice designed to secure that any resulting child will be of one sex rather than the other.

(2) Sub-paragraph (1) does not prevent the authorisation of any testing of embryos that is capable of being authorised under paragraph 1ZA.

(3) Sub-paragraph (1) does not prevent the authorisation of any other practices designed to secure that any resulting child will be of one sex rather than the other in a case where there is a particular risk that a woman will give birth to a child who will have or develop –

(a) a gender-related serious physical or mental disability,
(b) a gender-related serious illness, or
(c) any other gender-related serious medical condition.

(4) For the purposes of sub-paragraph (3), a physical or mental disability, illness or other medical condition is gender-related if the Authority is satisfied that –

(a) it affects only one sex, or
(b) it affects one sex significantly more than the other.

Amendments—Inserted by HFEA 2008, Sch 2, para 3.

1ZC Power to amend paragraphs 1ZA and 1ZB

(1) Regulations may make any amendment of paragraph 1ZA (embryo testing).

(2) Regulations under this paragraph which amend paragraph 1ZA may make any amendment of sub-paragraphs (2) to (4) of paragraph 1ZB (sex selection) which appears to the Secretary of State to be necessary or expedient in consequence of the amendment of paragraph 1ZA.

(3) Regulations under this paragraph may not enable the authorisation of –

(a) the testing of embryos for the purpose of establishing their sex, or
(b) other practices falling within paragraph 1ZB(1), except on grounds relating to the health of any resulting child.

(4) For the purposes of this paragraph, 'amend' includes add to and repeal, and references to 'amendment' are to be read accordingly.

Amendments—Inserted by HFEA 2008, Sch 2, para 3.

1A Licences for non-medical fertility services

(1) A licence under this paragraph may authorise any of the following in the course of providing non-medical fertility services –

(a) procuring sperm, and
(b) distributing sperm.

(1A) A licence under this paragraph cannot authorise the procurement or distribution of sperm to which there has been applied any process designed to secure that any resulting child will be of one sex rather than the other.

(2) Subject to the provisions of this Act, a licence under this paragraph may be granted subject to such conditions as may be specified in the licence and may authorise the performance of any of the activities referred to in sub-paragraph (1) above in such manner as may be so specified.

(3) A licence under this paragraph shall be granted for such period not exceeding five years as may be specified in the licence.

Amendments—SI 2007/1522; HFEA 2008, Sch 2, para 4.

****

SCHEDULE 3A
SUPPLEMENTARY LICENCE CONDITIONS: HUMAN APPLICATION

1 Traceability and coding system

Licence conditions shall require that all persons to whom a licence applies adopt such systems as the Authority considers appropriate to secure –

(a) in relation to traceability, compliance with the requirements of Article 8 (traceability) of the first Directive and Article 9 (traceability) of the third Directive, and
(b) in relation to the coding of information, compliance with the requirements of Article 25 (coding of information) of the first Directive and Article 10 (European coding system) of the third Directive.

2 Licence conditions imposed in accordance with paragraph 1 may specify the coding system which must be applied in relation to gametes and embryos intended for human application.

3 Serious adverse events and serious adverse reactions

Licence conditions shall require such –

(a) systems to report, investigate, register and transmit information about serious adverse events and serious adverse reactions, and
(b) accurate, rapid and verifiable procedures for recalling from distribution any product which may be related to a serious adverse event or serious adverse reaction,

to be in place as are necessary to secure compliance with the requirements of Article 11 (notification of serious adverse events and reactions) of the first Directive and Article 5 (notification of serious adverse reactions) and Article 6 (notification of serious adverse events) of the third Directive.

4 Third party agreements and termination of licensed activities

For the purpose of securing compliance with the requirements of Articles 21(5) (tissue and cell storage conditions) and 24 (relations between tissue establishments and third parties) of the first Directive, licence conditions shall specify the requirements that must be met in relation to the termination of storage activities authorised by the licence and in relation to third party agreements.

5 Requirements for procurement of gametes and embryos

Licence conditions shall require all persons to whom a licence applies who are authorised to procure gametes or embryos, or both, to comply with the requirements (including as to staff training, written agreements with staff, standard operating procedures, and appropriate facilities and equipment) laid down in Article 2 (requirements for the procurement of human tissues and cells) of the second Directive.

6 Selection criteria and laboratory tests required for donors of reproductive cells

In relation to partner-donated sperm which is not intended to be used without processing or storage, licence conditions shall require compliance with the selection criteria for donors and the requirements for laboratory tests laid down in section 2 (partner donation (not direct use)) of Annex III (selection criteria and laboratory tests required for donors of reproductive cells) to the second Directive.

7 In relation to donations of gametes or embryos other than partner-donated sperm or partner-created embryos, licence conditions shall require compliance with the selection criteria for donors and the requirements for laboratory tests laid down in section 3 (donations other than by partners) of Annex III to the second Directive.

8 Licence conditions shall require that the laboratory tests required by sections 2 and 3 of Annex III to the second Directive to be carried out for the purpose of selecting gametes or embryos for donation, meet the requirements of section 4 (general requirements to be met for determining biological markers) of Annex III to the second Directive.

9 Donation and procurement procedures and reception at the tissue establishment

In relation to –

(a) donation and procurement procedures, and
(b) the reception of gametes and embryos at the premises to which a licence relates or at relevant third party premises,

licence conditions shall require compliance with the requirements of Article 15(3) (selection, evaluation and procurement) and Article 19(4) to (6) (tissue and cell reception) of the first Directive and with the requirements laid down in the provisions of the second Directive listed in the right-hand column, the subject-matter of which are described in the left-hand column in respect of those provisions.

Amendments—Inserted by SI 2007/1522.

****

Human Fertilisation and Embryology Act 2008

ARRANGEMENT OF SECTIONS

PART II
PARENTHOOD IN CASES INVOLVING ASSISTED REPRODUCTION

Section		Page
	Meaning of 'mother'	
33	Meaning of 'mother'	978
	Application of sections 35 to 47	
34	Application of sections 35 to 47	978
	Meaning of 'father'	
35	Woman married to a man at time of treatment	978
36	Treatment provided to woman where agreed fatherhood conditions apply	979
37	The agreed fatherhood conditions	979
38	Further provision relating to sections 35 and 36	980
39	Use of sperm, or transfer of embryo, after death of man providing sperm	980
40	Embryo transferred after death of husband etc. who did not provide sperm	981
41	Persons not to be treated as father	982
	Cases in which woman to be other parent	
42	Woman in civil partnership or marriage to a woman at time of treatment	982
43	Treatment provided to woman who agrees that second woman to be parent	982
44	The agreed female parenthood conditions	983
45	Further provision relating to sections 42 and 43	983
46	Embryo transferred after death of civil partner or wife or intended female parent	984
47	Woman not to be other parent merely because of egg donation	985
	Effect of sections 33 to 47	
48	Effect of sections 33 to 47	985
	References to parties to marriage or civil partnership	
49	Meaning of references to parties to a marriage	986
50	Meaning of references to parties to a civil partnership	986
	Further provision about registration by virtue of section 39, 40 or 46	
51	Meaning of 'relevant register of births'	986
52	Late election by mother with consent of Registrar General	987
	Interpretation of references to father etc. where woman is other parent	
53	Interpretation of references to father etc	987
	Parental orders	
54	Parental orders	988

****

PART II
PARENTHOOD IN CASES INVOLVING ASSISTED REPRODUCTION

Meaning of 'mother'

33 Meaning of 'mother'

(1) The woman who is carrying or has carried a child as a result of the placing in her of an embryo or of sperm and eggs, and no other woman, is to be treated as the mother of the child.

(2) Subsection (1) does not apply to any child to the extent that the child is treated by virtue of adoption as not being the woman's child.

(3) Subsection (1) applies whether the woman was in the United Kingdom or elsewhere at the time of the placing in her of the embryo or the sperm and eggs.

Rights/status of the biological mother—A shared residence care arrangement order may in appropriate circumstances be a means of conferring parental responsibility to the genetic/biological mother in relation to children born as a result of egg donation between parties in a same-sex relationship where there has been a close relationship between the genetic mother and the children and the relationship between the couple breaks down and the legal mother subsequently enters into a civil partnership or a same-sex marriage with another woman: *Re G (Shared Residence Order: Biological Mother of Donor Egg)* [2014] 2 FLR 897, CA.

Application of sections 35 to 47

34 Application of sections 35 to 47

(1) Sections 35 to 47 apply, in the case of a child who is being or has been carried by a woman (referred to in those sections as 'W') as a result of the placing in her of an embryo or of sperm and eggs or her artificial insemination, to determine who is to be treated as the other parent of the child.

(2) Subsection (1) has effect subject to the provisions of sections 39, 40 and 46 limiting the purposes for which a person is treated as the child's other parent by virtue of those sections.

Meaning of 'father'

35 Woman married to a man at time of treatment

(1) If –

(a) at the time of the placing in her of the embryo or of the sperm and eggs or of her artificial insemination, W was a party to a marriage with a man, and

(b) the creation of the embryo carried by her was not brought about with the sperm of the other party to the marriage,

then, subject to section 38(2) to (4), the other party to the marriage is to be treated as the father of the child unless it is shown that he did not consent to the placing in her of the embryo or the sperm and eggs or to her artificial insemination (as the case may be).

(2) This section applies whether W was in the United Kingdom or elsewhere at the time mentioned in subsection (1)(a).

Amendments—Marriage (Same Sex Couples) Act 2013, s 17, Sch 7, para 38.

Meaning of 'father'—The definition is made subject to the common law presumption that the child is the legitimate child of the married couple, so that the husband will be treated as the father of the child even where the woman becomes pregnant with a child conceived through assisted reproduction and the fatherhood conditions set out in s 37 below have been satisfied in relation to another man. The distinction between whether the husband consented to artificial insemination (AI) of his wife or merely acquiesced will depend on the circumstances. The husband's failure to vocalise his objection or to have taken active steps to prevent the AI can only amount to consent if there were the outward signs of an inward consent. Where the husband did not consent to AI, the child will have no father but where the child was conceived as a result of sexual intercourse between the wife and the donor, the donor would not only be the biological father of the child but also the child's legal parent: *M v F and H (Legal Paternity)* [2014] 1 FLR 352, FD. Section 35 cannot be interpreted so that it does not apply to unlicensed AI. The issue of the surrogate mother's status at the relevant time is important to determine whether the father was as a matter of English law the child's father and thus it is essential that the conditions set out in s 35 are carefully considered. In *Re D (Surrogacy)* [2014] EWHC 2121 (Fam), the evidence of the surrogate mother's status was incomplete and she could not be traced. There was also no written agreement between the clinic and the parent until the birth. The evidence from the director of the clinic was unsatisfactory. The difficulties were overcome by warding the child and the court making a shared residence order.

36 Treatment provided to woman where agreed fatherhood conditions apply

If no man is treated by virtue of section 35 as the father of the child and no woman is treated by virtue of section 42 as a parent of the child but –

(a) the embryo or the sperm and eggs were placed in W, or W was artificially inseminated, in the course of treatment services provided in the United Kingdom by a person to whom a licence applies,

(b) at the time when the embryo or the sperm and eggs were placed in W, or W was artificially inseminated, the agreed fatherhood conditions (as set out in section 37) were satisfied in relation to a man, in relation to treatment provided to W under the licence,

(c) the man remained alive at that time, and

(d) the creation of the embryo carried by W was not brought about with the man's sperm,

then, subject to section 38(2) to (4), the man is to be treated as the father of the child.

'fatherhood conditions'—Section 36 must be read together with s 37 to identify all the criteria that need to be satisfied.

37 The agreed fatherhood conditions

(1) The agreed fatherhood conditions referred to in section 36(b) are met in relation to a man ('M') in relation to treatment provided to W under a licence if, but only if, –

(a) M has given the person responsible a notice stating that he consents to being treated as the father of any child resulting from treatment provided to W under the licence,

(b) W has given the person responsible a notice stating that she consents to M being so treated,

(c) neither M nor W has, since giving notice under paragraph (a) or (b), given the person responsible notice of the withdrawal of M's or W's consent to M being so treated,

(d) W has not, since the giving of the notice under paragraph (b), given the person responsible –

 (i) a further notice under that paragraph stating that she consents to another man being treated as the father of any resulting child, or

 (ii) a notice under section 44(1)(b) stating that she consents to a woman being treated as a parent of any resulting child, and

(e) W and M are not within prohibited degrees of relationship in relation to each other.

(2) A notice under subsection (1)(a), (b) or (c) must be in writing and must be signed by the person giving it.

(3) A notice under subsection (1)(a), (b) or (c) by a person ('S') who is unable to sign because of illness, injury or physical disability is to be taken to comply with the requirement of subsection (2) as to signature if it is signed at the direction of S, in the presence of S and in the presence of at least one witness who attests the signature.

Scope—The conditions set out and the requirements relating to consent are to ensure that both parties carefully consider and record in approved forms their intentions regarding fatherhood of the child and its implications, as well as their consent. Once the gametes or embryo are placed in the woman, neither party can withdraw consent in relation to that cycle of treatment.

Consent of M being treated as the father—Where the evidence indicates that the PP form in which the consent of the man to the treatment provided to W was completed but could not be found, or there is later found to be a clerical error in the completion of the consent forms such as incorrect forms being used or forms incorrectly completed or not signed, the court can correct a mistake that is obvious on the face of the document, if necessary applying the doctrine of rectification to satisfy the requirements of the Act and grant a declaration of parentage pursuant to FLA 1986, s 55A. To do otherwise would be inconsistent with the underlying intention to provide certainty simply because the clinic mislaid the document. 'Failure by the clinic to maintain records did not amount to a breach of the licence so as to invalidate it, so that the treatment was "provided under a licence" as required by s 37(1)': *X and Y v St Bartholomew's Hospital Centre for Reproductive Medicine)* [2016] 1 FLR 544, FD. It may be desirable in such cases to obtain a copy of the form when consent is given to treatment. Parole evidence may be adduced to prove that the consent forms required to be completed by the HFE Authority (i e Form WP and/or Form PP) had in fact been executed in compliance with HFEA 2008, Pt 2 before treatment was provided: *Re Human Fertilisation and Embryology Act 2008 (Cases A, B, C, D, E, F, G and H)* [2017] 1 FLR 366, FD, in which the statutory framework, legal principles and reasoning are set out in detail. This decision has been applied in a series of other cases: *Re J* [2016] EWHC 1330 (Fam); *Re M (HFEA 2008)* [2016] EWHC 1572 (Fam); *Re N* [2016] EWHC 1329 (Fam) (see also under s 44). Where the completed form shows that X's sperm was to be used but in fact the sperm of an anonymous donor is used but where it is clear to the parties and the clinic that there was no question of X's sperm being used, it was known from the outset that the treatment would involve donor sperm and it is obvious that there was an error in the completed form, the mistake can be corrected as a matter of construction.

38 Further provision relating to sections 35 and 36

(1) Where a person is to be treated as the father of the child by virtue of section 35 or 36, no other person is to be treated as the father of the child.

(2) In England and Wales and Northern Ireland, sections 35 and 36 do not affect any presumption, applying by virtue of the rules of common law, that a child is the legitimate child of the parties to a marriage.

(3) In Scotland, sections 35 and 36 do not apply in relation to any child who, by virtue of any enactment or other rule of law, is treated as the child of the parties to a marriage.

(4) Sections 35 and 36 do not apply to any child to the extent that the child is treated by virtue of adoption as not being the man's child.

39 Use of sperm, or transfer of embryo, after death of man providing sperm

(1) If –

(a) the child has been carried by W as a result of the placing in her of an embryo or of sperm and eggs or her artificial insemination,

(b) the creation of the embryo carried by W was brought about by using the sperm of a man after his death, or the creation of the embryo was brought about using the sperm of a man before his death but the embryo was placed in W after his death,

(c) the man consented in writing (and did not withdraw the consent) –

(i) to the use of his sperm after his death which brought about the creation of the embryo carried by W or (as the case may be) to the placing in W after his death of the embryo which was brought about using his sperm before his death, and

(ii) to being treated for the purpose mentioned in subsection (3) as the father of any resulting child,

(d) W has elected in writing not later than the end of the period of 42 days from the day on which the child was born for the man to be treated for the purpose mentioned in subsection (3) as the father of the child, and

(e) no-one else is to be treated –

(i) as the father of the child by virtue of section 35 or 36 or by virtue of section 38(2) or (3), or

(ii) as a parent of the child by virtue of section 42 or 43 or by virtue of adoption, then the man is to be treated for the purpose mentioned in subsection (3) as the father of the child.

(2) Subsection (1) applies whether W was in the United Kingdom or elsewhere at the time of the placing in her of the embryo or of the sperm and eggs or of her artificial insemination.

(3) The purpose referred to in subsection (1) is the purpose of enabling the man's particulars to be entered as the particulars of the child's father in a relevant register of births.

(4) In the application of this section to Scotland, for any reference to a period of 42 days there is substituted a reference to a period of 21 days.

Scope—This section replaces the provisions inserted into HFEA 1990 by the Human Fertilisation and Embryology (Deceased Fathers) Act 2003. It sets out the conditions that must be satisfied before the man who provided the sperm may be treated as the child's father for registration of birth only. The section must be read with HFEA 1990, ss 13 and 14 (provision of relevant information and the conditions that apply to storage of gametes and the regulations made pursuant to s 14).

40 Embryo transferred after death of husband etc. who did not provide sperm

(1) If –

(a) the child has been carried by W as a result of the placing in her of an embryo,

(b) the embryo was created at a time when W was a party to a marriage with a man,

(c) the creation of the embryo was not brought about with the sperm of the other party to the marriage,

(d) the other party to the marriage died before the placing of the embryo in W,

(e) the other party to the marriage consented in writing (and did not withdraw the consent) –

(i) to the placing of the embryo in W after his death, and

(ii) to being treated for the purpose mentioned in subsection (4) as the father of any resulting child,

(f) W has elected in writing not later than the end of the period of 42 days from the day on which the child was born for the man to be treated for the purpose mentioned in subsection (4) as the father of the child, and

(g) no-one else is to be treated –

(i) as the father of the child by virtue of section 35 or 36 or by virtue of section 38(2) or (3), or

(ii) as a parent of the child by virtue of section 42 or 43 or by virtue of adoption,

then the man is to be treated for the purpose mentioned in subsection (4) as the father of the child.

(2) If –

(a) the child has been carried by W as a result of the placing in her of an embryo,

(b) the embryo was not created at a time when W was a party to a marriage or a civil partnership but was created in the course of treatment services provided to W in the United Kingdom by a person to whom a licence applies,

(c) a man consented in writing (and did not withdraw the consent) –

(i) to the placing of the embryo in W after his death, and

(ii) to being treated for the purpose mentioned in subsection (4) as the father of any resulting child,

(d) the creation of the embryo was not brought about with the sperm of that man,

(e) the man died before the placing of the embryo in W,

(f) immediately before the man's death, the agreed fatherhood conditions set out in section 37 were met in relation to the man in relation to treatment proposed to be provided to W in the United Kingdom by a person to whom a licence applies,

(g) W has elected in writing not later than the end of the period of 42 days from the day on which the child was born for the man to be treated for the purpose mentioned in subsection (4) as the father of the child, and

(h) no-one else is to be treated –

(i) as the father of the child by virtue of section 35 or 36 or by virtue of section 38(2) or (3), or

(ii) as a parent of the child by virtue of section 42 or 43 or by virtue of adoption,

then the man is to be treated for the purpose mentioned in subsection (4) as the father of the child.

(3) Subsections (1) and (2) apply whether W was in the United Kingdom or elsewhere at the time of the placing in her of the embryo.

(4) The purpose referred to in subsections (1) and (2) is the purpose of enabling the man's particulars to be entered as the particulars of the child's father in a relevant register of births.

(5) In the application of this section to Scotland, for any reference to a period of 42 days there is substituted a reference to a period of 21 days.

Amendments—Marriage (Same Sex Couples) Act 2013, s 17, Sch 7, para 39.

Scope—This section deals with cases where a child is born as a result of posthumous use of donated sperm. It sets out the conditions that must be satisfied before the deceased husband/partner of the woman can be treated as the father/parent of the resulting child for registration of birth only.

41 Persons not to be treated as father

(1) Where the sperm of a man who had given such consent as is required by paragraph 5 of Schedule 3 to the 1990 Act (consent to use of gametes for purposes of treatment services or non-medical fertility services) was used for a purpose for which such consent was required, he is not to be treated as the father of the child.

(2) Where the sperm of a man, or an embryo the creation of which was brought about with his sperm, was used after his death, he is not, subject to section 39, to be treated as the father of the child.

(3) Subsection (2) applies whether W was in the United Kingdom or elsewhere at the time of the placing in her of the embryo or of the sperm and eggs or of her artificial insemination.

Scope—This section provides that the donor of the sperm is not to be treated as the father of the child, nor is a person who has not consented to the use of his sperm after his death (see under s 42 for the position regarding a known male donor who has developed a relationship with the child).

Cases in which woman to be other parent

42 Woman in civil partnership or marriage to a woman at time of treatment

(1) If at the time of the placing in her of the embryo or the sperm and eggs or of her artificial insemination, W was a party to a civil partnership or a marriage with another woman, then subject to section 45(2) to (4), the other party to the civil partnership or marriage is to be treated as a parent of the child unless it is shown that she did not consent to the placing in W of the embryo or the sperm and eggs or to her artificial insemination (as the case may be).

(2) This section applies whether W was in the United Kingdom or elsewhere at the time mentioned in subsection (1).

Amendments—Marriage (Same Sex Couples) Act 2013, s 17, Sch 7, para 40.

Scope—Similar provisions to those that apply to heterosexual couples and to same-sex married couples are made in ss 42–47 in relation to same-sex female couples in a civil partnership and those who have not entered into a civil partnership. The female couple is regarded in law as the legal parents of the child with full parental responsibility. The provisions of s 42(1) indicate that there is a presumption that the other party to the civil partnership or marriage will be treated as a parent of the child unless proved otherwise; for example, where the couple have separated and subsequently one of them forms a relationship with another person and treatment is provided to them without the knowledge and consent of the party to the marriage or civil partnership, evidence from the other party to the civil partnership or marriage that he/she was unaware of or did not consent to the treatment: *Re G & Others (HFEA 2008)* [2016] EWHC 729 (Fam) (see also under s 44). The biological father is denied this status but it does not prevent the female couple in whom legal parenthood is vested from encouraging or enabling the biological father to become a psychological parent. If such a relationship is encouraged and developed, this relationship is likely to fall within the scope of private family life within Art 8 of the European Convention on Human Rights. Depending on the circumstances, it is also likely to provide the biological father grounds under CA 1989, s 10(9) for seeking permission to apply for contact under s 8 of that Act: *Re G; Re Z (Children: Sperm Donors: Leave to Apply for Children Act Orders)* [2013] 1 FLR 1334, FD (and see also the judgment of Baroness Hale in *Re G (Children)* [2006] 2 FLR 629, HL.

Consent—See commentary under s 37.

43 Treatment provided to woman who agrees that second woman to be parent

If no man is treated by virtue of section 35 as the father of the child and no woman is treated by virtue of section 42 as a parent of the child but –

- (a) the embryo or the sperm and eggs were placed in W, or W was artificially inseminated, in the course of treatment services provided in the United Kingdom by a person to whom a licence applies,
- (b) at the time when the embryo or the sperm and eggs were placed in W, or W was artificially inseminated, the agreed female parenthood conditions (as set out in section 44) were met in relation to another woman, in relation to treatment provided to W under that licence, and
- (c) the other woman remained alive at that time,

then, subject to section 45(2) to (4), the other woman is to be treated as a parent of the child.

'under that licence'—In *Re Human Fertilisation and Embryology Act 2008 (Cases A, B, C, D, E, F, G and H)* [2017] 1 FLR 366, FD, Munby P construed the term as follows: 'It is noticeable that the statute does not, for example, use the words "in accordance with the licence", or "in compliance with the licence" or even, to pick up the language of section 23(3) of the 1990 Act, "in pursuance of the licence." The word 'under' is much less specific. It serves the important purpose of making sure that parenthood is conferred by virtue of ss 36 and 43 only where the child results from "treatment under the licence" of a licensed clinic, rather than treatment by an unlicensed clinic, or treatment outside the scope of the clinic's licence'.

44 The agreed female parenthood conditions

(1) The agreed female parenthood conditions referred to in section 43(b) are met in relation to another woman ('P') in relation to treatment provided to W under a licence if, but only if, –

(a) P has given the person responsible a notice stating that P consents to P being treated as a parent of any child resulting from treatment provided to W under the licence,

(b) W has given the person responsible a notice stating that W agrees to P being so treated,

(c) neither W nor P has, since giving notice under paragraph (a) or (b), given the person responsible notice of the withdrawal of P's or W's consent to P being so treated,

(d) W has not, since the giving of the notice under paragraph (b), given the person responsible –

(i) a further notice under that paragraph stating that W consents to a woman other than P being treated as a parent of any resulting child, or

(ii) a notice under section 37(1)(b) stating that W consents to a man being treated as the father of any resulting child, and

(e) W and P are not within prohibited degrees of relationship in relation to each other.

(2) A notice under subsection (1)(a), (b) or (c) must be in writing and must be signed by the person giving it.

(3) A notice under subsection (1)(a), (b) or (c) by a person ('S') who is unable to sign because of illness, injury or physical disability is to be taken to comply with the requirement of subsection (2) as to signature if it is signed at the direction of S, in the presence of S and in the presence of at least one witness who attests the signature.

Consent—Consent must be informed consent and obtained as set out in the guidance issued by the HFE Authority. If this is not properly complied with, it will be ineffective to grant parentage to the woman who does not carry the child. The Commencement Arrangements Guidance provides that partners of women undergoing treatment would only be recognised as legal parents of any child born from the treatment if written consent had been given before gamete or embryo transfer took place. If consents are not in place before such transfer, the partner of the woman receiving treatment would not be recognised as the second parent (see *AB v CD and the Z Fertility Clinic* [2013] 2 FLR 1357, FD for consequences where this procedure was not followed). The extent to which errors in completed consent forms can be corrected by way of construction or rectification or a wrong consent form being executed by the parties or a consent form used that is in form other than Form WP and Form PP can operate as a valid consent for the purposes of ss 37 and 44 was considered by Munby P in *Re Human Fertilisation and Embryology Act 2008 (Cases A, B, C, D, E, F, G and H)* [2017] 1 FLR 366, FD; *Re G & Others (HFEA 2008)* [2016] EWHC 729 (Fam); and *Re Human Fertilisation and Embryology Act 2008 (Case I)* [2017] 1 FLR 998, FD. In *(Cases A, B, C, D, E, F, G and H)*, Munby P ruled that there was no reason why Form WP or Form PP could not be rectified and if the mistake is obvious on the face of it and it is plain what was meant, the court can as a matter of construction correct the mistake. Where the consents by the parties were provided before the 2008 Act came into force on 6 April 2009 on the appropriate Form IC but the treatment commenced on or after 6 April 2009 when Forms WP and PP should have been executed, the issue 'is as a matter of content and construction apt to operate both as a Form PP and as a Form WP, complying with the requirements of both s 37(1)(a) and s 37((1)(b)' and Form IC is not precluded from operating as consent and the failure to use the appropriate forms does not invalidate a consent that would otherwise comply with the requirements of HFEA 2008: *Re I & Others (HFEA 2008)* (see also under s 37).

45 Further provision relating to sections 42 and 43

(1) Where a woman is treated by virtue of section 42 or 43 as a parent of the child, no man is to be treated as the father of the child.

(2) In England and Wales and Northern Ireland, sections 42 and 43 do not affect any presumption, applying by virtue of the rules of common law, that a child is the legitimate child of the parties to a marriage.

(3) In Scotland, sections 42 and 43 do not apply in relation to any child who, by virtue of any enactment or other rule of law, is treated as the child of the parties to a marriage.

(4) Sections 42 and 43 do not apply to any child to the extent that the child is treated by virtue of adoption as not being the woman's child.

Status of the biological father—This provision denies the biological father the status of a legal parent but where a relationship between him and the child is encouraged and enabled to be developed in an appropriate case it will be a relevant consideration with those under CA 1989, s 10(9) to support his application for permission to apply for an order under s 8 of that Act (see above under s 42).

46 Embryo transferred after death of civil partner or wife or intended female parent

(1) If –

- (a) the child has been carried by W as the result of the placing in her of an embryo,
- (b) the embryo was created at a time when W was a party to a civil partnership or marriage with another woman,
- (c) the other party to the civil partnership or marriage died before the placing of the embryo in W,
- (d) the other party to the civil partnership or marriage consented in writing (and did not withdraw the consent) –
  - (i) to the placing of the embryo in W after the death of the other party, and
  - (ii) to being treated for the purpose mentioned in subsection (4) as the parent of any resulting child,
- (e) W has elected in writing not later than the end of the period of 42 days from the day on which the child was born for the other party to the civil partnership or marriage to be treated for the purpose mentioned in subsection (4) as the parent of the child, and
- (f) no one else is to be treated –
  - (i) as the father of the child by virtue of section 35 or 36 or by virtue of section 45(2) or (3), or
  - (ii) as a parent of the child by virtue of section 42 or 43 or by virtue of adoption,

then the other party to the civil partnership or marriage is to be treated for the purpose mentioned in subsection (4) as a parent of the child.

(2) If –

- (a) the child has been carried by W as the result of the placing in her of an embryo,
- (b) the embryo was not created at a time when W was a party to a marriage or a civil partnership, but was created in the course of treatment services provided to W in the United Kingdom by a person to whom a licence applies,
- (c) another woman consented in writing (and did not withdraw the consent) –
  - (i) to the placing of the embryo in W after the death of the other woman, and
  - (ii) to being treated for the purpose mentioned in subsection (4) as the parent of any resulting child,
- (d) the other woman died before the placing of the embryo in W,
- (e) immediately before the other woman's death, the agreed female parenthood conditions set out in section 44 were met in relation to the other woman in relation to treatment proposed to be provided to W in the United Kingdom by a person to whom a licence applies,
- (f) W has elected in writing not later than the end of the period of 42 days from the day on which the child was born for the other woman to be treated for the purpose mentioned in subsection (4) as the parent of the child, and
- (g) no one else is to be treated –
  - (i) as the father of the child by virtue of section 35 or 36 or by virtue of section 45(2) or (3), or
  - (ii) as a parent of the child by virtue of section 42 or 43 or by virtue of adoption,

then the other woman is to be treated for the purpose mentioned in subsection (4) as a parent of the child.

(3) Subsections (1) and (2) apply whether W was in the United Kingdom or elsewhere at the time of the placing in her of the embryo.

(4) The purpose referred to in subsections (1) and (2) is the purpose of enabling the deceased woman's particulars to be entered as the particulars of the child's other parent in a relevant register of births.

(5) In the application of subsections (1) and (2) to Scotland, for any reference to a period of 42 days there is substituted a reference to a period of 21 days.

Amendments—Marriage (Same Sex Couples) Act 2013, s 17, Sch 7, para 41.

47 Woman not to be other parent merely because of egg donation

A woman is not to be treated as the parent of a child whom she is not carrying and has not carried, except where she is so treated –

(a) by virtue of section 42 or 43, or
(b) by virtue of section 46 (for the purpose mentioned in subsection (4) of that section), or
(c) by virtue of adoption.

Woman to be treated as the parent of the child—The genetic mother may, however, be granted parental responsibility by means of a shared care arrangement order when the relationship between parties in a same-sex relationship breaks down where there has been a close relationship between the genetic mother and the child: *Re G (Shared Residence Order: Biological Mother of Donor Egg)* [2014] 2 FLR 897, CA.

Effect of sections 33 to 47

48 Effect of sections 33 to 47

(1) Where by virtue of section 33, 35, 36, 42 or 43 a person is to be treated as the mother, father or parent of a child, that person is to be treated in law as the mother, father or parent (as the case may be) of the child for all purposes.

(2) Where by virtue of section 33, 38, 41, 45 or 47 a person is not to be treated as a parent of the child, that person is to be treated in law as not being a parent of the child for any purpose.

(3) Where section 39(1) or 40(1) or (2) applies, the deceased man –

(a) is to be treated in law as the father of the child for the purpose mentioned in section 39(3) or 40(4), but
(b) is to be treated in law as not being the father of the child for any other purpose.

(4) Where section 46(1) or (2) applies, the deceased woman –

(a) is to be treated in law as a parent of the child for the purpose mentioned in section 46(4), but
(b) is to be treated in law as not being a parent of the child for any other purpose.

(5) Where any of subsections (1) to (4) has effect, references to any relationship between two people in any enactment, deed or other instrument or document (whenever passed or made) are to be read accordingly.

(6) In relation to England and Wales and Northern Ireland, a child who –

(a) has a parent by virtue of section 42, or
(b) has a parent by virtue of section 43 who is at any time during the period beginning with the time mentioned in section 43(b) and ending with the time of the child's birth a party to a civil partnership with the child's mother,

is the legitimate child of the child's parents.

(7) In relation to England and Wales and Northern Ireland, nothing in the provisions of section 33(1) or sections 35 to 47, read with this section –

(a) affects the succession to any dignity or title of honour or renders any person capable of succeeding to or transmitting a right to succeed to any such dignity or title, or
(b) affects the devolution of any property limited (expressly or not) to devolve (as nearly as the law permits) along with any dignity or title of honour.

(8) In relation to Scotland –

(a) those provisions do not apply to any title, coat of arms, honour or dignity transmissible on the death of its holder or affect the succession to any such title, coat of arms or dignity or its devolution, and

(b) where the terms of any deed provide that any property or interest in property is to devolve along with a title, coat of arms, honour or dignity, nothing in those provisions is to prevent that property or interest from so devolving.

Effect of ss 33 to 47—See annotations to ss 42 and 45.

References to parties to marriage or civil partnership

49 Meaning of references to parties to a marriage

(1) The references in sections 35 to 47 to the parties to a marriage at any time there referred to –

(a) are to the parties to a marriage subsisting at that time, unless a judicial separation was then in force, but

(b) include the parties to a void marriage if either or both of them reasonably believed at that time that the marriage was valid; and for the purposes of those sections it is to be presumed, unless the contrary is shown, that one of them reasonably believed at that time that the marriage was valid.

(2) In subsection (1)(a) 'judicial separation' includes a legal separation obtained in a country outside the British Islands and recognised in the United Kingdom.

50 Meaning of references to parties to a civil partnership

(1) The references in sections 35 to 47 to the parties to a civil partnership at any time there referred to –

(a) are to the parties to a civil partnership subsisting at that time, unless a separation order was then in force, but

(b) include the parties to a void civil partnership if either or both of them reasonably believed at that time that the civil partnership was valid; and for the purposes of those sections it is to be presumed, unless the contrary is shown, that one of them reasonably believed at that time that the civil partnership was valid.

(2) The reference in section 48(6)(b) to a civil partnership includes a reference to a void civil partnership if either or both of the parties reasonably believed at the time when they registered as civil partners of each other that the civil partnership was valid; and for this purpose it is to be presumed, unless the contrary is shown, that one of them reasonably believed at that time that the civil partnership was valid.

(3) In subsection (1)(a), 'separation order' means –

(a) a separation order under section 37(1)(d) or 161(1)(d) of the Civil Partnership Act 2004,

(b) a decree of separation under section 120(2) of that Act, or

(c) a legal separation obtained in a country outside the United Kingdom and recognised in the United Kingdom.

Further provision about registration by virtue of section 39, 40 or 46

51 Meaning of 'relevant register of births'

For the purposes of this Part a 'relevant register of births', in relation to a birth, is whichever of the following is relevant –

(a) a register of live-births or still-births kept under the Births and Deaths Registration Act 1953,

(b) a register of births or still-births kept under the Registration of Births, Deaths and Marriages (Scotland) Act 1965, or

(c) a register of live-births or still-births kept under the Births and Deaths Registration (Northern Ireland) Order 1976 (S.I. 1976/1041 (N.I. 14)).

52 Late election by mother with consent of Registrar General

(1) The requirement under section 39(1), 40(1) or (2) or 46(1) or (2) as to the making of an election (which requires an election to be made either on or before the day on which the child was born or within the period of 42 or, as the case may be, 21 days from that day) is nevertheless to be treated as satisfied if the required election is made after the end of that period but with the consent of the Registrar General under subsection (2).

(2) The Registrar General may at any time consent to the making of an election after the end of the period mentioned in subsection (1) if, on an application made to him in accordance with such requirements as he may specify, he is satisfied that there is a compelling reason for giving his consent to the making of such an election.

(3) In this section 'the Registrar General' means the Registrar General for England and Wales, the Registrar General of Births, Deaths and Marriages for Scotland or (as the case may be) the Registrar General for Northern Ireland.

Interpretation of references to father etc. where woman is other parent

53 Interpretation of references to father etc

(1) Subsections (2) and (3) have effect, subject to subsections (4) and (6), for the interpretation of any enactment, deed or any other instrument or document (whenever passed or made).

(2) Any reference (however expressed) to the father of a child who has a parent by virtue of section 42 or 43 is to be read as a reference to the woman who is a parent of the child by virtue of that section.

(3) Any reference (however expressed) to evidence of paternity is, in relation to a woman who is a parent by virtue of section 42 or 43, to be read as a reference to evidence of parentage.

(4) This section does not affect the interpretation of the enactments specified in subsection (5) (which make express provision for the case where a child has a parent by virtue of section 42 or 43).

(5) Those enactments are –

(a) the Legitimacy Act (Northern Ireland) 1928,
(b) the Schedule to the Population (Statistics) Act 1938,
(c) the Births and Deaths Registration Act 1953,
(d) the Registration of Births, Deaths and Marriages (Special Provisions) Act 1957,
(e) Part 2 of the Registration of Births, Deaths and Marriages (Scotland) Act 1965,
(f) the Congenital Disabilities (Civil Liability) Act 1976,
(g) the Legitimacy Act 1976,
(h) the Births and Deaths Registration (Northern Ireland) Order 1976 (S.I. 1976/1041 (N.I. 14)),
(i) the British Nationality Act 1981,
(j) the Family Law Reform Act 1987,
(k) Parts 1 and 2 of the Children Act 1989,
(l) Part 1 of the Children (Scotland) Act 1995,
(m) section 1 of the Criminal Law (Consolidation) (Scotland) Act 1995, and
(n) Parts 2, 3 and 14 of the Children (Northern Ireland) Order 1995 (S.I. 1995/755 (N.I. 2)).

(6) This section does not affect the interpretation of references that fall to be read in accordance with section 1(2)(a) or (b) of the Family Law Reform Act 1987 or Article 155(2)(a) or (b) of the Children (Northern Ireland) Order 1995 (references to a person whose father and mother were, or were not, married to each other at the time of the person's birth).

Parental orders

54 Parental orders

(1) On an application made by two people ('the applicants'), the court may make an order providing for a child to be treated in law as the child of the applicants if –

- (a) the child has been carried by a woman who is not one of the applicants, as a result of the placing in her of an embryo or sperm and eggs or her artificial insemination,
- (b) the gametes of at least one of the applicants were used to bring about the creation of the embryo, and
- (c) the conditions in subsections (2) to (8) are satisfied.

(1A) For the purposes of this section, neither of the following is to be treated as a person whose gametes were used to create an embryo ('embryo E') –

- (a) where embryo E is a permitted embryo by virtue of regulations under section 3ZA(5) of the 1990 Act, the person whose mitochondrial DNA (not nuclear DNA) was used to bring about the creation of embryo E;
- (b) where embryo E has been created by the fertilisation of an egg which was a permitted egg by virtue of regulations under section 3ZA(5) of the 1990 Act, the person whose mitochondrial DNA (not nuclear DNA) was used to bring about the creation of that permitted egg.

(2) The applicants must be –

- (a) husband and wife,
- (b) civil partners of each other, or
- (c) two persons who are living as partners in an enduring family relationship and are not within prohibited degrees of relationship in relation to each other.

(3) Except in a case falling within subsection (11), the applicants must apply for the order during the period of 6 months beginning with the day on which the child is born.

(4) At the time of the application and the making of the order –

- (a) the child's home must be with the applicants, and
- (b) either or both of the applicants must be domiciled in the United Kingdom or in the Channel Islands or the Isle of Man.

(5) At the time of the making of the order both the applicants must have attained the age of 18.

(6) The court must be satisfied that both –

- (a) the woman who carried the child, and
- (b) any other person who is a parent of the child but is not one of the applicants (including any man who is the father by virtue of section 35 or 36 or any woman who is a parent by virtue of section 42 or 43),

have freely, and with full understanding of what is involved, agreed unconditionally to the making of the order.

(7) Subsection (6) does not require the agreement of a person who cannot be found or is incapable of giving agreement; and the agreement of the woman who carried the child is ineffective for the purpose of that subsection if given by her less than six weeks after the child's birth.

(8) The court must be satisfied that no money or other benefit (other than for expenses reasonably incurred) has been given or received by either of the applicants for or in consideration of –

- (a) the making of the order,
- (b) any agreement required by subsection (6),
- (c) the handing over of the child to the applicants, or
- (d) the making of arrangements with a view to the making of the order,

unless authorised by the court.

(9) For the purposes of an application under this section –

(a) in relation to England and Wales –

(i) 'the court' means the High Court or the family court, and

(ii) proceedings on the application are to be 'family proceedings' for the purposes of the Children Act 1989,

(b) in relation to Scotland, 'the court' means the Court of Session or the sheriff court of the sheriffdom within which the child is, and

(c) in relation to Northern Ireland, 'the court' means the High Court or any county court within whose division the child is.

(10) Subsection (1)(a) applies whether the woman was in the United Kingdom or elsewhere at the time of the placing in her of the embryo or the sperm and eggs or her artificial insemination.

(11) An application which –

(a) relates to a child born before the coming into force of this section, and

(b) is made by two persons who, throughout the period applicable under subsection (2) of section 30 of the 1990 Act, were not eligible to apply for an order under that section in relation to the child as husband and wife,

may be made within the period of six months beginning with the day on which this section comes into force.

Amendments—CCA 2013, s 17, Sch 11.

Modifications—Subsection 1A inserted for certain purposes by SI 2015/572.

Scope—Married couples, civil partners, unmarried heterosexual couples and same-sex couples in an enduring family relationship are eligible to apply for a parental order. Note, however, that where a child has been born following treatment services a person who donated mitochondria is not eligible to apply for a parental order on the basis of that donation alone. A single person cannot apply for a parental order (*B v C (Surrogacy: Adoption)* [2015] 1 FLR 1392, FD; *Re Z (A Child: Human Fertilisation and Embryology Act: Parental Order)* [2015] EWFC 73). However, in *Re Z (A Child) (No 2)* [2016] 2 FLR 327, FD, the court was invited to and made a declaration pursuant to HRA 1998, s 4 that this provision was incompatible with ECHR, Arts 8 and 14). Legal status can, however, be obtained by an adoption order. In *B v C*, the surrogate was the father's mother and therefore not a parent of the child within the meaning of s 42(2). It was therefore necessary for him to seek permission to apply for an adoption order, but see the implications of ACA 2002, ss 92 and 93 in respect of which Theis J pointed out that but for the familial relationship between the father and the child the actions taken would have left them liable to prosecution under s 93 and CA 1989, s 70. It is 'imperative that single parents contemplating parenthood through surrogacy obtain comprehensive legal advice as to how to proceed as adoption is the only means to ensure that they are the only legal parents of their child. The process under which they can achieve this is a legal minefield', at [33]. SI 2010/985, SI 2010/986 and SI 2010/987 make provisions for the commencement of the section and other related issues, consequential, transitional and savings provisions, and with appropriate modification for many sections of the ACA 2002 to apply to applications for a parental order. For procedure, see FPR 2010, r 13. Where foreign surrogacy arrangements are made, Hedley J in *Re IJ (Foreign Surrogacy Agreement: Parental Order)* [2011] 2 FLR 646, FD per curiam suggested that 'those who travel abroad to make these arrangements really should take advice from those skilled in our domestic law to be sure as to the problems that will confront them (not the least of which is immigration) and how they can be addressed. Reliance on advice from overseas agencies is dangerous as the provisions of our domestic and immigration law are often not fully understood'. This guidance has been reinforced in *Re Q (Parental Order: Domicile)* [2014] EWHC 1307 (Fam) and *Re Z (Foreign Surrogacy: Allocation of Work: Guidance on Parental Order Reports)* [2016] 2 FLR 803, FD, at [71]. Upon any application to revoke a parental order, the court will be guided by the authorities on revoking adoption orders. There is no statutory power or inherent power to set aside the order unless there are exceptional circumstances such as in *Re M (Minors) (Adoption)* [1991] 1 FLR 458, CA and *Re K (Adoption and Wardship)* [1997] 2 FLR 221, CA (*G v G (Parental Order: Revocation)* [2013] 1 FLR 286, FD). The court will need to be satisfied that revocation is in the best interests and welfare of the child.

Time limit of 6 months beginning with the day on which the child is born—It was understood that because of the mandatory nature of the provision, there is no discretionary power to extend this time limit. Where the parties are out of time, the way forward for the commissioning couples to regulate the use by the surrogate mother of her parental responsibility is to make the child a ward of court and to apply under Children Act 1989, s 8 for a shared care arrangement order in favour of the commissioning couple and a prohibited steps order against the surrogate mother prohibiting her from exercising her parental responsibility without leave of the court (*JP v LP and Others (Surrogacy Arrangement: Wardship)* [2015] 1 FLR 307, FD). However, in *Re X (A Child) (Surrogacy: Time Limit)* [2015] 1 FLR 349, FD, Sir James Munby P granted a parental order, although the application was made more than 2 years after the birth of the child and despite the fact that the commissioning parents had separated and were living apart when they made their application. The President applied a liberal and purposive approach and considered the effect of non-compliance and Parliament's assumed intention that the court would achieve a sensible outcome. He also took into consideration the fact that the provision of s 54 affected the fundamental aspects of a child's identity as a human being and the fact that a parental order had profound lifelong personal, emotional, psychological, social and possible cultural and religious consequences, as well as legal ones. In *AB and CD v CT (Parental Order: Consent of Surrogate*

Mother) [2016] 1 FLR 41, FD, Theis J applied *Re X* (above) to grant a parental order despite the fact that the application was not made within the 6 months' time limit and the fact that the only evidence of consent of the surrogate mother was her obtaining a child arrangements order in proceedings issued in Australia. In arriving at her decision, Theis J concluded from the perspective of the child's welfare a parental order was preferable to an adoption order because 'it confirms the important legal, practical and psychological reality' of the child's identity. In *A and Anr v C* [2016] EWFC 4, a parental order was made 10 years over the statutory limit of 6 months. See also *D and G v ED and DD* [2015] EWHC 911 (Fam), [2016] 2 FLR 530, FD.

Application made by two people (applicants) in an enduring relationship—The applicants must be a married couple, civil partners or two persons who are living as partners in an enduring family relationship. 'Enduring family relationship' is not defined; although attempts were made to set a minimum time period of the relationship to have existed this was not included in the Act. It is therefore fact-specific and dependant on the strength of the evidence to prove the quality and nature of the relationship rather than longevity: *P and B v Z* [2016] EWHC 1594 (Fam) (see also under ACA 2002, s 144(4)). It may be satisfied where the couple is maintaining two households, e g to enable one of them to exercise contact with his/her children from a former relationship: *DM & LK v SJ & OJ* [2016] EWHC 270 (Fam). Although s 54(1) requires the application to be made by two people, it does not require that there be two living applicants at the time when the order is made. Hence, where one of two applicants dies, since all of the relevant welfare considerations in s 54 relate to the child, as a matter of law the court retains jurisdiction to consider the application: *A v P (Surrogacy: Parental Order: Death of Applicant)* [2012] 2 FLR 145, FD. Where an application has been made jointly by two people who are eligible under s 54(2), if the evidence at the hearing suggests that their relationship is close to a breakdown and that the mother's consent would not be available if this fact was disclosed to her, it is unlikely that an order will be made as such a situation would be outside that contemplated by the section. Whether a parental order would be set aside if the breakdown occurs immediately after the parental order is very much fact-specific. As there is no statutory provision that deals with the criteria to be applied on such an application, the court will draw guidance from adoption cases and will consider the need for certainty. *G v G (Parental Order: Revocation)* [2013] 1 FLR 286, FD is an illustration of the principles that are relevant to such a case and the need to ensure that the procedure set out in the FPR 2010, Pt 13 is not short-circuited. Where the parties had separated when the application was made, the President in *Re X (A Child) (Surrogacy: Time Limit)* [2015] 1 FLR 349, FD ruled that since the child split his time between their two homes he could be said to be living with both his parents but he stressed that he was not laying down any new principles. See *Re C and D (Children) (Fact Finding Hearing)* [2015] EWHC 1059 (Fam) and *Re A and B (Parental Order)* [2016] 2 FLR 446, FD, where not only were the applicants separated when the application was made it was out of time and there was considerable ill-feeling between them. With regard to whether a foreign adoption order prevents the court considering an application for a parental order by reason of the fact that if valid the parties would be the child's legal parents, see *Re Q (Parental Order: Domicile)* [2014] EWHC 1307 (Fam).

Child's home with the applicants, applicants' domicile and jurisdiction—The fact that one of the applicants splits his/her time between two households does not mean that the child does not have a home with him/her and the other applicant. In any event, if the evidence suggests that the circumstances of the applicants results in family life being established within Art 8 of the European Convention, this criterion will be satisfied: *DM & LK v SJ & OJ* [2016] EWHC 270 (Fam). This home does not need to be within England and Wales (*Re X and Y (Foreign Surrogacy)* [2009] 1 FLR 733, FD) but one or both of the applicants must be domiciled in England and Wales (*Re G (Surrogacy: Foreign Domicile)* [2008] 1 FLR 1047, FD). The court has no jurisdiction to entertain the application where the child is outside the jurisdiction and has not been habitually resident in England and Wales: *Re K (Foreign Surrogacy)* [2011] 1 FLR 533, FD. Neither FLA 1986 nor the 2008 Act refers to the basis on which jurisdiction is founded in s 54 applications. It is assumed that the court applied Brussels IIA, Art 8, but see *Re Q (Parental Order: Domicile)* [2014] EWHC 1307 (Fam) in which Theis J held that a parental order is not a Pt I order as defined in FLA 1986, Ch 1 and therefore such an order is not governed by that Act. There is also no requirement in s 54 that the applicant or the child should be present in the jurisdiction when the application is heard. The court's jurisdiction rests solely on the requirement set out in s 54(4)(b) that at least one of the applicants has a domicile in the UK, the Channel Islands or the Isle of Man (Theis J in *Re Q (Parental Order: Domicile)* (above), at [20] and *Re Z (Foreign Surrogacy: Allocation of Work: Guidance on Parental Order Reports)* [2016] 2 FLR 803, FD). Where the UK etc is not the domicile of origin of the applicant(s), evidence that they or one of them had acquired a domicile of choice in England must be adduced (*Re A and B (Parental Order: Domicile)* [2014] 1 FLR 169, FD; *Re B-G (Parental Orders: Domicile)* [2014] 2 FLR 968, FD; *Re Q (Parental Order: Domicile)* [2014] EWHC 1307 (Fam)).

Agreement of the mother and any other person who is a parent of the child—It is essential that the consent is given freely and with full understanding of the process and its implication and must be unconditional and that the surrogate and her husband, if she is married, are fully informed of any change in the circumstances of the parties and especially of any genetic changes in the embryo prior to it being transferred to the surrogate. The court will need to be satisfied that any consent given by the surrogates has been given with the knowledge of the genetic details: *DM & LK v SJ & OJ* (above). The parental reporter's report must therefore be a full inquiry into the applicants' circumstances and must ensure that the basis on which the mother has given her consent remains valid, for example if it was given on the basis of a functional family when in fact the applicants' relationship is unstable and at breaking point (*G v G (Parental Order: Revocation)* [2013] 1 FLR 286, FD). It is also essential, particularly when the surrogacy arrangement is made overseas, that appropriate steps are taken 'to ensure that clear lines of communication with the surrogate are established before the birth to facilitate the giving of consent after the expiry of the six week period' (*Re D and L (Surrogacy)* [2013] 2 FLR 275, FD). If the consent is notarised, it must be by an independent notary, not the applicant's solicitor: *P and B v Z* (above). Consent given before the expiry of 6 weeks after the birth is not valid for the purposes of s 54 but in an exceptional case the court is entitled to take into account evidence that the woman did give consent at an earlier time to giving up the baby. The weight attached to such earlier consent is likely to be limited and the court is unlikely to allow such evidence, as to do so would undermine the legal requirement that consent is only valid when it is given after 6 weeks following the birth of the child. It is also advisable to ensure that the consent given is with the understanding that her legal status as a parent will cease and be transferred to the commissioning couple: *AB and CD v CT (Parental Order: Consent of Surrogate Mother)* [2016] 1 FLR 41, FD. The court will also require details of the circumstances of the signing of the documents by the surrogate mother and her understanding. If this essential information is not available and later the surrogate mother cannot be served and the clinic proves unhelpful, it will prove difficult to satisfy the requirement of consent having been given 'freely and with full understanding to the making of a parental order': *R and S v T (Surrogacy: Service, Consent and Payments)* [2015] EWFC 22 where eventually the court made an order on the basis that the mother 'cannot be found'. Where the surrogate mother genuinely changes her mind and refuses to hand over the child and proceedings are commenced under CA 1989, the court will deal with the matter applying the welfare checklist and weighing the respective factors set out in s 1(3) (see *H v S (Disputed Surrogacy Agreement)* [2016] 1 FLR 723, FD; *Re TT (Surrogacy)* [2011] 2 FLR 392, FD; *Re WT (Foreign Surrogacy)* [2014] EWHC 1303 (Fam)) but see *Re Z (Surrogacy Agreements: Child Arrangements Orders)* [2017] 1 FLR 946, FD, which was flawed in every respect and when refusing to make a child arrangement order the court held that had the application been for a parental order the court would have found that the mother did not have full understanding of what was involved. In *Re AB (Surrogacy: Consent)* [2016] EWHC 2643 (Fam), twins born to the surrogate were the biological children of the commissioning parents. Although all the applicants met all the criteria for a parental order, the surrogate refused to give her consent. A parental order could not be made and neither could the court grant an adoption order under ACA 2002, s 67(1) because it would in effect mean that the parents were adopting their own children. The application has been adjourned. The difficulties created as a result of surrogacy arrangements that are subject to varying regulations and the significant differences in their effect is illustrated in *Re D (Surrogacy)* (see under s 35).

No requirement of the agreement of a person who cannot be found—There is power to make a parental order without the mother's consent if she cannot be found, but the court will scrutinise the evidence as to the efforts that have been made to find her and it is only when all reasonable steps have been taken to locate her without success that a court is likely to dispense with the need for a valid consent (see *R and S v T (Surrogacy: Service, Consent and Payments)* [2015] EWFC 22). The court will take account of the welfare of the child as the paramount consideration when arriving at its decision: *Re D and L (Surrogacy)* [2013] 2 FLR 275, FD.

No money or other benefit (other than for expenses reasonably incurred) has been given—The provisions of s 54(8) are mandatory. The parental reporter's report must deal comprehensively with the matters set out in this subsection, applying the statutory checklist in ACA 2002 (see Hedley J's comments in *G v G*, below). The question of whether payments go beyond 'reasonable expense' is fact-specific but it is contrary to the principles embodied in s 54(8) to sanction excessive payments. However, applying the changes brought about by the Human Fertilisation and Embryology (Parental Orders) Regulations 2010, welfare considerations are paramount and will be balanced with public policy consideration but with the scales being weighted in favour of welfare: see *R and S v T (Surrogacy: Service, Consent and Payments)* [2015] EWFC 22, where the applicants were found to have acted in good faith, had been cooperative and provided the court will all the information it required, and *G v G (Parental Order: Revocation)* [2013] 1 FLR 286, FD). See also *Re S (Parental Order)* [2010] 1 FLR 1156, FD (applied in *Re L (Commercial Surrogacy)* [2011] 1 FLR 1423, FD, *Re X and Y (s 54 HFEA 2008)* [2012] 1 FLR 1347, FD and *Re D and L (Surrogacy)* [2013] 2 FLR 275, FD; *J v G (Parental Orders)* [2014] 1 FLR 297, FD) for the principles that the court will apply. 'It will only be in the clearest case of the abuse of public policy that the court will be able to withhold an order if otherwise welfare considerations supports its making'. The court should nevertheless continue carefully to scrutinise applications for authorisations under s 54(8) with a view to policing the public policy issues identified in *Re S* (above). As a matter of procedure, where an application is made in the first instance to the Family Court before lay justices, the matter should be referred to the High Court. See also *Re IJ (Foreign Surrogacy Agreement: Parental Order)* [2011] 2 FLR 646, FD, where retrospective approval of monies paid was granted. In *Re X and Y (s 54 HFEA 2008)* (above), the President confirmed the approach adopted in *Re X and Y (Foreign Surrogacy)* [2009] 1 FLR 733, FD: in such cases, the court should consider (a) the issue of welfare on the basis of lifelong perspective of welfare as in cases of adoption and not the 'minority' perspective of CA 1989; (b) as regards payments made to the surrogates and public policy issues, the sums involved together with the element of gain in the context of the surrogate's particular circumstances and the economic circumstances in the country where the surrogacy agreement was made to ensure that the payments made were not of such magnitude to overbear the will of the surrogate. It is also a vital part of the court's public-policy assessment to ensure that the surrogacy arrangement is not a mere purchase of a child overseas; and (c) the examination of these issues should be undertaken at an early stage in the proceedings rather than at the final hearing and preferably at the point of entry into the UK. See *Re P-M (Parental Order: Payments to Surrogacy Agency)* [2014] 1 FLR 725, FD for the need to consider all payments made and not merely those made to the surrogate mother. It assists the court if all payments made are itemised and set out (eg for egg donation, medical treatment etc). *Re A B and C (Surrogacy Expenses)* [2016] EWFC 33 illustrates how the 'surrogacy market' works on the basis that the court will usually authorise payments not related to reasonable expenses as the court has little alternative but to grant the order on the basis of the welfare of the child. Where the parties seek surrogacy in a country where commercial surrogacy is legal, there is no process to obtain authorisation for these payments in advance of the application for a parental order. Authorisation for payments made in excess of the reasonable needs of the surrogate mother will have to be sought.

★★★★

Human Rights Act 1998

ARRANGEMENT OF SECTIONS

Section Page

Introduction

1 The Convention Rights 992
2 Interpretation of Convention rights 993

Legislation

3 Interpretation of legislation 994
4 Declaration of incompatibility 995
5 Right of Crown to intervene 996

Public authorities

6 Acts of public authorities 997
7 Proceedings 998
8 Judicial remedies 999
9 Judicial acts 1001
12 Freedom of expression 1001
21 Interpretation, etc 1002

Schedule 1 – The Articles 1004
Part I – The Convention 1004
Part II – The First Protocol 1011

Introduction

1 The Convention Rights

(1) In this Act 'the Convention rights' means the rights and fundamental freedoms set out in –

(a) Articles 2 to 12 and 14 of the Convention,
(b) Articles 1 to 3 of the First Protocol, and
(c) Article 1 of the Thirteenth Protocol,

as read with Articles 16 to 18 of the Convention.

(2) Those Articles are to have effect for the purposes of this Act subject to any designated derogation or reservation (as to which see sections 14 and 15).

(3) The Articles are set out in Schedule 1.

(4) The Secretary of State may by order make such amendments to this Act as he considers appropriate to reflect the effect, in relation to the United Kingdom, of a protocol.

(5) In subsection (4) 'protocol' means a protocol to the Convention –

(a) which the United Kingdom has ratified; or
(b) which the United Kingdom has signed with a view to ratification.

(6) No amendment may be made by an order under subsection (4) so as to come into force before the protocol concerned is in force in relation to the United Kingdom.

Amendments—SI 2001/3500; SI 2003/1887; SI 2004/1574.

Scope—It is important to note that *only* those Articles of ECHR 1950 set out in Schedule 1 are to be read into domestic law. Articles not listed (eg Articles 1 and 13) are specifically excluded and are not formally incorporated into UK law.

Jurisdiction—Notwithstanding the exclusion of Article 1, dealing with jurisdiction, the House of Lords held that the principles of extraterritoriality developed by the ECtHR were applicable to claims under HRA 1998: *R (Mazim Jumaa Gatteh Al Skeina & Others) v The Secretary of State for Defence* [2008] 1 AC 153, HL; *Ghaidan v Godin-Mendoza* [2004] 2 FLR 600, HL. Thus, although the application of the Convention is usually limited to the jurisdiction of the contracting state, there may be an exception where a state is in 'effective control' of a foreign territory through military occupation, acquiescence or invitation. In such circumstances the territory could be within the jurisdiction of the state and the Convention would then apply to acts undertaken by the state within that territory. The ECtHR has held that extra-territorial jurisdiction can exist whenever a state through its agents exercises authority and control over an individual: *Al Skeini v UK* (2011) 53 EHRR 18, ECHR and *Jamaa v Italy* (2012) 55 EHRR 627, ECHR. Accordingly, Art 1 extends to securing the protection of Art 2 to members of the armed forces when they are serving outside the territory of the UK: *Smith & Ors v Ministry of Defence* [2013] UKSC 41.

2 Interpretation of Convention rights

(1) A court or tribunal determining a question which has arisen in connection with a Convention right must take into account any –

(a) judgment, decision, declaration or advisory opinion of the European Court of Human Rights,

(b) opinion of the Commission given in a report adopted under Article 31 of the Convention,

(c) decision of the Commission in connection with Article 26 or 27(2) of the Convention, or

(d) decision of the Committee of Ministers taken under Article 46 of the Convention,

whenever made or given, so far as, in the opinion of the court or tribunal, it is relevant to the proceedings in which that question has arisen.

(2) Evidence of any judgment, decision, declaration or opinion of which account may have to be taken under this section is to be given in proceedings before any court or tribunal in such manner as may be provided by rules.

(3) In this section 'rules' means rules of court or, in the case of proceedings before a tribunal, rules made for the purposes of this section –

(a) by the Lord Chancellor or Secretary of State, in relation to any proceedings outside Scotland;

(b) by the Secretary of State, in relation to proceedings in Scotland; or

(c) by a Northern Ireland department, in relation to proceedings before a tribunal in Northern Ireland –

(i) which deals with transferred matters; and

(ii) for which no rules made under paragraph (a) are in force.

Amendments—SI 2003/1887; SI 2005/3429.

'must take into account' (s 2(1))—The court is required to take account of Strasbourg case-law but is not required to follow it. However, the circumstances in which domestic courts would not follow Strasbourg will be rare (e g the decision is based on an unambiguous misunderstanding of domestic law or procedure: *Doherty v Birmingham City Council* [2009] AC 367, HL, at [20] and [82]). The purpose of the requirement is to ensure Convention rights are enforced under HRA 1998 as they would be enforced by the ECtHR (see *R (Al Jedda) v Secretary of State for Defence* [2008] 1 AC 332, HL), but that should not prohibit the UK courts from developing its domestic human rights jurisprudence under the common law: HRA 1998, s 11. However, the Supreme Court appears to have signalled a broadening of the circumstances in which the domestic courts will not follow decisions of the ECtHR. Lord Phillips said, 'There will, however, be rare occasions where this court has concerns as to whether a decision of the Strasbourg Court sufficiently appreciates or accommodates particular aspects of our domestic process. In such circumstances it is open to this court to decline to follow the Strasbourg decision, giving reasons for adopting this course. This is likely to give the Strasbourg Court the opportunity to reconsider the particular aspect of the decision that is in issue, so that there takes place what may prove to be a valuable dialogue between this court and the Strasbourg Court.' (*R v Horncastle* [2010] 2 AC 373, SC). Lord Neuberger, giving the judgment of the Supreme Court, said that 'this Court is not bound to follow every decision of the ECtHR. Not only would it be impractical to do so: it would sometimes be inappropriate, as it would destroy the ability of the Court to engage in the constructive dialogue with the ECtHR which is of value to the development of Convention law … Where, however, there is a clear and constant line of decisions whose effect is not inconsistent with some fundamental substantive or procedural aspect of our law, and whose reasoning does not appear to overlook or misunderstand some argument or point of principle, we consider that it would be wrong for this Court not to follow that line' *Manchester City Council v Pinnock* [2011] 2 AC 104, SC, at [48].

'a question which has arisen' (s 2(1))—A question may arise in ongoing proceedings, in which case the issue must be determined (if possible) within those proceedings (see annotations to s 7). Alternatively, a question may arise as an issue where there are no current proceedings. In this case, an application may be made by way of freestanding proceedings under HRA 1998 or by way of judicial review to determine the question (see annotations to s 7).

'Evidence of any judgment' (s 2(2))—By FPR PD29B the President has directed that when an authority is to be cited at a hearing, the authority must be an authoritative and complete report and copies of the report, with a list of authorities, must be filed in accordance with FPR PD27A, or otherwise not less than 2 days before the hearing. The *President's Direction* states that these must be copies of the complete original text issued by the European Court and Commission (either paper-based or through HUDOC which is available on the internet at *www.echr.coe.int/hudoc*).

Precedent—The court at first instance must adhere to the English rules of precedent. If a judge feels a decision is inconsistent with Strasbourg authority he has to follow the binding precedent but could give leave to appeal as appropriate: see *Kay and Ors v London Borough of Lambeth and Ors; Leeds City Council v Price and Ors* [2006] 2 AC 465, HL.

Competing Convention rights—Where competing Convention rights are in issue, neither has precedence over the other: *Campbell v MGN Ltd* [2004] 2 AC 457, HL and *R (L) v Commissioner of the Metropolis* [2010] 1 FLR 643, SC.

Legislation

3 Interpretation of legislation

(1) So far as it is possible to do so, primary legislation and subordinate legislation must be read and given effect in a way which is compatible with the Convention rights.

(2) This section –

(a) applies to primary legislation and subordinate legislation whenever enacted;

(b) does not affect the validity, continuing operation or enforcement of any incompatible primary legislation; and

(c) does not affect the validity, continuing operation or enforcement of any incompatible subordinate legislation if (disregarding any possibility of revocation) primary legislation prevents removal of the incompatibility.

Scope—This section is the lynchpin of the Act. It imposes a strong interpretative obligation in respect both of primary and secondary legislation whenever it was enacted.

'So far as it possible to do so' (s 3(1))—This has been held to mean that primary legislation and subordinate legislation must be read and given effect in a way that is compatible with the Convention rights 'unless it is plainly impossible to do so': *R v A* [2002] 1 AC 45, HL, at [44]. The section is not available where the suggested interpretation is contrary to express statutory words or is by implication necessarily contradicted by the statute: *Re S (Minors) (Care Order: Implementation of Care Plan)* [2002] 1 FLR 815, HL, at [40]. Lord Hope has said that 'In the face of such strong statutory language, any reading down of the section to enable the court to postpone the execution of an order for possession of a dwelling-house which was not let on a secure tenancy for a longer period than the statutory maximum would go well beyond what section 3(1) of the 1998 Act permits'. As Lord Nicholls of Birkenhead said in *Ghaidan v Godin-Mendoza* [2004] 2 FLR 600, HL, at [33], for the courts to adopt a meaning inconsistent with a fundamental feature of legislation would be to cross the constitutional boundary that section 3 of the 1998 Act seeks to demarcate and preserve: *Hounslow LBC v Powell* [2011] 2 AC 186, SC, at [62]. If it is unavailable, recourse must be had to s 4 and an application made for a declaration of incompatibility of legislation with a Convention right.

Effect of the provision—The strong interpretative obligation of s 3 is vital to the working of HRA 1998. 'What is necessary, however, is to emphasise that interpretation under s 3(1) is the prime remedial remedy and that resort to s 4 must always be an exceptional course. In practical effect there is a strong rebuttable presumption in favour of an interpretation consistent with Convention rights': per *Ghaidan v Godin-Mendoza* [2004] 2 FLR 600, HL, at [50]. In the first instance the court must decide whether the statute is consistent with a Convention right using the ordinary principles of statutory interpretation and identify the word or phrase that is or is claimed to be incompatible. A claimant should identify 'precisely (a) the words used by the legislature which would otherwise be incompatible with the Convention right and (b) how these words were to be construed, according to the rule which s 3 lays down, to make them compatible': *R v A* (above) at [110]. The obligation may require the courts to:

(a) give legislation a Convention-compliant meaning even where there is no ambiguity in the statute;
(b) on occasions adopt a linguistically strained interpretation of legislation;
(c) modify the meaning and effect of primary and secondary legislation (which may require the court to depart from the parliamentary intention behind the legislation);
(d) read in additional words to the legislation to achieve Convention compliance;
(e) read down the legislation so as to narrow the interpretation of the provision; or
(f) clarify the effect of the provision without altering the words used.

See *Re S (Care Order: Implementation of a Care Plan)* (above) at [36]–[41]; *Ghaidan v Godin-Mendoza* (above) paras 28–34; *R v A* (above) at [4]–[68]; and *R v Lambert* [2002] 2 AC 545, HL, at [79]–[81].

Limitations—Lord Hope identified the limitations on the use of s 3 when he observed, 'The rule of construction which section 3 lays down is quite unlike any previous rule of statutory interpretation ... But the rule is only a rule of interpretation. It does not entitle the judges to act as legislators ... Section 3 does not entitle the court to legislate; its task is still one of interpretation. The compatibility is to be achieved only so far as this is possible. Plainly this will not be possible if the legislation contains provisions that expressly contradict the meaning that the enactment would have to be given to make it compatible': *R v A* (above) at [108].

Victim—The obligation imposed by the section is a general one. There is no need to satisfy the test of being a victim (cf the provisions of s 7) to be entitled to seek a declaration of the meaning of legislation: *R (Rusbridger) v Attorney General* [2004] AC 357, HL, at [21].

4 Declaration of incompatibility

(1) Subsection (2) applies in any proceedings in which a court determines whether a provision of primary legislation is compatible with a Convention right.

(2) If the court is satisfied that the provision is incompatible with a Convention right, it may make a declaration of that incompatibility.

(3) Subsection (4) applies in any proceedings in which a court determines whether a provision of subordinate legislation, made in the exercise of a power conferred by primary legislation, is compatible with a Convention right.

(4) If the court is satisfied –

(a) that the provision is incompatible with a Convention right, and
(b) that (disregarding any possibility of revocation) the primary legislation concerned prevents removal of the incompatibility,

it may make a declaration of that incompatibility.

(5) In this section 'court' means –

(a) the Supreme Court;
(b) the Judicial Committee of the Privy Council;
(c) the Courts-Martial Appeal Court;
(d) in Scotland, the High Court of Justiciary sitting otherwise than as a trial court or the Court of Session;
(e) in England and Wales or Northern Ireland, the High Court or the Court of Appeal
(f) the Court of Protection, in any matter being dealt with by the President of the Family Division, the Vice-Chancellor or a puisne judge of the High Court.

(6) A declaration under this section ('a declaration of incompatibility') –

(a) does not affect the validity, continuing operation or enforcement of the provision in respect of which it is given; and
(b) is not binding on the parties to the proceedings in which it is made.

Amendments—MCA 2005, s 67(1), Sch 6, para 43; CRA 2005, Sch 9, para 66(2).

Scope—This section provides the higher courts (as defined in s 4(4)) with power to make a 'declaration of incompatibility' if satisfied that a provision of primary or subordinate legislation is incompatible with the Convention. Such a declaration is not binding upon the parties and it does not change the law, which the court is required to continue to apply (s 4(6)). This provision enables the Crown to take a different position from the court making the declaration if the matter proceeds to the ECtHR. The court therefore cannot set aside the primary legislation but can disapply subordinate legislation unless the terms of the enabling statute prevent this (s 3(2)(b),(c)). Such a declaration should have the effect of prompting the government to change the law.

Procedure—A claim for a declaration of incompatibility must be made on a claim form. The procedure for an application under s 4 is contained within FPR 2010, r 29.5 and PD29A. The court may not make a declaration of incompatibility unless 21 days' notice, or such other period as the court directs, has been given to the Crown (CPR 1998, r 19.4A and FPR 2010, r 29.5(3)). Where notice has been given to the Crown, a Minister, or other person permitted by the HRA, shall be joined as a party on giving notice to the court (CPR 1998, r 19.4A(2) and FPR 2010, r 29.5(4)).

Making a declaration—A court must use the rule of construction in s 3 to read and give effect to legislation so that it is Convention-compliant unless it is plainly impossible to do so. Where, however, the whole scheme of the legislation is incompatible with the Convention or where there are multiple incompatibilities, it is unlikely that s 3 could be used to remedy the defects. In *R (Wright & others) v Secretary of State for Health* [2009] 1 AC 739, HL, at [39], Baroness Hale said, when approving the first instance decision to make a declaration of incompatibility, 'However, I would not make any attempt to suggest ways in which the scheme could be made compatible … the incompatibility arises from the interaction between the three elements of the scheme – the procedure, the criterion and the consequences. It is not for us to attempt to rewrite the legislation. There is, as I have already said, a delicate balance to be struck … It is right that that balance be struck in the first instance by the legislature.'

A declaration of compatibility is a discretionary remedy. The court will consider a number of factors: that the matter has been fully argued before the court; the legislation cannot be read or given effect in a way that is compliant with Convention rights; the making of the declaration gives legitimacy to the court's order; and that the declaration will serve a legislative purpose under the 1998 Act, in that it provides a basis, under s 10(1)(a), for a Minister of the Crown to consider whether there are compelling reasons to make amendments to the

PART II

legislation by remedial order (under Schedule 2 to the Act) for the purpose of removing the incompatibility that the court has identified: *Wilson v First County Trust Ltd (No.2)* [2002] QB 74, CA, at [46] and [47].

Declarations of incompatibility—The Home Secretary's scheme to control the right of any person subject to immigration control to marry in the UK was the subject of a declaration of incompatibility as being inconsistent with the Convention rights enshrined in Art 12 (*R (Baiai) v Secretary of State for the Home Department* [2008] 2 FLR 1462, HL) and *Aguilar v Secretary of State for the Home Department* [2011] 1 FLR 1187, CA). The rejection of unmarried couples in Northern Ireland as prospective adopter parents was the subject of a declaration of incompatibility as being inconsistent with Convention rights of Art 14 (*Re P and Ors* [2008] 2 FLR 1084, HL). However, a school's decision to refuse to permit a pupil to wear a 'purity' ring as an expression of her Christian faith and as a sign of her belief of celibacy before marriage did not breach ECHR Art 9 (*R (Lydia Playfoot) v Millais School Governing Body* [2007] ELR 484, QBD). Further, although a school's decision to refuse to allow a pupil to wear a niqab veil at school engaged her ECHR Art 9 rights, it did not infringe that right and, even if it had, the decision was objectively justifiable under Art 9(2) (*R (X) v Governors of Y School* [2007] ELR 278, QBD). HFEA 2008, s 54 is incompatible with ECHR, Art 14 on the basis that it discriminates against a single applicant: *Re Z (A Child) (No 2)* [2016] 2 FLR 327, FD.

Lacuna in legislation—A lacuna in legislation cannot be the subject of a declaration of incompatibility: *Re S (Minors) (Care Order: Implementation of Care Plan)* [2002] 1 FLR 815, HL (concerning the Court of Appeal's attempt to create 'starred' care plans).

Effective remedy—The ECHR does not yet consider that a 'declaration of incompatibility' constitutes an effective remedy within Convention terms: *Burden v UK* [2008] 2 FLR 787, ECHR, at [35]–[40].

Hopeless applications—Where the court considers that a claim for a declaration of incompatibility has no chance of success, there is no need to transfer the case to the High Court (*Re V (Care Proceedings: Human Rights Claims)* [2004] 1 FLR 944, CA).

Rectification—The Government may remedy incompatibility, following a final declaration of incompatibility or following a decision of the ECtHR, by later primary legislation or by making a remedial order pursuant to HRA 1998, s 10 (either by the standard procedure (Sch 2, para 2(a)) or the emergency procedure (Sch 2, para 2(b))).

5 Right of Crown to intervene

(1) Where a court is considering whether to make a declaration of incompatibility, the Crown is entitled to notice in accordance with rules of court.

(2) In any case to which subsection (1) applies –

- (a) a Minister of the Crown (or a person nominated by him),
- (b) a member of the Scottish Executive,
- (c) a Northern Ireland Minister,
- (d) a Northern Ireland department,

is entitled, on giving notice in accordance with rules of court, to be joined as a party to the proceedings.

(3) Notice under subsection (2) may be given at any time during the proceedings.

(4) A person who has been made a party to criminal proceedings (other than in Scotland) as the result of a notice under subsection (2) may, with leave, appeal to the Supreme Court against any declaration of incompatibility made in the proceedings.

(5) In subsection (4) –

'criminal proceedings' includes all proceedings before the Courts-Martial Appeal Court; and

'leave' means leave granted by the court making the declaration of incompatibility or by the Supreme Court.

Amendments—CRA 2005, Sch 9, para 66(3).

Scope—Where consideration is being given to a 'declaration of incompatibility', the Crown, or in a case relating to Scotland or Northern Ireland the person mentioned in s 5(2)(b)–(d), should be notified and allowed to become a party to the proceedings. A court may not make a declaration unless 21 days' notice, or such other period as the court directs, has been given to the Crown (CPR 1998, r 19.4A and FPR 2010, r 29.5(3)). Where such notice has been given, a Minister, on giving notice to the court, will be joined as a party (CPR 1998, r 19.4A(2) and FPR 2010, r 29.5(4)).

Notice to the Crown—The notice must be served on the person named in the list published under the Crown Proceedings Act 1947, s 17. The list is annexed to CPR PD66 (see CPR PD19A, para 6.4(1)).

Criminal Proceedings—The Crown is given a right – subject to the grant of leave – to appeal against a declaration of incompatibility made in criminal proceedings direct to the Supreme Court (s 5(4)).

Public authorities

6 Acts of public authorities

(1) It is unlawful for a public authority to act in a way which is incompatible with a Convention right.

(2) Subsection (1) does not apply to an act if –

(a) as the result of one or more provisions of primary legislation, the authority could not have acted differently; or

(b) in the case of one or more provisions of, or made under, primary legislation which cannot be read or given effect in a way which is compatible with the Convention rights, the authority was acting so as to give effect to or enforce those provisions.

(3) In this section 'public authority' includes –

(a) a court or tribunal, and

(b) any person certain of whose functions are functions of a public nature,

but does not include either House of Parliament or a person exercising functions in connection with proceedings in Parliament.

(4) *(repealed)*

(5) In relation to a particular act, a person is not a public authority by virtue only of subsection (3)(b) if the nature of the act is private.

(6) 'An act' includes a failure to act but does not include a failure to –

(a) introduce in, or lay before, Parliament a proposal for legislation; or

(b) make any primary legislation or remedial order.

Amendments—CRA 2005, Sch 9, para 66(4).

Scope—It is unlawful for a public authority (meaning, inter alia, a court, tribunal or local authority) to act in a way which is incompatible with Convention rights unless it could not have acted differently because of primary legislation or the primary legislation could not be read in a manner compatible with Convention rights. Where the provision cannot be read as compatible, an application can be made for a declaration of incompatibility (pursuant to s 4). Accordingly, individuals have a direct cause of action against public authorities. There is no direct cause of action for acting incompatibly with Convention rights between private individuals although, of course, in all proceedings the courts are required to give effect to Convention rights and obligations: *Venables and Thompson v Newsgroup Newspapers and Associated Newspapers Ltd* [2001] 1 FLR 791, CA; *Campbell v MGN Ltd* [2004] 2 AC 457, HL.

Public authority—A distinction is to be drawn between 'core public authorities' (e g government departments, local authorities, NHS trusts and the police) and 'hybrid public authorities' (otherwise referred to as 'functional public authorities') some of whose functions may be of a public nature but others of which will be of a private nature (e g a private security company would be exercising public functions in relation to the management of a contracted-out prison but would be acting privately when guarding ordinary commercial premises). There is no single test of universal application to determine whether a body is a core public authority or a hybrid public authority given the diverse nature of governmental functions and the variety of means by which these functions are discharged. 'Factors to be taken into account include the extent to which in carrying out the relevant function the body is publicly funded, or is exercising statutory powers, or is taking the place of central government or local authorities, or is providing a public service': *Aston Cantlow and Wilmcote with Billesley Parochial Church Council v Wallbank* [2004] 1 AC 546, HL, at [12]. In *Aston* the House of Lords sought to narrow the scope of core public authorities (which cannot enjoy Convention rights) and to widen the scope of hybrid public authorities (which in relation to its private acts is not disabled from having Convention rights).

Duty to protect Art 6 rights—The state, including the courts, is under a duty to protect a litigant's Art 6(1) rights to a fair hearing: *RP and Others v UK (Application No 38245/08)* [2013] 1 FLR 744, ECHR and *Re D (A Child)* [2015] 1 FLR 531, FD.

Functions of a public/a private nature—In the leading case of *YL v Birmingham City Council* [2008] 1 AC 95, HL, the House of Lords interprets the meaning of 'functions of a public nature' more narrowly than that given in *Aston Cantlow* (above). The majority drew a distinction between a council's provision of services pursuant to a statutory duty and the like provision of services provided by a private company under a commercial contract paid for by public money: they emphasised the commercial nature of the operation of the private company. By contrast, the minority view was that if a private body performed functions by arrangement with a public body and at its expense, which functions if carried out by the latter would be a 'public function', then the private body was undertaking 'functions of a public nature' and was thus a hybrid public authority.

Primary legislation defence—The distinction between the two limbs of the statutory defence is neither obvious nor clear. In *R (Hooper) v Secretary of State for Work & Pensions* [2005] 1 WLR 1681, HL, two law lords thought the appropriate defence was s 6(2)(a) and two thought it was s 6(2)(b). In practice the defence is rarely relied upon because most powers and duties can be read to be Convention-compliant.

Parliament (s 6(3))—Parliament, as the legislature, is not a public authority for the purposes of the section and is not bound by s 6(1).

Exclusion of failure to legislate or make a remedial order—The failure to make primary legislation or a remedial order to remedy an incompatibility or to give effect to a Convention right is not 'an act' within the meaning of s 6(1) and thus may not be challenged in the UK courts (s 6(6)(b)): *Chester v Secretary of State for Justice & Anthr* [2011] 1 WLR 1436, CA and *Tovey & Othrs v Ministry of Justice* [2011] EWHC 271 (QB).

7 Proceedings

(1) A person who claims that a public authority has acted (or proposes to act) in a way which is made unlawful by section 6(1) may –

(a) bring proceedings against the authority under this Act in the appropriate court or tribunal, or

(b) rely on the Convention right or rights concerned in any legal proceedings,

but only if he is (or would be) a victim of the unlawful act.

(2) In subsection (1)(a) 'appropriate court or tribunal' means such court or tribunal as may be determined in accordance with rules; and proceedings against an authority include a counterclaim or similar proceeding.

(3) If the proceedings are brought on an application for judicial review, the applicant is to be taken to have a sufficient interest in relation to the unlawful act only if he is, or would be, a victim of that act.

(4) If the proceedings are made by way of a petition for judicial review in Scotland, the applicant shall be taken to have title and interest to sue in relation to the unlawful act only if he is, or would be, a victim of that act.

(5) Proceedings under subsection (1)(a) must be brought before the end of –

(a) the period of one year beginning with the date on which the act complained of took place; or

(b) such longer period as the court or tribunal considers equitable having regard to all the circumstances,

but that is subject to any rule imposing a stricter time limit in relation to the procedure in question.

(6) In subsection (1)(b) 'legal proceedings' includes –

(a) proceedings brought by or at the instigation of a public authority; and

(b) an appeal against the decision of a court or tribunal.

(7) For the purposes of this section, a person is a victim of an unlawful act only if he would be a victim for the purposes of Article 34 of the Convention if proceedings were brought in the European Court of Human Rights in respect of that act.

(8) Nothing in this Act creates a criminal offence.

(9) In this section 'rules' means –

(a) in relation to proceedings before a court or tribunal outside Scotland, rules made by the Lord Chancellor or Secretary of State for the purposes of this section or rules of court,

(b) in relation to proceedings before a court or tribunal in Scotland, rules made by the Secretary of State for those purposes,

(c) in relation to proceedings before a tribunal in Northern Ireland –

(i) which deals with transferred matters; and

(ii) for which no rules made under paragraph (a) are in force,

rules made by a Northern Ireland department for those purposes,

and includes provision made by order under section 1 of the Courts and Legal Services Act 1990.

(10) In making rules, regard must be had to section 9.

(11) The Minister who has power to make rules in relation to a particular tribunal may, to the extent he considers it necessary to ensure that the tribunal can provide an appropriate remedy in relation to an act (or proposed act) of a public authority which is (or would be) unlawful as a result of section 6(1), by order add to –

(a) the relief or remedies which the tribunal may grant; or
(b) the grounds on which it may grant any of them.

(12) An order made under subsection (11) may contain such incidental, supplemental, consequential or transitional provision as the Minister making it considers appropriate.

(13) 'The Minister' includes the Northern Ireland department concerned.

Amendments—SI 2003/1887; SI 2005/3429.

Scope—This section provides the mechanism for complaints about acts which are unlawful, being incompatible with Convention rights. There are two routes: under s 7(1)(b) in legal proceedings in any court or tribunal in which the proceedings are brought by or at the instigation of a public authority, or constitute an appeal against the decision of a court or tribunal (s 7(6)). The other route is a separate claim under s 7(1)(a). Where the claim under s 7(1)(a) relates to a judicial act, the claim must be way of judicial review or by way of an appeal (HRA 1998, s 9). Otherwise, it seems that a freestanding claim should be made under CPR 1998, Pt 8.

'public authority'—A claim under s 7(1)(a) in relation to a judicial act must be brought in the High Court. Otherwise a claim in relation to an act of a public authority may be brought in any court (CPR 1998, r 7.11) in ongoing proceedings. The more usual procedure in relation to a claim concerning a judicial act will be by way of appeal from the decision made. For assistance in determining what is a 'public authority' or when a body is 'exercising functions of a public nature' see the notes to s 6 above.

'victim'—A claim of breach of Convention rights can only be made by a victim or prospective victim. Articles 6, 8 and 14 are generally only applicable to those within the jurisdiction of the court (*Re J (Child Returned Abroad: Human Rights)* [2004] 2 FLR 85, CA) but there may be exceptions: see the note to s 1 above.

Procedure—Where the complaint is in relation to a local authority care plan, the application under this provision should be heard in the Family Division of the High Court, if possible by a judge with experience of sitting in the Administrative Court; see *CF v The Secretary of State for the Home Department* [2004] 2 FLR 517, FD and *Re S and W (Care Proceedings)* [2007] 2 FLR 275, CA. Oral evidence may be heard and this should be determined at a directions hearing (*C v Bury Metropolitan Borough Council* [2002] 2 FLR 868, FD). Where a freestanding application is made concerning a child the matter should be referred to Cafcass Legal. Where care proceedings are afoot and a party alleges a breach of his Art 6 and/or Art 8 Convention rights by a local authority, it may be appropriate to institute separate proceedings for judicial review but only where that party has no alternative remedy other than judicial review proceedings to challenge the decision in issue: *R (H) v Kingston upon Hull City Council* [2014] 1 FLR 1094, QBD.

Where a parent seeks to rely on a breach of Arts 6 and 8 within public law proceedings, he must act without delay and should seek interim relief as a matter of urgency (e g breach of care plan by a local authority: see *Re P (Adoption: Breach of Care Plan)* [2004] 2 FLR 1109, CA; and egregious failures and delays by a local authority in care planning and complying with court orders: *Northamptonshire County Council v AS, KS and DS* [2015] EWHC 199 (Fam)).

The provisions of the Convention may not be used to mount a collateral challenge to the decision of a court in public law proceedings (in particular where the original decision was not challenged on appeal) (*Hinds v Liverpool County Court and Ors* [2008] 2 FLR 63, QBD).

The mistaken judgments or assessments of professionals or medical experts as to the cause of child's injuries or presenting symptoms, did not of themselves establish a breach of Art 8. However, the absence of an effective remedy for any arguable violation of the child's parents' human rights constituted a breach of Art 13. (*RK and AK v UK* [2009] 1 FLR 274, ECHR). Note: Article 13 is not incorporated into domestic UK law by HRA 1998. Accordingly, a failure to afford a victim an effective remedy is not, of itself, actionable in this jurisdiction. Ex turpi causa – the principle that a person may not benefit from his own wrongdoing is not recognised under Convention law and is not a legitimate basis for denying a claimant relief to which he would otherwise be entitled: *Al Hassan-Daniel v Revenue and Customs Commissioners* [2011] QB 866, CA.

8 Judicial remedies

(1) In relation to any act (or proposed act) of a public authority which the court finds is (or would be) unlawful, it may grant such relief or remedy, or make such order, within its powers as it considers just and appropriate.

(2) But damages may be awarded only by a court which has power to award damages, or to order the payment of compensation, in civil proceedings.

(3) No award of damages is to be made unless, taking account of all the circumstances of the case, including –

PART II

(a) any other relief or remedy granted, or order made, in relation to the act in question (by that or any other court), and
(b) the consequences of any decision (of that or any other court) in respect of that act,

the court is satisfied that the award is necessary to afford just satisfaction to the person in whose favour it is made.

(4) In determining –

(a) whether to award damages, or
(b) the amount of an award,

the court must take into account the principles applied by the European Court of Human Rights in relation to the award of compensation under Article 41 of the Convention.

(5) A public authority against which damages are awarded is to be treated –

(a) in Scotland, for the purposes of section 3 of the Law Reform (Miscellaneous Provisions) (Scotland) Act 1940 as if the award were made in an action of damages in which the authority has been found liable in respect of loss or damage to the person to whom the award is made;
(b) for the purposes of the Civil Liability (Contribution) Act 1978 as liable in respect of damage suffered by the person to whom the award is made.

(6) In this section –

'court' includes a tribunal;
'damages' means damages for an unlawful act of a public authority; and
'unlawful' means unlawful under section 6(1).

Scope—This section does not grant additional powers. Damages can only be awarded by a court with jurisdiction to do so.

Act or proposed act—It is plain from the wording of the section that a claim may be brought in anticipation of an act that would be unlawful if carried out and the court may grant the appropriate relief or remedy.

Grant relief or remedy (s 8(1))—The court may quash a decision made by a local authority in the care planning for a child where the parents' Convention rights have been breached by the authority in coming to that decision: *Re M (Care: Challenging Decisions made by Local Authority)* [2001] 2 FLR 1300, FD. The court has jurisdiction in appropriate cases to make an injunction against a local authority preventing, for example, a child being removed from foster carers pending the full hearing of the matter (*Coventry CC v O (Adoption)* [2011] 2 FLR 936, CA) or to prevent the separation of a mother and child pending a full hearing (*Re H (Care Plan: Human Rights)* [2012] 1 FLR 191, CA).

Findings of breach of Convention rights—The Court of Appeal has given guidance on the approach that courts should adopt when invited to make findings that a local authority has breached a parent's or a child's Convention rights when, for example, it has removed a child from the parent's care. The court should focus on the issues in terms of the 1950 Convention. The court could pose the simple question 'What would an impartial observer be saying if the local authority had delayed and something had gone wrong?': *Re S (Care Proceedings: Human Rights)* [2012] 2 FLR 209, CA.

Where placement orders had been made in respect of two children but they had never been adopted, their ties with their natural family had been cut without a new family being found for them. Accordingly, the court made declarations that the local authority and the IRO had acted incompatibly with the Arts 3, 6 and 8 rights of the children: *A and S v Lancashire County Council* [2013] 2 FLR 803, FD.

Judicial review—The courts' traditional powers of review should be expanded to permit a court to assess any relevant facts which may be in issue in a case. The expansion of the court's powers was required by the jurisprudence of the ECtHR: *Manchester City Council v Pinnock* [2011] 2 AC 104, SC, per Lord Neuberger at [73].

Just satisfaction (s 8(3))—The court may decline to make an award of damages where the court decides that the declaratory or other relief granted is sufficient remedy for the breach of Convention rights. Wilson LJ observed in *Re C (Breach of Human Rights: Damages)* [2007] 1 FLR 1957, CA: 'In general the "principles" applied by the European Court, which we are thus enjoined to "take into account", are not clear or coherent ... What is clear, however, is that the European Court generally favours an award of damages in cases in which local authorities have infringed the right of parents under Article 8 to respect for their family life by shortcomings in the procedures by which they have taken children into care or kept them in care, whether temporarily or permanently'. In that case the infringement of the mother's human rights, as found by the court, was seen to be at the low end of the spectrum and it was unnecessary to award her damages to afford her just satisfaction.

The ECtHR assesses 'just satisfaction' under three heads: pecuniary loss, non-pecuniary loss and costs.

Award of damages—The Court of Appeal laid down procedural guidelines in respect of the award of damages and the circumstances in which maladministration will constitute a breach of Art 8: the guidelines are of general application:

(a) claims for damages alone may not be brought by way of judicial review but should be started in the Administrative Court by ordinary claim;
(b) courts should examine carefully attempts to recover damages for maladministration other than by way of judicial review;
(c) claimants must first exhaust all available complaints procedures including reference to an ombudsman;
(d) if there is a claim for relief in addition to a claim for damages, only the former should be granted permission and the latter should be adjourned or stayed pending determination of the substantive application; and
(e) citation of authorities in support of arguments about the quantum of damages should be limited to three and, save for exceptional cases, the hearing should be listed for no more than half a day: *Anufrijeva v Southwark LBC* [2004] 1 FLR 8, CA.

Quantum of damages—The court must take account of the principles applied by the ECtHR under Article 41 of the Convention when deciding whether to award damages and the quantum to be awarded: s 8(4) and see *Re C* (above). The awards of damages made by the ECtHR are generally modest. Lord Bingham said in *R (Greenfield) v Secretary of State for the Home Department* [2005] 1 WLR 673, HL, at [19] that courts 'should not aim to be significantly more or less generous that the [ECtHR] might be expected to be, in a case where it was willing to make an award at all'. In respect of a breach of Art 8 by a local authority and the award of damages, see *Kent County Council v M and K* [2016] EWFC 28.

9 Judicial acts

(1) Proceedings under section 7(1)(a) in respect of a judicial act may be brought only –

(a) by exercising a right of appeal;
(b) on an application (in Scotland a petition) for judicial review; or
(c) in such other forum as may be prescribed by rules.

(2) That does not affect any rule of law which prevents a court from being the subject of judicial review.

(3) In proceedings under this Act in respect of a judicial act done in good faith, damages may not be awarded otherwise than to compensate a person to the extent required by Article 5(5) of the Convention.

(4) An award of damages permitted by subsection (3) is to be made against the Crown; but no award may be made unless the appropriate person, if not a party to the proceedings, is joined.

(5) In this section –

'appropriate person' means the Minister responsible for the court concerned, or a person or government department nominated by him;
'court' includes a tribunal;
'judge' includes a member of a tribunal, a justice of the peace (or, in Northern Ireland, a lay magistrate) and a clerk or other officer entitled to exercise the jurisdiction of a court;
'judicial act' means a judicial act of a court and includes an act done on the instructions, or on behalf, of a judge; and
'rules' has the same meaning as in section 7(9).

Amendments—Justice (Northern Ireland) Act 2002, Sch 4, para 39; SI 2005/109.

Scope—Where there are freestanding proceedings in which a complaint is made of a judicial act, the appropriate procedure is to appeal. The objective of the provision is to prevent collateral attacks on the decisions of courts and tribunals. Where the judicial act is not within existing proceedings or there is no right of appeal, the appropriate procedure is by way of an application for judicial review under CPR 1998, Pt 54. Otherwise, a separate freestanding application under HRA 1998 should be by proceedings commenced under CPR 1998, Pt 8; however, see the case of *Hinds* (s 7 above).

Judicial act—The interpretation of the phrase is wide and includes any tribunal, any member of court or tribunal (including any legal advisor or other official entitled to exercise the powers of the court) and the act of any person acting on the instructions of or on behalf of any of the foregoing individuals.

Article 5(5)—This relates to the unlawful detention of the victim (eg continued detention after a bail application). In such circumstances damages are awarded against the Crown and not the court concerned. The government minister responsible for the court must be joined as a party to the proceedings: s 9(3),(4).

****

12 Freedom of expression

(1) This section applies if a court is considering whether to grant any relief which, if granted, might affect the exercise of the Convention right to freedom of expression.

(2) If the person against whom the application for relief is made ('the respondent') is neither present nor represented, no such relief is to be granted unless the court is satisfied –

(a) that the applicant has taken all practicable steps to notify the respondent; or
(b) that there are compelling reasons why the respondent should not be notified.

(3) No such relief is to be granted so as to restrain publication before trial unless the court is satisfied that the applicant is likely to establish that publication should not be allowed.

(4) The court must have particular regard to the importance of the Convention right to freedom of expression and, where the proceedings relate to material which the respondent claims, or which appears to the court, to be journalistic, literary or artistic material (or to conduct connected with such material), to –

(a) the extent to which –
  (i) the material has, or is about to, become available to the public; or
  (ii) it is, or would be, in the public interest for the material to be published;
(b) any relevant privacy code.

(5) In this section –

'court' includes a tribunal; and

'relief' includes any remedy or order (other than in criminal proceedings).

Applications for reporting restrictions order—Applications for reporting restriction orders are to be heard in the High Court and, if required, can be dealt with speedily and out of normal court hours (out of hours number 020 7947 6000). Service of an application on the national media can be effected via the Press Association's CopyDirect service, but note the *Financial Times* and *Sky News* do not subscribe to CopyDirect and must be served directly with the application. Similarly, if it is proposed to seek relief against a local newspaper, most do not subscribe to the CopyDirect service and must be served directly. A party who proposes to use CopyDirect to effect service on the national press and broadcast media should contact the service on 0870 837 6429.

Reporting Restrictions Orders—For guidance on the approach to applications for RROs, see: *Re J (Reporting Restriction: Internet: Video)* [2014] 1 FLR 523, FD; *Re Al Hilli (Children Reporting Restrictions)* [2014] 1 FLR 403, FD; *City and County of Swansea v XZ and YZ* [2014] 2 FLR 1091, FD; and *Birmingham City Council v Riaz and Others* [2015] 2 FLR 763, FD.

Without notice orders—The court retains the power to entertain without-notice applications but such cases will be exceptional and will permit those affected by the order to apply on short notice to vary or discharge the order made: see FPR PD12I. For further guidance, see CAFCASS Practice Note of 18 March 2005: *Applications for Reporting Restriction Orders* (updated 25 March 2015).

★★★★

21 Interpretation, etc

(1) In this Act –

'amend' includes repeal and apply (with or without modifications);

'the appropriate Minister' means the Minister of the Crown having charge of the appropriate authorised government department (within the meaning of the Crown Proceedings Act 1947);

'the Commission' means the European Commission of Human Rights;

'the Convention' means the Convention for the Protection of Human Rights and Fundamental Freedoms, agreed by the Council of Europe at Rome on 4 November 1950 as it has effect for the time being in relation to the United Kingdom;

'declaration of incompatibility' means a declaration under section 4;

'Minister of the Crown' has the same meaning as in the Ministers of the Crown Act 1975;

'Northern Ireland Minister' includes the First Minister and the deputy First Minister in Northern Ireland;

'primary legislation' means any –

(a) public general Act;
(b) local and personal Act;
(c) private Act;
(d) Measure of the Church Assembly;
(e) Measure of the General Synod of the Church of England;
(f) Order in Council –
  (i) made in exercise of Her Majesty's Royal Prerogative;

(ii) made under section 38(1)(a) of the Northern Ireland Constitution Act 1973 or the corresponding provision of the Northern Ireland Act 1998; or
(iii) amending an Act of a kind mentioned in paragraph (a), (b) or (c);

and includes an order or other instrument made under primary legislation (otherwise than by the Welsh Ministers, the First Minister for Wales, the Counsel General to the Welsh Assembly Government, a member of the Scottish Executive, a Northern Ireland Minister or a Northern Ireland department) to the extent to which it operates to bring one or more provisions of that legislation into force or amends any primary legislation;

'the First Protocol' means the protocol to the Convention agreed at Paris on 20th March 1952;

'the Eleventh Protocol' means the protocol to the Convention (restructuring the control machinery established by the Convention) agreed at Strasbourg on 11 May 1994;

'the Thirteenth Protocol' means the protocol to the Convention (concerning the abolition of the death penalty in all circumstances) agreed at Vilnius on 3 May 2002;

'remedial order' means an order under section 10;

'subordinate legislation' means any –

(a) Order in Council other than one –
(i) made in exercise of Her Majesty's Royal Prerogative;
(ii) made under section 38(1)(a) of the Northern Ireland Constitution Act 1973 or the corresponding provision of the Northern Ireland Act 1998; or
(iii) amending an Act of a kind mentioned in the definition of primary legislation;
(b) Act of the Scottish Parliament;
(ba) Measure of the National Assembly for Wales;
(bb) Act of the National Assembly for Wales;
(c) Act of the Parliament of Northern Ireland;
(d) Measure of the Assembly established under section 1 of the Northern Ireland Assembly Act 1973;
(e) Act of the Northern Ireland Assembly;
(f) order, rules, regulations, scheme, warrant, byelaw or other instrument made under primary legislation (except to the extent to which it operates to bring one or more provisions of that legislation into force or amends any primary legislation);
(g) order, rules, regulations, scheme, warrant, byelaw or other instrument made under legislation mentioned in paragraph (b), (c), (d) or (e) or made under an Order in Council applying only to Northern Ireland;
(h) order, rules, regulations, scheme, warrant, byelaw or other instrument made by a member of the Scottish Executive, Welsh Ministers, the First Minister for Wales, the Counsel General to the Welsh Assembly Government, a Northern Ireland Minister or a Northern Ireland department in exercise of prerogative or other executive functions of Her Majesty which are exercisable by such a person on behalf of Her Majesty;

'transferred matters' has the same meaning as in the Northern Ireland Act 1998; and

'tribunal' means any tribunal in which legal proceedings may be brought.

(2) The references in paragraphs (b) and (c) of section 2(1) to Articles are to Articles of the Convention as they had effect immediately before the coming into force of the Eleventh Protocol.

(3) The reference in paragraph (d) of section 2(1) to Article 46 includes a reference to Articles 32 and 54 of the Convention as they had effect immediately before the coming into force of the Eleventh Protocol.

(4) The references in section 2(1) to a report or decision of the Commission or a decision of the Committee of Ministers include references to a report or decision made as provided by paragraphs 3, 4 and 6 of Article 5 of the Eleventh Protocol (transitional provisions).

(5) Any liability under the Army Act 1955, the Air Force Act 1955 or the Naval Discipline Act 1957 to suffer death for an offence is replaced by a liability to imprisonment for life or any less punishment authorised by those Acts; and those Acts shall accordingly have effect with the necessary modifications.

Amendments—SI 2004/1574; Government of Wales Act 2006, Sch 10, para 56.

Primary legislation—This is not limited to Acts of Parliament (public general, local and personal or private) but includes Orders made in Council (a) under the Royal Prerogative and (b) amending Acts of Parliament.

Subordinate legislation—In the interests of maintaining the sovereignty of the UK Parliament, Acts and other measures passed by the Scottish Parliament, the National Assembly for Wales or the Northern Ireland Assembly are all subordinate and not primary legislation.

Remedial order—A remedial order pursuant to s 10 is the fast-track procedure by which a minister may amend primary or secondary legislation to remove its incompatibility with the Convention either as a result of a declaration of incompatibility or in consequence of a decision of the ECtHR, if there are 'compelling reasons' for so doing. The 'standard procedure' requires the minister to lay a draft statutory instrument before Parliament that will not come into effect unless approved by a resolution of both Houses: Sch 2, para 2(a). The emergency procedure requires the minister to lay a draft statutory instrument before Parliament but it has immediate effect and will cease to have effect 120 days after it was made unless approved by a resolution of both Houses: Schedule 2, para 2(b). The emergency procedure must only be used where it appears to the minister that the urgency of the matter requires it.

****

SCHEDULE 1
THE ARTICLES

PART I
THE CONVENTION

Rights and Freedoms

Article 2 – Right to life

1 Everyone's right to life shall be protected by law. No one shall be deprived of his life intentionally save in the execution of a sentence of a court following his conviction of a crime for which this penalty is provided by law.

2 Deprivation of life shall not be regarded as inflicted in contravention of this Article when it results from the use of force which is no more than absolutely necessary:

(a) in defence of any person from unlawful violence;
(b) in order to effect a lawful arrest or to prevent the escape of a person lawfully detained;
(c) in action lawfully taken for the purpose of quelling a riot or insurrection.

Death penalty—The use of the death penalty was abolished by Protocol 6, save during time of war or of imminent threat of war, and in all circumstances by Protocol 13. No derogations or reservations may be made in respect of the abolition of the death penalty.

Everyone's right to life—The issue arises of whether an unborn foetus has the right to life. In *Vo v France* [2004] ECHR 326, at [75] and [82], the Grand Chamber of the ECtHR held that in the absence of a European consensus on when human life begins, the issue falls within the margin of appreciation to be accorded to each state. In *Evans v United Kingdom* [2007] 1 FLR 1990, ECHR, at [55] and [56], the Grand Chamber referred to the English authorities that a foetus does not have a right to life and accordingly found there had been no breach of Art 2. In *A, B & C v Ireland* [2010] ECHR 2032, at [237] the Grand Chambers held that 'of central importance is the finding in the above-cited *Vo* case, referred to above, that the question of when the right to life begins came within the states' margin of appreciation because there was no European consensus on the scientific and legal definition of the beginning of life, so that it was impossible to answer the question whether the unborn was a person to be protected for the purposes of Article 2. Since the rights claimed on behalf of the foetus and those of the mother are inextricably interconnected ... the margin of appreciation accorded to a state's protection of the unborn necessarily translates into a margin of appreciation for that state as to how it balances the conflicting rights of the mother'.

Positive obligations—The Article imposes positive obligations on the state to protect the right to life. To be engaged the state authorities must have known or ought to have known that there was a real and immediate risk to life and yet failed to take measures within the scope of their power which, judged reasonably, might have been expected to avoid that risk: *Osman v UK* [1999] 1 FLR 193, ECHR; *Van Colle v Chief Constable of Hertfordshire Police* [2009] 1 AC 225, HL. The article imposed on the state operational obligations to protect mentally ill patients who were not detained under MHA 1983 where there was a real and immediate risk of suicide: *Rabone & Othrs v Pennine Care NHS Trust* [2012] UKSC 2.

Prohibition—The Article prohibits the taking of life intentionally or unintentionally, where the force used is more than absolutely necessary: *Osman* (above) and *McShane v UK* [2002] ECHR 469.

Right to die—The House of Lords and the ECtHR have held that the Article does not confer a right to die: *R (Pretty) v DPP* [2002] 1 FLR 268, HL; *Pretty v UK* [2002] 2 FLR 45, ECHR. However, the House of Lords and the ECtHR disagreed on whether Article 8 was engaged in 'right to die' cases: the former found not, whereas the latter found it was. The House of Lords has subsequently departed from the decision in *R (Pretty)* and found that Article 8 is engaged: *R (Purdy) v DPP* [2010] 1 AC 345, HL.

Article 3 – Prohibition of torture

No one shall be subjected to torture or to inhuman or degrading treatment or punishment.

Prohibited activities—Torture (inhuman treatment that causes very serious and cruel suffering); inhuman treatment (treatment that causes intense physical and mental suffering); and degrading treatment (treatment that arouses in the victim a feeling of fear, anguish and inferiority capable of humiliating and debasing the victim and possibly breaking his or her physical or moral resistance): *Ireland v UK* [1978] ECHR 1. The treatment must attain a 'minimum level of severity' to engage the Article (ie a high level of severity): *Chalal v UK* [1996] ECHR 54.

Negative and positive obligations—The Article imposes negative and positive obligations on the state. 'There must be some distinction between the scope of the state's duty not to take life or ill-treat people in a way which falls foul of Article 3 [the negative obligation] and its duty to protect people from the harm which others may do to them [the positive obligation]. In the one case, there is an absolute duty not to do it. In the other, there is a duty to do what is reasonable in all the circumstances to protect people from a real and immediate risk of harm': *Re E (A Child) (Northern Ireland)* [2009] AC 536, HL, per Baroness Hale at [10].

Prevention—The state is under a positive duty to protect children from chronic neglect and abuse. Where children have so suffered and where the authorities knew but failed to take any action or any timeous action, the state is likely to be found in breach of the Article and liable to the children for damages: *A v UK* [1998] 2 FLR 959, ECHR; *Z v UK* [2001] 2 FLR 612, ECHR; *E & Others v UK* [2003] 1 FLR 348, ECHR; *Mayeka v Belgium* [2007] 1 FLR 1726, ECHR.

Article 4 – Prohibition of slavery and forced labour

1 No one shall be held in slavery or servitude.

2 No one shall be required to perform forced or compulsory labour.

3 For the purpose of this Article the term 'forced or compulsory labour' shall not include:

(a) any work required to be done in the ordinary course of detention imposed according to the provisions of Article 5 of this Convention or during conditional release from such detention;
(b) any service of a military character or, in case of conscientious objectors in countries where they are recognised, service exacted instead of compulsory military service;
(c) any service exacted in case of an emergency or calamity threatening the life or well-being of the community;
(d) any work or service which forms part of normal civic obligations.

Article 5 – Right to liberty and security

1 Everyone has the right to liberty and security of person. No one shall be deprived of his liberty save in the following cases and in accordance with a procedure prescribed by law –

(a) the lawful detention of a person after conviction by a competent court;
(b) the lawful arrest or detention of a person for non-compliance with the lawful order of a court or in order to secure the fulfilment of any obligation prescribed by law;
(c) the lawful arrest or detention of a person effected for the purpose of bringing him before the competent legal authority on reasonable suspicion of having committed an offence or when it is reasonably considered necessary to prevent his committing an offence or fleeing after having done so;
(d) the detention of a minor by lawful order for the purpose of educational supervision or his lawful detention for the purpose of bringing him before the competent legal authority;
(e) the lawful detention of persons for the prevention of the spreading of infectious diseases, of persons of unsound mind, alcoholics or drug addicts or vagrants;
(f) the lawful arrest or detention of a person to prevent his effecting an unauthorised entry into the country or of a person against whom action is being taken with a view to deportation or extradition.

2 Everyone who is arrested shall be informed promptly, in a language which he understands, of the reasons for his arrest and of any charge against him.

3 Everyone arrested or detained in accordance with the provisions of paragraph 1(c) of this Article shall be brought promptly before a judge or other officer authorised by law to exercise judicial power and shall be entitled to trial within a reasonable time or to release pending trial. Release may be conditioned by guarantees to appear for trial.

4 Everyone who is deprived of his liberty by arrest or detention shall be entitled to take proceedings by which the lawfulness of his detention shall be decided speedily by a court and his release ordered if the detention is not lawful.

5 Everyone who has been the victim of arrest or detention in contravention of the provisions of this Article shall have an enforceable right to compensation.

Deprivation of liberty—Has three elements; (i) the objective element of a person's confinement to a certain limited place for a not negligible length of time; (ii) the additional subjective element that they had not validly consented to the confinement in question; and (iii) the confinement had to be imputable to the state: *Storck v Germany* (2006) 43 EHRR 6, ECHR.

The Supreme Court considered the issue of a deprivation of liberty in *P (By His Litigation Friend the Official Solicitor) v Cheshire West and Chester Council and Another; P and Q (By Their Litigation Friend the Official Solicitor) v Surrey County Council* [2014] COPLR 313, SC, where Lady Hale said 'It is very easy to focus upon the positive features of these placements for all three of the appellants. The local authorities who are responsible for them have no doubt done the best they could to make their lives as happy and fulfilled, as well as safe, as they possibly could be. But the purpose of article 5 is to ensure that people are not deprived of their liberty without proper safeguards, safeguards which will secure that the legal justifications for the constraints which they are under are made out: in these cases, the law requires that they do indeed lack the capacity to decide for themselves where they should live and that the arrangements made for them are in their best interests. It is to set the cart before the horse to decide that because they do indeed lack capacity and the best possible arrangements have been made, they are not in need of those safeguards. If P, MIG and MEG were under the same constraints in the sort of institution in which Mr Stanev was confined, we would have no difficulty in deciding that they had been deprived of their liberty. In the end, it is the constraints that matter', at [56] and [57].

Article 6 – Right to a fair trial

1 In the determination of his civil rights and obligations or of any criminal charge against him, everyone is entitled to a fair and public hearing within a reasonable time by an independent and impartial tribunal established by law. Judgment shall be pronounced publicly but the press and public may be excluded from all or part of the trial in the interest of morals, public order or national security in a democratic society, where the interests of juveniles or the protection of the private life of the parties so require, or to the extent strictly necessary in the opinion of the court in special circumstances where publicity would prejudice the interests of justice.

2 Everyone charged with a criminal offence shall be presumed innocent until proved guilty according to law.

3 Everyone charged with a criminal offence has the following minimum rights –

(a) to be informed promptly, in a language which he understands and in detail, of the nature and cause of the accusation against him;

(b) to have adequate time and facilities for the preparation of his defence;

(c) to defend himself in person or through legal assistance of his own choosing or, if he has not sufficient means to pay for legal assistance, to be given it free when the interests of justice so require;

(d) to examine or have examined witnesses against him and to obtain the attendance and examination of witnesses on his behalf under the same conditions as witnesses against him;

(e) to have the free assistance of an interpreter if he cannot understand or speak the language used in court.

Scope—The right to a fair trial is absolute but the constituent rights are not and may be limited: the only balancing permitted is what the concept of a fair trial entails. Any limitation must satisfy the test of proportionality: *R v A* [2002] 1 AC 45, HL, at [38].

Civil rights and obligations—Although they recognise that the meaning of the phrase is autonomous, the UK courts have tended to adopt a more restrictive interpretation than the ECtHR of what constitutes 'civil rights and obligations': *R (Kehoe) v Secretary of State for Work & Pensions* [2005] 2 FLR 1249, HL (no right to apply to court to recover child maintenance); *R (A) v Croydon LBC; R (M) v Lambeth LBC* [2009] 1 FLR 1324, CA, at [50]–[59] (asylum-seeker's 'right' to accommodation under CA 1989, s 20); and *Ali & Others v Birmingham City Council & Others* [2010] 2 AC 39, SC (cases where the award of services or benefits in kind was not an individual right of which the applicant could consider himself the holder, but rather was dependent upon a series of evaluative judgments by the provider did not engage Art 6(1)).

Rights protected—The rights protected by the Article include: (i) access to a court (*Golder v UK* (1975) 1 EHRR 524, ECHR); (ii) which is real and effective (*Steel & Morris v UK* [2005] ECHR 103); (iii) a hearing before an independent and impartial tribunal established by law (*McGonnell v UK* [2000] ECHR 62); (iv) in public; (v) within a reasonable time (*Adam v Germany* [2009] 1 FLR 560, ECHR); (vi) with a real opportunity to present a case, including 'equality of arms' or an oral hearing if required in the circumstances (*Ruiz-Mateos v Spain* (1993) 16 EHRR 505, ECHR); and (vii) a reasoned decision (*English v Emery, Reimbold & Strick* [2002] 1 WLR 2409, CA).

Public hearing—There are exceptions to the right to a public hearing and the ECtHR has accepted the general presumption of hearings concerning children being held in private (*B v UK* [2000] 1 FLR 1, ECHR). The requirement for judgment to be pronounced publicly does not necessarily require the judgment to be delivered in open court but simply that the decision is made public.

Provision of legal assistance—There is no automatic right under the Convention for legal aid or legal representation (save in respect of those charged with a criminal offence under Article 6.3(c)), but where fairness or the right of a party to put forward his case in a proper and effective manner so requires, the absence of a lawyer to represent the party may render the proceedings unfair (*P, C & S v UK* [2002] 2 FLR 631, ECHR (contested care and freeing for adoption proceedings)).

Requirements—'The single theme which runs through the whole of Article 6 is the right of a litigant or an accused to have a fair trial … But while there can be no doubt that the right to a fair trial is an absolute right, precisely what is comprised in the concept of fairness may be open to a varied analysis. It is not to be supposed that the content of the right is necessarily composed of rigid rules which provide an absolute protection for an accused person under every circumstance …The jurisprudence of the ECtHR demonstrates that several of the particular rights which … by implication fall within the scope of Article 6 are not absolute rights.': *Brown v Stott (Procurator Fiscal, Dunfermline) & Another* [2003] 1 AC 681, PC per Lord Clyde. For an overview of the principles for and requirements of a fair trial see *Re B (Disclosure to Other Parties)* [2001] 2 FLR 1017, FD, at [33]–[68]; *Re L (Care: Assessment: Fair Trial)* [2002] 2 FLR 730, FD, at [86]–[106].

The Court of Appeal has held that the failure to grant a vulnerable litigant in person an adjournment to enable him to obtain alternate legal representation, especially where the delay involved in doing so would be very short, was a breach of his Art 6 rights to a fair trial: *Re L (Application Hearing: Legal Representation)* [2013] 2 FLR 1444, CA. See also the notes to CPR 1998, r 52.3.

Article 7 – No punishment without law

1 No one shall be held guilty of any criminal offence on account of any act or omission which did not constitute a criminal offence under national or international law at the time when it was committed. Nor shall a heavier penalty be imposed than the one that was applicable at the time the criminal offence was committed.

2 This Article shall not prejudice the trial and punishment of any person for any act or omission which, at the time when it was committed, was criminal according to the general principles of law recognised by civilised nations.

Article 8 – Right to respect for private and family life

1 Everyone has the right to respect for his private and family life, his home and his correspondence.

2 There shall be no interference by a public authority with the exercise of this right except such as is in accordance with the law and is necessary in a democratic society in the interests of national security, public safety or the economic well-being of the country, for the prevention of disorder or crime, for the protection of health or morals, or for the protection of the rights and freedoms of others.

Scope—There are four elements protected by the Article: (i) private life; (ii) family life; (iii) home; and (iv) correspondence, but the effect of the Article, as interpreted by the ECtHR and domestic courts, protects a diverse range of rights most notably a right to privacy. The protection afforded by the Article is qualified: an interference with a right protected by Article 8(1) is only permissible insofar as it is (i) in accordance with the law; (ii) necessary in a democratic society; and (iii) the degree of interference is proportionate to the objective sought to be achieved by the state. The rights protected by this Article include the right to have measures taken by the state with a view to a parent being reunited with their child: *Pakhomova v Russia (Application No 22935/11)* [2014] 2 FLR 44, ECHR.

Private life—The extent of the meaning of the phrase 'private life' cannot be identified but it includes the notion of 'personal autonomy', 'physical & mental integrity', 'the protection of one's reputation' and extends to 'those features which are integral to a person's identity or ability to function socially as a person': *R (Razgar) v Secretary of State for the Home Department* [2004] 2 AC 368, HL. The House of Lords has held that the right to private life is engaged when an individual suffering from a terminal illness chooses death rather than life: *R (Purdy) v DPP* [2010] 1 AC 345, HL.

Family life—There is no clear definition of what is meant by 'family life'. 'The existence or non-existence of "family life" for the purposes of Art 8 is essentially a question of fact depending upon the real existence in practice of close personal ties', which 'has sufficient constancy and substance to create de facto "family ties"': *Lebbink v The Netherlands* [2004] 2 FLR 463, ECHR, at [36]. Family life is not confined to married couples or to cohabiting couples and can exist even where there is no biological relationship between parent and child: *Singh v Entry Clearance Officer, New Delhi* [2005] 1 FLR 308, CA, at [58]–[80]. The right to start a family is not protected by the right to respect for family life: *Evans v UK* [2007] 1 FLR 1990, ECHR.

Balancing of rights—Where the rights under Art 8 of parents and those of a child are at stake, the child's rights must be the paramount consideration. If any balancing of the interests of the child, on the one hand, and of the parents, on the other, is necessary, the interests of the child must prevail: *Yousef v The Netherlands* [2003] 1 FLR 210, ECHR. See also, *Re B (A Child)* [2015] 1 FLR 871, CA: compelling an under-age half-brother of an abducted child to give evidence about the same requires a careful evaluation of the Art 8 rights of the half-brother.

Home—Whether a place is or is not a 'home' is fact-specific and depends on there being sufficient and continuous links. 'Home' has been held to include a long-stay hospital and second homes: *R v North & East Devon District Health Authority, ex p Coughlan* [2001] QB 213, CA. An order for possession of a property does infringe Article 8(1) but the County Court may assume that domestic law satisfies the requirements of 8(2) and would not generally need to apply the proportionality test: *Kay v Lambeth LBC* [2006] 2 AC 465, HL.

Right to privacy—The approach of the domestic courts to an action for breach of confidence has dramatically changed in light of Article 8. The new approach 'focuses upon the protection of human autonomy and dignity – the right to control the dissemination of information about one's private life and the right to the esteem and respect of other people': *Campbell v MGN* [2004] 2 AC 457, HL, at [51]. See the notes below to Article 10 and the balance between the protection of private life and right to freedom of expression.

Fairness—Although the Article contains no explicit procedural requirements, it is clear that the provision affords significant procedural safeguards: thus 'the decision-making process leading to measures of interference must be fair and such as to afford due respect to the interests safeguard by Art 8': *McMichael v UK* (1995) 20 EHRR 205, ECHR, at [87]. Accordingly, local authorities must ensure that parents are sufficiently involved in the decision-making process before and during court proceedings and must make full and proper disclosure: *Re L (Care: Assessment: Fair Trial)* (above); *Re G (Care: Challenge to Local Authority's Decision)* [2003] 2 FLR 42, FD, at [28]–[60]. However, the mere failure to observe these precepts does not automatically or necessarily result in a finding that a parent's human rights have been breached or render the proceedings unfair: *Re V (Care: Pre-Birth Actions)* [2005] 1 FLR 627, CA, at [4], [24], [29] and [33]; *Re J (Care: Assessment: Fair Trial)* [2007] 1 FLR 77, CA, at [25]–[30].

Threshold criteria—Article 8 is not engaged when a court is considering whether the threshold criteria of CA 1989, s 31(2) are satisfied. It is fully engaged, however, when the court is considering whether to make a care order. Decisions about whether the threshold criteria are satisfied and whether a care order is necessary are evaluative exercises and not the exercise of a judicial discretion: *Re B (Care Proceedings: Appeal)* [2013] 2 FLR 1075, SC.

Care orders—A court must not sanction a care plan providing for the removal of a child from his family 'unless he is satisfied that that is both necessary and proportionate and that no other less radical form of order would achieve the essential end of promoting the welfare of the child': *Re B (Care: Interference with Family Life)* [2003] 2 FLR 813, at [34].

Adoption—A high degree of justification is required for the making of an adoption order. The court must carefully consider the proportionality of such an order: *Re B (Care Proceedings: Appeal)* [2013] 2 FLR 1075, SC. In order to consider the Art 8 proportionality of making an adoption order it is essential that the court has proper evidence before it, which must balance the advantages and disadvantages of all realistically possible options that meet the best interests of the child and the court must adopt a 'global, holistic evaluation' of all of those options: *Re B-S (Adoption: Application of s 47(5))* [2014] 1 FLR 1035, CA and *Re R* [2015] 1 FLR 715, CA.

Forced marriages—Under an amendment to the Immigration Rules, the age at which foreign spouses were banned from entering the UK for settlement was increased from 18 to 21. The Supreme Court held that the amendment pursued a legitimate aim of deterring forced marriage but was not necessary in a democratic society in that it was not a proportionate response to the problem caused by forced marriage: *R (Quila); R (Bibi) v Secretary of State for the Home Department* [2012] 1 FLR 788, SC; see also *Re E (Adoption Order: Proportionality of Outcome to Circumstances)* [2014] 2 FLR 514, CA.

Lack of capacity—The force-feeding of a patient who lacked capacity for the purposes of MCA 2005, s 2(1) was found to be in her best interests. The resulting interference in her Arts 3 and 8 rights was proportionate and necessary to protect her right to life: *A Local Authority v E and Others* [2012] COPLR 441, COP.

Immigration and extradition cases—*Norris v United States* [2010] UKSC 9 had not decided that the Art 8 rights of the family of a proposed extradite could never prevail unless an exceptionality test was satisfied: exceptionality was a prediction and not a test. The need to examine the way the process would interfere with the children's best interests was just as great in extradition cases as it was in cases of immigration control: *HH & PH v Italy; FK v Poland* [2013] 1 AC 338, SC.

Article 9 – Freedom of thought, conscience and religion

1 Everyone has the right to freedom of thought, conscience and religion; this right includes freedom to change his religion or belief and freedom, either alone or in community with others and in public or private, to manifest his religion or belief, in worship, teaching, practice and observance.

2 Freedom to manifest one's religion or beliefs shall be subject only to such limitations as are prescribed by law and are necessary in a democratic society in the interests of public safety, for the protection of public order, health or morals, or for the protection of the rights and freedoms of others.

Foster carers—A local authority did not discriminate against a couple on grounds of religion when refusing to approve them as foster carers because of their views on sexuality, namely that sexual relations other than those within marriage between one man and one woman were morally wrong: *R (Eunice Johns & Owen Johns) v Derby City Council & Othrs* [2011] 1 FLR 2094, QBD).

Article 10 – Freedom of expression

1 Everyone has the right to freedom of expression. This right shall include freedom to hold opinions and to receive and impart information and ideas without interference by public authority and regardless of frontiers. This Article shall not prevent States from requiring the licensing of broadcasting, television or cinema enterprises.

2 The exercise of these freedoms, since it carries with it duties and responsibilities, may be subject to such formalities, conditions, restrictions or penalties as are prescribed by law and are necessary in a democratic society, in the interests of national security, territorial integrity or public safety, for the prevention of disorder or crime, for the protection of health or morals, for the protection of the reputation or rights of others, for preventing the disclosure of information received in confidence, or for maintaining the authority and impartiality of the judiciary.

Scope—The rights protected under Article 10 are seen to be essential to a democratic society. The protection is afforded to natural and legal persons, including commercial companies. The rights are not limited to freedom of expression but include rights to receive information but the Article does not give rise to a general right to freedom of information: the latter may arise consequentially to protect another right: *Gaskin v UK* [1990] 1 FLR 167, ECHR.

Press freedom—The courts have long recognised the importance to be accorded to the freedom of the press. Lord Bingham noted that 'the proper functioning of a modern participatory democracy requires that the media be free, active, professional and inquiring. For this reason, the courts, here and elsewhere, have recognised the cardinal importance of press freedom': *Turkington & Others v Times Newspapers Ltd (Northern Ireland)* [2001] 2 AC 277, HL.

HRA 1998, s 12—The courts are enjoined to have 'particular regard' to the importance of the freedom of expression when considering the grant of injunctive relief. By ss 12(2),(3) courts should not grant without notice orders restraining freedom of expression without strong justification for so doing.

Limitations—Although the possible limitations on the rights are couched in wide terms, the ECtHR requires a strong justification for interfering with the right. To justify interference it must be (i) in accordance with law, (ii) in pursuance of a legitimate aim and (iii) necessary in a democratic society: *Sunday Times v UK (No.1)* (1979) 2 EHRR 245. The extent and duration of an obstruction of the highway and the public nuisance inherent in that obstruction may warrant an interference with protesters' rights under Arts 10 and 11 if lawful, necessary and proportionate (*City of London v Tammy Samede (Representative of those Persons Taking Part in a Protest Camp at St Paul's Churchyard, London EC4) & Othrs* [2012] EWHC 34 (QB)).

Court of Protection—Art 10 is engaged when the media first make an application to attend a hearing and not merely once a 'good reason' for the application had been established: *Independent News & Media v A* [2010] COPLR Con Vol 686, CA.

When determining issues under MCA 2005, a judge should first ascertain the best interests of the patient by applying the s 4 checklist of factors and only then consider whether the resulting conclusion amounted to a violation of the patient's rights under Art 8 and whether the violation was necessary and proportionate; Art 8 is not the starting point: *K v LBX and Others* [2012] COPLR 411, CA.

Conflict with other Convention rights—The leading case in domestic law is *Re S (A Child) (Identification Restrictions on Publication)* [2005] 1 FLR 591, HL. Lord Steyn said, at [17], 'First, neither Article has as such precedence over the other. Secondly, where the values under the two Articles are in conflict, an intense focus on the comparative importance of the specific rights being claimed in the individual case is necessary. Thirdly, the justifications for interfering with or restricting each right must be taken into account. Finally, the proportionality test must be applied to each. For convenience I will call this the ultimate balancing test.'

Contra mundum injunctions—The President has given guidance on the grounds for making injunctions to prevent parents and others speaking out about a case concerning a child and/or perceived deficiencies in the family justice system and the practice to be adopted in relation to the internet, in particular social media, and foreign defendants: *Re J (Reporting Restriction: Internet: Video)* [2014] 1 FLR 523, FD.

Injunctions preventing publication—Where a court proposed to make an injunction prohibiting the publication of information with a view to preventing an interference in the claimant's Art 8 rights, it was important that the order contained the undertakings required by CPR PD25A and the Master of the Rolls' Practice Guidance: *Interim Non-Disclosure Orders*: *AM v News Group Newspapers Ltd & Persons Unknown* [2012] EWHC 308 (QB).

Anonymisation of proceedings—When granting an injunction to restrain the publication of information in order to prevent an interference with a claimant's Art 8 rights, the general rule was that parties' names would be included in the court's orders and judgments; there was no general exception for cases where private matters were in issue. Anonymising the proceedings was an exceptional course to take: *Spelman (A Child by his Litigation Friends) v Express Newspapers* [2012] EWHC 239 (QB).

Article 11 – Freedom of assembly and association

1 Everyone has the right to freedom of peaceful assembly and to freedom of association with others, including the right to form and to join trade unions for the protection of his interests.

2 No restrictions shall be placed on the exercise of these rights other than such as are prescribed by law and are necessary in a democratic society in the interests of national security or public safety, for the prevention of disorder or crime, for the protection of health or morals or for the protection of the rights and freedoms of others. This Article shall not prevent the imposition of lawful restrictions on the exercise of these rights by members of the armed forces, of the police or of the administration of the State.

Article 12 – Right to marry

Men and women of marriageable age have the right to marry and to found a family, according to the national laws governing the exercise of this right.

Scope—Two rights are expressed in this Article: (i) the right to marry and (ii) the right to found a family. National states are, however, given a wide discretion to govern the exercise of these rights. The ECtHR has construed the provisions more narrowly than those under Article 8. An interference with family life that is justified under 8(2) cannot be a violation of Article 12: *Boso v Italy* [2002] ECHR 846.

National laws—There is a limit to the extent to which national laws may regulate the exercise of Article 12 rights – the rules must not be arbitrary or interfere with the essence of the right: *B v UK* (2004) 39 EHRR 30, ECHR (prohibition on father-in-law and daughter-in-law marrying save if waiver obtained by way of private Act of Parliament). The government is entitled to enact measures to prevent 'sham' marriages by those subject to immigration control, but the scheme must not disproportionately infringe the rights of non-nationals: *R (Baiai & Others) v Secretary of State for the Home Department* [2008] 2 FLR 1462, HL and *Aguilar v Secretary of State for the Home Department* [2011] 1 FLR 1187, CA). A ban on transsexuals, who had undergone gender reassignment, to marry was held not to be justified and in the UK led to the passing of the GRA 2004: *Goodwin v UK* [2002] 2 FLR 487, ECHR; *Bellinger v Bellinger* [2003] 1 FLR 1043, HL.

Same-sex marriages—These are not recognised or protected by the Article: *Wilkinson v Kitzinger* [2006] 2 FLR 397, FD and [2007] 1 FLR 295, FD.

Right to found a family—The Article does not create a freestanding right to found a family in the absence of a marital relationship: *Marckx v Belgium* (1979) 2 EHRR 330, ECHR.

****

Article 14 – Prohibition of discrimination

The enjoyment of the rights and freedoms set forth in this Convention shall be secured without discrimination on any ground such as sex, race, colour, language, religion, political or other opinion, national or social origin, association with a national minority, property, birth or other status.

Scope—The Article provides a limited degree of protection. It does not create a freestanding right of equal treatment but merely a right to equal treatment in the application of other rights afforded by the Convention. A breach of another Convention right is not a prerequisite for the finding of a breach of the Article but the facts relied on to demonstrate discrimination must come within the ambit of one or more other Convention rights: *Abdulaziz & Others v UK* (1985) 7 EHRR 471; *Ghaidan v Godin-Mendoza* [2004] 2 FLR 600, HL.

Foreign nationals—In the absence of exceptional circumstances, aliens could not claim any entitlement under the European Convention to remain in England to escape from the discriminatory effects of the system of family law in their country of origin and could not rely on the rights protected by Article 14. It was not enough to show that a child custody regime was arbitrary and discriminatory; an applicant had to show that return to such a regime would completely deny or nullify her own and the child's right to respect for family life together: *EM (Lebanon) v Secretary of State for the Home Department* [2008] 2 FLR 2067, HL.

European case-law—In cases where an applicant alleges a breach of a substantive Convention right and a breach of Article 14, the ECtHR invariably will not consider the claim under Article 14 if it finds a breach of the former (eg *S & Marper v UK* [2008] ECHR 1581).

****

Article 16 – Restrictions on political activity of aliens

Nothing in Articles 10, 11 and 14 shall be regarded as preventing the High Contracting Parties from imposing restrictions on the political activity of aliens.

Article 17 – Prohibition of abuse of rights

Nothing in this Convention may be interpreted as implying for any State, group or person any right to engage in any activity or perform any act aimed at the destruction of any of the rights and freedoms set forth herein or at their limitation to a greater extent than is provided for in the Convention.

Article 18 – Limitation on use of restrictions on rights

The restrictions permitted under this Convention to the said rights and freedoms shall not be applied for any purpose other than those for which they have been prescribed.

PART II

THE FIRST PROTOCOL

Article 1 – Protection of property

Every natural or legal person is entitled to the peaceful enjoyment of his possessions. No one shall be deprived of his possessions except in the public interest and subject to the conditions provided for by law and by the general principles of international law.

The preceding provisions shall not, however, in any way impair the right of a State to enforce such laws as it deems necessary to control the use of property in accordance with the general interest or to secure the payment of taxes or other contributions or penalties.

Scope—The Article comprises three distinct but not unconnected rules: the principle of the peaceful enjoyment of property; the deprivation of possessions subject to conditions; and the recognition that states are entitled to control the use of property (*Allard v Sweden* (2004) 39 EHRR 321).

Positive obligations—The ECtHR has held that a 'state may be responsible under Art 1 for interferences with peaceful enjoyment of possessions resulting from transactions between private individuals' (*Gustafson v Sweden* (1996) 22 EHRR 409).The court's approach to positive and negative obligations under Art 1 are similar. In both contexts, regard must be had 'to the fair balance to be struck between the competing interests of the individual and of the community as a whole' and 'the state enjoys a certain margin of appreciation in determining the steps to be taken to ensure compliance with the Convention' (*Broniowski v Poland* (2005) 40 EHRR 495).

Possessions—The term embraces a broad range of property rights. The concept, however, extends far beyond real and personal property to include all manner of things that have an economic value (e g planning permission: *Pine Valley Developments Ltd v Ireland* (1992) 14 EHRR 319).

Deprivation—Destruction of property constitutes a deprivation (*Isayeva v Russia* (2005) 41 EHRR 847. For a de facto deprivation through expropriation to arise, there must effectively be an extinction of property rights (*Papamichalopoulos v Greece* (1993) 16 EHRR 440).

Conditions for permitted deprivations—The measure must be in accordance with national law, respect the general principles of international law and be in the public interest, which requires a balancing of the public interest against individual rights. Thus, the measure must be sufficiently precise and foreseeable in its consequences and have appropriate procedural guarantees (*Hentrich v France* (1994) 18 EHRR 440; *R (Bizzy B Management Ltd) v Stockton-on-Tees Borough Council)* [2011] EWHC 2325 (Admin)).

Balancing public interest against individual rights—A compulsory purchase order for the acquisition of a derelict residential property by a local authority did not contravene the property owner's rights under the Article (*Terry Navarro Peart v Secretary of State for Transport, Local Government & Regions* [2003] EWCA Civ 295). Legislation banning the sale of tobacco from automatic vending machines pursued a legitimate public health aim and was not a disproportionate interference with the claimant's economic rights (*R (Sinclair Collis Ltd) v Secretary of State for Health* [2011] LLR 592, CA).

Article 2 – Right to education

No person shall be denied the right to education. In the exercise of any functions which it assumes in relation to education and to teaching, the State shall respect the right of parents to ensure such education and teaching in conformity with their own religious and philosophical convictions.

Scope—The negative formulation of the first sentence means that 'there is no obligation on a state to establish at its own expense, or to subsidise, education of any particular type or at any level' (*Belgian*

Linguistic Case (1979–80) 1 EHRR 252). The scope of the second sentence is far wider and the rights protected are those of parents. The objectives of this provision are to safeguard the possibility of pluralism in education and to prevent the state pursuing an aim of indoctrination that might be considered as not respecting parents' religious and philosophical convictions (*Kjeldsen & Othrs v Denmark* (1979–80) 1 EHRR 711; *Campbell & Cosans v UK* (1982) 4 EHRR 293).

Limitations—The Article does not confer a right to be educated at a particular school but rather confers a right not to be denied access to the general level of educational provision available in the Member State (*Ali v Headteacher and Governors of Lord Grey School* [2006] 2 AC 363, HL). The Article does not impose on contracting states a positive obligation to provide education that caters for the special needs of the small, if significant, portion of the population who could not profit from mainstream education (eg those with special education needs). The authorities assumed that all contracting states had an education system and limited the positive obligation imposed by the Article to regulating education in such a way as to give access without discrimination to that system (*A v Essex County Council* [2011] AC 280, SC).

****

Inheritance (Provision for Family and Dependants) Act 1975

ARRANGEMENT OF SECTIONS

Section		Page
	Powers of court to order financial provision from deceased's estate	
1	Application for financial provision from deceased's estate	1013
2	Powers of court to make orders	1019
3	Matters to which the court is to have regard in exercising powers under s 2	1021
4	Time-limit for applications	1024
5	Interim orders	1025
6	Variation, discharge, etc of orders for periodical payments	1026
7	Payment of lump sums by instalments	1027
	Property available for financial provision	
8	Property treated as part of 'net estate'	1027
9	Property held on a joint tenancy	1028
	Powers of court in relation to transactions intended to defeat applications for financial provision	
10	Dispositions intended to defeat applications for financial provision	1029
11	Contracts to leave property by will	1030
12	Provisions supplementary to ss 10 and 11	1031
13	Provisions as to trustees in relation to ss 10 and 11	1032
	Special provisions relating to cases of divorce, separation etc	
14	Provision as to cases where no financial relief was granted in divorce proceedings etc	1033
14A	Provision as to cases where no financial relief was granted in proceedings for the dissolution etc. of a civil partnership	1033
15	Restriction imposed in divorce proceedings etc on application under this Act	1033
15ZA	Restriction imposed in proceedings for the dissolution etc. of a civil partnership on application under this Act	1034
15A	Restriction imposed in proceedings under Matrimonial and Family Proceedings Act 1984 on application under this Act	1034
15B	Restriction imposed in proceedings under Schedule 7 to the Civil Partnership Act 2004 on application under this Act	1035
16	Variation and discharge of secured periodical payments orders made under Matrimonial Causes Act 1973	1035
17	Variation and revocation of maintenance agreements	1035
18	Availability of court's powers under this Act in applications under ss 31 and 36 of the Matrimonial Causes Act 1973	1036

18A Availability of court's powers under this Act in applications under paragraphs 60 and 73 of Schedule 5 to the Civil Partnership Act 2004 1036

Miscellaneous and supplementary provisions

19 Effect, duration and form of orders 1037
25 Interpretation 1037

Powers of court to order financial provision from deceased's estate

1 Application for financial provision from deceased's estate

(1) Where after the commencement of this Act a person dies domiciled in England and Wales and is survived by any of the following persons –

(a) the spouse or civil partner of the deceased;
(b) a former spouse or former civil partner of the deceased, but not one who has formed a subsequent marriage or civil partnership;
(ba) any person (not being a person included in paragraph (a) or (b) above) to whom subsection (1A) or (1B) below applies;
(c) a child of the deceased;
(d) any person (not being a child of the deceased) who in relation to any marriage or civil partnership to which the deceased was at any time a party, or otherwise in relation to any family in which the deceased at any time stood in the role of a parent, was treated by the deceased as a child of the family;
(e) any person (not being a person included in the foregoing paragraphs of this subsection) who immediately before the death of the deceased was being maintained, either wholly or partly, by the deceased;

that person may apply to the court for an order under section 2 of this Act on the ground that the disposition of the deceased's estate affected by his will or the law relating to intestacy, or the combination of his will and that law, is not such as to make reasonable financial provision for the applicant.

(1A) This subsection applies to a person if the deceased died on or after 1 January 1996 and, during the whole of the period of two years ending immediately before the date when the deceased died, the person was living –

(a) in the same household as the deceased, and
(b) as the husband or wife of the deceased.

(1B) This subsection applies to a person if for the whole of the period of two years ending immediately before the date when the deceased died the person was living –

(a) in the same household as the deceased, and
(b) as the civil partner of the deceased.

(2) In this Act 'reasonable financial provision' –

(a) in the case of an application made by virtue of subsection (1)(a) above by the husband or wife of the deceased (except where the marriage with the deceased was the subject of a decree of judicial separation and at the date of death the decree was in force and the separation was continuing), means such financial provision as it would be reasonable in all the circumstances of the case for a husband or wife to receive, whether or not that provision is required for his or her maintenance;
(aa) in the case of an application made by virtue of subsection (1)(a) above by the civil partner of the deceased (except where, at the date of death, a separation order under Chapter 2 of Part 2 of the Civil Partnership Act 2004 was in force in relation to the civil partnership and the separation was continuing), means such financial provision as it would be reasonable in all the circumstances of the case for a civil partner to receive, whether or not that provision is required for his or her maintenance;

(b) in the case of any other application made by virtue of subsection (1) above, means such financial provision as it would be reasonable in all the circumstances of the case for the applicant to receive for his maintenance.

(2A) The reference in subsection (1)(d) above to a family in which the deceased stood in the role of a parent includes a family of which the deceased was the only member (apart from the applicant).

(3) For the purposes of subsection (1)(e) above, a person is to be treated as being maintained by the deceased (either wholly or partly, as the case may be) only if the deceased was making a substantial contribution in money or money's worth towards the reasonable needs of that person, other than a contribution made for full valuable consideration pursuant to an arrangement of a commercial nature.

Amendments—Law Reform (Succession) Act 1995, s 2; CPA 2004, s 71, Sch 4, para 15(1)–(6); Inheritance and Trustees' Powers Act 2014, s 6, Sch 2. The amendments only apply to claims under the Act in respect of the estate of the deceased who died on or after 1 October 2014.

Defined terms—'former wife', 'former husband': s 25(1).

'person dies'—Proof of death must be proved. This is commonly done by the production of the death certificate. Where a person in the armed forces dies in action overseas, the Ministry of Defence issues a notification of death certificate. Where death occurs in unusual circumstances, a Coroner's inquest may be opened and a final certificate is issued when the inquest is concluded. Where a person has been missing for a period of 7 years or more, a presumption of death arises. It is now possible pursuant to the provisions of the Presumption of Death Act 2013 to apply for a declaration (see post). The procedure set out in CPR 1998, rr 57.17–57.23 and PD57B applies for making the application.

'domiciled in England and Wales' (s 1(1))—The issue of domicile of the deceased at the time of death is relevant and is the first precondition that must be established when applying for relief under the Act. Therefore, any determination of domicile in proceedings for a declaration of presumption of death may be relevant in proceedings under the Act. Domicile is a legal concept that is not easily defined. For a summary of the law and reported cases, see Andrew Francis: *Inheritance Act Claims Law Practice and Procedure* (Family Law) and Nasreen Pearce *Inheritance Act Claims* (Wildy, Simmonds & Hill Publishing) and *Wills, Probate and Administration Service* (Butterworths). In *Holliday v Musa* [2010] 2 FLR 702, CA, in a claim made by the deceased's partner under the Act, the Court of Appeal followed the decision in *Cyganik v Agulian* [2006] EWCA Civ 129 and the principles laid down in *Re Fuld's Estate (No 3)* [1968] P 675, PDAD. In relation to jurisdiction in divorce proceedings, see in *Olafisoye v Olafisoye* [2011] 2 FLR 553, FD. See also *Perdoni v Curati* [2011] EWHC 3442 (Ch); *Ray v Sekhri* [2014] 2 FLR 1168, CA; *Divall v Divall* [2014] 2 FLR 1104, FD. It is for the claimant to prove that the deceased died domiciled in England and Wales.

'spouse of the deceased' (s 1(1)(a))—For meaning see s 25(4). Pursuant to the Marriage (Same Sex Couples) Act 2013, this now includes a marriage between same-sex couples. A marriage has the same effect in relation to same-sex couples as it has in relation to opposite sex couples (s 11(1) of the 2013 Act). The law of England and Wales (including all England and Wales legislation) whenever passed or made has effect in accordance with s 11(1) (s 11(2)). In existing legislation a reference to marriage is to be read as including a reference to marriage of a same-sex couple and reference to a married couple is to be read as including a reference to a same-sex couple (Sch 3, paras (a),(b) of the 2013 Act).

Schedule 3, para 5(2) defines the meaning that applies to the expression 'husband', 'wife' 'widow' and 'widower' as follows:

'(2) The following expressions have the meanings given –

(a) "husband" includes a man who is married to another man;

(b) "wife" includes a woman who is married to another woman;

(c) "widower" includes a man whose marriage to another man ended with the other man's death;

(d) "widow" includes a woman whose marriage to another woman ended with the other woman's death;

and related expressions are to be construed accordingly.'

Same-sex couples who have entered in to a civil partnership have the same rights as those enjoyed by heterosexual couples and same-sex couples who enter into a marriage under CPA 2004. However, this situation may change in the future as pursuant to s 15 of the 2013 Act the Secretary of State is under a duty to arrange for the operation and future of CPA 2004 in England and Wales to be reviewed and for a report on the outcome of the review to be produced and published.

The meaning of a void marriage under s 25(4) is the same as in MCA 1973, s 11. For a ceremony of marriage to create a void marriage it has to at least purport to be a marriage contemplated by the Marriage Acts and it must have been entered into in good faith (*Gandhi v Patel* [2002] 1 FLR 603, ChD). Distinction should be made between a void marriage and a non-marriage (see *K v A (Marriage: Validity)* [2015] 2 FLR 461, FD; *Sharbatly v Shagroon* [2013] 1 FLR 1493, CA). Where a presumption of marriage by cohabitation and reputation is claimed, the presumption requires extended period of cohabitation, the couple's acquisition of reputation of being husband and wife and some positive evidence from which it could be inferred that the statutory requirements for marriage had been complied (*Al-Saedy v Musawi (Presumption of Marriage)* [2011] 2 FLR 287, FD).

In relation to a religious marriage generally, see *El Gamal v Al-Maktoum* [2012] 2 FLR 387, FD and *Dukali v Lamrani (Attorney-General Intervening)* [2012] 2 FLR 1099, FD, where the court declared a non-marriage. Contrast with *MA v JA and the Attorney-General* [2013] 2 FLR 68, FD, where the religious ceremony was recognised on the basis that the marriage ceremony was conducted by an authorised person, was celebrated in an authorised place and both parties genuinely believed that they had undergone a valid marriage recognised under English Law. In relation to marriages of convenience, see *Adetola v First-Tier Tribunal (Immigration and Asylum Chamber) and SSHD* [2011] 2 FLR 611, QBD and the cases cited therein). On customary marriage, see *GE v KE & AE (Nigerian Customary Marriage and Divorce)* [2013] EWHC 1938 (Fam), *MO v RO & Anor* [2013] EWHC 392 (Fam) and *M-T v T (Marriage: Strike-Out)* [2014] 1 FLR 1352, FD; *N v D (Customary Marriage)* [2015] EWFC 28. Although it is a case concerning succession on intestacy in relation to Administration of Estates Act 1925, s 46, *Official Solicitor to the Senior Courts v Yemoh and others* [2011] 2 FLR 371 may be relevant in cases under the Act where there are surviving polygamous spouses since it was held that for the purposes so s 46(2) of the 1925 Act surviving polygamous spouses lawfully married in accordance with the law of his or her domicile to someone dying intestate was entitled to be recognised in England and Wales as a surviving spouse in relation to the property of the intestate. By virtue of the Matrimonial Proceedings (Polygamous Marriages) Act 1972, a party to a polygamous marriage is a spouse of the deceased (*Re Sehota (dec'd), Kaur v Kaur* [1978] 1 WLR 1506, ChD). Where the marriage is polygamous and the deceased has more than one wife, each of the wives would become a widow on his death. However, their entitlement to financial provision may vary (*Bibi v Chief Adjudication Officer* [1998] 1 FLR 375, CA). Furthermore, see the provisions of s 14. The common law does not recognise same-sex marriage but pursuant to the Marriage (Same Sex Couples) Act 2013, such marriages will be recognised and have the same effect as heterosexual marriages (see above). The Gender Recognition Act 2004, which came into force on 4 April 2005, allows those who have obtained a certificate from the Gender Recognition Panel to enter into a valid marriage.

Civil partner of the deceased—For meaning see s 25(4A). CPA 2004, Sch 4 amends s 14 by extending the provisions to civil partners.

Former spouse of the deceased—Can only make a claim if s/he has not remarried before the death of the deceased and the financial provision order did not include an order under ss 15 and 15A. In relation to civil partners, see ss 15ZA and 15B. Where a decree nisi has not been made absolute, the claim should be made under s 1(1)(a). In *Barrass v Harding and Newman* [2001] 1 FLR 138, CA, where the ancillary relief proceedings were concluded 32 years before the death of the deceased and in the intervening years there was no ongoing relationship between the deceased and his first wife, it was held that there was no basis on which an order under the Act could be justified. Where following the dissolution of their marriage the couple resume living together, the former spouse may be able to make a claim as a cohabitant of the deceased under s 1(1A): *Chekov v Fryer & Fryer* [2015] EWHC 1642 (Ch).

'child of the deceased' (s 1(1)(c))—For meaning see s 25(1). An adopted child is treated as a legitimate child of his/her adopters (ACA 2002, s 67). An overseas adoption as defined in ACA 2002, s 87(1) is recognised as an adoption order without the need to issue proceedings (see ACA 2002, s 66 and Adoption (Intercountry Aspects) Act 1999) provided it comes within the specification of overseas adoption set out in Adoption (Designation of Overseas Adoptions) Order 1973 prior to 3 January 2014 and thereafter the Adoption (Recognition of Overseas Adoptions) Regulations 2013 (save with respect to adoptions designated as overseas adoption under the 1973 order prior to that date; see *A County Council v M and Others (No 4) (Foreign Adoption: Refusal of Recognition)* [2014] 1 FLR 881, FD for a case that fell outside the designated countries under the 1993 Convention and the specified countries set out in the schedule to the 1973 order). In relation to the rights of an illegitimate child of the deceased or an adopted child, whether under the Adoption and Children Act 1926, 1949, 1976 or 2002, the case must be settled not only on the basis of domestic law but alongside the rights protected under the provisions of the European Convention of Human Rights, especially those under Arts 8 and 14, the case-law of the ECtHR and the provisions of the Human Rights Act 1998. The European approach on the application of the Convention to illegitimate and adopted children has been settled in a number of cases. In *Marckx v Belgium* (1979) 2 EHRR 330, the ECtHR held that the Convention must be interpreted in the light of present-day conditions and that there was no objective or reasonable justification for the differences of treatment between a legitimate and illegitimate child even where the disposition in question was made before the Convention was drafted. In *Pla and Puncernau v Andorra* (Application No 69498/01) [2004] 2 FCR 630, ECHR, which concerned the rights of an adopted child, the ECtHR confirmed the decision in *Marckx*. It rejected the contention that the issue related to the free will of the testatrix. It held that domestic law should not be made exclusively in the light of the social conditions existing when the will was made or at the time of the testatrix's death, particularly where a long period has elapsed between when the will was made and the date on which the estate passed to the heirs. Where a long period has elapsed during which profound social, economic and legal changes have occurred, the courts cannot ignore these new realities (at [62]). The ECtHR held that an adopted child was in the same legal position as a biological child in all respects (see also *Brauer v Germany (Application No 3545/04)* (2009) 51 EHRR 574 and *Fabris v France (Application No 16574/08)* [2013] ECHR 16574/08). For the full discussion on the impact of these decisions and the Human Rights Act and domestic case-law, see *Hand and Anr v George and Anr* [2017] EWHC 533 (Ch), where the court considered the claim made by adopted grandchildren of the deceased under a will the deceased had made in 1946 when, under existing domestic law, adopted children were considered the child of their natural parents. The case confirms that in order for the claimants to rely on Convention rights to establish a claim, the claimant must show not only that they are 'victims of an infringement of the Convention but also that the Human Rights Act 1998 confers on them a right to seek a remedy for that infringement in the domestic court. The court concluded that, although under domestic law the claimants' claim would have failed, the court had to respect their rights under Arts 14 and 8 not to be discriminated against by the application of a legislative provisions that excludes them as adopted grandchildren. Although not a case under the Act, in *Re Erskine Trust* [2012] 2 FLR 725, ChD, the court when construing an existing trust fund applied the European Convention and followed *Pla and Puncernau v Andorra* (above) when granting a £3.2m trust fund to two adopted children of the deceased, but see the observations made by Rose J in *Hand*, at [62]–[68], on the approach adopted by the judge in *Re Erskine Trust*. Any interpretation of a will/testamentary disposition should, therefore, be made in the light of social, economic and legal changes and the application of the ECHR 1950, and not with regard to the conditions which existed at the time when the will or trust was made. A child who is adopted after his parent's death but before he makes his application is not a child of the deceased because, by virtue of ACA 2002, an adopted child is treated in law as the child of the adopters. The Act does not confer on such an applicant an interest expectant as he merely has a right to apply to the court for relief (*Re Collins (dec'd)* [1990] 2 FLR 72, FD). Note however that in relation to the estate of the deceased who died on or after 1 October 2014, the Inheritance and Trustees' Powers Act 2014 amends ACA 2002, s 69 (rules of interpretation) to extend the provisions of s 67(3) so that it does not prejudice any contingent interest (other than a contingent interest in remainder) in the estate of a deceased parent whether testate or intestate that the adopted person has immediately before the adoption. The Legitimacy Act 1976 provides that a child of a void marriage whenever born is, subject to s 2 of and Sch 1 to the Act, to be treated as a legitimate child of his parents if, at the time of the insemination resulting in the birth or, where there was no such insemination, the child's conception (or at the time of the celebration of the marriage, if later), both parties to the marriage or either of them reasonably believed that the marriage was valid. See also *Re Spence (dec'd)* [1990] 2 FLR 278, CA. See further the provisions of the Legitimacy Act 1976, FLRA 1987 and the HFEAs 1990 and 2008, ss 33–45, to determine who can be treated as the 'father', 'mother' and 'parent' of a child, and the decisions in *Re B (Minors) (Parentage)* [1996] 2 FLR 15, FD; *Re Q (Parental Order)* [1996] 1 FLR 369, FD; and *R v Human Fertilisation and Embryology Authority ex parte Blood* [1997] 2 FLR 742, CA. Where a child is conceived by artificial insemination before the commencement of HFEA 1990 and the provisions of FLRA 1987 apply, the reference in FLRA 1987, s 27(1)(b) to 'the other party to that marriage' refers to a man and not to same-sex relationship (*J v C (Void Marriage: Status of Children)* [2006] 2 FLR 1098, CA). Where parentage is in issue, paternity should be established by scientific means, ie, DNA (*Re H & A (Paternity: Blood Tests)* [2002] 1 FLR 1145, CA). Where the child is a minor, FLRA 1969, s 21(3) authorises the court to order that a bodily sample be taken from a person under the age of 16 who does not consent if the court considers that it would be in his interests for the sample to be taken. The court may also draw adverse inferences if a person fails to consent to such tests.

Pursuant to regulations made under HFEA 1990 and under HFEA 2008, where a parental order has been made under s 30 of the 1990 Act and s 54 of the 2008 Act, the child who is the subject of a parental order is treated as the child of the couple in whose favour the parental order is made.

Cohabitant of the deceased (s 1(1)(ba),(1A))—This includes a cohabitant of the deceased who has lived with him or her in the same household as the husband or wife or as a civil partner of the deceased for a period of 2 years immediately preceding the deceased's death (see the Law Commission's Report dated 14 December 2011 and the changes proposed in the Cohabitation Rights Bill to address the law that applies to cohabitants). In *Gully v Dix* [2004] 1 FLR 918, CA, although they had been living separately, the claimant was held to be living with the deceased in the same household at the moment of his death because their relationship had not come to an end. In exceptional circumstances, even a lengthy period of living apart may not preclude to the existence of a single shared household: *Kaur V Dhaliwal* [2014] EWHC 1991 (Ch). Where these conditions are not satisfied, the applicant can rely on s 1(1)(e). The question whether a person falls within s 1(1A) should be determined by asking whether in the opinion of a reasonable person with normal perceptions, it could be said that the two people in question were living together as husband and wife (*Re Watson (Deceased)* [1999] 1 FLR 878, ChD). Stability, financial support, sexual relationship, children and public acknowledgement are also relevant factors in determining whether a household has existed. The claimant's continued links with his/her country of origin, the fact that he/she has property there and a child by a previous relationship are also relevant considerations in determining whether the claim should be treated as one by a cohabitant or a dependant (*Witkowska v Kaminski* [2007] 1 FLR 1547, ChD). The mere fact that the deceased had retained a separate property, of which he made occasional use, is not in itself a barrier to establishing that he was living with the claimant in the same household. It could only be regarded as a barrier, if the fact and the extent to which the deceased maintained and made use of it and treated himself as still resident there, indicated that he and the claimant had not yet established a mutual home (*Kotke v Saffarini* [2005] 2 FLR 517, CA). In *Lindop v Agus, Bass and Hedley* [2010] 1 FLR 631, ChD, the claimant who had retained her postal address at her father's home was held to have been maintained for the purposes of the Act at least partly by the deceased before his death in that he provided a home for which he paid all the outgoings and for transport to and from work. He had also paid for her holidays and some of her wardrobe. For other reported cases, see *Cattle v Evans* [2011] 2 FLR 843, ChD (where the claimant received £100,000 to provide for her housing needs) and *Musa v Holliday* [2013] 1 FLR 806, CA.

'child of the family' (s 1(1)(d))—There is no definition of 'child of the family' nor any guidance in the Act as to when a person is regarded as having been treated as a child of the family. This category of claimants extends to any person who in relation to any marriage etc to which the deceased was at any time party or in relation to any family in which the deceased at any time stood in the role of a parent. The focus is on the relationship, which must be shown to be that of parent/child. It is wide enough to include one-parent situations (see subsection (2A)). An adult child is included. The nature of the relationship between the deceased and the applicant is the relevant factor (*Re Callaghan (dec'd)* [1985] FLR 116, FD; *Re Leach, Leach v Lindeman* [1984] FLR 590, CA. In each case the question will be judged by an objective test on the basis of all the facts, so that where grandparents had assumed primary responsibility for their grandchild for the foreseeable future the grandchild was a 'child of the family' (*Re A (Child of the Family)* [1998] 1 FLR 347, CA). A person may apply against the estate of his parent's civil partner if he was a child of the family (CPA 2004, Sch 4, para 15(4)).

'court'—Pursuant to CLSA 1990, s 1, CCA 1984, s 25 and HCCCJO 1991, art 2(1), unlimited jurisdiction is conferred on the County Court in respect of claims under the I(PFD)A 1975. However, under art 7 of the 1991 Order, subject to the criteria set out in art 7(5), any action where the value of the claim (the sum which the applicant has reasonable expectancy of recovering) is less than £25,000 must be tried in the County Court. Where the value of the claim is £50,000 or more, the action must be tried in the High Court unless it is commenced in the County Court and the court does not consider it ought to be transferred up to the High Court. Similarly, if the action has been commenced in the High Court, that court may transfer the action down to the County Court.

Other persons (s 1(1)(e))—An applicant under s 1(1)(e) must establish that he or she was being maintained, either wholly or partly, by the deceased immediately before the deceased's death (s 1(1)(e)), but see the provisions of subsection (3), which require proof only that the deceased was making a substantial contribution in money or money's worth. The applicant must establish some sort of obligation to be maintained by the deceased beyond the fact of a relationship (*Williams v Johns* [1988] 2 FLR 475, ChD). In determining whether the applicant had been maintained by the deceased, the court should have regard to the extent to which, the basis upon which and the length of time for which the deceased discharged that responsibility (s 3(4)). 'The court will look at the problem in the round, applying a common sense approach, avoiding fine balancing computations involving the value of normal exchanges of support in the domestic sense' (*Bishop v Plumley* [1991] 1 FLR 121, CA; see also *Rees v Newbery and the Institute of Cancer Research* [1998] 1 FLR 1041, ChD; *Graham v Murphy and Another* [1997] 1 FLR 860, ChD, where a male applicant succeeded in his claim, made before 1 January 1996, for financial provision from the estate of his cohabitant; as did the applicant in *Re Wilkinson, Neale v Newell* [1978] Fam 22, FD, who had left her employment at the age of 61 to look after her brother; *Harrington v Gill* (1983) 4 FLR 265, CA, where 8 years' cohabitation was held sufficient evidence of dependency; *Re Viner; Kreeger v Cooper* [1978] CLY 3091, where a weekly payment of £5 for 6 months before death was considered sufficient). In *Baynes v Hedger* [2009] 2 FLR 767, CA, the court dismissed a goddaughter's claim on the grounds that she was not eligible to make a claim under s 1(1)(e) as she had not been able to satisfy the court that the deceased had assumed responsibility for her maintenance. In any event there had been no failure to make reasonable financial provision for her.

The settled basis or general arrangement between the parties during the lifetime of the deceased has to be looked at, not the actual, perhaps fluctuating, variations of it which exist immediately before death. In determining the issue, the provisions of ss 1(3) and 3(4) should be considered together. The court has to consider whether the deceased was in fact making a substantial contribution in money or money's worth towards the reasonable needs of the applicant other than a contribution made for full valuable consideration pursuant to an arrangement of a commercial nature either immediately before death or to the time that the approach of death made it impossible for either party to continue to carry out the arrangement (*Jelley v Iliffe* [1981] Fam 128, CA). 'Whether one person makes a substantial gratuitous contribution to another person's needs is essentially a question of fact, and the benefactor's motives or intentions are irrelevant except so far as s 3(4) makes them relevant to the court's task in deciding whether to make provision for the claimant, and if so in what form and on what scale. Even when s 3(4) is taken into account this court has taken the view that actions speak louder than words' (per Robert Walker LJ in *Bouette v Rose* [2000] 1 FLR 363, CA). Maintenance is not necessarily confined to support of a person's cost of living. It is capable of referring to other forms of assistance with the requirements of daily life. The court has to make a value judgement of the claimant's need in the round: *Lewis v Warner* [2016] EWHC 1787 (Ch).

'immediately before the death' (s 1(1)(e))—See *Re Beaumont, Martin v Midland Bank Trust Ltd* [1980] Ch 444, ChD; *Kourkgy v Lusher* (1983) 4 FLR 65, FD, where the claim failed because cohabitation came to an end nine days before the deceased's death; and *Layton v Martin* [1986] 2 FLR 227, ChD, where cohabitation had ended 2 years before death.

Reasonable financial provision (s 1(2)(a),(b))—The Act does not distinguish between claims made by a surviving wife or husband of the deceased. In view of the decisions in *White v White* [2000] 2 FLR 981, HL and *Cowan v Cowan* [2001] 2 FLR 192, CA, there is no place for discrimination based on gender. This principle was applied in *Barron v Woodhead* [2009] 1 FLR 747, ChD.The court considered his case on the basis of what he might have expected to receive had the marriage terminated by divorce. It rejected the suggestion that his claim should be decreased by reason of his conduct during the marriage, and in awarding him a life interest in the sum of £100,000 to enable him to buy a house to live in together with a lump sum of £25,000, the court took into account the factors under s 3. In defining reasonable financial provision, the Act distinguishes between a surviving spouse/civil partner and the other categories of applicants. In the case of a surviving spouse/civil partner, it need not be an amount required for maintenance. The fictional 'deemed divorce' exercise has been applied when dealing with a claim by a surviving spouse/civil partner, making appropriate adjustments where the estate is insufficient to meet the needs of all the beneficiaries, but the amendments made to s 3 of the Act (see below) now clearly provide that when exercising its powers under s 2 in relation to a surviving spouse, the court is not required to treat such provision as setting an upper or lower limit on the provision made by the order. The objective must be to achieve a fair outcome. There is no presumption of equal division of assets, and caution needs to be exercised in using the divorce comparison in such cases (*P v G, P and P (Family Provision: Relevance of Divorce Provision)* [2006] 1 FLR 431, FD). See also *Aston v Aston* [2007] WTLR 1349, Cty Ct; *Baker v Baker (Financial Provision: Divorce Comparison)* [2008] 2 FLR 1956, ChD; and *Moore v Holdsworth* [2010] 2 FLR 1501, ChD where the application of the 'divorce fiction' was considered. The court has to strike a fair balance (*A v L* [2012] 1 FLR 985, FD). Where the marriage has been short, the widow is entitled to a 'reasonable expectation that her life again as a single woman need not revert to what it was before her marriage', but the brevity of the marriage and the limited nature of the widow's contribution are relevant factors that may affect issues of housing needs and the level of income: *Fielden v Cunliffe* [2006] 1 FLR 745, CA. There is also nothing in the 1975 Act to suggest that this factor should be given more weight than the other factors referred to in s 3 of the Act: in *Re Rowlands (dec'd)* [1984] FLR 813, CA, the widow was 90, had been separated from the deceased for 47 years and was unable to formulate what her needs were and what she would do if a substantial sum was awarded to her; she received £3000. See also *Re Bunning (dec'd), Bunning v Salmon* [1985] FLR 1, ChD and *Re Gregory, Gregory v Goodenough* [1970] 1 WLR 1455, CA. Where the former husband and wife settle their financial claims on divorce without a court order, the court will be slow to order further provision under the Act (*Re Fullard* [1982] Fam 42, CA). See also *T v T (An Agreement not embodied in a consent order)* [2013] EWHC B3). In matrimonial proceedings where an order for financial relief is made but it is then discovered that there has been material non-disclosure such as to vitiate any consent or it is established that the court would have made a substantially different order, it is possible to apply for the order to be set aside (*Gohil v Gohil* [2015] 2 FLR 1289, SC;

Sharland v Sharland [2015] 2 FLR 1367, SC; *Roocroft v Ball* [2016] EWCA Civ 1009). It is arguable, provided that a long period has not elapsed, that similar principles should apply in relation to an application under the Act by a former wife. Where a party to a consent order for financial relief dies shortly after the order is made it could be argued that the death of the other party was not a contemplated event when the order was made and was therefore a new event. In such a case the application to set aside the consent order must be made promptly. In relation to non-matrimonial property, property acquired before the marriage and post-separation or divorce, and inherited property and prenuptial agreements, see under MCA 1973, s 25.

In respect of any other applicant, including a judicially separated or divorced spouse/civil partner and a cohabitant as defined by ss 1(1A) or 1(1B) (but note the changes proposed in the Cohabitation Rights Bill), s 1(2)(b) makes it clear that reasonable financial provision is limited to what would be reasonable in all the circumstances for the applicant to receive for his maintenance. The Supreme Court's decision in *Illott v The Blue Cross & Others* [2017] UKSC 17 sets out some principles that will be applied in future cases but in all cases the court's decision is very much fact-specific and dependant on the court's assessment of those facts. It is also important to take account of the concerns and criticisms expressed by Lady Hale in her judgment that the current state of the law is unsatisfactory as it does not give any 'guidance as to the factors to be taken into account in deciding whether an adult child is deserving or undeserving of reasonable maintenance' and her regret that the Law Commission did not reconsider the fundamental principles underlying such claims when they considered this issue in 2011(at [66]). Lady Hale also referred to the fact that one factor not in the list of factors to be taken account of but that features elsewhere in family law is the public interest in family members discharging their responsibilities towards one another so that these do not fall upon the state (at [63]). The court, however, ruled that although the concept of maintenance is broad it 'cannot extend to any or everything that it would be desirable for a claimant to have. It must import provision to meet the everyday expenses of living' (at [14]) (*Re Jennings (deceased)*; *Harlow v National Westminster Bank plc and Others* [1994] 1 FLR 536, CA and *Re Dennis (Deceased)* [1981] 2 All ER 140 approved). It falls to be assessed on the facts of each case and that it is not limited to subsistence level. Nor, although it is by definition the provision of income rather than capital, 'need it necessarily be provided for by way of periodical payments. It will very often be more appropriate as well as cheaper and more convenient for other beneficiaries and for executors, if income is provided for by way of a lump sum from which both income and capital can be drawn for years, for example on the *Duxbury* model'. Maintenance may include the provision of housing in some cases but, if so, it should more often be provided by way of a life interest in a trust fund together with a power of advancement rather than a capital sum (at [15]) (*Re Dennis (Deceased)* (above) and *Myers v Myers* [2004] EWHC 1944 (Fam) approved). (See also *Martin v Williams* [2017] EWHC 491 (Ch), where an appeal against an order made at first instance transferring the deceased's half-share in the property in which he lived with Mrs Williams to her was partially allowed on the facts and applying similar principles by vesting the deceased's half-share in Mrs Williams for life with all other rights and specifically the reversion of that interest vesting in Mrs Martin, the deceased's widow). The Supreme Court also referred to the two-stage approach applied in a claim under the Act as set out in s 1(1),(2) of the Act and stated it could usually be applied by asking: '(1) did the will/intestacy make reasonable financial provision for the claimant and (2) if not, what reasonable financial provision ought now to be made for him?', at [23]. The first of these two distinct questions is often described as one of value judgment and the second as one of discretion. However, there is in most cases an overlap between the two stages and s 3 factors will be relevant under both stages. In relation to the question of whether reasonable financial provision was not made, although the issue will largely turn on the claimant's needs, this by itself may not be enough; it confirmed that the claimant will have to establish more than a qualifying relationship and some sort of moral claim beyond the claim of blood-relationship and some reason why it can be said that in the circumstances it was unreasonable that no or no greater provision was made by the deceased for the claimant. Where the court has concluded that the deceased has not made reasonable financial provision for the claimant, in determining what provision should be made the court will undoubtedly also have to consider the competing claims of others on the estate. Where the beneficiary is a charity, although their claim is not based on need the fact that they rely on bequests is 'by definition of public benefit and in many cases will be for humanitarian purposes' (at [46]) and therefore relevant and in any event the reduction of their benefit is relevant and it cannot be ignored that any orders the court makes will be at the expense of those whom the testator intended to benefit. In applying s 3, factors of relevance will also include the nature of the relationship between the deceased and the claimant to determine what would be a just order to make. Hence, conduct of the deceased and the claimant towards each other will also be a relevant factor in determining the provision if any and the extent to which should be made (at [22]) but care must be taken to avoid making awards that are rewards for good behaviour on the part of the claimant or penalties for the deceased's bad behaviour. Based on these principles, the following cases remain as good examples of the approach to be adopted in claims under the Act. In *Negus v Bahouse* [2008] 1 FLR 381, ChD, the court took account of the lifestyle provided by the deceased for his partner, his promises and the assurance he had given her that she would always have a roof over her head. This was balanced against the claims of the other beneficiaries. It was held that the applicant was entitled to a reasonable degree of financial security (see also *Baker v Baker* [2008] 2 FLR 767, ChD). In *Webster v Webster* [2009] 1 FLR 1240, ChD, on the basis of the cohabitant's indirect contribution to the family budget and applying the decision in *Lloyds Bank plc v Rosset* [1990] 2 FLR 155, HL, the court inferred that she had an interest in the family home. The long period of cohabitation, the claimant's age and needs and the needs of the other beneficiaries were taken into account. Applying the clean-break principle and *Duxbury* capitalisation, the court ordered the transfer of the home to her free of mortgage. Reasonable financial provision does not mean that the applicant should be provided for on a lavish scale (*Wooldridge v Wooldridge* (Case No 3CL1022132) [2016] Fam Law 451, or such as would relieve him from the need to earn a living or provide himself with a home (*Graham v Murphy and Another* [1997] 1 FLR 860, ChD). An adult child, towards whom the deceased failed to discharge his responsibility, is not entitled to make a claim where he is in comfortable circumstances in order to maintain his standard of living (*Re Jennings (deceased)*; *Harlow v National Westminster Bank plc and Others* [1994] 1 FLR 536, CA;

Re Hancock (dec'd) [1998] 2 FLR 346, CA; *Re Abram (dec'd)* [1996] 2 FLR 379, ChD). As regards a clamant who is on state benefits, the Supreme Court observed that benefits are part of the resources of the claimant and it will be relevant to consider whether they will continue to be received. Receipt of means-tested benefits is therefore likely to be a relevant indication of the claimant's financial position (at [45]). In such cases, it is imperative when preparing the claimant's case to obtain accurate and detailed information on the impact of any award on entitlement and receipt of the benefits paid to the claimant whether such benefits are by way of tax credit, child benefit, working tax credits and other benefits such as housing and council tax benefits. When advising a client to make a will, consideration should be given to the s 3 criteria so that the client can make an informed choice. However, the client should nevertheless be advised that there is no guarantee it will have the effect of preventing a claim being made and, if a claim is made of its success, as much will depend on the circumstances at the date of the hearing of the claim. In *Illott v Blue Cross & Others*, the Supreme Court confirmed that where the court has to assess whether reasonable financial provision has been made and what order, if any, should be made, the relevant date is the date of the hearing of the application (see also under s 3).

The court must have regard to all of the matters set out under s 3. Relevant to this issue is also the fact that the deceased's assets have been acquired from the inheritance of the applicant's mother (*Gora v Treasury Solicitor* [2003] Fam Law 93, Cty Ct). It is not necessary in every case for the applicant to establish 'a moral obligation'. For a discussion of this issue, see: *Re Coventry, Coventry v Coventry* (1979) FLR Rep 142, CA; *Re Jennings (deceased)* (above); *Re Pearce (deceased)* [1998] 2 FLR 705, CA; *Re Hancock (dec'd)* (above); and *Gora v Treasury Solicitor*. The Supreme Court's decision in *Illott v The Blue Cross & Others* clearly suggests that benefits from whatever source are part of the financial resources of the claimant (at [45]) but does not preclude a claim being made where the claimant is not on state benefits. In *Re Collins* [1990] 2 FLR 72, FD, Hollins J said 'I do not consider that the fact of support from the DSS precludes consideration of whether the intestacy has or has not made reasonable financial provision for her'.

2 Powers of court to make orders

(1) Subject to the provisions of this Act, where an application is made for an order under this section, the court may, if it is satisfied that the disposition of the deceased's estate effected by his will or the law relating to intestacy, or the combination of his will and that law, is not such as to make reasonable financial provision for the applicant, make any one or more of the following orders –

(a) an order for the making to the applicant out of the net estate of the deceased of such periodical payments and for such term as may be specified in the order;

(b) an order for the payment to the applicant out of that estate of a lump sum of such amount as may be so specified;

(c) an order for the transfer to the applicant of such property comprised in that estate as may be so specified;

(d) an order for the settlement for the benefit of the applicant of such property comprised in that estate as may be so specified;

(e) an order for the acquisition out of property comprised in that estate of such property as may be so specified and for the transfer of the property so acquired to the applicant or for the settlement thereof for his benefit;

(f) an order varying any ante-nuptial or post-nuptial settlement (including such a settlement made by will) made on the parties to a marriage to which the deceased was one of the parties, the variation being for the benefit of the surviving party to that marriage, or any child of that marriage, or any person who was treated by the deceased as a child of the family in relation to that marriage;

(g) an order varying any settlement made –

(i) during the subsistence of a civil partnership formed by the deceased, or

(ii) in anticipation of the formation of a civil partnership by the deceased,

on the civil partners (including such a settlement made by will), the variation being for the benefit of the surviving civil partner, or any child of both the civil partners, or any person who was treated by the deceased as a child of the family in relation to that civil partnership.

(h) an order varying for the applicant's benefit the trusts on which the deceased's estate is held (whether arising under the will, or the law relating to intestacy, or both).

(2) An order under subsection (1)(a) above providing for the making out of the net estate of the deceased of periodical payments may provide for –

(a) payments of such amount as may be specified in the order,

(b) payments equal to the whole of the income of the net estate or of such portion thereof as may be so specified,

(c) payments equal to the whole of the income of such part of the net estate as the court may direct to be set aside or appropriated for the making out of the income thereof of payments under this section,

or may provide for the amount of the payments or any of them to be determined in any other way the court thinks fit.

(3) Where an order under subsection (1)(a) above provides for the making of payments of an amount specified in the order, the order may direct that such part of the net estate as may be so specified shall be set aside or appropriated for the making out of the income thereof of those payments; but no larger part of the net estate shall be so set aside or appropriated than is sufficient, at the date of the order, to produce by the income thereof the amount required for the making of those payments.

(3A) In assessing for the purposes of an order under this section the extent (if any) to which the net estate is reduced by any debts or liabilities (including any inheritance tax paid or payable out of the estate), the court may assume that the order has already been made.

(4) An order under this section may contain such consequential and supplemental provisions as the court thinks necessary or expedient for the purpose of giving effect to the order or for the purpose of securing that the order operates fairly as between one beneficiary of the estate of the deceased and another and may, in particular, but without prejudice to the generality of this subsection –

(a) order any person who holds any property which forms part of the net estate of the deceased to make such payment or transfer such property as may be specified in the order;

(b) vary the disposition of the deceased's estate effected by the will or the law relating to intestacy, or by both the will and the law relating to intestacy, in such manner as the court thinks fair and reasonable having regard to the provisions of the order and all the circumstances of the case;

(c) confer on the trustees of any property which is the subject of an order under this section such powers as appear to the court to be necessary or expedient.

Amendments—CPA 2004, s 71, Sch 4, para 16; Inheritance and Trustees' Powers Act 2014, s 6, Sch 2.

'net estate'—Defined in s 25, and see ss 8, 9. A severable share in property in which the deceased held a joint tenancy may be treated as part of the net estate pursuant to s 9 (*Jessop v Jessop* [1992] 1 FLR 591, CA).

Periodical payments (s 2(1)(a))—Unless an application has been made for an interim order, the order for periodical payments will normally be made from the date of the deceased's death, even where the applicant has been in receipt of state benefits (*Re Goodwin, Goodwin v Goodwin* [1969] 1 Ch 283, ChD). The matter is one for the discretion of the court. The court may specify the amount to be paid under the order, express the amount to be paid to be such sum as is equivalent to the whole or a specified portion of the income of the net estate, direct that a specified part of the net estate be appropriated or set aside for meeting periodical payments and express the amount of such periodical payments to be equivalent to the whole of the income of such part of the net estate or provide for the amount of the payment to be determined in any other way it thinks fit (s 2(2)).

Lump sum (s 2(1)(b))—In the case of a lump sum order, particularly where the capital sum is provided to produce an income, the fact that the applicant will not be able to return to the court for further orders means that in assessing the amount the court should make allowances for inflation and possible future contingencies (*Re Besterman* [1984] FLR 503, CA); but see *A v A (Financial Provision)* [1998] 2 FLR 180, FD, a case concerning an application for financial provision under MCA 1973, where it was held that the concept of awarding a lump sum as a cushion had not survived the introduction of *Duxbury* calculations). See also *Fielden v Cunliffe* and *P v G, P and P (Family Provision: Relevance of Divorce Provision)* (above). A lump sum may also be made on an application for a variation of periodical payments order under s 6. The court has the power to order that the lump sum payment be made by instalments and may vary the number of instalments payable, the amount of the instalments and the date on which any instalment becomes payable (s 7(2)).

Order varying any antenuptial or postnuptial settlement—See **Nuptial agreements** under MCA 1973, s 25.

Settlement of property and the mentally disabled (s 2(1)(d))—It is not unusual to find that parents refrain from making provision for a mentally disabled child, particularly an adult child, in the belief that the child will be provided for adequately by the state and any benefit under a testamentary provision will have the effect of reducing the benefit. With the increasing tendency of care for such persons being provided within the community, some financial support could make a difference to the quality of life of that person. Although there are no decided cases on the subject it is submitted that under the wide powers given to the court by s 2, and in particular s 2(4), the court could make an order for the settlement of property for the benefit of a mentally handicapped claimant by setting up a discretionary trust so as to permit the whole or any part of the income of the trust fund to be applied for the maintenance, care and benefit of the claimant as the trustees in their absolute discretion deem fit. For further information on the provisions which may be included in the trust, see *Butterworths Wills, Probate and Administration Service*.

Order for costs—Costs in claims under the Act is governed by CPR 1998, Pts 36 and 44. In considering whether to make any orders in respect of costs, the court will have regard to any Pt 36 offers but it has the discretion to disapply the normal consequences if it considers that to do so would result in injustice. In exercising its discretion, the court will have regard to the factors set out in Pt 44 and to the overriding objective (see *Lilleyman v Lilleyman* [2013] 1 FLR 47, ChD, where the court, when making an order against the claimant after a Pt 36 offer took account of the defendant's conduct. See also *Graham v Murphy and Another* [1997] 1 FLR 860, ChD).

3 Matters to which the court is to have regard in exercising powers under s 2

(1) Where an application is made for an order under section 2 of this Act, the court shall, in determining whether the disposition of the deceased's estate effected by his will or the law relating to intestacy, or the combination of his will and that law, is such as to make reasonable financial provision for the applicant and, if the court considers that reasonable financial provision has not been made, in determining whether and in what manner it shall exercise its powers under that section, have regard to the following matters, that is to say –

(a) the financial resources and financial needs which the applicant has or is likely to have in the foreseeable future;

(b) the financial resources and financial needs which any other applicant for an order under section 2 of this Act has or is likely to have in the foreseeable future;

(c) the financial resources and financial needs which any beneficiary of the estate of the deceased has or is likely to have in the foreseeable future;

(d) any obligations and responsibilities which the deceased had towards any applicant for an order under the said section 2 or towards any beneficiary of the estate of the deceased;

(e) the size and nature of the net estate of the deceased;

(f) any physical or mental disability of any applicant for an order under the said section 2 or any beneficiary of the estate of the deceased;

(g) any other matter, including the conduct of the applicant or any other person, which in the circumstances of the case the court may consider relevant.

(2) This subsection applies, without prejudice to the generality of paragraph (g) of subsection (1) above, where an application for an order under section 2 of this Act is made by virtue of section 1(1)(a) or (b) of this Act. The court shall, in addition to the matters specifically mentioned in paragraphs (a) to (f) of that subsection, have regard to –

(a) the age of the applicant and the duration of the marriage or civil partnership;

(b) the contribution made by the applicant to the welfare of the family of the deceased, including any contribution made by looking after the home or caring for the family.

In the case of an application by the wife or husband of the deceased, the court shall also, unless at the date of death a decree of judicial separation was in force and the separation was continuing, have regard to the provision which the applicant might reasonably have expected to receive if on the day on which the deceased died the marriage, instead of being terminated by death, had been terminated by a decree of divorce; but nothing requires the court to treat such provision as setting an upper or lower limit on the provision which may be made by an order under section 2. In the case of an application by the civil partner of the deceased, the court shall also, unless at the date of the death a separation order under Chapter 2 of Part 2 of the Civil Partnership Act 2004 was in force and the separation was continuing, have regard to the provision which the applicant might reasonably have expected to receive if on the day on which the deceased died the civil partnership, instead of being terminated by death, had been terminated by a dissolution order; but nothing requires the court to treat such provision as setting an upper or lower limit on the provision which may be made by an order under section 2.

(2A) Without prejudice to the generality of paragraph (g) of subsection (1) above, where an application for an order under section 2 of this Act is made by virtue of section 1(1)(ba) of this Act, the court shall, in addition to the matters specifically mentioned in paragraphs (a) to (f) of that subsection, have regard to –

- (a) the age of the applicant and the length of the period during which the applicant lived as the husband or wife or civil partner of the deceased and in the same household as the deceased;
- (b) the contribution made by the applicant to the welfare of the family of the deceased, including any contribution made by looking after the home or caring for the family.

(3) Without prejudice to the generality of paragraph (g) of subsection (1) above, where an application for an order under section 2 of this Act is made by virtue of section 1(1)(c) or 1(1)(d) of this Act, the court shall, in addition to the matters specifically mentioned in paragraphs (a) to (f) of that subsection, have regard to the manner in which the applicant was being or in which he might expect to be educated or trained, and where the application is made by virtue of section 1(1)(d) the court shall also have regard –

- (a) to whether the deceased maintained the applicant and, if so, to the length of time for which and basis on which the deceased did so, and to the extent of the contribution made by way of maintenance;
- (aa) to whether and, if so, to what extent the deceased assumed responsibility for the maintenance of the applicant;
- (b) to whether in maintaining or assuming responsibility for maintaining the applicant the deceased did so knowing that the applicant was not his own child;
- (c) to the liability of any other person to maintain the applicant.

(4) Without prejudice to the generality of paragraph (g) of subsection (1) above, where an application for an order under section 2 of this Act is made by virtue of section 1(1)(e) of this Act, the court shall, in addition to the matters specifically mentioned in paragraphs (a) to (f) of that subsection, have regard –

- (a) to the length of time for which and basis on which the deceased maintained the applicant, and to the extent of the contribution made by way of maintenance;
- (b) to whether and, if so, to what extent the deceased assumed responsibility for the maintenance of the applicant.

(5) In considering the matters to which the court is required to have regard under this section, the court shall take into account the facts as known to the court at the date of the hearing.

(6) In considering the financial resources of any person for the purposes of this section the court shall take into account his earning capacity and in considering the financial needs of any person for the purposes of this section the court shall take into account his financial obligations and responsibilities.

Amendments—Law Reform (Succession) Act 1995, s 2; CPA 2004, s 71, Sch 4, paras 17(1)–(5), 18; Inheritance and Trustees' Powers Act 2014, s 6, Sch 2.

Matters to be considered in determining reasonable financial provision (s 3(1))—See **Reasonable financial provision** under s 1. In the case of an application by a cohabitant, the further specific matters that the court is required to take into account under s 3(2A) are identical to those which apply in the case of a spouse or former spouse who has not married.

'financial resources and financial needs' (s 3(1)(b))—'Financial needs' means reasonable requirements, including housing needs. The standard of living enjoyed by the applicant during the lifetime of the deceased and the extent to which the deceased contributed to that standard will be relevant (*Negus v Bahouse* [2008] 1 FLR 381, ChD; *Lewis v Warner* [2016] EWHC 1787 (Ch)). The court may also restrict the distribution of the liquid assets of the estate to ensure the preservation of the capital of the estate to cover unforeseen circumstances (*Stead v Stead* [1985] FLR 16, CA; see also *Malone v Harrison* [1979] 1 WLR 1353, FD). In considering the applicant's claim, the court may need to balance the applicant's needs and those of the beneficiaries, including charities (see **Reasonable financial provision** under s 1 and the effect of the Supreme Court's decision in *Illott v The Blue Cross & Others* [2017] UKSC 17 (above);(*Kusminow v Barclay's Bank Trust Co Ltd and Sokolow and Sitnikova* [1989] Fam Law 66, FD). In proceedings for financial remedy following a divorce, the court in future will exercise its discretion along the lines set out in the Family Justice Council 'Guidance on "Financial Needs" on Divorce' (June 2016). Although the guidance is stated to apply to divorce cases, it may also provide a guide to those dealing with needs cases in claims under the 1975 Act.

Obligations and responsibilities—'Obligations and responsibilities' in s 3(1)(d) extends beyond legal obligation and the deceased's obligations are not to be construed too narrowly, but in a broad sense (*Gora v Treasury Solicitor* [2003] Fam Law 93, Cty Ct; *Espinosa v Bourke* [1999] 1 FLR 747, CA). The court is entitled to have regard to the entire estate, including foreign property, when considering whether the estate has made reasonable provision for the applicant and assessing the financial resources and needs of any beneficiary of the estate (*Bheekhun v Williams* [1999] 2 FLR 229, CA). In this respect, consideration should be given to whether a claim should also be included based on whether trusts created by the deceased are 'sham' or whether it is necessary to add in a claim to bring in assets hidden behind the corporate veil in relation to transactions entered into by the deceased during his lifetime on the basis of the decision in *Prest v Petrodel Resources Ltd & Others* [2013] 2 FLR 732, SC to show a nominal holding or a resulting trust (successfully argued in *M v M and Others* [2014] 1 FLR 439, FD). The deceased's moral obligation and the morality of the applicant's claim may be relevant. (See *Re Goodchild (Deceased) and Another* [1997] 2 FLR 644, CA and see also *Re Debenham (dec'd)* [1986] 1 FLR 404, FD). The applicant must establish some sort of a moral claim to be maintained by the deceased beyond the mere fact of blood relationship (*Re Coventry (dec'd), Coventry v Coventry* (1979) FLR Rep 142, CA; *Re Abram (Deceased)* [1996] 2 FLR 379, ChD; approved and applied in *Illott v The Blue Cross & Others* [2017] UKSC 17). In *Re Debenham (dec'd)*, the court found that, although the deceased did not have any legal obligation to the applicant, she owed her a moral obligation; in *Re Jennings (deceased), Harlow v National Westminster Bank plc and Others* [1994] 1 FLR 536, CA, a claim made by an adult son of the deceased, which was based on the fact that the deceased had failed to discharge his responsibilities to the son during his minority, failed; see also *Re Wood, Wood v Wood* (1982) LS Gaz 774 and *Re Rowlands (dec'd)* [1984] FLR 813, CA and *Garland v Morris* [2007] 2 FLR 528, ChD where an adult child's claim against her father's estate failed on the facts.

Size and nature of the net estate—For meaning of net estate, see s 25(1). Note also the impact of Regulation (EU) No 650/2012 on jurisdiction, applicable law, recognition and enforcement of decisions and acceptance and enforcement of authentic instruments in matters of succession and on the creation of a European Certificate of Succession where the deceased's estate includes property within the EU (see *http://eur-lex.europa.eu/LexUriServ/LexUriServ.do?uri=OJ:L:2012:201:0107:0134:EN:PDF*). Where the size of the estate is limited, the court will be slow to deprive the deceased of his freedom to dispose of his estate as he willed (*Re Gregory, Gregory v Goodenough* [1970] 1 WLR 1455, CA; *Gora v Treasury Solicitor* [2003] Fam Law 93, Cty Ct).

Physical and mental disability—Old age may be a relevant factor in the overall assessment: *Lewis v Warner* [2016] EWHC 1787 (Ch). See final paragraph of **Reasonable financial provision** under s 1 and **Settlement of property and the mentally disabled** under s 2 and *Iqbal v Ahmed* [2012] 1 FLR 31, CA.

Conduct—In *Re Snoek (dec'd)* [1983] Fam Law 18, FD, Wood J said that he could see no reason why conduct under s 3 should be understood differently from that under MCA 1973, s 25. This decision was applied in *Barron v Woodhead* [2009] 1 FLR 747, ChD. See also *Miller v Miller; McFarlane v McFarlane* [2006] 1 FLR 1186, HL on the issue of conduct. Conduct that has been considered relevant includes: concealment by the applicant widow of her true financial position after her marriage had broken down and had been dissolved, resulting in her continuing to receive maintenance at a much higher level than she would have been entitled to (*Re Harker-Thomas* [1969] P 28, CA); the deceased being secretive about his financial position (*Re W (dec'd)* (1975) 119 SJ 439, ChD; *Roocroft v Ball* [2016] EWCA Civ 1009; and the deceased encouraging the applicant to believe that the applicant would acquire an interest in the estate and, on that belief, allowing her to act to her detriment, which can give rise to an estoppel (*Re Basham* [1987] 2 FLR 264, ChD). Where the applicant has unlawfully killed the deceased, the forfeiture rule applies (see below). See also **Reasonable financial provision** under s 1 and *Illott v The Blue Cross & Others* [2017] UKSC 17.

Deceased's reason—The Act does not specifically provide for the deceased's reason for making or not making any provision to be considered but this does not mean they do not carry any weight. The section is wide enough for the court to consider his reasons and can infer his intention from all the circumstances and weigh these against all other factors and can be overridden (see: *Illott v The Blue Cross & Others* [2017] UKSC 17; *Re Coventry (dec'd), Coventry v Coventry* (1979) FLR Rep 142, CA; *Re Leach (dec'd), Leach v Linderman* [1984] FLR 590, ChD). See *Myers v Myers* [2004] EWHC 1944 (Fam).

Any other matter—See *Re Wood, Wood v Wood* (1982) LS Gaz 774. Where the claim is made in respect of intestacy or partial intestacy, the changes made to the intestacy law with effect from 1 October 2014 by the Inheritance and Trustees' Powers Act 2014 should be considered (for a summary of the changes see [2014] Fam Law 1591).

Proprietary estoppel—The conduct of the deceased in encouraging the claimant to believe that he/she would acquire an interest in his/her estate and thereby, upon that belief, to act to his/her detriment, can give rise to estoppel on which a claim may be based. To establish such a claim, the claimant must prove that: (a) the claimant had a belief at all material times that he/she would receive the property that is the subject of the claim; (b) that belief was encouraged by the deceased; and (c) in reliance on that belief and assurance, the claimant acted to his/her detriment (*Re Basham* [1987] 2 FLR 264, ChD). For cases where the conditions that must be satisfied to found a claim in estoppel, see *HM Revenue and Customs v Benchdollar Ltd & others* [2009] EWHC 1310 (Ch) and *Thorner v Majors* [2009] 2 FLR 405, HL, where the House of Lords set out the conditions that must be satisfied, namely: (a) the relevant assurances must be clear and unequivocal and must appear to have been intended to be taken seriously and might reasonably be expected to be relied upon by the person to whom it was made; and (b) the assurances given to the claimant whether expressly, impliedly or tacitly should relate to identified property owned by the defendant. This doctrine was applied in *Wayling v Jones* [1995] 2 FLR 1029, CA, where the claimant and the deceased had been in a homosexual relationship. In *MacDonald & Anor v Frost* [2009] EWHC 2276 (Ch) a claim in estoppel made by the deceased's daughters failed on the facts. In *Evans v HSBC Trust Co (UK) Ltd* [2005] WTLR 1289, ChD, a claim brought by two brothers who were unrelated to the deceased but whom she had treated as her grandchildren was allowed as it was established that the deceased had given them assurances upon which they had acted to their detriment. In *Suggitt v Suggitt* [2011] 2 FLR 875, ChD, the deceased, who was a farmer with an agricultural estate worth £4m, left his estate to his daughter with the proviso that if his son should show himself capable of managing the farmland the daughter should transfer the farmland to him. The son, having attended agricultural college and assisted the deceased in the farming business, brought a successful claim on proprietary estoppel. It was held that once proprietary estoppel had been established, the court had to do what was necessary to avoid an unconscionable result. The court granted him the farmland and a home but no other assets. See *Moore v Moore* [2016] EWHC 2202 (Ch) and *Edgerton v Edgerton and Shaikh* [2012] 2 FLR 273, CA, in which the Master of the Rolls considered other authorities on estoppels and the effect of a determination of a Family Division judge on proceedings issued in the Chancery Division.

Mutual wills—The doctrine of mutual wills applies where the agreement to enter into mutual wills is reinforced by undertakings that the wills not be revoked. If the first testator dies having made a will in compliance with the agreement, the agreement is binding on the second testator and gives rise to an equitable obligation to give effect to the mutually agreed disposition. The legal principles that apply to mutual wills were summarised in *Charles & Ors v Fraser* [2010] EWHC 2154 (Ch). Where the legal formalities relating to mutual wills have not been complied with but the parties believed that they had created mutually binding wills, a constructive trust may be applied to prevent the second testator from dealing with the deceased's estate in a way that is incompatible with the agreement (*Healey v Brown* [2002] EWHC 1405 (Ch)). To avoid the need to apply for rectification of the will, practitioners should take care to supervise the execution of mutual wills to ensure that each client signs his/her own will and not that of the other spouse, as occurred in *Marley v Rawlings* [2012] 2 FLR 556, CA, notwithstanding the fact that on further appeal the Supreme Court has now ruled that in such a case the will should be treated in the same way as a commercial contract and it is what the parties intended that is relevant. The error should be treated as a 'clerical error' and capable of rectification (*Marley v Rawlings & Anor* [2014] UKSC 2), but in *Marley v Rawlings (No 2) (Costs)* [2015] 1 FLR 1063, SC, the Supreme Court held that the original solicitors' insurers ought to pay the costs of both parties in the lower courts. However, in relation to the costs arising from the litigation in the Supreme Court, due to the terms of the conditional fee agreements (CFAs), the insurers were only liable for the appellant's costs, the costs of the respondents' solicitors' disbursements and the costs of the respondents' counsels' fees. This was on the condition of the respondents' counsels disclaiming any entitlement to their success fees under the CFA (which they did).

Forfeiture rule—This rule disentitles a person from acquiring a benefit from the estate of another whom he has unlawfully killed. However, it does not preclude that person from making a claim under this Act since the Forfeiture Act 1982 gives the court a discretion to modify the application of the rule if it takes the view that the moral culpability of the applicant is such that it would be unjust to deny him any benefit (*Re K* [1985] FLR 558, ChD; *Re S (Deceased) (Forfeiture Rule)* [1996] 1 FLR 910, ChD). An application in respect of the unlawful killing must be made within 3 months of the applicant's conviction. The effect of the rule is to preclude the applicant from acquiring an interest in property (as defined in the Forfeiture Act 1982). When applying the forfeiture rule, and in exercising its discretion, the court does not draw any distinction between murder and manslaughter. In both cases the assailant remains criminally responsible for his actions (*Jones v Roberts* [1995] 2 FLR 422, ChD and *Re Jones (Deceased), Jones v Midland Bank Trust Co Ltd and Others* [1998] 1 FLR 246, CA). In *Chadwick v Chadwick* [2014] EWHC 3055 (Ch), the claimant killed his cohabitant and child. He sought a declaration that the rule did not apply, alternatively that it should be disapplied under s 2(2) of the Act. In holding that the rule should not be disapplied, the judge took into account factors such as the level of culpability of the claimant, the gravity of the offence and the fact that the deceased's interests in the jointly owned property had been funded with her resources. See also *Re Land (Deceased); Land v Land* [2007] 1 WLR 1009, ChD, where the claim was allowed and provision made for the deceased's son although his application was out of time under the Forfeiture Act 1982. The rule also applies to offences under the Suicide Act 1961, including aiding and abetting a suicide in pursuance of a suicide pact. Where one of the parties to a suicide pact succeeds in taking his life and the other survives, public policy would not normally require forfeiture by the survivor (*Dunbar v Plant* [1998] 1 FLR 157, CA). The decision whether to exercise the discretion, and in what manner, will depend upon the facts of each case. In *Dunbar v Plant* the circumstances of the suicide were extremely tragic and the events which occurred were horrific for the parties involved in the suicide pact and their families.

Provision which the deceased's spouse might have expected to receive on divorce—Any disposition by the deceased with the intention of defeating the spouse's claim would be a relevant factor (*Re Dawkins, Dawkins v Judd* [1986] 2 FLR 360, FD, as is the length of the marriage and the contribution made by the applicant (*Kusminow v Barclay's Bank Trust Co Ltd and Sokolow and Sitnikova* [1989] Fam Law 66, FD). However, it is not the duty of the court to alter the disposition so as to make an equitable redistribution of the available assets. The provision that the spouse might reasonably have expected to receive on divorce is only one of the matters which the court is required to consider. The major element is what is reasonable in all the circumstances of the case (*Re Krubert (Deceased)* [1997] 1 FLR 42, CA). See further **Reasonable financial provision** under s 1 above.

4 Time-limit for applications

An application for an order under section 2 of this Act shall not, except with the permission of the court, be made after the end of the period of six months from the date on which representation with respect to the estate of the deceased is first taken out (but nothing prevents the making of an application before such representation is first taken out).

Amendments—Inheritance and Trustees' Powers Act 2014, s 6, Sch 2.

Time-limit—Although the time limit for bringing a claim remains at 6 months from the date on which representation is taken out, an application can and should now be made before a grant is taken out because an extension of time will in future only be considered appropriate in exceptional circumstances. CPR 1998, r 57.16 has been amended to permit a claim to be made under the Act without naming the defendant/s and for an application for direction to be made and for the court to give direction of its own initiative as to the representation of the estate.

Standing searches—An application for a standing search is made in accordance with the Non-Contentious Probate Rules 1987, r 43 by completing the notice PA and sending it with the prescribed fee (currently £10) to the Postal Copies and Search Department, District Probate Registry, York House, 31 York Place, Leeds LS1 2BA, DX 26451 Leeds Park Place. The name and date of death of the deceased, as recorded in the Register of Deaths, must be included in the notice lodged for a standing search and in any case where the name of the deceased differs from that recorded in the Register, that name shall also be included in the oath or the notice, as appropriate (see *PD of 12 January 1999* in Part V). The court will then make an entry and acknowledge it. Once an entry is made the applicant for a standing search will receive an office copy of any grant which tallies with the particulars given and which either has been issued not more than 12 months before the receipt of the application for the search or is issued within a period of 6 months thereafter. An application for the search to be extended may be made within the last month of the 6 months' period by completing a request with the appropriate fee and sending it to the above address.

Application out of time—The court's power to extend time is discretionary (*Fielden v Cunliffe* (above)). An application for an extension must be expressly asked for in the claim form and the grounds on which the court's leave to entertain the application is sought must be included in the supporting witness statement or affidavit. If the application is opposed, the defendant must file an affidavit in answer, setting out the grounds of opposition and the personal representative is required to file a witness statement or affidavit in answer setting out the matters required by CPR 1998, r 57.16(5) and PD57, para 16. In exercising its discretion the court will look at all the circumstances and consider whether extension of time is required in the interests of justice (*Re Ruttie, Ruttie v Saul* [1970] 1 WLR 89, ChD). In *Re Salmon (dec'd), Coard v National Westminster Bank Ltd and Others* [1981] Ch 167, ChD, Sir Robert Megarry VC considered *Re Ruttie* and gave a full account of the matters which might be considered material on an application for permission to apply out of time.

Examples of cases where leave was granted are *Re Trott, Trott v Miles* [1958] 1 WLR 604, ChD, where the widow gave posthumous birth to a child; *Re McNare, McNare v McNare* [1964] 1 WLR 1255, ChD, where the widow, who was blind, crippled and aged 71, was unaware of the husband's death until five months after probate had been granted and had no information regarding the deceased's assets. Leave was refused in *Longley, Longley and Longley v Longley* [1981] CLY 2885 (but *cf Adams v Schofield* [1983] CLY 594, CA), *Escritt v Escritt* (1982) 3 FLR 280, CA, where there was a delay of more than 3 years, and *Vodanas v Kriaris* [2012] VSC 248 (a decision of the Victorian Supreme Court in Australia), where 25 days had elapsed after the time limitation period had expired.

The crucial factor in deciding whether to grant leave to apply out of time is the balance of prejudice over and above that which is inherent in the granting or withholding of leave (*Bouette v Rose* [1999] 2 FLR 466, ChD). The court will consider all the circumstances of the case, including whether it is in the interest of justice to allow an extension of time; the reasons for the delay; what efforts have been made to mitigate any effects of the delay; whether any negotiations are being carried out; whether the estate has been distributed before notice of the claim is given; whether the applicant would have a claim against the solicitors if the application were refused; whether refusal would cause hardship and operate unfairly against the applicant and, in particular, whether it would leave the applicant without redress against anyone; and whether the applicant has an arguable case (*Re Salmon (dec'd), Coard v National Westminster Bank* (above), *Re C (Deceased) (Leave to Apply for Provision)* [1995] 2 FLR 24, FD (where an 8-year-old illegitimate child of the deceased was granted leave, although her mother had taken no steps to make a claim for two and a half years)). See also *Stock v Brown* [1994] 1 FLR 840, FD (where the time-limit had been exceeded by 6 years). See *Hashtroodi v Hancock* [2004] 1 WLR 3206, CA for the possible effect of a solicitor's failure to serve the claim form before the due date and *Vodanas v Kriaris* (above), where the Australian court found that there was an arguable case, the applicant had acted promptly once H became aware of the his rights and there was no prejudice to the beneficiaries. The court should also consider any possible infringement of ECHR 1950, Art 6 rights.

5 Interim orders

(1) Where on an application for an order under section 2 of this Act it appears to the court –

- (a) that the applicant is in immediate need of financial assistance, but it is not yet possible to determine what order (if any) should be made under that section; and
- (b) that property forming part of the net estate of the deceased is or can be made available to meet the need of the applicant;

the court may order that, subject to such conditions or restrictions, if any, as the court may impose and to any further order of the court, there shall be paid to the applicant out of the net estate of the deceased such sum or sums and (if more than one) at such intervals at the court thinks reasonable; and the court may order that, subject to the provisions of this Act, such payments are to be made until such date as the court may specify, not being later than the date on which the court either makes an order under the said section 2 or decides not to exercise its powers under that section.

PART II

(2) Subsections (2), (3) and (4) of section 2 of this Act shall apply in relation to an order under this section as they apply in relation to an order under that section.

(3) In determining what order, if any, should be made under this section the court shall, so far as the urgency of the case admits, have regard to the same matters as those to which the court is required to have regard under section 3 of this Act.

(4) An order made under section 2 of this Act may provide that any sum paid to the applicant by virtue of this section shall be treated to such an extent and in such manner as may be provided by that order as having been paid on account of any payment provided for by that order.

Procedure—The rules do not prescribe the procedure for such an application. Since the application is made in the main proceedings, it should be made by summons in those proceedings and supported by affidavit. The applicant must show that the conditions in s 5(1)(a) and (b) are satisfied.

'in immediate need of financial assistance' (s 5(1)(a))—This power is discretionary and will depend on whether the claimant is in immediate need of financial assistance and there is sufficient property in the estate to meet that need. Note that the court is required to have regard to the matters set out in s 3 when determining an application for an interim order (see *Smith v Smith and others* [2012] 2 FLR 230, ChD. See also *M v M* [2011] EWHC 3574 (Fam), which although a case under MFPA 1984, Pt III it was held that 'immediate' means 'current' not 'urgent'.

Sanctioning interim payments—Personal representatives may find themselves in difficulties when such an application is made, particularly when the parties are on bad terms. In such cases they should form their own view, with the assistance of their legal advisers, as to the payments that can properly be made. Alternatively, they should ask the parties who might conceivably be affected – whether applicant or residuary legatee – for their consent. If such consent is not forthcoming the executors can apply to the court for leave to make the payment in question. In the event that the court finds that consent was unreasonably withheld it may order costs against the party who acted unreasonably (*Re Ralphs, Ralphs v District Bank* [1968] 1 WLR 1522, ChD).

6 Variation, discharge, etc of orders for periodical payments

(1) Subject to the provisions of this Act, where the court has made an order under section 2(1)(a) of this Act (in this section referred to as 'the original order') for the making of periodical payments to any person (in this section referred to as 'the original recipient'), the court, on an application under this section, shall have power by order to vary or discharge the original order or to suspend any provision of it temporarily and to revive the operation of any provision so suspended.

(2) Without prejudice to the generality of subsection (1) above, an order made on an application for the variation of the original order may –

(a) provide for the making out of any relevant property of such periodical payments and for such term as may be specified in the order to any person who has applied, or would but for section 4 of this Act be entitled to apply, for an order under section 2 of this Act (whether or not, in the case of any application, an order was made in favour of the applicant);

(b) provide for the payment out of any relevant property of a lump sum of such amount as may be so specified to the original recipient or to any such person as is mentioned in paragraph (a) above;

(c) provide for the transfer of the relevant property, or such part thereof as may be so specified, to the original recipient or to any such person as is so mentioned.

(3) Where the original order provides that any periodical payments payable thereunder to the original recipient are to cease on the occurrence of an event specified in the order (other than the formation of a subsequent marriage or civil partnership by a former spouse or former civil partner) or on the expiration of a period so specified, then, if, before the end of the period of six months from the date of the occurrence of that event or of the expiration of that period, an application is made for an order under this section, the court shall have power to make any order which it would have had power to make if the application had been made before that date (whether in favour of the original recipient or any such person as is mentioned in subsection (2)(a) above and whether having effect from that date or from such later date as the court may specify).

(4) Any reference in this section to the original order shall include a reference to an order made under this section and any reference in this section to the original recipient shall include a reference to any person to whom periodical payments are required to be made by virtue of an order under this section.

(5) An application under this section may be made by any of the following persons, that is to say –

(a) any person who by virtue of section 1(1) of this Act has applied, or would but for section 4 of this Act be entitled to apply, for an order under section 2 of this Act,

(b) the personal representatives of the deceased,

(c) the trustees of any relevant property, and

(d) any beneficiary of the estate of the deceased.

(6) An order under this section may only affect –

(a) property the income of which is at the date of the order applicable wholly or in part for the making of periodical payments to any person who has applied for an order under this Act, or

(b) in the case of an application under subsection (3) above in respect of payments which have ceased to be payable on the occurrence of an event or the expiration of a period, property the income of which was so applicable immediately before the occurrence of that event or the expiration of that period, as the case may be,

and any such property as is mentioned in paragraph (a) or (b) above is in subsections (2) and (5) above referred to as 'relevant property'.

(7) In exercising the powers conferred by this section the court shall have regard to all the circumstances of the case, including any change in any of the matters to which the court was required to have regard when making the order to which the application relates.

(8) Where the court makes an order under this section, it may give such consequential directions as it thinks necessary or expedient having regard to the provisions of the order.

(9) No such order as is mentioned in section 2(1)(d), (e) or (f), 9, 10 or 11 of this Act shall be made on an application under this section.

(10) For the avoidance of doubt it is hereby declared that, in relation to an order which provides for the making of periodical payments which are to cease on the occurrence of an event specified in the order (other than the formation of a subsequent marriage or civil partnership by a former spouse or former civil partner) or on the expiration of a period so specified, the power to vary an order includes power to provide for the making of periodical payments after the expiration of that period or the occurrence of that event.

Amendments—CPA 2004, s 71, Sch 4, para 19.

7 Payment of lump sums by instalments

(1) An order under section 2(1)(b) or 6(2)(b) of this Act for the payment of a lump sum may provide for the payment of that sum by instalments of such amount as may be specified in the order.

(2) Where an order is made by virtue of subsection (1) above, and court shall have power, on an application made by the person to whom the lump sum is payable, by the personal representatives of the deceased or by the trustees of the property out of which the lump sum is payable, to vary that order by varying the number of instalments payable, the amount of any instalment and the date on which any instalment becomes payable.

Property available for financial provision

8 Property treated as part of 'net estate'

(1) Where a deceased person has in accordance with the provisions of any enactment nominated any person to receive any sum of money or other property on his death and that nomination is in force at the time of his death, that sum of money, after deducting therefrom any capital transfer tax payable in respect thereof, or that other property, to the extent of the value thereof at the date of the death of the deceased after deducting therefrom any capital transfer tax so payable, shall be treated for the purposes of this Act as part of the net estate of the deceased; but this subsection shall not render any person liable for having paid that sum or transferred that other property to the person named in the nomination in accordance with the directions given in the nomination.

(2) Where any sum of money or other property is received by any person as a donatio mortis causa made by a deceased person, that sum of money, after deducting therefrom any capital transfer tax payable thereon, or that other property, to the extent of the value thereof at the date of the death of the deceased after deducting therefrom any capital transfer tax so payable, shall be treated for the purposes of this Act as part of the net estate of the deceased; but this subsection shall not render any person liable for having paid that sum or transferred that other property in order to give effect to that donatio mortis causa.

(3) The amount of capital transfer tax to be deducted for the purpose of this section shall not exceed the amount of that tax which has been borne by the person nominated by the deceased or, as the case may be, the person who has received a sum of money or other property as a donatio mortis causa.

Defined terms—'net estate': s 25(1) (see also under s 2).

'property'—This term includes a chose in action (s 25(1)).

'donatio mortis causa'—Land is capable of passing through a donatio mortis causa (*Sen v Headley* [1991] 2 FLR 449, CA).

9 Property held on a joint tenancy

(1) Where a deceased person was immediately before his death beneficially entitled to a joint tenancy of any property, then, if an application is made for an order under section 2 of this Act, the court for the purpose of facilitating the making of financial provision for the applicant under this Act may order that the deceased's severable share of that property shall, to such extent as appears to the court to be just in all the circumstances of the case, be treated for the purposes of this Act as part of the net estate of the deceased.

(1A) Where an order is made under subsection (1) the value of the deceased's severable share of the property concerned is taken for the purposes of this Act to be the value that the share would have had at the date of the hearing of the application for an order under section 2 had the share been severed immediately before the deceased's death, unless the court orders that the share is to be valued at a different date.

(2) In determining the extent to which any severable share is to be treated as part of the net estate of the deceased by virtue of any order under subsection (1) above, the court shall have regard to any capital transfer tax payable in respect of that severable share.

(3) Where an order is made under subsection (1) above, the provisions of this section shall not render any person liable for anything done by him before the order was made.

(4) For the avoidance of doubt it is hereby declared that for the purposes of this section there may be a joint tenancy of a chose in action.

Amendments—Inheritance and Trustees' Powers Act 2014, s 6, Sch 2.

Defined terms—'net estate': s 25(1).

Application for an order—Inheritance and Trustees' Powers Act 2014 removes any reference to a time limit. Nevertheless, if it is proposed to make an application under this section it should be made within the substantive application for financial provision.

'joint tenancy of any property' (s 9(1))—In the case of a joint life policy, in the absence of evidence to the contrary, the death benefit is taken to be intended by the parties to be payable to the survivor of the two policy-holders (*Murphy v Murphy & Others* [2003] EWCA Civ 1862). Where a husband and wife took out a policy of fixed-term life insurance that provided for death or terminal illness benefit, the deceased who died of a terminal illness was held to have a severable interest in the terminal illness benefit and the policy had to be valued taking into account the fact that the interest would cease to exist if death occurred before a claim was made. Therefore, the value of the deceased's interest was nil and there could be no interest that could be taken to be part of the deceased's estate on which a claim could be made: *Lim v Walia* [2015] 2 FLR 339, CA. In *Jessop v Jessop* [1992] 1 FLR 591, CA, the court ordered the deceased's severable share of his cohabitee's house which had been jointly owned before the deceased's death, to be treated as part of the net estate of the deceased and ordered the cohabitee to pay a lump sum to the widow. In *Re Crawford* (1983) 4 FLR 273, FD, a lump sum received by the deceased on his retirement had been paid into an account held jointly with his second wife. The court made an order under s 9 that the deceased's share of the lump sum should be treated as part of his estate. Note the change that applies in relation to the timing of assessment of the value of the deceased's share as from 1 October 2014. Where a deceased person's estate is found to be insolvent, administration takes place under Insolvency Act 1986, s 421 and the matter is governed by the Administration of Insolvent Estates of Deceased Persons Order 1986. However, the making of an insolvency administration order does not relate back to sever the deceased's beneficial interest in property owned by the deceased and his wife immediately before the deceased's death, as the deceased's interest in the property passes to the widow by survivorship at the moment of death (*Re Palmer (Deceased) (Insolvent Estate)* [1994] 2 FLR 609, CA). Where, on an application for ancillary relief following a divorce, an agreement is reached between the parties for the sale of the former matrimonial home and the division of the proceeds of sale, the joint tenancy is severed so that, if one of the parties dies before the agreement is approved by the court and an order made, the joint tenancy remains severed by the agreement. The agreement does not have to be enforceable, provided it indicates a common intention to sever (*Davis v Smith* [2012] 1 FLR 1177, CA; *Quigley v Masterson* [2011] EWHC 2529 (Ch)).

'at the value thereof immediately before his death'—For the meaning of this term see *Dingmar v Dingmar* [2007] 1 FLR 210, CA and *Lim v Walia* [2015] 2 FLR 339, CA.

'for the purpose of facilitating the making of financial provision' (s 9(1))—This should not be understood to narrow the broad discretionary power given by s 9 (*Kourkgy v Lusher* (1983) 4 FLR 65, FD), but the broad discretionary power is no more than a power to facilitate the making of an order under s 2 (*Jessop v Jessop* [1992] 1 FLR 591, CA).

Powers of court in relation to transactions intended to defeat applications for financial provision

10 Dispositions intended to defeat applications for financial provision

(1) Where an application is made to the court for an order under section 2 of this Act, the applicant may, in the proceedings on that application, apply to the court for an order under subsection (2) below.

(2) Where on an application under subsection (1) above the court is satisfied –

(a) that, less than six years before the date of the death of the deceased, the deceased with the intention of defeating an application for financial provision under this Act made a disposition, and

(b) that full valuable consideration for that disposition was not given by the person to whom or for the benefit of whom the disposition was made (in this section referred to as 'the donee') or by any other person, and

(c) that the exercise of the powers conferred by this section would facilitate the making of financial provision for the applicant under this Act,

then, subject to the provisions of this section and of sections 12 and 13 of this Act, the court may order the donee (whether or not at the date of the order he holds any interest in the property disposed of to him or for his benefit by the deceased) to provide, for the purpose of the making of that financial provision, such sum of money or other property as may be specified in the order.

(3) Where an order is made under subsection (2) above as respects any disposition made by the deceased which consisted of the payment of money to or for the benefit of the donee, the amount of any sum of money or the value of any property orders to be provided under that subsection shall not exceed the amount of the payment made by the deceased after deducting therefrom any capital transfer tax borne by the donee in respect of that payment.

(4) Where an order is made under subsection (2) above as respects any disposition made by the deceased which consisted of the transfer of property (other than a sum of money) to or for the benefit of the donee, the amount of any sum of money or the value of any property ordered to be provided under that subsection shall not exceed the value at the date of the death of the deceased of the property disposed of by him to or for the benefit of the donee (or if that property has been disposed of by the person to whom it was transferred by the deceased, the value at the date of that disposal thereof) after deducting therefrom any capital transfer tax borne by the donee in respect of the transfer of that property by the deceased.

(5) Where an application (in this subsection referred to as 'the original application') is made for an order under subsection (2) above in relation to any disposition, then, if on an application under this subsection by the donee or by any applicant for an order under section 2 of this Act the court is satisfied –

(a) that, less than six years before the date of the death of the deceased, the deceased with the intention of defeating an application for financial provision under this Act made a disposition other than the disposition which is the subject of the original application, and

(b) that full valuable consideration for that other disposition was not given by the person to whom or for the benefit of whom that other disposition was made or by any other person,

the court may exercise in relation to the person to whom or for the benefit of whom that other disposition was made the powers which the court would have had under subsection (2) above if the original application had been made in respect of that other disposition and the court had been satisfied as to the matters set out in paragraphs (a), (b) and (c) of that subsection; and where any application is made under this subsection, any reference in this section (except in subsection (2)(b)) to the donee shall include a reference to the person to whom or for the benefit of whom that other disposition was made.

(6) In determining whether and in what manner to exercise its powers under this section, the court shall have regard to the circumstances in which any disposition was made and any valuable consideration which was given therefor, the relationship, if any, of the donee to the deceased, the conduct and financial resources of the donee and all the other circumstances of the case.

(7) In this section 'disposition' does not include –

(a) any provision in a will, any such nomination as is mentioned in section 8(1) of this Act or any donatio mortis causa, or
(b) any appointment of property made, otherwise than by will, in the exercise of a special power of appointment,

but, subject to these exceptions, includes any payment of money (including the payment of a premium under a policy of assurance) and any conveyance, assurance, appointment or gift of property of any description, whether made by an instrument or otherwise.

(8) The provisions of this section do not apply to any disposition made before the commencement of this Act.

Defined terms—'valuable consideration': s 25.

Avoidance of disposition intended to defeat a claim—An applicant who applies for an order under s 2 may also apply for an order that the donee of a disposition made less than 6 years before the deceased's death with the intention of defeating a claim under the Act and without full valuable consideration should provide such sum or property as may be necessary for the making of reasonable financial provision for the applicant. The court's power under this section is subject to the matters referred to in ss 12 and 13.

See *Clifford v Tanner* [1987] CLY 3881, CA, where it was held that a deed releasing a donee from a covenant allowing the donor and his wife to occupy a house, which was the subject of a gift to the donee, is a disposition within s 10(7).

'intention of defeating an application' (s 10(2)(a),(5)(a))—It is not essential to show that the deceased had the provision of the Act in mind when the transaction in issue was made, but the evidence must show that he intended to defeat a claim against his estate made after his death (*Re Kennedy (dec'd)* [1980] CLY 2820, Cty Ct).

11 Contracts to leave property by will

(1) Where an application is made to a court for an order under section 2 of this Act, the applicant may, in the proceedings on that application, apply to the court for an order under this section.

(2) Where on an application under subsection (1) above the court is satisfied –

(a) that the deceased made a contract by which he agreed to leave by his will a sum of money or other property to any person or by which he agreed that a sum of money or other property would be paid or transferred to any person out of his estate, and
(b) that the deceased made that contract with the intention of defeating an application for financial provision under this Act, and
(c) that when the contract was made full valuable consideration for that contract was not given or promised by the person with whom or for the benefit of whom the contract was made (in this section referred to as 'the donee') or by any other person, and
(d) that the exercise of the powers conferred by this section would facilitate the making of financial provision for the applicant under this Act,

then, subject to the provisions of this section and of sections 12 and 13 of this Act, the court may make any one or more of the following orders, that is to say –

(i) if any money has been paid or any other property has been transferred to or for the benefit of the donee in accordance with the contract, an order directing the donee to provide, for the purpose of the making of that financial provision, such sum of money or other property as may be specified in the order;

(ii) if the money or all the money has not been paid or the property or all the property has not been transferred in accordance with the contract, an order directing the personal representatives not to make any payment or transfer any property, or not to make any further payment or transfer any further property, as the case may be, in accordance therewith or directing the personal representatives only to make such payment or transfer such property as may be specified in the order.

(3) Notwithstanding anything in subsection (2) above, the court may exercise its powers thereunder in relation to any contract made by the deceased only to the extent that the court considers that the amount of any sum of money paid or to be paid or the value of any property transferred or to be transferred in accordance with the contract exceeds the value of any valuable consideration given or to be given for that contract, and for this purpose the court shall have regard to the value of property at the date of the hearing.

(4) In determining whether and in what manner to exercise its powers under this section, the court shall have regard to the circumstances in which the contract was made, the relationship, if any, of the donee to the deceased, the conduct and financial resources of the donee and all the other circumstances of the case.

(5) Where an order has been made under subsection (2) above in relation to any contract, the rights of any person to enforce that contract or to recover damages or to obtain other relief for the breach thereof shall be subject to any adjustment made by the court under section 12(3) of this Act and shall survive to such extent only as is consistent with giving effect to the terms of that order.

(6) The provision of this section do not apply to a contract made before the commencement of this Act.

Avoidance of contracts to leave property by will—An applicant who applies for an order under s 2 may also apply for an order directing the donee under a contract which was made with the intention of defeating a claim under the Act and without full valuable consideration to provide such sum of money or other property as may be necessary for the making of reasonable financial provision for the applicant. Where the sum of money or the property has not been transferred, the order should direct that the personal representatives must not make the payment or transfer the property, or make any further payment or transfer any further property, or that they may make only such payment or transfer as the court may direct. Under this section the court has power to make such further consequential directions as it thinks fit for giving effect to any order it makes.

12 Provisions supplementary to ss 10 and 11

(1) Where the exercise of any of the powers conferred by section 10 or 11 of this Act is conditional on the court being satisfied that a disposition or contract was made by a deceased person with the intention of defeating an application for financial provision under this Act, that condition shall be fulfilled if the court is of the opinion that, on a balance of probabilities, the intention of the deceased (though not necessarily his sole intention) in making the disposition or contract was to prevent an order for financial provision being made under this Act or to reduce the amount of the provision which might otherwise be granted by an order thereunder.

(2) Where an application is made under section 11 of this Act with respect to any contract made by the deceased and no valuable consideration was given or promised by any person for that contract then, notwithstanding anything in subsection (1) above, it shall be presumed, unless the contrary is shown, that the deceased made that contract with the intention of defeating an application for financial provision under this Act.

(3) Where the court makes an order under section 10 or 11 of this Act it may give such consequential directions as it thinks fit (including directions requiring the making of any payment or the transfer of any property) for giving effect to the order or for securing a fair adjustment of the rights of the persons affected thereby.

(4) Any power conferred on the court by the said section 10 or 11 to order the donee, in relation to any disposition or contract, to provide any sum of money or other property shall be exercisable in like manner in relation to the personal representative of the donee, and –

(a) any reference in section 10(4) to the disposal of property by the donee shall include a reference to disposal by the personal representative of the donee, and

(b) any reference in section 10(5) to an application by the donee under that subsection shall include a reference to an application by the personal representative of the donee;

but the court shall not have power under the said section 10 or 11 to make an order in respect of any property forming part of the estate of the donee which has been distributed by the personal representative; and the personal representative shall not be liable for having distributed any such property before he has notice of the making of an application under the said section 10 or 11 on the ground that he ought to have taken into account the possibility that such an application would be made.

13 Provisions as to trustees in relation to ss 10 and 11

(1) Where an application is made for –

(a) an order under section 10 of this Act in respect of a disposition made by the deceased to any person as a trustee, or

(b) an order under section 11 of this Act in respect of any payment made or property transferred, in accordance with a contract made by the deceased, to any person as a trustee,

the powers of the court under the said section 10 or 11 to order that trustee to provide a sum of money or other property shall be subject to the following limitation (in addition, in a case of an application under section 10, to any provision regarding the deduction of capital transfer tax) namely, that the amount of any sum of money or the value of any property ordered to be provided –

(i) in the case of an application in respect of a disposition which consisted of the payment of money or an application in respect of the payment of money in accordance with a contract, shall not exceed the aggregate of so much of that money as is at the date of the order in the hands of the trustee and the value at that date of any property which represents that money or is derived therefrom and is at that date in the hands of the trustee;

(ii) in the case of an application in respect of a disposition which consisted of the transfer of property (other than a sum of money) or an application in respect of the transfer of property (other than a sum of money) in accordance with a contract, shall not exceed the aggregate of the value at the date of the order of so much of that property as is at that date in the hands of the trustee and the value at that date of any property which represents the first mentioned property or is derived therefrom and is at that date in the hands of the trustee.

(2) Where any such application is made in respect of a disposition made to any person as a trustee or in respect of any payment made or property transferred in pursuance of a contract to any person as a trustee, the trustee shall not be liable for having distributed any money or other property on the ground that he ought to have taken into account the possibility that such an application would be made.

(3) Where any such application is made in respect of a disposition made to any person as a trustee or in respect of any payment made or property transferred in accordance with a contract to any person as a trustee, any reference in the said section 10 or 11 to the donee shall be construed as including a reference to the trustee or trustees for the time being of the trust in question and any reference in subsection (1) or (2) above to a trustee shall be construed in the same way.

Special provisions relating to cases of divorce, separation etc

14 Provision as to cases where no financial relief was granted in divorce proceedings etc

(1) Where, within twelve months from the date on which a decree of divorce or nullity of marriage has been made absolute or a decree of judicial separation has been granted, a party to the marriage dies and –

(a) an application for a financial provision order under section 23 of the Matrimonial Causes Act 1973 or a property adjustment order under section 24 of that Act has not been made by the other party to that marriage, or

(b) such an application has been made but the proceedings thereon have not been determined at the time of the death of the deceased,

then, if an application for an order under section 2 of this Act is made by that other party, the court shall, notwithstanding anything in section 1 or section 3 of this Act, have power, if it thinks it just to do so, to treat that party for the purposes of that application as if the decree of divorce or nullity of marriage had not been made absolute or the decree of judicial separation had not been granted, as the case may be.

(2) This section shall not apply in relation to a decree of judicial separation unless at the date of the death of the deceased the decree was in force and the separation was continuing.

Defined terms—'financial provision': MCA 1973, s 23; 'property adjustment order': MCA 1973, s 24.

14A Provision as to cases where no financial relief was granted in proceedings for the dissolution etc. of a civil partnership

(1) Subsection (2) below applies where –

(a) a dissolution order, nullity order, separation order or presumption of death order has been made under Chapter 2 of Part 2 of the Civil Partnership Act 2004 in relation to a civil partnership,

(b) one of the civil partners dies within twelve months from the date on which the order is made, and

(c) either –

  (i) an application for a financial provision order under Part 1 of Schedule 5 to that Act or a property adjustment order under Part 2 of that Schedule has not been made by the other civil partner, or

  (ii) such an application has been made but the proceedings on the application have not been determined at the time of the death of the deceased.

(2) If an application for an order under section 2 of this Act is made by the surviving civil partner, the court shall, notwithstanding anything in section 1 or section 3 of this Act, have power, if it thinks it just to do so, to treat the surviving civil partner as if the order mentioned in subsection (1)(a) above had not been made.

(3) This section shall not apply in relation to a separation order unless at the date of the death of the deceased the separation order was in force and the separation was continuing.

Amendments—Inserted by CPA 2004, s 71, Sch 4, para 20.

15 Restriction imposed in divorce proceedings etc on application under this Act

(1) On the grant of a decree of divorce, a decree of nullity of marriage or a decree of judicial separation or at any time thereafter the court, if it considers it just to do so, may, on the application of either party to the marriage, order that the other party to the marriage shall not on the death of the applicant be entitled to apply for an order under section 2 of this Act.

In this subsection 'the court' means the High Court or the family court.

(2) In the case of a decree of divorce or nullity of marriage an order may be made under subsection (1) above before or after the decree is made absolute, but if it is made before the decree is made absolute it shall not take effect unless the decree is made absolute.

(3) Where an order made under subsection (1) above on the grant of a decree of divorce or nullity of marriage has come into force with respect to a party to a marriage, then, on the death of the other party to that marriage, the court shall not entertain any application for an order under section 2 of this Act made by the first-mentioned party.

(4) Where an order made under subsection (1) above on the grant of a decree of judicial separation has come into force with respect to any party to a marriage, then, if the other party to that marriage dies while the decree is in force and the separation is continuing, the court shall not entertain any application for an order under section 2 of this Act made by the first-mentioned party.

Amendments—MFPA 1984, s 8(1); CCA 2013, s 17, Sch 10.

15ZA Restriction imposed in proceedings for the dissolution etc. of a civil partnership on application under this Act

(1) On making a dissolution order, nullity order, separation order or presumption of death order under Chapter 2 of Part 2 of the Civil Partnership Act 2004, or at any time after making such an order, the court, if it considers it just to do so, may, on the application of either of the civil partners, order that the other civil partner shall not on the death of the applicant be entitled to apply for an order under section 2 of this Act.

(2) In subsection (1) above 'the court' means the High Court or the family court.

(3) In the case of a dissolution order, nullity order or presumption of death order ('the main order') an order may be made under subsection (1) above before (as well as after) the main order is made final, but if made before the main order is made final it shall not take effect unless the main order is made final.

(4) Where an order under subsection (1) above made in connection with a dissolution order, nullity order or presumption of death order has come into force with respect to a civil partner, then, on the death of the other civil partner, the court shall not entertain any application for an order under section 2 of this Act made by the surviving civil partner.

(5) Where an order under subsection (1) above made in connection with a separation order has come into force with respect to a civil partner, then, if the other civil partner dies while the separation order is in force and the separation is continuing, the court shall not entertain any application for an order under section 2 of this Act made by the surviving civil partner.

Amendments—Inserted by CPA 2004, s 71, Sch 4, para 21. Amended by CCA 2013, s 17, Sch 10.

15A Restriction imposed in proceedings under Matrimonial and Family Proceedings Act 1984 on application under this Act

(1) On making an order under section 17 of the Matrimonial and Family Proceedings Act 1984 (orders for financial provision and property adjustment) the court, if it considers it just to do so, may, on the application of either party to the marriage, order that the other party to the marriage shall not on the death of the applicant be entitled to apply for an order under section 2 of this Act.

In this subsection 'the court' means the High Court or the family court.

(2) Where an order under subsection (1) above has been made with respect to a party to a marriage which has been dissolved or annulled, then, on the death of the other party to that marriage, the court shall not entertain an application under section 2 of this Act made by the first-mentioned party.

(3) Where an order under subsection (1) above has been made with respect to a party to a marriage the parties to which have been legally separated, then, if the other party to the marriage dies while the legal separation is in force, the court shall not entertain an application under section 2 of this Act made by the first-mentioned party.

Amendments—Inserted by MFPA 1984, s 25. Amended by CCA 2013, s 17, Sch 10.

15B Restriction imposed in proceedings under Schedule 7 to the Civil Partnership Act 2004 on application under this Act

(1) On making an order under paragraph 9 of Schedule 7 to the Civil Partnership Act 2004 (orders for financial provision, property adjustment and pension-sharing following overseas dissolution etc. of civil partnership) the court, if it considers it just to do so, may, on the application of either of the civil partners, order that the other civil partner shall not on the death of the applicant be entitled to apply for an order under section 2 of this Act.

(2) In subsection (1) above 'the court' means the High Court or the family court.

(3) Where an order under subsection (1) above has been made with respect to one of the civil partners in a case where a civil partnership has been dissolved or annulled, then, on the death of the other civil partner, the court shall not entertain an application under section 2 of this Act made by the surviving civil partner.

(4) Where an order under subsection (1) above has been made with respect to one of the civil partners in a case where civil partners have been legally separated, then, if the other civil partner dies while the legal separation is in force, the court shall not entertain an application under section 2 of this Act made by the surviving civil partner.

Amendments—Inserted by CPA 2004, s 71, Sch 4, para 22. Amended by CCA 2013, s 17, Sch 10.

16 Variation and discharge of secured periodical payments orders made under Matrimonial Causes Act 1973

(1) Where an application for an order under section 2 of this Act is made to the court by any person who was at the time of the death of the deceased entitled to payments from the deceased under a secured periodical payments order made under the Matrimonial Causes Act 1973 or Schedule 5 to the Civil Partnership Act 2004, then, in the proceedings on that application, the court shall have power, if an application is made under this section by that person or by the personal representative of the deceased, to vary or discharge that periodical payments order or to revive the operation of any provision thereof which has been suspended under section 31 of that Act of 1973 or Part 11 of that Schedule.

(2) In exercising the powers conferred by this section the court shall have regard to all the circumstances of the case, including any order which the court proposes to make under section 2 or section 5 of this Act and any change (whether resulting from the death of the deceased or otherwise) in any of the matters to which the court was required to have regard when making the secured periodical payments order.

(3) The powers exercisable by the court under this section in relation to an order shall be exercisable also in relation to any instrument executed in pursuance of the order.

Amendments—CPA 2004, s 71, Sch 4, para 23.
Defined terms—'secured periodical payments': MCA 1973, s 23.

17 Variation and revocation of maintenance agreements

(1) Where an application for an order under section 2 of this Act is made to the court by any person who was at the time of the death of the deceased entitled to payments from the deceased under a maintenance agreement which provided for the continuation of payments under the agreement after the death of the deceased, then, in the proceedings on that application, the court shall have power, if an application is made under this section by that person or by the personal representative of the deceased, to vary or revoke that agreement.

(2) In exercising the powers conferred by this section the court shall have regard to all the circumstances of the case, including any order which the court proposes to make under section 2 or section 5 of this Act and any change (whether resulting from the death of the deceased or otherwise) in any of the circumstances in the light of which the agreement was made.

(3) If a maintenance agreement is varied by the court under this section the like consequences shall ensue as if the variation had been made immediately before the death of the deceased by agreement between the parties and for valuable consideration.

(4) In this section 'maintenance agreement', in relation to a deceased person, means any agreement made, whether in writing or not and whether before or after the commencement of this Act, by the deceased with any person with whom he formed a marriage or civil partnership, being an agreement which contained provisions governing the rights and liabilities towards one another when living separately of the parties to that marriage or of the civil partners (whether or not the marriage or civil partnership has been dissolved or annulled) in respect of the making or securing of payments or the disposition or use of any property, including such rights and liabilities with respect to the maintenance or education of any child, whether or not a child of the deceased or a person who was treated by the deceased as a child of the family in relation to that marriage or civil partnership.

Amendments—CPA 2004, s 71, Sch 4, para 24.

Scope—The provision is similar to that under s 16, to vary or revoke a maintenance agreement which provided for the continuation of payment under the agreement after the death of the deceased. MCA 1973, s 36 also provides for an application to be made for the alteration of a maintenance agreement after the death of one of the spouses, and FPR 2010, rr 8.6–8.11 prescribes the procedure that must be followed. When making an application under this section reference should be made to the annotation to MCA 1973, s 36 and FPR 2010, Pt 8, Ch 3.

18 Availability of court's powers under this Act in applications under ss 31 and 36 of the Matrimonial Causes Act 1973

(1) Where –

(a) a person against whom a secured periodical payments order was made under the Matrimonial Causes Act 1973 has died and an application is made under section 31(6) of that Act for the variation or discharge of that order or for the revival of the operation of any provision thereof which has been suspended, or

(b) a party to a maintenance agreement within the meaning of section 34 of that Act has died, the agreement being one which provides for the continuation of payments thereunder after the death of one of the parties, and an application is made under section 36(1) of that Act for the alteration of the agreement under section 35 thereof,

the court shall have power to direct that the application made under the said section 31(6) or 36(1) shall be deemed to have been accompanied by an application for an order under section 2 of this Act.

(2) Where the court gives a direction under subsection (1) above it shall have power, in the proceedings on the application under the said section 31(6) or 36(1), to make any order which the court would have had power to make under the provisions of this Act if the application under the said section 31(6) or 36(1), as the case may be, had been made jointly with an application for an order under the said section 2; and the court shall have power to give such consequential directions as may be necessary for enabling the court to exercise any of the powers available to the court under this Act in the case of an application for an order under section 2.

(3) Where an order made under section 15(1) of this Act is in force with respect to a party to a marriage, the court shall not give a direction under subsection (1) above with respect to any application made under the said section 31(6) or 36(1) by that party on the death of the other party.

18A Availability of court's powers under this Act in applications under paragraphs 60 and 73 of Schedule 5 to the Civil Partnership Act 2004

(1) Where –

(a) a person against whom a secured periodical payments order was made under Schedule 5 to the Civil Partnership Act 2004 has died and an application is made under paragraph 60 of that Schedule for the variation or discharge of that order or for the revival of the operation of any suspended provision of the order, or

(b) a party to a maintenance agreement within the meaning of Part 13 of that Schedule has died, the agreement being one which provides for the continuation of payments under the agreement after the death of one of the parties, and an application is made under paragraph 73 of that Schedule for the alteration of the agreement under paragraph 69 of that Schedule, the court shall have power to direct that the application made under paragraph 60 or 73 of that Schedule shall be deemed to have been accompanied by an application for an order under section 2 of this Act.

(2) Where the court gives a direction under subsection (1) above it shall have power, in the proceedings on the application under paragraph 60 or 73 of that Schedule, to make any order which the court would have had power to make under the provisions of this Act if the application under that paragraph had been made jointly with an application for an order under section 2 of this Act; and the court shall have power to give such consequential directions as may be necessary for enabling the court to exercise any of the powers available to the court under this Act in the case of an application for an order under section 2.

(3) Where an order made under section 15ZA(1) of this Act is in force with respect to a civil partner, the court shall not give a direction under subsection (1) above with respect to any application made under paragraph 60 or 73 of that Schedule by that civil partner on the death of the other civil partner.

Amendments—Inserted by CPA 2004, s 71, Sch 4, para 25.

Miscellaneous and supplementary provisions

19 Effect, duration and form of orders

(1) Where an order is made under section 2 of this Act then for all purposes, including the purposes of the enactments relating to inheritance tax, the will or the law relating to intestacy, or both the will and the law relating to intestacy, as the case may be, shall have effect and be deemed to have had effect as from the deceased's death subject to the provisions of the order.

(2) Any order made under section 2 or 5 of this Act in favour of –

(a) an applicant who was the former spouse or former civil partner of the deceased, or

(b) an applicant who was the husband or wife of the deceased in a case where the marriage with the deceased was the subject of a decree of judicial separation and at the date of death the decree was in force and the separation was continuing, or

(c) an applicant who was the civil partner of the deceased in a case where, at the date of death, a separation order under Chapter 2 of Part 2 of the Civil Partnership Act 2004 was in force in relation to their civil partnership and the separation was continuing,

shall, in so far as it provides for the making of periodical payments, cease to have effect on the remarriage of the applicant on the formation by the applicant of a subsequent marriage or civil partnership, except in relation to any arrears due under the order on the date of the formation of the subsequent marriage or civil partnership.

(3) A copy of every order made under this Act other than an order made under section 15(1) or 15ZA(1) of this Act shall be sent to the principal registry of the Family Division for entry and filing, and a memorandum of the order shall be endorsed on, or permanently annexed to, the probate or letters of administration under which the estate is being administered.

Amendments—AJA 1982, s 52; CPA 2004, s 71, Sch 4, para 26.

****

25 Interpretation

(1) In this Act –

'beneficiary', in relation to the estate of a deceased person, means –

(a) a person who under the will of the deceased or under the law relating to intestacy is beneficially interested in the estate or would be so interested if an order had not been made under this Act, and

(b) a person who has received any sum of money or other property which by virtue of section 8(1) or (2) of this Act is treated as part of the net estate of the deceased or would have received that sum or other property if an order had not been made under this Act;

'child' includes an illegitimate child and a child en ventre sa mere at the death of the deceased;

'the court' means, unless the context otherwise requires, the High Court, or where the county court has jurisdiction by virtue of section 25 of the County Courts Act 1984, the county court;

'former civil partner' means a person whose civil partnership with the deceased was during the lifetime of the deceased either –

(a) dissolved or annulled by an order made under the law of any part of the British Islands, or

(b) dissolved or annulled in any country or territory outside the British Islands by a dissolution or annulment which is entitled to be recognised as valid by the law of England and Wales;

'former spouse' means a person whose marriage with the deceased was during the lifetime of the deceased either –

(a) dissolved or annulled by a decree of divorce or a decree of nullity of marriage granted under the law of any part of the British Islands, or

(b) dissolved or annulled in any country or territory outside the British Islands by a divorce or annulment which is entitled to be recognised as valid by the law of England and Wales;

'net estate', in relation to a deceased person, means –

(a) all property of which the deceased had power to dispose by his will (otherwise than by virtue of a special power of appointment) less the amount of his funeral, testamentary and administration expenses, debts and liabilities, including any capital transfer tax payable out of his estate on his death;

(b) any property in respect of which the deceased held a general power of appointment (not being a power exercisable by will) which has not been exercised;

(c) any sum of money or other property which is treated for the purposes of this Act as part of the net estate of the deceased by virtue of section 8(1) or (2) of this Act;

(d) any property which is treated for the purposes of this Act as part of the net estate of the deceased by virtue of an order made under section 9 of the Act;

(e) any sum of money or other property which is, by reason of a disposition or contract made by the deceased, ordered under section 10 or 11 of this Act to be provided for the purpose of the making of financial provision under this Act;

'property' includes any chose in action;

'reasonable financial provision' has the meaning assigned to it by section 1 of this Act;

'valuable consideration' does not include marriage or a promise of marriage;

'will' includes codicil.

(2) For the purposes of paragraph (a) of the definition of 'net estate' in subsection (1) above a person who is not of full age and capacity shall be treated as having power to dispose by will of all property of which he would have had power to dispose by will if he had been of full age and capacity.

(3) Any references in this Act to provision out of the net estate of a deceased person includes a reference to provision extending to the whole of that estate.

(4) For the purposes of this Act any reference to a spouse, wife or husband shall be treated as including a reference to a person who in good faith entered into a void marriage with the deceased unless either –

(a) the marriage of the deceased and that person was dissolved or annulled during the lifetime of the deceased and the dissolution or annulment is recognised by the law of England and Wales, or

(b) that person has during the lifetime of the deceased formed a subsequent marriage or civil partnership.

(4A) For the purposes of this Act any reference to a civil partner shall be treated as including a reference to a person who in good faith formed a void civil partnership with the deceased unless either –

(a) the civil partnership between the deceased and that person was dissolved or annulled during the lifetime of the deceased and the dissolution or annulment is recognised by the law of England and Wales, or

(b) that person has during the lifetime of the deceased formed a subsequent civil partnership or marriage.

(5) Any reference in this Act to the formation of, or to a person who has formed, a subsequent marriage or civil partnership includes (as the case may be) a reference to the formation of, or to a person who has formed, a marriage or civil partnership which is by law void or voidable.

(5A) The formation of a marriage or civil partnership shall be treated for the purposes of this Act as the formation of a subsequent marriage or civil partnership, in relation to either of the spouses or civil partners, notwithstanding that the previous marriage or civil partnership of that spouse or civil partner was void or voidable.

(6) Any reference in this Act to an order or decree made under the Matrimonial Causes Act 1973 or under any section of that Act shall be construed as including a reference to an order or decree which is deemed to have been made under that Act or under that section thereof, as the case may be.

(6A) Any reference in this Act to an order made under, or under any provision of, the Civil Partnership Act 2004 shall be construed as including a reference to anything which is deemed to be an order made (as the case may be) under that Act or provision.

(7) Any reference in this Act to any enactment is a reference to that enactment as amended by or under any subsequent enactment.

Amendments—CPA 2004, s 71, Sch 4, para 27; CCA 2013, s 17, Sch 9.

Deductions out of the estate—Note the provisions of s 2(3A) in assessing the extent to which the net estate is reduced.

****

Judicial Proceedings (Regulation of Reports) Act 1926

1 Restriction on publication of reports of judicial proceedings

(1) It shall not be lawful to print or publish, or cause or procure to be printed or published –

(a) in relation to any judicial proceedings any indecent matter or indecent medical, surgical or physiological details being matter or details the publication of which would be calculated to injure public morals;

(b) in relation to any judicial proceedings for dissolution of marriage, for nullity of marriage, or for judicial separation, or for the dissolution or annulment of a civil partnership or for the separation of civil partners, any particulars other than the following, that is to say:

(i) the names, addresses and occupations of the parties and witnesses;

(ii) a concise statement of the charges, defences and countercharges in support of which evidence has been given;

(iii) submissions on any point of law arising in the course of the proceedings, and the decision of the court thereon;

(iv) the summing-up of the judge and the finding of the jury (if any) and the judgment of the court and observations made by the judge in giving judgment.

Provided that nothing in this part of this subsection shall be held to permit the publication of anything contrary to the provisions of paragraph (a) of this subsection.

(2) If any person acts in contravention of the provisions of this Act, he shall in respect of each offence be liable, on summary conviction, to imprisonment for a term not exceeding four months, or to a fine not exceeding level 5 on the standard scale, or to both such imprisonment and fine:

Provided that no person, other than a proprietor, editor, master printer or publisher, shall be liable to be convicted under this Act.

(3) No prosecution for an offence under this Act shall be commenced in England and Wales by any person without the sanction of the Attorney-General.

(4) Nothing in this section shall apply to the printing of any pleading, transcript of evidence or other document for use in connection with any judicial proceedings or the communication thereof to persons concerned in the proceedings, or to the printing or publishing of any notice or report in pursuance of the directions of the court; or to the printing or publishing of any matter in any separate volume or part of any bone fide series of law reports which does not form part of any other publication and consists solely of reports of proceedings in courts of law, or in any publication of a technical character bona fide intended for circulation among members of the legal or medical professions.

(5) *(repealed)*

Amendments—Criminal Justice Act 1982, s 46(1); CPA 2004, s 261(1),(4), Sch 27, para 8(1)–(3), Sch 30. See also under **Extension of s 1(1)(b)** below.

General note—The fact that a hearing takes place in chambers does not determine whether it should be regarded as subject to a ban on publication. Hearings relating to children and ancillary relief are covered by privacy and secrecy; information about such cases cannot be disclosed without leave of the court, but see *Lykiardopulo v Lykiardopulo and Lykiardopulo* [2011] 1 FLR 1427, CA where on appeal publication of the judgment without anonymisation but with redaction of sensitive commercial material was allowed. This may in part have been due to the false evidence and documents relied on which led the court to hold that where there has been fraud on the court the litigant who perpetrates that fraud loses the entitlement of confidentiality. Other family proceedings are not so protected. Whether or not they are protected depends on the applicability of AJA 1960, s 12 and Arts 8 and 10 of the European Convention or the existence of other circumstances which make disclosure prejudicial to the administration of justice, including consideration of the requirement of CCA 1981, s 11 (*Clibbery v Allan and Another* [2002] 1 FLR 565, CA). Section 12 does not prevent publication of the names of the parties or the children, nor does it prohibit discussion within certain bounds of the nature of the dispute, but it does prevent (unless directed by the court) the publication of what occurred before the court and of the documents filed in the proceedings and the evidence given (*Re B; X Council v B and Ors (No 2)* [2008] 1 FLR 1460, FD). However, see the impact of *Practice Guidance of 16 January 2014: Transparency in the Family Courts: Publication of Judgments*, which took effect on 3 February 2014 (set out in Part V). Practitioners' attention is drawn to the provisions of FPR 2010, r 27.11, which provide that save for certain exceptions accredited representatives of the media are by right entitled to access to family proceedings in all courts but reporting restriction under AJA 1960 and CA 1989, s 97(2) will continue to apply (see under FPR 2010, Pt 3). See also under FPR PD10A and FPR PD27B, the *Guidance of 22 April 2009* and *Practice Direction: Committal for Contempt of Court – Open Court* (26 March 2015), which reaffirms the general rule that all hearings including hearings for committal for contempt should be heard in public, save in exceptional circumstances (in which case the court must give a reasoned public judgment setting out the reasons for so doing) and makes provisions for how such applications should be listed in the public court list (see Part V). In *DE v AB (No 2) Permission Hearing: Publicity Protection)* [2015] 1 FLR 1119, CA, Ryder J used the appellate courts' powers to prevent publication of the prohibited information being disclosed while continuing to sit in public (see the analysis of authorities in the judgment). See also *Re Child X (Residence and Contact: Rights of Media Attendance)* [2009] 2 FLR 1467, FD. In relation to the prohibition contained in AJA 1960, s 12 on the publication of information relating to proceedings held in private in children cases and the expectation of anonymity by experts and witnesses, see *A v Ward* [2010] 1 FLR 1497, FD. See also *Coventry City Council v X, Y and Z (Identification of Local Authority)* [2011] 1 FLR 977, FD, where the court permitted identification of the local authority; *Re S (Reporting Restriction Order)* [2015] EWHC 4159 (Fam), where a reporting restriction order made in wardship proceedings to prevent publication of names of five family members in relation to terrorist offences was continued; *London Borough of Sutton v MH, RH and NH (No 2)* [2016] EWHC 1371 (Fam), where a reporting restriction order was made so as to report on the facts but protect the child's identity and his relationship to the 'public person'. Hearings of proceedings under TLATA 1996 are covered by CPR 1998 and hearings are held in public. Any application to restrain publicity will have to be supported by convincing evidence of any violation of Art 8 rights. Where the Art 8 rights engaged include those of children, the court will have regard to their interests in carrying out the balancing exercise between those rights and the rights of the media (*Surrey County Council v ME and Others* [2014] 2 FLR 1267, FD, applying the UKSC's approach in *Re S (Identification: Restrictions on Publication)* [2005] 1 FLR 591, HL; *W v M (TOLATA Proceedings: Anonymity)* [2013] 1 FLR 1513, FD). As regards balancing the competing rights under Arts 8 and 10, see *A Council v M and Others (No 3) (Reporting Restriction Order; Adoption; Artificial Insemination)* [2013] 2 FLR 1270, FD; *Z & Others v News Group Newspapers Ltd & Others* [2013] EWHC 1150 (Fam) and 1371 (Fam)(Fam), *Re X and Y (Executive Summary of Serious Case Review: Reporting Restrictions)* [2013] 2 FLR 628, CA, *Bristol City Council v NGN Ltd and Others* [2013] 1 FLR 1205, FD and *Cumbria CC v M & Ors* [2014] EWHC 2596 (Fam), FD. In relation to financial remedy proceedings, see *A v A (Reporting Restriction)* [2013] 2 FLR 947, FD and *Cooper-Hohn v Hohn* [2015] 1 FLR 19, FD. In *MXB v East Sussex Hospitals Trust* [2013] 1 FLR 1152, QBD, the court relied on CPR 1998, r 39.2(4) to make a wider order than that covered by the Children and Young Persons Act 1933, as amended to include digital media.

'in relation to any judicial proceedings for dissolution of marriage' (s 1(1)(b))—Proceedings are not concluded finally until any question arising as to the validity of any decree or order which might have been made is finally resolved; thus, proceedings concerning an application to render a decree of divorce null and void are covered by the 1926 Act and the evidence given at the hearing cannot be reported

(*Moynihan v Moynihan (Nos 1 and 2)* [1997] 1 FLR 59, FD), but 'there would appear to be ample scope in the context of the subparagraphs of subpara (b) for clear and full details to be given, though not necessarily a line-by-line account of what a particular witness says at any particular time' (at [62G]).

Extension of s 1(1)(b)—Although this section has not been amended textually, it has been extended, by virtue of amendments made to Domestic and Appellate Proceedings (Restriction of Publicity) Act 1968, s 2(3) by FLA 1986 and FLRA 1987, to cover proceedings under MCA 1973, s 27 (failure to maintain), proceedings under FLA 1986, Pt III (as from 4 April 1988), and applications for a declaration under FLA 1986, s 56(1) (as from 4 April 1988). The particulars specified in s 1(1)(b) are modified in their application to allow publication of the particulars of the declaration sought instead of a concise statement of charges, defences and countercharges. See further under DAP(RP)A 1968, s 2 above.

Procedure—See *Emergency Remedies in the Family Courts* (Family Law).

PART II

Law Reform (Miscellaneous Provisions) Act 1970

1 Engagements to marry not enforceable at law

(1) An agreement between two persons to marry one another shall not under the law of England and Wales have effect as a contract giving rise to legal rights and no action shall lie in England and Wales for breach of such an agreement, whatever the law applicable to the agreement.

(2) This section shall have effect in relation to agreements entered into before it comes into force, except that it shall not affect any action commenced before it comes into force.

2 Property of engaged couples

(1) Where an agreement to marry is terminated, any rule of law relating to the rights of husbands and wives in relation to property in which either or both has or have a beneficial interest, including any such rule as explained by section 37 of the Matrimonial Proceedings and Property Act 1970, shall apply, in relation to any property in which either or both of the parties to the agreement had a beneficial interest while the agreement was in force, as it applies in relation to property in which a husband or wife has a beneficial interest.

(2) Where an agreement to marry is terminated, section 17 of the Married Women's Property Act 1882 and section 7 of the Matrimonial Causes (Property and Maintenance) Act 1958 (which sections confer power on a judge of the High Court or the family court to settle disputes between husband and wife about property) shall apply, as if the parties were married, to any dispute between, or claim by, one of them in relation to property in which either or both had a beneficial interest while the agreement was in force; but an application made by virtue of this section to the judge under the said section 17, as originally enacted or as extended by the said section 7, shall be made within three years of the termination of the agreement.

Amendments—CCA 2013, s 17, Sch 11.

3 Gifts between engaged couples

(1) A party to an agreement to marry who makes a gift of property to the other party to the agreement on the condition (express or implied) that it shall be returned if the agreement is terminated shall not be prevented from recovering the property by reason only of his having terminated the agreement.

(2) The gift of an engagement ring shall be presumed to be an absolute gift; this presumption may be rebutted by proving that the ring was given on the condition, express or implied, that it should be returned if the marriage did not take place for any reason.

****

Legal Aid, Sentencing and Punishment of Offenders Act 2012

Public funding, funding and costs—Legal aid, like legal services orders (MCA 1973, s 22ZA: private law inter partes funding), concerns funding of court proceedings, as distinct from costs orders, which are regulated by SCA 1981, s 51 and CPR 1998, r 44.2 (mostly). It is not possible to raise public finance to fund proceedings, including for a parent in wardship proceedings (*Re K and H (Private Law: Public Funding)* [2015]

EWCA Civ 543, [2016] 1 FLR 754, sub nom *Re K and H (Children)* and *HB v A Local Authority & Anor (Wardship – Costs Funding Order)* [2017] EWHC 524 (Fam)).

****

25 Charges on property in connection with civil legal services

(1) Where civil legal services are made available to an individual under this Part, the amounts described in subsection (2) are to constitute a first charge on –

(a) any property recovered or preserved by the individual in proceedings, or in any compromise or settlement of a dispute, in connection with which the services were provided (whether the property is recovered or preserved for the individual or another person), and

(b) any costs payable to the individual by another person in connection with such proceedings or such a dispute.

(2) Those amounts are –

(a) amounts expended by the Lord Chancellor in securing the provision of the services (except to the extent that they are recovered by other means), and

(b) other amounts payable by the individual in connection with the services under section 23 or 24.

(3) Regulations may make provision for exceptions from subsection (1).

(4) Regulations may make provision about the charge under subsection (1) including, in particular –

(a) provision as to whether the charge is in favour of the Lord Chancellor or a person by whom the services were made available,

(b) provision modifying the charge for the purposes of its application in prescribed cases or circumstances, and

(c) provision about the enforcement of the charge.

(5) Regulations under subsection (4)(c) may, in particular, include –

(a) provision requiring amounts recovered by the individual in proceedings or as part of a compromise or settlement of a dispute, and costs payable to the individual, to be paid to the Lord Chancellor or a person by whom the services were made available,

(b) provision about the time and manner in which the amounts must be paid,

(c) provision about what the Lord Chancellor or the person by whom the services were made available must do with the amounts,

(d) provision for the payment of interest on all or part of the amounts,

(e) provision for the payment to the individual concerned of any amount in excess of the amounts described in subsection (2), and

(f) provision for the enforcement of requirements described in paragraph (a).

(6) Regulations under this section may include provision requiring information and documents to be provided.

Note on public funding, funding and costs—Legal aid, like legal services orders (MCA 1973, s 22ZA: private law inter partes funding), concerns funding of court proceedings, as distinct from costs orders (which are regulated by SCA 1981, s 51 and CPR 1998, r 44.2 (mostly)). It is not possible to raise public finance to fund proceedings, including for a parent in wardship proceedings (*Re K and H (Private Law: Public Funding)* [2015] EWCA Civ 543, [2016] 1 FLR 754, sub nom *Re K and H (Children)* and *HB v A Local Authority & Anor (Wardship – Costs Funding Order)* [2017] EWHC 524 (Fam)).

(1) OPERATION OF THE LEGAL AID STATUTORY CHARGE

'a first charge on any property recovered or preserved … in the proceedings' (s 25(1)(a))—The legal aid (or civil legal services (CLS) statutory charge is derived from the solicitor's lien on property recovered or preserved in proceedings as a result of the solicitor's instrumentality (eg see *Hanlon v Law Society* [1981] AC 124, HL, at [191A]; and see Solicitors Act 1974, s 73). This gives rise to four questions to be answered to define whether the charge applies to any property in issue in the proceedings:

(1) *What are the proceedings?* The starting point for definition of the 'extent of the charge' will be by reference to the CLS certificate; and to the proceedings referred to in that certificate (per Lord Scarman in *Hanlon v Law Society*, at [186G–H]: the proceedings in *Hanlon* were under Legal Aid Act 1974, s 9(6), but in all material respects s 25(1) and s 9(6) are the same). The scope of a CLS certificate is akin to the

solicitors' retainer for work to be done for a client. If there are separate proceedings, or a second certificate is issued (eg for 'civil proceedings' under HRA 1998, s 8(2)), then different principles for definition of 'proceedings' under s 25(1)(a) apply (see **SEPARATE PROCEEDINGS** below)).

(2) *What is the property?* Subject to the definition of 'property' below, property is any property that was in issue between the parties in the proceedings (or included as a 'compromise or settlement' (s 25(1)(a)) of any proceedings: *Van Hoorn v Law Society* [1984] FLR 203, QBD).

(3) *Was the property in issue in the proceedings (or part of a 'compromise or settlement' of the case)?* Whether or not the charge applies to particular property turns on whether or not it was in issue in the proceedings for which the certificate was granted (*Watkinson v Legal Aid Board* [1991] 2 FLR 26, CA). 'What has been in issue is to be collected as a matter of fact from pleadings, evidence, judgment and/or order' – even the correspondence between the parties (per Lord Simon in *Hanlon v Law Society*, at [180H]). It is the lis between two or more parties that defines the proceedings. In the case of HRA 1998, s 8(1) damages cases, the lis is between the claimant (parents and/or child) and the local authority, and the costs (subject to the 'separate proceedings' point below) are the costs only in the 'civil proceedings' under s 8(2) (eg see *R (Faulkner) v Director of Legal Aid Casework* [2016] EWHC 717 (Admin) and *P v A Local Authority* [2016] EWHC 2779 (Fam) (below)).

(4) *Was the 'property recovered or preserved'?* Property or money or 'possessions' can only be 'recovered or preserved' if they were in issue in, or part of a compromise etc of, proceedings (*Foxon v Gascoigne* (1874) LR 9 Ch App 654): 'A person recovers or preserves in legal proceedings only what is in issue between the parties' (Lord Scarman in *Hanlon*, at [187G]). Property is recovered if a person takes proceedings to convert it to his own use – eg a property adjustment order or a lump sum order (*Curling v Law Society* [1985] FLR 831, CA); property is preserved if a person successfully resists a claim to his property – eg an order for sale or a property adjustment order (*Parkes v Legal Aid Board* [1997] 1 FLR 77, CA).

'property'—'Property' means assets or possessions (akin to the definition of property or possessions in European Convention 1950, First Protocol, Art 1). It can include money, such as a MCA 1973, s 23 lump sum or HRA 1998 damages (subject to definition of the term 'proceedings'). It does not mean the same as in MCA 1973, s 24 (property adjustment order).

Amounts to be charged; 'services under section 23 or 24' (s 25(2))—The statutory charge applies in respect of costs paid for civil legal services to lawyers under a CLS certificate (LASPOA 2012, s 23) or any costs of enforcement of claims by the LAA against legally aided individuals (s 24), net of any costs actually received from costs payable to the individual (s 25(1)(b)).

(2) SEPARATE PROCEEDINGS

Separate proceedings—Only proceedings covered by a legal aid certificate are subject to the charge (*Hanlon v Law Society* (above)). While lawyers may not 'pull the wool over [the court's] eyes' (Lord Denning MR in *Manley v Law Society* (below), at [346C]) in application of legal aid principles, so too the court must follow statutory and common law principle in determining to what proceedings the s 25(1) charge can apply (eg see Civil Legal Aid (Procedure) Regulations 2012, reg 37(3); *Watkinson v Legal Aid Board* (below)).

Meaning of 'family proceedings' in regulations—'Family proceedings' is exhaustively defined in Civil Legal Aid (Statutory Charge) Regulations 2013, reg 2(1). This definition does not include any reference to damages or 'civil proceedings' under HRA 1998, s 8(1) and (2).

Children proceedings and HRA 1998 damages—The issue of the statutory charge and children proceedings arises especially if proceedings are taken by parents or children against a local authority that has involved them in care (CA 1989, s 31(2)) proceedings. Care proceedings are legally aided without regard to merit or means of the parties, but costs can be substantial. Can the CLS statutory charge apply in such cases? Yes, says Cobb J sitting in the Family Court in *CZ (Human Rights Claim: Costs)* [2017] EWFC 11, but no said the Lord Chancellor in *H (A Minor) v Northamptonshire County Council & Anor* [2017] EWHC 282 (Fam) because the HRA 1998 proceedings were 'separate' from the children proceedings (see under HRA 1998, s 8(2)).

Does a CLS certificate relate to separate proceedings—At the time of going to press, the following principles apply in relation to HRA 1998, s 8(1),(2) claims (pace eg *CZ (Human Rights Claim: Costs)*) and whether or not a separate proceedings certificate has been issued. Costs to be covered by the statutory charge relate only to those separate (ie not to any parallel or related) proceedings (eg costs of care proceedings could not, as a rule, be charged against HRA 1998 damages):

(1) HRA 1998 damages can only be claimed in 'civil proceedings' in a court that 'has power to award damages' (HRA 1998, s 8(2); *Anufrijeva v Southwark LBC* [2004] 1 FLR 8, CA (claims should generally be issued in the Administrative Court, at [81](ii))).

(2) The family courts have no power to award damages (Courts Act 2003, s 75, leading to SCA 1981, Sch 1, para 3 do not include HRA 1998 proceedings, HRA 1998, s 8(2)). Proceedings are under CPR 1998 (see commentary under CPR 1998, Pt 8).

(3) LASPOA 2012, s 8(1)(b) deals with the grant of civil legal services for advice, assistance and representation, and s 12(1)(b) with 'the matters in relation to which the services are to be available'. LASPOA, s 12(2) provides for the making of Civil Legal Aid (Procedure) Regulations 2012, which govern the conduct of civil legal services, and which includes reg 37(3) (in relation to CLS certificates) (emphasis added):

'(3) […] the Director must issue a *separate certificate* for each –

(a) form of civil legal services for which the individual qualifies; and

(b) set of proceedings to which a determination relates, unless the Director decides that the proceedings are so closely connected that they should be covered by a single certificate.'

Even if the Legal Aid Agency says HRA damages proceedings are 'closely connected' (per reg 38(3)(b)), they remain 'separate' within the terms of *Hanlon v Law Society* and should not be dealt with under an amended certificate if there is any doubt (*Watkinson v Legal Aid Board* [1991] 2 FLR 26, CA). The charge cannot apply to damages recovered in related wardship (legally aided) and separate HRA 1998 damages proceedings (unfunded: legal aid refused) where a legal aid certificate was refused to the claimant (*P v A Local Authority* [2016] EWHC 2779 (Fam)).

Civil proceedings (HRA 1998, s 8(2))—Different principles apply to civil proceedings, for example, in relation to striking out claims. Nor is there any reason why separate civil claims should not proceed in parallel with family proceedings (e g bankruptcy and ancillary relief claims (*Arif v Zar* [2012] EWCA Civ 986) or claims under TLATA 1996, s 14 and under Children Act 1989, Sch 1 in respect of the same family breakdown). Parties to the HRA 1998 damages case would be bound by findings in the children proceedings (issue estoppel: *Re S (Care Proceedings: Human Rights)* [2012] 2 FLR 209, CA, at [4]–[5]), so there would be no danger of extra costs from re-litigation.

(3) REGULATIONS

Regulations under s 25(3)–(6)—Civil Legal Aid (Statutory Charge) Regulations 2013 are made under s 25(3)–(6). These include (at reg 5) 'exceptions' from the charge in accordance with s 25(3): for example periodical payments and pension adjustment orders. The charge may be waived (reg 9) in cases of 'significant wider public interest', where others might benefit from the outcome of publically funded litigation.

Money or property subject to the charge—Any payment that is subject to the charge must be made to the legally aid party's lawyer (Civil Legal Aid (Statutory Charge) Regulations 2013, reg 13(1)). That lawyer must give notice of payment being due to the paying party (reg 14) and only that lawyer can give the payer a 'good discharge' (reg 13(1)). If property is the subject of the charge, the Lord Chancellor may postpone enforcement (reg 22) and if so the Lord Chancellor must secure the charge by registration (reg 22(2)).

(4) AVOIDANCE OR EVASION

Evasion of the charge: 'whether for himself or any other person' (s 25(1)(a))—The charge arises even though property or money is transferred to a third party, such as a child or the funded party's debtors, in an attempt to evade operation of the charge (*Manley v Law Society* [1981] 1 WLR 335, CA). The charge will apply if payment is made direct to the funded client personally.

Avoidance of the charge—Legal aid rules correctly applied (e g appropriate application for a separate certificate, or avoiding an amendment where the charge already operates: *Watkinson v Legal Aid Board* (above)) may avoid operation of the charge, but that is a permissible use of the legal aid scheme and in the interests of the client.

26 Costs in civil proceedings

(1) Costs ordered against an individual in relevant civil proceedings must not exceed the amount (if any) which it is reasonable for the individual to pay having regard to all the circumstances, including –

- (a) the financial resources of all of the parties to the proceedings, and
- (b) their conduct in connection with the dispute to which the proceedings relate.

(2) In subsection (1) 'relevant civil proceedings', in relation to an individual, means –

- (a) proceedings for the purposes of which civil legal services are made available to the individual under this Part, or
- (b) if such services are made available to the individual under this Part for the purposes of only part of proceedings, that part of the proceedings.

(3) Regulations may make provision for exceptions from subsection (1).

(4) In assessing for the purposes of subsection (1) the financial resources of an individual to whom civil legal services are made available, the following must not be taken into account, except so far as prescribed –

- (a) the individual's clothes and household furniture, and
- (b) the implements of the individual's trade.

(5) Subject to subsections (1) to (4), regulations may make provision about costs in relation to proceedings for the purposes of which civil legal services are made available under this Part.

(6) Regulations under subsection (5) may, in particular, make provision –

- (a) specifying the principles to be applied in determining the amount of any costs which may be awarded against a party to whom civil legal services are made available under this Part,
- (b) limiting the circumstances in which, or the extent to which, an order for costs may be enforced against such a party,

(c) as to the cases in which, and the extent to which, such a party may be required to give security for costs and the manner in which it is to be given,
(d) requiring the payment by the Lord Chancellor of the whole or part of any costs incurred by a party to whom civil legal services are not made available under this Part,
(e) specifying the principles to be applied in determining the amount of costs which may be awarded to a party to whom civil legal services are made available under this Part,
(f) as to the court, tribunal or other person by whom the amount of any costs is to be determined, and
(g) as to the extent to which any determination of that amount is to be final.

(7) Regulations may provide that an individual is to be treated, for the purposes of subsection (1) or regulations under subsection (3) or (5), as having or not having financial resources of a prescribed description (but such regulations have effect subject to subsection (4)).

(8) Regulations under subsection (7) may, in particular, provide that the individual is to be treated as having prescribed financial resources of a person of a prescribed description.

(9) Regulations under this section may include provision requiring information and documents to be provided.

****

Legal Services Act 2007

ARRANGEMENT OF SECTIONS

PART 3
RESERVED LEGAL ACTIVITIES

Section		Page
	Reserved legal activities	
12	Meaning of 'reserved legal activity' and 'legal activity'	1046
	Carrying on the activities	
13	Entitlement to carry on a reserved legal activity	1047
	Offences	
14	Offence to carry on a reserved legal activity if not entitled	1047
15	Carrying on of a reserved legal activity: employers and employees etc	1047
16	Offence to carry on reserved legal activity through person not entitled	1048
17	Offence to pretend to be entitled	1049
	Interpretation	
18	Authorised persons	1049
19	Exempt persons	1050
20	Approved regulators and relevant approved regulators	1050
21	Regulatory arrangements	1050
	Continuity of existing rights and transitional protection	
22	Continuity of existing rights to carry on reserved legal activities	1051
	Alteration of reserved legal activities	
24	Extension of the reserved legal activities	1051
25	Provisional designation as approved regulators and licensing authorities	1051
26	Recommendations that activities should cease to be reserved legal activities	1052
	Schedule 2 – The Reserved Legal Activities	1052
	Schedule 3 – Exempt Persons	1053

Rights of audience—The 2007 Act provides the regulatory framework for the provision of legal services, including the exercise of a right of audience. As of 1 January 2010, it replaced similar provisions in the Courts and Legal Services Act 1990. Whether or not a person has a right of audience must be determined solely in accordance with the provisions of the Act. A person must either be 'authorised' or 'exempt'. A person will be 'authorised' if granted a right of audience by an 'authorised body' (i e authorised by the Legal Services Board). Thus, for example, the General Council of the Bar and the Law Society will authorise barristers and solicitors. A person who is not authorised may be 'exempt' under Sch 3, para 1.

Schedule 3, para 1(2) enables the court, as a matter of discretion, to grant a right of audience to a particular person in relation to a specific case (not generally) and it is in this area that most of the case-law arises. Unqualified persons wishing to appear for a party have caused particular problems in family cases. In *Clarkson v Gilbert* [2000] 2 FLR 839, CA, Lord Woolf explained that a party to litigation has two options: first, he may instruct a lawyer with the appropriate rights; second, he can act in person. If he exercises the second option but then does not wish to exercise his right he cannot delegate it (not even to a person with a power of attorney (*Gregory v Turner; R (Morris) v North Somerset Council* [2003] 1 WLR 1149, CA)) and must invite the court (at the first inter partes hearing) to exercise its inherent jurisdiction preserved by para 1(2). However, this provision cannot be habitually relied on by unqualified persons who have set themselves up to provide advocacy services (whether for reward or not) and wishing to represent a litigant in person – that would be 'monstrously inappropriate' (per Lord Woolf in *D v S* [1997] 1 FLR 724, CA, at [19]) The court is inclined to look more favourably on a request that is clearly specific to the instant case, such as by a relative or family friend. But in all cases the court must have regard to the statutory framework, for it is essential not only to justice but to the administration of justice that the court has confidence in advocates. A 'right of audience' means the right to appear before and address a court, including the right to call and to cross-examine witnesses (s 2 and Sch 2, para 3(1)).

A 'McKenzie Friend' does not have a right of audience, but see further *Practice Guidance of 12 July 2010* (in Part V).

'Reserved family proceedings' are mentioned in Sch 3, para 1(10) and would be a category of proceedings to which the exemption referred to in para 1(7) would not apply. However, the Lord Chancellor has not exercised the power to prescribe any category of family proceedings as such.

****

PART 3
RESERVED LEGAL ACTIVITIES

Reserved legal activities

12 Meaning of 'reserved legal activity' and 'legal activity'

(1) In this Act 'reserved legal activity' means –

- (a) the exercise of a right of audience;
- (b) the conduct of litigation;
- (c) reserved instrument activities;
- (d) probate activities;
- (e) notarial activities;
- (f) the administration of oaths.

(2) Schedule 2 makes provision about what constitutes each of those activities.

(3) In this Act 'legal activity' means –

- (a) an activity which is a reserved legal activity within the meaning of this Act as originally enacted, and
- (b) any other activity which consists of one or both of the following –
  - (i) the provision of legal advice or assistance in connection with the application of the law or with any form of resolution of legal disputes;
  - (ii) the provision of representation in connection with any matter concerning the application of the law or any form of resolution of legal disputes.

(4) But 'legal activity' does not include any activity of a judicial or quasi-judicial nature (including acting as a mediator).

(5) For the purposes of subsection (3) 'legal dispute' includes a dispute as to any matter of fact the resolution of which is relevant to determining the nature of any person's legal rights or liabilities.

(6) Section 24 makes provision for adding legal activities to the reserved legal activities.

Carrying on the activities

13 Entitlement to carry on a reserved legal activity

(1) The question whether a person is entitled to carry on an activity which is a reserved legal activity is to be determined solely in accordance with the provisions of this Act.

(2) A person is entitled to carry on an activity ('the relevant activity') which is a reserved legal activity where –

(a) the person is an authorised person in relation to the relevant activity, or
(b) the person is an exempt person in relation to that activity.

(3) Subsection (2) is subject to section 23 (transitional protection for non-commercial bodies).

(4) Nothing in this section or section 23 affects section 84 of the Immigration and Asylum Act 1999 (which prohibits the provision of immigration advice and immigration services except by certain persons).

Offences

14 Offence to carry on a reserved legal activity if not entitled

(1) It is an offence for a person to carry on an activity ('the relevant activity') which is a reserved legal activity unless that person is entitled to carry on the relevant activity.

(2) In proceedings for an offence under subsection (1), it is a defence for the accused to show that the accused did not know, and could not reasonably have been expected to know, that the offence was being committed.

(3) A person who is guilty of an offence under subsection (1) is liable –

(a) on summary conviction, to imprisonment for a term not exceeding 12 months or a fine not exceeding the statutory maximum (or both), and
(b) on conviction on indictment, to imprisonment for a term not exceeding 2 years or a fine (or both).

(4) A person who is guilty of an offence under subsection (1) by reason of an act done in the purported exercise of a right of audience, or a right to conduct litigation, in relation to any proceedings or contemplated proceedings is also guilty of contempt of the court concerned and may be punished accordingly.

(5) In relation to an offence under subsection (1) committed before the commencement of section 154(1) of the Criminal Justice Act 2003, the reference in subsection (3)(a) to 12 months is to be read as a reference to 6 months.

15 Carrying on of a reserved legal activity: employers and employees etc

(1) This section applies for the interpretation of references in this Act to a person carrying on an activity which is a reserved legal activity.

(2) References to a person carrying on an activity which is a reserved legal activity include a person ('E') who –

(a) is an employee of a person ('P'), and
(b) carries on the activity in E's capacity as such an employee.

(3) For the purposes of subsection (2), it is irrelevant whether P is entitled to carry on the activity.

(4) P does not carry on an activity ('the relevant activity') which is a reserved legal activity by virtue of E carrying it on in E's capacity as an employee of P, unless the provision of relevant services to the public or a section of the public (with or without a view to profit) is part of P's business.

(5) Relevant services are services which consist of or include the carrying on of the relevant activity by employees of P in their capacity as employees of P.

(6) Where P is an independent trade union, persons provided with relevant services do not constitute the public or a section of the public where –

(a) the persons are provided with the relevant services by virtue of their membership or former membership of P or of another person's membership or former membership of P, and

(b) the services are excepted membership services.

(7) Subject to subsection (8), 'excepted membership services' means relevant services which relate to or have a connection with –

(a) relevant activities of a member, or former member, of the independent trade union;

(b) any other activities carried on for the purposes of or in connection with, or arising from, such relevant activities;

(c) any event which has occurred (or is alleged to have occurred) in the course of or in connection with such relevant activities or activities within paragraph (b);

(d) activities carried on by a person for the purposes of or in connection with, or arising from, the person's membership of the independent trade union;

and such other relevant services as the Lord Chancellor may by order specify.

(8) The Lord Chancellor may by order make provision about the circumstances in which relevant services do or do not relate to, or have a connection with, the matters mentioned in paragraphs (a) to (d) of subsection (7).

(9) Subject to that, the Lord Chancellor may by order make provision about –

(a) what does or does not constitute a section of the public;

(b) the circumstances in which the provision of relevant services to the public or a section of the public does or does not form part of P's business.

(10) The Lord Chancellor may make an order under subsection (7), (8) or (9) only on the recommendation of the Board.

(11) If P is a body, references to an employee of P include references to a manager of P.

(12) In subsection (7), 'relevant activities', in relation to a person who is or was a member of an independent trade union, means any employment (including self-employment), trade, occupation or other activity to which the person's membership of the trade union relates or related.

16 Offence to carry on reserved legal activity through person not entitled

(1) Where subsection (2) applies it is an offence for a person ('P') to carry on an activity ('the relevant activity') which is a reserved legal activity, despite P being entitled to carry on the relevant activity.

(2) This subsection applies if –

(a) P carries on the relevant activity by virtue of an employee of P ('E') carrying it on in E's capacity as such an employee, and

(b) in carrying on the relevant activity, E commits an offence under section 14.

(3) If P is a body, references in subsection (2) to an employee of P include references to a manager of P.

(4) In proceedings for an offence under subsection (1), it is a defence for the accused to show that the accused took all reasonable precautions and exercised all due diligence to avoid committing the offence.

(5) A person who is guilty of an offence under subsection (1) is liable –

(a) on summary conviction, to imprisonment for a term not exceeding 12 months or a fine not exceeding the statutory maximum (or both), and

(b) on conviction on indictment, to imprisonment for a term not exceeding 2 years or a fine (or both).

(6) A person who is guilty of an offence under subsection (1) by reason of an act done in the purported exercise of a right of audience, or a right to conduct litigation, in relation to any proceedings or contemplated proceedings is also guilty of contempt of the court concerned and may be punished accordingly.

(7) In relation to an offence under subsection (1) committed before the commencement of section 154(1) of the Criminal Justice Act 2003, the reference in subsection (5)(a) to 12 months is to be read as a reference to 6 months.

17 Offence to pretend to be entitled

(1) It is an offence for a person –

(a) wilfully to pretend to be entitled to carry on any activity which is a reserved legal activity when that person is not so entitled, or

(b) with the intention of implying falsely that that person is so entitled, to take or use any name, title or description.

(2) A person who is guilty of an offence under subsection (1) is liable –

(a) on summary conviction, to imprisonment for a term not exceeding 12 months or a fine not exceeding the statutory maximum (or both), and

(b) on conviction on indictment, to imprisonment for a term not exceeding 2 years or a fine (or both).

(3) In relation to an offence under subsection (1) committed before the commencement of section 154(1) of the Criminal Justice Act 2003, the reference in subsection (2)(a) to 12 months is to be read as a reference to 6 months.

Interpretation

18 Authorised persons

(1) For the purposes of this Act 'authorised person', in relation to an activity ('the relevant activity') which is a reserved legal activity, means –

(a) a person who is authorised to carry on the relevant activity by a relevant approved regulator in relation to the relevant activity (other than by virtue of a licence under Part 5), or

(b) a licensable body which, by virtue of such a licence, is authorised to carry on the relevant activity by a licensing authority in relation to the reserved legal activity.

(2) A licensable body may not be authorised to carry on the relevant activity as mentioned in subsection (1)(a).

(3) But where a body ('A') which is authorised as mentioned in subsection (1)(a) becomes a licensable body, the body is deemed by virtue of this subsection to continue to be so authorised from that time until the earliest of the following events –

(a) the end of the period of 90 days beginning with the day on which that time falls;

(b) the time from which the relevant approved regulator determines this subsection is to cease to apply to A;

(c) the time when A ceases to be a licensable body.

(4) Subsection (2) is subject to Part 2 of Schedule 5 (by virtue of which licensable bodies may be deemed to be authorised as mentioned in subsection (1)(a) in relation to certain activities during a transitional period).

(5) A person other than a licensable body may not be authorised to carry on the relevant activity as mentioned in subsection (1)(b).

(6) But where a body ('L') which is authorised as mentioned in subsection (1)(b) ceases to be a licensable body, the body is deemed by virtue of this subsection to continue to be so authorised from that time until the earliest of the following events –

(a) the end of the period of 90 days beginning with the day on which that time falls;

(b) the time from which the relevant licensing authority determines this subsection is to cease to apply to L;

(c) the time when L becomes a licensable body.

PART II

19 Exempt persons

In this Act, 'exempt person', in relation to an activity ('the relevant activity') which is a reserved legal activity, means a person who, for the purposes of carrying on the relevant activity, is an exempt person by virtue of –

(a) Schedule 3 (exempt persons), or
(b) paragraph 13 or 18 of Schedule 5 (additional categories of exempt persons during transitional period).

20 Approved regulators and relevant approved regulators

(1) In this Act, the following expressions have the meaning given by this section –

'approved regulator';
'relevant approved regulator'.

(2) 'Approved regulator' means –

(a) a body which is designated as an approved regulator by Part 1 of Schedule 4 or under Part 2 of that Schedule (or both) and whose regulatory arrangements are approved for the purposes of this Act, and
(b) if an order under section 62(1)(a) has effect, the Board.

(3) An approved regulator is a 'relevant approved regulator' in relation to an activity which is a reserved legal activity if –

(a) the approved regulator is designated by Part 1, or under Part 2, of Schedule 4 in relation to that reserved legal activity, or
(b) where the approved regulator is the Board, it is designated in relation to that reserved legal activity by an order under section 62(1)(a).

(4) An approved regulator is a 'relevant approved regulator' in relation to a person if the person is authorised by the approved regulator to carry on an activity which is a reserved legal activity.

(5) Schedule 4 makes provision with respect to approved regulators other than the Board.

In that Schedule –

(a) Part 1 designates certain bodies as approved regulators in relation to certain reserved legal activities,
(b) Part 2 makes provision for bodies to be designated by order as approved regulators in relation to one or more reserved legal activities, and
(c) Part 3 makes provision relating to the approval of changes to an approved regulator's regulatory arrangements.

(6) An approved regulator may authorise persons to carry on any activity which is a reserved legal activity in respect of which it is a relevant approved regulator.

21 Regulatory arrangements

(1) In this Act references to the 'regulatory arrangements' of a body are to –

(a) its arrangements for authorising persons to carry on reserved legal activities,
(b) its arrangements (if any) for authorising persons to provide immigration advice or immigration services,
(c) its practice rules,
(d) its conduct rules,
(e) its disciplinary arrangements in relation to regulated persons (including its discipline rules),
(f) its qualification regulations,
(g) its indemnification arrangements,
(h) its compensation arrangements,
(i) any of its other rules or regulations (however they may be described), and any other

arrangements, which apply to or in relation to regulated persons, other than those made for the purposes of any function the body has to represent or promote the interests of persons regulated by it, and

(j) its licensing rules (if any), so far as not within paragraphs (a) to (i),

(whether or not those arrangements, rules or regulations are contained in, or made under, an enactment).

...

Continuity of existing rights and transitional protection

22 Continuity of existing rights to carry on reserved legal activities

Schedule 5 makes provision for the continuity of existing rights and for certain persons to be deemed, during a transitional period, to be authorised by approved regulators to carry on certain activities.

****

Alteration of reserved legal activities

24 Extension of the reserved legal activities

(1) The Lord Chancellor may, by order, amend section 12 or Schedule 2 (reserved legal activities) so as to add any legal activity to the activities which are reserved legal activities for the purposes of this Act.

(2) An order under subsection (1) may be made only on the recommendation of the Board.

(3) Schedule 6 makes provision about the making of recommendations for the purposes of this section.

(4) Where a recommendation is made in relation to an activity, the Lord Chancellor must –

(a) consider the report containing the recommendation given to the Lord Chancellor under paragraph 16(3)(a) of that Schedule,

(b) decide whether or not to make an order under this section in respect of the activity, and

(c) publish a notice of that decision,

within the period of 90 days beginning with the day on which the report was given to the Lord Chancellor.

(5) Where the Lord Chancellor decides not to make an order under this section in respect of an activity, the notice under subsection (4)(c) must state the reasons for that decision.

25 Provisional designation as approved regulators and licensing authorities

(1) The Lord Chancellor may, by order, make provision –

(a) enabling applications to be made, considered and determined under Part 2 of Schedule 4 or Part 1 of Schedule 10 in relation to a provisional reserved activity, as if the activity were a reserved legal activity;

(b) enabling provisional designation orders to be made by the Lord Chancellor in respect of a provisional reserved activity, as if the activity were a reserved legal activity.

(2) An order under subsection (1) may, in particular, provide that Part 2 of Schedule 4 or Part 1 of Schedule 10 is to apply, in relation to such cases as may be specified by the order, with such modifications as may be so specified.

(3) The Lord Chancellor may also, by order, make provision –

(a) for the purpose of enabling applications for authorisation to carry on an activity which is a provisional reserved activity to be made to and considered and determined by –

(i) a body in respect of which a provisional designation order is made, or

(ii) the Board in its capacity as a licensing authority;

(b) for the purpose of enabling persons to be deemed to be authorised to carry on an

PART II

activity which is a new reserved legal activity by a relevant approved regulator in relation to the activity, or by the Board in its capacity as a licensing authority, for a period specified in the order.

(4) For this purpose –

'provisional reserved activity' means an activity in respect of which a provisional report under paragraph 10 of Schedule 6 states that the Board is minded to make a recommendation for the purposes of section 24;

'provisional designation order' means an order made by the Lord Chancellor under Part 2 of Schedule 4 or Part 1 of Schedule 10 which is conditional upon the Lord Chancellor making an order under section 24 in respect of the provisional reserved activity, pursuant to a recommendation made by the Board following the provisional report;

'new reserved legal activity' means a legal activity which has become a reserved legal activity by virtue of an order under section 24.

26 Recommendations that activities should cease to be reserved legal activities

(1) The Board may recommend that an activity should cease to be a reserved legal activity.

(2) Schedule 6 makes provision about the making of recommendations for the purposes of this section.

(3) The Lord Chancellor must consider any recommendation made by the Board for the purposes of this section (but nothing in section 208 (minor and consequential provision etc) authorises the Lord Chancellor to give effect to such a recommendation).

(4) Where the Lord Chancellor disagrees with a recommendation (or any part of it), the Lord Chancellor must publish a notice to that effect which must include the Lord Chancellor's reasons for disagreeing.

****

SCHEDULE 2
THE RESERVED LEGAL ACTIVITIES

1 Introduction

This Schedule makes provision about the reserved legal activities.

2 In this Schedule 'the appointed day' means the day appointed for the coming into force of section 13 (entitlement to carry on reserved legal activities).

3 Rights of audience

(1) A 'right of audience' means the right to appear before and address a court, including the right to call and examine witnesses.

(2) But a 'right of audience' does not include a right to appear before or address a court, or to call or examine witnesses, in relation to any particular court or in relation to particular proceedings, if immediately before the appointed day no restriction was placed on the persons entitled to exercise that right.

4 Conduct of litigation

(1) The 'conduct of litigation' means –

(a) the issuing of proceedings before any court in England and Wales,

(b) the commencement, prosecution and defence of such proceedings, and

(c) the performance of any ancillary functions in relation to such proceedings (such as entering appearances to actions).

(2) But the 'conduct of litigation' does not include any activity within paragraphs (a) to (c) of sub-paragraph (1), in relation to any particular court or in relation to any particular proceedings, if immediately before the appointed day no restriction was placed on the persons entitled to carry on that activity.

****

SCHEDULE 3
EXEMPT PERSONS

1 Rights of audience

(1) This paragraph applies to determine whether a person is an exempt person for the purpose of exercising a right of audience before a court in relation to any proceedings (subject to paragraph 7).

(2) The person is exempt if the person –

- (a) is not an authorised person in relation to that activity, but
- (b) has a right of audience granted by that court in relation to those proceedings.

(3) The person is exempt if the person –

- (a) is not an authorised person in relation to that activity, but
- (b) has a right of audience before that court in relation to those proceedings granted by or under any enactment.

(4) The person is exempt if the person is the Attorney General or the Solicitor General and –

- (a) the name of the person is on the roll kept by the Law Society under section 6 of the Solicitors Act 1974, or
- (b) the person has been called to the Bar by an Inn of Court.

(5) The person is exempt if the person is the Advocate General for Scotland and is admitted –

- (a) as a solicitor in Scotland under section 6 of the Solicitors (Scotland) Act 1980, or
- (b) to practise as an advocate before the courts of Scotland.

(6) The person is exempt if the person –

- (a) is a party to those proceedings, and
- (b) would have a right of audience, in the person's capacity as such a party, if this Act had not been passed.

(7) The person is exempt if –

- (a) the person is an individual whose work includes assisting in the conduct of litigation,
- (b) the person is assisting in the conduct of litigation –
  - (i) under instructions given (either generally or in relation to the proceedings) by an individual to whom sub-paragraph (8) applies, and
  - (ii) under the supervision of that individual, and
- (c) the proceedings are not reserved family proceedings and are being heard in chambers –
  - (i) in the High Court or county court, or .
  - (ii) in the family court by a judge who is not, or by two or more judges at least one of whom is not, within section 31C(1)(y) of the Matrimonial and Family Proceedings Act 1984 (lay justices).

(8) This sub-paragraph applies to –

- (a) any authorised person in relation to an activity which constitutes the conduct of litigation;
- (b) any person who by virtue of section 193 is not required to be entitled to carry on such an activity.

(9) The person is an exempt person in relation to the exercise of a right of audience in proceedings on an appeal from the Comptroller-General of Patents, Designs and Trade Marks to the Patents Court under the Patents Act 1977, if the person is a solicitor of the Court of Judicature of Northern Ireland.

(10) For the purposes of this paragraph –

'family proceedings' has the same meaning as in the Matrimonial and Family Proceedings Act 1984 and also includes any proceedings in the family court and any other proceedings which are family proceedings for the purposes of the Children Act 1989;

'reserved family proceedings' means such category of family proceedings as the Lord Chancellor may, after consulting the President of the Law Society and with the concurrence of the President of the Family Division, by order prescribe;

and any order made under section 27(9) of the Courts and Legal Services Act 1990 before the day appointed for the coming into force of this paragraph is to have effect on and after that day as if it were an order made under this sub-paragraph.

Amendments—CCA 2013, s 17, Sch 10.

2 Conduct of litigation

(1) This paragraph applies to determine whether a person is an exempt person for the purpose of carrying on any activity which constitutes the conduct of litigation in relation to any proceedings (subject to paragraph 7).

(2) The person is exempt if the person –

(a) is not an authorised person in relation to that activity, but
(b) has a right to conduct litigation granted by a court in relation to those proceedings.

(3) The person is exempt if the person –

(a) is not an authorised person in relation to that activity, but
(b) has a right to conduct litigation in relation to those proceedings granted by or under any enactment.

(4) The person is exempt if the person –

(a) is a party to those proceedings, and
(b) would have a right to conduct the litigation, in the person's capacity as such a party, if this Act had not been passed.

(5) The person is an exempt person in relation to any activity which is carried on in or in connection with proceedings on an appeal from the Comptroller-General of Patents, Designs and Trade Marks to the Patents Court under the Patents Act 1977, if the person is a solicitor of the Court of Judicature of Northern Ireland.

****

7 European lawyers

A European lawyer (within the meaning of the European Communities (Services of Lawyers) Order 1978 (SI 1978/1910)) is an exempt person for the purposes of carrying on an activity which is a reserved legal activity and which the European lawyer is entitled to carry on by virtue of that order.

****

9 Further exempt persons

(1) The Lord Chancellor may, by order, amend this Schedule so as to provide –

(a) for persons to be exempt persons in relation to any activity which is a reserved legal activity (including any activity which is a reserved legal activity by virtue of an order under section 24 (extension of reserved legal activities)),
(b) for persons to cease to be such persons, or
(c) for the amendment of any provision made in respect of an exempt person.

(2) The Lord Chancellor may make an order under sub-paragraph (1) only on the recommendation of the Board.

****

Legitimacy Act 1976

ARRANGEMENT OF SECTIONS

Section		Page
1	Legitimacy of children of certain void marriages	1055
2	Legitimation by subsequent marriage of mother and father	1056
2A	Legitimation by subsequent marriage or civil partnership of parents	1056
3	Legitimation by extraneous law	1056
4	Legitimation of adopted child	1057
5	Rights of legitimated persons and others to take interests in property	1057
6	Dispositions depending on date of birth	1057
7	Protection of trustees and personal representatives	1058
8	Personal rights and obligations	1058
9	Re-registration of birth of legitimated person	1058
10	Interpretation	1058

1 Legitimacy of children of certain void marriages

(1) The child of a void marriage, whenever born, shall, subject to subsection (2) below and Schedule 1 to this Act, be treated as the legitimate child of his parents if at the time of the insemination resulting in the birth or, where there was no such insemination, the child's conception (or at the time of the celebration of the marriage if later) both or either of the parties reasonably believed that the marriage was valid.

(2) This section only applies where –

(a) the father of the child was domiciled in England and Wales at the time of the birth, or if he died before the birth, was so domiciled immediately before his death, or

(b) if a woman is treated as the female parent of a child by virtue of section 42 or 43 of the Human Fertilisation and Embryology Act 2008, that female parent was domiciled in England and Wales at the time of the birth, or if she died before the birth, was so domiciled immediately before her death.

(3) It is hereby declared for the avoidance of doubt that subsection (1) above applies notwithstanding that the belief that the marriage was valid was due to a mistake as to law.

(4) In relation to a child born after the coming into force of section 28 of the Family Law Reform Act 1987, it shall be presumed for the purposes of subsection (1) above, unless the contrary is shown, that one of the parties to the void marriage reasonably believed at the time of the insemination resulting in the birth or, where there was no such insemination, the child's conception (or at the time of the celebration of the marriage if later) that the marriage was valid.

(5) Subsections (1) and (4) are to be read, in relation to the child of a void marriage which has resulted from the purported conversion of a civil partnership under section 9 of the Marriage (Same Sex Couples) Act 2013 and regulations made under that section, as if the reference to the time of the celebration of the marriage was a reference to the date of the purported conversion of the civil partnership into a marriage.

Amendments—FLRA 1987, s 28; SI 2014/560; SI 2014/3168.

Defined terms—'void marriage': s 10(1).

'child of a void marriage'—The decision in *Spence, Spence v Dennis* [1990] 2 FLR 278, CA suggests that this definition includes only a child who would be born *in wedlock* if the marriage were valid; there is a distinction between a child of a void marriage and a child legitimated by the subsequent marriage of its parents (see s 2). In the case of a child born *after* a void marriage, the child will be treated as a legitimate child, but a child born *before* the void marriage will be treated as illegitimate (see also *F and F v AG and F* [1980] Fam Law 60, FD).

2 Legitimation by subsequent marriage of mother and father

Subject to the following provisions of this Act, where the mother and father of an illegitimate person marry one another, the marriage shall, if the father of the illegitimate person is at the date of marriage domiciled in England and Wales, render that person, if living, legitimate from the date of the marriage.

Amendments—SI 2014/560.

2A Legitimation by subsequent marriage or civil partnership of parents

Subject to the following provisions of this Act, where –

(a) a person ('the child') has a parent ('the female parent') by virtue of section 43 of the Human Fertilisation and Embryology Act 2008 (treatment provided to woman who agrees that second woman to be parent),

(b) at the time of the child's birth, the female parent and the child's mother are neither married nor civil partners of each other,

(c) the female parent and the child's mother subsequently marry or enter into a civil partnership, and

(d) the female parent is at the date of the marriage or the formation of the civil partnership domiciled in England and Wales,

the marriage or the civil partnership shall render the child, if living, legitimate from the date of the marriage or the formation of the civil partnership.

Amendments—Inserted by HFEA 2008, s 56, Sch 6, Pt 1, para 16. Amended by SI 2014/560.

Scope—This provision extends the legitimation provision to same-sex female couples who have a child together by means of assisted reproduction (see HFEA 2008, ss 43–45) and they subsequently enter into a civil partnership so that they can legitimise the child as from the date of the civil partnership, provided the conditions set out in the section are met.

3 Legitimation by extraneous law

(1) Subject to the following provisions of this Act, where the mother and father of an illegitimate person marry one another and the father of the illegitimate person is not at the time of the marriage domiciled in England and Wales but is domiciled in a country by the law of which the illegitimate person became legitimated by virtue of such subsequent marriage, that person, if living, shall in England and Wales be recognised as having been so legitimated from the date of the marriage notwithstanding that, at the time of his birth, his father was domiciled in a country the law of which did not permit legitimation by subsequent marriage.

(2) Subject to the following provisions of this Act, where –

(a) a person ('the child') has a parent ('the female parent') by virtue of section 43 of the Human Fertilisation and Embryology Act 2008 (treatment provided to woman who agrees that second woman to be parent),

(b) at the time of the child's birth, the female parent and the child's mother are neither married nor civil partners of each other,

(c) the female parent and the child's mother subsequently marry or enter into a civil partnership, and

(d) the female parent is not at the time of the marriage or the formation of the civil partnership domiciled in England and Wales but is domiciled in a country by the law of which the child became legitimated by virtue of the marriage or civil partnership,

the child, if living, shall in England and Wales be recognised as having been so legitimated from the date of marriage or the formation of the civil partnership notwithstanding that, at the time of the child's birth, the female parent was domiciled in a country the law of which did not permit legitimation by subsequent marriage or civil partnership.

Amendments—HFEA 2008, s 56, Sch 6, Pt 1, para 17; SI 2014/560.

Scope—See above under s 2A.

4 Legitimation of adopted child

(1) Section 39 of the Adoption Act 1976 or section 67 of the Adoption and Children Act 2002 does not prevent an adopted child being legitimated under section 2 or 3 above if either natural parent is the sole adoptive parent.

(2) Where an adopted child (with a sole adoptive parent) is legitimated –

(a) subsection (2) of the said section 39 or subsection (3)(b) of the said section 67 shall not apply after the legitimation to the natural relationship with the other natural parent, and
(b) revocation of the adoption order in consequence of the legitimation shall not affect section 39, 41 or 42 of the Adoption Act 1976 or section 67, 68 or 69 of the Adoption and Children Act 2002 as it applies to any instrument made before the date of legitimation.

Amendments—AA 1976, s 73(2), Sch 3, para 23; ACA 2002, Sch 3, para 17.

5 Rights of legitimated persons and others to take interests in property

(1) Subject to any contrary indication, the rules of construction contained in this section apply to any instrument other than an existing instrument, so far as the instrument contains a disposition of property.

(2) For the purposes of this section, provisions of the law of intestate succession applicable to the estate of a deceased person shall be treated as if contained in an instrument executed by him (while of full capacity) immediately before his death.

(3) A legitimated person, and any other person, shall be entitled to take any interest as if the legitimated person had been born legitimate.

(4) A disposition which depends on the date of birth of a child or children of the parent or parents shall be construed as if –

(a) a legitimated child had been born on the date of legitimation,
(b) two or more legitimated children legitimated on the same date had been born on that date in the order of their actual births,

but this does not affect any reference to the age of a child.

(5) Examples of phrases in wills on which subsection (4) above can operate are –

1 Children of A 'living at my death or born afterwards'.
2 Children of A 'living at my death or born afterwards before any one of such children for the time being in existence attains a vested interest, and who attain the age of 21 years'.
3 As in example 1 or 2, but referring to grandchildren of A, instead of children of A.
4 A for life 'until he has a child' and then to his child or children.

Note. Subsection (4) above will not affect the reference to the age of 21 years in example 2.

(6) If an illegitimate person or a person adopted by one of his natural parents dies, or has died before the commencement of this Act, and –

(a) after his death his parents marry or have married; and
(b) the deceased would, if living at the time of the marriage, have become a legitimated person,

this section shall apply for the construction of the instrument so far as it relates to the taking of interests by, or in succession to, his spouse, children and remoter issue as if he had been legitimated by virtue of the marriage.

(7) In this section 'instrument' includes a private Act settling property, but not any other enactment.

Defined terms—'disposition', 'legitimated person': s 10(1).

6 Dispositions depending on date of birth

(1) Where a disposition depends on the date of birth of a child who was born illegitimate and who is legitimated (or, if deceased, is treated as legitimated), section 5(4) above does not affect entitlement under Part II of the Family Law Reform Act 1969 (illegitimate children).

(2) Where a disposition depends on the date of birth of an adopted child who is legitimated (or, if deceased, is treated as legitimated) section 5(4) above does not affect entitlement by virtue of section 42(2) of the Adoption Act 1976 or section 69(2) of the Adoption and Children Act 2002.

(3) This section applies for example where –

(a) a testator dies in 1976 bequeathing a legacy to his eldest grandchild living at a specified time,
(b) a daughter has an illegitimate child in 1977 who is the first grandchild,
(c) his married son has a child in 1978,
(d) subsequently the illegitimate child is legitimated,

and in all those cases the daughter's child remains the eldest grandchild of the testator throughout.

Amendments—AA 1976, s 73(2), Sch 3, para 24; ACA 2002, Sch 3, para 18.

7 Protection of trustees and personal representatives

(1) A trustee or personal representative is not under a duty, by virtue of the law relating to trusts or the administration of estates, to enquire, before conveying or distributing any property, whether any person is illegitimate or has been adopted by one of his natural parents, and could be legitimated (or if deceased be treated as legitimated), if that fact could affect entitlement to the property.

(2) A trustee or personal representative shall not be liable to any person by reason of a conveyance or distribution of the property made without regard to any such fact if he has not received notice of the fact before the conveyance or distribution.

(3) This section does not prejudice the right of a person to follow the property, or any property representing it, into the hands of another person, other than a purchaser, who has received it.

8 Personal rights and obligations

A legitimated person shall have the same rights, and shall be under the same obligations in respect of the maintenance and support of himself or of any other person as if he had been born legitimate, and, subject to the provisions of this Act, the provisions of any Act relating to claims for damages, compensation, allowance, benefit or otherwise by or in respect of a legitimate child shall apply in like manner in the case of a legitimated person.

9 Re-registration of birth of legitimated person

(1) It shall be the duty of the parents of a legitimated person or, in cases where re-registration can be effected on information furnished by one parent and one of the parents is dead, of the surviving parent to furnish to the Registrar General information with a view to obtaining the re-registration of the birth of that person within 3 months after the date of the marriage or of the formation of the civil partnership by virtue of which he was legitimated.

(2) The failure of the parents or either of them to furnish information as required by subsection (1) above in respect of any legitimated person shall not affect the legitimation of that person.

(3) This section does not apply in relation to a person who was legitimated otherwise than by virtue of the subsequent marriage or civil partnership of his parents.

(4) Any parent who fails to give information as required by this section shall be liable on summary conviction to a fine not exceeding level 1 on the standard scale.

Amendments—Criminal Justice Act 1982, ss 38, 46; HFEA 2008, s 56, Sch 6, Pt 1, para 18(b).

Scope—The provisions of s 9 have been extended to include the re-registration of birth of a legitimated child born to same-sex female couples who enter into a subsequent civil partnership.

10 Interpretation

(1) In this Act, except where the context otherwise requires, –

'disposition' includes the conferring of a power of appointment and any other disposition of an interest in or right over property;

'existing', in relation to an instrument, means one made before 1 January 1976;

'legitimated person' means a person legitimated or recognised as legitimated –

(a) under section 2, 2A or 3 above; or

(b) under section 1 or 8 of the Legitimacy Act 1926; or

(c) except in section 8, by a legitimation (whether or not by virtue of the subsequent marriage of his parents) recognised by the law of England and Wales and effected under the law of any other country:

and cognate expressions shall be construed accordingly;

'power of appointment' includes any discretionary power to transfer a beneficial interest in property without the furnishing of valuable consideration;

'void marriage' means a marriage, not being voidable only, in respect of which the High Court has or had jurisdiction to grant a decree of nullity, or would have or would have had such jurisdiction if the parties were domiciled in England and Wales.

(2) For the purposes of this Act 'legitimated person' includes, where the context admits, a person legitimated, or recognised as legitimated, before the passing of the Children Act 1975.

(3) For the purpose of this Act, except where the context otherwise requires, –

(a) the death of the testator is the date at which a will or codicil is to be regarded as made;

(b) an oral disposition of property shall be deemed to be contained in an instrument made when the disposition was made.

(4) *(repealed)*

(5) Except in so far as the context otherwise requires, any reference in this Act to an enactment shall be construed as a reference to that enactment as amended by or under any other enactment, including this Act.

Amendments—TLATA 1996, s 25(2),(4),(5), Sch 4; HFEA 2008, s 56, Sch 6, Pt 1, para 19.

Definition—'legitimated person' includes a child born to same-sex female couples to whom ss 2A and 3 apply.

****

Magistrates' Courts Act 1980

****

111A Appeals on ground of error of law etc in child support proceedings

(1) This section applies in relation to proceedings under the Child Support Act 1991 in a magistrates' court.

(2) Any person who was a party to any proceeding before the court, or is aggrieved by the order, determination or other proceeding of the court, may question the proceeding on the ground that it is wrong in law or is in excess of jurisdiction by appealing to the family court.

(3) But a person may not appeal under subsection (2) in respect of a decision if –

(a) the person has a right of appeal to the county court or the family court against the decision otherwise than under this section, or

(b) the decision is final by virtue of any enactment passed after 31 December 1879.

(4) A notice of appeal under subsection (2) shall be filed within 21 days after the day on which the decision of the magistrates' court was given.

(5) *(repealed)*

Amendments—Inserted by SI 2009/871. Amended by CCA 2013, s 17, Schs 9, 10.

Defined terms—'family court': ss 65, 111A(5).

Appeals from magistrate under CSA 1991—Child support cases are dealt with by the magistrates' courts in their civil jurisdiction (i e they are not family proceedings). Once notice of appeal has been filed, the appeal proceeds under FPR 2010, Pt 30 and PD30A, in particular paras 9.3–9.5. This combination of provisions creates a conflict between statute and rules. An appeal under s 111A(2) is on grounds that the decision was wrong in law (or in excess of jurisdiction), whereas an appeal, once in the Family Court, proceeds under

FPR 2010, Pt 30, where the appeal may be allowed on grounds that the decision below was wrong (FPR 2010, r 30.12(3)(a)): that is, it could be wrong in law (per s 111A(2)) but also on the facts or on a wrong exercise of discretion.

Permission to appeal—Permission to appeal is not required for an appeal under s 111A, which remains unaffected by the provisions of FPR 2010, r 30.3 as to permission to appeal.

Time for filing notice of appeal (s 111A(4))—The 21-day time-limit is fixed and cannot be extended (*Giltinane v Child Support Agency* [2006] 2 FLR 857, FD), although if a judge can be persuaded to transfer a meritorious out-of-time appeal to the High Court and then to deal with it as a judicial review application (as in *Giltinane*), time could be extended: CPR 1998, rr 3.9 (court's powers to give relief from sanctions, such as time limits), 54.5 (time limits for filing of a judicial review application).

****

Maintenance Enforcement Act 1991

The High Courts and family court

1 Maintenance orders in the High Court and family court: means of payment, attachment of earnings and revocation, variation, etc

(1) Where the High Court or the family court makes a qualifying periodical maintenance order, it may at the same time exercise either of its powers under subsection (4) below in relation to the order, whether of its own motion or on an application made under this subsection by an interested party.

(1A) Where the family court makes a qualifying periodical maintenance order, it may at the same time exercise any of its powers under subsection (4A) below in relation to the order, whether of its own motion or on an application made under this subsection by an interested party.

(2) For the purposes of this section, a periodical maintenance order is an order –

(a) which requires money to be paid periodically by one person ('the debtor') to another ('the creditor'); and

(b) which is a maintenance order;

and such an order is a 'qualifying periodical maintenance order' if, at the time it is made, the debtor is ordinarily resident in England and Wales.

(3) Where the High Court or the family court has made a qualifying periodical maintenance order, it may at any later time –

(a) on an application made under this subsection by an interested party, or

(b) of its own motion, in the course of any proceedings concerning the order,

exercise either of its powers under subsection (4) below in relation to the order.

(3A) Where the family court has made a qualifying periodical maintenance order, it may at any later time –

(a) on an application made under this subsection by an interested party, or

(b) of its own motion, in the course of any proceedings concerning the order,

exercise any of its powers under subsection (4A) below in relation to the order.

(4) The powers mentioned in subsections (1) and (3) above are –

(a) the power to order that payments required to be made by the debtor to the creditor under the qualifying periodical maintenance order in question shall be so made by such a method of payment falling within subsection (5) below as the court may specify in the particular case; or

(b) the power, by virtue of this section, to make an attachment of earnings order under the Attachment of Earnings Act 1971 to secure payments under the qualifying periodical maintenance order in question.

(4A) The powers mentioned in subsections (1A) and (3A) above are –

(a) the power to order that payments under the qualifying periodical maintenance order in question be made to the court;

(b) the power to order that payments under the qualifying periodical maintenance order in question required to be made to the court are to be so made by such method of payment falling within subsection (5) below as the court may specify in the particular case; or

(c) the power to order that payments under the qualifying periodical maintenance order in question be made in accordance with arrangements for their collection made by the Secretary of State under section 30 of the Child Support Act 1991 and regulations made under that section.

(5) The methods of payment mentioned in subsection (4)(a) above are –

(a) payment by standing order; or

(b) payment by any other method which requires the debtor to give his authority for payments of a specific amount to be made from an account of his to an account of the creditor's on specific dates during the period for which the authority is in force and without the need for any further authority from the debtor; or

(c) any method of payment specified in regulations made by the Lord Chancellor.

(6) In any case where –

(a) the court proposes to exercise its power under paragraph (a) of subsection (4) above or under paragraph (b) of subsection (4A) above, and

(b) having given the debtor an opportunity of opening an account from which payments under the order may be made in accordance with the method of payment proposed to be ordered under that paragraph, the court is satisfied that the debtor has failed, without reasonable excuse, to open such an account,

the court in exercising its power under that paragraph may order that the debtor open such an account.

(7) Where in the exercise of its powers under subsection (1), (1A), (3) or (3A) above, the High Court or the family court has made in relation to a qualifying periodical maintenance order such an order as is mentioned in subsection (4)(a) or (4A) above (a 'means of payment order'), it may at any later time –

(a) on an application made under this subsection by an interested party, or

(b) of its own motion, in the course of any proceedings concerning the qualifying periodical maintenance order,

revoke, suspend, revive or vary the means of payment order.

(8) In deciding whether to exercise any of its powers under this section the court in question having (if practicable) given every interested party an opportunity to make representations shall have regard to any representations made by any such party.

(8A) No order made by the family court under subsection (4) or (4A)(a) or (b) above has effect at any time when the Secretary of State is, under section 30 of the Child Support Act 1991 and regulations made under that section, arranging for the collection of payments under the qualifying periodical maintenance order in question.

(9) Nothing in this section shall be taken to prejudice –

(a) any power under the Attachment of Earnings Act 1971 which would, apart from this section, be exercisable by the High Court or the family court; or

(b) any right of any person to make any application under that Act;

and subsection (7) above is without prejudice to any other power of the High Court or the family court to revoke, suspend, revive or vary an order.

(10) For the purposes of this section –

'debtor' and 'creditor' shall be construed in accordance with subsection (2) above;

'interested party' means any of the following, that is to say –

(a) the debtor;

(b) the creditor; and

(c) in a case where the person who applied for the qualifying periodical maintenance order in question is a person other than the creditor, that other person;

'maintenance order' means any order specified in Schedule 8 to the Administration of Justice Act 1970 and includes any such order which has been discharged, if any arrears are recoverable under it;

'qualifying periodical maintenance order' shall be construed in accordance with subsection (2) above, and the references to such an order in subsections (3) and (7) above are references to any such order, whether made before or after the coming into force of this section;

and the reference in subsection (2) above to an order requiring money to be paid periodically by one person to another includes a reference to an order requiring a lump sum to be paid by instalments by one person to another.

(11) The power of the Lord Chancellor to make regulations under subsection (5)(c) above is exercisable by statutory instrument, and a statutory instrument containing regulations under subsection (5)(c) is subject to annulment in pursuance of a resolution of either House of Parliament.

Amendments—CCA 2013, s 17, Sch 10.

Defined terms—'creditor', 'debtor': s 1(2); 'interested party', 'maintenance order': s 1(10); 'qualifying maintenance order': s 1(2),(10).

'qualifying periodical maintenance order' (s 1(2))—The powers created or extended by this section apply only on making such an order or in relation to such an order already made.

'application … by an interested party' (s 1(3)(a))—The expression 'interested party' includes both the person who applied for the qualifying periodical maintenance order and, if different, the person entitled to receive the payments. Thus it would appear that the latter, though not a party, can apply directly and presumably would not need leave to intervene in the main proceedings or cause. The debtor is also an interested party; in the case of a qualifying periodical maintenance order s 1(3)(a) seems to enable the debtor to apply for an attachment of earnings order at any time, not only on the maintenance order being made or varied under FPR 2010, r 39.5.

'of its own motion' (s 1(3)(b))—The court may exercise its powers in the course of any proceedings relating to the qualifying periodical maintenance order. This provision is general so, for example, the powers may be exercised not only on an application to vary or discharge but also on an enforcement application or an application by the debtor to suspend a warrant of execution. Since the powers include the power to make an attachment of earnings order, s 1(3) has the effect of extending to such an occasion the powers to require information given by AEA 1971, s 14.

Methods of payment (s 1(5))—It is unlikely that banks would accept a direct debit authority (as distinct from a standing order) in favour of a personal maintenance creditor, but this power might be used where the person entitled to receive the payments had authorised an institution or Government department to collect them on his behalf.

'opportunity to make representations' (s 1(8))—This requirement will be satisfied if the debtor is present at the hearing at which the question is considered or if he has been given notice of the intention to apply for the order. Otherwise, the court must adjourn and cause notice to be given to him that it is minded to make the order.

Lump sums (s 1(10))—Although a lump sum order is a maintenance order, it is not a qualifying periodical maintenance order unless the lump sum has been ordered to be paid by instalments.

Maintenance Orders Act 1950

ARRANGEMENT OF SECTIONS

PART I
JURISDICTION

Section		Page
4	Contributions under the Children and Young Persons Act 1933, and National Assistance Act 1948	1063
15	Service of process	1063

PART II
ENFORCEMENT

16 Application of Part II 1064
17 Procedure for registration of maintenance orders 1066
18 Enforcement of registered orders 1066
19 Functions of collecting officer etc 1068
20 Arrears under registered maintenance orders 1068
21 Discharge and variation of maintenance orders registered in superior courts 1069
22 Discharge and variation of maintenance orders registered in summary or sheriff courts 1069
23 Notice of variation etc 1071
24 Cancellation of registration 1071
25 Rules as to procedure of courts of summary jurisdiction 1073

PART III
GENERAL

26 Proof of declarations etc 1073

PART I
JURISDICTION

****

4 Contributions under the Children and Young Persons Act 1933, and National Assistance Act 1948

(1) The family court shall have jurisdiction in proceedings against a person residing in Scotland or Northern Ireland –

(a), (b) (*repealed*)

(c) for an order under section 18 of the Supplementary Benefits Act 1976 (which provides for the recovery of expenditure on supplementary benefits from persons liable for maintenance)

(d) for an order under section 106 of the Social Security Administration Act 1992 (which provides for the recovery of expenditure on income support or universal credit from such persons).

(2) A court in England by which an order has been made under the said section 18 or the said section 106 shall have jurisdiction in proceedings by or against a person residing in Scotland or Northern Ireland for the revocation, revival or variation of that order.

Amendments—Supplementary Benefits Act 1976, s 35(2), Sch 7, para 8; Child Care Act 1980, s 89(3), Sch 6; Social Security Act 1986, s 86(1), Sch 10, para 35; Social Security (Consequential Provisions) Act 1992, s 4, Sch 2, para 3, Health and Social Care Act 2008, Sch 15; SI 2013/630; CCA 2013, s 17, Sch 11.

'revocation, revival or variation' (s 1(2))—MCA 1980, s 60 applies to such proceedings.

****

15 Service of process

(1) Where –

(a) proceedings are begun in a court having jurisdiction under or by virtue of the following, namely –

(i) this Part of this Act; or

(ii) sections 24(1) and 30(3) of the Domestic Proceedings and Magistrates' Courts Act 1978;

(iii) section 92 of and Schedule 11 to the Children Act 1989; or

(iv) section 93(2)(g) of that Act (including that provision as applied in relation to Northern Ireland by section 116(3) of the Courts and Legal Services Act 1990; or

(v) Article 164 of and Schedule 7 to the Children (Northern Ireland) Order 1995 or Article 165(2)(g) of that Order; or

(vi) Council Regulation (EC) No 4/2009 including as applied in relation to Denmark by virtue of the Agreement made on 19 October 2005 between the European Community and the Kingdom of Denmark and Schedule 6 to the Civil Jurisdiction and Judgments (Maintenance) Regulations 2011; or

(b) an action which contains a conclusion for aliment not falling within the scope of paragraph (a)(i) above is commenced in a sheriff court in Scotland,

and the person against whom the action or other proceedings is or are brought resides in another part of the United Kingdom, any summons or initial writ addressed to him in the proceedings may, if endorsed in accordance with the provisions of this section in that part of the United Kingdom, be served within that part of the United Kingdom as if it had been issued or authorised to be served, as the case may be, by the endorsing authority.

(2) A summons or writ may be endorsed under this section, in England by a judge of the family court, in Scotland by a sheriff, and in Northern Ireland by a resident magistrate; and the endorsement shall be made in the form numbered 1 in the Second Schedule to this Act, or any form to the like effect.

(3) In any proceedings in which a summons or writ is served under this section, the service may be proved by means of a declaration made in the form numbered 2 in the Second Schedule to this Act, or any form to the like effect, before a judge of the family court, sheriff, or resident magistrate, as the case may be.

(4) Nothing in this section shall be construed as authorising the service of a summons or writ otherwise than personally.

(5) Section four of the Summary Jurisdiction (Process) Act 1881 shall not apply to any process which may be served under this section; and nothing in this section or in any other enactment shall be construed as authorising the execution in one part of the United Kingdom of a warrant for the arrest of a person who fails to appear in answer to any such process issued in another part of the United Kingdom.

Amendments—Children Act 1975, s 108(1), Sch 3, para 10; AJA 1977, s 3, Sch 3, para 11; DPMCA 1978, s 89(2)(a), Sch 2, para 12; Child Care Act 1980, s 89, Sch 5, para 2; SI 1980/564; CJJA 1982, ss 16(5), 23(2), Sch 12, para 2; CLSA 1990, s 116, Sch 16, para 34; SI 1995/756; SI 2011/1484; CCA 2013, s 17, Sch 11.

'declaration' (s 15(3))—For proof of declarations, see s 26.

PART II
ENFORCEMENT

16 Application of Part II

(1) Any order to which this section applies (in this Part of this Act referred to as a maintenance order) made by a court in any part of the United Kingdom may, if registered in accordance with the provisions of this Part of this Act in a court in another part of the United Kingdom, be enforced in accordance with those provisions in that other part of the United Kingdom.

(2) This section applies to the following orders, that is to say –

(a) an order for alimony, maintenance or other payments made or deemed to be made by a court in England under any of the following enactments –

(i) sections 15 to 17, 19 to 22, 30, 34 and 35 of the Matrimonial Causes Act 1965 and sections 22, 23(1), (2) and (4) and 27 of the Matrimonial Causes Act 1973 and section 14 or 17 of the Matrimonial and Family Proceedings Act 1984;

(ii) Part I of the Domestic Proceedings and Magistrates' Courts Act 1978;

(iii) Schedule 1 to the Children Act 1989;

(iv) *(repealed)*

(v) paragraph 23 of Schedule 2 to the Children Act 1989;

(vi) section 18 of the Supplementary Benefits Act 1976;

(vii) *(repealed)*

(viii) section 106 of the Social Security Administration Act 1992;

(ix) Part 1, 8 or 9 of Schedule 5 to the Civil Partnership Act 2004, Schedule 6 to that Act or paragraph 5 or 9 of Schedule 7 to that Act;

(b) a decree for payment of aliment granted by a court in Scotland, including –

(i) an order for the payment of an annual or periodical allowance under section two of the Divorce (Scotland) Act 1938 or an order for the payment of a periodical allowance or a capital sum under section 26 of the Succession (Scotland) Act 1964 or section 5 of the Divorce (Scotland) Act 1976 or an order for financial provision in the form of a monetary payment under s 8 of the Family Law (Scotland) Act 1985;

(ii) an order for the payment of weekly or periodical sums under subsection (2) of section 3 or subsection (4) of section 5 of the Guardianship of Infants Act 1925;

(iii) an order for the payment of sums in respect of aliment under subsection (3) of section 1 of the Illegitimate Children (Scotland) Act 1930;

(iv) a decree for payment of aliment under section 44 of the National Assistance Act 1948, or under section 26 of the Children Act 1948; and

(v) *(repealed)*

(vi) a contribution order under section 80 of, or a decree or an order made under section 81 of, the Social Work (Scotland) Act 1968;

(vii) an order for the payment of weekly or other periodical sums under subsection (3) of section 11 of the Guardianship Act 1973;

(viii) an order made on an application under section 18 or section 19(8) of the Supplementary Benefits Act 1976;

(ix) an order made on an application under section 106 of the Social Security Administration Act 1992;

(x) an order made on an application under Schedule 11 to the Civil Partnership Act 2004;

(c) an order for alimony, maintenance or other payments made by a court in Northern Ireland under or by virtue of any of the following enactments: –

(i) subsection (2) of section 17, subsections (2) to (7) of section 19, subsection (2) of section 20, section 22 or subsection (1) of section 28 of the Matrimonial Causes Act (Northern Ireland) 1939;

(ii) Schedule 1 to the Children (Northern Ireland) Order 1995;

(iii) *(repealed)*

(iv) Article 41 of the Children (Northern Ireland) Order 1995 or Article 101 of the Health and Personal Social Services (Northern Ireland) Order 1972;

(v) any enactment of the Parliament of Northern Ireland containing provisions corresponding with section 22(1), 34 or 35 of the Matrimonial Causes Act 1965, with section 22, 23(1), (2) or (4) or 27 of the Matrimonial Causes Act 1973;

(vi) Article 23 or 24 of the Supplementary Benefits (Northern Ireland) Order 1977;

(vii) the Domestic Proceedings (Northern Ireland) Order 1980;

(viii) any enactment applying in Northern Ireland and corresponding to section 106 of the Social Security Administration Act 1992;

(ix) Articles 18 or 21 of the Matrimonial and Family Proceedings (Northern Ireland) Order 1989

(x) Part 1, 7 or 8 of Schedule 15 to the Civil Partnership Act 2004, Schedule 16 to that Act or paragraph 5 or 9 of Schedule 17 to that Act.

Amendments—Social Work (Scotland) Act 1968, s 95(1), Sch 8, para 34; Guardianship of Minors Act 1971, s 18(1), Sch 1; Guardianship Act 1973, ss 9(3), 14, 15(3), Sch 5, para 4; MCA 1973, s 54, Sch 2, para 3(1); Children Act 1975, s 108(1), Sch 3, para 11; Supplementary Benefits Act 1976, s 35(2), Sch 7, para 13; Divorce (Scotland) Act 1976, s 12(1), Sch 1, para 1; AJA 1977, s 3, Sch 3, para 12; SI 1977/2158; DPMCA 1978, s 89(2), Sch 2, para 13; Child Care Act 1980, s 89, Sch 5, para 3; SI 1980/564; Social Security and Housing Benefit Act 1982, s 48(5), Sch 4, para 2; CJJA 1982, s 54, Sch 14; MFPA 1984, s 46(1), Sch 1, para 1; Family Law (Scotland) Act 1985, s 28(1), Sch 1, para 3; Social Security Act 1986, Sch 10; FLRA 1987, Schs 2 and 4; SI 1989/678; CLSA 1990, Schs 16 and 20; Social Security (Consequential Provisions) Act 1992, s 4, Sch 2, para 3; SI 1995/756; CPA 2004, s 261(1), Sch 27, para 18(1)–(4); Health and Social Care Act 2008, Sch 15, Pt 5.

17 Procedure for registration of maintenance orders

(1) An application for the registration of a maintenance order under this Part of this Act shall be made in the prescribed manner to the appropriate authority, that is to say –

- (a) *(repealed)*
- (b) where the maintenance order was made by a court of summary jurisdiction in Northern Ireland, a resident magistrate acting for the same petty sessions district as the court which made the order;
- (c) in every other case, the prescribed officer of the court which made the order.

(2) If upon application made as aforesaid by or on behalf of the person entitled to payments under a maintenance order it appears that the person liable to make those payments resides in another part of the United Kingdom, and that it is convenient that the order should be enforceable there, the appropriate authority shall cause a certified copy of the order to be sent to the prescribed officer of a court in that part of the United Kingdom in accordance with the provisions of the next following subsection.

(3) The court to whose officer the certified copy of a maintenance order is sent under this section shall be –

- (a) where the maintenance order was made by a superior court, the Senior Courts, the Court of Session or the Court of Judicature, as the case may be;
- (b) in any other case –
  - (i) where the defendant appears to be in England and Wales, the family court;
  - (ii) where the defendant appears to be in Northern Ireland, a court of summary jurisdiction acting for the place in which the defendant appears to be;
  - (iii) where the defendant appears to be in Scotland, the sheriff court within the jurisdiction of which the defendant appears to be.

(4) Where the prescribed officer of any court receives a certified copy of a maintenance order sent to him under this section, he shall cause the order to be registered in that court in the prescribed manner, and shall give notice of the registration in the prescribed manner to the prescribed officer of the court which made the order.

(5) The officer to whom any notice is given under the last foregoing subsection shall cause particulars of the notice to be registered in his court in the prescribed manner.

(6) Where the sums payable under a maintenance order, being an order made by the family court or a court of summary jurisdiction in Northern Ireland, are payable to or through an officer of any court, that officer shall, if the person entitled to the payments so requests, make an application on behalf of that person for the registration of the order under this Part of this Act; but the person at whose request the application is made shall have the same liability for costs properly incurred in or about the application as if the application had been made by him.

(7) An order which is for the time being registered under this Part of this Act in any court shall not be registered thereunder in any other court.

Amendments—Courts Act 2003, s 109(1), Sch 8, para 87; CRA 2005, Sch 11, para 19(2); CCA 2013, s 17, Sch 11.

'maintenance order' (s 17(1))—See s 16(2).

'prescribed manner' (s 17(1))—The manner of application is prescribed, for cases in the High Court or Family Court, in FPR 2010, rr 32.2–32.12.

18 Enforcement of registered orders

(1) Subject to the provisions of this section, a maintenance order registered under this Part of this Act in a court in any part of the United Kingdom may be enforced in that part of the United Kingdom in all respects as if it had been made by that court and as if that court had had jurisdiction to make it; and proceedings for or with respect to the enforcement of any such order may be taken accordingly.

(1A) A maintenance order registered under this Part of this Act in the family court or a court of summary jurisdiction in Northern Ireland shall not carry interest; but where a maintenance order so registered is registered in the High Court under section 36 of the Civil Jurisdiction and

Judgments Act 1982, this subsection shall not prevent any sum for whose payment the order provides from carrying interest in accordance with section 11A of the Maintenance and Affiliation Orders Act (Northern Ireland) 1966.

(1B) A maintenance order made in Scotland which is registered under this Part of this Act in the Senior Courts or the Court of Judicature shall, if interest is by the law of Scotland recoverable under the order, carry the like interest in accordance with subsection (1) of this section.

(2)–(2ZB) *(repealed)*

(2A) Any person under an obligation to make payments under a maintenance order registered under this Part of this Act in a court of summary jurisdiction in Northern Ireland shall give notice of any change of address to the proper officer of the court; and any person who without reasonable excuse fails to give such a notice shall be liable on summary conviction to a fine not exceeding level 2 on the standard scale.

(2B) In subsection (2A) of this section 'proper officer' means –

(a) *(repealed)*

(b) in relation to a court of summary jurisdiction in Northern Ireland, the clerk of the court.

(3) Every maintenance order registered under this Part of this Act in a court of summary jurisdiction in Northern Ireland shall be enforceable as an order made by that court to which Article 98 of the Magistrates' Courts (Northern Ireland) Order 1981 applies, subject to the modifications of that Article specified in subsection (3ZA) of this section.

(3ZA) Article 98 (enforcement of sums adjudged to be paid) shall have effect –

(a) as if for paragraph (7)(a) there were substituted the following sub-paragraph –

'(a) if the court is of the opinion that it is appropriate –

(i) to make an attachment of earnings order; or

(ii) to exercise its power under paragraph (8C)(b)';

(b) as if for paragraphs (8B) to (8D) there were substituted the following paragraphs –

'(8B) Upon the appearance of a person or proof of service of the summons on him as mentioned in paragraph (4) for the enforcement of an order to which this Article applies, the court or resident magistrate may vary the order by exercising one of the powers under paragraph (8C).

(8C) The powers mentioned in paragraph (8B) are –

(a) the power to order that payments under the order be made directly to the collecting officer;

(b) the power to order that payments under the order be made to the collecting officer by such method of payment falling within Article 85(7) (standing order, etc) as may be specified;

(c) the power to make an attachment of earnings order under Part IX to secure payments under the order.

(8D) In deciding which of the powers under paragraph (8C) is to be exercised, the court or, as the case may be, a resident magistrate shall have regard to any representations made by the debtor (within the meaning of Article 85).

(8E) Paragraph (5) of Article 85 (power of court to require debtor to open account) shall apply for the purposes of paragraph (8C) as it applies for the purposes of that Article but as if for sub-paragraph (a) there were substituted –

"(a) the court proposes to exercise its power under sub-paragraph (b) of Article 98(8C), and"'.

(3A) Notwithstanding subsection (1) above, no court in England in which a maintenance, order is registered under this Part of this Act shall enforce that order to the extent that it is for the time being registered in another court in England under Part I of the Maintenance Orders Act 1958.

(3B) Notwithstanding subsection (1) above, no court in Northern Ireland in which a maintenance order is registered under this Part of this Act shall enforce that order to the extent that it is for the time being registered in another court in Northern Ireland under section 36 of the Civil Jurisdiction and Judgments Act 1982.

(4), (5) *(repealed)*

(6) Except as provided by this section, no proceedings shall be taken for or with respect to the enforcement of a maintenance order which is for the time being registered in any court under this Part of this Act.

Amendments—Ministry of Social Security Act 1966, s 39(3), Sch 8; AJA 1977, s 3, Sch 3, para 6; SI 1981/1675; CJJA 1982, ss 36(6), 37(1), Sch 11, paras 1, 5, Sch 12, para 1; MFPA 1984, s 46(1), Sch 1, para 2; FLRA 1987, Sch 2; SI 1989/678; MEA 1991, s 10, Sch 1, para 3; Statute Law (Repeals) Act 1993; SI 1993/1577; SI 1995/756; AJA 1999, s 90, Sch 13, para 13; Courts Act 2003, Sch 8, para 88; CRA 2005, Sch 11, para 19(3); CCA 2013, s 17, Sch 11.

'proceedings ... may be taken' (s 18(1))—In magistrates' courts in Northern Ireland (and formerly in England and Wales), enforcement proceedings may be taken by the court on behalf of the person entitled to payment. In Scotland, the sheriff's court will not act on behalf of the person entitled to payment, and legal representation is therefore advisable.

'level 2 on the standard scale' (s 18(2A))—Currently £500 (Criminal Justice Act 1982, s 37(2)).

19 Functions of collecting officer etc

(1) Where a maintenance order made in England by the family court or in Northern Ireland by a court of summary jurisdiction is registered in any court under this Part of this Act, any provision of the court by virtue of which sums payable thereunder are required to be paid through or to any court or officer or person on behalf of the person entitled thereto shall be of no effect so long as the order is so registered.

(2) Where a maintenance order is registered under this Part of this Act in a court of summary jurisdiction in Northern Ireland, the court shall order that all payments to be made under the maintenance order (including any arrears accrued before the date of the registration) shall be made through the collecting officer of the court or the collecting officer of some other court of summary jurisdiction in Northern Ireland.

(3) An order made under subsection (2) of this section –

(a) *(repealed)*

(b) by a court of summary jurisdiction in Northern Ireland may be varied or revoked by an exercise of the powers conferred by virtue of section 18(3ZA) or section 22(1F) or (1J) of this Act.

(4) Where by virtue of the provisions of this section or any order made thereunder payments under a maintenance order cease to be or become payable through or to any court or officer or person, the person liable to make the payments shall, until he is given the prescribed notice to that effect, be deemed to comply with the maintenance order if he makes payments in accordance with the maintenance order and any order under this section of which he had received such notice.

(5) *(repealed)*

Amendments—SI 1981/1675; MEA 1991, s 10, Sch 1, para 4; SI 1993/1577; CCA 2013, s 17, Sch 11.

Scope—This section prescribes the duties of court collecting officers in relation to the enforcement of orders registered under the Act. See, however, **'proceedings ... may be taken'** under s 18.

20 Arrears under registered maintenance orders

(1) Where application is made for the registration of a maintenance order under this Part of this Act, the applicant may lodge with the appropriate authority –

(a) if the payments under the order are required to be made to or through a court or an officer of any court, a certificate in the prescribed form, signed by an officer of that court or (as the case may be) that officer, as to the amount of any arrears due under the order;

(b) in any other case, a statutory declaration or affidavit as to the amount of those arrears;

and if a certified copy of the maintenance order is sent to the prescribed officer of any court in pursuance of the application, the certificate, declaration or affidavit shall also be sent to that officer.

(2) In any proceedings for or with respect to the enforcement of a maintenance order which is for the time being registered in any court under this Part of this Act, a certificate, declaration or affidavit sent under this section to the appropriate officer of that court shall be evidence, and in Scotland sufficient evidence, of the facts stated therein.

(3) Where a maintenance order made by a court in England or Northern Ireland is registered in a court in Scotland, a person shall not be entitled, except with the leave of the last-mentioned court, to enforce, whether by diligence or otherwise, the payment of any arrears accrued and due under the order before the commencement of this Act; and on any application for leave to enforce the payment of any such arrears, the court may refuse leave, or may grant leave subject to such restrictions and conditions (including conditions as to the allowing of time for payment or the making of payment by instalments) as the court thinks proper, or may remit the payment of such arrears or of any part thereof.

Amendments—CCA 2013, s 17, Sch 11.

'appropriate authority' (s 20(1))—See s 17(1).

21 Discharge and variation of maintenance orders registered in superior courts

(1) The registration of a maintenance order in a superior court under this Part of this Act shall not confer on that court any power to vary or discharge the order, or affect any jurisdiction of the court in which the order was made to vary or discharge the order.

(2) Where a maintenance order made in Scotland is for the time being –

(a) registered under this Part of this Act in a superior court and not registered under Part I of the Maintenance Orders Act 1958 or under section 36 of the Civil Jurisdiction and Judgments Act 1982, or

(b) registered in a court in England under that Part of that Act of 1958 by virtue of section 1(2) of that Act of 1958,

(c) registered in a court in Northern Ireland under section 36 of the Civil Jurisdiction and Judgments Act 1982,

the person liable to make payments under the order may, upon application made to that court in the prescribed manner, adduce before that court any evidence upon which he would be entitled to rely in any proceedings brought before the court by which the order was made for the variation or discharge of the order.

(3) A court before which evidence is adduced in accordance with the foregoing subsection shall cause a transcript or summary of that evidence, signed by the deponent, to be sent to the prescribed officer of the court by which the order was made; and in any proceedings before the last-mentioned court for the variation or discharge of the order, the transcript or summary shall be evidence of the facts stated therein.

Amendments—AJA 1977, s 3, Sch 3, para 7; CJJA 1982, s 36(6), Sch 12, Pt III, para 1(3).

'prescribed manner' (s 21(2))—See FPR 2010, rr 32.2–32.12.

22 Discharge and variation of maintenance orders registered in summary or sheriff courts

(1) Subject to subsection (1ZA), where a maintenance order is for the time being registered under this Part of this Act in the family court, a court of summary jurisdiction in Northern Ireland or a sheriff court, that court may, upon application made in the prescribed manner by or on behalf of the person liable to make periodical payments under the order or the person entitled to those payments, by order make such variation as the court thinks fit in the rate of the payments under the maintenance order; but no such variation shall impose on the person liable to make payments under the maintenance order a liability to make payments in excess of the maximum rate (if any) authorised by the law for the time being in force in the part of the United Kingdom in which the maintenance order was made.

(1ZA) *(repealed)*

(1A) The family court may exercise the same powers in relation to an order registered in the family court under this Part of this Act as are exercisable by the family court under section 1 of the Maintenance Enforcement Act 1991 in relation to a qualifying periodical maintenance order (within the meaning of that section) which has been made by the family court, including the power under subsection (7) of that section to revoke, suspend, revive or vary any means of payment order (within the meaning of that subsection) made by virtue of this subsection.

(1B)–(1E) *(repealed)*

(1F) The power of a court of summary jurisdiction in Northern Ireland to vary a maintenance order under subsection (1) of this section shall include power, if the court is satisfied that payment has not been made in accordance with the order, to vary the order by exercising one of its powers under subsection (1G) of this section.

(1G) The powers of the court are –

- (a) the power to order that payments under the order be made directly to the collecting officer;
- (b) the power to order that payments under the order be made to the collecting officer by such method of payment falling within Article 85(7) of the Magistrates' Courts (Northern Ireland) Order 1981 (standing order, etc) as may be specified;
- (c) the power to make an attachment of earnings order under Part IX of the Order of 1981 to secure payments under the order;

and in this subsection 'collecting officer' means the officer mentioned in Article 85(4) of the Order of 1981.

(1H) In deciding which of the powers under subsection (1G) of this section it is to exercise, the court shall have regard to any representations made by the person liable to make payments under the order.

(1I) Paragraph (5) of Article 85 of the Magistrates' Courts (Northern Ireland) Order 1981 (power of court to require debtor to open account) shall apply for the purposes of subsection (1G) of this section as it applies for the purposes of that Article but as if for sub-paragraph (a) there were substituted –

'(a) the court proposes to exercise its power under paragraph (b) of section 22(1G) of the Maintenance Orders Act 1950, and'.

(1J) Paragraphs (4) to (11) of Article 86 of the Magistrates' Courts (Northern Ireland) Order 1981 (power of clerk and court to vary maintenance order) shall apply in relation to a maintenance order for the time being registered under this Part of this Act in a court of summary jurisdiction in Northern Ireland as they apply in relation to a maintenance order made by a court of summary jurisdiction in Northern Ireland but –

- (a) as if in paragraph (4) for sub-paragraph (b) there were substituted –

  '(b) payments under the order are required to be made to the collecting officer by any method of payment falling within Article 85(7) (standing order, etc)';

  and as if after the words 'petty sessions' there were inserted 'for the petty sessions district for which the court which made the order acts';
- (b) as if in paragraph (5) for the words 'to the collecting officer' there were substituted 'in accordance with paragraph (a) of section 22(1G) of the Maintenance Orders Act 1950';
- (c) as if in paragraph (7), sub-paragraph (c) and the word 'and' immediately preceding it were omitted;
- (d) as if in paragraph (8) for the words 'sub-paragraphs (a) to (d) of Article 85(3)' there were substituted 'section 22(1G) of the Maintenance Orders Act 1950';
- (e) as if for paragraphs (9) and (10) there were substituted the following paragraphs –

  '(9) In deciding which of the powers under section 22(1G) of the Maintenance Orders Act 1950 it is to exercise, the court shall have regard to any representations made by the debtor.

(10) Paragraph (5) of Article 85 (power of court to require debtor to open account) shall apply for the purposes of paragraph (8) as it applies for the purposes of that Article but as if for sub-paragraph (a) there were substituted –

"(a) the court proposes to exercise its power under paragraph (b) of section 22(1G) of the Maintenance Orders Act 1950, and".'

(2) For the purposes of subsection (1) of this section, a court in any part of the United Kingdom may take notice of the law in force in any other part of the United Kingdom.

(3) Section 15 of this Act shall apply to the service of process for the purposes of this section as it applies to the service of process in proceedings begun in a court having jurisdiction by virtue of Part I of this Act.

(4) Except as provided by subsection (1) of this section, no variation shall be made in the rate of the payments under a maintenance order which is for the time being registered under this Part of this Act in the family court, a court of summary jurisdiction in Northern Ireland or a sheriff court, but without prejudice to any power of the court which made the order to discharge it or vary it otherwise than in respect of the rate of the payments thereunder.

(5) Where a maintenance order is for the time being registered under this Part of this Act in the family court, a court of summary jurisdiction in Northern Ireland or a sheriff court –

(a) the person entitled to payments under the order or the person liable to make payments under the order may, upon application made in the prescribed manner to the court by which the order was made, or in which the order is registered, as the case may be, adduce in the prescribed manner before the court in which the application is made any evidence on which he would be entitled to rely in proceedings for the variation or discharge of the order;

(b) the court in which the application is made shall cause a transcript or summary of that evidence, signed by the deponent, to be sent to the prescribed officer of the court in which the order is registered or of the court by which the order was made, as the case may be; and in any proceedings for the variation or discharge of the order the transcript or summary shall be evidence of the facts stated therein.

Amendments—DPMCA 1978, s 89(2), Sch 2, para 14; MEA 1991, s 10, Sch 1, para 5; SI 1993/1577; AJA 1999, s 90, Sch 13, para 14, Sch 15; Courts Act 2003, Sch 8, para 89; SI 2011/1484; CCA 2013, s 17, Sch 11.

'standing order etc' (s 22(1B),(1E),(1G))—This does not include the power to order payment by direct debit.

23 Notice of variation etc

(1) Where a maintenance order registered under this Part of this Act is discharged or varied by any court, the prescribed officer of that court shall give notice of the discharge or variation in the prescribed manner –

(a) to the prescribed officer of any court in which the order is registered; and

(b) if the order was made by another court, to the prescribed officer of that court.

(2) Any officer to whom a notice is given under this section shall cause particulars of the notice to be registered in his court in the prescribed manner.

Amendments—AJA 1977, s 3, Sch 3, para 8.

'prescribed manner' (s 23(1))—See FPR 2010, rr 32.5–32.7.

'prescribed officer' (s 23(1)(a))—See FPR 2010, rr 32.5–32.7.

24 Cancellation of registration

(1) At any time while a maintenance order is registered under this Part of this Act in any court, an application for the cancellation of the registration may be made in the prescribed manner to the prescribed officer of that court by or on behalf of the person entitled to payments under the order; and upon any such application that officer shall (unless proceedings for the variation of the order are pending in that court), cancel the registration, and thereupon the order shall cease to be registered in that court.

PART II

(2) Where, after a maintenance order has been registered under this Part of this Act in the family court, a court of summary jurisdiction in Northern Ireland or a sheriff court in Scotland, it appears to the appropriate authority (as defined by section seventeen of this Act), upon application made in the prescribed manner by or on behalf of the person liable to make payments under the order, that the person has ceased to reside in England, Northern Ireland or Scotland, as the case may be, the appropriate authority may cause a notice to that effect to be sent to the prescribed officer of any court in which the order is registered; and where such a notice is sent the prescribed officer shall cancel the registration of the maintenance order, and thereupon the order shall cease to be registered in that court.

(3) Where the prescribed officer of any court cancels the registration of a maintenance order under this section, he shall give notice of the cancellation in the prescribed manner –

(a) to the prescribed officer of the court by which the order was made; and
(b) to the prescribed officer of any court in which it is registered under Part I of the Maintenance Orders Act 1958 or section 36 of the Civil Jurisdiction and Judgments Act 1982.

(3A) On receipt of a notice under subsection 3 above –

(a) any such officer as is mentioned in paragraph (a) of that subsection shall cause particulars of the notice to be registered in his court in the prescribed manner; and
(b) any such officer as is mentioned in paragraph (b) of that subsection shall cause particulars of the notice to be registered in his court in the prescribed manner and shall cancel the registration of the order.

(4) Except as provided by subsection (5) of this section, the cancellation of the registration of a maintenance order shall not affect anything done in relation to the maintenance order while it was registered.

(5) On the cancellation of the registration of a maintenance order, any order made in relation thereto under subsection (2) of section 19 of this Act shall cease to have effect; but until the person liable to make payments under the maintenance order receives the prescribed notice of the cancellation, he shall be deemed to comply with the maintenance order if he makes payments in accordance with any order under the said subsection (2) which was in force immediately before the cancellation.

(5A) On the cancellation of the registration of a maintenance order registered in the family court in England and Wales, any order –

(a) made in relation thereto by virtue of the powers conferred by section 22(1A) of this Act, and
(b) requiring payment to the family court (whether or not by any method of payment falling within section 1(5) of the Maintenance Enforcement Act 1991),

shall cease to have effect; but until the person liable to make payments under the maintenance order receives the prescribed notice of the cancellation, he shall be deemed to comply with the maintenance order if he makes payments in accordance with any such order which was in force immediately before the cancellation.

(5B) On the cancellation of the registration of a maintenance order registered in a court of summary jurisdiction in Northern Ireland, any order –

(a) made in relation thereto by virtue of the powers conferred by section 18(3ZA) or section 22(1F) or (1J) of this Act, and
(b) requiring payment to the collecting officer in Northern Ireland (whether or not by any method of payment falling within Article 85(7) of the Magistrates' Court (Northern Ireland) Order 1981),

shall cease to have effect; but until the person liable to make payments under the maintenance order receives the prescribed notice of the cancellation, he shall be deemed to comply with the maintenance order if he makes payments in accordance with any such order which was in force immediately before the cancellation.

(6) Where, by virtue of an order made under subsection (2) of section nineteen of this Act, sums payable under a maintenance order registered in a court of summary jurisdiction in Northern Ireland are payable through the collecting officer of any court, that officer shall, if the person entitled to the payments so requests, make an application on behalf of that person for the cancellation of the registration.

Amendments—AJA 1977, s 3, Sch 3, para 9; CJJA 1982, s 36(6), Sch 12, para 1; MEA 1991, s 10, Sch 1, para 6; SI 1993/1577; AJA 1999, s 90, Sch 13, para 15; Courts Act 2003, Sch 8, para 90; CCA 2013, s 17, Sch 11.

'prescribed manner' (s 24(1),(3),(5))—For the High Court and the Family Court, see FPR 2010, rr 32.3–32.6.

25 Rules as to procedure of courts of summary jurisdiction

(1) *(repealed)*

(2) Rules made under section 23 of the Magistrates' Courts Act (Northern Ireland) 1964 may regulate the practice to be followed in courts of summary jurisdiction in Northern Ireland under this Part of this Act.

(2A) Without prejudice to the generality of the power to make rules under Article 13 of the Magistrates' Courts (Northern Ireland) Order 1981, for the purposes of giving effect to this Part of this Act such rules may make, in relation to any proceedings brought under or by virtue of this Part of this Act, any provision not covered by subsection (2) above which –

(a) falls within paragraph (2) of Article 165 of the Children (Northern Ireland) Order 1995, and

(b) may be made in relation to relevant proceedings under that Article.

(3) Rules of court made for the purposes of this Part of this Act may require that any order or other matter required under this Part of this Act to be registered in the family court or a court of summary jurisdiction in Northern Ireland shall be registered –

(a) in England, in accordance with the rules;

(b) *(repealed)*

Amendments—SI 1977/2158; Judicature (Northern Ireland) Act 1978, s 122(1), Sch 5, Pt II; MCA 1980, s 154, Sch 7, para 8; SI 1995/756; Courts Act 2003, Sch 8, para 91; CRA 2005, s 15(1), Sch 4, para 365(1); CCA 2013, s 17, Sch 11.

Duty to keep the register—The register is kept in pursuance of a duty imposed by MCR 1981, r 66.

PART III
GENERAL

26 Proof of declarations etc

(1) Any document purporting to be a declaration made under section 15 of this Act, or to be a certified copy, statutory declaration, affidavit, certificate, transcript or summary made for the purposes of this Act or of any rules made thereunder shall, unless the contrary is shown, be deemed without further proof to be the document which it purports to be, and to have been duly certified, made or signed by or before the person or persons by or before whom it purports to have been certified, made or signed.

(2) Paragraph 7 of the Second Schedule to the Emergency Laws (Miscellaneous Provisions) Act 1947 (which relates to the proof of affiliation orders and maintenance orders and of orders for the discharge or variation of such orders), shall apply to the registration of orders under Part II of this Act, and to the cancellation of such registration, as it applies to the variation of orders; and for the purposes of that paragraph –

(a) a maintenance order registered under the said Part II in a court of summary jurisdiction; and

(b) any proceedings under the said Part II relating to a maintenance order made by or registered in such a court, being a proceeding of which a memorandum is required to be entered in the register kept by the clerk of that court pursuant to section 22 of the Summary Jurisdiction Act 1879, shall be deemed to be an order made by that court.

****

Maintenance Orders Act 1958

ARRANGEMENT OF SECTIONS

PART I
REGISTRATION, ENFORCEMENT AND VARIATION OF CERTAIN MAINTENANCE ORDERS

Section		Page
1	Application of Part I	1074
2	Registration of orders	1075
2A	No interest on sums recoverable under registered orders	1076
3	Enforcement of registered orders	1076
4	Variation of orders registered in magistrates' courts	1076
4A	Variation etc of orders registered in the family court	1077
5	Cancellation of registration	1077

PART III
MISCELLANEOUS AND SUPPLEMENTAL

Miscellaneous

17	Prohibition of committal more than once in respect of same arrears	1078

Supplemental

20	Repeat applications to enforce payment of maintenance arrears	1079
21	Interpretation etc	1079

PART I
REGISTRATION, ENFORCEMENT AND VARIATION OF CERTAIN MAINTENANCE ORDERS

1 Application of Part I

(1) The provisions of this Part of this Act shall have effect for the purpose of enabling maintenance orders to which this Part of this Act applies be registered in the family court and, subject to those provisions, while so registered to be enforced in like manner as an order made by the family court and to be varied by that court.

(1A) In the following provisions of this Act 'maintenance order' means any order, decision, settlement, arrangement or instrument specified in Schedule 8 to the Administration of Justice Act 1970.

(2) For the purposes of subsection (1) above, a maintenance order made by a court in Scotland or Northern Ireland and registered in the High Court under Part II of the Maintenance Orders Act 1950 shall be deemed to have been made by the High Court.

(2A) This Part of this Act applies –

(a) to maintenance orders made by the High Court, other than orders registered in Scotland or Northern Ireland under Part II of the Maintenance Orders Act 1950, and

(b) to maintenance orders made by a court in Scotland or Northern Ireland and registered in the High Court under Part II of the Maintenance Orders Act 1950.

(3) Without prejudice to the provisions of section 21 of this Act, in this Part of this Act, unless the context otherwise requires, the following expressions have the following meanings –

'High Court order' means an order made by the High Court;

'order' means a maintenance order to which this Part of this Act applies;

'original court' and 'court of registration', in relation to an order mean the court by which the order was made or, as the case may be, the court in which the order is registered;

'registered' means registered in accordance with the provisions of this Part of this Act, and 'registration' shall be construed accordingly;

and for the purposes of this Part of this Act an order for the payment by the defendant of any costs incurred in proceedings relating to a maintenance order, being an order for the payment of costs made while the maintenance order is not registered, shall be deemed to form part of that maintenance order.

(4)–(6) *(repealed)*

Amendments—AJA 1970, s 27(3); MO(RE)A 1972, s 22(1), Sch, para 4; AJA 1977, s 3, Sch 3, para 1; CJJA 1982, s 15(4), Sch 12, para 3; SI 2001/3929; SI 2007/1655; SI 2011/1484; SI 2012/2814; CCA 2013, s 17, Sch 10.

Defined terms—'costs': s 21(4); 'defendant', 'England': s 21(1).

2 Registration of orders

(1) A person entitled to receive payments under a High Court order may apply to the High Court for registration of the order in the family court, and the High Court may, if it thinks fit, grant the application.

(2) Where an application for the registration of such an order is granted –

(a) no proceedings shall be begun, and no writ, warrant or other process shall be issued, for the enforcement of the order before the registration of the order or the expiration of the prescribed period from the grant of the application, whichever first occurs; and

(b) the High Court shall, on being satisfied within the period aforesaid by the person who made the application that no such proceedings or process begun or issued before the grant of the application remain pending or in force, cause a certified copy of the order to be sent to the family court;

but if at the expiration of the period aforesaid the High Court has not been so satisfied, the grant of the application shall become void.

(3)–(4) *(repealed)*

(5) An officer of the family court who receives a certified copy of an order sent to him under this section shall cause the order to be registered in that court.

(6) *(repealed)*

(6ZA) Where a High Court order is registered under this Part of this Act in the family court, then –

(a) if a means of payment order (within the meaning of section 1(7) of the Maintenance Enforcement Act 1991) has effect in relation to the order in question, it shall continue to have effect after registration.

(b) *(repealed)*

(6ZB) *(repealed)*

(6ZC) Where by virtue of the provisions of this section payments under an order cease to be or become payable to the family court, the person liable to make the payments shall, until he is given the prescribed notice to that effect, be deemed to comply with the order if he makes payments in accordance with the order and any order under subsection (6ZA)(b) of this section of which he has received such notice.

(6A) In this section –

'High Court order' includes a maintenance order deemed to be made by the High Court by virtue of section 1(2) above.

…

(7) In this section 'certified copy' in relation to an order of a court means a copy certified by the proper officer of the court to be a true copy of the order or of the official record thereof.

Amendments—AJA 1977, s 3, Sch 3, para 2; CJJA 1982, s 37(1), Sch 11, para 2; MEA 1991, s 10, Sch 1, para 7; AJA 1999, s 90, Sch 13, para 26, Sch 15; Courts Act 2003, Sch 8, para 98; CCA 2013, s 17, Sch 10.

Defined terms—'certified copy': s 2(7); 'county court order': s 1(3); 'defendant': s 21(1); 'High Court order': s 1(3); 'original court': s 1(3); 'person entitled to receive payments': s 21(2).

'The officer or clerk ... shall' (s 2(5))—If the original court has granted the application, the recipient court cannot decline to effect the registration.

'prescribed period' (s 2(2))—The prescribed period is 14 days (FPR 2010, r 32.14).

'person entitled to receive payments' (s 2(3))—Although this expression includes a court collecting officer, he or she is prevented from applying for registration except in accordance with the provisions of s 20.

'standing order, etc' (s 2(6)(a))—This does not include payment by direct debit.

2A No interest on sums recoverable under registered orders

(1)–(4) *(revoked)*

(5) Sums payable under registered orders shall not carry interest.

Amendments—Inserted by CJJA 1982, s 37(1), Sch 11, para 6; CCA 2013, s 17, Sch 10.

Defined terms—'certified copy': s 2(7); 'registered': s 1(3).

3 Enforcement of registered orders

(1) Subject to the provisions of section 2A of this Act and this section, a registered order shall be enforceable in all respects as it if had been made by the court of registration and as if that court had had jurisdiction to make it; and proceedings for or with respect to the enforcement of a registered order may be taken accordingly.

(2)–(2B) *(revoked)*

(3) Where an order remains or becomes registered after the discharge of the order, no proceedings shall be taken by virtue of that registration except in respect of arrears which were due under the order at the time of the discharge and have not been remitted.

(3A) *(revoked)*

(4) Except as provided by this section, no proceedings shall be taken for or with respect to the enforcement of a registered order.

Amendments—CJJA 1982, Sch 11; MFPA 1984, Sch 1; FLRA 1987, Sch 2; MEA 1991, s 10, Sch 1, para 8; Statute Law (Repeals) Act 1993; AJA 1999, s 90, Sch 13, para 27; Courts Act 2003, Sch 8, para 99; CCA 2013, s 17, Sch 10.

Defined terms—'court of registration', 'registered': s 1(3).

'shall be enforceable' (s 3(1))—For enforcement, see MCA 1980, ss 76 and 93.

4 Variation of orders registered in magistrates' courts

(1) The provisions of this section shall have effect with respect to the variation of High Court orders registered in the family court, and references in this section to registered orders shall be construed accordingly.

(2) Subject to the following provisions of this section –

(a) the family court may exercise the same jurisdiction to vary any rate of payments specified by a registered order (other than jurisdiction in a case where a party to the order is not present in England when the application for variation is made) as is exercisable, apart from this subsection, by the High Court; and

(b) a rate of payments specified by a registered order shall not be varied except by the family court.

(2A)–(3) *(repealed)*

(4) If an application is made by virtue of subsection (2) of this section for the variation of a rate of payments specified by a registered order and it appears to the family court that it is for any reason appropriate to remit the application to the High Court, the family court shall so remit the application, and the High Court shall thereupon deal with the application as if the order were not registered.

(5) Nothing in subsection (2) of this section shall affect the jurisdiction of the High Court to vary a rate of payments specified by a registered order if an application for the variation of that rate is made to that court –

- (a) in proceedings for a variation of provisions of the order which do not specify a rate of payments; or
- (b) at a time when a party to the order is not present in England.

(5A), (5B) *(repealed)*

(6) No application for any variation of a registered order shall be made to any court while proceedings for any variation of the order are pending in any other court.

(6A) Although such an order as is mentioned in this subsection may be varied under section 1 of the Maintenance Enforcement Act 1991 as applied by section 4A(2) of this Act, no application for any other variation in respect of a registered order shall be made to the family court in respect of an order made by the Court of Session or the High Court in Northern Ireland and registered in the family court in accordance with the provisions of this Part of this Act by virtue of sections 1(2) and 2(6A) above.

(6B) No application for any variation of a registered order shall be made to the family court in respect of an order for periodical or other payments made under Part III of the Matrimonial and Family Proceedings Act 1984 or under Schedule 7 to the Civil Partnership Act 2004.

(7) *(repealed)*

Amendments—AJA 1970, s 48, Sch 11; AJA 1977, ss 3, 32, Schs 3, 5; MFPA 1984, s 46(1), Sch 1, para 5; MEA 1991, s 10, Sch 1, para 9; AJA 1999, s 90, Sch 13, para 28, Sch 15; CPA 2004, s 261(1), Sch 27, para 22; SI 2009/871; CCA 2013, s 17, Sch 10.

Defined terms—'court of registration': s 1(3); 'England': s 21(1); 'original court', 'registered': s 1(3).

Scope—This section provides for the variation of the rate of payment under registered orders. The section does not allow the revocation or revival of registered orders, or the extension (after expiry) of a child periodical payments order where the child remains dependent. The section also allows the making of a means of payment order if satisfied that payment has not been made in accordance with the order. See FPR 2010, r 32.19.

Variation—In exercising the power of variation, the court must apply the same principles as the court which made the original order (*Miller v Miller* [1961] P 1, PDAD). Where the application is made a short time after the original order and there is no change of circumstances, the court should refuse the application (*Bromiley v Bromiley* [1987] 2 FLR 207, FD; *GN v MA (Child Maintenance: Children Act Sch 1)* [2017] 1 FLR 285, FD). The variation of the order may be backdated to the date of complaint (*Moon v Moon* (1980) 1 FLR 115, FD). The prohibition on variation in s 4(2) is subject to the exceptions contained in s 4(5).

4A Variation etc of orders registered in the family court

(1) *(repealed)*

(2) The family court may exercise the same powers in relation to a registered order as are exercisable by the family court under section 1 of the Maintenance Enforcement Act 1991 in relation to a qualifying periodical maintenance order (within the meaning of that section) which has been made by the family court, including the power under subsection (7) of that section to revoke, suspend, revive or vary –

- (a) *(repealed)*
- (b) any means of payment order (within the meaning of section 1(7) of that Act of 1991) made by virtue of the provisions of this section.

Amendments—Inserted by MEA 1991, s 10, Sch 1, para 10. Amended by SI 2011/1484; CCA 2013, s 17, Sch 10.

Defined terms—'registered': s 1(3).

5 Cancellation of registration

(1) If a person entitled to receive payments under a registered order desires the registration to be cancelled, he may give notice under this section.

(2) Where the original court varies or discharges an order registered in the family court, the original court may, if it thinks fit, give notice under this section.

(3) *(repealed)*

(4) Notice under this section shall be given to the court of registration; and where such notice is given –

(a) no proceedings for the enforcement of the registered order shall be begun before the cancellation of the registration and no writ, warrant or other process for the enforcement thereof shall be issued in consequence of any such proceedings begun before the giving of the notice; and

(b) *(repealed)*

(c) the court of registration shall cancel the registration on being satisfied in the prescribed manner –

(i) that no process for the enforcement of the registered order issued before the giving of the notice remains in force; and

(ii) in the case of an order registered in the family court, that no proceedings for the variation of the order are pending in the family court.

(4A) For the purposes of a notice under subsection (2) or (3) above –

'court of registration' includes any court in which an order is registered under Part II of the Maintenance Orders Act 1950, and

'registration' includes registration under that Act.

(5) On the cancellation of the registration of a High Court order –

(a) any order which requires payments under the order in question to be made by any method of payment falling within section 1(5) of the Maintenance Enforcement Act 1991 (standing order, etc), other than an order which requires payments to be made to the family court, is to continue to have effect, and

(b) any order which requires payments under the order in question to be made to the family court (whether or not by any method of payment falling within section 1(5) of the Maintenance Enforcement Act 1991) is to cease to have effect;

but, in a case falling within paragraph (b) of this subsection, until the defendant receives the prescribed notice of the cancellation he shall be deemed to comply with the High Court order if he makes payment in accordance with any such order as is referred to in paragraph (b) of this subsection which was in force immediately before the cancellation and of which he has notice.

(6) *(repealed)*

(7) In subsection (5) of this section 'High Court order' shall be construed in accordance with section 2(6A) of this Act.

Amendments—AJA 1977, s 3, Sch 3, para 4; MEA 1991, s 10, Sch 1, para 11; AJA 1999, s 90, Sch 13, para 29, Sch 15; Courts Act 2003, Sch 8, para 101; CCA 2013, s 17, Sch 10.

Defined terms—'court of registration': ss 1(3), 5(4A); 'defendant', 'original court': s 21(1); 'person entitled to receive payments': s 21(2).

****

PART III
MISCELLANEOUS AND SUPPLEMENTAL

Miscellaneous

17 Prohibition of committal more than once in respect of same arrears

Where a defendant has been imprisoned or otherwise detained under an order or warrant of commitment issued in respect of his failure to pay a sum due under a maintenance order, then, notwithstanding anything in this Act, no such order or warrant (other than a warrant of which the issue has been postponed under paragraph (ii) of subsection (5) of the next following section) shall thereafter be issued in respect of that sum or any part thereof.

Defined terms—'defendant': s 21(1).

****

Supplemental

20 Repeat applications to enforce payment of maintenance arrears

(1)–(7) *(repealed)*

(8) For the avoidance of doubt it is hereby declared that an application may be made to enforce payment of a sum due and unpaid under a maintenance order notwithstanding that a previous application has been made in respect of that sum or a part thereof and whether or not an order was made in pursuance of the previous application.

Amendments—AEA 1971, Sch 5; MCA 1980, s 154, Sch 9; AJA 1999, s 90, Sch 13, para 31; Courts Act 2003, Sch 8, para 103; CCA 2013, s 17, Sch 10.

21 Interpretation etc

(1) In this Act, unless the context otherwise requires, the following expressions have the following meanings –

…

'defendant', in relation to a maintenance order or a related attachment of earnings order, means the person liable to make payments under the maintenance order;

'England' includes Wales;

'prescribed' means prescribed by rules of court.

(2) Any reference in this Act to a person entitled to receive payments under a maintenance order is a reference to a person entitled to receive such payments either directly or through another person or for transmission to another person.

(3) Any reference in this Act to proceedings relating to an order includes a reference to proceedings in which the order may be made.

(4) Any reference in this Act to costs incurred in proceedings relating to a maintenance order shall be construed, in the case of a maintenance order made by the High Court, as a reference to such costs as are included in an order for costs relating solely to that maintenance order.

(5) *(repealed)*

(6) Any reference in this Act to any enactment is a reference to that enactment as amended by or under any subsequent enactment.

Amendments—AJA 1970, s 54(3), Sch 11; MCA 1980, s 154, Sch 7, para 24; FLRA 1987, s 33(4), Sch 4; AJA 1999, s 76, Sch 10, para 22, Sch 15; Courts Act 2003, Sch 8, para 104; CCA 2013, s 17, Sch 10.

****

Maintenance Orders (Facilities for Enforcement) Act 1920

ARRANGEMENT OF SECTIONS

Section		Page
1	Enforcement in England and Ireland of maintenance orders made in His Majesty's dominions outside the United Kingdom	1080
2	Transmission of maintenance orders made in England or Ireland	1080
3	Power to make provisional orders of maintenance against persons resident in His Majesty's dominions outside the United Kingdom	1081
4	Power of court of summary jurisdiction to confirm maintenance order made out of the United Kingdom	1082
4A	Variation and revocation of maintenance orders	1083
5	Power of Lord Chancellor to make regulations for facilitating communications between courts	1084
6	Mode of enforcing orders	1084

PART II

7	Application of Summary Jurisdiction Acts	1084
8	Proof of documents signed by officers of court	1084
9	Depositions to be evidence	1084
10	Interpretation	1085
12	Extent of Act	1085

1 Enforcement in England and Ireland of maintenance orders made in His Majesty's dominions outside the United Kingdom

(1) Where a maintenance order has, whether before or after the passing of this Act, been made against any person by any court in any part of His Majesty's dominions outside the United Kingdom to which this Act extends, and a certified copy of the order has been transmitted by the governor of that part of His Majesty's dominions to the Lord Chancellor, the Lord Chancellor shall send a copy of the order to the prescribed officer of a court in England or Ireland for registration; and on receipt thereof the order shall be registered in the prescribed manner, and shall, from the date of such registration, be of the same force and effect, and, subject to the provisions of this Act, all proceedings may be taken on such order as if it had been an order originally obtained in the court in which it is so registered, and that court shall have power to enforce the order accordingly.

(2) The Court in which an order is to be so registered as aforesaid shall, if the court by which the order was made was a court of superior jurisdiction, be the Family Division of the High Court, or in Ireland the King's Bench Division (Matrimonial) of the High Court of Justice in Ireland, and, if the court was not a court of superior jurisdiction, be the family court or, in Northern Ireland, a court of summary jurisdiction.

Amendments—AJA 1970, s 1(6), Sch 2, para 2; SI 1992/709; CCA 2013, s 17, Sch 11.

Defined terms—'certified copy', 'maintenance order': s 10.

Areas to which the Act extends—The Act remains in force only for Commonwealth countries that are not designated as reciprocating countries under MO(RE)A 1972. Although the 1972 Act provides for the repeal of the whole of this Act, that provision (s 22(2) of the 1972 Act) has been brought into force only as regards such designated countries. This Act currently applies to:

(a) *Africa* Botswana, Lesotho, Malawi, Mauritius, Nigeria, Seychelles, Sierra Leone, Swaziland, The Gambia, Uganda, Zambia, Zanzibar.
(b) *America* Antigua, Bahamas, Belize, Cayman Islands, Dominica, Grenada, Guyana, Jamaica, Montserrat, St Christopher and Nevis, St Lucia, St Vincent, Trinidad and Tobago, Virgin Islands, Yukon Territory and Prince Edward Island.
(c) *Asia* Malaysia, Sri Lanka.
(d) *Australasia* Solomon Islands, Kiribati, Tuvalu.
(e) *Europe* Cyprus, Guernsey.

See also s 12.
The REMO Unit maintains a list of countries with reciprocal arrangements at *www.gov.uk/government/uploads/system/uploads/attachment_data/file/489224/remo-countries-list.pdf*.

'shall be registered' (s 1(1))—For procedure in the High Court and the Family Court, see FPR 2010, rr 34.1–34.11. Registration is an administrative and not a judicial act, and the payer cannot object to or appeal against registration (*Pilcher v Pilcher* [1955] P 318, PDAD).

Date from which order takes effect—An order registered under this section takes effect from the date specified in the original order or from the date of the original order. Contrast the position for the confirmation of provisional orders under s 4.

'power to enforce' (s 1(1))—This does not include the power to vary or discharge the order (see *Pilcher v Pilcher* (above) and *R v Rose ex parte McGibbon* (1959) 123 JP 374, QBD).

2 Transmission of maintenance orders made in England or Ireland

Where a court in England or Ireland has, whether before or after the commencement of this Act, made a maintenance order against any person, and it is proved to that court that the person against whom the order was made is resident in some part of His Majesty's dominions outside the United Kingdom to which this Act extends, the court shall send to the Lord Chancellor for transmission to the governor of that part of His Majesty's dominions a certified copy of the order.

Amendments—SI 1992/709.

Defined terms—'certified copy', 'maintenance order': s 10.

3 Power to make provisional orders of maintenance against persons resident in His Majesty's dominions outside the United Kingdom

(1) Where an application is made to the family court, or in Northern Ireland to a court of summary jurisdiction, for a maintenance order against any person, and it is proved that that person is resident in a part of His Majesty's dominions outside the United Kingdom to which this Act extends, the court may, in the absence of that person, if after hearing the evidence it is satisfied of the justice of the application, make any such order as it might have made if that person had been habitually resident in England and Wales, had received reasonable notice of the date of the hearing of the application and had failed to appear at the hearing, but in such case the order shall be provisional only, and shall have no effect unless and until confirmed by a competent court in such part of His Majesty's dominions as aforesaid.

(2) The evidence of any witness who is examined on any such application shall be put into writing, and such deposition shall be read over to and signed by him.

(3) Where such an order is made, the court shall send to the Lord Chancellor for transmission to the governor of the part of His Majesty's dominions in which the person against whom the order is made is alleged to reside the depositions so taken and a certified copy of the order, together with a statement of the grounds on which the making of the order might have been opposed if the person against whom the order is made had been habitually resident in England and Wales, had received reasonable notice of the date of the hearing and had appeared at the hearing, and such information as the court possesses for facilitating the identification of that person, and ascertaining his whereabouts.

(4) Where any such provisional order has come before a court in a part of His Majesty's dominions outside the United Kingdom to which this Act extends for confirmation, and the order has by that court been remitted to the court which made the order for the purpose of taking further evidence, that court or, in Northern Ireland, any other court of summary jurisdiction shall, after the prescribed notice, proceed to take the evidence in like manner and subject to the like conditions as the evidence in support of the original application.

If upon the hearing of such evidence it appears to the court that the order ought not to have been made, the court may revoke the order, but in any other case the depositions shall be sent to the Lord Chancellor and dealt with in like manner as the original depositions.

(5) The confirmation of an order made under this section shall not affect any power of the family court, or a court of summary jurisdiction in Northern Ireland, to vary or revoke that order:

Provided that on the making of a varying or revoking order the court shall send a certified copy thereof to the Lord Chancellor for transmission to the governor of the part of His Majesty's dominions in which the original order was confirmed, and that in the case of an order varying the original order the order shall not have any effect unless and until confirmed in like manner as the original order.

(6) The applicant shall have the same right of appeal, if any, against a refusal to make a provisional order as he would have had against a refusal to make the order had the person against whom the order is sought to be made been habitually resident in England and Wales and received reasonable notice of the date of the hearing of the application.

(7) *(repealed)*

(8) In this section 'revoke' includes discharge.

Amendments—DPMCA 1978, s 89(2), Sch 2, para 2; Justices of the Peace Act 1979, s 71, Sch 2, para 1; MO(RE)A 1992, s 1, Sch 1, para 1; SI 1992/709; Justices of the Peace Act 1997, s 73(2), Sch 5, para 2; AJA 1999, s 106, Sch 15; Courts Act 2003, s 109(1), Sch 8, para 68; SI 2012/2814; CCA 2013, s 17, Sch 11.

'the order shall be provisional only' (s 3(1))—Liability to make payments cannot precede the date of registration.

PART II

'prescribed notice' (s 3(4))—The notice should specify the further evidence required and the date, time and place fixed for taking the evidence. The notice should be sent by the clerk to the person who applied for the provisional order.

4 Power of court of summary jurisdiction to confirm maintenance order made out of the United Kingdom

(1) Where a maintenance order has been made by a court in a part of His Majesty's dominions outside the United Kingdom to which this Act extends, and the order is provisional only and has no effect unless and until confirmed by the family court or by a court of summary jurisdiction in Ireland, and a certified copy of the order, together with the depositions of witnesses and a statement of the grounds on which the order might have been opposed has been transmitted to the Lord Chancellor, and it appears to the Lord Chancellor that the person against whom the order was made is resident in England or Ireland, the Lord Chancellor may send the said documents to the family court if it appears to the Lord Chancellor that the person is resident in England and Wales or to the prescribed officer of a court of summary jurisdiction in Northern Ireland if it appears to the Lord Chancellor that the person is resident in Northern Ireland, with a requisition that a notice be served on the person informing him that he may attend a hearing at the time and place specified in the notice to show cause why that order should not be confirmed, and upon receipt of such documents and requisition the court shall cause such a notice to be served upon such a person.

(2) A notice required to be served under this section may be served by post.

(3) At the hearing it shall be open to the person on whom the notice was served to oppose the confirmation of the order on any grounds on which he might have opposed the making of the order in the original proceedings had he been a party to them, but on no other grounds, and the certificate from the court which made the provisional order stating the grounds on which the making of the order might have been opposed if the person against whom the order was made had been a party to the proceedings shall be conclusive evidence that those grounds are grounds on which objection may be taken.

(4) If at the hearing the person served with the notice does not appear or, on appearing, fails to satisfy the court that the order ought not to be confirmed, the court may confirm the order either without modification or with such modifications as to the court after hearing the evidence may seem just.

(5) If the person served with the notice appears at the hearing and satisfies the court that for the purpose of establishing any grounds on which he opposes the confirmation of the order it is necessary to remit the case to the court which made the provisional order for the taking of any further evidence, the court may so remit the case and adjourn the proceedings for the purpose.

(5A) Where the family court confirms a provisional order under this section, it may at the same time exercise one of its powers under subsection (5B).

(5B) The powers of the court are –

(a) the power to order that payments under the order be made directly to the family court;

(b) the power to order that payments under the order be made to the family court by such method of payment falling within section 1(5) of the Maintenance Enforcement Act 1991 (standing order, etc) as may be specified;

(c) the power to make an attachment of earnings order under the Attachment of Earnings Act 1971 to secure payments under the order.

(5C) In deciding whether to exercise any of its powers under subsection (5B), the court shall have regard to any representations made by the person liable to make payments under the order.

(5D) Subsection (6) of section 1 of the Maintenance Enforcement Act 1991 (power of court to require debtor to open account) shall apply for the purposes of subsection (5B) as it applies for the purposes of that section but as if for paragraph (a) there were substituted –

'(a) the court proposes to exercise its power under paragraph (b) of section 4(5B) of the Maintenance Orders (Facilities for Enforcement) Act 1920, and'.

(6) Where a provisional order has been confirmed under this section, it may be varied or revoked in like manner as if it had originally been made by the confirming court.

(6A) *(repealed)*

(6B) Where on an application for variation or revocation the confirming court is satisfied that it is necessary to remit the case to the court which made the order for the purpose of taking any further evidence, the court may so remit the case and adjourn the proceedings for the purpose.

(7) Where an order has been so confirmed the person bound thereby shall have the same right of appeal, if any, against the confirmation of the order as he would have had against the making of the order had the order been an order made by the court confirming the order.

Amendments—MEA 1991, s 10, Sch 1, para 1; MO(RE)A 1992, s 1, Sch 1, para 2; SI 1992/709; AJA 1999, s 90, Sch 13, para 7, Sch 15; Courts Act 2003, s 109(1), Sch 8, para 69; CCA 2013, s 17, Sch 11.

Scope—If the relevant law of the foreign court permits the making of an order for custody and maintenance, this may also be confirmed under the Act.

Defences that may be raised (s 4(3))—Although the certificate is said to be conclusive as to the grounds of objection which may be taken, other defences have been allowed; in *Harris v Harris* 1949] WN 290, PDAD, a challenge on the grounds of want of jurisdiction was allowed (see also *Re Wheat* [1932] 2 KB 716).

Conversion to sterling—The order, on confirmation, should be converted to sterling. The rate of exchange applicable on the date of registration will continue to apply thereafter.

4A Variation and revocation of maintenance orders

(1) This section applies to –

(a) any maintenance order made by virtue of section 3 of this Act which has been confirmed as mentioned in that section; and

(b) any maintenance order which has been confirmed under section 4 of this Act.

(2) Where the respondent to an application for the variation or revocation of a maintenance order to which this section applies is residing in a part of Her Majesty's dominions outside the United Kingdom to which this Act extends, the family court shall have jurisdiction to hear the application (where it would not have such jurisdiction apart from this subsection) if that court would have had jurisdiction to hear it had the respondent been habitually resident in England and Wales.

(3) Where the respondent to an application for the variation or revocation of a maintenance order to which this section applies is residing in a part of Her Majesty's dominions outside the United Kingdom to which this Act extends, a court of summary jurisdiction in Northern Ireland shall have jurisdiction to hear the application (where it would not have such jurisdiction apart from this subsection) if that court would have had jurisdiction to hear it had the respondent been habitually resident in Northern Ireland.

(4) Where –

(a) the respondent to an application for the variation or revocation of a maintenance order to which this section applies does not appear at the time and place appointed for the hearing of the application by the family court, and

(b) the court is satisfied that the respondent is residing in a part of Her Majesty's dominions outside the United Kingdom to which this Act extends,

the court may proceed to hear and determine the application at the time and place appointed for the hearing or for any adjourned hearing in like manner as if the respondent had appeared at that time and place.

(5) Subsection (4) shall apply to Northern Ireland with the following modifications –

(a), (b) *(repealed)*

(c) for the words 'the family court' there shall be substituted 'a court of summary jurisdiction in Northern Ireland'.

(6) In this section 'revocation' includes 'discharge'.

Amendments—Inserted by MO(RE)A 1992, s 1, Sch 1, para 3. Amended by SI 1995/755; SI 2012/2814; CCA 2013, s 17, Sch 11.

PART II

5 Power of Lord Chancellor to make regulations for facilitating communications between courts

The Lord Chancellor may make regulations as to the manner in which a case can be remitted by a court authorised to confirm a provisional order to the court which made the provisional order, and generally for facilitating communications between such courts.

Amendments—SI 1992/709.

Regulations—No regulations have been made in exercise of this power.

6 Mode of enforcing orders

(1) A court in which an order has been registered under this Act or by which an order has been confirmed under this Act, and the officers of such court, shall take all such steps for enforcing the order as may be prescribed.

(2) Every such order registered in or confirmed by the family court is enforceable as if it were an order made by the family court and as if that court had had jurisdiction to make it.

(3) A warrant of distress, control or commitment issued by the family court or a court of summary jurisdiction for the purpose of enforcing any order so registered or confirmed may be executed in any part of the United Kingdom in the same manner as if the warrant had been originally issued or subsequently endorsed by a court of summary jurisdiction having jurisdiction in the place where the warrant is executed.

(4) For the purposes of its execution under subsection (3) in England and Wales, a warrant of distress has effect as a warrant of control.

(5) For the purposes of its execution under subsection (3) elsewhere than in England and Wales, a warrant of control has effect as a warrant of distress.

Amendments—MEA 1991, s 10, Sch 1, para 2; TCEA 2007, s 62(3), Sch 13, para 22; CCA 2013, s 17, Sch 11.

7 Application of Summary Jurisdiction Acts

(1) The Summary Jurisdiction Acts shall apply to proceedings before courts of summary jurisdiction under this Act in like manner as they apply to proceedings under those Acts.

(2) For the purpose of giving effect to this Act rules of court may make, in relation to any proceedings brought under or by virtue of this Act, any provision which –

(a) falls within subsection (2) of section 93 of the Children Act 1989, and

(b) may be made in relation to relevant proceedings under that section.

Amendments—Justices of the Peace Act 1949, s 46(2), Sch 7, Pt II; MO(RE)A 1992, s 1, Sch 1, para 4; Courts Act 2003, s 109(1), Sch 8, para 70.

8 Proof of documents signed by officers of court

Any documents purporting to be signed by a judge or officer of a court outside the United Kingdom shall, until the contrary is proved, be deemed to have been so signed without proof of the signature or judicial or official character of the person appearing to have signed it, and the officer of a court by whom a document is signed shall, until the contrary is proved, be deemed to have been the proper officer of the court to sign the document.

9 Depositions to be evidence

Depositions taken in a court in a part of His Majesty's dominions outside the United Kingdom to which this Act extends for the purposes of this Act, may be received in evidence in proceedings before courts of summary jurisdiction, or the family court, under this Act.

Amendments—CCA 2013, s 17, Sch 11.

10 Interpretation

For the purposes of this Act, the expression 'maintenance order' means an order other than an order of affiliation for the periodical payment of sums of money towards the maintenance of the wife or other dependants of the person against whom the order is made, and the expression 'dependants' means such persons as that person is, according to the law in force in the part of His Majesty's dominions in which the maintenance order was made, liable to maintain; the expression 'certified copy' in relation to an order of a court means a copy of the order certified by the proper officer of the court to be a true copy, and the expression 'prescribed' means prescribed by rules of court.

'rules of court'—The rules of court for the purposes of the Act are FPR 2010, rr 34.4–34.11.

****

12 Extent of Act

(1) Where His Majesty is satisfied that reciprocal provisions have been made by the legislature of any part of His Majesty's dominions outside the United Kingdom for the enforcement within that part of maintenance orders made by courts within England and Ireland, His Majesty may by Order in Council extend this Act to that part, and thereupon that part shall become a part of His Majesty's dominions to which this Act extends.

(2) His Majesty may by Order in Council extend this Act to any British protectorate and where so extended this Act shall apply as if any such protectorate was a party of His Majesty's dominions to which this Act extends.

'dominions to which this Act extends'—See **Areas to which the Act extends** under s 1.

****

Maintenance Orders (Reciprocal Enforcement) Act 1972

ARRANGEMENT OF SECTIONS

PART I
RECIPROCAL ENFORCEMENT OF MAINTENANCE ORDERS MADE IN UNITED KINGDOM OR RECIPROCATING COUNTRY

Section		Page
	Designation of reciprocating countries	
1	Orders in Council designating reciprocating countries	1087
	Orders made by courts in the United Kingdom	
2	Transmission of maintenance order made in United Kingdom for enforcement in reciprocating country	1088
3	Power of court to make provisional maintenance order against person residing in reciprocating country	1088
5	Variation and revocation of maintenance order made in United Kingdom	1089
	Orders made by courts in reciprocating countries	
6	Registration in United Kingdom court of maintenance order made in reciprocating country	1091
7	Confirmation by United Kingdom court of provisional maintenance order made in reciprocating country	1091
8	Enforcement of maintenance order registered in United Kingdom court	1093
9	Variation and revocation of maintenance order registered in United Kingdom court	1094
10	Cancellation of registration and transfer of order	1096

11 Steps to be taken by Lord Chancellor where payer under certain orders is not residing in the United Kingdom 1097

Appeals

12 Appeals 1097

Evidence

13 Admissibility of evidence given in reciprocating country 1098
14 Obtaining of evidence needed for purpose of certain proceedings 1098
15 Order etc made abroad need not be proved 1099

Supplemental

16 Payment of sums under orders made abroad: conversion of currency 1099
17 Proceedings in the family court in England and Wales or in magistrates' courts in Northern Ireland 1100
18 Rules of court 1101
20 Restriction on enforcement of arrears under maintenance order registered in Scotland 1101
21 Interpretation of Part I 1102

Amendments, repeals and transitional provisions

22 Amendments and repeals 1103
23 Maintenance order registered in High Court under the Maintenance Orders etc Act 1920 1103
24 Application of Part I to certain orders and proceedings under the Maintenance Orders etc Act 1920 1104

PART II

RECIPROCAL ENFORCEMENT OF CLAIMS FOR THE RECOVERY OF MAINTENANCE

Convention countries

25 Convention countries 1104

Application by person in the United Kingdom for recovery etc of maintenance in Convention country

26 Application by person in United Kingdom for recovery etc of maintenance in Convention country 1105

Application by person in Convention country for recovery of maintenance in England, Wales or Northern Ireland

27A Applications for recovery of maintenance in England and Wales 1105
27B Sending application to the family court 1106
27C Applications to which section 27A applies: general 1106
28 Applications by spouses under the Domestic Proceedings and Magistrates' Courts Act 1978 1107
28A Applications by former spouses under the Domestic Proceedings and Magistrates' Courts Act 1978 1107
28C Applications for recovery of maintenance in Northern Ireland 1108
28D Sending application to the appropriate magistrates' court 1108
28E Applications to which section 28C applies: general 1109

Transfer, enforcement, variation and revocation of registered orders

32 Transfer of orders 1109
33 Enforcement of orders 1110
34 Variation and revocation of orders 1111
34A Variation of orders by the family court in England and Wales 1111
34B Variation of orders by courts of summary jurisdiction in Northern Ireland 1112
35 Further provisions with respect to variation etc of orders by the family court in England and Wales 1113
35A Further provisions with respect to variation etc of orders by magistrates' courts in Northern Ireland 1114

Supplemental

36	Admissibility of evidence given in Convention country	1114
37	Obtaining of evidence for purpose of proceedings in United Kingdom court	1115
38	Taking of evidence at request of court in Convention country	1116
38A	Rules of court	1116
39	Interpretation of Part II	1117

PART III

MISCELLANEOUS AND SUPPLEMENTAL

Further provisions relating to enforcement of maintenance orders and to applications for recovery of maintenance

40	Power to apply Act to maintenance orders and applications for recovery of maintenance made in certain countries	1117

Provisions with respect to certain orders of magistrates' courts

42	Provisional order for maintenance of party to marriage made by court to cease to have effect on remarriage of party	1118

Supplemental provisions

44	Exclusion of certain enactments relating to evidence	1118
47	Interpretation: general	1118

Modifications—In relation to Hague Convention countries, to which the Maintenance Regulation (EC) No 4/2009 does not apply, the provisions of this Act are excepted, adapted and modified as summarised in FPR PD34A.

PART I

RECIPROCAL ENFORCEMENT OF MAINTENANCE ORDERS MADE IN UNITED KINGDOM OR RECIPROCATING COUNTRY

Designation of reciprocating countries

1 Orders in Council designating reciprocating countries

(1) Her Majesty, if satisfied that, in the event of the benefits conferred by this Part of this Act being applied to, or to particular classes of, maintenance orders made by the courts of any country or territory outside the United Kingdom, similar benefits will in that country or territory be applied to, or to those classes of, maintenance orders made by the courts of the United Kingdom, may by Order in Council designate that country or territory as a reciprocating country for the purposes of this Part of this Act; and, subject to subsection (2) below, in this Part of this Act 'reciprocating country' means a country or territory that is for the time being so designated.

(2) A country or territory may be designated under subsection (1) above as a reciprocating country either as regards maintenance orders generally, or as regards maintenance orders other than those of any specified class, or as regards maintenance orders of one or more specified classes only; and a country or territory which is for the time being so designated otherwise than as regards maintenance orders generally shall for the purposes of this Part of this Act be taken to be a reciprocating country only as regards maintenance orders of the class to which the designation extends.

Defined terms—'court', 'maintenance order': s 21(1); 'reciprocating country': s 1(1).

'may by Order in Council designate' (s 1(1))—The Reciprocal Enforcement of Maintenance Orders (Designation of Reciprocating Countries) Order 1974 has been made for this purpose. It is important to note that a country does not become a reciprocating country for the purposes of this Act merely by acceding to the 1956 UN Convention on the Recovery Abroad of Maintenance as, for example, the Ukraine did in 2006. It is necessary for the UK Government to make an Order under the Act designating the country in question. It is otherwise with the 2007 Hague Convention, which applies across the EU to states that have acceded to it.

Orders made by courts in the United Kingdom

2 Transmission of maintenance order made in United Kingdom for enforcement in reciprocating country

(1) Subject to subsection (2) below, where the payer under a maintenance order made, whether before or after the commencement of this Part of this Act, by a court in the United Kingdom is residing or has assets in a reciprocating country, the payee under the order may apply for the order to be sent to that country for enforcement.

(2) Subsection (1) above shall not have effect in relation to a provisional order or to an order made by virtue of a provision of Part II of this Act.

(3) Every application under this section shall be made in the prescribed manner to the prescribed officer of the court which made the maintenance order to which the application relates.

(4) If, on an application duly made under this section to the prescribed officer of a court in the United Kingdom, that officer is satisfied that the payer under the maintenance order to which the application relates is residing or has assets in a reciprocating country, the following documents, that is to say –

(a) a certified copy of the maintenance order;
(b) a certificate signed by that officer certifying that the order is enforceable in the United Kingdom;
(c) a certificate of arrears so signed;
(d) a statement giving such information as the officer possesses as to the whereabouts of the payer and the nature and location of his assets in that country;
(e) a statement giving such information as the officer possesses for facilitating the identification of the payer; and
(f) where available, a photograph of the payer;

shall be sent by that officer to the Lord Chancellor with a view to their being transmitted by the Lord Chancellor to the responsible authority in the reciprocating country if he is satisfied that the statement relating to the whereabouts of the payer and the nature and location of his assets in that country gives sufficient information to justify that being done.

(5) Nothing in this section shall be taken as affecting any jurisdiction of a court in the United Kingdom with respect to a maintenance order to which this section applies, and any such order may be enforced, varied or revoked accordingly.

Amendments—CJJA 1982, s 37(1), Sch 11, para 9; SI 1992/709.

Defined terms—'certificate of arrears', 'certified copy', 'court', 'maintenance order', 'payee', 'payer', 'provisional order': s 21(1); 'reciprocating country': s 1(1).

'habitually resident' (s 3(1)(a))—The Act is amended to refer to habitual residence as part of the exercise of bringing the law into line with the Hague Convention 2007.

'prescribed manner' (s 2(3))—See FPR 2010, rr 34.14 and PD34A.

'prescribed officer' (s 2(3),(4))—See FPR 2010, r 34.2.

3 Power of court to make provisional maintenance order against person residing in reciprocating country

(1) Where an application is made to the family court for a maintenance order against a person residing in a reciprocating country and the court would have jurisdiction to determine the application under the Domestic Proceedings and Magistrates' Courts Act 1978 or the Children Act 1989 if that person –

(a) were habitually resident in England and Wales, and
(b) received reasonable notice of the date of the hearing of the application,

the court shall (subject to subsection (2) below) have jurisdiction to determine the application.

(2) A maintenance order made by virtue of this section shall be a provisional order.

(3) *(repealed)*

(4) No enactment (or provision made under an enactment) requiring or enabling –

(za) a court to transfer proceedings from the family court to the High Court,
(a) a court to transfer proceedings from a magistrates' court in Northern Ireland to a county court or the High Court of Justice in Northern Ireland, or
(b) a magistrates' court in Northern Ireland to refuse to make an order on an application on the ground that any matter in question is one that would be more conveniently dealt with by the High Court of Justice in Northern Ireland,

shall apply in relation to an application to which subsection (1) above applies.

(5) Where a court makes a maintenance order which is by virtue of this section a provisional order, the following documents, that is to say –

(a) a certified copy of the maintenance order;
(b) a document, authenticated in the prescribed manner, setting out or summarising the evidence given in the proceedings;
(c) a certificate signed by the prescribed officer of the court certifying that the grounds stated in the certificate are the grounds on which the making of the order might have been opposed by the payer under the order;
(d) a statement giving such information as was available to the court as to the whereabouts of the payer;
(e) a statement giving such information as the officer possesses for facilitating the identification of the payer, and
(f) where available, a photograph of the payer;

shall be sent by that officer to the Lord Chancellor with a view to their being transmitted by the Lord Chancellor to the responsible authority in the reciprocating country in which the payer is residing if he is satisfied that the statement relating to the whereabouts of the payer gives sufficient information to justify that being done.

(6) A maintenance order made by virtue of this section which has been confirmed by a competent court in a reciprocating country shall be treated for all purposes as if the court which made the order had made it in the form in which it was confirmed and as if the order had never been a provisional order, and subject to section 5 of this Act, any such order may be enforced, varied or revoked accordingly.

(7) In the application of this section to Northern Ireland –

(a) for subsection (1) there shall be substituted –

'(1) Where an application is made to a magistrates' court against a person residing in a reciprocating country and the court would have jurisdiction to determine the application under the Domestic Proceedings (Northern Ireland) Order 1980 or the Children (Northern Ireland) Order 1995 if that person –

(a) were habitually resident in Northern Ireland, and
(b) received reasonable notice of the date of the hearing of the application,

the court shall (subject to subsection (2) below) have jurisdiction to determine the application.';

(b) *(repealed)*

Amendments—FLRA 1987, s 33(4), Sch 4; MO(RE)A 1992, s 1, Sch 1, para 6; SI 1992/709; SI 1995/755; SI 2012/2814; CCA 2013, s 17, Sch 11.

Defined terms—'certified copy', 'court': s 21(1); 'jurisdiction': s 47(3); 'maintenance order', 'payer', 'provisional order': s 21(1); 'reciprocating country': s 1(1); 'responsible authority': s 21(1).

'prescribed manner' (s 3(5)(b))—See FPR 2010, r 34.15.

'prescribed officer' (s 3(5))—See FPR 2010, r 34.2.

****

5 Variation and revocation of maintenance order made in United Kingdom

(1) This section applies to a maintenance order a certified copy of which has been sent to a reciprocating country in pursuance of section 2 of this Act and to a maintenance order made by virtue of section 3 or 4 thereof which has been confirmed by a competent court in such a country.

(2) A court in the United Kingdom having power to vary a maintenance order to which this section applies shall have power to vary that order by a provisional order.

(3) Where the court hearing an application for the variation of a maintenance order to which this section applies proposes to vary it by increasing the rate of the payments under the order then, unless either –

(a) both the payer and the payee under the order appear in the proceedings, or
(b) the applicant appears and the appropriate process has been duly served on the other party,

the order varying the order shall be a provisional order.

(3A) *(repealed)*

(3B) Where paragraph (1) of Article 86 of the Magistrates' Courts (Northern Ireland) Order 1981 applies in relation to a maintenance order to which this section applies, that paragraph shall have effect as if for the words 'by order on complaint,' there were substituted 'on an application being made, by order'.

(4) Where a court in the United Kingdom makes a provisional order varying a maintenance order to which this section applies, the prescribed officer of the court shall send in the prescribed manner to the court in a reciprocating country having power to confirm the provisional order a certified copy of the provisional order together with a document, authenticated in the prescribed manner, setting out or summarising the evidence given in the proceedings.

(5) Where a certified copy of a provisional order made by a court in a reciprocating country, being an order varying or revoking a maintenance order, to which this section applies, together with a document, duly authenticated, setting out or summarising the evidence given in the proceedings in which the provisional order was made, is received by the court in the United Kingdom which made the maintenance order, that court may confirm or refuse to confirm the provisional order and, if that order is an order varying the maintenance order, confirm it either without alteration or with such alterations as it thinks reasonable.

(6) For the purpose of determining whether a provisional order should be confirmed under subsection (5) above, the court shall proceed as if an application for the variation or revocation, as the case may be, of the maintenance order in question, had been made to it.

(7) Where a maintenance order to which this section applies has been varied by an order (including a provisional order which has been confirmed) made by a court in the United Kingdom or by a competent court in a reciprocating country, the maintenance order shall, as, from the date on which under the provisions of the order the variation is to take effect, have effect as varied by that order and, where that order was a provisional order, as if that order had been made in the form in which it was confirmed, and as if it had never been a provisional order.

(8) Where a maintenance order to which this section applies has been revoked by an order made by a court in the United Kingdom or by a competent court in a reciprocating country, including a provisional order made by the last-mentioned court which has been confirmed by a court in the United Kingdom, the maintenance order shall, as from the date on which under the provisions of the order the revocation is to take effect, be deemed to have ceased to have effect except as respects any arrears due under the maintenance order at that date.

(9) Where before a maintenance order made by virtue of section 3 or 4 of this Act is confirmed a document, duly authenticated, setting out or summarising evidence taken in a reciprocating country for the purpose of proceedings relating to the confirmation of the order is received by the court in the United Kingdom which made the order, or that court, in compliance with a request made to it by a court in such a country, takes the evidence of a person residing in the United Kingdom for the purpose of such proceedings, the court in the United Kingdom which made the order shall consider that evidence and if, having done so, it appears to it that the order ought not to have been made –

(a) it shall, in such manner as may be prescribed, give to the person on whose application the maintenance order was made an opportunity to consider that evidence, to make representations with respect to it and to adduce further evidence; and

(b) after considering all the evidence and any representations made by that person, it may revoke the maintenance order.

(10) …

Amendments—DPMCA 1978, s 54; MO(RE)A 1992, s 1, Sch 1, para 7; SI 1995/755; CCA 2013, s 17, Sch 11.

Defined terms—'certified copy', 'court', 'maintenance order', 'payee', 'payer', 'provisional order': s 21(1); 'reciprocating country': s 1(1).

'prescribed officer' (s 5(4))—See FPR 2010, rr 34.2, 34.15.

'prescribed manner' (s 5(4))—See FPR 2010, rr 34.15, 34.18, 34.22.

'court may confirm or refuse to confirm' (s 5(5))—The discretion is as wide as if the application had been made to that court (*Horn v Horn* [1985] FLR 984, FD).

'prescribed' (s 5(9)(a))—See FPR 2010, r 34.17.

PART II

Orders made by courts in reciprocating countries

6 Registration in United Kingdom court of maintenance order made in reciprocating country

(1) This section applies to a maintenance order made, whether before or after the commencement of this Part of this Act, by a court in a reciprocating country, including such an order made by such a court which has been confirmed by a court in another reciprocating country but excluding a provisional order which has not been confirmed.

(2) Where a certified copy of an order to which this section applies is received by the Lord Chancellor from the responsible authority in a reciprocating country, and it appears to the Lord Chancellor that the payer under the order is residing or has assets in the United Kingdom, he shall send the copy of the order to the prescribed officer of the appropriate court.

(3) Where the prescribed officer of the appropriate court receives from the Lord Chancellor a certified copy of an order to which this section applies, he shall, subject to subsection (4) below, register the order in the prescribed manner in that court.

(4) Before registering an order under this section an officer of a court shall take such steps as he thinks fit for the purpose of ascertaining whether the payer under the order is residing or has assets within the jurisdiction of the court, and if after taking those steps he is satisfied that the payer is not residing and has no assets within the jurisdiction of the court he shall return the certified copy of the order to the Lord Chancellor with a statement giving such information as he possesses as to the whereabouts of the payer and the nature and location of his assets.

Amendments—CJJA 1982, s 37(1), Sch 11, para 10; SI 1992/709.

Defined terms—'appropriate court', 'certified copy', 'court', 'maintenance order', 'payer', 'provisional order': s 21(1); 'reciprocating country': s 1(1); 'responsible authority': s 21(1).

'prescribed officer' (s 6(2))—See FPR 2010, r 34.2.

'prescribed manner' (s 6(3))—See FPR 2010, r 34.3.

7 Confirmation by United Kingdom court of provisional maintenance order made in reciprocating country

(1) This section applies to a maintenance order made, whether before or after the commencement of this Part of this Act, by a court in a reciprocating country being a provisional order.

(2) Where a certified copy of an order to which this section applies together with –

(a) a document, duly authenticated, setting out or summarising the evidence given in the proceedings in which the order was made; and

(b) a statement of the grounds on which the making of the order might have been opposed by the payer under the order, is received by the Lord Chancellor from the responsible authority in a reciprocating country, and it appears to the Lord Chancellor that the payer under the order is residing in the United Kingdom, he shall send the copy of the order and documents which accompanied it to the prescribed officer of the appropriate court, and that court shall –

(i) if the payer under the order establishes any grounds on which he might have opposed the making of the order in the proceedings in which the order was made, refuse to confirm the order; and

(ii) in any other case, confirm the order either without alteration or with such alterations as it thinks reasonable.

(3) In any proceedings for the confirmation under this section of a provisional order the statement received from the court which made the order of the grounds on which the making of the order might have been opposed by the payer under the order shall be conclusive evidence that the payer might have opposed the making of the order on any of those grounds.

(4) For the purpose of determining whether a provisional order should be confirmed under this section a magistrates' court in Northern Ireland shall proceed as if an application for a maintenance order against the payer under the provisional order had been made to it.

(5) The prescribed officer of a court having power under this section to confirm a provisional order shall, if the court confirms the order, register the order in the prescribed manner in that court, and shall, if the court refuses to confirm the order, return the certified copy of the order and the documents which accompanied it to the Lord Chancellor.

(5A) Where the family court confirms a provisional order under this section, it may at the same time exercise one of its powers under subsection (5B) below.

(5B) The powers of the court are –

(a) the power to order that payments under the order be made directly to the court;

(b) the power to order that payments under the order be made to the court by such method of payment falling within section 1(5) of the Maintenance Enforcement Act 1991 (standing order, etc) as may be specified;

(c) the power to make an attachment of earnings order under the Attachment of Earnings Act 1971 to secure payments under the order.

(5C) In deciding whether to exercise any of its powers under subsection (5B) above, the court shall have regard to any representations made by the payer under the order.

(5D) Subsection (6) of section 1 of the Maintenance Enforcement Act 1991 (power of court to require debtor to open account) shall apply for the purposes of subsection (5B) above as it applies for the purposes of that section but as if for paragraph (a) there were substituted –

'(a) the court proposes to exercise its power under paragraph (b) of section 7(5B) of the Maintenance Orders (Reciprocal Enforcement) Act 1972, and'.

(5E) Where a court of summary jurisdiction in Northern Ireland confirms a provisional order under this section, it shall at the same time exercise one of its powers under subsection (5F) below.

(5F) The powers of the court are –

(a) the power to order that payments under the order be made directly to the collecting officer;

(b) the power to order that payments under the order be made to the collecting officer, by such method of payment falling within Article 85(7) of the Magistrates' Court (Northern Ireland) Order 1981 (standing order, etc) as may be specified;

(c) the power to make an attachment of earnings order under Part IX of the Order of 1981 to secure payments under the order;

and in this subsection 'collecting officer' means the officer mentioned in Article 85(4) of the Order of 1981.

(5G) In deciding which of the powers under subsection (5F) above it is to exercise, the court shall have regard to any representations made by the payer under the order.

(5H) Paragraph (5) of Article 85 of the Magistrates' Courts (Northern Ireland) Order 1981 (power of court to require debtor to open account) shall apply for the purposes of subsection (5F) above as it applies for the purposes of that Article but as if for sub-paragraph (a) there were substituted –

'(a) the court proposes to exercise its powers under paragraph (b) of section 7(5F) of the Maintenance Orders (Reciprocal Enforcement) Act 1972, and'.

(6) If notice of the proceedings for the confirmation of the provisional order cannot be duly served on the payer under that order the officer by whom the certified copy of the order was received shall return that copy and the documents which accompanied it to the Lord Chancellor with a statement giving such information as he possesses as to the whereabouts of the payer.

(7) …

(8) *(repealed)*

Amendments—MEA 1991, s 10, Sch 1, para 12; MO(RE)A 1992, s 1, Sch 1, para 8; SI 1992/709; SI 1993/1576; SI 1995/755; AJA 1999, s 90, Sch 13, para 72; Courts Act 2003, s 109(1), Sch 8, para 151; CCA 2013, s 17, Sch 11.

Defined terms—'court', 'maintenance order', 'payer', 'provisional order': s 21(1); 'reciprocating country': s 1(1); 'responsible authority': s 21(1).

'prescribed officer' (s 7(2),(5))—See FPR 2010, r 34.2.

Alteration of order (s 7(2)(ii))—The laws of the reciprocating country are to be applied to the making of the order (*Peagram v Peagram* [1926] 2 KB 165; *Harris v Harris* [1949] WN 290, PDAD).

'statement … shall be conclusive evidence' (s 7(3))—The statement of possible grounds of opposition received from the reciprocating country does not prevent other defences being raised (*Re Wheat* [1932] 2 KB 716; see also *Harris v Harris* (above), where the payer was permitted to raise the issue of jurisdiction).

'prescribed manner' (s 7(5))—See FPR 2010, r 34.3.

'standing order, etc' (s 7(5B)(b),(5E)(b))—The methods of payment available do not include power to order payment by direct debit.

8 Enforcement of maintenance order registered in United Kingdom court

(1) Subject to subsection (2) below, a registered order may be enforced in the United Kingdom as if it had been made by the registering court and as if that court had had jurisdiction to make it; and proceedings for or with respect to the enforcement of any such order may be taken accordingly.

(2) Subsection (1) above does not apply to an order which is for the time being registered in the High Court of Justice in Northern Ireland under Part II of the Maintenance and Affiliation Orders Act (Northern Ireland) 1966.

(3) Any person for the time being under an obligation to make payments in pursuance of an order registered in a court in Northern Ireland shall give notice of any change of address to the clerk of that court, and any person failing without reasonable excuse to give such a notice shall be liable on summary conviction to a fine not exceeding level 2 on the standard scale.

(3A)–(4B) *(repealed)*

(5) A magistrates' court in Northern Ireland by which an order is enforceable by virtue of this section, and the officers thereof, shall take all such steps for enforcing the order as may be prescribed.

(6) In any proceedings for or with respect to the enforcement of an order which is for the time being registered in any court under this Part of this Act a certificate of arrears sent to the prescribed officer of the court shall be evidence of the facts stated therein.

(7) Subject to subsection (8) below, sums of money payable under a registered order shall be payable in accordance with the order as from the date on which they are required to be paid under the provisions of the order.

(8) The court having power under section 7 of this Act to confirm a provisional order may, if it decides to confirm the order, direct that the sums of money payable under it shall be deemed to have been payable in accordance with the order as from the date on which they are required to be paid under the provisions of the order or such later date as it may specify; and subject to any such direction, a maintenance order registered under the said section 7 shall be treated as if it had been made in the form in which it was confirmed and as if it had never been a provisional order.

(9) …

(10) *(repealed)*

Amendments—DPMCA 1978, s 54; SI 1981/1675; Criminal Justice Act 1982, s 46; CJJA 1982, s 37(1), Sch 11, para 11; FLRA 1987, s 33(1), Sch 2, para 45; MEA 1991, s 10, Sch 1, para 13; AJA 1999, s 90, Sch 13, para 73; Courts Act 2003, Sch 8, para 152; CCA 2013, s 17, Sch 11; SI 2014/605.

Defined terms—'certificate of arrears', 'maintenance order', 'provisional order', 'registered order', 'registering court': s 21(1).

Application to Northern Ireland—Enforcement in Northern Ireland is effected under a modified Magistrates' Court (Northern Ireland) Order 1981. The provisions are similar to the powers outlined here but reference should be made to the Family Law (Northern Ireland) Order 1993.

'standing order, etc' (s 8(4A))—The methods of payment available do not include power to order payment by direct debit.

'prescribed' (s 8(5))—See FPR 2010, r 34.24.

'prescribed officer' (s 8(6))—See FPR 2010, r 34.2.

Payment of monies collected—Monies collected are to be sent to the court that made the order, except for the following countries and territories: Gibraltar, Barbados, Bermuda, Ghana, Kenya, Fiji, Hong Kong, Singapore, Turks and Caicos Islands, Tanzania (except for Zanzibar), Anguilla, Falkland Islands and dependencies, St Helena. In the case of these territories, monies are payable through the Crown Agents for Overseas Governments and Territories – FPR PD34A, para 8.1.

9 Variation and revocation of maintenance order registered in United Kingdom court

(1) Subject to the provisions of this section, the registering court –

(a) shall have the like power, on an application made by the payer or payee under a registered order, to vary or revoke the order as if it had been made by the registering court and as if that court had had jurisdiction to make it; and

(b) shall have power to vary or revoke a registered order by a provisional order.

(1ZA) *(repealed)*

(1ZB) Where the registering court is a court of summary jurisdiction in Northern Ireland, Article 86 of the Magistrates' Courts (Northern Ireland) Order 1981 (revocation, variation etc, of orders for periodical payment) shall have effect in relation to the registered order –

(za) as if in paragraph (1) for the words 'by order on complaint,' there were substituted 'on an application being made, by order';

(a) as if in paragraph (3) for the words 'sub-paragraphs (a) to (d) of Article 85(3)' there were substituted 'paragraph (3A)' and after that paragraph there were inserted –

'(3A) The powers of the court are –

(a) the power to order that payments under the order be made directly to the collecting officer;

(b) the power to order that payments under the order be made to the collecting officer by such method of payment falling within Article 85(7) (standing order, etc) as may be specified;

(c) the power to make an attachment of earnings order under Part IX to secure payments under the order.';

(b) as if in paragraph (4) for sub-paragraph (b) there were substituted –

'(b) payments under the order are required to be made to the collecting officer by any method of payment falling within Article 85(7) (standing order, etc)';

and as if after the words 'petty sessions' there were inserted 'for the petty sessions district for which the court which made the order acts';

(c) as if in paragraph (5) for the words 'to the collecting officer' there were substituted 'in accordance with sub-paragraph (a) of paragraph (3A)';

(d) as if in paragraph (7), sub-paragraph (c) and the word 'and' immediately preceding it were omitted;

(e) as if in paragraph (8) for the words 'sub-paragraphs (a) to (d) of Article 85(3)' there were substituted 'paragraph (3A)';

(f) as if for paragraphs (9) and (10) there were substituted the following paragraphs –

'(9) In deciding, for the purposes of paragraphs (3) and (8), which of the powers under paragraph (3A) it is to exercise, the court shall have regard to any representations made by the debtor.

(10) Paragraph (5) of Article 85 (power of court to require debtor to open account) shall apply for the purposes of paragraph (3A) as it applies for the purposes of that Article but as if for sub-paragraph (a) there were substituted –

"(a) the court proposes to exercise its powers under sub-paragraph (b) of Article 86(3A), and".'.

(2) The registering court shall not vary a registered order otherwise than by a provisional order unless –

(a) both the payer and the payee under the registered order are for the time being residing in the United Kingdom; or
(b) the application is made by the payee under the registered order; or
(c) the variation consists of a reduction in the rate of the payments under the registered order and is made solely on the ground that there has been a change in the financial circumstances of the payer since the registered order was made or, in the case of an order registered under section 7 of this Act, since the registered order was confirmed, and the courts in the reciprocating country in which the maintenance order in question was made do not have power, according to the law in force in that country, to confirm provisional orders varying maintenance orders.

(3) The registering court shall not revoke a registered order otherwise than by a provisional order unless both the payer and the payee under the registered order are for the time being residing in the United Kingdom.

(4) On an application for the revocation of a registered order the registering court shall, unless both the payer and the payee under the registered order are for the time being residing in the United Kingdom, apply the law applied by the reciprocating country in which the registered order was made; but where by virtue of this subsection the registering court is required to apply that law, that court may make a provisional order if it has reason to believe that the ground on which the application is made is a ground on which the order could be revoked according to the law applied by the reciprocating country, notwithstanding that it has not been established that it is such a ground.

(5) Where the registering court makes a provisional order varying or revoking a registered order the prescribed officer of the court shall send in the prescribed manner to the court in the reciprocating country which made the registered order a certified copy of the provisional order together with a document, authenticated in the prescribed manner, setting out or summarising the evidence given in the proceedings.

(6) Where a certified copy of a provisional order made by a court in a reciprocating country, being an order varying a registered order, together with a document, duly authenticated, setting out or summarising the evidence given in the proceedings in which the provisional order was made, is received by the registering court, that court may confirm the order either without alteration or with such alterations as it thinks reasonable or refuse to confirm the order.

(7) For the purpose of determining whether a provisional order should be confirmed under subsection (6) above the court shall proceed as if an application for the variation of the registered order had been made to it.

(8) Where a registered order has been varied by an order (including a provisional order which has been confirmed) made by a court in the United Kingdom or by a competent court in a reciprocating country, the registered order shall, as from the date on which under the provisions of the order the variation is to take effect, have effect as varied by that order and, where that order was a provisional order, as if that order had been made in the form in which it was confirmed and as if it had never been a provisional order.

(9) Where a registered order has been revoked by an order made by a court in the United Kingdom or by a competent court in a reciprocating country, including a provisional order made

by the first-mentioned court which has been confirmed by a competent court in a reciprocating country, the registered order shall, as from the date on which under the provisions of the order the revocation is to take effect, be deemed to have ceased to have effect except as respects any arrears due under the registered order at that date.

(10) The prescribed officer of the registering court shall register in the prescribed manner any order varying a registered order other than a provisional order which is not confirmed.

(11) …

Amendments—DPMCA 1978, s 54; CJJA 1982, s 37(1), Sch 11, paras 4, 12; MEA 1991, s 10, Sch 1, para 14; MO(RE)A 1992, s 1, Sch 1, para 9; SI 1993/1576; SI 1995/755; AJA 1999, s 90, Sch 13, para 74, Sch 15; Courts Act 2003, Sch 8, para 153; CCA 2013, s 17, Sch 11.

Defined terms—'payee', 'payer', 'provisional order': s 21(1); 'reciprocating country': s 1(1); 'registered order', 'registering court': s 21(1).

'standing order, etc' (s 9(1ZA))—See under s 7.

'prescribed officer' (s 9(5),(10))—See FPR 2010, r 34.2.

'prescribed manner' (s 9(10))—See FPR 2010, rr 34.18, 34.19.

10 Cancellation of registration and transfer of order

(1) Where –

(a) a registered order is revoked by an order made by the registering court; or

(b) a registered order is revoked by a provisional order made by that court which has been confirmed by a court in a reciprocating country and notice of the confirmation is received by the registering court; or

(c) a registered order is revoked by an order made by a court in such a country and notice of the revocation is received by the registering court,

the prescribed officer of the registering court shall cancel the registration; but any arrears due under the registered order at the date when its registration is cancelled by virtue of this subsection shall continue to be recoverable as if the registration had not been cancelled.

(2) Where the prescribed officer of the registering court is of opinion that the payer under a registered order is not residing within the jurisdiction of that court and has no assets within that jurisdiction against which the order can be effectively enforced, he shall cancel the registration of the order and, subject to subsection (3) below, shall send the certified copy of the order to the Lord Chancellor.

(3) Where the prescribed officer of the registering court, being a magistrates' court in Northern Ireland, is of opinion that the payer is residing or has assets within the jurisdiction of another magistrates' court in Northern Ireland, he shall transfer the order to that other court by sending the certified copy of the order to the prescribed officer of that other court.

(4) On the transfer of the order under subsection (3) above the prescribed officer of the court to which it is transferred shall, subject to subsection (6) below, register the order in the prescribed manner in that court.

(5) Where the certified copy of an order is received by the Lord Chancellor under this section and it appears to him that the payer under the order is residing or has assets in the United Kingdom, he shall transfer the order to the appropriate court by sending the certified copy of the order together with the related documents to the prescribed officer of the appropriate court and, subject to subsection (6) below, that officer shall register the order in the prescribed manner in that court.

(6) Before registering an order in pursuance of subsection (4) or (5) above an officer of a court shall take such steps as he thinks fit for the purpose of ascertaining whether the payer is residing or has assets within the jurisdiction of the court, and if after taking those steps he is satisfied that the payer is not residing and has no assets within the jurisdiction of the court he shall send the certified copy of the order to the Lord Chancellor.

(7) The officer of a court who is required by any of the foregoing provisions of this section to send to the Lord Chancellor or to the prescribed officer of another court the certified copy of an order shall send with that copy –

(a) a certificate of arrears signed by him;

(b) a statement giving such information as he possesses as to the whereabouts of the payer and the nature and location of his assets; and

(c) any relevant documents in his possession relating to the case.

(8) …

Amendments—CJJA 1982, s 37(1), Sch 11, para 13; SI 1992/709; CCA 2013, s 17, Sch 11.

Defined terms—'certified copy', 'court': s 21(1); 'jurisdiction': s 47(3); 'provisional order': s 21(1); 'reciprocating country': s 1(1); 'registered order', 'registering court': s 21(1).

'prescribed officer' (s 10(1)–(3))—See FPR 2010, r 34.2.

'prescribed manner' (s 10(4),(5))—See FPR 2010, r 34.3.

11 Steps to be taken by Lord Chancellor where payer under certain orders is not residing in the United Kingdom

(1) If at any time it appears to the Lord Chancellor that the payer under a maintenance order, a certified copy of which has been received by him from a reciprocating country, is not residing and has no assets in the United Kingdom, he shall send to the responsible authority in that country or, if having regard to all the circumstances he thinks it proper to do so, to the responsible authority in another reciprocating country –

(a) the certified copy of the order in question and a certified copy of any order varying that order;

(b) if the order has at any time been a registered order, a certificate of arrears signed by the prescribed officer;

(c) a statement giving such information as the Lord Chancellor possesses as to the whereabouts of the payer and the nature and location of his assets; and

(d) any other relevant documents in his possession relating to the case.

(2) Where the documents mentioned in subsection (1) above are sent to the responsible authority in a reciprocating country other than that in which the order in question was made, the Lord Chancellor shall inform the responsible authority in the reciprocating country in which that order was made of what he has done.

Amendments—CJJA 1982, s 37(1), Sch 11, para 13; SI 1992/709.

Defined terms—'certified copy', 'maintenance order', 'payer': s 21(1); 'reciprocating country': s 1(1); 'registered order', 'responsible authority': s 21(1).

'prescribed officer' (s 11(1))—See FPR 2010, r 34.2.

Appeals

12 Appeals

(1) No appeal shall lie from a provisional order made in pursuance of any provision of this Part of this Act by a court in the United Kingdom.

(2) Where in pursuance of any such provision any such court confirms or refuses to confirm a provisional order made by a court in a reciprocating country, whether a maintenance order or an order varying or revoking a maintenance order, the payer or payee under the maintenance order shall have the like right of appeal (if any) from the confirmation of, or refusal to conform, the provisional order as he would have if that order were not a provisional order and the court which confirmed or refused to confirm it had made or, as the case may be, refused to make it.

(3) Where in pursuance of any such provision any such court makes, or refuses to make, an order varying or revoking a maintenance order made by a court in a reciprocating country, then, subject to subsection (1) above, the payer or payee under the maintenance order shall have the like right of appeal (if any) from that order or from the refusal to make it as he would have if the maintenance order had been made by the first-mentioned court.

(4) Nothing in this section (except subsection (1)) shall be construed as affecting any right of appeal conferred by any other enactment.

Defined terms—'court', 'payee', 'payer', 'provisional order': s 21(1); 'reciprocating country': s 1(1).

Evidence

13 Admissibility of evidence given in reciprocating country

(1) A statement contained in –

(a) a document, duly authenticated, which purports to set out or summarise evidence given in proceedings in a court in a reciprocating country; or

(b) a document, duly authenticated, which purports to set out or summarise evidence taken in such a country for the purpose of proceedings in a court in the United Kingdom under this Part of this Act, whether in response to a request made by such a court or otherwise; or

(c) a document, duly authenticated, which purports to have been received in evidence in proceedings in a court in such a country or to be a copy of a document so received,

shall in any proceedings in a court in the United Kingdom relating to a maintenance order to which this Part of this Act applies be admissible as evidence of any fact stated therein to the same extent as oral evidence of that fact is admissible in those proceedings.

(2) A document purporting to set out or summarise evidence given as mentioned in subsection (1)(a) above, or taken as mentioned in subsection (1)(b) above, shall be deemed to be duly authenticated for the purposes of that subsection if the document purports to be certified by the judge, magistrate or other person before whom the evidence was given, or, as the case may be, by whom it was taken, to be the original document containing or recording, or, as the case may be, summarising, that evidence or a true copy of that document.

(3) A document purporting to have been received in evidence as mentioned in subsection (1)(c) above, or to be a copy of a document so received, shall be deemed to be duly authenticated for the purposes of that subsection if the document purports to be certified by a judge, magistrate or officer of the court in question to have been, or to be a true copy of a document which has been, so received.

(4) It shall not be necessary in any such proceedings to prove the signature or official position of the person appearing to have given such a certificate.

(5) Nothing in this section shall prejudice the admission in evidence of any document which is admissible in evidence apart from this section.

Defined terms—'court', 'maintenance order': s 21(1); 'reciprocating country': s 1(1).

14 Obtaining of evidence needed for purpose of certain proceedings

(1) Where for the purpose of any proceedings in a court in a reciprocating country relating to a maintenance order to which this Part of this Act applies a request is made by or on behalf of that court for the taking in the United Kingdom of the evidence of a person residing therein relating to matters specified in the request, such court in the United Kingdom as may be prescribed shall have power to take that evidence and, after giving notice of the time and place at which the evidence is to be taken to such persons and in such manner as it thinks fit, shall take the evidence in such manner as may be prescribed.

Evidence taken in compliance with such a request shall be sent in the prescribed manner by the prescribed officer of the court to the court in the reciprocating country by or on behalf of which the request was made.

(2) Where any person, not being the payer or the payee under the maintenance order to which the proceedings in question relate, is required by virtue of this section to give evidence before a court in the United Kingdom, the court may order that there shall be paid –

(a) if the court is a court in England, Wales or Scotland, out of moneys provided by Parliament; and

(b) if the court is a court in Northern Ireland, out of moneys provided by the Northern Ireland Assembly,

such sums as appear to the court reasonably sufficient to compensate that person for the expense, trouble or loss of time properly incurred in or incidental to his attendance.

(3) Articles 118(1), (3) and (4), 119 and 120 of the Magistrates' Courts (Northern Ireland) Order 1981 (which provide for compelling the attendance of witnesses, etc) shall apply in relation to a magistrates' court in Northern Ireland having power under subsection (1) above to take the evidence of any person as if the proceedings in the court in a reciprocating country for the purpose of which a request for the taking of the evidence has been made were proceedings in the magistrates' court and had been begun by complaint.

(4) …

(5) A court in the United Kingdom may for the purpose of any proceedings in that court under this Part of this Act relating to a maintenance order to which this Part of this Act applies request a court in a reciprocating country to take or provide evidence relating to such matters as may be specified in the request and may remit the case to that court for that purpose.

(6) (*repealed*)

Amendments—SI 1973/2163; MCA 1980, s 154, Sch 7, para 105; SI 1981/1675; SI 2010/976; CCA 2013, s 17, Sch 11.

Defined terms—'court', 'maintenance order': s 21(1); 'reciprocating country': s 1(1).

'such court ... as may be prescribed' (s 14(1))—See FPR 2010, r 34.20.

'prescribed manner' (s 14(1))—See FPR 2010, r 34.20.

'prescribed officer' (s 14(1))—See FPR 2010, r 34.2.

15 Order etc made abroad need not be proved

For the purposes of this Part of this Act, unless the contrary is shown –

(a) any order made by a court in a reciprocating country purporting to bear the seal of that court or to be signed by any person in his capacity as a judge, magistrate or officer of the court, shall be deemed without further proof to have been duly sealed or, as the case may be, to have been signed by that person;

(b) the person by whom the order was signed shall be deemed without further proof to have been a judge, magistrate or officer, as the case may be, of that court when he signed it and, in the case of an officer, to have been authorised to sign it; and

(c) a document purporting to be a certified copy of an order made by a court in a reciprocating country shall be deemed without further proof to be such a copy.

Defined terms—'certified copy', 'court': s 21(1); 'reciprocating country': s 1(1).

Supplemental

16 Payment of sums under orders made abroad: conversion of currency

(1) Payment of sums due under a registered order shall, while the order is registered in a court in England, Wales or Northern Ireland, be made in such manner and to such person as may be prescribed.

(2) Where the sums required to be paid under a registered order are expressed in a currency other than the currency of the United Kingdom, then, as from the relevant date, the order shall be treated as if it were an order requiring the payment of such sums in the currency of the United Kingdom as, on the basis of the rate of exchange prevailing at that date, are equivalent to the sums so required to be paid.

(3) Where the sum specified in any statement, being a statement of the amount of any arrears due under a maintenance order made by a court in a reciprocating country is expressed in a currency other than the currency of the United Kingdom, that sum shall be deemed to be such sum in the currency of the United Kingdom as, on the basis of the rate of exchange prevailing at the relevant date, is equivalent to the sum so specified.

(4) For the purposes of this section a written certificate purporting to be signed by an officer of any bank in the United Kingdom certifying that a specified rate of exchange prevailed between currencies at a specified date and that at such rate a specified sum in the currency of the United

PART II

Kingdom is equivalent to a specified sum in another specified currency shall be evidence of the rate of exchange so prevailing on that date and of the equivalent sums in terms of the respective currencies.

(5) In this section 'the relevant date' means –

(a) in relation to a registered order or to a statement of arrears due under a maintenance order made by a court in a reciprocating country, the date on which the order first becomes a registered order or (if earlier) the date on which it is confirmed by a court in the United Kingdom;

(b) in relation to a registered order which has been varied, the date on which the last order varying that order is registered in a court in the United Kingdom or (if earlier) the date on which the last order varying that order is confirmed by such a court.

(6) …

Defined terms—'maintenance order', 'registered order': s 21(1); 'reciprocating country': s 1(1).

'to such person as may be prescribed' (s 16(1))—See FPR 2010, r 34.23.

17 Proceedings in the family court in England and Wales or in magistrates' courts in Northern Ireland

(1)–(3) *(repealed)*

(4) Anything authorised or required by this Part of this Act to be done by, to or before the magistrates' court in Northern Ireland by, to or before which any other thing was done may be done by, to or before any magistrates' court acting for the same petty sessions district as that court.

(5) *(repealed)*

(5A) Where the respondent to an application for the variation or revocation of –

(a) a maintenance order made by the family court, being an order to which section 5 of this Act applies; or

(b) a registered order which is registered in the family court,

is residing in a reciprocating country, the family court shall have jurisdiction to hear the application (where it would not have such jurisdiction apart from this subsection) if it would have had jurisdiction to hear it had the respondent been habitually resident in England and Wales.

(6) Where the respondent to an application for the variation or revocation of –

(a) a maintenance order made by a magistrates' court in Northern Ireland, being an order to which section 5 of this Act applies; or

(b) a registered order which is registered in such a court,

is residing in a reciprocating country, a magistrates' court in Northern Ireland shall have jurisdiction to hear the application (where it would not have jurisdiction apart from this subsection) if it would have had jurisdiction to hear it had the respondent been habitually resident in Northern Ireland.

(7) Where the respondent to an application for the variation or revocation –

(a) of a maintenance order made by the family court in England and Wales or a magistrates' court in Northern Ireland, being an order to which section 5 of this Act applies; or

(b) of a registered order registered in the family court in England and Wales or a magistrates' court in Northern Ireland,

does not appear at the time and place appointed for the hearing of the application, but the court is satisfied that the respondent is residing in a reciprocating country, the court may proceed to hear and determine the application at the time and place appointed for the hearing or for any adjourned hearing in like manner as if the respondent had appeared at that time and place.

(7A), (8) *(repealed)*

Amendments—DPMCA 1978, s 89(2), Sch 3; SI 1981/1675; MO(RE)A 1992, s 1, Sch 1, para 10; SI 1995/755; Courts Act 2003, Sch 8, para 154; SI 2012/2814; CCA 2013, s 17, Sch 11; SI 2014/605.

Defined terms—'maintenance order': s 21(1); 'reciprocating country': s 1(1); 'registered order': s 21(1).

18 Rules of court

(A1) Rules of court may make provision with respect to the matters that would be mentioned in any of paragraphs (b), (c), (e) and (f) of subsection (1) if references in those paragraphs to a magistrates' court, or to magistrates' courts, were references to the family court.

(1) The matters referred to in subsections (A1) and (2) are –

(a) Rules of court may make provision with respect to the circumstances in which anything authorised or required by this Part of this Act to be done by, to or before a magistrates' court acting in a particular petty sessions district or by, to or before an officer of that court may be done by, to or before a magistrates' court acting in such other petty sessions district as the rules may provide or by, to or before an officer of that court;

(b) the orders made, or other things done, by a magistrates' court, or an officer of such a court, under this Part of this Act, or by a court in a reciprocating country, notice of which is to be given to such persons as the rules may provide and the manner in which such notice shall be given;

(c) the cases and manner in which courts in reciprocating countries are to be informed of orders made, or other things done, by a magistrates' court under this Part of this Act;

(d) the cases and manner in which a justices' clerk may take evidence needed for the purpose of proceedings in a court in a reciprocating country relating to a maintenance order to which this Part of this Act applies;

(e) the circumstances and manner in which cases may be remitted by magistrates' courts to courts in reciprocating countries;

(f) the circumstances and manner in which magistrates' courts may for the purposes of this Part of this Act communicate with courts in reciprocating countries.

(1A) For the purpose of giving effect to this Part of this Act, rules of court may make, in relation to any proceedings brought under or by virtue of this Part of this Act, any provision not covered by subsection (A1) above which –

(a) falls within subsection (2) of section 93 of the Children Act 1989, and

(b) may be made in relation to relevant proceedings under that section.

(2) Rules with respect to the matter mentioned in subsection (1) above may be made in accordance with Article 13 of the Magistrates' Courts (Northern Ireland) Order 1981 in relation to proceedings or matters in magistrates' courts in Northern Ireland under this Part of this Act.

(2A) For the purpose of giving effect to this Part of this Act, rules made in accordance with Article 13 of the Magistrates' Courts (Northern Ireland) Order 1981 may make, in relation to any proceedings brought under or by virtue of this Part of this Act, any provision not covered by subsection (2) above which –

(a) falls within paragraph (2) of Article 165 of the Children (Northern Ireland) Order 1995, and

(b) may be made in relation to relevant proceedings under that Article.

Amendments—MCA 1980, s 154, Sch 7, para 106; SI 1981/1675; MO(RE)A 1992, s 1, Sch 1, para 11; SI 1995/755; Courts Act 2003, s 109(1), Sch 8, para 155; CCA 2013, s 17, Sch 11.

Defined terms—'maintenance order': s 21(1); 'reciprocating country': s 1(1).

****

20 Restriction on enforcement of arrears under maintenance order registered in Scotland

Where a maintenance order is for the time being registered in the sheriff court under this Part of this Act, a person shall not be entitled, except with the leave of the sheriff, to enforce, whether by diligence or otherwise, the payment of any arrears due under the order, if either –

(a) the sheriff has made a provisional order under section 9 of this Act revoking the said maintenance order and the arrears accrued after the making of the said provisional order, or

(b) the arrears accrued before the commencement of this Part of this Act;

and on any application for leave to enforce the payment of any such arrears, the sheriff may refuse leave, or may grant leave subject to such restrictions and conditions (including conditions as to the allowing of time for payment or the making of payment by instalments) as he thinks appropriate, or may remit the payment of such arrears or of any part thereof.

Defined terms—'maintenance order', 'provisional order': s 21(1).

21 Interpretation of Part I

(1) In this Part of this Act –

'affiliation order' means an order (however described) adjudging, finding or declaring a person to be the father of a child, whether or not it also provides for the maintenance of the child;

'the appropriate court' –

(a) in relation to a person residing or having assets in England and Wales means the family court; and

(b) in relation to a person residing or having assets in Northern Ireland means a magistrates' court, and in relation to a person residing or having assets in Scotland means a sheriff court, within the jurisdiction of which that person is residing or has assets;

'certificate of arrears', in relation to a maintenance order, means a certificate certifying that the sum specified in the certificate is to the best of the information or belief of the officer giving the certificate the amount of the arrears due under the order at the date of the certificate or, as the case may be, that to the best of his information or belief there are no arrears due thereunder at that date;

'certified copy', in relation to an order of a court, means a copy of the order certified by the proper officer of the court to be a true copy;

'court' includes any tribunal or person having power to make, confirm, enforce, vary or revoke a maintenance order;

'maintenance order' means an order (however described) of any of the following descriptions, that is to say –

(a) an order (including an affiliation order or order consequent upon an affiliation order) which provides for the payment of a lump sum or the making of periodical payments towards the maintenance of any person, being a person whom the person liable to make payments under the order is, according to the law applied in the place where the order was made, liable to maintain; and

(b) an affiliation order or order consequent upon an affiliation order, being an order which provides for the payment by a person adjudged, found or declared to be a child's father of expenses incidental to the child's birth or, where the child has died, of his funeral expenses,

and, in the case of a maintenance order which has been varied, means that order as varied;

'payee', in relation to a maintenance order, means the person entitled to the payments for which the order provides;

'payer', in relation to a maintenance order, means the person liable to make payments under the order;

'prescribed', in relation to a magistrates' court in Northern Ireland, means prescribed by rules made in accordance with Article 13 of the Magistrates' Courts (Northern Ireland) Order 1981, and in relation to any other court means prescribed by rules of court;

'provisional order' means (according to the context) –

(a) an order made by a court in the United Kingdom which is provisional only and has no effect unless and until confirmed, with or without alteration, by a competent court in a reciprocating country; or

(b) an order made by a court in a reciprocating country which is provisional only and has no effect unless and until confirmed, with or without alteration, by a court in the United Kingdom having power under this Part of this Act to confirm it;

'reciprocating country' has the meaning assigned to it by section 1 of this Act;

'registered order' means a maintenance order which is for the time being registered in a court in the United Kingdom under this Part of this Act;

'registering court', in relation to a registered order, means the court in which that order is for the time being registered under this Part of this Act;

'the responsible authority', in relation to a reciprocating country, means any person who in that country has functions similar to those of the Lord Chancellor under this Part of this Act;

'revoke' and 'revocation' include discharge.

(2) For the purposes of this Part of this Act an order shall be taken to be a maintenance order so far (but only so far) as it relates to the payment of a lump sum or the making of periodical payments as mentioned in paragraph (a) of the definition of 'maintenance order' in subsection (1) above or to the payment by a person adjudged, found or declared to be a child's father of any such expenses as are mentioned in paragraph (b) of that definition.

(3) Any reference in this Part of this Act to the payment of money for the maintenance of a child shall be construed as including a reference to the payment of money for the child's education.

Amendments—MCA 1980, s 154, Sch 7, para 107; SI 1981/1675; CJJA 1982, s 37(1), Sch 11, paras 4, 15; MO(RE)A 1992, s 1, Sch 1, para 12; SI 1992/709; Courts Act 2003, Sch 8, para 156; CCA 2013, s 17, Sch 11.

Amendments, repeals and transitional provisions

22 Amendments and repeals

(1) The enactments mentioned in the Schedule to this Act shall have effect subject to the minor and consequential amendments specified therein.

(2) The following are hereby repealed –

- (a) the Maintenance Orders (Facilities for Enforcement) Act 1920;
- (b) *(repealed)*
- (c) in the Maintenance Orders Act 1958, section 19 and, in section 23(2), the words 'section nineteen';
- (d) *(repealed)*

Amendments—MCA 1980, s 154, Sch 9; South Africa Act 1995, s 1, Sch, para 7(2).

23 Maintenance order registered in High Court under the Maintenance Orders etc Act 1920

(1) Where a country or territory, being a country or territory to which at the commencement of section 1 of this Act the Maintenance Orders (Facilities for Enforcement) Act 1920 extended becomes a reciprocating country, then, if immediately before the Order in Council made under section 12 of that Act extending that Act to that country or territory was revoked any maintenance order made by a court in that country or territory was registered in the High Court or the High Court of Justice in Northern Ireland under section 1 of that Act, the subsection (1A) applies in relation to the order.

(1A) Where the order was at that time registered in the High Court, that court may, on an application by the payer or the payee under the order or of its own motion, transfer the order to the family court, with a view to the order being registered in the family court under this Part of this Act; and where the order was at that time registered in the High Court of Justice in Northern Ireland, that court may, on an application by the payer or the payee under the order or of its own motion, transfer the order to such magistrates' court in Northern Ireland as having regard to the place where the payer is residing and to all the circumstances it thinks most appropriate, with a view to the order being registered in that magistrates' court under this Part of this Act.

(1B) Where the High Court transfers an order to the family court under this section it shall –

- (a) cause a certified copy of the order to be sent to an officer of the family court, and
- (b) cancel the registration of the order in the High Court.

(2) Where the High Court of Justice in Northern Ireland transfers an order to a magistrates' court under this section it shall –

(a) cause a certified copy of the order to be sent to the appropriate officer of that court, and
(b) cancel the registration of the order in the High Court.

(3) The officer of the court who receives a certified copy of an order sent to him under this section shall register the order in the prescribed manner in that court.

(4) On registering a maintenance order in a court by virtue of this section the officer registering it shall, if the order is registered in that court under Part I of the Maintenance Orders Act 1958 cancel that registration.

(5), 6 …

Amendments—AJA 1999, s 90, Sch 13, para 75; CCA 2013, s 17, Sch 11.

Defined terms—'certified copy', 'court', 'maintenance order', 'payee', 'payer': s 21(1); 'reciprocating country': s 1(1).
'prescribed manner' (s 23(3))—See FPR 2010, r 34.3.

24 Application of Part I to certain orders and proceedings under the Maintenance Orders etc Act 1920

Where Her Majesty proposes by an Order in Council under section 1 of this Act to designate as a reciprocating country a country or territory to which at the commencement of that section the Maintenance Orders (Facilities for Enforcement) Act 1920 extended, that Order in Council may contain such provisions as Her Majesty considers expedient for the purpose of securing –

(a) that the provisions of this Part of this Act apply, subject to such modifications as may be specified in the Order, to maintenance orders, or maintenance orders of a specified class –
  (i) made by a court in England, Wales or Northern Ireland against a person residing or having assets in that country or territory, or
  (ii) made by a court in that country or territory against a person residing or having assets in England, Wales or Northern Ireland,

  being orders to which immediately before the date of the coming into operation of the Order in Council the said Act of 1920 applied, except any order which immediately before that date is registered in the High Court or the High Court of Justice in Northern Ireland under section 1 of that Act;
(b) that any maintenance order, or maintenance order of a specified class, made by a court in that country or territory which has been confirmed by a court in England, Wales or Northern Ireland under section 4 of the said Act of 1920 and is in force immediately before that date is registered under section 7 of this Act;
(c) that any proceedings brought under or by virtue of a provision of the said Act of 1920 in a court in England, Wales or Northern Ireland which are pending at that date, being proceedings affecting a person resident in that country or territory, are continued as if they had been brought under or by virtue of the corresponding provision of this Part of this Act.

Amendments—CJJA 1982, s 37(1), Sch 11, para 16.
Defined terms—'court', 'maintenance order': s 21(1); 'reciprocating country': s 1(1).

PART II
RECIPROCAL ENFORCEMENT OF CLAIMS FOR THE RECOVERY OF MAINTENANCE

Convention countries

25 Convention countries

(1) Her Majesty may by Order in Council declare that any country or territory specified in the Order, being a country or territory outside the United Kingdom to which the Maintenance Convention extends, is a Convention country for the purposes of this Part of this Act.

(2) In this section 'the Maintenance Convention' means the United Nations Convention on the Recovery Abroad of Maintenance done at New York on 20 June 1956.

Scope—This section provides that a country or territory may be declared a Convention country for the purposes of Pt II by Order in Council. The Recovery Abroad of Maintenance (Convention Countries) Order 1975, as amended, has been made for this purpose. The countries to which the Order applies are: Algeria, Australia, Barbados, Bosnia and Herzegovina, Brazil, Burkina Faso, Cape Verde, Central African Republic, Chile, Croatia, Ecuador, Guatemala, Haiti, Holy See, Israel, Mexico, Monaco, Morocco, New Zealand, Niger, Norway, Pakistan, Philippines, Sri Lanka, Suriname, Switzerland, the former Yugoslav Republic of Macedonia, Tunisia, Turkey, Uruguay, Yugoslavia (sic).

Application by person in the United Kingdom for recovery etc of maintenance in Convention country

26 Application by person in United Kingdom for recovery etc of maintenance in Convention country

(1) Where a person in the United Kingdom ('the applicant') claims to be entitled to recover in a Convention country maintenance from another person, and that other person is for the time being subject to the jurisdiction of that country, the applicant may apply to the Lord Chancellor, in accordance with the provisions of this section, to have his claim for the recovery of maintenance from that other person transmitted to that country.

(2) Where the applicant seeks to vary any provision made in a Convention country for the payment by any other person of maintenance to the applicant, and that other person is for the time being subject to the jurisdiction of that country, the applicant may apply to the Lord Chancellor, in accordance with the provisions of this section, to have his application for the variation of that provision transmitted to that country.

(3) An application to the Lord Chancellor under subsection (1) or (2) above shall be made through the appropriate officer, and that officer shall assist the applicant in completing an application which will comply with the requirements of the law applied by the Convention country and shall send the application to the Lord Chancellor, together with such other documents, if any, as are required by that law.

(4) On receiving an application from the appropriate officer the Lord Chancellor shall transmit it, together with any accompanying documents, to the appropriate authority in the Convention country, unless he is satisfied that the application is not made in good faith or that it does not comply with the requirements of the law applied by that country.

(5) The Lord Chancellor may request the appropriate officer to obtain from the court of which he is an officer such information relating to the application as may be specified in the request, and it shall be the duty of the court to furnish the Lord Chancellor with the information he requires.

(6) …

Amendments—SI 1992/709; CCA 2013, s 17, Sch 11.
Defined terms—'Convention country': s 25(1).

Application by person in Convention country for recovery of maintenance in England, Wales or Northern Ireland

27 *(repealed)*

27A Applications for recovery of maintenance in England and Wales

(1) This section applies to any application which –

- (a) is received by the Lord Chancellor from the appropriate authority in a Convention country, and
- (b) is an application by a person in that country for the recovery of maintenance from another person who is for the time being residing in England and Wales.

(2) Subject to sections 27B to 28B of this Act, an application to which this section applies shall be treated for the purposes of any enactment as if it were an application for a maintenance order

under the relevant Act, made at the time when the application was received by the Lord Chancellor. This subsection does not confer jurisdiction on a court in England and Wales that it would not otherwise have.

(3) In the case of an application for maintenance for a child (or children) alone, the relevant Act is the Children Act 1989.

(4) In any other case, the relevant Act is the Domestic Proceedings and Magistrates' Courts Act 1978.

(5) In subsection (3) above, 'child' means the same as in Schedule 1 to the Children Act 1989.

Amendments—Inserted by MO(RE)A 1992, s 1, Sch 1, para 13. Amended by SI 2012/2814.
Defined terms—'Convention country': s 25(1).

27B Sending application to the family court

(1) On receipt of an application to which section 27A of this Act applies, the Lord Chancellor shall send it, together with any accompanying documents, to the family court.

(2) If notice of the hearing of the application by the family court cannot be duly served on the respondent, the family court shall return the application and the accompanying documents to the Lord Chancellor with a statement giving such information as the family court possesses as to the whereabouts of the respondent.

(3) If the application is returned to the Lord Chancellor under subsection (2) above, then, unless he is satisfied that the respondent is not residing in the United Kingdom, he shall deal with it in accordance with subsection (1) above or section 28D(1) of this Act or send it to the Secretary of State to be dealt with in accordance with section 31 of this Act (as the circumstances of the case require).

(4), (5) *(repealed)*

Amendments—Inserted by MO(RE)A 1992, s 1, Sch 1, para 13; SI 1995/756. Amended by AJA 1999, s 90, Sch 13, para 77; Courts Act 2003, Sch 8, para 159; CCA 2013, s 17, Sch 11.
Defined terms—'jurisdiction': s 47(3).

27C Applications to which section 27A applies: general

(1) This section applies where the family court makes an order on an application to which section 27A of this Act applies.

(2) *(repealed)*

(3) The court may, at the same time that it makes the order, exercise one of its powers under subsection (4) below.

(4) Those powers are –

(a) the power to order that payment under the order be made directly to the court;
(b) the power to order that payments under the order be made to the court, by such method of payment falling within section 1(5) of the Maintenance Enforcement Act 1991 (standing order, etc) as may be specified;
(c) the power to make an attachment of earnings order under the Attachment of Earnings Act 1971 to secure payments under the order.

(5) In deciding whether to exercise any of its powers under subsection (4) above, the court shall have regard to any representations made by the person liable to make payments under the order.

(6) Subsection (6) of section 1 of the Maintenance Enforcement Act 1991 (power of court to require debtor to open account) shall apply for the purposes of subsection (4) above as it applies for the purposes of that section, but as if for paragraph (a) there were substituted –

'(a) the court proposes to exercise its power under paragraph (b) of section 27C(4) of the Maintenance Orders (Reciprocal Enforcement) Act 1972, and'.

(7) The court shall register the order in the prescribed manner.

Amendments—Inserted by MO(RE)A 1992, s 1, Sch 1, para 13. Amended by AJA 1999, s 90, Sch 13, para 78; Courts Act 2003, Sch 8, para 160; CCA 2013, s 17, Sch 11.

28 Applications by spouses under the Domestic Proceedings and Magistrates' Courts Act 1978

(1) On hearing an application which by virtue of section 27A of this Act is to be treated as if it were an application for a maintenance order under the Domestic Proceedings and Magistrates' Courts Act 1978, the family court may make any order on the application which it has power to make under section 2 or 19(1) of that Act.

(2) Part I of that Act shall apply in relation to such an application, and to any order made on such an application, with the following modifications –

(a) sections 6 to 8, 16 to 18, 20ZA, 25, 26 and 28(2) shall be omitted, and
(b) *(repealed)*
(c) section 32(2) shall be omitted.

(3) Subsections (1) and (2) above do not apply where section 28A of this Act applies.

Amendments—MO(RE)A 1992, s 1, Sch 1, para 13; CCA 2013, s 17, Sch 11.

28A Applications by former spouses under the Domestic Proceedings and Magistrates' Courts Act 1978

(1) This section applies where in the case of any application which by virtue of section 27A of this Act is to be treated as if it were an application for a maintenance order under the Domestic Proceedings and Magistrates' Courts Act 1978 ('the 1978 Act') –

(a) the applicant and respondent were formerly married,
(b) their marriage was dissolved or annulled in a country or territory outside the United Kingdom by a divorce or annulment which is recognised as valid by the law of England and Wales,
(c) an order for the payment of maintenance for the benefit of the applicant or a child of the family has, by reason of the divorce or annulment, been made by a court in a Convention country, and
(d) where the order for the payment of maintenance was made by a court of a different country from that in which the divorce or annulment was obtained, either the applicant or the respondent was resident in the Convention country whose court made that order at the time that order was applied for.

(2) The family court shall have jurisdiction to hear the application notwithstanding the dissolution or annulment of the marriage.

(3) If the family court is satisfied that the respondent has failed to comply with the provisions of any order such as is mentioned in subsection (1)(c) above, it may (subject to subsections (4) and (5) below) make any order which it has power to make under section 2 or 19(1) of the 1978 Act.

(4) The court shall not make an order for the making of periodical payments for the benefit of the applicant or any child of the family unless the order made in the Convention country provides for the making of periodical payments for the benefit of the applicant or, as the case may be, that child.

(5) The court shall not make an order for the payment of a lump sum for the benefit of the applicant or any child of the family unless the order made in the Convention country provides for the payment of a lump sum to the applicant or, as the case may be, to that child.

(6) Part I of the 1978 Act shall apply in relation to the application, and to any order made on the application, with the following modifications –

(a) section 1 shall be omitted,
(b) for the reference in section 2(1) to any ground mentioned in section 1 of that Act there shall be substituted a reference to non-compliance with any such order as is mentioned in subsection (1)(c) of this section,
(c) for the references in section 3(2) and (3) to the occurrence of the conduct which is alleged as the ground of the application there shall be substituted references to the breakdown of the marriage,

PART II

(d) the reference in section 4(2) to the subsequent dissolution or annulment of the marriage of the parties affected by the order shall be omitted,

(e) sections 6 to 8, 16 to 18, 20ZA, 25, 26 and 28 shall be omitted, and

(f) *(repealed)*

(g) section 32(2) shall be omitted.

(7) A divorce or annulment obtained in a country or territory outside the United Kingdom shall be presumed for the purposes of this section to be one the validity of which is recognised by the law of England and Wales, unless the contrary is proved by the respondent.

(8) In this section, 'child of the family' has the meaning given in section 88 of the 1978 Act.

Amendments—Inserted by MO(RE)A 1992, s 1, Sch 1, para 13; CCA 2013, s 17, Sch 11.
Defined terms—'Convention country': s 25(1); 'jurisdiction': s 47(3).

28B *(repealed)*

28C Applications for recovery of maintenance in Northern Ireland

(1) This section applies to any application which –

(a) is received by the Lord Chancellor from the appropriate authority in a convention country, and

(b) is an application by a person in that country for the recovery of maintenance from another person who is for the time being residing in Northern Ireland.

(2) Subject to sections 28D to 29B of this Act, an application to which this section applies shall be treated for the purposes of any enactment as if it were an application for a maintenance order under the relevant Order, made at the time when the application was received by the Lord Chancellor. This subsection does not confer jurisdiction on a court in Northern Ireland that it would not otherwise have.

(3) In the case of an application for maintenance for a child (or children) alone, the relevant Order is the Children (Northern Ireland) Order 1995.

(4) In any other case, the relevant Order is the Domestic Proceedings (Northern Ireland) Order 1980.

(5) In subsection (3) above, 'child' means the same as in Schedule 1 to the Children (Northern Ireland) Order 1995.

Amendments—Inserted by MO(RE)A 1992, s 1, Sch 1, para 13; substituted by SI 1995/755. Amended by SI 2012/2814.
Defined terms—'Convention country': s 25(1).

28D Sending application to the appropriate magistrates' court

(1) On receipt of an application to which section 28C of this Act applies, the Lord Chancellor shall send it, together with any accompanying documents, to the clerk of a magistrates' court acting for the petty sessions district in which the respondent is residing.

(2) Subject to subsection (4) below, if notice of the hearing of the application by a magistrates' court having jurisdiction to hear it cannot be duly served on the respondent, the clerk of the court shall return the application and the accompanying documents to the Lord Chancellor with a statement giving such information as he possesses as to the whereabouts of the respondent.

(3) If the application is returned to the Lord Chancellor under subsection (2) above, then, unless he is satisfied that the respondent is not residing in the United Kingdom, he shall deal with it in accordance with subsection (1) above or section 27B of this Act or send it to the Secretary of State to be dealt with in accordance with section 31 of this Act (as the circumstances of the case require).

(4) If the clerk of a court to whom the application is sent under this section is satisfied that the respondent is residing within the petty sessions district for which another magistrates' court acts, he shall send the application and accompanying documents to the clerk of that other court and shall inform the Lord Chancellor that he has done so.

(5) If the application is sent to the clerk of a court under subsection (4) above, he shall proceed as if it had been sent to him under subsection (1) above.

Amendments—Inserted by SI 1995/755.

28E Applications to which section 28C applies: general

(1) This section applies where a magistrates' court makes an order on an application to which section 28C of this Act applies.

(2) Article 85 of the Magistrates' Courts (Northern Ireland) Order 1981 ('the 1981 Order') (orders for periodical payment: means of payment) shall not apply.

(3) The court shall, at the same time that it makes the order, exercise one of its powers under subsection (4) below.

(4) Those powers are –

(a) the power to order that payments under the order be made directly to the collecting officer;

(b) the power to order that payments under the order be made to the collecting officer, by such method of payment falling within Article 85(7) of the 1981 Order (standing order, etc.) as may be specified;

(c) the power to make an attachment of earnings order under Part IX of the 1981 Order to secure payments under the order;

and in this subsection 'collecting officer' means the officer mentioned in Article 85(4) of the 1981 Order.

(5) In deciding which of the powers under subsection (4) above it is to exercise, the court shall have regard to any representation made by the person liable to make payments under the order.

(6) Paragraph (5) of Article 85 of the 1981 Order (power of court to require debtor to open account) shall apply for the purposes of subsection (4) above as it applies for the purposes of that Article, but as if for sub-paragraph (a) there were substituted –

'(a) the court proposes to exercise its power under paragraph (b) of section 28E(4) of the Maintenance Orders (Reciprocal Enforcement) Act 1972, and'.

(7) The clerk of the court shall register the order in the prescribed manner in the court.

Amendments—Inserted by SI 1995/755.

****

Transfer, enforcement, variation and revocation of registered orders

32 Transfer of orders

(1) Where the prescribed officer of the registering court is of opinion that the payer under a registered order has ceased to reside within the jurisdiction of that court, then, unless he is of opinion that the payer has ceased to reside in the United Kingdom, he shall, subject to subsection (2) below, send a certified copy of the order and the related documents to the Lord Chancellor, and if he is of opinion that the payer has ceased to reside in the United Kingdom he shall send a notice to that effect to the Lord Chancellor.

(2) Where the clerk of the registering court, being a magistrates' court in Northern Ireland, is of opinion that the payer is residing within the jurisdiction of another magistrates' court in Northern Ireland, he shall transfer the order to that other court by sending a certified copy of the order and the related documents to the clerk of that other court and, subject to subsection (4) below, that clerk shall register the order in the prescribed manner in that court.

(2A) *(repealed)*

(3) Where a certified copy of an order is received by the Lord Chancellor under this section and it appears to him that the payer under the order is still residing in the United Kingdom, he shall transfer the order to the appropriate court by sending the copy of the order and the related

PART II

documents to the prescribed officer of the appropriate court and subject to subsection (4) below, that officer shall register the order in the prescribed manner in that court.

(4) Before registering an order in pursuance of subsection (2) or (3) above an officer of a court shall take such steps as he thinks fit for the purpose of ascertaining whether the payer under the order is residing within the jurisdiction of the court, and if after taking those steps he is satisfied that the payer is not so residing he shall return the certified copy of the order and the related documents to the officer of the court or the Lord Chancellor, as the case may be, from whom he received them, together with a statement giving such information as he possesses as to the whereabouts of the payer.

(5) Where a certified copy of an order is received by the Lord Chancellor under this section and it appears to him that the payer under the order has ceased to reside in the United Kingdom he shall return the copy of the order and the related documents to the registering court.

(6) An officer of a court on registering an order in the court in pursuance of subsection (2) or (3) above shall give notice of the registration in the prescribed manner to the prescribed officer of the court in which immediately before its registration under this section the order was registered.

(7) The officer to whom notice is given under subsection (6) above shall on receiving the notice cancel the registration of the order in that court.

(7A), (7B) …

(8) In this section –

'the appropriate court' –

(a) in relation to a person residing in England and Wales, means the family court; and

(b) in relation to a person residing in Northern Ireland, means a magistrates' court within the jurisdiction of which that person is residing;

'certificate of arrears' and 'certified copy' have the same meanings respectively as in Part I of this Act;

'payer', in relation to a registered order, means the person liable to make payments under the order; and

'related documents' means –

(a) the application on which the order was made;

(b) a certificate of arrears signed by the prescribed officer of the registering court;

(c) a statement giving such information as he possesses as to the whereabouts of the payer; and

(d) any relevant documents in his possession relating to the case.

(9) …

Amendments—SI 1992/709; AJA 1999, s 90, Sch 13, para 79; CCA 2013, s 17, Sch 11.

Defined terms—'certificate of arrears', 'certified copy': s 21(1); 'jurisdiction': s 47(3); 'part of the United Kingdom': s 47(2); 'registered order', 'registering court': s 39.

33 Enforcement of orders

(1) Subject to subsection (2) below, a registered order which is registered in a court other than the court by which the order was made may be enforced as if it had been made by the registered court and as if that court had had jurisdiction to make it; and proceedings for or with respect to the enforcement of any such order may be taken in accordance with this subsection but not otherwise.

(2) Subsection (1) above does not apply to an order which is for the time being registered in the High Court of Justice in Northern Ireland under Part II of the Maintenance and Affiliation Orders Act (Northern Ireland) 1966.

(3), (3A) *(repealed)*

(3B) …

(4) A magistrates' court in Northern Ireland in which an order is registered under this Part of this Act, and the officers thereof, shall take all such steps for enforcing the order as may be prescribed.

(5) In any proceedings for or with respect to the enforcement of an order which is for the time being registered in any court under this Part of this Act a certificate of arrears sent under section 32 of this Act to the prescribed officer of the court shall be evidence of the facts stated therein.

(6) Part II of the Maintenance Orders Act 1950 (enforcement of certain orders throughout the United Kingdom) shall not apply to a registered order.

(7) …

Amendments—FLRA 1987, s 33, Sch 2, para 50; MEA 1991, s 10, Sch 1, para 18; CCA 2013, s 17, Sch 11; SI 2014/605.

Defined terms—'certificate of arrears': s 21(1); 'registered order', 'registering court': s 39.

Application to Northern Ireland—In Northern Ireland, subsection (3) is modified and an additional subsection (3B) is added by Family Law (Northern Ireland) Order 1993 and Children (Northern Ireland) Order 1995.

34 Variation and revocation of orders

(1) Subject to section 34A of this Act, where a registered order is registered in a court other than the court by which the order was made, the registering court shall have the like power to vary or revoke the order as if it had been made by the registering court and as if that court had had jurisdiction to make it; and no court other than the registering court shall have power to vary or revoke a registered order.

(2) Where the registering court revokes a registered order it shall cancel the registration.

(3) Where the Lord Chancellor receives from the appropriate authority in a Convention country an application by a person in that country for the variation of a registered order, he shall –

(a) if the registering court is the family court, send the application together with any documents accompanying it to that court;

(b) if the registering court is a magistrates' court in Northern Ireland, send the application together with any documents accompanying it to the clerk of that court.

(3A) *(repealed)*

(4) Where a court in a part of the United Kingdom makes, or refuses to make, an order varying or revoking a registered order made by a court in another part thereof, any person shall have the like right of appeal (if any) against the order or refusal as he would have if the registered order had been made by the first-mentioned court.

(5) …

Amendments—MEA 1991, s 10, Sch 1, para 19(1); MO(RE)A 1992, s 1, Sch 1, para 14; SI 1992/709; AJA 1999, s 90, Sch 13, para 80; Courts Act 2003, s 109(1), Sch 8, para 162; CCA 2013, s 17, Sch 11.

Defined terms—'Convention country': s 25(1); 'part of the United Kingdom': s 47(2); 'registered order', 'registering court': s 39.

Application to Northern Ireland—See note under s 33.

34A Variation of orders by the family court in England and Wales

(1) The provisions of this section shall have effect in relation to a registered order which is registered in the family court (whether or not the court made the order) in place of the following enactments, that is to say –

(a) section 1(3A) of the Maintenance Enforcement Act 1991;

(b) section 20ZA of the Domestic Proceedings and Magistrates' Courts Act 1978; and

(c) paragraph 6A of Schedule 1 to the Children Act 1989.

(2) The power of the family court to vary a registered order shall include power, if the court is satisfied that payment has not been made in accordance with the order, to exercise one of its powers under subsection (3) below.

(3) The powers of the court are –

(a) the power to order that payments under the order be made directly to the court;

(b) the power to order that payments under the order be made to the court by such method of payment falling within section 1(5) of the Maintenance Enforcement Act 1991 (standing order, etc) as may be specified;

(c) the power to make an attachment of earnings order under the Attachment of Earnings Act 1971 to secure payments under the order.

(4)–(8) *(repealed)*

(9) In deciding, for the purposes of subsection (2) above, whether to exercise any of its powers under subsection (3) above, the court shall have regard to any representations made by the debtor or the creditor.

(10) Subsection (6) of section 1 of the Maintenance Enforcement Act 1991 (power of court to require debtor to open account) shall apply for the purposes of subsection (3) above as it applies for the purposes of that section but as if for paragraph (a) there were substituted –

> '(a) the court proposes to exercise its power under paragraph (b) of section 34A(3) of the Maintenance Orders (Reciprocal Enforcement) Act 1972, and'.

(11) In this section 'creditor' and 'debtor' have the same meaning as they have in section 1 of the Maintenance Enforcement Act 1991.

Amendments—Inserted by MEA 1991, s 10, Sch 1, para 19(2). Amended by AJA 1999, s 90, Sch 13, para 81; Courts Act 2003, Sch 8, para 163; CCA 2013, s 17, Sch 11.

Defined terms—'registered order': s 39.

'standing order, etc' (s 34A(3)(b))—The methods of payment available do not include power to order payment by direct debit.

34B Variation of orders by courts of summary jurisdiction in Northern Ireland

(1) The provisions of this section shall have effect in relation to a registered order which is registered in a court of summary jurisdiction in Northern Ireland (whether or not the court made the order) in place of the following enactments, that is to say –

(a) paragraphs (3) to (11) of Article 86 of the Magistrates' Courts (Northern Ireland) Order 1981; and

(b) Article 22A of the Domestic Proceedings (Northern Ireland) Order 1980.

(2) The power of a court of summary jurisdiction in Northern Ireland to vary a registered order shall include power, if the court is satisfied that payment has not been made in accordance with the order, to exercise one of its powers under subsection (3) below.

(3) The powers of the court are –

(a) the power to order that payments under the order be made directly to the collecting officer;

(b) the power to order that payments under the order be made to the collecting officer by such method of payment falling within Article 85(7) of the Magistrates' Courts (Northern Ireland) Order 1981 (standing order, etc) as may be specified;

(c) the power to make an attachment of earnings order under Part IX of the Order of 1981 to secure payments under the order;

and in this subsection 'collecting officer' means the officer mentioned in Article 85(4) of the Order of 1981.

(4) In any case where –

(a) a registered order is registered in a court of summary jurisdiction in Northern Ireland, and

(b) payments under the order are required to be made to the collecting officer in Northern Ireland, by any method of payment falling within Article 85(7) of the Magistrates' Courts (Northern Ireland) Order 1981 (standing order, etc),

an interested party may apply in writing to the clerk of petty sessions in which the order is registered for the order to be varied as mentioned in subsection (5) below.

(5) Subject to subsection (8) below, where an application has been made under subsection (4) above, the clerk, after giving written notice (by post or otherwise) of the application to any other interested party and allowing that party, within the period of 14 days beginning with the date of the giving of that notice, an opportunity to make written representations, may vary the order to provide that payments under the order shall be made in accordance with paragraph (a) of subsection (3) above.

(6) The clerk may proceed with an application under subsection (4) above notwithstanding that any such interested party as is referred to in subsection (5) above has not received written notice of the application.

(7) In subsections (4) to (6) above 'interested party', in relation to an order, means the debtor or the creditor.

(8) Where an application has been made under subsection (4) above, the clerk may, if he considers it inappropriate to exercise his power under subsection (5) above, refer the matter to the court which may vary the order by exercising one of its powers under subsection (3) above.

(9) In deciding, for the purposes of subsections (2) and (8) above, which of the powers under subsection (3) above it is to exercise, the court shall have regard to any representations made by the debtor.

(10) Paragraph (5) of Article 85 of the Magistrates' Courts (Northern Ireland) Order 1981 (power of court to require debtor to open account) shall apply for the purposes of subsection (3) above as it applies for the purposes of that Article but as if for sub-paragraph (a) there were substituted –

'(a) the court proposes to exercise its power under paragraph (b) of section 34B(3) of the Maintenance Orders (Reciprocal Enforcement) Act 1972, and'.

(11) In this section 'creditor' and 'debtor' have the same meaning as they have in Article 85 of the Magistrates' Courts (Northern Ireland) Order 1981.

Amendments—Inserted by SI 1993/1576.

35 Further provisions with respect to variation etc of orders by the family court in England and Wales

(1) Subsection (1A) applies in relation to an application for the variation or revocation of a registered order registered in the family court ('the registering court') made –

(a) by the person against whom or on whose application the registered order was made, and
(b) in circumstances where the person by or against whom the application is made is residing outside England and Wales.

(1A) The registering court has jurisdiction to hear the application even though –

(a) a party to the application is residing outside England and Wales.
(b) *(repealed)*

(1B) But if the application or part of it relates to a matter where jurisdiction falls to be determined by reference to the jurisdictional requirements of the Maintenance Regulation and Schedule 6 to the Civil Jurisdiction and Judgments (Maintenance) Regulations 2011, the registering court may not entertain the application or that part of it unless it has jurisdiction to do so by virtue of that Regulation and that Schedule.

(2) None of the powers of the court, under section 34A of this Act shall be exercisable in relation to such an application.

(3) Where the respondent to an application for the variation or revocation of a registered order which is registered in the family court does not appear at the time and place appointed for the hearing of the application, but the court is satisfied –

(a) that the respondent is residing outside England and Wales, and
(b) that the prescribed notice of the making of the application and of the time and place appointed for the hearing has been given to the respondent in the prescribed manner,

PART II

the court may proceed to hear and determine the application at the time and place appointed for the hearing or for any adjourned hearing in like manner as if the respondent had appeared at that time and place.

(4) In subsection (1B) 'the Maintenance Regulation' means Council Regulation (EC) No 4/2009 including as applied in relation to Denmark by virtue of the Agreement made on 19 October 2005 between the European Community and the Kingdom of Denmark.

Amendments—MO(RE)A 1992, s 1, Sch 1, para 16; SI 2012/2814; CCA 2013, s 17, Sch 11; SI 2014/605.
Defined terms—'registered order': s 39.

35A Further provisions with respect to variation etc of orders by magistrates' courts in Northern Ireland

(1) Subsection (1A) applies in relation to an application for the variation or revocation of a registered order registered in a magistrates' court in Northern Ireland ('the registering court') made –

(a) by the person against whom or on whose application the registered order was made, and
(b) in circumstances where the person by or against whom the application is made is residing outside Northern Ireland.

(1A) The registering court has jurisdiction to hear the application even though –

(a) a party to the application is residing outside England and Wales, and
(b) the requirement in Article 32 of the Domestic Proceedings (Northern Ireland) Order 1980, as applied by section 29(2) or 29A(6) of this Act, is not satisfied.

(1B) But if the application or part of it relates to a matter where jurisdiction falls to be determined by reference to the jurisdictional requirements of the Maintenance Regulation and Schedule 6 to the Civil Jurisdiction and Judgments (Maintenance) Regulations 2011, the registering court may not entertain the application or that part of it unless it has jurisdiction to do so by virtue of that Regulation and that Schedule.

(2) None of the powers of the court, or of the clerk, under section 34B of this Act shall be exercisable in relation to such an application.

(3) Where the respondent to an application for the variation or revocation of a registered order which is registered in a magistrates' court in Northern Ireland does not appear at the time and place appointed for the hearing of the application, but the court is satisfied –

(a) that the respondent is residing outside Northern Ireland, and
(b) that the prescribed notice of the making of the application and of the time and place appointed for the hearing has been given to the respondent in the prescribed manner,

the court may proceed to hear and determine the application at the time and place appointed for the hearing or for any adjourned hearing in like manner as if the respondent had appeared at that time and place.

(4) In subsection (1B) 'the Maintenance Regulation' means Council Regulation (EC) 4/2009 including as applied in relation to Denmark by virtue of the Agreement made on 19 October 2005 between the European Community and the Kingdom of Denmark.

Amendments—Inserted by MO(RE)A 1992, s 1, Sch 1, para 16. Substituted by SI 1995/755. Amended by SI 2012/2814.
Defined terms—'registered order': s 39.
Scope—A means of payment order may not be made under this section.

Supplemental

36 Admissibility of evidence given in Convention country

(A1) A statement contained in a document mentioned in subsection (1) shall –

(a) in any proceedings in the family court arising out of an application to which section 27A(1) of this Act applies or an application made by any person for the variation or revocation of a registered order, or

(b) in proceedings on appeal from proceedings within paragraph (a),

be admissible as evidence of any fact stated to the same extent as oral evidence of that fact is admissible in those proceedings.

(1) The documents referred to in subsections (A1) and (1A) are –

(a) a document, duly authenticated, which purports to set out or summarise evidence given in proceedings in a court in a Convention country;

(b) a document, duly authenticated, which purports to set out or summarise evidence taken in such a country for the purpose of proceedings in a court in the United Kingdom under this Part of this Act, whether in response to a request made on behalf of such a court or otherwise;

(c) a document, duly authenticated, which purports to have been received in evidence in proceedings in a court in such a country, or to be a copy of a document so received.

(1A) A statement contained in a document mentioned in subsection (1) shall, in any proceedings in a magistrates' court in Northern Ireland or in, or remitted from, a sheriff court arising out of an application to which section 28C(1) of this Act applies, an application received by the Secretary of State as mentioned in section 31(1) of this Act or an application made by any person for the variation or revocation of a registered order or in proceedings on appeal from any such proceedings, be admissible as evidence of any fact stated therein to the same extent as oral evidence of that fact is admissible in those proceedings.

(2) A document purporting to set out or summarise evidence given as mentioned in subsection (1)(a) above, or taken as mentioned in subsection (1)(b) above, shall be deemed to be duly authenticated for the purposes of that subsection if the document purports to be certified by the judge, magistrate or other person before whom the evidence was given or, as the case may be, by whom it was taken, to be the original document containing or recording, or, as the case may be, summarising, that evidence or a true copy of that document.

(3) A document purporting to have been received in evidence as mentioned in subsection (1)(c) above, or to be a copy of a document so received, shall be deemed to be duly authenticated for the purposes of that subsection if the document purports to be certified by a judge, magistrate or officer of the court in question to have been, or to be a true copy of a document which has been, so received.

(4) It shall not be necessary in any such proceedings to prove the signature or official position of the person appearing to have given such a certificate.

(5) Nothing in this section shall prejudice the admission in evidence of any document which is admissible in evidence apart from this section.

Amendments—DPMCA 1978, s 60(3); MO(RE)A 1992, s 1, Sch 1, para 17; SI 1992/709; SI 1995/755; CCA 2013, s 17, Sch 11.

Defined terms—'Convention country': s 25(1); 'registered order': s 39.

37 Obtaining of evidence for purpose of proceedings in United Kingdom court

(1) A court in the United Kingdom may for the purpose of any proceedings in that court under this Part of this Act arising out of an application received by the Lord Chancellor from a Convention country request the Lord Chancellor to make to the appropriate authority or court in the Convention country a request for the taking in that country of the evidence of a person residing therein relating to matters connected with the application.

(2) A request made by a court under this section shall –

(a) give details of the application in question;

(b) state the name and address of the person whose evidence is to be taken; and

(c) specify the matters relating to which the evidence of that person is required.

(3) If the Lord Chancellor is satisfied that a request made to him under this section contains sufficient information to enable the evidence of the person named in the request relating to the matters specified therein to be taken by a court or person in the Convention country, he shall transmit the request to the appropriate authority or court in that country.

Amendments—SI 1992/709.
Defined terms—'Convention country': s 25(1).

38 Taking of evidence at request of court in Convention country

(1) Where a request is made to the Lord Chancellor by or on behalf of a court in a Convention country to obtain the evidence of a person residing in the United Kingdom relating to matters connected with an application to which section 26 of this Act applies, the Lord Chancellor shall request such court, or such officer of a court, as he may determine to take the evidence of that person relating to such matters connected with that application as may be specified in the request.

(2) The court by which or officer by whom a request under subsection (1) above is received from the Lord Chancellor shall have power to take the evidence and, after giving notice of the time and place at which the evidence is to be taken to such persons and in such manner as it or he thinks fit, shall take the evidence of the person named in the request relating to the matters specified therein in such manner as may be prescribed; and the evidence so taken shall be sent in the prescribed manner by the prescribed officer to the court in the Convention country by or on behalf of which the request referred to in subsection (1) above was made.

(3) Where any person, not being the person by whom the application mentioned in subsection (1) above was made, is required by virtue of this section to give evidence before a court in the United Kingdom, the court may order that there shall be paid –

(a) if the court is a court in England, Wales or Scotland, out of moneys provided by Parliament; and
(b) if the court is a court in Northern Ireland, out of moneys provided by the Northern Ireland Assembly,

such sums as appear to the court reasonably sufficient to compensate that person for the expense, trouble or loss of time properly incurred in or incidental to his attendance.

(4) Articles 118(1), (3) and (4), 119 and 120 of the Magistrates' Courts (Northern Ireland) Order 1981 (which provide for compelling the attendance of witnesses, etc) shall apply in relation to a magistrates' court in Northern Ireland to which a request under subsection (1) above is made as if the application to which the request relates were a complaint to be heard by that court.

(5) …

(6) *(repealed)*

Amendments—SI 1973/2163; MCA 1980, s 154, Sch 7, para 109; SI 1981/1675; SI 1992/709; SI 2010/976; CCA 2013, s 17, Sch 11.
Defined terms—'Convention country': s 25(1).

38A Rules of court

(1) Rules of court may make provision with respect to the orders made or other things done by the family court or a magistrates' court, or an officer of such a court, by virtue of this Part of this Act, notice of which is to be given to such persons as the rules may provide and the manner in which such notice shall be given.

(2) For the purpose of giving effect to this Part of this Act, rules of court may make, in relation to any proceedings brought under or by virtue of this Part of this Act, any provision not covered by subsection (1) above which –

(a) falls within subsection (2) of section 93 of the Children Act 1989, and
(b) may be made in relation to relevant proceedings under that section.

(3) *(repealed)*

(4) For the purpose of giving effect to this Part of this Act, rules made under Article 13 of the Magistrates' Courts (Northern Ireland) Order 1981 may make, in relation to any proceedings brought under or by virtue of this Part of this Act, any provision not covered by subsection (1) above which –

(a) falls within paragraph (2) of Article 165 of the Children (Northern Ireland Order) 1995, and

(b) may be made in relation to relevant proceedings under that Article.

Amendments—Inserted by MO(RE)A 1992, s 1, Sch 1, para 18. Amended by SI 1995/755; SI 2004/2035; CCA 2013, s 17, Sch 11.

39 Interpretation of Part II

In this Part of this Act –

'maintenance order' has the same meaning as in Part I of this Act;

'prescribed' has the same meaning as in Part I of this Act;

'registered order' means an order which is for the time being registered in a court in the United Kingdom under this Part of this Act;

'registering court', in relation to a registered order, means the court in which that order is for the time being registered under this Part of this Act;

'revoke' and 'revocation' include 'discharge'.

Amendments—MO(RE)A 1992, s 1, Sch 1, para 19.

PART III
MISCELLANEOUS AND SUPPLEMENTAL

Further provisions relating to enforcement of maintenance orders and to applications for recovery of maintenance

40 Power to apply Act to maintenance orders and applications for recovery of maintenance made in certain countries

Where Her Majesty is satisfied –

(a) that arrangements have been or will be made in a country or territory outside the United Kingdom to ensure that maintenance orders made by courts in the United Kingdom can be enforced in that country or territory or that applications by persons in the United Kingdom for the recovery of maintenance from persons in that country or territory can be entertained by courts in that country or territory; and

(b) that in the interest of reciprocity it is desirable to ensure that maintenance orders made by courts in that country or territory can be enforced in the United Kingdom or, as the case may be, that applications by persons in that country or territory for the recovery of maintenance from persons in the United Kingdom can be entertained by courts in the United Kingdom,

Her Majesty may by Order in Council make provision for applying the provisions of this Act, with such exceptions, adaptations and modifications as may be specified in the Order, to such orders or applications as are referred to in paragraph (a) or (b) above and to maintenance and other orders made in connection with such applications by courts in the United Kingdom or in that country or territory.

Amendments—CJJA 1982, ss 37(1), 54, Sch 11, para 17, Sch 14.

Scope—In addition to s 25 regarding Convention countries, this section allows the application of the Act to be extended to other countries by Order in Council, with such modifications as may be necessary. Reference should be made to Procedural Guide C1.

★★★★

Provisions with respect to certain orders of magistrates' courts

42 Provisional order for maintenance of party to marriage made by court to cease to have effect on remarriage of party

(1) Where a court has, by virtue of section 3 of this Act, made a provisional maintenance order consisting of, or including, a provision such as is mentioned in section 2(1)(a) of the Domestic Proceedings and Magistrates' Courts Act 1978 (making of periodical payments by husband or wife) or Article 4(1)(a) of the Domestic Proceedings (Northern Ireland) Order 1980 and the order has been confirmed by a competent court in a reciprocating country, then, if after the making of that order the marriage of the parties to the proceedings in which the order was made is dissolved or annulled but the order continues in force, that order or, as the case may be, that provision thereof shall cease to have effect on the remarriage of the party in whose favour it was made, except in relation to any arrears due under it on the date of such remarriage and shall not be capable of being revived.

(2) For the avoidance of doubt it is hereby declared that reference in this section to remarriage include references to a marriage which is by law void and voidable.

(3) …

Amendments—DPMCA 1978, s 89(2), Sch 2, para 37; SI 1980/564; CCA 2013, s 17, Sch 11.

****

Supplemental provisions

44 Exclusion of certain enactments relating to evidence

(1) Section 20 of the Family Law Reform Act 1969 (power of court hearing certain proceedings to require use of blood tests to determine paternity) and any corresponding enactment of the Parliament of Northern Ireland shall not apply to any proceedings under this Act, but the foregoing provision is without prejudice to the power of a court to allow the report of any person who has carried out such tests to be given in evidence in those proceedings.

(2) The Evidence (Proceedings in Other Jurisdictions) Act 1975 shall not apply to the taking of evidence in the United Kingdom for the taking of which section 14 or section 38 of this Act provides.

Amendments—Evidence (Proceedings in Other Jurisdictions) Act 1975, s 8(1), Sch 1.

****

47 Interpretation: general

(1) In this Act –

'enactment' includes an enactment of the Parliament of Northern Ireland;

'magistrates' court', in relation to Northern Ireland, means a court of summary jurisdiction within the meaning of Article 2(2)(a) of the Magistrates' Courts (Northern Ireland) Order 1981.

(2) References in this Act to a part of the United Kingdom are references to England and Wales, to Scotland, or to Northern Ireland.

(3) Any reference in this Act to the jurisdiction of a court, where the reference is to assets being located or to a person residing within the jurisdiction of a court, shall be construed in relation to a magistrates' court in Northern Ireland as a reference to the petty sessions district for which the court acts.

(4) Any reference to this Act to any other enactment is a reference thereto as amended, and includes a reference thereto as extended or applied, by or under any other enactment.

Amendments—SI 1981/1675; CJJA 1982, ss 37(1), 54, Sch 11, para 18, Sch 14; Courts Act 2003, Sch 8, para 164; CCA 2013, s 17, Sch 11.

****

Marriage (Same Sex Couples) Act 2013

Scope—The vast majority of the Act's provisions came into force on 13 March 2014, permitting the first same-sex marriages to take place on 29 March 2014. It enables same-sex couples to marry in England and Wales only either in a civil ceremony (i e a civil ceremony in a register office or approved premises, e g a hotel) or, provided that the religious organisation concerned is in agreement, on religious premises, with the marriage being solemnised through a religious ceremony. The Act does not remove the availability of civil partnership for same-sex couples. Those in a civil partnership are able to convert that relationship to a marriage, if they choose to do so, from 10 December 2014 (s 9).

The Act enables a person to change their legal gender without ending their existing marriage (see the Gender Recognition Act 2004, as amended), contains provisions dealing with consular marriages and marriage on armed forces bases overseas and recognition of certain marriages of same-sex couples formed outside England and Wales.

The Act is largely an amending statute, amending various statutes, including MA 1949, the Equality Act 2010, the Marriage (Registrar General's Licence) Act 1970, MCA 1973, DMPA 1973, the Social Security Contributions and Benefits Act 1992, the Pension Schemes Act 1993, CPA 2004 and the GRA 2004. The full structure of the Act is as follows:

Pt 1 (ss 1–11 and Schs 1–4) contains the main provisions relating to marriage of same-sex couples.

Pt 2 (ss 12–16 and Schs 5 and 6) deals with the change of legal gender of a married person or civil partner and marriage overseas, as well as with reviews of marriage by belief organisations, of the operation and future of CPA 2004 in England and Wales and of survivor benefits under occupational pension schemes.

Pt 3 (ss 17–21 and Sch 7) contains the standard technical provisions of the Act, including order-making powers and procedures, interpretation, extent and commencement.

The Family Procedure (Amendment) Rules 2014 made consequential amendments to FPR 2010. The Marriage (Same Sex Couples) (Jurisdiction and Recognition of Judgments) Regulations 2014 make corresponding provision, as far as is possible in domestic law, for marriages of same-sex couples as to the jurisdiction and recognition elements of Brussels IIA for proceedings for divorce, annulment or judicial separation of a married same-sex couple as regards the law of England and Wales.

Same-sex marriage may have immigration law implications: *SB (India) v Secretary of State for the Home Department* [2016] EWCA Civ 451.

1 Extension of marriage to same sex couples

(1) Marriage of same sex couples is lawful.

(2) The marriage of a same sex couple may only be solemnized in accordance with –

- (a) Part 3 of the Marriage Act 1949,
- (b) Part 5 of the Marriage Act 1949,
- (c) the Marriage (Registrar General's Licence) Act 1970, or
- (d) an Order in Council made under Part 1 or 3 of Schedule 6.

(3) No Canon of the Church of England is contrary to section 3 of the Submission of the Clergy Act 1533 (which provides that no Canons shall be contrary to the Royal Prerogative or the customs, laws or statutes of this realm) by virtue of its making provision about marriage being the union of one man with one woman.

(4) Any duty of a member of the clergy to solemnize marriages (and any corresponding right of persons to have their marriages solemnized by members of the clergy) is not extended by this Act to marriages of same sex couples.

(5) A 'member of the clergy' is –

- (a) a clerk in Holy Orders of the Church of England, or
- (b) a clerk in Holy Orders of the Church in Wales.

Scope—Section 1 makes marriage of same-sex couples lawful in England and Wales and sets out the legislative provisions under which same-sex couples may marry, while ensuring that there is no obligation on the clergy of the Church of England and the Church in Wales to marry same-sex couples.

★★★★

Other provisions relating to marriages of same sex couples

9 Conversion of civil partnership into marriage

(1) The parties to an England and Wales civil partnership may convert their civil partnership into a marriage under a procedure established by regulations made by the Secretary of State.

(2) The parties to a civil partnership within subsection (3) may convert their civil partnership into a marriage under a procedure established by regulations made by the Secretary of State.

(3) A civil partnership is within this subsection if –

(a) it was formed outside the United Kingdom under an Order in Council made under Chapter 1 of Part 5 of the Civil Partnership Act 2004 (registration at British consulates etc or by armed forces personnel), and

(b) the part of the United Kingdom that was relevant for the purposes of section 210(2)(b) or (as the case may be) section 211(2)(b) of that Act was England and Wales.

(4) Regulations under this section may in particular make –

(a) provision about the making by the parties to a civil partnership of an application to convert their civil partnership into a marriage;

(b) provision about the information to be provided in support of an application to convert;

(c) provision about the making of declarations in support of an application to convert;

(d) provision for persons who have made an application to convert to appear before any person or attend at any place;

(e) provision conferring functions in connection with applications to convert on relevant officials, relevant armed forces personnel, the Secretary of State, or any other persons;

(f) provision for fees, of such amounts as are specified in or determined in accordance with the regulations, to be payable in respect of –

(i) the making of an application to convert;

(ii) the exercise of any function conferred by virtue of paragraph (e).

(5) Functions conferred by virtue of paragraph (e) of subsection (4) may include functions relating to –

(a) the recording of information on the conversion of civil partnerships;

(b) the issuing of certified copies of any information recorded;

(ba) the carrying out, on request, of searches of any information recorded and the provision, on request, of records of any information recorded (otherwise than in the form of certified copies);

(c) the conducting of services or ceremonies (other than religious services or ceremonies) following the conversion of a civil partnership.

(5A) Subsection (5B) applies where regulations under this section provide for a fee to be payable to a superintendent registrar or registrar.

(5B) The regulations may provide for such part of the fee as may be specified in or determined in accordance with the regulations to be payable by the superintendent registrar or registrar to the Registrar General in such circumstances as may be set out in the regulations.

(5C) The regulations may provide for the reduction, waiver or refund of part or all of a fee whether by conferring a discretion or otherwise.

(6) Where a civil partnership is converted into a marriage under this section –

(a) the civil partnership ends on the conversion, and

(b) the resulting marriage is to be treated as having subsisted since the date the civil partnership was formed.

(7) In this section –

'England and Wales civil partnership' means a civil partnership which is formed by two people registering as civil partners of each other in England or Wales (see Part 2 of the Civil Partnership Act 2004);

'relevant armed forces personnel' means –

(a) a member of Her Majesty's forces;

(b) a civilian subject to service discipline (within the meaning of the Armed Forces Act 2006);

and for this purpose 'Her Majesty's forces' has the same meaning as in the Armed Forces Act 2006;

'relevant official' means –

(a) the Registrar General;

(b) a superintendent registrar;

(c) a registrar;

(d) a consular officer in the service of Her Majesty's government in the United Kingdom;

(e) a person authorised by the Secretary of State in respect of the solemnization of marriages or formation of civil partnerships in a country or territory in which Her Majesty's government in the United Kingdom has for the time being no consular representative.

Amendments—Deregulation Act 2015, s 99(3); Immigration Act 2016, s 89, Sch 15.

Scope—The completed conversion process (s 9(1)) automatically ends the civil partnership and the couple are treated as having been married since the date the civil partnership was formed (s 9(6)). Conversion has been possible from 10 December 2014. It would appear that the effect of s 9(6) is that a petition for divorce may be presented within 1 year of the conversion to marriage providing that more than 1 year has elapsed from the date the civil partnership was formed.

10 Extra-territorial matters

(1) A marriage under –

(a) the law of any part of the United Kingdom (other than England and Wales), or

(b) the law of any country or territory outside the United Kingdom,

is not prevented from being recognised under the law of England and Wales only because it is the marriage of a same sex couple.

(2) For the purposes of this section it is irrelevant whether the law of a particular part of the United Kingdom, or a particular country or territory outside the United Kingdom –

(a) already provides for marriage of same sex couples at the time when this section comes into force, or

(b) provides for marriage of same sex couples from a later time.

(3) Schedule 2 (extra-territorial matters) has effect.

Schedule 2 (extra-territorial matters)—Schedule 2 provides for the treatment in Scotland and Northern Ireland of English and Welsh marriages of same-sex couples as civil partnerships (Pt 1), the dissolution, annulment or separation of a same-sex marriage treated as a civil partnership in Scotland or Northern Ireland when the civil partnership is dissolved, annulled or an order is made for the separation of the civil partners (Pt 2) and provision for the treatment of 'overseas relationships' as defined by CPA 2004 so that an overseas marriage of a same-sex couple will be treated as a marriage under the law of England and Wales, but as a civil partnership under the law of Scotland and Northern Ireland (Pt 3).

Effect of extension of marriage

11 Effect of extension of marriage

(1) In the law of England and Wales, marriage has the same effect in relation to same sex couples as it has in relation to opposite sex couples.

(2) The law of England and Wales (including all England and Wales legislation whenever passed or made) has effect in accordance with subsection (1).

(3) Schedule 3 (interpretation of legislation) has effect.

(4) Schedule 4 (effect of extension of marriage: further provision) has effect.

(5) For provision about limitations on the effects of subsections (1) and (2) and Schedule 3, see Part 7 of Schedule 4.

(6) Subsections (1) and (2) and Schedule 3 do not have any effect in relation to –

(a) Measures and Canons of the Church of England (whenever passed or made),

(b) subordinate legislation (whenever made) made under a Measure or Canon of the Church of England, or

(c) other ecclesiastical law (whether or not contained in England and Wales legislation, and, if contained in England and Wales legislation, whenever passed or made).

(7) In Schedules 3 and 4 –

'existing England and Wales legislation' means –

(a) in the case of England and Wales legislation that is primary legislation, legislation passed before the end of the Session in which this Act is passed (excluding this Act), or

(b) in the case of England and Wales legislation that is subordinate legislation, legislation made on or before the day on which this Act is passed (excluding legislation made under this Act);

'new England and Wales legislation' means –

(a) in the case of England and Wales legislation that is primary legislation, legislation passed after the end of the Session in which this Act is passed, or

(b) in the case of England and Wales legislation that is subordinate legislation, legislation made after the day on which this Act is passed.

Scope—Section 11 and Schs 3 and 4 provide that the marriage of a same-sex couple has the same effect in law in England and Wales in relation to such a couple as it does in relation to an opposite-sex couple, ensuring that existing and new legislation is interpreted accordingly, except where specific provision is made.

****

Married Women's Property Act 1882

****

17 Questions between husband and wife as to property to be decided in summary way

In any question between husband and wife as to the title to or possession of property, either party may apply by summons or otherwise in a summary way to the High Court or the family court and the court may, on such an application (which may be heard in private), make such order with respect to the property as it thinks fit.

In this section 'prescribed' means prescribed by rules of court.

Amendments—Statute Law (Repeals) Act 1969; MFPA 1984, s 43; CCA 2013, s 17, Sch 11.

Scope—This section enables the court to declare and enforce the proprietary rights of each party as they are found to exist in accordance with trust and common law principles. It does not give the court power to adjust those rights to produce a fair allocation of capital and income in the way that is done on an application for financial provision and property adjustment orders under MCA 1973, s 25. Where there is or will be an application for financial relief under MCA 1973 it is, generally speaking, a waste of time and money to apply under this section (*Fielding v Fielding* [1977] 1 WLR 1146, CA). Two situations where s 17 still has a useful purpose are:

(a) where it is believed that one party may shortly become bankrupt, a declaration as to each party's respective beneficial interest in an asset may be of some value against any claim that a trustee in bankruptcy may subsequently mount; and

(b) where it is desired to obtain a sale of property before the final ancillary relief hearing (although FPR 2010, r 20.2(1)(c)(v) now provides an express procedural route to sale).

Procedure—See FPR 2010, rr 8.12–8.17, which govern applications under MWPA 1882, s 17. The application may be made to the High Court or the Family Court under r 8.14. Where particulars of a mortgage are provided, the mortgagee must be served and may be made a party: r 8.15(1),(2).

Power of sale—Section 17 contains a power of sale: *Wicks v Wicks* [1998] 1 FLR 470, CA. This power of sale can be exercised on an interim basis, i e prior to the final financial remedy hearing and in relation to the former matrimonial home only if the court is satisfied that the other party's home rights should also be terminated (so as to allow vacant possession, if appropriate) after applying and balancing the factors in FLA 1996, s 33(6). See further, **Interim Orders** under MCA 1973, s 23.

'property'—Property is defined by s 24 to include a thing in action. The Matrimonial Causes (Property and Maintenance) Act 1958, an Act which enables the court to make orders in respect of property which a party has had in his possession or control, defines 'property' (in s 8) to mean any real or personal property, any money, any negotiable instrument, debt or other chose in action and any other right or interest whether in possession or not.

Extension of court's powers—Matrimonial Causes (Property and Maintenance) Act 1958, s 7 extends this section to enable the court to make orders where money or property has ceased to be in the possession or under the control of one of the parties. In such a case the court is able to order one party to pay to the other the value of the applicant's interest in the asset that has been disposed of or to transfer to the applicant any property which can be traced to the original asset. Section 7(7) of that Act confirms the court's power to order a sale of property but a sale may be ordered only if there is some question between the parties as to the title to or possession of the property other than the issue of whether the property should be sold (*Rawlings v Rawlings* [1964] P 398, CA).

Engaged parties—Law Reform (Miscellaneous Provisions) Act 1970, s 2(2) provides that an application under this section may be made by parties who have been engaged but not married. Jurisdiction exists even if the agreement to marry is unenforceable at common law, eg because it was made at a time when one of the parties was already married (*Shaw v Fitzgerald* [1992] 1 FLR 357, FD).

Civil partners—Subject to a limitation period of 3 years from dissolution or annulment, application may be made by civil partners for orders equivalent to the relief provided by this section (see CPA 2004, s 66).

Polygamous marriages—The reference to 'husband and wife' includes parties to a polygamous or potentially polygamous marriage (*Chaudhry v Chaudhry* [1976] Fam 148, CA).

Time-limit for making application—Under MPPA 1970, s 39, a husband or wife must apply within 3 years of decree absolute. Engaged parties must apply within 3 years after the termination of the engagement (Law Reform (Miscellaneous Provisions) Act 1970, s 2(2)).

Court's powers—The court's jurisdiction to declare and enforce proprietary rights includes the power to restrain by injunction one party from disposing of a matrimonial home while the other wishes to live in it (*Lee v Lee* [1952] 2 QB 489, CA; *Halden v Halden* [1966] 1 WLR 1481, CA), and the power to assess the monetary value of a party's interest in an asset and to order the other party to pay a lump sum in that amount (*Bothe v Amos* [1976] Fam 46, CA).

★★★★

Married Women's Property Act 1964

1 Money and property derived from housekeeping allowance

If any question arises as to the right of a husband or wife to money derived from any allowance made by the husband for the expenses of the matrimonial home or for similar purposes, or to any property acquired out of such money, the money or property shall, in the absence of any agreement between them to the contrary, be treated as belonging to the husband and the wife in equal shares.

★★★★

Matrimonial and Family Proceedings Act 1984

ARRANGEMENT OF SECTIONS

PART III

FINANCIAL RELIEF IN ENGLAND AND WALES AFTER OVERSEAS DIVORCE ETC

Section		Page
	Applications for financial relief	
12	Applications for financial relief after overseas divorce etc	1124
13	Leave of the court required for applications for financial relief	1125
14	Interim orders for maintenance	1125
15	Jurisdiction of the court	1126
16	Duty of the court to consider whether England and Wales is appropriate venue for application	1127
	Orders for Financial Provision and Property Adjustment	
17	Orders for financial provision and property adjustment	1127
18	Matters to which the court is to have regard in exercising its powers under s 17	1128
19	Consent orders for financial provision or property adjustment	1129
20	Restriction of powers of court where jurisdiction depends on matrimonial home in England or Wales	1129
21	Application to orders under ss 14 and 17 of certain provisions of Part II of Matrimonial Causes Act 1973	1130

Orders for transfer of tenancies

22	Powers of the court in relation to certain tenancies of dwelling-houses	1132

Avoidance of transactions intended to prevent or reduce financial relief

23	Avoidance of transactions intended to defeat applications for financial relief	1132
24	Prevention of transactions intended to defeat prospective applications for financial relief	1133

Interpretation

27	Interpretation of Part III	1134

PART 4A
THE FAMILY COURT

31B	Sittings	1134
31E	Family court has High Court and county court powers	1135
31F	Proceedings and decisions	1135
31G	Witnesses and evidence	1137
31H	Contempt of court: power to limit court's powers	1138
31I	Powers of the High Court in respect of family court proceedings	1139
31J	Overview of certain powers of the court under other Acts	1139
31K	Appeals	1140
31L	Enforcement	1141
31O	Justices' clerks and assistants: functions	1142
31P	Orders, regulations and rules under Part 4A	1143

PART V
FAMILY BUSINESS: DISTRIBUTION AND TRANSFER

Preliminary

32	What is family business	1144

Distribution and transfer of family business and proceedings

37	Directions as to distribution and transfer of family business and proceedings	1144
38	Transfer of family proceedings from High Court	1144
39	Transfer of family proceedings to High Court	1145

****

PART III
FINANCIAL RELIEF IN ENGLAND AND WALES AFTER OVERSEAS DIVORCE ETC

Applications for financial relief

12 Applications for financial relief after overseas divorce etc

(1) Where –

(a) a marriage has been dissolved or annulled, or the parties to a marriage have been legally separated, by means of judicial or other proceedings in an overseas country, and

(b) the divorce, annulment or legal separation is entitled to be recognised as valid in England and Wales,

either party to the marriage may apply to the court in the manner prescribed by rules of court for an order for financial relief under this Part of this Act.

(2) If after a marriage has been dissolved or annulled in an overseas country one of the parties to the marriage forms a subsequent marriage or civil partnership, that party shall not be entitled to make an application in relation to that marriage.

(3) The reference in subsection (2) above to the forming of a subsequent marriage or civil partnership includes a reference to the forming of a marriage or civil partnership which is by law void or voidable.

(4) In this Part of this Act except sections 19, 23, and 24 'order for financial relief' means an order under section 17 or 22 below of a description referred to in that section.

Amendments—CPA 2004, s 261(1), Sch 27, para 90(1)–(3).

Scope—This section enables a party whose marriage has been ended by proceedings taken overseas (including by talaq) that are recognised as valid in accordance with FLA 1986, Pt II to apply for financial relief in this country. In making the application, there must be compliance with the formal requirements of English law, in that there must have been a marriage under s 12(a), recognised under English law as valid, or at least void. In *Sharbatly v Shagroon* [2013] 1 FLR 1493, CA, a ceremony in a London hotel between Saudi nationals was not a marriage for the purposes of matrimonial relief under MCA 1973, approving *Dukali v Lamrani (Attorney-General Intervening)* [2012] 2 FLR 1099, FD (marriage ceremony within Moroccan consulate not a marriage). The orders by way of financial relief to which a party may be entitled are practically identical to the orders that may be made under MCA 1973, ss 22–24A and Matrimonial Homes Act 1983, Sch 1 except that, where the only ground conferring jurisdiction is the existence of a matrimonial home within the jurisdiction, special rules apply. Remarriage bars an application in the same way as under MCA 1973, s 28(3).

Costs—Applications under MFPA 1984, Pt III are financial remedy proceedings under FPR 2010, rr 2.3, 28.3(4)(b)(ii). Save where conduct arises, the general rule is that in financial remedy proceedings, the court will not make a costs order against a party: FPR 2010, r 28.3(6).

PART II

13 Leave of the court required for applications for financial relief

(1) No application for an order for financial relief shall be made under this Part of this Act unless the leave of the court has been obtained in accordance with rules of court; and the court shall not grant leave unless it considers that there is substantial ground for the making of an application for such an order.

(2) The court may grant leave under this section notwithstanding that an order has been made by a court in a country outside England and Wales requiring the other party to the marriage to make any payment or transfer any property to the applicant or a child of the family.

(3) Leave under this section may be granted subject to such conditions as the court thinks fit.

Defined terms—'child of the family': s 27; 'order for financial relief': s 12(4).

Scope—In *Agbaje v Agbaje* [2010] 1 FLR 1813, SC, the Supreme Court provided guidance on the operation of MFPA 1984 in the grant of financial relief in England, following overseas divorce. The threshold for leave under s 13 is 'a substantial ground for the making of an application', which meant 'a solid ground'; this is specifically a higher standard than 'a serious issue to be tried' or 'a good arguable case'. The guidance set down in *Agbaje* in the interpretation and application of s 13 should be followed. A test of a 50% probability of the claimant receiving a substantive order as in *CG v IF* [2010] 2 FLR 1790, FD was disapproved by the Court of Appeal in *Traversa v Freddi* [2011] 2 FLR 272, CA, applying *Agbaje* and granting leave to apply. See also *Schofield v Schofield* [2011] 1 FLR 2129, CA, where a wife's earnings were modest and her husband's army pension a significant resource.

In considering a leave application under s 13, the s 16 duty of the court to consider whether England and Wales is the appropriate venue for the application should be considered.

The procedure to obtain permission is set out in FPR 2010, rr 8.24–8.28. See commentary to FPR 2010, r 8.28 for allocation guidance.

Leave, once given, should be set aside only where there is a compelling reason to do so. An application to set aside leave should be heard with the substantive application, unless the respondent could deliver a 'knockout blow': *Traversa v Freddi*.

14 Interim orders for maintenance

(1) Where leave is granted under section 13 above for the making of an application for an order for financial relief and it appears to the court that the applicant or any child of the family is in immediate need of financial assistance, the court may make an interim order for maintenance, that is to say, an order requiring the other party to the marriage to make to the applicant or to the child such periodical payments, and for such term, being a term beginning not earlier than the date of the grant of leave and ending with the date of the determination of the application for an order for financial relief, as the court thinks reasonable.

(2) If it appears to the court that the court has jurisdiction to entertain the application for an order for financial relief by reason only of paragraph (c) of section 15(1) below the court shall not make an interim order under this section.

(3) An interim order under subsection (1) above may be made subject to such conditions as the court thinks fit.

Scope—Where jurisdiction arises solely through the ownership of a matrimonial home in England and Wales, the court shall not make interim orders under this section. However, this section enables the court to make an interim order for maintenance of the applicant and/or the children of the family, pending final hearing. The limitations imposed by s 14 were (i) no order for interim maintenance would be made until leave had been given to make a Pt III application; (ii) under s 14(2), the jurisdiction must be founded on domicile or habitual residence, as opposed to an interest in a former matrimonial home in the jurisdiction; (iii) the applicant must be in 'immediate need' and the provision must be reasonable in the sense of 'current' rather than 'urgent', as with application for interim maintenance under MCA 1973: *M v M (Financial Provision)* [2011] 1 FLR 1773, FD.

15 Jurisdiction of the court

(1) Subject to subsections (1A) and (2) below, the court shall have jurisdiction to entertain an application for an order for financial relief if any of the following jurisdictional requirements are satisfied that is to say –

(a) either of the parties to the marriage was domiciled in England and Wales on the date of the application for leave under section 13 above or was so domiciled on the date on which the divorce, annulment or legal separation obtained in the overseas country took effect in that country; or

(b) either of the parties to the marriage was habitually resident in England and Wales throughout the period of one year ending with the date of the application for leave or was so resident throughout the period of one year ending with the date on which the divorce, annulment or legal separation obtained in the overseas country took effect in that country; or

(c) either or both of the parties to the marriage had at the date of the application for leave a beneficial interest in possession in a dwelling-house situated in England or Wales which was at some time during the marriage a matrimonial home of the parties to the marriage.

(1A) If an application or part of an application relates to a matter where jurisdiction falls to be determined by reference to the jurisdictional requirements of the Maintenance Regulation and Schedule 6 to the Civil Jurisdiction and Judgments (Maintenance) Regulations 2011, those requirements are to determine whether the court has jurisdiction to entertain the application or that part of it.

(2) Where the jurisdiction of the court to entertain proceedings under this Part of this Act would fall to be determined by reference to the jurisdictional requirements imposed by virtue of Part I of the Civil Jurisdiction and Judgments Act 1982 (implementation of certain European conventions) then –

(a) satisfaction of the requirements of subsection (1) above shall not obviate the need to satisfy the requirements imposed by virtue of Part I of that Act; and

(b) satisfaction of the requirements imposed by virtue of Part I of that Act shall obviate the need to satisfy the requirements of subsection (1) above;

and the court shall entertain or not entertain the proceedings accordingly.

(3) In this section, 'the Maintenance Regulation' means Council Regulation (EC) No 4/2009 including as applied in relation to Denmark by virtue of the Agreement made on 19 October 2005 between the European Community and the Kingdom of Denmark.

Amendments—SI 2001/3929; SI 2007/1655; SI 2011/1484.

'matrimonial home' (s 15(1)(c))—Whether a property has been a matrimonial home is a question of fact, evidenced by any period of time spent living there or any agreement to so treat it (*King v King* [1942] P 1, PDAD).

Civil Jurisdiction and Judgments Act 1982, Pt I (s 15(2))—The 1982 Act applies only where the respondent is domiciled in a contracting state. With the exception of Greece, all the contracting states are in Western Europe; they include Belgium, Germany, France, Italy, Luxembourg, The Netherlands, Denmark, Republic of Ireland and the UK. By Sch 1, Art 1, the 1982 Act does not apply to rights in property arising out of a matrimonial relationship, but subject to that exception the basic theme of the 1982 Act, Pt I is that if a proposed respondent is domiciled in a contracting state he must be sued there. There is one further exception, namely that in matters relating to maintenance even though the respondent is domiciled in a contracting state he may nevertheless be sued in the courts of the country where the maintenance creditor is either domiciled or habitually resident. In summary, if the proposed respondent is resident outside the contracting states, CJJA, Pt I is irrelevant. If the respondent is resident within a contracting state, careful attention should be paid to the provisions of Pt I.

16 Duty of the court to consider whether England and Wales is appropriate venue for application

(1) Subject to subsection (3), before making an order for financial relief the court shall consider whether in all the circumstances of the case it would be appropriate for such an order to be made by a court in England and Wales, and if the court is not satisfied that it would be appropriate, the court shall dismiss the application.

(2) The court shall in particular have regard to the following matters –

- (a) the connection which the parties to the marriage have with England and Wales;
- (b) the connection which those parties have with the country in which the marriage was dissolved or annulled or in which they were legally separated;
- (c) the connection which those parties have with any other country outside England and Wales;
- (d) any financial benefit which the applicant or a child of the family has received or is likely to receive, in consequence of the divorce, annulment or legal separation, by virtue of any agreement or the operation of the law of a country outside England and Wales,
- (e) in a case where an order has been made by a court in a country outside England and Wales requiring the other party to the marriage to make any payment or transfer any property for the benefit of the applicant or a child of the family, the financial relief given by the order and the extent to which the order has been complied with or is likely to be complied with;
- (f) any right which the applicant has, or has had, to apply for financial relief from the other party to the marriage under the law of any country outside England and Wales and if the applicant has omitted to exercise that right the reason for that omission;
- (g) the availability in England and Wales of any property in respect of which an order under this Part of this Act in favour of the applicant could be made;
- (h) the extent to which any order made under this Part of this Act is likely to be enforceable;
- (i) the length of time which has elapsed since the date of the divorce, annulment or legal separation.

(3) If the court has jurisdiction in relation to the application or part of it by virtue of the Maintenance Regulation and Schedule 6 to the Civil Jurisdiction and Judgments (Maintenance) Regulations 2011, the court may not dismiss the application or that part of it on the ground mentioned in subsection (1) if to do so would be inconsistent with the jurisdictional requirements of that Regulation and that Schedule.

(4) In this section, 'the Maintenance Regulation' means Council Regulation (EC) No 4/2009 including as applied in relation to Denmark by virtue of the Agreement made on 19 October 2005 between the European Community and the Kingdom of Denmark.

Amendments—SI 2011/1484.

Scope—In seeking leave under the Act, ss 13 and 16 should be taken in conjunction. The court must consider whether under s 16(1), England and Wales is the appropriate venue for the application. Regard must be had for the principle of comity, which demands respect for overseas orders, and forum (non) conveniens: *Moore v Moore* [2007] 2 FLR 339, CA. In *Agbaje v Agbaje* [2010] 1 FLR 1813, SC, the Supreme Court said that the doctrine of forum conveniens did not apply, as no choice between the jurisdictions was involved.

Orders for Financial Provision and Property Adjustment

17 Orders for financial provision and property adjustment

(1) Subject to section 20 below, on an application by a party to a marriage for an order for financial relief under this section, the court may –

- (a) make any one or more of the orders which it could make under Part II of the 1973 Act if a decree of divorce, a decree of nullity of marriage or a decree of judicial separation in respect of the marriage had been granted in England and Wales, that is to say –

(i) any order mentioned in section 23(1) of the 1973 Act (financial provision orders); and

(ii) any order mentioned in section 24(1) of that Act (property adjustment orders); and

(b) if the marriage has been dissolved or annulled, make one or more orders each of which would, within the meaning of that Part of that Act, be a pension sharing order in relation to the marriage.

(c) if the marriage has been dissolved or annulled, make an order which would, within the meaning of that Part of that Act, be a pension compensation sharing order in relation to the marriage.

(2) Subject to section 20 below, where the court makes a secured periodical payments order, an order for the payment of a lump sum or a property adjustment order under subsection (1) above, then, on making that order or at any time thereafter, the court may make any order mentioned in section 24A(1) of the 1973 Act (orders for sale of property) which the court would have power to make if the order under subsection (1) above had been made under Part II of the 1973 Act.

Amendments—WRPA 1999, s 84(1), Sch 12, para 3; Pensions Act 2008, Sch 6, Pt 2.

Scope—This section incorporates the principles of MCA 1973, ss 25 and 25A, including the obligation to consider whether a clean break is appropriate, where the court is considering whether and in what manner to exercise its powers under the Act. In *Agbaje v Agbaje* [2010] 1 FLR 1813, SC, the Supreme Court said that MCA 1973, P t III contains no express reference to hardship, justice or exceptionality and these were not conditions for the making of an award but may make it appropriate for an award to be made and might affect the nature of the provision ordered. Mere disparity between a foreign award and what would be awarded on an English divorce would be insufficient to trigger the application of Pt III, but the presence of hardship or injustice might make it appropriate for an order to be made. In *Agbaje*, the case was characterised not by the disparity between what the wife would receive in Nigeria and England, but the large disparity between what the husband and wife had received in the Nigerian courts, such as to create a real hardship and a serious injustice for the wife. *Agbaje* has established that the amount of financial provision would depend on all the circumstances of the case, not the minimum amount required to overcome injustice. The Court has a broad jurisdiction, subject to three principles that (i) primary consideration must be given to the welfare of any child of the marriage, (ii) it is wrong in principle to award more than the English court would have awarded and (iii) where possible, the order should provide for the 'reasonable needs' of the spouse. Where the English connections are very strong, this might justify treating the application for financial relief as if it were 'made in purely English proceedings'; *Agbaje v Agbaje*, at [5].

Pension Sharing/Pension Attachment—For an overview of pension sharing and pension attachment see the annotations to MCA 1973, s 21.

18 Matters to which the court is to have regard in exercising its powers under s 17

(1) In deciding whether to exercise its powers under section 17 above and, if so, in what manner the court shall act in accordance with this section.

(2) The court shall have regard to all the circumstances of the case, first consideration being given to the welfare while a minor of any child of the family who has not attained the age of eighteen.

(3) As regards the exercise of those powers in relation to a party to the marriage, the court shall in particular have regard to the matters mentioned in section 25(2)(a) to (h) of the 1973 Act and shall be under duties corresponding with those imposed by section 25A(1) and (2) of the 1973 Act where it decides to exercise under section 17 above powers corresponding with the powers referred to in those subsections.

(3A) The matters to which the court is to have regard under subsection (3) above –

(a) so far as relating to paragraph (a) of section 25(2) of the 1973 Act, include any benefits under a pension arrangement which a party to the marriage has or is likely to have and any PPF compensation to which a party to the marriage is or is likely to be entitled (whether or not in the foreseeable future), and

(b) so far as relating to paragraph (h) of that provision, include –

(i) any benefits under a pension arrangement which, by reason of the dissolution or annulment of the marriage, a party to the marriage will lose the chance of acquiring, and

(ii) any PPF compensation which, by reason of the dissolution or annulment of the marriage, a party to the marriage will lose the chance of acquiring entitlement to.

(4) As regards the exercise of those powers in relation to a child of the family, the court shall in particular have regard to the matters mentioned in section 25(3)(a) to (e) of the 1973 Act.

(5) As regards the exercise of those powers against a party to the marriage in favour of a child of the family who is not the child of that party, the court shall also have regard to the matters mentioned in section 25(4)(a) to (c) of the 1973 Act.

(6) Where an order has been made by a court outside England and Wales for the making of payments or the transfer of property by a party to the marriage, the court in considering in accordance with this section the financial resources of the other party to the marriage or a child of the family shall have regard to the extent to which that order has been complied with or is likely to be complied with.

(7) In this section –

(a) 'pension arrangement' has the meaning given by section 25D(3) of the 1973 Act, and

(b) references to benefits under a pension arrangement include any benefits by way of pension, whether under a pension arrangement or not, and

(c) 'PPF compensation' means compensation payable under –

(i) Chapter 3 of Part 2 of the Pensions Act 2004 (pension protection) or any regulations or order made under it,

(ii) Chapter 1 of Part 3 of the Pensions Act 2008 (pension compensation sharing) or any regulations or order made under it, or

(iii) any provision corresponding to the provisions mentioned in sub-paragraph (i) or (ii) in force in Northern Ireland.

Amendments—WRPA 1999, s 22(2),(3); Pensions Act 2004, Sch 12, para 4; Pensions Act 2008, Sch 6, Pt 2.

Scope—See the commentary to s 17, above. The scale of the award and the degree of connection to the jurisdiction is discussed in *Z v A (Financial Remedy after Overseas Divorce)* [2014] 2 FLR 109, FD, where the marriage was short and only the wife had property in England. A case where the parties were truly international did not justify consideration of compensation or sharing; fair and reasonable provision for the needs of the wife and child and a capital clean break were appropriate orders. Foreign parties who had accrued very substantial wealth were nevertheless subject to the principles of MCA 1973, s 25(1) and (2), but an award could not exceed that which would be made in a conventional case under MCA 1973: *M v M and Five Others* [2014] 1 FLR 439, FD.

19 Consent orders for financial provision or property adjustment

(1) Notwithstanding anything in section 18 above, on an application for a consent order for financial relief the court may, unless it has reason to think that there are other circumstances into which it ought to inquire, make an order in the terms agreed on the basis only of the prescribed information furnished with the application.

(2) Subsection (1) above applies to an application for a consent order varying or discharging an order for financial relief as it applies to an application for an order for financial relief.

(3) In this section –

'consent order', in relation to an application for an order, means an order in the terms applied for to which the respondent agrees;

'order for financial relief' means an order under section 17 above; and

'prescribed' means prescribed by rules of court.

Scope—MFPA 1984, s 19 mirrors MCA 1973, s 33A(1). This section empowers the court to make a consent order without a full investigation and without hearing oral evidence. There is a requirement for up-to-date information of the parties' circumstances. This is provided in each party's separate or joint statement of information: if separate documents, each party must sign the other's statement. There is no requirement for the parties to attend court. See FPR 2010, r 9.26.

20 Restriction of powers of court where jurisdiction depends on matrimonial home in England or Wales

(1) Where the court has jurisdiction to entertain an application for an order for financial relief by reason only of the situation in England or Wales of a dwelling-house which was a matrimonial home of the parties, the court may make under section 17 above any one or more of the following orders (but no other) –

PART II

(a) an order that either party to the marriage shall pay to the other such lump sum as may be specified in the order;
(b) an order that a party to the marriage shall pay to such person as may be so specified for the benefit of a child of the family, or to such a child, such lump sum as may be so specified;
(c) an order that a party to the marriage shall transfer to the other party, to any child of the family or to such person as may be so specified for the benefit of such a child, the interest of the first-mentioned party in the dwelling-house or such part of that interest as may be so specified;
(d) an order that a settlement of the interest of a party to the marriage in the dwelling-house, or such part of that interest as may be so specified, be made to the satisfaction of the court for the benefit of the other party to the marriage and of the children of the family or either or any of them;
(e) an order varying for the benefit of the parties to the marriage and of the children of the family or either or any of them any ante-nuptial or post-nuptial settlement (including such a settlement made by will or codicil) made on the parties to the marriage so far as that settlement relates to an interest in the dwelling-house;
(f) an order extinguishing or reducing the interest of either of the parties to the marriage under any such settlement so far as that interest is an interest in the dwelling-house;
(g) an order for the sale of the interest of a party to the marriage in the dwelling-house.

(2) Where, in the circumstances mentioned in subsection (1) above, the court makes an order for the payment of a lump sum by a party to the marriage, the amount of the lump sum shall not exceed, or where more than one such order is made the total amount of the lump sums shall not exceed in aggregate, the following amount, that is to say –

(a) if the interest of that party in the dwelling-house is sold in pursuance of an order made under subsection (1)(g) above, the amount of the proceeds of the sale of that interest after deducting therefrom any costs incurred in the sale thereof;
(b) if the interest of that party is not so sold, the amount which in the opinion of the court represents the value of that interest.

(3) Where the interest of a party to the marriage in the dwelling-house is held jointly or in common with any other person or persons –

(a) the reference in subsection (1)(g) above to the interest of a party to the marriage shall be construed as including a reference to the interest of that other person, or the interest of those other persons in the dwelling-house, and
(b) the reference in subsection (2)(a) above to the amount of the proceeds of a sale ordered under subsection (1)(g) above shall be construed as a reference to that part of those proceeds which is attributable to the interest of that party to the marriage in the dwelling-house.

Scope—Where the only fact establishing jurisdiction is the existence of a matrimonial home in this country, the court cannot make any maintenance order and it must not make a capital order which exceeds the monetary value of the matrimonial home.

21 Application to orders under ss 14 and 17 of certain provisions of Part II of Matrimonial Causes Act 1973

(1) The following provisions of Part II of the 1973 Act (financial relief for parties to marriage and children of family) shall apply in relation to an order under section 14 or 17 above as they apply in relation to a like order under that Part of that Act, that is to say –

(a) section 23(3) (provisions as to lump sums);
(b) section 24A(2), (4), (5) and (6) (provisions as to orders for sale);
(ba) section 24B(3) to (5) (provisions about pension sharing orders in relation to divorce and nullity);
(bb) section 24C (duty to stay pension sharing orders);
(bc) section 24D (apportionment of pension sharing charges);

(bca) section 24E(3) to (10) (provisions about pension compensation orders in relation to divorce and nullity);
(bcb) section 24F (duty to stay pension compensation sharing orders);
(bcc) section 24G (apportionment of pension compensation sharing charges);
(bd) section 25B(3) to (7B) (power, by financial provision order, to attach payments under a pension arrangement, or to require the exercise of a right of commutation under such an arrangement);
(be) section 25C (extension of lump sum powers in relation to death benefits under a pension arrangement);
(bf) section 25E(2) to (10) (the Pension Protection Fund);
(bg) section 25F (power, by financial provision order, to attach pension compensation payments, or to require the exercise of a right of commutation of pension compensation);
(c) section 28(1) and (2) (duration of continuing financial provision orders in favour of party to marriage);
(d) section 29 (duration of continuing financial provision orders in favour of children, and age limit on making certain orders in their favour);
(e) section 30 (direction for settlement of instrument for securing payments or effecting property adjustment), except paragraph (b);
(f) section 31 variation, discharge etc of certain orders for financial relief), except subsection (2)(e) and subsection (4);
(g) section 32 (payment of certain arrears unenforceable without the leave of the court);
(h) section 33 (orders for repayment of sums paid under certain orders);
(i) section 38 (orders for repayment of sums paid after cessation of order by reason of remarriage);
(j) section 39 (settlements etc made in compliance with a property adjustment order may be avoided on bankruptcy of settlor); and
(k) section 40 (payments etc under order made in favour of person suffering from mental disorder).
(l) section 40A (appeals relating to pension sharing orders which have taken effect).
(m) section 40B (appeals relating to pension compensation sharing orders which have taken effect).

(2) Subsection (1)(bd), (be) and (bg) above shall not apply where the court has jurisdiction to entertain an application for an order for financial relief by reason only of the situation in England or Wales of a dwelling-house which was a matrimonial home of the parties.

(3) Section 25D(1) of the 1973 Act (effect of transfers on orders relating to rights under a pension arrangement) shall apply in relation to an order made under section 17 above by virtue of subsection (1)(bd) or (be) above as it applies in relation to an order made under section 23 of that Act by virtue of section 25B or 25C of the 1973 Act.

(4) The Lord Chancellor may by regulations make for the purposes of this Part of this Act provision corresponding to any provision which may be made by him under subsections (2) to (2B) of section 25D of the 1973 Act or under subsections (1) to (3) of section 25G of that Act.

(5) Power to make regulations under this section shall be exercisable by statutory instrument which shall be subject to annulment in pursuance of a resolution of either House of Parliament.

Amendments—WRPA 1999, ss 22(4),(5), 84(1), Sch 12, para 4, Sch 13, Pt II; Pensions Act 2004, Sch 12, para 4; Pensions Act 2008, Sch 6, Pt 2.

Scope—Subject to CSA 1991, which restricts the court's power to order child maintenance (see Procedural Guide B7), this section imports into the provisions for providing financial relief following an overseas divorce the vast majority of the powers of the court which apply where a financial application is brought following a divorce in this country. The three conspicuous absentees are the power to award interest on a lump sum under MCA 1973, s 23(6), the power to make a direction under s 25A(3) that there may be no further application for a periodical payments or secured periodical payments order, and the prohibition from applying to extend the term of a maintenance order under s 28(1A).

Mental disorder under s 21(1)(k)—See MCA 2005: a person who lacks capacity is defined in s 2(1) as a person who at the material time 'is unable to make a decision for himself … because of an impediment of, or a disturbance in the functioning of, the mind or brain'.

Orders for transfer of tenancies

22 Powers of the court in relation to certain tenancies of dwelling-houses

(1) This section applies if –

(a) an application is made by a party to a marriage for an order for financial relief; and
(b) one of the parties is entitled, either in his own right or jointly with the other party, to occupy a dwelling-house situated in England or Wales by virtue of a tenancy which is a relevant tenancy within the meaning of Schedule 7 to the Family Law Act 1996 (certain statutory tenancies).

(2) The court may make in relation to that dwelling-house any order which it could make under Part II of that Schedule if a decree of divorce, a decree of nullity of marriage or a decree of judicial separation has been granted in England and Wales in respect of the marriage.

(3) The provisions of paragraphs 10, 11 and 14(1) in Part III of that Schedule apply in relation to any order under this section as they apply to any order under Part II of that Schedule.

Amendments—Substituted by FLA 1996, s 66(1), Sch 8, para 52. Amended by SI 1997/1892.

Avoidance of transactions intended to prevent or reduce financial relief

23 Avoidance of transactions intended to defeat applications for financial relief

(1) For the purposes of this section 'financial relief' means relief under section 14 or 17 above and any reference to defeating a claim by a party to a marriage for financial relief from being granted is a reference to preventing financial relief from being granted or reducing the amount of relief which might be granted, or frustrating or impeding the enforcement of any order which might be or has been made under either of those provisions at the instance of that party.

(2) Where leave is granted under section 13 above for the making by a party to a marriage of an application for an order for financial relief under section 17 above, the court may, on an application by that party –

(a) if it is satisfied that the other party to the marriage is, with the intention of defeating the claim for financial relief, about to make any disposition or to transfer out of the jurisdiction or otherwise deal with any property, make such order as it thinks fit for restraining the other party from so doing or otherwise for protecting the claim;
(b) if it is satisfied that the other party has, with that intention, made a reviewable disposition and that if the disposition were set aside financial relief or different financial relief would be granted to the applicant, make an order setting aside the disposition.

(3) Where an order for financial relief under section 14 or 17 above has been made by the court at the instance of a party to a marriage, then, on an application made by that party, the court may, if it is satisfied that the other party to the marriage has, with the intention of defeating the claim for financial relief, made a reviewable disposition, make an order setting aside the disposition.

(4) Where the court has jurisdiction to entertain the application for an order for financial relief by reason only of paragraph (c) of section 15(1) above, it shall not make any order under subsection (2) or (3) above in respect of any property other than the dwelling-house concerned.

(5) Where the court makes an order under subsection (2)(b) or (3) above setting aside a disposition it shall give such consequential directions as it thinks fit for giving effect to the order (including directions requiring the making of any payments or the disposal of any property).

(6) Any disposition made by the other party to the marriage (whether before or after the commencement of the application) is a reviewable disposition for the purposes of subsections (2)(b) and (3) above unless it was made for valuable consideration (other than marriage) to a person who, at the time of the disposition, acted in relation to it in good faith and without notice of any intention on the part of the other party to defeat the applicant's claim for financial relief.

(7) Where an application is made under subsection (2) or (3) above with respect to a disposition which took place less than three years before the date of the application or with respect to a disposition or other dealing with property which is about to take place and the court is satisfied –

(a) in a case falling within subsection (2)(a) or (b) above, that the disposition or other dealing would (apart from this section) have the consequence, or

(b) in a case falling within subsection (3) above, that the disposition has had the consequence,

of defeating a claim by the applicant for financial relief, it shall be presumed unless the contrary is shown, that the person who disposed of or is about to dispose of or deal with the property did so or, as the case may be, is about to do so, with the intention of defeating the applicant's claim for financial relief.

(8) In this section 'disposition' does not include any provision contained in a will or codicil but, with that exception, includes any conveyance, assurance or gift of property of any description, whether made by an instrument or otherwise.

(9) The preceding provisions of this section are without prejudice to any power of the High Court to grant injunctions under section 37 of the Senior Courts Act 1981.

Amendments—CRA 2005, Sch 11, para 1(2).

Scope—This section is the equivalent of MCA 1973, s 37. It enables an applicant who has been granted leave to apply for financial relief to restrain future, and set aside past, disposals made with the intention of defeating the claim.

24 Prevention of transactions intended to defeat prospective applications for financial relief

(1) Where, on an application by a party to a marriage, it appears to the court –

(a) that the marriage has been dissolved or annulled, or that the parties to the marriage have been legally separated, by means of judicial or other proceedings in an overseas country; and

(b) that the applicant intends to apply for leave to make an application for an order for financial relief under section 17 above as soon as he or she has been habitually resident in England and Wales for a period of one year; and

(c) that the other party to the marriage is, with the intention of defeating a claim for financial relief, about to make any disposition or to transfer out of the jurisdiction or otherwise deal with any property,

the court may make such order as it thinks fit for restraining the other party from taking such action as is mentioned in paragraph (c) above.

(2) For the purposes of an application under subsection (1) above –

(a) the reference to defeating a claim for financial relief shall be construed in accordance with subsection (1) of section 23 above (omitting the reference to any order which has been made); and

(b) subsections (7) and (8) of section 23 above shall apply as they apply for the purposes of an application under that section.

(3) The preceding provisions of this section are without prejudice to any power of the High Court to grant injunctions under section 37 of the Senior Courts Act 1981.

Amendments—CRA 2005, Sch 11, para 1(2).

Defined terms—'the court', 'overseas country': s 27.

Scope—Although the major restraining provisions, equivalent to MCA 1973, s 37, are contained in s 23, this provides a remedy, equivalent to that contained in MCA 1973, s 37(2)(a), for an applicant who has not yet obtained leave but who intends to do so as soon as there has been 1 year's habitual residence. Without prejudice to the court's power under SCA 1981, s 37, this section enables an applicant to restrain anticipated dealings made with the intention of defeating the claim.

****

Interpretation

27 Interpretation of Part III

In this Part of this Act –

'the 1973 Act' means the Matrimonial Causes Act 1973;

'child of the family' has the meaning as in section 52(1) of the 1973 Act;

'the court' means the High Court or the family court;

'dwelling-house' includes any building or part thereof which is occupied as a dwelling, and any yard, garden, garage or outhouse belonging to the dwelling-house and occupied therewith;

'order for financial relief' has the meaning given by section 12(4) above;

'overseas country' means a country or territory outside the British Islands;

'possession' includes receipt of, or the right to receive, rents and profits;

'property adjustment order' means such an order as is specified in section 24(1)(a), (b), (c) or (d) of the 1973 Act;

'rent' does not include mortgage interest;

'secured periodical payments order' means such an order as is specified in section 23(1)(b) or (e) of the 1973 Act.

Amendments—CCA 2013, s 17, Sch 11.

****

PART 4A
THE FAMILY COURT

CCA 2013, s 17(3) and Sch 10—The effect of these amendments to MFPA 1984 is to create (alongside the child support administrative appeals system under TCEA 2007) three principal regimes for court proceedings on family breakdown:

(1) *High Court*

- 'High Court' refers to the jurisdiction of the Family Division that is defined by SCA 1981, Sch 1, para 3. The amendments to MFPA 1984 considered below do not specifically apply to the High Court (eg finality of family courts' orders after *Sharland v Sharland* [2015] 2 FLR 1367, SC, at [41] and evidence 'in the interests of' litigants in person (s 31G(6); although the common law is likely to adapt these provisions for use in the Family Division).
- Administrative law family proceedings (mostly judicial review, eg under HRA 1998, CSA 1991 etc, will often be dealt with in the Queen's Bench Division (Administrative Court)). TLATA 1996 (see Procedural Guide A4) and bankruptcy proceedings will be dealt with in the Chancery Division.

(2) *Family Court* Amalgamates former county court and magistrates' (civil-family) powers in FPR 2010 proceedings, but leaves certain powers that are not to be allocated to lay justices and some child support work with the magistrates.

(3) *County Court* Family proceedings not covered by FPR 2010 (ie by SCA 1981, Sch 1 para 3) remain in the separate County Court regulated entirely by CPR 1998 (eg proceedings under I(PFD)A 1975; TLATA 1996).

The County Court: CCA 1984—CCA 2013, s 17(1) creates a single County Court. CCA 1984 remains in force. A number of the provisions in ss 31A–31P are derived from CCA 1984 and a number of CCA 1984 provisions are directly applied to practice in the Family Court by ss 31A–31P.

A court of record (s 31A(2))—As a court of record – that is an 'inferior' court – the Family Court (where and if appropriate: eg on a human rights, delay or listing points) could be subject to judicial review. The basis for such application was defined by *R (Sivasubramaniam) v Wandsworth County Court* [2003] 1 WLR 475, CA and reviewed and narrowed in *Cart v The Upper Tribunal* [2012] 1 FLR 997, SC.

****

31B Sittings

(1) Sittings of the family court may be held, and any other business of the family court may be conducted, at any place in England and Wales.

(2) Sittings of the family court at any place may be continuous or intermittent or occasional.

(3) Sittings of the family court may be held simultaneously to take any number of different cases in the same place or different places, and the court may adjourn cases from place to place at any time.

(4) The places at which the family court sits, and the days and times at which it sits in any place, are to be determined in accordance with directions given by the Lord Chancellor after consulting the Lord Chief Justice.

(5) The Lord Chief Justice may nominate a judicial office holder (as defined in section 109(4) of the Constitutional Reform Act 2005) to exercise functions of the Lord Chief Justice under this section.

Amendments—Inserted by CCA 2013, s 17(6), Sch 10, para 1.

****

31E Family court has High Court and county court powers

(1) In any proceedings in the family court, the court may make any order –

(a) which could be made by the High Court if the proceedings were in the High Court, or
(b) which could be made by the county court if the proceedings were in the county court.

(2) In its application to a power of the High Court to issue a writ directed to an enforcement officer, subsection (1)(a) gives the family court power to issue a warrant, directed to an officer of the family court, containing provision corresponding to any that might be contained in the writ.

(3) Subsection (1) is subject to section 38(3) of the County Courts Act 1984.

(4) Subsection (1) is without prejudice to, and not limited by, any other powers of the family court.

(5) The Lord Chancellor may by regulations make provision, about or in connection with the effect or execution of warrants issued by the family court for enforcing any order or judgment enforceable by the court, that corresponds to any provision applying in relation to the effect or execution of writs issued by the High Court, or warrants issued by the county court, for the purpose of enforcing any order or judgment enforceable by that court.

Amendments—Inserted by CCA 2013, s 17(6), Sch 10, para 1.

Inherent powers—This section (especially s 31E(1)) is parallel to CCA 1984, s 38, which is treated as giving the County Court inherent and statutory powers akin to those of the High Court where the High Court has already exercised such powers: the injunction jurisdiction (especially that of the freezing order) is the obvious example (as explained in the commentary to CCA 1984, s 38).

Inherent jurisdiction—Beyond the powers given by s 31E(1), the Family Court has no inherent jurisdiction. However, as each step is taken in the High Court in the exercise of its inherent jurisdiction, so the Family Court judge can follow under s 31E(1).

Judicial review (s 31E(3))—The major exception to the above is CCA 1984, s 38(3), which prevents the Family Court and County Court making judicial review orders, or other prescribed orders (see, for example, CCRR 2014, which probably prevents the Family Court making a search order under Civil Procedure Act 1997, s 7).

Declarations and other inherent jurisdiction orders—Examples of the exercise of its inherent jurisdiction by the High Court can be found in, for example, *Birmingham City Council v Riaz and Others* [2015] 2 FLR 763, FD (reporting restriction order); *Re J (A Minor)* [2016] EWHC 2595 (Fam) (anonymity).

31F Proceedings and decisions

(1) The family court may adjourn a hearing, and may do so at any time including a time before the hearing has begun.

(2) Any order made by the family court –

(a) may be absolute or conditional;
(b) may be final or interim;
(c) may, subject to rules of court, be made without taking evidence.

(3) Every judgment and order of the family court is, except as provided by this or any other Act or by rules of court, final and conclusive between the parties.

(4) Where the family court has power to require the doing of anything other than the payment of money, or to prohibit the doing of anything, an order of the court made in exercising the power may contain provision –

(a) as to the manner in which anything is to be done,
(b) as to the time within which anything is to be done,

(c) as to the time during which anything is not to be done, and
(d) generally for giving effect to the order.

(5) Where the family court has power to require the payment of money, an order of the court made in exercising the power may allow time for payment or order payment by instalments; and where the court has ordered payment by instalments and default is made in the payment of any one instalment, proceedings may be taken as if the default had been made in the payment of all the instalments then unpaid.

(6) The family court has power to vary, suspend, rescind or revive any order made by it, including –

(a) power to rescind an order and re-list the application on which it was made,
(b) power to replace an order which for any reason appears to be invalid by another which the court has power to make, and
(c) power to vary an order with effect from when it was originally made.

(7) Subject to rules of court, the family court may proceed in the absence of one, some or all of the parties.

(8) The family court has the same power to enforce an undertaking given by a solicitor in relation to any proceedings in that court as the High Court has to enforce an undertaking given by a solicitor in relation to any proceedings in the High Court.

(9) In any case not expressly provided for by or in pursuance of this or any other Act, the general principles of practice in the High Court may be adopted and applied to proceedings in the family court.

Amendments—Inserted by CCA 2013, s 17(6), Sch 10, para 1.

Derivation—This section is derived from CCA 1984, ss 70–77 (sections entitled 'judgments and orders').

Orders of the Family Court (s 31F(2)(a),(b))—This provision is derived from CCA 1984, s 38(2).

'Any order… may be final or interim' (s 31F(2)(b))—This provision relates to 'any order' and cuts across the general rule, for example in financial remedy proceedings under MCA 1973, that capital orders are final (as explained in *Wicks v Wicks* [1998] 1 FLR 470, CA; but doubting Mostyn J in *BR v VT (Financial Remedies: Interim)* [2016] 2 FLR 519, FD). Periodical payments under MCA 1973 and CA 1989, Sch 1 can be varied, and as a matter of common law can be made interim (there is no specific provision for interim orders, although FPR 2010, r 9.7 provides a procedure for the Family Court to make such orders).

An order made 'without taking evidence' (s 31F(2)(c))—FPR 2010, r 22.2(1) provides that the 'general rule' for evidence to be proved is by oral evidence at a final hearing, but that 'any other hearing' (mostly interim or urgent hearings: FPR 2010, Pts 18 and 25) can be by 'evidence in writing'. Statutory force for r 22.2(1)(b) is provided here, although 'taking' in this context is not defined: it can perhaps be assumed to mean oral evidence, and that this is not always required as the basis for proof of a fact.

Interim financial remedy orders and the High Court—MFPA 1984, s 31E enables the Family Court to make orders that the High Court can make, but there is no reciprocal power in the High Court to make Family Court orders. Mostly, this will not matter, since the High Court relies on its inherent jurisdiction. Caution is needed in the area of, for example, MCA 1973 and CA 1989 because of the extensive statutory powers available to the courts (*Wicks v Wicks* [1998] 1 FLR 470, CA); but now see *BR v VT (Financial Remedies: Interim)* [2016] 2 FLR 519, FD where an order for sale was made interim to financial relief proceedings.

'Every judgment and order … is … final and conclusive between the parties' (s 31F(3))—This provision is derived from CCA 1984, s 70 and is immediately qualified in a way that s 70 is not (eg by s 31F(6), see *Sharland v Sharland* [2015] 2 FLR 1367, SC (below)). Statutory provisions applicable to the Family Court employ the following terminology for judgment, decision etc:

- *Decision* For example, in CPR 1998, r 52.4(2) (the date from which time runs for the filing of an appeal notice; also per FPR 2010, r 30.4(2)). MFPA 1984, s 31K(5)(c) requires 'a note' of the court's decision on law or findings of fact.
- *Decision made on appeal* For second appeals (AJA 1999, s 54; CPR 1998, r 52.13(2)).
- *Order* For example, in CPR 1998, r 52.10(2) (the appellate court can set aside the order made below. also per FPR 2010, r 30.11(2)); but see **Sealing the order** (below) for its conclusiveness.
- *Judgment* 'Judgment' is often used cumulatively with 'order' (as in s 31F(3) and see, for example, CPR 1998, r 40.7 and FPR 2010, r 29.15 (considered fully in *JP v NP* [2015] 1 FLR 659, FD, at [29]–[36])). The judgment provides the reasons for a decision, which is then recorded in an order and sealed, but may be additional to the 'note' prescribed by s 31K(5)(c)).
- *Direction* Case management directions (also called 'orders' (r 4.1(6), mostly under FPR 2010, Pt 4) can be 'varied or revoked' (FPR 2010, rr 4.1(7)(a) and 18.10(3)), whereas an order can only be appealed against.

Sealing the order: 'final and conclusive between the parties' (s 31F(3))—An order is only 'final' and therefore conclusive of the issues between the parties once it is sealed (*Re L-B (Reversal of Judgment)* [2013] 2 FLR 859, SC, at [44]: the judge changed her mind as to findings of fact in care proceedings and was able to change (i e 'vary for cause' per Lady Hale) her decision 2 months after it was made because – as it happened – the order, although drawn up, had not been sealed). Once sealed, the order dates back to the original decision.

Conditions on injunctions and other Family Court orders (s 31F(4))—The 'power to require the doing of anything … or prohibit the doing of anything' refers to all orders made in the Family Court, including:

(1) orders that can be made in the High Court, which translates, in terms of empowerment, to the Family Court by s 31E(1)(a). It includes injunctions, mandatory or prohibitory (the power to make an injunction is inherent in the High Court, codified by statute in SCA 1981, s 37); and

(2) Orders under the variety of statutes, which define family law and are provided for procedurally in FPR 2010.

Payment of a money order by instalments (s 31F(5))—Derived from CCA 1984, s 71, s 31F(5) includes provision to enable a receiving party to enforce for the full amount of a debt if default is made of one payment or more under an instalment order. Enforcement is under MFPA 1984, s 31L and procedures for enforcement under FPR 2010, Pt 33. This provision, by definition, cannot apply to periodical payments or other orders for unliquidated amounts.

Rescission of decrees of divorce and civil partnership (s 31F(6))—In *Lachaux v Lachaux* [2017] EWHC 385 (Fam), Mostyn J expressed the view that decrees of divorce could be rescinded under FPR 2010, r 4.1(6) or in the inherent jurisdiction of the court. His attention was perhaps not drawn to MFPA 1984, s 31F(6), which provides a statutory basis (alongside FPR 2010, r 7.28 for rescission of decrees nisi) for rescission of an order, such as a decree absolute.

'power to vary, suspend, rescind or revive any order' (s 31F(6))—At face value, s 31F(6) seems to undermine principles in relation to finality of judgments and orders. In *Sharland v Sharland* [2015] 2 FLR 1367, SC, at [41], Lady Hale confirmed this and that s 31F(6) does indeed provide the Family Court with a 'very wide power', which could include variation of lump sum and property adjustment orders. Although general, she said, the power is 'not unbounded', but it certainly gives the Family Court the power to set aside a final financial remedy order on established principles, such as non-disclosure (see Procedural Guide E7 for discussion and an outline of procedure) or to rescind an order (*Norman v Norman* [2017] EWCA Civ 120).

'undertaking given by a solicitor … as [in] the High Court' (s 31F(8))—The jurisdiction of the Family Court is based on the right of the High Court to see that a high standard of conduct is maintained by its officers (*John Fox v Bannister, King & Rigbeys* [1988] QB 925, CA; and see Solicitors Act 1974, s 50(1)). It is summary (i e by the former originating summons procedure, now FPR 2010, Pt 19 or Pt 18 in the proceedings 'in relation to' which the undertaking was given (per Sir John Donaldson MR in *John Fox v Bannister*).

'general principles of practice in the High Court' (s 31F(8))—Derived from CCA 1984, s 71, s 31F(8) ensures that any gap in practice in the Family Court (i e as this is provided for in FPR 2010, Pts 1–37) can be explained by reference to High Court practice principles (see application of this principle in family proceedings in *Tchenguiz-Imerman v Imerman* [2014] 1 FLR 232, FD (disclosure and procedure where legal professional privilege is claimed: CPR 1998, Pt 31) and *JP v NP* [2015] 1 FLR 659, FD (final order postponed until after decree nisi: CPR 1998, r 40.7(1)).

31G Witnesses and evidence

(1) Subsection (2) applies where the family court is satisfied that a person in England and Wales is likely to be able to give material evidence, or produce any document or thing likely to be material evidence, in proceedings in the court.

(2) The court may, if it is satisfied that it is in the interests of justice to do so, issue a summons –

(a) requiring the person to attend before the court, at the time and place specified in the summons, to give evidence,

(b) requiring the person to attend before the court, at the time and place specified in the summons, to produce the document or thing, or

(c) requiring the person to produce the document or thing to the court.

(3) Subsection (4) applies where without just excuse –

(a) a person fails to attend before the court in answer to a summons under subsection (2)(a) or (b),

(b) a person fails to produce a document or thing in answer to a summons under subsection (2)(b) or (c), or

(c) a person attending before the court, whether or not in answer to a summons under subsection (2), refuses to be sworn or give evidence.

(4) The court may –

(a) commit the person to custody until the expiry of a period not exceeding one month specified by the court or until the person sooner gives evidence or produces the document or thing, or

(b) impose on the person a fine not exceeding £2,500, or

(c) both.

(5) A fine imposed under subsection (4) is deemed, for the purposes of any enactment, to be a sum adjudged to be paid by a conviction of a magistrates' court.

(6) Where in any proceedings in the family court it appears to the court that any party to the proceedings who is not legally represented is unable to examine or cross-examine a witness effectively, the court is to –

(a) ascertain from that party the matters about which the witness may be able to depose or on which the witness ought to be cross-examined, and

(b) put, or cause to be put, to the witness such questions in the interests of that party as may appear to the court to be proper.

(7) Subject to the provisions of any Act or instrument made under an Act or rule of law authorising the reception of unsworn evidence, evidence given before the family court is to be given on oath.

(8) An affidavit to be used in the family court may be sworn before –

(a) a judge of the court, or

(b) an officer of the court appointed by a judge of the court for the purpose,

as well as before a commissioner for oaths or any other person authorised to take affidavits under the Commissioners for Oaths Acts 1889 and 1891.

(9) An affidavit sworn before any such judge or officer may be sworn without the payment of any fee.

Amendments—Inserted by CCA 2013, s 17(6), Sch 10, para 1.

Summons—The power to issue a witness summons is provided for by s 31G(1),(2). In practice (see FPR 2010, rr 24.1–24.10), the summons is issued as of right by court staff: there is no need for a judge (or equivalent) to be 'satisfied'. If issue is opposed by a witness, s/he can apply to set aside the summons (FPR 2010, r 24.3(4)). The penalties provisions in s 31G(3)–(5) are derived from CCA 1984, s 55, although s 31G is silent as to the provision in CCA 1984, s 55(3) for tendering conduct money:

'(3) No person summoned in pursuance of rules of court as a witness in the county court shall forfeit a fine under this section unless there has been paid or tendered to him at the time of the service of the summons such sum in respect of his expenses (including, in such cases as may be prescribed, compensation for loss of time) as may be prescribed for the purposes of this section.'

Section 31G(4) gives the court a discretion as to penalty. If a witness is not tendered attendance money, it might be that discretion should be exercised with s 55(3) very much in mind.

Witness summons for a child—It is likely that a competent child can be summoned to give evidence and compelled to give evidence in family proceedings. A summons can be issued accordingly under s 31G (*Re S (Children)* [2016] EWCA Civ 83).

Summons by court officer—Formal HMCTS procedures in relation to service of a summons by a court officer are dealt with by s 31N.

'any party … not legally represented' (s 31G(6))—It is understood that the civil justice authorities are looking at the subject of litigants in person in general and that Family Procedure Rules Committee (FPRC) are concerned about the subject. Section 31G(6) has imposed on judges – 'if it appears to the court' – a duty always to consider whether an unrepresented party is 'unable to examine etc' a witness effectively and if so, to decide what role the judge should take in assisting a party.

'put, or cause to be put, to the witness': HMCTS funding (s 31G(6)(b))—Family judges must rely on their own devices in ensuring that a witness is properly questioned 'in the interests of' the party concerned (*Re K and H (Private Law: Public Funding)* [2016] 1 FLR 754, CA; *sub nom Re K & H (Children)*), save in the rare circumstance that they can persuade the Attorney-General to assist (per the Attorney General's Memorandum of 19 December 2001, para 4 (see Part V) and in accordance with the rare example of *H v L and R* [2007] 2 FLR 162, FD; but see doubts as to this approach expressed in *Re K and H*).

Vulnerable witnesses and children—The FPRC are looking at working party recommendations for the introduction of rules to protect vulnerable witnesses and children. It may be that application to the court to protect a witness from an alleged abuser's cross-examination can be made already within the terms of the common law for protective measures akin to Youth Justice and Criminal Evidence Act 1999, Pt 2 (see the discussion at [2016] Fam Law 1025).

31H Contempt of court: power to limit court's powers

(1) The Lord Chancellor may by regulations made after consulting the Lord Chief Justice make provision limiting or removing, in circumstances specified in the regulations, any of the powers exercisable by the family court when dealing with a person for contempt of court.

(2) The Lord Chief Justice may nominate a judicial office holder (as defined in section 109(4) of the Constitutional Reform Act 2005) to exercise functions of the Lord Chief Justice under this section.

Amendments—Inserted by CCA 2013, s 17(6), Sch 10, para 1.

31I Powers of the High Court in respect of family court proceedings

(1) If the High Court, at any stage in proceedings in the family court, thinks it desirable that the proceedings, or any part of them, should be transferred to the High Court, it may order the transfer to the High Court of the proceedings or part.

(2) The power given by subsection (1) is without prejudice to section 29 of the Senior Courts Act 1981, and is to be exercised –

(a) in accordance with any directions given as to the distribution or transfer of proceedings, and

(b) subject to any provision made under section 1 of the Courts and Legal Services Act 1990 or made by or under any other enactment.

Amendments—Inserted by CCA 2013, s 17(6), Sch 10, para 1.

Scope—This provision is derived from CCA 1984, s 41. SCA 1981, s 29 enables the High Court to make prerogative orders (judicial review) and CLSA 1990, s 1 deals with distribution of business as between the High Court and the County Court.

31J Overview of certain powers of the court under other Acts

The powers of the family court include its powers under –

(a) section 33 of the Senior Courts Act 1981 (powers exercisable before commencement of action);

(b) section 34 of that Act (power to order disclosure or inspection of documents or property of non-party);

(c) section 37 of that Act (power to grant injunction or appoint receiver);

(d) section 39 of that Act (power to order documents to be executed or indorsed by nominated person);

(e) section 70(1) and (2) of that Act (assessors);

(f) section 57 of the County Courts Act 1984 (evidence of prisoners);

(g) section 71 of that Act (powers as to payment of costs).

Amendments—Inserted by CCA 2013, s 17(6), Sch 10, para 1.

'powers of the Family Court include'—Section 31J provides an inclusive list of remedies available in the Family Court that are available in other courts, and can be read alongside s 31F(9) for more general application of application of High Court principles in the Family Court. These powers are among those referred to as 'interim remedies' in FPR 2010, Pt 20. Allocation of these remedies to the judiciary and the appropriate court level is by FC(CDB)R 2014.

SCA 1981, s 33 (s 31J(a))—In relation to pre-action disclosure of documents, SCA 1981, s 33 provides as follows:

> **'33 Powers of High Court exercisable before commencement of action**
>
> …
>
> (2) On the application, in accordance with rules of court, of a person who appears to the High Court to be likely to be a party to subsequent proceedings in that court … the High Court shall, in such circumstances as may be specified in the rules, have power to order a person who appears to the court to be likely to be a party to the proceedings and to be likely to have or to have had in his possession, custody or power any documents which are relevant to an issue arising or likely to arise out of that claim –
>
> (a) to disclose whether those documents are in his possession, custody or power; and
>
> (b) to produce such of those documents as are in his possession, custody or power to the applicant or, on such conditions as may be specified in the order –
>
> (i) to the applicant's legal advisers; or
>
> (ii) to the applicant's legal advisers and any medical or other professional adviser of the applicant; or
>
> (iii) if the applicant has no legal adviser, to any medical or other professional adviser of the applicant.
>
> …'

SCA 1981, s 34 (s 31J(b))—In relation to disclosure of documents etc by a person not a party to the proceedings, SCA 1981, s 34 provides as follows:

> **'34 Power of High Court to order disclosure of documents**
>
> …
>
> (2) On the application, in accordance with rules of court, of a party to any proceedings …, the High Court shall, in such circumstances as may be specified in the rules, have power to order a person who is not a

party to the proceedings and who appears to the court to be likely to have in his possession, custody or power any documents which are relevant to an issue arising out of the said claim –
(a) to disclose whether those documents are in his possession, custody or power; and
(b) to produce such of those documents, as are in his possession, custody or power to the applicant or, on such conditions as may be specified in the order –
 (i) to the applicant's legal advisers; or
 (ii) to the applicant's legal advisers and any medical or other professional adviser of the applicant; or
 (iii) if the applicant has no legal adviser, to any medical or other professional adviser of the applicant.
...
(4) The preceding provisions of this section are without prejudice to the exercise by the High Court of any power to make orders which is exercisable apart from those provisions.
...'

Application under SCA 1981, ss 33 and 34

(1) FPR 2010, Pt 20 provides specifically for application for interim remedies including application under SCA 1981, ss 33 and 34 (r 20.2(2)). Such application will be by the FPR 2010, Pt 18 procedure (save as mentioned at 2)).
(2) Application under SCA 1981, s 33 is by the FPR 2010, Pt 19 procedure pending the issue of any later proceedings. (A s 33 application might be of value, for example, where mediation could only proceed successfully where the Family Court had made a preliminary decision on what documents should be disclosed (or other information provided: see reference to CPR 1998, Pt 18 under FPR 2010, r 21.2)).
(3) FPR 2010, r 21.2 provides for application by the FPR 2010, Pt 18 procedure in the existing proceedings, for disclosure and such application will predominantly be under SCA 1981, s 34(2).

Power to appoint assessors (s 31J(e))—See FPR 2010, r 25.20.

CCA 1974, s 71: payment of orders for costs (s 31J(g))—MFPA 1984, s 31F(5) gives the Family Court powers akin to CCA 1984, s 71, but does not extend those powers to costs. To provide the Family Court with such powers, s 31J(G) is therefore necessary. As material CCA 1984, s 71 provides:

'(1) Where a judgment is given or an order is made by the county court under which a sum of money of any amount is payable, whether by way of satisfaction of the claim or counterclaim in the proceedings or by way of costs or otherwise, the court may, as it thinks fit, order the money to be paid either –
 (a) in one sum, whether forthwith or within such period as the court may fix; or
 (b) by such instalments payable at such times as the court may fix.
(2) If at any time it appears to the satisfaction of the county court that any party to any proceedings in the court is unable from any cause to pay any sum recovered against him (whether by way of satisfaction of the claim or counterclaim in the proceedings or by way of costs or otherwise) or any instalment of such a sum, the court may, in its discretion, suspend or stay any judgment or order given or made in the proceedings for such time and on such terms as the court thinks fit, and so from time to time until it appears that the cause of inability has ceased.
...'

31K Appeals

(1) Subject to any order made under section 56(1) of the Access to Justice Act 1999 (power to provide for appeals to be made instead to the High Court or county court, or to the family court itself), if any party to any proceedings in the family court is dissatisfied with the decision of the court, that party may appeal from it to the Court of Appeal in such manner and subject to such conditions as may be provided by Family Procedure Rules.

(2) Subsection (1) does not –

 (a) confer any right of appeal from any decision where a right of appeal is conferred by some other enactment, or

 (b) take away any right of appeal from any decision where a right of appeal is so conferred,

and has effect subject to any enactment other than this Part; and in this subsection 'enactment' means an enactment whenever passed.

(3) The Lord Chancellor may, after consulting the Lord Chief Justice, by order make provision as to the circumstances in which appeals may be made against decisions taken by courts or judges on questions arising in connection with the transfer, or proposed transfer, of proceedings from or to the family court.

(4) Except to the extent provided for in any order made under subsection (3), no appeal may be made against any decision of a kind mentioned in that subsection.

(5) At the hearing of any proceedings in the family court in which there is a right of appeal or from which an appeal may be brought with permission, the judge, if requested to do so by any party, is to make a note –

 (a) of any question of law raised at the hearing,

(b) of the facts in evidence in relation to any such question, and
(c) of the court's decision on any such question and of the court's determination of the proceedings.

(6) Where such a note is made, and whether or not an appeal has been made, the court –

(a) on the application of any party to the proceedings, and
(b) on payment of the fee (if any) prescribed under section 92 of the Courts Act 2003,

is to provide that party with a copy of the note signed by the judge, and the copy so signed is to be used at the hearing of any appeal.

(7) Section 81 of the County Courts Act 1984 (powers of Court of Appeal on appeal from county court) applies to appeals from the family court to the Court of Appeal as it applies to appeals from the county court to the Court of Appeal.

(8) The Lord Chief Justice may nominate a judicial office holder (as defined in section 109(4) of the Constitutional Reform Act 2005) to exercise functions of the Lord Chief Justice under subsection (3).

Amendments—Inserted by CCA 2013, s 17(6), Sch 10, para 1.

'party to any family proceedings' (s 31K(1))—A 'party' to family proceedings who has a right to appeal under s 31K(1) can include a witness (eg social worker or police officer) against whom adverse findings were made in a judgment and where they had no opportunity to make representation to the court below as to those findings. The appeal court can consider their appeal on grounds that they assert the court acted in breach of their ECHR Art 6 (fair trial) and 8 (right to private and family life) rights under HRA 1998, ss 7–9.

'the judge ... is to make a note' (s 31K(5) and (6))—Derived from CCA 1984, s 80, s 31K(5) enables a party to proceedings in the Family Court to ask a judge to deal with certain matters there set out. In practice, it is likely that this will in any event be dealt with in any judgment and in the reasons for the court's decision recorded in that judgment.

31L Enforcement

(1) Payment of a fine or penalty imposed by the family court may be enforced upon the order of the court in like manner as a judgment of the court for the payment of money.

(2) Rules of court may, in relation to cases where under two or more orders made by or registered in the family court the same person is required to make periodical payments to the same recipient, make provision –

(a) for recovery of payments under more than one of the orders to be dealt with in the same proceedings;
(b) for apportioning, between some or all of the orders, payments made by the person required to make payments under the orders.

(3) Subsection (4) applies where –

(a) periodical payments are required to be made, or a lump sum is required to be paid, to a child under an order made by the family court, or
(b) periodical payments are required to be made to a child under an order registered in the family court.

(4) Any sum required under the order to be paid to the child may be paid to the person who looks after the child, and that person may proceed in that person's own name for –

(a) the variation, revival or revocation of the order, or
(b) the recovery of any sum required to be paid under the order.

(5) Where a child has a right under any Act or instrument made under an Act to apply for the revival of an order made by the family court which provided for the making of periodical payments to or for the benefit of the child, the person who looks after the child may proceed in the person's own name for the revival of the order.

(6) Where any person by whom periodical payments are required to be paid to a child under an order made by or registered in the family court applies for the variation or revocation of the order, the person who looks after the child may answer the application in the person's own name.

(7) Nothing in subsections (4) and (5) affects any right of a child to proceed in the child's own name for the variation, revival or revocation of an order or for the recovery of a sum payable under an order.

(8) In this section –

(a) a reference to the person who looks after a child is –

(i) in the case of a child who is being looked after by a local authority (within the meaning of section 22 of the Children Act 1989 or section 74 of the Social Services and Well-being (Wales) Act 2014), a reference to that local authority, and

(ii) in any other case, a reference to the person who, disregarding any absence of the child at a hospital or boarding school and any other temporary absence, has care of the child;

(b) 'child' means a person under the age of 18;

(c) a reference to an order registered in the family court is a reference to an order registered in the court under the Maintenance Orders (Facilities for Enforcement) Act 1920, Part 2 of the Maintenance Orders Act 1950, Part 1 of the Maintenance Orders Act 1958, the Maintenance Orders (Reciprocal Enforcement) Act 1972 or Part 1 of the Civil Jurisdiction and Judgments Act 1982.

Amendments—Inserted by CCA 2013, s 17(6), Sch 10, para 1; SI 2016/413.

Enforcement: 'proceed … (b) for recovery of any sum' (s 31L(4)(b))—It can be assumed that 'proceed … for recovery' encompasses not only (1) seeking and receiving payments from the paying party, but also (2) any form of enforcement thereof. That enforcement may include an application to commit (DA 1869, s 5). FPR 2010, Pt 37 makes definition of the term 'recovery' more significant (see above). However, the word 'enforcement' or any derivative of it does not appear in the operative part of s 31L (save in s 31L(8)(c) as part of the title to another statute). Parliament appears to use the word as a component of 'recovery' (although 'recovery' has wider connotations, such as seeking payment or payments short of enforcing through the courts: see, for example, CSA 1991, s 4).

Enforcement of Family Court orders—Most aspects of procedure for enforcement in the Family Court under a variety of statutory provisions are dealt with under FPR 2010, Pt 33 and for committal for breach of court orders or other contempt under Pt 37 (in both the High Court and the Family Court). Enforcement of a fine or other penalty imposed by the Family Court is specifically provided for by s 31L(1).

Enforcement of 'two or more orders' (s 31L(2))—FPR 2010, r 9.26E deals procedurally with s 31L(2).

'sum … to be paid to a child' (s 31L(3)-(7))—Two features of financial provision for a child, where it is required already to be paid, are dealt with under s 31L(4):

- That a local authority that looks after a child, or any other person having 'care of a child' (defined by s 31L(7)) (C) can receive money on behalf of the child; and
- C can apply, to the Family Court, in C's own name (s 31L(4)) to 'proceed for recovery' of payments of money (periodical payments or a lump sum, but not property) for the child.

'in that person's own name' (s 31L(4))—There is no need for C to characterise him/herself as representing the child in the sense of FPR 2010, Pt 16: C applies as a party in his/her own right in the proceedings, subject to the trustee point below.

Application in financial remedy proceedings—It is open to C to apply to join in the proceedings in which payment has arisen (common law as codified in CPR 1998, Pt 19.2: i e these are not 'proceedings for a financial remedy' but only enforcement thereof, and therefore not covered by FPR 2010, r 9.26B). C applies by FPR 2010, Pt 18 procedure (a) to be added to the proceedings and (b) to enforce by the means chosen. No clear provision for this is set out in FPR 2010, Pts 33 or 37

'to or for the benefit of the child' (s 31L(5))—C receives the money as a trustee for the child, but is able (as between the payer and the child) to give the payer a good receipt for any money recovered on behalf of the child.

****

31O Justices' clerks and assistants: functions

(1) The Lord Chancellor may by rules made with the agreement of the Lord Chief Justice and after consulting the Family Procedure Rule Committee –

(a) make provision enabling functions of the family court, or of a judge of the court, to be carried out by a justices' clerk;

(b) make provision enabling functions of a justices' clerk given under paragraph (a), or specified in subsection (2), to be carried out by an assistant to a justices' clerk.

(2) The functions of a justices' clerk include –

(a) giving advice to lay judges of the family court about matters of law (including procedure and practice) on questions arising in connection with the discharge by them of functions conferred on them or the court, including questions arising when the clerk is not personally attending on them, and

(b) power, at any time when the clerk thinks that the clerk should do so, to bring to the attention of lay judges of the family court any point of law (including procedure and practice) that is or may be involved in any question so arising;

and in this subsection 'lay judge of the family court' means a judge of the court who is within section 31C(1)(y).

(3) Subsection (2) does not limit –

(a) the functions of a justices' clerk, or

(b) the matters on which any judge of the family court may obtain assistance from a justices' clerk.

(4) A justices' clerk is not subject to the direction of the Lord Chancellor or any other person when carrying out –

(a) a function of the family court or of a judge of the court, or

(b) a function specified in subsection (2);

and an assistant to a justices' clerk when carrying out any such function is not subject to the direction of any person other than a justices' clerk.

(5) No action lies against a person in respect of anything done or not done in carrying out functions of the family court or of a judge of the court –

(a) in execution of the person's duties as a justices' clerk or an assistant to a justices' clerk, and

(b) in relation to matters within the person's jurisdiction.

(6) An action lies against a person in respect of anything done or not done in carrying out functions of the family court or of a judge of the court –

(a) in purported execution of the person's duties as a justices' clerk or an assistant to a justices' clerk, and

(b) in relation to a matter not within the person's jurisdiction,

if, but only if, it is proved that the person acted in bad faith.

(7) If an action is brought in circumstances in which subsection (5) or (6) provides that no action lies, the court in which the action is brought –

(a) may, on the application of the defendant, strike out the proceedings in the action, and

(b) if it does so, may if it thinks fit order the person bringing the action to pay costs.

(8) The Lord Chief Justice may nominate a judicial office holder (as defined in section 109(4) of the Constitutional Reform Act 2005) to exercise functions of the Lord Chief Justice under this section.

Amendments—Inserted by CCA 2013, s 17(6), Sch 10, para 1.

31P Orders, regulations and rules under Part 4A

(1) Any power of the Lord Chancellor to make an order, regulations or rules under this Part –

(a) is exercisable by statutory instrument,

(b) includes power to make different provision for different purposes, and

(c) includes power to make supplementary, incidental, consequential, transitional, transitory or saving provision.

(2) The Lord Chancellor may not make the first rules under section 31O(1) unless a draft of the statutory instrument containing the rules (whether alone or with other provisions) has been laid before, and approved by a resolution of, each House of Parliament.

(3) A statutory instrument that –

(a) contains an order, regulations or rules made under this Part by the Lord Chancellor other than regulations under section 31M, and
(b) is not subject to any requirement that a draft of the instrument be laid before, and approved by a resolution of, each House of Parliament,

is subject to annulment in pursuance of a resolution of either House of Parliament.

Amendments—Inserted by CCA 2013, s 17(6), Sch 10, para 1.

PART V
FAMILY BUSINESS: DISTRIBUTION AND TRANSFER

Preliminary

32 What is family business

In this Part of this Act –

'family business' means business of any description which in the High Court is for the time being assigned to the Family Division and to no other Division by or under section 61 of (and Schedule 1 to) the Senior Courts Act 1981;

'family proceedings' means proceedings which are family business;

…

'matrimonial cause' means an action for divorce, nullity of marriage or judicial separation.

…

Amendments—FLA 1986, s 68(1), Sch 1, para 27; CPA 2004, s 261(1), Sch 27, para 91; CRA 2005, Sch 11, para 1(2); CCA 2013, s 17, Sch 11.

33–36D (*repealed*)

Distribution and transfer of family business and proceedings

37 Directions as to distribution and transfer of family business and proceedings

The President of the Family Division may, with the concurrence of the Lord Chancellor, give directions with respect to the distribution and transfer between the High Court and the family court of family business and family proceedings.

Amendments—CCA 2013, s 17, Sch 11.

38 Transfer of family proceedings from High Court

(1) At any stage in any family proceedings in the High Court the High Court may, if the proceedings are transferable under this section, either of its own motion or on the application of any party to the proceedings, order the transfer of the whole or any part of the proceedings to the family court.

(2) The following family proceedings are transferable to the family court under this section, namely –

(a) all family proceedings commenced in the High Court which are within the jurisdiction of the family court;
(b) wardship proceedings, except applications for an order that a minor be made, or cease to be, a ward of court or any other proceedings which relate to the exercise and the inherent jurisdiction of the High Court with respect to minors; and
(c) all family proceedings transferred to the High Court under section 39 below or section 41 of the County Courts Act 1984 (transfer to High Court by order of High Court); and
(d) all matrimonial causes and matters transferred from a county court otherwise than as mentioned in paragraph (c) above.

(3)–(3B) (*repealed*)

(4) The transfer shall not affect any right of appeal from the order directing the transfer, or the right to enforce in the High Court any judgment signed, or order made, in that Court before the transfer.

(5) Where proceedings are transferred to the family court under this section, the family court –

- (a) if it has no jurisdiction apart from this paragraph, shall have jurisdiction to hear and determine those proceedings;
- (b) shall have jurisdiction to award any relief which could have been awarded by the High Court.

Amendments—Matrimonial Proceedings (Transfer) Act 1988, s 1(1); CA 1989, s 108(5), Sch 13, para 51; CPA 2004, s 261(1), Sch 27, para 93; SI 2005/3336; CCA 2013, s 17, Sch 11.

39 Transfer of family proceedings to High Court

(1) At any stage in any family proceedings in the family court, the family court may, if the proceedings are transferable under this section, either of its own motion or on the application of any party to the proceedings, order the transfer of the whole or any part of the proceedings to the High Court.

(2) The following family proceedings are transferable to the High Court under this section, namely –

- (a) all family proceedings commenced in the family court which are within the jurisdiction of the High Court, and
- (b) all family proceedings transferred from the High Court under section 38 above.

Amendments—CPA 2004, s 261(1), Sch 27, para 94; CCA 2013, s 17, Sch 11.

Proceedings allocated to a High Court Judge—See Procedural Guide B5 for guidance as to financial remedy proceedings allocated to a High Court judge and see Mostyn J's *Statement on the Efficient Conduct of Financial Remedy Proceedings Allocated to a High Court Judge Whether Sitting at the Royal Courts of Justice or Elsewhere*, revised 1 February 2016 and set out in Part V (the Statement deals with both matters of allocation and procedure thereafter).

★★★★

Matrimonial Causes Act 1973

ARRANGEMENT OF SECTIONS

PART I
DIVORCE, NULLITY AND OTHER MATRIMONIAL SUITS

Section		Page
	Divorce	
1	Divorce on breakdown of marriage	1147
2	Supplemental provisions as to facts raising presumption of breakdown	1149
3	Bar on petitions for divorce within one year of marriage	1149
4	Divorce not precluded by previous judicial separation	1150
5	Refusal of decree in five year separation cases on grounds of grave hardship to respondent	1151
6	Attempts at reconciliation of parties to marriage	1152
7	Consideration by the court of certain agreements or arrangements	1152
8	Intervention of Queen's Proctor	1154
9	Proceedings after decree nisi: general powers of court	1154
10	Proceedings after decree nisi: special protection for respondent in separation cases	1155
10A	Proceedings after decree nisi: religious marriage	1156
	Nullity	
11	Grounds on which a marriage is void	1156
12	Grounds on which a marriage is voidable	1157

12A Grounds on which a marriage converted from a civil partnership is void or voidable 1157
13 Bars to relief where marriage is voidable 1157
14 Marriages governed by foreign law or celebrated abroad under English law 1158
15 Application of ss 1(5), 8 and 9 to nullity proceedings 1159
16 Effect of decree of nullity in case of voidable marriage 1159

Other matrimonial suits

17 Judicial separation 1159
18 Effects of judicial separation 1159

General

20 Relief for respondent in divorce proceedings 1160

PART II
FINANCIAL RELIEF FOR PARTIES TO MARRIAGE AND CHILDREN OF FAMILY

Financial provision and property adjustment orders

21 Financial provision and property adjustment orders 1160
21A Pension sharing orders 1161
21B Pension compensation sharing orders 1162
21C Pension compensation: interpretation 1163

Ancillary relief in connection with divorce proceedings etc

22 Maintenance pending suit 1163
22ZA Orders for payment in respect of legal services 1164
22ZB Matters to which court is to have regard in deciding how to exercise power under section 22ZA 1165
23 Financial provision orders in connection with divorce proceedings etc 1167
24 Property adjustment orders in connection with divorce proceedings etc 1171
24A Orders for sale of property 1173
24B Pension sharing orders in connection with divorce proceedings etc 1174
24C Pension sharing orders: duty to stay 1175
24D Pension sharing orders: apportionment of charges 1175
24E Pension compensation sharing orders in connection with divorce proceedings 1176
24F Pension compensation sharing orders: duty to stay 1177
24G Pension compensation sharing orders: apportionment of charges 1177
25 Matters to which court is to have regard in deciding how to exercise its powers under ss 23, 24, 24A, 24B and 24E 1177
25A Exercise of court's powers in favour of party to marriage on decree of divorce or nullity of marriage 1184
25B Pensions 1186
25C Pensions: lump sums 1187
25D Pensions: supplementary 1188
25E The Pension Protection Fund 1190
25F Attachment of pension compensation 1192
25G Pension compensation: supplementary 1193
26 Commencement of proceedings for ancillary relief etc 1193

Financial provision in case of neglect to maintain

27 Financial provision orders etc in case of neglect by party to marriage to maintain other party or child of the family 1194

Additional provisions with respect to financial provision and property adjustment orders

28 Duration of continuing financial provision orders in favour of party to marriage, and effect of remarriage or formation of civil partnership 1196
29 Duration of continuing financial provision orders in favour of children, and age limit on making certain orders in their favour 1197

30 Direction for settlement of instrument for securing payments or effecting property adjustment 1198

Variation, discharge and enforcement of certain orders etc

31 Variation, discharge etc of certain orders for financial relief 1198
32 Payment of certain arrears unenforceable without the leave of the court 1203
33 Orders for repayment in certain cases of sums paid under certain orders 1204

Consent orders

33A Consent orders for financial provision or property adjustment 1205

Maintenance agreements

34 Validity of maintenance agreements 1205
35 Alteration of agreements by court during lives of parties 1206
36 Alteration of agreements by court after death of one party 1207

Miscellaneous and supplemental

37 Avoidance of transactions intended to prevent or reduce financial relief 1208
38 Orders for repayment in certain cases of sums paid after cessation of order by reason of remarriage or formation of civil partnership 1210
39 Settlement etc made in compliance with a property adjustment order may be avoided on bankruptcy of settlor 1211
40 Payments etc under order made in favour of person suffering from mental disorder 1212
40A Appeals relating to pension sharing orders which have taken effect 1212
40B Appeals relating to pension compensation sharing orders which have taken effect 1213

PART IV
MISCELLANEOUS AND SUPPLEMENTAL

47 Matrimonial relief and declarations of validity in respect of polygamous marriages 1213
48 Evidence 1214
52 Interpretation 1214

PART I
DIVORCE, NULLITY AND OTHER MATRIMONIAL SUITS

Divorce

1 Divorce on breakdown of marriage

(1) Subject to section 3 below, a petition for divorce may be presented to the court by either party to a marriage on the ground that the marriage has broken down irretrievably.

(2) The court hearing a petition for divorce shall not hold the marriage to have broken down irretrievably unless the petitioner satisfies the court of one or more of the following facts, that is to say –

(a) that the respondent has committed adultery and the petitioner finds it intolerable to live with the respondent;
(b) that the respondent has behaved in such a way that the petitioner cannot reasonably be expected to live with the respondent;
(c) that the respondent has deserted the petitioner for a continuous period of at least two years immediately preceding the presentation of the petition;
(d) that the parties of the marriage have lived apart for a continuous period of at least two years immediately preceding the presentation of the petition (hereafter in this Act referred to as 'two years' separation') and the respondent consents to a decree being granted;
(e) that the parties to the marriage have lived apart for a continuous period of at least five years immediately preceding the presentation of the petition (hereafter in this Act referred to as 'five years' separation').

(3) On a petition for divorce it shall be the duty of the court to inquire, so far as it reasonably can, into the facts alleged by the petitioner and into any facts alleged by the respondent.

(4) If the court is satisfied on the evidence of any such fact as is mentioned in subsection (2) above, then, unless it is satisfied on all the evidence that the marriage has not broken down irretrievably, it shall, subject to section 5 below, grant a decree of divorce.

(5) Every decree of divorce shall in the first instance be a decree nisi and shall not be made absolute before the expiration of six months from its grant unless the High Court by general order from time to time fixes a shorter period, or unless in any particular case the court in which the proceedings are for the time being pending from time to time by special order fixes a shorter period than the period otherwise applicable for the time being by virtue of this subsection.

(6) Only conduct between the respondent and a person of the opposite sex may constitute adultery for the purposes of this section.

Amendments—MFPA 1984, s 46(1), Sch 1, para 10; Marriage (Same Sex Couples) Act 2013, s 11, Sch 4, para 3.

Defined terms—'the court': s 52.

Procedure—Procedure for divorce and most other matrimonial causes is covered by FPR 2010, Pt 7; see also Procedural Guides B2 and B4.

'duty of the court to inquire ... into the facts alleged' (s 1(3))—Section 1(3) places on the court the duty to inquire into the fact or facts alleged, which duty must be discharged conscientiously, even though divorce is now a largely administrative exercise (*Lachaux v Lachaux* [2017] EWHC 385 (Fam)). If satisfied as the fact or facts, the court certifies that a decree – initially a decree nisi followed by a decree absolute – be granted, unless the court is not satisfied as to irretrievable breakdown. The court's duty is performed by a district judge under the procedure in FPR 2010, r 7.20, but it may be performed under the standard procedure in open court if the petition is defended or the district judge is not prepared to sign his certificate under r 7.20; and after a case-management hearing (FPR 2010, r 7.22).

'facts alleged by the petitioner [or] by the respondent' (s 1(3))—Where an answer has been filed with a cross-prayer, there will be cases where a decree is granted solely on the fact(s) in the answer. The respondent is therefore the spouse who has obtained the decree nisi.

Behaviour such 'that the petitioner cannot reasonably be expected to live with the respondent' (s 1(2)(b))—Where a party alleges that the other has behaved in a way contrary to s 1(2)(b), the court must 'evaluate what is proved to have happened' subjectively to the parties in the light of all the circumstances of the particular marriage and 'having regard to the cumulative effect of all the respondent's conduct' (*Owens v Owens* [2017] EWCA Civ 182, at [37]).

'decree of divorce' (s 1(4),(5))—In the first instance, a decree nisi is issued (FPR 2010, r 7.20(2)(a)). This decree can be made absolute on application by the spouse who obtained the decree (FPR 2010, r 7.32(2)) or, failing that, by the other spouse.

Time for application for decree absolute (s 1(5))—The time for application for a decree absolute is as follows:

(a) *Application by party who obtained the decree nisi* The general rule is that a decree nisi can be made absolute on application by the party who obtained the decree nisi after 6 weeks from grant of the decree. Application for decree absolute is under FPR 2010, r 7.32.

(b) *Expedited decree* Application may be made to the court to 'fix a shorter period' (s 1(5)) where grounds for expedition exist (eg impending death, birth of a child to one party or perhaps travel abroad). Application is made at the time of the decree nisi application or later if the urgency is not discovered until then (see **Application for expedited decree** under FPR 2010, r 7.32 and PD7A, paras 8.1–8.4).

(c) *Application by spouse against whom decree pronounced* The party against whom the decree was obtained can apply for a decree absolute on notice 3 months after the other spouse could have applied (MCA 1973, s 9(2)). Application is made under FPR 2010, r 7.33(2)(c). In *Re G (Decree Absolute: Prejudice)* [2003] 1 FLR 870, FD, Bennett J allowed a respondent husband's application for decree absolute, which was opposed by the wife petitioner. Although the husband might not be prejudiced by the delay, in the absence of good grounds to refuse a decree, it should issue. Had the wife applied, a decree would have been granted. Outstanding ancillary relief proceedings were not a reason to delay grant (but see *Thakker*, below).

Discretion to postpone decree absolute—See the commentary to s 9.

Parties named and not named—MCA 1973, s 49 requires that a person against whom adultery or other improper association is alleged be joined in any divorce, judicial separation proceedings or for any form of financial relief (FPR PD5A, Form F), although the section recognises that rules may disapply this requirement (s 49(2)). If there is insufficient evidence against a party, that party may be dismissed from the suit (s 49(3)). FPR 2010, r 7.10(3) permits removal of a co-respondent (eg they are dead or under 16) and PD7A, para 7.1 requires (so far as it has power so to do) that a prospective co-respondent should not be named unless 'likely to object to the making' of the matrimonial order.

2 Supplemental provisions as to facts raising presumption of breakdown

(1) One party to a marriage shall not be entitled to rely for the purposes of section 1(2)(a) above on adultery committed by the other if, after it became known to him that the other had committed that adultery, the parties have lived with each other for a period exceeding, or periods together exceeding, six months.

(2) Where the parties to a marriage have lived with each other after it became known to one party that the other had committed adultery, but subsection (1) above does not apply, in any proceedings for divorce in which the petitioner relies on that adultery the fact that the parties have lived with each other after that time shall be disregarded in determining for the purposes of section 1(2)(a) above whether the petitioner finds it intolerable to live with the respondent.

(3) Where in any proceedings for divorce the petitioner alleges that the respondent has behaved in such a way that the petitioner cannot reasonably be expected to live with him, but the parties to the marriage have lived with each other for a period or periods after the date of the occurrence of the final incident relied on by the petitioner and held by the court to support his allegation, that fact shall be disregarded in determining for the purposes of section 1(2)(b) above whether the petitioner cannot reasonably be expected to live with the respondent if the length of that period or of those periods together was six months or less.

(4) For the purposes of section 1(2)(c) above the court may treat a period of desertion as having continued at a time when the deserting party was incapable of continuing the necessary intention if the evidence before the court is such that, had that party not been so incapable, the court would have inferred that his desertion continued at that time.

(5) In considering for the purposes of section 1(2) above whether the period for which the respondent has deserted the petitioner or the period for which the parties to a marriage have lived apart has been continuous, no account shall be taken of any one period (not exceeding six months) or of any two or more periods (not exceeding six months in all) during which the parties resumed living with each other, but no period during which the parties lived with each other shall count as part of the period of desertion or of the period for which the parties to the marriage lived apart, as the case may be.

(6) For the purposes of section 1(2)(d) and (e) above and this section a husband and wife shall be treated as living apart unless they are living with each other in the same household, and references in this section to the parties to a marriage living with each other shall be construed as references to their living with each other in the same household.

(7) Provision shall be made by rules of court for the purpose of ensuring that where in pursuance of section 1(2)(d) above the petitioner alleges that the respondent consents to a decree being granted the respondent has been given such information as will enable him to understand the consequences to him of his consenting to a decree being granted and the steps which he must take to indicate that he consents to the grant of a decree.

Defined terms—'the court': s 52.

Scope—This section sets out a variety of provisions (s 2(1)–(5)) which have the effect of enabling the parties to live together for 6 months, or periods totalling 6 months, without jeopardising the evidence on which they may ultimately wish to found a divorce petition. It defines living apart as a state of not living together in the same household.

Rescission of decree nisi—The provisions of s 2(1) may apply if the court is asked to exercise any discretion it may have to rescind a decree nisi (*Kim v Morris* [2013] 2 FLR 1197, FD, at [63]), but only after 1 year from decree nisi (i e when provisions of FPR 2010, r 7.32(3) become effective) and requires rules to be made that will ensure that the respondent to a petition based on s 1(2)(d) is properly able to give informed consent. The FPR Committee is considering the subject of rescission, including in this context.

Information as to consent (s 2(7))—None has been included in FPR 2010.

3 Bar on petitions for divorce within one year of marriage

(1) No petition for divorce shall be presented to the court before the expiration of the period of one year from the date of the marriage.

(2) Nothing in this section shall prohibit the presentation of a petition based on matters which occurred before the expiration of that period.

PART II

Amendments—MFPA 1984, s 1.

Defined terms—'the court': s 52.

'matters which occurred before' (s 3(2))—Facts arising before the 1-year period can be pleaded as a basis for a divorce petition.

Judicial separation—Section 3 is no bar, for example, to a petition for judicial separation. Most other forms of relief under MCA 1973 (eg financial relief) are thus available to a petitioner, even though her marriage cannot be dissolved. If dissolution is subsequently sought, leave to present a petition is not necessary (FPR 2010, r 7.7(2)); however, leave is required to file a fresh petition even if the facts relied on pre-date the 1-year period and no decree in the judicial separation proceedings has been granted (*Butler v Butler, The Queen's Proctor Intervening* [1990] 1 FLR 114, FD).

4 Divorce not precluded by previous judicial separation

(1) A person shall not be prevented from presenting a petition for divorce, or the court from granting a decree of divorce, by reason only that the petitioner or respondent has at any time, on the same facts or substantially the same facts as those proved in support of the petition, been granted a decree of judicial separation or an order under, or having effect as if made under, the Matrimonial Proceedings (Magistrates' Courts) Act 1960 or Part I of the Domestic Proceedings and Magistrates' Courts Act 1978 or any corresponding enactments in force in Northern Ireland, the Isle of Man or any of the Channel Islands.

(2) On a petition for divorce in such a case as is mentioned in subsection (1) above, the court may treat the decree or order as sufficient proof of any adultery, desertion or other fact by reference to which it was granted, but shall not grant a decree of divorce without receiving evidence from the petitioner.

(3) Where a petition for divorce in such a case follows a decree of judicial separation or (subject to subsection (5) below) an order containing a provision exempting one party to the marriage from the obligation to cohabit with the other, for the purposes of that petition a period of desertion immediately preceding the institution of the proceedings for the decree or order shall, if the parties have not resumed cohabitation and the decree or order has been continuously in force since it was granted, be deemed immediately to precede the presentation of the petition.

(4) For the purposes of section 1(2)(c) above the court may treat as a period during which the respondent has deserted the petitioner any of the following periods, that is to say –

- (a) any period during which there is in force an injunction granted by the High Court, the family court or the county court which excludes the respondent from the matrimonial home;
- (b) any period during which there is in force an order made by the High Court or a county court under section 1 or 9 of the Matrimonial Homes Act 1983 which prohibits the exercise by the respondent of the right to occupy a dwelling-house in which the applicant and the respondent have or at any time have had a matrimonial home;
- (c) any period during which there is in force an order made by a magistrates' court under section 16(3) of the Domestic Proceedings and Magistrates' Courts Act 1978 which requires the respondent to leave the matrimonial home or prohibits the respondent from entering the matrimonial home.

(5) Where –

- (a) a petition for divorce is presented after the date on which Part I of the Domestic Proceedings and Magistrates' Courts Act 1978 comes into force, and
- (b) an order made under the Matrimonial Proceedings (Magistrates' Courts) Act 1960 containing a provision exempting the petitioner from the obligation to cohabit with the respondent is in force on that date,

then, for the purpose of section 1(2)(c) above, the court may treat a period during which such a provision was included in that order (whether before or after that date) as a period during which the respondent has deserted the petitioner.

Amendments—DPMCA 1978, ss 62, 89(2)(a), Sch 2, para 38; Matrimonial Homes Act 1983, s 12, Sch 2; CCA 2013, s 17, Sch 11.

Defined terms—'the court': s 52.

Scope—This section enables a spouse who has obtained a decree of judicial separation to seek a divorce on substantially the same facts and relying on findings in the previous proceedings. The section also sets out a number of factors which do not prevent the petitioner from seeking a decree under s 1(2)(c) (desertion).

Petition for divorce after decree of judicial separation (s 4(1))—If a decree of divorce is sought by a petitioner who has, or who is proceeding with, a judicial separation petition where the parties have not been married for a year, it is necessary to file a fresh petition (*Butler v Butler, The Queen's Proctor Intervening* [1990] 1 FLR 114, FD). If the petition is presented after the 1-year period has expired, it may be amended, provided no decree has already been granted.

No decree 'without receiving evidence from the petitioner' (s 4(2))—Not only is a fresh petition needed where there has already been a decree, but the petitioner will also need to prove formally that the facts have already been found by a court.

5 Refusal of decree in five year separation cases on grounds of grave hardship to respondent

(1) The respondent to a petition for divorce in which the petitioner alleges five years' separation may oppose the grant of a decree on the ground that the dissolution of the marriage will result in grave financial or other hardship to him and that it would in all the circumstances be wrong to dissolve the marriage.

(2) Where the grant of a decree is opposed by virtue of this section, then –

- (a) if the court finds that the petitioner is entitled to rely in support of his petition on the fact of five years' separation and makes no such finding as to any other fact mentioned in section 1(2) above, and
- (b) if apart from this section the court would grant a decree on the petition,

the court shall consider all the circumstances, including the conduct of the parties to the marriage and the interests of those parties and of any children or other persons concerned, and if of opinion that the dissolution of the marriage will result in grave financial or other hardship to the respondent and that it would in all the circumstances be wrong to dissolve the marriage it shall dismiss the petition.

(3) For the purposes of this section hardship shall include the loss of the chance of acquiring any benefit which the respondent might acquire if the marriage were not dissolved.

Scope—This section enables the respondent to a petition under s 1(2)(e) (5 years' living apart), if no other fact under s 1(2) is pleaded by the petitioner, to oppose the grant of a decree on the grounds that divorce will cause grave financial hardship and that it would in all the circumstances be wrong to dissolve the marriage. If, after consideration of all the circumstances including those in s 5(2)(b), the court finds the grounds established by the respondent then the petition must be dismissed. Proceedings under this section are to be distinguished from those under s 10(2)–(4), where the court's power is limited to delaying the grant of a decree absolute.

Procedure—To oppose the grant of a decree under this section the respondent must file an answer within 21 days from the date by which the acknowledgment of service is required to be filed. The answer must plead details of the financial hardship which the respondent will suffer and the circumstances which it is alleged would make it wrong to dissolve the marriage. The answer should conclude with a prayer that the petition be dismissed. The cause then proceeds as a defended cause; the court must direct that the case be listed for a case management hearing: FPR 2010, r 7.20(4). See r 7.22 for the duties of the court at case management, including deciding where the hearing should take place, setting a timetable for the filing of evidence, and giving directions in relation to disclosure and witnesses.

Financial provision for the respondent—While the petition subsists the respondent may seek maintenance pending suit; but upon 'determination of the suit' (which includes dismissal of the petition under s 5(2)(b)) the maintenance pending suit ceases (s 22). If the respondent seeks continuing financial provision and the petitioner has failed to provide her with reasonable maintenance, application may be made under s 27. The respondent may seek to have such an application consolidated with the petition and tried immediately thereafter in the event of dismissal (FPR 2010, r 4.1(3)(h),(i) permitting the court to consolidate proceedings and to hear two or more applications on the same occasion); if the petition is dismissed many of the factors considered by the court in its dismissal will be similar to those in a consideration of the respondent's financial circumstances under ss 25(2) and 27(3).

'grave financial or other hardship' (s 5(1))—The hardship, whether financial or otherwise, must be caused by the dissolution, as opposed to the breakdown, of the marriage. The usual case of financial hardship is where dissolution will result in one of the parties (usually the wife) losing a widow's pension (contingent upon her husband's death), the pension often being index-linked. In such a case, she must set out her case in her answer (probably referring to the Value of Lost Pension Table in *At A Glance*) and it is then for the husband in his reply to set out his proposals, if any, for compensating the wife for that financial hardship, for example by offering to fund a policy providing the wife with a lump sum should he predecease her, offering to agree a pension sharing order or, so as to cover the death in benefit lump sum, a pension attachment order – although both forms of relief may not be given against the same pension scheme. Additionally, he will point out that, while on decree absolute the wife will lose the chance of obtaining a widow's pension under the terms of his employer's scheme, the realisation of that chance depends on her outliving him and, by virtue of the divorce, she can rely on his national insurance contributions during the marriage, whereby she will receive the certainty of a state retirement pension at age 60 (for women who attain that age by 2010 and under the Government's current equalisation proposals staggered to age 65 up to 2020, and age 65 for those who attain that age after that date) whereas she would otherwise receive a much lesser amount by way of state retirement pension, i e the difference between a married couple's pension and a single person's pension. Pound for pound compensation for loss of contingent widow's pension rights is not appropriate (*Le Marchant v Le Marchant* [1977] 1 WLR 559, CA). Hardship other than financial hardship, such as being regarded as a social outcast in one's own community (*Banik v Banik* (1973) FLR Rep 65, CA), must also be pleaded in the answer but is very difficult to establish. If, for example, a wife petitions for divorce on the ground of the husband's behaviour and the husband then cross-petitions on the ground of 5 years' separation the wife is estopped from pleading that dissolution will result in grave financial or other hardship (*Grenfell v Grenfell* [1978] Fam 128, CA). If the party who is losing pension rights has substantial capital, grave financial hardship is unlikely to be made out (*Archer v Archer* [1999] 1 FLR 327, CA).

6 Attempts at reconciliation of parties to marriage

(1) Provision shall be made by rules of court for requiring the legal representative acting for a petitioner for divorce to certify whether he has discussed with the petitioner the possibility of a reconciliation and given him the names and addresses of persons qualified to help effect a reconciliation between parties to a marriage who have become estranged.

(2) If at any stage of proceedings for divorce it appears to the court that there is a reasonable possibility of a reconciliation between the parties to the marriage, the court may adjourn the proceedings for such period as it thinks fit to enable attempts to be made to effect such a reconciliation.

The power conferred by the foregoing provision is additional to any other power of the court to adjourn proceedings.

Amendments—Legal Services Act 2007, s 208(1), Sch 21, para 29.

Defined terms—'the court': s 52.

Scope—This section provides for any solicitor acting for a petitioner to certify that reconciliation has been discussed with his client, and enables the court to adjourn proceedings if reconciliation appears to be a possibility. As worded, it applies to divorce proceedings only, although s 17(3) applies it to judicial separation proceedings as well.

'Provision shall be made by rules of court' (s 6(1))—FPR 2010, r 7.6 requires the solicitor acting for a petitioner in divorce proceedings to file with the petition a 'statement of reconciliation'.

7 Consideration by the court of certain agreements or arrangements

Provision may be made by rules of court for enabling the parties to a marriage, or either of them, on application made either before or after the presentation of a petition for divorce, to refer to the court any agreement or arrangement made or proposed to be made between them, being an agreement or arrangement which relates to, arises out of, or is connected with, the proceedings for divorce which are contemplated or, as the case may be, have begun, and for enabling the court to express an opinion, should it think it desirable to do so, as to the reasonableness of the agreement or arrangement and to give such directions, if any, in the matter as it thinks fit.

Defined terms—'the court': s 52.

Rules of court—No rules have been made under this section, but practices have developed which have given some effect to what is proposed here:

(a) *Pounds v Pounds [1994] 1 FLR 775*, CA Where a consent application is lodged before decree, but after the filling of a petition, this can be made the subject of an order effective on grant of decree nisi or conditional order.

(b) *Agreement between the parties* In *Smith v McInerney* [1994] 2 FLR 1077, FD, Thorpe J (following *Edgar v Edgar* (1981) 2 FLR 19, CA) held that parties should be required to adhere to any 'contract (sic)' entered into by them at the time of separation:
'As a matter of general policy I think it is very important that what the parties themselves agree at the time of separation should be upheld by the courts unless there are overwhelmingly strong considerations for interference.' (at [1081A]).
However, see also Prohibition of any restriction on right to apply under MCA 1973, s 34.

(c) *Agreement at FDR* Where agreement is reached at FDR in terms agreed by the judge, but not incorporated immediately into a fully drafted consent order, the court will uphold that approved agreement as an order (*Rose v Rose* [2002] 1 FLR 978, CA).

(d) *Pre-proceedings approval of an agreement* FPR PD19A, para 1.5 suggests that it may be possible to use the Pt 19 procedure to seek the court's approval of a financial agreement between spouses, civil partners or unmarried parents at a pre-proceedings stage

Agreement as a preliminary issue—In *Xydhias v Xydhias* [1999] 1 FLR 683, CA, Thorpe LJ suggested that where one party thought there was an agreement (eg in a draft consent application) but the other party denied it, then the question of whether or not an agreement had been reached should be tried as a separate and preliminary issue. Below is a procedure for dealing with this question which avoids the full ancillary relief procedure until the agreement issue is resolved:

(i) File application in Form A.
(ii) Seek immediate directions:
 - to stay requirements of FPR 2010, r 9.14 that Form E etc be filed
 - to vacate first appointment
 - for trial of a preliminary issue: 'whether there is an agreement on the face of any documents produced which settles financial issues between the parties' subject to the subsequent consideration of the agreement in the light of MCA 1973, s 25.
(iii) List the preliminary issue as to whether there is agreement before a district judge (who, if he finds no agreement, cannot hear any final application if he has seen 'without prejudice' correspondence which is privileged from disclosure).

Agreement in correspondence covered by the without prejudice rule—If the agreement is contained in correspondence that is part of negotiations, it will be covered by without prejudice privilege, unless it provides evidence of an agreement when the privilege ceases (*Tomlin v Standard Telephones* [1969] 1 WLR 1378, CA). The court may then look at the correspondence to determine whether there is an agreement (*Brown v Rice and anor* [2007] EWHC 625 (Ch)). The correspondence will be produced as part of the application, but must be removed from the court file if – as in *Brown v Rice* – the court finds there was no agreement.

Antenuptial agreement—In *Radmacher (formerly Granatino) v Granatino* [2010] 2 FLR 1900, SC, the Supreme Court considered the effects of an antenuptial agreement on the outcome of financial remedy order proceedings and held that it should be taken into consideration, subject to suitable safeguards. The alleged existence of an antenuptial agreement (a pre-nup) or its effect would be a matter for evidence at the time of negotiations for settlement or of argument in any financial remedy order proceedings as to the weight to be given to it (and see *Z v Z (No 2)* [2012] 1 FLR 1100, FD and *V v V* [2012] 1 FLR 1315, FD for further guidance on the impact of *Radmacher*). Such agreement could not be caught by s 7.

Arbitral award—Parties may agree to submit their financial remedy proceedings to arbitration under the Institute of Family Law Arbitrators scheme (*www.ifla.org.uk*). An award may result. If the parties agree to be bound by this result, that agreement will be a 'magnetic' factor, which should, in the absence of some very compelling factor(s) be determinative of the order the court makes (*S v S (Financial Remedies: Arbitral Award)* [2014] 1 FLR 1257, FD, at [18]). In *S v S*, Sir James Munby P approved the streamlined process applied by Coleridge J in *S v P (Settlement by Collaborative Law Process)* [2008] 2 FLR 2040, FD, which should be followed:

- In confirming the proposed order the judge, while undertaking the role of 'watchdog' rather than 'ferret', must bear in mind the 'fundamental principles ... to achieve a fair outcome' (*White v White* [2000] 2 FLR 981, HL).
- If the law applied by arbitral process is based on other than English law, then different considerations may apply: eg in the event of 'gender-based discrimination' (and see European Convention 1950, Art 14).

The procedure for applications to stay financial remedy proceedings pending arbitration requires the urgent attention of the FPRC. It is suggested that the Pt 18 procedure should be engaged. Parties will wish to ensure that they have a decree nisi or conditional order before a consent order; but see *Pounds v Pounds* procedure (above) for pre-decree nisi applications.

If no MCA 1973 or CPA 2004 proceedings are underway, it is suggested that an application under the FPR 2010, Pt 19 procedure might be engaged (PD19A, para 1.5).

Setting aside—Parties seeking to resile from the agreement should apply to the court using the 'notice to show cause' procedure and should be met by an appropriately robust approach, per *S v S (Financial Remedies: Arbitral Award)* [2014] 1 FLR 1257, FD, at [25]. Application should be to a High Court judge whether to set aside for mistake or fraud, or because of supervening events (*DB v DLJ (Challenge to Arbitral Award)* [2016] 2 FLR 1308, at [90]).

Arbitral award consent order—Any consent order application, and any final order following an arbitral award, must include (per *S v S (Financial Remedies: Arbitral Award)* [2014] 1 FLR 1257, FD, at [24]):

- under FPR 2010, r 9.26, both the agreed submission to arbitration (eg for the IFLA Scheme, the completed Form ARB1) and the arbitrator's award; and
- the consent order should contain recitals to the following effect, suitably adapted:

'The documents lodged in relation to this application include the parties' arbitration agreement (Form ARB1), their Form(s) D81, a copy of the arbitrator's award, and a draft of the order which the court is requested to make.

'By their Form ARB1 the parties agreed to refer to arbitration the issues described in it which encompass some or all of the financial remedies for which applications are pending in this court; and the parties have invited the court to make an order in agreed terms which reflects the arbitrator's award.'

Early Neutral Evaluation (ENE)—Although these words are not used in s 7, Parliament, in the latter part of the provision, seems to have been envisaging something of the sort. CPR 1998, r 3.1(1)(m) has been amended (with effect from 1 October 2015) to include that ENE may help to further the overriding objective and 'with the aim of helping the parties settle the case'. It remains to be seen whether judges in the family courts treat this as part of the common law and apply it also to family proceedings, where ENE is perceived to be helpful to the parties in an individual case.

8 Intervention of Queen's Proctor

(1) In the case of a petition for divorce –

(a) the court may, if it thinks fit, direct all necessary papers in the matter to be sent to the Queen's Proctor, who shall under the directions of the Attorney-General instruct counsel to argue before the court any question in relation to the matter which the court considers it necessary or expedient to have fully argued;

(b) any person may at any time during the progress of the proceedings or before the decree nisi is made absolute give information to the Queen's Proctor on any matter material to the due decision of the case, and the Queen's Proctor may thereupon take such steps as the Attorney-General considers necessary or expedient.

(2) Where the Queen's Proctor intervenes or shows cause against a decree nisi in any proceedings for divorce, the court may make such order as may be just as to the payment by other parties to the proceedings of the costs incurred by him in so doing or as to the payment by him of any costs incurred by any of those parties by reason of his so doing.

(3) The Queen's Proctor shall be entitled to charge as part of the expenses of his office –

(a) the costs of any proceedings under subsection (1)(a) above;

(b) where his reasonable costs of intervening or showing cause as mentioned in subsection (2) above are not fully satisfied by any order under that subsection, the amount of the difference;

(c) if the Treasury so directs, any costs which he pays to any parties under an order made under subsection (2).

Defined terms—'the court': s 52.

Divorce and nullity—As worded, this section applies to divorce proceedings only, although s 15 applies it to nullity proceedings as well.

Procedure (s 8(1))—Despite the breadth of s 8(1), the rules apply only to an application by the Queen's Proctor to show cause against a decree nisi being made absolute (FPR 2010, r 7.31).

9 Proceedings after decree nisi: general powers of court

(1) Where a decree of divorce has been granted but not made absolute, then, without prejudice to section 8 above, any person (excluding a party to the proceedings other than the Queen's Proctor) may show cause why the decree should not be made absolute by reason of material facts not having been brought before the court; and in such a case the court may –

(a) notwithstanding anything in section 1(5) above (but subject to section 10(2) to (4) below) make the decree absolute; or

(b) rescind the decree; or

(c) require further inquiry; or

(d) otherwise deal with the case as it thinks fit.

(2) Where a decree of divorce has been granted and no application for it to be made absolute has been made by the party to whom it was granted, then, at any time after the expiration of three months from the earliest date on which that party could have made such an application, the party against whom it was granted may make an application to the court, and on that application the court may exercise any of the powers mentioned in paragraphs (a) to (d) of subsection (1) above.

Amendments—CFA 2014, s 17.

Defined terms—'the court': s 52.

Divorce and nullity—As worded, this section applies to divorce proceedings only, although s 15 applies it to nullity proceedings as well.

Applications under MCA 1973, s 9—Section 9 deals with two separate forms of application:

(1) *Application to show cause (s 9(1))* The procedure for the Queen's Proctor or 'any person' to apply to the court to assert why a decree nisi should not be made absolute is set out in FPR 2010, r 7.31.

(2) *Application for decree absolute by spouse against whom the decree nisi was obtained (s 9(2))* The procedure for the spouse who did not obtain the decree nisi to apply for a decree absolute is set out in FPR 2010, r 7.33(2)(c).

An application for a decree nisi to be made absolute that is made before the time-limit of 3 months renders void (as distinct from voidable) a decree made on that application, and the decree must be set aside (*Manchanda v Manchanda* [1995] 2 FLR 590, CA).

Discretion to postpone decree absolute (s 9(2))—Where application is made under s 9(2), the court has an absolute discretion as to whether to grant the application (*Dart v Dart* [1996] 2 FLR 286, CA). In a case where the existence of off-shore structures might cause 'very considerable prejudice' to the wife if the marriage was finally dissolved, an application might be refused (*Thakkar v Thakkar* [2016] EWHC 2488 (Fam)).

10 Proceedings after decree nisi: special protection for respondent in separation cases

(1) Where in any case the court has granted a decree of divorce on the basis of a finding that the petitioner was entitled to rely in support of his petition on the fact of two years' separation coupled with the respondent's consent to a decree being granted and has made no such finding as to any other fact mentioned in section 1(2) above, the court may, on an application made by the respondent at any time before the decree is made absolute, rescind the decree if it is satisfied that the petitioner misled the respondent (whether intentionally or unintentionally) about any matter which the respondent took into account in deciding to give his consent.

(2) The following provisions of this section apply where –

(a) the respondent to a petition for divorce in which the petitioner alleged two years' or five years' separation coupled, in the former case, with the respondent's consent to a decree being granted, has applied to the court for consideration under subsection (3) below of his financial position after the divorce; and

(b) the court has granted a decree on the petition on the basis of a finding that the petitioner was entitled to rely in support of his petition on the fact of two years' or five years' separation (as the case may be) and has made no such finding as to any other fact mentioned in section 1(2) above.

(3) The court hearing an application by the respondent under subsection (2) above shall consider all the circumstances, including the age, health, conduct, earning capacity, financial resources and financial obligations of each of the parties, and the financial position of the respondent as, having regard to the divorce, it is likely to be after the death of the petitioner should the petitioner die first; and, subject to subsection (4) below, the court shall not make the decree absolute unless it is satisfied –

(a) that the petitioner should not be required to make any financial provision for the respondent, or

(b) that the financial provision made by the petitioner for the respondent is reasonable and fair or the best that can be made in the circumstances.

(4) The court may if it thinks fit make the decree absolute notwithstanding the requirements of subsection (3) above if –

(a) it appears that there are circumstances making it desirable that the decree should be made absolute without delay, and

(b) the court has obtained a satisfactory undertaking from the petitioner that he will make such financial provision for the respondent as the court may approve.

Scope—This section contains two distinct provisions. First, s 10(1) enables a respondent who claims to have been misled when giving his consent to seek rescission of a decree of divorce, but not judicial separation, under MCA 1973, s 1(2)(d) (2 years' living apart with consent), provided that no other fact in MCA 1973, s 1(2) was proved by the petitioner. It makes no difference whether the petitioner misled him intentionally or unintentionally. The second aspect of the section is contained in s 10(2)–(4) which is a half-way house between the full defence to the grant of a decree nisi on the ground of financial (or other) hardship under s 5 and the range of income and capital orders available under ss 23 and 24. Where there is a loss of widow's pension rights, before issuing a s 10(2) application consideration should be given as to whether an application for a pension attachment and/or sharing order (although the two forms of relief may not be granted in respect of the same pension scheme) will meet the requirements of the applicant. In *Garcia v Garcia* [1992] Fam 83, CA, this section was successfully used when the petitioner was in breach of a past obligation to contribute equally to the maintenance of a child.

Procedure for application for rescission under s 10(1)—See FPR 2010, r 7.28. It is probable that a decree under MCA 1973, s 1(2)(d) obtained on a respondent's answer would also be covered by this procedure.

Procedure for application under s 10(2)—Where the court makes a decree absolute following an application under s 10(2), it must make a written record of the reasons for making the decree absolute.

Effect of s 10(2) application—Making the application has the effect that the decree cannot be made absolute until the application has been heard, unless there are both circumstances making it desirable for the decree to be made absolute before hearing the application and the petitioner has given an undertaking to make suitable financial provision. The undertaking must contain concrete specific proposals and not merely be a general undertaking to carry out whatever the court may consider appropriate at some future time (see *Grigson v Grigson* [1974] 1 WLR 228, CA).

10A Proceedings after decree nisi: religious marriage

(1) This section applies if a decree of divorce has been granted but not made absolute and the parties to the marriage concerned –

- (a) were married in accordance with –
  - (i) the usages of the Jews, or
  - (ii) any other prescribed religious usages; and
- (b) must co-operate if the marriage is to be dissolved in accordance with those usages.

(2) On the application of either party, the court may order that a decree of divorce is not to be made absolute until a declaration made by both parties that they have taken such steps as are required to dissolve the marriage in accordance with those usages is produced to the court.

(3) An order under subsection (2) –

- (a) may be made only if the court is satisfied that in all the circumstances of the case it is just and reasonable to do so; and
- (b) may be revoked at any time.

(4) A declaration of a kind mentioned in subsection (2) –

- (a) must be in a specified form;
- (b) must, in specified cases, be accompanied by such documents as may be specified; and
- (c) must, in specified cases, satisfy such other requirements as may be specified.

(5) The validity of a decree of divorce made by reference to such a declaration is not to be affected by any inaccuracy in that declaration.

(6) 'Prescribed' means prescribed in an order made by the Lord Chancellor after consulting the Lord Chief Justice and such an order –

- (a) must be made by statutory instrument;
- (b) shall be subject to annulment in pursuance of a resolution of either House of Parliament.

(7) 'Specified' means specified in rules of court.

(8) The Lord Chief Justice may nominate a judicial office holder (as defined in section 109(4) of the Constitutional Reform Act 2005) to exercise his functions under this section.

Amendments—Inserted by Divorce (Religious Marriages) Act 2002, s 1. Amended by CRA 2005, s 15(1), Sch 4, para 76.

Procedure—Applications under s 10A(2) are governed by FPR 2010, r 7.30, which determines the form of the declaration and the necessary documentation in support.

Nullity

11 Grounds on which a marriage is void

A marriage celebrated after 31 July 1971, other than a marriage to which section 12A applies, shall be void on the following grounds only, that is to say –

- (a) that it is not a valid marriage under the provisions of the Marriage Acts 1949 to 1986 (that is to say where –
  - (i) the parties are within the prohibited degrees of relationship;
  - (ii) either party is under the age of sixteen; or
  - (iii) the parties have intermarried in disregard of certain requirements as to the formation of marriage);
- (b) that at the time of the marriage either party was already lawfully married or a civil partner;
- (c) *(repealed)*

(d) in the case of a polygamous marriage entered into outside England and Wales, that either party was at the time of the marriage domiciled in England and Wales.

For the purposes of paragraph (d) of this subsection a marriage is not polygamous if at its inception neither party has any spouse additional to the other.

Amendments—Marriage (Prohibited Degrees of Relationship) Act 1986, s 6(4); Private International Law (Miscellaneous Provisions) Act 1995, s 8, Sch, para 2; CPA 2004, s 261(1), Sch 27, para 40; Marriage (Same Sex Couples) Act 2013, s 17, Sch 7, para 27; SI 2014/3168.

Procedure—The procedure for petitions for nullity of marriage are, as for divorce, set out in FPR 2010, Pt 7.

12 Grounds on which a marriage is voidable

(1) A marriage celebrated after 31 July 1971, other than a marriage to which section 12A applies, shall be voidable on the following grounds only, that is to say –

(a) that the marriage has not been consummated owing to the incapacity of either party to consummate it;

(b) that the marriage has not been consummated owing to the wilful refusal of the respondent to consummate it;

(c) that either party to the marriage did not validly consent to it, whether in consequence of duress, mistake, unsoundness of mind or otherwise;

(d) that at the time of the marriage either party, though capable of giving a valid consent, was suffering (whether continuously or intermittently) from mental disorder within the meaning of the Mental Health Act 1983 of such a kind or to such an extent as to be unfitted for marriage;

(e) that at the time of the marriage the respondent was suffering from venereal disease in a communicable form;

(f) that at the time of the marriage the respondent was pregnant by some person other than the petitioner;

(g) that an interim gender recognition certificate under the Gender Recognition Act 2004 has, after the time of the marriage, been issued to either party to the marriage;

(h) that the respondent is a person whose gender at the time of the marriage had become the acquired gender under the Gender Recognition Act 2004.

(2) Paragraphs (a) and (b) of subsection (1) do not apply to the marriage of a same sex couple.

Amendments—MHA 1983, s 148, Sch 4, para 34; GRA 2004, ss 4, 11, Sch 2, para 2, Sch 4, para 5; Marriage (Same Sex Couples) Act 2013, s 11, Sch 4, para 4; SI 2014/3168.

Procedure—The procedure for petitions for nullity of marriage is dealt with in FPR 2010, Pt 7. Rule 7.26 contains particular rules for medical evidence where the allegation is that a spouse has been incapable of consummating the marriage (s 12(a)).

'mental disorder' (s 12(d))—By virtue of MHA 1983, s 1(2), this means 'mental illness, arrested or incomplete development of mind, psychopathic disorder and any other disorder or disability of mind and 'mentally disordered' shall be construed accordingly'.

12A Grounds on which a marriage converted from a civil partnership is void or voidable

(1) This section applies to a marriage which has been converted, or is purported to have been converted, from a civil partnership under section 9 of the 2013 Act and regulations made under that section.

(2) A marriage which results from the purported conversion of a void civil partnership is void.

(3) A marriage which results from the conversion of a civil partnership is voidable if any of paragraphs (c) to (h) of section 12(1) applied at the date from which the marriage is treated as having subsisted in accordance with section 9(6) of the 2013 Act.

(4) In this section, the '2013 Act' means the Marriage (Same Sex Couples) Act 2013.

Amendments—Inserted by SI 2014/3168.

13 Bars to relief where marriage is voidable

(1) The court shall not, in proceedings instituted after 31 July 1971, grant a decree of nullity on the ground that a marriage is voidable if the respondent satisfies the court –

(a) that the petitioner, with knowledge that it was open to him to have the marriage avoided, so conducted himself in relation to the respondent as to lead the respondent reasonably to believe that he would not seek to do so; and
(b) that it would be unjust to the respondent to grant the decree.

(2) Without prejudice to subsection (1) above, the court shall not grant a decree of nullity by virtue of section 12 above on the grounds mentioned in paragraph (c), (d), (e), (f) or (h) of that section unless –

(a) it is satisfied that proceedings were instituted within the period of three years from the date of marriage, or
(b) leave for the institution of proceedings after the expiration of that period has been granted under subsection (4) below.

(2A) Without prejudice to subsection (1) above, the court shall not grant a decree of nullity by virtue of section 12 above on the ground mentioned in paragraph (g) of that section unless it is satisfied that proceedings were instituted within the period of six months from the date of issue of the interim gender recognition certificate.

(3) Without prejudice to subsections (1) and (2) above, the court shall not grant a decree of nullity by virtue of section 12 above on the grounds mentioned in paragraph (e), (f) or (h) of that section unless it is satisfied that the petitioner was at the time of the marriage ignorant of the facts alleged.

(4) In the case of proceedings for the grant of a decree of nullity by virtue of section 12 above on the grounds mentioned in paragraph (c), (d), (e), (f) or (h) of that section, a judge of the court may, on an application made to him, grant leave for the institution of proceedings after the expiration of the period of three years from the date of the marriage if –

(a) he is satisfied that the petitioner has at some time during that period suffered from mental disorder within the meaning of the Mental Health Act 1983, and
(b) he considers that in all the circumstances of the case it would be just to grant leave for the institution of proceedings.

(5) An application for leave under subsection (4) above may be made after the expiration of the period of three years from the date of the marriage.

Amendments—MFPA 1984, s 2; GRA 2004, ss 4, 11, Sch 2, para 3, Sch 4, para 6.

Defined terms—'the court': s 52.

Application for leave after 3 years (s 13(4))—No procedure is prescribed for application under this provision. The application is likely to be dealt with under FPR 2010, Pt 18 procedure to start Pt 7 nullity proceedings. Application should be made without notice with an affidavit in support containing the following:

(a) a draft nullity application (petition);
(b) the medical evidence on which the petitioner relies in support of her contention that she was a patient;
(c) a statement of the background to the marriage and application; and
(d) a statement of why the petitioner believes the interests of justice require that she be granted leave.

'mental disorder' (s 13(4)(a))—By virtue of MHA 1983, s 1(2), this means 'mental illness, arrested or incomplete development of mind, psychopathic disorder and any other disorder or disability of mind and 'mentally disordered' shall be construed accordingly'.

14 Marriages governed by foreign law or celebrated abroad under English law

(1) Subject to subsection (3), where, apart from this Act, any matter affecting the validity of a marriage would fall to be determined (in accordance with the rules of private international law) by reference to the law of a country outside England and Wales, nothing in section 11, 12 or 13(1) above shall –

(a) preclude the determination of that matter as aforesaid; or
(b) require the application to the marriage of the grounds or bar there mentioned except so far as applicable in accordance with those rules.

(2) In the case of a marriage which purports to have been celebrated under the Foreign Marriage Acts 1892 to 1947 or has taken place outside England and Wales and purports to be a marriage under common law, section 11 above is without prejudice to any ground on which the marriage may be void under those Acts or, as the case may be, by virtue of the rules governing the celebration of marriages outside England and Wales under common law.

(3) No marriage is to be treated as valid by virtue of subsection (1) if, at the time when it purports to have been celebrated, either party was already a civil partner.

Amendments—CPA 2004, s 261(1), Sch 27, para 41(1)–(3).

15 Application of ss 1(5), 8 and 9 to nullity proceedings

Sections 1(5), 8 and 9 above shall apply in relation to proceedings for nullity of marriage as if for any reference in those provisions to divorce there were substituted a reference to nullity of marriage.

16 Effect of decree of nullity in case of voidable marriage

A decree of nullity granted after 31 July 1971 in respect of a voidable marriage shall operate to annul the marriage only as respects any time after the decree has been made absolute, and the marriage shall, notwithstanding the decree, be treated as if it had existed up to that time.

Scope—This section provides that a voidable marriage (i e covered by one or more of the grounds under s 12) only becomes void on decree absolute and is deemed to subsist until that time.

Other matrimonial suits

17 Judicial separation

(1) A petition for judicial separation may be presented to the court by either party to a marriage on the ground that any such fact as is mentioned in section 1(2) above exists, and the provisions of section 2 above shall apply accordingly for the purposes of a petition for judicial separation alleging any such fact, as they apply in relation to a petition for divorce alleging that fact.

(2) On a petition for judicial separation it shall be the duty of the court to inquire, so far as it reasonably can, into the facts alleged by the petitioner and into any facts alleged by the respondent, but the court shall not be concerned to consider whether the marriage has broken down irretrievably, and if it is satisfied on the evidence of any such fact as is mentioned in section 1(2) above it shall grant a decree of judicial separation.

(3) Sections 6 and 7 above shall apply for the purpose of encouraging the reconciliation of parties to proceedings for judicial separation and of enabling the parties to a marriage to refer to the court for its opinion an agreement or arrangement relevant to actual or contemplated proceedings for judicial separation, as they apply in relation to proceedings for divorce.

Amendments—CFA 2014, s 17.

Defined terms—'the court': s 52.

'duty of the court to inquire ... into the facts alleged' (s 17(2))—The procedure for judicial separation is covered by FPR 2010, Pt 7; see also Procedural Guides B2 and B4. The court's duty is dealt with by a district judge under the procedure in FPR 2010, r 7.20(2)(a).

'decree of judicial separation' (s 17(2))—In the case of judicial separation only a single decree is issued, but this cannot be granted until after the court has dealt with any issues which may arise under s 41 (arrangements for the children of the family).

18 Effects of judicial separation

(1) Where the court grants a decree of judicial separation it shall no longer be obligatory for the petitioner to cohabit with the respondent.

(2) If while a decree of judicial separation is in force and the separation is continuing either of the parties to the marriage dies intestate as respects all or any of his or her real or personal property, the property as respects which he or she died intestate shall devolve as if the other party to the marriage had then been dead.

(3) Notwithstanding anything in section 2(1)(a) of the Matrimonial Proceedings (Magistrates' Courts) Act 1960, a provision in force under an order made, or having effect as if made, under that section exempting one party to a marriage from the obligation to cohabit with the other shall not have effect as a decree of judicial separation for the purposes of subsection (2) above.

Defined terms—'the court': s 52.

Divorce after judicial separation—If divorce is sought where there are judicial separation proceedings not yet disposed of by dismissal or decree, leave to present a further petition is necessary (FPR 2010, r 7.7(1));

save where the petition follows a judicial separation petition filed within 1 year of the marriage and the new petition is based on the same facts as the old (FPR 2010, r 7.7(2)).

19 *(repealed)*

General

20 Relief for respondent in divorce proceedings

If in any proceedings for divorce the respondent alleges and proves any such fact as is mentioned in subsection (2) of section 1 above (treating the respondent as the petitioner and the petitioner as the respondent for the purposes of that subsection) the court may give to the respondent the relief to which he would have been entitled if he had presented a petition seeking that relief.

Defined terms—'the court': s 52.

Where in divorce proceedings a respondent proves a fact, s/he can be granted a decree—This is to be read with FPR 2010, r 7.14(2), which provides that the respondent's separate application (petition) containing allegations under MCA 1973, s 1 shall be treated 'as an application in the same proceedings' (i e the application (petition) already filed by the other spouse or civil partner). The remaining words of s 20 enable s 1(2) to be read in such a way as to fit the situation of a decree-seeking respondent.

PART II
FINANCIAL RELIEF FOR PARTIES TO MARRIAGE AND CHILDREN OF FAMILY

Financial provision and property adjustment orders

21 Financial provision and property adjustment orders

(1) The financial provision orders for the purposes of this Act are the orders for periodical or lump sum provision available (subject to the provisions of this Act) under section 23 below for the purpose of adjusting the financial position of the parties to a marriage and any children of the family in connection with proceedings for divorce, nullity of marriage or judicial separation and under section 27(6) below on proof of neglect by one party to a marriage to provide, or to make a proper contribution towards, reasonable maintenance for the other or a child of the family, that is to say –

(a) any order for periodical payments in favour of a party to a marriage under section 23(1)(a) or 27(6)(a) or in favour of a child of the family under section 23(1)(d), (2) or (4) or 27(6)(d);

(b) any order for secured periodical payments in favour of a party to a marriage under section 23(1)(b) or 27(6)(b) or in favour of a child of the family under section 23(1)(e), (2) or (4) or 27(6)(e); and

(c) any order for lump sum provision in favour of a party to a marriage under section 23(1)(c) or 27(6)(c) or in favour of a child of the family under section 23(1)(f), (2) or (4) or 27(6)(f);

and references in this Act (except in paragraphs 17(1) and 23 of Schedule 1 below) to periodical payments orders, secured periodical payments orders, and orders for the payment of a lump sum are references to all or some of the financial provision orders requiring the sort of financial provision in question according as the context of each reference may require.

(2) The property adjustment orders for the purposes of this Act are the orders dealing with property rights available (subject to the provisions of this Act) under section 24 below for the purpose of adjusting the financial position of the parties to a marriage and any children of the family on or after the grant of a decree of divorce, nullity of marriage or judicial separation, that is to say –

(a) any order under subsection (1)(a) of that section for a transfer of property;

(b) any order under subsection (1)(b) of that section for a settlement of property; and

(c) any order under subsection (1)(c) or (d) of that section for a variation of settlement.

'Any children of the family'—For the statutory definition of 'child of the family' see MCA 1973, s 52. For practical purposes there must be a family in existence, and the relevant child must be treated as a child of that family by both parties. This is a question of fact and degree. In *Teeling* [1984] FLR 808, CA, a child of another man brought up within the matrimonial household for 6 months was a child of the family. In *Carron* [1984] FLR 805, CA, the wife's children by other men were still children of the family, despite being maintained by the birth fathers, because they had been treated as children of the family.

Judicial separation—This section deals with the court's global powers to adjust the financial position of the parties. The court's powers to make orders in a suit for judicial separation are more circumscribed than in divorce or nullity. A party seeking judicial separation may apply under s 23 (periodical payments) and s 24 (property adjustment). Section 25 considerations are therefore engaged. Other remedies available to the judicially separated are under s 22 (maintenance pending suit) and s 27 (neglect to maintain). There is no jurisdiction to make a clean break order under s 25A or a pension share under s 24B in judicial separation cases.

Relationship of financial proceedings with criminal compensation orders—Following the implementation of the Proceeds of Crime Act 2002, issues of confiscation and enforcement lie with the Crown Court (*Webber v Webber* [2007] 2 FLR 116, FD). Ancillary relief and applications for confiscation orders are no longer heard together. In *Stodgell v Stodgell* [2009] 2 FLR 244, CA, a wife's application for ancillary relief could not proceed until after a compensation order imposed on the husband following his conviction for tax evasion was discharged. Where the husband's assets are extinguished by moneys due under a confiscation order, a wife would fail in her ancillary relief claim, even where she was non-complicit in the husband's fraud. See also *W v W (Financial Remedies: Confiscation Order)* [2013] 2 FLR 359, FD.

PART II

Procedure—An application for financial orders under MCA 1973 is an application for a financial remedy. The procedure under FPR 2010, Pt 9 applies.

21A Pension sharing orders

(1) For the purposes of this Act, a pension sharing order is an order which –

(a) provides that one party's –

(i) shareable rights under a specified pension arrangement, or

(ii) shareable state scheme rights,

be subject to pension sharing for the benefit of the other party, and

(b) specifies the percentage value to be transferred.

(1A) Where section 25E(7) applies, the reference in subsection (1) –

(a) to shareable rights under a specified pension arrangement shall include a reference to entitlement to PPF compensation (as defined in section 25E(9)); and

(b) to pension sharing shall include a reference to sharing of that compensation.

(2) In subsection (1) above –

(a) the reference to shareable rights under a pension arrangement is to rights in relation to which pension sharing is available under Chapter I of Part IV of the Welfare Reform and Pensions Act 1999, or under corresponding Northern Ireland legislation,

(b) the reference to shareable state scheme rights is to rights in relation to which pension sharing is available under Chapter II of Part IV of the Welfare Reform and Pensions Act 1999, or under corresponding Northern Ireland legislation, and

(c) 'party' means a party to a marriage.

Amendments—Inserted by WRPA 1999, s 19, Sch 3, para 2.

Modifications—By virtue of the Divorce etc (Pension Protection Fund) Regulations 2006, reg 4, s 21A is modified so as to apply in certain circumstances (see s 25E(7)) as if after s 21A(1) there were inserted s 21A(1A). See SI 2006/1932 for further details.

Defined terms—'PPF compensation': s 21C.

'shareable rights under a specified pension arrangement' (s 21A(1)(a))—Widely defined in WRPA 1999, ss 19–46 to include all pension arrangements and unfunded public service pensions except for:

(i) The Great Offices of State (the Prime Minister, the Lord Chancellor and the Speaker) (Pension Sharing (Excepted Schemes) Order 2001 (SI 2001/358));

(ii) Those arising from being the widow, widower or other dependant of a deceased person and equivalent pension benefits when those rights are the only rights held by a person under a pension scheme (Pension Sharing (Valuation) Regulations 2000 (SI 2000/1052), reg 2).

'shareable state scheme rights' (s 21A(1)(a))—Defined by WRPA 1999, s 47 as the State Earnings Related Pension scheme ((SERPs) (subsequently the State Second Pension (S2P) or (compositely) the Additional State Pension (ASP)) and shared additional pension, i e rights derived from a pension share relating to ASP made in previous family proceedings. The old basic state retirement pension could not be shared. These are referred to as 'old state scheme rights' (WRPA 1999, s 47(1A)(a)). Shareable state scheme rights also include 'new state scheme rights' (WRPA 1999, s 47(1A)(b)), being the state scheme rights under the single tier pension that may be the subject of a pension sharing order discussed below. The single-tier state pension was introduced by the Pensions Act 2014 and applies to those who reach state pension age on or after 6 April 2016. The old state pension provision for those reaching state pension age before 6 April 2016 remains unchanged. The single-tier pension replaces the basic state pension and ASP for those reaching state pension age after 6 April 2016. National Insurance contributions made prior to the implementation of the reforms are to be accounted for by way of 'protected payments' above the flat rate of the single-tier pension, for those whose contributions bring them over the 'foundation level' for the flat rate. Pension sharing is not available in relation to the single-tier pension except that protected payments, where awarded, may be subject to a pension sharing order. Existing pension sharing orders in relation to ASP are honoured. From 6 April 2016, state pension provision is based upon individual qualification so that it is no longer possible to derive or inherit rights from a spouse's/civil partner's contribution record. See, further, the commentary in relation to the Sharing of State Scheme Rights (Provision of Information and Valuation) (No 2) Regulations 2000.

'percentage value' (s 21A(1)(b))—Although a court may calculate the percentage by taking the capital sum that seems appropriate and undertaking a calculation to determine the relevant percentage, the result contained in the pension sharing order annex must be specified only in percentage terms and not 'such sum as will give such percentage' (*H v H (Financial Relief: Pensions)* [2010] 2 FLR 173, FD).

Scope—Pension sharing enables the court to share a pension at the time of divorce so that (typically) the wife either becomes a member of (typically) the husband's pension scheme in her own right by provision of what has been termed 'shadow membership' ('internal transfer') or, alternatively, takes a transfer of a designated amount into her own pension ('external transfer'). Central to the concept of pension sharing is the creation of pension debits and pension credits. On the making of a pension sharing order, the transferor loses the percentage required to be transferred (the pension debit) so that his pension fund is reduced in value. The transferee acquires the right to require the pension arrangement to credit her with that amount (the pension credit) so that she gains a pension fund of that value (WRPA 1999, s 29(1)). In an unfunded public service scheme, only an internal transfer is possible. Otherwise, dependent on the position of the person responsible for managing the pension arrangements, there will be either an internal transfer within the scheme or an external transfer to some other pension arrangement. However, an external transfer must be offered. In either case, the applicant receives an indefeasible pension fund in her own right which does not end on remarriage and (subject to a limited exception, mentioned below) is not capable of variation. Broadly speaking, the charges are met by the parties and not by the pension arrangement (see annotations to s 24D). The court is not able to make a pension sharing order against any foreign pension (*Goyal v Goyal* [2016] EWFC 50): see commentary under MCA 1973, s 25 and 'International Pensions Orders After Goyal' [2016] Fam Law 1413.

21B Pension compensation sharing orders

(1) For the purposes of this Act, a pension compensation sharing order is an order which –

(a) provides that one party's shareable rights to PPF compensation that derive from rights under a specified pension scheme are to be subject to pension compensation sharing for the benefit of the other party, and

(b) specifies the percentage value to be transferred.

(2) In subsection (1) –

(a) the reference to shareable rights to PPF compensation is to rights in relation to which pension compensation sharing is available under Chapter 1 of Part 3 of the Pensions Act 2008 or under corresponding Northern Ireland legislation;

(b) 'party' means a party to a marriage;

(c) 'specified' means specified in the order.

Amendments—Inserted by Pensions Act 2008, Sch 6, Pt 1.

Defined terms—'PPF compensation': s 21C.

Scope—Reference should be made to the annotations to s 25E for a discussion of the Pension Protection Fund (PPF). Until the provisions of the Pensions Act 2008 (PA 2008) came into force, it was not possible to make pension sharing orders or pension attachment orders against PPF compensation because such compensation was not a pension. The PA 2008 amended MCA 1973 and CPA 2004, providing the necessary regulation-making powers to allow for PPF compensation to be treated in much the same way as pensions are treated on divorce, dissolution or annulment. The provision mirrors as closely as possible the legislation relating to pensions. The two main differences are that there is no death-in-service benefit as part of PPF compensation and that any 'credit member' created as a result of a pension compensation sharing order will not in any circumstances have the option of an external transfer from the PPF.

The relevant rules are FPR 2010, Pt 9, Ch 9, the Pension Protection Fund (Pension Compensation on Divorce etc) Regulations 2011 and the Divorce and Dissolution etc (Pension Protection Fund) Regulations 2011. The Rules and Regulations again closely mirror those for pensions with two differences due to the differing nature of PPF compensation. First, the valuation of PPF compensation entitlement to be used in financial remedy applications is only produced for that express purpose. Therefore, such a valuation must always be requested for use in proceedings, whereas (in the case of a pension) the member may already be in possession of a 'relevant valuation'. The second difference is that it is unnecessary to allow the PPF 21 days to lodge an objection with the court where it has received notice that an attachment order is being sought (FPR 2010, r 9.42, cf r 9.33).

21C Pension compensation: interpretation

In this Part –

'PPF compensation' means compensation payable under the pension compensation provisions;

'the pension compensation provisions' means –

(a) Chapter 3 of Part 2 of the Pensions Act 2004 (pension protection) and any regulations or order made under it,

(b) Chapter 1 of Part 3 of the Pensions Act 2008 (pension compensation on divorce etc) and any regulations or order made under it, and

(c) any provision corresponding to the provisions mentioned in paragraph (a) or (b) in force in Northern Ireland.

Amendments—Inserted by Pensions Act 2008, Sch 6, Pt 1.

Scope—This section defines terms in relation to pension compensation used in this Part. See, further, annotations to s 21B.

Ancillary relief in connection with divorce proceedings etc

22 Maintenance pending suit

(1) On a petition for divorce, nullity of marriage or judicial separation, the court may make an order for maintenance pending suit, that is to say, an order requiring either party to the marriage to make to the other such periodical payments for his or her maintenance and for such term, being a term beginning not earlier than the date of the presentation of the petition and ending with the date of the determination of the suit, as the court thinks reasonable.

(2) An order under this section may not require a party to a marriage to pay to the other party any amount in respect of legal services for the purposes of the proceedings.

(3) In subsection (2) 'legal services' has the same meaning as in section 22ZA.

Amendments—LASPOA 2012, s 49.

Procedure—The procedure on an application for maintenance pending suit is set out in FPR 2010, Pt 9; see Procedural Guide

Conversion to final order—The procedure for converting a maintenance pending suit order into a periodical payments order on decree absolute is prescribed by FPR 2010, r 9.8 and is governed by Pt 18 procedure.

Scope—This section applies to periodical payments in the period following the filing of the petition (for divorce, nullity or judicial separation) but before the grant of decree. The section is intended to address the immediate needs of a spouse by making income-based orders: issues of capital or long-term expenditure are better dealt with at the final hearing.

The principles derived from the leading cases are distilled in *TL v ML and others (Ancillary Relief: Claim against Assets of Extended Family)* [2006] 1 FLR 1263, FD, at [124]. The sole criterion to be applied is 'reasonableness', which is synonymous with 'fairness', and the marital standard of living is an important factor in determining fairness. Where a husband may historically derive his income from his family, care must be taken to establish whether there are regular payments from this source to the payer, and thence an established payment stream to the applicant, before making a s 22 order: *S v S (Maintenance Pending Suit)* [2013] 1 FLR 1173, FD. There should be a specific budget relating to immediate expenditure needs, which the court should examine critically. Where the information provided by the payer is deficient, the court may make robust assumptions on behalf of the applicant payee. Where there has historically been support from a third party, the court may assume that support will continue at least until trial. For maintenance pending suit following the dismissal of the suit, see *M v M (Maintenance Pending Suit: Enforcement on Dismissal of Suit)* [2009] 1 FLR 790, FD. Maintenance pending suit (MPS) is designed to deal with short-term cash-flow problems that arise during divorce proceedings. Its calculation has been described as 'sometimes somewhat rough and ready', as financial information is frequently in short supply at the early stages of the proceedings: *Moore v Moore* [2010] 1 FLR 1413, CA. This case is also authority for the proposition that MPS paid before trial is not refundable to the payer and unpaid maintenance in breach of a court order is an enforceable debt, absent special circumstances. MPS is to address a party's immediate needs between now and a later consideration of financial requirements. The nature of the order may be 'very short, interim and impressionistic': *Chai v Peng* [2014] 2 FLR 1189, FD.

MPS where prenuptial agreement—The court should apply the terms of the agreement strictly, unless the applicant can demonstrate to a convincing standard that there is a likely prospect of satisfying the court it should not be upheld: *BN v MA (MPS: Pre Nuptial Agreement)* [2013] EWHC 4250 (Fam).

MPS where jurisdictional issue—Where there is an arguable case that one party has residence in the jurisdiction, the court will have jurisdiction to determine an application for MPS: *CC v NC (Maintenance Pending Suit)* [2015] 1 FLR 404, FD.

MPS where permission to apply for financial remedy after foreign divorce—A party with a strong case for the grant of leave under MPFA 1984 has a strong case for MPS: *MET v HAT (No 2)* [2015] 1 FLR 576, FD, reversing *MET v HAT (Interim Maintenance)* [2014] 2 FLR 692, FD. Interim spousal maintenance may be refused where there is uncertainty about jurisdiction and the applicant fails to show need. See MPFA 1984, ss 13 and 16.

Segal Orders—On an application for MPS or interim periodical payments early in financial proceedings where there has been no CSA assessment or court-directed disclosure, a court may make a Segal Order in favour of a parent that includes an element of support for a child. In making a Segal Order, the court determines the amount necessary for the wife and children as a family unit, apportioning a sum for each of the children within this. The sum to be paid is reduced automatically by the amount of CSA assessment that exceeds the sum determined by the court as necessary for the child. This was approved by the CA in *Dorney-Kingdom*, in circumstances where a parent with primary care requires support, pending CSA assessment.

Costs orders following MPS hearing—The general rule in financial remedy proceedings is that, save where conduct arises, the court will not make a costs order against a party: FPR 2010, r 28.3(6). This rule does not apply to interim financial orders: r 28.3(4)(a). On an application under s 22 for maintenance pending suit or outcome, or interim periodical payments, a party may apply for a costs order. CPR 1998, r 44.2 therefore applies. See *Solomon v Solomon and Ors* [2013] EWCA Civ 1095, where costs in relation to interim orders are held to be in the discretion of the court, and CPR 1998, r 44 applied; *Gojkovic v Gojkovic (No 2)* [1991] 2 FLR 233, CA approved: the 'starting point ... is that costs prima facie follow the event'. The court has discretion as to whether costs are payable and in what amount, according to the guidelines in CPR 1998, r 44.2(4),(5) and may summarily assess costs under r 44.6.

22ZA Orders for payment in respect of legal services

(1) In proceedings for divorce, nullity of marriage or judicial separation, the court may make an order or orders requiring one party to the marriage to pay to the other ('the applicant') an amount for the purpose of enabling the applicant to obtain legal services for the purposes of the proceedings.

(2) The court may also make such an order or orders in proceedings under this Part for financial relief in connection with proceedings for divorce, nullity of marriage or judicial separation.

(3) The court must not make an order under this section unless it is satisfied that, without the amount, the applicant would not reasonably be able to obtain appropriate legal services for the purposes of the proceedings or any part of the proceedings.

(4) For the purposes of subsection (3), the court must be satisfied, in particular, that –

(a) the applicant is not reasonably able to secure a loan to pay for the services, and

(b) the applicant is unlikely to be able to obtain the services by granting a charge over any assets recovered in the proceedings.

(5) An order under this section may be made for the purpose of enabling the applicant to obtain legal services of a specified description, including legal services provided in a specified period or for the purposes of a specified part of the proceedings.

(6) An order under this section may –

(a) provide for the payment of all or part of the amount by instalments of specified amounts, and

(b) require the instalments to be secured to the satisfaction of the court.

(7) An order under this section may direct that payment of all or part of the amount is to be deferred.

(8) The court may at any time in the proceedings vary an order made under this section if it considers that there has been a material change of circumstances since the order was made.

(9) For the purposes of the assessment of costs in the proceedings, the applicant's costs are to be treated as reduced by any amount paid to the applicant pursuant to an order under this section for the purposes of those proceedings.

(10) In this section 'legal services', in relation to proceedings, means the following types of services –

(a) providing advice as to how the law applies in the particular circumstances,

(b) providing advice and assistance in relation to the proceedings,

(c) providing other advice and assistance in relation to the settlement or other resolution of the dispute that is the subject of the proceedings, and

(d) providing advice and assistance in relation to the enforcement of decisions in the proceedings or as part of the settlement or resolution of the dispute,

and they include, in particular, advice and assistance in the form of representation and any form of dispute resolution, including mediation.

(11) In subsections (5) and (6) 'specified' means specified in the order concerned.

Amendments—Inserted by LASPOA 2012, s 49.

Defined terms—'legal services': s 22ZA(10); 'specified': s 22ZA(11).

Scope—Hitherto, costs allowances have been a matter of common law (referred to specifically in FPR PD28A, para 4.6). Parliament has now (via amendments introduced by LASPOA 2012) both defined and restricted judicial discretion in two critical areas (costs and financial provision), but only under MCA 1973 and the parallel provisions of CPA 2004. The availability of orders for payment for legal services are interim orders and, as such, are dependent on the continuation of the main suit for divorce or dissolution of a civil partnership.

'legal services ... for the proceedings' and 'for financial relief' (s 22ZA(1),(2))—Legal services may be for a matrimonial cause (divorce, judicial separation etc, ie 'the proceedings': s 22ZA(1)) and for financial relief (s 22ZA(2)). 'Financial relief', as a term, is not defined in MCA 1973, which still uses 'ancillary relief' (although the term is used (undefined) in CPA 2004, Sch 5). In this context, it can perhaps be connoted with financial remedy proceedings under MCA 1973 and CPA 2004 (but not financial remedy proceedings under, for example, CA 1989, Sch 1).

'Financial relief' and 'financial remedy proceedings'—In the costs order lexicon (see notes to FPR 2010, r 28.3), there is a difference between (1) 'proceedings for a financial order' and (2) 'financial remedy proceedings'. It remains to be seen which of these two forms of 'financial relief' – or whether yet another – is judicially regarded as the preferred definition for 'financial relief' under s 22ZA(2).

Funding (costs) allowances—Costs allowances (in fact for funding proceedings, properly so-called 'costs' are orders under SCA 1981, s 51) remain available at common law in (for example) proceedings under CA 1989, Sch 1 (*PG v TW (No 1) (Child: Financial Provision: Legal Funding)* [2014] 1 FLR 508, FD, Theis J; *MET v HAT (Interim Maintenance)* [2014] 2 FLR 692, FD, Mostyn J; MFPA 1984, Pt III, DPMCA 1978 and possibly under I(PFD)A 1975. There is no fetter in law on the discretion of the court to grant such orders, although each statute concerned has its checklist (for example, see CA 1989, Sch 1, para 4). In *MG and JG v JF (Child Maintenance: Costs Allowance)* [2016] 1 FLR 424, FD, Mostyn J ordered a funding allowance in proceedings under CA 1989, s 8, but did not state the statutory source of the remedy or that the 'parents' must attempt to seek legal aid funding.

'specified description' and 'specified amounts' (s 22ZA(5) and (6))—The court may restrict the legal representation available to a party by defining, from the menu at s 22ZA(10), for what 'part of the proceedings' (s 22ZA(5)) an applicant will be able to secure funding and the 'amount' (s 22ZA(1),(6)(a)).

'assessment of costs' (s 22ZA(9))—If an order for costs is made in favour of the applicant, her award will be reduced by an amount paid to her under a costs allowance order.

Scope of 'legal services' (s 22ZA(10))—As with the scope of a legal aid certificate, so too with a legal services order: judges and parties will need to define the scope of the services to be covered within the terms of s 22ZA(10) and, for instance, the scope of 'enforcement of decisions' (s 22ZA(10)(a)) and a dispute resolution (s 22ZA(10)(d)). Caution is likely to continue to be exercised in relation to the amount and duration of an order for payment of legal services. Knowledge that the order may conclude at a financial dispute resolution (FDR) hearing may be a reasonable encouragement to settle. A judge at the FDR hearing should not hear an application to vary or extend a legal costs order under FPR 2010, r 9.17(2).

Repayment of money ordered to be paid on a legal services order—In *Wyatt v Vince* [2015] 1 FLR 972, SC, Lord Wilson explained (at [42]) how a legal services order and funding allowance payment should be dealt with in the event of successful appeal arising out of the main proceedings to which it related. The court has a discretion as to whether repayment should be made by a losing payee party (ie it is not for the lawyers to repay) and thus for example 'to order repayment unconditionally or subject to a prohibition against enforcement against her without further leave', but such discretion 'should certainly not be equated with that of determining the incidence of costs at the conclusion of an appeal'.

22ZB Matters to which court is to have regard in deciding how to exercise power under section 22ZA

(1) When considering whether to make or vary an order under section 22ZA, the court must have regard to –

(a) the income, earning capacity, property and other financial resources which each of the applicant and the paying party has or is likely to have in the foreseeable future,

(b) the financial needs, obligations and responsibilities which each of the applicant and the paying party has or is likely to have in the foreseeable future,

(c) the subject matter of the proceedings, including the matters in issue in them,

(d) whether the paying party is legally represented in the proceedings,

(e) any steps taken by the applicant to avoid all or part of the proceedings, whether by proposing or considering mediation or otherwise,

(f) the applicant's conduct in relation to the proceedings,

(g) any amount owed by the applicant to the paying party in respect of costs in the proceedings or other proceedings to which both the applicant and the paying party are or were party, and

(h) the effect of the order or variation on the paying party.

(2) In subsection (1)(a) 'earning capacity', in relation to the applicant or the paying party, includes any increase in earning capacity which, in the opinion of the court, it would be reasonable to expect the applicant or the paying party to take steps to acquire.

(3) For the purposes of subsection (1)(h), the court must have regard, in particular, to whether the making or variation of the order is likely to –

(a) cause undue hardship to the paying party, or

(b) prevent the paying party from obtaining legal services for the purposes of the proceedings.

(4) The Lord Chancellor may by order amend this section by adding to, omitting or varying the matters mentioned in subsections (1) to (3).

(5) An order under subsection (4) must be made by statutory instrument.

(6) A statutory instrument containing an order under subsection (4) may not be made unless a draft of the instrument has been laid before, and approved by a resolution of, each House of Parliament.

(7) In this section 'legal services' has the same meaning as in section 22ZA.

Amendments—Inserted by LASPOA 2012, s 50.

Defined terms—'legal services': MCA 1973, s 22ZA(10).

Scope—This section provides for orders for payment for legal services, following LASPO 2012. It replaced the discretionary remedies for costs allowances under s 22. The statute reflects the case-law principles in *Currey v Currey (No 2)* [2007] 1 FLR 946, CA, which can be treated as a case that assists the court when it has to decide whether to exercise its powers under s 22ZA (*AM v SS (Legal Services Order)* [2013] EWHC 4380 (Fam), at [22]).

Principles to be considered in application for legal services payment order—The merits of the substantive application will be considered by the court as part of its analysis: in *BN v MA (MPS: Pre Nuptial Agreement)* [2013] EWHC 4250 (Fam), where a wife's claim was described as 'extremely speculative ... borderline irresponsible' given the existence of a recent prenuptial agreement, the application for a costs order was dismissed. See *Rubin v Rubin* [2014] 2 FLR 1018, FD, at [13] for a guide to the substantive and procedural principles, and incorporating best practice. The application is governed by Pt 18 procedure and should be supported by written evidence and include a detailed estimate of current and future costs. Evidence of refusal to fund by two commercial lenders of repute, and from solicitors in relation to the availability of a *Sears Tooth* agreement, are likely to be determinative. If a payee is offered a litigation loan at a very high rate of interest, it is likely to be unreasonable for the payee to take such a loan unless the payer offers an undertaking to meet the interest payments. Funding should not last, in the first instance, beyond FDR stage, with a further post-FDR hearing to determine costs to trial. Monthly instalments are preferable to a single lump sum payment. Historic unpaid costs would not be met unless the court was satisfied that without such a payment appropriate legal services would not be obtained. It is suggested in *Rubin* that a legal services order may be made to assist in the costs of mediation and arbitration. In *AM v SS (Legal Services Order)*, above, a legal services order was made in the form of a charge on property not cash, as this was the only asset in the jurisdiction owned by the husband.

'must have regard to' (s 22ZB(1))—The list is exclusive: only the factors set out in s 22ZB(1) can be considered by the court when it decides whether to make an order. The first two mirror MCA 1973, s 25(2).

'subject matter of the proceedings' including matters in issue (s 22ZB(1)(c))—One of the more formidable tasks of the court will be to gauge what is the cost of the case. This subsection, if the parties provide the information to comply with it, will enable the court to conduct its enquiry on that particular aspect.

'the applicant's conduct in relation to the proceedings' (s 22ZB(1)(f))—It is likely that this subsection touches on 'conduct' as defined in the costs jurisdiction (see FPR 2010, r 28.3) and that the term should be construed accordingly.

'steps taken by the applicant to avoid all or part of the proceedings' (s 22ZB(1)(e))—This is a reference to alternative dispute resolution. It appears unnecessary for both parties to take steps to avoid litigation, only the applicant.

23 Financial provision orders in connection with divorce proceedings etc

(1) On granting a decree of divorce, a decree of nullity of marriage or a decree of judicial separation or at any time thereafter (whether, in the case of a decree of divorce or of nullity of marriage, before or after the decree is made absolute), the court may make any one or more of the following orders, that is to say –

(a) an order that either party to the marriage shall make to the other such periodical payments, for such term, as may be specified in the order;

(b) an order that either party to the marriage shall secure to the other to the satisfaction of the court such periodical payments, for such term, as may be so specified;

(c) an order that either party to the marriage shall pay to the other such lump sum or sums as may be so specified;

(d) an order that a party to the marriage shall make to such person as may be specified in the order for the benefit of a child of the family, or to such a child, such periodical payments, for such term, as may be so specified;

(e) an order that a party to the marriage shall secure to such person as may be so specified for the benefit of such a child, or to such a child, to the satisfaction of the court, such periodical payments, for such term, as may be so specified;

(f) an order that a party to the marriage shall pay to such person as may be so specified for the benefit of such a child, or to such a child, such lump sum as may be so specified;

subject, however, in the case of an order under paragraph (d), (e) or (f) above, to the restrictions imposed by section 29(1) and (3) below on the making of financial provision orders in favour of children who have attained the age of eighteen.

(2) The court may also, subject to those restrictions, make any one or more of the orders mentioned in subsection (1)(d), (e) and (f) above –

(a) in any proceedings for divorce, nullity of marriage or judicial separation, before granting a decree; and

(b) where any such proceedings are dismissed after the beginning of the trial, either forthwith or within a reasonable period after the dismissal.

(3) Without prejudice to the generality of subsection (1)(c) or (f) above –

(a) an order under this section that a party to a marriage shall pay a lump sum to the other party may be made for the purpose of enabling that other party to meet any liabilities or expenses reasonably incurred by him or her in maintaining himself or herself or any child of the family before making an application for an order under this section in his or her favour;

(b) an order under this section for the payment of a lump sum to or for the benefit of a child of the family may be made for the purpose of enabling any liabilities or expenses reasonably incurred by or for the benefit of that child before the making of an application for an order under this section in his favour to be met; and

(c) an order under this section for the payment of a lump sum may provide for the payment of that sum by instalments of such amount as may be specified in the order and may require the payment of the instalments to be secured to the satisfaction of the court.

(4) The power of the court under subsection (1) or (2)(a) above to make an order in favour of a child of the family shall be exercisable from time to time; and where the court makes an order in favour of a child under subsection (2)(b) above, it may from time to time, subject to the restrictions mentioned in subsection (1) above, make a further order in his favour of any of the kinds mentioned in subsection (1)(d), (e) or (f) above.

(5) Without prejudice to the power to give a direction under section 30 below for the settlement of an instrument by conveyancing counsel, where an order is made under subsection (1)(a), (b) or (c) above on or after granting a decree of divorce or nullity of marriage, neither the order nor any settlement made in pursuance of the order shall take effect unless the decree has been made absolute.

(6) Where the court –

(a) makes an order under this section for the payment of a lump sum; and
(b) directs –
(i) that payment of that sum or any part of it shall be deferred; or
(ii) that the sum or any part of it shall be paid by instalments,

the court may order that the amount deferred or the instalments shall carry interest at such rate as may be specified by the order from such date, not earlier than the date of the order, as may be so specified, until the date when payment of it is due.

Amendments—AJA 1982, s 16.

Scope—MCA 1973, s 23 sets out the principal financial provision orders available on divorce (for the benefit of adult parties and children). The court must also consider whether a clean break order under s 25A is possible. Whereas the severance of financial ties between parties to a marriage is encouraged, certain cases require orders for periodical payments to be made, mainly so as to meet a party's future budgetary needs – see Potter P: 'on the exit from the marriage the partnership ends and in ordinary circumstances a wife has no right or expectation of continuing economic parity ("sharing") unless and to the extent that consideration of her needs or compensation for relationship-generated disadvantage so require. A clean break is to be encouraged wherever possible': *VP v JB* [2008] 1 FLR 742, FD. See also the commentary on clean breaks under s 25A.

Procedure—The procedure for an application under s 23 is set out in FPR 2010, Pt 9 and see Procedural Guide

Jurisdiction—An order of the Chancery Division relating to the ownership of assets is a final determination of those issues between the parties and operates as an estoppel for the wife disputing the ownership of those assets in the Family Division: *Edgerton v Edgerton and Shaikh* [2012] 2 FLR 273, CA. Note that the court's jurisdiction may be excluded in relation to 'maintenance' (which is not necessarily limited to periodical payments) if the paying party remains resident in another EU Member State in which a decision as to maintenance, including a dismissal of a spouse's claim, has previously been made: Council Regulation (EC) No 4/2009 (Maintenance Regulation), Art 8. For a discussion as to what amounts to a 'decision' or 'court settlement' of a foreign court, see *Ramadani v Ramadani* [2015] EWCA Civ 1138. Jurisdiction may also be excluded if the parties have previously agreed in writing that another Member State shall have jurisdiction (Art 4).

Timing of application—If an order is made before there has been a decree, it is made without jurisdiction and cannot be validated either under the slip rule or the inherent jurisdiction of the court (*Board (Board Intervening) v Checkland* [1987] 2 FLR 257, CA), save in the case of a pure clerical error (*Pounds v Pounds* [1994] 1 FLR 775, CA). Further, by s 23(5), the order only takes effect on the decree being made absolute.

Although there is no jurisdiction to make an order under this section (or s 24) before decree nisi, in view of the time it will take to get the application ready for a final hearing, the application should normally be made as soon after the filing of the petition as possible. There is no statute of limitation in the matrimonial jurisdiction: see *Wyatt v Vince* [2015] UKSC 14 in which case the Supreme Court allowed an appeal by the wife against an order striking out her claim for financial provision brought some 18 years after decree absolute. See further *Briers v Briers* [2017] EWCA Civ 15, in which the Court of Appeal made it clear that (i) delay does not, in principle, place a burden on the applicant to justify a distributive remedy and (ii) an elision of the concepts of entitlement-sharing and needs provision is contrary to authority. Her claim had been brought some 18 years after decree absolute. See further the commentary to FPR 2010, r 4.4.

Number of applications for periodical payments (s 23(1)(a))—A party to the marriage may make any number of applications for a periodical payments order (but see the notes under s 25A). The earliest date on which the order can commence is the date when the claim is made; the order can continue until the death of either of the parties or the remarriage of the recipient, whichever is the earlier (see s 28(1)(a)).

Duration and form of periodical payments order—The options available to the court are:

(i) No order and a clean break as to the payment of maintenance;
(ii) A nominal order permitting the maintenance claim to be kept alive;
(iii) A joint lives order expressed to be until the death of either party, the remarriage or cohabitation for more than a stated period of the receiving party, or further order;
(iv) A term order until a defined event, such as the children completing education (before which, the receiving party may apply to extend the term); and
(v) A term order with a s 28(1A) bar preventing a party from applying for an extension of the order under s 31.

Step-down orders—The court has the power under s 23(1)(a) to make orders that go up or down at defined points to reflect anticipated future circumstances, commonly a step-down on return to employment. A step-down order was rejected in *Murphy v Murphy* [2014] EWHC 2263 (Fam), where the court found the wife's employment prospects at a set rate of remuneration at any given time to be 'totally speculative' and declined to implement an order for step-down periodical payments.

Nominal orders—The effect of a nominal order is to reduce the periodical payments to nil, while preserving the payee's ability to renew a claim. Whether there should be a nominal order or a clean break is a matter for judicial discretion on the facts of the case and the application of s 25 criteria. See the commentary on clean break orders under s 25A.

Segal Orders—The court may make an order for periodical payments on the conventional basis, providing that if the Child Support Agency or its successors make an assessment for child support in respect of the children of the family, the sum designated for periodical payments shall be reduced by the amount of such assessment each month. A so-called 'global' order may incorporate some of the costs of the children. However, the court has no power to include child periodical payments as part of a spousal order by the operation of CSA 1991, as the jurisdiction to make the assessment lies with the CSA. A Segal Order is correctly confined to applications early in financial proceedings where there is no CSA assessment, prior to first appointment or disclosure. See *Dorney-Kingdom v Dorney-Kingdom* [2000] 2 FLR 855, CA.

Joint lives orders—There are certain circumstances in which the court will consider that the dependant spouse is likely to require a joint lives order, notwithstanding the duty of the court to consider whether it is just and reasonable to terminate the financial obligations of each party to the other under s 25A. Joint lives maintenance may be appropriate where needs or, exceptionally, compensation are established, but not sharing, as sharing applies to the assets already acquired within the marriage, not future earnings. The most common rationale for imposing the obligation to maintain into the future is to meet needs that the relationship has generated:

(i) where the wife is at a disadvantage in economic terms through caring for young children, age, health or impaired earning capacity through lack of an employment history. This derives from decisions made by the parties during the marriage and may have lifelong consequences for the primary carer: see *G v G (Financial Remedies: Short Marriage: Trust Assets)* [2012] 2 FLR 48, FD. The CA in *Flavell v Flavell* [1997] 1 FLR 353, CA considered that it was not usually appropriate to provide for the termination of periodical payments where a woman was in her mid-50s: such orders would be only justified where the wife had her own substantial capital and a significant earning capacity. However, the courts have acknowledged the potential for unfairness where a wife who had received an equal division of capital may go on to make further income claims. See *D v D (Financial Provision: Periodical Payments)* [2004] 1 FLR 988, FD: wife's periodical payments to determine at the husband's retirement even if he had prospered relative to her. Term order substituted for joint lives order.

(ii) where there is real uncertainty whether and to what extent the wife may become financially self-supporting: in such circumstances, the CA has preferred not to impose a term, as it is open to the husband to seek a variation in the future: *C v C (Financial Relief: Short Marriage)* [1997] 2 FLR 26, CA.

(iii) where the wife requires compensation for the interruption from her career, and capital assets are not available for this purpose: *Miller v Miller; McFarlane v McFarlane* [2006] 1 FLR 1186, HL.

As the threshold needed for the extension of a term order is high, the burden should not be on the wife to make renewed applications to extend; it is better to make a joint lives order, so that it should be for the husband to apply for and justify termination or reduction, at which stage the court could consider a clean break among other options: *Miller; McFarlane* at [97]. Note that in *SS v NS (Spousal Maintenance)* [2015] 2 FLR 1124, FD, Mostyn J considered that the test of 'exceptionality' to justify an extension of a term of periodical payments has not survived subsequent case-law developments. Instead, such an application should examine whether the 'implicit premise of the original order of the ability of the payee to achieve independence had been impossible to achieve' (at [44]).

Joint lives orders may be expressed to be until death, remarriage or cohabitation. A period of settled cohabitation may be a factor ending the liability of a spouse to continued periodical payments. For the court's approach to cohabitation, see the commentary to MCA 1973, s 31. See also the commentary on clean breaks under s 25A.

Number of applications for secured periodical payments (s 23(1)(b))—Any number of applications may be made for a secured periodical payments order in the absence of a direction under s 25A(3) (see the notes under s 25A).

Duration and form of secured periodical payments order—The earliest date on which a secured periodical payments order can commence is the date when the claim is made but, by s 28(1)(b), it can be defined to continue beyond the death of the payer.

Capitalisation of income orders—Where there is sufficient wealth, the objective of achieving a clean break may permit the court to order a lump sum for income purposes. For guidance as to the rate of return and method of calculation, see *Duxbury v Duxbury* [1987] 1 FLR 7, CA; *F v F (Duxbury Calculation: Rate of Return)* [1996] 1 FLR 833, FD; *H v H* [2015] 2 FLR 447, CA.

Number of applications for lump sum order (s 23(1)(c))—Only one lump sum order may be made for a party to the marriage: *Coleman v Coleman* [1973] Fam 10, FD; *Banyard v Banyard* [1984] FLR 643, CA. The court has jurisdiction to extend time for the payment of the lump sum where the payer is not to blame for the delay and the extension of time did not prejudice the recipient: *Masefield v Alexander (Lump sum: Extension of time)* [1995] 1 FLR 100, CA.

Section 23(1)(c) gives the court power to order a lump sum or several lump sums at one time. Save for the limited exception as to timing as in *Masefield v Alexander*, orders under s 23 are not variable under s 31. However, where parties have agreed payment of lump sums by instalments over time in a consent order, the court retains jurisdiction in the event of disagreement about what was intended and may vary the order. A preamble to the order should set out the basis of the agreement, i e whether the lump sum orders are intended to be variable or not: see *Hamilton v Hamilton* [2014] 1 FLR 55, CA.

Lump sums to children are not subject to the same restriction (see s 23(4)). Difficulties in the mortgage market do not justify a delay in making lump-sum payments, especially without provision for interest (*Milton v Milton* [2009] 1 FLR 661, CA).

Rollover of statutory charge—The Legal Aid Agency may postpone the enforcement of the statutory charge as set out in CLS(F)R 2000, reg 52 where, 'by order of the court or agreement it relates to property to be used as a home by the client or his dependants, or, where the relevant proceedings were family proceedings, to money to pay for such a home'.

Outline of child support calculation—See under CSA 1991, s 4.

Duration and form of child periodical payments order (s 23(1)(d),(e))—This section provides that unless there are special circumstances (such as physical or mental disability), or the child remains in education, an order for child periodical payments should cease when a child reached 18: (s 29(1),(3)). Payments for tertiary education are increasingly sought and are permissible under the section. The court may permit payment for a gap year before or after tertiary education: see *Re N (Payments for Benefit of Child)* [2009] 1 FLR 1442, FD for the application of the principle in Sch 1 Children Act cases. Care should be taken to consider the needs of a child for future provision for tertiary education or a gap year, to avoid a child having to make his or her own application against a parent. By s 29(2)(a), the order should in the first instance be expressed not to extend beyond the age of 17. It is usual to have the following words: 'until the said child attains the age of 17 years or ceases full-time (secondary/tertiary) education, whichever is the later'.

School fees—A suggested form of wording for a school fees order is:

'As from … the Petitioner/Respondent do pay or cause to be paid to the Respondent/ Petitioner for the benefit of … until he/she shall attain the age of 17 years or cease full-time secondary education if later or further order periodical payments of an amount equivalent to the school fees (but not extras/including the following extras) at the school the said child shall from time to time attend by way of three payments at the start of each term and it is further directed that the school fees shall be paid to the headmaster/bursar/school secretary as agent for the Respondent/Petitioner and the receipt of that payee shall be sufficient discharge.'

There is power to order lump sums for school fees and for the property of the payer to be charged until payment in full (*T v T (Financial Provision: Private Education)* [2006] 1 FLR 903, FD).

Assignment of pensions by service personnel—Pensions Act 1995, s 166 provides that the statutory provisions that prohibit service personnel from assigning their pensions do not prevent a divorce court from making orders in respect of those pension benefits, thus overruling the line of cases, such as *Walker v Walker* (1983) 4 FLR 779, CA, which had previously prevented the court from exercising jurisdiction in respect of terminal grants and other pension rights. Section 166(4)–(6) provides as follows:

'(4) Nothing in the provisions mentioned in subsection (5) applies to a court exercising its powers under section 23 of MCA 1973 (financial provision orders in connection with divorce proceedings etc) in respect of any benefits under a pension scheme (within the meaning of section 25B of MCA 1973) which a party to the marriage has or is likely to have.

(5) The provisions referred to in subsection (4) are:

(a) section 203(1) and (2) of the Army Act 1955, s 203(1) and (2) of the Air Force Act 1955, s 128G(1) and (2) of the Naval Discipline Act 1957 or s 159(4) or (4A) of the Pension Schemes Act 1993 (which prevent assignment, or orders being made restraining a person from receiving anything which he is prevented from assigning),

(b) section 91 of this Act,

(c) any provision of any Act (whether passed or made before or after this Act is passed) corresponding to any of the enactments mentioned in paragraphs (a) and (b), and

(d) any provision in the scheme in question corresponding to any of those enactments.

(6) Subsections (3) to (7) of section 25B and section 25C of MCA 1973, as inserted by this section, do not affect the powers of the court under section 31 of that Act (variation, discharge etc) in relation to any order made before the commencement of this section.'.

Interim orders—While the court can make a maintenance pending suit order, it does not have power to make an interim lump sum order under s 23 (*Bolsom v Bolsom* (1983) 4 FLR 21, CA; *Barry v Barry* [1992] 2 FLR 233, FD), except under s 23(3)(a) for meeting expenses for maintaining an applicant or child before applying for an order under s 23(1)(c); but this limited type of order cannot be applied for before decree nisi and does not take effect until decree absolute. Under s 23(4), where the court has the power to make periodical payments orders in favour of a child of the family, that power shall be exercisable 'from time to time', giving the flexibility of making further orders, in line with a child's needs. In *Wicks v Wicks* [1998] 1 FLR 470, CA, the Court of Appeal held that the court does not have an administrative power of appropriation which it may exercise before the substantive hearing by allocating a particular asset, thus overruling *Barry v Barry*. To obtain a sale of property (including the former matrimonial home) before the final ancillary relief hearing, there appear to be three procedural alternatives (*BR v VT (Financial Remedies: Interim)* [2016] 2 FLR 519, FD):

(i) an application under MWPA 1882, s 17 with, if an order for possession is required, an application to terminate the home rights of the other party under FLA 1996, s 33 (see Procedural Guide A3);

(ii) an application under TLATA 1996 (see Procedural Guide A4) with an application to terminate the home rights of the other party under FLA 1996, s 33; or

(iii) an application pursuant to FPR 2010, r 20.2(1)(c)(v) for an order for sale of 'relevant property which is of a perishable nature or which for any other good reason it is desirable to sell quickly' with an application to terminate the home rights of the other party under FLA 1996, s 33.

Interest—A lump sum cannot take affect before decree absolute. An order may provide for payment to be made on or by a specific date, or the grant of decree absolute, whichever was later. Interest at judgment debt rate could only run from the date when the judgment became effective, that is, on grant of the decree absolute: *Robson v Robson* [2011] 1 FLR 751, CA.

Relationship with bankruptcy—There is a discretion under Insolvency Act 1986, s 281(5) to release a spouse from orders to pay lump sums in financial proceedings where the payer is a discharged bankrupt. The discretion may be exercised where the debt is unlikely to be satisfied or where release is necessary to allow the debtor to re-establish himself, but not for the purpose of reviewing or varying the debt: *McRoberts v McRoberts* [2013] BPIR 77, ChD, applying *Hayes v Hayes* [2012] BPIR 739, ChD. A trustee in bankruptcy, after the death of the bankrupt, is not entitled to an order for financial relief against the surviving spouse: the deceased's claims do not vest in the trustee (*Ian Roberts (Trustee in Bankruptcy of Jonathan Elichaoff, Deceased) v Woodall* [2016] EWHC 2987 (Ch)).

Guidance for litigants in person—The Family Justice Council guide 'Sorting out Finances on Divorce' provides information about financial settlements for unrepresented couples who are getting divorced or ending a civil partnership; see *www.judiciary.gov.uk/wp-content/uploads/2016/04/fjc-financial-needs-april-16-final.pdf*.

24 Property adjustment orders in connection with divorce proceedings etc

(1) On granting a decree of divorce, a decree of nullity of marriage or a decree of judicial separation or at any time thereafter (whether, in the case of a decree of divorce or of nullity of marriage, before or after the decree is made absolute), the court may make any one or more of the following orders, that is to say –

(a) an order that a party to the marriage shall transfer to the other party, to any child of the family or to such person as may be specified in the order for the benefit of such a child such property as may be so specified, being property to which the first-mentioned party is entitled, either in possession or reversion;

(b) an order that a settlement of such property as may be so specified, being property to which a party to the marriage is so entitled, be made to the satisfaction of the court for the benefit of the other party to the marriage and of the children of the family or either or any of them;

(c) an order varying for the benefit of the parties to the marriage and of the children of the family or either or any of them any ante-nuptial or post-nuptial settlement (including such a settlement made by will or codicil) made on the parties to the marriage, other than one in the form of a pension arrangement (within the meaning of section 25D below);

(d) an order extinguishing or reducing the interest of either of the parties to the marriage under any such settlement, other than one in the form of a pension arrangement (within the meaning of section 25D below);

subject, however, in the case of an order under paragraph (a) above, to the restrictions imposed by section 29(1) and (3) below on the making of orders for a transfer of property in favour of children who have attained the age of eighteen.

(2) The court may make an order under subsection (1)(c) above notwithstanding that there are no children of the family.

(3) Without prejudice to the power to give a direction under section 30 below for the settlement of an instrument by conveyancing counsel, where an order is made under this section on or after granting a decree of divorce or nullity of marriage, neither the order nor any settlement made in pursuance of the order shall take effect unless the decree has been made absolute.

Amendments—WRPA 1999, s 19, Sch 3, para 3.

Procedure—Applications under s 24 are governed by FPR 2010, Pt 9 and see Procedural Guide

Scope—The jurisdiction to make an order under this section arises only after decree nisi. This section defines a court's power to make a property adjustment order for a party to a marriage or any children. A wife in occupation of the matrimonial home seeking a transfer of property in preference to a sale, with primary regard for the children's need for a home, should ordinarily succeed, subject to securing the release of the husband's mortgage liability: *Fisher-Aziz v Aziz* [2010] 2 FLR 1053, CA. There is no jurisdiction to make an order to a child under s 24(1)(a) where the child is over 18, unless there are special circumstances such as disability or continuing education.

'property'—Property includes a council tenancy. In *Jones v Jones* [1997] 1 FLR 27, CA, the Court of Appeal gave guidance in the approach to the transfer of tenancies in needs cases. The court had to have regard to the effect on the parties, including what would happen to the party deprived of the right to live in the former matrimonial home, and the effect of the local authority's housing policy in relation to the timescale for rehousing. The possibility that the outgoing spouse could afford accommodation in the private sector was a consideration for the court. See also *Newlon Housing Trust v Alsulaimen* [1998] 2 FLR 690, HL. As the court may make an order under s 37 to restrain dealing with property outside the jurisdiction (*Hamlin v Hamlin* [1986] 1 FLR 61, CA) it has by implication power to make a property adjustment order in respect of overseas property. Where property in issue is a tenancy, an alternative way of obtaining a transfer is under FLA 1996, Sch 7. Where there is a covenant against assignment, such an application is the preferred option (see under Sch 7, para 7 of that Act).

Property may include company property, but only where there are legitimate grounds for piercing the corporate veil. The law is now as set down by the Supreme Court in *Prest v Petrodel Resources Ltd & Others* [2013] 2 FLR 732, SC, unanimously allowing a wife's appeal from the majority decision of the Court of Appeal.

There are three possible legal bases on which the assets of a company could be available to satisfy a lump sum order made in favour of a wife: (i) exceptionally and in very limited circumstances piercing the corporate veil where a party has deliberately evaded an obligation – *Salomon v Salomon and Co Ltd* [1897] AC 22, HL remains good law and *Ben Hashem v Ali Sharif* [2009] 1 FLR 115, FD approved; (ii) under s 24, which confers a distinct power to disregard the corporate veil in matrimonial cases; and (iii) where in the particular circumstances of the case the company could be said to be holding assets on trust for the husband, which was applied in Mrs Prest's case. A post-nuptial settlement, as a disposition in favour of one or both parties of the marriage in their capacity as husband and wife, and for their present or future benefit, could potentially be subject to variation under s 24. See *Li Quan v William Stuart Bray* [2015] 2 FLR 546, FD: a charitable trust for conserving tigers was held to be neither a post-nuptial settlement nor a resource of the husband's available for distribution to the wife.

In *Gowers v Gowers* [2012] 1 FLR 1040, FD, cash sums paid into court by a company subject to a freezing order could not be diverted to a wife without notice to the company: there was a risk of prejudice to third party interests and the corporate veil had not been pierced.

Obtaining office copy entries and registration of protective charges—LRA 2002, s 66 permits inspection and copying of entries on the register. At each stage in the proceedings, before and after decree absolute, the practitioner should check that he has registered the appropriate charge against the property subject to the claim. Thus, on decree absolute, any Class F land charge should be replaced by a pending action land charge or its registered land equivalent, ie a caution or restriction against dealings.

'settlement'—Settlement means any provision (other than an absolute gift) made for the benefit of the parties to the marriage by either one or both of them or by a third party (*Ulrich v Ulrich and Felton* [1968] 1 WLR 180, CA). A nuptial settlement is one that makes some form of continuing provision for both or either of the parties to a marriage with or without provision for their children: see *DR v GR and Others (Financial Remedy: Variation of Overseas Trust)* [2013] 2 FLR 1534, FD for a modern summary of the law as to what constitutes a variable nuptial settlement.

Variation of a settlement—Section 24(1)(c) permits a spouse to apply to vary a nuptial settlement in ancillary relief proceedings: *K v K (Ancillary Relief: Deed of Appointment)* [2009] 2 FLR 936, FD. The leading authority on the principles applicable to a variation of settlement application is *Ben Hashem v Ali Sharif* [2009] 1 FLR 115, FD: (a) the court's jurisdiction is unfettered and unlimited, and can extend to transferring an asset to a non-beneficiary free of a trust; (b) a settlement ought not to be interfered with further than is necessary to achieve the objective of fairness; and (c) the court should be slow to deprive innocent third parties of their rights under a settlement (see further below under **Rights of third parties**). For a good example of the application of these principles see *P v P (Variation of Post-Nuptial Settlement* [2016] 1 FLR 437, CA, on appeal from *AB v CB (Financial Remedy: Variation of Trust)* [2015] 2 FLR 25, FD.

Number of applications—In general terms, the fact that an order has been made under one subsection of this section does not preclude a later application for an order under another subsection (*Carson v Carson* (1981) 2 FLR 352, CA). However, on the subsequent application, any earlier order and any admissible material relating to it should be examined to establish whether it was intended as a final and conclusive financial settlement (either overall or in relation to a particular property). If it was intended to be a once and for all settlement of all claims any further claim under this section is precluded. It follows that if the earlier order was intended as a once and for all settlement in respect of one property only, a second application in respect of another property may be made (*Dinch v Dinch* [1987] 2 FLR 162, HL; *Sandford v Sandford* [1986] 1 FLR 412, CA).

No power to make interim property adjustment order—The court does not have power to make an interim property adjustment order. However, the court does have power, for example, to order an interim sale of property (including the former matrimonial home) if circumstances warrant and the other party's FLA 1996 home rights are properly terminated, if appropriate (see *BR v VT (Financial Remedies: Interim)* [2016] 2 FLR 519, FD and commentary relevant to interim orders under MCA 1973, s 23)).

Timing of application—An order under this section does not take effect until decree absolute, but there is good reason to make the application and prepare it for hearing as soon as the petition is filed. There is no time-limit for making an application. For greater detail see **Timing of application** under s 23.

Rollover of statutory charge—For a suggested form of wording for an order which is to be adopted to allow for rollover of the Legal Aid Agency's statutory charge where property is to be used as a home.

Rights of third parties—Whereas s 24A (in the context of applying for an order for sale where a property is owned by a party to the marriage and a third party) expressly provides for that third party to be served with the application so that he can be heard on it, there is no similar express provision on an application under this section where the property is owned jointly with another or is subject to third party rights. Two points should be noted:

(a) The court cannot adversely affect third party rights unless those third parties have been given notice of the proceedings and the opportunity to intervene, in which case they will be bound by the court's decision (*Tebbutt v Haynes* [1981] 2 All ER 238, CA). See also *P v P (Variation of Post-Nuptial Settlement* [2016] 1 FLR 437, CA for both a clear exposition of the principles applicable to an application for an order varying a settlement and a note of caution not to overstate the impact of any variation on other beneficiaries of a settlement. In *P v P* the matrimonial home farmhouse was held subject to a trust. The wife received a lump sum of £134,000 for life to enable her to rehouse. The following factors were important: first, had the parties remained married, the wife would have had the continued benefit of living in the farmhouse; secondly, the [children] beneficiaries were not overly prejudiced as the entire trust property (the farmhouse) would have provided a home to the parents during their marriage; and thirdly, the trust powers entitled the trustees to transfer the entire trust property to the husband absolutely.

(b) Where a third party does have such an interest there should be service under FPR 2010, r 9.13.

Third Party attacks on property transfers—The circumstances in which the state may claim the proceeds of crime under a confiscation order have been narrowed. In *R v Rastelli* [2008] EWCA Crim 373 a confiscation order was overturned by the Court of Appeal, where money fraudulently obtained by the husband and then paid to the former wife to pay off the mortgage on jointly owned property was held to be payment for good consideration and not a gift. In *Re B (Confiscation Order)* [2008] 2 FLR 1, QBD, a gift made by a husband to his wife on advice from financial institutions to place the family finances in order was made without consideration, and was therefore available to pay the husband's confiscation order.

Rights of trustees in bankruptcy—Transfers of property and settlements may be challenged by trustees in bankruptcy (see MCA 1973, s 39). A property transfer pursuant to s 24 gives consideration for the purpose of Insolvency Act 1986, s 339: *Hill v Haines* [2008] 1 FLR 1192, CA), followed in *Paulin v Paulin* [2009] 2 FLR 354, CA, where the CA said that there is very little risk that an ancillary relief award to a wife would be set aside at an undervalue in any subsequent bankruptcy proceedings.

Relationship between ancillary relief and bankruptcy—A spouse may apply to set aside the bankruptcy of the other spouse, in which case the bankruptcy proceedings may be heard together with ancillary relief proceedings: see *Paulin* (above), which provides a useful review of case-law and the relevant sections of the Insolvency Act 1986. Note also *Horton v Henry* [2016] EWCA Civ 989, in which the Court of Appeal held that there is no power for the court to order a bankrupt to draw down a tax-free entitlement from a pension scheme or to draw the pension income so as to satisfy an income payments order under Insolvency Act 1986, s 310.

Pension sharing—See under MCA 1973, s 21A.

24A Orders for sale of property

(1) Where the court makes an order under section 22ZA or makes under section 23 or 24 of this Act a secured periodical payments order, an order for the payment of a lump sum or a property adjustment order, then, on making that order or at any time thereafter, the court may make a further order for the sale of such property as may be specified in the order, being property in which or in the proceeds of sale of which either or both of the parties to the marriage has or have a beneficial interest, either in possession or reversion.

(2) Any order made under subsection (1) above may contain such consequential or supplementary provisions as the court thinks fit and, without prejudice to the generality of the foregoing provision, may include –

(a) provision requiring the making of a payment out of the proceeds of sale of the property to which the order relates, and

(b) provision requiring any such property to be offered for sale to a person, or class of persons, specified in the order.

(3) Where an order is made under subsection (1) above on or after the grant of a decree of divorce or nullity of marriage, the order shall not take effect unless the decree has been made absolute.

(4) Where an order is made under subsection (1) above, the court may direct that the order, or such provision thereof as the court may specify, shall not take effect until the occurrence of an event specified by the court or the expiration of a period so specified.

(5) Where an order under subsection (1) above contains a provision requiring the proceeds of sale of the property to which the order relates to be used to secure periodical payments to a party to the marriage, the order shall cease to have effect on the death or re-marriage of, or formation of a civil partnership by, that person.

(6) Where a party to a marriage has a beneficial interest in any property, or in the proceeds of sale thereof, and some other person who is not a party to the marriage also has a beneficial interest in that property or in the proceeds of sale thereof, then, before deciding whether to make an order under this section in relation to that property, it shall be the duty of the court to give that other person an opportunity to make representations with respect to the order; and any representations made by that other person shall be included among the circumstances to which the court is required to have regard under section 25(1) below.

Amendments—Inserted by Matrimonial Homes and Property Act 1981, s 7. Amended by MFPA 1984, s 46(1), Sch 1, para 11; CPA 2004, s 261(1), Sch 27, para 42; LASPOA 2012, s 51.

Procedure—Applications under s 24A are governed by FPR 2010, Pt 9 and see Procedural Guide

Scope—This section gives the court jurisdiction to make an order for sale if there has been a lump sum or property adjustment order. Pursuant to s 24A(3), an order for sale may only take effect upon decree absolute, which usually follows a final order in financial proceedings, although it may be made at an earlier stage. An interim order for sale of property – during the 'pendency of proceedings' – is not permitted under s 24A. The potential routes to achieve an interim order for sale of property are set out in the commentary to s 23 above under **Interim orders** and in *BR v VT (Financial Remedies: Interim)* [2016] 2 FLR 519, FD.

Where an order for sale is contemplated, the conventional costs of sale in England and Wales should be taken to be 3%, in the absence of evidence to the contrary: *Behzadi v Behzadi* [2009] 2 FLR 649, CA. An order for the sale of property under s 24A may be varied under s 31(2)(f). However, s 24A is a purely procedural section limited to matters of enforcement, implementation and procedure in respect of an underlying property adjustment order. Therefore, any application to vary a s 24A order will not be permitted if such variation 'revisits the territory', or undermines the substratum, of the primary property adjustment order under s 24: see *Birch v Birch* [2016] 2 FLR 467, CA, in which the wife unsuccessfully sought an order varying an undertaking made by her to sell a property by a certain date if she had not released the husband from the joint mortgage secured on it.

Enforcement—Where an order for sale has been made under s 24A, and a respondent is uncooperative, there is power to grant the other party sole conduct of the sale under s 24A(2). As vacant possession is necessary for the completion of the sale, the court may direct the delivery up of the property under FPR 2010, r 9.24(2). The matter may be transferred to the High Court for the purpose of enforcement by sheriffs. In the event that a party declines to cooperate in signing transfer documents in relation to the transfer of property, life policies etc, a judge has the power to sign the documents under SCA 1981, s 39.

Property jointly owned with third parties (s 24A(6))—Section 24(6) requires that a third party who has a beneficial interest in the property which it is proposed be sold must be given the opportunity to be heard on whether there should be a sale.

24B Pension sharing orders in connection with divorce proceedings etc

(1) On granting a decree of divorce or a decree of nullity of marriage or at any time thereafter (whether before or after the decree is made absolute), the court may, on an application made under this section, make one or more pension sharing orders in relation to the marriage.

(2) A pension sharing order under this section is not to take effect unless the decree on or after which it is made has been made absolute.

(3) A pension sharing order under this section may not be made in relation to a pension arrangement which –

(a) is the subject of a pension sharing order in relation to the marriage, or
(b) has been the subject of pension sharing between the parties to the marriage.

(4) A pension sharing order under this section may not be made in relation to shareable state scheme rights if –

(a) such rights are the subject of a pension sharing order in relation to the marriage, or
(b) such rights have been the subject of pension sharing between the parties to the marriage.

(5) A pension sharing order under this section may not be made in relation to the rights of a person under a pension arrangement if there is in force a requirement imposed by virtue of section 25B or 25C below which relates to benefits or future benefits to which he is entitled under the pension arrangement.

Amendments—Inserted by WRPA 1999, s 19, Sch 3, para 4.

Defined terms—'pension sharing order': ss 21A, 52(2); 'the court': s 52(1).

Scope—This section empowers the court in proceedings for divorce or nullity, but not judicial separation, to make on or at any time after a decree one or more pension sharing orders. (See also the annotations to s 21A.) Provided orders at different points in time relate to different schemes, the court, having made one pension sharing order, can subsequently make another in the absence of an appropriate dismissal. The order does not take effect until the later of the date of decree absolute (s 24B(2) or 7 days after the time for appealing the order (Divorce etc (Pensions) Regulations 2000, reg 9).

It is not possible to make a deferred pension sharing order to overcome what has been termed 'income gap syndrome'. Where therefore the pension of the pension debit member is already in payment, the amount of his pension will be adversely affected by a pension sharing order with no corresponding immediate benefit to the pension credit member, if she has not attained the age specified by the pension scheme for pension credit benefit (*Stevenson v Police Pension Scheme* [2004] (30 April), Pensions Ombudsman ref M00258; *Langley v Police Pension Scheme* [2006] (21 January), Pensions Ombudsman ref P00586; *Kerbel v Southwark Council* (2009) 26 January, ref 725771, Pensions Ombudsman). These provisions do not contravene ECHR 1950 (*R (Smith) v Secretary of State for Defence and Secretary of State for Work and Pensions* [2005] 1 FLR 97, QBD affirmed on appeal [2004] EWCA Civ 1664; *R (Thomas) v Ministry of Defence* [2008] 2 FLR 1385, QBD). However, by virtue of Occupational, Personal and Stakeholder Pensions (Miscellaneous Amendments) Regulations 2009, reg 15, which came into force on 6 April 2009, the age at which pension credit benefit will be paid is aligned in the case of occupational pension schemes with other pension rights (subject to amendment of the relevant scheme rules) from 6 April 2010. The position in relation to public sector schemes depends on the terms of the individual scheme. It may, nonetheless, be possible to overcome 'income gap syndrome' by undertaking not to supply the information required by the pension arrangement under the Pensions on Divorce etc (Provision of Information) Regulations 2000, reg 5 until the pension credit member is eligible to receive pension credit benefit. Providing the pension sharing order has taken effect, the pension credit member will still have an enforceable pension credit even if the pension debit member dies before implementation of the pension sharing order.

Prohibition if other pension sharing or attachment orders made (s 24B(3)–(5))—An order for pension sharing against a particular scheme or shareable state scheme rights cannot be made if there either is or has been a pension sharing order made in relation to the marriage before the court against that scheme. However, if the pension sharing order has been made in proceedings relating to a previous marriage, a further pension sharing order *can* be made. A pension attachment order which is in force for this or any previous marriage prevents a pension sharing order being made.

Valuation—The valuation of the pension benefits is prescribed by Pensions on Divorce etc (Provision of Information) Regulations 2000, reg 3 as the Cash Equivalent (CE) of the benefits acquired to date on the assumption that the member ceased employment on the date of the valuation. As set out in the annotations to the Pensions on Divorce etc (Provision of Information) Regulations, reg 3 (which contain a more detailed commentary in relation to valuation) including the applicable case-law, the CE does not include the value of the death in service package nor past service reserve.

Pensions in payment—Where a pension sharing order is made against a pension in payment, that payment ceases to be paid to the member at the former higher rate from the date the pension sharing order takes effect (being the later of the date of decree absolute and 7 days after the end of the period for filing notice of appeal against the pension sharing order) and any overpayment may be recouped by the pension scheme (*Shepherd v Trustees of the Air Products plc Pension Plan* [2006] (21 September), Pensions Ombudsman ref Q00278; *Pike v Teachers Pension Scheme* (2008) 26 March, ref 26355, Pensions Ombudsman; *Davis v Windsor Life Assurance Co Ltd* (2012) 6 March, ref 80998/1, Deputy Pensions Ombudsman; *Cleworth v Teacher's Pension Scheme* (2012) 21 December, ref 87725/2, Deputy Pensions Ombudsman; *Collinson v NHS Pension Scheme* (2013) 28 March, ref PO-128, Pensions Ombudsman; *Emson v Teachers' Pensions* (2013) 10 September, ref PO-168, Deputy Pensions Ombudsman).

The date of the CE to be used for valuation purposes is determined for evidential purposes by the Divorce etc (Pensions) Regulations 2000, reg 3 and for implementation purposes by WRPA 1999, s 29. As to 'moving target syndrome', see annotations to WRPA 1999, s 29.

24C Pension sharing orders: duty to stay

(1) No pension sharing order may be made so as to take effect before the end of such period after the making of the order as may be prescribed by regulations made by the Lord Chancellor.

(2) The power to make regulations under this section shall be exercisable by statutory instrument which shall be subject to annulment in pursuance of a resolution of either House of Parliament.

Amendments—Inserted by WRPA 1999, s 19, Sch 3, para 4.

Defined terms—'pension sharing order': ss 21A, 52(2).

Scope—A pension sharing order cannot take effect until, as provided by Divorce etc (Pensions) Regulations 2000, reg 9, 7 days have elapsed after the time for filing notice of appeal (21 days: FPR 2010, r 30.4). Subject to decree absolute, the order takes effect after 28 days, the 7-day period prescribed by the Divorce etc (Pensions) Regulations 2000, reg 9, not being subject to the computation of time provisions of FPR 2010, r 2.9(4).

24D Pension sharing orders: apportionment of charges

If a pension sharing order relates to rights under a pension arrangement, the court may include in the order provision about the apportionment between the parties of any charge under section 41 of the Welfare Reform and Pensions Act 1999 (charges in respect of pension sharing costs), or under corresponding Northern Ireland legislation.

Amendments—Inserted by WRPA 1999, s 19, Sch 3, para 4.

Defined terms—'the court': s 52(1); 'pension sharing order': ss 21A, 52(2).

Scope—This section enables the court to order who should pay the charges of the person responsible for the pension arrangement. This issue is dealt with in the annex to the pension sharing order (Form P1).The core features of WRPA 1999, s 41 and the Pensions on Divorce etc (Charging) Regulations 2000 are as follows:

(i) There is no charge for providing a CE provided that only one valuation is given in 12 months or it is not required in less than 3 months from the date of request/order.
(ii) Provided that the person responsible for the pension arrangement has stated his costs in writing in advance and that those costs are reasonable, the parties must pay for the cost of implementing the pension sharing order and not the arrangement itself.
(iii) If the court's order is silent as to who should pay the charges, the costs fall on the transferor (WRPA 1999, s 41(3)(b)).
(iv) The resolution of a dispute as to the amount of pension-sharing charges is an issue for the Pensions Ombudsman and not for the court, e g on a detailed assessment of costs.

See, further, the annotations to Pensions on Divorce etc (Provision of Information) Regulations 2000, reg 2 in Part IV.

The Pensions and Lifetime Savings Association (formerly the National Association of Pension Funds) (*www.plsa.co.uk*; tel 020 7601 1700) provides a recommended scale of charges for private sector occupational

PART II

pension schemes to use when providing information in relation to, and for the implementation of, pension sharing orders. The guidance also includes a flowchart showing the circumstances in which a charge may be made. The scale and flowchart may be downloaded from the website.

24E Pension compensation sharing orders in connection with divorce proceedings

(1) On granting a decree of divorce or a decree of nullity of marriage or at any time thereafter (whether before or after the decree is made absolute), the court may, on an application made under this section, make a pension compensation sharing order in relation to the marriage.

(2) A pension compensation sharing order under this section is not to take effect unless the decree on or after which it is made has been made absolute.

(3) A pension compensation sharing order under this section may not be made in relation to rights to PPF compensation that –

- (a) are the subject of pension attachment,
- (b) derive from rights under a pension scheme that were the subject of pension sharing between the parties to the marriage,
- (c) are the subject of pension compensation attachment, or
- (d) are or have been the subject of pension compensation sharing between the parties to the marriage.

(4) For the purposes of subsection (3)(a), rights to PPF compensation 'are the subject of pension attachment' if any of the following three conditions is met.

(5) The first condition is that –

- (a) the rights derive from rights under a pension scheme in relation to which an order was made under section 23 imposing a requirement by virtue of section 25B(4), and
- (b) that order, as modified under section 25E(3), remains in force.

(6) The second condition is that –

- (a) the rights derive from rights under a pension scheme in relation to which an order was made under section 23 imposing a requirement by virtue of section 25B(7), and
- (b) that order –
  - (i) has been complied with, or
  - (ii) has not been complied with and, as modified under section 25E(5), remains in force.

(7) The third condition is that –

- (a) the rights derive from rights under a pension scheme in relation to which an order was made under section 23 imposing a requirement by virtue of section 25C, and
- (b) that order remains in force.

(8) For the purposes of subsection (3)(b), rights under a pension scheme 'were the subject of pension sharing between the parties to the marriage' if the rights were at any time the subject of a pension sharing order in relation to the marriage or a previous marriage between the same parties.

(9) For the purposes of subsection (3)(c), rights to PPF compensation 'are the subject of pension compensation attachment' if there is in force a requirement imposed by virtue of section 25F relating to them.

(10) For the purposes of subsection (3)(d), rights to PPF compensation 'are or have been the subject of pension compensation sharing between the parties to the marriage' if they are or have ever been the subject of a pension compensation sharing order in relation to the marriage or a previous marriage between the same parties.

Amendments—Inserted by Pensions Act 2008, Sch 6, Pt 1.

Defined terms—'pension compensation sharing order': s 21B; 'the court': s 52(1); 'PPF compensation': s 21C.

Scope—See under s 25E for a discussion of the Pension Protection Fund (PPF) and under s 21B in relation to pension compensation sharing orders. This section is the counterpart of s 24B in relation to pension sharing orders.

Prohibition if other pension or sharing order attachment orders made (s 24E(3)–(10))—The restrictions contained in s 24B(3)–(5) are replicated so that the court may not make a pension compensation sharing order in relation to PPF compensation that is subject to pension attachment (as defined by s 24E(4)), pension compensation attachment, pension compensation sharing order or deriving from pension rights that have been subject to pension sharing. However, in the case of pension compensation sharing or PPF compensation derived from pension rights that had previously been the subject of pension sharing, the order will only preclude a pension compensation sharing order if it was between the parties to the marriage: if the prior pension sharing order or pension compensation sharing order related to a previous marriage between different parties, a further pension compensation sharing order may be made. A prior pension attachment order or pension compensation attachment order for this or any previous marriage prevents a pension compensation sharing order being made.

Valuation—The valuation of PPF compensation is prescribed by the Divorce and Dissolution etc (Pension Protection Fund) Regulations 2011, reg 3, which cross-refers to the Pension Protection Fund (Pension Compensation Sharing and Attachment on Divorce etc) Regulations 2011, regs 3 and 4, under which the value of shareable rights to PPF compensation is to be calculated in accordance with actuarial assumptions approved by the PPF Board on the date that the PPF Board receives the request for a valuation.

24F Pension compensation sharing orders: duty to stay

(1) No pension compensation sharing order may be made so as to take effect before the end of such period after the making of the order as may be prescribed by regulations made by the Lord Chancellor.

(2) The power to make regulations under this section shall be exercisable by statutory instrument which shall be subject to annulment in pursuance of a resolution of either House of Parliament.

Amendments—Inserted by Pensions Act 2008, Sch 6, Pt 1.

Defined term—'pension compensation sharing order': s 21B.

Scope—See under s 25E for a discussion of the Pension Protection Fund (PPF) and under s 21B in relation to pension compensation sharing orders. This section is the counterpart of s 24C in relation to pension sharing orders. A pension compensation sharing order cannot take effect until (as provided by the Divorce and Dissolution etc (Pension Protection Fund) Regulations 2011, reg 6) 7 days have elapsed after the time for filing notice of appeal (21 days: FPR 2010, r 30.4). Subject to decree absolute, the order takes effect after 28 days, the 7-day period prescribed by the Divorce and Dissolution etc (Pension Protection Fund) Regulations 2011, reg 6 not being subject to the computation of time provisions of FPR 2010, r 2.9(4).

24G Pension compensation sharing orders: apportionment of charges

The court may include in a pension compensation sharing order provision about the apportionment between the parties of any charge under section 117 of the Pensions Act 2008 (charges in respect of pension compensation sharing costs), or under corresponding Northern Ireland legislation.

Amendments—Inserted by Pensions Act 2008, Sch 6, Pt 1.

Defined terms—'pension compensation sharing order': s 21B; 'the court': s 52(1).

Scope—See under s 25E for a discussion of the Pension Protection Fund (PPF) and under s 21B in relation to pension compensation sharing orders. This section is the counterpart of s 24D in relation to the apportionment of charges on the making of the pension sharing order. Reference should be made to the annotations to s 24D.

See also the Pension Protection Fund (Pension Compensation Sharing and Attachment on Divorce etc) Regulations 2011, regs 16 and 17.

25 Matters to which court is to have regard in deciding how to exercise its powers under ss 23, 24, 24A, 24B and 24E

(1) It shall be the duty of the court in deciding whether to exercise its powers under section 23, 24, 24A, 24B and 24E above and, if so, in what manner, to have regard to all the circumstances of the case, first consideration being given to the welfare while a minor of any child of the family who has not attained the age of eighteen.

(2) As regards the exercise of the powers of the court under section 23(1)(a), (b) or (c), 24, 24A, 24B and 24E above in relation to a party to the marriage, the court shall in particular have regard to the following matters –

(a) the income, earning capacity, property and other financial resources which each of the parties to the marriage has or is likely to have in the foreseeable future, including in the case of earning capacity any increase in that capacity which it would in the opinion of the court be reasonable to expect a party to the marriage to take steps to acquire;

(b) the financial needs, obligations and responsibilities which each of the parties to the marriage has or is likely to have in the foreseeable future;

(c) the standard of living enjoyed by the family before the breakdown of the marriage;

(d) the age of each party to the marriage and the duration of the marriage;
(e) any physical or mental disability of either of the parties to the marriage;
(f) the contributions which each of the parties has made or is likely in the foreseeable future to make to the welfare of the family, including any contribution by looking after the home or caring for the family;
(g) the conduct of each of the parties, if that conduct is such that it would in the opinion of the court be inequitable to disregard it;
(h) in the case of proceedings for divorce or nullity of marriage, the value to each of the parties to the marriage of any benefit which, by reason of the dissolution or annulment of the marriage, that party will lose the chance of acquiring.

(3) As regards the exercise of the powers of the court under section 23(1)(d), (e) or (f), (2) or (4), 24 or 24A above in relation to a child of the family, the court shall in particular have regard to the following matters –

(a) the financial needs of the child;
(b) the income, earning capacity (if any), property and other financial resources of the child;
(c) any physical or mental disability of the child;
(d) the manner in which he was being and in which the parties to the marriage expected him to be educated or trained;
(e) the considerations mentioned in relation to the parties to the marriage in paragraphs (a), (b), (c) and (e) of subsection (2) above.

(4) As regards the exercise of the powers of the court under section 23(1)(d), (e) or (f), (2) or (4), 24 or 24A above against a party to a marriage in favour of a child of the family who is not the child of that party, the court shall also have regard –

(a) to whether that party assumed any responsibility for the child's maintenance, and, if so, to the extent to which, and the basis upon which, that party assumed such responsibility and to the length of time for which that party discharged such responsibility;
(b) to whether in assuming and discharging such responsibility that party did so knowing that the child was not his or her own;
(c) to the liability of any other person to maintain the child.

Amendments—MFPA 1984, s 3; Pensions Act 1995, s 166; WRPA 1999, s 19, Sch 3, para 5; Pensions Act 2008, Sch 6, Pt 1.

Section 25 and the inquisitorial jurisdiction—This section and s 25A (clean break) contain the statutory criteria for determining how claims by a party to a marriage for income and capital should be decided. 'It shall be the duty of the court' (s 25(1)) emphasises the quasi-inquisitorial duty of the court to investigate in ancillary relief litigation. The CA in *Grey v Grey* [2010] 1 FLR 1764, CA stated that 'in ancillary relief proceedings the judge is not confined in the search for fairness by the nature of counsels' submissions nor is he bound by the evidence the parties choose to adduce'. The judge must be satisfied that the court has or has sought all the information needed to discharge the duty to find the fairest solution: *Lykiardopulo v Lykiardopulo and Lykiardopulo* [2011] 1 FLR 1427, CA. The court has a duty to have meticulous regard to all the relevant circumstances pertaining to financial orders applications. This duty is inconsistent with any summary procedure to determine whether a party has a real prospect of success, as there is no power under FPR 2010, r 4.4 to strike out a financial order application: *Wyatt v Vince* [2015] UKSC 14. Accordingly, the parties owe the court the duty of full, frank and clear disclosure, which is absolute: *NG v SG (Appeal: Non-Disclosure)* [2012] 1 FLR 1211, FD.

Case-law has shaped the approach of the courts to the s 25 directed imperative. The analysis must be on the basis of gender equality and non-discrimination. In *White v White* [2000] 2 FLR 981, HL, 'in seeking to achieve a fair outcome, there was no place for discrimination between husband and wife and their respective roles. Fairness required that their division of labour should not prejudice or advantage either party when considering their contribution to the welfare of the family' (affirmed in *Young v Young* [2014] 2 FLR 786, FD, where there was to be no discrimination between breadwinner and homemaker). In considering the s 25 criteria, the House of Lords has considered three main distributive principles: needs, compensation and sharing, shaped by the overarching requirement of fairness; 'each [party] is entitled to an equal share of the assets of the partnership, unless there is good reason to the contrary', but the yardstick of equality is to be used as an aid not a rule: *Miller v Miller; McFarlane v McFarlane* [2006] 1 FLR 1186, HL.

In *Charman v Charman (No 4)* [2007] 1 FLR 1246, CA, the Court of Appeal has said that 'the starting point of every enquiry in applications for ancillary relief was the financial position of the parties, and was always in two stages, first computation, then distribution'. Extending the approach of *Charman*, a third stage after computation and distribution is to decide whether the result produced by the sharing principle meets the need (generously interpreted) of the parties and is, in overview, fair: *L v L* [2008] 1 FLR 142, FD.

The concept of sharing ends with the end of the marital partnership: 'on the exit from a marriage, the partnership ends, and in ordinary circumstances a wife has no right or expectation of continuing economic parity ('sharing') unless and to the extent that consideration of her needs, or compensation for relationship-generated disadvantage so require': *VP v JB* [2008] 1 FLR 742, FD. Only if the application of the sharing principle fails to meet the requirements of both parties would the unmet needs of one party then dictate a greater share. This approach means that the sharing principle is cross-checked against the other s.25 factors. In applying needs and sharing, the court is engaged in two separate exercises, involving different considerations; the higher of the two separate assessments should found the final award: *Jones v Jones* [2011] 1 FLR 1723, CA. Disparity in income or earning capacity in the future can justify an unequal split in matrimonial capital, where a wife has continuing income need and a limited capacity to earn it for herself: the court must give reasons for any significant departure from equality and demonstrate how the resulting capital order will fairly meet the needs of both parties: *A v L* [2012] 1 FLR 985, FD.

In *Tattersall v Tattersall* [2014] 1 FLR 997, CA, a judge had not erred in awarding an unequal distribution of assets and declining to make a *Mesher* order in favour of the husband, as the wife's day-to-day responsibility for a 3-year-old child, the husband's higher earning capacity and the potential for conflict if a *Mesher* order were made justified the wife receiving 70% of the capital. In *R v R (Financial Remedies)* [2013] 1 FLR 106, FD, a departure from equality was not justified where a husband's post-separation achievement was more than matched by a wife's earlier financial contribution. An unequal distribution of the assets, arising out of the special contribution of one party, had to be based on 'a striking evidential foundation which so clearly stood out that the question almost answered itself': *Evans v Evans* [2013] 2 FLR 999, FD. This principle was recognised in *Cooper-Hohn v Hohn* [2015] 1 FLR 745, FD, where in an application involving assets of $1.5 billion it was appropriate to depart from the principle of equality because the husband had made a special contribution in generating the wealth and there had been an exponential post-separation accrual.

The court, in its duty to see if fairness is being achieved, should embark on rough calculations to the extent of compiling a balance sheet as a basis for the financial award, so that the court understands the financial consequences of the exercise of its discretion: see *MD v D* [2009] 1 FLR 810, FD; *Behzadi v Behzadi* [2009] 2 FLR 649, CA.

Where the matrimonial assets comprise liquid and illiquid or risk-laden assets, fairness may require that consideration should be given to distributing these between each of the parties: *Wells v Wells* [2002] 2 FLR 97, CA; *P v P (Financial Relief: Illiquid Assets)* [2005] 1 FLR 548, FD. Where the entirety of the matrimonial assets have their origins in money brought into the marriage by one of the spouses, a departure from equality may be necessary in the interests of fairness: *Smith v Smith* [2007] 2 FLR 1103, CA. The Court of Appeal has commented that 'there was no rule that equal division was the starting point in all cases; on the contrary, the starting point in all cases was the financial position of the parties, and s 25 of the Act': see *B v B (Ancillary Relief: Distribution of Assets)* [2008] 2 FLR 1627, CA.

The concept of compensation raises the possibility that financial payment may be ordered, not just to meet financial needs, but as a measure of compensation to reflect that the spouse who stayed at home may have put his/her career on hold, to future economic disadvantage if the marriage ends. In *Lauder v Lauder* [2007] 2 FLR 802, FD, a wife aged 70 with disabilities and a long marriage was entitled to an element of compensation, because of relationship-generated disadvantage that went beyond need.

However, 'compensation' has been criticised as not being a statutory term under MCA 1973, s 25 nor a separate 'head of claim', as in a civil action. Parties who make lifestyle choices about careers or the domestic sphere may make a combined and equal contribution, entitling each to a full share of the fruits of the marriage, and to give an additional entitlement for 'compensation' for perceived loss of economic opportunity may risk double counting: *RP v RP* [2007] 1 FLR 2105, FD. The CA has said that 'contribution, not relationship generated disadvantage, was the language of the statute': *Hvorostovsky v Hvorostovsky* [2009] 2 FLR 1574, CA. For an example of a robust rejection of a wife's entitlement to compensation, see *SA v PA* [2014] EWHC 392 (Fam), in which a compensation claim by and for a wife who had been a lawyer was rejected by the court. However, in *H v H* [2014] 2 FLR 1338, FD, a wife who had been a qualified accountant before leaving her career to look after the children was entitled to a compensation element to be paid as lump sum by H upon his retirement. In cases in which the capital division is insufficient to meet a party's future maintenance needs, any outstanding compensatory element 'is best dealt with by a generous assessment of her continuing needs unrestricted by purely budgetary considerations, in the light of the contribution of the wife to the marriage and the broad effect of the sacrifice of her own earning capacity upon her ability [to provide for her own needs]': *VB v JP* [2008] 1 FLR 742, FD.

Nuptial agreements—The importance of the judge's discretionary powers has been emphasised by the Court of Appeal in *Crossley v Crossley* [2008] 1 FLR 1467, CA, followed in *S v S (Ancillary Relief)* [2009] 1 FLR 254, FD.

On nuptial agreements generally, agreements executed in a foreign jurisdiction following independent legal advice have been recognised by the English courts, to the extent that the English divorce petition has been stayed: *S v S (Divorce: Staying Proceedings)* [1997] 2 FLR 100, FD; *C v C (Divorce: Stay of English Proceedings)* [2001] 1 FLR 624, FD. See also *MacLeod v MacLeod* [2009] 1 FLR 641, PC, where a prenuptial agreement confirmed in principle by a postnuptial agreement 8 years into the marriage was held to be a valid and enforceable agreement.

The leading case is *Radmacher v Granatino* [2010] 2 FLR 1900, SC, the Supreme Court holding that prenuptial agreements would be given decisive weight as part of the s 25 exercise, if entered into willingly by the parties, with all material information available to them and each intending that the agreement should be applied should the marriage come to an end. Duress, fraud or misrepresentation will negate any effect the agreement might otherwise have, these being vitiating factors. Unconscionable conduct such as undue pressure (falling short of duress) will also be likely to eliminate the weight to be attached to the agreement, and other unworthy conduct, such as exploitation of a dominant position to secure an unfair advantage, would reduce or eliminate it. Finally, the court will investigate whether is it fair to hold the parties to the agreement in the circumstances prevailing. If parties have entered into a valid agreement with no vitiating factors but the agreement is held to be unfair in the circumstances prevailing, this does not necessarily lead to the conclusion that the agreement is set aside: instead, the court will look to 'step in' to alleviate the unfairness (see *DB v PB* [2016] EWHC 3431 (Fam)). For the law relating to undue influence, see *RBS v Etridge (No 2)* [2001] 2 FLR 1364, HL.

Nuptial agreements and need—The fact of a nuptial agreement itself may act to limit a party's claim to not being placed in a 'predicament of real need', as opposed to meeting 'reasonable [or other] needs' (*Radmacher v Granatino* [2010] 2 FLR 1900, SC, at [81]). The existence of a prenuptial agreement may 'feature prominently as a depressing factor' on a party's needs: *WW v HW (Prenuptial Agreement: Needs: Conduct)* [2016] 2 FLR 299, FD.

Post-*Radmacher*, the case-law has established that it is important to give weight to the autonomy of the parties who made the agreement. The fact of the agreement can alter what would otherwise be a fair award: *V v V (Pre-Nuptial Agreement)* [2012] 1 FLR 1315, FD. In *Z v Z (No 2)* [2012] 1 FLR 1100, FD, a French prenuptial agreement was upheld insofar as it excluded sharing; the wife had established a needs case that was recognised by the court and met by an award of 40% of the assets, representing a suitable departure from equality to reflect the agreement. Current and future need may outweigh the existence of a nuptial agreement: in *Luckwell v Limata* [2014] 2 FLR 168, FD, the agreement was unfair, as the husband had no provision in any circumstances; his need for accommodation for himself and the children resulted in a capital award on a *Mesher* basis, 45% reverting to the wife when the youngest was 22. In *GS v L (Financial Remedies: Pre-Acquired Assets: Needs)* [2013] 1 FLR 300, FD and *B v S (Financial Remedy: Marital Property Regime)* [2012] 2 FLR 502, FD, the court declined to uphold a separation of property agreement because neither party had had a full appreciation of its implications in the *Radmacher* sense. The court therefore applied the normal principles of sharing and need to the capital division. A prenuptial agreement may carry no weight: *F v F (Pre-nuptial Agreement)* [2010] 1 FLR 1743, FD, where a French prenuptial agreement was perceived by the parties to be merely an administrative inconvenience, imposed by the state, which they believed they had to comply with in order to marry, and placed no reliance on when divorcing after a 15-year marriage. A valid prorogation clause as to jurisdiction (pursuant to Art 4(1),(2) of the Maintenance Regulation EC No 4/2009) within a nuptial agreement may act to limit the court's powers to make financial remedy orders that relate to the claimant's maintenance and needs, see *DB v PB* [2016] EWHC 3431 (Fam).

Section 25 principles—In performing the inquisitorial task, first consideration must be given to the welfare of any minor child of the family under s 25(1). Thereafter, the factors listed under s 25(2) should be considered individually: 'confusion would be avoided if resort was had to the precise language of the statute': *Robson v Robson* [2011] 1 FLR 751, CA. The CA has emphasised that there is no order of importance in the s 25(2) factors – each had to be given its due weight in the exercise of the court's discretion, with the objective of reaching a just result.

The s 25(2)(a) resources will always be balanced against the s 25(2)(b) needs of each party. The court is also concerned with the foreseeable future, as well as with the past history and present position of the parties.

Income, earning capacity, property and other financial resources (s 25(2)(a))—This was extended in 1984 to include consideration of 'any increase in that capacity which it would in the in the opinion of the court be reasonable to expect a party to the marriage to take steps to acquire'. This implies a rebuttable presumption of future economic self-sufficiency. A primary task of the court is to identify what is matrimonial and non-matrimonial property. Non-matrimonial property may include property brought in by one party through gift or inheritance, or may be created or acquired post-separation. Pre-acquired non-matrimonial assets should be apportioned in the light of the 'sharing principle': see *Jones v Jones* [2011] 1 FLR 1723, CA.

The cut-off date for defining matrimonial property is the date when mutual support ends, usually but not necessarily when cohabitation ends. The weight to be given to post-separation assets is a matter for the court's discretion, but future earning capacity is expressly listed in s 25(2)(a), and therefore cannot be ignored: see *P v P (Post-separation Accruals and Earning Capacity)* [2008] 2 FLR 1135, FD; *H v H (Financial Provision)* [2009] 2 FLR 795, FD; *CR v CR* [2008] 1 FLR 323, FD. Income and bonuses accrued post-separation may be as a result of the husband's sole endeavours and there may be a reluctance to include them as marital property: *H v H* [2007] 2 FLR 548, FD; *Evans v Evans* [2013] 2 FLR 999, FD. See **Non-matrimonial resources – post-separation accruals**, below.

As a starting point, all assets should be valued at the date of trial (*Rossi v Rossi* [2007] 1 FLR 790, FD; *S v S (Ancillary Relief after Lengthy Separation)* [2007] 1 FLR 2120, FD). Residential property should be valued in net terms after deduction of mortgage and costs of sale, conventionally 3% in England in Wales in the absence of evidence to the contrary (*Behzadi v Behzadi* [2009] 2 FLR 649, CA). Valuations should be at present market value, not based on future optimism: *FZ v SZ and Others (Ancillary Relief: Conduct: Valuations)* [2011] 1 FLR 64, FD. The court must do its best on the valuation current and available at trial, even where a husband's assets have dramatically reduced in value: *Marano v Marano* [2010] 1 FLR 1903, CA.

Where disclosure is deficient, the court is required by adverse inferences to attempt 'realistic and reasonable quantification, even in the broadest terms of the hidden funds' – see *NG v SG (Appeal: Non-Disclosure)* [2012] 1 FLR 1211, FD; *Kremen v Agrest (Financial Remedy: Non-Disclosure: Post Nuptial Agreement)* [2012] 2 FLR 414, FD.

'Add backs'—It may be proper to 'add back' a notional sum into the assets of a spouse who has recklessly depleted the matrimonial assets, thereby potentially disadvantaging the other spouse: principle developed in *Norris v Norris* [2003] 1 FLR 1142, FD. The principle was applied to the wife in *McCartney v Mills McCartney* [2008] 1 FLR 1508, FD. In *Vaughan v Vaughan* [2008] 1 FLR 1108, CA 'add backs' were considered further: the requirement was of clear evidence of dissipation with a 'wanton element' and could not apply to sums expended in meeting living costs or needs. The court was not obliged to limit its orders to known resources of capital or income, but may infer the availability of other unidentified resources available to the husband. See also *BP, KP and NI (Financial Remedy Proceedings: Res Judicata)* [2013] 1 FLR 1310, FD; *AC v DC (No 2)*

[2013] 2 FLR 1499, FD. Where both parties are found to have spent at a prodigious rate, and the add back sought by the wife is a small percentage of the total assets, an add back may not be necessary for a fair result to be achieved: *Evans v Evans* [2013] 2 FLR 999, FD. Care, however, must be taken in pursuing a claim of 'add back'. Even if a spouse has spent considerable sums on, for example, drugs and prostitution, this may not result in the court adding back the sums expended: a spouse cannot take advantage of all the good characteristics of his or her partner while disavowing the bad, see *MAP v MFP (Financial Remedies: Add-Back)* [2016] 1 FLR 70, FD.

The matrimonial home is often the greatest asset; it has a central role in the marriage and is available for sharing, irrespective of the source of the funding, as it becomes over time treated by the parties as a central item of matrimonial property. See *Miller v Miller; McFarlane v McFarlane* [2006] 1 FLR 1186, HL; *K v L (Non-Matrimonial Property: Special Contribution)* [2011] 2 FLR 980, CA; *Lawrence v Gallagher* [2012] 2 FLR 643, CA. However, unequal financial contributions to the acquisition of a matrimonial home may justify an unequal division of its value on divorce; see for example, *S v AG (Financial Orders: Lottery Prize)* [2012] 1 FLR 651, FD.

Inherited wealth is a resource under s 25(2)(a), but may be treated differently from wealth generated by the parties' efforts during the marriage. The CA has stated that inherited wealth must be taken into account under s 25. The approach taken to inherited assets depends on the nature and source of the assets that might justify a departure from the sharing principle, the duration of the marriage, the length of time the inheritance had been enjoyed, the effect on the parties' standard of living and the way in which the inherited asset had been treated by the parties. Inherited property that has been applied within the marriage and long enjoyed by both parties may be more likely to be made available to meet a party's needs, although 'judges should be cautious and not invade inherited property unnecessarily': *Robson v Robson* [2011] 1 FLR 751, CA. See also *K v L (Non-Matrimonial Property: Special Contribution)* [2011] 2 FLR 980, CA, where an award to a husband of a small proportion of his wife's inheritance that was based on a generous assessment of need, but not sharing, was upheld on appeal. See also *AR v AR (Treatment of Inherited Wealth)* [2012] 2 FLR 1, FD, for the application of s 25 factors where almost the entirety of the parties' substantial resources were family gifts and properties inherited by the husband. In *Y v Y (Financial Orders: Inherited Wealth)* [2013] 2 FLR 924, FD, the husband had inherited very substantial resources built up by his forbears over generations. After a 26-year marriage, the wife was entitled to a housing fund and capital as this was primarily a needs case, but she was also entitled to a share of the resources, the husband retaining the major part of the inheritance.

Financial resources provided by parents to enable spouses to acquire a home may be inferred as being intended to be a gift to husband and wife jointly; a house acquired with parents' help may be held on trust for spouses in equal shares: *Abbot v Abbot* [2008] 1 FLR 1451, PC, following *Stack v Dowden* [2007] 1 FLR 1858, HL. Where the needs of the parties are the main consideration, it may be wrong to ringfence inherited assets, where all available assets are needed to meet the parties' requirements: *S v S (Ancillary Relief: Importance of FDR)* [2008] 1 FLR 944, FD.

'other financial resources'—The potential availability of wealth owned by others could be taken into account by the court. A trust may be a financial resource, where a husband's interest has vested, and there was a likelihood that the husband would ultimately receive a significant part of the trust fund: *C v C (Ancillary Relief: Trust Fund)* [2010] 1 FLR 337, FD; *B v B (Ancillary Relief)* [2010] 2 FLR 887, FD; *Whaley v Whaley* [2012] 1 FLR 735, CA. However, while the court could encourage trustees to act in the interests of a spouse, they could not be compelled, see *Thomas v Thomas* [1995] 2 FLR 668, CA; *A v A* [2007] 2 FLR 467, FD. In considering whether a [discretionary] trust is to be treated as a financial resource available to a party, the court will consider whether, if a request was made, a trustee would be likely to advance capital or income to the party (*Charman v Charman (No 4)* [2007] 1 FLR 1246, CA). The court could make an award that would put pressure on the husband's parents, who had historically provided bounty, as in *TL v ML (Ancillary Relief: Claim against Assets of Extended Family)* [2006] 1 FLR 1263, FD. Even when the court finds that a property is legally and beneficially owned by a third party, the facts of the case may support a conclusion that the asset is nevertheless available to the husband as a financial resource, as in *Gadhavi v Gadhavi* [2015] EWCA Civ 520 (property in India owned by husband's mother but funded from income of husband, who was 'head' of the family). Family shares held for the benefit of the husband's children were held to constitute a constructive trust and the proceeds of the shares were not matrimonial property: *De Bruyne v De Bruyne* [2010] 2 FLR 1240, CA. A husband's entitlement under a discretionary trust was a matrimonial resource: *SR v CR (Ancillary Relief: Family Trusts)* [2009] 2 FLR 1083, FD. Where there is a needs-based claim, the derivation of funds requires to be given some, but not great, weight: *G v B (Financial Remedies: Asset Beneficiaries)* [2014] 2 FLR 292, FD.

The family company is a potential resource, but valuation can present difficulties. Judges are required to consider the division of the assets using the yardstick of equality, so they should make specific findings about the value of a company, particularly where the parties disagree: *Re C (Divorce: Financial Relief)* [2008] 1 FLR 625, FD. Valuation should be by a single joint expert: *P v P (Financial Relief: Illiquid Assets)* [2005] 1 FLR 548, FD; *H v H* [2008] 2 FLR 2092, FD. The purpose of the valuation is to assist the court in testing the fairness of the proposed outcome; it should not be a detailed accounting exercise and should be proportionate to the overall value of the assets. A minority shareholding held by a spouse may attract a discounted value, unless the relationship between the spouse and other shareholders is a quasi-partnership, with shareholders cooperating and likely to sell together, so that full market value may apply: see *Re Bird Precision Bellows Ltd* [1984] 1 Ch 419, CA; *G v G (Financial Provision: Equal Division)* [2002] 2 FLR 1143, FD; *Irvine v Irvine* [2006] EWHC 583 (Ch); *Charman v Charman (No 2)* [2007] 1 FLR 593, FD; *NA v MA* [2007] 1 FLR 1760, FD. The court should be cautious about ordering a sale, because it is difficult to value and the best price is rarely obtainable: *A v A* [2006] 2 FLR 115, FD; *R v R (Financial Relief: Company Valuation)* [2005] 2 FLR 365, FD. A wife may not merit a share in the capital value of the business where the income stream is needed to finance her maintenance, and there is a danger of double counting: *V v V (Financial Relief)* [2005] 2 FLR 697, FD.

Personal injury awards—Damages received by one spouse may be a relevant factor to be considered in the s 25 exercise. Damages may not be sacrosanct against the needs of the other spouse. Each case turns on its facts: the application of the general sharing rule must be tempered to reflect the particular needs of the recipient of the damages and the fact that damages were acquired as compensation for pain, suffering or loss. See *Daubney v Daubney* [1976] Fam 267, CA, *Pritchard v Cobden Ltd and Another (No 1)* [1987] 2 FLR 30, CA, *Wagstaff v Wagstaff* [1992] 1 FLR 333, CA and *Mansfield v Mansfield* [2012] 1 FLR 117, CA.

Pensions—Pensions may be a significant element in the domestic economy of the parties, the cash equivalent (CE) value being clear and quantifiable at the end of the marriage. The CA has emphasised that the CE value of the parties' pension provision should be included on a balance sheet to assist in the computation of the available assets, and failure to do so may distort the distribution of assets: *Vaughan v Vaughan* [2008] 1 FLR 1108, CA; *Behzadi v Behzadi* [2009] 2 FLR 649, CA. Pensions can be 'offset' by the payment of a lump sum or transfer of property in lieu of a pension sharing order. The way to calculate the appropriate offsetting figure is without formula or discernible principle: in *WS v WS* [2015] EWHC 3941 (Fam) the court approached the calculation of the offsetting amount on the basis of a conventional Duxbury-based calculation. A court in England and Wales cannot make a pension sharing order in respect of a foreign pension: see the analysis of Mostyn J in *Goyal v Goyal* [2016] EWFC 50 following the Court of Appeal judgment in *Goyal v Goyal* [2016] EWCA Civ 792. MCA 1973, s 24B is directed towards domestic pension schemes and there is a general presumption against the extra-territorial application of domestic legislation. However, approval was given to agreements in consent orders – backed up by undertakings – to obtain orders dividing a pension in the courts in the country in which a foreign pension scheme is based. Care should be taken by the 'applicant' for such an approach to furnish the court with expert evidence as to the likelihood of the foreign court implementing and enforcing such orders.

The distinction between matrimonial and non-matrimonial property—The court is entitled to draw a distinction between matrimonial property (acquired by the parties during the marriage) and non-matrimonial property (acquired by one party prior to the marriage or gifted to, or inherited by, them during or after the marriage). There are two broad schools of thought as to the proper approach to the division of non-matrimonial property. The first adopts a more formulaic approach: categorising property as matrimonial or non-matrimonial; dividing the matrimonial property equally; and sharing the non-matrimonial property only insofar as it is necessary to meet the other party's needs (see *N v F (Financial Orders: Pre-Acquired Wealth)* [2011] 2 FLR 533, FD). The other is a more holistic approach that is less categoric in its assessment of the available property, adjusting the overall division of property on divorce from an equal to an unequal one to reflect the existence and source of non-matrimonial property (see, for example, *SK v WL (Ancillary Relief: Post-Separation Accrual)* [2011] 1 FLR 1471, FD).

Non-matrimonial resources – pre-acquired assets—The argument that pre-acquired assets should be excluded from distribution may be raised where parties marry later in life, or not for the first time, or where the length of the marriage is short. The existence of pre-acquired assets has previously been recognised by a percentage approach: in *C v C* [2009] 1 FLR 8, FD, the court should not undertake a precise account of the parties' premarital wealth, especially after a long marriage, but where a husband had a successful company with a substantial asset base, a departure from equality, to be expressed in percentage terms, was justified. The approach has been further developed by the CA in *Jones v Jones* [2011] 1 FLR 1723, CA: the non-matrimonial assets should be defined and valued where possible and may remain with the spouse who brought them into the marriage; the remaining matrimonial assets then fall to be divided in accordance with the sharing principle. The result should then be cross-checked by a reference to a percentage division of the assets to achieve a fair result. It remains the case that non-matrimonial property belonging to one spouse may be awarded to the other where need requires such an award. The approach in *Jones v Jones* is, however, a tool and not a rule (*Robertson v Robertson* [2017] 1 FLR 1174, FD). In *K v L (Non-matrimonial Property: Special Contribution)* [2011] 2 FLR 980, CA, the husband after a long marriage was entitled to £5 million (but no more) to meet his needs, the wife retaining the greater part of her shares in her family's business, worth £28 million, which were non matrimonial and not to be shared. See *N v F (Financial Orders: Pre-Acquired Wealth)* [2011] 2 FLR 533, FD for further refinement of the principle in *Jones* and some guidance as to the court's approach to dividing assets including pre-marital property: (i) Should the existence of pre-marital property be reflected at all? This depends on questions of duration and mingling; (ii) How much of the pre-marital property should be excluded from sharing?; (iii) Remaining matrimonial property should normally be divided equally; and (iv) The fairness of the overall award should be tested by considering the overall percentage division, reiterated in *JL v SL (No 2) (Appeal: Non-Matrimonial Property)* [2015] 2 FLR 1202, FD, per Mostyn J.

Non-matrimonial assets and 'mingling'—Non-matrimonial property may, by virtue of being 'mingled', lose its status as non-matrimonial property or the weight to be attached to such property within the discretionary exercise may be affected. Mingling can arise where, for example, non-matrimonial property is mixed with matrimonial property or used as a bedrock on which the financial success of the marriage is founded. This reflects the proposition that 'the importance of the source of assets may diminish over time': see Wilson LJ in *K v L (Non-matrimonial Property: Special Contribution)* [2011] 2 FLR 980, CA for the following explanation: where, over time, the non-matrimonial property 'has been mixed with matrimonial property in circumstances in which the contributor may be said to have accepted that it should be treated as matrimonial property or in which, at any rate, the task of identifying its current value is too difficult', at [18]. See also *Robson v Robson* [2011] 1 FLR 751, CA for direction to the court to consider the 'way the property was preserved, enhanced or depleted'; 'the more and longer that the [in that case, inherited wealth], has been enjoyed, the less fair it is that it should be ringfenced and excluded from distribution', at [43].

Non-matrimonial resources – post-separation accruals – companies—A valuable asset that comes to fruition after parties have separated may nevertheless on the facts be a matrimonial asset, where founded and developed during the marriage: 40% awarded to the wife in *SK v WL (Ancillary Relief: Post-Separation Accrual)* [2011] 1 FLR 1471, FD. In *Gordon (formerly Stefanou) v Stefanou* [2011] 1 FLR 1582, CA, a company created by a husband some years after separation but before divorce, to which the wife had made no contribution, was treated as a non-matrimonial asset not available for sharing. See also *S v S (Ancillary Relief* *after Lengthy Separation)* [2007] 1 FLR 2120, FD. In the case of a company that starts life as a matrimonial asset but increases significantly in value after separation, the court may have regard to the extent to which the increased value represents a 'continuum' [of development] as opposed to the fruits of a 'new venture' attributable to the efforts of one party and, therefore, justifying an unequal division: see, for example, *JB v MB* [2015] EWHC 1846 (Fam) and *Cooper-Hohn v Hohn* [2015] 1 FLR 745, FD.

Post-separation accruals – share schemes—In *SS v NS (Spousal Maintenance)* [2015] 2 FLR 1124, FD, the husband held vested shares that would be received in the future and taxed as income. Mostyn J observed that 'there would have to be special features present before money earned but that is "deferred in collection and conditional on performance" is excluded from the divisible pool', at [12]. In *B v B (Ancillary Relief: Post-Separation Income)* [2010] 2 FLR 1214, FD, the husband's assets had increased considerably through his performance-related bonuses post-separation, but before trial. The wife received 15% of additional sums if subsequently received, but an equal division of the assets at date of trial was not justified.

Post-separation accruals – bonus payments—For treatment of future bonuses see *H v W (Cap on Wife's Share of Bonus Payments)* [2015] 1 FLR 75, FD: the wife's basic needs should be met out of salary, together with a percentage of the post-separation bonus where this is needed to top up her maintenance, but subject to a cap to represent the wife's reasonable maintenance entitlement. Where a husband may expect an increase in the future value of the business and therefore in his income, such future income is not an asset that is susceptible to the sharing principle: *H v H (Financial Relief)* [2010] 1 FLR 1864, FD; *Evans v Evans* [2013] 2 FLR 999, FD. See also *Cooper-Hohn v Hohn* [2015] 1 FLR 745, FD under **Section 25 and the inquisitorial jurisdiction**, above.

PART II

Cohabitation as a resource—The court should be alive to the practical impact of cohabitation, including its financial consequences and duration. A cohabiting wife has no legal claim to be maintained by a third party, so the burden of maintenance may still rest with the husband. However, in the exercise of its s 25 discretion, the court must attach a significant weight to a settled relationship and should be able to conduct a full investigation of its financial consequences, to the extent of assessing what the third party is, or ought to be, contributing to the wife: *Grey v Grey* [2010] 1 FLR 1764, CA. See notes to MCA 1973, s 31 for commentary on cohabitation cases.

Needs and obligations (s 25(2)(b))—The needs of the parties are a question of fact for the court: they are invariably the driving force for calculating any financial award to both parties. The Family Justice Council has produced a useful document 'Guidance on "Financial Needs" on Divorce' (June 2016). The guidance is designed to clarify the meaning of 'financial needs' on divorce and to encourage a consistent approach by courts in England and Wales. Financial needs invariably focus on the provision of housing and meeting present and future income, including in retirement. The need to provide for the continuing care of children of the marriage is the responsibility of both parties and is part of the relationship-generated disadvantage of the primary carer, who may have given up work during the marriage, with lifelong consequences, which may need to be met by spousal maintenance: *G v G* [2012] EWHC 167 (Fam). The needs of the applicant may be the dominant factor in a case, but a husband was not liable for needs created by the wife's financial mismanagement and irresponsibility: *North v North* [2008] 1 FLR 158, CA. In small money cases, the focus will be on the parties' minimal future needs, rather than the strict division of the matrimonial acquest, *M-D v D* [2009] 1 FLR 810, FD. The moral obligation to maintain an elderly parent may reduce the level of legal obligation to an applicant spouse: *Judge v Judge* [2009] 1 FLR 1287, CA. Albeit that the requirement of securing housing for each party is likely to dominate smaller money cases, there is no requirement to achieve exact parity in each party's housing need: *Arbili v Arbili* [2016] 1 FLR 473, CA.

The need for the children to be securely rehoused where there is limited capital may cause a tension between need and the husband's own capital entitlement arising out of the concept of sharing. A *Mesher* order enables the husband to take his capital share at a future point, when the wife's responsibilities as a homemaker end. A *Mesher* order has been criticised as harsh for the primary carer, who has continued to discharge responsibilities to the children but has to rehouse with reduced capital and/or earning capacity later in life. See *White v White* [2000] 2 FLR 981, HL; *Dorney-Kingdom v Dorney-Kingdom* [2000] 2 FLR 855, CA; *Elliot v Elliot* [2001] 1 FCR 477, CA; a *Mesher* order may be inappropriate where there is a very short marriage and a very young child: *B v B (Mesher Order)* [2003] 2 FLR 285, FD.

The age of the parties and the duration of the marriage—The duration of the marriage is to be considered with the other s 25 factors. A period of settled and committed cohabitation immediately before the marriage may be treated as part of the overall length of the marriage for the purposes of s 25(2)(d): *GW v RW (Financial Provision: Departure from Equality)* [2003] 2 FLR 108, FD; *CO v CO (Ancillary Relief: Pre-marriage cohabitation)* [2004] 1 FLR 1095, FD. The principle of equal sharing [of family assets] is applicable as much to short marriages as to long ones. However, 'the difference is that a short marriage has been less enduring. In the nature of things, this will affect the quantum of the financial fruits of the partnership'; see *Miller v Miller; McFarlane v McFarlane* [2006] 1 FLR 1186, HL, per Lord Nicholls, at [17].

In a short marriage, the absence of children and consequent enhanced housing needs may mean that the nature and source of property brought to the marriage will be accorded a greater significance than in a longer marriage, justifying a departure from equality where one party has contributed significantly more than the other: *Foster v Foster* [2003] 2 FLR 299, CA, where the wife received 61% of the assets. The longer the marriage, the more likely that non-matrimonial property has become merged with matrimonial or inherited property: *Robson v Robson* [2011] 1 FLR 751, CA. In a short marriage, non-matrimonial or inherited property may be less likely to be shared, unless the needs of a spouse require it: *Rossi v Rossi* [2007] 1 FLR 790, FD. In a short marriage, spousal maintenance may provide a transition over an appropriate period to an independent lifestyle, which may be less than that enjoyed during the marriage: *G v G* [2012] EWHC 167 (Fam). Where a child has been born in a short marriage, periodical payments may nevertheless be required without term.

In short marriages, fairness may mean that a claimant is not entitled to a share of the other spouse's non-matrimonial property, and the parties will have less of a claim against the other, even if the resulting division of capital is unequal: *Miller v Miller; McFarlane v McFarlane* (above), which were directed at providing for the financial need of the wife. In a short marriage of 4 years, where the husband had acquired his capital after the marriage had ended, the transfer of 30% of his assets to the wife was held to be plainly excessive: *Fallon v Fallon* [2010] 1 FLR 910, CA. In *R v R (Financial Remedies: Needs and Practicalities)* [2013] 1 FLR 120, FD, a marriage of 7 years was regarded as a short marriage and accordingly pre-existing assets were excluded from sharing, and the wife's entitlement to continue to receive a very high income order after separation was held to be limited. In long-marriage cases, factors of substance are required to justify departing from broad equality, such as a substantial asset base pre-dating the relationship: see **Non-matrimonial resources – pre-acquired assets**, above.

Standard of living (s 25(2)(c))—Where there is sufficient money, the continuation of the marital lifestyle choices may be sanctioned by the court. In *S v S* [2008] 2 FLR 113, FD, the President upheld an award permitting the wife to keep horses, for so long as the husband could afford to finance it, equestrian activities having been integral to the parties' marriage. The lifestyle enjoyed in the marriage is a benchmark relevant to the consideration of the future lifestyles of the parties after separation: *G v G* [2012] EWHC 167 (Fam).

Contributions to the welfare of the family (s 25(2)(f))—The generation of wealth is to be regarded as a contribution to the welfare of the family, although care must be taken not to discriminate against the homemaker or the provider of a domestic contribution, which may be incommensurable, but is equally valuable. The court will also deprecate the parties indulging 'in a detailed and lengthy retrospective involving a general rummage through the attic of their marriage to discover relics from the past to enhance their role or diminish their spouse's'; see *G v G (Financial Provision: Equal Division)* [2002] 2 FLR 1143, FD, at [49]. Special, genius or stellar contributions may still be grounds for departing from equality. In a long marriage, the wife had done everything required of her, but the husband had the spark of genius which created the wealth, so he was nevertheless entitled to 60% of the capital: *Sorrell v Sorell* [2006] 1 FLR 497, FD. The wife's share of the assets in Charman was held at 36.5%, partly because of the special contribution of the husband: *Charman v Charman (No 4)* [2007] 1 FLR 1246, CA. It is suggested that where a special contribution is established, the departure from equality would not be less that 55:45 or greater than 66:33 in the circumstances of a long marriage. A special contribution is not necessarily demonstrated because the assets are substantial. In *G v G* (above) and *H v H (Financial Relief)* [2010] 1 FLR 1864, FD, the husband (although wealthy) was not a genius and was found to have made no special contribution.

Conduct (s 25(2)(g))—This is only to be considered if it would be 'inequitable to disregard it'. A broader approach to conduct, involving appraisals as to why the marriage broke down, was seen in *G v G (Financial Provision: Separation Agreement)* [2004] 1 FLR 1011, CA. This approach was disapproved by the HL in *Miller v Miller; McFarlane v McFarlane* [2006] 1 FLR 1186, HL: 'in most cases, misconduct is not relevant to the bases upon which financial ancillary relief is ordered today' (at [1202]). Conduct may include litigation conduct, through failure to disclose, although care must be taken to ensure that litigation misconduct is not unfairly reflected in substantive orders rather than being reflected on orders for costs, see *Ezair v Ezair* [2013] 1 FLR 281, CA. Litigation conduct through failure to disclose assets and to engage in proceedings resulted in wife being awarded 50% of assets, plus uplift in respect of husband's conduct: *A v A* [2012] All ER (D) 108 (Dec), FD. Financial dissipation through gambling has also been held to be conduct within the section: *M v M (Third Party Subpoena: Financial Conduct)* [2006] 2 FLR 1253, FD. Conduct will not normally extend beyond financial conduct or conduct with financial consequences, for example, physical assault may have financial consequences: in *H v H (Financial Relief: Attempted Murder as Conduct)* [2006] 1 FLR 990, FD, the conduct of a husband who stabbed his wife so that she was unable to work, and refused the sale or letting of the family home, was described as conduct at the very top end of the scale, because of its financial consequences, thus entitling the wife's needs to be given a higher priority than the husband's. Cohabitation may be seen as conduct: see *Atkinson v Atkinson* [1988] 2 FLR 353, CA. For cohabitation, see resources under **Section 25 principles**, above, and the commentary to MCA 1973, s 31. A false report by a wife to the police to obtain an occupation order has been considered to be conduct: *FZ v SZ and Others (Ancillary Relief: Conduct: Valuations)* [2011] 1 FLR 64, FD.

25A Exercise of court's powers in favour of party to marriage on decree of divorce or nullity of marriage

(1) Where on or after the grant of a decree of divorce or nullity of marriage the court decides to exercise its powers under section 23(1)(a), (b) or (c), 24, 24A, 24B or 24E above in favour of a party to the marriage, it shall be the duty of the court to consider whether it would be appropriate so to exercise those powers that the financial obligations of each party towards the other will be terminated as soon after the grant of the decree as the court considers just and reasonable.

(2) Where the court decides in such a case to make a periodical payments or secured periodical payments order in favour of a party to the marriage, the court shall in particular consider whether it would be appropriate to require those payments to be made or secured only for such term as would in the opinion of the court be sufficient to enable the party in whose favour the order is made to adjust without undue hardship to the termination of his or her financial dependence on the other party.

(3) Where on or after the grant of a decree of divorce or nullity of marriage an application is made by a party to the marriage for a periodical payments or secured periodical payments order in his or her favour, then, if the court considers that no continuing obligation should be imposed on either party to make or secure periodical payments in favour of the other, the court may dismiss the application with a direction that the applicant shall not be entitled to make any future application in relation to that marriage for an order under section 23(1)(a) or (b) above.

Amendments—Inserted by MFPA 1984, s 3. Amended by WRPA 1999, s 19, Sch 3, para 6; Pensions Act 2008, Sch 6, Pt 1.

Scope—The 'clean break' section is to be read with s 25(2)(a) to provide that earning capacity includes 'any increase in that capacity which it would in the opinion of the court be reasonable to expect a party to the marriage to take steps to acquire' with a view to a clean break. The court must consider:

(i) termination: whether it is appropriate to terminate the financial obligations as soon after the decree as is 'just and reasonable';
(ii) term: if periodical payments are to be made, whether they should be made or secured only for such period as to allow adjustment without undue hardship to termination (with or without a bar on the payee applying to extend the original term);
(iii) dismissal: if there is no continuing obligation for periodical payments, the court may dismiss the application, with a direction under s 28(1A) that there be no future application for an order under s 23(1)(a) or (b).

At any stage when the court is considering orders under s 23 or s 24, the court has a duty to consider whether an immediate or future clean break is appropriate. This principle was developed in *Minton v Minton* (1978) FLR Rep 461, HL and had survived *White v White* [2000] 2 FLR 981, HL to be reiterated in *Miller; McFarlane* [2006] 1 FLR 1186, HL. See also *Robson v Robson* [2011] 1 FLR 751, CA.

The statute is silent as to the circumstances in which it may be appropriate to make a clean break order. In *C v C (Financial Relief: Short Marriage)* [1997] 2 FLR 26, CA, the Court of Appeal summarised the proper approach to assessing whether a clean break order should be made, which depends on all the circumstances of the case, including the welfare of any minor child and the s 25 checklist factors. A short marriage will not of itself require a term order. If a term is appropriate, there must be evidence to support that conclusion, as opposed to hope or crystal ball gazing. If there is doubt about when self-sufficiency will be attained, it is wrong to require the payee to apply to extend the term. If there is uncertainty about the appropriate length of the term, the proper course is to impose no term but leave the payer to seek variation or discharge.

Therefore, a clean break order may be appropriate where there is evidence that the applicant is financially self-sufficient, or is expected to be in the near future, or where the parties are impecunious with no prospect of future financial contribution. In *L v L (Financial Remedies: Deferred Clean Break)* [2012] 1 FLR 1283, FD on appeal from the PRFD, a joint lives order was set aside in favour of a non-extendable term order of just over 2 years, where a 44-year-old wife worked in an established business and retained a valuable farm that was capable of generating income, the children were subject to shared care arrangements and the wife additionally expected to benefit from a family trust.

The Court of Appeal has expressed itself in favour of a clean break in *Matthews v Matthews* [2014] 2 FLR 1259, CA, where the imposition of a clean break was upheld on appeal. The wife's claim for a nominal spousal maintenance was rejected where the wife's earning capacity was found to be greater than the husband's, despite her difficulties in finding employment and her poor credit rating. The submission that it was wrong in principle to impose a clean break (subject to child support) where there were dependent children aged 6 and 3 was rejected, as there was a clear presumption in favour of a clean break and the trial judge had taken all relevant circumstances into account. In *Chiva v Chiva* [2014] EWCA Civ 1558, the Court of Appeal dismissed a wife's appeal, approving a clean break after 24 months where the wife's future earning power was such that she could be expected to make up the loss of periodical payments at the end of 2 years. In *Wright v Wright* [2015] EWCA Civ 201, a husband's variation application some years after a joint lives order, the Court of Appeal refused a wife permission to appeal against an order that reduced her spousal maintenance, with termination in December 2018 when the younger child reached 14, the wife having had since the divorce in 2006 to achieve self-sufficiency.

Therefore, clean break orders may no longer be thought to be inappropriate where there is a continuing responsibility to the housing and maintenance of dependent children.

For consolidated guidance on the approach to claims for spousal periodical payments, see Mostyn J in *SS v NS (Spousal Maintenance)* [2015] 2 FLR 1124, FD, at [46]:

(i) A spousal maintenance award is properly made where the evidence shows that choices made during the marriage have generated hard future needs on the part of the claimant. Here the duration of the marriage and the presence of children are pivotal factors.
(ii) An award should only be made by reference to needs, save in a most exceptional case where it can be said that the sharing or compensation principle applies. (Also note here that 'needs' is a very flexible concept and may, if the circumstances of a case allow, permit, for example, the 'stockpiling' of maintenance to generate a stronger capital base or to make future pension provision: see *Fields v Fields* [2016] 1 FLR 1186, FD.)
(iii) Where the needs in question are not causally connected to the marriage, the award should generally be aimed at alleviating significant hardship.
(iv) In every case, the court must consider a termination of spousal maintenance with a transition to independence as soon as it is just and reasonable. A term should be considered unless the payee would

be unable to adjust without undue hardship to the ending of payments. A degree of (not undue) hardship in making the transition to independence is acceptable.

(v) If the choice between an extendable term and a joint lives order is finely balanced, the statutory steer should militate in favour of the former.

(vi) The marital standard of living is relevant to the quantum of spousal maintenance but is not decisive. That standard should be carefully weighed against the desired objective of eventual independence.

(vii) The essential task of the judge is not merely to examine the individual items in the claimant's income budget but also to stand back and to look at the global total and to ask if it represents a fair proportion of the respondent's available income that should go to the support of the claimant.

(viii) Where the respondent's income comprises a base salary and a discretionary bonus, the claimant's award may be equivalently partitioned, with needs of strict necessity being met from the base salary and additional, discretionary, items being met from the bonus on a capped percentage basis.

(ix) There is no criterion of exceptionality on an application to extend a term order. On such an application, an examination should be made of whether the implicit premise of the original order of the ability of the payee to achieve independence had been impossible to achieve and, if so, why.

(x) On an application to discharge a joint lives order, an examination should be made of the original assumption that it was just too difficult to predict eventual independence.

(xi) If the choice between an extendable and a non-extendable term is finely balanced, the decision should normally be in favour of the economically weaker party.

Longer-term dependence on maintenance—The situation of a dependant party may still be relevant. In *Murphy v Murphy* [2014] EWHC 2263 (Fam), the court rejected a term order for a wife at 57 lacking capital and held that 'the fact of having children, and their obvious dependence in this particular case on their mother for their care, changes everything … The economic impact on this wife is likely to endure not only until they leave school but, indeed for the rest of her life'. In *Miller; McFarlane* [2006] 1 FLR 1186, HL, it was held that a clean break should not be imposed at the expense of a fair result: where a party is likely to need financial support or is entitled to compensation, and capital assets are not available, periodical payments might properly be ordered.

25B Pensions

(1) The matters to which the court is to have regard under section 25(2) above include –

(a) in the case of paragraph (a), any benefits under a pension arrangement which a party to the marriage has or is likely to have, and

(b) in the case of paragraph (h), any benefits under a pension arrangement which, by reason of the dissolution or annulment of the marriage, a party to the marriage will lose the chance of acquiring,

and, accordingly, in relation to benefits under a pension arrangement, section 25(2)(a) above shall have effect as if 'in the foreseeable future' were omitted.

(2) *(repealed)*

(3) The following provisions apply where, having regard to any benefits under a pension arrangement, the court determines to make an order under section 23 above.

(4) To the extent to which the order is made having regard to any benefits under a pension arrangement, the order may require the person responsible for the pension arrangement in question, if at any time any payment in respect of any benefits under the arrangement becomes due to the party with pension rights, to make a payment for the benefit of the other party.

(5) The order must express the amount of any payment required to be made by virtue of subsection (4) above as a percentage of the payment which becomes due to the party with pension rights.

(6) Any such payment by the person responsible for the arrangement –

(a) shall discharge so much of his liability to the party with pension rights as corresponds to the amount of the payment, and

(b) shall be treated for all purposes as a payment made by the party with pension rights in or towards the discharge of his liability under the order.

(7) Where the party with pension rights has a right of commutation under the arrangement, the order may require him to exercise it to any extent; and this section applies to any payment due in consequence of commutation in pursuance of the order as it applies to other payments in respect of benefits under the arrangement.

(7A) The power conferred by subsection (7) above may not be exercised for the purpose of commuting a benefit payable to the party with pension rights to a benefit payable to the other party.

(7B) The power conferred by subsection (4) or (7) above may not be exercised in relation to a pension arrangement which –

(a) is the subject of a pension sharing order in relation to the marriage, or

(b) has been the subject of pension sharing between the parties to the marriage.

(7C) In subsection (1) above, references to benefits under a pension arrangement include any benefits by way of pension, whether under a pension arrangement or not.

Amendments—Inserted by Pensions Act 1995, s 166. Amended by WRPA 1999, ss 21, 88, Sch 4, para 1, Sch 13, Pt II.

Modification—See the Divorce etc (Pension Protection Fund) Regulations 2006 for modifications to s 25B.

Defined terms—'the court': s 52(1); 'financial provision order': ss 21(1), 52(2); 'the other party': s 25D(3); 'the party with pension rights': s 25D(3); 'pension arrangement': s 25D(3); 'pension sharing order': ss 21A, 52(2); 'person responsible for the pension arrangement': s 25D(4).

Scope—This section, taken together with the following two sections, sets out the basis for pension attachment (previously known as earmarking), which is less favoured by applicants than pension sharing:

1 Applies to all forms of relief including judicial separation.

2 Attaches a percentage (rather than a cash amount) of:
  (a) member's pension in retirement (s 25B(4));
  (b) lump sum payable on retirement (s 25B(7): court can require commutation); or
  (c) lump sum payable on death in service, after leaving service but before retirement, and after retirement (s 25C: the court can require trustees to exercise discretion as regards lump sum or can require respondent to nominate for the benefit of the applicant, e g under a personal pension).

3 No power to create spouse's pension on member's death, i e an order for attached periodical payments lapses on member's death.

4 Court can order a member to take pension benefits by means of an injunction under SCA 1981, s 37 or the appointment of a receiver (*Blight v Brewster* [2012] EWHC 165 (Ch)).

5 Pension attachment is a species of financial provision order. Pension attachment periodical payment orders therefore end on remarriage and can be varied at any time. A pension attachment lump sum order can be varied (even as to amount) before either party's death.

6 Not available if pension arrangement is or has been subject to pension sharing between parties to this marriage.

7 Periodical payments element taxable in the hands of the member/payer, but not the recipient.

8 For the order to be effective, the person responsible for the pension arrangement must be given notice of the proceedings, order and subsequent changes of address of the applicant after the order is made.

9 An order for attached periodical payments or an attached lump sum is exempt from the Legal Aid Agency's statutory charge with effect from 1 April 2013 (Civil Legal Aid (Statutory Charge) Regulations 2013, reg 5(1)(b)(i))

10 The court must have regard to the benefits of all pension schemes, not just those in the foreseeable future (s 25B(1)), thus abrogating the rule in *Milne v Milne* (1981) 2 FLR 286, CA (which restricted foreseeable future to 10 years).

11 Armed Services pensions are amenable to pension attachment orders (Pensions Act 1995, s 166(4)–(6)), the full text to which is set out in **Assignment of pensions by service personnel** under s 23.

12 As to PPF compensation, see annotations to ss 21B and 25E.

13 Anomalies may arise where the member seeks to take advantage of the liberalisation of access to pension provisions of the Taxation of Pensions Act 2014, e g by withdrawing a lump sum greater than that allowed when the original pension attachment was made.

14 A foreign pension may not be attached (*Goyal v Goyal* [2016] EWFC 50).

T v T (Financial Relief: Pensions) [1998] 1 FLR 1072, FD and *Burrow v Burrow* [1999] 1 FLR 508, FD comprehensively review these sections.

'matters to which the court is to have regard' (s 25B(1))—Section 25B(1) is not restricted to pension attachment, but applies also to, for example, pension sharing and off-setting.

25C Pensions: lump sums

(1) The power of the court under section 23 above to order a party to a marriage to pay a lump sum to the other party includes, where the benefits which the party with pension rights has or is likely to have under a pension arrangement include any lump sum payable in respect of his death, power to make any of the following provision by the order.

(2) The court may –

(a) if the person responsible for the pension arrangement in question has power to determine the person to whom the sum, or any part of it, is to be paid, require him to pay the whole or part of that sum, when it becomes due, to the other party,

(b) if the party with pension rights has power to nominate the person to whom the sum, or any part of it, is to be paid, require the party with pension rights to nominate the other party in respect of the whole or part of that sum,

(c) in any other case, require the person responsible for the pension arrangement in question to pay the whole or part of that sum, when it becomes due, for the benefit of the other party instead of to the person to whom, apart from the order, it would be paid.

(3) Any payment by the person responsible for the pension arrangement under an order made under section 23 above by virtue of this section shall discharge so much of his liability in respect of the party with pension rights as corresponds to the amount of the payment.

(4) The powers conferred by this section may not be exercised in relation to a pension arrangement which –

(a) is the subject of a pension sharing order in relation to the marriage, or

(b) has been the subject of pension sharing between the parties to the marriage.

Amendments—Inserted by Pensions Act 1995, s 166. Amended by WRPA 1999, s 21, Sch 4, para 2.

Defined terms—'the court': s 52(1); 'the other party': s 25D(3); 'the party with pension rights': s 25D(3); 'pension arrangement': s 25D(3); 'pension sharing order': ss 21A, 52(2); 'person responsible for the pension arrangement': s 25D(4).

Scope—This section enables the court, except where there is or has been a pension sharing order in relation to this marriage, to attach the lump sum payable if the person with pension benefits dies before taking his benefits (eg death in service, death after leaving service but before retirement or the lump sum payable on death after retirement). This power may only be exercised for the benefit of a party to a marriage. An obligation in favour of a child of the family can only be created by a suitable undertaking in the preamble to a consent order. Lump sums defined as a multiple of pensionable salary are common in public service and occupational pension schemes. The terms of most personal pension and retirement annuity contracts allow for the return of the fund (with or without interest) in the event of the policyholder's death before taking his retirement benefits. See annotations to s 25B.

25D Pensions: supplementary

(1) Where –

(a) an order made under section 23 above by virtue of section 25B or 25C above imposes any requirement on the person responsible for a pension arrangement ('the first arrangement') and the party with pension rights acquires rights under another pension arrangement ('the new arrangement') which are derived (directly or indirectly) from the whole of his rights under the first arrangement, and

(b) the person responsible for the new arrangement has been given notice in accordance with regulations made by the Lord Chancellor,

the order shall have effect as if it had been made instead in respect of the person responsible for the new arrangement.

(2) The Lord Chancellor may by regulations –

(a) in relation to any provision of sections 25B or 25C above which authorises the court making an order under section 23 above to require the person responsible for a pension arrangement to make a payment for the benefit of the other party, make provision as to the person to whom, and the terms on which, the payment is to be made,

(ab) make, in relation to payment under a mistaken belief as to the continuation in force of a provision included by virtue of section 25B or 25C above in an order under section 23 above, provision about the rights or liabilities of the payer, the payee or the person to whom the payment was due,

(b) require notices to be given in respect of changes of circumstances relevant to such orders which include provision made by virtue of sections 25B and 25C above,

(ba) make provision for the person responsible for a pension arrangement to be discharged in prescribed circumstances from a requirement imposed by virtue of section 25B or 25C above,

(c), (d) *(repealed)*

(e) make provision about calculation and verification in relation to the valuation of –
 (i) benefits under a pension arrangement, or
 (ii) shareable state scheme rights,

for the purposes of the court's functions in connection with the exercise of any of its powers under this Part of this Act.

(2A) Regulations under subsection (2)(e) above may include –

(a) provision for calculation or verification in accordance with guidance from time to time prepared by a prescribed person, and

(b) provision by reference to regulations under section 30 or 49(4) of the Welfare Reform and Pensions Act 1999.

(2B) Regulations under subsection (2) above may make different provision for different cases.

(2C) Power to make regulations under this section shall be exercisable by statutory instrument which shall be subject to annulment in pursuance of a resolution of either House of Parliament.

(3) In this section and sections 25B and 25C above –

'occupational pension scheme' has the same meaning as in the Pension Schemes Act 1993;

'the party with pension rights' means the party to the marriage who has or is likely to have benefits under a pension arrangement and 'the other party' means the other party to the marriage;

'pension arrangement' means –

(a) an occupational pension scheme,

(b) a personal pension scheme,

(c) a retirement annuity contract,

(d) an annuity or insurance policy purchased, or transferred, for the purpose of giving effect to rights under an occupational pension scheme or a personal pension scheme, and

(e) an annuity purchased, or entered into, for the purpose of discharging liability in respect of a pension credit under section 29(1)(b) of the Welfare Reform and Pensions Act 1999 or under corresponding Northern Ireland legislation;

'personal pension scheme' has the same meaning as in the Pension Schemes Act 1993;

'prescribed' means prescribed by regulations;

'retirement annuity contract' means a contract or scheme approved under Chapter III of Part XIV of the Income and Corporation Taxes Act 1988;

'shareable state scheme rights' has the same meaning as in section 21A(1) above; and

'trustees or managers', in relation to an occupational pension scheme or a personal pension scheme, means –

(a) in the case of a scheme established under a trust, the trustees of the scheme, and

(b) in any other case, the managers of the scheme.

(4) In this section and sections 25B and 25C above, references to the person responsible for a pension arrangement are –

(a) in the case of an occupational pension scheme or a personal pension scheme, to the trustees or managers of the scheme,

(b) in the case of a retirement annuity contract or an annuity falling within paragraph (d) or (e) of the definition of 'pension arrangement' above, the provider of the annuity, and

(c) in the case of an insurance policy falling within paragraph (d) of the definition of that expression, the insurer.

Amendments—Inserted by Pensions Act 1995, s 166. Amended by WRPA 1999, ss 21, 88, Sch 4, para 3, Sch 13, Pt II.

Defined terms—'the court': s 52(1).

Scope—This section defines various terms and provides for regulations to be made, particularly for enabling pension benefits to be valued. As outlined in the annotations to MCA 1973, s 24B the method of calculating the value of the Cash Equivalent (CE) is prescribed by Pensions on Divorce etc (Provision of Information) Regulations 2000, reg 3. The prescribed method of valuation is calculated on the basis that the member's service ends at the date of valuation. For the constituent elements of the CE and the fact that the death in

PART II

service benefit is excluded, as are past service reserves, see annotations to the Pensions on Divorce etc (Provision of Information) Regulations 2000, reg 3, in Part IV.

A 'pension arrangement' does not include a foreign pension (*Goyal v Goyal* [2016] EWFC 50).

The only regulations that the reader need have a working knowledge of are the Pensions on Divorce etc (Provision of Information) Regulations 2000, the Divorce etc (Pensions) Regulations 2000 and the Sharing of State Scheme Rights (Provision of Information and Valuations) (No 2) Regulations 2000; see Part IV. As to PPF compensation, see under ss 21B and 25E.

25E The Pension Protection Fund

(1) The matters to which the court is to have regard under section 25(2) include –

- (a) in the case of paragraph (a), any PPF compensation to which a party to the marriage is or is likely to be entitled, and
- (b) in the case of paragraph (h), any PPF compensation which, by reason of the dissolution or annulment of the marriage, a party to the marriage will lose the chance of acquiring entitlement to,

and, accordingly, in relation to PPF compensation, section 25(2)(a) shall have effect as if 'in the foreseeable future' were omitted.

(2) Subsection (3) applies in relation to an order under section 23 so far as it includes provision made by virtue of section 25B(4) which –

- (a) imposed requirements on the trustees or managers of an occupational pension scheme for which the Board has assumed responsibility in accordance with Chapter 3 of Part 2 of the Pensions Act 2004 (pension protection) or any provision in force in Northern Ireland corresponding to that Chapter, and
- (b) was made before the trustees or managers of the scheme received the transfer notice in relation to the scheme.

(3) The order is to have effect from the time when the trustees or managers of the scheme receive the transfer notice –

- (a) as if, except in prescribed descriptions of case –
  - (i) references in the order to the trustees or managers of the scheme were references to the Board, and
  - (ii) references in the order to any pension or lump sum to which the party with pension rights is or may become entitled under the scheme were references to any PPF compensation to which that person is or may become entitled in respect of the pension or lump sum, and
- (b) subject to such other modifications as may be prescribed.

(4) Subsection (5) applies to an order under section 23 if –

- (a) it includes provision made by virtue of section 25B(7) which requires the party with pension rights to exercise his right of commutation under an occupational pension scheme to any extent, and
- (b) before the requirement is complied with the Board has assumed responsibility for the scheme as mentioned in subsection (2)(a).

(5) From the time the trustees or managers of the scheme receive the transfer notice, the order is to have effect with such modifications as may be prescribed.

(6) Regulations may modify section 25C as it applies in relation to an occupational pension scheme at any time when there is an assessment period in relation to the scheme.

(7) Where the court makes a pension sharing order in respect of a person's shareable rights under an occupational pension scheme, or an order which includes provision made by virtue of section 25B(4) or (7) in relation to such a scheme, the Board subsequently assuming responsibility for the scheme as mentioned in subsection (2)(a) does not affect –

- (a) the powers of the court under section 31 to vary or discharge the order or to suspend or revive any provision of it, or
- (b) on an appeal, the powers of the appeal court to affirm, reinstate, set aside or vary the order.

(8) Regulations may make such consequential modifications of any provision of, or made by virtue of, this Part as appear to the Lord Chancellor necessary or expedient to give effect to the provisions of this section.

(9) In this section –

'assessment period' means an assessment period within the meaning of Part 2 of the Pensions Act 2004 (pension protection) (see sections 132 and 159 of that Act) or an equivalent period under any provision in force in Northern Ireland corresponding to that Part;

'the Board' means the Board of the Pension Protection Fund;

'occupational pension scheme' has the same meaning as in the Pension Schemes Act 1993;

'prescribed' means prescribed by regulations;

'regulations' means regulations made by the Lord Chancellor;

'shareable rights' are rights in relation to which pension sharing is available under Chapter 1 of Part 4 of the Welfare Reform and Pensions Act 1999 or any provision in force in Northern Ireland corresponding to that Chapter;

'transfer notice' has the same meaning as in section 160 of the Pensions Act 2004 or any corresponding provision in force in Northern Ireland.

(10) Any power to make regulations under this section is exercisable by statutory instrument, which shall be subject to annulment in pursuance of a resolution of either House of Parliament.

Amendments—Inserted by Pensions Act 2004, Sch 12, para 3. Amended by Pensions Act 2008, Sch 6, Pt 1.

Defined terms—'the court': s 52(1).

'Regulations may make such consequential modifications' (s 25E(8))—The relevant regulations are the Divorce etc (Pension Protection Fund) Regulations 2006, which came into force on 8 August 2006.

Scope—This section (along with the Pensions Act 2004, s 220) makes provision for where a pension sharing or attachment order is made before the PPF assumes responsibility for a scheme (*cf* pension compensation sharing orders (s 21B) and pension compensation attachment orders (s 25F)). The PPF acts as a form of insurance to ensure the payment of certain defined benefit occupational scheme and hybrid scheme benefits, if the scheme has insufficient funds to pay them and the employer is insolvent (where there is no prospect of a corporate rescue or business rescue with pension liabilities attached) and the scheme was not in wind-up as at 6 April 2005. Certain schemes are exempt from the PPF. However, schemes that are not in wind-up will not be covered if a 'qualifying insolvency event' (voluntary administration, appointment of receiver, administration or winding up) has already taken place before 6 April 2005, unless a further insolvency event takes place after that date. Nonetheless, the Financial Assistance Scheme (FAS), established on 1 September 2005 by the Pensions Act 2004, s 286 and the Financial Assistance Scheme Regulations 2005 may provide assistance rather than compensation for those who cannot benefit from the PPF where a wind-up occurs between 1 January 1997 and 5 April 2005 or, alternatively, where the underfunded scheme started to wind up after 5 April 2005 but before 22 December 2008 having become insolvent before 6 April 2005. On 10 July 2009, the PPF became the FAS scheme manager. No separate statutory framework has as yet been created for pension sharing or pension attachment in relation to the FAS.

The PPF covers 100% of pension benefits in payment for those who have reached normal scheme retirement age (or earlier because of incapacity) and 90% (£34,655.04 applying the cap) of the accrued pensions for all others with spouses, civil partners or dependants receiving a percentage of the member's PPF benefit. PPF compensation is capped at £38,505.61 a year (PPF and Occupational Pension Schemes (Levy Ceiling and Compensation Cap) Order 2017), or less if the member retired early (such amount to be increased in line with average earnings). The cap is increased for those with pensionable service of 21 years or more from 6 April 2017. Pensions in payment derived from pensionable service on or after 6 April 1997 will be increased in line with RPI (or CPI from 1 January 2012) or 2.5% per annum, if less; pensions in deferment will be revalued in line with RPI (or CPI from 31 March 2011 with first payments being made on 1 January 2012) or 5% per annum for service before 6 April 2009 and 2.5% for service on or after that date, if less. Payments relating to service before 5 April 1997 will not increase. PPF compensation does not include payment of death-in-service lump sums.

If an insolvency practitioner is appointed in relation to a scheme sponsoring employer, he must inform the PPF that an insolvency event has occurred. If the insolvency practitioner concludes that a scheme rescue is not possible, he must so notify the PPF. There follows an assessment period (s 25E(9)), which will last for at least 1 year, with most assessments completed within 2 years, following which the PPF will assume responsibility for a scheme where the scheme cannot be rescued and cannot afford to pay its members at least the PPF level of benefits. The PPF assumes responsibility for a scheme under the Pensions Act 2004, s 161 when a transfer notice (s 25E(9)) is given to the trustees or managers under the Pensions Act 2004, s 160. When the PPF assumes responsibility, all of the scheme's assets transfer to the PPF along with all of the scheme's pensions obligations.

Details of schemes that have transferred into the PPF (as well as schemes that have completed assessment but will not be transferring into the PPF) may be accessed online at *www.pensionprotectionfund.org.uk/TransferredSchemes/pages/Transferred-Schemes.aspx*.

PPF compensation is included as a matter to which the court must have regard under MCA 1973, s 25(2)(a) or (h) (s 25E(1)).

Section 25E(2)–(6) address pension attachment; s 25E(7) addresses both pension sharing and attachment in the context of variations and appeals. Pension sharing is also addressed by the Pensions Act 2004, s 220 (see below). The broad regime is that pension attachment orders made before the PPF assumes responsibility for a scheme will be honoured. During the assessment period, it will be possible for pension attachment orders to be made, even if they will be implemented after the PPF assumes responsibility. Assumption of responsibility by the PPF will not affect the court's powers (limited as they are in the case of pension sharing) to vary a pension sharing or pension attachment order or the powers of an appeal court (s 25E(7)).

When a scheme is in the assessment period, it may only pay out benefits which would be payable under PPF compensation, which will not include death-in-service lump sums. If a person with pension benefits dies during an assessment period, the pension provider will not be able to pay out a death-in-service lump sum and any pension attachment order made under MCA 1973, s 25C will fail. This affects all pension attachment orders relating to death-in-service lump sums including those made before the introduction of the PPF. However, if the pension scheme is not taken over by the PPF, death-in-service benefits accrued, but not paid during the assessment period will be paid out at that stage and the order made under MCA 1973, s 25C will then become operative. It should be borne in mind that it is not possible to apply to vary an order under MCA 1973, s 25C on the death of either of the parties to the marriage (MCA 1973, s 31(2B)).

When the PPF assumes responsibility for a scheme, it is required under the Pension Protection Fund (Provision of Information) Regulations 2005 to inform both members and 'beneficiaries' of this fact. A 'beneficiary' is defined (reg 2(1)) as 'any person, other than a member of that scheme, who is entitled to compensation in accordance with the pension compensation provisions' and will therefore include the other party to a pension attachment order.

Pensions Act 2004, s 220 enables regulations to be made modifying the Pensions Act 2004 or WRPA 1999 in relation to pension sharing. The relevant regulations are the Pension Protection Fund (Pension Sharing) Regulations 2006. Broadly, the regulations make provision for the PPF to discharge liability for a pension sharing order made before the date on which the PPF assumes responsibility for the scheme, but which had either not come into effect or remained unimplemented as at that date. The PPF is substituted for the trustees or managers of the scheme and PPF compensation replaces any pension previously payable. The person entitled to the pension credit is to be treated as if he or she had been a member of the relevant scheme immediately before the assessment date in relation to the scheme and the PPF is obliged to determine the PPF compensation payable to that person from the effective date of the pension sharing order to which the credit relates. The valuation methodology remains the CE, even if the pension were in payment and would therefore be subject to the compensation cap (Pension Protection Fund (Pensions Sharing) Regulations 2006, reg 2(2)(b)).

Reference should also be made to FPR 2010, r 9.37.

25F Attachment of pension compensation

(1) This section applies where, having regard to any PPF compensation to which a party to the marriage is or is likely to be entitled, the court determines to make an order under section 23.

(2) To the extent to which the order is made having regard to such compensation, the order may require the Board of the Pension Protection Fund, if at any time any payment in respect of PPF compensation becomes due to the party with compensation rights, to make a payment for the benefit of the other party.

(3) The order must express the amount of any payment required to be made by virtue of subsection (2) as a percentage of the payment which becomes due to the party with compensation rights.

(4) Any such payment by the Board of the Pension Protection Fund –

(a) shall discharge so much of its liability to the party with compensation rights as corresponds to the amount of the payment, and

(b) shall be treated for all purposes as a payment made by the party with compensation rights in or towards the discharge of that party's liability under the order.

(5) Where the party with compensation rights has a right to commute any PPF compensation, the order may require that party to exercise it to any extent; and this section applies to any payment due in consequence of commutation in pursuance of the order as it applies to other payments in respect of PPF compensation.

(6) The power conferred by subsection (5) may not be exercised for the purpose of commuting compensation payable to the party with compensation rights to compensation payable to the other party.

(7) The power conferred by subsection (2) or (5) may not be exercised in relation to rights to PPF compensation that –

(a) derive from rights under a pension scheme that were at any time the subject of a pension sharing order in relation to the marriage, or a previous marriage between the same parties, or

(b) are or have ever been the subject of a pension compensation sharing order in relation to the marriage or a previous marriage between the same parties.

Amendments—Inserted by Pensions Act 2008, Sch 6, Pt 1.

Defined terms—'PPF compensation': s 21C; 'the other party': s 25G; 'the party with compensation rights': s 25G.

Scope—This section enables the court to make attachment orders in relation to pension compensation where a scheme has already entered the PPF. This section and s 25G are the counterparts of ss 25B, 25C and 25D, which permit pension attachment orders to be made against pensions. However, the court cannot attach death-in-service lump sums under this provision as PPF compensation does not include payment of such lump sums (see annotations to s 25E). It is not possible to make an order under this section in relation to PPF compensation derived from pension rights that have previously been the subject of pension sharing in relation to *any* marriage between the same parties or have previously been the subject of a pension compensation sharing order in relation to *any* marriage between the same parties (s 25F(7) *cf* s 25B(7B)).

25G Pension compensation: supplementary

(1) The Lord Chancellor may by regulations –

(a) make provision, in relation to any provision of section 25F which authorises the court making an order under section 23 to require the Board of the Pension Protection Fund to make a payment for the benefit of the other party, as to the person to whom, and the terms on which, the payment is to be made;

(b) make provision, in relation to payment under a mistaken belief as to the continuation in force of a provision included by virtue of section 25F in an order under section 23, about the rights or liabilities of the payer, the payee or the person to whom the payment was due;

(c) require notices to be given in respect of changes of circumstances relevant to orders under section 23 which include provision made by virtue of section 25F;

(d) make provision for the Board of the Pension Protection Fund to be discharged in prescribed circumstances from a requirement imposed by virtue of section 25F;

(e) make provision about calculation and verification in relation to the valuation of PPF compensation for the purposes of the court's functions in connection with the exercise of any of its powers under this Part.

(2) Regulations under subsection (1)(e) may include –

(a) provision for calculation or verification in accordance with guidance from time to time prepared by a prescribed person;

(b) provision by reference to regulations under section 112 of the Pensions Act 2008.

(3) Regulations under subsection (1) may make different provision for different cases.

(4) The power to make regulations under subsection (1) is exercisable by statutory instrument which shall be subject to annulment in pursuance of a resolution of either House of Parliament.

(5) In this section and section 25F –

'the party with compensation rights' means the party to the marriage who is or is likely to be entitled to PPF compensation, and 'the other party' means the other party to the marriage;

'prescribed' means prescribed by regulations.

Amendments—Inserted by Pensions Act 2008, Sch 6, Pt 1.

Defined terms—'PPF compensation': s 21C; 'the court': s 52(1).

Scope—This section defines the various terms and provides for regulations to be made. The relevant regulations are the Divorce and Dissolution etc (Pension Protection Fund) Regulations 2011.

26 Commencement of proceedings for ancillary relief etc

(1) Where a petition for divorce, nullity of marriage or judicial separation has been presented, then, subject to subsection (2) below, proceedings for maintenance pending suit under section 22

above, for a financial provision order under section 23 above, or for a property adjustment order may be begun, subject to and in accordance with rules of court, at any time after the presentation of the petition.

(2) Rules of court may provide, in such cases as may be prescribed by the rules –

(a) that applications for any such relief as is mentioned in subsection (1) above shall be made in the petition or answer; and

(b) that applications for any such relief which are not so made, or are not made until after the expiration of such period following the presentation of the petition or filing of the answer as may be so prescribed, shall be made only with the leave of the court.

Procedure—An application for a financial order may be made in an application for a matrimonial order (divorce, financial separation, nullity) or at any time after an application for a matrimonial order has been made, under FPR 2010, r 9.4.

Financial provision in case of neglect to maintain

27 Financial provision orders etc in case of neglect by party to marriage to maintain other party or child of the family

(1) Either party to a marriage may apply to the court for an order under this section on the ground that the other party to the marriage (in this section referred to as the respondent) –

(a) has failed to provide reasonable maintenance for the applicant, or

(b) has failed to provide, or to make a proper contribution towards, reasonable maintenance for any child of the family.

(2) The court may not entertain an application under this section unless it has jurisdiction to do so by virtue of the Maintenance Regulation and Schedule 6 to the Civil Jurisdiction and Judgments (Maintenance) Regulations 2011.

(3) Where an application under this section is made on the ground mentioned in subsection (1)(a) above, then, in deciding –

(a) whether the respondent has failed to provide reasonable maintenance for the applicant, and

(b) what order, if any, to make under this section in favour of the applicant,

the court shall have regard to all the circumstances of the case including the matters mentioned in section 25(2) above, and where an application is also made under this section in respect of a child of the family who has not attained the age of eighteen, first consideration shall be given to the welfare of the child while a minor.

(3A) Where an application under this section is made on the ground mentioned in subsection (1)(b) above then, in deciding –

(a) whether the respondent has failed to provide, or to make a proper contribution towards, reasonable maintenance for the child of the family to whom the application relates, and

(b) what order, if any, to make under this section in favour of the child,

the court shall have regard to all the circumstances of the case including the matters mentioned in section 25(3)(a) to (e) above, and where the child of the family to whom the application relates is not the child of the respondent, including also the matters mentioned in section 25(4) above.

(3B) In relation to an application under this section on the ground mentioned in subsection (1)(a) above, section 25(2)(c) above shall have effect as if for the reference therein to the breakdown of the marriage there were substituted a reference to the failure to provide reasonable maintenance for the applicant, and in relation to an application under this section on the ground mentioned in subsection (1)(b) above, section 25(2)(c) above (as it applies by virtue of section 25(3)(e) above) shall have effect as if for the reference therein to the breakdown of the marriage there were substituted a reference to the failure to provide, or to make a proper contribution towards, reasonable maintenance for the child of the family to whom the application relates.

(4) (*repealed*)

(5) Where on an application under this section it appears to the court that the applicant or any child of the family to whom the application relates is in immediate need of financial assistance, but it is not yet possible to determine what order, if any, should be made on the application, the court may make an interim order for maintenance, that is to say, an order requiring the respondent to make to the applicant until the determination of the application such periodical payments as the court thinks reasonable.

(6) Where on an application under this section the applicant satisfies the court of any ground mentioned in subsection (1) above, the court may make any one or more of the following orders, that is to say –

(a) an order that the respondent shall make to the applicant such periodical payments, for such term, as may be specified in the order;

(b) an order that the respondent shall secure to the applicant, to the satisfaction of the court, such periodical payments, for such term, as may be so specified;

(c) an order that the respondent shall pay to the applicant such lump sum as may be so specified;

(d) an order that the respondent shall make to such person as may be specified in the order for the benefit of the child to whom the application relates, or to that child, such periodical payments, for such term, as may be so specified;

(e) an order that the respondent shall secure to such person as may be so specified for the benefit of that child, or to that child, to the satisfaction of the court, such periodical payments, for such term, as may be so specified;

(f) an order that the respondent shall pay to such person as may be so specified for the benefit of that child, or to that child, such lump sum as may be so specified;

subject, however, in the case of an order under paragraph (d), (e) or (f) above, to the restrictions imposed by section 29(1) and (3) below on the making of financial provision orders in favour of children who have attained the age of eighteen.

(6A) An application for the variation under section 31 of this Act of a periodical payments order or secured periodical payments order made under this section in favour of a child may, if the child has attained the age of sixteen, be made by the child himself.

(6B) Where a periodical payments order made in favour of a child under this section ceases to have effect on the date on which the child attains the age of sixteen or at any time after that date but before or on the date on which he attains the age of eighteen, then, if at any time before he attains the age of twenty-one an application is made by the child for an order under this subsection, the court shall have power by order to revive the first-mentioned order from such date as the court may specify, not being earlier than the date of the making of the application, and to exercise its powers under section 31 of this Act in relation to any order so revived.

(7) Without prejudice to the generality of subsection (6)(c) or (f) above, an order under this section for the payment of a lump sum –

(a) may be made for the purpose of enabling any liabilities or expenses reasonably incurred in maintaining the applicant or any child of the family to whom the application relates before the making of the application to be met;

(b) may provide for the payment of that sum by instalments of such amount as may be specified in the order and may require the payment of the instalments to be secured to the satisfaction of the court.

(8) *(repealed)*

Amendments—DMPA 1973, s 6(1); DPMCA 1978, ss 63, 89(2)(b), Sch 3; MFPA 1984, ss 4, 46(1), Sch 1, para 12; FLRA 1987, s 33(1), Sch 2, para 52; SI 2011/1484.

Procedure—An application under s 27 is governed by FPR 2010, Pt 9.

Scope—Subject to CSA 1991, which restricts the court's power to order child maintenance (see further **Outline of child support calculation** under CSA 1991, s 4), this section enables an applicant (once he has established the domicile/residence requirement under s 27(2) and the fact that the other party has failed to provide reasonable maintenance) to obtain a financial provision order (i e periodical payments, secured periodical payments or lump sum) for herself/himself and any children of the family without petitioning. The same principles apply to an application under this section as to an application for ancillary relief where a

PART II

petition has been filed. The right to pursue an application under joint lives to judgment does not endure beyond the death of the respondent (*Harb v King Fahd Bin Abdul Aziz* [2006] 1 FLR 825, CA).

Interim orders—An interim order for periodical payments or secured periodical payments may be made under this section. However, only one lump sum order may be made, so an interim lump sum order cannot be made (see **Interim orders** under s 23).

Costs—The costs rule in FPR 2010, r 28.3 does not apply to applications under s 27. The court may exercise its discretion as to costs in the light of CPR 1998, r 44.2. See FPR PD28A.

Additional provisions with respect to financial provision and property adjustment orders

28 Duration of continuing financial provision orders in favour of party to marriage, and effect of remarriage or formation of civil partnership

(1) Subject in the case of an order made on or after the grant of a decree of a divorce or nullity of marriage to the provisions of sections 25A(2) above and 31(7) below, the term to be specified in a periodical payments or secured periodical payments order in favour of a party to a marriage shall be such term as the court thinks fit, except that the term shall not begin before or extend beyond the following limits, that is to say –

(a) in the case of a periodical payments order, the term shall begin not earlier than the date of the making of an application for the order, and shall be so defined as not to extend beyond the death of either of the parties to the marriage or, where the order is made on or after the grant of a decree of divorce or nullity of marriage, the remarriage, or formation of a civil partnership by, of the party in whose favour the order is made; and

(b) in the case of a secured periodical payments order, the term shall begin not earlier than the date of the making of an application for the order, and shall be so defined as not to extend beyond the death or, where the order is made on or after the grant of such a decree, the remarriage, or formation of a civil partnership by, of the party in whose favour the order is made.

(1A) Where a periodical payments or secured periodical payments order in favour of a party to a marriage is made on or after the grant of a decree of divorce or nullity of marriage, the court may direct that that party shall not be entitled to apply under section 31 below for the extension of the term specified in the order.

(2) Where a periodical payments or secured periodical payments order in favour of a party to a marriage is made otherwise than on or after the grant of a decree of divorce or nullity of marriage, and the marriage in question is subsequently dissolved or annulled but the order continues in force, the order shall, notwithstanding anything in it, cease to have effect on the remarriage of, or formation of a civil partnership by, that party, except in relation to any arrears due under it on the date of the remarriage or formation of the civil partnership.

(3) If after the grant of a decree dissolving or annulling a marriage either party to that marriage remarries whether at any time before or after the commencement of this Act or forms a civil partnership, that party shall not be entitled to apply, by reference to the grant of that decree, for a financial provision order in his or her favour, or for a property adjustment order, against the other party to that marriage.

Amendments—MFPA 1984, s 5; CPA 2004, s 261(1), Sch 27, para 43(1)–(5).

Maximum term of periodical payments order and secured periodical payments order (s 28(1))—This section is the source of the important difference that, while a periodical payments order must end on the death of the payer (or earlier remarriage of the payee), a secured periodical payments order can continue after the payer's death.

Power to prohibit extension of term (s 28(1A))—Section 28(1A) enables the court to prohibit a person who has the benefit of a maintenance order from applying to extend its term. See **Scope** under s 25A for the crucial importance of inserting this prohibition in an order where a complete clean break is required. Where capital had been equally divided, a term order until the husband's retirement was preferred to a joint lives order, but a s 28(1A) order would not be made, given the lengthy dependency of the wife: *D v D (Financial Provision: Periodical Payments)* [2004] 1 FLR 988, FD. A s 28(1A) direction is inappropriate where there are young children (*Mawson v Mawson* [1994] 2 FLR 985, FD). If the applicant's right to extend the term is to be excluded, the order must expressly state that fact (*Richardson v Richardson* [1994] 1 FLR 286, FD). Even if a court order does not contain this prohibition against applying to extend the term, any application to extend must be made before the order has expired. An order for periodical payments which ceased on a determined event cannot be varied after that event (*T v T (Financial Provision)* [1988] 1 FLR 480, FD). The application for variation must be made in the life of the order but the fact that the order has expired at the time of the hearing of the application to vary does not prevent jurisdiction (*Jones v Jones* [2000] 2 FLR 307, CA).

Prohibition on application after remarriage (s 28(3))—Section 28(3) imposes an almost absolute bar on the court's jurisdiction to entertain an application made after remarriage. However, s 28(3) does not apply to an application for a pension sharing order.

If the application is made before remarriage but is then proceeded with after remarriage, there is no jurisdictional problem, although the remarriage will be relevant on the merits. The prohibition is against a husband or wife making an application for their own benefit; applications for children are not affected. The fact that the other party has made an application for property adjustment does not enable the court to make an order in favour of the party who has not applied (*Robin v Robin* (1983) 4 FLR 632, CA, considered in *Whitehouse-Piper v Stokes* [2009] 1 FLR 983, CA).

The application has to be made either in the petition or answer (if it is an answer claiming relief) or by notice in Form A (with leave if the application ought to have been made in the petition or answer) in accordance with procedure specified in FPR 2010, r 9.4. See *Nixon v Fox (formerly Nixon)* [1978] Fam 173, FD; *Doherty v Doherty* [1976] Fam 71, CA and *Wilson v Wilson* [1976] Fam 142, CA. In *Hargood (formerly Jenkins) v Jenkins* [1978] Fam 148, FD, it was held that an answer in an acknowledgement of service did not amount to an application for ancillary relief.

It is therefore wise practice, in order to avoid the effect of this prohibition, always to include in the petition (or answer claiming relief) the full range of financial provision or, in the case of a respondent who has not filed an answer claiming relief, to file a Form A claiming the full range of financial provision as soon as possible.

PART II

29 Duration of continuing financial provision orders in favour of children, and age limit on making certain orders in their favour

(1) Subject to subsection (3) below, no financial provision order and no order for a transfer of property under section 24(1)(a) above shall be made in favour of a child who has attained the age of eighteen.

(2) The term to be specified in a periodical payments or secured periodical payments order in favour of a child may begin with the date of the making of an application for the order in question or any later date or a date ascertained in accordance with subsection (5) or (6) below but –

(a) shall not in the first instance extend beyond the date of the birthday of the child next following his attaining the upper limit of the compulsory school age (construed in accordance with section 8 of the Education Act 1996) unless the court considers that in the circumstances of the case the welfare of the child requires that it should extend to a later date; and

(b) shall not in any event, subject to subsection (3) below, extend beyond the date of the child's eighteenth birthday.

(3) Subsection (1) above, and paragraph (b) of subsection (2), shall not apply in the case of a child, if it appears to the court that –

(a) the child is, or will be, or if an order were made without complying with either or both of those provisions would be, receiving instruction at an educational establishment or undergoing training for a trade, profession or vocation, whether or not he is also, or will also be, in gainful employment; or

(b) there are special circumstances which justify the making of an order without complying with either or both of those provisions.

(4) Any periodical payments order in favour of a child shall, notwithstanding anything in the order, cease to have effect on the death of the person liable to make payments under the order, except in relation to any arrears due under the order on the date of the death.

(5) Where –

(a) a maintenance calculation ('the current calculation') is in force with respect to a child; and

(b) an application is made under Part II of this Act for a periodical payments or secured periodical payments order in favour of that child –

(i) in accordance with section 8 of the Child Support Act 1991, and

(ii) before the end of the period of 6 months beginning with the making of the current calculation, the term to be specified in any such order made on that application may be expressed to begin on, or at any time after, the earliest permitted date.

(6) For the purposes of subsection (5) above, 'the earliest permitted date' is whichever is the later of –

(a) the date 6 months before the application is made; or

(b) the date on which the current calculation took effect or, where successive maintenance calculations have been continuously in force with respect to a child, on which the first of those calculations took effect.

(7) Where –

(a) a maintenance calculation ceases to have effect by or under any provision of the Child Support Act 1991; and

(b) an application is made, before the end of the period of 6 months beginning with the relevant date, for a periodical payments or secured periodical payments order in favour of a child with respect to whom that maintenance calculation was in force immediately before it ceased to have effect,

the term to be specified in any such order made on that application may begin with the date on which that maintenance calculation ceased to have effect, or any later date.

(8) In subsection (7)(b) above, –

(a) where the maintenance calculation ceased to have effect, the relevant date is the date on which it so ceased

(b) *(repealed)*

Amendments—MFPA 1984, s 5; SI 1993/623; Education Act 1996, s 582(1), Sch 37, para 136; CSPSSA 2000, ss 26, 85, Sch 3, para 3, Sch 9.

Scope—This section provides that no financial provision order and no property adjustment order shall be made for children who have reached the age of 18 unless either they are continuing in education or there are special circumstances such as physical or mental disability. It also provides that in the first instance a child maintenance order should be specified to extend to the age of 17. The standard wording is 'until the said child shall attain the age of 17 years or ceases full time education if later or further order'.

'special circumstances' (s 29(3)(b))—Compare CA 1989, Sch 1, para 3(2)(b). Where there are special circumstances the order can continue beyond 18 years despite CSA 1991, ss 8 and 55. Special circumstances may include physical or other handicap, and the expenses attributed to the child's disability should be taken into account in the broadest sense (*C v F (Disabled Child: Maintenance Orders)* [1998] 2 FLR 1, CA).

30 Direction for settlement of instrument for securing payments or effecting property adjustment

Where the court decides to make a financial provision order requiring any payments to be secured or a property adjustment order –

(a) it may direct that the matter be referred to one of the conveyancing counsel of the court for him to settle a proper instrument to be executed by all necessary parties; and

(b) where the order is to be made in proceedings for divorce, nullity of marriage or judicial separation it may, if it thinks fit, defer the grant of the decree in question until the instrument has been duly executed.

Scope—This section provides for the relatively rare event of instructing conveyancing counsel. For the standard wording of a secured periodical payments order see **Duration and form of secured periodical payments order** under s 23.

Variation, discharge and enforcement of certain orders etc

31 Variation, discharge etc of certain orders for financial relief

(1) Where the court has made an order to which this section applies, then, subject to the provisions of this section and of section 28(1A) above, the court shall have power to vary or discharge the order or to suspend any provision thereof temporarily and to revive the operation of any provision so suspended.

(2) This section applies to the following orders, that is to say –

(a) any order for maintenance pending suit and any interim order for maintenance;
(b) any periodical payments order;
(c) any secured periodical payments order;
(d) any order made by virtue of section 23(3)(c) or 27(7)(b) above (provision for payment of a lump sum by instalments);
(dd) any deferred order made by virtue of section 23(1)(c) (lump sums) which includes provision made by virtue of –
 (i) section 25B(4),
 (ii) section 25C, or
 (iii) section 25F(2),
 (provision in respect of pension rights or pension compensation rights);
(e) any order for a settlement of property under section 24(1)(b) or for a variation of settlement under section 24(1)(c) or (d) above, being an order made on or after the grant of a decree of judicial separation;
(f) any order made under section 24A(1) above for the sale of property.
(g) a pension sharing order under section 24B above or a pension compensation sharing order under section 24E above which is made at a time before the decree has been made absolute.

(2A) Where the court has made an order referred to in subsection (2)(a), (b) or (c) above, then, subject to the provisions of this section, the court shall have power to remit the payment of any arrears due under the order or of any part thereof.

(2B) Where the court has made an order referred to in subsection (2)(dd)(ii) above, this section shall cease to apply to the order on the death of either of the parties to the marriage.

(3) The powers exercisable by the court under this section in relation to an order shall be exercisable also in relation to any instrument executed in pursuance of the order.

(4) The court shall not exercise the powers conferred by this section in relation to an order for a settlement under section 24(1)(b) or for a variation of settlement under section 24(1)(c) or (d) above except on an application made in proceedings –
(a) for the rescission of the decree of judicial separation by reference to which the order was made, or
(b) for the dissolution of the marriage in question.

(4A) In relation to an order which falls within paragraph (g) of subsection (2) above ('the subsection (2) order') –
(a) the powers conferred by this section may be exercised –
 (i) only on an application made before the subsection (2) order has or, but for paragraph (b) below, would have taken effect; and
 (ii) only if, at the time when the application is made, the decree has not been made absolute; and
(b) an application made in accordance with paragraph (a) above prevents the subsection (2) order from taking effect before the application has been dealt with.

(4B) No variation of a pension sharing order, or a pension compensation sharing order, shall be made so as to take effect before the decree is made absolute.

(4C) The variation of a pension sharing order, or a pension compensation sharing order, prevents the order taking effect before the end of such period after the making of the variation as may be prescribed by regulations made by the Lord Chancellor.

(5) Subject to subsections (7A) to (7G) below and without prejudice to any power exercisable by virtue of subsection (2)(d), (dd), (e) or (g) above or otherwise than by virtue of this section, no property adjustment order or pension sharing order, or pension compensation sharing order shall be made on an application for the variation of a periodical payments or secured periodical payments order made (whether in favour of a party to a marriage or in favour of a child of the family) under section 23 above, and no order for the payment of a lump sum shall be made on an

PART II

application for the variation of a periodical payments or secured periodical payments order in favour of a party to a marriage (whether made under section 23 or under section 27 above).

(6) Where the person liable to make payments under a secured periodical payments order has died, an application under this section relating to that order (and to any order made under section 24A(1) above which requires the proceeds of sale of property to be used for securing those payments) may be made by the person entitled to payments under the periodical payments order or by the personal representatives of the deceased person, but no such application shall, except with the permission of the court, be made after the end of the period of six months from the date on which representation in regard to the estate of that person is first taken out.

(7) In exercising the powers conferred by this section the court shall have regard to all the circumstances of the case, first consideration being given to the welfare while a minor of any child of the family who has not attained the age of eighteen, and the circumstances of the case shall include any change in any of the matters to which the court was required to have regard when making the order to which the application relates, and –

- (a) in the case of a periodical payments or secured periodical payments order made on or after the grant of a decree of divorce or nullity of marriage, the court shall consider whether in all the circumstances and after having regard to any such change it would be appropriate to vary the order so that payments under the order are required to be made or secured only for such further period as will in the opinion of the court be sufficient (in the light of any proposed exercise by the court, where the marriage has been dissolved, of its powers under subsection (7B) below) to enable the party in whose favour the order was made to adjust without undue hardship to the termination of those payments;
- (b) in a case where the party against whom the order was made has died, the circumstances of the case shall also include the changed circumstances resulting from his or her death.

(7A) Subsection (7B) below applies where, after the dissolution of a marriage, the court –

- (a) discharges a periodical payments order or secured periodical payments order made in favour of a party to the marriage; or
- (b) varies such an order so that payments under the order are required to be made or secured only for such further period as is determined by the court.

(7B) The court has power, in addition to any power it has apart from this subsection, to make supplemental provision consisting of any of –

- (a) an order for the payment of a lump sum in favour of a party to the marriage;
- (b) one or more property adjustment orders in favour of a party to the marriage;
- (ba) one or more pension sharing orders;
- (bb) a pension compensation sharing order;
- (c) a direction that the party in whose favour the original order discharged or varied was made is not entitled to make any further application for –
  - (i) a periodical payments or secured periodical payments order, or
  - (ii) an extension of the period to which the original order is limited by any variation made by the court.

(7C) An order for the payment of a lump sum made under subsection (7B) above may –

- (a) provide for the payment of that sum by instalments of such amount as may be specified in the order; and
- (b) require the payment of the instalments to be secured to the satisfaction of the court.

(7D) Section 23(6) above applies where the court makes an order for the payment of a lump sum under subsection (7B) above as it applies where the court makes such an order under section 23 above.

(7E) If under subsection (7B) above the court makes more than one property adjustment order in favour of the same party to the marriage, each of those orders must fall within a different paragraph of section 21(2) above.

(7F) Sections 24A and 30 above apply where the court makes a property adjustment order under subsection (7B) above as they apply where it makes such an order under section 24 above.

(7G) Subsections (3) to (5) of section 24B above apply in relation to a pension sharing order under subsection (7B) above as they apply in relation to a pension sharing order under that section.

(7H) Subsections (3) to (10) of section 24E above apply in relation to a pension compensation sharing order under subsection (7B) above as they apply in relation to a pension compensation sharing order under that section.

(8) The personal representatives of a deceased person against whom a secured periodical payments order was made shall not be liable for having distributed any part of the estate of the deceased after the expiration of the period of six months referred to in subsection (6) above on the ground that they ought to have taken into account the possibility that the court might permit an application under this section to be made after that period by the person entitled to payments under the order; but this subsection shall not prejudice any power to recover any part of the estate so distributed arising by virtue of the making of an order in pursuance of this section.

(9) The following are to be left out of account when considering for the purposes of subsection (6) above when representation was first taken out –

(a) a grant limited to settled land or to trust property,
(b) any other grant that does not permit any of the estate to be distributed,
(c) a grant limited to real estate or to personal estate, unless a grant limited to the remainder of the estate has previously been made or is made at the same time,
(d) a grant, or its equivalent, made outside the United Kingdom (but see subsection (9A) below).

(9A) A grant sealed under section 2 of the Colonial Probates Act 1892 counts as a grant made in the United Kingdom for the purposes of subsection (9) above, but is to be taken as dated on the date of sealing.

(10) Where the court, in exercise of its powers under this section, decides to vary or discharge a periodical payments or secured periodical payments order, then, subject to section 28(1) and (2) above, the court shall have power to direct that the variation or discharge shall not take effect until the expiration of such period as may be specified in the order.

(11) Where –

(a) a periodical payments or secured periodical payments order in favour of more than one child ('the order') is in force;
(b) the order requires payments specified in it to be made to or for the benefit of more than one child without apportioning those payments between them;
(c) a maintenance calculation ('the calculation') is made with respect to one or more, but not all, of the children with respect to whom those payments are to be made; and
(d) an application is made, before the end of the period of 6 months beginning with the date on which the assessment was made, for the variation or discharge of the order,

the court may, in exercise of its powers under this section to vary or discharge the order, direct that the variation or discharge shall take effect from the date on which the calculation took effect or any later date.

(12) Where –

(a) an order ('the child order') of a kind prescribed for the purposes of section 10(1) of the Child Support Act 1991 is affected by a maintenance calculation;
(b) on the date on which the child order became so affected there was in force a periodical payments or secured periodical payments order ('the spousal order') in favour of a party to a marriage having the care of the child in whose favour the child order was made; and
(c) an application is made, before the end of the period of 6 months beginning with the date on which the maintenance calculation was made, for the spousal order to be varied or discharged,

the court may, in exercise of its powers under this section to vary or discharge the spousal order, direct that the variation or discharge shall take effect from the date on which the child order became so affected or any later date.

(13) For the purposes of subsection (12) above, an order is affected if it ceases to have effect or is modified by or under section 10 of the Child Support Act 1991.

(14) Subsections (11) and (12) above are without prejudice to any other power of the court to direct that the variation of discharge of an order under this section shall take effect from a date earlier than that on which the order for variation or discharge was made.

(15) The power to make regulations under subsection (4C) above shall be exercisable by statutory instrument which shall be subject to annulment in pursuance of a resolution of either House of Parliament.

Amendments—Matrimonial Homes and Property Act 1981, s 8(2); AJA 1982, s 51; MFPA 1984, s 6; SI 1993/623; Pensions Act 1995, s 166; FLA 1996, Sch 8, para 16(5)(a),(6)(b),(7) (as modified by SI 1998/2572); WRPA 1999, s 19, Sch 3, para 7; CSPSSA 2000, s 26, Sch 3, para 3; Pensions Act 2008, Sch 6, Pt 1; Inheritance and Trustees' Powers Act 2014, s 6, Sch 2.

Procedure—An application for variation under s 31 follows the shorter procedure as set out in FPR 2010, rr 9.18–9.20, PD9A, para 1.2, and see Procedural Guide B5. In *Mutch v Mutch* [2017] 1 FLR 408, CA, a variation application that was set out in the solicitors' statement in support (but not expressly referred to in the application notice itself) was deemed sufficient to engage the variation powers of the court.

Extent of inquiry—An application for variation of a periodical payments order does not necessarily require the court to undertake a full re-analysis of all the MCA 1973, s 25 factors: a variation application may require a complete review but, equally, it may justify a 'light touch review', addressing only those factors specifically relevant to the variation application (*Morris v Morris* [2016] EWCA Civ 812).

Scope—This section gives the court the power to vary its own financial orders, as listed in s 31(2)(a)–(g). It follows that property orders under s 24 may not be varied, save for any order made under s 24A(1) for the sale of property (see **Scope** under MCA 1973, s 24A). Orders may be amended under the inherent jurisdiction of the court only to give effect to the intention of the court (*Swindale v Forder (Forder Intervening)* [2007] 1 FLR 1905, CA). There is jurisdiction under s 31(2)(d) to vary the timing of instalments and the manner of payment (*G v G (Role of FDR Judge)* [2007] 1 FLR 237, FD). The power to vary agreements is contained in ss 35 and 36.

Limits upon the court's power to vary—The court's power to vary under s 31 applies only to orders requiring the payment of income to another, and orders for the sale of property. There is no jurisdiction to vary capital orders, save in the following four exceptions:

(i) where the order is for a lump sum payable by instalments, see *Penrose v Penrose* [1994] 2 FLR 621, CA) – increased tax liability, no reason to vary lump sum order although there was jurisdiction to suspend remaining instalments due. For jurisdiction to extend time for the payment of lump sum in specified circumstances, see *Masefield v Alexander (Lump sum: Extension of time)* [1995] 1 FLR 100, CA. In *Richardson v Richardson* [2011] 2 FLR 244, CA, instalments of lump sum payments due to be paid by the husband to the wife were varied to be paid into court because of the death of the wife, and the joint liability of the parties to an unexpected personal injury claim. See commentary to s 23;

(ii) where settlement of property or variation of settlement order has been made in the course of judicial separation proceedings, and there is a subsequent petition for divorce, or the recission of the decree of judicial separation;

(iii) where a pension attachment lump sum order under s 25B(4) or s 25C has been made;

(iv) where a pension sharing order has been made and the application to vary is made both before the order has taken effect and before decree absolute.

Power to vary child periodical payments—The court has the power to vary a child maintenance order, even where the order is a nominal order by consent (*V v V (Child Maintenance)* [2001] 2 FLR 799, FD). However, if the parent with care is on benefits, the court only has power to vary if there is no application for a child support assessment, and notice of the application to vary should be given to the Child Support Agency.

Power to extend the term of a periodical payments order—The application for variation must be made during the life of the order. The fact that the order has expired at the time of the variation hearing does not prevent the court having jurisdiction, so long as the application to extend was made prior to the order's expiry (*Jones v Jones* [2000] 2 FLR 307, CA). Where parties agree and intend to be bound by a term order, the exercise of the power to extend the obligations has been held to require 'some exceptional justification': *Fleming v Fleming* [2004] 1 FLR 667, CA. In *Miller v Miller; McFarlane v McFarlane* [2006] 1 FLR 1186, HL, this was referred to as a 'high threshold'. However, in *SS v NS (Spousal Maintenance)* [2015] 2 FLR 1124, FD, Mostyn J considered that this 'higher hurdle' test had not survived subsequent case-law analysis. The Court of Appeal is yet to reconsider its *Fleming v Fleming* decision.

Power to vary due to death—If the application to vary a secured periodical payments order arises because of the payer's death, the application to vary requires leave, if it is made later that 6 months from the grant of probate or letters of administration. The personal representatives of the deceased will not be liable for distributing the estate before an application being made, if it is made after the 6-month period has elapsed.

Capitalisation of periodical payments on the application of either party for a clean break—Section 31(5) prohibits the making of a property adjustment or lump sum order on an application for the variation of maintenance, save in defined circumstances. Where no lump sum or property adjustment order has been made, an application may be made and heard at the same time as an application for the variation of periodical payments (*Pearce v Pearce* (1980) 1 FLR 261, CA).

The court has the power to make a pension sharing order upon a variation application. This power applies only to petitions filed after 1 December 2000 (WRPA 1999 s 85(3)(b)).

Under s 31(7A) and (7B), upon the application of either party for a clean break, the court may make a lump sum order, or a further property adjustment order. Where a party has achieved a variation of an order, s 31(7B)(c) prevents that party from making further application: in *Mann v Mann* [2015] 2 FLR 1116, CA, s 31(7B)(c) was held to apply to the whole of s 31(7), preventing applications for variation or discharge of orders other than periodical payments such as lump sums. The court has no power under s 31 to reopen capital claims, but may substitute such sum as would compensate the payee for the termination of periodical payments and achieve the clean break. There are three questions to consider: (i) what variation if any should be ordered to periodical payments? (ii) when the variation should take effect and (iii) whether the payments should be capitalized (*Pearce v Pearce* [2003] 2 FLR 1144, CA). In *Vaughan v Vaughan* [2010] 2 FLR 242, CA, these questions are reinterpreted as (i) whether periodical payments should terminate or continue, and if so, at what level; (ii) if continuing, the capital equivalent, applying the Duxbury formula; and (iii) whether it is fair to both parties to capitalise periodical payments and whether it is reasonably practical for the payer to pay a capital sum, as opposed to periodical payments. The CA has approved the payment of a lump sum derived from capitalised periodical payments in three instalments, but the wife would also receive periodical payments until the adjusted lump sum was paid off: *Grocholewska-Mullins v Mullins* [2014] EWCA Civ 148.

Capitalisation may be calculated from Duxbury Tables based upon interest rates of 3.75%, (see *At A Glance*, Family Law Bar Association, 2008). The court has the discretion to adopt the figure suggested in the tables, or to depart from it (*Harris v Harris* [2001] 1 FCR 68, CA). The issue is 'what is a fair capital sum?'. There is also a discretion to depart from the tables to reflect individual special factors, but it should be exercised narrowly.

Principles upon which the court will act in variation and capitalization cases (s 31(7))—The discretion has been described as 'almost unfettered', but the principles governing an original consent order should not be interfered with, so that where the principle of joint lives had been accepted, the quantum to be capitalised should not extend beyond the husband's death (*Harris v Harris* [2001] 1 FCR 68, CA).

The clean break provisions apply upon an application to vary and are set out in s 31(7)(a). The court has an ongoing statutory duty to consider whether the party in whose favour the order was made may adjust to the termination of those payments without undue hardship: *Boylan v Boylan* [1988] 1 FLR 282, FD; *Fleming* [2004] 1 FLR 667, CA. The desirability of bringing financial dependency to an end if it can be done fairly has been considered in *H v H* [2014] EWHC 760 (Fam), where the parties had been separated for 10 years and the court was scrutinising the parties' finances for the third time.

Changes in s 25(2) factors since the order was made should be considered. Cohabitation with a new partner may commonly arise to be considered as a 'circumstance of the case'. For the court's approach to cohabitation in variation applications, see *Atkinson v Atkinson* [1988] 2 FLR 353, CA, and *Fleming v Fleming*. In *K v K (Periodical Payments: Cohabitation)* [2006] 2 FLR 468, FD, a 3-year cohabitation was a factor in varying the term of periodical payments to a shorter period. The court should be alive to the practical implications of cohabitation, including its financial consequences and duration. In *W v W (Periodical Payments: Variation)* [2010] 2 FLR 985, FD, a wife's 6-year cohabitation was not material because the financial contribution of the cohabitee meant that the wife was not subsidising him to any significant extent. The wife received increased periodical payments that were capitalised, in part because of her ongoing contributions as a mother. The CA has stated that post-divorce cohabitation would not lead to an inevitable revaluation of a wife's claim for periodical payments: *Grey v Grey* [2010] 1 FLR 1764, CA. Where the payer has remarried, priority should not be given to the interests of the second wife, to the extent that the claims of the applicant first wife are undervalued: *Roberts v Roberts* [1970] P 1, PDAD, approved in *Vaughan v Vaughan* [2010] 2 FLR 242, CA.

The principles of both *Miller* and *McFarlane* [2006] 1 FLR 1186, HL have been specifically applied to variation and capitalization cases: *Lauder* [2007] 2 FLR 802, FD; *VB v JP* [2008] 1 FLR 742, FD.

In assessing the upward variation, the court will have regard to the original award. In *Lauder*, the fact that the original award had given the wife a high proportion of the husband's net income was not solely determinative in percentage terms, but was a relevant circumstance as one of the background factors. In *VB v JP*, the President found that the percentage of the husband's net income previously awarded was 'an appropriate cross check (if not a starting point)', in an application based on the substantial increase in the husband's income. In *Hvorostovsky v Hvorostovsky* [2009] 2 FLR 1574, CA, the Court of Appeal stressed the usefulness of a percentage comparison between the original order and the order on variation, to judge the overall proportionality of the conclusions. Consideration of the standard of living immediately before the breakdown of the marriage was not a determinative factor and it was unnecessary to assert relationship-generated disadvantage. The 'reasonable requirements' argument was expressly disapproved where a rich husband who had experienced a significant increase in income had the means to pay more than the wife's needs, even where interpreted generously. See *McFarlane v McFarlane* [2009] 2 FLR 1322, FD, where a husband's rising income in the light of the application of the principles of financial needs, compensation and sharing led to an order for payments to be paid to the wife as a percentage of his banded income.

32 Payment of certain arrears unenforceable without the leave of the court

(1) A person shall not be entitled to enforce through the High Court or the family court the payment of any arrears due under an order for maintenance pending suit, an interim order for

maintenance or any financial provision order without the leave of that court if those arrears became due more than twelve months before proceedings to enforce the payment of them are begun.

(2) The court hearing an application for the grant of leave under this section may refuse leave, or may grant leave subject to such restrictions and conditions (including conditions as to the allowing of time for payment or the making of payment by instalments) as that court thinks proper, or may remit the payment of the arrears or of any part thereof.

(3) An application for the grant of leave under this section shall be made in such manner as may be prescribed by rules of court.

Amendments—CCA 2013, s 17, Sch 11.

Procedure—An application for the issue of a judgment summons is governed by FPR 2010, rr 33.9–33.17. Where an attachment of earnings order is sought, it may be convenient to issue the summons or notice of application under this section simultaneously with and returnable on the same date as the attachment of earnings application. The same practice may be adopted on an application for the appointment of a receiver or on an application for a means of payment order under MEA 1991, s 1(4)(a). In the case of applications for third party debt orders (old garnishee orders) or charging orders where relief is given initially on an application without notice, leave must be sought under this section as a preliminary step.

'financial provision order' (s 32(1))—The High Court has suggested that this includes a foreign judgment for financial provision and in considering enforcement under this section the English court is not reviewing the foreign judgment as to its merits contrary to the Judgments Regulation: *O'Farrell v O'Farrell* [2013] 1 FLR 77, QBD.

'may refuse leave, or may grant leave' (s 32(2))—There is no presumption that leave should be granted only in special circumstances (*Lumsden v Lumsden* 11 November 1998, CA).

'application for the grant of leave' (s 32(3))—Leave to enforce accrued arrears due during a period in excess of 12 months can be sought by making an application in general form supported by a sworn statement/affidavit by the party applying setting out the arrears sought to be enforced and giving the reasons for failure to apply to enforce earlier together with any other relevant information which may assist the court.

33 Orders for repayment in certain cases of sums paid under certain orders

(1) Where on an application made under this section in relation to an order to which this section applies it appears to the court that by reason of –

(a) a change in the circumstances of the person entitled to, or liable to make, payments under the order since the order was made, or

(b) the changed circumstances resulting from the death of the person so liable,

the amount received by the person entitled to payments under the order in respect of a period after those circumstances changed or after the death of the person liable to make payments under the order, as the case may be, exceeds the amount which the person so liable or his or her personal representatives should have been required to pay, the court may order the respondent to the application to pay to the applicant such sum, not exceeding the amount of the excess, as the court thinks just.

(2) This section applies to the following orders, that is to say –

(a) any order for maintenance pending suit and any interim order for maintenance;

(b) any periodical payments order; and

(c) any secured periodical payments order.

(3) An application under this section may be made by the person liable to make payments under an order to which this section applies or his or her personal representatives and may be made against the person entitled to payments under the order or her or his personal representatives.

(4) An application under this section may be made in proceedings in the High Court or the family court for –

(a) the variation or discharge of the order to which this section applies, or

(b) leave to enforce, or the enforcement of, the payment of arrears under that order;

but when not made in such proceedings shall be made to the family court, and accordingly references in this section to the court are references to the High Court or the family court, as the circumstances require.

(5) *(repealed)*

(6) An order under this section for the payment of any sum may provide for the payment of that sum by instalments of such amount as may be specified in the order.

Amendments—CCA 2013, s 17, Sch 11.

Procedure—An application under s 33 is governed by FPR 2010, Pt 9.

Scope—This section empowers the court to order the party who has received maintenance to repay monies that have been received where there has been a change in circumstances of the payee or a change of circumstances which results from the payer's death. The power to order repayment relates to the period before the order is varied and is distinct from the court's powers to remit arrears and to vary the order itself. Section 38 covers the situation where payments have been made at a time when the order no longer existed because it had been determined by, for instance, the remarriage of the payee.

No repayment in respect of capital orders (s 33(2))—The power to order repayment applies only to orders for maintenance pending suit and periodical payments orders and not to capital orders. For the impeachability of a capital order where there has been a drastic change of circumstances, see the principles established by the House of Lords in *Barder v Barder* [1987] 2 FLR 480, HL. For a discussion of *Barder*-type events, see **Power to reopen or set aside consent orders** at FPR 2010, r 9.26 and, for the procedure that applies to an application to set aside an original order (whether by consent or after a contested hearing), see FPR 2010, r 9.9A and Procedural Guide E7(2).

Mode of application (s 33(4),(5))—Where application is made under this section, the Family Court's jurisdiction is unlimited. Normally the party applying will be seeking a discharge of the order and it is likely that there will be a linked application to vary the order so that the procedure set out in FPR 2010, Pt 9 applies. If there are no variation proceedings and the application stands on its own, no form of application is specified by FPR 2010.

Consent orders

33A Consent orders for financial provision or property adjustment

(1) Notwithstanding anything in the preceding provisions of this Part of this Act, on an application for a consent order for financial relief the court may, unless it has reason to think that there are other circumstances into which it ought to inquire, make an order in the terms agreed on the basis only of the prescribed information furnished with the application.

(2) Subsection (1) above applies to an application for a consent order varying or discharging an order for financial relief as it applies to an application for an order for financial relief.

(3) In this section –

'consent order', in relation to an application for an order, means an order in the terms applied for to which the respondent agrees;

'order for financial relief' means an order under any of sections 23, 24, 24A, 24B or 27 above; and

'prescribed' means prescribed by rules of court.

Amendments—Inserted by MFPA 1984, s 7. Amended by WRPA 1999, s 19, Sch 3, para 8.

Procedure—An application for a consent order is governed by FPR 2010, Pt 9.

Scope—This section empowers the court to make a consent order without a full investigation and without hearing oral evidence; however, it does not in any way inhibit its power to make further enquiries or to suggest amendments to the parties, see *Sharland v Sharland* [2015] 2 FLR 1367, SC. The court cannot exercise its mandatory duties under ss 25 and 25A without up-to-date information of the salient facts (*Jenkins v Livesey (formerly Jenkins)* [1985] FLR 813, HL). This is provided in each party's separate or joint statement of information: if separate documents, each party must sign the other's statement. There is no requirement for the parties to attend court. See FPR 2010, r 9.26. If there is dispute as to the meaning of any term in a consent order, the same principles of construction apply as in commercial contracts: the question is 'what a reasonable person, circumstanced as the actual parties were, would have understood the parties to have meant by the use of specific language. The answer to that question is to be gathered from the text under consideration and its relevant contextual scene' (*Besharova v Berezovsky* [2016] EWCA Civ 161).

Maintenance agreements

34 Validity of maintenance agreements

(1) If a maintenance agreement includes a provision purporting to restrict any right to apply to a court for an order containing financial arrangements, then –

(a) that provision shall be void; but

(b) any other financial arrangements contained in the agreement shall not thereby be rendered void or unenforceable and shall, unless they are void or unenforceable for any other reason (and subject to sections 35 and 36 below), be binding on the parties to the agreement.

(2) In this section and in section 35 below –

'maintenance agreement' means any agreement in writing made, whether before or after the commencement of this Act, between the parties to a marriage, being –

(a) an agreement containing financial arrangements, whether made during the continuance or after the dissolution or annulment of the marriage; or

(b) a separation agreement which contains no financial arrangements in a case where no other agreement in writing between the same parties contains such arrangements;

'financial arrangements' means provisions governing the rights and liabilities towards one another when living separately of the parties to a marriage (including a marriage which has been dissolved or annulled) in respect of the making or securing of payments or the disposition or use of any property, including such rights and liabilities with respect to the maintenance or education of any child, whether or not a child of the family.

Prohibition of any restriction on right to apply (s 34(1))—Section 34(1) provides that it is not possible for an agreement to restrict either party's right to apply for income or capital relief from the court. However, while it is impossible to restrict the theoretical right to apply, the fact that parties have come to an agreement carefully arrived at with the benefit of legal advice (in the absence of a vitiating factor such as set out in *Edgar v Edgar* (1981) 2 FLR 19, CA) will be an important factor but only one ingredient within a complex equation in determining whether the court should in fact make financial provision and property adjustment orders in identical terms to those that had been agreed (*Smith v Smith* [2000] 3 FCR 374, CA).

'maintenance agreement' (s 34(2))—This term is defined as either an agreement containing financial arrangements made at any time or a separation agreement which contains no such financial arrangements. It has been held to cover only agreements made with expressed or clearly implied purpose of governing the parties' financial affairs. Other than this, a term ought not to be implied unless equitable and reasonable in all the circumstances: *F v F (Financial Remedies: Premarital Wealth)* [2012] 2 FLR 1212, FD. A maintenance agreement can refer to the payment of maintenance after a recipient party's remarriage, despite the statutory dismissal of periodical payments after remarriage (*T v R (Maintenance After Remarriage – Agreement)* [2016] EWFC 26).

35 Alteration of agreements by court during lives of parties

(1) Where a maintenance agreement is for the time being subsisting and each of the parties to the agreement is for the time being either domiciled or resident in England and Wales, then, subject to subsections (1A) and (3) below, either party may apply to the court for an order under this section.

(1A) If an application or part of an application relates to a matter where jurisdiction falls to be determined by reference to the jurisdictional requirements of the Maintenance Regulation and Schedule 6 to the Civil Jurisdiction and Judgments (Maintenance) Regulations 2011 –

(a) the requirement as to domicile or residence in subsection (1) does not apply to the application or that part of it, but

(b) the court may not entertain the application or that part of it unless it has jurisdiction to do so by virtue of that Regulation and that Schedule.

(2) If the court is satisfied either –

(a) that by reason of a change in the circumstances in the light of which any financial arrangements contained in the agreement were made or, as the case may be, financial arrangements were omitted from it (including a change foreseen by the parties when making the agreement), the agreement should be altered so as to make different, or, as the case may be, so as to contain, financial arrangements, or

(b) that the agreement does not contain proper financial arrangements with respect to any child of the family,

then subject to subsections (4) and (5) below, the court may by order make such alterations in the agreement –

(i) by varying or revoking any financial arrangements contained in it, or

(ii) by inserting in it financial arrangements for the benefit of one of the parties to the agreement or of a child of the family, as may appear to the court to be just having regard to all the circumstances, including, if relevant, the matters mentioned in section 25(4) above; and the agreement shall have effect thereafter as if any alteration made by the order had been made by agreement between the parties and for valuable consideration.

(3) *(repealed)*

(4) Where the court decides to alter, by order under this section, an agreement by inserting provision for the making or securing by one of the parties to the agreement of periodical payments for the maintenance of the other party or by increasing the rate of the periodical payments which the agreement provides shall be made by one of the parties for the maintenance of the other, the term for which the payments or, as the case may be, the additional payments attributable to the increase are to be made under the agreement as altered by the order shall be such term as the court may specify, subject to the following limits, that is to say –

(a) where the payments will not be secured, the term shall be so defined as not to extend beyond the death of either of the parties to the agreement or the remarriage of, or formation of a civil partnership by, the party to whom the payments are to be made;

(b) where the payments will be secured, the term shall be so defined as not to extend beyond the death or remarriage of, or formation of a civil partnership by, that party.

(5) Where the court decides to alter, by order under this section, an agreement by inserting provision for the making or securing by one of the parties to the agreement of periodical payments for the maintenance of a child of the family or by increasing the rate of the periodical payments which the agreement provides shall be made or secured by one of the parties for the maintenance of such a child, then, in deciding the term for which under the agreement as altered by the order the payments, or as the case may be, the additional payments attributable to the increase are to be made or secured for the benefit of the child, the court shall apply the provisions of section 29(2) and (3) above as to age limits as if the order in question were a periodical payments or secured periodical payments order in favour of the child.

(6) For the avoidance of doubt it is hereby declared that nothing in this section or in section 34 above affects any power of a court before which any proceedings between the parties to a maintenance agreement are brought under any other enactment (including a provision of this Act) to make an order containing financial arrangements or any right of either party to apply for such an order in such proceedings.

Amendments—MFPA 1984, s 46(1), Sch 1, para 13; Justices of the Peace Act 1997, s 73(2), Sch 5, para 14; AJA 1999, s 106, Sch 15; CPA 2004, s 261(1), Sch 27, para 44; Courts Act 2003, Sch 8, para 169; SI 2011/1484; CCA 2013, s 17, Sch 11.

Procedure—An application under s 25 is governed by FPR 2010, Pt 9 and see Procedural Guide A5.

Scope—Subject to CSA 1991, this section empowers the court to alter a maintenance agreement during the lives of the parties. The power arises if either there is a change in circumstances or there are no proper financial arrangements for the children. To overturn an agreed post-nuptial settlement, the court had to be satisfied that the applicant wife's will was overborne by her husband exercising undue pressure or influence upon her (*NA v MA* [2007] 1 FLR 1760, FD). Post nuptial settlements clearly can be varied by the court, although the Privy Council has stated that prenuptial settlements might not be covered by the variation power in s 35 (*MacLeod v MacLeod* [2009] 1 FLR 641, PC).

36 Alteration of agreements by court after death of one party

(1) Where a maintenance agreement within the meaning of section 34 above provides for the continuation of payments under the agreement after the death of one of the parties and that party dies domiciled in England and Wales, the surviving party or the personal representatives of the deceased party may, subject to subsections (2) and (3) below, apply to the court for an order under section 35 above.

(2) An application under this section shall not, except with the permission of the court, be made after the end of the period of six months from the date on which representation in regard to the estate of the deceased is first taken out.

(3) *(repealed)*

(4) If a maintenance agreement is altered by the court on an application made in pursuance of subsection (1) above, the like consequences shall ensue as if the alteration had been made immediately before the death by agreement between the parties and for valuable consideration.

(5) The provisions of this section shall not render the personal representatives of the deceased liable for having distributed any part of the estate of the deceased after the expiration of the period of six months referred to in subsection (2) above on the ground that they ought to have taken into account the possibility that the court might permit an application by virtue of this section to be made by the surviving party after that period; but this subsection shall not prejudice any power to recover any part of the estate so distributed arising by virtue of the making of an order in pursuance of this section.

(6) Section 31(9) above shall apply for the purposes of subsection (2) above as it applies for the purposes of subsection (6) of section 31.

(7) *(repealed)*

Amendments—I(PFD)A 1975, s 26(1); CCA 2013, s 17, Sch 11.

Procedure—An application under s 36 is governed by FPR 2010, rr 8.6–8.11. Application is by notice of application on Form D50D.

Six-month time-limit (s 36(2))—Leave to apply is required if the application is made later than six months from the grant of probate or letters of administration.

Miscellaneous and supplemental

37 Avoidance of transactions intended to prevent or reduce financial relief

(1) For the purposes of this section 'financial relief' means relief under any of the provisions of sections 22, 23, 24, 24B, 27, 31 (except subsection (6)) and 35 above, and any reference in this section to defeating a person's claim for financial relief is a reference to preventing financial relief from being granted to that person, or to that person for the benefit of a child of the family, or reducing the amount of any financial relief which might be so granted, or frustrating or impeding the enforcement of any order which might be or has been made at his instance under any of those provisions.

(2) Where proceedings for financial relief are brought by one person against another, the court may, on the application of the first-mentioned person –

- (a) if it is satisfied that the other party to the proceedings is, with the intention of defeating the claim for financial relief, about to make any disposition or to transfer out of the jurisdiction or otherwise deal with any property, make such order as it thinks fit for restraining the other party from so doing or otherwise for protecting the claim;
- (b) if it is satisfied that the other party has, with that intention, made a reviewable disposition and that if the disposition were set aside financial relief or different financial relief would be granted to the applicant, make an order setting aside the disposition;
- (c) if it is satisfied, in a case where an order has been obtained under any of the provisions mentioned in subsection (1) above by the applicant against the other party, that the other party has, with that intention, made a reviewable disposition, make an order setting aside the disposition;

and an application for the purposes of paragraph (b) above shall be made in the proceedings for the financial relief in question.

(3) Where the court makes an order under subsection (2)(b) or (c) above setting aside a disposition it shall give such consequential directions as it thinks fit for giving effect to the order (including directions requiring the making of any payments or the disposal of any property).

(4) Any disposition made by the other party to the proceedings for financial relief in question (whether before or after the commencement of those proceedings) is a reviewable disposition for the purposes of subsection (2)(b) and (c) above unless it was made for valuable consideration (other than marriage) to a person who, at the time of the disposition, acted in relation to it in good faith and without notice of any intention on the part of the other party to defeat the applicant's claim for financial relief.

(5) Where an application is made under this section with respect to a disposition which took place less than three years before the date of the application or with respect to a disposition or other dealing with property which is about to take place and the court is satisfied –

(a) in a case falling within subsection (2)(a) or (b) above, that the disposition or other dealing would (apart from this section) have the consequence, or

(b) in a case falling within subsection (2)(c) above, that the disposition has had the consequence,

of defeating the applicant's claim for financial relief, it shall be presumed, unless the contrary is shown, that the person who disposed of or is about to dispose of or deal with the property did so or, as the case may be, is about to do so, with the intention of defeating the applicant's claim for financial relief.

(6) In this section 'disposition' does not include any provision contained in a will or codicil but, with that exception, includes any conveyance, assurance or gift of property of any description, whether made by an instrument or otherwise.

(7) This section does not apply to a disposition made before 1 January 1968.

Amendments—WRPA 1999, s 19, Sch 3, para 9.

Procedure—An application under s 37 preventing a disposition is governed by FPR 2010, Pt 18 (r 9.6(1)). An application may be made without notice to a respondent: r 9.6(2). See Procedural Guide B6.

Scope—This section has two separate functions. First, it empowers the court to restrain the future disposal of or future dealings with property in order to protect the applicant's pending claims (s 37(2)(a)). The court's inherent jurisdiction and its jurisdiction under SCA 1981, s 37(3) to freeze assets are in addition to the jurisdiction under this section (see Procedural Guide B6). Note that SCA 1981, s 37 does not include power to make a mandatory injunction (requiring a party to do a certain act) unless such an injunction is made as ancillary to, or in support of, a substantive legal or equitable right, see *Goyal v Goyal* [2016] EWCA Civ 792. A permitted example would be an injunction mandating the recipient of an annuity to take the maximum income available in support of an order for payment of a proportion of the annuity income to the other party to the marriage (see *Goyal v Goyal* [2016] EWFC 50). Second, it empowers the court to set aside dispositions that have already been made where, if the disposition were set aside, different financial relief would be granted to the applicant (s 37(2)(b)) or where following an order of the court a disposition has been made that impedes the enforcement of an order (s 37(2)(c)). The section applies retrospectively to void the transaction from the beginning and has been described as 'a bespoke alternative to the equitable right to seek rescission': *AC v DC and Others (Financial Remedy: Effect of s 37 Avoidance Order)* [2013] 2 FLR 1483, FD. See *UL v BK (Freezing Orders: safeguards: Standard Examples)* [2013] EWHC 1735 (Fam) for elementary principles relating to freezing orders, including the need for compliance with express requirements of FPR PD18A, para 5.1 in relation to notice, and the high duty of candour required for the application, including where documents used to found the application had been improperly obtained from the other side. In all cases, the applicant has to show the existence of an intention to defeat the claim for financial relief.

Essential preconditions (s 37(2),(5),(6))—Before an order may be made under s 37, there must be proceedings for financial remedy in existence. The jurisdiction to make s 37 orders ceases after final orders are made in the proceedings: *Ahmed v Mustafa* [2015] 1 FLR 139, CA. Section 37(1) defines 'financial relief' to mean an order for maintenance pending suit, financial provision, property adjustment, wilful neglect to maintain or a variation application. Thus, there must be a valid notice of application either in the application for a matrimonial order/divorce, judicial separation, nullity or by an application for a financial order in Form A: FPR 2010, r 9.4.

The applicant must also show that the act complained of was made with the intention of defeating the claim for financial relief. If the act complained of took place less than 3 years before the application (or is anticipated at the time of the application) then it shall be presumed until the contrary is shown that the person who disposed (will dispose) of the asset had (will have) the necessary intention if the disposition has (will have) the effect of reducing the amount of any financial relief which might be granted or frustrating or impeding the enforcement of any order. Otherwise, proving the necessary intention is a question of fact.

The definition of 'disposition' is wide but any provision in a will is excluded. The meaning of 'property' is not defined but it is not restricted to property in England and Wales, and includes real and personal property situated abroad (*Hamlin v Hamlin* [1986] 1 FLR 61, CA). It is usual to exclude a sum for the respondent's living expenses from the injunction, but this should not be used as a device to obtain periodical payments for the wife out of this allowance, who should apply under s 22 for maintenance pending suit (*Re M (Freezing Injunction)* [2006] 1 FLR 1031, FD). The court would generally unfreeze assets to discharge a genuine commercial debt, while preserving the home of the wife and children (*Paulin v Paulin* [2009] 2 FLR 354, CA).

To restrain an anticipated disposal under s 37(2)(a), the applicant should file a notice of application supported by a sworn statement. To obtain a s 37 order requires the applicant to demonstrate contemporaneous and factual evidence of the likelihood of the movement and dissipation of assets, with the intention of defeating the applicant's claim. A without notice order would be made only where there was positive evidence that to give notice would lead to irretrievable prejudice to the applicant. An applicant is fixed with a high duty of candour, which if breached would lead to the discharge of the order: *ND v KP (Freezing*

PART II

Order: Ex Parte Application) [2011] 2 FLR 662, FD. The freezing order should contain conventional provisions permitting the use of funds for day-to-day living and business expenses: *Harrison v Harrison* [2008] 2 FLR 35, QBD.

Power to extend without notice order—Where there has been no compliance with disclosure provisions in a without notice order, the order may be extended by the court to cover additional assets including funds held by solicitors and property: *Nightingale v Nightingale* [2014] COPLR 397, FD.

Effect on third parties—There is no jurisdiction to freeze the assets of a third party who is not a party to the application. Third parties, such as banks served with an injunction after a hearing without notice, are entitled to have the documents which disclose the evidence relied upon, in separate affidavits if necessary. It is a breach of Article 6 of the ECHR to give the judge information in a without notice hearing, which is not revealed to a party affected by the application: *C v C (Without Notice Orders)* [2006] 1 FLR 936, FD. A bank charge which continued to attach to a property sold on to defeat the wife's interest is not a reviewable disposition under s 37(1) where the husband had not been a party to the charge, and the bank was not a party to the wife's proceedings against the husband (*Ansari v Ansari* [2009] 1 FLR 1121, CA). Where a third party has actual or constructive knowledge/notice of the husband's intention to defeat a wife's claim, a third party charge may be set aside, as he had not acted in good faith, whether or not there had been valuable consideration: *Kremen v Agrest and Fishman* [2011] 2 FLR 478, FD: this extends to, for example, a party's solicitors' firm securing a charge over real property relevant to the proceedings, if those solicitors have constructive notice of an intention to defeat a claim to financial relief: *ABC v PM and Another* [2015] EWFC 32.

Restraining surrender of a tenancy—The surrender of a tenancy is not a disposition so, once made, it cannot be set aside under s 37(2)(b) or (c). If it is believed that a tenancy or joint tenancy is about to be surrendered then, in the absence of any undertaking, there should be an application under s 37(2)(a) to restrain the surrender. The undertaking/order should be served on the landlord (*Bater v Greenwich London Borough Council* [1999] 2 FLR 993, CA).

Impounding of a passport—The power to impound a respondent's passport is addressed in *Young v Young* [2012] 2 FLR 470, FD: see [26] for principles. Also, see SCA 1981, s 19.

Assignment of pensions by service personnel—Pensions Act 1995, s 166 enables the court to exercise jurisdiction in respect of terminal grants and other pension rights; see further under s 23 of this Act.

Breach of s 37 injunction—A husband who disposed of monies in his bank account in breach of a s 37 injunction was properly committed to prison for contempt: *Peyman-Fard v Peyman-Fard* [2011] EWCA Civ 959.

Costs—The costs rule in FPR 2010, r 28.3 does not apply to applications under s 37(2)(a) as it is not a financial order or remedy as defined in FPR 2010, r 2.3. The court may exercise its discretion as to costs in the light of CPR 1998, r 44.2. See FPR PD28A. Rule 28.3 does apply to applications under s 37(2)(b),(c) as these are for financial orders as defined in rr 2.3 and 9.3. For costs in relation to an application under s 37(2), see *Solomon v Solomon and Ors* [2013] EWCA Civ 1095, where an application under s 37(2) is an interim application, costs were then in the discretion of the court, and CPR 1998, Pt 44 applied. Costs 'prima facie follow the event', as in *Gojkovic v Gojkovic (No 2)* [1991] 2 FLR 233, CA.

38 Orders for repayment in certain cases of sums paid after cessation of order by reason of remarriage or formation of civil partnership

(1) Where –

- (a) a periodical payments or secured periodical payments order in favour of a party to a marriage (hereafter in this section referred to as 'a payments order') has ceased to have effect by reason of the remarriage of, or formation of a civil partnership by, that party, and
- (b) the person liable to make payments under the order or his or her personal representatives made payments in accordance with it in respect of a period after the date of the remarriage or formation of the civil partnership in the mistaken belief that the order was still subsisting,

the person so liable or his or her personal representatives shall not be entitled to bring proceedings in respect of a cause of action arising out of the circumstances mentioned in paragraphs (a) and (b) above against the person entitled to payments under the order or her or his personal representatives, but may instead make an application against that person or her or his personal representatives under this section.

(2) On an application under this section the court to which the application is made may order the respondent to pay to the applicant a sum equal to the amount of the payments made in respect of the period mentioned in subsection (1)(b) above or, if it appears to the court that it would be unjust to make that order, it may either order the respondent to pay to the applicant such lesser sum as it thinks fit or dismiss the application.

(3) An application under this section may be made in proceedings in the High Court or the family court for leave to enforce, or the enforcement of, payment of arrears under the order in question, but when not made in such proceedings shall be made to the family court; and accordingly references in this section to the court are references to the High Court or the family court, as the circumstances require.

(4) (*repealed*)

(5) An order under this section for the payment of any sum may provide for the payment of that sum by instalments of such amount as may be specified in the order.

(6) An officer of the family court, and the collecting officer under an attachment of earnings order made to secure payments under a payments order, shall not be liable –

(a) in the case of an officer of the family court, for any act done by him, in pursuance of a payments order requiring payments to be made to the court or an officer of the court, after the date on which that order ceased to have effect by reason of the remarriage of, or formation of a civil partnership by, the person entitled to payments under it, and

(b) in the case of the collecting officer, for any act done by him after that date in accordance with any enactment or rule of court specifying how payments made to him in compliance with the attachment of earnings order are to be dealt with,

if, but only if, the act was one which he would have been under a duty to do had the payments order not so ceased to have effect and the act was done before notice in writing of the fact that the person so entitled had remarried or formed a civil partnership was given to him by or on behalf of that person, the person liable to make payments under the payments order or the personal representatives of either of those persons.

(7) In this section 'collecting officer', in relation to an attachment of earnings order, means the officer of the High Court, or the officer of the family court to whom a person makes payments in compliance with the order.

Amendments—AJA 1999, s 90, Sch 13, para 82; CPA 2004, s 261(1), Sch 27, para 43(1)–(4); Courts Act 2003, Sch 8, para 170; CCA 2013, s 17, Sch 11.

Procedure—The application under s 38 is governed by FPR 2010, Pt 9.

Scope—This section empowers the court to order repayment of a maintenance order when payments have been made under it after the order had in fact ceased (e g because the payee has remarried without informing the payer of that fact). Section 33 will apply if the reason for seeking repayment arises from a change of circumstances such as, for instance, steady cohabitation. The jurisdiction of the County Court under this section is unlimited.

Usually the application will be linked with an application to vary or discharge the order and should therefore be made in the same way as a variation application, i e on Form A with a supporting affidavit. If it is not combined with any other application, no procedure is prescribed except that it should be made to the County Court.

39 Settlement etc made in compliance with a property adjustment order may be avoided on bankruptcy of settlor

The fact that a settlement or transfer of property had to be made in order to comply with a property adjustment order shall not prevent that settlement or transfer from being a transaction in respect of which an order may be made under section 339 or 340 of the Insolvency Act 1986 (transfers at an undervalue and preferences).

Amendments—Insolvency Act 1985, s 235(1), Sch 8, para 23; Insolvency Act 1986, s 439(2), Sch 14.

Scope—This section provides that the fact that a settlement or transfer of property is made pursuant to a property adjustment order does not prevent it from being attacked by a trustee in bankruptcy. A declaration of solvency as a recital to a property adjustment order may deter the trustee in bankruptcy from attacking the transfer. Since this section was amended in 1986, the ability of the trustee in bankruptcy to set aside an order made in matrimonial proceedings seems to be reduced. Concurrent bankruptcy proceedings may be transferred to the court hearing the ancillary relief application. The court has the power to annul the bankruptcy on the application of a party (*Paulin v Paulin* [2009] 2 FLR 354, CA).

'section 339 or 340 of the Insolvency Act 1986'—In essence, s 339 enables a transaction to be set aside on the application of a trustee in bankruptcy where an individual has been adjudged bankrupt and he has in the 5 years before the bankruptcy made a gift of property or transferred it at an undervalue. As s 339 requires a bankrupt individual to have entered into a transaction at an undervalue, it is difficult to see how this section would enable the trustee in bankruptcy to set aside a property adjustment order after genuinely contested proceedings. Insolvency Act 1986, s 340 enables a transaction to be set aside where a bankrupt individual does something or allows something to be done within 2 years of his bankruptcy which has the effect of putting one of his creditors into a better position than he otherwise would have been. After contested proceedings, it may be difficult for the trustee in bankruptcy to set aside a transfer of property which flows from the court exercising its mandatory duties under s 25. However, where there has been a consent order, a trustee in bankruptcy may set aside an order where a bankrupt husband transferred a property to a wife and had failed to disclose his interest in the property to the trustee (*R v R and S (Bankruptcy Jurisdiction Concerning Real Property Abroad: Setting Aside Consent Order)* [2008] 2 FLR 474, FD). See also MCA 1973, s 24 annotation **Third Party attacks on property transfers**.

40 Payments etc under order made in favour of person suffering from mental disorder

(1) Where the court makes an order under this Part of this Act requiring payments (including a lump sum payment) to be made, or property to be transferred, to a party to a marriage and the court is satisfied that the person in whose favour the order is made ('P') lacks capacity (within the meaning of the Mental Capacity Act 2005) in relation to the provisions of the order then, subject to any order, direction or authority made or given in relation to P under that Act, the court may order the payments to be made, or as the case may be, the property to be transferred, to such person ('D') as it may direct.

(2) In carrying out any functions of his in relation to an order made under subsection (1), D must act in P's best interests (within the meaning of that Act).

Amendments—MCA 2005, s 67(1), Sch 6, para 19.

MCA 2005—A relevant extract is contained in this Part.

'lacks capacity mental disorder'—This term is expressly defined as being 'within the meaning of MCA 2005' so as to incorporate the principles that apply within that legislation and the jurisprudence that develops in the new mental capacity jurisdiction. Nevertheless, many of the principles that have evolved under previous case-law are still relevant. MCA 2005, s 2(1) sets out the definition:

> 'A person lacks capacity in relation to a matter if at the material time he is unable to make a decision for himself in relation to the matter because of an impairment of, or a disturbance in the functioning of, the mind or brain'.

For a full explanation see the note to FPR 2010, r 15.1.

'order, direction or authority'—This is a reference to the powers of the Court of Protection pursuant to MCA 2005.

Use of this provision—This provision leaves considerable discretion to the court as to the future management of the financial provision but it will not always be appropriate to exercise the power conferred thereby (see notes below). The power will be useful where the incapacitated recipient has no capital or savings, only periodical payments are involved and there is an established carer who can receive and expend the money on his or her behalf. In that situation, any social security benefits will usually be dealt with under the appointeeship procedure and the person who is appointee may be suitable to handle additional weekly maintenance. But there will be no continuing supervision and it may be difficult to deal with a subsequent change of carer. Query whether this power might be used to direct payments to the local authority where the incapacitated recipient is in residential care funded by that authority.

Role of the Court of Protection—If the incapacitated party in whose favour an order is made already has income or assets which need to be administered, or if substantial provision is to be made, the Court of Protection should be left to administer the entire financial affairs. The jurisdiction of the County Court or High Court under this provision should not be allowed to conflict with that of the Court of Protection (see generally notes to FPR 2010, Pt 15).

Enduring or lasting power of attorney—Where there is such power of attorney, it would normally be appropriate for the attorney who is managing the affairs to receive all payments or property pursuant to the financial provision order, if the terms of the power are capable of extending to this.

Implications on the proceedings—A party who lacks capacity (within the meaning of MCA 2005) to conduct the proceedings will be a 'protected party' for whom a litigation friend must be appointed: see generally FPR 2010, Pt 15.

40A Appeals relating to pension sharing orders which have taken effect

(1) Subsections (2) and (3) below apply where an appeal against a pension sharing order is begun on or after the day on which the order takes effect.

(2) If the pension sharing order relates to a person's rights under a pension arrangement, the appeal court may not set aside or vary the order if the person responsible for the pension arrangement has acted to his detriment in reliance on the taking effect of the order.

(3) If the pension sharing order relates to a person's shareable state scheme rights, the appeal court may not set aside or vary the order if the Secretary of State has acted to his detriment in reliance on the taking effect of the order.

(4) In determining for the purposes of subsection (2) or (3) above whether a person has acted to his detriment in reliance on the taking effect of the order, the appeal court may disregard any detriment which in its opinion is insignificant.

(5) Where subsection (2) or (3) above applies, the appeal court may make such further orders (including one or more pension sharing orders) as it thinks fit for the purpose of putting the parties in the position it considers appropriate.

(6) Section 24C above only applies to a pension sharing order under this section if the decision of the appeal court can itself be the subject of an appeal.

(7) In subsection (2) above, the reference to the person responsible for the pension arrangement is to be read in accordance with section 25D(4) above.

Amendments—Inserted by WRPA 1999, s 19, Sch 3, para 10.

Defined terms—'the court': s 52(1); 'pension sharing order': ss 21A, 52(2).

Scope—As set out in MCA 1973, s 24C, a pension sharing order does not take effect until 7 days after the time for appealing has expired (i e in total 28 days), assuming that the decree nisi has been made absolute. Where a pension sharing order has already taken effect, any appeal will be out of time and the court will need to grant permission on the usual principles. The special provisions contained in this section will then apply. The appeal court is not able to set aside or vary a pension sharing order if the pension arrangement/the Department of Work and Pensions (in relation to shareable state scheme rights: see annotations to s 21A) has acted to its detriment in reliance on the taking effect of the order. Instead, the appeal court may make such further orders (including one or more pension sharing orders) as it thinks fit for the purpose of putting the parties into the position it considers appropriate. This could include in effect a reverse pension sharing order made against the pension credit created by the pension sharing order under appeal.

40B Appeals relating to pension compensation sharing orders which have taken effect

(1) This section applies where an appeal against a pension compensation sharing order is begun on or after the day on which the order takes effect.

(2) If the Board of the Pension Protection Fund has acted to its detriment in reliance on the taking effect of the order the appeal court –

(a) may not set aside or vary the order;
(b) may make such further orders (including a pension compensation sharing order) as it thinks fit for the purpose of putting the parties in the position it considers appropriate.

(3) In determining for the purposes of subsection (2) whether the Board has acted to its detriment the appeal court may disregard any detriment which in the court's opinion is insignificant.

(4) Section 24F (duty to stay) only applies to a pension compensation sharing order under this section if the decision of the appeal court can itself be the subject of an appeal.

Amendments—Inserted by Pensions Act 2008, Sch 6, Pt 1.

Defined terms—'the court': s 52(1); 'pension compensation order': s 21B(1).

Scope—This section provides a counterpart to s 40A in relation to a pension compensation sharing order, as to which see annotations to s 21B.

****

PART IV
MISCELLANEOUS AND SUPPLEMENTAL

47 Matrimonial relief and declarations of validity in respect of polygamous marriages

(1) A court in England and Wales shall not be precluded from granting matrimonial relief or making a declaration concerning the validity of a marriage by reason only that either party to the marriage is, or has during the subsistence of the marriage been, married to more than one person.

(2) In this section 'matrimonial relief' means –

(a) any decree under Part I of this Act;
(b) a financial provision order under section 27 above;
(c) an order under section 35 above altering a maintenance agreement;

(d) an order under any provision of this Act which confers a power exercisable in connection with, or in connection with proceedings for, such decree or order as is mentioned in paragraphs (a) to (c) above;

(dd) an order under Part III of the Matrimonial and Family Proceedings Act 1984;

(e) an order under Part I of the Domestic Proceedings and Magistrates' Courts Act 1978.

(3) In this section 'a declaration concerning the validity of a marriage' means any declaration under Part III of the Family Law Act 1986 involving a determination as to the validity of a marriage.

(4) Provision may be made by rules of court –

(a) for requiring notice of proceedings brought by virtue of this section to be served on any additional spouse of a party to the marriage in question; and

(b) for conferring on any such additional spouse the right to be heard in the proceedings,

in such cases as may be specified in the rules.

Amendments—DPMCA 1978, s 89(2)(a), Sch 2, para 39; MFPA 1984, s 46(1), Sch 1, para 15; FLA 1986, s 68(1), Sch 1, para 14; Private International Law (Miscellaneous Provisions) Act 1995, s 8, Sch, para 2.

Defined terms—'the court': s 52; 'matrimonial relief': s 47(2).

'provision may be made by rules of court' (s 47(4))—FPR PD7C makes provision for proceedings for matrimonial relief, as defined by s 47(2). The applicant for relief (eg petitioner) must state in their application (petition) that the marriage is polygamous (PD7C, para 2.1) and the court may then give notice to any additional spouse and to order that spouse to be made a party to the proceedings (para 2.4).

48 Evidence

(1) The evidence of a husband or wife shall be admissible in any proceedings to prove that marital intercourse did or did not take place between them during any period.

(2) In any proceedings for nullity of marriage, evidence on the question of sexual capacity shall be heard in camera unless in any case the court is satisfied that in the interests of justice any such evidence ought to be heard in open court.

Amendments—CCA 2013, s 17, Sch 10.

Scope—This section enables the admission of a spouse's evidence as to whether or not intercourse took place, and requires evidence of sexual capacity to be heard in private ('in camera') unless otherwise directed by the judge.

'evidence of a husband or wife' (s 48(1))—A husband and wife can give evidence against one another in all circumstances (Evidence Amendment Act 1853, s 1), including in respect of adultery and marital intercourse, or lack of it.

'shall be heard in camera' (s 48(2))—A hearing of a matrimonial case is in open court (FPR 2010, r 7.16) unless otherwise ordered, and save where s 48(2) applies.

****

52 Interpretation

(1) In this Act –

'child', in relation to one or both of the parties to a marriage, includes an illegitimate child of that party or, as the case may be, of both parties;

'child of the family', in relation to the parties to a marriage, means –

(a) a child of both of those parties; and

(b) any other child, not being a child who is placed with those parties as foster parents by a local authority or voluntary organisation, who has been treated by both of those parties as a child of their family;

'the court' (except where the context otherwise requires) means the High Court or the family court;

'education' includes training;

'maintenance calculation' has the same meaning as it has in the Child Support Act 1991 by virtue of section 54 of that Act as read with any regulations in force under that section.

'the Maintenance Regulation' means Council Regulation (EC) No 4/2009 including as applied in relation to Denmark by virtue of the Agreement made on 19 October 2005 between the European Community and the Kingdom of Denmark;

(2) In this Act –

(a) references to financial provision orders, periodical payments and secured periodical payments orders and orders for the payment of a lump sum, and references to property adjustment orders, shall be construed in accordance with section 21 above;

(aa) references to pension sharing orders shall be construed in accordance with section 21A above; and

(b) references to orders for maintenance pending suit and to interim orders for maintenance shall be construed respectively in accordance with section 22 and section 27(5) above.

(3) For the avoidance of doubt it is hereby declared that references in this Act to remarriage include references to a marriage which is by law void or voidable.

(3A) References in this Act to the formation of a civil partnership by a person include references to a civil partnership which is by law void or voidable.

(4) Except where the contrary intention is indicated, references in this Act to any enactment include references to that enactment as amended, extended or applied by or under any subsequent enactment, including this Act.

Amendments—Children Act 1975, s 108(1)(b), Sch 4; MFPA 1984, s 46(1), Sch 1, para 16; CA 1989, s 108(4), (7), Sch 12, para 33, Sch 15; SI 1993/623; WRPA 1999, s 19, Sch 3, para 11; CSPSSA 2000, s 26, Sch 3, para 3; CPA 2004, s 261(1), Sch 27, para 46; SI 2011/1484; CCA 2013, s 17, Sch 11, subject to saving provisions.

****

Matrimonial Proceedings and Property Act 1970

****

30 Order for maintenance of party to marriage made by magistrates' court to cease to have effect on remarriage of that party

(1) *(repealed)*

(2) Section 4(2) of the Domestic Proceedings and Magistrates' Courts Act 1978 shall apply in relation to an order consisting of or including a provision such as is mentioned in section 2(1)(a) of that Act made by the family court and confirmed in accordance with section 3 of the Maintenance Orders (Facilities for Enforcement) Act 1920 (which enables the family court to make a maintenance order against a person resident in a part of Her Majesty's dominions outside the United Kingdom but provides that the order shall have no effect unless and until confirmed by a competent court in that part) as it applies in relation to an order made under section 2(1)(a) of the Domestic Proceedings and Magistrates' Courts Act 1978.

Amendments—MO(RE)A 1972, s 42(3); DPMCA 1978, s 89(2), Sch 2, para 28, Sch 3; CCA 2013, s 17, Sch 11.

****

37 Contributions by spouse in money or money's worth to the improvement of property

It is hereby declared that where a husband or wife contributes in money or money's worth to the improvement of real or personal property in which or in the proceeds of sale of which either or both of them has or have a beneficial interest, the husband or wife so contributing shall, if the contribution is of a substantial nature and subject to any agreement between them to the contrary express or implied, be treated as having then acquired by virtue of his or her contribution a share or an enlarged share, as the case may be, in that beneficial interest of such an extent as may have been then agreed or, in default of such agreement, as may seem in all the circumstances just to any court before which the question of the existence or extent of the beneficial interest of the husband or wife arises (whether in proceedings between them or in any other proceedings).

****

39 Extension of s 17 of Married Women's Property Act 1882

An application may be made to the High Court or the family court under section 17 of the Married Women's Property Act 1882 (powers of the court in disputes between husband and wife about property) (including that section as extended by section 7 of the Matrimonial Causes (Property and Maintenance) Act 1958) by either of the parties to a marriage notwithstanding that their marriage has been dissolved or annulled so long as the application is made within the period of three years beginning with the date on which the marriage was dissolved or annulled; and references in the said section 17 and the said section 7 to a husband or a wife shall be construed accordingly.

Amendments—CCA 2013, s 17, Sch 11.

****

Mental Capacity Act 2005

ARRANGEMENT OF SECTIONS

PART 1

PERSONS WHO LACK CAPACITY

Section		Page
	The principles	
1	The principles	1216
	Preliminary	
2	People who lack capacity	1217
3	Inability to make decisions	1217
4	Best interests	1217
4A	Restriction on deprivation of liberty	1218
4B	Deprivation of liberty necessary for life-sustaining treatment etc	1219
5	Acts in connection with care or treatment	1219
6	Section 5 acts: limitations	1219
7	Payment for necessary goods and services	1220
8	Expenditure	1220

PART 1
PERSONS WHO LACK CAPACITY

The principles

1 The principles

(1) The following principles apply for the purposes of this Act.

(2) A person must be assumed to have capacity unless it is established that he lacks capacity.

(3) A person is not to be treated as unable to make a decision unless all practicable steps to help him to do so have been taken without success.

(4) A person is not to be treated as unable to make a decision merely because he makes an unwise decision.

(5) An act done, or decision made, under this Act for or on behalf of a person who lacks capacity must be done, or made, in his best interests.

(6) Before the act is done, or the decision is made, regard must be had to whether the purpose for which it is needed can be as effectively achieved in a way that is less restrictive of the person's rights and freedom of action.

Preliminary

2 People who lack capacity

(1) For the purposes of this Act, a person lacks capacity in relation to a matter if at the material time he is unable to make a decision for himself in relation to the matter because of an impairment of, or a disturbance in the functioning of, the mind or brain.

(2) It does not matter whether the impairment or disturbance is permanent or temporary.

(3) A lack of capacity cannot be established merely by reference to –

- (a) a person's age or appearance, or
- (b) a condition of his, or an aspect of his behaviour, which might lead others to make unjustified assumptions about his capacity.

(4) In proceedings under this Act or any other enactment, any question whether a person lacks capacity within the meaning of this Act must be decided on the balance of probabilities.

(5) No power which a person ('D') may exercise under this Act –

- (a) in relation to a person who lacks capacity, or
- (b) where D reasonably thinks that a person lacks capacity,

is exercisable in relation to a person under 16.

(6) Subsection (5) is subject to section 18(3).

3 Inability to make decisions

(1) For the purposes of section 2, a person is unable to make a decision for himself if he is unable –

- (a) to understand the information relevant to the decision,
- (b) to retain that information,
- (c) to use or weigh that information as part of the process of making the decision, or
- (d) to communicate his decision (whether by talking, using sign language or any other means).

(2) A person is not to be regarded as unable to understand the information relevant to a decision if he is able to understand an explanation of it given to him in a way that is appropriate to his circumstances (using simple language, visual aids or any other means).

(3) The fact that a person is able to retain the information relevant to a decision for a short period only does not prevent him from being regarded as able to make the decision.

(4) The information relevant to a decision includes information about the reasonably foreseeable consequences of –

- (a) deciding one way or another, or
- (b) failing to make the decision.

4 Best interests

(1) In determining for the purposes of this Act what is in a person's best interests, the person making the determination must not make it merely on the basis of –

- (a) the person's age or appearance, or
- (b) a condition of his, or an aspect of his behaviour, which might lead others to make unjustified assumptions about what might be in his best interests.

(2) The person making the determination must consider all the relevant circumstances and, in particular, take the following steps.

(3) He must consider –

- (a) whether it is likely that the person will at some time have capacity in relation to the matter in question, and
- (b) if it appears likely that he will, when that is likely to be.

(4) He must, so far as reasonably practicable, permit and encourage the person to participate, or to improve his ability to participate, as fully as possible in any act done for him and any decision affecting him.

(5) Where the determination relates to life-sustaining treatment he must not, in considering whether the treatment is in the best interests of the person concerned, be motivated by a desire to bring about his death.

(6) He must consider, so far as is reasonably ascertainable –

(a) the person's past and present wishes and feelings (and, in particular, any relevant written statement made by him when he had capacity),

(b) the beliefs and values that would be likely to influence his decision if he had capacity, and

(c) the other factors that he would be likely to consider if he were able to do so.

(7) He must take into account, if it is practicable and appropriate to consult them, the views of –

(a) anyone named by the person as someone to be consulted on the matter in question or on matters of that kind,

(b) anyone engaged in caring for the person or interested in his welfare,

(c) any donee of a lasting power of attorney granted by the person, and

(d) any deputy appointed for the person by the court,

as to what would be in the person's best interests and, in particular, as to the matters mentioned in subsection (6).

(8) The duties imposed by subsections (1) to (7) also apply in relation to the exercise of any powers which –

(a) are exercisable under a lasting power of attorney, or

(b) are exercisable by a person under this Act where he reasonably believes that another person lacks capacity.

(9) In the case of an act done, or a decision made, by a person other than the court, there is sufficient compliance with this section if (having complied with the requirements of subsections (1) to (7)) he reasonably believes that what he does or decides is in the best interests of the person concerned.

(10) 'Life-sustaining treatment' means treatment which in the view of a person providing health care for the person concerned is necessary to sustain life.

(11) 'Relevant circumstances' are those –

(a) of which the person making the determination is aware, and

(b) which it would be reasonable to regard as relevant.

4A Restriction on deprivation of liberty

(1) This Act does not authorise any person ('D') to deprive any other person ('P') of his liberty.

(2) But that is subject to–

(a) the following provisions of this section, and

(b) section 4B.

(3) D may deprive P of his liberty if, by doing so, D is giving effect to a relevant decision of the court.

(4) A relevant decision of the court is a decision made by an order under section 16(2)(a) in relation to a matter concerning P's personal welfare.

(5) D may deprive P of his liberty if the deprivation is authorised by Schedule A1 (hospital and care home residents: deprivation of liberty).

Amendments—Inserted by MHA 2007, s 50(2).

4B Deprivation of liberty necessary for life-sustaining treatment etc

(1) If the following conditions are met, D is authorised to deprive P of his liberty while a decision as respects any relevant issue is sought from the court.

(2) The first condition is that there is a question about whether D is authorised to deprive P of his liberty under section 4A.

(3) The second condition is that the deprivation of liberty –

- (a) is wholly or partly for the purpose of –
  - (i) giving P life-sustaining treatment, or
  - (ii) doing any vital act, or
- (b) consists wholly or partly of –
  - (i) giving P life-sustaining treatment, or
  - (ii) doing any vital act.

(4) The third condition is that the deprivation of liberty is necessary in order to –

- (a) give the life-sustaining treatment, or
- (b) do the vital act.

(5) A vital act is any act which the person doing it reasonably believes to be necessary to prevent a serious deterioration in P's condition.

Amendments—Inserted by MHA 2007, s 50(2).

5 Acts in connection with care or treatment

(1) If a person ('D') does an act in connection with the care or treatment of another person ('P'), the act is one to which this section applies if –

- (a) before doing the act, D takes reasonable steps to establish whether P lacks capacity in relation to the matter in question, and
- (b) when doing the act, D reasonably believes –
  - (i) that P lacks capacity in relation to the matter, and
  - (ii) that it will be in P's best interests for the act to be done.

(2) D does not incur any liability in relation to the act that he would not have incurred if P –

- (a) had had capacity to consent in relation to the matter, and
- (b) had consented to D's doing the act.

(3) Nothing in this section excludes a person's civil liability for loss or damage, or his criminal liability, resulting from his negligence in doing the act.

(4) Nothing in this section affects the operation of sections 24 to 26 (advance decisions to refuse treatment).

6 Section 5 acts: limitations

(1) If D does an act that is intended to restrain P, it is not an act to which section 5 applies unless two further conditions are satisfied.

(2) The first condition is that D reasonably believes that it is necessary to do the act in order to prevent harm to P.

(3) The second is that the act is a proportionate response to –

- (a) the likelihood of P's suffering harm, and
- (b) the seriousness of that harm.

(4) For the purposes of this section D restrains P if he –

- (a) uses, or threatens to use, force to secure the doing of an act which P resists, or
- (b) restricts P's liberty of movement, whether or not P resists.

(5) *(repealed)*

(6) Section 5 does not authorise a person to do an act which conflicts with a decision made, within the scope of his authority and in accordance with this Part, by –

(a) a donee of a lasting power of attorney granted by P, or
(b) a deputy appointed for P by the court.

(7) But nothing in subsection (6) stops a person –

(a) providing life-sustaining treatment, or
(b) doing any act which he reasonably believes to be necessary to prevent a serious deterioration in P's condition,

while a decision as respects any relevant issue is sought from the court.

Amendments—MHA 2007, s 50(4)(a).

7 Payment for necessary goods and services

(1) If necessary goods or services are supplied to a person who lacks capacity to contract for the supply, he must pay a reasonable price for them.

(2) 'Necessary' means suitable to a person's condition in life and to his actual requirements at the time when the goods or services are supplied.

8 Expenditure

(1) If an act to which section 5 applies involves expenditure, it is lawful for D –

(a) to pledge P's credit for the purpose of the expenditure, and
(b) to apply money in P's possession for meeting the expenditure.

(2) If the expenditure is borne for P by D, it is lawful for D –

(a) to reimburse himself out of money in P's possession, or
(b) to be otherwise indemnified by P.

(3) Subsections (1) and (2) do not affect any power under which (apart from those subsections) a person –

(a) has lawful control of P's money or other property, and
(b) has power to spend money for P's benefit.

General note—The Act creates an entirely new jurisdiction separate from the family jurisdiction but replacing (in part) the inherent jurisdiction. The principles are of general application but the Act establishes a new Court of Protection with a regional presence that deals with matters arising under the new jurisdiction. The scope of this legislation has been extended by MHA 2007, which introduces safeguards for the deprivation of liberty of a person who cannot consent to detention in a nursing or care home. Sections 1–8 are reproduced above because they are of general application and will on occasions need to be taken into account by family lawyers. An overview follows.

Background—For many years procedures for the delegation of decision-making powers comprised:

- *agency* – bank mandate; ordinary power of attorney;
- *specific* – appointee for state benefits; litigation friend for court proceedings;
- *statutory* – enduring power of attorney; jurisdiction of the Court of Protection to appoint a receiver;
- *trusts* – bare trust; settlement.

Each has its own limitations and normal agency concepts do not survive a loss of capacity. These all relate to financial decisions and there were no procedures for other types of decision (i e social welfare or healthcare) to be delegated or made on behalf of mentally incapacitated adults.

Overview of the mental capacity jurisdiction—The MCA 2005 establishes a comprehensive statutory framework setting out how decisions should be made by and on behalf of those whose capacity to make their own decisions is in doubt. It also clarifies what actions can be taken by others involved in the care and medical treatment of people lacking capacity.

The framework provides a hierarchy of processes, extending from informal day-to-day care, to decision-making requiring formal powers and ultimately to court decisions. An individual can anticipate lack of capacity by completing a lasting power of attorney for either financial affairs or personal welfare decisions (which includes healthcare). Failing this, the Court of Protection now has jurisdiction to make declarations or decisions or to appoint a deputy to make decisions on the incapacitated person's behalf.

The common law relating to advance refusals of medical treatment is also placed on a statutory footing and there is an offence of 'ill-treatment and neglect' on the part of carers, donees of lasting powers of attorney and deputies.

The Act's provisions apply in general only to people lacking capacity who are aged 16 years or over, but the property and financial affairs jurisdiction may be exercised in relation to a child who will lack capacity into adulthood.

A Code of Practice provides guidance for the courts, professionals and those concerned with the welfare of a mentally incapacitated adult and a Public Guardian is appointed to supervise and promote the new jurisdiction.

Fundamental concepts—There are two fundamental concepts that apply for the purposes of this Act, namely a definition of incapacity and clarification of best interests (the basis on which delegated decisions must be made).

1 *Incapacity*

Section 2(1) sets out the definition of a person who lacks capacity:

'A person lacks capacity in relation to a matter if at the material time he is unable to make a decision for himself in relation to the matter because of an impairment of, or a disturbance in the functioning of, the mind or brain.'

This is a two-stage test, because it must be established first, that there is an impairment of, or disturbance in the functioning of, the person's mind or brain (the diagnostic threshold); and secondly, that the impairment or disturbance is sufficient to render the person incapable of making that particular decision.

Capacity is thus decision-specific, but it does not matter whether the impairment or disturbance is permanent or temporary. A person is unable to make a decision if unable:

- to understand the information relevant to the decision;
- to retain that information;
- to use or weigh that information as part of the process of making the decision; or
- to communicate his decision (whether by talking, using sign language or any other means).

Explanations must be provided in ways that are appropriate to the person's circumstances.

2 *Best interests*

The Act sets out a checklist of factors which must be considered in deciding what is in a person's best interests aimed at identifying those issues most relevant to the individual who lacks capacity (as opposed to the decision-maker or any other persons). Not all the factors in the checklist will be relevant to all types of decisions or actions, but they must still be considered if only to be disregarded as irrelevant to that particular situation. They include:

- consideration of all relevant circumstances;
- whether the person will at some time have the required capacity;
- encouraging the person to participate in the decision;
- the person's past and present wishes and feelings;
- the beliefs and values that would be likely to influence the person's decision;
- the views of others who should be consulted.

Decision-making—There are three areas of decision-making (although the first and second are combined in the legislation):

1 personal welfare;
2 healthcare;
3 property and affairs.

There are four levels of decision-making:

(i) a person acting under ss 5–6 – the statutory defence (in effect a 'general authority to act' with restrictions) or ss 7–8, which cover payment for 'necessary' goods and services;
(ii) an attorney under a lasting power of attorney (or an earlier enduring power of attorney);
(iii) a deputy appointed by the Court;
(iv) the Court of Protection making decisions or declarations.

General principles—There are five general principles:

1 a decision-specific approach to capacity based on understanding and the ability to make and communicate a decision;
2 adults are presumed to have capacity so unjustified assumptions are outlawed and there is a 'balance of probabilities' approach;
3 individuals should be helped to make their own decisions with simple explanations, and they may make unwise decisions;
4 there must be participation in decision-making and consultation with others;
5 a 'least restrictive' approach is to be applied to any intervention.

The new public bodies

I *Court of Protection*

The current Court of Protection is a very different body to its predecessor of the same name. It is a Superior Court of Record with full status to deal with the entire range of decision-making on behalf of incapacitated persons (as defined). It takes over the financial jurisdiction of the former Court of Protection and extends this to personal welfare and healthcare decisions thus absorbing the existing declaratory jurisdiction of the Family Division of the High Court.

Most applications are dealt with 'on paper' by district judges sitting at First Avenue House, 42–49 High Holborn, London but hearings may be before nominated district judges based in a number of regional courts, with nominated circuit judges and High Court judges hearing more important cases and appeals.

The Court of Protection rules promote active case management drawing on CPR 1998.

II *Public Guardian*

The Public Guardian has a statutory appointment with an office and staff known as the Office of the Public Guardian (OPG). The new role of regulator is both administrative and supervisory and there are five key functions:

1 to maintain a register of lasting powers of attorney (and the former enduring powers that still remain valid);

2 to maintain a register of deputies;
3 to supervise and receive security from deputies;
4 to receive reports from and hear representations about attorneys and deputies;
5 to provide reports to the court and arrange reports from visitors;

The jurisdiction under the MCA—There is a wider range of cases under the new jurisdiction and a consequent increase in the volume of cases. The unmet need has now emerged (eg residence and contact disputes in respects of learning disabled adults) and there is a new variety of outcomes. The court is more accessible, but alternative dispute resolution may be imposed before contested hearings and the court should be seen as the last resort. There is a constant struggle to maintain the balance between protection and empowerment of these potentially vulnerable people, but the court and the Office of the Public Guardian have now attained greater prominence and wider influence.

Key points

- enduring powers of attorney previously executed are effective, but since 1 October 2007 only lasting powers of attorney may be completed and registration of these does not point towards lack of capacity;
- the Court of Protection is able to deal with the full range of decision-making on behalf of adults who lack capacity in accessible local courts;
- serious medical treatment decisions are dealt with by Family Division judges in the Court of Protection under the statutory jurisdiction rather than by the former declaratory procedure under the inherent jurisdiction;
- cases in the Family Court and County Court involving a significant mental capacity element may be transferred to a suitable nominated judge as a 'specialist' and a nominated judge may sit in a dual jurisdiction;
- a discrete body of law is developing in regard to the assessment of capacity with a more professional approach towards decision-making issues.

For a comprehensive explanation of the mental capacity jurisdiction, see *Mental Capacity: Law and Practice* and *Court of Protection Practice*, which is a companion volume to the present work, and *Civil Court Service* (all LexisNexis).

****

Presumption of Death Act 2013

Scope—The Act came into force on 1 October 2014 and extends to England and Wales only. Under the pre-existing law, a number of statutes (eg MCA 1973, s 19 and CPA 2004, s 37) contained specific procedures dealing with different aspects of a missing person's property and affairs under which a missing person might be presumed dead, some of which lead to the issue of a death certificate. Further, there was a common law rebuttable evidential presumption that a person was deemed to be dead after a 7-year absence. The Act introduces a court-based procedure enabling a declaration to be obtained from the High Court (Family Division or Chancery Division: CPR 1998, r 57.18(2)) that a missing person is deemed to have died. Such a declaration is conclusive as to the presumed death and effective for all purposes and against all persons. The application for a declaration may be made at any time following a disappearance if there is clear evidence that the missing person has died; alternatively, the application may be made after 7 years if there is no evidence that the missing person has been alive during this period (s 1(1)). The missing person's property will pass to others in the same way as if the missing person had died and had been certified dead in the normal way and his or her marriage or civil partnership will end as a marriage or civil partnership ends on death. Where a declaration is made, the court sends a copy of the declaration to the Registrar General for England and Wales who enters details of the death of the missing person in a Register of Presumed Deaths (s 15 and Sch 1). If, following the making of a declaration, facts emerge that require the declaration to be revoked or varied, the High Court may on application make a variation order (ss 5–8). When making a declaration or a variation order, the High Court may also decide questions and make orders relating to property acquired as a result of the declaration or the variation order and as to the domicile of the missing person at the time of his or her death (ss 4 and 7).

The procedure for applying for a declaration under the Act is dealt with in CPR 1998, rr 57.17–57.23 and PD57B (set out in Part III).

See, for example, *A v H (Presumption of Death)* [2016] EWHC 762 (Fam).

Declaration of presumed death

1 Applying for declaration

(1) This section applies where a person who is missing –

(a) is thought to have died, or

(b) has not been known to be alive for a period of at least 7 years.

(2) Any person may apply to the High Court for a declaration that the missing person is presumed to be dead.

(3) The court has jurisdiction to hear and determine an application under this section only if –

- (a) the missing person was domiciled in England and Wales on the day on which he or she was last known to be alive,
- (b) the missing person had been habitually resident in England and Wales throughout the period of 1 year ending with that day, or
- (c) subsection (4) is satisfied.

(4) This subsection is satisfied if the application is made by the spouse or civil partner of the missing person and –

- (a) the applicant is domiciled in England and Wales on the day on which the application is made, or
- (b) the applicant has been habitually resident in England and Wales throughout the period of 1 year ending with that day.

(5) The court must refuse to hear an application under this section if –

- (a) the application is made by someone other than the missing person's spouse, civil partner, parent, child or sibling, and
- (b) the court considers that the applicant does not have a sufficient interest in the determination of the application.

(6) This section has effect subject to section 21(2).

Defined terms—'the court': s 20(2); 'missing person': s 20(1); 'sibling': s 20(1).

2 Making declaration

(1) On an application under section 1, the court must make the declaration if it is satisfied that the missing person –

- (a) has died, or
- (b) has not been known to be alive for a period of at least 7 years.

(2) It must include in the declaration a finding as to the date and time of the missing person's death.

(3) Where the court –

- (a) is satisfied that the missing person has died, but
- (b) is uncertain at which moment during a period the missing person died,

the finding must be that the missing person is presumed to have died at the end of that period.

(4) Where the court –

- (a) is satisfied that the missing person has not been known to be alive for a period of at least 7 years, but
- (b) is not satisfied that the missing person has died,

the finding must be that the missing person is presumed to have died at the end of the period of 7 years beginning with the day after the day on which he or she was last known to be alive.

Defined terms—'the court': s 20(1); 'missing person': s 20(1).

3 Effect of declaration

(1) A declaration under this Act is conclusive of –

- (a) the missing person's presumed death, and
- (b) the date and time of the death.

(2) A declaration under this Act is effective against all persons and for all purposes, including for the purposes of –

- (a) the acquisition of an interest in any property, and
- (b) the ending of a marriage or civil partnership to which the missing person is a party.

(3) But subsections (1) and (2) apply to a declaration only if –

- (a) it has not been appealed against and the period for bringing an appeal has ended, or

(b) it has been appealed against and the appeal (and any further appeal) has been unsuccessful.

(4) For the purposes of subsection (3), an appeal has been unsuccessful if –

(a) it has been dismissed or withdrawn, and
(b) any period for bringing a further appeal has ended.

Defined terms—'missing person': s 20(1).

Scope—A declaration of presumed death is conclusive and effective against all persons and for all purposes. Section 15 and Sch 1, para 4 provide that a certified copy of a sealed or stamped entry in the Register of Presumed Deaths is to be received as evidence of the person's death without further or other proof. Section 15 and Sch 1, para 5 enable the court to direct the Registrar General to correct an error in the Register of Presumed Deaths.

Time for appeal—The standard period for making an appeal is 21 days (CPR 1998, r 52.4(2)(b)).

4 Other powers of court making declaration

(1) When making a declaration under this Act, the court may –

(a) determine any question which relates to an interest in property and arises as a result of the declaration, and
(b) determine the domicile of the missing person at the time of his or her presumed death.

(2) When making a declaration under this Act, the court may make such order as it considers reasonable in relation to any interest in property acquired as a result of the declaration.

(3) An order under subsection (2) may direct that the value of any interest in property acquired as a result of the declaration is not to be recoverable by virtue of an order made under section 7(2).

(4) It may, in particular, direct that the value of the interest –

(a) is not to be recoverable in any circumstances, or
(b) is not to be recoverable where conditions specified in the order are met.

Scope—When making such an order, the court may specify conditions or generally (s 4(4)) that the value of the asset acquired as a result of the declaration cannot in due course be recovered under an order made by the court when varying or revoking a declaration (ss 5 and 7(2)).

Defined terms—'the court': s 20(1); 'interest in property': s 20(1); 'missing person': s 20(1).

Variation order

5 Varying and revoking declaration

(1) On an application by any person, a declaration under this Act may be varied or revoked by an order of the High Court (a 'variation order').

(2) The court must refuse to hear an application for a variation order if it considers that the applicant does not have a sufficient interest in the determination of the application.

Scope—A variation order (eg where the missing person reappears) may be made on the application of any person. However, the court must refuse to consider an application if it considers that the applicant does not have sufficient interest in the outcome.

Defined term—'the court': s 20(1).

6 Effect of variation order

(1) A variation order does not affect an interest in property acquired as a result of a declaration under this Act (but see section 7).

(2) A variation order does not revive a marriage or civil partnership that was brought to an end by virtue of a declaration under this Act.

(3) Except as otherwise required by subsection (1) or (2) –

(a) where a variation order varies a declaration, subsections (1) and (2) of section 3 have effect in relation to the declaration as varied by the order, and
(b) where a variation order revokes a declaration, those subsections cease to have effect in relation to the declaration.

(4) But subsection (3) applies only if –

(a) the variation order has not been appealed against and the period for bringing an appeal has ended, or

(b) the variation order has been appealed against and the appeal (and any further appeal) has been unsuccessful.

(5) For the purposes of subsection (4), an appeal has been unsuccessful if –

(a) it has been dismissed or withdrawn, and

(b) any period for bringing a further appeal has ended.

Scope—A variation order does not of itself affect property acquired as a result of a declaration of presumed death, thereby protecting the position of those acquiring property in good faith (s 6(1); s 7(2),(6)). A variation order does not revive any marriage or civil partnership entered by a declaration of presumed death, ensuring that any subsequent marriage or civil partnership of the missing person's spouse/civil partner is not invalidated (s 6(2)). Subject to these qualifications, a declaration of presumed death as varied by a variation order is conclusive of the missing person's presumed death and the date and time of that presumed death and is effective for all purposes and against all persons (s 6(3)(a)). Where the variation order revokes a declaration of presumed death, the declaration ceases to be conclusive and effective (s 6(3)(b)). The consequences specified in s 6(3) are subject to any appeal (s 6(4)).

Defined term—'variation order': s 5(1).

7 Other functions of court making variation order

(1) When making a variation order, the court may –

(a) determine any question which relates to an interest in property and arises as a result of the variation order, and

(b) determine the domicile of the missing person at the time of his or her presumed death.

(2) When making a variation order, the court must make such further order (if any) as it considers reasonable in relation to any interest in property acquired as a result of the declaration varied or revoked by the order ('the original declaration') (but see subsections (3), (5) and (6)).

(3) The court must not make an order under subsection (2) if the application for the variation order was made after the end of the period of 5 years beginning with the day on which the original declaration was made, unless it considers that there are exceptional circumstances which make it appropriate to do so.

(4) In considering what order to make under subsection (2), the court must, as far as practicable, have regard to the principles in section 8.

(5) An order under subsection (2) does not affect income that accrued in the period –

(a) beginning with the day on which the original declaration was made, and

(b) ending with the day on which the variation order was made.

(6) An order under subsection (2) does not affect or provide grounds to challenge –

(a) a related good faith transaction, or

(b) an interest in property acquired under such a transaction.

(7) A 'related good faith transaction' is a transaction under which a person acquires an interest in the property that is the subject of the order (or any part of it) in good faith and for value from –

(a) a person who acquired an interest in the property (or any part of it) as a result of the original declaration, or

(b) a person who acquired an interest in the property (or any part of it) from a person described in paragraph (a), whether directly or indirectly.

(8) Where a person has entitlement under a trust by virtue of an order under subsection (2), the trustee is liable to that person for any loss suffered by that person on account of any breach of trust by the trustee in the administration or distribution of all or part of the property that is the subject of the order.

(9) Subsection (8) does not apply to the extent that the trustee's liability is restricted under any enactment or by any provision in a deed regulating the administration of the trust.

(10) In subsection (9) 'enactment' includes an enactment contained in –

(a) an instrument made under an Act, or

(b) an Act or Measure of the National Assembly for Wales or an instrument made under such an Act or Measure.

Defined terms—'court': s 20(1); 'interest in property': s 20(1); 'missing person': s 20(1); 'trustee': s 20(1); 'variation order': s 5(1).

8 Principles

(1) These are the principles referred to in section 7(4).

(2) The first principle is relevant where property ('the relevant property') is being or has been administered under a trust.

(3) The first principle is that –

(a) a person who, but for section 6(1), would have an interest in the relevant property by virtue of a variation order, and

(b) a person who, but for section 6(1), would have acquired an interest in the relevant property from a person described in paragraph (a),

should be entitled to have made over to him or her by the trustee in full satisfaction of that interest the things listed in subsection (4).

(4) Those things are –

(a) the interest in the relevant property or an equivalent interest in property representing the relevant property, to the extent that such property is still in the hands of the trustee when the variation order is made, and

(b) the value of the interest in the relevant property, to the extent that such property has been distributed.

(5) The second principle is relevant where an insurer has paid a capital sum as a result of a declaration varied or revoked by a variation order.

(6) The second principle is that the capital sum, or any part of the capital sum, should be repaid to the insurer if the facts in respect of which the variation order was made justify such repayment.

(7) The references in subsections (5) and (6) to a capital sum do not include a capital sum distributed by way of an annuity or other periodical payment.

Scope—Section 8 sets out the two principles to which the court must have regard as far as practicable in considering what order to make under s 7(2) (ss 7(4) and 8(1)). The first principle (s 8(3)) has two limbs and is relevant where property acquired as a result of the declaration to be varied or revoked is or has been held in trust (s 8(2)). The first limb is that where, but for the fact the variation order does not affect interests in property acquired as a result of a declaration of presumed death (s 6(1)), a person would have an interest in the property in question as a result of the variation order, that person should be entitled to receive the property or value specified in s 6(4) in full satisfaction of the interest from the trustee (s 8(3)(a)). The second limb is to the same effect except that the person entitled is a person who would, but for the limitation in s 6(1), have acquired an interest in property acquired as a result of the declaration to be varied or revoked from the person described in the first limb (s 8(3)(b)). The property or value to be made over by the trustee under the first principle depends on whether the trustee still holds the interest in the property acquired as a result of the declaration to be varied or revoked or an equivalent interest in property representing that property. If the trustee does, there is an entitlement to that interest. If the trustee does not, the entitlement is to the value of the interest in the property in question (s 8(4)). The second principle is relevant where an insurer has paid a capital sum (other than one distributed by way of an annuity or other periodical payment) as a result of a declaration varied or revoked by a variation order (s 8(5),(7)). The principle is that the whole or part of the capital sum should be repaid to the insurers if repayment is justified by the facts in respect of which the variation is made (s 8(6)). Section 14 allows insurers to require recipients of capital sums to insure against the consequences of a variation order.

Defined term—'interest in property': s 20(1).

Further provision about declarations and orders

9 Giving notice of application

(1) A person who makes an application under this Act for a declaration or a variation order must send to the persons specified by rules of court –

(a) notice of the application, and

(b) any other information specified by rules of court.

(2) An application under this Act for a declaration or a variation order must be advertised in accordance with rules of court.

(3) The court must refuse to hear an application under this Act for a declaration or a variation order if the requirements in this section have not been met.

Scope—Section 9 provides for an application for a declaration of presumed death or a variation order to be notified and advertised as required by CPR 1998, as amended. The giving of notice of such an application is intended to enable those with an interest to consider whether or not they need to intervene in the proceedings (s 11). If these requirements have not been met, the court must refuse to hear the application (s 9(3)).

Defined terms—'the court': s 20(1); 'variation order': s 5(1).

10 Attorney General

(1) In proceedings on an application under this Act for a declaration or a variation order, the court may at any stage direct that papers relating to the matter be sent to the Attorney General.

(2) It may do so on the application of a party to the proceedings or without such an application being made.

(3) Where the Attorney General incurs costs in connection with an application under this Act for a declaration or a variation order, the court may make such order as it considers appropriate as to the payment of the costs by parties to the proceedings.

(4) Subsection (3) applies whether the costs are incurred by virtue of a direction under subsection (1), an intervention under section 11(2) or otherwise.

Defined terms—'the court': s 20(1); 'party to proceedings': s 20(2); 'variation order': s 5(1).

11 Right to intervene

(1) The missing person's spouse, civil partner, parent, child or sibling may intervene in proceedings on an application under this Act for a declaration or a variation order.

(2) The Attorney General may intervene in such proceedings, whether or not the court directs papers relating to the application to be sent to the Attorney General.

(3) Any other person may intervene in such proceedings only with the permission of the court.

(4) References in this section to intervening in proceedings include –

- (a) arguing before the court any question in relation to the application which the court considers it necessary to have fully argued,
- (b) in proceedings on an application for a declaration under this Act, seeking a determination or order under section 4, and
- (c) in proceedings on an application for a variation order, seeking a determination or order under section 7.

Scope—Section 11 specifies who may intervene in an application for a declaration of presumed death or a variation order.

Defined terms—'missing person': s 20(1); 'sibling': s 20(1); 'variation order': s 5(1).

12 Information

(1) In proceedings on an application under this Act for a declaration or a variation order, the court may by order at any stage require a person who is not a party to the proceedings to provide it with specified information that it considers relevant to the question of whether the missing person is alive or dead.

(2) It may do so only where it considers it necessary for the purpose of disposing of the proceedings.

(3) It may do so on the application of a party to the proceedings or without such an application being made.

(4) The order may not require the provision of information –

- (a) which is permitted or required by any rule of law to be withheld on grounds of public interest immunity,
- (b) which any person would be entitled to refuse to provide on grounds of legal professional privilege, or

(c) whose provision might incriminate the person providing it, or that person's spouse or civil partner, of an offence.

(5) Before making an order under this section, the court must send notice of its intention to make the order to any person who, in its opinion, is likely to be affected by the order.

(6) The court may discharge or vary an order made under this section on an application made by any person who, in the opinion of the court, is affected by it.

(7) In this section 'specified' means specified in an order under this section.

Scope—In proceedings for a declaration of presumed death or a variation order, the court may, where it considers it necessary to dispose of the proceedings, order the provision of information by persons who are not party to the proceedings. The information sought must be relevant to the question of whether a missing person is alive or dead and must be specified in the order (s 12(1),(2),(7)). The court may make such an order on application by a party or of its own initiative (s 12(3)), but must give prior notice of its intention to make the order to anyone likely to be affected (s 12(5)). A person whom the court considers is affected by such an order may apply for it to be discharged or varied (s 12(6)). An order may not require the provision of certain information specified in s 12(4).

Defined terms—'the court': s 20(1); 'party to proceedings': s 20(2); 'variation order': s 5(1).

13 Insurance against claims: trustees

(1) If the court so directs, the trustee of a trust affected by a declaration under this Act must as soon as reasonably practicable take out an insurance policy in respect of any claim which may arise by virtue of an order under section 7(2).

(2) For the purposes of this section, a trust is affected by a declaration under this Act if –

(a) it arises as a result of the declaration, or
(b) property held under the trust is affected by the declaration.

(3) A premium payable by the trustee in accordance with a direction under this section may be paid out of money or other property held under the trust.

14 Insurance against claims: insurers paying capital sums

(1) Before paying a capital sum to a person as a result of a declaration under this Act, an insurer may require the person to take out an insurance policy in respect of any claim which the insurer may make in the event of a variation order being made.

(2) The policy must be taken out –

(a) in the person's own name, and
(b) for the benefit of the insurer.

(3) Subsection (1) does not apply where the sum is paid in respect of an annuity or other periodical payment.

(4) In this section 'insurer' means any person who provides for the payment of a benefit on a person's death.

Defined term—'variation order': s 5(1).

****

Other determinations

16 Other determinations about death of missing person

(1) No declaration which may be applied for under section 1 may be made otherwise than under this Act.

(2) Where a court or tribunal makes a declaration that a missing person is presumed to be dead (other

than on an application under this Act), subsections (2) to (4) of section 2 apply to the court or tribunal as they apply to the High Court when it makes a declaration under this Act.

(3) Schedule 2 (amendment of provisions about presumption of death) has effect.

(4) Apart from subsections (1) to (3) and Schedule 2, nothing in the preceding provisions of this Act affects any power or duty that a court or tribunal has other than under this Act to determine a question relating to the death of a missing person.

Scope—Section 16 defines the relationship of the Act with other legislation dealing with presumed death. Where a declaration of presumed death may be made under s 1, it must be made under the Act (s 16(1)). That apart and subject to Sch 2, which amends provisions about presumption of death, the Act does not affect other legislative powers to determine a question relating to the death of a missing person (s 16(4)). Where a declaration of presumed death is made other than on an application under other legislation, it must specify the time and date of death and the requirements in s 2(3)–(4) apply (s 16(2)).

Defined term—'missing person': s 20(1).

★★★★

20 Interpretation

(1) In this Act –

'the court' means the High Court (except in section 16(2));

'interest in property' means an interest in property of any description, including an estate in land and a right over property;

'the missing person', in relation to a declaration under this Act or an application, determination or order made in connection with such a declaration, means the person who is or would be the subject of the declaration;

'the Registrar General' means the Registrar General for England and Wales;

'sibling' means a sibling of the full blood or the half blood;

'trustee' includes an executor, administrator or personal representative;

'variation order' has the meaning given in section 5.

(2) References in this Act to a party to proceedings include a person intervening in the proceedings in accordance with section 11.

★★★★

Protection from Harassment Act 1997

England and Wales

1 Prohibition of harassment

(1) A person must not pursue a course of conduct –

(a) which amounts to harassment of another, and
(b) which he knows or ought to know amounts to harassment of the other.

(1A) A person must not pursue a course of conduct –

(a) which involves harassment of two or more persons, and
(b) which he knows or ought to know involves harassment of those persons, and
(c) by which he intends to persuade any person (whether or not one of those mentioned above) –
  (i) not to do something that he is entitled or required to do, or
  (ii) to do something that he is not under any obligation to do.

(2) For the purposes of this section, the person whose course of conduct is in question ought to know that it amounts to or involves harassment of another if a reasonable person in possession of the same information would think the course of conduct amounted to or involved harassment of the other.

(3) Subsection (1) does not apply to a course of conduct if the person who pursued it shows –

(a) that it was pursued for the purpose of preventing or detecting crime,
(b) that it was pursued under any enactment or rule of law or to comply with any condition or requirement imposed by any person under any enactment, or
(c) that in the particular circumstances the pursuit of the course of conduct was reasonable.

Amendments—Serious Organised Crime and Police Act 2005, s 125(2).

'harassment'—This term includes, but is not restricted to, 'alarming the person' and 'causing the person distress' (s 7(2)). 'Harassment ... includes within it an element of intent, intent to cause distress or harm' (*Johnson v Walton* [1990] 1 FLR 350, CA, at [352H]).

'course of conduct'—Harassment is a 'course of conduct' (s 1(1)) that 'must involve conduct on at least two occasions' (s 7(3)). However proceedings can be brought based on an 'apprehended breach of section 1' (see under s 3(1)). '"Conduct" includes speech' (s 7(4)). In *R v Hills* [2001] 1 FLR 580, CA it was held that assaults in April and October were not a 'course of conduct', particularly since the parties had been reconciled. On the facts, a charge of assault might have been more appropriate. In *AJR v Regina* [2013] 2 FLR 1383, CA, a 5-year restraining order was set aside as there was no 'course of conduct'. The Court of Appeal has criticised prosecutions under this Act where a charge of assault is more appropriate (*R v Widdows* [2011] 2 FLR 869, CA). In the family jurisdiction, parties should consider whether remedies under FLA 1996 may be more appropriate.

2 Offence of harassment

(1) A person who pursues a course of conduct in breach of section 1(1) or (1A) is guilty of an offence.

(2) A person guilty of an offence under this section is liable on summary conviction to imprisonment for a term not exceeding six months, or a fine not exceeding level 5 on the standard scale, or both.

(3) *(repealed)*

Amendments—Police Reform Act 2002, s 107(2), Sch 8; Serious Organised Crime and Police Act 2005, s 125(3).

****

3 Civil remedy

(1) An actual or apprehended breach of section 1(1) may be the subject of a claim in civil proceedings by the person who is or may be the victim of the course of conduct in question.

(2) On such a claim, damages may be awarded for (among other things) any anxiety caused by the harassment and any financial loss resulting from the harassment.

(3) Where –

(a) in such proceedings the High Court or the county court grants an injunction for the purpose of restraining the defendant from pursuing any conduct which amounts to harassment, and

(b) the plaintiff considers that the defendant has done anything which he is prohibited from doing by the injunction,

the plaintiff may apply for the issue of a warrant for the arrest of the defendant.

(4) An application under subsection (3) may be made –

(a) where the injunction was granted by the High Court, to a judge of that court, and

(b) where the injunction was granted by the county court, to a judge of that court.

(5) The judge to whom an application under subsection (3) is made may only issue a warrant if –

(a) the application is substantiated on oath, and

(b) the judge has reasonable grounds for believing that the defendant has done anything which he is prohibited from doing by the injunction.

(6) Where –

(a) the High Court or the county court grants an injunction for the purpose mentioned in subsection (3)(a), and

(b) without reasonable excuse the defendant does anything which he is prohibited from doing by the injunction,

he is guilty of an offence.

(7) Where a person is convicted of an offence under subsection (6) in respect of any conduct, that conduct is not punishable as a contempt of court.

(8) A person cannot be convicted of an offence under subsection (6) in respect of any conduct which has been punished as a contempt of court.

(9) A person guilty of an offence under subsection (6) is liable –

(a) on conviction on indictment, to imprisonment for a term not exceeding five years, or a fine, or both, or

(b) on summary conviction, to imprisonment for a term not exceeding six months, or a fine not exceeding the statutory maximum, or both.

Amendments—Serious Organised Crime and Police Act 2005, s 125(4); CCA 2013, s 17, Sch 9.

Scope—This section creates the statutory tort of harassment. In *Tuppen and anor v Microsoft Corporation Ltd and anor* (2000) *The Times*, 15 November, QBD, it was held, after referring to *Hansard*, that the Act was directed at the prevention of stalking, anti-social behaviour by neighbours and racial harassment and is not to be used to stifle litigation. The Act can be used to protect employees (*Huntingdon Life Sciences v Stop Huntingdon Animal Cruelty* [2003] EWHC 1139 (QB)).

'claim in civil proceedings', 'damages'—A claim for damages is not necessary if all the applicant seeks is an injunction. A freestanding application for an injunction can be made in the County Court in proceedings founded on any matter within the jurisdiction of the County Court: CCA 1984, s 38. However, in many cases it will be appropriate to seek damages and the court is given express power to award damages for anxiety and any financial loss (see s 3(2)). In *Singh v Bhakar* [2007] 1 FLR 880, Cty Ct, damages of £35,000 were awarded against the claimant's former mother-in-law.

Procedure—Proceedings under PHA 1997 are civil proceedings and are governed by CPR 1998, Pt 65. See further Procedural Guide A10. Enforcement of an order is governed by CPR 1998, Pt 81.

Service—Service should be effected in accordance with the Family Justice Council *Protocol for Process Servers: Non–Molestation Orders* (in Part V of this work); see the 'Introduction' in the Protocol, which applies it to 'harassment' cases despite the misleading title.

'apprehended breach of section 1'—Although the tort is incomplete until the course of conduct involves 'conduct on at least two occasions' (s 7(3)), an application for an injunction can be brought for a threatened tort, provided the evidence justifies a finding that commission of the tort is likely (*South Carolina Insurance Co v Assurantie Maatschappij 'De Zeven Provincien' NV* [1987] AC 24, HL; *Khorasandjian v Bush* [1993] 2 FLR 66, CA). However, see *R v A (AJ)* [2013] EWCA Crim 591.

Concurrent proceedings—Remedies under FLA 1996 may be more appropriate in a particular case. Damages can be awarded under PHA 1997 but not FLA 1996. Thus, exceptionally, concurrent proceedings under both statutes can be brought. They should be consolidated and tried together (*Lomas v Parle* [2004] 1 FLR 812, CA).

Ambit of injunction—An injunction can forbid the defendant from entering a defined area around the applicant's home, where this is needed to make the injunction effective (*Burris v Azadani* [1996] 1 FLR 266, CA) and from any other area such as a place of work (*Silverton v Gravett* [2001] All ER (D) 282, QBD).

'warrant of arrest'—A warrant of arrest can be obtained for the purpose of arresting the defendant and bringing him before the court following a breach of the injunction. See further Procedural Guide C14. Note that it is not possible for a power of arrest to be attached to the injunction itself.

'guilty of an offence'—By virtue of s 3(6)–(7), where the defendant has disobeyed an injunction forbidding harassment, he may be convicted of an offence, in which case contempt proceedings are no longer permissible. Where he has been punished for the contempt, criminal proceedings are no longer permissible (s 3(8)).

3A Injunctions to protect persons from harassment within section 1(1A)

(1) This section applies where there is an actual or apprehended breach of section 1(1A) by any person ('the relevant person').

(2) In such a case –

(a) any person who is or may be a victim of the course of conduct in question, or

(b) any person who is or may be a person falling within section 1(1A)(c),

may apply to the High Court or the county court for an injunction restraining the relevant person from pursuing any conduct which amounts to harassment in relation to any person or persons mentioned or described in the injunction.

(3) Section 3(3) to (9) apply in relation to an injunction granted under subsection (2) above as they apply in relation to an injunction granted as mentioned in section 3(3)(a).

Amendments—Inserted by Serious Organised Crime and Police Act 2005, s 125(5). Amended by CCA 2013, s 17, Sch 9.

****

7 Interpretation of this group of sections

(1) This section applies for the interpretation of sections 1 to 5.

(2) References to harassing a person include alarming the person or causing the person distress.

(3) A 'course of conduct' must involve –

(a) in the case of conduct in relation to a single person (see section 1(1)), conduct on at least two occasions in relation to that person, or

(b) in the case of conduct in relation to two or more persons (see section 1(1A)), conduct on at least one occasion in relation to each of those persons.

(3A) A person's conduct on any occasion shall be taken, if aided, abetted, counselled or procured by another –

(a) to be conduct on that occasion of the other (as well as conduct of the person whose conduct it is); and

(b) to be conduct in relation to which the other's knowledge and purpose, and what he ought to have known, are the same as they were in relation to what was contemplated or reasonably foreseeable at the time of the aiding, abetting, counselling or procuring.

(4) 'Conduct' includes speech.

(5) References to a person, in the context of the harassment of a person, are references to a person who is an individual.

Amendments—Criminal Justice and Police Act 2001, s 44; Serious Organised Crime and Police Act 2005, s 125(7).

****

Senior Courts Act 1981

ARRANGEMENT OF SECTIONS

PART II
JURISDICTION

Section		Page
	The Court of Appeal	
15	General jurisdiction of Court of Appeal	1233
16	Appeals from High Court	1234
17	Applications for new trial	1234
18	Restrictions on appeals to Court of Appeal	1234
	The High Court	
	General jurisdiction	
19	General jurisdiction of High Court	1235
	Other particular fields of jurisdiction	
29	Orders of mandamus, prohibition and certiorari	1236
30	Injunctions to restrain persons from acting in offices in which they are not entitled to act	1237
31	Application for judicial review	1237
31A	Transfer of judicial review applications to Upper Tribunal	1239
	Powers	
37	Powers of High Court with respect to injunctions and receivers	1240
39	Execution of instrument by person nominated by High Court	1243
40	Attachment of debts	1244

40A	Administrative and clerical expenses of garnishees	1244
41	Wards of court	1245
42	Restriction of vexatious legal proceedings	1245
	General Provisions	
	Law and equity	
49	Concurrent administration of law and equity	1246
	Costs	
51	Costs in civil division of Court of Appeal, High Court and county courts	1247
	PART III	
	PRACTICE AND PROCEDURE	
	The High Court	
67	Proceedings in court and in chambers	1248
151	Interpretation of this Act, and rules of construction for other Acts and documents	1249
	Schedule 1 – Distribution of Business in High Court	1250

****

PART II
JURISDICTION

The Court of Appeal

15 General jurisdiction of Court of Appeal

(1) The Court of Appeal shall be a superior court of record.

(2) Subject to the provisions of this Act, there shall be exercisable by the Court of Appeal –

(a) all such jurisdiction (whether civil or criminal) as is conferred on it by this or any other Act; and

(b) all such other jurisdiction (whether civil or criminal) as was exercisable by it immediately before the commencement of this Act.

(3) For all purposes of or incidental to –

(a) the hearing and determination of any appeal to the civil division of the Court of Appeal; and

(b) the amendment, execution and enforcement of any judgment or order made on such an appeal,

the Court of Appeal shall have all the authority and jurisdiction of the court or tribunal from which the appeal was brought.

(4) It is hereby declared that any provision in this or any other Act which authorises or requires the taking of any steps for the execution or enforcement of a judgment or order of the High Court applies in relation to a judgment or order of the civil division of the Court of Appeal as it applies in relation to a judgment or order of the High Court.

Amendments—CRA 2005, Sch 11, para 1.

Scope—This section establishes the general jurisdiction of the Court of Appeal. For the procedural regime governing appeals to the Court of Appeal see Procedural Guide E5.

'for all purposes of or incidental to' (s 15(3))—In relation to the hearing and determination of an appeal, this does not include maintenance pending suit where the appeal is subsequent to decree absolute (see *Cavendish-Bentinck v Cavendish-Bentinck* [1949] P 203, CA).

'all the authority and jurisdiction' (s 15(3))—This includes a power conferred on the High Court after the order being appealed was made (see *Attorney-General v Vernazza* [1960] AC 965, HL).

16 Appeals from High Court

(1) Subject as otherwise provided by this or any other Act (and in particular to the provision in section 13(2)(a) of the Administration of Justice Act 1969 excluding appeals to the Court of Appeal in cases where leave to appeal from the High Court directly to the Supreme Court is granted under Part II of that Act), or as provided by any order made by the Lord Chancellor under section 56(1) of the Access to Justice Act 1999 the Court of Appeal shall have jurisdiction to hear and determine appeals from any judgment or order of the High Court.

(2) An appeal from a judgment or order of the High Court when acting as a prize court shall not be to the Court of Appeal, but shall be to Her Majesty in Council in accordance with the Prize Acts 1864 to 1944.

Amendments—SI 2000/1071; CRA 2005, Sch 9, para 36(3); SI 2016/917.

Scope—Subject to certain exceptions, this section gives the Court of Appeal power to hear any appeal from a High Court judgment or order; for the procedure governing appeals to the Court of Appeal, see CPR 1998, Pt 52. This section must be read in conjunction with CPR 1998, r 52.3 which require permission (leave) to appeal for all appeals save for a few limited exceptions.

'judgment or order'—This phrase includes a decree (SCA 1981, s 151(1)), and a decree absolute of nullity (*Whitehead v Whitehead* [1963] P 117, CA). An appeal cannot be pursued against the reasons for a decision, only against the judgment or order (*Lake v Lake* [1955] P 336, CA), but it is possible to appeal findings of fact made after a split trial (*Re B (Split Hearings: Jurisdiction)* [2000] 1 FLR 334, CA). Appeals against ex parte orders should not be made as they are provisional and expected to be revisited by the court (*WEA Records Ltd v Visions Channel 4 Ltd* [1983] 1 WLR 721, CA).

17 Applications for new trial

(1) Where any cause or matter, or any issue in any cause or matter, has been tried in the High Court, any application for a new trial thereof, or to set aside a verdict, finding or judgment therein, shall be heard and determined by the Court of Appeal except where rules of court made in pursuance of subsection (2) provide otherwise.

(2) As regards cases where the trial was by a judge alone and no error of the court at the trial is alleged, or any prescribed class of such cases, rules of court may provide that any such application as is mentioned in subsection (1) shall be heard and determined by the High Court.

(3) Nothing in this section shall alter the practice in bankruptcy.

Scope—CPR 1998, r 52.10 sets out the powers of the Court of Appeal on hearing an appeal and specifically provides the power to order a new trial or hearing (r 52.10(2)). No rules have been made pursuant to s 17(2). Therefore any application for a new trial must be made to the Court of Appeal (see also *B-T v B-T (Divorce: Procedure)* [1990] 2 FLR 1, FD). It is important to distinguish between orders which are capable of review by the original court: for example ex parte orders (see notes to SCA 1981, s 18), interim orders and orders where there has been an error on the face (which may be corrected in accordance with CPR 1998, r 40.12); and those orders which are covered by this section, where an appeal must be made to obtain a fresh hearing. For the purpose of considering the requirement of permission to appeal under AJA 1999, s 54, an application for a new trial is treated as an appeal to the Court of Appeal.

18 Restrictions on appeals to Court of Appeal

(1) No appeal shall lie to the Court of Appeal –

- (a) except as provided by the Administration of Justice Act 1960, from any judgment of the High Court in any criminal cause or matter;
- (b) from any order of the High Court or any other court or tribunal allowing an extension of time for appealing from a judgment or order;
- (c) from any order, judgment or decision of the High Court or any other court or tribunal which, by virtue of any provision (however expressed) of this or any other Act, is final;
- (d) from a decree absolute of divorce or nullity of marriage, by a party who, having had time and opportunity to appeal from the decree nisi on which that decree was founded, has not appealed from the decree nisi;
- (e), (f) *(repealed)*
- (fa) from a dissolution order, nullity order or presumption of death order under Chapter 2 of Part 2 of the Civil Partnership Act 2004 that has been made final, by a party who, having had time and opportunity to appeal from the conditional order on which that final order was founded, has not appealed from the conditional order;

(g) except as provided by Part I of the Arbitration Act 1996, from any decision of the High Court under that Part;

(h) *(repealed)*

(1A)–(2) *(repealed)*

Amendments—CA 1989, s 108(5), Sch 13, para 45(1); CLSA 1990, s 7(1)–(3), Sch 20; Arbitration Act 1996, s 107(1), Sch 3, para 37(2); Civil Procedure Act 1997, s 10, Sch 2, para 1(1),(2); AJA 1999, s 106, Sch 15; CPA 2004, s 261(1), Sch 27, para 68.

Scope—This section sets out the restrictions which apply to the apparently wide-ranging right of appeal provided by s 16. In most cases, an appeal may be made only with permission (see CPR 1998, r 52.3). There is no appeal against the refusal of permission to appeal by a court below (where the court below would have been exercising an appellate jurisdiction, for example a judge from a district judge, see *Bulled v Khayat and Another* [2002] EWCA Civ 804 and *Slot v Isaac* [2002] EWCA Civ 481).

'extension of time for appealing' (s 18(1)(b))—There is no appeal against an order allowing an extension of time for appealing, but the Court of Appeal does have jurisdiction to hear an appeal against the refusal of an application for an extension of time (*Rickards v Rickards* [1990] Fam 194, CA).

'decree absolute' (s 18(1)(d))—A decree absolute should not be made if there is an appeal pending (*Lloyd-Davies v Lloyd-Davies* [1947] P 53, CA *Everitt v Everitt* [1948] WN 237, CA).

Costs—The Court of Appeal may interfere on an order for costs where the judge has not acted judicially, without exercising his discretion at all or without material with which to exercise his discretion (see *Jones v McKie* [1964] 1 WLR 960, CA; *Hellyer v Sheriff of Yorkshire* [1975] Ch 16, CA; *Alltrans Express Ltd v CVA Holdings Ltd* [1984] 1 WLR 394, CA; *Scherer v Counting Instruments Ltd* [1986] 1 WLR 615, CA; *Taylor v UKF Fertilisers Ltd and Harvey Plant Ltd* (1988) *The Independent*, 14 November, CA). There is a right of appeal where the appeal is genuinely as to other issues (*Crystall v Crystall* [1963] 1 WLR 564, CA), even where the outcome to those other issues is unsuccessful (*Wheeler v Somerfield* [1966] 2 QB 94, CA).

Ex parte orders—The Court of Appeal will not entertain appeals against ex parte orders; the proper course is to apply, if possible to the same judge, to vary or discharge the order (*WEA Records Ltd v Visions Channel 4 Ltd* [1983] 1 WLR 721, CA; *Re P (A Minor) (Ex Parte Interim Residence Order)* [1993] 1 FLR 915, CA).

Consent orders—In *Re R (Contact: Consent Order)* [1995] 1 FLR 123, CA, the Court of Appeal held that, where a mother gave consent to an order for contact after the judge had warned of a risk of costs being ordered against this (being a criticism of the trial judge), such an order was for the Court of Appeal, and not the court of first instance, to set aside (distinguishing *Re F (A Minor) (Custody: Consent Order: Procedure)* [1992] 1 FLR 561, CA). Bad advice is not a good basis to appeal a consent order (*Tibbs v Dick* [1998] 2 FLR 1118, CA).

Permission to appeal—By virtue of AJA 1999, s 54, permission to appeal to the Court of Appeal is required in all cases, save for a few limited exceptions (as prescribed by CPR 1998, r 52.3). The application for permission should be made to the trial judge and, if refused, thereafter to the Court of Appeal. Full details of the procedure are contained within CPR PD52A–PD52E (see Part III).

Finding of fact hearings—Where the lower court refuses to make findings of fact sought by a party, the Court of Appeal has no jurisdiction to entertain an appeal against that decision where the findings of fact sought were not 'pregnant with legal consequences': *Re M (Children)* [2013] EWCA Civ 1170.

In urgent cases where the judge had refused a stay of the order pending the application for permission to appeal, the prospective appellant may telephone the Court of Appeal to apply for a stay (during office hours the telephone number is 0207 947 6000 and out of hours contact is made to the security office at the RCJ on 0207 947 6260, who will refer the matter to the duty deputy master): see CPR PD52C, para 26). A deputy master will refer the matter to a Lord Justice who may grant the stay or list the matter urgently for consideration of the application for a stay (*Re S (Child Proceedings: Urgent Appeals)* [2007] 2 FLR 1044, CA; *Re A (A Child) (Residence Order)* [2007] EWCA Civ 899).

Reopening of final appeals—It is possible, in exceptional circumstances, to reopen a final determination of an appeal to avoid injustice where there is no alternative remedy (see CPR 1998, r 52.17; *Re U (Re-opening of Appeal)* [2005] 2 FLR 444, CA).

The High Court

General jurisdiction

19 General jurisdiction of High Court

(1) The High Court shall be a superior court of record.

(2) Subject to the provisions of this Act, there shall be exercisable by the High Court –

(a) all such jurisdiction (whether civil or criminal) as is conferred on it by this or any other Act; and

(b) all such other jurisdiction (whether civil or criminal) as was exercisable by it immediately before the commencement of this Act (including jurisdiction conferred on a judge of the High Court by any statutory provision).

(3) Any jurisdiction of the High Court shall be exercised only by a single judge of that court, except in so far as it is –

(a) by or by virtue of rules of court or any other statutory provision required to be exercised by a divisional court; or

(b) by rules of court made exercisable by a master, district judge or other officer of the court, or by any other person.

(4) The specific mention elsewhere in this Act of any jurisdiction covered by subsection (2) shall not derogate from the generality of that subsection.

Scope—Subject to the provisions of this Act, s 19(2) prescribes in general terms the jurisdiction of the High Court by defining its statutory and non-statutory jurisdiction. By virtue of s 19(2)(a), the High Court is empowered to exercise all the jurisdiction conferred by this Act or any Act passed after it. Thus, the High Court has jurisdiction as a court of first instance and as a court of appeal from decisions of district judges of the High Court and, as from October 2016, the decisions of circuit judges and recorders in private law proceedings (FPR 2010, Pt 30 and PD30A, as amended).

High Court—For the constitution and divisions of the High Court, see s 4 et seq.

'all such other jurisdiction' (s 19(2)(b))—Subject to the provisions of this Act, the High Court has retained all such jurisdiction, whether statutory or otherwise, which was exercisable by it immediately before the commencement of this Act. This includes the 'inherent jurisdiction' of the court, which has been exercisable by the superior court from the earliest days of the common law.

Inherent jurisdiction—The exercise of the court's powers under its inherent jurisdiction is unrestricted and unlimited, except where it has been specifically curtailed by statute. It is derived from the very nature of the court as a superior court of law and not from any statute or rule of law. It invests the court with power to maintain its authority and, as a reserve or residual source of power, to deal with and act effectively on any matter when it is just and equitable to do so. It can be exercised summarily, and may be invoked by or against any person, irrespective of whether they are party to the proceedings. Examples of situations where, in recent years, the court has assumed and exercised its inherent jurisdiction and made orders and declarations, and given directions, include cases relating to the administration or withdrawal of medical treatment, particularly in cases where the sterilisation of an adult mentally disabled person is considered necessary, and in cases of persistent vegetative state (PVS).

Writ ne exeat regno—The provisions of s 19(2)(b) subsume the High Court's jurisdiction to grant this prerogative writ, whereby a person may be prevented from leaving the jurisdiction of the court. Before the writ may be granted, the relevant conditions set out in Debtors Act 1869, s 6 must be satisfied: the applicant must show that he has a good cause of action against the defendant for a substantial award; there must be strong evidence for believing that the defendant is about to leave England unless he is arrested; and there must be evidence that the defendant's absence would materially prejudice the applicant in the prosecution of his case. It should be noted, however, that the issue of the writ is discretionary, and the standard and burden of proof imposed on the applicant is extremely high. The court will require convincing evidence, so that it can be sure that it is right to grant the writ. It will not generally be granted as an ancillary remedy to enforce a *Mareva* injunction or an *Anton Piller* order (see *Allied Arab Bank Ltd v Hajjar* [1988] QB 787, QBD and *Al Nahkel for Contracting and Trading v Lowe* [1986] QB 235, QBD). The relief was granted in *Thaha v Thaha* [1987] 2 FLR 142, FD by reason of the particular facts of the case. For a fuller consideration of the issue concerning the writ, see *Felton v Callis* [1969] 1 QB 200, QBD and *Emergency Remedies in the Family Courts* (Family Law). After judgment, an injunction restraining movement out of the jurisdiction cannot be made as a freestanding enforcement measure but must be linked to another measure and be time limited: *B v B (Injunction: Restraint on Leaving Jurisdiction)* [1997] 2 FLR 148, FD; *Bhura v Bhura* [2013] 2 FLR 44, FD.

Impounding of a respondent's passport—The exercise of the power to impound a passport is discussed in *Young v Young* [2012] 2 FLR 470, FD where Mostyn J sets out the relevant principles at [26].

****

Other particular fields of jurisdiction

****

29 Orders of mandamus, prohibition and certiorari

(1) The orders of mandamus, prohibition and certiorari shall be known instead as mandatory, prohibiting and quashing orders respectively.

(1A) The High Court shall have jurisdiction to make mandatory, prohibiting and quashing orders in those classes of case in which, immediately before 1 May 2004, it had jurisdiction to make orders of mandamus, prohibition and certiorari respectively.

(2) Every such order shall be final, subject to any right of appeal therefrom.

(3), (3A) …

(4) The power of the High Court under any enactment to require justices of the peace or a judge or officer of the county court to do any act relating to the duties of their respective offices, or to require a magistrates' court to state a case for the opinion of the High Court, in any case where the High Court formerly had by virtue of any enactment jurisdiction to make a rule absolute, or an order, for any of those purposes, shall be exercisable by mandatory order.

(5), (6) …

Amendments—Armed Forces Act 2001, s 23; SI 2004/1033; CCA 2013, s 17, Sch 9.

Scope—The procedure for an application for judicial review is contained within CPR 1998, Pt 54. In judicial review proceedings, the court can grant a mandatory order (formerly mandamus), a prohibiting order (formerly prohibition) or a quashing order (formerly certiorari) (SCA 1981, s 31(1), CPR 1998, r 54.2); it also has power to grant declarations and injunctions (SCA 1981, s 31, CPR 1998, r 54.3). Under SCA 1981, s 31 and CPR 1998, r 54.3, an application for a mandatory order, a prohibiting order or a quashing order must be by way of an application for judicial review; however, a declaration or injunction may be obtained in proceedings for judicial review or in other proceedings.

30 Injunctions to restrain persons from acting in offices in which they are not entitled to act

(1) Where a person not entitled to do so acts in an office to which this section applies, the High Court may –

- (a) grant an injunction restraining him from so acting; and
- (b) if the case so requires, declare the office to be vacant.

(2) This section applies to any substantive office of a public nature and permanent character which is held under the Crown or which has been created by any statutory provision or royal charter.

Scope—An application under this section must be made by way of judicial review in accordance with the provisions of CPR 1998, Pt 54. The application may be made in conjunction with an application for any prerogative order, i e a mandatory, prohibiting or quashing order (CPR 1998, r 54.3).

31 Application for judicial review

(1) An application to the High Court for one or more of the following forms of relief, namely –

- (a) a mandatory, prohibiting or quashing order;
- (b) a declaration or injunction under subsection (2); or
- (c) an injunction under section 30 restraining a person not entitled to do so from acting in an office to which that section applies,

shall be made in accordance with rules of court by a procedure to be known as an application for judicial review.

(2) A declaration may be made or an injunction granted under this subsection in any case where an application for judicial review, seeking that relief, has been made and the High Court considers that, having regard to –

- (a) the nature of the matters in respect of which relief may be granted by mandatory, prohibiting or quashing orders;
- (b) the nature of the persons and bodies against whom relief may be granted by such orders; and
- (c) all the circumstances of the case,

it would be just and convenient for the declaration to be made or for the injunction to be granted, as the case may be.

(2A) The High Court –

- (a) must refuse to grant relief on an application for judicial review, and
- (b) may not make an award under subsection (4) on such an application,

if it appears to the court to be highly likely that the outcome for the applicant would not have been substantially different if the conduct complained of had not occurred.

(2B) The court may disregard the requirements in subsection (2A)(a) and (b) if it considers that it is appropriate to do so for reasons of exceptional public interest.

(2C) If the court grants relief or makes an award in reliance on subsection (2B), the court must certify that the condition in subsection (2B) is satisfied.

(3) No application for judicial review shall be made unless the leave of the High Court has been obtained in accordance with rules of court; and the court shall not grant leave to make such an application unless it considers that the applicant has a sufficient interest in the matter to which the application relates.

(3C) When considering whether to grant leave to make an application for judicial review, the High Court –

(a) may of its own motion consider whether the outcome for the applicant would have been substantially different if the conduct complained of had not occurred, and
(b) must consider that question if the defendant asks it to do so.

(3D) If, on considering that question, it appears to the High Court to be highly likely that the outcome for the applicant would not have been substantially different, the court must refuse to grant leave.

(3E) The court may disregard the requirement in subsection (3D) if it considers that it is appropriate to do so for reasons of exceptional public interest.

(3F) If the court grants leave in reliance on subsection (3E), the court must certify that the condition in subsection (3E) is satisfied.

(4) On an application for judicial review the High Court may award to the applicant damages, restitution or the recovery of a sum due if –

(a) the application includes a claim for such an award arising from any matter to which the application relates; and
(b) the court is satisfied that such an award would have been made if the claim had been made in an action begun by the applicant at the time of making the application.

(5) If, on an application for judicial review, the High Court quashes the decision to which the application relates, it may in addition –

(a) remit the matter to the court, tribunal or authority which made the decision, with a direction to reconsider the matter and reach a decision in accordance with the findings of the High Court; or
(b) substitute its own decision for the decision in question.

(5A) But the power conferred by subsection (5)(b) is exercisable only if –

(a) the decision in question was made by a court or tribunal;
(b) the decision is quashed on the ground that there has been an error of law; and
(c) without the error, there would have been only one decision which the court or tribunal could have reached.

(5B) Unless the High Court otherwise directs, a decision substituted by it under subsection (5)(b) has effect as if it were a decision of the relevant court or tribunal.

(6) Where the High Court considers that there has been undue delay in making an application for judicial review, the court may refuse to grant –

(a) leave for the making of the application; or
(b) any relief sought on the application,

if it considers that the granting of the relief sought would be likely to cause substantial hardship to, or substantially prejudice the rights of, any person or would be detrimental to good administration.

(7) Subsection (6) is without prejudice to any enactment or rule of court which has the effect of limiting the time within which an application for judicial review may be made.

(8) In this section 'the conduct complained of', in relation to an application for judicial review, means the conduct (or alleged conduct) of the defendant that the applicant claims justifies the High Court in granting relief.

Amendments—SI 2004/1033; Tribunals, Courts and Enforcement Act 2007, s 141; Criminal Justice and Courts Act 2015, s 84 (subject to transitional provisions).

Scope—All applications for judicial review must be made in accordance with CPR 1998, Pt 54. CPR 1998, r 54.2 states that the procedure of judicial review must be used where the claimant is seeking a mandatory order (mandamus), a prohibiting order (prohibition), a quashing order (certiorari), or an injunction (under SCA 1981 restraining a person acting in an office in which he is not entitled). Further, r 54.3 provides that judicial review may also be used to claim a declaration or an injunction. The remedies, other than damages, may be claimed as alternatives or in addition to any other relief (CPR 1998, r 54.3). An application for judicial review may proceed only after permission has been granted (SCA 1981, s 31; CPR 1998, r 54.4).

There is an overlap between the supervisory jurisdiction of the High Court in judicial review proceedings and the inherent jurisdiction of the High Court to make orders in respect of children and incompetent adults. Where the court's task is to come to a decision for and on behalf of the child or incompetent adult, their welfare should be the court's paramount consideration and hence the inherent jurisdiction rather than judicial review would be the most appropriate procedure (*A (A Patient) v A Health Authority* [2002] 1 FLR 845, FD). For the interplay between judicial review and CA 1989, Pt III see *Re T* [2004] 1 FLR 601, QBD, *CF v The Secretary of State of the Home Department* [2004] 2 FLR 517, FD and *Re S and W (Care Proceedings)* [2007] 2 FLR 275, CA.

Where there is a right of appeal to the Care Standards Tribunal, judicial review is not appropriate (*R (M) v London Borough of Bromley* [2002] 2 FLR 802, CA). Judicial review is limited to a review of the local authority decision and not to a detailed examination of the evidence.

'just and convenient' (s 31(2))—The High Court has power to grant a declaration or injunction on an application for judicial review. Unlike the prerogative orders (mandatory, prohibiting or quashing orders), a declaration or injunction is available not only on an application for judicial review, but may also be obtained in other proceedings (CPR 1998, r 54.3).

'sufficient interest' (s 31(3))—The applicant for judicial review must have sufficient interest in the matter to which the application relates in order to proceed. 'Mere busybodies do not have sufficient interest' (*Inland Revenue Commissioners v Federation of Self-employed and Small Businesses Ltd* [1982] AC 617, HL, at [108B]; see also *Council of Civil Service Unions v Minister for the Civil Service* [1985] AC 374, HL, at [949F]).

'undue delay' (s 31(6))—If the court considers that there has been undue delay in making the application, it may refuse leave to move for judicial review. This provision must be read in conjunction with the time limitations imposed by CPR 1998, r 54.5, namely that the application must be made promptly and in any event within three months from the date when the grounds for the application first arose and the time limit cannot be extended by agreement of the parties.

31A Transfer of judicial review applications to Upper Tribunal

(1) This section applies where an application is made to the High Court –

(a) for judicial review, or

(b) for permission to apply for judicial review.

(2) If Conditions 1, 2 and 3 are met, the High Court must by order transfer the application to the Upper Tribunal.

(2A) *(repealed)*

(3) If Conditions 1, and 2 are met, but Condition 3 is not, the High Court may by order transfer the application to the Upper Tribunal if it appears to the High Court to be just and convenient to do so.

(4) Condition 1 is that the application does not seek anything other than –

(a) relief under section 31(1)(a) and (b);

(b) permission to apply for relief under section 31(1)(a) and (b);

(c) an award under section 31(4);

(d) interest;

(e) costs.

(5) Condition 2 is that the application does not call into question anything done by the Crown Court.

(6) Condition 3 is that the application falls within a class specified under section 18(6) of the Tribunals, Courts and Enforcement Act 2007.

(7), (8) *(repealed)*

Amendments—Inserted by Tribunals, Courts and Enforcement Act 2007, s 19(1). Amended by Borders, Citizenship and Immigration Act 2009, s 53; CCA 2013, s 22.

★★★★

Powers

★★★★

37 Powers of High Court with respect to injunctions and receivers

(1) The High Court may by order (whether interlocutory or final) grant an injunction or appoint a receiver in all cases in which it appears to the court to be just and convenient to do so.

(2) Any such order may be made either unconditionally or on such terms and conditions as the court thinks just.

(3) The power of the High Court under subsection (1) to grant an interlocutory injunction restraining a party to any proceedings from removing from the jurisdiction of the High Court, or otherwise dealing with, assets located within that jurisdiction shall be exercisable in cases where that party is, as well as in cases where he is not, domiciled, resident or present within that jurisdiction.

(4), (5) …

(6) This section applies in relation to the family court as it applies in relation to the High Court.

Amendments—CCA 2013, s 17, Sch 10.

Scope—This section restates the law governing the power of the court to grant injunctions and/or to appoint receivers. It does not fetter the court's powers (*Motorola Credit Corp v Uzan* (No 2) [2004] 1 WLR 113, CA). However, HRA 1998 requires a marginally higher threshold test in applications for interlocutory injunctions (*Imutran Ltd v Uncaged Campaigns* [2001] 2 All ER 385, ChD).

'whether interlocutory or final' (s 37(1))—These words confirm the practice which existed before the Act, and do not restrict the power to grant an injunction after judgment to assist in the process of enforcement. Thus, in family cases, an injunction can be obtained to prevent a respondent from disposing of assets to defeat enforcement (see *Orwell Steel (Erection and Fabrication) Ltd v Asphalt and Tarmac (UK) Ltd* [1984] 1 WLR 1097, QBD; *Roche v Roche* (1981) Fam Law 243, CA; *Shipman v Shipman* [1991] 1 FLR 250, FD).

Court's power to grant 'Freezing injunctions' and 'Search orders'—For clarification, see Civil Procedure Act 1997, s 7.

'Search order'—A search order is provided for by CPR 1998, r 25.1(1)(h). It is an interlocutory order which achieves disclosure and protection of documentary and real evidence. It was described by Lord Denning MR as a 'search warrant' (*Anton Piller KG v Manufacturing Processes Ltd* [1976] Ch 55, CA). *Imerman v Tchenguiz and Others* [2010] 2 FLR 814, CA, in holding that there is no right to 'self-help' in family cases, also held that the remedy where another party is likely to suppress relevant documents is to apply for a search order (see per Lord Neuberger MR, at [128]–[135]). An order is usually sought without notice. The search order is usually accompanied by a freezing injunction freezing the defendant's bank accounts and restraining any disposition of assets (see **Freezing injunctions** below). In matrimonial proceedings, it is very much an order of last resort, where all other methods of seeking the necessary information have failed. For example, where a wife maintained that her husband had failed to make full disclosure of his financial position and that he was a man of substantial means and had secreted his assets abroad, the court was prepared to make a search order (*Kepa v Kepa* (1983) 4 FLR 515, FD). Where a party to matrimonial proceedings seeks documents which are not themselves the subject matter of the proceedings, the Family Division still has jurisdiction to grant a search order provided that the applicant has a strong prima facie case that the relevant documents are essential for the case and are at serious risk of being removed or destroyed (*Emanuel v Emanuel* [1982] 1 WLR 669, FD). The order may permit a search of the defendant's premises and seizure of documents or other items found there which might form evidence in the applicant's action or proposed action against the defendant. The procedure must not be used oppressively. In *Burgess v Burgess* [1996] 2 FLR 34, CA, the husband obtained a search order, but the search yielded no relevant evidence; he was ordered to pay the wife's costs on the indemnity basis, and the court reiterated that, in family proceedings, search orders are to be used only in extreme or exceptional circumstances; see further the judgment of Mostyn J in *UL v BK* [2013] EWHC 1735 (Fam), where he criticised inappropriate applications.

Procedure for search order—Interim remedies in family proceedings are governed by FPR 2010, Pt 20. Rule 20.2 expressly refers to a 'search order' (r 20.2(1)(h)); see Pt 20 and the commentary thereon, in particular PD20A, which explains the procedure in detail.

Effect of search order—The search order is a draconian remedy and should be used with the utmost caution. An order made without notice must be given the earliest practicable return day. The court considering whether or not to make the order must strike a balance between the applicant's need for a remedy for a breach of his civil rights and the requirements of justice that a defendant should not be deprived of his property without being heard (*Columbia Picture Industries v Robinson* [1987] Ch 38, ChD). The order must contain a provision for the defendant to apply to vary or discharge the order, even though this will be of little immediate value because, when the order is served, he is under an obligation to allow entry and search of his premises and removal of the documents and items specified in the order. If he fails to comply, he risks the sanction of a committal order for contempt of court (*Wardle Fabrics Ltd v G Myristis Ltd* [1984] FSR 263, ChD). For the form of search order see the Annex to CPR PD25A in Part III.

Duty of disclosure—The applicant is under a duty to make a full and frank disclosure to the court in his affidavit in support of an application for a search order (*Lock International plc v Beswick* [1989] 1 WLR 1268,

ChD), even where the material comes to his knowledge after the order was obtained (*O'Regan v Iambic Productions Ltd* (1989) 139 NLJ 1378, HC). Failure to do so is likely to lead to the order being discharged without consideration of the merits (*Manor Electronics Ltd v Dickson* [1988] RPC 618, QBD) and refusal of a fresh order (*Arena Corp Ltd v Schroeder* [2003] EWHC 1089 (Ch)).

Safeguards for interests of defendant—See FPR PD20A. The order must be served by a 'supervising solicitor' and carried out in their presence and under their supervision. The supervising solicitor should be an experienced solicitor, having some familiarity with the operation of search orders, who is not a member or employee of the firm acting for the applicant. The evidence in support of the application should include the identity and experience of the proposed supervising solicitor.

Search and seizure of documents and articles—Where a search order is executed at business premises, it should be conducted by the supervising solicitor named in the order, and it should be carried out in the presence of the defendant or a person appearing to be a responsible employee of the defendant. The order may only be served on a weekday between 9.30 am and 5.30 pm. When the supervising solicitor and the applicant's solicitor attend at the premises to execute the order, the defendant (or any other person appearing to be in control of the premises) may seek legal advice, and may apply to the court to vary or discharge the order, provided they do so at once. See FPR PD20A.

Discharge of search order—An application for variation or discharge of a search order must be made immediately to the court that made the order. It should be made on notice (*Hallmark Cards Inc v Image Arts Ltd* [1977] FSR 150, CA). The application should be accompanied by sworn evidence. So far as practicable, any application for the discharge or variation of the order should be dealt with effectively on the inter partes return date. If the order is discharged on the return date, the judge should always consider whether it is appropriate to assess damages at once and direct immediate payment by the applicant. It is not possible to appeal against the order until the application to set aside has been made and refused (*WEA Records Ltd v Visions Channel 4 Ltd* [1983] 1 WLR 721, CA).

Jurisdiction (s 37(3))—Interlocutory applications for freezing injunctions and directions as to dealing with assets outside the jurisdiction should generally be dealt with in the High Court. However, the County Court does now have power to grant freezing orders as CCRR 2014 restrict only its power to grant search orders.

Freezing injunctions (s 37(3))—Section 37(3) embodies in statute the practice explained in *Mareva Compania Naviera SA v International Bulk Carriers SA* [1980] 1 All ER 213, CA. Initially, the practice was confined to cases where there was a risk of assets being transferred abroad but the practice of granting freezing injunctions has been extended to cover any situation where there are grounds for believing that the defendant may transfer or dissipate assets, whether inside or outside the jurisdiction, with a view to defeating the applicant's claim. See the judgment of Mostyn J in *UL v BK* [2013] EWHC 1735 (Fam), where he explains the principles relating to freezing orders and expresses concern at the widespread abuse of without notice applications.

Procedure for freezing injunctions—Interim remedies in family proceedings are governed by FPR 2010, Pt 20. Rule 20.2(1)(f) expressly refers to a 'freezing injunction'. See Pt 20 and the commentary thereon, in particular PD20A, which explains the procedure in detail.

Principles on which a freezing injunction is made—'It is an absolutely elementary tenet of English law that save in an emergency a court should hear both sides before giving a ruling. The only recognised exception to this rule ... is where there is a well-founded belief that the giving of notice would lead to irretrievable prejudice being caused to the applicant for relief' (*FZ v SZ and Others (Ancillary Relief: Conduct: Valuations)* [2011] 1 FLR 64, FD, at [32]). The principles on which a freezing injunction is made were clearly set out by Lord Denning MR in *Third Chandris Shipping Corporation v Unimarine SA* [1979] QB 645, CA. They include a duty on the applicant to make full and frank disclosure of all matters in his knowledge which are material for the judge to know. If material non-disclosure is established at a later stage, the court has a discretion to discharge the order. (See, for example, *ND v KP (Freezing Order: Ex Parte Application)* [2011] 2 FLR 662, FD, where the order was discharged.) The applicant must make proper inquiries before making the application, and this duty applies to any additional facts he would have known if he had made such inquiries (*Bank Mellat v Nikpour* [1985] FSR 87, CA). The applicant must give particulars of his claim against the respondent, stating his grounds and the amount involved, and fairly state the points made against the applicant by the respondent. The applicant must depose to some grounds for believing that there is a risk of the assets being removed or dissipated before the judgment or award is satisfied (*Z Ltd v A-Z and AA-LL* [1982] QB 558, CA). As without notice freezing orders are granted on the basis of urgency and on the basis that notice would defeat the ends of justice it is inappropriate to warn of the possibility of such an order by a letter before action. Indeed such a warning might defeat the application (*Oaktree Financial Services Ltd v Higham* [2004] EWHC 2098 (Ch)). The applicant must give an undertaking in damages in case he fails in his claim or the injunction turns out to have been unjustified. The undertakings to be given by the applicant are set out in FPR PD20A. An applicant should be required, in an appropriate case, to support his cross-undertaking in damages by a payment into court or the provision of a bond by an insurance company. Alternatively, the judge may order a payment by way of such security to the applicant's solicitor to be held by the solicitor as an officer of the court pending further order. (If a freezing injunction is discharged on the return date, the judge should always consider whether it is appropriate for him to assess damages at once and direct immediate payment by the applicant). Where the injunction affects third parties, the applicant may have to give an undertaking to indemnify those third parties against all expenses reasonably incurred in complying with the order. These elementary principles are explained by Mostyn J in *UL v BK* [2013] EWHC 1735 (Fam).

Matrimonial disputes—In addition to the principles set out above, in a matrimonial case an injunction should not extend to all the assets of the other party because it is unlikely that the applicant would be awarded all the assets. Thus the injunction should be limited to the size of the fund reasonably regarded as being in issue. For example, in *Paulin v Paulin* [2009] 2 FLR 354, CA, the wife obtained a specific order that the matrimonial home was not to be disposed of or charged and a freezing order against the husband's assets up to £4m. In *FZ v SZ* *and Others (Ancillary Relief: Conduct: Valuations)* [2011] 1 FLR 64, FD, Mostyn J said: 'I have been shocked by the volume of spurious ex parte applications that are made in the urgent applications list'. In *ND v KP (Freezing Order: Ex Parte Application)* [2011] 2 FLR 662, FD, the same judge set aside an ex parte freezing order for lack of candour in the application. But see also *Peyman-Fard v Peyman-Fard* [2011] EWCA Civ 959, where a sentence of imprisonment was upheld on a husband who had paid a sum to his sister in breach of a freezing order obtained during ancillary relief proceedings. Where an order is made requiring payment of a lump sum, the injunctive and receivership powers in s 37 can be used to make it effective. In *(1) Blight (2) Meredith (3) Lewis v Brewster* [2012] BPIR 476, ChD, the debtor was required to delegate to the judgment creditor's solicitor power to elect to receive a lump sum from a pension fund. In *O'Farrell v O'Farrell* [2013] 1 FLR 77, QBD, a freezing order was made to preserve a sum equal to the judgment made in German divorce proceedings.

Form of freezing injunction—FPR PD20A explains what the order must do but, unlike CPR PD25A, does not contain a specimen order. The standard order may need to be modified, eg to restrain transactions diminishing the value of the respondent's shares (*Group Seven Ltd v Allied Investment Corp Ltd* [2014] 1 WLR 735, ChD). The injunction may, in its widest form, include an order that the respondent disclose all his assets, which include chattels and choses in action (*CBS UK Ltd v Lambert* [1983] Ch 37, CA; *Z Ltd v A-Z and AA-LL* [1982] QB 558, CA), but at the inter partes hearing the court may consider whether the disclosure order against the respondent should be discharged (*Arab Monetary Fund v Hashim* [1989] 1 WLR 565, ChD). There is no general rule that a party against whom a freezing order is made is entitled to a stay or the disclosure obligations ancillary to that order until after it has been finally determined whether the freezing order should stand (*Motorola Credit Corp v Uzan* [2004] 1 WLR 113, CA). Where appropriate, and especially where the injunction relates to the rights of third parties, the injunction should extend to the specified maximum amount claimed by the applicant. Where there is a risk of the respondent disposing of money owed to him, the court may, with the approval of the creditor, order that sum to be paid into court or into an account frozen by the injunction (*Bank Mellat v Kazmi* [1989] QB 541, CA). The injunction takes effect, from the moment it is made, in respect of every asset of the respondent covered by the order. It is desirable to fix a return date when the continuation can be considered inter partes and third parties can have the opportunity to be heard. The order must be carefully drafted so as to make clear the date on which the order begins and ends. Where the court is concerned with injunctions imposing serious restrictions on the activities of litigants, the 'slip rule' will be invoked to remedy a defect in the order only in exceptional circumstances (*Langley v Langley* [1994] 1 FLR 383, CA). Because of its Draconian effect, the injunction must be clear and unequivocal and is strictly construed in favour of the respondent (see *JSC BTA Bank v Ablyazov* [2015] EWCA Civ 70). Although the language of the standard freezing order is evolving to meet new avoidance measures, the order must be clear and unambiguous. Suggested precedents are annexed to the judgment of Mostyn J in *UL v BK (Freezing Orders: safeguards: Standard Examples)* [2013] EWHC 1735 (Fam).

Notice of freezing injunction—Notice of the injunction should be given to banks and other financial institutions, where it is believed that the respondent has assets, and they must do what they can to preserve such assets; otherwise, they risk being in contempt of court. The applicant must give to the bank as much detail as possible about the account number, branch number and so forth. The specimen order set out in CPR PD25A contains a clause which provides that the injunction does not prevent any bank from exercising any right of set-off it may have in respect of any facility which it gave to the respondent before it was notified of the order, and this proviso should be included where appropriate (*Oceanica Castelana Armadora SA v Mineralimportexport, The Theotokos* [1983] 1 WLR 1302, CA). The bank is entitled to apply for a variation to enable it to exercise any right of facilities granted before it receives notice of the injunction and, in order to save court time, a proviso to that effect should be included in the injunction (*Oceanica Castelana Armadora SA v Mineralimportexport, The Theotokos*).

Respondent's access to assets—The respondent should be allowed access to sums for his normal living expenses, and the injunction should specify these. Those sums may include sums for medical expenses and legal expenses where appropriate. In *Zakharov v White* [2003] EWHC 2463 (Ch), because of the respondent's lack of frankness at an earlier hearing, the court revisited its previous order and inserted provisions more strictly policing his ability to spend.

Assets outside the jurisdiction—By virtue of CJJA 1982, s 25(1), it is clear that a freezing injunction can cover assets worldwide, even though the respondent is outside the jurisdiction (*Babanaft International Co SA v Bassatne* [1990] Ch 13, CA; *Republic of Haiti and Others v Duvaliers and Others* [1990] 1 QB 202, CA), provided that the personal effect of such an order is limited to the particular respondents against whom it was granted. A worldwide injunction will only be granted in exceptional circumstances and should be subject to strict undertakings and provisos to prevent the injunction from being more oppressive to the respondent than beneficial to the applicant. The specimen order contained in CPR PD25A should be used for an injunction to prevent the disposal of assets worldwide. The specimen order contains the undertakings to be given to the court by the applicant.

Limitations—A freezing injunction should not be granted unless the applicant can show a substantial case for saying that, unless it is granted, there will be a serious risk of the assets which might otherwise be available to meet judgment being dissipated (*Behbehani v Salem (Note)* [1989] 1 WLR 723, CA). Other pending proceedings against the respondent are relevant (*Jarvis Field Press v Chelton* [2003] EWHC 2674 (Ch)). In *Kanev-Lipinski v Aharon Lipinski* [2016] EWHC 475 (QB), May J refused to continue a freezing order over the husbands' assets.

Undertaking in lieu of injunction—At an inter partes hearing, the application can be compromised by an undertaking. The parties must be clear as to whether the application is disposed of or simply adjourned. This affects the right to apply for discharge or variation (see *Emailgen Systems Corp v Exclaimer Ltd & Anor* [2013] EWHC 167 (Comm)).

Contempt of court—Disobedience of a freezing order is a contempt of court. See further CCA 1981. The court has power to commit for up to 2 years and/or impose an unlimited fine. (See, for example, *W v W* [2011] 2 FLR 1268, FD – 1 year's imprisonment for Swedish banker suspended on terms including immediate payment.) In *Raja v Van Hoogstraten* [2004] EWCA Civ 968, it was held to be inconsistent with ECHR 1950, Art 6 for a judge to proceed with an effective hearing of an application to commit in circumstances where he knew the alleged contemnor wished to be heard in person but was prevented from being present by matters over which he had no control. The court should be astute to detect when contempt proceedings are not being pursued for legitimate aims. Adverse costs orders may follow where claimants bring disproportionate contempt applications (*PJSC Vseukrainskyi v Aktsionernyi Bank* [2014] EWHC 3771 (Comm)).

No jurisdiction to grant freezing injunctions in support of enforcement of assessments under CSA 1991—The High Court has no jurisdiction to grant a freezing injunction in support of, and as ancillary to, the enforcement procedure for maintenance assessments provided for by CSA 1991 (*Department of Social Security v Butler* [1996] 1 FLR 65, CA).

'or otherwise dealing with' (s 37(3))—These words include disposing of, selling or charging (see *CBS UK Ltd v Lambert* [1983] Ch 37, CA).

Writ ne exeat regno—This writ cannot be issued for the purpose of enforcing a freezing injunction (see further under s 19 above).

Impounding of a passport—The power to impound a respondent's passport is addressed in *Young v Young* [2012] 2 FLR 470, FD: see [26] for principles. Also, see s 19.

Section 46 LRA 2002—This section enables the court, for the purpose of protecting a right or claim in relation to a registered estate or charge, to make an order requiring a restriction to be entered in the register. The order may include a direction that the entry is to have overriding priority. It may be appropriate to obtain this order ancillary to a freezing order.

Appeals—Permission to appeal to the Court of Appeal from an order granting or refusing an interlocutory injunction is required pursuant to CPR 1998, r 52.3.

****

39 Execution of instrument by person nominated by High Court

(1) Where the High Court or family court has given or made a judgment or order directing a person to execute any conveyance, contract or other document, or to indorse any negotiable instrument, then, if that person –

(a) neglects or refuses to comply with the judgment or order; or
(b) cannot after reasonable inquiry be found,

that court may, on such terms and conditions, if any, as may be just, order that the conveyance, contract or other document shall be executed, or that the negotiable instrument shall be indorsed, by such person as the court may nominate for that purpose.

(2) A conveyance, contract, document or instrument executed or indorsed in pursuance of an order under this section shall operate, and be for all purposes available, as if it had been executed or indorsed by the person originally directed to execute or indorse it.

Amendments—CCA 2013, s 17, Sch 10.

'directing a person to execute' (s 39(1))—The person must of course be identified in the order, and he must have been ordered to execute a document, not merely (for example) to transfer a property. If an order has been made in the latter form, it is necessary first to secure an order requiring execution of the relevant document before an order can be made under this section.

'neglects or refuses' (s 39(1)(a))—In the case of neglect or refusal, this section provides a cheaper, more effective and less draconian remedy than an application to commit. If this ground is relied on it must be shown that the Respondent is aware of the order but personal service is not mandatory. It is normally required that he has been given the opportunity to execute the document, but not if it is patent that he refuses and will continue to refuse to do so (*Savage v Norton* [1908] 1 Ch 290, ChD).

'such person as the court may nominate' (s 39(1))—Any person may be nominated, but it is frequently the district judge (who may, it seems, nominate himself). The nominee signs not 'on behalf of' the respondent but merely pursuant to the order.

'as if it had been executed … by the person originally directed' (s 39(2))—The nominee assumes no personal liability under the document.

County court—The same power is exercised by the County Court by virtue of CCA 1984, s 38.

Procedure—Normally the application is made by summons or on notice to the district judge (FPR 2010, r 18.1). If the respondent cannot be found (and has no solicitor on record), the application will usually be made without notice, unless (rarely) the court directs substituted service (eg by advertisement).

Alternative procedure—Where what is sought to be achieved is the transfer of a property from one party to another, it may be possible to avoid the expense and inconvenience of preparing a document for signature, obtaining an order that the transferor sign it, obtaining an order under this section and then having the document signed by the named person. The court can be asked instead to make an order under Trustee

Act 1925, s 44(vii), vesting the property in the transferee. If such an order is available, it may be particularly appropriate where the whereabouts of the transferor are unknown or his co-operation otherwise seems unlikely.

40 Attachment of debts

(1) Subject to any order for the time being in force under subsection (4), this section applies to any deposit account, and any withdrawable share account, with a deposit-taker.

(2) In determining whether, for the purposes of the jurisdiction of the High Court to attach debts for the purpose of satisfying judgments or orders for the payment of money, a sum standing to the credit of a person in an account to which this section applies is a sum due or accruing to that person and, as such, attachable in accordance with rules of court, any condition mentioned in subsection (3) which applies to the account shall be disregarded.

(3) Those conditions are –

- (a) any condition that notice is required before any money or share is withdrawn;
- (b) any condition that a personal application must be made before any money or share is withdrawn;
- (c) any condition that a deposit book or share-account book must be produced before any money or share is withdrawn; or
- (d) any other prescribed condition.

(4) The Lord Chancellor may by order make such provision as he thinks fit, by way of amendment of this section or otherwise, for all or any of the following purposes, namely –

- (a) including in, or excluding from, the accounts to which this section applies accounts of any description specified in the order;
- (b) excluding from the accounts to which this section applies all accounts with any particular deposit-taker so specified or with any deposit-taker of a description so specified.

(5) Any order under subsection (4) shall be made by statutory instrument subject to annulment in pursuance of a resolution of either House of Parliament.

(6) 'Deposit-taker' means a person who may, in the course of his business, lawfully accept deposits in the United Kingdom.

(7) Subsection (6) must be read with –

- (a) section 22 of the Financial Services and Markets Act 2000;
- (b) any relevant order under that section; and
- (c) Schedule 2 to that Act.

Amendments—Banking Act 1987, s 108(1), Sch 6, para 11; SI 2001/3649.

Scope—This section extends the availability of third party debt order proceedings to bank and building society accounts which would otherwise not be vulnerable to such an order because of conditions attached to their operation (see CPR 1998, Pt 72 and particularly r 72.2(3)).

40A Administrative and clerical expenses of garnishees

(1) Where an interim third party debt order made in the exercise of the jurisdiction mentioned in subsection (2) of the preceding section is served on a deposit-taker, it may, subject to the provision of this section, deduct from the relevant debt or debts an amount not exceeding the prescribed sum towards its administrative and clerical expenses in complying with the order; and the right to make a deduction under this subsection shall be exercisable as from the time the interim third party debt order is served on it.

(1A) In subsection (1) 'the relevant debt or debts', in relation to an interim third party debt order served on a deposit-taker, means the amount, as at the time the order is served on it, of the debt or debts of which the whole or a part is expressed to be attached by the order.

(1B) A deduction may be made under subsection (1) in a case where the amount referred to in subsection (1A) is insufficient to cover both the amount of the deduction and the amount of the judgment debt and costs in respect of which the attachment was made, notwithstanding that the benefit of the attachment to the creditor is reduced as a result of the deduction.

(2) An amount may not in pursuance of subsection (1) be deducted or, as the case may be, retained in a case where, by virtue of section 346 of the Insolvency Act 1986 or section 183 of the Insolvency Act 1986 or otherwise, the creditor is not entitled to retain the benefit of the attachment.

(3) In this section –

'deposit-taker' has the meaning given by section 40(6); and

'prescribed' means prescribed by an order made by the Lord Chancellor.

(4) An order under this section –

(a) may make different provision for different cases;
(b) without prejudice to the generality of paragraph (a) of this subsection, may prescribe sums differing according to the amount due under the judgment or order to be satisfied;
(c) may provide for this section not to apply to deposit-takers of any prescribed description.

(5) Any such order shall be made by statutory instrument subject to annulment in pursuance of a resolution of either House of Parliament.

Amendments—Inserted by AJA 1982, s 55, Sch 4, Pt I. Amended by AJA 1985, s 52; Companies Consolidation (Consequential Provisions) Act 1985, s 30, Sch 2; Insolvency Act 1986, s 439(2), Sch 14; SI 2001/3649; SI 2002/439.

'the prescribed sum' (s 40A(1))—The current sum is £55: SI 1996/3098.

41 Wards of court

(1) Subject to the provisions of this section, no minor shall be made a ward of court except by virtue of an order to that effect made by the High Court.

(2) Where an application is made for such an order in respect of a minor, the minor shall become a ward of court on the making of the application, but shall cease to be a ward of court at the end of such period as may be prescribed unless within that period an order has been made in accordance with the application.

(2A) Subsection (2) does not apply with respect to a child who is the subject of a care order (as defined by section 105 of the Children Act 1989).

(3) The High Court may, either upon an application in that behalf or without such an application, order that any minor who is for the time being a ward of court shall cease to be a ward of court.

Amendments—CA 1989, s 108(5), Sch 13, para 45(2).

Defined terms—'minor': FLRA 1969, s 1.

Applications without notice—The court has the power to grant injunctions and emergency orders before the application is issued (*Re N (Infants) (No 2)* [1967] Ch 512, ChD). Applications without notice before the issue of proceedings should be used only as a matter of emergency (*Re O (Proposed Wardship Proceedings)* [1990] FCR 599, FD). Where an application without notice is made before the issue of the substantive application on undertakings given to file the process, although the child becomes a ward when proceedings are issued, it is essential that the court is asked at that stage to confirm the wardship, particularly if the emergency that occasioned the issue of the wardship has been adequately protected by the judge's order or the emergency has passed.

42 Restriction of vexatious legal proceedings

(1) If, on an application made by the Attorney General under this section, the High Court is satisfied that any person has habitually and persistently and without any reasonable ground –

(a) instituted vexatious civil proceedings, whether in the High Court or the family court or any inferior court, and whether against the same person or against different persons; or
(b) made vexatious applications in any civil proceedings, whether in the High Court or the family court or any inferior court, and whether instituted by him or another, or
(c) instituted vexatious prosecutions (whether against the same person or different persons),

the court may, after hearing that person or giving him an opportunity of being heard, make a civil proceedings order, a criminal proceedings order or an all proceedings order.

(1A) In this section –

'civil proceedings order' means an order that –

(a) no civil proceedings shall without the leave of the High Court be instituted in any court by the person against whom the order is made;

(b) any civil proceedings instituted by him in any court before the making of the order shall not be continued by him without the leave of the High Court; and

(c) no application (other than one for leave under this section) shall be made by him, in any civil proceedings instituted in any court by any person, without the leave of the High Court;

'criminal proceedings order' means an order that –

(a) no information shall be laid before a justice of the peace by the person against whom the order is made without the leave of the High Court; and

(b) no application for leave to prefer a bill of indictment shall be made by him without the leave of the High Court; and

'all proceedings order' means an order which has the combined effect of the two other orders.

(2) An order under subsection (1) may provide that it is to cease to have effect at the end of a specified period, but shall otherwise remain in force indefinitely.

(3) Leave for the institution or continuance of, or for the making of an application in, any civil proceedings by a person who is the subject of an order for the time being in force under subsection (1) shall not be given unless the High Court is satisfied that the proceedings or application are not an abuse of the process of the court in question and that there are reasonable grounds for the proceedings or application.

(3A) Leave for the laying of an information or for an application for leave to prefer a bill of indictment by a person who is the subject of an order for the time being in force under subsection (1) shall not be given unless the High Court is satisfied that the institution of the prosecution is not an abuse of the criminal process and that there are reasonable grounds for the institution of the prosecution by the applicant.

(4) No appeal shall lie from a decision of the High Court refusing leave required by virtue of this section.

(5) A copy of any order made under subsection (1) shall be published in the London Gazette.

Amendments—Prosecution of Offences Act 1985, s 24; CCA 2013, s 17, Sch 10.

'civil proceedings ... in the High Court or any inferior court' (s 42(1)(a))—The term 'civil proceedings' is not defined by SCA 1981; nor is there an obvious definition elsewhere. Civil proceedings are any proceedings which are not criminal.

Vexatious litigant—Section 42 enables the Attorney-General to apply to the High Court where a 'person has habitually and persistently and without reasonable ground instituted vexatious civil proceedings'. The court has the power to make a 'civil proceedings order', which prevents issue of further proceedings, stays any continuing proceedings and prevents any application by the defendant in any existing proceedings, without permission. In *Attorney-General v Barker* [2000] 1 FLR 759, QBD, Div Ct) suggested that the main characteristic of a vexatious litigant is that his applications have little or no basis in law; their effect is to subject the respondents to harassment, inconvenience and expense, and abuses the process of the court. In such circumstances, a s 42 order may be justified.

Civil restraint orders and orders under CA 1989, s 91(14)—Orders under s 42 are to be contrasted with civil restraint orders (see FPR 2010, r 4.8) and from orders under CA 1989, s 91(14).

****

General Provisions

Law and equity

49 Concurrent administration of law and equity

(1) Subject to the provisions of this or any other Act, every court exercising jurisdiction in England or Wales in any civil cause or matter shall continue to administer law and equity on the basis that, wherever there is any conflict or variance between the rules of equity and the rules of the common law with reference to the same matter, the rules of equity shall prevail.

(2) Every such court shall give the same effect as hitherto –

(a) to all equitable estates, titles, rights, reliefs, defences and counterclaims, and to all equitable duties and liabilities; and

(b) subject thereto, to all legal claims and demands and all estates, titles, rights, duties, obligations and liabilities existing by the common law or by any custom or created by any statute,

and, subject to the provisions of this or any other Act, shall so exercise its jurisdiction in every cause or matter before it as to secure that, as far as possible, all matters in dispute between the parties are completely and finally determined, and all multiplicity of legal proceedings with respect to any of those matters is avoided.

(3) Nothing in this Act shall affect the power of the Court of Appeal or the High Court to stay any proceedings before it, where it thinks fit to do so, either of its own motion or on the application of any person, whether or not a party to the proceedings.

Scope—This section provides for courts to act as courts of law and equity. The principle that equity prevails relates to substantive law and not practice (*La Grange v McAndrew* (1879) 4 QBD 210). The court has an inherent jurisdiction to stay any proceedings which are an abuse of its powers (see *Hinckley and South Leicestershire Permanent Benefit Building Society v Freeman* [1941] Ch 32, ChD).

****

Costs

51 Costs in civil division of Court of Appeal, High Court and county courts

(1) Subject to the provisions of this or any other enactment and to rules of court, the costs of and incidental to all proceedings in –

(a) the civil division of the Court of Appeal;

(b) the High Court;

(ba) the family court; and

(c) the county court,

shall be in the discretion of the court.

(2) Without prejudice to any general power to make rules of court, such rules may make provision for regulating matters relating to the costs of those proceedings including, in particular, prescribing scales of costs to be paid to legal or other representatives or for securing that the amount awarded to a party in respect of the costs to be paid by him to such representatives is not limited to what would have been payable by him to them if he had not been awarded costs.

(3) The court shall have full power to determine by whom and to what extent the costs are to be paid.

(4) In subsections (1) and (2) 'proceedings' includes the administration of estates and trusts.

(5) Nothing in subsection (1) shall alter the practice in any criminal cause, or in bankruptcy.

(6) In any proceedings mentioned in subsection (1), the court may disallow, or (as the case may be) order the legal or other representative concerned to meet, the whole of any wasted costs or such part of them as may be determined in accordance with rules of court.

(7) In subsection (6), 'wasted costs' means any costs incurred by a party –

(a) as a result of any improper, unreasonable or negligent act or omission on the part of any legal or other representative or any employee of such a representative; or

(b) which, in the light of any such act or omission occurring after they were incurred, the court considers it is unreasonable to expect that party to pay.

(8) Where –

(a) a person has commenced proceedings in the High Court; but

(b) those proceedings should, in the opinion of the court, have been commenced in the county court or family court in accordance with any provision made under section 1 of the Courts and Legal Services Act 1990 or by or under any other enactment, the person responsible for determining the amount which is to be awarded to that person by way of costs shall have regard to those circumstances.

(9) Where, in complying with subsection (8), the responsible person reduces the amount which would otherwise be awarded to the person in question –

(a) the amount of that reduction shall not exceed 25 per cent; and

(b) on any taxation of the costs payable by that person to his legal representative, regard shall be had to the amount of the reduction.

(10) The Lord Chancellor may by order amend subsection (9)(a) by substituting, for the percentage for the time being mentioned there, a different percentage.

(11) Any such order shall be made by statutory instrument and may make such transitional or incidental provision as the Lord Chancellor considers expedient.

(12) No such statutory instrument shall be made unless a draft of the instrument has been approved by both Houses of Parliament.

(13) In this section 'legal or other representative', in relation to a party to proceedings, means any person exercising a right of audience or right to conduct litigation on his behalf.

Amendments—CLSA 1990, s 4(1); AJA 1999, s 31; CCA 2013, s 17, Schs 9, 10.

Rules of court—The general rule, prescribed by CPR 1998, r 44.2 is that the unsuccessful party pays the costs of the successful party. This provision is specifically disapplied in relation to family appeals (by CPR 1998, r 44.2(3)). The court has a discretion as to costs and when exercising that discretion must have regard to the conduct of the parties, the success of the appeal and attempts or offers to settle the matter (r 44.2). The Supreme Court held that where it is reasonable that allegations of misconduct to a child should be investigated by a court 'justice does not demand that the local authority responsible for placing the allegations before the court should ultimately be responsible for the legal costs of the person against whom the allegations are made': *Re T (Costs: Care Proceedings: Serious Allegation Not Proved)* [2013] 1 FLR 133, SC, at [42] and see also *Re S (A Child) (Costs: Care Proceedings)* [2015] 2 FLR 208, SC.

Wasted costs orders—These orders are dealt with by CPR 1998, r 44.11.

Third party costs orders—See under CPR 1998, r 44.3.

****

PART III
PRACTICE AND PROCEDURE

****

The High Court

****

67 Proceedings in court and in chambers

Business in the High Court shall be heard and disposed of in court except in so far as it may, under this or any other Act, under rules of court or in accordance with the practice of the court, be dealt with in chambers.

Exercise of the court's discretion as to whether a hearing should take place in open court or in chambers—This section does not provide a statutory basis for making a direction that a particular hearing should be held in chambers. However, it was held in *Scott v Scott* (1913) FLR Rep 657, HL that, although business conducted in the High Court should normally be by way of public hearing to secure that justice is done, the court has jurisdiction in matrimonial proceedings to decide whether or not a particular hearing should be in chambers or in open court, where the case falls within the three exceptions identified by Viscount Haldane LC, that is to say: (i) wards; (ii) lunatics (in each of which the court is sitting primarily to safeguard the interests of the ward or lunatic); and (iii) litigation in respect of a secret process where the effect of publicity would be to destroy the subject matter. However, *Scott* (above) cannot be taken to prevent or restrict the enactment of rules for regulating the trial of family proceedings and there is no objection to hearing family cases in private and excluding the public where the rules permit it (*Clibbery v Allan and Another* [2002] 1 FLR 565, CA). In exercising its discretion in this matter, the court must conduct a balancing exercise between the genuine public interest in the case in holding the hearing in open court, and the competing interest of those people concerned in the case who seek the protection of a hearing in chambers (*Re G (Adult Patient: Publicity)* [1995] 2 FLR 528, FD – where an adult patient was maintained on life support machines in a persistent vegetative state, the court decided that the genuine public interest in the decision as to whether or not to allow the hospital to discontinue the life-sustaining treatment required that the hearing should be held in open court, but with safeguards to protect the positions and anonymity of the relatives, doctors and nursing staff involved). The general rule is that it is not a contempt of court to report what happened in a hearing in chambers unless AJA 1960, s 12 applies, or the case comes within the recognised categories of children or ancillary relief cases, or the administration of justice would otherwise be impeded or prejudiced by publication (*Clibbery v Allan and Another* [2002] 1 FLR 565, CA). See further under CCA 1981, s 11 and AJA 1960, s 12.

Attendance of the media—See the notes to AJA 1960, s 12.

****

151 Interpretation of this Act, and rules of construction for other Acts and documents

(1) In this Act, unless the context otherwise requires –

'action' means any civil proceedings commenced by writ or in any other manner prescribed by rules of court;

'appeal', in the context of appeals to the civil division of the Court of Appeal, includes –

(a) an application for a new trial, and

(b) an application to set aside a verdict, finding or judgment in any cause or matter in the High Court which has been tried, or in which any issue has been tried, by a jury;

'arbitration agreement' has the same meaning as it has in Part I of the Arbitration Act 1996;

'cause' means any action or any criminal proceedings;

'Division', where it appears with a capital letter, means a division of the High Court;

'judgment' includes a decree;

'jurisdiction' includes powers;

'matter' means any proceedings in court not in a cause;

'party', in relation to any proceedings, includes any person who pursuant to or by virtue of rules of court or any other statutory provision has been served with notice of, or has intervened in, those proceedings;

'prescribed' means –

(a) except in relation to fees, prescribed by rules of court;

(b) *(repealed)*

'qualifying judge advocate' means –

(a) the Judge Advocate General; or

(b) a person appointed under section 30(1)(a) or (b) of the Courts-Martial (Appeals) Act 1951 (assistants to the Judge Advocate General);

'senior judge', where the reference is to the senior judge of a Division, means the president of that Division;

'solicitor' means a solicitor of the Senior Courts;

'statutory provision' means any enactment, whenever passed, or any provision contained in subordinate legislation (as defined in section 21(1) of the Interpretation Act 1978), whenever made;

'this or any other Act' includes an Act passed after this Act.

(2) Section 128 contains definitions of expressions used in Part V and in the other provisions of this Act relating to probate causes and matters.

(3) Any reference in this Act to rules of court under section 84 includes a reference to rules of court in relation to the Supreme Court under any provision of this or any other Act which confers on the Civil Procedure Rule Committee or the Crown Court Rule Committee power to make rules of court.

(4) Except where the context otherwise requires, in this or any other Act –

'divisional court' (with or without capital letters) means a divisional court constituted under section 66;

'judge of the Senior Courts' means –

(a) a judge of the Court of Appeal other than an ex-officio judge within paragraph (b) or (c) of section 2(2), or

(b) a judge of the High Court,

and accordingly does not include, as such, a judge of the Crown Court;

'official referees' business' has the meaning given by section 68(6);

(5) The provisions of Schedule 4 (construction of references to superseded courts and officers) shall have effect.

Amendments—CLSA 1990, s 125(3), Sch 18, para 41; Arbitration Act 1996, s 107(1), Sch 3, para 37(1), (3); Civil Procedure Act 1997, s 10, Sch 2, para 2(1),(7); Courts Act 2003, s 109(1), (3), Sch 8, para 265, Sch 10; SI 2004/2035; CRA 2005, s 15(1), Sch 4, paras 114, 146, Sch 11, para 26(2); Armed Forces Act 2011, s 26, Sch 2, para 5.

SCHEDULE 1
DISTRIBUTION OF BUSINESS IN HIGH COURT

****

3 Family Division

To the Family Division are assigned –

(a) all matrimonial causes and matters (whether at first instance or on appeal);

(aa) applications for a writ of habeas corpus for release relating to a minor;

(b) all causes and matters (whether at first instance or on appeal) relating to –

  (i) legitimacy;

  (ii) the exercise of the inherent jurisdiction of the High Court with respect to minors, the maintenance of minors and any proceedings under the Children Act 1989, except proceedings solely for the appointment of a guardian of a minor's estate;

  (iii) adoption;

  (iv) non-contentious or common form probate business;

(c) applications for consent to the marriage of a minor or for a declaration under section 27B(5) of the Marriage Act 1949;

(d) *(repealed)*

(e) applications under Part III of the Family Law Act 1986;

(e) proceedings under the Children Act 1989;

(ea) proceedings under section 79 of the Childcare Act 2006;

…

(ec) proceedings under Part 6 of the Social Services and Well-being (Wales) Act 2014;

(f) all proceedings under –

  (i) Part IV or 4A of the Family Law Act 1996;

  (ii) the Child Abduction and Custody Act 1985;

  (iii) the Family Law Act 1986;

  (iv) section 30 of the Human Fertilisation and Embryology Act 1990;

  (v) Council Regulation (EC) No 2201/2003 of 27 November 2003 concerning jurisdiction and the recognition and enforcement of judgments in matrimonial matters and matters of parental responsibility, so far as that Regulation relates to jurisdiction, recognition and enforcement in parental responsibility matters;

  (vi) the Convention on Jurisdiction, Applicable Law, Recognition, Enforcement and Co-Operation in respect of Parental Responsibility and Measures for the Protection of Children that was signed at The Hague on 19 October 1996;

(fa) all proceedings relating to a debit or credit under section 29(1) or 49(1) of the Welfare Reform and Pensions Act 1999;

(g) all proceedings for the purpose of enforcing an order made in any proceedings of a type described in this paragraph;

(h) all proceedings under the Child Support Act 1991;

(ha) all proceedings under Part 1 of Schedule 2 to the Female Genital Mutilation Act 2003;

(i) all civil partnership causes and matters (whether at first instance or on appeal);

(j) applications for consent to the formation of a civil partnership by a minor or for a declaration under paragraph 7 of Schedule 1 to the Civil Partnership Act 2004;

(k) applications under section 58 of that Act (declarations relating to civil partnerships).

(l) proceedings under Regulation (EU) No 606/2013 of the European Parliament and of the

Council of 12 June 2013 on mutual recognition of protection measures in civil matters, so far as relating to the recognition and enforcement in England and Wales of a protection measure (within the meaning of that Regulation) ordered in a Member State other than the United Kingdom.

Amendments—Marriage (Prohibited Degrees of Relationship) Act 1986, s 5; FLA 1986, s 68(1), Sch 1, para 26; FLRA 1987, s 33(4), Sch 4; CA 1989, ss 92(11), 108(5), Sch 11, para 9, Sch 13, para 45(3); SI 1991/1210; SI 1993/622; FLA 1996, s 66(1), Sch 8, para 51; WRPA 1999, s 84(1), Sch 12, para 1; CPA 2004, s 261(1), Sch 27, para 70; SI 2005/265; Childcare Act 2006, Sch 2, para 3; Forced Marriage (Civil Protection) Act 2007, s 3(1), Sch 2, para 1; SI 2010/1898; CCA 2013, s 17, Sch 10; ;SI 2014/3257; SI 2014/3298; Serious Crime Act 2015, s 85, Sch 4, para 5; SI 2016/413.

Two sub-paragraphs (e)—A sub-paragraph (e) was inserted by FLA 1986, but the draftsman of the insertion made by CA 1989 seems to have been unaware of it; it is submitted that the words of amendment in CA 1989, Sch 11, para 9 ('In paragraph 3 … the following sub-paragraph shall be added at the end – (e)') mean that the second (e) has not inadvertently been substituted for the first (e), but merely added after it, so that both paragraphs (e) are fully effective, albeit that they inconveniently have the same name.

Two references to CA 1989—CA 1989 is referred to in both (b)(ii) and (the second) (e). This seems to have been simply a proverbial case of the 'left hand and the right hand', as the two references were inserted by different provisions of CA 1989 (Sch 13, para 45 and Sch 11, para 9, respectively). The result is overkill but nothing more; although (b)(ii) more obviously includes appeals from proceedings under the Act, it would seem that the effect of each reference is identical.

****

Social Security Administration Act 1992

ARRANGEMENT OF SECTIONS

Section		Page
78	Recovery of social fund awards	1251
106	Recovery of expenditure on benefit from person liable for maintenance	1252
108	Reduction of expenditure on income support: certain maintenance orders to be enforceable by the Secretary of State	1252
191	Interpretation – general	1254

****

78 Recovery of social fund awards

(1)–(5) …

(6) For the purposes of this section –

(a) a man shall be liable to maintain his wife or civil partner and any children of whom he is the father;

(b) a woman shall be liable to maintain her husband or civil partner and any children of whom she is the mother;

(c) a person shall be liable to maintain another person throughout any period in respect of which the first-mentioned person has, on or after 23 May 1980 (the date of the passing of the Social Security Act 1980) and either alone or jointly with a further person, given an undertaking in writing in pursuance of immigration rules within the meaning of the Immigration Act 1971 to be responsible for the maintenance and accommodation of the other person; and

(d) 'child' includes a person who has attained the age of 16 but not the age of 19 and in respect of whom either parent, or some person acting in the place of either parent, is receiving universal credit, income support or an income-based jobseeker's allowance.

(7) Any reference in subsection (6) above to children of whom the man or the woman is the father or the mother shall be construed in accordance with section 1 of the Family Law Reform Act 1987.

(8) Subsection (7) above does not apply in Scotland, and in the applications of subsection (6) above to Scotland any reference to children of whom the man or the woman is the father or the mother shall be construed as a reference to any such children whether or not their parents have ever been married to one another.

(9) A document bearing a certificate which –

- (a) is signed by a person authorised in that behalf by the Secretary of State; and
- (b) states that the document apart from the certificate is, or is a copy of, such an undertaking as is mentioned in subsection (6)(c) above,

shall be conclusive of the undertaking in question for the purposes of this section; and a certificate purporting to be so signed shall be deemed to be so signed until the contrary is proved.

Amendments—Jobseekers Act 1995, s 41, Sch 2, para 51; CPA 2004, s 254(1), Sch 24, para 61(1)–(4); WRA 2012, s 31, Sch 2, para 9.

****

106 Recovery of expenditure on benefit from person liable for maintenance

(1) Subject to the following provisions of this section, if income support or universal credit is claimed by or in respect of a person whom another person is liable to maintain or paid to or in respect of such a person, the Secretary of State may make an application against the liable person to the family court for an order under this section.

(2) On the hearing of an application under this section the court shall have regard to all the circumstances and, in particular, to the income of the liable person, and may order him to pay such sum, weekly or otherwise, as it may consider appropriate, except that in a case falling within section 78(6)(c) above that sum shall not include any amount which is not attributable to income support or universal credit (whether paid before or after the making of the order).

(3) In determining whether to order any payments to be made in respect of income support or universal credit for any period before the application was made, or the amount of any such payments, the court shall disregard any amount by which the liable person's income exceeds the income which was his during that period.

(4) Any payments ordered to be made under this section shall be made –

- (a) to the Secretary of State in so far as they are attributable to any income support or universal credit (whether paid before or after the making of the order);
- (b) to the person claiming income support or universal credit or (if different) the dependant; or
- (c) to such other person as appears to the court expedient in the interests of the dependant.

(5) *(repealed)*

(6) In the application of this section to Scotland, for the references to the family court there shall be substituted references to the sheriff.

(7) *(repealed)*

Amendments—CMOPA 2008, s 58, Sch 8; Welfare Reform Act 2012, s 31, Sch 2, para 11; CCA 2013, s 17, Sch 11.
Defined terms—'child', 'liable to maintain': s 78(6).

107 *(repealed)*

108 Reduction of expenditure on income support: certain maintenance orders to be enforceable by the Secretary of State

(1) This section applies where –

- (a) a person ('the claimant') who is the parent of one or more children is in receipt of income support or universal credit either in respect of those children or in respect of both himself and those children; and
- (b) there is in force a maintenance order made against the other parent ('the liable person') –
  - (i) in favour of the claimant or one or more of the children, or

(ii) in favour of some other person for the benefit of the claimant or one or more of the children;

and in this section 'the primary recipient' means the person in whose favour that maintenance order was made.

(2) If, in a case where this section applies, the liable person fails to comply with any of the terms of the maintenance order –

(a) the Secretary of State may bring any proceedings or take any other steps to enforce the order that could have been brought or taken by or on behalf of the primary recipient; and

(b) any court before which proceedings are brought by the Secretary of State by virtue of paragraph (a) above shall have the same powers in connection with those proceedings as it would have had if they had been brought by the primary recipient.

(3) The Secretary of State's powers under this section are exercisable at his discretion and whether or not the primary recipient or any other person consents to their exercise; but any sums recovered by virtue of this section shall be payable to or for the primary recipient, as if the proceedings or steps in question had been brought or taken by him or on his behalf.

(4) The powers conferred on the Secretary of State by subsection (2)(a) above include power –

(a) to apply for the registration of the maintenance order under –
  (i) section 17 of the Maintenance Orders Act 1950;
  (ii) section 2 of the Maintenance Orders Act 1958; or
  (iii) the Civil Jurisdiction and Judgments Act 1982;

(aa) to apply for recognition and enforcement of the maintenance order under the Maintenance Regulation, to the extent permitted by Article 64 of that Regulation;

(ab) to apply for recognition and enforcement of the maintenance order under the Convention on the International Recovery of Child Support and other forms of Family Maintenance done at The Hague on 23 November 2007, to the extent permitted by Article 36 of that Convention; and

(b) to make an application under section 2 of the Maintenance Orders (Reciprocal Enforcement) Act 1972 (application for enforcement in reciprocating country).

(5) Where this section applies, the prescribed person shall in prescribed circumstances give the Secretary of State notice of any application –

(a) to alter, vary, suspend, discharge, revoke, revive or enforce the maintenance order in question; or

(b) to remit arrears under that maintenance order;

and the Secretary of State shall be entitled to appear and be heard on the application.

(6) Where, by virtue of this section, the Secretary of State commences any proceedings to enforce a maintenance order, he shall, in relation to those proceedings, be treated for the purposes of any enactment or instrument relating to maintenance orders as if he were a person entitled to payment under the maintenance order in question (but shall not thereby become entitled to any such payment).

(7) Where, in any proceedings under this section in England and Wales, the court makes an order for the whole or any part of the arrears due under the maintenance order in question to be paid as a lump sum, the Secretary of State shall inform the Lord Chancellor of the amount of that lump sum if he knows –

(a) that the primary recipient either –
  (i) received legal aid under the Legal Aid Act 1974 in connection with the proceedings in which the maintenance order was made, or
  (ii) was an assisted party, within the meaning of the Legal Aid Act 1988, in those proceedings, or
  (iii) received services funded by the Legal Services Commission as part of the Community Legal Service; or

PART II

(iv) was provided with civil legal services (within the meaning of Part 1 of the Legal Aid, Sentencing and Punishment of Offenders Act 2012) under arrangements made for the purposes of that Part of that Act; and

(b) that a sum remains unpaid on account of the contribution required of the primary recipient –

(i) under section 9 of the Legal Aid Act 1974 in respect of those proceedings, or

(ii) under section 16 of the Legal Aid Act 1988 in respect of the costs of his being represented under Part IV of that Act in those proceedings, or

(iii) by virtue of section 10 of the Access to Justice Act 1999 in respect of services funded by the Legal Services Commission as part of the Community Legal Service, or

(iv) under regulations under section 23 or 24 of the Legal Aid, Sentencing and Punishment of Offenders Act 2012 in respect of civil legal services (within the meaning of Part 1 of that Act) provided under arrangements made for the purposes of that Part of that Act,

as the case may be.

(8) In this section 'maintenance order' –

(a) in England and Wales, means –

(i) any order for the making of periodical payments which is, or has at any time been, a maintenance order within the meaning of the Attachment of Earnings Act 1971;

(ii) any order under Part 3 of the Matrimonial and Family Proceedings Act 1984 (overseas divorce) for the making of periodical payments;

(iii) any order under Schedule 7 to the Civil Partnership Act 2004 for the making of periodical payments;

(b) in Scotland, means any order, except an order for the payment of a lump sum, falling within the definition of 'maintenance order' in section 106 of the Debtors (Scotland) Act 1987, but disregarding paragraph (h) (alimentary bond or agreement).

(9) In this section 'the Maintenance Regulation' means Council Regulation (EC) No 4/2009 including as applied in relation to Denmark by virtue of the Agreement made on 19 October 2005 between the European Community and the Kingdom of Denmark.

Amendments—AJA 1999, s 24, Sch 4, para 48; SI 2001/3929, SI 2007/1655; CMOPA 2008, s 57(1), Sch 7, para 2(1); SI 2011/1484; LASPOA 2012, s 39, Sch 5, para 41; Welfare Reform Act 2012, s 31, Sch 2, para 12; SI 2012/2814.

Defined terms—'claimant': s 191.

Note—The Legal Aid Agency replaced the Legal Services Commission on 1 April 2013.

****

191 Interpretation – general

In this Act, unless the context otherwise requires –

...

'claim' is to be construed in accordance with 'claimant';

'claimant' (in relation to contributions under Part I and to benefit under Parts II to IV of the Contributions and Benefits Act) means –

(a) a person whose right to be excepted from liability to pay, or to have his liability deferred for, or to be credited with, a contribution, is in question;

(b) a person who has claimed benefit;

and includes, in relation to an award or decision a beneficiary under the award or affected by the decision;

'claimant' (in relation to industrial injuries benefit) means a person who has claimed such a benefit and includes –

(a) an applicant for a declaration under section 44 above that an accident was or was not an industrial accident; and

(b) in relation to an award or decision, a beneficiary under the award or affected by the decision;

…

★★★★

Solicitors Act 1974

★★★★

73 Charging orders

(1) Subject to subsection (2), any court in which a solicitor has been employed to prosecute or defend any suit, matter or proceedings may at any time –

(a) declare the solicitor entitled to a charge on any property recovered or preserved through his instrumentality for his assessed costs in relation to that suit, matter or proceeding; and

(b) make such orders for the assessment of those costs and for raising money to pay or for paying them out of the property recovered or preserved as the court thinks fit;

and all conveyances and acts done to defeat, or operating to defeat, that charge shall, except in the case of a conveyance to a bona fide purchaser for value without notice, be void as against the solicitor.

(2) No order shall be made under subsection (1) if the right to recover the costs is barred by any statute of limitations.

Amendments—Legal Services Act 2007, s 177, Sch 16, paras 1, 68.

Origin of the charge—Like the legal aid statutory charge under LASPOA 2012, s 25, the charge under Solicitors Act 1974, s 73 is a statutory re-working of the equitable remedy of the solicitor's lien on property recovered or retained through his/her instrumentality – that is, the solicitor's work on the case in question. The same principles as to when the charge operates apply (see LASPOA 2012, s 25(1): **'a first charge on any property recovered or preserved'**). Under LASPOA 2012, s 25, the charge arises by operation of statute, whereas under Solicitors Act 1974, s 73 the solicitor must seek a declaration from the court, and the court has a discretion whether to make the declaration.

Section 73 and a *Sears Tooth* assignment—Practitioners may find it as straightforward to rely on s 73, rather than go to the trouble of a *Sears Tooth* assignment (*Sears Tooth v Payne Hicks Beach* [1997] 2 FLR 116, FD; and see under MCA 1973, s 22ZA(4)).

Declaration of a charge—Given the case-law surrounding the subject (see, for example, the old editions of *Cordery* (the modern looseleaf leaves out the case-law)), it seems likely that the declaration is an on notice matter (as between solicitor and paying party). The procedure implied by s 73(1) requires the court, if it is to grant the declaration to:

- assert the existence of the charge;
- deal with, or release appropriately (perhaps to a costs judge), assessment of the solicitors' bill;
- Case manage the question of 'raising money to pay or for paying [the costs] out of the property' charged.

The charge—The charge should be registered immediately (where the property to be charged comes within Charging Orders Act 1979, s 2), since if a client disposes of the property to a bona fide purchaser for value before registration, the solicitor's security will be lost. Upon the application being made, a pending action application can be made (the court can be asked to make an interim charging order: FPR 2010, Pt 40, Ch 2). This can be made absolute upon final assessment of costs.

Anti-evasion provisions—Provisions for preventing evasion of the charge (cf *Manley v Law Society* [1981] 1 WLR 335, CA) include:

- the proviso to s 73(1) above;
- the common law requirement (per legal aid regulations) that any third party, knowing of the charge who seeks to assist a paying party to evade it may take over that paying party's liability (*Khans Solicitors (a Firm) v Chifuntwe* [2014] 1 WLR 1185, CA).

Barrister's fees—Barristers do not apparently have the same right to a charge, but can be presumed to have such through their instructing solicitors. This may prove a problem for direct access barristers.

Procedure—No procedure is prescribed in, for example, CPR 1998 or FPR 2010. The parties are the solicitor and his/her (former) client. The application relates to business that is confidential as between them (ie not to any other party to the former proceedings). It is therefore suggested that the appropriate court process is a freestanding declaration application (Solicitors Act 1974 proceedings are not 'family proceedings': application cannot be under FPR 1991) under CPR 1998, Pt 8, as follows:

- Issue of CPR 1998, Pt 8 application with Pt 23 application and draft order for district judge to make (CPR 1998, r 23.8(c));
- The order is in terms akin to COA 1979, s 1 and should be registered at the first opportunity (where land was recovered or preserved and is to be charged);

PART II

- Include in the order a paragraph for a provisional detailed assessment, activated only if the paying party (former client) gives notice to the court within a specified time of service;
- Provisional directions (as with the previous point) for raising the money to pay the amount due under the declaration.

Property—Property is likely to be any property, real or personalty, within the terms of European Convention 1950, Art 1 (Protection of property) in the First Protocol (Human Rights Act 1998, Sch 1, Pt II).

****

Surrogacy Arrangements Act 1985

1 Meaning of 'surrogate mother', 'surrogacy arrangement' and other terms

(1) The following provisions shall have effect for the interpretation of this Act.

(2) 'Surrogate mother' means a woman who carries a child in pursuance of an arrangement –

(a) made before she began to carry the child, and

(b) made with a view to any child carried in pursuance of it being handed over to, and parental responsibility being met (so far as practicable) by, another person or other persons.

(3) An arrangement is a surrogacy arrangement if, were a woman to whom the arrangement relates to carry a child in pursuance of it, she would be a surrogate mother.

(4) In determining whether an arrangement is made with such a view as is mentioned in subsection (2) above regard may be had to the circumstances as a whole (and, in particular, where there is a promise or understanding that any payment will or may be made to the woman or for her benefit in respect of the carrying of any child in pursuance of the arrangement, to that promise or understanding).

(5) An arrangement may be regarded as made with such a view though subject to conditions relating to the handing over of any child.

(6) A woman who carries a child is to be treated for the purposes of subsection (2)(a) above as beginning to carry it at the time of the insemination or of the placing in her of an embryo, of an egg in the process of fertilisation or of sperm and eggs as the case may be, that results in her carrying the child.

(7) 'Body of persons' means a body of persons corporate or unincorporate.

(7A) 'Non-profit making body' means a body of persons whose activities are not carried on for profit.

(8) 'Payment' means payment in money or money's worth.

(9) This Act applies to arrangements whether or not they are lawful.

Amendments—CA 1989, s 108(5), Sch 13, para 56; HFEA 1990, s 36; SI 1995/755; HFEA 2008, s 59(2).

Surrogacy arrangement—The arrangement/agreement must be made before the surrogate mother begins to carry the child and made with a view to any child carried in pursuance of it being handed over and parental responsibility being met by another person or other persons especially where circumstances of the commissioning parties change: see *DM & LK v SJ & OJ* [2016] EWHC 270 (Fam) and **Agreement of the mother and any other person who is a parent of the child** under HFEA 2008, s 54.

1A Surrogacy arrangements unenforceable

No surrogacy arrangement is enforceable by or against any of the persons making it.

Amendments—Inserted by HFEA 1990, s 36.

Surrogacy arrangements unenforceable—See *Re TT (Surrogacy)* [2011] 2 FLR 392, FD, where the surrogate mother who had agreed to hand over the child to the couple changed her mind during the pregnancy and refused to hand over the child. On the application of the father for a residence order of the child the court granted the order to the mother. See *Re Z (Surrogacy Agreements: Child Arrangements Orders)* [2017] 1 FLR 946, FD and the commentary to HFEA 2008.

2 Negotiating surrogacy arrangements on a commercial basis etc

(1) No person shall on a commercial basis do any of the following acts in the United Kingdom, that is –

(a) initiate any negotiations with a view to the making of a surrogacy arrangement,
(aa) take part in any negotiations with a view to the making of a surrogacy arrangement,
(b) offer or agree to negotiate the making of a surrogacy arrangement, or
(c) compile any information with a view to its use in making, or negotiating the making of, surrogacy arrangements;

and no person shall in the United Kingdom knowingly cause another to do any of those acts on a commercial basis.

(2) A person who contravenes subsection (1) above is guilty of an offence; but it is not a contravention of that subsection –

(a) for a woman, with a view to becoming a surrogate mother herself, to do any act mentioned in that subsection or to cause such an act to be done, or
(b) for any person, with a view to a surrogate mother carrying a child for him, to do such an act or to cause such an act to be done.

(2A) A non-profit making body does not contravene subsection (1) merely because –

(a) the body does an act falling within subsection (1)(a) or (c) in respect of which any reasonable payment is at any time received by it or another, or
(b) it does an act falling within subsection (1)(a) or (c) with a view to any reasonable payment being received by it or another in respect of facilitating the making of any surrogacy arrangement.

(2B) A person who knowingly causes a non-profit making body to do an act falling within subsection (1)(a) or (c) does not contravene subsection (1) merely because –

(a) any reasonable payment is at any time received by the body or another in respect of the body doing the act, or
(b) the body does the act with a view to any reasonable payment being received by it or another person in respect of the body facilitating the making of any surrogacy arrangement.

(2C) Any reference in subsection (2A) or (2B) to a reasonable payment in respect of the doing of an act by a non-profit making body is a reference to a payment not exceeding the body's costs reasonably attributable to the doing of the act.

(3) For the purposes of this section, a person does an act on a commercial basis (subject to subsection (4) below) if –

(a) any payment is at any time received by himself or another in respect of it, or
(b) he does it with a view to any payment being received by himself or another in respect of making, or negotiating or facilitating the making of, any surrogacy arrangement.

In this subsection 'payment' does not include payment to or for the benefit of a surrogate mother or prospective surrogate mother.

(4) In proceedings against a person for an offence under subsection (1) above, he is not to be treated as doing an act on a commercial basis by reason of any payment received by another in respect of the act if it is proved that –

(a) in a case where the payment was received before he did the act, he did not do the act knowing or having reasonable cause to suspect that any payment had been received in respect of the act; and
(b) in any other case, he did not do the act with a view to any payment being received in respect of it.

(5) Where –

(a) a person acting on behalf of a body of persons takes any part in negotiating or facilitating the making of a surrogacy arrangement in the United Kingdom, and
(b) negotiating or facilitating the making of surrogacy arrangements is an activity of the body,

then, if the body at any time receives any payment made by or on behalf of –

(i) a woman who carries a child in pursuance of the arrangement,
(ii) the person or persons for whom she carries it, or
(iii) any person connected with the woman or with that person or those persons, the body is guilty of an offence.

For the purposes of this subsection, a payment received by a person connected with a body is to be treated as received by the body.

(5A) A non-profit making body is not guilty of an offence under subsection (5), in respect of the receipt of any payment described in that subsection, merely because a person acting on behalf of the body takes part in facilitating the making of a surrogacy arrangement.

(6) In proceedings against a body for an offence under subsection (5) above, it is a defence to prove that the payment concerned was not made in respect of the arrangement mentioned in paragraph (a) of that subsection.

(7) A person who in the United Kingdom takes part in the management or control –

(a) of any body of persons, or
(b) of any of the activities of any body of persons,

is guilty of an offence if the activity described in subsection (8) below is an activity of the body concerned.

(8) The activity referred to in subsection (7) above is negotiating or facilitating the making of surrogacy arrangements in the United Kingdom, being –

(a) arrangements the making of which is negotiated or facilitated on a commercial basis, or
(b) arrangements in the case of which payments are received (or treated for the purposes of subsection (5) above as received) by the body concerned in contravention of subsection (5) above.

(8A) A person is not guilty of an offence under subsection (7) if –

(a) the body of persons referred to in that subsection is a non-profit making body, and
(b) the only activity of that body which falls within subsection (8) is facilitating the making of surrogacy arrangements in the United Kingdom.

(8B) In subsection (8A)(b) 'facilitating the making of surrogacy arrangements' is to be construed in accordance with subsection (8).

(9) In proceedings against a person for an offence under subsection (7) above, it is a defence to prove that he neither knew nor had reasonable cause to suspect that the activity described in subsection (8) above was an activity of the body concerned; and for the purposes of such proceedings any arrangement falling within subsection (8)(b) above shall be disregarded if it is proved that the payment concerned was not made in respect of the arrangement.

Amendments—HFEA 2008, ss 59(3)–(8).

'negotiating surrogacy arrangements on a commercial basis'—A surrogacy agreement may be drawn up free of charge without contravening ss 1 and 2 of the Act. Where a fee is charged for the preparation of the agreement, solicitors or others doing so would be committing a criminal offence as it would amount to 'negotiating surrogacy arrangements on a commercial basis in contravention of s 2' (*JP v LP and Others (Surrogacy Arrangement: Wardship)* [2015] 1 FLR 307, FD).

3 Advertisements about surrogacy

(1) This section applies to any advertisement containing an indication (however expressed) –

(a) that any person is or may be willing to enter into a surrogacy arrangement or to negotiate or facilitate the making of a surrogacy arrangement, or
(b) that any person is looking for a woman willing to become a surrogate mother or for persons wanting a woman to carry a child as a surrogate mother.

(1A) This section does not apply to any advertisement placed by, or on behalf of, a non-profit making body if the advertisement relates only to the doing by the body of acts that would not contravene section 2(1) even if done on a commercial basis (within the meaning of section 2).

(2) Where a newspaper or periodical containing an advertisement to which this section applies is published in the United Kingdom, any proprietor, editor or publisher of the newspaper or periodical is guilty of an offence.

(3) Where an advertisement to which this section applies is conveyed by means of an electronic communications network so as to be seen or heard (or both) in the United Kingdom, any person who in the United Kingdom causes it to be so conveyed knowing it to contain such an indication as is mentioned in subsection (1) above is guilty of an offence.

(4) A person who publishes or causes to be published in the United Kingdom an advertisement to which this section applies (not being an advertisement contained in a newspaper or periodical or conveyed by means of an electronic communications network) is guilty of an offence.

(5) A person who distributes or causes to be distributed in the United Kingdom an advertisement to which this section applies (not being an advertisement contained in a newspaper or periodical published outside the United Kingdom or an advertisement conveyed by means of an electronic communications network) knowing it to contain such an indication as is mentioned in subsection (1) above is guilty of an offence.

(6) (*repealed*)

Amendments—Communications Act 2003, s 406, Schs 17, 19; HFEA 2008, s 59(7).

4 Offences

(1) A person guilty of an offence under this Act shall be liable on summary conviction –

- (a) in the case of an offence under section 2 to a fine not exceeding level 5 on the standard scale or to imprisonment for a term not exceeding 3 months or both,
- (b) in the case of an offence under section 3 to a fine not exceeding level 5 on the standard scale.

(2) No proceedings for an offence under this Act shall be instituted –

- (a) in England and Wales, except by or with the consent of the Director of Public Prosecutions; and
- (b) in Northern Ireland, except by or with the consent of the Director of Public Prosecutions for Northern Ireland.

(3) Where an offence under this Act committed by a body corporate is proved to have been committed with the consent or connivance of, or to be attributable to any neglect on the part of, any director, manager, secretary or other similar officer of the body corporate or any person who was purporting to act in any such capacity, he as well as the body corporate is guilty of the offence and is liable to be proceeded against and punished accordingly.

(4) Where the affairs of a body corporate are managed by its members, subsection (3) above shall apply in relation to the acts and defaults of a member in connection with his functions of management as if he were a director of the body corporate.

(5) In any proceedings for an offence under section 2 of this Act, proof of things done or of words written, spoken or published (whether or not in the presence of any party to the proceedings) by any person taking part in the management or control of a body of persons or of any of the activities of the body, or by any person doing any of the acts mentioned in subsection (1)(a) to (c) of that section on behalf of the body, shall be admissible as evidence of the activities of the body.

(6) In relation to an offence under this Act, section 127(1) of the Magistrates' Courts Act 1980 (information must be laid within six months of commission of offence), section 136(1) of the Criminal Procedure (Scotland) Act 1995 (proceedings must be commenced within that time) and Article 19(1) of the Magistrates' Courts (Northern Ireland) Order 1981 (complaint must be made within that time) shall have effect as if for the reference to six months there were substituted a reference to two years.

Amendments—Statute Law (Repeals) Act 1993; Criminal Procedure (Consequential Provisions) (Scotland) Act 1995, ss 4, 5, Sch 4, para 57.

****

Trusts of Land and Appointment of Trustees Act 1996

****

Right of beneficiaries to occupy trust land

12 The right to occupy

(1) A beneficiary who is beneficially entitled to an interest in possession in land subject to a trust of land is entitled by reason of his interest to occupy the land at any time if at that time –

(a) the purposes of the trust include making the land available for his occupation (or for the occupation of beneficiaries of a class of which he is a member or of beneficiaries in general), or

(b) the land is held by the trustees so as to be so available.

(2) Subsection (1) does not confer on a beneficiary a right to occupy land if it is either unavailable or unsuitable for occupation by him.

(3) This section is subject to section 13.

Scope—This section defines entitlement to occupy land as arising when a beneficiary is entitled to an interest in possession, and the purpose of the trust is to make the land available for his occupation. The right to occupy enjoyed by a spouse is not passed to her son, who was not a beneficiary under s 12, and therefore not entitled to protection under s 13 (*Omotajo v Omotajo* [2008] All ER (D) 156 (Oct), QBD).

13 Exclusion and restriction of right to occupy

(1) Where two or more beneficiaries are (or apart from this subsection would be) entitled under section 12 to occupy land, the trustees of land may exclude or restrict the entitlement of any one or more (but not all) of them.

(2) Trustees may not under subsection (1) –

(a) unreasonably exclude any beneficiary's entitlement to occupy land, or

(b) restrict any such entitlement to an unreasonable extent.

(3) The trustees of land may from time to time impose reasonable conditions on any beneficiary in relation to his occupation of land by reason of his entitlement under section 12.

(4) The matters to which trustees are to have regard in exercising the powers conferred by this section include –

(a) the intentions of the person or persons (if any) who created the trust,

(b) the purposes for which the land is held, and

(c) the circumstances and wishes of each of the beneficiaries who is (or apart from any previous exercise by the trustees of those powers would be) entitled to occupy the land under section 12.

(5) The conditions which may be imposed on a beneficiary under subsection (3) include, in particular, conditions requiring him –

(a) to pay any outgoings or expenses in respect of the land, or

(b) to assume any other obligation in relation to the land or to any activity which is or is proposed to be conducted there.

(6) Where the entitlement of any beneficiary to occupy land under section 12 has been excluded or restricted, the conditions which may be imposed on any other beneficiary under subsection (3) include, in particular, conditions requiring him to –

(a) make payments by way of compensation to the beneficiary whose entitlement has been excluded or restricted, or

(b) forgo any payment or other benefit to which he would otherwise be entitled under the trust so as to benefit that beneficiary.

(7) The powers conferred on trustees by this section may not be exercised –

(a) so as to prevent any person who is in occupation of land (whether or not by reason of an entitlement under section 12) from continuing to occupy the land, or

(b) in a manner likely to result in any such person ceasing to occupy the land,

unless he consents or the court has given approval.

(8) The matters to which the court is to have regard in determining whether to give approval under subsection (7) include the matters mentioned in subsection (4)(a) to (c).

Scope—This section provides that, where beneficiaries are entitled under s 12 to occupy land, the trustees of land may exclude a beneficiary's entitlement to occupy, provided they act reasonably. The trustees can impose conditions (including apportioning occupation – *Rodway v Landy* [2001] Ch 703, CA) and can compensate the beneficiary who has been excluded. A checklist of factors to be taken into account is set out; and the trustees cannot exclude without the person's consent or the court's approval.

Powers of court

14 Applications for order

(1) Any person who is a trustee of land or has an interest in property subject to a trust of land may make an application to the court for an order under this section.

(2) On an application for an order under this section the court may make any such order –

(a) relating to the exercise by the trustees of any of their functions (including an order relieving them of any obligation to obtain the consent of, or to consult, any person in connection with the exercise of any of their functions), or

(b) declaring the nature or extent of a person's interest in property subject to the trust,

as the court thinks fit.

(3) The court may not under this section make any order as to the appointment or removal of trustees.

(4) The powers conferred on the court by this section are exercisable on an application whether it is made before or after the commencement of this Act.

Provision—An application under TLATA 1996 is for a civil remedy and is therefore not governed by FPR 2010. CPR 1998 apply. See Procedural Guide A4.

Scope—Any trustee, or anyone who has an interest in property subject to a trust of land (which, by virtue of s 17(2), includes a beneficiary in the proceeds of sale of land), may apply for an order relating to the exercise by the trustees of any of their functions (including the power to exclude or the power of sale) or may apply for an order declaring the nature or extent of a person's interest in the trust of land. In cases of co-owners, the court does not have power under s 14 to order that one beneficiary under a trust of land sells or transfers his beneficial interest to another beneficiary. It does, however, have the power to order that trustees sell trust property to a particular beneficiary without the consent of another beneficiary to whom the land is not being sold: more usually, this power will be exercised by allowing all beneficiaries to bid for the property on sale but it is permissible, on an evaluation of factors in s 15, to give that opportunity first to only one beneficiary, see *Bagum v Hafiz and Another* [2016] 2 FLR 337, CA. The court's powers under this section are wide, but do not encompass the appointment or removal of trustees, which is provided for in ss 19–21. Commonly, applications are made by cohabitees, family members, trustees in bankruptcy and creditors with a charge secured on the property. Applications by a married party against a spouse are disapproved of. In principle, property issues between divorcing spouses should be resolved under MCA 1973: *Miller-Smith v Miller-Smith* [2010] 1 FLR 1402, CA. This is the case even where divorce proceedings are in a foreign jurisdiction: *Prazic v Prazic* [2006] 2 FLR 1128, CA.

15 Matters relevant in determining applications

(1) The matters to which the court is to have regard in determining an application for an order under section 14 include –

(a) the intentions of the person or persons (if any) who created the trust,

(b) the purposes for which the property subject to the trust is held,

(c) the welfare of any minor who occupies or might reasonably be expected to occupy any land subject to the trust as his home, and

(d) the interests of any secured creditor of any beneficiary.

(2) In the case of an application relating to the exercise in relation to any land of the powers conferred on the trustees by section 13, the matters to which the court is to have regard also include the circumstances and wishes of each of the beneficiaries who is (or apart from any previous exercise by the trustees of those powers would be) entitled to occupy the land under section 12.

(3) In the case of any other application, other than one relating to the exercise of the power mentioned in section 6(2), the matters to which the court is to have regard also include the circumstances and wishes of any beneficiaries of full age and entitled to an interest in possession in property subject to the trust or (in case of dispute) of the majority (according to the value of their combined interests).

(4) This section does not apply to an application if section 335A of the Insolvency Act 1986 (which is inserted by Schedule 3 and relates to applications by a trustee of a bankrupt) applies to it.

Scope—This section sets out the criteria to be applied under s 14. The four factors to which the court is to have regard include the intentions of the person who created the trust, the purposes for which the property subject to the trust is held, the welfare of any minor who occupies or may be expected to occupy the property as his home and the interests of any secured creditor of any beneficiary. The use of the word 'include' demonstrates that the four factors listed in s 15(1) are not inclusive. The welfare of any children is established as a relevant criterion, but no factor is overriding. This section is expressly excluded from consideration by the court in applications by trustees in bankruptcy under Insolvency Act 1986, s 335A.

Relationship with MCA 1973—In principle, property disputes between spouses are better dealt with under MCA 1973: *Miller-Smith v Miller-Smith* [2010] 1 FLR 1402, CA, which considers the guidelines to be considered in applications under TLATA between spouses. Where a party delays a divorce by defending it, a spouse who is bearing the running costs of the former matrimonial home may use TLATA to achieve an order for vacant possession under s 13, or an order for sale under s 14. Section 15(1) and (2) will be considered and where the joint intention to provide a home for the joint occupation of the spouses is no longer being achieved, orders under s 13 and s 14 may be made.

Application by cohabitees or family members—Former cohabitees may apply under s 14 to enforce a sale of property against the ex-partner. This jurisdiction is separate from but parallel to s 15 and Schedule 1 of CA 1989, where there is jurisdiction to transfer or settle property, but no power to order a sale.

Where a property has been acquired as an enterprise among family members or friends, an application may also be made under TLATA 1996. Typically, an application by a wife in respect of a property in the hands of the husband's family may be made alongside an application for financial ancillary relief under MCA 1973. It is usual to join the interested family members as defendants, and for the Trusts of Land and matrimonial applications to be heard together, the decision in the Trusts application governing the size of the pot available for distribution between the spouses.

Determination of applications under s 14 involves a two-stage process: first it is necessary to determine whether the parties expressly or by inference intended to share the beneficial ownership. If so, then it is necessary to determine the nature and extent of the parties' beneficial interests.

Principles of land law apply—An express declaration of trust is conclusive, and a defendant may not go behind it, in the absence of fraud or mistake (*Clarke v Harlow* [2007] 1 FLR 1, ChD). In the absence of an express declaration, the various routes to be followed in establishing an entitlement to property are those familiar to practitioners of land law:

(i) proprietary estoppel, where a representation or assurance by the owner must relate to a specific property or part of a property, which must be objectively ascertainable, and in reliance the claimant was induced to act to their detriment (*see Thorner v Majors* [2009] 2 FLR 405, HL). Whether an assurance is sufficiently clear to found a proprietary estoppel claim is 'hugely dependent on context' (at [56]): for a modern application of principles, see *Liden v Burton* [2017] 1 FLR 310, CA;
(ii) resulting trust, through direct or indirect contributions to the property; and
(iii) constructive trust at the time of purchase, or where parties formed a common intention that an incoming cohabitee would have a beneficial share in the property owned by the other.

Living together, a common business enterprise contributed to by the claimant and promises of future benefit were insufficiently specific to found an estoppel or a constructive trust (*James v Thomas* [2008] 1 FLR 1598, CA; *Morris v Morris* [2008] EWCA Civ 257; *Abbot v Abbott* [2008] 1 FLR 1451, PC), the Privy Council applying the principle of the constructive trust to a matrimonial case. In *Walsh v Singh* [2010] 1 FLR 1658, ChD, a claim for a beneficial interest failed where there was no financial contribution made, no representation that the claimant would have a share in the property, and no common intention giving rise to constructive trust or estoppel. For an overview of s 15 factors, see *Oxley v Hiscock* [2004] 2 FLR 669, CA. See *Q v Q* [2009] 1 FLR 935, FD for an explanation of the law relating to proprietary estoppel and constructive trusts, and the relationship between the doctrines. The leading case is *Stack v Dowden* [2007] 1 FLR 1858, HL, see below. Courts must apply strict legal principles and ignore 'fairness'. A claimant must show that it was jointly intended that she should have a share. A common intention that the man provide a home for the woman and children is not sufficient to establish the common intention that she should also have a share in the property: *Thomson v Humphrey* [2010] 2 FLR 107, Ch.

Registration in joint names—Where a property has been transferred into joint names after April 1998, the nature and extent of the beneficial interests should be determined by Form TR1, which provides for an express declaration of the beneficial interest.

Where the transfer of property into joint names was completed before 1 April 1998 or in circumstances where Form TR1 does not expressly declare the beneficial interests, there is a presumption in the case of domestic property that the beneficial interests are also held equally, until the contrary is proved on trust principles. In *Stack v Dowden* [2007] 1 FLR 1858, HL a couple had cohabited over 27 years and raised four children together, latterly in jointly owned property. The woman had made the greater capital contribution and had the higher earnings and established the beneficial entitlement of two thirds. However, 'cases in which the joint legal owners are to be taken to have intended their beneficial interest should be different from their legal interest will be very unusual' (and see *Fowler v Barron* [2008] 2 FLR 831, CA).The starting point where there is joint legal ownership is that there is joint beneficial ownership. The burden is on the party who wishes to show other than joint beneficial ownership. Baroness Hale identified a non-exhaustive list of factors, as evidence of the parties' intentions: including the reason the home was acquired, the nature of the relationship, how the purchase was financed initially and subsequently, and how the parties arranged their finances and discharged their outgoings. To this list can be added the financial contributions (or lack of them) to the maintenance of children, unless it is clear that to do so would result in double liability, eg arrears owed to the Child Maintenance Service: see *Barnes v Phillips* [2016] 2 FLR 1292, CA, at [41]. The Supreme Court has given further guidance in *Jones v Kernott* [2012] 1 FLR 45, SC. A family home was bought and registered in the joint names of the parties, paid for jointly and occupied by them and their two children for 8 years. Upon the relationship ending, they tried unsuccessfully to sell the property. An insurance policy was then divided equally and the man went on to buy his own property. He made no further contribution to the family home, which was thereafter solely funded by the woman. The Supreme Court has established the guiding principle that where a family home is in joint names of a cohabiting couple and both are responsible for the mortgage, without any express declaration as to beneficial interests (i) they are joint tenants in law and equity; (ii) the presumption may be displaced by a different common intention expressed when the home is purchased, or at a later stage; (iii) otherwise, a common intention may be inferred from their conduct, as in *Gissing v Gissing* [1971] 1 AC 886, HL, at [906] and *Stack v Dowden* at [69]; (iv) where there is no evidence as to their joint intentions at the outset, or that intention has changed but it is not possible to determine the new intention, each is entitled to such share as the court considers fair, having regard to the whole course of their dealings with regard to the property: *Oxley v Hiscock* [2004] 2 FLR 669, CA at [69] followed; and (v) each case turns on its facts. In *Jones v Kernott*, the Supreme Court determined that fairness involved an equal division between the parties of the value of the property at the conclusion of the relationship, the woman additionally retaining the value that had accrued since that date. In *Barnes v Phillips* (above), the fact that the man received the full benefit of monies released by way of a remortgage on the jointly owned property shortly before the relationship ended was good evidence of an inferred common intention to vary the parties' interests in the property. Different principles can apply to the ownership of commercial property, see *Laskar v Laskar* [2008] 2 FLR 589, CA, where shares of a rental property held by mother and daughter were defined as two-thirds: one-third because this was their respective financial contributions.

Registration in a sole name—Where a property is registered in the name of one party, but is occupied by both of them, they may have agreed to a sharing of the beneficial interest or each party may have made a financial contribution to purchase costs, mortgage costs and household bills, but there may be no express agreement or declaration of trust. In the case of such an asset (owned in law by one person but another claims to share a beneficial interest in it), a two-stage analysis is required to determine whether a common intention constructive trust arises. First, the person claiming the beneficial interest must show that there was an agreement (express or inferred from conduct) that he should have a beneficial interest in the property owned by his partner, even if there was no agreement as to the precise extent of that interest. Secondly, if such an agreement can be shown to have been made, then absent agreement or inference on the extent of the interest, the court may impute an intention that the person was to have a fair beneficial share in the asset and may assess the quantum of that fair share in the light of the whole course of dealing between them in relation to the property; see *Jones v Kernott* [2012] 1 FLR 45, SC, at [64]. The determining principles were set out by the HL in *Lloyds Bank plc v Rosset* [1990] 2 FLR 155, HL, subsequently applied by the Court of Appeal in *Oxley v Hiscock* [2004] 2 FLR 669, CA and *Parris v Williams* [2009] BPIR 96, CA. The principles where the family home is in the name of one party only has been considered in *Jones v Kernott*, at [52]. If on the evidence there is a common intention to share (stage 1), but not of what shares were intended (stage 2), the court will have to proceed as in (iv) and (v) above (see **Registration in joint names**). Care must be taken not to impute an intention within the first stage: imputation only applies to the second stage in determining the fair beneficial share: *Capehorn v Harris* [2016] 2 FLR 1026, CA. The imputations of particular intentions by way of a resulting trust are not appropriate to the ascertainment of beneficial interests in a family home. An intention to purchase in joint names, not acted upon because of financial advice, does not entitle the non-legal owner to a 50% beneficial interest: *Thompson v Hurst* [2014] 1 FLR 238, CA.

The requirement for the court to establish a fair share, having regard to the whole course of the parties' dealings in relation to the property, was established in *Stack v Dowden* [2007] 1 FLR 1858, HL. In *Kamarah Kathleen Inessah Graham-York v Adrian York (Personal Representative of the Estate of Norton Brian York) and Others* [2016] 1 FLR 407, CA, the Court of Appeal clarified that (a) in deciding what a party's fair share is in a property, the court is not concerned with some form of 'redistributive justice'; instead (b) the 'fair' share is decided only by considering the parties' dealings in relation to the property; and (c) there is no presumed starting point of equality of interests, even in cases involving a substantial financial contribution from a non-owner. For further authorities on this point, see *Holman v Howes* [2008] 1 FLR 1217, CA, a sole name case in which the Court of Appeal said that inferences will be drawn from the whole course of dealing between the parties both before and after purchase, including the arrangements made to meet the outgoings of the property. A substantial financial contribution by a man to building works on a barn owned by his former cohabitee entitled him to a 25% interest: *Aspden v Elvy* [2012] 2 FLR 807, ChD. There may be a change of beneficial ownership after the property has been acquired, but the court will be slow to infer this from conduct alone, without evidence of an express agreement (*James v Thomas* [2008] 1 FLR 1598, CA; *Morris v Morris* [2008] EWCA Civ 257, CA). The Court of Appeal has said on several occasions that fairness between the parties is not the basis for the court's decision; to argue what may be considered fair is the 'impermissible question', in the absence of evidence of the parties' intentions derived from a survey of their whole course of dealings (*Holman v Howes* [2008] 1 FLR 1217, CA); on 'fairness', see also *James v Thomas* [2008] 1 FLR 1598, CA; *Laskar v Laskar* [2008] 2 FLR 589, CA; *Thomson v Humphrey* [2010] 2 FLR 107, ChD.

Application by trustee in bankruptcy—The Insolvency Act 1986 s 335A provides that a trustee in bankruptcy may apply for an order under s 14 for a sale of land. The application must be made to the court having jurisdiction in relation to the bankruptcy. The court will make such order as is just and reasonable, having regard to (a) the interests of the creditors; (b) where the application is made in respect of a dwelling house which is or has been the home of the bankrupt, his spouse or former spouse, the court will consider (i) the conduct of the spouse or former spouse in contributing to the bankruptcy, (ii) the needs and financial resources of the spouse, and (iii) the needs of any children. The court will also consider (c) all the circumstances of the case other than the needs of the bankrupt. Where the application is made more than a year after the vesting of the bankrupt's estate in the trustee, the court is entitled to assume that the interests of the creditors outweigh all other considerations, unless the circumstances of the case are exceptional: see *Dean v Stout (Trustee in Bankruptcy)* [2006] 1 FLR 725, ChD. Even if circumstances of a case are characterised as 'exceptional', for example involving a disabled adult child at home aged 30 but with a mental age of 8 or 9, this may not be sufficient to prevent or postpone the sale of a property for an indefinite period of time, see *Grant & Another v Baker* [2016] EWHC 1782 (Ch). The court's discretion under s 15 has to be compatible with the European Convention rights of those affected by an order: a balance will be drawn between the creditor's rights under Article 1 and the Article 8 rights to family life of those affected by the sale: *National Westminster Bank Plc v Rushmer* [2010] 2 FLR 362, ChD.

A matrimonial consent order giving a two thirds interest in the matrimonial home to the wife upon a trust for sale upon future contingencies did not give an absolute right to the wife, where the husband was entitled to one third interest upon sale. The husband's right to apply under s 14 passes intact to the trustee in bankruptcy, entitling him to apply for sale under the Insolvency Act s 335A (*Avis v Turner* [2008] 1 FLR 1127, CA). The trustee was subsequently granted possession and an order for sale: the existence of the consent order did not constitute an 'exceptional circumstance' (*Turner v Avis and Avis* [2009] 1 FLR 74, ChD). A trustee in bankruptcy who secures an order for sale is entitled to compensation in the form of occupation rent (*Re Barcham (In Bankruptcy)* [2008] BPIR 857, ChD).

Costs—An application under TLATA 1996 is not for a financial order or financial remedy and is not governed by FPR 2010. CPR 1998, r 44.2 applies.

****

Welfare Reform and Pensions Act 1999

****

29 Creation of pension debits and credits

(1) On the application of this section –

(a) the transferor's shareable rights under the relevant arrangement become subject to a debit of the appropriate amount, and

(b) the transferee becomes entitled to a credit of that amount as against the person responsible for that arrangement.

(2) Where the relevant order or provision specifies a percentage value to be transferred, the appropriate amount for the purposes of subsection (1) is the specified percentage of the cash equivalent of the relevant benefits on the valuation day.

(3) Where the relevant order or provision specifies an amount to be transferred, the appropriate amount for the purposes of subsection (1) is the lesser of –

(a) the specified amount, and

(b) the cash equivalent of the relevant benefits on the valuation day.

(4) Where the relevant arrangement is an occupational pension scheme and the transferor is in pensionable service under the scheme on the transfer day, the relevant benefits for the purposes of subsections (2) and (3) are the benefits or future benefits to which he would be entitled under the scheme by virtue of his shareable rights under it had his pensionable service terminated immediately before that day.

(5) Otherwise, the relevant benefits for the purposes of subsections (2) and (3) are the benefits or future benefits to which, immediately before the transfer day, the transferor is entitled under the terms of the relevant arrangement by virtue of his shareable rights under it.

(6) The Secretary of State may by regulations provide for any description of benefit to be disregarded for the purposes of subsection (4) or (5).

(7) For the purposes of this section, the valuation day is such day within the implementation period for the credit under subsection (1)(b) as the person responsible for the relevant arrangement may specify by notice in writing to the transferor and transferee.

(8) In this section –

'relevant arrangement' means the arrangement to which the relevant order or provision relates;

'relevant order or provision' means the order or provision by virtue of which this section applies;

'transfer day' means the day on which the relevant order or provision takes effect;

'transferor' means the person to whose rights the relevant order or provision relates;

'transferee' means the person for whose benefit the relevant order or provision is made.

Defined terms—'implementation period': ss 34, 46(1); 'occupational pension scheme': s 46(1); 'pensionable service': s 46(1),(3); 'person responsible for a pension arrangement': s 46(2); 'shareable rights': ss 27(2), 46(1).

Scope—This section gives rise to what has become known as 'moving target syndrome': see *Cowland v Capita SIPP Services* [2007] (3 April), ref Q00244, Pensions Ombudsman, *Chaundy v James Hay Pension Trustees Limited* [2007] (22 May), ref Q00060, Pensions Ombudsman and *Crabtree v BAE Executive Pension Scheme* (2008) 19 May, ref S00522, Pensions Ombudsman; *Slattery v Cabinet Office (Civil Service Pensions)* [2009] 1 FLR 1365, ChD; *Staley v Marlborough Investment Management Limited Retirement Scheme* (2012) 31 July, ref 81482/2, Pensions Ombudsman; *Stocks v Hornbuckle Mitchell Trustee Limited* (2012) 13 November, ref 84269/1, Deputy Pensions Ombudsman. It is critical to recognise that the valuation used evidentially will not be the same as that used by the pension provider for implementation purposes. The three relevant dates giving rise to this syndrome are best explained diagrammatically:

Date	*Function*	*Source*
1 Valuation date	Evidential valuation for the purposes of negotiation or court hearing. The 'moving date syndrome' refers to the difference between this valuation and that on the valuation day.	Divorce etc (Pensions) Regulations 2000, reg 3
2 Transfer day	Establishes the relevant benefits to be valued for implementation purposes and is the date the pension sharing order takes effect.	WRPA 1999, s 29(4), (5) and (8)
3 Valuation day	Date chosen for actual implementation purposes, on which the relevant benefits are revalued to take account of market fluctuations (but not contributions and salary accruals)	WRPA 1999, s 29(7)

'Implementation period' (s 29(7))—For a pension credit, this is the period of 4 months beginning with the later of –

'(a) the day on which the relevant order or provision takes effect, and

(b) the first day on which the person responsible for the pension arrangement to which the relevant order or provision relates is in receipt of –

(i) the relevant documents, and

(ii) such information relating to the transferor and transferee as the Secretary of State may prescribe by regulations' (WRPA 1999, s 34(1)).

The relevant documents are 'copies of':

'(a) the relevant order or provision, and

(b) the order, decree or declarator responsible for the divorce, dissolution or annulment to which it relates [...]' (WRPA 1999, s 34(2)).

The 4-month period of implementation is a maximum period: unnecessary delays *within* that period by a scheme administrator or trustees may give rise to an award of compensation by the Pensions Ombudsman (*Boughton v Punter Southall* (2009) 22 September, ref 74851/1, Pensions Ombudsman).

★★★★

PART III

Procedure Rules

PART III: Procedure Rules

Contents

All relevant procedural provisions in the following legislation, as amended and fully annotated:

Family Procedure Rules 2010

Part 1 – Overriding Objective 1277

Part 2 – Application and Interpretation of the Rules 1278

Practice Direction – Practice Directions Relating to Family Proceedings In Force Before 6 April 2011 which Support the Family Procedure Rules 2010 1292

Practice Direction 2A – Functions of the Court in the Family Procedure Rules 2010 and Practice Directions which may be Performed by a Single Lay Justice 1297

Practice Direction 2B – References in the Rules to Actions done by the Court or by a Court Officer 1306

Part 3 – Non-court Dispute Resolution 1306

Practice Direction 3A – Family Mediation Information and Assessment Meetings (MIAMS) 1312

Part 4 – General Case Management Powers 1319

Practice Direction 4A – Striking Out a Statement of Case 1325

Practice Direction 4B – Civil Restraint Orders 1326

Part 5 – Forms and Start of Proceedings 1330

Practice Direction 5A – Forms 1332

Practice Direction 5B – Communication and Filing of Documents by E-Mail 1342

Part 6 – Service 1345

Practice Direction 6A – Service within the Jurisdiction 1362

Practice Direction 6B – Service out of the Jurisdiction 1368

Practice Direction 6C – Disclosure of Addresses by Government Departments 13 February 1989 [as amended by Practice Direction 20 July 1995] 1373

Part 7 – Procedure for Applications in Matrimonial and Civil Partnership Proceedings 1378

Practice Direction 7A – Procedure for Applications in Matrimonial and Civil Partnership Proceedings 1406

PART III

Practice Direction 7B – Medical Examinations on Applications for Annulment of a Marriage 1411

Practice Direction 7C – Polygamous Marriages 1411

Practice Direction 7D – Gender Recognition Act 2004 1412

Part 8 – Procedure for Miscellaneous Applications 1417

Practice Direction 8A – Where to Start Certain Proceedings 1427

Part 9 – Applications for a Financial Remedy 1427

Practice Direction 9A – Application for a Financial Remedy 1462

Practice Direction 9B – Communication of Information from Financial Remedy Proceedings 1468

Part 10 – Applications under Part 4 of the Family Law Act 1996 1469

Practice Direction 10A – Part 4 of the Family Law Act 1996 1475

Part 11 – Applications under Part 4A of the Family Law Act 1996 or Part 1 of Schedule 2 to the Female Genital Mutilation Act 2003 1476

Part 12 – Children Proceedings Except Parental Order Proceedings and Proceedings for Applications in Adoption, Placement and Related Proceedings 1485

Practice Direction 12A – Care, Supervision and Other Part 4 Proceedings: Guide to Case Management 1565

Practice Direction 12B – Child Arrangements Programme 1577

Practice Direction 12C – Service of Application in Certain Proceedings 1598

Practice Direction 12D – Inherent Jurisdiction (including Wardship) Proceedings 1602

Practice Direction 12E – Urgent Business 1605

Practice Direction 12F – International Child Abduction 1606

Practice Direction 12G – Communication of Information 1618

Practice Direction 12H – Contribution Orders 1623

Practice Direction 12I – Applications for Reporting Restriction Orders 1623

Practice Direction 12J – Child Arrangements & Contact Order: Domestic Violence and Harm 1624

Practice Direction 12K – Children Act 1989: Exclusion Requirement 1631

Practice Direction 12L – Children Act 1989: Risk Assessments under Section 16A 1631

Practice Direction 12M – Family Assistance Orders: Consultation 1632

Practice Direction 12N – Enforcement of Children Act 1989 Child Arrangements Orders: Disclosure of Information to Officers of the National Probation Service (High Court and County Court) 1632

Practice Direction 12O – Child: Arrival by Air 1633

Practice Direction 12P – Removal from Jurisdiction: Issue of Passports 1633

Part 13 – Proceedings under Section 54 of the Human Fertilisation and Embryology Act 2008 1633

Part 14 – Procedure for Applications in Adoption, Placement and Related Proceedings 1643

Practice Direction 14A – Who Receives a Copy of the Application Form for Orders in Proceedings 1663

Practice Direction 14B – The First Directions Hearing – Adoptions with a Foreign Element 1664

Practice Direction 14C – Reports by the Adoption Agency or Local Authority 1665

Practice Direction 14D – Reports by a Registered Medical Practitioner ('Health Reports') 1673

Practice Direction 14E – Communication of Information Relating to Proceedings 1675

Practice Direction 14F – Disclosing Information to an Adopted Adult 1679

Part 15 – Representation of Protected Parties 1680

Practice Direction 15A – Protected Parties 1689

Practice Direction 15B – Adults Who May Be Protected Parties and Children Who May Become Protected Parties in Family Proceedings 1691

Part 16 – Representation of Children and Reports in Proceedings Involving Children 1693

Practice Direction 16A – Representation of Children 1713

Part 17 – Statements of Truth 1721

Practice Direction 17A – Statements of Truth 1725

Part 18 – Procedure for Other Applications in Proceedings 1728

Practice Direction 18A – Other Applications in Proceedings 1732

Part 19 – Alternative Procedure for Applications 1736

Practice Direction 19A – Alternative Procedure for Applications 1739

Part 20 – Interim Remedies and Security for Costs 1741

Practice Direction 20A – Interim Remedies 1748

Part 21 – Miscellaneous Rules about Disclosure and Inspection of Documents 1752

Practice Direction 21A – Disclosure and Inspection 1759

Part 22 – Evidence 1759

Practice Direction 22A – Written Evidence 1768

Part 23 – Miscellaneous Rules about Evidence 1777

Part 24 – Witnesses, Depositions Generally and Taking of Evidence in Member States of the European Union 1781

Practice Direction 24A – Witnesses, Depositions and Taking of Evidence in Member States of the European Union 1787

Part 25 – Experts and Assessors 1793

Practice Direction 25A – Experts – Emergencies and Pre Proceedings Instructions 1801

Practice Direction 25B – The Duties of an Expert, the Expert's Report and Arrangements for an Expert to Attend Court 1803

Practice Direction 25C – Children Proceedings – The Use of Single Joint Experts and the Process Leading to an Expert Being Instructed or Expert Evidence Being Put Before the Court 1812

Practice Direction 25D – Financial Remedy Proceedings and Other Family Proceedings (Except Children Proceedings) – The Use of Single Joint Experts and the Process Leading to Expert Evidence Being Put Before the Court 1818

Practice Direction 25E – Discussions Between Experts in Family Proceedings 1823

Practice Direction 25F – Assessors in Family Proceedings 1825

Part 26 – Change of Solicitor 1825

Practice Direction 26A – Change of Solicitor 1828

Part 27 – Hearings and Directions Appointments 1829

Practice Direction 27A – Family Proceedings: Court Bundles (Universal Practice to be applied in the High Court and Family Court) 1837

Practice Direction 27B – Attendance of Media Representatives at Hearings in Family Proceedings (High Court and County Courts) 1843

Part 28 – Costs 1846

Practice Direction 28A – Costs 1849

Part 29 – Miscellaneous 1851

Practice Direction 29A – Human Rights, Joining the Crown 1860

Practice Direction 29B – Human Rights Act 1998 1861

Practice Direction 29C – Transfer of Proceedings from the Family Court to the High Court 1862

Part 30 – Appeals 1862

Practice Direction 30A – Appeals 1872

Part 31 – Registration of Orders under the Council Regulation, the Civil Partnership (Jurisdiction and Recognition of Judgments) Regulations 2005, The Marriage (Same Sex Couples) (Jurisdiction and Recognition of Judgments) Regulations 2014 and Under the Hague Convention 1996 1896

Practice Direction 31A – Registration of Orders under the Council Regulation, the Civil Partnership (Jurisdiction and Recognition of Judgments) Regulations 2005, the Marriage (Same Sex Couples) (Jurisdiction and Recognition of Judgments) Regulations 2014 and under the 1996 Hague Convention 1905

Part 32 – Registration and Enforcement of Orders 1909

Practice Direction 32A – Forms Relating to Part 32 1924

Part 33 – Enforcement 1926

Practice Direction 33A – Enforcement of Undertakings 1936

Part 34 – Reciprocal Enforcement of Maintenance Orders 1937

Practice Direction 34A – Reciprocal Enforcement of Maintenance Orders 1959

Practice Direction 34B – Practice Note (Tracing Payers Overseas) 1969

Practice Direction 34C – Applications for Recognition and Enforcement To or From European Union Member States 1970

Practice Direction 34D – Form Relating to Part 34 1973

Practice Direction 34E – Reciprocal Enforcement of Maintenance Orders – Designated Family Judge Areas 1973

Part 35 – Mediation Directive 1976

Practice Direction 35A – Mediation Directive 1979

Part 36 – Transitional Arrangements and Pilot Schemes 1979

Practice Direction 36D – Pilot Scheme: Procedure for Using an Online System to Generate Applications in Certain Proceedings for a Matrimonial Order 1980

Part 37 – Applications and Proceedings in relation to Contempt of Court 1981

Practice Direction 37A – Applications and Proceedings in Relation to Contempt of Court 1998

Part 38 – Recognition and Enforcement of Protection Measures 2002

Practice Direction 38A – Recognition and Enforcement of Protection Measures 2009

Part 39 – Attachment of Earnings 2014

Part 40 – Charging Order, Stop Order, Stop Notice 2021

Practice Direction 40A – Charging Orders, Stop Orders and Stop Notices 2028

Glossary 2030

Civil Procedure Rules 1998

Part 1 – Overriding Objective 2031

Part 2 – Application and Interpretation of the Rules 2032

Part 3 – The Court's Case and Costs Management Powers 2035

PART III

Part 7 – How to Start Proceedings – The Claim Form 2038
Practice Direction 7A – How to Start Proceedings 2042
Part 8 – Alternative Procedure for Claims 2047
Practice Direction 8A – Alternative Procedure for Claims 2051
Part 18 – Further Information 2054
Practice Direction 18 – Further Information 2055
Part 19 – Parties and Group Litigation 2057
Part 21 – Children and Protected Parties 2059
Practice Direction 21 – Children and Protected Parties 2070
Part 23 – General Rules about Applications for Court Orders 2077
Practice Direction 23A – Applications 2080
Practice Direction 23B – Applications under Particular Statutes 2085
Part 25 – Interim Remedies and Security for Costs 2086
Practice Direction 25A – Interim Injunctions 2088
Part 31 – Disclosure and Inspection of Documents 2104
Practice Direction 31A – Disclosure and Inspection 2111
Practice Direction 31B – Disclosure of Electronic Documents 2115
Part 32 – Evidence 2115
Practice Direction 32 – Evidence 2117
Part 35 – Experts and Assessors 2127
Practice Direction 35 – Experts and Assessors 2131
Part 36 – Offers to Settle 2135
Part 39 – Miscellaneous Provisions Relating to Hearings 2141
Part 44 – General Rules about Costs 2143
Practice Direction 44 – General Rules About Costs 2151
Part 46 – Costs – Special Cases 2156
Practice Direction 46 – Costs Special Cases 2162
Part 47 – Procedure for Detailed Assessment of Costs and Default Provisions 2165
Practice Direction 47 – Procedure for Detailed Assessment of Costs and Default Provisions 2176
Part 50 – Application of the Schedules 2191
Part 52 – Appeals 2191
Practice Direction 52A – Appeals: General Provisions 2208
Practice Direction 52B – Appeals in the County Court and High Court 2214

Practice Direction 52C – Appeals to the Court of Appeal 2220

Practice Direction 52D – Statutory Appeals and Appeals Subject to Special Provision 2233

Practice Direction 52E – Appeals by way of Case Stated 2251

Part 54 – Judicial Review and Statutory Review 2251

Practice Direction 54A – Judicial Review 2261

Practice Direction 54C – References by the Legal Services Commission 2266

Practice Direction 54D – Administrative Court (Venue) 2266

Part 57 – Probate, Inheritance and Presumption of Death 2268

Practice Direction 57A – Probate 2274

Practice Direction 57B – Proceedings under the Presumption of Death Act 2013 2275

Part 65 – Proceedings Relating to Anti-Social Behaviour and Harassment 2278

Part 69 – Court's Power to Appoint a Receiver 2279

Part 70 – General Rules about Enforcement of Judgments and Orders 2279

Practice Direction 70 – Enforcement of Judgments and Orders 2281

Part 71 – Orders to Obtain Information from Judgment Debtors 2284

Practice Direction 71 – Orders to Obtain Information from Judgment Debtors 2287

Part 72 – Third Party Debt Orders 2290

Practice Direction 72 – Third Party Debt Orders 2296

Part 73 – Charging Orders, Stop Orders and Stop Notices 2298

Part 74 – Enforcement of Judgments in Different Jurisdictions 2299

Part 81 – Applications and Proceedings in Relation to Contempt of Court 2300

Practice Direction 81 – Applications and Proceedings in relation to Contempt of Court 2314

Part 83 – Writs and Warrants – General Provisions 2319

Practice Direction 83 – Writs and Warrants – General Provisions 2336

Part 84 – Enforcement by Taking Control of Goods 2337

Practice Direction 84 – Enforcement by Taking Control of Goods 2344

Part 87 – Applications for Writ of Habeas Corpus 2346

Supreme Court Rules 2009

Part 1 – Interpretation and Scope 2350

Part 2 – Application for Permission to Appeal 2354

PART III

Part 3 – Commencement and Preparation of Appeal 2356

Part 4 – Hearing and Decision of Appeal 2359

Part 5 – Further General Provisions 2360

Part 6 – Particular Appeals and References 2362

Part 7 – Fees and Costs 2363

Part 8 – Transitional Arrangements 2366

Note—By virtue of CCA 2013, s 17, Sch 9, para 11, in relevant legislation: (i) any reference that is or is deemed to be a reference to a county court is to be read as a reference to the County Court; and (ii) any reference that is or is deemed to be a reference to a judge of a county court is, if the context permits, to be read as a reference to the County Court and otherwise is to be read as a reference to a judge of the County Court. Note that (ii) does not apply to a reference to a holder of a particular office (for example, a reference to a Circuit Judge).

Family Procedure Rules 2010, SI 2010/2955

PART 1
OVERRIDING OBJECTIVE

CONTENTS OF THIS PART

Rule		Page
1.1	The overriding objective	1277
1.2	Application by the court of the overriding objective	1277
1.3	Duty of the parties	1278
1.4	Court's duty to manage cases	1278

1.1 The overriding objective

(1) These rules are a new procedural code with the overriding objective of enabling the court to deal with cases justly, having regard to any welfare issues involved.

(2) Dealing with a case justly includes, so far as is practicable –

(a) ensuring that it is dealt with expeditiously and fairly;
(b) dealing with the case in ways which are proportionate to the nature, importance and complexity of the issues;
(c) ensuring that the parties are on an equal footing;
(d) saving expense; and
(e) allotting to it an appropriate share of the court's resources, while taking into account the need to allot resources to other cases.

Scope—The overriding objective is fundamental and the bedrock of the 2010 Rules and reflects a similar provision in CPR 1998, save that the wording differs to take account, in particular of 'any welfare issues involved'. The FPR are deliberately not designed to answer every possible procedural question that could arise and the overriding objective provides a compass to guide the courts, the parties and legal advisers.

'new procedural code' (r 1.1(1))—These words denote an intention to start afresh, procedurally speaking. Authorities on the interpretation of earlier rules may not be followed. However, it is the procedure that has changed, not the underlying law.

'an equal footing' (r 1.1(2)(c))—In *Maltez v Lewis* (2000) 16 Const LJ 65, ChD, Neuberger J, when applying the identical rule in the CPR, held that it did not mean that the court could prevent one party from employing leading counsel where the other could not afford to do so. However, the general rule that the unsuccessful party will be ordered to pay the costs of the successful party in CPR 1998, r 44.2(2) does not apply in family proceedings; see generally FPR 2010, Pt 28.

'saving expense' (r 1.1(2)(d))—The cost of taking a particular step has to be justified before the court can order it to be taken whether the cost will fall on the party or public funds. Clear examples of this are the court's duty to restrict expert evidence (see FPR 2010, r 25.4) and the power to control evidence (see FPR 2010, r 22.1) but saving expense is a general principle.

'the court's resources' (r 1.1(2)(e))—The identical words in the CPR have assumed increasing importance over the years. Parties and their advisers have a particular duty to keep the court informed of developments that may affect the use of court resources.

1.2 Application by the court of the overriding objective

The court must seek to give effect to the overriding objective when it –

(a) exercises any power given to it by these rules; or
(b) interprets any rule.

Scope—This rule indicates that a purposive approach is to be adopted. The overriding objective is the crucial aid to interpretation of the rules.

1.3 Duty of the parties

The parties are required to help the court to further the overriding objective.

'help the court'—FPR 2010, rr 1.1 and 1.2 suggest that achieving the overriding objective is the duty of the court and r 1.3 confirms this by not imposing a duty on the parties to further the overriding objective but instead requiring them to 'help the court' to further the overriding objective.

1.4 Court's duty to manage cases

(1) The court must further the overriding objective by actively managing cases.

(2) Active case management includes –

- (a) setting timetables or otherwise controlling the progress of the case;
- (b) identifying at an early stage –
  - (i) the issues; and
  - (ii) who should be a party to the proceedings;
- (c) deciding promptly –
  - (i) which issues need full investigation and hearing and which do not; and
  - (ii) the procedure to be followed in the case;
- (d) deciding the order in which issues are to be resolved;
- (e) controlling the use of expert evidence;
- (f) encouraging the parties to use a non-court dispute resolution procedure if the court considers that appropriate and facilitating the use of such procedure;
- (g) helping the parties to settle the whole or part of the case;
- (h) encouraging the parties to co-operate with each other in the conduct of proceedings;
- (i) considering whether the likely benefits of taking a particular step justify the cost of taking it;
- (j) dealing with as many aspects of the case as it can on the same occasion;
- (k) dealing with the case without the parties needing to attend at court;
- (l) making use of technology; and
- (m) giving directions to ensure that the case proceeds quickly and efficiently.

Amendments—SI 2012/3061; SI 2014/843.

Scope—The concept of 'case management' for civil proceedings was the single most important recommendation to emerge from Lord Woolf's 'Access to Justice' report, which led to CPR 1998. It is no surprise to find that r 1.4 is very similar, although not identical, to the same rule number in the CPR. Thus, FPR 2010, r 1.4 contains a list of various case-management elements but is not exhaustive. It summarises aims that are implemented in various ways throughout the FPR. The list was amended in 2012. Former para (g) is reworded and elevated to (a). Para (e) is a new additional factor. The key point is that the court is under a duty to manage cases. Robust case management has a place in family proceedings but in *Re B (Case Management)* [2013] 1 FLR 963, CA a judge erred in holding an unnecessarily truncated hearing and making a finding of fact on limited evidence. See also *Re J (Residence and Contact Dispute*) [2013] 1 FLR 716, CA, where the Recorder erred in stopping further cross-examination. But contrast *Re C (Family Proceedings: Case Management)* [2013] 1 FLR 1089, CA, where the judge did not err in stopping residence proceedings and giving judgment shortly after the father began his evidence. In family proceedings, the judge has an inquisitorial role and a duty to further the interests of the child.

PART 2
APPLICATION AND INTERPRETATION OF THE RULES

CONTENTS OF THIS PART

Rule		Page
2.1	Application of these Rules	1279
2.2	The glossary	1279
2.3	Interpretation	1279
2.4	Modification of rules in application to serial numbers etc.	1288
2.5	Power to perform functions conferred on the court by these rules and practice directions	1288
2.6	Powers of the single justice to perform functions under the 1989 Act, the 1996 Act, the 2002 Act and the Childcare Act 2006	1289

2.7	Single lay justice: power to refer to the family court	1290
2.8	Court's discretion as to where it deals with cases	1290
2.9	Computation of time	1291
2.10	Dates for compliance to be calendar dates and to include time of day	1291
	Practice Direction – Practice Directions Relating to Family Proceedings In Force Before 6 April 2011 which Support the Family Procedure Rules 2010	1292
	Practice Direction 2A – Functions of the Court in the Family Procedure Rules 2010 and Practice Directions which may be Performed by a Single Lay Justice	1297
	Practice Direction 2B – References in the Rules to Actions done by the Court or by a Court Officer	1306

2.1 Application of these Rules

Unless the context otherwise requires, these rules apply to family proceedings in –

(a) the High Court; and

(b) the family court.

Amendments—Substituted by SI 2013/3204.

'family proceedings'—The term is defined in MFPA 1984, s 32 and SCA 1981, s 61(1), which provide that 'business in the High Court of any description mentioned in Schedule 1, as for the time being in force, shall be distributed among the Divisions in accordance with that Schedule'. Sch 1 provides that the list in para 3 shall be assigned to the Family Division. Proceedings in that list will be subject to FPR 2010; CPR 1998 cannot apply to such proceedings (CPR 1998, r 2.1(2)).

'these rules apply to family proceedings'—Courts Act 2003, s 75(1) requires '[t]here ... to be rules of court (to be called "Family Procedure Rules") governing the practice and procedure to be followed in family proceedings'.

'family proceedings in ... the Family Court'—The Family Court was created, with effect from 22 April 2014 by Crime and Courts Act 2013, s 17(3) and Sch 10 and by amendment of MFPA 1984 by addition of ss 31A–31P. The Family Division of the High Court remains separate from the Family Court, although FPR 2010 apply to both. The new statutory provisions in MFPA 1984 alongside CFA 2014, Pts 1 and 2 together introduce a new scheme of family proceedings.

'the High Court'—This terminology is used in FPR 2010 and in all Family Court delegated legislation; although in practice (see SCA 1981, Sch 1, para 3), 'High Court' means the Family Division of the High Court and is separate from the Family Court.

2.2 The glossary

(1) The glossary at the end of these rules is a guide to the meaning of certain legal expressions used in the rules, but is not to be taken as giving those expressions any meaning in the rules which they do not have in the law generally.

(2) Subject to paragraph (3), words in these rules which are included in the glossary are followed by 'GL'.

(3) The word 'service', which appears frequently in the rules, is included in the glossary but is not followed by 'GL'.

Glossary in CPR 1998—The glossary in FPR 2010 is derived from that in CPR 1998. The following terms occur in the CPR 1998 glossary and apply in proceedings under FPR 2010 but do not appear in the family proceedings Glossary:

- **Alternative dispute resolution** Collective description of methods of resolving disputes otherwise than through the normal trial process.
- **Base rate** The interest rate set by the Bank of England which is used as the basis for other banks' rates.
- **Divisional Court** With or without capital letters, means a divisional court constituted under section 66 of the Senior Courts Act 1981.

2.3 Interpretation

(1) In these rules –

'the 1958 Act' means the Maintenance Orders Act 1958;

'the 1973 Act' means the Matrimonial Causes Act 1973;

'the 1978 Act' means the Domestic Proceedings and Magistrates' Courts 1978;

'the 1980 Hague Convention' means the Convention on the Civil Aspects of International Child Abduction which was signed at The Hague on 25 October 1980;

'the 1984 Act' means the Matrimonial and Family Proceedings Act 1984;

'the 1986 Act' means the Family Law Act 1986;

'the 1989 Act' means the Children Act 1989;

'the 1990 Act' means the Human Fertilisation and Embryology Act 1990;

'the 1991 Act' means the Child Support Act 1991;

'the 1996 Act' means the Family Law Act 1996;

'the 1996 Hague Convention' means the Convention on Jurisdiction, Applicable Law, Recognition, Enforcement and Co-Operation in Respect of Parental Responsibility and Measures for the Protection of Children;

'the 2002 Act' means the Adoption and Children Act 2002;

'the 2004 Act' means the Civil Partnership Act 2004;

'the 2005 Act' means the Mental Capacity Act 2005;

'the 2007 Hague Convention' means the Convention on the International Recovery of Child Support and other forms of Family Maintenance done at The Hague on 23 November 2007;

'the 2008 Act' means the Human Fertilisation and Embryology Act 2008;

'the 2014 Act' means the Children and Families Act 2014

'adoption proceedings' means proceedings for an adoption order under the 2002 Act;

...

'application form' means a document in which the applicant states his intention to seek a court order other than in accordance with the Part 18 procedure;

'application notice' means a document in which the applicant states his intention to seek a court order in accordance with the Part 18 procedure;

'Article 11 form' means a form published by the Permanent Bureau of the Hague Conference under Article 11(4) of the 2007 Hague Convention for use in relation to an application under Article 10 of that Convention, and includes a Financial Circumstances Form as defined in rule 9.3(1) which accompanies such an application;

'Assembly' means the National Assembly for Wales;

'bank holiday' means a bank holiday under the Banking and Financial Dealings Act 1971 –

(a) for the purpose of service of a document within the United Kingdom, in the part of the United Kingdom where service is to take place; and

(b) for all other purposes, in England and Wales.

'business day' means any day other than –

(a) a Saturday, Sunday, Christmas Day or Good Friday; or

(b) a bank holiday;

'care order' has the meaning assigned to it by section 31(11) of the 1989 Act;

'CCR' means the County Court Rules 1981, as they appear in Schedule 2 to the CPR;

'child' means a person under the age of 18 years who is the subject of the proceedings; except that –

(a) in adoption proceedings, it also includes a person who has attained the age of 18 years before the proceedings are concluded; and

(b) in proceedings brought under the Council Regulation, the 1980 Hague Convention or the European Convention, it means a person under the age of 16 years who is the subject of the proceedings;

'child arrangements order' has the meaning given to it by section 8(1) of the 1989 Act;

'child of the family' has the meaning given to it by section 105(1) of the 1989 Act;

'children and family reporter' means an officer of the Service or a Welsh family proceedings officer who has been asked to prepare a welfare report under section 7(1)(a) of the 1989 Act or section 102(3)(b) of the 2002 Act;

'children's guardian' means –

(a) in relation to a child who is the subject of and a party to specified proceedings or proceedings to which Part 14 applies, the person appointed in accordance with rule 16.3(1); and

(b) in any other case, the person appointed in accordance with rule 16.4;

'civil partnership order' means one of the orders mentioned in section 37 of the 2004 Act;

'civil partnership proceedings' means proceedings for a civil partnership order;

…

'civil restraint order' means an order restraining a party –

(a) from making any further applications in current proceedings (a limited civil restraint order);

(b) from making certain applications in specified courts (an extended civil restraint order); or

(c) from making any application in specified courts (a general civil restraint order);

…

'consent order' means an order in the terms applied for to which the respondent agrees;

…

'the Council Regulation' means Council Regulation (EC) No 2201/2003 of 27 November 2003 on jurisdiction and the recognition and enforcement of judgments in matrimonial matters and in matters of parental responsibility;

'court' means, subject to any rule or other enactment which provides otherwise, the High Court or the family court;

(rule 2.5 relates to the power to perform functions of the court.)

…

'court officer' means a member of court staff;

'CPR' means the Civil Procedure Rules 1998;

'deputy' has the meaning given in section 16(2)(b) of the 2005 Act;

…

'detailed assessment proceedings' means the procedure by which the amount of costs is decided in accordance with Part 47 of the CPR;

'directions appointment' means a hearing for directions;

…

'the European Convention' means the European Convention on Recognition and Enforcement of Decisions concerning Custody of Children and on the Restoration of Custody of Children which was signed in Luxembourg on 20 May 1980;

'filing', in relation to a document, means delivering it, by post or otherwise, to the court office;

'financial order' means –

(a) an avoidance of disposition order;

(b) an order for maintenance pending suit;

(c) an order for maintenance pending outcome of proceedings;

(d) an order for periodical payments or lump sum provision as mentioned in section 21(1) of the 1973 Act, except an order under section 27(6) of that Act;

(e) an order for periodical payments or lump sum provision as mentioned in paragraph 2(1) of Schedule 5 to the 2004 Act, made under Part 1 of Schedule 5 to that Act;

(f) a property adjustment order;

(g) a variation order;

(h) a pension sharing order;

(i) a pension compensation sharing order; or

(j) an order for payment in respect of legal services;

('variation order', 'pension compensation sharing order' and 'pension sharing order' are defined in rule 9.3)

'financial remedy' means –

(a) a financial order;

(b) an order under Schedule 1 to the 1989 Act;

(c) an order under Part 3 of the 1984 Act except an application under section 13 of the 1984 Act for permission to apply for a financial remedy;

PART III

(d) an order under Schedule 7 to the 2004 Act except an application under paragraph 4 of Schedule 7 to the 2004 Act for permission to apply for an order under paragraph 9 or 13 of that Schedule;
(e) an order under section 27 of the 1973 Act;
(f) an order under Part 9 of Schedule 5 to the 2004 Act;
(g) an order under section 35 of the 1973 Act;
(h) an order under paragraph 69 of Schedule 5 to the 2004 Act;
(i) an order under Part 1 of the 1978 Act;
(j) an order under Schedule 6 to the 2004 Act;
(k) an order under section 10(2) of the 1973 Act; or
(l) an order under section 48(2) of the 2004 Act;

'hearing' includes a directions appointment;

'hearsay' means a statement made, otherwise than by a person while giving oral evidence in proceedings, which is tendered as evidence of the matters stated, and references to hearsay include hearsay of whatever degree;

'incoming protection measure' means a protection measure that has been ordered in a Member State of the European Union other than the United Kingdom or Denmark;

'inherent jurisdiction' means the High Court's power to make any order or determine any issue in respect of a child, including in wardship proceedings, where it would be just and equitable to do so unless restricted by legislation or case law;

(Practice Direction 12D (Inherent Jurisdiction (including Wardship Proceedings)) provides examples of inherent jurisdiction proceedings.)

'judge' means –

(a) in the High Court, a judge or a district judge of that court (including a district judge of the principal registry) or a person authorised to act as such; and
(b) in the family court, a person who is –
  (i) the Lord Chief Justice;
  (ii) the Master of the Rolls;
  (iii) the President of the Queen's Bench Division;
  (iv) the President of the Family Division;
  (v) the Chancellor of the High Court;
  (vi) an ordinary judge of the Court of Appeal (including the vice-president, if any, of either division of that court);
  (vii) the Senior President of Tribunals;
  (viii) a puisne judge of the High Court;
  (ix) a deputy judge of the High Court;
  (x) a person who has been a judge of the Court of Appeal or a puisne judge of the High Court who may act as a judge of the family court by virtue of section 9 of the Senior Courts Act 1981;
  (xi) the Chief Taxing Master;
  (xii) a taxing master of the Senior Courts;
  (xiii) a person appointed to act as a deputy for the person holding office referred to in sub-paragraph (xii) or to act as a temporary additional officer for any such office;
  (xiv) a circuit judge;
  (xv) a Recorder;
  (xvi) the Senior District Judge of the Family Division;
  (xvii) a district judge of the principal registry;
  (xviii) a person appointed to act as a deputy for the person holding office referred to in sub-paragraph (xvii) or to act as a temporary additional office holder for any such office;
  (xix) a district judge;
  (xx) a deputy district judge appointed under section 102 of the Senior Courts Act 1981 or section 8 of the County Courts Act 1984;
  (xxi) a District Judge (Magistrates' Courts);

(xxii) a lay justice;

(xxiii) any other judge referred to in section 31C(1) of the 1984 Act who is authorised by the President of the Family Division to conduct particular business in the family court;

'jurisdiction' means, unless the context requires otherwise, England and Wales and any part of the territorial waters of the United Kingdom adjoining England and Wales;

'justices' clerk' has the meaning assigned to it by section 27(1) of the Courts Act 2003;

'lay justice' means a justice of the peace who is not a District Judge (Magistrates' Courts);

'legal representative' means a –

(a) barrister;

(b) solicitor;

(c) solicitor's employee;

(d) manager of a body recognised under section 9 of the Administration of Justice Act 1985; or

(e) person who, for the purposes of the Legal Services Act 2007, is an authorised person in relation to an activity which constitutes the conduct of litigation (within the meaning of the Act),

who has been instructed to act for a party in relation to proceedings;

'litigation friend' has the meaning given –

(a) in relation to a protected party, by Part 15; and

(b) in relation to a child, by Part 16;

'the Maintenance Regulation' means Council Regulation (EC) No 4/2009 of 18 December 2008 on jurisdiction, applicable law, recognition and enforcement of decisions and co-operation in matters relating to maintenance obligations, including as applied in relation to Denmark by virtue of the Agreement made on 19 October 2005 between the European Community and the Kingdom of Denmark;

'matrimonial cause' means proceedings for a matrimonial order;

'matrimonial order' means –

(a) a decree of divorce made under section 1 of the 1973 Act;

(b) a decree of nullity made on one of the grounds set out in section 11, 12 or 12A of the 1973 Act;

(c) a decree of judicial separation made under section 17 of the 1973 Act;

'non-court dispute resolution' means methods of resolving a dispute, including mediation, other than through the normal court process;

'note' includes a record made by mechanical means;

'officer of the Service' has the meaning given by section 11(3) of the Criminal Justice and Court Services Act 2000;

'order' includes directions of the court;

'order for maintenance pending outcome of proceedings' means an order under paragraph 38 of Schedule 5 to the 2004 Act;

'order for maintenance pending suit' means an order under section 22 of the 1973 Act;

'order for payment for legal services' means an order under section 22ZA of the 1973 Act or an order under paragraph 38A of Part 8 of Schedule 5 to the 2004 Act;

'parental order proceedings' has the meaning assigned to it by rule 13.1;

'parental responsibility' has the meaning assigned to it by section 3 of the 1989 Act;

'placement proceedings' means proceedings for the making, varying or revoking of a placement order under the 2002 Act;

'principal registry' means the principal registry of the Family Division of the High Court;

'proceedings' means, unless the context requires otherwise, family proceedings as defined in section 75(3) of the Courts Act 2003;

'professional acting in furtherance of the protection of children' includes –

(a) an officer of a local authority exercising child protection functions;

(b) a police officer who is –

(i) exercising powers under section 46 of the Act of 1989; or

(ii) serving in a child protection unit or a paedophile unit of a police force,

(c) any professional person attending a child protection conference or review in relation to a child who is the subject of the proceedings to which the information regarding the proceedings held in private relates;
(d) an officer of the National Society for the Prevention of Cruelty to Children; or
(e) a member or employee of the Disclosure and Barring Service, being the body established under section 87(1) of the Protection of Freedoms Act 2012;

'professional legal adviser' means a –
(a) barrister;
(b) solicitor;
(c) solicitor's employee;
(d) manager of a body recognised under section 9 of the Administration of Justice Act 1985; or
(e) person who, for the purposes of the Legal Services Act 2007, is an authorised person in relation to an activity which constitutes the conduct of litigation (within the meaning of that Act),

who is providing advice to a party but is not instructed to represent that party in the proceedings;

'property adjustment order' means –
(a) in proceedings under the 1973 Act, any of the orders mentioned in section 21(2) of that Act;
(b) in proceedings under the 1984 Act, an order under section 17(1)(a)(ii) of that Act;
(c) in proceedings under Schedule 5 to the 2004 Act, any of the orders mentioned in paragraph 7(1); or
(d) in proceedings under Schedule 7 to the 2004 Act, an order for property adjustment under paragraph 9(2) or (3);

'protected party' means a party, or an intended party, who lacks capacity (within the meaning of the 2005 Act) to conduct proceedings;

'protection measure' has the meaning given to it in the Protection Measures Regulation;

'Protection Measures Regulation' means the Regulation (EU) No 606/2013 of the European Parliament and of the Council of 12 June 2013 on mutual recognition of protection measures in civil matters;

'reporting officer' means an officer of the Service or a Welsh family proceedings officer appointed to witness the documents which signify a parent's or guardian's consent to the placing of the child for adoption or to the making of an adoption order or a section 84 order;

'risk assessment' has the meaning assigned to it by section 16A(3) of the 1989 Act;

…

'RSC' means the Rules of the Supreme Court 1965 as they appear in Schedule 1 to the CPR;

'section 8 order' has the meaning assigned to it by section 8(2) of the 1989 Act;

'section 84 order' means an order made by the High Court under section 84 of the 2002 Act giving parental responsibility prior to adoption abroad;

'section 89 order' means an order made by the High Court under section 89 of the 2002 Act –
(a) annulling a Convention adoption or Convention adoption order;
(b) providing for an overseas adoption or determination under section 91 of the 2002 Act to cease to be valid; or
(c) deciding the extent, if any, to which a determination under section 91 of the 2002 Act has been affected by a subsequent determination under that section;

'Service' has the meaning given by section 11 of the Criminal Justice and Court Services Act 2000;

'the Service Regulation' means Regulation (EC) No. 1393/2007 of the European Parliament and of the Council of 13 November 2007 on the service in the Member States of judicial and extrajudicial documents in civil or commercial matters (service of documents), and repealing Council Regulation (EC) No. 1348/2000, as amended from time to time and as applied by the Agreement made on 19 October 2005 between the European Community and the Kingdom of Denmark on the service of judicial and extrajudicial documents in civil and commercial matters;

'specified proceedings' has the meaning assigned to it by section 41(6) of the 1989 Act and rule 12.27;

'welfare officer' means a person who has been asked to prepare a report under section 7(1)(b) of the 1989 Act;

'Welsh family proceedings officer' has the meaning given by section 35(4) of the Children Act 2004.

(2) In these rules a reference to –

(a) an application for a matrimonial order or a civil partnership order is to be read as a reference to a petition for –

(i) a matrimonial order; or

(ii) …

(iii) a civil partnership order,

and includes a petition by a respondent asking for such an order;

(b) 'financial order' in matrimonial proceedings is to be read as a reference to 'ancillary relief';

(c) 'matrimonial proceedings' is to be read as a reference to a matrimonial cause.

(3) Where these rules apply the CPR, they apply the CPR as amended from time to time.

(4) *(revoked)*

PART III

Amendments—SI 2011/1328; SI 2012/679; SI 2012/2007; SI 2012/2046; SI 2012/2806; SI 2012/3006; SI 2013/1472; SI 2013/3204; SI 2014/667; SI 2014/843; SI 2014/3296; SI 2015/913.

Interpretation provisions in the rules—While FPR 2010, r 2.3 deals with 'interpretation' of certain terms within FPR 2010 as a whole, some individual Parts have their own internal sets of interpretation rules (eg FPR 2010, r 12.2 for children proceedings and FPR 2010, r 9.3 for financial remedy proceedings). Most of these apply only to the Part in question. In addition to the commentary to r 2.3 ((1) below), the terms in use in family proceedings under these rules will be divided also into (2) common terms not defined by r 2.3 and (3) a summary of costs and procedure provisions in particular forms of application and cause.

Ancillary relief—See **Financial remedy**, below.

(1) Rule 2.3

'application form' and 'application notice'—A party to FPR 2010 family proceedings applies for any remedy, either (1) by 'application form' (see FPR 2010, Pt 5) for an originating process (generic or FPR 2010, Pt 19)); or (2) by 'application notice' for an interim or pre/post-action remedy (FPR 2010, Pt 18; and see for example FPR 2010, Pt 20). In the body of the rules in Pt 5, the term 'application form' does not appear: it is used only in the heading to FPR 2010, r 5.3. The rules leave parties to imply the term into the process of issue of originating applications in Pt 5. This is significant because the rules seem deliberately to make no reference in each Part to issue of a specific form of process, so applicants will need to depend on Pt 5, the accompanying FPR PD5A and the list of forms for issue, and the definition terminology in FPR 2010, r 2.3(1). This in its turn depends on understanding the meaning of what is 'other than … the Part 18 procedure'.

'application form… other than in accordance with the Part 18 procedure'—If the application is not made within the terms of Pt 18 (ie an interim order application), then r 2.3(1) provides that the application must be issued by 'application form', that is to say in accordance with the applications provided for in FPR 2010, Pt 5.

Meaning of 'child' and 'child of the family'—The statutory provisions that deal with family law, including statutes that are relevant to FPR 2010, provide a variety of different definitions of 'child'. Only a restricted number of these is touched on by FPR 2010, r 2.3(1). A full list would include: CA 1989, s 105(10); CA 1989; Sch 1, paras 2 and 6 (over 18 for certain financial remedy proceedings); CSA 1991, s 55; MCA 1973, s 52 and CPA 2004; I(PFD)A 1975, s 25(1); and CPR 1998; rr 2.3(1) and 21.1(2).

Child of age and understanding—Any reference to 'child' in family proceedings must be seen also in the context of the child's age and understanding (CA 1989, s 1(3); see *Gillick v West Norfolk and Wisbech Area Health Authority and Another* [1986] 1 FLR 224, HL and the factors in Pt 16 (eg appointment of a litigation friend or not: eg *Re CT (A Minor) (Wardship: Representation)* [1993] 2 FLR 278, CA)).

'detailed assessment proceedings' and 'summary assessment'—Detailed assessment proceedings, but not either detailed assessment or summary assessment, are defined. These are to be found defined in CPR 1998, rr 44.1.

'Maintenance Regulation'—Council Regulation (EC) No 4/2009 came into effect on 18 June 2011.

'Financial remedy' proceedings and 'financial orders'—The main terms comprised in these two definitions are distributed among MCA 1973 and other statutory and common law sources, in FPR 2010, r 2.3 and 9.3.

The following notes are intended to accompany the table below, to explain the various terminologies and to provide a guide for financial remedy costs orders under Pt 28. (MCA 1973 remedies in all cases have parallel CPA 2004 remedies.)

'Financial remedy'—This is defined to include all statutory remedies available under family proceedings legislation. In addition, there are a number of common law remedies (eg interim periodical payments are referred to in the rules (see r 9.7(1)), but not in any statute save MFPA 1984, s 14 and under MFPA 1984, s 31F(2)(b)). 'Ancillary relief' remains the statutory term under MCA 1973 (which comprises most financial relief on relationship breakdown).

Financial remedy proceedings in Part 28—'Financial remedy proceedings' in r 28.3 means something different than in the rest of the rules, namely a restricted set of financial remedy proceedings set out in r 28.3(4)(b) not being proceedings for a financial remedy set out in this rule. All 'financial order' proceedings are included, except for the interim orders excepted from the definition of 'financial order' by r 28.3(4)(b)(i).

Financial orders—These are comprised within the definition of 'financial remedy' order, but for costs purposes, exclude from the 'financial order' definition most remedies interim to financial order proceedings.

'protected party'—The meaning of 'protected party' and a person 'who lacks capacity' is further explained in FPR 2010, r 15.1.

(2) Terms not defined in this rule or within individual Parts

Answer—Proceedings are started by application form (originating application, including by the FPR 2010, Pt 19 procedure) or application notice. There is no generic term – save possibly 'answer' – to describe the respondent's or another party's statement of case in reply to an application (ie 'defence' in other civil proceedings). FPR 2010, r 4.1(1) is probably the nearest that the rules get to a definition of a term that describes the application and answer forms that parties exchange (where the rules provide for it) to describe their claim and opposition to that claim, and in r 4.1(1) the term 'answer' is used.

Early Neutral Evaluation—This term is used frequently in practice by family lawyers. It has been incorporated into civil proceedings (CPR 1998, r 3.1(1)(m)). There is no reason why it should not be used in family proceedings.

Party—See SCA 1981, s 151(1) and CCA 1984, s 147(1), as explained in *Re W (A Child)* [2016] EWCA Civ 1140, at [21]–[24].

Set aside application—See Procedural Guide E7 and FPR 2010, r 9.9A for financial remedy proceedings.

Specific disclosure—See introduction to Pt 21.

Standard disclosure—See under Pt 21.

(3) Costs and procedure in particular forms of application and cause

Procedure for issue (Table: col 3)—A summary of the procedure for issue is set out in col 3 (and see notes to Pts 5 and 9 (especially Ch 2):

- MCA 1973/CPA 2004 applications (mostly) will be in the petition/application, and then ancillary to that a financial claim can be issued (FPR 2010, r 9.4) in Form A.
- Other originating claims will be by Form A1, which is the originating application (there is no specific authority for this: it is merely implied by reading PD5A).
- Applications in the magistrates' court are issued as originating applications by Form A2 (again by implication from Pt 5 and PD5A).
- The FPR 2010, Pt procedure applies to all applications made interim to existing proceedings (r 9.7; and see FPR 2010, Pt 20 for urgent applications).
- Application to prevent a disposition (MCA 1973, s 37(2)(a)) is in existing (or to be filed) MCA 1973/CPA 2004 proceedings (FPR 2010, r 9.6).
- A variation application is made by Form A, A1 or A2 in the proceedings in which the original order was made.

Costs: proceedings for a financial remedy and 'financial remedy proceedings' (Table: col 4)—Costs orders are defined and explained in Pt 28, especially in r 28.3. This table deals in summary form with costs in all proceedings for a financial remedy. The term 'financial remedy proceedings' has a special meaning in relation to applications for orders for costs. (Other costs questions are dealt with under SCA 1981, s 51, FPR 2010, Pt 28 and CPR 1998, Pt 44. For financial remedy proceedings, the rules prescribe a 'clean sheet' (as explained under r 28.3) or that there should be no order (subject to exceptions: r 28.3(5)). The table therefore divides applications between the former (O) and the latter (N):

- **N** — no order for costs (r 28.3(5)) save in accordance with r 28.3(6)-(7).
- **O** — 'clean sheet' costs order (per *Judge v Judge* [2009] 1 FLR 1287, CA): per CPR 1998, r 44.2, save for costs following the event and subject to *Gojkovic* (see under FPR 2010, r 28.3).

TABLE

1 **Form of financial remedy or financial order**	2 **Defined**	3 **Procedure for application**	4 **Costs**
Avoidance of disposition	MCA 1973, s 37(2)(b),(c); FPR 2010, r 9.3(1)	1	O
Consideration of financial position	MCA 1973, s 10(2)	1	N
Costs allowance	Common law and per CA 1989, Sch 1, para 5 and 10 (below), but not in MCA 1973 or CPA 2004 proceedings (per MCA 1973, s 22(3))	2	O
Financial relief after overseas divorce: MFPA 1984, Pt 3	MFPA 1984, s 12	5	O
– if permission granted	MFPA 1984, s 17	1	N
Interim lump sum: MCA 1973	MCA 1973, s 23(3)	2	N
Interim lump sum: CA 1989 *	CA 1989, Sch 1, para 5(1)	3	O
Interim periodical payments: MCA 1973	Common law (and see MFPA 1984, s 31F(2); FPR 2010, r 9.7(1)(c))	2	O
	MFPA 1984, s 14; FPR 2010, r 8.24	2	O
Interim periodical payments: CA 1989 *	CA 1989, Sch 1, para 9; and FPR 2010 r 9.7(1)(c))	2	O
Interim remedies, including:		2	O
– applications under CPA 1997, s 7 (search and freezing orders)	FPR 2010, rr 9.7, 20.3 and 20.4		
– application to join a party	FPR 2010, r 9.26B		
– application to strike out	FPR 2010, r 4.4		
Interim order; DPMCA 1978	DPMCA 1978, s 19	2	O
Interim variation order	Common law (and see MFPA 1984, s 31F(2); FPR 2010, r 9.7(1)(d))	2	O†
Interim maintenance: MFPA 1984	MFPA 1984, s 14	2	O
Legal services order	MCA 1973, s 22ZA	2	O
Legal services order sale order	MCA 1973, s 24A		
Lump sum – final: MCA 1973	MCA 1973 s 21, 23(1)(c),(f)	1	N
Lump sum – final: CA 1989	CA 1989, Sch 1, para 1(2)(c)	3	O
Lump sum: DPMCA 1978	DPMCA 1978, s 2(b),(d)	3	O
Maintenance pending suit	MCA 1973, s 22(1)	2	O
Neglect to maintain	MCA 1973, s 27	3	O
Pension adjustment or other pension order	MCA 1973, ss 25B–25G; FPR 2010, r 9.3(1)	1	N
Periodical payments: MCA 1973	MCA 1973, s 21, 23	1	N
Periodical payments: CA 1989*	CA 1989, Sch 1 para 1(2)(a),(b)	3	O

PART III

1 Form of financial remedy or financial order	2 Defined	3 Procedure for application	4 Costs
Periodical payments: DPMCA 1978	DPMCA 1978, s 2(a) and (c)	3	O
Property adjustment order: MCA 1973	MCA 1973, s 24(1)	1	N
Restraint of disposal	MCA 1973, s 37(2)(a)	4	O
Set aside application (financial remedy proceedings)	–	2	O
Variation order	FPR 2010, r 9.3(1)	4	O
Variation of maintenance agreement	MCA 1973, s 35	3	O

† PD28A, para 4.2(a) should not assert that r 28.3(5) applies to interim variations of periodical payments given that r 28.3(4)(b)(i) provides that it is not a financial order for the purposes of r 28.3(4)(b); that does not make it a financial order. Only a 'variation' order (which presumably means a final order) is a 'financial order'.

Procedure for:

1 Application in divorce petition; Form A
2 Application per FPR 2010, Pt 18 in existing financial remedy proceedings
3 Free-standing application by Form A, A1 or A2; or D50C
4 Application by Form A in existing MCA 1973, CPA 2004 or CA 1989, Sch 1 proceedings
5 Application under FPR 2010, Pt 8
* In these instances, application can be made for a costs allowance (a common law remedy), which is not available in MCA 1973/CPA 2004 proceedings for 'divorce' etc or 'financial relief' proceedings (not statutorily defined), but which is available in most other forms of family financial relief proceedings.

2.4 Modification of rules in application to serial numbers etc.

If a serial number has been assigned under rule 14.2 or the name or other contact details of a party is not being revealed in accordance with rule 29.1 –

(a) any rule requiring any party to serve any document will not apply; and
(b) the court will give directions about serving any document on the other parties.

2.5 Power to perform functions conferred on the court by these rules and practice directions

(1) Where these rules or a practice direction provide for the court to perform any function then, except where any rule or practice direction or any other enactment provides otherwise, that function may be performed –

(a) in relation to proceedings in the High Court or in a district registry, by any judge or district judge of that Court including a district judge of the principal registry;
(b) in relation to proceedings in the family court –
 (i) by the court composed in accordance with rules made under section 31D of the 1984 Act; or
 (ii) where Practice Direction 2A applies, by a single lay justice who is authorised as specified in rules made under section 31D of the 1984 Act.
(c) *(revoked)*

(Rules made under section 31O of the 1984 Act make provision for a justices' clerk to carry out certain functions of the family court or of a judge of the family court and for an assistant to a justices' clerk to carry out functions of a justices' clerk given under those rules, or by section 31O(2) of the 1984 Act.)

(2) A deputy High Court judge and a district judge, including a district judge of the principal registry, may not try a claim for a declaration of incompatibility in accordance with section 4 of the Human Rights Act 1998.

Amendments—SI 2013/3204; SI 2014/667.

Defined terms—'district judge', 'district registry', 'principal registry': r 2.3(1).

Declaration of compatibility (r 2.5(2))—HRA 1998, s 4(5) defines which court can deal with declarations of compatibility (e g Supreme Court, Court of Appeal and High Court), but sitting in the High Court a deputy judge or district judge cannot hear such an application.

2.6 Powers of the single justice to perform functions under the 1989 Act, the 1996 Act, the 2002 Act and the Childcare Act 2006

(1) A single lay justice who is authorised as specified in rules made under section 31D of the 1984 Act may perform the functions of the family court –

- (a) where an application without notice is made under sections 10, 44(1), 48(9), 50(4) and 102(1) of the 1989 Act;
- (b) subject to paragraph (2), under sections 11(3) or 38(1) of the 1989 Act;
- (c) under sections 4(3)(b), 4A(3)(b), 4ZA(6)(b), 7, 34(3)(b), 41, 44(9)(b) and (11)(b)(iii), 48(4), 91(15) or (17) or paragraph 11(4) of Schedule 14 of the 1989 Act;
- (d) *(revoked)*
- (e) where an application without notice is made under section 41(2) of the 2002 Act (recovery orders);
- (f) where an application without notice is made for an occupation order or a non-molestation order under Part 4 of the 1996 Act; or
- (g) where an application is made for a warrant under section 79 of the Childcare Act 2006;

(2) A single lay justice may make an order under section 11(3) or 38(1) of the 1989 Act where –

- (a) a previous such order has been made in the same proceedings;
- (b) the terms of the order sought are the same as those of the last such order made; and
- (c) a written request for such an order has been made and –
  - (i) the other parties and any children's guardian consent to the request and they or their legal representatives have signed the request; or
  - (ii) at least one of the other parties and any children's guardian consent to the request and they or their legal representatives have signed the request, and the remaining parties have not indicated that they either consent to or oppose the making of the order.

(3) The proceedings referred to in paragraph (1)(a) and (c) are proceedings which are prescribed for the purposes of section 93(2)(i) of the 1989 Act.

Amendments—SI 2014/667.

'section 93(2)(i) of the 1989 Act' (r 2.6(3))—This paragraph was repealed by CCA 2013, Sch 11, para 110.

Scope—This rule sets out the functions that may be performed by a single lay justice under CA 1989, FLA 1996, ACA 2002 and the Childcare Act 2006. FPR PD2A provides that a single lay justice can perform any function that may be performed by the court under FPR 2010 and the PDs supplementing those Rules, except for those functions listed in Tables 1 and 2 of FPR PD2A.

'application without notice' (r 2.6(1)(a),(f))—Only certain orders may be sought without notice. Most of these are listed in FPR 2010, rr 10.2 and 12.16, which also set out the procedure to be followed. The court may refuse to make an order on an application without notice and adjourn the proceedings with a direction that the application be heard on notice (FPR 2010, r 12.16(6)).

'sections 10, 44(1), 48(9), 50(4) and 102(1)' (r 2.6(1)(a))—These sections of CA 1989 deal with the following: s 10 (power of the court to make s 8 orders); s 44(1) (application for an emergency protection order); s 48(9) (application for a warrant authorising a constable to assist in the enforcement of an emergency protection order); s 50(4) (application for a recovery order in relation to a child who has been abducted, run away etc); and s 102(1) (application for a warrant authorising a constable to assist in the exercise of certain powers to search for children and inspect premises).

'sections 11(3) or 38(1)' (r 2.6(1)(b),(2))—CA 1989, s 11(3) empowers the court to make a s 8 order before it is in a position to dispose finally of the proceedings in question. For example, where the proceedings have to be adjourned for a period and the court feels it necessary to regulate where the child is going to live by making an interim child arrangements order for living arrangements pending the resumed hearing. Section 38(1) empowers the court to make an interim care or supervision order where an application for a full care or supervision order is adjourned or where the court gives a direction under s 37(1) that the local authority should investigate the child's circumstances with a view to it possibly making a care or supervision order. FPR 2010, r 2.6(2) sets out the conditions that must apply for a single justice to be able to make such orders.

Provisions specified in r 2.6(1)(c)—The provisions specified in r 2.6(1)(c) require leave of the court before certain proceedings may be commenced or certain steps may be taken. The drafting is ambiguous in that, in

PART III

relation to certain of the specified statutory provisions, it is not clear as to whether it is the leave application with which the single lay justice is empowered to deal (as was almost certainly intended) or the substantive application that will follow should leave be given. CA 1989, s 4(3)(b) authorises a child to seek an order terminating a parental responsibility order or agreement in respect of him provided that he has the leave of the court. CA 1989, s 7 empowers the court (which, by virtue of r 2.6(c), may comprise a single lay justice) to require a welfare report. Section 34 allows certain people to apply for orders with regard to contact with a child in care; under s 34(3)(b) certain applicants must first seek leave to apply. Section 41 provides for the appointment by the court of a children's guardian or a solicitor for a child concerned in specified proceedings such as care proceedings etc. CA 1989 s 44 enables the court to make emergency protection order and where it does so, it may under s 44(6) give directions as to medical, psychiatric or other assessment of the child or contact with him. Section 44(9)(b) makes provision for the variation of such directions on application.

Section 44(11) applies where, after the making of an emergency protection order, it is proposed to return a child or allow his removal from the place where he has been detained. It specifies the rules of precedence by reference to which the applicant is to determine to whom he must deliver the child. The first choice is the person from whom the child has been removed, but, if that is not reasonably practicable, one of the other possibilities is, in accordance with s 44(11)(b)(iii), such other person as the applicant (with the agreement of the court) considers appropriate. Rule 2.6(1)(c)) empowers a single justice to signify the requisite agreement.

Section 48 includes miscellaneous provisions to assist in finding children who may be in need of emergency protection. Under s 48(4), the court may authorise a search of premises for a child with respect to whom there is reasonable cause to believe that an emergency protection order ought to be made. Both s 91(15) and (17) prohibit the making of repeat applications within 6 months in certain cases without leave (for example, no application for the discharge of a care or supervision order may be made within 6 months of the last such application). A single lay justice is empowered by r 2.6(1)(c) to give such leave. Finally, CA 1989, Sch 14, para 11(4) prohibits a child from applying for the discharge of an existing order except with the leave of the court. Rule 2.6(1)(c) permits a single lay justice to give such leave.

Power of Justices' Clerks—JCAR 2014, rr 2, 3 prescribe that justices' clerks and assistants may perform all of the functions of the Family Court or a judge of the court specified in the first column in the Table in the Schedule to the 2014 Rules, subject to the exceptions or restrictions contained in the second column.

Satisfying the conditions in r 2.6(2)—All three conditions must be satisfied before the order can be made. It follows that a single lay justice or justices' clerk can never grant the first interim order in a case but only a second or subsequent interim order, and then only if the order is in identical terms to the last such order, there is a written request for such an order and either signed consent of all parties or signed consent of at least one of the other parties and any children's guardian and no indication of opposition from remaining parties.

As to the duties of local authorities and the courts' powers and duties in relation to the making of interim care orders, see *C v Solihull MBC* [1993] 1 FLR 290, FD, *Re G (Minors) (Interim Care Order)* [1993] 2 FLR 839, CA, *Re J (Minors) (Care: Care Plan)* [1994] 1 FLR 253, FD, *Re W (A Minor) (Interim Care Order)* [1994] 2 FLR 892, CA and **Nature of interim orders** under CA 1989, s 38. See also **Abolition of requirement to renew interim orders** under CA 1989, s 38.

Written and signed request—There is no prescribed form for the making of such a request. The *Handbook of Best Practice* (see above) contains a draft application form that is tailored to this situation. It will not always be practical for all parties who wish to do so to endorse their consent on the written request itself and, in these circumstances, it ought to suffice if copies are signed and filed with the original.

2.7 Single lay justice: power to refer to the family court

Where a single lay justice –

(a) is performing a function of the family court in accordance with rule 2.5(1)(b)(ii) or rule 2.6(1) or (2); and

(b) considers, for whatever reason, that it is inappropriate to perform the function,

the single lay justice must refer the matter to the family court.

Amendments—SI 2014/667.

Scope—This rule provides for a single lay justice to refer the matter to a full court in an appropriate case. Identical provision is made for a justices' clerk performing the powers of a single lay justice to refer the matter to the court by virtue of JCAR 2014, r 4.

2.8 Court's discretion as to where it deals with cases

The court may deal with a case at any place that it considers appropriate.

Defined terms—'court', 'hearing': r 2.3(1).

'hearing'—'Hearing' comprises any court appointment before any judge or court (eg hearing in a solicitors' office: in *Oral Contraceptive Group Litigation XYZ & Ors v Schering Health Care Ltd & Ors* [2004] EWHC 823 (QB) the scale of documents involved justified detailed assessment being dealt with in a solicitors' office).

Hearing 'at any place [which the court] considers appropriate'—The court is final arbiter of where the hearing should take place. A venue more appropriate to a child or a protected party might be fixed, even if only for part of a hearing. Application could be made, for example, for the hearing of a case that involved a large volume of documents, to be held where the documents are most conveniently held (FPR 2010, rr 21.2 and 24.2(4)(b); and see *Khanna v Lovell White Durrant* [1995] 1 WLR 121, ChD), perhaps as a preliminary issue hearing on carefully defined document-based issues.

Application—The order could be made on the initiative of the court (FPR 2010), r 4.3) or on application under the FPR 2010, Pt 18 procedure (see especially FPR 2010, rr 18.9 and 18.10: hearings without attendance). The court will be concerned with the overriding objective, especially of 'saving expense' to the parties, where it considers an alternative venue for a hearing. Where numerous witnesses and a child involved in the case are distant from the court, there may be an economic argument for a removed hearing. Alternatively, a hearing by video-link may assist (FPR 2010, r 22.3; eg *Black v Pastouna* [2005] EWCA Civ 1389, where the Court of Appeal discouraged Liverpool counsel from attending court personally (as distinct from by video-link) on an appeal renewal application (and see CPR PD32, Annex 3 and FPR PD22A, Annex 3 on video conferencing)).

2.9 Computation of time

(1) This rule shows how to calculate any period of time for doing any act which is specified –

- (a) by these rules;
- (b) by a practice direction; or
- (c) by a direction or order of the court.

(2) A period of time expressed as a number of days must be computed as clear days.

(3) In this rule 'clear days' means that in computing the numbers of days –

- (a) the day on which the period begins; and
- (b) if the end of the period is defined by reference to an event, the day on which that event occurs,

are not included.

(4) Where the specified period is 7 days or less and includes a day which is not a business day, that day does not count.

(5) When the period specified –

- (a) by these rules or a practice direction; or
- (b) by any direction or order of the court,

for doing any act at the court office ends on a day on which the office is closed, that act will be in time if done on the next day on which the court office is open.

Defined terms—'business day': r 2.3(1); 'clear days': rr 2.3(1), 2.9(3).

Use of a calendar date and time—Rule 2.9 must be read in conjunction with FPR 2010, r 2.10, which requires dates and times to be specified in orders. If r 2.10 is followed, it should avoid many of the pitfalls that r 2.9 seeks to mitigate or provide for.

'7 days or less' (r 2.9(4))—CPR 1998, r 2.8(4) retains the shorter period of '5 days or less'.

Calculation of 'within 7 days', or the application will be struck out—For example, where a step in proceedings must be completed 'within 7 days' (which means 'clear days': r 2.9(2)) of a Tuesday:

(1) The 7 days starts the next day (Wednesday), followed by 7 business days. This takes the period to Friday in the following week for filing and service (i e 7 clear business days).

(2) If the Tuesday is in the week before Easter, the document must be filed and served as follows:

- (a) Time starts to run on the Wednesday (r 2.9(3)(b)) and the Easter weekend 'does not count' (r 2.9(4)). There are 2 business days before, and 4 in the week after, Easter: total 6 days to the weekend after Easter).
- (b) The weekend 'does not count' (r 2.9(4)), Monday is the final day of the 7 clear business days.
- (c) The period being '7 days or less' (r 2.9(4)) and 'clear days' being specified by the order, time expires on the Tuesday 2 weeks after time began to run.

2.10 Dates for compliance to be calendar dates and to include time of day

(1) Where the court makes an order or gives a direction which imposes a time limit for doing any act, the last date for compliance must, wherever practicable –

- (a) be expressed as a calendar date; and
- (b) include the time of day by which the act must be done.

(2) Where the date by which an act must be done is inserted in any document, the date must, wherever practicable, be expressed as a calendar date.

(3) Where 'month' occurs in any order, direction or other document, it means a calendar month.

Defined terms—'month': r 2.10(3).

Practice Direction – Practice Directions Relating to Family Proceedings In Force Before 6 April 2011 which Support the Family Procedure Rules 2010

Introduction and the Existing Practice Directions

1.1 The Family Procedure Rules 2010 ('the FPR 2010') come into force on 6 April 2011. The purpose of this practice direction is to inform court users of the practice directions relating (only) to family proceedings which date from before 6 April 2011 ('existing Practice Directions') but will continue to apply after that date.

1.2 The table in the Annex to this practice direction lists those existing Practice Directions which will continue to apply. The listed existing Practice Directions will apply to family proceedings on and after 6 April 2011 –

(a) with the modifications outlined in the Annex (in particular that the numbering of the existing Practice Directions will be as set out in column one of the table in the Annex) and any other modifications necessary in consequence of the FPR 2010 coming into force; and

(b) subject to the FPR 2010 and any other practice directions supporting those rules.

Application of Practice Direction 23B of the Civil Procedure Rules 1998

2.1 Paragraphs 1.1, 1.2, 1.4 and 1.5 of CPR Practice Direction 23B apply to applications under Part III of the Family Law Reform Act 1969 for the use of scientific tests to determine parentage. These applications will be made using the procedure in Part 18 of the FPR 2010 (Procedure for Other Applications in Proceedings).

ANNEX

Number	Title	Date	Court	Updated rule references
PD6C	Practice Direction (Disclosure of Addresses by Government Departments) (amending Practice Direction of 13 February 1989) (NB this practice direction does not apply to requests for disclosure from HMRC and related agencies which are covered by 'Disclosure Orders against the Inland Revenue-Guidance from the President's Office (November 2003)'	20 July 1995	High Court, county court and magistrates' court	
PD7D	Gender Recognition Act 2004	5 April 2005	High Court and county court	
PD12A	Public Law Proceedings Guide to Case Management: April 2010	April 2010	High Court, county court and magistrates' court	

Number	Title	Date	Court	Updated rule references
PD12B	The Revised Private Law Programme	April 2010	High Court, county court and magistrates' court	
PD12I	Applications for Reporting Restriction Orders (nb this practice direction applies to information about children and protected parties)	18 March 2005	High Court	
PD12J	Residence and Contact Orders: Domestic Violence and Harm	14 January 2009	High Court, county court and magistrates' court	In paragraph 10, for 'the Family Proceedings Rules 1991, rule 4.17AA and by the Family Proceedings Courts (Children Act 1989) Rules 1991, rule 17AA', substitute, 'rule 12.34 of the Family Procedure Rules 2010'
PD12K	President's Direction (Children Act 1989: Exclusion Requirement)	17 December 1997	High Court, county court and magistrates' court	
PD12L	Children Act 1989:Risk Assessments under Section 16A	3 September 2007	High Court, county court and magistrates' court	
PD12M	Family Assistance Orders: Consultation	3 September 2007	High Court, county court and magistrates' court	
PD12N	Enforcement of Children Act 1989 Contact Orders: Disclosure of Information to Officers of the National Probation Service (High Court and county court)	6 November 2008	High Court and county court (The Lord Chief Justice issued a Practice Direction on this subject for the magistrates' courts mirroring the one for the High Court and county courts)	
PD12O	Practice Direction (Arrival of Child in England by Air)	18 January 1980	High Court and county court	

PART III

Number	Title	Date	Court	Updated rule references
PD12P	Registrar's Direction (Removal from jurisdiction: issue of Passports)	15 May 1987	High Court and county court	
PD14A	Who Receives a Copy of the Application Form for Orders in Proceedings		High Court, county court and magistrates' court	In the heading, for 'Part 5,rule 24(1)(b)(ii) of the Family Procedure (Adoption) Rules 2005', substitute 'Part 14, rule 14.6(1)(b)(ii) of the Family Procedure Rules 2010'
PD14B	The First Directions Hearing-Adoptions with a Foreign Element		High Court, county court and magistrates' court	In the heading, for 'Part 5,rule 26(3) of the Family Procedure (Adoption) Rules 2005', substitute 'Part 14, rule 14.8(3) of the Family Procedure Rules 2010'; and in paragraph 2, for 'rule 26(1)', substitute 'rule 14.8(1)'
PD14C	Reports by the Adoption Agency or Local Authority		High Court, county court and magistrates' court	In the heading for 'Part 5,rule 29(3) of the Family Procedure (Adoption) Rules 2005', substitute 'Part 14, rule 14.11(3) of the Family Procedure Rules 2010'
PD14D	Reports by a Registered Medical Practitioner ('Health Reports')		High Court, county court and magistrates' court	In the heading for 'Part 5,rule 30(2) of the Family Procedure(Adoption) Rules 2005', substitute 'Part 14, rule 14.12(2) of the Family Procedure Rules 2010'; and in paragraph 1.1, for 'rule 30(1)', substitute 'rule 14.12(1)'
PD14E	Communication of Information Relating to the Proceedings		High Court, county court and magistrates' court	In the heading for 'Part 8,rule 78(1)(b) of the Family Procedure (Adoption) Rules 2005', substitute 'Part 14, rule 14.14(b) of the Family Procedure Rules 2010'; and in paragraph 1.1, for 'rule 78', substitute 'rule 14.14'

Number	Title	Date	Court	Updated rule references
PD14F	Disclosing Information to an Adopted Adult		High Court, county court and magistrates' court	In the heading for 'Part 8,rule 84(1)(d) of the Family Procedure (Adoption) Rules 2005', substitute 'Part 14, rule 14.18(1)(d) of the Family Procedure Rules 2010'; in paragraphs 1,1 and 1.2, for 'rule 84', substitute 'rule 14.18'; and in paragraph 1.2, for 'rule 17', substitute 'rule 5'
PD27A	Family Proceedings: Court Bundles (Universal Practice to be applied in All Courts other than the Family Proceedings Court)	27 July 2006	High Court and county court	
PD27B	Attendance of Media Representatives at Hearings in Family Proceedings (High Court and county courts) (This practice direction should be read as if amended by *Re X (a child) (residence and contact: rights of media attendance)* (2009) EWHC 1728 (Fam) [87])	20 April 2009	High Court and county courts	For references to 'rule 10.28 of the Family Proceedings Rules 1991', substitute 'rule 27.11 of the Family Procedure Rules 2010'; in paragraph 2.2 for 'paragraphs (4) to (6)', substitute 'paragraphs (3) to (5)'; in paragraph 2.3, for 'Part 11 of the Family Proceedings Rules 1991', substitute 'Part 12, Chapter 7 of the Family Procedure Rules 2010 and Practice Direction 12G'; in paragraph 4.2, for 'paragraph (8)', substitute 'paragraph (7)'; in paragraph 4.3, for 'paragraph (3)(f)', substitute 'paragraph 2(f)' and for 'paragraph 3(g)', substitute 'paragraph (2)(g)';

PART III

Number	Title	Date	Court	Updated rule references
				in paragraph 5.1,for paragraph(4), substitute paragraph (3); in paragraph 5.2, for 'paragraph (4)', substitute 'paragraph (3)' and for 'paragraph (4)(a)', substitute 'paragraph 3(a)'; in paragraph 5.3, for 'paragraph 4(a)(iii)', substitute 'paragraph 3(a)(iii)'; in paragraph 5.4, for 'paragraph 4(b)', substitute 'paragraph 3(b)'; and in paragraph 6.1, for 'paragraph (6)' substitute 'paragraph (5)'
PD27C	Attendance of Media Representatives at Hearings in Family Proceedings (Family Proceedings Court) (This practice direction should be read as if amended by *Re X (a child) (residence and contact: rights of media attendance)* (2009) EWHC 1728 (Fam) at [87])	20 April 2009	Magistrates' courts	In paragraph 1.1, for 'rule 16A of the Family Proceedings Courts (Children Act 1989) Rules 1991 ("the Rules")', substitute 'rule 27.11 of the Family Procedure Rules 2010 ("the Rules")'; in paragraph 2.1, for references to 'rule 16A(2)' where it occurs, substitute 'rule 27.11(1)' and for 'paragraphs (3) to (5) of rule 16A', substitute; 'paragraphs (3) to (5) of rule 27.11'; in paragraph 2.2, for 'rule 16A(2)', substitute 'rule 27.11(1)'; in paragraph 2.3 for 'Part 11C (rules relating to disclosure to third parties)', substitute 'Part 12, Chapter 7 of the Family Procedure Rules 2010 and Practice Direction 12G'; in paragraph 2.4, for 'rule 16A', substitute 'rule 27.11'; and in paragraph 4.3, for 'paragraph (1)(f)', substitute 'paragraph 2(f)' and for 'paragraph (1)(g)' substitute 'paragraph 2(g)'

Number	Title	Date	Court	Updated rule references
PD29B	Human Rights Act 1998	24 July 2000	High Court, county court and magistrates' court	
PD34B	Practice Note Tracing Payers Overseas	10 February 1976	High Court and county court	

Note—The list of Practice Directions above is no longer up to date and has not been formally amended.

PART III

Practice Direction 2A – Functions of the Court in the Family Procedure Rules 2010 and Practice Directions which may be Performed by a Single Lay Justice

This Practice Direction supplements FPR Part 2, rule 2.5(1)(b)(ii) (Power to perform functions conferred on the court by these rules and practice directions)

1.1 Where the FPR or a practice direction provide for the court to perform any function, that function may be performed by a single lay justice who is authorised as specified in rules made under section 31D of the 1984 Act except that such a justice cannot perform the functions listed in:

(a) column 2 of Table 1 in accordance with the rules listed in column 1; and

(b) column 2 of Table 2 in accordance with the paragraph of the practice direction listed in column 1.

1.2 For the avoidance of doubt, unless a rule, practice direction or other enactment provides otherwise, a single lay justice cannot make the decision of the family court at the final hearing of an application for a substantive order. For example, a single lay justice cannot make a child arrangements order on notice, placement order, adoption or care order. However, a single lay justice can discharge the functions of the family court under the statutory provisions listed in rule 2.6 of the FPR.

Table 1

Rule	Nature of function
3.10	Determining whether a MIAM exemption has been validly claimed.
4.1(3)(g)	Stay the whole or part of any proceedings or judgment either generally or until a specified date or event.
4.1(3)(l)	Exclude an issue from consideration.
4.1(3)(m)	Dismiss or give a decision on an application after a decision on a preliminary issue.
4.1(4)(a)	When the court makes an order, making that order subject to conditions.
4.1(6)	Varying and revoking an order (other than directions which the court has made).
4.3(1)	Ability of the court to make orders (other than directions) of its own initiative.
4.3(7)	Recording a decision to strike out a statement of case or dismiss an application (including an application for permission to appeal) and considering whether it is appropriate to make a civil restraint order where the court considers that the application is totally without merit.

Rule	Nature of function
4.4, 4.5 and 4.6	All the powers of the family court under these rules (power to strike out statement of case, sanctions have effect unless defaulting party obtains relief from sanctions).
Part 7	The duties and powers of the family court in this Part.
Part 8	The duties and powers of the family court in this Part otherwise than specified in rule 8.20(4) and except in relation to applications for a declaration of parentage under section 55A of the 1986 Act.
8.20(4)	A direction that a child should be made a respondent to the application for a declaration of parentage under section 55A of the Family Law Act 1986, except where the parties consent to the child being made a respondent.
9.11(2)	Direction that a child be separately represented on an application.
9.12(1)	The duties of the family court upon the issue of an application for financial remedies for children.
9.15	The duties and powers of the family court in respect of the first appointment relating to applications for financial remedies for children.
9.16(1)	Giving permission for the production of further documents between the first appointment and FDR appointment in applications for financial remedies for children.
9.16(2)	Giving further directions or directing that parties attend an FDR appointment.
9.17(8)	Making an appropriate consent order at the conclusion of an FDR appointment.
9.17(9)	Giving directions for the future course of proceedings for financial remedies for children where it does not make an appropriate consent order.
9.17(10)	Giving directions that the parties need not personally attend an FDR appointment.
9.18A(3)	Determining whether to give a direction that the procedure in Chapter 4 or Chapter 5 of Part 9 of the FPR should apply and notifying parties of that determination.
9.22	All the powers of the family court under this rule (relating to proceedings by or against a person outside England and Wales for variation or revocation of orders under section 20 of the 1978 Act or paragraphs 30 to 34 of Schedule 6 to the 2004 Act).
9.26B	The powers of the family court in respect of adding parties to, or removing parties from, proceedings for a financial remedy.
9.33(6)	Giving notice of the date of the first appointment or other hearing in an application for a financial remedy where the applicant or respondent is the party with pension rights.
9.34(3)(b)	Giving directions that a person objecting to a consent order for pension attachment attends court of furnish written details of the objection.
9.36	The duties of the family court in respect of making a pension sharing order or a pension attachment order.
10.11(2)	Determining, following an arrest, whether the facts and circumstances leading to an arrest amount to breach of an occupation order or non-molestation order and deciding whether to adjourn proceedings.
10.14	Adjourning hearings for consideration of the penalty to be imposed for contempt of court.
10.17(1)	The taking of recognizance.
Part 11	The duties and powers of the family court in this Part.

Rule	Nature of function
12.3(2)	Where the person with parental responsibility is a child, a direction for that child be made a party, except where the parties consent to that child being made a party.
12.3(3)	Direction that a child be made a party to proceedings or that a child who is a party be removed, except where the parties consent to the child being made a party or to the removal of that party.
12.3(4)	Consequential directions following the addition or removal of a party except where a single justice is able to make such a direction under rule 12.3(2) and (3).
12.8(2)	Directing that an applicant effect service in section 8 private law proceedings.
12.22	Drawing up a timetable for public law proceedings.
12.25	The duties and powers of the family court in respect of case management hearings.
12.26	The duties and powers of the family court in respect of discussions between advocates.
12.26C(1)	Giving reasons for, and an explanation of the impact on the welfare of the child of, decisions to extend time limits.
12.61(1) and (2)	Considering the transfer of proceedings to the court of another member state, directions in relation to the manner in which parties may make representations and power to deal with question of transfer without a hearing with the consent of parties.
12.64(1)	Exercising court's powers under Article 15 of the Council Regulation or Article 8 of the 1996 Hague Convention.
12.68(1)	Staying the proceedings.
12.68(3)	Giving reasons for the court's decision, making a finding of fact and stating a finding of fact where such a finding has been made.
12.70(1)	Contemplating the placement of a child in another member state.
12.70(3)	Sending request directly to the central authority or other authority having jurisdiction in the other Member State.
12.70(4)	Sending request to Central Authority for England and Wales for onward transmission.
12.70(5)	Considering the documents which should accompany the request.
13.3(3)	Where the person with parental responsibility is a child, a direction for that child be made a party, except where the parties consent to that child being made a party.
13.3(4)	Direction that a child be made a party to proceedings or that a child who is a party be removed, except where the parties consent to the child being made a party or to the removal of that party.
13.3(5)	Consequential directions following the addition or removal of a party except where a single justice is able to make such a direction under rule 13.3(3) and (4).
13.9(7)	Variation or revocation of direction following transfer, except where a single justice would be able to make the direction in question under rule 13.9(1).
13.15(3)	Determination of the probable date of the child's birth.
13.20(1)	Specifying a later date by which a parental order takes effect.
14.2(4)	Giving directions regarding the removal of serial numbers.
14.3(2)	Direction that a child be made a respondent, except where the parties consent to the child being made a respondent.

Rule	Nature of function
14.3(3)(b)	Direction that a child who is a party be removed, except where the parties consent to the child being made a respondent.
14.3(4)	Consequential directions following the addition or removal of a party except where a single justice is able to make such a direction under rule 14.3(2) and (3)
14.8(3)	Any of the directions listed in PD14B in proceedings for – (a) a Convention adoption order (b) a section 84 order (c) a section 88 direction (d) a section 89 order; or (e) an adoption order where section 83(1) of the 2002 Act applies (restriction on bringing children in)
14.16(8)	Making an adoption order under section 50 of the 2002 Act after personal attendance of one only of the applicants if there are special circumstances.
14.16(9)	Not making a placement order unless the legal representative of the applicant attends the final hearing.
14.17(4)	Determination of the probable date of the child's birth.
14.25(1)	Specifying a later date by which an order takes effect.
15.3(1)	Permission to a person to take steps before the protected party has a litigation friend.
15.3(2)	Permission to a party to take steps (where during proceedings a person lacks capacity to continue to conduct proceedings) before the protected party has a litigation friend.
15.3(3)	Making an order that a step taken before a protected party has a litigation friend has effect.
15.6(1)	Making an order appointing a person as a litigation friend.
15.6(6)	Court may not appoint a litigation friend unless it is satisfied that the person complies with the conditions in rule 15.4(3).
15.7	Direction that a person may not act as a litigation friend, termination of an appointment, appointment of a litigation friend in substitution for an existing one.
16.2	Power of court to make a child a party to proceedings if it considers it is in the best interests of the child to do so.
16.6(3)(a)	Permission to a child to conduct proceedings without a children's guardian or litigation friend.
16.6(6)	Power of the court to grant an application under paragraph (3)(a) or (5) if the court considers that the child has sufficient understanding to conduct the proceedings.
16.6(7)	Power of the court to require the litigation friend or children's guardian to take such part in proceedings (referred to in paragraph (6)) as the court directs.
16.6(8)	Power of the court to revoke permission granted under paragraph (3) in specified circumstances.
16.6(10)	Power of the court, in specified circumstances, to appoint a person to be the child's litigation friend or children's guardian.
16.8(2)	Permission to a person to take steps before the child has a litigation friend.
16.8(3)	Making an order that a step taken before the child has a litigation friend has effect.
16.11(1)	Making an order appointing a person as a litigation friend.

Rule	Nature of function
16.12	Direction that a person may not act as a litigation friend, termination of an appointment, appointment of a litigation friend in substitution for an existing one.
16.23(2)	Permission to a person to take steps before the child has a children's guardian.
18.3(1)(c)	Direction that a child be a respondent to an application under Part 18.
18.9(1)(a)	Power of court to deal with a Part 18 application without a hearing.
18.12	Power of the court to proceed in absence of a party, except where a single justice has the power to make the relevant order applied for.
19.8(2)	The court's power to require or permit a party to give oral evidence at the hearing.
Part 20	The duties and powers of the family court in this Part.
21.3	Power of court relating to withholding inspection or disclosure of a document.
22.1(2) to (4)	Power to exclude evidence that would otherwise be admissible, power to permit a party to adduce evidence, or to seek to rely on a document, in respect of which that party has failed to comply with requirements of Part 22 and power to limit cross examination.
22.6	Court's powers relating to use at final hearing of witness statements which have been served.
22.12	Power of court to require evidence by affidavit instead of or in addition to a witness statement.
22.15(4)	Permission for a party to amend or withdraw any admission made by that party on such terms as the court thinks just.
22.20(3)(a)	Permission for a witness statement in proceedings in the family court under Part 9 to be used for a purpose other than the proceedings in which it is served.
24.16(2)	Ordering the issue of a request to a designated court.
24.16(5)	Order for the submission of a request under article 17 of the Taking of Evidence Regulation.
25.4	Giving permission to put expert evidence before the family court.
25.5(1)	Having regard to any failure to comply with rule 25.6 or any direction of the family court about expert evidence when deciding whether to give permission mentioned in section 13(1), (3) or (5) of the 2014 Act or to give a direction under section 38(6) of the 1989 Act.
25.6(1)	Giving directions in respect of permission mentioned in section 13(1), (3) or (5) of the 2014 Act or rule 25.4(2).
27.5	Granting applications to set aside judgments or orders following failure to attend.
27.10(1)(b)	Direction that proceedings to which the Rules apply will not be held in private, expect that a single justice may give such a direction in relation to a hearing which that single justice is conducting.
27.11(2)(g)	Power of the court to permit any other person to be present during any hearing, except that a single justice may give such permission in relation to a hearing which that single justice is conducting.
27.11(3)	Direction that persons within rule 27.11(2)(f) shall not attend the proceedings or any part of them.
28.3(6)	Making an order requiring one party to pay the costs of another party.

Rule	Nature of function
29.8(1)	Court's opinion that it would be prevented by section 8 or 9 of the Child Support Act 1991 from making an order.
29.8(2)	Court's consideration of the matter without a hearing.
29.8(10)	Power of the court to determine that it would be prevented by sections 8 or 9 of the 1991 Act from making an order, and to dismiss the application.
29.8(11)	The court must give written reasons for its decision.
29.9(2)	Direction that the document will be treated as if it contained the application and directions as the court considers appropriate as to the subsequent conduct of the proceedings.
29.12(1)	Permission for inspection of a document, except where no party to the proceedings to which that document relates objects.
29.13(1)	Direction for a court officer not to serve a copy of an order (other than directions that the single justice has made) to every party affected by it.
29.15	Specifying alternative date for an order to take effect, except an order which the single justice has made.
29.16	Correcting an accidental slip or omission in an order, except where that order was made by a single justice.
29.17	Functions in relation to the transfer of proceedings to another court.
29.19(3)	Giving directions in respect of requests for reconsideration of decisions on the allocation of proceedings.
29.91(5)	Reconsidering decisions in respect of allocation of proceedings.
Part 30	Any power of the magistrates' court (where it is the lower court) to grant or refuse permission to appeal, except where a single justice has the power to make the order which is subject to the appeal.
31.9	Power for court to stay the proceedings.
32.22B	Powers in relation to methods of payment for means of payment orders.
32.22C(2)	Notifying interested parties of the outcome of an application for a variation of a method of payment.
32.22C(3)	Recording variations of methods of payment on the order to which the variation relates.
Part 33	The duties and powers of the family court in this Part.
Part 34	The duties and powers of the family court in this Part in so far as they relate to enforcement.
Part 37	The duties and powers of the family court in this Part.
Part 38	Recognition and Enforcement of Protection Measures
Part 39	The duties and powers of the family court in this Part
Part 40	The duties and powers of the family court in this Part

Table 2

PD3A – Family Mediation Information and Assessment Meetings (MIAMS) – Paragraphs 7, 36 and 37	• Under paragraph 7 if an applicant claims a MIAM exemption, the family court will issue proceedings but will inquire into the exemption claimed. At the first hearing the family court may review any supporting evidence in order to ensure that the MIAM exemption was validly claimed. If a MIAM exemption has not been validly claimed, the family court may direct the applicant or the parties to attend a MIAM, and may adjourn proceedings for that purpose. • Under paragraph 36 the family court may adjourn proceedings where evidence is not available or may give directions about how and when evidence is to be filed. • Under paragraph 37, if the family court determines that the MIAM exemption was not validly claimed, the court may direct the applicant, or the parties, to attend a MIAM and may adjourn proceedings pending MIAM attendance.
PD4B – Civil Restraint Orders	• Generally, the family court's functions in respect of applications for civil restraint orders.
PD7A – Procedure for Applications in Matrimonial and Civil Partnership Proceedings – Paragraphs 3.4, 5.3 and 7.1	• Under paragraph 3.4 the family court may give permission to file an application without the required documentation. • Under paragraph 5.3 the family court may direct a period within which a party must file with the court an amended application for a matrimonial or civil partnership order or an amended answer. • Under paragraph 7.1 the family court may made an order for the disclosure of documents under rule 7.22(2)(c) where an application for a matrimonial or civil partnership order is not being dealt with as an undefended case.
PD7B – Medical Examinations on Applications for Annulment of a Marriage – Paragraph 1.1	• Under paragraph 1.1 where a defended application is made for the annulment of a marriage based on the incapacity of one of the parties to consummate, the family court should not appoint a medical examiner unless it appears necessary to do so for the proper disposal of the case.
PD7C – Polygamous Marriages – paragraph 2.4	• Under paragraph 2.4 the family court may give an additional spouse notice of any of the proceedings to which this practice direction applies and make an additional spouse a party to such proceedings.
PD8A – Where to Start Certain Proceedings – Paragraph 1.2	• Under paragraph 1.2 the family court may make a direction in respect of whether a matter will be heard in the same location of the family court as existing (or proposed) proceedings.
PD12J – Child Arrangements and Contact Order: Domestic Violence and Harm.	• Generally, the family court's functions in respect of applications in respect of child arrangements orders, about where a child should live or about contact between a child and a parent or other family member except the functions in the first three bullets points in paragraph 6 and paragraphs 8, 15 and 21.

PD12M – Family Assistance Orders: Consultation – paragraphs 1.2, 1.3 and 1.5	• Under paragraph 1.2 the family court must have obtained the opinion of the appropriate officer about whether it would be in the best interests of the child in question for a family assistance order to be made and, if so, how the family assistance order could operate and for what period • Under paragraph 1.3 the family court decides on the category of officer required to be made available under the family assistance order • Under paragraph 1.5 the family court must give to the person it proposes to name in the order an opportunity to comment
PD14B – The First Directions Hearing – adoptions with a Foreign Element – Paragraph 2	Under paragraph 2 the court's consideration of: (a) whether the requirements of the Adoption and Children Act 2002 and the Adoptions with a Foreign Element Regulations 2005 (S.I. 2005/392) appear to have been complied with and, if not, consider whether or not it is appropriate to transfer the case to the High Court; (b) whether all relevant documents are translated into English and, if not, fix a timetable for translating any outstanding documents; (c) whether the applicant needs to file an affidavit setting out the full details of the circumstances in which the child was brought to the United Kingdom, of the attitude of the parents to the application and confirming compliance with the requirements of The Adoptions with a Foreign Element Regulations 2005; and (d) give directions about: (i) the production of the child's passport and visa; (ii) the need for the Official Solicitor and a representative of the Home office to attend future hearings; and (iii) personal service on the parents (via the Central Authority in the case of an application for a Convention Adoption Order) including information about the role of the Official Solicitor and availability of legal aid to be represented within the proceedings; and (e) consider fixing a further directions no later than 6 weeks after the date of the first directions appointment and timetable a date by which the Official Solicitor should file an interim report in advance of that further appointment.
PD15A – Protected Parties – Paragraph 4.2(b)	Under paragraph 4.2(b) court directions on service on protected party.
PD16A – Representation of Children – Paragraph 6.8	Under paragraph 6.8 the children's guardian must – (a) unless the court otherwise directs, file a written report advising on the interests of the child in accordance with the timetable set by the court; and (b) in proceedings to which Part 14 applies, where practicable, notify any person the joining of whom as a party to those proceedings would be likely, in the opinion of the children's guardian, to safeguard the interests of the child, of the court's power to join that person as a party under rule 14.3 and must inform the court (i) of any notification; (ii) of anyone whom the child's guardian attempted to notify under this paragraph but was unable to contact; and (iii) of anyone whom the children's guardian believes may wish to be joined to the proceedings

	Under paragraph 7.5 the court may, at the same time as deciding whether to join the child as a party, consider whether the proceedings should be transferred to another court taking into account the provisions of Part 3 of the Allocation and Transfer of Proceedings Order 2008.
PD18A – Other Applications in Proceedings Paragraphs 4.1 to 4.4(a)	Under paragraph 4.1 on receipt of an application notice containing a request for a hearing, unless the court considers that the application is suitable for consideration without a hearing, the court officer will, if serving a copy of the application notice, notify the applicant of the time and date fixed for the hearing of the application. Under paragraph 4.2 on receipt of an application notice containing a request that the application be dealt with without a hearing, the court will decide whether the application is suitable for consideration without a hearing. Under paragraph 4.3 where the court considers that the application is suitable for consideration without a hearing but is not satisfied that it has sufficient material to decide the application immediately it may give directions for the filing of evidence and will inform the applicant and the respondent(s) of its decision. Under paragraph 4.4(a) where the court does not consider that the application is suitable for consideration without a hearing it may give directions as to the filing of evidence.
PD20A – Interim Remedies	Generally, the family court's functions in respect of applications for interim remedies.
PD22A – Written Evidence – Paragraphs 1.6, 14.1 and 14.2	Under paragraph 1.6 the court may give a direction under rule 22.12 that evidence shall be given by affidavit instead of or in addition to a witness statement on its own initiative; or after any party has applied to the court for such a direction. Under paragraph 14.1 where an affidavit, a witness statement or an exhibit to either an affidavit or a witness statement does not comply with Part 22 or PD22A in relation to its form, the court may refuse to admit it as evidence and may refuse to allow the costs arising from its preparation. Under paragraph 14.2 permission to file a defective affidavit or witness statement or to use a defective exhibit may be obtained from the court where the case is proceeding.
PD24A – Witnesses, Depositions and Taking of Evidence in Member States of the European Union – Paragraph 9.1 and 9.6	Under paragraph 9.1 where a person wishes to take a deposition from a person in another Regulation State, the court where proceedings are taking place may order the issue of a request to the designated court in the Regulation State (rule 24.16(2)). The form of request is prescribed as Form A in the Taking of Evidence Regulation. Under paragraph 9.6 Article 17 permits the court where proceedings are taking place to take evidence directly from a deponent in another Regulation State if the conditions of the article are satisfied. Direct taking of evidence can only take place if evidence is given voluntarily without the need for coercive measures. Rule 24.16(5) provides for the court to make an order for the submission of a request to take evidence directly. The form of request is Form I annexed to the Taking of Evidence Regulation and rule 24.16(6) makes provision for a draft of this form to be filed by the a party seeking the order. An application for an order under rule 24.16(5) should be by application notice in accordance with Part 18.

PD27A – Family Proceedings: Court Bundles (Universal Practice to be Applied in all Courts other than the Family Proceedings Court)	• Generally, the family court's functions in respect of court bundles.
PD27B – Attendance of Media Representatives at Hearings in Family Proceedings	• Generally the family court's discretion to exclude media representatives from attending hearings or part of hearings (other than where a Single Lay Justice is conducting the hearing).
PD37A – Applications and Proceedings in relation to contempt of court	• Generally, the family court's functions in respect of applications and proceedings in relation to contempt of court.
PD38A – Recognition and Enforcement of Protection Measures	
PD40A – Charging Orders, Stop Orders and Stop Notices	• Generally, the family court's functions in respect of applications and proceedings for charging orders, stop orders and stop notices.

Practice Direction 2B – References in the Rules to Actions done by the Court or by a Court Officer

This Practice Direction supplements FPR Part 2

In the past, where the Rules have provided for an action to be done by the court or by a court officer, they have often provided that the court or court officer 'will' do that action.

From and including 11 January 2015, and including amendments coming into force on that date, where an amendment is made to these Rules to insert a new provision or alter an existing one, and that amendment provides for an action to be done by the court, or by a court officer, the Rules will generally provide that the court or court officer 'must' do the action, rather than 'will'. This is to make it clearer where an obligation lies with the court or court officer to do something. Occasionally in the future, it may still be appropriate to use the word 'will', for example in a statement of future intent, and on those occasions, 'will' will be used.

This does not affect the meaning of 'will' and 'must' in the Rules before 11 January 2015.

PART 3
NON-COURT DISPUTE RESOLUTION

CONTENTS OF THIS PART

Chapter 1

Rule Page

Interpretation

3.1 1307

Chapter 2

The Court's Duty and Powers Generally

3.2 Scope of this Chapter 1308
3.3 The court's duty to consider non-court dispute resolution 1308
3.4 When the court will adjourn proceedings or a hearing in proceedings 1308

Chapter 3
Family Mediation Information and Assessment Meetings (MIAMs)

3.5	Scope of this Chapter	1309
3.6	Applications to which the MIAM requirement applies	1309
3.7	Making an application	1309
3.8	Circumstances in which the MIAM requirement does not apply (MIAM exemptions and mediator's exemptions)	1309
3.9	Conduct of MIAMs	1311
3.10	MIAM exemption not validly claimed	1312
	Practice Direction 3A – Family Mediation Information and Assessment Meetings (MIAMS)	1312

General note—This Part of the Rules represents an emphasis on what is here termed 'non-court dispute resolution' (NCDR), reflecting the fact that many family cases are best disposed of by NCDR, particularly by mediation. If no welfare or safeguarding considerations arise, many private law issues under CA 1989 are better resolved by agreement between those who actually know the child and who are going to have to make any arrangement work, rather than by a solution being imposed by a court. Similarly, in a great many financial cases where assets are modest, the real question is not 'What is the appropriate outcome having regard to the criteria in MCA 1973?' so much as 'Is there some division of what is actually there that we can both live with?'. But, as the rules make clear, mediation has to involve the agreement of the parties. 'It is one thing to encourage the parties to agree to mediation, even to encourage them in the strongest terms. It is another to order them to do so' (*Halsey v Milton Keynes General NHS Trust* [2004] EWCA Civ 576). However, in *PGF II SA v OMFS Company 1 Ltd* [2013] EWCA Civ 1288, a failure to respond to an invitation to mediate was regarded as unreasonable and penalised in costs, as was a refusal to mediate save on unreasonable terms in *H v W (Cap on Wife's Share of Bonus Payments) (No 2)* [2015] 2 FLR 161, FD, and it appears that a retreat from *Halsey* may be underway.

It has been suggested that there ought to be a power to compel parties to engage in NCDR, and specifically that there should be such a power in enforcement proceedings, but it appears that under the rules as they stand this is not possible (*Mann v Mann* [2014] 2 FLR 928, FD).

As FPR PD3A makes clear, before commencing private law proceedings relating to children or proceedings for a financial remedy, an applicant must, save in certain specified circumstances, attend a mediation information and assessment meeting (MIAM). It is obligatory when issuing proceedings to file confirmation from a mediator that a MIAM has been attended, or to claim a 'MIAM exemption' or 'mediator's exemption', as defined. If it appears that exemption has been wrongly claimed, the court may adjourn the proceedings for the applicant to attend a MIAM.

A striking illustration of the court supporting ADR, in this case non-binding arbitration by the New York Beth Din in a case involving a devout Orthodox Jewish couple, is *AI v MT (Alternative Dispute Resolution)* [2013] 2 FLR 371, FD. However, the court will not sanction an arbitral process based on any form of gender-based discrimination: President's *Practice Guidance* of 23 November 2015, para 2.

Chapter 1
Interpretation

3.1 In this Part –

'allocation' means allocation of proceedings other than appeal proceedings to a level of judge;

'authorised family mediator' means a person identified by the Family Mediation Council as qualified to conduct a MIAM;

'domestic violence' means any incident, or pattern of incidents, of controlling, coercive or threatening behaviour, violence or abuse (whether psychological, physical, sexual, financial or emotional) between the prospective applicant and another prospective party;

'family mediation information and assessment meeting' has the meaning given to it in section 10(3) of the 2014 Act.

'harm' has the meaning given to it in section 31 of the Children Act 1989;

'mediator's exemption' has the meaning given to it in Rule 3.8(2);

'MIAM' means a family mediation information and assessment meeting;

'MIAM exemption' has the meaning given to it in Rule 3.8(1);

'MIAM requirement' is the requirement in section 10(1) of the 2014 Act for a person to attend a MIAM before making a relevant family application;

'private law proceedings' has the meaning given to it in Rule 12.2;

'prospective applicant' is the person who is considering making a relevant family application;

'prospective party' is a person who would be likely to be a party to the proceedings in the relevant family application;

'prospective respondent' is a person who would be a likely respondent to the proceedings in the relevant family application; and

'relevant family application' has the meaning given to it in section 10(3) of the 2014 Act.

Amendments—Substituted by SI 2014/843. Amended by SI 2015/1868.

Chapter 2
The Court's Duty and Powers Generally

3.2 Scope of this Chapter

This Chapter contains the court's duty and powers to encourage and facilitate the use of non-court dispute resolution.

Amendments—Substituted by SI 2014/843.

'encourage'—As noted, the court cannot compel the parties to use non-court dispute resolution.

'facilitate'—Where parties have agreed to use the Institute of Family Law Arbitrators arbitration scheme, that fact is likely to be a single magnetic factor of determinative importance for the court in deciding whether to approve a consent order giving effect to the arbitrator's award. The order should contain recitals to the effect that: (a) the documents lodged include the arbitration agreement (Form ARB1), their Form(s) D81, a copy of the arbitrator's award and a draft of the proposed order; and (b) by their Form ARB1 the parties agreed to refer to arbitration the issues described in it that encompass some or all of the financial remedies for which applications are pending in this court; and the parties have invited the court to make an order in agreed terms that reflect the arbitrator's award (*S v S (Financial Remedies: Arbitral Award)* [2014] 1 FLR 1257, FD, Munby P). See, generally, the President's *Practice Guidance* of 23 November 2015 in Part V.

If following an arbitral award evidence emerges that would have entitled the court to set aside an order on the grounds of mistake or supervening event, then the court is entitled to refuse to incorporate the arbitral award in its order and instead to make a different order reflecting the new evidence. An assertion that the award was 'wrong' or 'unjust' without more 'will almost never get off the ground': *DB v DLJ (Challenge to Arbitral Award)* [2016] 2 FLR 1308, FD, per Mostyn J.

3.3 The court's duty to consider non-court dispute resolution

(1) The court must consider, at every stage in proceedings, whether non-court dispute resolution is appropriate.

(2) In considering whether non-court dispute resolution is appropriate in proceedings which were commenced by a relevant family application, the court must take into account –

(a) whether a MIAM took place;

(b) whether a valid MIAM exemption was claimed or mediator's exemption was confirmed; and

(c) whether the parties attempted mediation or another form of non-court dispute resolution and the outcome of that process.

Amendments—Substituted by SI 2014/843.

3.4 When the court will adjourn proceedings or a hearing in proceedings

(1) If the court considers that non-court dispute resolution is appropriate, it may direct that the proceedings, or a hearing in the proceedings, be adjourned for such specified period as it considers appropriate –

(a) to enable the parties to obtain information and advice about, and consider using, non-court dispute resolution; and

(b) where the parties agree, to enable non-court dispute resolution to take place.

(2) The court may give directions under this rule on an application or of its own initiative.

(3) Where the court directs an adjournment under this rule, it will give directions about the timing and method by which the parties must tell the court if any of the issues in the proceedings have been resolved.

(4) If the parties do not tell the court if any of the issues have been resolved as directed under paragraph (3), the court will give such directions as to the management of the case as it considers appropriate.

(5) The court or court officer will –

(a) record the making of an order under this rule; and

(b) arrange for a copy of the order to be served as soon as practicable on the parties.

(6) Where the court proposes to exercise its powers of its own initiative, the procedure set out in rule 4.3(2) to (6) applies.

Amendments—Substituted by SI 2014/843. Amended by SI 2014/3296.

'and consider using' (r 3.4(1)(a))—These words, inserted with effect from 5 April 2015, have no real effect but give a further emphasis to the policy of encouraging the parties to use NCDR.

'where the parties agree' (r 3.4(1)(b))—Apart from the FDR procedure (as to which it has been suggested that for a party to fail to attend would be a 'serious contempt of court'), there is no power to compel parties to engage in NCDR (*Mann v Mann* [2014] 2 FLR 928, FD).

Chapter 3
Family Mediation Information and Assessment Meetings (MIAMs)

3.5 Scope of this Chapter

This Chapter contains Rules about the requirement in section 10(1) of the 2014 Act to attend a MIAM.

Amendments—Substituted by SI 2014/843.

3.6 Applications to which the MIAM requirement applies

(1) The MIAM requirement applies to any application to initiate the proceedings specified in paragraph (2), unless a MIAM exemption or a mediator's exemption applies.

(2) The specified proceedings are –

(a) the private law proceedings relating to children specified in Practice Direction 3A; and

(b) the proceedings for a financial remedy specified in Practice Direction 3A.

Amendments—Substituted by SI 2014/843.

3.7 Making an application

An application to initiate any of the proceedings specified in Rule 3.8 must contain, or be accompanied by, a form containing, either –

(a) a confirmation from an authorised family mediator that the prospective applicant has attended a MIAM;

(b) a claim by the prospective applicant that one of the MIAM exemptions applies; or

(A list of MIAM exemptions is set out in Rule 3.8(1) below.)

(c) a confirmation from an authorised family mediator that a mediator's exemption applies.

(A list of mediator's exemptions is set out in Rule 3.8(2) below.)

Amendments—Substituted by SI 2014/843.

3.8 Circumstances in which the MIAM requirement does not apply (MIAM exemptions and mediator's exemptions)

The MIAM requirement does not apply if –

(1) a prospective applicant claims in the relevant form that any of the following circumstances (a 'MIAM exemption') applies –

Domestic violence

(a) there is evidence of domestic violence, as specified in Practice Direction 3A; or

Child protection concerns

(b)

(i) a child would be the subject of the application; and

(ii) that child or another child of the family who is living with that child is currently –

(aa) the subject of enquiries by a local authority under section 47 of the 1989 Act; or

(ab) the subject of a child protection plan put in place by a local authority; or

Urgency

(c) the application must be made urgently because –

(i) there is risk to the life, liberty or physical safety of the prospective applicant or his or her family or his or her home; or

(ii) any delay caused by attending a MIAM would cause –

(aa) a risk of harm to a child;

(ab) a risk of unlawful removal of a child from the United Kingdom, or a risk of unlawful retention of a child who is currently outside England and Wales;

(ac) a significant risk of a miscarriage of justice;

(ad) unreasonable hardship to the prospective applicant; or

(ae) irretrievable problems in dealing with the dispute (including the irretrievable loss of significant evidence); or

(iii) there is a significant risk that in the period necessary to schedule and attend a MIAM, proceedings relating to the dispute will be brought in another state in which a valid claim to jurisdiction may exist, such that a court in that other state would be seised of the dispute before a court in England and Wales; or

Previous MIAM attendance or MIAM exemption

(d)

(i) in the 4 months prior to making the application, the person attended a MIAM or participated in another form of non-court dispute resolution relating to the same or substantially the same dispute; or

(ii) at the time of making the application, the person is participating in another form of non-court dispute resolution relating to the same or substantially the same dispute; or

(e)

(i) in the 4 months prior to making the application, the person filed a relevant family application confirming that a MIAM exemption applied; and

(ii) that application related to the same or substantially the same dispute; or

(f)

(i) the application would be made in existing proceedings which are continuing; and

(ii) the prospective applicant attended a MIAM before initiating those proceedings; or

(g)

(i) the application would be made in existing proceedings which are continuing; and

(ii) a MIAM exemption applied to the application for those proceedings; or

Other

(h)

(i) there is evidence that the prospective applicant is bankrupt, as specified in Practice Direction 3A; and

(ii) the proceedings would be for a financial remedy; or

(i) the prospective applicant does not have sufficient contact details for any of the prospective respondents to enable a family mediator to contact any of the prospective respondents for the purpose of scheduling the MIAM; or

(j) the application would be made without notice; or

(Paragraph 5.1 of Practice Direction 18A sets out the circumstances in which applications may be made without notice.)

(k)

(i) the prospective applicant is or all of the prospective respondents are subject to a disability or other inability that would prevent attendance at a MIAM unless appropriate facilities can be offered by an authorised mediator;

(i) the prospective applicant has contacted as many authorised family mediators as have an office within fifteen miles of his or home (or three of them if there are three or more), and all have stated that they are unable to provide such facilities; and

(iii) the names, postal addresses and telephone numbers or e-mail addresses for such authorised family mediators, and the dates of contact, can be provided to the court if requested; or

(l) the prospective applicant or all of the prospective respondents cannot attend a MIAM because he or she is, or they are, as the case may be –

(i) in prison or any other institution in which he or she is or they are required to be detained;

(ii) subject to conditions of bail that prevent contact with the other person; or

(iii) subject to a licence with a prohibited contact requirement in relation to the other person; or

(m) the prospective applicant or all of the prospective respondents are not habitually resident in England and Wales; or

(n) a child is one of the prospective parties by virtue of Rule 12.3(1); or

(o)

(i) the prospective applicant has contacted as many authorised family mediators as have an office within fifteen miles of his or her home (or three of them if there are three or more), and all of them have stated that they are not available to conduct a MIAM within fifteen business days of the date of contact; and

(ii) the names, postal addresses and telephone numbers or e-mail addresses for such authorised family mediators, and the dates of contact, can be provided to the court if requested; or

(p) there is no authorised family mediator with an office within fifteen miles of the prospective applicant's home; or

(2) an authorised family mediator confirms in the relevant form (a 'mediator's exemption') that he or she is satisfied that –

(a) mediation is not suitable as a means of resolving the dispute because none of the respondents is willing to attend a MIAM; or

(b) mediation is not suitable as a means of resolving the dispute because all of the respondents failed without good reason to attend a MIAM appointment; or

(c) mediation is otherwise not suitable as a means of resolving the dispute.

Amendments—Substituted by SI 2014/843.

'evidence of domestic violence' (r 3.8(1)(a))—Note that while PD3A remains prescriptive about what evidence of violence is acceptable, the timing of that evidence has been relaxed; it must now relate to violence within the past 5 years rather than the past 2.

'unlawful retention of a child who is currently outside England and Wales' (r 3.8(1)(c)(ii)(ab))—This is a curious provision. It implies that the unlawful retention of a child within England and Wales is not an emergency justifying a MIAM exemption. But it is submitted that this remains, as was said in *Re H (Children)* [2007] EWCA Civ 529, 'a situation which call[s] for the court to act with urgency and to treat the matter as an emergency', and to do otherwise will create 'a significant risk of a miscarriage of justice' (r 3.8(1)(c)(ii)(ac)).

3.9 Conduct of MIAMs

(1) Only an authorised family mediator may conduct a MIAM.

(2) At the MIAM, the authorised family mediator must –

(a) provide information about the principles, process and different models of mediation, and information about other methods of non-court dispute resolution;

(b) assess the suitability of mediation as a means of resolving the dispute;

(c) assess whether there has been, or is a risk of, domestic violence; and

(d) assess whether there has been, or is a risk of, harm by a prospective party to a child that would be a subject of the application.

Amendments—Substituted by SI 2014/843.

'authorised family mediator' (r 3.9(1))—This expression is defined in r 3.1.

PART III

3.10 MIAM exemption not validly claimed

(1) If a MIAM exemption has been claimed, the court will, if appropriate when making a decision on allocation, and in any event at the first hearing, inquire into whether the exemption was validly claimed.

(2) If a court finds that the MIAM exemption was not validly claimed, the court will –

(a) direct the applicant, or direct the parties to attend a MIAM; and

(b) if necessary, adjourn the proceedings to enable a MIAM to take place;

unless the court considers that in all the circumstances of the case, the MIAM requirement should not apply to the application in question.

(3) In making a decision under Rule 3.10(2), the court will have particular regard to—

(a) any applicable time limits;

(b) the reason or reasons why the MIAM exemption was not validly claimed;

(c) the applicability of any other MIAM exemptions; and

(d) the number and nature of issues that remain to be resolved in the proceedings.

Amendments—Substituted by SI 2014/843.

'will direct the applicant, or direct the parties, to attend a MIAM ... unless the court considers that ... the MIAM requirement should not apply' (r 3.10(2)(a))—The court must direct the applicant, or both parties, to attend a MIAM unless there is good reason not to. In addition to the circumstances envisaged in r 3.10(3), it may transpire that following the issue of the proceedings the parties have started to talk constructively to one another. In such circumstances, it may be felt that having had to pay a substantial fee is a sufficient sanction on the applicant.

Practice Direction 3A – Family Mediation Information and Assessment Meetings (MIAMS)

This Practice Direction supplements FPR Part 3

Summary

1 The purpose of this Practice Direction is to supplement the MIAM Rules in the Family Procedure Rules and to set out good practice to be followed by prospective respondents who are expected to also attend a MIAM.

2 Under section 10(1) of the Children and Families Act 2014, it is now a requirement for a person to attend a MIAM before making certain kinds of applications to obtain a court order. (A list of these applications is set out in Rule 3.6 and in paragraphs 12 and 13 below.) The person who would be the respondent to the application is expected to attend the MIAM. The court has a general power to adjourn proceedings in order for non-court dispute resolution to be attempted, including attendance at a MIAM to consider family mediation and other options.

3 A MIAM is a short meeting that provides information about mediation as a way of resolving disputes. A MIAM is conducted by a trained mediator who will assess whether mediation is appropriate in the circumstances. A MIAM should be held within 15 business days of contacting the mediator.

4 There are exemptions to the MIAM requirement. These are set out in the MIAM Rules (see Chapter 3 to Part 3 of the Family Procedure Rules), and are explained in more detail in this Practice Direction.

5 The effect of the MIAM requirement and accompanying Rules is that a person who wishes to make certain kinds of applications to the court must first attend a MIAM unless a 'MIAM exemption' or a 'mediator's exemption' applies. These exemptions are set out in Rule 3.8.

6 When making certain kinds of applications (see paragraphs 12 and 13 below), an applicant must therefore provide on the application form, or on a separate form, one of the following: (i) confirmation from a mediator that she or he has attended a MIAM; (ii) confirmation from a

mediator that a 'mediator's exemption' applies; or (iii) a claim that a MIAM exemption applies. An applicant who claims an exemption from the MIAM requirement is not required to attach any supporting evidence with their application, but should bring any supporting evidence to the first hearing.

7 If an applicant claims a MIAM exemption, the court will issue proceedings but will inquire into the exemption claimed, either at the stage at which the case is allocated or at the first hearing. At the first hearing, the court may review any supporting evidence in order to ensure that the MIAM exemption was validly claimed. As set out in more detail below, if a MIAM exemption has not been validly claimed, the court may direct the applicant or the parties to attend a MIAM, and may adjourn proceedings for that purpose.

Background: Consideration of mediation and other non-court dispute resolution

8 The adversarial court process is not always best suited to the resolution of family disputes. Such disputes are often best resolved through discussion and agreement, where that can be managed safely and appropriately.

9 Family mediation is one way of settling disagreements. A trained mediator can help the parties to reach an agreement. A mediator who conducts a MIAM is a qualified independent facilitator who can also discuss other forms of dispute resolution if mediation is not appropriate.

10 Attendance at a MIAM provides an opportunity for the parties to a dispute to receive information about the process of mediation and to understand the benefits it can offer as a way to resolve disputes. At that meeting, a trained mediator will discuss with the parties the nature of their dispute and will explore with them whether mediation would be a suitable way to resolve the issues on which there is disagreement.

The applications to which the MIAM requirement applies

11 In accordance with section 10 of the 2014 Act, and Rule 3.6, the proceedings to which the MIAM requirement applies are the private law proceedings relating to children listed in paragraph 12 and the proceedings for a financial remedy listed in paragraph 13 below.

Private law proceedings relating to children

12 (1) The private law proceedings relating to children referred to in paragraph 11 are proceedings for the following orders, unless one of the circumstances specified in sub-paragraph (2) applies –

- (a) a child arrangements order and other orders with respect to a child or children under section 8 of the Children Act 1989;
- (b) a parental responsibility order (under sections 4(1)(c), 4ZA(1)(c) or 4A(1)(b) of the Children Act 1989) or an order terminating parental responsibility (under sections 4(2A), 4ZA(5) or 4A(3) of that Act);
- (c) an order appointing a child's guardian (under section 5(1) of the Children Act 1989) or an order terminating the appointment (under section 6(7) of that Act);
- (d) an order giving permission to change a child's surname or remove a child from the United Kingdom (under sections 13(1) or 14C of the Children Act 1989);
- (e) a special guardianship order; and
- (f) an order varying or discharging such an order (under section 14D of the Children Act 1989).

(2) The circumstances referred to in sub-paragraph (1) are that the proceedings –

- (a) are for a consent order;
- (b) are for an order relating to a child or children in respect of whom there are ongoing emergency proceedings, care proceedings or supervision proceedings; or
- (c) are for an order relating to a child or children who are the subject of an emergency protection order, a care order or a supervision order.

Proceedings for a financial remedy

13 (1) The proceedings for a financial remedy referred to in paragraph 11 are proceedings for the following orders, unless one of the circumstances specified in sub-paragraph (2) applies –

(a) the following financial orders:
   (i) an order for maintenance pending suit;
   (ii) an order for maintenance pending outcome of proceedings;
   (iii) an order for periodical payments or lump sum provision as mentioned in section 21(1) of the Matrimonial Causes Act 1973, except an order under section 27(6) of that Act;
   (iv) an order for periodical payments or lump sum provision as mentioned in paragraph 2(1) of Schedule 5 to the Civil Partnership Act 2004, made under Part 1 of Schedule 5 to that Act;
   (v) a property adjustment order;
   (vi) a variation order;
   (vii) a pension sharing order; or
   (viii) a pension compensation sharing order;

(b) an order for financial provision for children (under Schedule 1 to the Children Act 1989);

(c) an order for financial provision in a case of neglect to maintain (under section 27 of the Matrimonial Causes Act 1973 or under Part 9 of Schedule 5 to the Civil Partnership Act 2004);

(d) an order for alteration of a maintenance agreement (under section 35 of the Matrimonial Causes Act 1973 or under paragraph 69 of Schedule 5 to the 2004 Act);

(e) an order for financial provision for failure to maintain for parties to a marriage and children of the family (under Part 1 of the Domestic Proceedings and Magistrates' Courts Act 1978 or an order under Schedule 6 to the Civil Partnership Act 2004); and

(f) an order for special protection for respondent in certain separation cases (under section 10(2) of the Matrimonial Causes Act 1973 or under section 48(2) of the Civil Partnership Act 2004).

(2) The circumstances referred to in sub-paragraph (1) are that the proceedings –

(a) are for a consent order; or

(b) are for enforcement of any order made in proceedings for a financial remedy or of any agreement made in or in contemplation of proceedings for a financial remedy.

Making an application

14 An application to the court in any of the proceedings specified above must be on the relevant court form which must contain either: (a) a confirmation from a mediator that the applicant has attended a MIAM; (b) a claim by the applicant that a MIAM exemption applies (the list of MIAM exemptions is set out in Rule 3.8(1)); or (c) a confirmation from a mediator that a mediator's exemption applies (the list of circumstances that qualify for a mediator's exemption is in Rule 3.8(2)).

15 Relevant application forms are available from the HMCTS form finder service at www.justice.gov.uk/forms/hmcts. For matters concerning children you can find out which form to use by reading the leaflet CB1 – Making an application – Children and the Family Courts'. Leaflet CB7 – Guide for separated parents: children and the family courts also provides guidance on the court process.

16 The relevant form can be completed either by the applicant or his or her legal representative. Any reference in this Practice Direction or in the Rules to completion of the form by an applicant includes a reference to completion by a legal representative.

MIAM exemptions

17 FPR Rule 3.8(1) sets out the circumstances in which the MIAM requirement does not apply. These are called MIAM exemptions.

18 In order to claim that a MIAM exemption applies, an applicant will need to tick the appropriate MIAM exemption boxes on the relevant form.

19 Applicants should note that some of the MIAM exemptions require that certain evidence is available. The next section of the Practice Direction specifies those forms of evidence. This evidence does not need to be provided with the application but applicants should bring such evidence to the first hearing because the court will inquire into such evidence in order to determine whether the MIAM exemption has been validly claimed.

MIAM exemption – Domestic violence

20 (1) The forms of evidence referred to in Rule 3.8(1)(a) are –

(a) a relevant unspent conviction for a domestic violence offence;

(aa) a relevant conviction for a domestic violence offence where a prospective party was convicted of that offence within the sixty month period immediately preceding the date of the application;

(b) a relevant police caution for a domestic violence offence given within the sixty month period immediately preceding the date of the application;

(c) evidence of relevant criminal proceedings for a domestic violence offence which have not concluded;

(d) a relevant protective injunction which is in force or which was granted within the sixty month period immediately preceding the date of the application;

(e) an undertaking given in England and Wales under section 46 or 63E of the 1996 Act (or given in Scotland or Northern Ireland in place of a protection injunction) –
  (i) by any prospective party in relation to another prospective party; and
  (ii) within the sixty month period immediately preceding the date of the application;

(f) evidence that a prospective party is on relevant police bail for a domestic violence offence;

(g) a letter from any person who is a member of a multi-agency risk assessment conference confirming that –
  (i) any prospective party was referred to the conference as a victim of domestic violence; and
  (ii) the conference has, within the sixty month period immediately preceding the date of the application, put in place a plan to protect that party from a risk of harm by another prospective party;

(h) a copy of a finding of fact, made in proceedings in the United Kingdom within the sixty month period immediately preceding the date of the application, that there has been domestic violence giving rise to a risk of harm by one prospective party to another prospective party;

(j) a letter or report from a health professional who has access to the medical records of a prospective party confirming that that professional, or another health professional –
  (i) has examined any prospective party in person within the sixty month period immediately preceding the date of the application; and
  (ii) was satisfied following that examination that that party had injuries or a condition consistent with those of a victim of domestic violence;

(ja) a letter from a social services department in England or Wales (or its equivalent in Scotland or Northern Ireland) confirming that, within the sixty month period immediately preceding the date of the application, any prospective party was assessed as being, or at risk of being, a victim of domestic violence by another prospective party;

(k) a letter or report from a domestic violence support organisation in the United Kingdom confirming –
  (i) that within the sixty month period immediately preceding the date of the application, any prospective party had been accommodated in a refuge;
  (ii) the dates on which that prospective party was admitted to and, if applicable, left the refuge; and

(iii) that that party was admitted to the refuge because of allegations by that party of domestic violence;

(l) a letter or report from a domestic violence support organisation in the United Kingdom confirming –

(i) that a prospective party was, within the sixty month period immediately preceding the date of the application, refused admission to a refuge on account of there being insufficient accommodation available in the refuge; and

(ii) the date on which that prospective party was refused admission to the refuge;

(m) a letter or report from –

(i) the person to whom the referral described below was made;

(ii) the health professional who made the referral described below; or

(iii) a health professional who has access to the medical records of a prospective party,

confirming that there was, within the sixty month period immediately preceding the date of the application, a referral by a health professional of a prospective party to a person who provides specialist support or assistance for victims of, or those at risk of, domestic violence;

(n) a relevant domestic violence protection notice issued under section 24 of the Crime and Security Act 2010, or a relevant domestic violence protection order made under section 28 of that Act, against a prospective party within the sixty month period immediately preceding the date of the application;

(o) evidence of a relevant court order binding over a prospective party in connection with a domestic violence offence, which is in force or which was granted within the sixty month period immediately preceding the date of the application; or

(p) evidence which demonstrates that a prospective party has been, or is at risk of being, the victim of domestic violence by another prospective party in the form of abuse which relates to financial matters, where that evidence dates within the sixty month period immediately preceding the date of the application.

MIAM exemption – Bankruptcy

21 The forms of evidence referred to in Rule 3.8(1)(h) are –

(a) application by the prospective applicant for a bankruptcy order;

(b) petition by a creditor of the prospective applicant for a bankruptcy order; or

(c) a bankruptcy order in respect of the prospective applicant.

Finding an authorised family mediator

22 As set out in Rule 3.9, a MIAM must be conducted by an authorised family mediator. Under that rule, an authorised family mediator is a person identified by the Family Mediation Council as qualified to conduct a MIAM.

23 A list of authorised family mediators, including their location, can be found using the 'Find your local mediator' search engine at: www.familymediationcouncil.org.uk

24 The expectation is that a prospective applicant should be able to find an authorised family mediator within 15 miles of his or her home. As stated in Rule 3.8(1)(o) a MIAM exemption is available if:

(i) the prospective applicant has contacted as many authorised family mediators as have an office within fifteen miles of his or her home (or three of them if there are three or more), and all of them have stated that they are not available to conduct a MIAM within fifteen business days of the date of contact; and

(ii) the names, postal addresses and telephone numbers or e-mail addresses for such authorised family mediators, and the dates of contact, can be provided to the court if requested.

25 Rule 3.8(1)(p) also provides an exemption if there is no authorised family mediator with an office within fifteen miles of the prospective applicant's home.

26 To determine whether a mediator is within the distance of 15 miles from their home, applicants can use the 'Find your local mediator' search engine to type in their own post code and then use the distance option to display only family mediators within a 15 mile distance.

27 The applicant will need to be prepared to produce at the first hearing the names, contact information and details of the dates of contact with the authorised family mediators.

28 Information about the Family Mediation Council, including its code of conduct can also be found at www.familymediationcouncil.org.uk

Funding attendance at a MIAM

29 The cost of attending a MIAM will depend on whether the prospective parties attend separately or together and whether at least one of the prospective parties is eligible for Legal Aid. If at least one party is eligible for Legal Aid then the total cost of MIAM attendance can be met by the Legal Aid Agency, whether the parties attend the same MIAM or separate MIAMs.

30 If neither party is eligible for Legal Aid then the mediator will agree with the prospective parties how the cost of MIAM attendance is to be met.

31 Parties can find out whether they are eligible for Legal Aid by using the calculator tool available at www.gov.uk/legal-aid

Attending a MIAM

32 Prospective respondents are expected to attend a MIAM, either with the prospective applicant or separately. A respondent may choose to attend a MIAM separately but this should usually be with the same authorised family mediator.

33 The prospective applicant should provide contact details for the prospective respondent to an authorised family mediator for the purpose of the mediator contacting them to discuss their willingness to attend a MIAM and, if appropriate, to schedule their attendance at a MIAM.

34 If the mediator contacts the prospective respondent and determines that he or she is unwilling to attend a MIAM, a prospective applicant should ask the mediator to confirm this as a ground for MIAM exemption in the relevant section of the application form, which should then be returned signed to the applicant.

MIAM exemption: Inquiries by the court

35 Where a MIAM exemption requires that certain evidence is available, the evidence does not need to be provided with the application form. Applicants should instead bring any such evidence to the first hearing because the court will inquire into such evidence in order to determine whether the MIAM exemption was validly claimed.

36 The court may if appropriate adjourn proceedings where such evidence is not available or may give directions about how and when such evidence is to be filed with the court.

37 If the court determines that the MIAM exemption was not validly claimed, the court may direct the applicant, or the parties, to attend a MIAM and may adjourn proceedings pending MIAM attendance.

Definitions

38 For the purpose of this Practice Direction –

'accommodated' [in paragraph 20(1)(k)(i)] does not require a stay of a minimum time period;
'care order' has the meaning given to it in Rule 2.3 of the FPR;
'care proceedings' has the meaning given to it in Rule 12.2 of the FPR;
'consent order' has the meaning given to it in Rule 2.3 of the FPR;
'emergency proceedings' has the meaning given to it in Rule 12.2 of the FPR;
'emergency protection order' has the meaning given to it in Rule 12.2 of the FPR;
'FPR' means the Family Procedure Rules 2010;
'financial order' has the meaning given to it in Rule 2.3 of the FPR;

'financial remedy' has the meaning given to it in Rule 2.3 of the FPR;

'health professional' means a registered –

(a) medical practitioner who holds a licence to practise;
(b) nurse;
(c) midwife; or
(d) practitioner psychologist who holds a licence to practise;

'mediator's exemption' has the meaning given to it in Rule 3.1 of the FPR;

'MIAM' means a family mediation information and assessment meeting;

'MIAM exemption' has the meaning given to it in Rule 3.1 of the FPR;

'MIAM requirement' has the meaning given to it in Rule 3.1 of the FPR;

'non-court dispute resolution' has the meaning given to it in Rule 2.3 of the FPR;

'pension compensation sharing order' has the meaning given in Rule 9.3 of the FPR;

'pension sharing order' has the meaning given in Rule 9.3 of the FPR;

'private law proceedings' has the meaning given to it in Rule 12.2 of the FPR;

'prospective applicant' has the meaning given to it in Rule 3.1 of the FPR;

'prospective party' has the meaning given to it in Rule 3.1 of the FPR;

'prospective respondent' has the meaning given to it in Rule 3.1 of the FPR;

'protective injunction' means –

(a) a non-molestation order under section 42 of the 1996 Act or article 20 of the Family Homes and Domestic Violence (Northern Ireland) Order 1998;
(b) an occupation order under section 33, 35, 36, 37 or 38 of the 1996 Act or article 11, 13, 14, 15 or 16 of the Family Homes and Domestic Violence (Northern Ireland) Order 1998;
(c) an exclusion order under section 4 of the Matrimonial Homes (Family Protection) (Scotland) Act 1981 or section 104 of the 2004 Act;
(d) a forced marriage protection order or interim forced marriage protection order under any of the following provisions –
    (i) Part 4A of the 1996 Act;
    (ii) section 2 of, and paragraph 1 of Schedule 1 to, the Forced Marriage (Civil Protection) Act 2007;
    (iii) section 1 of the Forced Marriage etc. (Protection & Jurisdiction) (Scotland) Act 2011; and
    (iv) section 5 of the Forced Marriage etc. (Protection & Jurisdiction) (Scotland) Act 2011;
(da) an injunction under section 3A of the Protection from Harassment Act 1997;
(e) a restraining order under section 5 or 5A of the Protection from Harassment Act 1997;
(f) a restraining injunction under article 5 or a restraining order under article 7 or 7A of the Protection from Harassment (Northern Ireland) Order 1997;
(g) a non-harassment order under section 234A of the Criminal Procedure (Scotland) Act 1995 or section 8 or 8A of the Protection from Harassment Act 1997;
(h) a common law injunction;
(i) any of the following interdicts –
    (i) a matrimonial interdict within the meaning of section 14 of the Matrimonial Homes (Family Protection) (Scotland) Act 1981;
    (ii) a domestic interdict within the meaning of section 18A of the Matrimonial Homes (Family Protection) (Scotland) Act 1981;
    (iii) an interdict for civil partners within the meaning of section 113 of the Civil Partnership Act 2004;
    (iv) an interdict that has been determined to be a domestic abuse interdict within the meaning of section 3 of the Domestic Abuse (Scotland) Act 2001; and
    (v) a common law interdict;
(j) a female genital mutilation protection order under paragraph 1 or 18 of Schedule 2 to the Female Genital Mutilation Act 2003;

(j) a violent offender order within the meaning of section 98 of the Criminal Justice and Immigration Act 2008;

'refuge' means a refuge established for the purpose of providing accommodation for victims of, or those at risk of, domestic violence;

'relevant' in paragraph 20 of this Practice Direction means that the evidence –

(a) identifies a prospective party as being, or at risk of being, the victim of domestic violence unless the evidence –

(i) is in a form described in paragraph 20 (1)(a) to (c), (f), (n) or (o); and

(ii) relates to a domestic violence offence which does not identify the victim; and

(b) identifies another party as being –

(i) for evidence described in paragraph 20(1)(a) to (c) and (f), convicted of, cautioned with, on police bail for, or charged with the domestic violence offence; and

(ii) for evidence described in paragraph 20(1)(d), the respondent to the protective injunction;

(iii) for evidence described in paragraph 20(1)(n), the person against whom the notice or order has been issued or made; and

(iv) for evidence described in paragraph 20(1)(o), the person against whom the order binding over has been made.

'supervision order' has the meaning given to it in Rule 12.2 of the FPR;

'supervision proceedings' has the meaning given to it in Rule 12.2 of the FPR; and

'variation order' has the meaning given to it in Rule 9.3 of the FPR.

Note—Within the definition of 'protective injunction', there appears to be two paragraphs labelled '(i)'.

PART III

PART 4
GENERAL CASE MANAGEMENT POWERS

CONTENTS OF THIS PART

Rule		Page
4.1	The court's general powers of management	1319
4.2	Court officer's power to refer to the court	1321
4.3	Court's power to make order of its own initiative	1321
4.4	Power to strike out a statement of case	1322
4.5	Sanctions have effect unless defaulting party obtains relief	1323
4.6	Relief from sanctions	1323
4.7	General power of the court to rectify matters where there has been an error of procedure	1324
4.8	Power of the court to make civil restraint orders	1324
	Practice Direction 4A – Striking Out a Statement of Case	1325
	Practice Direction 4B – Civil Restraint Orders	1326

4.1 The court's general powers of management

(1) In this Part, 'statement of case' means the whole or part of, an application form or answer.

(2) The list of powers in this rule is in addition to any powers given to the court by any other rule or practice direction or by any other enactment or any powers it may otherwise have.

(3) Except where these rules provide otherwise, the court may –

(a) extend or shorten the time for compliance with any rule, practice direction or court order (even if an application for extension is made after the time for compliance has expired);

(b) make such order for disclosure and inspection, including specific disclosure of documents, as it thinks fit;
(c) adjourn or bring forward a hearing;
(d) require a party or a party's legal representative to attend the court;
(e) hold a hearing and receive evidence by telephone or by using any other method of direct oral communication;
(f) direct that part of any proceedings be dealt with as separate proceedings;
(g) stay(GL) the whole or part of any proceedings or judgment either generally or until a specified date or event;
(h) consolidate proceedings;
(i) hear two or more applications on the same occasion;
(j) direct a separate hearing of any issue;
(k) decide the order in which issues are to be heard;
(l) exclude an issue from consideration;
(m) dismiss or give a decision on an application after a decision on a preliminary issue;
(n) direct any party to file and serve an estimate of costs; and
(o) take any other step or make any other order for the purpose of managing the case and furthering the overriding objective.

(Rule 21.1 explains what is meant by disclosure and inspection.)

(4) When the court makes an order, it may –
(a) make it subject to conditions, including a condition to pay a sum of money into court; and
(b) specify the consequence of failure to comply with the order or a condition.

(5) Where the court gives directions it will take into account whether or not a party has complied with any relevant pre-action protocol(GL).

(6) A power of the court under these rules to make an order includes a power to vary or revoke the order.

(7) Any provision in these rules –
(a) requiring or permitting directions to be given by the court is to be taken as including provision for such directions to be varied or revoked; and
(b) requiring or permitting a date to be set is to be taken as including provision for that date to be changed or cancelled.

(8) The court may not extend the period within which an application for a section 89 order must be made.

Amendments—SI 2012/679.

'The court's general powers of management'—The powers set out in r 4.1(3) are almost identical to the powers accorded to the civil courts under CPR 1998, r 3.1 but following *Mitchell v News Group Newspapers Ltd* [2013] EWCA Civ 1537 decisions on the interpretation of the CPR are likely to be of limited assistance in construing them.

'adjourn ... a hearing' (r 4.1(3)(c))—The court is not required by HRA 1998, Sch 1, Pt I, Art 6 to adjourn a hopeless case to allow a party back into the fray simply because there has been some procedural unfairness along the way (*Lloyds Bank plc v Dix & anor* [2000] EWCA Civ 269). *Fitzroy Robinson v Mentmore Towers* [2009] EWHC 3070 (TCC) provides a useful checklist of factors to be taken into account when considering a contested last-minute application to adjourn a trial, although in dealing with family cases other considerations will also arise.

'telephone' (r 4.1(3)(e))—Parties are encouraged to save costs by taking advantage of telephone and video conferencing services. Care should be taken to organise these properly, cf *K v K (Financial Relief: Management of Difficult Cases)* [2005] 2 FLR 1137, FD, at [23]–[31].

'a separate trial of any issue' (r 4.1(3)(j))—In *McLoughlin v Grovers (A firm)* [2001] EWCA Civ 1743, guidelines were suggested, which included the following:

(a) Only issues that are decisive or potentially decisive should be identified.
(b) Issues should be decided on the basis of a schedule of agreed or assumed facts.
(c) The issues should be triable without significant delay, making full allowance for the implications of a possible appeal.
(d) Any order should be made by the court following a case-management conference.

'take any other step or make any other order' (r 4.1(4)(b))—It is doubtful that this extends to removing a judgment from the public domain or otherwise making orders restricting its use: *Re C (A Child)* [2016] EWCA Civ 798, doubting *H v A (No 2)* [2016] 2 FLR 723, FD.

'complied with any relevant pre-action protocol' (r 4.1(5))—In the civil courts, pre-action protocols have proved themselves to be a powerful agent of change for the better in daily practice. The Family Court is here given explicit encouragement to enforce good practice. Practitioners (and litigants) who persist in viewing family litigation as a species of warfare are likely to be firmly dealt with.

'a power to vary or revoke' (r 4.1(6))—In *Arif v Zar and anor* [2012] EWCA Civ 986, Patten LJ observed that this power was 'ordinarily limited to cases where there has been a material change of circumstances since the order was made or the original order can be shown to have been based on mis-stated facts or material non-disclosure'. While the power is not a substitute for an appeal (*Edwards v Golding* [2007] EWCA Civ 416), that approach was followed by Sir James Munby P in *CS v ACS (Consent Order: Non-Disclosure: Correct Procedure)* [2016] 1 FLR 131, FD, holding that an application to set aside a consent order in family proceedings could be made (with permission) by way of appeal or (with no requirement to seek permission) by application under this rule.

An application to set aside a consent order under this rule will be considered against the criteria set out in *Tibbles v SIG plc* [2012] EWCA Civ 518. Finality in litigation is desirable; litigants should not have 'two bites at the cherry'; the concept of appeal should not be undermined; application should be made promptly. Having borne those matters in mind, the court can set aside an order:

'(i) where there has been a material change of circumstances since the order was made;
(ii) where the facts on which the original decision were based have been misstated; or
(ii) where there has been a manifest mistake on the part of the judge in formulating the order.' (*Norman v Norman* [2017] EWCA Civ 120)'.

When the High Court concluded that a Dubai divorce was entitled to recognition, with the consequence that a subsequent purported English divorce was void, this rule was cited as a procedural basis for setting the English decree aside (*Lachaux v Lachaux* [2017] EWHC 385 (Fam)).

'the period within which an application for a section 89 order must be made' (r 4.1(8))—That is, an order by the High Court under ACA 2002, s 89 annulling an overseas or Convention adoption, see FPR 2010, rr 2.3(1) and 14.22.

'exclude an issue from consideration' (r 4.1(3)(l))—The court may achieve much with orders under r 4.1(3)(l) excluding particular issues, such as conduct, from consideration; or by orders directing, for example, that unless particular steps are taken the final hearing will proceed on the assumption that, e g the respondent has net earnings of not less than £X per annum, or free capital of £Y million. Cf the approach taken to an uncooperative and obstructive respondent in *Al-Baker v Al-Baker* [2016] EWHC 2510 (Fam), which culminated in an award of £61.5 million. If it is proposed to draw adverse inferences from a party's failure to attend a hearing, it has been said that this should be spelt out explicitly (*Iqbal v Iqbal* [2017] EWCA Civ 19).

4.2 Court officer's power to refer to the court

Where a step is to be taken by a court officer –

(a) the court officer may consult the court before taking that step;
(b) the step may be taken by the court instead of the court officer.

4.3 Court's power to make order of its own initiative

(1) Except where an enactment provides otherwise, the court may exercise its powers on an application or of its own initiative.

(Part 18 sets out the procedure for making an application.)

(2) Subject to rule 29.17, where the court proposes to make an order of its own initiative –

(a) it may give any person likely to be affected by the order an opportunity to make representations; and
(b) where it does so it must specify the time by and the manner in which the representations must be made.

(3) Where the court proposes –

(a) to make an order of its own initiative; and
(b) to hold a hearing to decide whether to make the order,

it must give each party likely to be affected by the order at least 5 days' notice of the hearing.

(4) The court may make an order of its own initiative without hearing the parties or giving them an opportunity to make representations.

(5) Where the court has made an order under paragraph 4 –

(a) a party affected by the order may apply to have it set aside(GL), varied or stayed(GL); and
(b) the order must contain a statement of the right to make such an application.

PART III

(6) An application under paragraph (5)(a) must be made –

(a) within such period as may be specified by the court; or

(b) if the court does not specify a period, within 7 days beginning with the date on which the order was served on the party making the application.

(7) If the court of its own initiative strikes out a statement of case or dismisses an application (including an application for permission to appeal) and it considers that the application is totally without merit –

(a) the court's order must record that fact; and

(b) the court must at the same time consider whether it is appropriate to make a civil restraint order.

Amendments—SI 2013/3204.

'subject to rule 29.17' (r 4.3(2))—That rule deals with the transfer of cases and provides that a court may transfer a case without a hearing if the court has notified the parties that it intends to do so and no party has within 14 days requested a hearing to determine the question. If the case for transfer is overwhelming (eg application issued in Birmingham relating to child living in Truro) it is not clear that the requirement to wait 14 days accords with Children Act 1989, s 1(2) and indeed r 1.1(2)(a).

4.4 Power to strike out a statement of case

(1) Except in proceedings to which Parts 12 to 14 apply, the court may strike out[(GL)] a statement of case if it appears to the court –

(a) that the statement of case discloses no reasonable grounds for bringing or defending the application;

(b) that the statement of case is an abuse of the court's process or is otherwise likely to obstruct the just disposal of the proceedings;

(c) that there has been a failure to comply with a rule, practice direction or court order; or

(d) in relation to applications for matrimonial and civil partnership orders and answers to such applications, that the parties to the proceedings consent.

(1A) When the court is considering whether to exercise the power to strike out a statement of case, it must take into account any written evidence filed in relation to the application or answer.

(2) When the court strikes out a statement of case it may make any consequential order it considers appropriate.

(3) Where –

(a) the court has struck out an applicant's statement of case;

(b) the applicant has been ordered to pay costs to the respondent; and

(c) before paying those costs, the applicant starts another application against the same respondent, arising out of facts which are the same or substantially the same as those relating to the application in which the statement of case was struck out,

the court may, on the application of the respondent, stay[(GL)] that other application until the costs of the first application have been paid.

(4) Paragraph (1) does not limit any other power of the court to strike out[(GL)] a statement of case.

(5) If the court strikes out an applicant's statement of case and it considers that the application is totally without merit –

(a) the court's order must record that fact; and

(b) the court must at the same time consider whether it is appropriate to make a civil restraint order.

Amendments—SI 2013/3204; SI 2016/355.

'Except in proceedings to which Parts 12 to 14 apply' (r 4.4(1))—If a statement of case discloses no reasonable grounds for bringing or defending a claim, or is an abuse of process – for example, 'a strategic [divorce] petition which is filed and left to hibernate for years while the parties carry on with their marriage' (per Mostyn J in *Thum v Thum* [2016] EWHC 2634 (Fam)) – the court is likely to deal with it summarily. The power to strike out a case under this rule does not apply to proceedings concerning children; however, in an appropriate case a civil restraint order may be made (*K v K* [2015] EWHC 1064 (Fam)).

'Power to strike out a statement of case' (r 4.4)—PD4A is self-explanatory. Claims that are incoherent and unintelligible are liable to be struck out even if the applicant is a litigant in person, although normally an opportunity to amend should be given – *Spencer v Barclays Bank plc* [2009] EWHC 2832 (Ch).

In *K v D and others* [1998] 1 FLR 700, Cty Ct, an order striking out a claim for ancillary relief was 'plainly intended to afford some protection to the respondent' and while the petitioner did not need leave as such to proceed with her application for ancillary relief, she needed an order reinstating it, and the matters relevant to the question whether she should be granted such an order included the lapse of time, the reasons for not pursuing the original application, the strength of the application and the effects on third parties.

Whereas the CPR also allow the court to give summary judgment, there is no equivalent power in FPR 2010 and this omission is deliberate. An application has 'no reasonable grounds' for the purposes of r 4.4(1)(a) only if it is not legally recognisable, e g because there has already been a final determination of the proceedings or because the applicant has remarried. An application is not to be viewed as an 'abuse of process' falling within r 4.4(1)(b) solely on the basis that it appears to have no real prospect of success (*Wyatt v Vince* [2015] 1 FLR 972, SC); but c f the power to dismiss summarily an application under CA 1989 if it is ', if not groundless, lacking enough merit to justify pursuing the matter': *Re Q (Implacable Contact Dispute)* [2016] 2 FLR 287, CA, per Munby P; and the power to dismiss summarily an application identical to one that has already been dismissed (*GN v MA (Child Maintenance: Children Act Sch 1)* [2017] 1 FLR 285, FD).

'must at the same time consider whether it is appropriate to make a civil restraint order' (r 4.4(5)(b))—Note, however, that by virtue of Sch 2, Table 2 of FC(CDB)R 2014 even a limited civil restraint order may not be made by a District Judge (c f the position in civil proceedings under CPR PD3C, para 2.1) and if the making of such an order does appear appropriate the matter will have to be referred to a Circuit Judge. How this accords with r 1.1(2)(d),(e) is not immediately apparent.

PART III

4.5 Sanctions have effect unless defaulting party obtains relief

(1) Where a party has failed to comply with a rule, practice direction or court order, any sanction for failure to comply imposed by the rule, practice direction or court order has effect unless the party in default applies for and obtains relief from the sanction.

(Rule 4.6 sets out the circumstances which the court may consider on an application to grant relief from a sanction.)

(2) Where the sanction is the payment of costs, the party in default may only obtain relief by appealing against the order for costs.

(3) Where a rule, practice direction or court order –

(a) requires a party to do something within a specified time; and

(b) specifies the consequence of failure to comply,

the time for doing the act in question may not be extended by agreement between the parties.

General note—The underlying idea is to maintain the momentum of judicial case management by making it unnecessary for the 'innocent' party to have to apply for a sanction imposed against a 'guilty' party to take effect; it will do so automatically, whatever the source of the sanction. The party in default must apply for relief under FPR 2010, r 4.6 (*Marcan Shipping (London) Ltd v George Kefalas & Candida Corporation* [2007] EWCA Civ 463). An agreement to extend time in such cases is of no effect.

'payment of costs' (r 4.5(2))—Relief against all other sanctions should, in the first place, be considered at the level at which the sanction was imposed. But if the payment of costs and some other sanction are imposed by the same order, an appeal is necessary, if it is desired to seek relief against both.

'may not be extended by agreement between the parties' (r 4.5(3))—To the apparent surprise of many, this provision means exactly what it says; see the irate observations of Munby P, accompanied by threats of orders for costs, in *Re W (Children) (Strict Compliance with Court Orders)* [2015] 1 FLR 1092, FD.

4.6 Relief from sanctions

(1) On an application for relief from any sanction imposed for a failure to comply with any rule, practice direction or court order the court will consider all the circumstances including –

(a) the interests of the administration of justice;

(b) whether the application for relief has been made promptly;

(c) whether the failure to comply was intentional;

(d) whether there is a good explanation for the failure;

(e) the extent to which the party in default has complied with other rules, practice directions, court orders and any relevant pre –action protocol(GL);

(f) whether the failure to comply was caused by the party or the party's legal representative;

(g) whether the hearing date or the likely hearing date can still be met if relief is granted;

(h) the effect which the failure to comply had on each party; and

(i) the effect which the granting of relief would have on each party or a child whose interest the court considers relevant.

(2) An application for relief must be supported by evidence.

General note—The importance of systematically considering the analogous checklist in the then CPR 1998, r 3.9 was emphasised in *CIBC Mellon Trust Co v Stolzenberg* [2004] EWCA Civ 827. However, in *Tarn Insurance Services Limited (in Administration) v Kirby* [2009] EWCA Civ 19, the Court of Appeal explained that, when considering the provisions of this rule on an application for relief from sanctions imposed by an unless order, the true test to be applied was whether, notwithstanding that the unless order was a proper order to make for the purpose of furthering the overriding objective in the circumstances known at the time it was made, it remained appropriate at the time of hearing the application for relief to allow the sanction to take effect. Since the amendment of CPR 1998 in April 2013, decisions on this subject in civil proceedings are not necessarily relevant to family proceedings.

The Court of Appeal indicated in *Vernon v Spoudeas* [2010] EWCA Civ 666 that to deal on paper with an application for relief from sanctions was not normally to be recommended. The Court reiterated the importance of giving reasons when deciding such an application.

'all the circumstances' (r 4.6(1))—Consistent with FPR 2010, r 1.1(2)(b), the Court of Appeal paid particular regard to the proportionality of the strike-out sanction in *London Borough of Southwark v Onayamoke* [2007] EWCA Civ 1426.

It has been said that the court should not accept that the mere fact of being unrepresented provides a good reason for not adhering to the rules (*R (Dinjan Hysaj) v The Home Secretary* [2014] EWCA Civ 1633, cited in *Re D (Appeal: Procedure: Evidence)* [2016] 1 FLR 249, CA).

'any sanction' (r 4.6(1))—This provision is unrestricted and applies to applications for relief from any sanction, whether payment for costs or other and however the application is made. When delay is under consideration, no distinction should be drawn between the litigant and his advisers (*Daryananii v Kumar and Gerry* (2000) (unreported) 12 December, CA).

'the interests of the administration of justice' (r 4.6(1)(a))—Thus, where H posted an answer to the court but it did not arrive, the certificate of entitlement to a decree, and the decree nisi, were set aside (*Price v Price* [2015] 1 FLR 1202, CA. 'Despite the strains on the system, the fundamental obligation to deal with cases justly has to prevail' (*Mr R v Mrs R* [2014] EWFC 48, where the court highlighted important principles applying to case management orders particularly in proceedings under FLA 1996).

'good explanation' (r 4.6(1)(d))—Pressure of work is unlikely to be regarded as a satisfactory excuse (*Mitchell v News Group Newspapers Ltd* [2013] EWCA Civ 1537).

'evidence' (r 4.6(2))—In particular, the court will need evidence as to the explanation for the failure (r 4.6(1)(d)) and as to who was responsible (r 4.6(1)(f)). In many cases, but not all, the other matters set out in the rule may be able to be established by argument based on the existing papers.

4.7 General power of the court to rectify matters where there has been an error of procedure

Where there has been an error of procedure such as a failure to comply with a rule or practice direction –

(a) the error does not invalidate any step taken in the proceedings unless the court so orders; and

(b) the court may make an order to remedy the error.

'error' (r 4.7)—Technical defects (eg the use of an incorrect form) should be looked at in the light of the overriding objective (*Hannigan v Hannigan & ors* [2000] 2 FCR 650, CA). The rule is not to be given a narrow meaning and the court's discretion will be used so as not to cause injustice to one party when relieving against another's error. However, the rule cannot be used to achieve something prohibited under another rule (*Steele v Mooney & ors* [2005] EWCA Civ 96).

4.8 Power of the court to make civil restraint orders

Practice Direction 4B sets out –

(a) the circumstances in which the court has the power to make a civil restraint order against a party to proceedings;

(b) the procedure where a party applies for a civil restraint order against another party; and

(c) the consequences of the court making a civil restraint order.

Amendments—SI 2013/3204.

Power of the court to make a civil restraint order (r 4.8)—This provision follows the familiar provisions of CPR 1998, r 3.11. In family proceedings involving money, the authorities on CPR 1998, r 3.11 are likely to be of assistance. In proceedings involving children, it is submitted that the authorities on the interpretation of CA 1989, s 91(14) are likely to prove a more reliable guide; but see on this point *K v K* [2015] EWHC 1064 (Fam).

Fees—A party who is subject to a restraint order is required to pay a fee if he seeks to appeal the order or seeks leave to make an application, even if he would otherwise qualify for fee remission, the fee being refunded if the application succeeds. This is not a breach of Art 6 of the European Convention on Human Rights: *Senior-Milne v Secretary of State* [2012] EWHC 3062 (Admin).

Practice Direction 4A – Striking Out a Statement of Case

This Practice Direction supplements FPR Part 4, rule 4.4 (Power to strike out a statement of case)

Introduction

1.1A Before exercising these powers the court must take into account any written evidence filed in relation to the application or answer (rule 4.4(1A)). For example, the court must take into account the financial statement (Form E) filed in relation to an application for a property adjustment order, pension sharing order and other financial orders.

1.1 Rule 4.4 enables the court to strike out the whole or part of a statement of case which discloses no reasonable grounds for bringing or defending the application (rule 4.4(1)(a)), or which is an abuse of the process of the court or otherwise likely to obstruct the just disposal of the proceedings (rule 4.4(1)(b)). These powers may be exercised on an application by a party or on the court's own initiative.

1.2 This practice direction sets out the procedure a party should follow to make an application for an order under rule 4.4.

Examples of cases within the rule

2.1 The following are examples of cases where the court may conclude that an application falls within rule 4.4(1)(a) –

(a) those which set out no facts indicating what the application is about;
(b) those which are incoherent and make no sense;
(c) those which contain a coherent set of facts but those facts, even if true, do not disclose any legally recognisable application against the respondent.

2.2 An application may fall within rule 4.4(1)(b) where it cannot be justified, for example because it is frivolous, scurrilous or obviously ill-founded.

2.3 An answer may fall within rule 4.4(1)(a) where it consists of a bare denial or otherwise sets out no coherent statement of facts.

2.4 *(omitted)*

2.5 The examples set out above are intended only as illustrations.

2.6 Where a rule, practice direction or order states 'shall be struck out or dismissed' or 'will be struck out or dismissed' this means that the order striking out or dismissing the proceedings will itself bring the proceedings to an end and that no further order of the court is required.

Applications which appear to fall within rule 4.4(1)(a) or (b)

3.1 A court officer who is asked to issue an application form but believes the application may fall within rule 4.4(1)(a) or (b) should issue the application form, but may then consult the court (under rule 4.2) before returning the form to the applicant or taking any other step to serve the respondent. The court may of its own initiative make an immediate order designed to ensure that the application is disposed of or (as the case may be) proceeds in a way that accords with the rules.

3.2 The court may allow the applicant a hearing before deciding whether to make such an order.

3.3 Orders the court may make include –

(a) an order that the application be stayed until further order;
(b) an order that the application form be retained by the court and not served until the stay is lifted;

(c) an order that no application by the applicant to lift the stay be heard unless the applicant files such further documents (for example a witness statement or an amended application form) as may be specified in the order.

3.4 Where the court makes any such order or, subsequently, an order lifting the stay, it may give directions about the service on the respondent of the order and any other documents on the court file.

3.5 The fact that the court allows an application referred to it by a court officer to proceed does not prejudice the right of any party to apply for any order against the applicant.

'should issue the application form' (para 3.1)—'Should' in this context clearly means 'must' because the court officer 'certainly has no discretion to make a judicial determination' that the application is an abuse of process or discloses no reasonable grounds: *Gwynedd Council v Grunshaw* [2000] 1 WLR 494, CA.

Answers which appear to fall within rule 4.4(1)(a) or (b)

4.1 A court officer may similarly consult the court about any document filed which purports to be an answer and which the officer believes may fall within rule 4.4(1)(a) or (b).

4.2 If the court decides that the document falls within rule 4.4(1)(a) or (b) it may on its own initiative make an order striking it out. Where the court does so it may extend the time for the respondent to file a proper answer.

4.3 The court may allow the respondent a hearing before deciding whether to make such an order.

4.4 Alternatively the court may make an order requiring the respondent within a stated time to clarify the answer or to give additional information about it. The order may provide that the answer will be struck out if the respondent does not comply.

4.5 The fact that the court does not strike out an answer on its own initiative does not prejudice the right of the applicant to apply for any order against the respondent.

General provisions

5.1 The court may exercise its powers under rule 4.4(1)(a) or (b) on application by a party to the proceedings or on its own initiative at any time.

5.2 Where the court at a hearing strikes out all or part of a party's statement of case it may enter such judgment for the other party as that party appears entitled to.

Applications for orders under rule 4.4(1)

6.1 Attention is drawn to Part 18 (Procedure for Other Applications in Proceedings) and to the practice direction that supplements it. The practice direction requires all applications to be made as soon as possible.

6.2 While many applications under rule 4.4(1) can be made without evidence in support, the applicant should consider whether facts need to be proved and, if so, whether evidence in support should be filed and served.

Practice Direction 4B – Civil Restraint Orders

This Practice Direction supplements FPR rule 4.8

Introduction

1.1 This practice direction applies where the court is considering whether to make –

(a) a limited civil restraint order;
(b) an extended civil restraint order; or
(c) a general civil restraint order,

against a party who has made applications which are totally without merit.

Rules 4.3(7), 4.4(5) and 18.13 provide that where a statement of case or application is struck out or dismissed and is totally without merit, the court order must specify that fact and the court must consider whether to make a civil restraint order. Rule 30.11(5) makes similar provision where the appeal court refuses an application for permission to appeal, strikes out an appellant's notice or dismisses an appeal.

The powers of the court to make civil restraint orders are separate from and do not replace the powers given to the court by section 91(14) of the Children Act 1989.

Limited civil restraint orders

2.1 A limited civil restraint order may be made where a party has made 2 or more applications which are totally without merit.

2.2 Where the court makes a limited civil restraint order, the party against whom the order is made –

(a) will be restrained from making any further applications in the proceedings in which the order is made without first obtaining the permission of a judge identified in the order;
(b) may apply for amendment or discharge of the order, but only with the permission of a judge identified in the order; and
(c) may apply for permission to appeal the order and if permission is granted, may appeal the order.

2.3 Where a party who is subject to a limited civil restraint order –

(a) makes a further application in the proceedings in which the order is made without first obtaining the permission of a judge identified in the order, such application will automatically be dismissed –
  (i) without the judge having to make any further order; and
  (ii) without the need for the other party to respond to it; and
(b) repeatedly makes applications for permission pursuant to that order which are totally without merit, the court may direct that if the party makes any further application for permission which is totally without merit, the decision to dismiss the application will be final and there will be no right of appeal, unless the judge who refused permission grants permission to appeal.

2.4 A party who is subject to a limited civil restraint order may not make an application for permission under paragraphs 2.2(a) or (b) without first serving notice of the application on the other party in accordance with paragraph 2.5.

2.5 A notice under paragraph 2.4 must –

(a) set out the nature and grounds of the application; and
(b) provide the other party with at least 7 days within which to respond.

2.6 An application for permission under paragraphs 2.2(a) or (b) –

(a) must be made in writing;
(b) must include the other party's written response, if any, to the notice served under paragraph 2.4; and
(c) will be determined without a hearing.

2.7 *(omitted)*

2.8 Where a party makes an application for permission under paragraphs 2.2(a) or (b) and permission is refused, any application for permission to appeal –

(a) must be made in writing; and
(b) will be determined without a hearing.

2.9 A limited civil restraint order –

(a) is limited to the particular proceedings in which it is made;
(b) will remain in effect for the duration of the proceedings in which it is made, unless the court orders otherwise; and

PART III

(c) must identify the judge or judges to whom an application for permission under paragraphs 2.2(a), 2.2(b) or 2.8 should be made.

Extended civil restraint orders

3.1 An extended civil restraint order may be made where a party has persistently made applications which are totally without merit.

3.2 Unless the court orders otherwise, where the court makes an extended civil restraint order, the party against whom the order is made –

(a) will be restrained from making applications in any court concerning any matter involving or relating to or touching upon or leading to the proceedings in which the order is made without first obtaining the permission of a judge identified in the order;
(b) may apply for amendment or discharge of the order, but only with the permission of a judge identified in the order; and
(c) may apply for permission to appeal the order and if permission is granted, may appeal the order.

3.3 Where a party who is subject to an extended civil restraint order –

(a) makes an application in a court identified in the order concerning any matter involving or relating to or touching upon or leading to the proceedings in which the order is made without first obtaining the permission of a judge identified in the order, the application will automatically be struck out or dismissed –
   (i) without the judge having to make any further order; and
   (ii) without the need for the other party to respond to it; and
(b) repeatedly makes applications for permission pursuant to that order which are totally without merit, the court may direct that if the party makes any further application for permission which is totally without merit, the decision to dismiss the application will be final and there will be no right of appeal, unless the judge who refused permission grants permission to appeal.

3.4 A party who is subject to an extended civil restraint order may not make an application for permission under paragraphs 3.2(a) or (b) without first serving notice of the application on the other party in accordance with paragraph 3.5.

3.5 A notice under paragraph 3.4 must –

(a) set out the nature and grounds of the application; and
(b) provide the other party with at least 7 days within which to respond.

3.6 An application for permission under paragraphs 3.2(a) or (b) –

(a) must be made in writing;
(b) must include the other party's written response, if any, to the notice served under paragraph 3.4; and
(c) will be determined without a hearing.

3.7 (*omitted*)

3.8 Where a party makes an application for permission under paragraphs 3.2(a) or (b) and permission is refused, any application for permission to appeal –

(a) must be made in writing; and
(b) will be determined without a hearing.

3.9 An extended civil restraint order –

(a) will be made for a specified period not exceeding 2 years;
(b) must identify the courts in which the party against whom the order is made is restrained from making applications; and
(c) must identify the judge or judges to whom an application for permission under paragraphs 3.2(a), 3.2(b) or 3.8 should be made.

3.10 The court may extend the duration of an extended civil restraint order, if it considers it appropriate to do so, but the duration of the order must not be extended for a period greater than 2 years on any given occasion.

General civil restraint orders

4.1 A general civil restraint order may be made where the party against whom the order is made persists in making applications which are totally without merit, in circumstances where an extended civil restraint order would not be sufficient or appropriate.

4.2 Unless the court otherwise orders, where the court makes a general civil restraint order, the party against whom the order is made –

(a) will be restrained from making any application in any court without first obtaining the permission of a judge identified in the order;
(b) may apply for amendment or discharge of the order, but only with the permission of a judge identified in the order; and
(c) may apply for permission to appeal the order and if permission is granted, may appeal the order.

4.3 Where a party who is subject to a general civil restraint order –

(a) makes an application in any court without first obtaining the permission of a judge identified in the order, the application will automatically be struck out or dismissed –
  (i) without the judge having to make any further order; and
  (ii) without the need for the other party to respond to it; and
(b) repeatedly makes applications for permission pursuant to that order which are totally without merit, the court may direct that if the party makes any further application for permission which is totally without merit, the decision to dismiss that application will be final and there will be no right of appeal, unless the judge who refused permission grants permission to appeal.

4.4 A party who is subject to a general civil restraint order may not make an application for permission under paragraphs 4.2(a) or (b) without first serving notice of the application on the other party in accordance with paragraph 4.5.

4.5 A notice under paragraph 4.4 must –

(a) set out the nature and grounds of the application; and
(b) provide the other party with at least 7 days within which to respond.

4.6 An application for permission under paragraphs 4.2(a) or (b) –

(a) must be made in writing;
(b) must include the other party's written response, if any, to the notice served under paragraph 4.4; and
(c) will be determined without a hearing.

4.7 *(omitted)*

4.8 Where a party makes an application for permission under paragraphs 4.2(a) or (b) and permission is refused, any application for permission to appeal –

(a) must be made in writing; and
(b) will be determined without a hearing.

4.9 A general civil restraint order–

(a) will be made for a specified period not exceeding 2 years;
(b) must identify the courts in which the party against whom the order is made is restrained from making applications; and
(c) must identify the judge or judges to whom an application for permission under paragraphs 4.2(a), 4.2(b) or 4.8 should be made.

PART III

4.10 The court may extend the duration of a general civil restraint order, if it considers it appropriate to do so, but he duration of the order must not be extended for a period greater than 2 years on any given occasion.

General

5.1 The other party or parties to the proceedings may apply for any civil restraint order.

5.2 An application under paragraph 5.1 must be made using the procedure in Part 18 unless the court otherwise directs and the application must specify which type of civil restraint order is sought.

PART 5
FORMS AND START OF PROCEEDINGS

CONTENTS OF THIS PART

Rule		Page
5.1	Forms	1330
5.2	Documents to be attached to a form	1331
5.3	Proceedings are started by issue of application form	1331
5.4	Where to start proceedings	1331
5.5	Filing documents with and sending documents to the court by e-mail	1332
	Practice Direction 5A – Forms	1332
	Practice Direction 5B – Communication and Filing of Documents by E-Mail	1342

5.1 Forms

(1) Subject to rule 14.10(2) and (3), the forms referred to in a practice direction, shall be used in the cases to which they apply.

(2) A form may be varied by the court or a party if the variation is required by the circumstances of a particular case.

(3) A form must not be varied so as to leave out any information or guidance which the form gives to the recipient.

(4) Where these rules require a form to be sent by the court or by a party for another party to use, it must be sent without any variation except such as is required by the circumstances of the particular case.

(5) Paragraph (2) does not apply to the forms annexed to the Maintenance Regulation, or to an Article 11 form.

(6) Nothing in this rule requires a party to reveal any particulars referred to in rule 29.1(1) if notice of those particulars is given to the court in accordance with rule 29.1(2).

Amendments—SI 2011/1328; SI 2012/679; SI 2012/2806.

Modifications—Where FPR PD36D applies, r 5.1 is modified to read:

'5.1

Where the Pilot Scheme referred to in Practice Direction 36D applies, the applicant must-

(a) complete all sections of the application process set out in the online system referred to in that Practice Direction;

(b) print or save the resulting application form which is generated by the online system;

(c) when filing that application, include all of the information, including any additional documents, that the online system requires to be included.'

Practice Direction—PD5A supplements Pt 5 and sets out the forms prescribed for issue of applications in family proceedings.

'subject to rule 14.10(2) and (3)' (r 5.1(1))—FPR 2010, Pt 14 deals with adoption proceedings; r 14.10 deals with the consent of a parent or guardian in such proceedings and r 14.10(3) requires consent to a Convention adoption to be in accordance with any form required by the country of the child's habitual residence.

5.2 Documents to be attached to a form

Subject to any rule or practice direction, unless the court directs otherwise, a form must have attached to it any documents which, in the form, are –

(a) stated to be required; or
(b) referred to.

Modifications—Where FPR PD36D applies, r 5.2 is omitted.

Modification of rules of evidence—This rule sits uncomfortably with the rule of evidence that only evidence relevant to an issue should be disclosed (eg where unnecessary documents such as bank statements or valuation evidence is required by a form; but see the rule-makers powers to modify rules of evidence in Courts Act 2003, s 76(3).

5.3 Proceedings are started by issue of application form

(1) Proceedings are started when a court officer issues an application at the request of the applicant.

(2) An application is issued on the date entered in the application form by the court officer.

(3) Where the application is made under Article 56 of the Maintenance Regulation, or under Article 10 of the 2007 Hague Convention, the applicant is deemed to have requested the issue of the application by virtue of making the application for establishment or modification of a maintenance decision forwarded on his or her behalf by the Lord Chancellor.

[The Lord Chancellor is the Central Authority for England and Wales in relation to the 2007 Hague Convention and the Maintenance Regulation]

(Rule 29.7 requires an application form to be authenticated with the stamp of the court when it is issued)

Amendments—SI 2012/2806.

Defined terms—'application form': r 2.3(1).

Start of proceedings—FPR 2010 distinguishes between the application form by which originating proceedings (either under a specific rule or under FPR 2010, Pt 19) are issued and the 'application notice' (which is a different document (often Form D11) by which application is made under the FPR 2010, Pt 18 procedure); and see definition of application forms and notices in FPR 2010, r 2.3(1).

Applications and applications in proceedings—To commence any originating process under the rules, an application form must be filed and must then be issued by a court officer. Applications under the rules come in three categories:

(1) Procedures prescribed by the rules for a particular process. These are commenced by an application form (defined by FPR 2010, r 2.3(1)), generally in a form prescribed by FPR PD5A (eg matrimonial and civil partnership proceedings by Form D8; financial remedy proceedings under FPR 2010, Pt 9 by Forms A, A1 or A2 and children proceedings by Form C1).
(2) The FPR 2010, Pt 19 procedure is for certain particular simplified processes (eg application for a declaration of parentage by Form C63) or where not otherwise prescribed (as at (1), above). Applications by the FPR 2010, Pt 19 procedure are freestanding or originating applications; or prescribed to be by that procedure.
(3) Applications in proceedings, the FPR 2010, Pt 18 procedure: interim applications in existing or applications in proposed proceedings (such as where permission is required to start an application: eg application for permission to apply for a forced marriage protection order (r 11.3(1)(a)(i)); or for interim remedies under FPR 2010, Pt 20 or FPR 2010, r 9.7).

The first two sets of application are originating processes. Each will attract an individual court number (and court fee), whereas the FPR 2010, Pt 18 procedure is issued out of another set of proceeding (or an anticipated application). The equivalent procedures under CPR 1998 are:

(1) that CPR 1998, Pt 7 provides for all claims (if in doubt a CPR 1998 claimant issues under CPR 1998, Pt 7);
(2) CPR 1998, Pt 8 (like FPR 2010, Pt 19) provides a simplified originating procedure (eg where a claim 'is unlikely to involve a substantial dispute of fact' or where the simplified CPR 1998, Pt 8 procedure is prescribed); and
(3) CPR 1998, Pt 23 is the equivalent of FPR 2010, Pt 18 and provides for applications in the course of proceedings ('an application … made to the court where the claim was started': CPR 1998, r 23.2(1)).

5.4 Where to start proceedings

(1) Where both the family court and the High Court have jurisdiction to deal with a matter, the proceedings relating to that matter must be started in the family court.

(2) Paragraph (1) does not apply where –

PART III

(a) proceedings relating to the same parties are already being heard in the High Court;
(b) any rule, other enactment or Practice Direction provides otherwise; or
(c) the court otherwise directs.

Amendments—Inserted by SI 2013/3204.

'Jurisdiction to deal with a matter' (r 5.4(1))—In the first instance, or if in doubt, application should be issued out of the Family Court. MFPA 1984, s 31P(1) enables the High Court to transfer family proceedings to itself.

5.5 Filing documents with and sending documents to the court by e-mail

(1) A practice direction may make provision for documents to be filed with or sent to the court by e-mail.

(2) Any such practice direction may –

(a) provide that only particular categories of documents may be filed with or sent to the court by such means;
(b) provide that particular provisions only apply in specified courts or court offices; and
(c) specify the requirements that must be fulfilled for any document filed with or sent to the court by such means.

Amendments—Inserted by SI 2015/1868.

Practice Direction—Practice Direction 5B has been made to comply with r 5.5. Chapter 2 applies to filing by email by specified organisations (local authorities, Cafcass etc), and Ch 3 for filing by all others (including solicitors on the court record). Recording of information on the emails is at Ch 4 and timing of filing at Ch 5. If a document contains a signed statement of truth, that must be filed at court in accordance with Ch 6.

Practice Direction 5A – Forms

This Practice Direction supplements FPR Part 5, rule 5.1 (Forms)

Note—All of the forms listed in FPR PD5A are available on the Family Law Online service, which is available by subscription.

Scope and interpretation

1.1 This Practice Direction lists the forms to be used in family proceedings on or after 6 April 2011. Table 1 lists the forms against the part of the FPR to which they are relevant, and Table 2 lists the forms individually with their description.

1.2 The forms may be –

(a) modified as the circumstances require, provided that all essential information, especially information or guidance which the form gives to the recipient, is included;
(b) expanded to include additional pages where that may be necessary, provided that any additional pages are also verified by a statement of truth.

1.3 Any reference in family proceedings forms to a Part, rule or Practice Direction is to be read as a reference to the equivalent Part, rule or Practice Direction in the FPR and any reference to a Practice Direction in any CPR form used in family proceedings is to be read as a reference to the equivalent Practice Direction in the FPR.

****

Application notices

2.2 Where an application under the Part 18 procedure is to be made by application notice, the forms to be used are:

(i) Form C2 where the application is made in the course of or in connection with proceedings under Part 12;
(ii) Subject to sub-paragraphs (iii) and (iv), Form D11 where the application is made in the course of or in connection with proceedings under Parts 7, 8 or 9;
(iii) Form D650 where the application is to vary or set aside a financial order where a Form E

calculator error has been identified in an online HMCTS FormFinder Form E and the applicant asserts that this has materially or significantly affected the order;

(iv) Form D651 where the application is to vary or set aside an order made in financial remedy proceedings where a Form E1 calculator error has been identified in an online HMCTS FormFinder Form E1 and the applicant asserts that this has materially or significantly affected the order;

(v) Form N244 where the application is made in the course of or in connection with appeal proceedings in the family court;

(vi) Form FP244 where the application is made in the course of or in connection with appeal proceedings in the High Court;

(vii) Form FP2 in any other case.

Other Forms

3.1 Other forms may be authorised by practice directions.

Table 1

Index to forms

FPR Part	**Forms**
Part 3 Alternative Dispute Resolution (Family Mediation)	FM1
Part 6 Service	C9, D5, D89, FL415, FP6
Part 7 Matrimonial and Civil Partnership Proceedings	C60, D6, D8, D8 Notes, D8A, D8B, D8D, D8D Notes, D8N, D8N Notes, D9B, D11, D13B, D20, D36, D80A, D80B, D80C, D80D, D80E, D80F, D80G, D81, D84,
Part 8 Miscellaneous Applications	D50, D50A, D50B, D50C, D50D, D50E, D50F, D50G, D50H, D50J, D50K
Part 8 Chapter 5 Applications for declarations	C63, C64, C65, D70
Part 9 Applications for a Financial Remedy	Form A, Form A1, Form B, Form E, Form E Notes, Form E1, Form E2, Form F, Form I, Form P, Form P1, Form P2, Form PPF, Form PPF1, Form PPF2
Part 10 Applications under Part 4 of the Family Law Act 1996	FL401, FL403, FL407, FL415
Part 11 Applications under Part 4A of the Family Law Act 1996 or Part 1 of Schedule 2 to the Female Genital Mutilation Act 2003	FGM001, FGM003, FGM005, FGM006, FGM007, FL401A, FL403A, FL407A, FL430, FL431
Part 12 Applications in respect of children	C1, C1A, C2, C3, C4, C5, C8, C9, C12, C13A, C14, C15, C16, C18, C19, C20, C61, C62, C66, C67, C68, C78, C79, C100, C110A, C(PRA1), C(PRA2) C(PRA3), PLO8, PLO9, PLP10 (PLO8 and PLO9 do not apply to Part 4 proceedings)
Part 13 Applications under section 54 of Human Fertilisation and Embryology Act 2008	C51, C52, A64A, A101A
Part 14 Adoption	A4, A5, A50, A51, A52, A53, A54, A55, A56, A57, A58, A59, A60, A61, A62, A63, A50 Notes, A51 Notes, A52 Notes, A53 Notes, A54 Notes, A55 Notes, A56 Notes, A57 Notes, A58 Notes, A59 Notes, A60 Notes, A61 Notes, A62 Notes, A63 Notes, A64, A65, A100, A101, A102, A103, A104, A105, A106, A107

PART III

FPR Part	Forms
Part 15 Representation of Protected Parties	FP9
Part 16 Representation of children	FP9
Part 18 Applications in proceedings	C2, D11, D650, D651, FP2
Part 19 Alternative Procedure for applications	FP1, FP1A, FP1B, FP3, FP5
Part 22 Evidence	N285
Part 24 Witnesses	FP25
Part 26 Notification of change of solicitor	FP8
Part 28 Costs	D252, D254, D258, D258A, D258B, D258C, D259, Form H, Form H1, N260
Part 30 Appeals	FP161, FP161A, FP162, FP162A, N161, N161A, N161B, N161D, N162, N162A, N162, N164
Part 31 Registration of Orders under the Council Regulation, The Civil Partnership (Jurisdiction and Recognition of Judgements) Regulations 2005 and under the Hague Convention 1996	C60, C61, C62, C69, D180
Part 32 Registration and Enforcement of Orders	D151
Part 33 Enforcement	D62, N323, N349
Part 34 Reciprocal Enforcement of Maintenance Orders	REMO 1, REMO 2
Part 37	Form No. 67
Part 39	FE15, FE16, FE17
Part 40	FE6, FE7

Table 2

List of Forms

Number	Name
A4	Application for Revocation of an Order Freeing a Child for Adoption
A5	Application for Substitution of One Adoption Agency for Another
A50	Application for a placement order Section 22 Adoption and Children Act 2002
A51	Application for variation of a placement order Section 23 Adoption and Children Act 2002
A52	Application for revocation of a placement order Section 24 Adoption and Children Act 2002
A53	Application for a contact order Section 26 of the Adoption and Children Act 2002 or an order for contact or prohibiting contact under section 51A of the Adoption and Children Act 2002
A54	Application for variation or revocation of a contact order Section 27(1)(b) or Section 51B(1)(c) Adoption and Children Act 2002
A55	Application for permission to change a child's surname Section 28 Adoption and Children Act 2002

Number	Name
A56	Application for permission to remove a child from the United Kingdom Section 28 Adoption and Children Act 2002
A57	Application for a recovery order Section 41 Adoption and Children Act 2002
A58	Application for an adoption order Section 46 Adoption and Children Act 2002
A59	Application for a Convention adoption order Section 46 Adoption and Children Act 2002
A60	Application for an adoption order (excluding a Convention adoption order) where the child is habitually resident outside the British Islands and is brought into the United Kingdom for the purposes of adoption Section 46 Adoption and Children Act 2002
A61	Application for an order for parental responsibility prior to adoption abroad Section 84 Adoption and Children Act 2002
A62	Application for a direction under section 88(1) of the Adoption and Children Act 2002
A63	Application for an order to annul a Convention adoption or Convention adoption order or for an overseas adoption or determination under section 91 to cease to be valid Section 89 Adoption and Children Act 2002
A50 Notes	Application for a placement order Section 22 Adoption and Children Act 2002 – Notes on completing the form
A51 Notes	Application for variation of a placement order Section 23 Adoption and Children Act 2002 – Notes on completing the form
A52 Notes	Application for revocation of a placement order Section 24 Adoption and Children Act 2002 – Notes on completing the form
A53 Notes	Application for a contact order Section 26 Adoption and Children Act 2002 or an order under section 51A of the Act – Notes on completing the form
A54 Notes	Application for variation or revocation of a contact order Section 27(1)(b) or section 51B(1)(c) Adoption and Children Act 2002 – Notes on completing the form
A55 Notes	Application for permission to change a child's surname Section 28 Adoption and Children Act 2002 – Notes on completing the form
A56 Notes	Application for permission to remove a child from the United Kingdom Section 28 Adoption and Children Act 2002 – Notes on completing the form
A57 Notes	Application for a recovery order Section 41 Adoption and Children Act 2002 – Notes on completing the form
A58 Notes	Application for an adoption order Section 46 Adoption and Children Act 2002 – Notes on completing the form
A59 Notes	Application for a Convention adoption order Section 46 Adoption and Children Act 2002 – Notes on completing the form
A60 Notes	Application for an adoption order (excluding a Convention adoption order) where the child is habitually resident outside the British Islands and is brought into the United Kingdom for the purposes of adoption Section 46 Adoption and Children Act 2002 – Notes on completing the form
A61 Notes	Application for an order for parental responsibility prior to adoption abroad Section 84 Adoption and Children Act 2002 – Notes on completing the form
A62 Notes	Application for a direction under section 88(1) of the Adoption and Children Act 2002 – Notes on completing the form

Number	Name
A63 Notes	Application for an order to annul a Convention adoption or Convention adoption order or for an overseas adoption or determination under section 91 to cease to be valid Section 89 Adoption and Children Act 2002 – Notes on completing the form
A64	Application to receive information from court records Section 60(4) Adoption and Children Act 2002
A64A	Application to receive information from court records about a parental order Section 60(4) Adoption and Children Act 2002
A65	Confidential information
A100	Consent to the placement of my child for adoption with any prospective adopters chosen by the Adoption Agency Section 19 of the Adoption and Children Act 2002
A101	Consent to the placement of my child for adoption with identified prospective adopters Section 19 of the Adoption and Children Act 2002
A101A	Agreement to the making of a parental order in respect of my child Section 54 of the Human Fertilisation and Embryology Act 2008
A102	Consent to the placement of my child for adoption with identified prospective adopter(s) and, if the placement breaks down, with any prospective adopter(s) chosen by the adoption agency Section 19 of the Adoption and Children Act 2002
A103	Advance Consent to Adoption Section 20 of the Adoption and Children Act 2002
A104	Consent to Adoption. The Adoption and Children Act 2002
A105	Consent to the making of an Order under Section 84 of the Adoption and Children Act 2002
A106	Withdrawal of Consent Sections 19 and 20 of the Adoption and Children Act 2002
A107	Consent by the child's parent to adoption by their partner The Adoption and Children Act 2002
C1	Application for an Order
C1A	Allegations of harm and domestic violence (Supplemental information form)
C2	Application For permission to start proceedings For an order or directions in existing proceedings To be joined as, or cease to be, a party in existing family proceedings under the Children Act 1989
C3	Application for an order authorising search for, taking charge of and delivery of child
C4	Application for an order for disclosure of a child's whereabouts
C5	Local Authority application concerning the registration of a child-minder or a provider of day care
C8	Confidential contact details
C9	Statement of service
C12	Supplement for an application for a warrant to assist a person authorised by an Emergency Protection Order
C13A	Supplement for an application for a Special Guardianship Order Section 14A Children Act 1989

Number	Name
C14	Supplement for an application for authority to refuse contact with a child in care
C15	Supplement for an application for contact with a child in care
C16	Supplement for an application for a Child Assessment Order
C18	Supplement for an application for a Recovery Order
C19	Application for a warrant of assistance
C20	Supplement for an application for an order to hold a child in Secure Accommodation
C51	Application for a Parental Order Section 54 Human Fertilisation and Embryology Act 2008
C52	Acknowledgement of an application for a Parental Order
C60	Certificate referred to in Article 39 of Council Regulation (EC) No. 2201/ 2003 of 27 November 2003 concerning judgments on parental responsibility
C61	Certificate referred to in Article 41(1) of Council Regulation (EC) No. 2201/2003 of 27 November 2003 concerning judgments on rights of access
C62	Certificate referred to in Article 42(1) of Council Regulation (EC) No. 2201/2003 of 27 November 2003 concerning the return of the child
C63	Application for declaration of parentage under section 55A of the Family Law Act 1986
C64	Application for declaration of legitimacy or legitimation under section 56(1)(b) and (2) of the Family Law Act 1986
C65	Application for declaration as to adoption effected overseas under section 57 of the Family Law Act 1986
C66	Application for inherent jurisdiction order in relation to children
C67	Application under the Child Abduction and Custody Act 1985 or Article 11 of Council Regulation (EC) 2201/2003
C68	Application for international transfer of jurisdiction to or from England and Wales
C69	Application for registration, recognition or non-recognition of a judgment under Council Regulation (EC) 2201/2003 or the 1996 Hague Convention
C78	Application for attachment of a warning notice to a child arrangements order
C79	Application related to enforcement of a child arrangements order
C100	Application under the Children Act 1989 for a child arrangements, prohibited steps or specific issue section 8 order or to vary or discharge a section 8 order
C110A	Application for a Care or Supervision Order and other orders under Part 4 of the Children Act 1989 or an Emergency Protection Order under section 44 of the Children Act 1989
C(PRA1)	Parental Responsibility Agreement
C(PRA2)	Step Parent Parental Responsibility Agreement
C(PRA3)	Parental Responsibility Agreement Section 4ZA Children Act 1989 (Acquisition of parental responsibility by second female parent)
D5	Notice to be indorsed on documents served in accordance with rule 6.14
D6	Statement of Reconciliation
D8	Divorce/dissolution/(judicial) separation petition

Number	Name
D8 Notes	Supporting notes for guidance on completing a divorce/dissolution/(judicial) separation petition
D8A	Statement of arrangements for children
D8B	Answer to a divorce/dissolution/(judicial) separation or nullity petition
D8D	Petition for a presumption of death order and dissolution of a civil partnership
D8D Notes	Supporting notes for guidance on completing a petition for a presumption of death order and dissolution of a civil partnership
D8N	Nullity petition
D8N Notes	Supporting notes for guidance on completing a nullity petition
D9B	Particulars of person whose address is being sought where details are unknown
D11	Application Notice
D13B	Statement in support of a request to dispense with service of the divorce/dissolution/nullity/(judicial) separation petition on the Respondent
D20	Medical Examination: statement of parties & examiner
D36	Notice of Application for Decree Nisi to be made Absolute or Conditional Order to be made final
D50	Notice of application under section 17 of the Married Women's Property Act 1882/section 66 of the Civil Partnership Act 2004
D50A	Notice of proceedings and acknowledgement of service under section 17 of the Married Women's Property Act 1882/section 66 of the Civil Partnership Act 2004
D50B	Application under section 17 of the Married Women's Property Act 1882/section 66 of the Civil Partnership Act 2004/Application to transfer a tenancy under the Family Law Act 1996
D50C	Application on ground of failure to provide maintenance
D50D	Application for alteration of maintenance agreement after the death of one of the parties, under section 36 of the Matrimonial Causes Act 1973/paragraph 73 of Schedule 5 to the Civil Partnership Act 2004
D50E	Application for permission to apply for financial relief after overseas divorce/dissolution etc under section 13 of the Matrimonial and Family Proceedings Act 1984 / paragraph 4 of Schedule 7 to the Civil Partnership Act 2004
D50F	Application for financial relief after overseas divorce etc under section 12 of the Matrimonial and Family Proceedings Act 1984/paragraph 4 to Schedule 7 to the Civil Partnership Act 2004
D50G	Application to prevent transactions intended to defeat prospective applications for financial relief
D50H	Application for alteration of maintenance agreement during parties lifetime
D50J	Application for an order preventing avoidance under section 32L of the Child Support Act 1991
D50K	Notice of Application for Enforcement by such method of enforcement as the court may consider appropriate
D62	Request for issue of Judgment Summons
D70	Application for Declaration of Marital/Civil Partnership Status

Number	Name
D80A	Statement in support of divorce/(judicial) separation – adultery
D80B	Statement in support of divorce/dissolution/(judicial) separation – unreasonable behaviour
D80C	Statement in support of divorce/dissolution/(judicial) separation – desertion
D80D	Statement in support of divorce/dissolution/(judicial) separation – 2 years consent
D80E	Statement in support of divorce/dissolution/(judicial) separation – 5 years separation
D80F	Statement in support of annulment -void marriage/civil partnership
D80G	Statement in support of annulment – voidable marriage/civil partnership
D81	Statement of information for a Consent Order in relation to a financial remedy
D84	Application for a decree nisi/conditional order or (judicial) separation decree/order
D89	Request for personal service by a court bailiff
D151	Application for registration of maintenance order in the family court
D180	Concerning judgements in matrimonial matters
D252	Notice of commencement of assessment of bill of costs.
D254	Request for a default costs certificate
D258	Request for a detailed assessment of hearing
D258A	Request for detailed assessment (legal aid only)
D258B	Request for detailed assessment (Costs payable out of a fund other than the Community Legal Service Fund)
D258C	Request for detailed assessment hearing pursuant to an order under Part III of the Solicitors Act 1974
D259	Notice of appeal against a detailed assessment (divorce)
D650	Notice of application to vary or set aside a financial order (Form E calculator error)
D651	Notice of application to vary or set aside a financial remedy (Form E1 calculator error)
FE6	Application for a charging order on land or property
FE7	Application for a charging order on securities
FE15	Request for attachment of earnings order
FE16	Request and result of search in the attachment of earnings index
FE17	Form for replying to an attachment of earnings application (statement of means)
FGM001	Application for a Female Genital Mutilation (FGM) Protection Order
FGM003	Application to vary, extend or discharge a Female Genital Mutilation (FGM) Protection Order
FGM005	Application for a warrant of arrest – Female Genital Mutilation Protection Order
FGM006	Application for leave to apply for a Female Genital Mutilation (FGM) Protection Order
FGM007	Application to be joined as, or cease to be, a party to a Female Genital Mutilation (FGM) Protection Order
FL401	Application for a non-molestation order/an occupation order

Number	Name
FL401A	Application for a Forced Marriage Protection Order
FL403	Application to vary, extend or discharge
FL403A	Application to vary, extend or discharge Forced Marriage Protection Orders
FL407	Applications for warrant of Arrest
FL407A	Application for warrant of arrest for a Forced Marriage Protection Order
FL415	Statement of service
FL430	Application for leave to apply for a Forced Marriage Protection Order
FL431	Application to join / cease as a party to Forced Marriage Protection Proceedings
FM1	Family Mediation Information and Assessment Form FM1
Form A	Notice of [intention to proceed with] an application for a financial order (NOTE: This form should be used whether the applicant is proceeding with an application in the petition or making a freestanding application)
Form A1	Notice of [intention to proceed with] an application for a financial remedy (other than a financial order) in the family or high court
Form B	Notice of an application to consider the financial position of the Respondent after the divorce/dissolution
Form E	Financial statement – For a financial order (other than a variation order) under the Matrimonial Causes Act 1973/Civil Partnership Act 2004 – For financial relief after an overseas divorce etc under Part 3 of the Matrimonial and Family Proceedings Act 1984/Schedule 7 to the Civil Partnership Act 2004
Form E Notes	Form E (Financial Statement for a financial order (other than a variation order) or for financial relief after an overseas divorce or dissolution etc) Notes for guidance
Form E1	Financial Statement for a financial remedy (other than a financial order or financial relief after an overseas divorce/dissolution etc) in the family or high court
Form E2	Financial Statement for a variation of an order for a financial remedy
Form F	Notice of allegation in proceedings for financial remedy
Form H	Estimate of costs (financial remedy)
Form H1	Statement of Costs (financial remedy)
Form I	Notice of request for periodical payments order at the same rate as order for interim maintenance pending outcome of proceeding
Form P	Pension inquiry form
Form P1	Pension sharing annex
Form P2	Pension attachment annex
Form PPF	Pension Protection Fund Inquiry Form
Form No 67	Writ of sequestration (rule 37.26)
Form PPF1	Pension Protection Fund sharing annex
Form PPF2	Pension Protection Fund attachment annex
FP1	Application under Part 19 of the Family Procedure Rules 2010

Number	Name
FP1A	Application under Part 19 of the Family Procedure Rules 2010 Notes for applicant on completing the application (Form FP1)
FP1B	Application under Part 19 of the Family Procedure Rules 2010 Notes for respondent
FP2	Application notice Part 18 of the Family Procedure Rules 2010
FP3	Application for injunction (General form)
FP5	Acknowledgment of service Application under Part 19 of the Family Procedure Rules 2010
FP6	Certificate of service
FP8	Notice of change of solicitor
FP9	Certificate of suitability of litigation friend
FP25	Witness Summons
FP161	Appellant's Notice
FP161A	Guidance Notes on completing the FP161 – Appellant's Notice
FP162	Respondent's Notice
FP162A	Guidance Notes on completing the FP162 – Respondent's Notice
FP244	Application Notice
FP244A	Application Notice (FP244) – Notes for Guidance
N161	Appellant's Notice
N161A	Guidance Notes on Completing the Appellant's Notice
N161B	Important Notes for Respondents
N161D	Guidance Notes on completing the form N161 – Appellant's notice (all family proceedings appeals in the Court of Appeal (Civil Division) and the family court)
N162	Respondent's Notice
N162A	Guidance Notes for Completing the Respondent's Notice
N163	Skeleton Argument
N164	Appellant's Notice
N244	Application Notice
N260	Statement of costs (summary assessment)
N285	General Affidavit
N323	Request for Warrant of Execution
N349	Application for a third party debt order
PLO8	Standard Directions on Issue
PLO9	Standard Directions at First Appointment
PLP10	Order Menu – Directions Revised Private Law Programme
REMO 1	Notice of Registration
REMO 2	Notice of Refusal of Registration.

Practice Direction 5B – Communication and Filing of Documents by E-Mail

This Practice Direction supplements FPR Part 5, rule 5.5

CHAPTER 1
SCOPE AND INTERPRETATION

1.1 This practice direction provides for communication and filing of documents with the court by e-mail.

1.2 Chapter 2 applies to specified organisations.

1.3 Chapter 3 applies to persons other than specified organisations.

1.4 Chapters 4, 5 and 6 apply to all persons, including specified organisations.

1.5 In this practice direction –

(a) 'specified document' is a document that is –
  (i) related to any family proceedings other than adoption proceedings; and
  (ii) listed in the e-mail guidance on Her Majesty's Courts and Tribunals Service website as a document that may be sent by e-mail to a specified e-mail address;

  (The e-mail guidance can be found at: https://www.justice.gov.uk/courts/email-guidance#canfile)

(b) 'specified e-mail address' is the e-mail address for a court office which has been listed on the Courts and Tribunals Finder website at: https://courttribunalfinder.service.gov.uk/courts/

(c) 'specified organisation' is any of –
  (i) a local authority;
  (ii) Cafcass;
  (iii) CAFCASS Cymru; and

(d) 'urgent application' means an application in which –
  (i) there is risk to the life, liberty or physical safety of a person who is the subject of the application or his or her family or his or her home;
  (ii) any delay in issuing the application could cause –
    (aa) a risk of harm to a child;
    (bb) a risk of unlawful removal of a child from the United Kingdom, or a risk of unlawful retention of a child who is currently outside England and Wales;
    (cc) a significant risk of a miscarriage of justice;
    (dd) unreasonable hardship to the applicant; or
    (ee) irretrievable problems in dealing with the dispute (including the irretrievable loss of significant evidence).

1.6 References in this practice direction to e-mailing a court mean e-mailing a court office at its specified e-mail address.

CHAPTER 2
SPECIFIED ORGANISATIONS

2.1 Subject to this Chapter, a specified organisation may e-mail a court at the court's specified e-mail address and may attach or include one or more specified documents to or in that e-mail.

2.2 If a fee is payable in order for a document to be filed with or accepted by the court, then subject to paragraph 2.3, the specified organisation must, when e-mailing the court –

(a) provide a Fee Account number, credit card number or debit card number which the person e-mailing the court has the authority to charge; and

(b) authorise the court to charge the applicable fee to that Account or card number.

2.3 When a specified organisation is e-mailing an urgent application to the court, the specified organisation may undertake to take the steps specified at paragraph 2.2(a) and (b) on the next business day.

(A list of applicable fees can be found here: http://www.justice.gov.uk/courts/fees)

(Further information about using the Fee Account service can be found at: https://www.justice.gov.uk/courts/fees/payment-by-account)

2.4 A court officer must refuse any application or other document, including any attachment, sent to the court by e-mail if –

(a) it does not comply with this Chapter; or
(b) a fee is payable and –
  (i) the court has not been able to charge the fee to the Account or card number provided by the sender; or
  (ii) in the case of an urgent application, the sender has not provided the undertaking specified in paragraph 2.3.

CHAPTER 3
PERSONS OTHER THAN SPECIFIED ORGANISATIONS

3.1 Subject to paragraphs 3.2–3.4, a person other than a specified organisation may e-mail the court or attach a specified document to an e-mail to the court.

3.2 If a fee is payable in order for an e-mailed document to be filed with or accepted by the court, the person must, when e-mailing the court –

(a) provide a Fee Account number, credit card number or debit card number which the person has authority to charge for the applicable fee; and
(b) authorise the court to charge the applicable fee to that Account or card number.

(A list of applicable fees can be found here: http://www.justice.gov.uk/courts/fees)

3.3 A person may e-mail the court or attach one or more specified documents to an e-mail to the court provided that –

(a) when printed out on both sides of A4 paper, the following documents together do not exceed 25 sheets of paper in total –
  (i) the e-mail;
  (ii) the attachments, including any document or e-mail embedded in any attachment; and
  (iii) copies of documents in (i) and (ii) that the court would be required to serve, if service by the court is requested or required under the rules;
(b) if the e-mail, including any attachments, is being sent to take a step in proceedings, that step is being taken by only that e-mail and attachments, and no other e-mail or hard copy is being sent as part of that step; and
(c) the total size of the e-mail, including any attachments, does not exceed 10.0 megabytes.

3.4 A court officer must refuse any application or other document, including any attachment, sent to the court by e-mail if –

(a) it does not comply with this Chapter; or
(b) a fee is payable and the court has not been able to charge the fee to the Account or card number provided by the sender.

CHAPTER 4
TECHNICAL SPECIFICATIONS

4.1 An e-mail sent to the court must –

(a) contain the name of the sender and an address for contact, which can be an e-mail address; and
(b) be in plain text or rich text format rather than HTML.

(Rule 29.1 specifies the information that a party is not required to reveal, and makes provision for notice by a party to the court where a party does not wish for particulars to be revealed by the court to another person.)

4.2 Subject to this practice direction, correspondence and documents may be sent as either text in the body of an e-mail, or as one or more attachments.

4.3 Completed forms that are prescribed by a rule or practice direction must be sent as attachments.

4.4 Where a prescribed form requires that one or more documents must be attached to that form, that document or documents must be attached to the e-mail to which the form is attached.

Court forms may be downloaded from HMCTS website at:

http://hmctsformfinder.justice.gov.uk/HMCTS/FormFinder.do

4.5 Attachments must be sent in a format supported by the software used by the court to which it is sent.

The format or formats which may be used in sending attachments to a particular specified court are listed in the e-mail guidance on Her Majesty's Courts and Tribunals website. The e-mail guidance can be found at:

https://www.justice.gov.uk/courts/email-guidance#canfile

4.6 Where an e-mail relates to existing proceedings, the person sending the e-mail must include the following information in the subject line of the e-mail, to the extent that space allows –

(a) the case number, if one exists;
(b) the parties' names (abbreviated if necessary);
(c) the name of the judge or other person before whom the case has been listed, if known by the person sending the e-mail; and
(d) if applicable, the date and time of any hearing to which the e-mail relates.

CHAPTER 5
FURTHER PROVISIONS

5.1 Where a person sends an e-mail to the court, that person must not send a hard copy of that e-mail or any attachment to the court.

5.2 Where an application is received by the court by e-mail –

(a) in accordance with Chapter 2 or Chapter 3 of this practice direction, whichever is applicable; and
(b) the e-mail is recorded by HMCTS e-mail software as received at or after 4:31pm and before or at 11:59pm;

the date of issue of the application will not be before the next day the court office is open.

5.3 Where an e-mail, including any attachment, is received by the court –

(a) in accordance with Chapter 2 or Chapter 3 of this practice direction, whichever is applicable; and
(b) the e-mail is recorded by HMCTS e-mail software as received at or after 4:31pm and before or at 11:59pm, the date of receipt is the next day the court office is open.

5.4 Where a time limit applies to the receipt or filing of a document or application, and the document or application is e-mailed to the court, it remains the responsibility of the person subject to that time limit to ensure that the document or application is sent within applicable time limits taking into account the operation of the practice direction.

5.5 A court officer may reply by e-mail to an e-mail received at a specified e-mail address, where the e-mail or any attachment received relates to proceedings which are not adoption proceedings.

5.6 If a document sent by e-mail requires urgent attention, the sender should contact the court by telephone.

CHAPTER 6
STATEMENTS OF TRUTH

6.1 Where a person wishes to file a specified document containing a statement of truth by e-mail, that person should retain the document containing the original signature and file with the court a version of the document satisfying one of the following requirements –

(a) the name of the person who has signed the statement of truth is typed underneath the statement; or

(b) the person who has signed the statement of truth has applied a facsimile of their signature to the statement in the document by mechanical means.

6.2 The court may require a person to produce the document containing the original signature.

PART 6
SERVICE

CONTENTS OF THIS PART

Chapter 1

Rule		Page
	Scope of this Part and Interpretation	
6.1	Part 6 rules about service apply generally	1346
6.2	Interpretation	1347
	Chapter 2	
	Service of the Application for a Matrimonial Order or Civil Partnership Order in the Jurisdiction	
6.3	Interpretation	1347
6.4	Methods of service	1347
6.5	Who is to serve the application	1347
6.6	Every respondent to be served	1347
6.7	Personal service	1347
6.8	Service of application by the court	1348
6.9	Service by the bailiff	1348
6.10	Where to serve the application – general provisions	1348
6.11	Service of the application on a solicitor within the jurisdiction or in any EEA state	1348
6.12	Service of the application where the respondent gives an address at which the respondent may be served	1349
6.13	Service of the application where the respondent does not give an address at which the respondent may be served	1349
6.14	Service of the application on children and protected parties	1349
6.15	Deemed service – receipt of acknowledgment of service	1351
6.16	Deemed service by post or alternative service where no acknowledgment of service filed	1351
6.17	Proof of personal service where no acknowledgment of service filed	1351
6.18	Proof of service by the court etc.	1352
6.19	Service of the application by an alternative method or at an alternative place	1352
6.20	Power of the court to dispense with service of the application	1352
6.21	Notification of failure of service by the court	1353
6.22	Notice of non-service by bailiff	1353
	Chapter 3	
	Service of Documents other than an Application for a Matrimonial Order or Civil Partnership Order in the United Kingdom	
6.23	Method of service	1353
6.24	Who is to serve	1353
6.25	Personal service	1354
6.26	Address for service	1354

6.27 Change of address for service 1354
6.28 Service of an application form commencing proceedings on children and protected parties 1354
6.29 Service of other documents on or by children and protected parties where a litigation friend has been or will be appointed 1355
6.30 Service on or by children where a children's guardian has been or will be appointed under rule 16.4 1355
6.31 Service on or by children where a children's guardian has been appointed under rule 16.3 1355
6.32 Supplementary provisions relating to service on children and protected parties 1355
6.33 Supplementary provision relating to service on children 1355
6.34 Deemed service 1356
6.35 Service by an alternative method or at an alternative place 1356
6.36 Power to dispense with service 1357
6.37 Certificate of service 1357
6.38 Notification of outcome of service by the court 1357
6.39 Notification of non-service by bailiff 1357

Chapter 4
Service Out of the Jurisdiction

6.40 Scope and interpretation 1357
6.41 Permission to serve not required 1358
6.42 Period for acknowledging service or responding to application where application is served out of the jurisdiction 1358
6.43 Method of service – general provisions 1359
6.44 Service in accordance with the Service Regulation 1359
6.45 Service through foreign governments, judicial authorities and British Consular authorities 1360
6.46 Procedure where service is to be through foreign governments, judicial authorities and British Consular authorities 1360
6.47 Translation of application form or other document 1361
6.48 Undertaking to be responsible for expenses of the Foreign and Commonwealth Office 1361

Practice Direction 6A – Service within the Jurisdiction 1362

Practice Direction 6B – Service out of the Jurisdiction 1368

Practice Direction 6C – Disclosure of Addresses by Government Departments 13 February 1989 as amended by Practice Direction 20 July 1995 1373

Scope—FPR 2010, Pt 6 provides a comprehensive code for the service of an application for a matrimonial order or civil partnership order and for other documents. Chapter 2 relates to the service of an application for a matrimonial order or civil partnership order *in the jurisdiction* as defined in FPR 2010. Chapter 3 provides for the service of other documents *in the UK*. Chapter 4 provides for service *out of the jurisdiction*. Part 6, Chs 2 and 3 are supplemented by FPR PD6A (service within the jurisdiction); Pt 6, Ch 4 is supplemented by FPR PD6B (service out of the jurisdiction).

Chapter 1
Scope of this Part and Interpretation

6.1 Part 6 rules about service apply generally

This Part applies to the service of documents, except where –

(a) another Part, any other enactment or a practice direction makes a different provision; or
(b) the court directs otherwise.

Scope—The court may 'direct otherwise' under r 6.19: service by an alternative method or at an alternative place.

'another Part' (r 6.1(a))—This includes FPR 2010, r 33.13 (judgment summons).

'any other enactment' (r 6.1(a))—These include: Companies Act 2006, s 1139; Crown Proceedings Act 1947, ss 17 and 18; and State Immunity Act 1978, s 12.

6.2 Interpretation

In this Part 'solicitor' includes any person who, for the purposes of the Legal Services Act 2007, is an authorised person in relation to an activity which constitutes the conduct of litigation (within the meaning of that Act).

Defined term—'authorised person': Legal Services Act 2007, s 18.

Chapter 2

Service of the Application for a Matrimonial Order or Civil Partnership Order in the Jurisdiction

6.3 Interpretation

In this Chapter, unless the context otherwise requires, a reference to an application –

(a) is a reference to an application for a matrimonial or civil partnership order; and
(b) includes an application by a respondent as referred to in rule 7.4.

(Part 7 deals with applications in matrimonial or civil partnership proceedings.)

Defined terms—'matrimonial order', 'civil partnership order': FPR 2010, r 2.3.

6.4 Methods of service

An application may be served by any of the following methods –

(a) personal service in accordance with rule 6.7;
(b) first class post, or other service which provides for delivery on the next business day, in accordance with Practice Direction 6A or
(c) where rule 6.11 applies, document exchange.

Scope—In the first instance, the application will normally be served by post. The option to serve personally is provided for as an alternative to postal service and is not obligatory. Service through a document exchange applies where a solicitor is acting for the respondent (FPR 2010, r 6.11 and FPR PD6A, para 2.1). It is also possible to effect service by another service which provides for delivery on the next business day by leaving the document with or delivering the document to the relevant service provider or having the document collected by the relevant service provider (FPR PD6A, para 3.1) (i e by a non-Royal Mail provider capable of next-day delivery service).

As to service on members of the Regular Forces and US Air Force, see FPR PD6A, para 5.1 and Annex.

6.5 Who is to serve the application

(1) Subject to the provisions of this rule, an application may be served by –

(a) the applicant; or
(b) a court officer, if so requested by the applicant.

(2) A court officer will not serve the application if the party to be served is a child or protected party.

(3) An application must not be served personally by the applicant himself or herself.

(Rule 6.14 deals with service of the application on children and protected parties)

Scope—Primary responsibility for service of the application falls upon the applicant, although the applicant may not serve it personally. However, unless the party to be served is a child or a protected party (FPR 2010, r 6.14), the applicant may on issuing the application request the court to serve the application by post under FPR 2010, r 6.8. Personal service by court bailiff is available under FPR 2010, r 6.9.

6.6 Every respondent to be served

The application must be served on every respondent.

6.7 Personal service

An application is served personally on a respondent by leaving it with that respondent.

'served personally'— FPR 2010, r 6.17 makes provision for proof of personal service where no acknowledgment of service has been filed.

PART III

6.8 Service of application by the court

(1) Where the application is to be served by a court officer, the applicant must give the court officer an address at which the respondent is to be served in accordance with rule 6.4.

(2) Where the court officer has sent a notification of failure of service to the applicant in accordance with rule 6.21, the applicant may request the court officer to serve the document on the respondent at an alternative address.

6.9 Service by the bailiff

(1) An applicant may request that an application be served by a bailiff delivering a copy of the application to the respondent personally.

(2) The request must be made in accordance with Practice Direction 6A.

(3) Where the bailiff is unable to serve the application, the applicant may apply to the court for an order under rule 6.19 (service by an alternative method or at an alternative place).

(Practice Direction 6A contains provision about when a request under this rule is appropriate.)

(Rule 6.22 provides for notice of non-service by a bailiff.)

Scope—An applicant may make a request to the court officer for personal service by the court bailiff. Such an application will only be considered where the address for service is in England and Wales and, normally, where postal service has already been attempted and failed. A request will rarely be granted where the applicant is legally represented, unless it can be shown why bailiff service is required rather than service by a process server (FPR PD6A, para 11). The request is made in accordance with FPR PD6A, para 11.3. Personal service by bailiff must be proved in accordance with FPR PD6A, para 12.

Defined term—'bailiff': CCA 1984, s 147(1).

6.10 Where to serve the application – general provisions

(1) The application must be served within the jurisdiction except as provided for by Chapter 4 of this Part (service out of the jurisdiction).

(2) The applicant must include in the application an address at which the respondent may be served.

(3) Paragraph (2) does not apply where an order made by the court under rule 6.19 (service by an alternative method or at an alternative place) specifies the place or method of service of the application.

Scope—The general rule is that the application must state an address at which the respondent may be served, unless (having taken the steps required by FPR 2010, r 6.13) an application is made under FPR 2010, r 6.19 for service by an alternative method or at an alternative place.

Defined term—'jurisdiction': FPR 2010, r 2.3.

6.11 Service of the application on a solicitor within the jurisdiction or in any EEA state

(1) Where a solicitor acting for the respondent has notified the applicant in writing that the solicitor is instructed by the respondent to accept service of the application on behalf of the respondent at a business address within the jurisdiction, the application must be served at the business address of that solicitor.

(2) Subject to the provisions of Chapter 4 of this Part, where a solicitor acting for the respondent has notified the applicant in writing that the solicitor is instructed by the respondent to accept service of the application on behalf of the respondent at a business address within any EEA state, the application must be served at the business address of that solicitor.

('Solicitor' has the extended meaning set out in rule 6.2 and 'EEA state' is defined in Schedule 1 to the Interpretation Act 1978.)

Scope—Where a solicitor within the jurisdiction or in any EEA state, who is acting for a respondent, has notified the applicant in writing that he/she is instructed to accept service, there is an obligation to serve the application at the business address of that solicitor. This rule makes explicit the principle established in *Nanglegan v Royal Free Hampstead NHS Trust* [2001] EWCA Civ 127 that, where solicitors have been nominated to accept service, the claim form (application) must be served on the solicitors.

6.12 Service of the application where the respondent gives an address at which the respondent may be served

Subject to rules 6.13, the respondent may be served with the application at an address within the jurisdiction which the respondent has given for the purpose of being served with the proceedings.

6.13 Service of the application where the respondent does not give an address at which the respondent may be served

(1) This rule applies where –

- (a) rule 6.11 (service of application on solicitor); and
- (b) rule 6.12 (respondent gives address at which respondent may be served),

do not apply and the applicant does not wish the application to be served personally under rule 6.7.

(2) Subject to paragraphs (3) to (5) the application must be served on the respondent at his usual or last known address.

(3) Where the applicant has reason to believe that the respondent no longer resides at his usual or last known address, the applicant must take reasonable steps to ascertain the current address of the respondent.

(4) Where, having taken the reasonable steps required by paragraph (3), the applicant –

- (a) ascertains the respondent's current address, the application must be served at that address; or
- (b) is unable to ascertain the respondent's current address, the applicant must consider whether there is –
  - (i) an alternative place where; or
  - (ii) an alternative method by which,

service may be effected.

(5) If, under paragraph (4)(b), there is such a place where or a method by which service could be effected, the applicant must make an application under rule 6.19.

'Usual or last known residence' (r 6.13(2),(3))—Service at the respondent's usual or last known address will be good service even where a respondent is no longer residing there, unless the applicant had, viewed objectively, reason to believe that the Respondent no longer resides at that address. In this event, reasonable steps must be taken to ascertain the respondent's current address.

Enquiries as to respondent's address—Enquiries should be made of at least the following people or organisations, where appropriate:

- (a) *Relatives, friends, neighbours, former employers* The district judge will want to know that, at the very least, letters have been sent to such of these as might know of the respondent's whereabouts.
- (b) *Bank, accountant, former solicitors, doctor, dentist, etc* Any of these may be willing to forward a stamped envelope containing the petition to a (former) customer/client/patient, even though they will not reveal his address.
- (c) *Government departments generally* In the case of applications concerning financial provision of tracing a child, certain government departments may be requested to provide a party's or a child's address. Requests for such information must be made officially by the district judge following FPR PD6C. An application for a matrimonial order containing an application for a financial order would satisfy the Practice Direction's requirement enabling an address to be requested. The departments concerned are the Department of Work and Pensions, the Office for National Statistics (which administers the National Health Service Central Register), the Passport Office and the Ministry of Defence (service personnel). The district judge asks the applicant to provide as much as possible of the information set out in the Practice Direction; the Passport Office require, in addition to the request, an undertaking that the information will be used only for the purposes of service of court process. As to HMRC, see annotations to FPR PD6C.
- (d) *Department for Work and Pensions* In addition to the facilities available under the Practice Direction (see (c) above), this department, if able to identify the respondent, will forward the application to him. Application may be made direct by the applicant to: Department for Work and Pensions, NICB, Special Section A, Newcastle-upon-Tyne NE98 1YU. As much information as possible about the respondent, by reference to the Practice Direction, should be given.

Service on members of the Regular Forces—See annex to FPR PD6A.

6.14 Service of the application on children and protected parties

(1) Where the respondent is a child, the application form must be served on –

(a) one of the child's parents or guardians; or
(b) if there is no parent or guardian, an adult with whom the child resides or in whose care the child is.

(2) Where the respondent is a protected party, the application must be served on –

(a) one of the following persons with authority in relation to the protected party –
(i) the attorney under a registered enduring power of attorney;
(ii) the donee of a lasting power of attorney; or
(iii) the deputy appointed by the Court of Protection; or
(b) if there is no such person, an adult with whom the protected party resides or in whose care the protected party is.

(3) Any reference in this Chapter to a respondent or party to be served includes the person to be served with the application form on behalf of a child or protected party under paragraph (1) or (2).

(4) The court may make an order permitting an application form to be served on a child or protected party, or on a person other than the person specified in paragraph (1) or (2).

(5) An application for an order under paragraph (4) may be made without notice.

(6) The court may order that, although an application form has been sent or given to someone other than the person specified in paragraph (1) or (2), it is to be treated as if it had been properly served.

(7) Where a document is served in accordance with this rule –

(a) it must be endorsed with the notice set out in Practice Direction 6A; and
(b) the person commencing the proceedings must file a witness statement by the person on whom the application form was served stating whether –
(i) the contents of the application form; or
(ii) the purpose and intention of the application,

were communicated to the child or protected party and, if not, why not.

(8) Paragraph (7)(b) does not apply where the Official Solicitor is, as the case may be –

(a) the litigation friend of the protected party; or
(b) the litigation friend or children's guardian of the child.

Scope—This rule makes special provision for service upon a child or protected party with service being effected in the normal way upon the category of persons specified.

Defined terms—'child', 'protected party': FPR 2010, r 2.3.

Person to be served—Where there is no parent or guardian for a child, the application is to be served on 'an adult with whom [he] resides or in whose care [he] is'.

In the case of a protected party, there may be an attorney under a registered enduring power of attorney, a donee under a lasting power of attorney or a deputy appointed by the Court of Protection. Each of these people would be suitable to accept service of proceedings upon the protected party. In the absence of any such persons, the application is to be served on 'an adult with whom [he] resides or in whose care [he] is'.

In either case, the court can provide for service to be on the child or protected party or on some other person (r 6.14(4)) and an application under this provision may be made without notice (r 6.14(5)).

'an adult with whom the child or protected party resides or in whose care the child or protected party is' (r 6.14(1)(b) and (2)(b))—The purpose of this provision is to reach a responsible adult who will be concerned to ensure that the child or protected party is properly represented in the proceedings and will initiate the appointment of a litigation friend (see FPR 2010, Pt 15 and PDs 15A and 15B). There will seldom be a problem in the case of a child. In case of difficulty involving a protected party, in addition to attempts at formal service, it may be prudent to communicate with any person concerned as to the welfare of the protected party in the hope that a suitable representative will emerge.

A person cannot be in the care of someone who is himself a protected party. Where several such persons share a home (eg under supervision), it will be necessary to look beyond the occupants of the home (eg to the persons who provide the supervision). Occupants of a residential care or nursing home will be in the care of the registered proprietor who should bring the proceedings to the attention of any concerned person. If such care is funded by the local authority, it would be appropriate to involve the social services department which will have carried out a community care assessment of need. Service on a proper officer of the local social services authority or other guardian when the protected party is under a guardianship order, or the district health authority when the protected party has been compulsorily admitted to hospital under the Mental Health Act 1983 (as amended by Mental Health Act 2007) may be sufficient. Where no one can be identified, it is possible to resort to the provision for deemed service (see note below) thereby ensuring that the problem is brought before the court. When there is no response to due service, the need for a litigation friend will have to be addressed by the court in any event. Reference may be made to the Official Solicitor in case of continuing difficulty as he may need to be appointed.

Deemed service (r 6.14(6))—The provision for deemed service enables the court to proceed with the appointment of a litigation friend when service is not otherwise possible.

Communication to the child or protected party (r 6.14(7))—Communication to the child or protected party is generally required, unless an explanation is provided.

'notice' (r 6.14(7)(a))—Form D5 set out in FPR PD6A, para 9.1.

6.15 Deemed service – receipt of acknowledgment of service

(1) Subject to paragraph (2), an application is deemed to be served if the acknowledgment of service, signed by the party served or the solicitor acting on that party's behalf, is returned to the court office.

(2) Where the signature on the acknowledgment of service purports to be that of the other party to the marriage or civil partnership, the applicant must prove that it is the signature of that party by –

(a) giving oral evidence to that effect at the hearing; or

(b) if the application is undefended, confirming it to be so in the statement the applicant files under rule 7.19(4).

Amendments—SI 2012/679.

6.16 Deemed service by post or alternative service where no acknowledgment of service filed

(1) Subject to paragraph (2), if –

(a) an application has been served on a respondent by post or other service which provides for delivery on the next business day;

(b) no acknowledgment of service has been returned to the court office; and

(c) the court is satisfied that the respondent has received the application,

the court may direct that the application is deemed to be served.

(2) Where –

(a) the application alleges 2 years' separation and the respondent consents to a matrimonial or civil partnership order being granted; and

(b) none of the other facts mentioned in section 1(2) of the 1973 Act or section 44(5) of the 2004 Act, as the case may be, is alleged,

paragraph (1) applies only if –

(i) the court is satisfied that the respondent has received notice of the proceedings; and

(ii) the applicant produces a written statement, signed by the respondent, containing the respondent's consent to the grant of an order.

Amendments—SI 2013/3204.

General note—A common example of this form of deemed service is by production of a letter from the respondent's solicitors which states that the application was brought to them by the respondent. Such a letter may be exhibited to the applicant's application under FPR 2010, r 7.19 (application for decree nisi) with an additional paragraph asking the district judge to deem service of the application in view of the contents of the letter.

6.17 Proof of personal service where no acknowledgment of service filed

(1) This rule applies where –

(a) an application has been served on a respondent personally; and

(b) no acknowledgment of service has been returned to the court office.

(2) The person serving the application must file a certificate of service stating the date and time of personal service.

(Practice Direction 6A makes provision for a certificate of service by a bailiff.)

(3) If the respondent served was the other party to the marriage or civil partnership, the certificate of service must show the means by which the person serving the application knows the identity of the party served.

Scope—If service is effected personally (other than by bailiff) and no acknowledgment of service is returned to the court, a certificate of service (Form FP6) must be filed. If, as is generally the case, the respondent is not known to the server, his means of identifying the respondent must be described in one of the following ways, eg:

(a) by means of a photograph;
(b) by personal knowledge of the process server or other person identifying the respondent; or
(c) by admission of the person served.

In (b) or (c), corroborative evidence will be necessary. In the first instance, the process server should be asked to seek the respondent's signature on the acknowledgment of service obviating the need for a certificate of service. In no circumstances may the applicant effect personal service (FPR 2010, r 6.5(3)).

6.18 Proof of service by the court etc.

(1) Where a court officer serves an application by post, or other service which provides for delivery on the next business day, the court officer must note in the court records the date of –

(a) posting; or
(b) leaving with, delivering to or collection by the relevant service provider.

(2) A record made in accordance with paragraph (1) is evidence of the facts stated in it.

(3) This rule does not affect the operation of section 31N of the 1984 Act.

(Section 31N of the 1984 Act provides that where a summons or other process issued from the family court is served by an officer of a court, service may be proved by a certificate in a prescribed form.)

Amendments—SI 2013/3204.

Defined term—'officer': CCA 1984, s 147(1).

6.19 Service of the application by an alternative method or at an alternative place

(1) Where it appears to the court that there is a good reason to authorise service by a method or at a place not otherwise permitted by this Part, the court may direct that service is effected by an alternative method or at an alternative place.

(2) On an application under this rule, the court may direct that steps already taken to bring the application form to the attention of the respondent by an alternative method or at an alternative place is good service.

(3) A direction under this rule must specify –

(a) the method or place of service;
(b) the date on which the application form is deemed served; and
(c) the period for filing an acknowledgment of service or answer.

Scope—This rule provides for what was previously known as 'substituted service'. The only issue to be decided on an application for service by an alternative method is whether service by the prescribed methods (FPR 2010, r 6.4) is impracticable. The court may then either direct that steps already taken to bring the application to the attention of the respondent constitute good service by way of retrospective authorisation (r 6.19(2)) or give further directions specifying the method or place of service, the date the application will be deemed to be served and the period for filing an acknowledgment of service or answer (r 6.19(3)). The method of service might be by advertisement or by posting to an address where the application might be expected to come to the respondent's attention. If validly obtained, such an order cannot be challenged, even if the party intended to be served did not receive the documents. However, the order cannot be said to be validly obtained if the district judge is not given all the necessary information relevant to the application (for example that, in the past, the respondent had a solicitor acting for him) (*Clifford v Clifford* [1985] FLR 732, CA). This rule may authorise service by email (*Maughan v Wilmot* [2016] 2 FLR 1349, FD (order for service by email was not a contravention of the Hague Service Convention 1965)). See, also, *E v E (BIIA: Arts 16 and 19)* [2017] 1 FLR 658, FD.

6.20 Power of the court to dispense with service of the application

(1) The court may dispense with service of the application where it is impracticable to serve the application by any method provided for by this Part.

(2) An application for an order to dispense with service may be made at any time and must be supported by evidence.

(3) The court may require the applicant to attend when it decides the application.

Scope—The court is given power to dispense with service of an application where it is impracticable to serve by any of the other methods provided by FPR 2010, Pt 6. The district judge must be satisfied that full enquiries as to the respondent's whereabouts have been made. By dispensing with service, the district judge accepts that a party cannot be served and, in doing so, he balances the need for the court to be satisfied that a party to proceedings has had notice of them against the applicant's wish or need to proceed with an application. The needs of any children involved might be a factor in the district judge's consideration. The application must be supported by evidence from the applicant or his solicitor. The district judge may require the personal attendance of the applicant to clarify points in the evidence in support of the application.

6.21 Notification of failure of service by the court

Where –

(a) the court serves the application by post or other service which provides for delivery on the next business day; and

(b) the application is returned to the court,

the court will send notification to the applicant that the application has been returned.

6.22 Notice of non-service by bailiff

Where –

(a) the bailiff is to serve an application; and

(b) the bailiff is unable to serve it on the respondent,

the court officer will send notification to the applicant.

Defined terms—'officer' (including 'bailiff'): CCA 1984, s 147(1).

Chapter 3

Service of Documents other than an Application for a Matrimonial Order or Civil Partnership Order in the United Kingdom

6.23 Method of service

A document may be served by any of the following methods –

(a) personal service, in accordance with rule 6.25;

(b) first class post, document exchange or other service which provides for delivery on the next business day, in accordance with Practice Direction 6A;

(c) leaving it at a place specified in rule 6.26; or

(d) fax or e-mail in accordance with Practice Direction 6A.

(Rule 6.35 provides for the court to permit service by an alternative method or at an alternative place.)

Amendments—SI 2015/1868.

6.24 Who is to serve

(1) A party to proceedings will serve a document which that party has prepared, or which the court has prepared or issued on behalf of that party, except where –

(a) a rule or practice direction provides that the court will serve the document; or

(b) the court directs otherwise.

(2) Where a court officer is to serve a document, it is for the court to decide which method of service is to be used.

(3) Where the court officer is to serve a document prepared by a party, that party must provide a copy for the court and for each party to be served.

6.25 Personal service

(1) Where required by another Part, any other enactment, a practice direction or a court order, a document must be served personally.

(2) In other cases, a document may be served personally except where the party to be served has given an address for service under rule 6.26(2)(a).

(3) A document is served personally on an individual by leaving it with that individual.

6.26 Address for service

(1) A party to proceedings must give an address at which that party may be served with documents relating to those proceedings.

(2) Subject to paragraph (4), a party's address for service must be –

- (a) the business address either within the United Kingdom or any other EEA state of a solicitor acting for the party to be served; or
- (b) where there is no solicitor acting for the party to be served, an address within the United Kingdom at which the party resides or carries on business.

('EEA state' is defined in Schedule 1 to the Interpretation Act 1978.)

(3) Where there is no solicitor acting for the party to be served and the party does not have an address within the United Kingdom at which that party resides or carries on business, the party must, subject to paragraph (4), give an address for service within the United Kingdom.

(4) A party who –

- (a) has been served with an application for a matrimonial or civil partnership order outside the United Kingdom; and
- (b) apart from acknowledging service of the application, does not take part in the proceedings,

need not give an address for service within the United Kingdom.

(5) Any document to be served in proceedings must be sent, or transmitted to, or left at, the party's address for service unless it is to be served personally or the court orders otherwise.

(6) Where, in accordance with Practice Direction 6A, a party indicates or is deemed to have indicated that they will accept service by fax, the fax number given by that party must be at the address for service.

(7) Where a party indicates in accordance with Practice Direction 6A, that they will accept service by e-mail, the e-mail address given by that party will be deemed to be the address for service.

(8) This rule does not apply where an order made by the court under rule 6.35 (service by an alternative method or at an alternative place) specifies where a document may be served.

Amendments—SI 2015/1868.

6.27 Change of address for service

Where the address for service of a party changes, that party must give notice in writing of the change, as soon as it has taken place, to the court and every other party.

6.28 Service of an application form commencing proceedings on children and protected parties

(1) This rule applies to the service of an application form commencing proceedings other than an application for a matrimonial or civil partnership order.

(2) An application form commencing proceedings which would otherwise be served on a child or protected party must be served –

- (a) where the respondent is a child, in accordance with rule 6.14(1); and
- (b) where the respondent is a protected party, in accordance with rule 6.14(2).

Child—If a litigation friend has been or will be appointed, the service of documents other than the application form must be served as set out in FPR 2010, r 6.29 below. If a children's guardian pursuant to FPR 2010, r 16.4 has been or will be appointed or a children's guardian pursuant to FPR 2010, r 16.3 has been appointed, the provisions for service on or by children are set out in FPR 2010, rr 6.30 and 6.31 below.

6.29 Service of other documents on or by children and protected parties where a litigation friend has been or will be appointed

(1) This rule applies to –

(a) a protected party; or
(b) a child to whom the provisions of rule 16.5 and Chapter 5 of Part 16 apply (litigation friends).

(2) An application for an order appointing a litigation friend where a protected party or child has no litigation friend must be served in accordance with rule 15.8 or rule 16.13 as the case may be.

(3) Any other document which would otherwise be served on or by a child or protected party must be served on or by the litigation friend conducting the proceedings on behalf of the child or protected party.

6.30 Service on or by children where a children's guardian has been or will be appointed under rule 16.4

(1) This rule applies to a child to whom the provisions of rule 16.4 and Chapter 7 apply.

(2) An application for an order appointing a children's guardian where a child has no children's guardian must be served in accordance with rule 16.26.

(3) Any other document which would otherwise be served on or by a child must be served on or by the children's guardian conducting the proceedings on behalf of the child.

Rule 16.4 children's guardian—Applies when the child is the subject of or a party to specified proceedings (as defined by CA 1989, s 41(6) and FPR 2010, r 12.27) or adoption or placement order proceedings etc.

6.31 Service on or by children where a children's guardian has been appointed under rule 16.3

(1) This rule applies where a children's guardian has been appointed for a child in accordance with rule 16.3.

(2) Any document which would otherwise be served on the child must be served on –

(a) the solicitor appointed by the court in accordance with section 41(3) of the 1989 Act; and
(b) the children's guardian.

(3) Any document which would otherwise be served by the child must be served by –

(a) the solicitor appointed by the court in accordance with section 41(3) of the 1989 Act or by the children's guardian; or
(b) if no solicitor has been appointed as mentioned in paragraph (a), the children's guardian.

Rule 16.3 children's guardian—Applies where the child is not the subject of proceedings referred in FPR 2010, r 16.3 but is an applicant in the proceedings, or the rules provide for the child to be a party or the court has made the child a party.

6.32 Supplementary provisions relating to service on children and protected parties

(1) The court may direct that a document be served on a protected party or child or on some person other than a person upon whom it would be served under rules 6.28 to 6.31 above.

(2) The court may direct that, although a document has been sent or given to someone other than a person upon whom it should be served under rules 6.28 to 6.31 above, the document is to be treated as if had been properly served.

(3) This rule and rules 6.28 to 6.31 do not apply where the court has made an order under rule 16.6 allowing a child to conduct proceedings without a children's guardian or litigation friend.

6.33 Supplementary provision relating to service on children

(1) This rule applies to proceedings to which Part 12 applies.

PART III

(2) Where a rule requires –

(a) a document to be served on a party;
(b) a party to be notified of any matter; or
(c) a party to be supplied with a copy of a document,

in addition to the persons to be served in accordance with rules 6.28 to 6.32, the persons or bodies mentioned in paragraph (3) must be served, notified or supplied with a copy of a document, as applicable, unless the court directs otherwise.

(3) The persons or bodies referred to in paragraph (2) are –

(a) such of the following who are appointed in the proceedings –
 (i) the children's guardian (if the children's guardian is not otherwise to be served);
 (ii) the welfare officer;
 (iii) the children and family reporter;
 (iv) the officer of the Service, Welsh family proceedings officer or local authority officer acting under a duty referred to in rule 16.38; and
(b) a local authority preparing a report under section 14A(8) or (9) of the 1989 Act.

Part 12 proceedings—Proceedings relating to children except parental order proceedings and applications for adoption, placement and related proceedings (i e Pt 12 applies to emergency proceedings, private and public proceedings, applications relating to the court's exercise of the inherent jurisdiction, child abduction proceedings and proceedings relating to Brussels IIb or the 1996 Hague Convention).

6.34 Deemed service

A document, other than an application for a matrimonial or civil partnership order, served in accordance with these rules or a practice direction is deemed to be served on the day shown in the following table –

Method of service	*Deemed day of service*
First class post (or other service which provides for delivery on the next business day)	The second day after it was posted, left with, delivered to or collected by the relevant service provider, provided that day is a business day; or, if not, the next business day after that day
Document exchange	The second day after it was left with, delivered to or collected by the relevant service provider, provided that day is a business day; or, if not, the next business day after that day.
Delivering the document to or leaving it at a permitted address	If it is delivered to or left at the permitted address on a business day before 4.30p.m., on that day; or in any other case, on the next business day after that day.
Fax	If the transmission of the fax is completed on a business day before 4.30p.m., on that day; or, in any other case, the next business day after the day on which it was transmitted.
Other electronic method	If the e-mail or other electronic transmission is sent on a business day before 4.30p.m., on that day; or in any other case, on the next business day after the day on which it was sent.
Personal service	If the document is served personally before 4.30p.m. on a business day, on that day; or, in any other case, on the next business day after that day.

(Practice Direction 6A contains examples of how the date of deemed service is calculated.)

6.35 Service by an alternative method or at an alternative place

Rule 6.19 applies to any document in proceedings as it applies to an application for a matrimonial or civil partnership order and reference to the respondent in that rule is modified accordingly.

6.36 Power to dispense with service

The court may dispense with the service of any document which is to be served in proceedings.

6.37 Certificate of service

(1) Where a rule, practice direction or court order requires a certificate of service, the certificate must state the details set out in the following table –

Method of service	*Details to be certified*
Personal service	Date and time of personal service and method of identifying the person served.
First class post, document exchange or other service which provides for delivery on the next business day	Date of posting, leaving with, delivering to or collection by the relevant service provider.
Delivery of document to or leaving it at a permitted place	Date and time when the document was delivered to or left at the permitted place.
Fax	Date and time of completion of transmission.
Other electronic method	Date and time of sending the email or other electronic transmission.
Alternative method or place permitted by court	As required by the court.

(2) An applicant who is required to file a certificate of service of an application form must do so at or before the earlier of –

(a) the first directions appointment in; or
(b) the hearing of,

the proceedings unless a rule or practice direction provides otherwise.

(Rule 17.2 requires a certificate of service to contain a statement of truth.)

6.38 Notification of outcome of service by the court

Where –

(a) a document to be served by a court officer is served by post or other service which provides for delivery on the next working day; and
(b) the document is returned to the court,

the court officer will send notification to the party who requested service that the document has been returned.

6.39 Notification of non-service by bailiff

Where –

(a) the bailiff is to serve a document; and
(b) the bailiff is unable to serve it,

the court officer must send notification to the party who requested service.

Chapter 4
Service Out of the Jurisdiction

6.40 Scope and interpretation

(1) This Chapter contains rules about –

(a) service of application forms and other documents out of the jurisdiction; and

PART III

(b) the procedure for service.

('Jurisdiction' is defined in rule 2.3.)

(2) In this Chapter –

'application form' includes an application notice;

'Commonwealth State' means a State listed in Schedule 3 to the British Nationality Act 1981; and

'the Hague Convention' means the Convention on the service abroad of judicial and extra-judicial documents in civil or commercial matters signed at the Hague on November 15, 1965.

Scope—This Chapter should be read in conjunction with PD6B, which contains provisions in relation to service out of the jurisdiction. For service within the EU, reference should be made to the Service Regulation (r 6.44). For service outside the EU, reference should be made to the Hague Service Convention (The Hague Convention on the Service Abroad of Judicial and Extra Judicial Documents in Civil or Commercial Matters 1965): *Maughan v Wilmot* [2016] 2 FLR 1349, FD.

6.41 Permission to serve not required

Any document to be served for the purposes of these rules may be served out of the jurisdiction without the permission of the court.

'may be served out of the jurisdiction without the permission of the court'—The fact that proceedings may be served out of the jurisdiction does not necessarily mean that they should be. Choice of forum is a critical factor at the outset of any international case. The court will consider (other than where Brussels IIA or DMPA 1973, Sch 1, para 8 apply) whether England and Wales is the proper place to conduct the proceedings (*The Spiliada* [1987] AC 460, HL). See annotations to DMPA 1973, s 5. Despite the epithet forum *non conveniens*, the question is not one of convenience so much as whether the proceedings are in the appropriate forum. As family proceedings can be served out of England and Wales as of right, it will be for the respondent to show that another forum is clearly more appropriate (*Ella v Ella* [2007] 2 FLR 35, CA; *Prazic v Prazic* [2006] 2 FLR 1128, CA).

6.42 Period for acknowledging service or responding to application where application is served out of the jurisdiction

(1) This rule applies where, under these rules, a party is required to file –

(a) an acknowledgment of service; or

(b) an answer to an application,

and sets out the time period for doing so where the application is served out of the jurisdiction.

(2) Where the applicant serves an application on a respondent in –

(a) Scotland or Northern Ireland; or

(b) a Member State or Hague Convention country within Europe,

the period for filing an acknowledgment of service or an answer to an application is 21 days after service of the application.

(3) Where the applicant serves an application on a respondent in a Hague Convention country outside Europe, the period for filing an acknowledgment of service or an answer to an application is 31 days after service of the application.

(4) Where the applicant serves an application on a respondent in a country not referred to in paragraphs (2) and (3), the period for filing an acknowledgment of service or an answer to an application is set out in Practice Direction 6B.

'Member State' (r 6.42(2))—See PD6B, para 2.

'period for filing an acknowledgment of service' (r 6.42(2))—The period for filing an acknowledgment of service or an answer to an application, where the respondent is in a country other than Scotland, Northern Ireland, a Member State or Hague Convention country, is prescribed by FPR PD6B, para 5.1 and the Table in FPR PD6B.

Application notices and orders—The provisions of FPR 2010, Pt 6, Ch 4 also apply to the service out of the jurisdiction of an application notice or order (FPR PD6B, para 6). Where an application notice or order is served out of the jurisdiction, the period for responding is 7 days less than the number of days listed in the Table (FPR PD6B, para 7.1).

6.43 Method of service – general provisions

(1) This rule contains general provisions about the method of service of an application for a matrimonial or civil partnership order, or other document, on a party out of the jurisdiction.

Where service is to be effected on a party in Scotland or Northern Ireland

(2) Where a party serves an application form or other document on a party in Scotland or Northern Ireland, it must be served by a method permitted by Chapter 2 (and references to 'jurisdiction' in that Chapter are modified accordingly) or Chapter 3 of this Part and rule 6.26(5) applies.

Where service is to be effected on a respondent out of the United Kingdom

(3) Where the applicant wishes to serve an application form, or other document, on a respondent out of the United Kingdom, it may be served by any method –

provided for by –

rule 6.44 (service in accordance with the Service Regulation);

rule 6.45 (service through foreign governments, judicial authorities and British Consular authorities); or

permitted by the law of the country in which it is to be served.

(4) Nothing in paragraph (3) or in any court order authorises or requires any person to do anything which is contrary to the law of the country where the application form, or other document, is to be served.

'permitted by the law of the country in which it is to be served' (r 6.43(3)(b))—Although it has been held under CPR 1998, r 6.40 that this provision 'should be applied with a reasonable degree of flexibility' (*Arros Invest Limited v Rafik Nishanov* [2004] EWHC 576 (Ch)), the onus is on the claimant to show, by expert evidence if necessary, that the local rules have been complied with. An alternative method of service may be permitted so long as it does not contravene the law of the country of service (*Habib Bank v Central Bank of Sudan* [2006] EWHC 1767 (Comm); *Bentinck v Bentinck* [2007] 2 FLR 1, CA).

6.44 Service in accordance with the Service Regulation

(1) This rule applies where the applicant wishes to serve the application form, or other document, in accordance with the Service Regulation.

(2) The applicant must file –

(a) the application form or other document;
(b) any translation; and
(c) any other documents required by the Service Regulation.

(3) When the applicant files the documents referred to in paragraph (2), the court officer will –

(a) seal[(GL)], or otherwise authenticate with the stamp of the court, the copy of the application form; and
(b) forward the documents to the Senior Master of the Queen's Bench Division.

(4) In addition to the documents referred to in paragraph (2), the applicant may file a photograph of the person to be served if the applicant considers that it would assist in ensuring effective service.

(The Service Regulation is annexed to Practice Direction 6B.)

(Article 20(1) of the Service Regulation provides that the Regulation prevails over other provisions contained in any other agreement or arrangement concluded by Member States.)

Amendments—SI 2011/1328.

'the Service Regulation' (r 6.44 generally)—The Service Regulation is an attempt to establish an efficient system for the service of documents within the European Union. Its use is complicated by the fact that states may opt out of a number of its provisions. The Regulation set out in Part VI and is also annexed to FPR PD6B. Reference should also be made to FPR PD6B, para 2. Up-to-date information on the implementation of the Regulation may be found on the Europa website at *http://eur-lex.europa.eu*. It will often be prudent to seek the advice of a practitioner in the state in which service is to be effected. Such practitioners may be located by visiting *www.iaml.org*. The Foreign Process Section (Room E16) at the Royal Courts of Justice, Strand, London WC2A 2LL (DX 44450 Strand) (tel: 020 7947 7786/6488/6691/1741/6682; fax: 0870 324 0025; email: foreignprocess.rcj@hmcts.gsi.gov.uk) will also offer guidance.

'the applicant must file' (r 6.44(2))—See FPR PD6B, para 3.

PART III

6.45 Service through foreign governments, judicial authorities and British Consular authorities

(1) Where the applicant wishes to serve an application form, or other document, on a respondent in any country which is a party to the Hague Convention, it may be served –

(a) through the authority designated under the Hague Convention in respect of that country; or

(b) if the law of that country permits –

(i) through the judicial authorities of that country; or

(ii) through a British Consular authority in that country.

(2) Where the applicant wishes to serve an application form, or other document, on a respondent in any country which is not a party to the Hague Convention, it may be served, if the law of that country so permits –

(a) through the government of that country, where that government is willing to serve it; or

(b) through a British Consular authority in that country.

(3) Where the applicant wishes to serve an application form, or other document, in –

(a) any Commonwealth State which is not a party to the Hague Convention;

(b) the Isle of Man or the Channel Islands; or

(c) any British Overseas Territory,

the methods of service permitted by paragraphs (1)(b) and (2) are not available and the applicant or the applicant's agent must effect service on a respondent in accordance with rule 6.43 unless Practice Direction 6B provides otherwise.

(4) This rule does not apply where service is to be effected in accordance with the Service Regulation.

(A list of British overseas territories is reproduced in Practice Direction 6B.)

'Hague Convention' (r 6.45(3)(a))—FPR 2010, r 6.40(2).

'British Overseas Territories' (r 6.45(3)(c))—FPR PD6B, para 4.2.

6.46 Procedure where service is to be through foreign governments, judicial authorities and British Consular authorities

(1) This rule applies where the applicant wishes to serve an application form, or other document, under rule 6.45(1) or (2).

(2) Where this rule applies, the applicant must file –

(a) a request for service of the application form, or other document, by specifying one or more of the methods in rule 6.45(1) or (2);

(b) a copy of the application form or other document;

(c) any other documents or copies of documents required by Practice Direction 6B; and

(d) any translation required under rule 6.47.

(3) When the applicant files the documents specified in paragraph (2), the court officer will –

(a) seal(GL), or otherwise authenticate with the stamp of the court, the copy of the application form or other document; and

(b) forward the documents to the Senior Master of the Queen's Bench Division.

(4) The Senior Master will send documents forwarded under this rule –

(a) where the application form, or other document, is being served through the authority designated under the Hague Convention, to that authority; or

(b) in any other case, to the Foreign and Commonwealth Office with a request that it arranges for the application form or other document to be served.

(5) An official certificate which –

(a) states that the method requested under paragraph (2)(a) has been performed and the date of such performance;

(b) states, where more than one method is requested under paragraph (2)(a), which method was used; and

(c) is made by –

(i) a British Consular authority in the country where the method requested under paragraph (2)(a) was performed;

(ii) the government or judicial authorities in that country; or

(iii) the authority designated in respect of that country under the Hague Convention,

is evidence of the facts stated in the certificate.

(6) A document purporting to be an official certificate under paragraph (5) is to be treated as such a certificate, unless it is proved not to be.

'the applicant wishes to serve the application form, or other document' (r 6.44(1))—Where service is effected through the Foreign Office, service is not being effected by the court but by the applicant and, if there is a delay, the onus is on the applicant to show that all reasonable steps have been taken.

6.47 Translation of application form or other document

(1) Except where paragraphs (4) and (5) apply, every copy of the application form, or other document, filed under rule 6.45 (service through foreign governments, judicial authorities and British Consular authorities) must be accompanied by a translation of the application form or other document.

(2) The translation must be –

(a) in the official language of the country in which it is to be served; or

(b) if there is more than one official language of that country, in any official language which is appropriate to the place in the country where the application form or other document is to be served.

(3) Every translation filed under this rule must be accompanied by a statement by the person making it that it is a correct translation, and the statement must include that person's name, address and qualifications for making the translation.

(4) The applicant is not required to file a translation of the application form, or other document, filed under rule 6.45 where it is to be served in a country of which English is an official language.

(5) The applicant is not required to file a translation of the application form or other document filed under rule 6.45 where –

(a) the person on whom the document is to be served is able to read and understand English; and

(b) service of the document is to be effected directly on that person.

(This rule does not apply to service in accordance with the Service Regulation which contains its own provisions about the translation of documents.)

6.48 Undertaking to be responsible for expenses of the Foreign and Commonwealth Office

Every request for service filed under rule 6.46 (procedure where service is to be through foreign governments, judicial authorities etc.) must contain an undertaking by the person making the request –

(a) to be responsible for all expenses incurred by the Foreign and Commonwealth Office or foreign judicial authority; and

(b) to pay those expenses to the Foreign and Commonwealth Office or foreign judicial authority on being informed of the amount.

PART III

Practice Direction 6A – Service within the Jurisdiction

This Practice Direction supplements FPR Part 6, Chapters 2 and 3

GENERAL PROVISIONS

Scope of this Practice Direction

1.1 This Practice Direction supplements the following provisions of Part 6 –

(a) Chapter 2 (service of the application for a matrimonial order or civil partnership order in the jurisdiction);
(b) Chapter 3 (service of documents other than an application for a matrimonial order or civil partnership order in the United Kingdom); and
(c) rule 6.43(2) in relation to the method of service on a party in Scotland or Northern Ireland.

(Practice Direction B supplementing Part 6 contains provisions relevant to service on a party in Scotland or Northern Ireland, including provisions about the period for responding to an application notice.)

When service may be by document exchange

2.1 Subject to the provisions of rule 6.4 (which provides when an application for a matrimonial or civil partnership order may be served by document exchange) service by document exchange (DX) may take place only where –

(a) the address at which the party is to be served includes a numbered box at a DX; or
(b) the writing paper of the party who is to be served or of the solicitor acting for that party sets out a DX box number; and
(c) the party or the solicitor acting for that party has not indicated in writing that they are unwilling to accept service by DX.

How service is effected by post, an alternative service provider or DX

3.1 Service by post, DX or other service which provides for delivery on the next business day is effected by –

(a) placing the document in a post box;
(b) leaving the document with or delivering the document to the relevant service provider; or
(c) having the document collected by the relevant service provider.

Service by fax or e-mail

4.1 Paragraphs 4.2 to 4.6 apply to the service by the court or by a party of a document other than an application for a matrimonial or civil partnership order and documents in adoption proceedings and parental order proceedings.

4.2 Subject to the provisions of rule 6.26(6) and (7), where a document is to be served by fax or e-mail –

(a) the party who is to be served or the solicitor acting for that party must previously have indicated in writing to the court or party serving, whichever is applicable –
  (i) that the party to be served or the solicitor is willing to accept service by fax or e-mail; and
  (ii) the fax number or e-mail address to which it must be sent; and
(b) the following are to be taken as sufficient written indications for the purposes of paragraph 4.2(a) –
  (i) a fax number set out on the letterhead or website of the solicitor acting for the party to be served;

(ii) an e-mail address set out on the letterhead or website of the solicitor acting for the party to be served but only where it is stated that the e-mail address may be used for service;

(iii) a fax number or e-mail address set out on a statement of case or an answer to a claim filed with the court by the party to be served; or

(iv) an e-mail or other correspondence from the party to be served, to the court or party serving, confirming that they are willing to accept service by e-mail.

4.3 Where a party intends to –

(a) serve a document by e-mail; or

(b) request that the court serve a document by e-mail

that party must first ask the party who is to be served whether there are any limitations to the recipient's agreement to accept service by such means (for example, the format in which documents are to be sent and the maximum size of attachments that may be received).

4.4 Where a document is served by e-mail, the party serving the document need not in addition send or deliver a hard copy.

4.5 Where a party requests the court to serve a document by e-mail and has received notification of limitations to the recipient's agreement to accept service pursuant to paragraph 4.3, that party must communicate those limitations to the court when requesting the court to serve.

4.6 Where limitations have been communicated by a party pursuant to paragraph 4.3, service on that party must comply with those limitations.

Service on members of the Regular Forces and United States Air Force

5.1 The provisions that apply to service on members of the regular forces (within the meaning of the Armed Forces Act 2006) and members of the United States Air Force are annexed to this practice direction.

Application for an order for service by an alternative method or at an alternative place

6.1 An application for an order under rule 6.19 may be made without notice.

6.2 Where an application for an order under rule 6.19 is made before the document is served, the application must be supported by evidence stating –

(a) the reason why an order is sought;

(b) what alternative method or place is proposed; and

(c) why the applicant believes that the document is likely to reach the person to be served by the method or at the place proposed.

6.3 Where the application for an order is made after the applicant has taken steps to bring the document to the attention of the person to be served by an alternative method or at an alternative place, the application must be supported by evidence stating –

(a) the reason why the order is sought;

(b) what alternative method or alternative place was used;

(c) when the alternative method or place was used; and

(d) why the applicant believes that the document is likely to have reached the person to be served by the alternative method or at the alternative place.

6.4 Examples –

(a) an application to serve by posting or delivering to an address of a person who knows the other party must be supported by evidence that if posted or delivered to that address, the document is likely to be brought to the attention of the other party;

(b) an application to serve by sending a SMS text message or leaving a voicemail message at a particular telephone number saying where the document is must be accompanied by evidence that the person serving the document has taken, or will take, appropriate steps to ensure that the party being served is using that telephone number and is likely to receive the message.

Applications for an order to dispense with service

7.1 An application for an order under rule 6.36 (power to dispense with service) may be made without notice.

Deemed service of a document other than an application for a matrimonial or civil partnership order

8.1 Rule 6.34 contains provisions about deemed service of a document other than an application for a matrimonial or civil partnership order. Examples of how deemed service is calculated are set out below.

Example 1

8.2 Where the document is posted (by first class post) on a Monday (a business day), the day of deemed service is the following Wednesday (a business day).

Example 2

8.3 Where the document is left in a numbered box at the DX on a Friday (a business day), the day of deemed service is the following Monday (a business day).

Example 3

8.4 Where the document is sent by fax on a Saturday and the transmission of that fax is completed by 4.30p.m. on that day, the day of deemed service is the following Monday (a business day).

Example 4

8.5 Where the document is served personally before 4.30p.m. on a Sunday, the day of deemed service is the next day (Monday, a business day).

Example 5

8.6 Where the document is delivered to a permitted address after 4.30p.m. on the Thursday (a business day) before Good Friday, the day of deemed service is the following Tuesday (a business day) as the Monday is a bank holiday.

Example 6

8.7 Where the document is posted (by first class post) on a bank holiday Monday, the day of deemed service is the following Wednesday (a business day).

Service of application on children and protected parties

9.1 Rule 16.14(1) and (2) are applied to service of an application form (other than an application for a matrimonial or civil partnership order) commencing proceedings on children and protected parties by rule 6.28. Rule 6.14(7) makes provision as to how an application form must be served where the respondent is a child or protected party. A document served in accordance with rule 6.14(7) must be endorsed with the following notice which is set out in Form D5 –

Important Notice

The contents or purport of this document are to be communicated to the Respondent
[or as the case may be], [full name of Respondent]
if s/he is over 16 [add if the person to be served lacks capacity within the meaning of the Mental Capacity Act 2005 to conduct the proceedings] unless you are satisfied [after consultation with the responsible medical officer within the meaning of the Mental Health Act 1983 or, if s/he is not liable to be detained or subject to guardianship under that Act, his/her medical attendant]* that communication will be detrimental to his/her mental condition].

PROVISIONS RELATING TO APPLICATIONS FOR MATRIMONIAL AND CIVIL PARTNERSHIP ORDERS

Acknowledgment of service to be sent to applicant

10.1 Where the court office receives an acknowledgment of service the court officer must send a photographic or scanned copy of it to the applicant.

Personal service of application by bailiff

11.1 The court will only consider a request for personal service of the application by a bailiff if the address for service is in England and Wales.

11.2 In normal circumstances, a request should only be made if postal service has been attempted. In this case, if –

(a) a signed acknowledgment of service is not returned to the court within 14 days after posting; and
(b) the applicant reasonably believes the respondent is still living at the stated address,

the applicant may make a request to the court for personal service by a bailiff.

11.3 A request for personal service by a bailiff should be made in writing to the court officer on the prescribed form and accompanied by the relevant fee. The request should also be accompanied by-

(a) evidence that postal service has been attempted and failed; or
(b) if postal service has not been attempted, an explanation as to why postal service is not considered appropriate in the circumstances of the case.

11.4 A request will rarely be granted where the applicant is legally represented and it will be necessary for the representative to show why service by bailiff is required rather than by a process server.

Proof of personal service by bailiff

12.1 Once service of the application has been effected or attempted by the bailiff he must file a certificate of service in the issuing court.

12.2 If the respondent fails to sign and return an acknowledgment of service to the court office and –

(a) the certificate contains a signature of receipt of the application by the respondent; or
(b) the identity of the respondent is to be proved by a photograph supplied by the applicant,

the applicant must prove the signature or photograph in the statement filed by the applicant under rule 7.19(4).

****

Service of application on children and protected parties

14.1 A document served in accordance with rule 6.14(7) must be endorsed with the notice contained in paragraph 9.1.

ANNEX

Service on Members of the Regular Forces

1 The following information is for litigants and legal representatives who wish to serve legal documents in civil proceedings in the courts of England and Wales on parties to the proceedings who are (or who, at the material time, were) members of the regular forces (as defined in the Armed Forces Act 2006).

2 The proceedings may take place in the family court or the High Court, and the documents to be served may be claim forms, interim application notices and pre-action application notices. Proceedings for divorce or maintenance and proceedings in the Family Courts generally are subject to special rules as to service which are explained in a practice direction issued by the Senior District Judge of the Principal Registry on 26 June 1979.

> (now see Practice Direction 1 Maintenance Orders: Service Personnel; 2 Disclosure of Addresses [1995] 2 FLR 813.)

3 In this Annex, the person wishing to effect service is referred to as the 'claimant' and the member of the regular forces to be served is referred to as 'the member'; the expression 'overseas' means outside the United Kingdom.

Enquiries as to address

4 As a first step, the claimant's legal representative will need to find out where the member is serving, if this is not already known. For this purpose the claimant's legal representative should write to the appropriate officer of the Ministry of Defence as specified in paragraph 10 below.

5 The letter of enquiry should in every case show that the writer is a legal representative and that the enquiry is made solely with a view to the service of legal documents in civil proceedings.

6 In all cases the letter must give the full name, service number, rank or rate, and Ship, Arm or Trade, Regiment or Corps and Unit or as much of this information as is available. Failure to quote the service number and the rank or rate may result either in failure to identify the member or in considerable delay.

7 The letter must contain an undertaking by the legal representative that, if the address is given, it will be used solely for the purpose of issuing and serving documents in the proceedings and that so far as is possible the legal representative will disclose the address only to the court and not to the claimant or to any other person or body. A legal representative in the service of a public authority or private company must undertake that the address will be used solely for the purpose of issuing and serving documents in the proceedings and that the address will not be disclosed so far as is possible to any other part of the legal representative's employing organisation or to any other person but only to the court. Normally on receipt of the required information and undertaking the appropriate office will give the service address.

8 If the legal representative does not give the undertaking, the only information that will be given is whether the member is at that time serving in England or Wales, Scotland, Northern Ireland or overseas.

9 It should be noted that a member's address which ends with a British Forces Post Office address and reference (BFPO) will nearly always indicate that the member is serving overseas.

10 The letter of enquiry should be addressed as follows –

Royal Navy and Royal Marine Officers, Ratings and Other Ranks

> Director Naval Personnel
> Fleet Headquarters
> MP 3.1
> Leach Building
> Whale Island
> Portsmouth
> Hampshire
> PO2 8BY

Army Officers and other Ranks –

Army Personnel Centre
Disclosures 1
MP 520
Kentigern House
65 Brown Street
Glasgow
G2 8EX

Royal Air Force Officers and Other Ranks –

Manning 22E
RAF Disclosures
Room 221B
Trenchard Hall
RAF Cranwell
Sleaford
Lincolnshire
NG34 8HB

Assistance in serving documents on members

11 Once the claimant's legal representative has ascertained the member's address, the legal representative may use that address as the address for service by post, in cases where this method of service is allowed by the Civil Procedure Rules. There are, however, some situations in which service of the proceedings, whether in the High Court or in the family court, must be effected personally; in these cases an appointment will have to be sought, through the Commanding Officer of the Unit, Establishment or Ship concerned, for the purpose of effecting service. The procedure for obtaining an appointment is described below, and it applies whether personal service is to be effected by the claimant's legal representative or the legal representative's agent or by a court bailiff, or, in the case of proceedings served overseas (with the leave of the court) through the British Consul or the foreign judicial authority.

12 The procedure for obtaining an appointment to effect personal service is by application to the Commanding Officer of the Unit, Establishment or Ship in which the member is serving. The Commanding Officer may grant permission for the document server to enter the Unit, Establishment or Ship but if this is not appropriate the Commanding Officer may offer arrangements for the member to attend at a place in the vicinity of the Unit, Establishment or Ship in order that the member may be served. If suitable arrangements cannot be made the legal representative will have evidence that personal service is impracticable, which may be useful in an application for service by an alternative method or at an alternative place.

General

13 Subject to the procedure outlined in paragraphs 11 and 12, there are no special arrangements to assist in the service of legal documents when a member is outside the United Kingdom. The appropriate office will, however, give an approximate date when the member is likely to return to the United Kingdom.

14 It sometimes happens that a member has left the regular forces by the time an enquiry as to address is made. If the claimant's legal representative confirms that the proceedings result from an occurrence when the member was in the regular forces and the legal representative gives the undertaking referred to in paragraph 7, the last known private address after discharge will normally be provided. In no other case, however, will the Ministry of Defence disclose the private address of a member of the regular forces.

Service on Members of United States Air Force

15 In addition to the information contained in the memorandum of 26 July 1979, and after some doubts having been expressed as to the correct procedure to be followed by persons having civil

claims against members of the United States Air Force in England and Wales, the Lord Chancellor's Office (as it was then) issued the following notes for guidance with the approval of the appropriate United States authorities.

16 Instructions have been issued by the United States authorities to the commanding officers of all their units in England and Wales that every facility is to be given for the service of documents in civil proceedings on members of the United States Air Force. The proper course to be followed by a creditor or other person having a claim against a member of the United States Air Force is for that person to communicate with the commanding officer or, where the unit concerned has a legal officer, with the legal officer of the defendant's unit requesting the provision of facilities for the service of documents on the defendant. It is not possible for the United States authorities to act as arbitrators when a civil claim is made against a member of their forces. It is, therefore, essential that the claim should either be admitted by the defendant or judgment should be obtained on it, whether in the High Court or the family court. If a claim has been admitted or judgment has been obtained and the claimant has failed to obtain satisfaction within a reasonable period, the claimant's proper course is then to write to: Office of the Staff Judge Advocate, Headquarters, Third Air Force, R.A.F. Mildenhall, Suffolk, enclosing a copy of the defendant's written admission of the claim or, as the case may be, a copy of the judgment. Steps will then be taken by the Staff Judge Advocate to ensure that the matter is brought to the defendant's attention with a view to prompt satisfaction of the claim.

Practice Direction 6B – Service out of the Jurisdiction

This Practice Direction supplements FPR Part 6, Chapter 4

Scope of this Practice Direction

1.1 This Practice Direction supplements Chapter 4 (service out of the jurisdiction) of Part 6.

(Practice Direction 6A contains relevant provisions supplementing rule 6.43(2) in relation to the method of service on a party in Scotland or Northern Ireland.)

Service in other Member States of the European Union

2.1 Where service is to be effected in another Member of State of the European Union, the Service Regulation applies.

2.2 The Service Regulation is Regulation (EC) No. 1393/2007 of the European Parliament and of the Council of 13 November 2007 on the service in the Member States of judicial and extrajudicial documents in civil or commercial matters (service of documents), and repealing Council Regulation (EC) no. 1348/2000, as amended from time to time and as applied by the Agreement made on 19 October 2005 between the European Community and the Kingdom of Denmark on the service of judicial and extrajudicial documents in civil and commercial matters.

2.3 The Service Regulation is annexed to this Practice Direction.

(Article 20(1) of the Service Regulation provides that the Regulation prevails over other provisions contained in bilateral or multilateral agreements or arrangements concluded by the Member of States and in particular Article IV of the protocol to the Brussels Convention of 1968 and the Hague Convention of 15 November 1965)

Documents to be filed under rule 6.46(2)

3.1 A duplicate of –

(a) the application form or other document to be served under rule 6.45(1) or (2);
(b) any documents accompanying the application or other document referred to in paragraph (a); and
(c) any translation required by rule 6.47;

must be provided for each party to be served out of the jurisdiction, together with forms for responding to the application.

3.2 Some countries require legalisation of the document to be served and some require a formal letter of request which must be signed by the Senior Master. Any queries on this should be addressed to the Foreign Process Section (Room E02) at the Royal Courts of Justice.

Note—The Foreign Process Section is in Room E16 at the Royal Courts of Justice.

Service in a Commonwealth State or British Overseas Territory

4.1 The judicial authorities of certain Commonwealth States which are not a party to the Hague Convention require service to be in accordance with rule 6.45(1)(b)(i) and not 6.45(3). A list of such countries can be obtained from the Foreign Process Section (Room E02) at the Royal Courts of Justice.

Note—The Foreign Process Section is in Room E16 at the Royal Courts of Justice.

4.2 The list of British overseas territories is contained in Schedule 6 to the British Nationality Act 1981. For ease of reference these are –

(a) Anguilla;
(b) Bermuda;
(c) British Antarctic Territory;
(d) British Indian Ocean Territory;
(e) Cayman Islands;
(f) Falkland Islands;
(g) Gibraltar;
(h) Montserrat;
(i) Pitcairn, Henderson, Ducie and Oeno Islands;
(j) St. Helena, Ascension and Tristan da Cunha;
(k) South Georgia and the South Sandwich Islands;
(l) Sovereign Base Areas of Akrotiri and Dhekelia;
(m) Turks and Caicos Islands;
(n) Virgin Islands.

Period for responding to an application form

5.1 Where rule 6.42 applies, the period within which the respondent must file an acknowledgment of service or an answer to the application is the number of days listed in the Table after service of the application.

5.2 Where an application is served out of the jurisdiction any statement as to the period for responding to the claim contained in any of the forms required by the Family Procedure Rules to accompany the application must specify the period prescribed under rule 6.42.

Service of application notices and orders

6.1 The provisions of Chapter 4 of Part 6 (special provisions about service out of the jurisdiction) also apply to service out of the jurisdiction of an application notice or order.

6.2 Where an application notice is to be served out of the jurisdiction in accordance with Chapter 4 of Part 6 the court must have regard to the country in which the application notice is to be served in setting the date for the hearing of the application and giving any direction about service of the respondent's evidence.

Period for responding to an application notice

7.1 Where an application notice or order is served out of the jurisdiction, the period for responding is 7 days less than the number of days listed in the Table.

Further information

8.1 Further information concerning service out of the jurisdiction can be obtained from the Foreign Process Section, Room E02, Royal Courts of Justice, Strand, London WC2A 2LL (telephone 020 7947 6691).

Note—The Foreign Process Section is in Room E16 at the Royal Courts of Justice.

Table

Place or country	Number of days
Afghanistan	23
Albania	25
Algeria	22
Andorra	21
Angola	22
Anguilla	31
Antigua and Barbuda	23
Antilles (Netherlands)	31
Argentina	22
Armenia	21
Ascension Island	31
Australia	25
Austria	21
Azerbaijan	22
Azores	23
Bahamas	22
Bahrain	22
Balearic Islands	21
Bangladesh	23
Barbados	23
Belarus	21
Belgium	21
Belize	23
Benin	25
Bermuda	31
Bhutan	28
Bolivia	23
Bosnia and Herzegovina	21
Botswana	23
Brazil	22
British Virgin Islands	31
Brunei	25
Bulgaria	23
Burkina Faso	23
Burma	23
Burundi	22
Cambodia	28
Cameroon	22
Canada	22
Canary Islands	22
Cape Verde	25
Caroline Islands	31
Cayman Islands	31
Central African Republic	25
Chad	25
Chile	22
China	24
China (Hong Kong)	31
China (Macau)	31
China (Taiwan)	23
China (Tibet)	34
Christmas Island	27
Cocos (Keeling) Islands	41
Colombia	22
Comoros	23
Congo (formerly Congo Brazzaville or French Congo)	25
Congo (Democratic Republic)	25
Corsica	21
Costa Rica	23
Croatia	21
Cuba	24
Cyprus	31
Czech Republic	21

Place or country	Number of days
Denmark	21
Djibouti	22
Dominica	23
Dominican Republic	23
East Timor	25
Ecuador	22
Egypt	22
El Salvador	25
Equatorial Guinea	23
Eritrea	22
Estonia	21
Ethiopia	22
Falkland Islands and Dependencies	31
Faroe Islands	31
Fiji	23
Finland	24
France	21
French Guyana	31
French Polynesia	31
French West Indies	31
Gabon	25
Gambia	22
Georgia	21
Germany	21
Ghana	22
Gibraltar	31
Greece	21
Greenland	31
Grenada	24
Guatemala	24
Guernsey	21
Guinea	22
Guinea-Bissau	22
Guyana	22
Haiti	23
Holland (Netherlands)	21

Place or country	Number of days
Honduras	24
Hungary	22
Iceland	22
India	23
Indonesia	22
Iran	22
Iraq	22
Ireland (Republic of)	21
Ireland (Northern)	21
Isle of Man	21
Israel	22
Italy	21
Ivory Coast	22
Jamaica	22
Japan	23
Jersey	21
Jordan	23
Kazakhstan	21
Kenya	22
Kiribati	23
Korea (North)	28
Korea (South)	24
Kosovo	21
Kuwait	22
Kyrgyzstan	21
Laos	30
Latvia	21
Lebanon	22
Lesotho	23
Liberia	22
Libya	21
Liechtenstein	21
Lithuania	21
Luxembourg	21
Macedonia	21
Madagascar	23
Madeira	31

PART III

Place or country	Number of days
Malawi	23
Malaysia	24
Maldives	26
Mali	25
Malta	21
Mariana Islands	26
Marshall Islands	32
Mauritania	23
Mauritius	22
Mexico	23
Micronesia	23
Moldova	21
Monaco	21
Mongolia	24
Montenegro	21
Montserrat	31
Morocco	22
Mozambique	23
Namibia	23
Nauru	36
Nepal	23
Netherlands	21
Nevis	24
New Caledonia	31
New Zealand	26
New Zealand Island Territories	50
Nicaragua	24
Niger (Republic of)	25
Nigeria	22
Norfolk Island	31
Norway	21
Oman (Sultanate of)	22
Pakistan	23
Palau	23
Panama	26
Papua New Guinea	26
Paraguay	22

Place or country	Number of days
Peru	22
Philippines	23
Pitcairn, Henderson, Ducie and Oeno Islands	31
Poland	21
Portugal	21
Portuguese Timor	31
Puerto Rico	23
Qatar	23
Reunion	31
Romania	22
Russia	21
Rwanda	23
Sabah	23
St. Helena	31
St. Kitts and Nevis	24
St. Lucia	24
St. Pierre and Miquelon	31
St. Vincent and the Grenadines	24
Samoa (U.S.A. Territory) (See also Western Samoa)	30
San Marino	21
Sao Tome and Principe	25
Sarawak	28
Saudi Arabia	24
Scotland	21
Senegal	22
Serbia	21
Seychelles	22
Sierra Leone	22
Singapore	22
Slovakia	21
Slovenia	21
Society Islands (French Polynesia)	31
Solomon Islands	29
Somalia	22
South Africa	22

Place or country	Number of days
South Georgia (Falkland Island Dependencies)	31
South Orkneys	21
South Shetlands	21
Spain	21
Spanish Territories of North Africa	31
Sri Lanka	23
Sudan	22
Surinam	22
Swaziland	22
Sweden	21
Switzerland	21
Syria	23
Tajikistan	21
Tanzania	22
Thailand	23
Togo	22
Tonga	30
Trinidad and Tobago	23
Tristan Da Cunha	31
Tunisia	22

Place or country	Number of days
Turkey	21
Turkmenistan	21
Turks & Caicos Islands	31
Tuvalu	23
Uganda	22
Ukraine	21
United Arab Emirates	22
United States of America	22
Uruguay	22
Uzbekistan	21
Vanuatu	29
Vatican City State	21
Venezuela	22
Vietnam	28
Virgin Islands – U.S.A	24
Wake Island	25
Western Samoa	34
Yemen (Republic of)	30
Zaire	25
Zambia	23
Zimbabwe	22

PART III

ANNEX – SERVICE REGULATION (RULE 6.44)

http://www.justice.gov.uk/courts/procedure-rules/family/practice_directions/pd_form_imgs/pd_06b_pdf_eps/pd_06b_ecreg2007.pdf

Note—EC Regulation 1393/2007 is set out in Part VI.

Practice Direction 6C – Disclosure of Addresses by Government Departments 13 February 1989 [as amended by Practice Direction 20 July 1995]

This Practice Direction supplements FPR Part 6

NB—This practice direction does not apply to requests for disclosure from HMRC and related agencies that are covered by 'Disclosure Orders against the Inland Revenue-Guidance from the President's Office (November 2003)'. Practice Direction of 20 July 1995 (*Disclosure of Addresses by Government Departments*), amending Practice Direction of 13 February 1989, still applies to family proceedings – see PD29C.

The arrangements set out in the Registrar's Direction of 26 April 1988 whereby the court may request the disclosure of addresses by government departments have been further extended. These arrangements will now cover:

(a) tracing the address of a person in proceedings against whom another person is seeking to obtain or enforce an order for financial provision either for himself or herself or for the children of the former marriage; and,

(b) tracing the whereabouts of a child, or the person with whom the child is said to be, in proceedings under the Child Abduction and Custody Act 1985 or in which a [Part I order] is being sought or enforced.

Requests for such information will be made officially by the [district judge]. The request, in addition to giving the information mentioned below, should certify:

1 *In financial provision applications either*

(a) that a financial provision order is in existence, but cannot be enforced because the person against whom the order has been made cannot be traced; or

(b) that the applicant has filed or issued a notice, petition or originating summons containing an application for financial provision which cannot be served because the respondent cannot be traced.

[A 'financial provision order' means any of the orders mentioned in s 21 of the Matrimonial Causes Act 1973, except an order under s 27(6) of that Act].

2 *In wardship proceedings* that the child is the subject of wardship proceedings and cannot be traced, and is believed to be with the person whose address is sought.

3 *(deleted)*

The following notes set out the information required by those departments which are likely to be of the greatest assistance to an applicant.

(1) Department of Social Security

The department most likely to be able to assist is the Department of Social Security, whose records are the most comprehensive and complete. The possibility of identifying one person amongst so many will depend on the particulars given. An address will not be supplied by the department unless it is satisfied from the particulars given that the record of the person has been reliably identified.

The applicant or his solicitor should therefore be asked to supply as much as possible of the following information about the person sought:

(i) National Insurance number;
(ii) surname;
(iii) forenames in full;
(iv) date of birth (or, if not known, approximate age);
(v) last known address, with date when living there;
(vi) any other known address(es) with dates;
(vii) if the person sought is a war pensioner, his war pension and service particulars (if known);

and in applications for financial provision:

(viii) the exact date of the marriage and the wife's forenames.

Enquiries should be sent by the [district judge] to:

Contribution Agency
Special Section A, Room 101B
Longbenton
Newcastle upon Tyne
NE98 1YX

The department will be prepared to search if given full particulars of the person's name and date of birth, but the chances of accurate identification are increased by the provision of more identifying information.

Second requests for records to be searched, provided that a reasonable interval has elapsed, will be met by the Department of Social Security.

Income Support [/Supplementary Benefit]

Where, in the case of applications for financial provision, the wife is or has been in receipt of [income support/supplementary benefit], it would be advisable in the first instance to make enquiries of the manager of the local Social Security office for the area in which she resides in order to avoid possible duplication of enquiries.

(2) [Office for National Statistics]

National Health Service Central Register

[The Office for National Statistics] administers the National Health Service Central Register for the Department of Health. The records held in the Central Register include individuals' names, with dates of birth and National Health Service number, against a record of the Family Practitioner Committee area where the patient is currently registered with a National Health Service doctor. The Central Register does not hold individual patients' addresses, but can advise courts of the last Family Practitioner Committee area registration. Courts can then apply for information about addresses to the appropriate Family Practitioner Committee for independent action.

When application is made for the disclosure of Family Practitioner Committee area registrations from these records the applicant or his solicitor should supply as much as possible of the following information about the person sought:

(i) National Health Service number;
(ii) surname;
(iii) forenames in full;
(iv) date of birth (or, if not known, approximate age);
(v) last known address;
(vi) mother's maiden name.

Enquiries should be sent by the [district judge] to:

[The Office for National Statistics]
National Health Service Central Register
Smedley Hydro, Trafalgar Road
Southport
Merseyside PR8 2HH

(3) Passport Office

If all reasonable enquiries, including the aforesaid methods, have failed to reveal an address, or if there are strong grounds for believing that the person sought may have made a recent application for a passport, enquiries may be made to the Passport Office. The applicant or his solicitor should provide as much of the following information about the person as possible:

(i) surname;
(ii) forenames in full;
(iii) date of birth (or, if not known, approximate age);
(iv) place of birth;
(v) occupation;
(vi) whether known to have travelled abroad, and, if so, the destination and dates;
(vii) last known address, with date living there;
(viii) any other known address(es), with dates.

The applicant or his solicitor must also undertake in writing that information given in response to the enquiry will be used solely for the purpose for which it was requested, i e to assist in tracing the husband in connection with the making or enforcement of a financial provision order or in tracing a child in connection with a [Part 1 order] or wardship proceedings, as the case may be.

PART III

Enquiries should be sent to:

The Chief Passport Officer
[UK Passport Agency]
Home Office
Clive House, Petty France
London SW1H 9HD

(4) *Ministry of Defence*

In cases where the person sought is known to be serving or to have recently served in any branch of HM Forces, the solicitor representing the applicant may obtain the address for service of financial provision or [Part I] and wardship proceedings direct from the appropriate service department. In the case of army servicemen, the solicitor can obtain a list of regiments and of the various manning and record offices from the Officer in Charge, Central Manning Support Office, Higher Barracks, Exeter EC4 4ND.

The solicitor's request should be accompanied by a written undertaking that the address will be used for the purpose of service of process in those proceedings and that so far as is possible the solicitor will disclose the address only to the court and not to the applicant or any other person, except in the normal course of the proceedings.

Alternatively, if the solicitor wishes to serve process on the person's commanding officer under the provisions contained in s 101 of the Naval Act 1957, s 153 of the Army Act 1955 and s 153 of the Air Force Act 1955 (all of which as amended by s 62 of the Armed Forces Act 1971) he may obtain that officer's address in the same way.

Where the applicant is acting in person the appropriate service department is prepared to disclose the address of the person sought, or that of his commanding officer, to a [district judge] on receipt of an assurance that the applicant has given an undertaking that the information will be used solely for the purpose of serving process in the proceedings.

In all cases, the request should include details of the person's full name, service number, rank or rating, and his ship, arm or trade, corps, regiment or unit or as much of this information as is available. The request should also include details of his date of birth, or, if not known, his age, his date of entry into the service and, if no longer serving, the date of discharge, and any other information, such as his last known address. Failure to quote the service number and the rank or rating may result in failure to identify the serviceman or at least in considerable delay.

Enquiries should be addressed as follows:

[(a)	Officers of Royal Navy and Women's Royal Naval Service	The Naval Secretary, Room 161, Victory Building, HM Naval Base, Portsmouth, Hants PO1 3LS
	Ratings in the Royal Navy, WRNS Ratings, QARNNS Ratings	Captain, Naval Drafting, Centurion Building, Grange Road, Gosport, Hants PO13 9XA
	RN Medical and Dental Officers	The Medical Director General (Naval), Room 114, Victory Building, HM Naval Base, Portsmouth, Hants PO1 3LS

	Naval Chaplains	Director General, Naval Chaplaincy Service, Room 201, Victory Building, HM Naval Base, Portsmouth, Hants PO1 3LS
(b)	Royal Marine Officers	The Naval Secretary, Room 161, Victory Building, HM Naval Base, Portsmouth, Hants PO1 3LS
	Royal Marine Ranks	HQRM (DRORM), West Battery, Whale Island, Portsmouth, Hants PO2 8DX
(c)	Army Officers (including WRAC and QARANC)	Army Officer Documentation Office, Index Department, Room F7, Government Buildings, Stanmore, Middlesex
	Other Ranks, Army	The Manning and Record Office which is appropriate to the Regiment or Corps
(d)	Royal Air Force Officers and Other Ranks, Women's Royal Air Force Officers and Other Ranks (including PMRA FNS)	Ministry of Defence, RAF Personnel Management, 2b1(a) (RAF), Building 248, RAF Innsworth, Gloucester, GL3 1EZ]

General notes

Records held by other departments are less likely to be of use, either because of their limited scope or because individual records cannot readily be identified. If, however, the circumstances suggest that the address may be known to another department, application may be made to it by the [district judge], all relevant particulars available being given.

When the department is able to supply the address of the person sought to the [district judge], it will be passed on by him to the applicant's solicitor (or, in proper cases, direct to the applicant if acting in person) on an understanding to use it only for the purpose of the proceedings.

Nothing in this practice direction affects the service in matrimonial causes of petitions which do not contain any application for financial provision, etc. The existing arrangements whereby the Department of Social Security will at the request of the solicitor forward a letter by ordinary post to a party's last known address remain in force in such cases.

The Registrar's Direction of 26 April 1988 is hereby revoked.

Issued [in its original form] with the concurrence of the Lord Chancellor.

Note—Words in square brackets reflect text that has been amended to bring the PD up to date.

Inland Revenue—Concerns arising from the Data Protection legislation and the HRA 1998 have led the Inland Revenue to withdraw from these arrangements. They will, however, comply with a disclosure order made by the High Court exercising its inherent jurisdiction. In November 2003, an approved draft form of order was supplied to courts by the office of the President with the explanatory note. That note has not been revised since the coming into operation of FPR 2010 and of MFPA 1984 and its amendments, which set up the Family Court. PD29C confirms that the Family Court is permitted to transfer proceedings to the High Court where the proceedings are transferred solely for the purpose of making a disclosure order under the inherent jurisdiction of the High Court addressed to a Government Department or agency. Ordinary principles of disclosure against a third party apply (FPR 2010, r 21.2).

All disclosure orders against the Inland Revenue/HMRC should be sent to the following addresses:

1 Where the request is for information about an adult, it should be sent to: Inland Revenue, National Insurance Contributions Office, Special Section A, Longbenton, Newcastle upon Tyne NE98 1YX;
2 Where the request is for information about a child (which may include information about the whereabouts of the relevant adult in receipt of child benefit), it should be sent to: Child Benefits Office (GB) Internal Security, Waterview Park, District 15, Mandarin Way, Paterson, Washington NE38 8QA.

Other agencies—It is not clear whether the other agencies referred to in the PD are taking the same stance. Application can be made by Pt 18 application on principles in FPR 2010, r 21.2 (disclosure against third parties).

PART 7
PROCEDURE FOR APPLICATIONS IN MATRIMONIAL AND CIVIL PARTNERSHIP PROCEEDINGS

CONTENTS OF THIS PART

Chapter 1

Rule		Page
	Application and Interpretation	
7.1	Application and interpretation	1379
7.4	References to respondents	1381

Chapter 2
Rules about Starting and Responding to Proceedings

7.6	Statement of reconciliation	1381
7.7	Limitation on applications in respect of same marriage or civil partnership	1381
7.8	Service of application	1382
7.9	Withdrawal of application before service	1382
7.10	Who the parties are	1382
7.11	Nullity: Interim and full gender recognition certificates	1383
7.12	What the respondent and co-respondent should do on receiving the application	1384
7.13	Supplemental application and amendment of application and answer	1387
7.14	How the respondent can make an application	1389
7.15	Further information about the contents of the application and the answer	1390

Chapter 3
How the Court Determines Matrimonial and Civil Partnership Proceedings

7.16	General rule – hearing to be in public	1390
7.18	Notice of hearing	1391
7.19	Applications for a decree nisi or a conditional order	1391
7.20	What the court will do on an application for a decree nisi, a conditional order, a decree of judicial separation or a separation order	1392
7.21	Further provisions about costs	1395
7.22	What the court must do for the case management hearing	1395
7.26	Medical examinations in proceedings for nullity of a marriage of an opposite sex couple	1397
7.27	Stay of proceedings	1398

Chapter 4
Court Orders

7.28	The circumstances in which an order may be set aside (rescission)	1399
7.29	Applications under section 10(2) of 1973 Act or section 48(2) of 2004 Act	1400
7.30	Orders under section 10A(2) of the 1973 Act	1400
7.31	Applications to prevent decrees nisi being made absolute or conditional orders being made final	1401

7.32	Making decrees nisi absolute or conditional orders final by giving notice	1402
7.33	Applications to make decrees nisi absolute or conditional orders final	1404
7.34	What the court officer must do when a decree nisi is made absolute	1405
7.35	What the court officer must do when a conditional order is made final	1406
7.36	Records of decrees absolute and final orders	1406
	Practice Direction 7A – Procedure for Applications in Matrimonial and Civil Partnership Proceedings	1406
	Practice Direction 7B – Medical Examinations on Applications for Annulment of a Marriage	1411
	Practice Direction 7C – Polygamous Marriages	1411
	Practice Direction 7D – Gender Recognition Act 2004	1412

INTRODUCTORY NOTE

Structure of Pt 7 and its PD—FPR PD7A prescribes use of the form for application for a matrimonial decree absolute or civil partnership order (Form D8, and Form D8N (nullity), with supporting 'notes for guidance'). FPR 2010, Pt 7 deals with all forms of application in matrimonial proceedings or causes under MCA 1973; and with the various forms application in civil partnership proceedings under CPA 2004. In this context, an 'application' has the same meaning as a petition. **It** deals with all proceedings whether defended or undefended, although the procedures run in parallel.

Simplification, semantics and statutory provision—Courts Act 2003, s 75(5)(b) requires that the 2010 Rules be expressed in 'simple and simply expressed' terms. To this end some terminology in Part 7 has been simplified. However, where procedure is provided for by statute – such as that a divorce 'petition' shall start divorce proceedings – then use of the term 'application' (although apt to CPA 2004 proceedings) does not always accommodate the legislative description.

Online divorce pilot scheme—FPR 2010, PD36D: *Pilot Scheme: Procedure for using an online system to generate applications in certain proceedings for a matrimonial order* has been added as part of the transitional provisions Practice Direction. It represents a first step towards digitalisation of the procedure for dissolution of marriage and civil partnership (although it applies only to divorce at present). The Practice Direction uses 'application' and 'matrimonial order' where the statute (MCA 1973) uses petition and decree (as does the commentary below).

Chapter 1
Application and Interpretation

7.1 Application and interpretation

(1) The rules in this Part apply to matrimonial and civil partnership proceedings.

(2) (*revoked*)

(3) In this Part –

'defended case' means matrimonial proceedings or civil partnership proceedings in which –

(a) an answer has been filed opposing the grant of a matrimonial or civil partnership order on the application, and has not been struck out; or

(b) the respondent has filed an application for a matrimonial or civil partnership order in accordance with rule 7.14 and neither party's application has been disposed of; or

(c) rule 7.12(11A) applies, in light of paragraph (11) of that rule, notice has been given of intention to rebut and that notice has not been withdrawn,

and in which no matrimonial or civil partnership order has been made; and

'undefended case' means matrimonial proceedings or civil partnership proceedings other than a defended case.

(4) In this Part –

(a) a reference to a conditional order is a reference to a civil partnership order (other than a separation order) which has not been made final; and

(b) a reference to a final order is a reference to a conditional order which has been made final.

Amendments—SI 2013/3204; SI 2015/913.

Defined terms—'civil partnership proceedings', 'civil partnership order', 'matrimonial order': FPR 2010, r 2.3(1).

Terminology—Rule 7.1(4) introduces the terminology for civil partnership proceedings, but does not give the equivalent terms for matrimonial proceedings. For example, a decree nisi is the same as a conditional order and a decree absolute the same as a final order (see MCA 1973, s 1(5)).

Matrimonial and civil partnership proceedings—The proceedings covered by FPR 2010, Pt 7 are matrimonial and civil partnership proceedings, which are defined as follows:

(1) A 'matrimonial cause' means proceedings for a matrimonial order (FPR 2010, r 2.3(1)). 'Matrimonial proceedings' is not defined in FPR 2010, r 2.3(1) or Pt 7, but such proceedings may be assumed to be proceedings for a matrimonial order. 'Matrimonial order' (r 2.3(1)) means:
   (a) a decree of divorce (i e decree nisi and decree absolute) made under MCA 1973, s 1;
   (b) a decree of nullity (i e decree nisi and decree absolute) made on one of the grounds set out in MCA 1973, ss 11 or 12;
   (c) a decree of judicial separation made under MCA 1973, s 17;

(2) A 'civil partnership order' is defined by reference to CPA 2004, s 37(1), which enables the court to make the civil partnership equivalent of each of those.

'Defended case'—A case becomes defended when a respondent files an answer (FPR 2010, r 7.12(8)) or, having failed to do so in time (r 7.12(8)) obtains permission from the court so to do. The consequence of that is that the court fixes a case management hearing (rr 7.20(4) and 7.22). If matrimonial or civil partnership proceedings are to be defended and if the respondent seeks to oppose the application for a matrimonial or civil partnership order (as the case may be), an answer must be filed.

Circumstances in which an answer must be filed—FPR 1991, r 2.12(1) set out in terms the circumstances in which an answer must be filed and this remains the law since the coming into operation of FPR 2010. By contrast, the 2010 Rules do not provide any procedure for certain statutory provisions (e g defence under MCA 1973, s 5 (with CPA 2004 s 47(1)): right to respond for a co-respondent). Thus, an answer should be filed by a respondent in the following circumstances:

(1) Defending an application or disputing facts in it:
   (a) If a respondent wishes to oppose the grant of a matrimonial and civil partnership order, or a co-respondent wishes to dispute facts in an application (the rights of a co-respondent here are not referred to in r 7.1(3)), he must file an answer.
   (b) If a respondent accepts that the marriage has irretrievably broken down but disputes certain particulars, he may wish to file an answer. However, if the purpose of doing so is to answer allegations that might be raised again in children or ancillary relief proceedings, it may be sufficient for him to write to the petitioner or her solicitors, at the time of filing his acknowledgement of service, in the following terms: 'The respondent accepts that the marriage has irretrievably broken down but does not accept certain of the allegations in the petition. He reserves the right to reply to those allegations if raised in any subsequent proceedings relating to the children or for ancillary relief.'
   (c) If the respondent seeks to deny irretrievable breakdown on the grounds alleged, but seeks a decree himself, he may file his/her own application (petition) seeking a decree (see below and r 7.14(2)).

(2) Respondent wishing to cross-apply or to make any charge against the petitioner – If a respondent wishes to make allegations against a petitioner or to cross-apply for an order on facts that he alleges, he must file an answer (FPR 2010, r 7.14). It is not necessary to file an answer if the respondent seeks relief other than a decree (see below, filing of answer not required).

(3) Respondent under MCA 1973, s 5(1) or CPA 2004, s 47(1) who wishes to oppose the grant of decree – Where the respondent to a petition under MCA 1973, s 1(2)(e) or CPA 2004, s 4 (5 years' living apart) wishes to oppose the grant of an order on grounds that it will result in grave financial or other hardship, she must file an answer containing particulars of the hardship alleged (and see under FPR 2010, r 7.12(8) below).

Circumstances where filing of answer not required—There is no need to file an answer where the respondent –

(1) seeks or opposes an order in respect of children;
(2) seeks an order or to be heard on an application for a financial order; or
(3) wishes to be heard only on the question of costs (FPR 2010, r 7.21).

Respondent wishing to proceed on his/her own application (petition)—Where a respondent seeks a decree on his/her own application (petition) s/he will have to file an answer denying breakdown on the facts pleaded by the petitioner, and file a separate application (petition) making his/her own separate allegations and seeking a separate decree (MCA 1973, s 20; FPR 2010, r 7.14(2)).

'in which no matrimonial and civil partnership order has been made' (r 7.1(3)(d))—Rule 7.1(3)(d) recalls the fact that no proceedings can be defended until a decree absolute or final order is made. However, if a respondent wishes to defend, his chances of so doing recede as the date when a decree absolute or final order can finally be made approaches. Such defences and other avenues that may delay the proceedings (including involvement of the Queen's Proctor) are in MCA 1973, ss 8–10(1), CPA 2004, ss 46–48(1), and are dealt with in FPR 2010, rr 7.28 and 7.31.

7.2–7.3 *(revoked)*

7.4 References to respondents

(1) Where a respondent makes an application for a matrimonial order or a civil partnership order, unless the context otherwise requires, the rules in this Part shall apply with necessary modifications as if the reference to a respondent is a reference to the applicant in the other party's application for a matrimonial order or a civil partnership order.

(2) Where a respondent makes an application for a matrimonial order, unless the context otherwise requires, the rules in this Part shall apply with necessary modifications as if the reference to a co-respondent is a reference to a party cited in the respondent's application for a matrimonial order.

Defined terms—'civil partnership order'; 'matrimonial order': FPR 2010, r 2.3(1).

Chapter 2
Rules about Starting and Responding to Proceedings

7.5 *(revoked)*

7.6 Statement of reconciliation

(1) Where the applicant is legally represented, the legal representative must, unless the court directs otherwise, complete and file with the application a statement in the form for this purpose referred to in Practice Direction 5A, certifying whether the legal representative has discussed with the applicant the possibility of a reconciliation and given the applicant the names and addresses of persons qualified to help effect a reconciliation.

(2) This rule applies to an application for –

(a) a decree of divorce made under section 1 of the 1973 Act;
(b) a decree of judicial separation made under section 17 of the 1973 Act;
(c) a dissolution order as mentioned in section 37(1)(a) of the 2004 Act; or
(d) a separation order as mentioned in section 37(1)(d) of the 2004 Act.

Amendments—SI 2012/679.

Defined terms—'legal representative': FPR 2010, s 2.3(1).

Certificate of discussion of reconciliation by legal representative—Rule 7.6 confirms the requirement under MCA 1973, s 6 and CPA 2004, s 42 that, where a petitioner/applicant is legally represented, then that representative must file a statement in accordance with Form D6.

7.7 Limitation on applications in respect of same marriage or civil partnership

(1) Subject to paragraph (2), a person may not make more than one application for a matrimonial or civil partnership order in respect of the same marriage or civil partnership unless –

(a) the first application has been dismissed or finally determined; or
(b) the court gives permission.

(2) Where a person –

(a) has, within one year of the date of the marriage or civil partnership, made an application for, as the case may be, a decree of judicial separation or an order for separation; and
(b) then, after that one-year period has passed, wishes to apply for a decree of divorce or a dissolution order on the same facts as those mentioned in the first application,

that person does not need the court's permission to make the application referred to in sub-paragraph (b).

Defined terms—'civil partnership order', 'matrimonial order': FPR 2010, r 2.3(1).

Further applications for a matrimonial or civil partnership order—This rule deals with the following in relation to petitions or civil partnership applications:

(a) the court giving permission for a fresh application where a petition/application has not been disposed of (r 7.7(1)(b));
(b) amendment of an existing petition/application (see r 7.13 below);
(c) the filing, without permission, of a fresh petition/application where there is an existing application for judicial separation or a civil partnership separation order application filed before the expiry of 1 year from the date of the marriage or civil partnership (r 7.7(2)).

PART III

Application by respondent: permission not required—There is no need for a respondent to proceedings to seek permission to file his/her own application (petition), which step is specifically envisaged by FPR 2010, r 7.14.

Permission for a second application (r 7.7(1))—Application notice to the court to file a further application (petition) will be made in the existing proceedings under the FPR 2010, Pt 18 procedure. Three options arise:

(a) If the application has not been served it can be withdrawn (r 7.9), in which case no question of permission for a fresh application arises;
(b) The parties themselves may wish to consider whether there is some way to deal with and for the court to determine the original petition/application (r 7.7(1)(a): this is not possible, for example, if the parties have resumed cohabitation for more than 6 months) if only to save the court fee and dealing with further paperwork.
(c) If it comes to dealing with the application for permission, the court will want to consider whether the original petition/application can be formally dismissed (r 7.7(1)(a)).

Amendment of judicial separation petition or application—An application (petition) for a judicial separation filed before the parties have been married for a year may not be amended, after that year, for a petition for divorce (*Butler v Butler, The Queen's Proctor Intervening* [1990] 1 FLR 114, FD; see also FPR 2010, r 2.6(4)). A fresh petition can be filed (r 7.7(2)), for which permission is not needed.

Applications: amended petitions, further evidence or permission under r 7.7—MCA 1973, s 2 and CPA 2004, s 45 have parallel provisions that enable parties to resume cohabitation for a period or periods up to 6 months during the time of their living apart or while behaviour is alleged (although in cases of living apart periods of living together do not count towards the total living apart period). These periods may, for example, give a couple a chance to attempt reconciliation. Once together for more than 6 months, time must run all over again or fresh behaviour facts be pleaded. Mention has already been made of the need for care in pleading these periods (see under FPR 2010, r 7.5). Where such circumstances occur, up-to-date evidence must be filed (perhaps with the affidavit in support of an application for a certificate) or, if time under s 2 or s 45 has been exceeded, for seeking permission to file a second application (petition) or for dismissal of the first application (petition).

7.8 Service of application

(1) After an application for a matrimonial or civil partnership order has been issued by the court, a copy of it must be served on the respondent and on any co-respondent.

(Rule 6.5 provides for who may serve an application for a matrimonial or civil partnership order.)

(2) When the application is served on a respondent or co-respondent it must be accompanied by –

(a) a form for acknowledging service; and
(b) a notice of proceedings.

Amendments—SI 2014/843; SI 2014/3296.

Service of the application—FPR 2010, r 6.5 prescribes that service may be by an applicant (other than personal service: r 6.5(3)) or by the court (if requested: r 6.5(1)(b)). In the past, the forms of acknowledgement of service and notice of proceedings have been provided by the court and, in the first instance, the court has served documents by post.

Consent to a decree—Documents served on the respondent that require his consent to a decree under MCA 1973, s 1(2)(d) or CPA 2004, s 44(5)(b) must enable him 'to understand the consequences of consenting to a decree'. MCA 1973, s 2(7) and CPA 2004, s 45(4)(a) requires that provision for this be made by rules of court. It is not clear where this rule is in FPR 2010.

7.9 Withdrawal of application before service

An application for a matrimonial or civil partnership order may be withdrawn at any time before it has been served by giving notice in writing to the court where the proceedings were started.

7.10 Who the parties are

(1) The parties to matrimonial proceedings or civil partnership proceedings are –

(a) the parties to the marriage or civil partnership concerned; and
(b) any other person who is to be a party in accordance with a provision of the rules in this Part.

(2) Subject to paragraph (3), where an application for a matrimonial order or an answer to such an application alleges that the other party to the marriage has committed adultery with a named person, that named person is to be the co-respondent.

(3) The named person referred to in paragraph (2) is not to be a co-respondent where –

(a) the court so directs;

(b) that person has died; or

(c) unless the court directs otherwise –

(i) that person is under 16 years of age; or

(ii) the other party to the marriage is alleged in the application or answer to have committed rape on the named person.

(4) Where an application for a matrimonial or civil partnership order or an answer alleges that the other party to the marriage or civil partnership has had an improper association with a named person, the court may direct that the named person is to be the co-respondent to the application, unless the named person has died.

(5) An application for directions under paragraph (3)(a) or (c) may be made without notice if the acknowledgment of service indicates that no party intends to defend the case.

Amendments—SI 2012/679.

Defined terms—'Answer': r 7.1(3)(a); 'civil partnership proceedings', 'matrimonial proceedings': FPR 2010, r 2.3(1).

'Parties' to the proceedings—'Parties' under r 7.10 are parties in the matrimonial or civil partnership proceedings (and see Pt 7 **Introductory note**). They are parties only to the FPR 2010, Pt 7 proceedings. In other ancillary or subsidiary proceedings (e g financial order proceedings – see, for example, FPR 2010, r 9.12) the parties may have different party status names; additional parties may be joined who are not parties to the matrimonial and civil partnership proceedings at all.

Parties: statutory provision—Statute law (namely MCA 1973, s 49 and CPA 2004, s 64) and the rules do not align over the naming of parties. MCA 1973, s 49 is prescriptive and takes a more stern line than the 2010 Rules (and the PD) on the naming of co-respondents. By contrast, CPA 2004, s 64 is an empowering provision only: it leaves questions dealt with in s 49 (i e by statute) to the rules. Dismissal, addition of parties to the proceedings and naming of parties in civil partnership proceedings (CPA 2004, s 64(1)) is left to rules. In matrimonial and civil partnership proceedings (as distinct from any proceedings alongside such proceedings), the parties will be the petitioner/applicant and any one or more of the following:

- the respondent (the other spouse or civil partner)
- the co-respondent (if any)
- the party-cited (if any: FPR 2010, r 7.4(2)); and
- any parties formally added as parties to the proceedings (likely to be rare at this stage; and see MCA 1973, s 49(5) below).

Respondent and other parties—The respondent remains so called, even though he files an answer. Others may be added to the proceedings as co-respondent (MCA 1973, s 49(1) and see below). However, the mere service of proceedings does not make the person served a party to proceedings unless the person is formally added as a party by the court (*Re T (Divorce: Interim Maintenance: Discovery)* [1990] 1 FLR 1, FD).

Practice Direction 7A— FPR PD7A, para 2.1 and r 7.10 read together confine the naming of a co-respondent in matrimonial and civil partnership proceedings and exclude certain categories of co-respondent (r 7.10(3)).

'named person is to be the co-respondent' (r 7.10(2))—Rule 7.10(3) excludes a narrow category of possible co-respondents from being named in the proceedings (MCA 1973, s 49(1)); but otherwise a named person is required to be a party to the proceedings. The approach of the rule is at odds with FPR PD7A, which discourages the naming of co-respondents. Under the heading 'Respondents: restrictions' FPR PD7A, para 2.1 directs (so far as it is able so to do) that an applicant should not name the prospective co-respondent (i e they are strongly discouraged from naming a co-respondent) unless it is thought that the respondent is likely to defend the proceedings.

'improper association' (r 7.10(4))—Anyone named in an application as having had 'an improper association' with the respondent may, by direction of the court, be named as a co-respondent. The rules do not dictate what, in either a hetero- or homosexual marital or civil partnership relationship, is regarded as an 'improper association' in this context.

Intervener co-respondent—MCA 1973, s 49(5) enables a person against whom adultery is alleged to apply to be joined (added) as a party in matrimonial proceedings.

Dismissal of a party from the suit—A party against whom an allegation is made, can be 'dismissed from the suit' (proceedings) if the court considers the evidence against them is unjustified (MCA 1973, s 49(3)).

7.11 Nullity: Interim and full gender recognition certificates

(1) Where the application is for –

(a) nullity of marriage under section 12(1)(g) of, or paragraph 11(1)(e) of Schedule 1 to, the 1973 Act;

(aa) nullity of marriage under section 12A(3) of the 1973 Act in a case where section 12(1)(g) of the 1973 Act applies; or

(b) an order of nullity of civil partnership under section 50(1)(d) of the 2004 Act, the court officer must send to the Secretary of State a notice in writing that the application has been made.

(2) Where a copy of an interim gender recognition certificate has been filed with the application, that certificate must be attached to the notice.

(3) Where no copy of an interim gender recognition certificate has been filed the notice must also state –

(a) in matrimonial proceedings –

(i) the names of the parties to the marriage and the date and place of the marriage, and

(ii) the last address at which the parties to the marriage lived together as a married couple;

(b) in civil partnership proceedings –

(i) the names of the parties to the civil partnership and the date on, and the place at which, the civil partnership was formed, and

(ii) the last address at which the parties to the civil partnership lived together as civil partners of each other; and

(c) in either case, such further particulars as the court officer considers appropriate.

(4) Where –

(a) the application is for –

(i) a decree of nullity of marriage under section 12(1)(h) of the 1973 Act;

(ii) a decree of nullity of marriage under section 12A(3) of the 1973 Act in a case where section 12(1)(h) of the 1973 Act applies; or

(iii) an order of nullity of civil partnership under section 50(1)(e) of the 2004 Act; and

(b) a full gender recognition certificate has been issued to the respondent,

the applicant must file a copy of that full certificate with the application unless the court, on an application made without notice, directs otherwise.

(In relation to paragraphs (1)(aa), (3)(a) and (4)(a)(ii), section 9(6) of the Marriage (Same Sex Couples) Act 2013 provides that where a civil partnership is converted into a marriage, the civil partnership ends on the conversion, and the resulting marriage is to be treated as having subsisted since the date the civil partnership was formed.)

Amendments—SI 2014/524; SI 2015/913.

Scope—This rule is the counterpart of FPR 1991, rr 2.6A, 2.12A and 2.12B. See, generally, the annotations to the Gender Recognition Act 2004. In the circumstances provided for by GRA 2004, s 4(3) (as amended), the Gender Recognition Panel must issue an interim gender recognition certificate. An interim certificate permits either party to the marriage to apply for a decree of nullity under MCA 1973, s 12(1)(g) (marriages celebrated after 31 July 1971) or Sch 1, para 11(1)(e) (marriages celebrated before 1 August 1971) on the ground that the marriage is voidable. The CPA 2004, s 50(1)(d) makes comparable provision for nullity of civil partnerships. When the court makes absolute a decree of nullity granted on the ground that an interim gender recognition certificate has been issued to either party, the court must issue a full gender recognition certificate to that party. The Secretary of State must be notified of the proceedings, which could act as a trigger for proceedings for a reference under Gender Recognition Act 2004, s 8(5) (applications secured by fraud). MCA 1973, s 12(1)(h) permits an application to be made for a decree of nullity on the ground that the marriage is voidable because the respondent is a person whose gender at the time of the marriage had become the acquired gender under GRA 2004, s 1(2). The CPA 2004, s 50(1)(e) makes comparable provision for nullity of civil partnerships.

Defined terms—'interim gender recognition certificate' (r 7.11(2)): Gender Recognition Act 2004, ss 4(3) and 25; 'full gender recognition certificate' (r 7.11(4)): Gender Recognition Act 2004, ss 4(2) and 25.

7.12 What the respondent and co-respondent should do on receiving the application

(1) The respondent, and any co-respondent, must file an acknowledgment of service within 7 days beginning with the date on which the application for a matrimonial or civil partnership order was served.

(2) This rule is subject to rule 6.42 (which specifies how the period for filing an acknowledgment of service is calculated where the application is served out of the jurisdiction).

(3) The acknowledgment of service must –

(a) subject to paragraph (4), be signed by the respondent or the respondent's legal representative or, as the case may be, the co-respondent or the co respondent's legal representative;

(b) include the respondent's or, as the case may be, the co-respondent's address for service; and

(c) where it is filed by the respondent, indicate whether or not the respondent intends to defend the case.

(4) Where paragraph (5) or (6) applies, the respondent must sign the acknowledgment of service personally.

(5) This paragraph applies where –

(a) the application for a matrimonial order alleges that the respondent has committed adultery; and

(b) the respondent admits the adultery.

(6) This paragraph applies where –

(a) the application for a matrimonial or civil partnership order alleges that the parties to the marriage or civil partnership concerned have been separated for more than 2 years; and

(b) the respondent consents to the making of the matrimonial or civil partnership order.

(7) *(revoked)*

(8) A respondent who wishes to defend the case must file and serve an answer within 21 days beginning with the date by which the acknowledgment of service is required to be filed.

(9) An answer is not required where the respondent does not object to the making of the matrimonial or civil partnership order but objects to paying the costs of the application.

(10) A respondent may file an answer even if the intention to do so was not indicated in the acknowledgment of service.

(11) Paragraph (11A) applies where –

(a) the application is for –

(i) nullity of marriage under section 12(1)(d) of the 1973 Act;

(ii) nullity of marriage under section 12A(3) of the 1973 Act in a case where section 12(1)(d) of the 1973 Act applies; or

(iii) nullity of civil partnership under section 50(1)(b) of the 2004 Act; and

(b) the respondent files an answer containing no more than a simple denial of the facts stated in the application.

(11A) The respondent must, if intending to rebut the matters stated in the application, give notice to the court of that intention when filing the answer.

(12) A respondent to an application for a matrimonial or civil partnership order alleging 2 years' separation and the respondent's consent may –

(a) indicate consent to the making of the matrimonial or civil partnership order in writing at any time after service of the application, whether in the acknowledgment of service or otherwise;

(b) indicate lack of consent to the making of that order, or withdraw any such consent already given, by giving notice to the court.

(13) Where a respondent gives a notice under paragraph (12)(b) and no other relevant fact is alleged, the proceedings must be stayed[(GL)], and notice of the stay[(GL)] given to the parties by the court officer.

(14) In this rule, a 'relevant fact' is –

(a) in matrimonial proceedings, one of the facts mentioned in section (1)(2) of the 1973 Act; and

PART III

(b) in civil partnership proceedings, one of the facts mentioned in section 44(5) of the 2004 Act.

(15) In paragraphs (3)(c), (8), (9) and (10), any reference to a respondent is to be read as including a reference to a co-respondent where the context so requires.

(The form of the answer is referred to in Practice Direction 5A.)

(In relation to paragraph (11)(a)(ii), section 9(6) of the Marriage (Same Sex Couples) Act 2013 provides that where a civil partnership is converted into a marriage, the civil partnership ends on the conversion, and the resulting marriage is to be treated as having subsisted since the date the civil partnership was formed.)

Amendments—SI 2012/679; SI 2014/843; SI 2015/913.

Defined terms—'civil partnership order', 'matrimonial order': r 2.3(1); 'defended case': FPR 2010, r 7.1(3).

Introduction—Rule 7.12 deals with requirements as to what a respondent does on service of the petition/application. It contains two separate components:

(1) The acknowledgement of service: the requirements of a respondent if he wishes to sign it; and
(2) Proceedings becoming defended by the filing of an answer (briefly referred to in r 7.12(8)).

Structure of the rules: defended and undefended proceedings—Rule 7.12 deals with the divide between defended and undefended proceedings. Rules and procedure for the two forms of process are intermingled in FPR 2010, Pt 7, but the real divide between defended and undefended proceedings has the following procedural consequences.

(i) Once an answer is filed, rules of pleading (e g amendment of pleadings: FPR 2010, r 7.13; ordering of further information: FPR 2010, r 7.15) become relatively formal (akin to CPR 1998 proceedings).
(ii) Undefended cases will generally proceed without any further attendance at court required by the parties.

(1) The acknowledgement of service

Response to matrimonial and civil partnership order application (petition)—If a respondent chooses to sign an acknowledgement of service and if he wants it (1) to stand as an admission of adultery or (2) as his consent to the parties having lived apart for 2 years or more, then he must personally sign the acknowledgement of service.

Costs claimed in application (petition) (r 7.12(9))—If the respondent's only formal reply to the application is that he objects to paying costs, there is no need for a formal answer to be filed, although the respondent can file a short reply on costs in the acknowledgement of service when it is returned to the court (e g to admit to pay half the costs limited to a figure of (say) £350). Other opportunities will arise for objection to be taken in court to payment of costs (r 7.21).

Notice of consent (r 7.12(12)(a))—The fact of living apart for 2 years (MCA 1973, s 1(2)(d), CPA 2004, s 44(5)(b)) is the only fact that requires a respondent's consent to a decree or order. Thus the court needs to know not only that the respondent has received the application (petition) but also that he consents to a decree. The acknowledgement of service asks if the respondent consents to a decree being granted. Consent will be given if the respondent answers this affirmatively and signs the form personally (r 7.12(6)). Any other form of notice filed at court by the respondent and indicating his consent would appear to suffice.

No consent or withdrawal of consent (r 7.12(12)(b))—A respondent may indicate to the court that he does not consent or that he withdraws his consent, although no date by which this is to be done is specified in the rule. Once the district judge has signed his certificate under the special procedure, it may be difficult to set up the withdrawal (*Day v Day* (1980) 1 FLR 341, CA: certificate of registrar (district judge: certificate then is the same as a certificate under r 7.20(2)) under divorce rules held to be tantamount to a decree nisi).

Stay on proceedings (r 7.12(13),(14))—When the respondent gives an indication of no consent or withdrawal of consent (if this notice is in time (see previous note)), then if there is no other fact under MCA 1973, s 1(2) or CPA 2004, s 44(5) (r 7.12(14)), the proceedings must be stayed. The application remains on file and can be proceeded with only if permission is granted by the court. If there is no consent, the petitioner will be unable to proceed since consent is an essential component for proof of the fact under MCA 1973, s 1(2)(d). Where the respondent withdraws consent, the court may be able to resurrect the original consent when considering an application to remove the stay (*N v N (Divorce: Agreement not to Defend)* [1992] 1 FLR 266, CA: husband who agreed not to defend was held to his original agreement). Application to remove the stay is by the FPR 2010, Pt 18 procedure; but in effect an application to remove could only be made by consent of the respondent (save in the unusual circumstances of *N v N*).

Withdrawal of consent after r 7.20 certificate signed—Once a district judge's r 7.20 certificate has been signed or decree nisi (or conditional order) has been obtained, withdrawal of consent is unlikely to be effective (and see *Day v Day* (above)), unless a respondent can appeal against the order, can successfully apply for it to be set aside (e g because notice was not given under MCA 1973, s 2(7)), or he can apply for rescission of the decree (FPR 2010, r 7.28)). A general rule of appeals is that it is rare to be able to appeal against an order made by consent (consent in the acknowledgement of service is not the same, but the principle is clear).

(2) Proceedings becoming defended by the filing of an answer

Filing of answer: rules of pleading—Once an answer is filed the case becomes defended (FPR 2010, r 7.1(3)). In effect rules of pleading apply (e g amendment of pleadings: FPR 2010, r 7.13; ordering of further information: FPR 2010, r 7.15; disclosure: FPR 2010, r 7.22(2)(c)).

Answer: defended proceedings (r 7.12(8))—Rule 7.12(8) requires that a respondent who wishes to defend matrimonial or civil partnership proceedings must file an answer to the application. The term 'answer' is not defined in the Rules. It is a term that has been carried over from the former procedure and (like a defence in proceedings under CPR 1998) it indicates that a party does not agree – for whatever reason, but mostly it will be on the facts in matrimonial and civil partnership proceedings – to the application. Upon an answer being filed, the case becomes defended (see defended case under FPR 2010, r 7.1). If a respondent wishes to defend the proceedings and make separate allegations as a basis for a decree, a separate application (petition) must be filed by him/her (r 7.14).

Time for filing an answer (r 7.12(8))—Computation of time for filing an answer remains as it was under FPR 1991. It is calculated from the date on which the application was served on the respondent (a date that only the respondent will know for certain), by reference to two periods:

(a) The date for filing the acknowledgement of service: by r 7.12(1) this is '7 days beginning with the date on which the application … was served'; and
(b) 21 days from the last of the days in (a), above.
   (i) *Date of service of application* Calculation of the correct period under r 7.12(1) depends on a calculation of the exact date on which service took effect and how time runs from there. FPR 2010, Pt 6, Ch 2 creates a set of rules for service of matrimonial and civil partnership proceedings that are particular to those proceedings. No formal date for service is defined by Pt 6, Ch 2, so that where an acknowledgement of service is not returned to the court, the court may be asked to deem service and on a particular date (FPR 2010, rr 6.15, 6.16). Therefore, it must be assumed that the date for service is as for other documents: that is, 2 days after posting by first-class post avoiding non-business days (FPR 2010, r 6.34).
   (ii) *Date for filing answer* The date is calculated by a combination of two periods to which different rules apply – the time for filing an answer is the aggregate of the time limited for giving notice to defend (7 days) and the 21 days following that. Therefore, the time for giving notice to defend is 7 days after service of the application (petition). To this moving target is then added 21 days, i e 21 days regardless of what holidays, weekends etc may intervene.

Permission out of time to file an answer—Rule 7.12(8) is in mandatory terms. Permission from the court, by the FPR 2010, Pt 18 procedure (application notice in Form D11), is therefore required if an answer is to be filed once the time limits referred to above have expired. The court is likely to draw a distinction between an answer filed a few days late and one filed considerably out of time (see *Lawlor v Lawlor* [1995] 1 FLR 269, CA).

Test for permission application

(1) FPR 2010, r 4.6 – The court will bear in mind the factors in r 4.6 (relief from sanctions) when deciding whether or not to give permission relief to a respondent who has failed to comply with the time limit in r 7.12(8); this will include the prospects of success at trial of the matters raised by the proposed answer to the application.
(2) The prospect of success in the context of family proceedings (especially MFPA 1984, Pt III) has been considered by the Supreme Court in *Agbaje v Agbaje* [2010] 1 FLR 1813, SC,, at [33]: essentially that 'wholly unmeritorious claims' are not pursued. Perhaps the criterion is that a respondent should show he has a 'good arguable case' for permission to be granted (lower for example than for an appeal: r 30.3(7): the 'threshold [need not] be high').

Procedure for a permission application:—No procedure is prescribed for obtaining permission and the detail of FPR 2010, Pt 18 does not assist. Procedure for a permission application in MFPA 1984, Pt III proceedings (which may assist with permission applications generally) was considered by Munby LJ in the Court of Appeal in *Traversa v Freddi* [2011] 2 FLR 272, CA, at [54] and [58].

(1) An application for permissions 'should be listed ex parte for a hearing which can be appropriately brief' (as with appeals (FPR PD30A, para 4.14) and judicial review applications (CPR 1998, r 54.12)).
(2) If the respondent attends the hearing she will not be heard or have any costs for so doing (as in the Court of Appeal etc). The respondent's case will be heard at any substantive hearing (if permission is given).
(3) An applicant can apply to set aside a grant of permission, but only if she can demonstrate some 'knock-out blow' (a compelling reason: on analogy with CPR 1998, r 52.9(2)) why permission should be set aside (per *Agbaje* (at [33]).
(4) Subject to these points the applicant will be able to argue the merits of the answer at the final hearing.

Permission where r 7.20 certificate signed—If the district judge has already signed his certificate under r 7.20(2), permission to file an answer out of time is unlikely to be given (*Day v Day* (1980) 1 FLR 341, CA), unless the respondent (Pt 18 applicant for permission) is able successfully to apply for the certificate to be set aside. This area of law and the status of the certificate (as against the status of a formal order) may be appropriate for re-consideration by the courts under the current law: the requirement for the Family Court to deal with 'cases justly' and the entitlement of respondents in Mr Day's position to a fair trial of an issue reasonably raised by him before the court. At present, the law is as stated by the Court of Appeal in *Day v Day*.

MCA 1973, s 5(1); CPA 2004, s 47(1)—If a respondent to an application under MCA 1973, s 1(2)(e) or CPA 2004, s 44(5)(c) wishes to say that she may suffer grave financial hardship if a matrimonial or civil partnership order is made, she must file an answer.

7.13 Supplemental application and amendment of application and answer

(1) In this rule –

(a) paragraphs (2)(a) and (b) and (3) set out when a supplemental application may or may not be made or an application may or may not be amended before an answer has been filed and before an application has been made under rule 7.19(1);

(b) paragraphs (2)(c) and (3) set out when an answer may or may not be amended before an application has been made under rule 7.19(1);

(c) paragraph (5) sets out when a supplemental application may be made or an application may be amended after an answer has been filed or after an application has been made under rule 7.19(1); and

(d) paragraph (6) sets out when an answer may be amended after an application has been made under rule 7.19(1).

(2) Unless paragraph (3) applies –

(a) a party making an application for a matrimonial or civil partnership order may amend the application at any time before an answer to it has been filed;

(b) a party making an application for a matrimonial or civil partnership order may make a supplemental application at any time before an answer has been filed;

(c) a party who has filed an answer may amend the answer.

(3) No supplemental application may be made and no amendment to an application for a matrimonial or civil partnership order or to an answer may be made under paragraph (2) if an application under rule 7.19(1) has been made in relation to the marriage or civil partnership concerned.

(4) Where an amendment is made or a supplemental application is made under paragraph (2) –

(a) if the document amended is the application or if a supplemental application is made –

(i) it must be served in accordance with rule 7.8; and

(ii) rule 7.12 applies;

(b) rule 7.10 applies; and

(c) any person who becomes a co-respondent to the proceedings in accordance with rule 7.10 as a consequence of such an amendment or supplemental application must be served with the documents required to be served on a co-respondent with an application for a matrimonial or civil partnership order.

(5) Where an answer has been filed, or an application has been made under rule 7.19(1), an amendment may not be made to an application and a supplemental application may not be made except –

(a) with the written consent of all the other parties; or

(b) with the permission of the court.

(6) Where an answer has been filed and an application has been made under rule 7.19(1), an amendment may not be made to the answer except –

(a) with the written consent of all the other parties; or

(b) with the permission of the court.

(7) Where paragraph (5) or (6) applies, the court may give directions as to –

(a) the service of the amended application, the amended answer or the supplemental application, as the case may be, and the service of any accompanying documents;

(b) the joining of any additional parties in accordance with rule 7.10; and

(c) the extent to which rule 7.12 must be complied with in respect of any amended application or any supplemental application.

(8) The court may direct that any person cease to be a party if, in consequence of any amendment made or supplemental application made under this rule, that person –

(a) no longer falls within rule 7.10(2) or (4); or

(b) falls within rule 7.10(4), but it is no longer desirable for that person to be a party to the proceedings.

(Practice Direction 7A contains information regarding amending applications, making supplemental applications and making second (or further) applications.)

Amendments—Substituted by SI 2014/3296.

Application for decree nisi or conditional order: FPR 2010, r 7.19 (r 7.13(2))—No application to amend a pleading can be made (save with permission from the court) once application has been made (under r 7.19(1)) for a decree nisi or conditional order.

Supplemental and amended applications (petitions)—A supplemental application (petition) dates from the date of the supplemental application (petition), whereas an amended application (petition) dates from the date of the original earlier pleading. For example, if a couple agree that they will proceed on an application (petition) under MCA 1973, s 1(2)(d) instead of on unreasonable behaviour they would file, in the same cause, a supplemental application (petition). They cannot amend since the facts they are now pleading did not exist at the time of the original application (petition). The supplemental application (petition) may prove to be of assistance to the mediator. All other issues are resolved, but things said in the original application (petition) can remain unproved and time can become the only fact on which the decree proceeds.

Amendment of an answer (r 7.13(1)(b))—A respondent who has filed an answer is able to amend without permission until an application is made under FPR 2010, r 7.19(1), whereas the applicant, once the answer has been filed, can only amend her application with permission of the court or the consent of the respondent (r 7.13(4)).

Application to amend; Practice Direction 7A—Application to amend, where there is no consent to amend, is by the FPR 2010, Pt 18 procedure (Form D11). For further guidance on procedure for amendment and other detailed requirements, assistance may be drawn from CPR PD17 (from which parts of FPR PD7A are drawn). The rules relating to the original pleading (statements of truth, signing etc) will apply to the amended pleading. FPR PD7A para 5.2 explains that the application and the proposed amendments incorporated into the existing pleading should be filed at court. If permission is given then the amended pleading should be filed at court (and served, perhaps) within 14 days (FPR PD7A, para 5.3).

Direction: cease to be a party (r 7.13(6))—The court may direct that a co-respondent or other party cease to be a party (r 7.10(2) or (4)) where allegations are no longer made against them (for example, because a petition/application is amended from adultery to unreasonable behaviour, or a respondent agrees finally to a decree nisi or conditional order based on 2 years living apart rather than unreasonable behaviour where an 'improper association' had been alleged). The drafting of the rule suggests that such a direction would be made on the court's initiative; but in principle there is no reason why it should not be done on the application of a party (i e including the co-respondent) and save where the point was contentious it could presumably be done by letter to the court.

Costs of amendment—It does not follow automatically that the costs of an amendment should be borne by the amender. If a request is made to amend by consent (r 7.13(4)(a)) and that is refused by the other party but the amendment is then permitted by the court, in principle there is no reason why costs should not be awarded to the party who amends (*La Chemise Lacoste SA v Sketchers USA Ltd* [2006] EWHC 3642 (Ch)).

7.14 How the respondent can make an application

(1) A respondent who wishes to make an application for a matrimonial or civil partnership order must make the application for that order within 21 days beginning with the date by which the respondent's acknowledgment of service is required to be filed, unless the court gives permission to make the application after that time has passed.

(2) Where the respondent makes an application under this rule, that application is to be treated as an application in the same proceedings for the purposes of this Part.

MCA 1973, s 20; CPA 2004, s 62—MCA 1973, s 20 (with its parallel in CPA 2004, s 62) provides that if a respondent obtains a decree or order in matrimonial or civil partnership proceedings then he does so as if it were his application that had started the proceedings, and then the party names, as between applicant and respondent, are reversed. Rule 7.14 deals with the way that the position on which ss 20 and 62 are predicated is reached.

'must make the application … within 21 days' (r 7.14(1))—This provision only partly sets out the steps that a respondent may take to make his own application. If a respondent seeks a matrimonial or civil partnership order (and thus bring himself within MCA 1973, s 20 or CPA 2004, s 62), as the law stands, he can do so in one of the following ways:

(1) File and serve an answer outside the time limit in FPR 2010, rr 7.14(1) and 7.12(8), but seek permission to proceed out of time under FPR 2010, r 7.13(4).
(2) File a separate application (petition) (i e a separate set of matrimonial or civil partnership proceedings) seeking a separate matrimonial decree or civil partnership order (FPR 2010, r 7.14(1)). In the second application (petition), the respondent will make reference to the existing application (petition) already filed; the further application will be treated as in the existing proceedings (r 7.14(2)).

'application in the same proceedings' (r 7.14(2))—This provision restates MCA 1973, s 20 and CPA 2004, s 62 and enables the respondent to obtain any of the remedies available to an applicant. Thus, for example, an application for a financial order (the matrimonial and civil partnership proceedings equivalent of a financial remedy) is made in an application for a matrimonial or civil partnership order (FPR 2010, r 9.4(a)).

'date by which the respondent's acknowledgement of service is to be filed' (r 7.14(1))—See FPR 2010, r 7.12(8) and commentary.

PART III

7.15 Further information about the contents of the application and the answer

(1) The court may at any time order a party –

(a) to clarify any matter which is in dispute in the proceedings; or

(b) to give additional information in relation to any such matter,

whether or not the matter is contained or referred to in the application for a matrimonial or civil partnership order or in the answer.

(2) Paragraph (1) is subject to any rule of law to the contrary.

(3) Where the court makes an order under paragraph (1), the party against whom it is made must –

(a) file the reply to the order made under paragraph (1); and

(b) serve a copy of it on each of the other parties,

within the time specified by the court.

(4) The court may direct that information provided by a party to another party (whether given voluntarily or following an order made under paragraph (1)) must not be used for any purpose except for the proceedings in which it is given.

Further information—The scheme is that in the first instance a party should be asked for the information (FPR PD7A, paras 6.1 and 6.2) and only if the information is not provided may application then be made to the court.

Application for information—Application (where information is not provided) will be by the FPR 2010, Pt 18 procedure (Form D11) and will be accompanied by the documents thus far exchanged in attempts to obtain the information. In exercising its discretion as to whether or not to grant an application, and if so to what extent, the judge will have in mind what is necessary and proportionate for a fair disposal of the case (*King v Telegraph Group Ltd* [2004] EWCA Civ 613), as against what is needed by the parties efficiently and justly to deal with the matters in dispute between them (*Harcourt v Griffin* [2007] EWHC 1500 (QB)). In particular, the court will be concerned to ensure that a party is in a position, as far as possible, to know the case he is meeting (*Butterworth v Butterworth* [1997] 2 FLR 336, CA).

Information and disclosure—Disclosure in the context of defended matrimonial and civil partnership proceedings is dealt with under FPR 2010, r 7.22 and generally under FPR 2010, Pt 21. Certain of the same principles for opposing an order for disclosure applies to an order to give information (such as rules in matrimonial proceedings relating to oppressive enquiry: *Hildebrand v Hildebrand* [1992] 1 FLR 244, FD, refusal of permission for excessive or oppressive inquiry or interrogatories). The information request provisions in FPR PD7A, para 6.1–6.5 are similar to those in CPR 1998, r 18.1.

Chapter 3
How the Court Determines Matrimonial and Civil Partnership Proceedings

Introductory note—Ch 3 leads the parties through the undefended and the defended process for matrimonial and civil partnership proceedings; mostly it will be necessary, in respect of each of the main rules, to disentangle the defended and the undefended aspects to the procedure.

Procedural guides—The steps for each process are summarised in Procedural Guide B2 (undefended) and Procedural Guide B4 (defended). Critical stages in the procedure are:

(1) application for decree nisi or conditional order (FPR 2010, r 7.19);
(2) directions for decree nisi or conditional order hearing (FPR 2010, r 7.20(2));
(3) directions for defended hearing with prior case-management hearing (FPR 2010, r 7.20(4));
(4) the case-management hearing (FPR 2010, r 7.22).

7.16 General rule – hearing to be in public

(1) The general rule is that a hearing to which this Part applies is to be in public.

(2) The requirement for a hearing to be in public does not require the court to make special arrangements for accommodating members of the public.

(3) A hearing, or any part of it, may be in private if –

(a) publicity would defeat the object of the hearing;

(b) it involves matters relating to national security;

(c) it involves confidential information (including information relating to personal financial matters) and publicity would damage that confidentiality;

(d) a private hearing is necessary to protect the interests of any child or protected party;

(e) it is a hearing of an application made without notice and it would be unjust to any respondent for there to be a public hearing; or

(f) the court considers this to be necessary, in the interests of justice.

(4) A hearing of an application for rescission of an order by consent under rule 7.28 is, unless the court directs otherwise, to be in private.

(5) The court may order that the identity of any party or witness must not be disclosed if it considers non-disclosure necessary in order to protect the interests of that party or witness.

Defined terms—'child': FPR 2010, r 2.3(1) (and see MCA 1973, s 54); 'hearing': FPR 2010, r 2.3(1); hearing 'in private': FPR 2010, r 27.10(2); 'protected party': FPR 2010, r 2.3(1).

Hearings—Rule 7.16 is addressed mostly to defended proceedings, but in principle it applies to all hearings under FPR 2010, Pt 7. A 'hearing' includes a directions appointment, but whether this will include paperwork exercises by a district judge under FPR 2010, r 7.20 when directions are given for the decree nisi or conditional order hearing, (when the certificate for a decree or order is made) remains to be seen. A person 'need not attend' the decree nisi or conditional order hearing consequent upon that certificate being signed (FPR 2010, r 7.18(b)).

Hearing in public: right to a transcript—A hearing in public normally carries a right to a transcript (CPR 1998, PD39A, para 1.11) and a hearing may be held in private, but judgment given in public, anonymised as need be.

'a hearing to which this Part applies is to be in public'—Rule 7.16(3) is derived from CPR 1998, r 39.2 and brings FPR 2010, Pt 7 into line with European Convention 1950, Art 6(1) and its requirement for public court hearings. It incorporates for matrimonial and civil partnership proceedings only (ie not for all family proceedings).

'personal financial matters' (r 7.16(3)(c))—CPR PD39A, para 1.5 lists a number of forms of financial proceedings that 'shall in the first instance be listed by the court as hearings in private', which suggests that in the civil jurisdiction a relatively wide meaning is given to personal financial matters. In matrimonial and civil partnership proceedings, finance in that context may have a narrower meaning (*Clibbery v Allan* [2002] 1 FLR 565, CA).

'necessary to protect the interests of any child or protected party' (r 7.16(3)(d))—The court is likely to see this basis for hearing a case in private in terms similar to FPR 2010, r 27.10, but as with 'personal financial matters' it may be necessary for the parties to distinguish clearly what the issues are before the court and the extent to which protection of children might be affected by matrimonial and civil partnership proceedings being heard in public.

Order that a hearing be in private—Application by a party for a private hearing should be made in advance of the hearing by the FPR 2010, Pt 18 procedure, although in practice it may often be that the application is made on the first day of a hearing or during its course. Hearing 'in private' for the purposes of FPR 2010 means 'proceedings at which the general public have no right to be present' (FPR 2010, r 27.10(2)).

7.17 *(revoked)*

7.18 Notice of hearing

The court officer will give notice to the parties –

(a) of the date, time and place of every hearing which is to take place in a case to which they are a party; and

(b) in the case of a hearing following a direction under rule 7.20(2)(a), of the fact that, unless the person wishes or the court requires, the person need not attend.

Direction under r 7.20(2)(a)—This hearing is the list hearing of decrees nisi and conditional orders. Costs issues at this hearing will arise separately: see FPR 2010, r 7.21 below.

7.19 Applications for a decree nisi or a conditional order

(1) An application may be made to the court for it to consider the making of a decree nisi, a conditional order, a decree of judicial separation or a separation order in the proceedings –

(a) at any time after the time for filing the acknowledgment of service has expired, provided that no party has filed an acknowledgment of service indicating an intention to defend the case; and

(b) in any other case, at any time after the time for filing an answer to every application for a matrimonial or civil partnership order made in the proceedings has expired.

(2) An application under paragraph (1) may be made –

(a) in a case within paragraph (1)(a), by the applicant; and

(b) in any other case, by either party to the marriage or civil partnership in question.

PART III

(3) An application under this rule must, if the information which was required to be provided by the application form is no longer correct, be accompanied by a statement setting out particulars of the change.

(4) If no party has filed an answer opposing the making of a decree nisi, a conditional order, a decree of judicial separation or a separation order on another party's application then an application under this rule must be accompanied by a statement –

- (a) stating whether there have been any changes in the information given in the application;
- (b) confirming that, subject to any changes stated, the contents of the application are true; and
- (c) where the acknowledgment of service has been signed by the other party to the marriage or civil partnership, confirming that party's signature on the acknowledgment of service.

(5) A statement under paragraph (4) must be verified by a statement of truth.

Amendments—SI 2012/679; SI 2014/843.

Defined terms—'decree nisi': r 2.3(1).

Application for consideration of making a decree nisi or conditional order (r 7.19(1),(2))—The 2010 rules do away with the former 'request for directions for trial' (FPR 1991, r 2.24: defended or undefended, with undefended causes going into the 'special procedure list': r 2.24(3)). Rule 7.19 replaces the 'request for directions' with an application for a decree nisi or conditional order. Such application is made within time limits as fixed for filing of the acknowledgement of service and answer. It is likely that r 7.19(2)(b) intends (although it does not say so) that an application for consideration can only be made by a respondent where he seeks directions for a final hearing in the case of defended proceedings. That either party may apply in this way is new in these rules.

Application under r 7.19: consideration statement (r 7.19(4))—The application process commences with the filing of the application with a statement (prescribed by Forms D80A–D80G; Table 2 to FPR PD5A). The information required by the court is prescribed in r 7.19(4) and the question of 'changes' recurs there and in r 7.19(3). The statement under r 7.19(4), which applies for consideration of the making of a decree or conditional order, is required to include confirmation of the other party's signature on the acknowledgement of service, which then provides evidence as to service of the application (and of any admitted adultery).

Application and statement (r 7.19(4) and (5)—Since the April 2012 amendments to FPR 2010, the application is to be in the form of a statement verified by a statement of truth.

7.20 What the court will do on an application for a decree nisi, a conditional order, a decree of judicial separation or a separation order

(1) This rule applies where an application is made under rule 7.19.

(2) If at the relevant time the case is an undefended case, the court must –

- (a) if satisfied that the applicant is entitled to –
  - (i) in matrimonial proceedings, a decree nisi or a decree of judicial separation (as the case may be); or
  - (ii) in civil partnership proceedings, a conditional order or a separation order (as the case may be),

so certify and direct that the application be listed before a judge for the making of the decree or order at the next available date;

- (b) if not so satisfied, direct –
  - (i) that any party to the proceedings provide such further information, or take such other steps, as the court may specify; or
  - (ii) that the case be listed for a case management hearing.

(3) If the applicant has applied for costs, the court may, on making a direction under paragraph (2)(a) –

- (a) if satisfied that the applicant is entitled to an order for costs, so certify; or
- (b) if not so satisfied, make no direction about costs.

(4) If at the relevant time the case is a defended case, the court must direct that the case be listed for a case management hearing.

(5) The court may, when giving a direction under paragraph (2)(b), direct that the further information provided be verified by an affidavit or a statement of truth.

(6) The court must not give directions under this rule unless at the relevant time it is satisfied –

(a) that a copy of each application for a matrimonial or civil partnership order or answer (including any amended application or answer) has been properly served on each party on whom it is required to be served; and

(b) that –

(i) in matrimonial proceedings, the application for a decree nisi or a decree of judicial separation; or

(ii) in civil partnership proceedings, the application for a conditional order or separation order,

was made at a time permitted by rule 7.19(1).

(7) In this rule, 'the relevant time' means the time at which the court is considering an application made under rule 7.19(1).

(8) Where a decree or order is made in accordance with a certificate under paragraph (2)(a), any person may, within 14 days after the making of the decree or order, inspect the certificate and the evidence filed under rule 7.19(4) and may obtain copies.

(9) Paragraph (8) does not apply to a certificate which relates to –

(a) a decree of nullity of marriage under section 12(1)(g) of, or paragraph 11(1)(e) of Schedule 1 to, the 1973 Act;

(aa) a decree of nullity of marriage under section 12A(3) of the 1973 Act in a case where section 12(1)(g) of the 1973 Act applies; or

(b) an order for nullity of civil partnership under section 50(1)(d) of the 2004 Act,

unless the court has given permission.

Amendments—SI 2012/679; SI 2013/3204; SI 2014/843; SI 2015/913.

Defined terms—'defended case', 'undefended case': FPR 2010, r 7.1(3); 'hearing': FPR 2010, r 2.3(1); 'relevant time': FPR 2010, r 7.20(7).

Courts duties on application for consideration under r 7.19 (r 7.20(1))—The steps to be taken by the court under r 7.20 on application for consideration of a decree nisi or conditional order under FPR 2010, r 7.19 fall into these categories:

(1) Certificate under 7.20(2)(a) leading directly to the hearing of the decree or order application;
(2) Direction that the court is not satisfied on the application for consideration (r 7.20(2)(b));
(3) Direction for case management hearing on a defended case (rr 7.20(4), 7.22).

Evidence for decree nisi or conditional order—The standard of evidence in the statement under r 7.19(4) that the court is entitled to expect is to enable it 'to inquire, so far as it reasonably can, into the facts alleged by the petitioner and into any facts alleged by the respondent' (MCA 1973, s 1(3),(4): CPA 2004, s 44(2)–(4) is in terms that are to similar effect). On the face of the statute itself, there is therefore a duty on the court to 'inquire' within reason into the facts alleged by the applicant and satisfy itself as to the evidence before it. This duty must be balanced against the need for proportionality (FPR 2010, r 1.1) and the duty of the court not to seek to be 'over-meticulous' (*R v Nottinghamshire County Court ex parte Byers* [1985] FLR 695, QBD).

Determination of the proceedings—The 2010 Rules do nothing to lay the controversy in FPR 1991 as to when a decree nisi (or later a conditional order) becomes fully effective. The question is important since it affects:

(1) Whether or not an intended respondent can file an answer out of time (see eg *Day v Day* (1980) 1 FLR 341, CA);
(2) What is the date in law of any decree nisi or conditional order for appeal or set-aside purposes; and
(3) What is the status of any certificate under r 7.20(2)(a) (as distinct from a decree nisi or conditional order (eg for the purposes of an application to set it aside)).

The variety of terminology in FPR 2010, Pt 7, Ch 2 makes the issue more critical than before. In legal terms, the concepts that bear on the problem are considered more fully under FPR 2010, r 7.28 and Court Orders in FPR 2010, Pt 7 Ch 4.

(1) Certificate under r 7.20(2)(a): list for hearing

Certificate of entitlement to a decree nisi or conditional order (r 7.20(2)(a) and 7.20(6))—The court can only issue a certificate under r 7.20(2)(b) if satisfied as to the following:

(1) That the application for the order (divorce petition etc) or answer with application for a cross-decree or cross-order has been 'properly served' (r 7.20(6)(a)): normally this will be done by the applicant having confirmed in the consideration statement identification of the respondent's signature on the acknowledgement of service (FPR 2010, rr 7.12 and 7.19(4)) and his admission there that he has received the application or answer.
(2) That the application for a decree nisi or conditional order was made at a time permitted by FPR 2010, r 7.19(1) (r 7.20(6)(b)).

PART III

(3) That the court's inquiry under MCA 1973, s 1(3) and (4) or CPA 2004, s 44(2)–(4) enable it to be 'satisfied that the applicant is entitled to' the decree or order (r 7.20(2)(a)).

Court 'satisfied that the applicant is entitled' to a decree or order (r 7.20(2)(a))—If the court is satisfied as to the entitlement of the applicant or respondent to a decree or order it 'must … so certify' and the court then directs a routine listing in open court before a district judge. The court will give notice of the resultant appointment to the parties (FPR 2010, r 7.18). At this stage no decree or final order has been made, but this intermediate phase has been characterised by the Court of Appeal as tantamount to an order (*Day v Day*, above; and see further FPR 2010, Pt 7, Ch 4).

Standard or detail of evidence—Although MCA 1973, s 1(3) and CPA 2004, s 44(2) place on the court a duty to inquire, it is likely still to be the case that the procedure under r 7.20(2) does not envisage a high standard for the detail of the evidence to be provided. The court can only expect to be 'satisfied' within the terms of the procedure set up in FPR 2010, rr 7.19 and 7.20(2)(a), and there should be no room for excessive technicality of approach by district judges (*R v Nottinghamshire County Court ex parte Byers* [1985] FLR 695, QBD). That said, parties should anticipate areas of possible controversy (and see **(2) Court not satisfied**, below) such as to explain where they appear still to be living together but plead that they are not, or where a chronology might help explain issues under MCA 1973, s 2 or CPA 2004, s 46.

Hearing of decree nisi or conditional order application—Save for any pre-warned issue of costs (see FPR 2010, r 7.21) the hearing is a block hearing: a list is read out and decrees/orders made en bloc by the court. In the case of an undefended case there is no need for the parties to attend unless 'the court requires' (FPR 2010, r 7.18(b)) or there is an issue as to costs (FPR 2010, r 7.21).

Costs (r 7.20(3))—See further FPR 2010, r 7.21.

(2) Court not satisfied

If the court is 'not so satisfied'—Rule 7.20(2)(b) deals with the position where the district judge is not satisfied as to the applicant's entitlement to a decree or order (in undefended proceedings). The court has two options:

(1) The district judge may direct that 'any party to the proceedings' should provide further information or take such other steps as the court requires that party to do (r 7.20(2)(b)(i)). The court may direct that the information be provided by statement (r 7.20(5)); or
(2) The district judge may direct that the case is listed for a case-management hearing (r 7.20(2)(b)(ii)).

Further information required by the court: case management hearing (r 7.20(2)(b))—In cases where more clarification is needed, the court can fix a case-management appointment. FPR 2010, r 7.22(3) prescribes what the court 'must' do at the r 7.20(2)(b) case-management hearing, namely to consider whether further evidence is required (FPR 2010, r 7.22(3)(a)). It is likely that the appointment will only be attended by the applicant for the decree or order, and in principle there is no reason why the appointment should not be by telephone (FPR 2010, r 1.4(2)(k)) (and see further consideration of case management hearing under FPR 2010, r 7.22).

(3) Direction for case management hearing: defended case

Defended cases (r 7.20(4))—If at the time that the court considers an application for decree or order the case remains defended, then a case-management hearing 'must … be listed' (see under FPR 2010, r 7.22 below). If the defended case had been compromised by this time, there would appear to be no reason why the district judge should not adjourn consideration of the papers under r 7.20 to give one of the parties time to file a under FPR 2010, r 7.19(4) to enable the application then to proceed undefended.

(4) Setting aside a district judge's certificate

Setting aside the district judge's certificate—If a respondent fails to file an answer within 28 days of service of the petition (FPR 2010, r 7.12(8)) and the petitioner has obtained a certificate under the special procedure or if, after the certificate has been signed, the respondent decides that he wants to defend the proceedings, application must be made to the district judge to set aside his certificate and to seek permission to file an answer out of time (for permission to file an answer out of time, see under FPR 2010, r 7.12).

Application to set aside a certificate—The application is made by the FPR 2010, Pt 18 procedure (Form D11) and should be supported by a statement giving reasons (e g for the delay in filing or for the change of mind) and should exhibit a draft answer. If the set-aside application is made to enable the respondent to file an answer (as will generally be the case) the author of the statement will need to bear in mind the factors in FPR 2010, r 4.6 and the need to make a good arguable case (see *Agbaje v Agbaje* [2010] 1 FLR 1813, SC, at [33] and the discussion under FPR 2010, r 7.12 above).

Grounds for setting aside a certificate—The court will be concerned that the applicant for set aside (respondent to the application) has good arguable grounds and the court must be alert to the particular problems encountered by respondents under the r 7.20(2) procedure in that they are not given notice of when the district judge will be considering his r 7.20(2)(a) certificate (*Day v Day* (1980) 1 FLR 341, CA). To that extent they have no notice of any hearing, neither do they see what is put before the district judge when he considers signing his certificate.

Setting aside for vitiating factor—Where a respondent can show that he was not served or was in some way deceived about the proceedings, the certificate should be set aside almost automatically, and where, for example, an adviser failed to act on the respondent's instructions or where through ignorance the respondent failed to take the necessary procedural steps to file an answer, the grounds for setting aside a r 7.20(2)(a) certificate may exist (*Mitchell v Mitchell* [1984] FLR 50, CA). In the latter instance, the court must also be satisfied that, if the certificate were not set aside, the respondent would be prevented from putting forward a defence with merit: the court must consider the respondent's prospects of success on his answer.

Appeal or set aside a decree nisi or conditional order—Once a decree nisi or conditional order has been granted, the respondent may apply by the FPR 2010, Pt 18 procedure to set it aside and seek a rehearing (FPR 2010, r 7.28) or appeal against the decree (FPR 2010, Pt 30); although note limitations on appeal against any later decree absolute in SCA 1981, s 18(1)(d).

Procedure for application—An application to set aside the certificate proceeds by the FPR 2010, Pt 18 procedure.

(1) The applicant to set aside should ensure that the court stays any further steps on the decree nisi or conditional order hearing and takes the hearing appointment out of the court list.

(2) FPR 2010, Pt 18 provides its own internal procedural steps that will lead to a hearing of the set-aside application. The court can deal with the application on the papers, so that if, upon first consideration of the application, the district judge could set aside or stay his certificate (FPR 2010, r 18.9(1)(a): eg if the district judge sees an obvious error that was missed on his original consideration), although that without notice order can then be sought to be set aside (FPR 2010, r 18.11).

(3) The hearing should be before the district judge who signed the original certificate (if available).

(4) Other matters on decree nisi or conditional order application

The *Pounds* procedure—In *Pounds v Pounds* [1994] 1 FLR 775, CA (at [790B]) the Court of Appeal held that a consent order could be approved by a district judge 'as part of his "directions for trial"' when approving the special procedure documents for divorce. This procedure would apply equally to the certificate under FPR 2010, r 7.22(2)(a). This pre-decree order can be made, even though the order is not drawn up and perfected until a date after decree nisi. Once the certificate was granted under the special procedure the decree nisi is all but made (*Day v Day* (1980) 1 FLR 341, CA).

PART III

7.21 Further provisions about costs

(1) Subject to paragraph (2), any party to matrimonial or civil partnership proceedings may be heard on any question as to costs at the hearing of the proceedings.

(2) In the case of a hearing following a direction under rule 7.20(2)(a), a party will not be heard unless that party has, not less than 14 days before the hearing –

(a) given written notice to the court of that party's intention to attend the hearing and apply for, or oppose the making of, an order for costs; and

(b) served that notice on every other party.

(3) On receipt of such a written notice, the court may make such directions in relation to the hearing as it sees fit.

Amendments—SI 2015/913.

Applications for costs—Rule 7.20(3) enables the court to deal with costs at the decree or order hearing (which otherwise is likely to be unattended by the parties). In principle costs, orders are made in accordance with SCA 1981, s 51(1) and CPR 1998, r 44.1 (as modified by FPR 2010, r 28.2). In practice, most courts are likely to follow a broad rule that fault applications (MCA 1973, s 1(2)(a)–(c); CPA 2004, s 44(5)(a),(d)) may attract an order for costs, but that living-apart applications only attract an order much more rarely.

Certificate for costs—Although neither FPR 2010, r 7.20(3) nor r 7.21 say it, it may be reasonable to assume that if a certificate is made by the district judge under r 7.20(3)(a) and there is no opposition to it at the hearing of the decree or order, then an order for costs will be made; the intended beneficiary of the order need do no more to secure her order at the decree/order hearing.

Application for costs on a direction under r 7.20(2)(a)—FPR 2010, r 7.20(3) enables the court to take a preliminary view on costs (although r 7.20(3) expresses this as a certificate or 'no direction', neither of which are orders).

Application for costs at the hearing (r 7.21(1))—Either party can attend the hearing on any application for costs (subject to appropriate notice being given to the other party: r 7.21(2)). The respondent to a costs application has the opportunity to come to the block hearing of the decree or order to make representation as to why an order should not be made. An applicant who has been deprived of costs (as he sees it) by the district judge under FPR 2010, r 7.20(3)(b) can make representation as to why an order should be made.

Although the rule does not require it, it would be prudent for the party who intends to attend on a costs application to inform the court, as well as the other party (not applicable from 1 July 2015: see rule 7.21(2)(b)).

Application for costs at the hearing (r 7.21(2),(3))—From 1 July 2015, the time prior to the hearing for notice of an intention to apply for or oppose an order for costs under r 7.21 is extended so that the parties must give 2 weeks' notice to the court and to the other party. The implication of r 7.21(3) is that the court may, in appropriate circumstances, give further directions, eg to the other party to reply in writing to any application under r 7.21(2)(a).

7.22 What the court must do for the case management hearing

(1) This rule applies to a case in which the court has directed a case management hearing under rule 7.20.

(2) Where a hearing has been directed under rule 7.20(4) the court must –

(a) decide where the hearing in the case should take place;

(b) set a timetable for the filing and service of evidence;

(c) make such order for the disclosure and inspection of documents as it considers appropriate; and

(d) give directions as to the conduct of the final hearing and the attendance of witnesses.

(Rule 21.1 explains what is meant by disclosure and inspection.)

(3) Where a hearing has been directed under rule 7.20(2)(b)(ii), the court must –

(a) consider what further evidence is required properly to dispose of the proceedings and give directions about the filing and service of such evidence;

(b) *(revoked)*

(c) give directions for the further conduct of the proceedings including –

(i) giving a direction that on compliance with any directions under sub-paragraph (a) a further application may be made under rule 7.19(1) for the proceedings to be dealt with under rule 7.20(2)(a); or

(ii) giving a direction that the case is not suitable for determination under that rule.

(4) Where the court gives a direction under paragraph (3)(c)(ii) it may also give directions under paragraph (2) or direct that the case be listed for a further hearing at which such directions will be given.

(5) Any party to proceedings which are not being dealt with under rule 7.20(2)(a) may apply to the court for further directions at any time.

(Part 3 sets out the court's powers to encourage the parties to use non-court dispute resolution and Part 4 sets out the court's general case management powers.)

Amendments—SI 2014/843.

Case-management under FPR 2010—FPR 2010, rr 1.4 and 4.1 contain duties of the court on case management (r 1.4) and its powers alongside (r 4.1). These case-management duties and powers are extensive and there are, in addition, parallel mandatory case-management provisions for matrimonial and civil partnership proceedings in r 7.22(2).

Case-management hearing—The listing of a case-management hearing under r 7.22 will be in relation to:

(1) Defended matrimonial or civil partnership proceedings; or

(2) Undefended proceedings – As directed under FPR 2010, r 7.20(2)(b)(ii) where a r 7.20(2) certificate has been refused (e g because the district judge wants further information).

(1) Defended hearing

Case management for a defended hearing (r 7.22(2))—In the giving of directions for a defended matrimonial or civil partnership hearing, r 7.22(2) will be only one of the aspects of case management that will concern the court. The court may have in mind the following provisions in FPR 2010:

(1) the overriding objective, especially the need to dispose of the case expeditiously and fairly and in a way that is 'proportionate to the nature … of the issues' (FPR 2010, r 1.1(2));

(2) the duty to manage the case (FPR 2010, r 1.4(2) and see below);

(3) the duty to consider 'whether alternative dispute resolution is appropriate' (FPR 2010, r 3.2);

(4) the court's general powers of case management (FPR 2010, r 4.1(3)); and

(5) the court's case management duties under r 7.22(2).

Alternative dispute resolution—Before taking any steps to prolong the progress of a defended matrimonial and civil partnership case, the court will be concerned to pursue any avenues that permit alternative dispute resolution (and see FPR 2010, r 1.4(2)(f): helping parties to settle a case). The 2010 Rules impose on the courts a duty 'at every stage of proceedings, whether alternative dispute resolution is appropriate', notwithstanding that defended matrimonial and civil partnership proceedings are not one of the 'relevant family proceedings' for the purposes of the mediation practice direction, FPR PD3A (see Annex B to PD3A).

Overriding objective—The overriding objective requires that all cases be dealt with justly, so that a respondent who insists that he wishes to defend decree proceedings must be entitled to do so. (It should always be remembered that decree nisi or conditional order proceedings have two components: that certain facts are proved and that a marriage/civil partnership has irretrievably broken down. The second may be obvious and the more so in the course of contested proceedings; but if the facts cannot be proved (e g adultery is denied, or behaviour not unreasonable (see *Butterworth v Butterworth* [1997] 2 FLR 336, CA)), then irretrievable breakdown does not come into issue before the court.

Case management hearing duties—The duties referred to by r 7.22(2) are likely to be a last resort for the court where all else (including alternative dispute resolution) has failed. The components of these duties are as follows:

(1) *Place of hearing (r 7.22(2)(a))*

(2) *Timetable for filing and service of evidence (r 7.22(2)(b))* This rule echoes FPR 2010, r 1.4(2)(g) and in

litigation such as defended matrimonial and civil partnership proceedings the court is as likely as in any jurisdiction to fix timetables and to guillotine the evidence of witnesses (and see **Evidence and a final hearing**, below).

(3) *Directions for disclosure and inspection of documents (r 7.22(2)(c))* The subjects of (1) requests for further information and (2) disclosure and inspection of documents are separated in Pt 7: for matrimonial and civil partnership proceedings (whether defended or undefended), the first is dealt with in FPR 2010, r 7.15. Disclosure and inspection is touched upon in r 7.22(2) and the subject elaborated upon in FPR PD7A, paras 7.1-7.6, and then also in FPR 2010, Pt 21. For current purposes the subject is dealt with more fully in the commentary to Pt 21 (should a disclosure issue arise in defended proceedings). The court will wish to keep a tight rein on disclosure (bearing in mind what is meant by disclosure in family proceedings (see FPR 2010, r 21.1), and in the light of the overriding objective as to proportionality).

(4) *Directions as to conduct of the final hearing (r 7.22(2)(d))* In setting down the final hearing the court may look to its case management powers under FPR 2010, r 4.1(3). The district judge will be aware of his powers to make orders, not only on application, but also on his own initiative (FPR 2010, r 4.3, subject to a party's right to ask for the order to be re-listed: FPR 2010, r 18.12(2)). A number of the powers in r 4.1(3) will enable the court to control the final hearing (even to excluding issues from trial: r 4.1(3)(j)).

Power to strike out a case—FPR 2010, r 4.4 enables the court to strike out a statement of case. That would include a pleading – application or answer, or part of either – in defended matrimonial and civil partnership proceedings. The court can do this on its own initiative (FPR 2010, r 4.3(1)) subject to proper notice being given to the parties (FPR 2010, r 4.3(3) and (4)); or on Pt 18 application of a party. (It can also strike out matrimonial and civil partnership proceedings by consent: FPR 2010, rr 4.4(1)(d) and 7.9, although this is an altogether different jurisdiction to the mainstream of r 4.4.)

PART III

(2) Court not satisfied on decree or order application

Directions under r 7.20(2)(b)(ii)—Under r 7.22(3), the district judge must give directions for further conduct of the application, including that on compliance with any case management hearing directions a further application under FPR 2010, r 7.19 can be made for a decree nisi or conditional order. Alternatively a direction can be made that the case 'is not suitable for determination under that rule' (r 7.22(3)(c)(ii)), in which case the application can be set down for a further directions. Presumably if this fails, or if the application seems otherwise to be stalled, an applicant could ask for a hearing of the decree nisi or conditional order issue. The only opposition to a decree or order would then come from the court: there is no issue between the parties, nor any issue between the parties for the court to resolve. The hearing would enable a judge finally to resolve in the presence of the applicant (or both parties) whatever it was that was delaying the court's certificate and decree nisi or conditional order.

Application for further directions: Pt 18 procedure—Rule 7.22(5) permits any party to proceedings referred by r 7.20 for case management to seek, at any time, further directions, which application would be dealt with by the FPR 2010, Pt 18 procedure.

7.23–7.25 *(revoked)*

7.26 Medical examinations in proceedings for nullity of a marriage of an opposite sex couple

(1) Where the application is for a decree of nullity of a marriage of an opposite sex couple on the ground of incapacity to consummate or wilful refusal to do so, the court must determine whether medical examiners should be appointed to examine the parties or either of them.

(2) The court must only appoint medical examiners under paragraph (1) where it considers that it is necessary for the proper disposal of the case.

(3) The person to be examined must, in the presence of the medical examiner, sign a statement identifying that person as the party to whom the order for examination applies.

(4) The medical examiner must certify on the same statement that it was signed in his or her presence by the person who has been examined.

(5) The person who carries out the examination must prepare a report and file it with the court by the date directed by the court.

(6) Either party is entitled to see a copy of a report filed under paragraph (5).

Amendments—SI 2014/524.

PD7B—Rule 7.26 is accompanied by FPR PD7B.

Application for appointment—Rule 7.26(1) requires the court to 'determine' the issue of whether a medical examiner should be appointed. Application is by the FPR 2010, Pt 18 procedure, with grounds to be provided in an accompanying statement and particular reasons why a report is necessary in undefended proceedings.

Medical examiner as expert—The examiner will be giving opinion evidence and his report will be subject to the requirements of a report under FPR 2010, Pt 25 (especially the information required by FPR PD25A). There, duty is to the court (FPR 2010, r 25.4) with whom they are required to file their report (FPR 2010, r 7.26(5)).

Appointment of a medical examiner—The appointment of an examiner should only be made where necessary for proper disposal of the case (FPR 2010, r 7.26(2)). For example, appointment will not normally be necessary where a nullity application is undefended (FPR PD7B, para 1.1). The party who seeks an appointment must deal with her attendance at the final hearing at the case-management hearing appointment (FPR PD7B, para 1.4).

7.27 Stay of proceedings

(1) Where –

(a) the court is considering an application in accordance with rule 7.20 or gives directions under rule 7.22;

(b) it appears to the court that there are proceedings continuing in any country outside England and Wales which are in respect of the marriage or civil partnership in question or which are capable of affecting its validity or subsistence; and

(c) the court considers that the question whether the proceedings should be stayed(GL) under paragraph 9 of Schedule 1 to the Domicile and Matrimonial Proceedings Act 1973 or, for civil partnership proceedings, under rules made under sections 75 and 76 of the Courts Act 2003 ought to be determined by the court,

the court must give directions for the hearing of that question.

(2) Where at any time after the making of an application under this Part it appears to the court in matrimonial proceedings that, under Articles 16 to 19 of the Council Regulation, the court does not have jurisdiction to hear the application and is or may be required to stay(GL) the proceedings, the court will –

(a) stay(GL) the proceedings; and

(b) fix a date for a hearing to determine the questions of jurisdiction and whether there should be a further stay(GL) or other order.

(3) The court must give reasons for its decision under Articles 16 to 19 of the Council Regulation and, where it makes a finding of fact, state such finding of fact.

(4) An order under Article 17 of the Council Regulation that the court has no jurisdiction over the proceedings will be recorded by the court or the court officer in writing.

(5) The court may, if all parties agree, deal with any question about the jurisdiction of the court without a hearing.

Amendments—SI 2012/679.

Defined terms—'the Council Regulation', 'court': FPR 2010, r 2.3(1).

Stay of matrimonial or civil partnership proceedings—Rule 7.27 sets up a procedure by which a district judge, on considering his certificate under FPR 2010, r 7.20(2)(a) or under FPR 2010, r 7.22, imposes an obligatory stay on pending matrimonial or civil partnership proceedings. It also applies where the court exercises a discretion to impose a stay on any matrimonial or civil partnership proceedings, where other proceedings are pending outside the jurisdiction.

Stay under DMPA 1973—DMPA 1973, s 5(6) gives the court power to stay matrimonial proceedings (as defined in Sch 1, para 2) where there are concurrent proceedings in another jurisdiction in respect of the same marriage.

Application for a discretionary stay—An application for a discretionary stay under DMPA 1973, Sch 1, para 9 is heard by a judge. Application is made by the FPR 2010, Pt 18 procedure. The supporting statement should state as clearly as possible the grounds for seeking a stay. If a party seeks to persuade the court on the basis that another jurisdiction is the more appropriate or convenient for deciding the issue ('forum non conveniens'), it is important that the application be made at the outset of proceedings or at the first opportunity, before steps have been taken in the application and costs are incurred by either party (*Mansour v Mansour* [1989] 1 FLR 418, CA; *Krenge v Krenge* [1999] 1 FLR 969, FD).

Referral at time of giving directions (r 7.27(1)(a),(2))—If the court considers, when looking at a case under FPR 2010, rr 7.20(2) or 7.22(2), that there is information in the statements of case of the parties that refer to other proceedings relating to the marriage or capable of affecting its validity or subsistence and that might lead to a discretionary stay, then the district judge does the following:

(1) imposes a stay on the present proceedings (r 7.27(2)(a));
(2) fixes an appointment before the judge and give notice of this to the parties (r 7.27(2)(b)).

Stay of proceedings: directions (r 7.27(1)(b) or (2))—Where the court is considering grant of a certificate under r 7.20 but it appears there are proceedings continuing in any country outside England and Wales in respect of the marriage or civil partnership, the court must give directions for the hearing of that question of whether there are other proceedings or whether to stay proceedings to decide whether the court has jurisdiction due to Council Regulation Arts 16–19 (*Lachaux v Lachaux* [2017] EWHC 385 (Fam)).

Stay during the trial—If a party fails to provide particulars of other proceedings as required by the rules and the Act, the court can stay proceedings even after the start of the trial (DMPA 1973, Sch 1, para 9(4)).

Removal of stay—An application for removal of a stay can be made on grounds that the other proceedings are stayed or concluded, or that a party has delayed unreasonably in prosecuting them (DMPA 1973, Sch 1, para 10(1)). The application is made by the Pt 18 procedure (Form D11). The application should state the grounds on which removal of the stay is sought.

Chapter 4
Court Orders

Forms of court determination under Pt 7—FPR 2010, Pt 7 deals with three separate forms of determination by the court:

(1) *Directions orders* Directions for the conduct of proceedings or at a case-management hearing will be recorded in an 'order'. 'Order' within the terms of FPR 2010 includes 'directions of the court' (FPR 2010, r 2.3(1)).

(2) *Certificate of satisfaction as to entitlement to a decree nisi or conditional order* A certificate under FPR 2010, r 7.20(2)(a) (akin to the former special procedure certificate) that results in a case being listed for hearing in the block list for decree nisi or conditional order. It is possible that the decision in *Day v Day* (1980) 1 FLR 341, CA (above: based on the certificate being, in effect, the disposal of the application) would be decided differently since the coming into operation of Human Rights Act 1998 and European Convention 1950, Art 6(1). The certificate is not an order in the sense intended by the rules generally or by FPR 2010, Ch 4 in particular.

(3) *Orders: decree nisi or conditional order* Orders made on application for a decree nisi or conditional order whether (a) on an undefended application or (b) following contested proceedings. It is these orders that are dealt with in FPR 2010, Ch 4.

PART III

Applications and orders—Practitioners and parties will find that under FPR 2010, Pt 7, Ch 2 the rules relate to orders, and occasionally to applications. That is to say, the rules sometimes indicate how application is to be made for the order (see for example FPR 2010, r 7.31(2)), but more often they are silent (eg under FPR 2010, r 7.28(1), 7.29 and 7.30(1)), so that the applicant must assume that the FPR 2010, Pt 18 procedure applies for the particular application.

Review or re-hearing of orders and certificates—Orders may be appealed against. A certificate, as a judicial disposal of an application, can be set aside (eg *Mitchell v Mitchell* [1984] FLR 50, CA, where permission was given to file an answer and the registrar's certificate was set aside, albeit on appeal against the decree nisi granted following the certificate), but possibly not appealed against. Certain directions can be reviewed (eg as under FPR 2010, rr 18.9 and 18.12) or appealed against (FPR 2010, Pt 30).

Appeals, set aside or re-hearing—Appeals from a district judge's grant of a decree following the r 7.22 procedure are in accordance with the appeals procedures under FPR 2010, Pt 30, but note limitations on appeal against decrees absolute in SCA 1981, s 18(1)(d), where the appellant respondent had time to appeal against the decree nisi.

7.28 The circumstances in which an order may be set aside (rescission)

(1) The court must not hear an application by a respondent for –

(a) the rescission of a decree of divorce under section 10(1) of the 1973 Act;
(b) the rescission of a dissolution order under section 48(1) of the 2004 Act,

less than 14 days after service of the application.

(2) Either party to the marriage concerned may apply –

(a) after the decree nisi has been made but before it has been made absolute; or
(b) after a decree of judicial separation has been made

for the rescission of the decree on the grounds that the parties are reconciled and both consent to the rescission.

(3) Either party to the civil partnership concerned may apply –

(a) after a conditional order has been made but before it has been made final; or
(b) after a separation order has been made,

for the rescission of the order on the grounds that the parties are reconciled and both consent to the rescission.

MFPA 1984, s 31F(6)—Section 31F(6) gives the Family Court powers, including to rescind orders at any time and the court's power to rescind must be read alongside.

Setting aside of decree nisi or conditional order—In r 7.28, rescission of decrees nisi or conditional orders in two very different sets of circumstances is elided. There is no means prescribed by the 2010 Rules (cf FPR 1991, r 2.42) for setting aside a decree where no error of the court is alleged. If the court is alleged to be in error, a party is obliged to appeal (FPR 2010, Pt 30)).

(1) Rescission under MCA 1973, s 10(1) or CPA 2004, s 48(1)
Under MCA 1973, s 10(1) or CPA 2004, s 48(1) the court is asked to exercise a set-aside jurisdiction (as the heading to the rule implies). The rules do not prescribe any procedure for the rescission application, although it is likely to be by the FPR 2010, Pt 18 procedure (Form D11). The application will be heard in open court.

Grounds of application for rescission under s 10(1) or s 48(1)—In the drafting of grounds for the application, the applicant will bear in mind that the application can only be made within the terms of MCA 1973, s 10(1) or CPA 2004, s 48(1): namely that the respondent was misled by the petitioner, whether intentionally or unintentionally. The factors that influenced the respondent in consenting can be elaborated on in his statement in support of the application. If intentional misleading is alleged, it must be borne in mind that this is a serious allegation and, as a result, the court is likely to require a high standard of proof from the respondent (eg fraud may only be alleged in drafting by an advocate if the client gives clear instructions). Since this is an application to set aside a consent order (a decree obtained on the basis of the respondent's consent) the respondent will need to explain clearly how his consent was obtained and why he was 'misled … (whether intentionally or unintentionally)' (MCA 1973, s 10(1)) or his consent is otherwise vitiated.

(2) Setting aside of a decree or order in other circumstances
A decree nisi or conditional order may be able to be set aside for other reasons. The set aside jurisdiction of the County Court under CCR 1981, Ord 37 has not been reproduced in FPR 2010, so the applicant is left to apply on general or common law principles (i e that no error of the court is alleged: e g *Peek v Peek* [1948] P 46, PDAD). In none of these instances would it be open to a party to appeal (no judge was in error), yet the errors must by some means be put right.

Procedure—Application is by the FPR 2010, Pt 18 procedure. When the circumstances come to light, the court should be asked to list the matter urgently on notice to both parties to show good reason why the decree should not be set aside as a nullity. It may be wise for the parties to be alerted by telephone to minimise the risk of one of them taking steps to arrange remarriage. The matter should be listed in open court (because the decree nisi was pronounced in open court) before either a district judge (if the decree was pronounced by a district judge) or a circuit judge (if pronounced by a circuit judge). The designated family judge should be alerted and may wish the matter to be listed before him/her in any event.

7.29 Applications under section 10(2) of 1973 Act or section 48(2) of 2004 Act

Where the court makes –

(a) in the case of divorce, a decree absolute following an application under section 10(2) of the 1973 Act; or

(b) in the case of dissolution, a final order following an application under section 48(2) of the 2004 Act,

it must make a written record of the reasons for deciding to make that decree absolute or final order.

MCA 1973, s 10(2) or CPA 2004, s 48(2)—MCA 1973, s 10(4) and CPA 2004, s 48(5) enable the court to make a decree nisi or conditional order absolute or final (as the case may be), notwithstanding a respondent's application under ss 10(2) or 48(2) (respondent's application to the court to consider her financial position) and this rule provides that a proper record of the judge's reasons under ss 10(4) and 48(5) for allowing a final decree/order be made: any ss 10(2) or 48(2) application will be contested and heard in open court and a record of the judgment will be available by tape-recording (eg CPR PD39A, para 1.11).

7.30 Orders under section 10A(2) of the 1973 Act

(1) Where the court has made an order under section 10A(2) of the 1973 Act, the declaration referred to in that section must –

(a) be made and signed by both parties to the marriage concerned;

(b) give particulars of the proceedings in which the order was obtained;

(c) confirm that the steps required to dissolve the marriage in accordance with the religious usages appropriate to the parties have been taken;

(d) be accompanied by –

(i) a certificate from a relevant religious authority that all such steps have been taken; or

(ii) such other documents showing the relevant steps have been taken as the court may direct; and

(iii) be filed at the court either before or together with an application to make the decree nisi absolute,

under rule 7.32 or 7.33.

(2) Where the certificate referred to in paragraph (1)(d)(i) is not in English it must be accompanied by a translation of that certificate into English, certified by a notary public or authenticated by statement of truth.

(3) The court may direct that the declaration need not be accompanied by the material mentioned in paragraph (1)(d).

(4) In this rule a religious authority is 'relevant' if the party who made the application for the order under section 10A(2) of the 1973 Act considers that authority competent to confirm that the steps referred to in paragraph (1)(c) have been taken.

Context of provision—MCA 1973, s 10A(1) provides that, where a couple were married in accordance with 'the usages of the Jews' or other religious usages and these prescribe final dissolution, an application can be made under s 10A(2) for an order that stays the grant of a decree absolute. The stay will continue until the court is satisfied by a declaration of both parties that the marriage is also dissolved in accordance with 'those [Jewish or other] usages'. Rule 7.30 provides the regulatory framework for such application.

Application under s 10A(2)—No specific means of making the r 7.30 application under s 10A(2) is prescribed (as it was by FPR 1991, r 2.45A). It must be assumed that the rule-maker intends an application for the order delaying decree absolute shall be made by the Pt 18 procedure (Form D11; and see **Timing of application**, below). The application will be supported by the declaration as to Jewish dissolution required by s 10A(2),(4) and as further prescribed by r 7.30(1).

Timing of application—MCA 1973, s 10A(1) is engaged as soon as 'a decree of divorce has been granted' (i e upon decree nisi, but not before). This will demand vigilance from practitioners, since the importance of s 10A(2) to a Jewish wife will be lost if the decree nisi is made absolute. An early return date will be needed (for a respondent wife, before the end of the 6-week period for decree absolute). If a husband manages to persuade the court to expedite a decree absolute, it is possible that little can be done, unless he has in some way misled the court.

7.31 Applications to prevent decrees nisi being made absolute or conditional orders being made final

(1) This rule applies to an application under section 8 or 9 of the 1973 Act or under section 39 or 40 of the 2004 Act to prevent –

- (a) in the case of divorce or nullity of marriage, a decree nisi being made absolute; or
- (b) in the case of dissolution or nullity of civil partnership, a conditional order being made final.

(2) An application to which this rule applies must be made using the Part 18 procedure, subject to paragraphs (3) to (6) of this rule.

(3) The person making an application to which this rule applies must within 28 days of filing the application apply to the court to give directions for the hearing of the application.

(4) Where the person making an application to which this rule applies does not apply for directions under paragraph (3), then the person in whose favour the decree nisi or conditional order (as the case may be) was made may do so.

(5) Rule 7.22(2) applies to an application to which this rule applies as it applies to an application for a matrimonial or civil partnership order.

(6) Where an application to which this rule applies is made by the Queen's Proctor –

- (a) the Queen's Proctor may give written notice, to the court and to the party in whose favour the decree nisi or conditional order (as the case may be) was made, of the Queen's Proctor's intention to make an application to prevent the decree nisi being made absolute or the conditional order being made final; and
- (b) where the Queen's Proctor does so the application under paragraph (1) must be made within 21 days beginning with the date on which the notice is given.

Application under MCA 1973, ss 8 and 9(1) and CPA 2004, ss 39 and 40(1)—Rule 7.31 deals with two separate sets of application:

(1) MCA 1973, s 8 and CPA 2004, s 39 enable the Queen's Proctor to show cause why a decree nisi or conditional order should not be made absolute or final (ss 8(2) and 39(4)); and

(2) MCA 1973, s 9(1) and CPA 2004, s 40(1) enable 'any person' to bring 'material facts' before the court to show that a decree nisi or conditional order should not be made absolute or final. (This has nothing to do with the entitlement of a respondent to apply for a decree absolute or final order under s 9(2) and 40(2): for which see r 7.33.)

PART III

Procedure for application (r 7.31(2)–(5))—Application is made by the Pt 18 procedure (r 7.31(2): application notice Form D11) as extended by r 7.31(3)–(6):

(1) The applicant will wish to ensure that his application (r 18.7) sets out clearly the basis of what will be serious allegations ('material facts': e g that a couple who claim to be living apart are living together; that there was no such claimed 'improper association' and so on. The allegations will need to be set out to a high degree of credibility).
(2) The applicant, including the Queen's Proctor, should consider including application for a stay of the decree absolute or final order in the application notice (see reference to **Stay of application for decree absolute or final order** below and in r 7.32(2)).
(3) Service of the application and accompanying is in accordance with r 18.8 and Pt 6.
(4) The duty is on the applicant (the Queen's Proctor or other person who applies under s 9(1) or 40(1)) to apply within 28 days of its filing, for directions on his application (r 7.31(3)). (This provision is not consistent with the FPR 2010, Pt 18 procedure and in particular r 18.8. The provision is not as clear as it might be; but the implication at least of FPR 2010, r 18.8 (read alongside FPR 2010, r 18.9(1)) is that upon issue of the application a hearing date will be fixed before its service.)
(5) Failing application under r 7.31(3) (and if no date is fixed under FPR 2010, r 18.8 by the court) the spouse or civil partner who obtained the decree nisi or conditional order can apply (r 7.31(4)); or they may wish to apply to have the application (especially if by a private individual) struck out, e g as disclosing no grounds for the application (FPR 2010, r 4.4(1)(a)) or being an abuse of process if not pursued (FPR 2010, r 4.4(1)(b)).
(6) Upon application to the court under r 7.31(3) or (4) a case-management hearing is fixed in accordance with the procedures under FPR 2010, r 7.22(2).

Case management: 'Rule 7.22(2) applies' (r 7.31(5))—This provision may be thought redundant: FPR 2010, Pt 18 has its own procedures. These are enhanced, in case-management hearing terms by FPR 2010, rr 1.4 and 4.1 (and see **Case management hearing duties** under FPR 2010, r 7.22). There should be no need for the further procedural gloss of r 7.22(2) to be added for this single issue application.

Stay of application for decree absolute or final order—The is no express provision in statute or rule to say that an application under this rule stays the grant of a decree absolute or final order, although FPR 2010, r 7.32(2) provides that a decree nisi or conditional order shall be made absolute or a final order, if no ss 8/9(1) or 39/40(1) application has been made.

7.32 Making decrees nisi absolute or conditional orders final by giving notice

(1) Unless rule 7.33 applies –

(a) in matrimonial proceedings, a spouse in whose favour a decree nisi has been made may give notice to the court that he or she wishes the decree nisi to be made absolute; or
(a) in civil partnership proceedings, a civil partner in whose favour a conditional order has been made may give notice to the court that he or she wishes the conditional order to be made final.

(2) Subject to paragraphs (3) and (4), where the court receives a notice under paragraph (1) it will make the decree nisi absolute or the conditional order final (as the case may be) if it is satisfied that –

(a) no application for rescission of the decree nisi or the conditional order is pending;
(b) no appeal against the making of the decree nisi or the conditional order is pending;
(c) no order has been made by the court extending the time for bringing an appeal of the kind mentioned in sub-paragraph (b), or if such an order has been made, that the time so extended has expired;
(d) no application for an order of the kind mentioned in sub-paragraph (c) is pending;
(e) no application to prevent the decree nisi being made absolute or the conditional order being made final is pending;
(f) *(revoked)*
(g) the provisions of section 10(2) to (4) of the 1973 Act or section 48(2) to (4) of the 2004 Act do not apply or have been complied with;
(h) any order under section 10A(2) of the 1973 Act has been complied with; and
(i) where the decree nisi was made on the ground in section 12(1)(g) of, or paragraph 11(1)(e) of Schedule 1 to, the 1973 Act, or was made under section 12A(3) of the 1973 Act in a case where section 12(1)(g) of the 1973 Act applies, or the conditional order was made under section 50(1)(d) of the 2004 Act –
    (i) there is not pending a reference under section 8(5) of the Gender Recognition

Act 2004, or an application under section 8(5A) of that Act, in respect of the application on which the interim gender recognition certificate to which the application relates was granted;

(ii) that interim certificate has not been revoked under section 8(6)(b) of that Act; and

(iii) no appeal is pending against an order under section 8(6)(a) of that Act.

(3) Where the notice is received more than 12 months after the making of the decree nisi or the conditional order, it must be accompanied by an explanation in writing stating –

(a) why the application has not been made earlier;

(b) whether the applicant and respondent have lived together since the decree nisi or the conditional order was made, and, if so, between what dates;

(c) if the applicant is female, whether she has given birth to a child since the decree nisi or the conditional order was made and whether it is alleged that the child is or may be a child of the family;

(d) if the respondent is female, whether the applicant has reason to believe that she has given birth to a child since the decree nisi or the conditional order was made and whether it is alleged that the child is or may be a child of the family.

(4) Where paragraph (3) applies, the court may –

(a) require the applicant to file an affidavit verifying the explanation or to verify the explanation with a statement of truth; and

(b) make such order on the application as it thinks fit, but where it orders the decree nisi to be made absolute or the conditional order to be made final that order is not to take effect until the court is satisfied that none of the matters mentioned in paragraph (2)(a) to (i) applies.

Amendments—SI 2012/679; SI 2014/843; SI 2015/913.

Defined terms—'child of the family': r 2.3(1).

Application by spouse or civil partner in whose favour [a decree or order] has been made (r 7.32(1))—In the first instance, the application can only be by the spouse who obtained the decree nisi. After the final date for applying has passed (see **Time for notice**, below), the other spouse or civil partner can apply.

Application by 'notice under paragraph (1)' (r 7.32(2))—The applicant under r 7.32 'applies' for a decree absolute or final order on prescribed Form D36. Application under r 7.32(2) is by 'notice' (as distinct from an application made by 'application' for decree absolute or final order made, e g under FPR 2010, r 7.33). The first is a request to the court to do something: the second a formal application to be dealt with on notice.

Time for notice—An application for decree absolute or final order must generally be made 6 weeks or later from decree nisi or conditional order. Application may be made to expedite the decree absolute or final order and if application is not made by the decree nisi or conditional order applicant. The respondent can apply for a decree absolute or final order (MCA 1973, s 9(2); CPA 2004, s 40(2)) if no application is made by the party who obtained the decree nisi or conditional order.

Procedure for applications—The procedure for each of these applications is as follows:

(1) *Application by party who obtained the decree nisi or conditional order* In accordance with this rule:
   (a) The period prescribed by MCA 1973, s 1(5) for applying for a decree absolute has been shortened to 6 weeks by the Matrimonial Causes (Decree Absolute) Order 1972.
   (b) The period prescribed by CPA 2004, s 38(1) is 6 weeks.

(2) *Expedited decree nisi or final order* Application may be made to the court, in appropriate circumstances, to 'fix a shorter period' for grant of decree absolute or final order (MCA 1973, s 1(5); CPA 2004, s 38(4)).

(3) *Application by spouse against whom decree pronounced* The party against whom the decree nisi or conditional order was obtained can apply for a decree absolute on notice 3 months after the other spouse could have applied (MCA 1973, s 9(2); CPA 2004, s 40(2); and see r 7.33).

Application for expedited decree—Application may be made to the court to 'fix a shorter period' than 6 weeks for grant of a decree absolute or final order (MCA 1973, s 1(5); CPA 2004, s 38(4)) where grounds for expedition exist (e g impending death or birth of a child, or perhaps a permanent move abroad). Procedure is governed by FPR PD7A, paras 8.1–8.4, as follows:

(1) *Prior to application for decree nisi* If the application can be made prior to application for decree nisi or conditional order then application can be made to the district judge for early directions at the time the district judge gives directions under FPR 2010, r 7.19 (FPR PD7A, para 8.1).

(2) *After decree nisi or conditional order application* Where the need for expedition emerges after decree nisi or conditional order then application can be made to the court using FPR 2010, Pt 18 procedure (Form D11; FPR PD7A, paras 8.2 and 8.4).

Search of court records (r 7.32(2))—The purpose of the search conducted under r 7.32(2) is to check that there is no outstanding application or question affecting the decree nisi or conditional order or preventing the grant of the decree absolute or final order, and in particular:

(1) *Compliance with MCA 1973, s 41 or CPA 2004, s 63(1) (r 7.32(f))* A stay on the decree being made absolute until satisfaction has been expressed by the judge is no longer available, but MCA 1973, s 41(2) (as substituted by CA 1989) and CPA 2004, s 63(2) enable the court in the instances set out in the respective subsections to stay the grant of a decree until further order of the court (i e until application is made to the court to lift the stay).

(2) *'the provisions of section 10(2) to (4) of the Act of 1973' (r 2.49(2)(g))* MCA 1973, s 10(2)–(4) concerns applications for consideration of the respondent's financial position in divorce proceedings under MCA 1973, s 1(2)(d),(e) (2 years' living apart with consent and 5 years' living apart) and enables the court to delay the decree absolute (MCA 1973, s 10(3)), subject to the provisions of MCA 1973, s 10(4).

'[the court] will make the decree nisi absolute or the conditional order final' (r 7.32(2))—The court is required to make the decree nisi absolute or the conditional order final if the court office is satisfied that none of the factors listed in the rule applies, subject to the proviso (in r 7.32(3) and (4)) where the application is made 12 months after decree nisi.

Court action if one or more factors in r 7.32(2) apply—Rule 7.32 does not state what the court shall do if one of the factors in r 7.32(2) applies: it only tells the court what to do (i e make the decree absolute or order final if none of the factors applies). For example, an appeal does not stay the order appealed against (a stay must be applied for: r 30.8). It is not clear from this that a stay in other circumstances in r 7.32(2) must be applied for, or whether the decree absolute or final order application remains in procedural limbo.

Stay on grant of decree absolute—It may be possible to stay grant of a decree absolute if its grant might prejudice financial rights of a party in another jurisdiction (in this case, the USA; *Evans v Evans* [2013] 2 FLR 295, CA) or where the structure of a party's finances were such that dissolution of the marriage might prejudice the other spouse (see *Thakkar v Thakkar* [2016] EWHC 2488 (Fam) within **Discretion to postpone decree absolute** under MCA 1973, s 1).

Where notice is lodged more than 12 months after decree nisi (r 7.32(3))—Where application is made more than 12 months after decree nisi, an explanation in writing must be provided to the district judge. This could be by letter from the applicant (if acting in person) or his solicitor. The court can call for an affidavit by the applicant to verify the explanation (r 7.32(4)), for example where the court has doubts as to the explanation or where an unusual state of affairs is described. Where there has been cohabitation in excess of 6 months, the court has a discretion as to whether a decree absolute is granted and as to whether the decree nisi should be rescinded (*Kim v Morris* [2013] 2 FLR 1197, FD).

Explanation for delay (r 7.32(3))—The explanation must deal with the factors mentioned in the paragraph, including:

(1) *'whether the parties have lived with each other'* Living with each other means living together in the same household and sharing a common life (MCA 1973, s 2(6)). If the parties have lived together for less than 6 months during the previous 12 months MCA 1973, s 2(5) (or CPA 2004, s 45) apply; however, where the parties have lived together for longer than 6 months during that period, there is likely to be a presumption that the marriage has not irretrievably broken down, a decree absolute may be refused and the decree nisi rescinded (*Biggs v Biggs and Wheatley* [1977] Fam 1, FD).

(2) *'relevant facts' concerning any child born to the wife* Such facts would include the date of birth and the child's parentage and, if the parties are themselves the parents, they will need to give a clear explanation concerning cohabitation (if any).

'the court … may (b) make such order … as it thinks fit' (r 7.32(4)(b))—The court has a discretion as to the order that is made on the late application: whether to grant a decree absolute or final order; to refuse a decree (in which case the judge is likely to consider rescinding the decree nisi or conditional order and, where appropriate, dismissing the application: (*Kim v Morris* [2013] 2 FLR 1197, FD); or to make another order, e g as to filing further affidavit evidence (r 7.32(4)(a)).

7.33 Applications to make decrees nisi absolute or conditional orders final

(1) An application must be made –

(a) in matrimonial proceedings, for the decree nisi to be made absolute; or

(b) in civil partnership proceedings, for the conditional order to be made final,

where the conditions set out in paragraph (2) apply.

(2) The conditions referred to in paragraph (1) are –

(a) the Queen's Proctor gives notice to the court under rule 7.31(6)(a) and has not withdrawn that notice;

(b) there are other circumstances which ought to be brought to the attention of the court before the application is granted; or

(c) the application is made –

(i) in matrimonial proceedings, by the spouse against whom the decree nisi was made; or

(ii) in civil partnership proceedings, by the civil partner against whom the conditional order was made.

(3) An application under this rule to which paragraph (2)(a) applies must be served on the Queen's Proctor.

(4) Where the court orders –

(a) in matrimonial proceedings, a decree to be made absolute under this rule; or
(b) in civil partnership proceedings, a conditional order to be made final under this rule,

that order is not to take effect until the court is satisfied about the matters mentioned in rule 7.32(2)(a) to (i).

Amendments—SI 2013/3204.

Defined terms—'civil partnership proceedings', 'court', 'district judge', 'matrimonial proceedings': FPR 2010, r 2.3(1).

Application to make decree nisi or conditional order absolute or final—Rule 7.33 deals with two separate matters:

(1) *Delay of grant of decree absolute or final order* Application for a decree nisi or conditional order to be made absolute or final, where the Queen's Proctor has intervened or where 'there are other circumstances which ought to be brought to the attention of the court' (r 7.33(2)(a),(3),(4));
(2) *Application for decree absolute or final order by the respondent spouse or civil partner* The wholly different, and generally uncontroversial question, of application for a decree absolute or final order by the non-applicant spouse or civil partner (r 7.33(2)(c)).

Application on notice—Application under r 7.33 is on notice to the other parties (including the Queen's Proctor, if it is a Queen's Proctor case) under the FPR 2010, Pt 18 procedure (by Form D11). The statement in support of the application under (1) will be extensive, but under (2) can be more or less routine (and see cases referred to below).

Hearing of the application (r 7.33(3))—An application involving the Queen's Proctor (in (1) above) – which will be essentially to warn off the Queen's Proctor – must be heard by a judge (r 7.33(3)(a)). An application (at (2)) for a respondent's decree or order will be heard by a district judge. Any application involving 'other circumstances' (see below) will be likely to be dealt with, in the first instance by a district judge.

Powers of the court—The powers of the court on dealing with an application by the Queen's Proctor are prescribed by MCA 1973, s 9(1) and CPA 2004, s 40(3). In summary these powers are:

(1) To make the decree nisi or conditional order absolute or final in any event;
(2) To rescind the decree nisi or conditional order;
(3) To require further inquiry and information; or
(4) Deal with the case in such other way as the court thinks fit.

'there are other circumstances which ought to be brought to the attention of the court' (r 7.33(2)(b))—There is no evidence on the face of the statute that indicates a power in the court to refer an issue of this nature to a judge. It is possible that what the rule anticipates is referral to a judge in circumstances such as those set out in FPR 2010, r 7.32(2), but this is unclear.

Application for decree absolute or final order by original applicant—There appears to be nothing in r 7.33(2)(c) to prevent the spouse or civil partner who obtained the decree nisi or conditional order filing a routine decree absolute application (under FPR 2010, r 7.32(2)) on receipt of the application notice under r 7.33 (unless 12 months have elapsed since the date of the decree nisi). If that happens, the spouse or civil partner applying under r 7.33(2)(c) should maintain his application if he wishes to seek an order for costs against the spouse who obtained the decree nisi.

Grant of decree or order under MCA 1973, s 9(2) or CPA 2004, s 40(2): discretion—Grant of a decree on the respondent's application is a matter for the court's discretion (MCA 1973, s 9(2); CPA 2004, s 40(2)), although if application is made before the 3 month period in MCA 1973, s 9(2) any decree will be void (*Manchanda v Manchanda* [1995] 2 FLR 590, CA). In *Re G (Decree Absolute: Prejudice)* [2003] 1 FLR 870, FD, Bennett J allowed a respondent husband's application for decree absolute. Although the husband might not be prejudiced by the delay, in the absence of good grounds to refuse a decree, it should issue. Had the wife applied, a decree would have been granted. Such application gives the court a discretion to grant a decree absolute or final order to the other spouse or civil partner, although the court may refuse to exercise discretion in appropriate circumstances (*Smith v Smith* [1990] 1 FLR 438, FD). The decree will not be made absolute (or a conditional order final) if the refusal to do so is the only way to ensure that a party complies with an ancillary relief order (*Wickler v Wickler* [1998] 2 FLR 326, FD).

Service on the Queen's Proctor—The Queen's Proctor is served by the Treasury Solicitor.

7.34 What the court officer must do when a decree nisi is made absolute

In matrimonial proceedings, where a decree nisi is made absolute the court officer must –

(a) endorse that fact on the decree nisi together with the precise time at which the decree was made absolute; and

PART III

(b) send a certificate that a decree nisi has been made absolute to the applicant, the respondent, any co-respondent and any other party.

Defined terms—'matrimonial proceedings': FPR 2010, r 2.3(1).

7.35 What the court officer must do when a conditional order is made final

Where a conditional order is made final the court officer must –

(a) endorse that fact on the conditional order together with the precise time at which the order was made final; and

(b) send the final order to the applicant, the respondent and any other party.

Defined terms—'matrimonial proceedings': FPR 2010, r 2.3(1).

7.36 Records of decrees absolute and final orders

(1) A central index of decrees absolute and final orders must be kept under the control of the principal registry.

(2) Any person may require a search to be made of that index and to be provided with a certificate showing the results of that search.

(3) Any person who requests it must be issued with a copy of the decree absolute or final order.

Amendments—SI 2012/679.

Defined terms—'principal registry': FPR 2010, r 2.3(1).

Practice Direction 7A – Procedure for Applications in Matrimonial and Civil Partnership Proceedings

This Practice Direction supplements FPR Part 7

Applications for matrimonial and civil partnership orders: general

1.1 An application for a matrimonial or civil partnership order must be made in the form referred to in Practice Direction 5A. The application form sets out the documents which must accompany the application.

Modifications—Where FPR PD36D applies, para 1.1 is modified to read:

'1.1 Where the pilot scheme referred to in Practice Direction 36D applies, an application for a matrimonial order must be made in the form generated by the online system referred to in that Practice Direction. The online system sets out the documents which must accompany the application.'

1.2 The application for a matrimonial order or a civil partnership order must be completed according to the detailed notes which accompany the form. It is especially important that the particulars provide evidence to show why the applicant is entitled to –

(a) in matrimonial proceedings, a dissolution or annulment of the marriage or a decree of judicial separation;

(b) in civil partnership proceedings, a dissolution or annulment of the civil partnership or a separation order.

The particulars should, however, be as concise as possible consistent with providing the necessary evidence.

Modifications—Where FPR PD36D applies, paras 1.2 is modified to read:

'1.2 The application must be completed according to the detailed guidance contained in the online system. It is especially important that the particulars provide evidence to show why the applicant is entitled to a decree of divorce. The particulars should, however, be as concise as possible consistent with providing the necessary evidence.'

1.3 Where it is necessary in some way to amend an application for a matrimonial order or a civil partnership order, there are distinctions to be drawn between an amended application, a supplemental application and a further application –

(a) an amended application might be used to add or amend particulars, allegations or acts which occurred before the date of the application, or to make alterations and additions not connected with the allegations (including, for example, substituting a prayer for divorce instead of judicial separation or stating the birth of a child after the date of the application);

(b) a supplemental application might be used to add particulars, allegations or acts which occurred after the date of the original application. A supplemental application forms part of the original application and effects an amendment to it;

(c) a further (or second) application may only be presented with permission under FPR 2010, r 7.7(1)(b) except that no permission is required where the purpose of the further application is to seek a divorce, or dissolution, following the expiration of one year from the date of the marriage, or civil partnership, on the basis of the same facts contained in an original application for judicial separation, or for an order for separation (FPR 2010, r 7.7(2)). An example of where a further application might be filed with permission is where the further petition is based on consent after 2 years' separation and the applicant wishes to preserve the original application in case the respondent withdraws his consent to the further application before decree nisi. In such a case, permission may be given to file a further application and an order made that the original application will stand dismissed on the granting of a decree nisi on the further application. There may also be cases where certain orders for financial remedies on the original application should not be disturbed until orders are made on the further application.

Amended and supplemental applications operate on a principle of relation back to the date of issue of the original application. This means it is not possible to allege in a supplemental application, for example, a period of desertion or separation expiring after the date of the original application. A further application will be required for this purpose. Nonetheless, a supplemental application may contain further allegations of unreasonable behaviour or adultery postdating the date of the original application.

Modifications—Where FPR PD36D applies, paras 1.1 and 1.2 are modified to read:

'1.1 Where the pilot scheme referred to in Practice Direction 36D applies, an application for a matrimonial order must be made in the form generated by the online system referred to in that Practice Direction. The online system sets out the documents which must accompany the application.

1.2 The application must be completed according to the detailed guidance contained in the online system. It is especially important that the particulars provide evidence to show why the applicant is entitled to a decree of divorce. The particulars should, however, be as concise as possible consistent with providing the necessary evidence.'

PART III

Respondents: restrictions

2.1 Where the application refers to adultery or to an improper association with another person, that other person should not be named in the application unless the applicant believes the other party to the marriage or civil partnership in question is likely to object to the making of a matrimonial or civil partnership order on the application. Furthermore, such a person should not be a respondent if under the age of 16 or alleged to have been the victim of rape committed by the other party to the marriage or civil partnership, unless the court gives permission.

Proof of marriage or civil partnership to accompany the application

3.1 The application form for a matrimonial order or a civil partnership order sets out the documents which must accompany the application. Where the existence and validity of a marriage or civil partnership is not disputed, its validity will be proved by the application being accompanied by –

(a) one of the following –

(i) a certificate of the marriage or civil partnership to which the application relates issued under the law in force in the country where the marriage or civil partnership registration took place;

(ii) a similar document issued under the law in force in the country where the marriage or civil partnership registration took place; or

(iii) a certified copy of such a certificate or document obtained from the appropriate register office; and

(b) where the certificate, document or certified copy is not in English (or, where the court is in Wales, in Welsh), a translation of that document certified by a notary public or authenticated by a statement of truth.

Modifications—Where FPR PD36D applies, para 3.1 and the heading are modified to read:

'Proof of marriage

3.1 The online system referred to in Practice Direction 36D sets out the documents which must accompany the application for a matrimonial order. Where the existence and validity of a marriage is not disputed, its validity will be proved by the application being accompanied by –

(a) one of the following –

(i) a certificate of the marriage to which the application relates issued under the law in force in the country where the marriage took place;

(ii) a similar document issued under the law in force in the country where the marriage registration took place; or

(iii) a certified copy of such a certificate or document obtained from the appropriate register office; and

(b) where the certificate, document or certified copy is not in English (or, where the court is in Wales, in Welsh), a translation of that document certified by a notary public or authenticated by a statement of truth.'

Filing without accompanying proof of marriage or civil partnership

3.2 If –

(a) the applicant cannot produce –

(i) the certificate, similar document or a certified copy; and

(ii) (where necessary) an authenticated translation;

at the time of filing the application; and

(b) it is urgent that the application be filed,

the applicant may apply to the court without notice for permission to file the application without the certificate, document, certified copy or authenticated translation.

3.3 The applicant or the applicant's solicitor must in such a case file with the application a statement explaining why –

(a) the required document is not available; and

(b) the application is urgent.

3.4 The court may give permission to file the application without the required document if the applicant gives an undertaking to file that document at the very earliest opportunity and within any time limit set by the court.

Other methods of proof of the marriage or civil partnership

3.5 The requirements of this Practice Direction do not prevent the existence and validity of a marriage, or of an overseas relationship which is not a marriage, being proved in accordance with –

(a) the Evidence (Foreign, Dominion and Colonial Documents) Act 1933; or

(b) any other method authorised in any other Practice Direction, rule or Act.

Information required where evidence of a conviction or finding is to be relied on

4.1 An applicant for a matrimonial or civil partnership order who wishes to rely on evidence –

(a) under section 11 of the Civil Evidence Act 1968 of a conviction of an offence; or

(b) under section 12 of that Act of a finding or adjudication of adultery or paternity,

must include in the application form a statement to that effect and give the following details –

(i) the type of conviction, finding or adjudication and its date;

(ii) the court or Court-Martial which made the conviction, finding or adjudication; and

(iii) the issue in the proceedings to which it relates.

Modifications—Where FPR PD36D applies, para 4.1 is modified to read:

'4.1 Where the pilot scheme referred to in Practice Direction 36D applies, an applicant who wishes to rely on evidence –
(a) under section 11 of the Civil Evidence Act 1968 of a conviction of an offence; or
(b) under section 12 of that Act of a finding or adjudication of adultery or paternity,
must include in the application a statement to that effect and give the following details –
(i) the type of conviction, finding or adjudication and its date;
(ii) the court or Court-Martial which made the conviction, finding or adjudication; and
(iii) the issue in the proceedings to which it relates.'

Supplemental applications and amendments to applications and answers

5.1 An application for permission, where required, to file a supplemental application for a matrimonial or civil partnership order or to amend an application or answer may be dealt with at a hearing.

5.2 When making an application for permission for the purposes of paragraph 5.1, the applicant should file at court –

(a) the notice of application for permission; and
(b) the proposed supplemental application or a copy of the application for a matrimonial or civil partnership order or the answer showing the proposed amendments.

5.3 Where permission has been given for the purposes of paragraph 5.1, the applicant should within 14 days of the date of the order, or within such other period as the court directs, file with the court the amended application for a matrimonial or a civil partnership order, the amended answer or the supplemental application for a matrimonial or civil partnership order.

5.4 A supplemental application should be made on form D8. It should contain the same details of the parties as the original application, set out the supplemental allegations the party seeks to rely upon, state that 'The [Petitioner/Respondent] prays as before', include an address for service and be dated.

PART III

Summary of applications etc. which may be made

5A.1 An applicant may make (i) an application (ii) an amended application (iii) a supplemental application (iv) a further (or second) application. By virtue of being served with such applications, a respondent may file (i) an answer (ii) an answer to an amended application (iii) an answer to a supplemental application (iv) an answer to a further (or second) application. Separately, a respondent may file an amended answer. Rule 7.14 sets out when a respondent may make an application

Requests for further information under rule 7.15 (further information)

6.1 Before making an application under rule 7.15, the party seeking clarification or information ('the requesting party') should first serve a written request for it on the party from whom the clarification or information is sought, giving a date by which a reply should be served. The date should be such as to allow the requested party a reasonable time to respond.

6.2 A request should be made by letter or in a separate document, should contain no other subject matter, and should make clear that it is made under rule 7.15. It must be concise and confined to matters which are reasonably necessary and proportionate to enable the requesting party to prepare his or her own case or understand the case of the party to whom the request is directed.

6.3 The reply to the request must be in writing, dated and signed by the requested party or that party's legal representative.

6.4 The reply may be made by letter or in a separate document, should contain no other subject matter, and should make clear that it is a reply to the request concerned. It should repeat each request together with the reply to it. It must be served on every party to the proceedings.

6.5 A party who objects to replying to all or part of a request under rule 7.15, or who is unable to do so, must inform the requesting party promptly, and in any event within the time within which a reply has been requested, and give reasons for objecting or being unable to reply (as the case may be).

Disclosure and inspection

7.1 Where an application for a matrimonial or civil partnership order is not being dealt with as an undefended case the court may make an order for the disclosure of documents under rule 7.22(2)(c).

7.2 When an order for disclosure is made, the disclosing party must, in order to comply, make a reasonable search for the documents required to be disclosed. The extent of the search will depend upon the circumstances of the case and parties should bear in mind the overriding principle of proportionality.

7.3 Documents should be disclosed in a list which should normally list the documents in date order, numbering them consecutively and giving each a concise description. Where there are a large number of documents falling into a particular category they may be grouped together (e.g. 50 bank statements relating to x account from y date to z date).

7.4 The obligations imposed by a disclosure order continue until the proceedings come to an end. If, after the list of documents has been prepared and served, the existence of further documents to which the order applies comes to the attention of the disclosing party, that party must prepare and serve a supplemental list.

7.5 A list of documents must contain the following statement:

> I, [insert name] state that I have carried out a reasonable and proportionate search to locate all the documents which I am required to disclose under the disclosure order made by the court on [insert date]. [I did not search for [insert here any limitations on search by reference to date, location, nature of documents etc]]. I understand the duty of disclosure and to the best of my knowledge I have carried out that duty. I certify that the list above is a complete list of all the documents which are or have been in my control and which I am obliged under the order to disclose.

7.6 If the disclosing party wishes to claim a right or duty to withhold inspection of a document or part of a document, that party must indicate in writing in the disclosure statement that such a right or duty is claimed, and the grounds on which it is claimed.

Decrees absolute and final orders: need for expedition

8.1 Where a party in an application for a matrimonial order has grounds for expediting the making of the decree absolute, that party should ordinarily seek directions with a view to an early hearing of the case. Where such an application has not been possible, an application should be made to the district judge making the decree nisi for the time between the decree nisi and the making absolute of that decree to be shortened.

8.2 Where the need for expedition only becomes obvious after the making of the decree nisi, or where (exceptionally) it arises in an undefended case to which the summary procedure applies, an application, on notice to the other parties to the proceedings, should be made using the procedure in Part 18 for an order shortening the time before which the decree nisi may be made absolute.

8.3 Where a party in an application for a civil partnership order has grounds for expediting the making of the final order, that party should ordinarily seek directions with a view to an early hearing of the case. Where such an application has not been possible, an application should be made to the district judge making the conditional order for the time between the conditional and final order to be shortened.

8.4 Where the need for expedition only becomes obvious after the making of the conditional order, or where (exceptionally) it arises in an undefended case to which the summary procedure applies, an application, on notice to the other parties to the proceedings, should be made using the procedure in Part 18 for an order shortening the time before which the final order may be made.

Practice Direction 7B – Medical Examinations on Applications for Annulment of a Marriage

This Practice Direction supplements FPR Part 7, rule 7.26 (Medical examinations in proceedings for nullity of marriage)

1.1 Where an application is made for the annulment of a marriage based on the incapacity of one of the parties to consummate, it will not usually be necessary to appoint a medical examiner where the application is undefended. Where the application is defended the court should not appoint a medical examiner unless it appears necessary to do so for the proper disposal of the case.

1.2 A medical examination ordered under rule 7.26 must, if the party to be examined so requests, be conducted by a doctor of the same gender as the person to be examined. Unless both parties are to be examined, each by a doctor of their own gender, it should not normally be necessary to appoint more than one medical examiner.

1.3 The costs of any medical examination ordered under rule 7.26 will be borne, in the first instance, by the party on whose application the medical examiner is appointed. Such costs form part of the costs of the proceedings.

1.4 It is the responsibility of the party on whose application the medical examiner is appointed to address, at the case management hearing, the question of whether any medical examiner is required to attend the final hearing of the proceedings. A medical examiner who is to give evidence at the proceedings is to be treated as an expert witness and the relevant rules in Part 25 (Experts and Assessors) will apply. The relevant rules in Part 25 will also apply to the medical examiner's report.

1.5 Nothing in this Practice Direction or in rule 7.26 affects the parties' right to adduce other evidence relevant to the proper disposal of the case. Such evidence must be verified by a statement of truth.

PART III

Practice Direction 7C – Polygamous Marriages

This Practice Direction supplements FPR Part 7 (procedure for applications in matrimonial and civil partnership proceedings), Part 9 (applications for a financial remedy) and Part 18 (procedure for other applications in proceedings)

Scope of this Practice Direction

1.1 This practice direction applies where an application is made for –

(a) a matrimonial order;
(b) an order under section 27 of the 1973 Act;
(c) an order under section 35 of the 1973 Act;
(d) an order under the 1973 Act which is made in connection with, or with proceedings for any of the above orders; or
(e) an order under Part 3 of the 1984 Act,

and either party to the marriage is, or has during the course of the marriage, been married to more than one person (a polygamous marriage).

Polygamous marriages

2.1 Where this practice direction applies the application must state –

(a) that the marriage is polygamous;

(b) whether, as far as the party to the marriage is aware, any other spouse (that is, a spouse other than the spouse to whom the application relates) of that party is still living (the 'additional spouse'); and

(c) if there is such an additional spouse –

   (i) the additional spouse's name and address;

   (ii) the date and place of the marriage to the additional spouse.

2.2 A respondent who believes that the marriage is polygamous must include the details referred to in paragraph 2.1 above in the acknowledgment of service if they are not included in the application.

2.3 The applicant in any proceedings to which this practice direction applies must apply to the court for directions as soon as possible after the filing of the application or the receipt of an acknowledgment of service mentioning an additional spouse.

2.4 On such an application or of its own initiative the court may –

(a) give the additional spouse notice of any of the proceedings to which this practice direction applies; and

(b) make the additional spouse a party to such proceedings.

2.5 In any case where the application or acknowledgment of service states that the marriage is polygamous (whether or not there is an additional spouse) a court officer must clearly mark the file with the words 'Polygamous Marriage'. The court officer must also check whether an application under paragraph 2.4 has been made in the case and, where no application has been made, refer the file to the court for consideration.

References in decrees to section 47 of the 1973 Act

3.1 Every decree nisi and decree absolute which is made in respect of a polygamous marriage must refer to the fact that the order is made with reference to section 47 of the 1973 Act.

Practice Direction 7D – Gender Recognition Act 2004

This Practice Direction supplements FPR Part 7

1 Introduction

The Gender Recognition Act 2004 ('the Act') provides transsexual people with the opportunity to obtain legal recognition in their acquired gender. Legal recognition follows from the issue of a full gender recognition certificate by a Gender Recognition Panel. Section 4 of the Act requires that where a Panel has granted an application to a married applicant, the gender recognition certificate that it must issue shall be an interim gender recognition certificate. The interim certificate may then be used by either party to the marriage as evidence in support of an application to annul the marriage under section 12(g) of, or paragraph 11(1)(e) of Schedule 1 to, the Matrimonial Causes Act 1973 (*'that an interim gender recognition certificate has, after the time of the marriage, been issued to either party to the marriage'*).

2 Application

2.1 This Practice Direction applies to proceedings for divorce, judicial separation and annulment of marriage commenced on or after **4 April 2005**.

2.2 Where proceedings for divorce, judicial separation or annulment of marriage have been commenced prior to this date, paragraphs 3.2 to 3.5 below shall also apply to those proceedings if, but only if, the court acquires protected information (as defined by section 22 of the Act) in respect of a party to those proceedings.

3 *Title of the cause*

3.1 When a party to a matrimonial cause has changed his or her name since marriage, by deed poll or otherwise, the name currently being used by the party should appear first on any petition, answer and statement of arrangements followed by 'formerly known as .... (married name)'.

3.2 Subject to paragraph 3.3, when describing the parties in any Decree, Order, Notice or other document issued by the court, the parties should be described by their full current names only.

3.3 When giving details of the parties in any court list (including a special procedure cause list) they should be described by the initials and surname of their current names only. (For example, A B Jones v C D Jones).

3.4 For the sake of clarity, in any document or court list mentioned in paragraphs 3.2 and 3.3 above party titles (ie Mr, Mrs, Miss, etc.) should be omitted.

3.5 The Practice Note of 2 May 1940 (Title of Cause) shall cease to have effect.

4 *Evidence at trial of cause*

4.1 This part of the Practice Direction applies where the following conditions are met:

(a) proceedings for annulment of marriage are brought under Section 12(g) of, or paragraph 11(1)(e) of Schedule 1 to, the Matrimonial Causes Act 1973 and paragraph 11 of Schedule 1 to, that Act; and

(b) the cause is an undefended cause.

4.2 Any party requesting directions for trial may, in addition to the requirements of FPR rule 2.25(2), state in their request that they would wish to give their evidence at the trial of the cause in accordance with the provisions of this Practice Direction; and in that event, the request must be accompanied by an affidavit setting out the information required by the appendix to this Practice Direction.

4.3 Where directions for trial are given in accordance with FPR rule 2.24(5) in respect of a request to which paragraph 4.2 applies, a direction may also be given under Rule 2.28(3) that the affidavit lodged with the request for directions shall be treated as the evidence of that party at the trial of the cause (unless otherwise directed).

4.4 In the case of an undefended cause proceeding on the respondent's answer, this part of the Practice Direction and the contents of the appendix shall apply with appropriate modifications.

4.5 The appendix sets out a form of affidavit that may be used for the purposes of paragraph 4.2.

5 Issued with the approval and concurrence of the Lord Chancellor.

APPENDIX

A FORM OF AFFIDAVIT FOR THE PURPOSES OF PARAGRAPH 4.2

Affidavit by Petitioner in support of petition for annulment under Section 12(g) of the Matrimonial Causes Act 1973

No. of matter:

* Delete as appropriate.

IN THE COUNTY COURT*
[PRINCIPAL REGISTRY OF THE FAMILY DIVISION*]

Between (Petitioner)

and (Respondent)

and (Co-Respondent)

QUESTION	ANSWER
About the Petition 1. Have you read the petition in this case?	
2. Do you wish to alter or to add to any statement in the petition? If so, state the alterations or additions.	
3. Subject to these alterations or additions (if any) is everything stated in your petition true? If any statement is not within your own knowledge, indicate this and say whether it is true to the best of your information and belief.	
About the interim gender recognition certificate 4. State the date on which the interim gender recognition certificate was issued: State the serial number of the interim certificate: State the name of the person to whom the certificate has been issued:	

State the date on which you commenced proceedings to annul your marriage: **You must attach a copy of the interim gender recognition certificate to this form.**	
About other proceedings 5. To the best of your knowledge and belief has there been or is there continuing any of the following proceedings; • an application to amend an error in the interim certificate; • an appeal against a decision to amend (or not to amend) an error in the interim certificate; • a reference under section 8(5) of the Gender Recognition Act 2004; or • an appeal against a decision made following a reference under section 8(5)? If so, please give details of those proceedings and any order made. (You should also attach copies of any orders made).	
About the children of the family 6. Has a Statement of Arrangements been filed in this case? If so, answer questions 7, 8 and 9.	
7. Have you read the Statement of Arrangements filed in this case?	
8. Do you wish to alter anything in the Statement of Arrangements or add to it? If so, state the alterations or additions.	
9. Subject to these alterations and additions (if any) is everything stated in the **Statement of Arrangements** true? If any statement is not within your own knowledge, indicate this and say whether it is true and correct to the best of your information and belief.	

I, (full name)

of (full residential address)

(occupation)

make oath and say as follows:-

1. I am the petitioner in this cause.

2. **The answers to Questions 1 to 9 above are true.**

3.[1] I identify the signature ....[2]
appearing in the copy acknowledgement of service now produced to me and marked "A" as the signature of my husband / wife, the respondent in this cause.

4. I exhibit marked "B" a copy of the interim gender recognition certificate issued to myself / the respondent in this cause.

5. [3]

6. I identify the signature..[2]
appearing at Part IV of the Statement of Arrangements dated....................................
now produced to me and marked "C" as the signature of the respondent.

7. I ask the court to grant a decree annulling my marriage with the respondent on the ground stated in my petition [and to order the respondent / co-respondent to pay the costs of this suit]. [4]

(1) Delete if the acknowledgement is signed by a solicitor.

(2) Insert name of the respondent exactly as it appears on the acknowledgement signed by him or her.

(3) If you have answered "Yes" to question 5, exhibit any document on which you wish to rely.

(4) Amend or delete as appropriate.

Sworn at

In the County of

this day of 20

Before me, ...

A Commissioner for Oaths [5]
Officer of the Court appointed by the Judge to take Affidavits

(5) Delete as the case may be.

PART 8
PROCEDURE FOR MISCELLANEOUS APPLICATIONS

CONTENTS OF THIS PART

Chapter 1

Rule		Page
	Procedure	
8.1	Procedure	1418
	Chapter 2 *Application for Corrected Gender Recognition Certificate*	
8.2	Scope of this Chapter	1418
8.3	Where to start proceedings	1418
8.4	Who the parties are	1418
8.5	Delivery of copy certificate to Secretary of State	1418
	Chapter 3 *Application for Alteration of Maintenance Agreement after Death of One Party*	
8.6	Scope of this Chapter	1419
8.8	Who the parties are	1419
8.9	Representative parties	1419
8.10	Acknowledgment of service	1420
8.11	Hearings may be in private	1420
	Chapter 4 *Application for Question as to Property to be Decided in Summary Way*	
8.12	Scope of this Chapter	1420
8.13	Procedure	1420
8.14	Where to start proceedings	1420
8.15	Mortgagees as parties	1420
8.16	Injunctions	1421
8.17	Application of other rules	1421
	Chapter 5 *Declarations*	
8.18	Scope of this Chapter	1421
8.20	Who the parties are	1423
8.21	The role of the Attorney General	1424
8.22	Declarations of parentage	1424
	Chapter 6 *Application for Permission to Apply for a Financial Remedy after Overseas Proceedings*	
8.23	Scope of this Chapter	1424
8.24	How to start proceedings	1424
8.25	Application without notice	1425
8.26	Notification of hearing date	1425
8.27	Hearings to be in private unless the court directs otherwise	1425
8.28	Direction that application be dealt with by a district judge of the principal registry	1425
	Chapter 7 *Application for the Transfer of a Tenancy under Section 53 of, and Schedule 7 to, the 1996 Act*	
8.29	Scope of this Chapter	1426
8.30	Where to start proceedings	1426
8.31	Service of the application	1426
8.32	Who the parties are	1426
8.33	Orders for disclosure	1426

PART III

8.34 Injunctions 1426

Chapter 9
Application for Consent to Marriage of a Child or to Registration of Civil Partnership of a Child

8.41 Scope of this Chapter 1426
8.42 Child acting without a children's guardian 1427
8.43 Who the respondents are 1427

Practice Direction 8A –
Where to Start Certain Proceedings 1427

Chapter 1
Procedure

8.1 Procedure

Subject to rules 8.13 and 8.24, applications to which this Part applies must be made in accordance with the Part 19 procedure.

General note—FPR 2010, Pt 19 provides an alternative procedure for applications, where the FPR 2010, Pt 18 procedure does not apply. See, generally, annotations to FPR 2010, r 19.1 and FPR PD19A. FPR 2010, r 8.13 relates to MWPA 1882, s 17/CPA 2004, s 66 and r 8.24 relates to MFPA 1984, Pt III/CPA 2004, Sch 7, where specific procedures and forms apply.

Chapter 2
Application for Corrected Gender Recognition Certificate

General note—This chapter makes provision for an application to the court under the Gender Recognition Act 2004, s 6 to correct an error in a gender recognition certificate issued by the court. The application is made to the court only where the application was determined by the court. In any other case, the application to correct is to a Gender Recognition Panel.

8.2 Scope of this Chapter

The rules in this Chapter apply to an application under section 6(1) of the Gender Recognition Act 2004 for the correction of a full gender recognition certificate issued under section 5(1) or 5A(1) of that Act.

8.3 Where to start proceedings

The application must be made to the court which issued the original certificate unless the court directs otherwise.

8.4 Who the parties are

Where the applicant is –

(a) the person to whom the original certificate was issued, the Secretary of State must be a respondent;
(b) the Secretary of State, the person to whom the original certificate was issued must be a respondent.

8.5 Delivery of copy certificate to Secretary of State

Where the court issues a corrected full gender recognition certificate, a court officer must send a copy of the corrected certificate to the Secretary of State.

Chapter 3
Application for Alteration of Maintenance Agreement after Death of One Party

8.6 Scope of this Chapter

The rules in this Chapter apply to an application under section 36 of the 1973 Act or paragraph 73 of Schedule 5 to the 2004 Act to alter a maintenance agreement after the death of one of the parties.

Defined terms—'maintenance agreement': MCA 1973, s 34(2).

8.7 *(revoked)*

8.8 Who the parties are

(1) Where the applicant is –

- (a) the surviving party to the agreement, the personal representative of the deceased must be a respondent;
- (b) the personal representative of the deceased, the surviving party to the agreement must be a respondent.

(2) The court may at any time direct that –

- (a) any person be made a party to proceedings; or
- (b) a party be removed.

8.9 Representative parties

(1) The court may, before or after the application has been filed at court, make an order appointing a person to represent any other person or persons in the application where the person or persons to be represented –

- (a) are unborn;
- (b) cannot be found;
- (c) cannot easily be ascertained; or
- (d) are a class of persons who have the same interest in an application and –
  - (i) one or more members of that class are within sub-paragraphs (a), (b) or (c); or
  - (ii) to appoint a representative would further the overriding objective.

(2) An application for an order under paragraph (1) may be made by –

- (a) any person who seeks to be appointed under the order; or
- (b) any party to the application.

(3) An application for an order under paragraph (1) must be served on –

- (a) all parties to the application to alter the maintenance agreement, if that application has been filed at court;
- (b) the person sought to be appointed, if that person is not the applicant or a party to the application; and
- (c) any other person as directed by the court.

(4) The court's approval is required to settle proceedings in which a party is acting as a representative.

(5) The court may approve a settlement where it is satisfied that the settlement is for the benefit of all the represented persons.

(6) Unless the court directs otherwise, any order made on an application in which a party is acting as a representative –

- (a) is binding on all persons represented in the proceedings; and
- (b) may only be enforced by or against a person who is not a party with the permission of the court.

PART III

(7) An application may be brought by or against trustees, executors or administrators without adding as parties any persons who have a beneficial interest in the trust or estate and any order made on the application is binding on the beneficiaries unless the court orders otherwise.

8.10 Acknowledgment of service

(1) A respondent who is a personal representative of the deceased must file with the acknowledgment of service a statement setting out –

- (a) full particulars of the value of the deceased's estate for probate after providing for the discharge of the funeral, testamentary and administration expenses, debts and liabilities (including inheritance tax and interest); and
- (b) the people (including names, addresses and details of any persons under disability) or classes of people beneficially interested in the estate and the value of their interests so far as ascertained.

(2) The respondent must file the acknowledgment of service and any statement required under this rule within 28 days beginning with the date on which the application is served.

8.11 Hearings may be in private

The court may decide to hear any application to which this Chapter applies in private.

Chapter 4

Application for Question as to Property to be Decided in Summary Way

8.12 Scope of this Chapter

The rules in this Chapter apply to an application under section 17 of the Married Women's Property Act 1882 or section 66 of the 2004 Act.

8.13 Procedure

Where an application for an order under section 17 of the Married Women's Property Act 1882 or section 66 of the 2004 Act is made in any proceedings for a financial order, the application must be made in accordance with the Part 18 procedure.

Defined terms—'financial order' is defined in FPR 2010, r 2.3, which provides a list of nine orders defined as a 'financial order'. This is drawn more widely than previously under FPR 1991, r 2.51B.

Procedure—The application may be made in the Family Court, in accordance with FPR 2010, Pt 18 procedure. Where particulars of a mortgage are provided with the application, a mortgagee must be served with a copy of the application, and must be made a party if requested by the mortgagee. Injunctions may be granted only if ancillary or incidental to the assistance sought by the applicant.

8.14 Where to start proceedings

Where any matrimonial proceedings or civil partnership proceedings have been started, or are intended to be started, by the applicant or the respondent, the application must be made in the same court as those matrimonial proceedings or civil partnership proceedings.

(Practice Direction 8A makes provision in respect of the particular location where the application should be made.)

Amendments—Substituted by SI 2013/3204.

8.15 Mortgagees as parties

(1) Where particulars of a mortgage are provided with the application –

- (a) the applicant must serve a copy of the application on the mortgagee; and
- (b) the mortgagee may, within 14 days beginning with the date on which the application was received, file an acknowledgment of service and be heard on the application.

(2) The court must direct that a mortgagee be made a party to the proceedings where the mortgagee requests to be one.

8.16 Injunctions

(1) The court may grant an injunction(GL) only if the injunction(GL) is ancillary or incidental to the assistance sought by the applicant.

(2) Applications for injunctive relief must be made in accordance with the procedure in rule 20.4 (how to apply for an interim remedy) and the provisions of rule 20.5 (interim injunction(GL) to cease if application is stayed(GL)) apply.

8.17 Application of other rules

Rule 9.24 applies where the court has made an order for sale under section 17 of the Married Women's Property Act 1882 or section 66 of the 2004 Act.

Chapter 5

Declarations

Introductory note: declarations and the inherent jurisdiction as an originating jurisdiction—The declaration is a common law remedy (perhaps mostly associated with the prerogative jurisdiction of the High Court (SCA 1981, s 31(2)). The declaration may be applied for in family (especially children) proceedings (see discussion under CA 1989, s 100(2) and in *Gillick v West Norfolk and Wisbech Area Health Authority and Another* [1986] 1 FLR 224, HL, esp per Lord Scarman). The declaration is associated particularly with publicity or immunisation of children in care (*LCC v A & Ors* [2011] EWHC 4033 (Fam)). In *Rolls-Royce plc v Unite the Union* [2009] EWCA Civ 387, the Court of Appeal explained when an application for a declaration would be appropriate in civil proceedings. The inherent jurisdiction of the High Court was utilised by Keehan J in *Birmingham City Council v Riaz and Others* [2015] 2 FLR 763, FD and its limits delineated, as he saw it, by Hayden J in *London Borough of Redbridge v SNA* [2016] 1 FLR 994, FD.

'originating summons' application in inherent jurisdiction—Typically, application will be made in the High Court, but so far as the High Court has the jurisdiction so too does the Family Court (MFPA 1984, s 31E(1)(a)). In *CM v The Executor of the Estate of EJ (Deceased) and Her Majesty's Coroner* [2013] 2 FLR 1410, FD (application under Human Tissues Act 2004) the applicant used what Cobb J described as 'the originating summons procedure under the inherent jurisdiction' probably best adapted from the FPR 2010, Pt 19 procedure.

Procedure: Part 19—The general rule is that all applications under FPR 2010, Pt 8 are by the FPR 2010, Pt 19 procedure and this includes applications under Pt 8, Ch 5 for declarations in relation to status (FLA 1986, Pt 3 and CPA 2004, s 58). Whereas each of the applications for a declaration had a separate rule in FPR 1991, the four under consideration here are incorporated together in Ch 5.

Part 19 requirements—FPR 2010, Pt 19 applies to the declaration application (r 19.3(a)). A document filed with the FPR PD5A application form (see above) will be required to state:

- the issue the applicant wants the court to decide (r 19.3(b)(i));
- the 'enactment' under which the application is being made, i e FLA 1986, s 55A (r 19.3(c));
- details of any representative capacity in which the application is made (r 19.3(d)) and of any representative capacity in which a respondent might appear (r 19.3(e));
- the 'sufficient personal interest' of the applicant in the application (FLA 1986, s 55A(3),(4)) or that CSA 1991, s 27(2) applies, that is:
  - (a) that the applicant is the person with care of the child (i e looking after the child for child support purposes); or
  - (b) that (where applicable) the applicant is the Secretary of State for Work and Pensions;
- the grounds on which the applicant relies for his assertion that he is entitled to seek the declaration and, if he is asserting that he is not a parent, why none of the cases in CSA 1991, s 26 applies to him;
- the 'legal basis of the application' made by the applicant (r 19.3(b)(ii)) or the terms of the order sought;
- details of any directions sought by the applicant (FPR 2010, Pt 18), e g as to disclosure of documents, scientific tests (see below).

Progress of the application—FPR 2010, Pt 19 deals with progress of the application (rr 19.5–19.7) and, in particular, with evidence (rr 19.7, 19.8). Rule 19.5 requires that each respondent who wishes to take part at a final hearing (compare r 19.6(2)) must file an acknowledgement of service, together with any evidence on which he intends to rely (r 19.7(1)).

8.18 Scope of this Chapter

The rules in this Chapter apply to applications made in accordance with –

(a) section 55 of the 1986 Act (declarations as to marital status) and section 58 of the 2004 Act (declarations as to civil partnership status);

(b) section 55A of the 1986 Act (declarations of parentage);

(c) section 56(1)(b) and (2) of the 1986 Act (declarations of legitimacy or legitimation); and

(d) section 57 of the 1986 Act (declaration as to adoptions effected overseas).

PART III

Application form—Application for a declaration is by application form, i e 'other than under the Part 18 procedure' (FPR 2010, r 2.3(1)). FPR PD5A prescribes the following application forms:

- C63 – declaration of parentage under FLA 1986, s 55A (new form from 6 April 2017);
- C64 – declaration of legitimacy or legitimation under FLA 1986, s 56(1)(b) and (2) (new form from 6 April 2017);
- C65 – declaration as to adoption effected overseas under FLA 1986, s 57;
- D70 – declaration of marital/civil partnership status.

Requirements of r 19.3—The requirements of FPR 2010, Pt 19 and specifically of r 19.3 must be borne in mind alongside the form's disclosure requirements, for example:

– Form C63 (Section 3) asks for 'brief details about why you are making this application' and forbids the filing of a 'full statement'. FPR 2010, Pt 19 requires the applicant to state either the question to be decided or a draft order and its legal basis (r 19.3(b)) and also to file all 'written evidence on which the applicant intends to rely' (r 19.7(1)). In a declaration as to marital status or adoption this may be copious.
– No section is left in comparable CPR 1998, Pt 8 applications for an application by the applicant for a scientific test direction, which will be the inevitable consequence of certain declaration applications (see FLRA 1969, s 20).
– If an alleged non-resident parent is asserting that he is not a parent, he should say somewhere in Form C63 why none of the cases in CSA 1991, s 26 apply to him.

Answer to the application—This must be by acknowledgment of service (FPR 2010, r 19.5). No form is prescribed for this. The acknowledgment of service must be accompanied by any evidence on which the respondent intends to rely (FPR 2010, r 19.7(3)). An answer might include an application by the respondent, for example:

– to apply the application to be struck out (FPR 2010, r 4.4), e g (1) where another court has already made a declaration or made a finding which proves parentage; or (2) the respondent denies that the applicant has sufficient personal interest (FLA 1986, s 55A(3)) to make application;
– to seek disclosure of particular documents.

Parentage and parenthood in issue—The procedure distinguishes between person whose parentage is in issue (i e the child, who may be an adult by the time of the application); and a person whose parenthood is in issue (i e the father or putative father, or fathers).

Parties to a parentage declaration application (r 8.20(1))—The parties to an application under FLA 1986, s 55A will depend on by whom the issue is raised and by whom and how it is responded to. For example:

(1) On an application by a father, the child will be 'the person whose parentage is in issue' and the mother will also be a respondent.
(2) On an application by the Secretary of State for Work and Pensions, under CSA 1991, both parents and the child will be respondents.

Application for a parentage declaration—The remedy provided by FLA 1986, s 55A (which was inserted into the 1986 Act by CSPSSA 2000 and is closely interdependent on CSA 1991, s 27) is a declaration as to whether one person (it will always be a father) 'is or was the parent of another person' named in the application (FLA 1986, s 55A). Application for a declaration may be by others than members of the immediate family: e g a government department, local authority, Child Support Agency or other party with 'sufficient interest'. The statutory ground for obtaining a scientific test is FLRA 1969, s 20.

Applications in parentage declaration proceedings—In the application the applicant would be advised to draft into the document prepared a formal application for scientific tests. In principle, the application proceeds as a FPR 2010, Pt 18 application. An early, short court appointment (normally before a district judge) should be fixed for application for a direction to be dealt with (see **The tests direction** under FLRA 1969, s 20).

Respondent's acknowledgement of service and any applications— FPR 2010, Rule 19.5(3) deals with the respondent's opposition to the application. Any acknowledgement of service can indicate whether the respondent 'contests the application' (r 19.5(3)(a); and see FPR 2010, r 8.20(3)); and the extent of and basis for that opposition. It will be necessary for the respondent to apply for any of these issues to be considered or tried by the court under the FPR 2010, Pt 18 procedure. Any witness statement in support would need to be supported by full grounds for the application. For example:

(1) A respondent may challenge whether the applicant has 'sufficient interest' to bring the application (see FLA 1986, s 55A(3)).
(2) Application to strike out on grounds that the applicant (say) has no grounds for bringing the application or as an abuse of process (or res judicata: see for example *Law v Ahumuda & ors* [2011] 1 FLR 708, CA).

If either of these preliminary applications succeeded, there would be no basis for the court to direct blood tests.

Case management and representation of any child respondent—If preliminary issues are raised the court will direct the order in which they are dealt with (and see FPR 2010, r 1.4(2)(c)). If the 'person named', i e the child whose parentage is in issue, is still a child, consideration may be needed for the child to be joined as a party and be represented by a litigation friend (FPR 2010, Pt 16, Ch 5).

Appeals to a court under CSA 1991, s 20 and Ch 5— FPR PD30A, para 12.1 directs that 'the rules in Chs 1 and 5 of Pt 8 will apply as appropriate to an appeal' under CSA 1991, s 20. All appeals under s 20 go to the First-Tier Tribunal, save for appeals that raise a question of parentage, which go to the Family Court (Child Support Appeals (Jurisdiction of Courts) Order 2002). The two sets of provisions (i e FPR 2010, Pt 8, Ch 5 and FPR PD30A, paras 12.1–12.3) have in common that the result of the process that they describe may be a declaration of parentage. It is difficult to see how Ch 5 can assist the parties. Procedure for a s 20 child support appeal is dealt with fully under Tribunal Procedure (First-tier Tribunal) (Social Entitlement Chamber) Rules 2008 and the magistrates only provide a venue for trial of the issues (i e all of the issues per Art 4 of the 2002 Order), whereas Ch 5 is procedural for a different set of application issues. Further, Ch 5 is governed by the FPR 2010, Pt 19 procedure, which need have nothing to do with CSA 1991, s 20 appeals. The justices will hear issues such as directing a scientific test report, but they do not need the FPR 2010, Pt 19 procedure for this. They will rely on the Pt 18 procedure for such a direction (CPR PD30A, paras 13.1 and 13.2).

8.19 *(revoked)*

8.20 Who the parties are

(1) In relation to the proceedings set out in column 1 of the following table, column 2 sets out who the respondents to those proceedings will be.

Proceedings	*Respondent*
Applications for declarations as to marital or civil partnership status.	The other party to the marriage or civil partnership in question or, where the applicant is a third party, both parties to the marriage or civil partnership.
Applications for declarations of parentage.	(i) The person whose parentage is in issue except where that person is a child; and (ii) any person who is or is alleged to be the parent of the person whose parentage is in issue, except where that person is the applicant or is a child.
Applications for declarations of legitimacy or legitimation.	The applicant's father and mother or the survivor of them.
Applications for declarations as to adoption effected overseas.	The person(s) whom the applicant is claiming are or are not the applicant's adoptive parents.

(Under rule 16.2 the court may make a child a party to certain proceedings (including applications for declarations of parentage) where it considers that to be in the best interests of the child.)

(2) The applicant must include in his application particulars of every person whose interest may be affected by the proceedings and his relationship to the applicant.

(3) The acknowledgment of service filed under rule 19.5 must give details of any other persons the respondent considers should be made a party to the application or be given notice of the application.

(4) Upon receipt of the acknowledgment of service, the court must give directions as to any other persons who should be made a respondent to the application or be given notice of the proceedings.

(5) A person given notice of proceedings under paragraph (4) may, within 21 days beginning with the date on which the notice was served, apply to be joined as a party.

(6) No directions may be given as to the future management of the case under rule 19.9 until the expiry of the notice period in paragraph (5).

Amendments—SI 2012/679; SI 2016/901.

Adding parties to the application—Rule 8.20(3)–(5) deals with the question of who might be required to be joined as a party to the application. It is likely that the court will treat CPR r 19.2 as representing the common law on this subject, in the absence of any specific general family proceedings provision for joinder of addition of parties.

Child not to be respondent—With effect from 3 October 2016, the table in r 8.20(1) has been amended to provide that any child concerned in the proceedings is excluded from the class of possible respondents.

'respondent considers should be made a party' (r 8.20(3))—This rule gives the respondent no indication as to on what ground anyone else might be added as a party; but see the note above.

'directions as to who should be made a respondent' (r 8.20(4))—This rule requires a person to be made a party. For an assessment of grounds for this to be done, see the note above. A party added as a respondent will have to apply to have the order set aside on grounds analogous to setting aside a witness summons (see FPR 2010, r 24.2).

'apply to be joined as a party' (r 8.20(5))—FPR 2010, r 9.26B has been inserted (see above). This rule may be permitted as a criterion for joining as a party.

Application involving person who lacks capacity—An application under FLA 1986, s 55A involving a person who lacks capacity cannot be issued in the Court of Protection, but since the respondent to such an application must be a third party, probably the Official Solicitor, the application is likely to be transferred to the High Court and heard by a judge with Court of Protection jurisdiction (*LG v DK* [2012] COPLR 80, Sir Nicholas Wall P). This decision considers the approach to declarations as to paternity in different circumstances.

8.21 The role of the Attorney General

(1) The applicant must, except in the case of an application for a declaration of parentage, send a copy of the application and all accompanying documents to the Attorney General at least one month before making the application.

(2) The Attorney General may, when deciding whether to intervene in the proceedings, inspect any document filed at court relating to any family proceedings mentioned in the declaration proceedings.

(3) If the court is notified that the Attorney General wishes to intervene in the proceedings, a court officer must send the Attorney General a copy of any subsequent documents filed at court.

(4) The court must, when giving directions under rule 8.20(4), consider whether to ask the Attorney General to argue any question relating to the proceedings.

(5) If the court makes a request to the Attorney General under paragraph (4) and the Attorney General agrees to that request, the Attorney General must serve a summary of the argument on all parties to the proceedings.

'send a copy of the application to the Attorney General' (r 8.21(1))—This complies with the requirements of FLA 1986, s 59, but in requiring that the application be sent to the Attorney General before it is filed, r 8.21(1) goes further than s 59.

8.22 Declarations of parentage

(1) If the applicant or the person whose parentage or parenthood is in issue, is known by a name other than that which appears in that person's birth certificate, that other name must also be stated in any order and declaration of parentage.

(2) A court officer must send a copy of a declaration of parentage and the application to the Registrar General within 21 days beginning with the date on which the declaration was made.

Delay in registration—The time for registration could be delayed by order of the court but by a limited period only. FLA 1996, s 55A(7) provides that a period for registration of a declaration be prescribed and r 8.22 restricts this to 21 days. This should be the norm and any divergence should only occur in exceptional circumstances (*Re F (Children: Declaration of Parentage)* [2013] 2 FLR 1036, CA: 4 months is permissible; 4 years was plainly too long).

Chapter 6
Application for Permission to Apply for a Financial Remedy after Overseas Proceedings

8.23 Scope of this Chapter

Subject to rule 9.26(6) the rules in this Chapter apply to an application for permission to apply for a financial remedy under section 13 of the 1984 Act and paragraph 4 of Schedule 7 to the 2004 Act.

> (Rule 9.26(6) enables the application for permission to apply for a financial remedy under section 13 of the 1984 Act or paragraph 4 of Schedule 7 to the 2004 Act to be heard at the same time as the application for a financial remedy under Part 3 of the 1984 Act or Schedule 7 to the 2004 Act where that application is an application for a consent order.)

8.24 How to start proceedings

The application must be made in accordance with the Part 18 procedure.

Amendments—Substituted by SI 2013/3204.

Defined terms—'Financial remedy' (r 2.3).

Application—Application is for permission under MFPA 1984, Pt III in Form D50E and Form D50F. The application must be accompanied by a statement by the applicant. Form D50F sets out the matters that the court expects to see in the statement and this must be supplemented by the factors set out in the checklist in

MFPA 1984, s 16(2). If permission is granted, the substantive application proceeds under FPR 2010, Pt 9, as if Form A had been issued and subject to any case-management directions given at the time of permission being granted.

The hearing of the application—The practice in London has been for a without notice hearing in the RCJ before a judge of the Division, with a time estimate of 30 minutes, to filter out unmeritorious claims that may oppress or blackmail a former spouse: *Agbaje v Agbaje* [2010] 1 FLR 1813, SC. The practice of giving notice to respondents has been disapproved by the Court of Appeal in *Traversa v Freddi* [2011] 2 FLR 272, CA. In *Barnett v Barnett* [2014] EWHC 2678 (Fam), it was proposed that it was in the interest of efficient use of both High Court and local judicial resources that suitable applications for leave, and also substantive hearings, could be heard within the Family Court outside London, including by district judges. See r 8.26 below in respect of the leave application.

Draft order—It is central to the FPR 2010, Pt 18 procedure that a draft order accompanies the application. This should include disposal of the application and any case-management directions sought by the applicant if permission is granted.

8.25 Application without notice

(1) The court may grant an application made without notice if it appears to the court that there are good reasons for not giving notice.

(2) If the applicant makes an application without giving notice, the applicant must state the reasons why notice has not been given.

Amendments—SI 2014/3296.

Made without notice—Munby LJ in *Traversa v Freddi* [2011] 2 FLR 272, CA (at [57]) describes the wording of this provision as 'slightly odd', but he explains what it means in the context of this rule and FPR 2010, Pt 18. He holds that the sense of the rule, in conjunction with *Agbaje v Agbaje* [2010] 1 FLR 1813, SC, means that the application in the first instance is without notice and that the court can refuse to make an order when the application is listed on notice to the applicant ('not, it may be noted, to the respondent', at [57]).

8.26 Notification of hearing date

The court officer must –

(a) fix a date, time and place for the hearing of the application; and

(b) give notice of the date of the hearing to the applicant.

Amendments—SI 2014/3296.

Notification of hearing—Rule 8.26 previously excluded a district judge from hearing of the leave application for financial remedy after overseas divorce (*Barnett v Barnett* [2014] EWHC 2678 (Fam)). See r 8.24, above.

8.27 Hearings to be in private unless the court directs otherwise

An application under this Chapter must be heard in private unless the court directs otherwise.

8.28 Direction that application be dealt with by a district judge of the principal registry

In the High Court, if the application is granted, the judge may direct that the application for a financial remedy under Part 3 of the 1984 Act or Schedule 7 to the 2004 Act may be heard by a district judge of the principal registry.

Amendments—SI 2013/3204.

Allocation—Under FC(CDB)R 2014, r 15(1) and Sch 1, para 4(a), proceedings where the permission application is opposed or where there is consent to the permission application but not to the substantive order sought should be allocated to a judge of High Court level. However, FC(CDB)R 2014, r 15(2) makes it clear that allocation to High Court level is 'subject to the need to take into account the need to make the most effective and efficient use of local judicial resource and the resource of the High Court bench that it appropriate given the nature and type of the application'. In *Barnett v Barnett* [2014] EWHC 2678 (Fam), Holman J stated that contested applications for permission and for a substantive order under MFPA 1984 should be dealt with at district judge level unless the matter involves 'some special feature, or complexity, or very substantial assets', at [22].

Chapter 7
Application for the Transfer of a Tenancy under Section 53 of, and Schedule 7 to, the 1996 Act

Scope—This rule regulates the procedure for transfer of tenancies on divorce or the separation of cohabitants under FLA 1996, s 53 and Sch 7. See commentary to s 53 and Procedural Guide A11.

Procedure—The application may be made to the High Court or the County Court, or to the court in which there are pending divorce or civil partnership proceedings, if applicable. The application will be served on the respondent and normally upon the landlord who will be made a party if he requests it. The court has the power to grant an injunction.

8.29 Scope of this Chapter

This Chapter applies to an application for the transfer of a tenancy under section 53 of, and Schedule 7 to, the 1996 Act.

8.30 Where to start proceedings

Where any matrimonial proceedings or civil partnership proceedings have been started by the applicant or the respondent, the application must be made in the same court as those matrimonial proceedings or civil partnership proceedings.

(Practice Direction 8A makes provision in respect of the particular location where the application should be made.)

Amendments—Substituted by SI 2013/3204.

8.31 Service of the application

(1) The court will serve a copy of the application on –

(a) the respondent; and
(b) the landlord (as defined by paragraph 1 of Schedule 7 to the 1996 Act),

unless the court directs that the applicant must do so.

(2) Where service is effected by the applicant, the applicant must file a certificate of service.

8.32 Who the parties are

The court will direct that a landlord be made a party to the proceedings where the landlord requests to be one.

8.33 Orders for disclosure

Any party may apply to the court under rule 21.2 for an order that any person must attend an appointment before the court and produce any documents that are specified or described in the order.

8.34 Injunctions

(1) The court may grant an injunction(GL) only if the injunction(GL) is ancillary or incidental to the assistance sought by the applicant.

(2) Applications for injunctive relief must be made in accordance with the procedure in rule 20.4 (how to apply for an interim remedy) and the provisions of rule 20.5 (interim injunction(GL) to cease if application is stayed(GL)) apply accordingly.

****

Chapter 9
Application for Consent to Marriage of a Child or to Registration of Civil Partnership of a Child

8.41 Scope of this Chapter

The rules in this Chapter apply to an application under –

(a) section 3 of the Marriage Act 1949; or
(b) paragraph 3, 4 or 10 of Schedule 2 to the 2004 Act.

Scope—This rule makes provision for the procedure for an application under either the Marriage Act 1949, s 3 (consent of the court to the marriage of a minor) or under CPA 2004, Sch 2, para 3 (where the required consent of a person to the registration of a civil partnership of a child is unobtainable due to absence, inaccessibility or disability, where the special procedure for registration does not apply), para 4 (where the required consent has been refused, where the special procedure does not apply) and para 10 (where the required consent is unobtainable or has been refused, where the special procedure does not apply).

8.42 Child acting without a children's guardian

The child may bring an application without a children's guardian, unless the court directs otherwise.

8.43 Who the respondents are

Where an application follows a refusal to give consent to –

(a) the marriage of a child; or
(b) a child registering as the civil partner of another person,

every person who has refused consent will be a respondent to the application.

Practice Direction 8A – Where to Start Certain Proceedings

This Practice Direction supplements rules 8.14 and 8.30 FPR

1.1 Provision for the court (that is, the family court or the High Court) in which proceedings should be started is made in –

(a) rule 8.14 FPR as regards an application under section 17 of the Married Women's Property Act 1882 or section 66 of the 2004 Act; and
(b) rule 8.30 FPR as regards an application for the transfer of a tenancy under section 53 of, and Schedule 7 to, the 1996 Act.

1.2 Where rule 8.14 or rule 8.30 FPR means that an application must be made in the family court, then-

(a) the application must be made to the same Designated Family Judge area as the existing (or proposed) matrimonial proceedings or civil partnership proceedings; and
(b) subject to any direction of the court, the matter will be heard in the same location of the family court as those existing (or proposed) proceedings.

PART 9
APPLICATIONS FOR A FINANCIAL REMEDY

CONTENTS OF THIS PART

Chapter 1

Rule		Page
	Application and Interpretation	
9.1	Application	1429
9.3	Interpretation	1429
	Chapter 2	
	Procedure for Applications	
9.4	When an application for a financial order may be made	1432
9.5	Where to start proceedings	1432
9.6	Application for an order preventing a disposition	1432
9.7	Application for interim orders	1432
9.8	Application for periodical payments order at same rate as an order for maintenance pending suit	1433
9.9	Application for periodical payments order at same rate as an order for maintenance pending outcome of proceedings	1433
9.9A	Application to set aside a financial remedy order	1433

PART III

Chapter 3
Applications for Financial Remedies for Children

9.10	Application by parent, guardian etc for financial remedy in respect of children	1434
9.11	Children to be separately represented on certain applications	1435

Chapter 4
Procedure after Filing an Application

9.12	Duties of the court and the applicant upon issuing an application	1435
9.13	Service of application on mortgagees, trustees etc	1436
9.14	Procedure before the first appointment	1436
9.15	Duties of the court at the first appointment	1438
9.16	After the first appointment	1441
9.17	The FDR appointment	1441

Chapter 5
Procedure After Filing Particular Applications

9.18	Duties of the court and the applicant upon filing an application	1443
9.18A	Request for change of procedure	1444
9.19	Procedure before the first hearing	1444
9.20	Power of the court to direct filing of evidence and set dates for further hearings	1445
9.21	Who the respondent is on an application under section 20 or section 20A of the 1978 Act or Part 6 of Schedule 6 to the 2004 Act	1445
9.21A	Duty to make entries in the court's register	1445

Chapter 5A
Certain applications

9.22	Application for a maintenance order, or revocation of a maintenance order to which the 1982 Act, the Lugano Convention, the 1988 Convention or the Maintenance Regulation applies	1445

Chapter 6
General Procedure

9.24	Power to order delivery up of possession etc.	1446
9.25	Where proceedings may be heard	1446
9.26	Applications for consent orders for financial remedy	1446
9.26A	Questions as to the court's jurisdiction or whether the proceedings should be stayed	1449
9.26AA	International Maintenance Obligations: Communication with the Central Authority for England and Wales	1449
9.26B	Adding or removing parties	1450
9.26C	Method of making periodical payments	1450
9.26D	Court officer to notify subsequent marriage or formation of civil partnership of a person entitled to payments under a maintenance order	1451
9.26E	Enforcement and apportionment where periodical payments are made under more than one order	1451

Chapter 7
Estimates of Costs

9.27	Estimates of Costs	1452
9.28	Duty to make open proposals	1452

Chapter 8
Pensions

9.29	Application and interpretation of this Chapter	1455
9.30	What the party with pension rights must do when the court fixes a first appointment	1455
9.31	Applications for pension sharing orders	1455
9.32	Applications for consent orders for pension sharing	1455

9.33 Applications for pension attachment orders 1456
9.34 Applications for consent orders for pension attachment 1456
9.35 Pension sharing orders or pension attachment orders 1457
9.36 Duty of the court upon making a pension sharing order or a pension attachment order 1457
9.37 Procedure where Pension Protection Fund becomes involved with the pension scheme 1458

Chapter 9
Pension Protection Fund Compensation

9.38 Application and interpretation of this Chapter 1459
9.39 What the party with compensation rights must do when the court fixes a first appointment 1459
9.40 Applications for pension compensation sharing orders 1460
9.41 Applications for consent orders for pension compensation sharing 1460
9.42 Applications for pension compensation attachment orders 1460
9.43 Applications for consent orders for pension compensation attachment 1460
9.44 Pension compensation sharing orders or pension compensation attachment orders 1460
9.45 Duty of the court upon making a pension compensation sharing order or a pension compensation attachment order 1461

Chapter 10
Communication of Information from Financial Remedy Proceedings

9.46 Communication of information: Practice Direction 9B 1461

Practice Direction 9A –
Application for a Financial Remedy 1462

Practice Direction 9B –
Communication of Information from Financial Remedy Proceedings 1468

PART III

Chapter 1
Application and Interpretation

9.1 Application

The rules in this Part apply to an application for a financial remedy.

('Financial remedy' and 'financial order' are defined in rule 2.3)

Scope—FPR 2010, Rule 2.3 provides a list of orders defined as a 'financial remedy' or 'financial order'. An order under MWPA 1882, TLATA 1996, I(PFD)A 1975 or for a tenancy transfer under FLA 1996, Pt IV is not a 'financial remedy' or a 'financial order'.

9.2 (*revoked*)

9.3 Interpretation

(1) In this Part –

'avoidance of disposition order' means –

(a) in proceedings under the 1973 Act, an order under section 37(2)(b) or (c) of that Act;

(b) in proceedings under the 1984 Act, an order under section 23(2)(b) or 23(3) of that Act;

(c) in proceedings under Schedule 5 to the 2004 Act, an order under paragraph 74(3) or (4); or

(d) in proceedings under Schedule 7 to the 2004 Act, an order under paragraph 15(3) or (4);

'the Board' means the Board of the Pension Protection Fund;

'FDR appointment' means a Financial Dispute Resolution appointment in accordance with rule 9.17;

'Financial Circumstances Form' means the Financial Circumstances Form published by the Permanent Bureau of the Hague Conference under Article 11(4) of the 2007 Hague Convention for use in relation to applications under Article 10 of that Convention;

'order preventing a disposition' means –

(a) in proceedings under the 1973 Act, an order under section 37(2)(a) of that Act;
(b) in proceedings under the 1984 Act, an order under section 23(2)(a) of that Act;
(c) in proceedings under Schedule 5 to the 2004 Act, an order under paragraph 74(2); or
(d) in proceedings under Schedule 7 to the 2004 Act, an order under paragraph 15(2);

'pension arrangement' means –

(a) an occupational pension scheme;
(b) a personal pension scheme;
(c) shareable state scheme rights;
(d) a retirement annuity contract;
(e) an annuity or insurance policy purchased, or transferred, for the purpose of giving effect to rights under an occupational pension scheme or a personal pension scheme; and
(f) an annuity purchased, or entered into, for the purpose of discharging liability in respect of a pension credit under section 29(1)(b) of the Welfare Reform and Pensions Act 1999 or under corresponding Northern Ireland legislation;

'pension attachment order' means –

(a) in proceedings under the 1973 Act, an order making provision under section 25B or 25C of that Act;
(b) in proceedings under the 1984 Act, an order under section 17(1)(a)(i) of that Act making provision equivalent to an order referred to in paragraph (a);
(c) in proceedings under Schedule 5 to the 2004 Act, an order making provision under paragraph 25 or paragraph 26; or
(d) in proceedings under Schedule 7 to the 2004 Act, an order under paragraph 9(2) or (3) making provision equivalent to an order referred to in paragraph (c);

'pension compensation attachment order' means –

(a) in proceedings under the 1973 Act, an order making provision under section 25F of that Act;
(b) in proceedings under the 1984 Act, an order under section 17(1)(a)(i) of that Act making provision equivalent to an order referred in to paragraph (a);
(c) in proceedings under Schedule 5 to the 2004 Act, an order under paragraph 34A; and
(d) in proceedings under Schedule 7 to the 2004 Act, an order under paragraph 9(2) or (3) making provision equivalent to an order referred to in paragraph (c);

'pension compensation sharing order' means –

(a) in proceedings under the 1973 Act, an order under section 24E of that Act;
(b) in proceedings under the 1984 Act, an order under section 17(1)(c) of that Act;
(c) in proceedings under Schedule 5 to the 2004 Act, an order under paragraph 19A; and
(d) in proceedings under Schedule 7 to the 2004 Act, an order under paragraph 9(2) or (3) making provision equivalent to an order referred to in paragraph (c);

'pension sharing order' means –

(a) in proceedings under the 1973 Act, an order making provision under section 24B of that Act;
(b) in proceedings under the 1984 Act, an order under section 17(1)(b) of that Act;
(c) in proceedings under Schedule 5 to the 2004 Act, an order under paragraph 15; or
(d) in proceedings under Schedule 7 to the 2004 Act, an order under paragraph 9(2) or (3) making provision equivalent to an order referred to in paragraph (c);

'pension scheme' means, unless the context otherwise requires, a scheme for which the Board has assumed responsibility in accordance with Chapter 3 of Part 2 of the Pensions Act 2004 (pension protection) or any provision in force in Northern Ireland corresponding to that Chapter;

'PPF compensation' has the meaning given to it –

(a) in proceedings under the 1973 Act, by section 21C of the 1973 Act;

(b) in proceedings under the 1984 Act, by section 18(7) of the 1984 Act; and

(c) in proceedings under the 2004 Act, by paragraph 19F of Schedule 5 to the 2004 Act;

'relevant valuation' means a valuation of pension rights or benefits as at a date not more than 12 months earlier than the date fixed for the first appointment which has been furnished or requested for the purposes of any of the following provisions –

(a) the Pensions on Divorce etc (Provision of Information) Regulations 2000;

(b) regulation 5 of and Schedule 2 to the Occupational Pension Schemes (Disclosure of Information) Regulations 1996 and regulation 11 of and Schedule 1 to the Occupational Pension Schemes (Transfer Value) Regulations 1996;

(c) section 93A or 94(1)(a) or (aa) of the Pension Schemes Act 1993;

(d) section 94(1)(b) of the Pension Schemes Act 1993 or paragraph 2(a) (or, where applicable, 2(b)) of Schedule 2 to the Personal Pension Schemes (Disclosure of Information) Regulations 1987;

(e) the Dissolution etc. (Pensions) Regulations 2005;

'variation order' means –

(a) in proceedings under the 1973 Act, an order under section 31 of that Act; or

(b) in proceedings under the 2004 Act, an order under Part 11 of Schedule 5 to that Act.

(2) *(revoked)*

(3) (a) Where an application is made under Article 56 of, and using the form in Annex VII to, the Maintenance Regulation, references in this Part to 'financial statement' apply to the applicant as if for the words 'financial statement' were substituted 'the form in Annex VII to the Maintenance Regulation';

(aa) where an application for establishment or modification of maintenance is made under Article 10 of the 2007 Hague Convention, references in this Part to 'financial statement' apply to the applicant as if for 'financial statement' there were substituted 'Financial Circumstances Form';

(b) Sub-paragraphs (a) and (aa) do not apply where the relief sought includes relief which is of a type to which the Maintenance Regulation or the 2007 Hague Convention, as the case may be, does not apply.

Amendments—SI 2011/1328; SI 2012/2806; SI 2013/3204.

Chapter 2
Procedure for Applications

Defined terms—'financial order' is defined in FPR 2010, r 2.3, which provides a list of nine orders defined as a 'financial order'.

Pre-application protocol—This is annexed to FPR PD9A, which outlines the steps that must be taken to provide information before the commencement of all applications for a financial remedy. The 'overriding objective' should be borne in mind: 'applications should be resolved and a just outcome achieved as speedily as possible without costs being unreasonably incurred ... in a manner designed to promote as good a continuing relationship between the parties and any children affected as is possible'. There is an ongoing obligation to make 'full and frank disclosure of all material facts, documents and other information relevant to the issues'. The principle of proportionality in relation to costs must be borne in mind at all times.

Practice Direction 9B—PD9B supplements FPR 2010, r 9.46 and governs the information relating to financial remedy proceedings that a party or another person in receipt of such information may communicate for the purpose of appeals to the Child Support Appeal Tribunal or the Child Support Commissioner.

Procedure—An application may be made within or following an application for a matrimonial or civil partnership order and is lodged in the appropriate Divorce Centre (see Procedural Guide B5).

Subject to the prohibition on application after remarriage under MCA 1973, s 28, and consistent with 'the potentially life-long obligations which attend a marriage' (*Wyatt v Vince* [2015] 1 FLR 972, SC), there is no time limit for the application. Delay in issuing proceedings for a financial remedy does not in principle exclude the sharing of non-matrimonial post-separation accrual (*Briers v Briers* [2017] EWCA Civ 15). However, substantial delay may reduce or even eliminate the financial provision awarded to the applicant; see *Wyatt v Vince*. It is not an abuse of process for one party to seek an order making provision for the other: *Dart v Dart* [1996] 2 FLR 286, CA, at [296].

Applications for an order preventing a party from disposing of assets and for interim orders including maintenance pending suit and interim orders may be made and are governed by FPR 2010, Pt 18 procedure.

9.4 When an application for a financial order may be made

An application for a financial order may be made –

(a) in an application for a matrimonial or civil partnership order; or
(b) at any time after an application for a matrimonial or civil partnership order has been made.

'An application for a financial order may be made'—Despite the wide terms of this rule, the court's jurisdiction may be excluded in relation to 'maintenance' (although not child maintenance) if the parties have agreed in writing that the courts of another Member State shall have jurisdiction: Council Regulation (EC) No 4/2009 (Maintenance Regulation), Art 4. If the paying party remains resident in another Member State in which a decision as to maintenance (including child maintenance), including a dismissal of a spouse's claim, has previously been made, the court's jurisdiction will generally be excluded (Art 8), unlike the position under Brussels I. *M v V (Child Maintenance: Jurisdiction: Brussels I)* [2011] 1 FLR 109, FD is no longer good law. See also *Ramadani v Ramadani* [2015] EWCA Civ 1138 for a discussion as to what – in the context of the Maintenance Regulation – may amount to a previous 'decision' or 'court settlement' of another Member State that can prohibit an applicant from pursuing a claim for spousal maintenance in England and Wales.

Note that 'maintenance' for the purposes of the Maintenance Regulation can extend to lump sums and transfers of property if they are for the purpose of providing maintenance or meeting needs: *Van den Boogard v Laumen* [1997] 2 FLR 399, ECJ.

9.5 Where to start proceedings

(1) An application for a financial remedy must be filed –

(a) if there are proceedings for a matrimonial order or a civil partnership order which are proceeding in the family court, in that court; or
(b) if there are proceedings for a matrimonial order or a civil partnership order which are proceeding in the High Court, in the registry in which those proceedings are taking place.

(2) *(revoked)*

(3) An application for a financial remedy under Part 3 of the 1984 Act or Schedule 7 to the 2004 Act which is proceeding in the High Court must be heard by a judge, but not a district judge, of that court unless a direction has been made that the application may be heard by a district judge of the principal registry.

(Rule 8.28 enables a judge to direct that an application for a financial remedy under Part 3 of the 1984 Act or Schedule 7 to the 2004 Act which is proceeding in the High Court may be heard by a district judge of the principal registry.)

Amendments—SI 2013/3204.

Proceedings allocated to a High Court Judge—See Procedural Guide 5B for guidance as to financial remedy proceedings allocated to a High Court judge and see Mostyn J's *Statement on the Efficient Conduct of Financial Remedy Proceedings Allocated to a High Court Judge Whether Sitting at the Royal Courts of Justice or Elsewhere*, revised 1 February 2016 and set out in Part V (the Statement deals with both matters of allocation and procedure thereafter).

9.6 Application for an order preventing a disposition

(1) The Part 18 procedure applies to an application for an order preventing a disposition.

(2) An application for an order preventing a disposition may be made without notice to the respondent.

('Order preventing a disposition' is defined in rule 9.3.)

9.7 Application for interim orders

(1) A party may apply at any stage of the proceedings for –

(a) an order for maintenance pending suit;

(b) an order for maintenance pending outcome of proceedings;
(c) an order for interim periodical payments;
(d) an interim variation order;
(da) an order for payment in respect of legal services; or
(e) any other form of interim order.

(2) An application for an order mentioned in paragraph (1) shall be made using the Part 18 procedure.

(3) Where a party makes an application before filing a financial statement, the written evidence in support must –

(a) explain why the order is necessary; and
(b) give up to date information about that party's financial circumstances.

(4) Unless the respondent has filed a financial statement, the respondent must, at least 7 days before the court is to deal with the application, file a statement of his means and serve a copy on the applicant.

(5) An application for an order mentioned in paragraph (1)(e) may be made without notice.

Amendments—SI 2013/1472.

Application for interim orders—The various types of interim orders are defined here, but the operation of r 9.7(1)(e) means that r 9.7 will also apply to other interim orders, such as legal services orders in relation to costs. Part 18 procedure applies: see FPR 2010, Pt 18 and PD18A. It is envisaged that an applicant may make their application at the beginning of proceedings before filing their Form E and a without notice application is permissible. Where there is no financial statement, the written evidence in support must state why the order is necessary and provide up-to-date information about that party's current financial circumstances; if the application is prior to the filing of the respondent's financial statement, the respondent must file and serve a statement of means.

9.8 Application for periodical payments order at same rate as an order for maintenance pending suit

(1) This rule applies where there are matrimonial proceedings and –

(a) a decree nisi of divorce or nullity of marriage has been made;
(b) at or after the date of the decree nisi an order for maintenance pending suit is in force; and
(c) the spouse in whose favour the decree nisi was made has made an application for an order for periodical payments.

(2) The spouse in whose favour the decree nisi was made may apply, using the Part 18 procedure, for an order providing for payments at the same rate as those provided for by the order for maintenance pending suit.

9.9 Application for periodical payments order at same rate as an order for maintenance pending outcome of proceedings

(1) This rule applies where there are civil partnership proceedings and –

(a) a conditional order of dissolution or nullity of civil partnership has been made;
(b) at or after the date of the conditional order an order for maintenance pending outcome of proceedings is in force;
(c) the civil partner in whose favour the conditional order was made has made an application for an order for periodical payments.

(2) The civil partner in whose favour the conditional order was made may apply, using the Part 18 procedure, for an order providing for payments at the same rate as those provided for by, the order for maintenance pending the outcome of proceedings.

9.9A Application to set aside a financial remedy order

(1) In this rule –

(a) 'financial remedy order' means an order or judgment that is a financial remedy, and includes –
(i) part of such an order or judgment; or

(ii) a consent order; and

(b) 'set aside' means –

(i) in the High Court, to set aside a financial remedy order pursuant to section 17(2) of the Senior Courts Act 1981 and this rule;

(ii) in the family court, to rescind or vary a financial remedy order pursuant to section 31F(6) of the 1984 Act.

(2) A party may apply under this rule to set aside a financial remedy order where no error of the court is alleged.

(3) An application under this rule must be made within the proceedings in which the financial remedy order was made.

(4) An application under this rule must be made in accordance with the Part 18 procedure, subject to the modifications contained in this rule.

(5) Where the court decides to set aside a financial remedy order, it shall give directions for the rehearing of the financial remedy proceedings or make such other orders as may be appropriate to dispose of the application.

Amendments—Inserted by SI 2016/901.

Scope—This new rule applies to an application to set aside a financial remedy order and attempts to unify the applicable procedure (see the comments of Sir James Munby P in *CS v ACS (Consent Order: Non-Disclosure: Correct Procedure)* [2016] 1 FLR 131, FD). If the original financial remedy order was made before 22 April 2014, application is made to the Family Court. If the original order was made after that date, the set aside application is to be made to the court that made the original order. Rule 9.9A came into force on 3 October 2016. Where reasonably possible, the set aside application should be dealt with by the judge who made the original order. Rule 9.9A applies to both a financial remedy order made after a contested hearing and one made by consent and the application can be made to set aside all or part of the original order. The set aside application is treated as an application pursuant to FPR 2010, Pt 18 and requires, therefore, an application notice and a draft of the order sought (r 18.7).

See also the accompanying Practice Direction, paras 13.1–13.9 and Procedural Guide E7(2).

Financial remedy—'Financial remedy' is defined in FPR 2010, r 2.3 and includes a financial order (relief under MCA 1973) and an order made pursuant to CA 1989, Sch 1.

No error of the court—A set aside application is permitted 'where no error of the court is alleged'. If the applicant argues that the court was wrong in its decision on the facts or the law, the correct application is for an appeal. The Practice Direction expands on this single ground to include (i) fraud, (ii) material non-disclosure, (iii) limited types of mistake and (iv) subsequent events, unforeseen and unforeseeable at the time the original order was made, which invalidate the basis on which the order was made. As can be seen, ground (iv) is the basis, hitherto, of an application for an appeal (usually out of time) pursuant to the case of *Barder v Barder* [1987] 2 FLR 480, HL. It appears, therefore, that r 9.9A seeks expressly to alter the procedural route for seeking to challenge an original order on the basis of a 'supervening event' (*Barder*). Prior to r 9.9A, a supervening event would be returned to court by an application for permission to appeal (out of time). Although it is not clear how r 9.9A purports to alter the procedural route confirmed by the Court of Appeal in *Barder*, in cases of a subsequent supervening event, the express wording of the PD9A, para 13.5 would appear to make a set aside application the appropriate route of challenge in such cases, rather than an application to appeal (out of time). Note also the additional jurisdiction to set aside an order that is executory: the court may set aside an executor order if it would be inequitable not to do so because of or in light of some significant change in circumstances since the order was made, see *Bezeliansky v Bezelianskaya* [2016] EWCA Civ 76 following *Thwaite v Thwaite* (1981) 2 FLR 280.

Set aside—According to PD9A, para 13.8, the court, once satisfied that the original order should be set aside, may either direct a re-hearing or, 'if it is satisfied that it has sufficient information to do so … may proceed to determine the original application at the same time as setting aside the financial remedy order'.

Chapter 3
Applications for Financial Remedies for Children

9.10 Application by parent, guardian etc for financial remedy in respect of children

(1) The following people may apply for a financial remedy in respect of a child –

(a) a parent, guardian or special guardian of any child of the family;

(b) any person who is named in a child arrangements order as a person with whom a child of the family is to live, and any applicant for such an order;

(c) any other person who is entitled to apply for a child arrangements order which names that person as a person with whom a child is to live;

(d) a local authority, where an order has been made under section 31(1)(a) of the 1989 Act placing a child in its care;
(e) the Official Solicitor, if appointed the children's guardian of a child of the family under rule 16.24; and
(f) subject to paragraph (1A), a child of the family who has been given permission to apply for a financial remedy.

(1A) Where the application is –

(a) for the variation of an order under section 2(1)(c), 6 or 7 of the 1978 Act or paragraph 2(1)(c) of, or Part 2 or 3 of, Schedule 6 to the 2004 Act for periodical payments in respect of a child;
(b) the application is made by the child in question; and
(c) the child in question is aged 16 or over,

the child does not require permission to make the application.

(2) *(revoked)*

Amendments—SI 2013/3204; SI 2014/843.

Defined terms—'financial remedy' is defined in FPR 2010, r 2.2 as a 'financial order' made under MCA 1973 and the 2004 Act, together with orders under other specified statutes. The statutes are defined in FPR 2010, r 2.3.

Scope—This rule sets out the categories of people who may apply for a financial remedy in respect of a child. Where the application includes an application for a variation of settlement, the court must (unless satisfied that the child is not adversely affected) direct that the child be separately represented, see FPR 2010, r 9.11.

9.11 Children to be separately represented on certain applications

(1) Where an application for a financial remedy includes an application for an order for a variation of settlement, the court must, unless it is satisfied that the proposed variation does not adversely affect the rights or interests of any child concerned, direct that the child be separately represented on the application.

(2) On any other application for a financial remedy the court may direct that the child be separately represented on the application.

(3) Where a direction is made under paragraph (1) or (2), the court may if the person to be appointed so consents, appoint –

(a) a person other than the Official Solicitor; or
(b) the Official Solicitor,

to be a children's guardian and rule 16.24(5) and (6) and rules 16.25 to 16.28 apply as appropriate to such an appointment.

Chapter 4
Procedure after Filing an Application

Amendments—SI 2013/3204.

9.12 Duties of the court and the applicant upon issuing an application

(1) When an application under this Part is issued , except where Chapter 5 of this Part applies –

(a) the court will fix a first appointment not less than 12 weeks and not more than 16 weeks after the date of the filing of the application; and
(b) subject to paragraph (2), within 4 days beginning with the date on which the application was filed, a court officer will –
   (i) serve a copy of the application on the respondent; and
   (ii) give notice of the date of the first appointment to the applicant and the respondent.

(2) Where the applicant wishes to serve a copy of the application on the respondent and on filing the application so notifies the court –

(a) paragraph (1)(b) does not apply;

PART III

(b) a court officer will return to the applicant the copy of the application and the notice of the date of the first appointment; and
(c) the applicant must, –
 (i) within 4 days beginning with the date on which the copy of the application is received from the court, serve the copy of the application and notice of the date of the first appointment on the respondent; and
 (ii) file a certificate of service at or before the first appointment.

(Rule 6.37 sets out what must be included in a certificate of service)

(3) The date fixed under paragraph (1), or for any subsequent appointment, must not be cancelled except with the court's permission and, if cancelled, the court must immediately fix a new date.

(4) In relation to an application to which the Maintenance Regulation or the 2007 Hague Convention applies, where the applicant does not already know the address of the respondent at the time the application is issued, paragraph (2) does not apply and the court will serve the application in accordance with paragraph (1).

Amendments—SI 2011/1328; SI 2012/2806; SI 2013/3204.

Scope—This rule deals with the duties of the court upon the issuing of an application. The application is in the prescribed form referred to in FPR PD5A, namely by a document entitled Form A. A first appointment shall be fixed within 12–16 weeks after the date of the filing of the application. Service upon the respondent may be by the court or the applicant and must be within 4 days beginning on the date that the application was filed. Pre-action disclosure of information and negotiations that are cost effective and issue-based are still required by the Pre-Application Protocol: see FPR PD9A.

Hearing dates may not be cancelled save with the court's permission: the court, not the parties, is in control of the timetable.

9.13 Service of application on mortgagees, trustees etc

(1) Where an application for a financial remedy includes an application for an order for a variation of settlement, the applicant must serve copies of the application on –

(a) the trustees of the settlement;
(b) the settlor if living; and
(c) such other persons as the court directs.

(2) In the case of an application for an avoidance of disposition order, the applicant must serve copies of the application on the person in whose favour the disposition is alleged to have been made.

(3) Where an application for a financial remedy includes an application relating to land, the applicant must serve a copy of the application on any mortgagee of whom particulars are given in the application.

(4) Any person served under paragraphs (1), (2) or (3) may make a request to the court in writing, within 14 days beginning with the date of service of the application, for a copy of the applicant's financial statement or any relevant part of that statement.

(5) Any person who –

(a) is served with copies of the application in accordance with paragraphs (1), (2) or (3); or
(b) receives a copy of a financial statement, or a relevant part of that statement, following an application made under paragraph (4),

may within 14 days beginning with the date of service or receipt file a statement in answer.

(6) Where a copy of an application is served under paragraphs (1), (2) or (3), the applicant must file a certificate of service at or before the first appointment.

(7) A statement in answer filed under paragraph (5) must be verified by a statement of truth.

9.14 Procedure before the first appointment

(1) Not less than 35 days before the first appointment both parties must simultaneously exchange with each other and file with the court a financial statement in the form referred to in Practice Direction 5A.

(2) The financial statement must –

(a) be verified by a statement of truth; and

(b) accompanied by the following documents only –

(i) any documents required by the financial statement;

(ii) any other documents necessary to explain or clarify any of the information contained in the financial statement; and

(iii) any documents provided to the party producing the financial statement by a person responsible for a pension arrangement, either following a request under rule 9.30 or as part of a relevant valuation; and

(iv) any notification or other document referred to in rule 9.37(2), (4) or (5) which has been received by the party producing the financial statement.

(2ZA) Paragraph (2A) applies where the court has determined that the procedure in this Chapter should apply to an application under Article 56 of the Maintenance Regulation or Article 10 of the 2007 Hague Convention.

(2A) The requirement of paragraph (2)(a) relating to verification by a statement of truth does not apply to the financial statement of either party where the application has been made under –

(a) Article 56 of the Maintenance Regulation, using the form in Annex VII to that Regulation; or

(b) Article 10 of the 2007 Hague Convention, using the Financial Circumstances Form,

and the relief sought is limited to a type to which that Regulation or that Convention, as appropriate, applies, but the court may at any time direct that the financial statement of either party shall be verified by a statement of truth.

(3) Where a party was unavoidably prevented from sending any document required by the financial statement, that party must at the earliest opportunity –

(a) serve a copy of that document on the other party; and

(b) file a copy of that document with the court, together with a written explanation of the failure to send it with the financial statement.

(4) No disclosure or inspection of documents may be requested or given between the filing of the application for a financial remedy and the first appointment, except –

(a) copies sent with the financial statement, or in accordance with paragraph (3); or

(b) in accordance with paragraphs (5) and (6).

(Rule 21.1 explains what is meant by disclosure and inspection.)

(5) Not less than 14 days before the hearing of the first appointment, each party must file with the court and serve on the other party –

(a) a concise statement of the issues between the parties;

(b) a chronology;

(c) a questionnaire setting out by reference to the concise statement of issues any further information and documents requested from the other party or a statement that no information and documents are required; and

(d) a notice stating whether that party will be in a position at the first appointment to proceed on that occasion to a FDR appointment.

(6) Not less than 14 days before the hearing of the first appointment, the applicant must file with the court and serve on the respondent confirmation –

(a) of the names of all persons served in accordance with rule 9.13(1) to (3); and

(b) that there are no other persons who must be served in accordance with those paragraphs.

Amendments—SI 2011/1328; SI 2012/679; SI 2012/2806; SI 2014/667.

Procedure before first appointment—This governs what the parties must do leading up to the first appointment. By 35 days before the first appointment, the parties must simultaneously exchange a financial statement in the prescribed form referred to in PD5A, namely Form E, verified by a statement of truth, accompanied by a limited category of documents. No disclosure or inspection of the parties' documents may be given between the filing of the application and the first appointment, save as laid down in r 9.14(4).

Documents to be exchanged and filed before first appointment—Rule 9.14(6) stipulates that by 14 days before the first directions appointment, each party must file and serve a concise statement, chronology, questionnaire and a notice stating whether that party will be in a position to use the hearing as a financial dispute resolution appointment. In addition, the parties should if possible exchange additional documents as defined in FPR PD9A. These are an agreed case summary, a schedule of assets and details of any directions sought by the parties, including, where appropriate, the name of any proposed expert.

9.15 Duties of the court at the first appointment

(1) The first appointment must be conducted with the objective of defining the issues and saving costs.

(2) At the first appointment the court must determine –

- (a) the extent to which any questions seeking information under rule 9.14(5)(c) must be answered; and
- (b) what documents requested under rule 9.14(5)(c) must be produced,

and give directions for the production of such further documents as may be necessary.

(3) The court must give directions where appropriate about –

- (a) the valuation of assets (including the joint instruction of joint experts);
- (b) obtaining and exchanging expert evidence, if required;
- (c) the evidence to be adduced by each party; and
- (d) further chronologies or schedules to be filed by each party.

(4) If the court decides that a referral to a FDR appointment is appropriate it must direct that the case be referred to a FDR appointment.

(5) If the court decides that a referral to a FDR appointment is not appropriate it must direct one or more of the following –

- (a) that a further directions appointment be fixed;
- (b) that an appointment be fixed for the making of an interim order;
- (c) that the case be fixed for a final hearing and, where that direction is given, the court must determine the judicial level at which the case should be heard.

(Under Part 3 the court may also direct that the case be adjourned if it considers that non-court dispute resolution is appropriate.)

(6) In considering whether to make a costs order under rule 28.3(5), the court must have particular regard to the extent to which each party has complied with the requirement to send documents with the financial statement and the explanation given for any failure to comply.

(7) The court may –

- (a) where an application for an interim order has been listed for consideration at the first appointment, make an interim order;
- (b) having regard to the contents of the notice filed by the parties under rule 9.14(5)(d), treat the appointment (or part of it) as a FDR appointment to which rule 9.17 applies;
- (c) in a case where a pension sharing order or a pension attachment order is requested, direct any party with pension rights to file and serve a Pension Inquiry Form, completed in full or in part as the court may direct; and
- (d) in a case where a pension compensation sharing order or a pension compensation attachment order is requested, direct any party with PPF compensation rights to file and serve a Pension Protection Fund Inquiry Form, completed in full or in part as the court may direct.

(8) Both parties must personally attend the first appointment unless the court directs otherwise.

Amendments—SI 2014/843.

Scope—At the first appointment, the court in pursuance of the overriding objective in FPR 2010, Pt 1 will actively manage the financial application in relation to defining the issues and saving costs: disclosure, expert evidence and the extent of other evidence will be considered. The next hearing will be timetabled, normally to the financial dispute resolution (FDR) appointment. Costs will be considered. Both parties must attend in person. After the first appointment, there is no further provision for the disclosure of documents except with permission of the court.

Preliminary oral hearing—The court has the power to order a preliminary oral discovery hearing as a trial of a preliminary issue to assist oral discovery or the first part of a split final hearing. There are advantages where financial complexity require elucidation, early testing of factual issues and explanations and to assist in negotiations: *OS v DS (Oral Disclosure: Preliminary Hearing)* [2005] 1 FLR 675, FD; *CR v MZ (Financial Remedies: Beneficial Ownership)* [2014] 1 FLR 22, FD. The usefulness of preliminary hearings, given their expense, was criticised in *Young v Young* [2014] 2 FLR 786, FD.

Directions at the first appointment—Replies to questionnaires, requests for documents, expert evidence including valuation evidence will be directed by the court, in line with the overriding objective.

(i) *Questionnaires seeking information* The overriding objective determines that only relevant and necessary information will be ordered. The judge will go through the questionnaires, determining which questions should be answered, and in what manner. Questions that are irrelevant, oppressive or more appropriately asked in cross-examination will be disallowed. Conversely, issues that may prove fatal to an FDR hearing if not addressed in advance may be properly directed in questionnaires.

(ii) *Disclosure of documents* The overriding objective suggests that only documents that are relevant, necessary and proportionate will be directed to be disclosed.

(iii) *Valuation of assets* The use of experts in financial proceedings is now governed by amendments to Practice Directions (see FPR PD25D). Specific guidance is given for the use of single joint experts. In financial proceedings, there is no requirement for the court's permission to be obtained before the instruction of an expert. Permission is required for the report of a single joint expert to be placed before the court. The test for permission in r 3.1 follows current practice in financial remedy proceedings: the expert evidence must be in the opinion of the court necessary to assist the court to resolve the proceedings. See also FPR PD25A–PD25F.

(iv) *Other evidence* At the first appointment, the court may give directions in relation to what other evidence may be called and the form that evidence should take. Directions may be given where a party wishes to assert a prenuptial agreement: *Crossley v Crossley* [2008] 1 FLR 1467, CA.

(v) *Joinder and other case management issues* As part of the case-management function of the court, the position of third parties and interveners should be considered as early as possible. Provision for the joinder of parties derives from RSC 1965, Ord 15, r 6(2)(b) and CPR 1998, r 19.2(2), and is now expressly provided for under r 9.26B.

Where property is in a respondent's name but is held by a third party, there is a clear obligation to the applicant to join that party as a party at an early stage: *TL v ML (Ancillary Relief: Claims against Assets of Extended Family)* [2006] 1 FLR 1263, FD, followed in *Fisher Meredith v JH and PH (Financial Remedy: Appeal: Wasted Costs)* [2012] 2 FLR 536, FD. Conversely, where a respondent has legal title to property that is subject to a third-party claim, prima facie the legal and beneficial interests lie with the respondent: *Stack v Dowden* [2007] 1 FLR 1858, HL applying. The applicant could seek to join the non-legal owner if she wished, but is under no obligation to do so: *Fisher Meredith v JH and PH* (Rev 2), above.

Trustees need not routinely be joined as parties just because the case involves a trust issue, for example, a party's potential resources under a discretionary trust arrangement; however, a hostile trust dispute will require the joinder of the trustees: *A v A (No 2)* [2008] 1 FLR 1428, FD. A company alleged to be the depository of most of a husband's wealth was held by the Court of Appeal to have been correctly joined in financial proceedings and the decision of the judge to apply the FPR not the CPR and to order a trial of the preliminary issue in relation to the company was 'wise and well founded on authority': *Goldstone v Goldstone* [2011] 1 FLR 1926, CA. There is power to depart from standard procedures: in *Crossley v Crossley* [2008] 1 FLR 1467, CA the court approved directions for a preliminary trial on the issue of a prenuptial agreement: a Form E should be filed without documentation and questionnaires be dispensed with, pending a hearing in which the wife should demonstrate why the prenuptial agreement should not stand. The addition or removal of parties is governed by FPR 2010, r 9.26B.

(vi) *Jurisdiction* Proceedings under MCA 1973 are allocated to a judge of district judge level within the Family Court: FC(CDB)R 2014, Sch 1, 2(b). Complex matters involving high-value assets, significant non-disclosure, international elements, complex family or offshore holdings may be listed before a High Court Judge within the Family Court or before a judge sitting in the Financial Remedy Unit in the Central Family Court, London, upon the application of the parties and upon filing the appropriate certificate (see Procedural Guide B5). Management at an early stage by a High Court judge may prevent delay and limit costs: *P v P (Financial Relief: Procedure)* [2009] 1 FLR 696, FD.

Fixing the next stage—The court will usually fix a FDR appointment, but may fix a final hearing, fix a further directions appointment, treat the hearing as FDR with the consent of the parties or adjourn for mediation or negotiation.

Attendance of media representatives at a first appointment—Provided for by FPR 2010, r 27.11. Representatives of accredited media have the right to attend the first appointment. The court may exclude the media, where this is necessary under r 27.11(3) or where justice would be impeded or prejudiced. The press must have the opportunity to make representations: *D v D (Divorce: Media Presence*) [2009] 2 FLR 324, FD; *Spencer v Spencer* [2009] 2 FLR 1416, FD, where the court refused to exclude the press. See commentary under r 27.11.

Ongoing duty of disclosure: first appointment—The duty to disclose and the standard to be expected has long been established by the Court of Appeal in *J v J* [1955] P 215, CA: disclosure is to be 'full, frank and clear'. PD9A (Application for a Financial Remedy) underlines the obligation of the parties to make full disclosure of all material facts, documents and information relevant to the issues. Solicitors have a duty to tell their clients in clear terms of this obligation and of the possible consequences of a breach. This duty of disclosure is an ongoing obligation, especially as the final hearing approaches, and includes the duty to disclose any material changes after initial disclosure has been given: FPR PD9A and CPR 1998, r 31.11. In *Bokor-Ingram v Bokor-Ingram* [2009] 2 FLR 922, CA the court reminded practitioners that the principle of full

PART III

and frank disclosure in *J v J* had never varied. Furthermore, 'the duty to disclose in ancillary relief cases extends beyond what is certain … to any fact relevant to the court's review of the foreseeable future': *I v I (Ancillary Relief: Disclosure)* [2009] 1 FLR 201, FD disapproved. See also *V v V (Financial Relief)* [2010] 2 FLR 516, FD. Where an order for ancillary relief has been vitiated by non-disclosure, the court may make such additional or different provision as would have been made at the time had proper disclosure been given: *Kingdon v Kingdon* [2011] 1 FLR 1409, CA. For a recent review of the authorities in relation to the duty of disclosure see *NG v SG (Appeal: Non-Disclosure)* [2012] 1 FLR 1211, FD. Full disclosure to the wife, including sensitive documents connected with the husband's criminal conviction for money-laundering was ordered, subject to the condition of her undertaking not to disclose the documents further, save for use in her financial applications: *P v P (Financial Remedies: Disclosure)* [2013] 1 FLR 1003, FD.

Disclosure: the millionaire's defence—A wealthy respondent may avoid giving full disclosure by asserting that he could meet any order that the court could reasonably make: *Thyssen-Bornemisza v Thyssen-Bornemisza* [1985] FLR 670, CA; *Dart v Dart* [1996] 2 FLR 286, CA. This approach was limited in *White v White* [2000] 2 FLR 981, HL and *Lambert v Lambert* [2003] 1 FLR 139, CA. The emphasis by the Supreme Court on 'fairness' rather than 'reasonable needs' in *Miller v Miller; McFarlane v McFarlane* [2006] 1 FLR 1186, HL, and the overriding objective under FPR 2010 to deal with a case 'justly', balancing proportionality and saving expense, while ensuring that both parties are on an equal footing has rendered the millionaire's defence obsolete. However, in *AH v PH (Scandinavian Marriage Settlement)* [2014] 2 FLR 251, FD, a short marriage case with assets solely non-matrimonial, sharing did not engage and the wife's claim were limited to reasonable needs; the husband's wealth was subject only to a broad outline, effectively approving the millionaire's defence. See also *Cooper-Hohn v Hohn* [2015] 1 FLR 19, FD and *Re A (A Child: Financial Provision)* [2015] 2 FLR 625, CA.

Disclosure: self-help—The circumstances in which a party may acquire and use for the purpose of litigation documents belonging to the other party have long been subject to so-called '*Hildebrand* Rules' (*Hildebrand v Hildebrand* [1992] 1 FLR 244, FD), requiring the prompt disclosure of such documents. The use of such material was permitted where non-disclosure was reasonably anticipated (*T v T (Interception of Documents)* [1994] 2 FLR 1083, FD) and could include the recovery of documents deleted from a computer hard drive (*L v L* [2007] 2 FLR 171, QBD). However, in *White v Withers LLP and Dearle* [2010] 1 FLR 859, CA, the court would not sanction the use of force to obtain documents or the interception of documents. The CA has given guidance in *Imerman v Tchenguiz* [2010] 2 FLR 814, QBD, where the wife was in possession of confidential documents downloaded by her brothers from the husband's password-protected computer. The husband's Article 8 rights to privacy had been breached by an unlawful act. *Hildebrand* Rules are 'not good law and could not be justified on any basis including lawful excuse, self-help or public interest'. The duty of full and frank disclosure still lies with the parties. Fear that the other side might conceal documents does not justify illegal self-help that breached confidence. Where there is concern that evidence should not be wrongly destroyed or concealed, the remedy lies in search and seize orders in the High Court, and in freezing orders. Where a party has had recourse to documents by unlawful means, the court has the power to exclude such documents and would be guided by what was necessary for disposing of the case fairly and would take into account the importance of the evidence and the conduct of the parties. A party's failure to describe the unlawful means used to obtain materials upon which they seek to rely after judgment may lead to a refusal by the court to reconsider its judgment: *Arbili v Arbili* [2016] 1 FLR 473, CA.

Disclosure from third parties—Disclosure of documents held by third parties will be considered, if necessary or proportionate to the case. For principles applied in determining such applications, see *M v M (Third Party Subpoena: Financial Conduct)* [2006] 2 FLR 1253, FD. A third party who attends court under a subpoena duces tecum is entitled to the costs of compliance and conduct money. Where information may be held by a third party, the party seeking its disclosure may be ordered to use his best endeavours to obtain information: *G v G (Financial Provision: Discovery)* [1992] 1 FLR 40, FD. In contrast to ordinary civil litigation, a request by a wife for documents held by a non-party is not limited to those whose existence is already known, as a wife would be unlikely to have that knowledge: '… the wife is entitled to go fishing in the Family Division within the limits of law and practice': *Charman v Charman* [2006] 2 FLR 422, CA, following *Parra v Parra* [2003] 1 FLR 942, CA. The power of the court to order disclosure extends to offshore discretionary trusts: trusts held in Jersey, deemed to be nuptial settlements for the purposes of MCA 1973, s 24 and the resources of which were financial resources potentially available for distribution under s 25, could be subject to disclosure, notwithstanding strong concerns expressed in the Royal Court of Jersey and the demands of comity: *Tchenguiz-Imerman v Imerman (Disclosure)* [2014] 2 FLR 939, FD. See FPR 2010, rr 20.2(1)(i) (orders for disclosure of documents against a non-party as an interim remedy) and 21.2 (orders for disclosure against a person not a party).

Enforcement of order to provide information or documents—If an order made for the disclosure of information or documents is not complied with by the designated date, an application may be made for an order that the defaulting party files and serves the document within a specified date from service of the order, endorsed with a penal notice. The order endorsed with the penal notice should be served by a process server with an affidavit of service lodged at court. In default of compliance, application may be made to commit.

Power to make a costs order—See FPR 2010, r 28.3(5),(6). In considering whether to make a costs order, the court must have regard to the extent to which a party has complied with the requirement to send documents with the financial statement, and the explanation given for any failure to comply.

Pension sharing and attachment—If a pension order is sought, the person responsible for the pension arrangement must be served under FPR 2010, rr 9.31 and 9.33. Information as to the cash equivalent transfer value of any pension is required in the statement of financial information. Directions may be needed at the first appointment in relation to evidence from a pensions expert in relation to the appropriate pension share or attachment. A party with pension rights may be directed to file a Pension Inquiry Form, or a Pension Protection Fund Inquiry Form, as appropriate.

9.16 After the first appointment

(1) Between the first appointment and the FDR appointment, a party is not entitled to the production of any further documents except –

(a) in accordance with directions given under rule 9.15(2); or

(b) with the permission of the court.

(2) At any stage –

(a) a party may apply for further directions or a FDR appointment;

(b) the court may give further directions or direct that parties attend a FDR appointment.

No further production of documents without permission—The request for the disclosure of information and documents 14 days before the first appointment, together with the directions made at the hearing, is intended as a one-window opportunity to request disclosure. Permission is needed for further disclosure of documents after the first appointment, sought by separate application on notice for a directions appointment under r 9.16.

9.17 The FDR appointment

(1) The FDR appointment must be treated as a meeting held for the purposes of discussion and negotiation.

(2) The judge hearing the FDR appointment must have no further involvement with the application, other than to conduct any further FDR appointment or to make a consent order or a further directions order.

(3) Not less than 7 days before the FDR appointment, the applicant must file with the court details of all offers and proposals, and responses to them.

(4) Paragraph (3) includes any offers, proposals or responses made wholly or partly without prejudice[(GL)], but paragraph (3) does not make any material admissible as evidence if, but for that paragraph, it would not be admissible.

(5) At the conclusion of the FDR appointment, any documents filed under paragraph (3), and any filed documents referring to them, must, at the request of the party who filed them, be returned to that party and not retained on the court file.

(6) Parties attending the FDR appointment must use their best endeavours to reach agreement on matters in issue between them.

(7) The FDR appointment may be adjourned from time to time.

(8) At the conclusion of the FDR appointment, the court may make an appropriate consent order.

(9) If the court does not make an appropriate consent order as mentioned in paragraph (8), the court must give directions for the future course of the proceedings including, where appropriate –

(a) the filing of evidence, including up to date information; and

(b) fixing a final hearing date.

(10) Both parties must personally attend the FDR appointment unless the court directs otherwise.

Scope—The FDR is normally the second court hearing in a claim for a financial order. It is defined in FPR PD9A as a 'meeting held for the purpose of discussion and negotiation'. The rules do not provide for FDRs to take place in the magistrates' courts. See the Family Justice Council's *FDR Appointments: Best Practice Guidance* (December 2012) for valuable guidance on all aspects of FDRs, including preparation, documentation, conduct of the FDR, the role of the judge, agreements and costs. The court expects both parties to approach the FDR hearing openly and without reserve and to make and respond to offers in a genuine attempt to reach a settlement. All offers, whether expressed to be 'open' or 'without prejudice', must be disclosed to the court, so that the judge can advise the parties of the likely outcome if the matter were contested and examine how the issues between them may be resolved in the light of the costs implications and delay in waiting for a final hearing. A FDR-style hearing has been recommended to assist in the determination of a preliminary issue and save costs in a bitterly fought dispute involving other family members and companies: *Shield v Shield* [2014] 2 FLR 1422, FD.

Admissibility—So that the parties approach the FDR openly and without reservation, anything said at the FDR appointment is not admissible in any subsequent proceedings, (except where an offence is committed at the hearing). See FPR PD9A.

Further judicial involvement—Where agreement is not reached, r 9.17(2) directs that the judge who conducts the appointment has no further involvement with the financial application. A judge who made a consent order at the conclusion of a successful FDR could not then decide subsidiary issues that the parties had

PART III

subsequently failed to agree: *Myerson v Myerson* [2009] 1 FLR 826, CA. Once the issues are determined and the order is made, a FDR judge may hear an application for variation of that order: *G v G (Role of FDR Judge)* [2007] 1 FLR 237, FD.

Requirement to file details of offers—Seven days before the FDR appointment, the applicant must file details of all offers and proposals and responses to them. At the end of the appointment, the parties should request the return of the schedule of offers and proposals and any other privileged documents submitted during the course of the FDR.

Attendance of media representatives is not permitted at FDR—By FPR 2010, r 27.11(1)(a), the right of the media to be present at private hearings is specifically excluded from 'judicially assisted conciliation or negotiation'.

Active case management where failure to reach agreement—Rule 9.17(9) provides that if the FDR does not result in a consent order, the court will fix a date for the final hearing and give all the necessary case-management directions. The importance of the FDR is such that where a FDR has not been effective, the court may permit another appointment as soon as is practicable, so an experienced tribunal could engage with the matter: *S v S (Ancillary Relief: Importance of FDR)* [2008] 1 FLR 944, FD. The duty of full and frank disclosure continues after FDR. Where a final hearing is unavoidable, the court should direct s 25 narrative statements to identify the issues upon which the court is being asked to adjudicate and for the broader presentation of the factual background relevant to the s 25 exercise. This is particularly important where there are factual disputes or allegations in relation to conduct or dishonesty, so that the basis of each party's case is clear and to reduce the extent of oral evidence: *J v J* [2009] EWHC 2654 (Fam). The court may also consider the need to list further hearings upon the application of the parties, to deal with maintenance pending suit/interim maintenance and applications for legal services orders, to be listed before another judge in compliance with r 9.17(2).

Steps to be taken if agreement is reached at FDR—The judge should be told in full the terms of the agreement. If at all possible, a detailed consent order signed by both parties and their legal representatives should be handed to the judge, so that the order may be approved and sealed immediately. Where agreement is reached, the court may dispense with the filing of a statement of information: FPR 2010, r 9.26(5)(a). If the issues are complicated, written Heads of Agreement should be signed by the parties and their legal representatives and handed to the judge. The Heads of Agreement are important evidence of consensus and will carry weight if a party subsequently resiles from the agreement. Practitioners must be clear in explaining to their clients when making the Heads of Agreement that either (i) the agreement is understood and agreed to be a binding agreement but not yet expressed in the form of an order, because the parties are awaiting a point of drafting or detail: *Xydhias v Xydhias* [1999] 1 FLR 683, CA; or (ii) the agreement is approved as an unperfected order of the court: *Rose v Rose* [2002] 1 FLR 978, CA. The FJC's *Best Practice Guidance* (December 2012) recommends that where appropriate, it should be recorded on the face of the signed and dated Agreement whether it is understood to be a binding agreement (*Xydhias*) or an approved agreement that is an order of the court (*Rose*). Where a final or perfected order is unavailable, it is the duty of the court to case manage the application to its conclusion, by listing for a 5-minute Mention in an appropriate time frame such as 2–4 weeks to be vacated upon the lodging of a typed draft order signed by the parties. The mention hearing may be adjourned as necessary, or further directions may be given.

Issues about agreements—In the event of a dispute about whether an agreement has been reached, and whether there is jurisdiction to make a subsequent order in those terms, a hearing will be necessary, but must not be before the judge who conducted the FDR hearing, to determine the point. The court will consider all of the circumstances, but formal agreements properly arrived at with competent legal advice should not be displaced unless there are 'good and substantial grounds for concluding that an injustice would be done' by upholding the agreement. See also *Edgar v Edgar* (1981) 2 FLR 19, CA and *Xydhias v Xydhias* [1999] 1 FLR 683, CA: 'ordinarily, heads of agreement signed by the parties or a clear exchange of solicitors' letters would establish consensus', although the agreement may still be vitiated by material non-disclosure. See also *Smith v McInerney* [1994] 2 FLR 1077, FD; *X v X (Y and Z intervening)* [2002] 1 FLR 508, FD. The same principles apply to agreements made through court-directed mediation: *Rothwell v Rothwell* [2009] 2 FLR 96, CA. In *TW v PL (Agreement)* [2014] 2 FLR 106, FD, a draft order and undertakings had been signed by one side only and not approved by the court. It was held it was not possible for there to be a formal breach of undertakings and the parties were held to their agreement.

Agreements and enforceability—Ordinary contractual principles do not apply to an agreement for the compromise of an application for financial relief (*Xydhias v Xydhias* [1999] 1 FLR 683, CA). However, an agreement between parties that is sufficiently distinct from the overall compromise of an application for financial relief may be viewed as giving rise to a separate agreement, which itself may be enforceable according to normal contractual principles, for example, by specific performance: *DN v HN* [2016] 1 FLR 1171, FD.

See commentary to MCA 1973, s 7 for the procedure where there is an issue about whether an agreement has been made. Without prejudice documents will usually have to be seen by the court to determine the issue of whether an agreement has been made, and should be lodged in a sealed envelope: then, if no agreement is found, the hearing should be listed before another judge.

Bundles—In compliance with r 9.17(3),(4), the court must see written evidence of the parties' offers, proposals and responses, which should be filed by the applicant. As the FDR hearing is conventionally listed for 1 hour, PD27A, para 2.4 applies: in hearings in the PRFD and in family proceedings in all other courts, cases listed for an hour or less do not require bundles. However, it is good practice to provide a concise bundle for the judge, to include skeleton arguments, asset schedules, written offers and responses and Forms E without their attached documentation. Rule 9.17(5) provides that documents filed under r 9.17(3) shall be returned to the parties at the conclusion of the hearing so that without prejudice material does not lie on the court file.

Costs at FDR stage—FPR 2010 r 28.3(5),(6) applies. The general rule is that one party will not be required to pay the costs of another party, but a costs order may be appropriate because of the conduct of a party in relation to the proceedings. Costs against a party may be ordered at FDR stage for a refusal to negotiate, or any failure to comply with the FPRs and any order of the court or practice direction. See FPR 2010, r 28(3) and FPR PD28A in relation to costs.

Chapter 5
Procedure After Filing Particular Applications

Amendments—SI 2013/3204.

Procedure—The procedure under Pt 9, Ch 5 applies to the orders for financial remedy listed in r 9.18(A1) and envisages a shorter procedure than that for financial orders with the aim of early resolution. Applicants are required to attend a mediation information assessment meeting (MIAM) before making the application: CFA 2014, s 10(1); FPR 2010, r 3.6(2)(b) and PD3A, para 13(1)(b),(e) subject to exemptions (FPR 2010, r 3.8).

9.18 Duties of the court and the applicant upon filing an application

(A1) This Chapter applies where an application is made –

(a) under –
  (i) the 1978 Act;
  (ii) Schedule 6 to the 2004 Act;
  (iii) Schedule 1 to the 1989 Act;
  (iv) Article 56 of the Maintenance Regulation; or
  (v) Article 10 of the 2007 Hague Convention.
(b) for the variation of an order for a financial remedy.

(1) Where an application is issued –

(a) the court will fix a first hearing date not less than 4 weeks and not more than 8 weeks after the date of the filing of the application; and
(b) subject to paragraph (2), within 4 days beginning with the date on which the application was filed, a court officer will –
  (i) serve a copy of the application on the respondent;
  (ii) give notice of the date of the first hearing to the applicant and the respondent; and
  (iii) send a blank financial statement to both the applicant and the respondent.

(2) Where the applicant wishes to serve a copy of the application on the respondent and, on filing the application, so notifies the court –

(a) paragraph (1)(b) does not apply;
(b) a court officer will return to the applicant the copy of the application and the notice of the date of the first hearing; and
(c) the applicant must –
  (i) within 4 days beginning with the date on which the copy of the application is received from the court, serve the copy of the application and notice of the date of the first hearing on the respondent;
  (ii) send a blank financial statement to the respondent; and
  (iii) file a certificate of service at or before the first hearing.

(3) The date fixed under paragraph (1), or for any other subsequent hearing or appointment must not be cancelled except with the court's permission and, if cancelled, the court must immediately fix a new date.

(4) The requirement in paragraph (1)(b)(iii) for the court officer to send a blank financial statement to the applicant does not apply where the application has been made under –

(a) Article 56 of the Maintenance Regulation, using the form in Annex VII to that Regulation; or
(b) Article 10 of the 2007 Hague Convention, using the Financial Circumstances Form.

(5) In relation to an application to which the Maintenance Regulation or the 2007 Hague Convention applies, where the applicant does not already know the address of the respondent at the time the application is issued, paragraph (2) does not apply and the court will serve the application in accordance with paragraph (1).

Amendments—SI 2011/1328; SI 2012/2806; SI 2013/3204; SI 2014/667.

Maintenance Regulation and 2007 Hague Convention proceedings (r 9.18(4),(5))—An applicant for maintenance from another Member State of the EU must apply using forms annexed to the Maintenance Regulation rather than the usual domestic forms. Similarly, applicants from non-EU Contracting States under the 2007 Hague Convention will use the prescribed forms of application and the financial circumstances form published under Art 11(4) of the 2007 Convention. The court is required to serve the issued application and accompanying documentation where the applicant does not know the respondent's address so as to reduce the potential risk of domestic violence resulting from the applicant discovering the whereabouts of the respondent as a result of the service process.

9.18A Request for change of procedure

(1) This rule applies if the applicant wishes to seek a direction from the court that the procedure in Chapter 4 of this Part should apply to an application for an order in proceedings referred to in rule 9.18(A1).

(2) The application for the order must state –

(a) that the applicant seeks a direction that the procedure in Chapter 4 of this Part should apply; and
(b) the applicant's reasons for seeking such a direction.

(3) The court will –

(a) determine without notice to the parties and before the first hearing whether the procedure in Chapter 4 or Chapter 5 of this Part should apply to the application; and
(b) notify the parties of its determination and any directions made in consequence of that determination.

Amendments—Inserted by SI 2013/3204.

9.19 Procedure before the first hearing

(1) Not more than 14 days after the date of the issue of the application both parties must simultaneously exchange with each other and file with the court a financial statement referred to in Practice Direction 5A.

(2) The financial statement must –

(a) be verified by a statement of truth; and
(b) contain the following documents only –
 (i) any documents required by the financial statement; and
 (ii) any other documents necessary to explain or clarify any of the information contained in the financial statement.

(2A) The requirement of paragraph (2)(a) relating to verification by statement of truth does not apply to the financial statement of either party where the application has been made under –

(a) Article 56 of the Maintenance Regulation, using the form in Annex VII to that Regulation; or
(b) Article 10 of the 2007 Hague Convention, using the Financial Circumstances Form, but the court may at any time direct that the financial statement of either party shall be verified by a statement of truth.

(3) Where a party was unavoidably prevented from sending any document required by the financial statement, that party must at the earliest opportunity –

(a) serve a copy of that document on the other party; and
(b) file a copy of that document with the court, together with a statement explaining the failure to send it with the financial statement.

(4) No disclosure or inspection of documents may be requested or given between the filing of the application for a financial remedy and the first hearing except copies sent with the financial statement or in accordance with paragraph (3).

(Rule 21.1 explains what is meant by disclosure and inspection.)

Amendments—SI 2011/1328; SI 2012/679; SI 2012/2806.

'verified by a statement of truth' (r 9.19(2)(a))—FPR 2010, Pt 17 and FPR PD17A prescribe the form that a statement of truth must take and who may sign it. This requirement does not apply, unless directed by the court, where the application is made by a party from another EU Member State under the Maintenance Regulation or from a non-EU Contracting State under the 2007 Hague Convention as the forms to be used are those prescribed by the relevant Regulation or Convention.

9.20 Power of the court to direct filing of evidence and set dates for further hearings

Unless the court is able to determine the application at the first hearing the court may direct that further evidence be filed and set a date for a directions hearing or appointment or final hearing.

9.21 Who the respondent is on an application under section 20 or section 20A of the 1978 Act or Part 6 of Schedule 6 to the 2004 Act

In relation to proceedings set out in column 1 of the following table, column 2 sets out who the respondents to those proceedings will be.

Proceedings	*Respondent*
Application under section 20 of the 1978 Act.	The other party to the marriage; and where the order to which the application relates requires periodical payments to be made to, or in respect of, a child who is 16 years of age or over, that child.
Application under paragraphs 30 to 34 of Schedule 6 to the 2004 Act.	The other party to the civil partnership; and where the order to which the application relates requires periodical payments to be made to, or in respect of, a child who is 16 years of age or over, that child.
Application for the revival of an order under section 20A of the 1978 Act or paragraph 40 of Schedule 6 to the 2004 Act.	The parties to the proceedings leading to the order which it is sought to have revived.

Amendments—SI 2013/3204.

9.21A Duty to make entries in the court's register

Where a court officer receives notice of any direction made in the High Court or family court under section 28 of the 1978 Act by virtue of which an order made under that Act or the 2004 Act ceases to have effect, particulars of the direction must be noted in the court's records.

Amendments—Inserted by SI 2014/667.

Chapter 5A
Certain applications

Amendments—Inserted by SI 2014/667.

9.22 Application for a maintenance order, or revocation of a maintenance order to which the 1982 Act, the Lugano Convention, the 1988 Convention or the Maintenance Regulation applies

(1) This rule applies where a person makes an application for a maintenance order, or for the variation or the revocation of a maintenance order, in relation to which the court has jurisdiction by virtue of the 1982 Act, the Lugano Convention, the 1988 Convention or the Maintenance Regulation, and the respondent is outside the United Kingdom.

(2) Where the respondent does not enter an appearance and is not represented at the hearing –

- (a) the court will apply the provisions of Article 20 of the 1968 Convention, Article 20 of the 1988 Convention, Article 26 of the Lugano Convention, or Article 11 of the Maintenance Regulation as appropriate;
- (b) where the court proceeds to hear the application having applied the appropriate

provision referred to in sub-paragraph (a), the court will take into account any written representations made and any evidence given by the respondent under these rules.

(3) *(revoked)*

(4) In this rule –

(a) 'the 1982 Act', 'the Lugano Convention' and 'the 1988 Convention' have the meanings given to them in rule 34.1(2);

(b) 'the 1968 Convention' has the meaning given to it in the Civil Jurisdiction and Judgments Act 1982.

Amendments—Substituted by SI 2011/1328. Amended by SI 2013/3204.

Scope—This rule prescribes the procedure where a respondent who is outside the UK does not attend a hearing on an application for maintenance in a cross-border case to which the 1982 Act, the Lugano Convention, the 1988 Convention or the Maintenance Regulation applies. The countries concerned are the Members States of the EU, Iceland, Norway and Switzerland.

9.23 *(revoked)*

Chapter 6
General Procedure

9.24 Power to order delivery up of possession etc.

(1) This rule applies where the court has made an order under –

(a) section 24A of the 1973 Act;
(b) section 17(2) of the 1984 Act;
(c) Part 3 of Schedule 5 to the 2004 Act; or
(d) paragraph 9(4) of Schedule 7 to the 2004 Act.

(2) When the court makes an order mentioned in paragraph (1), it may order any party to deliver up to the purchaser or any other person –

(a) possession of the land, including any interest in, or right over, land;
(b) receipt of rents or profits relating to it; or
(c) both.

Scope—When the court makes an order for the sale or transfer of property, it may order any party to deliver up to the purchaser or any other person possession of land and/or receipt of rents and profits.

9.25 Where proceedings may be heard

(1) Paragraph (2) applies to an application –

(a) for a financial order;
(b) under Part 3 of the 1984 Act; or
(c) under Schedule 7 to the 2004 Act.

(2) An application mentioned in paragraph (1) must be heard –

(a) *(revoked)*
(b) where the case is proceeding in the High Court –
 (i) at the Royal Courts of Justice; or
 (ii) in matrimonial or civil partnership proceedings, any court at which sittings of the High Court are authorised.

(3)–(5) *(revoked)*

Amendments—SI 2013/3204.

Proceedings allocated to a High Court Judge—See Procedural Guide 5B for guidance as to financial remedy proceedings allocated to a High Court judge and see Mostyn J's *Statement on the Efficient Conduct of Financial Remedy Proceedings Allocated to a High Court Judge Whether Sitting at the Royal Courts of Justice or Elsewhere*, revised 1 February 2016 and set out in Part V (the Statement deals with both matters of allocation and procedure thereafter).

9.26 Applications for consent orders for financial remedy

(1) Subject to paragraph (5) and to rule 35.2 in relation to an application for a consent order –

(a) the applicant must file two copies of a draft of the order in the terms sought, one of which must be endorsed with a statement signed by the respondent to the application signifying agreement; and

(b) each party must file with the court and serve on the other party, a statement of information in the form referred to in Practice Direction 5A.

(2) Where each party's statement of information is contained in one form, it must be signed by both the applicant and respondent to certify that they have read the contents of the other party's statement.

(3) Where each party's statement of information is in a separate form, the form of each party must be signed by the other party to certify that they have read the contents of the statement contained in that form.

(4) Unless the court directs otherwise, the applicant and the respondent need not attend the hearing of an application for a consent order.

(5) Where all or any of the parties attend the hearing of an application for a financial remedy the court may –

(a) dispense with the filing of a statement of information; and

(b) give directions for the information which would otherwise be required to be given in such a statement in such a manner as it thinks fit.

(6) In relation to an application for a consent order under Part 3 of the 1984 Act or Schedule 7 to the 2004 Act, the application for permission to make the application may be heard at the same time as the application for a financial remedy if evidence of the respondent's consent to the order is filed with the application.

(The following rules contain provision in relation to applications for consent orders – rule 9.32 (pension sharing order), rule 9.34 (pension attachment order), rule 9.41 (pension compensation sharing orders) and rule 9.43 (pension compensation attachment orders).

Scope—The draft order: this rule provides for the procedure to be followed for the court to be able to exercise its discretion under MCA 1973, s 25 by making an order in accordance with the terms agreed by the parties. Two copies of the proposed order are to be lodged, one of which should be endorsed by the respondent to the application signifying agreement. It is a wise precaution to insert at the end of the proposed order a statement that each party has read and understood the terms of the agreement, and for each party to sign personally. Until a draft order is perfected, approved by the judge and sealed, the court retains jurisdiction: *Sharland v Sharland* [2014] 2 FLR 89, CA.

Preambles and drafting—Where the agreed provisions contain terms beyond the jurisdiction of the statute, those terms should be set out as recitals to the order. The body of the order may state that the court approves the recitals and directs that they be made a rule of court and filed as such. This permits the terms to be enforced in the suit without the need to bring a separate action. The Family Orders Project has provided an omnibus of draft orders and undertakings – both substantive and procedural – to regularise the drafting of financial remedy orders. These are available to download at *www.judiciary.gov.uk/publications/family-orders-project/*.

Statements of information—The Rules provide that the court must receive information in the prescribed form setting out the necessary personal information about the parties, their means and resources, so that the court may properly exercise its powers. There are requirements to ensure that the court can be satisfied that each party at the time of consenting to an order is aware of the details of the other's resources. Under r 9.26(2), where the statement of information is contained in one form, it must be signed by both parties to certify that they have read the contents. Under r 9.26(3), there may be separate forms, but each side must sign the form of the other party.

Clean break—Where the parties intend to be subject to a joint capital and/or income clean break, it is good practice, as followed at the Principal Registry of the Family Division, for the respondent to the financial application to have lodged on his behalf a Form A; without this, the respondent's claim does not exist and therefore cannot be dismissed. The Form A should be marked 'For dismissal purposes only' to prevent inadvertent issue and so that the purpose of the Form A is apparent on its face. If a prayer for financial orders has been included in the petition (or cross-petition), a separate Form A from that party is not required for dismissal purposes.

Undertakings—Consent orders may commonly contain undertakings given by the parties on the face of the order for the payment of money, or doing or abstaining from any act other than the payment of money. In each case, the undertaking must be endorsed with a notice setting out the consequence of disobedience and must contain a signed statement that the person giving the undertaking understands its terms and the consequences of failing to comply: see FPR PD33A. Undertakings dealing with matters outside the powers of the court under MCA 1973 are enforceable as effectively as direct orders [of the court]: *Livesey v Jenkins* [1985] FLR 813, HL; *Birch v Birch* [2016] 2 FLR 467, CA.

Powers of the court—The judge has full discretion to approve or reject a draft order lodged for approval. It is open to the court to decline to make the order and to list a hearing with the attendance of the parties. The court in its inquisitorial jurisdiction is not a 'rubber stamp' and must always exercise a discretion, but not to the extent of acting 'as a bloodhound or a ferret': *L v L* [2008] 1 FLR 26, FD. The applicant and the respondent need not attend the hearing of an application for a consent order, unless the court otherwise directs. Where agreement had been reached as a result of arbitration by religious authorities, court proceedings having been stayed for this purpose, the High Court approved a consent order in relation to children and matrimonial finance where a non-binding agreement had been reached under the auspices of the Beth Din, the court respecting the agreement reached by the parties and finding the terms of the financial settlement 'unobjectionable': *AI v MT (Alternative Dispute Resolution)* [2013] 2 FLR 371, FD.

Power to set aside consent order—In certain circumstances, it may be possible to set aside a consent order. The procedural basis for doing so is now set out in FPR 2010, r 9.9A and PD9A, paras 13.1–13.8. See the commentary to r 9.9A. The main grounds for challenging a consent order are:

(i) an erroneous basis of fact at the time of the consent order, such as misrepresentation, material non-disclosure or fraud;

(ii) an unforeseen supervening event after the consent order, such as to invalidate the basis upon which the consent order was made.

Erroneous basis of fact: the duty owed to the court of providing full and frank disclosure before an agreement is axiomatic: see *Livesey v Jenkins* [1985] FLR 813, HL. The power to set aside a financial order – whether by consent or by order after a contested hearing – arises where there is material non-disclosure by a party. Non-disclosure may be inadvertent (mistaken or negligent) or fraudulent. The leading cases are *Gohil v Gohil* [2015] 2 FLR 1289, SC and *Sharland v Sharland* [2015] 2 FLR 1367, SC. Where a party's non-disclosure is inadvertent, there is no presumption that it is 'material' and the onus is on the other party to show that proper disclosure would, on the balance of probabilities, have led to a different order being made. However, where a party's non-disclosure was intentional (fraudulent), it is deemed to be 'material', such that it is presumed that proper disclosure would have led to a different order, unless that party can show, on the balance of probabilities, that it would not have done so; see Lord Neuberger in *Gohil v Gohil*, at [44]. An applicant must act without unreasonable delay upon a discovery of alleged non-disclosure: *Burns v Burns* [2004] EWCA Civ 1258. Whether or not there has been non-disclosure by one party is a question of fact, which involves an evaluative assessment of the available admissible evidence, see *Gohil*, at [49]. The principles applicable to the admissibility of fresh evidence on appeal (*Ladd v Marshall* (1954) FLR Rep 422, CA) have no relevance to the determination of an application to set aside a financial order on the ground of fraudulent non-disclosure (*Gohil v Gohil*, at [32]).

Supervening event: the principles derive from *Barder v Barder* [1987] 2 FLR 480, HL, where the husband agreed to transfer his interest in the former matrimonial home to the wife, who then killed the children and committed suicide. Prior to r 9.9A, it was necessary to apply for leave to appeal out of time if the *Barder* principles were engaged (rather than applying to set aside the order). Leave to appeal may have been given where (i) a new event occurred, (ii) the basis upon which the consent order was made was invalidated, (iii) the event was close in time, (iv) there was a prompt application and (v) there was no third-party prejudice. *Barder* events are likely to be unforeseeable at the time of the consent order. Pursuant to r 9.9A, it now appears that a supervening event (*Barder v Barder*) requires an application to set aside rather than to appeal out of time. It is assumed that the factors ((i)–(v), above) will still be relevant in determining whether the court should set aside all or part of the original order. Foreseeable events, such as dramatic fluctuations in the value of assets such as shares, which had been properly valued and taken into account, have been held not to be a *Barder* event: *Cornick v Cornick* [1994] 2 FLR 530, FD; *Myerson v Myerson (No 2)* [2009] 2 FLR 147, CA; *Walkden v Walkden* [2010] 1 FLR 174, CA. A change in the law must be unforeseeable to constitute a *Barder* event: *S v S (Ancillary Relief: Consent Order)* [2002] 1 FLR 992, FD. In *Dixon v Marchant* [2008] 1 FLR 655, CA the wife's rapid remarriage was held not to be a *Barder* event. The parties had agreed the capitalisation of periodical payments to achieve a clean break. There was no fundamental assumption between the parties to be invalidated by the wife's remarriage. For a case in which a husband's receipt of an inheritance upon his father's death just 1 month after an FDR consent order was classed as a *Barder* event, see *Critchell v Critchell* [2016] 1 FLR 400, CA. In *Richardson v Richardson* [2011] 2 FLR 244, CA, justice required that both the husband and his late wife's estate bear equally the liability for an unforeseen damages claim against their company, where the insurance claim was voided. This case is also an example of the appeal court refusing to interfere with the original distributive award, despite the death of the wife 2 months after final order, as her award was based on 'sharing' the matrimonial resources rather than on her 'needs'. Thorpe LJ said that cases with a *Barder* factor as opposed to a vitiating factor are extremely rare. The principles of *Barder* should not be thought to be extendable by ingenuity or the lowering of the judicially created bar. Mistake as to value of an asset has been discounted as falling within the *Barder* principle: *Judge v Judge* [2009] 1 FLR 1287, CA: for guidance as to the principles applicable to a mistake as a ground for setting aside an order, see *DB v DLJ (Challenge to Arbitral Award)* [2016] 2 FLR 1308, FD.

Procedure to reopen or set aside consent order—See FPR 2010, r 9.9A and Procedural Guide E7(2).

Relationship between arbitration and consent orders—Arbitration can be a cost-effective, proportionate and confidential form of alternative dispute resolution. There is now comprehensive Practice Guidance as to Arbitration in the Family Court dealing with financial remedy claims (as defined in FPR 2010, r 2.3), which is replicated in Part V. Where the parties have bound themselves to accept an arbitral award under the Institute of Family Lawyers Arbitration Scheme, the order should be approved by the court, in the absence of compelling countervailing factors that would fundamentally vitiate the award: *S v S (Financial Remedies: Arbitral Award)* [2014] 1 FLR 1257, FD. In *DB v DLJ (Challenge to Arbitral Award)* [2016] 2 FLR 1308, FD, Mostyn J considered an application by a husband to show cause why an arbitral award should not be made an order of the court. The wife claimed that the award had been vitiated by mistake. See para [57] for guidance as to setting aside an order on the ground of mistake. Mostyn J also stated obiter that in the future any notice to show cause why an arbitral award should not be made an order of the court must, for London and the South Eastern Circuit, be issued in the Royal Courts of Justice and immediately placed before Mostyn J for allocation to a High Court judge. If the application is issued on a different Circuit, it must be placed immediately before the Family Division Liaison Judge for speedy hearing before that judge or another High Court judge (including a s 9 judge).

Negligence and drafting consent orders—If a solicitor is instructed simply to draft a consent order to obtain the court's approval to an agreement, that solicitor is not necessarily negligent for failing to advise on the appropriateness of the settlement. The extent of the solicitor's duty to advise will be determined by the retainer, although it is implicit in the retainer that a solicitor will give advice that is reasonably incidental to the retainer. For guidance, see *Minkin v Landsberg* [2015] EWCA Civ 1152.

9.26A Questions as to the court's jurisdiction or whether the proceedings should be stayed

(1) This rule applies to applications for maintenance where a question as to jurisdiction arises under –

(a) the 1968 Convention;
(b) the 1988 Convention;
(c) the Lugano Convention;
(d) the Maintenance Regulation; or
(e) Article 18 of the 2007 Hague Convention.

(2) If at any time after the issue of the application it appears to the court that it does not or may not have jurisdiction to hear an application, or that under the instruments referred to in paragraph (1) it is or may be required to stay the proceedings or to decline jurisdiction, the court must –

(a) stay the proceedings, and
(b) fix a date for a hearing to determine jurisdiction or whether there should be a stay or other order.

(3) The court officer will serve notice of the hearing referred to at paragraph (2)(b) on the parties to the proceedings.

(4) The court must, in writing –

(a) give reasons for its decision under paragraph (2), and
(b) where it makes a finding of fact, state such finding.

(5) The court may with the consent of all the parties deal with any question as to the jurisdiction of the court, or as to whether the proceedings should be stayed, without a hearing.

(6) In this rule –

(a) 'the 1968 Convention' has the meaning given to it in the Civil Jurisdiction and Judgments Act 1982;
(b) 'the 1988 Convention' and 'the Lugano Convention' have the meanings given to them in rule 34.1(2).

Amendments—Inserted by SI 2011/1328. Amended by SI 2012/2806.

9.26AA International Maintenance Obligations: Communication with the Central Authority for England and Wales

(1) Where the Lord Chancellor requests information or a document from the court officer for the relevant court for the purposes of Article 58 of the Maintenance Regulation or Articles 12 or 25(2) of the 2007 Hague Convention, the court officer shall provide the requested information or document to the Lord Chancellor forthwith.

(2) In this rule, 'relevant court' means the court at which an application under Article 56 of the Maintenance Regulation or Article 10 of the 2007 Hague Convention has been filed.

[The Lord Chancellor is the Central Authority for England and Wales in relation to the 2007 Hague Convention and the Maintenance Regulation]

Amendments—Inserted by SI 2012/2806.

9.26B Adding or removing parties

(1) The court may direct that a person or body be added as a party to proceedings for a financial remedy if –

- (a) it is desirable to add the new party so that the court can resolve all the matters in dispute in the proceedings; or
- (b) there is an issue involving the new party and an existing party which is connected to the matters in dispute in the proceedings, and it is desirable to add the new party so that the court can resolve that issue.

(2) The court may direct that any person or body be removed as a party if it is not desirable for that person or body to be a party to the proceedings.

(3) If the court makes a direction for the addition or removal of a party under this rule, it may give consequential directions about –

- (a) the service of a copy of the application form or other relevant documents on the new party; and
- (b) the management of the proceedings.

(4) The power of the court under this rule to direct that a party be added or removed may be exercised either on the court's own initiative or on the application of an existing party or a person or body who wishes to become a party.

(5) An application for an order under this rule must be made in accordance with the Part 18 procedure and, unless the court directs otherwise, must be supported by evidence setting out the proposed new party's interest in or connection with the proceedings or, in the case of removal of a party, the reasons for removal.

Amendments—Inserted by SI 2012/679.

Scope—This rule addresses the issue of joinder, but is specific to financial remedy proceedings, following the decision of the CA in *Goldstone v Goldstone* [2011] 1 FLR 1926, CA. It therefore has no application to other family proceedings. The principles of joinder under r 9.26B have been explored in *DR v GR and Others (Financial Remedy: Variation of Overseas Trust)* [2013] 2 FLR 1534, FD. The substantive terms and procedure under FPR 2010, r 9.26B must be carefully complied with. There has to be evidence that joinder actually would make a difference: mere assertions of belief will not suffice. An application for joinder has to be made under FPR 2010, Pt 18, which requires 7 days' notice and must be supported by clear evidence. The advantages of joinder are set out in *Tchenguiz-Imerman v Imerman* [2012] EWHC 4277 (Fam): joinder assists the court in the investigation and resolution of key issues, as the parties so joined are subject to direct disclosure obligations deriving from party status and may be cross-examined.

9.26C Method of making periodical payments

(1) This rule applies where under section 1(4) or (4A) of the Maintenance Enforcement Act 1991 the court orders that payments under a qualifying periodical maintenance order are to be made by a particular means.

(2) The court officer will record on a copy of the order the means of payment that the court has ordered.

(3) The court officer will notify in writing the person liable to make payments under the order how the payments are to be made.

(4) Where under section 1(4A) of the Maintenance Enforcement Act 1991 the court orders payment to the court by a method of payment under section 1(5) of that Act, the court officer will notify the person liable to make payments under the order of sufficient details of the account into which payments should be made to enable payments to be made into that account.

(5) Where payments are made to the court, the court officer will give or send a receipt to any person who makes such a payment and who asks for a receipt.

(6) Where payments are made to the court, the court officer will make arrangements to make the payments to –

- (a) the person entitled to them; or
- (b) if the person entitled to them is a child, to the child or to the person with whom the child has his or her home.

(7) The Part 18 procedure applies to an application under section 1(7) of the Maintenance Enforcement Act 1991 (application from an interested party to revoke, suspend, revive or vary the method of payment).

(8) Where the court makes an order under section 1(7) of the Maintenance Enforcement Act 1991 or dismisses an application for such an order, the court officer will, as far as practicable, notify in writing all interested parties of the effect of the order and will take the steps set out in paragraphs (2), (3) and (4), as appropriate..

(9) In this rule, 'interested party' and 'qualifying periodical maintenance order' have the meanings given in section 1(10) of the Maintenance Enforcement Act 1991.

Amendments—Inserted by SI 2014/667.

9.26D Court officer to notify subsequent marriage or formation of civil partnership of a person entitled to payments under a maintenance order

(1) This rule applies where –

- (a) there is an order of a type referred to in paragraph (4) which requires payments to be made to the court or to an officer of the court; and
- (b) the court is notified in writing by –
  - (i) the person entitled to receive payments under the order;
  - (ii) the person required to make payments under the order; or
  - (iii) the personal representative of such a person,

that the person entitled to receive payments under the order has subsequently married or formed a civil partnership.

(2) The court officer will, where practicable, notify in writing the courts referred to in paragraph (3) of the notification of the subsequent marriage or formation of a civil partnership.

(3) The courts to be notified are –

- (a) any other court which has made an order of a type referred to in paragraph (4);
- (b) in the case of a provisional order made under section 3 of the 1920 Act or section 3 of the 1972 Act, the court which confirmed the order;
- (c) if an order of a type referred to in paragraph (4) has been transmitted abroad for registration under section 2 of the 1920 Act or section 2 of the 1972 Act, the court in which the order is registered; and
- (d) any other court in which an application to enforce the order has been made.

(4) The orders are –

- (a) those to which the following provisions apply –
  - (i) section 38 of the 1973 Act;
  - (ii) section 4(2) of the 1978 Act;
  - (iii) paragraph 65 of Schedule 5 to the 2004 Act; and
  - (iv) paragraph 26(2) of Schedule 6 to the 2004 Act; and
- (b) an attachment of earnings order made to secure payments under an order referred to in sub-paragraph (a).

(5) In this rule –

'the 1920 Act' means the Maintenance Orders (Facilities for Enforcement) Act 1920; and
'the 1972 Act' means the Maintenance Orders (Reciprocal Enforcement) Act 1972.

Amendments—Inserted by SI 2014/667.

Requesting a search of the attachment of earnings index—The appropriate form is Form FE17.

9.26E Enforcement and apportionment where periodical payments are made under more than one order

(1) This rule applies where periodical payments are required to be made by a payer to a payee under more than one periodical payments order.

(2) Proceedings for the recovery of payments under more than one order may be made in one application by the payee, which must indicate the payments due under each order.

(3) Paragraphs (4) and (5) apply where any sum paid to the court on any date by a payer who is liable to make payments to the court under two or more periodical payments orders is less than the total sum that the payer is required to pay to the court on that date in respect of those orders.

(4) The payment made will be apportioned between the orders in proportion to the amounts due under each order over a period of one year.

(5) If, as a result of the apportionment referred to in paragraph (4), the payments under any periodical payments order are no longer in arrears, the residue shall be applied to the amount due under the other order or, if there is more than one other order, shall be apportioned between the other orders in accordance with paragraph (4).

(6) In this rule –

'payee' means a person entitled to receive payments under a periodical payments order; and 'payer' means a person required to make payments under a periodical payments order.

Amendments—Inserted by SI 2014/667.

Chapter 7
Estimates of Costs

9.27 Estimates of Costs

(1) Subject to paragraph (2), at every hearing or appointment each party must produce to the court an estimate of the costs incurred by that party up to the date of that hearing or appointment.

(2) Not less than 14 days before the date fixed for the final hearing of an application for a financial remedy, each party ('the filing party') must (unless the court directs otherwise) file with the court and serve on each other party a statement giving full particulars of all costs in respect of the proceedings which the filing party has incurred or expects to incur, to enable the court to take account of the parties' liabilities for costs when deciding what order (if any) to make for a financial remedy.

(3) (*revoked*)

(Rule 28.3 makes provision for orders for costs in financial remedy proceedings.)

Amendments—SI 2013/3204.

Scope—At every hearing a costs estimate must be produced to the judge (Form H). However, the requirement for the final hearing is for a statement giving full particulars of all costs incurred or envisaged. This is in the form of a more detailed and comprehensive document. The court is entitled to take into account the parties' liabilities for costs before deciding what order to make. The weight to be given to costs expended is for the discretion of the individual judge on s 25 principles. The court may credit back into the parties' assets any costs incurred by them, in accordance with the guidance in *Leadbetter v Leadbetter* [1985] FLR 789, FD. But see comments in *TL v ML (Ancillary Relief: Claims against Assets of Extended Family)* [2006] 1 FLR 1263, FD.

9.28 Duty to make open proposals

(1) Not less than 14 days before the date fixed for the final hearing of an application for a financial remedy, the applicant must (unless the court directs otherwise) file with the court and serve on the respondent an open statement which sets out concise details, including the amounts involved, of the orders which the applicant proposes to ask the court to make.

(2) Not more than 7 days after service of a statement under paragraph (1), the respondent must file with the court and serve on the applicant an open statement which sets out concise details, including the amounts involved, of the orders which the respondent proposes to ask the court to make.

Scope—This rule applies only to final hearings. There is no requirement to make open offers ahead of interim hearings.

'Open' proposals—The concept of the 'open' proposal is distinct from a proposal made within negotiation that is privileged, i e it cannot be disclosed to the court. It remains public policy that parties are to be encouraged to negotiate; it is thought that they will do so more readily if they can do so privately: *Rush & Tompkins Ltd v Greater London Council* [1989] AC 1280, HL. The rules do not alter the ability to negotiate privately. Reference should not be made in financial proceedings to correspondence between the parties that is privileged, except where both parties waive that privilege. By FPR 2010, r 28.3, no offer to settle that is not an open offer is admissible at any stage, except in FDRs under r 9.17. Take note that, if a party proposes an open settlement less advantageous to himself than that which the court considers to be his 'true' entitlement, the court is not under an obligation to make the [higher] award (*JS v RS* [2016] 2 FLR 839, FD). Only open proposals to settle can be taken into account by the court in determining whether to make an order for costs under FPR 2010, r 28.3. This rule does not apply to hearings on appeal when a '*Calderbank*' offer (without prejudice save as to costs) can be taken into account when determining an application for costs of the appeal (*WD v HD* [2017] 1 FLR 160, FD).

Chapter 8
Pensions

Scope—Part 9, Ch 8 (rr 9.29–9.37) governs the procedure for pension sharing and pension attachment (as well as disclosure by a party with benefits under a pension arrangement (whether or not pension sharing or attachment is applied for) in relation to pension arrangements including where the Pension Protection Fund (PPF) becomes involved. However, where the PPF has already assumed responsibility for a pension arrangement so that either party is entitled to PPF compensation, FPR 2010, Pt 9, Ch 9 (rr 9.38–9.45) applies.

Outline of procedural framework for pension sharing applications—For pension sharing applications, this is:

1 The application is made in the application for a matrimonial or civil partnership order (petition) or at any time thereafter (FPR 2010, r 9.4).
2 The person with pension benefits must apply for a CE within 7 days of notice of the First Appointment, unless there is already one in existence dated not earlier than 12 months before the date of the First Appointment (a 'relevant valuation': FPR 2010, r 9.30).
3 The person responsible for the pension arrangement must be served and given 21 days to provide information including details of any obstacles to a pension sharing order being made (FPR 2010, r 9.31 and Pensions on Divorce etc (Provision of Information) Regulations 2000, regs 2(7) and 4).
4 The form of the order must:
   (i) be expressed as a percentage (MCA 1973, s 21A; *H v H (Financial Relief: Pensions)* [2010] 2 FLR 173, FD) of the CE calculated in accordance with the Pensions on Divorce etc (Provision of Information) Regulations 2000, reg 3;
   (ii) state in the body of the order that there is to be provision by way of pension sharing in accordance with the annex(es) (Form P1 (pension sharing annex)) for each pension arrangement (FPR 2010, r 9.35). The order must not take effect until 7 days after the time has expired for appealing or the date of decree absolute (whichever is the later) (MCA 1973, ss 24B(2) and 24C);
   (iii) Direct whether the court or other party is to send the pension sharing order, annex(es) and the relevant decree/order to the pension arrangement (FPR 2010, r 9.36).
5 The final stage is implementation. The court or one of the parties serves the order (FPR 2010, r 9.36). The information needed from the parties for implementation to take place is set out in the Pension on Divorce etc (Provision of Information) Regulation 2000, reg 5 et seq.

Outline of procedural framework for consent pension sharing applications—A special procedural framework for dealing with consent pension sharing applications, where there has been no prior service of a formal application (Form A) under FPR 2010, r 9.31, is provided for by FPR 2010, r 9.32. This procedure will apply where, for example, the parties have been in negotiations and have reached an agreement without any formal application having been made. Unless the information set out in Section C of the Pension Inquiry Form has already been provided in relation to the pension arrangement in question, that information must be requested and, on receipt, a copy sent to the other party. There is no formal requirement to seek the approval of the pension arrangement to a consent pension sharing order whether an application has been served under r 9.31 or is made under r 9.32. However, if there is any doubt as to the ability of the pension arrangement to implement the proposed order, it is good practice to seek such approval.

Outline of procedural framework for pension attachment applications—For pension attachment applications this is:

1 The application is made in the application for a matrimonial or civil partnership order (petition) or at any time thereafter (FPR 2010, r 9.4).
2 The person with pension benefits must apply for a CE within 7 days of notice of the First Appointment, unless there is already one in existence dated not earlier than 12 months before the date of the First Appointment (a 'relevant valuation': FPR 2010, r 9.30).
3 The person responsible for the pension arrangement must be served with the application and the addresses referred to in FPR 2010, r 9.33(1). The person responsible for the pension arrangement may then within 21 days of service request the provision of the pension section of Form E from the party with pension rights which must be provided on exchange of Forms E or within 21 days of the date of the request (whichever is the later) (FPR 2010, r 9.33(2)–(4)).
4 The person responsible for the pension arrangement, who has received a copy of the requested section of Form E, may send to the court and to the parties a statement in answer within 21 days of receipt of the pensions section of Form E (FPR 2010, r 9.33(5)).
5 Where the person responsible for the pension arrangement files a statement in answer, that person is entitled to be given notice of the First Appointment and to be represented at that appointment (FPR 2010, r 9.33(6)).

PART III

6 The form of the order must:
- (i) be expressed as a percentage (MCA 1973, s 25B(5)) of the payment which becomes due to the party with pension rights;
- (ii) state in the body of the order that there is to be provision by way of pension attachment in accordance with an annex(es) (Form P2 (pension attachment annex)) for each arrangement (FPR 2010, r 9.35);
- (iii) within 21 days of service direct whether the court or one of the parties is to send the pension attachment order, annex(es) and accompany documents to the pension arrangement (FPR 2010, r 9.36).

7 The court or one of the parties serves the order (FPR 2010, r 9.36).

Outline of procedural framework for consent pension attachment applications—A special procedural framework is created for applications for consent pension attachment orders where an application has not been already served under FPR 2010, r 9.33(1). In these circumstances, the parties must serve on the pension arrangement a copy of the application for a consent order, a draft of the proposed order and pension attachment annex and particulars of the addresses referred to in r 9.33(1). The pension arrangement then has 21 days from the date of service of the consent order application in which to object (FPR 2010, r 9.34(3)).

Provision of information (r 9.30)—This rule provides that if one party has benefits under a pension arrangement (as opposed to shareable state scheme rights: see annotations to MCA 1973, s 21A) then, irrespective of whether a pension sharing or attachment order is being sought, that person must within 7 days of being notified of the date of the First Appointment apply to the pension arrangement for information about the scheme. That information, as set out in the Pensions on Divorce etc (Provision of Information) Regulations 2000, reg 2(2), is simply the CE. Where further information is required because of pension sharing or an attachment order is sought, that information will be obtained in response to the Pension Inquiry Form (Form P) directed on the First Appointment (FPR 2010, r 9.15(7)(c)). As regards shareable state scheme rights, these rules do not require similar information to be obtained. It is suggested that it is good practice to obtain the information at this stage. Sharing of State Scheme Rights (Provision of Information and Valuation) (No 2) Regulations 2000, reg 2) requires the Secretary of State to provide the person with shareable state scheme rights or the court with a valuation of that person's shareable state scheme rights and with an explanation of how a pension sharing order will affect that person and his spouse. See the annotations to these Regulations for details of the procedures involved and to MCA 1973, s 21A.

Valuation—See annotations in Part IV to PD(PI)R 2000, reg 3.

Service and objection by pension provider—The pension arrangement must be given notice of an application for a pension sharing or attachment order (FPR 2010, r 9.31). However, in the case of a consent application for a pension sharing order, the application need not be served on the pension arrangement provided FPR 2010, r 9.32 is complied with. Further, no specific provision is given in relation to pension sharing (whether or not the order is made by consent) for the pension arrangement to require or be given further information about the application or to take any part in the proceedings. The facility for the pension arrangement to object applies only to pension attachment orders (FPR 2010, rr 9.33 and 9.34). The rationale for this distinction is that the pension attachment order imposes a continuing obligation on a pension arrangement in a way that a pension sharing order does not.

Form of order (r 9.35)—This rule sets out formalities for the form of the pension sharing or attachment order. This order must be accompanied by an annex(es) (Form P1 (pension sharing annex); Form P2 (pension attachment annex)). Important points are that:

- (i) the order is expressed as a percentage (MCA 1973, ss 21A and 25B(5); *H v H (Financial Relief: Pensions)* [2010] 2 FLR 173, FD) of (pension sharing) the CE calculated in accordance with the Pensions on Divorce etc (Provision of Information) Regulations 2000, reg 3, (shareable state scheme rights: see annotations to MCA 1973, s 21A) as provided by the Sharing of State Scheme Rights (Provision of Information and Valuation) (No 2) Regulations 2000, reg 2 or (pension attachment) the payment which becomes due to the party with pension rights;
- (ii) the date of the valuation of the cash equivalent is, for evidential purposes, as specified by the court between 1 year before the application for a matrimonial or civil partnership order and the date of the order (Divorce etc (Pensions) Regulations 2000, reg 3). This is not, however, the valuation date used for implementation purposes, which is governed by WRPA 1999, s 29. For 'moving target syndrome', see annotations to WRPA 1999, s 29;
- (iii) responsibility between the parties for payment of the charges must be set out in the annex(es). If the annex(es) is silent, the transferor will pay (WRPA 1999, s 41(3)(i)). See, further, annotations to MCA 1973, s 24D and PD(PI)R 2000, reg 2;
- (iv) a pension sharing order must not take effect until the expiry of 7 days after the time for appealing has elapsed or the date of decree absolute (whichever is the later) (MCA 1973, ss 24B(2) and 24C).

Service of order and implementation (r 9.36)—Within 7 days of the order or decree absolute, whichever is the later, the court or one of the parties (as directed by the court) sends to the pension arrangement the order including the annex(es) and a copy of the relevant decree/order.

Both parties must provide the pension arrangement with the formal information (date of birth, national insurance number, etc) set out in the Pensions on Divorce etc (Provision of Information) Regulations 2000, reg 5. Service of the order on the pension arrangement and provision by the parties of the above formal information triggers the start of the 4-month period which the pension arrangement has to implement the order (WRPA 1999, s 34(1)). The pension arrangement must, if it has not already done so, provide details of the charges within 3 weeks of receiving the order and must issue a notice of discharge within three weeks of its implementation (Pensions on Divorce etc (Provision of Information) Regulations 2000, regs 7 and 8).

9.29 Application and interpretation of this Chapter

(1) This Chapter applies

(a) where an application for a financial remedy has been made; and

(b) the applicant or respondent is the party with pension rights.

(2) In this Chapter –

(a) in proceedings under the 1973 Act and the 1984 Act, all words and phrases defined in sections 25D(3) and (4) of the 1973 Act have the meaning assigned by those subsections;

(b) in proceedings under the 2004 Act –

all words and phrases defined in paragraphs 16(4) to (5) and 29 of Schedule 5 to that Act have the meanings assigned by those paragraphs; and

'the party with pension rights' has the meaning given to 'civil partner with pension rights' by paragraph 29 of Schedule 5 to the 2004 Act;

(c) all words and phrases defined in section 46 of the Welfare Reform and Pensions Act 1999 have the meanings assigned by that section.

9.30 What the party with pension rights must do when the court fixes a first appointment

(1) Where the court fixes a first appointment as required by rule 9.12(1)(a) the party with pension rights must request the person responsible for each pension arrangement under which the party has or is likely to have benefits to provide the information referred to in regulation 2(2) of the Pensions on Divorce etc (Provision of Information) Regulations 2000.

(The information referred to in regulation 2 of the Pensions on Divorce etc (Provision of Information) Regulations 2000 relates to the valuation of pension rights or benefits.)

(2) The party with pension rights must comply with paragraph (1) within 7 days beginning with the date on which that party receives notification of the date of the first appointment.

(3) Within 7 days beginning with the date on which the party with pension rights receives the information under paragraph (1) that party must send a copy of it to the other party, together with the name and address of the person responsible for each pension arrangement.

(4) A request under paragraph (1) need not be made where the party with pension rights is in possession of, or has requested, a relevant valuation of the pension rights or benefits accrued under the pension arrangement in question.

Scope—This rule provides for the provision of information in relation to benefits under a pension arrangement. See, further the notes to FPR 2010, Pt 9, Ch 8.

9.31 Applications for pension sharing orders

Where an application for a financial remedy includes an application for a pension sharing order, or where a request for such an order is added to an existing application for a financial remedy, the applicant must serve a copy of the application on the person responsible for the pension arrangement concerned.

Scope—This rule provides for the service of an application for a pension sharing order on the pension arrangement. See further the notes to FPR 2010, Pt 9, Ch 8.

9.32 Applications for consent orders for pension sharing

(1) This rule applies where –

(a) the parties have agreed on the terms of an order and the agreement includes a pension sharing order;

(b) service has not been effected under rule 9.31; and

(c) the information referred to in paragraph (2) has not otherwise been provided.

(2) The party with pension rights must –

(a) request the person responsible for the pension arrangement concerned to provide the information set out in Section C of the Pension Inquiry Form; and

(b) on receipt, send a copy of the information referred to in sub-paragraph (a) to the other party.

Scope—This rule provides for the special procedure for consent applications for a pension sharing order where there has been no prior service of an application under FPR 2010, r 9.31 (Form A). See further the notes to FPR 2010, Pt 9, Ch 8.

9.33 Applications for pension attachment orders

(1) Where an application for a financial remedy includes an application for a pension attachment order, or where a request for such an order is added to an existing application for a financial remedy, the applicant must serve a copy of the application on the person responsible for the pension arrangement concerned and must at the same time send –

(a) an address to which any notice which the person responsible is required to serve on the applicant is to be sent;
(b) an address to which any payment which the person responsible is required to make to the applicant is to be sent; and
(c) where the address in sub-paragraph (b) is that of a bank, a building society or the Department of National Savings, sufficient details to enable the payment to be made into the account of the applicant.

(2) A person responsible for a pension arrangement who receives a copy of the application under paragraph (1) may, within 21 days beginning with the date of service of the application, request the party with the pension rights to provide that person with the information disclosed in the financial statement relating to the party's pension rights or benefits under that arrangement.

(3) If the person responsible for a pension arrangement makes a request under paragraph (2), the party with the pension rights must provide that person with a copy of the section of that party's financial statement that relates to that party's pension rights or benefits under that arrangement.

(4) The party with the pension rights must comply with paragraph (3) –

(a) within the time limited for filing the financial statement by rule 9.14(1); or
(b) within 21 days beginning with the date on which the person responsible for the pension arrangement makes the request,

whichever is the later.

(5) A person responsible for a pension arrangement who receives a copy of the section of a financial statement as required pursuant to paragraph (4) may, within 21 days beginning with the date on which that person receives it, send to the court, the applicant and the respondent a statement in answer.

(6) A person responsible for a pension arrangement who files a statement in answer pursuant to paragraph (5) will be entitled to be represented at the first appointment, or such other hearing as the court may direct, and the court must within 4 days, beginning with the date on which that person files the statement in answer, give the person notice of the date of the first appointment or other hearing as the case may be.

Scope—This rule sets out the procedure for applying for a pension attachment order, including provision for objection by a pension arrangement. See further the notes to FPR 2010, Pt 9, Ch 8.

9.34 Applications for consent orders for pension attachment

(1) This rule applies where service has not been effected under rule 9.33(1).

(2) Where the parties have agreed on the terms of an order and the agreement includes a pension attachment order, then they must serve on the person responsible for the pension arrangement concerned –

(a) a copy of the application for a consent order;
(b) a draft of the proposed order, complying with rule 9.35; and
(c) the particulars set out in rule 9.33(1).

(3) No consent order that includes a pension attachment order must be made unless either –

(a) the person responsible for the pension arrangement has not made any objection within 21 days beginning with the date on which the application for a consent order was served on that person; or

(b) the court has considered any such objection, and for the purpose of considering any objection the court may make such direction as it sees fit for the person responsible to attend before it or to furnish written details of the objection.

Scope—This rule makes special provision for consent applications for pension attachment orders. See further the notes to FPR 2010, Pt 9, Ch 8.

9.35 Pension sharing orders or pension attachment orders

An order for a financial remedy, whether by consent or not, which includes a pension sharing order or a pension attachment order, must –

(a) in the body of the order, state that there is to be provision by way of pension sharing or pension attachment in accordance with the annex or annexes to the order; and

(b) be accompanied by a pension sharing annex or a pension attachment annex as the case may require, and if provision is made in relation to more than one pension arrangement there must be one annex for each pension arrangement.

Scope—This rule lays down the formal requirements for pension sharing or attachment orders. See further the notes to FPR 2010, Pt 9, Ch 8.

9.36 Duty of the court upon making a pension sharing order or a pension attachment order

(1) A court which varies or discharges a pension sharing order or a pension attachment order, must send, or direct one of the parties to send –

(a) to the person responsible for the pension arrangement concerned; or

(b) where the Board has assumed responsibility for the pension scheme or part of it, the Board;

the documents referred to in paragraph (4).

(2) A court which makes a pension sharing order or pension attachment order, must send, or direct one of the parties to send to the person responsible for the pension arrangement concerned, the documents referred to in paragraph (4).

(3) Where the Board has assumed responsibility for the pension scheme or part of it after the making of a pension sharing order or attachment order but before the documents have been sent to the person responsible for the pension arrangement in accordance with paragraph (2), the court which makes the pension sharing order or the pension attachment order, must send, or direct one of the parties to send to the Board the documents referred to in paragraph (4).

(4) The documents to be sent in accordance with paragraph (1) to (3) are –

(a) in the case of –

(i) proceedings under the 1973 Act, a copy of the decree of judicial separation;

(ii) proceedings under Schedule 5 to the 2004 Act, a copy of the separation order;

(iii) proceedings under Part 3 of the 1984 Act, a copy of the document of divorce, annulment or legal separation;

(iv) proceedings under Schedule 7 to the 2004 Act, a copy of the document of dissolution, annulment or legal separation;

(b) in the case of divorce or nullity of marriage, a copy of the decree absolute under rule 7.31 or 7.32 or

(c) in the case of dissolution or nullity of civil partnership, a copy of the order making the conditional order final under rule 7.31 or 7.32; and

(d) a copy of the pension sharing order or the pension attachment order, or as the case may be of the order varying or discharging that order, including any annex to that order relating to that pension arrangement but no other annex to that order.

(5) The documents referred to in paragraph (4) must be sent –

(a) in proceedings under the 1973 Act and the 1984 Act, within 7 days beginning with the date on which –

(i) the relevant pension sharing or pension attachment order, or any order varying or discharging such an order, is made; or

(ii) the decree absolute of divorce or nullity or decree of judicial separation is made,

whichever is the later; and

(b) in proceedings under the 2004 Act, within 7 days beginning with the date on which –

(i) the relevant pension sharing or pension attachment order, or any order varying or discharging such an order, is made; or

(ii) the final order of dissolution or nullity or separation order is made,

whichever is the later.

Amendments—SI 2012/679.

Scope—This rule lays down duties upon the court when a pension sharing or attachment order is made, including the service of the order and accompanying documents. See further the notes to FPR 2010, Pt 9, Ch 8.

9.37 Procedure where Pension Protection Fund becomes involved with the pension scheme

(1) This rule applies where –

(a) rules 9.30 to 9.34 or 9.36 apply; and

(b) the party with the pension rights ('the member') receives or has received notification in compliance with the Pension Protection Fund (Provision of Information) Regulations 2005 ('the 2005 Regulations') –

(i) from the trustees or managers of a pension scheme, that there is an assessment period in relation to that scheme; or

(ii) from the Board that it has assumed responsibility for the pension scheme or part of it.

(2) If the trustees or managers of the pension scheme notify or have notified the member that there is an assessment period in relation to that scheme, the member must send to the other party, all the information which the Board is required from time to time to provide to the member under the 2005 Regulations including –

(a) a copy of the notification; and

(b) a copy of the valuation summary,

in accordance with paragraph (3).

(3) The member must send the information or any part of it referred to in paragraph (2) –

(a) if available, when the member sends the information received under rule 9.30(1); or

(b) otherwise, within 7 days of receipt.

(4) If the Board notifies the member that it has assumed responsibility for the pension scheme, or part of it, the member must –

(a) send a copy of the notification to the other party within 7 days of receipt; and

(b) comply with paragraph (5).

(5) Where paragraph (4) applies, the member must –

(a) within 7 days of receipt of the notification, request the Board in writing to provide a forecast of the member's compensation entitlement as described in the 2005 Regulations; and

(b) send a copy of the forecast of the member's compensation entitlement to the other party within 7 days of receipt.

(6) In this rule –

'assessment period' means an assessment period within the meaning of Part 2 of the Pensions Act 2004; and 'valuation summary' has the meaning assigned to it by the 2005 Regulations.

Scope—This rule governs the procedure for pension sharing and pension attachment where there is a supervening Pension Protection Fund (PPF) involvement. As to the PPF generally, reference should be made to the annotations to MCA 1973, ss 21B, 25E and 25F. Where there is an application for a pension sharing or attachment order, and the party with pension rights has received notification that a PPF assessment period is in operation, he/she must provide certain information and documentation (namely, a copy of the notification and a copy of the valuation summary) to the other party at the same time as the documentation required by FPR 2010, r 9.30(1) or otherwise within 7 days of receipt. If the pension arrangement is in an assessment period and the PPF notifies the member that it has assumed responsibility for the scheme or part of it, the member must send a copy of the notification to the other party (within 7 days of receipt) and also, again within 7 days of receipt, request the PPF under the Pension Protection Fund (Provision of Information) Regulations 2005 to provide a forecast of his compensation entitlement, which must be sent to the other party within 7 days of receipt. There is no obligation to notify the other party if the PPF does not take over responsibility for the scheme (eg, where the scheme is wound up or rescued) simply because there is no obligation on the PPF to notify members in such circumstances. Furthermore, there is no notification provision in relation to winding up in non-PPF cases.

Where the PPF has assumed responsibility for a pension arrangement *before* the issue of an application for a pension sharing or attachment order, reference should be made to FPR 2010, Pt 9, Ch 9.

PART III

Chapter 9
Pension Protection Fund Compensation

General note—This chapter provides the procedural framework for applications for pension compensation sharing orders and pension compensation attachment orders. Such orders may only be made where the Pension Protection Fund (PPF) has already assumed responsibility for a scheme. See, generally, annotations to MCA 1973, ss 21B, 25E and 25F. The procedure follows as closely as possible that in relation to pension sharing and attachment in relation to pensions contained in FPR 2010, Pt 9, Ch 8; reference might usefully be made to the notes to Ch 8. See, also, the Divorce and Dissolution etc (Pension Protection Fund) Regulations 2011 and the Pension Protection Fund (Pension Compensation Sharing and Attachment on Divorce etc) Regulations 2011.

9.38 Application and interpretation of this Chapter

(1) This Chapter applies –

(a) where an application for a financial remedy has been made; and
(b) the applicant or respondent is, the party with compensation rights.

(2) In this Chapter 'party with compensation rights' –

(a) in proceedings under the 1973 Act and the 1984 Act, has the meaning given to it by section 25G(5) of the 1973 Act;
(b) in proceedings under the 2004 Act, has the meaning given to 'civil partner with compensation rights' by paragraph 37(1) of Schedule 5 to the 2004 Act.

9.39 What the party with compensation rights must do when the court fixes a first appointment

(1) Where the court fixes a first appointment as required by rule 9.12(1)(a) the party with compensation rights must request the Board to provide the information about the valuation of entitlement to PPF compensation referred to in regulations made by the Secretary of State under section 118 of the Pensions Act 2008.

(2) The party with compensation rights must comply with paragraph (1) within 7 days beginning with the date on which that party receives notification of the date of the first appointment.

(3) Within 7 days beginning with the date on which the party with compensation rights receives the information under paragraph (1) that party must send a copy of it to the other party, together with the name and address of the trustees or managers responsible for each pension scheme.

(4) Where the rights to PPF Compensation are derived from rights under more than one pension scheme, the party with compensation rights must comply with this rule in relation to each entitlement.

9.40 Applications for pension compensation sharing orders

Where an application for a financial remedy includes an application for a pension compensation sharing order or where a request for such an order is added to an existing application for a financial remedy, the applicant must serve a copy of the application on the Board.

9.41 Applications for consent orders for pension compensation sharing

(1) This rule applies where –

(a) the parties have agreed on the terms of an order and the agreement includes a pension compensation sharing order;

(b) service has not been effected under rule 9.40; and

(c) the information referred to in paragraph (2) has not otherwise been provided.

(2) The party with compensation rights must –

(a) request the Board to provide the information set out in Section C of the Pension Protection Fund Inquiry Form; and

(b) on receipt, send a copy of the information referred to in sub-paragraph (a) to the other party.

9.42 Applications for pension compensation attachment orders

Where an application for a financial remedy includes an application for a pension compensation attachment order or where a request for such an order is added to an existing application for a financial remedy, the applicant must serve a copy of the application on the Board and must at the same time send –

(a) an address to which any notice which the Board is required to serve on the applicant is to be sent;

(b) an address to which any payment which the Board is required to make to the applicant is to be sent; and

(c) where the address in sub-paragraph (b) is that of a bank, a building society or the Department of National Savings, sufficient details to enable the payment to be made into the account of the applicant.

9.43 Applications for consent orders for pension compensation attachment

(1) This rule applies where service has not been effected under rule 9.42.

(2) Where the parties have agreed on the terms of an order and the agreement includes a pension compensation attachment order, then they must serve on the Board –

(a) a copy of the application for a consent order;

(b) a draft of the proposed order, complying with rule 9.44; and

(c) the particulars set out in rule 9.42.

9.44 Pension compensation sharing orders or pension compensation attachment orders

An order for a financial remedy, whether by consent or not, which includes a pension compensation sharing order or a pension compensation attachment order, must –

(a) in the body of the order, state that there is to be provision by way of pension compensation sharing or pension compensation attachment in accordance with the annex or annexes to the order; and

(b) be accompanied by a pension compensation sharing annex or a pension compensation attachment annex as the case may require, and if provision is made in relation to entitlement to PPF compensation that derives from rights under more than one pension scheme there must be one annex for each such entitlement.

9.45 Duty of the court upon making a pension compensation sharing order or a pension compensation attachment order

(1) A court which makes, varies or discharges a pension compensation sharing order or a pension compensation attachment order, must send, or direct one of the parties to send, to the Board –

(a) in the case of –

(i) proceedings under Part 3 of the 1984 Act, a copy of the document of divorce, annulment or legal separation;

(ii) proceedings under Schedule 7 to the 2004 Act, a copy of the document of dissolution, annulment or legal separation;

(b) in the case of –

(i) divorce or nullity of marriage, a copy of the decree absolute under rule 7.32 or 7.33;

(ii) dissolution or nullity of civil partnership, a copy of the order making the conditional order final under rule 7.32 or 7.33;

(c) in the case of separation –

(i) in the matrimonial proceedings, a copy of the decree of judicial separation;

(ii) in civil partnership proceedings, a copy of the separation order; and

(d) a copy of the pension compensation sharing order or the pension compensation attachment order, or as the case may be of the order varying or discharging that order, including any annex to that order relating to that PPF compensation but no other annex to that order.

(2) The documents referred to in paragraph (1) must be sent –

(a) in proceedings under the 1973 Act and the 1984 Act, within 7 days beginning with the date on which –

(i) the relevant pension compensation sharing or pension compensation attachment order is made; or

(ii) the decree absolute of divorce or nullity or the decree of judicial separation is made,

whichever is the later; and

(b) in proceedings under the 2004 Act, within 7 days beginning with the date on which –

(i) the relevant pension compensation sharing or pension compensation attachment order is made; or

(ii) the final order of dissolution or nullity or separation order is made,

whichever is the later.

Chapter 10
Communication of Information from Financial Remedy Proceedings

Amendments—Chapter title inserted by SI 2015/1868.

9.46 Communication of information: Practice Direction 9B

(1) For the purposes of the law relating to contempt of court, information from financial remedy proceedings may be communicated in accordance with Practice Direction 9B.

(2) Paragraph (1) is subject to any direction of the court.

(3) Nothing in this rule permits the communication to the public at large, or any section of the public, of any information relating to the proceedings.

(Rule 29.2 makes provision about disclosure of information under the 1991 Act.)

Amendments—Inserted by SI 2015/1868.

Scope—For the purposes of the law relating to contempt of court, information from financial remedy proceedings may, subject to any court direction, be communicated in accordance with FPR PD9B, which sets out who may communicate specified information to whom for a specified purpose.

Practice Direction 9A – Application for a Financial Remedy

This Practice Direction supplements FPR Part 9

Introduction

1.1 Part 9 of the Family Procedure Rules sets out the procedure applicable to the financial proceedings that are included in the definition of a 'financial remedy'.

1.2 The shorter procedure set out in Chapter 5 of Part 9 of the Family Procedure Rules applies in respect of –

- proceedings under:
  - the 1978 Act,
  - Schedule 6 to the 2004 Act,
  - Schedule 1 to the 1989 Act;
  - Article 56 of the Maintenance Regulation; and
  - Article 10 of the 2007 Hague Convention
- any application for the variation of an order for a financial remedy.

The longer procedure set out in Chapter 4 of Part 9 applies in respect of all other applications for a financial remedy. In a case to which the shorter Chapter 5 procedure applies, the initial application can include a request for the court instead to apply the longer Chapter 4 procedure. Examples of cases in which it may be appropriate to make such a request include an application under Schedule 1 to the 1989 Act in which there are contested issues about the settlement of property, or a variation application in which a capital payment or pension sharing order is proposed.

1.3 Where an application for a financial remedy includes an application relating to land, details of any mortgagee must be included in the application.

Pre-application protocol

2.1 The 'pre-application protocol' annexed to this Direction outlines the steps parties should take to seek and provide information from and to each other prior to the commencement of any application for a financial remedy. The court will expect the parties to comply with the terms of the protocol.

Costs

3.1 Rule 9.27 requires each party to produce to the court, at every hearing or appointment, an estimate of the costs incurred by the party up to the date of that hearing or appointment.

3.2 The purpose of this rule is to enable the court to take account of the impact of each party's costs liability on their financial situations. Parties should ensure that the information contained in the estimate is as full and accurate as possible and that any sums already paid in respect of a party's financial remedy costs are clearly set out. Where relevant, any liability arising from the costs of other proceedings between the parties should continue to be referred to in the appropriate section of a party's financial statement; any such costs should not be included in the estimates under rule 9.27.

3.3 Rule 28.3 provides that the general rule in financial remedy proceedings is that the court will not make an order requiring one party to pay the costs of another party. However the court may make such an order at any stage of the proceedings where it considers it appropriate to do so because of the conduct of a party in relation to the proceedings.

3.4 Any breach of this practice direction or the pre-application protocol annexed to it will be taken into account by the court when deciding whether to depart from the general rule as to costs.

Procedure before the first appointment

4.1 In addition to the matters listed at rule 9.14(5), the parties should, if possible, with a view to identifying and narrowing any issues between the parties, exchange and file with the court –

(a) a summary of the case agreed between the parties;
(b) a schedule of assets agreed between the parties; and
(c) details of any directions that they seek, including, where appropriate, the name of any expert they wish to be appointed.

4.2 Where a party is prevented from sending the details referred to in (c) above, the party should make that information available at the first appointment.

Financial Statements and other documents

5.1 Practice Direction 22A (Written Evidence) applies to any financial statement filed in accordance with rules 9.14 or 9.19 and to any exhibits to a financial statement. In preparing a bundle of documents to be exhibited to or attached to a financial statement, regard must be had in particular to paragraphs 11.1 to 11.3 and 13.1 to 13.4 of that Direction. Where on account of their bulk, it is impracticable for the exhibits to a financial statement to be retained on the court file after the First Appointment, the court may give directions as to their custody pending further hearings.

5.2 Where the court directs a party to provide information or documents by way of reply to a questionnaire or request by another party, the reply must be verified by a statement of truth. Unless otherwise directed, a reply to a questionnaire or request for information and documents shall not be filed with the court.

(Part 17 and Practice Direction 17A make further provision about statements of truth)

Financial Dispute Resolution (FDR) Appointment

6.1 A key element in the procedure is the Financial Dispute Resolution (FDR) appointment. Rule 9.17 provides that the FDR appointment is to be treated as a meeting held for the purposes of discussion and negotiation. Such meetings have been developed as a means of reducing the tension which inevitably arises in family disputes and facilitating settlement of those disputes.

6.2 In order for the FDR to be effective, parties must approach the occasion openly and without reserve. Non-disclosure of the content of such meetings is vital and is an essential prerequisite for fruitful discussion directed to the settlement of the dispute between the parties. The FDR appointment is an important part of the settlement process. As a consequence of *Re D (Minors) (Conciliation: Disclosure of Information)* [1993] Fam 231, evidence of anything said or of any admission made in the course of an FDR appointment will not be admissible in evidence, except at the trial of a person for an offence committed at the appointment or in the very exceptional circumstances indicated in *Re D*.

6.3 Courts will therefore expect –

(a) parties to make offers and proposals;
(b) recipients of offers and proposals to give them proper consideration; and
(c) (subject to paragraph 6.4), that parties, whether separately or together, will not seek to exclude from consideration at the appointment any such offer or proposal.

6.4 Paragraph 6.3(c) does not apply to an offer or proposal made during non-court dispute resolution.

6.5 In order to make the most effective use of the first appointment and the FDR appointment, the legal representatives attending those appointments will be expected to have full knowledge of the case.

6.6 (*omitted*)

(Provision relating to experts in financial remedy proceedings is contained in Practice Direction 25D (Financial Remedy Proceedings and Other Family Proceedings (Except Children Proceedings) – The Use of Single Joint Experts and the Process Leading to Expert Evidence Being Put Before The Court).)

Consent orders

7.1 Rule 9.26(1)(a) requires an application for a consent order to be accompanied by two copies of the draft order in the terms sought, one of which must be endorsed with a statement signed by the respondent to the application signifying the respondent's agreement. The rule is considered to have been properly complied with if the endorsed statement is signed by solicitors on record as acting for the respondent; but where the consent order applied for contains undertakings, it should be signed by the party giving the undertakings as well as by that party's solicitor.

(Provision relating to the enforcement of undertakings is contained in the Practice Direction 33A supplementing Part 33 of the FPR)

7.2 Rule 9.26(1)(b) requires each party to file with the court and serve on the other party a statement of information. Where this is contained in one form, both parties must sign the statement to certify that each has read the contents of the other's statement.

7.3 Rule 35.2 deals with applications for a consent order in respect of a financial remedy where the parties wish to have the content of a written mediation agreement to which the Mediation Directive applies made the subject of a consent order.

Section 10(2) of the Matrimonial Causes Act 1973 and section 48(2) of the Civil Partnership Act 2004

8.1 Where a respondent who has applied under section 10(2) of the Matrimonial Causes Act 1973, or section 48(2) of the Civil Partnership Act 2004, for the court to consider his or her financial position after a divorce or dissolution elects not to proceed with the application, a notice of withdrawal of the application signed by the respondent or by the respondent's solicitor may be filed without leave of the court. In this event a formal order dismissing or striking out the application is unnecessary. Notice of withdrawal should also be given to the applicant's solicitor.

8.2 An application under section 10(2) or section 48(2) which has been withdrawn is not a bar to making in matrimonial proceedings, the decree absolute and in civil partnership proceedings, the final order.

Maintenance Orders – registration in the family court

9.1 Where periodical payments are required to be made to a child under an order registered in the family court, section 31L(3) and (4) of the1984 Act permits the payments to be made instead to the person with whom the child has his home. That person may proceed in his own name for variation, revival or revocation of the order and may enforce payment in his own name.

9.2 The registration in the family court of an order made direct to a child entails a considerable amount of work. Accordingly, when the High Court is considering the form of an order where there are children, care should be taken not to make orders for payment direct where such orders would be of no benefit to the parties.

Pensions

10.1 The phrase 'party with pension rights' is used in FPR Part 9, Chapter 8. For matrimonial proceedings, this phrase has the meaning given to it by section 25D(3) of the Matrimonial Causes Act 1973 and means 'the party to the marriage who has or is likely to have benefits under a pension arrangement'. There is a definition of 'civil partner with pension rights' in paragraph 29 of Schedule 5 to the Civil Partnership Act 2004 which mirrors the definition of 'party with pension rights' in section 25D(3) of the 1973 Act. The phrase 'is likely to have benefits' in these definitions refers to accrued rights to pension benefits which are not yet in payment.

PPF Compensation

11.1 The phrase 'party with compensation rights' is used in FPR Part 9, Chapter 9. For matrimonial proceedings, the phrase has the meaning given to it by section 25G(5) of the Matrimonial Causes Act 1973 and means the party to the marriage who is or is likely to be entitled to PPF compensation. There is a definition of 'civil partner with compensation rights' in paragraph 37(1) of Schedule 5 to the Civil Partnership Act 2004 which mirrors the definition of 'party with compensation rights' in section 25G(5). The phrase 'is likely to be entitled to PPF Compensation' in those definitions refers to statutory entitlement to PPF Compensation which is not yet in payment.

Orders for payment in respect of legal services

12.1 An application for an order for payment in respect of legal services under section 22ZA of the 1973 Act or paragraph 38A of Part 8 of Schedule 5 to the 2004 Act must be made in accordance with FPR 9.7 using the Part 18 procedure. Where the application is made at the same time as an application for an order for maintenance pending suit or maintenance pending outcome, the applications may be included in one application notice, and evidence in support of or in response to the applications may be contained in one witness statement.

(Where an application is made for an order under FPR 9.7, a copy of the application notice must be served in accordance with the provisions of FPR Part 6 at least 14 days before the court is to deal with the application: FPR 18.8(1)(b).)

12.2 The evidence filed in support of an application for an order for payment in respect of legal services must, in addition to the matters referred to in rule 9.7(3), include a concise statement of the applicant's case on –

(a) the criteria set out in section 22ZA(3) and (4) of the 1974 Act or paragraph 38A(3) and (4) of Part 8 of Schedule 5 to the 2004 Act as applicable; and

(b) the matters set out in section 22ZB(1) of the 1973 Act or paragraph 38B(1) of Part 8 of Schedule 5 to the 2004 Act as applicable.

Applications to set aside a financial remedy

13.1 As set out in rule 9.9A(4), the Part 18 procedure applies to applications to set aside a financial remedy. Where such an application was made before rule 9.9A came into force, the Part 18 procedure will still apply subject to any directions that the court might make for the purpose of ensuring the proceedings are dealt with fairly (see the Family Procedure (Amendment No 2) Rules 2016, rule 5).

13.2 If the financial remedy order was made before 22 April 2014, by any court, an application to set it aside under rule 9.9A is to be made to the family court. This is the combined effect of rule 9.9A(3), which provides that the application is made within the original proceedings, and the Crime and Courts Act 2013 (Family Court: Transitional and Savings Provision) Order 2014, which provides that any such proceedings became family court proceedings as of 22 April 2014.

13.3 If the financial remedy order was made on or after 22 April 2014, an application to set it aside under rule 9.9A is to be made to the court that made the order.

13.4 An application under rule 9.9A is to be dealt with by the same level of judge that dealt with the original application, by virtue of rule 17 of the Family Court (Composition and Distribution of Business) Rules 2014. Where reasonably possible, the application will be dealt with by the same judge that dealt with the original application.

13.5 An application to set aside a financial remedy order should only be made where no error of the court is alleged. If an error of the court is alleged, an application for permission to appeal under Part 30 should be considered. The grounds on which a financial remedy order may be set aside are and will remain a matter for decisions by judges. The grounds include (i) fraud; (ii) material non-disclosure; (iii) certain limited types of mistake; (iv) a subsequent event, unforeseen and unforeseeable at the time the order was made, which invalidates the basis on which the order was made.

13.6 The effect of rules 9.9A(1)(a) and (2) is that an application may be made to set aside all or only part of a financial remedy order, including a financial remedy order that has been made by consent.

13.7 The family court has the power under section 31F(6) of the Matrimonial and Family Proceedings Act 1984 to vary or set aside a financial remedy order. The High Court has the power under rule 9.9A and section 17(2) of the Senior Courts Act 1981 to set aside a financial remedy order. The difference in the wording of the legislative provisions is the reason that "set aside" has been defined as it has in rule 9.9A(1)(b).

13.8 In applications under rule 9.9A, the starting point is that the order which one party is seeking to have set aside was properly made. A mere allegation that it was obtained by, eg, non-disclosure, is not sufficient for the court to set aside the order. Only once the ground for setting aside the order has been established (or admitted) can the court set aside the order and rehear the original application for a financial remedy. The court has a full range of case management powers and considerable discretion as to how to determine an application to set aside a financial remedy order, including where appropriate the power to strike out or summarily dispose of an application to set aside. If and when a ground for setting aside has been established, the court may decide to set aside the whole or part of the order there and then, or may delay doing so, especially if there are third party claims to the parties' assets. Ordinarily, once the court has decided to set aside a financial remedy order, the court would give directions for a full rehearing to re-determine the original application. However, if the court is satisfied that it has sufficient information to do so, it may proceed to re-determine the original application at the same time as setting aside the financial remedy order.

13.9 The effect of rule 28.3(9) is that the Part 28 rules relating to costs do not apply to applications under rule 9.9A.

ANNEX – PRE-APPLICATION PROTOCOL

Notes of guidance

Scope of the Protocol

1 This protocol is intended to apply to all applications for a financial remedy as defined by rule 2.3. It is designed to cover all classes of case, ranging from a simple application for periodical payments to an application for a substantial lump sum and property adjustment order. The protocol is designed to facilitate the operation of the procedure for financial remedy applications.

2 In considering the options of pre-application disclosure and negotiation, solicitors should bear in mind the advantage of having a court timetable and court managed process. There is sometimes an advantage in preparing disclosure before proceedings are commenced. However, solicitors should bear in mind the objective of controlling costs and in particular the costs of discovery and that the option of pre-application disclosure and negotiation has risks of excessive and uncontrolled expenditure and delay. This option should only be encouraged where both parties agree to follow this route and disclosure is not likely to be an issue or has been adequately dealt with in mediation or otherwise.

3 Solicitors should consider at an early stage and keep under review whether it would be appropriate to suggest mediation and/or collaborative law to the clients as an alternative to solicitor negotiation or court based litigation.

4 Making an application to the court should not be regarded as a hostile step or a last resort, rather as a way of starting the court timetable, controlling disclosure and endeavouring to avoid the costly final hearing and the preparation for it.

First letter

5 The circumstances of parties to an application for a financial remedy are so various that it would be difficult to prepare a specimen first letter. The request for information will be different in every case. However, the tone of the initial letter is important and the guidelines in paragraphs 14 and 15

should be followed. It should be approved in advance by the client. Solicitors writing to an unrepresented party should always recommend that he seeks independent legal advice and enclose a second copy of the letter to be passed to any solicitor instructed. A reasonable time limit for an answer may be 14 days.

Negotiation and settlement

6 In the event of pre-application disclosure and negotiation, as envisaged in paragraph 12 an application should not be issued when a settlement is a reasonable prospect.

Disclosure

7 The protocol underlines the obligation of parties to make full and frank disclosure of all material facts, documents and other information relevant to the issues. Solicitors owe their clients a duty to tell them in clear terms of this duty and of the possible consequences of breach of the duty, which may include criminal sanctions under the Fraud Act 2006. This duty of disclosure is an ongoing obligation and includes the duty to disclose any material changes after initial disclosure has been given. Solicitors are referred to the Good Practice Guides available to Resolution members at www.resolution.org.uk and can also contact the Law Society's Practice Advice Service on 0870 606 2522.

The Protocol

General principles

8 All parties must always bear in mind the overriding objective set out at rules 1.1 to 1.4 and try to ensure that applications should be resolved and a just outcome achieved as speedily as possible without costs being unreasonably incurred. The needs of any children should be addressed and safeguarded. The procedures which it is appropriate to follow should be conducted with minimum distress to the parties and in a manner designed to promote as good a continuing relationship between the parties and any children affected as is possible in the circumstances.

9 The principle of proportionality must be borne in mind at all times. It is unacceptable for the costs of any case to be disproportionate to the financial value of the subject matter of the dispute.

10 Parties should be informed that where a court is considering whether to make an order requiring one party to pay the costs of another party, it will take into account pre-application offers to settle and conduct of disclosure.

Identifying the issues

11 Parties must seek to clarify their claims and identify the issues between them as soon as possible. So that this can be achieved, they must provide full, frank and clear disclosure of facts, information and documents, which are material and sufficiently accurate to enable proper negotiations to take place to settle their differences. Openness in all dealings is essential.

Disclosure

12 If parties carry out voluntary disclosure before the issue of proceedings the parties should exchange schedules of assets, income, liabilities and other material facts, using the financial statement as a guide to the format of the disclosure. Documents should only be disclosed to the extent that they are required by the financial statement. Excessive or disproportionate costs should not be incurred.

Correspondence

13 Any first letter and subsequent correspondence must focus on the clarification of claims and identification of issues and their resolution. Protracted and unnecessary correspondence and 'trial by correspondence' must be avoided.

14 The impact of any correspondence upon the reader and in particular the parties must always be considered. Any correspondence which raises irrelevant issues or which might cause the other party to adopt an entrenched, polarised or hostile position is to be discouraged.

Summary

15 The aim of all pre-application proceedings steps must be to assist the parties to resolve their differences speedily and fairly or at least narrow the issues and, should that not be possible, to assist the court to do so.

Practice Direction 9B – Communication of Information from Financial Remedy Proceedings

This Practice Direction supplements FPR rule 9.46

1.1 Subject to any direction of the court, information from financial remedy proceedings may be communicated for the purposes of the law relating to contempt of court in accordance with this Practice Direction.

Communication of information by a party etc. for purposes relating to appeals under the Child Support Act 1991

2.1 A person specified in the first column of the following table may communicate to a person listed in the second column such information as is specified in the third column for the purpose specified in the fourth column –

A party	The Secretary of State, a McKenzie Friend, a lay adviser or the First-tier Tribunal dealing with an appeal under section 20 of the Child Support Act 1991	Any information relating to financial remedy proceedings	For the purposes of making or responding to an appeal under section 20 of the Child Support Act 1991 or the determination of such an appeal
A party or any other person lawfully in receipt of information	The Secretary of State, a McKenzie Friend, a lay adviser or the Upper Tier Tribunal dealing with an appeal under section 24 of the Child Support Act 1991 in respect of a decision of the First-tier Tribunal that was made under section 20 of that Act	Any information relating to financial remedy proceedings	For a purpose connected with an appeal under section 24 of the Child Support Act 1991 in respect of a decision of the First-tier Tribunal that was made under section 20 of that Act

Onward communication

3.1 A person in the second column of the table at paragraph 2.1 may only communicate information relating to the proceedings received from a person in the first column for the purpose for which he or she received that information.

Interpretation

4.1 In this Practice Direction –

'lay adviser' means a non-professional person who gives lay advice on behalf of an organisation in the lay advice sector; and

'McKenzie Friend' means any person permitted by the court or tribunal to sit beside an unrepresented litigant in court or in a tribunal to assist that litigant by prompting, taking notes and giving advice to that litigant.

PART 10
APPLICATIONS UNDER PART 4 OF THE FAMILY LAW ACT 1996

CONTENTS OF THIS PART

Rule		Page
10.1	Scope and interpretation of this Part	1469
10.2	Applications for an occupation order or a non-molestation order	1469
10.3	Service of the application	1470
10.5	Privacy	1470
10.6	Service of an order	1470
10.7	Representations made by a mortgagee or landlord	1471
10.8	Applications to vary, extend or discharge an order	1471
10.9	Orders containing provisions to which a power of arrest is attached	1471
10.10	Service of an order on the officer for the time being in charge of a police station	1471
10.11	Proceedings following arrest	1472
10.12	Enforcement of an order: requirement for a penal notice	1473
10.13	Enforcement of an undertaking	1473
10.14	Power to adjourn the hearing for consideration of the penalty	1474
10.15	Hospital orders or guardianship orders under the Mental Health Act 1983	1474
10.16	Transfer directions under section 48 of the Mental Health Act 1983	1474
10.17	Recognizances	1474
	Practice Direction 10A – Part 4 of the Family Law Act 1996	1475

PART III

10.1 Scope and interpretation of this Part

The rules in this Part apply to proceedings under Part 4 of the 1996 Act.

'Part 4 of the 1996 Act'—FLA 1996, Pt IV has the title 'Family Homes and Domestic Violence'. The Act is set out with detailed commentary in Part II of this work. FPR 2010, Pt 10 deals with all procedural aspects and includes provisions derived from FPR 1991, rr 3.8, 3.9, 3.9A and 3.10 and their equivalent rules in FPC(MP etc)R 1991. However, these four rules are replaced by 17 rules. The provisions are essentially the same, but clearer drafting makes the 2010 Rules much easier to follow.

10.2 Applications for an occupation order or a non-molestation order

(1) An application for an occupation order or a non-molestation order must be supported by a witness statement.

(2) An application for an occupation order or a non-molestation order may be made without notice.

(3) *(revoked)*

(4) Where an application is made without notice, the witness statement in support of the application must state the reasons why notice has not been given.

(Section 45 of the 1996 Act sets out the criteria for making an order without notice.)

Amendments—SI 2013/3204.

'witness statement'—A witness statement, which must contain a statement of truth (see Pt 17), has replaced the 'sworn statement' of the former rule.

'without notice'—In the rule, although not in the 1996 Act, the term 'without notice' replaces 'ex parte'. Such an application is often necessary (see s 45 and commentary).

'must state the reasons why notice has not been given'—Natural justice dictates that where an order, especially an order that might affect liberty of the subject, is made in the absence of a party without that party having even been told of the application, that party is entitled to know why. Thus reasons must be given in the witness statement for the dual purpose of persuading the court to make the order without notice and then explaining to the respondent. Written evidence used not to be required in the magistrates' court (oral evidence used to suffice) but the rule applies to all courts.

Fee—A policy decision has been made that no fee will be charged on an application for an occupation or non-molestation order from 22 April 2014 (Family Proceedings Fees (Amendment) Order 2014).

10.3 Service of the application

(1) In an application made on notice, the applicant must serve –

(a) a copy of the application together with any statement in support; and
(b) notice of any hearing or directions appointment set by the court,

on the respondent personally –

(i) not less than 2 days before the hearing; or
(ii) within such period as the court may direct.

(1A) An application must not be served personally by the applicant himself or herself.

(2) Where the applicant is acting in person, the applicant may request the court officer to serve the application on the respondent.

(3) In an application for an occupation order under section 33, 35 or 36 of the 1996 Act, the applicant must serve on the mortgagee and any landlord of the dwelling-house in question –

(a) a copy of the application; and
(b) notice of the right to make representations in writing or orally at any hearing.

(4) The applicant must file a certificate of service after serving the application.

(Rule 6.23 makes provision for the different methods of serving a document and rule 6.35 provides for the court to authorise service by an alternative method.)

Amendments—SI 2017/413.

'on notice'—The applicant must effect service 'not less than 2 days before the hearing' or 'within such period as the court may direct', which could be shorter. FPR 2010, Pt 6 deals with service of the application (cf service of the order: r 10.6). The signpost in r 10.3 points to FPR 2010, r 6.23 for the various methods of service. Personal service is not essential, although it is often the best method in FLA cases. An applicant cannot effect service personally (r 10.3(1A)) but an applicant acting in person can request the court to effect service (r 10.3(2)), which it will generally do by post.

'the mortgagee and any landlord'—Note the requirement to serve the application and notice on the mortgagee/landlord if an occupation order is sought.

'certificate of service'—Use Form FL415. This form, like all forms, is prescribed by FPR 2010, Pt 5.

10.4 *(revoked)*

10.5 Privacy

Any hearing relating to an application for an occupation order or a non-molestation order will be in private unless the court directs otherwise.

Amendments—SI 2013/3204.

'in private'—Statutes (eg Legal Services Act 2007) tend to refer to 'chambers' and 'open court', whereas rules refer to 'in private' and 'in public', which are more accurate and more helpful terms. The general rule is that hearings of civil proceedings are in public, but family proceedings covered by FPR 2010 are in private, save as provided for by FPR 2010, r 27.10.

10.6 Service of an order

(1) The applicant must, as soon as reasonably practicable, serve on the respondent personally –

(a) a copy of the order; and
(b) where the order is made without notice –
  (i) a copy of the application together with any statement supporting it; and
  (ii) where the order is made by lay justices, a copy of the written record of the reasons for the court's decision.

(Rule 27.2 makes provision in respect of lay justices giving written reasons in the family court.)

(1A) The documents listed in paragraph (1) must not be served personally by the applicant himself or herself.

(2) The court must serve the documents listed in paragraph (1) if –

(a) an applicant, acting in person, so requests; or

(b) the court made the order of its own initiative.

(3) In an application for an occupation order under section 33, 35 or 36 of the 1996 Act, the applicant must serve a copy of any order made on the mortgagee and any landlord of the dwelling-house in question.

Amendments—SI 2014/667; SI 2017/413.

'serve on the respondent personally'—The rule requires personal service of the order and, in without notice cases, of the further documents specified in r 10.6(1)(b). No injunctive order is enforceable unless it is proved that the respondent is aware of it (see further the commentary on enforcement and CCA 1981). Service should be effected in accordance with the Family Justice Council *Protocol for Process Servers: Non-Molestation Orders*, November 2011 (see Part V). Litigants in person can require the court to effect service (r 10.6(2)(a)). Although an applicant cannot serve personally (r 10.6(1A)), an applicant acting in person can require the court to effect service under r 10.6(2)(a).

10.7 Representations made by a mortgagee or landlord

The court may direct that a hearing be held in order to consider any representations made by a mortgagee or a landlord.

10.8 Applications to vary, extend or discharge an order

Rules 10.5 to 10.7 apply to applications to vary, extend or discharge an order.

10.9 Orders containing provisions to which a power of arrest is attached

Where the court makes an occupation order containing one or more provisions to which a power of arrest is attached ('relevant provisions') –

(a) each relevant provision must be set out in a separate paragraph in the order; and

(b) a paragraph containing a relevant provision must not include a provision of the order to which the power of arrest is not attached.

'power of arrest'—The law on powers of arrest is in FLA 1996, s 47. The power can only be attached to an occupation order (not a non-molestation order) and if it is, both the respondent who is being injuncted and the police who may have to use the power need to know precisely what it is that the respondent can be arrested for if he does it (or does not do it as the case may be). Clarity ought to be a feature of all court orders but is absolutely essential in injunctions and especially so in those that contain a power of arrest. Hence, the clear requirements of r 10.9.

10.10 Service of an order on the officer for the time being in charge of a police station

(1) Where the court makes –

(a) an occupation order to which a power of arrest is attached; or

(b) a non-molestation order,

a copy of the order must be delivered to the officer for the time being in charge of –

(i) the police station for the applicant's address; or

(ii) such other police station as the court may specify.

(2) A copy of the order delivered under paragraph (1) must be accompanied by a statement showing that the respondent has been served with the order or informed of its terms (whether by being present when the order was made or by telephone or otherwise).

(3) The documentation referred to in paragraphs (1) and (2) must be delivered by –

(a) the applicant; or

(b) the court officer, where the order was served following a request under rule 10.6(2).

(4) Paragraph (5) applies where an order is made varying or discharging –

(a) a provision of an occupation order to which a power of arrest is attached; or

(b) a provision of a non-molestation order.

PART III

(5) The court officer must –

(a) immediately inform –

(i) the officer who received a copy of the order under paragraph (1); and

(ii) if the applicant's address has changed, the officer for the time being in charge of the police station for the new address; and

(b) deliver a copy of the order referred to in paragraph (4)(a) or (b) and the order referred to in paragraph (1) to any officer so informed.

Service on the police—Breach of a non-molestation order is a crime (see FLA 1996, s 42A). Thus, the police need to know of all such orders so that they can deal with any breach. The police do not need to know of occupation orders unless they contain a power of arrest so that the power can be exercised if necessary (and note FPR 2010, r 10.9, above). See the Family Justice Council *Protocol for Process Servers: Non-Molestation Orders*, November 2011 in Part V.

Generally, orders must be delivered to the officer in charge of the police station for the applicant's address, but a different station can be specified and the court should be asked to specify a more appropriate station if there is one: for example, the police may have a domestic violence unit based at a particular police station.

Note the requirements of r 10.10(2) and that the effect of it is to require service on the respondent before notification to the police so that there is no risk of the police effecting an unlawful arrest based on an order of which the respondent knows nothing.

'the court officer must' (r 10.10(5))—As stated above, the police need to be aware of relevant orders. The court has power to vary or discharge FLA 1996 orders (s 49) and if an order notified to the police is varied or discharged, the police must be notified of that. However, the duty to do so is on the court officer not the party who obtained the variation or discharge.

10.11 Proceedings following arrest

(1) This rule applies where a person is arrested pursuant to –

(a) a power of arrest attached to a provision of an occupation order;

(b) a warrant of arrest issued on an application under section 47(8) of the 1996 Act; or

(c) a warrant of arrest issued on an application for enforcement of an incoming protection measure.

(The Civil Jurisdiction and Judgments (Protection Measures) Regulations 2014 make provision in relation to the powers of the family court and the High Court to enforce incoming protection measures under the Protection Measures Regulation.)

(2) The court before which a person is brought following arrest may –

(a) determine whether the facts, and the circumstances which led to the arrest, amounted to disobedience of the order; or

(b) adjourn the proceedings.

(3) Where the proceedings are adjourned and the arrested person is released –

(a) unless the court directs otherwise, the matter must be dealt with within 14 days beginning with the date of arrest; and

(b) the arrested person must be given not less than 2 days' notice of the hearing.

(4) An application notice seeking the committal for contempt of court of the arrested person may be issued if the arrested person is not dealt with within the period mentioned in paragraph (3)(a).

(The powers of the court to remand in custody or on bail are contained in section 47 of and Schedule 5 to the Family Law Act 1996.)

Amendments—SI 2013/3204; SI 2014/3296.

Practice Direction—See the Practice Direction of 26 March 2015: *Committal for Contempt of Court – Open Court*, in Part V.

'where a person is arrested' (r 10.11(1))—There are three ways that a person said to be in breach of an FLA 1996 order can be brought before the court: arrest under a power of arrest; arrest under a warrant of arrest; and in answer to an application notice. This rule applies to the first two only, i e the procedure following arrest.

The rule contains provisions formerly in FPR 1991, r 3.9A but in terms much easier to follow. It even contains a signpost to the relevant statutory provisions, namely FLA 1996, s 47 and Sch 5 (see those provisions and commentary thereon).

'determine ... the facts' (r 10.11(2)(a))—A trial is required to determine the facts. Where the facts are disputed, the evidence of the applicant will be required (and, if represented, submissions from the legal representative) but the applicant is unlikely to be present and may not even know of the arrest. Even if the facts are admitted, the court is unlikely to be able to proceed as it may not have the full facts. The respondent must be brought before the court within 24 hours of arrest pursuant to a power of arrest (s 47(7)) and is most unlikely to have had the opportunity to reflect or take legal advice. (The 24 hour rule does not apply to warrants but in practice is usually followed.) Further, an alleged contemnor is entitled to notice in writing, setting out clearly what he is alleged to have done (*Newman (t/a Mantella Publishing) v Modern Bookbinders Ltd* [2000] 1 WLR 2559, CA). If it proceeded, the court could deal only with the alleged breach that led to the arrest, whereas the applicant may wish to issue an application alleging other breaches (Form N78 should be used) to be considered at the trial. For all of these reasons the court is unlikely to be able to proceed as envisaged by r 10.11(2)(a) and is much more likely to have to adjourn, as permitted by r 10.11(2)(b).

Contempt of court—Breach of an FLA 1996 order is a contempt of court. The powers of the High Court and the County Court to punish are contained in the Contempt of Court Act 1981: see that Act and commentary thereon.

Relevant judicial authority—By FLA 1996, s 58 the power to punish contempt is exercisable by the 'relevant judicial authority', which is defined in s 63(1).

'adjourn the proceedings' (r 10.11(2)(b))—Following the arrest the court can adjourn and, for the reasons explained above, often has to do so. If it adjourns, the court has to decide whether just to adjourn or also to remand. If the court decides to remand it has to decide whether to remand in custody or on bail. FLA 1996, s 47 and Sch 5 contain the powers of the High Court and the County Court to remand (see those provisions and commentary thereon). The maximum period of a remand in custody is 8 days if remanded to prison and 3 days if remanded to police cells.

'within 14 days' (r 10.11(3)(a))—Dealing with a committal application promptly is desirable in all cases and r 10.11(3) states the basic rule that a respondent should be dealt with within 14 days of the arrest 'unless the court directs otherwise'. The rule only applies where 'the arrested person is released', so would cover both a mere adjournment and a remand on bail but not a remand in custody, where the maximum period of remand is 8 days (although there is express power to further remand in FLA 1996, Sch 5, paras 2(2) and 3).

PART III

'not less than 2 days' notice of the hearing' (r 10.11(3)(b))—If the arrested person is released (whether on bail or not) and the hearing is adjourned, he must be given at least 2 days' notice of the new date. The better practice is for the judge to fix the date and announce it in court so that there is no doubt about it. Notice of the new date should still be served, but posting it would then be sufficient.

'application notice' (r 10.11(4))—There are three reasons why an application notice (Form N78) may be required where the respondent has been arrested: one is mentioned in r 10.11(4) and speaks for itself; the second is where the applicant wishes to put before the court for consideration other alleged breaches in addition to that which gave rise to the arrest; and the third is where the judge requires it to give effect to the requirement that a person alleged to be in breach is entitled to written notice of what he is alleged to have done (*Newman (t/a Mantella Publishing) v Modern Bookbinders Ltd* [2000] 1 WLR 2559, CA).

'incoming protection measure' (r 10.11(1)(c))—See Pt 38 and commentary.

10.12 Enforcement of an order: requirement for a penal notice

At the time when the order is drawn up, the court officer will –

(a) where the order made is (or includes) a non-molestation order; or

(b) where the order made is an occupation order and the court so directs,

issue a copy of the order, endorsed with or incorporating a notice as to the consequences of disobedience, for service in accordance with rule 10.6.

(For enforcement of an order by way of committal see Part 37 (rule 37.9 concerns the requirement for a judgment or order to do or not to do an act to contain a penal notice if it is to be enforceable by way of committal).)

Amendments—Substituted by SI 2014/667.

Penal notice—The effect of r 10.12 is to require that a penal notice is endorsed on FLA orders. A penal notice, which warns the respondent of the consequences of disobedience, is an essential prerequisite to enforcement. Particular wording is prescribed by FPR PD37A. A defective penal notice makes the order unenforceable: *Re Dad* [2015] EWHC 2655 (Fam).

10.13 Enforcement of an undertaking

Chapter 2 of Part 37 applies with the necessary modifications where an application is made to commit a person for breach of an undertaking.

(For enforcement of an undertaking by way of committal see rule 37.4(4).)

Amendments—Substituted by SI 2014/667.

Undertakings—The court can accept an undertaking instead of making an order: see FLA 1996, s 46 and commentary. As to enforcement of undertakings, see FPR PD33A and the rules indicated in r 10.13.

10.14 Power to adjourn the hearing for consideration of the penalty

The court may adjourn the hearing for consideration of the penalty to be imposed for any contempt of court found proved and such a hearing may be restored if the respondent does not comply with any conditions specified by the court.

Amendments—SI 2013/3204.

'may adjourn the hearing for consideration of the penalty'—The standard form (Form N79) used by sentencing judges includes provision for adjourning penalty as permitted by r 10.14. There are many reasons why this may be appropriate. For example, the judge may adjourn on terms (including strict compliance with the injunction) to give the respondent a final opportunity to comply. However, there is a trap here: it is not possible to remand in custody while the judge considers the appropriate penalty, as no statute has conferred such a power (*Delaney v Delaney* [1996] 1 FLR 458, CA).

10.15 Hospital orders or guardianship orders under the Mental Health Act 1983

(1) Where the court makes a hospital order under the Mental Health Act 1983 the court officer must –

- (a) send to the hospital any information which will be of assistance in dealing with the patient; and
- (b) inform the applicant when the respondent is being transferred to hospital.

(2) Where the court makes a guardianship order under the Mental Health Act 1983, the court officer must send any information which will be of assistance in dealing with the patient to –

- (a) the patient's guardian; and
- (b) where the guardian is a person other than the local services authority, the local services authority.

Amendments—SI 2013/3204.

'hospital order'—The powers of the court to make a hospital order are found in CCA 1981, s 14: see that Act, the commentary thereon and the sections of MHA 1983 referred to. First, the court will normally have used the powers to remand for medical examination and report in FLA 1996, s 48. See further FPR PD10A.

10.16 Transfer directions under section 48 of the Mental Health Act 1983

(1) Where a transfer direction given by the Secretary of State under section 48 of the Mental Health Act 1983 is in force in respect of a person remanded in custody by the court, the court officer must notify –

- (a) the governor of the prison to which that person was remanded; and
- (b) the hospital where that person is detained,

of any committal hearing which that person is required to attend.

(2) The court officer must also give notice in writing of any further remand to the hospital where that person is detained.

Amendments—SI 2013/3204.

10.17 Recognizances

(1) Where, in accordance with paragraph 2(1)(b)(ii) of Schedule 5 to the 1996 Act, the court fixes the amount of any recognizance with a view to it being taken subsequently, the recognizance may be taken by –

- (a) a judge of the court;
- (b) a police officer of the rank of inspector or above or in charge of a police station; or
- (c) the governor or keeper of a prison where the arrested person is in custody.

(2) The person having custody of an applicant for bail must release that applicant if satisfied that the required recognizances have been taken.

Amendments—SI 2013/3204.

Recognizance—Recognizances by defendants in criminal proceedings were abolished by the Bail Act 1976, which created the offence of failure to answer to bail. But that offence only arises in criminal proceedings, so FLA 1996, Sch 5, para 2(1)(b) requires a recognizance to be taken where a person is remanded on bail under FLA 1996, s 47.

A recognizance is an obligation or bond acknowledged before a court. The person acknowledging it, that is the person bound by it, is the cognisor or conusor. The object of a recognizance is to secure the performance of an act by the cognisor, such as to appear at court on a particular day. If the obligation is not performed the recognizance is estreated.

Practice Direction 10A – Part 4 of the Family Law Act 1996

This Practice Direction supplements FPR Part 10

★★★★

Applications for an occupation order or non-molestation order made by a child under the age of sixteen

2.1 If an application for an occupation order or non-molestation order is made by a child under the age of sixteen attention is drawn to section 43 of the 1996 Act. This provides that leave of the court is required for an application made by a child under the age of sixteen. The application should be made in accordance with Part 18.

Privacy

3.1 If at a hearing which has been held in private –

(a) a non-molestation order is made or an occupation order is made to which a power of arrest is attached; and

(b) the person to whom it is addressed was not given notice of the hearing and was not present at the hearing,

the terms of the order and the name of the person to whom it is addressed shall be announced in open court at the earliest opportunity.

3.2 This announcement may be either on the same day when the court proceeds to hear cases in open court or where there is no further business in open court on that day at the next listed sitting of the court.

3.3 When a person arrested under a power of arrest attached to an occupation order cannot conveniently be brought before the relevant judicial authority sitting in a place normally used as a courtroom within 24 hours after the arrest, that person may be brought before the relevant judicial authority at any convenient place. As the liberty of the subject is involved, the press and public should be permitted to be present, unless security needs make this impracticable.

Warrant of arrest on an application under section 47(8) of the 1996 Act

4.1 In accordance with section 47(9) of the 1996 Act, a warrant of arrest on an application under section 47(8) shall not be issued unless –

(a) the application is substantiated on oath; and

(b) the court has reasonable grounds for believing that the respondent has failed to comply with the order.

Attendance of arresting officer

5.1 Attention is drawn to section 47(7) of the 1996 Act. This provides that a person arrested under a power of arrest attached to an occupation order must be brought before a judge within the period of 24 hours beginning at the time of arrest.

5.2 When the arrested person is brought before the judge the attendance of the arresting officer will not be necessary, unless the arrest itself is in issue. A written statement from the arresting officer as to the circumstances of the arrest should normally be sufficient.

5.3 In those cases where the arresting officer was also a witness to the events leading to the arrest and his or her evidence regarding those events is required, arrangements should be made for the arresting officer to attend at a subsequent hearing to give evidence.

Application for Bail

6.1 An application for bail by a person arrested under –

(a) a power of arrest attached to an occupation order under section 47(2) or (3) of the 1996 Act; or

(b) a warrant of arrest issued on an application under section 47(8) or the 1996 Act,

may be made orally or in writing.

6.2 The court will require the following information, which an application in writing should therefore contain –

(a) the full name of the person making the application;

(b) the address of the place where the person making the application is detained at the time when the application is made;

(c) the address where the person making the application would reside if granted bail;

(d) the amount of the recognizance in which the person making the application would agree to be bound; and

(e) the grounds on which the application is made and, where a previous application has been refused, full particulars of any change in circumstances which has occurred since that refusal.

6.3 An application made in writing must be signed –

(a) by the person making the application or by a person duly authorised by that person in that behalf; or

(b) where the person making the application is a child or is for any reason incapable of acting, by a children's guardian or litigation friend acting on that person's behalf.

6.4 A copy of the application must be served on the person who obtained the injunction.

6.5 A copy of the bail notice must be given to a respondent who is remanded on bail.

Remand for Medical Examination and Report

7.1 Section 48(4) of the 1996 Act provides that the judge has power to make an order under section 35 of the Mental Health Act 1983 (remand to hospital for report on accused's mental condition) in certain circumstances. If the judge does so attention is drawn to section 35(8) of that Act, which provides that a person remanded to hospital under that section may obtain at his or her own expense an independent report on his or her mental condition from a registered medical practitioner or approved clinician of his or her choice and apply to the court on the basis of it for the remand to be terminated under section 35(7).

PART 11
APPLICATIONS UNDER PART 4A OF THE FAMILY LAW ACT 1996 OR PART 1 OF SCHEDULE 2 TO THE FEMALE GENITAL MUTILATION ACT 2003

Amendments—SI 2015/1420.

CONTENTS OF THIS PART

Rule		Page
11.1	Scope and interpretation	1477
11.2	Applications	1477
11.2A	Directions about service	1478
11.3	Permission to apply	1478
11.4	Service of applications on notice	1479
11.6	Parties	1479

11.7	Hearings and service of orders	1480
11.8	Orders made by the court of its own initiative	1481
11.9	Representations in respect of orders	1482
11.10	Applications to vary, extend or discharge an order	1482
11.12	Service of an order on the officer for the time being in charge of a police station	1482
11.13	Application for issue of warrant for arrest	1482
11.14	Proceedings following arrest	1483
11.15	Enforcement of orders and undertakings	1484
11.16	Power to adjourn the hearing for consideration of the penalty	1484
11.17	Hospital orders or guardianship orders under the Mental Health Act 1983	1484
11.18	Transfer directions under section 48 of the Mental Health Act 1983	1484
11.19	Recognizances	1485

11.1 Scope and interpretation

(1) The rules in this Part apply to proceedings under Part 4A of the 1996 Act and under Part 1 of Schedule 2 to the 2003 Act.

(2) In this Part –

'the 2003 Act' means the Female Genital Mutilation Act 2003;

'a FGM protection order' means an order under paragraph 1(1) of Part 1 of Schedule 2 to the 2003 Act;

'a forced marriage protection order' means an order under section 63A of the 1996 Act;

'an individual' means a person (whether legally represented or not) who is not applying for an order on behalf of an organisation, and includes the person who is the subject of the proceedings;

'a protection order' means a forced marriage protection order or a FGM protection order; and

'the person who is the subject of the proceedings' means the person who will be protected by the protection order applied for or being considered by the court of its own initiative, if that order is made, or who is being protected by the protection order.

Amendments—SI 2013/3204; SI 2015/1420; SI 2017/413.

Rules apply to proceedings in the High Court and the Family Court (District Judge or Circuit Judge level)—See FPR 2010, r 2.3. An application for a FMPO may be allocated to a judge of district or circuit judge level authorised to deal with such cases. Lay justices do not have jurisdiction to hear such cases (FC(CDB)R 2014).

11.2 Applications

(1) An application for a protection order may be made without notice.

(2) Where an application is made without notice, it must be supported by a witness statement explaining why notice has not been given.

(3) An application for a protection order made by an organisation must state –

(a) the name and address of the person submitting the application; and

(b) the position which that person holds in the organisation.

Amendments—SI 2015/1420.

Application/forms—Form FL401A is the prescribed form for an application for a FMPO. Form FGM001 should be used to make an application for a FGM protection order. Proceedings for a FMPO or FGM protection order are started when the court issues an application form, which means a document in which the applicant states his intention to seek a court order other than in accordance with the FPR 2010, Pt 18 procedure (see FPR 2010, rr 2.3, 5.3). A without notice application should be made under Pt 18 in Form FL430 (PD5A). Pt 18 and PD18A procedure will apply to the application.

Statement in support—It must be a sworn statement and must set out the reasons for applying without notice. The statement should deal with the reasons for the urgency and why notice to the respondent is inappropriate, demonstrate how the overriding objective will best be furthered and refer to this rule, which permits such an application to be made (FPR PD18A, para 5.1, FLA 1996, s 63D and FGMA 2003, Sch 2, para 5). If an order is made, it must contain a statement required under FPR 2010, r 18.11 and the court must list the application for a hearing on notice as soon as just and convenient (Sch 2, para 5(1),(3),(4) in the case of a FGM protection order).

Service—See FPR 2010, r 6 for service generally and for service out of jurisdiction.

11.2A Directions about service

(1) Where rules within this Part require the person who is the subject of proceedings to be served with any documents or informed of any action taken by the court, and that person is not the applicant and is –

(a) a child;

(b) a person, not being a party, who lacks or may lack capacity within the meaning of the 2005 Act; or

(c) a protected party;

the court must give directions about the persons who are to be served or informed.

(2) This rule applies to rules 11.3(3)(c), 11.4(1)(b), 11.6(3)(c) and 11.7(3).

Amendments—Inserted by SI 2015/1420.

11.3 Permission to apply

(A1) An application for permission to apply for a protection order may be made without notice.

(1) Where the permission of the court is required to apply for a protection order, the person seeking permission must file –

(a) a Part 18 application notice setting out –

(i) the reasons for the application, for the making of which permission is sought ('the proposed application');

(ii) the applicant's connection with the person to be protected;

(iii) the applicant's knowledge of the circumstances of the person to be protected; and

(iv) in relation to an application for permission to apply for a forced marriage protection order only, the applicant's knowledge of the wishes and feelings of the person to be protected; and

(b) a draft of the proposed application, together with sufficient copies for one to be served on each respondent and (if different) the person to be protected.

(2) As soon as practicable after receiving an application under paragraph (1), the court must –

(a) grant the application; or

(b) direct that a date be fixed for the hearing of the application and fix the date.

(3) The court officer must inform the following persons of the court's action under paragraph (2) –

(a) the applicant;

(b) the respondent;

(c) (if different) the person to be protected; and

(d) any other person directed by the court.

(4) Where permission is granted to apply for a protection order, the application must proceed in accordance with rule 11.2.

Amendments—SI 2015/1420.

Application for permission—The application should be made by a FPR 2010, Pt 18 notice (r 11.3(1)(a)) and therefore the procedure set out in r 18 and FPR PD18A should be followed. The application notice in Form FL430 for permission to apply for a FMPO and in Form FGM006 for a FGM protection order must set out the details set out in r 11.3(1)(a)(i)–(iv).

Service of the order made—For service generally, see FPR 2010, r 6. Care should be taken to ensure that an appropriate penal notice under Pt 37 and PD37A is attached to the FMPO and FGM protection order. The order should be served personally on the persons to whom it is addressed.

Permission to apply—The PTBP and a local authority may apply for a FMPO without permission. All other persons require permission. In the case of a FGM protection order, FGMA 2003, Sch 2, para 2(2) provides that the girl to be protected and a relevant third party may apply without permission but as yet no regulation has been made specifying who the relevant third party may be. In *Re E (Children) (Female Genital Mutilation Protection Orders)* [2015] 2 FLR 997, FD, the mother of the girls needed permission to apply for such an order without notice.

11.4 Service of applications on notice

(1) Subject to paragraph (3), where an application is made on notice, the applicant must serve a copy of the application, together with the notice of proceedings, personally on –

(a) the respondent,
(b) the person who is the subject of the proceedings (if that person is neither the applicant nor a respondent); and
(c) any other person directed by the court,

not less than 2 days before the date on which the application will be heard.

(1A) Where the applicant is an individual, the application must not be served personally by the applicant himself or herself.

(2) The court may abridge the period specified in paragraph (1).

(3) Service of the application must be effected by the court if the applicant, acting in person, so requests (this does not affect the court's power to order substituted service).

(4) Where the application is served on the person who is the subject of the proceedings, it must be accompanied by a notice informing that person –

(a) how to apply to become a party to the proceedings; and
(b) of that person's right to make representations in writing or orally at any hearing.

(5) *(revoked)*

(6) Where an application is served by the applicant, the applicant must file a certificate of service stating the date and time of personal service on each party served.

Amendments—SI 2012/679; SI 2015/1420; SI 2017/413.

Person to be protected who lacks capacity is a vulnerable person or is a protected person—See the implications of the decision in *Re X (A Child)* [2012] 2 FLR 456, FD under FPR 2010, r 15.1. Where the Official Solicitor is invited to represent the person to be protected (PTBP) who lacks capacity or where the person is a vulnerable person or has learning difficulties or mental health issues, the court should consider giving directions under its case management powers under FPR 2010, r 4.1(3)(o) that the person's independent mental health professional or social worker should be informed of the case and any orders made and that the independent mental health professional or social worker should attend with the person to provide support. Where the person has other disabilities (eg is hard of hearing or has a speech impediment) directions should be sought for the instruction of an appropriate person to assist the person during the whole court process. It is highly unlikely that any member of the family would be an appropriate person to offer such assistance as he/she is not likely to be sufficiently able or independent to offer support and assistance.

Service of application on notice—The respondent must be personally served unless the court directs otherwise. The PTBP must also be served if he/she is neither the applicant nor a respondent to the application. The court may direct that a person who is not a party to the proceedings be served. In any case where the applicant is an individual (whether legally represented or not), it is now prohibited for the application to be served personally by the individual. In this case, the court should be asked to give directions for service to be effected by the court under r 11.4(3) or for an order for substituted service (for meaning of 'individual', see r 11.1(1)). Where the PTBP is a child or lacks capacity or is a protected person the court should be asked to give direction about service. See further under FPR 2010, Pt 15 and the notes above.

Evidence of service—Although the rule provides that it must be by filing a certificate of service that sets out the date and time of service, the certificate should also provide details of how the person served was identified (see FPR 2010, r 6.37). Prescribed Form FL415 should be used (FPR PD5A). The statement of service must be verified by a statement of truth (FPR 2010, r 17.2).

11.5 *(revoked)*

11.6 Parties

(A1) Where the person who is the subject of proceedings is not the applicant and is a child, the court must consider, at every stage in the proceedings, whether to make that child a party to proceedings.

(For when a child should be made a party to proceedings generally see paragraph 7 of Practice Direction 16A).

(1) In proceedings under this Part, a person may file a Part 18 application notice for that person or another person to –

(a) be joined as a party; or

PART III

(b) cease to be a party.

(2) As soon as practicable after receiving an application under paragraph (1), the court must do one of the following –

(a) in the case only of an application under paragraph (1)(a), grant the application;
(b) order that the application be considered at a hearing, and fix a date for the hearing; or
(c) invite written representations, as to whether the application should be granted, to be filed within a specified period, and upon expiry of that period act under sub-paragraph (a) or (b) as it sees fit.

(3) The court officer must inform the following persons of the court's action under paragraph (2) –

(a) the applicant under paragraph (1);
(b) (if different) the applicant for the protection order and the respondent to that application;
(c) (if different) the person who is the subject of the proceedings; and
(d) any other person directed by the court.

(4) The court may at any time direct –

(a) that a person who would not otherwise be a respondent under these rules be joined as a party to the proceedings; or
(b) that a party to the proceedings cease to be a party,

and such a direction may be made by the court of its own initiative as well as upon an application under paragraph (1).

(5) Where the court directs the addition or removal of a party, it may give consequential directions about –

(a) service on a new party of a copy of the application for the protection order and other relevant documents; and
(b) the management of the proceedings.

Amendments—SI 2015/1420.

Note—Although rule 11.6(1) provides the use of a FPR 2010, Pt 18 application notice, FPR PD5A prescribes Form FL431 for such an application in FMPO proceedings and Form FGM007 in FGM protection order proceedings. The application may be considered and granted without a hearing or on written representation but the court may direct an oral hearing.

Consequential directions and case management—The court may consider giving consequential directions and any other directions for the management of the case at this stage of the proceedings (r 11.6(5)). The court should apply the overriding objective principle and its case-management duties robustly.

11.7 Hearings and service of orders

(1) Any hearing relating to an application for a protection order must be in private unless the court otherwise directs.

(2) The court may direct the withholding of any submissions made, or any evidence adduced, for or at any hearing in proceedings to which this Part applies –

(a) in order to protect the person who is the subject of the proceedings or any other person; or
(b) for any other good reason.

(3) The applicant must, as soon as reasonably practical, serve personally –

(a) a copy of the order;
(b) a copy of the record of the hearing; and
(c) where the order is made without notice, a copy of the application together with any statement supporting it,

on the respondent, the person who is the subject of the proceedings (if neither the applicant nor a respondent), and any other person named in the order.

(3A) Where the applicant is an individual, the documents listed in paragraph (3) must not be served personally by the applicant himself or herself.

(4) The court must serve the documents listed in paragraph (3) if –

(a) an applicant, acting in person, so requests; or
(b) the court made the order of its own initiative.

Amendments—SI 2015/1420; SI 2017/413.

Hearing must be in private unless the court otherwise directs—FPR 2010, r 27.11 provides that, save for certain exceptions, accredited representatives of the media are by right entitled to access to family proceedings in all courts. However, reporting restrictions under AJA 1960 and if appropriate under the CA 1989, s 97(2) will continue to apply (see further under r 27.11 and *Practice Guidance on Transparency in the Family Courts: Publications of Judgments* (Part V)).

Disclosure against a third party and MARACs—See the commentary under FLA 1996, s 63D and *Family Law* [2012] page 331.

Withholding of any submissions etc—Rules 11.7(2) and 21.3 should be considered together when the issue of withholding of information is under consideration. In determining any application for withholding information or documents, consideration should be given not only to the grounds set out in the said two rules but the court should also balance the Arts 2, 3 and 8 Convention rights of the applicant/PTBP and the Arts 6 and 8 rights of the respondents. See *A Chief Constable v YK and Others* [2011] 1 FLR 1493, FD, *A County Council v SB & Others* [2011] 1 FLR 651, FD and *A (A Child) v Chief Constable of Dorset Police* [2011] 1 FLR 11, QBD. See *Re T (Wardship: Impact of Police Intelligence)* [2010] 1 FLR 1048, FD and *A Chief Constable v YK* on the issue of when the appointment of a special advocate might be appropriate. The provision relating to orders for disclosure against a person who is not a party to the proceedings is set out in FPR 2010, r 21.2. Where an order is made without notice giving permission to withhold information, the court should include in the order the right of the person to whom it is addressed to apply to have the order varied or discharged, to make representations and where appropriate to consider listing the case for a hearing in any event so that the court can case manage the proceedings and give directions if necessary (see FPR 2010, r 11.9, below). One way of dealing with the issue of non-disclosure is to direct that the party seeking to withhold information should set out in summary the gist of the harm and the nature of the sensitive and confidential information that it is sought to withhold. Although the court cannot compel the person affected to give his legal advisers instructions permitting them to see the material that was not supplied to him, if such agreement is forthcoming the material could then be disclosed to the legal representatives on their written undertaking not to disclose it to their client. If this course was taken, the court must be satisfied that the agreement was given freely and voluntarily and that the person concerned had made an informed decision to give his consent to this procedure (*Re A (a child) v Chief Constable of Dorset & B* [2011] 1 FLR 11, QBD). The media should be excluded only as a last resort and, if there is reason to believe that the situation cannot be adequately protected, a reporting restrictions order should be made: *Re M (Wardship: Jurisdiction and Powers)* [2016] 1 FLR 1055, FD).

Service of the order ... on any other person named in the order—It is now prohibited for an applicant who is an individual (see r 11.1 for meaning) personally to serve the documents set out in r 11.7(3). In such cases, the court should be asked to give directions by the court pursuant to r 11.7(4) or for substituted service. If legally represented, a process server should be instructed to serve the respondent(s) or any other person directed by the court to be served. Service must be effected in accordance with the FJC Protocol of November 2011: *Process Servers: Non-Molestation Orders*. The statement of service must be a sworn statement and must contain all the information set out in the Protocol. To provide the maximum protection to the PTBP, particularly because of the foreign element in such cases and the serious risk of the person being removed, kidnapped or abducted from the UK, as a matter of course the applicant should invite the court and the court should direct that the order must be served on: (i) the Forced Marriage Unit/Foreign and Commonwealth Office; (ii) the UK Border Agency (via the Foreign Marriage Unit); (iii) the Identity and Passport Service; (iv) the Children's Services/Adult Services; (v) the appropriate Police Authority; and (vi) where appropriate, the relevant embassy.

11.8 Orders made by the court of its own initiative

(1) Where the court makes a protection order of its own initiative under section 63C of the 1996 Act or under paragraph 2 of Part 1 of Schedule 2 to the 2003 Act, it must set out in the order –

(a) a summary of its reasons for making the order; and
(b) the names of the persons who are to be served with the order.

(2) The court may order service of the order on –

(a) any of the parties to the current proceedings;
(b) (if different) the person who is the subject of the proceedings; and
(c) any other person whom the court considers should be served.

(3) The court must give directions as to how the order is to be served.

Amendments—SI 2015/1420.

Scope—Note that the specific provision for the court to direct a further hearing to consider any representation is set out in FPR 2010, r 11.9.

11.9 Representations in respect of orders

Where the court makes an order of a type referred to in rule 11.7 or 11.8, it may direct that a hearing (or further hearing) be held in order to consider any representations made by any of the persons named in, or directed to be served with, the order.

Amendments—SI 2012/679.

11.10 Applications to vary, extend or discharge an order

Rules 11.7 and 11.9 apply to applications to vary, extend or discharge a protection order.

Amendments—SI 2015/1420.

Scope—This rule reinforces the provisions of FLA 1996, s 63G in relation to FMPO and FGMA 2003, Sch 2, para 6. The application should be made on Form FL403A in respect of FMPO and on Form FGM003 in respect of FGM protection orders (PD5A).

11.11 *(revoked)*

11.12 Service of an order on the officer for the time being in charge of a police station

(1) Where the court makes a protection order a copy of the order must be delivered to the officer for the time being in charge of –

(a) the police station for the address of the person who is the subject of the proceedings; and

(b) such other police station as the court may specify.

(2) A copy of the order delivered under paragraph (1) must be accompanied by a statement showing that the respondent(s) and any other person whose breach of the order would be an offence have been served with the order or informed of its terms (whether by being present when the order was made or by telephone or otherwise).

(3) The documents referred to in paragraphs (1) and (2) must be delivered by –

(a) the applicant; or

(b) the court officer, where the order was served following a request under rule 11.7(4).

(4) Where an order is made varying, extending or discharging a protection order the court officer must –

(a) immediately inform –

(i) the officer who received a copy of the order under paragraph (1); and

(ii) if the address of the person who is the subject of the proceedings has changed, the officer for the time being in charge of the police station for the new address; and

(b) deliver a copy of the order made varying, extending or discharging a protection order, together with a copy of the order referred to in paragraph (1) to any officer so informed.

Amendments—Rule substituted by SI 2015/913. Amended by SI 2015/1420.

Delivery to the police—The relevant provision of the order made must be delivered to the police only after the order has been served on the respondent/s. (For mode and evidence of service, see the notes to FPR 2010, r 11.7.) It is best practice to ask the court to specify in the order that it should be delivered to the police station that has a domestic violence unit. If any relevant provision of the order is subsequently varied or discharged the police must be notified. Similarly, if the address of the person to whom the order is addressed or that of the person to be protected has changed, the police must be informed and if necessary the court should be informed so that any relevant provision of the order may be amended/varied if necessary.

11.13 Application for issue of warrant for arrest

(1) An application under section 63J(2) of the 1996 Act or under paragraph 7(1) of Part 1 of Schedule 2 to the 2003 Act for the issue of a warrant for the arrest of a person must be supported by a sworn statement.

(2) An application for the issue of a warrant for arrest made by a person who is neither the person who is the subject of the proceedings nor (if different) the person who applied for the order shall be treated, in the first instance, as an application for permission to apply for the warrant to be issued, and the court shall either –

(a) grant the application; or
(b) direct that a date be fixed for the hearing of the application and fix a date.

(3) The court officer must inform the following persons of the court's action under paragraph (2) –

(a) the person applying for the issue of the warrant;
(b) the person being protected by the order; and
(c) any other person directed by the court.

Amendments—SI 2015/1420.

Scope—This rule reinforces the provisions of FLA 1996, s 63J(2) in respect of a FMPO and FGMA 2003, Sch 2, para 7.

Application for a warrant—Pursuant to FLA 1996, s 63J(4) in respect of a FMPO and FGMA 2003, Sch 2, para 7 in respect of a FGM protection order, permission is required to make an application if made by a person other than the applicant or the person to be protected. The application must be made on Form FL407 in respect of FMPO and Form FGM005 in respect of FGMPO using FPR 2010, Pt 18 procedure and must be supported by a sworn statement (previously an affidavit) setting out the interest or connection of the person applying for the warrant in making the application. It should exhibit a copy of the order, the terms that it is alleged have been breached and identify the breach or non-compliance with the terms or how it is alleged that the respondent is stated to be in contempt of court in relation to that order (s 63J(3); see also FPR PD10A, para 4.1).

PART III

11.14 Proceedings following arrest

(1) This rule applies where a person is arrested pursuant to –

(a) a power of arrest attached to a provision of a forced marriage protection order; or
(b) a warrant of arrest issued on an application under section 63J(2) of the 1996 Act or under paragraph 7(1) of Part 1 of Schedule 2 to the 2003 Act.

(2) The court before whom a person is brought following his arrest may –

(a) determine whether the facts and the circumstances which led to the arrest amounted to disobedience of the order; or
(b) adjourn the proceedings.

(3) Where the proceedings are adjourned, the arrested person may be released and –

(a) unless the court directs otherwise, be dealt with within 14 days of the day on which the person was arrested; and
(b) be given not less than 2 days' notice of the adjourned hearing.

(4) An application notice seeking the committal for contempt of court of the arrested person may be issued if the arrested person is not dealt with within the period mentioned in paragraph (3)(a).

(The powers of the court to remand in custody or on bail are contained in section 47 of and Schedule 5 to the 1996 Act and in paragraphs 8 to 14 of Part 1 of Schedule 2 to the 2003 Act.)

Amendments—SI 2013/3204; SI 2015/1420.

Committal for breach of order—Note that if the person in breach of the protection order is not arrested and charged by the police, the applicant will have to issue committal proceedings for contempt of court. For procedure of committal hearings see FPR PD37A.

The court's power on committal for contempt—See the Contempt of Court Act 1981 (see note under that Act) and FLA 1996, s 58.

Power to grant bail—These are contained in FLA 1996, ss 47 and 63K and Sch 5. For the procedure on making an application for bail, see FPR PD10A, paras 6.1–6.5.

Power to remand in custody—The court's power to remand in custody is set out in FLA 1996, s 63K and Sch 5 and FGMA 2003, Sch 2, paras 8, 10–14. The period of remand cannot exceed 8 clear days (FLA 1996, Sch 5, para 2(5) and Sch 2, para 12 of the 2003 Act), although the court can remand the person for a further 8 days (Sch 5, paras 2(2) and 3).

Power to remand for medical examination and report—See FLA 1996, s 63L and FGMA 2003, Sch 2, para 9. If the court considers it necessary to obtain a medical report it may remand the person in custody but the adjournment must not be for more than 3 weeks at a time. In the case of a remand on bail, the adjournment must not be for more than 4 weeks at a time.

11.15 Enforcement of orders and undertakings

(1) At the time when the order is drawn up, the court officer will, where the order made is (or includes) a protection order, issue a copy of the order, endorsed with or incorporating a notice as to the consequences of disobedience, for service in accordance with rule 11.7.

(2) Chapter 2 of Part 37 applies with the necessary modifications where an application is made to commit a person for breach of an undertaking.

> (For enforcement of an order generally see Part 37 (rule 37.9 concerns the requirement for a judgment or order to do or not to do an act to contain a penal notice if it is to be enforceable by way of committal). For undertakings, see section 63E of the 1996 Act and rule 37.4(4).)

Amendments—Substituted by SI 2014/667. Amended by SI 2015/1420.

Enforcement of orders and undertakings—The provisions set out in FPR 2010, Pt 37 and PD37A now set out the procedure that must be followed. Case-law in relation to service or orders and application to commit, the content of that application, the burden and standard of proof and penalty if breach is established may still be relevant. See also rr 11.16 and 11.17.

11.16 Power to adjourn the hearing for consideration of the penalty

The court may adjourn the hearing for consideration of the penalty to be imposed for any contempt of court found proved and such hearing may be restored if the contemnor does not comply with any conditions specified by the court.

Power to adjourn—Where the court finds the contempt proved, instead of sentencing the contemnor immediately, the court may adjourn the consideration of the penalty. The court may consider this as an option (where it is satisfied that the contemnor's remorse is sincere and there is evidence of change in his/her behaviour) to see whether the change is real, maintained and enduring. In addition and or in the alternative, it may extend and/or vary the terms of the injunction or make a new order.

11.17 Hospital orders or guardianship orders under the Mental Health Act 1983

(1) Where the court makes a hospital order under the Mental Health Act 1983, the court officer must –

- (a) send to the hospital any information which will be of assistance in dealing with the patient; and
- (b) inform the persons directed by the court to be informed about when the patient is being transferred to hospital.

(2) Where the court makes a guardianship order under the Mental Health Act 1983, the court officer must send any information which will be of assistance in dealing with the patient to –

- (a) the patient's guardian; and
- (b) where the guardian is a person other than the local services authority, the local services authority.

Hospital/guardianship order—For the court's power to make orders, see FLA 1996, ss 48 and 63L(4),(5). Where the court has reason to suspect that a person who is arrested is suffering from a mental illness or severe mental impairment it has power to make an order under Mental Health Act 1983, s 35 (remand for report on the accused's mental health) similar to the power of the Crown Court. FPR PD10A, para 7.1 also draws attention to s 35(8) of the Act, which provides that a person remanded to hospital under that section may obtain (at his own expense) an independent report on his mental condition from a registered medical practitioner or approved clinician of his choice and apply to the court on the basis of it for the remand to be terminated under s 35(7).

11.18 Transfer directions under section 48 of the Mental Health Act 1983

(1) Where a transfer direction given by the Secretary of State under section 48 of the Mental Health Act 1983 is in force in respect of a person remanded in custody by the court, the court officer must notify –

- (a) the governor of the prison to which that person was remanded; and
- (b) the hospital where that person is detained,

of any committal hearing which that person is required to attend.

(2) The court officer must also give notice in writing of any further remand to the hospital where that person is detained.

11.19 Recognizances

(1) Where, in accordance with paragraph 2(1)(b)(ii) of Schedule 5 to the 1996 Act or paragraph 10(3)(b) of Part 1 of Schedule 2 to the 2003 Act, the court fixes the amount of any recognizance with a view to it being taken subsequently, the recognizance may be taken by –

(a) a judge of the court;

(b) a police officer of the rank of inspector or above or in charge of a police station; or

(c) the governor or keeper of a prison where the arrested person is in the custody of that governor or keeper.

(2) The person having custody of an applicant for bail must release him if satisfied that the required recognizances have been taken.

Amendments—SI 2013/3204; SI 2015/1420.

Recognizance—See FLA 1996, Sch 5 and the commentary thereon.

PART 12
CHILDREN PROCEEDINGS EXCEPT PARENTAL ORDER PROCEEDINGS AND PROCEEDINGS FOR APPLICATIONS IN ADOPTION, PLACEMENT AND RELATED PROCEEDINGS

Amendments—SI 2012/3061.

CONTENTS OF THIS PART

Chapter 1

Rule		Page
	Interpretation and Application of this Part	
12.1	Application of this Part	1488
12.2	Interpretation	1488
	Chapter 2	
	General Rules	
12.3	Who the parties are	1490
12.4	Notice of proceedings to person with foreign parental responsibility	1503
12.5	What the court will do when the application has been issued	1503
12.6	Children's guardian, solicitor and reports under section 7 of the 1989 Act	1504
12.7	What a court officer will do	1505
12.8	Service	1505
12.12	Directions	1506
12.13	Setting dates for hearings and setting or confirming the timetable and date for the final hearing	1517
12.14	Attendance at hearings	1517
12.15	Steps taken by the parties	1521
12.16	Applications without notice	1521
12.17	Investigation under section 37 of the 1989 Act	1524
12.18	Disclosure of a report under section 14A(8) or (9) of the 1989 Act	1525
12.19	Additional evidence	1525
12.21	Hearings	1526
	Chapter 3	
	Special Provisions about Public Law Proceedings	
12.22	Timetable for the proceedings	1533
12.23	Application of rules 12.24 to 12.26C	1533
12.24	Directions	1533
12.25	The Case Management Hearing and the Issues Resolution Hearing	1534
12.26	Discussion between advocates	1535
12.26A	Application for extension of the time limit for disposing of the application	1535

12.26B Disapplication of rule 4.1(3)(a) court's power to extend or shorten the time for compliance with a rule 1536
12.26C Extension of time limit: reasons for court's decision 1536
12.27 Matters prescribed for the purposes of the Act 1536
12.28 Exclusion requirements: interim care orders and emergency protection orders 1537
12.29 Notification of consent 1539
12.30 Proceedings for secure accommodation orders: copies of reports 1540

Chapter 4

Special Provisions about Private Law Proceedings

12.31 The First Hearing Dispute Resolution Appointment 1541
12.32 Answer 1541
12.33 Applications for warning notices or applications to amend enforcement orders by reason of change of residence 1541
12.34 Service of a risk assessment 1542
12.35 Service of enforcement orders or orders amending or revoking enforcement orders 1542

Chapter 5

Special Provisions about Inherent Jurisdiction Proceedings

12.36 Where to start proceedings 1542
12.37 Child as respondent to wardship proceedings 1548
12.38 Registration requirements 1548
12.39 Notice of child's whereabouts 1548
12.40 Enforcement of orders in wardship proceedings 1549
12.41 Child ceasing to be ward of court 1549
12.42 Adoption of a child who is a ward of court 1549
12.42A Application for a writ of habeas corpus for release in relation to a minor 1550

Chapter 6

Proceedings under the 1980 Hague Convention, the European Convention, the Council Regulation, and the 1996 Hague Convention

12.43 Scope 1550

Section 1

Proceedings under the 1980 Hague Convention or the European Convention

12.44 Interpretation 1550
12.45 Where to start proceedings 1551
12.46 Evidence in support of application 1551
12.47 Without-notice applications 1551
12.48 Directions 1552
12.49 Answer 1553
12.50 Filing and serving written evidence 1553
12.51 Adjournment 1554
12.52 Stay of proceedings upon notification of wrongful removal etc. 1555
12.53 Stay of proceedings where application made under s 16 of the 1985 Act (registration of decisions under the European Convention) 1555
12.54 Transfer of proceedings 1556
12.55 Revocation and variation of registered decisions 1556
12.56 The central index of decisions registered under the 1985 Act 1557
12.57 Disclosure of information in proceedings under the European Convention 1557

Section 2

Applications relating to the Council Regulation and the 1996 Hague Convention

12.58 Interpretation 1557
12.59 Procedure under Article 11(6) of the Council Regulation where the court makes a non-return order under Article 13 of the 1980 Hague Convention 1558

12.60 Procedure under Article 11(7) of the Council Regulation where the court receives a non-return order made under Article 13 of the 1980 Hague Convention by a court in another Member State 1558
12.61 Transfer of proceedings under Article 15 of the Council Regulation or under Article 8 of the 1996 Hague Convention 1559
12.62 Application by a party for transfer of the proceedings 1559
12.63 Application by a court of another Member State or another Contracting State for transfer of the proceedings 1560
12.64 Exercise by the court of its own initiative of powers to seek to transfer the proceedings 1560
12.65 Application to High Court to make request under Article 15 of the Council Regulation or Article 9 of the 1996 Hague Convention to request transfer of jurisdiction 1560
12.66 Procedure where the court receives a request from the authorities of another Member State or Contracting State to assume jurisdiction in a matter concerning a child 1561
12.67 Service of the court's order or request relating to transfer of jurisdiction under the Council Regulation or the 1996 Hague Convention 1561
12.68 Questions as to the court's jurisdiction or whether the proceedings should be stayed 1561
12.69 Request for consultation as to contemplated placement of child in England and Wales 1561
12.70 Request made by court in England and Wales for consultation as to contemplated placement of child in another Member State or Contracting State 1562
12.71 Application for a declaration as to the extent, or existence, of parental responsibility in relation to a child under Article 16 of the 1996 Hague Convention 1562

Chapter 7
Communication of Information: Children Proceedings

12.72 Interpretation 1563
12.73 Communication of information: general 1563
12.75 Communication of information for purposes connected with the proceedings 1564

Practice Direction 12A –
Care, Supervision and Other Part 4 Proceedings: Guide to Case Management 1565

Practice Direction 12B –
Child Arrangements Programme 1577

Practice Direction 12C –
Service of Application in Certain Proceedings 1598

Practice Direction 12D –
Inherent Jurisdiction (including Wardship) Proceedings 1602

Practice Direction 12E –
Urgent Business 1605

Practice Direction 12F –
International Child Abduction 1606

Practice Direction 12G –
Communication of Information 1618

Practice Direction 12H –
Contribution Orders 1623

Practice Direction 12I –
Applications for Reporting Restriction Orders 1623

Practice Direction 12J –
Child Arrangements & Contact Order: Domestic Violence and Harm 1624

Practice Direction 12K –
Children Act 1989: Exclusion Requirement 1631

Practice Direction 12L –
Children Act 1989: Risk Assessments under Section 16A 1631

Practice Direction 12M –
Family Assistance Orders: Consultation 1632

Practice Direction 12N –
Enforcement of Children Act 1989 Child Arrangements Orders: Disclosure of Information to Officers of the National Probation Service (High Court and County Court) 1632

Practice Direction 12O –
Child: Arrival by Air 1633

Practice Direction 12P –
Removal from Jurisdiction: Issue of Passports 1633

Chapter 1
Interpretation and Application of this Part

12.1 Application of this Part

(1) The rules in this Part apply to –

(a) emergency proceedings;
(b) private law proceedings;
(c) public law proceedings;
(d) proceedings relating to the exercise of the court's inherent jurisdiction (other than applications for the court's permission to start such proceedings);
(e) proceedings relating to child abduction and the recognition and enforcement of decisions relating to custody under the European Convention;
(f) proceedings relating to the Council Regulation or the 1996 Hague Convention in respect of children; and
(g) any other proceedings which may be referred to in a practice direction.

(Part 18 sets out the procedure for making an application for permission to bring proceedings.)

(Part 31 sets out the procedure for making applications for recognition and enforcement of judgments under the Council Regulation or the 1996 Hague Convention.)

(2) The rules in Chapter 7 of this Part also apply to family proceedings which are not within paragraph (1) but which otherwise relate wholly or mainly to the maintenance or upbringing of a minor.

Chapter 7 (r 12.1(2))—The rules in Pt 12, Ch 7, deal with the communication of information in proceedings relating to children. They set out the categories of persons to whom information relating to proceedings held in private may be communicated (FPR 2010, r 12.73) and the categories of persons to whom a party or his legal representative may communicate information relating to the proceedings where necessary for support, advice, assistance, mediation, non-court dispute resolution or to pursue a complaint (FPR 2010, r 12.75). See FPR PD12G for tables showing who may communicate information, to whom and for what purpose.

12.2 Interpretation

In this Part –

'the 2006 Act' means the Childcare Act 2006;
'activity condition' has the meaning given to it by section 11C(2) of the 1989 Act;
'activity direction' has the meaning given to it by section 11A(3) of the 1989 Act;
'advocate' means a person exercising a right of audience as a representative of, or on behalf of, a party;
'care proceedings' means proceedings for a care order under section 31(1)(a) of the 1989 Act;
'Case Management Order' means an order in the form referred to in Practice Direction 12A;
'child assessment order' has the meaning assigned to it by section 43(2) of the 1989 Act;

...

'contribution order' has the meaning assigned to it by paragraph 23(2) of Schedule 2 to the 1989 Act;

'education supervision order' has the meaning assigned to it by section 36(2) of the 1989 Act;

'emergency proceedings' means proceedings for –

(a) the disclosure of information as to the whereabouts of a child under section 33 of the 1986 Act;

(b) an order authorising the taking charge of and delivery of a child under section 34 of the 1986 Act;

(c) an emergency protection order;

(d) an order under section 44(9)(b) of the 1989 Act varying a direction in an emergency protection order given under section 44(6) of that Act;

(e) an order under section 45(5) of the 1989 Act extending the period during which an emergency protection order is to have effect;

(f) an order under section 45(8) of the 1989 Act discharging an emergency protection order;

(g) an order under section 45(8A) of the 1989 Act varying or discharging an emergency protection order in so far as it imposes an exclusion requirement on a person who is not entitled to apply for the order to be discharged;

(h) an order under section 45(8B) of the 1989 Act varying or discharging an emergency protection order in so far as it confers a power of arrest attached to an exclusion requirement;

(i) warrants under sections 48(9) and 102(1) of the 1989 Act and under section 79 of the 2006 Act; or

(j) a recovery order under section 50 of the 1989 Act;

'emergency protection order' means an order under section 44 of the 1989 Act;

'enforcement order' has the meaning assigned to it by section 11J(2) of the 1989 Act;

'financial compensation order' means an order made under section 11O(2) of the 1989 Act;

'interim order' means an interim care order or an interim supervision order referred to in section 38(1) of the 1989 Act;

'Part 4 proceedings' means proceedings for –

(a) a care order, or the discharge of such an order, under section 39(1) of the 1989 Act;

(b) an order giving permission to change a child's surname or remove a child from the United Kingdom under section 33(7) of the 1989 Act;

(c) a supervision order, the discharge or variation of such an order under section 39(2) of the 1989 Act, or the extension of such an order under paragraph 6(3) of Schedule 3 to that Act;

(d) an order making provision regarding contact under section 34(2) to (4) of the 1989 Act or an order varying or discharging such an order under section 34(9) of that Act;

(e) an education supervision order, the extension of an education supervision order under paragraph 15(2) of Schedule 3 to the 1989 Act, or the discharge of such an order under paragraph 17(1) of Schedule 3 to that Act;

(f) an order varying directions made with an interim care order or interim supervision order under section 38(8)(b) of the 1989 Act;

(g) an order under section 39(3) of the 1989 Act varying a supervision order in so far as it affects a person with whom the child is living but who is not entitled to apply for the order to be discharged;

(h) an order under section 39(3A) of the 1989 Act varying or discharging an interim care order in so far as it imposes an exclusion requirement on a person who is not entitled to apply for the order to be discharged;

(i) an order under section 39(3B) of the 1989 Act varying or discharging an interim care order in so far as it confers a power of arrest attached to an exclusion requirement; or

(j) the substitution of a supervision order for a care order under section 39(4) of the 1989 Act;

'private law proceedings' means proceedings for –

(a) a section 8 order except a child arrangements order to which section 9(6B) of the 1989 Act applies with respect to a child who is in the care of a local authority;
(b) a parental responsibility order under sections 4(1)(c), 4ZA(1)(c) or 4A(1)(b) of the 1989 Act or an order terminating parental responsibility under sections 4(2A), 4ZA(5) or 4A(3) of that Act;
(c) an order appointing a child's guardian under section 5(1) of the 1989 Act or an order terminating the appointment under section 6(7) of that Act;
(d) an order giving permission to change a child's surname or remove a child from the United Kingdom under sections 13(1) or 14C(3) of the 1989 Act;
(e) a special guardianship order except where that order relates to a child who is subject of a care order;
(f) an order varying or discharging such an order under section 14D of the 1989 Act;
(g) an enforcement order;
(h) a financial compensation order;
(i) an order under paragraph 9 of Schedule A1 to the 1989 Act following a breach of an enforcement order;
(j) an order under Part 2 of Schedule A1 to the 1989 Act revoking or amending an enforcement order; or
(k) an order that a warning notice be attached to a child arrangements order;

'public law proceedings' means Part 4 proceedings and proceedings for –

(a) a child arrangements order to which section 9(6B) of the 1989 Act applies with respect to a child who is in the care of a local authority;
(b) a special guardianship order relating to a child who is the subject of a care order;
(c) a secure accommodation order under section 25 of the 1989 Act;
(d)–(m) *(revoked)*
(n) a child assessment order, or the variation or discharge of such an order under section 43(12) of the 1989 Act;
(o) an order permitting the local authority to arrange for any child in its care to live outside England and Wales under paragraph 19(1) of Schedule 2 to the 1989 Act;
(p) a contribution order, or revocation of such an order under paragraph 23(8) of Schedule 2 to the 1989 Act;
(q) an appeal under paragraph 8(1) of Schedule 8 to the 1989 Act;

'special guardianship order' has the meaning assigned to it by section 14A(1) of the 1989 Act;

'supervision order' has the meaning assigned to it by section 31(11) of the 1989 Act;

'supervision proceedings' means proceedings for a supervision order under section 31(1)(b) of the 1989 Act;

'warning notice' means a notice attached to an order pursuant to section 8(2) of the Children and Adoption Act 2006.

(The 1980 Hague Convention, the 1996 Hague Convention, the Council Regulation, and the European Convention are defined in rule 2.3.)

Amendments—SI 2014/843.

Chapter 2
General Rules

12.3 Who the parties are

(1) In relation to the proceedings set out in column 1 of the following table, column 2 sets out who may make the application and column 3 sets out who the respondents to those proceedings will be.

Proceedings for	*Applicants*	*Respondents*
A parental responsibility order (section 4(1)(c), 4ZA(1)(c), or section 4A(1)(b) of the 1989 Act).	The child's father; the step parent; or the child's parent (being a woman who is a parent by virtue of section 43 of the Human Fertilisation and Embryology Act 2008 and who is not a person to whom section 1(3) of the Family Law Reform Act 1987 applies) (sections 4(1)(c), 4ZA(1)(c) and 4A(1)(b) of the 1989 Act).	Every person whom the applicant believes to have parental responsibility for the child; where the child is the subject of a care order, every person whom the applicant believes to have had parental responsibility immediately prior to the making of the care order; in the case of an application to extend, vary or discharge an order, the parties to the proceedings leading to the order which it is sought to have extended, varied or discharged; in the case of specified proceedings, the child.
An order terminating a parental responsibility order or agreement (section 4(2A), 4ZA(5) or section 4A(3) of the 1989 Act).	Any person who has parental responsibility for the child; or with the court's permission, the child (section 4(3), 4ZA(6) and section 4A(3) of the 1989 Act).	As above.
An order appointing a guardian (section 5(1) of the 1989 Act).	An individual who wishes to be appointed as guardian (section 5(1) of the 1989 Act).	As above.
An order terminating the appointment of a guardian (section 6(7) of the 1989 Act).	Any person who has parental responsibility for the child; or with the court's permission, the child (section 6(7) of the 1989 Act).	As above.
A section 8 order.	Any person who is entitled to apply for a section 8 order with respect to the child (section 10(4) to (7) of the 1989 Act); or with the court's permission, any person (section 10(2)(b) of the 1989 Act).	As above.
An enforcement order (section 11J of the 1989 Act).	A person who is, for the purposes of the child arrangements order, a person with whom the child concerned lives or is to live; any person whose contact with the child concerned is provided for in the child arrangements order; any individual subject to a condition under section 11(7)(b) of the 1989 Act or an activity condition imposed by a child arrangements order; or	The person the applicant alleges has failed to comply with the child arrangements order.

PART III

Proceedings for	*Applicants*	*Respondents*
	with the court's permission, the child (section 11J(5) of the 1989 Act).	
A financial compensation order (section 11O of the 1989 Act).	Any person who is, for the purposes of the child arrangements order, a person with whom the child concerned lives or is to live; any person whose contact with the child concerned is provided for in the child arrangements order; any individual subject to a condition under section 11(7)(b) of the 1989 Act or an activity condition imposed by a child arrangements order; or with the court's permission, the child (section 11O(6) of the 1989 Act).	The person the applicant alleges has failed to comply with the child arrangements order.
An order permitting the child's name to be changed or the removal of the child from the United Kingdom (section 13(1), 14C(3) or 33(7) of the 1989 Act).	Any person (section 13(1), 14C(3), 33(7) of the 1989 Act).	As for a parental responsibility order.
A special guardianship order (section 14A of the 1989 Act).	Any guardian of the child; any individual who is named in a child arrangements order as a person with whom the child is to live; any individual listed in subsection (5)(b) or (c) of section 10 (as read with subsection (10) of that section) of the 1989 Act; a local authority foster parent with whom the child has lived for a period of at least one year immediately preceding the application; or any person with the court's permission (section 14A(3) of the 1989 Act) (more than one such individual can apply jointly (section 14A(3) and (5) of that Act)).	As above, and if a care order is in force with respect to the child, the child.
Variation or discharge of a special guardianship order (section 14D of the 1989 Act).	The special guardian (or any of them, if there is more than one); any individual who is named in a child arrangements order as a person with whom the child is to live;	As above.

Proceedings for	Applicants	Respondents
	the local authority designated in a care order with respect to the child; any individual within section 14D(1)(d) of the 1989 Act who has parental responsibility for the child; the child, any parent or guardian of the child and any step-parent of the child who has acquired, and has not lost, parental responsibility by virtue of section 4A of that Act with the court's permission; or any individual within section 14D(1)(d) of that Act who immediately before the making of the special guardianship order had, but no longer has, parental responsibility for the child with the court's permission.	
A secure accommodation order (section 25 of the 1989 Act).	The local authority which is looking after the child; or the Health Authority, Secretary of State, National Health Service Commissioning Board, clinical commissioning group, National Health Service Trust established under section 25 of the National Health Service Act 2006 or section 18(1) of the National Health Service (Wales) Act 2006, National Health Service Foundation Trust or any local authority providing or arranging accommodation for the child (unless the child is looked after by a local authority).	As above.
A care or supervision order (section 31 of the 1989 Act).	Any local authority; the National Society for the Prevention of Cruelty to Children and any of its officers (section 31(1) of the 1989 Act); or any authorised person.	As above.
An order varying directions made with an interim care or interim supervision order (section 38(8)(b) of the 1989 Act).	The parties to proceedings in which directions are given under section 38(6) of the 1989 Act; or any person named in such a direction.	As above.

PART III

Proceedings for	*Applicants*	*Respondents*
An order discharging a care order (section 39(1) of the 1989 Act).	Any person who has parental responsibility for the child; the child; or the local authority designated by the order (section 39(1) of the 1989 Act).	As above.
An order varying or discharging an interim care order in so far as it imposes an exclusion requirement (section 39(3A) of the 1989 Act).	A person to whom the exclusion requirement in the interim care order applies who is not entitled to apply for the order to be discharged (section 39(3A) of the 1989 Act).	As above.
An order varying or discharging an interim care order in so far as it confers a power of arrest attached to an exclusion requirement (section 39(3B) of the 1989 Act).	Any person entitled to apply for the discharge of the interim care order in so far as it imposes the exclusion requirement (section 39(3B) of the 1989 Act).	As above.
An order substituting a supervision order for a care order (section 39(4) of the 1989 Act).	Any person entitled to apply for a care order to be discharged under section 39(1) (section 39(4) of the 1989 Act).	As above.
A child assessment order (section 43(1) of the 1989 Act).	Any local authority; the National Society for the Prevention of Cruelty to Children and any of its officers; or any person authorised by order of the Secretary of State to bring the proceedings and any officer of a body who is so authorised (section 43(1) and (13) of the 1989 Act).	As above.
An order varying or discharging a child assessment order (section 43(12) of the 1989 Act).	The applicant for an order that has been made under section 43(1) of the 1989 Act; or the persons referred to in section 43(11) of the 1989 Act (section 43(12) of that Act).	As above.
An emergency protection order (section 44(1) of the 1989 Act).	Any person (section 44(1) of the 1989 Act).	As for a parental responsibility order.
An order extending the period during which an emergency protection order is to have effect (section 45(4) of the 1989 Act).	Any person who – has parental responsibility for a child as the result of an emergency protection order; and is entitled to apply for a care order with respect to the child (section 45(4) of the 1989 Act).	As above.

Proceedings for	*Applicants*	*Respondents*
An order discharging an emergency protection order (section 45(8) of the 1989 Act).	The child; a parent of the child; any person who is not a parent of the child but who has parental responsibility for the child; or any person with whom the child was living before the making of the emergency protection order (section 45(8) of the 1989 Act).	As above.
An order varying or discharging an emergency protection order in so far as it imposes the exclusion requirement (section 45(8A) of the 1989 Act).	A person to whom the exclusion requirement in the emergency protection order applies who is not entitled to apply for the emergency protection order to be discharged (section 45(8A) of the 1989 Act).	As above.
An order varying or discharging an emergency protection order in so far as it confers a power of arrest attached to an exclusion requirement (section 45(8B) of the 1989 Act).	Any person entitled to apply for the discharge of the emergency protection order in so far as it imposes the exclusion requirement (section 45(8B) of the 1989 Act).	As above.
An emergency protection order by the police (section 46(7) of the 1989 Act).	The officer designated officer for the purposes of section 46(3)(e) of the 1989 Act (section 46(7) of the 1989 Act).	As above.
A warrant authorising a constable to assist in exercise of certain powers to search for children and inspect premises (section 48 of the 1989 Act).	Any person attempting to exercise powers under an emergency protection order who has been or is likely to be prevented from doing so by being refused entry to the premises concerned or refused access to the child concerned (section 48(9) of the 1989 Act).	As above.
A warrant authorising a constable to assist in exercise of certain powers to search for children and inspect premises (section 102 of the 1989 Act).	Any person attempting to exercise powers under the enactments mentioned in section 102(6) of the 1989 Act who has been or is likely to be prevented from doing so by being refused entry to the premises concerned or refused access to the child concerned (section 102(1) of that Act).	As above.
An order revoking an enforcement order (paragraph 4 of Schedule A1 to the 1989 Act).	The person subject to the enforcement order.	The person who was the applicant for the enforcement order; and where the child was a party to the proceedings in which the enforcement order was made, the child.

Proceedings for	*Applicants*	*Respondents*
An order amending an enforcement order (paragraphs 5 to 7 of Schedule A1 to the 1989 Act).	The person subject to the enforcement order.	The person who was the applicant for the enforcement order. (Rule 12.33 makes provision about applications under paragraph 5 of Schedule A1 to the 1989 Act.)
An order following breach of an enforcement order (paragraph 9 of Schedule A1 to the 1989 Act).	Any person who is, for the purposes of the child arrangements order, the person with whom the child lives or is to live; any person whose contact with the child concerned is provided for in the child arrangements order; any individual subject to a condition under section 11(7)(b) of the 1989 Act or an activity condition imposed by a child arrangements order; or with the court's permission, the child (paragraph 9 of Schedule A1 to the 1989 Act).	The person the applicant alleges has failed to comply with the unpaid work requirement imposed by an enforcement order; and where the child was a party to the proceedings in which the enforcement order was made, the child.
An order permitting the local authority to arrange for any child in its care to live outside England and Wales (Schedule 2, paragraph 19(1), to the 1989 Act).	The local authority (Schedule 2, paragraph 19(1), to the 1989 Act).	As for a parental responsibility order.
A contribution order (Schedule 2, paragraph 23(1), to the 1989 Act).	The local authority (Schedule 2, paragraph 23(1), to the 1989 Act).	As above and the contributor.
An order revoking a contribution order (Schedule 2, paragraph 23(8), to the 1989 Act).	The contributor; or the local authority.	As above.
An order relating to contact with the child in care and any named person (section 34(2) of the 1989 Act) or permitting the local authority to refuse contact (section 34(4) of that Act).	The local authority; or the child (section 34(2) or 34(4) of the 1989 Act).	As above; and the person whose contact with the child is the subject of the application.
An order relating to contact with the child in care (section 34(3) of the 1989 Act).	The child's parents; any guardian or special guardian of the child; any person who by virtue of section 4A of the 1989 Act has parental responsibility for the child;	As above; and the person whose contact with the child is the subject of the application.

Proceedings for	*Applicants*	*Respondents*
	where there was a child arrangements order in force with respect to the child immediately before the care order was made, any person named in that order as a person with whom the child was to live; a person who by virtue of an order made in the exercise of the High Court's inherent jurisdiction with respect to children had care of the child immediately before the care order was made (section 34(3)(a) of the 1989 Act); or with the court's permission, any person (section 34(3)(b) of that Act).	
An order varying or discharging an order for contact with a child in care under section 34 (section 34((9) of the 1989 Act).	The local authority; the child; or any person named in the order (section 34(9) of the 1989 Act).	As above; and the person whose contact with the child is the subject of the application.
An education supervision order (section 36 of the 1989 Act).	Any local authority (section 36(1) of the 1989 Act).	As above; and the child.
An order varying or discharging a supervision order (section 39(2) of the 1989 Act).	Any person who has parental responsibility for the child; the child; or the supervisor (section 39(2) of the 1989 Act).	As above; and the supervisor.
An order varying a supervision order in so far as it affects the person with whom the child is living (section 39(3) of the 1989 Act).	The person with whom the child is living who is not entitled to apply for the order to be discharged (section 39(3) of the 1989 Act).	As above; and the supervisor.
An order varying a direction under section 44(6) of the 1989 Act in an emergency protection order (section 44(9)(b) of that Act).	The parties to the application for the emergency protection order in respect of which it is sought to vary the directions; the children's guardian; the local authority in whose area the child is ordinarily resident; or any person who is named in the directions.	As above, and the parties to the application for the order in respect of which it is sought to vary the directions; any person who was caring for the child prior to the making of the order; and any person named in a child arrangements order as a person with whom the child is to spend time or otherwise have contact and who is affected by the direction which it is sought to have varied.

PART III

Proceedings for	*Applicants*	*Respondents*
A recovery order (section 50 of the 1989 Act).	Any person who has parental responsibility for the child by virtue of a care order or an emergency protection order; or where the child is in police protection the officer designated for the purposes of section 46(3)(e) of the 1989 Act (section 50(4) of the 1989 Act).	As above; and the person whom the applicant alleges to have effected or to have been or to be responsible for the taking or keeping of the child.
An order discharging an education supervision order (Schedule 3, paragraph 17(1), to the 1989 Act).	The child concerned; a parent of the child; or the local authority concerned (Schedule 3, paragraph 17(1), to the 1989 Act).	As above; and the local authority concerned; and the child.
An order extending an education supervision order (Schedule 3, paragraph 15(2), to the 1989 Act).	The local authority in whose favour the education supervision order was made (Schedule 3, paragraph 15(2), to the 1989 Act).	As above; and the child.
An appeal under paragraph (8) of Schedule 8 to the 1989 Act.	A person aggrieved by the matters listed in paragraph 8(1) of Schedule 8 to the 1989 Act.	The appropriate local authority.
An order for the disclosure of information as to the whereabouts of a child under section 33 of the 1986 Act.	Any person with a legitimate interest in proceedings for an order under Part 1 of the 1986 Act; or a person who has registered an order made elsewhere in the United Kingdom or a specified dependent territory.	Any person alleged to have information as to the whereabouts of the child.
An order authorising the taking charge of and delivery of a child under section 34 of the 1986 Act.	The person to whom the child is to be given up under section 34(1) of the 1986 Act.	As above; and the person who is required to give up the child in accordance with section 34(1) of the 1986 Act.
An order relating to the exercise of the court's inherent jurisdiction (including wardship proceedings).	A local authority (with the court's permission); any person with a genuine interest in or relation to the child; or the child (wardship proceedings only).	The parent or guardian of the child; any other person who has an interest in or relationship to the child; and the child (wardship proceedings only and with the court's permission as described at rule 12.37).

Proceedings for	*Applicants*	*Respondents*
A warrant under section 79 of the 2006 Act authorising any constable to assist Her Majesty's Chief Inspector for Education, Children's Services and Skills in the exercise of powers conferred on him by section 77 of the 2006 Act.	Her Majesty's Chief Inspector for Education, Children's Services and Skills.	Any person preventing or likely to prevent Her Majesty's Chief Inspector for Education, Children's Services and Skills from exercising powers conferred on him by section 77 of the 2006 Act.
An order in respect of a child under the 1980 Hague Convention.	Any person, institution or body who claims that a child has been removed or retained in breach of rights of custody or claims that there has been a breach of rights of access in relation to the child.	The person alleged to have brought the child into the United Kingdom; the person with whom the child is alleged to be; any parent or guardian of the child who is within the United Kingdom and is not otherwise a party; any person in whose favour a decision relating to custody has been made if that person is not otherwise a party; and any other person who appears to the court to have sufficient interest in the welfare of the child.
An order concerning the recognition and enforcement of decisions relating to custody under the European Convention.	Any person who has a court order giving that person rights of custody in relation to the child.	As above.
An application for the High Court to request transfer of jurisdiction under Article 15 of the Council Regulation or Article 9 of the 1996 Hague Convention (rule 12.65).	Any person with sufficient interest in the welfare of the child and who would be entitled to make a proposed application in relation to that child, or who intends to seek the permission of the court to make such application if the transfer is agreed.	As directed by the court in accordance with rule 12.65.
An application under rule 12.71 for a declaration as to the existence, or extent, of parental responsibility under Article 16 of the 1996 Convention.	Any interested person including a person who holds, or claims to hold, parental responsibility for the child under the law of another State which subsists in accordance with Article 16 of the 1996 Hague Convention following the child becoming habitually resident in a territorial unit of the United Kingdom.	Every person whom the applicant believes to have parental responsibility for the child; any person whom the applicant believes to hold parental responsibility for the child under the law of another State which subsists in accordance with Article 16 of the 1996 Hague Convention following the child becoming habitually resident in a territorial unit of the United Kingdom; and

Proceedings for	*Applicants*	*Respondents*
		where the child is the subject of a care order, every person whom the applicant believes to have had parental responsibility immediately prior to the making of the care order
A warning notice.	The person who is, for the purposes of the child arrangements order, the person with whom the child concerned lives or is to live; the person whose contact with the child concerned is provided for in the child arrangements order; any individual subject to a condition under section 11(7)(b) of the 1989 Act or an activity condition imposed by the child arrangements order; or with the court's permission, the child.	Any person who was a party to the proceedings in which the child arrangements order was made. (Rule 12.33 makes provision about applications for warning notices).

(2) The court will direct that a person with parental responsibility be made a party to proceedings where that person requests to be one.

(3) Subject to rule 16.2, the court may at any time direct that –

(a) any person or body be made a party to proceedings; or
(b) a party be removed.

(4) If the court makes a direction for the addition or removal of a party under this rule, it may give consequential directions about –

(a) the service of a copy of the application form or other relevant documents on the new party;
(b) the management of the proceedings.

(5) In this rule –

'a local authority foster parent' has the meaning assigned to it by section 23(3) of the 1989 Act; and

'care home', 'independent hospital', 'local authority' and 'clinical commissioning group' have the meanings assigned to them by section 105 of the 1989 Act.

(Part 16 contains the rules relating to the representation of children.)

Amendments—SI 2013/235; SI 2014/843.

Public Law Outline (FPR PD12A)—Under the PLO any decisions as to the joinder of parties and the making of directions as to party status will be considered by the court at the case management hearing. See further under FPR 2010, r 12.25.

Factors in decision whether to join or discharge a party—There is no guidance in the rules or CA 1989 as to the factors that the court should take into account in making decisions about parties. The court is required to apply the overriding objective in FPR 2010, r 1.1, so as to deal with cases justly and in ways that are expeditious, fair and proportionate. The court is asked to save expense and to ensure that it allots an appropriate share of the court's resources to the case. The following propositions can be extracted from the authorities, but practitioners are warned that a court considering similar cases in future might decide them differently in the light of the overriding objective:

(a) It appears that CA 1989, s 1(1) does not apply in this context. Where the request is for joinder, see *North Yorkshire County Council v G* [1993] 2 FLR 732, FD. As to discharge, in *Re W (Discharge of Party to Proceedings)* [1997] 1 FLR 128, FD, Hogg J held that, in considering an application by a mother that the father cease to be a party to her proceedings for the discharge of a care order, the welfare of the children was important but not paramount. In exceptional circumstances the court has power to make a declaration that the local authority be absolved from the duty to provide information to a parent and from the duty to consult him or her in any way about the child (*Re C (Care: Consultation with Parents not in Child's Best Interests)* [2006] 2 FLR 787, FD).

(b) Where an applicant seeks to become a party in existing proceedings in order to apply for a s 8 order, the factors in s 10(9) are applicable even though he does not expressly seek leave to apply for a s 8 order (*W v Wakefield City Council* [1995] 1 FLR 170, FD – an aunt sought a residence order (now a child arrangements order) in respect of her niece and applied to become a party to separate care proceedings relating to her nephew).

(c) Where a natural father without parental responsibility for the child concerned applies for leave to be joined as a party to care proceedings concerning the child, albeit at a late stage, there is a presumption that his application should be granted unless there is some justifiable reason for refusing it. There is no requirement for the court to consider the CA 1989, s 10(9) factors for granting leave to seek a s 8 order in this context: *Re B (Care Proceedings: Notification of Father Without Parental Responsibility)* [1999] 2 FLR 408, FD; *Re F (Care: Party Status: Directions)* [1999] Fam Law 294, FD; cf *Re P (Care Proceedings: Father's Application to be Joined as Party)* [2001] 1 FLR 781, FD – father's application refused as he had had every opportunity to participate in the care proceedings at an early stage and had chosen not to. This was not a breach of ECHR 1950, Art 6 (right to fair trial), because it was the father's fault that he had not applied earlier. Furthermore, there was no breach of Art 8 (right to respect for private and family life) as the father's rights had to be balanced against those of the children and the children needed a speedy conclusion to the proceedings.

(d) Where a grandparent applies to become a party to care proceedings, the Court of Appeal in *Re B (Paternal Grandmother: Joinder as Party)* [2012] 2 FLR 1358, CA has given guidance as to the approach to be taken. It held that it is appropriate to refer to the factors in CA 1989, s 10(9), albeit that no order under CA 1989, s 8 is being sought by the grandparent. Section 10(9) does not contain a test; by picking out some factors to which the court should have particular regard, it is acknowledged by implication that there may be other factors the court has to consider and it would be wrong to try to list or limit those. The prospects of success of the proposed application are relevant and leave will not be given for an application that is not arguable. However, the fact that a person has an arguable case might not necessarily be sufficient to entitle him to leave under s 10 or joinder as a party, since there may be other factors that outweigh this. The court has a broad discretion to conduct the case as is most appropriate given the issues involved and the evidence available. Some cases may properly be determined on submissions alone. It will not always be necessary for findings to be made in relation to disputed facts, perhaps because the result would not depend on them or because there are enough undisputed facts to form the basis of the decision that has to be taken. Furthermore, there is no absolute entitlement to an assessment with a view to caring for a child. The observation of Thorpe LJ in *Re J (Leave to Issue Application for Residence Order)* [2003] 1 FLR 114, CA that judges should be careful not to dismiss the possibility of a child being cared for by grandparents 'without full inquiry' should be read in the context of the facts of that case. There are various levels of investigation that may be appropriate, ranging from a full hearing with reports and oral evidence at one end of the spectrum, to a careful but limited examination of the situation by the local authority that may disclose overwhelming reasons why care by the grandparent is clearly not an option. The court must also consider the risk of delay occasioned by or associated with the application (s 10(9)(c)).

(e) The court may consider the overall merits of the applicant's case, but a good arguable case may suffice (contrasting *Re M (Care: Contact: Grandmother's Application for Leave)* [1995] 2 FLR 86, CA).

(f) If the applicant for leave does not have independent or separate views to put forward he might not be joined (*North Yorkshire County Council v G*, above, and see **Separate representation of parties**, below). The court will seek to control wasted time and costs in making its decision on joinder (*Re B and H (Minors) (Costs: Legal Aid)* [1994] 1 FLR 327, FD).

(g) By analogy with the decision in *Re A (A Minor) (Residence Order: Leave to Apply)* [1993] 1 FLR 425, FD (determining an application for leave to apply for a residence order (now a child arrangements order)), no doubt the wishes of the child can also be part of the relevant circumstances.

(h) There may be situations in which current foster-parents are joined as respondents to care proceedings but, in ordinary circumstances, the court would not regard it as appropriate because, in most cases, it would run counter to the policy of CA 1989, ss 9(3) and 10(3) (*Re G (Minors) (Interim Care Order)* [1993] 2 FLR 839, CA; see further **Separate representation of parties**, below).

(i) It is not correct (given the restrictions on applications by local authorities for private law orders) to join a local authority as a party to a father's s 8 application following its decision (pursuant to s 37) not to apply for a care or supervision order (*F v Cambridgeshire County Council* [1995] 1 FLR 516, FD).

(j) It is not always necessary to add an individual to proceedings as a party simply to make a prohibited steps order against him, nor is it necessary for him even to be present in court, although the court should make it clear that if any person served with the order disagreed with any part of it and wished to seek to set aside or vary it, they should make an immediate application to the court to do so under s 11(7)(d) (*LLBC v TG, JG and KR* [2009] 1 FLR 414, FD; *Re H (Prohibited Steps Order)* [1995] 1 FLR 638, CA).

(k) As to the appropriate parties to an application for sanction for the sterilisation of a minor, see FPR 2010, Pt 16 and PD16A, which govern the representation of children in family proceedings.

(l) It may be appropriate to give leave to intervene for a specific purpose rather than joining a person as a party (*Re S (Care: Residence: Intervener)* [1997] 1 FLR 497, CA). However, there is no right for satellite parties against whom allegations are being made in care proceedings to intervene and each case must be looked at on its own merits (*Re H (Care Proceedings: Intervener)* [2000] 1 FLR 775, CA). In *Re H (Children) (Care Proceedings: Sexual Abuse)* [2000] 2 FCR 499, CA the court held that where, in the course of care proceedings, specific allegations of child sexual abuse are made against a non-party and brought for

PART III

preliminary issue trial, it is vital that that person's evidence is before the court at that stage, even if he is unlikely to have party status at the substantive hearing. See also *Re L (Police Investigation: Privilege)* [1996] 1 FLR 731, HL, in which an application by the police for disclosure of medical reports was determined without the police being joined as a party to the care proceedings.

(m) Courts will not sanction the withholding of information about the existence of a child from his parent, or dispense with service on that parent of proceedings relating to the child, in anything other than exceptional circumstances (*Re A (Father: Knowledge of Child's Birth)* [2011] 2 FLR 123, CA). The test simply requires a high degree of exceptionality and is not limited to significant physical risk; when evaluating the risk of future harm there is no minimum requirement (*Re A*). Where the mother challenges the legitimacy of the child concerned in care proceedings it is still necessary to serve notice of the proceedings on her husband (*Re AB (Care Proceedings: Service on Husband Ignorant of Child's Existence)* [2004] 1 FLR 527, CA).

(n) In exceptional circumstances it may be appropriate to exclude a father with parental responsibility from care proceedings (*A Local Authority v M and F; The Children (by their Guardian)* [2010] 1 FLR 1355, FD – where the father presented a real and substantial risk to the children and the mother).

Joinder of child—Where a child seeks to make an application concerning himself, he must seek leave under CA 1989, s 10 and must start the proceedings in the Family Court (FC(CDB)R 2014; President's Guidance on *Allocation and Gatekeeping*); the Schedule to the Guidance indicates that such cases will be dealt with at District Judge level or above and not by lay justice. In certain situations, the child is automatically a respondent to proceedings begun by others, notably where the proceedings are specified (see CA 1989, s 41). Where this is not the case, a child who seeks to become a respondent must apply under r 12.3 (*Re N (A Minor)* (unreported) 25 September 1997, CA). Where the application to be joined as a respondent succeeds, rr 16.4 and 16.6 will dictate whether the child can instruct his solicitor independently or whether he must do so through a children's guardian. See FPR PD16A, paras 7.1–7.19 for further information about the appointment of a children's guardian under FPR 2010, r 16.4.

Separate representation of parties—Guidance as to the representation of parties is given in *Re M (Minors) (Sexual Abuse: Evidence)* [1993] 1 FLR 822, CA, where the Court of Appeal held that grandparents should not intervene in CA 1989 proceedings unless they have a separate point of view to put forward. In *North Yorkshire County Council v G* [1993] 2 FLR 732, FD, magistrates were wrong to permit the brother of a child subject to care proceedings to be joined as a party in the proceedings when he had no independent point of view to present. In *Re BJ (Care: Third Party Intervention)* [1999] Fam Law 613, CA, the court refused to join a 12-year-old boy as intervener to protect his own interests where allegations had been made that he had sexually abused one of the two children who were the subjects of the care proceedings in question. The current care proceedings did not directly involve the boy, his situation was being considered in another local authority area and his interests were being properly safeguarded by his mother. Furthermore, the court observed that intervener status brings with it onerous responsibilities which it would be inappropriate to impose on a child of his age. See also *Re G*, in **Factors in decision whether to join or discharge a party** (sub-paragraph (g)), above. Where a number of parties are putting forward essentially the same case, serious consideration should be given to the degree of separate representation of those parties that is strictly necessary (*Birmingham City Council v H (No 3)* [1994] 1 FLR 224, HL). As to the de-merits of local authorities using employed solicitors rather than specialist local counsel as representatives in contested child care cases, see *Re B (Local Authorities: Representation) (Note)* [1996] 1 FLR 56, CA. Public funds should not be used to enable parties to be represented unless they have a positive case to put before the court (*Merton London Borough Council v K; Re K (Care: Representation: Public Funding)* [2005] 2 FLR 422, FD) or to duplicate representation (*Oxfordshire County Council v X, Y and J* [2011] 1 FLR 272, CA; *Re B and H Minors (Costs: Legal Aid)* [1994] 1 FLR 327, FD). Where legal representation is unnecessarily duplicated, there may be adverse costs consequences (*Re TG (Care Proceedings: Case Management: Expert Evidence)* [2013] 1 FLR 1250, CA). As to representation on appeal, it should be borne in mind that it may be justifiable for a party to play an active role at first instance but not on appeal and, in those circumstances, costs might be ordered against him in relation to the appeal (*Re O (Costs: Liability of Legal Aid Board)* [1997] 1 FLR 465, CA).

Children as parties where separately represented—See FPR 2010, r 16.2 for the circumstances when the court may make a child a party to the proceedings. FPR PD16A, paras 7.1–7.5 set out the matters that the court will take into consideration before making a child a party. As to whether there is jurisdiction to order separate representation for children who are the subject of proceedings without adding them as parties, see *L v L (Minors) (Separate Representation)* [1994] 1 FLR 156, CA.

Request to be joined as a party—Where a person wishes to apply for permission to be made a party in the course of existing proceedings the procedure in FPR 2010, rr 18.1–18.13 and FPR PD18A should be used. Note that PD18A, para 3.5 requires the application notice to include a draft of the application for the making of which permission is sought, together with sufficient copies for one to be served on each respondent. The request to be joined as a party should be made on Form C2. The reasons for the request to be joined as a party, or to cease to be a party, should be set out in as much detail as possible and, where the person making a request to be joined as a party has parental responsibility, this should be clearly stated because it will entitle him to have his request granted as of right (r 12.3(2)). The rule is wide enough to entitle a person to request that someone else be joined or cease to be a party. So, for example, where a respondent's interest in the proceedings has come to an end, perhaps because the child ceased to live with him some time ago, the applicant may apply for him to be removed as a party. Where the request is by one person that another be joined as a party, r 12.3(3) makes no provision for him to be consulted in advance as to his views with the result that a person might find himself a party to proceedings without knowing of the possibility in advance. Bearing in mind that participation in proceedings can have serious financial and other implications, the court should be alive to this danger and make what enquiries it can as to the willingness of the person concerned to be a party. Form C2 has been amended to include an additional question related to harm, which must be completed where an application is made under CA 1989, s 8 (for child arrangements, specific issue or prohibited steps orders) or s 4(1)(c) (for a parental responsibility order). Question 4 on Form C2 asks whether the child who is the subject of the application has suffered or is at risk of suffering any harm from (a) any form of domestic abuse; (b) violence within the household; (c) child abduction; or (d) other conduct or behaviour. If this question is answered in the affirmative, supplemental Form C1A must also be completed. It is intended that cases in which an allegation of harm is made should be identified as early as possible in the court process. See further under r 12.3.

Granting request without a hearing—The court has power under r 12.3(3) to direct at any time that a person be made a party to the proceedings. FPR PD18A, para 4.2 gives the court power to consider a request for an application to be made without a hearing if it considers it appropriate to do so. However, applications should, wherever possible, be made so that they are considered at the next hearing for which a date has been fixed (see PD18A, paras 4.7–4.9).

12.4 Notice of proceedings to person with foreign parental responsibility

(1) This rule applies where a child is subject to proceedings to which this Part applies and –

- (a) a person holds or is believed to hold parental responsibility for the child under the law of another State which subsists in accordance with Article 16 of the 1996 Hague Convention following the child becoming habitually resident in a territorial unit of the United Kingdom; and
- (b) that person is not otherwise required to be joined as a respondent under rule 12.3.

(2) The applicant shall give notice of the proceedings to any person to whom the applicant believes paragraph (1) applies in any case in which a person whom the applicant believed to have parental responsibility under the 1989 Act would be a respondent to those proceedings in accordance with rule 12.3.

(3) The applicant and every respondent to the proceedings shall provide such details as they possess as to the identity and whereabouts of any person they believe to hold parental responsibility for the child in accordance with paragraph (1) to the court officer, upon making, or responding to the application as appropriate.

(4) Where the existence of a person who is believed to have parental responsibility for the child in accordance with paragraph (1) only becomes apparent to a party at a later date during the proceedings, that party must notify the court officer of those details at the earliest opportunity.

(5) Where a person to whom paragraph (1) applies receives notice of proceedings, that person may apply to the court to be joined as a party using the Part 18 procedure.

'parental responsibility' (r 12.4(1)(a))—See definition in Hague Convention 1996, Art 1(2) and the commentary under Art 16 (see Part VI). The Hague Convention came into force in the UK on 1 November 2012.

Jurisdiction and international issues—See *R v R (Jurisdiction and Acquiescence)* [2016] EWHC 1339 (Fam), where the court highlighted the need for legal practitioners to pay proper regard to the question of jurisdiction when issuing private law proceedings under CA 1989 in any case that has, or appears to have, an international element, particularly where a parent had recently arrived in the jurisdiction with the children.

12.5 What the court will do when the application has been issued

(1) When proceedings other than public law proceedings have been issued the court will consider –

- (a) setting a date for –
  - (i) a directions appointment;
  - (ii) in private law proceedings, a First Hearing Dispute Resolution Appointment; or
  - (iii) *(revoked)*
  - (iv) the hearing of the application,

  and if the court sets a date it will do so in accordance with rule 12.13 and Practice Direction 12B;
- (b) giving any of the directions listed in rule 12.12 or, where Chapter 6, section 1 applies, rule 12.48; and
- (c) doing anything else which is set out in Practice Direction 12B or any other practice direction.

(2) When Part 4 proceedings and in so far as practicable other public law proceedings have been issued the court will –

PART III

(a) set a date for the Case Management Hearing in accordance with Practice Direction 12A;
(b) set a date for the hearing of an application for an interim order if necessary;
(c) give any directions listed in rule 12.12; and
(d) do anything else which is set out in Practice Direction 12A.

(Practice Direction 12A sets out details relating to the Case Management Hearing. Practice Direction 12B supplementing this Part sets out details relating to the First Hearing Dispute Resolution Appointment.)

Amendments—SI 2014/843.

Child Arrangements Programme (CAP)—The CAP is in FPR PD12B and applies to disputes between separated parents and/or families about the arrangements concerning children. It is designed to assist them to reach safe agreements, where possible, out of the court setting and without the involvement of professionals or the court. If parents are unable to reach agreement, the CAP encourages swift resolution through the court. The general approach is now that private law cases should be actively case managed so as to bring them to a conclusion as soon as possible. The previous practice of listing cases for review is no longer encouraged, save in exceptional cases. Therefore, it will not be appropriate to list cases for review to see, for example, how contact is progressing. Instead, the CAP envisages final orders being made providing for stepped progression of contact as advised by the s 7 report.

Before making a 'relevant family application' to the court (defined in CAP, para 23.1 and in FPR 2010, r 3.6 and PD3A, paras 12, 13), the applicant must attend a family mediation information and assessment meeting (MIAM) to find out about and consider mediation or other forms of dispute resolution, unless that person meets limited criteria exempting them from this requirement. They will be required to confirm attendance on the amended form C100 (for s 8 applications) or on form FM1 together with form C1 or form C2 (for other applications requiring a MIAM, for example applications for parental responsibility orders, special guardianship orders, orders for appointment as a child's guardian under s 5, financial orders). The exemptions are set out in FPR 2010, r 3.8 and PD3A, paras 17–21 and include, for example, cases that are urgent, or where a MIAM cannot be arranged within a specified time, or where there is evidence of domestic violence. The purpose is to encourage and facilitate the use of non-court dispute resolution in appropriate cases and to ensure, so far as possible, that all parties have considered mediation as an alternative way of resolving their disputes. In *Re W (Direct Contact)* [2013] 1 FLR 494, the Court of Appeal held that it is an integral aspect of parental responsibility that parents should work to put aside differences and ensure that their children have relationships with both parents. There will be an increased emphasis on dispute resolution outside the court process, and the court is obliged to consider, at every stage, whether this is appropriate (CAP, para 1). The First Hearing Dispute Resolution Appointment (FHDRA) should take place between weeks 5 and 6 following the issuing of the application (para 14.1), and a Cafcass officer will be in attendance, together with a mediator (where available) to assist the parties in conciliation and resolution of all or any of the issues between them. Any remaining issues will be identified and directions will be given for their future resolution. The FHDRA is not privileged, so that what is said there may be referred to at later hearings (para 14.9). If it would be helpful in the interests of the child, the court will list the application for a Dispute Resolution Appointment (DRA) to follow the preparation of a s 7 report, or attendance by the parties at a Separated Parents Information Programme (SPIP) (para 14.13). There are Standard form Orders, namely form CAP01 (for Directions on Issue), form CAP02 (for Directions at the FHDRA), form CAP03 (for an order at DRA) and form CAP04 (for a final order).

President's Guidance to support the CAP—To support these arrangements, see the *President's Guidance on Allocation and Gatekeeping (Private Law)* (with Allocation Schedule); *President's Guidance on Deployment (Private Law)*; *President's Guidance on Use of Prescribed Documents (Private Law)*; *Flowchart for private law (a visual aid for judges and litigants)*; and the *Expectation Document (Cafcass)*.

Leaflet CB7—Leaflet CB7 is a *Guide for Separated Parents: Children and the Family Courts* and contains a great deal of useful information for anyone who may be considering an application to court, or is already involved in a court case. Further information is to be found at *www.sortingoutseparation.org.uk*.

Forms and start of proceedings—For the general rules about forms and the start of proceedings see FPR 2010, rr 5.1–5.3 and FPR PD5A. However, for certain proceedings the relevant forms to be used are specified in the appropriate PD governing that type of application.

12.6 Children's guardian, solicitor and reports under section 7 of the 1989 Act

Within a day of the issue of Part 4 proceedings or the transfer of Part 4 Proceedings to the court and as soon as practicable after the issue of other proceedings or the transfer of the other proceedings to the court, the court will –

(a) in specified proceedings, appoint a children's guardian under rule 16.3(1) unless –
  (i) such an appointment has already been made by the court which made the transfer and is subsisting; or
  (ii) the court considers that such an appointment is not necessary to safeguard the interests of the child;
(b) where section 41(3) of the 1989 Act applies, consider whether a solicitor should be appointed to represent the child, and if so, appoint a solicitor accordingly;

(c) consider whether to ask an officer of the service or a Welsh family proceedings officer for advice relating to the welfare of the child;

(d) consider whether a report relating to the welfare of the child is required, and if so, request such a report in accordance with section 7 of the 1989 Act.

(Part 16 sets out the rules relating to representation of children.)

Amendments—SI 2014/843.

Defined terms—'child', 'children's guardian', 'court', 'officer of the service', 'Welsh family proceedings officer': FPR 2010, r 2.3(1): 'specified proceedings': FPR 2010, r 12.27 and CA 1989, s 41(6).

Appointment—The obligation to appoint a children's guardian in specified proceedings unless the circumstances are as described in r 12.6(a)(ii) is imposed by CA 1989, s 41(1). CJCSA 2000, ss 11 and 12 established the Children and Family Court Advisory and Support Service (Cafcass), which is responsible for fulfilling the requirements of courts in respect of investigating and reporting; see further the annotations under those sections and CA 1989, ss 7 and 37. The purpose of r 12.6 is to require the appointment to be made as soon as practicable after the commencement of the proceedings, or the arrival of transferred proceedings if the transferring court has not already made an appointment. The phrase 'as soon as practicable' is not restricted to matters internal to the court but includes problems relating to the identification and availability of an officer of the service for appointment as guardian. The reference in r 12.6(a)(i) to an existing appointment by the transferring court is not confined to the possibility that that court did not request Cafcass to make an officer of the service available for appointment, but includes the possibility that such a request was made and has not been complied with at the time of transfer (*R v Children and Family Court Advisory and Support Service* [2003] 1 FLR 953, QBD). See also the *Best Practice Guide of August 2009 (Preparing for Care and Supervision Proceedings* in Part V) and the PLO (FPR PD12A). The appointment is likely to be made by way of a direction under FPR 2010, r 12.12(2)(e) (which can be done quickly and without a hearing as long as the parties are given the opportunity to make written representations; this would have the advantage of enabling the guardian to be in place in time to attend the case management hearing). Where proceedings in which a guardian has already been appointed are transferred, the appointment continues to subsist unless terminated in accordance with r 12.6.

The focus on 'issue of proceedings' and 'transfer' in r 12.6 seems inappropriate for some types of specified proceedings. Any non-specified family proceedings will become 'specified' at any time while they are pending if a direction under CA 1989, s 37(1) (investigation of the child's circumstances) is given, or if the court begins to consider making a s 8 order in respect of a child who is in care (see CA 1989, s 41(6)(b),(e)). In those circumstances, the requirement really means as soon as practicable after the proceedings become specified.

Appointment of guardian as a result of a s 37 direction—See 'direction under section 37(1)' under CA 1989, s 41.

Appointment not necessary (r 12.6(a)(ii))—See, for example, *Re J (A Minor) (Change of Name)* [1993] 1 FLR 699, FD.

Duties of the children's guardian—See FPR 2010, Pt 16 for the rules relating to the representation of children, and FPR PD16A, paras 6.1–6.11 for details of the duties of a children's guardian appointed under FPR 2010, r 16.3. Note that these include a duty in cases involving unrepresented parties to ensure that there is procedural fairness (*Re G (Shared Residence)* [2013] 1 FLR 1323, CA).

Where interests of children conflict—There is usually no reason why a guardian ad litem (children's guardian) should not properly represent children whose interests conflict (*Re T and E (Proceedings: Conflicting Interests)* [1995] 1 FLR 581, FD).

12.7 What a court officer will do

(1) As soon as practicable after the issue of proceedings the court officer will return to the applicant the copies of the application together with the forms referred to in Practice Direction 5A.

(2) As soon as practicable after the issue of proceedings or the transfer of proceedings to the court or at any other stage in the proceedings the court officer will –

(a) give notice of any hearing set by the court to the applicant; and

(b) do anything else set out in Practice Directions 12A or 12B or any other practice direction.

12.8 Service

(1) After the issue of proceedings under this Part, the documents specified in paragraph (5) must be served on the respondent or respondents.

(2) In section 8 private law proceedings, service under paragraph (1) will be effected by the court officer, unless –

(a) the applicant requests to do so; or

(b) the court directs the applicant to do so.

PART III

(3) In this Rule, 'section 8 private law proceedings' are proceedings for a section 8 order except proceedings for a child arrangements order to which section 9(6B) of the 1989 Act applies with respect to a child who is in the care of a local authority.

(4) In any other proceedings to which this Part applies, service under paragraph (1) must be effected by the applicant.

(5) The documents are –

(a) the application together with the documents referred to in Practice Direction 12C; and
(b) notice of any hearing set by the court.

(6) Service under this rule must be carried out in accordance with Practice Direction 12C.

(7) The general rules about service in Part 6 apply but are subject to this rule.

(Practice Direction 12C (Service of Application in Children Proceedings) provides that in Part 4 proceedings (except proceedings for an interim order) the minimum number of days prior to the Case Management Hearing for service of the application and accompanying documents is 7 days. The Court has discretion to extend or shorten this time (see rule 4.1(3)(a))

Amendments—Substituted by SI 2014/843.

Practice Direction 12C—FPR PD12C supplements r 12.8 and sets out tables showing those persons who are to receive a copy of the application form (para 1), the time for serving the application (para 2) and the persons who are to receive a copy of Form C6A (Notice to Non-Parties) (para 3).

12.9–12.11 *(revoked)*

12.12 Directions

(1) This rule does not apply to proceedings under Chapter 6 of this Part.

(2) At any stage in the proceedings, the court may give directions about the conduct of the proceedings including –

(a) the management of the case;
(b) the timetable for steps to be taken between the giving of directions and the final hearing;
(c) the joining of a child or other person as a party to the proceedings in accordance with rules 12.3(2) and (3);
(d) the attendance of the child;
(e) the appointment of a children's guardian or of a solicitor under section 41(3) of the 1989 Act;
(f) the appointment of a litigation friend;
(g) the service of documents;
(h) the filing of evidence including experts' reports; and
(i) the exercise by an officer of the Service, Welsh family proceedings officer or local authority officer of any duty referred to in rule 16.38(1).

(3) Paragraph (4) applies where –

(a) an officer of the Service or a Welsh family proceedings officer has filed a report or a risk assessment as a result of exercising a duty referred to in rule 16.38(1)(a); or
(b) a local authority officer has filed a report as a result of exercising a duty referred to in rule 16.38(1)(b).

(4) The court may –

(a) give directions setting a date for a hearing at which that report or risk assessment will be considered; and
(b) direct that the officer who prepared the report or risk assessment attend any such hearing.

(5) The court may exercise the powers in paragraphs (2) and (4) on an application or of its own initiative.

(6) Where the court proposes to exercise its powers of its own initiative the procedure set out in rule 4.3(2) to (6) applies.

(7) Directions of a court which are still in force immediately prior to the transfer of proceedings to another court will continue to apply following the transfer subject to –

(a) any changes of terminology which are required to apply those directions to the court to which the proceedings are transferred; and

(b) any variation or revocation of the direction.

(8) The court or court officer will –

(a) take a note of the giving, variation or revocation of a direction under this rule; and

(b) as soon as practicable serve a copy of the note on every party.

(Rule 12.48 provides for directions in proceedings under the 1980 Hague Convention and the European Convention.)

Defined terms—'child', 'children and family reporter', 'children's guardian', 'court', 'directions appointment', 'section 8 order': FPR 2010, r 2.3(1).

Non-application to Chapter 6—FPR 2010, Pt 12, Ch 6 deals with applications under the Hague Convention 1980, the European Convention, The Council Regulations and the Hague Convention 1996; for directions in these applications see FPR 2010, r 12.48.

Non-court dispute resolution—Pursuant to FPR 2010, r 3.2, the court has a duty, at every stage in family proceedings, to consider whether non-court dispute resolution (NCDR) is appropriate. It has power to direct, at any stage of the proceedings, that the matter be adjourned for such specified period as it considers appropriate to enable the parties to obtain information and advice about NCDR, and, where they agree, to enable NCDR to take place (FPR 2010, r 3.4(1)). The court may give directions about this either on application or of its own initiative (FPR 2010, r 3.4(2)). See further **Child Arrangements Programme (CAP)** under FPR 2010, r 12.5.

General case management powers—See also FPR 2010, r 4.1, which lists the general case management powers that the court has in addition to those mentioned specifically in r 12.12 (except where the rules provide otherwise). These include: extending or shortening time; making orders for disclosure and inspection; adjourning or bringing forward hearings; requiring the attendance at court of parties or their legal representatives; holding telephone hearings; directing that there be separate proceedings or separate hearings; staying proceedings; consolidating proceedings; deciding the order in which issues are to be heard; excluding issues from consideration; dismissing or giving a decision on a preliminary issue; directing parties to file and serve an estimate of costs; taking any other step or making any other order for the purpose of managing the case and furthering the overriding objective. See also **Delay generally** under CA 1989, s 1(2).

Court's power to make an order of its own initiative—The court has power to make orders either on an application or of its own initiative (see r 4.3).

The Public Law Outline (PLO)—The PLO in FPR PD12A governs all applications in public law proceedings for care and supervision orders under CA 1989, Pt IV. Rules dealing specifically with public law proceedings are to be found in FPR 2010, rr 12.23–12.30.

Child Arrangements Programme (CAP)—The CAP in FPR PD12B applies to any private law applications issued under CA 1989, Pt II. It sets out the structure for the management of such cases. See further under FPR 2010, r 12.5. Special provisions dealing with private law proceedings are to be found in FPR 2010, rr 12.31–12.35.

Case management—The *Best Practice Guidance (Handbook of Best Practice in Children Act Cases)* (June 1997) produced by the Children Act Advisory Committee (see Part V) gives great assistance in relation to the preparation for and conduct of hearings.

Judicial continuity in private law proceedings—The CAP in FPR PD12B imposes strict rules so as to ensure judicial continuity in private law cases to streamline the proceedings and cut down delay. See also *President's Guidance on Continuity and Deployment (Private Law)* (see Part V).

Judicial continuity in public law proceedings—The PLO in FPR PD12A imposes strict rules so as to ensure judicial continuity in public law cases, to streamline the proceedings and to cut down delay. See also *President's Guidance on Continuity and Deployment (Public Law)* (see Part V). There are a number of cases reported before the implementation of the old Protocol prior to the PLO that contain useful guidelines as to judicial continuity. However, where they conflict with the PLO, the PLO should take precedence: *Re G (Care Proceedings: Split Trials)* [2001] 1 FLR 872, CA; *A Health Authority v X and Others* [2002] 1 FLR 1045, CA. There is also a need for continuity of counsel and solicitors advising the various parties (*Re CB and JB (Care Proceedings: Guidelines)* [1998] 2 FLR 211, FD).

Preparation of public law cases—There is useful guidance in relation to public law cases in *Re R (Care: Disclosure: Nature of Proceedings)* [2002] 1 FLR 755, FD (dealt with more fully in **Preparation of public law cases** under CA 1989, s 31). For guidance as to the conduct and recording of meetings and the provision of documents in care proceedings, see the judgment in *Re L (Care: Assessment: Fair Trial)* [2002] 2 FLR 730, FD, which is referred to in more detail in **Disclosure – impact of ECHR 1950** (below). See also the note to FPR PD27A.

Flexible powers of court to give directions in public law cases—Where an application is made under CA 1989, Pt IV, the PLO in FPR PD12A provides the court with flexible powers to make appropriate directions following the issue of the application, the transfer of the case or at any other stage. The court may give directions without a hearing, including setting a date for the final hearing. The court may cancel or repeat a particular hearing if appropriate (PLO, paras 2.1–2.3).

Need to file care plan—In public law cases, CA 1989, s 31A places the local authority under a duty to file a care plan in every case in which it seeks a care order (see CA 1989, ss 31, 31A and *Manchester City Council v F (Note)* [1993] 1 FLR 419, FD).

Fact-finding hearings - domestic violence and harm—FPR PD12J came into force on 22 April 2014. It supersedes the President's *Guidance in Relation to Split Hearings* of May 2010. PD12J applies to both private and public law proceedings. The factors that the court should take into account when determining whether it is necessary to conduct a fact-finding hearing are set out in para 17. Allegations of violence do not automatically justify a preliminary fact-finding hearing. The court must consider the nature of the allegations and the extent to which, if admitted or proved, they would be relevant in making its decision. If they are unlikely to have any impact on the court's order, there is no need for a separate fact-finding hearing. For the rationale for split hearings, see *Re S (Care Proceedings: Split Hearing)* [1996] 2 FLR 773, FD. When a split hearing is ordered in care proceedings it is essential for the court and the parties to be absolutely clear about the purpose of the hearing, the issues to be decided and the nature of the relief sought (*Somerset County Council v D & Others* [2008] 1 FLR 399, CA; *Re F (Care Proceedings)* [2007] EWCA Civ 810; *Re P (Care Proceedings: Split Hearing)* [2007] EWCA Civ 1265). Consideration should be given to whether questions of fact, such as an allegation of physical or sexual abuse, might need to be determined at a preliminary stage, so that the substantive hearing can proceed more speedily and focus on the child's welfare with greater clarity. Local authorities and children's guardians, in particular, should give assistance to the court in identifying cases that are suited to such a split hearing. Useful guidance as to the directions to be given in relation to fact-finding hearings can be found in *Re A (Children: Split Hearing)* [2007] 1 FLR 905, CA. All public law applications issued by local authorities under Pt IV (care and supervision orders) are subject to the time limits contained in the PLO in FPR PD12A. See FPR 2010, r 12.25 **Case management hearing** and **Issues resolution hearing** and PD12A. See also, **Split hearings** under CA 1989, s 31. The importance of judicial continuity was emphasised in *Re G (Care Proceedings: Split Trials)* [2001] 1 FLR 872, CA. Even where the parents make limited concessions that mean that the threshold criteria are proved, the court still has a discretion, as part of the proper management of the proceedings in the child's best interests, to order that there be a trial in relation to the threshold criteria where this is necessary to resolve a core factual issue without the determination of which the experts involved in the case are unable to advise on child protection (*Re D (Child: Threshold Criteria)* [2001] 1 FLR 274, CA). Where an expert is asked to express an opinion, he must have all the relevant information, including a copy of any judgment given earlier in the case; the summary of a judgment is not sufficient (*Re G (Care Proceedings: Split Trials)* (above)). *Re T (A Minor) (Procedure: Alleged Sexual Abuse) (No 1)* [1996] 2 FCR 370, CA, however, sounds a cautionary note about splitting the evidence on the primary facts as to sexual abuse from the evidence as to what risk there will be in the future if it is established. The Court of Appeal has jurisdiction to hear an appeal against findings of fact on preliminary issues made at the first part of a split hearing in care proceedings where those findings are of crucial importance to the final care decision to be made (*Re B (Split Hearing: Jurisdiction)* [2000] 1 FLR 334, CA). Parents can be compelled to give evidence in any care proceedings. They have no right to refuse to do so, or to refuse to answer questions that may incriminate them (per curiam, *Re Y and K (Split Hearing: Evidence)* [2003] 2 FLR 273, CA).

Timetable for public law cases—The PLO in FPR PD12A requires the court to set down a strict timetable for the disposal of public law cases with the aim of resolving then within 26 weeks. There must be timely crystallisation of the issues on which the case turns and a resolution of those issues without any unacceptable delay. The timetable for the case is set by the court and must be appropriate for the child who is the subject of the proceedings. It should take account of all significant steps in the child's life that are likely to take place during the proceedings, not just legal steps, and could include social, health and education steps (para 5).

Timetable for the proceedings and time estimates (r 12.2(2)(b))—The court is put firmly in control of the timetable for proceedings under CA 1989 in an effort to avoid delay that CA 1989, s 1(2) stresses is likely to be prejudicial to the welfare of a child. Section 11(1) obliges the court, when dealing with proceedings in which any question of making a s 8 order arises, to draw up a timetable with a view to determining the question at issue without delay and to give such directions as it considers appropriate to ensure adherence to the timetable; s 32(1) is a similar provision relating to proceedings under CA 1989, Pt IV. Rule 12.13(1) obliges the court dealing with any proceedings to which Pt IV applies to fix a date for the next hearing upon the transfer of such proceedings, or adjourning or concluding an interlocutory hearing or appointment. In relation to the timetable for public law proceedings, see FPR 2010, rr 12.23–12.26 and FPR PD12A. In relation to the timetable for the first hearing dispute resolution appointment in private law proceedings see r 12.31. Subject to these positive duties, however, the court has a wide discretion as to how the timetable for a case is set. In reaching decisions about timetabling, the time limits set by the rules for various steps should be observed. The court has wide powers under FPR 2010, r 12.12(2)(a),(b) to give directions for the management of the case and the timetable, which allow it to adjust time limits as and when necessary. The court can exercise these powers either on application or on its own initiative (r 12.12(5)). What is required is a timetable that prevents the case from drifting, without sacrificing the interests of the parties and the welfare of the child. For comments on the benefits of planned and purposeful delay, see *C v Solihull MBC* [1993] 1 FLR 290, FD and *Hounslow LBC v A* [1993] 1 FLR 702, FD. See also **Interim care order or full care order?** under CA 1989, s 38 and **Delay generally** under CA 1989, s 1(2).

In determining any application to adjourn a case involving children, as well as in fixing the timetable for the proceedings, the court has to consider delay and the interests of the other parties have to be assessed in the light of the principle that delay in determining a question concerning a child's upbringing is likely to prejudice his welfare (*Re SW (A Minor) (Care Proceedings)* [1993] 2 FLR 609, FD, noted more fully in **Hearing in the**

absence of applicant under FPR 2010, r 12.14). Where orders are not produced by the court and/or there are delays in compliance with these orders, directions should be sought from the court at an early stage (*Re K (Order Delay)* [2008] 1 FLR 572, FD); however, see *London Borough of Redbridge v A, B and E (Failure to Comply with Directions)* [2016] EWHC 2627 (Fam), where the court reiterated the importance of compliance with case management directions to the fair administration of justice, stating that such directions were the key tool by which the court maintained fidelity to the statutory principle in s 1(2). An application for an adjournment can be granted without notice, but such application should only be made in exceptional circumstances and where it would be in the best interests of the children to justify such a course. Even then, those representing the parties should be in attendance, either having given undertakings or subject to a direction of the court not to pass on the information to their clients (*Re B (Minors) (Care: Procedure)* [1994] Fam Law 72, FD).

Urgent hearings and applications without notice—See FPR 2010, r 12.16 and FPR PD12E (Urgent Business).

Electronic exchange of documents, video and telephone conferencing—The court is required to further the overriding objective in FPR 2010, r 1.1 by actively managing cases; this includes making use of technology (FPR 2010, r 1.4(2)(k)) and giving directions to ensure that the case proceeds quickly and efficiently (FPR 2010, r 1.4(2)(l)). The court may allow a witness to give evidence through a video link or by other means (FPR 2010, r 22.3). Video conferencing facilities are available in the Royal Courts of Justice and the procedure to be adopted where it is desired to use these facilities is specified in FPR PD22A, para 17.1 and Annex 3. In cases to which the PLO in FPR PD12A applies, the court will specifically consider whether any arrangements for video and telephone conferencing are required at the case management conference hearing and at the issues resolution hearing (see **Case management conference** and **Issues resolution hearing** under FPR 2010, r 12.25). The PLO in FPR PD12A requires that where facilities are available to the court and the parties, the court should consider making full use of technology, including electronic information exchange and video or telephone conferencing (FPR PD12A, para 24).

Care proceedings: more than one local authority involved—Where the applicant local authority will not be the authority responsible for operating the arrangements for the child once an order is made, the need for the second local authority to attend court to deal with issues arising must be borne in mind (*Re C (Care Order: Appropriate Local Authority)* [1997] 1 FLR 544, FD).

Disclosure by a party, inspection and production—Disclosure (meaning that a party states the existence of a document: FPR 2010, Pt 21.1(1)) is left by the rule-makers to the procedures under common law, although FPR 2010, r 4.1(3)(b) gives the High Court and the Family Court power to make orders 'for disclosure and inspection, including specific disclosure'. Applications for discovery should precede the trial and be part of the preparatory process rather than taking place during the trial (*Re JC (Care Proceedings: Procedure)* [1995] 2 FLR 77, FD). If public interest immunity arises, the procedure to be followed is set out in **Public interest immunity** (below). For guidance as to the conduct and recording of meetings and the provision of documents in care proceedings, see the judgment in *Re L (Care: Assessment: Fair Trial)* [2002] 2 FLR 730, FD and **Disclosure – impact of ECHR 1950** (below). For guidance as to the factors to be taken into account when the court considers whether or not to order disclosure see **Submission of evidence**, **Public interest immunity (PII)** and **Rejection of blanket public interest immunity (PII)** (below).

Submission of evidence (r 12.12(2)(h))—Rule 12.12 gives the court a broad power to deal with questions concerning the submission of evidence. For example, such directions may be given as are necessary for the purposes of FPR 2010, r 12.19, which lays down the rules about the filing and service of written and oral evidence in proceedings for a s 8 order or a special guardianship order (see *R v Nottinghamshire CC* [1993] Fam Law 625, FD, discussed in **Non-compliance with r 12.19(2)** under FPR 2010, r 12.19). See *Re W-M (Children)* [2015] EWCA Civ 1201, where it was held proportionate for a judge to limit the length of statements for use at a hearing to determine the frequency of contact with a child where she was very familiar with the case and the parties had a habit of ranging widely over all aspects of the case; there was a duty to assist the parties to focus the issues on the current welfare topics for determination. Questions of relevance/admissibility should normally be referred to the judge who will be conducting the final hearing (*Re CB and JB (Care Proceedings: Guidelines)* [1998] 2 FLR 211, FD). All public law applications under CA 1989, Pt IV are subject to the PLO in PD12A and any issues as to disclosure will be addressed at the case management conference and the issues resolution hearing (see FPR 2010, rr 12.24, 12.25).Where disclosure of material to a party may be damaging to the child concerned in the proceedings, the court has power, in an appropriate case, to direct that the information should be withheld. Such a direction will only be given in exceptional circumstances. The principles have been set out in a number of cases including *Official Solicitor v K* (1963) FLR Rep 520, HL, *Re B (A Minor) (Disclosure of Evidence)* [1993] 1 FLR 191, CA, *Re G (Minors) (Welfare Report: Disclosure)* [1993] 2 FLR 293, CA, and *Re M (Minors) (Disclosure of Evidence)* [1994] 1 FLR 760, CA. In *Re D (Adoption Reports: Confidentiality)* [1995] 2 FLR 687, HL, the House of Lords gave full consideration to the whole question of disclosure. Although this was in the context of an adoption application, Lord Mustill's formulation of the test for non-disclosure is the test in Children Act proceedings as well, and was applied in care proceedings in *Re C (Disclosure)* [1996] 1 FLR 797, FD and endorsed in *Re M (Disclosure)* [1998] 2 FLR 1028, CA. Accordingly, the position is as follows:

(a) It is a fundamental principle of fairness that a party is entitled to disclosure of all materials that might be taken into account by a court when reaching a decision adverse to that party – non-disclosure is the exception and not the rule.
(b) When faced with a non-disclosure application, the court should first consider whether disclosure would involve a real possibility of significant harm to the child.
(c) If so, the court should next consider whether the overall interests of the child would benefit from non-disclosure, weighing the interest of the child in having the material properly tested against the magnitude of risk that harm would occur and the gravity of that harm.
(d) If the court is satisfied that the interests of the child point towards non-disclosure, it should finally weigh

that consideration against the interest of the parent or other party in having an opportunity to see and respond to the material, taking into account the importance of the material to the issues in the case.

(e) The court should be rigorous in its examination of the risk and gravity of the feared harm to the child, and should order non-disclosure only where the case for it is compelling. To say that harm must be certain is to pitch the test too high, but 'a powerful combination of likelihood and seriousness of harm will be required before the requirements for a fair trial can be overridden' (*Re D* at [694H]).

As *Re M* stresses, welfare of the child is not the paramount consideration. A proper balance has to be struck between the welfare consideration and the requirements of the administration of fair justice. See *Re BR and C (Care: Duty of Disclosure: Appeals)* [2003] Fam Law 305, CA, where the Court of Appeal reinstated an order requiring disclosure of medical reports by the mother in family proceedings, emphasising that the court will only withhold evidence from disclosure to another party if such disclosure would be so detrimental to the children's welfare as to outweigh the normal requirements of a fair trial. In *Re X (Adoption: Confidential Procedure)* [2002] 2 FLR 476, CA, Hale LJ added to these principles to provide that the ECHR 1950, Art 8 rights of adults may also justify non-disclosure where the risk is of harm to them rather than the child. In *A Local Authority v A* [2010] 1 FLR 545, FD, the court refused their application for non-disclosure, holding that disclosure is the norm and non-disclosure should only be permitted where the case for doing so is compelling. In the context of this case, non-disclosure would only be justified if there were a real risk of death or really serious bodily harm. In *KM v Lambeth MBC* [2012] 1 FLR 1278, CA, the court held that it would not be right to allow only partial disclosure of the mother's psychiatric report to the father when the child's guardian and the local authority had had access to the whole report. However, the father was prohibited from disclosing it to anyone but his legal advisers, and this was backed by a penal notice. See *Commissioner of Police of the Metropolis v A Local Authority and Ors* [2016] EWHC 2400 (Fam), where the court gave permission to disclose to the Metropolitan Police Service (MPS) information revealed in the care proceedings where parents were suspected of involvement in terrorism; however, such permission was subject to a condition that the information should not be disclosed to or discussed with any person outside the MPS, the CPS or the Security Service without the court's further permission.

Re C (Disclosure) (above) considered the procedure to be followed where an application for non-disclosure is made. Johnson J declined to lay down rigid rules, taking the view that the procedure in each case will be determined by the court in the light of the particular circumstances and demands of the case, so as to enable the court to carry out the appropriate balancing exercise. This approach was endorsed by the Court of Appeal in *Re M (Disclosure)* [1998] 2 FLR 1028, CA and should be the norm, subject to any necessary variations in individual cases. Accordingly:

(1) The application should be transferred to the High Court.
(2) Notice of the application should be given to the party from whom the material is intended to be withheld.
(3) It is essential that any party to whom the information was not to be revealed should have the opportunity of making representations to the court.
(4) In many cases it will be appropriate to follow the practice endorsed in *Official Solicitor v K* (1963) FLR Rep 520, HL, namely disclosure in the first instance to counsel only and thereafter counsel would have the opportunity to apply for onward transmission to the client.

Where disclosure is resisted in complex family proceedings it may be possible to use Special Advocates to 'filter' the evidence (*Re T (Wardship: Impact of Police Intelligence)* [2010] 1 FLR 1048, FD). See **Special Advocates**, below.

The possibility of hearings or part of hearings being held without notice is not excluded but should arise only rarely. For example, where there is material in a document upon which the judge is asked to make a decision whether to disclose but the judge needs assistance from a party in some way to ascertain the meaning of the document, he could properly ask for such help before making his decision as to whether the document should be disclosed (*Re M*). The procedure for without notice hearings is in FPR 2010, r 12.16.

Where certain information is to have limited distribution, special arrangements will have to be made with regard to filing it in court (in *Re C*, the children's guardian was to provide the restricted information to the judge in a confidential supplementary report dealing only with that information) and the court will have to take administrative steps to ensure that it is not disclosed inadvertently. See *Re K (Adoption: Disclosure of Information)* [1997] 2 FLR 74, FD, in which the procedure in adoption cases was distinguished from that contemplated by *Re C (Disclosure)* for care cases and it was also pointed out that, where the party from whom it is sought to conceal information is not represented, giving notice of the application about the evidence may defeat the object of the exercise.

As *Re C* contemplates, circumstances can change, and the importance of maintaining confidentiality decline. *Re B (A Minor) (Disclosure of Evidence)* (above) stresses the importance of any order for non-disclosure being only for the shortest period possible consonant with preserving the child's welfare.

Disclosure – waiver of legal professional privilege—Where a mother had waived her legal professional privilege in care proceedings by stating in a witness statement the reasons why, after a number of legal conferences, she had changed her account of how her child's injuries were sustained, fairness required full disclosure of the attendance notes of those conferences. The undesirability of breaching confidentiality between the mother and her legal representatives had to be balanced against the unfairness to the father if it was not breached (*Re D (Care Proceedings: Legal Privilege)* [2011] 2 FLR 1183, CA). Counsel and solicitors ought to be aware that advice might have been given to prompt a change of attitude by their client and they should be on guard to protect their client from revealing that advice in either written or oral evidence. Judges must also be astute to anticipate an unintentional observation that may result in privilege being waived and must be ready to warn a witness of any such danger. See further under FPR 2010, r 21.1.

Disclosure by a person not a party—The court can only order disclosure against a non-party where statute permits this (FPR 2010, r 21.1(1); and see CPR 1998, r 31.18). In *A London Borough Council v K and Others*

[2009] EWHC 850 (Fam), Baker J considered (at [159]) deficiencies in 'police disclosure' (meaning production of evidence, since the police were not parties). In that case, the police suggested a 'meeting with that officer and the lead solicitor, usually the Local Authority's solicitor, to ensure that disclosure has taken place as ordered (sic)'. He suggested that any production order made should include a 'liberty to apply clause' and that 'This is a matter which should be reviewed urgently by the Family Justice Council'. Four years later, the law remains the same: an order for disclosure by police is not possible (the limitations in law on production of documents were not, it seems, drawn to the judge's attention). In October 2013, a Protocol and Good Practice Model came into force governing the *Disclosure of Information in Cases of Alleged Child Abuse and Linked Criminal and Care Directions Hearings* (see Part V).

Directions as to production and inspection—Rule 12.12(2) enables the court to give case management directions 'at any stage in the proceedings'. This would include requests for inspection and production. Disclosure and requests for inspection (considered more fully under FPR 2010, Pt 21) are likely to arise in the following ways:

- that a party seeks a specific document or information;
- that a party seeks confirmation of its view that a document is covered by legal professional privilege and need not therefore be produced (it must still be disclosed: r 21.1(1));
- that a public body (mostly) seeks public interest immunity.

Translation of documents—The cost of translating documents produced during family proceedings should be paid by the party requiring the translation, provided that the party is publicly funded. Only documents necessary for the party to understand the case need to be translated and the party's solicitor can provide his client with a summary only of some documents where appropriate: *Re R (Translation of Documents in Proceedings); sub nom Suffolk County Council v M, F and child* [2015] EWFC B112.

Production of documents by a witness—On application by a party, a witness summons will be issued by the court that requires a witness (which includes the police) to produce documents (r 24.2(1)(b)). They can be required to produce only those documents that could be required to be produced at a hearing (r 24.2(5): e g not documents covered by public interest immunity (see below) or confidential documents). If a witness objects to production, he (or they: e g the police) can apply to set aside the order for production (r 24.3(4)).

Public interest immunity (PII)—The modern law on PII derives from *R v Chief Constable of West Midlands Police ex parte Wiley* [1995] 1 AC 274, HL (*exp Wiley*). Production is always the starting point, save for specific documents: that is, rarely will a whole class of documents be exempt from disclosure. Each document will generally be expected to be assessed for materiality (*Bank Mellat v Her Majesty's Treasury (No 1)* [2013] UKSC 38, at [3]: 'fundamental to any justice system in a modern, democratic society is the principle of natural justice, whose most important aspect is that every party has a right to know the full case against him, and the right to test and challenge that case fully' (see further Introduction to FPR 2010, Pt 21).

Rejection of blanket public interest immunity (PII)—In *Re R (Care: Disclosure: Nature of Proceedings)* [2002] 1 FLR 755, FD, Charles J proposed that any PII case that precedes, or does not fully take it into account (if later) the House of Lords decision in *exp Wiley* (above) 'should be regarded with caution and carefully reconsidered' (including, for example, *Re M (A Minor) (Disclosure of Material)* [1990] 2 FLR 36, CA in the Court of Appeal). He emphasised the point made in *Re B (Disclosure to Other Parties)* [2001] 2 FLR 1017, FD (see **Disclosure – impact of ECHR 1950**, above), in respect of claims for non-disclosure based on ECHR 1950, Art 8, that a compelling case for non-disclosure based on PII needs to be made out and any non-disclosure must go no further than is strictly necessary, having regard to the competing public interests. Furthermore, he expressed the view that 'both local authorities and guardians ad litem should be more willing than they seem to be at present to exhibit their notes of relevant conversations and incidents that are relied on as evidence for findings at the threshold or welfare stage of proceedings, rather than to embark on what is a time-consuming and difficult exercise of preparing summaries of those notes'. Charles J commended the Official Solicitor's practice of exhibiting attendance records to his report and said that it would have been beneficial if this practice had been adopted by both the local authority and the guardian in that case and, indeed, it would be likely to be beneficial in many other cases. In *Re R* (above) the failure of the foster-parent, the children's guardian and further witnesses to disclose their contemporaneous notes until called for by the judge during the hearing led to the local authority having to abandon allegations of serious sexual abuse and to rely on other allegations to support its case for care orders. However, local authorities should abstain from introducing into proceedings, and sending to experts, material that would inevitably be perceived as unfair in the sense of being purely prejudicial (*Re S (Expert Evidence)* [2008] 2 FLR 1163, CA).

Further guidance was given in *Re Chapman* (2002) Lawtel, 9 April, a case in which the local authority received information that the father was involved in serious criminal activity and likely to harm and abduct the child and so sought directions on disclosure from the police of information about the father. The police agreed to disclose information about the father's convictions and arrests but not otherwise, contending that to disclose further material about the father's possible criminal activity was likely to seriously harm the proper functioning of the police and the strong public interest in proper investigation and persecution of crime. Charles J held, inter alia, that:

(1) The parties to the care proceedings would not be prejudiced by not being given further detail from the police, whereas the public interest could have been harmed by it.
(2) *Nottinghamshire County Council v H* [1995] 1 FLR 115, FD had to be reconsidered in the light of *R v Chief Constable of West Midlands Police, ex parte Wiley* [1995] 1 AC 274, HL.
(3) A person was entitled to disclosure of all material taken into account by a decision-maker when reaching a decision adverse to that person. Non-disclosure of relevant material to one party was exceptional.
(4) The general position was that confidentiality was not a valid reason for non-disclosure of material that passed the relevant threshold test.
(5) The stages of any issue relating to disclosure were:

PART III

(a) whether the relevant threshold test was satisfied; and
(b) if so, whether there were nevertheless grounds for refusing disclosure.

In *Re W (Disclosure to Police)* [1998] 2 FLR 135, CA, the court considered the status of local authority working papers, such as information and notes used to prepare an assessment report for court. The assessment report had been filed at court but the notes had not. Unless there is an order of the court to the contrary, such confidential information has to be dealt with by the local authority in accordance with the guide *Working Together to Safeguard Children 2010*. It is protected by PII from general publication but should be shared with the police without prior reference to the court where necessary for the protection of children. This decision is expressly confined, however, to documents held by and information known to social workers and has no application to the position of a children's guardian or children and family reporter appointed for court proceedings. It should also be noted that leave must be sought in the normal way to show documents that have been filed with the court (such as the assessment report here) to the police.

As to the confidentiality of adoption files, see *Re H (Criminal Proceedings: Disclosure of Adoption Records)* [1995] 1 FLR 964, FD and for a case concerning disclosure of Crown Prosecution Service documents, see *Nottinghamshire County Council v H* [1995] 1 FLR 115, FD. In the latter case, attention was drawn to the children's guardian's power under CA 1989, s 42 to examine the local authority's social work records. The court's discretion in Children Act proceedings will be exercised in the light of this power.

Re C (Expert Evidence: Disclosure: Practice) [1995] 1 FLR 204, FD provides guidance as to the procedure to be followed where an issue arises, because of PII, as to whether certain material should or should not be disclosed. If documents held by the local authority are apparently relevant but appear to be protected from disclosure by PII, a letter should be written by the local authority to the parties' legal advisers and to the children's guardian, drawing general attention to the existence of the documents and inviting an application to the court if disclosure of the relevant documents is required. The appropriate procedure would be to seek directions as to the service of documents pursuant to r 12.12(2)(g) or directions as to the filing of evidence pursuant to r 12.12(2)(h). The local authority should identify and flag the documents that they believe are, or may be, relevant and, if possible, a short précis of the information should be prepared to assist the court that is to make the decision. If the court orders disclosure of the documents and if the nature of the précis satisfies the party affected that the material identified and disclosed is sufficient, the directions hearing can proceed on a short basis. If the précis does not achieve agreement and the other party wishes to see more of the files, some further guide to the file should be provided so that the court can carry out the balancing exercise envisaged in *Re M (A Minor) (Disclosure of Material)* (above), taking into account the comments in *Re R* (above) and *Re B (Disclosure to Other Parties)* (above). It is for the court to make the decision as to disclosure of documents covered by PII. It is important for the local authority to draw the attention of the children's guardian to any matters of concern within the documents, since his full knowledge of the material may enable him to assist the court as to its relevance. In *Re T (Wardship: Impact of Police Intelligence)* [2010] 1 FLR 1048, FD, Special Advocates were used to 'filter' evidence the disclosure of which was resisted. See further **Special Advocates** (below). The approach to be applied when deciding whether to order the disclosure of third party allegations against the father of sexual abuse in child contact proceedings was summarised by the Supreme Court in *Re A (Sexual Abuse: Disclosure)* [2013] 1 FLR 948, SC. Here, the undisclosed information was at the core of the case and represented the entirety of the material relating to the only issue that had generated the mother's application to vary the contact regime. The judge at first instance had erred in conflating the issue of whether the complainant should give oral evidence with the question of disclosure of the substance of her allegations. On the facts of this case, the balance of rights under ECHR 1950, Arts 3, 6 and 8 came down in favour of disclosure by the local authority to the parents and the children's guardian of the complainant's identity and of the records of the substance of her allegations.

As to the difficult issue of the extent to which the local authority is free to waive PII without leave of the court, see inter alia, *D v NSPCC* (1977) FLR Rep 181, HL, *Re M (A Minor) (Disclosure of Material)* (above), *R v Chief Constable of the West Midland Police ex p Wiley* (above), *Re C (Expert Evidence: Disclosure: Practice)* (above).

Application for PII—Application is by Pt 18 procedure by the public body that seeks immunity (FPR 2010, r 21.3).

Special Advocates—Special Advocates were used for (probably) the first time in *Re T (Wardship: Impact of Police Intelligence)* [2010] 1 FLR 1048, FD to 'filter' evidence, the disclosure of which was resisted. The police informed the court dealing with the father's contact application in respect of the ward that there was credible intelligence to the effect that he had taken out a contract to have the mother murdered while at court. However, the police had decided not to investigate further. The police requested that this information not be disclosed to the father, his family or any of his family's representatives. The police took the mother and child into police protection but stated that this would be withdrawn if interim contact with the father were established. McFarlane J described the procedure to be adopted in appointing Special Advocates and extracted the lessons to be learned. The lack of understanding between the police and the family justice system had delayed, and at times risked thwarting, the discharge of the Family Court's duty to act in accordance with the welfare needs of the ward. Any issue of public interest immunity material that raises issues of complexity should trigger a transfer to the High Court (see further under **Public interest immunity (PII)**, above). In *BCC v FZ, AZ, HZ and TVP* [2013] 1 FLR 974, FD, Pauffley J gave judicial sanction to withholding from the parents the entire evidential basis for the making of an interim care order and decided that there was no need for a Special Advocate to assist with basic disclosure or issues of public interest immunity. However, she held that as a consequence of her judgment this became one of those exceptional cases in which it was essential, to give the parents proper protection of their rights under ECHR 1950, Arts 6 and 8, that a Special Advocate(s) be brought into the case forthwith to represent their interests both in relation to continuing and future disclosure and, in the event that there was to be no disclosure going forward, in the testing of the evidence at any subsequent trial.

Multi-agency risk assessment conferences (MARACs) – disclosure in public law and private law proceedings—MARAC meetings collate information about high-risk cases of domestic abuse with a view to creating a coordinated safety plan for the victim and children (if any). The work is case-specific and all relevant agencies will attend or contribute to the conference. MARACs may be a valuable source of information in both public law and private law proceedings where domestic abuse towards an adult or a child may be an issue. Clearly, it important that generally the details of the safety plan devised by the MARAC are kept confidential if it is to be effective. A request for disclosure of documents or other information is most likely to come from the person whose conduct is under scrutiny at the MARAC. Therefore, there is a tension between the potential existence of relevant information and the need for confidentiality. In December 2011, the Working Party of the Family Justice Council issued guidance on *MARACs and Disclosure into Court Proceedings* (see Part V). The question of disclosure should always be considered well in advance of a contested hearing and be dealt with by an order for directions (para 7). If a request for disclosure will interfere significantly with a safety plan or may cause harm to a child, the chair of the MARAC has a duty to raise a formal objection (para 8). The chair will not normally be from a legal background and therefore it is important that his attention is drawn to the guidance and he is encouraged to take legal advice before he decides whether or not to object. If, however, there is no objection, the chair should follow the procedure in para 8(a)–(f). It will sometimes happen that the MARACs hold information that they believe would be useful to a court but that they do not want to disclose to all parties. In those circumstances, they should disclose the information to the relevant statutory body (the local authority, police, Cafcass) for them to use as appropriate in court proceedings. MARAC workers and independent domestic violence advisors (IDVAs) should not ordinarily be called as witnesses in court proceedings (para 10). See also the notes under FPR 2010, rr 21.2 and 21.3 and under FLA 1996, s 63A.

Disclosure – impact of ECHR 1950—It is essential that a parent be placed in a position where he may obtain access to information that is relied on by the authorities in taking measures of protective care (*TP and KM v United Kingdom* [2001] 2 FLR 549, ECHR). See further under **Public interest immunity (PII)** (above). Issues concerning the disclosure of confidential information involve the consideration of rights under ECHR 1950, Arts 6 and 8 and HRA 1998. The guidelines relevant to these issues are set out in *Re B (Disclosure to Other Parties)* [2001] 2 FLR 1017, FD.

Confidentiality of statements by parties to non-court dispute resolution (mediation)—In CA 1989 proceedings, statements by parties during mediation or other confidential non-court dispute resolution (NCDR) are not admissible, save where what is said suggests that the maker may cause future harm including to the welfare of a child (*W v Egdell* [1990] Ch 359, CA; and see *Re D (Minors) (Conciliation: Disclosure of Information)* [1993] 1 FLR 932, CA). There is no separate NCDR privilege (see note to FPR 2010, r 21.1).

Bundles and other particular matters—It is good practice to observe FPR PD27A in *all applications* concerning the preparation of court bundles. However, it applies specifically in: (i) all hearings before a High Court judge of the Family Division, wherever the court may be sitting; (ii) all hearings in the Family Court. The PD does not apply to the hearing of any urgent application if and to the extent that it is impossible to comply with it. PD27A is to be read, where appropriate, in conjunction with the PLO (FPR PD12A) and the CAP (PD12B). However, the PD is subject to any directions that may be given in a particular case by the case-management judge. In *Re X and Y (Bundles)* [2008] 2 FLR 2053, FD, Munby J issued a stern warning in open court to all practitioners, pointing out that far too often the requirements of FPR PD27A are not observed and that this is unacceptable. Orders for costs can be made against either the party in default or against the defaulting lawyers (see para 12 of the PD). Furthermore, he warned that in particularly flagrant cases defaulters may be publicly identified in open court. In *Re L (Procedure: Bundles: Translation)* [2015] 1 FLR 1417, FD, the President warned practitioners that the Family Division and the Family Court had had enough of failures to comply with PD27A and that from now on defaulters could expect to be exposed to sanctions, including public condemnation, the disallowance of fees or suffer the sanction meted out in *Seagrove v Sullivan* [2015] 2 FLR 602, FD, where the parties were told to take away a non-compliant bundle and produce a compliant bundle the following day.

Citation of Authorities—Practice Direction of 24 March 2012: *Citation of Authorities* clarifies the practice and procedure governing the citation of authorities and applies throughout the Senior Courts of England and Wales, including the Crown Court and the Family Court. See Part V.

Public Law Outline (PLO) – instructing and calling experts—See under FPR 2010, Pt 25 and PD25A–PD25F.

Deciding whether case should be heard in the Administrative Court or Family Division—Where cases plainly involve only issues of public law, although they concern the welfare of either children or incompetent adults, then the proper course is to apply to the Administrative Court for judicial review (*A (A Patient) v A Health Authority; Re J; The Queen on the Application of S v Secretary of State for the Home Department* [2002] 1 FLR 845, FD). But if cases may, in part, involve some issues of public law but are also private law cases about the best interests of a child or an incompetent adult then the proper course is to apply to the Family Division. Exactly the same principle applies in 'family' cases where a freestanding application is made for relief in accordance with HRA 1998, s 7; such cases should be heard in the Family Division and, if possible, by judges with experience of sitting in the Administrative Court (*Re S (Habeas Corpus): S v Haringey London Borough Council* [2004] 1 FLR 590, QBD). Recourse to judicial review in the area of child protection will be rare (*A and S v London Borough of Enfield* [2008] 2 FLR 1945, QBD). Where the conduct of a local authority in care proceedings is fundamentally flawed and its decision-making process is a key issue, the court may direct a rehearing of the care proceedings before a High Court judge of the Family Division who is also authorised to sit in the Administrative Court. In this way, the care proceedings can run concurrently with judicial review proceedings, since the subject matter in each is essentially the same (*Re S and W (Care Proceedings)* [2007] 2 FLR 275, CA).

'directions for the conduct of the proceedings' (r 12.12(2))—The court has a wide discretion to grant directions. The matters listed in r 12.12(2) are only examples of the types of issue that might arise. A directions hearing will almost inevitably be required in a case of any substance and a date for it is fixed by the court office in accordance with FPR 2010, r 12.5 when the application is commenced or when it is received from the transmitting court. Care proceedings are non-adversarial in character (see *Re L (Police Investigation: Privilege)* [1996] 1 FLR 731, HL) and, in practice, judges dealing with directions hearings in such cases adopt an interventionist style. Directions hearings should not be treated as a formality; they enable the court to come firmly to grips with the case and ensure that it is tightly timetabled and prepared for its final hearing at the earliest opportunity. Where a party feels that the case is not making satisfactory progress, he should apply for directions to ensure that progress is made (*B v B (Child Abuse: Contact)* [1994] 2 FLR 713, FD; see also *Re A and B (Minors) (No 2)* [1995] 1 FLR 351, FD, and the notes on the timetable for the proceedings, above. In public law proceedings, the court will give directions under FPR 2010, r 12.24 for the conduct of the case at the case management hearing and at the issues resolution hearing. See further under FPR 2010, rr 12.22–12.26 and FPR PD12A.

Parties who receive notice of the directions appointment are normally required to attend (see FPR 2010, r 12.14(2)). As to directions for the conduct of cases involving expert witnesses, see FPR 2010, Pt 25 and PD25A–PD25F.

Agreement between parties as to proposals for management of proceedings—If the parties or any children's guardian agree proposals for the management of the proceedings, and the court considers that the proposals are suitable, it may approve them without a hearing and give directions in the terms proposed (FPR 2010, r 12.15).

Repeated applications—As to the possibility of renewing an application previously refused by the court, see *Re F (A Minor) (Care Proceedings: Directions)* [1995] 3 FCR 601, FD.

Dismissal of proceedings at directions stage—In *Re B (Contact: Stepfather's Opposition)* [1997] 2 FLR 579, CA, the court held that, in an appropriate case, a contact application can be dismissed at a directions hearing. The CA pointed out that, in the exercise of that power, the court must bear in mind that the more Draconian the order and the more unique the situation, the greater the need for the court to be satisfied that grave harm is virtually certain to befall the child if the court follows its usual procedure and investigates the matter on its merits. In *Re A (Application for Leave)* [1998] 1 FLR 1, CA, the court reaffirmed the view that, in appropriate cases, an application may be determined at a directions appointment if the content of the statements and the children and family reporter's report indicate that it should go no further. This principle is clearly demonstrated in *Re W (Minors)* (unreported) 15 December 1998, CA, where the CA upheld the first instance decision, observing:

> 'Of course, it is normally the case that children's cases are heard on oral evidence … which is tested under cross-examination. But it is quite clear from a number of decisions of this court and decisions at first instance that a judge does have a discretion as to whether or not there should be a full hearing permitted with oral evidence. This is particularly the case when there has already been one full investigation by the court which has produced a particular result, as here. The judge in so acting would obviously have to look carefully at the case and weigh a number of important considerations: Was the material available before the court sufficient to enable him to take that particular course? Was the outcome likely to be affected by fresh evidence or cross-examination? Would the denial of the opportunity for the mother to cross-examine witnesses or produce evidence of her own be likely to produce a skewed result and be unfair to her? Was the expert evidence available before the court sufficient? Would it be likely to be changed in the light of cross-examination or further evidence? and, above all, the welfare of the children and the likely effect on them of continuing litigation. If that was likely to be detrimental to the welfare of the children that would be a factor which would weigh very heavily in the scales. Finally, of course, the ultimate question for the judge: Would the full hearing be likely realistically to produce any different result to that which had already been reached?'.

For further examples of situations in which an application may be brought to a premature end, see **Full hearing not always appropriate** under FPR 2010, r 12.21.

Attendance of the child (r 12.12(2)(d))—As to the attendance of the child at directions appointments and hearings, see FPR 2010, r 12.14(3),(4).

Appointment of a children's guardian (r 12.12(2)(e))—CA 1989, s 41 obliges the court to appoint a children's guardian for a child concerned in specified proceedings (such as care and supervision order proceedings) unless satisfied that it is not necessary to do so in order to safeguard his interest; FPR 2010, r 16.3 sets out the normal procedure for the appointment of such a guardian. There is no provision in CA 1989 for the appointment of a children's guardian for a child involved in non-specified proceedings. ACA 2002, s 122(1)(b),(2) inserts into CA 1989, s 41 subsection (6A) so as to include within the category of proceedings that may be 'specified for the time being … by rules of court' any proceedings for the making, varying or discharging of an order under CA 1989, s 8 (i e child arrangements, specific issue and prohibited steps orders). As far as the rules are concerned, a children's guardian can be appointed in non-specified proceedings under FPR 2010, r 16.4 (see for example *L v L (Minors) (Separate Representation)* [1994] 1 FLR 156, CA). It appears that it is to such an appointment that the words 'or otherwise' in r 12.12(2)(e) refer (*Essex CC v B* [1993] 1 FLR 866, FD); see also *Re S (A Minor) (Independent Representation)* [1993] 2 FLR 437, CA, at [445C], where Sir Thomas Bingham MR suggests that, where the court has dismissed a children's guardian earlier in the relevant proceedings in order to enable the child to participate as a party in his own right but then later decides that the child lacks the necessary understanding so as to participate, it can use its 'general power to appoint under r 4.14(2)(d) [FPR 2010, r 12.12(2)] (and r 9.5) [FPR 2010, r 16.4]'. Whether r 12.12(2)(e) might ever have a wider application, however, remains somewhat uncertain. A children's guardian appointed in non-specified proceedings will not receive funding from the Legal Aid Agency and probably not from his own panel. Where a guardian has been appointed in the course of an investigation under CA 1989, s 37 at the conclusion of which the local authority decides not to apply for a care or supervision order, it would be possible for the High Court or the County Court to direct that the guardian should continue to be involved under FPR 2010, r 16.4. However, this should only be done where the guardian consents, where funding is available and where the guardian has a continuing role to play despite the changed status of the proceedings (*Re CE (Section 37 Direction)* [1995] 1 FLR 26, FD).

Appointment of a solicitor under s 41(3) (r 12.12(2)(e))—CA 1989, s 41(3) enables the court to appoint a solicitor to represent a child concerned in specified proceedings where he has no children's guardian, where he is of sufficient understanding to instruct a solicitor and wants to do so or where it appears that it would be in his best interests for him to be represented by a solicitor (see *Re H (A Minor) (Care Proceedings: Child's Wishes)* [1993] 1 FLR 440, FD). In contrast to the position with regard to the appointment of a children's guardian, there is no rule dealing specifically with the procedure for the appointment of such a solicitor so this must be carried out under this rule, although r 12.12(8) imposes a duty on the court to record the appointment. Where there is a children's guardian, he generally has a duty to appoint a solicitor for the child under FPR PD16A, para 6.2(a). An appointment by the children's guardian is not made under s 41(3) and the court cannot therefore give directions with regard to it. However, it is presumed that should the court's assistance be required at a later stage (for example, if a question arises as to how the solicitor should carry out his duties under FPR 2010, r 16.29), directions under this rule could be sought on the basis that the matter arises in connection with the conduct of the proceedings. An application by the child or the children's guardian for termination of the solicitor's appointment would, however, have to be made under r 16.29(7),(8).

There is no power to appoint a solicitor for a child under s 41(3) in non-specified proceedings (*Re W (A Minor) (Contact)* [1994] 1 FLR 843, FD).

Appointment of a litigation friend (r 12.12(2)(f))—Where a child is a party to proceedings, but not the subject of those proceedings, the child must have a litigation friend to conduct them on his behalf: see rr 16.5 and 16.7–16.15. For the circumstances in which a child does not need a children's guardian or a litigation friend, see r 16.6.

Appointment of the Official Solicitor—In recent times there has been a marked increase in the number of public law children cases in which the Official Solicitor (OS) is invited to act as guardian ad litem or litigation friend of a protected party. In December 2010, the President of the Family Division issued *Guidance in cases involving protected parties in which the Official Solicitor is being invited to act as guardian ad litem or litigation friend* (see Part V). It sets out the Official Solicitor's acceptance criteria, which remain: (1) satisfactory evidence or a finding by the court that the party lacks capacity to conduct the proceedings and is therefore a protected party; (2) confirmation that there is security for the costs of legal representation; (3) that there is no other person who is suitable and willing to act as guardian ad litem/litigation friend. When the Official Solicitor does consent to act, Standard Instructions to the solicitor whom he instructs for the protected party can be found at *www.gov.uk/government/uploads/system/uploads/attachment_data/file/587031/ospt-practice-note.doc*. The Public Law Family telephone number for the Official Solicitor is 020 3681 2755 and the website is *www.justice.gov.uk/about/ospt*.

Litigants in person—See notes to FPR 2010, r 12.21 and PD27A.

McKenzie Friend—See notes to FPR 2010, r 12.21.

Service of documents (r 12.12(2)(g))—As to service generally, see FPR 2010, rr 6.23–6.39, 12.8 and FPR PD12C. The power to give directions about service under this rule is supplementary to the power of the court to give directions under FPR 2010, r 12.8. See also the note to FPR PD27A and the guidance in *Re B (Litigants In Person: Timely Service of Documents)* [2016] EWHC 2365 (Fam).

Preparation of welfare reports (r 12.12(2)(i))—As to welfare reports generally, see CA 1989, s 7 and FPR 2010, r 16.33 and FPR PD16A. Directions may be sought under this rule where, for example, there are problems in complying with the request for a welfare report, either because of time constraints or for other reasons, or where the children and family reporter or welfare officer considers that part of his report contains sensitive material that ought not to be shown to the parties in the normal way.

Transfer of proceedings—The transfer of proceedings between courts is governed by FC(CDB)R 2014 and the *President's Guidance on Allocation and Gatekeeping (Private Law)* and *President's Guidance on Allocation and Gatekeeping (Public Law)*.

Consolidation with other proceedings—It is desirable wherever possible for directions to be given as to transfer between courts, consolidation etc, so that all linked proceedings can be heard and determined together; this will be the case, for example, where there are separate applications with regard to several children of the same family (see for example *W v Wakefield City Council* [1995] 1 FLR 170, FD) or more than one set of proceedings concerning an individual child that ought logically to be heard together.

Notice of court's intention to give directions of its own initiative (r 12.12(5),(6))—The court may exercise its powers on its own initiative, but where it proposes to do so it must follow the procedure in FPR 2010, r 4.3. This means that it may give any person likely to be affected by the order an opportunity to make representations (r 4.3(2)). Where the court proposes to hold a hearing to decide whether to make the order, it must give the parties affected at least 5 days' notice (r 4.3(3)). However, there will be situations in which the court may make an order without hearing the parties or giving them an opportunity to make representations (r 4.3(4)); in this event, the party affected by the order may apply to have it set aside, varied or stayed (r 4.3(6)).

Written directions in difficult child care cases—As a general rule, it is bad practice for directions in difficult child care cases to be sought and given in writing without the attendance of the parties (*Re A and B (Minors) (No 2)* [1995] 1 FLR 351, FD).

Service—See FPR 2010, rr 12.8 and FPR PD12C.

Request of or order against Home Office—In October 2014, the President of the Family Division reissued a protocol *Communicating with the Home Office in Family Proceedings* (see FPR PD12F, Annex 1). It sets out the appropriate procedure for the Family Court to communicate with the Home Office to obtain information in relation to immigration, visa and passport information for family proceedings. It gives guidance about the timescale within which a response from the Home Office may be expected and includes a sample court order requesting information and a sample completed form EX660 (request for information). Further guidance as to the approach to be taken when family proceedings are running concurrently with other proceedings was given in *Re M and N (Parallel Family and Immigration Proceedings)* [2008] 2 FLR 2030, FD, where Munby J held that:

(1) practitioners acting for parents in family proceedings have an ongoing duty to remain up to date with other related proceedings;
(2) parents are under a duty to instruct their advisers in other related proceedings to keep their family solicitors informed of progress. Those other advisers then have a duty to keep the family solicitors informed accordingly;
(3) family proceedings practitioners have a duty to take adequate steps before each hearing to find out what has been going on in the related proceedings and where a formal decision is anticipated, when that decision is likely to be given;
(4) it is preferable to obtain copies of correspondence and other documents of the other solicitors' files rather than attempting to find out what is going on through correspondence;
(5) if practitioners experience difficulty in obtaining the relevant information from the other advisers, prompt consideration should be given, as early as possible, to asking the court to make a peremptory order that the other advisers deliver a complete copy of their file to the family proceedings solicitors, or to make an order pursuant to the President's protocol; and
(6) where the outcome in family proceedings is dependent upon or likely to be affected by a third party's decision, early consideration should be given to whether, and if so how, that decision-maker should be brought into some appropriate form of direct engagement with the family proceedings.

Where immigration applications or proceedings are ongoing at the same time as an application for the summary return of children to the country from which they came, it is highly desirable for there to be communication and collaboration between the Secretary of State and the judge who is dealing with the latter application (*Re F (Abduction: Removal Outside Jurisdiction)* [2008] 2 FLR 1649, CA). When considering the welfare of children who have been in the UK illegally for more than 7 years, the local authority must take into account the Secretary of State's policy in such cases and the reasons underlying it. Careful consideration should be given to joining the Home Office in an attempt to ascertain the Secretary of State's views in an individual case; this would reduce the risk of relevant central and public authority decision-makers reaching different conclusions and contain unnecessary expenditure in respect of persons in the jurisdiction unlawfully who would not be given leave to remain (*R (AC) v Birmingham City Council* [2009] 1 FLR 838, QBD).

Protocol between judges of the Family Court and Immigration and Asylum Chambers—The Protocol of 19 July 2013 on Communications between Judges of the Family Court and Immigration and Asylum Chambers (see Part V) is designed to enable judges in each jurisdiction to communicate to obtain information about proceedings in their respective jurisdictions that may affect the outcome of the proceedings before them, and to make better informed decisions.

Guidance in cases of stranded spouses—See *Re S (Wardship: Stranded Spouses)* [2011] 1 FLR 305, FD for guidance as to the approach to be adopted by the court in cases in which one parent has been left stranded abroad by the other parent. It aims to ensure that the relevant ECHR 1950, Arts 6 and 8 rights are upheld, that there is a fair trial of the factual allegations and that the child/children have contact with both parents pending a final welfare-based determination of the issues of residence and contact.

Attendance of the media in family proceedings—For the rules relating to the attendance of the media at hearings in family proceedings, see FPR 2010, r 27.11.

Court of Appeal standing instructions against identification of child—While it is highly desirable that appellate proceedings, wherever possible, should be in open court, in the great majority of cases involving children this could have adverse consequences for the children. It has been accepted therefore by the Court of Appeal that in general the identity of the child should be protected by means of an order restricting publication of information that could lead to his identity. Under standing instructions of the Court of Appeal, orders in such terms have almost invariably been made in cases involving children. Without standing instructions, there would always be a risk that the court might fail, through oversight, to give the direction that the restriction should be included. If there were unusual circumstances which made publicity desirable then the court could decide to depart from standing instructions (*Re R (Court of Appeal: Order Against Identification)* [1999] 2 FLR 145, CA). Hearing children cases in England and Wales in private, without public pronouncement of judgment, does not breach ECHR 1950, Art 6 (*B v UK and P v UK* [2001] 2 FLR 261, ECHR): if judgment were pronounced publicly that would to a large extent frustrate the aims of holding the proceedings in chambers. In *Pelling v Bruce-Williams (Secretary of State for Constitutional Affairs Intervening)* [2004] 2 FLR 823, CA, the Court of Appeal followed *B v UK and P v UK*, but acknowledged that it was not clear that either the inherent or the statutory jurisdiction justified the imposition of an automatic restriction without the exercise of a specific discretion in the individual case. It was held to be desirable for the Master of the Rolls and the President of the Family Division to review the standard practice of the court to reflect the developments since *Re R (Court of Appeal: Order Against Identification)*, above, in which the Court of Appeal indicated that the automatic application of restrictions in all appeals involving children had been developed or confirmed by the court with the approval of the Master of the Rolls nearly 10 years before. In *Pelling v Bruce-Williams* counsel for the Secretary of State for Constitutional Affairs suggested that for the future the court should consider, both at the outset and at the conclusion of each appeal concerning children, exercising a specific discretion either to impose or to refuse prohibition on the identification of the parties to the appeal.

12.13 Setting dates for hearings and setting or confirming the timetable and date for the final hearing

(1) At the –

(a) transfer to a court of proceedings;
(b) postponement or adjournment of any hearing; or
(c) conclusion of any hearing at which the proceedings are not finally determined,

the court will set a date for the proceedings to come before the court again for the purposes of giving directions or for such other purposes as the court directs.

(2) At any hearing the court may –

(a) confirm a date for the final hearing or the week within which the final hearing is to begin (where a date or period for the final hearing has already been set);
(b) set a timetable for the final hearing unless a timetable has already been fixed, or the court considers that it would be inappropriate to do so; or
(c) set a date for the final hearing or a period within which the final hearing of the application is to take place.

(3) The court officer will notify the parties of –

(a) the date of a hearing fixed in accordance with paragraph (1);
(b) the timetable for the final hearing; and
(c) the date of the final hearing or the period in which it will take place.

(4) Where the date referred to in paragraph (1) is set at the transfer of proceedings, the date will be as soon as possible after the transfer.

(5) The requirement in paragraph (1) to set a date for the proceedings to come before the court again is satisfied by the court setting or confirming a date for the final hearing.

Defined terms—'children and family reporter', 'children's guardian', 'court', 'directions appointment': r 2.3(1).

Related provisions—Other provisions affecting the timing of proceedings include CA 1989, ss 1(2) (general principle that delay is likely to be prejudicial to the welfare of a child), 11(1) (obligation of the court in s 8 proceedings to draw up a timetable) and 32(1) (obligation of the court in proceedings under Pt IV of the Act to draw up a timetable) and FPR 2010, rr 12.12 and 12.13 (power of the court to give directions as to time-limits, timetabling etc).

Computation of time—See r 2.9.

Variation of time-limits—Time-limits may not be extended except by direction of the court. However, if the parties or any children's guardian agree proposals for the management of the proceedings, and the court considers that the proposals are suitable, it may approve them without a hearing and give directions in the terms proposed (FPR 2010, r 12.15).

Failure to observe time-limits—Where a local authority failed to submit written evidence as directed by the court and to comply with a direction to serve documents, the court was correct in giving leave for statements to be filed out of time because it was vital in the interests of the children that the court should have the best information available. The sanction for failure to comply with directions was a costs order, where appropriate (*R v Nottinghamshire CC* [1993] Fam Law 625, FD). See *London Borough of Redbridge v A, B and E (Failure to Comply with Directions)* [2016] EWHC 2627 (Fam), where the court adjourned a final hearing in care proceedings concerning a 2-year old child where the local authority had failed comprehensively to comply with case management directions. The court reiterated the importance of compliance with case management directions to the fair administration of justice, stating that such directions were the key tool by which the court maintained fidelity to the statutory principle in s 1(2).

Urgent hearings on Circuit before Family Division judges—See FPR PD12E and under FPR 2010, r 12.16.

Fixing a new date (r 12.13(1))—The court must keep a tight rein on the proceedings, ensuring that a new date is fixed, either at the end of the interim hearing or directions appointment while the parties are still at court or as soon as practicable thereafter. Fixing a new date is not only a question of finding an appropriate court slot for the matter to be heard. CA 1989, s 1(2) must always be kept in mind and other provisions of the Act may also impose constraints (see, for example, s 38(4), which limits the duration of interim care orders). Parties and their legal representatives must be in a position to inform the court of their availability for future hearings and that of their witnesses.

Notice—As to the giving of notice, see FPR 2010, rr 6.23–6.39, 29.3.

12.14 Attendance at hearings

(1) This rule does not apply to proceedings under Chapter 6 of this Part except for proceedings for a declaration under rule 12.71.

(2) Unless the court directs otherwise and subject to paragraph (3), the persons who must attend a hearing are –

(a) any party to the proceedings;
(b) any litigation friend for any party or legal representative instructed to act on that party's behalf; and
(c) any other person directed by the court or required by Practice Directions 12A or 12B or any other practice direction to attend.

(3) Proceedings or any part of them will take place in the absence of a child who is a party to the proceedings if –

(a) the court considers it in the interests of the child, having regard to the matters to be discussed or the evidence likely to be given; and
(b) the child is represented by a children's guardian or solicitor.

(4) When considering the interests of the child under paragraph (3) the court will give –

(a) the children's guardian;
(b) the solicitor for the child; and
(c) the child, if of sufficient understanding,

an opportunity to make representations.

(5) Subject to paragraph (6), where at the time and place appointed for a hearing, the applicant appears but one or more of the respondents do not, the court may proceed with the hearing.

(6) The court will not begin to hear an application in the absence of a respondent unless the court is satisfied that –

(a) the respondent received reasonable notice of the date of the hearing; or
(b) the circumstances of the case justify proceeding with the hearing.

(7) Where, at the time and place appointed for a hearing one or more of the respondents appear but the applicant does not, the court may –

(a) refuse the application; or
(b) if sufficient evidence has previously been received, proceed in the absence of the applicant.

(8) Where at the time and place appointed for a hearing neither the applicant nor any respondent appears, the court may refuse the application.

(9) Paragraphs (5) to (8) do not apply to a hearing where the court –

(a) is considering –
  (i) whether to make a contact activity direction or to attach an activity condition to a child arrangements order; or
  (ii) an application for a financial compensation order, an enforcement order or an order under paragraph 9 of Schedule A1 to the 1989 Act following a breach of an enforcement order; and
(b) has yet to obtain sufficient evidence from, or in relation to, the person who may be the subject of the direction, condition or order to enable it to determine the matter.

(10) Nothing in this rule affects the provisions of Article 18 of the Council Regulation in cases to which that provision applies.

(The Council Regulation makes provision in Article 18 for the court to stay proceedings where the respondent is habitually resident in another Member State of the European Union and has not been adequately served with the proceedings as required by that provision.)

Amendments—SI 2014/843.

Non-application to Chapter 6—Pt 12, Ch 6 relates to proceedings under the 1980 Hague Convention, the European Convention, the Council Regulation and the 1996 Hague Convention; for directions in these applications see FPR 2010, r 12.48.

Defined terms—'child', 'children's guardian', 'court': FPR 2010, r 2.3(1).

Related provisions—Other provisions relating to attendance include: FPR 2010, r 16.20(2), which imposes a duty on the children's guardian to provide the court with such assistance as it may require; FPR PD16A, which sets out his other duties – including attending all directions hearings unless the court orders otherwise (para 6.5) and advising on the attendance of the child at court (para 6.6(b)); FPR 2010, r 12.12(2)(d), which is a general power enabling the court to give directions as to the attendance of the child; and CA 1989, s 95, which empowers a court hearing proceedings under Pt IV or V of the Act (or considering whether to make an order under those Parts) to require the attendance of the child and to make supplementary orders to secure that attendance.

'unless the court directs otherwise' (r 12.14(2))—The court is given a complete discretion as to the circumstances in which to dispense with the attendance of a party at a directions hearing and can do so either of its own initiative (for example when sending out notice of the hearing) or on the request of a party.

Seeking a direction dispensing with attendance at a hearing—It would seem that the appropriate procedure for seeking a direction dispensing with attendance at a hearing would be that set out in FPR 2010, rr 18.1–18.13.

Medical evidence required to justify non-attendance—Where a party wishes to demonstrate that he is unable to attend and participate in a hearing, he should provide medical evidence that: identifies the medical attendant and gives details of his familiarity with the party's medical condition, detailing all recent consultations; identifies with particularity his condition and the features of that condition preventing participation in the trial process; provides a reasoned prognosis; and gives the court confidence that the evidence expressed was an independent opinion following proper examination (*Levy (Trustee in Bankruptcy of Ellis-Carr) v Ellis-Carr and Another* [2012] BPIR 347, ChD).

Use of the power to exclude (r 12.14(2),(3))—Generally, all parties (including the child himself if he is a party) are entitled to be present throughout the proceedings. Rule 12.14(3) empowers the court to exclude any child who is a party where the criteria laid down are satisfied; it is in mandatory terms and contrasts with r 12.14(5),(6), which confers on the court a discretion as to whether to proceed with a hearing or appointment where a party fails to attend. Rule 12.14(3) will no doubt normally come into play when the child should be excluded for his own good. For the attitude of the courts towards the attendance of children at hearings, see **Child at court**, below. The court's power in r 12.14(2) to 'direct otherwise' would presumably be used to exclude attendance where, for some reason, another party's presence would impede a proper hearing, for example in the very rare case where an older child is to give evidence and would find it distressing to do so in the presence of a parent who is alleged to be guilty of a serious sexual assault on him or her. However, in such a situation, the giving of the child's evidence by video link or behind a screen may be a better course. Exceptionally, an application for an adjournment can be granted without notice, but only where the best interests of the children justify such a course of action. Even then, those representing the parties should be in attendance, either having given undertakings or being subject to a direction of the court not to pass on the information to their clients (*Re B (Minors) (Care: Procedure)* [1994] Fam Law 72, FD). As to the procedure to be followed where an application is made to withhold material from a party to proceedings, see *Re C (Disclosure)* [1996] 1 FLR 797, FD, which is considered fully in **Submission of evidence** under FPR 2010, r 12.12.

Child at court—The effect of r 12.14(2) is to require the child, if he is a party, to be present at hearings unless the court otherwise directs under r 12.14(3). Under the CAP in FPR PD12B, which applies to all applications issued under CA 1989, Pt II, para 4.5(4) provides that the court will consider how best the child's view should be ascertained; this may include the judge meeting with the child, in accordance with the *FJC Guidelines for Judges Meeting Children Subject to Family Proceedings* (April 2010) (see Part V).

However, the attitude of the court towards the attendance of children has consistently been cautious (*Re C (A Minor) (Care: Child's Wishes)* [1993] 1 FLR 832, FD). In *Re W (Secure Accommodation Order: Attendance at Court)* [1994] 2 FLR 1092, FD, Ewbank J said that attending court is likely to be harmful for a child and should only be permitted if the court is satisfied that it is in the child's interests. He held that r 4.16(2) (FPR 2010, r 12.14(3)) applies only to one set of circumstances. In other circumstances, the child's interests will prevail. In addition to the consideration of the interests of the child, the court has an inherent power to control its own proceedings that entitles it to decide to proceed in the child's absence. The fact that the child would need to be physically restrained during the hearing to control him (as in *Re W*) would, in itself, be sufficient ground for refusing to allow the child to be in court. Further examples given in *Re W* of situations in which the court would not allow a child to be present are where there is a prospect of disturbance or unruliness in court or the possibility of the child being educationally subnormal or where the child is much younger than the 10-year-old boy in that case. The presence of older children in court is unusual, but by no means unheard of in cases where a child has sufficient maturity to give instructions directly to a solicitor. Likewise, the Supreme Court has done away with the presumption that children should not give evidence: *Re W (Children) (Abuse: Oral Evidence)* [2010] 1 FLR 1485, SC (see notes to CA 1989, s 96). In *A City Council v T, J and K* [2011] 2 FLR 803, FD, a case concerning secure accommodation, the court held that although it has the power to exclude a child who wants to attend court, on the grounds that it would be bad for him to be there, the rules do not contain any in-built presumption; it is a question of what is in the best interests of the child. It can no longer be presumed that a child's attendance in court is likely to be harmful, nor should children have to prove that their attendance at proceedings about them is in their interests. The starting point should be an open evaluation of the consequences of attendance or non-attendance. The relevant factors would generally include: (1) the age and level of understanding of the child; (2) the nature and strength of the child's wishes; (3) the child's emotional and psychological state; (4) the effect of influence from others; (5) the matters to be discussed; (6) the evidence to be given; (7) the child's behaviour; (8) practical and logistical considerations; and (9) the integrity of the proceedings. An evaluation of these factors may well lead to the conclusion that a child of sufficient understanding who wants to attend an important hearing about his future should be allowed to do so for at least part of the time, unless there are clear reasons justifying refusal. This situation is most likely to arise in public law proceedings. In cases in which attendance at the hearing itself is not thought appropriate, a meeting with the judge is a possible alternative (see **Judge seeing child** under FPR 2010, r 12.21). The court, per curiam, added that in any case in which a child wishes to attend a hearing, or where he might wish to do so if told that was possible, the parties must ensure that the court is informed of any arrangements proposed. In the event of disagreement, the parties must, where possible, ensure that the matter is formally brought before the court as a preliminary issue for decision in good time before the relevant hearing; disagreement should not be resolved by informal communications between the parties and the court.

'the party is represented by a children's guardian or solicitor' (r 12.14(3)(b))—The rule appears to suggest that a party is represented only if the solicitor is actually in attendance at the relevant hearing. In *Re AS (Secure Accommodation Order)* [1999] 1 FLR 103, FD, considering the requirement for legal representation of the child concerned in secure accommodation proceedings (CA 1989, s 25(6)), the court held that to be effective, legal representation must involve the taking of instructions. It was not sufficient for the child to be represented at the hearing by a solicitor and counsel who had not been able to take any instructions because the child had not been informed of the hearing.

Child of sufficient understanding to make representations (r 12.14(4)(c))—There are a number of situations in which the rules or the Act oblige the court to evaluate the understanding of the child (see, for example, s 4(4) with regard to parental responsibility agreements, s 10(8) with regard to leave to apply for a s 8 order, and s 43(8) with regard to medical and other examinations). No criteria are laid down as to what constitutes sufficient understanding and what is sufficient for one purpose may not, of course, be sufficient for another; the court will have to take a decision on the particular facts of each case. The authorities on the understanding of a child are collected together under 'able … to give such instructions on his own behalf' under FPR 2010, r 16.29. Where there is a children's guardian he will advise the court as to the level of the child's understanding and the child's wishes in accordance with FPR 2010, r 16.20 and FPR PD16A, para 6.6, and where there is a children and family reporter he can be asked to assist (para 9.4). Alternatively, the assessment will have to be based on how the child appears and what he (or his legal representative on his behalf) says in court or the judge or district judge could, presumably, exercise his discretion to see him privately if appropriate (see **Judge seeing child** under r 12.21). In certain cases, it may be necessary for evidence to be heard on the question from the expert or experts already involved in the case.

'opportunity to make representations' (r 12.14(4))—The rules do not require that there should be an opportunity for oral representations so, although oral representations will be usual, presumably an opportunity to make written representations will suffice.

Hearing in the absence of a respondent (r 12.14(5),(6))—Rule 12.14(5),(6) gives the court a wide discretion to entertain proceedings in the absence of a respondent and even goes so far as to permit the court, in an appropriate case, to proceed to hear an application where the respondent is absent because he has not had reasonable notice of the hearing date. The court is not likely to go to this extreme very often but, where it is prepared to do so, it may be inclined to safeguard the position of the respondent by providing, for example, that he shall be entitled to apply within a certain number of days of service of the order upon him to have it varied or discharged (for a similar sort of order, see *Re D (A Minor) (Child: Removal from Jurisdiction)* [1992] 1 FLR 637, CA). Where an application is made at the hearing itself for an order that is different in kind from that previously applied for, the respondent must be given the opportunity to be present at the hearing and should be given the chance to cross-examine witnesses called by the applicant (*Re W (A Minor) (Interim Care Order)* [1994] 2 FLR 892, CA). In particular, a wholly different order should not be made without giving the parties an opportunity to make representations or to call evidence (*Re M (Judge's Discretion)* [2002] 1 FLR 730, CA). *Re SW (A Minor) (Care Proceedings)* [1993] 2 FLR 609, FD, a care order application, is an example of the type of situation in which the court may decide to proceed in the absence of a respondent.

Dismissal of proceedings at directions stage—See further under FPR 2010, r 12.12.

'reasonable notice of the date of the hearing' (r 12.14(6)(a))—Where it is the court's obligation to give notice to the respondents of a hearing date, proof will be found in the court file. Where it is the applicant's responsibility, he will have to prove that the respondent has had reasonable notice. FPR 2010, r 29.2 makes provision as to the appropriate method of giving notice and FPR 2010, rr 6.23–6.39 and 12.8 with regard to service and the filing of a statement as to service in Form C9. However, it is possible that the respondent may have had reasonable notice of the hearing date even if it has not been given (or cannot be proved) in accordance with these rules. Rule 12.14(6) does not specify that the notice has to be in writing to be reasonable and oral notice may suffice where, for example, the respondent was present at the last hearing when the new date was fixed. Alternatively, he may have shown in some way that he knows of the date of the hearing, for example by writing to the court about it or by telling one of the parties that he has no intention of coming to court on such and such a day. For a further example, see *Re SW (A Minor) (Care Proceedings)* [1993] 2 FLR 609, FD. Where there has been an interim care or supervision order and no change in this is sought, a notification in the antecedent order that the renewal hearing will take place on a certain day is sufficient; there is no need to go through the formality of serving another piece of paper. However, if a change is intended in the nature of the order that is being sought on the subsequent occasion, then normally specific notice of at least 2 clear days should be given by the party who seeks the new form of order (*Re W (A Minor) (Interim Care Order)* [1994] 2 FLR 892, CA).

For certain applications, minimum notice periods are laid down in the rules themselves or in FPR PD12C, para 2.1, and it may be difficult in such cases to satisfy the court that a lesser period of notice is 'reasonable'.

Hearing in the absence of applicant (r 12.14(5))—The court has a discretion as to whether or not to proceed with a hearing in the absence of the applicant. However, there will be many cases (for example where there is doubt as to whether the applicant has had reasonable notice of the time and place of a hearing) where the appropriate course is to adjourn the application, fixing another date for it to be heard. If the applicant fails to turn up for no good reason on more than one occasion or has indicated that he no longer wishes to proceed with his case, the court will no doubt give very serious consideration to refusing the application. However, it must be borne in mind that such a course of action would be tantamount to permitting the withdrawal of an application, and such leave is not granted as a matter of course (see under FPR 2010, r 29.4).

Where neither applicant nor respondent attends (r 12.14(8))—Although r 12.14(8) refers only to the court's discretion to refuse the application, it must also have power in an appropriate case either to adjourn it or to grant it.

12.15 Steps taken by the parties

If – (a) the parties or any children's guardian agree proposals for the management of the proceedings (including a proposed date for the final hearing or a period within which the final hearing is to take place); and

(b) the court considers that the proposals are suitable,

it may approve them without a hearing and give directions in the terms proposed.

(Practice Direction 12A gives guidance as to the application of this rule to Part 4 proceedings in the light of the period that is for the time being allowed under section 32(1)(a)(ii) of the 1989 Act)

Amendments—SI 2014/843.

12.16 Applications without notice

(1) This rule applies to –

(a) proceedings for a section 8 order;

(b) emergency proceedings; and

(c) proceedings relating to the exercise of the court's inherent jurisdiction (other than an application for the court's permission to start such proceedings and proceedings for collection, location and passport orders where Chapter 6 applies).

(2) An application in proceedings referred to in paragraph (1) may be made without notice in which case the applicant must file the application –

(a) where the application is made by telephone, the next business day after the making of the application; or

(b) in any other case, at the time when the application is made.

(3) *(revoked)*

(4) Where –

(a) a section 8 order;

(b) an emergency protection order;

(c) an order for the disclosure of information as to the whereabouts of a child under section 33 of the 1986 Act; or

(d) an order authorising the taking charge of and delivery of a child under section 34 of the 1986 Act,

is made without notice, the applicant must serve a copy of the application on each respondent within 48 hours after the order is made.

(5) Within 48 hours after the making of an order without notice, the applicant must serve a copy of the order on –

(a) the parties, unless the court directs otherwise;

(b) any person who has actual care of the child or who had such care immediately prior to the making of the order; and

(c) in the case of an emergency protection order and a recovery order, the local authority in whose area the child lives or is found.

(6) Where the court refuses to make an order on an application without notice it may direct that the application is made on notice in which case the application will proceed in accordance with rules 12.3 to 12.15.

(7) Where the hearing takes place outside the hours during which the court office is normally open, the court or court officer will take a note of the proceedings.

(Practice Direction 12E (Urgent Business) provides further details of the procedure for out of hours applications. See also Practice Direction 12D (Inherent Jurisdiction (including Wardship Proceedings).)

PART III

(Rule 12.47 provides for without-notice applications in proceedings under Chapter 6, section 1 of this Part, (proceedings under the 1980 Hague Convention and the European Convention).)

Amendments—SI 2013/3204.

Non-application to Chapter 6 (r 12.16(1)(c))—FPR 2010, Pt 12, Ch 6 relates to proceedings under the 1980 Hague Convention, the European Convention, the Council Regulation and the 1996 Hague Convention; for directions in these applications see r 12.48.

Out-of-hours hearings – President's Guidance—See FPR PD12E and FPR PD18A, which give details of how telephone hearings should be conducted (paras 8.1–8.5).

Urgent hearings before Court of Appeal for immediate relief—See *Re S (Authorising children's immediate removal)* [2010] 2 FLR 873, CA for the steps that can be taken to seek an urgent hearing before the Court of Appeal (CA) for immediate relief. In *Re A (A Child) (Residence Order)* [2007] EWCA Civ 899, at [27], the CA held that when a judge considers that a significant change in the arrangements for a child needs to be made forthwith and learns that there is an aspiration to appeal to the CA, he should always give serious consideration to making an order that affords the aspiring appellant a narrow opportunity to approach the CA for further, temporary relief before his order takes effect. The welfare of the child remains paramount, but, subject thereto, the judge needs to consider whether a refusal to afford this narrow opportunity unfairly erodes the facility for effective appeal. If he decides to afford it, he can do so either by directing that the change in the arrangements should occur only at the end (say) of the following working day or by directing that the change should occur forthwith but that execution of his order be stayed until the end (say) of the following working day. When, however, a judge declines to take either of these courses, there remains the opportunity for the aspiring appellant to approach the CA by telephone, and usually on notice to the other party. The approach can even be made out of court hours, first through the security officers of the CA (on 020 7947 6260) and then through a Deputy Master, to a Lord Justice. He may decide to grant a stay, for example until the end of the following working day, to enable documents, such as a note of the judgment and draft grounds of appeal, to be faxed or emailed to the court, for his consideration of the merits of a further stay.

Unlawful removal of a child from his usual place of residence—The seemingly unlawful removal of a child from his usual place of residence ordinarily calls for a peremptory order for his return. An application for such an order should be made without notice and at once to any court that has a 24-hour service, or at least a judge available every court day (*Re R (Children: Peremptory Return)* [2011] 2 FLR 863, CA).

Power to make without notice orders (r 12.16(4))—It is clear that without notice orders will not be granted readily, see for example *Re G (Minors) (Ex Parte Interim Residence Order)* [1993] 1 FLR 910, CA; *Re P (A Minor) (Ex Parte Interim Residence Order)* [1993] 1 FLR 915, CA; *M v C (Children Orders: Reasons)* [1993] 2 FLR 584, CA (all with regard to the limited circumstances in which an interim residence order (now a child arrangements order) should be made without notice); *R v St Albans Magistrates' Court ex parte J* [1993] Fam Law 518, QBD (CA 1989, s 75 application to cancel registration as childminder not normally to be dealt with without notice); *Re R (A Minor) (Blood Transfusion)* [1993] 2 FLR 757, FD (on application for authority to give a blood transfusion, strenuous efforts should be made to arrange a with notice hearing). In *Re B (Minors) (Care: Procedure)* [1994] Fam Law 72, FD, Bracewell J held that a court should only allow without notice applications for adjournment of proceedings for reduction of contact in exceptional circumstances; if a hearing was to take place without the parents being present, their legal representatives should be permitted access, subject to undertakings or directions not to pass the information to their clients. Save in exceptional circumstances, it is highly undesirable that a without notice order should be allowed to stand for more than 7 days; a 12-week without notice child arrangements order for living arrangements in favour of a grandmother was plainly wrong (*Re Y (A Minor) (Ex Parte Interim Orders)* [1994] 1 FLR 172, FD). In *Re J (Children: Ex Parte Orders)* [1997] 1 FLR 606, FD, Hale J made certain observations about without notice orders following consultation with the President of the Family Division. She stressed that the courts have a special responsibility to ensure that without notice orders that could harm the interests of an adult or child are not made without a good reason. Orders requiring the handing over of a very young child to a parent with whom he has not lived for some time should only be made in exceptional circumstances. Applicants for without notice orders and their legal advisers must be scrupulously careful in relation to the application itself and to the implementation of any order that might be made. It is incumbent on the applicant's legal advisers to understand any order and to represent it accurately to others. If there is some doubt about their interpretation, urgent clarification should be sought from the court on a with notice basis. The police should always have a clear understanding of their role in relation to the order. Counsel should never advise on the effect of an order made in their absence without being satisfied of the exact terms of the order, which will generally involve reading it.

Procedure for without notice orders—Where without notice orders are sought, Munby J has set out in *Re S (Ex Parte Orders)* [2001] 1 FLR 308, FD guidelines that state:

(1) It is appropriate, generally, in the Family Division for the court to require the applicant (and, where appropriate, the applicant's solicitors) to give the following undertakings:
   (a) where proceedings have not yet been issued, to issue and serve on the respondent, either by some specified time or as soon as practicable, proceedings either in the form of the draft produced to the court or otherwise as may be appropriate;
   (b) where the application has been made otherwise than on sworn evidence, to cause to be sworn, filed and served on the respondent as soon as practicable an affidavit substantially in the terms of that produced to the court or, as the case may be, confirming the substance of what was said to the court by the applicant's counsel or solicitors; and
   (c) subject to (a) and (b), to serve on the respondent as soon as practicable: (i) the proceedings; (ii) a

sealed copy of the order; (iii) copies of the affidavit(s) and exhibit(s) containing the evidence relied on by the applicant; and (iv) notice of the return date and details of the application to be made on that date.

(2) Whether or not express undertakings have been given, and subject to any order to the contrary, an applicant who obtains without notice injunctive relief is under an obligation to the court, and his solicitor is under an obligation both to the court and his client, to carry out the steps referred to above.

(3) A person who finds himself unable to comply timeously with his undertaking should apply for an extension of time before the time for compliance has expired, or pass the task to someone who has available the time in which to do it.

(4) Persons injuncted are entitled to be given, if they ask, proper information as to what happened at the hearing and told what documents etc were lodged with the court and what legal authorities were cited to the judge. The applicant's lawyers should respond forthwith to any reasonable request from the respondent or his lawyers, for copies of the materials read by the judge or for information about what took place at the hearing. It would therefore be prudent for those acting for the applicant to keep a proper note of the proceedings.

Three additional points of guidance for all without notice applications (and of particular importance if the relief involves the grant of a Tipstaff order) were given in *KY v DD* [2012] 2 FLR 200, FD:

(1) Where information is put before the court to substantiate a without notice order, it should be the subject of the closest scrutiny and, if the applicant is not present to verify it in person, it should be substantiated by the production of a contemporaneous note of the instructions. Otherwise, a short adjournment might be necessary to verify that information.

(2) If additional information is put before the court orally, there must be a direction for the filing of sworn evidence to confirm the information within a very short period of time.

(3) It is incumbent on those giving advice in relation to the making of such an application to consider rigorously whether the application is justified and to be clear as to the evidential basis for it.

Flagrant breaches of these principles and procedures may well lead to a wasted costs order (*B v A (Wasted Costs Order)* [2013] 2 FLR 958, FD). Ryder LJ gave further guidance in relation to without notice applications in *Re C (A Child)* [2014] 1 FLR 1239, CA. Referring to without notice applications that had been made in the absence of the father, he emphasised, among other things, that:

(a) where, in private law child proceedings, there is often no written evidence in support, it is an essential procedural protection that the court order the applicant to file and serve a statement setting out the matters relied upon orally in the absence of the respondent and/or, where appropriate, obtain and serve a transcript of the proceedings;

(b) the father's right to apply to set aside or vary the order was absolute and should have been set out in a statement on face of the order in accordance with FPR 2010, r 18.10(3). The phrase 'liberty to apply on 24 hours' notice' is inapt for a litigant in person;

(c) the without notice prohibited steps order without limit of time was an error of principle and was not corrected by an early return date; the finite nature of the order must be expressed on the face of the order.

(d) it is in the nature of due process that where 'exceptional urgency' is relied upon (FPR PD18A, para 5.1), steps should be taken to notify a respondent informally and/or to give him short notice rather than no notice at all (FPR PD20A, para 4.3(c));

(e) where parties are litigants in person, the court will have to offer a lawyer's analysis, without assistance, if the dispute is not susceptible to conciliation or out of court mediation;

(f) a more inquisitorial process may help judges who need to deal with difficult cases involving litigants in person.

He recommended that, in view of the increased number of litigants in person, the relevant court forms should be amended to ensure that sufficient information is before the court dealing with such applications. In addition, the precedent forms of order currently used by the Family Court in such cases, which helpfully prompt the court to give reasons for the order on the face of the order, should in future be regarded as good practice in the Family Court where written reasons or a judgment are not otherwise readily available. He expressly approved the repeated guidance of the judges of the Family Division in relation to these cases and the summary of that guidance as collated by Charles J in *B v A* (above).

Munby J gave guidance in *Re W (Ex Parte Orders)* [2000] 2 FLR 927, FD as to the procedure to be followed in seeking a without notice injunction in the Family Division.

Without notice application on notice—Although no provision is made for it in the Rules, a procedure has evolved, as a matter of practice and fairness, whereby a without notice application can be made on informal notice (see for example *Croydon LBC v A (No 3)* [1992] 2 FLR 350, FD). This procedure must not be used, however, as a way of getting what should be a proper with notice hearing more quickly than would otherwise be the case.

Application on short notice as alternative to without notice application—Where possible, it is preferable for an application to be served and for notice to be abridged than for a without notice application to be made (see for example *Re B (A Minor) (Residence Order: Ex Parte)* [1992] 2 FLR 1, CA). As to the giving of notice, see FPR 2010, r 29.2 and as to service see FPR 2010, rr 6.23–6.39, 12.8 and FPR PD12C.

Service of the without notice orders (r 12.16(4))—Service of an order of the kind specified in r 12.16(4) within the period of 48 hours there prescribed is mandatory. Failure to serve within the period might generate argument as to enforceability of the order and therefore, to avoid problems, an applicant who knows that there is likely to be difficulty in complying with the time limit for service should seek directions at the same time as the initial without notice application is made. Rule 6.36 gives the court power to dispense with service, and

PART III

FPR 2010, rr 6.19 and 6.35 give the court power to order that service shall be effected in an alternative manner. FPR 2010, r 12.12(2)(a),(b) provides a general power to give directions about the management of the case and the timetable for steps to be taken between the giving of directions and the final hearing. As to the computation of time, see FPR 2010, r 2.9; as to the extension of time limits, see FPR 2010, rr 4.1(3)(a), 12.12(2)(a),(b) and 12.13(1).

Refusal of an application for a without notice order (r 12.16(6))—Where it is directed that the application is to be heard with notice before there can be a hearing the applicant will have to file the application, if this has not already been done, serve copies in accordance with FPR 2010, r 12.8 and give notice in Form C6A in accordance with FPR 2010, r 12.3(1) and FPR PD12C.

Application to set aside without notice order—Where a without notice order has been made and the absent party wishes to challenge it, the appropriate course is to apply to the judge who made it to vary or rescind the order. There is no purpose, in anything other than a wholly exceptional case, in making such an application without notice. Notice (albeit short notice if justified by the urgency of the situation) should be given to the other parties (*Re P (A Minor) (Ex Parte Interim Residence Order)* [1993] 1 FLR 915, CA; see also *Re H (Wardship: Ex Parte Orders)* [1994] 2 FLR 981, CA).

Interim remedies—See also FPR 2010, Pt 20, which deals with certain other interim remedies not otherwise dealt with in the rules, and with security for costs.

12.17 Investigation under section 37 of the 1989 Act

(1) This rule applies where a direction is given to an appropriate authority by the court under section 37(1) of the 1989 Act.

(2) On giving the direction the court may adjourn the proceedings.

(3) As soon as practicable after the direction is given the court will record the direction.

(4) As soon as practicable after the direction is given the court officer will –

- (a) serve the direction on –
  - (i) the parties to the proceedings in which the direction is given; and
  - (ii) the appropriate authority where it is not a party;
- (b) serve any documentary evidence directed by the court on the appropriate authority.

(5) Where a local authority informs the court of any of the matters set out in section 37(3)(a) to (c) of the 1989 Act it will do so in writing.

(6) Unless the court directs otherwise, the court officer will serve a copy of any report to the court under section 37 of the 1989 Act on the parties.

(Section 37 of the 1989 Act refers to the appropriate authority and section 37(5) of that Act sets out which authority should be named in a particular case.)

Guidance on use of CA 1989, s 37—See **Best Practice Guidance on s 37(1) Directions** under CA 1989, s 37, which stresses the importance of the local authority being informed as quickly as possible of a s 37 direction and advises that an immediate telephone notification should be made, then confirmed in writing in compliance with r 12.17(5). See also *CAAC Handbook of Best Practice in Children Act Cases*, App A, item IV (set out in Part V of this work as *Best Practice Guidance of June 1997*).

Public Law Outline (PLO)—Applications for care and supervision orders under CA 1989, s 31 are subject to the relevant provisions of FPR 2010, Pt 12 and PD12A and the PLO contained therein. See in particular Case management hearing, Further case management hearing and Issues resolution hearing in FPR PD12A. On the same day that the court makes such a direction, it must identify the local authority that is to prepare the s 37(1) report, fix a date for the next hearing and give directions as to filing and service of the report. Following a direction under s 37, the local authority must report back within 8 weeks unless the court otherwise directs: s 37(4). The date for the next hearing must be fixed: FPR 2010, r 12.13(1). The date for the report should also be specified under FPR 2010, r 12.12(2). At the conclusion of their enquiries social services must consult the family, the child and all relevant agencies before making decisions about a plan for the child. The local authority must record the response of each person and agency consulted, decide whether to apply to the court for an order, file the report with the court and serve it on the parties on or before the date specified in the court's order. Where social services decide not to apply for a care or supervision order they should set out in their report their decisions and reasons and any plan they have made for the child, including any services to be provided in accordance with Government guidance. Note that a local authority's hard-pressed financial position will not release it from its statutory responsibility under s 37. Where an order under s 37 is made, the local authority will be sufficiently closely connected to the litigation to justify a non-party costs order against it in circumstances where any failings on the part of the local authority reach the threshold of exceptionality for making such an order (*Re HB, PB, OB and Croydon London Borough Council* [2016] 1 FLR 92, FD).

'appropriate authority' (r 12.17(1))—This phrase refers back to CA 1989, s 37; s 37(5) sets out which authority should be named in any given case.

'record the direction' (r 12.17(3))—The direction is to be recorded and constitutes a direction to a specified local authority to undertake an investigation under s 37(1). The record should set out the full name and date of birth of the child concerned.

'parties' (r 12.17(3))—As r 12.17 does not widen the normal meaning of 'parties' to the proceedings so as to include the welfare officer as a party, it appears that the parties are simply the applicant and the respondents.

Documentary evidence that may accompany copy of direction (r 12.17(4)(b))—Rule 12.17(4) is important because it enables the court to ensure that the local authority carrying out the investigation receives the documentary evidence that it will need to do its job properly. However, the authority does not simply have access to the whole court file; the court has a discretion as to precisely which documents should be provided and must give a direction about this when making the s 37(1) direction.

Service—As to service, see FPR 2010, rr 6.23–6.39, 12.8 and FPR PD12C.

12.18 Disclosure of a report under section 14A(8) or (9) of the 1989 Act

(1) In proceedings for a special guardianship order, the local authority must file the report under section 14A(8) or (9) of the 1989 Act within the timetable fixed by the court.

(2) The court will consider whether to give a direction that the report under section 14A(8) or (9) of the 1989 Act be disclosed to each party to the proceedings.

(3) Before giving a direction for the report to be disclosed, the court must consider whether any information should be deleted from the report.

(4) The court may direct that the report must not be disclosed to a party.

(5) The court officer must serve a copy of the report in accordance with any direction under paragraph (2).

(6) In paragraph (3), information includes information which a party has declined to reveal under rule 29.1(1).

Definitions—'special guardianship order': r 12.2.

Rule 29.1 (r 12.18(6))—This rule states that a party is not required to reveal certain personal details such as his home address, contact details and so forth unless the court directs otherwise (FPR 2010, r 29.1(1)). If he does not wish to reveal these particulars he must give notice of them to the court and they will not be revealed to any person unless the court directs otherwise (r 29.1(2)). However, the party concerned must notify the court of any change of address (r 29.1(3)).

12.19 Additional evidence

(1) This rule applies to proceedings for a section 8 order or a special guardianship order.

(2) Unless the court directs otherwise, a party must not –

- (a) file or serve any document other than in accordance with these rules or any practice direction;
- (b) in completing a form prescribed by these rules or any practice direction, give information or make a statement which is not required or authorised by that form; or
- (c) file or serve at a hearing –
  - (i) any witness statement of the substance of the oral evidence which the party intends to adduce; or
  - (ii) any copy of any document (including any experts' report) which the party intends to rely on.

(3) Where a party fails to comply with the requirements of this rule in relation to any witness statement or other document, the party cannot seek to rely on that statement or other document unless the court directs otherwise.

Defined terms—'section 8 order': CA 1989, s 8(2).

Child Arrangements Programme (CAP)—The CAP is contained in FPR PD12B; it applies to all applications issued under CA 1989, Pt II and sets out the structure for the management of such cases (see FPR 2010, r 12.31).

Case management—See the CAAC *Handbook of Best Practice in Children Act Cases* (set out in Part V of this work as *Best Practice Guidance of June 1997*) and **Bundles and other particular matters** under FPR 2010, r 12.12. For the detailed rules about bundles see FPR PD27A.

Parties—Broadly speaking, the parties to proceedings are the applicant and the respondents set out in the relevant table entry in r 12.3(1). As to the power of the court to order that a person be joined as or cease to be a party, see FPR 2010, r 12.3(3).

Time for filing statements and documents (r 12.19(2))—Directions will normally be given under FPR 2010, r 12.12 for all but the very early stages of the proceedings. It is suggested that directions should be specific. Solicitors should identify the deponents of proposed statements and the relevance of their evidence, and a timetable for the filing of statements should be drawn up. This has the additional advantage that the court is in a far better position to assess the reasonableness of any estimate of the length of the final hearing.

PART III

Non-compliance with r 12.19(2) (r 12.19(3))—Rule 12.19(3) not only prevents a witness who has not filed a statement at all from giving evidence without permission, it also requires an application for permission before a witness who has filed a statement can give evidence on matters outside its scope. If the court feels that any party has been prejudiced by not receiving advance notice in accordance with r 12.19(1), it may refuse permission. However, as a matter of practice, most courts are reluctant to refuse to entertain evidence that has a bearing on the welfare of a child purely because of a breach of procedural rules (*R v Nottinghamshire CC* [1993] Fam Law 625, FD). The alternative is to adjourn the proceedings for an appropriate period so that proper instructions can be taken etc. In such circumstances, an application for a costs order against the party who is in breach or for a wasted costs order may be appropriate. An application for permission should be made using the FPR 2010, Pt 18 procedure; FPR 2010, rr 18.1–18.13 provide a simplified process for straightforward applications made within existing proceedings, which in some cases may be determined summarily and without a hearing. The Pt 18 procedure will generally apply to applications for the court's permission unless the rules or PDs state otherwise.

Forms and documentary evidence in s 8 and special guardianship cases (r 12.19(2))—The documentation to be filed and served in s 8 cases is strictly controlled to prevent matters becoming inflamed by comments and allegations in forms, statements and reports before the parties have had an opportunity to resolve matters amicably by negotiation. Broadly summarised, the position is as follows:

(a) In a normal case, certain documents are required by the rules to be filed and served and do not require leave. These include the application form (FPR 2010, r 5.1 and FPR PD5A), a statement of service in Form C9 (PD5A)) and the acknowledgement of the application. Care must be taken in each case to include only such information as is required by the form.
(b) An answer is not required or authorised by the rules and should not be filed or served without leave.
(c) Statements or copies of other documents (including experts' reports) on which a party intends to rely should not be filed or served until the court so directs. The court will normally address questions as to the filing of statements and documents at an early directions hearing to ensure that all relevant evidence is exchanged and filed with the court in advance of the hearing to which it relates, but not so early in proceedings that it jeopardises the possibility of an amicable resolution of the issues between the parties. Where advance planning of this kind is not possible, e g where a party wishes to rely on a statement for which leave has not yet been granted to support an urgent interim application, the statement should be prepared and taken to the hearing, and the court should be invited to give leave for it to be filed forthwith.

In *Re W-M (Children)* [2015] EWCA Civ 1201, the Court of Appeal upheld a judge's decision to limit the length of statements for use at a hearing to determine the frequency of contact with a child where she was very familiar with the case and the parties had a habit of ranging widely over all aspects of the case. The judge had acted proportionately and had a duty to assist the parties to focus the issues on the current welfare topics for determination.

Secure editing of documents—Where the court makes an order permitting the omission of certain identifying information from documents and evidence, the legal representatives must adhere to the guidelines approved by the President of the Family Division and set out in *Re R (Secure Editing of Documents)* [2007] 2 FLR 759, FD.

Service—See FPR 2010, rr 6.23–6.39, 12.8 and FPR PD12C.

12.20 *(revoked)*

12.21 Hearings

(1) The court may give directions about the order of speeches and the evidence at a hearing.

(2) Subject to any directions given under paragraph (1), the parties and the children's guardian must adduce their evidence at a hearing in the following order –

(a) the applicant;
(b) any party with parental responsibility for the child;
(c) other respondents;
(d) the children's guardian;
(e) the child, if the child is a party to proceedings and there is no children's guardian.

Defined terms—'child', 'children's guardian', 'court', 'directions appointment': FPR 2010, r 2.3(1); 'parental responsibility': CA 1989, s 3.

Case management—Great assistance is to be derived from the *Handbook of Best Practice in Children Act cases* produced by the Children Act Advisory Committee (set out in Part V of this work as *Best Practice Guidance of June 1997*). See also **Bundles and other particular matters** under FPR 2010, r 12.12 and for detailed guidance about bundles see FPR PD27A. See the practical guidance given as to the proper preparation of cases brought under CA 1989 in *Re R (Care: Disclosure: Nature of Proceedings)* [2002] 1 FLR 755, FD. For further useful guidance as to the conduct and recording of meetings and the provision of documents in care proceedings see *Re L (Care: Assessment: Fair Trial)* [2002] 2 FLR 730, FD, which is referred to in more detail in **Disclosure – impact of ECHR 1950** under FPR 2010, r 12.12.

Interim hearings—*Hampshire County Council v S* [1993] 1 FLR 559, FD, provides valuable guidance as to the conduct of interim hearings. The justices in that case had, on submissions only and without reading the statements filed or the children's guardian's report, made an interim order reducing the contact that the parents had to a child in care. On appeal, it was held that they had made a number of serious errors and Cazalet J also gave some general guidance with the approval of the President. Guidance as to interim hearings can also be derived from *Re W (A Minor) (Interim Care Order)* [1994] 2 FLR 892, CA, which endorses the *Hampshire* case. As to the making of interim orders for contact on the basis of the papers only, without hearing oral evidence and/or having the advice of a children and family reporter or other experts, see *Re D (Contact: Interim Order)* [1995] 1 FLR 495, FD), further noted under **Full hearing not always appropriate** (below). For information as to interim orders in care proceedings, see under CA 1989, s 38. In *RE v North Yorkshire County Council, LO and A (A Child)* [2015] EWCA Civ 1169, the Court of Appeal gave guidance about procedure at issues resolution hearings. Although in family proceedings it would only be appropriate occasionally to make final orders at a case management hearing, the court would and always had to consider making final orders at the issues resolution hearing. It is the professional duty of the advocates and lawyers in every case to direct their attention to the obligation to achieve finality at the issues resolution hearing wherever possible. It follows that lay parties are always required to attend the issues resolution hearing and that, if a party is in custody, a Home Office production order should be obtained. See also *Re M (A Child)* [2015] EWCA Civ 1296, where the refusal of a father's application for direct contact was overturned where he had been ambushed at a directions hearing when the judge unexpectedly decided to hear evidence and determine the substantive application.

Orders generally—Since January 2016, the orders in private law cases under the Child Arrangements Programme (CAP) have been amended to make them as concise as possible and easier to understand by the parties. The new orders now incorporate simpler language and are less prescriptive as to recitals, leaving it to the discretion of the individual judge in any particular case what they choose to include or exclude. All penal and warning notices are now prominently displayed together on the front of the order. The expectation is now that all parties should leave court with a copy of the order made at the hearing whenever possible. See note under FPR PD12B.

Agreed orders—Although the court has an overriding judicial duty to investigate proposals that are put before it by consent, the depth of that investigation must reflect the consensus between the parties. Where the court intends to depart from the agreed terms, it must first tell the parties the nature of the proposed departure and allow submissions: *Devon CC v S and Others* [1992] 2 FLR 244, FD. The practice adopted in the higher courts, whereby the parties submit a draft consent order setting out the agreed terms, was commended. Such a draft order cannot, of course, bind the court but it does serve to concentrate the minds of the parties on the terms they are agreeing, thus reducing the possibility of mistakes and misunderstandings, and makes it easier for the justices to define the points at which they might tentatively depart from the agreed package (*M v Warwickshire County Council* [1994] 2 FLR 593, FD). *S v E (Access to Child)* [1993] Fam Law 407, FD (decided under the pre-CA 1989 law but still relevant) stressed that, while magistrates are not bound to rubber stamp what the parties agree, there must be truly exceptional circumstances for justices to discard arrangements sensitively negotiated between the parties with the assistance of legal advice (here intended as provisional during a period when the natural father was being reintroduced to his child after an extensive break in contact).

As to the extent of the court's duty to investigate where either of the parties are agreed that there should be a care order or the parents are prepared to concede that there should be a care order, see **Agreed orders** under CA 1989, s 31.

Hearings in private—FPR 2010, r 27.10 states that proceedings to which FPR 2010 apply will be held in private, except where the rules or any other enactment provide otherwise, and subject to any enactment, where the court directs otherwise. The rules relating to attendance at private hearings are covered by FPR 2010, r 27.11.

Children's hearings in private do not breach ECHR 1950, Art 6—See under r 12.14.

Full hearing not always appropriate—There can be limited situations in which the application before the court has so remote a prospect of a positive outcome that it is wrong to allow it to go any further and the appropriate course is to dismiss it without hearing oral evidence or further investigation (*Cheshire County Council v M* [1993] 1 FLR 463, FD; *W v Ealing London Borough Council* [1993] 2 FLR 788, CA).

In cases that do not fall within the limited *Cheshire County Council v M* category, the court nonetheless has a broad discretion to conduct the case as is most appropriate for the issues involved and the evidence available (*Re C (Contact: Conduct of Hearings)* [2006] 2 FLR 289, CA). Indeed, the overriding objective in FPR 2010, r 1.1(2)(b) requires the court to deal with cases in ways that are proportionate to the nature, importance and complexity of the issues. In family proceedings, a judge has an inquisitorial role and his duty is to further the welfare of the children, which is his paramount consideration. For that reason, he exercises a far broader discretion than in a civil jurisdiction to determine how an application should be pursued (*Re C (Family Proceedings: Case Management)* [2013] 1 FLR 1089, CA). It will not necessarily hold a full hearing with the parties permitted to call oral evidence and cross-examine any witnesses that they may choose. Applications for child arrangements orders to determine with whom a child will live, care orders or for the revocation of a care order are likely to be decided on full oral evidence, although not invariably; applications for contact may be and are heard sometimes with, and sometimes without, oral evidence or with a limited amount of oral evidence. In *Re N; A v G and N* [2010] 1 FLR 272, FD, a case in which acrimonious family proceedings had been ongoing for more than 5 years, Munby J held that there was no need for a full hearing of either parent's applications because there was already more than enough evidence and other material before the court to enable it to make a fair and proper decision. The prospects of either parent succeeding at full trial were remote and the justice of the case did not require a full investigation with oral evidence. Moreover, the further prolongation of this litigation could only be seriously detrimental to the child's welfare, and to do otherwise than to dismiss both parents' applications would be an abdication of the court's responsibilities to the child. Important factors for the court to consider include: (a) whether there is sufficient evidence on which to make the decision; (b) whether the proposed evidence that the applicant for a full trial wishes to adduce and whether the opportunity to cross-examine the witnesses is likely to affect the outcome of the proceedings; (c) the welfare of the child and the effect of further litigation; (d) whether the delay will be so detrimental to the child's well-being that exceptionally there should not be a full hearing; (e) the prospects of success of the applicant for a full trial; and (f) whether the justice of the case requires a full investigation with oral evidence. In *Re H (Contact Order: Permissibility of Judge's Actions)* [2012] 2 FLR 1114, CA, a variation of contact was sought in a case with a considerable litigation history; the parents and the child were all represented. An agreed note from all three counsel was submitted to the judge before the hearing, indicating that the parties, who had been negotiating, required more time; following a discussion with the judge, all counsel agreed that the matter would be dealt with by submissions rather than by oral evidence and further time was thus allowed for negotiation. The Court of Appeal held that everything the judge did on the day of the hearing was not only permissible but sensible and consistent with the general approach of judges in the trial courts to case management where the parties were engaged in lengthy negotiations that threatened to prevent the completion of a contested issue in the time permitted. While a judge should stop irrelevant or time-wasting cross-examination, he should always bear in mind that however carefully he has read the papers beforehand, counsel is likely to have a better grasp of the inner forensic realities of the case (*Re J (Residence and Contact Dispute*) [2013] 1 FLR 716, CA).

For a further example of a curtailed hearing, see *Re B (Contact: Stepfather's Opposition)* [1997] 2 FLR 579, CA noted under **Dismissal of proceedings at directions stage** under FPR 2010, r 12.12 and the further comments of the CA in *Re A (Application for Leave)* [1998] 1 FLR 1, CA, at p 4F. A judge has not only the right but the duty to bring proceedings to an end if he reaches the conclusion that the proceedings can go no further (*Re C-P (A Child*) (2006) *Lawtel* 24 January, CA). Where there is a split hearing there is nothing wrong with the court determining at the preliminary hearing, in advance of the local authority's final care plan, that a particular individual will not be in a position to care for a child safely within the timescale that the child needs, provided, of course, that the evidence substantiates this conclusion (*North Yorkshire CC v B* [2008] 1 FLR 1645, FD).

However, the court has to be careful not to deal with the matter in too peremptory a way (*Re J (Residence and Contact Dispute*) [2013] 1 FLR 716, CA – where the recorder was wrong to curtail the cross-examination of the mother) and where there are disputed matters that go to the heart of the issue, the court must determine them rather than try to bypass them to progress the case (*Re S (Contact Order)* [2013] 1 FLR 825, CA). See also *Re L (A Child)* [2016] EWCA Civ 871, where a contact order was set aside where it had been made without the children's special guardians having the opportunity to hear the evidence of other witnesses or to make submissions on the issue of contact.

Robust case management very much has a place in family proceedings, but it also has its limits (*Re B (Case Management)* [2013] 1 FLR 963, CA – where the judge held an unnecessarily truncated hearing and made a crucial finding of fact on the basis of limited evidence). Where a preliminary fact-finding hearing involves serious allegations of domestic violence, the judge should not terminate the case without hearing all the available evidence (*Re R (Family Proceedings: No Case to Answer)* [2009] 2 FLR 83, CA). In *Re I and H (Contact: Right to Give Evidence)* [1998] 1 FLR 876, CA, it was said that an applicant under CA 1989 has a fundamental right to be heard. Similarly, in *H v West Sussex CC* [1998] 1 FLR 862, FD, Johnson J said that evidence in such cases ought to be regulated by weight rather than admissibility, particularly in a case where a parent was at risk of being separated permanently from his child. He expressed a view that such a parent ought, surely, to be allowed to present his case in the way that he chose, subject to the evidence being tendered in a responsible and professional manner. In *Re W (Contact Application: Procedure)* [2000] 1 FLR 263, FD, Wilson J roundly criticised a procedure that had been generally adopted by lay justices in one particular court in respect of applications for leave to apply for contact where the matter was dealt with summarily, neither party was invited to attend, no order was drawn up granting leave and no reasons were given in writing or orally.

It is clear that, where the court hears oral evidence from one side, it is wholly inappropriate not to hear from the other (*Re F (A Minor) (Care Order: Procedure)* [1994] 1 FLR 240, FD). Reasons for a decision to refuse to hear oral evidence from a party should be given by the justices. In contrast to *Re F*, however, it was permissible for the lay justices to stop proceedings for the discharge of a care order/defined contact in *Re S and P (Discharge of Care Order)* [1995] 2 FLR 782, FD, after hearing only the mother's evidence, there being no reasonable prospect of her application succeeding. In *Re M (Contact)* [1995] 1 FLR 1029, FD, it was acknowledged that there were cases in which an application was so hopeless that the court would be entitled to dismiss it effectively out of hand, but the lay justices had been wrong to dismiss this application by a father for staying contact on the papers only and without hearing oral evidence. It is difficult to envisage circumstances in which an order for interim contact could properly be made, where the principle of contact was genuinely in dispute and where there were substantial factual issues relating to the child that were unresolved without the court hearing oral evidence or having the advice of an expert such as the children and family reporter (*Re D (Contact: Interim Order)* [1995] 1 FLR 495, FD). However, see *Re B (Contact: Stepfather's Opposition*), above, for a case in which the judge took the exceptional course of dismissing an application for contact at the directions stage without hearing evidence.

As to the possibility of estoppel, see *Re B (Children Act Proceedings: Issue Estoppel)* [1997] 1 FLR 285, FD and *Re W (Care Proceedings: Litigation Capacity)* [2010] 1 FLR 1176, FD.

Judge not to make unannounced visits—A judge cannot seek to determine who is telling the truth by a surprise or unannounced visit in relation to disputed facts; a judge's job is to consider the facts presented, weigh up that evidence after cross-examination, make findings and a determination (*AMV v RM (Children: Judge's Visit to Private Home)* [2013] 2 FLR 150, FD – it was wrong for the judge to make surprise visits to the homes of the mother and grandmother in a disputed residence case).

Organising expert evidence: private law – public law—See FPR 2010, Pt 25 and PD25A–PD25F.

Facilitated communication—It is dangerous for a court in family proceedings to rely on evidence provided by facilitated communication, a process in which a helper supports the hand or arm of the person with communication difficulties while using a keyboard or typing device, in support of allegations of abuse made by the individual (*Re D (Evidence: Facilitated Communication)* [2001] 1 FLR 148, FD).

Wearing of veils in court—Guidance on the wearing of the niqab (the full veil worn by Muslim women) was published in 2007 by the Equal Treatment Advisory Committee (ETAC) of the Judicial Studies Board (JSB). For victims and complainants, it may be possible for evidence to be given in court by a woman wearing a veil, or for the woman to agree to remove it while giving evidence. Other measures are available to the court, such as screens, video links and clearing the public gallery. A decision on these matters should ideally be reached after discussion at a preliminary hearing. For witnesses and defendants, a sensitive request to remove a veil may be appropriate. However, it may be possible to properly assess the evidence of a woman wearing a niqab in some cases. For advocates, the starting point is that an advocate wearing a full veil should be entitled to appear while wearing it. It will be a matter for the judge to decide whether in the particular circumstances the interests of justice are being impeded or not by the fact that the advocate's face cannot be seen, or that they cannot be heard clearly. The Judicial Studies Board's *Equal Treatment Advisory Committee's Guidance on Religious Dress (December 2007)* can be viewed in Part V of this work and future updates will be found at *www.judiciary.gov.uk*. In *Re S (Practice: Muslim Women Giving Evidence)* [2007] 2 FLR 461, FD, a Muslim woman was granted a decree of nullity nisi on the grounds of duress. When giving evidence, the witness agreed to remove her veil before the female judge, provided that she was screened from the view of her male counsel, the only male member of the particular court. Macur J held that it was a matter of extreme importance that witnesses in sensitive cases were permitted to present their case to the satisfaction of the court while maintaining their religious observance of dress. The facility of screens and the ability, if at all possible, to list such cases before a female judge would obviate the objections of litigants or witnesses, subject to an assessment of the genuine nature of their unwillingness to appear before the court without the veil. In that case counsel had spoken to the Clerk to the Rules 2 days before the hearing to alert the court to the problem and this enabled proper thought to be given as to the best way to conduct the hearing.

Citation of authorities—See note to FPR 2010, r 12.12.

Order of speeches (r 12.21(1))—Whereas r 12.21(2) establishes a normal order in which the parties and children's guardian will adduce their evidence, this rule is silent as to the normal order for speeches. The court may give directions under r 12.21(1) if necessary, but tradition generally dictates that all the respondents have their say first, the applicant goes next and the children's guardian last. Where one legal representative has made oral representations, the others in the case should not be confined to written representations (*Re E (Minors)* [1991] TLR 300, CA).

Continuing duty of advocates—Where an advocate's submissions on the primary issue fail, it is very important that he continues to present the views of his client during the ensuing debate as to the implementation and drawing of the order (*Buckinghamshire County Council v M* [1994] 2 FLR 506, CA).

Legal representation at hearing – the right to a fair trial under ECHR 1950, Art 6—Generally, it is important for parents in cases where the outcome could be the permanent loss of their children, to have equality of representation and to have a sense that a full and sympathetic hearing has taken place (*Re G (Adoption Proceedings: Representation of Children)* [2001] 1 FCR 353, CA). The loss by parents of legal representation on the first day of care proceedings (leaving them to conduct their own case) will not necessarily amount to a breach of Art 6 (the right to a fair trial) (*Re B and T (Care Proceedings: Legal Representation)* [2001] 1 FLR 485, CA – where the parents had had skilled legal advice in the preparation of the case and had changed lawyers on four previous occasions, the judge had supported the parents at the final hearing and had a duty not only to the parents but also to the children who were entitled to an early determination of their future). However, in care proceedings the complexity of the case, the importance of what is at stake and the highly emotive nature of the subject matter mean that the principles of litigants having effective access to the court and of fairness require that they should receive the assistance of a lawyer (*P, C and S v UK* [2002] 2 FLR 631, ECHR).

Litigants in person (LIPs)—Since litigants in person (LIPs) are now the rule rather than the exception, judges should have every party sworn in before they make their submissions so that what is said by them becomes a matter of evidence (*Re H (A Child)* [2014] EWCA Civ 271). Important guidance as to the way in which courts manage cases involving LIPs is to be found in *Re C (A Child)* [2013] EWCA Civ 1412 (see further under FPR 2010, r 12.16). The Law Society has published Practice Note: *Litigants in Person*, providing guidance to all solicitors who may need to deal with litigants in person as part of their work. This can be found in [2012] Family Law 727 and on the Law Society website: *www.lawsociety.org.uk*. The HMCS leaflet CB7 'Guide for separated parents: children and the family Courts' contains useful information for those wishing to make applications without representation. The report of the Judicial Working Group on Litigants in Person was published in July 2013; Annex B, contains *Draft Guidance (Family Proceedings)* for judges conducting hearings involving litigants in person. It can be found at *www.judiciary.gov.uk*. The Bar Council has published *A Guide to Representing Yourself in Court*, which can be found at *www.barcouncil.org.uk*. Online assistance for LIPs is available at the government information hub *www.sortingoutseparation.org.uk*. HMCTS has developed three videos for LIP about the court process ('Making your application'; 'Attending the first hearing'; and 'Attending a full hearing'), which can be seen at *www.bit.ly/guides_for_separating_parents*. Some courts have a Personal Support Unit (PSU) attached, which can provide invaluable assistance. The Ministry of Justice is helping the PSUs to expand their coverage. See also the notes to FPR PD27A.

McKenzie friend (MF)—In 2010, the President issued *Practice Guidance: McKenzie Friends (Civil and Family Courts)* (see Part V and the CAP in FPR PD12B, para 14.5). It is intended to act as a reminder of the principles set out in the authorities. In appropriate cases, the court has a power to grant an application under CLSA 1990, ss 27 and 28 to allow a MF to have rights of audience. Whereas the court will be slow to grant such an application, it should be prepared to do so for good reason bearing in mind all of the circumstances of the case; such circumstances are likely to vary greatly (*Re N (A Child) (McKenzie Friend: Rights of Audience)* [2008] 2 FLR 1899, FD). The assistance of a MF is available for the benefit of the litigant in person (LIP) and whether or not a MF is paid or unpaid for his services he has no right to provide those services; the court is solely concerned with the interests of the LIP. There is a strong presumption in family proceedings in favour of permitting a MF to be present unless the judge is satisfied that fairness and the interests of justice do not require it (*In the Matter of the Children of Mr O'Connell, Mr Whelan and Mr Watson* [2005] 2 FLR 967, CA). However, the court can prevent a MF from continuing to act where the assistance given is inimical to the efficient administration of justice, for example, where the friend is indirectly running the case or using the litigant as a puppet (*Noueiri v Paragon Finance plc* [2001] 1 WLR 2357, CA). Where the MF has intimidated the other party, the judge may exclude him from acting as a MF in future (*Re H (Appeal: Case Management Decisions)* [2013] 1 FLR 1234, CA). The judge is entitled to refuse an application for a particular person to act as a MF without allowing that person to be present in court for the application (*Re F (Children)* [2013] EWCA Civ 726). The report of the Judicial Working Group on Litigants in Person was published in July 2013 and it made certain recommendations in relation to MFs, given that since the withdrawal of legal aid for most family work there are likely to be more MFs involved in court proceedings.

Advocate to the court (amicus curiae)—The Attorney-General, Lord Goldsmith QC, in conjunction with Lord Woolf CJ, issued a *Memorandum of 19 December 2001 – Requests for the Appointment of an Advocate to the Court* (see Pt V), which details the provisions for the appointment of an advocate to the court (amicus curiae) in appropriate cases. In most cases, an advocate to the court is appointed by the Attorney-General following a request by the court. However, in some cases, an advocate to the court will be appointed by the Official Solicitor or Cafcass where the issue is one in which their experience of representing children and adults under a disability gives them special experience. The representation of children is governed by FPR 2010, Pt 16 and PD16A. The procedure and circumstances for requesting an advocate to the court to be appointed by the Official Solicitor or Cafcass are the same as those applying to requests to the Attorney-General. In cases of extreme urgency, telephone requests may be made (NB the *Memorandum* contains all relevant contact telephone numbers, addresses etc). In some cases, the Official Solicitor himself will be appointed as advocate to the court. He may be given directions by the court authorising him to obtain documents, conduct investigations and enquiries and to advise the court. He may appear by counsel or an in-house advocate (see para 12 of the *Memorandum*). Where an advocate to the court has been involved in a first instance hearing, he can often make a vital contribution to any appeal, and judges giving directions for an oral hearing or an appeal should consider his role. If nothing has been said by the supervising Lord Justice then he should seek directions as to his future role (*Re A (Father: Knowledge of Child's Birth)* [2011] 2 FLR 123, CA).

'parties' (r 12.21(2))—Broadly speaking, the parties to proceedings are the applicant and the respondents set out in the relevant entry in the table in FPR 2010, r 12.3(1). As to the power of the court to order that a person be joined as or cease to be a party, see FPR 2010, r 12.3(3). The children's guardian is not personally a party (although the child whose interests he represents may be) but, to an extent, he participates in the proceedings as if he were.

'child, if he is a party to the proceedings' (r 12.21(2)(e))—If the child is bringing the application, no doubt his status as applicant (within FPR 2010, r 20.21(2)(a)) will prevail over his status as child (within r 12.21(2)(e)) and he will adduce his evidence first. A child who is responding to an application and has a FPR 2010, r 16.4 children's guardian but no s 41 children's guardian will fall within r 12.21(2)(e), as a r 16.4 children's guardian is not the same as a children's guardian for the purposes of r 16.3 (see the definition in r 2.3(1)). The duties of the children's guardian are set out in FPR PD16A.

Role of National Youth Advocacy Service (NYAS)—The role of NYAS is becoming increasingly important in the separate representation of children, particularly in acrimonious contact cases. See note under CA 1989, s 7.

Where the child and his children's guardian part company (r 12.21(2))—Rule 12.21(2) does not expressly cover the situation where the child and the children's guardian part company because the child is instructing his solicitor direct (see FPR 2010, r 16.29(2)) or intends and is able to conduct the proceedings on his own behalf. In this case, r 16.21(2) dictates that the children's guardian takes such part in the proceedings as the court may direct and may, with the leave of the court, have his own legal representation. When it comes to the order of adducing evidence, the guardian falls within r 12.21(2)(d) but the child does not fall within r 12.21(2)(e) so the court will have to give directions.

Questioning the children's guardian (r 12.21(2)(d))—The children's guardian cannot simply put in his written report; he must submit to questioning on this and on any other oral or written advice that he tenders to the court if any party so requires (FPR PD16A); see also *Hampshire County Council v S* [1993] 1 FLR 559, FD.

Court calling witness—As the semi-inquisitorial nature of Children Act proceedings has increasingly become accepted, the practice has developed of the court itself occasionally calling a witness where fairness dictates that an advocate should be able to cross-examine the witness and normal procedure would confine him to examination-in-chief (*Re P (Witness Summons)* [1997] 2 FLR 447, CA).

Witness anonymity—A court will give anonymity to a professional social worker witness in care proceedings only in highly exceptional cases (*Re W (Care Proceedings: Witness Anonymity)* [2003] 1 FLR 329, CA – where it was held that the guidance as to witness anonymity given in the criminal jurisdiction has parallels for public law cases such as care proceedings; in this case the threat of violence from adults who faced permanent separation from their children was held to be a professional hazard of social work, and not exceptional).

Judge seeing child for purposes of communication—There is a very clear distinction to be made between a meeting between the child and the judge for the purposes of communicating without the aim of evidence-gathering and a meeting with a view to evidence-gathering: these two different processes should be distinguished with care. (See also **Judge seeing child** under CA 1989, s 96.) Where the judge is listening to the child's point of view, his or her role should be largely that of a passive recipient of whatever communication the child wishes to transmit; where the purpose of the meeting is not to gather evidence, the judge should not probe or seek to test whatever the child wishes to say; and where the child does volunteer evidence, the judge should report back to the parties and determine whether, and if so how, that evidence should be adduced – see *Re KP (Abduction: Child's Objections)* [2014] 2 FLR 660, CA and *Re K (Breakdown of Arrangements: Urgent Hearing)* [2015] 1 FLR 95, CA.

Although the United Nations Convention on the Rights of the Child 1989 has not been made part of English law, the court is obliged to have regard to it when considering matters to which it relates. Article 12 recognises that a child who is capable of forming his own views has the right to express those views freely in all matters affecting him and that the voice of the child might be conveyed either directly or through a representative or appropriate body. Accordingly, while children have a right to be heard in proceedings, that right does not specify how they are to be heard. It does not seem to be essential that it must be the judge who hears directly from the child; it may be enough that a social worker, that is to say the Cafcass officer or guardian, hears their views. So, while the child must be listened to, there is nothing in the Convention that entitles him to a 'right' to give evidence (*Re P-S* [2014] 2 FLR 27, CA, at [28], [32], [35]–[36]). In *Re P-S*, the Court of Appeal reminded judges that they must be very cautious when they see children in the absence of the other parties. Ward LJ said by way of footnote that he would encourage the judge to explain the judgment he is about to give, or has just or recently given, in order to reassure the child that his wishes have been given proper weight and respect by the court. If the judge cannot accede to the child's wishes, the judge can take that useful opportunity to explain why. However, that meeting should not be used to take evidence from the child because if that evidence is given in the absence of the other parties, they could legitimately claim that their right to a fair trial has been invaded because a part of it was not undertaken in public (at [42]).

It is becoming more common for judges to see children in private in the course of proceedings affecting the child's welfare. In April 2010 the President issued *Guidelines for Judges Meeting Children who are Subject to Family Proceedings* (see Part V). The judge's decision whether or not personally to interview a child is, above all, a question for the exercise of judicial discretion and the judge is under no obligation to see a child in private before deciding what order to make (*Re R (A Minor) (Residence: Religion)* [1993] 2 FLR 163, CA). ECHR 1950, Art 12 provides that a child should be heard in any judicial proceedings affecting him, either directly or through a representative. Similarly, the United Nations Convention on the Rights of the Child 1989, Art 12 requires that a child who is capable of forming his own views has the right to express them freely in all matters affecting him. *Mabon v Mabon* [2005] 2 FLR 1011, CA reviewed the principles that apply when the court considers how best to ensure that the child's views are heard in such cases. Further important guidance from the Court of Appeal is contained in *Re W (Leave to Remove)* [2008] 2 FLR 1170, CA, *B v B (Minors) (Interviews and Listing Arrangements)* [1994] 2 FLR 489, CA and *Re A (Fact-Finding Hearing: Judge Meeting with Child)* [2012] 2 FLR 369, CA. In *Re A*, the Court of Appeal gave cautions and guidance in a case in which the judge saw the child after hearing evidence but before giving judgment. The parents appealed against his finding that the children had been sexually abused on the basis that they had been denied the opportunity to make representations regarding the meeting with the child and that the judge had used that meeting to gather evidence, in breach of the 2010 *Guidelines*. The CA dismissed the appeal but augmented the judge's order to clarify what he had found, holding, inter alia, that: (1) It would be quite disproportionate to allow the appeal and order a retrial. The process, properly analysed, had been full and complete; (2) Much more care should be taken in defining the judicial task at a preliminary trial; this should be contained in an early directions order so that the parties know precisely what it is that the applicants are seeking to be determined, by a simple direction that at the trial the court will determine the issues contained within the schedule. Then when the process is complete and judgment given, the order drawn needs specifically to state which of the items within the schedule have been found proved; (3) There is a useful distinction between two levels of participation and involvement of children in proceedings: (a) meeting with children under the April 2010 *Guidelines* and (b) children giving evidence under the December 2011 *Guidelines in Relation to Children Giving Evidence in Family Proceedings* (as to which see further under CA 1989, s 96). If an application governed by (b) results in a direction for oral evidence, the risk of contamination of the proceedings is no greater than with the involvement of any other witness. However, if an application governed by (a) results in a decision from the meeting between judge and child, the risk of contamination is increased. So, a range of distinctions needs to be drawn and the judge must consider whether the objective of the proceedings is to establish what happened in the past or what should happen in the future, and the stage the proceedings have reached; (4) In this case, the objective was to establish what had happened and the proceedings were at a stage where the evidence was concluded but judgment reserved. This is the most dangerous situation in which a judge is likely to meet a child. Much safer is the ground when the issue is what should happen in the future and the judge is anxious to ascertain for himself the strength of the child's wishes and feelings and perhaps what has contributed to the formation of those wishes and feelings; (5) The judge would have been far wiser to have explained to the child at the outset that the process was complete and that all that remained was the formal expression of his reasons for his conclusion. To give the child the impression that his mind was still open and that he was susceptible to influence, was to give completely the wrong impression. Equally, when he came to recording the meeting in his judgment, it was unguarded of him to say that he had found the child to be truthful in his recollection and statement; (6) It was not enough for the appellants to show that an irregularity had taken place. The critical question was whether its effect was sufficiently serious to undermine the integrity of the judge's conclusions on the factual issues. If his judgment were read as a whole, it was clear that he had made all his findings of fact without reliance on his meeting with the child. In *Re KP (Abduction: Child's Objections)* [2014] 2 FLR 660, CA, the Court of Appeal found that the judge, at the conclusion of Hague Convention proceedings, had crossed the line between simply meeting with the child under the 2010 Guidelines and actually eliciting evidence from the child. Moore-Bick LJ, in giving reasons for the court's judgment, also set out further guidance about judicial meetings with children:

(i) During that part of any meeting between a child and a judge in which the judge is listening to the child's point of view and hearing what they have to say, the judge's role should be largely that of a passive recipient of whatever communication the child wishes to transmit.

PART III

(ii) The purpose of the meeting is not to obtain evidence and the judge should not probe or seek to test whatever it is that the child wishes to say. The meeting is primarily for the benefit of the child, rather than for the benefit of the forensic process by providing additional evidence to the judge. As the Guidelines state, the task of gathering evidence is for the specialist CAFCASS officers who have developed an expertise in this field.

(iii) A meeting that takes place prior to the judge deciding upon the central issues should be for the dual purposes of allowing the judge to hear what the child may wish to volunteer and for the child to hear the judge explain the nature of the court process. While not wishing to be prescriptive, it would be difficult to imagine circumstances in which such a meeting would last for more than 20 minutes or so.

(iv) If the child volunteers evidence that would or might be relevant to the outcome of the proceedings, the judge should report back to the parties and determine whether, and if so how, that evidence should be adduced.

(The process adopted by the judge in that case, in which she sought to 'probe' the child's wishes and feelings, and did so over the course of more than an hour by asking some 87 questions, strayed significantly over the line and into the process of gathering evidence upon which she then relied in coming to her decision. The judge was in error in regarding the meeting as being an opportunity for the child to make representations or submissions to the judge. The purpose of any judicial meeting is not for the child to argue their case; it is simply, but importantly, to provide an opportunity for the child to state whatever it is that they wish to state directly to the judge who is going to decide an important issue in their lives.)

In *Re K (Breakdown of Arrangements: Urgent Hearing)* [2015] 1 FLR 95, CA, the Court of Appeal found that the judge had impermissibly relied on her own assessment of two teenage boys in a discussion she had with them at the beginning of the hearing. Despite the judge's best intentions, her discussions with the boys had strayed beyond reassurance, explanation and listening. The CA confirmed that it remains an essential principle that a meeting with a child is not for the purpose of gathering evidence. The judge's reliance on her own assessment of the boys was procedurally unfair and, to the extent that her primary concern was that they were out of control, it had dominated her thinking; that was a value judgment gathered from a discussion not intended for that purpose and which could not be challenged effectively.

For further detail as to how the court manages the process of hearing the child's views in Hague Convention proceedings, see further under CACA 1985, Sch 1, which sets out the relevant Articles of the Convention on the Civil Aspects of International Child Abduction; see in particular the commentary to Art 13. Note the guidance in *Re S (Abduction: Hearing the Child)* [2015] 2 FLR 588, CA, where the Court of Appeal cautioned that the policies that were relevant to Hague Convention and European abduction cases were not to be imported into the inherent jurisdiction to the exclusion of the obligation to hear the child, which was both an integral part of the welfare evaluation and the guarantee of the child's effective access to justice. Therefore, as a matter of principle, there is an obligation on the High Court sitting in its inherent jurisdiction in relation to an abduction application to consider whether and how to hear the child concerned.

The judge will decide who should be present during an interview with children, but he cannot promise the children absolute confidentiality and he must tell the parties what the child has said to him so that they may deal with it (*H v H (Child: Judicial Interview)* [1974] 1 WLR 595, CA; *Elder v Elder* [1986] 1 FLR 610, CA). Any interview between the judge and the child should take place at the court (*L v L (Access: Contempt)* [1991] 2 FLR 43, CA).

Judge seeing advocates—Thorpe LJ observed in *Re CH (Care or Interim Care Order)* [1998] 1 FLR 402, CA that it seemed to him undesirable that judges should encourage or permit significant exchanges between the advocates unrecorded in the privacy of the judge's room. If it is thought desirable by the advocates or by the judge that exchanges should take place without the clients and other persons being present, those exchanges can be in the court room in chambers where they will be fully recorded.

Judge recusing himself from a case—Applications to a judge to recuse himself from a case must be taken seriously, even if they are, in part, wild and extravagant (*Re F (Contact)* [2008] 1 FLR 1163, FD). The test to be applied is whether all of the circumstances bearing on the suggestion that the judge could be biased would lead a fair-minded and informed observer, adopting a balanced approach, to conclude that there was a real possibility that the tribunal was biased. In *Re F* (above) neither the judge's approach nor manner had reached a level where he should recuse himself and Sumner J set out some useful principles to be considered in such applications.

Departing from an expert's opinion—The court is entitled to depart from the opinion of an expert although, if it does so, it must explain its reasons (*Re B (Care: Expert Witnesses)* [1996] 1 FLR 667, CA). Where there is a conflict between experts, the court must address and resolve that conflict insofar as it is relevant to the issues before the court and it is entitled to give greater weight to the opinion of one expert as against that of another, provided that proper reasons are given (*Re J (Expert Evidence: Hearsay)* [1999] 2 FLR 661, FD; *Re W and P (Children)* (2002) Lawtel, 30 April). Where there is a stark conflict of forensic medical evidence, a judge should not decline to choose between the medical opinions; instead he should invite the parties to agree a tertiary referral. To leave the evidence unresolved makes the disposal stage problematic (*Re W and P*, above). Where experts are unanimous in their opinion as to a person's core personality and emotional state, it is not open to the judge to reject that expert evidence purely on the basis of his own appraisal of the person when giving oral evidence (*Re M (Residence)* [2002] 2 FLR 1059, CA). However, the role of the expert and the court are distinct. The court must make its findings based on the totality of the evidence. Expert evidence is but one part of the evidence available to the court at the fact-finding stage. It is open to the court on the totality of the evidence, to reach a decision that is different from those of the experts (*A County Council v K, D and L* [2005] 1 FLR 851, FD; *A County Council v A Mother, A Father and X, Y and Z (by their Guardian)* [2005] 2 FLR 129, FD).

Hearings in care proceedings—*Oxfordshire CC v M* [1994] 1 FLR 175, CA highlights the fact that care proceedings do not have an essentially adversarial character (*Re L (Police Investigation: Privilege)* [1996] 1 FLR

731, HL; *Re S (Contact: Evidence)* [1998] 1 FLR 798, CA). In all public law proceedings under CA 1989, Pt IV the PLO must be followed (see FPR PD12A and FPR 2010, rr 12.23–12.30). Proceedings by a childminder challenging the refusal of a local authority to register her are, however, adversarial (*London Borough of Sutton v Davis (Costs) (No 2)* [1994] 2 FLR 569, FD).

Split hearings—For guidance about split hearings in public law proceedings, see the notes to CA 1989, s 31 and under FPR 2010, r 12.12.

Judicial reasoning—It is an advocate's responsibility, whether invited or not, to draw the attention of the judge to any ambiguity or deficiency in the reasoning (*English v Emery, Reimbold & Strick* [2002] 1 WLR 2409, CA; *Re T (Contact: Alienation: Permission to Appeal)* [2003] 1 FLR 531, CA). Where permission to appeal is sought on the ground of lack of reasons, the trial judge should reconsider and, if necessary, provide additional reasons. If neither happens, an appeal court will normally remit the case to the trial judge, with a list of specific questions to be addressed (*Re A and L (Children)* [2012] 1 FLR 134, CA). However, although the court positively encourages tight, succinct judgments with good selectivity of relevant and necessary issues, judgments that leave readers unable to trace the reasoning underpinning the judge's conclusion would be susceptible to a successful appeal. In *Li Quan v Stuart Bray & Save China's Tigers* [2015] EWCA Civ 1253, permission to appeal was granted where it was considered too late to ask the judge to review his judgment and expand upon his reasons, especially as he had been asked to do so at the time and had refused.

Change of mind by judge prior to order being perfected—Where the judge makes a decision in civil or family proceedings, he has the power to reverse it at any time before the order is sealed. While this power must be exercised judicially rather than capriciously, it is not limited to exceptional circumstances. In family proceedings a judge is not to be bound by his earlier judgment to decide the future placement of a child upon what he has come to believe is a false basis (*Re L-B (Reversal of Judgment)* [2013] 2 FLR 859, SC).

Reasons for a decision by lay justices—FPR 2010, r 27.2 requires that after a hearing before lay justices their decision should be made as soon as is practicable and they must give written reasons for the decision (r 27.3). The Justices' Clerks' Society and Magistrates' Association have issued revised guidance *Provision of Justices' Reasons in Uncontested Cases* dated March 2014 that has been approved by the President of the Family Division; it follows from the decision in *Re NL (Appeal: Interim Care Order: Facts and Reasons)* [2014] 1 FLR 1384, FD. In particular, it emphasises that under no circumstances should any of the parties to the proceedings be involved in drafting the justices' written reasons, irrespective of whether orders are said to be agreed or 'not opposed'.

Chapter 3
Special Provisions about Public Law Proceedings

12.22 Timetable for the proceedings

In public law proceedings other than Part 4 proceedings, in so far as practicable the court will draw up the timetable for the proceedings or revise that timetable with a view to disposing of the application without delay and in any event within 26 weeks beginning with the date on which the application is issued.

(In relation to Part 4 proceedings, section 32(1)(a) of the 1989 Act requires the court to draw up a timetable with a view to disposing of the application without delay and in any event within 26 weeks beginning with the day on which the application is issued.)

Amendments—Substituted by SI 2014/843.

Public Law Outline (PLO)—Pursuant to amendments brought about by CFA 2014, applications for care and supervision orders must now be disposed of without delay and are subject a default timetable of 26 weeks. The length by which and the circumstances in which the applicable time-limits may be extended are strictly circumscribed by reference to the child's welfare and the impact on the duration and conduct of the proceedings (CA 1989, s 32(1)(a)). This rule applies these time limits to public law proceedings that are not subject to FPR PD12A and the PLO contained therein, for example, applications for emergency protection orders or recovery orders. See **Avoidance of delay** under CA 1989, s 32. Agreements between the parties to amend the timetable set by the Family Court are forbidden by FPR 2010, r 4.5(3). See **Case management and the Public Law Outline** under CA 1989, s 31.

12.23 Application of rules 12.24 to 12.26C

Rules 12.24 to 12.26C apply to Part 4 proceedings and in so far as practicable other public law proceedings.

Amendments—SI 2014/843.

Application—This rule applies rr 12.24–12.26C to public law proceedings that are not subject to FPR PD12A and the PLO contained therein, for example, applications for emergency protection orders or recovery orders.

12.24 Directions

The court will direct the parties to –

(a) monitor compliance with the court's directions; and

(b) tell the court or court officer about –
   (i) any failure to comply with a direction of the court; and
   (ii) any other delay in the proceedings.

Timetable for public law cases—Pursuant to amendments brought about by CFA 2014, applications for care and supervision orders must now be disposed of without delay and are subject a default timetable of 26 weeks. The length by which and the circumstances in which the applicable time-limits may be extended are strictly circumscribed by reference to the child's welfare and the impact on the duration and conduct of the proceedings (CA 1989, s 32(1)(a)). Within this context the PLO in PD12A sets down a strict timetable for the progress of public law cases. It is vital that all parties adhere to this, and that if there is any prospect of delay the court is informed immediately so that the case does not drift. See **Case management and the Public Law Outline** under CA 1989, s 31 and **Avoidance of delay** under CA 1989, s 32.

Care monitoring system—The care monitoring system (CMS) is a judicially led management information programme intended to provide accurate ongoing information about case volumes, case progress and allocation. It is intended to assist judges, legal advisers and magistrates to focus on avoiding delay for children and to help identify the real causes of delay. The system has been piloted nationwide from 2 April 2012 from when all new care and supervision cases have been entered onto the system and orders have been required to contain information that will be monitored by the system, in particular the timetable for the child expressed as the expected number of weeks necessary to conclude the proceedings. In preparation for the reforms contemplated by the family modernisation programme, all cases will be given a 26-week timetable on issue.

12.25 The Case Management Hearing and the Issues Resolution Hearing

(1) The court will conduct the Case Management Hearing with the objective of –
   (a) confirming the level of judge to which the proceedings have been allocated;
   (b) drawing up a timetable for the proceedings including the time within which the proceedings are to be resolved;
   (c) identifying the issues; and
   (d) giving directions in accordance with rule 12.12 and Practice Direction 12A to manage the proceedings.

(2) The court may hold a further Case Management Hearing only where this hearing is necessary to fulfil the objectives of the Case Management Hearing set out in paragraph (1).

(3) The court will conduct the Issues Resolution Hearing with the objective of –
   (a) identifying the remaining issues in the proceedings;
   (b) as far as possible resolving or narrowing those issues; and
   (c) giving directions to manage the proceedings to the final hearing in accordance with rule 12.12 and Practice Direction 12A.

(4) Where it is possible for all the issues in the proceedings to be resolved at the Issues Resolution Hearing, the court may treat the Issues Resolution Hearing as a final hearing and make orders disposing of the proceedings.

(5) The court may set a date for the Case Management Hearing, a further Case Management Hearing and the Issues Resolution Hearing at the times referred to in Practice Direction 12A.

(6) The matters which the court will consider at the hearings referred to in this rule are set out in Practice Direction 12A.

(Rule 25.6 (experts: when to apply for the court's permission) provides that unless the court directs otherwise, parties must apply for the court's permission as mentioned in section 13(1), (3) and (5) of the 2014 Act as soon as possible and in Part 4 proceedings and in so far as practicable other public law proceedings no later than the Case Management Hearing.)

Amendments—Substituted by SI 2014/843.

Derivation—This rule is derived from the PLO in FPR PD12A. In applications for care and supervision orders under CA 1989, the procedural stages will be those set out in the PLO. See in particular Pre-proceedings checklist, Case management hearing, Further case management hearing and Issues resolution hearing in FPR PD12A.

Case management in public law proceedings—Before the implementation of the PLO, there were a number of cases that gave useful guidance as to the preparation of public law cases, although where that guidance conflicts with the PLO, the PLO must take precedence. See *Re G, S and M (Wasted Costs)* [2000] 1 FLR 52, FD; *Re EC (Disclosure of Material)* [1996] 2 FLR 123, FD; *Re R (Care: Disclosure: Nature of Proceedings)* [2002] 1 FLR 755, FD. For further useful guidance, see **Case management and the Public Law Outline** under CA 1989, s 31 and **Disclosure – impact of ECHR 1950** under FPR 2010, r 12.12 and in particular the judgment in *Re L (Care: Assessment: Fair Trial)* [2002] 2 FLR 730, FD.

Case management hearing—In accordance with Stage 2 of the PLO (FPR PD12A), the court will fix a case management hearing to take place not before day 12 and no later than day 18, at which the court will identify the issues and give full case-management directions, including whether or not experts are to be instructed and, if so, why and how this is to be done. No later than 2 days before the case management hearing there must be an advocates' meeting, the aim of which is to facilitate agreement, narrow down the issues and prepare a draft case management order. There should be ongoing consideration of the draft case management order throughout the proceedings. The local authority will take the lead in preparing and adjusting the order, which must then be filed with the court by 11.00 am 1 working day before the case management hearing (paras 5.9 and 14.6). Note that only one order should be filed with the court. A Further Case Management Conference is to be held only if necessary and must be listed as soon as possible and in any event no later than day 25.

Issues resolution hearing—In accordance with Stage 3 of the PLO (FPR PD12A), the court will fix an issues resolution hearing (IRH) to take place as directed by the court and at which the court will try to resolve and narrow the issues and identify any remaining key issues. There must be an advocates' meeting no later than 7 days before the IRH, the aim of which is to update the draft case management order. Once the updated order has been drafted, it must be filed with the court by 11.00 am 1 working day before the IRH. At the IRH the court will identify the key issues and consider whether the IRH can be used as the final hearing. Where a contested final hearing is required, the court will give final case management directions including for the filing of evidence, skeleton arguments, bundles, agreements relating to satisfaction of the CA 1989, s 31 criteria and time estimates. It will then issue a case management order in preparation for the final hearing.

Final hearing—The final hearing is expected to take place by week 26 or earlier (*Re B-S (Adoption: Application of s 47(5))* [2014] 1 FLR 1035, CA). The timing will be fixed in accordance with the needs of the child. The object of the hearing is to determine the remaining issues. All parties will file and serve updated case-management documents and the bundle, together with the draft final order(s) in approved form. At the conclusion of the hearing the court will give its judgment and reasons for its decision and then make appropriate orders for disclosure of documents as required after the hearing. Cases that are suitable for an early final hearing are those in which all of the evidence necessary to determine issues of fact and welfare is immediately or shortly available to be filed. The court will identify such cases at the Case Management Hearing and set a date for the final hearing.

PART III

12.26 Discussion between advocates

(1) When setting a date for the Case Management Hearing or the Issues Resolution Hearing the court will direct a discussion between the parties' advocates to –

- (a) discuss the provisions of a draft of the Case Management Order; and
- (b) consider any other matter set out in Practice Direction 12A.

(2) Where there is a litigant in person the court will give directions about how that person may take part in the discussions between the parties' advocates.

(3) Unless the court directs otherwise –

- (a) any discussion between advocates must take place no later than 2 days before the Case Management Hearing; and
- (b) a draft of the Case Management Order must be filed with the court no later than 11a.m. on the day before the Case Management Hearing.

(4) Unless the court directs otherwise –

- (a) any discussion between advocates must take place no later than 7 days before the Issues Resolution Hearing; and
- (b) a draft of the Case Management Order must be filed with the court no later than 11a.m. on the day before the Issues Resolution Hearing.

(5) For the purposes of this rule 'advocate' includes a litigant in person.

Amendments—Substituted by SI 2014/843.

12.26A Application for extension of the time limit for disposing of the application

(1) An application requesting the court to grant an extension must state –

- (a) the reasons for the request;
- (b) the period of extension being requested; and
- (c) a short explanation of –
  - (i) why it is necessary for the request to be granted to enable the court to resolve the proceedings justly;
  - (ii) the impact which any ensuing timetable revision would have on the welfare of the child to whom the application relates;

(iii) the impact which any ensuing timetable revision would have on the duration and conduct of the proceedings; and

(iv) the reasons for the grant or refusal of any previous request for extension.

(2) Part 18 applies to an application requesting the grant of an extension.

(3) In this rule

'ensuing timetable revision' has the meaning given to it by section 32(6) of the 1989 Act;

'extension' means an extension of the period for the time being allowed under section 32(1)(a)(ii) of the 1989 Act which is to end no more than 8 weeks after the later of the times referred to in section 32(8) of that Act.

Amendments—Inserted by SI 2014/843.

12.26B Disapplication of rule 4.1(3)(a) court's power to extend or shorten the time for compliance with a rule

Rule 4.1(3)(a) does not apply to any period that is for the time being allowed under section 32(1)(a)(ii) of the 1989 Act.

Amendments—Inserted by SI 2014/843.

12.26C Extension of time limit: reasons for court's decision

(1) When refusing or granting an extension of the period that is for the time being allowed under section 32(1)(a)(ii) in the case of the application, the court will announce its decision and –

(a) the reasons for that decision; and

(b) where an extension is granted or refused, a short explanation of the impact which the decision would have on the welfare of the child.

(2) The court office will supply a copy of the order granting or refusing the extension including the reasons for the court's decision and the period of any extension and short explanation given under paragraph (1)(b) to –

(a) the parties; and

(b) any person who has actual care of the child who is the subject of the proceedings.

Amendments—Inserted by SI 2014/843.

12.27 Matters prescribed for the purposes of the Act

(1) Proceedings for an order under any of the following provisions of the 1989 Act –

(a) a secure accommodation order under section 25;

(b) an order giving permission to change a child's surname or remove a child from the United Kingdom under section 33(7);

(c) an order permitting the local authority to arrange for any child in its care to live outside England and Wales under paragraph 19(1) of Schedule 2;

(d) the extension or further extension of a supervision order under paragraph 6(3) of Schedule 3;

(e) appeals against the determination of proceedings of a kind set out in sub-paragraphs (a) to (d);

are specified for the purposes of section 41 of that Act in accordance with section 41(6)(i) of that Act.

(2) The persons listed as applicants in the table set out in rule 12.3 to proceedings for the variation of directions made with interim care or interim supervision orders under section 38(8) of the 1989 Act are the prescribed class of persons for the purposes of that section.

(3) The persons listed as applicants in the table set out in rule 12.3 to proceedings for the variation of a direction made under section 44(6) of the 1989 Act in an emergency protection order are the prescribed class of persons for the purposes of section 44(9) of that Act.

'specified' (r 12.27(1))—CA 1989, s 41 imposes a duty on the court in any 'specified proceedings' to appoint a children's guardian for the child concerned, unless it is satisfied that it is not necessary to do so to safeguard his interests. Section 41(6) specifies many of the proceedings in which this duty arises and s 41(6)(i) provides for rules of court to specify further proceedings.

'section 38(8)' (r 12.27(2))—CA 1989, s 38(8) empowers the court to vary a direction made under s 38(6) on the application of a person within any class prescribed by rules of court. Section 38(6) empowers the court to make directions regarding medical or psychiatric examination or other assessment of a child where it makes an interim care or supervision order.

Section 44(6),(9) (r 12.27(3))—CA 1989, s 44 enables the court to make emergency protection orders and, where it does so, it may, under s 44(6), give directions as to the medical, psychiatric or other assessment of the child or contact with him. Section 44(9) provides that such directions can be varied at any time on the application of a person falling within any class of person prescribed by rules of court.

12.28 Exclusion requirements: interim care orders and emergency protection orders

(1) This rule applies where the court includes an exclusion requirement in an interim care order or an emergency protection order.

(2) The applicant for an interim care order or emergency protection order must –

- (a) prepare a separate statement of the evidence in support of the application for an exclusion requirement;
- (b) serve the statement personally on the relevant person with a copy of the order containing the exclusion requirement (and of any power of arrest which is attached to it);
- (c) inform the relevant person of that person's right to apply to vary or discharge the exclusion requirement.

(3) Where a power of arrest is attached to an exclusion requirement in an interim care order or an emergency protection order, the applicant will deliver –

- (a) a copy of the order; and
- (b) a statement showing that the relevant person has been served with the order or informed of its terms (whether by being present when the order was made or by telephone or otherwise),

to the officer for the time being in charge of the police station for the area in which the dwelling-house in which the child lives is situated (or such other police station as the court may specify).

(4) Rules 10.6(2) and 10.10 to 10.17 will apply, with the necessary modifications, for the service, variation, discharge and enforcement of any exclusion requirement to which a power of arrest is attached as they apply to an order made on an application under Part 4 of the 1996 Act.

(5) The relevant person must serve the parties to the proceedings with any application which that person makes for the variation or discharge of the exclusion requirement.

(6) Where an exclusion requirement ceases to have effect whether –

- (a) as a result of the removal of a child under section 38A(10) or 44A(10) of the 1989 Act;
- (b) because of the discharge of the interim care order or emergency protection order; or
- (c) otherwise,

the applicant must inform –

- (i) the relevant person;
- (ii) the parties to the proceedings;
- (iii) any officer to whom a copy of the order was delivered under paragraph (3); and
- (iv) (where necessary) the court.

(7) Where the court includes an exclusion requirement in an interim care order or an emergency protection order of its own motion, paragraph (2) will apply with the omission of any reference to the statement of the evidence.

(8) In this rule, 'the relevant person' has the meaning assigned to it by sections 38A(2) and 44A(2) of the 1989 Act.

Defined terms—'care order': CA 1989, ss 31(11), 105(1); 'child'; 'court': r 2.3(1); 'emergency protection order': r 12.2; 'exclusion requirement': CA 1989, s 38A(3); 'relevant person': CA 1989, s 38A(2)(a).

Applicant for interim care order or emergency protection order (r 12.28(2))—The applicant in the case of an interim care order will generally be the local authority (or other authorised person) who has made the original application under CA 1989, s 31(1). Section 38 gives the court power to make an interim care order where the care/supervision proceedings are adjourned and also gives the court power to make an interim care order where it gives a direction under s 37(1) for the local authority to investigate the child's circumstances. It is unclear who is the applicant for the purpose of r 12.28(2) in such a situation or, indeed, whether there is one at all. It may be that this is unlikely to cause a problem given that it is difficult to foresee the court being in a position to incorporate an exclusion requirement anyway at such an early stage. If the court did consider such a course appropriate, it could act of its own motion in including the requirement, in which case r 12.28(7) would dispense with the need for a statement of the evidence.

The applicant in the case of an emergency protection order can be any person (s 44(1)) though it is most likely to be a local authority.

Public Law Outline—See **Public Law Outline (PLO)** under CA 1989, s 44.

Separate statement of evidence (r 12.28(2))—The applicant will already have completed forms with regard to the application for an interim care order/emergency protection order. The statement of evidence in support of the exclusion requirement must be separate. There is no prescribed form. Reference must be made to the provisions of CA 1989, s 38A or 44A and in particular to the conditions for the inclusion of an exclusion requirement, which are set out in ss 38A(2) and 44A(2). The question of the ability of another person living in the home to care for the child and the consent of that person to the exclusion requirement (ss 38A(2)(b) and 44A(2)(b)) will no doubt be covered in the statement but it should be noted that it is also the subject of a separate procedural rule, FPR 2010, r 12.29. Best practice in respect of the separate statement of evidence to be served in support of an application for an exclusion requirement demands that the statement should:

(1) be separate and self-standing;
(2) set out in a concise form the factual material upon which the applicant relies;
(3) state the statutory requirements for obtaining an exclusion order, under CA 1989, s 38A(2) (for interim care orders) or s 44A(2) (for emergency protection orders), in particular the relevant subsections, with a summary of the evidence in support; and
(4) make it clear that the exclusion requirement sought is a requirement that a particular person should leave the dwelling-house in which the child is living, and/or prohibit the person from entering the dwelling house in which the child is living, and/or exclude the person from a defined area surrounding the dwelling-house in which the child is living (*Re W (Exclusion: Statement of Evidence)* [2000] 2 FLR 666, FD).

If the court orders an exclusion requirement of its own motion, in the absence of the relevant person, it will usually be appropriate for the court to direct that a concise statement be prepared of the evidence laid at the hearing, with the other matters set out above, to be served personally on the relevant person. If the hearing was before justices then it will be desirable also to serve their findings and reasons on the relevant person. This will ensure that he receives the appropriate information to allow him to make an application to vary or discharge the order. If the person was present in court and heard the evidence laid against him, the court might, in appropriate circumstances, disapply any requirements as to service of the relevant statement. The consent of the other person living in the dwelling-house can be given either orally in court or in writing, signed by that person; written consent should provide the necessary details of the person able and willing to give the child the care that it would be reasonable to expect a parent to give, and it should state that that person understood that the giving of consent could lead to the exclusion of the relevant person from the dwelling-house in which the child was living. Once the appropriate statement has been served, it will not be necessary at subsequent renewals of the order to serve the separate statement again, unless there has been a further hearing, and the grounds have changed (*Re W* (above)).

Serve on relevant person (r 12.28(2))—The 'relevant person' is the person who is excluded. Service on this person of the supporting statement is only required once an order has been made; there is no specific requirement that he be given advance notice that there is a question of such a provision being included. The 'relevant person' may be a party to the proceedings in any event. Even if not, he is likely to know of the possibility of an exclusion requirement being imposed because an approach will have been made to another person living in the home to ensure that the requisite consent etc will be forthcoming for CA 1989, s 38A(2)(b) or 44A(2)(b). It remains to be seen to what extent the courts consider it appropriate to join as a party a relevant person, who is not a party, for the purpose of arguing the issue of an exclusion requirement or perhaps to allow him or her to intervene for this limited purpose without becoming a party. It may be that the relevant person will be excluded from the home almost summarily and then left to rely on his or her right to seek a variation or discharge of the order under s 39(3A)(3B) or s 45(8A),(8B).

'inform the relevant person of his right to apply to vary or discharge' (r 12.28(2)(c))—The rules do not say whether the 'relevant person' should be informed orally or in writing. Given that personal service of the statement and order is required, it would seem sensible for the information to be given orally at the time of service but for the documents also to be accompanied by a written notice of the right to apply to vary or discharge. Where the exclusion requirement is included in an interim care order, the right to seek variation/discharge is contained in CA 1989, s 39(3A) (with regard to the exclusion requirement itself) and s 39(3B) (with regard to any attendant power of arrest). For an emergency protection order, the relevant provisions are s 45(8A) and (8B).

Power of arrest (r 12.28(3))—If a power of arrest is attached to an order, FPR PD12K requires that, unless the person to whom the exclusion requirement refers was given notice of the hearing and attended it, the name of that person and the fact that an order has been made including an exclusion requirement to which a power of arrest has been attached shall be announced in open court at the earliest opportunity. Note that, by virtue of r 12.28(3), a copy of an order including a power of arrest is only to be delivered to the police station once the relevant person is aware of its terms. This may be because he was present when it was made or because he has subsequently been told about it or service has been effected.

Rules 10.6(2) etc (r 12.28(4))—FPR 2010, r 10.6(2) dictates service of a copy of any order by the court where the applicant is acting in person and requests this. Rules 10.10–10.16 deal with enforcement of orders that have powers of arrest attached, including also the duty to inform the police where an order with a power of arrest is subsequently varied or discharged. FPR 2010, r 10.17 deals with bail after arrest. FLA 1996, Pt IV contains the provisions dealing with family homes and domestic violence.

Application for variation/discharge (r 12.28(5))—FPR 2010, r 5.3 would seem to apply given that the relevant person is making 'an application'. There does not appear to be a notice period for the variation/discharge application. The periods required for discharge applications under ss 39 and 45 do not apply because they refer specifically to certain subsections of ss 39 and 45 but do not mention s 39(3A) or 45(8A). Presumably, in the absence of any specific form, Form C2 should be used for the relevant person's application. The parties to the proceedings who must be served will be the parties to the care proceedings or to the emergency protection order application, as appropriate. This may not include the person who is caring for the child in the absence of the relevant person but common sense dictates that he or she is likely to be affected by any discharge or variation and ought to be notified of the application. Indeed, it may be that the court will consider it desirable that when an exclusion requirement is included in reliance upon care to be delivered by someone who is not presently a party to the proceedings, that person should be joined so that he or she is entitled to be kept aware of developments and to make representations. Alternatively, he or she may be eligible for notice under FPR 2010, r 12.3 as a person 'who [is] caring for the child at the time when the proceedings are commenced'.

Parties to the proceedings (r 12.28(6)(c)(ii))—This phrase refers to the parties to the care proceedings or emergency protection proceedings, depending on the type of order to which the exclusion requirement was attached. This may not include the person caring for the child in the absence of the excluded person but it would seem necessary to inform him or her as well.

'(where necessary) the court' (r 12.28(6)(c)(iv))—It is suggested that it would be sensible to inform the court as a matter of course.

12.29 Notification of consent

(1) Consent for the purposes of the following provisions of the 1989 Act –

(a) section 16(3);

(b) section 38A(2)(b)(ii) or 44A(2)(b)(ii); or

(c) paragraph 19(3)(c) or (d) of Schedule 2,

must be given either –

(i) orally to the court; or

(ii) in writing to the court signed by the person giving consent.

(2) Any written consent for the purposes of section 38A(2) or 44A(2) of the 1989 Act must include a statement that the person giving consent –

(a) is able and willing to give to the child the care which it would be reasonable to expect a parent to give; and

(b) understands that the giving of consent could lead to the exclusion of the relevant person from the dwelling-house in which the child lives.

Defined terms—'court': r 2.3.

Scope—This rule sets out the procedure for signifying consent in certain cases under CA 1989. It does not apply to all consents that are required under the Act, only to those specified.

'section 16(3)'—This provision states that the court may not make a family assistance order unless it has obtained the consent of every person to be named in the order other than the child.

'section 38A(2)(b)(ii) or 44A(2)(b)(ii)'—Section 38A(2)(b)(ii) sets out a condition for the making of an exclusion requirement in an interim care order that another person living in the house consents to the inclusion of the exclusion requirement. Section 44A(2)(b)(ii) sets out a similar condition for the making of an exclusion requirement in an emergency protection order.

'paragraph 19(3)(c) or (d) of Schedule 2'—This provision states that a local authority may only arrange for a child in care to live outside England and Wales if the child has consented to living in that country.

'orally in court' (r 12.29(1)(c)(i))—There is no requirement that the consent should be given in evidence, and so it appears that the person giving consent need not be sworn. Indeed, where the person who is consenting orally is represented by a lawyer, it is likely to be the general practice that the legal representative will tell the court of the consent rather than the person himself, who will simply confirm what has been said. There are no provisions that require a note to be made of the giving of consent, but it is quite plain that such a note will have to be taken by the court.

Written consent (r 12.29(2))—There is no prescribed form of written consent; the only guidance in the rules is that the consent should be signed by the person consenting. Clearly, as well as identifying the consenting party and including the signed (and dated) consent, the document must refer to any order or proceedings that are relevant (such as the family proceedings where the consent is given under CA 1989, r 16, or the care order where the consent is given under Sch 2, para 19), giving the number thereof. However, r 12.29(2) does stipulate certain matters that must be included in the written consent to be given under CA 1989, ss 38A(2) and 44A(2).

Where the making of a court order depends on the giving of consent—The giving of consent is a condition precedent to the making of a family assistance order under CA 1989, s 16(3) and also the inclusion of an exclusion requirement in an interim care order or emergency protection order (CA 1989, ss 38A(1) and 44A(1)). Although the prescribed form of family assistance order does not require it, it is therefore suggested that, for the avoidance of doubt, the order should recite the requisite consents and state whether they were given orally or in writing. The same should also be done where the court gives approval under Sch 2, para 19(1). Form C23 and Form C33 provide for the recital of the requisite consents for the inclusion of an exclusion requirement in an emergency protection order and an interim care order.

12.30 Proceedings for secure accommodation orders: copies of reports

In proceedings under section 25 of the 1989 Act, the court will, if practicable, arrange for copies of all written reports filed in the case to be made available before the hearing to –

(a) the applicant;
(b) the parent or guardian of the child to whom the application relates;
(c) any legal representative of the child;
(d) the children's guardian; and
(e) the child, unless the court directs otherwise,

and copies of the reports may, if the court considers it desirable, be shown to any person who is entitled to notice of any hearing in accordance with Practice Direction 12C.

'parent'—This term is not defined in the rules or CA 1989 (see meaning of 'parent' under CA 1989, s 10).

'any person who is entitled to notice of any hearing in accordance with Practice Direction 12C'—Namely the local authority providing accommodation for the child, persons caring for the child at the time when proceedings are commenced and in the case of proceedings brought in respect of a child who is alleged to be staying in a refuge which is certified under s 51(1) or (2) of the 1989 Act, the person who is providing the refuge.

Copies of reports—There appears to be a distinction between those persons listed in r 12.30(a)–(e) and persons who are simply entitled to notice in accordance with the rules. The former must have copies of reports made available to them if practicable, whereas the latter are allowed only sight of the reports, and then only if the court considers it desirable.

Form of application—Pt IV applies to secure accommodation proceedings, which must therefore be started in accordance with Pt 12. The prescribed forms are Form C1 and supplementary Form C20. Form C1 requires the applicant to give the name and date of birth of the child concerned, to identify himself and to give details of his relationship to the child. The form requires details of: any other proceedings which concern the child; the respondents to the application; other persons to whom notice is to be given; the present arrangements for the care of the child; any involvement with the child by Social Services; the arrangements for the health and education of the child; the identity of the child's parents; the family of the child, i e siblings etc; and other adults who live at the child's address. The applicant must then fill in the supplementary Form C20 in which he is required to set out the grounds for the application, the reasons for applying and the length of order applied for. Copies of reports or other documentary evidence on which the applicant relies should be enclosed with the prescribed forms, together with details as to the dates and authors of the documents. The respondents and the persons who are to receive notice of the proceedings are set out in FPR 2010, r 12.3 and FPR PD12C, respectively.

An application for remand in secure accommodation may also be made in criminal proceedings under CYPA 1969, s 25.

Hearsay—Proceedings under CA 1989, s 25 are 'family proceedings', and hearsay evidence contained in reports and statements is admissible, although its weight will be a matter for judicial discretion (see *Re W (Fact-Finding Hearing: Hearsay Evidence)* [2014] 2 FLR 703, CA).

Delay—It is essential that there should be no delay whatsoever in the hearing of a case which concerns the liberty of the subject, such as an appeal in a secure accommodation case. In any appeal from the justices in a matter of urgency, the procedure set out in *Oxfordshire County Council v R* [1992] 1 FLR 648, FD, at [651H]–[652A] should be followed. Thus if, when the appeal is entered in the district registry of the appropriate care centre, no High Court judge is available to hear it, it is the duty of the appellant's solicitor to make the district registry aware of the need for urgency and to invite the district registry or the district judge to list the matter at the nearest court where an early hearing can take place before a High Court judge. Where any difficulty is encountered, an application for directions can always be made to a High Court judge sitting either at the appropriate care centre or in London (*Re W (A Minor) (Secure Accommodation Order)* [1993] 1 FLR 692, FD).

Interim orders—A freestanding application for an interim secure accommodation order cannot be made. Where the court was satisfied it had all the information needed to determine the issues raised by the application and that it would be procedurally fair to proceed, it is unlikely there would be grounds upon which the court could properly adjourn the application. Prolonging secure accommodation proceedings simply to keep a children's guardian involved for the purposes of assisting the child or overseeing the performance of the local authority's statutory duties is not a proper use of the court's power (*Birmingham City Council v M* [2008] 2 FLR 542, FD).

Other procedural matters—See CA 1989, s 25 and the notes to that section; see also C(SA)R 1991 (as amended by SI 2015/1883) and C(SA)(No 2)R 1991 (see Part IV).

Chapter 4

Special Provisions about Private Law Proceedings

12.31 The First Hearing Dispute Resolution Appointment

(1) The court may set a date for the First Hearing Dispute Resolution Appointment after the proceedings have been issued.

(2) The court officer will give notice of any of the dates so fixed to the parties.

(Provisions relating to the timing of and issues to be considered at the First Hearing Dispute Resolution Appointment are contained in Practice Direction 12B.)

Child Arrangements Programme (CAP)—The CAP is contained in FPR PD12B. It provides a framework for private law proceedings within which local arrangements should be made to ensure its effective operation. It is fundamental to the provisions of the CAP that the timescales be observed rigidly in all courts.

Judicial continuity—Judicial continuity is central to the CAP in FPR PD12B, which applies where a dispute arises between separated parents and/or families about the arrangements concerning children.

12.32 Answer

A respondent must file and serve on the parties an answer to the application for an order in private law proceedings within 14 days beginning with the date on which the application is served.

Defined terms—'section 8 order': CA 1989, s 8(2).

'within 14 days'—As to the computation of time, see FPR 2010, r 2.9; as to the extension of time, see FPR 2010, rr 12.12(2), 12.13(1).

Service—See FPR 2010, rr 6.23–6.39, 12.8 and FPR PD12C.

Parties—See FPR 2010, r 12.3.

Form C7—Each respondent to an application for a s 8 order or an order under CA 1989, Sch 1 must serve on the other parties to the proceedings an acknowledgement in Form C7. Form C7 requires the respondent to give details identifying himself and his solicitor (if he has one) and to give an address to which correspondence may be sent. The respondent must state when he received the application, whether he opposes it and whether he intends to apply to the court for an order. If the respondent indicates that he does wish to apply for an order himself, that indication is not tantamount to making the application, which must be launched using an application form in the normal way (see r 5.1 and FPR PD5A). Form C7 allows only a small space for the respondent to say whether or not he opposes the application. He is not invited to give his side of the picture at this early stage. This is deliberate, because in s 8 cases the filing of evidence and giving of information is strictly controlled (see FPR 2010, r 12.19(2),(3)). The acknowledgement should therefore restrict itself to the fact of opposition. However, Form C7 has been amended to include an additional question related to harm, which must be completed where the relevant application is made under CA 1989, s 8 (for child arrangements, specific issue or prohibited steps orders) or ss 4(1)(c), 4ZA(1)(c), 4A(1)(b) (for a parental responsibility order). Question 7 on Form C7 asks whether the child who is the subject of the application has suffered or is at risk of suffering any harm. If this question is answered in the affirmative, supplemental Form C1A must also be completed by the respondent. If the applicant has asked the court to order the respondent to make a payment for a child under CA 1989, Sch 1, the respondent must also fill in a statement of his financial means in Form C10A.

Written answer—Where the prescribed forms are not applicable, the respondent's written answer must be drafted from scratch. It is suggested that a similar format to that used in the prescribed form is adopted and the same sort of matters covered. It is the respondent who must serve the answer.

12.33 Applications for warning notices or applications to amend enforcement orders by reason of change of residence

(1) This rule applies in relation to an application for –

(a) a warning notice to be attached to a child arrangements order; or

(b) an order under paragraph 5 of Schedule A1 to the 1989 Act to amend an enforcement order by reason of change of residence.

(2) The application must be made without notice.

(3) The court may deal with the application without a hearing.

(4) If the court decides to deal with the application at a hearing, rules 12.5, 12.7 and 12.8 will apply.

Amendments—SI 2013/3204; SI 2014/843.

Warning notices—See under CA 1989, s 8, **Warning notices on child arrangements orders** and **Care required when drafting child arrangements orders to which warning notices are to be attached**, and see Procedural Guide D8.

12.34 Service of a risk assessment

(1) Where an officer of the Service or a Welsh family proceedings officer has filed a risk assessment with the court, subject to paragraph (2), the court officer will as soon as practicable serve copies of the risk assessment on each party.

(2) Before serving the risk assessment, the court must consider whether, in order to prevent a risk of harm to the child, it is necessary for –

(a) information to be deleted from a copy of the risk assessment before that copy is served on a party; or

(b) service of a copy of the risk assessment (whether with information deleted from it or not) on a party to be delayed for a specified period,

and may make directions accordingly.

Practice direction—CA 1989, s 16A requires a Cafcass officer carrying out any function in private law CA 1989 proceedings to carry out a risk assessment if he has cause to suspect that the child concerned is at risk of harm, and to provide that assessment to the court. See further under s 16A, FPR 2010, r 16.38 and Form C42. See also FPR PD16A, paras 11.1–11.7.

12.35 Service of enforcement orders or orders amending or revoking enforcement orders

(1) Paragraphs (2) and (3) apply where the court makes –

(a) an enforcement order; or

(b) an order under paragraph 9(2) of Schedule A1 to the 1989 Act (enforcement order made following a breach of an enforcement order).

(2) As soon as practicable after an order has been made, a copy of it must be served by the court officer on –

(a) the parties, except the person against whom the order is made;

(b) the officer of the Service or the Welsh family proceedings officer who is to comply with a request under section 11M of the 1989 Act to monitor compliance with the order; and

(c) the responsible officer.

(3) Unless the court directs otherwise, the applicant must serve a copy of the order personally on the person against whom the order is made.

(4) The court officer must send a copy of an order made under paragraph 4, 5, 6 or 7 of Schedule A1 to the 1989 Act (revocation or amendment of an enforcement order) to –

(a) the parties;

(b) the officer of the Service or the Welsh family proceedings officer who is to comply with a request under section 11M of the 1989 Act to monitor compliance with the order;

(c) the responsible officer; and

(d) in the case of an order under paragraph 5 of Schedule A1 to the 1989 Act (amendment of enforcement order by reason of change of residence), the responsible officer in the former local justice area.

(5) In this rule, 'responsible officer' has the meaning given in paragraph 8(8) of Schedule A1 to the 1989 Act.

Amendments—SI 2013/3204.

Chapter 5

Special Provisions about Inherent Jurisdiction Proceedings

12.36 Where to start proceedings

(1) An application for proceedings under the Inherent Jurisdiction of the court must be started in the High Court.

(2) Wardship proceedings, except applications for an order that a child be made or cease to be a ward of court, may be transferred to the family court unless the issues of fact or law make them more suitable for hearing in the High Court.

(The question of suitability for hearing in the High Court is explained in Practice Direction 12D (Inherent Jurisdiction (including Wardship Proceedings)).)

Amendments—SI 2013/3204.

The nature of inherent jurisdiction—The inherent jurisdiction of the court relates to its general jurisdiction as a court of superior record and as a trustee of the Crown's duty to protect all of its subjects. In appropriate circumstances, it may be used to supplement or fill gaps in statutory provisions where this is necessary in the interests of society but 'should not be exercised in a manner which cuts across the statutory scheme': *Re B (A Child) (Habitual Residence: Inherent Jurisdiction)* [2016] 1 FLR 561, SC. It may also, therefore, be used to supplement Convention and European provisions, especially in an emergency situation: *Re Z (Recognition of Foreign Order)* [2017] 1 FLR 1236, FD and *Re K and D (Wardship Without Notice Return Order)* [2017] EWHC 153 (Fam). The jurisdiction in respect of children and in particular its wardship jurisdiction is only one facet of the court's inherent jurisdiction. It is not synonymous with, but has many of the characteristics of, wardship. It is the duty of the court under its inherent jurisdiction to ensure that a child who is the subject of proceedings is protected and taken care of. See further under FPR PD12D, paras 1.1 and 1.3.

Distinguishing characteristics of wardship—These are set out in FPR PD12D, para 1.3. Good examples of the need for obtaining permission are set out in FPR PD12D, paras 5 and 6. Removal of a ward from the jurisdiction requires the court's permission (PD12D, para 4.1).

Ward and criminal proceedings—FPR PD12D, para 5 sets out the procedure that must be followed to obtain permission where there is a need to interview a ward in relation to criminal investigations and proceedings. It also makes provision for the procedure to be followed in those cases where the police need to take urgent action without prior permission of the court.

Application to the Criminal Injuries Compensation Authority (CICA)—See FPR PD12D, para 6 for the procedure to be followed when an application to the CICA is proposed and disclosure of documents in the wardship proceedings is being considered.

Publicity and disclosure of evidence—AJA 1960, s 12(1) provides that the publication of information relating to wardship proceedings before any court sitting in private is a contempt of court (see also CCA 1981, s 12; CA 1989, ss 2, 97(2); and *Harris v Harris; Attorney-General v Harris* [2001] 2 FLR 895, FD). In all other respects, the ward enjoys no greater protection against unwelcome publicity than other children. If the information relates to the ward but not to the proceedings, there is no contempt. No contempt is committed by the media in interviewing a ward or publishing or broadcasting such an interview. The issue in each case will be whether a reporting restriction injunction is necessary to protect the child from clear and identifiable harm and whether the injunction sought is proportionate to that aim. If a wider protection is required, application should be made for an order specifically providing for the wider protection. In such cases, the court will balance the rights of the media to publish information against the need to protect the welfare of the child to uphold the effective functioning of the court's wardship jurisdiction. See *Re M (Wardship: Jurisdiction and Powers)* [2016] 1 FLR 1055, FD, where reporting restrictions were initially imposed in terms similar to those in *Re KR (Abduction: Forcible Removal by Parents)* [1999] 2 FLR 542, FD but once the family returned to the UK with the children the reporting restrictions were discharged. Transparency nevertheless remains an important principle. Careful consideration needs to be given to the extent of any reporting restrictions sought in advance of the hearing and a draft provided to the court: *London Borough of Tower Hamlets v M and Others* [2015] 2 FLR 1431, FD. For an analysis of all other relevant cases, the competing issues of the child's rights under ECHR 1950, Art 8 and the rights of the press to freedom of expression under Art 10 see *X County Council v M & Others* [2014] EWHC 2262 (Fam); *Re Al Hilli (Children Reporting Restrictions)* [2014] 1 FLR 403, FD, where unusually the issue was whether the child's Article 2 rights were engaged; *Re J (Reporting Restriction: Internet: Video)* [2014] 1 FLR 523, FD, where the court had to consider that all identifying information would be available indefinitely and accessible; *Re K (Wardship: Publicity)* [2014] 1 FLR 548, FD, where the balance was struck in favour of allowing the parents to discuss information relating to the breakdown of an adoption placement with the media; *Re P (Enforced Caesarean: Reporting Restrictions)* [2014] 2 FLR 410, FD, where in granting restrictions of publication of information relating to the identity and whereabouts of the child, the court confirmed that the interests of the child, although not paramount, is a primary consideration; and *Practice Guidance on Transparency in the Family Courts: Publications of Judgments* (see Part V)). For the effect of s 12 on a child who is not a ward of court see *Re B, X Council v B (No 2)* [2008] 1 FLR 1460, FD and Judicial Proceedings (Regulation of Reports) Act 1926. Reference should also be made to the FPR PD27B. For further details see [2010] Fam Law 708, [2011] Fam Law 670 and also the decision of the ECtHR in *Tarasag a Szabadsagjogokert v Hungary* (App No 37374/05) [2009] EHRR 130.

Where an injunction is sought, the effect of which would be to impose a restraint on the freedom of the press and the media generally, the application should be transferred to the High Court and the Official Solicitor should be invited to represent the child (*Re H (Minors) (Injunction: Public Interest)* [1994] 1 FLR 519, CA). FPR PD12E, paras 3.1 and 3.2 set out the procedure that should be followed, particularly where it is intended to restrict publication in urgent or out-of-hours applications.

When considering such an application, the court will balance the right of a person and of the media to publish information and matters of public interest against the need to protect the welfare of the child and the risk of harm to the child (see *Re X, Y and Z (Expert Witness)* [2011] 2 FLR 1437, FD and *Clayton v Clayton* [2007] 1 FLR 11, CA, at [77] and [145]). See also: *Norfolk County Council v Webster & ors* [2007] 2 FLR 415, FD, where the restrictions were found to be too wide; *British Broadcasting Corporation v CAFCASS Legal & ors* [2007] 2 FLR 765, FD, where limited publicity was permitted in the public interest; *BBC v Coventry CC and Others (Care Proceedings: Costs: Identification of Local* Authority [2011] 1 FLR 977, FD, where permission was given for the local authority to be identified; *Re LM (Reporting Restrictions: Coroner's Inquest)* [2008] 1 FLR 1360, FD, where reporting of an inquest into the death of a child was permitted; *Re S (Identification: Restrictions on Publication)* [2005] 1 FLR 591, HL, where restrictions relating to the identity of a defendant in a

PART III

murder trial to protect the privacy of the defendant's child were considered inappropriate on the ground that the freedom of the press to report a criminal trial without restraint outweighed the child's rights (applied in *Surrey County Council v ME and Others* [2014] 2 FLR 1267, FD); and *Leeds County Council & ors v Channel 4 Television Corporation* [2007] 1 FLR 678, FD. The welfare of the child is not the paramount consideration but, when public interest turns into public curiosity, public interest in the protection of the child becomes the greater public interest and the interest of the child becomes 'the more important factor' (*Re Manda (Wardship: Disclosure of Evidence)* [1993] 1 FLR 205, CA; see also *A v M (Family Proceedings: Publicity)* [2000] 1 FLR 562, FD and *Re G (Celebrities: Publicity)* [1999] 1 FLR 409, CA). The court's jurisdiction, however, can only be invoked where the child concerned is the subject of the proceedings before the court and the court is concerned with the care and upbringing of the child (*R v Central Independent Television plc* [1994] 2 FLR 151, CA). See also the commentary under AJA 1960, s 12. For standard forms on press/publicity orders see *Emergency Remedies in the Family Courts* (Family Law), App 8 and *Practice Note of 18 March 2005 (Official Solicitor: Deputy Director of Legal Services: CAFCASS: Applications for Reporting Restrictions Orders)* (see Part V). Reference should also be made to FPR PD12I in relation to applications for restricting publication of information about children or incapacitated adults.

Restrictions under CA 1989—CA 1989, s 100 restricts the use of the wardship jurisdiction by local authorities in relation to children (see under CA 1989, s 100 for cases in which the court has warded the child where the situation has been unusual and also where the child has been accommodated voluntarily pursuant to CA 1989, s 20). Where a care order is made in respect of a child who is a ward of court, the making of the care order discharges the wardship (s 91(4)). The court may, however, grant an injunction as an ancillary to care orders under SCA 1981, s 37, as part of its general jurisdiction. FPR PD12D, para 1.1 requires that issues concerning children in the first instance should be resolved under CA 1989. Where the issue cannot be resolved under CA 1989 or the powers of the court under its inherent jurisdiction are required for the local authority to exercise its statutory functions, the local authority may apply for permission to seek relief under the inherent jurisdiction of the court (*Re S (Wardship: Peremptory Return)* [2010] 2 FLR 1960, CA; see further under CA 1989, s 100). Where there have been suspicions that children with their parents or on their own are planning, attempting or being groomed with a view to travel to Syria controlled by ISIS or where they have been or are at risk of being radicalised or involved in terrorist activities, proceedings have been brought under the inherent jurisdiction and the children have been made wards of court (*Re M (Wardship: Jurisdiction and Powers)* [2016] 1 FLR 1055, FD; *Re Y (Risk of Young Person Travelling to Join IS) (No 1)* [2016] 2 FLR 225, FD and *Re Y (Risk of Young Person Travelling to Join IS) (No 2)* [2016] 2 FLR 229, FD and *London Borough of Tower Hamlets v M and Others* [2015] 2 FLR 1431, FD). Usually it is the local authority that makes the application but the President in his Guidance of 8 October 2015 on *Radicalisation Cases in the Family Courts* (see **Cases of alleged radicalisation** under CA 1989, s 31) stated that 'there is no reason why in a case where it seems to the police to be necessary to do so, the police should not start such proceedings for the purposes, for example, of making a child a ward of court' (para 3), obtaining injunctions and other ancillary orders to protect and locate a child.

Commencement of application—An application to ward a child may only be made after its birth; an unborn child cannot be warded (*Re F (In Utero) (Wardship)* [1988] 2 FLR 307, CA. However, the inherent jurisdiction of the court may be invoked to obtain an anticipatory declaratory relief in respect of an unborn child (see *Re D (Unborn Baby)* [2009] 2 FLR 313, FD or a non-disclosure order and reporting restriction order in relation to an unborn child but limited in time: *X County Council v M & Others* [2014] EWHC 2262 (Fam)).

Where to start proceedings—All applications under the inherent jurisdiction of the court must be started in the High Court (FPR 2010, r 12.36). No child shall be made a ward of court or cease to be a ward of court except by an order of the High Court.

Transfer of proceedings—The provision for transfer is dealt with in FPR PD12D, para 2. The Family Court does not have jurisdiction to deal with applications that a child be made or cease to be a ward of court, but the case in whole or in part may be transferred to the Family Court once a direction has been given confirming the wardship and directing that the child remain a ward of court during his minority or until further order (para 2.1). If a decision is required as to whether the child should remain a ward, the Family Court must retransfer the case to the High Court (para 2.2) or to a judge of the High Court.

Proceedings that should be dealt with in the High Court—FPR PD12D, para 2.3 identifies the proceedings in relation to a ward of court that will be dealt with in the High Court unless the nature of the issues of fact or law makes them more suitable for hearing in the Family Court. These include proceedings in which: (a) an officer of the Cafcass High Court Team or the Official Solicitor is or becomes the litigation friend or children's guardian of the ward or a party to the proceedings; (b) a local authority is or becomes a party; (c) an application for paternity testing is made; (d) there is a dispute about medical treatment; (e) an application is opposed on the grounds of lack of jurisdiction; (f) there is a substantial foreign element; and (g) there is an opposed application for leave to take the child permanently out of the jurisdiction or where there is an application for temporary removal of a child from the jurisdiction and it is opposed on the ground that the child may not be returned. See also FC(CDB)R 2014 and FPR PD12E, para 3.1. The President in his Guidance of 8 October 2015 on *Radicalisation Cases in the Family Courts* (see **Cases of alleged radicalisation** under CA 1989, s 31) has decided that all radicalisation cases that fall within the description set out in para 1 of the Guidance (see **Restrictions under CA 1989**, above) are to be heard by High Court Judges of the Family Division, which does not include a judge or other person authorised to sit as a High Court judge under SCA 1981, s 9. Where proceedings have been issued in the Family Court, steps must be taken to notify the designated family judge who in turn must notify the Liaison Judge with a view to listing the case before a High Court Judge. Cases that raise issues of PII require a closed hearing or use of a special advocate or, where electronic tagging is proposed, must be dealt with by a judge of the Family Division. The Guidance also sets out some of the factors that the court may need to consider in radicalisation cases.

Jurisdiction—In the exercise of its inherent jurisdiction the High Court has jurisdiction only if the child is habitually resident in England and Wales or is present in England and Wales and is not habitually resident in any other part of the UK and provided that jurisdiction is not excluded by FLA 1986, s 3(2) (*H v H (Jurisdiction to Grant Wardship)* [2012] 1 FLR 23, CA; see also *Re A (Children)* [2014] 1 FLR 111, SC). Jurisdiction under the inherent jurisdiction may also be invoked to protect a child or vulnerable adult who has British nationality and has been abducted or where the circumstances of the case justify such intervention (*Re K and D (Wardship Without Notice Return Order)* [2017] EWHC 153 (Fam); *Al-Jeffery v Al-Jeffery (Vulnerable adult; British citizen)* [2016] EWHC 2151 (Fam); *Re A (Children)*; *Re B (Habitual Residence: Inherent Jurisdiction)* [2015] EWCA Civ 886; and *Re B (A Child) (Habitual Residence: Inherent Jurisdiction)* [2016] 1 FLR 561, SC, where in refusing jurisdiction the court explored the use of the inherent jurisdiction and especially its protective aspects necessary to meet exceptional circumstances; see also *Re N (Abduction: Appeal)* [2013] 1 FLR 457, CA, where the court refused to exercise the jurisdiction to make an order for the return to the jurisdiction of the child who was not habitually resident or present in the jurisdiction). The cases indicate that the court can and will exercise its inherent jurisdiction in respect of a British child/vulnerable person who is outside the jurisdiction based on nationality where the court is satisfied that the child or vulnerable person is at risk and requires the protection of the court. Where it is excluded by the 1986 Act, provided the child is present in England and Wales on the relevant date (for meaning see s 3(6)) and the court considers that the immediate exercise of its powers is necessary for the child's protection the court will exercise jurisdiction. (For the meaning of habitual residence see note under CACA 1985, Sch 1, Art 4.) Where the child is habitually resident in a State within the European Union or a Contracting State that has ratified the Hague Convention 1996, the provisions of Brussels IIA and the Convention, respectively, will need to be considered to determine jurisdiction and applicable law. If a Member State or a Contracting State has jurisdiction, the court may (if the situation is urgent) take necessary measures for the protection of a child and in some instances take provisional measures, for example in urgent cases to make orders that provide for the immediate recognition and enforcement of orders of a court of a Member State of the EU pending the application under FPR 2010, Pt 31, to comply with its obligation under European provisions (*Re Z (Recognition of Foreign Order)* [2017] 1 FLR 1236, FD). However, in invoking the inherent jurisdiction in these circumstances the court must ensure compliance with relevant European provisions. In *Re Z*, for example, the court considered the provisions of Brussels IIA, Art 23 and ensured that the child had been given the opportunity to be heard and that the order made by the Member State did not infringe the parental responsibility of any person and that those with parental responsibility for the child had been given the opportunity to be heard in the original Member State. (See Brussels IIA and the 1996 Convention in Part VI and the PRMPC(IO)(EWNI)R 2010 in Part IV.) The issue of habitual residence is usually to be determined on proper evidence and where there is a challenge on full argument. The court may proceed to hear a case and provide the necessary protection under its inherent jurisdiction where the evidence discloses that the child has lived in England for all of her life before removal out of the jurisdiction of the court and requires protection (*Re S (Wardship: Peremptory Return)* [2010] 2 FLR 1960, CA and *Re K and D (Wardship Without Notice Return Order)* [2017] EWHC 153 (Fam)). Before commencing proceedings, consideration should be given to the nature of the issues on which a determination is sought. If the court is required to review the decision of a public authority taken in the exercise of its statutory power, the governing principles that will apply will be those of public law and not those governed by reference to the inherent jurisdiction of the court. In such cases the application should be made in the Administrative Court for judicial review and not in the Family Division (*A (A Patient) v A Health Authority; Re J; The Queen on the Application of S v Secretary of State for the Home Department* [2002] 1 FLR 845, FD). Note also that the court has exercised its inherent jurisdiction in relation to vulnerable adults and cases of stranded spouses.

Powers of the court—The court under its inherent jurisdiction has power to make any order or determine any issue in respect of a child or an adult unless restricted by legislation. See FPR PD12D, para 2.3 for some examples. The court may also make a collection and location order, port alerts, passport orders or injunctive order, e g prohibiting the removal of a child from the jurisdiction. The court ensures that its orders are complied with by directing the Tipstaff to enforce the order. The role of the Tipstaff is set out in FPR PD12D, para 7.1 (see also *Emergency Remedies in the Family Courts* (Family Law) at B[5.56]; see B[1.7], B[1.8] and B[2.4A] for direction orders to the Tipstaff). If any of these orders is applied for and it is intended to register the prohibited steps order and/or the port alert with the National Ports Office (Tel: 0208 721 6000), the order should be carefully drafted to ensure that it identifies the child, the person to whom the order is directed and details of the person(s) or organisation(s) who should be contacted in the event of an attempted removal of the child. See also under PD12F, Pt 4 in relation to police assistance to prevent removal from England and Wales. In addition to all of the orders that can be made in family proceedings the court may make a wide range of injunctions for the protection of a child, of which the most common are orders: (a) to restrain publicity, e g see *Thompson and Venables v News Group Newspapers, Associated Newspapers Ltd and MGN Ltd* [2001] 1 FLR 791, CA but, because of the need to balance the freedom of the press against the protection of a child any such order must be drawn in clear and precise terms; (b) to prevent an undesirable association; (c) relating to medical treatment; (d) to protect abducted children or children where the case has another substantial foreign element; (e) for the return of children to and from another state; and (f) to grant an injunction pursuant to SCA 1981, s 37 restraining the local authority from removing children from placement with foster carers, who had given notice of their intention to adopt the children, pending the full hearing by the court (*Coventry CC v O (Adoption)* [2011] 2 FLR 936, CA). The inherent jurisdiction has also been sought to extend an injunction, granted during wardship proceedings, beyond the child's 18th birthday irrespective of the fact that the ward had become habitually resident in another country where there was clearly a risk that the child would continue to suffer harm: *Re SO (Wardship: Extension of Protective Injunction Orders)* [2016] 1 FLR 1144 , FD. GPS electronic tagging may be ordered in exceptional circumstances: see *Re X (Children) and Y (Children) (No 1)* [2015] 2 FLR 1487, FD, at [100] for guidance and procedure (the Guidance is also set out in Part V); *Re X (Children) and Y (Children) (No 2)* [2015] 2 FLR 1515, FD. (See also under HRA 1998, s 9, FPR 2010, r 29.5 and

PART III

CPR 1998, r 19.4A.) The court has the power to make an order for the summary return of a British child in abduction cases pursuant to its inherent jurisdiction on an application made without notice but will exercise its powers with 'great caution or circumspection for the protection of the child' where there are exceptional circumstances. (See *Re A (A Child)* [2016] EWCA Civ 572 for the principles that apply to all applications made without notice. For a recent example of an exceptional case where an order was granted on a without notice application, see *Re K and D (Wardship Without Notice Return Order)* [2017] EWHC 153 (Fam).) Where a without notice order is sought, the information to be put before the court in support of the order should be the subject of the closest scrutiny and those advising the making of a without notice application should consider rigorously whether the application is justified and whether there is clear evidence to support the application. If the applicant is not present when the application is made, a contemporaneous note of the instructions given should be available for production to the court. If material other than that disclosed in a written statement is relied on, the court should give direction for the filing of sworn evidence to confirm the information within a very short time: see *KY v DD* [2012] 2 FLR 200, FD.

Undesirable association—Where the child has formed or is seeking to form an association considered to be undesirable with another person, that other person should not be made a party to an application within the proceedings for an injunction or committal and should not be added to the title of the proceedings or allowed to see any documents other than those relating directly to the proceedings for the injunction or committal. The person should be allowed time to obtain representation and any injunction should in the first instance extend over a few days only (FPR PD12D, para 3.1).

Medical treatment—It is only in cases concerning children or a vulnerable adult (i e those with capacity) that the High Court's inherent jurisdiction can be invoked. When dealing with such cases the court will apply the 'patient's best interests' principle and will have to be satisfied that the proposed treatment is necessary (*Re TM (Medical Treatment)* [2013] EWHC 4103 (Fam); *Portsmouth NHS Trust v Wyatt* [2006] 1 FLR 652, FD; *Re Wyatt* [2006] 2 FLR 111, FD; MCA 2005, s 4). Where there are serious medical issues such as surgery for a serious medical condition, initially it is for the parents who have parental responsibility for the child to seek to resolve the issue with the hospital. Although medical professionals can act on the consent of either parent with parental responsibility, if the matter is very serious and the parents do not accept the advice offered by the medical team, it will be appropriate to invoke the inherent jurisdiction, provided that the issue is properly formulated (see *An NHS Trust v SR (Radiotherapy and Chemotherapy)* [2013] 1 FLR 1297, FD). In such cases, and especially where the medical advice is for withdrawal or withholding of treatment, the hospital should be invited to intervene. The medical guidance from the Royal College of Paediatrics and Child Health *Making Decisions to Limit Treatment in Life – Limiting and Life Treating Conditions: A Framework for Practice* indicates that in such circumstances the child's best interests demand that an order should be sought from the court.(See also *Bolton NHS Foundation Trust v C (by her Guardian) and LB & BT* [2015] EWHC 2920 (Fam), where the compatibility of the aforesaid Guidance with ECHR rights was considered, approved and applied.) Where the local authority shares parental responsibility, it should not give its consent to such serious medical interventions. It is inappropriate to seek to resolve such issues within care proceedings or by seeking permission to apply for a specific issue order under CA 1989, s 8: *A Local Authority v SB, AB & MB* [2010] 2 FLR 1203, FD; *Re Jake (Withholding of Medical Treatment)* [2015] EWHC 2442 (Fam), where the medical team treating a gravely ill 1-year-old child sought a declaration that it was lawful if the child's condition deteriorated to withhold invasive medical treatment and intravenous nutrition; *Re A (Medical Treatment: Removal of Artificial Ventilation)* [2016] 1 FLR 241, FD, where the evidence pointed overwhelmingly to the child having suffered brain stem death but the parents contended that this was not synonymous with clinical/legal death and they wished to remove the child to Saudi Arabia while still on ventilation. The court applied the definition of death in the *Code of Practice* applicable to those who were comatose and being ventilated and was satisfied that the criteria of death had been established. The Court also held that the hospital trust had acted properly in bringing the matter to the High Court to resolve the issue. In *A Local Health Board v Y (A Child)* [2016] EWHC 206 (Fam), the health board was granted a declaration permitting the withdrawal and withholding of treatment of a very profoundly ill child and in *County Durham and Darlington NHS Foundation Trust v SS* [2016] EWHC 535 (Fam) a declaration was granted that it was lawful and in the profoundly disabled child's best interests to treat her in accordance with the clinicians discretion, including whether or not to resuscitate the child. Although in *Re JM (A Child) (Medical Treatment)* [2016] 2 FLR 235, FD – a case where the hospital trust applied for authorisation for a child of 10 to undergo surgery for an aggressive form of cancer against the wishes of the child and his parents – Mostyn J took the view that the issue that had been raised was concerned with aspects of parental responsibility and therefore that the application for the relief sought should have been under CA 1989, s 8. It is suggested that this is not supported by case-law. In most serious medical treatment cases a declaration is sought that the treatment proposed is in the best interests of the child and for authorisation for the treatment to be given or withdrawn. This can only be granted by the High Court. Where a child is in care, the local authority cannot apply for a specific issue order. The nature of the issues that arise is not within the scope of a s 8 order. It also does not take into account: the delay that this procedure would entail; the need for the child's interests to be independently considered by being made a party to the proceedings and for the child to be represented; the hurdles that would have to be overcome to obtain legal funding and representation for the child; and the fact that the case would have to be dealt with by a judge of the Family Division, thus requiring a transfer to the High Court. In relation to children aged 16–18 and adults who lack capacity, MCA 2005 and its *Code of Practice* will apply. The decision of the UKSC in *Aintree University Hospitals NHS Foundation Trust v James* [2013] COPLR 492, SC confirms and in some respects clarifies the principles that should apply to cases where the patient who lacks capacity is seriously ill. However, similar principles apply to cases involving children where life-sustaining treatment in the circumstances of the case is regarded as futile, with no evidence of any discernible improvement and where there is a risk of other deteriorating factors, including persistent intense and invasive treatment (*NHS Trust v Baby X* [2013] 1 FLR 225, FD; see also *Re KH (Medical Treatment: Advanced Care Plan)* [2013] 1 FLR 1471, FD, where similar principles were adopted when making a declaration of lawfulness of the advanced care plan put forward by the medical team; *An NHS Foundation Trust v Mr and Mrs R* [2014] 2 FLR 955, FD; *NHS Foundation Trust v AB & Ors* [2014] EWHC 1031 (Fam)). In *An NHS Trust v MB (A Child Represented by CAFCASS as Guardian ad Litem)* [2006] 2 FLR 319, FD the court directed that a list specifically identifying the benefits/advantages and burdens/disadvantages of continuing or discontinuing treatment should be submitted by each party as part of the preparation of the case. In *Re B (Medical Treatment)* [2009] 1 FLR 1264, FD, when making a declaration allowing for the withholding of resuscitation if the child's condition deteriorated, the court suggested that a short, joint experts' report be attached to the order so that in the event of a crisis any new doctor coming to that situation would have the information needed to make this difficult, sensitive and finely balanced clinical judgment. The court has given its consent: to medical treatment where the parents have refused to do so (*NHS Trust v A* [2008] 1 FLR 70, FD, where applying an objective test based on the best interests of the child and discounting the religious faith of the parents, the court held that a 50% prospect of full normal life even with the risk of infertility, outweighed all other considerations); to medical treatment where the patient, whether a child or an adult, has refused to consent (*Re E (A Minor) (Wardship: Medical Treatment)* [1993] 1 FLR 386, FD; *Re R (A Minor) (Wardship: Consent to Treatment)* [1992] 1 FLR 190, CA; *Re J (A Minor) (Medical Treatment)* [1992] 2 FLR 165, CA; *Re H (Mental Patient: Diagnosis)* [1993] 1 FLR 28, FD); to the termination of a pregnancy (*Re P (A Minor)* [1986] 1 FLR 272, FD). For cases relating to issues of withholding or withdrawing treatment, the principles set out in *Aintree* (above) will apply. For sterilisation, see *Re P (A Minor) (Wardship: Sterilisation)* [1989] 1 FLR 182, FD; for the approach adopted in respect of male sterilisation, see *Re A (Male Sterilisation)* [2000] 1 FLR 549, CA where the application was refused, and *A NHS Trust v DE* [2013] COPLR 531 where it was authorised. For cases involving making a choice between two alternative surgical interventions, see *Re S (Sterilisation: Patient's Best Interests)* [2000] 2 FLR 389, CA; *Re ZM and OS (Sterilisation: Patient's Best Interests)* [2000] 1 FLR 523, FD.

However, where a patient is an adult and of sound mind and, in anticipation of entering into a condition such as persistent vegetative state or other life-threatening condition, permanent mental impairment or unconsciousness, has given clear instructions that in such an event he is not to be given medical care designed to keep him alive, the court will respect his wishes (*Re AK (Medical Treatment: Consent)* [2001] 1 FLR 129, FD and *Re B (Consent to Treatment: Capacity)* [2002] 1 FLR 1090, FD). In such cases, the patient can make an advanced decision, provided it complies with MCA 2005, ss 24–26. With regard to the patient's right to choose, see the President's guidelines in *Re B*, above. Where an urgent or out-of-hours application has to be made, the procedure set out in FPR PD12E should be followed.

Detention of a child or vulnerable adult—The court also has power to direct the placement/detention of a child or a vulnerable or incapacitated adult in a specified institution, subject to the principle that the jurisdiction must be exercised in compliance with ECHR 1950, Art 5 rights (for the tests that apply in such cases, see *P (By His Litigation Friend the Official Solicitor) v Cheshire West and Chester Council and Another; P and Q (By Their Litigation Friend the Official Solicitor) v Surrey County Council* [2014] COPLR 313, SC). Where a child has a mental disorder or lacks capacity of a nature and degree that warrants detention in hospital to receive treatment and there is real risk and immediate risk of death to the child without such detention and treatment, authorisation from the court should be sought: to take all proportionate and reasonable steps to detain the child in hospital and prevent the child from absconding from the hospital; for the police to search for, arrest and detain the child in their custody if he/she absconds; and for the medical team to use proportionate and reasonable force and/or restraint by trained professionals to administer treatment and medical procedures in the child's best interests. The existence of a remedy under mental health legislation does not preclude the court exercising its inherent jurisdiction in appropriate cases. As to when it is appropriate to invoke the court's inherent jurisdiction as opposed to an application for a specific issue order under CA 1989, see *A Local Authority v D and Others* [2016] 2 FLR 601, FD, where the local authority sought to place a 14-year-old boy in a residential unit under conditions that would have amounted to deprivation of liberty and it was held that the local authority was right to seek authorisation by invoking the inherent jurisdiction of the court pursuant to CA 1989, s 100(4). The local authority could not consent to the deprivation of liberty as it would constitute a breach of Art 5 of the ECHR. Of the two routes available, ie secure accommodation under s 25 or the inherent jurisdiction, the latter was the appropriate route. In *Re D (A Child: Deprivation of Liberty)* [2015] COPLR 209, FD, the consent of the parents to the placement of their 15-year-old son in a residential unit, which amounted to deprivation of liberty, was approved as an appropriate exercise of parental responsibility. See also *A Local Authority v SB, AB & MB* [2010] 2 FLR 1203, FD, *Devon County Council v S* [1993] 1 FLR 842, FD and *Re O (A Minor) (Medical Treatment)* [1993] 2 FLR 149, FD; cf *Re R (A Minor) (Blood Transfusion)* [1993] 2 FLR 757, FD. Such an application should be heard inter partes where possible in the High Court. The procedure set out in Pt 19 should be followed.

Vulnerable adults and adults lacking capacity—Applications in relation to adults who lack capacity are governed by the provisions of MCA 2005 and the rules and directions issued under the Act. FPR PD12E, para 4.4 confirms this by providing that medical and welfare issues relating to an adult lacking capacity are brought in the Court of Protection. Enquires about such cases should be addressed to a Court of Protection healthcare and welfare lawyer at the offices of the Official Solicitor.

MCA 2005, s 2(1) defines those who lack capacity in relation to a matter: '… if at the material time he is unable to make a decision for himself in relation to the matter because of an impairment of, or disturbance in the functioning of, the mind or brain'. Capacity is therefore subject- and issue-specific and is not limited to mental disability. MCA 2005, s 3 sets out the test to be applied for assessing whether a person is unable to make an informed decision on the relevant matter. Practitioners are advised to refer to MCA 2005 in relevant cases. (See also: Gordon Ashton et al *Mental Capacity – The New Law*; *Court of Protection Practice*; and *Urgent Applications in the Court of Protection* (all LexisNexis)). All applications in relation to a vulnerable adult lacking capacity should in future be made to the Court of Protection, which will then refer the matter to the appropriate level of judiciary/court. For practice and procedure refer to the Court of Protection Rules, PDs and Codes of Practice. Where an adult is considered to have capacity for the purposes of MCA 2005 but is incapacitated by external forces outside his/her control from reaching a decision and is vulnerable, the court's inherent jurisdiction may still be invoked to protect the vulnerable adult (*A Local Authority v DL, RL, and ML* [2011] 1 FLR 957, FD, in which Local Government Act 1972, s 222 was also relied on for seeking relief) but not to impose a decision as to welfare or finance (*LBL v RYJ and VJ* [2010] COPLR Con Vol 795, COP).

Experimental medical treatment—The court has permitted experimental and pioneering treatment to be carried out where the benefits and risks were unknown, but where there was no increased risk of suffering to the patient and some chance of benefit, and where there was a responsible body of relevant professional opinion that supported the treatment (*JS v An NHS Trust; JA v An NHS Trust* [2003] 1 FLR 879, FD).

Exercise of the court's powers is discretionary—The court may refuse to exercise its powers if it considers it inappropriate to do so. There are numerous examples of cases where the court has declined to exercise its inherent jurisdiction. These include: where the sole object of the application was to gain publicity (*Re Dunhill (An Infant)* (1967) 111 Sol Jo 11, ChD); where proceedings were issued to frustrate immigration laws or to prevent the exercise of statutory powers (*S v S* [2009] 1 FLR 241, FD); to prevent a boy soldier being arrested under military law (*Re JS (A Minor) (Wardship: Boy Soldier)* [1991] 1 FLR 7, FD); where relief is available under CA 1989 (*C v C (Access Order: Enforcement)* [1990] 1 FLR 462, CA); and to direct a school to educate a child against his/her wishes (*Re C (A Minor) (Wardship: Jurisdiction)* [1991] 2 FLR 168, CA).

Order for costs—Under FPR 2010, r 28.1, the court has a wide discretion to make such an order if it thinks it just. Where a party to the proceedings has advanced a case that amounts to 'litigation conduct', the court may order that party to pay the costs (*R and R v A (Costs in Children Proceedings)* [2011] 2 FLR 672, FD).

12.37 Child as respondent to wardship proceedings

(1) A child who is the subject of wardship proceedings must not be made a respondent to those proceedings unless the court gives permission following an application under paragraph (2).

(2) Where nobody other than the child would be a suitable respondent to wardship proceedings, the applicant may apply without notice for permission to make the wardship application –

(a) without notice; or

(b) with the child as the respondent.

Ward as a party to proceedings—See FPR 2010, rr 16.1–16.15 and FPR PD16A for representation of children and appointment of litigation friend. In cases relating to medical treatment and press injunction, it may be desirable for a child who is the subject of such proceedings to be made a party and represented by a children's guardian. Where an application is made out of hours, the urgent business officer will contact a representative of Cafcass. A child of sufficient understanding to instruct a solicitor should be made a party and given notice of the application (FPR PD12E, para 3.1).

12.38 Registration requirements

The court officer will send a copy of every application for a child to be made a ward of court to the principal registry for recording in the register of wards.

Defined terms—'principal registry': FPR 2010, r 2.3.

Scope—This provision is related to cases that are issued in the District Registry.

12.39 Notice of child's whereabouts

(1) Every respondent, other than a child, must file with the acknowledgment of service a notice stating –

(a) the respondent's address; and

(b) either –

(i) the whereabouts of the child; or

(ii) that the respondent is unaware of the child's whereabouts if that is the case.

(2) Unless the court directs otherwise, the respondent must serve a copy of that notice on the applicant.

(3) Every respondent other than a child must immediately notify the court in writing of –

(a) any subsequent changes of address; or

(b) any change in the child's whereabouts,

and, unless the court directs otherwise, serve a copy of that notice on the applicant.

(4) In this rule a reference to the whereabouts of a child is a reference to –

(a) the address at which the child is living;

(b) the person with whom the child is living; and

(c) any other information relevant to where the child may be found.

Whereabouts of the child—There is a duty on the Respondent to disclose the child's whereabouts. A solicitor is under a duty to disclose information that may assist in locating a ward even if such information has been conveyed to him in confidence by his client (*Ramsbotham v Senior* (1869) FLR Rep 591, CE). Information about the child's whereabouts may also be obtained through government departments (but in the first instance usually through HM Customs and Excise) by applying to the High Court (or a judge authorised to sit as a judge of the High Court) for an order for disclosure (see FPR PD6C for the information required and procedure to be followed). The order will direct that the department to whom the order is addressed should disclose the information to the court. Where the information is disclosed to the applicant's solicitor, an undertaking will be required that the information given in response to the inquiry will be used solely for the purpose of assisting in tracing the person concerned or the child. A collection and/or a location order may be sought in the prescribed form directing the tipstaff to ascertain the child's whereabouts, to search for and recover the child and if necessary to arrest any person who fails to comply with the order. Where such an order is obtained, the tipstaff must be provided with all available information as to the child's possible whereabouts. See also PD12D and PD12F and the court's powers under FLA 1986, ss 33 and 34.) Where an order is sought for the return of a child about to arrive by air and the applicant requires information to enable him to meet the aeroplane, the court should be asked to direct that the airline and (if he has the information) the immigration officer at the appropriate airport should supply the necessary information to the applicant. Where the applicant has an order for the return of the child, application should be made for such a direction. Where the child has been abducted, consideration should be given as to whether a press publicity order is required to trace the child (see FPR PD12F, paras 4.15, 4.16). If a child is believed to be in a state that has ratified the Hague Convention 1996, a request may be made for assistance in discovering the whereabouts of the child if it appears that the child may be present in that state and in need of protection and the Central Authority of a Contracting State, either directly or through public authorities or other bodies, is under a duty to provide the information (Hague Convention 1996, Art 31).

12.40 Enforcement of orders in wardship proceedings

The High Court may secure compliance with any direction relating to a ward of court by an order addressed to the tipstaff.

(The role of the tipstaff is explained in Practice Direction 12D (Inherent Jurisdiction (including Wardship Proceedings)).)

Tipstaff—For the purposes of FLA 1986, s 34 the tipstaff is the officer of the court to whom orders should be directed. FPR PD12D, para 7.1 sets out the extent and nature of the role of the tipstaff in family matters. All appropriate orders made in the High Court will be addressed to the tipstaff. The tipstaff has two assistants but he can call on any constable or bailiff to assist him. The tipstaff has authority to effect an arrest and inform the police. The tipstaff has the authority to make a forced entry but in practice the tipstaff will obtain the assistance of the police to ensure that there is no breach of the peace. Standard forms of orders addressed to the tipstaff should be used.

Committal—Where there has been a deliberate attempt to thwart the child's return to England in breach of an order made by the court, the breach may, as in all other cases of breach of an order, be punished by committal to prison (see *Re X (A Child by His Litigation Friend)* [2011] 2 FLR 793, CA, where an 8-month prison sentence was upheld by the CA).

12.41 Child ceasing to be ward of court

(1) A child who, by virtue of section 41(2) of the Senior Courts Act 1981, automatically becomes a ward of court on the making of a wardship application will cease to be a ward on the determination of the application unless the court orders that the child be made a ward of court.

(2) Nothing in paragraph (1) affects the power of the court under section 41(3) of the Senior Courts Act 1981 to order that any child cease to be a ward of court.

Confirmation of wardship—The child will become a ward immediately on the application being issued. It is, however, essential to ensure that at the first opportunity thereafter a direction hearing is applied for and an order is sought that the child should remain a ward during his/her minority or until further order. In the absence of such an order the wardship will lapse.

12.42 Adoption of a child who is a ward of court

An application for permission –

(a) to start proceedings to adopt a child who is a ward of court;
(b) to place such a child for adoption with parental consent; or
(c) to start proceedings for a placement order in relation to such a child,

may be made without notice in accordance with Part 18.

Procedure—The application must be made in accordance with the procedure set out in FPR 2010, Pt 18 and FPR PD18A, which supplements the rule.

12.42A Application for a writ of habeas corpus for release in relation to a minor

(1) Part 87 of the CPR applies in respect of an application for a writ of habeas corpus for release in relation to a minor –

(a) as if –

(i) for rule 87.2(1)(a) of the CPR there were substituted –

'(a) an application notice; and'; and

(ii) for rule 87.2(4) of the CPR there were substituted –

'(4) The application notice must be filed in the Family Division of the High Court.'; and

(b) subject to any additional necessary modifications.

(2) Rules 12.5 to 12.8, 12.12 to 12.16, 12.21 and 12.39 do not apply to an application to which this rule applies.

(The term 'application notice' is defined in rule 2.3(1).)

Amendments—Inserted by SI 2014/3296.

Application for a writ of habeas corpus and CPR 1998, r 87—As from 1 April 2014, CPR 1998, r 87 is incorporated into family proceedings. Applications can therefore be made to the Family Division of the High Court for the writ under this rule. Parallel amendment is made to FPR 2010, r 30. The application should be made in accordance with Pt 18 procedure.

Chapter 6

Proceedings under the 1980 Hague Convention, the European Convention, the Council Regulation, and the 1996 Hague Convention

12.43 Scope

This Chapter applies to –

(a) children proceedings under the 1980 Hague Convention or the European Convention; and

(b) applications relating to the Council Regulation or the 1996 Hague Convention in respect of children.

Amendments—SI 2012/3061.

Section 1

Proceedings under the 1980 Hague Convention or the European Convention

12.44 Interpretation

In this section –

'the 1985 Act' means the Child Abduction and Custody Act 1985;

'Central Authority' means, in relation to England and Wales, the Lord Chancellor;

'Contracting State' has the meaning given in –

(a) section 2 of the 1985 Act in relation to the 1980 Hague Convention; and

(b) section 13 of the 1985 Act in relation to the European Convention; and

'decision relating to custody' has the same meaning as in the European Convention.

('the 1980 Hague Convention' and the 'the European Convention' are defined in rule 2.3.)

The 1980 Hague Convention—This is the Convention on the Civil Aspects of International Child Abduction signed at The Hague on 25 October 1980 and is set out in Sch 1 to the 1985 Act (see the commentary thereunder). (See also FPR 2010, r 2.3.)

'the European Convention'—This is the European Convention on Recognition and Enforcement of Decisions Concerning Custody of Children and on the Restoration of Custody of Children signed in Luxembourg on 20 May 1980 and is set out in CACA 1985, Sch 2 in Part II (see also FPR 2010, r 2.3).

The 1996 Hague Convention—This is the Convention on Jurisdiction, Applicable Law, Recognition, Enforcement and Co-operation in Respect of Parental Responsibility and Measures for the Protection of Children signed at the Hague on 19 October 1996, which came into force in the UK on 1 November 2012 (see Part VI). The PRMPC(IO)(EWNI)R 2010 contain provisions relevant to applications under this Convention and the 1980 Hague Convention. For procedure for recognition, registration and enforcement of orders, see FPR 2010, Pt 31.

12.45 Where to start proceedings

Every application under the 1980 Hague Convention or the European Convention must be –

(a) made in the High Court and issued in the principal registry; and

(b) heard by a Judge of the High Court unless the application is;

(i) to join a respondent; or

(ii) to dispense with service or extend the time for acknowledging service.

Which court—This rule and FPR PD12F, para 2.10 set out two interlocutory applications that may be heard by a judge other than a High Court Judge.

12.46 Evidence in support of application

Where the party making an application under this section does not produce the documents referred to in Practice Direction 12F, the court may –

(a) fix a time within which the documents are to be produced;

(b) accept equivalent documents; or

(c) dispense with production of the documents if the court considers it has sufficient information.

Application—Must be made on Form C67 (FPR PD5A) and include the information set out in FPR PD12F para 2.11. The heading on the application form must comply with the provisions set out in PD12F, para 2.14 and the guidance given in *Vigreux v Michel* [2006] 2 FLR 1180, CA. Where habitual residence may be in issue, lawyers responsible for the preparation of the statements should familiarise themselves with recent case-law, which emphasises the scope and ambit of the enquiry. If the statement does not address the salient issues, counsel instructed should bring the failure to the attention of the instructing solicitors and an application should be made expeditiously to the court for permission to file an amended statement (Hayden J in *Re B (A Minor) (Habitual Residence)* [2016] EWHC 2174 (Fam)). See also *Re J (A Child) (Finland) (Habitual Residence)* [2017] EWCA Civ 80, at [64].

Documents that must be filed with the application—See FPR PD12F, paras 2.12 and 2.13.

12.47 Without-notice applications

(1) This rule applies to applications –

(a) commencing or in proceedings under this section;

(b) for interim directions under section 5 or 19 of the 1985 Act;

(c) for the disclosure of information about the child and for safeguarding the child's welfare, under rule 12.57;

(d) for the disclosure of relevant information as to where the child is, under section 24A of the 1985 Act; or

(e) for a collection order, location order or passport order.

(2) Applications under this rule may be made without notice, in which case the applicant must file the application –

(a) where the application is made by telephone, the next business day after the making of the application; or

(b) in any other case, at the time when the application is made.

(3) Where an order is made without notice, the applicant must serve a copy of the order on the other parties as soon as practicable after the making of the order, unless the court otherwise directs.

(4) Where the court refuses to make an order on an application without notice, it may direct that the application is made on notice.

(5) Where any hearing takes place outside the hours during which the court office is usually open –

(a) if the hearing takes place by telephone, the applicant's solicitors will, if practicable, arrange for the hearing to be recorded; and

(b) in all other cases, the court or court officer will take a note of the proceedings.

(Practice Direction 12E (Urgent Business) provides further details of the procedure for out of hours applications. See also Practice Direction 12D (Inherent Jurisdiction (including Wardship Proceedings)).)

PART III

Defined terms—'application form' and 'application notice': FPR 2010, r 2.3.

Scope—This rule applies to all emergency applications made before and after proceedings have commenced and specifically those that relate to the court's interim powers on disclosure of information relating to a child, in applications under the European Convention, the disclosure of a child's whereabouts and applications for a location and collection order (see commentary under FPR 2010, rr 12.36 and 12.48). An application under this rule may be justified where the evidence indicates that a child who is a British national has been abducted and needs protection and that the appropriate means of conferring that protection is to order the return of the child within the jurisdiction but, if notice is given to the parent who has abducted the child, that parent will seek to frustrate any steps taken by the court to protect the child's welfare and attempt to manipulate the child. In *Re K and D (Wardship Without Notice Return Order)* [2017] EWHC 153 (Fam), an order was made under the court's inherent jurisdiction based on the children's British nationality but MacDonald J observed that 'the court will always be cautious before it accedes to a without notice application for the summary return pursuant to the court's inherent jurisdiction. This is not least because to do so will necessarily involve the court having either to reach an interim conclusion on the question of habitual residence as a precursor to making a return order (with the attendant difficulties inherent in basing the summary return of a child on a provisional view as to jurisdiction) or to exercise its jurisdiction based on the child's nationality', at [49]; see also [40]–[43]. Where the emergency application is made by telephone before commencement of the proceedings, the substantive application must be issued on the next business day (for meaning of 'business day', see FPR 2010, r 2.3). In any other case, the substantive application should be filed at the time when the without notice application is made. Provision is made for the court to give directions for an on notice hearing. A without notice application should be made under FPR 2010, Pt 18 procedure. See further under FPR PD18A, para 5.1, which lists the circumstances in which an application without notice may be made, and *Re A (A Child)* [2016] EWCA Civ 572 for the principles that apply to all applications made without notice.

Out of hours – urgent applications—For procedure, see FPR PD12E.

Service—Unless the court otherwise directs, service of any order made without notice must be effected as soon as practicable after the order is made. In appropriate cases, application should be made for the court to direct alternative methods of service, eg by email, text message or other electronic means or other form of substituted service. For service generally, see FPR 2010, r 6.

Evidence of service—An appropriate certificate of service must be prepared and filed as soon as practicable after service, setting out the date, time and place of service and describe how the person served was identified (FPR 2010, r 6.37). The certificate of service must be verified by a statement of truth (FPR 2010, r 17.2). Preferably, Form FL415 (the prescribed form for a statement of service) should be used.

12.48 Directions

(1) As soon as practicable after an application to which this section applies has been made, the court may give directions as to the following matters, among others –

(a) whether service of the application may be dispensed with;

(b) whether the proceedings should be transferred to another court under rule 12.54;

(c) expedition of the proceedings or any part of the proceedings (and any direction for expedition may specify a date by which the court must issue its final judgment in the proceedings or a specified part of the proceedings);

(d) the steps to be taken in the proceedings and the time by which each step is to be taken;

(e) whether the child or any other person should be made a party to the proceedings;

(f) if the child is not made a party to the proceedings, the manner in which the child's wishes and feelings are to be ascertained, having regard to the child's age and maturity and in particular whether an officer of the Service or a Welsh family proceedings officer should report to the court for that purpose;

(g) where the child is made a party to the proceedings, the appointment of a children's guardian for that child unless a children's guardian has already been appointed;

(h) the attendance of the child or any other person before the court;

(i) the appointment of a litigation friend for a child or for any protected party, unless a litigation friend has already been appointed;

(j) the service of documents;

(k) the filing of evidence including expert evidence; and

(l) whether the parties and their representatives should meet at any stage of the proceedings and the purpose of such a meeting.

(Rule 16.2 provides for when the court may make the child a party to the proceedings and rule 16.4 for the appointment of a children's guardian for the child who is made a party. Rule 16.5 (without prejudice to rule 16.6) requires a child who is a party to the proceedings but not the subject of those proceedings to have a litigation friend.)

(2) Directions of a court which are in force immediately prior to the transfer of proceedings to another court under rule 12.54 will continue to apply following the transfer subject to –

(a) any changes of terminology which are required to apply those directions to the court to which the proceedings are transferred; and

(b) any variation or revocation of the directions.

(3) The court or court officer will –

(a) take a note of the giving, variation or revocation of directions under this rule; and

(b) as soon as practicable serve a copy of the directions order on every party.

Scope—Other matters, save in relation to directions, will be covered where appropriate by the general provisions set out in FPR 2010, Pt 12 and under the court's general case management powers set out in FPR 2010, Pt 4. The court is required to address the issues that arise under Brussels IIA, Art 11 regarding the representation of children and the avoidance of delay. On this issue, attention is drawn to the Lady Hale's views in *Re M (Abduction: Zimbabwe)* [2008] 1 FLR 251, HL and *Re LC (Reunite: International Child Abduction Centre Intervening)* [2014] 1 FLR 1486, SC, and Black LJ in In *Re M (Republic of Ireland) (Child's Objections) (Joinder of Children as Parties to Appeal)* [2015] 2 FLR 1074, CA (see under CACA 1985, Sch 1). The provisions in FPR 2010, rr 16.2–16.6 deal with the issues of whether a child should be made a party to the proceedings and the appointment of a guardian and litigation friend for a child who is either a party to the proceedings or the subject of the proceedings. In addition, the court is obliged to consider giving further directions under its case management powers under FPR 2010, rr 4.1–4.8 and to consider whether non-court dispute resolution is appropriate and take account of whether a family mediation information and assessment meeting (MIAM) took place or whether exemption to that procedure was claimed or confirmed or whether the parties attempted mediation or non-court dispute resolution and the outcome of that process under FPR 2010, rr 3.1–3.3. For the court's powers to strike out/dismiss proceedings and deal with them 'ultra-summarily', see *Re D (Children) (Child Abduction: Practice)* [2016] EWHC 504 (Fam) under CACA 1985, Art 12. For the court's powers if it considers non-court dispute resolution appropriate, see r 3.4. As to representation of children, see further under CACA 1985, Sch 1, Art 12, FPR 2010, Pt 16 and *Emergency Remedies in the Family Courts* (Family Law), Div D. For the court's general powers to make orders see under 'inherent jurisdiction' and also FPR PD12F, which specifies some of the ways in which removal of a child may be prevented without a court order and the orders that may be made to obtain information from government departments.

Interim directions—CACA 1985, ss 5 and 19 empower the court at any time before the application is determined to give such interim directions as it thinks fit for the purpose of securing the welfare of the child concerned or preventing changes in the circumstances relevant to the determination of the application. The provision of CACA 1985, Sch 1, Arts 7 and 10 and Sch 2, Art 5 require all appropriate steps to be taken to ascertain the whereabouts of the child and to ensure his return (see further CACA 1985, s 5). The court may also grant injunctions, request a report from Cafcass (ss 6 and 21), give specific directions for trial, order publicity (see PD12F, paras 4.15, 4.16 and *Re D (A Minor) (Child Abduction)* [1989] 1 FLR 97, FD), dispense with service (r 12.48) or abridge time under its case management powers under r 4.1 and adjourn the hearing (r 12.51). Where appropriate the court may direct a local housing authority to provide accommodation for an abductor and the abducted child and direct the local authority to accommodate the child (*Re C (Abduction: Interim Directions: Accommodation by Local Authority)* [2004] 1 FLR 653, FD; *Re A (Abduction: Interim Directions: Accommodation by Local Authority)* [2011] 1 FLR 1, CA and see under CACA 1985, s 50 in Part II.

On the directions hearing, the court should consider including a provision in the order that each party should identify any undertakings that they seek and any undertakings that they are prepared to give for the purpose of paving the way for the child's return (*Re M (Child Abduction: Existence of Undertaking)* [2000] 3 FCR 693, FD).

12.49 Answer

(1) Subject to paragraph (2) and to any directions given under rule 12.48, a respondent must file and serve on the parties an answer to the application within 7 days beginning with the date on which the application is served.

(2) The court may direct a longer period for service where the respondent has been made a party solely on one of the following grounds –

(a) a decision relating to custody has been made in the respondent's favour; or

(b) the respondent appears to the court to have sufficient interest in the welfare of the child.

Time for filing answer—The court may under its power to give/make interim directions/orders abridge time for service to deal with any issue that requires urgent directions or orders.

12.50 Filing and serving written evidence

(1) The respondent to an application to which this section applies may file and serve with the answer a statement verified by a statement of truth, together with any further evidence on which the respondent intends to rely.

PART III

(2) The applicant may, within 7 days beginning with the date on which the respondent's evidence was served under paragraph (1), file and serve a statement in reply verified by a statement of truth, together with any further evidence on which the applicant intends to rely.

Respondent's evidence—If the respondent wishes to file a statement and/or other evidence, he must file and serve it with his answer, i e within 7 days after service of the application. The statement must be verified by a statement of truth (see FPR 2010, r 17.2 and FPR PD17A for the form and verification of a witness statement generally and FPR 2010, rr 22.4–22.7 and FPR PD22A).

If the respondent wishes to defend the application, the statement must set out any defence to the application (e g that the removal or retention was not wrongful, that the applicant does not have custody rights or that Art 13 applies or challenge the issue of habitual residence of the child) at the earliest opportunity and in any event within the time limit directed by the court (FPR PD12F, paras 2.21–2.24). In cases under the European Convention, the defendant's statement should show that the grounds set out in CACA 1985, Sch 2, Arts 9 and 10 apply and the relevant provisions of Brussels IIA and the 1996 Hague Convention, where appropriate. (See further, Part VI.)

Preparation—Care should be taken to ensure that statements in support are succinct and confined to the issues, which must be identified, excluding the inevitable emotions that underlie such cases to provoke 'irrelevance, prejudice and prolixity' (*Re S (Abduction: Intolerable Situation: Beth Din)* [2000] 1 FLR 454, FD and the President's *House Rules*). The rules and PDs relating to evidence and hearings should be followed in all hearings, irrespective of the duration of the hearing (see FPR 2010, Pt 27 and PD27A) In relation to the preparation of the court bundles, it is only in cases of urgency where it is not reasonably practicable to prepare a bundle that the court may excuse the absence of a proper court bundle.

Oral evidence—The provisions of FPR 2010, Pt 27 apply to oral hearings. Once a child has been found and surrendered, there is no power to order a person to give evidence. The desirability of introducing such a power by way of amendment was considered in *Re D (A Minor) (Child Abduction) Note* [1989] 1 FLR 97, FD and *Re E (A Minor) (Abduction)* [1989] 1 FLR 135, CA. The evidence in proceedings under CACA 1985 is by way of affidavit. Oral evidence is only admitted at the discretion of the court. In *Re K (Abduction: Case Management)* [2011] 1 FLR 1268, CA, Thorpe LJ emphasised this principle and directed that 'not only should orders for oral evidence be extremely rare' but that they should 'never be made in advance of the filing of written statements on the point in issue … If there were to be exceptional provision for oral evidence, it should be strongly expressed to ensure that the parties understood that this was not an opportunity to express their cases on the generality. It was strictly limited in its ambit and should be limited in its duration'.

The proceedings under the Convention are summary in nature and designed to provide a speedy resolution of disputes over children and secure the prompt return of children wrongfully removed from the country of habitual residence. The admission of oral evidence runs the risk of delaying and frustrating the purpose of the Convention. The admission of oral evidence was refused in *Re K (Abduction: Child's Objections)* [1995] 1 FLR 977, FD. The court held that it was not necessary for there to be specific findings of fact for the defence under Art 13(b) to succeed. In exceptional circumstances, oral evidence from experts may be permitted, e g medical, psychological or psychiatric (see under CACA 1985).

Introduction of evidence after hearing—New and additional evidence in support of an application for the reversal or reconsideration of a judgment may be permitted if that evidence could not have been obtained with reasonable diligence before the conclusion of the case and if the court is satisfied that the additional evidence would materially affect the court's decision. If such an application is made after judgment has been given, it would have to satisfy the test in *Ladd v Marshall* (see below) but if made after the hearing was concluded but before judgment the applicant does not have to show strong reasons for so doing (*TF v PJ* [2015] 1 FLR 861, FD and the cases cited therein; *K v K (No 2) (Hague Convention Adjournment)* [2010] 1 FLR 1310, FD; *K v K (Abduction) (No 1)* [2010] 1 FLR 1295, FD).

As to the introduction on appeal of additional evidence (particularly evidence that was available at the trial), see *Re S (Minors) (Abduction)* [1993] 1 FCR 789, CA; the principles laid down in *Ladd v Marshall* (1954) FLR Rep 422, CA were relaxed because the mother and her legal advisers had had only 3 days to prepare the evidence and the case was one that was difficult by reason of the fact that it dealt with children of dual nationality. The court held that, in appropriate cases, the *Ladd v Marshall* rules should be relaxed where the welfare of children required the court to see additional evidence.

Applicant's reply—The applicant has 7 days after service of the respondent's evidence to file and serve a statement in reply, which also must be verified by a statement of truth, together with any further evidence on which the applicant intends to rely.

12.51 Adjournment

The court will not adjourn the hearing of an application to which this section applies for more than 21 days at any one time.

Adjournment—Where an adjournment results in delay, the court will be required to give reasons for any delay beyond 6 weeks in reaching a decision under CACA 1985, Sch 1, Art 11. Once a draft judgment has been handed down, the sealed order must be sent out with expedition (*Re M (Child Abduction: Delay)* (2007) *The Times* August 28, CA). Brussels IIA, Art 11 requires the court, save where exceptional circumstances make this impossible, to issue its judgment within 6 weeks of the issue of the application. See further *Emergency Proceedings in the Family Courts* (Family Law).

12.52 Stay of proceedings upon notification of wrongful removal etc.

(1) In this rule and in rule 12.53 –

(a) 'relevant authority' means –
  (i) the High Court;
  (ii) the family court;
  (iii) …
  (iv) the Court of Session;
  (v) a sheriff court;
  (vi) a children's hearing within the meaning of section 93 of the Children (Scotland) Act 1995;
  (vii) the High Court in Northern Ireland;
  (viii) a county court in Northern Ireland;
  (ix) a court of summary jurisdiction in Northern Ireland;
  (x) the Royal Court of Jersey;
  (xi) a court of summary jurisdiction in Jersey;
  (xii) the High Court of Justice of the Isle of Man;
  (xiii) a court of summary jurisdiction in the Isle of Man; or
  (xiv) the Secretary of State; and

(b) 'rights of custody' has the same meaning as in the 1980 Hague Convention.

(2) Where a party to proceedings under the 1980 Hague Convention knows that an application relating to the merits of rights of custody is pending in or before a relevant authority, that party must file within the proceedings under the 1980 Hague Convention a concise statement of the nature of that application, including the relevant authority in or before which it is pending.

(3) On receipt of a statement filed in accordance with paragraph (2) above, a court officer will notify the relevant authority in or before which the application is pending and will subsequently notify the relevant authority of the result of the proceedings.

(4) On receipt by the relevant authority of a notification under paragraph (3) from the High Court or equivalent notification from the Court of Session, the High Court in Northern Ireland or the High Court of Justice of the Isle of Man –

(a) all further proceedings in the action will be stayed(GL) unless and until the proceedings under the 1980 Hague Convention in the High Court, Court of Session, the High Court in Northern Ireland or the High Court of Justice of the Isle of Man are dismissed; and

(b) the parties to the action will be notified by the court officer of the stay(GL) and dismissal.

Amendments—SI 2013/3204.

Modifications—Rule 12.52(1)(a) is modified for certain purposes by SI 2013/1465, art 17, Sch 1, para 28.

Defined terms—'court officer': r 2.3.

Scope of the provision—This provision ensures that parties notify the court dealing with an application under the 1980 Convention of any other proceedings that may be pending in any other court and that such court stays the proceedings before it until the 1980 Convention proceedings have been concluded.

12.53 Stay of proceedings where application made under s 16 of the 1985 Act (registration of decisions under the European Convention)

(1) A person who –

(a) is a party to –
  (i) proceedings under section 16 of the 1985 Act; or
  (ii) proceedings as a result of which a decision relating to custody has been registered under section 16 of the 1985 Act; and

(b) knows that an application is pending under –
  (i) section 20(2) of the 1985 Act;
  (ii) Article 21(2) of the Child Abduction and Custody (Jersey) Law 2005; or
  (iii) section 42(2) of the Child Custody Act 1987 (an Act of Tynwald),

must file within the proceedings under section 16 of the 1985 Act a concise statement of the nature of the pending application.

(2) On receipt of a statement filed in accordance with paragraph (1) above, a court officer will notify the relevant authority in or before which the application is pending and will subsequently notify the relevant authority of the result of the proceedings.

(3) On receipt by the relevant authority of a notification under paragraph (2) from the High Court or equivalent notification from the Court of Session, the High Court in Northern Ireland or the High Court of Justice of the Isle of Man, the court officer will notify the parties to the action.

Defined terms—'court officer': FPR 2010, r 2.3; 'relevant authority': FPR 2010, r 12.52(1).

Scope—This rule makes similar provisions to those under FPR 2010, r 12.52 in relation to an application made for registration of decisions under the European Convention.

12.54 Transfer of proceedings

(1) At any stage in proceedings under the 1985 Act the court may –

- (a) of its own initiative; or
- (b) on the application of a party with a minimum of two days' notice;

order that the proceedings be transferred to a court listed in paragraph (4).

(2) Where the court makes an order for transfer under paragraph (1) –

- (a) the court will state its reasons on the face of the order;
- (b) a court officer will send a copy of the order, the application and the accompanying documents (if any) and any evidence to the court to which the proceedings are transferred; and
- (c) the costs of the proceedings both before and after the transfer will be at the discretion of the court to which the proceedings are transferred.

(3) Where proceedings are transferred to the High Court from a court listed in paragraph (4), a court officer will notify the parties of the transfer and the proceedings will continue as if they had been commenced in the High Court.

(4) The listed courts are the Court of Session, the High Court in Northern Ireland, the Royal Court of Jersey or the High Court of Justice of the Isle of Man.

Scope—Rule 12.54(2) makes it clear that the court must state its reason for the transfer on the face of the order.

'two days' notice'—The court has power to dispense with service of an application under FPR 2010, r 12.48 or abridge time under its case management powers contained in r 4.1. As to computation of time, see FPR 2010, r 2.3.

12.55 Revocation and variation of registered decisions

(1) This rule applies to decisions which –

- (a) have been registered under section 16 of the 1985 Act; and
- (b) are subsequently varied or revoked by an authority in the Contracting State in which they were made.

(2) The court will, on cancelling the registration of a decision which has been revoked, notify –

- (a) the person appearing to the court to have care of the child;
- (b) the person on whose behalf the application for registration of the decision was made; and
- (c) any other party to the application.

(3) The court will, on being informed of the variation of a decision, notify –

- (a) the party appearing to the court to have care of the child; and
- (b) any party to the application for registration of the decision;

and any such person may apply to make representations to the court before the registration is varied.

(4) Any person appearing to the court to have an interest in the proceedings may apply for the registration of a decision for the cancellation or variation of the decision referred to in paragraph (1).

Scope—This rule should be read together with CACA 1985, s 17, which places a duty on the person on whose behalf the application for registration was made to notify the court in which the decision of the variation or revocation is registered. Where the decision is revoked, the court will cancel the registration and will give notice to the parties of the cancellation. There is no provision for the parties to make representations before cancellation takes place. In a case where the decision has been varied, the court will notify the parties and they have the right to make representations before the registration is varied. In addition, under r 12.55(4) any person who has an interest in the matter is given the right to apply for the registration of a variation or the cancellation of a decision that has been registered under CACA 1985, s 16.

12.56 The central index of decisions registered under the 1985 Act

A central index of decisions registered under section 16 of the 1985 Act, together with any variation of those decisions made under section 17 of that Act, will be kept by the principal registry.

Central index—This provision was introduced to keep a record of such decisions.

12.57 Disclosure of information in proceedings under the European Convention

At any stage in proceedings under the European Convention the court may, if it has reason to believe that any person may have relevant information about the child who is the subject of those proceedings, order that person to disclose such information and may for that purpose order that the person attend before it or file affidavit(GL) evidence.

Defined terms—'child': CACA 1985, Sch 2, Art 1(a) and FPR 2010, r 2.3; 'European Convention' CACA 1985, s 12(1) and FPR 2010, r 2.3.

Scope—This rule reinforces the provisions of CACA 1985, s 24A. A person is not excused from complying with an order under s 24A on the ground that to do so may incriminate him or his spouse of an offence (s 24A(2)). A statement or admission made in compliance with such an order will not be admissible in evidence against the person or his spouse in proceedings for any offence other than perjury. The court has power to order the attendance of a witness (see FPR 2010, r 24 and FPR PD24A, para 1) to give information about the whereabouts of a child (see *Re D (A Minor) (Child Abduction) Note* [1989] 1 FLR 97, FD). Where an order for disclosure is made, the form of order should provide for the disclosure of 'all information possessed by [the named person] as to the past movements and present whereabouts of the child or of the defendant' (see *Re D*, above, at [100]).

'in proceedings under the European Convention'—This rule applies only to proceedings under the European Convention, although CACA 1985, s 24A applies to proceedings under both Conventions.

Section 2
Applications relating to the Council Regulation and the 1996 Hague Convention

Scope—Part 12, Ch 6, Section 2 makes provision for certain applications under Brussels IIA and the Hague Convention 1996:

(a) Procedure under Brussels IIA, art 11(6), where a non-return order has been made under the Hague Convention 1980, art 13 (FPR 2010, r 12.59);
(b) Procedure under Brussels IIA, art 11(7), where a non-return order made under the Hague Convention 1980, art 13 by a court in another Member State is received (FPR 2010, r 12.60);
(c) Transfer of proceedings under Brussels IIA, art 15 or the Hague Convention 1996, arts 8 and 9 (FPR 2010, rr 12.61–12.65 and 12.67 (service of order or request relating to transfer));
(d) Request from another Member/Contracting State to assume jurisdiction in relation to a child (FPR 2010, r 12.66);
(e) Questions as to the court's jurisdiction under Brussels IIA, arts 16–18 or whether proceedings should be stayed under Brussels IIA, art 19 or the Hague Convention 1996, art 13 (FPR 2010, r 12.68);
(f) Request for consultation on or consent to the contemplated placement of a child in England and Wales under Brussels IIA, art 56 or the Hague Convention 1996, art 33 (FPR 2010, r 12.69);
(g) Request made by court in England or Wales for consultation on or consent to the contemplated placement of a child in another Member/Contracting State under Brussels IIA, art 56 or the Hague Convention 1996, art 33 (FPR 2010, r 12.70); and
(h) Application for a declaration regarding parental responsibility under the Hague Convention 1996, art 16 (FPR 2010, r 12.71).

References should be made to the annotations to Brussels IIA and to the Hague Convention 1996, both in Part VI.

12.58 Interpretation

(1) In this section –

…

'Contracting State' means a State party to the 1996 Hague Convention;

'domestic Central Authority' means –

PART III

(a) where the matter relates to the Council Regulation, the Lord Chancellor;
(b) where the matter relates to the 1996 Hague Convention in England, the Lord Chancellor;
(c) where the matter relates to the 1996 Hague Convention in Wales, the Welsh Ministers;

'judgment' has the meaning given in Article 2(4) of the Council Regulation;

'Member State' means a Member State bound by the Council Regulation or a country which has subsequently adopted the Council Regulation;

'parental responsibility' has the meaning given in –
(a) Article 2(7) of the Council Regulation in relation to proceedings under that Regulation; and
(b) Article 1(2) of the 1996 Hague Convention in relation to proceedings under that Convention; and

'seised' has the meaning given in Article 16 of the Council Regulation.

(2) In rules 12.59 to 12.70, references to the court of another member State or Contracting State include authorities within the meaning of 'court' in Article 2(1) of the Council Regulation, and authorities of Contracting States which have jurisdiction to take measures directed to the protection of the person or property of the child within the meaning of the 1996 Hague Convention.

Amendments—SI 2012/2046.

12.59 Procedure under Article 11(6) of the Council Regulation where the court makes a non-return order under Article 13 of the 1980 Hague Convention

(1) Where the court makes an order for the non-return of a child under Article 13 of the 1980 Hague Convention, it must immediately transmit the documents referred to in Article 11(6) of the Council Regulation –
(a) directly to the court with jurisdiction or the central authority in the Member State where the child was habitually resident immediately before the wrongful removal to, or wrongful retention in, England and Wales; or
(b) to the domestic Central Authority for onward transmission to the court with jurisdiction or the central authority in the other Member State mentioned in sub-paragraph (a).

(2) The documents required by paragraph (1) must be transmitted by a method which, in the case of direct transmission to the court with jurisdiction in the other Member State, ensures and, in any other case, will not prevent, their receipt by that court within one month of the date of the non-return order.

Amendments—SI 2012/2046.

12.60 Procedure under Article 11(7) of the Council Regulation where the court receives a non-return order made under Article 13 of the 1980 Hague Convention by a court in another Member State

(1) This rule applies where the court receives an order made by a court in another Member State for the non-return of a child.

(2) In this rule, the order for non-return of the child and the papers transmitted with that order from the court in the other Member State are referred to as 'the non-return order'.

(3) Where, at the time of receipt of the non-return order, the court is already seised of a question of parental responsibility in relation to the child, –
(a) the court officer shall immediately –
(i) serve copies of the non-return order on each party to the proceedings in which a question of parental responsibility in relation to the child is at issue; and
(ii) where the non-return order was received directly from the court or the central authority in the other Member State, transmit to the domestic Central Authority a copy of the non-return order.
(b) the court shall immediately invite the parties to the 1980 Hague Convention proceedings

to file written submissions in respect of the question of custody by a specified date, or to attend a hearing to consider the future conduct of the proceedings in the light of the non-return order.

(4) Where, at the time of receipt of the non-return order, the court is not already seised of the question of parental responsibility in relation to the child, it shall immediately –

(a) open a court file in respect of the child and assign a court reference to the file;

(b) serve a copy of the non-return order on each party to the proceedings before the court in the Member State which made that order;

(c) invite each party to file, within 3 months of notification to that party of receipt of the non-return order, submissions in the form of –

(i) an application for an order under –

(aa) the 1989 Act; or

(bb) (in the High Court only) an application under the inherent jurisdiction in respect of the child; or

(ii) where permission is required to make an application for the order in question, an application for that permission;

(d) where the non-return order was received directly from the court or central authority in the other Member State, transmit to the domestic Central Authority a copy of the non-return order.

(5) In a case to which paragraph (4) applies where no application is filed within the 3 month period provided for by paragraph (4)(c) the court must close its file in respect of the child.

(Enforcement of a subsequent judgment requiring the return of the child, made under Article 11(8) by a court examining custody of the child under Article 11(7), is dealt with in Part 31 below.)

Amendments—SI 2012/2046.

12.61 Transfer of proceedings under Article 15 of the Council Regulation or under Article 8 of the 1996 Hague Convention

(1) Where the court is considering the transfer of proceedings to the court of another Member State or Contracting State under rules 12.62 to 12.64 it will –

(a) fix a date for a hearing for the court to consider the question of transfer; and

(b) give directions as to the manner in which the parties may make representations.

(2) The court may, with the consent of all parties, deal with the question of transfer without a hearing.

(3) Directions which are in force immediately prior to the transfer of proceedings to a court in another Member State or Contracting State under rules 12.62 to 12.64 will continue to apply until the court in that other State accepts jurisdiction in accordance with the provisions of the Council Regulation or the 1996 Hague Convention (as appropriate), subject to any variation or revocation of the directions.

(4) The court or court officer will –

(a) take a note of the giving, variation or revocation of directions under this rule; and

(b) as soon as practicable serve a copy of the directions order on every party.

(5) A register of all applications and requests for transfer of jurisdiction to or from another Member State or Contracting State will be kept by the principal registry.

12.62 Application by a party for transfer of the proceedings

(1) A party may apply to the court under Article 15(1) of the Council Regulation or under Article 8(1) of the 1996 Hague Convention –

(a) to stay[(GL)] the proceedings or a specified part of the proceedings and to invite the parties to introduce a request before a court of another Member State or Contracting State; or

(b) to make a request to a court of another Member State or another Contracting State to assume jurisdiction for the proceedings, or a specified part of the proceedings.

PART III

(2) An application under paragraph (1) must be made –

(a) to the court in which the relevant parental responsibility proceedings are pending; and
(b) using the Part 18 procedure.

(3) The applicant must file the application notice and serve it on the respondents –

(a) where the application is also made under Article 11 of the Council Regulation, not less than 5 days, and
(b) in any other case, not less than 42 days,

before the hearing of the application.

12.63 Application by a court of another Member State or another Contracting State for transfer of the proceedings

(1) This rule applies where a court of another Member State or another Contracting State makes an application under Article 15(2)(c) of the Council Regulation or under Article 9 of the 1996 Hague Convention that the court having jurisdiction in relation to the proceedings transfer the proceedings or a specific part of the proceedings to the applicant court.

(2) When the court receives the application, the court officer will –

(a) as soon as practicable, notify the domestic Central Authority of the application; and
(b) serve the application, and notice of the hearing on all other parties in England and Wales not less than 5 days before the hearing of the application.

Amendments—SI 2012/2046.

12.64 Exercise by the court of its own initiative of powers to seek to transfer the proceedings

(1) The court having jurisdiction in relation to the proceedings may exercise its powers of its own initiative under Article 15 of the Council Regulation or Article 8 of the 1996 Hague Convention in relation to the proceedings or a specified part of the proceedings.

(2) Where the court proposes to exercise its powers, the court officer will give the parties not less than 5 days' notice of the hearing.

12.65 Application to High Court to make request under Article 15 of the Council Regulation or Article 9 of the 1996 Hague Convention to request transfer of jurisdiction

(1) An application for the court to request transfer of jurisdiction in a matter concerning a child from another Member State or another Contracting State under Article 15 of the Council Regulation, or Article 9 of the 1996 Hague Convention (as the case may be) must be made to the principal registry and heard in the High Court.

(2) An application must be made without notice to any other person and the court may give directions about joining any other party to the application.

(3) Where there is agreement between the court and the court or competent authority to which the request under paragraph (1) is made to transfer the matter to the courts of England and Wales, the court will consider with that other court or competent authority the specific timing and conditions for the transfer.

(4) Upon receipt of agreement to transfer jurisdiction from the court or other competent authority in the Member State, or Contracting State to which the request has been made, the court officer will serve on the applicant a notice that jurisdiction has been accepted by the courts of England and Wales.

(5) The applicant must attach the notice referred to in subparagraph (3) to any subsequent application in relation to the child.

(6) Nothing in this rule requires an application with respect to a child commenced following a transfer of jurisdiction to be made to or heard in the High Court.

(7) Upon allocation, the court to which the proceedings are allocated must immediately fix a directions hearing to consider the future conduct of the case.

12.66 Procedure where the court receives a request from the authorities of another Member State or Contracting State to assume jurisdiction in a matter concerning a child

(1) Where any court other than the High Court receives a request to assume jurisdiction in a matter concerning a child from a court or other authority which has jurisdiction in another Member State or Contracting State, that court must immediately refer the request to a Judge of the High Court for a decision regarding acceptance of jurisdiction to be made.

(2) Upon the High Court agreeing to the request under paragraph (1), the court officer will notify the parties to the proceedings before the other Member State or Contracting State of that decision, and the case must be allocated as if the application had been made in England and Wales.

(3) Upon allocation, the court to which the proceedings are allocated must immediately fix a directions hearing to consider the future conduct of the case.

(4) The court officer will serve notice of the directions hearing on all parties to the proceedings in the other Member State or Contracting State no later than 5 days before the date of that hearing.

12.67 Service of the court's order or request relating to transfer of jurisdiction under the Council Regulation or the 1996 Hague Convention

The court officer will serve an order or request relating to transfer of jurisdiction on all parties, the Central Authority of the other Member State or Contracting State, and the domestic Central Authority.

Amendments—SI 2012/2046.

12.68 Questions as to the court's jurisdiction or whether the proceedings should be stayed

(1) If at any time after issue of the application it appears to the court that under any of Articles 16 to 18 of the Council Regulation it does not or may not have jurisdiction to hear an application, or that under Article 19 of the Council Regulation or Article 13 of the 1996 Hague Convention it is or may be required to stay(GL) the proceedings or to decline jurisdiction, the court must –

(a) stay(GL) the proceedings; and
(b) fix a date for a hearing to determine jurisdiction or whether there should be a stay(GL) or other order.

(2) The court officer will serve notice of the hearing referred to at paragraph (1)(b) on the parties to the proceedings.

(3) The court must, in writing –

(a) give reasons for its decision under paragraph (1); and
(b) where it makes a finding of fact, state such finding.

(4) The court may with the consent of all the parties deal with any question as to the jurisdiction of the court, or as to whether the proceedings should be stayed(GL), without a hearing.

12.69 Request for consultation as to contemplated placement of child in England and Wales

(1) This rule applies to a request made –

(a) under Article 56 of the Council Regulation, by a court in another Member State; or
(b) under Article 33 of the 1996 Hague Convention by a court in another Contracting State

for consultation on or consent to the contemplated placement of a child in England and Wales.

(2) Where the court receives a request directly from a court in another Member State or Contracting State, the court shall, as soon as practicable after receipt of the request, notify the domestic Central Authority of the request and take the appropriate action under paragraph (4).

(3) Where it appears to the court officer that no proceedings relating to the child are pending before a court in England and Wales, the court officer must inform the domestic Central Authority of that fact and forward to the Central Authority all documents relating to the request sent by the court in the other Member State or Contracting State.

(4) Where the court receives a request forwarded by the domestic Central Authority, the court must, as soon as practicable after receipt of the request, either –

(a) where proceedings relating to the child are pending before the court, fix a directions hearing; or
(b) where proceedings relating to the child are pending before another court in England and Wales, send a copy of the request to that court.

Amendments—SI 2012/2046.

12.70 Request made by court in England and Wales for consultation as to contemplated placement of child in another Member State or Contracting State

(1) This rule applies where the court is contemplating the placement of a child in another Member State under Article 56 of the Council Regulation or another Contracting State under Article 33 of the 1996 Hague Convention, and proposes to send a request for consultation with or for the consent of the central authority or other authority having jurisdiction in the other State in relation to the contemplated placement.

(2) In this rule, a reference to 'the request' includes a reference to a report prepared for purposes of Article 33 of the 1996 Hague Convention where the request is made under that Convention.

(3) Where the court sends the request directly to the central authority or other authority having jurisdiction in the other State, it shall at the same time send a copy of the request to the domestic Central Authority.

(4) The court may send the request to the domestic Central Authority for onward transmission to the central authority or other authority having jurisdiction in the other Member State.

(5) The court should give consideration to the documents which should accompany the request.

(See Chapters 1 to 3 of this Part generally, for the procedure governing applications for an order under paragraph 19(1) of Schedule 2 to the 1989 Act permitting a local authority to arrange for any child in its care to live outside England and Wales.)

(Part 14 sets out the procedure governing applications for an order under section 84 (giving parental responsibility prior to adoption abroad) of the Adoption and Children Act 2002.)

Amendments—SI 2012/2046.

12.71 Application for a declaration as to the extent, or existence, of parental responsibility in relation to a child under Article 16 of the 1996 Hague Convention

(1) Any interested person may apply for a declaration –

(a) that a person has, or does not have, parental responsibility for a child; or
(b) as to the extent of a person's parental responsibility for a child,

where the question arises by virtue of the application of Article 16 of the 1996 Hague Convention.

(2) An application for a declaration as to the extent, or existence of a person's parental responsibility for a child by virtue of Article 16 of the 1996 Hague Convention must be made in the principal registry and heard in the High Court.

(3) An application for a declaration referred to in paragraph (1) may not be made where the question raised is otherwise capable of resolution in any other family proceedings in respect of the child.

Chapter 7

Communication of Information: Children Proceedings

Amendments—SI 2012/3061.

12.72 Interpretation

In this Chapter 'independent reviewing officer' means a person appointed in respect of a child in accordance with regulation 2A of the Review of Children's Cases Regulations 1991, or regulation 3 of the Review of Children's Cases (Wales) Regulations 2007.

Amendments—SI 2012/679.

12.73 Communication of information: general

(1) For the purposes of the law relating to contempt of court, information relating to proceedings held in private (whether or not contained in a document filed with the court) may be communicated –

- (a) where the communication is to –
  - (i) a party;
  - (ii) the legal representative of a party;
  - (iii) a professional legal adviser;
  - (iv) an officer of the service or a Welsh family proceedings officer;
  - (v) the welfare officer;
  - (vi) the Director of Legal Aid Casework (within the meaning of section 4 of the Legal Aid, Sentencing and Punishment of Offenders Act 2012);
  - (vii) an expert whose instruction by a party has been authorised by the court for the purposes of the proceedings;
  - (viii) a professional acting in furtherance of the protection of children;
  - (ix) an independent reviewing officer appointed in respect of a child who is, or has been, subject to proceedings to which this rule applies;
- (b) where the court gives permission; or
- (c) subject to any direction of the court, in accordance with rule 12.75 and Practice Direction 12G.

(2) Nothing in this Chapter permits the communication to the public at large, or any section of the public, of any information relating to the proceedings.

(3) Nothing in rule 12.75 and Practice Direction 12G permits the disclosure of an unapproved draft judgment handed down by any court.

Amendments—SI 2013/534, subject to savings.

General communication—There is no limitation on the communication of information to those people or bodies specified in r 12.73(1)(a).

Court prohibition or limitation—The wider communication of information relating to the proceedings as permitted by r 12.75 is subject to the direction of the court prohibiting or limiting the disclosure of information that would otherwise be permitted by the rules: r 12.73(1)(c). However, the power to prohibit or limit disclosure should be exercised with caution and only in limited circumstances because (i) the 2010 Rules represent a dramatic and radical change in the law, giving effect to a new public policy that it is not for the judges to whittle away, and (ii) the balance struck by r 12.73 plainly meets the requirements mandated by the Strasbourg court, even though it contains no requirement for prior judicial sanction: *Re N (Family Proceedings: Disclosure)* [2009] 2 FLR 1152, FD. In undertaking the balancing exercise, it is essential that the court has regard to the various human rights to be protected, particularly Art 8 of the Convention; the welfare of the children, although important, is not paramount: *Lewisham LBC v D (Local Authority Disclosure of DNA Samples to Police)* [2011] 1 FLR 895, FD.

Reporting Restrictions Orders—For guidance on the approach to applications for RROs, see *Re J (Reporting Restriction: Internet: Video)* [2014] 1 FLR 523, FD, *Re Al Hilli (Children Reporting Restrictions)* [2014] 1 FLR 403, FD, *City and County of Swansea v XZ and YZ* [2014] 2 FLR 1091, FD and *Birmingham City Council v Riaz and Others* [2015] 2 FLR 763, FD.

Professional legal adviser—Bodey J has held that the phrase 'professional legal adviser' includes a solicitor representing a party to family proceedings in related criminal proceedings: *Re B (A Child) (Disclosure of Evidence in Care Proceedings)* [2012] 1 FLR 142, FD. For the avoidance of any doubt, this provision does not apply to disclosure sought by the police.

Routine disclosure of experts' reports—The President has observed that he would like to see a practice develop in which expert reports would be routinely disclosed: the practice would aid the need for the family justice system to be as transparent as possible and encourage informed debate about the quality and content of expert evidence: *Re X, Y and Z (Expert Witness)* [2011] 2 FLR 1437, FD.

Release of information—In exceptional cases, the court may permit the disclosure of information into the public domain about the proceedings to correct inaccurate or false versions of events given by a party to the proceedings: *Doncaster MBC v Haigh, Tune and X (by the Children's Guardian)* [2012] 1 FLR 577, FD.

12.74 *(revoked)*

12.75 Communication of information for purposes connected with the proceedings

(1) A party or the legal representative of a party, on behalf of and upon the instructions of that party, may communicate information relating to the proceedings to any person where necessary to enable that party –

- (a) by confidential discussion, to obtain support, advice or assistance in the conduct of the proceedings;
- (b) to attend a mediation information and assessment meeting, or to engage in mediation or other forms of non-court dispute resolution;
- (c) to make and pursue a complaint against a person or body concerned in the proceedings; or
- (d) to make and pursue a complaint regarding the law, policy or procedure relating to a category of proceedings to which this Part applies.

(2) Where information is communicated to any person in accordance with paragraph (1)(a) of this rule, no further communication by that person is permitted.

(3) When information relating to the proceedings is communicated to any person in accordance with paragraphs (1)(b), (c) or (d) of this rule –

- (a) the recipient may communicate that information to a further recipient, provided that –
  - (i) the party who initially communicated the information consents to that further communication; and
  - (ii) the further communication is made only for the purpose or purposes for which the party made the initial communication; and
- (b) the information may be successively communicated to and by further recipients on as many occasions as may be necessary to fulfil the purpose for which the information was initially communicated, provided that on each such occasion the conditions in sub-paragraph (a) are met.

Amendments—SI 2014/843.

The safeguards—This rule introduces sweeping changes to the disclosure of information without the prior sanction of the court, especially r 12.75(1)(c),(d). Nevertheless, the rules contain safeguards against the improper dissemination of information relating to the proceedings –

- (i) the communication of the information must be 'necessary', which in 'the Strasbourg sense, has a meaning lying somewhere between "essential" or "indispensable", on the one hand, and "useful", "reasonable" or "desirable" on the other hand': *Spencer v Spencer* [2009] 2 FLR 1416, FD, at [31];
- (ii) r 12.75(3) imposes limitations on the use to which disclosed information may be put and to whom it may be further communicated; and
- (iii) the third limitation and safeguard – and this is fundamental – is that imposed by r 12.73(2), namely that communication to the public at large, or any section of the public, is not permitted.

See *Re N (A Child)* (above), at [64]–[70], and *Lewisham LBC v D (Local Authority Disclosure of DNA Samples to Police)* [2011] 1 FLR 895, FD and *Commissioner of Police of the Metropolis v A Local Authority and Ors* [2016] EWHC 2400 (Fam).

Note—Note the amendment to PD12G and PD14E to permit disclosure by a legal representative or a professional legal adviser to a professional indemnity insurer to notify the insurer of a claim or complaint or a potential claim or complaint and to obtain advice about the same.

Contempt of court—It may no longer be necessary to obtain prior judicial sanction for disclosures permitted by r 12.75, but someone communicating information in circumstances that would otherwise involve a contempt of court because of the operation of the AJA 1960, s 12, will be able to rely on FPR 2010, Pt 12, Ch 7 and FPR PD12G as disapplying s 12, and thus as exonerating him from the penalties of contempt, only if s 12(4) of the 1960 Act applies, that is, if he has acted in a manner 'authorised' by FPR 2010, Pt 12, Ch 7 and/or FPR PD12G.

Practice Direction 12A – Care, Supervision and Other Part 4 Proceedings: Guide to Case Management

This Practice Direction supplements FPR Part 12

1 The key stages of the court process

1.1 The Public Law Outline set out in the Table below contains an outline of –

(1) the order of the different stages of the process;
(2) the matters to be considered at the main case management hearings;
(3) the latest timescales within which the main stages of the process should take place in order to resolve the proceedings within 26 weeks.

1.2 In the Public Law Outline –

(1) 'CMH' means the Case Management Hearing;
(2) 'FCMH' means Further Case Management Hearing;
(3) 'ICO' means interim care order;
(4) 'IRH' means the Issues Resolution Hearing;
(5) 'LA' means the Local Authority which is applying for a care or supervision order or a final order in other Part 4 proceedings;
(6) 'OS' means the Official Solicitor.

1.3 In applying the provisions of FPR Part 12 and the Public Law Outline the court and the parties must also have regard to –

(1) all other relevant rules and Practice Directions and in particular –
- FPR Part 1 (Overriding Objective);
- FPR Part 4 (General Case Management Powers);
- FPR Part 15 (Representation of Protected Parties) and Practice Direction 15B (Adults Who May Be Protected Parties and Children Who May Become Protected Parties in Family Proceedings);
- FPR Part 18 (Procedure for Other Applications in Proceedings);
- FPR Part 22 (Evidence);
- FPR Part 24 (Witnesses, depositions generally and taking of evidence in Member States of the European Union);
- FPR Part 25 (Experts) and the Experts Practice Directions;
- FPR 27.6 and Practice Direction 27A (Court Bundles);
- FPR 30 (Appeals) and Practice Direction 30A (Appeals);

(2) the Allocation Rules;
(3) the Justices' Clerks Rules;
(4) President's Guidance issued from time to time on
- Distribution of business of the family court;
- Judicial continuity and deployment;
- Prescribed templates and orders;

(5) International instruments
- The Council Regulation (EC) No 2201/2003 (Brussels 2 revised);
- The 1996 Hague Convention;

(6) Guidance relating to protected parties and others with a disability –
- Protected Parties in Family Proceedings: Checklist For the Appointment of a Litigation Friend (including the Official Solicitor) (published in Family Law (January 2014);
- The Mental Capacity Act 2005 (Transfer of Proceedings) Order 2007 SI 2007/1899, relating to young people over 16 where they are likely to lack decision-making capacity at age 18.

PART III

Public Law Outline

PRE-PROCEEDINGS	
PRE-PROCEEDINGS CHECKLIST	
Annex Documents are the documents specified in the Annex to the Application Form which are to be attached to that form and filed with the court: • Social Work Chronology • Social Work Statement and Genogram • The current assessments relating to the child and/or the family and friends of the child to which the Social Work Statement refers and on which the LA relies • Care Plan • Index of Checklist Documents	Checklist documents (already existing on the LA's files) are – (a) Evidential documents including – • Previous court orders including foreign orders and judgments/reasons • Any assessment materials relevant to the key issues including capacity to litigate, section 7 and 37 reports • Single, joint or inter-agency materials (e.g., health and education/Home Office and Immigration Tribunal documents); (b) Decision-making records including – • Records of key discussions with the family • Key LA minutes and records for the child • Pre-existing care plans (e.g., child in need plan, looked after child plan and child protection plan) • Letters Before Proceedings Only Checklist documents in *(a) are to be served* with the application form Checklist Documents in *(b) are to be disclosed on request* by any party Checklist documents are *not* to be – • filed with the court unless the court directs otherwise; and • older than 2 years before the date of issue of the proceedings unless reliance is placed on the same in the LA's evidence

STAGE 1 – ISSUE AND ALLOCATION

DAY 1 AND DAY 2 (see interpretation section)

On Day 1 (Day of issue):

- The LA files the Application Form and Annex Documents and sends copies to Cafcass/CAFCASS Cymru
- The LA notifies the court of the need for an urgent preliminary case management hearing or an urgent contested ICO hearing where this is known or expected

Court officer issues application

Within a day of issue (Day 2):

- Court considers jurisdiction in a case with an international element
- Court considers initial allocation to specified level of judge, in accordance with the Allocation Rules and any President's Guidance on the distribution of business
- LA serves the Application Form, Annex Documents and evidential Checklist Documents on the parties together with the notice of date and time of CMH and any urgent hearing

- Court gives standard directions on Issue and Allocation including:
  - Checking compliance with Pre-Proceedings Checklist including service of any missing Annex Documents
  - Appointing Children's Guardian (to be allocated by Cafcass/CAFCASS Cymru)
  - Appointing solicitor for the child only if necessary
  - Appointing (if the person to be appointed consents) a litigation friend for any protected party or any non-subject child who is a party, including the OS where appropriate
  - Identifying whether a request has been made or should be made to a Central Authority or other competent authority in a foreign state or a consular authority in England and Wales in a case with an international element
  - Filing and service of a LA Case Summary
  - Filing and service of a Case Analysis by the Children's Guardian
  - Filing and Serving the Parents' Response
  - Sending a request for disclosure to, e.g., the police or health service body
  - Filing and serving an application for permission relating to experts under Part 25 on a date prior to the advocates meeting for the CMH
  - Directing the solicitor for the child to arrange an advocates' meeting no later than 2 business days before the CMH
  - Listing the CMH
- Court considers any request for an urgent preliminary case management hearing or an urgent contested ICO hearing and where necessary lists the hearing and gives additional directions.
- Court officer sends copy Notice of Hearing of the CMH and any urgent hearing by email to Cafcass/CAFCASS Cymru.

STAGE 2 – CASE MANAGEMENT HEARING

ADVOCATES' MEETING (including any litigants in person)	**CASE MANAGEMENT HEARING**
No later than 2 business days before CMH (or FCMH if it is necessary)	CMH: Not before day 12 and not later than day 18 A FCMH is to be held only if necessary, it is to be listed as soon as possible and in any event no later than day 25
• Consider information on the Application Form and Annex documents, the LA Case Summary, and the Case Analysis • Identify the parties' positions to be recited in the draft Case Management Order • Identify the parties' positions about jurisdiction, in particular arising out of any international element • If necessary, identify proposed experts and draft questions in accordance with Part 25 and the Experts Practice Directions • Identify any disclosure that in the advocates' views is necessary • Immediately notify the court of the need for a contested ICO hearing and any issue about allocation • LA advocate to file a draft Case Management Order in prescribed form with court by 11a.m. on the business day before the CMH and/or FCMH	• Court gives detailed case management directions, including: – Considering jurisdiction in a case with an international element; – Confirming allocation – Drawing up the timetable for the child and the timetable for the proceedings and considering if an extension is necessary – Identifying additional parties, intervenors and representation (including confirming that Cafcass/CAFCASS Cymru have allocated a Children's Guardian and that a litigation friend is appointed for any protected party or non-subject child) – Giving directions for the determination of any disputed issue about litigation capacity

PART III

	– Identifying the key issues – Identifying the evidence necessary to enable the court to resolve the key issues – Deciding whether there is a real issue about threshold to be resolved – Determining any application made under Part 25 and otherwise ensuring compliance with Part 25 where it is necessary for expert(s) to be instructed – Identifying any necessary disclosure and if appropriate giving directions – Giving directions for any concurrent or proposed placement order proceedings – Ensuring compliance with the court's directions – If a FCMH is necessary, directing an advocates' meeting and Case Analysis if required – Directing filing of any threshold agreement, final evidence and Care Plan and responses to those documents for the IRH – Directing a Case Analysis for the IRH – Directing an advocates' meeting for the IRH – Listing (any FCMH) IRH, Final Hearing (including early Final Hearing), as appropriate – Giving directions for special measures and/or interpreters and intermediaries – Issuing the Case Management Order

STAGE 3 – ISSUES RESOLUTION HEARING	
ADVOCATES' MEETING (including any litigants in person)	**IRH**
No later than 7 business days before the IRH	As directed by the court, in accordance with the timetable for the proceedings
• Review evidence and the positions of the parties • Identify the advocates' views of – – the remaining key issues and how the issues may be resolved or narrowed at the IRH including by the making of final orders – the further evidence which is required to be heard to enable the key issues to be resolved or narrowed at the IRH – the evidence that is relevant and the witnesses that are required at the final hearing – the need for a contested hearing and/or time for oral evidence to be given at the IRH	• Court identifies the key issue(s) (if any) to be determined and the extent to which those issues can be resolved or narrowed at the IRH • Court considers whether the IRH can be used as a final hearing • Court resolves or narrows the issues by hearing evidence • Court identifies the evidence to be heard on the issues which remain to be resolved at the final hearing • Court gives final case management directions including: – Any extension of the timetable for the proceedings which is necessary

• LA advocate to – – notify the court immediately of the outcome of the discussion at the meeting – file a draft Case Management Order with the court by 11a.m. on the business day before the IRH	– Filing of the threshold agreement or a statement of facts/issues remaining to be determined – Filing of: o Final evidence and Care Plan o Case Analysis for Final Hearing (if required) o Witness templates o Skeleton arguments – Judicial reading list/reading time, including time estimate and an estimate for judgment writing time – Ensuring Compliance with PD27A (the Bundles Practice Direction) – Listing the Final Hearing • Court issues Case Management Order

2 Flexible powers of the court

2.1 Attention is drawn to the flexible powers of the court either following the issue of the application or at any other stage in the proceedings.

2.2 The court may give directions without a hearing including setting a date for the Final Hearing or a period within which the Final Hearing will take place. The steps, which the court will ordinarily take at the various stages of the proceedings provided for in the Public Law Outline, may be taken by the court at another stage in the proceedings if the circumstances of the case merit this approach.

2.3 The flexible powers of the court include the ability for the court to cancel or repeat a particular hearing. For example, if the issue on which the case turns can with reasonable practicability be crystallised and resolved by taking evidence at an IRH then such a flexible approach must be taken in accordance with the overriding objective and to secure compliance with section 1(2) of the 1989 Act and resolving the proceedings within 26 weeks or the period for the time being specified by the court.

2.4 Where a party has requested an urgent hearing a) to enable the court to give immediate directions or orders to facilitate any case management issue which is to be considered at the CMH, or b) to decide whether an ICO is necessary, the court may list such a hearing at any appropriate time before the CMH and give directions for that hearing. It is anticipated that an urgent preliminary case management hearing will only be necessary to consider issues such as jurisdiction, parentage, party status, capacity to litigate, disclosure and whether there is, or should be, a request to a Central Authority or other competent authority in a foreign state or consular authority in England and Wales in an international case. It is not intended that any urgent hearing will delay the CMH.

2.5 Where it is anticipated that oral evidence may be required at the CMH, FCMH or IRH, the court must be notified in accordance with Stages 2 and 3 of the Public Law Outline well in advance and directions sought for the conduct of the hearing.

2.6 It is expected that full case management will take place at the CMH. It follows that the parties must be prepared to deal with all relevant case management issues, as identified in Stage 2 of the Public Law Outline. A FCMH should only be directed where necessary and must not be regarded as a routine step in proceedings.

3 Compliance with pre-proceedings checklist

3.1 It is recognised that in a small minority of cases the circumstances are such that the safety and welfare of the child may be jeopardised if the start of proceedings is delayed until all of the

PART III

documents appropriate to the case and referred to in the Pre-proceedings Checklist are available. The safety and welfare of the child should never be put in jeopardy by delaying issuing proceedings whether because of lack of documentation or otherwise. (Nothing in this Practice Direction affects an application for an emergency protection order under section 44 of the 1989 Act). Also, where an application for an interim order is urgent, then the hearing of that application is NOT expected to be postponed until the Case Management Hearing. The Case Management Hearing is still to be held not before day 12 and not later than day 18 in accordance with the Public Law Outline and guidance in this Practice Direction. If an urgent preliminary Case Management Hearing or an urgent contested ICO hearing is held before the CMH, the court should not dispense with the CMH unless all of the parties have been sufficiently prepared and the court has been able to deal with all case management issues which would have come before it at the CMH.

3.2 The court recognises that preparation may need to be varied to suit the circumstances of the case. In cases where any of the Annex Documents required to be attached to the Application Form are not available at the time of issue of the application, the court will consider making directions on issue about when any missing documentation is to be filed. The expectation is that there must be a good reason why one or more of the documents are not available. Further directions relating to any missing documentation will also be made at the Case Management Hearing.

4 Allocation

4.1 The court considers the allocation of proceedings in accordance with the Allocation Rules and any Guidance issued by the President on distribution of business of the family court. The justices' clerk or assistant justices' clerk (with responsibility for gatekeeping and allocation of proceedings) will discuss initial allocation with a district judge (with responsibility for allocation and gatekeeping of proceedings) as provided for in any Guidance issued by the President on distribution of business of the family court. The expectation is that, wherever possible, any question relating to allocation of the proceedings will be considered at the CMH.

5 The timetable for the child and the timetable for proceedings

5.1 The timetable for the proceedings:

(1) The court will draw up a timetable for the proceedings with a view to disposing of the application –
  (a) without delay; and
  (b) in any event within 26 weeks beginning with the day on which the application was issued in accordance with section 32(1)(a)(ii) of the Children Act 1989.

(2) The court, when drawing up or revising a timetable under paragraph (1), will in particular have regard to –
  (a) the impact which the timetable or any revised timetable would have on the welfare of the child to whom the application relates; and
  (b) the impact which the timetable or any revised timetable would have on the duration and conduct of the proceedings.

5.2 The impact which the timetable for the proceedings, any revision or extension of that timetable would have on the welfare of the child to whom the application relates are matters to which the court is to have particular regard. The court will use the Timetable for the Child to assess the impact of these matters on the welfare of the child and to draw up and revise the timetable for the proceedings.

5.3 The 'Timetable for the Child' is the timetable set by the court which takes into account dates which are important to the child's welfare and development.

5.4 The timetable for the proceedings is set having particular regard to the Timetable for the Child and the Timetable for the Child needs to be reviewed regularly. Where adjustments are made to the Timetable for the Child, the timetable for the proceedings will have to be reviewed consistently with resolving the proceedings within 26 weeks or the period for the time being specified by the court.

5.5 Examples of the dates the court will record and take into account when setting the Timetable for the Child are the dates of –

(1) any formal review by the Local Authority of the case of a looked after child (within the meaning of section 22(1) of the 1989 Act);
(2) any significant educational steps, including the child taking up a place at a new school and, where applicable, any review by the Local Authority of a statement of the child's special educational needs;
(3) any health care steps, including assessment by a paediatrician or other specialist;
(4) any review of Local Authority plans for the child, including any plans for permanence through adoption, Special Guardianship or placement with parents or relatives;
(5) any change or proposed change of the child's placement;
(6) any significant change in the child's social or family circumstances; or
(7) any timetable for the determination of an issue in a case with an international element.

5.6 To identify the Timetable for the Child, the applicant is required to provide the information needed about the significant steps in the child's life in the Application Form and the Social Work Statement and to update this information regularly taking into account information received from others involved in the child's life such as the parties, members of the child's family, the person who is caring for the child, the children's guardian, the Independent Reviewing Officer , the child's key social worker and any Central Authority or competent authority in a foreign state or a consular authority in England and Wales in a case with an international element.

5.7 Where more than one child is the subject of the proceedings, the court should consider and will set a Timetable for the Child for each child. The children may not all have the same timetable, and the court will consider the appropriate progress of the proceedings in relation to each child.

5.8 Where there are parallel care proceedings and criminal proceedings against a person connected with the child for a serious offence against the child, linked directions hearings should where practicable take place as the case progresses. The timing of the proceedings in a linked care and criminal case should appear in the Timetable for the Child. The time limit of resolving the proceedings within 26 weeks applies unless a longer timetable has been set by the court in order to resolve the proceedings justly in accordance with section 32(1)(a)(ii) and (5) of the 1989 Act. Early disclosure and listing of hearings is necessary in proceedings in a linked care and criminal case.

6 *Extensions to the timetable for proceedings*

6.1 The court is required to draw up a timetable for proceedings with a view to disposing of the application without delay and in any event within 26 weeks. If proceedings can be resolved earlier, then they should be. A standard timetable and process is expected to be followed in respect of the giving of standard directions on issue and allocation and other matters which should be carried out by the court on issue, including setting and giving directions for the Case Management Hearing.

6.2 Having regard to the circumstances of the particular case, the court may consider that it is necessary to extend the time by which the proceedings are to be resolved beyond 26 weeks to enable the court to resolve the proceedings justly (see section 32 (5) of the 1989 Act). When making this decision, the court is to take account of the guidance that extensions are not to be granted routinely and are to be seen as requiring specific justification (see section 32(7) of the 1989 Act). The decision and reason(s) for extending a case should be recorded in writing (in the Case Management Order) and orally stated in court, so that all parties are aware of the reasons for delay in the case (see FPR 12.26C). The Case Management Order must contain a record of this information, as well as the impact of the court's decision on the welfare of the child.

PART III

6.3 The court may extend the period within which proceedings are intended to be resolved on its own initiative or on application. Applications for an extension should, wherever possible, only be made so that they are considered at any hearing for which a date has been fixed or for which a date is about to be fixed. Where a date for a hearing has been fixed, a party who wishes to make an application at that hearing but does not have sufficient time to file an application notice should as soon as possible inform the court (if possible in writing) and, if possible, the other parties of the nature of the application and the reason for it. The party should then make the application orally at the hearing.

6.4 If the court agrees an extension is necessary, an initial extension to the time limit may be granted for up to eight weeks (or less if directed) in order to resolve the case justly (see section 32(8) of the 1989 Act). If more time is necessary, in order to resolve the proceedings justly, a further extension of up to eight weeks may be agreed by the court. There is no limit on the number of extensions that may be granted in a particular case.

6.5 If the court considers that the timetable for the proceedings will require an extension beyond the next eight week period in order to resolve the proceedings justly, the Case Management Order should –

(1) state the reason(s) why it is necessary to have a further extension;
(2) fix the date of the next effective hearing (which might be in a period shorter than a further eight weeks); and
(3) indicate whether it is appropriate for the next application for an extension of the timetable to be considered on paper.

6.6 The expectation is that, subject to paragraph 6.5, extensions should be considered at a hearing and that a court will not approve proposals for the management of a case under FPR 12.15 where the consequence of those proposals is that the case is unlikely to be resolved within 26 weeks or other period for the time being allowed for resolution of the proceedings. In accordance with FPR 4.1(3)(e), the court may hold a hearing and receive evidence by telephone or by using any other method of direct oral communication. When deciding whether to extend the timetable, the court must have regard to the impact of any ensuing timetable revision on the welfare of the child (see section 32(6) of the 1989 Act).

7 *Interpretation*

7.1 In this Practice Direction –

'Allocation Rules' mean any rules relating to composition of the court and distribution of business made under section 31D of the Matrimonial and Family Proceedings Act 1984;

'Care Plan' is a separate document from the evidence that is filed by the local authority. It is a 'section 31A plan' referred to in section 31A of the 1989 Act which complies with guidance as to content issued by the Secretary of State;

'Case Analysis' means a written or, if there is insufficient time for a written, an oral outline of the case from the perspective of the child's guardian or Welsh family proceedings officer for the CMH or FCMH (where one is necessary) and IRH or as otherwise directed by the court, incorporating an analysis of the key issues that need to be resolved in the case including –

(a) a threshold analysis;
(b) a case management analysis, including an analysis of the timetable for the proceedings, an analysis of the Timetable for the Child and the evidence which any party proposes is necessary to resolve the issues;
(c) a parenting capability analysis;
(d) a child impact analysis, including an analysis of the ascertainable wishes and feelings of the child and the impact on the welfare of the child of any application to adjourn a hearing or extend the timetable for the proceedings;

(e) an early permanence analysis including an analysis of the proposed placements and contact framework; by reference to a welfare and proportionality analysis;

(f) whether and if so what communication it is proposed there should be during the proceedings with the child by the court;

'Case Management Order' is the prescribed form of order referred to in any Guidance issued by the President from time to time on prescribed templates and orders;

'Day' means 'business day'. 'Day 1' is the day of issue and 'Day 2' is the next business day following the day of issue of proceedings. 'Day 12', 'Day 18' and 'Day 25' are respectively the 11th, 17th and the 24th business days after the day of issue of proceedings (Day 1). '26 weeks' means 26 calendar weeks beginning on the day of issue of proceedings (Day 1);

'Experts Practice Directions' mean –

(a) Practice Direction 25A (Experts – Emergencies and Pre Proceedings Instructions);

(b) Practice Direction 25B (The Duties of An Expert, The Expert's Report and Arrangements For An Expert To Attend Court);

(c) Practice Direction 25C (Children's Proceedings – The Use Of Single Joint Experts and The Process Leading to An Expert Being Instructed or Expert Evidence Being Put Before the Court);

(d) Practice Direction 25E (Discussions Between Experts in Family Proceedings);

'Genogram' means a family tree, setting out in diagrammatic form the child's family and extended family members and their relationship with the child;

'Index of Checklist Documents' means a list of Checklist Documents referred to in the Public Law Outline Pre-Proceedings Checklist which is divided into two parts with Part A being the documents referred to in column 2, paragraph (a) of the Pre- Proceedings Checklist and Part B being those referred to in column 2, paragraph (b) of the Pre-proceedings Checklist;

'International instruments'

'the Council Regulation (EC) No 2201/2003 (Brussels 2 revised)' means Council Regulation (EC) No 2201/2003 of 27 November 2003 on jurisdiction and the recognition and enforcement of judgments in matrimonial matters and in matters of parental responsibility;

'The 1996 Hague Convention' means the Convention on Jurisdiction, Applicable Law, Recognition, Enforcement and Co-operation in Respect of Parental Responsibility and Measures for the Protection of Children;

'Justices' Clerks Rules' means any rules made under section 310 of the Matrimonial and Family Proceedings Act 1984 enabling functions of the family court or judge of that court to be carried out by a justices' clerk or assistant to a justices' clerk;

'Letter Before Proceedings' means any letter from the Local Authority containing written notification to the parents and others with parental responsibility for the child of the Local Authority's likely intention to apply to court for a care or supervision order and any related subsequent correspondence confirming the Local Authority's position;

'Local Authority Case Summary' means a document prepared by the Local Authority legal representative for each case management hearing in the form referred to in any Guidance issued by the President from time to time on prescribed templates and orders;

'Parents' Response' means a document from either or both of the parents containing

(a) in no more than two pages, the parents' response to the Threshold Statement, and

(b) the parents' placement proposals including the identity and whereabouts of all relatives and friends they propose be considered by the court;

(c) Information which may be relevant to a person's capacity to litigate including information about any referrals to mental health services and adult services;

'Section 7 report' means any report under section 7 of the 1989 Act;

'Section 37 report' means any report by the Local Authority to the court as a result of a direction under section 37 of the 1989 Act;

'Social Work Chronology' means a schedule containing –

(a) a succinct summary of the length of involvement of the local authority with the family and in particular with the child;

(b) a succinct summary of the significant dates and events in the child's life in chronological order – i.e. a running record up to the issue of the proceedings; providing such information under the following headings –

(i) serial number;

(ii) date;

(iii) event-detail;

(iv) witness or document reference (where applicable);

'Social Work Statement' means a statement prepared by the Local Authority limited to the following evidence –

Summary

(a) The order sought;

(b) Succinct summary of reasons with reference as appropriate to the Welfare Checklist;

Family

(c) Family members and relationships especially the primary carers and significant adults/other children;

(d) Genogram;

Threshold

(e) Precipitating events;

(f) Background circumstances;

(i) summary of children's services involvement cross-referenced to the chronology;

(ii) previous court orders and emergency steps;

(iii) previous assessments;

(g) Summary of significant harm and or likelihood of significant harm which the LA will seek to establish by evidence or concession;

Parenting capability

(h) Assessment of child's needs;

(i) Assessment of parental capability to meet needs;

(j) Analysis of why there is a gap between parental capability and the child's needs;

(k) Assessment of other significant adults who may be carers;

Child impact

(l) Wishes and feelings of the child(ren);

(m) Timetable for the Child;

(n) Delay and timetable for the proceedings;

Permanence and contact

(o) Parallel planning;

(p) Realistic placement options by reference to a welfare and proportionality analysis;

(q) Contact framework;

Case Management

(r) Evidence and assessments necessary and outstanding;

(s) Any information about any person's litigation capacity, mental health issues, disabilities or vulnerabilities that is relevant to their capability to participate in the proceedings; and

(t) Case management proposals.

'Standard Directions on Issue and Allocation' means directions given by the court on issue and upon allocation in the prescribed form referred to in any Guidance issued by the President from time to time on prescribed templates and orders;

'Threshold Statement' means a written outline by the legal representative of the LA in the application form of the facts which the LA will seek to establish by evidence or concession to satisfy the threshold criteria under s 31(2) of the 1989 Act limited to no more than 2 pages;

'Welfare Checklist' means the list of matters which is set out in section 1(3) of the 1989 Act and to which the court is to have particular regard in accordance with section (1)(3) and (4).

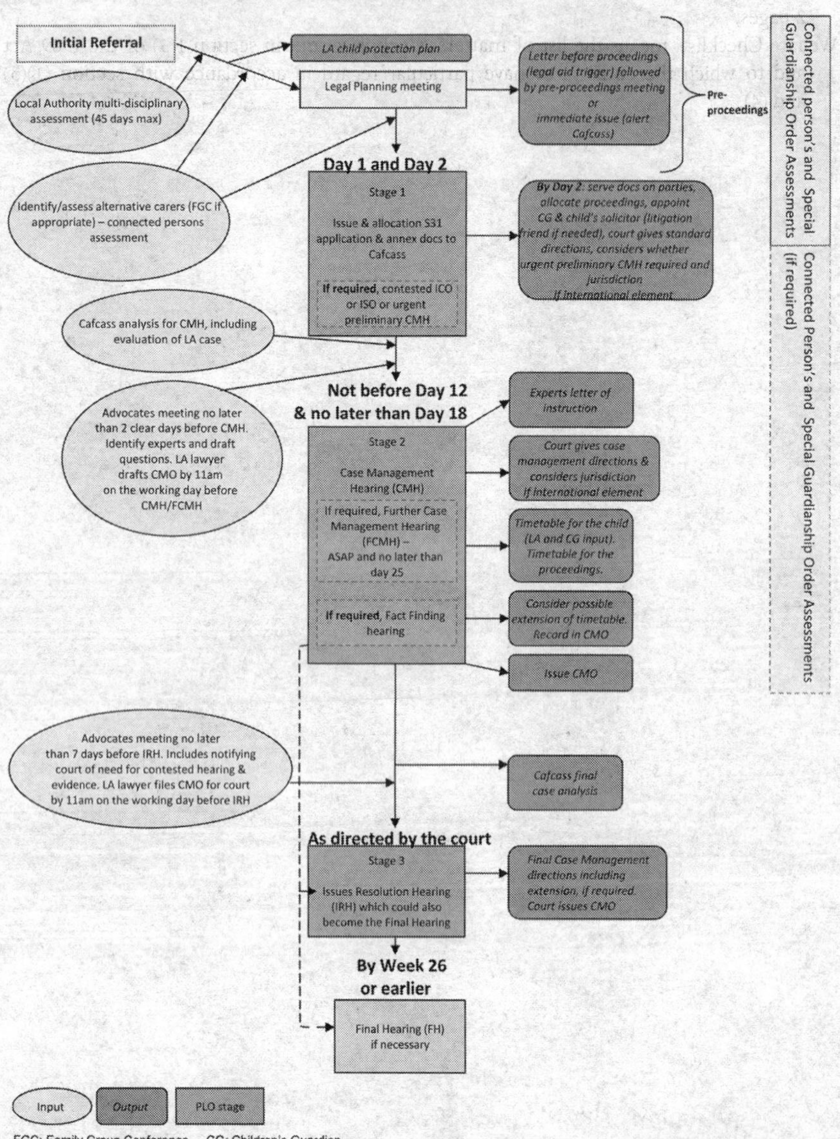

FGC: Family Group Conference CG: Children's Guardian
CMO: Case Management Order ICO: Interim Care Order ISO: Interim Supervision Order
Note: The court may give directions without a hearing, including setting a date or period for the FH.
Reference to Cafcass includes CAFCASS CYMRU

Practice Direction 12B – Child Arrangements Programme

This Practice Direction supplements FPR Part 12

1 *When does the Child Arrangements Programme Apply?*

1.1 The Child Arrangements Programme (the 'CAP') applies where a dispute arises between separated parents and/or families about arrangements concerning children.

1.2 The CAP is designed to assist families to reach safe and child-focused agreements for their child, where possible out of the court setting. If parents / families are unable to reach agreement, and a court application is made, the CAP encourages swift resolution of the dispute through the court.

1.3 It is well-recognised that negotiated agreements between adults generally enhance long-term co-operation, and are better for the child concerned. Therefore, separated parents and families are strongly encouraged to attempt to resolve their disputes concerning the child outside of the court system. This may also be quicker and cheaper.

2 *Signposting Services, Parenting Plans, & Public Funding*

2.1 **Services**: Where a dispute arises in relation to a child, or children, parents and families are encouraged to obtain advice and support as soon as possible.

2.2 There are many services available for such families, who seek advice about resolving disputes concerning their child.

2.3 The following services are recommended:

(1) For more information about family mediation and to find the nearest mediation service (including those providing a MIAM): www.familymediationcouncil.org.uk;

(2) For a Guide about children and the family courts for separating parents (including representing yourself in court): the form 'CB7': http://www.cafcass.gov.uk/media/168195/cb7-eng.pdf

(3) For Cafcass (England): www.cafcass.gov.uk;

(4) For CAFCASS Cymru (Wales): www.wales.gov.uk/cafcasscymru;

(5) To find a legal adviser or family mediator: http://find-legal-advice.justice.gov.uk;

(6) To check whether you can get financial help (legal aid) to pay for non-court dispute resolution, &/or advice and representation at court, and to find a legal aid solicitor or mediator: https://www.gov.uk/check-legal-aid

(7) For general advice about sorting out arrangements for children, the use of post-separation mediation, &/or going to court: http://www.advicenow.org.uk; http://www.advicenow.org.uk/advicenow-guides/family/sorting-out-arrangements-for-your-children/

(8) For general advice on separation services and options for resolving disputes: www.sortingoutseparation.org.uk;

(9) For general advice about sorting out arrangements for children: http://theparentconnection.org.uk/

(10) For advice about Contact Centres, which are neutral places where children of separated families can enjoy contact with their non-resident parents and sometimes other family members, in a comfortable and safe environment; and information about where they are: www.naccc.org.uk;

(11) For the form to apply for a child arrangements order: https://www.gov.uk/looking-after-children-divorce/apply-for-court-order;

(12) For help with taking a case to court without a lawyer, the Personal Support Unit: http://thepsu.org/;

(13) For guidance on representing yourself at court, including a list of commonly used terms that you may come across: http://www.barcouncil.org.uk/instructing-a-barrister/representing-yourself-in-court/;

(14) For advice about finding and using a family law solicitor see: Law Society http://www.lawsociety.org.uk, and Resolution (family law solicitors): http://www.resolution.org.uk;

(15) For advice about finding using a family law barrister: see http://www.barcouncil.org.uk/about-the-bar/find-a-barrister/, and for arrangements for using a barrister directly see http://www.barcouncil.org.uk/instructing-a-barrister/public-access/.

Note—The web address in para 2.2(2) is no longer valid, but useful resources can be found at *www.cafcass.gov.uk/grown-ups/supporting-separating-parents-in-dispute-pilot.aspx*. The web address in para 2.2(13) is now *www.barcouncil.org.uk/using-a-barrister/representing-yourself-in-court/*. The web addresses in para 2.2(15) are now *www.barcouncil.org.uk/using-a-barrister/find-a-barrister/* and *www.barcouncil.org.uk/using-a-barrister/public-access/*.

2.4 **Parenting Plan**: A Parenting Plan is widely recognised as being a useful tool for separated parents to identify, agree and set out in writing arrangements for their children; such a plan could appropriately be used as the basis for discussion about a dispute which has arisen. It is likely to be useful in any event for assisting arrangements between separated parents.

2.5 The Parenting Plan should cover all practical aspects of care for the child, and should reflect a shared commitment to the child and his/her future, with particular emphasis on parental communication (learning how to deal with differences), living arrangements, money, religion, education, health care and emotional well-being.

2.6 A Parenting Plan is designed to help separated parents (and their families) to work out the best possible arrangements for the child; the plan should be understood by everyone, including (where the child is of an appropriate age and understanding) the child concerned.

2.7 For help on preparing a Parenting Plan, see:

(1) Cafcass 'Putting Your Children First: A Guide for Separated Parents' (see also paragraph 4 below);

(2) A draft of a Parenting Plan for parents or families to complete: http://www.cafcass.gov.uk/media/190788/parenting_plan_final_web.pdf.

(3) A draft of a Parenting Plan prepared by CAFCASS Cymru for parents or families to complete:
http://gov.wales/docs/cafcass/publications/071015ParentingPlanEn.pdf (this links to the draft plan in English) or
http://gov.wales/docs/cafcass/publications/071015ParentingPlanCy.pdf (this links to the draft plan in Welsh).

2.8 **Publicly funded mediation and/or legal advice**: If parents need access to mediation, and legal advice in support of that mediation, they may be eligible for public funding. The Legal Aid Agency (LAA) will provide funding for Mediation Information and Assessment Meetings (MIAMs) and family mediation for all those who are eligible:

(1) Where at least one party is eligible, the LAA will cover the costs of both parties to attend a MIAM to encourage any non-eligible client to find out about the benefits and suitability of mediation without incurring any costs.

(2) The LAA will provide public funding for eligible parties to participate in family mediation and they may also receive some independent legal advice connected to the mediation process and where a settlement is reached can receive legal assistance to draft and issue proceedings to obtain a consent order.

(3) Parties may find out if they are likely to be eligible for legal aid at the following link: https://www.gov.uk/check-legal-aid

(4) To find the nearest publicly funded mediation service a client can use the search at familymediationcouncil.org.uk. Publicly funded legal advisors can be found at: https://www.gov.uk/check-legal-aid

2.9 Public funding for legal advice and/or representation at court is available in limited circumstances. Further information can be found here: http://www.justice.gov.uk/legal-aid-for-private-family-matters

3 Explanation of terms

3.1 Some of the terms used in this document, and in the websites referred to above, may not be familiar to those who seek help and support.

3.2 A guide to some of the relevant terms is attached in the Annex at the end of this document.

4 The child in the dispute

4.1 In making any arrangements with respect to a child, the child's welfare must be the highest priority.

4.2 Children and young people should be at the centre of all decision-making. This accords with the Family Justice Young People's Board Charter (https://www.cafcass.gov.uk/media/179714/fjypb_national_charter_1013.pdf).

4.3 The child or young person should feel that their needs, wishes and feelings have been considered in the arrangements which are made for them.

4.4 Children should be involved, to the extent which is appropriate given their age and level of understanding, in making the arrangements which affect them. This is just as relevant where:

(1) the parties are making arrangements between themselves (which may be recorded in a Parenting Plan),

as when:

(2) arrangements are made in the context of dispute resolution outside away from the court,

and/or

(3) the court is required to make a decision about the arrangements for the child.

4.5 If an application for a court order has been issued, the judge may want to know the child's view. This may be communicated to the judge in one of a number of ways:

(1) By a Cafcass officer (in Wales, a Welsh Family Proceedings Officer (WFPO)) providing a report to the court which sets out the child's wishes and feelings;

(2) By the child being encouraged (by the Cafcass officer or WFPO, or a parent or relative) to write a letter to the court;

(3) In the limited circumstances described in paragraph 18 below, by the child being a party to the proceedings;

and/or:

(4) By the judge meeting with the child, in accordance with approved Guidance (currently the FJC Guidelines for Judges Meeting Children subject to Family Proceedings (April 2010)). http://www.judiciary.gov.uk/JCO%2fDocuments%2fFJC%2fvoc%2fGuidelines_+Judges_seeing_+Children.pdf

Note—The web address is *www.judiciary.gov.uk/wp-content/uploads/JCO/Documents/FJC/voc/Guidelines_+Judges_seeing_+Children.pdf*.

5 Non-court resolution of disputed arrangements for children

5.1 Dispute resolution services, including mediation, are available to provide opportunities for parents and families to work in a positive and constructive way, and should be actively considered and attempted where it is safe and appropriate to do so. Information about mediation and other non-court dispute resolution is available widely (see 'Signposting Services for Families' – paragraph 2 above).

5.2 It is not expected that those who are the victims of domestic violence should attempt to mediate or otherwise participate in forms of non-court dispute resolution. It is also recognised that drug and/or alcohol misuse and/or mental illness are likely to prevent couples from making safe use of mediation or similar services; these risk factors (which can be discussed at a MIAM – see below, paragraph 5.3) are likely to have an impact on arrangements for the child. Court Orders, including those made by consent, must be scrutinised to ensure that they are safe and take account of any risk factors, in accordance with Practice Direction 12J FPR.

5.3 **Attendance at Mediation Information and Assessment Meeting ('MIAM')**: Subject to paragraph 5.6 (below), before making a family application to the court (a 'relevant family application' as defined in paragraph 23 below), the person who is considering making such application must attend a family MIAM. A prospective respondent is expected to attend a MIAM – whether this is a separate MIAM or the same MIAM attended by the prospective applicant. At the MIAM, information will be provided about mediation of disputes of the kind to which the application relates, ways in which the dispute may be resolved otherwise than by the court, and the suitability of mediation (or any other way of resolving the dispute) for trying to resolve the dispute. The mediator will also assess whether there has been, or is a risk of,

(1) domestic violence, and/or
(2) harm by a prospective party to a child that would be the subject of the application.

5.4 It is the responsibility of the prospective applicant (or that person's legal representative) to contact a family mediator to arrange attendance at a MIAM.

5.5 Only an authorised family mediator can carry out a MIAM. An authorised family mediator is a person identified by the Family Mediation Council as qualified to conduct a MIAM.

5.6 A prospective applicant is not required to attend a MIAM where one of the circumstances set out in rule 3.8(1) or 3.8(2) FPR applies.

5.7 Information on how to find an authorised family mediator may be obtained from www.familymediationcouncil.org.uk website which hosts the 'find a local family mediator' database (see also 'Signposting Services for Families' – paragraph 2 above).

5.8 The prospective applicant (or the prospective applicant's legal representative) should provide the mediator with contact details for the other party or parties to the dispute ('the prospective respondent(s)'), so that the mediator can contact the prospective respondent(s) to discuss their willingness and availability to attend a MIAM.

5.9 The prospective applicant and, where they agree to do so, the prospective respondent(s), should then attend a MIAM arranged by the mediator. If the parties are willing to attend together and where it is assessed by the mediator to be safe, the meeting may be conducted jointly; otherwise, separate meetings will be held.

5.10 The Family Mediation Council sets the requirements for mediators who conduct MIAMs. In summary, a mediator who arranges a MIAM with one or more parties to a dispute should consider any risk factors present and how these should be managed, and should also consider with the party or parties concerned whether public funding may be available to meet the cost of the meeting and any subsequent mediation. Where neither of the parties is eligible for, or wishes to seek, public funding, any charge made by the mediator for the MIAM will be the responsibility of the party or parties attending, in accordance with any agreement made with the mediator.

5.11 Mediation is a confidential process; none of the parties to the mediation may provide information to the court as to the content of any discussions held in mediation and/or the reasons why agreement was not reached. Similarly, the mediator may not provide such information, unless the mediator considers that a safeguarding issue arises.

5.12 However, it is important that the parties, or either of them, introduce at the MIAM (or any subsequent court application) any other evidence of attempts to resolve a dispute and to focus on the needs of the child.

6 *Resolution of disputed arrangements for children through the Court*

6.1 The judge is obliged to consider, at every stage of court proceedings, whether non-court dispute resolution is appropriate.

6.2 The parties should also actively consider non-court dispute resolution even if proceedings are issued and are ongoing.

6.3 If the court considers that another form of dispute resolution is appropriate, the court may direct that the proceedings, or a hearing in the proceedings, be adjourned for such specified period as it considers appropriate:

(1) to enable the parties to obtain information and advice about non-court dispute resolution; and
(2) where the parties agree, to enable non-court dispute resolution to take place.

6.4 Where the court adjourns proceedings, it shall give directions about the timing and method by which the parties must tell the court if any of the issues in the proceedings have been resolved.

6.5 It is to be noted that some courts operate an at-court mediation scheme, and at-court MIAMs, with providers contracted to the Legal Aid Agency. Some mediators may prefer to conduct mediation outside of the court premises. A mediation assessment may be possible at court; alternatively, the court may help in making an appointment with a local mediator for a MIAM or for mediation. Information about mediation arrangements should be advertised in the local court.

7 *Local Good Practice*

7.1 The CAP is designed to provide a framework for a consistent approach to the resolution of the issues in private family law in England & Wales.

7.2 Local practices and initiatives can be operated in addition to, and within, the framework

8 *Application to court*

8.1 Unless one of the MIAM exemptions applies (see rule 3.8 FPR), an application to court for determination of most issues concerning a child (see the definition of 'relevant family application' in rule 3.6 FPR and paragraphs 11 and 12 of PD3A) can be made only after a MIAM has taken place (at which meeting mediation and other forms of non-court dispute resolution will have been considered). One of the exemptions may be that the case is urgent, in which case see 'Urgent and Without Notice Applications' in paragraph 12 below. The grounds for urgency are defined in rule 3.8(c) FPR.

8.2 The application for a child arrangements order or other Children Act 1989 private law order shall be made on the relevant prescribed form.

8.3 For section 8 Children Act 1989 applications, the applicant will be required, on the form C100, to confirm attendance at a MIAM or specify that an exemption applies **unless** the application is for a consent order, or if the application concerns a child who is the subject of ongoing emergency proceedings, care proceedings or supervision proceedings, or if the child concerned is already the subject of an emergency protection order, care order or supervision order (see paragraphs 11 and 12 of PD3A).

8.4 The relevant part of the form C100 must be completed showing that either:

(1) the applicant has attended a MIAM; or
(2) the applicant has not attended a MIAM and claims one of the exemptions (rule 3.8(1) FPR) – exemptions include (but are not limited to) evidence of domestic violence, child protection concerns, urgency, previous MIAM attendance or exemption; or
(3) an authorised family mediator confirms in the form that he or she is satisfied that
   (a) mediation is not suitable because the respondents is (if more than one respondent, any one of them is) unwilling to attend a MIAM;
   (b) mediation is not suitable as a means of resolving the dispute because the respondent (if more than one, any of them) failed without good reason to attend a MIAM; or
   (c) mediation is otherwise not suitable as a means of resolving the dispute.

8.5 The C100 form may be obtained from the Family Court or from www.gov.uk.

8.6 If the parties have previously prepared a Parenting Plan, this shall be attached to the Form C100.

8.7 If possible at the time of issue, and in any event by no later than one working day after issue, or in courts where applications are first considered on paper by no later than two working days after issue, the court shall send or hand to the Applicant the following:

- (i) A copy of the application form C100 (together with the Supplemental Information Form C1A),
- (ii) The Notice of Hearing;
- (iii) The Acknowledgment Form C7;
- (iv) A blank Form C1A, (if required);
- (v) Information leaflets for the parties (which must include the CB7 leaflet)

8.8 Unless the applicant requests to do so, or the court directs the applicant to do so, the Court will serve the respondent(s) with:

- (i) A copy of the application form C100 (together with Supplemental Information Form C1A)(if provided);
- (ii) The Notice of Hearing;
- (iii) The Acknowledgement Form C7;
- (iv) A blank form C1A;
- (v) Information leaflet for the parties (which must include the CB7 leaflet).

8.9 The court shall send to Cafcass/CAFCASS Cymru a copy of the Form C100 (and the form C1A, if supplied), and the C6 Notice of Hearing no later than 2 working days after the date of issue. This will be in electronic format where possible.

8.10 The court shall not send to Cafcass/CAFCASS Cymru any other application under the Children Act 1989, or any other private law application, unless the Court has made a specific direction requesting the assistance of Cafcass/CAFCASS Cymru. Therefore, any application which is not in Form C100 or which does not contain a direction to Cafcass/CAFCASS Cymru will be returned to the court at which the application has been issued.

9 Allocation and Gatekeeping

9.1 It is important that the form C100 is fully completed (including the provision of telephone numbers of the relevant parties), otherwise there may be a delay in processing the application; where the form is not fully completed, the court staff may request further information before the application form is accepted for issue.

9.2 The application shall be considered by a nominated Legal Adviser &/or nominated District Judge ('the Gatekeeper(s)') within one working day of the date of receipt in accordance with the appropriate Rules of Procedure.

9.3 An application for a relevant family order shall be allocated to a level of judge in the Family Court in accordance with the Guidance issued by the President on Allocation and Gatekeeping for Proceedings under Part II of the Children Act 1989 (Private Law Proceedings) and the Family Court (Composition and Distribution of Business) Rules 2014, together with the Allocation Schedule.

9.4 Gatekeepers shall be able to issue Directions on Issue in the following circumstances:

- (1) where, on the basis of information provided on the application form and any additional information provided on a C1A Supplemental Information Form, the Gatekeeper finds that the exemption from attending a MIAM has not validly been claimed, the Gatekeeper will direct the applicant, or direct the parties to attend a MIAM before the FHDRA, unless the Gatekeeper considers that in all the circumstances of the case the MIAM requirement should not apply to the application in question; the Gatekeeper will have particular regard to the matters set out in rule 3.10(3) FPR when making this decision;

(2) where it appears that an urgent issue requires determination, the Gatekeeper may give directions for an accelerated hearing;
(3) exceptionally, where it appears that directions need to be given for the service and filing of evidence, he/she may give directions for the filing of evidence.

10 Judicial continuity

10.1 All private law cases will be allocated to a level of judge within the Family Court upon issue.

10.2 Continuity of Judicial involvement in the conduct of proceedings from the FHDRA to the making of a final order should be the objective in all cases.

10.3 Where the case has been allocated to be heard before lay justices, the expectation of judicial continuity should apply where:

(1) There has been a hearing to determine findings of fact,
(2) A decision yet to be made in the interests of a child by a court depends upon rulings or judicial assessments already made in the proceedings,

in which case, wherever possible, the hearing shall be listed before the same lay justices; alternatively, it shall be listed before the same legal adviser and at least one lay justice (preferably the chairman) to provide that continuity. Where a case is adjourned part-heard the court which resumes the hearing shall, wherever possible, be composed of the same lay justices as dealt with the previous part of the hearing (see rule 8 of the Family Court (Composition and Distribution of Business) Rules 2014).

11 Key welfare principles

11.1 Section 1 of the Children Act 1989 applies to all applications for orders concerning the upbringing of children. This means that:

(1) the child's welfare is the court's paramount consideration;
(2) delay is likely to be prejudicial to the welfare of the child, and
(3) a court order shall not be made unless the court considers that making an order would be better for the child than making no order at all.

11.2 Parties, and the court, must also have regard to the FPR in particular the following:

(1) FPR Rule 1. The 'overriding objective' will apply, so that the court will deal with a case justly, having regard to the welfare issues involved and specifically will:
  (a) Ensure that the case is dealt with expeditiously and fairly;
  (b) Deal with the case in ways which are proportionate to the nature, importance and complexity of the issues;
  (c) Ensure that the parties are on an equal footing;
  (d) Save expense;
  (e) Allot to each case an appropriate share of the court's resources, while taking account of the need to allot resources to other cases.
(2) Rule 3, and Practice Direction 3A;
(3) FPR Part 4 'General Case Management Powers';
(4) FPR Part 15 (Representation of Protected Parties) and Practice Direction 15B (Adults Who May Be Protected Parties and Children Who May Become Protected Parties in Family Proceedings);
(5) FPR Part 16 (Representation of Children) (and see also paragraph 18 below);
(6) FPR Part 18 (procedure for Other Applications in proceedings);
(7) FPR Part 22 (Evidence);
(8) FPR Part 24 (Witnesses, depositions generally and taking of evidence in Member States of the European Union);
(9) FPR Part 25 (Experts) and the Experts Practice Directions;
(10) FPR 27.6 and Practice Direction 27A (Court Bundles).

PART III

11.3 Where a fact-finding hearing is required, this shall take place in accordance with revised Practice Direction 12J FPR.

11.4 The court shall exercise its powers flexibly. The flexible powers of the court include the ability for the court to cancel or repeat a particular hearing.

12 Urgent and Without Notice Applications

12.1 **Urgent**: Where an order is sought as a matter of urgency, an application may be made to the Court for an emergency order without the requirement for the Applicant to have attended at a MIAM. The categories of urgent application justifying such an exemption are set out in rule 3.8(c) FPR and include cases in which:

(1) There is a risk to the life, liberty, or the physical safety of the prospective applicant or his or her family, or his or her home;
(2) Any delay caused by attending a MIAM would cause:
  (1) A risk of harm to the child;
  (2) A risk of unlawful removal of a child from the United Kingdom or a risk of unlawful retention of a child who is currently outside England and Wales;
  (3) A significant risk of a miscarriage of justice;
  (4) Unreasonable hardship to the prospective applicant;
  (5) Irretrievable problems in dealing with the dispute (including the irretrievable loss of significant evidence).
(3) There is a significant risk that in the period necessary to schedule and attend a MIAM, proceedings relating to the dispute will be brought in another state in which a valid claim to jurisdiction may exist, such that a court in that other State would be seised of the dispute before a court in England and Wales.

12.2 '**Without Notice'**: Applications to court made 'Without Notice' to the respondent(s) shall be allocated in accordance with the Family Court (Composition and Distribution of Business) Rules 2014, and determined by reference to the provisions of Practice Direction 18A, paragraph 5.1, with further regard to the principles set out in Practice Direction 20A, paragraph 4.3–4.5 FPR (noting particularly paragraph 4.3(c)).

12.3 Without Notice Orders should be made only exceptionally, and where:

(1) If the applicant were to give notice to the respondent(s) this would enable the respondent(s) to take steps to defeat the purpose of the injunction; cases where the application is brought without notice in order to conceal the step from the respondent(s) are very rare indeed; or
(2) The case is one of exceptional urgency; that is to say, that there has been literally no time to give notice (either by telephone, text or e-mail or otherwise) before the injunction is required to prevent the threatened wrongful act; or
(3) If the applicant gives notice to the respondent(s), this would be likely to expose the applicant or relevant child to unnecessary risk of physical or emotional harm.

12.4 Any Order which follows an emergency 'without notice' hearing should specify:

(1) the reason(s) why the order has been made without notice to the respondent(s),
(2) the outline facts alleged which have been relied upon by the court in making the order, unless the facts are clearly contained in the statement in support; and
(3) the right of the respondent(s) to apply to vary or discharge the order.

12.5 **Gatekeeping decisions**: Following any urgent or 'without notice' hearing, unless all issues have been determined or the application has been dismissed without any further directions given, the judge may make gatekeeping decisions, including allocation and venue of future hearing, (and if so, shall notify the Gatekeeping team responsible for the area in which the child resides), or shall refer the application to the relevant Gatekeeping team for a decision on allocation and venue of future hearing; in either event, a copy of the C100 shall be sent to Cafcass for safeguarding checks, and (depending on the Gatekeeping decision) the file shall be sent to the court where future hearings will take place (if at a different court centre from the court where the urgent hearing occurred).

13 Safeguarding

13.1 Where an application is made for a child arrangements order (but not necessarily for specific issue or prohibited steps orders), before the FHDRA (see paragraph 14 below) Cafcass/CAFCASS Cymru shall identify any safety issues by the steps outlined below.

13.2 Such steps shall be confined to matters of safety. The Cafcass Officer or (in Wales) the Welsh Family Proceedings Officer (WFPO) shall not discuss with either party before the FHDRA any matter other than one which relates to safety. The parties will not be invited to talk about other issues, for example relating to the substance of applications or replies or about issues concerning matters of welfare or the prospects of resolution. If such issues are raised by either party, they will be advised that such matters will be deferred to the FHDRA when there is equality between the parties and full discussion can take place which will be a time when any safety issues that have been identified can also be taken into account.

13.3 In order to inform the court of possible risks of harm to the child Cafcass/CAFCASS Cymru will carry out safeguarding enquiries. For all child arrangements orders this will include seeking information from local authorities, and carrying out police checks on the parties. For all other applications received from the court on the form C100, Cafcass/CAFCASS Cymru will carry out a screening process and will undertake those checks if in the professional judgment of the Cafcass officer, or the WFPO in Wales, such checks are necessary.

13.4 Cafcass/CAFCASS Cymru will, if possible, undertake telephone risk identification interviews with the parties and if risks of harm are identified, may invite parties to meet separately with the Cafcass Officer, or WFPO in Wales, before the FHDRA to clarify any safety issue.

13.5 Cafcass/CAFCASS Cymru shall record and outline any safety issues for the court, in the form of a Safeguarding letter (in Wales, this is called a 'Safeguarding report').

13.6 The Cafcass officer, or WFPO, will not initiate contact with the child prior to the FHDRA. If contacted by a child, discussions relating to the issues in the case will be postponed to the day of the hearing or after when the Cafcass officer or WFPO will have more knowledge of the issues.

13.7 Within 17 working days of receipt by Cafcass/CAFCASS Cymru of the application, and at least 3 working days before the hearing, the Cafcass Officer or WFPO shall report to the court, in a Safeguarding letter / report, the outcome of the risk identification work which has been undertaken.

13.8 Further, Cafcass and CAFCASS Cymru are required, under section 16A Children Act 1989, to undertake (and to provide to the court) risk assessments where an officer of the Service ('Cafcass Officer' or WFPO) suspects that a child is at risk of harm.

14 First Hearing Dispute Resolution Appointment (FHDRA)

14.1 The FHDRA may (where time for service on the respondent(s) has been abridged) take place within 4 weeks, but should ordinarily take place in week 5 following the issuing of the application; at the latest it will take place in week 6 following the issuing of the application.

14.2 The respondent(s) shall have at least 10 working days' notice of the hearing where practicable, but the court may abridge this time.

14.3 The respondent(s) should file a response on the Forms C7/C1A no later than 10 working days before the hearing, unless the court has abridged this time.

14.4 Unless the court otherwise directs, any party to proceedings, and any litigation friend of the parties must attend this (and any other) hearing. If a child is a party and represented by a children's guardian, the children's guardian need not attend directions hearings if represented.

14.5 A party may choose to be accompanied at this (or any) hearing by a McKenzie Friend to support them (a McKenzie Friend is someone who can provide moral support at court for the party; take notes; help with case papers; quietly give advice on any aspect of the conduct of the case.) If so, the McKenzie Friend must comply with the relevant Guidance (currently set out in the Practice Guidance: McKenzie Friends (Civil and Family Courts): July 2010: http://www.judiciary.gov.uk/Resources/JCO/Documents/Guidance/mckenzie-friends-practice-guidance-july-2010.pdf).

Note—The web address is no longer valid, but the Practice Guidance is set out in Part V.

14.6 A Cafcass Officer or WFPO shall attend this hearing. A mediator may attend where available.

14.7 The Cafcass Officer or WFPO shall, where practicable, speak separately to each party at court before the hearing in particular where it has not been possible to conduct a risk identification interview with either party.

14.8 The FHDRA provides an opportunity for the parties to be helped to an understanding of the issues which divide them, and to reach agreement. If agreement is reached:

(1) The Court will be able to make an order (which in many cases will be a final order) reflecting that agreement;

(2) The Court will assist the parties (so far as it is able) in putting into effect the agreement/order in a co-operative way.

14.9 The FHDRA is not privileged. That is to say that what is said at the FHDRA may be referred to at later court hearings.

14.10 By the time of the hearing, the Court should have the following documents:

(a) C100 application, and C1A (if any);
(b) Notice of Hearing;
(c) C7 response and C1A (if any);
(d) Cafcass/CAFCASS Cymru safeguarding letter/report.

14.11 At the FHDRA the judge, working with the Cafcass Officer, or WFPO, will seek to assist the parties in conciliation and in resolution of all or any of the issues between them. Any remaining issues will be identified, the Cafcass Officer or WFPO will advise the court of any recommended means of resolving such issues, and directions will be given for the future resolution of such issues. At all times the decisions of the Court and the work of the Cafcass Officer or WFPO will take account of any risk or safeguarding issues that have been identified.

14.12 The court should have information obtained through safeguarding checks carried out by Cafcass/CAFCASS Cymru, to ensure that any agreement between the parties, or any dispute resolution process selected, is in the interests of the child and safe for all concerned.

14.13 The FHDRA will be conducted in the most appropriate way in the interests of the child. In particular the court shall consider the following matters:

- **Safeguarding**, in this respect:

  (a) The court shall inform the parties of the content of the safeguarding letter/report provided by Cafcass/CAFCASS Cymru, where it has not already been sent by Cafcass/CAFCASS Cymru to the parties, unless it considers that to do so would create a risk of harm to a party or the child. The court may need to consider whether, and if so how, any information contained in the checks should be disclosed to the parties if Cafcass/CAFCASS Cymru have not disclosed the letter/report.

  The court will further consider:

  (b) Whether a fact finding hearing is needed to determine allegations which are not accepted, and whose resolution is likely to affect the decision of the court.

  (c) Risk identification followed by active case management including risk assessment, and compliance with the Practice Direction 12J.

Further:

(d) If the safeguarding information is (contrary to the arrangements set out in the CAP) not available at the FHDRA, the court should adjourn the application until the safeguarding checks are available. Interim orders (unless to protect the safety of a child) should not be made in the absence of safeguarding checks.

And further:

(e) Where the court so directs, a safeguarding letter/report ought to be attached to any referral to a supported or supervised child contact centre in the event the court directs supported or supervised contact.

- **MIAM**, specifically:
  - (a) Whether, if a MIAM exemption has been claimed, the Applicant has validly claimed the exemption;
  - (b) Whether the Respondent has attended a MIAM;
  - (c) If the court finds that a MIAM exemption has not been validly claimed the court will direct the applicant or direct the parties to attend a MIAM and if necessary adjourn the proceedings to enable a MIAM to take place, unless the court considers that in all the circumstances of the case, the MIAM requirement should not apply to the application in question; when making the decision the court will have particular regard to the matters contained in rule 3.10(3) FPR.
- **Mediation, At-Court Mediation assessment, and other Dispute Resolution**: allowing the parties the time and opportunity to engage in non-court dispute resolution.
  - (a) At the FHDRA, the judge will specifically consider whether, and the extent to which, the parties can safely resolve some or all of the issues with the assistance of the Cafcass Officer, WFPO, or a mediator.
  - (b) There will be, at every FHDRA, a period in which the Cafcass Officer, or WFPO, will seek to conciliate and explore with the parties the resolution of all or some of the issues between them if safe to do so. The procedure to be followed in this connection at the hearing will be determined by local arrangements between the Cafcass manager, or equivalent in Wales, and the Designated Family Judge or the Justices' Clerk where appropriate.

  The court will further consider:
  - (c) What is the result of any such meeting at Court?
  - (d) What other options there are for resolution e.g. may the case be suitable for further intervention by Cafcass/CAFCASS Cymru; Should a referral for mediation be made? Is collaborative law appropriate? Should the parties be advised to complete a Parenting Plan?
  - (e) Would the parties be assisted by attendance at an Activity Separated Parents Information Programme, (or in Wales, Working Together For Children (WT4C)) or other Activity or intervention, whether by formal statutory provision under section 11 Children Act 1989 or otherwise;
  - (f) An at-court assessment of the suitability of the parties for mediation.
- **Consent Orders**:
  - (a) Where agreement is reached at any hearing or submitted in writing to the court, no order will be made without scrutiny by the court.
  - (b) Where safeguarding checks or risk assessment work remain outstanding, the making of a final order may be deferred for such work. In such circumstances the court shall adjourn the case for no longer than 28 days to a fixed date. A written notification of this work is to be provided by Cafcass/CAFCASS Cymru in the form of an updating Safeguarding letter/report, or if deemed relevant by Cafcass/CAFCASS Cymru, a section 16A risk assessment in accordance with the timescale specified by the court. If satisfactory information is then available, the order may be made at the adjourned hearing in the agreed terms without the need for attendance by the parties. If satisfactory information is not available, the order will not be made, and the case will be adjourned for further consideration with an opportunity for the parties to make further representations

- **Reports:**

(a) Reports may be ordered where there are welfare issues or other specific considerations which should be addressed in a report by Cafcass/CAFCASS Cymru or the Local Authority. Before a report is ordered, the court should consider alternative ways of working with the parties such as are referred to in paragraph 5 ('non-court resolution of disputed arrangements') above.

(b) If a report is ordered in accordance with section 7 of the Children Act 1989, the Court should direct which specific matters relating to the welfare of the child are to be addressed. Welfare reports will generally only be ordered in cases where there is a dispute as to with whom the child should live, spend time, or otherwise have contact with. A report can also be ordered:

(i) If there is an issue concerning the child's wishes, and/or

(ii) If there is an alleged risk to the child, and/or

(iii) Where information and advice is needed which the court considers to be necessary before a decision can be reached in the case.

(c) General requests for a report on an application should be avoided; the Court should state on the face of the Order the specific factual and/or other issue which is to be addressed in the focused report.

(d) In determining whether a request for a report should be directed to the relevant local authority or to Cafcass/CAFCASS Cymru, the court should consider such information as Cafcass/CAFCASS Cymru has provided about the extent and nature of the local authority's current or recent involvement with the subject of the application and the parties, and any relevant protocol between Cafcass and the Association of Directors of Children's Services.

(e) The court may further consider whether there is a need for an investigation under section 37 Children Act 1989.

(f) A copy of the Order requesting the report and any relevant court documents are to be sent to Cafcass/CAFCASS Cymru or, in the case of the Local Authority to the Legal Adviser to the Director of the Local Authority Children's Services and, where known, to the allocated social worker by the court forthwith.

(g) Is any expert evidence required? If so, section 13 Children and Families Act 2014, and Part 25 of the FPR must be complied with. This is the latest point at which consideration should be given to the instruction of an expert in accordance with Rule 25.6(b) of the FPR; the court will need to consider carefully the future conduct of proceedings where the preparation of an expert report is necessary but where the parties are unrepresented and are unable to fund the preparation of such a report.

- **Wishes and feelings of the child:**

(a) In line with the Family Justice Young People's Board Charter, children and young people should be at the centre of all proceedings.

(b) The child or young person should feel that their needs, wishes and feelings have been considered in the court process.

(c) Each decision should be assessed on its impact on the child.

(d) The court must consider the wishes and feelings of the child, ascertainable so far as is possible in light of the child's age and understanding and circumstances. Specifically, the Court should ask:

(i) Is the child aware of the proceedings?

(ii) Are the wishes and feelings of the child available, and/or to be ascertained (if at all)?

(iii) How is the child to be involved in the proceedings, and if so, how; for example, should they meet the judge/lay justices? Should they be encouraged to write to the court, or have their views reported by Cafcass/CAFCASS Cymru or by a local authority?

(iv) Who will inform the child of the outcome of the case, where appropriate?

- **Case Management**:
  (a) What, if any, issues are agreed and what are the key issues to be determined?
  (b) Should the matter be listed for a fact-finding hearing?
  (c) Are there any interim orders which can usefully be made (e.g. indirect, supported or supervised contact) pending Dispute Resolution Appointment or final hearing?
  (d) What directions are required to ensure the application is ready for a Dispute Resolution Appointment or final hearing – statements, reports etc?
  (e) Should the application be listed for a Dispute Resolution Appointment (it is envisaged that most cases will be so listed)?
  (f) Should the application be listed straightaway for a final hearing?
  (g) Judicial continuity should be actively considered (especially if there has been or is to be a fact finding hearing or a contested interim hearing).
- **Allocation**:
  (a) The Allocation decision will be considered by the Court;
  (b) If it is necessary to transfer the case to another court within the DFJ area or another area, or re-allocate it, the court shall state the reasons for transfer/re-allocation, and shall specifically make directions for the next hearing in the court.
- **Order (other than a final order)**: Where no final agreement is reached, and the court is required to give case management directions, the following shall be included on the order:
  (a) the date, time and venue of the next hearing;
  (b) whether the author of any section 7 report is required to attend the hearing, in order to give oral evidence. A direction for the Cafcass officer or WFPO to attend court will not be made without first considering the reason why attendance is necessary, and upon what issues the Cafcass officer or WFPO will be providing evidence;
  (c) such other matters as may be included in President's guidance from time to time.

  Where both parties are Litigants in Person, the court may direct HMCTS to produce a Litigant in Person bundle.

  The judge will, as far as possible, provide a copy of the order to both parties before they leave the courtroom, and will, if necessary, go through and explain the contents of the order to ensure they are clearly understood by both parties. The parties should know the date, time and venue of any further hearing before they leave the court.

15 Timetable for the child

15.1 Court proceedings should be timetabled so that the dispute can be resolved as soon as safe and possible in the interests of the child.

15.2 The judge shall, at all times during the proceedings, have regard to the impact which the court timetable will have on the welfare and development of the child to whom the application relates. The judge and the parties shall pay particular attention to the child's age, and important landmarks in the immediate life of the child, including:

(a) the child's birthday;
(b) the start of nursery/schooling;
(c) the start/end of a school term/year;
(d) any proposed change of school;
and/or
(e) any significant change in the child's family, or social, circumstances.

15.3 While it is acknowledged that an interim order may be appropriate at an early stage of court proceedings, cases should not be adjourned for a review (or reviews) of contact or other orders/arrangements, &/or for addendum section 7 report, unless such a hearing is necessary and for a clear purpose that is consistent with the timetable for the child and in the child's best interests.

15.4 When preparing a section 7 report, Cafcass / CAFCASS Cymru (or, where appropriate, the local authority) is encouraged to make recommendations for the stepped phasing-in of child arrangements (i.e. recommendations for the medium and longer term future for the child) insofar as they are able to do so safely in the interests of the child concerned;

15.5 Where active involvement or monitoring is needed, the court may consider making:

(1) An order under section 11H Children Act 1989 (Monitoring);

(2) A Family Assistance Order under section 16 Children Act 1989) (in accordance with the Practice Direction 12M FPR, and if all the named adults in the order agree to the making of such an order and if the order is directed to a local authority, the child lives (or will live) within that local authority area or the local authority consents to the making of the order.

16 Capacity of Litigants

16.1 In the event that the judge has concerns about the capacity of a litigant before the court, the judge shall consider

(1) the Guidance issued by the Family Justice Council in relation to assessing the capacity of litigants;

(2) Practice Direction 15B (Adults Who May Be Protected Parties and Children Who May Become Protected Parties In Family Proceedings).

17 Evidence

17.1 No evidence shall be filed in relation to an application until after the FHDRA unless:

(1) It has been filed in support of a without notice application;

(2) It has been directed by the Court by the Directions on Issue;

(3) It has been directed by the Court for the purposes of determining an interim application.

18 Rule 16.4 children's guardians

18.1 The Court should be vigilant to identify the cases where a rule 16.4 children's guardian should be appointed. This should be considered initially at the FHDRA.

18.2 Where the court is considering the appointment of a children's guardian from Cafcass/CAFCASS Cymru, it should first ensure that enquiries have been made of the appropriate Cafcass/CAFCASS Cymru manager in accordance with paragraph 7.4, Part 4 of the Practice Direction 16A. This should either be in writing before the hearing or by way of case discussion with the relevant Cafcass service manager; for cases in Wales, the 'hotline' protocol agreed with CAFCASS Cymru will ensure that such a discussion can take place. The court should consult with Cafcass / CAFCASS Cymru, so as to consider any advice in connection with the prospective appointment, and the timescale involved.

18.3 When the court decides to appoint a children's guardian, consideration should first be given to appointing an Officer of the Service or WFPO. If Cafcass/CAFCASS Cymru is unable to provide a children's guardian without delay, or if there is some other reason why the appointment of a Cafcass officer is not appropriate, the court should (further to rule 16.24 of the FPR) appoint a person other than the Official Solicitor, unless the Official Solicitor expressly consents.

18.4 In considering whether to make such an appointment the Court shall take account of the demands on the resources of Cafcass/CAFCASS Cymru that such an appointment would make. The court should also make clear on the face of any order the purpose of the appointment and the timetable of any work to be undertaken.

19 Dispute Resolution Appointment (DRA)

19.1 The Court shall list the application for a Dispute Resolution Appointment ('DRA') to follow the preparation of section 7 or other expert report, or Separated Parenting Information Programme (SPIP) (or WT4C in Wales), if this is considered likely to be helpful in the interests of the child.

19.2 The author of the section 7 report will only attend this hearing if directed to do so by the Court.

19.3 At the DRA the Court will:

(1) Identify the key issue(s) (if any) to be determined and the extent to which those issues can be resolved or narrowed at the DRA;
(2) Consider whether the DRA can be used as a final hearing;
(3) Resolve or narrow the issues by hearing evidence;
(4) Identify the evidence to be heard on the issues which remain to be resolved at the final hearing;
(5) Give final case management directions including:
    (a) Filing of further evidence;
    (b) Filing of a statement of facts/issues remaining to be determined;
    (c) Filing of a witness template and / or skeleton arguments;
    (d) Ensuring Compliance with Practice Direction 27A (the Bundles Practice Direction);
    (e) Listing the Final Hearing.

20 Fact-finding hearing

20.1 If the court considers that a fact-finding hearing is necessary it shall conduct that hearing in accordance with revised Practice Direction 12J.

21 Enforcement of Child Arrangements

21.1 On any application for enforcement of a child arrangements order, the court shall:

- consider whether the facts relevant to the alleged non-compliance are agreed, or whether it is necessary to conduct a hearing to establish the facts;
- consider the reasons for any non-compliance;
- consider how the wishes and feelings of the child are to be ascertained;
- consider whether advice is required from Cafcass/CAFCASS Cymru on the appropriate way forward;
- assess and manage any risks of making further or other child arrangements order;
- consider whether a SPIP or referral for dispute resolution is appropriate;
- consider whether an enforcement order may be appropriate, and
- consider the welfare checklist.

21.2 The Gatekeepers shall list any application for enforcement of a child arrangements order for hearing, before the previously allocated judge if possible, within 20 working days of issue. Enforcement cases should be concluded without delay.

21.3 An application made within existing proceedings in the family court shall be allocated to the level of judge in accordance with rule 17 of the Family Court (Composition and Distribution of Business) Rules 2014.

21.4 The Gatekeepers shall, if considered necessary, direct that further safeguarding checks are required from Cafcass/CAFCASS Cymru. On any application for enforcement issued more than three months after the order which is the subject of the enforcement, safeguarding checks shall be ordered.

21.5 The court has a wide range of powers in the event of a breach of a child arrangements order without reasonable excuse.

PART III

21.6 This range of powers includes (but is not limited to):

(a) referral of the parents to a SPIP, or in Wales a WT4C, or mediation;
(b) variation of the child arrangements order (which could include a more defined order and/or reconsidering the contact provision or the living arrangements of the child);
(c) a contact enforcement order or suspended enforcement order under section 11J Children Act 1989 ('Enforcement order' for unpaid work), (see paragraph 21.7 below);
(d) an order for compensation for financial loss (under section 11O Children Act 1989);
(e) committal to prison or
(f) a fine.

21.7 In the event that the court is considering an enforcement order for alleged non-compliance with a court order (under section 11J Children Act 1989) or considering a Compensation order in respect of financial loss (under section 11O Children Act 1989), the court shall (in the absence of agreement between the parties about the relevant facts) determine the facts in order to establish the cause of the alleged failure to comply.

21.8 Section 11L Children Act 1989 provides that if the court finds that a breach has occurred without reasonable excuse it may order the non-compliant party to undertake unpaid work if that is necessary to secure compliance, and if the effect on the non-compliant party is proportionate to the seriousness of the breach. The court must also consider whether unpaid work is available in the locality and the likely effect on the non-compliant party. It is good practice to ask Cafcass/CAFCASS Cymru to report on the suitability of this order. Section 11L(7) also requires the court to take into account the welfare of the child who is the subject of the order for contact.

22 Court timetable

22.1 Working Day 1: Paperwork received. Court office checks whether the revised form C100 has been completed correctly. The application will not be issued unless the form has been completed correctly.

22.2 Working Day 2: Case considered by Gatekeeping team. Case allocated by Gatekeepers in accordance with the President's Guidance on allocation and the Family Court (Composition and Distribution) Rules 2014. The Gatekeeper(s) undertaking allocation to check whether form C100 has been completed. If there has been no MIAM, and there are reasons to believe that the applicant should have attended a MIAM, the Gatekeeping judge can direct that a MIAM should take place before the FHDRA.

22.3 17 working days from the date of its receipt of the application Cafcass/CAFCASS Cymru will provide the safeguarding letter / report to the Court (20 working days in the area of CAFCASS Cymru).

22.4 Week 5 (or latest, week 6): Case listed for FHDRA (before week 5 if requirements of notice have been abridged).

22.5 Thereafter, case may be listed for fact-finding hearing, DRA &/or final hearing.

23 Relevant Family Application (definition)

23.1 A relevant family application for the purposes of the CAP is an application that

(1) Is made to the court in, or to initiate, family proceedings, and
(2) Is of a description specified in the Family Procedure Rules.

ANNEX – EXPLANATION OF TERMS

Abuse	Any behaviour which causes harm
Adjourn/ Adjournment	Where the case, or a hearing, is directed to take place or continue at a later time (which might be on the same day or another day)

Allegation	A claim that someone has done something wrong
Applicant	The name given to someone who is asking the court for a court order
Application	How a person asks the court to do something
Cafcass	Cafcass stands for the 'Children and Family Court Advisory and Support Service'. Cafcass is independent of the courts, social services, education and health authorities and all similar agencies. Cafcass workers (sometimes called 'Family Court Advisers' or 'officers') are specialist social workers who help the court by making safeguarding checks, helping parties at the FHDRA to consider solutions, and if necessary writing reports for the court &/or monitoring arrangements after court.
CAFCASS Cymru	This is Cafcass in Wales. CAFCASS Cymru is part of the Department of Health and Social Services in the Welsh Government.
Child Arrangements Order	This is an order which will set out arrangements relating to (a) ***with whom*** a child is to live, spend time or otherwise have contact, and (b) ***when*** a child is to live, spend time or otherwise have contact with any other person.
Collaborative law	One of the ways of trying to sort out disputes away from court; each party appoints their own lawyer, and you and your lawyers all meet together to work things out face to face.
Consent order	When you have reached an agreement with the other parent, which resolves the dispute, the judge may agree to make that agreement into an order called a consent order
Contact centre	A place for a parent to see their child in a neutral and 'safe' environment. 'Supervised' contact centres provide a safe and neutral place for contact. 'Supported' contact centres, which are often run by volunteers, offer a neutral place for contact in cases where no safety concerns exist
Designated Family Judge	This is the judge who has responsibility to provide leadership to the family judiciary within the court centre or group of courts
Dispute Resolution	The method of solving disagreements
Domestic violence	This phrase is used to describe a wide range of behaviours including any incident or pattern of incidents of controlling, coercive or threatening behaviour, violence or abuse between those aged 16 or over who are or have been intimate partners or family members regardless of gender or sexuality. This can encompass, but is not limited to, the following types of abuse: psychological, physical, sexual, financial, or emotional. Controlling behaviour is: a range of acts designed to make a person subordinate and/or dependent by isolating them from sources of support, exploiting their resources and capacities for personal gain, depriving them of the means needed for independence, resistance and escape and regulating their everyday behaviour. Coercive behaviour is: an act or a pattern of acts of assault, threats, humiliation and intimidation or other abuse that is used to harm, punish, or frighten their victim.
DRA	Dispute Resolution Appointment. This is a court hearing which takes place towards the end of the court's involvement, and is another opportunity to see if the dispute can be sorted out with the help of a judge.
Enforcement	Making sure that an order is complied with
Expert evidence	Evidence and opinions provided by someone with special skills and knowledge (but, for these purposes, does not refer to a social worker employed by, and giving evidence on behalf of, a local authority who is a party to the case).

PART III

Fact finding hearing	A court hearing set up for the court to decide on issues of fact or allegations which are in dispute.
Family Assistance order	An order of the court which allows Cafcass or local authorities to provide social-work support to help parties to establish contact arrangements which might otherwise fail
FHDRA	First Hearing Dispute Resolution Appointment. This is a court hearing which takes place at the beginning of the court's involvement.
File	This means to send/deliver to the court office
FPR	Family Procedure Rules 2010; the rules of court which govern family cases.
Gatekeeper(s)	The nominated District Judge and/or nominated Legal Adviser responsible for deciding which level of judge in the family court should initially deal with an application
Hearing	The name given to a meeting or court appointment with a judge
Indirect contact	Any contact which is not face-to-face (for example, letters, birthday cards, phone calls).
Interim contact	Contact that takes place between the first court hearing and the final hearing
Investigation under section 37	Where it appears to a judge that a child is or may be at risk of significant harm and it may be appropriate for local authority children's services to apply for a court order giving them responsibilities towards a family, the judge can direct the local authority to investigate the child's circumstances
Judge	Where the term 'Judge' is used, this refers to any judge of the Family Court including lay justices (magistrates)and judges of the High Court
Judgment	The decision of the Judge, and the reasons why the decision has been made
LAA	Legal Aid Agency; this is the body responsible for providing public funding for legal representation.
Litigant in Person or LiP	This is the name given to a person in court proceedings who does not have a lawyer
Litigant in Person Bundle	A bundle of court documents, contained in a file, which contains the following: Section A: Applications, Section B: Orders, Section C: Statements, Section D: Cafcass safeguarding letter, analyses and any expert reports, and Section E: Police, medical, other documents
McKenzie Friend	A friend or other person who can help you prepare your case and go to court with you to give you support and take notes
MIAM	Mediation Information and Assessment Meeting. At this meeting, a trained mediator will explain what mediation is and how it works, explain the benefits of mediation and the likely costs, answer questions, assess whether the person is eligible for legal aid for mediation, assess whether mediation is suitable in the case. A MIAM should be held within 15 working days of contacting the mediator.
NACCC	National Association of Child Contact Centres: NACCC has in its membership about 350 child contact centres and services throughout England (including the Channel Isles), Wales and Northern Ireland. Child contact centres and services are neutral places where children of separated families can enjoy contact with the parent with whom the child does not live and sometimes with other family members, in a comfortable and safe environment.

Parental responsibility	All the legal rights and responsibilities normally associated with being a parent
Part-heard	Means a hearing which has started but which has not been finished within the day, and then continues on another day
Party	Someone involved in the court proceedings – either the person who has made the application, or the person(s) against whom the application has been made.
Practice Direction	This is a document which sets out good practice in supporting the FPR (Family Procedure Rules) or other Rules (see above) and/or may contain provisions which could otherwise be contained in rules of court and have same effect as rules
Private family law/private law	Family disputes between individuals about arrangements for children.
Respondent(s)	This is the name given to the person or people who receive the court application
Review	To look at something again
Rule 16.4 children's guardian	A person (usually a specialist social worker) appointed by the court to look after the interests of a child in the case
Safeguarding	Making sure that people are safe
Section 7 report	A welfare report, prepared under section 7 of the Children Act 1989; the report will be on such matters relating to the welfare of that child as are required to be dealt with in the report; the report may be in writing or oral.
Serve	Delivery of court documents
SPIP	Separated Parents Information Programme; this is available across England, and is for both parents and for grandparents.
Statement or Witness Statement	A document setting out what you want to say to the Judge about the case. You should sign it and date it. What you say in the statement must be true.
Undertaking	A solemn promise to the court to do, or not do, something
WFPO	Welsh Family Proceedings Officer. A Cafcass officer in Wales.
WT4C	The Working Together For Children programme which runs in Wales – and is the equivalent of the SPIP (see above)

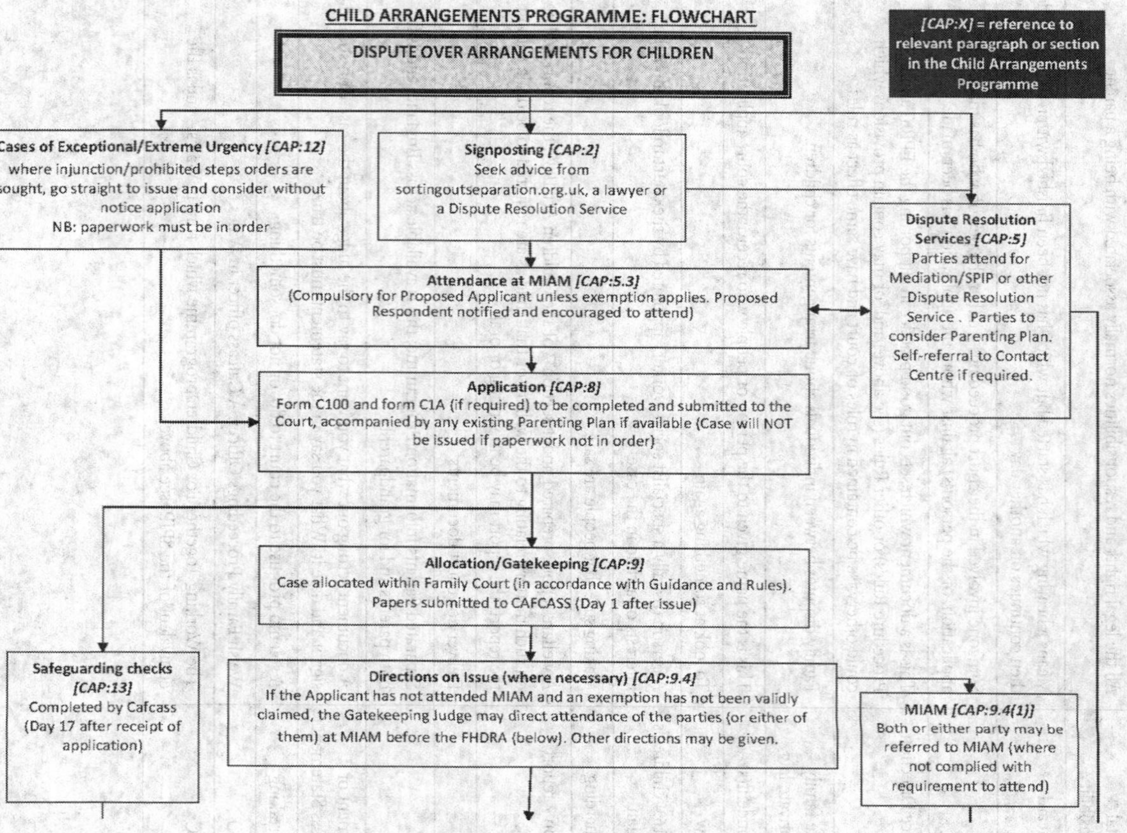
CHILD ARRANGEMENTS PROGRAMME: FLOWCHART
[CAP:X] = reference to relevant paragraph or section in the Child Arrangements Programme
DISPUTE OVER ARRANGEMENTS FOR CHILDREN
Cases of Exceptional/Extreme Urgency [CAP:12]
where injunction/prohibited steps orders are sought, go straight to issue and consider without notice application
NB: paperwork must be in order
Signposting [CAP:2]
Seek advice from sortingoutseparation.org.uk, a lawyer or a Dispute Resolution Service
Dispute Resolution Services [CAP:5]
Parties attend for Mediation/SPIP or other Dispute Resolution Service . Parties to consider Parenting Plan. Self-referral to Contact Centre if required.
Attendance at MIAM [CAP:5.3]
(Compulsory for Proposed Applicant unless exemption applies. Proposed Respondent notified and encouraged to attend)
Application [CAP:8]
Form C100 and form C1A (if required) to be completed and submitted to the Court, accompanied by any existing Parenting Plan if available (Case will NOT be issued if paperwork not in order)
Allocation/Gatekeeping [CAP:9]
Case allocated within Family Court (in accordance with Guidance and Rules). Papers submitted to CAFCASS (Day 1 after issue)
Safeguarding checks [CAP:13]
Completed by Cafcass (Day 17 after receipt of application)
Directions on Issue (where necessary) [CAP:9.4]
If the Applicant has not attended MIAM and an exemption has not been validly claimed, the Gatekeeping Judge may direct attendance of the parties (or either of them) at MIAM before the FHDRA (below). Other directions may be given.
MIAM [CAP:9.4(1)]
Both or either party may be referred to MIAM (where not complied with requirement to attend)

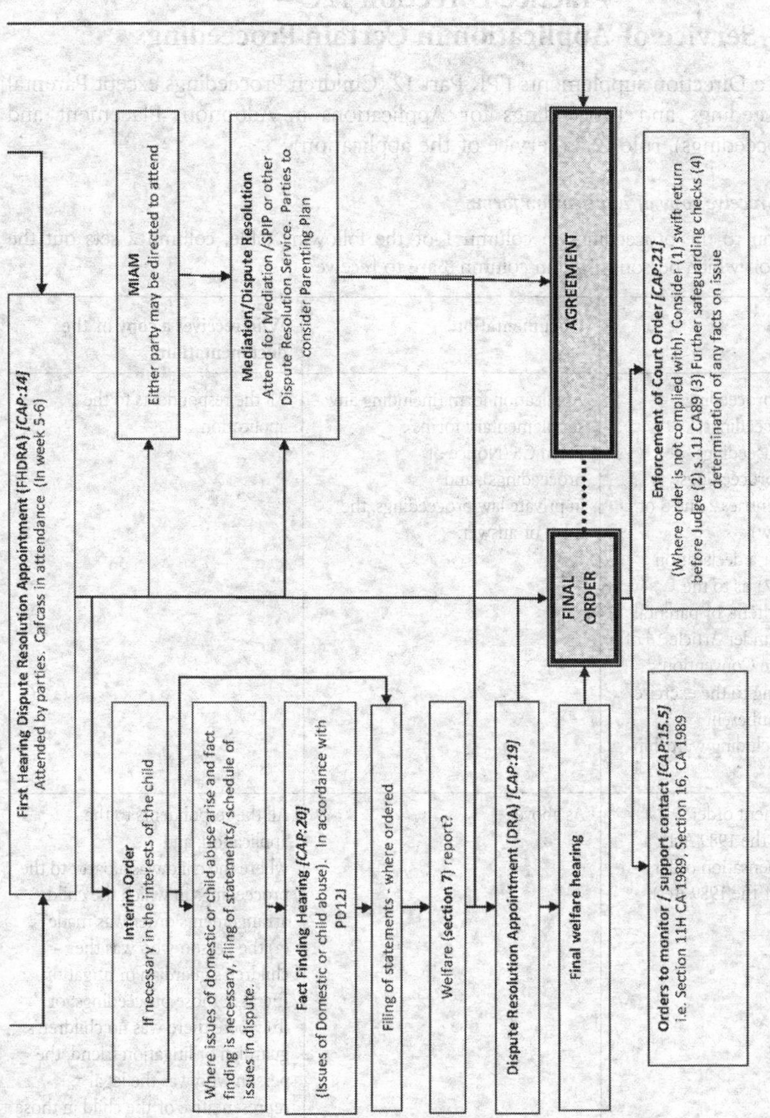
First Hearing Dispute Resolution Appointment (FHDRA) [CAP:14]
Attended by parties. Cafcass in attendance (In week 5-6)
MIAM
Either party may be directed to attend
Mediation/Dispute Resolution
Attend for Mediation /SPIP or other Dispute Resolution Service. Parties to consider Parenting Plan
AGREEMENT
Enforcement of Court Order [CAP:21]
(Where order is not complied with). Consider (1) swift return before Judge (2) s.11J CA89 (3) Further safeguarding checks (4) determination of any facts on issue
FINAL ORDER
Interim Order
If necessary in the interests of the child
Where issues of domestic or child abuse arise and fact finding is necessary, filing of statements/ schedule of issues in dispute.
Fact Finding Hearing [CAP:20]
(Issues of Domestic or child abuse). In accordance with PD12J
Filing of statements - where ordered
Welfare (section 7) report?
Dispute Resolution Appointment (DRA) [CAP:19]
Final welfare hearing
Orders to monitor / support contact [CAP:15.5]
I.e. Section 11H CA 1989, Section 16, CA 1989

Practice Direction 12C – Service of Application in Certain Proceedings

This Practice Direction supplements FPR Part 12 (Children Proceedings except Parental Order Proceedings and Proceedings for Applications in Adoption, Placement and Related Proceedings), rule 12.8 (Service of the application)

Persons who receive copy of application form

1.1 In relation to the proceedings in column 1 of the following table, column 2 sets out the documentation which persons listed in column 3 are to receive –

Proceedings	Documentation	Who receives a copy of the documentation
1 Private law proceedings; public law proceedings; emergency proceedings (except those proceedings referred to in entries 2 and 3 of the Table below); proceedings for a declaration under rule 12.71 as to the existence, or extent, of parental responsibility under Article 16 of the 1996 Hague Convention; an order relating to the exercise of the court's inherent jurisdiction (including wardship proceedings).	Application form (including any supplementary forms); Form C6 (Notice of proceedings); and in private law proceedings, the form of answer.	All the respondents to the application.
2 An enforcement order (section 11J of the 1989 Act); a financial compensation order (section 11O of the 1989 Act).	As above	All the respondents to the application; and where the child was a party to the proceedings in which the child arrangements order was made – (a) the person who was the children's guardian or litigation friend in those proceedings; or (b) where there was no children's guardian or litigation friend, the person who was the legal representative of the child in those proceedings.
3 A care or a supervision order (section 31 of the 1989 Act) and other Part 4 proceedings.	As above and such of the documents specified in the Annex to Form C110A as are available.	All the respondents to the application; and Cafcass or CAFCASS Cymru.
4 Proceedings for an order for the return of a child under the 1980 Hague Convention or registration of an order under the European Convention.	As above and the documents referred to in part 2 of the Practice Direction 12F (International Child Abduction).	All the respondents to the application.

(Rule 12.3 sets out who the parties to the proceedings are.)

1.2 When filing the documents referred to in column 2 of the Table in paragraph 1.1, the applicant must also file sufficient copies for one to be served on each respondent and, except for

Part 4 proceedings, Cafcass or CAFCASS Cymru. In relation to Part 4 proceedings, the applicant need not file a copy of the documents for Cafcass or CAFCASS Cymru as it is the applicant who sends copies of these documents to Cafcass or CAFCASS Cymru in accordance with Practice Direction 12A.

1.3 Where the application for an order in proceedings referred to in column 1 of the Table in paragraph 1.1 is made in respect of more than one child all the children must be included in the same application form.

1.4 Form C6A (notice to non-parties) must be served on the persons referred to in the Table in paragraph 3.1 at the same time as serving the documents in column 2 of the Table in paragraph 1.1.

Time for serving application

2.1 In relation to the proceedings in column 1 of the following table, column 2 sets out the time period within which the application and accompanying documents must be served on each respondent –

Proceedings	**Minimum number of days prior to hearing or directions appointment for service**
1 Private law proceedings; and proceedings for – an order relating to the exercise of the court's inherent jurisdiction (including wardship proceedings); a declaration under rule 12.71 as to the existence, or extent, of parental responsibility under Article 16 of the 1996 Hague Convention.	14 days.
2 Public law proceedings except proceedings for an interim care order, an interim supervision order or other proceedings referred to in Box 3 below.	7 days.
3 Proceedings for – an interim care order, or the discharge of such an order under section 39(1) of the 1989 Act; an interim supervision order under section 38(1) of the 1989 Act, the discharge or variation of such an order under section 39(2) of the 1989 Act, or the extension or further extension of such an order under paragraph 6(3) of Schedule 3 to that Act; an order varying directions made with an interim care order or interim supervision order under section 38(8)(b) of the 1989 Act; an order under section 39(3) of the 1989 Act varying an interim supervision order in so far as it affects a person with whom the child is living but who is not entitled to apply for the order to be discharged; an order under section 39(3A) of the 1989 Act varying or discharging an interim care order in so far as it imposes an exclusion requirement on a person who is not entitled to apply for the order to be discharged; an order under section 39(3B) of the 1989 Act varying or discharging an interim care order in so far as it confers a power of arrest attached to an exclusion requirement.	3 days.

PART III

Proceedings	Minimum number of days prior to hearing or directions appointment for service
4 Proceedings for an order for the return of a child under the 1980 Hague Convention or registration of an order under the European Convention.	4 days.
5 Emergency proceedings.	1 day.

2.2 The court may extend or shorten the time period referred to in column 2 of the table in paragraph 2.1 (see rule 4.1(3)(a)).

2.3 Where the application is to be served on a child, rule 6.33 provides that, in addition to the persons to be served in accordance with rules 6.28 and 6.32, the application must also be served on the persons or bodies listed in rule 6.33(3) unless the court orders otherwise.

Persons who receive a copy of Form C6A (Notice to Non-Parties)

3.1 In relation to each type of proceedings in column 1 of the following table, the persons listed in column 2 are to receive a copy of Form C6A (Notice of Proceedings/Hearing/Directions Appointment to Non-Parties) –

Proceedings	Persons to whom notice is to be given
1 All applications.	Subject to separate entries below: local authority providing accommodation for the child; persons who are caring for the child at the time when the proceedings are commenced; and in the case of proceedings brought in respect of a child who is alleged to be staying in a refuge which is certified under section 51(1) or (2) of the 1989 Act, the person who is providing the refuge.
2 An order appointing a guardian (section 5(1) of the 1989 Act).	As for all applications; and the father or parent (being a woman who is a parent by virtue of section 43 of the Human Fertilisation and Embryology Act 2008) of the child if that person does not have parental responsibility.
3 A section 8 order (section 8 of the 1989 Act).	As for all applications; and, every person whom the applicant believes – (i) to be named in a court order with respect to the same child, which has not ceased to have effect; (ii) to be party to pending proceedings in respect of the same child; or (iii) to be a person with whom the child has lived for at least 3 years prior to the application, unless, in a case to which (i) or (ii) applies, the applicant believes that the court order or pending proceedings are not relevant to the application.

Proceedings	Persons to whom notice is to be given
4 A special guardianship order (section 14A of the 1989 Act); variation or discharge of a special guardianship order (section 14D of the 1989 Act).	As for all applications; and every person whom the applicant believes – (i) to be named in a court order with respect to the same child, which has not ceased to have effect; (ii) to be party to pending proceedings in respect of the same child; or (iii) to be a person with whom the child has lived for at least 3 years prior to the application, unless, in a case to which (i) or (ii) applies, the applicant believes that the court order or pending proceedings are not relevant to the application; if the child is not being accommodated by the local authority, the local authority in whose area the applicant is ordinarily resident; and in the case of an application under section 14D of the 1989 Act, the local authority that prepared the report under section 14A(8) or (9) in the proceedings leading to the order which it is sought to have varied or discharged, if different from any local authority that will otherwise be notified.
5 An order permitting the local authority to arrange for any child in its care to live outside England and Wales (Schedule 2, paragraph 19(1) of the 1989 Act).	As for all applications; and the parties to the proceedings leading to the care order.
6 A care or supervision order (section 31 of the 1989 Act).	As for all applications; and every person whom the applicant believes to be a party to pending relevant proceedings in respect of the same child; and every person whom the applicant believes to be a parent without parental responsibility for the child.
7 A child assessment order (section 43(1) of the 1989 Act).	As for all applications; and every person whom the applicant believes to be a parent of the child; every person whom the applicant believes to be caring for the child; every person in whose favour a child arrangements order is in force with respect to the child; and every person who is allowed to have contact with the child by virtue of an order under section 34 of the 1989 Act.
8 An order varying or discharging a child assessment order (section 43(12) of the 1989 Act).	The persons referred to in section 43(11)(a) to (e) of the 1989 Act who were not party to the application for the order which it is sought to have varied or discharged.
9 An emergency protection order (section 44(1) of the 1989 Act).	As for all applications above; and every person whom the applicant believes to be a parent of the child.

PART III

Proceedings	Persons to whom notice is to be given
10 An order varying a direction under section 44(6) in an emergency protection order (section 44(9)(b) of the 1989 Act).	As for all applications; and the local authority in whose area the child is living; and any person whom the applicant believes to be affected by the direction which it is sought to have varied.
11 A warrant authorising a constable to assist in the exercise of certain powers to search for children and inspect premises (section 102 of the 1989 Act).	The person referred to in section 102(1) of the 1989 Act; and any person preventing or likely to prevent such a person from exercising powers under enactments mentioned in subsection (6) of that section.
12 An enforcement order (section 11J of the 1989 Act); a financial compensation order (section 11O of the 1989 Act).	Any officer of the Service or Welsh family proceedings officer who is monitoring compliance with a child arrangements order (in accordance with section 11H(2) of the 1989 Act).
13 An order revoking or amending an enforcement order (Schedule A1, paragraphs 4 to 7 of the 1989 Act) (rule 12.33 makes provision regarding applications under Schedule A1, paragraph 5 of the 1989 Act); an order following a breach of an enforcement order (Schedule A1, paragraph 9 of the 1989 Act).	Any officer of the Service or Welsh family proceedings officer who is monitoring compliance with the enforcement order (in accordance with section 11M(1) of the 1989 Act); the responsible officer (as defined in section 197 of the Criminal Justice Act 2003, as modified by Schedule A1 to the 1989 Act).
14 A declaration under rule 12.71 as to the existence, or extent, of parental responsibility under Article 16 of the 1996 Hague Convention.	A person who the applicant believes is a parent of the child.

Practice Direction 12D – Inherent Jurisdiction (including Wardship) Proceedings

This Practice Direction supplements FPR Part 12, Chapter 5

The nature of inherent jurisdiction proceedings

1.1 It is the duty of the court under its inherent jurisdiction to ensure that a child who is the subject of proceedings is protected and properly taken care of. The court may in exercising its inherent jurisdiction make any order or determine any issue in respect of a child unless limited by case law or statute. Such proceedings should not be commenced unless it is clear that the issues concerning the child cannot be resolved under the Children Act 1989.

1.2 The court may under its inherent jurisdiction, in addition to all of the orders which can be made in family proceedings, make a wide range of injunctions for the child's protection of which the following are the most common –

(a) orders to restrain publicity;
(b) orders to prevent an undesirable association;
(c) orders relating to medical treatment;
(d) orders to protect abducted children, or children where the case has another substantial foreign element; and
(e) orders for the return of children to and from another state.

1.3 The court's wardship jurisdiction is part of and not separate from the court's inherent jurisdiction. The distinguishing characteristics of wardship are that –

(a) custody of a child who is a ward is vested in the court; and
(b) although day to day care and control of the ward is given to an individual or to a local authority, no important step can be taken in the child's life without the court's consent.

Transfer of proceedings to family court

2.1 Whilst the family court does not have jurisdiction to deal with applications that a child be made or cease to be a ward of court, consideration should be given to transferring the case in whole or in part to the family court where a direction has been given confirming the wardship and directing that the child remain a ward of court during his minority or until further order.

2.2 The family court must transfer the case back to the High Court if a decision is required as to whether the child should remain a ward of court.

2.3 The following proceedings in relation to a ward of court will be dealt with in the High Court unless the nature of the issues of fact or law makes them more suitable for hearing in the family court –

(a) those in which an officer of the Cafcass High Court Team or the Official Solicitor is or becomes the litigation friend or children's guardian of the ward or a party to the proceedings;
(b) those in which a local authority is or becomes a party;
(c) those in which an application for paternity testing is made;
(d) those in which there is a dispute about medical treatment;
(e) those in which an application is opposed on the grounds of lack of jurisdiction;
(f) those in which there is a substantial foreign element;
(g) those in which there is an opposed application for leave to take the child permanently out of the jurisdiction or where there is an application for temporary removal of a child from the jurisdiction and it is opposed on the ground that the child may not be duly returned.

PART III

Parties

3.1 Where the child has formed or is seeking to form an association, considered to be undesirable, with another person, that other person should not be made a party to the application. Such a person should be made a respondent only to an application within the proceedings for an injunction or committal. Such a person should not be added to the title of the proceedings nor allowed to see any documents other than those relating directly to the proceedings for the injunction or committal. He or she should be allowed time to obtain representation and any injunction should in the first instance extend over a few days only.

Removal from jurisdiction

4.1 A child who is a ward of court may not be removed from England and Wales without the court's permission. Practice Direction 12F (International Child Abduction) deals in detail with locating and protecting children at risk of unlawful removal.

Criminal Proceedings

5.1 Where a child has been interviewed by the police in connection with contemplated criminal proceedings and the child subsequently becomes a ward of court, the permission of the court deciding the wardship proceedings ('the wardship court') is not required for the child to be called as a witness in the criminal proceedings.

5.2 Where the police need to interview a child who is already a ward of court, an application must be made for permission for the police to do so. Where permission is given the order should, unless there is some special reason to the contrary, give permission for any number of interviews which may be required by the prosecution or the police. If a need arises to conduct any interview beyond the permission contained in the order, a further application must be made.

5.3 The above applications must be made with notice to all parties.

5.4 Where a person may become the subject of a criminal investigation and it is considered necessary for the child who is a ward of court to be interviewed without that person knowing that the police are making inquiries, the application for permission to interview the child may be made without notice to that party. Notice should, however, where practicable be given to the children's guardian.

5.5 There will be other occasions where the police need to deal with complaints, or alleged offences, concerning children who are wards of court where it is appropriate, if not essential, for action to be taken straight away without the prior permission of the wardship court, for example –

(a) serious offences against the child such as rape, where a medical examination and the collection of forensic evidence ought to be carried out promptly;
(b) where the child is suspected by the police of having committed a criminal act and the police wish to interview the child in respect of that matter;
(c) where the police wish to interview the child as a potential witness.

5.6 In such instances, the police should notify the parent or foster parent with whom the child is living or another 'appropriate adult' (within the Police and Criminal Evidence Act 1984 – Code of Practice C for the Detention, Treatment and Questioning of Persons by Police Officers) so that that adult has the opportunity of being present when the police interview the child. Additionally, if practicable the child's guardian (if one has been appointed) should be notified and invited to attend the police interview or to nominate a third party to attend on the guardian's behalf. A record of the interview or a copy of any statement made by the child should be supplied to the children's guardian. Where the child has been interviewed without the guardian's knowledge, the guardian should be informed at the earliest opportunity of this fact and (if it be the case) that the police wish to conduct further interviews. The wardship court should be informed of the situation at the earliest possible opportunity thereafter by the children's guardian, parent, foster parent (through the local authority) or other responsible adult.

Applications to the Criminal Injuries Compensation Authority

6.1 Where a child who is a ward of court has a right to make a claim for compensation to the Criminal Injuries Compensation Authority ('CICA'), an application must be made by the child's guardian, or, if no guardian has been appointed, the person with care and control of the child, for permission to apply to CICA and disclose such documents on the wardship proceedings file as are considered necessary to establish whether or not the child is eligible for an award plus, as appropriate, the amount of the award.

6.2 Any order giving permission should state that any award made by CICA should normally be paid into court immediately upon receipt and, once that payment has been made, application should made to the court as to its management and administration. If it is proposed to invest the award in any other way, the court's prior approval must be sought

The role of the tipstaff

7.1 The tipstaff is the enforcement officer for all orders made in the High Court. The tipstaff's jurisdiction extends throughout England and Wales. Every applicable order made in the High Court is addressed to the tipstaff in children and family matters (e g 'The Court hereby directs the Tipstaff of the High Court of Justice, whether acting by himself or his assistants or a police officer as follows…').

7.2 The tipstaff may effect an arrest and then inform the police. Sometimes the local bailiff or police will detain a person in custody until the tipstaff arrives to collect that person or give further directions as to the disposal of the matter. The tipstaff may also make a forced entry although there will generally be a uniformed police officer standing by to make sure there is no breach of the peace.

7.3 There is only one tipstaff (with two assistants) but the tipstaff can also call on any constable or bailiff to assist in carrying out the tipstaff's duties.

7.4 The majority of the tipstaff's work involves locating children and taking them into protective custody, including cases of child abduction abroad.

Contacting the tipstaff—The tipstaff can be contacted on 0207 947 6713. See also **Powers of the court** under r 12.36 and see PD12F, paras 4.7–4.14.

Practice Direction 12E – Urgent Business

This Practice Direction supplements FPR Part 12

Introduction

1.1 This Practice Direction describes the procedure to be followed in respect of urgent and out of hours cases in the Family Division of the High Court. For the avoidance of doubt, it does not relate to cases in respect of adults.

1.2 Urgent or out of hours applications, particularly those which have become urgent because they have not been pursued sufficiently promptly, should be avoided. A judge who has concerns that the urgent or out of hours facilities may have been abused may require a representative of the applicant to attend at a subsequent directions hearing to provide an explanation.

1.3 Urgent applications should whenever possible be made within court hours. The earliest possible liaison is required with the Clerk of the Rules who will attempt to accommodate genuinely urgent applications (at least for initial directions) in the Family Division applications court, from which the matter may be referred to another judge.

1.4 When it is not possible to apply within court hours, contact should be made with the security office at the Royal Courts of Justice (020 7947 6000 or 020 7947 6260) who will refer the matter to the urgent business officer. The urgent business officer can contact the duty judge. The judge may agree to hold a hearing, either convened at court or elsewhere, or by telephone.

1.5 When the hearing is to take place by telephone it should, unless not practicable, be by tape-recorded conference call arranged (and paid for in the first instance) by the applicant's solicitors. Solicitors acting for potential applicants should consider having standing arrangements with their telephone service providers under which such conference calls can be arranged. All parties (especially the judge) should be informed that the call is being recorded by the service provider. The applicant's solicitors should order a transcript of the hearing from the service provider. Otherwise the applicant's legal representative should prepare a note for approval by the judge.

General Issues

2.1 Parents, carers or other necessary respondents should whenever possible be given the opportunity to have independent legal advice or at least to have access to support or counselling.

2.2 In suitable cases, application may be made for directions providing for anonymity of the parties and others involved in the matter in any order or subsequent listing of the case. Exceptionally, a reporting restriction order may be sought.

2.3 Either the Official Solicitor or Cafcass, or CAFCASS Cymru, as the case may be, may be invited by the court to be appointed as advocate to the court.

Medical treatment and press injunction cases

3.1 It may be desirable for a child who is the subject of such proceedings to be made a party and represented through a children's guardian (usually an officer of Cafcass or a Welsh Family Proceedings Officer). Cafcass and CAFCASS Cymru stand ready to arrange for an officer to accept appointment as a children's guardian. They should be contacted at the earliest opportunity where an urgent application is envisaged. For urgent out of hours applications, the urgent business officer will contact a representative of Cafcass. CAFCASS Cymru is not able to deal with cases that arise out of office hours and those cases should be referred to Cafcass who will deal with the matter on behalf of CAFCASS Cymru until the next working day. A child of sufficient understanding to instruct his or her own solicitor should be made a party and given notice of any application.

3.2 Interim declarations/orders under the wardship jurisdiction or Children Act 1989 may be made on application either by an NHS trust, a local authority, an interested adult (where necessary with the leave of the court) or by the child if he or she has sufficient understanding to make the application.

Consultation with Cafcass, CAFCASS Cymru and Official Solicitor

4.1 Cafcass, CAFCASS Cymru and members of the Official Solicitor's legal staff are prepared to discuss cases before proceedings are issued. In all cases in which the urgent and out of hours procedures are to be used it would be helpful if the Official Solicitor, Cafcass or CAFCASS Cymru have had some advance notice of the application and its circumstances.

4.2 Enquiries about children cases should be directed to the High Court Team Duty Manager at Cafcass National Office, 3rd Floor, 21 Bloomsbury Street, London, WC1B 3HF. DX: Cafcass DX 310101 Bloomsbury 11. Telephone 01753 235273 (Cafcass High Court Team) or 01753 235295 (Cafcass Legal Duty Lawyer). Email HighCourtGM@Cafcass.gsi.gov.uk (office hours only). Enquiries should be marked 'FAO High Court Team' or 'FAO HCT'.

Cafcass Legal Duty Lawyer—The telephone is 07776 470065.

4.3 Enquiries about children cases in Wales should be directed to:

Social Care Team
Legal Services
Welsh Assembly Government
Cathays Park
Cardiff
CF10 3NQ
telephone 02920 370888,
fax 0872 437 7306.

4.4 Medical and welfare cases relating to an adult lacking capacity in relation to their medical treatment or welfare are brought in the Court of Protection. Enquiries about adult medical and welfare cases should be addressed to the Court of Protection Healthcare and Welfare Team, Office of the Official Solicitor, Victory House, 30–34 Kingsway, London, WC2B 6EX, telephone 020 3681 2751, fax 020 3681 2762, email enquiries@offsol.gsi.gov.uk.

Reference should also be made to Practice Direction E, accompanying Part 9 of the Court of Protection Rules 2007, and to Practice Direction B accompanying Part 10 of those Rules. Information for parties and practitioners is available on the website of the Ministry of Justice www.justice.gov.uk and general information for members of the public is available on www.direct.gov.uk.

Note—For general information for members of the public, see *www.gov.uk*.

Practice Direction 12F – International Child Abduction

This Practice Direction supplements FPR Part 12, Chapters 5 and 6

Part I – Introduction

1.1 This Practice Direction explains what to do if a child has been brought to, or kept in, England and Wales without the permission of anyone who has rights of custody in respect of the child in the country where the child was habitually resident immediately before the removal or retention. It also explains what to do if a child has been taken out of, or kept out of, England and Wales[(a)] without the permission of a parent or someone who has rights of custody in respect of the child. These cases are called 'international child abduction cases' and are dealt with in the High Court. This Practice Direction also explains what to do if you receive legal papers claiming that you have abducted a child. You can find the legal cases which are mentioned in this Practice Direction, and other legal material, on the website http://www.bailii.org (British and Irish Legal Information Institute).

(a) The child must be taken or kept out of the United Kingdom without the permission of a parent or someone who has rights of custody for it to be an international child abduction. This practice direction relates to the law as it applies in England and Wales. If the child has been taken or kept out of the United Kingdom when the child was habitually resident in Scotland, you should contact the Central Authority for Scotland, Scottish Government Justice Directorate, Civil Law Division, St Andrew's House, Regent Road, Edinburgh EH1 3DG. Tel: +44 (0) 131 244 4827/4832 Fax: +44 (0)131 244 4848 Website: http://www.gov.scot/Topics/Justice/law/17867/fm-children-root/18533.

If the child has been taken or kept out of the United Kingdom when the child was habitually resident in Northern Ireland, you should contact the Central Authority for Northern Ireland, Northern Ireland Courts and Tribunals Service, Civil Policy and Tribunal Reform Division, 3rd Floor Laganside House, 23-27 Oxford Street, Belfast BT1 3LA. Tel: +44 (0)28 9072 8808 or + 44 (0) 28 9072 8819; fax +44 (0) 28 9072 8945. Website: http://www.nics.gov.uk or http://www.courtsni.gov.uk/en-GB/Services/ChildAbduction.

1.2 If you have rights of custody in respect of a child and the child has been brought to England or Wales without your permission, or has been brought here with your permission but the person your child is staying with is refusing to return the child, then you can apply to the High Court of Justice, which covers all of England and Wales, for an order for the return of the child.

1.3 How you make an application to the High Court, what evidence you need to provide and what orders you should ask the court to make are all explained in this Practice Direction.

1.4 If your child is under 16 years of age and has been brought to England or Wales from a country which is a party (a 'State party') to the 1980 Hague Convention on the Civil Aspects of International Child Abduction ('the 1980 Hague Convention') then you can make an application to the High Court for an order under that Convention for the return of your child to the State in which he or she was habitually resident immediately before being removed or being kept away. This is explained in Part 2 below.

1.5 If your child is over 16 years of age and under 18, or has been brought to England or Wales from a country which is not a State party to the 1980 Hague Convention, then you can make an application for the return of your child under the inherent jurisdiction of the High Court with respect to children. In exercising this jurisdiction over children, the High Court will make your child's welfare its paramount consideration. How to make an application under the inherent jurisdiction of the High Court with respect to children is explained in Part 3 below.

1.6 It might be necessary for you to make an urgent application to the court if you are not sure where your child is, or you think that there is a risk that the person who is keeping your child away from you might take the child out of the United Kingdom or hide them away. Part 4 below explains how to make an urgent application to the High Court for orders to protect your child until a final decision can be made about returning the child and also how to ask for help from the police and government agencies if you think your child might be taken out of the country.

Rights of Access

1.7 Rights of access to children (also called contact or visitation) may be enforced in England and Wales. Access orders made in other Member States of the European Union can be enforced under EU law, and the 1980 Hague Convention expects State parties to comply with orders and agreements concerning access as well as rights of custody. If you have an access order and you want to enforce it in England or Wales, you should read Part 5 below.

Part 2 – Hague Convention Cases

2.1 States which are party to the 1980 Hague Convention have agreed to return children who have been either wrongfully removed from, or wrongfully retained away from, the State where they were habitually resident immediately before the wrongful removal or retention. There are very limited exceptions to this obligation.

2.2 'Wrongfully removed' or 'wrongfully retained' means removed or retained in breach of rights of custody in respect of the child attributed to a person or a body or an institution. 'Rights of custody' are interpreted very widely (see paragraph 2.16 below).

2.3 The text of the 1980 Hague Convention and a list of Contracting States (that is, State parties) can be found on the website of the Hague Conference on Private International Law at http://www.hcch.net. All Member States of the European Union are State parties to the 1980 Hague Convention, and all but Denmark are bound by an EU Regulation which supplements the operation of the 1980 Hague Convention between the Member States of the EU (Council Regulation (EC) No 2201/2003, see paragraph 2.6).

2.4 In each State party there is a body called the Central Authority whose duty is to help people use the 1980 Hague Convention.

2.5 If you think that your child has been brought to, or kept in, England or Wales, and your State is a State party to the 1980 Hague Convention, then you should get in touch with your own Central Authority who will help you to send an application for the return of your child to the Central Authority for England and Wales. However, you are not obliged to contact your own Central Authority. You may contact the Central Authority for England and Wales directly, or you may simply instruct lawyers in England or Wales to make an application for you. The advantage of making your application through the Central Authority for England and Wales if you are applying from outside the United Kingdom is that you will get public funding ('legal aid') to make your application, regardless of your financial resources.

The Central Authority for England and Wales

2.6 The Child Abduction and Custody Act 1985 brings the 1980 Hague Convention into the law of England and Wales and identifies the Lord Chancellor as the Central Authority. His duties as the Central Authority are carried out by the International Child Abduction and Contact Unit (ICACU). ICACU also carries out the duties of the Central Authority for two other international instruments. These are the European Convention on Recognition and Enforcement of Decisions concerning Custody of Children signed at Luxembourg on 20 May 1980 (called 'the European Convention' in this Practice Direction but sometimes also referred to as 'the Luxembourg Convention') and the European Union Council Regulation (EC) No 2201/2003 of 27 November 2003 on jurisdiction and the recognition and enforcement of judgments in matrimonial matters and in matters of parental responsibility ('the Council Regulation[(b)]'). The Council Regulation has direct effect in the law of England and Wales.

(b) The Council Regulation (EC) No 2201/2003 of 27 November 2003 concerning jurisdiction and the recognition and enforcement of judgments in matrimonial matters and the matters of parental responsibility, repealing Regulation (EC) No 1347/2000 is also known as Brussels IIa, or Brussels II Revised, or Brussels II bis.

2.7 ICACU is open Mondays to Fridays from 9.00 a.m. to 5.00 p.m. It is located in the Office of the Official Solicitor and Public Trustee and its contact details are as follows:

International Child Abduction and Contact Unit
Office of the Official Solicitor
Victory House
30–34 Kingsway
London
WC2B 6EX
Email: ICACU@offsol.gsi.gov.uk
Tel: + 44 (20) 3681 2608 (10.00am to 4.00pm)
Fax: +44 (20) 3681 2763

In an emergency (including out of normal working hours) contact should be made with the Royal Courts of Justice on one of the following telephone numbers:

+ 44 (0)20 7947 6000, or
+ 44 (0)20 7947 6260.

In addition, in an emergency or outside normal working hours advice on international child abduction can be sought from reunite International Child Abduction Centre on +44 (0)1162 556 234. Outside office hours you will be directed to the 24 hour emergency service. You can also see information on Reunite's website http://www.reunite.org.

What ICACU Will Do

2.8 When ICACU receives your application for the return of your child, unless you already have a legal representative in England and Wales whom you want to act for you, it will send your application to a solicitor whom it knows to be experienced in international child abduction cases and ask them to take the case for you. You will then be the solicitor's client and the solicitor will make an application for public funding to meet your legal costs. The solicitor will then apply to the High Court for an order for the return of your child.

2.9 You can find out more about ICACU and about the 1980 Hague Convention and the other international instruments mentioned at paragraph 2.6 on two websites: Information for parties and practitioners is available on http://www.justice.gov.uk and general information for members of the public is available on www.gov.uk.

Applying to the High Court – the Form and Content of Application

2.10 An application to the High Court for an order under the 1980 Hague Convention must be made in the Principal Registry of the Family Division in Form C67. If the Council Regulation applies, then the application must be headed both 'in the matter of the Child Abduction and Custody Act 1985' and 'in the matter of Council Regulation (EC) 2201/2003'. This is to ensure that the application is handled quickly (see paragraph 2.14 below) and to draw the court's attention to its obligations under the Council Regulation.

2.11 The application must include –

(a) the names and dates of birth of the children;
(b) the names of the children's parents or guardians;
(c) the whereabouts or suspected whereabouts of the children;
(d) the interest of the applicant in the matter (e.g. mother, father, or person with whom the child lives and details of any order placing the child with that person);
(e) the reasons for the application;
(f) details of any proceedings (including proceedings not in England or Wales, and including any legal proceedings which have finished) relating to the children;
(g) where the application is for the return of a child, the identity of the person alleged to have removed or retained the child and, if different, the identity of the person with whom the child is thought to be;
(h) in an application to which the Council Regulation also applies, any details of measures of which you are aware that have been taken by courts or authorities to ensure the protection of the child after its return to the Member State of habitual residence.

2.12 The application should be accompanied by all relevant documents including (but not limited to) –

(a) an authenticated copy of any relevant decision or agreement;
(b) a certificate or an affidavit from a Central Authority, or other competent authority of the State of the child's habitual residence, or from a qualified person, concerning the relevant law of that State.

2.13 As the applicant you may also file a statement in support of the application, although usually your solicitor will make and file a statement for you on your instructions. The statement must contain and be verified by a statement of truth in the following terms:

> 'I make this statement knowing that it will be placed before the court, and I confirm that to the best of my knowledge and belief its contents are true.'
>
> (Further provisions about statements of truth are contained in Part 17 of these Rules and in Practice Direction 17A).

The Timetable for the Case

2.14 Proceedings to which the Council Regulation applies must be completed in 6 weeks 'except where exceptional circumstances make this impossible'. The following procedural steps are intended to ensure that applications under the 1980 Hague Convention and the Council Regulation are handled quickly –

(a) the application must be headed both 'in the matter of the Child Abduction and Custody Act 1985' and 'in the matter of Council Regulation (EC) 2201/2003';
(b) the court file will be marked to –
 (i) draw attention to the nature of the application; and
 (ii) state the date on which the 6 week period will expire (the 'hear-by date');
(c) listing priority will, where necessary, be given to such applications;
(d) the trial judge will expedite the transcript of the judgment and its approval and ensure that it is sent to the Central Authority without delay.

(The above is taken from the judgment of the Court of Appeal, Civil Division in *Vigreux v Michel & anor* [2006] EWCA Civ 630, [2006] 2 FLR 1180).

Applications for Declarations

2.15 If a child has been taken from England and Wales to another State party, the judicial or administrative authorities of that State may ask for a declaration that the removal or retention of the child was wrongful. Or it might be thought that a declaration from the High Court that a child has been wrongfully removed or retained away from the United Kingdom would be helpful in securing his return. The High Court can make such declarations under section 8 of the Child Abduction and Custody Act 1985. An application for a declaration is made in the same way as an application for a return order, the only difference being that the details of relevant legal proceedings in respect of which the declaration is sought (if any), including a copy of any order made relating to the application, should be included in the documentation.

Rights of Custody

2.16 'Rights of custody' includes rights relating to the care of the person of the child and, in particular, the right to determine the child's place of residence. Rights of custody may arise by operation of law (that is, they are conferred on someone automatically by the legal system in which they are living) or by a judicial or administrative decision or as a result of an agreement having legal effect. The rights of a person, an institution or any other body are a matter for the law of the State of the child's habitual residence, but it is for the State which is being asked to return the child to decide: if those rights amount to rights of custody for the purposes of the 1980 Hague Convention; whether at the time of the removal or retention those rights were actually being exercised; and whether there has been a breach of those rights.

2.17 In England and Wales a father who is not married to the mother of their child does not necessarily have 'rights of custody' in respect of the child. An unmarried father in England and Wales who has parental responsibility for a child has rights of custody in respect of that child. In the case of an unmarried father without parental responsibility, the concept of rights of custody may include more than strictly legal rights and where immediately before the removal or retention of the child he was exercising parental functions over a substantial period of time as the only or main carer for the child he may have rights of custody. An unmarried father can ask ICACU or his legal representative for advice on this. It is important to remember that it will be for the State which is being asked to return the child to decide if the father's circumstances meet that State's requirements for the establishment of rights of custody.

Custody rights and unmarried fathers—For case-law pre-2003, see *Practice Note of 14 October 1997* (set out in *The Family Court Practice 2011*) and post-December 2003, see under CACA 1985, Sch 1, Art 5 in Part II.

2.18 Sometimes, court orders impose restrictions on the removal of children from the country in which they are living. These can be orders under the Children Act 1989 ('section 8' orders) or orders under the inherent jurisdiction of the High Court (sometimes called 'injunctions'). Any removal of a child in breach of an order imposing such a restriction would be wrongful under the 1980 Hague Convention.

2.19 The fact that court proceedings are in progress about a child does not of itself give rise to a prohibition on the removal of the child by a mother with sole parental responsibility from the country in which the proceedings are taking place unless:

(a) the proceedings are Wardship proceedings in England and Wales (in which case removal would breach the rights of custody attributed to the High Court and fathers with no custody rights could rely on that breach); or

(b) the court is actually considering the custody of the child, because then the court itself would have rights of custody.

Particular provisions for European Convention applications

2.20 The European Convention provides for the mutual recognition and enforcement of decisions relating to custody and access, so if a child has been brought here or retained here in breach of a custody order, then that order can be enforced. The European Convention has now been superseded to a very great extent by the Council Regulation. If however you want to make an application under the European Convention, then you make it in the same way as is described in paragraphs 2.10 and 2.11 above, but in addition you must include a copy of the decision relating to custody (or rights of access – see paragraph 5.1 below) which you are seeking to register or enforce, or about which you are seeking a declaration by the court.

Defending Abduction Proceedings

2.21 If you are served with an application – whether it is under the 1980 Hague or the European Convention or the inherent jurisdiction of the High Court – you must not delay. You must obey any directions given in any order with which you have been served, and you should seek legal advice at the earliest possible opportunity, although neither you nor the child concerned will automatically be entitled to legal aid.

2.22 It is particularly important that you tell the court where the child is, because the child will not be permitted to live anywhere else without the permission of the court, or to leave England and Wales, until the proceedings are finished.

2.23 It is also particularly important that you present to the court any defence to the application which you or the child might want to make at the earliest possible opportunity, although the orders with which you will have been served are likely to tell you the time by which you will have to do this.

2.24 If the child concerned objects to any order sought in relation to them, and if the child is of an age and understanding at which the court will take account of their views, the court is likely to direct that the child is seen by an officer of the Children and Family Court Advisory and Support Service (Cafcass) or in Wales CAFCASS Cymru. You should cooperate in this process. Children are not usually made parties to abduction cases, but in certain exceptional circumstances the court can make them parties so that they have their own separate legal representation. These are all matters about which you should seek legal advice.

(Provisions about the power of the court to join parties are contained in rule 12.3 and provisions about the joining and representation of children are contained in Part 16 of these Rules and the Practice Direction 16A (Representation of Children).

Part 3 – Non-Convention Cases

3.1 Applications for the return of children wrongfully removed or retained away from States which are not parties to the 1980 Hague Convention or in respect of children to whom that Convention does not apply, can be made to the High Court under its inherent jurisdiction with respect to children. Such proceedings are referred to as 'non-Convention' cases. In proceedings under the inherent jurisdiction of the High Court with respect to children, the child's welfare is the court's paramount consideration. The extent of the court's enquiry into the child's welfare will depend on the circumstances of the case; in some cases the child's welfare will be best served by a summary hearing and, if necessary, a prompt return to the State from which the child has been removed or retained. In other cases a more detailed enquiry may be necessary (see *Re J (Child Returned Abroad: Convention Rights)* [2005] UKHL 40; [2005] 2 FLR 802).

3.2 Every application for the return of a child under the inherent jurisdiction must be made in the Principal Registry of the Family Division and heard in the High Court.

Provision about the inherent jurisdiction is made at Chapter 5 of Part 12 of the Rules and in Practice Direction 12D (Inherent Jurisdiction (including Wardship) Proceedings).

The Form and content of the application

3.3 An application for the return of a child under the inherent jurisdiction must be made in Form C66 and must include the information in paragraph 2.11 above.

3.4 You must file a statement in support of your application, which must exhibit all the relevant documents. The statement must contain and be verified by a statement of truth in the following terms:

> 'I make this statement knowing that it will be placed before the court, and confirm that to the best of my knowledge and belief its contents are true.'
>
> (Further provisions about statements of truth are contained in Part 17 of these Rules and Practice Direction 17A).

Timetable for Non-Convention Cases

3.5 While the 6 week deadline referred to in paragraph 2.14 is set out in the 1980 Hague Convention and in the Council Regulation, non-Convention child abduction cases must similarly be completed in 6 weeks except where exceptional circumstances make this impossible. Paragraph 2.14 applies to these cases as appropriate for a non-Convention case.

Part 4 – General Provisions

Urgent applications, or applications out of business hours

4.1 Guidance about urgent and out of hours applications is in Practice Direction 12E (Urgent Business).

Police assistance to prevent removal from England and Wales

4.2 The Child Abduction Act 1984 sets out the circumstances in which the removal of a child from this jurisdiction is a criminal offence. The police provide the following 24 hour service to prevent the unlawful removal of a child:

(a) they inform ports directly when there is a real and imminent threat that a child is about to be removed unlawfully from the country; and

(b) they liaise with Immigration Officers at the ports in an attempt to identify children at risk of removal.

4.3 Where the child is under 16, it is not necessary to obtain a court order before seeking police assistance. The police do not need an order to act to protect the child. If an order has already been obtained it should however be produced to the police. Where the child is between 16 and 18, an order must be obtained restricting or restraining removal before seeking police assistance.

4.4 Where the child is a ward of court (see Practice Direction 12D (Inherent Jurisdiction (including Wardship) Proceedings) the court's permission is needed to remove that child from the jurisdiction. When the court has not given that permission and police assistance is sought to prevent the removal of the ward, the applicant must produce evidence that the child is a ward such as:

(a) an order confirming wardship;

(b) an injunction; or
(c) where the matter is urgent and no order has been made, a certified copy of the wardship application.

4.5 The application for police assistance must be made by the applicant or his legal representative to the applicant's local police station except that applications may be made to any police station:

(a) in urgent cases;
(b) where the wardship application has just been issued; or
(c) where the court has just made the order relied on.

4.6 The police will, if they consider it appropriate, institute the 'port alert' system (otherwise known as 'an all ports warning') to try to prevent removal from the jurisdiction where the danger of removal is:

(a) real (ie not being sought merely by way of insurance); and
(b) imminent (ie within 24 to 48 hours).

4.7 The request for police assistance must be accompanied by as much of the following information as possible:

(a) *the child:* the name, sex, date of birth, physical description, nationality and passport number; if the child has more than one nationality or passport, provide details;
(b) *the person likely to remove:* the name, age, physical description, nationality, passport number, relationship to the child, and whether the child is likely to assist him or her; if the person has more than one nationality or passport, provide details;
(c) *person applying for a port alert:* the name, relationship to the child, nationality, telephone number and (if appropriate) solicitor's or other legal representative's name and contact details; if the person has more than one nationality, provide details;
(d) likely destination;
(e) likely time of travel and port of embarkation and, if known, details of travel arrangements;
(f) grounds for port alert (as appropriate) –
  (i) suspected offence under section 1 or section 2 of the Child Abduction Act 1984;
  (ii) the child is subject to a court order.
(g) details of person to whom the child should be returned if intercepted.

4.8 If the police decide that the case is one in which the port-alert system should be used, the child's name will remain on the stop list for **four weeks**. After that time it will be removed automatically unless a further application is made.

HM Passport Office

4.9 Where the court makes an order prohibiting or otherwise restricting the removal of a child from the United Kingdom, or from any specified part of it, or from a specified dependent territory, the court may make an order under section 37 of the Family Law Act 1986 requiring any person to surrender any UK passport which has been issued to, or contains particulars of, the child.

4.10 HM Passport Office ('HMPO') will take action to prevent a United Kingdom passport or replacement passport being issued only where HMPO has been served with a court order expressly requiring a United Kingdom passport to be surrendered, or expressly prohibiting the issue of any further United Kingdom passport facilities to the child without the consent of the court, or the holder of such an order. Accordingly, in every case in which such an order has been made, HMPO must be served the same day if possible, or at the latest the following day, with a copy of the order. It is the responsibility of the applicant to do this. The specimen form of letter set out below should be used and a copy of the court order must be attached to the letter. Delay in sending the letter to HMPO must be kept to an absolute minimum.

PART III

'Intelligence Hub
Her Majesty's Passport Office
3 Northgate
96 Milton Street
Glasgow
G4 0BT

Dear Sir/Madam

……………………v…………………

Case no: ………………………………

This is to inform you that the court has today made an order

*prohibiting the issue of a passport/passports to [name(s)] [date of birth (if known)] of [address] without the consent of the holder of the order.

*requiring [name(s)] [date of birth (if known)] of [address] to surrender the passport(s) issued to him/her/them/the following child[ren] / or which contain(s) particulars of the following child[ren]:

Name Date of Birth

*and has granted an injunction/*made an order restraining the removal of the child[ren] from the jurisdiction.

(*Delete as appropriate)

Please add these names to your records to prevent the issue of further passport facilities for the child[ren]. I enclose a copy of the court order.

Yours faithfully

Applicant's name / Applicant's Solicitor's name'

4.11 Following service on HMPO of an order either expressly requiring a United Kingdom passport to be surrendered by, or expressly prohibiting the issue of any further United Kingdom passport facilities to the child, HMPO will maintain a prohibition on issuing a passport, or further passport facilities until the child's 16th birthday. The order should state that a passport must not be granted/applied for without the consent of the court or the holder of the order.

Note: These requests may also be sent to any of the regional Passport Offices.

4.12 Further information on communicating with HMPO where the court has made a request of, or an order against, HMPO, may be found in The President's Guidance reissued in October 2014: *Communicating with the Home Office in Family Proceedings*. Annex 1 to this Practice Direction contains that Guidance and Annex 2 contains the current version (as at June 2015) of the relevant court form.

4.13 Information about other circumstances, in which HMPO will agree not to issue a passport to a child if HMPO receives an application, or an order in more general terms than set out at 4.11 above, from a person who claims to have parental responsibility for the child, is available from HMPO or at www.gov.uk.

The Home Office

4.14 Information about communicating with the Home Office, where a question of the immigration status of a party arises in family proceedings, may be found in the Protocol: Communicating with the Home Office in Family Proceedings (revised and re-issued October 2010).

Note—The Protocol has been reissued as of October 2014 (see para 4.12).

Press Reporting

4.15 When a child has been abducted and a judge considers that publicity may help in tracing the child, the judge may adjourn the case for a short period to enable representatives of the Press to attend to give the case the widest possible publicity.

4.16. If a Child Rescue Alert has been used concerning a child, within the UK or abroad, it will give rise to media publicity. The court should be informed that this has happened. If there are already court proceedings concerning a child, it is advisable to obtain the agreement of the court before there is publicity to trace a missing child. If the court has not given its permission for a child who is the subject of children proceedings to be identified as the subject of proceedings, to do so would be contempt of court.

Other Assistance

4.17 The Missing Persons Bureau will be participating for the UK in the European Union wide 116 000 hotline for missing children. Parents and children can ring this number for assistance. (It is primarily intended to deal with criminal matters, for example stranger kidnapping.)

4.18 It may also be possible to trace a child by obtaining a court order under the inherent jurisdiction or the wardship jurisdiction of the High Court addressed to certain government departments, as set out in Practice Direction 6C.

PART III

Part 5 – Applications about rights of access

5.1 Access orders made in another Member State of the European Union (except Denmark) can be enforced in England or Wales under the Council Regulation.

5.2 Chapter III of the Council Regulation sets out provision for recognition and enforcement of parental responsibility orders, which include orders for custody and access (child arrangements) between Member States. Under Article 41 of the Council Regulation you can enforce an access order in your favour from another Member State directly, provided you produce the certificate given under Article 41(2) by the court which made the order. This is a quick procedure. The unsuccessful party is not allowed to oppose recognition of the order.

5.3 The rules on recognition and enforcement of parental responsibility orders are in Part 31. You should apply to the High Court using Form C69. Rule 31.8 covers applications for Article 41 of the Council Regulation. You can make the application without notice.

5.4 If the Council Regulation does not apply, and the access order was made by a State party to the European Convention, an application can be made to enforce the order under Article 11 of the European Convention. Paragraph 2.20 above gives further information about how to make the application.

5.5 Article 21 of the 1980 Hague Convention requires the States parties to respect rights of access. However, in the case of *Re G (A Minor) (Hague Convention: Access)* [1993] 1 FLR 669, the Court of Appeal took the view that Article 21 conferred no jurisdiction to determine matters relating to access, or to recognise or enforce foreign access orders (see Practice Note of 5 March 1993: Child Abduction Unit: Lord Chancellor's Department set out in Annex 3 to this Practice Direction). (The Child Abduction Unit is now called ICACU see paragraph 2.6.) An access order which does not fall within the Council Regulation or the (very limited) application of the European Convention may only be enforced by applying for a 'child arrangements order' under section 8 of the Children Act 1989.

5.6 This means that if, during the course of proceedings under the 1980 Hague Convention for a return order, the applicant decides to ask for access (contact) instead of the return of the child, but no agreement can be reached, a separate application for a contact order will have to be made, or the court invited to make a child arrangements order without an application being made (Children Act 1989, s 10(1)(b)).

Part 6 – Child abduction cases between the United Kingdom and Pakistan

6.1 A consensus was reached in January 2003 between the President of the Family Division and the Hon. Chief Justice of Pakistan as to the principles to be applied in resolving child abduction cases between the UK and Pakistan.

The Protocol setting out that consensus can be accessed at:

http://www.fco.gov.uk/resources/en/pdf/2855621/3069133

Note—The Protocol can be found at *www.reunite.org/edit/files/Library%20-%20International%20Regulations/UK-Pakistan%20Protocol.pdf*.

ANNEX 1

Communicating with the Home Office in Family Proceedings

Originally issued December 2002

Re-issued October 2014

1 The 'Communicating with the Home Office in Family Proceedings' protocol enables the family courts to communicate with the Home Office (UK Visas & Immigration/HM Passport Office) to obtain immigration, visa and passport information for family court proceedings.

2 This guidance has been reissued to replace & amalgamate previous guidance issued in 2002, 2004, 2006, 2010 and 2014 (including the Communicating with the Passport Service 2004) to reflect the new contact details for the Home Office Liaison Officer who has responsibility for administering requests made under the Protocol. It does not alter the nature or purpose of the Protocol.

3 Where an order is made against the Home Office in Family Proceedings, the court shall draw up the relevant order. The HMCTS form EX660 should be fully completed (including specifying the details of the relevant family members and their relationship to the child). Parties should provide details of both mother and father if known, whether or not they are involved in the proceedings.

4 The sealed order and the completed EX660 should be sent immediately to:

Home Office Liaison Officer
Her Majesty's Courts and Tribunal Service
Arnhem House
PO Box 6987 Leicester
LE1 6ZX
Email: homeofficeliaison@hmcts.gsi.gov.uk
Telephone: 0116 249 4177
Fax: 0116 249 4302

5 Please note that all information provided in the EX660 will be forwarded to the Home Office. Parties should ensure that any additional information, such as a case synopsis, which it wishes the Home Office to view, has the required leave of the court, set out in the order, to be disclosed to the Home Office. (Note that it is a contempt of court to disclose this information otherwise).

6 Where the query relates to the proposed adoption of a foreign national minor, the Home Office Liaison Officer can advise as to the additional information which will be required.

7 The order and EX660 should clearly state the time by which the information is required. In order to comply with the agreed four (4) week period in for the Home Office to provide a response to the court, parties and court staff should ensure that the Home Office Liaison Officer receives the court order on the day the order is made.

8 Where it will not be possible for court to send the sealed order to the Home Office Liaison Officer on the day it is made, the court when stating the required date of receipt by the court of the information should allow any additional time necessary for the preparation and sending of the order. This is in order to ensure that Home Office has 4 weeks to provide a response from the time it receives the order from the Home Office Liaison Officer. Any reduction in this period may result in a request by the Home Office for further time in which to reply.

9 The request or order should identify the questions it wishes to be answered by the Home Office.

10 Parties should provide the name and contact details of someone who has agreed and is able to provide further information should it be needed.

11 The order and EX660 should be forwarded to the Home Office Liaison Officer together with such information as is sufficient to enable the Home Office to understand the nature of the case, to identify whether the case involves an adoption, and to identify whether the immigration issues raised might relate to an asylum or non-asylum application.

12 The Home Office Liaison Officer will then send to an appropriate officer in the Home Office the enquiry, together with a copy of any order made. The Home Office official will be personally responsible for either:

(a) answering the query themselves, by retrieving the file and preparing a statement for the court; or

(b) forwarding the request to a caseworker or relevant official with carriage of that particular file.

13 The Home Office Liaison Officer will follow up as required in order to ensure that the information is received by the court in time, and will receive the information before forwarding it on as instructed by the judge or court making the request.

14 Attached is a sample court order and completed EX660 which should provide further useful guidance.

****

Note—For the latest version of Form C21, see *www.familylaw.co.uk/news_and_comment/communicating-with-the-home-office-in-family-proceedings*.

ANNEX 2

****

Note—For the latest version of Form EX660, see *www.familylaw.co.uk/news_and_comment/communicating-with-the-home-office-in-family-proceedings*.

ANNEX 3

See paragraph 5.5

Practice Note

5 March 1993

Citations: [1993] 1 FLR 804

Child Abduction Unit: Lord Chancellor's Department

Duties of the Central Authority for England and Wales under Article 21 of the Hague Convention on the Civil Aspects of International Child Abduction

CHILD ABDUCTION AND CUSTODY ACT 1985

In the case of *Re G (A Minor) (Hague Convention: Access)* [1993] 1 FLR 669 the Court of Appeal considered the duties of the Central Authority for England and Wales on receiving an application in respect of rights of access under Art 21 of the Hague Convention.

The Court of Appeal took the view that Art 21 conferred no jurisdiction to determine matters relating to access, or to recognise or enforce foreign access orders. It provides, however, for executive co-operation in the enforcement of such recognition as national law allows.

Accordingly, the duty of the Central Authority is to make appropriate arrangements for the applicant by providing solicitors to act on his behalf in applying for legal aid and instituting proceedings in the High Court under s 8 of the Children Act 1989.

If, during the course of proceedings under Art 21 of the Convention, the applicant decides to seek access instead of the return of the child, but no agreement can be reached and the provisions of the European Convention on the Recognition and Enforcement of Decisions Concerning Custody of Children and on Restoration of Custody of Children are not available, a separate application under s 8 of the Children Act 1989 will have to be made.

Central Authority for England and Wales

NOTE: The Child Abduction Unit is now called ICACU, see paragraph 2.6.

Practice Direction 12G – Communication of Information

This Practice Direction supplements FPR Part 12, Chapter 7

1.1 Chapter 7 deals with the communication of information (whether or not contained in a document filed with the court) relating to proceedings which relate to children.

1.2 Subject to any direction of the court, information may be communicated for the purposes of the law relating to contempt in accordance with paragraphs 2.1, 3.1 or 4.1.

Communication of information by a party etc for other purposes

2.1 A person specified in the first column of the following table may communicate to a person listed in the second column such information as is specified in the third column for the purpose or purposes specified in the fourth column –

A party	A lay adviser, a McKenzie Friend, or a person arranging or providing pro bono legal services	Any information relating to the proceedings	To enable the party to obtain advice or assistance in relation to the proceedings
A party	A health care professional or a person or body providing counselling services for children or families		To enable the party or any child of the party to obtain health care or counselling
A party	The Secretary of State, a McKenzie Friend, a lay adviser or the First-tier Tribunal dealing with an appeal made under section 20 of the Child Support Act 1991		For the purposes of making or responding to an appeal under section 20 of the Child Support Act 1991 or the determination of such an appeal

A party or other person lawfully in receipt of information	The Secretary of State, a McKenzie Friend, a lay adviser or the Upper Tier Tribunal dealing with an appeal under section 24 of the Child Support Act 1991 in respect of a decision of the First-tier Tribunal that was made under section 20 of that Act		For a purpose connected with an appeal under section 24 of the Child Support Act 1991 in respect of a decision of the First-tier Tribunal that was made under section 20 of that Act
A party	An adoption panel		To enable the adoption panel to discharge its functions as appropriate
A party	A local authority's medical adviser appointed under the Adoption Agencies Regulations 2005 or the Adoption Agencies (Wales) Regulations 2005		To enable the medical adviser to discharge his or her functions as appropriate
A party	The European Court of Human Rights		For the purpose of making an application to the European Court of Human Rights
A party or any person lawfully in receipt of information	The Children's Commissioner or the Children's Commissioner for Wales		To refer an issue affecting the interests of children to the Children's Commissioner or the Children's Commissioner for Wales
A party, any person lawfully in receipt of information or a proper officer	A person or body conducting an approved research project		For the purpose of an approved research project
A legal representative or a professional legal adviser	A person or body responsible for investigating or determining complaints in relation to legal representatives or professional legal advisers		For the purposes of the investigation or determination of a complaint in relation to a legal representative or a professional legal adviser

A legal representative or a professional legal adviser	A professional indemnity insurer		To enable the professional indemnity insurer to be notified of a claim or complaint, or potential claim or complaint, in relation to the legal representative or a professional legal adviser, and the legal representative or professional legal adviser to obtain advice in respect of that claim or complaint
A legal representative or a professional legal adviser	A person or body assessing quality assurance systems		To enable the legal representative or professional legal adviser to obtain a quality assurance assessment
A legal representative or a professional legal adviser	An accreditation body	Any information relating to the proceedings providing that it does not, or is not likely to, identify any person involved in the proceedings	To enable the legal representative or professional legal adviser to obtain accreditation
A party	A police officer	The text or summary of the whole or part of a judgment given in the proceedings	For the purpose of a criminal investigation
A party or any person lawfully in receipt of information	A member of the Crown Prosecution Service		To enable the Crown Prosecution Service to discharge its functions under any enactment

Communication for the effective functioning of Cafcass and CAFCASS Cymru

3.1 An officer of the Service or a Welsh family proceedings officer, as appropriate, may communicate to a person listed in the second column such information as is specified in the third column for the purpose or purposes specified in the fourth column –

A Welsh family proceedings officer	A person or body exercising statutory functions relating to inspection of CAFCASS Cymru	Any information relating to the proceedings which is required by the person or body responsible for the inspection	For the purpose of an inspection of CAFCASS Cymru by a body or person appointed by the Welsh Ministers

An officer of the Service or a Welsh family proceedings officer	The Health and Care Professions Council or the Care Council for Wales	Any information relating to the proceedings providing that it does not, or is not likely to, identify any person involved in the proceedings	For the purpose of initial and continuing accreditation as a social worker of a person providing services to Cafcass or CAFCASS Cymru in accordance with section 13(2) of the Criminal Justice and Courts Services Act 2000 or section 36 of the Children Act 2004 as the case may be
An officer of the Service or a Welsh family proceedings officer	A person or body providing services relating to professional development or training to Cafcass or CAFCASS Cymru	Any information relating to the proceedings providing that it does not, or is not likely to, identify any person involved in the proceedings without that person's consent	To enable the person or body to provide the services, where the services cannot be effectively provided without such disclosure
An officer of the Service or a Welsh family proceedings officer	A person employed by or contracted to Cafcass or CAFCASS Cymru for the purposes of carrying out the functions referred to in column 4 of this row	Any information relating to the proceedings	Engagement in processes internal to Cafcass or CAFCASS Cymru which relate to the maintenance of necessary records concerning the proceedings, or to ensuring that Cafcass or CAFCASS Cymru functions are carried out to a satisfactory standard

PART III

Communication to and by Ministers of the Crown and Welsh Ministers

4.1 A person specified in the first column of the following table may communicate to a person listed in the second column such information as is specified in the third column for the purpose or purposes specified in the fourth column –

A party or any person lawfully in receipt of information relating to the proceedings	A Minister of the Crown with responsibility for a government department engaged, or potentially engaged, in an application before the European Court of Human Rights relating to the proceedings	Any information relating to the proceedings of which he or she is in lawful possession	To provide the department with information relevant, or potentially relevant, to the proceedings before the European Court of Human Rights

A Minister of the Crown	The European Court of Human Rights		For the purpose of engagement in an application before the European Court of Human Rights relating to the proceedings
A Minister of the Crown	Lawyers advising or representing the United Kingdom in an application before the European Court of Human Rights relating to the proceedings		For the purpose of receiving advice or for effective representation in relation to the application before the European Court of Human Rights
A Minister of the crown or a Welsh Minister	Another Minister, or Ministers, of the Crown or a Welsh Minister		For the purpose of notification, discussion and the giving or receiving of advice regarding issues raised by the information in which the relevant departments have, or may have, an interest

5.1 This paragraph applies to communications made in accordance with paragraphs 2.1, 3.1 and 4.1 and the reference in this paragraph to 'the table' means the table in the relevant paragraph.

5.2 A person in the second column of the table may only communicate information relating to the proceedings received from a person in the first column for the purpose or purposes –

(a) for which he or she received that information; or

(b) of professional development or training, providing that any communication does not, or is not likely to, identify any person involved in the proceedings without that person's consent.

6.1 In this Practice Direction –

'accreditation body' means –

(a) The Law Society,

(b) Resolution, or

(c) the Lord Chancellor in exercise of the Lord Chancellor's functions in relation to legal aid;

'adoption panel' means a panel established in accordance with regulation 3 of the Adoption Agencies Regulations 2005 or regulation 3 of the Adoption Agencies (Wales) Regulations 2005;

'approved research project' means a project of research –

(a) approved in writing by a Secretary of State after consultation with the President of the Family Division,

(b) approved in writing by the President of the Family Division, or

(c) conducted under section 83 of the Act of 1989 or section 13 of the Criminal Justice and Court Services Act 2000;

'body assessing quality assurance systems' includes –

(a) The Law Society,

(b) the Lord Chancellor in exercise of the Lord Chancellor's functions in relation to legal aid, or

(c) The General Council of the Bar;

'body or person responsible for investigating or determining complaints in relation to legal representatives or professional legal advisers' means –

(a) The Law Society,
(b) The General Council of the Bar,
(c) The Institute of Legal Executives,
(d) The Legal Services Ombudsman; or
(e) The Office of Legal Complaints.

'Cafcass' has the meaning assigned to it by section 11 of the Criminal Justice and Courts Services Act 2000;

'CAFCASS Cymru' means the part of the Welsh Assembly Government exercising the functions of Welsh Ministers under Part 4 of the Children Act 2004;

'criminal investigation' means an investigation conducted by police officers with a view to it being ascertained –
(a) whether a person should be charged with an offence, or
(b) whether a person charged with an offence is guilty of it;

'health care professional' means –
(a) a registered medical practitioner,
(b) a registered nurse or midwife,
(c) a clinical psychologist, or
(d) a child psychotherapist;

'lay adviser' means a non-professional person who gives lay advice on behalf of an organisation in the lay advice sector;

'McKenzie Friend' means any person permitted by the court to sit beside an unrepresented litigant in court to assist that litigant by prompting, taking notes and giving him advice; and

'social worker' has the meaning assigned to it by section 55 of the Care Standards Act 2000.

PART III

Practice Direction 12H – Contribution Orders

This Practice Direction supplements FPR Part 12

1.1 Paragraph 23(6) of Schedule 2 to the 1989 Act provides that where –
(a) a contribution order is in force;
(b) the local authority serve another contribution notice; and
(c) the contributor and the local authority reach an agreement under paragraph 22(7) in respect of that other contribution notice,

the effect of the agreement shall be to discharge the order from the date on which it is agreed that the agreement shall take effect.

1.2 Where a local authority notifies the court of an agreement reached under paragraph 23(6) of Schedule 2 to the 1989 Act, the notification must be sent in writing to the designated officer of the court.

Practice Direction 12I – Applications for Reporting Restriction Orders

This Practice Direction supplements FPR Part 12

1 This direction applies to any application in the Family Division founded on Convention rights for an order restricting publication of information about children or incapacitated adults.

2 Applications to be heard in the High Court

Orders can only be made in the High Court and are normally dealt with by a Judge of the Family Division. If the need for an order arises in existing proceedings in the family court, judges should either transfer the application to the High Court or consult their Family Division Liaison Judge. Where the matter is urgent, it can be heard by the Urgent Applications Judge of the Family Division (out of hours contact number 020 7947 6000).

3 *Service of application on the national news media*

Section 12(2) of the Human Rights Act 1998 means that an injunction restricting the exercise of the right to freedom of expression must not be granted where the person against whom the application is made is neither present nor represented unless the court is satisfied (a) that the applicant has taken all practicable steps to notify the respondent, or (b) that there are compelling reasons why the respondent should not be notified.

Service of applications for reporting restriction orders on the national media can now be effected via the Press Association's CopyDirect service, to which national newspapers and broadcasters subscribe as a means of receiving notice of such applications.

The court will bear in mind that legal advisers to the media (i) are used to participating in hearings at very short notice where necessary; and (ii) are able to differentiate between information provided for legal purposes and information for editorial use. Service of applications via the CopyDirect service should henceforth be the norm.

The court retains the power to make without notice orders, but such cases will be exceptional, and an order will always give persons affected liberty to apply to vary or discharge it at short notice.

4 *Further guidance*

The *Practice Note Applications for Reporting Restriction Orders* dated 18 March 2005 and issued jointly by the Official Solicitor and the Deputy Director of Legal Services, provides valuable guidance and should be followed.

5 Issued with the concurrence and approval of the Lord Chancellor.

Practice Direction 12J – Child Arrangements & Contact Order: Domestic Violence and Harm

This Practice Direction supplements FPR Part 12

Summary

This Practice Direction supplements FPR Part 12, and incorporates and supersedes the President's Guidance in Relation to Split Hearings (May 2010) as it applies to proceedings for child arrangements orders.

1 This Practice Direction applies to any family proceedings in the Family Court under the relevant parts of the Children Act 1989 or the relevant parts of the Adoption and Children Act 2002 ('the 2002 Act') in which an application is made for a child arrangements order, or in which any question arises about where a child should live, or about contact between a child and a parent or other family member, where the court considers that an order should be made.

2 The purpose of this Practice Direction is to set out what the Family Court should do in any case in which it is alleged or admitted, or there is other reason to believe, that the child or a party has experienced domestic violence or abuse perpetrated by another party or that there is a risk of such violence or abuse.

3 For the purpose of this Practice Direction –

'Domestic violence' includes any incident or pattern of incidents of controlling, coercive or threatening behaviour, violence or abuse between those aged 16 or over who are or have been intimate partners or family members regardless of gender or sexuality. This can encompass, but is not limited to, psychological, physical, sexual, financial, or emotional abuse.

'Controlling behaviour' means an act or pattern of acts designed to make a person subordinate and/or dependent by isolating them from sources of support, exploiting their resources and capacities for personal gain, depriving them of the means needed for independence, resistance and escape and regulating their everyday behaviour.

'Coercive behaviour' means an act or a pattern of acts of assault, threats, humiliation and intimidation or other abuse that is used to harm, punish, or frighten the victim.

General principles

4 The Family Court presumes that the involvement of a parent in a child's life will further the child's welfare, so long as the parent can be involved in a way that does not put the child or other parent at risk of suffering harm.

5 Domestic violence and abuse is harmful to children, and/or puts children at risk of harm, whether they are subjected to violence or abuse, or witness one of their parents being violent or abusive to the other parent, or live in a home in which violence or abuse is perpetrated (even if the child is too young to be conscious of the behaviour). Children may suffer direct physical, psychological and/or emotional harm from living with violence or abuse, and may also suffer harm indirectly where the violence or abuse impairs the parenting capacity of either or both of their parents.

6 The court must, at all stages of the proceedings, and specifically at the First Hearing Dispute Resolution Appointment ('FHDRA'), consider whether domestic violence is raised as an issue, either by the parties or by Cafcass or CAFCASS Cymru or otherwise, and if so must–

- identify at the earliest opportunity (usually at the FHDRA) the factual and welfare issues involved;
- consider the nature of any allegation, admission or evidence of domestic violence or abuse, and the extent to which it would be likely to be relevant in deciding whether to make a child arrangements order and, if so, in what terms;
- give directions to enable contested relevant factual and welfare issues to be tried as soon as possible and fairly;
- ensure that where violence or abuse is admitted or proven, that any child arrangements order in place protects the safety and wellbeing of the child and the parent with whom the child is living, and does not expose them to the risk of further harm. In particular, the court must be satisfied that any contact ordered with a parent who has perpetrated violence or abuse is safe and in the best interests of the child; and
- ensure that any interim child arrangements order (i.e. considered by the court before determination of the facts, and in the absence of admission) is only made having followed the guidance in paragraphs 25–27 below.

7 In all cases it is for the court to decide whether a child arrangements order accords with Section 1(1) of the Children Act 1989; any proposed child arrangements order, whether to be made by agreement between the parties or otherwise must be scrutinised by the court accordingly. The court shall not make a child arrangements order by consent or give permission for an application for a child arrangements order to be withdrawn, unless the parties are present in court, all initial safeguarding checks have been obtained by the court, and an officer of Cafcass or CAFCASS Cymru has spoken to the parties separately, except where it is satisfied that there is no risk of harm to the child in so doing.

8 In considering, on an application for a child arrangements order by consent, whether there is any risk of harm to the child, the court shall consider all the evidence and information available. The court may direct a report under Section 7 of the Children Act 1989, to be provided either orally or in writing, before it makes its decision; in such a case, the court may ask for information about any advice given by the officer preparing the report to the parties and whether they, or the

child, have been referred to any other agency, including local authority children's services. If the report is not in writing, the court shall make a note of its substance on the court file.

Before the FHDRA

9 Where any information provided to the court before the FHDRA or other first hearing (whether as a result of initial safeguarding enquiries by Cafcass or CAFCASS Cymru or on form C1A or otherwise) indicates that there are issues of domestic violence or abuse which may be relevant to the court's determination, the court must ensure that the issues are addressed at the hearing, and that the parties are not expected to engage in conciliation or other forms of dispute resolution which are not suitable.

10 If at any stage the court is advised by the applicant, by Cafcass or CAFCASS Cymru or otherwise that there is a need for special arrangements to secure the safety of any party or child attending any hearing, the court shall ensure that appropriate arrangements are made for the hearing and for all subsequent hearings in the case, unless it considers that these are no longer necessary.

First hearing/FHDRA

11 At the FHDRA, if the parties have not been provided with the safeguarding letter/report by Cafcass/CAFCASS Cymru, the court shall inform the parties of the content of any safeguarding letter or report or other information which has been provided by Cafcass or CAFCASS Cymru, unless it considers that to do so would create a risk of harm to a party or the child.

12 Where the results of Cafcass or CAFCASS Cymru safeguarding checks are not available at the FHDRA, and no other reliable safeguarding information is available, the court shall adjourn the FHDRA until the results of safeguarding checks are available. The court shall not generally make an interim child arrangements order, or orders for contact, in the absence of safeguarding information, unless it is to protect the safety of the child.

13 There is a continuing duty on the Cafcass Officer/Welsh FPO which requires them to provide a risk assessment for the court under section 16A Children Act 1989 if they are given cause to suspect that the child concerned is at risk of harm. Specific provision about service of a risk assessment under section 16A of the 1989 Act is made by rule 12.34 of the FPR 2010.

14 The court must ascertain at the earliest opportunity whether domestic violence or abuse is raised as an issue of risk of harm to the child which is likely to be relevant to any decision of the court relating to the welfare of the child, and specifically on the making of any child arrangements order.

Admissions

15 Where at any hearing an admission of domestic violence or abuse toward another person or the child is made by a party, the admission should be recorded in writing and retained on the court file. A copy of any record of admissions must be made available as soon as possible to any Cafcass officer or officer of CAFCASS Cymru or local authority officer preparing a report under section 7 of the Children Act 1989.

Directions for a fact-finding hearing

16 The court should determine as soon as possible whether it is necessary to conduct a fact-finding hearing in relation to any disputed allegation of domestic violence or abuse –

(a) in order to provide a factual basis for any welfare report or for assessment of the factors set out in paragraphs 36 and 37 (below);
(b) in order to provide a basis for an accurate assessment of risk; or
(c) before it can consider any final welfare-based order(s) in relation to child arrangements; or
(d) before it considers the need for a domestic violence-related Activity (such as a Domestic Violence Perpetrator Programme (DVPP)).

17 In determining whether it is necessary to conduct a fact-finding hearing, the court should consider –

(a) the views of the parties and of Cafcass or CAFCASS Cymru;
(b) whether there are admissions by a party which provide a sufficient factual basis on which to proceed;
(c) if a party is in receipt of legal aid, whether the evidence required to be provided to obtain legal aid provides a sufficient factual basis on which to proceed;
(d) whether there is other evidence available to the court that provides a sufficient factual basis on which to proceed;
(e) whether the factors set out in paragraphs 36 and 37 below can be determined without a fact-finding hearing;
(f) the nature of the evidence required to resolve disputed allegations;
(g) whether the nature and extent of the allegations, if proved, would be relevant to the issue before the court; and
(h) whether a separate fact-finding hearing would be necessary and proportionate in all the circumstances of the case.

18 Where the court determines that a finding of fact hearing is not necessary, the order shall record the reasons for that decision.

19 Where the court considers that a fact-finding hearing is necessary, it must give directions as to how the proceedings are to be conducted to ensure that the matters in issue are determined as soon as possible, fairly and proportionately, and within the capabilities of the parties. In particular it should consider –

(a) what are the key facts in dispute;
(b) whether it is necessary for the fact-finding to take place at a separate (and earlier) hearing than the welfare hearing;
(c) whether the key facts in dispute can be contained in a schedule or a table (known as a Scott Schedule) which sets out what the applicant complains of or alleges, what the respondent says in relation to each individual allegation or complaint; the allegations in the schedule should be focused on the factual issues to be tried; and if so, whether it is practicable for this schedule to be completed at the first hearing, with the assistance of the judge;
(d) what evidence is required in order to determine the existence of a pattern of coercive, controlling or threatening behaviour, violence or abuse;
(e) directing the parties to file written statements giving details of such behaviour and of any response;
(f) whether documents are required from third parties such as the police or health services and giving directions for those documents to be obtained;
(g) whether oral evidence may be required from third parties and if so, giving directions for the filing of written statements from such third parties;
(h) whether any other evidence is required to enable the court to decide the key issues and giving directions for that evidence to be provided;
(i) what evidence the alleged victim of violence is able to give and what support the alleged victim may require at the fact-finding hearing in order to give that evidence;
(j) what support the alleged perpetrator may need in order to have a reasonable opportunity to challenge the evidence; and
(k) whether a pre-hearing review would be useful prior to the fact-finding hearing to ensure directions have been complied with and all the required evidence is available.

20 Where the court fixes a fact-finding hearing, it must at the same time fix a Dispute Resolution Appointment to follow. Subject to the exception in paragraph 31 below, the hearings should be arranged in such a way that they are conducted by the same judge or, wherever possible, by the same panel of lay justices; where it is not possible to assemble the same panel of justices, the resumed hearing should be listed before at least the same chairperson of the lay justices. Judicial continuity is important.

Reports under Section 7

21 In any case where a risk of harm to a child resulting from domestic violence or abuse is raised as an issue, the court should consider directing that a report on the question of contact, or any other matters relating to the welfare of the child, be prepared under section 7 of the Children Act 1989 by an Officer of Cafcass or a Welsh family proceedings officer (or local authority officer if appropriate), unless the court is satisfied that it is not necessary to do so in order to safeguard the child's interests.

22 If the court directs that there shall be a fact-finding hearing on the issue of domestic violence or abuse, the court will not usually request a section 7 report until after that hearing. In that event, the court should direct that any judgment is provided to Cafcass/CAFCASS Cymru; if there is no transcribed judgment, an agreed list of findings should be provided.

23 Any request for a section 7 report should set out clearly the matters the court considers need to be addressed.

Representation of the child

24 Subject to the seriousness of the allegations made and the difficulty of the case, the court shall consider whether it is appropriate for the child who is the subject of the application to be made a party to the proceedings and be separately represented. If the court considers that the child should be so represented, it shall review the allocation decision so that it is satisfied that the case proceeds before the correct level of judge in the Family Court.

Interim orders before determination of relevant facts

25 Where the court gives directions for a fact-finding hearing, the court should consider whether an interim child arrangements order is in the interests of the child; and in particular whether the safety of the child and (bearing in mind the impact which domestic violence against a parent can have on the emotional well-being of the child) the parent who has made the allegation and is at any time caring for the child can be secured before, during and after any contact.

26 In deciding any interim child arrangements question pending a full hearing the court should –

(a) take into account the matters set out in section 1(3) of the Children Act 1989 or section 1(4) of the Adoption and Children Act 2002 ('the welfare check-list'), as appropriate; and

(b) give particular consideration to the likely effect on the child, and on the care given to the child by the parent who has made the allegation of domestic violence, of any contact and any risk of harm, whether physical, emotional or psychological, which the child and that parent is likely to suffer as a consequence of making or declining to make an order.

27 Where the court is considering whether to make an order for interim contact, it should in addition consider –

(a) the arrangements required to ensure, as far as possible, that any risk of harm to the child and the parent who is at any time caring for the child is minimised and that the safety of the child and the parties is secured; and in particular:

  (i) whether the contact should be supervised or supported, and if so, where and by whom; and

  (ii) the availability of appropriate facilities for that purpose;

(b) if direct contact is not appropriate, whether it is in the best interests of the child to make an order for indirect contact; and

(c) whether contact will be beneficial for the child.

The fact-finding hearing

28 While ensuring that the allegations are properly put and responded to, the fact-finding hearing can be an inquisitorial (or investigative) process, which at all times must protect the interests of all involved. At the fact-finding hearing–

- Each party can be asked to identify what questions they wish to ask of the other party, and to set out or confirm in sworn evidence their version of the disputed key facts.
- The judge or lay justices should be prepared where necessary and appropriate to conduct the questioning of the witnesses on behalf of the parties, focusing on the key issues in the case.

Victims of violence are likely to find direct cross-examination by their alleged abuser frightening and intimidating, and thus it may be particularly appropriate for the judge or lay justices to conduct the questioning on behalf of the other party in these circumstances, in order to ensure both parties are able to give their best evidence.

29 The court should, wherever practicable, make findings of fact as to the nature and degree of any domestic violence or abuse which is established and its effect on the child, the child's parents and any other relevant person. The court shall record its findings in writing, and shall serve a copy on the parties. A copy of any record of findings of fact or of admissions must be sent to any officer preparing a report under Section 7 of the 1989 Act.

30 At the conclusion of any fact-finding hearing, the court shall consider, notwithstanding any earlier direction for a section 7 report, whether it is in the best interests of the child for the court to give further directions about the preparation or scope of any report under section 7; where necessary, it may adjourn the proceedings for a brief period to enable the officer to make representations about the preparation or scope of any further enquiries. The court should also consider whether it would be assisted by any social work, psychiatric, psychological or other assessment of any party or the child (such as an expert risk assessment), and if so (subject to any necessary consent) make directions for such assessment to be undertaken and for the filing of any consequent report. Any section 7 or other report should address the factors set out in paragraphs 36 and 37, unless the court directs otherwise.

31 Where the court has made findings of fact on disputed allegations, any subsequent hearing in the proceedings should be conducted by the same judge or by at least the same chairperson of the justices. Exceptions may be made only where observing this requirement would result in delay to the planned timetable and the judge or chairperson is satisfied, for reasons recorded in writing, that the detriment to the welfare of the child would outweigh the detriment to the fair trial of the proceedings.

In all cases where domestic violence or abuse has occurred

32 The court should take steps to obtain (or direct the parties or an Officer of Cafcass or a Welsh family proceedings officer to obtain) information about the facilities available locally to assist any party or the child in cases where domestic violence or abuse has occurred.

33 Following any determination of the nature and extent of domestic violence or abuse, whether or not following a fact-finding hearing, the court should consider whether any party should seek advice, treatment or other intervention as a precondition to any child arrangements order being made or as a means of assisting the court in ascertaining the likely risk of harm to the child and to the parent with whom the child is living from that person, and may (with the consent of that party) give directions for such attendance and the filing of any consequent report.

34 Further or as an alternative to the advice, treatment or other intervention referred to in paragraph 33 above, the court may make an Activity Direction under section 11A and 11B Children Act 1989. Any intervention directed pursuant to this provision should be one commissioned and approved by Cafcass. It is acknowledged that acceptance on a DVPP is subject to a suitability assessment by the service provider, and that completion of a DVPP will take time in order to achieve the aim of risk-reduction for the long-term benefit of the child and the parent with whom the child is living.

Factors to be taken into account when determining whether to make child arrangements orders in all cases where domestic violence or abuse has occurred

35 When deciding the issue of child arrangements the court should ensure that any order for contact will be safe and in the best interests of the child.

PART III

36 In the light of any findings of fact the court should apply the individual matters in the welfare checklist with reference to those findings; in particular, where relevant findings of domestic violence or abuse have been made, the court should in every case consider any harm which the child and the parent with whom the child is living has suffered as a consequence of that violence or abuse, and any harm which the child and the parent with whom the child is living, is at risk of suffering if a child arrangements order is made. The court should only make an order for contact if it can be satisfied that the physical and emotional safety of the child and the parent with whom the child is living can, as far as possible, be secured before during and after contact, and that the parent with whom the child is living will not be subjected to further controlling or coercive behaviour by the other parent.

37 In every case where a finding of domestic violence or abuse is made, the court should consider the conduct of both parents towards each other and towards the child; in particular, the court should consider –

(a) the effect of the domestic violence or abuse on the child and on the arrangements for where the child is living;
(b) the effect of the domestic violence or abuse on the child and its effect on the child's relationship with the parents;
(c) whether the applicant parent is motivated by a desire to promote the best interests of the child or is using the process to continue a process of violence, abuse, intimidation or harassment or controlling or coercive behaviour against the other parent;
(d) the likely behaviour during contact of the parent against whom findings are made and its effect on the child; and
(e) the capacity of the parents to appreciate the effect of past violence or abuse and the potential for future violence or abuse.

Directions as to how contact is to proceed

38 Where the court has made findings of domestic violence or abuse but, having applied the welfare checklist, nonetheless considers that direct contact is safe and beneficial for the child, the court should consider what, if any, directions or conditions are required to enable the order to be carried into effect and in particular should consider–

(a) whether or not contact should be supervised, and if so, where and by whom;
(b) whether to impose any conditions to be complied with by the party in whose favour the order for contact has been made and if so, the nature of those conditions, for example by way of seeking intervention (subject to any necessary consent);
(c) whether such contact should be for a specified period or should contain provisions which are to have effect for a specified period; and
(d) whether it will be necessary, in the child's best interests, to review the operation of the order; if so the court should set a date for the review consistent with the timetable for the child, and shall give directions to ensure that at the review the court has full information about the operation of the order.

39 Where the court does not consider direct contact to be appropriate, it shall consider whether it is safe and beneficial for the child to make an order for indirect contact.

The reasons of the court

40 In its judgment or reasons the court should always make clear how its findings on the issue of domestic violence or abuse have influenced its decision on the issue of arrangements for the child. In particular, where the court has found domestic violence or abuse proved but nonetheless makes an order which results in the child having future contact with the perpetrator of domestic violence or abuse, the court should always explain, whether by way of reference to the welfare check-list the factors in paragraphs 36 and 37 or otherwise, why it takes the view that the order which it has made is safe and beneficial for the child.

This Practice Direction is issued by the President of the Family Division, as the nominee of the Lord Chief Justice, with the agreement of the Lord Chancellor.

Practice Direction 12K – Children Act 1989: Exclusion Requirement

This Practice Direction supplements FPR Part 12

Under s 38A(5) and s 44A(5) of the Children Act 1989 the court may attach a power of arrest to an exclusion requirement included in an interim care order or an emergency protection order. In cases where an order is made which includes an exclusion requirement, the following shall apply:

(1) If a power of arrest is attached to the order then unless the person to whom the exclusion requirement refers was given notice of the hearing and attended the hearing, the name of that person and that an order has been made including an exclusion requirement to which a power of arrest has been attached shall be announced in open court at the earliest opportunity. This may be either on the same day when the court proceeds to hear cases in open court or where there is no further business in open court on that day at the next listed sitting of the court.

(2) When a person arrested under a power of arrest cannot conveniently be brought before the relevant judicial authority sitting in a place normally used as a courtroom within 24 hours after the arrest, he may be brought before the relevant judicial authority at any convenient place but, as the liberty of the subject is involved, the press and the public should be permitted to be present, unless security needs make this impracticable.

(3) Any order of committal made otherwise than in public or in a courtroom open to the public, shall be announced in open court at the earliest opportunity. This may be either on the same day when the court proceeds to hear cases in open court or where there is no further business in open court on that day at the next listed sitting of the court. The announcement shall state –

(a) the name of the person committed,

(b) in general terms the nature of the contempt of the court in respect of which the order of committal has been made, and

(c) the length of the period of committal.

Practice Direction 12L – Children Act 1989: Risk Assessments under Section 16A

This Practice Direction supplements FPR Part 12

1 This Practice Direction applies to any family proceedings in the High Court or the family court in which a risk assessment is made under section 16A of the Children Act 1989 ('the 1989 Act'). It has effect from 1 October 2007.

2 Section 16A(2) of the 1989 Act provides that, if in carrying out any function to which the section applies (as set out in section 16A(1)), an officer of the Service or a Welsh family proceedings officer is given cause to suspect that the child concerned is at risk of harm, the officer must make a risk assessment in relation to the child and provide the risk assessment to the court.

3 The duty to provide the risk assessment to the court arises irrespective of the outcome of the assessment. Where an officer is given cause to suspect that the child concerned is at risk of harm and makes a risk assessment in accordance with section 16A(2), the officer must provide the assessment to the court, even if he or she reaches the conclusion that there is no risk of harm to the child.

4 The fact that a risk assessment has been carried out is a material fact that should be placed before the court, whatever the outcome of the assessment. In reporting the outcome to the court, the officer should make clear the factor or factors that triggered the decision to carry out the assessment.

5 Issued by the President of the Family Division, as the nominee of the Lord Chief Justice, with the agreement of the Lord Chancellor.

Practice Direction 12M – Family Assistance Orders: Consultation

This Practice Direction supplements FPR Part 12

1 This Practice Direction applies to any family proceedings in the High Court or the family court in which the court is considering whether to make a family assistance order under section 16 of the Children Act 1989, as amended ('the 1989 Act'). It has effect from 1 October 2007.

2 Before making a family assistance order the court must have obtained the opinion of the appropriate officer about whether it would be in the best interests of the child in question for a family assistance order to be made and, if so, how the family assistance order could operate and for what period.

3 The appropriate officer will be an officer of the Service, a Welsh family proceedings officer or an officer of a local authority, depending on the category of officer the court proposes to require to be made available under the family assistance order.

4 The opinion of the appropriate officer may be given orally or in writing (for example, it may form part of a report under section 7 of the 1989 Act).

5 Before making a family assistance order the court must give any person whom it proposes be named in the order an opportunity to comment upon any opinion given by the appropriate officer.

6 Issued by the President of the Family Division, as the nominee of the Lord Chief Justice, with the agreement of the Lord Chancellor.

Practice Direction 12N – Enforcement of Children Act 1989 Child Arrangements Orders: Disclosure of Information to Officers of the National Probation Service (High Court and County Court)

This Practice Direction supplements FPR Part 12

1 This Practice Direction applies to proceedings in the High Court or the family court where:

(a) the court is considering an application for an enforcement order[1] or for an order following an alleged breach of an enforcement order[2] and asks an officer of the Service or a Welsh family proceedings officer to provide information to the court in accordance with section 11L(5) of the Children Act 1989; or

1 Under section 11J of the Children Act 1989.
2 Under paragraph 9 of Schedule A1 to the Children Act 1989.

(b) the court makes an enforcement order or an order following an alleged breach of an enforcement order and asks an officer of the Service or a Welsh family proceedings officer to monitor compliance with that order and to report to the court in accordance with section 11M of the Children Act 1989.

2 In all cases in which paragraph 1 applies, the officer of the Service or Welsh family proceedings officer will need to discuss aspects of the court case with an officer of the National Probation Service.

3 In order to ensure that the officer of the Service or Welsh family proceedings officer will not potentially be in contempt of court by virtue of such discussions, the court should, when making a request under section 11L(5) or section 11M of the Children Act 1989, give leave to that officer to disclose to the National Probation Service such information (whether or not contained in a document filed with the court) in relation to the proceedings as is necessary.

4 This Practice Direction comes into force on 8 December 2008.

Practice Direction 12O – Child: Arrival by Air

This Practice Direction supplements FPR Part 12

Where a person seeks an order for the return to him of children about to arrive in England by air and desires to have information to enable him to meet the aeroplane, the judge should be asked to include in his order a direction that the airline operating the flight, and, if he has the information, the immigration officer at the appropriate airport, should supply such information to that person.

To obtain such information in such circumstances in a case where a person already has an order for the return to him of children, that person should apply to a judge ex parte for such a direction.

Practice Direction 12P – Removal from Jurisdiction: Issue of Passports

This Practice Direction supplements FPR Part 12

1 Removal from jurisdiction

The President has directed that on application for leave to remove from the jurisdiction for holiday periods a ward of court who has been placed by a local authority with foster-parents whose identity the court considers should remain confidential, for example because they are prospective adopters, it is important that such foster-parents should not be identified in the court's order. In such cases the order should be expressed as giving leave to the local authority to arrange for the child to be removed from England and Wales for the purpose of holidays.

It is also considered permissible, where care and control has been given to a local authority, or to an individual, for the court to give general leave to make such arrangements in suitable cases, thereby obviating the need to make application for leave each time it is desired to remove the child from the jurisdiction.

2 Issue of passports

It is the practice of the Passport Department of the Home Office to issue passports for wards in accordance with the court's direction. This frequently results in passports being restricted to the holiday period specified in the order giving leave. It is the President's opinion that it is more convenient for wards' passports to be issued without such restriction.

The Passport Department has agreed to issue passports on this basis unless the court otherwise directs. It will, of course, still be necessary for the leave of the court to be obtained for the child's removal.

PART 13
PROCEEDINGS UNDER SECTION 54 OF THE HUMAN FERTILISATION AND EMBRYOLOGY ACT 2008

CONTENTS OF THIS PART

Rule		Page
13.1	Interpretation and application	1634
13.2	Application of Part 12	1634
13.3	Who the parties are	1635
13.4	Notice of proceedings to person with foreign parental responsibility	1635
13.5	What the court or a court officer will do when the application has been issued	1636
13.6	Service of the application and other documents	1637
13.7	Acknowledgement	1637

PART III

13.8	Date for first directions hearing	1637
13.9	The first directions hearing	1637
13.10	Where the agreement of the other parent or the woman who carried the child is not required	1638
13.11	Agreement	1639
13.12	Reports of the parental order reporter and disclosure to the parties	1639
13.13	Notice of final hearing	1640
13.14	The final hearing	1640
13.15	Proof of identity of the child	1640
13.16	Disclosing information to an adult who was subject to a parental order	1640
13.17	Application for recovery orders	1641
13.18	Keeping of registers, custody, inspection and disclosure of documents and information	1641
13.19	Documents held by the court not to be inspected or copied without the court's permission	1641
13.20	Orders	1642
13.21	Copies of orders	1642
13.22	Amendment and revocation of orders	1642

13.1 Interpretation and application

(1) A reference in this Part to the 2002 Act is a reference to that Act as applied with modifications by the Human Fertilisation and Embryology (Parental Order) Regulations 2010.

(2) In this Part –

'the other parent' means any person who is a parent of the child but is not one of the applicants or the woman who carried the child (including any man who is the father by virtue of section 35 or 36 of the 2008 Act or any woman who is a parent by virtue of section 42 or 43 of that Act);

'parental order' means an order under section 54 of the 2008 Act;

'parental order proceedings' means proceedings for the making of a parental order under the 2008 Act or an order under any provision of the 2002 Act;

'parental order reporter' means an officer of the service or a Welsh family proceedings officer appointed to act on behalf of a child who is the subject of parental order proceedings;

'provision for contact' means –

(i) contact provision contained in a child arrangements order under section 8 of the 1989 Act, or

(ii) an order under section 34 of the 1989 Act;

'contact provision' has the meaning given to it in section 26(5A) of the 2002 Act.

(3) Except where the contrary intention appears, the rules in this Part apply to parental order proceedings.

Amendments—SI 2014/843.

Defined terms—'2002 Act', '2008 Act': r 2.3(1).

Scope—Pursuant to FC(CDB)R 2014, applications for a parental order should be commenced in the Family Court and allocated to a lay justice. Where the child's place of birth was outside England and Wales, the case should be allocated to a High Court judge of the Family Division (not a deputy or s 9 judge) (Sch 1, paras 1, 4(f); *Re Z (Foreign Surrogacy: Allocation of Work: Guidance on Parental Order Reports)* [2016] 2 FLR 803, FD, at [73]; see Procedural Guide A12 in Part I). Consideration of transfer to another court may be considered at the first directions appointment (see r 13.9).

13.2 Application of Part 12

Rules 12.19 and 12.21 apply as appropriate, with any necessary modifications, to parental order proceedings.

Amendments—SI 2013/3204.

Scope—This rule confirms that the provisions set out in FPR 2010, rr 12.19 and 12.21 relating to the prohibition on filing of any additional evidence in whatever form without the direction of the court and the conduct of the hearing also apply to applications under s 54 of the 2008 Act.

13.3 Who the parties are

(1) An application for a parental order may be made by such of the following who satisfy the conditions set out in section 54(1) of the 2008 Act –

- (a) a husband and wife;
- (b) civil partners of each other; or
- (c) two persons who are living as partners in an enduring family relationship and are not within the prohibited degrees of relationship in relation to each other.

(2) The respondents to an application for a parental order are –

- (a) the woman who carried the child;
- (b) the other parent (if any);
- (c) any person in whose favour there is provision for contact; and
- (d) any other person or body with parental responsibility for the child at the date of the application.

(3) The court will direct that a person with parental responsibility for the child be made a party to proceedings where that person requests to be one.

(4) The court may at any time direct that –

- (a) any other person or body be made a respondent to the proceedings; or
- (b) a respondent be removed from the proceedings.

(5) If the court makes a direction for the addition or removal of a party, it may give consequential directions about –

- (a) serving a copy of the application form on any new respondent;
- (b) serving relevant documents on the new party; and
- (c) the management of the proceedings.

Defined Terms—'other parent': r 13.1.

Application for a parental order—The application should be made on Form C51 (FPR PD5A).

'any other person with parental responsibility'—This category includes: (i) the birth mother; (ii) the birth father if he was married to the child's mother when the child was born, or if not married to the birth mother he registered the birth jointly with the birth mother or a person who has been granted parental responsibility for the child pursuant to a formal parental responsibility agreement with the child's birth mother or court order or he has since the child's birth married the child's birth mother; (iii) a guardian of the child; (iv) a person who has been granted a child arrangements order for living arrangements in respect of the child or a local authority under an emergency protection order or a care order; (v) the adoptive parent(s) of the child; (vi) a second female who was the civil partner of the child's birth mother when the child was born or if she was not a civil partner she has been granted a parental responsibility order, a child arrangements order for living arrangements in her favour or parental responsibility by the birth mother by a formal parental responsibility agreement or she has since the child's birth become a civil partner of the birth mother; or (vii) any person who has been appointed a special guardian of the child. See also, the Hague Convention 1996, Arts 16–18 (in Part VI) on the issue of attribution and extinction of parental responsibility and FPR 2010, r 13.4, below.

Husband and wife—This includes married same-sex couples (Marriage (Same Sex Couples) Act 2013, s 11, Sch 3).

13.4 Notice of proceedings to person with foreign parental responsibility

(1) This rule applies where a child is subject to proceedings to which this Part applies and at the date of the application –

- (a) a person holds or is believed to hold parental responsibility for the child under the law of another State which subsists in accordance with Article 16 of the 1996 Hague Convention following the child becoming habitually resident in a territorial unit of the United Kingdom; and
- (b) that person is not otherwise required to be joined as a respondent under rule 13.3.

(2) The applicant shall give notice of the proceedings to any person to whom the applicant believes paragraph (1) applies.

PART III

(3) The applicant and every respondent to the proceedings shall provide such details as they possess as to the identity and whereabouts of any person they believe to hold parental responsibility for the child in accordance with paragraph (1) to the court officer, upon making, or responding to the application as appropriate.

(4) Where the existence of such a person only becomes apparent to a party at a later date during the proceedings, that party must notify the court officer of those details at the earliest opportunity.

(5) Where a person to whom paragraph (1) applies receives notice of proceedings, that person may apply to the court to be joined as a party using the Part 18 procedure.

Scope—This provision deals with situations where there is a foreign element and Brussels IIA and the 1996 Hague Convention apply. Under the law of a number of EU countries and Contracting States to the 1996 Convention, for example, unmarried fathers have parental responsibility or other legal rights without the need for an order or agreement. The rule requires the applicant to give notice to such a person and gives that person the right to apply to be joined as a party using the FPR 2010, Pt 18 procedure (see below). It is important therefore to ensure that the notice of proceedings itself or a letter accompanying it draws the attention of the person concerned to his/her right to make an application to be joined as a party.

Procedure for making an application to be joined—The application should be made on a FPR 2010, Pt 18 application notice, which if not supported by a statement in support must be verified by a statement of truth (FPR 2010, r 17.2). FPR 2010, Pt 18 and PD18A procedure should be followed (see further FPR 2010, r 18.1).

13.5 What the court or a court officer will do when the application has been issued

(1) As soon as practicable after the issue of proceedings –

- (a) the court will –
  - (i) if section 48(1) of the 2002 Act applies (restrictions on making parental orders), consider whether it is proper to hear the application;
  - (ii) subject to paragraph (2), set a date for the first directions hearing;
  - (iii) appoint a parental order reporter; and
  - (iv) set a date for the hearing of the application; and
- (b) a court officer will –
  - (i) return to the applicants the copies of the application together with any other documents the applicant is required to serve; and
  - (ii) send a certified copy of the entry in the register of live births to the parental order reporter.

(2) Where it considers it appropriate the court may, instead of setting a date for a first directions appointment, give the directions provided for in rule 13.9.

Defined terms—'court officer': FPR 2010, r 2.3.

First directions hearing—Although this rule is not drafted in mandatory terms, to avoid delay it is suggested that the court should list the application for a first directions hearing, appoint a parental reporter and give such other directions as may appear to be appropriate, e g consider whether a litigation friend needs to be appointed for any of the parties to the application or whether an interpreter may be required at the first hearing and consider whether video link facilities and evidence taken via Skype (see *Re S (Relocation: Parental Responsibility)* [2013] 2 FLR 1453, FD and *Re ML (Use of Skype Technology)* [2013] EWHC 2091 (Fam)) may be required to prepare for and then utilise at the final hearing or other special arrangements are likely to be needed. If payment has been made to the surrogate mother, particularly where the arrangements were made outside the UK, the court may also need to consider whether a preliminary hearing to determine the issue set out in s 54(6),(8) of the 2008 Act is required. The issue of whether the woman who carried the child or the other parent or a respondent to the application is a protected person (and thus incapable of giving consent) may not be apparent on the face of the application and documents filed in the proceedings. Therefore, the question of the appointment of a litigation friend under r 15.6(3) may only be identified and appropriately dealt with at an oral hearing (see further under Pt 2).

Timing of the first direction hearing—Unless the court otherwise directs, a first directions hearing must take place within 4 weeks of the date of issue of the application (see above for the reason why the application should be listed for a first directions hearing and r 13.8).

Directions without a hearing—Rule 13.5(2) authorises the court, if it considers it appropriate to do so, to give the comprehensive directions set out in FPR 2010, r 13.9 without a hearing. However, it is suggested that if the court adopts this procedure, the order made should include a clause that the order was made without a hearing and that any party or person who is affected by the terms of the order and disagrees with it has the right to make an application to be heard and/or for the order or any of its terms to be varied, set aside or discharged within a time specified in the order (see FPR 2010, rr 4.3(2)–(7), 13.9(5)).

13.6 Service of the application and other documents

(1) The applicants must, within 14 days before the hearing or first directions hearing, serve on the respondents –

(a) the application;
(b) a form for acknowledging service; and
(c) a notice of proceedings.

(2) The applicants must serve a notice of proceedings on any local authority or voluntary organisation that has at any time provided accommodation for the child.

Duty for service—This rule makes it clear that it is for the applicant(s) and not the court to serve the application in form C51, an acknowledgment of service (form C52) and notice of the proceedings on the respondent(s).

13.7 Acknowledgement

Within 7 days of the service of an application for a parental order, each respondent must file an acknowledgment of service and serve it on all the other parties.

Defined terms—'parental order': FPR 2010, r 13.1; 'legal representatives': FPR 2010, r 2.3.

Time for service—The time for filing and service of the acknowledgment of service is 7 days and any statement in support should accompany the acknowledgment of service. If there is a genuine difficulty in doing so, application should be made for an extension of time (see FPR 2010, r 13.9(1)(f),(4)(b)) supported by good grounds for seeking an extension. The application should be made on a FPR 2010, Pt 18 application notice and the appropriate procedure set out in Pt 18 and FPR PD18A should be followed.

13.8 Date for first directions hearing

Unless the court directs otherwise, the first directions hearing must be within 4 weeks beginning with the date on which the application is issued.

Unless the court otherwise directs—Instead of listing the application for a first directions appointment the court may give directions without a hearing but if it elects to do so, the order must provide for any party or person who is affected by the terms of the order to make an application to be heard or to vary or discharge the order or any of its terms (see r 13.5).

13.9 The first directions hearing

(1) At the first directions hearing in the proceedings the court will –

(a) fix a timetable for the filing of –
  (i) any report from a parental order reporter;
  (ii) if a statement of facts has been filed, any amended statement of facts; and
  (iii) any other evidence;
(b) give directions relating to the report of the parental order reporter and other evidence;
(c) consider whether any other person should be a party to the proceedings and, if so, give directions in accordance with rule 13.3(3) or (4) joining that person as a party;
(d) give directions relating to the appointment of a litigation friend for any protected party unless a litigation friend has already been appointed;
(e) consider, in accordance with rule 29.17, whether the case needs to be transferred to another court and, if so, give appropriate directions;
(f) give directions about –
  (i) tracing the other parent or the woman who carried the child;
  (ii) service of documents;
  (iii) subject to paragraph (2), disclosure as soon as possible of information and evidence to the parties; and
  (iv) the final hearing.

(2) Rule 13.12 (reports of the parental order reporter and disclosure to parties) applies to any direction given under paragraph (1)(f)(iii) as it applies to a direction given under rule 13.12(1).

(3) The parties or their legal representatives must attend the first directions hearing unless the court directs otherwise.

(4) Directions may also be given at any stage in the proceedings –

(a) of the court's own initiative; or

PART III

(b) on the application of a party or the parental order reporter.

(5) Where the court proposes to exercise its powers in paragraph (1) of its own initiative the procedure set out in rule 4.3(2) to (7) applies.

(6) For the purposes of giving directions or for such purposes as the court directs –

(a) the court may set a date for a further directions hearing or other hearing; and
(b) the court officer will give notice of any date so fixed to the parties and to the parental order reporter.

(7) Directions of a court which are still in force immediately prior to the transfer of proceedings to another court shall continue to apply following the transfer subject to –

(a) any changes of terminology which are required to apply those directions to the court to which the proceedings are transferred; and
(b) any variation or revocation of the direction.

(8) The court or court officer will –

(a) take a note of the giving, variation or revocation of a direction under this rule; and
(b) as soon as practicable serve a copy of the note on every party.

(9) After the first directions hearing the court will monitor compliance by the parties with the court's timetable and directions.

Amendments—SI 2013/3204.

Defined terms—'parental order reporter': FPR 2010, r 13.1; 'protected party': FPR 2010, r 2.3(1), MCA 2005, ss 1, 2(1) and CPR 1998, r 21.1(2)(d); 'litigation friend': FPR 2010, r 2.3(1), FPR 2010, Pt 15 and in relation to a child, FPR 2010, Pt 16.

Directions—Apart from those listed in r 13.9(1), the court should consider making any other appropriate additional directions under its case management powers under FPR 2010, Pt 4 and to give effect to the overriding objective under FPR 2010, Pt 1. See also **First directions hearing** under FPR 2010, r 13.5.

Transfer of proceedings—See FPR 2010, rr 12.12 and 29.7.

Tracing the other parent or person who carried the child—In view of the increase in surrogate mothers from overseas being used to carry a child, this issue is likely to arise more frequently (eg *Re WT (Foreign Surrogacy)* [2014] EWHC 1303 (Fam); *Re D and L (Surrogacy)* [2012] EWHC 2631 (Fam)).

Service—See FPR 2010, r 6; consideration should also be given as to whether service needs to be effected on any party or person outside the jurisdiction, eg where the birth mother lives overseas.

13.10 Where the agreement of the other parent or the woman who carried the child is not required

(1) This rule applies where the agreement of the other parent or the woman who carried the child to the making of the parental order is not required as the person in question cannot be found or is incapable of giving agreement.

(2) The applicants must –

(a) state that the agreement is not required in the application form, or at any later stage by filing a written note with the court;
(b) file a statement of facts setting out a summary of the history of the case and any other facts to satisfy the court that the other parent or the woman who carried the child cannot be found or is incapable of giving agreement.

(3) On receipt of the application form or written note –

(a) a court officer will –
    (i) unless the other parent or the woman who carried the child cannot be found, inform the other parent or the woman who carried the child that their agreement is not required;
    (ii) send a copy of the statement of facts filed in accordance with paragraph (2)(b) to –
        (aa) the other parent unless the other parent cannot be found;
        (bb) the woman who carried the child unless the woman cannot be found; and
        (cc) the parental order reporter; and
(b) if the applicants consider that the other parent or the woman who carried the child is incapable of giving agreement the court will consider whether to –

(i) appoint a litigation friend for the other parent or the woman who carried the child under rule 15.6(1) or

(ii) give directions for an application to be made under rule 15.6(3),

unless a litigation friend is already appointed for the other parent or the woman who carried the child.

Consent of the woman who carried the child is not required—The applicants and their advisors must take steps to ensure that clear lines of communication with the surrogate are established before the birth to facilitate the giving of consent (see under r 13.9). The use of Skype or other e-technology should be considered to obtain the required information (see under r 13.5). When consent is obtained it is essential to ensure that it records the surrogate mother's understanding of the consequences of not only giving the consent but its long-term consequences in terms of losing all parental responsibility for and familial ties to the child (see further under CACA 1985, Sch 1).

13.11 Agreement

(1) Unless the court directs otherwise, the agreement of the other parent or the woman who carried the child to the making of the parental order may be given in the form referred to Practice Direction 5A or a form to the like effect.

(2) Any form of agreement executed in Scotland must be witnessed by a Justice of the Peace or a Sheriff.

(3) Any form of agreement executed in Northern Ireland must be witnessed by a Justice of the Peace.

(4) Any form of agreement executed outside the United Kingdom must be witnessed by –

(a) any person for the time being authorised by law in the place where the document is executed to administer an oath for any judicial or other legal purpose;

(b) a British Consular officer;

(c) a notary public; or

(d) if the person executing the document is serving in any of the regular armed forces of the Crown, an officer holding a commission in any of those forces.

Form of agreement—This provision mirrors that which applies in an application for an adoption order under FPR 2010, r 14.10. The agreement must be given on Form A101A (FPR PD5A). In the absence of a formal agreement (eg because the mother cannot be found), consent given (whether formal or informal, at an earlier stage or in an acknowledgement of service) may in exceptional circumstances be taken into account: *Re D and L (Surrogacy)* [2012] EWHC 2631 (Fam); *G v G (Parental Order: Revocation)* [2013] 1 FLR 286, FD; and under r 13.5. For recent cases on the issue of consent, see CACA 1985, Sch 1.

13.12 Reports of the parental order reporter and disclosure to the parties

(1) The court will consider whether to give a direction that a confidential report of the parental order reporter be disclosed to each party to the proceedings.

(2) Before giving such a direction the court will consider whether any information should be deleted including information which discloses the particulars referred to in rule 29.1(1) where a party has given notice under rule 29.1(2) (disclosure of personal details).

(3) The court may direct that the report shall not be disclosed to a party.

Scope—The report of the parental order reporter is confidential and should not be disclosed without permission of the court. Before permitting disclosure, the court must consider whether any information, including any personal details of a party, contained in the report should be redacted. In addition, the court is empowered to direct that the report be not disclosed to a party. When considering the withholding of information contained in the report or redacting it, the court will need to consider the Convention rights of the parties under Arts 6 and 8. (For case-law, see **Publicity and disclosure of evidence** under FPR 2010, r 12.36.)

Powers and duties of the parental order reporter—The parental order reporter has a duty to: (i) act on behalf of the child with the duty of safeguarding the interests of the child and must attend all directions hearings unless the court directs otherwise; (ii) investigate the issues that are set out in s 54(1)–(8) of the 2008 Act and any other matter contained in the application form or any other matter that may be relevant to the making of a parental order and in so doing must contact and seek to interview such persons as the parental reporter thinks appropriate or as the court directs and obtain such professional assistance as may be appropriate; (iii) advise the court if there is any reason to refuse the application; (iv) provide the court with such assistance as the court may require, including advice on the appropriate forum for the proceedings, the appropriate timing of the proceedings, the options available and the suitability of each option (including what order should be made in determining the application) and any other matter of which the parental order reporter considers that the court should be informed; (v) file a written report; and (vi) where practicable, identify any

PART III

person who should be joined as a party. See further FPR 2010, rr 16.34, 16.35 and FPR PD16A, paras 10.1–10.5. The application for a parental order requires the same care and caution as an application for an adoption order and the requirement of a parental order should not be dispensed with: *Re D and L (Surrogacy)* [2012] EWHC 2631 (Fam); *G v G (Parental Order: Revocation)* [2013] 1 FLR 286, FD.

Disclosure—See **Scope**, above.

13.13 Notice of final hearing

A court officer will give notice to the parties and to the parental order reporter –

(a) of the date and place where the application will be heard; and

(b) of the fact that, unless the person wishes or the court requires, the person need not attend.

13.14 The final hearing

(1) Any person who has been given notice in accordance with rule 13.13 may attend the final hearing and be heard on the question of whether an order should be made.

(2) The court may direct that any person must attend a final hearing.

13.15 Proof of identity of the child

(1) Unless the contrary is shown, the child referred to in the application will be deemed to be the child referred to in the form of agreement to the making of the parental order where the conditions in paragraph (2) apply.

(2) The conditions are –

(a) the application identifies the child by reference to a full certified copy of an entry in the registers of live-births;

(b) the form of agreement identifies the child by reference to a full certified copy of an entry in the registers of live-births attached to the form; and

(c) the copy of the entry in the registers of live-births referred to in sub-paragraph (a) is the same or relates to the same entry in the registers of live-births as the copy of the entry in the registers of live-births attached to the form of agreement.

(3) Where the precise date of the child's birth is not proved to the satisfaction of the court, the court will determine the probable date of birth.

(4) The probable date of the child's birth may be specified in the parental order as the date of the child's birth.

(5) Where the child's place of birth cannot be proved to the satisfaction of the court –

(a) the child may be treated as having been born in the registration district and sub-district in which the court is sitting where it is probable that the child may have been born in –

(i) the United Kingdom;

(ii) the Channel Islands; or

(iii) the Isle of Man; or

(b) in any other case, the particulars of the country of birth may be omitted from the parental order.

Amendments—SI 2013/3204.

13.16 Disclosing information to an adult who was subject to a parental order

(1) Subject to paragraph (2), the person who is subject to the parental order has the right to receive from the court which made the parental order a copy of the following –

(a) the application form for a parental order (but not the documents attached to that form);

(b) the parental order and any other orders relating to the parental order proceedings;

(c) a transcript of the court's decision; and

(d) a report made to the court by the parental order reporter.

(2) The court will not provide a copy of a document or order referred to in paragraph (1) unless the person making the request has completed the certificate relating to counselling in the form for that purpose referred to in Practice Direction 5A.

(3) This rule does not apply to a person under the age of 18 years.

13.17 Application for recovery orders

(1) An application for any of the orders referred to in section 41(2) of the 2002 Act (recovery orders) may be made without notice, in which case the applicant must file the application –

(a) where the application is made by telephone, the next business day after the making of the application; or

(b) in any other case, at the time when the application is made.

(2) Where the court refuses to make an order on an application without notice it may direct that the application is made on notice in which case the application shall proceed in accordance with rules 13.1 to 13.14.

(3) The respondents to an application under this rule are –

(a) in a case where parental order proceedings are pending, all parties to those proceedings;

(b) any person having parental responsibility for the child;

(c) any person in whose favour there is provision for contact;

(d) any person who was caring for the child immediately prior to the making of the application; and

(e) any person whom the applicant alleges to have effected, or to have been or to be responsible for, the taking or keeping the child.

Amendments—SI 2013/3204.

Note—Reference is made to ACA 2002 and so it follows that the matters raised in s 41(2) of the 2002 Act will be relevant to such an application (see Part II).

Procedure—Where the court refuses the application, direction will usually be given for the application to be made on notice and in this case the procedure set out in FPR 2010, rr 13.1–13.14 should be followed and the persons who should be made respondents to the application should be those that are listed in r 13.17(3). See also the commentary under s 41(2) of the 2002 Act and r 14.20. A without notice application should be made under FPR 2010, Pt 18 and the procedure set out in the rule and FPR PD18A (in particular para 5 should be complied with).

13.18 Keeping of registers, custody, inspection and disclosure of documents and information

(1) *(revoked)*

(2) All documents relating to parental order proceedings and related proceedings under the 2002 Act must, while they are in the custody of the court, be kept in a place of special security.

(3) Any person who obtains any information in the course of, or relating to, parental order proceedings must treat that information as confidential and must only disclose it if –

(a) the disclosure is necessary for the proper exercise of that person's duties; or

(b) the information is requested by –

(i) a court or public authority (whether in Great Britain or not) having power to determine parental order proceedings and related matters, for the purpose of that court or authority discharging its duties relating to those proceedings and matters; or

(ii) a person who is authorised in writing by the Secretary of State to obtain the information for the purposes of research.

Amendments—SI 2013/3204.

13.19 Documents held by the court not to be inspected or copied without the court's permission

Subject to the provisions of these rules, any practice direction or any direction given by the court –

(a) no document or order held by the court in parental order proceedings and related proceedings under the 2002 Act will be open to inspection by any person; and

(b) no copy of any such document or order, or of an extract from any such document or order, shall be taken by or given to any person.

13.20 Orders

(1) A parental order takes effect from the date when it is made, or such later date as the court may specify.

(2) In proceedings in Wales a party may request that an order be drawn up in Welsh as well as English.

13.21 Copies of orders

(1) Within 7 days beginning with the date on which the final order was made in proceedings, or such shorter time as the court may direct, a court officer will send –

(a) a copy of the order to the applicant;

(b) a copy, which is sealed(GL), authenticated with the stamp of the court or certified as a true copy of a parental order, to the Registrar General;

(c) a notice of the making or refusal of –

(i) the final order; or

(ii) an order quashing or revoking a parental order or allowing an appeal against an order in proceedings,

to every respondent and, with the permission of the court, any other person.

(2) The court officer will also send notice of the making of a parental order to –

(a) any court in Great Britain which appears to the court officer to have made any such order as is referred to in section 46(2) of the 2002 Act (order relating to parental responsibility for, and maintenance of, the child); and

(b) the principal registry, if it appears to the court officer that a parental responsibility agreement has been recorded at the principal registry.

(3) A copy of any final order may be sent to any other person with the permission of the court.

(4) The court officer will send a copy of any order made during the course of the proceedings to all the parties to those proceedings unless the court directs otherwise.

(5) If an order has been drawn up in Welsh as well as in English in accordance with rule 13.20(2), any reference in this rule to sending an order is to be taken as a reference to sending both the Welsh and English orders.

Defined terms—'court officer', '2002 Act', 'principal registry': FPR 2010, r 2.3(1); 'parental responsibility agreement': r 2.3(1) and CA 1989, ss 4(1)(b),(2), 4ZA(1)(b), 4A(1)(a),(2).

13.22 Amendment and revocation of orders

(1) This rule applies to an application under paragraph 4 of Schedule 1 to the 2002 Act (amendment of a parental order and revocation of direction).

(2) *(revoked)*

(3) Subject to paragraph (4), an application may be made without serving a copy of the application notice.

(4) The court may direct that an application notice be served on such persons as it thinks fit.

(5) Where the court makes an order granting the application, a court officer shall send the Registrar General a notice –

(a) specifying the amendments; or

(b) informing the Registrar General of the revocation,

giving sufficient particulars of the order to enable the Registrar General to identify the case.

Amendments—SI 2013/3204.

Defined terms—See under FPR 2010, r 13.21, above.

PART 14
PROCEDURE FOR APPLICATIONS IN ADOPTION, PLACEMENT AND RELATED PROCEEDINGS

CONTENTS OF THIS PART

Rule		Page
14.1	Application of this Part and interpretation	1643
14.2	Assignment of a serial number	1645
14.3	Who the parties are	1645
14.4	Notice of proceedings to person with foreign parental responsibility	1651
14.5	Who is to serve	1651
14.6	What the court or a court officer will do when the application has been issued	1651
14.7	Date for first directions hearing	1653
14.8	The first directions hearing	1653
14.9	Requesting the court to dispense with the consent of any parent or guardian	1654
14.10	Consent	1655
14.11	Reports by the adoption agency or local authority	1656
14.12	Health reports	1656
14.13	Confidential reports to the court and disclosure to the parties	1656
14.14	Communication of information relating to proceedings	1657
14.15	Notice of final hearing	1658
14.16	The final hearing	1658
14.17	Proof of identity of the child	1659
14.18	Disclosing information to an adopted adult	1659
14.19	Translation of documents	1660
14.20	Application for recovery orders	1660
14.21	Inherent jurisdiction and fathers without parental responsibility	1660
14.22	Timing of applications for section 89 order	1661
14.23	Custody of documents	1661
14.24	Documents held by the court not to be inspected or copied without the court's permission	1661
14.25	Orders	1661
14.26	Copies of orders	1661
14.27	Amendment and revocation of orders	1662
	Practice Direction 14A – Who Receives a Copy of the Application Form for Orders in Proceedings	1663
	Practice Direction 14B – The First Directions Hearing – Adoptions with a Foreign Element	1664
	Practice Direction 14C – Reports by the Adoption Agency or Local Authority	1665
	Practice Direction 14D – Reports by a Registered Medical Practitioner ('Health Reports')	1673
	Practice Direction 14E – Communication of Information Relating to Proceedings	1675
	Practice Direction 14F – Disclosing Information to an Adopted Adult	1679

PART III

14.1 Application of this Part and interpretation

(1) The rules in this Part apply to the following proceedings –

(a) adoption proceedings;

(b) placement proceedings; and

(c) proceedings for –
 (i) the making of a an order under section 26 or an order under section 51A(2)(a) of the 2002 Act;
 (iaa) the making of an order under section 51A(2)(b) of the 2002 Act;
 (ii) the variation or revocation of –
  (aa) an order under section 27 of the 2002 Act; or
  (bb) an order under section 51A(2) of the 2002 Act in accordance with section 51B(1)(c);
 (iii) an order giving permission to change a child's surname or remove a child from the United Kingdom under section 28(2) and (3) of the 2002 Act;
 (iv) a section 84 order;
 (v) a section 88 direction;
 (vi) a section 89 order; or
 (vii) any other order that may be referred to in a practice direction.

(2) In this Part –

'Central Authority' means –
 (a) in relation to England, the Secretary of State; and
 (b) in relation to Wales, the Welsh Ministers;

'Convention adoption order' means an adoption order under the 2002 Act which, by virtue of regulations under section 1 of the Adoption (Intercountry Aspects) Act 1999 (regulations giving effect to the Convention on Protection of Children and Co-operation in Respect of Intercountry Adoption, concluded at the Hague on 29 May 1993), is made as a Convention adoption order;

'guardian' means –
 (a) a guardian (other than the guardian of the estate of a child) appointed in accordance with section 5 of the 1989 Act; and
 (b) a special guardian within the meaning of section 14A of the 1989 Act;

'provision for contact' has the meaning given to it in rule 13.1(2);

'section 88 direction' means a direction given by the High Court under section 88 of the 2002 Act that section 67(3) of that Act (status conferred by adoption) does not apply or does not apply to any extent specified in the direction.

Amendments—SI 2014/843.

Defined terms—'adoption proceedings', 'child', 'placement proceedings', 'section 84 order', 'section 89 order': FPR 2010, r 2.3(1).

Which court—Save for the following exceptions, an application under ACA 2002 may be commenced in the Family Court. If there are pending or concluded proceedings relating to the same child, any additional application will be allocated to the level of judge dealing with the original case. FC(CDB)R 2014, Sch 1 makes provision for the allocation of certain applications under ACA 2002 where there are *no* current or concluded proceedings relating to the same child. In such cases, the following proceedings will be allocated to lay justices:

- a placement order (ACA 2002, s 21);
- an order varying a placement order (ACA 2002, s 23);
- a contact order (ACA 2002, s 26);
- an order varying a contact order (ACA 2002, s 27);
- an order permitting child's name to be changed or removal from UK (ACA 2002, s 28(2) or (3));
- an adoption order (ACA 2002, s 46), except where:
  - a local authority is a party;
  - the application is for an overseas adoption under ACA 2002, s 87; or
  - the application is for a Convention adoption under ACA 2002, s 66(1)(c));
- a post-adoption contact order (ACA 2002, s 51A);
- an order revoking adoption on legitimacy (ACA 2002, s 55);
- an order amending an order under ACA 2002, Sch 1, para 4.

Where there are *no* current or concluded proceedings relating to the subject child, the following applications under ACA 2002 will be allocated to a judge of district judge level:

- proceedings under ACA 2002, s 46 for an adoption order where:
  - a local authority is a party;
  - the application is for an overseas adoption under ACA 2002, s 87; or
  - the application is for a Convention adoption under ACA 2002, s 66(1)(c)).

High Court—ACA 2002, s 88 applies to Hague Convention adoptions.

14.2 Assignment of a serial number

(1) This rule applies where –

(a) any application in proceedings is made by a person who intends to adopt a child; or

(b) an adoption order in respect of the child has been made and an application is made for –

(i) a contact order under section 51A(2)(a) of the 2002 Act;

(ii) an order prohibiting contact with the child under section 51A(2)(b) of the 2002 Act; or

(iii) the variation or revocation of an order under section 51A(2) of the 2002 Act in accordance with section 51B(1)(c).

(2) In a case under paragraph (1)(a), a serial number must be assigned to identify the person intending to adopt the child in connection with the proceedings in order for the person's identity to be kept confidential in those proceedings.

(3) In a case under paragraph (1)(b), a serial number must be assigned to the person in whose favour the adoption order has been made to keep the identity of the person confidential in proceedings referred to in paragraph (1)(b).

(4) The court may at any time direct that a serial number assigned to a person under paragraph (2) or (3) must be removed.

(5) When a serial number has been assigned to a person under paragraph (2) or (3) –

(a) the court officer will ensure that any notice sent in accordance with these rules does not contain information which discloses, or is likely to disclose, the identity of that person to any other party to that application who is not already aware of that person's identity; and

(b) the proceedings on the application will be conducted with a view to securing that the person is not seen by or made known to any party who is not already aware of the person's identity except with the person's consent.

Amendments—Substituted by SI 2014/843. Amended by SI 2016/1013.

Defined terms—'application form/notice', 'child', 'court', 'court officer', 'proceedings': FPR 2010, r 2.3(1).

14.3 Who the parties are

(1) In relation to the proceedings set out in column 1 of the following table, column 2 sets out who the application may be made by and column 3 sets out who the respondents to those proceedings will be.

Proceedings for	*Applicants*	*Respondents*
An adoption order (section 46 of the 2002 Act).	The prospective adopters (sections 50 and 51 of the 2002 Act).	Each parent who has parental responsibility for the child unless that parent has given notice under section 20(4)(a) of the 2002 Act (statement of wish not to be informed of any application for an adoption order) which has effect; any guardian of the child unless that guardian has given notice under section 20(4)(a) of the 2002 Act (statement of wish not to be informed of any application for an adoption order) which has effect; any person in whose favour there is provision for contact; any adoption agency having parental responsibility for the child under section 25 of the 2002 Act;

Proceedings for	*Applicants*	*Respondents*
		any adoption agency which has taken part at any stage in the arrangements for adoption of the child; any local authority to whom notice under section 44 of the 2002 Act (notice of intention to adopt or apply for a section 84 order) has been given; any local authority or voluntary organisation which has parental responsibility for, is looking after or is caring for, the child; and the child where – – permission has been granted to a parent or guardian to oppose the making of the adoption order (section 47(3) or 47(5) of the 2002 Act); – the child opposes the making of an adoption order; – a children and family reporter recommends that it is in the best interests of the child to be a party to the proceedings and that recommendation is accepted by the court; – the child is already an adopted child; – any party to the proceedings or the child is opposed to the arrangements for allowing any person contact with the child, or a person not being allowed contact with the child after the making of the adoption order; – the application is for a Convention adoption order or a section 84 order; – the child has been brought into the United Kingdom in the circumstances where section 83(1) of the 2002 Act applies (restriction on bringing children in); – the application is for an adoption order other than a Convention adoption order and the prospective adopters intend the child to live in a country or territory outside the British Islands after the making of the adoption order; or

Proceedings for	*Applicants*	*Respondents*
		– the prospective adopters are relatives of the child.
A section 84 order.	The prospective adopters asking for parental responsibility prior to adoption abroad.	As for an adoption order.
A placement order (section 21 of the 2002 Act).	A local authority (section 22 of the 2002 Act).	Each parent who has parental responsibility for the child: any guardian of the child; any person in whose favour an order under the 1989 Act is in force in relation to the child; any adoption agency or voluntary organisation which has parental responsibility for, is looking after, or is caring for, the child; the child; and the parties or any persons who are or have been parties to proceedings for a care order in respect of the child where those proceedings have led to the application for the placement order.
An order varying a placement order (section 23 of the 2002 Act).	The joint application of the local authority authorised by the placement order to place the child for adoption and the local authority which is to be substituted for that authority (section 23 of the 2002 Act).	The parties to the proceedings leading to the placement order which it is sought to have varied except the child who was the subject of those proceedings; and any person in whose favour there is provision for contact.
An order revoking a placement order (section 24 of the 2002 Act).	The child; the local authority authorised to place the child for adoption; or where the child is not placed for adoption by the authority, any other person who has the permission of the court to apply (section 24 of the 2002 Act).	The parties to the proceedings leading to the placement order which it is sought to have revoked; and any person in whose favour there is provision for contact.
An order under section 26 of the 2002 Act.	The child; the adoption agency; any parent, guardian or relative;	The adoption agency authorised to place the child for adoption or which has placed the child for adoption;

PART III

Proceedings for	*Applicants*	*Respondents*
	any person in whose favour there was provision for contact under the 1989 Act which ceased to have effect on an adoption agency being authorised to place a child for adoption, or placing a child for adoption who is less than six weeks old (section 26(1) of the 2002 Act); if a child arrangements order was in force immediately before the adoption agency was authorised to place the child for adoption or (as the case may be) placed the child for adoption at a time when he or she was less than six weeks old, any person named in the order as a person with whom the child was to live; a person who by virtue of an order made in the exercise of the High Court's inherent jurisdiction with respect to children had care of the child immediately before that time; or any person who has the permission of the court to make the application (section 26 of the 2002 Act).	the person with whom the child lives or is to live; each parent with parental responsibility for the child; any guardian of the child; and the child where – – the adoption agency authorised to place the child for adoption or which has placed the child for adoption or a parent with parental responsibility for the child opposes the making of the order under section 26 of the 2002 Act; – the child opposes the making of the order under section 26 of the 2002 Act; – existing provision for contact is to be revoked; – relatives of the child do not agree to the arrangements for allowing any person contact with the child, or a person not being allowed contact with the child; or – the child is suffering or is at risk of suffering harm within the meaning of the 1989 Act.
An order varying or revoking an order under section 26 of the 2002 Act (section 27 of the 2002 Act).	The child; the adoption agency; or any person named in the order (section 27(1) of the 2002 Act).	The parties to the proceedings leading to the order which it is sought to have varied or revoked; and any person named in the order.
An order permitting the child's name to be changed or the removal of the child from the United Kingdom (section 28(2) and (3) of the 2002 Act).	Any person including the adoption agency or the local authority authorised to place, or which has placed, the child for adoption (section 28(2) of the 2002 Act).	The parties to proceedings leading to any placement order; the adoption agency authorised to place the child for adoption or which has placed the child for adoption; any prospective adopters with whom the child is living; each parent with parental responsibility for the child; and any guardian of the child.

Proceedings for	*Applicants*	*Respondents*
A contact order under section 51A(2)(a) of the 2002 Act.	The child; or any person who has obtained the court's leave to make the application.	A person who has applied for the adoption order or in whose favour the adoption order is or has been made; and Any adoption agency having parental responsibility for the child under section 25 of the 2002 Act.
An order prohibiting the person named in the order from having contact with the child (section 51A(2)(b) of the 2002 Act).	any person who has obtained the court's leave to make the application. the child; or any person who has obtained the court's leave to make the application.	A person against whom an application is made who – (but for the child's adoption) would be related to the child by blood (including half-blood), marriage or civil partnership; is a former guardian of the child; is a person who had parental responsibility for the child immediately before the making of the adoption order; is a person who was entitled to make an application for an order under section 26 of the 2002 Act in respect of the child (contact with children placed or to be placed for adoption) by virtue of subsection (3)(c), (d) or (e) of that section; is a person with whom the child has lived for a period of at least one year; and any adoption agency having parental responsibility for the child under section 25 of the 2002 Act.
The variation or revocation of a contact order or an order prohibiting contact under section 51A(2) of the 2002 Act (section 51B(1)(c) of that Act).	The child; a person in whose favour the adoption order was made; or	The parties to the proceedings leading to the contact order or an order prohibiting contact which it is sought to have varied or revoked; and any person named in the contact order or the order prohibiting contact.
A section 88 direction.	The adopted child; the adopters; any parent; or	The adopters; the parents; the adoption agency;

PART III

Proceedings for	*Applicants*	*Respondents*
	any other person.	the local authority to whom notice under section 44 of the 2002 Act (notice of intention to apply for a section 84 order) has been given; and the Attorney-General.
A section 89 order.	The adopters; the adopted person; any parent; the relevant Central Authority; the adoption agency; the local authority to whom notice under section 44 of the 2002 Act (notice of intention to adopt or apply for a section 84 order) has been given; the Secretary of State for the Home Department; or any other person.	The adopters; the parents; the adoption agency; and the local authority to whom notice under section 44 of the 2002 Act (notice of intention to adopt or apply for a section 84 order) has been given.

(2) The court may at any time direct that a child, who is not already a respondent to proceedings, be made a respondent to proceedings where –

- (a) the child –
  - (i) wishes to make an application; or
  - (ii) has evidence to give to the court or a legal submission to make which has not been given or made by any other party; or
- (b) there are other special circumstances.

(3) The court may at any time direct that –

- (a) any other person or body be made a respondent to proceedings; or
- (b) a party be removed.

(4) If the court makes a direction for the addition or removal of a party, it may give consequential directions about –

- (a) serving a copy of the application form on any new respondent;
- (b) serving relevant documents on the new party; and
- (c) the management of the proceedings.

Amendments—SI 2014/843.

Defined terms—'the 1989 Act', 'child', 'children and family reporter', 'jurisdiction', 'proceedings', 'section 84 order', 'section 89 order': FPR 2010, r 2.3(1); 'Central Authority', 'provision for contact', 'section 88 direction': FPR 2010, r 14.1.

Importance of giving notice to respondents—The court should ensure that each respondent is given notice of each hearing and that they are kept informed of the progress of the case (*X and Y v A Local Authority (Adoption: Procedure)* [2009] 2 FLR 984, FD).

Father without parental responsibility—A father who does not have parental responsibility is not automatically a respondent to proceedings (unless there is a provision for contact in his favour). The court must consider the question at the first directions hearing and may direct that he be made a respondent (FPR 2010, rr 14.3(3)(a) and 14.8(1)(b)). For discussion of position of father without parental responsibility, see note to ACA 2002, s 47.

Former parent of child freed for adoption—There is no requirement to give the former parents of a child freed for adoption under AA 1976 notice of an adoption application under ACA 2002 (*Re F (Adoption: Natural Parents)* [2007] 1 FLR 363, CA).

Removing child or children's guardian—Clear justification is required before removing a child as a party or removing his children's guardian in contested proceedings (*Re S (Adoption and Contact Applications: Representation of the Child)* [2016] 2 FLR 81, CA).

14.4 Notice of proceedings to person with foreign parental responsibility

(1) This rule applies where a child is subject to proceedings to which this Part applies and –

(a) a parent of the child holds or is believed to hold parental responsibility for the child under the law of another State which subsists in accordance with Article 16 of the 1996 Hague Convention following the child becoming habitually resident in a territorial unit of the United Kingdom; and

(b) that parent is not otherwise required to be joined as a respondent under rule 14.3.

(2) The applicant shall give notice of the proceedings to any parent to whom the applicant believes paragraph (1) applies in any case in which a person who was a parent with parental responsibility under the 1989 Act would be a respondent to the proceedings in accordance with rule 14.3.

(3) The applicant and every respondent to the proceedings shall provide such details as they possess as to the identity and whereabouts of any parent they believe to hold parental responsibility for the child in accordance with paragraph (1) to the court officer, upon making, or responding to the application as appropriate.

(4) Where the existence of such a parent only becomes apparent to a party at a later date during the proceedings, that party must notify the court officer of those details at the earliest opportunity.

(5) Where a parent to whom paragraph (1) applies receives notice of proceedings, that parent may apply to the court to be joined as a party using the Part 18 procedure.

Defined terms—'child', 'court officer', 'parental responsibility', 'the 1989 Act', 'the 1996 Hague Convention': FPR 2010, r 2.3(1).

14.5 Who is to serve

(1) The general rules about service in Part 6 are subject to this rule.

(2) In proceedings to which this Part applies, a document which has been issued or prepared by a court officer will be served by the court officer except where –

(a) a practice direction provides otherwise; or

(b) the court directs otherwise.

(3) Where a court officer is to serve a document, it is for the court to decide which of the methods of service specified in rule 6.23 is to be used.

Defined terms—'court officer': FPR 2010, r 2.3(1).

Service generally—See notes to FPR 2010, Pt 6.

Importance of service on parent—It is fundamental to the making of an adoption order that the natural parent should be informed of the application; the requirement for service is mandatory and the court will be very reluctant to dispense with service on a natural parent (*Re B (Adoption: Jurisdiction to Set Aside)* [1995] 2 FLR 1, CA; *Re G (Foreign Adoption: Consent)* [1995] 2 FLR 534, FD). Where a parent has given advance consent to adoption under ACA 2002, s 20 he may state that he does not wish to be informed of any application for an adoption order; such a parent is not required to be served with notice of any adoption proceedings.

14.6 What the court or a court officer will do when the application has been issued

(1) As soon as practicable after the application has been issued in proceedings –

(a) the court will –

(i) if section 48(1) of the 2002 Act (restrictions on making adoption orders) applies, consider whether it is proper to hear the application;

(ii) subject to paragraph (4), set a date for the first directions hearing;

(iii) appoint a children's guardian in accordance with rule 16.3(1);

(iv) appoint a reporting officer in accordance with rule 16.30;

(v) consider whether a report relating to the welfare of the child is required, and if so, request such a report in accordance with rule 16.33;

(vi) set a date for the hearing of the application; and

(vii) do anything else that may be set out in a practice direction; and

(b) a court officer will –

(i) subject to receiving confirmation in accordance with paragraph (2)(b)(ii), give

PART III

notice of any directions hearing set by the court to the parties and to any children's guardian, reporting officer or children and family reporter;

(ii) serve a copy of the application form (but, subject to sub-paragraphs (iii) and (iv), not the documents attached to it) on the persons referred to in Practice Direction 14A;

(iii) send a copy of the certified copy of the entry in the register of live-births or Adopted Children Register and any health report attached to an application for an adoption order to –

(aa) any children's guardian, reporting officer or children and family reporter; and

(bb) the local authority to whom notice under section 44 of the 2002 Act (notice of intention to adopt or apply for a section 84 order) has been given;

(iv) if notice under rule 14.9(2) has been given (request to dispense with consent of parent or guardian), in accordance with that rule inform the parent or guardian of the request and send a copy of the statement of facts to –

(aa) the parent or guardian;

(bb) any children's guardian, reporting officer or children and family reporter;

(cc) any local authority to whom notice under section 44 of the 2002 Act (notice of intention to adopt or apply for a section 84 order) has been given; and

(dd) any adoption agency which has placed the child for adoption; and

(v) do anything else that may be set out in a practice direction.

(2) In addition to the matters referred to in paragraph (1), as soon as practicable after an application for an adoption order or a section 84 order has been issued the court or the court officer will –

(a) where the child is not placed for adoption by an adoption agency –

(i) ask either the Service or the Assembly to file any relevant form of consent to an adoption order or a section 84 order; and

(ii) ask the local authority to prepare a report on the suitability of the prospective adopters if one has not already been prepared; and

(b) where the child is placed for adoption by an adoption agency, ask the adoption agency to –

(i) file any relevant form of consent to –

(aa) the child being placed for adoption;

(bb) an adoption order;

(cc) a future adoption order under section 20 of the 2002 Act; or

(dd) a section 84 order;

(ii) confirm whether a statement has been made under section 20(4)(a) of the 2002 Act (statement of wish not to be informed of any application for an adoption order) and if so, to file that statement;

(iii) file any statement made under section 20(4)(b) of the 2002 Act (withdrawal of wish not to be informed of any application for an adoption order) as soon as it is received by the adoption agency; and

(iv) prepare a report on the suitability of the prospective adopters if one has not already been prepared.

(3) In addition to the matters referred to in paragraph (1), as soon as practicable after an application for a placement order has been issued –

(a) the court will consider whether a report giving the local authority's reasons for placing the child for adoption is required, and if so, will direct the local authority to prepare such a report; and

(b) the court or the court officer will ask either the Service or the Assembly to file any form of consent to the child being placed for adoption.

(4) Where it considers it appropriate the court may, instead of setting a date for a first directions hearing, give the directions provided for by rule 14.8.

Defined terms—'court', 'court officer', 'child', 'children and family reporter', 'children's guardian', 'proceedings', 'reporting officer': FPR 2010, r 2.3(1).

Who receives a copy of the application for orders in proceedings (r 14.6(1)(b)(ii))—See FPR PD14A.

Form of consent (r 14.6(2)(b))—The form of consent must be in the relevant form (A100–A106) or a form to like effect (FPR 2010, r 14.10).

Children's guardian—For children's guardian in adoption or placement proceedings generally, see FPR 2010, rr 16.3 and 16.6–16.21 and see FPR PD16A.

A children's guardian who interviews a child should be very careful not to make promises of complete confidentiality; in unusually sensitive cases affecting older children, it is not unreasonable for a children's guardian to promise a child that he would tell the judge that the child would prefer that a party was not told details of the conversation (*Re D (Minors) (Adoption Reports: Confidentiality)* [1995] 1 FLR 631, CA).

The children's guardian must also, where practicable, notify any person the joining of whom as a party to those proceedings would be likely, in his opinion, to safeguard the interests of the child, of the court's power to join that person as a party under FPR 2010, r 14.3(3) and must inform the court:

(i) of any notification;
(ii) of anyone whom he attempted to notify under this paragraph but was unable to contact; and
(iii) of anyone whom he believes may wish to be joined to the proceedings (see FPR PD16A, para 6.8(b)).

The children's guardian has a duty to ensure that, in relation to a decision made by the court in the proceedings, the child is notified of the decision (if the guardian considers that to do so is appropriate to the child's age and understanding) and that if the child is so notified, it is explained to him in an age-appropriate manner (FPR PD16A, para 6.11).

Inter-country adoptions—See note to FPR 2010, r 14.18.

Involvement of children's guardian in decision-making—While a case is proceeding, the local authority ought not to take any major decisions relating to the child or his adoption without informing the children's guardian and listening to his views (*R v North Yorkshire County Council ex parte M* [1989] 1 FLR 203, QBD). However, a guardian has no right to dictate how an adoption panel conducts its business or to insist on attending meetings (*R v North Yorkshire County Council ex parte M (No 2)* [1989] 2 FLR 79, QBD). The views of a children's guardian should be communicated to any adoption panel that is considering a proposal concerning the child (*Re R (Adoption: Disclosure)* [1999] 2 FLR 1123, FD).

Inspection of records—A children's guardian has a right to inspect local authority records and adoption agency records (CA 1989, s 42; ACA 2002, s 103). Where the children's guardian inspects local authority or adoption agency records, he must bring all records and documents that may, in his opinion, assist in the proper determination of the proceedings to the attention of the court and (unless the court otherwise directs) the other parties (FPR PD16A, para 6.10).

14.7 Date for first directions hearing

Unless the court directs otherwise, the first directions hearing must be within 4 weeks beginning with the date on which the application is issued.

14.8 The first directions hearing

(1) At the first directions hearing in the proceedings the court will –

(a) fix a timetable for the proceedings including a timetable for the filing of –
  (i) any report relating to the suitability of the applicants to adopt a child;
  (ii) any report from the local authority;
  (iii) any report from a children's guardian, reporting officer or children and family reporter;
  (iv) if a statement of facts has been filed, any amended statement of facts;
  (v) any other evidence, and
  (vi) give directions relating to the reports and other evidence;

(b) consider whether the child or any other person should be a party to the proceedings and, if so, give directions in accordance with rule 14.3(2) or (3) joining that child or person as a party;

(c) give directions relating to the appointment of a litigation friend for any protected party or child who is a party to, but not the subject of, proceedings unless a litigation friend has already been appointed;

(d) consider in accordance with rule 29.17 whether the case needs to be transferred to another court and, if so, give directions to transfer the proceedings to another court;

(e) give directions about –
  (i) tracing parents or any other person the court considers to be relevant to the proceedings;
  (ii) service of documents;
  (iii) subject to paragraph (2), disclosure as soon as possible of information and evidence to the parties; and

(iv) the final hearing.

(Under Part 3 the court may also direct that the case be adjourned if it considers that non-court dispute resolution is appropriate.)

(2) Rule 14.13(2) applies to any direction given under paragraph (1)(e)(iii) as it applies to a direction given under rule 14.13(1).

(3) In addition to the matters referred to in paragraph (1), the court will give any of the directions listed in Practice Direction 14B in proceedings for –

(a) a Convention adoption order;
(b) a section 84 order;
(c) a section 88 direction;
(d) a section 89 order; or
(e) an adoption order where section 83(1) of the 2002 Act applies (restriction on bringing children in).

(4) The parties or their legal representatives must attend the first directions hearing unless the court directs otherwise.

(5) Directions may also be given at any stage in the proceedings –

(a) of the court's own initiative; or
(b) on the application of a party or any children's guardian or, where the direction concerns a report by a reporting officer or children and family reporter, the reporting officer or children and family reporter.

(6) For the purposes of giving directions or for such purposes as the court directs –

(a) the court may set a date for a further directions hearing or other hearing; and
(b) the court officer will give notice of any date so fixed to the parties and to any children's guardian, reporting officer or children and family reporter.

(7) After the first directions hearing the court will monitor compliance by the parties with the court's timetable and directions.

Amendments—SI 2013/3204; SI 2014/843.

Defined terms—'the 1989 Act', 'child', 'children and family reporter', 'children's guardian', 'court officer', 'filing', 'legal representative', 'litigation friend', 'proceedings', 'protected party', 'reporting officer', 'section 84 order', 'section 89 order': FPR 2010, r 2.3(1); 'section 88 direction': FPR 2010, r 14.1(2).

First directions hearing—The court may, if it considers it appropriate, give the directions provided for in r 14.8 at the time that the application is issued, rather than waiting for the first directions hearing (FPR 2010, r 14.6(4)).

Appointment of litigation friend (r 14.8(1)(c))—See FPR 2010, Pt 15.

First directions hearing: adoptions with a foreign element (r 14.8(3))—See FPR PD14B.

Intercountry adoptions—Guidance given in *Re R (Inter-Country Adoptions: Practice)* [1999] 1 FLR 1042, FD regarding intercountry adoption includes:

(a) drawing up a timetable to determine the application without delay;
(b) never accepting documents that do not have an English translation;
(c) early transfer to the High Court where there is a doubt concerning parental consent or adherence to proper pre-application procedures;
(d) before the directions hearing, the applicant should be directed to file and serve an affidavit setting out full details of the circumstances of the application;
(e) cross-examination of the applicants may take place at the directions hearing;
(f) directions should be given for personal service on the natural parents within 28 days, including the provision of information about the role of the children's guardian and the availability of public funding;
(g) further directions should be fixed before a judge within 6 weeks, with provision for filing an interim report from the children's guardian;
(h) at the next directions hearing, if it appears that the natural parents never consented and seek the return of the child, the court should consider whether to dismiss the adoption application summarily and consider proceeding in wardship.

14.9 Requesting the court to dispense with the consent of any parent or guardian

(1) This rule applies where the applicant wants to ask the court to dispense with the consent of any parent or guardian of a child to –

(a) the child being placed for adoption;

(b) the making of an adoption order except a Convention adoption order; or
(c) the making of a section 84 order.

(2) The applicant requesting the court to dispense with the consent must –

(a) give notice of the request in the application form or at any later stage by filing a written request setting out the reasons for the request; and
(b) file a statement of facts setting out a summary of the history of the case and any other facts to satisfy the court that –
(i) the parent or guardian cannot be found or is incapable of giving consent; or
(ii) the welfare of the child requires the consent to be dispensed with.

(3) If a serial number has been assigned to the applicant under rule 14.2, the statement of facts supplied under paragraph (2)(b) must be framed so that it does not disclose the identity of the applicant.

(4) On receipt of the notice of the request –

(a) a court officer will –
(i) inform the parent or guardian of the request unless the parent or guardian cannot be found; and
(ii) send a copy of the statement of facts filed in accordance with paragraph (2)(b) to –
(aa) the parent or guardian unless the parent or guardian cannot be found;
(bb) any children's guardian, reporting officer or children and family reporter;
(cc) any local authority to whom notice under section 44 of the 2002 Act (notice of intention to adopt or apply for a section 84 order) has been given; and
(dd) any adoption agency which has placed the child for adoption; and
(b) if the applicant considers that the parent or guardian is incapable of giving consent, the court will consider whether to –
(i) appoint a litigation friend for the parent or guardian under rule 15.6(1); or
(ii) give directions for an application to be made under rule 15.6(3);
(iii) unless a litigation friend is already appointed for that parent or guardian.

Defined terms—'child', 'children and family reporter', 'children's guardian', 'court officer', 'filing', 'litigation friend', 'reporting officer', 'section 84 order': FPR 2010, r 2.3(1).

Statement of facts (r 14.9(2)(b))—As a matter of practice the statement of facts will be of most use if it sets out succinctly in numbered paragraphs the history that is relied upon.

14.10 Consent

(1) Consent of any parent or guardian of a child –

(a) under section 19 of the 2002 Act, to the child being placed for adoption; and
(b) under section 20 of the 2002 Act, to the making of a future adoption order,

must be given in the form referred to in Practice Direction 5A or a form to the like effect.

(2) Subject to paragraph (3), consent –

(a) to the making of an adoption order; or
(b) to the making of a section 84 order,

may be given in the form referred to in Practice Direction 5A or a form to the like effect or otherwise as the court directs.

(3) Any consent to a Convention adoption order must be in a form which complies with the internal law relating to adoption of the Convention country of which the child is habitually resident.

(4) Any form of consent executed in Scotland must be witnessed by a Justice of the Peace or a Sheriff.

(5) Any form of consent executed in Northern Ireland must be witnessed by a Justice of the Peace.

(6) Any form of consent executed outside the United Kingdom must be witnessed by –

PART III

(a) any person for the time being authorised by law in the place where the document is executed to administer an oath for any judicial or other legal purpose;
(b) a British Consular officer;
(c) a notary public; or
(d) if the person executing the document is serving in any of the regular armed forces of the Crown, an officer holding a commission in any of those forces.

Defined terms—'child', 'section 84 order': FPR 2010, r 2.3(1).

Consequences of giving consent to placement or future adoption—Once consent has been given to placement for adoption (or to future adoption) and if that consent has not been withdrawn the consenting parent will be unable to oppose any subsequent adoption application unless there has been a subsequent change of circumstances and the court gives leave to oppose (see notes to ACA 2002, ss 47 and 52). As a result, for a consent to be validly given 'with full understanding of what is involved' (ACA 2002, s 52(5)) the parent must understand that, while the consent may be to placement, it fundamentally alters the parents' ability to oppose any subsequent adoption.

Forms of consent—The form of consent must be in the relevant form (A100–A106) or a form to like effect (FPR 2010, r 5.1 and PD5A).

14.11 Reports by the adoption agency or local authority

(1) The adoption agency or local authority must file the report on the suitability of the applicant to adopt a child within the timetable fixed by the court.

(2) A local authority that is directed to prepare a report on the placement of the child for adoption must file that report within the timetable fixed by the court.

(3) The reports must cover the matters specified in Practice Direction 14C.

(4) The court may at any stage request a further report or ask the adoption agency or local authority to assist the court in any other manner.

(5) A court officer will send a copy of any report referred to in this rule to any children's guardian, reporting officer or children and family reporter.

(6) A report to the court under this rule is confidential.

Defined terms—'child', 'children and family reporter', 'children's guardian', 'court officer', 'reporting officer': FPR 2010, r 2.3(1).

Reports by the adoption agency or local authority (r 14.11(3))—See FPR PD14C. These 'Annex A' reports provide an important welfare safeguard for a child (*Re S (Adoption: Annex A Report)* [2015] EWCA Civ 1345). These confidential reports (r 14.11(6)) may be disclosed to the parties (see r 14.13).

14.12 Health reports

(1) Reports by a registered medical practitioner ('health reports') made not more than 3 months earlier on the health of the child and of each applicant must be attached to an application for an adoption order or a section 84 order except where –

(a) the child was placed for adoption with the applicant by an adoption agency;
(b) the applicant or one of the applicants is a parent of the child; or
(c) the applicant is the partner of a parent of the child.

(2) Health reports must contain the matters set out in Practice Direction 14D.

(3) A health report is confidential.

Defined terms—'child', 'section 84 order': FPR 2010, r 2.3(1).

Health reports (r 14.12(2))—See FPR PD14D. These confidential reports (r 14.12(3)) may be disclosed to the parties (see r 14.13).

14.13 Confidential reports to the court and disclosure to the parties

(1) The court will consider whether to give a direction that a confidential report be disclosed to each party to the proceedings.

(2) Before giving such a direction the court will consider whether any information should be deleted including information which –

(a) discloses, or is likely to disclose, the identity of a person who has been assigned a serial number under rule 14.2(2) or (3); or

(b) discloses the particulars referred to in rule 29.1(1) where a party has given notice under rule 29.1(2) (disclosure of personal details).

(3) The court may direct that the report will not be disclosed to a party.

Amendments—SI 2014/843.

Defined terms—'proceedings': FPR 2010, r 2.3(1).

Confidentiality of reports—Any report provided to the court by the adoption agency or local authority, a children's guardian, reporting officer or children and family reporter is confidential.

Under the earlier law there was a presumption in the rules (Adoption Rules 1984, r 53(2)) in favour of a party being entitled to inspect that part of any confidential report that related to them. That presumption has been replaced by an open discretion, but the leading authorities on the earlier provision may still be of relevance.

In *Re D (Minors) (Adoption Reports: Confidentiality)* [1995] 2 FLR 687, HL, the House of Lords set out the principles on which issues about the disclosure of confidential adoption reports should be determined:

> 'It is a fundamental principle of fairness that a party is entitled to the disclosure of all materials which may be taken into account by the court when reaching a decision adverse to that party. This principle applies with particular force to proceedings designed to lead to an order for adoption, since the consequences of such an order are so lasting and far-reaching.
>
> When deciding whether to direct that notwithstanding Adoption Rules 1984, r 53(2) a party referred to in a confidential report supplied by an adoption agency, a local authority, a reporting officer or a guardian ad litem shall not be entitled to inspect that part of the report which refers to him or her, the court should first consider whether disclosure of the material would involve a real possibility of significant harm to the child. If it would, the court should next consider whether the overall interests of the child would benefit from non-disclosure, weighing on the one hand the interests of the child in having the material properly tested, and on the other both the magnitude of the risk that harm will occur and the gravity of the harm if it does occur.
>
> If the court is satisfied that the interests of the child point towards non-disclosure, the next and final step is for the court to weigh that consideration, and its strength in the circumstances of the case, against the interest of the parent or other party in having an opportunity to see and respond to the material. In the latter regard the court should take into account the importance of the material to the issues in the case.
>
> Non-disclosure should be the exception and not the rule. The court should be rigorous in its examination of the risk and gravity of the feared harm to the child, and should order non-disclosure only when the case for doing so is compelling.'

Following the implementation of the HRA 1998, the Court of Appeal has held that the House of Lords decision in *Re D* must be extended to include, not solely those of the children, but also the interests of the adult parties (*Re B (Disclosure to Other Parties)* [2001] 2 FLR 1017, FD, approved in *Re X (Adoption: Confidential Procedure)* [2002] 2 FLR 476, CA).

It would seem sensible that the court should consider the extent of the inspection to be allowed far enough in advance of the hearing for instructions to be taken and any necessary evidence prepared for the hearing. Practitioners are advised to keep in touch with the court and apply as soon as possible after the reports are filed for facilities for inspection, to avoid delay. There is no provision in the rules to cause parties to be notified that a report has been filed.

The duty of confidentiality applies to documents in the custody and control of an adoption agency that have never been placed before the court (*Re H (Criminal Proceedings: Disclosure of Adoption Records)* [1995] 1 FLR 964, FD).

An adoption agency must maintain the confidentiality and safekeeping of any adoption information and case records (Adoption Agencies Regulations 2005, regs 41 and 42 and Disclosure of Adoption Information (Post Commencement) Regs 2005, Pt 2).

Where information that is confidential to the adoption proceedings may be relevant in criminal proceedings, normally an application for disclosure should be made within the criminal proceedings, so that the judge may balance the high degree of confidentiality attaching to adoption proceedings against the benefits of disclosure (*Re H* above); an alternative course is to issue an originating summons in the High Court to determine whether disclosure should be made (*Re An Adoption Application* [1990] 1 FLR 412, FD; *Re C (A Minor) (Disclosure of Adoption Reports)* [1994] 2 FLR 525, FD). If appropriate, the Attorney-General should be represented before the court.

Communicating information relating to the proceedings—For the restrictions on a person communicating information relating to the proceedings to representatives and other persons, see FPR 2010, r 14.14.

14.14 Communication of information relating to proceedings

For the purposes of the law relating to contempt of court, information (whether or not it is recorded in any form) relating to proceedings held in private may be communicated –

(a) where the court gives permission;

(b) unless the court directs otherwise, in accordance with Practice Direction 14E; or

(c) where the communication is to –

(i) a party;

(ii) the legal representative of a party;

(iii) a professional legal adviser;

(iv) an officer of the service or a Welsh family proceedings officer;

(v) a welfare officer;

(vi) the Director of Legal Aid Casework (within the meaning of section 4 of the Legal Aid, Sentencing and Punishment of Offenders Act 2012);

(vii) an expert whose instruction by a party has been authorised by the court for the purposes of the proceedings; or

(viii) a professional acting in furtherance of the protection of children.

Amendments—SI 2013/534, subject to savings.

Defined terms—'the 1989 Act', 'child', 'legal representative', 'officer of the Service', 'proceedings', 'Welsh family proceedings officer': FPR 2010, r 2.3(1).

Communication of information relating to proceedings (r 14.14(1)(b))—See FPR PD14E.

14.15 Notice of final hearing

A court officer will give notice to the parties, any children's guardian, reporting officer or children and family reporter and to any other person to whom a practice direction may require such notice to be given –

(a) of the date and place where the application will be heard; and

(b) of the fact that, unless the person wishes or the court requires, the person need not attend.

Defined terms—'children and family reporter', 'children's guardian', 'court officer', 'reporting officer': FPR 2010, r 2.3(1).

14.16 The final hearing

(1) Any person who has been given notice in accordance with rule 14.15 may attend the final hearing and, subject to paragraph (2), be heard on the question of whether an order should be made.

(2) A person whose application for the permission of the court to oppose the making of an adoption order under section 47(3) or (5) of the 2002 Act has been refused is not entitled to be heard on the question of whether an order should be made.

(3) Any member or employee of a party which is a local authority, adoption agency or other body may address the court at the final hearing if authorised to do so.

(4) The court may direct that any person must attend a final hearing.

(5) Paragraphs (6) and (7) apply to –

(a) an adoption order;

(b) a section 84 order; or

(c) a section 89 order.

(6) Subject to paragraphs (7) and (8), the court cannot make an order unless the applicant and the child personally attend the final hearing.

(7) The court may direct that the applicant or the child need not attend the final hearing.

(8) In a case of adoption by a couple under section 50 of the 2002 Act, the court may make an adoption order after personal attendance of one only of the applicants if there are special circumstances.

(9) The court cannot make a placement order unless a legal representative of the applicant attends the final hearing.

Defined terms—'child', 'legal representative', 'section 84 order', 'section 89 order': FPR 2010, r 2.3(1).

Serial number case (r 14.2(4))—The operation of this rule will inevitably mean that the applicant and those who do not know the applicant's identity may not be in the courtroom at the same time. The normal approach of courts is to conduct most of the hearing in the absence of the applicant. In some cases, particularly in the High Court, arrangements can be made for the absent applicant to listen to the proceedings without being present in the courtroom. If the applicant is called to give evidence, the roles are reversed and those who do not know the applicant's identity will leave the courtroom. The practice of splitting a final hearing so that the child and adopters may attend for a short ceremony at a time after the court has decided to make an adoption order has been expressly approved (*Re F (Adoption: Natural Parents)* [2007] 1 FLR 363, CA).

Attendance of the child (r 14.16(6))—The default position is that the child must attend a FPR 2010, Pt 14 final hearing. In practice, in placement cases the court is likely to dispense with the child's attendance, but in adoption cases it is normal for the child to attend before the court either at the final hearing or at a later hearing. The underlying purpose of the provision is to ensure that a child in respect of whom an order is about to be made understands fully, as far as he or she can, the nature of the order (*Re P (Minors) (Adoption)* [1989] 1 FLR 1, CA).

14.17 Proof of identity of the child

(1) Unless the contrary is shown, the child referred to in the application will be deemed to be the child referred to in the form of consent –

(a) to the child being placed for adoption;
(b) to the making of an adoption order; or
(c) to the making of a section 84 order,

where the conditions in paragraph (2) apply.

(2) The conditions are –

(a) the application identifies the child by reference to a full certified copy of an entry in the registers of live-births;
(b) the form of consent identifies the child by reference to a full certified copy of an entry in the registers of live-births attached to the form; and
(c) the copy of the entry in the registers of live-births referred to in sub-paragraph (a) is the same or relates to the same entry in the registers of live-births as the copy of the entry in the registers of live-births attached to the form of consent.

(3) Where the child is already an adopted child paragraph (2) will have effect as if for the references to the registers of live-births there were substituted references to the Adopted Children Register.

(4) Subject to paragraph (7), where the precise date of the child's birth is not proved to the satisfaction of the court, the court will determine the probable date of birth.

(5) The probable date of the child's birth may be specified in the placement order, adoption order or section 84 order as the date of the child's birth.

(6) Subject to paragraph (7), where the child's place of birth cannot be proved to the satisfaction of the court –

(a) the child may be treated as having been born in the registration district and sub-district in which the court sits where it is probable that the child may have been born in –
  (i) the United Kingdom;
  (ii) the Channel Islands; or
  (iii) the Isle of Man; or
(b) in any other case, the particulars of the country of birth may be omitted from the placement order, adoption order or section 84 order.

(7) A placement order identifying the probable date and place of birth of the child will be sufficient proof of the date and place of birth of the child in adoption proceedings and proceedings for a section 84 order.

Amendments—SI 2013/3204.
Defined terms—'adoption proceedings', 'child', 'proceedings', 'section 84 order': FPR 2010, r 2.3(1).

14.18 Disclosing information to an adopted adult

(1) The adopted person has the right, on request, to receive from the court which made the adoption order a copy of the following –

(a) the application form for an adoption order (but not the documents attached to that form);
(b) the adoption order and any other orders relating to the adoption proceedings;
(c) orders containing any provision for contact with the child after the adoption order was made; and
(d) any other document or order referred to in Practice Direction 14F.

(2) The court will remove any protected information from any copy of a document or order referred to in paragraph (1) before the copies are given to the adopted person.

PART III

(3) This rule does not apply to an adopted person under the age of 18 years.

(4) In this rule 'protected information' means information which would be protected information under section 57(3) of the 2002 Act if the adoption agency gave the information and not the court.

Amendments—SI 2014/843.

Defined terms—'adoption proceedings', 'child', 'proceedings': FPR 2010, r 2.3(1).

Disclosing information to an adopted adult (r 14.18(1)(d))—See FPR PD14F.

14.19 Translation of documents

(1) Where a translation of any document is required for the purposes of proceedings for a Convention adoption order the translation must –

(a) unless the court directs otherwise, be provided by the applicant; and
(b) be signed by the translator to certify that the translation is accurate.

(2) This rule does not apply where the document is to be served in accordance with the Service Regulation.

Defined terms—'proceedings', 'the Service Regulation': FPR 2010, r 2.3(1).

14.20 Application for recovery orders

(1) An application for any of the orders referred to in section 41(2) of the 2002 Act (recovery orders) may be made without notice, in which case the applicant must file the application –

(a) where the application is made by telephone, the next business day after the making of the application; or
(b) in any other case, at the time when the application is made.

(2) Where the court refuses to make an order on an application without notice it may direct that the application is made on notice in which case the application will proceed in accordance with rules 14.1 to 14.17.

(3) The respondents to an application under this rule are –

(a) in a case where –
  (i) placement proceedings;
  (ii) adoption proceedings; or
  (iii) proceedings for a section 84 order,

  are pending, all parties to those proceedings;
(b) any adoption agency authorised to place the child for adoption or which has placed the child for adoption;
(c) any local authority to whom notice under section 44 of the 2002 Act (notice of intention to adopt or apply for a section 84 order) has been given;
(d) any person having parental responsibility for the child;
(e) any person in whose favour there is provision for contact;
(f) any person who was caring for the child immediately prior to the making of the application; and
(g) any person whom the applicant alleges to have effected, or to have been or to be responsible for, the taking or keeping of the child.

Amendments—SI 2013/3204.

Defined terms—'adoption proceedings', 'business day', 'child', 'court officer', 'placement proceedings', 'proceedings', 'section 84 order': FPR 2010, r 2.3(1); 'provision for contact': FPR 2010, r 14.1(2).

14.21 Inherent jurisdiction and fathers without parental responsibility

Where no proceedings have started an adoption agency or local authority may ask the High Court for directions on the need to give a father without parental responsibility notice of the intention to place a child for adoption.

Defined terms—'child', 'jurisdiction', 'proceedings': FPR 2010, r 2.3(1).

14.22 Timing of applications for section 89 order

An application for a section 89 order must be made within 2 years beginning with the date on which –

(a) the Convention adoption or Convention adoption order; or
(b) the overseas adoption or determination under section 91 of the 2002 Act,

to which it relates was made.

Defined terms—'section 89 order': FPR 2010, r 2.3(1).

High Court—Application for a s 89 order (annulment of overseas or Hague Convention orders) is in the High Court (ACA 2002, s 89).

14.23 Custody of documents

All documents relating to proceedings under the 2002 Act must, while they are in the custody of the court, be kept in a place of special security.

Defined terms—'the 2002 Act', 'proceedings': FPR 2010, r 2.3(1).

14.24 Documents held by the court not to be inspected or copied without the court's permission

Subject to the provisions of these rules, any practice direction or any direction given by the court –

(a) no document or order held by the court in proceedings under the 2002 Act will be open to inspection by any person; and
(b) no copy of any such document or order, or of an extract from any such document or order, will be taken by or given to any person.

Defined terms—'the 2002 Act', 'proceedings': FPR 2010, r 2.3(1).

Disclosure of court adoption records—Rule 14.24 applies in relation to adoptions made under ACA 2002; in relation to earlier adoption orders, the relevant rules, which are in similar terms to r 14.24, (Adoption Rules 1984, r 53(4) or Magistrates' Courts (Adoption) Rules 1984, r 32(4)), remain in force. The court must exercise discretion by considering all the circumstances, including public policy in maintaining confidentiality, the time elapsed, the relationships involved, the impact on third parties and any available safeguards (*Re X (Adoption Child: Access to Court File)* [2015] 1 FLR 375, FD).

14.25 Orders

(1) An order takes effect from the date when it is made, or such later date as the court may specify.

(2) In proceedings in Wales a party may request that an order be drawn up in Welsh as well as English.

(Rule 37.9 makes provision for the court to endorse an order prohibiting contact under section 51A(2)(b) of the 2002 Act with a penal notice on the application of the person entitled to enforce the order.)

Amendments—SI 2014/843.

Defined terms—'proceedings': FPR 2010, r 2.3(1).

14.26 Copies of orders

(1) Within 7 days beginning with the date on which the final order was made in proceedings, or such shorter time as the court may direct, a court officer will send –

(a) a copy of the order to the applicant;
(b) a copy, which is sealed(GL), authenticated with the stamp of the court or certified as a true copy, of –
  (i) an adoption order;
  (ii) a section 89 order; or
  (iii) an order quashing or revoking an adoption order or allowing an appeal against an adoption order,

  to the Registrar General;
(c) a copy of a Convention adoption order to the relevant Central Authority;
(d) a copy of a section 89 order relating to a Convention adoption order or a Convention adoption to the –

(i) relevant Central Authority;
(ii) adopters;
(iii) adoption agency; and
(iv) local authority;

(e) unless the court directs otherwise, a copy of an order under section 26 of the 2002 Act or a variation or revocation of such order under section 27 of the 2002 Act to the –
(i) person with whom the child is living;
(ii) adoption agency; and
(iii) local authority;

(ee) unless the court directs otherwise, a copy of a contact order under section 51A(2)(a) of the 2002 Act, an order prohibiting contact under section 51A(2)(b) of that Act or a variation or revocation of such orders under section 51B(1)(c) of that Act to the parties to the proceedings; and

(f) a notice of the making or refusal of –
(i) the final order; or
(ii) an order quashing or revoking an adoption order or allowing an appeal against an order in proceedings,

to every respondent and, with the permission of the court, any other person.

(2) The court officer will also send notice of the making of an adoption order or a section 84 order to –

(a) any court in Great Britain which appears to the court officer to have made any such order as is referred to in section 46(2) of the 2002 Act (order relating to parental responsibility for, and maintenance of, the child); and
(b) the principal registry, if it appears to the court officer that a parental responsibility agreement has been recorded at the principal registry.

(3) A copy of any final order may be sent to any other person with the permission of the court.

(4) The court officer will send a copy of any order made during the course of the proceedings to the following persons or bodies, unless the court directs otherwise –

(a) all the parties to those proceedings;
(b) any children and family reporter appointed in those proceedings;
(c) any adoption agency or local authority which has prepared a report on the suitability of an applicant to adopt a child;
(d) any local authority which has prepared a report on placement for adoption.

(5) If an order has been drawn up in Welsh as well as English in accordance with rule 14.25(2) any reference in this rule to sending an order is to be taken as a reference to sending both the Welsh and English orders.

Amendments—SI 2014/843.

Defined terms—'child', 'court officer', 'proceedings', 'section 84 order', 'section 89 order': FPR 2010, r 2.3(1). 'Central Authority': FPR 2010, 14.1(2).

14.27 Amendment and revocation of orders

(1) Subject to paragraph (2), an application under –

(a) section 55 of the 2002 Act (revocation of adoptions on legitimation); or
(b) paragraph 4 of Schedule 1 to the 2002 Act (amendment of adoption order and revocation of direction),

may be made without serving a copy of the application notice.

(2) The court may direct that an application notice be served on such persons as it thinks fit.

(3) Where the court makes an order granting the application, a court officer will send the Registrar General a notice –

(a) specifying the amendments; or
(b) informing the Registrar General of the revocation,

giving sufficient particulars of the order to enable the Registrar General to identify the case.

Defined terms—'application notice', 'court officer': FPR 2010, r 2.3(1).

14.28 *(revoked)*

Practice Direction 14A – Who Receives a Copy of the Application Form for Orders in Proceedings

This Practice Direction supplements FPR Part 14, rule 14.6(1)(b)(ii)

Persons who receive copy of application form

1 In relation to each type of proceedings in column 1 of the following table, column 2 sets out which persons are to receive a copy of the application form:

Proceeding for	Who Receives a Copy of the Application Form
An adoption order (section 46 of the Act); or a section 84 order	Any appointed children's guardian, children and family reporter and reporting officer; the local authority to whom notice under section 44 (notice of intention to apply to adopt or apply for a section 84 order) has been given; the adoption agency which placed the child for adoption with the applicants; any other person directed by the court to receive a copy.
A placement order (section 21 of the Act); or an order varying a placement order (section 23 of the Act)	Each parent with parental responsibility for the child or guardian of the child; any appointed children's guardian, children and family reporter and reporting officer; any other person directed by the court to receive a copy.
An order revoking a placement order (section 24 of the Act)	Each parent with parental responsibility for the child or guardian of the child; any appointed children's guardian and children and family reporter; the local authority authorised by the placement order to place the child for adoption; any other person directed by the court to receive a copy.

PART III

Proceeding for	Who Receives a Copy of the Application Form
A contact order (section 26 of the Act); an order varying or revoking a contact order (section 27 of the Act); an order permitting the child's name to be changed or the removal of the child from the United Kingdom (section 28(2) of the Act); a recovery order (section 41(2) of the Act); a contact order under section 51A(2)(a) of the Act; the making of an order prohibiting contact with the child under section 51A(2)(b) of the Act; the variation or revocation of an order under section 51A(2) of the Act in accordance with section 51B(1)(c) of the Act; a section 89 order; and a section 88 direction	All the parties; any appointed children's guardian and children and family reporter; any other person directed by the court to receive a copy.

Practice Direction 14B – The First Directions Hearing – Adoptions with a Foreign Element

This Practice Direction supplements FPR Part 14, rule 14.8(3)

Application

1 This Practice Direction applies to proceedings for:

(a) a Convention adoption order;
(b) a section 84 order;
(c) a section 88 direction;
(d) a section 89 order; and
(e) an adoption order where the child has been brought into the United Kingdom in the circumstances where section 83(1) of the Act applies.

The first directions hearing

2 At the first directions hearing the court will, in addition to any matters referred to in rule 14.8(1):

(a) consider whether the requirements of the Act and the Adoptions with a Foreign Element Regulations 2005 (S.I. 2005/392) appear to have been complied with and, if not, consider whether or not in a case in the family court, it is appropriate that the case should be considered by a puisne judge of the High Court sitting in the family court (who may in turn consider whether or not it is appropriate to transfer the case to the High Court);

(b) consider whether all relevant documents are translated into English and, if not, fix a timetable for translating any outstanding documents;
(c) consider whether the applicant needs to file an affidavit setting out the full details of the circumstances in which the child was brought to the United Kingdom, of the attitude of the parents to the application and confirming compliance with the requirements of The Adoptions with A Foreign Element Regulations 2005;
(d) give directions about:
 (i) the production of the child's passport and visa;
 (ii) the need for an officer of the Service or a Welsh family proceedings officer and a representative of the Home Office to attend future hearings; and
 (iii) personal service on the parents (via the Central Authority in the case of an application for a Convention Adoption Order) including information about the role of the officer of the Service or the Welsh family proceedings officer and availability of legal aid to be represented within the proceedings; and
(e) consider fixing a further directions appointment no later than 6 weeks after the date of the first directions appointment and timetable a date by which the officer of the Service or the Welsh family proceedings officer should file an interim report in advance of that further appointment.

Practice Direction 14C – Reports by the Adoption Agency or Local Authority

This Practice Direction supplements FPR Part 14, rule 14.11(3)

Matters to be contained in reports

1.1 The matters to be covered in the report on the suitability of the applicant to adopt a child are set out in Annex A to this Practice Direction.

1.2 The matters to be covered in a report on the placement of the child for adoption are set out in Annex B to this Practice Direction.

1.3 Where a matter to be covered in the reports set out in Annex A and Annex B does not apply to the circumstances of a particular case, the reasons for not covering the matter should be given.

ANNEX A – REPORT TO THE COURT WHERE THERE HAS BEEN AN APPLICATION FOR AN ADOPTION ORDER OR AN APPLICATION FOR A SECTION 84 ORDER

Section A: The Report and Matters for the Proceedings

Section B: The Child and the Birth Family

Section C: The Prospective Adopter of the Child

Section D: The Placement

Section E: Recommendations

Section F: Further information for proceedings relating to Convention Adoption Orders, Convention adoptions, section 84 Orders or adoptions where section 83(1) of the 2002 Act applies.

SECTION A: THE REPORT AND MATTERS FOR THE PROCEEDINGS

Part 1 – The report

For each of the principal author/s of the report:

(i) name;
(ii) role in relation to this case;
(iii) sections completed in this report;
(iv) qualifications and experience;

(v) name and address of the adoption agency; and
(vi) adoption agency case reference number.

Part 2 – Matters for the proceedings

(a) Whether the adoption agency considers that any other person should be made a respondent or a party to the proceedings, including the child.
(b) Whether any of the respondents is under the age of 18.
(c) Whether a respondent is a person who, by reason of mental disorder within the meaning of the Mental Health Act 1983, is incapable of managing and administering his or her property and affairs. If so, medical evidence should be provided with particular regard to the effect on that person's ability to make decisions in the proceedings.

SECTION B: THE CHILD AND THE BIRTH FAMILY

Part 1

(i) Information about the child

(a) Name, sex, date and place of birth and address including local authority area.
(b) Photograph and physical description.
(c) Nationality.
(d) Racial origin and cultural and linguistic background.
(e) Religious persuasion (including details of baptism, confirmation or equivalent ceremonies).
(f) Details of any siblings, half-siblings and step-siblings, including dates of birth.
(g) Whether the child is looked after by a local authority.
(h) Whether the child has been placed for adoption with the prospective adopter by a UK adoption agency.
(i) Whether the child was being fostered by the prospective adopter.
(j) Whether the child was brought into the UK for adoption, including date of entry and whether an adoption order was made in the child's country of origin.
(k) Personality and social development, including emotional and behavioural development and any related needs.
(l) Details of interests, likes and dislikes.
(m) A summary, written by the agency's medical adviser, of the child's health history, his current state of health and any need for health care which is anticipated, and date of the most recent medical examination.
(n) Any known learning difficulties or known general medical or mental health factors which are likely to have, or may have, genetic implications.
(o) Names, addresses and types of nurseries or schools attended, with dates.
(p) Educational attainments.
(q) Any special needs in relation to the child (whether physical, learning, behavioural or any other) and his emotional and behavioural development.
(r) Whether the child is subject to a statement under the Education Act 1996.
(s) Previous orders concerning the child:
 (i) the name of the court;
 (ii) the order made; and
 (iii) the date of the order.
(t) Inheritance rights and any claim to damages under the Fatal Accidents Act 1976 the child stands to retain or lose if adopted.
(u) Any other relevant information which might assist the court.

(ii) Information about each parent of the child

(a) Name, date and place of birth and address (date on which last address was confirmed current) including local authority area.
(b) Photograph, if available, and physical description.

(c) Nationality.
(d) Racial origin and cultural and linguistic background.
(e) Whether the mother and father were married to each other at the time of the child's birth or have subsequently married.
(f) Where the parent has been previously married or entered into a civil partnership, dates of those marriages or civil partnerships.
(g) Where the mother and father are not married, whether the father has parental responsibility and, if so, how it was acquired.
(h) If the identity or whereabouts of the father are not known, the information about him that has been ascertained and from whom, and the steps that have been taken to establish paternity.
(i) Past and present relationship with the other parent.
(j) Other information about the parent, where available:
  (i) health, including any known learning difficulties or known general medical or mental health factors which are likely to have, or may have, genetic implications;
  (ii) religious persuasion;
  (iii) educational history;
  (iv) employment history; and
  (v) personality and interests.
(k) Any other relevant information which might assist the court.

Part 2

Relationships, contact arrangements and views.

THE CHILD

(a) If the child is in the care of a local authority or voluntary organisation, or has been, details (including dates) of any placements with foster parents, or other arrangements in respect of the care of the child, including particulars of the persons with whom the child has had his home and observations on the care provided.
(b) The child's wishes and feelings (if appropriate, having regard to the child's age and understanding) about adoption, the application and its consequences, including any wishes in respect of religious and cultural upbringing.
(c) The child's wishes and feelings in relation to contact (if appropriate, having regard to the child's age and understanding).
(d) The child's wishes and feelings recorded in any other proceedings.
(e) Date when the child's views were last ascertained.

THE CHILD'S PARENTS (OR GUARDIAN) AND RELATIVES

(a) The parents' wishes and feelings before the placement, about the placement and about adoption, the application and its consequences, including any wishes in respect of the child's religious and cultural upbringing.
(b) Each parent's (or guardian's) wishes and feelings in relation to contact.
(c) Date/s when the views of each parent or guardian were last ascertained.
(d) Arrangements concerning any siblings, including half-siblings and step-siblings, and whether any are the subject of a parallel application or have been the subject of any orders. If so, for each case give:
  (i) the name of the court;
  (ii) the order made, or (if proceedings are pending) the order applied for; and
  (iii) the date of order, or date of next hearing if proceedings are pending.
(e) Extent of contact with the child's mother and father and, in each case, the nature of the relationship enjoyed.
(f) The relationship which the child has with relatives, and with any other person considered relevant, including:
  (i) the likelihood of any such relationship continuing and the value to the child of its doing so; and

(ii) the ability and willingness of any of the child's relatives, or of any such person, to provide the child with a secure environment in which the child can develop, and otherwise to meet the child's needs.

(g) The wishes and feelings of any of the child's relatives, or of any such person, regarding the child.

(h) Whether the parents (or members of the child's family) have met or are likely to meet the prospective adopter and, if they have met, the effect on all involved of such meeting.

(i) Dates when the views of members of the child's wider family and any other relevant person were last ascertained.

Part 3

A summary of the actions of the adoption agency

(a) Brief account of the agency's actions in the case, with particulars and dates of all written information and notices given to the child and his parents and any person with parental responsibility.

(b) If consent has been given for the child to be placed for adoption, and also consent for the child to be adopted, the names of those who gave consent and the date such consents were given. If such consents were subsequently withdrawn, the dates of these withdrawals.

(c) If any statement has been made under section 20(4)(a) of the Adoption and Children Act 2002 (the '2002 Act') that a parent or guardian does not wish to be informed of any application for an adoption order, the names of those who have made such statements and the dates the statements were made. If such statements were subsequently withdrawn, the dates of these withdrawals.

(d) Whether an order has been made under section 21 of the 2002 Act, section 18 of the Adoption (Scotland) Act 1978 or Article 17(1) or 18(1) of the Northern Ireland Order 1987.

(e) Details of the support and advice given to the parents and any services offered or taken up.

(f) If the father does not have parental responsibility, details of the steps taken to inform him of the application for an adoption order.

(g) Brief details and dates of assessments of the child's needs, including expert opinions.

(h) Reasons for considering that adoption would be in the child's best interests (with date of relevant decision and reasons for any delay in implementing the decision).

SECTION C: THE PROSPECTIVE ADOPTER OF THE CHILD

Part 1

Information about the prospective adopter, including suitability to adopt

(a) Name, date and place of birth and address (date on which last address was confirmed current) including local authority area.

(b) Photograph and physical description.

(c) Whether the prospective adopter is domiciled or habitually resident in a part of the British Islands and, if habitually resident, for how long they have been habitually resident.

(d) Racial origin and cultural and linguistic background.

(e) Marital status or civil partnership status, date and place of most recent marriage (if any) or civil partnership (if any).

(f) Details of any previous marriage, civil partnership, or relationship where the prospective adopter lived with another person as a partner in an enduring family relationship.

(g) Relationship (if any) to the child.

(h) Where adopters wish to adopt as a couple, the status of the relationship and an assessment of the stability and permanence of their relationship.

(i) If a married person or a civil partner is applying alone, the reasons for this.

(j) Description of how the prospective adopter relates to adults and children.

(k) Previous experience of caring for children (including as a step-parent, foster parent, child-minder or prospective adopter) and assessment of ability in this respect, together where appropriate with assessment of ability in bringing up the prospective adopter's own children.

(l) A summary, written by the agency's medical adviser, of the prospective adopter's health history, current state of health and any need for health care which is anticipated, and date of most recent medical examination.

(m) Assessment of ability and suitability to bring up the child throughout his childhood.

(n) Details of income and comments on the living standards of the household with particulars of the home and living conditions (and particulars of any home where the prospective adopter proposes to live with the child, if different).

(o) Details of other members of the household, including any children of the prospective adopter even if not resident in the household.

(p) Details of the parents and any siblings of the prospective adopter, with their ages or ages at death.

(q) Other information about the prospective adopter:
  (i) religious persuasion;
  (ii) educational history;
  (iii) employment history; and
  (iv) personality and interests.

(r) Confirmation that the applicants have not been convicted of, or cautioned for, a specified offence within the meaning of regulation 23(3) of the Adoption Agencies Regulations 2005 (S.I. 2005/389).

(s) Confirmation that the prospective adopter is still approved.

(t) Confirmation that any referees have been interviewed, with a report of their views and opinion of the weight to be placed thereon and whether they are still valid.

(u) Details of any previous family court proceedings in which the prospective adopter has been involved (which have not been referred to elsewhere in this report.)

Part 2

Wishes, views and contact arrangements

PROSPECTIVE ADOPTER

(a) Whether the prospective adopter is willing to follow any wishes of the child or his parents or guardian in respect of the child's religious and cultural upbringing.

(b) The views of other members of the prospective adopter's household and wider family in relation to the proposed adoption.

(c) Reasons for the prospective adopter wishing to adopt the child and extent of understanding of the nature and effect of adoption. Whether the prospective adopter has discussed adoption with the child.

(d) Any hope and expectations the prospective adopter has for the child's future.

(e) The prospective adopter's wishes and feelings in relation to contact.

Part 3

Actions of the adoption agency

(a) Brief account of the Agency's actions in the case, with particulars and dates of all written information and notices given to the prospective adopter.

(b) The Agency's proposals for contact, including options for facilitating or achieving any indirect contact or direct contact.

(c) The Agency's opinion on the likely effect on the prospective adopter and on the security of the placement of any proposed contact.

(d) Where the prospective adopter has been approved by an agency as suitable to be an adoptive parent, the agency's reasons for considering that the prospective adopter is suitable to be an adoptive parent for this child (with dates of relevant decisions).

SECTION D: THE PLACEMENT

(a) Where the child was placed for adoption by an adoption agency (section 18 of the 2002 Act), the date and circumstances of the child's placement with prospective adopter.
(b) Where the child is living with persons who have applied for the adoption order to be made (section 44 of the 2002 Act), the date when notice of intention to adopt was given.
(c) Where the placement is being provided with adoption support, this should be summarised and should include the plan and timescales for continuing the support beyond the making of the adoption order.
(d) Where the placement is not being provided with adoption support, the reasons why.
(e) A summary of the information obtained from the Agency's visits and reviews of the placement, including whether the child has been seen separately to the prospective adopter and whether there has been sufficient opportunity to see the family group and the child's interaction in the home environment.
(f) An assessment of the child's integration within the family of the prospective adopter and the likelihood of the child's full integration into the family and community.
(g) Any other relevant information that might assist the court.

SECTION E: RECOMMENDATIONS

(a) The relative merits of adoption and other orders with an assessment of whether the child's long term interests would be best met by an adoption order or by other orders (such as child arrangements and special guardianship orders).
(b) Recommendations as to whether or not the order sought should be made (and, if not, alternative proposals).
(c) Recommendations as to whether there should be future contact arrangements (or not).

SECTION F: FURTHER INFORMATION FOR PROCEEDINGS RELATING TO CONVENTION ADOPTION ORDERS, CONVENTION ADOPTIONS, SECTION 84 ORDERS OR AN ADOPTION WHERE SECTION 83(1) OF THE 2002 ACT APPLIES.

(a) The child's knowledge of their racial and cultural origin.
(b) The likelihood of the child's adaptation to living in the country he/she is to be placed.
(c) Where the UK is the State of origin, reasons for considering that, after possibilities for placement of the child within the UK have been given due consideration, intercountry adoption is in the child's best interests.
(d) Confirmation that the requirements of regulations made under sections 83(4), (5), (6) and (7) and 84(3) and (6) of the 2002 Act have been complied with.
(e) For a Convention adoption or a Convention Adoption Order where the United Kingdom is either the State of origin or the receiving State, confirmation that the Central Authorities of both States have agreed that the adoption may proceed.
(f) Where the State of origin is not the United Kingdom, the documents supplied by the Central Authority of the State of origin should be attached to the report, together with translation if necessary.
(g) Where a Convention adoption order is proposed, details of the arrangements which were made for the transfer of the child to the UK and that they were in accordance with the Adoptions with a Foreign Element Regulations 2005 (S.I. 2005/392).

ANNEX B – REPORT TO THE COURT WHERE THERE HAS BEEN AN APPLICATION FOR A PLACEMENT ORDER

Section A: The Report and Matters for the Proceedings
Section B: The Child and the Birth Family
Section C: Recommendations

SECTION A: THE REPORT AND MATTERS FOR THE PROCEEDINGS

Part 1

The report

For each of the principal author/s of the report:

- (i) name;
- (ii) role in relation to this case;
- (iii) section completed in this report;
- (iv) qualifications and experience;
- (v) name and address of the adoption agency; and
- (vi) adoption agency case reference number.

Part 2

Matters for the proceedings

- (a) Whether the adoption agency considers that any other person should be made a respondent or a party to the proceedings.
- (b) Whether any of the respondents is under the age of 18.
- (c) Whether a respondent is a person who, by reason of mental disorder within the meaning of the Mental Health Act 1983, is incapable of managing and administering his or her property and affairs. If so, medical evidence should be provided with particular regard to the effect on that person's ability to make decisions in the proceedings.

SECTION B: THE CHILD AND THE BIRTH FAMILY

Part 1

(i) Information about the child

- (a) Name, sex, date and place of birth and address including local authority area.
- (b) Photograph and physical description.
- (c) Nationality.
- (d) Racial origin and cultural and linguistic background.
- (e) Religious persuasion (including details of baptism, confirmation or equivalent ceremonies).
- (f) Details of any siblings, half-siblings and step-siblings, including dates of birth.
- (g) Whether the child is looked after by a local authority.
- (h) Personality and social development, including emotional and behavioural development and any related needs.
- (i) Details of interests, likes and dislikes.
- (j) A summary, written by the agency's medical adviser, of the child's health history, his current state of health and any need for health care which is anticipated, and date of the most recent medical examination.
- (k) Any known learning difficulties or known general medical or mental health factors which are likely to have, or may have, genetic implications.
- (l) Names, addresses and types of nurseries or schools attended, with dates.
- (m) Educational attainments.
- (n) Any special needs in relation to the child (whether physical, learning, behavioural or any other) and his emotional and behavioural development.
- (o) Whether the child is subject to a statement under the Education Act 1996.
- (p) Previous orders concerning the child:
  - (i) the name of the court;
  - (ii) the order made; and
  - (ii) the date of the order.
- (q) Inheritance rights and any claim to damages under the Fatal Accidents Act 1976 the child stands to retain or lose if adopted.

PART III

(r) Any other relevant information which might assist the court.

(ii) Information about each parent of the child

(a) Name, date and place of birth and address (date on which last address was confirmed current) including local authority area.
(b) Photograph, if available, and physical description.
(c) Nationality.
(d) Racial origin and cultural and linguistic background.
(e) Whether the mother and father were married to each other at the time of the child's birth, or have subsequently married.
(f) Where the parent has been previously married or entered into a civil partnership, dates of those marriages or civil partnerships.
(g) Where the mother and father are not married, whether the father has parental responsibility and, if so, how it was acquired.
(h) If the identity or whereabouts of the father are not known, the information about him that has been ascertained and from whom, and the steps that have been taken to establish paternity.
(i) Past and present relationship with the other parent.
(j) Other information about the parent, where available:
  (i) health, including any known learning difficulties or known general medical or mental health factors which are likely to have, or may have, genetic implications;
  (ii) religious persuasion;
  (iii) educational history;
  (iv) employment history; and
  (v) personality and interests.
(k) Any other relevant information which might assist the court.

Part 2

Relationships, contact arrangements and views

THE CHILD

(a) If the child is in the care of a local authority or voluntary organisation, or has been, details (including dates) of any placements with foster parents, or other arrangements in respect of the care of the child, including particulars of the persons with whom the child has had his home and observations on the care provided.
(b) The child's wishes and feelings (if appropriate, having regard to the child's age and understanding) about the application, its consequences, and adoption, including any wishes in respect of religious and cultural upbringing.
(c) The child's wishes and feelings in relation to contact (if appropriate, having regard to the child's age and understanding).
(d) The child's wishes and feelings recorded in any other proceedings.
(e) Date when the child's views were last ascertained.

THE CHILD'S PARENTS (OR GUARDIAN) AND RELATIVES

(a) The parents' wishes and feelings about the application, its consequences, and adoption, including any wishes in respect of the child's religious and cultural upbringing.
(b) Each parent's (or guardian's) wishes and feelings in relation to contact.
(c) Date/s when the views of each parent or guardian were last ascertained.
(d) Arrangements concerning any siblings, including half-siblings and step-siblings, and whether any are the subject of a parallel application or have been the subject of any orders. If so, for each case give:
  (i) the name of the court;
  (ii) the order made, or (if proceedings are pending) the order applied for; and
  (iii) the date of order, or date of next hearing if proceedings are pending.

(e) Extent of contact with the child's mother and father and in each case the nature of the relationship enjoyed.
(f) The relationship which the child has with relatives, and with any other person considered relevant, including:
  (i) the likelihood of any such relationship continuing and the value to the child of its doing so; and
  (ii) the ability and willingness of any of the child's relatives, or of any such person, to provide the child with a secure environment in which the child can develop, and otherwise to meet the child's needs.
(g) The wishes and feelings of any of the child's relatives, or of any such person, regarding the child.
(h) Dates when the views of members of the child's wider family and any other relevant person were last ascertained.

Part 3

Summary of the actions of the adoption agency

(a) Brief account of the Agency's actions in the case, with particulars and dates of all written information and notices given to the child and his parents and any person with parental responsibility.
(b) If consent has been given for the child to be placed for adoption, and also consent for the child to be adopted, the names of those who gave consent and the date such consents were given. If such consents were subsequently withdrawn, the dates of these withdrawals.
(c) If any statement has been made under section 20(4)(a) of the 2002 Act that a parent or guardian does not wish to be informed of any application for an adoption order, the names of those who have made such statements and the dates the statements were made. If such statements were subsequently withdrawn, the dates of these withdrawals.
(d) Details of the support and advice given to the parents and any services offered or taken up.
(e) If the father does not have parental responsibility, details of the steps taken to inform him of the application for a placement order.
(f) Brief details and dates of assessments of the child's needs, including expert opinions.
(g) Reasons for considering that adoption would be in the child's best interests (with date of relevant decision and reasons for any delay in implementing the decision).

SECTION C: RECOMMENDATIONS

(a) The relative merits of a placement order and other orders (such as a child arrangements or special guardianship order) with an assessment of why the child's long term interests are likely to be best met by a placement order rather than by any other order.
(b) Recommendations as to whether there should be future contact arrangements (or not), including whether a contact order under section 26 of the 2002 Act should be made.

Practice Direction 14D – Reports by a Registered Medical Practitioner ('Health Reports')

This Practice Direction supplements FPR Part 14, rule 14.12(2)

Matters to be contained in health reports

1.1 Rule 14.12(1) requires that health reports must be attached to an application for an adoption order or a section 84 order except where:

(a) the child was placed for adoption with the applicant by an adoption agency;
(b) the applicant or one of the applicants is a parent of the child; or

(c) the applicant is the partner of a parent of the child.

1.2 The matters to be contained in the health reports are set out in the Annex to this Practice Direction.

1.3 Where a matter to be contained in the health report does not apply to the circumstances of a particular case, the reasons for not covering the matter should be given.

ANNEX – CONTENTS OF HEALTH REPORTS

This information is required for reports on the health of children and their prospective adopter(s). Its purpose is to build up a full picture of each child's health history and current state of health, including strengths and weaknesses. This will enable local authorities' medical adviser to base their advice to the court on the fullest possible information when commenting on the health implications of the proposed adoption. The reports made by the examining doctor should cover, as far as practicable, the following matters.

1 *The child*

Name, date of birth, sex, weight and height.

A A health history of each natural parent, so far as is possible, including:

(i) name, date of birth, sex, weight and height;
(ii) a family health history, covering the parents, the brothers and sisters and the other children of the natural parent, with details of any serious physical or mental illness and inherited and congenital disease;
(iii) past health history, including details of any serious physical or mental illness, disability, accident, hospital admission or attendance at an out-patient department, and in each case any treatment given;
(iv) a full obstetric history of the mother, including any problems in the ante-natal, labour and post-natal periods, with the results of any tests carried out during or immediately after pregnancy;
(v) details of any present illness including treatment and prognosis;
(vi) any other relevant information which might assist the medical adviser; and
(vii) the name and address of any doctor(s) who might be able to provide further information about any of the above matters.

B A neo-natal report on the child, including:

(i) details of the birth, and any complications;
(ii) results of a physical examination and screening tests;
(iii) details of any treatment given;
(iv) details of any problem in management and feeding;
(v) any other relevant information which might assist the medical adviser; and
(vi) the name and address of any doctor(s) who might be able to provide further information about any of the above matters.

C A full health history and examination of the child, including:

(i) details of any serious illness, disability, accident, hospital admission or attendance at an out-patient department, and in each case any treatment given;
(ii) details and dates of immunisations;
(iii) a physical and developmental assessment according to age, including an assessment of vision and hearing and of neurological, speech and language development and any evidence of emotional or conduct disorder;
(iv) details, if relevant, of the impact of any addiction or substance use on the part of the natural mother before, during or following the pregnancy, and its impact or likely future impact on the child;
(v) the impact, if any, on the child's development and likely future development of any past exposure to physical, emotional or sexual abuse or neglectful home conditions and/or any non-organic failure to thrive;

(vi) for a child of school age, the school health history (if available);
(vii) any other relevant information which might assist the medical adviser; and
(viii) the name and address of any doctor(s) who might be able to provide further information about any of the above matters.

D The signature, name, address and qualifications of the registered medical practitioner who prepared the report, and the date of the report and of the examinations carried out.

2 The applicant

(If there is more than one applicant, a report on each applicant should be supplied covering all the matters listed below.)

A (i) name, date of birth, sex, weight and height;
(ii) a family health history, covering the parents, the brothers and sisters and the children of the applicant, with details of any serious physical or mental illness and inherited and congenital disease;
(iii) marital history, including (if applicable) reasons for inability to have children, and any history of domestic violence;
(iv) past health history, including details of any serious physical or mental illness, disability, accident, hospital admission or attendance at an out-patient department, and in each case any treatment given;
(v) obstetric history (if applicable);
(vi) details of any present illness, including treatment and prognosis;
(vii) a full medical examination;
(viii) details of any consumption of alcohol, tobacco and habit-forming drugs;
(ix) any other relevant information which might assist the medical adviser; and
(x) the name and address of any doctor(s) who might be able to provide further information about any of the above matters.

B The signature, name, address and qualifications of the registered medical practitioner who prepared the report, and the date of the report and of the examinations carried out.

PART III

Practice Direction 14E – Communication of Information Relating to Proceedings

This Practice Direction supplements FPR Part 14, rule 14.14(b)

Communication of information relating to proceedings

1.1 Rule 14.14 deals with the communication of information (whether or not it is recorded in any form) relating to proceedings.

1.2 Subject to any direction of the court, information may be communicated for the purposes of the law relating to contempt in accordance with paragraphs 1.3 or 1.4.

1.3 A person specified in the first column of the following table may communicate to a person listed in the second column such information as is specified in the third column for the purpose or purposes specified in the fourth column.

Communication of information without permission of the court

Communicated by	To	Information	Purpose
A party	A lay adviser or a McKenzie Friend	Any information relating to the proceedings	To enable the party to obtain advice or assistance in relation to the proceedings.

Communicated by	To	Information	Purpose
A party	The party's spouse, civil partner, cohabitant or close family member		For the purpose of confidential discussions enabling the party to receive support from his spouse, civil partner, cohabitant or close family member.
A party	A health care professional or a person or body providing counselling services for children or families		To enable the party or any child of the party to obtain health care or counselling.
A party	The Secretary of State, a McKenzie Friend, a lay adviser or an appeal tribunal dealing with an appeal made under section 20 of the Child Support Act 1991		For the purposes of making or responding to an appeal under section 20 of the Child Support Act 1991 or the determination of such an appeal.
A party or other person lawfully in receipt of information	The Secretary of State, a McKenzie Friend, a lay adviser or the Upper Tier Tribunal dealing with an appeal under section 24 of the Child Support Act 1991 in respect of a decision of the First-tier Tribunal that was made under section 20 of that Act		For a purpose connected with an appeal under section 24 of the Child Support Act 1991 in respect of a decision of the First-tier Tribunal that was made under section 20 of that Act
A party	An adoption panel		To enable the adoption panel to discharge its functions as appropriate.
A party	A local authority's medical adviser appointed under the Adoption Agencies Regulations 2005 or the Adoption Agencies (Wales) Regulations 2005		To enable the medical adviser to discharge his or her functions as appropriate
A party or any person lawfully in receipt of information	The Children's Commissioner or the Children's Commissioner for Wales		To refer an issue affecting the interests of children to the Children's Commissioner or the Children's Commissioner for Wales.

Communicated by	**To**	**Information**	**Purpose**
A party or a legal representative	A mediator		For the purpose of mediation in relation to the proceedings.
A party, any person lawfully in receipt of information or a proper officer	A person or body conducting an approved research project		For the purpose of an approved research project.
A party, a legal representative or a professional legal adviser	A person or body responsible for investigating or determining complaints in relation to legal representatives or professional legal advisers		For the purposes of making a complaint or the investigation or determination of a complaint in relation to a legal representative or a professional legal adviser.
A legal representative or a professional legal adviser	A professional indemnity insurer		To enable the professional indemnity insurer to be notified of a claim or complaint, or potential claim or complaint, in relation to the legal representative or a professional legal adviser, and the legal representative or professional legal adviser to obtain advice in respect of that claim or complaint
A legal representative or a professional legal adviser	A person or body assessing quality assurance systems		To enable the legal representative or professional legal adviser to obtain a quality assurance assessment.
A legal representative or a professional legal adviser	An accreditation body	Any information relating to the proceedings providing that it does not, or is not likely to, identify any person involved in the proceedings	To enable the legal representative or professional legal adviser to obtain accreditation.
A party	An elected representative or peer	The text or summary of the whole or part of a judgment given in the proceedings	To enable the elected representative or peer to give advice, investigate any complaint or raise any question of policy or procedure.
A party	The General Medical Council		For the purpose of making a complaint to the General Medical Council.
A party	A police officer		For the purpose of a criminal investigation.

Communicated by	To	Information	Purpose
A party or any person lawfully in receipt of information	A member of the Crown Prosecution Service		To enable the Crown Prosecution Service to discharge its functions under any enactment.

1.4 A person in the second column of the table in paragraph 1.3 may only communicate information relating to the proceedings received from a person in the first column for the purpose or purposes:

(a) for which he received that information, or
(b) of professional development or training, providing that any communication does not, or is not likely to, identify any person involved in the proceedings without that person's consent.

1.5 In this Practice Direction:

(1) 'accreditation body' means:
(a) The Law Society,
(b) Resolution, or
(c) the Lord Chancellor in exercise of the Lord Chancellor's functions in relation to legal aid;

(1A) 'adoption panel' means a panel established in accordance with regulation 3 of the Adoption Agencies Regulations 2005 or regulation 3 of the Adoption Agencies (Wales) Regulations 2005;

(2) 'approved research project' means a project of research:
(a) approved in writing by a Secretary of State after consultation with the President of the Family Division,
(b) approved in writing by the President of the Family Division, or
(c) conducted under section 83 of the Act of 1989 or section 13 of the Criminal Justice and Court Services Act 2000;

(3) 'body assessing quality assurance systems' includes:
(a) The Law Society,
(b) the Lord Chancellor in exercise of the Lord Chancellor's functions in relation to legal aid, or
(c) The General Council of the Bar;

(4) 'body or person responsible for investigating or determining complaints in relation to legal representatives or professional legal advisers' means:
(a) The Law Society,
(b) The General Council of the Bar,
(c) The Institute of Legal Executives, or
(d) The Legal Services Ombudsman;

(5) 'cohabitant' means one of two persons who are neither married to each other nor civil partners of each other but are living together as husband and wife or as if they were civil partners;

(6) 'criminal investigation' means an investigation conducted by police officers with a view to it being ascertained:
(a) whether a person should be charged with an offence, or
(b) whether a person charged with an offence is guilty of it;

(7) 'elected representative' means:
(a) a member of the House of Commons,
(b) a member of the National Assembly for Wales, or
(c) a member of the European Parliament elected in England and Wales;

(8) 'health care professional' means:
(a) a registered medical practitioner,
(b) a registered nurse or midwife,

(c) a clinical psychologist, or
(d) a child psychotherapist;

(9) 'lay adviser' means a non-professional person who gives lay advice on behalf of an organisation in the lay advice sector;

(10) 'McKenzie Friend' means any person permitted by the court to sit beside an unrepresented litigant in court to assist that litigant by prompting, taking notes and giving him advice;

(11) 'mediator' means a family mediator who is:
(a) undertaking, or has successfully completed, a family mediation training course approved by the United Kingdom College of Family Mediators, or
(b) a member of the Law Society's Family Mediation Panel;

(12) 'peer' means a member of the House of Lords as defined by the House of Lords Act 1999.

Practice Direction 14F – Disclosing Information to an Adopted Adult

This Practice Direction supplements FPR Part 14, rule 14.18(1)(d)

How to request for information

1.1 Rule 14.18 states that an adopted person who is over the age of 18 has the right to receive from the court which made the adoption order a copy of:

(a) the application form for an adoption order (but not the documents attached to that form);
(b) the adoption order and any other orders relating to the adoption proceedings; and
(c) orders allowing any person contact with the child after the adoption order was made.

1.2 An application under rule 14.18 must be made in form A64 which is contained in the practice direction supplementing rule 5 and must have attached to it a full certified copy of the entry in the Adopted Children Register relating to the applicant.

1.3 The completed application form must be taken to the court which made the adoption order along with evidence of the applicant's identity showing a photograph and signature, such as a passport or driving licence.

Additional documents that the adopted person is also entitled to receive from the court

2 The adopted adult is also entitled to receive the following documents:

(a) any transcript or written reasons of the court's decision; and
(b) a report made to the court by:
(i) a children's guardian, reporting officer or children and family reporter;
(ii) a local authority; or
(iii) an adoption agency.

Before the documents are sent to the adopted adult

3 The court will remove protected information from documents before they are sent to the adopted adult.

PART 15
REPRESENTATION OF PROTECTED PARTIES

CONTENTS OF THIS PART

Rule		Page
15.1	Application of this Part	1680
15.2	Requirement for litigation friend in proceedings	1684
15.3	Stage of proceedings at which a litigation friend becomes necessary	1685
15.4	Who may be a litigation friend for a protected party without a court order	1685
15.5	How a person becomes a litigation friend without a court order	1686
15.6	How a person becomes a litigation friend by court order	1687
15.7	Court's power to change litigation friend and to prevent person acting as litigation friend	1688
15.8	Appointment of litigation friend by court order – supplementary	1688
15.9	Procedure where appointment of litigation friend comes to an end	1689
	Practice Direction 15A – Protected Parties	1689
	Practice Direction 15B – Adults Who May Be Protected Parties and Children Who May Become Protected Parties in Family Proceedings	1691

15.1 Application of this Part

This Part contains special provisions which apply in proceedings involving protected parties.

Scope—This Part deals with protected parties (as defined) who were previously known as 'patients' and together with children (minors) referred to as 'persons under a disability'. The terminology changed to protected parties in 2007 following the implementation of MCA 2005. The remainder of this rule regulates the conduct of proceedings by and against such persons, and ensures that they are represented by a 'litigation friend'. Proceedings involving a child as a party are dealt with under FPR 2010, Pt 16, Ch 5. For non-family proceedings, reference should be made to CPR 1998, Pt 21, which contains similar, although not identical, provisions.

Practice Direction—See FPR PD15A. See also FPR PD15B, which provides guidance as to litigation capacity, fluctuating capacity, ability to give evidence as a witness, the use of experts in regard to capacity issues and children who are likely to lack capacity on attaining 18.

'protected party'—This means 'a party, or an intended party, who lacks capacity (within the meaning of MCA 2005) to conduct the proceedings' (FPR 2010, r 2.3(1)). It is possible for a child also to be a protected party and this may be relevant if that condition will continue following attainment of legal majority (e g in regard to the disposal of money awarded to the child). Thus, a child who has severe learning disabilities may continue to be a protected party even after attaining the age of 18.

The rules assume that it is known whether the party is a protected party but that will not always be the case and the annotations below illustrate just how difficult the assessment of capacity may be. Where there is doubt it is important to notify the party so as to provide an opportunity for representations to be made either on the issue of capacity or as to the identity of the litigation friend. It is good practice for anyone intending to become a litigation friend to serve upon or draw to the intention of the intended protected party the notice of intention to act as litigation friend and certificate of suitability, unless there is no prospect of a relevant response – see *Masterman-Lister v Brutton & Co and Jewell & Home Counties Dairies* [2003] 1 WLR 1511, CA.

MCA 2005—This legislation established from 1 October 2007 a comprehensive statutory framework for decisions to be made by and on behalf of those whose capacity to make their own decisions is in doubt. A regional Court of Protection has jurisdiction to make declarations or decisions or to appoint a deputy to make decisions on the person's behalf. A number of district judges and circuit judges are nominated to sit in the Court of Protection and difficult capacity issues may be referred to them.

The general principles that apply within the mental capacity jurisdiction are to be found in MCA 2005, ss 1–4. They include the test of 'incapacity' and a 'best interests' approach to any delegated decision-making according to a checklist of factors. (For an overview of MCA 2005, see Part II of this work.)

Persons who lack capacity—There are basically three categories of person who may come within the definition of a protected party, namely those with:

(1) a mental illness. The largest group comprises elderly people who become mentally impaired (e g by senile dementia or Alzheimer's disease);
(2) learning disabilities. The previous term was 'mental handicap'; and
(3) brain damage. The courts generally encounter persons with an acquired brain injury. If the damage was caused during the developmental years (e g in childbirth) this will be classed as learning disabilities.

'lacks capacity'—This term is expressly defined as being 'within the meaning of MCA 2005' and therefore the test (and the principles) set out in MCA 2005, Pt 1 apply. MCA 2005, s 2(1) sets out the definition:

'A person lacks capacity in relation to a matter if at the material time he is unable to make a decision for himself in relation to the matter because of an impairment of, or a disturbance in the functioning of, the mind or brain.'

This is a two-stage test because it must be established first, that there is an impairment of, or disturbance in the functioning of, the person's mind or brain (the diagnostic threshold); and second, that the impairment or disturbance is sufficient to render the person incapable of making that particular decision. The impairment or disturbance may be permanent or temporary and no reference is made to the degree of impairment or disturbance. This provides a useful screening process – merely being eccentric is not a basis for being deprived of one's right to conduct litigation.

'Unable to make a decision'—MCA 2005, s 3(1) provides that a person is unable to make a decision if unable to:

- understand the information relevant to the decision;
- retain that information;
- use or weigh that information as part of the process of making the decision; or
- communicate his decision (whether by talking, using sign language or any other means).

Explanations must be provided in ways appropriate to the person's circumstances (using simple language, visual aids or any other means). This is not a significant change of approach because it was previously held (in regard to medical treatment, although the test was no doubt universal) that the individual must be able to: (a) understand and retain information, and (b) weigh that information in the balance to arrive at a choice (*Re MB* [1997] 2 FLR 426, CA).

'conduct the proceedings'—The test of capacity under MCA 2005, s 2 is decision-specific, so it is the capacity of the party to conduct the particular proceedings that is relevant rather than capacity to manage and administer his property and affairs in general (as defined under the former test). Thus a person might be a protected party for complex personal injury proceedings, yet not for a simultaneous small claim. The Supreme Court in *Dunhill (A Protected Party By Her Litigation Friend Tasker) v Burgin (Nos 1 and 2)* [2014] COPLR 199, SC, applying the test under CPR 1998, r 21.1, endorsed the (common law) approach adopted by the Court of Appeal in *Masterman-Lister* (above) to determining capacity to conduct proceedings. This was set out most clearly by Chadwick LJ:

'[T]he test to be applied … is whether the party to legal proceedings is capable of understanding, with the assistance of such proper explanation from legal advisers and experts in other disciplines as the case may require, the issues on which his consent or decision is likely to be necessary in the course of those proceedings. If he has capacity to understand that which he needs to understand in order to pursue or defend a claim, I can see no reason why the law – whether substantive or procedural – should require the interposition of a next friend or guardian ad litem (or, as such a person is described in the CPR, a litigation friend).'

Presumptions as to capacity—There is a legal presumption that adults are competent until the contrary is proved. This presumption is relevant to the burden of proof. In general, the person who alleges that an individual lacks capacity must prove this, but the standard of proof is the civil standard, namely on the balance of probabilities rather than beyond reasonable doubt. Capacity must be assessed at the time that the decision is to be taken because it can vary. If an individual has previously been found to lack capacity there is no presumption of continuance, but if there is clear evidence of incapacity for a considerable period then the burden of proof may be more easily discharged even though it remains on whoever asserts incapacity.

Doubts about capacity may arise for several reasons, but these should not be confused with tests of capacity. Thus, the status of the individual (being elderly and living in a nursing home), the outcome of a decision (one that no person in his right mind would be expected to reach) or appearance, behaviour or conversation may cause capacity to be questioned, but these factors do not determine capacity. It is not unusual for outward appearances to create a false impression of lack of capacity (e g physical disabilities may obstruct the power of speech or movement) even where mental capacity is not affected. Conversely, a person may appear capable through social training and experience when in reality he/she lacks the understanding needed to make decisions. In all of these situations a proper assessment of capacity should be made.

Mental disorder—The existence of a mental disorder is no longer a criterion for a person being treated as incapable of conducting proceedings. The new diagnostic threshold of 'an impairment of, or a disturbance in the functioning of, the mind or brain' was introduced because the term 'mental disorder' had acquired distinct interpretations in the context of treatment under the Mental Health Acts. Being mentally disordered does not necessarily result in a person being a protected party, and an assessment of capacity must still be made. Thus:

(a) an individual may be sectioned under the provisions of the Mental Health Act 1983, yet not be a protected party as regards court proceedings because the criteria are different (consider *Re C (Refusal of Medical Treatment)* [1994] 1 FLR 31, FD);

(b) an individual with learning disabilities may still have the capacity to conduct litigation depending on the complexity and the support available.

Communication difficulties—Physical disabilities may obstruct the power of speech or movement even where mental capacity is not affected, and other methods of communication must then be attempted. An interpreter may be provided for those with communication difficulties in the same way as for those who do not understand the language used in court.

Physical disabilities—Where the ability of an individual to conduct or participate in proceedings is impaired due to physical disabilities, steps can be taken by the court to overcome these. Thus the loop system may be

PART III

provided for those who are hard of hearing, and enlarged print may be used on all documents for those whose sight is impaired. If necessary, hearings should be conducted in a courtroom or chambers with disabled access but they may be conducted elsewhere should the need arise (FPR 2010, r 2.8).

Tests of capacity—There is no universal test of capacity. Legal capacity depends on understanding rather than wisdom; the quality of the decision is irrelevant as long as the person understands what he is deciding. Legal tests vary according to the particular transaction or act involved but are generally issue-specific, i e they relate to the matters that the individual is required to understand. As capacity depends on time and context, a decision as to capacity in one context does not bind a court that has to consider the same issue in a different context.

A person found to be a protected party may nevertheless be capable of getting married, signing an enduring power of attorney (*Re K; Re F (Enduring Powers of Attorney)* [1988] 2 FLR 15, ChD) or consenting to medical treatment (*Re MB* above) because the matters to be taken into account are different. For a full explanation of the various tests that apply for different purposes reference should be made to the joint Law Society and BMA publication, *Assessment of Mental Capacity: A Practical Guide for Doctors and Lawyers* (The Law Society, 4th edn, 2015).

Assessment of capacity—Mental capacity is a question of fact so any issue of capacity can only be determined by a judge in legal proceedings acting not as a medical expert, but as a lay person influenced by personal observation and on the basis of evidence not only from doctors, but also those who know the individual. For comprehensive guidance as to the manner in which capacity should be assessed reference should be made to *Assessment of Mental Capacity: A Practical Guide for Doctors and Lawyers* (above). The mental abilities required to conduct litigation have been identified as comprising: the ability to recognise a problem, obtain and receive, understand and retain relevant information, including advice; the ability to weigh the information (including that derived from advice) in the balance in reaching a decision; and the ability to communicate that decision (*Masterman-Lister*, above). The Supreme Court in *Dunhill v Burgin* (above) placed a gloss upon the test (at [18]) by emphasising that the focus must be upon the individual's capacity to understand the claim or cause of action they in fact have, rather than to conduct the claim as formulated by their lawyers. This might be thought to raise the bar substantially in terms of the level of functional ability required.

The approach adopted by Boreham J in *White v Fell* (1987) 12 November, QBD (unreported) was referred to by the Court of Appeal with approval and may still be of assistance:

> 'The expression "incapable of managing her own affairs and property" must be construed in a common sense way as a whole. It does not call for proof of complete incapacity. On the other hand it is not enough to prove that the Plaintiff is now substantially less capable of managing her own affairs and property than she would have been had the accident not occurred.'

But understanding is not by itself sufficient because the individual needs to be able to use or apply that understanding in making decisions. Thus, in *Mitchell v Alasia* [2005] EWHC 11 (QB), Cox J relied on qualities such as impulsiveness and volatility when deciding that the claimant was, by reason of his mental disorder, incapable of managing and administering his own affairs.

In *Lindsay v Wood* [2006] EWHC 2895 (QB), Stanley Burnton J observed that:

> 'When considering the question of capacity, psychiatrists and psychologists will normally wish to take into account all aspects of the personality and behaviour of the person in question, including vulnerability to exploitation.'

For an early decision on the test of capacity under the MCA 2005 jurisdiction in regard to a brain-injured claimant, see *Saulle v Nouvet* [2007] EWHC 2902 (QB). Guidance on the approach to capacity issues (in childcare proceedings but of more general application) is to be found in *RP v Nottingham City Council & Official Solicitor* [2008] 2 FLR 1516, CA.

Time-specific assessment—In *Saulle v Nouvet* (above), Andrew Edis QC, sitting as a deputy judge of the High Court, dealt with the fact that circumstances might change and made the following observations at [51]–[54]:

> 'the Court must focus on the matters which arise for decision now, and on the Claimant's capacity to deal with them now. I am required not to attempt to foretell the future and provide for situations which may arise when he may have to take some other decision at some other time when his mental state may be different … I consider that [Dr X] may well be right when he suggests that there may be times in the future when the Claimant will lack capacity to make particular decisions, and note his concern that if that happens when he does not have the support of his family for any reason, he may not come to the attention of the Court of Protection until it is too late. This is a risk against which the old test for capacity used by the Court of Protection under Part VII of the 1983 Act used to guard. The modern law is different.'

The appointment of a litigation friend is not a once-for-all matter and it is possible in some cases that a person may either gain or regain capacity to conduct proceedings. In such a case, steps should be taken to discharge the litigation friend, but only (it is suggested) where it is clear that the (re)gaining of capacity is likely to be permanent. In an unusual case where the claimant's capacity fluctuated depending upon his drug usage, the court held that his advisers had been right not to return to court despite his regaining of capacity, but rather to take instructions from both the litigation friend and C in a pragmatic way, see *AB v Royal Devon & Exeter NHS Foundation Trust* [2016] EWHC 1024 (QB), at [67].

Ability to rely upon advice—The extent to which an individual with impaired capacity may rely upon the advice of others was considered by Boreham J in *White v Fell* (1987) 12 November, QBD (unreported, but quoted by Wright J in *Masterman-Lister v Jewell & anor* [2002] EWHC 417 (QB) at first instance):

> 'Few people have the capacity to manage all their affairs unaided. In matters of law, particularly litigation, medicine, and given sufficient resources, financial professional advice is almost universally needed and

sought ... she may not understand all the intricacies of litigation, or of a settlement, or of a wise investment policy ... But if that were the appropriate test then quite a substantial proportion of the adult population might be regarded as under disability.'

It is suggested that these dicta now need to be read in light of the gloss placed upon *Masterman v Lister* test by the Supreme Court in *Dunhill v Burgin* (above), at [18].

Medical evidence—In civil and family proceedings (and by contrast, perhaps, to proceedings before the Court of Protection), there almost invariably needs to be medical evidence for purposes of establishing lack of capacity. In *Masterman-Lister* (above) Kennedy LJ said that 'even where the issue does not seem to be contentious, a district judge who is responsible for case management will almost certainly require the assistance of a medical report before being able to be satisfied that incapacity exists'. In the absence of medical evidence, a court should be cautious before concluding that a litigant was suffering from a disturbance of the mind preventing him from participating in litigation – *Baker Tilly (A Firm) v Makar* [2013] COPLR 245, QB. Although expert evidence is likely to be of very considerable importance, the court may reach a different conclusion by weighing such evidence against findings on other evidence: *WBC (Local Authority) v Z and others* [2016] EWCOP 4.

Usually this expert will be a person with medical qualifications and ideally a psychiatrist. However, a psychologist, especially if of an appropriate speciality, may be better qualified in respect of a person with learning disabilities. Such opinion is merely part of the evidence and the factual evidence of a carer, social worker or family member may also be relevant and even more persuasive. Caution should be exercised when seeking evidence from general medical practitioners as most will have little knowledge of mental capacity and the various legal tests that apply, so the appropriate test should be spelt out, and it should be explained that different tests apply to different types of decision. Any doctor or other medical witness asked to assist in relation to capacity needs to know the area of the alleged protected party's activities in relation to which his advice is sought (*Masterman-Lister*, above). All relevant information should be provided, so when the test is whether the individual is incapable of conducting civil proceedings the doctor must be given some idea of the nature and complexity of those proceedings. The doctor will need to know what decisions the individual will be called upon to make for the conduct of that litigation. Only then can he express an opinion whether the individual is capable of giving instructions.

Issues as to capacity—The rules make no express provision as to issues regarding whether a party is a protected party. Such an issue may be raised by the court or one of the parties, or by a litigation friend if there is doubt about whether a party has recovered capacity. It will then be necessary for the proceedings to be stayed until the issue is resolved and the court may order an inquiry to be made in the proceedings to determine the issue. Notice should be given to the party alleged to be a protected party in case he wishes to contest this or arrange representation. This inquiry would normally be heard before a district judge who can compel the attendance of witnesses (including medical attendants and the claimant or defendant himself) and the production of documents. Where there are practical difficulties in obtaining medical evidence the Official Solicitor may be consulted. The court can also direct the Official Solicitor to make inquiries and to report about such matters as the court thinks fit (*Harbin v Masterman* [1896] 1 Ch 351, CA).

Courts should always, as a matter of practice, at the first convenient opportunity investigate the question of capacity whenever there is any reason to suspect that it may be absent (eg significant head injury) other than in cases where the Court of Protection has already accepted jurisdiction. Although medical evidence will be required (see above), the judge may consider that he would be assisted by seeing the person alleged to lack capacity (*Masterman-Lister*, above). A court cannot, however, compel an individual to comply with an assessment of capacity. In some cases, the judge will have to form a view as to capacity without the benefit of any external expertise, although the courts have emphasised that judges should be slow to do so because of the seriousness of the consequences for the person: *Baker Tilly (A Firm) v Makar* [2013] COPLR 245, QBD.

Where, understandably, a claimant's legal team is unable to present a positive case as to whether their client is a protected party, consideration should be given to seeking an order of the court directing the Official Solicitor to review the evidence, to appoint his own medical expert, and to appear and make such submissions as he considers appropriate (*Lindsay v Wood* [2006] EWHC 2895 (QB)). The *Masterman-Lister* decision has been explored by the Court of Appeal in a subsequent case where a 50/50 settlement was agreed and proceedings later commenced with a litigation friend to assess quantum (*Bailey v Warren* [2006] EWCA Civ 51).

While evidence is required to support an application for the appointment of a litigation friend, it does not follow that the other party to the litigation is then entitled to put in evidence disputing the basis for the appointment. It cannot properly be contended that a defendant is at risk of suffering prejudice from the appointment of a litigation friend for the claimant (*Folks v Faizey* [2006] EWCA Civ 381).

Default orders—Where there is doubt as to the capacity of a respondent it would not be appropriate for the court to make an order that unless he submitted to an examination by a particular psychiatrist by a specified date he was to be treated as capable because such order may have been made against a protected party who needed a litigation friend (see *Carmarthenshire County Council v Lewis* [2010] EWCA Civ 1567). In the case of a petitioner or applicant the proceedings would normally be stayed until the doubt was resolved because they should not be allowed to continue without a litigation friend if capacity was lacking.

Official Solicitor—The Official Solicitor to the Senior Courts provided for by SCA 1981, s 90 may be contacted at Victory House, 30–34 Kingsway, London WC2B 6EX, DX 141423 Bloomsbury 7; tel 020 7911 7127; fax 020 7911 7105. Where there are practical difficulties in obtaining medical evidence, the Official Solicitor may be consulted.

Care proceedings—In care proceedings the local authority is required to identify any concerns about the mental capacity of a parent to care for the child or to prepare for the proceedings. In *RP v Nottingham City Council and the Official Solicitor* [2008] 2 FLR 1516, CA the court gave guidance on the steps to be taken before and during care proceedings where there was an issue as to a parent's capacity. If a parent is

PART III

considered to lack capacity the authority should refer the individual to the local adult learning disability team or its equivalent for help and advice. Judgments about capacity should not be made by social workers engaged in child protection. Any issue as to the capacity of an adult to conduct the proceedings must be determined before the court gives any directions relevant to that adult's role within the proceedings (See FPR PD12A, para 8).

Need for Court of Protection involvement—See the note under CPR 1998, r 21.11.

Human rights—When a person is treated as a protected party, whether or not as a result of an order of the court, he is thereby deprived of important rights, long cherished by English law and safeguarded by ECHR 1950. Although CPR 1998 do not contain any requirement for a judicial determination of the question, the High Court and Family Court should always, as a matter of practice, at the first convenient opportunity investigate the question of capacity whenever there is any reason to suspect that it may be absent, other than in cases where the Court of Protection is already involved (*Masterman-Lister*, above).

Withdrawal of proceedings—The permission of the court is required for withdrawal of an application where any party is a protected party – see FPR 2010, r 29.4, which sets out the procedure.

Approval of settlements—Unlike FPR 1991 and the CPR, no provision is made for the approval of any compromise or settlement where a party is a protected party, although the permission of the court is required for withdrawal (see above). In most cases, the approval of the court will in any event be required to an order, but approval on behalf of a protected party is a different (and possibly more onerous) concept and may mean an inquiry into the best interests of that party, including looking at counsel's advice. In the absence of an express requirement, there is a danger that this aspect may be overlooked.

A consent order approved by the court may be set aside if it transpires that one of the parties lacked capacity at the relevant time. An application to set aside the order in such circumstances should be made pursuant to FPR 2010, r 4.1(6) rather than by way of appeal pursuant to FPR PD30A, para 14.1 (*MAP v RAP* [2015] 2 FLR 67, FD). The final sentence in FPR PD30A, para 14.1 was held by Sir James Munby P in *CS v ACS (Consent Order: Non-Disclosure: Correct Procedure)* [2016] 1 FLR 131, FD to be ultra vires and wrong.

Costs—Although a 'solicitor must be bound at the outset to consider the question whether a client might be eligible for legal aid' (*Truex v Kitchin* [2007] 2 FLR 1203, CA), there is no obligation on the Official Solicitor to seek public funding when acting for a protected party in matrimonial proceedings (*B v B* [2012] COPLR 480, FD).

Witnesses—In *Re X (A Child)* [2012] 2 FLR 456, FD application was made in care proceedings for a 17 year old with Asperger's syndrome who had given an ABE interview to give oral evidence. Theis J held that:

Capacity First, the court has to consider whether he is competent in accordance with CA 1989, s 96(2) (i e understands that it is his duty to speak the truth and has sufficient understanding to justify his evidence being heard).

Vulnerability The objective is to achieve a fair trial but the court must balance the advantages that the giving of oral evidence will bring to the determination of the truth and the damage it may do to the welfare of the witness and any other child – see *Re W (Children)* [2010] 1 FLR 1485, SC, at [24]–[31]. (Nine criteria were identified in the judgment.)

Intermediary's costs Where support is required to enable the witness to give evidence, the LSC takes the view that is not 'representation' but a mechanism analogous to translation that should be funded by the court. However, there is no provision for the use of registered intermediaries outside the scope of the Youth Justice and Criminal Evidence Act 1999, so there are obstacles to the funding of such support (unless there is a direct link to a criminal case in which the witness is involved).

15.2 Requirement for litigation friend in proceedings

A protected party must have a litigation friend to conduct proceedings on that party's behalf.

Scope—Rule 15.2 sets out the general rule that a protected party may only conduct proceedings by a litigation friend. There are no exceptions, although the court can waive the rule (see FPR 2010, r 15.3). FPR 2010, rr 15.5–15.8 set out the procedures for acquiring a litigation friend in various circumstances. The rule only refers to 'a litigation friend', so a protected party may not have more than one in any particular proceedings but there is nothing to prevent such party having a different litigation friend in other proceedings of a different nature.

'litigation friend'—Under the former Rules the term was 'next friend' for a petitioner or applicant and 'guardian ad litem' for a respondent. It is now 'litigation friend' for both.

Title of proceedings—In the proceedings, the protected party should be referred to in the title as 'A.B. (by C.D. his/her litigation friend)' – PD15A. A similar approach was formerly adopted by the CPR, but the most recent PD provides that the tile shall be 'A.B. (a protected party by C.D. his/her litigation friend)'. This is more helpful because it draws attention to the reason why there is a litigation friend.

Status of litigation friend—The specific powers of the litigation friend are not expressly set out in the Rules, but as the appointment is to 'conduct proceedings ... on behalf' of the protected party, subject to the provisions of the rules, it is assumed that any act that in the ordinary conduct of any proceedings is required or authorised to be done by a party shall or may be done by the litigation friend. (That was the position under the former CCR Ord 10, r 12).

Administration of funds—Unless the litigation friend is also a deputy appointed by the Court of Protection or an attorney under a registered lasting or enduring power of attorney, he will have no status in regard to the affairs of the protected party outside the proceedings in which he is appointed. So in that situation, if money is awarded to the protected party and this party is also incapable of handling that money (under the

CPR described as a 'protected beneficiary'), the Court of Protection will have to become involved unless the discretionary power referred to in the above note has been exercised. The money should not simply be paid to the litigation friend with no further guidance, thereby creating a potential for uncertainty and abuse, but the court is given an express discretion to permit small sums of money to be paid to someone (eg a relative or carer) so that a receipt may be obtained from that person rather than requiring Court of Protection involvement. This discretion may not be available in proceedings under CA 1989, Sch 1 relating to a mentally disabled child.

Power to pay monies to another person—In financial remedy (ancillary relief) proceedings, the court may order transfer of property or payment (periodical payments or a lump sum) to another person where a party lacks capacity to handle that money. The other person must then act in the incapacitated party's best interests (MCA 1973, s 40).

Enduring power of attorney—An enduring power of attorney created under the Enduring Powers of Attorney Act 1985 – for the criteria and the requirement to register see MCA 2005, Sch 4.

Lasting power of attorney—A power of attorney under which the donor (P) confers on the donee (or donees) authority to make decisions about all or any of the following, namely: (a) P's personal welfare or specified matters concerning P's personal welfare; and (b) P's property and affairs or specified matters concerning P's property and affairs, and which includes authority to make such decisions in circumstances where P no longer has capacity. For the criteria and the requirement to register see MCA 2005.

Need for a solicitor—A litigation friend is not required to act by a solicitor but failure to instruct one may result in questions being raised as to the suitability of the litigation friend.

PART III

15.3 Stage of proceedings at which a litigation friend becomes necessary

(1) A person may not without the permission of the court take any step in proceedings except –

(a) filing an application form; or

(b) applying for the appointment of a litigation friend under rule 15.6,

until the protected party has a litigation friend.

(2) If during proceedings a party lacks capacity (within the meaning of the 2005 Act) to continue to conduct proceedings, no party may take any step in proceedings without the permission of the court until the protected party has a litigation friend.

(3) Any step taken before a protected party has a litigation friend has no effect unless the court orders otherwise.

Scope—This rule expands upon the general rule that a protected party may only conduct proceedings by a litigation friend. The only steps that may be taken following the issue of the proceedings and before such appointment are the filing of an application form including for appointment of a litigation friend. Any other step will be of no effect. But the court is given some discretion (see below).

Court's discretion—The court may permit proceedings involving a protected party to continue to a limited extent even though a litigation friend has not been appointed ('without the permission of the court': r 15.3(1),(2)) and may validate proceedings that have continued in breach of the requirements ('unless the court orders otherwise': r 15.3(3)).

Implications—It is possible to make urgent orders in proceedings involving a protected party before the appointment of a litigation friend, but the court should be made fully aware of all relevant circumstances. Where it is realised during the course of proceedings that a party is (and has been) a protected party, provided everyone has acted in good faith and there has been no manifest disadvantage to the party subsequently found to have been a protected party, it is likely that the court will regularise the position retrospectively (*Masterman-Lister*, above). This might be the case where the proceedings have effectively been guided throughout by the person being appointed as litigation friend. Proceedings inappropriately conducted by a protected party or an unsuitable person on his behalf will be treated as being of no effect and further proceedings may then be commenced in proper form. In the context of care proceedings, the Court of Appeal in *Re D (Children)* [2015] EWCA Civ 749 found that there had been procedural failings in the assessment of the mother's litigation capacity. Notwithstanding those failings, the mother was not adversely affected and there was no practical difference to the outcome as a consequence. The proceedings were validated retrospectively and the care and placement orders confirmed.

Recovery of capacity—If the protected party recovers capacity, the appointment of the litigation friend may be terminated by court order under FPR 2010, r 15.9.

15.4 Who may be a litigation friend for a protected party without a court order

(1) This rule does not apply if the court has appointed a person to be a litigation friend.

(2) A person with authority as a deputy to conduct the proceedings in the name of a protected party or on that party's behalf is entitled to be the litigation friend of the protected party in any proceedings to which that person's authority extends.

(3) If there is no person with authority as a deputy to conduct the proceedings in the name of a protected party or on that party's behalf, a person may act as a litigation friend if that person –

(a) can fairly and competently conduct proceedings on behalf of the protected party;
(b) has no interest adverse to that of the protected party; and
(c) subject to paragraph (4), undertakes to pay any costs which the protected party may be ordered to pay in relation to the proceedings, subject to any right that person may have to be repaid from the assets of the protected party.

(4) Paragraph (3)(c) does not apply to the Official Solicitor.

('deputy' is defined in rule 2.3.)

Scope—This rule identifies a hierarchy for appointment as a litigation friend and the requirement of suitability for a person if not empowered under MCA 2005 as an attorney or deputy.

'Deputy'—Deputy is defined in FPR 2010, r 2.3 as having the meaning given in MCA 2005, s 16(2)(b), ie a person appointed by the Court of Protection to make decisions on the individual's behalf in relation to specified matters. In this context it means a deputy who has been authorised by the Court of Protection to conduct the proceedings in question.

Who is appointed—A duly authorised deputy takes precedence. An office copy of the order or other authorisation sealed with the official seal of the Court of Protection should be filed. Care should be taken to examine this document because simply being appointed a deputy does not by itself give authority to conduct proceedings. It is not clear if the court has power to appoint someone else (as under the former rules), but this situation is unlikely to arise and conflict between the court dealing with the litigation and the Court of Protection should be avoided.

There is no reference to an attorney under a registered lasting or enduring power but such attorney would normally be best placed to be a litigation friend because he will control the financial affairs of the protected party and there may, in consequence, be no need for a deputy. An ordinary power of attorney is of no significance because it ceases to have effect upon the incapacity of the donor, but of course the person acting may otherwise be suitable as litigation friend. If an EPA is registered this would normally indicate that the donor is a protected party, but that is not the case for an LPA because registration may take place at an earlier stage.

Suitability—There is no express restriction on who may be appointed apart from those stated in this rule, but obviously the person must not be a child or protected party. The litigation friend should not have any personal involvement in the proceedings, but see *Spurling v Broadhurst* [2012] EWHC 2883 (Ch). If the court becomes aware of the person's unsuitability, it may remove him under FPR 2010, r 15.9 and substitute another person as litigation friend, but there is no express duty to monitor the situation.

Official Solicitor—The Official Solicitor to the Senior Courts is only appointed by the court and the requirements of suitability do not apply.

Duty of litigation friend—The litigation friend must 'fairly and competently conduct proceedings on behalf of the protected party' and have 'no interest adverse to that of the protected party'. FPR PD15A, para 2.1 also provides that all steps and decisions the litigation friend takes in the proceedings must be taken for the benefit of the protected party. It is not clear whether this direction is at variance with the duty imposed upon delegated decision-makers under MCA 2005 to act in the 'best interests' of an incapacitated adult. A similar provision was initially included in CPR PD21, para 2.1 but removed following implementation of MCA 2005.

Costs undertaking—The prospective litigation friend (unless a deputy or the Official Solicitor) must undertake to pay any costs which the protected party may be ordered to pay in relation to the proceedings, subject to any right to be repaid from the assets of the protected party. This amounts to a severe disincentive especially in cases where the protected party is without funds, and may create problems in finding a suitable litigation friend, especially for a respondent.

Under the CPR (and the previous Rules) such indemnity is only required from the party bringing the proceedings and not from a defendant or respondent. It may be avoided by obtaining authority from the Court of Protection but that court may be cautious about granting authority where there are not sufficient funds to finance litigation. The court has a general discretion as to costs and will take into account the role of the litigation friend but may have power to impose a personal costs liability in case of misconduct quite apart from the undertaking.

15.5 How a person becomes a litigation friend without a court order

(1) If the court has not appointed a litigation friend, a person who wishes to act as a litigation friend must follow the procedure set out in this rule.

(2) A person with authority as a deputy to conduct the proceedings in the name of a protected party or on that party's behalf must file an official copy[(GL)] of the order, declaration or other document which confers that person's authority to act.

(3) Any other person must file a certificate of suitability stating that that person satisfies the conditions specified in rule 15.4(3).

(4) A person who is to act as a litigation friend must file –

(a) the document conferring that person's authority to act; or
(b) the certificate of suitability,

at the time when that person first takes a step in the proceedings on behalf of the protected party.

(5) A court officer will send the certificate of suitability to every person on whom, in accordance with rule 6.28, the application form should be served.

(6) This rule does not apply to the Official Solicitor.

Scope—This rule facilitates the appointment of a litigation friend by simply filing the required documents at the court office. It will be relied upon in most cases but does not apply if the court has already made such appointment.

Documents to be filed—A deputy merely needs to file the document issued by the Court of Protection authorising him to conduct the proceedings: FPR 2010, r 15.4(2). Any other person must file a certificate of suitability: r 15.5(2). The Official Solicitor does not need to file any of these documents but his consent to act is required.

Certificate of suitability—This states that the person signing can 'fairly and competently conduct proceedings on behalf of the protected party' and has 'no interest adverse to that of the protected party'. It also contains the required undertaking as to costs. The certificate of suitability will be sent by the court to the persons to be served under FPR 2010, r 6.28.

Form N235 is used for civil proceedings and this confirms the maker's consent to act and belief that the party is a protected party (with reasons/medical evidence). Form FP9 is specified for family proceedings in FPR PD5A.

Time for filing—The required documents must be filed before any steps are taken as litigation friend: r 15.5(4).

Persons to be served (FPR 2010, r 6.14(2))—In the case of a protected party, service is to be on one of the following persons with authority in relation to that party, namely an attorney under a registered enduring or lasting power of attorney or a deputy appointed by the Court of Protection. If there is no such person, service must be on an adult with whom the protected party resides or in whose care the protected party is. The assumption is that such person will then take appropriate steps to arrange a representative (litigation friend). Service on a proper officer of the local social services authority or other guardian when the protected party is under a guardianship order, or the district health authority when the protected party has been compulsorily admitted to hospital under MHA 1983, may be sufficient. The court has a wide discretion as to service and may vary the general rule or dispense with service in a particular instance (see FPR 2010, Pt 6).

Notice to protected party—No provision is made for the certificate of suitability to be sent to the protected party, so under this procedure the proceedings may be commenced without the knowledge of the party stated to be incapable, notwithstanding that such party may dispute the lack of capacity or wish to make representations as to the identity of the litigation friend.

Official Solicitor—The Official Solicitor is not appointed under this provision.

15.6 How a person becomes a litigation friend by court order

(1) The court may, if the person to be appointed so consents, make an order appointing –

(a) a person other than the Official Solicitor; or
(b) the Official Solicitor,

as a litigation friend.

(2) An order appointing a litigation friend may be made by the court of its own initiative or on the application of –

(a) a person who wishes to be a litigation friend; or
(b) a party to the proceedings.

(3) The court may at any time direct that a party make an application for an order under paragraph (2).

(4) An application for an order appointing a litigation friend must be supported by evidence.

(5) Unless the court directs otherwise, a person appointed under this rule to be a litigation friend for a protected party will be treated as a party for the purpose of any provision in these Rules requiring a document to be served on, or sent to, or notice to be given to, a party to the proceedings.

(6) Subject to rule 15.4(4), the court may not appoint a litigation friend under this rule unless it is satisfied that the person to be appointed complies with the conditions specified in rule 15.4(3).

Scope—This rule sets out the process whereby the court appoints a litigation friend.

The person appointed—Any adult who can 'fairly and competently conduct proceedings on behalf of the protected party' and has 'no interest adverse to that of the protected party' may be appointed. It is not necessary to approach the Official Solicitor in all cases, and the court will not be concerned to ascertain whether he has declined to consent before appointing someone else.

Official Solicitor—Where the circumstances justify the involvement of the Official Solicitor, the guidance set out in the Practice Note issued by the Official Solicitor in January 2017 (see Part V) should be followed. He will usually consent to act, subject to:

(a) satisfactory evidence in the form of an expert's opinion accepted by the party that he or she lacks capacity to conduct the proceedings, OR a finding by the court that the party is a protected party;
(b) confirmation that the Official Solicitor is litigation friend of last resort; and
(c) confirmation that there is security for the costs of legal representation.

Any order making such appointment should be expressed as being subject to the Official Solicitor's consent. Save in the most urgent of cases, it is unlikely that the Official Solicitor will be able to complete his enquiries in less than 3 months. Accordingly, a lengthy adjournment of the proceedings may be necessary and a substantive hearing should not be fixed within such period of his initial appointment without consulting him.

The Official Solicitor to the Senior Courts may be contacted at Victory House, 30–34 Kingsway, London WC2B 6EX, DX 141423 Bloomsbury 7; tel 020 3681 2751 (healthcare and welfare) or 020 3681 2758 (property and affairs); fax 020 3681 2762.

Service—Once appointed, the litigation friend is treated as a party for the purpose of service of documents.

15.7 Court's power to change litigation friend and to prevent person acting as litigation friend

(1) The court may –

(a) direct that a person may not act as a litigation friend;
(b) terminate a litigation friend's appointment; or
(c) appoint a new litigation friend in substitution for an existing one.

(2) An application for an order or direction under paragraph (1) must be supported by evidence.

(3) Subject to rule 15.4(4), the court may not appoint a litigation friend under this rule unless it is satisfied that the person to be appointed complies with the conditions specified in rule 15.4(3).

Scope—The court may prevent a person from being a litigation friend or replace a litigation friend during the course of proceedings. The court must be satisfied that the person to be appointed is suitable for appointment in accordance with the criteria set out in FPR 2010, r 15.4(3).

15.8 Appointment of litigation friend by court order – supplementary

(1) A copy of the application for an order under rule 15.6 or 15.7 must be sent by a court officer to –

(a) every person on whom, in accordance with rule 6.28, the application form should be served; and
(b) unless the court directs otherwise, the protected party.

(2) A copy of an application for an order under rule 15.7 must also be sent to –

(a) the person who is the litigation friend, or who is purporting to act as the litigation friend, when the application is made; and
(b) the person, if not the applicant, who it is proposed should be the litigation friend.

Scope—This rule makes provision for service of an application for the appointment of a litigation friend or the change of a litigation friend. In addition to being sent by the court to the persons to be served under FPR 2010, r 6.28, it must be sent to the purported protected party unless the court otherwise directs. The court has a wide discretion as to service and may vary the general rule or dispense with service in a particular instance (see FPR 2010, Pt 6).

Persons to be served (FPR 2010, r 6.28)—See note to FPR 2010, r 15.5 above.

Service of application for matrimonial order or civil partnership order—Special provisions apply to service of these proceedings on a protected party although the court has a general discretion. Neither the court nor the applicant personally must effect service: FPR 2010, r 6.5. The form must be endorsed with the notice set out in FPR PD6A, para 9.1 and the person commencing the proceedings must file a witness statement by the person on whom the application form was served stating whether the contents of the application form or the purpose and intention of the application were communicated to the protected party and, if not, why not: FPR 2010, r 6.14(7). This does not apply when the Official Solicitor is to be the litigation friend (presumably because his enquiries will have included the circumstances of the party): FPR 2010, r 6.14(8).

Although these provisions as to service are designed to ensure that the purported protected party may participate, it is not clear how the required witness statement may be obtained, although lack of co-operation would indicate that the person served was not suitable and the court would then wish to give further directions.

15.9 Procedure where appointment of litigation friend comes to an end

(1) When a party ceases to be a protected party, the litigation friend's appointment continues until it is brought to an end by a court order.

(2) An application for an order under paragraph (1) may be made by –

(a) the former protected party;
(b) the litigation friend; or
(c) a party.

(3) On the making of an order under paragraph (1), the court officer will send a notice to the other parties stating that the appointment of the protected party's litigation friend to act has ended.

Scope—This rule makes provision for a party ceasing to be a protected party. The litigation friend will only be removed by court order following an application under r 15.9(3) and evidence will be required as to capacity.

Liability of litigation friend for costs—The litigation friend may have had to give an undertaking as to costs pursuant to r 15.4(3)(c). This liability continues until the court order discharging the litigation friend. It is not clear whether, when discharged, the litigation friend is released from all liability for costs or only costs incurred from that date, although it is probably the latter.

Practice Direction 15A – Protected Parties

This Practice Direction supplements FPR Part 15

General

1.1 A protected party must have a litigation friend to conduct proceedings on the protected party's behalf.

1.2 In the proceedings the protected party should be referred to in the title as 'A.B. (by C.D. his/her litigation friend)'.

Duties of the Litigation Friend

2.1 It is the duty of a litigation friend fairly and competently to conduct proceedings on behalf of a protected party. The litigation friend must have no interest in the proceedings adverse to that of the protected party and all steps and decisions the litigation friend takes in the proceedings must be taken for the benefit of the protected party.

Becoming a Litigation Friend without a court order

3.1 In order to become a litigation friend without a court order the person who wishes to act as litigation friend must –

(a) file an official copy of the order, declaration or other document which confers the litigation friend's authority as a deputy to conduct the proceedings in the name of a protected party or on his/her behalf; or
(b) file a certificate of suitability –
   (i) stating that the litigation friend consents to act;
   (ii) stating that the litigation friend knows or believes that the [applicant][respondent] lacks capacity (within the meaning of the 2005 Act) to conduct proceedings;
   (iii) stating the grounds of that belief and if the belief is based upon medical opinion attaching any relevant document to the certificate;
   (iv) stating that the litigation friend can fairly and competently conduct proceedings on behalf of the protected party and has no interest adverse to that of the protected party;
   (v) undertaking to pay any costs which the protected party may be ordered to pay in

relation to the proceedings, subject to any right the litigation friend may have to be repaid from the assets of the protected party; and
(vi) which the litigation friend has verified by a statement of truth.

3.2 Paragraph 3.1 does not apply to the Official Solicitor.

3.3 The court officer will send the certificate of suitability to the person who is the attorney of a registered enduring power of attorney, donee of a lasting power of attorney or deputy or, if there is no such person, to the person with whom the protected party resides or in whose care the protected party is.

3.4 The court officer is not required to send the documents referred to in paragraph 3.1(b)(iii) when sending the certificate of suitability to the person to be served under paragraph 3.3.

3.5 The litigation friend must file either the certificate of suitability or the authority referred to in paragraph 3.1(a) at a time when the litigation friend first takes a step in the proceedings on behalf of the protected party.

Application for a court order appointing a litigation friend

4.1 An application for a court order appointing a litigation friend should be made in accordance with Part 18 and must be supported by evidence.

4.2 The court officer must serve the application notice –

(a) on the persons referred to in paragraph 3.3; and
(b) on the protected party unless the court directs otherwise.

4.3 The evidence in support must satisfy the court that the proposed litigation friend –

(a) consents to act;
(b) can fairly and competently conduct proceedings on behalf of the protected party;
(c) has no interest adverse to that of the protected party; and
(d) undertakes to pay any costs which the protected party may be ordered to pay in relation to the proceedings, subject to any right the litigation friend may have to be repaid from the assets of the protected party.

4.4 Paragraph 4.3(d) does not apply to the Official Solicitor.

4.5 The proposed litigation friend may be one of the persons referred to in paragraph 3.3 where appropriate, or otherwise may be the Official Solicitor. Where it is sought to appoint the Official Solicitor, provision must be made for payment of his charges.

Change of litigation friend and prevention of person acting as litigation friend.

5.1 Where an application is made for an order under rule 15.7, the application must set out the reasons for seeking it and must be supported by evidence.

5.2 Subject to paragraph 4.4, if the order sought is substitution of a new litigation friend for an existing one, the evidence must satisfy the court of the matters set out in paragraph 4.3.

5.3 The court officer will serve the application notice on –

(a) the persons referred to in paragraph 3.3; and
(b) the litigation friend or person purporting to act as litigation friend.

Procedure where the need for a litigation friend has come to an end

6.1 Where a person who was a protected party regains or acquires capacity (within the meaning of the 2005 Act) to conduct the proceedings, an application under rule 15.9(2) must be made for an order under rule 15.9(1) that the litigation friend's appointment has ceased.

6.2 The application must be supported by the following evidence –

(a) a medical report or other suitably qualified expert's report indicating that the protected party has regained or acquired capacity (within the meaning of the 2005 Act) to conduct the proceedings; and

(b) a copy of any relevant order or declaration of the Court of Protection.

Practice Direction 15B – Adults Who May Be Protected Parties and Children Who May Become Protected Parties in Family Proceedings

This Practice Direction supplements FPR Part 15

What the court will do where an adult may be a protected party

Litigation capacity

1.1 The court will investigate as soon as possible any issue as to whether an adult party or intended party to family proceedings lacks capacity (within the meaning of the Mental Capacity Act 2005) to conduct the proceedings. An adult who lacks capacity to conduct the proceedings is a protected party and must have a litigation friend to conduct the proceedings on his or her behalf. The expectation of the Official Solicitor is that the Official Solicitor will only be invited to act for the protected party as litigation friend if there is no other person suitable or willing to act. Attention is drawn to the Checklist 'Protected Parties in Family Proceedings: Checklist For the Appointment of a Litigation Friend (including the Official Solicitor)' (published in *Family Law* (January 2014)).

1.2 Any issue as to the capacity of an adult to conduct the proceedings must be determined before the court gives any directions relevant to that adult's role in the proceedings. Where a party has a solicitor, it is the solicitor who is likely to first identify that the party may lack litigation capacity. Expert evidence as to whether a party lacks such capacity is likely to be necessary for the court to make a determination relating to the party's capacity to conduct proceedings. However, there are some cases where the court may consider that evidence from a treating clinician such as a treating psychiatrist is all the evidence of lack of litigation capacity which may be necessary. There may also be cases where it will be clear that a party does not have litigation capacity such as where the party is in a coma, minimally conscious or in a persistent vegetative state. In those cases the court may well consider that a letter from a treating doctor confirming the party's condition is sufficient evidence of lack of litigation capacity and not need a report from an expert.

1.3 If at any time during the proceedings there is reason to believe that a party may lack capacity to conduct the proceedings, then the court must be notified and directions sought to ensure that this issue is investigated without delay. The presumption of capacity should not be forgotten. For example, where a person has an identified difficulty such as a learning disability or a mental illness, that difficulty should not automatically lead to an investigation about that party's capacity to litigate. Where a party has a solicitor, the starting point is whether that solicitor has concerns about the party's capacity to litigate.

Ability to give evidence as a witness

1.4 Where the court determines that a party does not have capacity to conduct the proceedings, the court may well also have to determine whether that party is able to give evidence and if so whether 'special measures' are required. Expert evidence is also likely to be necessary for the court to make such determinations. However, as in relation to the question of litigation capacity, the court may consider that evidence from a treating clinician who has a good understanding of the party's difficulties may be sufficient. If the treating clinician is provided with information about the legal framework, the clinician may be able to provide that evidence more readily and more quickly than an expert instructed to give an opinion as to the party's ability to give evidence.

1.5 Where the protected party is able to give evidence, the representative will wish to consider (and ask the expert to consider) the impact on that party of giving evidence. When making a determination as to whether that protected party should give evidence, the court may need to consider whether the impact of giving evidence would be so adverse to their condition that it

PART III

would not be in that party's best interests to do so. The representative may put forward an argument on behalf of the protected party that the protected party should not give evidence.

Instruction of an expert where an adult is a protected party

2.1 Where there is concern that a party or intended party may lack capacity to conduct the proceedings, that party's representative must take the lead in any instruction of an expert for the purpose of assessment of the party's capacity to conduct the proceedings. In the event that the assessment is that the party does lack capacity to conduct the proceedings, it may be appropriate to ask that the expert advise about a party's ability to give evidence as a witness. Such expert evidence would relate to the party's particular difficulties and vulnerabilities (in particular in the context of cross-examination) including the techniques or measures which could be used to assist the party to give his or her evidence to the best of his or her ability and to ensure that the party's support needs are identified and addressed in advance of any final hearing.

Factors to be considered when the court is deciding whether to give permission as mentioned in FPR 25.4(1) or (2)

3.1 FPR 25.5 lists factors to which the court is to have particular regard when deciding whether to give permission in all family proceedings for expert evidence to be put before the court, and in children proceedings also for an expert to be instructed or for a child to be medically or psychiatrically examined or assessed for the purposes of obtaining expert evidence. In relation to children proceedings, one factor to be considered by the court is whether evidence could be given by another person on matters on which the expert would give evidence. For the avoidance of doubt this factor is not intended to suggest that evidence of another party to the proceedings is a substitute for expert evidence relating to a party's capacity to conduct the proceedings, ability to give evidence or special measures as mentioned in paragraphs 1.2, 1.4 and 2.1 above.

3.2 In addition, in children proceedings, it should be noted that expert evidence or other evidence from a treating clinician about a party's litigation capacity in previous proceedings is no substitute for such evidence in current proceedings. Litigation capacity has to be considered in relation to the proceedings before the court. For example, a parent may have been found to lack litigation capacity in care proceedings about child A three years before the current proceedings. That finding about litigation capacity in previous proceedings is not evidence that the parent lacks litigation capacity in subsequent proceedings about child B. It may be that the subsequent proceedings are simpler in terms of the issues and evidence before the court or that the parent's previous difficulty leading to lack of litigation capacity has improved.

Fluctuation in a party's capacity to conduct litigation

4.1 A party's capacity to conduct the litigation may fluctuate over the course of the proceedings. Litigation capacity may be lost or regained during the proceedings as a result of deterioration or improvement in the impairment of, or disturbance in the functioning of, the party's mind or brain. The necessity for expert evidence or evidence of a treating clinician as to a party's capacity can therefore arise at any time during the proceedings.

4.2 Fluctuation in a party's capacity to conduct litigation means that a litigation friend may not represent that party throughout the proceedings. It is expected that where the litigation friend has been appointed or reappointed, the court will be likely to make a direction in accordance with FPR 25.10(2) permitting such a litigation friend to put written questions to the expert after the 10 day period referred to in FPR 25.10(2)(c)where the 10 days referred to in that rule would be insufficient time for the litigation friend to become familiar with the case or latest developments in the case while assimilating the expert's report and formulating any questions.

Single joint experts

5.1 FPR 25.11 and 25.12 and paragraphs 2.1 to 2.7 of Practice Direction 25C and of Practice Direction 25D make provision for two or more parties to put expert evidence before the court from a single joint expert. 'Single joint expert' ('SJE') is defined by FPR 25.2(1) as a person who provides expert evidence for use in proceedings on behalf of two or more parties (including the applicant) to the proceedings. No provision of the FPR nor the Practice Directions compel the use of an SJE. Paragraph 2.1 of Practice Direction 25C and of Practice Direction 25D provide that a SJE should be used 'wherever possible'. The expectation is that expert evidence as mentioned in paragraphs 1.2, 1.4 and 2.1 above, including on whether a party lacks capacity to conduct the proceedings, would not be evidence which is likely to be appropriately given by a SJE. However, there may be circumstances where expert evidence is needed by two or more parties relating to, for example, the capacity of a party when he or she gave consent to the making of a consent order made by the court in financial remedy proceedings and such evidence may be considered by the court to be appropriately given by a SJE. But these are circumstances where the expert evidence relates to an issue in the proceedings.

Child aged 16–17 who is the subject of the proceedings likely to lack relevant decision making capacity at age 18

6.1 Where the child who is the subject of the proceedings is aged l6 to 17 consideration should be given as to whether it is necessary to obtain expert evidence on whether that child will lack capacity (within the meaning of the Mental Capacity Act 2005) to make one or more of the decisions relevant to the proceedings (for example, in relation to residence, contact with family or about care arrangements) when that child reaches 18.

6.2 Attention is drawn to the fact that the Mental Capacity Act 2005 provides for a framework for decision making in respect of persons over 16 who lack capacity to makes decisions about their own finances, health and welfare. The Mental Capacity Act 2005 (Transfer of Proceedings) Order 2007 (SI 2007/1899) includes provision for the transfer of proceedings from a court having jurisdiction under the Children Act 1989 to the Court of Protection.

Child who is not the subject of proceedings likely to lack capacity to conduct the proceedings when he or she reaches 18

7.1 Where it appears that a child is –

(a) a party to the proceedings and not the subject of them;
(b) nearing age 18; and
(c) considered likely to lack capacity to conduct the proceedings when 18,

the court will consider giving directions for the child's capacity in this respect to be investigated.

Definition of 'expert' and 'children proceedings'

8.1 The definitions of 'expert' and 'children proceedings' in FPR 25.2(1) apply to this Practice Direction and the explanation of an expert team in paragraph 2.2 of Practice Direction 25B also applies.

PART 16
REPRESENTATION OF CHILDREN AND REPORTS IN PROCEEDINGS INVOLVING CHILDREN

CONTENTS OF THIS PART

Chapter 1

Rule		Page
	Application of this Part	
16.1	Application of this Part	1695
	Chapter 2 *Child as Party in Family Proceedings*	
16.2	When the court may make a child a party to proceedings	1695

PART III

Chapter 3
When a Children's Guardian or Litigation Friend will be Appointed

16.3 Appointment of a children's guardian in specified proceedings or proceedings to which Part 14 applies 1696
16.4 Appointment of a children's guardian in proceedings not being specified proceedings or proceedings to which Part 14 applies 1696
16.5 Requirement for a litigation friend 1697

Chapter 4
Where a Children's Guardian or Litigation Friend is Not Required

16.6 Circumstances in which a child does not need a children's guardian or litigation friend 1698

Chapter 5
Litigation Friend

16.7 Application of this Chapter 1700
16.8 Stage of proceedings at which a litigation friend becomes necessary 1700
16.9 Who may be a litigation friend for a child without a court order 1701
16.10 How a person becomes a litigation friend without a court order 1701
16.11 Appointment of litigation friend by the court 1702
16.12 Court's power to change litigation friend and to prevent person acting as litigation friend 1702
16.13 Appointment of litigation friend by court order – supplementary 1702
16.14 Powers and duties of litigation friend 1703
16.15 Procedure where appointment of litigation friend comes to an end 1703

Chapter 6
Children's Guardian Appointed under Rule 16.3

16.16 Application of this Chapter 1703
16.17 Who may be a children's guardian 1703
16.18 What the court or a court officer will do once the court has made a decision about appointing a children's guardian 1704
16.19 Termination of the appointment of the children's guardian 1704
16.20 Powers and duties of the children's guardian 1704
16.21 Where the child instructs a solicitor or conducts proceedings on the child's own behalf 1706

Chapter 7
Children's Guardian Appointed under Rule 16.4

16.22 Application of this Chapter 1706
16.23 Stage of proceedings at which a children's guardian becomes necessary 1706
16.24 Appointment of a children's guardian 1707
16.25 Court's power to change children's guardian and to prevent person acting as children's guardian 1707
16.26 Appointment of children's guardian by court order – supplementary 1708
16.27 Powers and duties of children's guardian 1708
16.28 Procedure where appointment of children's guardian comes to an end 1708

Chapter 8
Duties of Solicitor Acting for the Child

16.29 Solicitor for child 1708

Chapter 9
Reporting Officer

16.30 When the court appoints a reporting officer 1710
16.31 Appointment of the same reporting officer in respect of two or more parents or guardians 1710
16.32 The duties of the reporting officer 1710

Chapter 10
Children and Family Reporter and Welfare Officer

16.33 Request by court for a welfare report in respect of the child 1710

Chapter 11
Parental Order Reporter

16.34 When the court appoints a parental order reporter 1711
16.35 Powers and duties of the parental order reporter 1711

Chapter 12
Supplementary Appointment Provisions

16.36 Persons who may not be appointed as children's guardian, reporting officer or children and family reporter 1711
16.37 Appointment of the same person as children's guardian, reporting officer and children and family reporter 1712

Chapter 13
Officers of the Service, Welsh Family Proceedings Officers and Local Authority Officers: Further Duties

16.38 Officers of the Service, Welsh family proceedings officers and local authority officers acting under certain duties 1712

Chapter 14
Enforcement Orders and Financial Compensation Orders: Persons Notified

16.39 Application for enforcement orders and financial compensation orders: duties of the person notified 1713

Practice Direction 16A –
Representation of Children 1713

Chapter 1
Application of this Part

16.1 Application of this Part

This Part –

(a) sets out when the court will make a child a party in family proceedings; and
(b) contains special provisions which apply in proceedings involving children.

Chapter 2
Child as Party in Family Proceedings

16.2 When the court may make a child a party to proceedings

(1) The court may make a child a party to proceedings if it considers it is in the best interests of the child to do so.

(2) This rule does not apply to a child who is the subject of proceedings –

(a) which are specified proceedings; or
(b) to which Part 14 applies.

(The Practice Direction 16A sets out the matters which the court will take into consideration before making a child a party under this rule.)

PD16A—When a child should be made a party to proceedings and the circumstances which the court may consider to justify the making of an order are set out in FPR PD16A, paras 7.1–7.5.

Child joined as a party—In respect of articulate teenagers, their right to freedom of expression and participation may well outweigh the paternalistic judgment of their welfare best interests: *Cambra v Jones (Contempt Proceedings: Child Joined as Party)* [2015] 1 FLR 263, FD.

PART III

Chapter 3

When a Children's Guardian or Litigation Friend will be Appointed

16.3 Appointment of a children's guardian in specified proceedings or proceedings to which Part 14 applies

(1) Unless it is satisfied that it is not necessary to do so to safeguard the interests of the child, the court must appoint a children's guardian for a child who is –

(a) the subject of; and

(b) a party to,

proceedings –

(i) which are specified proceedings; or

(ii) to which Part 14 applies.

(Rules 12.6 and 14.6 set out the point in the proceedings when the court will appoint a children's guardian in specified proceedings and proceedings to which Part 14 respectively.)

(2) At any stage in the proceedings –

(a) a party may apply, without notice to the other parties unless the court directs otherwise, for the appointment of a children's guardian; or

(b) the court may of its own initiative appoint a children's guardian.

(3) Where the court refuses an application under paragraph (2)(a) it will give reasons for the refusal and the court or a court officer will –

(a) record the refusal and the reasons for it; and

(b) as soon as practicable, notify the parties and either the Service or the Assembly of a decision not to appoint a children's guardian.

(4) When appointing a children's guardian the court will consider the appointment of anyone who has previously acted as a children's guardian of the same child.

(5) Where the court appoints a children's guardian in accordance with this rule, the provisions of Chapter 6 of this Part apply.

Appointment—The obligation to appoint a children's guardian in specified proceedings unless the circumstances are as described in r 16.3(1) is imposed by CA 1989, s 41(1). CJCSA 2000, ss 11 and 12 established the Children and Family Court Advisory and Support Service which is responsible for fulfilling the requirements of courts in respect of investigating and reporting; see further the annotations under those sections and CA 1989, ss 7 and 37. Cafcass has a duty to appoint a guardian as soon as reasonably practicable, taking into account its general functions, duties and resources, but it does not owe a specific duty to an individual child: *R and Others v Cafcass* [2012] 2 FLR 1432, CA.

Status of a Children's Guardian—Macur LJ has observed that 'arguments advanced in this appeal have revealed the continuing misconception that the evidence and opinion of a children's guardian, however demonstrably poorly rooted or reasoned, carries additional weight by virtue of their "special" status. It must be firmly squashed. The children's guardian is required to proffer advice to the court but in doing so becomes a witness subject to the same judicial scrutiny as any other. A children's guardian starts with no special advantage': *MW and Hertfordshire County Council v A & V and Mr & Mrs J* [2014] EWCA Civ 405.

Where interests of children conflict—There is usually no reason why a children's guardian should not properly represent children whose interests conflict (*Re T and E (Proceedings: Conflicting Interests)* [1995] 1 FLR 581, FD).

Refusal to make an appointment (r 16.3(3))—The concept of a refusal imports a request to act in the way refused, but it is submitted that it is appropriate for the prescribed form to be completed not only where the court refuses an application under r 16.3(2)(a) but also where the court initially decides not to make an appointment under r 16.3(1).

16.4 Appointment of a children's guardian in proceedings not being specified proceedings or proceedings to which Part 14 applies

(1) Except in proceedings under section 55A of the 1986 Act and without prejudice to rule 8.42 or 16.6, the court must appoint a children's guardian for a child who is the subject of proceedings, which are not proceedings of a type referred to in rule 16.3(1), if –

(a) the child is an applicant in the proceedings;

(b) a provision in these rules provides for the child to be a party to the proceedings; or

(c) the court has made the child a party in accordance with rule 16.2.

(1A) Without prejudice to rule 16.6, in proceedings under section 55A of the 1986 Act, the court must appoint a children's guardian for a child where –

(a) the court has made the child a party in accordance with rule 16.2; and
(b) the child is the person whose parentage is in dispute in those proceedings.

(2) The provisions of Chapter 7 of this Part apply where the appointment of a children's guardian is required in accordance with paragraph (1) or paragraph (1A).

('children's guardian' is defined in rule 2.3.)

Amendments—SI 2016/901.

'rule 2.3'—A 'children's guardian' means a person appointed in accordance with FPR 2010, r 16.3 or 16.4.

'rule 8.42 or 16.6' (r 16.4(1))—Rule 8.42 allows a child to apply for consent to marry or to register a civil partnership and r 16.6 allows a child to participate in proceedings without a guardian respectively. Therefore, a guardian should not be appointed under r 16.4 if the child wishes to act without one and the condition in FPR 2010, r 16.6 as to his capacity is satisfied.

PD16A—Pt 4 of FPR PD16A, para 7.1 makes plain that making a child a party to proceedings is a step that will be taken only in cases which involve an issue of significant difficulty and consequently will occur in only a minority of cases. The circumstances which the court may consider to justify the making of an order are set out in para 7.2: the guidance includes 10 circumstances which may justify the making of an order.

Declarations of parentage—Note the insertion of r 16.4(1A). In applications for a declaration of parentage, the court must appoint a guardian where the child is a party and is the subject of the application.

Hague Convention proceedings—A child will not ordinarily be joined as a party to Hague Convention proceedings. When considering how a child's views were to be obtained and the circumstances in which a child should be joined as a party, Baroness Hale observed in *Re D (Abduction: Rights of Custody)* [2007] 1 FLR 961, HL, at [60] that 'The most common method is therefore an interview with a CAFCASS officer, who is not only skilled and experienced in talking with children but also, if practising in the High Court, aware of the limited compass within which the child's views are relevant in Hague Convention cases. In most cases, this should be enough. In others, and especially where the child has asked to see the judge, it may also be necessary for the judge to hear the child. Only in a few cases will full scale legal representation be necessary. But whenever it seems likely that the child's views and interests may not be properly presented to the court, and in particular where there are legal arguments which the adult parties are not putting forward, then the child should be separately represented'. See also *Re M (Abduction: Zimbabwe)* [2008] 1 FLR 251, HL and *Re M (Republic of Ireland) (Child's Objections) (Joinder of Children as Parties to Appeal)* [2015] 2 FLR 1074, CA. The Court of Appeal has more recently, however, in *Re D (A Child) (International Recognition)* [2016] 2 FLR 347, CA observed that 'the rule of law in England and Wales includes the right of the child to participate in the process that is about him or her. That is the fundamental principle that is reflected in our legislation, our rules and practice directions and jurisprudence. At its most basic level it involves asking at an early stage in family proceedings whether and how that child is going to be given the opportunity to be heard. The qualification in section 1(3)(a) [of the Children Act 1989] like that in article 12(1) [of the United Nations Convention on the Rights of the Child 1989] relates to the weight to be put upon a child's wishes and feelings, not their participation', at [44]: see **Separate representation for the child** under Art 12 of the Hague Convention (set out in CACA 1985, Sch 1).

Cafcass/Official Solicitor—The child should only be made a party in a minority of cases featuring issues of significant difficulty. Where it is felt that a child needs separate representation, consideration should first be given to appointing an officer of Cafcass as guardian. If Cafcass is unable to provide a guardian, r 16.24(1) makes further provision for the appointment of a guardian. See **'some other proper person'** under r 16.24. See *Practice Note of January 2017 (The Official Solicitor to the Senior Courts: Appointment in Family Proceedings and Proceedings under the Inherent Jurisdiction in Relation to Adults)* and *CAFCASS and the National Assembly for Wales Practice Note of June 2006 (Appointment of Guardians in Private Law Proceedings)*.

Continuing role of children's guardian when 'specified proceedings' cease to be 'specified'—It is possible for the High Court or the Family Court to direct that a guardian ad litem continue to be involved under r 16.4 even though proceedings which had been 'specified proceedings', within the meaning of CA 1989, s 41(6)(b), have ceased to be 'specified' (for example, where a local authority, as a result of a s 37 direction by the court, investigates the circumstances of a child but decides to make no application for a public law order in respect of him). However, this course can only be taken if: (i) the children's guardian consents to it; (ii) there is funding available; and (iii) the children's guardian has a continuing role to play in the matter despite the changed status of the proceedings (*Re CE (Section 37 Direction)* [1995] 1 FLR 26, FD).

16.5 Requirement for a litigation friend

(1) Except in proceedings under section 55A of the 1986 Act and without prejudice to rule 16.6, where a child is –

(a) a party to proceedings; but
(b) not the subject of those proceedings,

the child must have a litigation friend to conduct proceedings on the child's behalf.

PART III

(1A) Without prejudice to rule 16.6, where a child is –

(a) a party to proceedings under section 55A of the 1986 Act; but
(b) not the person whose parentage is in dispute in those proceedings,

the child must have a litigation friend to conduct proceedings on the child's behalf.

(2) The provisions of Chapter 5 of this Part apply where a litigation friend is required in accordance with paragraph (1) or paragraph (1A).

Amendments—SI 2016/901.

Scope—This rule introduces the provisions set out in FPR 2010, Pt 16, Ch 5, which relate to the appointment of a litigation friend for a child (cf FPR 2010, Pt 15, which makes similar provision for a protected party).

Declaration of parentage (r 16.5(1A))—A child is not automatically a party to proceedings for a declaration of parentage under FLA 1986, s 55A: FPR 2010, r 8.20. A child who is made a respondent to such an application, but is not the person whose parentage is in dispute, must have a litigation friend unless one of the conditions set out in r 16.6(3) is satisfied.

Chapter 4
Where a Children's Guardian or Litigation Friend is Not Required

16.6 Circumstances in which a child does not need a children's guardian or litigation friend

(1) Subject to paragraph (2), a child may conduct proceedings without a children's guardian or litigation friend where the proceedings are proceedings –

(a) under the 1989 Act;
(b) to which Part 11 (applications under Part 4A of the Family Law Act 1996 or Part 1 of Schedule 2 to the Female Genital Mutilation Act 2003) or Part 14 (applications in adoption, placement and related proceedings) of these rules apply;
(c) relating to the exercise of the court's inherent jurisdiction with respect to children; or
(d) under section 55A of the 1986 Act,

and one of the conditions set out in paragraph (3) is satisfied.

(2) Paragraph (1) does not apply where the child is the subject of and a party to proceedings –

(a) which are specified proceedings; or
(b) to which Part 14 applies.

(3) The conditions referred to in paragraph (1) are that either –

(a) the child has obtained the court's permission; or
(b) a solicitor –
  (i) considers that the child is able, having regard to the child's understanding, to give instructions in relation to the proceedings; and
  (ii) has accepted instructions from that child to act for that child in the proceedings and, if the proceedings have begun, the solicitor is already acting.

(4) An application for permission under paragraph (3)(a) may be made by the child without notice.

(5) Where a child –

(a) has a litigation friend or children's guardian in proceedings to which this rule applies; and
(b) wishes to conduct the remaining stages of the proceedings without the litigation friend or children's guardian,

the child may apply to the court, on notice to the litigation friend or children's guardian, for permission for that purpose and for the removal of the litigation friend or children's guardian.

(6) The court will grant an application under paragraph (3)(a) or (5) if it considers that the child has sufficient understanding to conduct the proceedings concerned or proposed without a litigation friend or children's guardian.

(7) In exercising its powers under paragraph (6) the court may require the litigation friend or children's guardian to take such part in the proceedings as the court directs.

(8) The court may revoke any permission granted under paragraph (3)(a) where it considers that the child does not have sufficient understanding to participate as a party in the proceedings concerned without a litigation friend or children's guardian.

(9) Where a solicitor is acting for a child in proceedings without a litigation friend or children's guardian by virtue of paragraph (3)(b) and either of the conditions specified in paragraph (3)(b)(i) or (ii) cease to be fulfilled, the solicitor must inform the court immediately.

(10) Where –

(a) the court revokes any permission under paragraph (8); or
(b) either of the conditions specified in paragraph (3)(b)(i) or (ii) is no longer fulfilled,

the court may, if it considers it necessary in order to protect the interests of the child concerned, appoint a person to be that child's litigation friend or children's guardian.

Amendments—SI 2016/901; SI 2017/413.

'entitled to begin, prosecute or defend any proceedings'—This rule does not confer any rights to party status which a child would not otherwise enjoy but merely affects whether a litigation friend or guardian ad litem is required when a child is a party. Unlike 'begin', 'prosecute or defend' refers to a continuing course of action; therefore, if in the course of proceedings which a child had been prosecuting or defending without a litigation friend or guardian ad litem in reliance on one (or both) of the grounds in r 16.6(3), the ground (or both of them) ceases to apply, the child is unable to continue prosecuting or defending the remaining stages of the proceedings unless and until he acquires a litigation friend or guardian ad litem. The provisions of r 16.6(1) ceases to apply only if the permission is revoked by the court under r 16.6(8), in which case the court would be able to appoint a litigation friend or guardian ad litem under r 16.6(10). Where r 16.6(3)(b) ceases to apply, the solicitor concerned must so inform the court under r 16.6(9) and the court is similarly able to make an appointment under r 16.6(10).

Declarations of parentage—Note the inclusion of applications for a declaration of parentage in r 16.6(1).

Permission of the court (r 16.6(3)(a))—The criterion for granting permission is set out in r 16.6(6). Where a child wishes to act as a litigant in person, the court's permission must be obtained under r 16.6(5). Even where a child has retained a solicitor, the solicitor may still wish the court's permission to be sought if he is unsure of whether r 16.6(3)(b)(i) is satisfied, or he is unwilling to shoulder the responsibility of deciding that it is satisfied. The court, rather than the solicitor, always has the ultimate right to decide whether a child who comes before it as a party without a next friend or guardian ad litem has the necessary ability, having regard to his understanding, to instruct his solicitor (*Re CT (A Minor) (Wardship: Representation)* [1993] 2 FLR 278, CA). The test in relation to an application to dispense with a guardian is a one-stage test, the essence of which is that the court has to consider whether or not the minor has 'sufficient understanding to participate as a party in the proceedings concerned' (r 16.6(6); *Re N (Contact: Minor Seeking Leave to Defend and Removal of Guardian)* [2003] 1 FLR 652, FD).

Solicitor's acceptance of instructions (r 16.6(3)(1)(b))—The test which applies under r 16.6(3)(b)(i) is, in substance, the same as that which governs whether a solicitor should accept instructions from a child who is the subject of specified proceedings (see FPR 2010, r 16.29(2)(b)). See also *Re CT (A Minor) (Wardship: Representation)* [1993] 2 FLR 278, CA (above) and 'sufficient understanding' below.

Ex parte nature of request (r 16.6(5))—Whether a child should be allowed to dispense with a litigation friend or guardian ad litem is a matter between the minor and the court (and the litigation friend or guardian ad litem if one is already acting). It is implicit that the other parties to the proceedings (or proposed parties to proceedings which the minor wishes to begin) have no standing in relation to questions under this rule, even though they may have their own reasons for wishing a particular outcome. The rules do not expressly or implicitly confer any right on the parents of the child or anyone else to be heard on the child's application. However, the judge always has a discretion (not conferred by the rules), in the course of hearing such an application, to hear the representations of the child's parents or others in the interests of justice (*Re S (A Minor) (Independent Representation)* [1993] 2 FLR 437, CA).

'sufficient understanding' (r 16.6(6))—In *Mabon v Mabon* [2005] 2 FLR 1011, CA, the Court of Appeal reviewed the older authorities and recognised the growing acknowledgement of the autonomy and consequential rights of children, both nationally and internationally. Thorpe LJ stated that r 16.6 (then r 9.2A) was sufficiently widely framed to meet the UK's obligations under Art 12 of the United Nations Convention on the Rights of the Child 1989 and that Art 8 of ECHR 1950 provided that judges, when measuring the sufficiency of a child's understanding, reflected the extent to which in the 21st century there was a keener appreciation of the child's autonomy and consequential right to participate in decision-making processes that fundamentally affected his or her life. The courts must, in the case of articulate teenagers, accept that the right to freedom of expression and participation outweighed the paternalistic judgement of welfare. However, welfare had a place in testing the sufficiency of a child's understanding. If direct participation would lead to a risk of harm to the child and if the child was incapable of comprehending that risk then a judge could find that sufficient understanding had not been demonstrated. However, judges also had to be aware of the risk of emotional harm that might arise from denying the child knowledge of, and participation in, the continuing proceedings.

Judge seeing children—The Court of Appeal has emphasised that seeing children in private in the course of proceedings is not to be used for the purposes of evidence gathering: *Re KP (Abduction: Child's Objections)* [2014] 2 FLR 660, CA.

Revocation of leave (r 16.6(8))—The court may wish to revoke leave in two main types of case. First, the complexity of the proceedings may materially increase during the course of the interlocutory process by the making of new applications in the course of them, the joinder of new parties or the raising of new and complicated factual or evidential issues that were not originally foreseen. Without altering its assessment of the child's level of understanding, the court may conclude that it is insufficient in the changed circumstances (see 'sufficient understanding' above). Second, through experiencing how the child conducts the interlocutory stages of the proceedings, the court may simply conclude that it was wrong to grant the leave in the first place. Where this occurs the court may appoint a litigation friend or guardian pursuant to the provisions of FPR 2010, Pt 16.

Chapter 5
Litigation Friend

16.7 Application of this Chapter

This Chapter applies where a child must have a litigation friend to conduct proceedings on the child's behalf in accordance with rule 16.5.

Scope—Rule 16.7 applies where a child is not excused from having a litigation friend by r 16.6. FPR 2010, rr 16.8–16.11 set out the procedures for acquiring a litigation friend in various circumstances.

Practice direction—See FPR PD16A.

'Litigation friend'—Under the former Rules the term was 'next friend' for a petitioner or applicant and 'guardian ad litem' for a respondent. It is now 'litigation friend' for both.

Need for a solicitor—A litigation friend is not required to act by a solicitor but failure to instruct one may result in questions being raised as to the suitability of the litigation friend.

Withdrawal of proceedings—The permission of the court is likely to be required for withdrawal of an application where any party is a child – see FPR 2010, r 29.4, which sets out the procedure.

Approval of settlements—Unlike FPR 1991 and CPR 1998, there is no provision for the approval of any compromise or settlement where a party is a child. However, in most, if not all, cases the approval of the court will in any event be required to an order.

16.8 Stage of proceedings at which a litigation friend becomes necessary

(1) This rule does not apply in relation to a child who is conducting proceedings without a litigation friend in accordance with rule 16.6.

(2) A person may not without the permission of the court take any step in proceedings except –

- (a) filing an application form; or
- (b) applying for the appointment of a litigation friend under rule 16.11,

until the child has a litigation friend.

(3) Any step taken before a child has a litigation friend has no effect unless the court orders otherwise.

Scope—This rule expands on the general rule that a child may only conduct proceedings by a litigation friend. The only steps that may be taken following the issue of the proceedings and before such appointment are the filing of an application form including for appointment of a litigation friend. Any other step will be of no effect. But the court is given some discretion (see below).

Title of proceedings—The child should be referred to in the title as 'A.B. (a child by C.D. his/her litigation friend)' – FPR PD16A. A similar approach is adopted by the CPR.

Court's discretion—The court may permit proceedings involving a child to continue to a limited extent even though a litigation friend has not been appointed ('without the permission of the court': r 16.8(2)) and may validate proceedings that have continued in breach of the requirements ('unless the court orders otherwise'; r 16.8(3)).

Implications—It is possible to make urgent orders in proceedings involving a child before the appointment of a litigation friend, but the court should be made fully aware of all relevant circumstances. Where it is realised during the course of proceedings that a party is a child, provided everyone has acted in good faith and there has been no manifest disadvantage to the child, it is likely that the court will regularise the position retrospectively (*Masterman-Lister*, above). This might be the case where the proceedings have effectively been guided throughout by the person being appointed as litigation friend. Proceedings inappropriately conducted by a child or an unsuitable person on his behalf will be treated as being of no effect and further proceedings may then be commenced in proper form.

Attainment of majority—When the child attains majority, the appointment of the litigation friend comes to an end: FPR 2010, r 16.15.

16.9 Who may be a litigation friend for a child without a court order

(1) This rule does not apply if the court has appointed a person to be a litigation friend.

(2) A person may act as a litigation friend if that person –

- (a) can fairly and competently conduct proceedings on behalf of the child;
- (b) has no interest adverse to that of the child; and
- (c) subject to paragraph (3), undertakes to pay any costs which the child may be ordered to pay in relation to the proceedings, subject to any right that person may have to be repaid from the assets of the child.

(3) Paragraph (2)(c) does not apply to the Official Solicitor, an officer of the Service or a Welsh family proceedings officer.

Scope—This rule identifies the requirement of suitability for a person to be appointed as litigation friend.

Suitability—There is no other express restriction on who may be appointed, but the person must not be a child or protected party. The litigation friend should not have any personal involvement in the proceedings, but see *Spurling v Broadhurst* [2012] EWHC 2883 (Ch). If the court becomes aware of the person's unsuitability, it may remove him under r 16.12 and substitute another person as litigation friend, but there is no express duty to monitor the situation.

Official Solicitor—The Official Solicitor to the Senior Courts is only appointed by the court and the requirements of suitability do not apply.

Duty of litigation friend—The litigation friend must 'fairly and competently conduct proceedings on behalf of the child' and have 'no interest adverse to that of the child'. FPR PD16A, para 2.1 also provides that all steps and decisions the litigation friend takes in the proceedings must be taken for the benefit of the child.

Costs undertaking—The prospective litigation friend (unless the Official Solicitor or an officer as defined) must undertake to pay any costs that the child may be ordered to pay in relation to the proceedings, subject to any right to be repaid from the assets of the child. This amounts to a severe disincentive especially in cases where the child is without funds, and may create problems in finding a suitable litigation friend.

Under the CPR (and the previous Rules) such indemnity is only required from the party bringing the proceedings and not from a defendant or respondent. The court has a general discretion as to costs and will take into account the role of the litigation friend but may have power to impose a personal costs liability in case of misconduct quite apart from the undertaking.

16.10 How a person becomes a litigation friend without a court order

(1) If the court has not appointed a litigation friend, a person who wishes to act as such must file a certificate of suitability stating that that person satisfies the conditions specified in rule 16.9(2).

(2) The certificate of suitability must be filed at the time when the person who wishes to act as litigation friend first takes a step in the proceedings on behalf of the child.

(3) A court officer will send the certificate of suitability to every person on whom, in accordance with rule 6.28, the application form should be served.

(4) This rule does not apply to the Official Solicitor, an officer of the Service or a Welsh family proceedings officer.

Scope—This rule facilitates the appointment of a litigation friend by simply filing the required documents at the court office. It will be relied upon in most cases but does not apply if the court has already made such appointment.

Documents to be filed—The intended litigation friend must file a certificate of suitability: r 16.10(1). The Official Solicitor does not need to file any of these documents but his consent to act is required.

Certificate of suitability—This states that the person signing can 'fairly and competently conduct proceedings on behalf of the child' and has 'no interest adverse to that of the child'. It also contains the required undertaking as to costs. The certificate of suitability will be sent by the court to the persons to be served (which do not include the child).

Form N235 is used for civil proceedings and this confirms the maker's consent to act and belief that the party is a child. Form FP9 is specified for family proceedings in PD5A.

Time for filing—The required documents must be filed before any steps is taken as litigation friend: r 16.10(2).

Persons to be served (FPR 2010, r 6.28)—In the case of a child, these are a parent or guardian, or, if none, an adult with whom the child resides or in whose care he or she is: FPR 2010, r 6.14(1). The assumption is that such person will then take appropriate steps to arrange a representative (litigation friend). Service on a proper officer of the local social services authority when the child is in care may be sufficient.

Notice to child—No provision is made for the certificate of suitability to be sent to the child.

Official Solicitor—The Official Solicitor to the Senior Courts is not appointed under this provision.

PART III

16.11 Appointment of litigation friend by the court

(1) The court may, if the person to be appointed consents, make an order appointing as a litigation friend –

(a) the Official Solicitor;
(b) an officer of the Service or a Welsh family proceedings officer; or
(c) some other person.

(2) An order appointing a litigation friend may be made by the court of its own initiative or on the application of –

(a) a person who wishes to be a litigation friend; or
(b) a party to the proceedings.

(3) The court may at any time direct that a party make an application for an order under paragraph (2).

(4) An application for an order appointing a litigation friend must be supported by evidence.

(5) Unless the court directs otherwise, a person appointed under this rule to be a litigation friend for a child will be treated as a party for the purpose of any provision in these rules requiring a document to be served on, or sent to, or notice to be given to, a party to the proceedings.

(6) Subject to rule 16.9(3), the court may not appoint a litigation friend under this rule unless it is satisfied that the person to be appointed complies with the conditions specified in rule 16.9(2).

(7) This rule is without prejudice to rule 16.6.

Scope—This rule sets out the process whereby the court appoints a litigation friend.

The person appointed—Any adult who can 'fairly and competently conduct proceedings on behalf of the child' and has 'no interest adverse to that of the child' may be appointed. It is not necessary to approach the Official Solicitor in all cases and the court will not be concerned to ascertain whether he has declined to consent before appointing someone else.

Official Solicitor—See note under FPR 2010, r 15.6. The Official Solicitor to the Senior Courts may be contacted at Victory House, 30–34 Kingsway, London WC2B 6EX, DX 141423 Bloomsbury 7; tel 020 3681 2751 (healthcare and welfare) or 020 3681 2758 (property and affairs); fax 020 3681 2762.

Service—Once appointed the litigation friend is treated as a party for the purpose of service of documents.

16.12 Court's power to change litigation friend and to prevent person acting as litigation friend

(1) The court may –

(a) direct that a person may not act as a litigation friend;
(b) terminate a litigation friend's appointment; or
(c) appoint a new litigation friend in substitution for an existing one.

(2) An application for an order or direction under paragraph (1) must be supported by evidence.

(3) Subject to rule 16.9(3), the court may not appoint a litigation friend under this rule unless it is satisfied that the person to be appointed complies with the conditions specified in rule 16.9(2).

Scope—The court may prevent a person from being a litigation friend or replace a litigation friend during the course of proceedings. The court must be satisfied that the person to be appointed is suitable for appointment in accordance with the criteria set out in FPR 2010, r 16.9(2).

16.13 Appointment of litigation friend by court order – supplementary

(1) A copy of the application for an order under rule 16.11 or 16.12 must be sent by a court officer to every person on whom, in accordance with rule 6.28, the application form should be served.

(2) A copy of an application for an order under rule 16.12 must also be sent to –

(a) the person who is the litigation friend, or who is purporting to act as the litigation friend when the application is made; and
(b) the person, if not the applicant, who it is proposed should be the litigation friend.

Scope—This rule makes provision for service of an application for the appointment of a litigation friend or the change of a litigation friend. It must be sent by the court to the persons to be served under FPR 2010, r 6.28 but need not be sent to the child. The court has a wide discretion as to service and may vary the general rule or dispense with service in a particular instance (see FPR 2010, Pt 6).

Persons to be served (FPR 2010, r 6.28)—The application must be served on one of the child's parents or guardians or, if there is no such person, an adult with whom the child resides or in whose care the child is: FPR 2010, r 6.14(1). See note to FPR 2010, r 16.10 above.

Service of application for matrimonial order or civil partnership order—Special provisions apply to service of these proceedings on a child although the court has a general discretion. Neither the court nor the applicant personally must effect service: FPR 2010, r 6.5. The form must be endorsed with the notice set out in FPR PD6A, para 9.1 and the person commencing the proceedings must file a witness statement by the person on whom the application form was served stating whether the contents of the application form or the purpose and intention of the application were communicated to the child and, if not, why not: FPR 2010, r 6.14(7). This does not apply when the Official Solicitor is to be the litigation friend (presumably because his enquiries will have included the circumstances of the party): FPR 2010, r 6.14(8).

16.14 Powers and duties of litigation friend

(1) The litigation friend –

(a) has the powers and duties set out in Practice Direction 16A; and
(b) must exercise those powers and duties in accordance with Practice Direction 16A.

(2) Where the litigation friend is an officer of the Service or a Welsh family proceedings officer, rule 16.20 applies as it applies to a children's guardian appointed in accordance with Chapter 6.

Powers of litigation friend—The specific powers of the litigation friend are not expressly set out in the Rules or FPR PD16A, Pt 2, but as the appointment is to 'conduct proceedings ... on behalf' of the child, it is assumed that any act that in the ordinary conduct of any proceedings is required or authorised to be done by the child shall or may be done by the litigation friend. (That was the position under the former CCR Ord 10, r 12.)

Duties of litigation friend—FPR PD16A, Pt 2, para 2.1 merely restates that the litigation friend must 'fairly and competently conduct proceedings on behalf of the child', have 'no interest adverse to that of the child' and that all steps and decisions the litigation friend takes in the proceedings must be taken for the benefit of the child.

Administration of funds—The litigation friend will have no status in regard to the affairs of the child outside the proceedings in which he is appointed. So in that situation, if money is awarded to the child, to whom should it be paid? There is a danger that the money will simply be paid to the litigation friend with no further guidance, thereby creating a potential for uncertainty and abuse. Should the court not be given an express discretion to permit money to be paid to someone (eg a relative or carer) so that a receipt may be obtained from that person?

16.15 Procedure where appointment of litigation friend comes to an end

(1) When a child who is not a protected party reaches the age of 18, a litigation friend's appointment comes to an end.

(2) A court officer will send a notice to the other parties stating that the appointment of the child's litigation friend to act has ended.

Scope—Unlike the position in respect of a protected party who regains capacity, the appointment of a litigation friend for a child ceases automatically when the child attains 18 years.

Liability of litigation friend for costs—An individual who was appointed litigation friend will have had to give an undertaking as to costs pursuant to FPR 2010, r 16.9(2)(c). It is not clear whether, when discharged, the litigation friend is released from all liability for costs or only costs incurred from that date, although it is probably the latter.

Chapter 6
Children's Guardian Appointed under Rule 16.3

16.16 Application of this Chapter

This Chapter applies where the court must appoint a children's guardian in accordance with rule 16.3.

16.17 Who may be a children's guardian

Where the court is appointing a children's guardian under rule 16.3 it will appoint an officer of the Service or a Welsh family proceedings officer.

Who may be appointed—The children's guardian must either be an officer of Cafcass or a Welsh family proceedings officer. FPR 2010, r 16.36 provides that in adoption proceedings certain individuals are ineligible for selection to act as children's guardian in particular proceedings if they have a close connection with the local authority concerned in the case or with any local authority if they have actually been involved with the arrangements for the child in that capacity within the previous 5 years and probation officers unless they have not been involved with the child or his family in that capacity. FPR 2010, r 16.3(4) requires the court to consider re-appointing anyone who has acted as the children's guardian in previous proceedings; the requirement is to do no more than consider re-appointing such a person, but the court will usually lean in favour of such a re-appointment as the previous knowledge of the child and the earlier proceedings will tend to enable the guardian better to safeguard the child's interests in the new proceedings.

Duration of appointment—When appointing a guardian, the court may specify the length of the appointment; otherwise the appointment will last until terminated by the court (r 16.19). The latter will be the more usual course. The rule does not specify what procedure is to be followed to terminate an appointment except to require the reasons to be given once the decision has been taken (FPR 2010, r 16.19(2)). If a guardian does act manifestly contrary to the child's best interests, the court will remove him even though neither his good faith nor his diligence is in issue. In reaching a responsible and considered decision, on which another mind might possibly take a different view, a guardian does not act manifestly contrary to the child's best interests (*Re A (Conjoined Twins: Medical Treatment) (No 2)* [2001] 1 FLR 267, CA). Derivative applications, such as those to discharge a care order or to regulate contact with a child in care, are separate proceedings and not a continuation of the original care proceedings for this purpose (see the structure of s 41(6)); therefore the original guardian's appointment will not automatically carry over into the new proceedings. Once a care order has been made, the court has no power to add a direction that the guardian continue his involvement with the child (*Kent County Council v C* [1993] 1 FLR 308, FD). However, see Adoption & Children Act 2002 – review of cases of looked-after children under CA 1989, s 26A for the role of a guardian where an Independent Reviewing Officer makes a referral to Cafcass. Following the repeal of CJCSA 2000, s 12(5)(b) by ACA 2002, there is no longer jurisdiction for a court to provide for a continuing role for a children's guardian following the making of a supervision order and therefore *Re MH (A Child) and Re SB and MB (Children)* [2001] 2 FLR 1334, FD is no longer a correct statement of the law.

16.18 What the court or a court officer will do once the court has made a decision about appointing a children's guardian

(1) Where the court appoints a children's guardian under rule 16.3 a court officer will record the appointment and, as soon as practicable, will –

(a) inform the parties and either the Service or the Assembly; and

(b) unless it has already been sent, send the children's guardian a copy of the application and copies of any document filed with the court in the proceedings.

(2) A court officer has a continuing duty to send the children's guardian a copy of any other document filed with the court during the course of the proceedings.

16.19 Termination of the appointment of the children's guardian

(1) The appointment of a children's guardian under rule 16.3 continues for such time as is specified in the appointment or until terminated by the court.

(2) When terminating an appointment in accordance with paragraph (1), the court will give reasons for doing so, a note of which will be taken by the court or a court officer.

16.20 Powers and duties of the children's guardian

(1) The children's guardian is to act on behalf of the child upon the hearing of any application in proceedings to which this Chapter applies with the duty of safeguarding the interests of the child.

(2) The children's guardian must also provide the court with such other assistance as it may require.

(3) The children's guardian, when carrying out duties in relation to specified proceedings, other than placement proceedings, must have regard to the principle set out in section 1(2) and the matters set out in section 1(3)(a) to (f) of the 1989 Act as if for the word 'court' in that section there were substituted the words 'children's guardian'.

(4) The children's guardian, when carrying out duties in relation to proceedings to which Part 14 applies, must have regard to the principle set out in section 1(3) and the matters set out in section 1(4)(a) to (f) of the 2002 Act as if for the word 'court' in that section there were substituted the words 'children's guardian'.

(5) The children's guardian's duties must be exercised in accordance with Practice Direction 16A.

(6) A report to the court by the children's guardian is confidential.

Duties of children's guardian—CA 1989, s 41(2)(b) places the children's guardian under a duty to safeguard the interests of the child in the manner prescribed by rules of court. This rule prescribes how this general duty is to be performed and lays far more specific duties on the children's guardian In *R v Cornwall County Council ex parte G* [1992] 1 FLR 270, QBD, it was emphasised that guardians are independent in the performance of their duties; and it was accordingly held that a local authority had acted unlawfully in seeking to restrict the number of hours spent by guardians on each individual case.

Tandem model—In his View of 19 September 2016, the President considered the tandem model of a solicitor and a guardian for the child(ren) to be 'fundamental to a fair and just care system. Only the tandem model can ensure that the child's interests, wishes and feelings are correctly identified and properly represented. Without the tandem model the potential for injustice is much increased. I would therefore be strongly opposed to any watering down of this vital component of care proceedings' ([2016] Fam Law 1227). Guardians are now required to adopt a proportionate approach to their duties (e g are they required to attend every directions hearing or each day of a fact-finding hearing?).

PD16A—The further duties of a children's guardian are set out in FPR PD16A, paras 6.1–6.11. If a care order is made, the guardian has no role in relation to the way in which the local authority performs its duties under the order, and the court has no power to direct the continuing involvement of the guardian (*Kent County Council v C* [1993] 1 FLR 308, FD). The guardian may find himself requested to act as a collator of expert reports and to produce for the court a schedule of the areas of agreement and dispute (*Re C (Expert Evidence: Disclosure: Practice)* [1995] 1 FLR 204, FD). In *Re L (Care Proceedings: Disclosure to Third Party)* [2000] 1 FLR 913, FD, the guardian was asked, as an officer of the court, to disclose information concerning the psychiatric condition of a mother to the UK Central Council for Nursing, Midwifery and Health Visiting.

Duties of children's guardian where local authority documents appear to be protected by public interest immunity—See public interest immunity under CA 1989, s 42.

Guardian detached from child—Where the child's solicitor is taking instructions from the child himself, the children's guardian must inform the court and the role of the children's guardian remains wholly in the discretion of the court (FPR 2010, r 16.21). The court may feel that it would be beneficial, particularly if the detachment occurred at a late stage in the course of the proceedings, for the guardian to have full liberty to present a case as if he were a party to the proceedings (by calling evidence, cross-examining other parties' witnesses, addressing argument etc, for which purposes he would probably wish his own legal representation to be authorised under r 16.21(2)(c))) and by making a report in the usual way. This ensures that a neutral view of the best interests of the child is advanced since, where the guardian does retain a role, CA 1989, s 41(1)(b) continues to require him to perform it for the purpose of safeguarding the interests of the child. However, the court may think it right to permit only a smaller role or even to terminate the guardian's appointment altogether under FPR 2010, r 16.19.

In the ordinary case where conflict arises, the solicitor first appointed continues in the case putting the views, wishes and feelings of the child, and the guardian finds a fresh advocate to assist him in his continuing role as defined by the court; however, see *Re P (Representation)* [1996] 1 FLR 486, CA.

'the children's guardian must advise the court' (FPR PD16A, para 6.6)—It is not part of the children's guardian function to adopt a judicial role or to seek to assess material which he does not have the expertise to assess (*B v B (Child Abuse: Contact)* [1994] 2 FLR 713, FD). However, it is proper for the guardian to offer his opinion on child care and related matters to the court where he has the experience in his background to justify offering such an opinion (*G v A Borough Council* [2000] Fam Law 11, Cty Ct). Presumably the guardian can rely on such admissible expert evidence in forming his conclusions and recommendations, while acknowledging that the final decision is that of the court.

In *Re K (Supervision Orders)* [1999] 2 FLR 303, FD, Wall J held that a guardian's opinions about threshold criteria could not be ruled inadmissible, even if they were at odds with all the other parties. However, the guardian must be careful not to usurp the function of the court and would be wise to predicate any recommendations on the premise that the court will make certain findings of fact. The guardian had a duty to represent the child and put all matters relevant to the child's welfare before the court. The guardian is the child's protection against poor social work practice, procedural delay and collusive agreements. However, where the local authority and the mother had reached a sensible agreement which clearly protected the child and was in no sense collusive, the guardian should think long and hard before seeking to upset that agreement or before putting forward contentious alternative proposals.

Child's capacity to refuse to be examined etc (FPR 2010, r 4.11A(4)(a))—CA 1989, s 38(6) provides that a child of sufficient understanding may refuse to submit to an examination or assessment directed by a court making an interim care or supervision order; s 43(8) allows a child who is of sufficient understanding to make an informed decision to refuse to submit to a medical or psychiatric examination or other assessment which would otherwise have been authorised by a child assessment order. In *Re H (A Minor) (Care Proceedings: Child's Wishes)* [1993] 1 FLR 440, FD, at [449A], Thorpe J said, in relation to the child's capacity under CA 1989, s 38(6) to make an informed decision whether to refuse to submit to a psychiatric examination, that 'the level of understanding that enables a child to make an informed decision whether to refuse to submit to a psychiatric examination is in all practical senses a much higher level of understanding than is required to enable him to give instructions to a solicitor on his own behalf'. It is useful to compare this with the power of the court, in exercising the inherent jurisdiction of the High Court, to override the child's wishes in respect of medical treatment (see *Re W (A Minor) (Consent to Medical Treatment)* [1993] 1 FLR 1, CA).

Confidentiality—The guardian's report presumably comes within the ambit of 'any information relating to the proceedings' within the provisions of FPR 2010, r 12.73(1) and therefore can be communicated by the parties and other specified people to other specified people for specified purposes without needing the permission of the court – see further rr 12.73, 12.75 and PD12G.

Where a children's guardian becomes aware of information that the child does not wish to be revealed to another party in the proceedings, it can never be proper for the guardian to promise the child that the information will be withheld from the court. In an unusually sensitive case involving an older child, a guardian could properly tell the child that the judge would be told that the child did not wish the information to be disclosed to a particular party, and why. In such a case, the court was required to balance the right of a properly concerned party to disclosure of information submitted to the court on which the judge's conclusion might in some measure be based, against the paramount interest of the child (*Re C (Disclosure)* [1996] 1 FLR 797, FD). Such cases should be transferred to the High Court.

Written report by children's guardian—It is a matter for the discretion of the court whether a report of a children's guardian in public law proceedings can be made available to a court hearing related private law proceedings and to the parties thereto. If two courts are dealing with different sets of proceedings concerning siblings (an exceptional situation, as it is normally right for one court to deal with all proceedings where siblings are concerned), the report should normally be made available to both (*W v Wakefield City Council* [1995] 1 FLR 170, FD).

Attendance of child at court—While the court can allow the child who is the subject of an application to attend court, it must always bear in mind that attendance is likely to be harmful to the child and should only permit it if satisfied that it is in the interests of the child (*Re W (Secure Accommodation Order: Attendance at Court)* [1994] 2 FLR 1092, FD set out under CA 1989, s 25 and see, further, **Use of the power to exclude** under FPR 2010, r 12.14).

'notify' and 'notification' (FPR 2010, r 4.11A(6))—It is submitted that these words do not attract FPR 2010, r 10.7 (mode of giving notice) because, although it might have been argued that 'notify' was cognate with 'notice', the use of 'notification' rather than 'notice' in conjunction with it indicates the contrary.

Inspection of records (FPR 2010, r 4.11A(9))—See also CA 1989, ss 41 and 42. A children's guardian is entitled to see case records prepared by the local authority giving detailed information concerning prospective adopters and to include the relevant information derived from it in his report to the court (*Re T (A Minor) (Guardian ad Litem: Case Record)* [1994] 1 FLR 632, CA).

Where court differs from children's guardian's advice—The court is not bound to follow the recommendation of the children's guardian but, just as with a welfare officer or children and family reporter, must give careful consideration to any argument advanced by him and, where it differs, must explain its reasons carefully (*S v Oxfordshire County Council* [1993] 1 FLR 452, FD).

Duties of children's guardian and local authority to consult one another—Guardians should think long and hard before opposing an agreement between the local authority and the parents of a child subject to care proceedings if it appears to be sensible and appears to protect the child. However, where the guardian has considered the matter carefully and has reached the conclusion that the course proposed by the local authority does not protect the child, the guardian's duty is to safeguard the interests of the child and to put before the court her view as to how best the child's welfare is to be promoted (*Re N (Leave to Withdraw Care Proceedings)* [2000] 1 FLR 134, FD; *Re K (Supervision Orders)* [1999] 2 FLR 303, FD). Note, however, the observations of Macur LJ in *MW and Hertfordshire County Council v A & V and Mr & Mrs J* [2014] EWCA Civ 405 set out in the notes to r 16.3 under **Status of a Children's Guardian**.

16.21 Where the child instructs a solicitor or conducts proceedings on the child's own behalf

(1) Where it appears to the children's guardian that the child –

- (a) is instructing a solicitor direct; or
- (b) intends to conduct and is capable of conducting the proceedings on that child's own behalf,

the children's guardian must inform the court of that fact.

(2) Where paragraph (1) applies the children's guardian –

- (a) must perform such additional duties as the court may direct;
- (b) must take such part in the proceedings as the court may direct; and
- (c) may, with the permission of the court, have legal representation in the conduct of those duties.

Chapter 7
Children's Guardian Appointed under Rule 16.4

16.22 Application of this Chapter

This Chapter applies where the court must appoint a children's guardian under rule 16.4.

PD16A—The circumstances when a child should be made a party to proceedings, the appointment of a children's guardian and the duties once appointed are set out in FPR PD16A, paras 7.1–7.19.

16.23 Stage of proceedings at which a children's guardian becomes necessary

(1) This rule does not apply in relation to a child who is conducting proceedings without a children's guardian in accordance with rule 16.6.

(2) A person may not without the permission of the court take any step in proceedings except –

- (a) filing an application form; or

(b) applying for the appointment of a children's guardian under rule 16.24,

until the child has a children's guardian.

(3) Any step taken before a child has a children's guardian has no effect unless the court orders otherwise.

16.24 Appointment of a children's guardian

(1) The court may make an order appointing as a children's guardian, an officer of the Service or a Welsh family proceedings officer or, if the person to be appointed consents –

(a) a person other than the Official Solicitor; or
(b) the Official Solicitor.

(2) An order appointing a children's guardian may be made by the court of its own initiative or on the application of –

(a) a person who wishes to be a children's guardian; or
(b) a party to the proceedings.

(3) The court may at any time direct that a party make an application for an order under paragraph (2).

(4) An application for an order appointing a children's guardian must be supported by evidence.

(5) The court may not appoint a children's guardian under this rule unless it is satisfied that that person –

(a) can fairly and competently conduct proceedings on behalf of the child;
(b) has no interest adverse to that of the child; and
(c) subject to paragraph (6), undertakes to pay any costs which the child may be ordered to pay in relation to the proceedings, subject to any right that person may have to be repaid from the assets of the child.

(6) Paragraph (5)(c) does not apply to the Official Solicitor, an officer of the Service or a Welsh family proceedings officer.

(7) This rule is without prejudice to rule 16.6 and rule 9.11.

(Rule 9.11 provides for a child to be separately represented in certain applications for a financial remedy.)

PD16A—The duties of the children's guardian once appointed are set out in FPR PD16A, paras 7.6, 7.7. A children's guardian who is an officer of Cafcass or a Welsh family proceedings officer has, in addition, the duties set out in paras 6.1–6.11.

Hague Convention proceedings—A child should only be made party to Convention proceedings in exceptional circumstances (*Re H (Abduction)* [2007] 1 FLR 242, CA). See also 'the child's objections' under CACA 1985, Sch 1, Art 13.

Cafcass/Official Solicitor—Where it is felt that a child needs separate representation, consideration should first be given to appointing an officer of Cafcass as guardian. If Cafcass is unable to provide a guardian, r 16.24(1) makes further provision for the appointment of a guardian. See **'some other proper person'**, below. See *Practice Note of January 2017 (The Official Solicitor to the Senior Courts: Appointment in Family Proceedings and Proceedings under the Inherent Jurisdiction in Relation to Adults)* and *CAFCASS and the National Assembly for Wales Practice Note of June 2006 (Appointment of Guardians in Private Law Proceedings)*.

'some other proper person' (r 16.24(1)(a))—This sub-rule permits a solicitor to act as solicitor and guardian (*Re N (Residence: Appointment of Solicitor: Placement with Extended Family)* [2001] 1 FLR 1028, CA). In *Re K (Replacement of Guardian ad Litem)* [2001] 1 FLR 663, CA, it was held that such a course is generally undesirable. The use of the National Youth Advocacy Service (NYAS) has been endorsed in recent Court of Appeal decisions such as *Re H (National Youth Advocacy Service)* [2007] 1 FLR 1028, CA and *Re B (A Child)* [2006] EWCA Civ 716.

16.25 Court's power to change children's guardian and to prevent person acting as children's guardian

(1) The court may –

(a) direct that a person may not act as a children's guardian;
(b) terminate the appointment of a children's guardian; or
(c) appoint a new children's guardian in substitution for an existing one.

PART III

(2) An application for an order or direction under paragraph (1) must be supported by evidence.

(3) Subject to rule 16.24(6), the court may not appoint a children's guardian under this rule unless it is satisfied that the person to be appointed complies with the conditions specified in rule 16.24(5).

PD16A—The change of a children's guardian and to prevent a person acting as a children's guardian are set out in FPR PD16A, paras 7.17–7.19.

16.26 Appointment of children's guardian by court order – supplementary

(1) A copy of the application for an order under rule 16.24 or 16.25 must be sent by a court officer to every person on whom, in accordance with rule 6.28, the application form should be served.

(2) A copy of an application for an order under rule 16.25 must also be sent to –

(a) the person who is the children's guardian, or who is purporting to act as the children's guardian when the application is made; and

(b) the person, if not the applicant, who it is proposed should be the children's guardian.

16.27 Powers and duties of children's guardian

(1) The children's guardian –

(a) has the powers and duties set out in Practice Direction 16A; and

(b) must exercise those powers and duties in accordance with Practice Direction 16A.

(2) Where the children's guardian is an officer of the Service or a Welsh family proceedings officer, rule 16.20 applies to a children's guardian appointed in accordance with this Chapter as it applies to a children's guardian appointed in accordance with Chapter 6.

PD16A—The powers and duties of a children's guardian appointed under FPR 2010, r 16.4 are set out in FPR PD16A, paras 7.6, 7.7. A children's guardian who is an officer of Cafcass or a Welsh family proceedings officer has, in addition, the duties set out in paras 6.1–6.11: see the notes to FPR 2010, r 16.20 above.

16.28 Procedure where appointment of children's guardian comes to an end

(1) When a child reaches the age of 18, the appointment of a children's guardian comes to an end.

(2) A court officer will send a notice to the other parties stating that the appointment of the child's children's guardian to act has ended.

Chapter 8
Duties of Solicitor Acting for the Child

16.29 Solicitor for child

(1) Subject to paragraphs (2) and (4), a solicitor appointed –

(a) under section 41(3) of the 1989 Act; or

(b) by the children's guardian in accordance with the Practice Direction 16A,

must represent the child in accordance with instructions received from the children's guardian.

(2) If a solicitor appointed as mentioned in paragraph (1) considers, having taken into account the matters referred to in paragraph (3), that the child –

(a) wishes to give instructions which conflict with those of the children's guardian; and

(b) is able, having regard to the child's understanding, to give such instructions on the child's own behalf,

the solicitor must conduct the proceedings in accordance with instructions received from the child.

(3) The matters the solicitor must take into account for the purposes of paragraph (2) are –

(a) the views of the children's guardian; and

(b) any direction given by the court to the children's guardian concerning the part to be taken by the children's guardian in the proceedings.

(4) Where –

(a) no children's guardian has been appointed; and

(b) the condition in section 41(4)(b) of the 1989 Act is satisfied,

a solicitor appointed under section 41(3) of the 1989 Act must represent the child in accordance with instructions received from the child.

(5) Where a solicitor appointed as mentioned in paragraph (1) receives no instructions under paragraphs (1), (2) or (4), the solicitor must represent the child in furtherance of the best interests of the child.

(6) A solicitor appointed under section 41(3) of the 1989 Act or by the children's guardian in accordance with Practice Direction 16A must serve documents, and accept service of documents, on behalf of the child in accordance with rule 6.31 and, where the child has not been served separately and has sufficient understanding, advise the child of the contents of any document so served.

(7) Where the child wishes an appointment of a solicitor –

(a) under section 41(3) of the 1989 Act; or
(b) by the children's guardian in accordance with the Practice Direction 16A,

to be terminated –

(i) the child may apply to the court for an order terminating the appointment; and
(ii) the solicitor and the children's guardian will be given an opportunity to make representations.

(8) Where the children's guardian wishes an appointment of a solicitor under section 41(3) of the 1989 Act to be terminated –

(a) the children's guardian may apply to the court for an order terminating the appointment; and
(b) the solicitor and, if of sufficient understanding, the child, will be given an opportunity to make representations.

(9) When terminating an appointment in accordance with paragraph (7) or (8), the court will give its reasons for so doing, a note of which will be taken by the court or a court officer.

(10) The court or a court officer will record the appointment under section 41(3) of the 1989 Act or the refusal to make the appointment.

PART III

Solicitors to whom the rule applies—This rule applies to two types of solicitor –

(a) those appointed under CA 1989, s 41(3) which, in combination with s 41(4), enables the court to appoint a solicitor for a child who does not already have one if:
(i) no children's guardian has yet been appointed;
(ii) the child has sufficient understanding to instruct a solicitor and wishes to do so; and
(iii) it appears to the court that it would be in the child's best interests for him to be represented by a solicitor.

(b) those appointed by the child's guardian in accordance with FPR 2010, r 16.21.

'able … to give such instructions on his own behalf' (FPR 2010, r 4.12(1)(a))—Guidance on the application of the test in r 16.29(2) was given in *Re H (A Minor) (Care Proceedings: Child's Wishes)* [1993] 1 FLR 440, FD. Assistance may also be obtained from authorities dealing with the understanding of a child in other contexts under CA 1989 and the associated rules; in particular see *Mabon v Mabon* [2005] 2 FLR 1011, CA, set out in 'sufficient understanding' under r 16.6. In April 2010, the President issued *Guidelines for Judges Meeting Children who are Subject to Family Proceedings* (see Part V). The judge's decision whether or not personally to interview a child is, above all, a question for the exercise of judicial discretion. It is becoming more common for judges to see children in private in the course of proceedings affecting the child's welfare. ECHR 1950, Art 12 provides that a child should be heard in any judicial proceedings affecting him, either directly or through a representative. Similarly, the United Nations Convention on the Rights of the Child 1989, Art 12 requires that a child who is capable of forming his own views has the right to express them freely in all matters affecting him. *Mabon v Mabon* reviewed the principles that apply when the court considers how best to ensure that the child's views are heard in such cases. Further important guidance from the Court of Appeal is contained in *Re W (Leave to Remove)* [2008] 2 FLR 1170, CA and in *B v B (Minors) (Interviews and Listing Arrangements)* [1994] 2 FLR 489, CA.

Opportunity to make representations (r 16.29(7),(8))—The 'opportunity to make representations' is a flexible concept that leaves the question of whether they should be oral or written, and the time within which they should be made, to be determined by the court according to the context in which the question arises.

Reasons for terminating appointment of solicitor or children's guardian to be given by the court (r 16.29(9))—Where the court terminates the appointment of a solicitor or children's guardian, this rule requires the court to give its reasons for doing so, and requires that a note of the reasons be taken by the court or by the proper officer. The simple fact that the court has ordered a termination of the solicitor's appointment is to be formally recorded in Form C48. No doubt the court's written reasons will therefore form an appendix to the duly completed Form C48.

Appeal hearings—The general admonition against unnecessary representation should not be taken to bar or fetter the responsibility of the children's representatives to take a firm line at the appeal hearing: *Re H (Children)* [2012] EWCA Civ 743.

Chapter 9
Reporting Officer

16.30 When the court appoints a reporting officer

In proceedings to which Part 14 applies, the court will appoint a reporting officer where –

(a) it appears that a parent or guardian of the child is willing to consent to the placing of the child for adoption, to the making of an adoption order or to a section 84 order; and
(b) that parent or guardian is in England or Wales.

16.31 Appointment of the same reporting officer in respect of two or more parents or guardians

The same person may be appointed as the reporting officer for two or more parents or guardians of the child.

16.32 The duties of the reporting officer

(1) The reporting officer must witness the signature by a parent or guardian on the document in which consent is given to –

(a) the placing of the child for adoption;
(b) the making of an adoption order; or
(c) the making of a section 84 order.

(2) The reporting officer must carry out such other duties as are set out in Practice Direction 16A.

(3) A report to the court by the reporting officer is confidential.

(4) The reporting officer's duties must be exercised in accordance with Practice Direction 16A.

Chapter 10
Children and Family Reporter and Welfare Officer

16.33 Request by court for a welfare report in respect of the child

(1) Where the court is considering an application for an order in proceedings, the court may ask –

(a) in proceedings to which Parts 12 and 14 apply, a children and family reporter; or
(b) in proceedings to which Part 12 applies, a welfare officer,

to prepare a report on matters relating to the welfare of the child, and, in this rule, the person preparing the report is called 'the officer'.

(2) It is the duty of the officer to –

(a) comply with any request for a report under this rule; and
(b) provide the court with such other assistance as it may require.

(3) A report to the court under this rule is confidential.

(4) The officer, when carrying out duties in relation to proceedings under the 1989 Act, must have regard to the principle set out in section 1(2) and the matters set out in section 1(3)(a) to (f) of that Act as if for the word 'court' in that section there were substituted the words 'children and family reporter' or 'welfare officer' as the case may be.

(5) A party may question the officer about oral or written advice tendered by that officer to the court.

(6) The court officer will notify the officer of a direction given at a hearing at which –

(a) the officer is not present; and

(b) the welfare report is considered.

(7) The officer's duties must be exercised in accordance with Practice Direction 16A

('children and family reporter' and 'welfare officer' are defined in rule 2.3)

Meaning of 'welfare officer' (r 16.33(1)(b))—The CJCSA 2000 introduced the Children and Family Court Advisory and Support Service (Cafcass). The term 'officer of the service' is defined in CJCSA 2000, s 11(3), and is used to denote the various categories of people appointed to undertake investigations and prepare reports for the court in children and family cases. Where a court directs, pursuant to s 7(1)(b), a local authority to report upon matters relating to the welfare of the child, the author of the report is described as a 'welfare officer'. The term 'welfare officer' is retained only for the purpose of describing that local authority officer in those specified circumstances. Where the court appoints an officer of the service to report to it under CA 1989, s 7(1)(a) he is called a 'children and family reporter'.

PD16A—FPR PD16A, paras 9.1–9.4 set out the powers and duties of a children and family reporter and welfare officer.

Chapter 11
Parental Order Reporter

PART III

16.34 When the court appoints a parental order reporter

In proceedings to which Part 13 applies, the court will appoint a parental order reporter in accordance with rule 13.5.

16.35 Powers and duties of the parental order reporter

(1) The parental order reporter is to act on behalf of the child upon the hearing of any application in proceedings to which Part 13 applies with the duty of safeguarding the interests of the child.

(2) The parental order reporter must –

(a) investigate the matters set out in sections 54(1) to (8) of the 2008 Act;

(b) so far as the parental order reporter considers necessary, investigate any matter contained in the application form or other matter which appears relevant to the making of the parental order; and

(c) advise the court on whether there is any reason under section 1 of the 2002 Act (as applied with modifications by the Human Fertilisation and Embryology (Parental Orders) Regulations 2010) to refuse the parental order.

(3) The parental order reporter must also provide the court with such other assistance as it may require.

(4) The parental order reporter's duties must be exercised in accordance with Practice Direction 16A.

(5) A report to the court by the parental order reporter is confidential.

Parental order report—See also, under FPR 2010, r 13.12 and HFEA 2008, s 54.

Chapter 12
Supplementary Appointment Provisions

16.36 Persons who may not be appointed as children's guardian, reporting officer or children and family reporter

(1) In specified proceedings (except where paragraph (2) applies), adoption proceedings or proceedings for a section 84 order or a section 89 order, no person may be appointed as a children's guardian, reporting officer or children and family reporter who –

(a) is a member, officer or servant of a local authority which is a party to the proceedings;

(b) is, or has been, a member, officer or servant of a local authority or voluntary organisation who has been directly concerned in that capacity in arrangements relating to the care, accommodation or welfare of the child during the 5 years prior to the start of the proceedings; or

(c) is a serving probation officer who has, in that capacity, been previously concerned with the child or the child's family.

(2) In placement proceedings, a person described in paragraph (1)(b) or (c) may not be appointed as a children's guardian, reporting officer or children and family reporter.

Amendments—SI 2012/679.

16.37 Appointment of the same person as children's guardian, reporting officer and children and family reporter

The same person may be appointed to act as one or more of the following –

(a) the children's guardian;
(b) the reporting officer; and
(c) the children and family reporter.

Chapter 13
Officers of the Service, Welsh Family Proceedings Officers and Local Authority Officers: Further Duties

16.38 Officers of the Service, Welsh family proceedings officers and local authority officers acting under certain duties

(1) This rule applies when –

(a) an officer of the Service or a Welsh family proceedings officer is acting under a duty in accordance with –
   (i) section 11E(7) of the 1989 Act (providing the court with information as to the making of an activity direction or an activity condition);
   (ii) section 11G(2) of the 1989 Act (monitoring compliance with an activity direction or an activity condition);
   (iii) section 11H(2) of the 1989 Act (monitoring compliance with a child arrangements order);
   (iv) section 11L(5) of the 1989 Act (providing the court with information as to the making of an enforcement order);
   (v) section 11M(1) of the 1989 Act (monitoring compliance with an enforcement order);
   (vi) section 16(6) of the 1989 Act (providing a report to the court in accordance with a direction in a family assistance order); and
   (vii) section 16A of the 1989 Act (making a risk assessment); and
(b) a local authority officer is acting under a duty in accordance with section 16(6) of the 1989 Act (providing a report to the court in accordance with a direction in a family assistance order).

(2) In this rule, –

(a) 'activity direction', 'activity condition' and 'enforcement order' have the meanings given in rule 12.2; and
(b) references to 'the officer' are to the officer of the Service, Welsh family proceedings officer or local authority officer referred to in paragraph (1).

(3) In exercising the duties referred to in paragraph (1), the officer must have regard to the principle set out in section 1(2) of the 1989 Act and the matters set out in section 1(3)(a) to (f) of the 1989 Act as if for the word 'court' in that section there were substituted the words 'officer of the Service, Welsh family proceedings officer or local authority officer'.

(4) The officer's duties referred to in paragraph (1) must be exercised in accordance with Practice Direction 16A.

Amendments—SI 2014/843.

Definitions—'activity condition', 'activity direction', 'enforcement order': FPR 2010, r 12.2. See also CA 1989, ss 11E–11M.

Family assistance order report—See **Practice Direction** under CA 1989, s 16.

Risk assessments—See **Risk assessments** under CA 1989, s 16 and see s 16A. See also FPR PD16A, paras 11.1–11.7.

'the principle set out in section 1(2)' (r 16.38(3))—'The delay principle'.

'the matters set out in section 1(3)(a) to (f)' (r 16.38(3))—This rule makes it clear that officers must have regard to the welfare checklist when carrying out all aspects of their duties under this rule. See CA 1989, s 1(3)(a)–(f).

Practice Direction 16A—FPR PD16A sets out what is required of officers in the performance of their duties.

Chapter 14
Enforcement Orders and Financial Compensation Orders: Persons Notified

16.39 Application for enforcement orders and financial compensation orders: duties of the person notified

(1) This rule applies where a person who was the child's children's guardian, litigation friend or legal representative in the proceedings in which a child arrangements order was made has been notified of an application for an enforcement order or for a financial compensation order as required by Practice Direction 12C.

(2) The person who has been notified of the application must –

(a) consider whether it is in the best interests of the child for the child to be made a party to the proceedings for an enforcement order or a financial compensation order (as applicable); and

(b) before the date fixed for the first hearing in the case notify the court, orally or in writing, of the opinion reached on the question, together with the reasons for this opinion.

(3) In this rule, 'enforcement order' and 'financial compensation order' have the meanings given in rule 12.2.

Amendments—SI 2014/843.

Definitions—'child', 'children's guardian', 'litigation friend', 'legal representative': r 2.3.

Enforcement orders—See CA 1989, s 11J–11N.

Financial compensation orders—See CA 1989, ss 11O–11P

Practice Direction 12C—FPR PD12C supplements r 12.8 and sets out the following requirements for the service of an application in certain proceedings relating to children: the persons who are to receive a copy of the application form (para 1.1); the time for serving the application (para 2.1); and the persons who are to receive a copy of Form C6A (Notice to Non-Parties).

Procedure—See Procedural Guide D8.

Practice Direction 16A – Representation of Children

This Practice Direction supplements FPR Part 16

PART 1: GENERAL

Reference in title of proceedings

1.1 Where a litigation friend represents a child in family proceedings in accordance with rule 16.5 and Chapter 5 of Part 16, the child should be referred to in the title of the proceedings as 'A.B. (a child by C.D. his/her litigation friend)'.

1.2 Where a children's guardian represents a child in family proceedings in accordance with rule 16.4 and Chapter 7 of Part 16, the child should be referred to in the title as 'A.B. (a child by C.D. his/her children's guardian)'.

1.3 A child who is conducting proceedings on that child's own behalf should be referred to in the title as 'A.B. (a child)'.

PART 2: LITIGATION FRIEND

Duties of the litigation friend

2.1 It is the duty of a litigation friend fairly and competently to conduct proceedings on behalf of the child. The litigation friend must have no interest in the proceedings adverse to that of the child and all steps and decisions the litigation friend takes in the proceedings must be taken for the benefit of the child.

2.2 …

Becoming a litigation friend without a court order

3.1 In order to become a litigation friend without a court order the person who wishes to act as litigation friend must file a certificate of suitability –

- (a) stating that the litigation friend consents to act;
- (b) stating that the litigation friend knows or believes that the [applicant][respondent] is a child to whom rule 16.5 and Chapter 5 of Part 16 apply;
- (c) stating that the litigation friend can fairly and competently conduct proceedings on behalf of the child and has no interest adverse to that of the child;
- (d) undertaking to pay any costs which the child may be ordered to pay in relation to the proceedings, subject to any right the litigation friend may have to be repaid from the assets of the child; and
- (e) which the litigation friend has verified by a statement of truth.

3.2 Paragraph 3.1 does not apply to the Official Solicitor, an officer of the Service or a Welsh family proceedings officer.

3.3 The court officer will send the certificate of suitability to one of the child's parents or guardians or, if there is no parent or guardian, to the person with whom the child resides or in whose care the child is.

3.4 The litigation friend must file the certificate of suitability at a time when the litigation friend first takes a step in the proceedings on behalf of the child.

Application for a court order appointing a litigation friend

4.1 An application for a court order appointing a litigation friend should be made in accordance with Part 18 and must be supported by evidence.

4.2 The court officer must serve the application notice on the persons referred to in paragraph 3.3.

4.3 The evidence in support must satisfy the court that the proposed litigation friend –

- (a) consents to act;
- (b) can fairly and competently conduct proceedings on behalf of the child;
- (c) has no interest adverse to that of the child; and
- (d) undertakes to pay any costs which the child may be ordered to pay in relation to the proceedings, subject to any right the litigation friend may have to be repaid from the assets of the child.

4.4 Paragraph 4.3(d) does not apply to the Official Solicitor, an officer of the Service of a Welsh family proceedings officer.

4.5 The proposed litigation friend may be one of the persons referred to in paragraph 3.3 where appropriate, or otherwise may be the Official Solicitor, an officer of the Service or a Welsh family proceedings officer. Where it is sought to appoint the Official Solicitor, an officer of the Service or a Welsh family proceedings officer, provision should be made for payment of that person's charges.

Change of litigation friend and prevention of person acting as litigation friend.

5.1 Where an application is made for an order under rule 16.12, the application must set out the reasons for seeking it and the application must be supported by evidence.

5.2 Subject to paragraph 4.4, if the order sought is substitution of a new litigation friend for an existing one, the evidence must satisfy the court of the matters set out in paragraph 4.3.

5.3 The court officer will serve the application notice on –

(a) the persons referred to in paragraph 3.3; and
(b) the litigation friend or person purporting to act as litigation friend.

PART 3: CHILDREN'S GUARDIAN APPOINTED UNDER RULE 16.3

How the children's guardian exercises duties – investigations and appointment of solicitor

6.1 The children's guardian must make such investigations as are necessary to carry out the children's guardian's duties and must, in particular –

(a) contact or seek to interview such persons as the children's guardian thinks appropriate or as the court directs; and
(b) obtain such professional assistance as is available which the children's guardian thinks appropriate or which the court directs be obtained.

6.2 The children's guardian must –

(a) appoint a solicitor for the child unless a solicitor has already been appointed;
(b) give such advice to the child as is appropriate having regard to that child's understanding; and
(c) where appropriate instruct the solicitor representing the child on all matters relevant to the interests of the child arising in the course of proceedings, including possibilities for appeal.

6.3 Where the children's guardian is authorised in the terms mentioned by and in accordance with section 15(1) of the Criminal Justice and Court Services Act 2000 or section 37(1) of the Children Act 2004 (right of officer of the Service or Welsh family proceedings officer to conduct litigation or exercise a right of audience), paragraph 6.2(a) will not apply if the children's guardian intends to have conduct of the proceedings on behalf of the child unless –

(a) the child wishes to instruct a solicitor direct; and
(b) the children's guardian or the court considers that the child is of sufficient understanding to do so.

6.4 Where rule 16.21 (Where the child instructs a solicitor or conducts proceedings on the child's own behalf) applies, the duties set out in paragraph 6.2(a) and (c) do not apply.

How the children's guardian exercises duties – attendance at court, advice to the court and reports

6.5 The children's guardian or the solicitor appointed under section 41(3) of the 1989 Act or in accordance with paragraph 6.2(a) must attend all directions hearings unless the court directs otherwise.

6.6 The children's guardian must advise the court on the following matters –

(a) whether the child is of sufficient understanding for any purpose including the child's refusal to submit to a medical or psychiatric examination or other assessment that the court has the power to require, direct or order;
(b) the wishes of the child in respect of any matter relevant to the proceedings including that child's attendance at court;
(c) the appropriate forum for the proceedings;
(d) the appropriate timing of the proceedings or any part of them;
(e) the options available to it in respect of the child and the suitability of each such option including what order should be made in determining the application; and
(f) any other matter on which the court seeks advice or on which the children's guardian considers that the court should be informed.

PART III

6.7 The advice given under paragraph 6.6 may, subject to any direction of the court, be given orally or in writing. If the advice is given orally, a note of it must be taken by the court or the court officer.

6.8 The children's guardian must –

(a) unless the court directs otherwise, file a written report advising on the interests of the child in accordance with the timetable set by the court; and

(b) in proceedings to which Part 14 applies, where practicable, notify any person the joining of whom as a party to those proceedings would be likely, in the opinion of the children's guardian, to safeguard the interests of the child, of the court's power to join that person as a party under rule 14.3 and must inform the court –

(i) of any notification;

(ii) of anyone whom the children's guardian attempted to notify under this paragraph but was unable to contact; and

(iii) of anyone whom the children's guardian believes may wish to be joined to the proceedings.

(Part 18 sets out the procedure for making an application to be joined as a party in proceedings.)

How the children's guardian exercises duties – service of documents and inspection of records

6.9 The children's guardian must serve and accept service of documents on behalf of the child in accordance with rule 6.31 and, where the child has not himself been served and has sufficient understanding, advise the child of the contents of any document so served.

6.10 Where the children's guardian inspects records of the kinds referred to in –

(a) section 42 of the 1989 Act (right to have access to local authority records); or

(b) section 103 of the 2002 Act (right to have access to adoption agency records)

the children's guardian must bring all records and documents which may, in the opinion of the children's guardian, assist in the proper determination of the proceedings to the attention of –

(i) the court; and

(ii) unless the court directs otherwise, the other parties to the proceedings.

How the children's guardian exercises duties – communication of a court's decision to the child

6.11 The children's guardian must ensure that, in relation to a decision made by the court in the proceedings –

(a) if the children's guardian considers it appropriate to the age and understanding of the child, the child is notified of that decision; and

(b) if the child is notified of the decision, it is explained to the child in a manner appropriate to that child's age and understanding.

PART 4: APPOINTMENT OF CHILDREN'S GUARDIAN UNDER RULE 16.4

Section 1 – When a child should be made a party to proceedings

7.1 Making the child a party to the proceedings is a step that will be taken only in cases which involve an issue of significant difficulty and consequently will occur in only a minority of cases. Before taking the decision to make the child a party, consideration should be given to whether an alternative route might be preferable, such as asking an officer of the Service or a Welsh family proceedings officer to carry out further work or by making a referral to social services or, possibly, by obtaining expert evidence.

7.2 The decision to make the child a party will always be exclusively that of the court, made in the light of the facts and circumstances of the particular case. The following are offered, solely by way of guidance, as circumstances which may justify the making of such an order –

(a) where an officer of the Service or Welsh family proceedings officer has notified the court that in the opinion of that officer the child should be made a party;

(b) where the child has a standpoint or interest which is inconsistent with or incapable of being represented by any of the adult parties;

(c) where there is an intractable dispute over residence or contact, including where all contact has ceased, or where there is irrational but implacable hostility to contact or where the child may be suffering harm associated with the contact dispute;

(d) where the views and wishes of the child cannot be adequately met by a report to the court;

(e) where an older child is opposing a proposed course of action;

(f) where there are complex medical or mental health issues to be determined or there are other unusually complex issues that necessitate separate representation of the child;

(g) where there are international complications outside child abduction, in particular where it may be necessary for there to be discussions with overseas authorities or a foreign court;

(h) where there are serious allegations of physical, sexual or other abuse in relation to the child or there are allegations of domestic violence not capable of being resolved with the help of an officer of the Service or Welsh family proceedings officer;

(i) where the proceedings concern more than one child and the welfare of the children is in conflict or one child is in a particularly disadvantaged position;

(j) where there is a contested issue about scientific testing.

7.3 It must be recognised that separate representation of the child may result in a delay in the resolution of the proceedings. When deciding whether to direct that a child be made a party, the court will take into account the risk of delay or other facts adverse to the welfare of the child. The court's primary consideration will be the best interests of the child.

7.4 When a child is made a party and a children's guardian is to be appointed –

(a) consideration should first be given to appointing an officer of the Service or Welsh family proceedings officer. Before appointing an officer, the court will cause preliminary enquiries to be made of Cafcass or CAFCASS Cymru. For the relevant procedure, reference should be made to the practice note issued by Cafcass in June 2006 and any modifications of that practice note.

(b) If Cafcass or CAFCASS Cymru is unable to provide a children's guardian without delay, or if for some other reason the appointment of an officer of the Service of Welsh family proceedings officer is not appropriate, rule 16.24 makes further provision for the appointment of a children's guardian.

7.5 *(omitted)*

Section 2 – Children's guardian appointed under rule 16.4

DUTIES OF THE CHILDREN'S GUARDIAN

7.6 It is the duty of a children's guardian fairly and competently to conduct proceedings on behalf of the child. The children's guardian must have no interest in the proceedings adverse to that of the child and all steps and decisions the children's guardian takes in the proceedings must be taken for the benefit of the child.

7.7 A children's guardian who is an officer of the Service or a Welsh family proceedings officer has, in addition, the duties set out in Part 3 of this Practice Direction and must exercise those duties as set out in that Part.

BECOMING A CHILDREN'S GUARDIAN WITHOUT A COURT ORDER

7.8 In order to become a children's guardian without a court order the person who wishes to act as children's guardian must file a certificate of suitability –

(a) stating that the children's guardian consents to act;

(b) stating that the children's guardian knows or believes that the [applicant][respondent] is a child to whom rule 16.4 and Chapter 7 of Part 16 apply;
(c) stating that the children's guardian can fairly and competently conduct proceedings on behalf of the child and has no interest adverse to that of the child;
(d) undertaking to pay any costs which the child may be ordered to pay in relation to the proceedings, subject to any right the children's guardian may have to be repaid from the assets of the child; and
(e) which the children's guardian has verified by a statement of truth.

7.9 Paragraph 7.8 does not apply to the Official Solicitor, an officer of the Service or a Welsh family proceedings officer.

7.10 The court officer will send the certificate of suitability to one of the child's parents or guardians or, if there is no parent or guardian, to the person with whom the child resides or in whose care the child is.

7.11 The children's guardian must file either the certificate of suitability at a time when the children's guardian first takes a step in the proceedings on behalf of the child.

APPLICATION FOR A COURT ORDER APPOINTING A CHILDREN'S GUARDIAN

7.12 An application for a court order appointing a children's guardian should be made in accordance with Part 18 and must be supported by evidence.

7.13 The court officer must serve the application notice on the persons referred to in paragraph 7.10.

7.14 The evidence in support must satisfy the court that the proposed children's guardian –

(a) consents to act;
(b) can fairly and competently conduct proceedings on behalf of the child;
(c) has no interest adverse to that of the child; and
(d) undertakes to pay any costs which the child may be ordered to pay in relation to the proceedings, subject to any right the children's guardian may have to be repaid from the assets of the child.

7.15 Paragraph 7.14 does not apply to the Official Solicitor, an officer of the Service of a Welsh family proceedings officer.

7.16 The proposed children's guardian may be one of the persons referred to in paragraph 7.10 where appropriate, or otherwise may be the Official Solicitor, an officer of the Service or a Welsh family proceedings officer. Where it is sought to appoint the Official Solicitor, an officer of the Service or a Welsh family proceedings officer, provision should be made for payment of that person's charges.

CHANGE OF CHILDREN'S GUARDIAN AND PREVENTION OF PERSON ACTING AS CHILDREN'S GUARDIAN

7.17 Where an application is made for an order under rule 16.25, the application must set out the reasons for seeking it and must be supported by evidence.

7.18 Subject to paragraph 7.15, if the order sought is substitution of a new children's guardian for an existing one, the evidence must satisfy the court of the matters set out in paragraph 7.14.

7.19 The court officer will serve the application notice on –

(a) the persons referred to in paragraph 7.10; and
(b) the children's guardian or person purporting to act as children's guardian.

PART 5: REPORTING OFFICER

How the reporting officer exercises duties

8.1 The reporting officer must –

(a) ensure so far as reasonably practicable that the parent or guardian is –
  (i) giving consent unconditionally to the placing of the child for adoption or to the making of an adoption order (as defined in section 46 of the Adoption and Children Act 2002) or a section 84 order; and
  (ii) with full understanding of what is involved;
(b) investigate all the circumstances relevant to a parent's or guardian's consent; and
(c) on completing the investigations the reporting officer must –
  (i) make a report in writing to the court in accordance with the timetable set by the court, drawing attention to any matters which, in the opinion of the reporting officer, may be of assistance to the court in considering the application; or
  (ii) make an interim report to the court if a parent or guardian of the child is unwilling to consent to the placing of the child for adoption or to the making of an adoption order or section 84 order.

8.2 On receipt of an interim report under paragraph 8.1(1)(c)(ii) a court officer must inform the applicant that a parent or guardian of the child is unwilling to consent to the placing of the child for adoption or to the making of an adoption order or section 84 order.

8.3 The reporting officer may at any time before the final hearing make an interim report to the court if the reporting officer considers it necessary and ask the court for directions.

8.4 The reporting officer must attend hearings as directed by the court.

PART 6: CHILDREN AND FAMILY REPORTER AND WELFARE OFFICER

How the children and family reporter or welfare officer exercises powers and duties

9.1 In this Part, the person preparing the welfare report in accordance with rule 16.33 is called 'the officer'.

9.2 The officer must make such investigations as may be necessary to perform the officer's powers and duties and must, in particular –

(a) contact or seek to interview such persons as appear appropriate or as the court directs; and
(b) obtain such professional assistance as is available which the children and family reporter thinks appropriate or which the court directs be obtained.

9.3 The officer must –

(a) notify the child of such contents of the report (if any) as the officer considers appropriate to the age and understanding of the child, including any reference to the child's own views on the application and the recommendation; and
(b) if the child is notified of any contents of the report, explain them to the child in a manner appropriate to the child's age and understanding.

9.4 The officer must –

(a) attend hearings as directed by the court;
(b) advise the court of the child's wishes and feelings;
(c) advise the court if the officer considers that the joining of a person as a party to the proceedings would be likely to safeguard the interests of the child;
(d) consider whether it is in the best interests of the child for the child to be made a party to the proceedings, and if so, notify the court of that opinion together with the reasons for that opinion; and
(e) where the court has directed that a written report be made –
  (i) file the report; and

(ii) serve a copy on the other parties and on any children's guardian,

in accordance with the timetable set by the court.

PART 7: PARENTAL ORDER REPORTER

How the parental order reporter exercises duties – investigations and reports

10.1 The parental order reporter must make such investigations as are necessary to carry out the parental order reporter's duties and must, in particular –

(a) contact or seek to interview such persons as the parental order reporter thinks appropriate or as the court directs; and
(b) obtain such professional assistance as is available which the parental order reporter thinks appropriate or which the court directs be obtained.

How the parental order reporter exercises duties – attendance at court, advice to the court and reports

10.2 The parental order reporter must attend all directions hearings unless the court directs otherwise.

10.3 The parental order reporter must advise the court on the following matters –

(a) the appropriate forum for the proceedings;
(b) the appropriate timing of the proceedings or any part of them;
(c) the options available to it in respect of the child and the suitability of each such option including what order should be made in determining the application; and
(d) any other matter on which the court seeks advice or on which the parental order reporter considers that the court should be informed.

10.4 The advice given under paragraph 10.3 may, subject to any direction of the court, be given orally or in writing. If the advice is given orally, a note of it must be taken by the court or the court officer.

10.5 The parental order reporter must –

(a) unless the court directs otherwise, file a written report advising on the interests of the child in accordance with the timetable set by the court; and
(b) where practicable, notify any person the joining of whom as a party to those proceedings would be likely, in the opinion of the parental order reporter, to safeguard the interests of the child, of the court's power to join that person as a party under rule 13.3 and must inform the court –
  (i) of any notification;
  (ii) of anyone whom the parental order reporter attempted to notify under this paragraph but was unable to contact; and
  (iii) of anyone whom the parental order reporter believes may wish to be joined to the proceedings.

(Part 18 sets out the procedure for making an application to be joined as a party in proceedings.)

PART 8: OFFICERS OF THE SERVICE, WELSH FAMILY PROCEEDINGS OFFICERS AND LOCAL AUTHORITY OFFICERS: FURTHER DUTIES

How officers of the Service, Welsh family proceedings officers and local authority officers exercise certain further duties

11.1 This Part applies when an officer of the Service, a Welsh family proceedings officer or a local authority officer is acting under a duty referred to in rule 16.38(1). In this Part, the person acting under a duty referred to in rule 16.38(1) is referred to as 'the officer'.

11.2 The officer must make such investigations as may be necessary to perform the officer's duties and must, in particular –

(a) contact or seek to interview such persons as the officer thinks appropriate or as the court directs; and

(b) obtain such professional assistance as the officer thinks appropriate or which the court directs.

11.3 The officer must –

(a) notify the child of such (if any) of the contents of any report or risk assessment as the officer considers appropriate to the age and understanding of the child;

(b) if the child is notified of any contents of a report or risk assessment, explain them to the child in a manner appropriate to the child's age and understanding;

(c) consider whether to recommend in any report or risk assessment that the court lists a hearing for the purposes of considering the report or risk assessment;

(d) consider whether it is in the best interests of the child for the child to be made a party to the proceedings, and, if so, notify the court of that opinion together with the reasons for that opinion.

11.4 When making a risk assessment, the officer must, if of the opinion that the court should exercise its discretion under rule 12.34(2), state in the risk assessment –

(a) the way in which the officer considers the court should exercise its discretion (including the officer's view on the length of any suggested delay in service); and

(b) the officer's reasons for that reaching that view.

11.5 The officer must file any report or risk assessment with the court –

(a) at or by the time directed by the court;

(b) in the absence of any direction, at least 14 days before a relevant hearing; or

(c) where there has been no direction from the court and there is no relevant hearing listed, as soon as possible following the completion of the report or risk assessment.

11.6 In paragraph 11.5, a hearing is relevant if the court officer has given the officer notice that a report prepared by the officer is to be considered at it.

11.7 A copy of any report prepared as a result of acting under a duty referred to in rule 16.38(1)(a)(i) to (vi) or (b) (but not any risk assessment) must, as soon as practicable, be served by the officer on the parties.

(Rule 12.34 makes provision for the service of risk assessments.)

PART 17
STATEMENTS OF TRUTH

CONTENTS OF THIS PART

Rule		Page
17.1	Interpretation	1721
17.2	Documents to be verified by a statement of truth	1722
17.3	Failure to verify a statement of case	1724
17.4	Failure to verify a witness statement	1724
17.5	Power of the court to require a document to be verified	1724
17.6	False statements	1725
	Practice Direction 17A – Statements of Truth	1725

17.1 Interpretation

(1) In this Part 'statement of case' has the meaning given to it in Part 4 except that a statement of case does not include –

(a) an application for a matrimonial or a civil partnership order or an answer to such an application;
(b) an application under Article 56 of the Maintenance Regulation made on the form in Annex VI or VII to that Regulation;
(c) an application under Article 10 of the 2007 Hague Convention using the Financial Circumstances Form.

(2) In this rule, 'Financial Circumstances Form' has the meaning given to it in rule 9.3(1).

(Rule 4.1 defines 'statement of case' for the purposes of Part 4.)

Amendments—Substituted by SI 2011/1328. Amended by SI 2012/2806.

Defined terms—'statement of case': FPR 2010, rr 4.1(1), 17.1.

Statement of truth—The statement of truth is defined by FPR 2010, r 17.2(4) as a statement that the party to proceedings, witness or person who signs it 'believes the facts stated in the document [to be] true'. It comes in probative value, it comes between the document that is signed by the document's maker, on the one hand, and a document which is sworn to be true (an affidavit) on the other. It was introduced first in civil proceedings by CPR 1998, Pt 22 and provides some guarantee that the maker of the statement confirms an honest belief in the content of the statement. In certain circumstances a statement signed with a statement of truth may be used as evidence (eg FPR 2010, r 22.7(2)). A false statement may be the subject of contempt proceedings (FPR 2010, r 17.6). There is no penalty for including a statement of truth and signing it where it was not needed, so a party in doubt as to whether a document requires a statement of truth should include one.

PD—FPR PD17A accompanies FPR 2010, Pt 17 and, in particular, prescribes the forms of words to be used in statements of truth (especially at paras 2.1 to 2.3). An annex to PD17A provides a form of words for a statement of truth where a person cannot read.

Affidavit and signed documents distinguished—Affidavit is defined in the Glossary as a 'written, sworn, statement of evidence'. A narrow range of documents are required to be sworn (eg certain interim remedies statements: see FPR PD20A, para 3.1; and, for example, under FPR 2010, r 7.32(4)); others are required to be verified by statement of truth (ie the documents listed in FPR 2010, r 17.2(1) or otherwise referred to in a rule or PD).

'statement of case'—Defined in FPR 2010, r 4.1(1) as 'the whole or part of, an application form or answer'. The statements of case and answer (if the definition of 'answer' in the next note is accepted) are the pleadings in a FPR 2010 application. Arrangements for signing of these documents are dealt with in FPR 2010, r 17.2.

Statement of case in family proceedings—'Statement of case' is defined in CPR 1998, r 2.3(1) in positive terms as a claim form, particulars of claim (if separate from the claim form), defence of reply to a defence; it includes any further information given to the court in respect of such documents. The effect of FPR 2010, rr 2.3(1) and 4.1(1) is that the equivalent documents, for the purposes of family proceedings, are defined in partly negative terms: that they are 'an application form' (FPR 2010, r 4.1(1): 'answer' is dealt with below). An application form is any document by which an applicant states an intention to seek a 'court order other than in accordance with the [FPR 2010] Part 18 procedure' (ie the negative content). Any document that starts proceedings and can be thus categorised is a statement of case and requires to be verified by a statement of truth under r 17.2(1)(a).

Answer: defence or reply to an application form—The term 'answer' (above: from FPR 2010, r 4.1(1)) is not defined by the rules. It has a particular meaning in matrimonial and civil partnership proceedings (it must be filed if a respondent is to defend to such proceedings: FPR 2010, r 7.12(8)). It will be assumed for current purposes that it is the defence, reply or other answer to an application form (ie formal claim; document by which proceedings (other than under FPR 2010, Pt 18) are commenced: FPR 2010, r 2.3(1)) under FPR 2010 proceedings.

17.2 Documents to be verified by a statement of truth

(1) Subject to paragraph (9), the following documents must be verified by a statement of truth –

(a) a statement of case;
(b) a witness statement;
(c) an acknowledgement of service in a claim begun by the Part 19 procedure;
(d) a certificate of service;
(e) *(revoked)*
(f) a statement of information filed under rule 9.26(1)(b); and
(g) any other document where a court order, rule or practice direction requires it.

(2) Where a statement of case is amended, the amendments must be verified by a statement of truth unless the court orders otherwise.

(3) Subject to paragraph (10), if an applicant wishes to rely on matters set out in the application form or application notice as evidence, the application form or notice must be verified by a statement of truth.

(4) Subject to paragraph (5), a statement of truth is a statement that –

(a) the party putting forward the document;
(b) in the case of a witness statement, the maker of the witness statement; or
(c) in the case of a certificate of service, the person who signs the certificate,

believes the facts stated in the document are true.

(5) If a party is conducting proceedings with a litigation friend, the statement of truth in –

(a) a statement of case; or
(b) an application notice,

is a statement that the litigation friend believes the facts stated in the document being verified are true.

(6) The statement of truth must be signed by –

(a) in the case of a statement of case –
  (i) the party or litigation friend; or
  (ii) the legal representative on behalf of the party or litigation friend; and
(b) in the case of a witness statement, the maker of the statement.

(7) A statement of truth, which is not contained in the document which it verifies, must clearly identify that document.

(8) A statement of truth in a statement of case may be made by –

(a) a person who is not a party; or
(b) by two parties jointly,

where this is permitted by a practice direction.

(9) An application that does not contain a statement of facts need not be verified by a statement of truth.

(10) Notwithstanding paragraph (3), and subject to any direction given under rule 9.14(2A) or rule 9.19(2A), the court may permit a party to rely upon matters set out in an application form which has not been verified by a statement of truth as evidence where the application has been made under –

(a) Article 56 of the Maintenance Regulation on the form in Annex VI or VII to that Regulation; or
(b) Article 10 of the 2007 Hague Convention on an Article 11 form.

(Practice Direction 17A sets out the form of statement of truth.)

Amendments—SI 2012/2806; SI 2014/843.

Defined terms—'statement of case': FPR 2010, r 17.1.

'verified by a statement of truth' (r 17.2(1))—Rules as to when a document should or should not be signed by a statement of truth are complex (e g an application in matrimonial and civil partnership proceedings cases or a document with no facts stated in it (r 17.2(9)) need not contain a statement of truth; only acknowledgements of service only in FPR 2010, Pt 19 proceedings (but no other) need have a statement of truth). The general rule must therefore be that, if in doubt, a statement of truth should be included in a document and it should be signed in accordance with r 17.2(3)–(6).

Documents to be verified or not:

(1) *Application or answer in matrimonial and civil partnership proceedings* Although these documents are not to be verified by a statement of truth, parties will need to have any document verified later if an interim application notice is filed.
(2) *Acknowledgement of service in Pt 19 proceedings* The acknowledgement of service in FPR 2010, Pt 19 proceedings partly performs the role of an answer or defence (FPR 2010, r 19.5(3)) and unlike other acknowledgements of service it is required to be verified by a statement of truth (r 17.2(1)(c)).
(3) *Statement of information for a financial remedy consent order* Although FPR 2010, r 9.26(1) does not say so, r 17.2(1)(f) requires that the financial information forms for a consent order be verified by a statement of truth, although there are also (new from the old rules) requirements also as to signing by the parties in FPR 2010, r 9.26(2),(3).
(4) *Enforcement documents* FPR PD17A, para 1.4 has added the following enforcement application documents as being required to be verified by a statement of truth:
  (i) an attachment of earnings order (FPR 2010, rr 33.3(1)(b) and 39.5(2)(a))
  (ii) a third party debt order (CPR Pt 72, as modified by FPR 2010, r 33.24);
  (iii) a hardship payment order (CPR Pt 72, as modified by FPR 2010, r 33.24); or
  (iv) a charging order (FPR 2010, r 40.4(4)(b)).

'matters set out … as evidence' (r 17.2(3))—Rule 17.2(3) refers to both an application form and application notice: if either are to be relied upon as evidence (other than at trial) they must be verified by a statement of truth (see also FPR 2010, rr 18.7 and 22.7(2)). This refers predominantly to interim hearings and has added relevance because such hearings, unless otherwise ordered or another rule says otherwise, will be based on written evidence only (FPR 2010, r 22.7(1)) and the court can only rely on the application form (or notice, if applicable) or the 'answer' (r 22.7(2)(c)) if they are verified by a statement of truth (r 22.7(2)).

Statement of truth as to facts (FPR 2010, r 17.2(4),(9))—Paras (4) and (9) confirm that a statement of truth need relate only to facts. A statement of opinion or as to the law will not require (in logic as well as under the rules) to be signed. It will be rare for a party to disentangle fact from opinion or law (say) in a r 17.2(1) document. Again, if in doubt a party should endorse a statement of truth and arrange for it to be signed.

Expert's report—FPR PD17A (para 1.3) draws attention to the need for an expert's report to be verified by a statement of truth. For the form of the statement of truth verifying an expert's report (which differs from that set out below) see PD25A, para 3.3(i).

Signature—Generally the statement can be signed by a legal representative (r 17.2(6)(a) and see FPR PD17A, para 3.7) and children's representative, save in the case of a statement of arrangements where it must be signed by the applicant parent who makes the statement (r 17(6)(b)).

17.3 Failure to verify a statement of case

(1) If a party fails to verify that party's statement of case by a statement of truth –

(a) the statement of case shall remain effective unless struck out; but

(b) the party may not rely on the statement of case as evidence of any of the matters set out in it.

(2) The court may strike out(GL) a statement of case which is not verified by a statement of truth.

(3) Any party may apply for an order under paragraph (2).

Defined terms—'statement of case': FPR 2010, r 17.1.

Failure to verify: 'effective unless struck out'—The statement of truth remains effective (i e it is not a nullity) unless court action is taken in respect of it (e g to strike it out: FPR 2010, r 4.4). The court may order that the error be remedied (FPR 2010, r 4.7(b)). Any application to strike out (r 17.3(3)) would be in the proceedings by FPR 2010, Pt 18 procedure application.

Evidence at interim hearing—In practice, the striking out of a document not properly verified is likely to be rare in family proceedings, but at an interim stage (where only evidence in writing generally is considered by the court (FPR 2010, r 22.7(1)) and the judge is not being asked to make a decision on the final issue), an application to strike out or at least suspend or ignore an imperfectly verified statement might be successful.

Verification—The effect of FPR 2010, r 17.2(7) is to enable a statement of truth to be included in a separate document provided that that separate document 'clearly identifies [the] document' that it is intended to verify. Failure to verify by statement of truth can be rectified under this provision by a separate and subsequent short document being signed and filed with the original dealing with verification.

17.4 Failure to verify a witness statement

If the maker of a witness statement fails to verify the witness statement by a statement of truth, the court may direct that it shall not be admissible as evidence.

Defined terms—'statement of case': FPR 2010, r 17.1.

'the court may direct [that a statement] shall not be admissible'—Any evidence that is relevant is admissible. There are procedures that dictate how that evidence be adduced (e g in FPR 2010, Pts 17 and 23). It is difficult to imagine circumstance where, on a final hearing, otherwise admissible evidence was excluded because a document was not signed, especially if the witness or party to proceedings were there to sign at the final hearing (see also rules on hearsay evidence at FPR 2010, rr 23.2–23.5).

17.5 Power of the court to require a document to be verified

(1) The court may order a person who has failed to verify a document in accordance with rule 17.2 to verify the document.

(2) Any party may apply for an order under paragraph (1).

'verify a document in [r 17.2]'—The list of documents in FPR 2010, r 17.2 are specific, so the court does not have power, for example, to order a party to sign or verify an application notice.

Application for verification—The court may order a party to verify on its own initiative, or a party can make application for this. Proportionality in the making of such applications, and the need for them, will be borne in mind (and see **Verification** under FPR 2010, r 17.3).

17.6 False statements

(1) Proceedings for contempt of court may be brought against a person who makes, or causes to be made, a false statement in a document verified by a statement of truth without an honest belief in its truth.

(2) Proceedings under this rule may be brought only –

(a) by the Attorney General, or

(b) with the permission of the court.

(3) *(revoked)*

Amendments—SI 2013/3204.

Practice Direction 17A – Statements of Truth

This Practice Direction supplements FPR Part 17

Documents to be verified by a statement of truth

1.1 Rule 17.2 sets out the documents which must be verified by a statement of truth.

1.2 If an applicant wishes to rely on matters set out in his application notice as evidence, the application notice must be verified by a statement of truth.

1.3 An expert's report should also be verified by a statement of truth. For the form of the statement of truth verifying an expert's report (which differs from that set out below), see paragraph 9.1(j) of Practice Direction 25B (The Duties of an Expert, The Expert's Report and Arrangements for an Expert to Attend Court).

1.4 In addition, the following documents must be verified by a statement of truth –

(a) an application notice for –

(i) a third party debt order (CPR Part 72 as modified by rule 33.24);

(ii) a hardship payment order (CPR Part 72 as modified by rule 33.24); or

(iii) a charging order (CPR Part 73 as modified by rule 33.25); and

(b) a notice of objections to an account being taken by the court, unless verified by an affidavit or witness statement.

1.5 The statement of truth may be contained in the document it verifies or it may be in a separate document served subsequently, in which case it must identify the document to which it relates.

1.6 Where the form to be used includes a jurat for the content to be verified by an affidavit, then a statement of truth is not required in addition.

1.7 In this Practice Direction, 'statement of case' has the meaning given to it by rule 17.1.

Form of the statement of truth

2.1 The form of the statement of truth verifying a statement of case or an application notice should be as follows:

'[I believe] [the (applicant or as may be) believes] that the facts stated in this [name document being verified] are true.'

2.2 The form of the statement of truth verifying a witness statement should be as follows:

'I believe that the facts stated in this witness statement are true.'

2.3 Where the statement of truth is contained in a separate document, the document containing the statement of truth must be headed with the title of and court reference for the proceedings. The document being verified should be identified in the statement of truth as follows –

(a) application form: 'the application form issued on [date]';

(b) statement of case: 'the (application or answer as may be) served on [name of party] on [date]';

(c) application notice: 'the application notice issued on [date] for [set out the remedy sought]';

(d) witness statement: 'the witness statement filed on [date] or served on [party] on [date]'.

Who may sign the statement of truth

3.1 In a statement of case or an application notice, the statement of truth must be signed by –

(a) the party or his litigation friend; or

(b) the legal representative of the party or litigation friend.

3.2 A statement of truth verifying a witness statement must be signed by the witness.

3.3 A statement of truth verifying a notice of objections to an account must be signed by the objecting party or his or her legal representative.

3.4 Where a document is to be verified on behalf of a company or corporation, subject to paragraph 3.7 below, the statement of truth must be signed by a person holding a senior position in the company or corporation. That person must state the office or position he or she holds.

3.5 Each of the following persons is a person holding a senior position:

(a) in respect of a registered company or corporation, a director, the treasurer, secretary, chief executive, manager or other officer of the company or corporation; and

(b) in respect of a corporation which is not a registered company, in addition to those persons set out in (a), the major, chairman, president, chief executive of a local authority or town clerk or other similar officer of the corporation.

3.6 Where the document is to be verified on behalf of a partnership, those who may sign the statement of truth are –

(a) any of the partners; or

(b) a person having the management or control of the partnership business.

3.7 Where a party is legally represented, the legal representative may sign the statement of truth on his or her behalf. The statement signed by the legal representative will refer to the client's belief, not his or her own. In signing he or she must state the capacity in which he or she signs and the name of his or her firm where appropriate.

3.8 Where a legal representative has signed a statement of truth, his or her signature will be taken by the court as his or her statement –

(a) that the client on whose behalf he or she has signed had authorised him or her to do so;

(b) that before signing he or she had explained to the client that in signing the statement of truth he or she would be confirming the client's belief that the facts stated in the document were true; and

(c) that before signing he or she had informed the client of the possible consequences to the client if it should subsequently appear that the client did not have an honest belief in the truth of those facts (see rule 17.6).

3.9 A legal representative who signs a statement of truth must print his or her full name clearly beneath his or her signature.

3.10 The individual who signs a statement of truth must sign in his or her own name and not that of his or her firm or employer.

3.11 The following are examples of the possible application of this practice direction describing who may sign a statement of truth verifying statements in documents other than a witness statement. These are only examples and not an indication of how a court might apply the practice direction to a specific situation.

Managing Agent

An agent who manages property or investments for the party cannot sign a statement of truth. It must be signed by the party or by the legal representative of the party.

Trusts

Where some or all of the trustees comprise a single party one, some or all of the trustees comprising the party may sign a statement of truth. The legal representative of the trustees may sign it.

Companies

Paragraphs 3.4 and 3.5 apply. The word 'manager' will be construed in the context of the phrase 'a person holding a senior position' which it is used to define. The court will consider the size of the company and the importance and nature of the proceedings. It would expect the manager signing the statement of truth to have personal knowledge of the content of the document or to be responsible for those who have that knowledge of the content. A small company may not have a manager, apart from the directors, who holds a senior position. A large company will have many such managers. In a large company with specialist claims, insurance or legal departments the statement may be signed by the manager of such a department if he or she is responsible for handling the claim or managing the staff handling it.

Inability of persons to read or sign documents to be verified by a statement of truth

4.1 Where a document containing a statement of truth is to be signed by a person who is unable to read or sign the document, it must contain a certificate made by an authorised person.

4.2 An authorised person is a person able to administer oaths and take affidavits but need not be independent of the parties or their representatives.

4.3 The authorised person must certify –

- (a) that the document has been read to the person signing it;
- (b) that the person appeared to understand it and approved its content as accurate;
- (c) that the declaration of truth has been read to that person;
- (d) that that person appeared to understand the declaration and the consequences of making a false declaration; and
- (e) that that person signed or made his mark in the presence of the authorised person.

4.4 The form of the certificate is set out at the Annex to this Practice Direction.

Consequences of failure to verify

5.1 If a statement of case is not verified by a statement of truth, the statement of case will remain effective unless it is struck out, but a party may not rely on the contents of a statement of case as evidence until it has been verified by a statement of truth.

5.2 Any party may apply to the court for an order that unless within such period as the court may specify the statement of case is verified by the service of a statement of truth, the statement of case will be struck out.

5.3 The usual order for the costs of an application referred to in paragraph 5.2 will be that the costs be paid by the party who had failed to verify, in any event and immediately.

Penalty

6 Attention is drawn to rule 17.6 which sets out the consequences of verifying a statement of case containing a false statement without an honest belief in its truth, and to the procedures set out in Chapter 5 of Part 37 and in paragraphs 4.1 to 4.7 of Practice Direction 37A (Applications and proceedings in relation to contempt of court).

ANNEX

Certificate to be used where a person is unable to read or sign a document to be verified by a statement of truth

I certify that I [name and address of authorised person] have read the contents of this document and the declaration of truth to the person signing the document [if there are exhibits, add 'and explained the nature and effect of the exhibits referred to in it'] who appeared to understand (a) the document and approved its content as accurate and (b) the declaration of truth and the consequences of making a false declaration, and made his or her mark in my presence.

PART 18
PROCEDURE FOR OTHER APPLICATIONS IN PROCEEDINGS

CONTENTS OF THIS PART

Rule		Page
18.1	Types of application for which Part 18 procedure may be followed	1728
18.2	Applications for permission to start proceedings	1729
18.3	Respondents to applications under this Part	1729
18.4	Application notice to be filed	1729
18.5	Notice of an application	1729
18.6	Time when an application is made	1730
18.7	What an application notice must include	1730
18.8	Service of a copy of an application notice	1730
18.9	Applications which may be dealt with without a hearing	1730
18.10	Service of application notice following court order where application made without notice	1731
18.11	Application to set aside or vary order made without notice	1731
18.12	Power of the court to proceed in the absence of a party	1731
18.13	Dismissal of totally without merit applications	1731
	Practice Direction 18A – Other Applications in Proceedings	1732

Derivation—FPR 2010, Pt 18 is derived from Pt 9 of the Family Procedure (Adoption) Rules 2005 but is wider and makes general provision for making applications to the court. Unless a rule requires otherwise (as does, for example, FPR 2010, r 30.3 dealing with permission to appeal) all applications for permission should be made under Pt 18.

Forms—FPR PD5A (Forms) prescribes all forms to be used under FPR 2010. Table 1 of PD5A states that form C2, D11 and FP2 are for use in FPR 2010, Pt 18 applications. Table 2 describes these forms: form C2 is the application for permission to start proceedings, for an order or directions in existing proceedings and to be joined as, or cease to be, a party in existing family proceedings under CA 1989; form D11 is an application notice; and form FP2 is described as 'application notice under Pt 18, FPR 2010'. Thus (regrettably) there is no one form to be used in all Pt 18 applications and the relevant form will depend on the nature of the application.

Structure of Pt 18—The basic structure of FPR 2010, Pt 18 is that, unless excused from doing so by a rule, practice direction or court order, the applicant must submit an application notice which states what order is being sought with brief reasons and attaches a draft of the order being sought (FPR 2010, r 18.7). Any written evidence in support must be filed with the application notice (FPR 2010, r 18.8). The general rule is that the application notice must be served (FPR 2010, r 18.5). Pt 18 is well drafted and is clear and generally the rules speak for themselves.

Practice Direction—FPR 2010, Pt 18 is supplemented by FPR PD18A. It is essential to refer to this PD before making any application under Pt 18. Fortunately, PD18A is particularly clear and helpful and, in effect, provides all necessary commentary on Pt 18.

Committal applications—An application to commit for contempt of court must be made using the Pt 18 procedure: see r 37.10.

18.1 Types of application for which Part 18 procedure may be followed

(1) The Part 18 procedure is the procedure set out in this Part.

(2) An applicant may use the Part 18 procedure if the application is made –

(a) in the course of existing proceedings;

(b) to start proceedings except where some other Part of these rules prescribes the procedure to start proceedings; or
(c) in connection with proceedings which have been concluded.

(3) Paragraph (2) does not apply –

(a) to applications where any other rule in any other Part of these rules sets out the procedure for that type of application;
(b) if a practice direction provides that the Part 18 procedure may not be used in relation to the type of application in question.

18.2 Applications for permission to start proceedings

An application for permission to start proceedings must be made to the court where the proceedings will be started if permission is granted.

(Rule 5.4 makes general provision in relation to the court in which proceedings should be started.)

Amendments—SI 2013/3204.

18.3 Respondents to applications under this Part

The following persons are to be respondents to an application under this Part –

(a) where there are existing proceedings or the proceedings have been concluded –
  (i) the parties to those proceedings; and
  (ii) if the proceedings are proceedings under Part 11, the person who is the subject of those proceedings;
(b) where there are no existing proceedings –
  (i) if notice has been given under section 44 of the 2002 Act (notice of intention to adopt or apply for an order under section 84 of that Act), the local authority to whom notice has been given; and
  (ii) if an application is made for permission to apply for an order in proceedings, any person who will be a party to the proceedings brought if permission is granted; and
(c) any other person as the court may direct.

18.4 Application notice to be filed

(1) Subject to paragraph (2) the applicant must file an application notice.

(2) An applicant may make an application without filing an application notice if –

(a) this is permitted by a rule or practice direction; or
(b) the court dispenses with the requirement for an application notice.

18.5 Notice of an application

(1) Subject to paragraph (2), a copy of the application notice must be served on –

(a) each respondent;
(b) in relation to proceedings under Part 11, the person who is, or, in the case of an application to start proceedings, it is intended will be, the subject of the proceedings; and
(c) in relation to proceedings under Parts 12 and 14, the children's guardian (if any).

(2) An application may be made without serving a copy of the application notice if this is permitted by –

(a) a rule;
(b) a practice direction; or
(c) the court.

(Rule 18.8 deals with service of a copy of the application notice.)

PART III

18.6 Time when an application is made

When an application must be made within a specified time, it is so made if the court receives the application notice within that time.

18.7 What an application notice must include

(1) An application notice must state –

(a) what order the applicant is seeking; and
(b) briefly, why the applicant is seeking the order.

(2) A draft of the order sought must be attached to the application notice.

(Part 17 requires an application notice to be verified by a statement of truth if the applicant wishes to rely on matters set out in his application as evidence.)

18.8 Service of a copy of an application notice

(1) Subject to rule 2.4, a copy of the application notice must be served in accordance with the provisions of Part 6 –

(a) as soon as practicable after it is filed; and
(b) in any event –
  (i) where the application is for an order under rule 9.7 at least 14 days; and
  (ii) in any other case, at least 7 days;
  before the court is to deal with the application.

(2) The applicant must, when filing the application notice, file a copy of any written evidence in support.

(3) If a copy of an application notice is served by a court officer it must be accompanied by –

(a) a notice of the date and place where the application will be heard;
(b) a copy of any witness statement in support; and
(c) a copy of the draft order which the applicant has attached to the application.

(4) If –

(a) an application notice is served; but
(b) the period of notice is shorter than the period required by these rules or a practice direction,

the court may direct that, in the circumstances of the case, sufficient notice has been given and hear the application.

(5) This rule does not require written evidence –

(a) to be filed if it has already been filed; or
(b) to be served on a party on whom it has already been served.

Amendments—SI 2013/1472.

18.9 Applications which may be dealt with without a hearing

(1) The court may deal with an application without a hearing if –

(a) the court does not consider that a hearing would be appropriate; or
(b) the parties agree as to the terms of the order sought or the parties agree that the court should dispose of the application without a hearing and the court does not consider that a hearing would be appropriate.

(2) Where –

(a) an application is made for permission to make an application in proceedings under the 1989 Act; and
(b) the court refuses the application without a hearing in accordance with paragraph (1)(a),

the court must, at the request of the applicant, re-list the application and fix a date for a hearing.

(3) *(revoked)*

Amendments—SI 2013/3204.

18.10 Service of application notice following court order where application made without notice

(1) This rule applies where the court has disposed of an application which it permitted to be made without service of a copy of the application notice.

(2) Where the court makes an order, whether granting or dismissing the application, a copy of the application notice and any evidence in support must unless the court orders otherwise, be served with the order on –

(a) all the parties in proceedings; and

(b) in relation to proceedings under Part 11, the person who is, or, in the case of an application to start proceedings, it is intended will be, the subject of the proceedings.

(3) The order must contain a statement of the right to make an application to set aside[(GL)] or vary the order under rule 18.11.

18.11 Application to set aside or vary order made without notice

(1) A person who was not served with a copy of the application notice before an order was made under rule 18.10 may apply to have the order set aside[(GL)] or varied.

(2) An application under this rule must be made within 7 days beginning with the date on which the order was served on the person making the application.

18.12 Power of the court to proceed in the absence of a party

(1) Where the applicant or any respondent fails to attend the hearing of an application, the court may proceed in the absence of that person.

(2) Where –

(a) the applicant or any respondent fails to attend the hearing of an application; and

(b) the court makes an order at the hearing,

the court may, on application or of its own initiative, re-list the application.

(3) *(revoked)*

Amendments—SI 2013/3204.

18.13 Dismissal of totally without merit applications

If the court dismisses an application (including an application for permission to appeal) and it considers that the application is totally without merit –

(a) the court's order must record that fact; and

(b) the court must at the same time consider whether it is appropriate to make a civil restraint order.

Amendments—SI 2013/3204.

'totally without merit'—These are key words which trigger the procedure for a civil restraint order and thus must be included in the order itself.

Power of the court to make civil restraint orders—FPR 2010, Rule 4.8 deals with the power of the court to make a civil restraint order. There are three types: limited, extended and general.

Practice Direction 4B—FPR PD4B sets out the circumstances in which the High Court or the County Court has power to make a civil restraint order and the procedure and consequences.

Practice Direction 18A – Other Applications in Proceedings

This Practice Direction supplements FPR Part 18

Application of Part 18

1.1 Part 18 makes general provision for a procedure for making applications. All applications for the court's permission should be made under this Part, with the exception of applications for permission for which specific provision is made in other Parts of the FPR, in which case the application should be made under the specific provision. Examples of where specific provision has been made in another Part of the FPR for applications for permission are rule 11.3 (Permission to apply for a forced marriage protection order) and rule 30.3 (Permission to appeal).

****

Additional requirements in relation to application notices

3.1 In addition to the requirements set out in rule 18.7, the following requirements apply to the applications to which the respective paragraph refers.

3.2 An application notice must be signed and include –

(a) the title of the case (if available);
(b) the reference number of the case (if available);
(c) the full name of the applicant;
(d) where the applicant is not already a party, the applicant's address for service, including a postcode. Postcode information may be obtained from www.royalmail.com or the Royal Mail Address Management Guide; and
(e) either a request for a hearing or a request that the application be dealt with without a hearing.

3.3 An application notice relating to an application under section 42(6) of the Adoption and Children Act 2002 (permission to apply for an adoption order) must include –

(a) the child's name, sex, date of birth and nationality;
(b) in relation to each of the child's parents or guardians, their name, address and nationality;
(c) the length of time that the child has had his or her home with the applicant;
(d) the reason why the child has had his or her home with the applicant;
(e) details of any local authority or adoption agency involved in placing the child in the applicant's home; and
(f) if there are or have been other court proceedings relating to the child, the nature of those proceedings, the name of the court in which they are being or have been dealt with, the date and type of any order made and, if the proceedings are still ongoing, the date of the next hearing.

3.4 An application notice relating to an application in the High Court by a local authority for permission under section 100(3) of the Children Act 1989 must include a draft of the application form.

3.5 Where permission is required to take any step under the Children Act 1989 (for example an application to be joined as a party to the proceedings) the application notice must include a draft of the application for the making of which permission is sought together with sufficient copies for one to be served on each respondent.

3.6 In an application for permission to bring proceedings under Schedule 1 of the Children Act 1989, the draft application for the making of which permission is sought must be accompanied by a statement setting out the financial details which the person seeking permission believes to be relevant to the request and contain a declaration that it is true to the maker's best knowledge and belief, together with sufficient copies for one to be served on each respondent.

3.7 The provisions in Schedule 1 which require an application for permission to bring proceedings are –

(a) paragraph 7(2) – permission is required to make an application for variation of a secured periodical payments order after the death of the parent liable to make the payments if a period of 6 months has passed from the date on which representation in regard to that parent's estate is first taken out; and

(b) paragraph 11(3) – permission is required to make an application to alter a maintenance agreement following the death of one of the parties if a period of 6 months has passed beginning with the day on which representation in regard to the estate of the deceased is first taken out.

Other provisions in relation to application notices

4.1 On receipt of an application notice containing a request for a hearing, unless the court considers that the application is suitable for consideration without a hearing, the court officer will, if serving a copy of the application notice, notify the applicant of the time and date fixed for the hearing of the application.

4.2 On receipt of an application notice containing a request that the application be dealt with without a hearing, the court will decide whether the application is suitable for consideration without a hearing.

4.3 Where the court –

(a) considers that the application is suitable for consideration without a hearing; but

(b) is not satisfied that it has sufficient material to decide the application immediately,

it may give directions for the filing of evidence and will inform the applicant and the respondent(s) of its decision. (Rule 18.11 enables a party to apply for an order made without notice to be set aside or varied.)

4.4 Where the court does not consider that the application is suitable for consideration without a hearing –

(a) it may give directions as to the filing of evidence; and

(b) the court officer will notify the applicant and the respondent of the time, date and place for the hearing of the application and any directions given.

4.5 *(omitted)*

4.6 Every application should be made as soon as it becomes apparent that it is necessary or desirable to make it.

4.7 Applications should, wherever possible, be made so that they are considered at any directions hearing or other hearing for which a date has been fixed or for which a date is about to be fixed.

4.8 The parties must anticipate that at any hearing (including any directions hearing) the court may wish to review the conduct of the case as a whole and give any necessary directions. They should be ready to assist the court in doing so and to answer questions the court may ask for this purpose.

4.9 Where a date for a hearing has been fixed, a party who wishes to make an application at that hearing but does not have sufficient time to file an application notice should as soon as possible inform the court (if possible in writing) and, if possible, the other parties of the nature of the application and the reason for it. That party should then make the application orally at the hearing.

Applications without service of application notice

5.1 An application may be made without service of an application notice only –

(a) where there is exceptional urgency;

(b) where the overriding objective is best furthered by doing so;

(c) by consent of all parties;

(d) with the permission of the court;

(e) where paragraph 4.9 applies; or
(f) where a court order, rule or practice direction permits.

Giving notice of an application

6.1 Unless the court otherwise directs or paragraph 5.1 of this practice direction applies, the application notice must be served as soon as practicable after it has been issued and, if there is to be a hearing, at least 7 days before the hearing date.

6.2 Where an application notice should be served but there is not sufficient time to do so, informal notification of the application should be given unless the circumstances of the application require no notice of the application to be given.

Pre-action applications

7.1 All applications made before proceedings are commenced should be made under this Part.

Telephone hearings

8.1 The court may direct that an application be dealt with by a telephone hearing.

8.2 The applicant should, if seeking a direction under paragraph 8.1, indicate this on the application notice. Where the applicant has not indicated such an intention but nevertheless wishes to seek a direction the request should be made as early as possible.

8.3 A direction under paragraph 8.1 will not normally be made unless every party entitled to be given notice of the application and to be heard at the hearing has consented to the direction.

8.4 No representative of a party to an application being heard by telephone may attend the court in person while the application is being heard unless the other party to the application has agreed that the representative may do so.

8.5 If an application is to be heard by telephone the following directions will apply, subject to any direction to the contrary –

(a) the applicant's legal representative is responsible for arranging the telephone conference for precisely the time fixed by the court. The telecommunications provider used must be one of the approved panel of service providers (see HMCS website at www.hmcourts-service.gov.uk);
(b) the applicant's legal representative must tell the operator the telephone numbers of all those participating in the conference call and the sequence in which they are to be called;
(c) it is the responsibility of the applicant's legal representative to ascertain from all the other parties whether they have instructed counsel and, if so the identity of counsel, and whether the legal representative and counsel will be on the same or different telephone numbers;
(d) the sequence in which those involved are to be called will be –
    (i) the applicant's legal representative and (if on a different number) his counsel;
    (ii) the legal representative (and counsel) for all other parties; and
    (iii) the judge or justices, as the case may be;
(e) each speaker is to remain on the line after being called by the operator setting up the conference call. The call may be 2 or 3 minutes before the time fixed for the application;
(f) when the judge has been connected the applicant's legal representative (or counsel) will introduce the parties in the usual way;
(g) if the use of a 'speakerphone' by any party causes the court or any other party any difficulty in hearing what is said the judge may require that party to use a hand held telephone;
(h) the telephone charges debited to the account of the party initiating the conference call will be treated as part of the costs of the application.

Note—For HMCTS, see *www.hmcourts-service.gov.uk*.

Video conferencing

9.1 Where the parties to a matter wish to use video conferencing facilities, and those facilities are available in the relevant court, the parties should apply to the court for directions.

(Practice Direction 22A provides guidance on the use of video conferencing)

Note of proceedings

10.1 The court or court officer should keep, either by way of a note or a tape recording, brief details of all proceedings before the court, including the dates of the proceedings and a short statement of the decision taken at each hearing.

Evidence

11.1 The requirement for evidence in certain types of applications is set out in some of the rules in the FPR and practice directions. Where there is no specific requirement to provide evidence it should be borne in mind that, as a practical matter, the court will often need to be satisfied by evidence of the facts that are relied on in support of or for opposing the application.

11.2 The court may give directions for the filing of evidence in support of or opposing a particular application. The court may also give directions for the filing of evidence in relation to any hearing that it fixes on its own initiative. The directions may specify the form that evidence is to take and when it is to be served.

11.3 Where it is intended to rely on evidence which is not contained in the application itself, the evidence, if it has not already been served, should be served with the application.

11.4 Where a respondent to an application wishes to rely on evidence, that evidence must be filed in accordance with any directions the court may have given and a court officer will serve the evidence on the other parties, unless the court directs otherwise.

11.5 If it is necessary for the applicant to serve any evidence in reply the court officer will serve it on the other parties unless the court directs otherwise.

11.6 Evidence must be filed with the court as well as served on the parties.

11.7 The contents of an application notice may be used as evidence provided the contents have been verified by a statement of truth.

Consent orders

12.1 The parties to an application for a consent order must ensure that they provide the court with any material it needs to be satisfied that it is appropriate to make the order. Subject to any rule in the FPR or practice direction a letter will generally be acceptable for this purpose.

12.2 Where a judgment or order has been agreed in respect of an application where a hearing date has been fixed, the parties must inform the court immediately.

Other applications considered without a hearing

13.1 Where rule 18.9(1)(b) applies the court will treat the application as if it were proposing to make an order on its own initiative.

13.2 Where the parties agree that the court should dispose of the application without a hearing they should so inform the court in writing and each should confirm that all evidence and other material on which he or she relies has been disclosed to the other parties to the application.

Miscellaneous

14.1 If the case is proceeding in the High Court and the draft order is unusually long or complex it should also be supplied in electronic form on such storage medium as shall be agreed with the judge or court staff, for use by the court office.

14.2 Where rule 18.12 applies the power to re-list the application in rule 18.12(2) is in addition to any other powers of the court with regard to the order (for example to set aside, vary, discharge or suspend the order).

Costs

15.1 Attention is drawn to the CPR costs practice direction and, in particular, to the court's power to make a summary assessment of costs.

15.2 Attention is also drawn to rule 44.13(1) of the CPR which provides that if an order makes no mention of costs, none are payable in respect of the proceedings to which it relates.

PART 19
ALTERNATIVE PROCEDURE FOR APPLICATIONS

CONTENTS OF THIS PART

Rule		Page
19.1	Types of application for which Part 19 procedure may be followed	1736
19.2	Applications for which the Part 19 procedure must be followed	1737
19.3	Contents of the application	1737
19.4	Issue of application without naming respondents	1737
19.5	Acknowledgment of service	1737
19.6	Consequence of not filing an acknowledgment of service	1738
19.7	Filing and serving written evidence	1738
19.8	Evidence – general	1738
19.9	Procedure where respondent objects to use of the Part 19 procedure	1738
	Practice Direction 19A – Alternative Procedure for Applications	1739

19.1 Types of application for which Part 19 procedure may be followed

(1) The Part 19 procedure is the procedure set out in this Part.

(2) An applicant may use the Part 19 procedure where the Part 18 procedure does not apply and –

- (a) there is no form prescribed by a rule or referred to in Practice Direction 5A in which to make the application;
- (b) the applicant seeks the court's decision on a question which is unlikely to involve a substantial dispute of fact; or
- (c) paragraph (5) applies.

(3) The court may at any stage direct that the application is to continue as if the applicant had not used the Part 19 procedure and, if it does so, the court may give any directions it considers appropriate.

(4) Paragraph (2) does not apply if a practice direction provides that the Part 19 procedure may not be used in relation to the type of application in question.

(5) A rule or practice direction may, in relation to a specified type of proceedings –

- (a) require or permit the use of the Part 19 procedure; and
- (b) disapply or modify any of the rules set out in this Part as they apply to those proceedings.

Derivation—FPR 2010, Pt 19 is derived from Family Proceedings (Adoption) Rules 2005, Pt 10 which, in turn, was based on CPR 1998, Pt 8 but is now of general application. Pt 19 is used where the FPR 2010, Pt 18 procedure does not apply and either there is no form prescribed by rule or in PD5A or the applicant seeks the court's decision on a question which is unlikely to involve a substantial dispute of fact. An applicant may also use the Pt 19 procedure if a practice direction permits or requires its use. It must be used for applications under s 60(3) or s 79(4) of the 2002 Act and for orders under FPR 2010, r 14.21.

Forms—Table 1 of FPR PD5A (Forms) lists the forms relevant to FPR 2010, Pt 19 and Table 2 describes those forms as follows:

- Form FP1 – Application under Part 19 FPR 2010
- Form FP1A – Application under Part 19 FPR 2010 – notes for applicant on completing form FP1
- Form FP1B – Application under Part 19 FPR 2010 – notes for respondent
- Form FP3 – Application for Injunction (General Form)
- Form FP5 – Acknowledgement of Service under Part 19 FPR 2010
- Form FP6 – Certificate of Service

Structure of Pt 19—The procedure permits an application without naming a respondent (FPR 2010, r 19.4 and FPR PD19A, para 2.2) but where a respondent is named an acknowledgement of service is required (FPR 2010, r 19.5) and any written evidence must be filed with it. A respondent who contends that the FPR 2010, Pt 19 procedure is not appropriate must say so and give reasons when filing the acknowledgement of service (FPR 2010, r 19.9). On receipt of the acknowledgement of service the court will give directions (r 19.9(2)). No written evidence may be relied on at a hearing unless it has been served or the court gives permission FPR 2010, (r 19.8). A respondent who does not file an acknowledgement of service may attend the hearing but may not take part unless the court gives permission (FPR 2010, r 19.6). Pt 19 is clearly drafted and speaks for itself. Note the formal requirements as to contents of a Pt 19 application in FPR 2010, r 19.3.

Practice Direction—FPR 2010, Pt 19 is supplemented by FPR PD19A, which, in effect, provides all necessary commentary.

19.2 Applications for which the Part 19 procedure must be followed

(1) The Part 19 procedure must be used in an application made in accordance with –

- (a) section 60(3) of the 2002 Act (order to prevent disclosure of information to an adopted person);
- (b) section 79(4) of the 2002 Act (order for Registrar General to give any information referred to in section 79(3) of the 2002 Act); and
- (c) rule 14.21 (directions of High Court regarding fathers without parental responsibility).

(2) The respondent to an application made in accordance with paragraph (1)(b) is the Registrar General.

PART III

19.3 Contents of the application

Where the applicant uses the Part 19 procedure, the application must state –

- (a) that this Part applies;
- (b) either –
  - (i) the question which the applicant wants the court to decide; or
  - (ii) the order which the applicant is seeking and the legal basis of the application for that order;
- (c) if the application is being made under an enactment, what that enactment is;
- (d) if the applicant is applying in a representative capacity, what that capacity is; and
- (e) if the respondent appears or is to appear in a representative capacity, what that capacity is.

(Part 17 requires a statement of case to be verified by a statement of truth.)

19.4 Issue of application without naming respondents

(1) A practice direction may set out circumstances in which an application may be issued under this Part without naming a respondent.

(2) The practice direction may set out those cases in which an application for permission must be made by application notice before the application is issued.

(3) The application for permission –

- (a) need not be served on any other person; and
- (b) must be accompanied by a copy of the application which the applicant proposes to issue.

(4) Where the court gives permission, it will give directions about the future management of the application.

19.5 Acknowledgment of service

(1) Subject to paragraph (2), each respondent must –

- (a) file an acknowledgment of service within 14 days beginning with the date on which the application is served; and
- (b) serve the acknowledgment of service on the applicant and any other party.

(2) If the application is to be served out of the jurisdiction, the respondent must file and serve an acknowledgment of service within the period set out in Practice Direction 6B.

(3) The acknowledgment of service must –

(a) state whether the respondent contests the application;

(b) state, if the respondent seeks a different order from that set out in the application, what that order is; and

(c) be signed by the respondent or the respondent's legal representative.

19.6 Consequence of not filing an acknowledgment of service

(1) This rule applies where –

(a) the respondent has failed to file an acknowledgment of service; and

(b) the time period for doing so has expired.

(2) The respondent may attend the hearing of the application but may not take part in the hearing unless the court gives permission.

19.7 Filing and serving written evidence

(1) The applicant must, when filing the application, file the written evidence on which the applicant intends to rely.

(2) The applicant's evidence must be served on the respondent with the application.

(3) A respondent who wishes to rely on written evidence must file it when filing the acknowledgment of service.

(4) A respondent who files written evidence must also, at the same time, serve a copy of that evidence on the other parties.

(5) Within 14 days beginning with the date on which a respondent's evidence was served on the applicant, the applicant may file further written evidence in reply.

(6) An applicant who files further written evidence must also, within the same time limit, serve a copy of that evidence on the other parties.

19.8 Evidence – general

(1) No written evidence may be relied on at the hearing of the application unless –

(a) it has been served in accordance with rule 19.7; or

(b) the court gives permission.

(2) The court may require or permit a party to give oral evidence at the hearing.

(3) The court may give directions requiring the attendance for cross-examination[(GL)] of a witness who has given written evidence.

(Rule 22.1 contains a general power for the court to control evidence.)

19.9 Procedure where respondent objects to use of the Part 19 procedure

(1) A respondent who contends that the Part 19 procedure should not be used because –

(a) there is a substantial dispute of fact; and

(b) the use of the Part 19 procedure is not required or permitted by a rule or practice direction,

must state the reasons for that contention when filing the acknowledgment of service.

(2) When the court receives the acknowledgment of service and any written evidence, it will give directions as to the future management of the case.

(Rule 19.7 requires a respondent who wishes to rely on written evidence to file it when filing the acknowledgment of service.)

(Rule 19.1(3) allows the court to make an order that the application continue as if the applicant had not used the Part 19 procedure.)

Practice Direction 19A – Alternative Procedure for Applications

This Practice Direction supplements FPR Part 19

Types of application in which Part 19 procedure must be used

1.1 An applicant must use the Part 19 procedure if the application is for an order under –

(a) section 60(3) of the 2002 Act, to prevent disclosure of information to an adopted person;
(b) section 79(4) of the 2002 Act, to require the Registrar General to provide information; or
(c) rule 14.21 (Inherent jurisdiction and fathers without parental responsibility) in Part 14, to request directions of the High Court regarding fathers without parental responsibility.

Types of application in which Part 19 procedure may be used

1.2 An applicant may use the Part 19 procedure if Part 18 does not apply and if –

(a) there is no prescribed form in which to make the application; or
(b) the applicant seeks the court's decision on a question which is unlikely to involve a substantial dispute of fact.

1.3 An applicant may also use the Part 19 procedure if a practice direction permits or requires its use for the type of proceedings concerned.

1.4 The practice directions referred to in paragraph 1.3 may in some respects modify or disapply the Part 19 procedure and, where that is so, it is those practice directions, rather than this one, which must be complied with.

1.5 The types of application for which the Part 19 procedure may be used include an application for an order or direction which is unopposed by each respondent before the commencement of the proceedings and the sole purpose of the application is to obtain the approval of the court to the agreement.

1.6 Where it appears to a court officer that an applicant is using the Part 19 procedure inappropriately, the officer may refer the application to the court for consideration of the point.

1.7 The court may at any stage order the application to continue as if the applicant had not used the Part 19 procedure and, if it does so, the court will give such directions as it considers appropriate (see rule 19.1(3)).

The application

2.1 Where an applicant uses the Part 19 procedure, the application form referred to in Practice Direction 5A should be used and must state the matters set out in rule 19.3 and, if paragraphs 1.3 and 1.4 apply, must comply with the requirements of the practice direction in question. In particular, the application form must state that Part 19 applies. A Part 19 application form means an application form which so states.

2.2 An application –

(a) in accordance with rule 19.4, to ask the High Court for directions on the need to give a father without parental responsibility notice of the intention to place a child for adoption; or
(b) under section 60(3) of the 2002 Act for an order to prevent disclosure of information to an adopted person,

may be issued without naming a respondent.

PART III

Responding to the application

3.1 Where a respondent who wishes to respond to a Part 19 application is required to file an acknowledgement of service, that acknowledgement of service should be in form FP5 which is referred to in Practice Direction 5A but can, alternatively be given in an informal document such as a letter.

3.2 Rule 19.5 sets out provisions relating to an acknowledgement of service of a Part 19 application.

3.3 Rule 19.6 sets out the consequence of failing to file an acknowledgement of service.

3.4 A respondent who believes that the Part 19 procedure should not be used because there is a substantial dispute of fact or, as the case may be, because its use is not authorised by any rule in the FPR or any practice direction, must state the reasons for that belief in writing when filing the acknowledgement of service (see rule 19.9). If the statement of reasons includes matters of evidence, it should be verified by a statement of truth.

Managing the application

4.1 The court may give directions immediately a Part 19 application is issued either on the application of a party or of its own initiative. The directions may include fixing a hearing date where –

(a) there is no dispute; or

(b) where there may be a dispute, but a hearing date could conveniently be given.

4.2 Where the court does not fix a hearing date when the application is issued, it will give directions for the disposal of the application as soon as practicable after the respondent has acknowledged service of the application or, as the case may be, after the period for acknowledging service has expired.

4.3 Certain applications may not require a hearing.

4.4 The court may convene a directions hearing before giving directions.

Evidence

5.1 An applicant wishing to rely on written evidence should file it when the Part 19 application form is issued.

5.2 Evidence will normally be in the form of a witness statement or an affidavit but an applicant may rely on the matters set out in the application form provided it has been verified by a statement of truth.

(For information about statements of truth see Part 7 and Practice Direction 17A, and about written evidence see Part 22 and Practice Direction 22A.)

5.3 A respondent wishing to rely on written evidence should file it with the acknowledgement of service (see rule 19.7(3)).

5.4 Rule 19.7 sets out the times and provisions for filing and serving written evidence.

5.5 A party may apply to the court for an extension of time to serve and file evidence under rule 19.7 or for permission to serve and file additional evidence under rule 19.8(1).

(For information about applications see Part 18 and Practice Direction 18A.)

5.6 The parties may, subject to paragraphs 5.7 and 5.8, agree in writing on an extension of time for serving and filing evidence under rule 19.7(3) or rule 19.7(5).

5.7 An agreement extending time for a respondent to file evidence in reply under rule 19.7(3) –

(a) must be filed by the respondent at the same time as the acknowledgement of service; and

(b) must not extend time by more than 17 days after the respondent files the acknowledgement of service.

5.8 An agreement extending time for an applicant to file evidence in reply under rule 19.7(5) must not extend time to more than 28 days after service of the respondent's evidence on the applicant.

Hearing

6.1 The court may on the hearing date –

(a) proceed to hear the case and dispose of the application;
(b) give case management directions.

PART 20
INTERIM REMEDIES AND SECURITY FOR COSTS

CONTENTS OF THIS PART

Chapter 1

Rule		Page
	Interim Remedies	
20.2	Orders for interim remedies	1742
20.3	Time when an order for an interim remedy may be made	1745
20.4	How to apply for an interim remedy	1746
20.5	Interim injunction to cease if application is stayed	1746
	Chapter 2	
	Security for Costs	
20.6	Security for costs	1746
20.7	Conditions to be satisfied	1747
20.8	Security for costs of an appeal	1747
	Practice Direction 20A – Interim Remedies	1748

Interim remedies: terminology—FPR 2010 uses the terms 'any other hearing' (i e other than a 'final hearing': e g FPR 2010, r 22.2(1)) and 'interim', interchangeably. The final hearing disposes of the issue before the court; whereas the interim hearing is preparatory for that. The injunction is interim to the extent that it does not dispose of a final issue (by definition) but it is often final in effect, since it provides the remedy sought by the applicant (e g FLA 1996, Pts IV and 4A; PFHA 1997). MFPA 1984, s 31F(2) confirms that orders in the Family Court can be interim. In the Family Division, and in the absence of specific statutory provision, the power to make interim orders is inherent.

Scope—FPR 2010, Pt 20 deals with two separate subjects: application (supplementing the FPR 2010, Pt 18 procedure) for certain interim remedies not otherwise provided for in the rules; and security for costs.

Inherent jurisdiction—Injunctions originate from the equitable jurisdiction of the High Court, and declarations are a creation of the mid-19th century. The Family Court has no inherent jurisdiction, so that, for example, any powers to grant injunctive relief depends on MFPA 1984, s 31E(1)(a) and the power conferred thereby on the Family Court to make orders that can be made by the High Court.

Pt 18 jurisdiction—Interim remedy applications (whether listed in FPR 2010, r 20.2(1) or not) are made by the FPR 2010, Pt 18 procedure: applications under Pt 20, by definition, will be parasitic on existing or proposed proceedings (see FPR 2010, r 18.1(2)), save in the case of, for example, proceedings under SCA 1981, s 33 (disclosure prior to issue of proceedings, when the Pt 19 procedure is likely to apply). The provisions of Pt 20 add to the Pt 18 procedure particular steps which are appropriate to seeking an interim remedy and confirm, for example, that an interim remedy can be applied for 'without notice if it appears to the court that there are good reasons for not giving notice' (FPR 2010, r 20.4(1)).

Remedy defines procedure—It is the remedy which defines or demands the procedure. Pts IV and 4A of FLA 1996 have created their own procedures (FPR 2010, Pts 10 and 11). Civil Procedure Act 1997, s 7 procedures exist independently of CPR 1998, Pt 25 (and FPR 2010, Pt 20) by which they are obtained. If the law provides a remedy, procedure must find a means to provide it. FPR 2010, r 20.2(3) confirms that the fact that a remedy is not listed in Pt 20 does not 'affect any power the court may have to grant that remedy'.

Other interim remedies—FPR 2010, Pt 20 merely elaborates FPR 2010, Pt 18 and is specific to no particular aspect of family proceedings. Other interim remedies, which are likely to impact more frequently on the family lawyer's practice and which have their own procedures in the rules are to be found as follows:

- Interim financial remedy – FPR 2010, r 9.7
- FLA 1996, Pt IV – FPR 2010, Pt 10
- FLA 1996, Pt 4A – FPR 2010, Pt 11

- Interim orders in private law children proceedings (except those forms of proceedings referred in FPR PD20A, para 1.1)
- Costs allowances where not available as LSPOs under MCA 1973: s 22ZA (eg in CA 1989, Sch 1 proceedings)
- Scientific tests direction: FLRA 1969, s 20 and CPR PD23B.

Chapter 1
Interim Remedies

20.1 *(revoked)*

20.2 Orders for interim remedies

(1) The court may grant the following interim remedies –

(a) an interim injunction(GL);
(b) an interim declaration;
(c) an order –
   (i) for the detention, custody or preservation of relevant property;
   (ii) for the inspection of relevant property;
   (iii) for the taking of a sample of relevant property;
   (iv) for the carrying out of an experiment on or with relevant property;
   (v) for the sale of relevant property which is of a perishable nature or which for any other good reason it is desirable to sell quickly; and
   (vi) for the payment of income from relevant property until an application is decided;
(d) an order authorising a person to enter any land or building in the possession of a party to the proceedings for the purposes of carrying out an order under sub-paragraph (c);
(e) an order under section 4 of the Torts (Interference with Goods) Act 1977 to deliver up goods;
(f) an order (referred to as a 'freezing injunction(GL)') –
   (i) restraining a party from removing from the jurisdiction assets located there; or
   (ii) restraining a party from dealing with any assets whether located within the jurisdiction or not;
(g) an order directing a party to provide information about the location of relevant property or assets or to provide information about relevant property or assets which are or may be the subject of an application for a freezing injunction(GL);
(h) an order (referred to as a 'search order') under section 7 of the Civil Procedure Act 1997 (order requiring a party to admit another party to premises for the purpose of preserving evidence etc.);
(i) an order under section 34 of the Senior Courts Act 1981 or section 53 of the County Courts Act 1984 (order in certain proceedings for disclosure of documents or inspection of property against a non-party);
(j) an order for a specified fund to be paid into court or otherwise secured, where there is a dispute over a party's right to the fund;
(k) an order permitting a party seeking to recover personal property to pay money into court pending the outcome of the proceedings and directing that, if money is paid into court, the property must be given up to that party;
(l) an order directing a party to prepare and file accounts relating to the dispute;
(m) an order directing any account to be taken or inquiry to be made by the court.

(2) In paragraph (1)(c) and (g), 'relevant property' means property (including land) which is the subject of an application or as to which any question may arise on an application.

(3) The fact that a particular kind of interim remedy is not listed in paragraph (1) does not affect any power that the court may have to grant that remedy.

Interim remedies—The term 'interim remedies' for the purposes of FPR 2010, Pt 20 is not defined. The remedies listed in FPR 2010, r 20.2(1) are taken from CPR 1998, r 25.1(1). Three of the civil proceedings remedies have been removed from the CPR 1998 list, but otherwise the list is not tailored to family proceedings.

Urgency—There is nothing to say that FPR 2010, Pt 20 is exclusive to remedies which are unusual or urgent, but they are mostly geared to urgency (eg without notice applications in FPR 2010, r 20.4).

Powers of High Court to grant injunctions—Section 37 of SCA 1981 confirms the inherent power of the High Court to make injunctions: 'The High Court may by order (whether [interim] or final) grant an injunction ... in all cases in which it appears to the court to be just and convenient to do so.'

Allocation of emergency applications—FC(CDB)R 2014, rr 16, 17 deals with allocation of interim and emergency applications:

- in existing proceedings: generally allocation is to the level of judge already dealing with the case (r 17(1));
- in the majority of the types of proceedings referred to in FPR 2010, r 20.2, allocation is in negative terms (ie the reader is told which judge may not deal with the application) in accordance with r 17(3) and Sch 2 (eg by Sch 2, Table 3, para 2 a search order (CPA 1997, s 7) cannot be dealt with by any judges of the Family Court so must be dealt with by a High Court Judge or higher from the list at MFPA 1984, s 31C(1)(a)–(i));
- in children proceedings (r 16(3)) and under FLA 1996, Pts 4 (domestic abuse) and 4A (forced marriage) (r 16(5)).

A discretionary remedy—The grant of an injunction is a matter for the court's discretion (SCA 1981, s 37(1): see *National Commercial Bank of Jamaica Ltd v Olint Corp Ltd (Jamaica)* [2009] 1 WLR 1405, PC, per Lord Hoffmann, especially in the context of an urgent order. He emphasised, first, that the court must adopt a course which seemed 'likely to cause the least irremediable prejudice to one party or the other'; and, second, in doing so the court should carry out an assessment in which, said Lord Hoffmann (adopting the words of Lord Diplock in *American Cyanamid Co v Ethicon Ltd* [1975] AC 396, HL): 'It would be unwise to attempt even to list all the various matters which may need to be taken into consideration in deciding where the balance lies, let alone to suggest the relative weight to be attached to them.' In terms of justice to the parties the court must 'assess whether granting or withholding an injunction is more likely to produce a just result'. Ultimately, can the court be satisfied, at the time of hearing the final application, that 'it will [then] appear that ... the injunction was rightly granted'?

PART III

JURISDICTION TO MAKE A WITHOUT NOTICE ORDER

Without notice applications—Judicial concern at the extent of without notice applications (r 20.4(3)) has been expressed in particular for without notice orders in *B v A (Wasted Costs Order)* [2013] 2 FLR 958, FD, *KY v DD* [2012] 2 FLR 200, FD (with approval of the then President) and *UL v BK (Freezing Orders: safeguards: Standard Examples)* [2013] EWHC 1735 (Fam). The following factors have been emphasised:

1 An interim remedy may be granted at any time, including 'before proceedings are started' (FPR 2010, r 20.3(1)(a)). The court must give directions requiring issue of an application (r 20.3(3) and FPR PD20A, para 4.4(a)).

2 The application must be supported by evidence (r 20.4(2)) and must include a statement as to why the application cannot be made on notice (r 20.4(3)).

3 An order under r 20.3(1)(a) can only be made (i) if urgent or (ii) 'desirable ... in the interests of justice' (r 20.3(2)(b)).

4 An order not on notice can only be made if there are good reasons for not giving notice (r 20.4(1)) (eg notice would cause the subject matter of the order to be destroyed: see, for example, *Olint* (below)).

5 Generally, there should always be some notice, even a telephone call: '... audi alterem partem [hear the other side] is a salutary and important principle.... Any notice is better than none' (*National Commercial Bank of Jamaica Ltd v Olint Corp Ltd (Jamaica)* [2009] 1 WLR 1405, PC per Lord Hoffman; *Moat Housing Group-South Ltd v Harris* [2005] 2 FLR 551, CA).

6 The applicant must make the fullest disclosure of all the relevant circumstances known to them – for and against their case, and whether of fact or law (*R v Kensington Income Tax Commissioners, ex p Princess Edmond de Polignac* [1917] 1 KB 486, CA).

7 An applicant must bring to the attention of the respondent, at the earliest practicable opportunity, the evidential and other materials on which the injunction was granted (FPR PD20A, para 5.1(b)).

8 In a without notice order, the court generally requires the applicant (and solicitors, as appropriate) to give the following undertakings (and see FPR PD20A, para 5.1(b)):
   (a) Where proceedings have not yet been issued, to issue and serve proceedings on the respondent, either by some specified time or as soon as practicable (and see r 20.3(3));
   (b) To file and serve sworn evidence where the application had been made on oral evidence or a draft affidavit (and see FPR PD20A, para 3.3); and
   (c) Subject to (a) and (b) above to serve on the respondent as soon as practicable (i) the proceedings, (ii) a sealed copy of the order, (iii) copies of the affidavit(s) and exhibit(s) containing the evidence relied on by the applicant (evidence must be by affidavit (FPR PD20A, para 3.1); and
   (d) notice of the return date including details of the application to be made on the return date (and see FPR PD20A, para 5.1(c)).

9 Good practice, fairness and indeed common sense demand (per Theis J and Charles J in *B Borough Council v S (by the Official Solicitor)* [2007] 1 FLR 1600, FD): on any application the applicant should provide the court with:
   (a) a balanced, fair and particularised account of the events leading up to the application; and in many cases this should include a brief account of what the applicant thinks the respondent's case is, or is likely to be (*R v Kensington Income Tax Commissioners*, above);
   (b) where available and appropriate, independent evidence should be filed;
   (c) a clear and particularised explanation of the reasons why the application is made without notice

(FPR 2010, r 20.4(3)) should be stated, and the reasons why any permission to apply to vary or discharge the injunction granted should be on notice; and
(d) in many cases, an account of the steps the applicant proposes concerning service, the giving of an explanation of the order and the implementation of an order.

10 Undertakings as to damages must be considered in appropriate (mostly financial) cases (FPR PD20A, para 5.1(a)), as considered further by Mostyn J in *ND v KP (Freezing Order: Ex Parte Application)* [2011] 2 FLR 662, FD).

11 In the case of a freezing order that covered all the respondent's assets, all principles and safeguards appropriate to such orders must be scrupulously adhered to (*UL v BK (Freezing Orders)* (above)).

FORMS OF ORDER

(1) Search order – Civil Procedure Act 1997, s 7

Search order in family proceedings—CPA 1997, s 7 provides for search orders. In *Imerman v Tchenguiz and Others* [2010] 2 FLR 814, CA, the court considered the availability of the search order in family proceedings (at [127]–[140]). They are as readily available in family, as in any other civil, proceedings, subject to issues such a proportionality: 'Such applications should be seriously considered where there are substantial reasons for believing that a husband is concealing or dissipating assets, or intending to conceal or destroy documents.' Removal of documents (or the freezing of electronic documents) should only be permitted by order of the High Court and under its supervision. It is not therefore open to the courts in any way to condone removal of confidential documents by spouses (at [136] and [137]). A spouse (or civil partner) was under no duty to disclose documents or information until such time as required to do so by FPR 2010, r 9.14(1) (filing and service of Form E) (and see **Introductory note** to Pt 21).

Practice Direction 20A and search orders—FPR PD20A, paras 6.1–6.9 provides detailed directions as to the application for and working out of a search order. It creates the concept of 'The Supervising Solicitor' (cf the parallel CPR PD25A for more explanation and information).

(2) Freezing injunction

Freezing orders and family proceedings—The spouse, parent (in CA 1989, Sch 1 proceedings), or civil partner involved in financial remedy proceedings where a restraint of disposal or other freezing order is sought from the court will consider precisely what order is sought alongside the powers of the particular court (if in the County Court) to grant the order; and the extent of the urgency of the order if sought on an interim basis and with or without notice to the other party. There is a distinction between freezing orders in support of a proprietary claim and freezing orders where the claim is in debt. In the latter case (which will include claims for arrears of maintenance), it is not legitimate to use a freezing injunction to secure advance security for the claim or to seek to prohibit reasonable expenditure by the respondent: *O'Farrell v O'Farrell* [2013] 1 FLR 77, QBD.

Freezing orders and matrimonial financial order proceedings—In financial order proceedings the court has power to make one of the following orders:

(1) *Order preventing a disposition* Restraining disposal where satisfied that a spouse (or civil partner) is about to make a disposition 'with intent to defeat' the other party's claim (MCA 1973, s 37(2)(a); MFPA 1984, s 23; CPA 2004, s 74(2) and Sch 7, para 15).
(2) *Shipman order* The High Court (and county court if CCA 1984, s 38 applies) can make an inherent jurisdiction order in terms of *Shipman v Shipman* [1991] 1 FLR 250, FD (Anthony Lincoln J, as a High Court judge, made an order in his inherent jurisdiction where he felt unable to make an order under MCA 1973, s 37(2)(a)).
(3) *Freezing injunction* The court can make the wider freezing injunction order where the facts of the case and the seriousness of the risk of disposal of assets justifies it.

Family proceedings where prevention of disposition orders are unavailable—Under CA 1989, Sch 1, the order preventing disposition is not available under statute; so any order would need to be in the inherent jurisdiction (per *Shipman*) or as a freezing injunction (under CPA 1997, s 7(1)(b)). This position applies also to the freezing of assets, or prevention of their disposal, under TOLATA 1996, s 14 (eg where a constructive trust declaration is sought), when application would be in accordance with CPR 1998, Pt 25.

(3) Other applications under Part 20

SCA 1981, s 34—Section 34 of SCA 1981 deals with disclosure of documents by a third party (for more detail, see MFPA 1984, s 31J; FPR 2010, r 22.12).

Writ ne exeat regno—The writ ne exeat regno is applied for under FPR 2010, Pt 20 (r 20.2(3)) in the High Court and in the existing case or matter (which must be transferred to a District Registry). The FPR 2010, Pt 18 application (on an urgent basis, as need be: FPR 2010, rr 20.3 and 20.4) is supported by an affidavit (FPR PD20A, para 3.1), which will include reference to (iii)–(v) of the provisos set out in *Young v Young* [2012] 2 FLR 470, FD, at [26] (see further **Writ ne exeat regno** and **Impounding of a respondent's passport** under SCA 1981, s 19).

Duration of a without notice order

Duration of orders made without notice in family proceedings—The subject of how long an interim order made without notice lasts can be divided into orders under the following (most of which are listed in r 20.2):

(a) Inherent injunctions and declaration;
(b) Civil Procedure Act 1997 (search and freezing orders);
(c) Children proceedings orders;
(d) Orders under FLA 1996, Pt IV (mostly non-molestation orders);
(e) Orders under FLA 1996, Pt 4A (forced marriage protection orders) and under FGMA 2003.

Return date—PD20A, para 5.1 states that if an order is made against a party without notice to that party, 'Any [interim] order … unless the court orders otherwise, must contain: … a return date for a further hearing at which the other party can be present'. This provision applies to all interim orders covered by FPR 2010, Pt 20. Although the Practice Guidance of 18 January 2017 (see below) states that without notices must have a return date (e g see para 5(i)), this is not entirely in line with PD20A, which enables a judge to make an order without a return date if 'the court [so] orders'.

Procedure under statute: particular statutory provisions—In the case of without notice orders under FLA 1996, ss 45 and 63D and FGMA 2003, s 5, the court must 'afford the respondent an opportunity to make representation about an order' (FLA 1996, s 63D(3) and FGMA 2003, s 5(3)) which, in the case of s 45, must be at a hearing' (s 45(3)).

FPR 2010, Pt 18—If the above without notice applications are dealt with in similar terms to other applications under FPR 2010, Pt 18 – all interim applications under Pt 20 are made under the Pt 18 procedure – then the court is bound by FPR 2010, rr 18.10(3) and 18.11(1). These provisions require only that a respondent to a without notice be told of his/her right to apply to have the order set aside.

Practice guidance—The Practice Guidance of 18 January 2017: *Family Court – Duration of Ex Parte (Without Notice) Orders* applies to without notice orders in family proceedings (other than freezing and search orders: para 8), but must be read subject to FLA 1996, ss 45(3) and 63D(3) and FGMA 2003, s 5(3), FPR 2010, Pts 18 and 20 and PD20A, para 5.1.

PART III

20.3 Time when an order for an interim remedy may be made

(1) An order for an interim remedy may be made at any time, including –

(a) before proceedings are started; and
(b) after judgment has been given.

(Rule 5.3 provides that proceedings are started when the court issues an application form.)

(2) However –

(a) paragraph (1) is subject to any rule, practice direction or other enactment which provides otherwise; and
(b) the court may grant an interim remedy before an application has been started only if –
 (i) the matter is urgent; or
 (ii) it is otherwise desirable to do so in the interests of justice.

(3) Where the court grants an interim remedy before an application has been started, it will give directions requiring an application to be started.

(4) The court need not direct that an application be started where the application is made under section 33 of the Senior Courts Act 1981 or section 52 of the County Courts Act 1984 (order for disclosure, inspection etc. before starting an application).

Procedure for an interim remedy: urgent applications—Procedure for an interim remedy is governed by rules in relation to the FPR 2010, Pt 18 procedure supplemented by FPR 2010, rr 20.3 and 20.4 and FPR PD20A. An interim remedy can be applied for at any time:

- before issue of proceedings (e g to protect assets or documents or otherwise to preserve the status quo) and with suitable undertakings given to the court by the applicant;
- during (i e interim, formerly interlocutory) to proceedings; and
- after judgment has been given (e g to protect disposal of assets as part of enforcement of an order).

'proceedings are started'—Proceedings are started where an 'application' is issued by the court office (FPR 2010, r 5.3(1)).

Service of the application—Application and supporting evidence must be served 'as soon as practicable after issue and in any event not less than 7 days before the application is heard' (FPR PD20A, para 2.2). Because 7 days excludes the day of hearing, the day of service and non-business days (r 2.8), it will always be 1 day under a fortnight (longer if Bank Holidays intervene), save where non-service is justified, such as:

- where service of the application might frustrate the action the court is being asked to take by the injunction (e g to protect a child's welfare, such as by encouraging a child to abscond (*Re K and D (Wardship Without Notice Return Order)* [2017] EWHC 153 (Fam)); or
- where service might enable a respondent to defeat the purpose of the application (*National Commercial Bank of Jamaica Ltd v Olint Corp Ltd (Jamaica)* [2009] 1 WLR 1405, PC).

'interim remedy … before an application has been started, [the court] will give directions' (r 20.3(3))—If the court makes an order before the substantive application has been issued, it must give directions as to the filing of application forms and (perhaps) any other evidence. This provision enables the court (as appropriate) to give full case management directions (FPR 2010, rr 1.4 and 4.1).

Senior Courts Act 1981, ss 33 (r 20.3(4))—See under MFPA 1984, s 31I.

20.4 How to apply for an interim remedy

(1) The court may grant an interim remedy on an application made without notice if it appears to the court that there are good reasons for not giving notice.

(2) An application for an interim remedy must be supported by evidence, unless the court orders otherwise.

(3) If the applicant makes an application without giving notice, the evidence in support of the application must state the reasons why notice has not been given.

(Part 4 lists general case-management powers of the court.)

(Part 18 contains general rules about making an application.)

'without notice' applications and evidence in support (r 20.4(1) and (3))—Whereas application for an order is under FPR 2010, Pt 18 (see above), r 20.4 deals with:

(1) applications for an interim remedy 'made without notice'; and
(2) the need to support any application 'with evidence', a provision which is extended substantially by common law.

Without notice applications: order 'desirable ... in the interests of justice' (r 20.3(2)(b))—Before issue of proceedings, the court may only grant an injunction on grounds of urgency or if 'it is otherwise desirable to do so in the interests of justice', which will depend on the facts of each case, as explained in *National Commercial Bank of Jamaica Ltd v Olint Corp Ltd (Jamaica)* [2009] 1 WLR 1405, PC. Whether to permit the hearing of a without notice (ex parte) application is entirely a matter for the individual judge, but:

> '[*A*]*udi alterem partem* [hear the other party] is a salutary and important principle ... [A] judge should not entertain an application of which no notice has been given unless either giving notice would enable the defendant to take steps to defeat the purpose of the injunction (as in the case of a *Mareva* or *Anton Piller* order [i e freezing injunction or search order]) or there has been literally no time to give notice before the injunction is required to prevent the threatened wrongful act'.

Applicant's duties to the court and other parties: full and fair disclosure—Any affidavit or witness statement in support of an application made without notice must provide the court with full and fair disclosure of the party's case and of the evidence to support it (see e g reference (for all interim remedy applications) in PD20A, para 3.3). The applicant is asking the court to exercise what originates in an equitable jurisdiction. The applicant therefore owes to the court (and to the party to be subject to any order) a duty to provide to the court not only evidence in support of, but any with information adverse to, his case (*R v Kensington Income Tax Commissioners, ex p Princess Edmond de Polignac* [1917] 1 KB 486, CA, at [514]).

Evidence in support of an application—Applications for search orders and freezing injunctions must be supported by affidavit evidence (FPR PD20A, para 3.1), whereas other applications should be supported by witness statement with statement of truth (FPR PD20A, para 3.2: if in doubt file affidavit evidence).

20.5 Interim injunction to cease if application is stayed

If – (a) the court has granted an interim injunction(GL) other than a freezing injunction(GL); and
(b) the application is stayed(GL) other than by agreement between the parties,

the interim injunction(GL) will be set aside(GL) unless the court orders that it should continue to have effect even though the application is stayed(GL).

'the court has granted an injunction' (r 20.5(a))—This wording logically refers to any injunction. Thus, where the injunction only is the intent of the proceedings, if the application is taken no further once the order is made, there is a real possibility that, unless application (at further cost) is made to continue the order, it may be set aside under this provision.

'application'—An application may be in the form of an 'application form' (i e the proceedings as a whole) or 'application notice' (i e the FPR Pt 18 application for the injunction).

Chapter 2
Security for Costs

20.6 Security for costs

(1) A respondent to any application may apply under this Chapter of this Part for security for costs of the proceedings.

(Part 4 provides for the court to order payment of sums into court in other circumstances.)

(2) An application for security for costs must be supported by written evidence.

(3) Where the court makes an order for security for costs, it will –

(a) determine the amount of security; and

(b) direct –
(i) the manner in which; and
(ii) the time within which,
the security must be given.

Defined terms—'court': r 2.3(1).

Application for security for costs—Application is by the FPR 2010, Pt 18 procedure (*Charman v Charman (No 3)* [2007] 1 FLR 1237, CA provides a rare example in family proceedings where the husband was resident out of the jurisdiction).

20.7 Conditions to be satisfied

(1) The court may make an order for security for costs under rule 20.6 if –

(a) it is satisfied, having regard to all the circumstances of the case, that it is just to make such an order; and
(b) either –
(i) one or more of the conditions in paragraph (2) applies; or
(ii) an enactment permits the court to require security for costs.

(2) The conditions are –

(a) the applicant is –
(i) resident out of the jurisdiction; but
(ii) not resident in a Brussels Contracting State, a State bound by the Lugano Convention, a State bound by the 2007 Hague Convention which is an EEA State, a Regulation State or a Maintenance Regulation State, as defined in section 1(3) of the Civil Jurisdiction and Judgments Act 1982, or a Member State bound by the Council Regulation;
(b) the applicant has changed address since the application was started with a view to evading the consequences of the litigation;
(c) the applicant failed to give an address in the application form, or gave an incorrect address in that form;
(d) the applicant has taken steps in relation to the applicant's assets that would make it difficult to enforce an order for costs against the applicant.

(3) The court may not make an order for security for costs under rule 20.6 in relation to the costs of proceedings under the 1980 Hague Convention.

(Rule 4.4 allows the court to strike out(GL) a statement of case.)

('EEA State' is defined in Schedule 1 to the Interpretation Act 1978).

Amendments—SI 2011/1328; SI 2012/679; SI 2012/2806.

Security for costs in family proceedings—This rule has been taken directly from CPR 1998, Pt 25, which relates to a jurisdiction where costs orders are the rule, whereas in family proceedings costs are the exception.

20.8 Security for costs of an appeal

The court may order security for costs of an appeal against –

(a) an appellant;
(b) a respondent who also appeals,

on the same grounds as it may order security for costs against an applicant under this Part.

Practice Direction 20A – Interim Remedies

This Practice Direction supplements FPR Part 20

Scope and jurisdiction

1.1 This Practice Direction does not apply to an order under section 48 (Powers to assist in discovery of children who may be in need of emergency protection), section 50 (Recovery of abducted children, etc.) of the Children Act 1989 or section 33(Power to order disclosure of child's whereabouts) or section 34 (Power to order recovery of child) of the Family Law Act 1986.

1.2 The Family Court (Composition and Distribution of Business) Rules 2014 make provision in relation to which judges may not grant certain remedies in the family court.

1.3 In a case in the High Court, district judges have the power to grant injunctions –

(a) by consent;
(b) in connection with charging orders and appointments of receivers;
(c) in aid of execution of judgments.

1.4–1.5 (*omitted*)

Making an application

2.1 The application notice must state –

(a) the order sought; and
(b) the date, time and place of the hearing.

2.2 The application notice and evidence in support must be served as soon as practicable after issue and in any event not less than 7 days before the court is due to hear the application unless the court directs otherwise.

2.3 Where the court is to serve, sufficient copies of the application notice and evidence in support for the court and for each respondent should be filed for issue and service.

2.4 Whenever possible a draft of the order sought should be filed with the application notice and an electronic version of the draft should also be available to the court in a format compatible with the word processing software used by the court and on such storage medium as shall be agreed by the court. This will enable the court officer to arrange for any amendments to be incorporated and for the speedy preparation and sealing of the order.

Evidence

3.1 Applications for search orders and freezing injunctions must be supported by affidavit evidence.

3.2 Applications for other interim injunctions must be supported by evidence set out in either –

(a) a witness statement; or
(b) the application notice provided that it is verified by a statement of truth,

unless the court, an Act, a rule in the FPR or a practice direction requires evidence by affidavit.

3.3 The evidence must set out the facts on which the applicant relies for the application being made against the respondent, including all material facts of which the court should be made aware.

3.4 Where an application is made without notice to the respondent, the evidence must also set out why notice was not given.

(See Part 22 and the practice direction that supplements it for information about evidence.)

Urgent applications and applications without notice

4.1 These fall into two categories –

(a) applications where an application in proceedings has already been issued; and
(b) applications where an application in proceedings has not yet been issued,

and, in both cases, where notice of the application has not been given to the respondent.

4.2 These applications are normally dealt with at a court hearing but cases of extreme urgency may be dealt with by telephone.

4.3 In relation to applications dealt with at a court hearing after issue of an application form –

(a) the application notice, evidence in support and a draft order (as in paragraph 2.4) should be filed with the court two hours before the hearing wherever possible;
(b) if an application is made before the application notice has been issued, a draft order (as in paragraph 2.4) should be provided at the hearing, and the application notice and evidence in support must be filed with the court on the same or next working day or as ordered by the court; and
(c) except in cases where it is essential that the respondent must not be aware of the application, the applicant should take steps to notify the respondent informally of the application.

4.4 In relation to applications made before the issue of an application –

(a) in addition to the provisions set out at paragraph 4.3, unless the court orders otherwise, either the applicant must undertake to the court to issue an application notice immediately or the court will give directions for the commencement of the application (see rule 20.3(3));
(b) where possible the application should be served with the order for the injunction;
(c) an order made before the issue of an application should state in the title after the names of the applicant and respondent 'the Applicant and Respondent in Intended Proceedings'.

4.5 In relation to applications made outside normal working hours –

(a) the applicant should either –
    (i) telephone the Royal Courts of Justice on 020 7947 6000 to be put in contact with the clerk to the appropriate duty judge in the High Court (or the appropriate area Circuit Judge where known); or
    (ii) telephone the Urgent Court Business Officer of the appropriate Circuit who will contact the local duty judge;
(b) where the facility is available it is likely that the judge will require a draft order to be faxed to him;
(c) the application notice and evidence in support must be filed with the court on the same or next working day or as ordered, together with two copies of the order for sealing;
(d) injunctions will be heard by telephone only where the applicant is acting by counsel or solicitors.

4.6 Each Designated Family Judge area of the family court will have its own scheme for out of hours applications, details of which will be given locally to:

– the police;
– any local Law Society and Bar organisation; and
– the local authority Social Services Department.

Orders for injunctions

5.1 Any order for an injunction, unless the court orders otherwise, must contain –

(a) an undertaking by the applicant to the court to pay any damages which the respondent sustains which the court considers the applicant should pay;

PART III

(b) if the order is made without notice to any other party, an undertaking by the applicant to the court to serve on the respondent the application notice, evidence in support and any order made as soon as practicable;
(c) if the order is made without notice to any other party, a return date for a further hearing at which the other party can be present;
(d) if the order is made before filing the application notice, an undertaking to file and pay the appropriate fee on the same or next working day; and
(e) if the order is made before issue of an application in proceedings –
(i) an undertaking to issue and pay the appropriate fee on the same or next working day; or
(ii) directions for the commencement of the application.

5.2 When the court makes an order for an injunction, it should consider whether to require an undertaking by the applicant to pay any damages sustained by a person other than the respondent, including another party to the proceedings or any other person who may suffer loss as a consequence of the order.

5.3 An order for an injunction made in the presence of all parties to be bound by it or made at a hearing of which they have had notice, may state that it is effective until final hearing or further order.

5.4 Any order for an injunction must set out clearly what the respondent must do or not do.

SEARCH ORDERS

Orders for the preservation of evidence and property

6.1 The following provisions apply to search orders in addition to those listed above.

The Supervising Solicitor

6.2 The Supervising Solicitor must be experienced in the operation of search orders. A Supervising Solicitor may be contacted either through the Law Society or, for the London area, through the London Solicitors Litigation Association.

Evidence

6.3 (1) The affidavit must state the name, firm and its address, and experience of the Supervising Solicitor, also the address of the premises and whether it is a private or business address.
(2) The affidavit must disclose very fully the reason the order is sought, including the probability that relevant material would disappear if the order were not made.

Service

6.4 (1) The order must be served personally by the Supervising Solicitor, unless the court directs otherwise, and must be accompanied by the evidence in support and any documents capable of being copied.
(2) Confidential exhibits need not be served but they must be made available for inspection by the respondent in the presence of the applicant's solicitors while the order is carried out and afterwards be retained by the respondent's solicitors on their undertaking not to permit the respondent –
(a) to see them or copies of them except in their presence; and
(b) to make or take away any note or record of them.
(3) The Supervising Solicitor may be accompanied only by the persons mentioned in the order.
(4) The Supervising Solicitor must explain the terms and effect of the order to the respondent in everyday language and advise the respondent –
(a) of the respondent's right to take legal advice, and to apply to vary or discharge the order; and

(b) that the respondent may be entitled to avail himself of –
(i) legal professional privilege; and
(ii) the privilege against self-incrimination.

(5) Where the Supervising Solicitor is a man and the respondent is likely to be an unaccompanied woman, at least one other person named in the order must be a woman and must accompany the Supervising Solicitor.

(6) The order may only be served between 9.30 a.m. and 5.30 p.m. Monday to Friday unless the court directs otherwise.

Search and custody of materials

6.5 (1) No material shall be removed unless clearly covered by the terms of the order.

(2) The premises must not be searched and no items shall be removed from them except in the presence of the respondent or a person who appears to be a responsible employee of the respondent.

(3) Where copies of documents are sought, the documents should be retained for no more than 2 days before return to the owner.

(4) Where material in dispute is removed pending hearing, the applicant's solicitors should place it in the custody of the respondent's solicitors on their undertaking to retain it in safekeeping and to produce it to the court when required.

(5) In appropriate cases the applicant should insure the material retained in the respondent's solicitors' custody.

(6) The Supervising Solicitor must make a list of all material removed from the premises and supply a copy of the list to the respondent.

(7) No material shall be removed from the premises until the respondent has had reasonable time to check the list.

(8) If any of the listed items exists only in computer readable form, the respondent must immediately give the applicant's solicitors effective access to the computers, with all necessary passwords, to enable them to be searched, and cause the listed items to be printed out.

(9) The applicant must take all reasonable steps to ensure that no damage is done to any computer or data.

(10) The applicant and his representatives may not themselves search the respondent's computers unless they have sufficient expertise to do so without damaging the respondent's system;

(11) the Supervising Solicitor shall provide a report on the carrying out of the order to the applicant's solicitors.

(12) As soon as the report is received the applicant's solicitors shall –
(a) serve a copy of it on the respondent; and
(b) file a copy of it with the court.

(13) Where the Supervising Solicitor is satisfied that full compliance with paragraph 6.5(7) and (8) above is impracticable, that Solicitor may permit the search to proceed and items to be removed without compliance with the impracticable requirements.

General

6.6 The Supervising Solicitor must not be an employee or member of the applicant's firm of solicitors.

6.7 If the court orders that the order need not be served by the Supervising Solicitor, the reason for so ordering must be set out in the order.

6.8 The search order must not be carried out at the same time as a police search warrant.

6.9 There is no privilege against self-incrimination in proceedings in which a court is hearing an application for an order under Part 4 or 5 of the Children Act 1989 (see section 98 of the Children Act 1989).

Delivery up orders

7.1 The following provision applies to orders, other than search orders, for delivery up or preservation of evidence or property where it is likely that such an order will be executed at the premises of the respondent or a third party.

7.2 In such cases the court will consider whether to include in the order for the benefit or protection of the parties similar provisions to those specified above in relation to injunctions and search orders.

Injunctions against third parties

8.1 The following provision applies to orders which will affect a person other than the applicant or respondent, who –

(a) did not attend the hearing at which the order was made; and
(b) is served with the order.

8.2 Where such a person served with the order requests –

(a) a copy of any materials read by the court, including material prepared after the hearing at the direction of the court or in compliance with the order; or
(b) a note of the hearing,

the applicant, or the applicant's legal representative, must comply promptly with the request, unless the court directs otherwise.

PART 21
MISCELLANEOUS RULES ABOUT DISCLOSURE AND INSPECTION OF DOCUMENTS

CONTENTS OF THIS PART

Rule		Page
21.1	Interpretation	1756
21.2	Orders for disclosure against a person not a party	1756
21.3	Claim to withhold inspection or disclosure of a document	1757
	Practice Direction 21A – Disclosure and Inspection	1759

Introductory note

FPR 2010 and disclosure—FPR 2010 does not provide a disclosure code for parties to family proceedings (as Moylan J points out in *Tchenguiz-Imerman v Imerman* [2014] 1 FLR 232, FD). Parties must refer to the common law, which is best summarised in CPR 1998, Pt 31. FPR 2010, Pt 21 deals only with definition of terms (r 21.1) and two other aspects of disclosure (disclosure against a third party under statute (r 21.2) and claims to withhold disclosure (r 21.3)). The remainder of rules as to disclosure must be found in common law, mostly in CPR 1998. This note deals with the subject of disclosure procedurally and comprises two main components: (1) disclosure between the parties to proceedings; and (2) release of court documents to non-parties or other publication ('collateral use').

Duty of disclosure: general—The general rule is that a fair trial demands that the court makes its decision on the basis of all available relevant evidence, which includes documentary evidence (to which disclosure is addressed). Certain documents may be exempt from disclosure, being covered by confidentiality or privacy (including privilege) or by public interest immunity. It is these exemptions or immunity that balance the general rule as to disclosure.

Duty of disclosure arises—The law is unclear as to when the duty to disclose arises: perhaps when proceedings begin; perhaps when parties jointly consent to mediate. In financial remedy proceedings, the duty has been held not to arise (mediation apart) until Form E is filed (*Imerman v Tchenguiz and Others* [2010] 2 FLR 814, CA). This has consequences as to when a person may be enjoined from unlawfully taking documents (and see, for example, conflict between the CA in *Lifely v Lifely* [2008] EWCA Civ 904 and Mostyn J in *UL v BK (Freezing Orders: safeguards: Standard Examples)* [2013] EWHC 1735 (Fam).

Continuing duty of disclosure—Once proceedings are begun, a duty of disclosure continues throughout. CPR 1998, r 31.11 stresses the common law rule that 'disclosure continues until the proceedings are concluded' (as explained by Stuart Smith LJ in *Vernon v Bosley (No 2)* [1998] 1 FLR 304, CA) and that common law applies equally to family, as to any other, civil proceedings.

Disclosure and the appellate process—In *N v N* [2015] 1 FLR 241, CA, McFarlane LJ considered the extent to which a duty to disclose arose in the period up to the hearing of an appeal. He considered he need not decide the point (at [53]), but made clear his own view that although there was no clear case-law on the point, he considered that 'the first instance process and the appellate process are very different and it does not follow as night follows day that what is essential for one is also essential for the other'. While any duty to disclose lies upon the person with the relevant documents and information, proof of an allegation that there has been non-disclosure is upon the applicant (see e g McFarlane LJ in *N v N* (above), at [72]).

New evidence before the appellate court—Where new evidence comes to light, it will be for the person who wishes to rely upon the fresh evidence to persuade the court to receive it (*Mulholland v Mitchell* [1971] AC 666, HL).

Terminology

(1) Disclosure

Disclosure—In law, 'disclosure' means only that a party states that s/he knows that a document 'exists or has existed' (CPR 1998, r 31.2; FPR 2010, r 21.1(1)). Any duty to produce does not arise until later. The requirement of forms to attach documents is in conflict with r 21.1(1) and the common law. Documents include electronic documents (and see CPR PD36B).

Inspection—Disclosure is accompanied by the right to inspect what is disclosed (CPR 1998, r 31.3(1); FPR 2010, r 21.1(2)). CPR 1998, r 31.3(1) sets out the exemptions to the rule as to inspection (FPR 2010, Pt 21 fails to do this, save by implication: FPR 2010, r 21.3; but r 31.3 can be assumed to represent the common law) as follows:

(1) Documents no longer in the possession or control of the disclosing party (see below)
(2) Documents to which a right to withhold is said to attach (e g privilege, confidentiality and PII and see FPR 2010, r 21.3 below)
(3) Documents the inspection of which the party claims would be disproportionate to the issues in the case (CPR 1998, r 31.3(2))

Production—Production means the act of producing documents that have been inspected at court (e g see terminology of FPR 2010, r 9.15(2)), mostly in a court bundle.

Possession or control—The meaning of 'control' is clarified in CPR 1998, r 31.8(2) and its meaning (especially in the context of committal proceedings) was explained in *North Shore Ventures Limited v Anstead Holdings Inc* [2012] EWCA Civ 11.

(2) Immunity from disclosure and privilege

Confidentiality—Confidentiality arises where one person reposes confidence in another. In *Att Gen v Guardian Newspapers Ltd (No 2)* [1990] 1 AC 109, HL (Spycatcher case) Lord Goff (at [281]) said confidentiality arose where 'information comes to the knowledge of a person (the confidant) in circumstances where he has notice, or is held to have agreed, that the information is confidential, with the effect that it would be just in all the circumstances that he should be precluded from disclosing the information to others'. The confider entrusts the confidant with their confidence and it must be respected. There is a public interest in confidentiality being maintained, but it may be overridden, for example, by a competing right (e g to a fair trial, see *Re A (Sexual Abuse: Disclosure)* [2013] 1 FLR 948, SC); or by statutory requirement (*Parry-Jones v Law Society* [1969] 1 Ch 1, CA and, for example, certain legal aid regulations). Confidentiality of itself does not give rise to privilege.

Privilege—'Privilege' entitles a party to court proceedings to withhold from the court otherwise relevant evidence. The most common forms of privilege are legal professional privilege (LPP; see below), self-incrimination privilege (not of immediate relevance in this guidance) and the immunity from disclosure that is derived from the without prejudice rule.

Legal professional privilege—LPP confers an absolute right, on the person entitled to it, not to have produced in court relevant information or documents (*R v Derby Magistrates' Court ex parte B* [1996] 1 FLR 513, HL). It comprises legal advice privilege (LAP) and litigation privilege (LP).

Legal advice privilege—LAP applies to advice in any 'relevant legal context' (*Balabel v Air India* [1988] Ch 317, CA) and whether or not court proceedings are in prospect. It enables any client to obtain advice in complete privacy (*Anderson v Bank of British Columbia* (1876) 2 ChD 644, CA).

Litigation privilege—LP applies only where proceedings are in prospect or are already under way and the dominant purpose of the evidence to which it attaches is the proceedings (*Waugh v British Railways Board* [1980] AC 521, HL; but see *Re L (Police Investigation: Privilege)* [1996] 1 FLR 731, HL, where the privilege is claimed in care proceedings).

Materials for litigation privilege—Where a party acts in person and has no lawyer, a similar privilege to LP may be said to exist in relation to evidence prepared by him/her in connection with forthcoming proceedings (and see *R (Kelly) v Warley Magistrates Court* [2007] EWHC Admin 1836).

Self-incrimination privilege—Self-incrimination privilege is the right to silence or the right of a party not to provide evidence against him/herself (*R v Director of Serious Fraud Office, ex parte Smith* [1993] AC 1, HL). It may be overridden in the public interest (*Brown v Stott* [2003] 1 AC 681, PC). See also, for example, CA 1989, s 98(2).

Without prejudice rule immunity—WP immunity is based on the public policy that parties should be encouraged to settle their litigation (or disputes that might lead to litigation) and on an implied contractual term that they agree that any admissions by either of them against their own interest cannot be disclosed to the court. The immunity is subject to a number of exceptions (summarised in *Unilever PLC v The Procter & Gamble Company* [2000] 1 WLR 2436, CA).

PART III

Privilege for non-court dispute resolution (including mediation)—There is no specific privilege for mediation or other non-court dispute resolution, although the proceedings may be confidential as between mediator and the parties (*Farm Assist Ltd v Secretary of State for the Environment, Food and Rural Affairs (No 2)* [2009] EWHC 1102 (TCC)). The parties can waive privilege as between themselves and the mediator will be fixed by this, subject to any court order overriding confidentiality.

Confidentiality and children—The confidentiality of children's evidence, whether as witnesses (potential or otherwise) or as parties to any proceedings or to mediation, is subject to no clear rules as to when their disclosures are or are not confidential, or even when legal professional privilege applies to them. Much may depend on to whom information was passed by a child (e g to a social worker, or to a lawyer for advice (when advice privilege applies)) and on the age and understanding of the child (when doctors and mediators are likely to be bound by principles arising from *Gillick v West Norfolk & Wisbech Area Health Authority* [1986] 1 FLR 224, HL).

Without prejudice rule and children proceedings—In *Re D (Minors) (Conciliation: Disclosure of Information)* [1993] 1 FLR 932, CA, the Court of Appeal considered the WP rule in children proceedings. (Despite FPR PD9A, para 6.2, *Re D* has nothing to do with financial remedy proceedings: but see *W v Egdell* (below)). Where mediation ('conciliation') was in progress, immunity from that evidence being placed before the court applied as much in children proceedings as in any other litigation: 'evidence may not be given in [CA 1989] proceedings ... of statements made by one or other of the parties in the course of meetings held or communications made for the purpose of conciliation save in the very unusual case where a statement is made clearly indicating that the maker has in the past caused or is likely in the future to cause serious harm to the well-being of a child'.

***Egdell* and overriding confidentiality**—*W v Egdell* [1990] Ch 359, CA identifies a public interest in professionals – doctors, lawyers, mediators, social workers etc – keeping confidences, which should not be broken lightly. Sometimes public safety may demand a breach. Bingham LJ held that if it is 'in the interests of public safety or the prevention of crime' then it may be appropriate to override confidentiality and report on to the relevant authorities. Each individual professional must make the decision.

Waiver of privilege—The privilege (or confidentiality) is that of the client. It can be waived expressly; it can be waived impliedly (see, for example, *Re D (Care Proceedings: Legal Privilege)* [2011] 2 FLR 1183, CA, where a mother in care proceedings had, by referring to part of the documents and notes that arose from an interview with her lawyers, impliedly waived privilege in respect of the rest). Confidentiality may be waived by a child, the subject of proceedings, with permission from the court (*Re Roddy (A Child) (Identification: Restriction on Publication)* [2004] 2 FLR 949, FD). In no circumstances (save *Egdell*, above) can it be dispensed with unilaterally by the confidant (e g counsel in wasted costs orders proceedings: *Medcalf v Weatherhill* [2003] 1 AC 120, HL).

Waiver of without prejudice immunity—Immunity is joint and can only be waived by both parties. A mediator is bound by any such waiver and can be called by summons to give evidence in separate proceedings (*Farm Assist Ltd v Secretary of State for the Environment, Food and Rural Affairs (No 2)* [2009] EWHC 1102 (TCC)), subject to any issue of confidentiality as between him/her and the parties, which can then be overridden by the court. There is no independent 'mediation privilege'.

(3) Public interest immunity

Public interest immunity (PII)—PII arises as a matter of public law (*Conway v Rimmer* [1968] AC 910, HL). It is a right that belongs almost exclusively to public bodies (*D v National Society for the Prevention of Cruelty to Children* (1977) FLR Rep 181, HL provides a rare private law exception), by which they ask the court to withhold disclosure of documents on grounds that disclosure might harm the public interest. The modern law on PII derives from *R v Chief Constable of West Midlands Police ex parte Wiley* [1995] 1 AC 274, HL (*ex p Wiley*). Production is always the starting point, save for specific documents: that is, rarely will a whole class of documents be exempt from disclosure. Each document will generally be expected to be assessed for materiality (*Bank Mellat v Her Majesty's Treasury (No 1)* [2013] UKSC 38, at [3]: 'fundamental to any justice system in a modern, democratic society is the principle of natural justice, whose most important aspect is that every party has a right to know the full case against him, and the right to test and challenge that case fully'.

Rejection of blanket immunity—In *Durham County Council v Dunn* [2012] EWCA Civ 1654 (a civil claim arising from alleged abuse of a person at a young people's centre) Munby LJ provided, obiter, a historical overview of PII. In the course of his review he specifically endorsed Charles J's assessment of blanket immunity and the role of *ex p Wiley* in *Re R (Care: Disclosure: Nature of Proceedings)* [2002] 1 FLR 755, FD: that is, that any PII case that precedes, or does not fully take it into account (if later) 'should be regarded with caution and carefully reconsidered' (including e g *Re M (A Minor) (Disclosure of Material)* [1990] 2 FLR 36, CA).

Public interest immunity or closed material procedures—If documents are immune from disclosure due to PII then only the party to which they belong sees them: neither the court nor other parties to proceedings see them. If a closed material procedure is adopted, at least it is only the excluded party (and perhaps his/her special advocate) who does not see sensitive material.

(4) Procedure for disclosure

Disclosure in family proceedings—In the absence of disclosure rules for family proceedings, prescribed documents are to be provided to the court (FPR 2010, r 5.2). This rule does not distinguish between documents that are irrelevant to any issue before the court and those that are relevant, even though not prescribed to be produced. Even where information or documents are not prescribed by Pt 5, there remains a duty on a party to disclose to other parties all evidence relevant to an issue to be tried. In *Imerman* (above), Moylan J urged parties to use the CPR 1998, r 31.10(3) procedure and CPR PD31A, paras 3.1 and 4.1 for guidance in family proceedings.

Disclosure: a procedure for family proceedings—CPR 1998, rr 31.5–31.15 provide a procedure that can be followed in family proceedings. FPR 2010, r 4.1(3)(b) enables the court to order 'such disclosure and inspection, including specific disclosure, as it sees fit'; but the CPR 1998 scheme seeks to deal with the process voluntarily as between the parties ('standard disclosure': rr 31.5, 31.6 and 31.10). Parties need only have recourse to the court:

(1) where they seek specific inspection (CPR 1998, r 31.12);
(2) where they seek production of a document withheld from disclosure (eg privilege: CPR 1998, r 31.19; FPR 2010, r 21.3).

Specific disclosure or inspection—If family courts are asked to order specific disclosure (FPR 2010, r 4.1(3)(b)), the law is summarised in CPR 1998, rr 31.5–31.12; and see FPR PD21A paras 2.1 and 2.4, which confirm how 'specific disclosure' works in family proceedings (other than ancillary relief). 'Inspection' is explained by CPR 1998, r 31.5(1) (see above) and includes the right to copies of documents (CPR 1998, r 31.15).

Disclosure against a third party—Disclosure and inspection orders against third parties is dealt with under r 21.2.

Procedure to withhold disclosure—The procedure for withholding inspection of confidential documents, and in relation to public interest immunity is set out in FPR 2010, r 21.3 and CPR 1998, r 31.19 (see below).

***Imerman* documents**—Documents that have been unlawfully taken by one spouse or partner have become known as *Imerman* documents after *Imerman v Tchenguiz and Others* [2010] 2 FLR 814, CA. In *UL v BK (Freezing Orders: safeguards: Standard Examples)* [2013] EWHC 1735 (Fam), Mostyn J (at [56]) gave guidance to lawyers as to how they should deal with such documents if presented to them, and to litigants in person if the issue arose for one of them. The guidance is controversial and should be treated with caution. It raises questions of advice privilege (the right to a client to seek advice, and the ability of a solicitor to advise unhampered). The guidance is directly contrary to *Lifely v Lifely* [2008] EWCA Civ 904 (although Mostyn J does not seem to have been referred to *Lifely*: in that case, a confidential document that should have been disclosed was the subject of a successful application for permission to appeal out of time and was admitted at the retrial below). Nor was there any reference in *UL v BK* to the human rights balancing exercise required in a case of this nature (eg *Lifely* at [22]–[30] applying *Re S (Identification: Restrictions on Publication)* [2005] 1 FLR 591, HL).

(5) Release of court documents to third parties

Release of documents: public and private hearings—There will be a difference in approach by the courts to the release of court documents according to whether a hearing is in public or in private. Family proceedings, unless otherwise directed, are in private (FPR 2010, r 27.10). That does not mean documents cannot be released later (*Clibbery v Allan* [2002] 1 FLR 565, CA). Despite FPR PD27B, para 2.3, those entitled to attend court (r 27.11(2)) may be able to seek court documents to enable them to make sense of the proceedings (*Harman v Secretary of State for the Home Department* [1983] 1 AC 280, HL; *Re Webster; Norfolk County Council v Webster and Others (No 2)* [2007] 2 FLR 415, FD) subject to appropriate conditions to protect confidentiality.

Court documents—Court documents for release to third parties (ie not entitled to 'disclosure') in family proceedings can be categorised as follows (and see more fully *Evidence in Family Proceedings* (David Burrows; Family Law) at Ch 13):

(1) *Court documents* Court documents for which a non-party is entitled to apply as a matter of formality (CPR 1998, r 5.4C; and see FPR 2010, r 29.12), although the court may accede to a request from a party to prevent release to a non-party (CPR 1998, r 5.4C(4)–(6));
(2) *Hearing documents* Court documents for which a non-party is entitled to apply, eg to make sense of the proceedings (*R (Guardian News and Media Ltd) v City of Westminster Magistrates' Court* [2013] QB 618, CA) or for a particular journalistic purpose (*NAB v Serco Ltd & Anor* [2014] EWHC 1225 (QB)).
(3) *Disclosed documents* Use, publication or other release, of documents whose production has been compelled by disclosure rules (CPR 1998, r 31.22(1): the 'implied undertaking' as to disclosed documents), and the release of which or other use the law restricts or may prevent, in cases of breach (r 31.22(2)).
(4) *Documents in children proceedings* See the provisions in FPR 2010, Pt 12 (below).

Release of court documents in children proceedings—FPR 2010, Pt 12, Ch 7 provides for communication or information in relation to children proceedings to third parties. PD12G provides a table of those to whom and by whom information can be provided without court order (AJA 1960, s 12(4); *Re X and Y (Disclosure of Judgment to Police)* [2015] 1 FLR 1218, FD).

Release to non-parties not listed (eg security services)—Where a non-party is not included in the list in PD12G (eg the security services, MI5), application can be made by or on their behalf for release (*Re X, Y and Z (Disclosure to the Security Service)* [2016] EWHC 2400 (Fam)) (if need be, by an appropriate form of closed material procedure: see under r 21.3). In making any order for release, the court will be concerned to preserve, as far as possible, the parties' rights and any confidentiality in documents (*Re X, Y and Z*).

Disclosure: children proceedings and joint investigation—The responsibilities of local authorities to share information derive from CA 2004, ss 10 (co-operation to improve well-being of children) and 11 (arrangements to safeguard welfare of children), and from departmental guidance under *Working Together*, March 2015, which includes the requirement for each public authority (under CA 2004, s 11(4)) to collaborate effectively, to be aware of the role that each has to play and to understand the role of other professionals. The local authority has a statutory duty to comply with this guidance (Local Authority Social Services Act 1970, s 7). Compliance with *Working Together* must be prompt and complete, and once underway it must be strategically coordinated

(*GD and BD (Children) and ors v Wakefield MDC and West Yorks Police* [2016] EWHC 3312 (Fam)). CA 2004, s 11 and FPR PD12G in effect provide for overriding of confidentiality of children but may conflict with duties in relation to confidentiality for the mature child (*Gillick v West Norfolk & Wisbech Area Health Authority* [1986] 1 FLR 224, HL).

***Working Together* and the sharing of information**—The duty to 'share' information, or to disclose to third parties covered by CA 2004, s 11, must be read in the light of further guidance: *Information sharing: Advice for practitioners providing safeguarding services to children, young people, parents and carers* (March 2015) contains further essential advice and information (as explained in *GD and BD (Children) and ors v Wakefield MDC and West Yorks Police* (above)). Limitations on disclosure that may be caused by rules in relation to confidentiality or professional privilege may affect sharing principles (eg, see the confidentiality of mature children and *Gillick* (above)). If criminal proceedings are in contemplation, release of information is covered also by the October 2013 protocol (see below).

Court documents and criminal proceedings—It is important that the courts encourage cooperation between agencies (see, for example, the *2013 Protocol and Good Practice Model: Disclosure of information in cases of alleged child abuse and linked criminal and care directions hearings*: *www.cps.gov.uk/publications/docs/third_party_protocol_2013.pdf*). Any release of documents may be conditional, eg to preserve confidentiality (*Re X, Y and Z* (above), at [69]–[71]).

Release of court documents to the press: 'full understanding' of the case—The press may be entitled to attend family court proceedings (FPR 2010, r 27.11(2)(f)) but the question remains as to what they may see of court documents and read to make full sense of a case (*Harman v Secretary of State for the Home Department* [1983] 1 AC 280, HL). For example, documents will be read by a judge (eg statements, skeleton arguments) but without sight of these any non-party (eg a member of the press) who attends court will be 'unable to obtain a full understanding of … the arguments on which the case was to be decided' (*Smithkline Beecham Biologicals SA v Connaught Laboratories Inc* [1999] EWCA Civ 1781). There is a range of judicial views: those who wish to permit or enhance understanding (*R (Guardian News and Media Ltd) v City of Westminster Magistrates' Court* [2013] QB 618, CA; *Re Webster; Norfolk County Council v Webster and Others (No 2)* [2007] 2 FLR 415, FD); and those who are less enthusiastic (eg *DL v SL* [2015] EWHC 2621 (Fam), at [16]). FPR PD27B, para 2.3, so far as it limits disclosure of documents, is likely to have to be treated with caution (*Guardian v Westminster* (above); *NAB v Serco Ltd & Anor* (above), at [29]), even for hearings in private (*Norfolk County Council v Webster and Others* (above)).

Collateral use of disclosed documents—Release or other publication of court documents is dealt with under CPR 1998, r 31.22.

21.1 Interpretation

(1) A party discloses a document by stating that the document exists or has existed.

(2) Inspection of a document occurs when a party is permitted to inspect a document disclosed by another person.

(3) For the purposes of disclosure and inspection –

(a) 'document' means anything in which information of any description is recorded; and

(b) 'copy' in relation to a document, means anything onto which information recorded in the document has been copied, by whatever means and whether directly or indirectly.

Disclosure, inspection and privilege—See **Introductory note** above for consideration of a definition of these terms.

21.2 Orders for disclosure against a person not a party

(1) This rule applies where an application is made to the court under any Act for disclosure by a person who is not a party to the proceedings.

(2) The application –

(a) may be made without notice; and

(b) must be supported by evidence.

(3) The court may make an order under this rule only where disclosure is necessary in order to dispose fairly of the proceedings or to save costs.

(4) An order under this rule must –

(a) specify the documents or the classes of documents which the respondent must disclose; and

(b) require the respondent, when making disclosure, to specify any of those documents –

(i) which are no longer in the respondent's control; or

(ii) in respect of which the respondent claims a right or duty to withhold inspection.

(5) Such an order may –

(a) require the respondent to indicate what has happened to any documents which are no longer in the respondent's control; and
(b) specify the time and place for disclosure and inspection.

(6) An order under this rule must not compel a person to produce any document which that person could not be compelled to produce at the final hearing.

(7) This rule does not limit any other power which the court may have to order disclosure against a person who is not a party to proceedings.

(Rule 35.3 contains provisions in relation to the disclosure and inspection of evidence arising out of mediation of cross-border disputes.)

Orders against non-parties—Orders for individuals or bodies who are not parties to proceedings can be made (1) for production of documents and (2) for information as to the whereabouts of a child, in four main categories:

1 Witness summons requiring production of documents (FPR 2010, r 24.2(1)(b));
2 Application to court by the procedure in FPR 2010, r 21.2 where statute permits an order against a third party (including information as to the whereabouts of a child);
3 Applications in respect of a child under FLA 1996, s 33 and CA 1989, ss 48 and 50 (see below); and
4 Orders under *Norwich Pharmacal v Commissioners of Customs & Excise* [1974] AC 133 (rarely applicable in family proceedings).

Disclosure under r 21.2—Applications can only be made where permitted by statute, eg under SCA 1981, s 34 (see above and under MFPA 1984, s 31J), CA 1989 and under Bankers Book Evidence Act 1879, s 7. The latter provision is the appropriate procedure to adopt for production of entries in bankers' books. Privilege may be claimed by a third party (*Waterhouse v Barker* [1924] 2 KB 759, CA), but a bank does not breach confidentiality to its customer if it produces his bank statements when ordered so to do (*Robertson v Canadian Imperial Bank of Commerce* [1994] 1 WLR 1493, PC).

Application—An application is made under the FPR 2010 procedure supported by evidence (for example as to why the documents are 'necessary' (r 21.2(3)(3)). The application must specify, as far as possible, what documents the court is being asked to order the third party to produce (r 21.2(4)).

'only where disclosure is necessary' (r 21.2(3))—Use of 'only' confirms that disclosure under the CPR 1998 equivalent of this rule is the exception rather than the rule (*Rowe & Ors v Fryers & Anor* [2003] 1 WLR 1952, CA; and see *A Health Authority v X (Discovery: Medical Conduct)* [2001] 2 FLR 673, Munby J). If a High Court judge has ordered disclosure it can be accepted that it is needed for disposal of proceedings and therefore 'necessary' to ensure a fair trial for parents and child (*Re C* [2016] EWHC 3171 (Fam)).

Information as to the whereabouts of a child: inherent jurisdiction—The High Court (and the Family Court: MFPA 1984, s 31E(1)) has an inherent power to order information to be provided from third parties, quite apart from the statutory powers of the court (*Re HM (Vulnerable Adult: Abduction)* [2010] 2 FLR 1057, FD, at [36]). Application for an order under the inherent jurisdiction can be made without notice (FPR 2010, r 20.4) and on an emergency basis in appropriate circumstances.

Information as to the whereabouts of a child: statutory jurisdiction

(1) FLA 1986, s 33 and CA 1989, s 48 provide examples covered procedurally by FPR 2010, r 21.2. An order under s 33(1) can be addressed to individuals who are not parties to the proceedings, including the manager of a women's refuge, a person's doctor or the police, as well as relatives or friends of a person. The address of a ward (ie of a child in proceedings) held by a solicitor is not covered by any form of confidentiality as against a court order (*Ramsbotham v Senior* (1869) FLR Rep 591, CE; *Re T (Wardship: Impact of Police Intelligence)* [2010] 1 FLR 1048, FD).
(2) CA 1989, ss 48 and 50 each provide family courts with powers to order that information be provided as to the whereabouts of children who may be in need of emergency protection or who it is thought have been abducted and in respect of whom the court has ordered recovery. In each case, the orders for providing information are ancillary to existing children proceedings.

Application under r 21.2—Any application under r 21.2 or under the inherent jurisdiction is by the FPR 2010, Pt 18 procedure and must include any information required by r 21.2(4),(5).

21.3 Claim to withhold inspection or disclosure of a document

(1) A person may apply, without notice, for an order permitting that person to withhold disclosure of a document on the ground that disclosure would damage the public interest.

(2) Unless the court otherwise orders, an order of the court under paragraph (1) –

(a) must not be served on any other person; and
(b) must not be open to inspection by any other person.

(3) A person who wishes to claim a right or a duty to withhold inspection of a document, or part of a document, must state in writing –

(a) the right or duty claimed; and
(b) the grounds on which that right or duty is claimed.

(4) The statement referred to in paragraph (3) must be made to the person wishing to inspect the document.

(5) A party may apply to the court to decide whether a claim made under paragraph (3) should be upheld.

(6) Where the court is deciding an application under paragraph (1) or (5) it may –

(a) require the person seeking to withhold disclosure or inspection of a document to produce that document to the court; and
(b) invite any person, whether or not a party, to make representations.

(7) An application under paragraph (1) or (5) must be supported by evidence.

(8) This Part does not affect any rule of law which permits or requires a document to be withheld from disclosure or inspection on the ground that its disclosure or inspection would damage the public interest.

Withholding inspection or disclosure—This rule conflates three separate aspects of the right to withhold inspection, production or disclosure:

(1) Public interest immunity (r 21.3(1))
(2) Privilege: 'a right … to withhold inspection' (r 21.3(3)–(5))
(3) Confidentiality: a 'duty to withhold inspection' (r 21.3(3)–(5)) – confidentially generally, and privacy and public policy (the right to withhold evidence improperly obtained (eg *Imerman v Tchenguiz and Others* [2010] 2 FLR 814, CA)).

Procedure –

(1) *Public interest immunity* Application is by the Pt 18 procedure by the public body (or other applicant) seeking immunity and can be without notice in the case of highly sensitive material. The court may restrict production of documents on its own initiative (*Duncan v Cammell Laird* [1942] AC 624, HL, at [641]) by the procedure under FPR 2010, r 4.4.
(2) *Privilege, confidentiality and privacy* Application is made in the proceedings in question by the Pt 18 procedure by the person who seeks inspection, after he has been notified that a party asserts the right or the duty not to produce documents.

'supported by evidence' (r 21.3(7))—In *West London Pipeline and Storage Ltd v Total UK Ltd* [2008] EWHC 1729 (Comm), Beatson J provides guidance as to the content of the affidavit in reply to an application to determine whether privilege applies and summarises the law on overriding privilege and on the factors to be considered by the court on an application.

Special advocate to the court—Appointment of a special advocate is by application to the Attorney-General (although not under the Attorney-General's *Memorandum* of 19 December 2001 – as stressed by the President's Guidance of 25 March 2015, considered under the 2001 memorandum). In *Re T (Wardship: Impact of Police Intelligence)* [2010] 1 FLR 1048, FD, McFarlane J (as he then was) gave guidance as to how the procedure might operate (at [31]–[34], [112]). In *A Chief Constable v YK and Others* [2011] 1 FLR 1493, FD, appointment of a special advocate was refused but it was anticipated that the appointment of a special advocate in the family court would occur in the future ([112]).

Procedure for disclosure (r 21.1)—As Moylan J records in *Tchenguiz-Imerman v Imerman* [2014] 1 FLR 232, FD, there is no procedure for disclosure in FPR 2010. He therefore explains (without considering CPR 1998, r 2.1(2): CPR 1998 not to apply to FPR 2010 proceedings) that CPR 1998, r 31.10(3) and PD31A, paras 3.1, 4.1 should provide guidance in family proceedings. In particular, he is concerned with the form in which documents should be listed and categorised where privilege is claimed (see FPR 2010, r 21.3(4), not considered by Moylan J). (It is understood that the Family Procedure Rules Committee take the view that procedure for disclosure should be left to the common law.)

Confidentiality owed by a party to third parties—If a party's duty of confidentiality to third parties conflicts with a duty of disclosure to the court (as with the wife in *AB v CD (Financial Remedy Consent Order: Non-Disclosure)* [2017] 1 FLR 13, FD), it is open to him/her under r 21.3(3) to state this in writing as part of the disclosure process and, if challenged, to make application (Pt 18 procedure, and see the *West London Pipeline* procedure (above)) to withhold production under r 21.3(5).

Practice Direction 21A – Disclosure and Inspection

This Practice Direction supplements FPR Part 21

CHAPTER 1
ORDERS FOR DISCLOSURE AND INSPECTION OF DOCUMENTS

Interpretation

1.1 A party discloses a document by stating that the document exists or has existed. Inspection occurs when a party is permitted to inspect a document disclosed by another party.

1.2 For the purposes of disclosure and inspection in family proceedings –

'document' means anything in which information of any description is recorded and any copy of a document which contains a modification, obliteration or other marking or feature shall be treated as a separate document; and

'copy', in relation to a document, means anything on which information recorded in the document has been copied, by whatever means and whether directly or indirectly.

Types of order for disclosure in family proceedings

2.1 In family proceedings other than proceedings for a financial remedy, where the court orders disclosure, the normal order will be for disclosure by each party setting out, in a list or questionnaire, the documents material to the proceedings, of the existence of which that party is aware and which are or have been in that party's control. This process is known as 'standard disclosure'.

2.2 In proceedings for a financial remedy, the process of disclosure is staged. First, Form E (the financial statement referred to in rule 9.14(1)) is served together with the documents which are required to be attached to it. The second stage occurs by the parties requesting (further) disclosure of each other by a questionnaire served before the first appointment; the questionnaire can request both information and documents. With the court's permission, a further questionnaire can be served later in the proceedings.

2.3 In matrimonial and civil partnership proceedings, under rule 7.15, the court – either on its own initiative or on the application of the other party – may order a party to clarify any matter which is in dispute in the proceedings or give additional information in relation to any such matter, whether or not the matter is contained in or referred to in the application or in the answer.

2.4 In any family proceedings, the court may order 'specific disclosure', which is an order that a party must –

(a) disclose documents or classes of documents specified in the order;
(b) carry out a search to the extent stated in the the order; or
(c) disclose any documents located as a result of that search.

PART 22
EVIDENCE

CONTENTS OF THIS PART

Chapter 1

Rule Page

General Rules

22.1 Power of court to control evidence 1761
22.2 Evidence of witnesses – general rule 1762
22.3 Evidence by video link or other means 1763

22.4	Witness statements	1763
22.5	Service of witness statements for use at the final hearing	1764
22.6	Use at the final hearing of witness statements which have been served	1764
22.7	Evidence at hearings other than the final hearing	1765
22.8	Order for cross-examination	1765
22.9	Witness summaries	1766
22.10	Consequence of failure to serve witness statement	1766
22.11	Cross-examination on a witness statement	1766
22.12	Affidavit evidence	1766
22.13	Form of affidavit	1766
22.14	Affidavit made outside the jurisdiction	1766
22.15	Notice to admit facts	1767
22.16	Notice to admit or produce documents	1767
22.17	Notarial acts and instruments	1767

Chapter 2
Rules Applying Only to Particular Proceedings

22.18	Scope of this Chapter	1767
22.19	Availability of witness statements for inspection during the final hearing	1767
22.20	Use of witness statements for other purposes	1768

Practice Direction 22A –
Written Evidence 1768

Evidence in family courts

(1) Witnesses and evidence

Evidence in the Family Court—MFPA 1984, s 31G formally deals with 'witnesses and evidence' in the Family Court, mostly in relation to summonses (s 31G(2)–(5)), evidence on oath (s 31G(7)), affidavits (s 31G(8)–(9)) and taking of evidence where a party is not represented (s 31G(6)). Most FPR 2010 procedural rules in relation to evidence in family proceedings are to be found as follows:

- Pt 21 – disclosure and public interest immunity;
- Pt 22 – general matters, statements and affidavits, attendance at court;
- Pt 23 – hearsay evidence;
- Pt 24 – witness summonses and depositions;
- Pt 25 – opinion ('expert') evidence.

Rules of evidence—Common law rules of evidence, applicable in all civil proceedings, apply equally in family proceedings subject to statutory variants (e g see CFA 2014, s 13 and expert evidence).

Format of witness statements—FPR PD22A, paras 3.1 et seq deal with format and presentation of statements and affidavits, how to deal with the inability of a deponent to read or sign (paras 7.1–7.4 and see Annexes 1 and 2) and exhibits (paras 9.1–13.4).

Evidence and the overriding objective: identification of issues—The overriding objective (FPR 2010, r 1.1) stresses the need to identify issues in a case, including dealing with a case 'in ways which are proportionate to … the complexity of the issues', to identifying those issues at an early stage and to 'deciding promptly which issues need full investigation' (FPR 2010, rr 1.1(2)(b) and 1.4(2)(b)(i),(c)(i)).

Relevance and admissibility—Only evidence that is relevant to an issue before the court is admissible. It follows from this that a definition of issues is critical to costs saving and to proportionate preparation of the case, and thus to effective case management. The court's case management powers include generally to control evidence (FPR 2010, r 22.1) and specifically to control expert evidence (FPR 2010, r 1.4(2)(e); Part 25).

(2) Evidence and witnesses in court

Examination of witnesses—The giving of evidence by witnesses and their examination in court arises in the following ways in FPR 2010:

- The evidence of a witness is to be oral at a final hearing, in writing 'at any other hearing' (r 22.2(1));
- Where a witness statement has been served, that witness must be available at the final hearing (r 22.6(1)), subject to hearsay rules (rr 23.2–23.4);
- Evidence-in-chief: a witness statement is to stand as that witness' evidence-in-chief (r 22.6(2));
- Cross-examination, which may be limited (r 22.1(4)).

Evidence at hearings—Hearings are either final or 'other' (mostly interim hearings under the FPR 2010, Pt 18 procedure): e g FPR 2010, r 22.2(1). FPR 2010 aims to provide a consistent set of evidence rules for these hearings, which will be the culmination of the process for:

(1) Originating processes – a variety of different originating applications;
(2) Pt 19 procedure cases – for an undefined smaller group of Pt 19 'alternative' applications; and
(3) Pt 18 interim procedure cases – for 'other', mostly interim, hearings under the Pt 18 procedure – 'other' hearings are dealt with on written evidence (subject to permission to cross-examine: r 22.8).

Chapter 1
General Rules

22.1 Power of court to control evidence

(1) The court may control the evidence by giving directions as to –

(a) the issues on which it requires evidence;

(b) the nature of the evidence which it requires to decide those issues; and

(c) the way in which the evidence is to be placed before the court.

(2) The court may use its power under this rule to exclude evidence that would otherwise be admissible.

(3) The court may permit a party to adduce evidence, or to seek to rely on a document, in respect of which that party has failed to comply with the requirements of this Part.

(4) The court may limit cross-examination[(GL)].

(1) Control of evidence

'power ... to exclude evidence' (r 22.1(2))—In *Re S-W (Children)* [2015] 2 FLR 136, CA (at [55]–[58]), the Court of Appeal re-asserted the rights of litigants (especially parents 'facing removal of their child', or children, as in *Re S-W*) that:

- they have an absolute entitlement to put their case to the court; and
- they have the right to 'confront [their] accusers' and thus to cross-examine 'important' witnesses relied upon by the applicant (local authority in care proceedings).

Exclusion of evidence—There may be instances where the court may feel justified in excluding evidence as a matter of procedure. For example:

- where a party has been culpably neglectful in failing to serve, either in time or at all, any appropriate notices of the intention to rely on hearsay evidence under Civil Evidence Act 1995, s 2(1) and FPR 2010, r 23.2 (but see r 22.1(3));
- evidence has been obtained illegally (*Imerman v Tchenguiz and Others* [2010] 2 FLR 814, CA). By contrast, in *Lifely v Lifely* [2008] EWCA Civ 904, the Court of Appeal permitted illegally obtained evidence (a diary), which should have been disclosed by its author, and re-opened proceedings on the basis of the evidence contained in the diary.

'power ... to exclude evidence': ECHRI balance—It is a serious matter for the court to exclude relevant evidence. To do so, the court will need to balance (1) both parties' rights to a fair trial against, for example (*Lifely*, above), (2) a parties' right to respect for family life and privacy.

Limits on cross-examination (r 22.1(4))—Limits on cross-examination might occur in two ways:

(1) The court may limit the issues to be explored: this would be consistent with r 22.1(1)(a) (*Watson v Chief Constable of Cleveland* [2001] EWCA Civ 1547).

(2) The court may limit the time available for cross-examination of a particular witness: a 'guillotine' order, which is unquestionably in line with the overriding objective, but see *Hayes v Transco plc* [2003] EWCA Civ 1261, at [58].

(2) Evidence relevant to the issues

'issues on which [the court] requires evidence': relevant evidence (r 22.1(1)(a))—The main rule governing the relevance and admissibility of evidence is that 'all evidence that is sufficiently relevant to an issue before the court is admissible and all that is irrelevant, or insufficiently relevant, should be excluded' (*Cross & Tapper on Evidence*, Colin Tapper (2010) at p 64). The importance of defining the issues for trial as part of case management is clear from r 1.4. Without that definition, parties cannot decide what evidence they need to prove their case, neither can they be sure – to prove an issue that is essential to the outcome of the case – that they have the evidence that the court will need and in a form that proves the point that the party wishes to make.

Burden of proof—The party who asserts a fact must prove it. The burden is on him to adduce the evidence and to prove the fact asserted. It falls once more to competent case management (FPR 2010, r 1.4 and Pt 4) to define what factual issues remain in dispute and on whom the burden lies (where there are disputed facts) to prove those facts. It is for the parties then to identify the evidence that they wish to adduce to prove those facts, subject to any power that the court may have under r 22.1(2) to 'exclude evidence'.

Standard of proof—The standard of proof refers to the level of probability required to prove a fact (*Bater v Bater* [1951] P 35, CA, at [36]–[37]). In family cases, this will be the civil standard, that is to say 'the simple balance of probabilities' (*Re B (Children)* [2008] 2 FLR 141, HL). The working of this principle is explained in *Re B*, at [2]: 'If a legal rule requires a fact to be proved (a 'fact in issue'), a judge or jury must decide whether or not it happened. There is no room for a finding that it might have happened. The law operates a binary system in which the only values are 0 and 1. The fact either happened or it did not. If the tribunal is left in doubt, the doubt is resolved by a rule that one party or the other carries the burden of proof. If the party who bears the burden of proof fails to discharge it, a value of 0 is returned and the fact is treated as not having happened. If he does discharge it, a value of 1 is returned and the fact is treated as having happened.'

Proof to criminal standard—Where family proceedings are such that a person may be subject to a criminal penalty (see *Engel and Others v The Netherlands (No 1)* (1979) 1 EHRR 647, at [80] and [81]) and ECHR 1950, Art 6(3)(c)), the standard of proof will be to the criminal standard of beyond reasonable doubt (eg on an application to commit and the judgment summons procedure under DA 1869, s 5, FPR 2010, rr 33.9—33.17; and CSA 1991, s 39A; and as explained in *Prest v Prest (Judgment Summons: Appeal)* [2016] 1 FLR 773, CA, at [55]).

(3) Evidence and issues

Defining issues for trial and preliminary issues—Defining issues for trial involves control of evidence and case management of procedure:

(1) *Preliminary issue* In such cases as *KSO v MJO, JMO and PSO* [2009] 1 FLR 1036, FD, *Young v Young* [2014] 2 FLR 786, FD and *J v J* [2014] EWHC 3654 (Fam), the High Court has been critical of costs expenditure. In each it could be argued that failure at an early case management stage to identify the cardinal issues and to define for preliminary trial any issues blocking settlement was partially to blame. For example, in *J v J* (above) until the value of the husband's shares had been defined, any FDR (of which there were two) would fail. Consideration should be given to the possibility of an FDR prior to the hearing of a preliminary issue (*Shield v Shield* [2014] 2 FLR 1422, FD).

(2) *Separate hearing of evidence* In *OS v DS (Oral Disclosure: Preliminary Hearing)* [2005] 1 FLR 675, FD Coleridge J heard evidence at a separate hearing: see also use of this procedure in *Arif v Anwar and Rehan* [2016] 1 FLR 359, FD and the *Khanna* hearing (under FPR 2010, r 24.2) for consideration of documents in advance of a final hearing.

Mediation, narrowing of issues and evidence—Case management includes encouraging parties to use NCDR, such as mediation (FPR 2010, r 1.4(2)(f)). The costs consequences of using mediation to help to define what issues need to be litigated, and thus to identify what evidence the court may wish to permit may be assisted in mediation.

Issue estoppel and the rule in *Henderson v Henderson*—In children proceedings, issue estoppel may give way to other demands (eg, see *Re B (Children Act Proceedings: Issue Estoppel)* [1997] 1 FLR 285, FD). In ancillary relief proceedings, issue estoppel is more strict (*N v N (Child Maintenance: Res Judicata and Strike Out)* [2015] 2 FLR 1441, FD). The rule in *Henderson v Henderson* (1843) 3 Hare 100 was summarised in *Virgin Atlantic Airways Ltd v Zodiac Seats UK Ltd* [2013] UKSC 46 as precluding 'a party from raising in subsequent proceedings matters which were not, but could and should have been, raised in the earlier' proceedings (and see FPR 2010, r 4.4(1)). It was applied in financial proceedings by the Court of Appeal in *Norman v Norman* [2017] EWCA Civ 120.

(4) Evidence where a party is not represented

Party not legally represented—MFPA 1984, s 31G(6) enables the Family Court, where a party (A) is not legally represented and is 'unable to examine or cross-examine a witness effectively', to proceed as follows:

- to find out from A the matters about which the witness may give evidence in chief or on which the witness of another party 'ought to be cross-examined' (s 31G(6)(a)); and then
- to 'put, or *cause to be put*, to the witness such questions in [A's interests] as may appear to the court to be proper' (emphasis added) (s 31G(6)(b)).

MFPA 1984, s 31G(6) and the vulnerable witness—The issue of cross-examination of a vulnerable witness by an unrepresented party (eg an alleged abuser: ie in the position of A above) has been considered by the courts (*H v L and R* [2007] 2 FLR 162, FD). This becomes more acute with legal aid or other funding being increasingly unavailable to A and where it is thought inappropriate for A to cross-examine the vulnerable witness (but now see Courts and Prisons Bill, cl 47).

(5) Care proceedings: family courts' control and parallel criminal proceedings

Evidence in family courts and the Crown Court: control of evidence—Where the CPS requires evidence that has been filed in care proceedings, the procedure is likely to be dealt with in the Crown Court (under Criminal Procedure Rules 2014) on application there and in accordance with *Protocol and Good Practice Model: Disclosure of information in cases of alleged child abuse and linked criminal and care directions hearings* (October 2013; *www.cps.gov.uk/publications/docs/third_party_protocol_2013.pdf*).

Requirement for a prosecuted parent's evidence—In *A Local Authority v DG and Others* [2014] 2 FLR 713, FD, Keehan J gave guidance on the provision of evidence in care proceedings where a party – the father in this case – is also being prosecuted. See **Concurrent care and criminal proceedings** under CA 1989, s 31.

22.2 Evidence of witnesses – general rule

(1) The general rule is that any fact which needs to be proved by the evidence of witnesses is to be proved –

(a) at the final hearing, by their oral evidence; and

(b) at any other hearing, by their evidence in writing.

(2) The general rule does not apply –

(a) to proceedings under Part 12 for secure accommodation orders, interim care orders or interim supervision orders; or

(b) where an enactment, any of these rules, a practice direction or a court order provides to the contrary.

(Section 45(7) of the Children Act 1989 (emergency protection orders) is an example of an enactment which makes provision relating to the evidence that a court may take into account when hearing an application.)

Derivation—CPR 1998, r 32.2.

'oral evidence' at a final hearing (r 22.2(1)(b))—The general rule for proof of an application or case is that the evidence of a witness be given orally and in public (FPR 2010, r 32.2(1) and see European Convention 1950, Art 6(1)). In family proceedings, this rule is altered, so that all hearings are in private (FPR 2010, r 27.10), subject as provided in FPR 2010, r 27.11 and unless otherwise provided (e g final defended matrimonial and civil partnership proceedings: FPR 2010, r 7.16(1), and all committal hearings, which are held in public).

Exceptions to general rule—Rules of evidence provide various exclusionary exceptions to this rule. Certain evidence need not be proved. This evidence can be treated as if it had been already formally proved before the court and includes: judicial notice, issue estoppel, formal admissions and existing judicial findings.

(1) *Judicial notice* Judicial notice establishes that a fact exists even where formal proof of it has not been called and even though that fact is in issue before the court. Judicial notice may be the general knowledge that can be imputed to the judge, just as it can be to other people. For example, in most financial remedy cases the courts are likely to take judicial notice of the content of a number of the tables in *At a Glance* (FLBA).

(2) *Estoppel: issue and cause of action estoppel (res judicata)* Evidential estoppels (issue and cause of action) prevent a party from denying what has already been tried and established against that party, either as part of the case (issue estoppel) or as to the final decision(s) in a case (cause of action). It operates where factors have been proved in a court of competent jurisdiction following a trial between the parties involved in the present litigation, where the earlier court was one of competent jurisdiction, and the trial – that decided the earlier proceedings – was on the merits, as between the parties. It rarely applies in children proceedings (*Re B (Children Act Proceedings: Issue Estoppel)* [1997] 1 FLR 285, FD) but it can apply in family proceedings generally, for example where there is a conflict as between family and other jurisdictions (*Edgerton v Edgerton and Zaffirili Shaikh* [2012] 2 FLR 273, CA, at [36]).

(3) *Admissions* The general rule is that a party is bound by his or her admission (and see under FPR 2010, r 22.15 for notices to admit facts), save in the case of admissions made against interest that are part of negotiations for settlement and therefore covered by the without prejudice rule.

(4) *Judicial findings* For example, Civil Evidence Act 1968, s 11 enables a party to civil proceedings to rely on the conviction of another party as evidence that the offence was committed 'unless the contrary is proved' (CEA 1968, s 11(2)(a)). A statutory presumption arises that the offence has been committed, so that a convicted party has the almost impossible task of seeking to persuade a judge that the conviction should not stand as evidence in the family proceedings (e g *Hunter v Chief Constable of West Midlands* [1982] AC 529, HL). A finding of adultery or paternity in relevant matrimonial proceedings will be admissible as evidence in other civil proceedings, where such evidence is relevant (CEA 1968, s 12).

22.3 Evidence by video link or other means

The court may allow a witness to give evidence through a video link or by other means.

Video link—This provision is in line with r 1.4(2)(k): that in managing and (as here) in hearing a case, the court should make 'use of technology'. In *Polanski v Conde Nast* [2005] 1 WLR 637, HL, the House of Lords permitted the claimant, a French resident who feared arrest by US authorities if he came to England, to give evidence from France by video link.

Children and vulnerable witnesses—Provision for the taking of evidence from children and vulnerable witnesses by videolink may be of assistance to the court. It is among special measures available under the present vulnerable witnesses working group recommendations and is automatic in criminal proceedings (Youth Justice and Criminal Evidence Act 1999 Pt 2; and see *R v Lubemba & Ors* [2014] EWCA (Crim) 2064, *Re A (Sexual Abuse: Disclosure)* [2013] 1 FLR 948, SC fully considered in 'Evidence of the child in family proceedings' at [2016] Fam Law 1025). Organisations such as Triangle (http://triangle.org.uk/services) work to assist children and the courts with ABE interviews and provide other assistance in children proceedings.

PD—Annex 3 to FPR PD22A provides guidance as to how video conferencing should be dealt with in court.

22.4 Witness statements

(1) A witness statement is a written statement signed by a person which contains the evidence which that person would be allowed to give orally.

(2) A witness statement must comply with the requirements set out in the Practice Direction 22A.

(Part 17 requires a witness statement to be verified by a statement of truth.)

'evidence which that person would be allowed to give' (r 22.4(1))—A witness statement is that of the witness; it is not, for example, a pleading, a skeleton argument or a chronology (although a chronology may help it). The likelihood is that in family cases a witness will be permitted to 'amplify his witness statement' or give updating evidence (FPR 2010, r 22.6(3)).

PART III

'evidence ... allowed to give' (r 22.4(1))—Every effort must be taken to ensure that a statement prepared by a legal representative complies with all relevant rules of evidence:

(1) Relevance – only evidence that is relevant to an issue before the court is admissible (i e 'allowed');
(2) Privilege – no information covered by privilege should be included, save where the privilege is that of a witness and he is willing to waive his own privilege;
(3) Hearsay – see further under FPR 2010, rr 23.2–23.5;
(4) Frivolous or abusive evidence must be excluded.

Foreign and translated witness statements—*NN v ZZ and ors* [2013] EWHC 2261 (Fam) provides guidance on obtaining evidence from non-English speaking witnesses:

(1) An affidavit or statement by a non-English-speaking witness must be prepared in the witness' own language before being translated into English (see PD22A, para 8.2).
(2) There must be clarity about the process by which a statement has been created (i e a statement as to the process by which it has been taken (e g face-to-face, by telephone, by Skype or based on a document written in the witness's own language).
(3) If a solicitor has been instructed by the litigant, s/he should be fully involved in the process and should not subcontract it to the client.
(4) If presented with a statement in English from a witness who cannot read or speak English, the solicitor should question its provenance and not simply use the document as a proof of evidence.
(5) The witness should be spoken to wherever possible, using an interpreter, and a draft statement should be prepared in the native language for them to read and sign. The solicitor can be the interpreter if fluent in the witness' language, but this must be made clear in the statement or in a separate affidavit.
(6) A litigant in person should where possible use a certified interpreter when preparing a witness statement.
(7) If the witness cannot read or write in their own native language, the interpreter must carefully read the statement to the witness in his/her own language and set this out in the translator's jurat or affidavit, using the words provided by PD22A, Annexes 1 or 2.
(8) Once the statement has been completed and signed in the native language, it should be translated by a certified translator who should so certify and that s/he has faithfully translated the statement.
(9) If a witness is to give live evidence either in person or by video-link, a copy of the original statement in the witness's own language and the English translation should be provided to them well in advance of the hearing.
(10) Any statement obtained/prepared abroad in compliance with the relevant country's laws, a certified translation must be filed together with the original document.

22.5 Service of witness statements for use at the final hearing

(1) The court may give directions as to service on the other parties of any witness statement of the oral evidence on which a party intends to rely in relation to any issues of fact to be decided at the final hearing.

(2) The court may give directions as to –

(a) the order in which witness statements are to be served; and
(b) whether or not the witness statements are to be filed.

(3) Where the court directs that a court officer is to serve a witness statement on the other parties, any reference in this Chapter to a party serving a witness statement is to be read as including a reference to a court officer serving the statement.

Defined terms—'court': r 2.3(1).

Service of statements in specific applications—Note that r 22.5(1) does not disapply the requirements of individual applications to be accompanied by their own evidences as required by other rules or (where required) by sworn statement (and see r 22.12).

22.6 Use at the final hearing of witness statements which have been served

(1) If a party –

(a) has served a witness statement; and
(b) wishes to rely at the final hearing on the evidence of the witness who made the statement,

that party must call the witness to give oral evidence unless the court directs otherwise or the party puts the statement in as hearsay evidence.

(Part 23 (miscellaneous rules about evidence) contains provisions about hearsay evidence.)

(2) The witness statement of a witness called to give oral evidence under paragraph (1) is to stand as the evidence in chief[(GL)] of that witness unless the court directs otherwise.

(3) A witness giving oral evidence at the final hearing may with the permission of the court –

(a) amplify his witness statement; and

(b) give evidence in relation to new matters which have arisen since the witness statement was served on the other parties.

(4) The court will give permission under paragraph (3) only if it considers that there is good reason not to confine the evidence of the witness to the contents of the witness statement.

(5) If a party who has served a witness statement does not –

(a) call the witness to give evidence at the final hearing; or
(b) put the witness statement in as hearsay evidence,

any other party may put the witness statement in as hearsay evidence.

Hearsay evidence (r 22.6(5)(b))—See under FPR 2010, Pt 23.

22.7 Evidence at hearings other than the final hearing

(1) Subject to paragraph (2), the general rule is that evidence at hearings other than the final hearing is to be by witness statement unless the court, any other rule, a practice direction or any other enactment requires otherwise.

(2) At hearings other than the final hearing, a party may rely on the matters set out in that party's –

(a) application form;
(b) application notice; or
(c) answer,

if the application form, application notice or answer, as the case may be, is verified by a statement of truth or if the court gives that party permission to do so without such verification.

Amendments—SI 2012/2806.

Statements of case as evidence—FPR 2010, PD22A, para 1.3 confirms the availability of statements of case (see definition in FPR 2010, rr 4.1 and 17.1(1)) provided that they are verified by a statement of truth (FPR 2010, Pt 17).

'verified by a statement of truth' (r 22.7(2))—This provision does not prevent a party relying on other evidence (e g a written statement; r 22.7(2)), but it is intended to provide only that the documents referred to can be relied on if verified by a statement of truth. This provision repeats FPR 2010, r 17.2(3) but in the context only of 'other hearings'.

22.8 Order for cross-examination

(1) Where, at a hearing other than the final hearing, evidence is given in writing, any party may apply to the court for permission to cross-examine(GL) the person giving the evidence.

(2) If the court gives permission under paragraph (1) but the person in question does not attend, that person's evidence may not be used unless the court directs otherwise.

(Rules 35.3 and 35.4 contain rules in relation to evidence arising out of mediation of cross-border disputes.)

Pt 18 procedure—The probability is that the circumstances to which r 22.8 is mostly addressed will be FPR 2010, Pt 20 proceedings. Difficult issues may be at stake and in many cases the interim remedy will, in effect, be the final remedy – certainly on the declaration or injunction issue. The ability to test – or not – the evidence against a party may go to important questions of fairness as between the parties or as to third parties drawn into the litigation.

Part 19 procedure—The court may give directions for attendance of a witness for cross-examination (FPR 2010, r 19.8(3)). The implication and context of this provision is that it refers to a final hearing, but the sub-rule does not so state. It may also refer to an interim hearing, or hearing other than the final hearing, in FPR 2010, Pt 19 procedure proceedings (e g a hearing on a parent's FPR 2010, Pt 18 procedure application for a DNA test direction).

Hearsay evidence—This rule should be read alongside the hearsay provisions considered in FPR 2010, Pt 23, as to what becomes of a statement or affidavit if a party ordered to attend does not do so.

Examination 'in the interests of' litigants in person—MFPA 1984, s 31G(6) imposes upon the Family Court (but not expressly the High Court) a duty to 'ascertain' from litigants in person matters they may want to give evidence about themselves, cross-examination to which other witnesses 'ought' to be subjected and put to that witness (for the litigant in person, or for another party) such questions as seem to 'the court to be proper'. No procedure for recording that this step has been taken by the judge or lay justices is set down.

22.9 Witness summaries

(1) A party who –

(a) is required to serve a witness statement for use at any hearing; but
(b) is unable to obtain one,

may apply, without notice, for permission to serve a witness summary instead.

(2) A witness summary is a summary of –

(a) the evidence, if known, which would otherwise be included in a witness statement; or
(b) if the evidence is not known, the matters about which the party serving the witness summary proposes to question the witness.

(3) Unless the court directs otherwise, a witness summary must include the name and address of the intended witness.

(4) Unless the court directs otherwise, a witness summary must be served within the period in which a witness statement would have had to be served.

(5) Where a party serves a witness summary, so far as practicable rules 22.4(2) (form of witness statements), 22.5 (service of witness statements for use at the final hearing) and 22.6(3) (amplifying witness statements) apply to the summary.

22.10 Consequence of failure to serve witness statement

If a witness statement for use at the final hearing is not served in respect of an intended witness within the time specified by the court, then the witness may not be called to give oral evidence unless the court gives permission.

'a witness statement not served'—The court has a discretion to permit a witness to be called, even though their statement has not been served. This discretion should be exercised in accordance with case management principles in FPR 2010, Pt 4 generally, and in FPR 2010, r 4.6 (relief from sanctions) in particular (eg *Durrant v Avon & Somerset Constabulary* [2013] EWCA Civ 1624 (statements not permitted to be adduced by defendants); *Chartwell Estate Agents Ltd v Fergies Properties SA & Anor* [2014] EWCA Civ 506 (statement allowed in: principles in CPR 1998, r 3.9 explained)). To avoid sanctions, it is essential that parties make timely application to the court for extension of time for service (*A Local Authority v DG and Others* [2014] 2 FLR 713, FD, Keehan J) per Pt 18 procedure.

22.11 Cross-examination on a witness statement

A witness who is called to give evidence at the final hearing may be cross-examined(GL) on the witness statement, whether or not the statement or any part of it was referred to during the witness's evidence in chief(GL).

Examination by the court 'in the interests' of a litigant in person—See MFPA 1984, s 31G(6) under r 22.8.

22.12 Affidavit evidence

(1) Evidence must be given by affidavit(GL) instead of or in addition to a witness statement if this is required by the court, a provision contained in any other rule, a practice direction or any other enactment.

(2) *(revoked)*

Amendments—SI 2013/3204.

Affidavit evidence under court order—FPR PD22A, para 1.4 and 1.6 make supplementary provision concerning affidavits and when they must be used as evidence (eg FPR 2010, r 9.14(2): Form E, Form E1 and Form E2; affidavits in FPR 2010, Pt 7 proceedings). Para 1.6 suggests that the court may direct the filing of affidavit evidence, on its own initiative or on application.

Affirmation—The term affidavit applies equally to affirmations (FPR PD22A, para 1.7).

22.13 Form of affidavit

An affidavit(GL) must comply with the requirements set out in the Practice Direction 22A.

22.14 Affidavit made outside the jurisdiction

A person may make an affidavit (GL) outside the jurisdiction in accordance with –

(a) this Part; or

(b) the law of the place where the affidavit(GL) is made.

22.15 Notice to admit facts

(1) A party may serve notice on another party requiring the other party to admit the facts, or the part of the case of the serving party, specified in the notice.

(2) A notice to admit facts must be served no later than 21 days before the final hearing.

(3) Where the other party makes any admission in answer to the notice, the admission may be used against that party only –

(a) in the proceedings in which the notice to admit is served; and
(b) by the party who served the notice.

(4) The court may allow a party to amend or withdraw any admission made by that party on such terms as it thinks just.

'notice ... to admit the facts' (r 22.15(1))—No form is prescribed for notice to admit. It is a notice as between the parties: i e there is no requirement of filing at court, although the notice and any response may be included in the court bundle.

Admission by the serving party 'only ... in the proceedings' (r 22.15(3))—The consequences of the admission do not carry forward to other proceedings between the parties.

Costs on failure to admit facts—The former rule that costs incurred by a party in proving a fact of which he had given notice to admit (RSC 1965, Ord 62, r 6(7)) is no longer included in costs rules generally. However, the court is likely to take such costs into account if unnecessarily incurred by a party who has given notice (CPR 1998, r 44.2).

22.16 Notice to admit or produce documents

(1) A party to whom a document is disclosed is deemed to admit the authenticity of that document unless notice is served by that party that the party wishes the document to be proved at the final hearing.

(2) A notice to prove a document must be served –

(a) by the latest date for serving witness statements; or
(b) within 7 days beginning with the date of service of the document, whichever is later.

Notice to admit or prove documents—If a party discloses a document – that is to say, he or she 'states that the document exists or has existed' (FPR 2010, r 21.1) – then the party provided with disclosure is deemed to admit 'the authenticity of that document' unless notice to prove the document is given under r 22.16. The 'authenticity' of a document is a separate question from the truthfulness or probative value of a document. It is not evidence of the facts it seeks to contain unless proved in some way: e g by its author preparing, filing and serving a witness statement (FPR 2010, r 22.5).

22.17 Notarial acts and instruments

A notarial act or instrument may be received in evidence without further proof as duly authenticated in accordance with the requirements of law unless the contrary is proved.

Chapter 2
Rules Applying Only to Particular Proceedings

22.18 Scope of this Chapter

This Chapter of this Part applies to affidavits(GL) and affirmations as it applies to witness statements.

22.19 Availability of witness statements for inspection during the final hearing

(1) This rule applies to proceedings under Part 7 (matrimonial and civil partnership proceedings).

(2) A witness statement which stands as evidence in chief(GL) is open to inspection during the course of the final hearing unless the court directs otherwise.

(3) Any person may ask for a direction that a witness statement is not open to inspection.

(4) The court will not make a direction under paragraph (2) unless it is satisfied that a witness statement should not be open to inspection because of –

(a) the interests of justice;

(b) the public interest;
(c) the nature of any expert medical evidence in the statement;
(d) the nature of any confidential information (including information relating to personal financial matters) in the statement; or
(e) the need to protect the interests of any child or protected party.

(5) The court may exclude from inspection words or passages in the witness statement.

'witness statement ... open to inspection' (r 22.19(2))—Rule 22.19 applies to public hearing in civil proceedings (CPR 1998, r 22.19) and in the same circumstances applies to FPR 2010, Pt 7 defended matrimonial and civil partnership proceedings hearings. It reflects concern for open justice, where statements are served and form a witness's evidence-in-chief. A member of the public, who is entitled to hear the case in open court, can inspect that part of the written evidence that is taken as read by FPR 2010, r 22.6(2).

22.20 Use of witness statements for other purposes

(1) This rule applies to proceedings under Part 7 (matrimonial and civil partnership proceedings) or Part 9 (financial remedies).

(2) Except as provided by this rule, a witness statement may be used only for the purpose of the proceedings in which it is served.

(3) Paragraph (2) does not apply if and to the extent that –

(a) the court gives permission for some other use; or
(b) the witness statement has been put in evidence at a hearing held in public.

Practice Direction 22A – Written Evidence

This Practice Direction supplements FPR Part 22

Evidence in general

1.1 Rule 22.2(1) sets out the general rule as to how evidence is to be given and facts are to be proved. This is that, at the final hearing, witnesses will normally give oral evidence and, at any hearing other than the final hearing, by evidence in writing (which under rule 22.7(1) will usually be by witness statement).

1.2 Rule 22.2(2) excludes the general rule –

(a) from proceedings under Part 12 (Children) for secure accommodation orders, interim care orders or interim supervision orders; or
(b) where an enactment, any rule in the FPR, a practice direction or a court order provides to the contrary.

1.3 Application forms, application notices and answers except an application for a matrimonial order or a civil partnership order or an answer to such an application may also be used as evidence provided that their contents have been verified by a statement of truth (see Part 17 for information about statements of truth).

(For information regarding evidence by deposition see Part 24 and the practice direction which supplements it.)

1.4 Affidavits must be used as evidence –

(a) where sworn evidence is required by an enactment, rule, order or practice direction; and
(b) in any application for an order against anyone for alleged contempt of court.

1.5 If a party believes that sworn evidence is required by a court in another jurisdiction for any purpose connected with the proceedings, he may apply to the court for a direction that evidence shall be given only by affidavit on any applications to be heard before the final hearing.

1.6 The court may give a direction under rule 22.12 that evidence shall be given by affidavit instead of or in addition to a witness statement –

(a) on its own initiative; or
(b) after any party has applied to the court for such a direction.

1.7 An affidavit, where referred to in the FPR or a practice direction, also means an affirmation unless the context requires otherwise.

AFFIDAVITS AND WITNESS STATEMENTS

Meaning of 'deponent' and 'witness'

2.1 For the purposes of the FPR –

a 'deponent' is a person who gives evidence by affidavit, affirmation or deposition; and
a 'witness' is a person who gives evidence by witness statement.

2.2 References in the following paragraphs to 'the maker of', or 'making', an affidavit, affirmation, deposition or witness statement are to be construed accordingly.

Heading and format

3.1 The affidavit/statement should be headed with the title of the proceedings where the proceedings are between several parties with the same status it is sufficient to identify the parties, subject to paragraph 4.2, as follows –

Number:

A.B. (and others)	Applicants
C.D. (and others)	Respondents

3.2 Subject to paragraph 4.2, at the top right-hand corner of the first page (and on the backsheet) there should be clearly written –

(a) the party on whose behalf it is made;
(b) the initials and surname of the maker;
(c) the number of the affidavit/statement in relation to its maker;
(d) the identifying initials and number of each exhibit referred to; and
(e) the date made.

3.3 The affidavit/statement should –

(a) be produced on durable quality A4 paper with a 3.5 cm margin;
(b) be fully legible and should normally be typed on one side of the paper only;
(c) where possible, should be bound securely in a manner which would not hamper filing or, where secure binding is not possible, each page should be endorsed with the case number and should bear the following initials –
 (i) in the case of an affidavit, of the maker and of the person before whom it is sworn; or
 (ii) in the case of a witness statement, of the maker and, where the maker is unable to read or sign the statement, of the authorised person (see paragraphs 7.3 and 7.4 below);
(d) have the pages numbered consecutively as a separate document (or as one of several documents contained in a file);
(e) be divided into numbered paragraphs;
(f) have all numbers, including dates, expressed in figures; and
(g) give the reference to any document or documents mentioned either in the margin or in bold text in the body of the affidavit/statement.

Body

4.1 Subject to paragraph 4.2 and rules 14.2 and 29.1, the affidavit/statement must, if practicable, be in the maker's own words, it should be expressed in the first person, and the maker should –

(a) commence –
 (i) in an affidavit, 'I (full name) of (residential address) state on oath ....';

PART III

(ii) in a statement, by giving his or her full name and residential address;

(b) if giving evidence in a professional, business or other occupational capacity, give the address at which he or she works in (a) above, the position held and the name of the firm or employer;

(c) give his or her occupation or (if none) description; and

(d) if it be the case that the maker is a party to the proceedings or is employed by a party to the proceedings, state that fact.

4.2 If, in proceedings to which Part 14 (Adoption, placement and related proceedings) applies, a serial number has been assigned under rule 14.2, the affidavit/statement must be framed so that it does not disclose the identity of the applicant.

(Rule 29.1 provides that, unless the court directs otherwise, a party to family proceedings is not required to reveal the address of his or her private residence or other contact details.)

4.3 An affidavit/statement must indicate –

(a) which of the statements in it are made from the maker's own knowledge and which are matters of information and belief; and

(b) the source for any matters of information and belief.

4.4 It is usually convenient to follow the chronological sequence of events or matters dealt with. Each paragraph should as far as possible be confined to a distinct portion of the subject.

4.5 The maker should, when referring to an exhibit or exhibits, state 'there is now shown to me marked "..." the (description of exhibit)'.

Alterations to affidavits and witness statements

5.1 Any alteration to an affidavit must be initialled by both the maker and the person before whom the affidavit is sworn.

5.2 Any alteration to a witness statement must be initialled by the maker or by the authorised person where appropriate (see paragraphs 7.3 and 7.4 below).

5.3 An affidavit/statement which contains an alteration that has not been initialled in accordance with paragraphs 5.1 and 5.2 may be filed or used in evidence only with the permission of the court.

Swearing an affidavit or verifying a witness statement

6.1 An affidavit is the testimony of the person who swears it. A witness statement is the equivalent of the oral evidence which the maker would, if called, give in evidence.

6.2 The jurat of an affidavit is a statement set out at the end of the document which authenticates the affidavit. It must –

(a) be signed by all deponents;

(b) be completed and signed by the person before whom the affidavit was sworn whose name and qualification must be printed beneath his signature;

(c) contain the full address of the person before whom the affidavit was sworn; and

(d) follow immediately on from the text and not be put on a separate page.

6.3 An affidavit must be sworn before a person independent of the parties or their representatives. Only the following may administer oaths and take affidavits –

(a) a Commissioner for Oaths (Commissioners for Oaths Acts 1889 and 1891);

(b) other persons specified by statute (sections 12 and 18 of, and Schedules 2 and 4 to, the Legal Services Act 2007);

(c) certain officials of the Senior Courts (section 2 of the Commissioners for Oaths Act 1889);

(d) a judge of the family court (section 31G(8) of the Matrimonial and Family Proceedings Act 1984);

(e) an officer of the family court appointed by a judge of the family court for the purpose (section 31G(8) of the Matrimonial and Family Proceedings Act 1984).

6.4 A witness statement must include a statement of truth by the intended maker as follows:

'I believe that the facts stated in this witness statement are true.'

(Attention is drawn to rule 17.6 which sets out the consequences of verifying a witness statement containing a false statement without an honest belief in its truth.)

(For information regarding statements of truth, see Part 17 (Statements of truth) and Practice Direction 17A.)

(Paragraphs 7.1 to 7.4 below set out the procedures to be followed where the intended maker of an affidavit or witness statement is unable to read or sign the affidavit/statement.)

6.5 If, in proceedings under Part 14 (Adoption, placement and related proceedings), a serial number has been assigned under rule 14.2 or the name of the maker of the affidavit/statement is not being revealed in accordance with rule 29.1, the signature of the maker will be edited from the affidavit/statement before it is served on the other party.

Inability of maker to read or sign affidavit/statement

7.1 Where an affidavit is sworn by a deponent who is unable to read or sign it, the person before whom the affidavit is sworn must certify in the jurat that –

(a) that person read the affidavit to the deponent;
(b) the deponent appeared to understand it; and
(c) the deponent signed, or made his mark, in that person's presence.

7.2 If that certificate is not included in the jurat, the affidavit may not be used in evidence unless the court is satisfied that it was read to the deponent and that the deponent appeared to understand it. Annex 1 to this practice direction sets out forms of the jurat with the certificate for an affidavit and an affirmation respectively.

7.3 Where a witness statement is made by a person who is unable to read or sign the statement, it must contain a certificate made by an authorised person. An authorised person is a person able to administer oaths and take affidavits but need not be independent of the parties or their representatives.

7.4 The authorised person must certify –

(a) that the witness statement has been read to the witness;
(b) that the witness appeared to understand it and approved its content as accurate;
(c) that the statement of truth has been read to the witness;
(d) that the witness appeared to understand the statement of truth and the consequences of making a false witness statement; and
(e) that the witness signed or made his or her mark in the presence of the authorised person.

The form of the certificate is set out at Annex 2 to this practice direction.

Filing of affidavits and witness statements

8.1 If the court directs that an affidavit/statement is to be filed, it must be filed in the court or Division, or office or Registry of the court or Division, where the action in which it was or is to be used, is proceeding or will proceed.

8.2 Where the affidavit/statement is in a foreign language –

(a) the party wishing to rely on it must –
  (i) have it translated; and
  (ii) must file the foreign language affidavit/statement with the court; and
(b) the translator must sign the translation to certify that it is accurate.

EXHIBITS

Manner of Exhibiting Documents

9.1 A document used in conjunction with an affidavit/statement should be –

(a) shown to and verified by the maker, and remain separate from the affidavit/statement; and

(b) identified by a declaration of the person before whom the affidavit/statement was sworn.

9.2 The declaration should be headed with the name of the proceedings in the same way as the affidavit/statement is headed.

9.3 The first page of each exhibit should be marked –

(a) as in paragraph 3.2 above; and

(b) with the exhibit mark referred to in the affidavit/statement in accordance with paragraph 4.5 above.

9.4 Where the maker makes more than one affidavit/statement, to which there are exhibits, in the same proceedings, the numbering of the exhibits should run consecutively throughout and not start again with each affidavit/statement.

Letters

10.1 Copies of individual letters should be collected together and exhibited in a bundle or bundles. They should be arranged in chronological order with the earliest at the top, and firmly secured.

10.2 When a bundle of correspondence is exhibited, the exhibit should have a front page attached stating that the bundle consists of original letters and copies. They should be arranged and secured as above and numbered consecutively.

Other documents

11.1 Photocopies instead of original documents may be exhibited provided the originals are made available for inspection by the other parties before the hearing and by the court at the hearing.

11.2 Court documents must not be exhibited (official copies of such documents prove themselves).

11.3 Where an exhibit contains more than one document, a front page should be attached setting out a list of the documents contained in the exhibit. The list should contain the dates of the documents.

Exhibits other than documents

12.1 Items other than documents should be clearly marked with an exhibit number or letter in such a manner that the mark cannot become detached from the exhibit.

12.2 Small items may be placed in a container and the container appropriately marked.

General provisions

13.1 Where an exhibit contains more than one document –

(a) the bundle should not be stapled but should be securely fastened in a way that does not hinder the reading of the documents; and

(b) the pages should be numbered consecutively at bottom centre.

13.2 Every page of an exhibit should be clearly legible; typed copies of illegible documents should be included, paginated with 'a' numbers.

13.3 Where affidavits/statements and exhibits have become numerous, they should be put into separate bundles and the pages numbered consecutively throughout.

13.4 Where on account of their bulk the service of exhibits or copies of exhibits on the other parties would be difficult or impracticable, the directions of the court should be sought as to arrangements for bringing the exhibits to the attention of the other parties and as to their custody pending trial.

MISCELLANEOUS

Defects in affidavits, witness statement and exhibits

14.1 Where –

(a) an affidavit;
(b) a witness statement; or
(c) an exhibit to either an affidavit or a witness statement,

does not comply with Part 22 or this practice direction in relation to its form, the court may refuse to admit it as evidence and may refuse to allow the costs arising from its preparation.

14.2 Permission to file a defective affidavit or witness statement or to use a defective exhibit may be obtained from the court where the case is proceeding.

Affirmations

15.1 All provisions in this or any other practice direction relating to affidavits apply to affirmations with the following exceptions –

(a) the deponent should commence 'I (full name) of (residential address) do solemnly and sincerely affirm ...'; and
(b) in the jurat the word 'sworn' is replaced by the word 'affirmed'.

Certificate of court officer

16.1 In proceedings under Part 7 (Matrimonial and Civil Partnership Proceedings), where the court has ordered that a witness statement, affidavit, affirmation or deposition is not be open to inspection by the public (see rule 22.19(2) and (3)) or that words or passages in the statement etc are not to be open to inspection (see rule 22.19(5)), the court officer will so certify on the statement etc and make any deletions directed by the court under rule 22.19(3).

Video Conferencing

17.1 Guidance on the use of video conferencing in the family courts is set out at Annex 3 to this practice direction.
A list of the sites which are available for video conferencing can be found on Her Majesty's Court Service's website at www.hm-courts-service.gov.uk.

Note—See now *www.gov.uk/government/organisations/hm-courts-and-tribunals-service*.
Use of video conferencing and court hearing—In *Black v Pastouna* [2005] EWCA Civ 1389, the Court of Appeal made recommendations as to the use of video hearings for distant advocates at unopposed hearings (e g permission to appeal: see FPR 2010, r 30.3).

ANNEX 1

Certificate to be used where a deponent to an affidavit is unable to read or sign it

Sworn at ... this ... day of ... Before me, I having first read over the contents of this affidavit to the deponent [if there are exhibits, add 'and explained the nature and effect of the exhibits referred to in it'] who appeared to understand it and approved its content as accurate, and made his/her* mark on the affidavit in my presence. Or, (after 'Before me') the witness to the mark of the deponent having been first sworn that the witness had read over etc. (as above) and that the witness saw the deponent make his/her* mark on the affidavit. (Witness must sign.)

* delete as appropriate

Certificate to be used where a deponent to an affirmation is unable to read or sign it

Affirmed at … this … day of … Before me, I having first read over the contents of this affirmation to the deponent [if there are exhibits, add 'and explained the nature and effect of the exhibits referred to in it'] who appeared to understand it and approved its content as accurate, and made his/her* mark on the affirmation in my presence. Or, (after 'Before me') the witness to the mark of the deponent having been first sworn that the witness had read over etc. (as above) and that the witness saw the deponent make his/her* mark on the affirmation. (Witness must sign.)

* delete as appropriate

ANNEX 2

Certificate to be used where a witness is unable to read or sign a witness statement

I certify that I [name and address of authorised person] have read over the contents of this witness statement and the statement of truth to the witness [if there are exhibits, add 'and explained the nature and effect of the exhibits referred to in it'] who (a) appeared to understand the witness statement and approved its content as accurate and (b) appeared to understand the statement of truth and the consequences of making a false witness statement, and [signed the statement] [made his/her mark]* in my presence.

* delete as appropriate.

ANNEX 3

Video conferencing guidance

1 This guidance is for the use of video conferencing (VCF) in proceedings to which the Family Procedure Rules apply. It is in part based, with permission, upon the protocol of the Federal Court of Australia. It is intended to provide a guide to all persons involved in the use of VCF, although it does not attempt to cover all the practical questions which might arise.

Any reference in this guide to a judge is to be taken as including any judge of the family court.

Video conferencing generally

2 The guidance covers the use of VCF equipment both (a) in a courtroom, whether via equipment which is permanently placed there or via a mobile unit, and (b) in a separate studio or conference room. In either case, the location at which the judge sits is referred to as the 'local site'. The other site or sites to and from which transmission is made are referred to as 'the remote site' and in any particular case any such site may be another courtroom. The guidance applies to cases where VCF is used for the taking of evidence and also to its use for other parts of any legal proceedings

3 VCF may be a convenient way of dealing with any part of proceedings – it can involve considerable savings in time and cost. Its use for the taking of evidence from overseas witnesses will, in particular, be likely to achieve a material saving of costs, and such savings may also be achieved by its use for taking domestic evidence. It is, however, inevitably not as ideal as having the witness physically present in court. Its convenience should not therefore be allowed to dictate its use. A judgment must be made in every case in which the use of VCF is being considered not only as to whether it will achieve an overall cost saving but as to whether its use will be likely to be beneficial to the efficient, fair and economic disposal of the litigation. In particular, it needs to be recognised that the degree of control a court can exercise over a witness at the remote site is or may be more limited than it can exercise over a witness physically before it.

4 When used for the taking of evidence, the objective should be to make the VCF session as close as possible to the usual practice in court where evidence is taken in open court. To gain the maximum benefit, several differences have to be taken into account. Some matters, which are taken for granted when evidence is taken in the conventional way, take on a different dimension

when it is taken by VCF – for example, the administration of the oath, ensuring that the witness understands who is at the local site and what their various roles are, the raising of any objections to the evidence and the use of documents.

5 It should not be presumed that all foreign governments are willing to allow their nationals or others within their jurisdiction to be examined before a court in England or Wales by means of VCF. If there is any doubt about this, enquiries should be directed to the Foreign and Commonwealth Office (International Legal Matters Unit, Consular Division) with a view to ensuring that the country from which the evidence is to be taken raises no objection to it at diplomatic level. The party who is directed to be responsible for arranging the VCF (see paragraph 8) will be required to make all necessary inquiries about this well in advance of the VCF and must be able to inform the court what those inquiries were and of their outcome.

6 Time zone differences need to be considered when a witness abroad is to be examined in England or Wales by VCF. The convenience of the witness, the parties, their representatives and the court must all be taken into account. The cost of the use of a commercial studio is usually greater outside normal business hours.

7 Those involved with VCF need to be aware that, even with the most advanced systems currently available, there are the briefest of delays between the receipt of the picture and that of the accompanying sound. If due allowance is not made for this, there will be a tendency to 'speak over' the witness, whose voice will continue to be heard for a millisecond or so after he or she appears on the screen to have finished speaking.

8 With current technology, picture quality is good, but not as good as a television picture. The quality of the picture is enhanced if those appearing on VCF monitors keep their movements to a minimum.

Preliminary arrangements

9 The court's permission is required for any part of any proceedings to be dealt with by means of VCF. Before seeking a direction, the applicant should notify the listing officer, diary manager or other appropriate court officer of the intention to seek it, and should enquire as to the availability of court VCF equipment for the day or days of the proposed VCF. If all parties consent to a direction, permission can be sought by letter, fax or e-mail, although the court may still require an oral hearing. All parties are entitled to be heard on whether or not such a direction should be given and as to its terms. If a witness at a remote site is to give evidence by an interpreter, consideration should be given at this stage as to whether the interpreter should be at the local site or the remote site. If a VCF direction is given, arrangements for the transmission will then need to be made. The court will ordinarily direct that the party seeking permission to use VCF is to be responsible for this. That party is hereafter referred to as 'the VCF arranging party'.

10 Subject to any order to the contrary, all costs of the transmission, including the costs of hiring equipment and technical personnel to operate it, will initially be the responsibility of, and must be met by, the VCF arranging party. All reasonable efforts should be made to keep the transmission to a minimum and so keep the costs down. All such costs will be considered to be part of the costs of the proceedings and the court will determine at such subsequent time as is convenient or appropriate who, as between the parties, should be responsible for them and (if appropriate) in what proportions.

11 The local site will, if practicable, be a courtroom but it may instead be an appropriate studio or conference room. The VCF arranging party must contact the listing officer, diary manager or other appropriate officer of the court which made the VCF direction and make arrangements for the VCF transmission. Details of the remote site, and of the equipment to be used both at the local site (if not being supplied by the court) and the remote site (including the number of ISDN lines and connection speed), together with all necessary contact names and telephone numbers, will have to be provided to the listing officer, diary manager or other court officer. The court will need to be satisfied that any equipment provided by the parties for use at the local site and also that at the remote site is of sufficient quality for a satisfactory transmission. The VCF arranging party must ensure that an appropriate person will be present at the local site to supervise the operation

PART III

of the VCF throughout the transmission in order to deal with any technical problems. That party must also arrange for a technical assistant to be similarly present at the remote site for like purposes.

12 It is recommended that the judge, practitioners and witness should arrive at their respective VCF sites about 20 minutes prior to the scheduled commencement of the transmission.

13 If the local site is not a courtroom, but a conference room or studio, the judge will need to determine who is to sit where. The VCF arranging party must take care to ensure that the number of microphones is adequate for the speakers and that the panning of the camera for the practitioners' table encompasses all legal representatives so that the viewer can see everyone seated there.

14 If the local site is to be a studio or conference room, the VCF arranging party must ensure that it provides sufficient accommodation to enable a reasonable number of members of the public to attend if appropriate.

15 In cases where the local site is a studio or conference room, the VCF arranging party should make arrangements, if practicable, for the royal coat of arms to be placed above the judge's seat.

16 In cases in which the VCF is to be used for the taking of evidence, the VCF arranging party must arrange for recording equipment to be provided by the court which made the VCF direction so that the evidence can be recorded. An associate will normally be present to operate the recording equipment when the local site is a courtroom. The VCF arranging party should take steps to ensure that an associate is present to do likewise when it is a studio or conference room. The equipment should be set up and tested before the VCF transmission. It will often be a valuable safeguard for the VCF arranging party also to arrange for the provision of recording equipment at the remote site. This will provide a useful back-up if there is any reduction in sound quality during the transmission. A direction from the court for the making of such a back-up recording must, however, be obtained first. This is because the proceedings are court proceedings and, save as directed by the court, no other recording of them must be made. The court will direct what is to happen to the back-up recording.

17 Some countries may require that any oath or affirmation to be taken by a witness accord with local custom rather than the usual form of oath or affirmation used in England and Wales. The VCF arranging party must make all appropriate prior inquiries and put in place all arrangements necessary to enable the oath or affirmation to be taken in accordance with any local custom. That party must be in a position to inform the court what those inquiries were, what their outcome was and what arrangements have been made. If the oath or affirmation can be administered in the manner normal in England and Wales, the VCF arranging party must arrange in advance to have the appropriate holy book at the remote site. The associate will normally administer the oath.

18 Consideration will need to be given in advance to the documents to which the witness is likely to be referred. The parties should endeavour to agree on this. It will usually be most convenient for a bundle of the copy documents to be prepared in advance, which the VCF arranging party should then send to the remote site.

19 Additional documents are sometimes quite properly introduced during the course of a witness's evidence. To cater for this, the VCF arranging party should ensure that equipment is available to enable documents to be transmitted between sites during the course of the VCF transmission. Consideration should be given to whether to use a document camera. If it is decided to use one, arrangements for its use will need to be established in advance. The panel operator will need to know the number and size of documents or objects if their images are to be sent by document camera. In many cases, a simpler and sufficient alternative will be to ensure that there are fax transmission and reception facilities at the participating sites.

The hearing

20 The procedure for conducting the transmission will be determined by the judge. He will determine who is to control the cameras. In cases where the VCF is being used for an application in the course of the proceedings, the judge will ordinarily not enter the local site until both sites

are on line. Similarly, at the conclusion of the hearing, he will ordinarily leave the local site while both sites are still on line. The following paragraphs apply primarily to cases where the VCF is being used for the taking of the evidence of a witness at a remote site.

21 At the beginning of the transmission, the judge will probably wish to introduce himself or herself and the advocates to the witness. He will probably want to know who is at the remote site and will invite the witness to introduce himself or herself and anyone else who is with the witness. The judge may wish to give directions as to the seating arrangements at the remote site so that those present are visible at the local site during the taking of the evidence and to explain to the witness the method of taking the oath or of affirming, the manner in which the evidence will be taken, and who will be conducting the examination and cross-examination. The judge will probably also wish to inform the witness of the matters referred to in paragraphs 7 and 8 (co-ordination of picture with sound, and picture quality).

22 The examination of the witness at the remote site should follow as closely as possible the practice adopted when a witness is in the courtroom. During examination, cross-examination and re-examination, the witness must be able to see the legal representative asking the question and also any other person (whether another legal representative or the judge) making any statements in regard to the witness's evidence. It will in practice be most convenient if everyone remains seated throughout the transmission.

PART 23
MISCELLANEOUS RULES ABOUT EVIDENCE

CONTENTS OF THIS PART

Rule		Page
23.1	Scope and interpretation of this Part	1777
23.2	Notice of intention to rely on hearsay evidence	1777
23.3	Circumstances in which notice of intention to rely on hearsay evidence is not required	1778
23.4	Power to call witness for cross-examination on hearsay evidence	1778
23.5	Credibility	1779
23.6	Use of plans, photographs and models etc as evidence	1779
23.7	Evidence of finding on question of foreign law	1780
23.8	Evidence of consent of trustee to act	1780
23.9	Note of oral evidence	1780

23.1 Scope and interpretation of this Part

Rules 23.2 to 23.6 apply to evidence to which the Children (Admissibility of Hearsay Evidence) Order 1993 does not apply.

23.2 Notice of intention to rely on hearsay evidence

(1) Where a party intends to rely on hearsay evidence at the final hearing and either –

- (a) that evidence is to be given by a witness giving oral evidence; or
- (b) that evidence is contained in a witness statement of a person who is not being called to give oral evidence,

that party complies with section 2(1)(a) of the Civil Evidence Act 1995 by serving a witness statement on the other parties in accordance with the court's directions.

(2) Where paragraph (1)(b) applies, the party intending to rely on the hearsay evidence must, when serving the witness statement –

- (a) inform the other parties that the witness is not being called to give oral evidence; and
- (b) give the reason why the witness will not be called.

(3) In all other cases where a party intends to rely on hearsay evidence at the final hearing, that party complies with section 2(1)(a) of the Civil Evidence Act 1995 by serving a notice on the other parties which –

(a) identifies the hearsay evidence;
(b) states that the party serving the notice proposes to rely on the hearsay evidence at the final hearing; and
(c) gives the reason why the witness will not be called.

(4) The party proposing to rely on the hearsay evidence must –

(a) serve the notice no later than the latest date for serving witness statements; and
(b) if the hearsay evidence is to be in a document, supply a copy to any party who requests it.

Definition of hearsay evidence—FPR 2010, rr 23.1–23.6 are closely modelled on CPR 1998, rr 33.1–33.6, but omit the definition of 'hearsay' in CPR 1998, r 33.1. Thus, normal rules as to hearsay apply to all family proceedings, except those proceedings exempted by Children (Admissibility of Hearsay Evidence) Order 1993, Art 2. Civil Evidence Act 1995, s 1(2) defines hearsay as:

'(a) "hearsay" means a statement made otherwise than by a person while giving oral evidence in the proceedings which is tendered as evidence of the matters stated; and
(b) references to hearsay include hearsay of whatever degree.'

Civil Evidence Act 1995: weight of evidence—The 1995 Act steers a course between technical rules of hearsay evidence and the need in civil proceedings to take a proportionate view as to the forms of evidence that may be admitted. Thus hearsay evidence, merely because hearsay, will not be inadmissible. Thus, s 1(1) provides: 'In civil proceedings evidence shall not be excluded on the ground that it is hearsay'. Its cogency and the weight to be given to it can be considered by the court under s 4. The court will want to deal with all cases justly and ensure that all evidence is before it to make a decision, but the court retains the power to exclude otherwise admissible evidence (FPR 2010, r 22.1(2)).

'civil proceedings'—Civil proceedings are defined by Civil Evidence Act 1995, s 11 and depend on the proceedings taking place before 'any tribunal in relation to which the strict rules of evidence apply'. This includes all family proceedings covered by FPR 2010.

Notice of reliance on hearsay evidence—A party who wishes to rely on hearsay evidence must give notice in accordance with Civil Evidence Act 1995, s 2(1) and to do so must comply with r 23.2. Rule 23.2(1),(3) distinguishes between notice of hearsay evidence expected to be given at a 'final hearing' (r 23.2(1)) and of notice 'in all other cases' (r 23.2(3)).

(1) Notice is given, in the case of a final hearing, by the party intending to call hearsay evidence: first by indicating the intention to do so, or by saying that a witness whose evidence is before the court will not be called.
(2) In the case of all other cases of hearsay evidence, notice is given by the party intending to rely on hearsay evidence, by him or her saying what evidence is to be relied on and why the witness will not be called.

23.3 Circumstances in which notice of intention to rely on hearsay evidence is not required

Section 2(1) of the Civil Evidence Act 1995 (duty to give notice of intention to rely on hearsay evidence) does not apply –

(a) to evidence at hearings other than final hearings;
(b) to an affidavit[(GL)] or witness statement which is to be used at the final hearing but which does not contain hearsay evidence; or
(c) where the requirement is excluded by a practice direction.

Civil Evidence Act 1995, s 2(1)—Civil Evidence Act 1995, s 2(1) provides as follows:

'(1) A party proposing to adduce hearsay evidence in civil proceedings shall, subject to the following provisions of this section, give to the other party or parties to the proceedings –
(a) such notice (if any) of that fact, and
(b) on request, such particulars of or relating to the evidence,
as is reasonable and practicable in the circumstances for the purpose of enabling him or them to deal with any matters arising from its being hearsay.'

The requirement for hearsay evidence notice under s 2(1) is excluded by r 23.3 in the case of interim hearings (and see FPR 2010, r 22.2(1)(b)) and for witness statements and affidavits that do not contain hearsay evidence. On a hearsay notice being given such further information concerning it shall be given (s 2(1)(b)).

23.4 Power to call witness for cross-examination on hearsay evidence

(1) Where a party –

(a) proposes to rely on hearsay evidence; and

(b) does not propose to call the person who made the original statement to give oral evidence,

the court may, on the application of any other party, permit that party to call the maker of the statement to be cross-examined(GL) on the contents of the statement.

(2) An application for permission to cross-examine(GL) under this rule must be made within 14 days beginning with the date on which a notice of intention to rely on the hearsay evidence was served on the applicant.

(Rules 35.3 and 35.4 contain rules in relation to evidence arising out of mediation of cross-border disputes.)

Application to cross-examine—A party to whom notice is given under FPR 2010, r 23.2 may apply to the court (under the FPR 2010, Pt 18 procedure) for an order that he be able to have called the witness concerned for their cross-examination on their statement. The court has a discretion as to whether to admit the evidence. Its importance of the evidence in the context of the case, the extent and relevance of the cross-examination and the proportionality of calling the witness as against the need to deal with the case fairly may all weigh in the judge's mind in the exercise of that discretion.

23.5 Credibility

(1) Where a party proposes to rely on hearsay evidence, but –

(a) does not propose to call the person who made the original statement to give oral evidence; and

(b) another party wishes to call evidence to attack the credibility of the person who made the statement,

the party who so wishes must give notice of that intention to the party who proposes to give the hearsay statement in evidence.

(2) A party must give notice under paragraph (1) within 14 days after the date on which a hearsay notice relating to the hearsay evidence was served on that party.

Weight of hearsay evidence—The counter-balance to Civil Evidence Act 1995, s 1(1) as to admissibility of hearsay evidence is to give the responsibility to the courts to assess the weight, or cogency, of the hearsay evidence. Accordingly, s 4 provides as follows:

'4 Considerations relevant to weighing of hearsay evidence

(1) In estimating the weight (if any) to be given to hearsay evidence in civil proceedings the court shall have regard to any circumstances from which any inference can reasonably be drawn as to the reliability or otherwise of the evidence.

(2) Regard may be had, in particular, to the following –

(a) whether it would have been reasonable and practicable for the party by whom the evidence was adduced to have produced the maker of the original statement as a witness;

(b) whether the original statement was made contemporaneously with the occurrence or existence of the matters stated;

(c) whether the evidence involves multiple hearsay;

(d) whether any person involved had any motive to conceal or misrepresent matters;

(e) whether the original statement was an edited account, or was made in collaboration with another or for a particular purpose;

(f) whether the circumstances in which the evidence is adduced as hearsay are such as to suggest an attempt to prevent proper evaluation of its weight.'

Civil Evidence Act 1995, s 4: judicial findings on hearsay—Civil Evidence Act 1995, s 4 places on the court a positive duty to assess the weight of any hearsay evidence, to have regard to 'any circumstances' in assessing the weight of that evidence and in particular to take into account the factors set out in s 4(2). If any evidence is hearsay, within the definition in s 1(2) then the judge must so state and make specific findings as to the weight to be given to that evidence in the court's decision.

23.6 Use of plans, photographs and models etc as evidence

(1) This rule applies to –

(a) evidence (such as a plan, photograph or model) which is not –

(i) contained in a witness statement, affidavit(GL) or expert's report;

(ii) to be given orally at the final hearing; or

(iii) evidence of which prior notice must be given under rule 23.2; and

(b) documents which may be received in evidence without further proof under section 9 of the Civil Evidence Act 1995.

PART III

(2) Except as provided below, section 2(1)(a) of the Civil Evidence Act 1995 (notice of proposal to adduce hearsay evidence) does not apply to evidence falling within paragraph (1).

(3) Such evidence is not receivable at the final hearing unless the party intending to rely on it (in this rule, 'the party') has –

(a) served it or, in the case of a model, a photograph of it with an invitation to inspect the original, on the other party in accordance with this rule; or
(b) complied with such directions as the court may give for serving the evidence on, or for giving notice under section 2(1)(a) of the Civil Evidence Act 1995 in respect of the evidence to, the other party.

(4) Where the party intends to use the evidence as evidence of any fact then, except where paragraph (6) applies, the party must serve the evidence not later than the latest date for serving witness statements.

(5) The party must serve the evidence at least 21 days before the hearing at which the party proposes to rely on it if –

(a) there are not to be witness statements; or
(b) the party intends to put in the evidence solely in order to disprove an allegation made in a witness statement.

(6) Where the evidence forms part of expert evidence, the party must serve the evidence when the expert's report is served on the other party.

(7) Where the evidence is being produced to the court for any reason other than as part of factual or expert evidence, the party must serve the evidence at least 21 days before the hearing at which the party proposes to rely on it.

(8) Where the court directs a party to give notice that the party intends to put in the evidence, the court may direct that every other party be given an opportunity to inspect it and to agree to its admission without further proof.

23.7 Evidence of finding on question of foreign law

(1) This rule sets out the procedure which must be followed by a party (in this rule, 'the party') who intends to put in evidence a finding on a question of foreign law by virtue of section 4(2) of the Civil Evidence Act 1972.

(2) The party must give any other party notice of that intention.

(3) The party must give the notice –

(a) if there are to be witness statements, not later than the latest date for serving them; or
(b) otherwise, not less than 21 days before the hearing at which the party proposes to put the finding in evidence.

(4) The notice must –

(a) specify the question on which the finding was made; and
(b) enclose a copy of a document where it is reported or recorded.

23.8 Evidence of consent of trustee to act

In proceedings to which Part 9 (financial remedies) applies, a document purporting to contain the written consent of a person to act as trustee and to bear that person's signature verified by some other person is evidence of such consent.

23.9 Note of oral evidence

In proceedings in the family court before a lay justice or lay justices, the justices' clerk or the court shall keep a note of the substance of the oral evidence given at a directions appointment or at a hearing of any proceedings.

Amendments—SI 2014/667.

PART 24
WITNESSES, DEPOSITIONS GENERALLY AND TAKING OF EVIDENCE IN MEMBER STATES OF THE EUROPEAN UNION

CONTENTS OF THIS PART

Chapter 1

Rule		Page
	Witnesses and Depositions	
24.1	Scope of this Chapter	1782
24.2	Witness summonses	1782
24.3	Issue of a witness summons	1782
24.4	Time for serving a witness summons	1783
24.5	Who is to serve a witness summons	1783
24.6	Right of witness to travelling expenses and compensation for loss of time	1783
24.7	Evidence by deposition	1783
24.8	Conduct of examination	1784
24.9	Enforcing attendance of witness	1784
24.10	Use of deposition at a hearing	1785
24.11	Restrictions on subsequent use of deposition taken for the purpose of any hearing except the final hearing	1785
24.12	Where a person to be examined is out of the jurisdiction – letter of request	1785
24.13	Fees and expenses of examiner of the court	1786
24.14	Examiners of the court	1786

Chapter 2
Taking of Evidence – Member States of the European Union

24.15	Interpretation	1786
24.16	Where a person to be examined is in another Regulation State	1787
	Practice Direction 24A – Witnesses, Depositions and Taking of Evidence in Member States of the European Union	1787

Note—FPR 2010, Pt 24 and FPR PD24A make provision for evidence in Member States of the EU. Chapter 1 makes provision for witnesses and dispositions; Chapter 2 makes provision for the taking of evidence in Member States of the EU.

Chapter 1
Witnesses and Depositions

Defined terms—'proceedings', 'jurisdiction': FPR 2010, r 2.3(1).

Scope—FPR 2010, rr 24.2–24.6 and PD24A, paras 1–3 make provision for the circumstances in which a person may be required to attend court to give evidence or to produce a document. The form of witness summons is set out in PD24A. The court's permission to issue a witness summons is required in certain circumstances (r 24.3(2)). A witness summons is issued either by the court where the case is proceeding or the court where the hearing in question will be held (r 24.3(3)). Time for serving a witness summons is regulated by r 24.4, the general rule being that a witness summons is binding if served at least 7 days before the hearing date. A witness summons is served by the issuing party except in proceedings to which Part 14 applies, where it must be served by the court unless otherwise directed (r 24.5). Provision for travelling expenses and compensation for loss of time is made by rr 24.5(3) and 24.6 and PD24A, para 3.

Evidence by deposition is provided for by rr 24.7–24.14 and PD24A, paras 4 and 5. The procedure enables a party to apply for an order that a person be examined before the hearing takes place before a judge, an examiner of the court (rr 24.13, 24.14) or such other person as the court appoints. The procedure where depositions are to be taken in England and Wales for use as evidence in proceedings in courts in England and Wales is set out in PD24A, para 4. The conduct of the examination is regulated by r 24.8. The court has powers to enforce the attendance of a witness before an examiner (r 24.9). The use of depositions is regulated by rr 24.10, 24.11. Where the deposition is to be taken out of the jurisdiction for use as evidence in proceedings before a court in England and Wales and where Council Regulation (EC) No 1206/2001 of 28 May 2011 ('the Taking of Evidence Regulation') does not apply (i e in the case of all Member States except

Denmark)), r 24.12 and PD24A, para 5 apply. The High Court may order the issue of a letter of request (PD24A, Annex A) to the judicial authorities of the country in which the proposed deponent is for arrangements to be made for a deposition to be taken.

24.1 Scope of this Chapter

(1) This Chapter provides –

(a) for the circumstances in which a person may be required to attend court to give evidence or to produce a document; and
(b) for a party to obtain evidence before a hearing to be used at the hearing.

(2) *(revoked)*

(Rules 34.16 to 34.21 and 34.24 of the CPR apply to incoming requests for evidence.)

Amendments—SI 2013/3204.

CPR 1998, rr 34.16–34.21, 34.24—Evidence (Proceedings in Other Jurisdictions) Act 1975, s 1 enables application to be made to the High Court by request from a court or tribunal outside the jurisdiction where proceedings are underway, or are contemplated, for the obtaining of evidence for use in that court. CPR 1998, rr 34.16–34.21 provides a procedure for such application, and – as applied here – for proceedings in the Family Court and Family Division. Rule 34.24 applies where a court in a country to which Council Regulation (EC) No 1206/2001 of 28 May 2001 (co-operation between the courts of the Member States in the taking of evidence in civil and commercial matters) applies, issues a request for evidence to be taken from a person who is within the jurisdiction.

24.2 Witness summonses

(1) A witness summons is a document issued by the court requiring a witness to –

(a) attend court to give evidence; or
(b) produce documents to the court.

(2) A witness summons must be in the form set out in Practice Direction 24A.

(3) There must be a separate witness summons for each witness.

(4) A witness summons may require a witness to produce documents to the court either –

(a) on the date fixed for a hearing; or
(b) on such date as the court may direct.

(5) The only documents that a summons under this rule can require a person to produce before a hearing are documents which that person could be required to produce at the hearing.

(Rules 35.3 and 35.4 contain rules in relation to evidence arising out of mediation of cross-border disputes.)

Witness summons in the Family Court—MFPA 1984, s 31G(1),(2) deals with the issue and s 31N with court service of witness summonses. Section 31G(3)–(5) deals with penalties for failure to answer to a witness summons.

'such date as the court may direct' (r 24.2(4)(b))—For production of documents, this rule gives regulatory effect to *Khanna v Lovell White Durrant (A Firm)* [1995] 1 WLR 121, ChD (applied in family proceedings in *Roker International Properties Inc* [2000] 2 FLR 976, FD). Rule 24.3(2)(b) adds to the *Khanna* appointment that, with permission, the court may require also that oral evidence (only documents could be dealt with under *Khanna*) be dealt with at a preliminary hearing. That hearing may be at a place other than the court itself (FPR 2010, r 2.8, e g at a venue where the documents are held).

Restrictions on production—Rule 24.2(5) (and c f r 21.2(5)) prevents a witness being required to produce a document where that witness could not be compelled to produce the document at any hearing (e g because it is covered by confidentiality or public interest immunity). Similar principles will then arise, as are considered at FPR 2010, r 21.3: the need for evidence to be before the court to ensure a fair trial balanced against the private interests of the third party, or of the relevance of the evidence to the issues before the court. A witness will also not be required to produce documents where they are not relevant to an issue before the court (see also **'set aside or vary a witness summons'** under r 24.3).

24.3 Issue of a witness summons

(1) A witness summons is issued on the date entered on the summons by the court.

(2) A party must obtain permission from the court where that party wishes to –

(a) have a summons issued less than 7 days before the date of the final hearing;
(b) have a summons issued for a witness to attend court to give evidence or to produce documents on any date except the date fixed for the final hearing; or

(c) have a summons issued for a witness to attend court to give evidence or to produce documents at any hearing except the final hearing.

(3) A witness summons must be issued by –

(a) the court where the case is proceeding; or
(b) the court where the hearing in question will be held.

(4) The court may set aside[(GL)] or vary a witness summons issued under this rule.

'set aside or vary a witness summons' (r 24.3(4))—The court has a discretion – on application being made – to 'set aside or vary a witness summons' on grounds similar to those for refusing disclosure (eg to require production of a document or attendance is oppressive; evidence not relevant to an issue before the court; not necessary to fair disposal; confidentiality; and see *South Tyneside Borough Council v Wickes Building Supplies Ltd* [2004] EWHC 2428 (Comm) for what is 'necessary for the fair disposal' of a case). In *Morgan v Morgan* (1976) FLR Rep 473, FD, Watkins J put the test as: the court must balance the need to have the information necessary to get the answer as near as possible right – that is, to ensure 'that the lump sum awarded is the correct figure' so far as it can be calculated; as against the 'rights of the citizen … to keep to himself … details of his wealth and what he intends to do with it' (wife's father had been subpoenaed to produce his will).

Application for permission to set aside or to vary—Applications under r 24.3 are by FPR 2010, Pt 18 procedure (Form D11).

24.4 Time for serving a witness summons

(1) The general rule is that a witness summons is binding if it is served at least 7 days before the date on which the witness is required to attend before the court.

(2) The court may direct that a witness summons is binding although it is served less than 7 days before the date on which the witness is required to attend before the court.

(3) A witness summons which is –

(a) served in accordance with this rule; and
(b) requires the witness to attend court to give evidence,

is binding until the conclusion of the hearing at which the attendance of the witness is required.

(Rules 35.3 and 35.4 contain rules in relation to evidence arising out of mediation of cross-border disputes.)

24.5 Who is to serve a witness summons

(1) Subject to paragraph (2), a witness summons is to be served by the party on whose behalf it is issued unless that party indicates in writing, when asking the court to issue the summons, that that party wishes the court to serve it instead.

(2) In proceedings to which Part 14 (procedure for applications in adoption, placement and related proceedings) applies, a witness summons is to be served by the court unless the court directs otherwise.

(3) Where the court is to serve the witness summons, the party on whose behalf it is issued must deposit, in the court office, the money to be paid or offered to the witness under rule 24.6.

Money to be paid to a witness—Whereas CCA 1984 and SCA 1981 provide that the court should impose no penalty if a witness fails to attend court if no attendance money is tendered to them at the time of service of a witness summons for the County Court and High Court (including the Family Division), there is no such relief specifically provided for in the Family Court (MFPA 1984, s 31G is silent on the point).

24.6 Right of witness to travelling expenses and compensation for loss of time

At the time of service of a witness summons the witness must be offered or paid –

(a) a sum reasonably sufficient to cover the expenses of the witness in travelling to and from the court; and
(b) such sum by way of compensation for loss of time as may be specified in Practice Direction 24A.

24.7 Evidence by deposition

(1) A party may apply for an order for a person to be examined before the hearing takes place.

PART III

(2) A person from whom evidence is to be obtained following an order under this rule is referred to as a 'deponent' and the evidence is referred to as a 'deposition'.

(3) An order under this rule is for a deponent to be examined on oath before –

(a) a judge;
(b) an examiner of the court; or
(c) such other person as the court appoints.

(Rule 24.14 makes provision for the appointment of examiners of the court.)

(4) The order may require the production of any document which the court considers is necessary for the purposes of the examination.

(5) The order must state the date, time and place of the examination.

(6) At the time of service of the order the deponent must be offered or paid –

(a) a sum reasonably sufficient to cover the expenses of the deponent in travelling to and from the place of examination; and
(b) such sum by way of compensation for loss of time as may be specified in Practice Direction 24A.

(7) Where the court makes an order for a deposition to be taken, it may also order the party who obtained the order to serve a witness statement or witness summary in relation to the evidence to be given by the person to be examined.

(Part 22 (evidence) contains the general rules about witness statements and witness summaries.)

(Rules 35.3 and 35.4 contain rules in relation to evidence arising out of mediation of cross-border disputes.)

24.8 Conduct of examination

(1) Subject to any directions contained in the order for examination, the examination must be conducted in the same way as if the witness were giving evidence at a final hearing.

(2) If all the parties are present, the examiner may conduct the examination of a person not named in the order for examination if all the parties and the person to be examined consent.

(3) In defended proceedings under Part 7 (matrimonial and civil partnership proceedings), the examiner may conduct the examination in private if of the view that it is appropriate to do so.

(4) Save in proceedings to which paragraph (3) applies, the examiner will conduct the examination in private unless of the view that it is not appropriate to do so.

(5) The examiner must ensure that the evidence given by the witness is recorded in full.

(6) The examiner must send a copy of the deposition –

(a) to the person who obtained the order for the examination of the witness; and
(b) to the court where the case is proceeding.

(7) The court will give directions as to service of the deposition on the other party.

24.9 Enforcing attendance of witness

(1) If a person served with an order to attend before an examiner –

(a) fails to attend; or
(b) refuses to be sworn for the purpose of the examination or to answer any lawful question or produce any document at the examination,

a certificate of that person's failure or refusal, signed by the examiner, must be filed by the party requiring the deposition.

(2) On the certificate being filed, the party requiring the deposition may apply to the court for an order requiring that person to attend or to be sworn or to answer any question or produce any document, as the case may be.

(3) An application for an order under this rule may be made without notice.

(4) The court may order the person against whom an order is made under this rule to pay any costs resulting from that person's failure or refusal.

(Rules 35.3 and 35.4 contain rules in relation to evidence arising out of mediation of cross-border disputes. Rule 35.4(1)(d) relates specifically to this rule.)

24.10 Use of deposition at a hearing

(1) A deposition ordered under rule 24.7 may be given in evidence at a hearing unless the court orders otherwise.

(2) A party intending to put in evidence a deposition at a hearing must file notice of intention to do so on the court and the court will give directions about serving the notice on every other party.

(3) The party must file the notice at least 21 days before the day fixed for the hearing.

(4) The court may require a deponent to attend the hearing and give evidence orally.

(5) Where a deposition is given in evidence at the final hearing, it is treated as if it were a witness statement for the purposes of rule 22.19 (availability of witness statements for inspection).

(Rules 35.3 and 35.4 contain rules in relation to evidence arising out of mediation of cross-border disputes. Rule 35.4(1)(e) relates specifically to this rule.)

24.11 Restrictions on subsequent use of deposition taken for the purpose of any hearing except the final hearing

(1) This rule applies to proceedings under Part 7 (matrimonial and civil partnership proceedings) or Part 9 (financial remedies).

(2) Where the court orders a party to be examined about that party's or any other assets for the purpose of any hearing except the final hearing, the deposition may be used only for the purpose of the proceedings in which the order was made.

(3) However it may be used for some other purpose –

(a) by the party who was examined;
(b) if the party who was examined agrees; or
(c) if the court gives permission.

24.12 Where a person to be examined is out of the jurisdiction – letter of request

(1) This rule applies where a party wishes to take a deposition from a person who is –

(a) out of the jurisdiction; and
(b) not in a Regulation State within the meaning of Chapter 2 of this Part.

(2) The High Court may order the issue of a letter of request to the judicial authorities of the country in which the proposed deponent is.

(3) A letter of request is a request to a judicial authority to take the evidence of that person, or arrange for it to be taken.

(4) The High Court may make an order under this rule in relation to family court proceedings.

(5) If the government of a country allows a person appointed by the High Court to examine a person in that country, the High Court may make an order appointing a special examiner for that purpose.

(6) A person may be examined under this rule on oath or affirmation or in accordance with any procedure permitted in the country in which the examination is to take place.

(7) If the High Court makes an order for the issue of a letter of request, the party who sought the order must file –

(a) the following documents and, except where paragraph (8) applies, a translation of them –
  (i) a draft letter of request;
  (ii) a statement of the issues relevant to the proceedings; and

PART III

(iii) a list of questions or the subject matter of questions to be put to the person to be examined; and

(b) an undertaking to be responsible for the Secretary of State's expenses.

(8) There is no need to file a translation if –

(a) English is one of the official languages of the country where the examination is to take place; or

(b) a practice direction has specified that country as a country where no translation is necessary.

(Rules 35.3 and 35.4 contain rules in relation to evidence arising out of mediation of cross-border disputes. Rule 35.4(1)(f) relates specifically to this rule.)

Amendments—SI 2013/3204.

24.13 Fees and expenses of examiner of the court

(1) An examiner of the court may charge a fee for the examination.

(2) The examiner need not send the deposition to the court unless the fee is paid.

(3) The examiner's fees and expenses must be paid by the party who obtained the order for examination.

(4) If the fees and expenses due to an examiner are not paid within a reasonable time, the examiner may report that fact to the court.

(5) The court may order the party who obtained the order for examination to deposit in the court office a specified sum in respect of the examiner's fees and, where it does so, the examiner will not be asked to act until the sum has been deposited.

(6) An order under this rule does not affect any decision as to the party who is ultimately to bear the costs of the examination.

24.14 Examiners of the court

(1) The Lord Chancellor will appoint persons to be examiners of the court.

(2) The persons appointed must be barristers or solicitor-advocates who have been practising for a period of not less than 3 years.

(3) The Lord Chancellor may revoke an appointment at any time.

Chapter 2

Taking of Evidence – Member States of the European Union

Scope—FPR 2010, Pt 24, Ch 2 and FPR PD24A, paras 6–9 regulate the taking of evidence between EU Member States. Where evidence is to be taken from a person in another Member State of the EU for use as evidence in proceedings before a court in England and Wales, Council Regulation (EC) No 1206/2001 of 28 May 2001 on cooperation between the courts of the Member States in the taking of evidence in civil or commercial matters ('the Taking of Evidence Regulation') applies. The Taking of Evidence Regulation (PD24A, Annex B) is set out in Part VI. The Taking of Evidence Regulation does not apply to Denmark, in relation to which r 24.12 applies. Each Regulation State (i e all Member States except Denmark) has prepared a list of designated courts competent to take evidence in accordance with the Taking of Evidence Regulation. The designated courts for England and Wales are listed in Annex C to PD24A (PD24A, para 7). The Taking of Evidence Regulation requires each Regulation State to nominate a Central Body responsible for, for example, supplying information to courts. The Central Body for the UK is the Senior Master, Queen's Bench Division (PD24A, para 8). The procedure for taking evidence in another Regulation State for use in England and Wales is set out in FPR 2010, r 24.16 and PD24A, para 9.

24.15 Interpretation

In this Chapter –

'designated court' has the meaning given in Practice Direction 24A;

'Regulation State' has the same meaning as 'Member State' in the Taking of Evidence Regulation, that is all Member States except Denmark;

'the Taking of Evidence Regulation' means Council Regulation (EC) No. 1206/2001 of 28 May 2001 on co-operation between the courts of the Member States in the taking of evidence in civil or commercial matters.

24.16 Where a person to be examined is in another Regulation State

(1) This rule applies where a party wishes to take a deposition from a person who is –

- (a) outside the jurisdiction; and
- (b) in a Regulation State.

(2) The court may order the issue of a request to a designated court ('the requested court') in the Regulation State in which the proposed deponent is.

(3) If the court makes an order for the issue of a request, the party who sought the order must file –

- (a) a draft Form A as set out in the annex to the Taking of Evidence Regulation (request for the taking of evidence);
- (b) except where paragraph (4) applies, a translation of the form;
- (c) an undertaking to be responsible for costs sought by the requested court in relation to –
  - (i) fees paid to experts and interpreters; and
  - (ii) where requested by that party, the use of special procedures or communications technology; and
- (d) an undertaking to be responsible for the court's expenses.

(4) There is no need to file a translation if –

- (a) English is one of the official languages of the Regulation State where the examination is to take place; or
- (b) the Regulation State has indicated, in accordance with the Taking of Evidence Regulation, that English is a language which it will accept.

(5) Where article 17 of the Taking of Evidence Regulation (direct taking of evidence by the requested court) allows evidence to be taken directly in another Regulation State, the court may make an order for the submission of a request in accordance with that article.

(6) If the court makes an order for the submission of a request under paragraph (5), the party who sought the order must file –

- (a) a draft Form I as set out in the annex to the Taking of Evidence Regulation (request for direct taking of evidence);
- (b) except where paragraph (4) applies, a translation of the form; and
- (c) an undertaking to be responsible for the court's expenses.

PART III

Practice Direction 24A – Witnesses, Depositions and Taking of Evidence in Member States of the European Union

This Practice Direction supplements FPR Part 24

WITNESS SUMMONSES

Issue of witness summons

1.1 A witness summons may require a witness to –

- (a) attend court to give evidence;
- (b) produce documents to the court; or
- (c) both,

on either a date fixed for the hearing or such date as the court may direct (see rule 24.2).

> (In relation to cases to which the Mediation Directive applies, rules 35.3 and 35.4 contain rules in relation to mediation evidence)

1.2 Two copies of the witness summons should be filed with the court for sealing, one of which will be retained on the court file.

1.3 A mistake in the name or address of a person named in a witness summons may be corrected if the summons has not been served.

1.4 The corrected summons must be re-sealed by the court and marked 'Amended and Re-Sealed'.

****

Travelling expenses and compensation for loss of time

3.1 When a witness is served with a witness summons the witness must be offered a sum to cover travelling expenses to and from the court and compensation for loss of time (see rule 24.6).

3.2 If the witness summons is to be served by the court, the party issuing the summons must deposit with the court –

(a) a sum sufficient to pay for the witness's expenses in travelling to the court and in returning to his or her home or place of work; and
(b) a sum in respect of the period during which earnings or benefit are lost, or such lesser sum as it may be proved that the witness will lose as a result of attendance at court in answer to the witness summons.

3.3 The sum referred to in paragraph 3.2(b) is to be based on the sums payable to witnesses attending the Crown Court (fixed pursuant to the Prosecution of Offences Act 1985 and Costs in Criminal Cases (General) Regulations 1986).

Depositions to be taken in England and Wales for use as evidence in proceedings in courts in England and Wales

4.1 A party may apply for an order for a person to be examined on oath before –

(a) a judge;
(b) an examiner of the court; or
(c) such other person as the court may appoint (see rule 24.7(3)).

(This is subject to rules about mediation evidence in cases to which the Mediation Directive applies: see rules 35.3 and 35.4)

4.2 The party who obtains an order for the examination of a deponent (see rule 24.7(2)) before an examiner of the court must –

(a) apply to the Foreign Process Section of the Masters' Secretary's Department at the Royal Courts of Justice for the allocation of an examiner;
(b) when allocated, provide the examiner with copies of all documents in the proceedings necessary to inform the examiner of the issues; and
(c) pay the deponent a sum to cover travelling expenses to and from the examination and compensation for loss of time (see rule 24.7(6)).

4.3 In ensuring that the deponent's evidence is recorded in full, the court or the examiner may permit it to be recorded on audiotape or videotape, but the deposition (see rule 24.7(2)) must always be recorded in writing by the examiner or by a competent shorthand writer or stenographer.

4.4 If the deposition is not recorded word for word, it must contain, as nearly as may be, the statement of the deponent. The examiner may record word for word any particular questions and answers which appear to have special importance.

4.5 If a deponent objects to answering any question or where any objection is taken to any question, the examiner must –

(a) record in the deposition or a document attached to it –
  (i) the question;
  (ii) the nature of and grounds for the objection;
  (iii) any answer given; and
(b) give the examiner's opinion as to the validity of the objection and must record it in the deposition or a document attached to it.

The court will decide as to the validity of the objection and any question of costs arising from it.

4.6 Documents and exhibits must –

(a) have an identifying number or letter marked on them by the examiner; and
(b) be preserved by the party or legal representative (see rule 2.3) who obtained the order for the examination, or as the court or the examiner may direct.

4.7 The examiner may put any question to the deponent as to –

(a) the meaning of any of the deponent's answers; or
(b) any matter arising in the course of the examination.

4.8 Where a deponent –

(a) fails to attend the examination; or
(b) refuses to –
 (i) be sworn; or
 (ii) answer any lawful question; or
 (iii) produce any document,

the examiner will sign a certificate (see rule 24.9) of such failure or refusal and may include in the certificate any comment as to the conduct of the deponent or of any person attending the examination.

4.9 The party who obtained the order for the examination must file the certificate with the court and may apply for an order that the deponent attend for examination or produce any document, as the case may be (see rule 24.9(2) and (3)). The application may be made without notice.

4.10 The court will make such order on the application as it thinks fit including an order for the deponent to pay any costs resulting from the failure or refusal (see rule 24.9(4)).

4.11 A deponent who wilfully refuses to obey an order of the High Court or the family court made under Part 24 may be proceeded against for contempt of court.

4.12 A deposition must –

(a) be signed by the examiner;
(b) have any amendments to it initialled by the examiner and the deponent;
(c) be endorsed by the examiner with –
 (i) a statement of the time occupied by the examination; and
 (ii) a record of any refusal by the deponent to sign the deposition and of the deponent's reasons for not doing so; and
(d) be sent by the examiner to the court where the proceedings are taking place for filing on the court file.

4.13 Rule 24.13 deals with the fees and expenses of an examiner.

Depositions to be taken abroad for use as evidence in proceedings before courts in England and Wales (where the Taking of Evidence Regulation does not apply)

5.1 Where a party wishes to take a deposition from a person outside the jurisdiction, the High Court may order the issue of a letter of request to the judicial authorities of the country in which the proposed deponent is (see rule 24.12).

(Rule 35.4(1)(f) deals with letters of request where the Mediation Directive applies)

5.2 An application for an order referred to in paragraph 5.1 should be made by application notice in accordance with Part 18 (Procedure for other applications in proceedings).

5.3 The documents which a party applying for an order for the issue of a letter of request must file with the application notice are set out in rule 24.12(7). They are as follows –

(a) a draft letter of request in the form set out in Annex A to this practice direction;
(b) a statement of the issues relevant to the proceedings;
(c) a list of questions or the subject matter of questions to be put to the proposed deponent;

PART III

(d) a translation of the documents in (a), (b) and (c), unless the proposed deponent is in a country of which English is an official language; and

(e) an undertaking to be responsible for the expenses of the Secretary of State.

In addition to the documents listed above the party applying for the order must file a draft order.

5.4 The above documents should be filed with the Masters' Secretary in Room E214, Royal Courts of Justice, Strand, London WC2A 2LL.

5.5 The application will be dealt with by the Senior Master of the Queen's Bench Division of the Senior Courts who will, if appropriate, sign the letter of request.

5.6 Attention is drawn to the provisions of rule 18.11 (Application to set aside or vary order made without notice).

5.7 If parties are in doubt as to whether a translation under paragraph 5.3(d) is required, they should seek guidance from the Foreign Process Section of the Masters' Secretary's Department.

5.8 A special examiner appointed under rule 24.12(5) may be the British Consul or the Consul-General or his deputy in the country where the evidence is to be taken if –

(a) there is in respect of that country a Civil Procedure Convention providing for the taking of evidence in that country for the assistance of proceedings in the High Court or other court in this country; or

(b) the Secretary of State has consented.

5.9 The provisions of paragraphs 4.1 to 4.12 apply to the depositions referred to in this paragraph.

TAKING OF EVIDENCE BETWEEN EU MEMBER STATES

Taking of Evidence Regulation

6.1 Where evidence is to be taken from a person in another Member State of the European Union for use as evidence in proceedings before courts in England and Wales Council Regulation (EC) No 1206/2001 of 28 May 2001 on co-operation between the courts of the Member States in the taking of evidence in civil or commercial matters ('the Taking of Evidence Regulation') applies.

6.2 The Taking of Evidence Regulation is annexed to this practice direction as Annex B.

6.3 The Taking of Evidence Regulation does not apply to Denmark. In relation to Denmark, therefore, rule 24.12 will continue to apply.

(Article 21(1) of the Taking of Evidence Regulation provides that the Regulation prevails over other provisions contained in bilateral or multilateral agreements or arrangements concluded by the Member States.)

Originally published in the official languages of the European Community in the Official Journal of the European Communities by the Office for Official Publications of the European Communities.

Meaning of 'designated court'

7.1 In accordance with the Taking of Evidence Regulation, each Regulation State has prepared a list of courts competent to take evidence in accordance with the Regulation indicating the territorial and, where appropriate, special jurisdiction of those courts.

7.2 Where Chapter 2 of this Part refers to a 'designated court' in relation to another Regulation State, the reference is to the court, referred to in the list of competent courts of that State, which is appropriate to the application in hand.

7.3 Where the reference is to the 'designated court' in England and Wales, the reference is to the appropriate competent court in the jurisdiction. The designated courts for England and Wales are listed in Annex C to this practice direction.

Central Body

8.1 The Taking of Evidence Regulation stipulates that each Regulation State must nominate a Central Body responsible for –

(a) supplying information to courts;
(b) seeking solutions to any difficulties which may arise in respect of a request; and
(c) forwarding, in exceptional cases, at the request of a requesting court, a request to the competent court.

8.2 The United Kingdom has nominated the Senior Master of the Queen's Bench Division, to be the Central Body for England and Wales.

8.3 The Senior Master, as Central Body, has been designated responsible for taking decisions on requests pursuant to Article 17 of the Regulation. Article 17 allows a court to submit a request to the Central Body or a designated competent authority in another Regulation State to take evidence directly in that State.

Evidence to be taken in another Regulation State for use in England and Wales

9.1 Where a person wishes to take a deposition from a person in another Regulation State, the court where the proceedings are taking place may order the issue of a request to the designated court in the Regulation State (rule 24.16 (2)). The form of request is prescribed as Form A in the Taking of Evidence Regulation.

9.2 An application to the court for an order under rule 24.16(2) should be made by application notice in accordance with Part 18 (Procedure for other applications in proceedings).

9.3 Rule 24.16(3) provides that the party applying for the order must file a draft form of request in the prescribed form. Where completion of the form requires attachments or documents to accompany the form, these must also be filed.

9.4 If the court grants an order under rule 24.16(2), it will send the form of request directly to the designated court.

9.5 Where the taking of evidence requires the use of an expert, the designated court may require a deposit in advance towards the costs of that expert. The party who obtained the order is responsible for the payment of any such deposit which should be deposited with the court for onward transmission. Under the provisions of the Taking of Evidence Regulation, the designated court is not required to execute the request until such payment is received.

9.6 Article 17 permits the court where proceedings are taking place to take evidence directly from a deponent in another Regulation State if the conditions of the article are satisfied. Direct taking of evidence can only take place if evidence is given voluntarily without the need for coercive measures. Rule 24.16(5) provides for the court to make an order for the submission of a request to take evidence directly. The form of request is Form I annexed to the Taking of Evidence Regulation and rule 24.16(6) makes provision for a draft of this form to be filed by the party seeking the order. An application for an order under rule 24.16(5) should be by application notice in accordance with Part 18.

9.7 Attention is drawn to the provisions of rule 18.11 (Application to set aside or vary order made without notice).

ANNEX A – DRAFT LETTER OF REQUEST (WHERE THE TAKING OF EVIDENCE REGULATION DOES NOT APPLY) (SEE PARAGRAPH 5.3(A) ABOVE)

1 To the Competent Judicial Authority of in the of

[name] Senior Master of the Queen's Bench Division of the Senior Courts of England and Wales respectfully request the assistance of your court with regard to the following matters.

2 An application is now pending in the Division of the High Court of Justice in England and Wales entitled as follows [set out full title and case number] in which [name] of [address] is the applicant and [name] of [address] is the respondent.

PART III

3 The names and addresses of the representatives or agents of [set out names and addresses of representatives of the parties].

4 The application by the applicant is for –

(a) [set out the nature of the application]
(b) [the order sought] and
(c) [a summary of the facts.]

5 It is necessary for the purposes of justice between the parties that you cause the following witnesses, who are resident within your jurisdiction, to be examined. The names and addresses of the witnesses are as follows:

6 The witnesses should be examined on oath or if that is not possible within your laws or is impossible of performance by reason of the internal practice and procedure of your court or by reason of practical difficulties, they should be examined in accordance with whatever procedure your laws provide for in these matters.

7 Either:

The witnesses should be examined in accordance with the list of questions annexed hereto.
Or:
The witnesses should be examined regarding [set out full details of evidence sought]
N.B. Where the witness is required to produce documents, these should be clearly identified.

8 I would ask that you cause me, or the agents of the parties (if appointed), to be informed of the date and place where the examination is to take place.

9 Finally, I request that you will cause the evidence of the said witnesses to be reduced into writing and all documents produced on such examinations to be duly marked for identification and that you will further be pleased to authenticate such examinations by the seal of your court or in such other way as is in accordance with your procedure and return the written evidence and documents produced to me addressed as follows –

Senior Master of the Queen's Bench Division
Royal Courts of Justice
Strand
London
WC2A 2LL
England

ANNEX B – TAKING OF EVIDENCE REGULATION

Note—Council Regulation (EC) No 1206/2001 is set out in Part VI.

ANNEX C – DESIGNATED COURTS IN ENGLAND AND WALES UNDER THE TAKING OF EVIDENCE REGULATION (SEE PARAGRAPH 7.3)

Area	Designated court
London and South Eastern Circuit	Royal Courts of Justice (Queen's Bench Division)
Midland Circuit	The Family Court sitting at Birmingham
Western Circuit	The Family Court sitting at Bristol
Wales and Chester Circuit	The Family Court sitting at Cardiff
Northern Circuit	The Family Court sitting at Manchester
North Eastern Circuit	The Family Court sitting at Leeds

PART 25
EXPERTS AND ASSESSORS

CONTENTS OF THIS PART

Rule		Page
25.2	Interpretation	1794
25.3	Experts – overriding duty to the court	1795
25.4	Control of expert evidence in proceedings other than children proceedings	1795
25.5	Further provisions about the court's power to restrict expert evidence	1795
25.6	When to apply for the court's permission	1796
25.7	What an application notice requesting the court's permission must include	1797
25.8	Where permission is granted	1797
25.9	General requirement for expert evidence to be given in a written report	1797
25.10	Written questions to experts	1798
25.11	Court's power to direct that evidence is to be given by a single joint expert	1798
25.12	Instructions to a single joint expert	1799
25.13	Power of court to direct a party to provide information	1799
25.14	Contents of report	1799
25.15	Use by one party of expert's report disclosed by another	1799
25.16	Discussions between experts	1799
25.17	Expert's right to ask court for directions	1800
25.18	Copies of orders and other documents	1800
25.19	Action after final hearing	1800
25.20	Assessors	1801
	Practice Direction 25A – Experts – Emergencies and Pre Proceedings Instructions	1801
	Practice Direction 25B – The Duties of an Expert, the Expert's Report and Arrangements for an Expert to Attend Court	1803
	Practice Direction 25C – Children Proceedings – The Use of Single Joint Experts and the Process Leading to an Expert Being Instructed or Expert Evidence Being Put Before the Court	1812
	Practice Direction 25D – Financial Remedy Proceedings and Other Family Proceedings (Except Children Proceedings) – The Use of Single Joint Experts and the Process Leading to Expert Evidence Being Put Before the Court	1818
	Practice Direction 25E – Discussions Between Experts in Family Proceedings	1823
	Practice Direction 25F – Assessors in Family Proceedings	1825

Amendments—FPR 2010, Pt 25 substituted by SI 2012/3061.

INTRODUCTION

Codes for expert evidence in family proceedings—CFA 2014, s 13 creates a statutory code for opinion evidence in children proceedings only. There are now three codes for expert evidence in civil and family proceedings, created variously by the common law (codified in rules) and by statute:

(1) Civil proceedings (including eg under TOLATA 1996) under common law and CPR 1998, Pt 35. This represents the default position in all civil proceedings where there is no other statutory or common law provision.
(2) Children proceedings (partly CFA 2014, s 13, partly FPR 2010, Pt 25).
(3) All other family proceedings per common law and under FPR 2010, Pt 25.

Opinion ('expert') evidence—The general rule is that a witness may only give evidence as to fact observed by them. This rule is overridden in the case of opinion evidence given by a person whose expertise justifies the court in receiving that opinion (Civil Evidence Act 1972, s 3). Such evidence can only be given with the court's permission (eg CFA 2014, s 13(1); FPR 2010, r 25.4(1)).

Common law—Save where expressly provided for by statute, the rules cannot change the common law, although they may represent a codification of law (eg with joint instruction of experts). Thus, for example, CFA 2014, s 13(1) and r 25.4(2) preserve the common law position (see also CPR 1998, r 35.1) that opinion evidence can only be given with the court's permission.

Impartiality of opinion—Nothing in CFA 2014, s 13 affects the rule of law that the essence of an expert's opinion is impartiality (as explained by *The Ikarian Reefer* (see below r 25.3) and as expressed by CPR 1998, r 35.3 and FPR 2010, r 25.3). Parties must therefore be wary of seeking permission to adduce evidence from, for example:

- Their own employee;
- A medical witness who also treats a party (eg *Vernon v Bosley (No 2)* [1998] 1 FLR 304, CA);
- A witness who worked for them before issue of the proceedings (eg their own or their company's accountant).

Control of expert evidence—Strictly speaking, any provision that seeks to give the court power to control opinion evidence (CFA 2014, s 13(1); FPR 2010, rr 1.4(2)(e), 25.5) is redundant, since at common law it is only with the court's permission that such evidence can be adduced. An expert gives evidence only to assist the court and it is therefore the court – not, for example, the parties – that decides whether such evidence can be adduced, although (subject to exceptions in the case of examination of children: CFA 2014, s 13) parties are free at any time to instruct their own expert (for whose report they have litigation privilege: *Waugh v British Railways Board* [1980] AC 521, HL; and see under FPR 2010, Pt 21).

Judge differing from expert's opinion—If a judge is to differ from the view of an expert, especially with a unanimous body of experts, he must give good reasons for so doing (eg *Re W (A Child)* [2005] EWCA Civ 649).

Protected parties and maturity of children—FPR PD25A, paras 2.6–2.10 make specific reference to appointment of an expert to deal with issues as to capacity or a child's maturity where protected parties or children may be parties to proceedings.

Expert evidence and veracity of children's evidence—An assessment of the capacity of children to give evidence is a proper subject for 'expert advice where necessary' (*Wigan Borough Council v M and Others (Veracity Assessments)* [2016] 1 FLR 126, FD, at [7]) but this is subject to the following principles (at [9] and [12]):

- There is no bar in law against admission of veracity evidence including the ultimate issue under Civil Evidence Act 1972, s 3 (*Re M and R (Child Abuse: Evidence)* [1996] 2 FLR 195, CA);
- Permission is a matter of judicial discretion in each case, but this discretion must be seen through the more restrictive regime under CFA 2014, s 13(6); and
- Cases where permission for veracity evidence will be granted are likely to be rare (see also *A London Borough Council v K and Others* [2009] EWHC 850 (Fam)).

25.1 *(revoked)*

25.2 Interpretation

(1) In this Part –

…

'children proceedings' means –

(a) proceedings referred to in rules 12.1 and 14.1 and any other proceedings which relate wholly or mainly to the maintenance or upbringing of a minor;

(b) applications for permission to start proceedings mentioned in paragraph (a); and

(c) applications made in the course of proceedings mentioned in paragraph (a);

'expert' means a person who provides expert evidence for use in proceedings;

(Section 13(8) of the 2014 Act provides for what is not included in reference to providing expert evidence or putting expert evidence before the court in children proceedings)

…

'single joint expert' means a person who provides expert evidence for use in proceedings on behalf of two or more of the parties (including the applicant) to the proceedings.

(2) The meaning of 'children proceedings' in paragraph (1) is the prescribed meaning for the purposes of section 13(9) of the 2014 Act.

(Regulation 3 of the Restriction on the Preparation of Adoption Reports Regulations 2005 (SI 2005/1711) sets out which persons are within a prescribed description for the purposes of section 94(1) of the 2002 Act.)

Amendments—SI 2014/843.

Expert gives expert evidence—The chief characteristic in law (and see Civil Evidence Act 1972) of expert evidence is the ability to give evidence of both fact and opinion.

Interpretation for children proceedings—Terminology for expert evidence in children proceedings is set out in CFA 2014, s 13(8).

'Children proceedings'—Definition of the term 'children proceedings' is by CFA 2014, s 13 deputed to FPR 2010 as set out in r 25.2, that is proceedings as follows

- listed in FPR 2010, rr 12.1, 12.2 (children proceedings: private law and public law (including emergency applications), wardship and the inherent jurisdiction, child abduction)
- listed in FPR 2010, r 14.1 (adoption proceedings)
- applications to commence such proceedings
- applications in the course of such proceedings
- applications in any other proceedings which relate to the maintenance or upbringing of a child (cf CA 1989, s 1), the emphasis here being on the financial claims of children in family proceedings.

25.3 Experts – overriding duty to the court

(1) It is the duty of experts to help the court on matters within their expertise.

(2) This duty overrides any obligation to the person from whom experts have received instructions or by whom they are paid.

(Particular duties of an expert are set out in Practice Direction 25B (The Duties of an Expert, the Expert's Report and Arrangements for an Expert to Attend Court.)

Overriding duty to the court: impartiality—Opinion evidence must be impartial as between the parties (whoever the expert may be instructed by: r 25.3(2); and see, for example, *National Justice Compania Naviera SA v Prudential Assurance Co; the Ikarian Reefer* [1993] 2 Lloyd's Rep 68, Comm Ct, affirmed in *Kennedy v Cordia (Services) LLP* [2016] 1 WLR 597, SC). The impartiality of an expert witness is essential to their evidence and if an expert has a view that is controversial as between experts or that might be derived from partiality, he must declare the extent of the interest (eg *Re C (Welfare of Child: Immunisation)* [2003] 2 FLR 1095, CA).

Duties of an expert—FPR PD25A sets out the duties of an expert in family proceedings.

Costs and the expert witness—See under CPR 1998, r 44.2, and see *Phillips v Symes* [2005] 1 WLR 2043, ChD, where an expert whose report lacked objectivity was ordered to be joined in wasted costs order proceedings. The expert may be ordered to pay costs within the court's powers under SCA 1981, s 51(3).

25.4 Control of expert evidence in proceedings other than children proceedings

(1) This rule applies to proceedings other than children proceedings.

(2) A person may not without the permission of the court put expert evidence (in any form) before the court.

(3) The court may give permission as mentioned in paragraph (2) only if the court is of the opinion that the expert evidence is necessary to assist the court to resolve the proceedings.

(Provision relating to the control of expert evidence in children proceedings is contained in section 13 of the 2014 Act.)

Amendments—Substituted by SI 2014/843.

Control of expert evidence in all family proceedings: permission where the report is 'necessary'—Rule 25.4 confirms the common law position for all expert evidence (also provided for by CFA 2014, s 13 for children proceedings). Such evidence may only be adduced where it is thought to be 'necessary' (see *Re H-L (Expert Evidence: Test for Permission)* [2013] 2 FLR 1434, CA and discussion of 'necessary' under CFA 2014, s 13).

Restrictions on disclosure of expert evidence—Whereas there is a strong presumption in favour of disclosing all relevant evidence, the court has powers to restrict disclosure, for example because of fears for the welfare of a child (*Re D (Adoption Reports: Confidentiality)* [1995] 2 FLR 687, HL; *A Local Authority v A* [2010] 2 FLR 1757, CA; and see **Submission of evidence** under FPR 2010, r 12.12 and restrictions on disclosure under FPR 2010, r 21.3).

25.5 Further provisions about the court's power to restrict expert evidence

(1) When deciding whether to give permission as mentioned in section 13(1), (3) or (5) of the 2014 Act or to give a direction under 38(6) of the 1989 Act in children proceedings, the court is to have regard in particular to any failure to comply with rule 25.6 or any direction of the court about expert evidence.

(1A) The matter referred to in paragraph (1) is a prescribed matter for the purposes of section 13(7)(h) of the 2014 Act and section 38(7B) of the 1989 Act.

(2) When deciding whether to give permission as mentioned in rule 25.4(1) in proceedings other than children proceedings, the court is to have regard in particular to –

PART III

(a) the issues to which the expert evidence would relate;
(b) the questions which the court would require the expert to answer;
(c) the impact which giving permission would be likely to have on the timetable, duration and conduct of the proceedings;
(d) any failure to comply with rule 25.6 or any direction of the court about expert evidence; and
(e) the cost of the expert evidence.

Amendments—SI 2014/843.

Scheme under CFA 2014, s 13(1), (3) and (5) and FPR 2010, r 25.4(2), 25.5 and 25.6—The scheme for seeking permission to adduce expert evidence in all family proceedings is as follows:

(1) The common law specifies no particular date for application to put evidence before the court, although the nearer trial approaches the less likely will it be that a court will give permission, especially if it endangers a final hearing (European Convention 1950, Art 6(1): trial must be 'within a reasonable' time; and see CA 1989, s 1(2) (delay likely to prejudice welfare of a child)).
(2) In family proceedings and subject to (1), an applicant party must proceed in under FPR 2010, r 25.6, namely by seeking permission to put the evidence before the court 'as soon as possible'.
(3) Unless directed otherwise (and subject to application), parties must apply for the court's permission 'as soon as possible'. Rule 25.6(a)–(e) sets out the time limits that apply in certain proceedings.
(4) Failure to comply with the above provisions or with any other relevant direction of the court (see FPR 2010, r 25.5(1A)) comprises a 'matter' under CFA 2014, s 13(7)(h) and CA 1989, s 38(7B) (the checklist of factors in CFA 2014, s 13).
(5) In all other family proceedings (eg forced marriage, declaration etc): No 'later than' date is specified; so the court must decide whether the application is timely, and deal with it accordingly.
(6) Statute and rules provide three inclusive checklists for all family proceedings based on the following hierarchy and the following lists of statutory and other factors:
   - Medical, psychiatric or other assessment of a child under CA 1989, s 38(6) (interim care orders): checklist at CA 1989, s 38(7B) (as amended by CFA 2014, s 13(11));
   - All forms of opinion evidence in all other forms of children proceedings: list at s 13(7);
   - All other forms of family proceedings covered by the list at r 25.5(2).
(7) If application is made for the presentation of evidence before the court despite its having been obtained contrary to the provisions of CFA 2014, s 13(1),(3), the court has a discretion to admit it. The likelihood is that a judge will then consider the existing statutory factors alongside, in particular, the welfare of any child affected.
(8) In particular, if an issue arises between parties as to whether a report should be permitted to be put before the court, European Convention 1950, Arts 6(1) (eg interference with the principle that cases should be disposed of within a 'reasonable time'), the overriding objective (FPR 2010, r 1.1) and CA 1989, s 1(2) (in children proceedings or those which affect their maintenance and upbringing: avoidance of delay) will need to be balanced against any other relevant factors.

25.6 When to apply for the court's permission

Unless the court directs otherwise, parties must apply for the court's permission as mentioned in section 13(1), (3) or (5) of the 2014 Act or rule 25.4(2) as soon as possible and –

(a) in Part 4 proceedings referred to in rule 12.2 and in so far as practicable other public law proceedings referred to in that rule, no later than a Case Management Hearing;
(b) in private law proceedings referred to in rule 12.2, no later than the First Hearing Dispute Resolution Appointment;
(c) in adoption proceedings and placement proceedings, no later than the first directions hearing;
(d) in proceedings for a financial remedy, no later than the first appointment; and
(e) in a defended case referred to in rule 7.1(3), no later than any Case Management Hearing directed by the court under rule 7.20.

Amendments—Substituted by SI 2014/843.

Practice Directions—FPR 2010, r 25.6 must be read in conjunction with PD25C (children proceedings: paras 3.7 to 3.9) and PD25D (other forms of family proceedings: paras 3.6 to 3.10). The starting point for an application for the court's permission to instruct an expert or adduce expert evidence must be the dates referred to in the rule. The practice directions have the effect of providing examples of where the court may 'direct otherwise', eg where application is thought necessary but a hearing date has already been fixed (PD25C, para 3.9; PD25D, para 3.8) or where delay arises for reasons outside the applicant's control (PD25D, para 3.10).

25.7 What an application notice requesting the court's permission must include

(1) Part 18 applies to an application for the court's permission as mentioned in section 13(1), (3) or (5) of the 2014 Act or rule 25.4(2).

(2) In any proceedings –

(a) the application notice requesting the court's permission as mentioned in section 13(1), (3) or (5) of the 2014 Act or rule 25.4(2) must state –
  (i) the field in which the expert evidence is required;
  (ii) where practicable, the name of the proposed expert;
  (iii) the issues to which the expert evidence is to relate;
  (iv) whether the expert evidence could be obtained from a single joint expert;
  (v) the other matters set out in Practice Direction 25C or 25D, as the case may be; and

(b) a draft of the order sought is to be attached to the application notice requesting the court's permission and that draft order must set out the matters specified in Practice Direction 25C or 25D, as the case may be.

(3) In children proceedings, an application notice requesting the court's permission as mentioned in section 13(1), (3) or (5) of the 2014 Act must, in addition to the matters specified in paragraph (2)(a), state the questions which the expert is to be required to answer.

Amendments—SI 2014/843.

Formal court 'application for the court's permission' (r 25.7(1))—Formal application 'for the court's permission as mentioned in rule 25.4' must be made at any case management appointment (e g the appointments referred to in FPR 2010, r 25.6). Application is by FPR 2010, Pt 18 procedure and must be accompanied by grounds and a draft order in the usual way (repeated in r 25.7(2)). The court can make the order without a hearing (FPR 2010, r 18.9) in advance of the case management conference (e g if there is any urgency or the order is not controversial and the court agrees to it). The court may also dismiss the application at the outset (r 4.3).

'other matters set out in Practice Direction 25C or 25D'—PD25C, para 3.10 and PD25D, para 3.11 set out further requirements of the applicant for an order, some of which are duplicated in the list in r 25.7(2).

Form of order—PD25C, para 3.11 and PD25D, para 3.11 set out the matters that are to be included in any order made for the putting of expert evidence before the court (it is r 18.7 that requires the drafting of the order, not as para 3.11 states).

25.8 Where permission is granted

(1) In any proceedings, where the court grants permission as mentioned in section 13(1), (3) or (5) of the 2014 Act or rule 25.4(2) –

(a) it will grant permission only in relation to the expert named or the field identified in the application notice requesting the court's permission; and

(b) the court will give directions specifying the date by which the expert is to provide a written report.

(2) In children proceedings, in addition to the directions in paragraph (1)(b), the court will give directions –

(a) approving the questions which the expert is required to answer;

(b) specifying the date by which the expert is to receive the letter of instruction.

Amendments—SI 2014/843.

Children proceedings—It is only in children proceedings that the court is required to be prescriptive about the questions to be answered and time limits as to instruction, although in practice case management judges may impose similar requirements in other family proceedings.

25.9 General requirement for expert evidence to be given in a written report

(1) Expert evidence is to be given in a written report unless the court directs otherwise.

(2) The court will not direct an expert to attend a hearing unless it is necessary to do so in the interests of justice.

Form of the report: expert's evidence—The form of the expert's report must be addressed to the court and it must comply with the requirements of FPR PD25A, para 3.3. It must be verified by a statement of truth.

Interests of justice (r 25.5(2))— FPR 2010, r 25.5(2) requires that the court should not direct the attendance of an expert witness save 'in the interests of justice'. An expert witness should only be called where a judge has found expressly that the evidence is required. Brief reasons should therefore be given by the court where a

PART III

direction is given that an expert is to be called. If an expert's report is not challenged, his report should be received in evidence without an attendance being required. The issue of his attendance or the narrowing of issues arising out of his report by the submission of questions (r 25.10) can be addressed at any case management hearings.

Video-link—Evidence may be given by video-link (FPR 2010, r 22.3).

25.10 Written questions to experts

(1) A party may put written questions about an expert's report to

(a) an expert instructed by another party; or
(b) a single joint expert appointed under rule 25.11.

(2) Unless the court directs otherwise or a practice direction provides otherwise, written questions under paragraph (1) –

(a) must be proportionate;
(b) may be put once only;
(c) must be put within 10 days beginning with the date on which the expert's report was served;
(d) must be for the purpose only of clarification of the report; and
(e) must be copied and sent to the other parties at the same time as they are sent to the expert.

(3) An expert's answers to questions put in accordance with paragraph (1) –

(a) must be given within the timetable specified by the court; and
(b) are treated as part of the expert's report.

(4) Where –

(a) a party has put a written question to an expert instructed by another party; and
(b) the expert does not answer that question,

the court may make one or both of the following orders in relation to the party who instructed the expert –

(i) that the party may not rely on the evidence of that expert; or
(ii) that the party may not recover the fees and expenses of that expert from any other party.

25.11 Court's power to direct that evidence is to be given by a single joint expert

(1) Where two or more parties wish to put expert evidence before the court on a particular issue, the court may direct that the evidence on that issue is to be given by a single joint expert.

(2) Where the parties who wish to put expert evidence before the court ('the relevant parties') cannot agree who should be the single joint expert, the court may –

(a) select the expert from a list prepared or identified by the relevant parties; or
(b) direct that the expert be selected in such other manner as the court may direct.

Evidence from single joint expert— FPR 2010, r 25.7 enables the court to direct that evidence 'on a particular' issue can be directed to be provided by 'a single joint expert' (SJE) and if parties do not agree as to the identity of the expert the court can chose the expert or direct how he is to be appointed. In *Daniels v Walker (Practice Note)* [2000] 1 WLR 1382, CA, Lord Woolf MR explained the working of CPR 1998, r 35.8.

Dissatisfaction with joint expert's report – for reasons 'not fanciful'— *Daniels v Walker* (above), Lord Woolf MR explained what a party might do if dissatisfied with the report of a SJE. In appropriate circumstances and for reason 'which are not fanciful', the court has a discretion to order another report. The steps to be taken before objection is taken to a report:

(1) Joint instruction of the expert.
(2) If a joint letter is not agreed, then in civil cases each party sends separate instructions, but see above for the consequences of FPR 2010, r 25.8(2).
(3) If a party is dissatisfied with the report, then within 10 days of service of the report (r 25.6(2)(b)) that party can raise questions of the expert (FPR 2010, r 25.10(1)(b)).
(4) If both parties seek expert evidence and the court agrees then the experts should discuss their reports before a decision as to whether either, or both, should be called to give evidence is made.
(5) Calling both to be cross-examined should be a 'last resort'.

25.12 Instructions to a single joint expert

(1) Where the court gives a direction under rule 25.11(1) for a single joint expert to be used, the instructions are to be contained in a jointly agreed letter unless the court directs otherwise.

(2) Where the instructions are to be contained in a jointly agreed letter, in default of agreement the instructions may be determined by the court on the written request of any relevant party copied to the other relevant parties.

(3) Where the court permits the relevant parties to give separate instructions to a single joint expert, each instructing party must, when giving instructions to the expert, at the same time send a copy of the instructions to the other relevant parties.

(4) The court may give directions about –

(a) the payment of the expert's fees and expenses; and
(b) any inspection, examination or assessments which the expert wishes to carry out.

(5) The court may, before an expert is instructed, limit the amount that can be paid by way of fees and expenses to the expert.

(6) Unless the court directs otherwise, the relevant parties are jointly and severally liable for the payment of the expert's fees and expenses.

Cost saving and the joint expert—CPR 1998, r 35.8(1) envisages that the parties can deliver separate letters of instruction to a single joint expert (noted also by the Court of Appeal in *Yorke v Katra* [2003] EWCA Civ 867, at [14]). Rule 25.8 creates the potential for extra expense to the parties by requiring the court to be involved in settling joint instructions (FPR 2010, r 25.8(2)). CPR 1998 and those under FPR 2010 on this point proceed a little differently (and see commentary on CPR 1998, r 35.8).

'limit the amount that can be paid' (r 25.12(5))—This provision deals with funding of proceedings. When it comes to costs, any direction under r 25.12(5) will not affect any provision that is later made under SCA 1981, s 51 (eg *Calderdale MBC v S and Legal Services Commission* [2005] 1 FLR 751, FD).

25.13 Power of court to direct a party to provide information

(1) Subject to paragraph (2), where a party has access to information which is not reasonably available to another party, the court may direct the party who has access to the information to –

(a) prepare and file a document recording the information; and
(b) serve a copy of that document on the other party.

(2) In proceedings under Part 14 (procedure for applications in adoption, placement and related proceedings), a court officer will send a copy of the document recording the information to the other party.

In-house expertise—The derivation rule (CPR 1998, r 35.9) was designed to ensure that defendants with in-house access to expertise (eg a hospital or a large company), could be compelled to produce information. In family proceedings it might be preferable to obtain a report from an outside source (*Field v Leeds City Council* [2001] CPLR 129, CA).

25.14 Contents of report

(1) An expert's report must comply with the requirements set out in Practice Direction 25B.

(2) At the end of an expert's report there must be a statement that the expert understands and has complied with the expert's duty to the court.

(3) The instructions to the expert are not privileged against disclosure.

(Rule 21.1 explains what is meant by disclosure.)

25.15 Use by one party of expert's report disclosed by another

Where a party has disclosed an expert's report, any party may use that expert's report as evidence at any hearing where an issue to which the report relates is being considered.

25.16 Discussions between experts

(1) The court may, at any stage, direct a discussion between experts for the purpose of requiring the experts to –

(a) identify and discuss the expert issues in the proceedings; and

PART III

(b) where possible, reach an agreed opinion on those issues.

(2) The court may specify the issues which the experts must discuss.

(3) The court may direct that following a discussion between the experts they must prepare a statement for the court setting out those issues on which –

(a) they agree; and
(b) they disagree, with a summary of their reasons for disagreeing.

Discussions between experts—Consistent with the overriding objective and with the court's concerns to keep costs to a minimum, the rules and the court are concerned to define any controversy that needs to be resolved. Where possible, the expert's bases for the controversy must be summarised for the court. If the court thinks it appropriate it can specify issues for the experts to discuss and it may direct that they prepare a summary identifying issues on which they agree and on which they disagree.

Experts' agreement—FPR PD25A, para 7.1 asserts a controversial proposition: (a) that experts can bind parties at their meeting; and (b) that the parties can be compelled to 'inform the court ... in writing why they do not agree with the agreement'. This provision is likely to be outside any powers in the rule-makers. The law is correctly stated by CPR 1998, r 35.12 (two sub-rules not included in FPR 2010):

'(4) The content of the discussion between the experts shall not be referred to at the trial unless the parties agree.

(5) Where experts reach agreement on an issue during their discussions, the agreement shall not bind the parties unless the parties expressly agree to be bound by the agreement.'

As a matter of law, experts have no agency from any party. Indeed, FPR 2010, r 25.3 does what it can to distance the expert from the party who instructs them, and to that extent FPR PD25A, para 7.1 is in direct conflict with FPR 2010, r 25.3. In any 'agreement' that experts reach, they are not speaking for a party to the proceedings (as does a party's lawyer).

25.17 Expert's right to ask court for directions

(1) Experts may file written requests for directions for the purpose of assisting them in carrying out their functions.

(2) Experts must, unless the court directs otherwise, provide copies of the proposed requests for directions under paragraph (1) –

(a) to the party instructing them, at least 7 days before they file the requests; and
(b) to all other parties, at least 4 days before they file them.

(3) The court, when it gives directions, may also direct that a party be served with a copy of the directions.

Expert's right to ask for directions—If an expert requires assistance from the court 'in carrying out [his] functions' he may file a written request for directions. The expert must give notice of the request for directions to all parties. There is no clear procedure within the rules or the court administration as to how these directions are to be requested or dealt with.

25.18 Copies of orders and other documents

Unless the court directs otherwise, a copy of any order or other document affecting an expert filed with the court after the expert has been instructed, must be served on the expert by the party who instructed the expert or, in the case of a single joint expert, the party who was responsible for instructing the expert, within 2 days of that party receiving the order or other document.

25.19 Action after final hearing

(1) Within 10 business days after the final hearing, the party who instructed the expert or, in the case of a single joint expert, the party who was responsible for instructing the expert, must inform the expert in writing about the court's determination and the use made by the court of the expert's evidence.

(2) Unless the court directs otherwise, the party who instructed the expert or, in the case of the single joint expert, the party who was responsible for instructing the expert, must send to the expert a copy of the court's final order, any transcript or written record of the court's decision, and its reasons for reaching its decision, within 10 business days from the date when the party received the order and any such transcript or record.

Amendments—SI 2014/843.

25.20 Assessors

(1) This rule applies where the court appoints one or more persons under section 70 of the Senior Courts Act 1981 as an assessor.

(2) An assessor will assist the court in dealing with a matter in which the assessor has skill and experience.

(3) The assessor will take such part in the proceedings as the court may direct and in particular the court may direct an assessor to –

(a) prepare a report for the court on any matter at issue in the proceedings; and
(b) attend the whole or any part of the hearing to advise the court on any such matter.

(4) If the assessor prepares a report for the court before the hearing has begun –

(a) the court will send a copy to each of the parties; and
(b) the parties may use it at the hearing.

(5) Unless the court directs otherwise, an assessor will be paid at the daily rate payable for the time being to a fee-paid deputy district judge of the principal registry and an assessor's fees will form part of the costs of the proceedings.

(6) The court may order any party to deposit in the court office a specified sum in respect of an assessor's fees and, where it does so, the assessor will not be asked to act until the sum has been deposited.

(7) Paragraphs (5) and (6) do not apply where the remuneration of the assessor is to be paid out of money provided by Parliament.

Amendments—SI 2014/667.

Assessors—Rule 25.20 is supplemented by FPR PD25F.

Senior Courts Act 1981, s 70—SCA 1981, s 70 provides as follows:

'70 Assessors and scientific advisers

(1) In any cause or matter before the High Court the court may, if it thinks it expedient to do so, call in the aid of one or more assessors specially qualified, and hear and dispose of the cause or matter wholly or partially with their assistance.

(2) The remuneration, if any, to be paid to an assessor for his services under subsection (1) in connection with any proceedings shall be determined by the court, and shall form part of the costs of the proceedings.

…'

County Courts Act 1984—CCA 1984, s 63 is in slightly different terms to SCA 1981, s 70 and goes beyond the different ages of the Parliamentary drafting. In the latter for example, it seems the assessor has a choice as to whether to act:

'63 Assessors

(1) In any proceedings the judge may, if he thinks fit, summon to his assistance, in such manner as may be prescribed, one or more persons of skill and experience in the matter to which the proceedings relate who may be willing to sit with the judge and act as assessors.

(2) …

(3) Subject to subsection (4), the remuneration of assessors for sitting under this section shall be determined by the judge and shall be costs in the proceedings unless otherwise ordered by the judge.

…'

Practice Direction 25A – Experts – Emergencies and Pre Proceedings Instructions

This Practice Direction supplements FPR Part 25

Introduction

1.1 This Practice Direction and Practice Directions 25B to E relate to expert evidence and supplement FPR Part 25. This Practice Direction applies to children proceedings and all other family proceedings.

PART III

Emergency and urgent cases

2.1 In emergency or urgent cases – for example, where, before formal issue of proceedings, a without-notice application is made to the court during or out of business hours; or where, after proceedings have been issued, a previously unforeseen need for (further) expert evidence arises at short notice – a party may wish to put expert evidence before the court without having complied with all or any part of Practice Directions 25B to E. In such circumstances, the party wishing to put the expert evidence before the court must apply forthwith to the court – where possible or appropriate, on notice to the other parties – for directions as to the future steps to be taken in respect of the expert evidence in question.

Note—On the making of an interim order 'before an application has been started' the court must give directions (including, as here, opinion evidence) for issue of the application (FPR 2010, r 20.3(3)).

Pre-application instruction of experts

3.1 When experts' reports are commissioned before the commencement of proceedings, it should be made clear to the expert that he or she may in due course be reporting to the court and should therefore consider himself or herself bound by the duties of an expert set out in Practice Direction 25B (The Duties of An Expert, the Expert's Report and Arrangements for An Expert To Attend Court). In so far as possible the enquiries of the expert and subsequent letter of instruction should follow either Practice Direction 25C (Children Proceedings – the Use of Single Joint Experts and the Process Leading to an Expert Being Instructed or Expert Evidence Being Put Before The Court) or 25D (Financial Remedy Proceedings and other Family Proceedings (except Children Proceedings) – the Use of Single Joint Experts and the Process Leading to Expert Evidence Being Put Before The Court).

3.2 In particular, a prospective party to children proceedings (for example, a local authority) should always write a letter of instruction when asking a potential witness for a report or an opinion, whether that request is within proceedings or pre-proceedings (for example, when commissioning specialist assessment materials, reports from a treating expert or other evidential materials); and the letter of instruction should conform to the principles set out in Practice Direction 25C.

3.3 It should be noted that the court's permission is required to put expert evidence (in any form) before the court in all family proceedings (see section 13(5) of the 2014 Act and FPR 25.4(2)). In children proceedings, the court's permission is also required for an expert to be instructed and for a child to be medically or psychiatrically examined or otherwise assessed for the purposes of the provision of expert evidence in the proceedings (section 13(1) and (3) of the 2014 Act). Where the court's permission has not been given in accordance with section 13(1) and (3) of the 2014 Act, evidence resulting from such instructions or examination or other assessment is inadmissible unless the court rules otherwise (section 13(2) and (4) of the 2014 Act). The court's permission will be needed to put any expert evidence before the court which was obtained before proceedings have started.

3.4 Attention is drawn to Practice Direction 15B (*Adults Who May Be Protected Parties and Children Who May Become Protected Parties In Family Proceedings*) which gives guidance relating to proceedings where an adult party may not have capacity to conduct the litigation or to instruct an expert.

Practice Direction 25B – The Duties of an Expert, the Expert's Report and Arrangements for an Expert to Attend Court

This Practice Direction supplements FPR Part 25

Scope of this Practice Direction

1.1 This Practice Direction focuses on the duties of an expert including the contents of the expert's report and, where an expert is to attend court, the arrangements for such attendance. Other Practice Directions supporting FPR Part 25 deal with different aspects of experts in family proceedings. The relevant Practice Directions are –

(a) Practice Direction 25A (Experts – Emergencies and Pre proceedings Instructions);
(b) Practice Direction 25C (Children Proceedings – The Use of Single Joint Experts and the Process Leading to an Expert Being Instructed or Expert Evidence Being Put Before the Court);
(c) Practice Direction 25D (Financial Remedy Proceedings and Other Family Proceedings (except Children Proceedings) – The Use of Single Joint Experts and the Process Leading to Expert Evidence Being Put Before The Court); and
(d) Practice Direction 25E (Discussions Between Experts in Family Proceedings).

1.2 Practice Direction 15B (Adults Who May Be Protected Parties and Children Who May Become Protected Parties In Family Proceedings) gives guidance relating to proceedings where an adult party may not have capacity to conduct the litigation or to instruct an expert.

1.3 In accordance with FPR 25.2(1), 'children proceedings' means –

(a) proceedings referred to in FPR 12.1 and 14.1 and any other proceedings which relate wholly or mainly to the maintenance or upbringing of a minor;
(b) applications for permission to start proceedings mentioned in paragraph (a);
(c) applications made in the course of proceedings mentioned in paragraph (a).

The meaning of 'expert'

2.1 In accordance with FPR 25.2(1), 'expert' means a person who provides expert evidence for use in family proceedings. section 13(8) of the 2014 Act expressly refers to evidence that is not expert evidence. For example, evidence given by a children's guardian is not expert evidence.

Note—For the admissibility of expert evidence, see commentary to FPR 2010, r 25.2. A guardian's opinion in law may well be 'expert evidence'.

2.2 An expert includes a reference to an expert team which can include ancillary workers in addition to experts. In an expert team, an 'ancillary' worker may be, for example, a play therapist or similar who undertakes work with the child or family for the purpose of the expert assessment. It is perfectly possible that such workers will be experts in their own right and in their own field, but it would be cumbersome to name everyone in that position in an order giving permission for an expert to be instructed, a child to be medically or psychiatrically examined or otherwise assessed or expert evidence to be put before the court or in a letter of instruction to an expert. The purpose of the term 'expert team' is to enable a multi-disciplinary team to undertake the assessment without the order having to name everyone who may be involved. The final expert's report must, however, give information about those persons who have taken part in the assessment and their respective roles and who is responsible for the report.

Note—Assertions of law in this passage are controversial. See commentary to FPR 2010, r 25.2.

The expert's overriding duty

3.1 An expert in family proceedings has an overriding duty to the court that takes precedence over any obligation to the person from whom the expert has received instructions or by whom the expert is paid.

Particular duties of the expert

4.1 An expert shall have regard to the following, among other, duties:

(a) to assist the court in accordance with the overriding duty;

(aa) in children proceedings, to comply with the Standards for Expert Witnesses in Children Proceedings in the Family Court which are set out in the Annex to this Practice Direction;

(b) to provide advice to the court that conforms to the best practice of the expert's profession;

(c) to answer the questions about which the expert is required to give an opinion (in children proceedings, those questions will be set out in the order of the court giving permission for an expert to be instructed, a child to be examined or otherwise assessed or expert evidence to be put before the court);

(d) to provide an opinion that is independent of the party or parties instructing the expert;

(e) to confine the opinion to matters material to the issues in the case and in relation only to the questions that are within the expert's expertise (skill and experience);

(f) where a question has been put which falls outside the expert's expertise, to state this at the earliest opportunity and to volunteer an opinion as to whether another expert is required to bring expertise not possessed by those already involved or, in the rare case, as to whether a second opinion is required on a key issue and, if possible, what questions should be asked of the second expert;

(g) in expressing an opinion, to take into consideration all of the material facts including any relevant factors arising from ethnic, cultural, religious or linguistic contexts at the time the opinion is expressed;

(h) to inform those instructing the expert without delay of any change in the opinion and of the reason for the change.

Note—None of these duties is provided for by law (see FPR 2010, rr 25.4, 25.5), which restricts duties.

The requirement for the court's permission

5.1 The general rule in family proceedings is that the court's permission is required to put expert evidence (in any form) before the court (see section 13(5) of the 2014 Act for children proceedings and FPR 25.4(2) for other family proceedings). The court is under a duty to restrict expert evidence to that which in the opinion of the court is necessary to assist the court to resolve the proceedings. The overriding objective in FPR1.1 applies when the court is exercising this duty. In children proceedings, the court's permission is required to instruct an expert and for a child to be medically or psychiatrically examined or otherwise assessed for the purposes of the provision of expert evidence in the proceedings (section 13(1) and (3) of the 2014 Act).

Preliminary enquiries which the expert should expect to receive

6.1 **In good time for the information requested to be available for –**

(a) **the court hearing** when the court will decide whether to give permission for the expert evidence to be put before the court (or also in children proceedings, for the expert to be instructed or the child to be examined or otherwise assessed); or

(b) **the advocates' meeting or discussion** where one takes place before such a hearing,

the party or parties intending to instruct the expert shall approach the expert with some information about the case.

6.2 The details of the information to be given to the expert are set out in Practice Direction 25C, paragraph 3.2 and Practice Direction 25D paragraph 3.3 and include the nature of the proceedings, the questions for the expert, the time when the expert's report is likely to be required, the timing of any hearing at which the expert may have to give evidence and how the expert's fees will be funded.

6.3 Children proceedings are confidential which means in those proceedings parties raising preliminary enquiries of an expert who has not yet been instructed can only tell the expert information which he or she will need about the case to be able to answer the preliminary questions raised.

Balancing the needs of the court and those of the expert

7.1 It is essential that there should be proper co-ordination between the court and the expert when drawing up the case management timetable: the needs of the court should be balanced with the needs of the expert whose forensic work is undertaken as an adjunct to his or her main professional duties.

The expert's response to preliminary enquiries

8.1 **In good time for the court hearing when the court will decide whether or not to give permission for the expert evidence to be put before the court (or also in children proceedings, for the expert to be instructed or the child to be examined or otherwise assessed) or for the advocates' meeting or discussion where one takes place before that hearing**, the party or parties intending to instruct the expert will need confirmation from the expert –

- (a) that acceptance of the proposed instructions will not involve the expert in any conflict of interest;
- (b) that the work required is within the expert's expertise;
- (c) that the expert is available to do the relevant work within the suggested time scale;
- (d) when the expert is available to give evidence, of the dates and times to avoid and, where a hearing date has not been fixed, of the amount of notice the expert will require to make arrangements to come to court (or to give evidence by telephone conference or video link) without undue disruption to his or her normal professional routines;
- (e) of the cost, including hourly or other charging rates, and likely hours to be spent attending experts' meetings, attending court and writing the report (to include any examinations and interviews);
- (f) of any representations which the expert wishes to make to the court about being named or otherwise identified in any public judgment given by the court.

PART III

Content of the expert's report

9.1 The expert's report shall be addressed to the court and prepared and filed **in accordance with the court's timetable** and must –

- (a) give details of the expert's qualifications and experience;
- (b) include a statement identifying the document(s) containing the material instructions and the substance of any oral instructions and, as far as necessary to explain any opinions or conclusions expressed in the report, summarising the facts and instructions which are material to the conclusions and opinions expressed;
- (c) state who carried out any test, examination or interview which the expert has used for the report and whether or not the test, examination or interview has been carried out under the expert's supervision;
- (d) give details of the qualifications of any person who carried out the test, examination or interview;
- (e) answer the questions about which the expert is to give an opinion and which relate to the issues in the case;
- (f) in expressing an opinion to the court –
  - (i) take into consideration all of the material facts including any relevant factors arising from ethnic, cultural, religious or linguistic contexts at the time the opinion is expressed, identifying the facts, literature and any other material, including research material, that the expert has relied upon in forming an opinion;
  - (ii) describe the expert's own professional risk assessment process and process of

differential diagnosis, highlighting factual assumptions, deductions from the factual assumptions, and any unusual, contradictory or inconsistent features of the case;

(iii) indicate whether any proposition in the report is an hypothesis (in particular a controversial hypothesis), or an opinion deduced in accordance with peer-reviewed and tested technique, research and experience accepted as a consensus in the scientific community;

(iv) indicate whether the opinion is provisional (or qualified, as the case may be), stating the qualification and the reason for it, and identifying what further information is required to give an opinion without qualification;

(g) where there is a range of opinion on any question to be answered by the expert –

(i) summarise the range of opinion;

(ii) identify and explain, within the range of opinions, any 'unknown cause', whether arising from the facts of the case (for example, because there is too little information to form a scientific opinion) or from limited experience or lack of research, peer review or support in the relevant field of expertise;

(iii) give reasons for any opinion expressed: the use of a balance sheet approach to the factors that support or undermine an opinion can be of great assistance to the court;

(h) contain a summary of the expert's conclusions and opinions;

(i) contain a statement that the expert –

(i) has no conflict of interest of any kind, other than any conflict disclosed in his or her report;

(ii) does not consider that any interest disclosed affects his or her suitability as an expert witness on any issue on which he or she has given evidence;

(iii) will advise the instructing party if, between the date of the expert's report and the final hearing, there is any change in circumstances which affects the expert's answers to (i) or (ii) above;

(iv) understands their duty to the court and has complied with that duty; and

(v) is aware of the requirements of FPR Part 25 and this practice direction;

(vi) in children proceedings, has complied with the Standards for Expert Witnesses in Children Proceedings in the Family Court which are set out in the Annex to this Practice Direction;

(j) be verified by a statement of truth in the following form –

'I confirm that I have made clear which facts and matters referred to in this report are within my own knowledge and which are not. Those that are within my own knowledge I confirm to be true. The opinions I have expressed represent my true and complete professional opinions on the matters to which they refer.'

Where the report relates to children proceedings the form of statement of truth must include –

'I also confirm that I have complied with the Standards for Expert Witnesses in Children Proceedings in the Family Court which are set out in the Annex to Practice Direction 25B – The Duties of an Expert, the Expert's Report and Arrangements for an Expert to Attend Court'

(FPR Part 17 deals with statements of truth. Rule 17.6 sets out the consequences of verifying a document containing a false statement without an honest belief in its truth.)

Arrangements for experts to give evidence

Preparation

10.1 Where the court has directed the attendance of an expert witness, the party who instructed the expert or party responsible for the instruction of the expert shall, **by a date specified by the court prior to the hearing at which the expert is to give oral evidence ('the specified date') or, where in care or supervision proceedings an Issues Resolution Hearing ('the IRH') is to be held, by the IRH**, ensure that –

(a) a date and time (if possible, convenient to the expert) are fixed for the court to hear the expert's evidence, substantially in advance of the hearing at which the expert is to give oral evidence and no later than a specified date prior to that hearing or, where an IRH is to be held, than the IRH;

(b) if the expert's oral evidence is not required, the expert is notified as soon as possible;

(c) the witness template accurately indicates how long the expert is likely to be giving evidence, in order to avoid the inconvenience of the expert being delayed at court;

(d) consideration is given in each case to whether some or all of the experts participate by telephone conference or video link, or submit their evidence in writing, to ensure that minimum disruption is caused to professional schedules and that costs are minimised.

Experts attending court

10.2 Where expert witnesses are to be called, all parties shall, **by the specified date or, where an IRH is to be held, by the IRH**, ensure that –

(a) the parties' advocates have identified (whether at an advocates' meeting or by other means) the issues which the experts are to address;

(b) wherever possible, a logical sequence to the evidence is arranged, with experts of the same discipline giving evidence on the same day;

(c) the court is informed of any circumstance where all experts agree but a party nevertheless does not accept the agreed opinion, so that directions can be given for the proper consideration of the experts' evidence and opinion;

(d) in the exceptional case the court is informed of the need for a witness summons.

ANNEX

Standards for Expert Witnesses in Children Proceedings in the Family Court

Subject to any order made by the court, expert witnesses involved in family proceedings (involving children) in England and Wales, whatever their field of practice or country of origin, must comply with the standards (1–11).

1 The expert's area of competence is appropriate to the issue(s) upon which the court has identified that an opinion is required, and relevant experience is evidenced in their CV.

2 The expert has been active in the area of work or practice, (as a practitioner or an academic who is subject to peer appraisal), has sufficient experience of the issues relevant to the instant case, and is familiar with the breadth of current practice or opinion.

3 The expert has working knowledge of the social, developmental, cultural norms and accepted legal principles applicable to the case presented at initial enquiry, and has the cultural competence skills to deal with the circumstances of the case.

4 The expert is up-to-date with Continuing Professional Development appropriate to their discipline and expertise, and is in continued engagement with accepted supervisory mechanisms relevant to their practice.

5 If the expert's current professional practice is regulated by a UK statutory body (See Appendix 1) they are in possession of a current licence to practise or equivalent.

6 If the expert's area of professional practice is not subject to statutory registration (eg child psychotherapy, systemic family therapy, mediation, and experts in exclusively academic appointments) the expert should demonstrate appropriate qualifications and/ or registration with a relevant professional body on a case by case basis. Registering bodies usually provide a code of conduct and professional standards and should be accredited by the Professional Standards Authority for Health and Social Care (See Appendix 2). If the expertise is academic in nature (eg regarding evidence of cultural influences) then no statutory registration is required (even if this includes direct contact or interviews with individuals) but consideration should be given to appropriate professional accountability.

7 The expert is compliant with any necessary safeguarding requirements, information security expectations, and carries professional indemnity insurance.

8 If the expert's current professional practice is outside the UK they can demonstrate that they are compliant with the FJC 'Guidelines for the instruction of medical experts from overseas in family cases'[1].

1 December 2011. See *www.judiciary.gov.uk/about-the-judiciary/advisory-bodies/fjc*.

9 The expert has undertaken appropriate training, updating or quality assurance activity – including actively seeking feedback from cases in which they have provided evidence – relevant to the role of expert in the family courts in England and Wales within the last year.

10 The expert has a working knowledge of, and complies with, the requirements of Practice Directions relevant to providing reports for and giving evidence to the family courts in England and Wales. This includes compliance with the requirement to identify where their opinion on the instant case lies in relation to other accepted mainstream views and the overall spectrum of opinion in the UK.

Expectations in relation to experts' fees

11 The expert should state their hourly rate in advance of agreeing to accept instruction, and give an estimate of the number of hours the report is likely to take. This will assist the legal representative to apply expeditiously to the Legal Aid Agency if prior authority is to be sought in a publicly funded case.

APPENDIX 1 TO THE STANDARDS

UK Health and Social Care Professions and Statutory Regulators with responsibilities within England and Wales

The Professional Standards Authority for Health and Social Care[2] (PSA) (formerly the Council for Healthcare Regulatory Excellence) oversees statutory bodies that regulate health and social care professionals in the UK. It assesses their performance, conducts audits, scrutinises their decisions and reports to Parliament. It also sets standards for organisations holding voluntary registers for health and social care occupations and accredits those that meet them. It shares good practice and knowledge, conducts research and introduces new ideas to the sector including the concept of right-touch regulation. It monitors policy developments in the UK and internationally and provides advice on issues relating to professional standards in health and social care.

2 *www.professionalstandards.org.uk*

The General Medical Council[3] (GMC) is the independent regulator for doctors in the UK. The GMC's statutory purpose is to protect, promote and maintain the health and safety of the public by ensuring proper standards in the practice of medicine through the Medical Register.

3 *www.gmc-uk.org*

The General Dental Council[4] regulates dental professionals in the UK. All dentists, dental nurses, dental technicians, clinical dental technicians, dental hygienists, dental therapists and orthodontic therapists must be registered with the GDC to work in the UK.

4 *www.gdc-uk.org*

The Nursing and Midwifery Council[5] regulates nurses and midwives in the UK, setting standards for work, education and a code of conduct for all registered nurses and midwives.

5 *www.nmc-uk.org*

Care Council for Wales: The Care Council for Wales is the social care workforce regulator in Wales responsible for promoting and securing high standards across the social services and social care workforce. It regulates social workers in Wales and managers of care services, including residential care homes for children, care homes for adults and domiciliary care for both adults and children. It also regulates social work students and residential child care workers.

Note—The website is at *www.ccwales.org.uk/*.

The General Optical Council[6] is the regulator for the optical professions in the UK. Its purpose is to protect the public by promoting high standards of education, performance and conduct amongst opticians.

6 www.optical.org

The General Pharmacy Council[7] is the independent regulator for pharmacists, pharmacy technicians and pharmacy premises in Great Britain. Its role is to protect, promote and maintain the health, safety and wellbeing of members of the public by upholding standards and public trust in pharmacy.

7 www.pharmacyregulation.org/about-us

The General Chiropractic Council[8] is a UK-wide statutory body with regulatory powers established by the Chiropractors Act 1994. Its duties are to protect the public by establishing and operating a scheme of statutory regulation for chiropractors, to set the standards of chiropractic education, conduct and practice and to ensure the development of the profession of chiropractic, using a model of continuous improvement in practice.

8 www.gcc-uk.org/page.cfm

The General Osteopathic Council[9] regulates the practice of osteopathy in the United Kingdom. By law osteopaths must be registered with the Council in order to practise in the UK. It works with the public and osteopathic profession to promote patient safety by registering qualified professionals and sets, maintain and develop standards of osteopathic practice and conduct.

9 www.osteopathy.org.uk

The Health and Care Professions Council regulates health and social care professionals with protected titles[10]. Further information is set out in the table below.

10 www.hpc-uk.org/aboutregistration/protectedtitles

Profession	Protected title(s)
Arts therapist An art, music or drama therapist encourages people to express their feelings and emotions through art, such as painting and drawing, music or drama.	• Art psychotherapist • Art therapist • Drama therapist • Music therapist
Biomedical scientist A biomedical scientist analyses specimens from patients to provide data to help doctors diagnose and treat disease.	• Biomedical scientist
Chiropodist/Podiatrist A chiropodist/podiatrist diagnoses and treats disorders, diseases and deformities of the feet.	• Chiropodist • Podiatrist
Clinical scientist A clinical scientist oversees specialist tests for diagnosing and managing disease. They advise doctors on using tests and interpreting data and they also carry out research to understand diseases.	• Clinical scientist
Dietician A dietician uses the science of nutrition to devise eating plans for patients to treat medical conditions, and to promote good health.	• Dietician
Hearing aid dispenser Hearing aid dispensers assess, fit and provide aftercare for hearing aids.	• Hearing aid dispenser
Occupational therapist An occupational therapist uses specific activities to limit the effects of disability and promote independence in all aspects of daily life.	• Occupational therapist
Operating department practitioner Operating department practitioners participate in the assessment of the patient prior to surgery and provide individualised care.	• Operating department practitioner
Orthoptist Orthoptists specialise in diagnosing and treating visual problems involving eye movement and alignment.	• Orthoptist

Profession	Protected title(s)
Paramedic Paramedics provide specialist care and treatment to patients who are either acutely ill or injured. They can administer a range of drugs and carry out certain surgical techniques.	• Paramedic
Physiotherapist Physiotherapists deal with human function and movement and help people to achieve their full physical potential. They use physical approaches to promote, maintain and restore wellbeing.	• Physiotherapist • Physical therapist
Practitioner psychologist Psychology is the scientific study of people, the mind and behaviour. Psychologists attempt to understand the role of mental functions in individual and social behaviour.	• Practitioner psychologist • Registered psychologist • Clinical psychologist • Counselling psychologist • Educational psychologist • Forensic psychologist • Health psychologist • Occupational psychologist • Sport and exercise psychologist
Prosthetist/Orthotist Prosthetists and orthotists are responsible for all aspects of supplying prostheses and orthoses for patients. A prosthesis is a device that replaces a missing body part. An orthosis is a device fixed to the body.	• Prosthetist • Orthotist
Radiographer Therapeutic radiographers plan and deliver treatment using radiation. Diagnostic radiographers produce and interpret high-quality images of the body to diagnose injuries and diseases.	• Radiographer • Diagnostic radiographer • Therapeutic radiographer
Social workers in England	• Social worker
Speech and language therapist Speech and language therapists assess, treat and help to prevent speech, language and swallowing difficulties.	• Speech and language therapist • Speech therapist

APPENDIX 2 TO THE STANDARDS

Examples of professional bodies/associations relating to non-statutorily regulated work

Resolution UK

www.resolution.org.uk/

Resolution's members are family lawyers committed to the constructive resolution of family disputes. Members follow a Code of Practice that promotes a non-confrontational approach to family problems, encourage solutions that consider the needs of the whole family and in particular the best interests of children.

Association of Child Psychotherapists (Psychoanalytic)

www.childpsychotherapy.org.uk

The Association of Child Psychotherapists is the professional organisation for Child and Adolescent Psychoanalytic Psychotherapy in the UK. The Association recognises and monitors five training schools in Child and Adolescent Psychotherapy (e g the Tavistock and Portman NHS Foundation Trust). Child Psychotherapists who have qualified in one of these trainings (minimum 4 years in-service clinical training, doctoral or doctoral equivalent) are eligible for full membership of the Association and are able to work as autonomous professionals within the NHS or in independent practice. Child Psychotherapists are appointed at similar grades to Clinical Psychologists.

The UK Council for Psychotherapy (UKCP)

www.psychotherapy.org.uk

The UKCP is a membership organisation with over 75 training and listing organisations, and over 7,000 individual practitioners. UKCP holds the national register of psychotherapists and psychotherapeutic counsellors, listing those practitioner members who meet exacting standards and training requirements. Organisational members/associations are grouped together in modality colleges representing all the main traditions in the practice of psychotherapy in the UK including:

- Association for Cognitive Analytic Therapy
- Association for Family Therapy and Systemic Practice
- Gestalt Psychotherapy and Training Institute
- Institute of Transactional Analysis
- Institute for Arts in Therapy and Education

The British Association for Counselling & Psychotherapy (BACP)

www.bacp.co.uk

BACP is a membership organisation and a registered charity that sets standards for a wide variety of therapeutic practice and provides information for therapists, clients of therapy, and the general public. It has over 37,000 members and is the largest professional body representing counselling and psychotherapy in the UK. BACP accredits training courses for counsellors and psychotherapists and is dedicated to ensuring its members practice responsibly, ethically and to the highest of standards.

The British Association for Behavioural and Cognitive Psychotherapies (BABCP)

www.babcp.com

The BABCP is the lead organisation for Cognitive Behavioural Therapy in the UK. It is a multi-disciplinary interest group for people involved in the practice and theory of behavioural and cognitive psychotherapy. The BABCP maintain standards for practitioners of Behavioural & Cognitive Psychotherapy by providing the opportunity for members who meet minimum criteria to become accredited.

British Psychoanalytic Council

www.psychoanalytic-council.org

Psychoanalytic or psychodynamic psychotherapy draws on theories and practices of analytical psychology and psychoanalysis. It is a therapeutic process which helps patients understand and resolve their problems by increasing awareness of their inner world and its influence over relationships both past and present. It differs from most other therapies in aiming for deep seated change in personality and emotional development. Psychoanalytic and psychodynamic psychotherapy aim to help people with serious psychological disorders to understand and change complex, deep-seated and often unconsciously based emotional and relationship problems thereby reducing symptoms and alleviating distress.

NAGALRO

www.nagalro.com

Professional association for Family Court Advisers, Children's Guardians and Independent Social Workers.

British Association of Social Workers (BASW);

www.basw.co.uk

UK professional association of social workers.

Confederation of Independent Social Work Agencies UK (CISWA)

www.ciswa-uk.org

Note—This web address is no longer valid.

CISWA-UK is a not for profit organisation which brings independent social work providers together with the aim of improving the professionalism and expertise of agencies providing services to children and families.

Practice Direction 25C – Children Proceedings – The Use of Single Joint Experts and the Process Leading to an Expert Being Instructed or Expert Evidence Being Put Before the Court

This Practice Direction supplements FPR Part 25

Scope of this Practice Direction

1.1 This Practice Direction applies to children proceedings and contains guidance on –

- (a) the use of single joint experts;
- (b) how to prepare for the hearing at which the court will consider whether to give permission for an expert to be instructed, a child to be medically or psychiatrically examined or otherwise assessed for the purposes of provision of expert evidence in the proceedings or for putting expert evidence (in any form) before the court including –
  - (i) preliminary enquiries of experts;
  - (ii) the content of an application for the court's permission in addition to matters mentioned in FPR 25.7;
  - (iii) matters to be set out in the draft order to be attached to the application for permission; and
- (c) the letter of instruction to the expert.

1.2 'Children proceedings' includes proceedings under Schedule 1 to the 1989 Act as those proceedings are proceedings which relate wholly or mainly to the maintenance or upbringing of a minor referred to in FPR 25.2(1).

Single joint experts

2.1 Section 13(1),(3) and (5) of the 2014 Act applies to a single joint expert ('SJE') in addition to an expert instructed by one party. This means that the court's permission is required to put expert evidence from an SJE (in any form) before the court (section 13(5) of the 2014 Act). The court's permission is also required to instruct an SJE and for a child to be medically or psychiatrically examined or otherwise assessed for the purposes of provision of evidence from an SJE (section 13(1) and (3) of the 2014 Act). Wherever possible, expert evidence should be obtained from an SJE instructed by both or all the parties. To that end, a party wishing to instruct an expert should as soon as possible after the start of the proceedings first give the other party or parties a list of the names of one or more experts in the relevant speciality whom they consider suitable to be instructed.

2.2 **Within 5 business days after receipt of the list of proposed experts**, the other party or parties should indicate any objection to one or more of the named experts and, if so, supply the name(s) of one or more experts whom they consider suitable.

2.3 Each party should disclose whether they have already consulted any of the proposed experts about the issue(s) in question.

2.4 Where the parties cannot agree on the identity of the expert, each party should think carefully before seeking the permission of the court to instruct their own expert because of the costs implications. Disagreements about the use and identity of an expert may be better managed by the court in the context of the application for the court's permission to instruct the expert and for directions for the use of an SJE (see paragraph 2.6 below).

Instructing separate experts

2.5 If the parties seek the permission of the court to instruct separate experts –

(a) they should agree in advance that the reports will be disclosed; and

(b) the instructions to each expert should comply, so far as appropriate, with paragraphs 4.1 and 6.1 below (Letter of instruction).

Where two or more parties wish to instruct an SJE

2.6 If two or more parties wish to instruct an SJE, before applying to the court for permission and directions for the use of an SJE, the parties should –

(a) so far as appropriate, comply with the guidance in paragraphs 3.2 (Preliminary enquiries of the expert) and paragraphs 3.10 and 3.11 below;

(b) receive the expert's confirmation in response to preliminary enquiries referred to in paragraph 8.1 of Practice Direction 25B;

(c) have agreed in what proportion the SJE's fee is to be shared between them (at least in the first instance) and when it is to be paid; and

(d) if applicable, have obtained agreement for public funding.

2.7 The instructions to the SJE should comply, so far as appropriate, with paragraphs 4.1 and 6.1 below (Letter of instruction).

Preparation for the permission hearing

3.1 Paragraphs 3.2 to 3.11 give guidance on how to prepare for the hearing at which the court will consider whether to give permission for an expert to be instructed, a child to be examined or otherwise assessed or expert evidence to be put before the court. The purpose of the preparation is to ensure that the court has the information required to enable it to exercise its powers under section 13(1), (3), (5) and (7) of the 2014 Act and FPR 25.5.

Preliminary enquiries of the expert

3.2 In good time for the information requested to be available for the hearing at which the court will consider whether to give permission for an expert to be instructed, a child to be examined or otherwise assessed or expert evidence to be put before the court or for the advocates' meeting or discussion where one takes place before that hearing, the party or parties intending to instruct the expert shall approach the expert with the following information –

(a) the nature of the proceedings and the issues likely to require determination by the court;

(b) the issues in the proceedings to which the expert evidence is to relate;

(c) the questions about which the expert is to be asked to give an opinion (including any ethnic, cultural, religious or linguistic contexts) and which relate to the issues in the case;

(d) the date when the court is to be asked to give permission for the instruction (or if – unusually – permission has already been given, the date and details of that permission);

(e) whether permission is to be asked of the court for the instruction of another expert in the same or any related field (that is, to give an opinion on the same or related questions);

(f) the volume of reading which the expert will need to undertake;

(g) whether or not permission has been applied for or given for the expert to examine the child;

(h) whether or not it will be necessary for the expert to conduct interviews – and, if so, with whom;

(i) the likely timetable of legal and social work steps;

(j) in care and supervision proceedings, any dates in the Timetable for the Child which would be relevant to the proposed timetable for the assessment;

(k) when the expert's report is likely to be required;

(l) whether and, if so, what date has been fixed by the court for any hearing at which the expert may be required to give evidence (in particular the Final Hearing); and whether it may be possible for the expert to give evidence by telephone conference or video link: see paragraphs 10.1 and 10.2 (Arrangements for experts to give evidence) of Practice Direction 25B;

(m) the possibility of making, through their instructing solicitors, representations to the court about being named or otherwise identified in any public judgment given by the court;

(n) whether the instructing party has public funding and the legal aid rates of payment which are applicable.

Confidentiality of children proceedings and making preliminary enquiries of an expert

3.3 For the purposes of the law of contempt of court, information relating to children proceedings (whether or not contained in a document filed with the court or recorded in any form) may be communicated only to an expert whose instruction by a party has been permitted by the court (see FPR 12.73(1)(a)(vii) and 14.14(c)(vii)) as children proceedings are confidential.

3.4 Before permission is obtained from the court to instruct an expert in children proceedings, the party seeking permission needs to make the enquiries of the expert referred to above in order to provide the court with information to enable it to decide whether to give permission. In practice, enquiries may need to be made of more than one expert for this purpose. This will in turn require each expert to be given sufficient information about the case to decide whether or not he or she is in a position to accept instructions. Such preliminary enquiries, and the disclosure of information about the case which is a necessary part of such enquiries, will not require the court's permission and will not amount to a contempt of court.

Expert's response to preliminary enquiries

3.5 In good time for the hearing at which the court will consider whether to give permission for an expert to be instructed, a child to be examined or otherwise assessed or expert evidence to be put before the court, **the party or parties** intending to instruct the expert must obtain the confirmations from the expert referred to in paragraph 8.1 of Practice Direction 25B. These confirmations include that the work is within the expert's expertise, the expert is available to do the work within the relevant timescale and the expert's costs.

3.6 Where the parties **cannot agree who should be the single joint expert** before the hearing at which the court will consider whether to give permission for an expert to be instructed, a child to be examined or otherwise assessed or expert evidence to be put before the court, they should obtain the above confirmations in respect of all experts whom they intend to put to the court for the purposes of FPR 25.11(2)(a) as candidates for the appointment.

The application for the court's permission mentioned in section 13(1), (3) and (5) of the 2014 Act

TIMING AND ORAL APPLICATIONS FOR THE COURT'S PERMISSION MENTIONED IN FPR 25.4

3.7 An application for the court's permission for an expert to be instructed, a child to be examined or otherwise assessed or expert evidence to be put before the court should be made as soon as it becomes apparent that it is necessary to make it. FPR 25.6 makes provision about the time by which applications for the court's permission should be made.

3.8 Applications should, wherever possible, be made so that they are considered at any directions hearing or other hearing for which a date has been fixed or for which a date is about to be fixed. It should be noted that one application notice can be used by a party to make more than one application for an order or direction at a hearing held during the course of proceedings. An application for the court's permission for an expert to be instructed, a child to be examined or otherwise assessed or expert evidence to be put before the court may therefore be included in an application notice requesting other orders to be made at such a hearing.

3.9 Where a date for a hearing has been fixed, a party who wishes to make an application at that hearing but does not have sufficient time to file an application notice should as soon as possible inform the court (if possible in writing) and, if possible, the other parties of the nature of the application and the reason for it. The party should provide the court and the other party with as much as possible of the information referred to in FPR 25.7 and paragraph 3.10 below. That party should then make the application orally at the hearing. An oral application of this kind should be the exception and reserved for genuine cases where circumstances are such that it has only become apparent shortly before the hearing that an expert opinion is necessary.

THE APPLICATION

3.10 In addition to the matters specified in FPR 25.7(2)(a) and (3), an application for the court's permission for an expert to be instructed, a child to be examined or otherwise assessed or expert evidence to be put before the court, must state-

(a) the discipline, qualifications and expertise of the expert (by way of C.V. where possible);
(b) the expert's availability to undertake the work;
(c) the timetable for the report;
(d) the responsibility for instruction;
(e) whether the expert evidence can properly be obtained by only one party (for example, on behalf of the child);
(f) why the expert evidence proposed cannot properly be given by an officer of the service, Welsh family proceedings officer or the local authority (social services undertaking a core assessment) in accordance with their respective statutory duties or any other party to the proceedings or an expert already instructed in the proceedings;
(g) the likely cost of the report on an hourly or other charging basis;
(h) the proposed apportionment (at least in the first instance) of any jointly instructed expert's fee; when it is to be paid; and, if applicable, whether public funding has been approved.

THE TERMS OF THE DRAFT ORDER TO BE ATTACHED TO THE APPLICATION FOR THE COURT'S PERMISSION

3.11 FPR 25.7(2)(b) provides that a draft of the order giving the court's permission as mentioned in section 13(1), (3) and (5) of the 2014 Act is to be attached to the application for the court's permission. That draft order must set out the following matters –

(a) the issues in the proceedings to which the expert evidence is to relate and which the court is to identify;
(b) the questions relating to the issues in the case which the expert is to answer and which the court is to approve ensuring that they
  (i) are within the ambit of the expert's area of expertise;
  (ii) do not contain unnecessary or irrelevant detail;
  (iii) are kept to a manageable number and are clear, focused and direct;
(c) the party who is responsible for drafting the letter of instruction and providing the documents to the expert;
(d) the timetable within which the report is to be prepared, filed and served;
(e) the disclosure of the report to the parties and to any other expert;
(f) the organisation of, preparation for and conduct of any experts' discussion (see Practice Direction 25E – *Discussions between Experts in Family Proceedings*);
(g) the preparation of a statement of agreement and disagreement by the experts following an experts' discussion;
(h) making available to the court at an early opportunity the expert reports in electronic form;
(i) the attendance of the expert at court to give oral evidence (alternatively, the expert giving his or her evidence in writing or remotely by video link), whether at or for the Final Hearing or another hearing; unless agreement about the opinions given by the expert is reached at or before the Issues Resolution Hearing ('IRH') or, if no IRH is to be held, by a date specified by the court prior to the hearing at which the expert is to give oral evidence.

PART III

Letter of instruction

4.1 The party responsible for instructing the expert shall prepare (in agreement with the other parties where appropriate), a letter of instruction to the expert and shall –

(a) set out the context in which the expert's opinion is sought (including any ethnic, cultural, religious or linguistic contexts);

(b) set out the questions approved by the court and which the expert is required to answer and any other linked questions ensuring that they –

(i) are within the ambit of the expert's area of expertise;

(ii) do not contain unnecessary or irrelevant detail;

(iii) are kept to a manageable number and are clear, focused and direct; and

(iv) reflect what the expert has been requested to do by the court

(Annex A to this Practice Direction sets out suggested questions in letters of instruction to (1) child mental health professionals or paediatricians, and (2) adult psychiatrists and applied psychologists, in Children Act 1989 proceedings);

(c) list the documentation provided, or provide for the expert an indexed and paginated bundle which shall include –

(i) an agreed list of essential reading; and

(ii) a copy of this Practice Direction and Practice Directions 25B and E and where appropriate Practice Direction 15B;

(d) identify any materials provided to the expert which have not been produced either as original medical (or other professional) records or in response to an instruction from a party, and state the source of that material (such materials may contain an assumption as to the standard of proof, the admissibility or otherwise of hearsay evidence, and other important procedural and substantive questions relating to the different purposes of other enquiries, for example, criminal or disciplinary proceedings);

(e) identify all requests to third parties for disclosure and their responses in order to avoid partial disclosure, which tends only to prove a case rather than give full and frank information;

(f) identify the relevant people concerned with the proceedings (for example, the treating clinicians) and inform the expert of his or her right to talk to them provided that an accurate record is made of the discussions;

(g) identify any other expert instructed in the proceedings and advise the expert of their right to talk to the other experts provided that an accurate record is made of the discussions;

(h) subject to any public funding requirement for prior authority, define the contractual basis upon which the expert is retained and in particular the funding mechanism including how much the expert will be paid (an hourly rate and overall estimate should already have been obtained), when the expert will be paid, and what limitation there might be on the amount the expert can charge for the work which they will have to do. In cases where the parties are publicly funded, there may also be a brief explanation of the costs and expenses excluded from public funding by Funding Code criterion 1.3 and the detailed assessment process.

Adult who is a protected party

5.1 Where the adult is a protected party, that party's representative shall be involved in any instruction of an expert, including the instruction of an expert to assess whether the adult, although a protected party, is competent to give evidence (see Practice Direction 15B – *Adults Who May Be Protected Parties and Children Who May Become Protected Parties in Family Proceedings*).

Asking the court to settle the letter of instruction to a single joint expert

6.1 Where possible, the written request for the court to consider the letter of instruction referred to in rule 25.12(2) should be set out in an e-mail to the court and copied by e-mail to the other instructing parties. The request should be sent to the relevant court or (by prior arrangement only) directly to the judge dealing with the proceedings. Where a legal adviser has been appointed as the case manager, the request should also be sent to the appointed legal adviser. The court will settle the letter of instruction, usually without a hearing to avoid delay; and will send (where practicable, by e-mail) the settled letter to the lead solicitor for transmission forthwith to the expert, and copy it to the other instructing parties for information.

ANNEX A

(drafted by the Family Justice Council)

Suggested questions in letters of instruction to child mental health professional or paediatrician in Children Act 1989 proceedings

A. The Child(ren)

1. Please describe the child(ren)'s current health, development and functioning (according to your area of expertise), and identify the nature of any significant changes which have occurred

- Behavioural
- Emotional
- Attachment organisation
- Social/peer/sibling relationships
- Cognitive/educational
- Physical
  - Growth, eating, sleep
  - Non-organic physical problems (including wetting and soiling)
  - Injuries
  - Paediatric conditions

2. Please comment on the likely explanation for/aetiology of the child(ren)'s problems/difficulties/injuries

- History/experiences (including intrauterine influences, and abuse and neglect)
- Genetic/innate/developmental difficulties
- Paediatric/psychiatric disorders

3. Please provide a prognosis and risk if difficulties not addressed above.

4. Please describe the child(ren)'s needs in the light of the above

- Nature of care-giving
- Education
- Treatment

in the short and long term (subject, where appropriate, to further assessment later).

B. The parents/primary carers

5. Please describe the factors and mechanisms which would explain the parents' (or primary carers) harmful or neglectful interactions with the child(ren) (if relevant).

6. What interventions have been tried and what has been the result?

7. Please assess the ability of the parents or primary carers to fulfil the child(ren)'s identified needs now.

8. What other assessments of the parents or primary carers are indicated?

- Adult mental health assessment
- Forensic risk assessment
- Physical assessment
- Cognitive assessment

9. What, if anything, is needed to assist the parents or primary carers now, within the child(ren)'s time scales and what is the prognosis for change?

- Parenting work

- Support
- Treatment/therapy

C. Alternatives

10. Please consider the alternative possibilities for the fulfilment of the child(ren)'s needs

- What sort of placement
- Contact arrangements

Please consider the advantages, disadvantages and implications of each for the child(ren).

Suggested questions in letters of instruction to adult psychiatrists and applied psychologists in Children Act 1989 proceedings

1. Does the parent/adult have – whether in his/her history or presentation – a mental illness/disorder (including substance abuse) or other psychological/emotional difficulty and, if so, what is the diagnosis?

2. How do any/all of the above (and their current treatment if applicable) affect his/her functioning, including interpersonal relationships?

3. If the answer to Q1 is yes, are there any features of either the mental illness or psychological/emotional difficulty or personality disorder which could be associated with risk to others, based on the available evidence base (whether published studies or evidence from clinical experience)?

4. What are the experiences/antecedents/aetiology which would explain his/her difficulties, if any, (taking into account any available evidence base or other clinical experience)?

5. What treatment is indicated, what is its nature and the likely duration?

6. What is his/her capacity to engage in/partake of the treatment/therapy?

7. Are you able to indicate the prognosis for, time scales for achieving, and likely durability of, change?

8. What other factors might indicate positive change?

(It is assumed that this opinion will be based on collateral information as well as interviewing the adult).

Practice Direction 25D – Financial Remedy Proceedings and Other Family Proceedings (Except Children Proceedings) – The Use of Single Joint Experts and the Process Leading to Expert Evidence Being Put Before the Court

This Practice Direction supplements FPR Part 25

Scope of this Practice Direction

1.1 This Practice Direction applies to financial remedy proceedings and other family proceedings except children proceedings and contains guidance on –

(a) the use of single joint experts;

(b) how to prepare for the hearing at which the court will consider whether to give permission for putting expert evidence (in any form) before the court including –

(i) preliminary enquiries of experts;

(ii) information to be given to the court before the hearing;

(c) the letter of instruction to the expert.

Single joint experts

2.1 FPR 25.4 applies to a single joint expert ('SJE') in addition to an expert instructed by one party. This means that the court's permission is required to put expert evidence from an SJE (in any form) before the court. However, in family proceedings (except children proceedings) there is no requirement for the court's permission to be obtained before instructing an expert. Wherever possible, expert evidence should be obtained from a single joint expert instructed by both or all the parties ('SJE'). To that end, a party wishing to instruct an expert should first give the other party or parties a list of the names of one or more experts in the relevant speciality whom they consider suitable to be instructed.

2.2 **Within 10 business days after receipt of the list of proposed experts**, the other party or parties should indicate any objection to one or more of the named experts and, if so, supply the name(s) of one or more experts whom they consider suitable.

2.3 Each party should disclose whether they have already consulted any of the proposed experts about the issue(s) in question.

2.4 Where the parties cannot agree on the identity of the expert, each party should think carefully before instructing their own expert and seeking the permission of the court to put that expert evidence before it because of the costs implications. Disagreements about the use and identity of an expert may be better managed by the court in the context of an application for the court's permission to put the expert evidence before the court and for directions for the use of an SJE (see paragraph 2.6 below).

Agreement to instruct separate experts

2.5 If the parties agree to instruct separate experts and to seek the permission of the court to put the separate expert evidence before it –

(a) they should agree in advance that the reports will be disclosed; and

(b) the instructions to each expert should comply, so far as appropriate, with paragraphs 4.1 and 6.1 below (Letter of instruction).

Agreement to instruct an SJE

2.6 If there is agreement to instruct an SJE, **before applying to the court for permission to put the expert evidence before it and directions for the use of an SJE**, the parties should –

(a) so far as appropriate, comply with the guidance in paragraphs 3.3 (Preliminary enquiries of the expert) and paragraphs 3.11 and 3.12 below;

(b) receive the expert's confirmation in response to preliminary enquiries referred to in paragraph 8.1 of Practice Direction 25B;

(c) have agreed in what proportion the SJE's fee is to be shared between them (at least in the first instance) and when it is to be paid; and

(d) if applicable, have obtained agreement for public funding.

2.7 The instructions to the SJE should comply, so far as appropriate, with paragraphs 4.1 and 6.1 below (Letter of instruction).

The test for permission and preparation for the permission hearing

3.1 The test in FPR 25.4(3) which the court is to apply to determine whether permission should be given for expert evidence to be put before the court has been altered from one which refers to expert evidence being restricted by the court to that which is reasonably required to resolve the proceedings to one which refers to the expert evidence being in the opinion of the court necessary to assist the court to resolve the proceedings. The overriding objective of the FPR, which is to enable the court to deal with cases justly, having regard to any welfare issues involved, continues to apply when the court is making the decision whether to give permission. In addition, the rules (FPR 25.5(2)) now tell the court what factors it is to have particular regard to when deciding whether to give permission.

PART III

3.2 Paragraphs 3.3 to 3.12 below give guidance on how to prepare for the hearing at which the court will apply the test in FPR 25.4(3) and the factors in FPR 25.5(2) and decide whether to give permission for expert evidence to be put before the court. The purpose of the preparation is to ensure that the court has the information required to enable it to exercise its powers under FPR 25.4(2) and 25.5(2) in line with FPR 25.4(3).

Preliminary enquiries of the expert

3.3 **In good time for the information requested to be available for the hearing** at which the court will consider whether to give permission for expert evidence to be put before the court, the party or parties intending to instruct the expert shall approach the expert with the following information –

(a) the nature of the proceedings and the issues likely to require determination by the court;
(b) the issues in the proceedings to which the expert evidence is to relate;
(c) the questions about which the expert is to be asked to give an opinion and which relate to the issues in the case;
(d) whether permission is to be asked of the court for the use of another expert in the same or any related field (that is, to give an opinion on the same or related questions);
(e) the volume of reading which the expert will need to undertake;
(f) whether or not it will be necessary for the expert to conduct interviews and, if so, with whom;
(g) the likely timetable of legal steps;
(h) when the expert's report is likely to be required;
(i) whether and, if so, what date has been fixed by the court for any hearing at which the expert may be required to give evidence (in particular the Final Hearing); and whether it may be possible for the expert to give evidence by telephone conference or video link: see paragraphs 10.1 and 10.2 (Arrangements for experts to give evidence) of Practice Direction 25B;
(j) the possibility of making, through their instructing solicitors, representations to the court about being named or otherwise identified in any public judgment given by the court;
(k) whether the instructing party has public funding and the legal aid rates of payment which are applicable.

Expert's response to preliminary enquiries

3.4 In good time for the hearing at which the court will consider whether to give permission for expert evidence to be put before the court, the solicitors or party intending to instruct the expert must obtain the confirmations from the expert referred to in paragraph 8.1 of Practice Direction 25B. These confirmations include that the work is within the expert's expertise, the expert is available to do the work within the relevant timescale and the expert's costs.

3.5 Where parties **cannot agree who should be the single joint expert** before the hearing at which the court will consider whether to give permission for expert evidence to be put before the court, they should obtain the above confirmations in respect of all experts whom they intend to put to the court for the purposes of rule 25.11(2)(a) as candidates for the appointment.

The application for the court's permission to put expert evidence before the court

TIMING AND ORAL APPLICATIONS FOR THE COURT'S PERMISSION

3.6 An application for the court's permission to put expert evidence before the court should be made as soon as it becomes apparent that it is necessary to make it. FPR 25.6 makes provision about the time by which applications for the court's permission should be made.

3.7 Applications should, wherever possible, be made so that they are considered at any directions hearing or other hearing for which a date has been fixed or for which a date is about to be fixed. It should be noted that one application notice can be used by a party to make more than one application for an order or direction at a hearing held during the course of proceedings. An application for the court's permission to put expert evidence before the court may therefore be included in an application notice requesting other orders to be made at such a hearing.

3.8 Where a date for a hearing has been fixed, a party who wishes to make an application at that hearing but does not have sufficient time to file an application notice should as soon as possible inform the court (if possible in writing) and, if possible, the other parties of the nature of the application and the reason for it. The party should provide the court and the other party with as much as possible of the information referred to in FPR 25.7 and paragraph 3.11 below. That party should then make the application orally at the hearing. An oral application of this kind should be the exception and reserved for genuine cases where circumstances are such that it has only become apparent shortly before the hearing that an expert opinion is necessary.

3.9 In financial remedy proceedings, unless the court directs otherwise, parties must apply for permission to put expert evidence before the court as soon as possible and no later than the first appointment. The expectation is that the court will give directions extending the time by which permission should be obtained where there is good reason for parties to delay the decision whether to use expert evidence and make an application for the court's permission.

3.10 Examples of situations where the time for requesting permission to put expert evidence before the court is likely to be extended are where –

(a) a decision about the need for expert evidence cannot be made until replies to questionnaires in relation to Forms E have been fully considered; or
(b) valuations of property are agreed for the purposes of the Financial Dispute Resolution appointment but no agreement is reached to resolve the proceedings at that appointment and the court cannot make a consent order as mentioned in FPR 9.17(8). In these circumstances, it may become clear to a party that he or she will want to use expert valuations of property and an application for the court's permission for such valuation to be put before it may be made orally at the end of the appointment to avoid the need for a separate hearing about this issue. As with other oral applications, the party should provide the court and the other party with as much as possible of the information referred to in FPR 25.7 and paragraph 3.11 below. FPR 9.17(9) requires the court to give directions for the future course of the proceedings where it has not made a consent order including, where appropriate, the filing of evidence.

THE APPLICATION

3.11 In addition to the matters specified in FPR 25.7(2)(a), an application for the court's permission to put expert evidence before the court must state –

(a) the discipline, qualifications and expertise of the expert (by way of C.V. where possible);
(b) the expert's availability to undertake the work;
(c) the timetable for the report;
(d) the responsibility for instruction;
(e) whether the expert evidence can properly be obtained by only one party;
(f) why the expert evidence proposed cannot properly be given by an expert already instructed in the proceedings;
(g) the likely cost of the report on an hourly or other charging basis:
(h) the proposed apportionment (at least in the first instance) of any jointly instructed expert's fee; when it is to be paid; and, if applicable, whether public funding has been approved.

THE DRAFT ORDER TO BE ATTACHED TO THE APPLICATION FOR THE COURT'S PERMISSION

3.12 FPR 25.7(2)(b) provides that a draft of the order giving the court's permission to put expert evidence before the court is to be attached to the application for the court's permission. That draft order must set out the following matters –

(a) the issues in the proceedings to which the expert evidence is to relate;
(b) the party who is to be responsible for drafting the letter of instruction and providing the documents to the expert;
(c) the timetable within which the report is to be prepared, filed and served;
(d) the disclosure of the report to the parties and to any other expert;
(e) the organisation of, preparation for and conduct of any experts' discussion (see Practice Direction 25E – *Discussions between Experts in Family Proceedings*);
(f) the preparation of a statement of agreement and disagreement by the experts following an experts' discussion;
(g) making available to the court at an early opportunity the expert reports in electronic form;
(h) the attendance of the expert at court to give oral evidence (alternatively, the expert giving his or her evidence in writing or remotely by video link), whether at or for the Final Hearing or another hearing; unless agreement about the opinions given by the expert is reached by a date specified by the court prior to the hearing at which the expert is to give oral evidence.

Letter of instruction

4.1 The party responsible for instructing the expert shall, **within 5 business days after the permission hearing**, prepare (in agreement with the other parties where appropriate), file and serve a letter of instruction to the expert which shall –

(a) set out the context in which the expert's opinion is sought (including any ethnic, cultural, religious or linguistic contexts);
(b) set out the questions which the expert is required to answer and ensuring that they –
    (i) are within the ambit of the expert's area of expertise;
    (ii) do not contain unnecessary or irrelevant detail;
    (iii) are kept to a manageable number and are clear, focused and direct; and
    (iv) reflect what the expert has been requested to do by the court;
(c) list the documentation provided, or provide for the expert an indexed and paginated bundle which shall include –
    (i) an agreed list of essential reading; and
    (ii) a copy of this Practice Direction and Practice Directions 25B, 25E and where appropriate Practice Direction 15B;
(d) identify any materials provided to the expert which have not been produced either as original medical (or other professional) records or in response to an instruction from a party, and state the source of that material (such materials may contain an assumption as to the standard of proof, the admissibility or otherwise of hearsay evidence, and other important procedural and substantive questions relating to the different purposes of other enquiries);
(e) identify all requests to third parties for disclosure and their responses in order to avoid partial disclosure, which tends only to prove a case rather than give full and frank information;
(f) identify the relevant people concerned with the proceedings and inform the expert of his or her right to talk to them provided that an accurate record is made of the discussions;
(g) identify any other expert instructed in the proceedings and advise the expert of their right to talk to the other experts provided that an accurate record is made of the discussions;
(h) subject to any public funding requirement for prior authority, define the contractual basis upon which the expert is retained and in particular the funding mechanism including how much the expert will be paid (an hourly rate and overall estimate should already have been obtained), when the expert will be paid, and what limitation there might be on the amount the expert can charge for the work which they will have to do.

In cases where the parties are publicly funded, there may also be a brief explanation of the costs and expenses excluded from public funding by Funding Code criterion 1.3 and the detailed assessment process.

Adult who is a protected party

5.1 Where the adult is a protected party, that party's representative shall be involved in any instruction of an expert, including the instruction of an expert to assess whether the adult, although a protected party, is competent to give evidence (see Practice Direction 15B – *Adults Who May Be Protected Parties and Children Who May Become Protected Parties in Family Proceedings*).

Asking the court to settle the letter of instruction to a single joint expert

6.1 Where possible, the written request for the court to consider the letter of instruction referred to in rule 25.12(2) should be set out in an e-mail to the court and copied by e-mail to the other instructing parties. The request should be sent to the relevant court or (by prior arrangement only) directly to the judge dealing with the proceedings. Where a legal adviser has been appointed as the case manager, the request should also be sent to the appointed legal adviser. The court will settle the letter of instruction, usually without a hearing to avoid delay; and will send (where practicable, by e-mail) the settled letter to the party responsible for instructing the expert for transmission forthwith to the expert, and copy it to the other instructing parties for information.

Practice Direction 25E – Discussions Between Experts in Family Proceedings

This Practice Direction supplements FPR Part 25

Scope

1.1 This Practice Direction supports FPR 25.16 by providing details about how and when experts discussions are to be arranged, their purpose and content. This Practice Direction applies to children proceedings and all other family proceedings.

Experts' discussion or meeting: purpose

2.1 In accordance with FPR 25.16, the court may, at any stage, direct a discussion between experts for the purpose outlined in paragraph (1) of that rule. FPR 25.16(2) provides that the court may specify the issues which the experts must discuss. The expectation is that those issues will include –

(a) the reasons for disagreement on any expert question and what, if any, action needs to be taken to resolve any outstanding disagreement or question;

(b) an explanation of existing evidence or additional evidence in order to assist the court to determine the issues.

One of the aims of specifying the issues for discussion is to limit, wherever possible, the need for the experts to attend court to give oral evidence.

Experts' discussion or meeting: arrangements

3.1 Subject to the directions given by the court under FPR 25.16, the solicitor or other professional who is given the responsibility by the court ('the nominated professional') shall **within 15 business days after the experts' reports have been filed and copied to the other parties**, make arrangements for the experts to have discussions. Subject to any specification by the court of the issues which experts must discuss under FPR 25.16(2), the following matters should be considered as appropriate –

(a) where permission has been given for the instruction of experts from different disciplines, a global discussion may be held relating to those questions that concern all or most of them;

(b) separate discussions may have to be held among experts from the same or related disciplines, but care should be taken to ensure that the discussions complement each other so that related questions are discussed by all relevant experts;

(c) 5 business days prior to a discussion or meeting, the nominated professional should formulate an agenda including a list of questions for consideration. The agenda should, subject always to the provisions of FPR 25.16(1), focus on those questions which are intended to clarify areas of agreement or disagreement.

Questions which repeat questions asked in the court order giving permission for an expert to be instructed or expert evidence to be put before the court or the letter of instruction or which seek to rehearse cross-examination in advance of the hearing should be rejected as likely to defeat the purpose of the meeting. The agenda may usefully take the form of a list of questions to be circulated among the other parties in advance and should comprise all questions that each party wishes the experts to consider.

The agenda and list of questions should be sent to each of the experts **not later than 2 business days before the discussion**;

(d) the nominated professional may exercise his or her discretion to accept further questions after the agenda with the list of questions has been circulated to the parties. **Only in exceptional circumstances should questions be added to the agenda within the 2-day period before the meeting. Under no circumstances should any question received on the day of or during the meeting be accepted**. This does not preclude questions arising during the meeting for the purposes of clarification. Strictness in this regard is vital, for adequate notice of the questions enables the parties to identify and isolate the expert issues in the case before the meeting so that the experts' discussion at the meeting can concentrate on those issues;

(e) the discussion should be chaired by the nominated professional. A minute must be taken of the questions answered by the experts. Where the court has given a direction under FPR 25.16(3) and subject to that direction, a Statement of Agreement and Disagreement must be prepared which should be agreed and signed by each of the experts who participated in the discussion. In accordance with FPR 25.16(3) the statement must contain a summary of the experts' reasons for disagreeing. The statement should be served and filed **not later than 5 business days after the discussion has taken place**;

(f) in each case, whether some or all of the experts participate by telephone conference or video link to ensure that minimum disruption is caused to professional schedules and that costs are minimised.

Meetings or conferences attended by a jointly instructed expert

4.1 Jointly instructed experts should not attend any meeting or conference which is not a joint one, unless all the parties have agreed in writing or the court has directed that such a meeting may be held, and it is agreed or directed who is to pay the expert's fees for the meeting or conference. Any meeting or conference attended by a jointly instructed expert should be proportionate to the case.

(Practice Direction 25C, paragraphs 2.1 to 2.7 deals generally with single joint experts in children proceedings and Practice Direction 25D paragraphs 2.1 to 2.7 deals with single joint experts in relation to other family proceedings).

Court-directed meetings involving experts in public law Children Act cases

5.1 In public law Children Act proceedings, where the court gives a direction that a meeting shall take place between the local authority and any relevant named experts for the purpose of providing assistance to the local authority in the formulation of plans and proposals for the child, the meeting shall be arranged, chaired and minuted in accordance with the directions given by the court.

Practice Direction 25F – Assessors in Family Proceedings

This Practice Direction supplements FPR Part 25

Scope of this Practice Direction

1.1 This Practice Direction applies to the appointment of assessors in family proceedings in England and Wales.

Appointment of assessors in family proceedings

2.1 The power to appoint one or more assessors to assist the court is conferred by section 70(1) of the Senior Courts Act 1981, which applies to the family court via section 31E(1) of the Matrimonial and Family Proceedings Act 1984 (and section 31J(e) of that Act confirms that this is the case). In practice, these powers have been used in appeals from a district judge or costs judge in costs assessment proceedings – although, in principle, the statutory powers permit one or more assessors to be appointed in any family proceedings where the High Court or the family court sees fit.

2.2 Not less than 21 days before making any such appointment, the court will notify each party in writing of the name of the proposed assessor, of the matter in respect of which the assistance of the assessor will be sought and of the qualifications of the assessor to give that assistance.

2.3 Any party may object to the proposed appointment, either personally or in respect of the proposed assessor's qualifications.

2.4 Any such objection must be made in writing and filed and served within 7 business days of receipt of the notification from the court of the proposed appointment, and will be taken into account by the court in deciding whether or not to make the appointment.

Scope—FPR 2010, r 25.20 makes provision for the appointment, duties and remuneration of one or more assessors. As indicated by para 2.1, the appointment of assessors normally takes place in appeals from a district judge or costs judge in costs assessment proceedings when, typically, a district judge and senior practising solicitor will be appointed as assessors to sit on the appeal alongside a High Court or circuit judge. FPR PD25F makes provision for an objection to be taken to any such appointment in appropriate circumstances. These provisions are derived from CPR 1998, r 35.15 and CPR PD35, para 10.

PART III

PART 26
CHANGE OF SOLICITOR

CONTENTS OF THIS PART

Rule		Page
26.1	Solicitor acting for a party	1825
26.2	Change of solicitor – duty to give notice	1826
26.3	Order that a solicitor has ceased to act	1827
26.4	Removal of solicitor who has ceased to act on application of another party	1828
	Practice Direction 26A – Change of Solicitor	1828

26.1 Solicitor acting for a party

Where the address for service of a party is the business address of that party's solicitor, the solicitor will be considered to be acting for that party until the provisions of this Part have been complied with.

(Part 6 contains provisions about the address for service.)

Practice Direction—See generally FPR PD26A.

Scope—In family proceedings, Pt 26 reproduces CPR 1998, Pt 42 with minor amendments. In other proceedings CPR 1998, Pt 42 applies.

Where a party employs a solicitor, the solicitor's business address will be the address for service (FPR 2010, r 6.11). All documents served by the court or another party are properly served at that address. The solicitor will be considered to be acting for that party until a notice of change has been filed with the court by the party concerned or his new solicitor and served on the other party (FPR PD26A, para 1.1).

26.2 Change of solicitor – duty to give notice

(1) This rule applies where –

(a) a party for whom a solicitor is acting wants to change solicitor;
(b) a party, after having conducted the application in person, appoints a solicitor to act for that party (except where the solicitor is appointed only to act as an advocate for a hearing); or
(c) a party, after having conducted the application by a solicitor, intends to act in person.

(2) Where this rule applies, the party or the party's solicitor (where one is acting) must –

(a) serve notice of the change on –
every other party; and
where paragraph (1)(a)or (c) applies, the former solicitor; and
(b) file notice of the change.

(3) Except where a serial number has been assigned under rule 14.2 or the name or address of a party is not being revealed in accordance with rule 29.1, the notice must state the party's new address for service.

(4) The notice filed at court must state that notice has been served as required by paragraph (2)(a) or, where rule 2.4 applies, in accordance with the court's directions given under that rule.

(5) Subject to paragraph (6), where a party has changed solicitor or intends to act in person, the former solicitor will be considered to be the party's solicitor unless and until –

(a) notice is filed and served in accordance with paragraph (2)(a) or, where rule 2.4 applies, in accordance with the court's directions given under that rule; or
(b) the court makes an order under rule 26.3 and the order is served as required by paragraph (3) of that rule.

(6) Where the certificate of a legally aided person (in this rule 'C') is revoked or withdrawn –

(a) the solicitor who acted for C will cease to be the solicitor acting in the case as soon as the retainer is determined under regulation 24 or 41 of the Civil Legal Aid (Procedure) Regulations 2012; and
(b) if C wishes to continue –
   (i) where C appoints a solicitor to act on C's behalf, paragraph (2) will apply as if C had previously conducted the application in person; and
   (ii) where C wants to act in person, C must give an address for service, in accordance with rule 6.26, unless the court directs otherwise.

(7) In this rule –

…

'certificate' means a certificate issued under the Civil Legal Aid (Procedure) Regulations 2012; and

…

'legally aided person' means a person to whom civil legal services (within the meaning of Part 1 of the Legal Aid, Sentencing and Punishment of Offenders Act 2012) have been made available under arrangements made for the purposes of that Part of that Act).

Amendments—SI 2013/534, subject to savings.

Practice Direction—See generally FPR PD26A, in particular para 2 (notice of change of solicitor).

Scope—In the three situations referred to in r 26.2(1), it is mandatory for the party or his solicitor:

(a) to file notice of change; and
(b) to serve notice of change on every other party and (where appropriate) the former solicitor.

No order of the court is required in the circumstances set out in r 26.2(1). Rule 26.2(5) makes it clear that, once a solicitor is appointed to act, he is considered to be the party's solicitor unless or until the requirements of Pt 26 are complied with. The notice of change of solicitor must state the party's new address for service, subject to the exceptions in r 26.2(3). The notice filed with the court must also state that the notice has been served on every other party and (where appropriate) the former solicitor.

The court cannot order a party to appoint a new solicitor; the court may only forbid solicitors from acting and grant a stay for new solicitors to be appointed (*SMC Engineering (Bristol) Limited v Fraser* (2001) *The Times*, 26 January, CA).

'Notice of change'—PD26A, para 2.6: Form FP8.

Revocation or discharge of certificate (r 26.2(6))—A solicitor's retainer under a legal aid certificate ends upon receipt by the solicitor of a notice of revocation or discharge of the certificate. The solicitor must serve notice of the revocation or discharge on all other parties and to the court. No further notice or order is required by the solicitor to come off the court record. If the legally aided person wishes to continue with the proceedings and appoints either the solicitor who was acting for him under the certificate or another solicitor, he must file notice of change and serve the notice on every other party. Alternatively, if the party who formerly had the benefit of a certificate wishes to act in person, then he must give an address for service within the jurisdiction.

26.3 Order that a solicitor has ceased to act

(1) A solicitor may apply for an order declaring that that solicitor has ceased to be the solicitor acting for –

(a) a party; or

(b) a children's guardian.

(2) Where an application is made under this rule –

(a) notice of the application must be given to the party, or children's guardian, for whom the solicitor is acting, unless the court directs otherwise; and

(b) the application must be supported by evidence.

(3) Where the court makes an order declaring that a solicitor has ceased to act, a court officer will serve a copy of the order on –

(a) every party to the proceedings; and

(b) where applicable, a children's guardian.

Practice Direction—See generally FPR PD26A and, in particular, para 3. It should be noted that an order made under r 26.3 must be served on every party and takes effect only when it is served. If the order is not served by the court, the solicitor or person serving the order must file proof of service.

Scope—A solicitor's retainer is usually an entire contract to conduct or defend the action to the end. See, however, *Cawdrey Kaye Fireman & Taylor v Minkin* [2012] EWCA Civ 546. Whether it has determined is a matter of fact. It will usually continue until one of the following occurs: the client discharges the solicitor; the solicitor discharges himself; death (but not necessarily) (*Donsland Limited v Van Hoogstraten* [2002] EWCA Civ 253); incapacity of the party; a change in the solicitor's firm; the final conclusion of the case or matter. The retainer is subject to implied terms allowing the solicitor to withdraw for good cause, e g where the client fails to provide a reasonable sum of money for disbursements (Solicitors Act 1974, s 65(2)) and upon reasonable notice (*Cawdrey Kaye Fireman & Taylor v Minkin*, above). As to the scope of the retainer, see *Inventors Friend Limited v Leathes Prior* [2011] EWHC 711 (QB) (fixed-fee legal advice) and *Minkin v Landsberg* [2015] EWCA Civ 1152 (limited retainer: unbundled legal services). The client may end the retainer at any time. If the former client or his new solicitor has not given notice of change under FPR 2010, r 26.2, the solicitor whose retainer has determined should apply promptly for an order under this rule. Where solicitors are plainly unwilling to continue to act due to a serious breakdown in the relationship between themselves and their client, they cannot be forced to continue to act and an order removing them from the record should be made (*UCB Bank plc v Hedworth* [2003] EWCA Civ 705).

An application under this rule is made in accordance with FPR 2010, Pt 18 and must state why the applicant is seeking the order and be supported by evidence (FPR 2010, r 18.7 and FPR PD26A, para 3.2). It is the party who is the respondent to the application. The court may direct other persons to be added as respondents but, unless this occurs, the other parties to the claim must not be served. It is appropriate in a simple case to allow a solicitor to make an application pursuant to r 26.3 in writing. To require attendance would take up court time and lead to an increase in costs (*Miller v Allied Sainif* (UK) (2000) *The Times*, 31 October, ChD). Solicitors wishing to come off the record in a more complex case would be well advised to attend court. If applying in writing, they will still normally have to file evidence that the application notice has been served on the former client (r 26.3(2)(a)).

The court may direct that notice of the application need not be given to the party for whom the solicitor is or was acting e g where that party has changed address without giving the solicitor details. It is useful practice for the order declaring that the solicitor has ceased to act to set out the address for service of the party concerned. A copy of the order must be served on every party to the claim.

An order for costs on the granting of an application that a solicitor cease to act should be unnecessary, as the costs form part of the solicitor's retainer and the order made does not affect the rights of either the solicitor or the client.

26.4 Removal of solicitor who has ceased to act on application of another party

(1) Where –

(a) a solicitor who has acted for a party –

(i) has died;

(ii) has become bankrupt;

(iii) has ceased to practise; or

(iv) cannot be found; and

(b) the party has not given notice of a change of solicitor or notice of intention to act in person as required by rule 26.2(2),

any other party may apply for an order declaring that the solicitor has ceased to be the solicitor acting for the other party in the case.

(2) Where an application is made under this rule, notice of the application must be given to the party to whose solicitor the application relates unless the court directs otherwise.

(3) Where the court makes an order made under this rule, a court officer will serve a copy of the order on every other party to the proceedings.

Practice Direction—See generally FPR PD26A, in particular para 4.

Practice Direction 26A – Change of Solicitor

This Practice Direction supplements FPR Part 26

Solicitor acting for a party

1.1 Rule 26.1 states that where the address for service of a party is the business address of his solicitor, the solicitor will be considered to be acting for that party until the provisions of Part 26 have been complied with.

1.2 Subject to rule 26.2(6) (where the certificate of a legally aided person or assisted person is revoked or withdrawn), where a party has changed his solicitor or intends to act in person, the former solicitor will be considered to be the party's solicitor unless or until –

(a) a notice of the change is –

(i) served on every other party (see rule 26.2(2)(a)); and

(ii) filed with the court (see rule 26.2(2)(b)); or

(b) the court makes an order under rule 26.3 and the order is served on the former solicitor and every other party in accordance with directions of the court (see rule 26.2(5)).

1.3 A solicitor appointed to represent a party only as an advocate at a hearing will not be considered to be acting for that party within the meaning of Part 26.

Notice of change of solicitor

2.1 Rule 26.2(1) sets out the circumstances following which a notice of the change must be filed and served.

2.2 A notice of the change giving the last known address of the former assisted person must also be filed and served on every party where, under rule 26.2(6) –

(a) the certificate of a legally aided person or assisted person is revoked or withdrawn; and

(b) the legally aided person or the assisted person wishes either to act in person or appoint another solicitor to act on his behalf.

2.3 Where a solicitor has given notice that he or she acts for a child directly, and an officer of the Service, a Welsh family proceedings officer or the Official Solicitor continues with the permission of the court to have legal representation, notice of that legal representation must be given to the court.

2.4 In addition, where a party or solicitor changes his address for service, a notice of that change should be filed and served on every party.

2.5 A party who, having conducted an application by a solicitor, intends to act in person must give in his notice an address for service that is within the United Kingdom (see rule 6.26).

2.6 The form giving notice of any change is referred to in Practice Direction 5A. The notice should be filed in the court office in which the application is proceeding.

Application for an order that a solicitor has ceased to act

3.1 A solicitor may apply under rule 26.3 for an order declaring that he has ceased to be the solicitor acting for a party.

3.2 The application should be made in accordance with Part 18 and must be supported by evidence (see Part 18 and the Practice Direction 18A). Unless the court directs otherwise the application notice must be served on the party (see rule 26.3(2)).

3.3 An order made under rule 26.3 will be served on every party by the court officer and takes effect when it is served.

Application by another party to remove a solicitor

4.1 Rule 26.4 sets out circumstances in which any other party may apply for an order declaring that a solicitor has ceased to be the solicitor acting for another party in the proceedings.

4.2 The application should be made in accordance with Part 18 and must be supported by evidence. Unless the court directs otherwise the application notice must be served on the party to whose solicitor the application relates.

4.3 An order made under rule 26.4 will be served on every party by the court officer.

New address for service where order made under rules 26.3 or 26.4

5.1 Where the court has made an order under rule 26.3 that a solicitor has ceased to act or under rule 26.4 declaring that a solicitor has ceased to be the solicitor for a party, the party for whom the solicitor was acting must give a new address for service to comply with rule 6.26.

> (Rule 6.26 provides that a party must give an address for service within the United Kingdom, or where a solicitor is acting for a party, an address for service either in the United Kingdom or any other EEA state, at which that party resides or carries on business. Where that party does not have such an address, an address within the United Kingdom must generally be given (see rule 6.26(3) and (4)).
>
> (Until such time as a new address for service is given directions may be needed under rule 6.19.)

PART 27
HEARINGS AND DIRECTIONS APPOINTMENTS

CONTENTS OF THIS PART

Rule		Page
27.1	Application of this Part	1830
27.2	Reasons for a decision: proceedings before a lay justice or justices	1830
27.3	Attendance at hearing or directions appointment	1832
27.4	Proceedings in the absence of a party	1832
27.5	Application to set aside judgment or order following failure to attend	1834
27.6	Court bundles and place of filing of documents and bundles	1834
27.7	Representation of companies or other corporations	1835
27.8	Impounded documents	1835
27.9	Official shorthand note etc of proceedings	1835
27.10	Hearings in private	1835
27.11	Attendance at private hearings	1836

Practice Direction 27A –
Family Proceedings: Court Bundles (Universal Practice to be applied in the High Court and Family Court) 1837

Practice Direction 27B –
Attendance of Media Representatives at Hearings in Family Proceedings (High Court and County Courts) 1843

27.1 Application of this Part

This Part is subject to any enactment, any provision in these rules or a practice direction.

(Rule 27.4(7) makes additional provision in relation to requirements to stay proceedings where the respondent does not appear and a relevant European regulation or international convention applies)

27.2 Reasons for a decision: proceedings before a lay justice or justices

(1) This rule applies to proceedings in the family court before a lay justice or justices.

(2) After a hearing, the court will make its decision as soon as is practicable.

(3) The court must give written reasons for its decision.

(4) Paragraphs (5) and (6) apply where the functions of the court are being performed by –

- (a) two or three lay justices; or
- (b) by a single lay justice in accordance with these rules and Practice Direction 2A.

(5) The justices' clerk must, before the court makes an order or refuses an application or request, make notes of –

- (a) the names of the lay justice or justices constituting the court by which the decision is made; and
- (b) in consultation with the lay justice or justices, the reasons for the court's decision.

(6) The justices' clerk must make a written record of the reasons for the court's decision.

(7) When making an order or refusing an application, the court, or one of the lay justices constituting the court by which the decision is made, will announce its decision and –

- (a) the reasons for that decision; or
- (b) a short explanation of that decision.

(8) Subject to any other rule or practice direction, the court officer will supply a copy of the order and the reasons for the court's decision to the persons referred to in paragraph (9) –

- (a) by close of business on the day when the court announces its decision; or
- (b) where that time is not practicable and the proceedings are on notice, no later than 72 hours from the time when the court announced its decision.

(9) The persons referred to in paragraph (8) are –

- (a) the parties (unless the court directs otherwise);
- (b) any person who has actual care of a child who is the subject of proceedings, or who had such care immediately prior to the making of the order;
- (c) in the case of an emergency protection order and a recovery order, the local authority in whose area the child lives or is found;
- (d) in proceedings to which Part 14 applies –
  - (i) an adoption agency or local authority which has prepared a report on the suitability of the applicant to adopt a child;
  - (ii) a local authority which has prepared a report on the placement of the child for adoption;
- (e) any other person who has requested a copy if the court is satisfied that it is required in connection with an appeal or possible appeal.

(10) *(revoked)*

(Rule 12.16(5) provides for the applicant to serve a section 8 order and an order in emergency proceedings made without notice within 48 hours after the making of the order. Rule 10.6(1) provides for the applicant to serve the order in proceedings under Part 4 of the 1996 Act. Rule 4.1(3)(a) permits the court to extend or shorten the time limit for compliance with any rule. Rule 6.33 provides for other persons to be supplied with copy documents under paragraph (8).)

Amendments—SI 2014/667.

The decision and the reasons for it—The Justices' Clerks' Society and the Magistrates' Association published joint guidance on the giving of justices' reasons in CA 1989 cases in November 2007; see *www.familieslink.co.uk/download/sept07/guidance_on_family_justices%27_reasons.pdf*. Revised guidance in respect of the provision of justices' reasons in uncontested cases was issued in March 2014 following comments made by Pauffley J in *Re NL (Appeal: Interim Care Order: Facts and Reasons)* [2014] 1 FLR 1384, FD (see Part V). Reasons must be given whenever an order is made or an application refused including, for example, interim orders ((*Hampshire County Council v S* [1993] 1 FLR 559, FD), a refusal to shorten a prescribed notice period or to make a without notice order (*Essex CC v F* [1993] 1 FLR 847, FD), the determination of the length of a secure accommodation order (*Re W (A Minor) (Secure Accommodation Order)* [1993] 1 FLR 692, FD), a decision to proceed to determine an application for leave under CA 1989, s 10 without notice and the decision whether to grant such leave (*Re M (Prohibited Steps Order: Application for Leave)* [1993] 1 FLR 275, FD), a refusal to give leave for a child psychiatrist to become involved in the case and to transfer the matter to the High Court (*London Borough of Croydon v R* [1997] 2 FLR 675, FD, where there was particular need to give reasons as the application for directions had been referred to the court by the justices' clerk). For consideration of whether there may be a class of quite exceptional cases in which reasons need not be given, see *T v W (Contact: Reasons for Refusing Leave)* [1996] 2 FLR 473, FD and see *London Borough of Croydon v R* (above) in which Wall J, not wishing to place an intolerable burden on justices, expressed his view that not every order for directions requires reasons to be given but that where the issue is contentious and requires a ruling from the court after full argument, it is good practice for succinct reasons to be given.

Although the rules require the decision to be made as soon as practicable (r 27.2(2), and see *Devon CC v S and Others* [1992] 2 FLR 244, FD), it can be better in certain circumstances (eg where the hearing lasts beyond normal hours) to adjourn the making of the order or the giving of the decision until the following court day or the earliest possible other date, on which subsequent occasion only one justice need return to court to state the decision, findings of fact and reasons (see *Oxfordshire County Council v R* [1992] 1 FLR 648, FD; *Hampshire CC v S* [1993] 1 FLR 559, FD). What is not permissible, however, is for the justices to announce their order before they have finished writing down their reasons (or by virtue of r 27.2(7(b), a short explanation of their decision) and then to give reasons and announce their findings on the following day (*Re W (A Minor) (Contact)* [1994] 1 FLR 843, FD). Justices must either complete their written reasons or draft a short explanation before announcing their decision and in any event provide a full copy of the written reasons within 72 hours (r 27.2(7),(8)). The findings of fact and reasons stated in court must tally with those recorded in writing (*S v S (Children: Periodical Payments)* [1993] 1 FLR 606, FD).

Failure to observe the requirements of r 27.2(5)–(7) can vitiate the decision of the justices and lead to their orders being set aside on appeal (*Re W (A Minor) (Contact)*, above). There are a number of cases in which the higher courts have given guidance as to how it should be done. The Court of Appeal in *Re B (Procedure: Family Proceedings Court)* [1993] Fam Law 209, CA stated that it was helpful if the justices first set out the relevant facts in chronological order or under convenient headings, making it clear what was in dispute and what was not, and then make findings on any disputed matters. It was also said to be helpful if, in giving reasons for their decision, the justices mentioned the factors that they had brought into the balancing exercise, even if obvious. This was not to say that every point, however trivial, had to be dealt with, but an appellate court would need to know the basis for the decision. On the format of reasons, see *Re D (Contact: Interim Order)* [1995] 1 FLR 495, FD as to the need to deal with matters set out in CA 1989. If, in the case of an interim application, the justices decide that they cannot make findings of fact and deliberately refrain from detailed investigation as part of the overall strategy of reaching a final conclusion only on the final hearing, this is a reasoning process that should be explained in their reasons (*F v R (Contact: Justices' Reasons)* [1995] 1 FLR 227, FD). Where the justices give inadequate reasons for their decision, they cannot retrieve the situation by sending extended reasons to the appeal court on receiving notice of appeal (see *Hillingdon LBC v H* [1992] 2 FLR 372, FD) or by corresponding with the appellate court (*Re F (A Minor) (Care Order: Withdrawal of Application)* [1993] 2 FLR 9, FD). It is also inappropriate for the justices to solicit general guidance from, or to communicate with, the appellate court, particularly in the submission of considerations that they believed justified their determination; anything that supported the justices' order must be contained within their stated reasons and it was not open to them further to reason their conclusion in response to the knowledge that there was an appeal (*Re WB (Residence Orders)* [1995] 2 FLR 1023, FD). The Court of Appeal commented in *Re M (Section 94 Appeals)* [1995] 1 FLR 546, CA that an appellate court might be less ready to assume that magistrates have taken relevant factors into account if they have not referred to them in their reasons than it might in the case of an experienced judge, but that the justices' reasons are not intended to be a judgment and that an appellate court should be slow to interfere with magistrates' decisions as it would be to interfere with any other tribunal charged with the duty to make decisions in the exercise of discretion. See also *Re C (Care or Supervision Order)* [1999] 2 FLR 621, FD, where Sir Stephen Brown P upheld the decision of the magistrates to follow the recommendation of the children's guardian to make a care order instead of the supervision order sought by the local authority, saying that the case revolved around the exercise of discretion by the magistrates. In *Re P (Contact: Discretion)* [1998] 2 FLR 696, FD it was recognised that the requirement that a decision to make or refuse an order could only be announced in court after the findings and reasons in support had been recorded in writing was an onerous one and it was said to be important that the appellate court did not take too pedantic an approach to a document produced in such circumstances. The key issues for the appellate court were whether the legal principles had been correctly identified, whether the material factors, particularly any under s 1(3), had been afforded sufficient weight in the balancing exercise and whether the decision was plainly wrong. For a case in which the court, dealing with an appeal in which the magistrates had failed to give adequate reasons, filled in the gaps and upheld the magistrates' decision, see *Oxfordshire CC v R* [1997] Fam Law 828, FD.

The June 1997 *CAAC Handbook of Best Practice in Children Act Cases*, App A, item X contains detailed guidance compiled by Mr Justice Cazalet as to the preparation of justices' written findings and reasons (see Part V).

Announcing the decision (r 27.2(7))—In *Oxfordshire CC v S* [2004] 1 FLR 426, FD, it was not clear from the justices' reasons that they had correctly applied the CA 1989, s 38 test relevant to the making of an interim care order. Munby J held that there is no legal obligation on justices to read out verbatim the whole of the document in which their reasons and findings of fact have been recorded. Rule 27.2(7)(b) provides that magistrates can choose to announce the decision and to summarise their written reasons by reading out a short explanation only. Consequently, Munby J's guidance remains valid and of particular relevance in such circumstances. Although the decision is not likely to be invalidated by a mere slip of the tongue, care should be taken that any summary does not involve a material or significant departure or deviation from the written document. Any such departure or deviation of substance rather than mere form is almost bound to lead to the decision being quashed. However, any litigant seeking to demonstrate that any such material or significant departure or deviation from the written reasons had taken place bears a heavy evidential burden and, absent admission or clear evidence, the court will be slow to find that justices have erred in this way.

Departing from an expert's opinion—The court is entitled to depart from the opinion of an expert although, if it does so, it must explain its reasons (*Re B (Care: Expert Witnesses)* [1996] 1 FLR 667, CA). Where there is a conflict between experts, the court must address and resolve that conflict insofar as it is relevant to the issues before the court and it is entitled to give greater weight to the opinion of one expert as against that of another, provided that proper reasons are given (*Re J (Expert Evidence: Hearsay)* [1999] 2 FLR 661, FD). It is unusual for lay justices to hear a case involving a real possibility of conflict of expert evidence (see the Schedule to the President's Guidance of 22 April 2014 on *Allocation and Gatekeeping for Care, Supervision and other proceedings under Part IV of the Children Act 1989 (Public Law)* (set out in Part V).

'a copy of the order' (r 27.2(8))—The order has to be made on whichever of the prescribed forms is appropriate to the case (see PD5A) or, in default of an appropriate form, in writing. Where the order is by consent, it should say so (see *Chandless-Chandless v Nicholson* [1942] 2 KB 321, CA). Where the justices make no order on the application, there should still be a written order to that effect (*S v R (Parental Responsibility)* [1993] 1 FCR 331, FD). If appropriate, it is possible for the order to recite the intention of the parties at the time of the order, as a preliminary to stating that the court considered an order unnecessary (*M v M (Defined Contact Application)* [1998] 2 FLR 244, FD, in which there was an order of 'no order as to defined contact' but with the parents' joint wishes and expectations set out in the preamble). The justices should give careful consideration to the practical effect of making no order (*D v D (Application for Contact)* [1994] 1 FCR 694, FD). As to the possibility of recording the agreement of a parent to seek treatment as a preamble to a supervision order, see *Re B (Supervision Order: Parental Undertaking)* [1996] 1 FLR 676, CA.

27.3 Attendance at hearing or directions appointment

Unless the court directs otherwise, a party shall attend a hearing or directions appointment of which that party has been given notice.

'a party shall attend'—It is a fundamental aspect of family procedure that, whatever aspect is before the court, the parties should be present as well as their legal advisers. This is an instance of the parties' duty under FPR 2010, r 1.3 to help the court further the overriding objective. If a party fails to attend, see FPR 2010, r 27.4.

'has been given notice'—Service is dealt with in FPR 2010, Pt 6. Service on a party's solicitor is, of course, good service on the party. But whereas 'service' has a technical meaning, 'notice' does not.

'unless the court directs otherwise'—The court has a complete discretion as to the circumstances in which to dispense with the attendance of a party and can do so either on request of a party or of its own initiative. For example, where a court is fixing the next appointment at the conclusion of a directions hearing it could, in special circumstances, excuse a party from attending that appointment.

27.4 Proceedings in the absence of a party

(1) Proceedings or any part of them shall take place in the absence of any party, including a party who is a child, if –

(a) the court considers it in the interests of the party, having regard to the matters to be discussed or the evidence likely to be given; and

(b) the party is represented by a children's guardian or solicitor,

and when considering the interests of a child under sub-paragraph (a) the court shall give the children's guardian, the solicitor for the child and, if of sufficient understanding and the court thinks it appropriate, the child, an opportunity to make representations.

(2) Subject to paragraph (3), where at the time and place appointed for a hearing or directions appointment the applicant appears but one or more of the respondents do not, the court may proceed with the hearing or appointment.

(3) The court shall not begin to hear an application in the absence of a respondent unless –

(a) it is proved to the satisfaction of the court that the respondent received reasonable notice of the date of the hearing; or

(b) the court is satisfied that the circumstances of the case justify proceeding with the hearing.

(4) Where, at the time and place appointed for a hearing or directions appointment, one or more of the respondents appear but the applicant does not, the court may refuse the application or, if sufficient evidence has previously been received, proceed in the absence of the applicant.

(5) Where, at the time and place appointed for a hearing or directions appointment, neither the applicant nor any respondent appears, the court may refuse the application.

(6) Paragraphs (2) to (5) do not apply to a hearing to which paragraphs (5) to (8) of rule 12.14 do not apply by virtue of paragraph (9) of that rule.

(7) Nothing in this rule affects any provision of a European regulation or international convention by which the United Kingdom is bound which requires a court to stay proceedings where a respondent in another State has not been adequately served with proceedings in accordance with the requirements of that regulation or convention.

'proceedings ... shall take place in the absence of a party ... if'—Parties are under a duty to attend all hearings unless the court directs otherwise (see FPR 2010, r 27.3). But this raises the question 'what if a party does not attend?' and that question is answered by r 27.4. If a child is also a party then the basic rule in r 27.3 applies to that child too but note the specific provisions in r 27.4(1), especially r 27.4(1)(b).

'the party is represented by a children's guardian or solicitor'—This rule (which merely reproduces the former r 4.16(2)(b)) is worded oddly. The words 'is represented' must surely mean 'is represented at the hearing'. But the rule makes no mention of representation by counsel. It is submitted that if a child who is a party is not present but is represented by fully instructed counsel that is sufficient to enable the court to proceed as the court must give effect to the overriding objective when it interprets any rule (FPR 2010, r 1.2). In *Re AS (Secure Accommodation Order)* [1999] 1 FLR 103, FD, when considering the requirement for legal representation of a child in secure accommodation proceedings, the court held that this involves the taking of instructions. Thus it was not sufficient for a child to be 'represented' by solicitor and counsel who had not been able to take instructions as the child had not been informed of the hearing.

Child of sufficient understanding to make representations—Rule 27.4 is one of many situations when the court is required to assess whether a child has 'sufficient understanding' to make representations in person rather than just through the guardian or legal representative. No criteria are laid down as much turns on not only the nature of the proceedings but also of the particular application before the court. Both the guardian and legal representative will be expected to assist the court in making the assessment.

Proceeding in the absence of the respondent—Paras (2) and (3) of r 27.4 must be read together. The rule refers to 'reasonable notice' rather than 'service' and this can take many forms. Where it is the court's obligation to give notice, proof will be on the court file. Otherwise the applicant will have to prove that the respondent has had reasonable notice. Clearly formal proof of service suffices but it would be sufficient also if the respondent was present at the previous hearing when the new date was fixed. Alternatively, for example, the respondent may have written to the court about the hearing or told the applicant that he will not be attending. Note that for certain applications (see for example FPR 2010, Pt 10 dealing with non-molestation orders etc) a particular rule requires a minimum period of notice and that, unless the court abridges time for service, anything less than the prescribed minimum would not be 'reasonable notice'.

Proceeding in the absence of the applicant—If the applicant does not attend, r 27.4(4) refers only to the court being able to 'refuse the application' or, alternatively, proceeding with it in the absence of the applicant if 'sufficient evidence has previously been received'. However, the use of the word 'may' clearly indicates that the court could instead adjourn to another day if it considered that to be more appropriate. The court will be reluctant to waste the time set aside to hear the application and would try to proceed if possible although the circumstances in which it could do so are prescribed by the rule: but to refuse an application which on the face of it has merit (*aliter* if it does not) may be draconian and lead to yet more court time being taken up by an application under r 27.5. Therefore, there will inevitably be occasions when the better course is to adjourn. However, if the applicant fails to attend on a second occasion the court would no doubt refuse the application.

'sufficient evidence has previously been received'—The best example of the court being able to proceed under r 27.4(4) is the part-heard case where the applicant's case has been closed or, at least, the applicant's own evidence has been concluded. The rule refers to 'evidence' and a witness statement is not evidence until the maker swears or affirms to it (before that it is merely an advance indication of the evidence which the maker intends to give).

Where neither applicant nor respondent attends—Rule 27.4(5) gives the court a discretion to refuse the application. The use of 'may' indicates that the court could adjourn and the court may prefer to do so if, for example, there is a suspicion that inappropriate pressure has been applied to keep a party away. However, where neither attends generally the application would be refused leaving either party to apply under FPR 2010, r 27.5.

Proceedings relating to children (except parental order proceedings and proceedings for applications in adoption, placement and related proceedings)—This sub-heading is the title to FPR 2010, Pt 12. FPR 2010, Rule 12.14 is titled 'Attendance at hearings' and thus needs to be read in conjunction with Pt 27 in proceedings relating to children. Rule 12.14 is expressly referred to in r 27.4(6). Paragraph (9) of r 12.14 is concerned with the enforcement of child arrangements orders.

27.5 Application to set aside judgment or order following failure to attend

(1) Where a party does not attend a hearing or directions appointment and the court gives judgment or makes an order against him, the party who failed to attend may apply for the judgment or order to be set aside(GL).

(2) An application under paragraph (1) must be supported by evidence.

(3) Where an application is made under paragraph (1), the court may grant the application only if the applicant –

- (a) acted promptly on finding out that the court had exercised its power to enter judgment or make an order against the applicant;
- (b) had a good reason for not attending the hearing or directions appointment; and
- (c) has a reasonable prospect of success at the hearing or directions appointment.

(4) *(revoked)*

Amendments—SI 2013/3204.

'set aside judgment or order'—Rule 27.5 enables a party who failed to attend a hearing or directions appointment to apply to have the judgment or order to be set aside. This provision had no equivalent in the former rules. It is clearly based on CPR 1998, r 39.3 and thus cases on that rule will aid interpretation. All cases cited in commentary on r 27.5 are cases on CPR 1998, r 39.3. It remains to be seen whether the different nature of family proceedings requires a more generous approach.

'must be supported by evidence'—At the very least a witness statement giving a full explanation and satisfying the strict requirements of r 27.5(3) will be necessary.

'the court may grant the application only'—The three criteria in r 27.5(3) have to be met. The court has no residual discretion (*Regency Rolls Ltd v Carnall* [2000] EWCA Civ 379).

'acted promptly'—'I would construe "promptly" here to require, not that an applicant has been guilty of no needless delay whatever, but rather that he has acted with all reasonable celerity in the circumstances' per Simon Brown LJ in *Regency Rolls Ltd v Carnall* [2000] EWCA Civ 379 where an application made over four weeks after the hearing was dismissed because the applicant had not acted promptly.

'had a good reason for not attending'—The court has to consider each application in the light of all relevant factors for non-attendance and, looking at the matter in the round, decide whether the reasons are sufficient to exercise the discretion to set aside (*Brazil v Brazil* [2002] EWCA Civ 1135). The court must be satisfied that the reason is genuine and honest but that, of itself, does not mean that the reason is 'good'. There are no fixed reasons that are 'good' or 'bad' and an over analytical approach is inconsistent with the overriding objective. The mere assertion that a party was unaware of the hearing is unlikely to be sufficient of itself. The court will enquire why this was so. Once a party is aware that proceedings are underway communications from the court and the other party are to be expected. A party who knows of proceedings is not entitled as of right to have an order set aside simply because he was not aware of a new hearing date (*Hackney London Borough Council v Driscoll* [2003] 1 WLR 2602, CA).

'has a reasonable prospect of success'—The reasonable prospect of success condition of r 27.5(3)(c) is just as important as the other two conditions and does not offend any fundamental principle of justice or any principle of the ECHR (see both *Hackney London Borough Council v Driscoll* and *Regency Rolls Ltd v Carnall* above).

27.6 Court bundles and place of filing of documents and bundles

(1) The provisions of Practice Direction 27A must be followed for the preparation of court bundles and for other related matters in respect of hearings and directions appointments.

(2), (3) *(revoked)*

Amendments—SI 2013/3204.

Trial bundles—It 'is standard practice for the parties in a care case to receive a contents list from which to make up their own bundle for court rather than for the local authority to provide a copy of the bundle for each party', per Black LJ in *Re J (Appeal from Care Order)* [2014] 2 FLR 1351, CA, at [60].

27.7 Representation of companies or other corporations

A company or other corporation may be represented at a hearing or directions appointment by an employee if –

(a) the employee has been authorised by the company or corporation to appear at the hearing or directions appointment on its behalf; and

(b) the court gives permission.

27.8 Impounded documents

(1) Documents impounded by order of the court must not be released from the custody of the court except in compliance with –

(a) a court order; or

(b) a written request made by a Law Officer or the Director of Public Prosecutions.

(2) A document released from the custody of the court under paragraph (1)(b) must be released into the custody of the person who requested it.

(3) Documents impounded by order of the court, while in the custody of the court, may not be inspected except by a person authorised to do so by a court order.

'impounded by order' (r 27.8(1))—The intent of this rule is to ensure only that while documents in a case are in the custody of the court they should not leave its custody, save by court order or formal request under this rule.

27.9 Official shorthand note etc of proceedings

(1) Unless the judge directs otherwise, an official shorthand note will be taken at the hearing in open court of proceedings pending in the High Court.

(2) An official shorthand note may be taken of any other proceedings before a judge if directions for the taking of such a note are given by the Lord Chancellor.

(3) The shorthand writer will sign the note and certify it to be a correct shorthand note of the proceedings and will retain the note unless directed by the district judge to forward it to the court.

(4) On being so directed, the shorthand writer will furnish the court with a transcript of the whole or such part of the shorthand note as may be directed.

(5) Any party, any person who has intervened in the proceedings, the Queen's Proctor or, where a declaration of parentage has been made under section 55A of the 1986 Act, the Registrar General is entitled to require from the shorthand writer a transcript of the shorthand note, and the shorthand writer will, at the request of any person so entitled, supply that person with a transcript of the whole or any part of the note on payment of the shorthand writer's charges authorised by any scheme in force providing for the taking of official shorthand notes of legal proceedings.

(6) Save as permitted by this rule, the shorthand writer will not, without the permission of the court, furnish the shorthand note or a transcript of the whole or any part of it to anyone.

(7) In these rules, references to a shorthand note include references to a record of the proceedings made by mechanical means and in relation to such a record references to the shorthand writer include the person responsible for transcribing the record.

27.10 Hearings in private

(1) Proceedings to which these rules apply will be held in private, except –

(a) where these rules or any other enactment provide otherwise;

(b) subject to any enactment, where the court directs otherwise.

(2) For the purposes of these rules, a reference to proceedings held 'in private' means proceedings at which the general public have no right to be present.

Hearings in private—In *Luckwell v Limata* [2014] 2 FLR 168, FD, Holman J held that this rule created no presumption in favour of family matters being heard in private. In *DL v SL* [2015] EWHC 2621 (Fam), however, Mostyn J came to a diametrically opposed conclusion. On balance, it is suggested that the majority of family judges favour the latter analysis and approach.

27.11 Attendance at private hearings

(1) This rule applies when proceedings are held in private, except in relation to –

(a) hearings conducted for the purpose of judicially assisted conciliation or negotiation;
(b) proceedings to which the following provisions apply –
(i) Part 13 (proceedings under section 54 of the Human Fertilisation and Embryology Act 2008);
(ii) Part 14 (procedure for applications in adoption, placement and related proceedings); and
(iii) any proceedings identified in a practice direction as being excepted from this rule.

(2) When this rule applies, no person shall be present during any hearing other than –

(a) an officer of the court;
(b) a party to the proceedings;
(c) a litigation friend for any party, or legal representative instructed to act on that party's behalf;
(d) an officer of the service or Welsh family proceedings officer;
(e) a witness;
(f) duly accredited representatives of news gathering and reporting organisations; and
(g) any other person whom the court permits to be present.

(3) At any stage of the proceedings the court may direct that persons within paragraph (2)(f) shall not attend the proceedings or any part of them, where satisfied that –

(a) this is necessary –
(i) in the interests of any child concerned in, or connected with, the proceedings;
(ii) for the safety or protection of a party, a witness in the proceedings, or a person connected with such a party or witness; or
(iii) for the orderly conduct of the proceedings; or
(b) justice will otherwise be impeded or prejudiced.

(4) The court may exercise the power in paragraph (3) of its own initiative or pursuant to representations made by any of the persons listed in paragraph (5), and in either case having given to any person within paragraph (2)(f) who is in attendance an opportunity to make representations.

(5) At any stage of the proceedings, the following persons may make representations to the court regarding restricting the attendance of persons within paragraph (2)(f) in accordance with paragraph (3) –

(a) a party to the proceedings;
(b) any witness in the proceedings;
(c) where appointed, any children's guardian;
(d) where appointed, an officer of the service or Welsh family proceedings officer, on behalf of the child the subject of the proceedings;
(e) the child, if of sufficient age and understanding.

(6) This rule does not affect any power of the court to direct that witnesses shall be excluded until they are called for examination.

(7) In this rule 'duly accredited' refers to accreditation in accordance with any administrative scheme for the time being approved for the purposes of this rule by the Lord Chancellor.

General note—Reference should be made to the *President's Guidance in Relation to Applications Consequent Upon the Attendance of the Media in Family Proceedings* (issued 22 April 2009; see Part V) and FPR PD27B. This rule provides for the attendance of persons, especially particular members of the press, at family proceedings heard 'in private' (r 27.11(2)). It gives effect, for proceedings in the Family Court, to policy changes arising out of 'Confidence and Confidentiality: Openness in Family Courts – A New Approach' (Ministry of Justice, Cm 7131) and outlined in the response to Family Justice in View (Cm 7502). The court may direct the exclusion of the media from all or a part of the proceedings for one of the reasons in r 27.11(3).

'Duly accredited' media representatives—Only 'duly accredited' representatives of the media are entitled to attend family proceedings. The production of a card issued by the UK Press Card Authority provides sufficient evidence of accreditation. An unaccredited representative of the media may nevertheless be permitted to attend the hearing at the court's discretion: r 27.11(2)(g).

There are limited grounds on which the court may direct that representatives of the media shall not attend the proceedings: r 27.11(3). Before exercising its power to exclude the media the court should give a party and any representatives of the media in attendance the opportunity to make representations: r 27.11(4). The *President's Guidance* (see above) sets out the principled approach courts should adopt in relation to applications under this rule: paras 20–22.

Confidentiality—The provisions permitting the attendance of the media at family proceedings do not affect or alter the statutory provisions and the rules prohibiting the publication of information relating to family proceedings: in particular AJA 1960, s 12.

'proceedings held "in private"' (r 27.11(1))— This means proceedings at which the general public have no right to be present.

'general public … no right to be present' (r 27.11(1))—While the general public may not attend 'in private' hearings, certain individuals, as listed in r 27.11(2), are entitled to be in court, including '(f) duly accredited' members of the press and '(g) any other person whom the court permits to be present'. The court appears to have an unfettered discretion as to those other persons whom it may permit to be present at a hearing held in private (which may include unaccredited members of the media: para 4.3 of FPR PD27B).

However, the power to direct that members of the media may not attend all or any part of the proceedings is not the exercise of a discretion (references to the exercise of a discretion in FPR PD27B and 27C, paras 3.1 and 5 and in the President's Guidance of 22 April 2009, para 10, are a misnomer). The court may only make a direction to exclude the media if one or more of the criteria set out in r 27.11(3) is satisfied. The burden of satisfying the court that one of the relevant criteria is satisfied rests on the party who seeks the direction to exclude the media.

The grounds for exclusion are –

(a) it is necessary (i) in the interests of any child concerned with or connected with the proceedings; (ii) for the safety or protection of a party, a witness or a person connected with a party or a witness; or (iii) for the orderly conduct of the proceedings; or
(b) justice will otherwise be impeded or prejudiced.

The President observed that where the Court has a duty to apply a test of necessity in relation to a series of questions as to legitimacy and proportionality, the duty of the Court is to proceed though the balancing exercise making a value judgment as to the conflicts that arise rather than to regard the matter simply as an exercise of discretion as between two equally legitimate courses. The court must balance the Art 8 rights of the children, the parties and of any witnesses (which may be competing) against the Art 10 rights of the media: *Re Child X (Residence and Contact – Rights of Media Attendance – FPR 10.28(4))* [2009] 2 FLR 1467, FD, at [51]–[58].

Reasons for exclusion—Reasons for exclusion should be given. No provision is made in the rules for the media to seek a review or to appeal a decision to exclude them from proceedings and there is as yet no authoritative guidance on the matter. It is suggested that the media will be entitled to seek permission to appeal against direction made to exclude them: it is unlikely that the media would be limited to seeking a judicial review or that that would be an appropriate route of challenge.

'may make representations to the court' (r 27.11(4))—That is to say, there is no need for formal application (and see FPR PD27A and FPR PD27B, para 6, especially 6.2). An application to exclude can be made at 'any stage' of proceedings: r 27.11(3).

Accredited representative—See r 27.11(7).

Statutory restrictions on publication—The provisions restricting the publication of information relating to proceedings, principally AJA 1960, s 12, and CA 1989, s 97(2), are unaffected by this rule.

Court documents—The provisions of this rule do not entitle media representatives to receive or peruse court documents referred to in the course of evidence, submissions or judgment without the permission of the court or otherwise in accordance with FPR 2010, rr 12.73–12.75 and FPR PD12G (rules relating to disclosure to third parties).

Practice Direction 27A – Family Proceedings: Court Bundles (Universal Practice to be applied in the High Court and Family Court)

This Practice Direction supplements FPR Part 27

Note 1—PD27A is applied in public law proceedings in the High Court with certain adjustments as made by FPR PD12A, para 25.2.

Note 2—In *Re X and Y (Bundles)* [2008] 2 FLR 2053, FD, Munby J issued a stern warning in open court to all practitioners, pointing out that far too often the requirements of PD27A are not observed and that this is unacceptable. Orders for costs can be made against either the party in default or against the defaulting lawyers (see para 12 of the PD). Furthermore, he warned that in particularly flagrant cases, defaulters may be publicly identified in open court. In *Re L (Procedure: Bundles: Translation)* [2015] 1 FLR 1417, FD, the President warned practitioners that the Family Division and the Family Court had had enough of failures to comply with PD27A and that from now on defaulters could expect to be exposed to sanctions, including public condemnation, the disallowance of fees or suffer the sanction meted out in *Seagrove v Sullivan* [2015]

2 FLR 602, FD, where the parties were told to take away a non-compliant bundle and produce a compliant bundle the following day. See **Bundles and other particular matters** under r 12.12.

Note 3—See *Re B (Litigants In Person: Timely Service of Documents)* [2016] EWHC 2365 (Fam) for general guidance about the service of documents on litigants in person. In family proceedings, the documents in PD27A should be served on litigants in person at least 3 days before the final hearing. The court should also consider directing that key documents be served with a translation where the litigant does not speak English, or adjourning the hearing where late service could cause genuine unfairness.

Note 4—With effect from 1 January 2016, case management orders have routinely contained the requirement that a party filing a hearing bundle has attached a certificate of compliance with PD27A in the form set out by the court. The certificate must be signed by the solicitor with overall responsibility for the case.

1.1 The President of the Family Division has issued this practice direction to achieve consistency across the country in the Family Court and the Family Division of the High Court in the preparation of court bundles and in respect of other related matters.

Application of the practice direction

2.1 Except as specified in paragraph 2.4, and subject to specific directions given in any particular case, the following practice applies to:

(a) all hearings before a judge sitting in the Family Division of the High Court wherever the court may be sitting; and
(b) all hearings in the Family Court.

2.2 'Hearing' includes all appearances before the court, whether with or without notice to other parties and whether for directions or for substantive relief.

2.3 This practice direction applies whether a bundle is being lodged for the first time or is being re-lodged for a further hearing (see paragraph 9.2).

2.4 This practice direction does not apply to the hearing of any urgent application if and to the extent that it is impossible to comply with it.

Responsibility for the preparation of the bundle

3.1 A bundle for the use of the court at the hearing shall be provided by the party in the position of applicant at the hearing (or, if there are cross-applications, by the party whose application was first in time) or, if that person is a litigant in person, by the first listed respondent who is not a litigant in person. Where all the parties are litigants in person none of them shall, unless the court otherwise directs, be obliged to provide a bundle, but any bundle which they choose to lodge must be prepared and lodged so as to comply with this practice direction.

3.2 The party preparing the bundle shall paginate it using Arabic numbering throughout. If possible the contents of the bundle shall be agreed by all parties.

Contents of the bundle

4.1 The bundle shall contain copies of only those documents which are relevant to the hearing and which it is necessary for the court to read or which will actually be referred to during the hearing. In particular, copies of the following classes of documents must not be included in the bundle unless specifically directed by the court:

(a) correspondence (including letters of instruction to experts);
(b) medical records (including hospital, GP and health visitor records);
(c) bank and credit card statements and other financial records;
(d) notes of contact visits;
(e) foster carer logs;
(f) social services files (with the exception of any assessment being relied on by any of the parties);
(g) police disclosure.

This does not prevent the inclusion in the bundle of specific documents which it is necessary for the court to read or which will actually be referred to during the hearing.

4.2 The documents in the bundle shall be arranged in chronological order from the front of the bundle, paginated individually and consecutively (starting with page 1 and using Arabic numbering throughout), indexed and divided into separate sections (each section being separately paginated) as follows:

(a) preliminary documents (see paragraph 4.3) and any other case management documents required by any other practice direction;
(b) applications and orders;
(c) statements and affidavits (which must be dated in the top right corner of the front page) but without exhibiting or duplicating documents referred to in para 4.1;
(d) care plans (where appropriate);
(e) experts' reports and other reports (including those of a guardian, children's guardian or litigation friend); and
(f) other documents, divided into further sections as may be appropriate.

All statements, affidavits, care plans, experts' reports and other reports included in the bundle must be copies of originals which have been signed and dated.

4.3 At the commencement of the bundle there shall be inserted the following documents (the preliminary documents):

(a) an up to date case summary of the background to the hearing confined to those matters which are relevant to the hearing and the management of the case and limited, if practicable, to four A4 pages;
(b) a statement of the issue or issues to be determined (1) at that hearing and (2) at the final hearing;
(c) a position statement by each party including a summary of the order or directions sought by that party (1) at that hearing and (2) at the final hearing;
(d) an up to date chronology, if it is a final hearing or if the summary under (i) is insufficient;
(e) skeleton arguments, if appropriate;
(f) a list of essential reading for that hearing; and
(g) the time estimate (see paragraph 10.1).

Copies of all authorities relied on must be contained in a separate composite bundle agreed between the advocates.

4.4 Each of the preliminary documents shall be as short and succinct as possible and shall state on the front page immediately below the heading the date when it was prepared and the date of the hearing for which it was prepared. Where proceedings relating to a child are being heard by magistrates the summary of the background shall be prepared in anonymised form, omitting the names and identifying information of every person referred to other than the parties' legal representatives, and stating the number of pages contained in the bundle. Identifying information can be contained in all other preliminary documents.

4.5 The summary of the background, statement of issues, chronology, position statement and any skeleton arguments shall be cross-referenced to the relevant pages of the bundle.

4.6 The summary of the background, statement of issues, chronology and reading list shall in the case of a final hearing, and shall so far as practicable in the case of any other hearing, each consist of a single document in a form agreed by all parties. Where the parties disagree as to the content the fact of their disagreement and their differing contentions shall be set out at the appropriate places in the document.

4.7 Where the nature of the hearing is such that a complete bundle of all documents is unnecessary, the bundle (which need not be repaginated) may comprise only those documents necessary for the hearing, but

(a) the summary of the background must commence with a statement that the bundle is limited or incomplete; and
(b) the bundle shall if reasonably practicable be in a form agreed by all parties.

4.8 Where the bundle is re-lodged in accordance with paragraph 9.2, before it is re-lodged:

(a) the bundle shall be updated as appropriate; and
(b) all superseded documents (and in particular all outdated summaries, statements of issues, chronologies, skeleton arguments and similar documents) shall be removed from the bundle.

Format of the bundle

5.1 Unless the court has specifically directed otherwise, being satisfied that such direction is necessary to enable the proceedings to be disposed of justly, the bundle shall be contained in one A4 size ring binder or lever arch file limited to no more than 350 sheets of A4 paper and 350 sides of text.

5.2 All documents in the bundle shall (a) be copied on one side of paper only, unless the court has specifically directed otherwise, and (b) be typed or printed in a font no smaller than 12 point and with 1½ or double spacing.

5.3 The ring binder or lever arch file shall have clearly marked on the front and the spine:

(a) the title and number of the case;
(b) the place where the case has been listed;
(c) the hearing date and time;
(d) if known, the name of the judge hearing the case; and
(e) where in accordance with a direction of the court there is more than one ring binder or lever arch file, a distinguishing letter (A, B, C etc).

Timetable for preparing and lodging the bundle

6.1 The party preparing the bundle shall, whether or not the bundle has been agreed, provide a paginated index to all other parties not less than 4 working days before the hearing.

6.2 Where counsel is to be instructed at any hearing, a paginated bundle shall (if not already in counsel's possession) be delivered to counsel by the person instructing that counsel not less than 3 working days before the hearing.

6.3 The bundle (with the exception of the preliminary documents if and insofar as they are not then available) shall be lodged with the court not less than 2 working days before the hearing, or at such other time as may be specified by the court.

6.4 The preliminary documents shall be lodged with the court no later than 11 am on the day before the hearing and, where the hearing is before a judge of the High Court and the name of the judge is known, shall (with the exception of the authorities, which are to be lodged in hard copy and not sent by email) at the same time be sent by email to the judge's clerk.

Lodging the bundle

7.1 The bundle shall be lodged at the appropriate office. If the bundle is lodged in the wrong place the court may:

(a) treat the bundle as having not been lodged; and
(b) take the steps referred to in paragraph 12.

7.2 Unless the court has given some other direction as to where the bundle in any particular case is to be lodged (for example a direction that the bundle is to be lodged with the judge's clerk) the bundle shall be lodged:

(a) for hearings at the RCJ, in the office of the Clerk of the Rules, 1st Mezzanine (Rm 1M), Queen's Building, Royal Courts of Justice, Strand, London WC2A 2LL (DX 44450 Strand);
(b) for hearings at any other place, at such place as may be designated by the designated family judge responsible for that place and in default of any such designation at the court office for the place where the hearing is to take place.

7.3 Any bundle sent to the court by post, DX or courier shall be clearly addressed to the appropriate office and shall show the date and place of the hearing on the outside of any packaging as well as on the bundle itself.

7.4 Unless the court has given some other direction or paragraph 7.5 applies only one copy of the bundle shall be lodged with the court but the party who is responsible for lodging the bundle shall bring to court at each hearing at which oral evidence may be called a copy of the bundle for use by the witnesses.

7.5 In the case of a hearing listed before a bench of magistrates four copies of the bundle shall be lodged with the court.

7.6 In the case of hearings at the RCJ or at any other place where the designated family judge responsible for that place has directed that this paragraph shall apply, parties shall:

(a) if the bundle or preliminary documents are delivered personally, ensure that they obtain a receipt from the clerk accepting it or them; and
(b) if the bundle or preliminary documents are sent by post or DX, ensure that they obtain proof of posting or despatch.

The receipt (or proof of posting or despatch, as the case may be) shall be brought to court on the day of the hearing and must be produced to the court if requested. If the receipt (or proof of posting or despatch) cannot be produced to the court the judge may: (a) treat the bundle as having not been lodged; and (b) take the steps referred to in paragraph 12.

PART III

Lodging the bundle – additional requirements for Family Division or Family Court cases being heard at the RCJ

8.1 Bundles or preliminary documents delivered after 11 am on the day before the hearing may not be accepted by the Clerk of the Rules and if not shall be delivered:

(a) in a case where the hearing is before a judge of the High Court, directly to the clerk of the judge hearing the case;
(b) in a case where the hearing is before any other judge, to such place as may be specified by the Clerk of the Rules.

8.2 Upon learning before which judge a hearing is to take place, the clerk to counsel, or other advocate, representing the party in the position of applicant shall no later than 3 pm the day before the hearing:

(a) in a case where the hearing is before a judge of the High Court, telephone the clerk of the judge hearing the case;
(b) in a case where the hearing is before any other judge email the Clerk of the Rules at RCJ.familyhighcourt@hmcts.gsi.gov.uk;

to ascertain whether the judge has received the bundle (including the preliminary documents) and, if not, shall organise prompt delivery by the applicant's solicitor.

Removing and re-lodging the bundle

9.1 Unless either the court wishes to retain the bundle or specific alternative arrangements have been agreed with the court, the party responsible for the bundle shall, following completion of the hearing, retrieve the bundle from the court immediately or, if that is not practicable, collect it from the court within 5 working days. Bundles which are not collected in due time are liable to be destroyed without further notice.

9.2 The bundle shall be re-lodged for the next and any further hearings in accordance with the provisions of this practice direction and in a form which complies with para 4.7.

Time estimates

10.1 In every case a time estimate (which shall be inserted at the front of the bundle) shall be prepared which shall so far as practicable be agreed by all parties and shall:

(a) specify separately: (i) the time estimated to be required for judicial pre-reading; and

(ii) the time required for hearing all evidence and submissions; and (iii) the time estimated to be required for preparing and delivering judgment;

(b) be prepared on the basis that before they give evidence all witnesses will have read all relevant filed statements and reports; and

(c) take appropriate account of any additional time likely to be incurred by the use of interpreters or intermediaries.

10.2 Once a case has been listed, any change in time estimates shall be notified immediately by telephone (and then immediately confirmed in writing):

(a) in the case of hearings in the RCJ, to the Clerk of the Rules; and

(b) in the case of hearings elsewhere, to the relevant listing officer.

Taking cases out of the list

11.1 As soon as it becomes known that a hearing will no longer be effective, whether as a result of the parties reaching agreement or for any other reason, the parties and their representatives shall immediately notify the court by telephone and email which shall be confirmed by letter. The letter, which shall wherever possible be a joint letter sent on behalf of all parties with their signatures applied or appended, shall include:

(a) a short background summary of the case;

(b) the written consent of each party who consents and, where a party does not consent, details of the steps which have been taken to obtain that party's consent and, where known, an explanation of why that consent has not been given;

(c) a draft of the order being sought; and

(d) enough information to enable the court to decide (i) whether to take the case out of the list and (ii) whether to make the proposed order.

Penalties for failure to comply with the practice direction

12.1 Failure to comply with any part of this practice direction may result in the judge removing the case from the list or putting the case further back in the list and may also result in a 'wasted costs' order or some other adverse costs order.

Commencement of the practice direction and application of other practice directions

13.1 Subject to paragraph 13.2 this practice direction shall have effect from 22 April 2014.

13.2 Sub-paragraphs (a)–(c) and (e)–(g) of paragraph 4.1 and paragraphs 5.1 and 5.3(e) shall have effect from 31 July 2014. In the meantime paragraphs 5.1 and 5.3(e) shall have effect as if:

(a) paragraph 5.1 read 'The bundle shall be contained in one or more A4 size ring binders or lever arch files (each lever arch file being limited to no more than 350 pages).'; and

(b) in paragraph 5.3(e) the words 'in accordance with a direction of the court' were omitted.

14.1 This practice direction should where appropriate be read in conjunction with the Public Law Outline 2014 (PD12A) and the Child Arrangements Programme 2014 (PD12B). In particular, nothing in this practice direction is to be read as removing or altering any obligation to comply with the requirements of the Public Law Outline 2014 and the Child Arrangements Programme 2014.

Practice Direction 27B – Attendance of Media Representatives at Hearings in Family Proceedings (High Court and County Courts)

This Practice Direction supplements FPR Part 27

1 Introduction

1.1 This Practice Direction supplements rule 27.11 of the Family Procedure Rules 2010 ('FPR 2010') and deals with the right of representatives of news gathering and reporting organisations ('media representatives') to attend at hearings of family proceedings which take place in private subject to the discretion of the court to exclude such representatives from the whole or part of any hearing on specified grounds[1] It takes effect on 27 April 2009.

1 It does not, accordingly, apply where hearings are held in open court where the general public including media representatives may attend as of right, such as committal hearings or the hearing of matrimonial or civil partnership causes.

2 Matters unchanged by the rule

2.1 Rule 27.11(1) contains an express exception in respect of hearings which are conducted for the purpose of judicially assisted conciliation or negotiation and media representatives do not have a right to attend these hearings. Financial Dispute Resolution hearings will come within this exception. First Hearing Dispute Resolution appointments in private law Children Act cases will also come within this exception to the extent that the judge plays an active part in the conciliation process. Where the judge plays no part in the conciliation process or where the conciliation element of a hearing is complete and the judge is adjudicating upon the issues between the parties, media representatives should be permitted to attend, subject to the discretion of the court to exclude them on the specified grounds. Conciliation meetings or negotiation conducted between the parties with the assistance of an officer of the service or a Welsh Family Proceedings officer, and without the presence of the judge, are not 'hearings' within the meaning of this rule and media representatives have no right to attend such appointments.

The exception in rule 27.11(1) does not operate to exclude media representatives from:

- Hearings to consider applications brought under Parts IV and V of the Children Act 1989, including Case Management Hearings, any Further Case Management Hearings and Issues Resolution Hearings
- Hearings relating to findings of fact
- Interim hearings
- Final hearings.

The rights of media representatives to attend such hearings are limited only by the powers of the court to exclude such attendance on the limited grounds and subject to the procedures set out in paragraphs (3)–(5) of rule 27.11.

2.2 During any hearing, courts should consider whether the exception in rule 27.11(1) becomes applicable so that media representatives should be directed to withdraw.

2.3 The provisions of the rules permitting the attendance of media representatives and the disclosure to third parties of information relating to the proceedings do not entitle a media representative to receive or peruse court documents referred to in the course of evidence, submissions or judgment without the permission of the court or otherwise in accordance with Part 12, Chapter 7 of the Family Procedure Rules 2010 and Practice Direction 12G (rules relating to disclosure to third parties). (This is in contrast to the position in civil proceedings, where the court sits in public and where members of the public are entitled to seek copies of certain documents[1]).

1 See *GIO Services Ltd v Liverpool and London Ltd* [1999] 1 WLR 984.

PART III

2.4 The question of attendance of media representatives at hearings in family proceedings to which rule 27.11 and this guidance apply must be distinguished from statutory restrictions on publication and disclosure of information relating to proceedings, which continue to apply and are unaffected by the rule and this guidance.

2.5 The prohibition in section 97(2) of the Children Act 1989, on publishing material intended to or likely to identify a child as being involved in proceedings or the address or school of any such child, is limited to the duration of the proceedings[1]. However, the limitations imposed by section 12 of the Administration of Justice Act 1960 on publication of information relating to certain proceedings in private[2] apply during and after the proceedings. In addition, in proceedings to which s 97(2) of the Children Act 1989 applies the court should continue to consider at the conclusion of the proceedings whether there are any outstanding welfare issues which require a continuation of the protection afforded during the course of the proceedings by that provision.

1 See *Clayton v Clayton* [2006] EWCA Civ 878.
2 In particular proceedings which
(a) relate to the exercise of the inherent jurisdiction of the High Court with respect to minors;
(b) are brought under the Children Act 1989; or
(c) otherwise relate wholly or mainly to the maintenance or upbringing of a minor.

3 *Aims of the guidance*

3.1 This Practice Direction is intended to provide guidance regarding:

- the handling of applications to exclude media representatives from the whole or part of a hearing; and
- the exercise of the court's discretion to exclude media representatives whether upon the court's own motion or any such application.

3.2 While the guidance does not aim to cover all possible eventualities, it should be complied with so far as consistent in all the circumstances with the just determination of the proceedings.

'discretion to exclude'—The reference in para 3.1 to a 'discretion' to exclude the media is a misnomer. The President observed that where the Court has a duty to apply a test of necessity in relation to a series of questions as to legitimacy and proportionality, the duty of the Court is to proceed though the balancing exercise making a value judgment as to the conflicts that arise rather than to regard the matter simply as an exercise of discretion as between two equally legitimate courses: *Re Child X (Residence and Contact: Rights of Media Attendance – FPR r 10.28(4))* [2009] 2 FLR 1467, FD, at [51]–[58].

4 *Identification of media representatives as 'accredited'*

4.1 Media representatives will be expected to carry with them identification sufficient to enable court staff, or if necessary the court itself, to verify that they are 'accredited' representatives of news gathering or reporting organisations within the meaning of the rule.

4.2 By virtue of paragraph (7) of the rule, it is for the Lord Chancellor to approve a scheme which will provide for accreditation. The Lord Chancellor has decided that the scheme operated by the UK Press Card Authority provides sufficient accreditation; a card issued under that scheme will be the expected form of identification, and production of the Card will be both necessary and sufficient to demonstrate accreditation.

4.3 A media representative unable to demonstrate accreditation in accordance with the UK Press Card Authority scheme, so as to be able to attend by virtue of paragraph (2)(f) of the rule, may nevertheless be permitted to attend at the court's discretion under paragraph (2)(g).

5 *Exercise of the discretion to exclude media representatives from all or part of the proceedings*

5.1 The rule anticipates and should be applied on the basis that media representatives have a right to attend family proceedings throughout save and to the extent that the court exercises its discretion to exclude them from the whole or part of any proceedings on one or more of the grounds set out in paragraph (3) of the rule.

5.2 When considering the question of exclusion on any of the grounds set out in paragraph (3) of the rule the court should –

- specifically identify whether the risk to which such ground is directed arises from the mere fact of media presence at the particular hearing or hearings the subject of the application or whether the risk identified can be adequately addressed by exclusion of media representatives from a part only of such hearing or hearings;

- consider whether the reporting or disclosure restrictions which apply by operation of law, or which the court otherwise has power to order will provide sufficient protection to the party on whose behalf the application is made or any of the persons referred to in paragraph (3)(a) of the rule;
- consider the safety of the parties in cases in which the court considers there are particular physical or health risks against which reporting restrictions may be inadequate to afford protection;
- in the case of any vulnerable adult or child who is unrepresented before the court, consider the extent to which the court should of its own motion take steps to protect the welfare of that adult or child.

5.3 Paragraph (3)(a)(iii) of the rule permits exclusion where necessary 'for the orderly conduct of proceedings'. This enables the court to address practical problems presented by media attendance. In particular, it may be difficult or even impossible physically to accommodate all (or indeed any) media representatives who wish to attend a particular hearing on the grounds of the restricted size or layout of the court room in which it is being heard. Court staff will use their best efforts to identify more suitable accommodation in advance of any hearing which appears likely to attract particular media attention, and to move hearings to larger court rooms where possible. However, the court should not be required to adjourn a hearing in order for larger accommodation to be sought where this will involve significant disruption or delay in the proceedings.

5.4 Paragraph (3)(b) of the rule permits exclusion where, unless the media are excluded, justice will be impeded or prejudiced for some reason other than those set out in sub-paragraph (a). Reasons of administrative inconvenience are not sufficient. Examples of circumstances where the impact on justice of continued attendance might be sufficient to necessitate exclusion may include:

- a hearing relating to the parties' finances where the information being considered includes price sensitive information (such as confidential information which could affect the share price of a publicly quoted company); or
- any hearing at which a witness (other than a party) states for credible reasons that he or she will not give evidence in front of media representatives, or where there appears to the court to be a significant risk that a witness will not give full or frank evidence in the presence of media representatives.

5.5 In the event of a decision to exclude media representatives, the court should state brief reasons for the decision.

Note—The reference in the title of this paragraph to a 'discretion' to exclude the media is a misnomer: see *Re Child X* (above).

6 Applications to exclude media representatives from all or part of proceedings

6.1 The court may exclude media representatives on the permitted grounds of its own motion or after hearing representations from the interested persons listed at paragraph (5) of the rule. Where exclusion is proposed, any media representatives who are present are entitled to make representations about that proposal. There is, however, no requirement to adjourn proceedings to enable media representatives who are not present to attend in order to make such representations, and in such a case the court should not adjourn unless satisfied of the necessity to do so having regard to the additional cost and delay which would thereby be caused.

6.2 Applications to exclude media representatives should normally be dealt with as they arise and by way of oral representations, unless the court directs otherwise.

6.3 When media representatives are expected to attend a particular hearing (for example, where a party is encouraging media interest and attendance) and a party intends to apply to the court for the exclusion of the media, that party should, if practicable, give advance notice to the court, to the other parties and (where appointed) any children's guardian, officer of the service or Welsh

Family Proceedings officer, NYAS or other representative of the child of any intention to seek the exclusion of media representatives from all or part of the proceedings. Equally, legal representatives and parties should ensure that witnesses are aware of the right of media representatives to attend and should notify the court at an early stage of the intention of any witness to request the exclusion of media representatives

6.4 Prior notification by the court of a pending application for exclusion will not be given to media interests unless the court so directs. However, where such an application has been made, the applicant must where possible, notify the relevant media organisations [and should do so by means of the Press Association CopyDirect service, following the procedure set out in the Official Solicitor / CAFCASS *Practice Note* dated 18 March 2005][1].

1 The additional words in square brackets were added by the President in *Re Child X (Residence and Contact: Rights of Media Attendance* – FPR r 10.28(4)) [2009] 2 FLR 1467, FD, at [87].

PART 28
COSTS

CONTENTS OF THIS PART

Rule		Page
28.1	Costs	1846
28.2	Application of other rules	1846
28.3	Costs in financial remedy proceedings	1847
	Practice Direction 28A – Costs	1849

Framework of commentary—The main operative parts of costs rules in family proceedings are in CPR 1998, Pt 44 and the main part of the commentary for all civil proceedings (especially in context in family proceedings under FPR 2010) is considered there. In this section, costs in family proceedings in general terms are considered under r 28.2 and specifically to financial remedy proceedings under r 28.3. An issue that is other than in relation to a family remedy will be considered under CPR 1998, Pt 44.

28.1 Costs

The court may at any time make such order as to costs as it thinks just.

SCA 1981, s 51—Section 51(1) of SCA 1981 provides that 'subject to rules of court, costs ... shall be in the discretion of the court'. Rule 28.1 is such a rule.

28.2 Application of other rules

(1) Subject to rule 28.3, Parts 44 (except rules 44.2(2) and (3) and 44.10(2) and (3)), 46 and 47 and rule 45.8 of the CPR apply to costs in proceedings, with the following modifications –

(a) in the definition of 'authorised court officer' in rule 44.1(1), for the words in sub-paragraph (i) substitute 'the family court';

(b) *(revoked)*

(c) in accordance with any provisions in Practice Direction 28A; and

(d) any other necessary modifications.

(2) *(revoked)*

Amendments—SI 2013/530; SI 2013/3204.

Defined terms—'the CPR': r 2.3(1).

'the CPR apply to costs in proceedings' (r 28.2(1))—The effect of incorporation of CPR 1998, Pts 44 (except rr 44.2(2),(3) and 44.10(2),(3)), 46 and 47 and r 45.8 is that costs provisions relevant to family proceedings from CPR 1998 remain applicable, and that, as before, the exclusion of CPR 1998, r 44.2(2) (formerly r 44.3(2)) exempts all family proceedings covered by FPR 2010 from the general rule 'that the unsuccessful party [should pay] the costs of the successful party' (subject to what was said in the Court of Appeal in *Gojkovic v Gojkovic (No 2)* [1991] 2 FLR 233, CA: the court needs to start somewhere and that should be that 'costs follow the event').

Costs in family proceedings—The costs rules under FPR 2010 and CPR 1998 apply as follows:

(1) *Financial remedy proceedings ('no order')* For 'financial remedy proceedings' as defined by FPR 2010,

r 28.3(4)(b) the no order for costs rule at FPR 2010, r 28.3(5) applies, subject to the court being required to 'have regard' to conduct issues in FPR 2010, r 28.3(7).

(2) *Proceedings for a financial remedy ('clean sheet')* Financial remedy proceedings that are outside FPR 2010, r 28.3(4)(b) are not covered by the exemptions from orders for costs in FPR 2010, r 28.3(5). The court has 'a clean sheet' as to what order to make. The applicant for costs and the court must be clear under which heading – 'no order' or 'clean sheet' – the application proceeds and whether the proceedings are 'in', 'in connection with' or 'for' (each preposition makes a difference) financial remedy proceedings, as explained in *Judge v Judge* [2009] 1 FLR 1287, CA, at [51] and in *Baker v Rowe* [2010] 1 FLR 761, CA, at [35]; and see the commentary to r 28.3. Unless the financial remedy application is for a final, first instance, inter partes financial order (as defined by FPR 2010, rr 2.3(1) and 28.3(4)(b)) – as most applications will be – then either (or any) party may apply for, or may be subject to, an order for costs.

(3) *Public law children proceedings* In *Re T (Costs: Care Proceedings: Serious Allegation Not Proved)* [2013] 1 FLR 133, SC, the Supreme Court drew attention to the rarity of orders for costs being made in children cases unless a party's conduct had been reprehensible (*London Borough of Sutton v Davis (Costs) (No 2)* [1994] 2 FLR 569, FD) or that party's stance had been beyond the band of what was reasonable. Costs orders should not be made, for example, because the local authority could afford to pay where grandparents were called upon to clear their name (*Re T*, above) or because a father (who was not legally aided in appellate proceedings) was successful in the Court of Appeal (*Re S (A Child) (Costs: Care Proceedings)* [2015] 2 FLR 208, SC). Exceptionally, an order might be made where a 'best outcome' for the child could be shown by the costs applicant in cases of 'real hardship' to the child's family: 'If the best outcome for the child is to be brought up by her own family, there may be cases where real hardship would be caused if the family had to bear their own costs of achieving that outcome' (at [33]). On the other hand, an order might be made in care proceedings where a parent's reprehensible conduct had caused the court to join a third party as intervenor to answer the parent's allegations (*Re F (Children)* [2016] EWCA Civ 353).

(4) *Hague Convention proceedings* In *SB v MB (Costs in Hague Convention proceedings)* [2014] EWHC 3721 (Fam), Hayden J suggested principles on which the court's discretion should be exercised if costs are to be awarded in Hague Convention proceedings.

(5) *Other children proceedings* Orders for costs in children proceedings generally will be rare (subject to the position of the Official Solicitor referred to below), but the starting point is likely to be *R v R (Costs: Child Case)* [1997] 2 FLR 95, CA (approved by the Supreme Court in passing in *Re T*, above), explained by Staughton LJ as that the judge 'found that the father had behaved unreasonably in the litigation. I do not doubt that Mr R genuinely believes that his arguments are perfectly reasonable. I do not question his good faith, but I am afraid I do agree with the judge that they did not, in reality, represent a reasonable attitude for the father to take'.

(6) *Other family proceedings under FPR 2010* The remainder of family proceedings under FPR 2010 – mostly divorce, civil partnership and other matrimonial causes, declaration applications etc – are covered by the general family proceedings costs principles at (2), above ('clean sheet'). Where the proceedings are parasitic on other proceedings (e g interim applications, appeals and enforcement), those parasitic proceedings will be covered by the 'clean sheet rule', even if other rules (e g FPR 2010, r 28.3(5)) apply to the original decision or main proceedings.

Costs where the Official Solicitor acts for a party—The costs of the Official Solicitor are entirely a matter for the discretion of the court, but a general rule has developed, which is that the Official Solicitor should have half his costs in the absence of special features that override this 'rule' (see *Re D (Costs)* [2012] COPLR 499, COP).

Conduct—In assessment of costs, the court may take into account 'conduct' of the parties (*K v K* [2016] EWHC 2002 (Fam) and see CPR 1998, r 44.2(4)(a),(5)).

28.3 Costs in financial remedy proceedings

(1) This rule applies in relation to financial remedy proceedings.

(2) Rule 44.2(1), (4) and (5) of the CPR do not apply to financial remedy proceedings.

(3) Rules 44.2(6) to (8) and 44.12 of the CPR apply to an order made under this rule as they apply to an order made under rule 44.3 of the CPR.

(4) In this rule –

(a) 'costs' has the same meaning as in rule 44.1(1)(c) of the CPR; and

(b) 'financial remedy proceedings' means proceedings for –

(i) a financial order except an order for maintenance pending suit, an order for maintenance pending outcome of proceedings, an interim periodical payments order, an order for payment in respect of legal services or any other form of interim order for the purposes of rule 9.7(1)(a), (b), (c) and (e);

(ii) an order under Part 3 of the 1984 Act;

(iii) an order under Schedule 7 to the 2004 Act;

(iv) an order under section 10(2) of the 1973 Act;

(v) an order under section 48(2) of the 2004 Act.

(5) Subject to paragraph (6), the general rule in financial remedy proceedings is that the court will not make an order requiring one party to pay the costs of another party.

(6) The court may make an order requiring one party to pay the costs of another party at any stage of the proceedings where it considers it appropriate to do so because of the conduct of a party in relation to the proceedings (whether before or during them).

(7) In deciding what order (if any) to make under paragraph (6), the court must have regard to –

(a) any failure by a party to comply with these rules, any order of the court or any practice direction which the court considers relevant;

(b) any open offer to settle made by a party;

(c) whether it was reasonable for a party to raise, pursue or contest a particular allegation or issue;

(d) the manner in which a party has pursued or responded to the application or a particular allegation or issue;

(e) any other aspect of a party's conduct in relation to proceedings which the court considers relevant; and

(f) the financial effect on the parties of any costs order.

(8) No offer to settle which is not an open offer to settle is admissible at any stage of the proceedings, except as provided by rule 9.17.

(9) For the purposes of this rule 'financial remedy proceedings' do not include an application under rule 9.9A.

Amendments—SI 2013/530; SI 2013/1472; SI 2016/901.

Defined terms—'costs': CPR 1998, r 44.1; 'financial remedy': FPR 2010, r 2.3(1); 'financial remedy proceedings': FPR 2010, r 28.3(4). See also the Table under FPR 2010, r 2.3(1).

'applies in financial remedy proceedings' (r 28.3(1))—Save in the case of 'conduct' (FPR 2010, r 28.3(6)), the rule excludes costs orders in the case of a prescribed list of matrimonial and civil partnership financial proceedings (FPR 2010, r 28.3(4)) and disallows *Calderbank* correspondence as a basis for seeking costs (FPR 2010, r 28.3(8)). In order to be effective to justify costs, all negotiations must be open.

'Financial remedy proceedings' defined—For costs rules purposes 'financial remedy proceedings' is defined differently from proceedings for a 'financial remedy'. The list in FPR 2010, r 28.3(4) specifically excludes orders for interim financial provision, maintenance pending suit, maintenance pending outcome of proceedings and any other form of interim financial provision. It includes only a defined number of financial relief applications specified as family proceedings in the list in r 2.3(1).

Financial remedy proceedings subject to orders for costs—Examples of proceedings which are not financial remedy proceedings for the purposes of FPR 2010, r 28.3:

(1) Applications under CA 1989, Sch 1

(2) Appeals – Under FPR 2010, Pt 30 and (to the Court of Appeal) under CPR 1998, Pt 52

(3) Interim applications – Interim applications, including for periodical payments, are specifically excluded by FPR 2010, r 28.3(4) from its application

(4) Applications to set aside financial remedy orders – In *Judge v Judge* [2009] 1 FLR 1287, CA (and see below) Wilson LJ held that an application to set aside, though not ancillary relief proceedings and therefore outside FPR 1991, r 2.71(1), were 'family proceedings', so that costs did not automatically follow the event (FPR 1991, r 2.71(1)(b)). The position is likely to be the same under FPR 2010, Pt 28, subject to any *Gojkovic* question.

(5) Preliminary issue application – In *KSO v MJO, JMO and PSO* [2009] 1 FLR 1036, FD, especially at [65], Munby J took the view that in the case of preliminary issue applications in the ancillary relief jurisdiction it was appropriate to make an order for costs; see also *Sharbatly v Shagroon* [2014] 2 FLR 209, FD (whether or not issue estoppel applied where a subsequent appeal had overturned the decision below (it did not) and under which regime should a costs order be made: CPR 1998 or FPR 2010: Parker J made an order but considered she need not decide under which regime).

(6) Intervener proceedings – Where a person intervenes in financial remedy proceedings, they will be 'family proceedings' so that FPR 2010, r 28.2(1) applies and CPR 1998, r 44.2 (costs follow the event) cannot formally apply. In any consideration of costs, the success of a party must be an important factor in consideration of an order for costs (*Baker v Rowe* (above)).

(7) Strike out applications (FPR 2010, r 4.4) – See *Wyatt v Vince* [2014] 1 FLR 246, CA.

(8) Relief from sanctions (FPR 2010, r 4.6) – The r 4.6 scheme under FPR 2010 now diverges from that under CPR 1998, r 3.9.

(9) Other applications – Further, the term 'financial remedy proceedings' for the purpose of FPR 2010, r 28.3 does not include the following (and, so far as these are family proceedings covered by FPR 2010, CPR 1998, r 44.2 does not formally apply either), so the 'clean sheet' principle applies:

- all appeals in family proceedings (including to the Court of Appeal);
- applications for restraint of disposal (MCA 1973, s 37(2)(a)) or *Shipman* orders (*Shipman v Shipman* [1991] 1 FLR 250, FD; and see Pt 20 interim remedies));

- enforcement in family proceedings (FPR 2010, Pt 33; *X v Y (Repayment of Overpaid Maintenance)* [2012] EWCC 2 (Fam));
- applications under CA 1989, s 15 and Sch 1.

'Clean sheet' principle: 'for' or 'about' a financial remedy—In *Judge v Judge* [2009] 1 FLR 1287, CA and *Baker v Rowe* [2010] 1 FLR 761, CA, the Court of Appeal had to decide the question: are proceedings 'for a financial remedy' or 'about a financial remedy'. *Judge* concerned an unsuccessful application and appeal by a wife to set aside an order in which she asserted that the order had been vitiated by non-disclosure on the part of the husband. The court considered whether the judge, in dealing with costs, had correctly concluded that the application before him (FPR 2010 terminology is here adopted) was not financial remedy proceedings (as distinct from proceedings for a financial remedy within the meaning of FPR 2010, r 28.3(5)) and that therefore the general rule in CPR 1998, r 44.2 applied; also that the unsuccessful party should pay the costs of the successful party. It was held:

- These were not ancillary relief proceedings (per Wilson LJ at [51]), they were merely in connection with such proceedings. Therefore, FPR 2010, r 28.3(5) (as now is) does not apply.
- Instead, the judge has a clean sheet (per Wilson LJ at [52] and [53]), because FPR 2010, r 28.2(1) disapplies CPR 1998, r 44.2 in family proceedings.

Search for a starting point: *Gojkovic (No 2)*—When a much earlier Court of Appeal considered the same – or a very similar – point (the disapplication for family proceedings of the rule that costs follow the event) under RSC 1965, Ord 62, which applied to the costs appeal then before the court in *Gojkovic v Gojkovic (No 2)* [1991] 2 FLR 233, CA and which in effect was in very similar terms to the present 'clean sheet' rules, Butler-Sloss LJ said:

> '… in the Family Division there still remains the necessity for some starting point. That starting point, in my judgment, is that costs prima facie follow the event (see Cumming-Bruce LJ in *Singer (formerly Sharegin) v Sharegin* [1984] FLR 114, CA, at [119]) but may be displaced much more easily than, and in circumstances which would not apply, in other divisions of the High Court.'

In *Solomon v Solomon and Ors* [2013] EWCA Civ 1095, the Court of Appeal (although refusing permission to appeal) affirmed the correctness of the approach to costs adopted by the court in *Gojkovic (No 2)*, above.

'conduct … in relation to the proceedings' (r 28.3(6),(7))—FPR 2010, r 28.3(7)(d),(e) are taken directly from CPR 1998, r 44.2. Examples of 'conduct' might include (in addition to the list in FPR 2010, r 28.3(7)):

- oppressive enquiry (see, for example, *Hildebrand v Hildebrand* [1992] 1 FLR 244, FD);
- disproportionate pursuit of a particular issue which turns out to of peripheral or of no relevance (and see FPR 1991, r 2.71(5)(c),(d)); and see for example *KSO v MJO, JMO and PSO* [2009] 1 FLR 1036, FD; and, for examples, see costs cases referred to at [76]–[81]; *A v A (No 2) (Ancillary Relief: Costs)* [2008] 1 FLR 1428, FD;
- persistent or unnecessary pursuit of interim applications such as for restraint of disposal (costs can be awarded in any event: see above) or for interim financial provision;
- tardy or non-disclosure of documents or information.

Ability of the intended payer to pay—It is not necessarily an impediment to making an order for costs against a party that they do not have the obvious means to pay (*Joy v Joy-Morancho (Rev 1)* [2015] EWHC 2507 (Fam)).

Costs of a financial relief set aside application—From 3 October 2016, the new r 28.3(9) confirms that an application to set aside under r 9.9A is not proceedings that generally will not attract an order for costs under r 28.3(5). The 'clean sheet' principle explained above applies.

Non-party costs claims—SCA 1981, s 51(3) can, in 'exceptional circumstances' (*Deutsche Bank AG v Sebastian Holdings Inc & Anor* [2016] EWCA Civ 23), give the court power to award costs against a non-party (third party) as explained under CPR 1998, r 46.2.

28.4 *(revoked)*

Practice Direction 28A – Costs

This Practice Direction supplements FPR Part 28

Application and modification of the CPR

1.1 Rule 28.2 provides that subject to rule 28.3 of the FPR, Parts 44 (except rules 44.2(2) and (3) and 44.10(2) and (3)), 46 and 47 and rule 45.8 of the CPR apply to costs in family proceedings with the modifications listed in rule 28.2(1)(a), (c) and (d). Rule 28.2(1)(c) refers to modifications in accordance with this Practice Direction.

1.2–1.3 *(omitted)*

PART III

Application and modification of the Practice Directions supplementing CPR Parts 44 to 47

2.1 For the purpose of proceedings to which these Rules apply, the Practice Directions which supplement Parts 44 to 47 of the CPR will apply, but with the exclusions and modifications explained below to reflect the exclusions and modifications to those Parts of the CPR as they are applied by Part 28 of these Rules.

2.2 Rule 28.2(1) applies, with modifications and certain exceptions, Parts 44 to 47 of the CPR to costs in family proceedings. Rule 28.3, by way of exception, disapplies CPR rule 44.2(1), (4) and (5) in the case of financial remedy proceedings.

2.3 CPR Practice Directions 44 to 47 do not, therefore, apply in their entirety but with the exclusion of Practice Direction 45 and of certain sections of the other Practice Directions, reflecting the non-application of Part 45 and of certain rules of the CPR which those sections of the other Practice Directions supplement.

2.4 CPR Practice Directions 44, 46 and 47 apply as follows –

- to family proceedings including financial remedy proceedings with the exception of paragraphs 3.1 to 3.5 of Practice Direction 44 and paragraphs 7.1 and 9.1 to 9.12 of Practice Direction 46.

2.5 All subsequent editions of CPR Practice Directions 44, 46 and 47 as and when they are published and come into effect shall in the same way extend to all family proceedings.

2.6 CPR Practice Directions 44, 46, 47 and 48 include provisions applicable to proceedings following changes in the manner in which legal services are funded pursuant to the Access to Justice Act 1999. It should be noted that family proceedings (within section 58A(2) of the Courts and Legal Services Act 1990) cannot be the subject of an enforceable conditional fee agreement.

2.7 Paragraph 1.1 of CPR Practice Direction 44 shall be modified as follows –

in the definition of 'counsel' for 'High Court or in the county courts' substitute 'High Court or in the family court.

2.8 Paragraphs 4.1 and 4.2 of CPR Practice Direction 47 shall be modified as follows:

– for paragraphs 4.1 and 4.2 substitute:

'4.1 For the purposes of rule 47.4(1), 'appropriate office' means the court office of the Designated Family Court for the Designated Family Judge area in which the case was being dealt with when the judgment or order was made, or the event occurred which gave rise to the right to assessment, or to which the case has subsequently been moved

(Her Majesty's Courts and Tribunals Service will publish information to enable Designated Family Judge areas and Designated Family Courts to be identified).'

General interpretation of references in CPR

3.1 References in the costs practice direction to 'claimant' and 'defendant' are to be read as references to equivalent terms used in proceedings to which these Rules apply and other terms and expressions used in the costs practice direction shall be similarly treated.

3.2 References in CPR Parts 44 to 47 to other rules or Parts of the CPR shall be read, where there is an equivalent rule or Part in these Rules, to that equivalent rule or Part.

Costs in financial remedy proceedings

4.1 Rule 28.3 relates to the court's power to make costs orders in financial remedy proceedings. For the purposes of rule 28.3, 'financial remedy proceedings' are defined in accordance with rule 28.3(4)(b). That definition, which is more limited than the principal definition in rule 2.3(1), includes:

(a) an application for a financial order, except:

(i) an order for maintenance pending suit or an order for maintenance pending outcome of proceedings;

(ii) an interim periodical payments order or any other form of interim order for the purposes of rule 9.7(1)(a), (b), (c) and (e);

(iii) an order for payment in respect of legal services.

(b) an application for an order under Part 3 of the Matrimonial and Family Proceedings Act 1984 or Schedule 7 to the Civil Partnership Act 2004; and

(c) an application under section 10(2) of the Matrimonial Causes Act 1973 or section 48(2) of the Civil Partnership Act 2004.

4.2 Accordingly, it should be noted that:

(a) while most interim financial applications are excluded from rule 28.3, the rule does apply to an application for an interim variation order within rule 9.7(1)(d),

(b) rule 28.3 does not apply to an application for any of the following financial remedies:

(i) an order under Schedule 1 to the Children Act 1989;

(ii) an order under section 27 of the Matrimonial Causes Act 1973 or Part 9 of Schedule 5 to the Civil Partnership Act 2004;

(iii) an order under section 35 of the Matrimonial Causes Act 1973 or paragraph 69 of Schedule 5 to the Civil Partnership Act 2004; or

(iv) an order under Part 1 of the Domestic Proceedings and Magistrates' Courts Act 1978 or Schedule 6 to the Civil Partnership Act 2004.

4.3 Under rule 28.3 the court only has the power to make a costs order in financial remedy proceedings when this is justified by the litigation conduct of one of the parties. When determining whether and how to exercise this power the court will be required to take into account the list of factors set out in that rule. The court will not be able to take into account any offers to settle expressed to be 'without prejudice' or 'without prejudice save as to costs' in deciding what, if any, costs orders to make.

4.4 In considering the conduct of the parties for the purposes of rule 28.3(6) and (7) (including any open offers to settle), the court will have regard to the obligation of the parties to help the court to further the overriding objective (see rules 1.1 and 1.3) and will take into account the nature, importance and complexity of the issues in the case. This may be of particular significance in applications for variation orders and interim variation orders or other cases where there is a risk of the costs becoming disproportionate to the amounts in dispute.

4.5 Parties who intend to seek a costs order against another party in proceedings to which rule 28.3 applies should ordinarily make this plain in open correspondence or in skeleton arguments before the date of the hearing. In any case where summary assessment of costs awarded under rule 28.3 would be appropriate parties are under an obligation to file a statement of costs in CPR Form N260.

4.6 An order for payment in respect of legal services under section 22ZA of the Matrimonial Causes Act 1973 or paragraph 38A of Part 8 of Schedule 5 to the Civil Partnership Act 2004 is not a 'costs order' within the meaning of rule 28.3.

4.7 By virtue of rule 28.2(1), where rule 28.3 does not apply, the exercise of the court's discretion as to costs is governed by the relevant provisions of the CPR and in particular rule 44.2 (excluding r 44.2(2) and (3)).

PART III

PART 29
MISCELLANEOUS

CONTENTS OF THIS PART

Rule		Page
29.1	Personal details	1852
29.2	Disclosure of information under the 1991 Act	1852
29.3	Method of giving notice	1853
29.4	Withdrawal of applications in proceedings	1853
29.5	The Human Rights Act 1998	1854

29.6	Documents in proceedings concerning gender recognition	1855
29.7	Stamping or sealing court documents	1855
29.8	Applications for relief which is precluded by the 1991 Act	1855
29.9	Modification of rule 29.8 where the application is not freestanding	1856
29.10	Standard requirements	1857
29.11	Drawing up and filing of judgments and orders	1857
29.12	Access to and inspection of documents retained in court	1858
29.13	Service of judgments and orders	1858
29.14	Power to require judgment or order to be served on a party as well as the party's solicitor	1858
29.15	When judgment or order takes effect	1858
29.16	Correction of errors in judgments and orders	1859
29.17	Transfer of proceedings	1859
29.18	Application for change of area	1859
29.19	Allocation of proceedings to another level of judge	1860
	Practice Direction 29A – Human Rights, Joining the Crown	1860
	Practice Direction 29B – Human Rights Act 1998	1861
	Practice Direction 29C – Transfer of Proceedings from the Family Court to the High Court	1862

29.1 Personal details

(1) Unless the court directs otherwise, a party is not required to reveal –

- (a) the party's home address or other contact details;
- (b) the address or other contact details of any child;
- (c) the name of a person with whom the child is living, if that person is not the applicant; or
- (d) in relation to an application under section 28(2) of the 2002 Act (application for permission to change the child's surname), the proposed new surname of the child.

(2) Where a party does not wish to reveal any of the particulars in paragraph (1), that party must give notice of those particulars to the court and the particulars will not be revealed to any person unless the court directs otherwise.

(3) Where a party changes home address during the course of proceedings, that party must give notice of the change to the court.

29.2 Disclosure of information under the 1991 Act

Where the Secretary of State requires a person mentioned in regulation 3(1), 4(2) or 6(2)(a) of the Child Support Information Regulations 2008 to furnish information or evidence for a purpose mentioned in regulation 4(1) of those Regulations, nothing in these rules will –

- (a) prevent that person from furnishing the information or evidence sought; or
- (b) require that person to seek permission of the court before doing so.

Amendments—SI 2012/2007.

Defined terms—'the 1991 Act': r 2.3(1).

Child Support Information Regulations 2008—The Child Support Information Regulations 2008, reg 4(1) provides for the disclosure to the Secretary of State for Work and Pensions of certain information or evidence required by it to perform its duties under CSA 1991 (especially calculation of child support maintenance or enforcement of arrears). This rule prevents any prohibitive measures being applied to a parent with care (reg 3(1)) or non-resident parent (reg 4(2)(a)) if they are required to produce, and do produce to the Secretary of State, documents arising in court proceedings. It enables the court to produce such documents directly to the Secretary of State (reg 6(2)(a)).

No contempt by parent who releases 'required' information or evidence—The release of the parent with care to disclose information and evidence ends any possibility of contempt proceedings for a parent with care who, when requested so to do under Child Support Information Regulations 2008, reg 3(1) ('must furnish such information as the Secretary of State requires'), passes court documents (eg Form E or other financial information) to the Secretary of State.

Legal representatives—There is no mention of a party's legal representative in the list in Child Support Information Regulations 2008, reg 4(2) of those required to disclose documents to the Secretary of State. Documents held by a lawyer remain confidential and many will be covered by privilege. A client's file, or any part of it, should only be released to the Secretary of State with the written authority of the client.

Child Support Act 1991, s 50—CSA 1991, s 50 prevents disclosure of information by the Secretary of State to third parties; save that they are entitled to release documents for use in court proceedings (s 50(6)).

29.3 Method of giving notice

(1) Unless directed otherwise, a notice which is required by these rules to be given to a person must be given –

(a) in writing; and

(b) in a manner in which service may be effected in accordance with Part 6.

(2) Rule 6.33 applies to a notice which is required by these rules to be given to a child as it applies to a document which is to be served on a child.

Rule 6.33—In FPR 2010, Pt 12 proceedings where a rule requires a document to be served on a party who is a child, then unless the court directs otherwise, the following additional persons or bodies must be served, notified or supplied with a copy of the document (in addition to those specified in FPR 2010, rr 6.28–6.32) namely the children's guardian, the welfare officer, the children and family reporter or the person acting under a duty referred to in r 16.38 and the local authority preparing a report under CA 1989, s 14A(8),(9).

29.4 Withdrawal of applications in proceedings

(1) This rule applies to applications in proceedings –

(a) under Part 7;

(b) under Parts 10 to 14 or under any other Part where the application relates to the welfare or upbringing of a child or;

(c) where either of the parties is a protected party.

(2) Where this rule applies, an application may only be withdrawn with the permission of the court.

(3) Subject to paragraph (4), a person seeking permission to withdraw an application must file a written request for permission setting out the reasons for the request.

(4) The request under paragraph (3) may be made orally to the court if the parties are present.

(5) A court officer will notify the other parties of a written request.

(6) The court may deal with a written request under paragraph (3) without a hearing if the other parties, and any other persons directed by the court, have had an opportunity to make written representations to the court about the request.

Court's approach to application—An application under r 29.4(2) involves the determination of a 'question with respect to the upbringing of a child', and so the paramountcy principle in CA 1989, s 1(1) applies. The paramount consideration for the court is whether the withdrawal of the proceedings would promote or conflict with the welfare of the child concerned. The court must look at each case on its facts to see if there is some 'solid advantage to the child to be derived from continuing the proceedings'. For examples, see *Re N (Leave to Withdraw Care Proceedings)* [2000] 1 FLR 134, FD and *Re W (Care Proceedings: Functions of Court and Local Authority)* [2014] 2 FLR 431, CA.

Withdrawal of proceedings – ECHR 1950—Where an application is made to withdraw public law child care proceedings on the basis that to continue them would amount to an interference with the right of the parents of the child concerned under Art 8(1) of the ECHR to respect for their private and family life, the court must assess whether such interference is necessary to protect one of the interests set out in Art 8(2) (*Re N (Leave to Withdraw Care Proceedings)* [2000] 1 FLR 134, FD). Where there is a serious conflict between the interests of the child and one of its parents which can only be resolved to the disadvantage of one of them, the interests of the child must prevail under Art 8(2) (*Yousef v The Netherlands* [2003] 1 FLR 210, ECHR).

'written request for permission'—The written request for permission to withdraw proceedings should be made in Form C2. The form requires the names and date of birth of the child concerned, and details as to the identity of the person making the request and as to his relationship with the child. The reasons for seeking permission to withdraw the proceedings must be clearly set out, and particular attention should be paid to the effect that withdrawal will have on the child.

Service—See FPR 2010, Pt 6, Ch 3.

Oral application in the presence of the parties—The court must not entertain an oral request for leave to withdraw proceedings in the absence of the children's guardian either, even if his legal representative is present (*Re F (A Minor) (Care Order: Withdrawal of Application)* [1993] 2 FLR 9, FD). It is possible that the applicant may change his mind almost immediately after filing the application and wish to raise the question of withdrawing the proceedings orally at the first directions hearing. At this stage, it may be that neither the children's guardian nor the children and family reporter will have been appointed, so neither could be present. This ought not to debar the making of an oral request. FPC(CA 989)R 1991, r 5(3), the equivalent provision for magistrates' courts, is much clearer on this point. It is not impossible (although it is very unusual) to have both a children's guardian and a children and family reporter in the same case. Where this occurs, the wording of the rule suggests that it will suffice if the oral application is made in the presence of one or the other though it is doubted whether, in practice, it would normally be prudent to proceed to determine the application without notification to both.

29.5 The Human Rights Act 1998

(1) In this rule –

'the 1998 Act' means the Human Rights Act 1998;

'Convention right' has the same meaning as in the 1998 Act; and

'declaration of incompatibility' means a declaration of incompatibility under section 4 of the 1998 Act.

(2) A party who seeks to rely on any provision of or right arising under the 1998 Act or seeks a remedy available under that Act must inform the court in that party's application or otherwise in writing specifying –

(a) the Convention right which it is alleged has been infringed and details of the alleged infringement; and

(b) the relief sought and whether this includes a declaration of incompatibility.

(3) The High Court may not make a declaration of incompatibility unless 21 days' notice, or such other period of notice as the court directs, has been given to the Crown.

(4) Where notice has been given to the Crown, a Minister, or other person permitted by the 1998 Act, will be joined as a party on giving notice to the court.

(5) Where a claim is made under section 7(1) of the 1998 Act (claim that public authority acted unlawfully) in respect of a judicial act –

(a) that claim must be set out in the application form or the appeal notice; and

(b) notice must be given to the Crown.

(6) Where paragraph (4) applies and the appropriate person (as defined in section 9(5) of the 1998 Act) has not applied within 21 days, or such other period as the court directs, beginning with the date on which the notice to be joined as a party was served, the court may join the appropriate person as a party.

(7) On any application concerning a committal order, if the court ordering the release of the person concludes that that person's Convention rights have been infringed by the making of the order to which the application or appeal relates, the judgment or order should so state, but if the court does not do so, that failure will not prevent another court from deciding the matter.

(8) Where by reason of a rule, practice direction or court order the Crown is permitted or required –

(a) to make a witness statement;

(b) to swear an affidavit(GL);

(c) to verify a document by a statement of truth; or

(d) to discharge any other procedural obligation,

that function will be performed by an appropriate officer acting on behalf of the Crown, and the court may if necessary nominate an appropriate officer.

(Practice Direction 29A (Human Rights – Joining the Crown) makes provision for the notices mentioned in this rule.)

Scope—An application in relation to a human rights point may be before the court as a freestanding issue, which will be by way of judicial review proceedings to the Administrative Court (see CPR 1998, Pt 54) or in existing proceedings (see the President's observation in *Re L (Care Proceedings: Human Rights Claims)* [2003] 2 FLR 160, FD). This rule applies to the latter. Where a human rights issue is to be raised, it should be included within the application or originating documentation. If the issue arises after the commencement of the proceedings, the application or originating documentation should be amended to include the human rights point.

Declaration of incompatibility—An application may be made under HRA 1998, s 4 to declare primary or secondary legislation incompatible with the provisions of ECHR 1950 (as defined under HRA 1998, s 1). If such an issue is raised the application must be dealt with in the High Court (HRA 1998, s 4(5)). This means the application must be made to the High Court or transferred there. Where such an application is made, notice must also be given to the Crown to consider joinder as a party to the application (FPR 2010, r 29.5(3),(4),(6)).

Judicial acts—An application may be made claiming that there has been a failure to act in a way which is compatible with the provisions of ECHR 1950 (as defined under HRA 1998, s 1). Such a claim may only be made by way of appeal, or judicial review where an appeal may not be made (HRA 1998, s 9). On such an application, where damages are sought, notice must be given to the Crown with a view to joinder (FPR 2010, r 29.5(5)). The notice given under r 29.5(5) must be served on the person named in the list published under Crown Proceedings Act 1947, s 17, namely the Lord Chancellor and should be served on the Treasury Solicitor (FPR PD29A, paras 1.1–1.6, 2.1–2.3). The full list published under Crown Proceedings Act 1947, s 17 is annexed to CPR PD66 (set out in *Civil Court Service*, LexisNexis).

Injunctions—The court has jurisdiction in appropriate cases to grant an injunction restraining a local authority from, for example, seeking to remove a child from a placement pending a full hearing by the court: *Coventry CC v O (Adoption)* [2011] 2 FLR 936, CA.

29.6 Documents in proceedings concerning gender recognition

(1) This rule applies to all documents in proceedings brought under –

(a) section 12(1)(g) or (h) of, or paragraph 11(1)(e) of Schedule 1 to, the 1973 Act;

(aa) section 12A(3) of the 1973 Act in a case where section 12(1)(g) or (h) of the 1973 Act applies; or

(b) the Gender Recognition Act 2004.

(2) Documents to which this rule applies must, while they are in the custody of the court, be kept in a place of special security.

(In relation to paragraph (1)(aa), section 9(6) of the Marriage (Same Sex Couples) Act 2013 provides that where a civil partnership is converted into a marriage, the civil partnership ends on the conversion, and the resulting marriage is to be treated as having subsisted since the date the civil partnership was formed.)

Amendments—SI 2015/913.

Scope—This rule provides for the security of documents in the custody of the court in proceedings concerning gender recognition.

29.7 Stamping or sealing court documents

(1) A court officer must, when issuing the following documents, seal(GL), or otherwise authenticate them with the stamp of the court –

(a) the application form;

(b) an order; and

(c) any other document which a rule or practice direction requires the court officer to seal(GL) or stamp.

(2) The court officer may place the seal(GL) or the stamp on the document –

(a) by hand; or

(b) by printing a facsimile of the seal(GL) on the document whether electronically or otherwise.

(3) A document purporting to bear the court's seal(GL) or stamp will be admissible in evidence without further proof.

29.8 Applications for relief which is precluded by the 1991 Act

(1) This rule applies where an application is made for an order which, in the opinion of the court, it would be prevented from making under section 8 or 9 of the 1991 Act and in this rule, 'the matter' means the question of whether or not the court would be so prevented.

(2) The court will consider the matter without holding a hearing.

(3) Where the court officer receives the opinion of the court, as mentioned in paragraph (1), the court officer must send a notice to the applicant of that opinion.

(4) Paragraphs (5) to (11) apply where the court officer sends a notice under paragraph (3).

(5) Subject to paragraph (6), no requirement of these rules apply except the requirements –

(a) of this rule;

(b) as to service of the application by the court officer; and
(c) as to any procedural step to be taken following the making of an application of the type in question.

(6) The court may direct that the requirements of these rules apply, or apply to such extent or with such modifications as are set out in the direction.

(7) If the applicant informs the court officer, within 14 days of the date of the notice, that the applicant wishes to persist with the application, the court will give appropriate directions for the matter to be heard and determined and may provide for the hearing to be without notice.

(8) Where directions are given in accordance with paragraph (7), the court officer must –
(a) inform the applicant of the directions;
(b) send a copy of the application to the other parties;
(c) if the hearing is to be without notice, inform the other parties briefly –
  (i) of the nature and effect of the notice given to the applicant under paragraph (3);
  (ii) that the matter is being resolved without a hearing on notice; and
  (iii) that they will be notified of the result; and
(d) if the hearing is to be on notice, inform the other parties of –
  (i) the circumstances which led to the directions being given; and
  (ii) the directions.

(9) If the applicant does not inform the court officer as mentioned in paragraph (7), the application shall be treated as having been withdrawn.

(10) Where –
(a) the matter is heard in accordance with directions given under paragraph (7); and
(b) the court determines that it would be prevented, under section 8 or 9 of the 1991 Act, from making the order sought by the applicant,

the court will dismiss the application.

(11) Where the court dismisses the application –
(a) the court must give its reasons in writing; and
(b) the court officer must send a copy of the reasons to the parties.

Defined terms—'the 1991 Act', 'court officer': FPR 2010, r 2.3(1); 'matter': FPR 2010, r 29.8(1).

'section 8 or 9 of the 1991 Act' (r 29.8(1))—Sections 8(3) and 9(5) of CSA 1991 prevent any court from making, varying or reviving any orders for periodical payments for children and from varying any agreement for child maintenance. These applications are financial remedy proceedings under FPR 2010, Pt 9, either with periodical payments as the sole object (r 29.8); or with periodical payments as part of a wider application for financial remedies (r 29.9). Where a party appears to have made an application precluded by CSA 1991, r 29.8 enables the court to give that party an opportunity to justify why he considers that the application should proceed.

'applicant wishes to persist' (r 29.8(7))—It is possible that the draftsman of r 29.8 has overlooked the crucial fact (to FPR 2010, rr 28.9 and 29.8) that all applications to which the rule applies will be financial remedy proceedings (not, for example, as before also under CA 1989, Sch 1 or MFPA 1984, with their bespoke procedures) and will therefore be covered by the first directions appointment procedure under FPR 2010, Pt 9 (r 9.15). Once a party has indicated a 'wish to persist', there seems to be no reason why this intent cannot be picked up on directions at the r 9.15 appointment. That would also obviate any separate court appointment under r 29.8(10).

29.9 Modification of rule 29.8 where the application is not freestanding

(1) Where the court officer sends a notice under rule 29.8(3) in relation to an application which is contained in another document ('the document') which contains material extrinsic to the application –

(a) subject to paragraph (2), the document will be treated as if it did not contain the application in respect of which the notice was served; and
(b) the court officer, when sending copies of the documents to the respondents under any provision of these rules, must attach –
  (i) a copy of the notice under rule 29.8(3); and
  (ii) a notice informing the respondents of the effect of paragraph (1)(a).

(2) If the court determines that it is not prevented by section 8 or 9 of the 1991 Act from making the order sought by the application, the court –

(a) must direct that the document shall be treated as if it contained the application; and

(b) may give such directions as it considers appropriate for the subsequent conduct of the proceedings.

Application for periodical payments included in a composite financial remedy application—This provision, like FPR 2010, r 29.8, may have been drafted without account of the points made in the note to r 29.8(7) above. So far as it is of continuing real effect, the rule deals with 'material extrinsic to the application' for child periodical payments. It enables the financial remedy application to proceed without the periodical payments application; and, if it is restored, to proceed with it.

'by the court'—The order will need to be clear, in proceedings under these rules, whether the court was the High Court or the Family Court.

29.10 Standard requirements

(1) Every judgment or order must state the name and judicial title of the person who made it.

(2) Every judgment or order must –

(a) bear the date on which it is given or made; and

(b) be sealed(GL) by the court.

Standard requirements (r 29.10)—This and the following rules, and the corresponding PD, follow CPR 1998, Pt 40 in seeking to standardise practice in drawing up and serving judgments and orders.

'the name and judicial title of the person who made it' (r 29.10(1))—It is necessary in dealing with appeals and applications to review or set aside orders to identify the judge of first instance. Judges frequently deal with lists back to back, and in the Family Court may be sitting back to back with benches of justices, and it is advisable to check who the adjudicator was before drawing up an order or judgment. Draft judgments should leave space for the judge's name and title to be inserted (compare CPR PD40B, para 3.3(2)).

29.11 Drawing up and filing of judgments and orders

(1) Except as provided by a rule or a practice direction, every judgment or order will be drawn up by the court unless –

(a) the court orders a party to draw it up;

(b) a party, with the permission of the court, agrees to draw it up; or

(c) the court dispenses with the need to draw it up.

(2) The court may direct that –

(a) a judgment or an order drawn up by a party must be checked by the court before it is sealed(GL); or

(b) before a judgment or an order is drawn up by the court, the parties must file an agreed statement of its terms.

(3) Where a judgment or an order is to be drawn up by a party –

(a) that party must file it no later than 7 days after the date on which the court ordered or gave permission for the order to be drawn up so that it can be sealed by the court; and

(b) if that party fails to file it within that period, any other party may draw it up and file it.

'drawn up' (r 29.11)—A judge has jurisdiction to re-consider his decision before an order is drawn up (*Re Barrell Enterprises* [1973] 1 WLR 19, CA; *Stewart v Engel & Anor* [2000] 1 WLR 2268, CA), although this power must be exercised sparingly, for, as observed in *Barrell*: 'When oral judgments have been given, either in a court of first instance or on appeal, the successful party ought, save in the most exceptional circumstances, to be able to assume that the judgment is a valid and effective one.' The law is conveniently summarised in *Paulin v Paulin* [2009] 2 FLR 354, CA, at [30].

However, a judge who has given an indication at the hearing is entitled to reflect upon her reasoning and perfect her judgment and even (see *Re L-B (Reversal of Judgment)* [2013] 2 FLR 859, SC) change her mind if justice so requires (*Surrey County Council v S* [2014] EWCA Civ 601). The judge's confidential draft circulated to the parties is not his judgment; the judgment as handed down is (*H v H* [2015] 2 FLR 447, CA).

'must file it no later than 7 days' (r 29.11(3)(a))—As this time limit exceeds 5 days, it includes weekends and public holidays (FPR 2010, r 2.9). It is particularly important to ensure that urgent orders are drawn up and served immediately to ensure that the time limit imposed in the order does not elapse. Even in non-urgent cases, this rule makes it clear that orders should be filed far more rapidly than often occurs in practice.

29.12 Access to and inspection of documents retained in court

(1) Except as provided by this rule or by any other rule or Practice Direction, no document or copy of a document filed or lodged in the court office shall be open to inspection by any person without the permission of the court, and no copy of any such document or copy shall be taken by, or issued to, any person without such permission.

(2) A copy of an order made in open court will be issued to any person who requests it.

(3) Subject to rules 14.24 and 29.1(2) and to any direction given by the court, a party to any family proceedings, or the legal representative, children's guardian or litigation friend for a party in any family proceedings, may have a search made for, and may inspect, and obtain a copy of, any document or copy of a document filed or lodged in the court office in those proceedings.

(4) Any person who intends to make an application in relation to a child under the 1980 Hague Convention in a Contracting State (as defined in rule 12.44) other than the United Kingdom shall, if the court is satisfied that that person intends to make such an application, be entitled to obtain a copy bearing the seal(GL) of the court of any order made in relation to the child under the 1989 Act or under the inherent jurisdiction, whether or not that person was a party to the proceedings in which the order was made.

(5) For the purposes of this rule, 'document' and 'copy' have the meanings given in rule 21.1(3).

Amendments—Substituted by SI 2012/679. Amended by SI 2015/1868.

'no document filed or lodged in the court office shall be open to inspection by any person' (r 29.12(1))—Although r 27.11(2)(f) permits the Press to attend hearings held in private, journalists are not allowed access to documents and their role is that of a watchdog: *Appleton and Gallagher v News Group Newspapers and PA* [2016] 2 FLR 1, FD.

'will be issued to any person who requests it' (r 29.12(2))—Any person may obtain a copy of a committal order from the court office: *Justice for Families Ltd v Secretary of State for Justice* [2015] 2 FLR 321, CA.

29.13 Service of judgments and orders

(1) The court officer must, unless the court directs otherwise, serve a copy of a judgment or an order made in family proceedings to every party affected by it.

(2) Where a judgment or an order has been drawn up by a party and is to be served by the court officer the party who drew it up must file a copy to be retained at court and sufficient copies for service on all the parties.

(3) A party in whose favour an order is made need not prove that a copy of the order has reached a party to whom it is required to be sent under this rule.

(4) This rule does not affect the operation of any rule or enactment which requires an order to be served in a particular way

29.14 Power to require judgment or order to be served on a party as well as the party's solicitor

Where the party on whom a judgment or order is served is acting by a solicitor, the court may order the judgment or order to be served on the party as well as on the party's solicitor.

'served on the party as well as on his solicitor' (r 29.14)—There is no guidance as to the circumstances in which such an order will be made. It is likely to be made only in exceptional circumstances, eg to ensure that it is brought to the lay party's attention that an adverse costs order has been made or that an order is penal.

29.15 When judgment or order takes effect

A judgment or order takes effect from the day when it is given or made, or such later date as the court may specify.

'takes effect' (r 29.15)—An order to do an act cannot be enforced unless and until a date for the act to be done is fixed. If a period of time is incorporated, the order should state the date from which the period of time is to run, but FPR 2010, r 2.10 (mirroring CPR 1998, r 2.9) requires that wherever practicable, the order should state a day and time by which an act is to be done. (Time and again, parties go to the trouble of obtaining 'unless orders', which are then drafted to require compliance 'within 7 days', say, but unless the order makes it clear *from when the 7 days runs*, getting the order is a wasted effort.)

If a party is not present when the order is made, sufficient time should, of course, be allowed for the order to be sealed and served, and, thereafter, for compliance.

29.16 Correction of errors in judgments and orders

(1) The court may at any time correct an accidental slip or omission in a judgment or order.

(2) A party may apply for a correction without notice.

'The court may at any time correct an accidental slip or omission' (r 29.16)(1))—This, the well-known 'slip rule', is not limited to errors of the court or its officials but it *is* limited to genuine slips and cannot be used to correct an error of substance. It cannot enable a court to have second or additional thoughts. Once the order is drawn up, any mistakes must be corrected by an appellate court. It is sometimes possible under the slip rule to amend an order to give effect to the intention of the court (*Bristol-Myers Squibb Co v (1) Baker Norton Pharmaceuticals Inc (2) Napro Biotherapeutics Inc* [2001] EWCA Civ 414, but cf *R v Cripps ex parte Muldoon* [1984] 1 QB 686, CA (where an order for costs had a clear meaning in law, although a different one from that which the judge intended, and could not be 'corrected' under the Slip Rule)).

29.17 Transfer of proceedings

(1) Subject to paragraph (3), a court may transfer a case to another court, either of its own initiative or on the application of one of the parties if –

- (a) the parties consent to the transfer;
- (b) the court has held a hearing to determine whether a transfer should be ordered; or
- (c) paragraph (2) applies.

(2) A court may transfer a case without a hearing if –

- (a) the court has notified the parties in writing that it intends to order a transfer; and
- (b) no party has, within 14 days of the notification being sent, requested a hearing to determine whether a transfer should be ordered.

(3) A case may not be transferred from the family court to the High Court unless –

- (a) the decision to transfer was made by a judge sitting in the family court who is a person to whom paragraph (4) applies; or
- (b) one or more of the circumstances specified in Practice Direction 29C applies.

(4) This paragraph applies to a person who is –

- (a) the President of the Family Division;
- (b) an ordinary judge of the Court of Appeal (including the vice-president, if any, of either division of that court);
- (c) a puisne judge of the High Court.

Amendments—Inserted by SI 2013/3204.

Allocation and Gatekeeping—See FC(CDB)R 2014 and the President's Guidance on *Allocation and Gatekeeping (Public Law)* and the attached Schedule for the factors to be considered when allocating cases. See also the procedure set out in the President's Guidance of December 2016: *Allocation of Work to Section 9 Judges* (set out in Part V). Proceedings should not be allocated or transferred to a s 9 judge without first informing the DFJ, who must then obtain the agreement of the FDLJ (or in the case of urgency from the Urgent Application Judge of the Family Division or other Judge of the Family Division before any hearing in proceedings allocated to High Court Level is conducted by a s 9 judge. Attention is also drawn to the President's Guidance of 8 October 2015 on *Radicalisation Cases in the Family Courts* (see **Cases of alleged radicalisation** under CA 1989, s 31). These cases should be heard by a judge of the Family Division and therefore should be issued in the High Court. Where the proceedings are issued in the Family Court and it later transpires that it falls within the description of a radicalisation case set out in para 1 of the Guidance, the designated judge must be notified immediately, who in turn must take immediate steps to notify the Family Division Liaison Judge and urgent steps must be taken to list and allocate the case to a High Court Judge. It is only in exceptional circumstances that a case falling within the description in para 1 of the Guidance may be heard by a designated judge or a judge authorised under SCA 1981, s 9.

29.18 Application for change of area

The Part 18 procedure applies to an application to the family court for existing proceedings to be heard in a different Designated Family Judge area.

(Her Majesty's Courts and Tribunals Service publishes information to enable Designated Family Judge areas to be identified.)

Amendments—Inserted by SI 2013/3204.

PART III

29.19 Allocation of proceedings to another level of judge

(1) Paragraphs (2) and (3) apply where there has been allocation without a hearing.

(2) A party may request the court to reconsider allocation at a hearing.

(3) Unless the court directs otherwise, a party may make a request referred to in paragraph (2) –

- (a) at any hearing where that party first has notice of allocation; or
- (b) in writing no later than 2 days before the first hearing in the proceedings after the party receives notice of allocation.

(4) When the party requests the court to reconsider allocation in accordance with paragraph (3)(b), the party must at the same time notify other parties of the request in writing.

(5) The court may reconsider allocation of its own initiative.

(6) Rule 4.3 does not apply to allocation without a hearing.

(7) In this rule 'allocation' means allocation of proceedings other than appeal proceedings to a level of judge.

Amendments—Inserted by SI 2014/667.

Procedure for Allocation of Work to s 9 judge—See the President's Guidance of December 2016: *Allocation of Work to Section 9 Judges* (set out in Part V), which requires that before re-allocating the case for hearing by a High Court Judge or a s 9 judge, the judge conducting the case should discuss the matter with the DFJ, who in turn must (if necessary) consult the FDLJ.

Practice Direction 29A – Human Rights, Joining the Crown

This Practice Direction supplements FPR Part 29, rule 29.5 (The Human Rights Act 1998)

Note—Any reference in this practice direction to 'the court' is to the High Court (HRA 1998, s 4(5)): the Family Court has no jurisdiction in this field.

Section 4 of the Human Rights Act 1998

1.1 Where a party has informed the court about –

- (a) a claim for a declaration of incompatibility in accordance with section 4 of the Human Rights Act 1998; or
- (b) an issue for the court to decide which may lead to the court considering making a declaration,

then the court may at any time consider whether notice should be given to the Crown as required by that Act and give directions for the content and service of the notice. The rule allows a period of 21 days before the court will make the declaration but the court may vary this period of time.

1.2 The court will normally consider the issues and give the directions referred to in paragraph 1.1 at a directions hearing.

1.3 The notice must be served on the person named in the list published under section 17 of the Crown Proceedings Act 1947.

1.4 The notice will be in the form directed by the court and will normally include the directions given by the court. The notice will also be served on all the parties.

1.5 The court may require the parties to assist in the preparation of the notice.

1.6 Unless the court orders otherwise, the Minister or other person permitted by the Human Rights Act 1998 to be joined as a party must, if he or she wishes to be joined, give notice of his or her intention to be joined as a party to the court and every other party. Where the Minister has nominated a person to be joined as a party the notice must be accompanied by the written nomination.

(Section 5(2)(a) of the Human Rights Act 1998 permits a person nominated by a Minister of the Crown to be joined as a party. The nomination may be signed on behalf of the Minister.)

Section 9 of the Human Rights Act 1998

2.1 The procedure in paragraphs 1.1 to 1.6 also applies where a claim is made under sections 7(1)(a) and 9(3) of the Human Rights Act 1998 for damages in respect of a judicial act.

2.2 Notice must be given to the Lord Chancellor and should be served on the Treasury Solicitor on his behalf.

2.3 The notice will also give details of the judicial act, which is the subject of the claim for damages, and of the court that made it.

(Section 9(4) of the Human Rights Act 1998 provides that no award of damages may be made against the Crown as provided for in section 9(3) unless the appropriate person is joined in the proceedings. The appropriate person is the Minister responsible for the court concerned or a person or department nominated by him or her (section 9(5) of the Act).

Practice Direction 29B – Human Rights Act 1998

This Practice Direction supplements FPR Part 29

1 It is directed that the following practice shall apply as from 2 October 2000 in all family proceedings:

Citation of authorities

2 When an authority referred to in s 2 of the Human Rights Act 1998 ('the Act') is to be cited at a hearing:

(a) the authority to be cited shall be an authoritative and complete report;

(b) the court must be provided with a list of authorities it is intended to cite and copies of the reports:

  (i) in cases to which *Practice Direction (Family Proceedings: Court Bundles)* (10 March 2000) [2000] 1 FLR 536 applies, as part of the bundle;

  (ii) otherwise, not less than 2 clear days before the hearing; and

(c) copies of the complete original texts issued by the European Court and Commission, either paper based or from the Court's judgment database (HUDOC) which is available on the internet, may be used.

Note—*PD Family Proceedings: Court Bundles* of 10 March 2000, [2000] 1 FLR 536 has been replaced by FPR PD27A (formerly *PD Family Proceedings: Court Bundles (Universal Practice to be Applied in all Courts other than the Family Proceedings Court)* of 27 July 2006, [2006] 2 FLR 199, and any reference in any other PD to *PD Family Proceedings: Court Bundles* shall be read as if substituted by a reference to PD27A.

Allocation to judges

3 (1) The hearing and determination of the following will be confined to a High Court judge and in the family court to a judge of High Court level:

  (a) a claim for a declaration of incompatibility under s 4 of the Act; or

  (b) an issue which may lead to the court considering making such a declaration.

(2) The hearing and determination of a claim made under the Act in respect of a judicial act shall be confined in the High Court to a High Court judge.

Practice Direction 29C – Transfer of Proceedings from the Family Court to the High Court

This Practice Direction supplements rule 29.17(3)(b) FPR

1 Rule 29.17(3)(b) FPR provides that a judge other than one to whom rule 29.17(4) applies may make a decision to transfer proceedings from the family court to the High Court where the circumstances specified in this Practice Direction apply.

1.2 The circumstances are that the proceedings are to be transferred solely for the purpose of making an order under the inherent jurisdiction of the High Court to require a Government Department or agency to disclose an address to the court.

Transfer of proceedings where relief under the inherent jurisdiction is sought—See the commentary set out under FPR 2010, rr 29.17 and 29.19 and the President's Guidance of December 2016: *Allocation of Work to Section 9 Judges* (set out in Part V).

PART 30
APPEALS

CONTENTS OF THIS PART

Rule		Page
30.1	Scope and interpretation	1862
30.2	Parties to comply with the practice direction	1863
30.3	Permission	1864
30.4	Appellant's notice	1866
30.5	Respondent's notice	1867
30.6	Grounds of appeal	1868
30.7	Variation of time	1868
30.8	Stay	1869
30.9	Amendment of appeal notice	1869
30.10	Striking out appeal notices and setting aside or imposing conditions on permission to appeal	1869
30.11	Appeal court's powers	1869
30.12	Hearing of appeals	1871
30.13	Assignment of appeals to the Court of Appeal	1871
30.14	Reopening of final appeals	1872
	Practice Direction 30A – Appeals	1872

30.1 Scope and interpretation

(1) The rules in this Part apply to appeals to –

(a) the High Court; and
(b) the family court.

(2) This Part does not apply to an appeal in detailed assessment proceedings against a decision of an authorised court officer.

(Rules 47.21 to 47.24 of the CPR deal with appeals against a decision of an authorised court officer in detailed assessment proceedings.)

(3) In this Part –

'appeal court' means the court to which an appeal is made;
'appeal notice' means an appellant's or respondent's notice;
'appellant' means a person who brings or seeks to bring an appeal;
'costs judge' means –

(a) the Chief Taxing Master;

(b) a taxing master of the Senior Courts; or

(c) a person appointed to act as deputy for the person holding office referred to in paragraph (b) or to act as temporary additional officer for any such office;

'district judge' means –

(a) the Senior District Judge of the Family Division

(b) a district judge of the Principal Registry of the Family Division;

(c) a person appointed to act as deputy for the person holding office referred to in paragraph (b) or to act as temporary additional officer for any such office;

(d) a district judge;

(e) a deputy district judge appointed under section 102 of the Senior Courts Act 1981 or section 8 of the County Courts Act 1984; or

(f) a District Judge (Magistrates' Courts);

'lower court' means the court from which, or the person from whom, the appeal lies; and

'respondent' means –

(a) a person other than the appellant who was a party to the proceedings in the lower court and who is affected by the appeal; and

(b) a person who is permitted by the appeal court to be a party to the appeal.

(4) This Part is subject to any rule, enactment or practice direction which sets out special provisions with regard to any particular category of appeal.

PART III

Amendments—SI 2014/667.

Appeals (FPR 2010, Pt 30)—See FPR PD30A.

Scope—The rules in this Part apply to all appeals in family proceedings from:

(i) lay justices to a judge of Circuit Judge level;

(ii) judges of District Judge level (including a district judge (magistrates' court)) to a judge of Circuit Judge level;

(iii) district judges of the High Court and district judges of the Principal Registry of the Family Division in financial remedy proceedings to a judge of High Court level; and

(iv) as from October 2016, appeals from a Circuit Judge and from a Recorder in private law children's matters, which are to be heard by a High Court judge rather than the Court of Appeal.

See ACA 2002, s 100, Access to Justice 1999 (Destination of Appeals) (Family Proceedings) Order 2014 and FC(CDB)R 2014.

Part 30 replicates the provisions of CPR 1998, Pt 52 with necessary and minor modifications: reference should be made to the notes to Pt 52 for guidance.

Procedure—All appeals must comply with the provisions of Pt 30 and PD30A.

Compliance with the rules—The Court of Appeal has held that litigants in person as much as a represented party are required to comply with the procedural rules on appeals. McFarlane LJ said: 'The fact that an applicant for permission to appeal is a litigant in person may cause a judge to spend more time explaining the process and the requirements, but that fact is not, and should not be, a reason for relaxing or ignoring the ordinary procedural structure of an appeal or the requirements of the rules. Indeed, as I have suggested, adherence to the rules should be seen as a benefit to all parties, including litigants in person, rather than an impediment': *Re D (Appeal: Procedure: Evidence)* [2016] 1 FLR 249, CA, at [40].

Applications—Where a party makes an application in an appeal, the provisions of FPR 2010, Pt 18 will apply (FPR PD30A, rr 13.1 and 13.2)

Interim orders—Where events changed or developed after the making of an interim order, the appropriate course was to seek a variation of the order from the judge, rather than seek to appeal against the order: *Re H (A Child)* [2011] EWCA Civ 762.

Special provisions—Special provisions are made for appeals (i) under MCA 1980, s 111A (FPR 2010, rr 9.2–9.12, FPR PD30A), (ii) Child Maintenance and Enforcement Commission (CMEC) deduction order appeals (FPR 2010, rr 9.13–9.34, FPR PD30A; note that CMEC was abolished on 30 July 2012), (iii) appeals against decisions under rr 31.10, 31.11 or 31.14 (FPR 2010, rr 10.1–10.5, FPR PD30A, (iv) appeals against pension orders and pension sharing orders (FPR 2010, rr 11.1–11.3, FPR PD30A) and (v) appeals in respect of parentage determinations pursuant to CSA 1991, s 20 (FPR 2010, rr 12.1–12.3, PD30A)

Lay justices—Lay justices may not order an appeal to be transferred to the Court of Appeal (FPR 2010, r 30.13).

Appeal to Court of Appeal—Appeals from the County Court and the High Court to the Court of Appeal are still governed by CPR 1998, Pt 52 and, as from 1 October 2012, CPR PD52A–PD52E.

30.2 Parties to comply with the practice direction

All parties to an appeal must comply with Practice Direction 30A.

30.3 Permission

(1) Paragraphs (1B) and (2) of this rule set out when permission to appeal is, or is not, required under these rules to appeal against a decision or order of the family court.

(1A) This rule does not apply where the route of appeal from a decision or order of the family court is to the Court of Appeal, namely where the appeal is against a decision or order made by a circuit judge or Recorder –

(a) in proceedings under –
  (i) Part 4 of the 1989 Act (care and supervision);
  (ii) Part 5 of the 1989 Act (protection of children);
  (iii) paragraph 19(1) of Schedule 2 to the 1989 Act (approval by the court of local authority arrangements to assist children to live abroad); or
  (iv) the 2002 Act (adoption, placement etc);
(b) in exercise of the family court's jurisdiction in relation to contempt of court where that decision or order was made in, or in connection with, proceedings referred to in sub-paragraph (a); or
(c) where that decision or order was itself made on an appeal to the family court.

(Appeals in the cases referred to in this paragraph are outside the scope of these rules. The CPR make provision requiring permission to appeal in those cases.)

(1B) Permission to appeal is required under these rules –

(a) unless paragraph (2) applies, where the appeal is against a decision made by a circuit judge, Recorder, district judge or costs judge; or
(b) as provided by Practice Direction 30A.

(2) Permission to appeal is not required where the appeal is against –

(a) a committal order;
(b) a secure accommodation order under section 25 of the 1989 Act; or
(c) a refusal to grant habeas corpus for release in relation to a minor.

(3) An application for permission to appeal may be made –

(a) to the lower court at the hearing at which the decision to be appealed was made; or
(b) to the appeal court in an appeal notice.

(Rule 30.4 sets out the time limits for filing an appellant's notice at the appeal court. Rule 30.5 sets out the time limits for filing a respondent's notice at the appeal court. Any application for permission to appeal to the appeal court must be made in the appeal notice (see rules 30.4(1) and 30.5(3).)

(4) Where the lower court refuses an application for permission to appeal, a further application for permission to appeal may be made to the appeal court.

(5) Subject to paragraph (5A), where the appeal court, without a hearing, refuses permission to appeal, the person seeking permission may request the decision to be reconsidered at a hearing.

(5A) Where a judge of the High Court or in the family court, a judge of the High Court or a Designated Family Judge refuses permission to appeal without a hearing and considers that the application is totally without merit, the judge may make an order that the person seeking permission may not request the decision to be reconsidered at a hearing.

(5B) Rule 4.3(5) will not apply to an order that the person seeking permission may not request the decision to be reconsidered at a hearing made under paragraph (5A).

(6) A request under paragraph (5) must be filed within 7 days beginning with the date on which the notice that permission has been refused was served.

(7) Permission to appeal may be given only where –

(a) the court considers that the appeal would have a real prospect of success; or
(b) there is some other compelling reason why the appeal should be heard.

(8) An order giving permission may –

(a) limit the issues to be heard; and

(b) be made subject to conditions.

(9) *(revoked)*

Amendments—SI 2013/530; SI 2014/667; SI 2014/3296; SI 2016/891.

Permission to appeal—FPR PD30A does not set out any other circumstances in which permission to appeal is required. Permission to appeal is required from a decision made by a district judge or a costs judge (save where FPR 2010, r 30.3(2) applies) and as from 22 April 2014 a district judge (magistrates' courts).

Application to lower court for permission to appeal—If an application for permission to appeal is not made at the hearing when judgment is given or handed down or at a later hearing adjourned for the purpose of considering any application made for permission to appeal, the lower court has no jurisdiction to grant permission to appeal. If an application is not made at one or other of those hearings, it can only be made to the appeal court: *Monroe v Hopkins* [2017] EWHC 645 (QB).

Permission not required—Permission to appeal is not required against (i) a committal order, (ii) a secure accommodation order under CA 1989, s 25, (iii) a refusal to grant habeas corpus for release in relation to a minor or (iv) a decision made by lay justices.

Applications for writ of habeas corpus for release in relation to a minor—The rules are set out in CPR 1998, Pt 87, as amended by FPR 2010, r 12.42A.

Material omission—Where a party's advocate considers there is a material omission from a judgment or written reasons, the advocate should before drawing the order give the lower court the opportunity to consider whether there is an omission (FPR PD30A, para 4.6).

Where the application for permission to appeal is made to the lower court, that court must consider whether there is a material omission from the judgment and if it concludes there is, to provide additions to the judgment. Where the application is made to the appeal court, it must consider whether there is a material omission from the judgment and if it concludes there is, it may remit the matter to the lower court with an invitation to provide additions to the judgment (FPR PD30A, paras 4.7-4.9). Where an alleged lack of reasons in the judgment had not been drawn to the attention of the trial judge or the judge had subsequently failed to elaborate on his reasons, the normal procedure was remittal to the judge at first instance with a list of specific questions: *Re A and L (Children)* [2012] 1 FLR 134, CA.

Power to change judgment after handing down—A judge has the power to change his mind after delivering a judgment at the conclusion of a fact-finding hearing: *Re L-B (Reversal of Judgment)* [2013] 2 FLR 859, SC and the notes to CPR 1998, r 52.3.

Appeal bundle—In an appeal to the High Court, the appeal bundle must contain the documents set out in PD30A, paras 5.10A–5.10C, an appeal to the Family Court must contain the documents set out in PD30A, paras 5.8–5.10 and in respect of both routes of appeal the documents set out in PD30A paras 5.11, 5.12, 6.4, 6.5 and 7.16–7.18 must be included in the appeal bundle or, as the case may be, a respondent's supplemental bundle.

Permission without a hearing (r 30.3(5))—The general rule is that permission to appeal will be considered without a hearing (ie on paper: FPR PD30A, para 4.10; and see **Determination by the appeal court of an application for permission to appear** under CPR 1998, r 52.3 in *Civil Court Service* (LexisNexis)). This procedure will be applicable also to applications for permission to appeal out of time under *Barder v Barder* [1987] 2 FLR 480, HL (see Baron J in *O v O (Procedure for Listing Applications for Permission to Appeal to the High Court)* [2011] EWHC 14 July 2011 (unreported)). In *Black v Pastouna* [2005] EWCA Civ 1389, the Court of Appeal referred to CPR PD32, Annex 3 (video conferencing; reproduced in FPR PD22A, Annex 3): it would expect applications under 30 minutes to be disposed of with Annex 3 in mind. Where the appeal court (ie a High Court judge in the High Court or a High Court judge or a Designated Family Judge in the Family Court) refuses permission to appeal on paper, an appellant may request that the decision be reconsidered at a hearing but not if the appeal judge considers the application to be totally without merit and orders that the appellant may not request an oral hearing: r 30.3(5A),(5B).

Litigants in person—Where, in public law proceedings, the party seeking permission to appeal is a litigant in person, the local authority should file a short position statement setting out its argument why permission to appeal should be refused: see CPR PD52C, para 19 and *Re B (A Child)* [2015] EWCA Civ 1053.

Permission to appeal out of time—When considering an application for permission to appeal out of time, the appellate court may have regard to the underlying merits of the proposed appeal, especially where the grounds of appeal are either very strong or very weak: *Re H (Children) (Application to Extend Time: Merits of Proposed Appeal)* [2016] 1 FLR 952, CA.

Request for an oral hearing—Where an appeal court refuses permission to appeal on paper, the appellant may request, subject to an order being made under r 30.3(5A),(5B), the decision to refuse permission to appeal be reconsidered at an oral hearing within 7 days of service of the notice of refusal. The request must at the same time be served on the respondents (FPR PD30A, para 4.13). The appellant's advocate must, at least 4 days before the oral hearing, set out in a brief written statement (i) the points the appellant proposes to raise at the hearing (ii) the reasons why permission to appeal should be granted and (iii) in the case of a publicly funded litigant confirm that a copy of the reasons given by the appeal court for refusing permission to appeal was sent to the relevant office of the Legal Aid Agency (FPR PD30A, paras 4.14 and 4.17). The respondent should not attend the oral hearing unless requested to do so by the appeal court (FPR PD30A, para 4.15). A refusal of permission to appeal at an oral hearing cannot be renewed: *McHugh v McHugh* [2014] EWCA Civ 1671.

Transcripts of the hearing or of the evidence—See notes to CPR 1998, r 52.14.

Limited permission—Where a court gives permission to appeal on some issues only it will either (i) refuse permission on remaining issues or (ii) reserve the question of permission on those remaining issues to the court hearing the appeal. If the court reserves the question of permission on the remaining issues, the appellant must within 14 days after service of the court's order notify the court and the respondent in writing whether the appellant intends to pursue the reserved issues. If the appellant intends to pursue the same, the parties must include in the time estimate for the appeal hearing their time estimate for the reserved issues (FPR PD30A, paras 4.18 and 4.19).

Once permission is granted—The appeal bundle must be served on each respondent within 7 days of receiving the order giving permission to appeal (FPR PD30A, para 6.2). Where the appeal court grants permission the appellant must add specified documents to the appeal bundle, namely (i) the respondent's notice and skeleton argument (if any), (ii) those parts of transcripts of evidence which are directly relevant to the appeal, (iii) the order granting permission to appeal and (iv) any other document which the parties have agreed should be added to the appeal bundle (FPR PD30A, para 6.4) The advocate for an appellant must give a time estimate for the hearing of the appeal: a respondent must notify the court within 7 days whether he disagrees with the appellant's time estimate (FPR PD30A, paras 6.6–6.8).

Case management appeals and appeals against discretionary decisions—See *Re W (Relocation: Removal Outside Jurisdiction)* [2011] 2 FLR 409, CA, at [7]–[12]. Appeals against case management orders should be dealt with in such a way as to avoid the adjournment of any substantive hearing already listed in the court below: *Re L (Case Management: Child's Evidence)* [2014] 2 FLR 972, CA.

Procedure for listing applications for permission to appeal—Practice guidance was given on the proper procedure for listing applications for permission to appeal to the High Court. It is akin to the procedure followed in the Court of Appeal: *O v O (Procedure for Listing Applications for Permission to Appeal to the High Court)* [2011] EWHC 14 July 2011 (unreported).

Real prospect of success—There are two conflicting authorities on the meaning of a 'real prospect of success'. In *NLW v ARC* [2012] 2 FLR 129, FD, Mostyn J held that 'real prospect of success' meant it was more likely than not that the appeal would be allowed at the substantive hearing 'anything less than a 50/50 threshold could only mean there was a real prospect of failure'. Moor J, however, has held that a 'real prospect of success' is one that is realistic rather than fanciful and does not mean a greater than 50/50 chance of success. He commented that a practice direction was required to clarify the procedure for applications for permission to appeal: *AV v RM (Appeal)* [2012] 2 FLR 709, FD. The weight of current first instance authority follows the approach of Moor J: see Jackson J in *H v G (Adoption: Appeal)* [2014] 1 FLR 691, FD and Moylan J in *CR v SR (Financial Remedies: Permission to Appeal)* [2014] 1 FLR 186, FD in a judgment that compares the two approaches.

Respondent's attendance at permission hearing (r 30.3(5))—Rule 30.3(5) permits reconsideration of a paper refusal of permission by the court. The respondent is permitted to attend, but FPR PD30A, paras 4.15, 4.22 and 4.23 in effect discourage such attendance. In *Livock v Livock* [2012] 1 FLR 776, FD, Coleridge J was critical of the lack of notice given to the wife respondent of the permission application and that she had not been able to respond to any fresh evidence application (per *Ladd v Marshall* (1954) FLR Rep 422, CA).

Appeals against decisions under rr 31.10, 31.11 and 31.14—Note that special provisions apply to appeals against certain FPR 2010, Pt 31 decisions. The provisions set out in FPR 2010, rr 30.3, 30.7, 30.8, 30.10 and 30.12 do not apply to these appeals. The time for filing an appellant's notice of appeal and provisions for extending or shortening time for compliance are set out in FPR 2010, r 31.15 (FPR PD30A, paras 10.1–10.5).

Appeals from a judge of district judge level—The Court of Appeal determined in *Cordle v Cordle* [2002] 1 FLR 207, CA that in the light of AJA 1999, s 55 appeals from district judges should henceforth only be allowed if it were demonstrated that there was procedural irregularity, or that in conducting the necessary balancing exercise, the district judge took into account matters that were irrelevant, or ignored matters that were relevant, or had otherwise arrived at a decision that was plainly wrong. These factors are reflected in r 30.3(7) 'real prospect of success or … some other compelling reason why the appeal should be heard', which is the necessary filter for permission to appeal. See *DE v AB (Financial Provision for Child)* [2012] 2 FLR 1396, FD.

30.4 Appellant's notice

(1) Where the appellant seeks permission from the appeal court it must be requested in the appellant's notice.

(2) Subject to paragraph (3), the appellant must file the appellant's notice at the appeal court within –

(a) such period as may be directed by the lower court (which may be longer or shorter than the period referred to in sub-paragraph (b)); or

(b) where the court makes no such direction, 21 days after the date of the decision of the lower court against which the appellant wishes to appeal.

(3) Where the appeal is against –

(a) a case management decision; or

(b) an order under section 38(1) of the 1989 Act,

the appellant must file the appellant's notice within 7 days beginning with the date of the decision of the lower court.

(4) Unless the appeal court orders otherwise, an appellant's notice must be served on each respondent and the persons referred to in paragraph (5) –

- (a) as soon as practicable; and
- (b) in any event not later than 7 days,

after it is filed.

(5) The persons referred to in paragraph (4) are –

- (a) any children's guardian, welfare officer, or children and family reporter;
- (b) a local authority who has prepared a report under section 14A(8) or (9) of the 1989 Act;
- (c) an adoption agency or local authority which has prepared a report on the suitability of the applicant to adopt a child;
- (d) a local authority which has prepared a report on the placement of the child for adoption; and
- (e) *(revoked)*

Amendments—SI 2014/667.

MCA 1980, s 111A appeal—The time for filing and service of the notice of appeal pursuant to s 111A is fixed at 21 days and may not be extended under FPR 2010, r 4.1(3)(a) or varied under r 30.4(2).

HRA 1998—Where an appellant seeks for the first time to rely on an issue under HRA 1998 or a remedy available under that Act he must include in the appeal notice the information required by FPR 2010, r 29.5(2) and FPR PD29A (Human Rights, Joining the Crown) will apply as if references to the directions hearing were to the application for permission to appeal (FPR PD30A, paras 5.2 and 5.3).

Incidental applications—Notice to the appeal court of an incidental application may be included in the notice of appeal or in a Pt 18 (Procedure for Other Applications in Proceedings) application notice (FPR PD30A, para 5.7).

Documents—FPR PD30A, para 5.8 sets out the documents which must be filed with the appellant's notice and para 5.9 sets out the documents which must be included in the appeal bundle (see Procedural Guide E2). All extraneous documents must be excluded and only material which is directly relevant to the subject matter of the appeal should be included in the bundle (FPR PD30A, para 5.10). The appeal bundle must contain a certificate signed by the party's counsel, solicitor or representative that the appellant has read and understood para 5.10 and the appeal bundle filed complies with it. Where it is not possible to file any of the required documents, the appellant must indicate the same, provide an estimate of when the same can be filed and then file as soon as practicable (FPR PD30A, paras 5.11, 5.12).

Skeleton arguments—The skeleton argument may be included in the appellant's notice or filed and served with the notice. Where it is impracticable to do so, the skeleton argument must be filed and served within 14 days of the filing of the notice. A skeleton argument must contain 'a numbered list of the points which the party wishes to make. These should both define and confine the areas of controversy. Each point should be stated as concisely as the nature of the case allows'. The skeleton argument must set out, in respect of each authority cited, the proposition of law that it demonstrates and identify the relevant page or paragraph. Where more than one authority is cited in support of a proposition, brief reasons must be given for doing so (FPR PD30A, paras 5.13–5.22, 7.7–7.12 and 7.14–7.15). Where the appeal is against a case management decision and the skeleton argument cannot accompany the appellant's notice, it must be filed as soon as practicable or as directed by the court but, in any event, not less than 3 days before the hearing of the appeal (FPR PD30A, para 5.14A).

Citation of authorities—On 24 March 2012, the Lord Chief Justice issued a practice direction: *Citation of Authorities* (see Part V). For a summary of the requirements, see the notes to Procedural Guide E5.

Transcripts—If an approved transcript of the judgment is not available, the following documents are acceptable: (i) a written copy of the judgment endorsed with the judge's signature; (ii) in the magistrates' court, a copy of the written reasons; (iii) an agreed note of the judgment submitted to the judge for approval or, if no agreement, copies of the rival versions should be submitted to the judge with an explanatory letter; and (iv) an advocates' note of the judgment where the appellant is unrepresented (FPR PD30A, paras 5.23 and 5.24).

30.5 Respondent's notice

(1) A respondent may file and serve a respondent's notice.

(2) A respondent who –

- (a) is seeking permission to appeal from the appeal court; or
- (b) wishes to ask the appeal court to uphold the order of the lower court for reasons different from or additional to those given by the lower court,

must file a respondent's notice.

(3) Where the respondent seeks permission from the appeal court it must be requested in the respondent's notice.

(4) Subject to paragraph (4A), a respondent's notice must be filed within –

(a) such period as may be directed by the lower court; or

(b) where the court makes no such direction, 14 days beginning with the date referred to in paragraph (5).

(4A) Where the appeal is against a case management decision, a respondent's notice must be filed within –

(a) such period as may be directed by the lower court; or .

(b) where the court makes no such direction, 7 days beginning with the date referred to in paragraph (5).

(5) The date referred to in paragraph (4) is –

(a) the date on which the respondent is served with the appellant's notice where – permission to appeal was given by the lower court; or permission to appeal is not required;

(b) the date on which the respondent is served with notification that the appeal court has given the appellant permission to appeal; or

(c) the date on which the respondent is served with notification that the application for permission to appeal and the appeal itself are to be heard together.

(6) Unless the appeal court orders otherwise, a respondent's notice must be served on the appellant, any other respondent and the persons referred to in rule 30.4(5) –

(a) as soon as practicable; and

(b) in any event not later than 7 days,

after it is filed.

(7) Where there is an appeal against an order under section 38(1) of the 1989 Act –

(a) a respondent may not, in that appeal, bring an appeal from the order or ask the appeal court to uphold the order of the lower court for reasons different from or additional to those given by the lower court; and

(b) paragraphs (2) and (3) do not apply.

Amendments—SI 2014/667.

Respondent's notice—A respondent who wishes to ask the appeal court to vary in any way the order of the lower court must appeal and obtain permission to appeal (if required, see FPR 2010, r 30.3(1),(2) above) on the same basis as for an appellant. A respondent who wishes to appeal or to invite the appeal court to uphold the order of the lower court but for different or additional reasons, must file a respondent's notice: in the absence of which a respondent will not be entitled, without permission of the appeal court, to rely on any reason not relied on by the lower court (FPR PD30A, paras 7.1–7.3). Note the reduced time limit where the appeal is against a case a management decision: 7 days (FPR 2010, r 30.5).

Skeleton arguments—For the content and form of skeleton arguments see the notes to FPR 2010, r 30.4, above. A party who files a respondent's notice but does not include a skeleton argument must file one within 14 days of filing the notice. A party who does not file a respondent's notice but who proposes to file a skeleton argument must do so at least 7 days before the appeal hearing. The respondent's skeleton argument should, where appropriate, answer the arguments set out in the appellant's skeleton argument (FPR PD30A, para 7.7–7.12).

Documents—Where a respondent considers additional documents should be included in the appeal bundle, the parties should agree amendments to the appeal bundle it possible. If unable to reach agreement, the respondent may prepare a supplemental bundle which bundle, with the requisite number of copies, must be filed at the appeal court: (i) with the respondent's notice; or (ii) within 21 days after being served with the appeal bundle (FPR PD30A, paras 7.16–7.18).

30.6 Grounds of appeal

The appeal notice must state the grounds of appeal.

30.7 Variation of time

(1) An application to vary the time limit for filing an appeal notice must be made to the appeal court.

(2) The parties may not agree to extend any date or time limit set by –

(a) these rules;
(b) Practice Direction 30A; or
(c) an order of the appeal court or the lower court.

(Rule 4.1(3)(a) provides that the court may extend or shorten the time for compliance with a rule, practice direction or court order (even if an application for extension is made after the time for compliance has expired).)

(Rule 4.1(3)(c) provides that the court may adjourn or bring forward a hearing.)

Extension of time—The application for an extension of time for filing the appellant's notice must be made in that notice with reasons for the delay. A respondent has the right to be heard on an application for an extension of time but a party who unreasonably opposes an extension of time is at risk of being ordered to pay the appellant's costs of the application (FPR PD30A, paras 5.4–5.6). An application to extend the time for filing a respondent's notice must be requested in that notice with reasons (FPR PD30A, para 7.6).

30.8 Stay

Unless the appeal court or the lower court orders otherwise, an appeal does not operate as a stay(GL) of any order or decision of the lower court.

Scope—An appeal (meaning an application for permission or following the grant of permission) does not automatically operate to stop the order which is the subject of the appeal taking effect. An application must be made for a stay of the order. A stay should normally be sought at the time of the application for permission to appeal, if not immediately following the decision which is to be appealed.

Imposition of conditions to grant of stay—The Supreme Court has criticised the imposition by the Court of Appeal of conditions to the grant of a stay pending determination of an application for permission to appeal by the Supreme Court. Lord Kerr said: 'as a general rule, conditions such as were imposed by the Court of Appeal in this case should not be made where a party seeks permission to appeal, not least because these might be seen as an unwarranted disincentive to the pursuit of what proved in this case to be a fully merited application': *Re B (A Child)* [2010] 1 FLR 551, SC.

30.9 Amendment of appeal notice

An appeal notice may not be amended without the permission of the appeal court.

Amendment—An application to amend should normally be made at the appeal hearing unless that would cause unnecessary expense or delay in which case a request should be made for it to be head in advance (FPR PD30A, para 5.44).

30.10 Striking out appeal notices and setting aside or imposing conditions on permission to appeal

(1) The appeal court may –

(a) strike out(GL) the whole or part of an appeal notice;
(b) set aside(GL) permission to appeal in whole or in part;
(c) impose or vary conditions upon which an appeal may be brought.

(2) The court will only exercise its powers under paragraph (1) where there is a compelling reason for doing so.

(3) Where a party was present at the hearing at which permission was given that party may not subsequently apply for an order that the court exercise its powers under paragraphs (1)(b) or (1)(c).

Compelling reasons—These are required to impose conditions under this rule and under FPR 2010, r 30.3(8). This rule applies where permission to appeal has already been granted on some previous occasion: *Radmacher v Granatino* [2009] 1 FLR 1566, CA.

30.11 Appeal court's powers

(1) In relation to an appeal the appeal court has all the powers of the lower court.

(Rule 30.1(4) provides that this Part is subject to any enactment that sets out special provisions with regard to any particular category of appeal.)

(2) The appeal court has power to –

(a) affirm, set aside(GL) or vary any order or judgment made or given by the lower court;
(b) refer any application or issue for determination by the lower court;
(c) order a new hearing;

PART III

(d) make orders for the payment of interest;
(e) make a costs order.

(3) The appeal court may exercise its powers in relation to the whole or part of an order of the lower court.

(Rule 4.1 contains general rules about the court's case management powers.)

(4) If the appeal court –

(a) refuses an application for permission to appeal;
(b) strikes out an appellant's notice; or
(c) dismisses an appeal,

and it considers that the application, the appellant's notice or the appeal is totally without merit, the provisions of paragraph (5) must be complied with.

(5) Where paragraph (4) applies –

(a) the court's order must record the fact that it considers the application, the appellant's notice or the appeal to be totally without merit; and
(b) the court must at the same time consider whether it is appropriate to make a civil restraint order.

'all the powers of the lower court' (r 30.11(1))—This includes the power to re-hear the matter. This is a power seldom used. The appeal is determined in accordance with the principles of *G v G (Minors: Custody Appeal)* [1985] FLR 894, HL. The appeal court does not hear the evidence and does not exercise a discretion afresh but must consider whether the court that heard the evidence erred in principle or was otherwise plainly wrong (see *Re W, Re A, Re B* [1999] 2 FLR 930, CA and *Re C (Leave to remove from jurisdiction)* [2000] 2 FLR 457, CA). However, where the court allows an appeal it may exercise the judicial discretion afresh rather than remitting the matter to the court below (*Fallon v Fallon* [2010] 1 FLR 910, CA). The Court of Appeal has given guidance on the limited grounds on which the court may grant an application for permission to appeal and to allow an appeal (particularly for the benefit of litigants in person) (*Re W (Permission to Appeal)* [2008] 1 FLR 406, CA).

Chronology—The Court of Appeal has observed that it would be 'enormously helpful' if a chronology was provided in all family appeals as they are for most first instance hearings: *Re H (Interim Contact: Domestic Violence Allegations)* [2014] 1 FLR 41, CA.

Fresh evidence—There is a presumption that the appeal court will determine the appeal on the basis of the evidence that was before the lower court. Fresh evidence will not be admitted without an order to that effect. Fresh evidence may be evidence of events since the decision which was the subject of the appeal or evidence relating to matters before the hearing that is the subject of the appeal but was not available at the hearing in the lower court. There is no specific requirement to be satisfied in respect of an application to admit fresh evidence. The former requirements laid down in *Ladd v Marshall* (1954) FLR Rep 422, CA are relevant as matters which should be considered in an exercise of the discretion whether to allow an appellant to rely on evidence not before the court below. These factors are:

(a) the evidence could not have been obtained with reasonable diligence at the trial;
(b) the evidence must be such that, if given, it would probably have had an important influence on the result of the case, though it need not be decisive; and
(c) the evidence must be such as would presumably be believed, or in other words, it must be apparently credible though it need not be incontrovertible (see *Hickey v Marks* (2000) 6 July, (unreported), CA and *Gillingham v Gillingham* [2001] EWCA Civ 906). There are dicta to suggest that in any case involving the welfare of a child fresh evidence would be admitted (*M v M (Transfer of Custody: Appeal)* [1987] 2 FLR 146, CA, at [150B]; *Re B (Minors) (Custody)* [1991] 1 FLR 137, CA, at [149B]; but see also *B v P (Access)* [1992] 2 FCR 576, FD).

These conditions do not apply to evidence in relation to matters that have occurred after the trial or where there was no trial on the facts. In such a situation the question of receiving the new evidence is a matter for the discretion of the appeal court. In deciding whether to admit fresh evidence as to events since the date of the trial, the appeal court will consider the matter without the benefit of the fresh evidence and, if the decision was wrong in accordance with the principles of *G v G (Minors: Custody Appeal)* [1985] FLR 894, HL, the court will consider the evidence and consider what weight to attach to it (*M v M (Transfer of Custody: Appeal)* [1987] 2 FLR 146, CA and *Re G (A Minor) (Wardship: Access)* [1988] 1 FLR 305, CA).

Proportionality—In exceptional but appropriate cases the appeal court may decline to hear an appeal on the basis that further litigation is disproportionate to the costs and/or issues in the case (*Cook v Plummer* [2008] 2 FLR 989, CA and *HH v BLW (Appeal: Costs: Proportionality)* [2013] 1 FLR 420, FD).

Welfare evaluation on appeal—The appeal court may substitute its own evaluation of the child's welfare for that of the lower court in the event that the appeal is allowed: *Re B (A Child)* [2015] 1 FLR 884, CA.

Second appeals—The unlawful removal of a child from his usual place of residence called for a peremptory order to be sought for his return, rather than to seek to challenge the dismissal of an appeal for an interim child arrangements order for living arrangements by way of a second appeal to the Court of Appeal: *Re R (Children)* [2011] 2 FLR 863, CA and AJA 1999, s 55.

Finding of fact hearings—Where the lower court refuses to make findings of fact sought by a party, the appeal court has no jurisdiction to entertain an appeal against that decision where the findings of fact sought were not 'pregnant with legal consequences': *Re M (Children)* [2013] EWCA Civ 1170, CA.

Challenging findings of fact after order is sealed—See the notes to CPR 1998, r 52.1.

Reopening an appeal—In exceptional circumstances, the High Court may reopen the final determination of an appeal if there is no alternative effective remedy and it would avoid real injustice (FPR 2010, r 30.14) The jurisdiction to reopen an appeal should only be permitted where the process of justice has been corrupted. It is insufficient for these purposes to establish that there is fresh evidence available which might have had a significant impact on the result (*Re U (Re-opening of Appeal)* [2005] 2 FLR 444, CA).

Hopeless appeals—Where the appeal court considers the application or appeal is totally without merit, it must record that fact in the court order and consider making a civil restraint order: see CPR 1998, Pt 3.

30.12 Hearing of appeals

(1) Every appeal will be limited to a review of the decision of the lower court unless –

(a) an enactment or practice direction makes different provision for a particular category of appeal; or

(b) the court considers that in the circumstances of an individual appeal it would be in the interests of justice to hold a re-hearing.

(2) Unless it orders otherwise, the appeal court will not receive –

(a) oral evidence; or

(b) evidence which was not before the lower court.

(3) The appeal court will allow an appeal where the decision of the lower court was –

(a) wrong; or

(b) unjust because of a serious procedural or other irregularity in the proceedings in the lower court.

(4) The appeal court may draw any inference of fact which it considers justified on the evidence.

(5) At the hearing of the appeal a party may not rely on a matter not contained in that party's appeal notice unless the appeal court gives permission.

Modifications—Modified for certain proceedings by FPR PD30A, para 9.30.

Separate representation—The Master of the Rolls has emphasised 'in the strongest possible terms that it is only where it is clear that there is an unavoidable conflict of interest, as a matter of law, between two parties in the same interest that they should have separate legal representation, especially where public money is involved. The fact that the parties may have different factual points, or that one party's case may be seen as stronger than the other's, or that the parties' legal advisers may see the legal arguments or the prospects somewhat differently, are not good reasons for their incurring the expense and the court time of separate representation': *Oxfordshire County Council v X, Y and J* [2011] 1 FLR 272, CA.

Fresh experts on appeal—The Court of Appeal emphasised that there was an obligation on an applicant seeking permission to appeal, or on an appellant who had obtained permission, to seek the appeal court's leave before instructing a fresh expert and releasing court papers to him: see notes to CPR 1998, r 52.11 (*Re McC (Care Proceedings: Fresh Evidence of Foreign Expert)* [2012] 2 FLR 121, CA and the Family Justice Council Guidelines of December 2011, *Instruction of Medical Experts from Overseas in Family Cases* (see Part V)).

Grounds for allowing an appeal—The test is whether the decision was wrong and not whether it was plainly wrong. Whether the threshold criteria of CA 1989, s 31(2) are satisfied and whether the court should make a care order are evaluative exercises and not the exercise of a discretion. Accordingly, the approach set out in *G v G (Minors: Custody Appeal)* [1985] FLR 894, HL is not appropriate: *Re B (Care Proceedings: Appeal)* [2013] 2 FLR 1075, SC; *Re P (A Child)* [2014] 1 FLR 824, CA.

Appeal against findings of fact—For Mostyn J's observations in *NG v SG (Appeal: Non-Disclosure)* [2012] 1 FLR 1211, FD, see the introduction to Guide E5.

Role of appellate court—For further guidance on the approach that an appellate court should adopt to (a) appeals where the adequacy of a trial judge's reasoning is in issue and (b) appeals against the exercise of a discretion by a trial judge, see the notes to CPR 1998, Pt 52.

Appeal court to re-make decision or to remit—See the notes to CPR 1998, r 52.10.

Litigants in person—Where the party seeking to appeal an order in the Court of Appeal in public law proceedings is a litigant in person, the local authority has the responsibility to ensure the appeal court is properly provided with appeal bundles: *Re R (A Child)* [2014] EWCA Civ 597.

30.13 Assignment of appeals to the Court of Appeal

(1) Where the court from or to which an appeal is made or from which permission to appeal is sought ('the relevant court') considers that –

(a) an appeal which is to be heard by a county court or the High Court would raise an important point of principle or practice; or

(b) there is some other compelling reason for the Court of Appeal to hear it,

the relevant court may order the appeal to be transferred to the Court of Appeal.

(2) Paragraph (1) does not allow an application for permission to appeal to be transferred to the Court of Appeal.

Amendments—SI 2014/667.

Scope—Where an appeal is to be heard in the County Court or the High Court, that court may transfer the appeal to be heard by the Court of Appeal. If that court (the County Court or High Court) hears and determines the appeal, there can be an appeal to the Court of Appeal from that decision only if there is some important point of principle or other compelling reason.

30.14 Reopening of final appeals

(1) The High Court will not reopen a final determination of any appeal unless –

(a) it is necessary to do so in order to avoid real injustice;

(b) the circumstances are exceptional and make it appropriate to reopen the appeal; and

(c) there is no alternative effective remedy.

(2) In paragraphs (1), (3), (4) and (6), 'appeal' includes an application for permission to appeal.

(3) This rule does not apply to appeals to the family court.

(4) Permission is needed to make an application under this rule to reopen a final determination of an appeal.

(5) There is no right to an oral hearing of an application for permission unless, exceptionally, the judge so directs.

(6) The judge will not grant permission without directing the application to be served on the other party to the original appeal and giving that party an opportunity to make representations.

(7) There is no right of appeal or review from the decision of the judge on the application for permission, which is final.

(8) The procedure for making an application for permission is set out in Practice Direction 30A.

Amendments—SI 2014/667.

Limitations—The jurisdiction to reopen an appeal should only be permitted where the process of justice has been corrupted. It is insufficient for these purposes to establish that there is fresh evidence available which might have had a significant impact on the result (*Re U (Re-opening of Appeal)* [2005] 2 FLR 444, CA).

Family Court—The Family Court does not have jurisdiction to reopen a final appeal (r 30.14(3)).

Procedure—The term 'appeal' includes an application for permission to appeal. The application for permission must be sought from the court whose decision the applicant wishes to re-open and must be made by application notice and supported by written evidence verified by a statement of truth. The application must not be served on any other party to the original appeal unless the courts so directs. Where such a direction is given that party may file within 14 days a written statement supporting or opposing the application. The application for permission will be considered by a single judge on paper and will only be allowed to proceed if the judge so directs (FPR PD30A, paras 18.1–18.7).

Practice Direction 30A – Appeals

This Practice Direction supplements FPR Part 30

Application and interpretation

1.1 This practice direction applies to all appeals to which Part 30 applies.

1.2 In this Practice Direction in relation to the family court –

'the 1984 Act' means the Matrimonial and Family Proceedings Act 1984;

'assistant to a justices' clerk' has the meaning given in section 27(5) of the Courts Act 2003;

'authorised' means authorised by the President of the Family Division or nominated by or on behalf of the Lord Chief Justice to conduct particular business in the family court, in accordance with Part 3 of rules relating to the composition of the court and distribution of business made in accordance with section 31D of the 1984 Act;

'costs judge' means –

(a) the Chief Taxing Master;
(b) a taxing master of the Senior Courts; or
(c) a person appointed to act as deputy for the person holding office referred to in paragraph (b) or to act as a temporary additional officer for any such office;

'judge of circuit judge level' means –

(a) a circuit judge who, where applicable, is authorised;
(b) a Recorder who, where applicable, is authorised;
(c) any other judge of the family court authorised to sit as a judge of circuit judge level in the family court;

'judge of district judge level' means –

(a) the Senior District Judge of the Family Division;
(b) a district judge of the Principal Registry of the Family Division ('PRFD');
(c) a person appointed to act as deputy for the person holding office referred to in paragraph (b) or to act as a temporary additional officer for any such office;
(d) a district judge who, where applicable, is authorised;
(e) a deputy district judge appointed under section 102 of the Senior Courts Act 1981 or section 8 of the County Courts Act 1984 who, where applicable, is authorised;
(f) an authorised District Judge (Magistrates' Courts);
(g) any other judge of the family court authorised to sit as a judge of district judge level in the family court.

'judge of High Court judge level' means –

(a) a deputy judge of the High Court;
(b) a puisne judge of the High Court;
(c) a person who has been a judge of the Court of Appeal or a puisne judge of the High Court who may act as a judge of the family court by virtue of section 9 of the Senior Courts Act 1981;
(d) the Senior President of Tribunals;
(e) the Chancellor of the High Court;
(f) an ordinary judge of the Court of Appeal (including the vice-president, if any, of either division of that court);
(g) the President of the Queen's Bench Division;
(h) the President of the Family Division;
(i) the Master of the Rolls;
(j) the Lord Chief Justice;

'justices' clerk' has the meaning given in section 27(1) of the Courts Act 2003; and

'lay justice' means an authorised justice of the peace who is not a District Judge (Magistrates' Courts).

Routes of appeal

2.1 The following table sets out to which court or judge an appeal is to be made (subject to obtaining any necessary permission) from decisions of the family court –

Decision of judge sitting in the family court	Permission generally required (subject to exception in rules of court, for example, no permission required to appeal against a committal order)	Appeal to
1 A bench of – • two or three lay magistrates; or • a lay justice	No	a judge of circuit judge level sitting in the family court; a judge of High Court judge level sitting in the family court where a Designated Family Judge or a judge of High Court Judge level considers that the appeal would raise an important point of principle or practice. (NB a judge of High Court judge level may hear the appeal in interests of effective and efficient use of local judicial resource and the resource of the High Court bench)
2 A judge of district judge level (except the Senior District Judge of the Family Division or a District Judge (PRFD) in proceedings for a financial remedy)	Yes	As above
3 District Judge (PRFD) in proceedings for financial remedy	Yes	Judge of High Court judge level sitting in the family court
4 Senior District Judge of the Family Division in proceedings for financial remedy	Yes	Judge of High Court judge level sitting in the family court
4A Circuit judge or Recorder, except where paragraph 5 of this table applies.	Yes	High Court Judge (sitting in the High Court)

Decision of judge sitting in the family court	Permission generally required (subject to exception in rules of court, for example, no permission required to appeal against a committal order)	Appeal to
5 Circuit judge or Recorder, where the appeal is from: (a) a decision or order in proceedings under – (i) Part 4 or 5 of, or paragraph 19(1) of Schedule 2 to, the Children Act 1989; or (ii) the Adoption and Children Act 2002; (b) a decision or order in exercise of the court's jurisdiction in relation to contempt of court, where that decision or order was made in, or in connection with, proceedings of a type referred to in sub-paragraph (a); or (c) a decision or order made on appeal to the family court.	Yes	Court of Appeal
6 Costs Judge	Yes	Judge of High Court judge level sitting in the family court
7 Judge of High Court judge level	Yes	Court of Appeal
8 Any other judge of the family court not referred to in paragraphs 1 to 7 of this table.	Yes	Court of Appeal

(Provisions setting out routes of appeal include section 31K(1) of the 1984 Act for appeals against decisions from the family court and section 13(2A) of the Administration of Justice Act 1960 for appeals against decisions or orders from the family court relating to contempt of court.

The Access to Justice Act 1999 (Destination of Appeals) (Family Proceedings) Order 2014 (S.I. 2014/602) routes appeals from certain judges and office holders to the family court instead of to the Court of Appeal and rules relating to the composition of the court and distribution of business made in accordance with section 31 D of the 1984 Act make provision for appeals within the family court. Amendments to the 2014 Order (made by the Access to Justice Act 1999 (Destination of Appeals) (Family Proceedings) (Amendment) Order 2016) route certain appeals from Circuit Judges or Recorders to the High Court instead of the Court of Appeal. These appeals are heard by a High Court judge sitting in the High Court (see paragraph 8.4 below).

The leapfrogging provision in section 57 of the Access to Justice Act 1999 applies to appeals where in any proceedings in the family court a person appeals or seeks permission to appeal to a court other than the Court of Appeal or the Supreme Court.)

2.2 The following table sets out to which court or judge an appeal is to be made (subject to obtaining any necessary permission) from decisions of the High Court –

Decision of judge	**Permission generally required (subject to exception in rules of court, for example, no permission required to appeal against a committal order)**	**Appeal to**
1 District Judge of the High Court; or • a deputy district judge appointed under section 102 of the Senior Courts Act 1981	Yes	High Court Judge
2 The Senior District Judge of the Family Division; • District Judge of the PRFD; or • a person appointed to act as deputy for a District Judge of the PRFD or to act as a temporary additional officer for such office	Yes	High Court Judge
3 Costs judge; or • a person appointed to act as deputy for a costs judge who is a taxing master of the senior courts or to act as a temporary additional officer for such office	Yes	High Court Judge
4 Judge of the High Court (including a person acting as a judge of the High Court in accordance with section 9(1) or section 9(4) of the Senior Courts Act 1981)	Yes	Court of Appeal

(Provisions setting out routes of appeal include section 16(1) of the Senior Courts Act 1981 (as amended) for appeals against decisions from the High Court and section 13 of the Administration of Justice Act 1960 for appeals against an order or decision of the High Court relating to contempt of court. The Access to Justice Act 1999 (Destination of Appeals)(Family

Proceedings) Order 2011 (S.I. 2011/1044) routes appeals against decisions of certain judges to the High Court instead of the Court of Appeal. The leapfrogging provision in section 57 of the Access to Justice Act 1999 referred to above applies.

The general rule is that appeals under section 8(1) of the Gender Recognition Act 2004 must be started in the family court as both the High Court and the family court have jurisdiction to hear the appeal (see section 8 of the 2004 Act and FPR 5.4). The procedure for appeals to the Court of Appeal is governed by the Civil Procedure Rules 1998, in particular CPR Part 52.).

2.3 A justices' clerk and assistant to a justices' clerk are not judges of the family court but they perform functions of the court in accordance with rules made under section 31O of the 1984 Act (see, for example, the Justices' Clerks and Assistants Rules 2014 (S.I. 2014/603)). Appeals against decisions of a justices' clerk or an assistant to a justices' clerk are to a judge of circuit judge level sitting in the family court. However, it is expected that such appeals will be rare as a justices' clerk and an assistant to a justices' clerk may refer a matter to the court as appropriate before making a decision.

2.4 Where the decision to be appealed is a decision in a Part 19 (Alternative Procedure For Applications) application on a point of law in a case which did not involve any substantial dispute of fact, the court to which the appeal lies, where that court is the High Court or the family court and unless the appeal would lie to the Court of Appeal in any event, must consider whether to order the appeal to be transferred to the Court of Appeal under FPR 30.13 (Assignment of Appeals to the Court of Appeal).

PART III

Grounds for appeal

3.1 Rule 30.12 (hearing of appeals) sets out the circumstances in which the appeal court will allow an appeal.

3.2 The grounds of appeal should –

(a) set out clearly the reasons why rule 30.12(3)(a) or (b) is said to apply; and
(b) specify in respect of each ground, whether the ground raises an appeal on a point of law or is an appeal against a finding of fact.

Permission to appeal

4.1 FPR 30.3 (Permission) sets out the circumstances in which permission to appeal is required. At present, permission to appeal is generally required under that provision where the decision of the family court appealed against was made by-

(a) a Circuit Judge or Recorder, except where the appeal is against a decision or order made in proceedings referred to in paragraph 4.1A;
(b) a district judge (including a District Judge (Magistrates' Courts)); or
(c) a costs judge.

However, permission to appeal is not required where FPR 30.3(2) applies (appeals against a committal order, a secure accommodation order under section 25 of the Children Act 1989, or a refusal to grant habeas corpus for release in relation to a minor).

In proceedings in the High Court, permission to appeal is required under FPR 30.3 where the decision appealed against is a decision of a district judge or a costs judge, except where FPR 30.3(2) applies.

4.1A FPR Part 30 does not apply to an appeal against the decision or order of a Circuit Judge or Recorder in the family court where the decision or order was made –

(a) in proceedings under-
  (i) Part 4 or 5 of, or paragraph 19(1) of Schedule 2 to, the Children Act 1989; or
  (ii) the Adoption and Children Act 2002;
(b) in exercise of the court's jurisdiction in relation to contempt of court, where that decision or order was made in, or in connection with, proceedings of a type referred to in paragraph (a); or
(c) on appeal to the family court.

(An appeal against a decision by a Circuit Judge or Recorder, where the appeal is from a decision or order referred to in paragraph 4.1A, is to the Court of Appeal and the Civil Procedure Rules 1998 apply.)

4.1B The court should not ordinarily grant permission to appeal where the matters complained of would be better dealt with on an application to set aside a financial remedy order under rule 9.9A. Such an application would be appropriate if the proposed appeal does not in fact allege an error of the court on the materials that were before the court at the time the order was made. However, by way of exception, permission to appeal may still be given where (i) a litigant alleges both that the court erred on the materials before it and that a ground for setting aside under rule 9.9A exists; or (ii) the order which it is sought to set aside includes a pension sharing order or pension compensation sharing order and the court may be asked to consider making orders under s 40A(5) or s 40B(2)(b) of the Matrimonial Causes Act 1973.

Court to which permission to appeal application should be made

4.2 An application for permission should be made orally at the hearing at which the decision to be appealed against is made.

4.3 Where –

(a) no application for permission to appeal is made at the hearing; or
(b) the lower court refuses permission to appeal,

an application for permission to appeal may be made to the appeal court in accordance with rules 30.3(3) and (4) (Permission).

(Rule 30.1(3) defines 'lower court'.)

4.4 Where no application for permission to appeal has been made in accordance with rule 30.3(3)(a) (Permission) but a party requests further time to make such an application the court may adjourn the hearing to give that party an opportunity to do so.

4.5 There is no appeal from a decision of the appeal court to allow or refuse permission to appeal to that court. However, where the appeal court, without a hearing, refuses permission to appeal, the person seeking permission may request that decision to be reconsidered at a hearing, unless an order has been made under rule 30.3(5A) that the person seeking permission may not do so (where the application for permission is considered to be totally without merit) – see section 54(4) of the Access to Justice Act 1999 and rule 30.3(5), (5A) (Permission).

Permission and case management decisions

4.5A Where the application is for permission to appeal from a case management decision, the factors to which the court is to have particular regard include whether –

(a) the issue is of sufficient significance to justify an appeal;
(b) the procedural consequences of an appeal (e.g. the impact upon the timetable) outweigh the significance of the case management decision;
(c) it would be more convenient to adjourn the determination of the issue.

4.5B Case management decisions include decisions made under FPR 4.1(3) and decisions about disclosure, filing of witness statements or experts' reports, directions about the timetable of the proceedings and adding a party to the proceedings.

Material omission from a judgment of the lower court

4.6 Where a party's advocate considers that there is a material omission from a judgment of the lower court or, where the decision is made by a lay justice or justices, the written reasons for the decision of the lower court (including inadequate reasons for the lower court's decision), the advocate should before the drawing of the order give the lower court which made the decision the opportunity of considering whether there is an omission and should not immediately use the omission as grounds for an application to appeal.

4.7 Paragraph 4.8 below applies where there is an application to the lower court for permission to appeal on the grounds of a material omission from a judgment or written reasons (where a decision is made in the family court by a lay justice or justices) of the lower court. Paragraph 4.9 below applies where there is an application for permission to appeal to the appeal court on the grounds of a material omission from a judgment or written reasons (where a decision is made in the family court by a lay justice or justices) of the lower court.

4.8 Where the application for permission to appeal is made to the lower court, the court which made the decision must –

(a) consider whether there is a material omission and adjourn for that purpose if necessary; and

(b) where the conclusion is that there has been such an omission, provide additions to the judgment.

4.9 Where the application for permission to appeal is made to the appeal court, the appeal court –

(a) must consider whether there is a material omission; and

(b) where the conclusion is that there has been such an omission, may adjourn the application and remit the case to the lower court with an invitation to provide additions to the judgment.

Consideration of Permission without a hearing

4.10 An application for permission to appeal may be considered by the appeal court without a hearing.

4.11 If permission is granted without a hearing the parties will be notified of that decision and the procedure in paragraphs 6.1 to 6.8 will then apply.

4.12 If permission is refused without a hearing the parties will be notified of that decision with the reasons for it. The decision is subject to the appellant's right to have it reconsidered at an oral hearing. This may be before the same judge. However the appellant has no right to have the application considered at an oral hearing where a High Court Judge or Designated Family Judge refused permission to appeal without a hearing and made an order under rule 30.3(5A) that the appellant may not request the decision to be reconsidered at a hearing because he or she considered the application for permission to be totally without merit.

4.13 A request for the decision to be reconsidered at an oral hearing must be filed at the appeal court within 7 days after service of the notice that permission has been refused. A copy of the request must be served by the appellant on the respondent at the same time. This does not apply where an order has been made under rule 30.3(5A) that the appellant may not request the decision to be reconsidered at a hearing.

Video conferencing—In *Black v Pastouna* [2005] EWCA Civ 1389 at [13]–[15], Brooke LJ issued guidance on the use of video conferencing under Annex 3, which urges parties always to consider when video arrangements might save cost (and see CPR 1998, rr 1.1 and 1.3, and the same rules in FPR 2010). Where cases in the Court of Appeal are likely to last 30 minutes or less, the Court will expect the parties or their advisers to consider the use of video conferencing. At [15] Brooke LJ concluded: 'If the Court is not satisfied that there are any features of the application which warrant an oral hearing … it may direct that any recoverable costs may be limited to the cost of conducting the hearing by video conference [where] less than the cost of attending court and any associated travel expenses.'

Permission hearing

4.14 Where an appellant, who is represented, makes a request for a decision to be reconsidered at an oral hearing, the appellant's advocate must, at least 4 days before the hearing, in a brief written statement –

(a) inform the court and the respondent of the points which the appellant proposes to raise at the hearing;

(b) set out the reasons why permission should be granted notwithstanding the reasons given for the refusal of permission; and

(c) confirm, where applicable, that the requirements of paragraph 4.17 have been complied with (appellant in receipt of legal aid).

4.15 The respondent will be given notice of a permission hearing, but is not required to attend unless requested by the court to do so.

4.16 If the court requests the respondent's attendance at the permission hearing, the appellant must supply the respondent with a copy of the appeal bundle (see paragraph 5.9 or 5.9A, as applicable) within 7 days of being notified of the request, or such other period as the court may direct. The costs of providing that bundle shall be borne by the appellant initially, but will form part of the costs of the permission application.

Appellants in receipt of services funded by legal aid: applying for permission to appeal

4.17 Where the appellant is in receipt of legal aid and permission to appeal has been refused by the appeal court without a hearing, the appellant must send a copy of the reasons the appeal court gave for refusing permission to the Director of legal aid casework as soon as it has been received from the court. The court will require confirmation that this has been done if a hearing is requested to re-consider the question of permission.

Limited permission

4.18 Where a court under rule 30.3 (Permission) gives permission to appeal on some issues only, it will –

(a) refuse permission on any remaining issues; or
(b) reserve the question of permission to appeal on any remaining issues to the court hearing the appeal.

4.19 If the court reserves the question of permission under paragraph 4.18(b), the appellant must, within 14 days after service of the court's order, inform the appeal court and the respondent in writing whether the appellant intends to pursue the reserved issues. If the appellant does intend to pursue the reserved issues, the parties must include in any time estimate for the appeal hearing, their time estimate for the reserved issues.

4.20 If the appeal court refuses permission to appeal on the remaining issues without a hearing and the applicant wishes to have that decision reconsidered at an oral hearing, the time limit in rule 30.3(6) (Permission) shall apply. Any application for an extension of this time limit should be made promptly. The court hearing the appeal on the issues for which permission has been granted will not normally grant, at the appeal hearing, an application to extend the time limit in rule 30.3(6) for the remaining issues.

4.21 If the appeal court refuses permission to appeal on remaining issues at or after an oral hearing, the application for permission to appeal on those issues cannot be renewed at the appeal hearing (see section 54(4) of the Access to Justice Act 1999).

Respondents' costs of permission applications

4.22 In most cases, applications for permission to appeal will be determined without the court requesting –

(a) submissions from; or
(b) if there is an oral hearing, attendance by,

the respondent.

4.23 Where the court does not request submissions from or attendance by the respondent, costs will not normally be allowed to a respondent who volunteers submissions or attendance.

4.24 Where the court does request –

(a) submissions from; or
(b) attendance by the respondent,

the court will normally allow the costs of the respondent if permission is refused.

Allocation – appropriate procedure

4A.1 Where a party is dissatisfied with allocation that party may appeal or request the court to reconsider allocation at a hearing under FPR 29.19.

4A.2 Where allocation was made at a hearing, the party who is dissatisfied may appeal.

4A.3 Where allocation was made without a hearing, the party who is dissatisfied should request the court to reconsider allocation at a hearing.

Allocation and Gatekeeping—See FC(CDB)R 2014 and the President's Guidance on *Allocation and Gatekeeping (Public Law)* and the attached Schedule for the factors to be considered when allocating cases.

Appellant's notice

5.1 An appellant's notice must be filed and served in all cases. Where an application for permission to appeal is made to the appeal court it must be applied for in the appellant's notice. Practice Direction 5A specifies the forms to be used to make an appeal: different forms are to be used, depending on the court to which the appeal lies.

Human Rights

5.2 Where the appellant seeks –

(a) to rely on any issue under the Human Rights Act 1998; or
(b) a remedy available under that Act,

for the first time in an appeal the appellant must include in the appeal notice the information required by rule 29.5(2).

5.3 Practice Direction 29A (Human Rights, Joining the Crown) will apply as if references to the directions hearing were to the application for permission to appeal.

Extension of time for filing appellant's notice

5.4 If an extension of time is required for filing the appellant's notice the application must be made in that notice. The notice should state the reason for the delay and the steps taken prior to the application being made.

5.5 Where the appellant's notice includes an application for an extension of time and permission to appeal has been given or is not required the respondent has the right to be heard on that application and must be served with a copy of the appeal bundle (see paragraph 5.9). However, a respondent who unreasonably opposes an extension of time runs the risk of being ordered to pay the appellant's costs of that application.

5.6 If an extension of time is given following such an application the procedure at paragraphs 6.1 to 6.8 applies.

Applications

5.7 Notice of an application to be made to the appeal court for a remedy incidental to the appeal (e.g. an interim injunction under rule 20.2 (Orders for interim remedies)) may be included in the appeal notice or in a Part 18 (Procedure For Other Applications in Proceedings) application notice.

(Paragraph 13 of this practice direction contains other provisions relating to applications.).

Documents: appeals to the family court

5.8 Where the appeal lies to the family court, the appellant must file the following documents together with an appeal bundle (see paragraph 5.9) with his or her appellant's notice –

(a) …
(b) one copy of the appellant's notice for each of the respondents;
(c) one copy of the appellant's skeleton argument for each of the respondents;
(d), (e) …

PART III

(f) any witness statements or affidavits in support of any application included in the appellant's notice.

5.9 Where the appeal lies to the family court, an appellant must include the following documents in his or her appeal bundle –

(a) a sealed or stamped copy of the appellant's notice;
(b) a sealed or stamped copy of the order being appealed, or a copy of the notice of the making of an order;
(c) a copy of any order giving or refusing permission to appeal, together with a copy of the court's reasons for allowing or refusing permission to appeal;
(d) any affidavit or witness statement filed in support of any application included in the appellant's notice;
(e) where the appeal is against a consent order, a statement setting out the change in circumstances since the order was agreed or other circumstances justifying a review or re-hearing;
(f) a copy of the appellant's skeleton argument;
(g) a transcript or note of judgment or, in a magistrates' court, written reasons for the court's decision (see paragraph 5.23), and in cases where permission to appeal was given by the lower court or is not required those parts of any transcript of evidence which are directly relevant to any question at issue on the appeal;
(h) the application form;
(i) any application notice (or case management documentation) relevant to the subject of the appeal;
(j) any other documents which the appellant reasonably considers necessary to enable the appeal court to reach its decision on the hearing of the application or appeal; and
(k) such other documents as the court may direct.

5.10 All documents that are extraneous to the issues to be considered on the application or the appeal must be excluded. The appeal bundle may include affidavits, witness statements, summaries, experts' reports and exhibits but only where these are directly relevant to the subject matter of the appeal.

Documents: appeals to the High Court

5.10A Where an appeal lies to the High Court, the appellant must file the following documents, in the following sequence, as the appeal bundle:

(a) a sealed or stamped copy of the appellant's notice (including the grounds of appeal);
(b) a sealed or stamped copy of the order being appealed [or a copy of the notice of the making of an order];
(c) a transcript or note of the judgment (see also paragraphs 5.23 and 5.24);
(d) copies of any documents specifically referred to in the judgment;
(e) a copy of the appellant's skeleton argument (see also paragraphs 5.14 and 5.15).

5.10B Subject to paragraphs 5.11 and 6.4(1) and (c), no further documents may be included in the appeal bundle without an order of a High Court Judge sitting in the High Court.

5.10C In addition to the appeal bundle, the appellant must file the following duplicate documents-

(a) one copy of the appellant's notice for each of the respondents;
(b) one copy of the appellant's skeleton argument for each of the respondents (see also paragraphs 5.14 and 5.15).

Documents: appeals to the family court or the High Court

5.11 Where the appellant is represented, the appeal bundle must contain a certificate signed by the appellant's solicitor, counsel or other representative to the effect that the appellant has read and understood paragraph 5.10 and that the composition of the appeal bundle complies with it.

5.12 Where it is not possible to file all the above documents, the appellant must indicate which documents have not yet been filed and the reasons why they are not currently available. The appellant must then provide a reasonable estimate of when the missing document or documents can be filed and file them as soon as reasonably practicable.

Skeleton arguments

5.13 As noted in paragraphs 5.9 and 5.10A, the appellant's notice must, subject to paragraphs 5.14 and 5.15, be accompanied by a skeleton argument. Alternatively the skeleton argument may be included in the appellant's notice. Where the skeleton argument is so included it will not form part of the notice for the purposes of rule 30.9 (Amendment of appeal notice).

5.14 Subject to paragraph 5.14A, where it is impracticable for the appellant's skeleton argument to accompany the appellant's notice it must be filed and served on all respondents within 14 days of filing the notice.

5.14A In appeals against case management decisions, where the appellant's skeleton argument cannot accompany the appellant's notice it must be filed as soon as practicable or as directed by the court, but in any event not less than 3 days before the hearing of the appeal.

5.15 An appellant who is not represented need not file a skeleton argument but is encouraged to do so since this will be helpful to the court.

5.16 A skeleton argument must contain a numbered list of the points which the party wishes to make. These should both define and confine the areas of controversy. Each point should be stated as concisely as the nature of the case allows.

5.17 A numbered point must be followed by a reference to any document on which the party wishes to rely.

5.18 A skeleton argument must state, in respect of each authority cited –

(a) the proposition of law that the authority demonstrates; and
(b) the parts of the authority (identified by page or paragraph references) that support the proposition.

5.19 If more than one authority is cited in support of a given proposition, the skeleton argument must briefly state the reason for taking that course.

5.20 The statement referred to in paragraph 5.19 should not materially add to the length of the skeleton argument but should be sufficient to demonstrate, in the context of the argument –

(a) the relevance of the authority or authorities to that argument; and
(b) that the citation is necessary for a proper presentation of that argument.

5.21 The cost of preparing a skeleton argument which –

(a) does not comply with the requirements set out in this paragraph; or
(b) was not filed within the time limits provided by this Practice Direction (or any further time granted by the court),

will not be allowed on assessment except to the extent that the court otherwise directs.

5.22 The appellant should consider what other information the appeal court will need. This may include a list of persons who feature in the case or glossaries of technical terms. A chronology of relevant events will be necessary in most appeals.

Suitable record of the judgment

5.23 Where the judgment to be appealed has been officially recorded by the court, an approved transcript of that record should accompany the appellant's notice. Photocopies will not be accepted for this purpose. However, where there is no officially recorded judgment, the following documents will be acceptable –

Written judgments – Where the judgment was made in writing a copy of that judgment endorsed with the judge's signature.

Written reasons – where a decision is made by a lay justice or justices in the family court, a copy of the written reasons for the court's decision.

Note of judgment – When judgment was not officially recorded or made in writing a note of the judgment (agreed between the appellant's and respondent's advocates) should be submitted for approval to the judge whose decision is being appealed. If the parties cannot agree on a single note of the judgment, both versions should be provided to that judge with an explanatory letter. For the purpose of an application for permission to appeal the note need not be approved by the respondent or the lower court judge.

Advocates' notes of judgments where the appellant is unrepresented – When the appellant was unrepresented in the lower court it is the duty of any advocate for the respondent to make the advocate's note of judgment promptly available, free of charge to the appellant where there is no officially recorded judgment or if the court so directs. Where the appellant was represented in the lower court it is the duty of the appellant's own former advocate to make that advocate's note available in these circumstances. The appellant should submit the note of judgment to the appeal court.

5.24 An appellant may not be able to obtain an official transcript or other suitable record of the lower court's decision within the time within which the appellant's notice must be filed. In such cases the appellant's notice must still be completed to the best of the appellant's ability on the basis of the documentation available. However it may be amended subsequently with the permission of the appeal court in accordance with rule 30.9 (Amendment of appeal notice).

Advocates' notes of judgments

5.25 Advocates' brief (or, where appropriate, refresher) fee includes –

(a) remuneration for taking a note of the judgment of the court;
(b) having the note transcribed accurately;
(c) attempting to agree the note with the other side if represented;
(d) submitting the note to the judge for approval where appropriate;
(e) revising it if so requested by the judge,
(f) providing any copies required for the appeal court, instructing solicitors and lay client; and
(g) providing a copy of the note to an unrepresented appellant.

****

Appeals under section 8(1) of the Gender Recognition Act 2004

5.27 Paragraph 5.28 to 5.30 apply where the appeal is brought under section 8(1) of the Gender Recognition Act 2004 on a point of law against a decision by the Gender Recognition Panel to reject the application under sections 1(1), 4A, 5(2), 5A(2) or 6(1) of the 2004 Act. The appeal is to the High Court or to the family court. However, FPR 5.4 provides that where the family court has jurisdiction to deal with a matter, the proceedings relating to that matter must be started in the family court except where the court otherwise directs, any rule, other enactment or Practice Direction provides otherwise or proceedings relating to the same parties are already being heard by the High Court. Most appeals under section 8(1) of the Gender Recognition Act 2004 are therefore likely to be to the family court and be heard by a judge of High Court Judge level sitting in that court in accordance with the rules relating to the composition of the court and distribution of business made in accordance with section 31D of the 1984 Act.

5.28 Where the appeal is to the High Court, the appeal notice must be –

(a) filed in the PRFD; and
(b) served on the Secretary of State and the President of the Gender Recognition Panels.

5.28A Where the appeal is to the family court the appeal notice must be served on the Secretary of State and the President of the Gender Recognition Panels.

5.29 The Secretary of State may appear and be heard in the proceedings on the appeal.

5.30 Where the High Court issues a gender recognition certificate under section 8(3)(a) of the Gender Recognition Act 2004, the court officer must send a copy of that certificate to the Secretary of State.

Transcripts or Notes of Evidence

5.31 When the evidence is relevant to the appeal an official transcript of the relevant evidence must be obtained. Transcripts or notes of evidence are generally not needed for the purpose of determining an application for permission to appeal.

Notes of evidence

5.32 If evidence relevant to the appeal was not officially recorded, a typed version of the judge's or justices' clerk's / assistant clerk's notes of evidence must be obtained.

Transcripts at public expense

5.33 Where the lower court or the appeal court is satisfied that –

(a) an unrepresented appellant; or
(b) an appellant whose legal representation is provided free of charge to the appellant and not funded by the Community Legal Service,

is in such poor financial circumstances that the cost of a transcript would be an excessive burden the court may certify that the cost of obtaining one official transcript should be borne at public expense.

5.34 In the case of a request for an official transcript of evidence or proceedings to be paid for at public expense, the court must also be satisfied that there are reasonable grounds for appeal. Whenever possible a request for a transcript at public expense should be made to the lower court when asking for permission to appeal.

Filing and service of appellant's notice

5.35 Rule 30.4 (Appellant's notice) sets out the procedure and time limits for filing and serving an appellant's notice. Subject to paragraph 5.36, the appellant must file the appellant's notice at the appeal court within such period as may be directed by the lower court, which should not normally exceed 14 days or, where the lower court directs no such period within 21 days of the date of the decision that the appellant wishes to appeal.

5.36 Rule 30.4(3) (Appellant's notice) provides that unless the appeal court orders otherwise, where the appeal is against an order under section 38(1) of the 1989 Act or a case management decision in any proceedings, the appellant must file the appellant's notice within 7 days beginning with the date of the decision of the lower court.

5.37 Where the lower court announces its decision and reserves the reasons for its judgment or order until a later date, it should, in the exercise of powers under rule 30.4(2)(a)) (Appellant's notice), fix a period for filing the appellant's notice at the appeal court that takes this into account.

5.38 Except where the appeal court orders otherwise a sealed or stamped copy of the appellant's notice, including any skeleton arguments must be served on all respondents and other persons referred to in rule 30.4(5) (Appellant's notice) in accordance with the timetable prescribed by rule 30.4(4)) (Appellant's notice) except where this requirement is modified by paragraph 5.14 or 5.14A in which case the skeleton argument should be served as soon as it is filed.

5.39 Where the appellant's notice is to be served on a child, then rule 6.33 (supplementary provision relating to service on children) applies and unless the appeal court orders otherwise a sealed or stamped copy of the appellant's notice, including any skeleton arguments must be served on the persons or bodies mentioned in rule 6.33(3). For example, the appeal notice must be served on any children's guardian, welfare officer or children and family reporter who is appointed in the proceedings.

5.40 Unless the court otherwise directs, a respondent need not take any action when served with an appellant's notice until such time as notification is given to the respondent that permission to appeal has been given.

5.41 The court may dispense with the requirement for service of the notice on a respondent.

PART III

5.42 Unless the appeal court directs otherwise, the appellant must serve on the respondent the appellant's notice and skeleton argument (but not the appeal bundle),where the appellant is applying for permission to appeal in the appellant's notice.

5.43 Where permission to appeal –

(a) has been given by the lower court; or
(b) is not required,

the appellant must serve the appeal bundle on the respondent and the persons mentioned in paragraph 5.39 with the appellant's notice.

Amendment of Appeal Notice

5.44 An appeal notice may be amended with permission. Such an application to amend and any application in opposition will normally be dealt with at the hearing unless that course would cause unnecessary expense or delay in which case a request should be made for the application to amend to be heard in advance.

Procedure after permission is obtained

6.1 This paragraph sets out the procedure where –

(a) permission to appeal is given by the appeal court; or
(b) the appellant's notice is filed in the appeal court and –
  (i) permission was given by the lower court; or
  (ii) permission is not required.

6.2 If the appeal court gives permission to appeal, the appeal bundle must be served on each of the respondents within 7 days of receiving the order giving permission to appeal.

6.3 The appeal court will send the parties –

(a) notification of the date of the hearing or the period of time (the 'listing window') during which the appeal is likely to be heard;
(b) where permission is granted by the appeal court a copy of the order giving permission to appeal; and
(c) any other directions given by the court.

6.4 Where the appeal court grants permission to appeal, the appellant must add the following documents to the appeal bundle –

(a) the respondent's notice and skeleton argument (if any);
(b) those parts of the transcripts of evidence which are directly relevant to any question at issue on the appeal;
(c) the order granting permission to appeal and, where permission to appeal was granted at an oral hearing, the transcript (or note) of any judgment which was given; and
(d) any document which the appellant and respondent have agreed to add to the appeal bundle in accordance with paragraph 7.16.

6.5 Where permission to appeal has been refused on a particular issue, the appellant must remove from the appeal bundle all documents that are relevant only to that issue.

Time estimates

6.6 If the appellant is legally represented, the appeal court must be notified, in writing, of the advocate's time estimate for the hearing of the appeal.

6.7 The time estimate must be that of the advocate who will argue the appeal. It should exclude the time required by the court to give judgment.

6.8 A court officer will notify the respondent of the appellant's time estimate and if the respondent disagrees with the time estimate the respondent must inform the court within 7 days of the notification. In the absence of such notification the respondent will be deemed to have accepted the estimate proposed on behalf of the appellant.

Respondent

7.1 A respondent who wishes to ask the appeal court to vary the order of the lower court in any way must appeal and permission will be required on the same basis as for an appellant.

(Paragraph 3.2 applies to grounds of appeal by a respondent.)

7.2 A respondent who wishes to appeal or who wishes to ask the appeal court to uphold the order of the lower court for reasons different from or additional to those given by the lower court must file a respondent's notice.

7.3 A respondent who does not file a respondent's notice will not be entitled, except with the permission of the court, to rely on any reason not relied on in the lower court. This paragraph and paragraph 7.2 do not apply where the appeal is against an order under section 38(1) of the 1989 Act (see rule 30.5(7) (Respondent's notice)).

7.4 Paragraphs 5.3 (Human Rights and extension for time for filing appellant's notice) and 5.4 to 5.6 (extension of time for filing appellant's notice) of this practice direction also apply to a respondent and a respondent's notice.

Time limits

7.5 The time limits for filing a respondent's notice are set out in rule 30.5(4) and (5) (Respondent's notice).

7.6 Where an extension of time is required the extension must be requested in the respondent's notice and the reasons why the respondent failed to act within the specified time must be included.

7.7 Except where paragraphs 7.8, 7.9A and 7.10 apply, the respondent must file a skeleton argument for the court in all cases where the respondent proposes to address arguments to the court. The respondent's skeleton argument may be included within a respondent's notice. Where a skeleton argument is included within a respondent's notice it will not form part of the notice for the purposes of rule 30.9 (Amendment of appeal notice).

7.8 Subject to paragraph 7.9A, a respondent who –

(a) files a respondent's notice; but
(b) does not include a skeleton argument with that notice,

must file the skeleton argument within 14 days of filing the notice.

7.9 Subject to paragraph 7.9A, a respondent who does not file a respondent's notice but who files a skeleton argument must file that skeleton argument at least 7 days before the appeal hearing.

(Rule 30.5(4) (Respondent's notice) sets out the period for filing a respondent's notice.)

7.9A In appeals against case management decisions, where –

(a) the respondent's skeleton argument cannot accompany the respondent 's notice; or
(b) a respondent does not file a respondent's notice but files a skeleton argument,

the skeleton argument must be filed as soon as practicable or as directed by the court, but in any event not less than 3 days before the hearing of the appeal.

7.10 A respondent who is not represented need not file a skeleton argument but is encouraged to do so in order to assist the court.

7.11 The respondent must serve the skeleton argument on –

(a) the appellant; and
(b) any other respondent;

at the same time as the skeleton argument is filed at court. Where a child is an appellant or respondent the skeleton argument must also be served on the persons listed in rule 6.33(3) unless the court directs otherwise.

7.12 A respondent's skeleton argument must conform to the directions at paragraphs 5.16 to 5.22 with any necessary modifications. It should, where appropriate, answer the arguments set out in the appellant's skeleton argument.

PART III

Applications within respondent's notices

7.13 A respondent may include an application within a respondent's notice in accordance with paragraph 5.7.

Filing respondent's notices and skeleton arguments

7.14 The respondent must file the following documents with the respondent's notice in every case –

(a) two additional copies of the respondent's notice for the appeal court; and
(b) one copy each for the appellant, any other respondents and any persons referred to in paragraph 5.39.

7.15 The respondent may file a skeleton argument with the respondent's notice and –

(a) where doing so must file two copies; and
(b) where not doing so must comply with paragraph 7.8.

7.16 If the respondent considers documents in addition to those filed by the appellant to be necessary to enable the appeal court to reach its decision on the appeal and wishes to rely on those documents, any amendments to the appeal bundle should be agreed with the appellant if possible.

7.17 If the representatives for the parties are unable to reach agreement, the respondent may prepare a supplemental bundle.

7.18 The respondent must file any supplemental bundle so prepared, together with the requisite number of copies for the appeal court, at the appeal court –

(a) with the respondent's notice; or
(b) if a respondent's notice is not filed, within 21 days after the respondent is served with the appeal bundle.

7.19 The respondent must serve –

(a) the respondent's notice;
(b) the skeleton argument (if any); and
(c) the supplemental bundle (if any),

on

(i) the appellant; and
(ii) any other respondent;

at the same time as those documents are filed at the court. Where a child is an appellant or respondent the documents referred to in paragraphs (a) to (c) above must also be served on the persons listed in rule 6.33(2) unless the court directs otherwise.

Appeals to the High Court

Application

8.1 The appellant's notice must be filed at the Family Division of the High Court at the Royal Courts of Justice, Strand, London, WC2A 2LL.

8.2 A respondent's notice must be filed at the court where the appellant's notice was filed.

8.3 In the case of appeals from district judges of the High Court, applications for permission and any other applications in the appeal, appeals may be heard and directions in the appeal may be given by a High Court Judge.

8.4 In cases where paragraph 8.5 applies, appeals, applications for permission to appeal and any other applications in the appeal may be heard, and directions in the appeal or application may be given, by a High Court judge only.

8.5 This paragraph applies in the case of appeals from a Circuit judge or Recorder, except where the appeal is from:

(a) a decision or order in proceedings under –
(i) Part 4 or 5 of, or paragraph 19(1) of Schedule 2 to, the Children Act 1989; or

(ii) the Adoption and Children Act 2002;

(b) a decision or order in exercise of the court's jurisdiction in relation to contempt of court, where that decision or order was made in, or in connection with, proceedings of a type referred to in sub-paragraph (a); or

(c) a decision or order made on appeal to the family court

****

Appeals to the family court from decisions in child support proceedings under section 111A of the Magistrates' Courts Act 1980 ('the 1980 Act')

9.3 Section 111A of the 1980 Act, provides that in proceedings under the Child Support Act 1991 a person may appeal to the family court on the ground that a decision is wrong in law or is in excess of jurisdiction. Section 111A(3)(a) provides that no appeal may be brought under section 111A if there is a right of appeal to the family court against the decision otherwise than under that section. Such an appeal is usually heard by a judge of circuit judge level court in accordance with the rules relating to the composition of the court and distribution of business made in accordance with section 31D of the 1984 Act.

9.4 Subject to section 111A of the 1980 Act and any other enactment, the following rules in Part 30 apply to appeals under section 111A of the 1980 Act –

(a) 30.1 (scope and interpretation);
(b) 30.2 (parties to comply with the practice direction);
(c) 30.4 (appellant's notice);
(d) 30.6 (grounds of appeal);
(e) 30.8 (stay); and
(f) 30.9 (amendment of appeal notice).

9.5 Section 111A(4) of the 1980 Act provides that the notice of appeal must be filed within 21 days after the day on which the decision of the magistrates' court was given. The notice of appeal should also be served within this period of time. The time period for filing the appellant's notice in rule 30.4(2) and (3) does not apply. There can be no extension of this 21 day time limit under rule 4.1(3)(a).

Other statutory rights of appeal from a magistrates' court and the court at which the appellant's notice is to be filed-provisions applying to those appeals and appeals under section 111A of the 1980 Act

9.6, 9.7 *(omitted)*

9.8 Subject to any enactment, a district judge may –

(a) dismiss an appeal;
  (i) for want of prosecution; or
  (ii) with the consent of the parties; or
(b) give leave for the appeal to be withdrawn,

and may deal with any question of costs arising out of the dismissal or withdrawal.

Unless the court directs otherwise, any interlocutory application in an appeal under section 111A of the 1980 Act may be made to a district judge sitting in the family court in accordance with the rules relating to the composition of the court and distribution of business made in accordance with section 31D of the 1984 Act.

9.9–9.11 *(omitted)*

9.12 This practice direction applies to appeals under section 111A of the 1980 Act with the following modifications and any other necessary modifications –

(a) after paragraph 5.6 insert –
'5.6A Paragraphs 5.4 to 5.6 do not apply to an appeal to the family court under section 111A of the Magistrates' Courts Act 1980.'

(b) in paragraph 5.35, insert 'and 5.36A' after 'subject to paragraph 5.36';

PART III

(c) after paragraph 5.36 insert –

'5.36A Where the appeal is to a judge of the family court under section 111A of the Magistrates' Courts Act 1980, the appellant's notice must be filed and served within 21 days after the day on which the decision of the lower court was given.'.

Appeals to the family court from the Secretary of State: Deduction order appeals

9.13 A 'deduction order appeal' is an appeal under regulation 25AB(1)(a) to (d) of the Child Support (Collection and Enforcement) Regulations 1992 (S.I. 1992/1989)('the Collection and Enforcement Regulations'). A deduction order appeal is an appeal against –

(a) the making of a regular deduction order under section 32A of the Child Support Act 1991 ('the 1991 Act');
(b) a decision on an application to review a regular deduction order;
(c) a decision to withhold consent to the disapplication of sections 32G(1) and 32H(2)(b) of the 1991 Act which has the effect of unfreezing funds in the liable person's account; or
(d) the making of a final lump sum deduction order under section 32F of the 1991 Act.

A deduction order appeal lies to a county court from the Secretary of State as a result of regulation 25AB(1) of the Collection and Enforcement Regulations.

9.14 The rules in Part 30 apply to deduction order appeals with the amendments set out in paragraphs 9.15 to 9.27 and 9.29 and 9.30 below. The rules in Part 30 also apply to appeals against the decision of a district judge in proceedings relating to a deduction order appeal with the amendments set out in paragraph 9.28 below.

9.15 'The respondent' means –

(a) the Secretary of State and any person other than the appellant who was served with an order under section 32A(1), 32E(1) or 32F(1) of the 1991 Act; and
(b) a person who is permitted by the appeal court to be a party to the appeal.

9.16 The appellant will serve the appellant's notice on the Secretary of State and any other respondent.

9.17 The appellant shall file and serve the appellant's notice, within 21 days of –

(a) where the appellant is a deposit-taker, service of the order;
(b) where the appellant is a liable person, receipt of the order; or
(c) where the appellant is either a deposit-taker or a liable person, the date of receipt of notification of the decision.

9.18 For the purposes of paragraph 9.17 –

(a) references to 'liable person' and 'deposit-taker' are to be interpreted in accordance with section 32E of the 1991 Act and regulation 25A(2) of the Collection and Enforcement Regulations and section 54 of the 1991 Act, respectively; and
(b) the liable person is to be treated as having received the order or notification of the decision 2 days after it was posted by the Secretary of State.

9.19 Rule 4.1(3)(a) (court's power to extend or shorten the time for compliance with a rule, practice direction or court order) does not apply to an appeal against the making of a lump sum deduction order under section 32F of the 1991 Act in so far as that rule gives the court power to extend the time set out in paragraph 9.17 for filing and serving an appellant's notice after the time for filing and serving the that notice set out in paragraph 9.17 has expired.

9.20 The Secretary of State shall provide to the court and serve on all other parties to the appeal any information and evidence relevant to the making of the decision or order being appealed, within 14 days of receipt of the appellant's notice.

9.21 Subject to paragraph 9.23, a respondent who wishes to ask the appeal court to uphold the order or decision of the Secretary of State for reasons different from or in additional to those given by the Secretary of State must file a respondent's notice.

9.22 A respondent's notice must be filed within 14 days of receipt of the appellant's notice.

9.23 Where the Secretary of State as a respondent, wishes to contend that the Secretary of State's order or decision should be –

(a) varied, either in any event or in the event of the appeal being allowed in whole or in part; or
(b) affirmed on different grounds from those on which the Secretary of State relied when making the order or decision,

the Secretary of State shall, within 14 days of receipt of the appellant's notice, file and serve on all other parties to the appeal a respondent's notice.

9.24 In so far as rule 30.7 (Variation of time) may permit any application for variation of the time limit for filing an appellant's notice after the time for filing the appellant's notice has expired, that rule shall not apply to an appeal made against an order under section 32F(1) of the Act of 1991.

9.25 Rule 30.8 (stay) shall not apply to an appeal made against an order under section 32F(1) of the Act of 1991.

9.26 *(omitted)*

9.27 Rule 30.11 (appeal court's powers) does not apply to deduction order appeals.

9.28 Rule 30.11(2)(d) (making orders for payment of interest) does not apply in the case of an appeal against a decision of a district judge in proceedings relating to a deduction order appeal.

9.29 In the case of a deduction order appeal –

(a) the appeal court has power to –
   (i) affirm or set aside the order or decision;
   (ii) remit the matter to the Secretary of State for the order or decision to be reconsidered, with appropriate directions;
   (iii) refer any application or issue for determination by the Secretary of State;
   (iv) make a costs order; and
(b) the appeal court may exercise its powers in relation to the whole or part of an order or decision of the Secretary of State.

9.30 In rule 30.12 (Hearing of appeals) –

(a) at the beginning of paragraph (1), for 'Every' substitute 'Subject to paragraph (2A), every';
(b) at the beginning of paragraph (2), for 'Unless' substitute 'Subject to paragraph (2A), unless';
(c) after paragraph (2), insert –
'(2A) In the case of a deduction order appeal, the appeal will be a re-hearing, unless the appeal court orders otherwise.';
(d) in paragraph (3), after 'lower court' insert 'or, in a deduction order appeal, the order or decision of the Secretary of State'; and
(e) for sub-paragraph (b) of paragraph (3), substitute –
'(b) unjust because of a serious procedural or other irregularity in –
   (i) the proceedings in the lower court; or
   (ii) the making of an order or decision by the Secretary of State.'

Information about the Secretary of State's decision

9.31 In relation to the deduction order appeals listed in column 1 of the table in Schedule 2 to this Practice Direction –

(a) the documents to be filed and served by the appellant include the documents set out in Column 3; and
(b) the relevant information to be provided by the Secretary of State in accordance with paragraph 9.20 above includes the information set out in Column 4.

PART III

The court at which the appeal notice is to be filed

9.32 In relation to a deduction order appeal, the appellant's notice and other documents required to be filed with that notice shall be filed in the family court (the Collection and Enforcement Regulations 25AB(1)). In accordance with the rules relating to the composition of the court and distribution of business made in accordance with section 31D of the 1984 Act , deduction order appeals will be heard at district judge level.

The Secretary of State's address for service

9.33 For the purposes of a deduction order appeal the Secretary of State's address for service is –

Freepost DWP Child Support Agency 19

All notices or other documents for Secretary of State relating to a deduction order appeal should be sent to the above address.

9.34 This practice direction applies to deduction order appeals and appeals against the decision of a district judge in proceedings relating to a deduction order appeal with the following modifications and any other necessary modifications-

(a) in paragraph 5.35, insert 'and 5.36B' after 'subject to paragraph 5.36A';
(b) after paragraph 5.36A insert –

'5.36A Where the appeal is a deduction order appeal, the appellant's notice must be filed and served within 21 days of –

(a) where the appellant is a deposit-taker, service of the order;
(b) where the appellant is a liable person, receipt of the order; or
(c) where the appellant is either a deposit-taker or a liable person, the date of receipt of notification of the decision the lower court was given.'.

Appeal against the court's decision under rules 31.10, 31.11 or 31.14

10.1 The rules in Part 30 apply to appeals against the court's decision under rules 31.10, 31.11 or 31.14 with the amendments set out in paragraphs 10.2 to 10.5 below. Rules 31.15 and 31.16 apply to these appeals. These modifications do not apply to appeals against the decision made on appeal under rule 31.15.

10.2 Rule 30.3 (permission to appeal) does not apply.

10.3 The time for filing an appellant's notice at the appeal court in rule 30.4(2) does not apply. Rule 31.15 sets out the time within which an appeal against the court's decision under rules 31.10, 31.11 or 31.14 must be made to a judge of the High Court.

10.4 Rule 4.1(3)(a) (court's power to extend or shorten the time for compliance with a rule, practice direction or court order) does not apply to an appeal against the court's decision under rules 31.10, 31.11 or 31.14 in so far as that rule gives the court power to extend the time set out in rules 31.15 for filing an appellant's notice.

10.5 Rules 30.7 (variation), 30.8 (stay of proceedings), 30.10 (striking out appeal notices, setting aside or imposing conditions on permission to appeal) and 30.12 (hearing of appeals) do not apply.

Appeals against pension orders and pension compensation sharing orders

11.1 Paragraph 11.2 below applies to appeals against –

(a) a pension sharing order under section 24B of the Matrimonial Causes Act 1973 or the variation of such an order under section 31 of that Act;
(b) a pension sharing order under Part 4 of Schedule 5 to the Civil Partnership Act 2004 or the variation of such an order under Part 11 of Schedule 5 to that Act;
(c) a pension compensation sharing order under section 24E of the Matrimonial Causes Act 1973 or a variation of such an order under section 31 of that Act; and
(d) a pension compensation sharing order under Part 4 of Schedule 5 to the Civil Partnership Act 2004 or a variation of such an order under Part 11 of Schedule 5 to that Act.

11.2 Rule 4.1(3)(a) (court's power to extend or shorten the time for compliance with a rule, practice direction or court order) does not apply to an appeal against the making of the orders referred to in paragraph 11.1 above in so far as that rule gives the court power to extend the time set out in rule 30.4 for filing and serving an appellant's notice after the time for filing and serving that notice has expired.

11.3 In so far as rule 30.7 (Variation of time) may permit any application for variation of the time limit for filing an appellant's notice after the time for filing the appellant's notice has expired, that rule shall not apply to an appeal made against the orders referred to in paragraph 11.1 above.

Appeals to a court under section 20 of the 1991 Act (appeals in respect of parentage determinations)

12.1 The rules in Chapters 1 and 5 of Part 8 will apply as appropriate to an appeal under section 20(1) of the 1991 Act where that appeal must be made to a court in accordance with the Child Support Appeals (Jurisdiction of Courts) Order 2002.

12.2 The respondent to such an appeal will be the Secretary of State. In accordance with the rules relating to the composition of the court and distribution of business made in accordance with section 31D of the 1984 Act, appeals under section 20 of the 1991 Act will be heard at district judge level.

12.3 *(omitted)*

Applications

13.1 Where a party to an appeal makes an application whether in an appeal notice or by Part 18 (Procedure For Other Applications in Proceedings) application notice, the provisions of Part 18 will apply.

13.2 *(omitted)*

Appeals against consent orders

14.1 The rules in Part 30 and the provisions of this Practice Direction apply to appeals relating to orders made by consent in addition to orders which are not made by consent.

Disposing of applications or appeals by consent

15.1 An appellant who does not wish to pursue an application or an appeal may request the appeal court for an order that the application or appeal be dismissed. Such a request must state whether the appellant is a child, or a protected person.

15.2 The request must be accompanied by a consent signed by the other parties stating whether the respondent is a child, or a protected person and consents to the dismissal of the application or appeal.

Allowing unopposed appeals or applications on paper

16.1 The appeal court will not normally make an order allowing an appeal unless satisfied that the decision of the lower court was wrong, but the appeal court may set aside or vary the order of the lower court with consent and without determining the merits of the appeal, if it is satisfied that there are good and sufficient reasons for doing so. Where the appeal court is requested by all parties to allow an application or an appeal the court may consider the request on the papers. The request should state whether any of the parties is a child, or protected person and set out the relevant history of the proceedings and the matters relied on as justifying the proposed order and be accompanied by a copy of the proposed order.

Summary assessment of costs

17.1 Costs are likely to be assessed by way of summary assessment at the following hearings –

(a) contested directions hearings;

(b) applications for permission to appeal at which the respondent is present;
(c) appeals from case management decisions or decisions made at directions hearings; and
(d) appeals listed for one day or less.

(Provision for summary assessment of costs is made by section 13 of the Practice Direction supplementing CPR Part 44)

17.2 Parties attending any of the hearings referred to in paragraph 17.1 should be prepared to deal with the summary assessment.

Reopening of final appeals

18.1 This paragraph applies to applications under rule 30.14 (Reopening of final appeals) for permission to reopen a final determination of an appeal.

18.2 In this paragraph, 'appeal' includes an application for permission to appeal.

18.3 Permission must be sought from the court whose decision the applicant wishes to reopen.

18.4 The application for permission must be made by application notice and supported by written evidence, verified by a statement of truth.

18.5 A copy of the application for permission must not be served on any other party to the original appeal unless the court so directs.

18.6 Where the court directs that the application for permission is to be served on another party, that party may within 14 days of the service on him or her of the copy of the application file a written statement either supporting or opposing the application.

18.7 The application for permission, and any written statements supporting or opposing it, will be considered on paper by a single judge, and will be allowed to proceed only if the judge so directs.

****

SCHEDULE 2

Appeal	**Relevant legislation**	**Appellant information**	**Secretary of State information**
Appeal against the making of a regular deduction order (under section 32A of the 1991 Act)	• Section 32C(4)(a) of the 1991 Act The Collection and Enforcement Regulations 25AB(1)(a) (appeals)	• A copy of the order; • A covering letter explaining that the order has been made and the reasons for the order namely that there are arrears of child maintenance and/or no other arrangements have been made for the payment of child maintenance, including arrears	• The amount of the current maintenance calculation, the period of debt and the total amount of arrears (including account breakdown if appropriate) and the reasons for the Secretary of State's decision, details of all previous attempts to negotiate payment i.e. phone calls and letters to the non-resident parent, details of any previous enforcement action taken

Appeal	Relevant legislation	Appellant information	Secretary of State information
Appeal against a decision on an application for a review of a regular deduction order	• Sections 32C(4)(b), 32C(2)(k) of the 1991 Act • The Collection and Enforcement Regulations 25G (review of a regular deduction order) and 25AB(1)(b) (appeals)	• A decision notification setting out whether or not the review has been agreed by the Secretary of State and the resulting action to be taken if agreed; with an enclosure setting out the specific reasons for the Secretary of State's decision	• The reasons for the Secretary of State's decision in respect of the application for review and any evidence supporting that decision
Appeal against the withholding of consent to the disapplication of sections 32G(1) and 32H(2)(b) of the 1991 Act	• Section 32I(4) of the 1991 Act • The Collection and Enforcement Regulations 25N (disapplication of sections 32G(1) and 32H(2)(b) of the 1991 Act) and 25AB(1)(c) (appeals)	• A decision notification setting out that either: (a) consent has been refused; or (b) consent has been given in relation to part of the application i.e. that only some of the funds which were requested to be released have been agreed to be released (the right of appeal will lie in respect of the part of the application which has been refused). • There will be an enclosure with the notification setting out the reasons for the decision on the application.	• The reasons for the Secretary of State's decision in respect of the application for consent and any evidence supporting that decision

Appeal	Relevant legislation	Appellant information	Secretary of State information
Appeal against the making of a final lump sum deduction order (under section 32F of the 1991 Act)	• Section 32J(5) of the 1991 Act Collection and Enforcement Regulations 25AB(1)(d) (appeals)	• A copy of the order; • A covering letter explaining that the order has been made and the reasons for the order namely that there are arrears of child maintenance and/or no other arrangements have been made for the payment of child maintenance, including arrears	• The amount of the current maintenance calculation (if applicable), the period of debt and the total amount of arrears (including account breakdown if appropriate) and the reasons for the Secretary of State's decision, details of all previous attempts to negotiate payment i.e. phone calls and letters to the non-resident parent, details of any previous enforcement action taken.

PART 31
REGISTRATION OF ORDERS UNDER THE COUNCIL REGULATION, THE CIVIL PARTNERSHIP (JURISDICTION AND RECOGNITION OF JUDGMENTS) REGULATIONS 2005, THE MARRIAGE (SAME SEX COUPLES) (JURISDICTION AND RECOGNITION OF JUDGMENTS) REGULATIONS 2014 AND UNDER THE HAGUE CONVENTION 1996

Amendments—SI 2014/524.

CONTENTS OF THIS PART

Rule		Page
31.1	Scope	1897
31.2	Interpretation	1897
31.3	Where to start proceedings	1898
31.4	Application for registration, recognition or non-recognition of a judgment	1898
31.5	Documents – supplementary	1899
31.6	Directions	1899
31.7	Recognition and enforcement under the Council Regulation of a judgment given in another Member State relating to rights of access or under Article 11(8) for the return of the child to that State	1899
31.8	Registration for enforcement or order for non-recognition of a judgment	1900
31.9	Stay of recognition proceedings by reason of an appeal	1901
31.10	Effect of refusal of application for a decision that a judgment should not be recognised	1901
31.11	Notification of the court's decision on an application for registration or non-recognition	1901
31.12	Effect of registration under rule 31.11	1902
31.13	The central index of judgments registered under rule 31.11	1902
31.14	Decision on recognition of a judgment only	1902
31.15	Appeal against the court's decision under rules 31.10, 31.11 or 31.14	1902
31.16	Stay of enforcement where appeal pending in state of origin	1903
31.17	Enforcement of judgments registered under rule 31.11	1903
31.18	Request for a certificate or a certified copy of a judgment	1903

31.19	Certificates issued in England and Wales under Articles 41 and 42 of the Council Regulation	1904
31.20	Rectification of certificate issued under Article 41 or 42 of the Council Regulation	1904
31.21	Authentic instruments and agreements under Article 46 of the Council Regulation	1904
31.22	Application for provisional, including protective measures	1904

Practice Direction 31A –
Registration of Orders under the Council Regulation, the Civil Partnership (Jurisdiction and Recognition of Judgments) Regulations 2005, the Marriage (Same Sex Couples) (Jurisdiction and Recognition of Judgments) Regulations 2014 and under the 1996 Hague Convention 1905

Scope—FPR 2010, Pt 31 makes provision for proceedings for the recognition, non-recognition and registration of the following incoming orders:

(a) Judgments as defined by Brussels IIA, art 2(4) (divorce, legal separation, marriage annulment or a judgment relating to parental responsibility pronounced by a court of a Member State);
(b) Measures taken by an authority with jurisdiction under the Hague Convention 1996, Chapter II (measures directed to the protection of a child's person or property); and
(c) Judgments to which the Civil Partnership (Jurisdiction and Recognition of Judgments) Regulations 2005 apply (dissolution or annulment of overseas relationships entitled to be treated as a civil partnership or legal separation of such a relationship, making corresponding provision to the relevant parts of Brussels IIA).

In relation to judgments to which Brussels IIA applies, reference should be made to the annotations to Brussels IIA, arts 11, 21, 28, 41 and 42.

31.1 Scope

This Part applies to proceedings for the recognition, non-recognition and registration of –

(a) judgments to which the Council Regulation applies;
(b) measures to which the 1996 Hague Convention applies;
(c) judgments to which the Jurisdiction and Recognition of Judgments Regulations apply, and which relate to dissolution or annulment of overseas relationships entitled to be treated as a civil partnership, or legal separation of the same; and
(d) judgments to which the 2014 Regulations apply and which relate to divorce, or annulment of a marriage of a same sex couple or the judicial separation of the same.

Amendments—SI 2014/524.

31.2 Interpretation

(1) In this Part –

(a) 'judgment' is to be construed –
  (i) in accordance with the definition in Article 2(4) of the Council Regulation where it applies;
  (ii) in accordance with regulation 6 of the Jurisdiction and Recognition of Judgments Regulations where those Regulations apply;
  (iii) as meaning any measure taken by an authority with jurisdiction under Chapter II of the 1996 Hague Convention where that Convention applies; or
  (iv) in accordance with regulation 4(1)(a) of The Marriage (Same Sex Couples) (Jurisdiction and Recognition of Judgments) Regulations 2014 where those Regulations apply.
(b) 'the Jurisdiction and Recognition of Judgments Regulations' means the Civil Partnership (Jurisdiction and Recognition of Judgments) Regulations 2005;
(ba) 'the 2014 Regulations' means the Marriage (Same Sex Couples) (Jurisdiction and Recognition of Judgments) Regulations 2014;
(c) 'Member State' means –
  (i) where registration, recognition or non-recognition is sought of a judgment under the Council Regulation, a Member State of the European Union which is bound by that Regulation or a country which has subsequently adopted it;
  (ii) where recognition is sought of a judgment to which the Jurisdiction and

Recognition of Judgments Regulations apply, a Member State of the European Union to which Part II of those Regulations applies;

(iii) where recognition is sought of a judgment to which the 2014 Regulations apply, a member State of the European Union to which Part II of those Regulations applies;

(d) 'Contracting State' means a State, other than a Member State within the meaning of (c) above, in relation to which the 1996 Hague Convention is in force as between that State and the United Kingdom; and

(e) 'parental responsibility' –

(i) where the Council Regulation applies, has the meaning given in Article 2(7) of that Regulation; and

(ii) where the 1996 Hague Convention applies, has the meaning given in Article 1(2) of that Convention.

(2) References in this Part to registration are to the registration of a judgment in accordance with the provisions of this Part.

Amendments—SI 2014/524.

Articles of the Council Regulation and the 1996 Hague Convention—See Part VI.

31.3 Where to start proceedings

(1) Every application under this Part, except for an application under rule 31.18 for a certified copy of a judgment, or under rule 31.20 for rectification of a certificate issued under Articles 41 or 42, must be made to the principal registry.

(2) Nothing in this rule prevents the determination of an issue of recognition as an incidental question by any court in proceedings, in accordance with Article 21(4) of the Council Regulation.

(3) Notwithstanding paragraph (1), where recognition of a judgment is raised as an incidental question in proceedings under the 1996 Hague Convention, the Jurisdiction and Recognition of Judgments Regulations or the 2014 Regulations the court hearing those proceedings may determine the question of recognition.

Amendments—SI 2014/524.

Jurisdiction to hear proceedings—The High Court in England and Wales, the Court of Session in Scotland and the High Court of Northern Ireland have jurisdiction to hear applications for recognition and non-recognition under Arts 24 and 26 of the 1966 Convention (PRMPC(IO)(EWNI)R 2010, reg 7, set out in Part IV) but if such an issue is raised as an incidental question in another court, that court may determine the issue of recognition. See Part VI for the Council Regulations and 1996 Convention.

31.4 Application for registration, recognition or non-recognition of a judgment

(1) Any interested person may apply to the court for an order that the judgment be registered, recognised or not recognised.

(2) Except for an application under rule 31.7, an application for registration, recognition or non-recognition must be –

(a) made to a district judge of the principal registry; and

(b) in the form, and supported by the documents and the information required by a practice direction.

Any interested person may apply—Contrast with the provisions of the Hague Convention 1980 and applications under Art 26 (which deals with enforcements provisions) and Brussels IIA, both of which refer to 'any interested party' rather than 'person'. This seems to restrict those entitled to apply to a person rather than a public body or institution.

Form of application—Must be made using the FPR 2010, Pt 19 procedure and Form C69. Where the application is for recognition only of an order, it should be made clear that the application does not extend to registration for enforcement. See FPR PD31A, para 1.

Supported by documents etc required by a PD—The documents etc to be submitted are set out in PD31A. In *Re P (Recognition and Registration of Orders under the Hague Child Protection Convention)* [2014] EWHC 2845 (Fam), Moylan J expressed concern that the requirements imposed by PD31A challenge the concept of a procedure that is required to be 'simple and rapid' (Art 26(2)), especially having regard to the increasing number of litigants in person. While recognising the importance of due process, he suggested that 'these requirements need to be applied with a light touch' by reference to whether the court has sufficient information for the essentially administrative purposes of recognising and registering the order. Where the application is in effect for a mirror order, the raft of documents and information as required by the rules will often not be necessary and they can be dispensed with pursuant to rule 31.5(c). This will be more so when the application follows a direct request for assistance from a judge of the International Hague Network of Judges (see [25], [26] and [34]–[36] of the judgment).

31.5 Documents – supplementary

(1) Except as regards a copy of a judgment required by Article 37(1)(a) of the Council Regulation, where the person making an application under this Part does not produce the documents required by rule 31.4(2)(b) the court may –

- (a) fix a time within which the documents are to be produced;
- (b) accept equivalent documents; or
- (c) dispense with production of the documents if the court considers it has sufficient information.

(2) This rule does not apply to applications under rule 31.7.

Documents required by r 31.4(2)(b)—These are identified in FPR PD31A.

Dispensation of documents—See the guidance given by Moylan J in *Re P* (see under r 31.4).

31.6 Directions

(1) As soon as practicable after an application under this Part has been made, the court may (subject to the requirements of the Council Regulation) give such directions as it considers appropriate, including as regards the following matters –

- (a) whether service of the application may be dispensed with;
- (b) expedition of the proceedings or any part of the proceedings (and any direction for expedition may specify a date by which the court must give its decision);
- (c) the steps to be taken in the proceedings and the time by which each step is to be taken;
- (d) the service of documents; and
- (e) the filing of evidence.

(2) The court or court officer will –

- (a) record the giving, variation or revocation of directions under this rule; and
- (b) as soon as practicable serve a copy of the directions order on every party.

Every party—In the case of an application for registration, recognition or order for non-recognition, service of the directions order will be on the person against whom registration is sought or in the case of non-recognition in whose favour the judgment was given (FPR 2010, rr 31.8 and 31.14).

Directions—The list set out above is not exhaustive. When considering an application for recognition and enforcement of a foreign order, the court can and should consider whether it is appropriate to join the child as a party to the proceedings. Where the child has been a party and is represented before the court of the Member State, in most cases it will not be necessary for the child to be made a party. Where it is considered that the child should be given an opportunity to be heard, the court may consider the new r 3A of the Court of Protection Rules 2007, which provides a range of options on how representation can be achieved, although the proposed amendments to the FPR 2010 (Pt 3A) have not yet been implemented (see *Re Z (Recognition of Foreign Order)* [2017] 1 FLR 1236, FD, at [25–28]).

31.7 Recognition and enforcement under the Council Regulation of a judgment given in another Member State relating to rights of access or under Article 11(8) for the return of the child to that State

(1) This rule applies where a judgment has been given in another Member State –

- (a) relating to rights of access: or
- (b) under Article 11(8) of the Council Regulation for the return of a child to that State,

which has been certified, in accordance with Article 41(2) or 42(2) as the case may be, by the judge in the court of origin.

(2) An application for recognition or enforcement of the judgment must be –

- (a) made in writing to a district judge of the principal registry; and
- (b) accompanied by a copy of the certificate issued by the judge in the court of origin.

(3) The application may be made without notice.

(4) Rules 31.5 and 31.8 to 31.17 do not apply to an application made under this rule.

(5) Nothing in this rule shall prevent a holder of parental responsibility from seeking recognition and enforcement of a judgment in accordance with the provisions of rules 31.8 to 31.17.

31.8 Registration for enforcement or order for non-recognition of a judgment

(1) This rule applies where an application is made for an order that a judgment given in another Member State, or a Contracting State, should be registered, or should not be recognised, except where rule 31.7 applies.

(2) Where the application is made for an order that the judgment should be registered –

- (a) upon receipt of the application, and subject to any direction given by the court under rule 31.6 the court officer will serve the application on the person against whom registration is sought;
- (b) the court will not accept submissions from either the person against whom registration is sought or any child in relation to whom the judgment was given.

(3) Where the application is for an order that the judgment should not be recognised –

- (a) upon receipt of the application, and subject to any direction given by the court under rule 31.6, the court officer will serve the application on the person in whose favour judgment was given;
- (b) the person in whose favour the judgment was given must file an answer to the application and serve it on the applicant –
  - (i) within 1 month of service of the application; or
  - (ii) if the applicant is habitually resident in another Member State, within two months of service of the application.

(4) In cases to which the 1996 Hague Convention applies and the Council Regulation does not apply, the court may extend the time set out in subparagraph (3)(b)(ii) on account of distance.

(5) The person in whose favour the judgment was given may request recognition or registration of the judgment in their answer, and in that event must comply with 31.4(2)(b) to the extent that such documents, information and evidence are not already contained in the application for non-recognition.

(6) If, in a case to which the Council Regulation applies, the person in whose favour the judgment was given fails to file an answer as required by paragraph (3), the court will act in accordance with the provisions of Article 18 of the Council Regulation.

(7) If, in a case to which the 1996 Hague Convention applies and the Service Regulation does not, the person in whose favour the judgment was given fails to file an answer as required by paragraph (3) –

- (a) where the Hague Convention of 15 November 1965 on the service abroad of judicial and extrajudicial documents in civil or commercial matters applies, the court shall apply Article 15 of that Convention; and
- (b) in all other cases, the court will not consider the application unless –
  - (i) it is proved to the satisfaction of the court that the person in whose favour judgment was given was served with the application within a reasonable period of time to arrange his or her response; or
  - (ii) the court is satisfied that the circumstances of the case justify proceeding with consideration of the application.

(8) In a case to which the Jurisdiction and Recognition of Judgments Regulations or the 2014 Regulations apply, if the person in whose favour judgment was given fails to file an answer as required by paragraph (3), the court will apply the Service Regulation where that regulation applies, and if it does not –

- (a) where the Hague Convention of 15 November 1965 on the service abroad of judicial and extrajudicial documents in civil or commercial matters applies, the court shall apply Article 15 of that Convention; and
- (b) in all other cases, the court will apply the provisions of paragraph (7)(b).

Amendments—SI 2014/524.

Scope—This rule applies to both the Council Regulation and the 1996 Convention. It (i) identifies the person on whom service should be effected where application is made for registration or non-recognition, (ii) provides for an answer to contain a cross-request for registration and recognition and sets out the evidence documents and information that should be filed to support such a cross-application, (iii) sets out the time limits for filing the answer and (iv) sets out the circumstances in which the court may consider the application where an answer is not filed.

31.9 Stay of recognition proceedings by reason of an appeal

Where recognition or non-recognition of a judgment given in another Member State or Contracting State is sought, or is raised as an incidental question in other proceedings, the court may stay the proceedings –

(a) if an ordinary appeal against the judgment has been lodged; or

(b) if the judgment was given in the Republic of Ireland, if enforcement of the judgment is suspended there by reason of an appeal.

Scope—Where an appeal is pending in the court of origin, the court is authorised to stay the proceedings, but in any event see FPR 2010, r 31.17, which provides that the court will not enforce a registered judgment until after the expiration of the time for lodging an appeal or any extension of time granted by the court unless an urgent enforcement of the judgment is necessary to secure the welfare of the child who is the subject to the proceedings. The rule applies to both the Council Regulations and the 1996 Convention. This rule should be read with FPR 2010, r 31.22, which provides for protective measures to be taken in an urgent situation notwithstanding that the time for appeal has not expired or where the appeal is pending.

PART III

31.10 Effect of refusal of application for a decision that a judgment should not be recognised

Where the court refuses an application for a decision that a judgment should not be recognised, the court may –

(a) direct that the decision to refuse the application is to be treated as a decision that the judgment be recognised; or

(b) treat the answer under paragraph (3)(b) of rule 31.8 as an application that the judgment be registered for enforcement if paragraph (5) of that rule is complied with and order that the judgment be registered for enforcement in accordance with rule 31.11.

31.11 Notification of the court's decision on an application for registration or non-recognition

(1) Where the court has –

(a) made an order on an application for an order that a judgment should be registered for enforcement; or

(b) refused an application that a judgment should not be recognised and ordered under rule 31.10 that the judgment be registered for enforcement,

the court officer will as soon as practicable take the appropriate action under paragraph (2) or (3).

(2) If the court refuses the application for the judgment to be registered for enforcement, the court officer will serve the order on the applicant and the person against whom judgment was given in the state of origin.

(3) If the court orders that the judgment should be registered for enforcement, the court officer will –

(a) register the judgment in the central index of judgments kept by the principal registry;

(b) confirm on the order that the judgment has been registered; and

(c) serve on the parties the court's order endorsed with the court officer's confirmation that the judgment has been registered.

(4) A sealed order of the court endorsed in accordance with paragraph (3)(b) will constitute notification that the judgment has been registered under Article 28(2) of the Council Regulation or under Article 26 of the 1996 Hague Convention, as the case may be, and in this Part 'notice of registration' means a sealed order so endorsed.

(5) The notice of registration must state –

(a) full particulars of the judgment registered and the order for registration;

(b) the name of the party making the application and his address for service within the jurisdiction;
(c) the right of the person against whom judgment was given to appeal against the order for registration; and
(d) the period within which an appeal against the order for registration may be made.

Scope—This rule sets out the procedure that must be followed to record, seal and serve the order made on an application for registration or non-recognition.

Effect of a sealed copy of the court order—A sealed copy of the court order endorsed in accordance with FPR 2010, r 31.11(3)(b) will constitute notification that the judgment has been registered under Art 26 of the 1996 Convention or recognised under Art 24, as the case may be. Registration of a judgment under FPR 2010, r 31.11 will serve for the purposes of Art 24 of the 1996 Convention as a decision that the judgment is recognised.

31.12 Effect of registration under rule 31.11

Registration of a judgment under rule 31.11 will serve for the purpose of Article 21(3) of the Council Regulation, Article 24 of the 1996 Hague Convention, regulation 7 of the Jurisdiction and Recognition of Judgments Regulations or regulation 5 of the 2014 Regulations (as the case may be) as a decision that the judgment is recognised.

Amendments—SI 2014/524.

31.13 The central index of judgments registered under rule 31.11

The central index of judgments registered under rule 31.11 will be kept by the principal registry.

31.14 Decision on recognition of a judgment only

(1) Where an application is made seeking recognition of a judgment only, the provisions of rules 31.8 and 31.9 apply to that application as they do to an application for registration for enforcement.

(2) Where the court orders that the judgment should be recognised, the court officer will serve a copy of the order on each party as soon as practicable.

(3) A sealed order of the court will constitute notification that the judgment has been recognised under Article 21(3) of the Council Regulation, Article 24 of the 1996 Hague convention, regulation 7 of the Jurisdiction and Recognition of Judgments Regulations or regulation 5 of the 2014 Regulations, as the case may be.

(4) The sealed order shall indicate –
(a) full particulars of the judgment recognised;
(b) the name of the party making the application and his address for service within the jurisdiction;
(c) the right of the person against whom judgment was given to appeal against the order for recognition; and
(d) the period within which an appeal against the order for recognition may be made.

Amendments—SI 2014/524.

31.15 Appeal against the court's decision under rules 31.10, 31.11 or 31.14

(1) An appeal against the court's decision under rules 31.10, 31.11 or 31.14 must be made to a judge of the High Court –
(a) within one month of the date of service of the notice of registration; or
(b) if the party bringing the appeal is habitually resident in another Member State, or a Contracting State, within two months of the date of service.

(2) The court may not extend time for an appeal on account of distance unless the matter is one to which the 1996 Hague Convention applies and the Council Regulation does not apply.

(3) If, in a case to which the 1996 Hague Convention applies and the Service Regulation does not, the appeal is brought by the applicant for a declaration of enforceability or registration and the respondent fails to appear –

(a) where the Hague Convention of 15 November 1965 on the service abroad of judicial and extrajudicial documents in civil or commercial matters applies, the court shall apply Article 15 of that Convention; and

(b) in all other cases, the court will not consider the appeal unless –

(i) it is proved to the satisfaction of the court that the respondent was served with notice of the appeal within a reasonable period of time to arrange his or her response; or

(ii) the court is satisfied that the circumstances of the case justify proceeding with consideration of the appeal.

(4) This rule is subject to rule 31.16.

(The procedure for applications under rule 31.15 is set out in Practice Direction 30A (Appeals).)

31.16 Stay of enforcement where appeal pending in state of origin

(1) A party against whom enforcement is sought of a judgment which has been registered under rule 31.11 may apply to the court with which an appeal is lodged under rule 31.15 for the proceedings to be stayed where –

(a) that party has lodged an ordinary appeal in the Member State or Contracting State of origin; or

(b) the time for such an appeal has not yet expired.

(2) Where an application for a stay is filed in the circumstances described in paragraph (1)(b), the court may specify the time within which an appeal must be lodged.

31.17 Enforcement of judgments registered under rule 31.11

(1) Subject to paragraph (1A), the court will not enforce a judgment registered under rule 31.11 until after –

(a) the expiration of any applicable period under rules 31.15 or 31.16; or

(b) if that period has been extended by the court, the expiration of the period so extended.

(1A) The court may enforce a judgment registered under rule 31.11 before the expiration of a period referred to in paragraph (1) where urgent enforcement of the judgment is necessary to secure the welfare of the child to whom the judgment relates.

(2) A party applying to the court for the enforcement of a registered judgment must produce to the court a certificate of service of –

(a) the notice of registration of the judgment; and

(b) any order made by the court in relation to the judgment.

(Service out of the jurisdiction, including service in accordance with the Service Regulation, is dealt with in chapter 4 of Part 6 and in Practice Direction 6B.)

Amendments—SI 2012/1462.

31.18 Request for a certificate or a certified copy of a judgment

(1) An application for a certified copy of a judgment, or for a certificate under Articles 39, 41 or 42 of the Council Regulation, must be made to the court which made the order or judgment in respect of which certification is sought and without giving notice to any other party.

(2) The application must be made in the form, and supported by the documents and information required by a practice direction.

(3) The certified copy of the judgment will be an office copy sealed with the seal of the court and signed by a court officer. It will be issued with a certified copy of any order which has varied any of the terms of the original order.

(4) Where the application is made for the purposes of applying for recognition or recognition and enforcement of the order in another Contracting State, the court must indicate on the certified copy of the judgment the grounds on which it based its jurisdiction to make the order, for the purposes of Article 23(2)(a) of the 1996 Hague Convention.

Amendments—SI 2013/3204.

Application for a certified copy—To avoid delay and additional costs, an application for a certified copy of the judgment and sealed order should be made at the conclusion of the proceedings to which it relates.

Application form and supporting documents—Where an application is not made at the conclusion of the proceedings, the application should be made using the Pt 18 procedure and form. In the case of all applications under Arts 39, 41 and 42, the application must be supported by a witness statement or an affidavit containing the information and attaching the documents set out in PD31A, para 6.3. In addition, further information and documents must be provided as follows: (a) in relation to proceedings under Art 39, those set out in PD31A, para 6.5; (b) in relation to judgement/order under Arts 41 and 42, those under para 6.4.

Application in relation to recognition/enforcement of order—It is essential to ensure that the judgment indicates the grounds on which jurisdiction to make the order was relied on. In such cases, the information and documents which will be required to support the application are those set out in PD31A, para 6.6.

31.19 Certificates issued in England and Wales under Articles 41 and 42 of the Council Regulation

The court officer will serve –

(a) a certificate issued under Article 41 or 42; or
(b) a certificate rectified under rule 31.20,

on all parties and will transmit a copy to the Central Authority for England and Wales.

Central Authority—The Central Authority for England and Wales is the Lord Chancellor but the function will be discharged by the International Child Abduction and Contact Unit, in Wales by the Welsh Ministers, in Scotland by the Scottish Ministers and in Northern Ireland by the Department of Justice.

31.20 Rectification of certificate issued under Article 41 or 42 of the Council Regulation

(1) Where there is an error in a certificate issued under Article 41 or 42, an application to rectify that error must be made to the court which issued the certificate.

(2) A rectification under paragraph (1) may be made –

(a) by the court of its own initiative; or
(b) on application by –
  (i) any party to the proceedings; or
  (ii) the court or Central Authority of another Member State.

(3) An application under paragraph (2)(b) may be made without notice being served on any other party.

31.21 Authentic instruments and agreements under Article 46 of the Council Regulation

This Chapter applies to an authentic instrument and an agreement to which Article 46 of the Council Regulation applies as it applies to a judgment.

31.22 Application for provisional, including protective measures

An application for provisional, including protective, measures under Article 20 of the Council Regulation or Articles 11 or 12 of the 1996 Hague Convention may be made notwithstanding that the time for appealing against an order for registration of a judgment has not expired or that a final determination of any issue relating to enforcement of the judgment is pending.

Scope—This rule authorises the court to take such measures as may be necessary to protect the welfare of a child who is the subject of the proceedings as a matter of urgency. The Convention does not define what may be deemed to be an urgent situation but the *Handbook* suggests that the test should be: were a state not to take the necessary measures, it would result in irreparable harm being caused to the child or the protection of the child or where the interests of the child might be compromised. See further under Art 20 of the Council Regulations or Arts 11 and 12 of the 1996 Convention (both in Part VI).

Practice Direction 31A – Registration of Orders under the Council Regulation, the Civil Partnership (Jurisdiction and Recognition of Judgments) Regulations 2005, the Marriage (Same Sex Couples) (Jurisdiction and Recognition of Judgments) Regulations 2014 and under the 1996 Hague Convention

This Practice Direction supplements FPR Part 31

Form of application

1.1 An application under rule 31.4 must be made using the Part 19 procedure, except that the provisions of rules 31.8 to 31.14 and of this Practice Direction shall apply in place of rules 19.4 to 19.9.

1.2 Where the application is for recognition only of an order, it should be made clear that the application does not extend to registration for enforcement.

Evidence in support of all applications for registration, recognition or non-recognition

2.1 The requirements for information and evidence for applications differ according to whether the application is made under the Council Regulation, the Jurisdiction and Recognition of Judgments Regulations, the 2014 Regulations, or the 1996 Hague Convention.

2.2 All applications to which rule 31.4(2) applies must be supported by a statement that is sworn to be true or an affidavit, exhibiting the judgment, or a verified, certified or otherwise duly authenticated copy of the judgment. In the case of an application under the Jurisdiction and Recognition of Judgments Regulations, the 2014 Regulations or under the 1996 Hague Convention, a translation of the judgment should be supplied.

2.3 Where any other document required by this Practice Direction or by direction of the court under rule 31.5 is not in English, the applicant must supply a translation of that document into English certified by a notary public or a person qualified for the purpose, or accompanied by witness statement or affidavit confirming that the translation is accurate.

Evidence required in support of application for registration, recognition or non-recognition of a judgment under the Council Regulation

3.1 An application for a judgment to be registered, recognised or not recognised under the Council Regulation must be accompanied by a witness statement or an affidavit exhibiting the following documents and giving the information required by 3.2 or 3.3 below, as appropriate.

3.2 In the case of an application for recognition or registration –

(a) the certificate in the form set out in Annex I or Annex II of the Council Regulation, issued by the Member State in which judgment was given;

(b) in the case of a judgment given in default, the documents referred to in Article 37(2);

(c) whether the judgment provides for the payment of a sum or sums of money;

(d) whether interest is recoverable on the judgment or part of the judgment in accordance with the law of the State in which the judgment was given, and if that is the case, the rate of interest, the date from which interest is recoverable, and the date on which interest ceases to accrue;

(e) an address within the jurisdiction of the court for service of process on the party making the application and stating, in so far as is known to the applicant, the name and usual or last known address or place of business of the person against whom judgment was given; and

(f) where appropriate, whether Article 56 has been complied with, and the identity and address of the authority or authorities from whom consent has been obtained, together with evidence of that consent.

PART III

3.3 In the case of an application for an order that a judgment should not be recognised under Article 21(3) –

(a) the certificate referred to at paragraph 3.2(a);

(b) in relation to the documents identified at paragraph 3.2(b), those documents or a statement that no such service or acceptance occurred if that is the case;

(c) an address within the jurisdiction of the court for service of process on the applicant and stating, in so far as is known to the applicant, the name and usual or last known address or place of business of the person in whose favour judgment was given; and

(d) a statement of the ground or grounds under Articles 22 or 23 (as the case may be) on which it is requested that the judgment should not be recognised, the reasons why the applicant asserts that such ground or grounds is, or are, made out, and any documentary evidence on which the applicant relies.

Evidence required in support of an application for registration, recognition or non-recognition of a judgment under the 1996 Hague Convention.

4.1 An application for an order for a judgment to be registered under Article 26 or not recognised under Article 24 of the 1996 Hague Convention must be accompanied by a witness statement or affidavit exhibiting the following documents and giving the information required by 4.2, 4.3 or 4.4 below as appropriate.

4.2 In the case of an application for registration –

(a) those documents necessary to show that the judgment is enforceable according to the law of the Contracting State in which it was given;

(b) a description of the opportunities provided by the authority which gave the judgment in question for the child to be heard, except where that judgment was given in a case of urgency;

(c) where the judgment was given in a case of urgency, a statement as to the circumstances of the urgency that led to the child not having the opportunity to be heard;

(d) details of any measures taken in the non-Contracting State of the habitual residence of the child, if applicable, specifying the nature and effect of the measure, and the date on which it was taken;

(e) in as far as not apparent from the copy of the judgment provided, a statement of the grounds on which the authority which gave the judgment based its jurisdiction, together with any documentary evidence in support of that statement;

(f) where appropriate, a statement regarding whether Article 33 of the 1996 Hague Convention has been complied with, and the identity and address of the authority or authorities from which consent has been obtained, together with evidence of that consent; and

(g) the information referred to at 3.2(c) to (e) above.

4.3 In the case of an application for an order that a judgment should not be recognised –

(a) a statement of the ground or grounds under Article 23 of the 1996 Hague Convention on which it is requested that the judgment be not recognised, the reasons why the applicant asserts that such ground or grounds is or are made out, and any documentary evidence on which the Applicant relies; and

(b) an address within the jurisdiction of the court for service of process on the applicant and stating, in so far as is known to the applicant, the name and usual or last known address or place of business of the person in whose favour judgment was given.

4.4 Where is it sought to apply for recognition only of a judgment under the 1996 Hague Convention, the provisions of paragraph 4.2 apply with the exception that the applicant is not required to produce the document referred to in subparagraph 4.2(a).

Evidence required in support of an application for recognition or non-recognition of a judgment under the Jurisdiction and Recognition of Judgments Regulations or the 2014 Regulations

5.1 An application for recognition of a judgment under regulation 7 of the Jurisdiction and Recognition of Judgments Regulations or under regulation 4 of the 2014 Regulations or for non-recognition of a judgment under regulation 8 of the Jurisdiction and Recognition of Judgments Regulations or regulation 5 of the 2014 Regulations must be accompanied by a witness statement or affidavit exhibiting the following documents and giving the information at 5.2 or 5.3 below, as appropriate.

5.2 In the case of an application for recognition of a judgment –

(a) where applicable, details of any decision determining the question of the substance or validity of the civil partnership or marriage previously given by a court of civil jurisdiction in England and Wales, or by a court elsewhere;
(b) where the judgment was obtained otherwise than by means of proceedings –
 (i) an official document certifying that the judgment is effective under the law of the country in which it was obtained;
 (ii) where either civil partner or spouse was domiciled in another country from that in which the judgment was obtained at the relevant date, an official document certifying that the judgment is recognised as valid under the law of that country; or
 (iii) a verified, certified or otherwise duly authenticated copy of the document at (i) or (ii) above, as appropriate;
(c) in relation to a judgment obtained by means of proceedings and given in default, the original or a certified true copy of the document which establishes that the party who did not respond was served with the document instituting the proceedings or with an equivalent document, or any document indicating that the respondent has accepted the judgment unequivocally; and
(d) the information referred to at paragraph 3.2(c) to (e) above.

5.3 In the case of an application for non-recognition of a judgment –

(a) an address within the jurisdiction of the court for service of process on the applicant and stating, in so far as is known to the applicant, the name and usual or last known address or place of business of the person in whose favour judgment was given;
(b) a statement of the ground or grounds under regulation 8 of the Jurisdiction and Recognition of Judgments Regulations or regulation 5 of the 2014 Regulations on which it is requested that the judgment should not be recognised together with any documentary evidence on which the applicant relies; and
(c) where the judgment was obtained by means of proceedings, the document referred to at paragraph 5.2(c) or a statement that no such service or acceptance occurred if that is the case.

Evidence in support of application for a certificate under Articles 39, 41 or 42 of the Council Regulation, or for a certified copy of a judgment

6.1 The procedure described in the following paragraphs should be used where the application for the certified copy of the judgment or relevant certificate under the Council Regulation has not been made at the conclusion of the proceedings to which it relates.

6.2 An application for a certified copy of a judgment, or for a certificate under Articles 39, 41 or 42 of the Council Regulation must be made by witness statement or affidavit, containing the information and attaching the documents required under paragraph 6.3, and paragraphs 6.4, 6.5 or 6.6 below, as appropriate.

6.3 All applications must –

(a) provide details of the proceedings in which the judgment was obtained;
(b) attach a copy of the application by which the proceedings were begun;
(c) attach a copy of all statements of case filed in the proceedings; and

(d) state –
   (i) whether the judgment provides for the payment of a sum of money; and
   (ii) whether interest is recoverable on the judgment or part of it and if so, the rate of interest, the date from which interest is recoverable, and the date on which interest ceases to accrue.

Further, where the application relates to the Council Regulation, the applicant must attach a document showing that he or she benefitted from legal aid in the proceedings to which the judgment relates, if that is the case.

6.4 An application for a certified copy of the judgment and a certificate under Article 41 or 42 of the Council Regulation must –

(a) contain a statement of whether the certificate is sought under Article 41 or Article 42;
(b) attach a document evidencing the service of the application by which the proceedings were begun on all respondents, and if no such service occurred, details of all opportunities provided to each respondent to put their case before the court;
(c) provide information regarding the age of the child at the time of the judgment and the opportunities given during the proceedings, if any, for the child's wishes and feelings to be ascertained;
(d) state the full names, addresses and dates and places of birth (where available) of all persons holding parental responsibility in relation to the child or children to whom the judgment relates; and
(e) state the full names and dates of birth of each child to whom the judgment relates.

6.5 An application for a certified copy of the judgment and a certificate under Article 39 of the Council Regulation must –

(a) state whether the certificate sought relates to a parental responsibility matter or a matrimonial matter;
(b) in relation to a parental responsibility matter, attach evidence that the judgment has been served on the respondent;
(c) in the case of a judgment given in default, attach a document which establishes that the respondent was served with the petition or application by which the proceedings were commenced, or a document indicating that the respondent accepted the judgment unequivocally;
(d) state that the time for appealing has expired, or give the date on which it will expire, as appropriate, and state whether a notice of appeal against the judgment has been given;
(e) in relation to a matrimonial matter, give the full name, address, country and place of birth, and date of birth of each party, and the country, place and date of the marriage;
(f) in relation to a parental responsibility matter, give the full name, address, place and date of birth of each person who holds parental responsibility;
(g) as appropriate, give the name, address, and date and place of birth of the person with access rights, or to whom the child is to be returned.

6.6 An application for a certified copy of a judgment for the purposes of recognition and enforcement of the judgment under the 1996 Hague Convention must –

(a) provide a statement of the grounds on which the court based its jurisdiction to make the orders in question;
(b) indicate the age of the child at the time of the judgment and the measures taken, if any, for the child's wishes and feelings to be ascertained; and
(c) indicate which persons were provided with notice of the proceedings and, where such persons were served with the proceedings, attach evidence of such service.

PART 32
REGISTRATION AND ENFORCEMENT OF ORDERS

CONTENTS OF THIS PART

Chapter 1

Rule		Page
	Scope and Interpretation of this Part	
32.1	Scope and interpretation	1910
	Chapter 2 *Registration etc of Orders under the 1950 Act*	
	Section 1 *Interpretation of this Chapter*	
32.2	Interpretation	1911
	Section 2 *Registration etc of High Court and Family Court Orders*	
32.3	Registration of a High Court order	1911
32.4	Notice of Variation etc. of a High Court order	1912
32.5	Cancellation of registration of a High Court order by the court of registration	1912
32.5A	Cancellation of registration of a High Court order by the High Court	1912
32.6	Application of this Chapter to a family court order	1912
32.6A	Variation of a family court order: section 22(1) of the 1950 Act	1912
32.6B	Application to adduce evidence: section 22(5) of the 1950 Act	1912
	Section 3 *Registration etc. of Scottish and Northern Irish Orders*	
32.7	Registration of Scottish and Northern Irish orders	1913
32.8	Application to adduce evidence: sections 21(2) and 22(5) of the 1950 Act	1913
32.9	Notice of variation etc. of Scottish and Northern Irish orders	1913
32.9A	Variation of Scottish and Northern Irish orders by the family court	1913
32.10	Cancellation of registration of Scottish and Northern Irish orders	1914
32.10A	Payments under a maintenance order registered in the family court	1914
32.11	Enforcement	1915
32.12	Inspection of register and copies of order	1915
32.12A	Notices and certificates: section 19(4), 20(1) and 24(5) and (5A) of the 1950 Act	1915
	Chapter 3 *Registration of Maintenance Orders under the 1958 Act*	
32.13	Interpretation	1916
32.14	Registration of orders – prescribed period	1916
32.15	Application for registration of a maintenance order in the family court – procedure in the High Court	1916
32.15A	Application for registration of a maintenance order in the family court – procedure in the family court	1916
32.16	Registration in the family court of an order registered in the High Court – procedure in the High Court	1916
32.16A	Registration in the family court of an order registered in the High Court – procedure in the family court	1916
32.19	Variation or discharge of an order registered in the family court – procedure in the High Court	1917
32.19A	Variation, remission, discharge or cancellation of registration of an order registered in the family court – procedure in the family court	1917
32.22	Cancellation of registration – orders registered in the family court	1918
32.22A	Notices: payments made through the family court	1918

PART III

32.22B	Method of payment	1918
32.22C	Variation of method of payment	1919
32.22D	Notices received from another court or from a person entitled to payments	1919

Chapter 4
Registration and Enforcement of Custody Orders under the 1986 Act

32.23	Interpretation	1919
32.24	Prescribed officer and functions of the court	1919
32.25	Application for the registration of an order made by the High Court or the family court	1920
32.26	Registration of orders made in Scotland, Northern Ireland or a specified dependent territory	1921
32.27	Revocation and variation of an order made in the High Court or the family court	1921
32.28	Registration of varied, revoked or recalled orders made in Scotland, Northern Ireland or a specified dependent territory	1921
32.29	Interim directions	1922
32.30	Staying and dismissal of enforcement proceedings	1922
32.31	Particulars of other proceedings	1922
32.32	Inspection of register	1922

Chapter 5
Ability of a Court Officer to Take Enforcement Proceedings in Relation to Certain Orders for Periodical Payments

32.33	Court officers and enforcement proceedings	1923
	Practice Direction 32A – Forms Relating to Part 32	1924

Chapter 1
Scope and Interpretation of this Part

32.1 Scope and interpretation

(1) This Part contains rules about the registration and enforcement of maintenance orders and custody orders.

(2) In this Part, 'the 1950 Act' means the Maintenance Orders Act 1950.

(3) Chapter 2 of this Part relates to –

- (a) the registration of a maintenance order, made in the High Court or the family court, in a court in Scotland or Northern Ireland in accordance with the 1950 Act; and
- (b) the registration of a maintenance order, made in Scotland or Northern Ireland, in the High Court in accordance with the 1950 Act.

(4) Chapter 3 of this Part contains rules to be applied in the family court in relation to the registration in the family court of a maintenance order made in the High Court, in accordance with the 1958 Act.

(5) Chapter 4 of this Part relates to the registration and enforcement of custody orders in accordance with the 1986 Act.

(6) Chapter 5 of this Part relates to the ability of a court officer to take enforcement proceedings in relation to certain orders for periodical payments.

Amendments—SI 2011/1328; SI 2012/679; SI 2013/3204.

Chapter 2
Registration etc of Orders under the 1950 Act

Section 1
Interpretation of this Chapter

32.2 Interpretation

In this Chapter –

'the clerk of the Court of Session' means the deputy principal clerk in charge of the petition department of the Court of Session;

'the clerk of the court which made the order' means, in the case of a county court in Northern Ireland, the Chief Clerk for the appropriate court in Northern Ireland;

…

'family court order' means a maintenance order made in the family court;

'High Court order' means a maintenance order made in the High Court;

'maintenance order' means a maintenance order to which section 16 of the 1950 Act applies;

'Northern Irish order' means a maintenance order made by a court in Northern Ireland;

'the register' means the register kept for the purposes of the 1950 Act;

'the registrar in Northern Ireland' means the chief registrar of the Queen's Bench Division (Matrimonial) of the High Court of Justice in Northern Ireland;

'registration' means registration under Part 2 of the 1950 Act and 'registered' is to be construed accordingly; and

'Scottish order' means a maintenance order made by a court in Scotland.

Amendments—SI 2013/3204.

Section 2
Registration etc of High Court and Family Court Orders

Amendments—SI 2013/3204.

32.3 Registration of a High Court order

(1) An application for the registration of a High Court order may be made by sending to a court officer at the court which made the order –

(a) a certified copy of the order; and

(b) a statement which –

  (i) contains the address in the United Kingdom, and the occupation, of the person liable to make payments under the order;

  (ii) contains the date on which the order was served on the person liable to make payments, or, if the order has not been served, the reason why service has not been effected;

  (iii) contains the reason why it is convenient for the order to be enforced in Scotland or Northern Ireland, as the case may be;

  (iv) contains the amount of any arrears due to the applicant under the order;

  (v) confirms that the order is not already registered; and

  (vi) is verified by a statement of truth.

(2) If it appears to the court that –

(a) the person liable to make payments under the order resides in Scotland or Northern Ireland; and

(b) it is convenient for the order to be enforced there,

the court officer will send the documents filed under paragraph (1) to the clerk of the Court of Session or to the registrar in Northern Ireland, as the case may be.

(3) On receipt of a notice of the registration of a High Court order in the Court of Session or the Court of Judicature of Northern Ireland, the court officer (who is the prescribed officer for the purposes of section 17(4) of the 1950 Act) will –

PART III

(a) enter particulars of the notice of registration in the register;
(b) note the fact of registration in the court records; and
(c) send particulars of the notice to the principal registry.

32.4 Notice of Variation etc. of a High Court order

(1) This rule applies where a High Court order, which is registered in the Court of Session or the Court of Judicature of Northern Ireland, is discharged or varied.

(2) A court officer in the court where the order was discharged or varied will send a certified copy of that order to the clerk of the Court of Session or the registrar in Northern Ireland, as the case may be.

32.5 Cancellation of registration of a High Court order by the court of registration

(1) This rule applies where –

(a) the registration of a High Court order registered in the Court of Session or the Court of Judicature of Northern Ireland is cancelled under section 24(1) of the 1950 Act; and
(b) notice of the cancellation is given to a court officer in the court in which the order was made (who is the prescribed officer for the purposes of section 24(3)(a) of the 1950 Act).

(2) On receipt of a notice of cancellation of registration, the court officer will enter particulars of the notice in the register.

Amendments—SI 2013/3204.

32.5A Cancellation of registration of a High Court order by the High Court

The Part 19 procedure applies to an application to the High Court under section 24(2) of the 1950 Act.

Amendments—Inserted by SI 2013/3204.

32.6 Application of this Chapter to a family court order

Rules 32.3 to 32.5A apply to a family court order as if –

(a) references to a High Court order were references to a family court order;
(aa) in rule 32.5A, references to the High Court were to the family court;
(b) where the order is to be registered in Scotland, references to the Court of Session and the clerk of the Court of Session were references to the sheriff court and the sheriff-clerk of the sheriff court respectively; and
(c) where the order is to be registered in Northern Ireland, references to the Court of Judicature of Northern Ireland and the registrar of Northern Ireland were references to the court of summary jurisdiction and the clerk of the court of summary jurisdiction respectively.

Amendments—SI 2013/3204.

32.6A Variation of a family court order: section 22(1) of the 1950 Act

Where a family court order, which is registered in a court in Scotland or Northern Ireland, is varied under section 22(1) of the 1950 Act by the court in which it is registered –

(a) the court officer for the court which made the order will be the prescribed officer to whom notice of the variation must be given under section 23(1) of the 1950 Act; and
(b) on receipt of a notice under section 23(1) of the 1950 Act, the court officer will enter particulars of the notice in the register.

Amendments—Inserted by SI 2013/3204.

32.6B Application to adduce evidence: section 22(5) of the 1950 Act

(1) The Part 18 procedure applies to an application under section 22(5) of the 1950 Act where a maintenance order was made by the family court.

(2) The family court will send a transcript or summary of any evidence taken to the clerk of the court in which the order is registered.

(3) The court officer for the court in England and Wales which made the maintenance order will be the prescribed officer to whom any transcript or summary of evidence adduced in the court in Scotland or Northern Ireland must be sent under section 22(5) of the 1950 Act.

Amendments—Inserted by SI 2013/3204.

Section 3
Registration etc. of Scottish and Northern Irish Orders

32.7 Registration of Scottish and Northern Irish orders

On receipt of a certified copy of a Scottish order or a Northern Irish order for registration, a court officer in the principal registry (who is the prescribed officer in the High Court for the purposes of section 17(2) of the 1950 Act) or a court officer in the family court (who is the prescribed officer in the family court for the purposes of section 17(2) of the 1950 Act) will –

(a) enter particulars of the order in the register;
(b) notify the clerk of the court which made the order or the registrar in Northern Ireland, as the case may be, that the order has been registered; and
(c) file the certified copy of the order and any statutory declaration, affidavit(GL) or statement as to the amount of any arrears due under the order.

(Section 17(3) of the 1950 Act makes provision as to the court in England and Wales to which a Northern Irish order or a Scottish order should be sent, which depends on which court originally made the order.)

Amendments—SI 2013/3204.

32.8 Application to adduce evidence: sections 21(2) and 22(5) of the 1950 Act

(1) The Part 18 procedure applies to the applications under these provisions of the 1950 Act –

(a) an application to the High Court to adduce evidence under section 21(2) by a person liable to make payments under a Scottish order registered in the High Court;
(b) an application to the family court to adduce evidence under section 21(2) by a person liable to make payments under a Scottish order registered in the High Court under the 1950 Act and registered in the family court under Part 1 of the 1958 Act; and
(c) an application to the family court to adduce evidence under section 22(5) by a person entitled to payments or a person liable to make payments under a Scottish order or a Northern Irish order registered in the family court under Part 1 of the 1950 Act.

(2) The court officer for the family court (being the court in which the order is registered) will be the prescribed officer under section 22(5) of the 1950 Act to whom any transcript or summary of evidence adduced in the court in Scotland or Northern Ireland by which the order was made must be sent.

Amendments—Substituted by SI 2013/3204.

32.9 Notice of variation etc. of Scottish and Northern Irish orders

(1) This rule applies where –

(a) a Scottish order or a Northern Irish order, which is registered in the High Court or the family court, is discharged or varied by the court in Scotland or Northern Ireland; and
(b) notice of the discharge or variation is given to the court officer in the High Court or in the family court, as the case may be (who is the prescribed officer for the purposes of section 23(1)(a) of the 1950 Act).

(2) On receipt of a notice of discharge or variation, the court officer will enter particulars of the notice in the register.

Amendments—SI 2013/3204.

32.9A Variation of Scottish and Northern Irish orders by the family court

(1) The Part 18 procedure applies to an application to the family court under section 22(1) of the 1950 Act to vary a Scottish order or a Northern Irish order which is registered in the family court.

PART III

(2) Where a Scottish order or a Northern Irish order is varied by the family court on an application under section 22(1) of the 1950 Act, the court officer will give notice of the variation to the clerk of the court in Scotland or Northern Ireland which made the order by sending a certified copy of the order of variation.

Amendments—Inserted by SI 2013/3204.

32.10 Cancellation of registration of Scottish and Northern Irish orders

(1) The Part 18 procedure applies to an application under section 24(1) of the 1950 Act for the cancellation of the registration of a Scottish order or a Northern Irish order in the High Court or the family court.

(2) The application must be made without notice to the person liable to make payments under the order.

(3) If the registration of the order is cancelled, the court officer will –

- (a) note the cancellation in the register; and
- (b) send written notice of the cancellation to –
  - (i) the clerk of the court which made the order or the registrar in Northern Ireland, as the case may be; and
  - (ii) the court officer of the family court if the order has been registered in the family court in accordance with section 2(5) of the 1958 Act.

(4) Where a maintenance order is registered under the 1950 Act in the family court, the court officer for the family court is the prescribed officer for the purposes of section 24(2) of the 1950 Act, and in paragraphs (5) and (6) references to the court officer are to the court officer of the family court.

(5) If a notice under section 24(2) of the 1950 Act is received, the court officer will –

- (a) cancel the registration of the order; and
- (b) send written notice of the cancellation to the clerk of the court which made the order.

(6) Where a maintenance order is registered in the family court under Part 1 of the 1958 Act and the court officer receives a notice of cancellation under section 24(3) of the 1950 Act from the appropriate officer of the High Court, the court officer will –

- (a) enter the details of the notice in the register;
- (b) cancel the registration under Part 1 of the 1958 Act; and
- (c) give notice of the cancellation to the appropriate officer of the court which made the order, being –
  - (i) the Deputy Principal Clerk of Session, in the case of the Court of Session; or
  - (ii) the Chief Registrar of the Queen's Bench Division (Matrimonial), in the case of the High Court of Justice in Northern Ireland.

Amendments—SI 2013/3204.

32.10A Payments under a maintenance order registered in the family court

(1) This rule applies where section 22(1A) of the 1950 Act applies and the family court orders that payments under a maintenance order registered in the family court are to be made by a particular means.

(2) The court officer will record on a copy of the order the means of payment that the court has ordered.

(3) The court officer will notify, in writing, the person liable to make payments under the order how the payments are to be made.

(4) Where under section 1(4A) of the Maintenance Enforcement Act 1991 the family court orders payment to the court by a method of payment specified in section 1(5) of that Act, the court officer will notify the person liable to make payments under the order of sufficient details of the account into which the payments should be made to enable payments to be made into that account.

(5) The Part 18 procedure applies to an application under section 1(7) of the Maintenance Enforcement Act 1991 (application from an interested party to revoke, suspend, revive or vary a means of payment order).

(6) Where the court makes an order under section 1(7) of the Maintenance Enforcement Act 1991 or dismisses an application for such an order, the court officer will, as far as practicable, notify in writing all interested parties of the effect of the order and will take the steps set out in paragraphs (2), (3) and (4), as appropriate.

(7) In this rule, 'interested party' has the meaning given in section 1(10) of the Maintenance Enforcement Act 1991.

Amendments—Inserted by SI 2013/3204. Amended by SI 2014/667.

32.11 Enforcement

(1) Subject to paragraph (2), Part 33 applies to an application for or with respect to the enforcement of a Scottish order or a Northern Irish order registered in the High Court or the family court.

(2) The application may be made without notice to the person liable to make payments under the order.

Amendments—SI 2013/3204.

32.12 Inspection of register and copies of order

Any person –

- (a) who is entitled to receive, or liable to make, payments under a Scottish order or a Northern Irish order registered in the High Court or the family court under the 1950 Act; or
- (b) with the permission of the court,

may –

- (i) inspect the register; or
- (ii) request a copy of any order registered in the High Court or the family court under Part 2 of the 1950 Act and any statutory declaration, affidavit(GL) or statement filed with the order.

Amendments—SI 2013/3204.

32.12A Notices and certificates: section 19(4), 20(1) and 24(5) and (5A) of the 1950 Act

(1) Practice Direction 32A contains the form of –

- (a) a notice under section 19(4) of the 1950 Act that payments under a maintenance order made by a sheriff court in Scotland or a court of summary jurisdiction in Northern Ireland have become payable through or to any officer or person;
- (b) a notice under section 19(4) of the 1950 Act that the payments under a maintenance order made by the family court have, on its registration under Part 2 of the 1950 Act in a court in Scotland or Northern Ireland, ceased to be payable to or through the court or any person;
- (c) a certificate lodged under section 20(1) of the 1950 Act as to the amount of any arrears due under a maintenance order made by the family court; and
- (d) a notice under section 24(5) or (5A) of the 1950 Act of the cancellation of the registration under Part 2 of the 1950 Act of a maintenance order in the family court.

(2) The court officer will send a notice referred to in paragraph (1)(a), (b) or (d) to the person liable to make the payments under the order at that person's last known address.

Amendments—Inserted by SI 2013/3204.

Chapter 3
Registration of Maintenance Orders under the 1958 Act

32.13 Interpretation

In this Chapter 'the register' means the register kept for the purposes of the 1958 Act.

32.14 Registration of orders – prescribed period

The prescribed period for the purpose of section 2(2) of the 1958 Act is 14 days.

(Section 2(2) sets out the period during which an order, which is to be registered in a magistrates' court, may not be enforced)

'registered in a magistrates' court'—These words are now obsolete following the amendment of the 1958 Act. The section now refers to the registration of High Court orders in the Family Court.

32.15 Application for registration of a maintenance order in the family court – procedure in the High Court

(1) An application under section 2(1) of the 1958 Act may be made by sending to the court officer at the court which made the order –

(a) a certified copy of the maintenance order; and
(b) two copies of the application.

(2) When, on the grant of an application, the court officer sends the certified copy of the maintenance order to the family court in accordance with section 2(2), the court officer must –

(a) note on the order that the application for registration has been granted; and
(b) send to the family court a copy of the application for registration of the order.

(3) On receiving notice that the family court has registered the order, the court officer of the High Court must enter particulars of the registration in the court records.

Amendments—SI 2013/3204.

Method of and grounds supporting application (r 32.15(1))—The court may grant the application if it thinks fit (MOA 1958, s 2(1)); there is no absolute right to registration.

32.15A Application for registration of a maintenance order in the family court – procedure in the family court

(1) This rule applies where the court officer for the family court receives from the court officer of the High Court a certified copy of a High Court order, in accordance with section 2(2)(b) of the 1958 Act.

(2) The court officer of the family court will –

(a) register the order in the family court by entering particulars in the register; and
(b) send notice to the court officer of the High Court that the order has been registered.

Amendments—Inserted by SI 2013/3204.

32.16 Registration in the family court of an order registered in the High Court – procedure in the High Court

(1) This rule applies where –

(a) a maintenance order is registered in the High Court in accordance with section 17(4) of the 1950 Act; and
(b) the court officer of the High Court receives notice that the family court has registered the order in accordance with section 2(5) of the 1958 Act.

(2) The court officer of the High Court must enter particulars of the registration in the register.

Amendments—SI 2013/3204.

32.16A Registration in the family court of an order registered in the High Court – procedure in the family court

(1) This rule applies where –

(a) a maintenance order is registered in the High Court in accordance with section 17(4) of the 1950 Act; and
(b) the court officer of the family court, in accordance with section 2(2)(b) of the 1958 Act, receives from the appropriate officer of the original court in Scotland or Northern Ireland a certified copy of an order made by the court in Scotland or Northern Ireland.

(2) The court officer of the family court will –

(a) register the order in the family court by entering particulars in the register; and
(b) send written notice to the court officer of the High Court and to the appropriate officer of the original court in Scotland or in Northern Ireland that the order has been registered.

Amendments—Inserted by SI 2013/3204.

32.17–32.18 *(revoked)*

32.19 Variation or discharge of an order registered in the family court – procedure in the High Court

(1) This rule applies where a maintenance order is registered in the family court under Part 1 of the 1958 Act.

(2) If the court which made the order makes an order varying or discharging that order the court officer of the High Court must send a certified copy of the order of variation or discharge to the family court.

(3) If the court officer of the High Court receives from the family court a certified copy of an order varying the maintenance order the court officer must –

(a) file the copy of the order; and
(b) enter the particulars of the variation in the place where the details required by rule 32.15(3) were entered.

Amendments—SI 2013/3204.

Variation of order (r 32.19)—Applications to vary the rate of payment must be made to the Family Court (MOA 1958, s 4(2)), unless made in proceedings to vary some other provision in the order (s 4(5)(a)) or unless either party is not present in England or Wales (s 4(5)(b)). If variation proceedings are pending in one court, no variation application may be made to the other (s 4(6)). The Family Court may remit a variation application to be heard by the High Court (s 4(4) and see r 32.19A(2)).

Discharge of order (r 32.19)—The MOA 1958 does not give the Family Court power to discharge a registered order made by the High Court. An application for discharge must be made to the original court. It is suggested, however, that the Family Court could in an appropriate case vary an order to a nominal figure.

32.19A Variation, remission, discharge or cancellation of registration of an order registered in the family court – procedure in the family court

(1) Where under section 4(2) of the 1958 Act a High Court order registered in the family court is varied by the family court, the court officer for the family court will give notice of the variation to the High Court.

(2) Where under section 4(4) of the 1958 Act an application for the variation of a High Court order registered in the family court is remitted to the High Court by the family court, the court officer for the family court will give notice of its having been remitted to the High Court.

(3) Where under section 5(4) of the 1958 Act the registration of a High Court order in the family court is cancelled by the family court, the court officer for the family court will give notice of cancellation to the High Court, stating (if applicable) that the cancellation is a result of a notice given under section 5(1) of the 1958 Act.

(4) Where under section 5(4) of the 1958 Act the registration in the family court of an order made in Scotland or Northern Ireland is cancelled by the family court, the court officer for the family court will give notice of the cancellation to –

(a) the appropriate officer of the court which made the order; and
(b) where the order is registered under Part 2 of the 1950 Act, to the appropriate officer of the High Court.

(5) Where under section 5(4) of the 1958 Act the registration in the family court of an order under Part 2 of the 1950 Act is cancelled by the family court, the court officer for the family court will give notice of the cancellation to the appropriate officer of the original court.

(6) Where under section 5 of the 1958 Act the cancellation of the registration of a High Court order means that any order which requires payment to be made to the family court is to cease to have effect, the court officer will give notice to the defendant in the form set out in Practice Direction 32A (Form 7).

Amendments—Inserted by SI 2013/3204.

32.20–32.21 (*revoked*)

32.22 Cancellation of registration – orders registered in the family court

(1) Where the court gives notice under section 5(2) of the 1958 Act, the court officer must endorse the notice on the certified copy of the order of variation or discharge sent to the family court in accordance with rule 32.19(2).

(2) Where notice is received from a magistrates' court that registration of an order made by the High Court under Part 1 of the 1958 Act has been cancelled, the court officer must enter particulars of the cancellation in the place where the details required by rule 32.15(3) were entered.

Amendments—SI 2013/3204.

32.22A Notices: payments made through the family court

(1) Paragraph (2) applies where a notice is given under section 2(6ZC) of the 1958 Act that payments under an order registered in the family court are payable to the family court.

(2) The notice will be in the form set out in Practice Direction 32A (Form 5) and will be given by the court officer of the family court.

(3) Paragraph (4) applies where a notice is given under section 2(6ZC) of the 1958 Act that payments under an order registered in the family court have ceased to be payable to the family court.

(4) The notice will be in the form set out in Practice Direction 32A (Form 6) and will be given by the court officer of the family court.

Amendments—Inserted by SI 2013/3204.

32.22B Method of payment

(1) This rule applies where the family court exercises its duties or powers under section 4A(2) of the 1958 Act to make, revive or vary any means of payment order within the meaning of section 1(7) of the Maintenance Enforcement Act 1991.

(2) Where the court orders that payments under a registered order are to be made by a particular means –

- (a) the court will record on a copy of the order the means of payment which the court has ordered; and
- (b) the court officer will notify, in writing, the person liable to make payments under the order how the payments are to be made.

(3) Paragraph (4) applies where the court orders that payments be made –

- (a) by the debtor to the creditor; or
- (b) by the debtor to the court;

by a method falling within section 1(5) of the Maintenance Enforcement Act 1991.

(4) The court officer will notify the person liable to make payments under the order of sufficient details of the account into which payments should be made to enable payments to be made into that account.

Amendments—Inserted by SI 2013/3204.

32.22C Variation of method of payment

(1) The Part 18 procedure applies to an application under section 1(3)(a) of the Maintenance Enforcement Act 1991 received from an interested party for the method of payment to be varied under section 4A of the 1958 Act.

(2) The court will notify the interested party who made the application and, where practicable, any other interested party, of the result of the application.

(3) The court will record any variation on a copy of the order.

Amendments—Inserted by SI 2013/3204.

32.22D Notices received from another court or from a person entitled to payments

(1) This rule applies where any notice is received –

- (a) of the discharge or variation by the High Court of a High Court order registered in the family court;
- (b) of the discharge or variation by a court in Scotland or Northern Ireland of an order made by such a court and registered in the family court; or
- (c) under section 5(1) or (2) of the 1958 Act.

(2) The court officer for the family court will enter details of any such notice in the register.

(3) In the case of a notice under section 5(1) or (2) of the 1958 Act, the court officer for the family court will ensure that the person in possession of any warrant of commitment, issued but not executed, for the enforcement of the order is informed of the giving of that notice.

Amendments—Inserted by SI 2013/3204.

Chapter 4

Registration and Enforcement of Custody Orders under the 1986 Act

32.23 Interpretation

In this Chapter –

'appropriate court' means, in relation to –

- (a) Scotland, the Court of Session;
- (b) Northern Ireland, the High Court in Northern Ireland; and
- (c) a specified dependent territory, the corresponding court in that territory;

'appropriate officer' means, in relation to –

- (a) the Court of Session, the Deputy Principal Clerk of Session;
- (b) the High Court in Northern Ireland, the Master (Care and Protection) of that court; and
- (c) the appropriate court in a specified dependent territory, the corresponding officer of that court;

'Part 1 order' means an order under Part 1 of the 1986 Act;

'the register' means the register kept for the purposes of Part 1 of the 1986 Act; and

'specified dependent territory' means a dependent territory specified in column 1 of Schedule 1 to the Family Law Act 1986 (Specified Dependent Territories) Order 1991.

Scope—The interpretation clause of this rule is in addition to FPR 2010, r 2.3(1). It deals with the terminology found in FLA 1986, ss 25–31 and in FPR 2010, rr 32.24–32.32 relating to the registration of 'custody orders' within the UK. References to the Isle of Man are included within the term 'specified dependant territory' pursuant to the Family Law Act 1986 (Dependent Territories) Order 1991, which brought orders made in the Isle of Man in relation to children within the reciprocal recognition and enforcement provision of FLA 1986. It also includes the Channel Island of Jersey and hence the Royal Court of Jersey (see FPR 2010, r 12.52).

32.24 Prescribed officer and functions of the court

(1) The prescribed officer for the purposes of sections 27(4) and 28(1) of the 1986 Act is the family proceedings department manager of the principal registry.

PART III

(2) The function of the court under sections 27(3) and 28(1) of the 1986 Act shall be performed by a court officer.

Defined terms—'court officer', 'appropriate officer': FPR 2010, r 2.3(1).

32.25 Application for the registration of an order made by the High Court or the family court

(1) An application under section 27 of the 1986 Act for the registration of an order made in the High Court or the family court may be made by sending to a court officer at the court which made the order –

(a) a certified copy of the order;

(b) a copy of any order which has varied the terms of the original order;

(c) a statement which –

(i) contains the name and address of the applicant and the applicant's interest under the order;

(ii) contains –

(aa) the name and date of birth of the child in respect of whom the order was made;

(bb) the whereabouts or suspected whereabouts of the child; and

(cc) the name of any person with whom the child is alleged to be;

(iii) contains the name and address of any other person who has an interest under the order and states whether the order has been served on that person;

(iv) states in which of the jurisdictions of Scotland, Northern Ireland or a specified dependent territory the order is to be registered;

(v) states that to the best of the applicant's information and belief, the order is in force;

(vi) states whether, and if so where, the order is already registered;

(vii) gives details of any order known to the applicant which affects the child and is in force in the jurisdiction in which the order is to be registered;

(viii) annexes any document relevant to the application; and

(ix) is verified by a statement of truth; and

(d) a copy of the statement referred to in paragraph (c).

(2) On receipt of the documents referred to in paragraph (1), the court officer will, subject to paragraph (4) –

(a) keep the original statement and send the other documents to the appropriate officer;

(b) record in the court records the fact that the documents have been sent to the appropriate officer; and

(c) file a copy of the documents.

(3) On receipt of a notice that the document has been registered in the appropriate court the court officer will record that fact in the court records.

(4) The court officer will not send the documents to the appropriate officer if it appears to the court officer that –

(a) the order is no longer in force; or

(b) the child has reached the age of 16.

(5) Where paragraph (4) applies –

(a) the court officer must, within 14 days of the decision, notify the applicant of the decision of the court officer in paragraph (4) and the reasons for it; and

(b) the applicant may apply to the court in private for an order that the documents be sent to the appropriate court.

Amendments—SI 2013/3204.

Defined terms—'specified territory': FPR 2010, r 32.23, but also includes Jersey.

Verified by statement of truth—For documents to be verified by statement of truth, see FPR 2010, r 17 and FPR PD17A, para 1.

Form of statement of truth—See FPR 2010, r 17.2 and FPR PD17A, paras 2–4.4.

32.26 Registration of orders made in Scotland, Northern Ireland or a specified dependent territory

(1) This rule applies where the prescribed officer receives, for registration, a certified copy of an order made in Scotland, Northern Ireland or a specified dependent territory.

(2) The prescribed officer will –

(a) enter in the register –

(i) the name and address of the applicant and the applicant's interest under the order;

(ii) the name and date of birth of the child and the date the child will attain the age of 16;

(iii) the whereabouts or suspected whereabouts of the child; and

(iv) the terms of the order, its date and the court which made it;

(b) file the certified copy and accompanying documents; and

(c) notify –

(i) the court which sent the order; and

(ii) the applicant,

that the order has been registered.

Defined terms—'specified territory', 'the register': r 32.23; 'prescribed officer': r 32.24.

Scope—This rule sets out what the prescribed officer has to do to register the order.

32.27 Revocation and variation of an order made in the High Court or the family court

(1) Where a Part 1 order, registered in an appropriate court, is varied or revoked, the court officer of the court making the order of variation or revocation will –

(a) send a certified copy of the order of variation or revocation to –

(i) the appropriate officer; and

(ii) if a different court, the court which made the Part 1 order;

(b) record in the court records the fact that a copy of the order has been sent; and

(c) file a copy of the order.

(2) On receipt of notice from the appropriate court that its register has been amended, this fact will be recorded by the court officer of –

(a) the court which made the order of variation or revocation; and

(b) if different, the court which made the Part 1 order.

Amendments—SI 2013/3204.

Defined terms—'appropriate court', 'appropriate officer': r 32.23; 'Part 1 order': FLA 1986, s 32 and FPR 2010, r 32.23.

Scope—This rule should be read together with FLA 1986, s 28, which makes provision for the cancellation and variation of registered orders. Similar provision is made for registration of Scottish and Northern Ireland orders and orders made in the Isle of Man in FPR 2010, r 32.28. Unlike r 32.28, there is no provision for the court of its own motion to cancel an order that ceased to have effect, other than by revocation or variation.

32.28 Registration of varied, revoked or recalled orders made in Scotland, Northern Ireland or a specified dependent territory

(1) This rule applies where the prescribed officer receives a certified copy of an order made in Scotland, Northern Ireland or a specified dependent territory which varies, revokes or recalls a registered Part 1 order.

(2) The prescribed officer shall enter particulars of the variation, revocation or recall in the register and give notice of the entry to –

(a) the court which sent the certified copy;

(b) if different, the court which made the Part 1 order;

(c) the applicant for registration; and

(d) if different, the applicant for the variation, revocation of recall of the order.

(3) An application under section 28(2) of the 1986 Act must be made in accordance with the Part 19 procedure.

PART III

(4) The applicant for the Part 1 order, if not the applicant under section 28(2) of the 1986 Act, must be made a defendant to the application.

(5) Where the court cancels a registration under section 28(2) of the 1986 Act, the court officer will amend the register and give notice of the amendment to the court which made the Part 1 order.

Defined terms—'specified territory', 'the register': FPR 2010, r 32.23; 'prescribed officer': FPR 2010, r 32.24; 'Part 1 Order': FLA 1986, s 32 and FPR 2010, r 32.23.

Procedure—FPR 2010, Pt 19 procedure must be followed.

Cancellation—Cancellation may take place only where the court acts of its own initiative or on an application of any person who has an interest in the matter (FLA 1986, s 28(2)).

32.29 Interim directions

The following persons will be made parties to an application for interim directions under section 29 of the 1986 Act –

(a) the parties to the proceedings for enforcement; and
(b) if not a party to those proceedings, the applicant for the Part 1 order.

Section 29 of the 1986 Act—The section relates to enforcement of a registered order. See further the commentary under the provisions of that section.

32.30 Staying and dismissal of enforcement proceedings

(1) The following persons will be made parties to an application under section 30(1) or 31(1) of the 1986 Act –

(a) the parties to the proceedings for enforcement which are sought to be stayed(GL); and
(b) if not a party to those proceedings, the applicant for the Part 1 order.

(2) Where the court makes an order under section 30(2) or (3) or section 31(3) of the 1986 Act, the court officer will amend the register and give notice of the amendment to –

(a) the court which made the Part 1 order; and
(b) the applicants for –
  (i) registration;
  (ii) enforcement; and
  (iii) stay(GL) or dismissal of the enforcement proceedings.

Defined terms—'court officer', 'Part 1 order': FLA 1986, s 32 and FPR 2010, r 32.23.

32.31 Particulars of other proceedings

A party to proceedings for or relating to a Part 1 order who knows of other proceedings which relate to the child concerned (including proceedings out of the jurisdiction and concluded proceedings) must file a witness statement which –

(a) states in which jurisdiction and court the other proceedings were begun;
(b) states the nature and current state of the proceedings and the relief claimed or granted;
(c) sets out the names of the parties to the proceedings and their relationship to the child;
(d) if applicable and if known, states the reasons why relief claimed in the proceedings for or relating to the Part 1 order was not claimed in the other proceedings; and
(e) is verified by a statement of truth.

Defined terms—'Part 1 order': FLA 1986, s 32 and r 32.23; 'witness statement': r 22.4.

Witness statement—See FPR 2010, r 17, FPR PD17A, FPR 2010, r 22.4 and FPR PD22A.

32.32 Inspection of register

The following persons may inspect any entry in the register relating to a Part 1 order and may request copies of the order any document relating to it –

(a) the applicant for registration of the Part 1 order;
(b) a person who, to the satisfaction of a district judge, has an interest under the Part 1 order; and
(c) a person who obtains the permission of a district judge.

Defined terms—'the register': FPR 2010, r 32.23; 'Part 1 order': FLA 1986, s 32 and FPR 2010, r 32.23; 'district judge': FPR 2010, r 2.3(1).

Chapter 5
Ability of a Court Officer to Take Enforcement Proceedings in Relation to Certain Orders for Periodical Payments

32.33 Court officers and enforcement proceedings

(1) In this rule –

'the 1972 Act' means the Maintenance Orders (Reciprocal Enforcement) Act 1972;
'relevant order' means –

(a) any order made by the family court for periodical payments, other than an order made by virtue of Part 2 of the 1972 Act;

(b) any order for periodical payments made by the High Court (including an order deemed to be made by the High Court by virtue of section 1(2) of the 1958 Act) and registered under Part 1 of the 1958 Act in the family court; and

(c) an order made by a court in Scotland or in Northern Ireland which is registered in the family court under Part 2 of the 1950 Act; and

'the payee' means the person for whose benefit payments under a relevant order are required to be made.

(2) Where –

(a) payments under a relevant order are required to be made periodically to the family court; and

(b) any sums payable under the order are in arrears,

a court officer will, if the payee so requests in writing, and unless it appears to the court officer that it is unreasonable in the circumstances to do so, proceed in the officer's own name for the recovery of those sums.

(3) Where payments under a relevant order are required to be made periodically to the court, the payee may, at any time during the period in which the payments are required to be so made, give authority in writing to a court officer for the officer to proceed as mentioned in paragraph (4).

(4) Where authority is given under paragraph (3) to a court officer, that officer will, unless it appears unreasonable in the circumstances to do so, proceed in the officer's own name for the recovery of any sums payable to the court under the order in question which, on or after the date of the giving of the authority, fall into arrears.

(5) In any case where –

(a) authority under paragraph (3) has been given to a court officer; and

(b) the payee gives notice in writing to that court officer cancelling the authority,

the authority will cease to have effect and so the court officer will not continue any proceedings already commenced by virtue of the authority.

(6 The payee shall have the same liability for all of the costs properly incurred in, or in relation to, proceedings taken under paragraph (2) at the payee's request, or under paragraph (3) by virtue of the payee's authority, including any court fees and any costs incurred as a result of any proceedings commenced not being continued, as if the proceedings had been commenced by the payee.

(7) Nothing in paragraph (2) or (4) shall affect any right of a payee to proceed in his or her own name for the recovery of sums payable under an order of any court.

Amendments—Inserted by SI 2013/3204.

'will ... proceed in the officer's own name' (r 32.33(2))—Before April 2014, the collecting officer in the magistrates' court frequently sought to enforce payment by way of the threat of committal before magistrates. Since the advent of the Family Court, the expense and procedural difficulty of proceeding by way of judgment summons appears to have caused this remedy to fall into disuse.

PART III

Practice Direction 32A – Forms Relating to Part 32

This Practice Direction supplements rules 32.12A(1)(a), (b), (c) and (d), 32.19A(6) and 32.22A(2) and (4)

1 The form referred to in rule 32.12A(1)(a) is –

Form 1

Notice to person liable to make payments that sums payable under a maintenance order registered in the family court become payable through the court: Maintenance Orders Act 1950

Family Court sitting at ....

Date:

To:

Address:

You are given notice that the sums payable by you under (*insert particulars of maintenance order*) made on the ..... day of....... 20..., by (*state court in Scotland or Northern Ireland by which order was made*) and registered in this Court under Part 2 of the Maintenance Orders Act 1950, have, under an order of this Court dated the..... day of ...... 20...., become payable through (*or* to) this Court.

From the date of this notice, payments under the order (including payments in respect of any sums due at the date of the receipt by you of this notice) should be only sent to (*state address*).

If payments are not sent in this way, then, unless the contrary is proved, you may be assumed not to have made the payments under the order.

A.B,

[Court Officer]

2 The form referred to in rule 32.12A(1)(b) is:

Form 2

Notice to person liable to make payments that sums payable under a maintenance order made by the family court have ceased to be payable to or through the court: Maintenance Orders Act 1950

Family Court sitting at .... (*Code*)

Date:

To:

Address:

You are given notice that the sums payable by you under (*insert particulars of maintenance order*) made on the .... day of ...... 20..., by this Court have, by reason of the registration of the said order in (*state court in Scotland or Northern Ireland in which order is registered*), ceased to be payable through (*or* to) the court.

From the date of this notice, payments under the order (including payments in respect of any sums due at the date of the receipt by you of this notice) should be only paid to (*state name and address of person entitled to payments under the order*) (, unless you receive, or have meanwhile received, notice from the clerk of the said court in Scotland or Northern Ireland that they are to be paid to any other person).

If payments are not paid in this way, then, unless the contrary is proved, you may be assumed not to have made the payments under the order.

A.B,

Court Officer

3 The form referred to in rule 32.12A(1)(c) is –

Form 3

Certificate of arrears: Maintenance Orders Act 1950

I hereby certify that the arrears due at the date of this certificate under (*insert particulars of maintenance order*) made on the .... day of ...... 20...., by the family court sitting at ...., the payments under which are at present required to be made to (*or* through) the court, amount to ....

Dated the .... day of .... 20....

A.B.

Court officer

4 The form referred to in rule 32.12A(1)(d) is –

Form 4

Notice of cancellation of registration of maintenance order in the family court

Family court sitting at .... *(Code)*

Date:

To:

Address:

You are given notice that the registration in this Court under Part 2 of the Maintenance Orders Act 1950 of (*insert particulars of maintenance order*) made on the .... day of ..... 20..., by (*state court in Scotland or Northern Ireland by which order was made*) has been cancelled.

(Sums payable by you under the order have, by reason of the cancellation of the registration of the order, ceased to be payable through the court (by the following method of payment falling within section 1 of the Maintenance Enforcement Act 1991 (standing order etc.), namely ....), (by an attachment of earnings order).

From the date of this notice, payments under the order (including payments in respect of any sums due at the date of receipt by you of this notice) should be only paid to (*state name and address of person entitled to payments under the order*), unless you receive, or meanwhile have received, notice from the court officer for a competent court that they are to be paid to any other person.

If payments are not paid in this way, then, unless the contrary is proved, you may be assumed not to have made the payments under the order.

A.B.

Court officer

5 The form referred to in rule 32.22A(2) is –

Form 5

Notice that payments have become payable through the family court
(Maintenance Orders Act 1958, section 2(6ZC))

Family Court sitting at .... *(Code)*

Date:

To:

Address:

You are given notice that the sums payable by you under (*insert particulars of maintenance order*) made on the .... day of .... 20.... by the (High Court) (Court of Session) (High Court in Northern Ireland) and registered in this Court under Part 1 of the Maintenance Orders Act 1958, have under an order of this Court dated the .... day of .... 20....., become payable through the family court.

From the date of this notice, payments under the order (including payments in respect of any sums due at the date of the receipt by you of this notice) should be only sent to the court at (*state address*).

If payments are not sent in this way, then, unless the contrary is proved, you may be assumed not to have made the payments under the order.

A.B.

Court officer, family court

6 The form referred to in rule 32.22A(4) is –

Form 6

Notice to person liable to make payments that sums payable under a maintenance order made by the family court have ceased to be payable to or through the court: Maintenance Orders Act 1958

Family Court sitting at .... (*Code*)

Date:

To:

Address:

You are given notice that the sums payable by you under (*insert particulars of maintenance order*) made on the .... day of ...... 20..., by the (High Court) (Court of Session) (High Court in Northern Ireland) and registered in this Court under Part 1 of the Maintenance Orders Act 1958, have under an Order of this Court dated the .... day of .... 20...., ceased to be payable to or through the family court.

From the date of this notice, payments under the order (including payments in respect of any sums due at the date of the receipt by you of this notice) should be paid only to (*state name and address of person entitled to payments under the order*) (, unless you receive, or have meanwhile received, notice from the clerk of the said High Court, Court of Session or High Court in Northern Ireland that they are to be paid to any other person).

If payments are not made in this way, then, unless the contrary is proved, you may be assumed not to have made the payments under the order.

A.B,

Court Officer

7 The form referred to at rule 32.19A(6) is –

Form 7

Notice of cancellation of registration

(Maintenance Orders Act 1958, section 5(5))

Family Court sitting at ....

Date:

To:

Address:

You are hereby given notice that the registration in this Court under Part 1 of the Maintenance Orders Act 1958, of (*insert particulars of maintenance order*) made on the .... day of .... 20....., by the (High Court) (Court of Session) (High Court in Northern Ireland) has been cancelled.

Sums payable by you under the said order have by reason of the cancellation of the registration of the order ceased to be payable through the family court, (by the following method of payment falling within section 1 of the Maintenance Enforcement Act 1991 (standing order etc), namely ....), (by an attachment of earnings order) (by direct payment to).

From the date of this notice, payments under the order (including payments in respect of any sums due on the date of the receipt by you of this notice) should be paid only to (*state name and address of person entitled to payments under the order*).

If payments are not sent in this way, then, unless the contrary is proved, you may be assumed not to have made the payments under the order.

A.B.

Court Officer

PART 33
ENFORCEMENT

CONTENTS OF THIS PART

Chapter 1

Rule		Page
	General Rules	
33.1	Application	1927
	Section 1 *Enforcement of Orders for the Payment of Money*	
33.2	Application of the Civil Procedure Rules	1928

33.3 How to apply 1928
33.4 Transfer of orders 1929

Section 2
Committal and Injunction

33.5 Enforcement of orders by way of committal 1929

Chapter 2
Committal by Way of Judgment Summons

33.9 Interpretation 1930
33.10 Application 1931
33.11 Judgment summons 1931
33.12 Successive judgment summonses 1932
33.13 Order or summons to attend adjourned hearing: requirement for personal service 1932
33.14 Committal on application for judgment summons 1932
33.14A Expenses 1933
33.15 Orders for the benefit of different persons 1933
33.16 Hearing of judgment summons 1933
33.17 Special provisions as to judgment summonses in the High Court 1934

Chapter 3
Attachment of Earnings

33.19 Enforcement by attachment of earnings order 1935

Chapter 4
Warrant of Control

33.20 Applications to vary existing orders 1935

Chapter 5
Court's Power to Appoint a Receiver

33.22 Application of the CPR 1935

Chapter 6
Orders to Obtain Information from Judgment Debtors

33.23 Application of the CPR 1935

Chapter 7
Third Party Debt Orders

33.24 Application of the CPR 1936

Chapter 8
Charging Order, Stop Order, Stop Notice

33.25 Application for a charging order, stop order or stop notice 1936

Practice Direction 33A –
Enforcement of Undertakings 1936

PART III

Chapter 1
General Rules

33.1 Application

(1) The rules in this Part apply to an application made in the High Court and the family court to enforce an order made in family proceedings.

(2) Parts 50, 83 and 84 of, and Schedules 1 and 2 to, the CPR apply, as far as they are relevant and with necessary modification, to an application made in the High Court and the family court to enforce an order made in family proceedings.

Amendments—SI 2014/667.

'an application ... to enforce an order made in family proceedings' (r 33.1(1))—In December 2016, the Law Commission published proposals for the reform of the enforcement of family financial orders (Law Comm no 370). It is impossible to disagree with the Commission's observations that 'the rules governing the enforcement of family financial orders are difficult to access and understand, and are inefficient ... and ... in need of revision', and it is to be hoped that Parliament and the Rule Committee give the subject urgent attention.

'as far as they are relevant and with necessary modification' (r 33.1(2))—The Commission observes with justice: 'This rule appears incomprehensible to a litigant in person, who must not only read the different provisions referred to, but be able to understand their relevance and ascertain whether (and what) modifications are required – a task that is difficult even for a judge'.

'Schedules 1 and 2 to the CPR' (r 33.1(2))—Some parts of the former RSC and CCR survive as part of the CPR 1998, as Schs 1 and 2, respectively, but none of the rules in question are now relevant to family proceedings.

'apply, as far as they are relevant' (r 33.1(2))—The reference to Pt 83 is slightly deceptive, because the Family Court cannot directly issue a writ of control directed to a High Court Enforcement Officer. See the **General Note** to Pt 83.

Section 1

Enforcement of Orders for the Payment of Money

33.2 Application of the Civil Procedure Rules

Part 70 of the CPR applies to proceedings under this Section as if –

(a) in rule 70.1, in paragraph (2)(d), 'but does not include a judgment or order for the payment of money into court' is omitted;

(a1) in rule 70.3(1), for 'County Court' there is substituted 'family court'; and

(b) rule 70.5 is omitted.

Amendments—SI 2014/667.

Note—Part 70 of the CPR is reproduced as modified.

33.3 How to apply

(1) Except where a rule or practice direction otherwise requires, an application for an order to enforce an order for the payment of money must be made in a notice of application accompanied by a statement which must –

(a) state the amount due under the order, showing how that amount is arrived at; and

(b) be verified by a statement of truth.

(2) The notice of application may either –

(a) apply for an order specifying the method of enforcement; or

(b) apply for an order for such method of enforcement as the court may consider appropriate.

(3) If an application is made under paragraph (2)(b), an order to attend court will be issued and rule 71.2 (6) and (7) of the CPR will apply as if the application had been made under that rule.

'Except where a rule or practice direction otherwise requires' (r 33.3(1))—Freestanding applications for third party debt orders (CPR 1998, Pt 72, as applied to family proceedings by FPR 2010, r 33.24) and charging orders (FPR 2010, Pt 40) do 'otherwise require'. An application for a third party debt order 'must be in the form, and contain the information, required by PD72' (CPR 1998, r 72.3(2)(a)); an application for a charging order 'must be in the form, and contain the information, required by FPR PD40A' (FPR 2010, r 40.4(a)). However, a judge considering making a third party debt order or charging order under an application under r 33.3(2)(b) merely needs to ensure that he has the requisite information.

'the amount due under the order' (r 33.3(1)(a))—It appears that interest cannot be charged on arrears of periodical payments (*TW v TM (Minors) (Child Maintenance: Jurisdiction and Departure from Formula)* [2016] 2 FLR 1386, FD).

'such means of enforcement as the court may consider appropriate' (r 33.3(2)(b))—This provision will result in an order to attend court for questioning to which certain provisions of CPR 1998, Pt 71 will apply. It should be noted that this provision is separate and distinct from the procedure for obtaining information from judgment debtors, which is also available in family proceedings (see r 33.23). As was pointed out by Thorpe LJ in *Corbett v Corbett* [2003] 2 FLR 385, CA, at [32], the intention of this provision is that it should be 'the issue of an enforcement summons to a ... judge who would be empowered to apply whatever power or remedy seemed most likely to yield satisfaction and conclusion'. As it is directed to the court considering what means of enforcement are appropriate, the questioning should take place before a judge, who may make an attachment of earnings order, direct the issue of a warrant of control, or make a charging order or third party debt order (as was done in *Kaur v Randhawa* [2015] EWHC 1592 (Fam) where the interim stage of the normal procedure was dispensed with) without further formality or fee; or before lay justices, who may make an attachment of earnings order. As lay justices cannot issue warrants of control or make charging orders or third party debt orders, the case will need to be reallocated to a District Judge if those remedies are thought appropriate. Note that information secured under compulsion in this way cannot be used as the basis for committal, although disclosed documents can be (*Mohan v Mohan* [2014] 1 FLR 717, CA).

If the respondent fails to attend, as CPR 1998, r 71.8 does not appear to be incorporated into this rule, the most appropriate way of securing attendance would seem to be the issue of a bench warrant. As to the power of a Family Court judge (including a bench of lay justices) to issue a bench warrant, consider the analysis of HHJ Birss (as he then was) in *Westwood v Knight* [2012] EWPCC 14, starting at [136]. He concluded that there was jurisdiction for a CJ in the County Court to issue a bench warrant. It arose from the inherent jurisdiction of the High Court but CCA 1984, s 38(1) allowed the County Court to make any order that could be made by the High Court if the proceedings were in the High Court. MFPA 1984, s 31E(1) similarly allows the Family Court to make any order that could be made by the High Court if the proceedings were in the High Court. FC(CDB)R 2014, r 14 provides that the jurisdiction of the Family Court may be exercised (unless specifically provided otherwise) by any judge of the Family Court.

'an order to attend court will be issued' (r 33.3(3))—Form D50K has been issued for this purpose.

'rule 71.2(6) and (7) of the CPR will apply' (r 33.3(3))—This provision is frequently ignored in practice in that although the hearing is before a judge or justices the payee is generally not expected to conduct the questioning in accordance with CPR 1998, r 71.2(6)(3)(b). The other provisions of Pt 71 do not appear to be incorporated into the procedure under this rule. Rule 33.23 refers to 'proceedings under this part' rather than 'under this rule', but if that wording incorporated the whole of CPR 1998, Pt 71 into r 33.3 it would render r 33.3(3) otiose.

33.4 Transfer of orders

(1) This rule applies to an application for the transfer –

(a) to the High Court of an order made in the family court; and
(b) to the family court of an order made in the High Court.

(2) The application must be –

(a) made without notice; and
(b) accompanied by a statement which complies with rule 33.3(1).

(3) The transfer will have effect upon the filing of the application.

(4) Where an order is transferred from the family court to the High Court –

(a) it will have the same force and effect; and
(b) the same proceedings may be taken on it,

as if it were an order of the High Court.

(5) This rule does not apply to the transfer of orders for periodical payments or for the recovery of arrears of periodical payments.

Amendments—SI 2014/667.

'transfer to the High Court of an order made in the family court' (r 33.4(1))—The proceedings themselves may not be transferred by the Family Court by reason of r 29.17(3).

'as if it were an order of the High Court' (r 33.4(4))—Note that if it is sought to enforce an English judgment abroad under AJA 1920 or FJ(RE)A 1933, it should be borne in mind that foreign courts may well not regard a Family Court order transferred to the High Court as being 'an order of the High Court'. See for example *Re Hardwick* [1995] Jersey LR 245.

'the transfer of orders for periodical payments' (r 33.4(5))—If it were ever appropriate to enforce such an order by instructing a High Court Enforcement Officer, a puisne judge of the High Court would have to be requested to transfer the proceedings to the High Court under r 29.17.

Section 2
Committal and Injunction

33.5 Enforcement of orders by way of committal

Part 37 applies as appropriate for the enforcement by way of committal of an order made in family proceedings.

Amendments—Substituted by SI 2014/667.

33.6–33.8 *(revoked)*

Chapter 2
Committal by Way of Judgment Summons

33.9 Interpretation

In this Chapter, unless the context requires otherwise –

'order' means an order made in family proceedings for the payment of money;

'judgment creditor' means a person entitled to enforce an order under section 5 of the Debtors Act 1869;

'debtor' means a person liable under an order; and

'judgment summons' means a summons under section 5 of the Debtors Act 1869 requiring a debtor to attend court.

Amendments—SI 2015/1420.

'section 5 of the Debtors Act 1869' (r 33.9)—The section provides:

'Subject to the provisions hereinafter mentioned, and to the prescribed rules, any court may commit to prison for a term not exceeding 6 weeks, or until payment of the sum due, any person who makes default in payment of any debt or instalment of any debt due from him in pursuance of any order or judgment of that or any other competent court. Provided –

(1) That the jurisdiction by this section given of committing a person to prison shall, in the case of any court other than the superior courts of law and equity, be exercised only subject to the following restrictions; that is to say

(a) be exercised only by a judge or his deputy, and by an order made in open court and showing on its face the ground on which it is issued;

(b) (*repealed*)

(c) be exercised only as respects a judgment of a county court by a county court judge or his deputy.

(2) That such jurisdiction shall only be exercised where it is proved to the satisfaction of the court that the person making default either has or has had since the date of the order or judgment the means to pay the sum in respect of which he has made default, and has refused or neglected, or refuses or neglects, to pay the same.

Proof of the means of the person making default may be given in such manner as the court thinks just.

For the purpose of considering whether to commit a debtor to prison under this section, the debtor may be summoned in accordance with the prescribed rules.

For the purposes of this section any court may direct any debt due from any person in pursuance of any order or judgment of that or any other competent court to be paid by instalments, and may from time to time rescind or vary such order.

No imprisonment under this section shall operate as a satisfaction or extinguishment of any debt or demand or cause of action, or deprive any person of any right to take out execution against the lands, goods or chattels of the person imprisoned, in the same manner as if such imprisonment had not taken place.

Any person imprisoned under this section shall be discharged out of custody upon a certificate signed in the prescribed manner to the effect that he has satisfied a debt or instalment of a debt in respect of which he was imprisoned, together with the prescribed costs (if any).'

The former provision that proof of the debtor's means may be given by summoning him to be examined on oath was removed as a consequence of the finding in *Mubarak v Mubarak and others* [2001] 1 FLR 698, CA that the provision was incompatible with the HRA 1998, the proceedings being of a penal character and the requirement amounting to compulsory self-incrimination. It is for the creditor to prove the necessary facts (see **'the judgment creditor proves'**, under FPR 2010, r 33.14) by such other evidence as he can muster.

The jurisdiction, which the section confers may be exercised by the High Court only in respect of a High Court maintenance order (i e a maintenance order enforceable by the High Court (AJA 1970, s 28(1)), which includes an order registered in or transferred to the High Court) and by the Family Court in respect of a High Court or Family Court maintenance order (the latter, of course, including orders originally made in the County Court or a magistrates' court), as well as in respect of certain orders for payment of taxes etc (AJA 1970, s 11). A judgment summons will initially be allocated to the level of judge who last dealt with the proceedings (FC(CDB)R 2014, r 17). While a case may be re-allocated, only a judge of the same level as made the original order or higher may commit for breach of an order (r 17(5)). A District Judge now has the same powers in this respect as a Circuit Judge. The term 'maintenance order' is defined by AJA 1970, s 28 and Sch 8; in addition to periodical payments the definitions in Sch 8 include 'other payments made or having effect as if made under' the provisions there referred to, including, for example, MCA 1973, Pt II, which provides for lump sum and other orders for payment of money that would not normally be thought of as maintenance orders.

An obligation to pay pursuant to an undertaking may be enforced by this procedure if it is equivalent to a maintenance order (*Symmons v Symmons* [1993] 1 FLR 317, FD) but not otherwise – *Farrant v Farrant* [1957] P 188, PDAD (school fees); *Nwogbe v Nwogbe* [2000] 2 FLR 744, CA (rent ordered to be paid under an occupation order)). An undertaking to pay money may not be enforced by committal except as permitted under DA 1869, s 5 (*Buckley v Crawford* [1893] 1 QB 105, QBD).

As to the formalities that are required if an undertaking, and in particular an undertaking to pay money, is to be enforceable by committal, see FPR PD33A.

33.10 Application

(1) An application for the issue of a judgment summons may be made –

(a) in the case of an order of the High Court, to –

(i) the principal registry;

(ii) a district registry; or

(iii) the family court,

whichever in the opinion of the judgment creditor is most convenient, and if to the family court, to whichever Designated Family Judge area is in the opinion of the judgment creditor most convenient; and

(b) in the case of an order of the family court, to whichever Designated Family Judge area is in the opinion of the judgment creditor most convenient,

having regard (in any case) to the place where the debtor resides or carries on business and irrespective of the location of the court or registry in which the order was made.

(For the way in which information will be provided to enable Designated Family Judge areas and Designated Family Courts to be identified, see Practice Direction 34E.)

(2) An application must be accompanied by a statement which –

(a) complies with rule 33.3(1);

(b) contains all the evidence on which the judgment creditor intends to rely; and

(c) has exhibited to it a copy of the order.

Amendments—SI 2014/667.

Venue—Which venue is 'convenient' depends inter alia on the debtor's residence or place of business.

Evidence (r 33.10(2)(b))—The requirement is to file all of the written evidence on which the creditor intends to rely. Copies will be served on the debtor (FPR 2010, r 33.13(2)). The object is to secure compliance with HRA 1998 as applied in *Mubarak v Mubarak* [2001] 1 FLR 698, CA. Thus, the written statements of witnesses on whose oral evidence it is intended to rely should be included. No doubt, if additional evidence came to light before the hearing, it would be admitted provided that it had been copied to the debtor promptly and in sufficient time before the hearing to enable him to deal with it.

33.11 Judgment summons

(1) If the debtor is in default under an order of committal made on a previous judgment summons in respect of the same order, a judgment summons must not be issued without the court's permission.

(2) A judgment summons must be accompanied by the statement referred to in rule 33.10(2).

(3) A judgment summons must be served on the debtor –

(a) personally; or

(b) by the court sending it to the debtor by first class post –

(i) at the address stated in the application for the issue of a judgment summons; or

(ii) in a case where a court officer is proceeding for the recovery of a debt in accordance with rule 32.33, at the last known address for the debtor shown on court records.

(4) In a case to which paragraph (3)(b)(i) applies, the judgment creditor must file with the court a certificate for postal service.

(5) A judgment summons must be served on the debtor not less than 14 days before the hearing.

(6) Paragraph (3) is subject to any direction of the court that the judgment summons must be served personally on the debtor.

Amendments—SI 2014/667; SI 2015/1420.

General note—This rule has been amended with effect from 24 August 2015 to allow judgment summonses to be served by post and to remove the requirement to offer travelling expenses for the initial hearing, which is intended to make it practicable to use the judgment summons in REMO cases (where the policy is that creditors should not be required to pay fees). If the debtor does not attend the first hearing, however, notice of the adjourned hearing must be personally served (r 33.13) and the debtor can only be committed for failing to attend the adjourned hearing if travelling expenses have been tendered (r 33.14A).

'a certificate for postal service' (r 33.11(4))—There is no prescribed form for such a certificate but PD6A, para 6.4 makes it clear that what is required is evidence that if posted or delivered to the proposed address, the document is likely to be brought to the attention of the debtor.

33.12 Successive judgment summonses

Subject to rule 33.11(1), successive judgment summonses may be issued even if the debtor has ceased to reside or carry on business at the address stated in the application for the issue of a judgment summons since the issue of the original judgment summons.

33.13 Order or summons to attend adjourned hearing: requirement for personal service

(1) Paragraph (2) applies in proceedings for committal by way of judgment summons where –

(a) the family court has ordered under section 110(1) of the County Courts Act 1984 that the debtor must attend an adjourned hearing; or

(b) the High Court has summonsed the debtor to attend an adjourned hearing following the debtor's failure to attend the hearing of the judgment summons.

(2) The following documents must be served personally on the debtor –

(a) the notice of the date and time fixed for the adjourned hearing; and

(b) copies of the judgment summons and the documents mentioned in rule 33.10(2).

Amendments—Substituted by SI 2015/1420.

33.14 Committal on application for judgment summons

(1) Subject to paragraph (2), on a hearing of an application for a judgment summons the debtor may be committed for making default on payment of a debt if the judgment creditor proves that the debtor –

(a) has, or has had, since the date of the order the means to pay the sum in respect of which the debtor has made default; and

(b) has refused or neglected, or refuses or neglects, to pay that sum.

(2) A debtor may not be committed in accordance with paragraph (1) where the judgment summons was served by post, unless the debtor attends the hearing.

(3) Where the debtor has been ordered or summonsed to attend an adjourned hearing in accordance with rule 33.13, the debtor may be committed –

(a) for failure to attend the adjourned hearing; or

(b) for making default on payment of a debt, if the judgment creditor proves that the debtor –

(i) has, or has had, since the date of the order the means to pay the sum in respect of which the debtor has made default; and

(ii) has refused or neglected, or refuses or neglects, to pay that sum.

(4) The debtor may not be compelled to give evidence.

Amendments—Substituted by SI 2015/1420.

'the debtor may be committed' (r 33.14(1))—Note that only a judge of at least the same level as the judge who made the original order may exercise the power to commit for breach of it: FC(CDB)R 2014, r 17(5).

'failure to attend the adjourned hearing' (r 33.14(3(a))—Note that the maximum sentence that can be imposed is 14 days under CCA 1984, s 110(2). However, as the debtor cannot be compelled to give evidence and the power to commit under DA 1869 can be exercised in his absence, it will be unusual for a debtor to be committed simply for failing to attend.

'the judgment creditor proves' (r 33.14(b))—The creditor must satisfy the judge that the judgment summons, the notice of hearing and the other documents referred to in r 33.10(2) have been personally served and the purpose of the hearing made clear (*Iqbal v Iqbal* [2017] EWCA Civ 19) and that the debtor has or has had the means to pay and neglects or refuses (or has neglected or refused) to pay.

The evidence must show that the debtor has or had the means to pay and the fact that the original order was made by consent was described as an 'obvious starting point' in *Topping v Topping* [2008] EWCA Civ 1142, but the judge's findings at a contested hearing will not suffice as they will have been made on the balance of probability (*Young v Young* [2014] 2 FLR 786, FD). The debtor's conduct must be in the nature of a contempt (*Re Edgcome, ex parte Edgcome* [1902] 2 KB 403, CA). The standard of proof of the debtor's means is the criminal standard, i e beyond reasonable doubt (*Woodley v Woodley* [1992] 2 FLR 417, CA). After the making of a bankruptcy order, the debtor will usually no longer have the means to pay and, in those circumstances, a committal order will not be made unless his failure to pay before the bankruptcy was such as to merit punishment (*Woodley v Woodley (No 2)* [1993] 2 FLR 477, CA). The debtor's means include gifts received (*Re Park, ex parte Koster* (1885) 14 QBD 597, CA), but not future sums that may be received such as a husband's allowance to his wife (*Barefoot v Clarke* [1949] 2 KB 97, CA) nor 'earning capacity' generally (*Constantinides v Constantinides* [2014] 2 FLR 736, FD). Child benefit and certain social security benefits paid in respect of children must be ignored.

Gaps in the evidence as to the debtor's means can no longer be made good by requiring him to submit to questioning (r 33.14(4)). Evidence given, under compulsion, on examination under r 33.23 or in the course of an application under r 33.3(2)(b), will not be admissible on the hearing of a judgment summons, although documents obtained during the process may be relied upon (*Mohan v Mohan* [2014] 1 FLR 717, CA).

As an alternative to a committal order the court may make an attachment of earnings order (AEA 1971, s 3(4)). For this purpose, proof of the debtor's means to the civil standard only would be needed. A further alternative is to make a new order under FPR 2010, r 33.16(1). If the proceedings concern a 'qualifying periodical maintenance order' within the meaning of MEA 1991, s 1 then, under s 1(4)(a), the court may of its own motion make a 'means of payment order', whether as an alternative to or in aid of a suspended committal order or a new order.

'the debtor may not be compelled to give evidence' (r 33.14(4))—While this remains correct, if the creditor advances a sufficient case, a debtor who fails to adduce convincing evidence does so at his peril – 'there is no proper affidavit of means from him which demonstrates the truth of what he says' (*Topping*, above); neither did 'generalised assertions, unsupported by any documentary evidence to which any weight could be properly applied' avail in *Prest v Prest* [2014] EWHC 3430 (Fam).

Note that if a variation application is wrongly listed to be heard together with a judgment summons, this will effectively deprive the debtor of his right to silence and any committal order (and associated order for costs) will be set aside – *Morris v Morris* [2016] EWCA Civ 812.

PART III

33.14A Expenses

(1) A debtor must not be committed to prison under section 110(2) of the County Courts Act 1984 unless the debtor has been paid or offered a sum reasonably sufficient to cover the expenses of travelling to and from the court building at which the debtor is summoned or ordered to appear.

(2) The sum must be paid or offered at the time of service of –

(a) the judgment summons; or

(b) the order to attend under section 110(1) of the County Courts Act 1984.

Amendments—Inserted by SI 2015/1420.

'under section 110(2) of the County Courts Act 1984' (r 33.14A(1))—That is, for disobeying an order to attend the adjourned hearing. It appears that the tender of travelling expenses is no longer an essential pre-requisite to committal under DA 1869, s 5.

'the debtor has been paid … expenses' (r 33.14A(1))—It has been said that conduct money tendered to the debtor is irrecoverable either directly or indirectly by a term of suspension of a committal order, provided that it has actually been spent on travel to court (*Migliaccio v Migliaccio (Rev 2)* [2016] EWHC 1055 (Fam)), although the observations of Mostyn J were obiter and not easy to reconcile with r 33.17(2).

33.15 Orders for the benefit of different persons

Where an applicant has obtained one or more orders in the same application but for the benefit of different persons –

(a) where the judgment creditor is a child, the applicant may apply for the issue of a judgment summons in respect of those orders on behalf of the judgment creditor without seeking permission to act as the child's litigation friend; and

(b) only one judgment summons need be issued in respect of those orders.

'only one judgment summons need be issued' (r 33.15(b))—A creditor who insists on issuing multiple judgment summonses in this situation (cf a familiar situation with charging orders) is unlikely to recover the costs of doing so.

33.16 Hearing of judgment summons

(1) On the hearing of the judgment summons the court may –

(a) where the order is for lump sum provision or costs; or

(b) where the order is an order for maintenance pending suit, an order for maintenance pending outcome of proceedings or an order for other periodical payments and it appears to the court that the order would have been varied or suspended if the debtor had made an application for that purpose,

make a new order for payment of the amount due under the original order, together with the costs of the judgment summons, either at a specified time or by instalments.

(2) If the court makes an order of committal, it may direct its execution to be suspended on terms that the debtor pays to the judgment creditor –

(a) the amount due;
(b) the costs of the judgment summons; and
(c) any sums accruing due under the original order,

either at a specified time or by instalments.

(3) All payments under a new order or an order of committal must be made to the judgment creditor unless the court directs otherwise.

(4) Where an order of committal is suspended on such terms as are mentioned in paragraph (2) –

(a) all payments made under the suspended order will be deemed to be made –
  (i) first, in or towards the discharge of any sums from time to time accruing due under the original order; and
  (ii) secondly, in or towards the discharge of a debt in respect of which the judgment summons was issued and the costs of the summons; and
(b) the suspended order must not be executed until the judgment creditor has filed a statement of default on the part of the debtor.

New order (r 33.16(1))—This alternative to a committal order effectively gives the periodical payments debtor further time to pay the arrears. It is available only if the judge believes that an application to vary or suspend would have succeeded. It allows time for such an application to be made and for the question then to be considered whether some or all of the arrears should be remitted. Preferably, the debtor should issue an application to vary the periodical payments order and (if appropriate) remit arrears so that this can be heard before an adjourned hearing of, the judgment summons (*Corbett v Corbett* [2003] 2 FLR 385, CA). As noted under r 33.14, the variation application and the judgment summons must not be listed to be heard together. The new order (or, indeed, any committal order) will then relate only to such of the arrears as remain after the application has been determined. A new order may of course also be made in respect of a lump sum order.

An order of committal (r 33.16(2))—It is important to note that the limit of the court's jurisdiction under this rule is to commit for up to 6 weeks in accordance with DA 1869, s 5: *Zuk v Zuk* [2013] 2 FLR 1466, CA, where 'the proceedings were peppered with errors'. Also, see *Bhura v Bhura* [2013] 2 FLR 44, FD, where wilful refusal to pay, accompanied by the giving of 'completely false evidence' (dishonesty in proceedings), attracted only a suspended sentence. Semble, an approach to the Attorney-General under FPR 2010, r 17.6 may be appropriate in such a case; cf recent decisions under CPR 1998, r 32.14 discussed in *Civil Court Service* (LexisNexis). In *Prest v Prest* [2014] EWHC 3430 (Fam), wilful refusal to pay over £360,000 attracted a 4-week sentence, suspended if payment were made within 3 months. On unusual facts, in *Bezeliansky v Bezelianskaya* [2016] EWCA Civ 76 a committal order in respect of child maintenance was suspended on terms that H comply with a capital order (which would allow the arrears to be discharged).

This must be distinguished from the power to commit for disobedience to other orders or for breach of an undertaking – for example *Cherwayko v Cherwayko (No 3) (Contempt in financial remedy proceedings and costs)* [2015] EWHC 2482 (Fam) (Parker J) (9 months' immediate imprisonment for failure to attend and failure to supply information; 12 months consecutively for breach of an undertaking to provide security).

Continued default after committal—Only one term of imprisonment can be imposed in respect of an unpaid amount (*Evans v Wills* (1876) 1 CPD 229). This would not prevent a second judgment summons in respect of fresh arrears under the same periodical payments order. Note that serving a term of imprisonment does not discharge the debt – s 5 above (*Re Edgcome, ex parte Edgcome* [1902] 2 KB 403, CA).

33.17 Special provisions as to judgment summonses in the High Court

(1) The High Court may summons witnesses to give evidence to prove the means of the debtor and may issue a witness summons for that purpose.

(2) Where the debtor appears at the hearing, the High Court may direct that the travelling expenses paid to the debtor be allowed as expenses of a witness.

(3) Where the debtor appears at the hearing and no order of committal is made, the High Court may allow the debtor's proper costs including compensation for any loss of earnings.

(4) When the High Court makes –

(a) a new order; or
(b) an order of committal,

a court officer must send notice of the order to the debtor and, if the original order was made in another court, to that court.

(5) An order of committal must be directed –

(a) where the order is to be executed by the tipstaff, to the tipstaff; or

(b) where the order is to be executed by a deputy tipstaff, to the Designated Family Judge area within which the debtor is to be found.

Amendments—SI 2014/667; SI 2015/1420.

33.18 *(revoked)*

Chapter 3

Attachment of Earnings

33.19 Enforcement by attachment of earnings order

Part 39 applies to applications for an attachment of earnings order to secure payments under a maintenance order.

Amendments—Last substituted by SI 2016/355.

33.19A *(revoked)*

Chapter 4

Warrant of Control

Amendments—SI 2014/667.

33.20 Applications to vary existing orders

Where an application is pending for a variation of –

(a) a financial order;

(b) an order under section 27 of the 1973 Act; or

(c) an order under Part 9 of Schedule 5 to the 2004 Act,

no warrant of control may be issued to enforce payment of any sum due under those orders, except with the permission of the court.

Amendments—SI 2014/667.

33.21 *(revoked)*

Chapter 5

Court's Power to Appoint a Receiver

33.22 Application of the CPR

Part 69 of the CPR applies to proceedings under this Part.

Chapter 6

Orders to Obtain Information from Judgment Debtors

33.23 Application of the CPR

(1) Part 71 of the CPR applies to proceedings under this Part with the following modifications.

(2) In rule 71.2(2), for paragraph (b) substitute –

'(b) must be –

(i) issued in the High Court if the High Court made the judgment or order which it is sought to enforce; or

(ii) made to the Designated Family Court for the Designated Family Judge area within which the judgment or order was made,

except that if the proceedings have since been transferred to a different court or Designated Family Judge area, it must be issued in that court or made to that area.'

Amendments—Substituted by SI 2014/667.

PART III

'Part 71 of the CPR applies to proceedings under this Part' (r 33.23(1))—Part 71, as slightly amended by r 33.23(2), applies in full to orders to obtain information from debtors. It cannot apply in full to the procedure under r 33.3(2)(b) (as to which see Procedural Guide C11) because that would render r 33.3(3) otiose.

Chapter 7
Third Party Debt Orders

33.24 Application of the CPR

(1) Part 72 of the CPR applies to proceedings under this Part with the following modifications.

(1A) In rule 72.3, for paragraph (1)(b) there is substituted –

'(b) must be issued in the court which made the judgment or order which it is sought to enforce, or made to the Designated Family Judge area within which that judgment or order was made, except that if the proceedings have since been transferred to a different court or Designated Family Judge area, it must be issued in that court or made to that area.'

(2) In rule 72.4 –

(a) in paragraph (1), for 'a judge' there is substituted 'the court'; and
(b) in paragraph (2), for 'judge' there is substituted 'court'.

(3) In rule 72.7 –

(a) in paragraph (2)(a), after 'the Royal Courts of Justice' there is inserted 'or the principal registry'; and
(b) in paragraph (2)(b), for 'in County Court proceedings, to any County Court hearing centre' there is substituted 'in family court proceedings, to any Designated Family Judge area'.

(4) Rule 72.10 is omitted.

Amendments—SI 2014/667.

Chapter 8
Charging Order, Stop Order, Stop Notice

33.25 Application for a charging order, stop order or stop notice

Part 40 applies for the enforcement of a judgment or order made in family proceedings by way of a charging order, stop order or stop notice.

Amendments—Amended by SI 2014/667. Substituted by SI 2016/355.

Practice Direction 33A – Enforcement of Undertakings

This Practice Direction supplements FPR Part 33

Enforcement of undertaking to do or abstain from doing any act other than the payment of money

1 Attention is drawn to the provisions of Chapter 2 of Part 37, and paragraphs 2.1 to 2.3 of Practice Direction 37A, about the enforcement of undertakings by way of committal.

Enforcement of undertaking for the payment of money

2.1 Any undertaking for the payment of money that has effect as if it was an order made under Part 2 of the Matrimonial Causes Act 1973 may be enforced as if it was an order and Part 33 and Part 37 apply accordingly.

2.2 The form of an undertaking for the payment of money that has effect as if it were an order under Part 2 of the Matrimonial Causes Act 1973 must be endorsed with a notice setting out the consequences of disobedience, as follows:

'If you fail to pay any sum of money which you have promised the court that you will pay, a person entitled to enforce the undertaking may apply to the court for an order. You may be sent to prison if it is proved that you –

(a) have, or have had since the date of your undertaking, the means to pay the sum; and
(b) have refused or neglected, or are refusing or neglecting, to pay that sum'.

2.3 The person giving the undertaking must make a signed statement to the effect that he or she understands the terms of the undertaking being given and the consequences of failure to comply with it, as follows:

'I understand the undertaking that I have given, and that if I break my promise to the court to pay any sum of money, I may be sent to prison'.

2.4 The statement need not be given before the court in person. It may be endorsed on the court copy of the undertaking or may be filed in a separate document such as a letter.

PART 34
RECIPROCAL ENFORCEMENT OF MAINTENANCE ORDERS

CONTENTS OF THIS PART

Rule		Page
34.1	Scope and interpretation of this Part	1939
34.2	Meaning of prescribed officer in the family court	1940
34.3	Registration of maintenance orders in the family court	1940
	Chapter 1 *Enforcement of Maintenance Orders under the Maintenance Orders (Facilities for Enforcement) Act 1920*	
34.4	Interpretation	1940
34.5	Confirmation of provisional orders made in a reciprocating country	1940
34.6	Payment of sums due under registered orders	1941
34.7	Collection and enforcement of sums due under registered orders	1941
34.8	Prescribed notice for the taking of further evidence	1941
34.9	Transmission of maintenance orders made in a reciprocating country to the High Court	1941
34.10	Transmission of maintenance orders made in the High Court to a reciprocating country	1941
34.11	Inspection of the register in the High Court	1942
	Chapter 2 *Enforcement of Maintenance Orders under Part 1 of the 1972 Act*	
34.12	Interpretation	1942
34.13	Scope	1942
	Section 1 *Reciprocal Enforcement of Maintenance Orders under Part 1 of the 1972 Act*	
34.14	Application for transmission of maintenance order to reciprocating country	1943
34.15	Certification of evidence given on provisional orders	1943
34.16	Confirmation of a provisional order made in a reciprocating country	1943
34.17	Consideration of revocation of a provisional order made by the family court	1943
34.18	Notification of variation or revocation of a maintenance order by the High Court or the family court	1944
34.19	Notification of confirmation, variation or revocation of a maintenance order by the family court	1944
34.20	Taking of evidence for court in reciprocating country	1944

34.21 Request for the taking of evidence by a court in a reciprocating country 1945
34.22 Transmission of documents 1945
34.23 Method of payment under registered orders 1945
34.24 Enforcement of payments under registered orders 1946
34.25 Notification of registration and cancellation 1946

Section 2
Modification of rules in Section 1 of this Chapter

Sub-section 2
Hague Convention Countries

34.27 Application of Section 1 of this Chapter to the Hague Convention Countries 1946

Sub-section 3
United States of America

34.28 Application of Section 1 of this Chapter to the United States of America 1948

Section 3
Proceedings in a Hague Convention Country or in the United States of America

34.28ZA Notification of proceedings in a Hague Convention Country or in the United States of America 1949

Section 4
Reciprocal Enforcement of Claims for the Recovery of Maintenance

34.28ZB Interpretation 1949
34.28ZC Dismissal of an application under section 27A of the 1972 Act or application for variation 1949
34.28ZD Application for recovery of maintenance in England and Wales: section 27B of the 1972 Act 1950
34.28ZE Application under section 26(1) or (2) of the 1972 Act and certificate under section 26(3A) of the 1972 Act: registration 1950
34.28ZF Registration of an order: sections 27C(7) and 32(3) and (6) of the 1972 Act 1950
34.28ZG Payments made to the family court 1950
34.28ZH Method of payment 1951
34.28ZI Application under section 34 of the 1972 Act: variation or revocation 1951
34.28ZJ Application under section 35 of the 1972 Act: variation or revocation 1951
34.28ZK Request under section 38(1) of the 1972 Act to the family court 1951
34.28ZL Request under section 38(1) of the 1972 Act to the officer of the court 1952
34.28ZM Onward transmission of documents 1952

Chapter 3
Enforcement of Maintenance Orders under the Civil Jurisdiction and Judgments Act 1982, the Judgments Regulation, the Maintenance Regulation, the 2007 Hague Convention and the Lugano Convention

34.28A Application of this Chapter 1952

Section 1
Registration and Enforcement in a Magistrates' Court of Maintenance Orders made in a Contracting State to the 1968 Convention, a Contracting State to the 1988 Convention, a Regulation State, a State bound by the 2007 Hague Convention other than a Member State of the European Union or a State bound by the Lugano Convention

34.29 Interpretation 1953
34.30 Registration of maintenance orders 1953
34.31 Appeal from a decision relating to registration 1954
34.32 Payment of sums due under a registered order 1954
34.33 Enforcement of payments under registered orders 1954
34.34 Variation and revocation of registered orders 1955
34.35 Registered order: payer residing in an area covered by a different Maintenance Enforcement Business Centre 1955
34.36 Cancellation of registered orders 1955
34.36A Directions as to stays, documents and translations 1956

34.36B International Maintenance Obligations; Communication with the Central Authority for England and Wales 1956
34.36C The Maintenance Regulation: applications for enforcement or for refusal or suspension of enforcement 1956

Section 2

Reciprocal enforcement in a Contracting State or a Member State of the European Union of Orders of a court in England and Wales

34.38 Admissibility of documents 1957
34.39 Enforcement of orders of the family court 1958
34.40 Enforcement of orders of the High Court or the family court 1959

Practice Direction 34A –
Reciprocal Enforcement of Maintenance Orders 1959

Practice Direction 34B –
Practice Note (Tracing Payers Overseas) 1969

Practice Direction 34C –
Applications for Recognition and Enforcement To or From European Union Member States 1970

Practice Direction 34D –
Form Relating to Part 34 1973

Practice Direction 34E –
Reciprocal Enforcement of Maintenance Orders – Designated Family Judge Areas 1973

34.1 Scope and interpretation of this Part

(1) This Part contains rules about the reciprocal enforcement of maintenance orders.

(2) In this Part –

'the 1920 Act' means the Maintenance Orders (Facilities for Enforcement) Act 1920;

'the 1972 Act' means the Maintenance Orders (Reciprocal Enforcement) Act 1972;

'the 1982 Act' means the Civil Jurisdiction and Judgments Act 1982;

'the 1988 Convention' means the Convention on jurisdiction and the enforcement of judgments in civil and commercial matters done at Lugano on 16 September 1988;

'the Judgments Regulation' means Council Regulation (EC) No. 44/2001 of 22 December 2000 on jurisdiction and the recognition and enforcement of judgments in civil and commercial matters; and

'the Lugano Convention' means the Convention on jurisdiction and the recognition and enforcement of judgments in civil and commercial matters, between the European Community and the Republic of Iceland, the Kingdom of Norway, the Swiss Confederation and the Kingdom of Denmark signed on behalf of the European Community on 30 October 2007.

(3) Chapter 1 of this Part relates to the enforcement of maintenance orders in accordance with the 1920 Act.

(4) Chapter 2 of this Part relates to the enforcement of maintenance orders in accordance with Parts 1 and 2 of the 1972 Act.

(5) Chapter 3 of this Part relates to the enforcement of maintenance orders in accordance with –

(a) the 1982 Act;
(b) the Judgments Regulation;
(c) the Lugano Convention;
(d) the Maintenance Regulation; and
(e) the 2007 Hague Convention.

Amendments—SI 2011/1328; SI 2012/2806; SI 2013/3204.

34.2 Meaning of prescribed officer in the family court

(1) For the purposes of the 1920 Act, the prescribed officer in relation to the family court is the court officer.

(2) For the purposes of Part 1 of the 1972 Act and section 5(2) of the 1982 Act, the prescribed officer in relation to the family court is the court officer.

(3) For the purposes of an application under Article 30 of the Maintenance Regulation for a declaration of enforceability of a maintenance order or under Article 23(2) or (3) of the 2007 Hague Convention for registration of a maintenance order, the prescribed officer in relation to the family court is the court officer.

Amendments—SI 2013/3204.

34.3 Registration of maintenance orders in the family court

Where the family court is required by any of the enactments referred to in rule 34.1(2) or by virtue of the Maintenance Regulation or the 2007 Hague Convention to register a foreign order the court officer must –

(a) enter a memorandum of the order in the register; and
(b) state on the memorandum the statutory provision or international instrument under which the order is registered.

Amendments—SI 2011/1328; SI 2012/679; SI 2012/2806; SI 2013/3204.

Chapter 1
Enforcement of Maintenance Orders under the Maintenance Orders (Facilities for Enforcement) Act 1920

34.4 Interpretation

(1) In this Chapter –

'payer', in relation to a maintenance order, means the person liable to make the payments for which the order provides; and
'reciprocating country' means a country or territory to which the 1920 Act extends.

(2) In this Chapter, an expression defined in the 1920 Act has the meaning given to it in that Act.

34.5 Confirmation of provisional orders made in a reciprocating country

(1) This rule applies where, in accordance with section 4(1) of the 1920 Act, the court officer receives a provisional maintenance order.

(2) The court must fix the date, time and place for a hearing.

(3) The court officer must register the order in accordance with rule 34.3.

(4) The court officer must serve on the payer –

(a) certified copies of the provisional order and accompanying documents; and
(b) a notice –
  (i) specifying the time and date fixed for the hearing; and
  (ii) stating that the payer may attend to show cause why the order should not be confirmed.

(5) The court officer must inform –

(a) the court which made the provisional order; and
(b) the Lord Chancellor,

whether the court confirms, with or without modification, or decides not to confirm, the order.

34.6 Payment of sums due under registered orders

Where an order made by a reciprocating country is registered in the family court under section 1 of the 1920 Act, the court must order payments due to be made to the court.

(Practice Direction 34A contains further provisions relating to the payment of sums due under registered orders.)

Amendments—SI 2013/3204.

34.7 Collection and enforcement of sums due under registered orders

(1) This rule applies to –

(a) an order made in a reciprocating county which is registered in the family court; and

(b) a provisional order made in a reciprocating country which has been confirmed by the family court,

where the court has ordered that payments due under the order be made to the court.

(2) The court officer must –

(a) collect the monies due under the order; and

(b) send the monies collected to –

(i) the court in the reciprocating country which made the order; or

(ii) such other person or authority as that court or the Lord Chancellor may from time to time direct.

(3) The court officer may take proceedings in that officer's own name for enforcing payment of monies due under the order.

(Rule 32.33 makes provision in relation to a court officer taking such proceedings.)

Amendments—SI 2013/3204.

'the Lord Chancellor may from time to time direct' (r 34.7(2)(b))—In Home Office Circular 139/1970 it is directed that payments under a New Zealand court order are to be made to the New Zealand Department of Social Security. The relevant addresses are listed in the appendix to the Circular.

34.8 Prescribed notice for the taking of further evidence

(1) This rule applies where a court in a reciprocating country has sent a provisional order to the family court for the purpose of taking further evidence.

(2) The court officer must send a notice to the person who applied for the provisional order specifying –

(a) the further evidence required; and

(b) the time and place fixed for taking the evidence.

Amendments—SI 2013/3204.

34.9 Transmission of maintenance orders made in a reciprocating country to the High Court

A maintenance order to be sent by the Lord Chancellor to the High Court in accordance with section 1(1) of the 1920 Act will be –

(a) sent to the senior district judge who will register it in the register kept for the purpose of the 1920 Act; and

(b) filed in the principal registry.

34.10 Transmission of maintenance orders made in the High Court to a reciprocating country

(1) This rule applies to maintenance orders made in the High Court.

(2) An application for a maintenance order to be sent to a reciprocating country under section 2 of the 1920 Act must be made in accordance with this rule.

(3) The application must be made to a district judge in the principal registry unless paragraph (4) applies.

(4) If the order was made in the course of proceedings in a district registry, the application may be made to a district judge in that district registry.

(5) The application must be –

(a) accompanied by a certified copy of the order; and
(b) supported by a record of the sworn written evidence.

(6) The written evidence must give –

(a) the applicant's reason for believing that the payer resides in the reciprocating country;
(b) such information as the applicant has as to the whereabouts of the payer; and
(c) such other information as may be set out in Practice Direction 34A.

34.11 Inspection of the register in the High Court

(1) A person may inspect the register and request copies of a registered order and any document filed with it if the district judge is satisfied that that person is entitled to, or liable to make, payments under a maintenance order made in –

(a) the High Court; or
(b) a court in a reciprocating country.

(2) The right to inspect the register referred to in paragraph (1) may be exercised by –

(a) a solicitor acting on behalf of the person entitled to, or liable to make, the payments referred to in that paragraph; or
(b) with the permission of the district judge, any other person.

Chapter 2
Enforcement of Maintenance Orders under Part 1 of the 1972 Act

34.12 Interpretation

(1) In this Chapter –

(a) 'reciprocating country' means a country to which Part 1 of the 1972 Act extends; and
(b) 'relevant court in the reciprocating country' means, as the case may be –
  (i) the court which made the order which has been sent to England and Wales for confirmation;
  (ii) the court which made the order which has been registered in a court in England and Wales;
  (iii) the court to which an order made in England and Wales has been sent for registration; or
  (iv) the court to which a provisional order made in England and Wales has been sent for confirmation.

(2) In this Chapter, an expression defined in the 1972 Act has the meaning given to it in that Act.

(3) In this Chapter, 'Hague Convention Countries' means the countries listed in Schedule 1 to the Reciprocal Enforcement of Maintenance Orders (Hague Convention Countries) Order 1993.

Amendments—SI 2011/1328.

34.13 Scope

(1) Section 1 of this Chapter contains rules relating to the reciprocal enforcement of maintenance orders under Part 1 of the 1972 Act.

(2) Section 2 of this Chapter modifies the rules contained in Section 1 of this Chapter in their application to –

(a) *(revoked)*
(b) the Hague Convention Countries; and
(c) the United States of America.

(3) Section 3 of this Chapter contains a rule in relation to notification of proceedings in a Hague Convention Country or the United States of America.

(4) Section 4 of this Chapter contains rules in relation to proceedings under Part 2 of the 1972 Act (reciprocal enforcement of claims for the recovery of maintenance).

(Practice Direction 34A sets out in full the rules for the Hague Convention Countries and the United States of America as modified by Section 2 of this Chapter.)

Amendments—SI 2011/1328; SI 2013/3204.

Hague Convention countries—In effect, this means Australia, Switzerland and Turkey, as Norway now only reciprocates with the UK under the 2007 Hague Convention and Lugano Convention. See note to r 34.27 for the effect of the Maintenance Regulation (EC) No 4/2009 (set out in Part VI), which takes precedence over the Hague Convention regime for EU countries. Turkey now also reciprocates under the 2007 Hague Convention and applications will be transmitted under the simplified and more modern procedures of that Convention rather than for determination under the provisions of the 1972 Act.

Section 1
Reciprocal Enforcement of Maintenance Orders under Part 1 of the 1972 Act

34.14 Application for transmission of maintenance order to reciprocating country

An application for a maintenance order to be sent to a reciprocating country under section 2 of the 1972 Act must be made in accordance with Practice Direction 34A.

34.15 Certification of evidence given on provisional orders

A document setting out or summarising evidence is authenticated by a court in England and Wales by a certificate signed by the judge before whom that evidence was given.

(Section 3(5)(b), 5(4) and 9(5) of the 1972 Act require a document to be authenticated by the court.)

Amendments—SI 2013/3204.

34.16 Confirmation of a provisional order made in a reciprocating country

(1) This rule applies to proceedings for the confirmation of a provisional order made in a reciprocating country.

(2) Paragraph (3) applies on receipt by the court of –

(a) a certified copy of the order; and

(b) the documents required by the 1972 Act to accompany the order.

(3) On receipt of the documents referred to in paragraph (2) –

(a) the court must fix the date, time and place for a hearing or a directions appointment; and

(b) the court officer must send to the payer notice of the date, time and place fixed together with a copy of the order and accompanying documents.

(4) The date fixed for the hearing must be not less than 21 days beginning with the date on which the court officer sent the documents to the payer in accordance with paragraph (2).

(5) The court officer will send to the relevant court in the reciprocating country a certified copy of any order confirming or refusing to confirm the provisional order.

(6) (*revoked*)

(Section 5(5) and 7 of the 1972 Act provide for proceedings for the confirmation of a provisional order.)

(Rule 34.22 provides for the transmission of documents to a court in a reciprocating country.)

Amendments—SI 2013/3204.

34.17 Consideration of revocation of a provisional order made by the family court

(1) This rule applies where –

(a) the family court has made a provisional order by virtue of section 3 of the 1972 Act;

(b) before the order is confirmed, evidence is taken by the court or received by it as set out in section 5(9) of the 1972 Act; and

(c) on consideration of the evidence the court considers that the order ought not to have been made.

(Section 5(9) of the 1972 Act provides that the family court may revoke a provisional order made by it, before the order has been confirmed in a reciprocating country, if it receives new evidence.)

(2) The court officer must serve on the person who applied for the provisional order ('the applicant') a notice which must –

(a) set out the evidence taken or received by the court;
(b) inform the applicant that the court considers that the order ought not to have been made; and
(c) inform the applicant that the applicant may –
make representations in relation to that evidence either orally or in writing; and
adduce further evidence.

(3) If an applicant wishes to adduce further evidence –

(a) the applicant must notify the court officer at the court which made the order;
(b) the court will fix a date for the hearing of the evidence; and
(c) the court officer will notify the applicant in writing of the date fixed.

Amendments—SI 2013/3204.

34.18 Notification of variation or revocation of a maintenance order by the High Court or the family court

(1) This rule applies where –

(a) a maintenance order has been sent to a reciprocating country in pursuance of section 2 of the 1972 Act; and
(b) the court makes an order, not being a provisional order, varying or revoking that order.

(2) The court officer must send a certified copy of the order of variation or revocation to the relevant court in the reciprocating country.

(Rule 34.22 provides for the transmission of documents to a court in a reciprocating country.)

Amendments—SI 2013/3204.

34.19 Notification of confirmation, variation or revocation of a maintenance order by the family court

(1) This rule applies where the family court makes an order –

(a) not being a provisional order, revoking or varying a maintenance order to which section 5 of the 1972 Act applies;
(b) under section 9 of the 1972 Act, revoking or varying a registered order; or
(c) under section 7(2) of the 1972 Act, confirming an order to which section 7 of that Act applies.

(2) The court officer must send written notice of the making, variation, revocation or confirmation of the order, as appropriate, to the relevant court in the reciprocating country.

(3) (*revoked*)

(Section 5 of the 1972 Act applies to a provisional order made by the family court in accordance with section 3 of that Act which has been confirmed by a court in a reciprocating country.)

(Rule 34.22 provides for the transmission of documents to a court in a reciprocating country.)

Amendments—SI 2013/3204.

34.20 Taking of evidence for court in reciprocating country

(1) This rule applies where a request is made by or on behalf of a court in a reciprocating country for the taking of evidence for the purpose of proceedings relating to a maintenance order to which Part 1 of the 1972 Act applies.

(Section 14 of the 1972 Act makes provision for the taking of evidence needed for the purpose of certain proceedings.)

(2) The High Court has power to take the evidence where –

(a) the request for evidence relates to a maintenance order made by a superior court in the United Kingdom; and

(b) the witness resides in England and Wales.

(3) The family court has power to take evidence where –

(a) the request for evidence relates to a maintenance order –

(i) made by the family court; or

(ii) registered in the family court; or

(b) the Lord Chancellor sends to the family court a request to take evidence.

(Practice Direction 34E makes further provision on this matter)

(4)–(5) *(revoked)*

(6) The evidence is to be taken in accordance with Part 22.

Amendments—SI 2011/1328; SI 2013/3204.

34.21 Request for the taking of evidence by a court in a reciprocating country

(1) This rule applies where a request is made by the family court for the taking of evidence in a reciprocating country in accordance with section 14(5) of the 1972 Act.

(2) The request must be made in writing to the court in the reciprocating country.

(Rule 34.22 provides for the transmission of documents to a court in a reciprocating country.)

Amendments—SI 2013/3204.

34.22 Transmission of documents

(1) This rule applies to any document, including a notice or request, which is required to be sent to a court in a reciprocating country by –

(a) Part 1 of the 1972 Act; or

(b) Section 1 of Chapter 2 of this Part of these rules.

(2) The document must be sent to the Lord Chancellor for transmission to the court in the reciprocating country.

34.23 Method of payment under registered orders

(1) Where an order is registered in the family court in accordance with section 6(3) of the 1972 Act, the court must order that the payment of sums due under the order be made –

(a) to the registering court; and

(b) at such time and place as the court officer directs.

(Section 6(3) of the 1972 Act makes provision for the registration of maintenance orders made in a reciprocating country.)

(2) Where the court orders payments to be made to the court, whether in accordance with paragraph (1) or otherwise, the court officer must send the payments –

(a) by post to either –

(i) the court which made the order; or

(ii) such other person or authority as that court, or the Lord Chancellor, directs; or

(b) if the court which made the order is a country or territory specified in the Practice Direction 34A –

(i) to the Crown Agents for Overseas Governments and Administrations for transmission to the person to whom they are due; or

(ii) as the Lord Chancellor directs.

(Practice Direction 34A contains further provisions relating to the payment of sums due under registered orders.)

PART III

Amendments—SI 2013/3204.

'Crown Agents for Overseas Governments and Administrations' (r 34.23(2)(b)(i))—The address of the Crown Agents is St Nicholas House, St Nicholas Road, Sutton, Surrey, SM1 1EL. See PD34A, para 8.1 for a list of the relevant countries and territories.

34.24 Enforcement of payments under registered orders

(1) This rule applies where a court has ordered periodical payments under a registered maintenance order to be made to the court.

(2) The court officer must take reasonable steps to notify the payee of the means of enforcement available.

(3) Paragraph (4) applies where periodical payments due under a registered order are in arrears.

(4) The court officer, on that officer's own initiative –

(a) may; or
(b) if the sums due are more than 4 weeks in arrears, must,

proceed in that officer's own name for the recovery of the sums due unless of the view that it is unreasonable to do so.

Amendments—SI 2013/3204.

'where periodical payments ... are in arrears' (r 34.24(3))—Applying the principle established in *Vogel v Lothschütz* [2012] EWHC 3411 (QB) in respect of registration of a European Enforcement Order, registration will not be invalidated by any miscalculation of arrears if registration has been effected in accordance with the proper procedure, as any miscalculation can be corrected.

34.25 Notification of registration and cancellation

(1) The court officer must send written notice to the Lord Chancellor of the due registration of orders registered in accordance with section 6(3), 7(5), or 10(4) of the 1972 Act.

(2) The court officer must, when registering an order in accordance with section 6(3), 7(5), 9(10), 10(4) or (5) or 23(3) of the 1972 Act, send written notice to the payer stating –

(a) that the order has been registered;
(b) that payments under the order should be made to the court officer; and
(c) the hours during which and the place at which the payments should be made.

(3) The court officer must, when cancelling the registration of an order in accordance with section 10(1) of the 1972 Act, send written notice of the cancellation to the payer.

Section 2
Modification of rules in Section 1 of this Chapter

****

Sub-section 2
Hague Convention Countries

34.27 Application of Section 1 of this Chapter to the Hague Convention Countries

Note—This subsection contains detailed provision for the application of the Maintenance Orders (Reciprocal Enforcement) Act 1972 to the countries listed in the Reciprocal Enforcement of Maintenance Orders (Hague Convention Countries) Order 1993, Sch 1 (i e 'the Hague Convention Countries'). However, where the country concerned is also a country to which the Maintenance Regulation (EC) No 4/2009 applies (EU member states), that regulation takes precedence over other reciprocal arrangements in Conventions and agreements and reference should be made instead to the provisions at Ch 3 of FPR 2010, Pt 34. The Maintenance Regulation therefore replaces the separate reciprocal regime between the UK and the Republic of Ireland. Although originally a 1973 Hague Convention Country, Norway now only reciprocates under the revised Lugano Convention 2007 and under the 2007 Hague Convention.

(1) In relation to the Hague Convention Countries, Section 1 of this Chapter has effect as modified by this rule.

(2) A reference in this rule, and in any rule which has effect in relation to the Hague Convention Countries by virtue of this rule to –

(a) the 1972 Act is a reference to the 1972 Act as modified by Schedule 2 to the Reciprocal Enforcement of Maintenance Orders (Hague Convention Countries) Order 1993; and
(b) a section under the 1972 Act is a reference to the section so numbered in the 1972 Act as so modified.

(3) A reference to a reciprocating country in rule 34.12(1) and Section 1 of this Chapter is a reference to a Hague Convention Country.

(4) Rules 34.15 (certification of evidence given on provisional orders), 34.16 (confirmation of provisional orders), 34.19 (notification of confirmation, variation or revocation of a maintenance order by the family court) and 34.21 (request for the taking of evidence by a court in a reciprocating country) do not apply.

(5) For rule 34.17 (consideration of revocation of a provisional order made by the family court) substitute –

'34.17 Consideration of variation or revocation of a maintenance order made by the family court

(1) This rule applies where –

(a) an application has been made to the family court by a payee for the variation or revocation of an order to which section 5 of the 1972 Act applies; and
(b) the payer resides in a Hague Convention Country.

(2) The court officer must serve on the payee, by post, a copy of any representations or evidence adduced by or on behalf of the payer.'

(6) For rule 34.18 (notification of variation or revocation of a maintenance order by the High Court or the family court) substitute –

'34.18 Notification of variation or revocation of a maintenance order by the High Court or the family court

(1) This rule applies if the High Court or the family court makes an order varying or revoking a maintenance order to which section 5 of the 1972 Act applies.

(2) If the time for appealing has expired without an appeal having been entered, the court officer will send to the Lord Chancellor –

(a) the documents required by section 5(8) of the 1972 Act; and
(b) a certificate signed by a judge stating that the order of variation or revocation is enforceable and no longer subject to the ordinary forms of review.

(3) A party who enters an appeal against the order of variation or revocation must, at the same time, give written notice to the court officer.'.

(7) For rule 34.23(2) (method of payment under registered orders) substitute –

'(2) Where the court orders payment to be made to the court, the court officer must send the payments by post to the payee under the order.'.

(8) For rule 34.25 (notification of registration and cancellation) substitute –

'34.25 Notification of registration and cancellation

The court officer must send written notice to –

(a) the Lord Chancellor, on the due registration of an order under section 10(4) of the 1972 Act; and
(b) the payer under the order,

on –

(i) the registration of an order under section 10(4) of the 1972 Act; or
(ii) the cancellation of the registration of an order under section 10(1) of the 1972 Act.'.

(9) After rule 34.25 insert –

'34.25A General provisions as to notices

(1) A notice to a payer of the registration of an order in the family court in accordance with section 6(3) of the 1972 Act must be in the form referred to in a practice direction.

(Section 6(8) of the 1972 Act requires notice of registration to be given to the payer.)

(2) If the court sets aside the registration of a maintenance order following an appeal under section 6(9) of the 1972 Act, the court officer must send written notice of the decision to the Lord Chancellor.

(3) A notice to a payee that the court officer has refused to register an order must be in the form referred to in a practice direction.

(Section 6(11) of the 1972 Act requires notice of refusal of registration to be given to the payee.)

(4) Where, under any provision of Part 1 of the 1972 Act, a court officer serves a notice on a payer who resides in a Hague Convention Country, the court officer must send to the Lord Chancellor a certificate of service.'.

Amendments—SI 2013/3204.

Modifications—See FPR PD34A, Annex 2.

Sub-section 3
United States of America

34.28 Application of Section 1 of this Chapter to the United States of America

(1) In relation to the United States of America, Section 1 of this Chapter has effect as modified by this rule.

(2) A reference in this rule and in any rule which has effect in relation to the United States of America by virtue of this rule to –

(a) the 1972 Act is a reference to the 1972 Act as modified by Schedule 1 to the Reciprocal Enforcement of Maintenance Orders (United States of America) Order 2007; and

(b) a section under the 1972 Act is a reference to the section so numbered in the 1972 Act as so modified.

(3) A reference to a reciprocating country in rule 34.12(1) and Section 1 of this Chapter is a reference to the United States of America.

(4) Rules 34.15 (certification of evidence given on provisional orders), 34.16 (confirmation of provisional orders), 34.19 (notification of confirmation, variation or revocation of a maintenance order made by the family court) and 34.21 (request for the taking of evidence in a reciprocating country) do not apply.

(5) For rule 34.17 (consideration of revocation of a provisional order made by the family court) substitute –

'34.17 Consideration of variation or revocation of a maintenance order made by the family court

(1) This rule applies where –

(a) an application has been made to the family court by a payee for the variation or revocation of an order to which section 5 of the 1972 Act applies; and

(b) the payer resides in the United States of America.

(2) The court officer must serve on the payee by post a copy of any representations or evidence adduced by or on behalf of the payer.'

(6) For rule 34.18 (notification of variation or revocation), substitute –

'34.18 Notification of variation or revocation

If the High Court or the family court makes an order varying or revoking a maintenance order to which section 5 of the 1972 Act applies, the court officer will send to the Lord Chancellor the documents required by section 5(7) of that Act.'.

(7) For rule 34.23(2) (method of payment under registered orders) substitute –

'(2) Where the court orders payment to be made to the court, the court officer must send the payments by post to the payee under the order.'.

(8) For rule 34.25 (notification of registration and cancellation) substitute –

'34.25 Notification of registration and cancellation

The court officer must send written notice to –

(a) the Lord Chancellor, on the due registration of an order under section 10(4) of the 1972 Act; or

(b) the payer under the order, on –

(i) the registration of an order under section 10(4) of the 1972 Act; or

(ii) the cancellation of the registration of an order under section 10(1) of that Act.'

Amendments—SI 2013/3204.

Modifications—See FPR PD34A, Annex 3.

Application to the USA—With effect from 1 October 2007 (SI 2007/2005 and SI 2007/2006) the provisions of the 1972 Act apply, with modifications, to the whole of the USA. The principal modification is that a maintenance order made in the USA and registered for enforcement in the UK may not be varied or revoked in the UK and a maintenance order made in the UK and registered for enforcement in the USA may not be varied or revoked in the USA. From 1 January 2017, the 2007 Hague Convention came into effect for the USA and the more modern and simplified procedures under that Convention will be used rather than those under Pt 1 of the 1972 Act.

Section 3
Proceedings in a Hague Convention Country or in the United States of America

34.28ZA Notification of proceedings in a Hague Convention Country or in the United States of America

Practice Direction 34E applies where the court officer receives from the Lord Chancellor notice of the institution of proceedings, including notice of the substance of a claim, in a Hague Convention Country or in the United States of America in relation to the making, variation or revocation of a maintenance order.

Amendments—Inserted by SI 2013/3204.

Section 4
Reciprocal Enforcement of Claims for the Recovery of Maintenance

34.28ZB Interpretation

In this Section –

'convention country' means a country or territory specified in an Order in Council made under section 25 of the 1972 Act; and

an expression defined in the 1972 Act has the meaning given to it in that Act.

Amendments—Inserted by SI 2013/3204.

34.28ZC Dismissal of an application under section 27A of the 1972 Act or application for variation

(1) Where the family court dismisses an application under –

(a) section 27A of the 1972 Act (application for recovery of maintenance); or

(b) an application by a person in a convention country for the variation of a registered order, the court officer will send a written notice of the court's decision to the Lord Chancellor.

(2) The notice will include a statement of the court's reasons for its decision.

Amendments—Inserted by SI 2013/3204.

34.28ZD Application for recovery of maintenance in England and Wales: section 27B of the 1972 Act

(1) Where the family court receives an application for the recovery of maintenance sent from the Lord Chancellor under section 27B of the 1972 Act, the court will –

- (a) fix the date, time and place for a hearing or directions appointment, allowing sufficient time for service under this rule to be effected at least 21 days before the date fixed; and
- (b) serve copies of the application and any accompanying documents, together with a notice stating the date, time and place so fixed, on the respondent.

(2) Within 14 days of service under this rule, the respondent must file an answer to the application in the form referred to in Practice Direction 5A.

Amendments—Inserted by SI 2013/3204.

34.28ZE Application under section 26(1) or (2) of the 1972 Act and certificate under section 26(3A) of the 1972 Act: registration

Where –

- (a) an application under section 26(1) or (2) of the 1972 Act; or
- (b) a certificate under section 26(3A) of the 1972 Act,

is required to be registered in the family court by virtue of the Recovery of Maintenance (United States of America) Order 2007, the court officer will enter a minute or memorandum of the application or certificate in the register.

Amendments—Inserted by SI 2013/3204.

34.28ZF Registration of an order: sections 27C(7) and 32(3) and (6) of the 1972 Act

(1) Where the family court makes an order which is required under section 27C(7) of the 1972 Act to be registered, the court officer will enter a minute or memorandum of the order in the register.

(2) Where a court officer receives under section 32(3) of the 1972 Act a certified copy of an order, the court officer will register the order by means of a minute or memorandum in the register.

(3) Every minute or memorandum entered under paragraph (1) or (2) will specify the section and subsection of the 1972 Act under which the order in question is registered.

(4) Where a court officer registers an order as required by section 27C(7) or 32(3) of the 1972 Act, the court officer will send written notice to the Lord Chancellor that the order has been registered.

(5) Where a court officer is required by section 32(6) of the 1972 Act to give notice of the registration of an order, the court officer will do this by sending written notice to the officer specified in that subsection that the order has been registered.

Amendments—Inserted by SI 2013/3204.

34.28ZG Payments made to the family court

(1) Where payments are made to the family court by virtue of section 27C or 34A of the 1972 Act, the court officer will send those payments by post to such person or authority as the Lord Chancellor may from time to time direct.

(2) Subject to paragraph (3), if it appears to a court officer that any sums payable under a registered order are in arrears, the officer may proceed in the officer's own name for the recovery of those sums.

(3) Where it appears to the officer that sums payable under the order are in arrears to an amount equal –

- (a) in the case of payments to be made monthly or less frequently, to twice the sum payable periodically; or

(b) in any other case, to four times the sum payable periodically,

the officer will proceed in the officer's own name for the recovery of those sums, unless it appears to the officer that it is unreasonable in the circumstances to do so.

Amendments—Inserted by SI 2013/3204.

34.28ZH Method of payment

(1) This rule applies where the family court exercises its duties or powers under section 27C or 34A of the 1972 Act.

(2) Where the court orders that payments under the order are to be made by a particular means –

- (a) the court will record on the copy of the order the means of payment that the court has ordered; and
- (b) the court officer will, as soon as practicable, notify, in writing, the person liable to make the payments under the order how payments are to be made.

(3) Paragraph (4) applies where the court orders that payments be made to the court by a method of payment falling within section 1(5) of the Maintenance Enforcement Act 1991.

(4) The court officer will notify the person liable to make the payments under the order of sufficient details of the account into which the payments should be made to enable payments to be made into that account.

Amendments—Inserted by SI 2013/3204.

34.28ZI Application under section 34 of the 1972 Act: variation or revocation

(1) This rule applies in relation to an application under section 34 of the 1972 Act for the variation or revocation of a registered order.

(2) An application which is made directly to the registering court must be filed in the form referred to in Practice Direction 5A.

(3) Where the court receives an application, either filed in accordance with paragraph (2) or sent from the Lord Chancellor under section 34(3) of the 1972 Act –

- (a) the court will set the date, time and place for a hearing or directions appointment; and
- (b) the court officer will notify the applicant of the date, time and place.

Amendments—Inserted by SI 2013/3204.

34.28ZJ Application under section 35 of the 1972 Act: variation or revocation

(1) This rule applies in relation to an application under section 35 of the 1972 Act for the variation or revocation of a registered order.

(2) Notice under section 35(3)(b) of the 1972 Act of the time and place appointed for the hearing of the application will be in the form specified in Practice Direction 34D.

(3) The court officer will send the notice by post to the Lord Chancellor for onward transmission to the appropriate authority in the convention country in which the respondent is residing.

(4) The time appointed for the hearing of the application will not be less than six weeks later than the date on which the notice is sent to the Lord Chancellor.

Amendments—Inserted by SI 2013/3204.

34.28ZK Request under section 38(1) of the 1972 Act to the family court

(1) This rule applies where the family court receives from the Lord Chancellor a request under section 38(1) of the 1972 Act (taking evidence at the request of a court in a convention country) to take the evidence of any person.

(2) Subject to paragraph (3) –

- (a) the evidence will be taken in the same manner as if the person concerned were a witness in family proceedings;
- (b) any oral evidence so taken will be put into writing and read to the person who gave it, who must sign the document; and

(c) the judge who takes any such evidence of any person will certify at the foot of the document setting out the evidence of, or produced in evidence by, that person that such evidence was taken, or document received in evidence, as the case may be, by that judge.

(3) Where the request referred to in section 38(2) of the 1972 Act includes a request that the evidence be taken in a particular manner, the court by which the evidence is taken will, so far as circumstances permit, comply with that request.

Amendments—Inserted by SI 2013/3204.

34.28ZL Request under section 38(1) of the 1972 Act to the officer of the court

(1) This rule applies where an officer of the court receives from the Lord Chancellor a request under section 38(1) of the 1972 Act to take the evidence of any person.

(2) Subject to paragraph (3) –

(a) the person whose evidence is to be taken will be examined on oath by or before a justices' clerk or any other court officer determined by the Lord Chancellor; .

(b) any oral evidence will be put into writing and read to the person who gave it, who must sign the document; and .

(c) the justices' clerk or other officer will certify at the foot of the document setting out the evidence of, or produced by, that person, that such evidence was taken, or document received in evidence, as the case may be, by that justices' clerk or other officer. .

(3) Where the request referred to in section 38(1) of the 1972 Act includes a request that the evidence be taken in a particular manner, the justices' clerk or other officer by whom the evidence is taken will, so far as circumstances permit, comply with that request.

(4) For the purposes of this rule, the justices' clerk or other officer has the same power to administer oaths as a single justice of the peace.

Amendments—Inserted by SI 2013/3204.

34.28ZM Onward transmission of documents

Any document mentioned in rule 34.28ZK(2)(c) or rule 34.28ZL(2)(c) will be sent to the Lord Chancellor for onward transmission to the appropriate authority in the convention country in which the request referred to in section 38(1) of the 1972 Act originated.

Amendments—Inserted by SI 2013/3204.

Chapter 3

Enforcement of Maintenance Orders under the Civil Jurisdiction and Judgments Act 1982, the Judgments Regulation, the Maintenance Regulation, the 2007 Hague Convention and the Lugano Convention

Amendments—SI 2011/1328; SI 2012/2806.

Note—The relevant orders to which this Chapter applies are orders made in one of the other Member States of the EU, one of the non-EU signatories to the 2007 Hague Convention being Albania, Bosnia-Herzegovina, Montenegro, Norway, Turkey, the USA and Ukraine, or orders made in Iceland or Switzerland sent for enforcement in England and Wales or vice versa.

34.28A Application of this Chapter

(1) In this Chapter –

(a) references to a maintenance order include –

(i) a decision, a court settlement or an authentic instrument within the meaning of Article 2 of the Maintenance Regulation where that Regulation applies;

(ii) a maintenance decision to which Chapter V of the 2007 Hague Convention applies by virtue of Article 19(1) of that Convention;

(iii) a maintenance arrangement (as defined in Article 3(e) of the 2007 Hague Convention) which is to be recognised and enforceable in the same way as a maintenance decision by virtue of Article 30 of that Convention;

(b) references to the Hague Protocol are to the Protocol on the Law Applicable to Maintenance Obligations done at The Hague on 23 November 2007;

(c) 'the 1968 Convention' has the meaning given in the 1982 Act.

(2) In relation to the Maintenance Regulation –

(a) Section 1 applies to maintenance orders to which Sections 2 and 3 of Chapter IV of the Maintenance Regulation apply (decisions given in a Member State which does not apply the rules of the Hague Protocol, that is, Denmark, and decisions to which Sections 2 and 3 of Chapter IV of that Regulation apply by virtue of Article 75(2)(a) or (b));

(b) Section 2 applies to all maintenance orders made in a magistrates' court in England and Wales for which reciprocal enforcement is sought in any Member State of the European Union, including Denmark.

Amendments—Inserted by SI 2011/1328. Amended by SI 2012/679; SI 2012/2806; SI 2013/3204.

Section 1

Registration and Enforcement in a Magistrates' Court of Maintenance Orders made in a Contracting State to the 1968 Convention, a Contracting State to the 1988 Convention, a Regulation State, a State bound by the 2007 Hague Convention other than a Member State of the European Union or a State bound by the Lugano Convention

Amendments—SI 2012/2806.

Note—EU Member States will use the 2007 Hague Convention with non-EU Contracting States only; the Maintenance Regulation will be used as between Member States. See the list of non-EU Contracting States to the 2007 Hague Convention under the general note to Ch 3, above.

34.29 Interpretation

In this Section –

(a) an expression defined in the 1982 Act has the meaning given to it in that Act, subject to paragraph (b); and

(b) 'Regulation State' means a Member State of the European Union which does not apply the rules of the Hague Protocol, or, where registration is sought for a maintenance order to which Article 75(2)(a) or (b) of the Maintenance Regulation applies, the Member State of the European Union from which the order originated.

Amendments—SI 2011/1328.

34.29A *(revoked)*

34.30 Registration of maintenance orders

(1) *(revoked)*

(2) This rule and Practice Direction 34E apply where the family court receives –

(a) an application under Article 31 of the 1968 Convention for the enforcement of a maintenance order made in a Contracting State other than the United Kingdom;

(b) an application under Article 31 of the 1988 Convention for the enforcement of a maintenance order made in a State bound by the 1988 Convention other than a Member State of the European Union;

(c) an application under Article 26 of the Maintenance Regulation for a declaration of enforceability of a maintenance order made in a Regulation State other than the United Kingdom;

(d) an application under Article 38 of the Lugano Convention for the enforcement of a maintenance order made in a State bound by the Lugano Convention other than a Member State of the European Union; or

(e) an application under Article 23 of the 2007 Hague Convention for registration of a maintenance order made in a State bound by that Convention other than a Member State of the European Union.

(3)–(5) *(revoked)*

PART III

(6) Except where Practice Direction 34E provides otherwise, the court must register the order unless –

(a) in the case of an application under Article 31 of the 1968 Convention, Articles 27 or 28 of that Convention apply;
(b) in the case of an application under Article 31 of the 1988 Convention, Articles 27 or 28 of that Convention apply; and
(c) in the case of an application under Article 23(2) or (3) of the 2007 Hague Convention, Article 22(a) of that Convention applies.

(7) If the court refuses to register an order to which this rule relates the court officer must notify the applicant.

(8) If the court registers an order the court officer must send written notice of that fact to –

(a) the Lord Chancellor;
(b) the payer; and
(c) the applicant.

(9) *(revoked)*

Amendments—SI 2011/1328; SI 2012/2806; SI 2013/3204.

34.31 Appeal from a decision relating to registration

(1) This rule applies to an appeal under –

(a) Article 36 or Article 40 of the 1968 Convention;
(b) Article 36 or Article 40 of the 1988 Convention;
(c) Article 32 of the Maintenance Regulation;
(d) Article 43 of the Lugano Convention; or
(e) Article 23(5) of the 2007 Hague Convention.

(2) The appeal must be to the family court.

(Practice Direction 34E makes provision in relation to such cases.)

Amendments—SI 2011/1328; SI 2012/2806; SI 2013/3204.

34.32 Payment of sums due under a registered order

(1) Where an order is registered in accordance with section 5(3) of the 1982 Act, Article 38 of the Judgments Regulation, Article 38 of the Lugano Convention or Article 23 of the 2007 Hague Convention, or declared enforceable under Article 26 of the Maintenance Regulation by virtue of registration, the court may order that payment of sums due under the order be made to the court, at such time and place as directed.

(2) Where the court orders payments to be made to the court, whether in accordance with paragraph (1) or otherwise, the court officer must send the payments by post either –

(a) to the court which made the order; or
(b) to such other person or authority as that court, or the Lord Chancellor, directs.

(Practice Direction 34A contains further provisions relating to the payment of sums due under registered orders.)

Amendments—SI 2011/1328; SI 2012/2806; SI 2013/3204.

34.33 Enforcement of payments under registered orders

(1) This rule applies where a court has ordered periodical payments under a registered maintenance order to be made to the family court.

(2) The court officer must take reasonable steps to notify the payee of the means of enforcement available.

(3) Paragraph (4) applies where periodical payments due under a registered order are in arrears.

(4) The court officer, on that officer's own initiative –

(a) may; or
(b) if the sums due are more than 4 weeks in arrears, must,

proceed in that officer's own name for the recovery of the sums due unless of the view that it is unreasonable to do so.

Amendments—SI 2013/3204.

'where periodical payments ... are in arrears' (r 34.33(3))—Applying the principle established in *Vogel v Lothschütz* [2012] EWHC 3411 (QB) in respect of registration of a European Enforcement Order, registration will not be invalidated by any miscalculation of arrears if registration has been effected in accordance with the proper procedure, as any miscalculation can be corrected.

34.34 Variation and revocation of registered orders

(1) This rule applies where the court officer for a registering court receives notice that a registered maintenance order has been varied or revoked by a competent court in a Contracting State to the 1968 Convention, a Contracting State to the 1988 Convention (other than a Member State of the European Union), a Regulation State or a State bound by the Lugano Convention or by the 2007 Hague Convention, other than a Member State of the European Union.

(2) The court officer for the registering court must –

- (a) register the order of variation or revocation; and
- (b) send notice of the registration by post to the payer and payee under the order.

(3) Where the court officer for a registering court receives notice that a maintenance order registered in that court by virtue of the provisions of the Judgments Regulation has been varied or revoked by a competent court in another Member State of the European Union, the court officer must –

- (a) note against the entry in the register that the original order so registered has been varied or revoked, as the case may be; and
- (b) send notice of the noting of the variation or revocation, as the case may be, by post to the payer and payee under the order.

Amendments—SI 2011/1328; SI 2012/2806.

34.35 Registered order: payer residing in an area covered by a different Maintenance Enforcement Business Centre

Practice Direction 34E makes provision for cases where a court officer in the Maintenance Enforcement Business Centre for the Designated Family Judge area where an order is registered considers that the payer is residing in a Designated Family Judge area covered by a different Maintenance Enforcement Business Centre.

(For the way in which information will be provided to enable Maintenance Enforcement Business Centres to be identified, see Practice Direction 34E.)

Amendments—Last substituted by SI 2015/1420.

Maintenance Enforcement Business Centre (MEBC)—REMO work for England and Wales is administered through three Maintenance Enforcement Business Centres. Reciprocal enforcement work for England (except London) is administered from the Bury St Edmunds MEBC, Triton House, St Andrews Street North, Bury St Edmunds IP33 1TR; the London MEBC is located at the Central Family Court, First Avenue House, 42–49 High Holborn, London WC1V 6NP; and the MEBC for Wales is based at The Law Courts, Sunnyside, Bridgend CF31 4AJ.

34.36 Cancellation of registered orders

(1) Where the court officer for the registering court –

- (a) has no reason to send papers to another Maintenance Enforcement Business Centre under Practice Direction 34E; and
- (b) considers that the payer under the registered order is not residing within the area covered by the Maintenance Enforcement Business Centre for the Designated Family Judge area where the order is registered and has no assets in England and Wales,

the court officer must cancel the registration.

(2) The court officer must –

- (a) give notice of cancellation to the payee; and
- (b) send to the Lord Chancellor –

(i) the information and documents relating to the registration;
(ii) a certificate of arrears, if applicable, signed by the court officer;
(iii) a statement giving such information as the court officer possesses as to the whereabouts of the payer and the nature and location of the payer's assets; and
(iv) any other relevant documents which the court officer has relating to the case.

(Practice Direction 34E makes further provision on this matter.)

Amendments—SI 2013/3204; SI 2015/913; SI 2015/1420.

Maintenance Enforcement Business Centre (MEBC)—See note under r 34.36, above.

34.36A Directions as to stays, documents and translations

At any stage in proceedings for registration of a maintenance order under this Section of this Chapter, the court may give directions about the conduct of the proceedings, including –

(a) staying of proceedings in accordance with –
  (i) Article 30 or 38 of the 1968 Convention,
  (ii) Article 30 or 38 of the 1988 Convention,
  (iii) Article 37 or 46 of the Lugano Convention,
  (iv) Article 25 or 35 of the Maintenance Regulation, or
  (v) Article 30(6) of the 2007 Hague Convention;
(b) the provision of documents in accordance with –
  (i) Article 48 of the 1968 Convention,
  (ii) Article 48 of the 1988 Convention,
  (iii) Article 55 of the Lugano Convention,
  (iv) Article 29 of the Maintenance Regulation, or
  (v) Article 25 or 30 of the 2007 Hague Convention;
(c) the provision of translations in accordance with –
  (i) Article 48 of the 1968 Convention,
  (ii) Article 48 of the 1988 Convention,
  (iii) Article 55 of the Lugano Convention,
  (iv) Article 28 of the Maintenance Regulation, or
  (v) in relation to an application under this Section relating to the 2007 Hague Convention, without prejudice to Article 44 of that Convention.

Amendments—Inserted by SI 2011/1328. Amended by SI 2012/2806.

34.36B International Maintenance Obligations; Communication with the Central Authority for England and Wales

(1) Where the Lord Chancellor requests information or a document from the court officer for the relevant court for the purposes of Article 58 of the Maintenance Regulation, or Article 12 or 25(2) of the 2007 Hague Convention, the court officer shall provide the requested information or document to the Lord Chancellor forthwith.

(2) In this rule, 'relevant court' means the court at which an application under Article 56 of the Maintenance Regulation or Article 10 of the 2007 Hague Convention has been filed.

[The Lord Chancellor is the Central Authority for the 2007 Hague Convention and the Maintenance Regulation]

Amendments—Inserted by SI 2012/2806.

34.36C The Maintenance Regulation: applications for enforcement or for refusal or suspension of enforcement

Practice Direction 34E makes provision regarding –

(a) an application for enforcement of a maintenance decision to which section 1 of Chapter IV of the Maintenance Regulation applies; and .
(b) an application by a debtor under Article 21 of the Maintenance Regulation for refusal or suspension of enforcement.

Amendments—Inserted by SI 2013/3204.

Section 2
Reciprocal enforcement in a Contracting State or a Member State of the European Union of Orders of a court in England and Wales

34.37 *(revoked)*

34.38 Admissibility of documents

(1) This rule applies to a document, referred to in paragraph (2) and authenticated in accordance with paragraph (3), which comprises, records or summarises evidence given in, or information relating to, proceedings in a court in another part of the UK, another Contracting State to the 1968 Convention or the 1988 Convention, Member State of the European Union or State bound by the Lugano Convention, or by the 2007 Hague Convention, and any reference in this rule to 'the court', without more, is a reference to that court.

(2) The documents referred to at paragraph (1) are documents which purport to –

- (a) set out or summarise evidence given to the court;
- (b) have been received in evidence to the court;
- (c) set out or summarise evidence taken in the court for the purpose of proceedings in a court in England and Wales to which the 1982 Act, the Judgments Regulation, the Maintenance Regulation or the 2007 Hague Convention applies; or
- (d) record information relating to payments made under an order of the court.

(3) A document to which paragraph (1) applies shall, in any proceedings in the family court relating to a maintenance order to which the 1982 Act, the Judgments Regulation, the Maintenance Regulation or the 2007 Hague Convention applies, be admissible as evidence of any fact stated in it to the same extent as oral evidence of that fact is admissible in those proceedings.

(4) A document to which paragraph (1) applies shall be deemed to be authenticated –

- (a) in relation to the documents listed at paragraph 2(a) or (c), if the document purports to be –
  - (i) certified by the judge or official before whom the evidence was given or taken; or
  - (ii) the original document recording or summarising the evidence, or a true copy of that document;
- (b) in relation to a document listed at paragraph (2)(b), if the document purports to be certified by a judge or official of the court to be, or to be a true copy of, the document received in evidence; and
- (c) in relation to the document listed at paragraph (2)(d), if the document purports to be certified by a judge or official of the court as a true record of the payments made under the order.

(5) It shall not be necessary in any proceedings in which evidence is to be received under this rule to prove the signature or official position of the person appearing to have given the certificate referred to in paragraph (4).

(6) Nothing in this rule shall prejudice the admission in evidence of any document which is admissible in evidence apart from this rule.

(7) Any request by the family court for the taking or providing of evidence by a court in a State listed in paragraph (8) for the purposes of proceedings to which an instrument listed in that paragraph applies, or by a court in another part of the United Kingdom, shall be communicated in writing to the court in question.

(8) The States and instruments referred to in paragraph (7) are –

- (a) a Contracting State to the 1968 Convention;
- (b) a Contracting State to the 1988 Convention;
- (c) a State bound by the Lugano Convention;
- (d) Denmark, in relation to proceedings to which the Maintenance Regulation applies;
- (e) a State bound by the 2007 Hague Convention,

but this paragraph and paragraph (7) do not apply where the State in question is a Member State of the European Union to which the Taking of Evidence Regulation (as defined in rule 24.15) applies.

(Chapter 2 of Part 24 makes provision for taking of evidence by a court in another Member State of the European Union).

Amendments—SI 2011/1328; SI 2012/2806; SI 2013/3204.

34.39 Enforcement of orders of the family court

(1) A person who wishes to enforce a maintenance order obtained in the family court in a State to which paragraph (2) applies must apply for a certified copy of the order and, where required by Practice Direction 34A, a certificate giving particulars relating to the judgment and proceedings in which it was given.

(2) The States referred to in paragraph (1) are –

(a) a Contracting State to the 1968 Convention;
(b) a Contracting State to the 1988 Convention (other than a Member State of the European Union);
(c) a Member State of the European Union;
(d) a State bound by the Lugano Convention (other than a Member State of the European Union); or
(e) a State bound by the 2007 Hague Convention (other than a Member State of the European Union).

(3) An application under this rule must be made in writing to the court officer and must specify –

(a) the names of the parties to the proceedings;
(b) the date, or approximate date, of the proceedings in which the maintenance order was made and the nature of those proceedings;
(c) the State in which the application for recognition or enforcement has been made or is to be made; and
(d) the postal address of the applicant.

(4) The court officer must, on receipt of the application, send a copy of the order to the applicant certified in accordance with practice direction 34A, together with a copy of any certificate required by that practice direction.

(5) Paragraph (6) applies where –

(a) a maintenance order is registered in the family court; and
(b) a person wishes to obtain a certificate giving details of any payments made or arrears accrued under the order while it has been registered, for the purposes of an application made or to be made in connection with that order in –
   (i) another Contracting State to the 1968 Convention;
   (ii) another Contracting State to the 1988 Convention (other than a Member State of the European Union);
   (iii) another Member State of the European Union;
   (iv) another State bound by the Lugano Convention (other than a Member State of the European Union);
   (v) another part of the United Kingdom; or
   (vi) another State bound by the 2007 Hague Convention (other than a Member State of the European Union).

(6) The person wishing to obtain the certificate referred to in paragraph (5) may make a written application to the court officer for the registering court.

(7) On receipt of an application under paragraph (6) the court officer must send to the applicant a certificate giving the information requested.

(Rule 74.12 (application for certified copy of a judgment) and 74.13 (evidence in support) of the CPR apply in relation to the application for a certified copy of a judgment obtained in the High Court or a county court.)

Amendments—SI 2011/1328; SI 2012/679; SI 2012/2806; SI 2013/3204.

34.40 Enforcement of orders of the High Court or the family court

(1) This rule applies where a person wishes to enforce a maintenance order obtained in the High Court or the family court in a Member State of the European Union or a State bound by the 2007 Hague Convention (other than a Member State of the European Union).

(2) Subject to the requirements of Practice Direction 34A, rules 74.12 (application for a certified copy of a judgment) and 74.13 (evidence in support) of the CPR apply in relation to –

(a) an application under Article 40(2) of the Maintenance Regulation for a certified copy of a judgment and an extract relating to that judgment in the form of Annex II to that Regulation;

(b) an application for a certified copy of a judgment and a certificate giving particulars relating to the judgment and the proceedings in which it was given.

Amendments—Inserted by SI 2011/1328. Substituted by SI 2012/2806. Amended by SI 2013/3204.

PART III

Practice Direction 34A – Reciprocal Enforcement of Maintenance Orders

This Practice Direction supplements FPR Part 34

Note—FPR PD34A remains in force unamended, notwithstanding the application of the EU Maintenance Regulation (Council Regulation (EC) No 4/2009) from 18 June 2011. For cases concerning the Republic of Ireland, or those European Union Member States that are Contracting Parties to the 1973 Hague Convention on the Recognition and Enforcement of Decisions Relating to Maintenance Obligations, reference should be had to FPR PD34C, which identifies the transitional arrangements for these cases.

Noting Record of Means of Payment

1.1 Where the family court orders payments under a maintenance order to which Part 34 applies to be made in a particular way, the court must record that on a copy of the order.

1.2 If the court orders payment to be made to the court by a method referred to in section 1(5) of the Maintenance Enforcement Act 1991, the court may vary the method of payment on the application of an interested party and where it does so the court must record the variation on a copy of the order.

(Section 1(5) refers to payment by standing order or other methods which require transfer between accounts of a specific amount on a specific date during the period for which the authority to make the payment is in force.)

Notification by court officer

2.1 The court officer must, as soon as practicable, notify in writing the person liable to make the payments of the method by which they must be made.

2.2 If the court orders payment to be made to the court by a method referred to in section 1(5) of the Maintenance Enforcement Act 1991 the court officer must inform the person liable to make the payments of the number and location of the account to which the payments must be made.

2.3 If, on application, the court varies the method of payment, the court officer will notify all parties of the result of the application, in writing and as soon as possible.

Applications under section 2 of the 1920 Act

3.1 This paragraph refers to an application for the transmission of a maintenance order to a reciprocating country under section 2 of the 1920 Act in accordance with rule 34.10.

3.2 The applicant's written evidence must include such information as may be required by the law of the reciprocating country for the purpose of enforcement of the order.

3.3 If, in accordance with section 2 of the 1920 Act, the court sends a maintenance order to the Lord Chancellor for transmission to a reciprocating country, it shall record the fact in the court records.

Applications under section 2 of the 1972 Act (rule 34.14)

Introduction

4.1 An application for a maintenance order to be sent to a reciprocating country under section 2 of the 1972 Act is made by lodging specified documents with the court. The documents to be lodged vary according to which country it is intended that the maintenance order is be sent and the requirements are set out in this paragraph.

General provision

4.2 The general requirement is that the following documents should be lodged with the court –

(a) an affidavit by the applicant stating –
  (i) the reason that the applicant has for believing that the payer under the maintenance order is residing in the reciprocating country; and
  (ii) the amount of any arrears due to the applicant under the order, the date to which those arrears have been calculated and the date on which the next payment under the order falls due;

(b) a certified copy of the maintenance order;

(c) a statement giving such information as the applicant has as to the whereabouts of the payer;

(d) a statement giving such information as the applicant has for facilitating the identification of the payer, (including, if known to the applicant, the name and address of any employer of the payer, his occupation and the date and place of issue of any passport of the payer); and

(e) if available to the applicant, a photograph of the payer.

…

Hague Convention Country

4.5 If the country to which it is intended to send the maintenance order is a Hague Convention country (as defined in rule 34.12), then the following changes to the general requirements apply.

4.6 In addition to the matters stated in that paragraph, the affidavit referred to in paragraph 4.2(a) must also state whether the time for appealing against the maintenance order has expired and whether an appeal is pending.

4.7 The applicant must lodge the following documents with the court in addition to those set out in paragraph 4.2 –

(a) a statement as to whether or not the payer appeared in the proceedings in which the maintenance order was made;

(b) if the payer did not so appear –
  (i) the original of a document which establishes that notice of the institution of proceedings, including notice of the substance of the claim, was served on the payer; or
  (ii) a copy of such a document certified by the applicant or the applicant's solicitor to be a true copy;

(c) a document which establishes that notice of the order was sent to the payer;

(d) a written statement as to whether or not the payee received legal aid in the proceedings in which the order was made, or in connection with the application under section 2 of the 1972 Act; and

(e) if the payee did receive legal aid, a copy certified by the applicant or the applicant's solicitor to be a true copy of the legal aid certificate.

United States of America

4.8 If the country to which it is intended to send the maintenance order is the United States of America, then the following changes to the general requirements apply.

4.9 There is no requirement to lodge a statement giving information as to the whereabouts of the payer since this information must be contained in the affidavit as mentioned in paragraph 4.10.

4.10 In addition to the matters stated in that paragraph, the affidavit referred to in paragraph 4.2(*a*) must also state –

(a) the address of the payee;
(b) such information as is known as to the whereabouts of the payer; and
(c) a description, so far as is known, of the nature and location of any assets of the payer available for execution.

4.11 The applicant must lodge three certified copies of the maintenance order.

Transitional Provision in respect of the United States of America

4A.1 Where, by virtue of article 6(2) of the Reciprocal Enforcement of Maintenance Orders (United States of America) Order 2007, the Reciprocal Enforcement of Maintenance Orders (United States of America) Order 1995 continues in full force and effect, the FPR shall apply with such modifications as are necessary.

Notification to the Lord Chancellor

5.1 Where, in accordance with Part 1 of the 1972 Act, the family court registers a maintenance order sent to it from a Hague Convention Country, the court officer must send written notice of the registration to the Lord Chancellor.

Notification of means of enforcement

6.1 The court officer of the family court must take reasonable steps to notify the person to whom payments are due under a registered order of the means of enforcement available in respect of it.

6.2 (*omitted*)

Certified copies of orders issued under rule 34.39 or 34.40

7.1 In an application under rule 34.39 or 34.40 by a person wishing to enforce abroad a maintenance order, the certified copy of the order will be a sealed copy and will be accompanied by a certificate signed by the court officer.

7.2 In an application under the 1982 Act, the certificate signed by the court officer must state that it is a true copy of the order concerned and must give particulars of the proceedings in which it was made.

7.3 In an application under the Judgments Regulation, the certificate will be in the form of Annex V to the Regulation.

7.4 In an application under the Lugano Convention, the certificate will be in the form of Annex V to the Convention.

7.5 In an application under the Maintenance Regulation, the certificate will be in the form of Annex II to that Regulation.

7.6 In an application under the 2007 Hague Convention, the certificate will be comprised of the following Article 11 forms duly completed by the court officer –

(a) the Abstract of a Decision;
(b) the Statement of Enforceability; and
(c) the Statement of Proper Notice.

7.7 In an application under the 2007 Hague Convention, the certificate will additionally state the jurisdictional basis upon which the order was made, with reference to the jurisdictional criteria in Article 20(1) of that Convention to be applied by the State in which recognition and/or enforcement is to be sought.

Countries and Territories in which Sums are Payable through Crown Agents for Overseas Governments and Territories (rule 34.23)

8.1 Gibraltar, Barbados, Bermuda, Ghana, Kenya, Fiji, Hong Kong, Singapore, Turks and Caicos Islands, United Republic of Tanzania (except Zanzibar), Anguilla, Falkland Islands and Dependencies, St Helena.

Part 1 of the 1972 Act – Modified Rules

9.1 The annexes to this Practice Direction set out rules 34.14 to 34.25 as they are modified –

(a) in relation to the Republic of Ireland, by rule 34.26 (Annex 1) (but see the note in that Annex regarding the ongoing relevance of those rules following revocation of rule 34.26);
(b) in relation to the Hague Convention Countries, by rule 34.27 (Annex 2); and
(c) in relation to the United States of America, by rule 34.28 (Annex 3).

9.2 The statutory references in the annexes are construed in accordance with rule 34.26(2), 34.27(2) or 34.28(2) as the case may be.

ANNEX 1 – APPLICATION OF SECTION 1 OF CHAPTER 2 OF PART 34 TO THE REPUBLIC OF IRELAND

NOTE—Rule 34.26 was revoked by SI 2011/1328. Reciprocal enforcement of maintenance as between the UK and the Irish Republic has been governed by the Maintenance Regulation (Council Regulation (EC) no 4/2009) since 18 June 2011 and the relevant rules for that Regulation are contained in Chapter 3 of Part 34 of the Rules. The provisions of this Annex are therefore of relevance only where either –

(a) the application for registration of an order relating to an Irish maintenance order was made on or before 18 June 2011 and was still pending on that date; or
(b) the order was registered prior to 18 June 2011.

All other applications are governed by the Maintenance Regulation. Practice Direction 34C provides further information regarding which rules apply to applications relating to other European Union Member States.

34.14 Application for transmission of maintenance order to the Republic of Ireland

An application for a maintenance order to be sent to the Republic of Ireland under section 2 of the 1972 Act must be made in accordance with Practice Direction 34A.

34.15 Certification of evidence given on provisional orders

A document setting out or summarising evidence is authenticated by a court in England and Wales by a certificate signed, as appropriate, by –

(a) one of the justices; or
(b) the District Judge (Magistrates' Courts),

before whom that evidence was given.

(Section 3(5)(b) or 5(3) of the 1972 Act require a document to be authenticated by the court.)

34.16 Confirmation of a provisional order…

[This rule does not apply to the Republic of Ireland]

34.17 Consideration of confirmation of a provisional order made by a magistrates' court

(1) This rule applies where–

(a) a magistrates' court has made a provisional order by virtue of section 3 of the 1972 Act;
(b) the payer has made representations or adduced evidence to the court; and

(c) the court has fixed a date for the hearing at which it will consider confirmation of the order.

(2) The court officer must serve on the applicant for the provisional order –

(a) a copy of the representations or evidence; and
(b) written notice of the date fixed for the hearing.

34.18 Notification of variation or revocation of a maintenance order by the High Court

Where the High Court makes an order varying or revoking an order to which section 5 of the 1972 Act applies the court officer must send –

(a) a certified copy of the order of variation or revocation; and
(b) a statement as to the service on the payer of the documents mentioned in section 5(3) of the 1972 Act;

to the court in the Republic of Ireland.

(Rule 34.22 provides for the transmission of documents to a court in a reciprocating country.)

34.19 Notification of revocation of a maintenance order by a magistrates' court

Where a magistrates' court makes an order revoking an order to which section 5 of the 1972 Act applies, the court officer must send written notice of the making of the order to the Lord Chancellor.

(Section 5 of the 1972 Act applies to a maintenance order sent to the Republic of Ireland in accordance with section 2 of that Act and a provisional order made by a magistrates' court in accordance with section 3 of that Act which has been confirmed by such a court.)

(Provision in respect of notification of variation of a maintenance order by a magistrates' court under the 1972 Act is made in Rules made under section 144 of the Magistrates' Courts Act 1980.)

34.20 Taking of evidence for court in the Republic of Ireland

(1) This rule applies where a request is made by or on behalf of a court in the Republic of Ireland for the taking of evidence for the purpose of proceedings relating to a maintenance order to which Part 1 of the 1972 Act applies.

(Section 14 of the 1972 Act makes provision for the taking of evidence needed for the purpose of certain proceedings.)

(2) The High Court has power to take the evidence where –

(a) the request for evidence relates to a maintenance order made by a superior court in the United Kingdom; and
(b) the witness resides in England and Wales.

(3) The county court has power to take the evidence where –

(a) the request for evidence relates to a maintenance order made by a county court; and
(b) the maintenance order has not been registered in a magistrates' court under the 1958 Act.

(4) The following magistrates' courts have power to take the evidence, that is –

(a) where the proceedings in the Republic of Ireland relate to a maintenance order made by a magistrates' court, the court which made the order;
(b) where the proceedings relate to an order which is registered in a magistrates' court, the court in which the order is registered; and
(c) a magistrates' court to which the Secretary of State sends the request to take evidence.

(5) A magistrates' court not mentioned in paragraph (4) has power to take the evidence if the magistrates' court which would otherwise have that power consents because the evidence could be taken more conveniently.

PART III

(6) The evidence is to be taken in accordance with Part 22.

34.21 Request for the taking of evidence by a court

[This rule does not apply to the Republic of Ireland]

34.22 Transmission of documents

(1) This rule applies to any document, including a notice or request, which is required to be sent to a court in the Republic of Ireland by –

(a) Part 1 of the 1972 Act; or
(b) Section 1 of Chapter 2 of this Part of these Rules.

(2) The document must be sent to the Lord Chancellor for transmission to the court in the Republic of Ireland.

34.23 Method of payment under registered orders

(1) Where an order is registered in a magistrates' court in accordance with section 6(3) of the 1972 Act, the court must order that the payment of sums due under the order be made –

(a) to the court officer for the registering court; and
(b) at such time and place as the court officer directs.

(Section 6(3) of the 1972 Act makes provision for the registration of maintenance orders made in the Republic of Ireland.)

(2) Where the court orders payment to be made to the court officer, the court officer must send the payments by post –

(a) to the payee under the order; or
(b) where a public authority has been authorised by the payee to receive the payments, to that public authority.

(Practice Direction 34A contains further provisions relating to the payment of sums due under registered orders.)

34.24 Enforcement of payments under registered orders

(1) This rule applies where periodical payments under a registered order are in arrears.

(2) The court officer must, on the written request of the payee, proceed in that officer's own name for the recovery of the sums due unless of the view that it is unreasonable to do so.

(3) If the sums due are more than 4 weeks in arrears the court officer must give the payee notice in writing of that fact stating the particulars of the arrears.

34.25 Notification of registration and cancellation

The court officer must send written notice to –

(a) the Lord Chancellor, on the due registration of an order under section 6(3) or 10(4) of the 1972 Act; and
(b) to the payer under the order, on –
    (i) the registration of an order under section 10(4) of the 1972 Act; or
    (ii) the cancellation of the registration of an order under section 10(1) of that Act.

34.25A Other notices under section 6 of the 1972 Act

(1) A notice required under section 6(6) or (10) of the 1972 Act must be in the form referred to in a practice direction.

(2) Where a magistrates' court sets aside the registration of an order following an appeal under section 6(7) of the 1972 Act, the court officer must send written notice of the court's decision to the payee.

(Section 6(6) of the 1972 Act provides for notice of registration in a United Kingdom court of a maintenance order made in the Republic of Ireland, and section 6(10) of that Act for notice that a maintenance order made in the Republic of Ireland has not been registered in a United Kingdom court.)

ANNEX 2 – APPLICATION OF SECTION 1 OF CHAPTER 2 OF PART 34 TO THE HAGUE CONVENTION COUNTRIES

34.14 Application for transmission of maintenance order to a Hague Convention Country

An application for a maintenance order to be sent to a Hague Convention Country under section 2 of the 1972 Act must be made in accordance with Practice Direction 34A.

34.15 Certification of evidence given on provisional orders

[This rule does not apply to the Hague Convention Countries]

34.16 Confirmation of a provisional order made in a reciprocating country

[This rule does not apply to the Hague Convention Countries]

34.17 Consideration of revocation of a maintenance order made by a magistrates' court

(1) This rule applies where –

- (a) an application has been made to a magistrates' court by a payee for the revocation of an order to which section 5 of the 1972 Act applies; and
- (b) the payer resides in a Hague Convention Country.

(2) The court officer must serve on the payee, by post, a copy of any representations or evidence adduced by or on behalf of the payer.

(Provision relating to consideration of variation of a maintenance order made by a magistrates' court to which section 5 of the 1972 Act applies is made in Rules made under section 144 of the Magistrates' Courts Act 1980.)

34.18 Notification of variation or revocation of a maintenance order by the High Court or a county court

(1) This rule applies if the High Court or a county court makes an order varying or revoking a maintenance order to which section 5 of the 1972 Act applies.

(2) If the time for appealing has expired without an appeal having been entered, the court officer will send to the Lord Chancellor –

- (a) the documents required by section 5(8) of the 1972 Act; and
- (b) a certificate signed by the district judge stating that the order of variation or revocation is enforceable and no longer subject to the ordinary forms of review.

(3) A party who enters an appeal against the order of variation or revocation must, at the same time, give written notice to the court officer.

34.19 Notification of confirmation or revocation of a maintenance order by a magistrates' court

[This rule does not apply to the Hague Convention Countries]

34.20 Taking of evidence for court in a Hague Convention Country

(1) This rule applies where a request is made by or on behalf of a court in a Hague Convention Country for the taking of evidence for the purpose of proceedings relating to a maintenance order to which Part 1 of the 1972 Act applies.

(Section 14 of the 1972 Act makes provision for the taking of evidence needed for the purpose of certain proceedings.)

PART III

(2) The High court has power to take the evidence where –

(a) the request for evidence relates to a maintenance order made by a superior court in the United Kingdom: and
(b) the witness resides in England and Wales.

(3) The county court has power to take the evidence where –

(a) the request for evidence relates to a maintenance order made by a county court; and
(b) the maintenance order has not been registered in a magistrates' court under the 1958 Act.

(4) The following magistrates' courts have power to take the evidence, that is –

(a) where the proceedings in the Hague Convention Country relate to a maintenance order made by a magistrates' court, the court which made the order;
(b) where the proceedings relate to an order which is registered in a magistrates' court, the court in which the order is registered; and
(c) a magistrates' court to which the Secretary of State sends the request to take evidence.

(5) A magistrates' court not mentioned in paragraph (4) has power to take the evidence if the magistrates' court which would otherwise have that power consents because the evidence could be taken more conveniently.

(6) The evidence is to be taken in accordance with Part 22.

34.21 Request for the taking of evidence by a court in a Hague Convention country
[This rule does not apply to the Hague Convention countries.]

34.22 Transmission of documents
(1) This rule applies to any document, including a notice or request, which is required to be sent to a court in a Hague Convention country by –

(a) Part 1 of the 1972 Act; or
(b) Section 1 of Chapter 2 of this Part of these Rules.

(2) The document must be sent to the Lord Chancellor for transmission to the court in the Hague Convention country.

34.23 Method of payment under registered orders
(1) Where an order is registered in a magistrates' court in accordance with section 6(3) of the 1972 Act, the court must order that the payment of sums due under the order be made –

(a) to the court officer for the registering court; and
(b) at such time and place as the court officer directs.

(Section 6(3) of the 1972 Act makes provision for the registration of maintenance orders made in a Hague Convention country.)

(2) Where the court orders payment to be made to the court officer, the court officer must send the payments by post to the payee under the order.

(Practice Direction 34A contains further provision relating to the payment of sums due under registered orders.)

34.24 Enforcement of payments under registered orders

(1) This rule applies where a court has ordered periodical payments under a registered maintenance order to be made to the court officer.

(2) The court officer must take reasonable steps to notify the payee of the means of enforcement available.

(3) Paragraph (4) applies where periodical payments due under a registered order are in arrears.

(4) The court officer, on that officer's own initiative –

(a) may; or
(b) if the sums due are more than 4 weeks in arrears, must,

proceed in that officer's own name for the recovery of the sums due unless of the view that it is unreasonable to do so.

34.25 Notification of registration and cancellation

The court officer must send written notice to –

(a) the Lord Chancellor, on the due registration of an order under section 10(4) of the 1972 Act; and
(b) the payer under the order, on –
  (i) the registration of an order under section 10(4) of the 1972 Act; or
  (ii) the cancellation of the registration of an order under section 10(1) of the 1972 Act.

34.25A General provisions as to notices

(1) A notice to a payer of the registration of an order in a magistrates' court in accordance with section 6(3) of the 1972 Act must be in the form referred to in a practice direction.

(Section 6(8) of the 1972 Act requires notice of registration to be given to the payer.)

(2) If the court sets aside the registration of a maintenance order following an appeal under section 6(9) of the 1972 Act, the court officer must send written notice of the decision to the Lord Chancellor.

(3) A notice to a payee that the court officer has refused to register an order must be in the form referred to in a practice direction.

(Section 6(11) of the 1972 Act requires notice of refusal of registration to be given to the payee.)

(4) Where, under any provision of Part 1 of the 1972 Act, a court officer serves a notice on a payer who resides in a Hague Convention Country, the court officer must send to the Lord Chancellor a certificate of service.

ANNEX 3 – APPLICATION OF SECTION 1 OF CHAPTER 2 OF PART 34 TO THE UNITED STATES OF AMERICA

34.14 Application for transmission of maintenance order to the United States of America

An application for a maintenance order to be sent to the United States of America under section 2 of the 1972 Act must be made in accordance with Practice Direction 34A.

34.15 Certification of evidence given on provisional orders

[This rule does not apply to the United States of America]

34.16 Confirmation of a provisional order made in a reciprocating country

[This rule does not apply to the United States of America]

34.17 Consideration of revocation of a maintenance order made by a magistrates' court

(1) This rule applies where –

(a) an application has been made to a magistrates' court by a payee for the revocation of an order to which section 5 of the 1972 Act applies; and
(b) the payer resides in the United States of America.

(2) The court officer must serve on the payee by post a copy of any representations or evidence adduced by or on behalf of the payer.

(Provision relating to consideration of variation of a maintenance order made by a magistrates' court to which section 5 of the 1972 Act applies is made in rules made under section 144 of the Magistrates' Courts Act 1980.)

34.18 Notification of variation or revocation

If the High Court or a county court makes an order varying or revoking a maintenance order to which section 5 of the 1972 Act applies, the court officer will send to the Lord Chancellor the documents required by section 5(7) of that Act.

34.19 Notification of confirmation or revocation of a maintenance order by a magistrates' court

[This rule does not apply to the United States of America]

34.20 Taking of evidence for court in United States of America

(1) This rule applies where a request is made by or on behalf of a court in the United States of America for the taking of evidence for the purpose of proceedings relating to a maintenance order to which Part 1 of the 1972 Act applies.

(Section 14 of the 1972 Act makes provision for the taking of evidence needed for the purpose of certain proceedings.)

(2) The High Court has power to take the evidence where –

(a) the request for evidence relates to a maintenance order made by a superior court in the United Kingdom; and
(b) the witness resides in England and Wales.

(3) The county court has power to take the evidence where –

(a) the request for evidence relates to a maintenance order made by a county court; and
(b) the maintenance order has not been registered in a magistrates' court under the 1958 Act.

(4) The following magistrates' courts have power to take the evidence, that is –

(a) where the proceedings in the United States of America relate to a maintenance order made by a magistrates' court, the court which made the order;
(b) where the proceedings relate to an order which is registered in a magistrates' court, the court in which the order is registered; and
(c) a magistrates' court to which the Secretary of State sends the request to take evidence.

(5) A magistrates' court not mentioned in paragraph (4) has power to take the evidence if the magistrates' court which would otherwise have that power consents because the evidence could be taken more conveniently.

(6) The evidence is to be taken in accordance with Part 22.

34.21 Request for the taking of evidence by a court in a reciprocating country

[This rule does not apply to the United States of America]

34.22 Transmission of documents

(1) This rule applies to any document, including a notice or request, which is required to be sent to a court in the United States of America by –

(a) Part 1 of the 1972 Act; or
(b) Section 1 of Chapter 2 of this Part of these Rules.

(2) The document must be sent to the Lord Chancellor for transmission to the court in the United States of America.

34.23 Method of payment under registered orders

(1) Where an order is registered in a magistrates' court in accordance with section 6(3) of the 1972 Act, the court must order that the payment of sums due under the order be made –

(a) to the court officer for the registering court; and
(b) at such time and place as the court officer directs.

(Section 6(3) of the 1972 Act makes provision for the registration of maintenance orders made in the United States of America.)

(2) Where the court orders payment to be made to the court officer, the court officer must send the payments by post to the payee under the order.

(Practice Direction 34A contains further provisions relating to the payment of sums due under registered orders.)

34.24 Enforcement of payments under registered orders

(1) This rule applies where a court has ordered periodical payments under a registered maintenance order to be made to the court officer.

(2) The court officer must take reasonable steps to notify the payee of the means of enforcement available.

(3) Paragraph (4) applies where periodical payments due under a registered order are in arrears.

(4) The court officer, on that officer's own initiative –

(a) may; or
(b) if the sums due are more than 4 weeks in arrears, must,

proceed in that officer's own name for the recovery of the sums due unless of the view that it is unreasonable to do so.

34.25 Notification of registration and cancellation

The court officer must send written notice to –

(a) the Lord Chancellor, on the due registration of an order under section 10(4) of the 1972 Act; or
(b) the payer under the order, on –
  (i) the registration of an order under section 10(4) of the 1972 Act; or
  (ii) the cancellation of the registration of an order under section 10(1) of that Act.

Practice Direction 34B – Practice Note (Tracing Payers Overseas)

This Practice Direction supplements FPR Part 34

Difficulties can arise where a person in this country wishes to take proceedings under the Maintenance Orders (Facilities for Enforcement) Act 1920 or Part I of the Maintenance Orders (Reciprocal Enforcement) Act 1972 to obtain or enforce a maintenance order against a payer living overseas whose address is unknown to the applicant.

To mitigate these difficulties, arrangements have now been made with the appropriate authorities in Australia, Canada, New Zealand and South Africa, whereby the court may on request ask the authorities in those countries to make enquiries with a view to tracing the whereabouts of the payer. The following procedure should be followed.

On or before an application is made for a provisional maintenance order, or for transmission of an absolute maintenance order under the above Acts by an applicant who does not know the payer's actual address in either Australia, Canada, New Zealand or South Africa, there should be completed and lodged with the [court] a questionnaire, in duplicate, ([Principal] Registry Form D312 or family court Form D85 as appropriate) obtainable from the registry or court office, together with a written undertaking from the solicitor (or from the applicant if acting in person) that any address of the payer received in response to the enquiries will not be disclosed or used except for the purpose of the proceedings.

This Note is issued [in its original form] with the concurrence of the Lord Chancellor.

Practice Direction 34C – Applications for Recognition and Enforcement To or From European Union Member States

This Practice Direction supplements FPR Part 34

This Practice Direction supplementing the Family Procedure Rules 2010 is made by the President of the Family Division under the powers delegated to him by the Lord Chief Justice under Schedule 2, Part 1, paragraph 2(2) of the Constitutional Reform Act 2005, and is agreed by Lord McNally, Minister of State, by the authority of the Lord Chancellor.

This Practice Direction comes into force on 31 October 2011.

1 *Introduction*

1.1 The Maintenance Regulation (Council Regulation (EC) No 4/2009 of 18 December 2008 on jurisdiction, applicable law, recognition and enforcement of decisions and cooperation in matters relating to maintenance obligations) ('the Maintenance Regulation') applies across the European Union from 18 June 2011. It applies to all cases for recognition and enforcement in or from a European Union Member State from that date. The domestic legislation facilitating the application of the Maintenance Regulation is the Civil Jurisdiction and Judgments (Maintenance) Regulations 2011[1] ('the CJJMR').

1 SI 2011/1484.

2 The Member States of the European Union are: Austria, Belgium, Bulgaria, Cyprus, Czech Republic, Denmark, Estonia, Finland, France, Germany, Greece, Hungary, Ireland, Italy, Latvia, Lithuania, Luxembourg, Malta, The Netherlands, Poland, Portugal, Romania, Slovakia, Slovenia, Spain, Sweden, and the United Kingdom.

2 *Relationship between the Maintenance Regulation and other international instruments*

2.1 The Maintenance Regulation replaces the relevant provisions of Regulation (EC) No 44/2001 of 22 December 2000 on jurisdiction and the recognition and enforcement of judgments in civil and commercial matters (known as 'Brussels I'), subject to the transitional provisions of Article 75. It will also take precedence over any other international conventions and agreements concerning matters which the Maintenance Regulation governs as regards relations between Member States. In particular (and subject to the relevant transitional provisions (discussed below)), the Maintenance Regulation must be applied between Member States instead of the following:

- (a) The Convention on the Recognition and Enforcement of Decisions Relating to Maintenance Obligations done at The Hague on 2 October 1973 ('the 1973 Convention');[2]
- (b) the arrangements for reciprocal enforcement of maintenance between the United Kingdom and the Republic of Ireland reflected in the Reciprocal Enforcement of Maintenance Orders (Republic of Ireland) Order 1993[3] ('the Republic of Ireland Order');
- (c) as regards Malta, the provisions of the Maintenance Orders (Reciprocal Enforcement) Act 1972 Part 1 ('the 1972 Act');

(d) the United Nations Convention on the Recovery Abroad of Maintenance done at New York on 20 June 1956 ('the 1956 New York Convention') (applied in England and Wales by Part II of the Maintenance Orders (Reciprocal Enforcement) Act 1972) (this Convention is concerned with the reciprocal treatment of applications for maintenance rather than reciprocal enforcement of orders, but is included here for clarity).

2 This Convention previously governed relations between the UK and other European Union Member States which were Contracting Parties to it, rather than Brussels I. Those Member States were – the Czech Republic, Denmark, Germany, Finland, France, Italy, Luxembourg, the Netherlands, Portugal, Estonia, Poland, Slovakia, Spain, and Sweden. The arrangements in the Reciprocal Enforcement of Maintenance Orders (Hague Convention Countries) Order 1993 (SI 1993/593) ('the Hague Convention Countries Order') no longer apply in relations with these countries.

3 SI 1993/594.

3 Application of the Maintenance Regulation rules to recognition, registration and enforcement in England and Wales of an order from another Member State

3.1 For an application for enforcement of a maintenance order from another European Union Member State which applies the 2007 Hague Protocol on the Law Applicable to Maintenance Orders (all other Member States except Denmark), the court will apply the rules in Sections 1 and 3 of Chapter IV of the Maintenance Regulation. Orders from such Member States are not subject to registration and benefit from direct enforceability in the family court in the same manner as an order for maintenance which had been made in proceedings in England and Wales. Rule 34.36C of the Family Procedure Rules 2010 and Practice Direction 34E make provision for such cases.

3.2 For an application from another European Union Member State which does not apply the 2007 Hague Protocol on the Law Applicable to Maintenance Orders (namely Denmark), the court will apply the rules in Sections 2 and 3 of Chapter IV of the Maintenance Regulation. These orders do require registration before they can be enforced and Section 1 of Chapter 3 of Part 34 of the Family Procedure Rules 2010 applies to these cases.

4 Application of the Maintenance Regulation to recognition and enforcement of a maintenance order from England and Wales in another Member State

4.1 Where recognition and enforcement of an England and Wales maintenance order is sought in another European Union Member State, the courts and authorities of that Member State will apply Sections 2 and 3 of Chapter IV of the Maintenance Regulation, because the United Kingdom is not a State Party to the 2007 Hague Protocol (and consequently courts and authorities of the United Kingdom are not bound to apply 'applicable law' rules to the initial decision). Section 2 of Chapter 3 of Part 34 of the Family Procedure Rules 2010 applies to those decisions.

5 Transitional cases

5.1 The Maintenance Regulation makes specific provision for transitional cases in Article 75. The general rule is provided by Article 75(1), whereby the Regulation applies only to proceedings instituted after its date of application (18 June 2011). However, special rules apply in relation to applications from another European Union Member State for recognition or recognition and enforcement:

(a) Where the maintenance decision was given in any Member State prior to 18 June 2011, but recognition and enforcement are sought after that date, the court will apply the rules of Sections 2 and 3 of Chapter IV.

(b) Where the maintenance decision was given in any Member State after 18 June 2011 but the proceedings for that decision were commenced prior to that date, the court will also apply the rules of Sections 2 and 3 of Chapter IV.

(c) Where there is an application in progress on 18 June 2011 for recognition and enforcement under Council Regulation (EC) No 44/2001 (Brussels I) relating to a maintenance decision from a Member State, the court will apply the rules of Chapter III of Brussels I.

PART III

5.2 It will therefore be seen that, for transitional cases (a) and (b) above, Section 1 of Chapter IV will not be used, regardless of whether the Member State in question applies the 2007 Hague Protocol – the arrangements are the same for all Member States.

5.3 As stated in paragraph 2.1 above, the Maintenance Regulation will apply as between Member States instead of other existing international agreements dealing with the same matters. The provisions of 5.1(a) and (b) above apply in all cases. Where relations in maintenance matters between the United Kingdom and another Member State were governed by Brussels I prior to the application of the Maintenance Regulation, the transitional arrangements in paragraph 5.1(c) above will apply, and transitional arrangements regarding rules of court for such cases are made in rule 38 of the Family Procedure (Amendment) Rules 2011[5].

5 SI 2011/1328.

5.4 Where maintenance matters between the United Kingdom and another Member State were governed by the 1973 Convention or the Republic of Ireland Order prior to 18 June 2011, the following provision is made for transitional cases:

(a) As regards cases governed by the 1973 Convention, the references in the Hague Convention Countries Order to those Member States which are party to that Convention have been revoked[6]. However, those Member States continue to be treated under that Order as Hague Convention Countries for transitional purposes[7] under the CJJMR, including those proceedings for establishment, variation, or revocation of a maintenance order, or for registration of a maintenance order, which are continuing on 18 June 2011. In those circumstances, the rules at Part 34, Chapter 2, Section 2 sub-section 2 of the Family Procedure Rules 2010 will continue to apply to those proceedings.

(b) In relation to cases concerning the Republic of Ireland, the Republic of Ireland Order has been revoked[8]. Transitional provision is made by paragraph 28 of Schedule 7 to the CJJMR. Again, this includes provision for proceedings for establishment of maintenance, variation or revocation of an order, or for registration of an order, which are continuing on 18 June 2011. The Family Procedure Rules 2010 have been amended so that Part 34, Chapter 2, Section 2 sub-section 1 has been revoked. Provision is made for the application of those rules in transitional cases in the Family Procedure (Amendment) Rules 2011 at rule 38. Annex 1 to Practice Direction 34A (which sets out rules 34.14 to 34.25 as modified by Part 34, Chapter 2, section 2 sub- section 1 prior to its revocation) should therefore be applied in accordance with the provision in rule 38 of those Amendment Rules.

6 The Civil Jurisdiction and Judgments (Maintenance) Regulations 2011 Schedule 7 paragraph 25(2) (SI 2011/1484).

7 Schedule 7 paragraph 26 ibid.

8 Schedule 7 paragraph 27 ibid.

5.5 No specific provision is currently made in domestic law for transitional provision relating to Malta or in relation to the 1956 New York Convention as it relates to applications from European Union Member States. The position is directly governed by Article 75(1) of the Maintenance Regulation. Where proceedings have been instituted by virtue of the 1956 New York Convention or the operation of Part I of the 1972 Act on or prior to 18 June 2011 and are continuing on that date, those proceedings are not affected by Maintenance Regulation rules. Such proceedings would include applications for variation and revocation of orders as well as for establishment of a maintenance order. However, recognition and enforcement in another Member State of any resulting order would occur in accordance with the Maintenance Regulation (and the transitional provisions of Article 75(2) should be considered). Enforcement in England and Wales of orders registered under either part of the 1972 Act on or prior to 18 June 2011 will not be affected by the Maintenance Regulation.

Practice Direction 34D – Form Relating to Part 34

This Practice Direction supplements rule 34.28ZJ

1 The form referred to in rule 34.28ZJ is –

Form of Notice

Notice under section 35(3) of the Maintenance Orders (Reciprocal Enforcement) Act 1972

Family Court sitting at ....

Date:

To the defendant ....

of ....

....

[application] has been made by

The applicant ....

of ....

..... who states that by an order made on

...... under the................Act

...... by the family court

...... you were ordered as follows:-

...... and applies for that order to be [revoked] [varied by an order requiring ....]

...... on the ground that

The hearing of the application will be on:

Date of hearing............... at .... [am/pm]

at the family court sitting at ....

A.B.

Court Officer

Practice Direction 34E – Reciprocal Enforcement of Maintenance Orders – Designated Family Judge Areas

This Practice Direction supplements FPR Part 34

Maintenance Enforcement Business Centres (MEBC)—REMO work for England and Wales is administered through three Maintenance Enforcement Business Centres. Reciprocal enforcement work for the whole of England except London is administered from the Bury St Edmunds MEBC, Triton House, St Andrews Street North, Bury St Edmunds IP33 1TR; the London MEBC is located at the Central Family Court, First Avenue House, 42–49 High Holborn, London WC1V 6NP; and the MEBC for Wales is based at The Law Courts, Sunnyside, Bridgend CF31 4AJ.

Maintenance Enforcement Business Centres, Designated Family Judge areas and Designated Family Courts

1.1 Her Majesty's Courts and Tribunals Service will publish information to enable Maintenance Enforcement Business Centres of the family court, Designated Family Judge areas and Designated Family Courts to be identified.

Taking of evidence for court in reciprocating country

2.1 Rule 34.20(3) FPR sets out where the family court has power to take evidence when a request is made by or on behalf of a court in a reciprocating country for the taking of evidence for the purpose of proceedings relating to a maintenance order to which Part 1 of the 1972 Act applies.

2.2 Where rule 34.20(3) applies, the evidence will be taken by the family court sitting in the Designated Family Judge area in which the maintenance order is made or registered, or to which the Lord Chancellor sends the request to take evidence.

Notification of proceedings in a Hague Convention Country or in the United States of America

3.1 Rule 34.28ZA FPR applies where the court officer receives from the Lord Chancellor a notice of the institution of proceedings, including notice of the substance of a claim, in a Hague Convention Country or in the United States of America in relation to the making, variation or revocation of a maintenance order.

3.2 Where rule 34.28ZA applies –

(a) if it appears to the court officer that the person against whom the proceedings were instituted is residing within the area covered by the Maintenance Enforcement Business Centre in which the court officer acts, the court officer will serve the notice on that person by sending it to that person's last known or usual address;
(b) if it appears to the court officer that the person concerned is not residing within that area, the court officer must inform the Lord Chancellor and return the notice.

Registration of maintenance orders

4.1 Paragraphs 4.2 to 4.5 apply where the family court receives an application of a type referred to in rule 34.30 FPR.

4.2 The court officer will –

(a) take such steps as appear appropriate for ascertaining whether the payer resides within the area covered by the Maintenance Enforcement Business Centre to which the application has been sent; and
(b) consider any available information as to the nature and location of the payer's assets.

4.3 If the court officer is satisfied that the payer –

(a) does not reside within the area covered by the Maintenance Enforcement Business Centre to which the application has been sent; and
(b) does not have assets in that area against which the maintenance order could be enforced,

the court officer will refuse the application and return the application to the Lord Chancellor stating the information the court officer has as to the whereabouts of the payer and the nature and location of the payer's assets.

4.4 Paragraph 4.5 applies if the court officer is satisfied that the payer-

(a) does not reside within the area covered by the Maintenance Enforcement Business Centre to which the application has been sent; but
(b) has assets in that area against which the maintenance order could be enforced.

4.5 Where this paragraph applies, then either –

(a) the court officer must register the order; or
(b) if the court officer believes that the payer is residing in an area covered by a different Maintenance Enforcement Business Centre, the court officer may refuse the application and return the documents to the Lord Chancellor stating the information the court officer has as to the whereabouts of the payer and the nature and location of the payer's assets.

Appeal from a decision relating to registration

5.A1 Where rule 34.31(2) FPR applies (certain appeals to be to the family court), the appeal should be sent to the Maintenance Enforcement Business Centre that has been in most recent communication with the parties.

5.1 Where rule 34.31(2) FPR applies (certain appeals to be to the family court), the appeal should be heard in the same Designated Family Judge area in which –

(a) the order is registered; or
(b) the application for registration has been refused,

as the case may be.

Registered order: payer residing in an area covered by a different Maintenance Enforcement Business Centre

6.1 Paragraphs 6.2 to 6.5 apply where a court officer in the Maintenance Enforcement Business Centre for the Designated Family Judge area where an order is registered considers that the payer is residing in a Designated Family Judge area covered by a different Maintenance Enforcement Business Centre (rule 34.35 FPR refers).

6.2 The court officer will send to the Maintenance Enforcement Business Centre for that other area –

(a) the information and documents relating to the registration;
(b) a certificate of arrears, if applicable, signed by the court officer;
(c) a statement giving such information as the court officer possesses as to the whereabouts of the payer and the nature and location of the payer's assets; and
(d) any other relevant documents which the court officer has relating to the case.

6.3 The information and documents referred to in paragraph 6.2(a) are those required, as appropriate, under –

(a) Articles 46 and 47 of the 1968 Convention;
(b) Articles 46 and 47 of the 1988 Convention;
(c) Article 53 of the Judgments Regulation;
(d) Article 53 of the Lugano Convention;
(e) Article 28 or 29 of the Maintenance Regulation; or
(f) Article 25 or 30 of the 2007 Hague Convention.

6.4 The court officer must give notice to the payee and the Lord Chancellor that the papers have been sent to the Maintenance Enforcement Business Centre for another area.

6.5 If the papers are sent to the Maintenance Enforcement Business Centre for another area, the court officer in that Maintenance Enforcement Business Centre must note that the order has been, and remains, registered in the family court.

Application for enforcement of a maintenance decision to which Section 1 of Chapter IV of the Maintenance Regulation (rule 34.36C FPR)

7.1 An application for the enforcement of a decision (within the meaning of Article 2 of the Maintenance Regulation) to which Section 1 of Chapter IV of the Maintenance Regulation applies (that is, a decision made in any other Member State of the European Union except Denmark) will be heard by the family court sitting in the Designated Family Judge area in which-

(a) the person against whom enforcement is sought resides;
(b) that person has assets against which the decision could be enforced; or
(c) any other matter relating to enforcement arises.

7.2 Where –

(a) the applicant is the person in whose favour the order was made or, if that person is a child, is the child or the person with whom the child has his or her home;
(b) the applicant resides in a different Designated Family Judge area to the area in which the application would be heard if paragraph 7.1 applied; and
(c) payment is directed to be made to the applicant,

the application may be heard in the Designated Family Court area in which the applicant resides.

7.3 Where an application for enforcement is made under Article 56 of the Maintenance Regulation in the form at Annex VI to that Regulation, the application must be made using that form,

PART III

Application by debtor under Article 21 of the Maintenance Regulation for refusal or suspension of enforcement

8.A1 An application by a debtor under Article 21 of the Maintenance Regulation for the refusal or suspension of enforcement of a decision should be sent to the Maintenance Enforcement Business Centre which has been in most recent communication with the debtor.

8.1 An application by a debtor under Article 21 of the Maintenance Regulation for the refusal or suspension of enforcement of a decision will be heard in –

(a) the Designated Family Judge area to which an application for enforcement of that decision has been made in accordance with paragraph 7.2 or 7.3, or

(b) where no such application has been made at the date at which the debtor makes an application to which this paragraph applies, the Designated Family Judge area to which an application for enforcement would be required to be made under paragraph 7.2 or 7.3.

PART 35
MEDIATION DIRECTIVE

CONTENTS OF THIS PART

Rule		Page
35.1	Scope and interpretation	1976
35.2	Relevant disputes: applications for consent orders in respect of financial remedies	1977
35.3	Mediation evidence: disclosure and inspection	1978
35.4	Mediation evidence: witnesses and depositions	1978
	Practice Direction 35A – Mediation Directive	1979

35.1 Scope and interpretation

(1) This Part applies to mediated cross-border disputes that are subject to Directive 2008/52/EC of the European Parliament and of the Council of 21 May 2008 on certain aspects of mediation in civil and commercial matters ('the Mediation Directive').

(2) In this Part –

'cross-border dispute' has the meaning given by article 2 of the Mediation Directive;

'mediation' has the meaning given by article 3(a) of the Mediation Directive;

'mediation administrator' means a person involved in the administration of the mediation process;

'mediation evidence' means evidence regarding information arising out of or in connection with a mediation process;

'mediator' has the meaning given by article 3(b) of the Mediation Directive; and

'relevant dispute' means a cross-border dispute that is subject to the Mediation Directive.

Scope—This Part applies only to mediated cross-border disputes subject to Directive 2008/52/EC of 21 May 2008 on certain aspects of mediation in civil and commercial matters ('the Mediation Directive'). The purpose of the Mediation Directive is to facilitate access to ADR and to promote the amicable settlement of cross-border disputes by encouraging the use of mediation and by ensuring a balanced relationship between mediation and judicial proceedings (Mediation Directive, Art 1.1). The Mediation Directive does not apply to Denmark (Mediation Directive, Art 1.3). FPR 2010, Pt 35 implements the Mediation Directive by ensuring that it is possible for the parties, or for one of them with the explicit consent of the others, to request that the content of a written agreement resulting from mediation is made enforceable. FPR 2010, Pt 3 is part of the implementation process of the Mediation Directive. The relevant parts of the Mediation Directive are set out below:

Article 2: Cross-border disputes

1 For the purposes of this Directive a cross-border dispute shall be one in which at least one of the parties is domiciled or habitually resident in a Member State other than that of any other party on the date on which:

(a) the parties agree to use mediation after the dispute has arisen;

(b) mediation is ordered by a court;

(c) an obligation to use mediation arises under national law; or
(d) for the purposes of Article 5 an invitation is made to the parties.

2 Notwithstanding paragraph 1, for the purposes of Articles 7 and 8 a cross-border dispute shall also be one in which judicial proceedings or arbitration following mediation between the parties are initiated in a Member State other than that in which the parties were domiciled or habitually resident on the date referred to in paragraph 1(a),(b) or (c).

3 For the purposes of paragraphs 1 and 2, domicile shall be determined in accordance with Articles 59 and 60 of Regulation (EC) No 44/2001 (see, now, the Maintenance Regulation (Council Regulation (EC) No 4/2009), art 2.3 and annotations to Ch III (Applicable Law)).

Article 3: Definitions

For the purposes of this Directive the following definitions shall apply:

(a) 'Mediation' means a structured process, however named or referred to, whereby two or more parties to a dispute attempt by themselves, on a voluntary basis, to reach an agreement on the settlement of their dispute with the assistance of a mediator. This process may be initiated by the parties or suggested or ordered by a court or prescribed by the law of a Member State.

It includes mediation conducted by a judge who is not responsible for any judicial proceedings concerning the dispute in question. It excludes attempts made by the court or the judge seised to settle a dispute in the course of judicial proceedings concerning the dispute in question.

(b) 'Mediator' means any third person who is asked to conduct a mediation in an effective, impartial and competent way, regardless of the denomination or profession of that third person in the Member State concerned and of the way in which the third person has been appointed or requested to conduct the mediation.

Article 6: Enforceability of agreements resulting from mediation

1 Member States shall ensure that it is possible for the parties, or for one of them with the explicit consent of the others, to request that the content of a written agreement resulting from mediation be made enforceable. The content of such an agreement shall be made enforceable unless, in the case in question, either the content of that agreement is contrary to the law of the Member State where the request is made or the law of that Member State does not provide for its enforceability.

2 The content of the agreement may be made enforceable by a court or other competent authority in a judgment or decision or in an authentic instrument in accordance with the law of the Member State where the request is made.

3 Member States shall inform the Commission of the courts or other authorities competent to receive requests in accordance with paragraphs 1 and 2.

4 Nothing in this Article shall affect the rules applicable to the recognition and enforcement in another Member State of an agreement made enforceable in accordance with paragraph 1.

Article 7: Confidentiality of mediation

1 Given that mediation is intended to take place in a manner which respects confidentiality, Member States shall ensure that, unless the parties agree otherwise, neither mediators nor those involved in the administration of the mediation process shall be compelled to give evidence in civil and commercial judicial proceedings or arbitration regarding information arising out of or in connection with a mediation process, except:

(a) where this is necessary for overriding considerations of public policy of the Member State concerned, in particular when required to ensure the protection of the best interests of children or to prevent harm to the physical or psychological integrity of a person; or
(b) where disclosure of the content of the agreement resulting from mediation is necessary in order to implement or enforce that agreement.

2 Nothing in paragraph 1 shall preclude Member States from enacting stricter measures to protect the confidentiality of mediation.

35.2 Relevant disputes: applications for consent orders in respect of financial remedies

(1) This rule applies in relation to proceedings for a financial remedy where the applicant, with the explicit consent of the respondent, wishes to make an application that the content of a written agreement resulting from mediation of a relevant dispute be made enforceable by being made the subject of a consent order.

(2) The court will not include in a consent order any matter which is contrary to the law of England and Wales or which is not enforceable under that law.

(3) The applicant must file two copies of a draft of the order in the terms sought.

(4) Subject to paragraph (5), the application must be supported by evidence of the explicit consent of the respondent.

(5) Where the respondent has written to the court consenting to the making of the order sought, the respondent is deemed to have given explicit consent to the order and paragraph (4) does not apply.

(6) Paragraphs (1)(b) and (2) to (6) of rule 9.26 apply to an application to which this rule applies.

PART III

Scope—This rule gives effect to the Mediation Directive, art 6. The rule does not make specific provision that the court must make the content of a cross-border mediated agreement enforceable, but rather relies upon the courts' existing powers to make consent orders (for example, FPR 2010, r 9.26 (applications for consent orders for a financial remedy)) and to enforce the content of a consent order (for example, in relation to child arrangements orders made by consent under CA 1989, s 8). This rule addresses the requirement of the Mediation Directive, art 6 that a respondent should give 'explicit consent'. Without this provision, FPR 2010, r 9.25(1)(a) would apply in default. FPR 2010, r 9.25(1)(a) requires that one copy of any draft consent order must be endorsed with a statement signed by the respondent signifying agreement. FPR PD9A, para 6.1 states that this requirement is properly complied with if the endorsed statement is signed by solicitors on record as acting for the respondent. Rule 35.2 addresses any potential limitation on the opportunities for providing explicit consent contained in FPR 2010, r 9.25(1)(a) and FPR PD9A, para 6.1. An application under r 35.2 must be completed in English or accompanied by a translation into English. The respondent's explicit consent must similarly be in English or accompanied by a translation into English (FPR PD35A).

Defined terms—'consent order' (FPR 2010, r 2.3); 'relevant dispute' (FPR 2010, r 35.1(2)).

35.3 Mediation evidence: disclosure and inspection

(1) Where a party to proceedings seeks disclosure or inspection of mediation evidence that is in the control of a mediator or mediation administrator, that party must first obtain the court's permission to seek the disclosure or inspection, by an application made in accordance with Part 18.

(2) The mediator or mediation administrator who has control of the mediation evidence must be named as a respondent to the application and must be served with a copy of the application notice.

(3) Evidence in support of the application must include evidence that –

- (a) all parties to the mediation agree to the disclosure or inspection of the mediation evidence;
- (b) disclosure or inspection of the mediation evidence is necessary for overriding considerations of public policy, in accordance with article 7(1)(a) of the Mediation Directive; or
- (c) the disclosure of the content of an agreement resulting from mediation is necessary to implement or enforce that agreement.

(4) Where this rule applies, Parts 21 to 24 apply to the extent they are consistent with this rule.

Defined terms—'mediation', 'mediation administrator', 'mediation evidence': FPR 2010, r 35.1(2); 'public policy': Mediation Directive, art 7.1(a) (a distinction is to be drawn between the narrow interpretation of 'public policy' used in European law and the wider meaning in domestic law of 'public interest').

Scope—FPR 2010, rr 35.3 and 35.4 relate to the implementation of the Mediation Directive, art 7 concerning the confidentiality of mediation other than in excepted cases. Where an application for disclosure and inspection is made in an excepted case, r 35.3 requires an application in accordance with FPR 2010, Pt 18 to be made.

35.4 Mediation evidence: witnesses and depositions

(1) This rule applies where a party wishes to obtain mediation evidence from a mediator or mediation administrator by –

- (a) a witness summons;
- (b) cross-examination with permission of the court under rule 22.8 or 23.4;
- (c) an order under rule 24.7 (evidence by deposition);
- (d) an order under rule 24.9 (enforcing attendance of witness);
- (e) an order under rule 24.10(4) deponent's evidence to be given orally); or
- (f) an order under rule 24.12 (order for the issue of a letter of request).

(2) When applying for a witness summons, permission under rule 22.8 or 23.4 or order under rule 24.7, 24.9, 24.10(4) or 24.12, the party must provide the court with evidence that –

- (a) all parties to the mediation agree to the obtaining of the mediation evidence;
- (b) obtaining the mediation evidence is necessary for overriding considerations of public policy in accordance with article 7(1)(a) of the Mediation Directive; or
- (c) the disclosure of the content of an agreement resulting from mediation is necessary to implement or enforce that agreement.

(3) When considering a request for a witness summons, permission under rule 22.8 or 23.4 or order under rule 24.7, 24.9, 24.10(4) or 24.12, the court may invite any person, whether or not a party, to make representations.

(4) Where this rule applies, Parts 21 to 24 apply to the extent they are consistent with this rule.

Scope—See the notes to FPR 2010, r 35.3.

Practice Direction 35A – Mediation Directive

This Practice Direction supplements FPR rule 35.2 (Relevant disputes: applications for consent orders in respect of financial remedies)

1.1 An application for an order to which rule 35.2 applies must be completed in English or accompanied by a translation into English.

1.2 Where the application is supported by evidence of explicit consent to the application by a party, the evidence must also be in English or accompanied by a translation into English.

1.3 Where a party chooses to write to the court consenting to the making of the order the correspondence must be in English or accompanied by a translation into English.

PART 36
TRANSITIONAL ARRANGEMENTS AND PILOT SCHEMES

CONTENTS OF THIS PART

Rule		Page
36.1	Transitional provisions	1979
36.2	Pilot schemes	1979
	Practice Direction 36D – Pilot Scheme: Procedure for Using an Online System to Generate Applications in Certain Proceedings for a Matrimonial Order	1980

Scope—As well as making provision for pilot schemes (FPR 2010, r 36.2), FPR 2010, Pt 36 and FPR PD36A make provision for transitional arrangements dealing with the application of the FPR to proceedings started before 6 April 2011 ('existing proceedings'). The general scheme (FPR PD36A, para 2.1) is to apply the FPR to existing proceedings so far as is practicable but, where this is not practicable, to apply the previous rules (as set out in FPR PD36A, para 1.2) to such proceedings. Where proceedings have been commenced before 6 April 2011, the case will proceed in the first instance under the previous rules with subsequent pleadings being filed and served in accordance with the previous rules. However, when proceedings come before a court (whether at a hearing, including a hearing of a substantive issue, or on paper) for the first time on or after 6 April 2011 (whether or not the application was issued before 6 April 2011), the court may direct how FPR 2010 are to apply to the proceedings on the general presumption that the FPR will apply to the proceedings from then on (FPR PD36A, para 4.4). Where a new step is to be taken in any existing proceedings on or after 6 April 2011, it is to be taken under the FPR (FPR PD36A, para 4.1). The overriding objective (FPR 2010, Pt 1) applies to all existing proceedings from 6 April 2011 (FPR PD36A, para 4.2). Any assessment of costs taking place on or after 6 April 2011 is in accordance with FPR 2010, Pt 28 (and the CPR as applied by FPR 2010, Pt 28). However, the general presumption that no costs for work undertaken before 6 April 2011 will be disallowed if those costs would have been allowed on detailed assessment before that date (FPR PD36A, para 4.5).

36.1 Transitional provisions

Practice Direction 36A shall make provision for the extent to which these rules shall apply to proceedings started before the day on which they come into force.

36.2 Pilot schemes

Practice directions may modify or disapply any provision of these rules –

(a) for specified periods; and

(b) in relation to proceedings in specified courts,

during the operation of pilot schemes for assessing the use of new practices and procedures in connection with proceedings.

Practice Direction 36C—FPR PD36C – Pilot Scheme: Care and Supervision Proceedings and other proceedings under Pt 4 of the Children Act 1989, which came into force on 1 July 2013 until 22 April 2014, is an example of such a pilot scheme, in this instance assessing the procedures to support the 26-week time limit for proceedings under CA 1989, Pt 4 now contained in FPR 2010, Pt 12 and PD12A. For FPR PDs 36A and 36C, see *The Family Court Practice 2014*.

****

Practice Direction 36D – Pilot Scheme: Procedure for Using an Online System to Generate Applications in Certain Proceedings for a Matrimonial Order

This Practice Direction supplements rule 36.2 FPR (Transitional arrangements and pilot schemes).

Scope—This Practice Direction represents the first step towards a completely digitalised divorce process. It is to be noted that the Pilot Scheme is restricted in scope. It applies only to divorce and not to nullity or judicial separation; it does not apply to civil partnerships. The Pilot Scheme will enable the divorce petition only at this stage to be generated via the online system. Once generated, the petition will need to be saved or printed off for filing at court under current procedures. The MoJ has confirmed that the East Midlands regional divorce centre at Nottingham will host the pilot scheme.

Potential users will be personally invited to use the first phase of the pilot and given access following a screening process at the pilot site. Access to the pilot is, therefore, controlled initially.

Scope and interpretation

1.1 This Practice Direction is made under rule 36.2 FPR and sets up a Pilot Scheme to allow for certain applications to be filled in via an online process.

1.2 The Pilot Scheme applies to applications where all of the following conditions are met:

(a) the application is for a matrimonial order which is a decree of divorce made under section 1 of the 1973 Act;

(b) access to the online system for making such applications is permitted;

(c) all stages of the process provided for in the online system can be fully completed;

(d) the application is started in the family court; and

(e) the application is filed in the period commencing 25 January 2017 and ending 28 July 2017.

1.3 In this Practice Direction, 'the online system' means Her Majesty's Courts and Tribunal Service's online system to allow for specified stages in for matrimonial proceedings to be dealt with online.

Purpose of the Pilot Scheme

2.1 The purpose of this Pilot Scheme is to assess new practices and procedures to allow for certain applications for certain matrimonial orders to be generated via the online system. For the purposes of this Pilot Scheme, once the application has been generated the applicant will need to save or print off the generated application. It will then need to be filed at court, in accordance with the procedure currently provided for in the FPR and Practice Directions. It is intended that future Practice Directions will establish other Pilot Schemes which will allow for later stages in matrimonial proceedings to take place via the online system, for example for making the application online.

Modification of the FPR and Practice Directions during the operation of the Pilot Scheme

3.1 During the operation of the Pilot Scheme, the FPR and the Practice Directions supporting the FPR will apply to cases falling within the Pilot Scheme as modified by paragraphs 4.1 to 5.4.

Modification of Part 5 FPR

4.1 For rule 5.1, substitute –

'5.1 Where the Pilot Scheme referred to in Practice Direction 36D applies, the applicant must –

(a) complete all sections of the application process set out in the online system referred to in that Practice Direction;
(b) print or save the resulting application form which is generated by the online system;
(c) when filing that application, include all of the information, including any additional documents, that the online system requires to be included.'.

4.2 Omit rule 5.2.

Modification of PD7A

5.1 For paragraph 1.1, substitute –

'1.1 Where the pilot scheme referred to in Practice Direction 36D applies, an application for a matrimonial order must be made in the form generated by the online system referred to in that Practice Direction. The online system sets out the documents which must accompany the application.'.

5.2 For paragraph 1.2 substitute –

'1.2 The application must be completed according to the detailed guidance contained in the online system. It is especially important that the particulars provide evidence to show why the applicant is entitled to a decree of divorce. The particulars should, however, be as concise as possible consistent with providing the necessary evidence.'.

5.3 In paragraph 3.1 –

(a) for the heading and the first sentence of paragraph 3.1 substitute –

'Proof of marriage

3.1 The online system referred to in Practice Direction 36D sets out the documents which must accompany the application for a matrimonial order.';

(b) in the second sentence of paragraph 3.1 omit 'or civil partnership';
(c) in sub-paragraph (a)(i) –
  (i) for 'marriage or civil partnership to' substitute 'marriage to'; and
  (ii) omit 'or civil partnership registration'; and
(d) in sub-paragraph (a)(ii), omit 'or civil partnership registration'.

5.4 In paragraph 4.1 –

(a) for 'An applicant for a matrimonial or civil partnership order' substitute –

'Where the pilot scheme referred to in Practice Direction 36D applies, an applicant'; and

(b) omit 'form'.

PART 37
APPLICATIONS AND PROCEEDINGS IN RELATION TO CONTEMPT OF COURT

Amendments—Inserted by SI 2014/667.

CONTENTS OF THIS PART

Chapter 1

Rule | Page

Scope and interpretation

37.1 Scope 1983
37.2 Saving for other powers 1985

PART III

37.3 Interpretation 1985

Chapter 2
Committal for breach of a judgment, order or undertaking to do or abstain from doing an act

37.4 Enforcement of judgment, order or undertaking to do or abstain from doing an act 1986
37.5 Requirement for service of a copy of the judgment or order and time for service 1986
37.6 Method of service – copies of judgments or orders 1987
37.7 Method of service – copies of undertakings 1987
37.8 Dispensation with personal service 1987
37.9 Requirement for a penal notice on judgments and orders 1988
37.10 How to make the committal application 1988
37.11 Committal for breach of a solicitor's undertaking 1989

Chapter 3
Contempt in the face of the court

37.12 Contempt in the face of the court 1989

Chapter 4
Committal for interference with the due administration of justice

37.13 Scope 1989
37.14 Court to which application for permission under this Chapter is to be made 1990
37.15 Application for permission 1990

Chapter 5
Committal for making a false statement of truth (Rule 17.6)

37.16 Scope and interaction with other Chapters of this Part 1991
37.17 Committal application in relation to a false statement of truth 1991

Chapter 6
Writ of sequestration to enforce a judgment, order or undertaking

37.18 Scope 1992
37.19 Writ of sequestration to enforce a judgment, order or undertaking 1992
37.20 Requirement for service of a copy of the judgment or order and time for service 1992
37.21 Method of service – copies of judgments or orders 1993
37.22 Method of service – copies of undertakings 1993
37.23 Dispensation with personal service 1993
37.24 Requirement for a penal notice on judgments and orders 1993
37.25 How to make an application for permission to issue a writ of sequestration 1993
37.26 Form of writ of sequestration 1994

Chapter 7
General rules about committal applications, orders for committal and writs of sequestration

37.27 The hearing 1994
37.28 Power to suspend execution of a committal order 1995
37.29 Warrant of committal 1995
37.30 Discharge of a person in custody 1995
37.31 Discharge of a person in custody where a writ of sequestration has been issued 1996

Chapter 8
Penal and disciplinary provisions under the County Courts Act 1984

37.32 Scope 1996
37.33 Offences under sections 14, 92 or 118 of the Act 1996
37.34 Offences under section 124 of the Act 1997
37.35 Notice to give evidence before or after a fine is imposed under section 31G of the 1984 Act 1997
37.36 Non-payment of fine 1997
37.37 Repayment of fine 1997
37.38 Section 118 of the Act and the tipstaff 1998

Practice Direction 37A – Applications and Proceedings in Relation to Contempt of Court 1998

Scope—FPR Pt 37 came into force on 22 April 2014. It applies only to family proceedings where the order sought to be enforced by committal was made under the provisions of the FPR (such as an application to commit for breach of an order under the Family Law Act 1996 obtained under Pt 10). It does not apply to civil proceedings, which have their own code under CPR 1998, Pt 81.

Before making any application to commit for contempt, it is necessary to have in mind the relevant law: see *Zuk v Zuk* [2013] 2 FLR 1466, CA, where the sentence was quashed as the contemnor had been sentenced under CCA 1981, whereas it should have been under DA 1869. Rules of procedure do not confer power to commit but merely regulate how the application is made and dealt with. The law on contempt is a complicated mixture of common law, statute and (in the case of the High Court) the inherent jurisdiction.

CPR 1998, Pt 81 came into force on 1 October 2012 and FPR 2010, Pt 37 is clearly modelled on it. Therefore, where there is a cognate rule in the CPR it is given in the commentary. Part 37 is divided into eight chapters, each being structured to deal with a specific type of contempt. This has the disadvantage that the Part is long and repetitive but that is outweighed by the advantage that there is less cross-referring and each chapter is clear and self-contained.

Part 37 is supplemented by PD37. The PD is important and, in effect, provides commentary on the various rules. The PD is, like Pt 37, divided into chapters and the corresponding chapter of the PD needs to be studied before making an application.

In all cases, the general rules in Ch 7 of Pt 37 and PD37 need to be considered in addition to the specific chapter dealing with the type of contempt in question.

Chapter 1
Scope and interpretation

37.1 Scope

(1) This Part sets out the procedure in respect of –

(a) committal for breach of a judgment, order, undertaking to do or abstain from doing an act or of an incoming protection measure;
(b) contempt in the face of the court;
(c) committal for interference with the due administration of justice;
(d) committal for making a false statement of truth;
(e) sequestration to enforce a judgment, order or undertaking; and
(f) the penal, contempt and disciplinary provisions of the County Courts Act 1984.

(2) So far as applicable, and with the necessary modifications, this Part applies in relation to an order requiring a person –

(a) guilty of contempt of court; or
(b) punishable by virtue of any enactment as if that person had been guilty of contempt of the High Court,

to pay a fine or to give security for good behaviour, as it applies in relation to an order of committal.

(3) Unless otherwise stated, this Part applies to procedure in the High Court and family court.

Amendments—Inserted by SI 2014/667. Amended by SI 2014/3296.
Parallel rule—CPR 1998, r 81.1.

Enforcement of orders or undertakings to pay money—See FPR PD33A. An order to pay money, or an undertaking to do so, cannot be enforced by committal proceedings, except in the very limited circumstances permitted under DA 1869, s 5, as limited by AJA 1970, s 11 and Sch 8 (*Symmons v Symmons* [1993] 1 FLR 317, FD). An application to commit for non-payment requires not merely proof of non-payment but proof (beyond reasonable doubt) that the non-payer had the means to pay but refused or neglected to pay. In *Mohan v Mohan* [2014] 1 FLR 717, CA, it was held that, as it is given under compulsion, information obtained on a general application for enforcement of a financial order cannot be used as evidence in a Debtors Act application to commit. By DA 1869, s 5, '... any court may commit to prison for a term not exceeding six weeks, or until payment of the sum due'. Although the Act does not say 'earlier payment', that is what it means, because the main purpose of the Act was to abolish indefinite imprisonment until payment (which was possible, without proof of means, before the Act). Imprisonment does not satisfy or extinguish the debt.

Production in court of person arrested under FLA 1996, s 47 and attendance of the victim—A person arrested by virtue of a power of arrest under s 47(6) must be brought before the court within 24 hours of the arrest (s 47(7)(a)). A warrant of arrest authorises the immediate arrest of the respondent for failing to comply with the provisions of a non-molestation or occupation order but, unlike the requirement in s 47(7)(a), there is no provision that a person arrested on a warrant must be brought before the court within 24 hours of the arrest. In practice, a person arrested under a warrant will be produced before the court as soon as reasonably practicable, regard being given to enabling the applicant to attend, unless the respondent is arrested some distance from the court which issued the warrant. When an arrested respondent is brought before the court, the attendance of the applicant will almost always be needed to enable the court to deal with the alleged breach, and if not available within a reasonable time the court may have to adjourn the matter, and consider whether to remand the respondent.

Procedural powers of court when person arrested under FLA 1996, s 47 is brought before the court—When a respondent is brought before the court following arrest, whether under a power of arrest or a warrant, the court may hear and deal with the alleged breach, or adjourn the hearing. The court may adjourn without having determined whether a breach has been proved, or after finding a breach proved. If the hearing is adjourned, the arrested person may be (i) released without remand, in which case additional injunctive directions may be appropriate; (ii) remanded in custody under s 47(7)(b) or s 47(10), and s 47(11) and Sch 5, para 2(1)(a); (iii) remanded on bail under s 47(7)(b) or s 47(10), and s 47(11) and (12) and Sch 5, para 2(1)(b); or (iv) remanded for the purpose of enabling a medical examination to be made under s 48(1) or for a report on his mental condition under s 48(4). See further commentary to FPR 2010, Pt 10 and to CCA 1981.

Remand under FLA 1996, s 47(7)(b),(10),(11) or s 48—A person arrested and brought before the court can be remanded under s 47(7)(b) or s 47(10), and s 47(11), (12) and Sch 5, in custody or on bail, or remanded for a medical report under s 48, in custody or on bail (s 47(11),(12) and Sch 5).

Committal hearing while criminal proceedings pending—Breach of an injunction can lead to concurrent civil proceedings to commit and criminal proceedings for an offence. The first court to sentence must not anticipate or allow for a likely further sentence; it is for the second court to reflect the prior sentence in its judgment (see *Lomas v Parle* [2004] 1 FLR 812, CA). There is never any need for the civil court to adjourn to await the outcome of criminal proceedings (which are not in any event under the control of the victim). Sentencing courts have different objectives and different powers. An important objective of contempt proceedings is to uphold the authority of the court by demonstrating that its orders should not be flouted with impunity (see further, per Thorpe LJ in *Lomas v Parle*). Concurrent civil and criminal proceedings are less likely now that breach of a non-molestation order is itself a crime and, in any event, it is not possible for the same breach to be dealt with in both civil and criminal courts; see FLA 1996, s 42A(3) and 42A(4). If a civil judge regards the punishment given by a criminal court as too lenient it is not permitted to 'top up' the punishment. The civil judge must sentence only for such conduct which was not the subject of criminal proceedings: *Slade v Slade* [2010] 1 FLR 160, CA.

Unrepresented contemnors—It is generally desirable that a person alleged to be in contempt of court be legally represented but, as with any other litigant, a contemnor is entitled to act in person (with or without a McKenzie friend). The court has no power to compel representation. However, persons in danger of losing their liberty are, subject to means, eligible for legal aid under LASPOA 2012. See *Brown v London Borough of Haringey* [2015] EWCA Civ 483, where the Court of Appeal gives guidance on how legal aid is obtained in committal proceedings. Accordingly, the court should always consider adjourning (and, in FLA cases, remanding) to enable the alleged contemnor to seek legal representation. If a hearing proceeds without the contemnor being represented, the judge should ensure that he understands his right to cross-examine, give evidence and call witnesses (*Shoreditch County Court Bailiffs v Madeiros* (1988) *The Times*, 24 February, CA).

The importance of abiding by correct procedure—The Court of Appeal has stressed in several cases that, because committal for contempt of court is concerned with offences of a quasi-criminal nature and the liberty of the subject is at stake, the relevant rules of court must be complied with and the prescribed forms must be used. However, FPR PD37, para 15.2 provides that 'The court may waive any procedural defect in the commencement or conduct of a committal application if satisfied that no injustice has been caused to the respondent by the defect'. In *Nicholls v Nicholls* [1997] 1 FLR 649, CA, Lord Woolf MR, giving the judgment of the Court of Appeal, stated (at [655D]) that 'While the … requirements of Ord 29, r 1 are there to be observed, in the absence of authority to the contrary, even though the liberty of the subject is involved, we would not expect the requirements to be mandatory, in the sense that any non-compliance with the rule means that a committal for contempt is irredeemably invalid.' Lord Woolf gave the following guidance (at [661E]):

'(1) As committal orders involve the liberty of the subject it is particularly important that the relevant rules are duly complied with. It remains the responsibility of the judge when signing the committal order to ensure that it is properly drawn and that it adequately particularises the breaches which have been proved and for which the sentence has been imposed.

(2) As long as the contemnor has had a fair trial and the order has been made on valid grounds the existence of a defect either in the application to commit or in the committal order served will not result in the order being set aside except insofar as the interests of justice require this to be done.

(3) Interests of justice will not require an order to be set aside where there is no prejudice caused as the result or errors in the application to commit or in the order to commit. When necessary the order can be amended.

(4) When considering whether to set aside the order, the court should have regard to the interests of any other party and the need to uphold the reputation of the justice system.

(5) If there has been a procedural irregularity or some other defect in the conduct of the proceedings which has occasioned injustice, the court will consider exercising its powers to order a new trial unless there are circumstances which indicate that it would not be just to do so.'

In *Devjee v Patel* [2006] EWCA Civ 1211 the fact that the exact process for bringing committal proceedings for breach of a non-molestation order had not been followed did not render the proceedings unfair as no injustice was caused to the contemnor: 6 months' imprisonment was upheld. But see *Re Dad* [2015] EWHC 2655 (Fam), where omission of a penal notice was fatal to the committal application.

Committal hearing procedure—In general terms, hearings of committal proceedings are in many respects similar to hearings of criminal charges. The burden of proof rests on the person making the allegation of contempt. The standard of proof is the criminal standard (*Cambra v Jones* [2014] EWHC 2264 (Fam), Munby P). The respondent must be allowed to cross-examine witnesses and to call evidence. The respondent is entitled to submit that there is no case to answer (*Savings and Investment Bank v Gasco Investments (Netherlands)* (1986) 136 NLJ 657, ChD). If a contempt is found proved, the contemnor must be allowed to address the court by way of mitigation or seeking to purge his contempt (*Stilwell v Williamson* (1986) *The Times*, 1 September, CA). Autrefois acquit and autrefois convict apply.

Evidence and witnesses at hearing—An alleged contemnor is not a compellable witness (*Comet Products UK Ltd v Hawkex Plastics Ltd* [1971] 2 QB 67, CA). The court can issue a witness summons to a person who witnessed an alleged contempt to attend committal proceedings although no application has been made by a party (*Yianni v Yianni* [1966] 1 WLR 120, ChD). Hearsay evidence is admissible but caution should be exercised (*Savings and Investment Bank v Gasco Investments (Netherlands) BV (No 2)* [1988] Ch 422, CA). Respondents to a motion to commit can be required by the court to swear, file and serve affidavits, or produce statements of witnesses of fact upon which they might wish to rely before the hearing, in order to enable proper preparation of the evidence in reply (*Re B (Contempt: Evidence)* [1996] 1 FLR 239, FD). However, the applicant must prove his case on the evidence filed in support of the application, supplemented by any admissions made by the alleged contemnor upon which the applicant was entitled to rely, and the applicant can make no use of the respondent's evidence until it has been deployed by the respondent. A respondent who complies with a direction from the court in the foregoing terms is not in peril of cross-examination until such time as he deploys the evidence in his own case (*Re B (Contempt: Evidence)*, above).

'Legal aid'—Legal aid can be granted by the court to an alleged contemnor. The Court of Appeal in *Brown v London Borough of Haringey* [2015] EWCA Civ 483 held that the Crown Court, the High Court and the Court of Appeal all have power to make determinations under LASPOA 2012, s 6 as to whether an individual qualifies for representation for the purposes of criminal proceedings (which includes committal applications) before them. There is no similar power in the County Court so, by s 18, it is for the Director of the Legal Aid Agency to make determinations in committal applications in the County Court. The judge may have to adjourn to enable this to be done.

37.2 Saving for other powers

(1) This Part is concerned only with procedure and does not itself confer upon the court the power to make an order for –

(a) committal;
(b) sequestration; or
(c) the imposition of a fine in respect of contempt of court.

(2) Nothing in this Part affects the power of the court to make an order requiring a person –

(a) guilty of contempt of court; or
(b) punishable by virtue of any enactment as if that person had been guilty of contempt of the High Court,

to pay a fine or to give security for good behaviour.

(3) Nothing in this Part affects any statutory or inherent power of the court to make a committal order of its own initiative against a person guilty of contempt of court.

Amendments—Inserted by SI 2014/667.

Parallel rule—CPR 1998, r 81.2.

Fines—The House of Lords held in *Heatons Transport (St Helens) Ltd v TGWU* [1973] AC 15, HL that the High Court may impose a fine in lieu of or in addition to committal. The County Court also has this power (*Rose v Laskington* [1990] 1 QB 562, QBD). There is no statutory limit to the amount of such a fine imposed by a judge of the High Court but Family Court (Contempt of Court) (Powers) Regulations 2014, reg 5 provides that the fine 'must not exceed level 5 on the standard scale' when imposed by a judge of the Family Court other than a High Court judge.

37.3 Interpretation

In this Part –

(a) 'applicant' means a person making –
  (i) an application for permission to make a committal application;
  (ii) a committal application; or
  (iii) an application for a writ of sequestration;
(b) 'committal application' means any application for an order committing a person to prison;
(c) 'judge of High Court judge level' means a person in sub-paragraphs (i) to (x) of paragraph (b) in the definition of 'judge' in rule 2.3;
(d) 'respondent' means a person –

(i) against whom a committal application is made or is intended to be made; or
(ii) against whose property it is sought to issue a writ of sequestration;

(e) 'undertaking' means an undertaking to the court; and

(f) references to a writ of sequestration are, in relation to the family court, to be read as references to a warrant containing provision corresponding to that which may be contained in a writ of sequestration.

(See section 31E of the Matrimonial and Family Proceedings Act 1984 (Family court has High Court and county court powers), in particular subsections (1) and (2) of that section.)

Amendments—Inserted by SI 2014/667.

Parallel rule—CPR 1998, r 81.3.

Chapter 2
Committal for breach of a judgment, order or undertaking to do or abstain from doing an act

37.4 Enforcement of judgment, order or undertaking to do or abstain from doing an act

(1) If a person –

(a) required by a judgment or order to do an act does not do it within the time fixed by the judgment or order; or

(b) disobeys a judgment or order not to do an act,

then, subject to the Debtors Acts 1869 and 1878 and to the provisions of these Rules, the judgment or order may be enforced under the court's powers by an order for committal.

(2) If the time fixed by the judgment or order for doing an act has been varied by a subsequent order, then references in paragraph (1)(a) to the time fixed are references to the time fixed by that subsequent order or agreement.

(3) If the person referred to in paragraph (1) is a company or other corporation, the committal order may be made against any director or other officer of that company or corporation.

(4) So far as applicable, and with the necessary modifications, this Chapter applies to undertakings given by a party as it applies to judgments or orders.

(Specific provision in relation to judgment summonses is contained in Chapter 2 of Part 33.)

Amendments—Inserted by SI 2014/667.
Parallel rule—CPR 1998, r 81.4.
Breach of judgment, order or undertaking—In practice, most applications to commit will be under Ch 2.
Undertaking—This means an undertaking to the court.

37.5 Requirement for service of a copy of the judgment or order and time for service

(1) Unless the court dispenses with service under rule 37.8, a judgment or order may not be enforced under rule 37.4 unless a copy of it has been served on the person required to do or not do the act in question, and in the case of a judgment or order requiring a person to do an act –

(a) the copy has been served before the end of the time fixed for doing the act, together with a copy of any order fixing that time;

(b) where the time for doing the act has been varied by a subsequent order, a copy of that subsequent order has also been served; and

(c) where the judgment or order was made pursuant to an earlier judgment or order requiring the act to be done, a copy of the earlier judgment or order has also been served.

(2) Where the person referred to in paragraph (1) is a company or other corporation, a copy of the judgment or order must also be served on a director or officer of the company or corporation before the end of the time fixed for doing the act.

(3) Copies of the judgment or order and any orders or agreements fixing or varying the time for doing an act must be served in accordance with rule 37.6 or 37.7, or in accordance with an order for alternative service made under rule 37.8(2)(b).

Amendments—Inserted by SI 2014/667.

Parallel rule—CPR 1998, r 81.5.

Service—The general rule is that an order may not be enforced by committal unless it has been served on the person required to do, or not to do, the act in question. Further, the order must have been endorsed with the appropriate penal notice warning of the consequences of disobedience.

37.6 Method of service – copies of judgments or orders

Subject to rules 37.7 and 37.8, copies of judgments or orders and any orders or agreements fixing or varying the time for doing an act must be served personally.

Amendments—Inserted by SI 2014/667.

Parallel rule—CPR 1998, r 81.6.

37.7 Method of service – copies of undertakings

(1) Subject to paragraph (2) and rule 37.8, a copy of any document recording an undertaking will be delivered by the court to the person who gave the undertaking –

(a) by handing to that person a copy of the document before that person leaves the court building;

(b) by posting a copy to that person at the residence or place of business of that person where this is known; or

(c) by posting a copy to that person's solicitor.

(2) If delivery cannot be effected in accordance with paragraph (1), the court officer will deliver a copy of the document to the party for whose benefit the undertaking was given and that party must serve it personally on the person who gave the undertaking as soon as practicable.

(3) Where the person referred to in paragraph (1) is a company or other corporation, a copy of the judgment or order must also be served on a director or officer of the company or corporation.

Amendments—Inserted by SI 2014/667.

Parallel rule—CPR 1998, r 81.7.

Copy of undertaking—The options listed in r 37.7(1) should be read as being in order of preference. Traditionally, because an undertaking to the court is freely and knowingly given, it was not necessary to serve it (*D v A & Co* [1900] 1 Ch 484, ChD) but that has not been the practice in family cases since *Hussain v Hussain* [1986] 2 FLR 271, CA and r 37.7(1) now clearly requires service, albeit not necessarily personal service.

37.8 Dispensation with personal service

(1) In the case of a judgment or order requiring a person not to do an act, the court may dispense with service of a copy of the judgment or order in accordance with rules 37.5 to 37.7 if it is satisfied that the person has had notice of it –

(a) by being present when the judgment or order was given or made; or

(b) by being notified of its terms by telephone, email or otherwise.

(2) In the case of any judgment or order the court may –

(a) dispense with service under rules 37.5 to 37.7 if the court thinks it just to do so; or

(b) make an order in respect of service by an alternative method or at an alternative place.

Amendments—Inserted by SI 2014/667.

Parallel rule—CPR 1998, r 81.8.

History of rule—Paragraph (1) of r 37.8 is based on former RSC Ord 45, r 7(6) and CCR Ord 29, r 1(6) and para (2)(a) follows former RSC Ord 45, r 7(7) and CCR Ord 29, r 1(7).

Dispense with service—The general rule is that the order should be served. But where the court is satisfied that there is no doubt that the respondent knew what the order said and knew the consequences of disobedience a failure to dispense with service would encourage offenders to use technicalities to defeat the purpose of the order (*Benson v Richards* [2002] EWCA Civ 1402; *Serious Organised Crime Agency v Hymans* [2011] EWHC 3599).

37.9 Requirement for a penal notice on judgments and orders

(1) Subject to paragraph (2), a judgment or order to do or not do an act may not be enforced under rule 37.4 unless there is prominently displayed, on the front of the copy of the judgment or order served in accordance with this Chapter, a warning to the person required to do or not do the act in question that disobedience to the order would be a contempt of court punishable by imprisonment, a fine or sequestration of assets.

(2) The following may be enforced under rule 37.4 notwithstanding that the judgment or order does not contain the warning described in paragraph (1) –

(a) an undertaking to do or not do an act which is contained in a judgment or order; and
(b) an incoming protection measure.

(3) In the case of –

(a) a section 8 order (within the meaning of section 8(2) of the Children Act 1989);
(b) an order under section 14A, 14B(2)(b), 14C(3)(b) or 14D of the Children Act 1989 enforceable by committal order;
(c) an order prohibiting contact with a child under section 51A(2)(b) of the 2002 Act,

the court may, on the application of the person entitled to enforce the order, direct that the court officer issue a copy of the order, endorsed with or incorporating a notice as to the consequences of disobedience, for service in accordance with this rule, and no copy of the order shall be issued with any such notice endorsed or incorporated save in accordance with such a direction.

Amendments—Inserted by SI 2014/667. Amended by SI 2014/843; SI 2014/3296.

Parallel rule—CPR 1998, r 81.9.

Wording of penal notice—The form of words to be used in a penal notice endorsed on a judgment or order are set out in PD37. These should be followed. However, it has long been recognised that the form of a penal notice prescribed by rules of court are not rigid and may be adapted to the facts of a particular case so long as it clear and substantially accords with the standard wording (*Iberian Trust Ltd v Founders Trust and Investment Co Ltd* [1932] 2 KB 87, KBD). A clear penal notice is an essential prerequisite to enforcement (*Re S-C (Contempt)* [2010] 1 FLR 1478, CA, *Re Dad* [2015] EWHC 2655 (Fam)).

Undertakings—Notwithstanding r 37.9(2), it is good practice to endorse a penal notice on an order containing an undertaking. Indeed, PD37, para 2.1 contains a form of words. But the rule is clear and such an undertaking is enforceable notwithstanding the lack of a penal notice.

37.10 How to make the committal application

(1) A committal application is made by an application notice using the Part 18 procedure in the proceedings in which the judgment or order was made or the undertaking was given.

(2) Where the committal application is made against a person who is not an existing party to the proceedings, it is made against that person by an application notice using the Part 18 procedure.

(3) The application notice must –

(a) set out in full the grounds on which the committal application is made and must identify, separately and numerically, each alleged act of contempt including, if known, the date of each of the alleged acts; and
(b) be supported by one or more affidavits containing all the evidence relied upon.

(4) Subject to paragraph (5), the application notice and the evidence in support must be served personally on the respondent.

(5) The court may –

(a) dispense with service under paragraph (4) if it considers it just to do so; or
(b) make an order in respect of service by an alternative method or at an alternative place.

Amendments—Inserted by SI 2014/667.

Parallel rule—CPR 1998, r 81.10.

Application—Application is made using the Pt 18 procedure. Note the clear requirements of r 37.10(3)(a). The criminal standard of proof applies to committal applications and the application is the equivalent of an indictment.

Application/evidence—Clearly distinguish the application itself (see r 37.10(3)(a)) from the evidence in support of the application (see r 37.10(3)(b)).

Affidavit—The modern trend is to use witness statements endorsed with a statement of truth. But exceptionally the greater solemnity of an affidavit is prescribed to emphasise the serious nature of the application. Note that all the evidence relied upon must be in affidavit form.

37.11 Committal for breach of a solicitor's undertaking

(1) This rule applies where an order for committal is sought in respect of a breach by a solicitor of an undertaking given by the solicitor to the court in connection with family proceedings.

(2) The applicant must obtain permission form the court before making a committal application under this rule.

(3) The application for permission must be made by filing an application notice using the Part 18 procedure.

(4) The application for permission must be supported by an affidavit setting out –

(a) the name, description and address of the respondent;
(b) the grounds on which the committal order is sought.

(5) The application for permission may be made without notice.

(6) Rules 18.10 and 18.11 do not apply.

(7) Unless the applicant makes the committal application within 14 days after permission has been granted under this rule, the permission will lapse.

Amendments—Inserted by SI 2014/667.

Parallel rule—CPR 1998, r 81.11.

Permission—Following its cognate CPR, a 'permission stage' is introduced by r 37.11 before applying to commit a solicitor for breach of an undertaking. Solicitors Act 1974, s 50 preserves the inherent jurisdiction of the High Court to commit a solicitor as an officer of the court. County Court Act 1984, s 142 gives the County Court the same power as the High Court.

Chapter 3

Contempt in the face of the court

37.12 Contempt in the face of the court

Where –

(a) contempt has occurred in the face of the court; and
(b) that court has power to commit for contempt,

the court may deal with the matter of its own initiative and give such directions as it thinks fit for the disposal of the matter.

Amendments—Inserted by SI 2014/667.

Parallel rule—CPR 1998, r 81.16.

PD37—Contempt in the face of the court is dealt with in detail in FPR PD37, paras 3.1–3.5, which are distilled from a series of cases. Although a judge can deal 'summarily' with a contempt in the face of the court (ie without formal trial procedures), the requirements of the PD have considerably reduced the summary nature of the procedure. 'In the face of the court' was a colloquial expression that has become a term of art. The nature of the jurisdiction to commit for this type of contempt was reviewed by the Court of Appeal in *Balogh v St Albans Crown Court* [1975] QB 73, CA. Unfortunately, there are more such cases in family proceedings than in other areas. Although a judge can often do much to defuse a potential incident in court, all judges need to be familiar with the PD as situations invariably have to be dealt with immediately (see *Wilkinson v S* [2003] 1 WLR 1254, CA).

Chapter 4

Committal for interference with the due administration of justice

37.13 Scope

(1) This Chapter regulates committal applications in relation to interference with the due administration of justice in connection with family proceedings, except where the contempt is committed in the face of the court or consists of disobedience to an order of the court or a breach of an undertaking to the court.

(2) A committal application under this Chapter may not be made without the permission of the court.

(The procedure for applying for permission to make a committal application is set out in rule 37.15.)

(Rules 37.16(3) and (4) make provision for cases in which both this Chapter and Chapter 5 (Committal for making a false statement of truth) may be relevant.)

Amendments—Inserted by SI 2014/667.

Parallel rule—CPR 1998, r 81.12.

Scope—See commentary to rule 37.14.

37.14 Court to which application for permission under this Chapter is to be made

(1) Where the contempt of court is committed in connection with any family proceedings, the application for permission may be made only to a single judge of the Family Division.

(2) Where the contempt of court is committed otherwise than in connection with any proceedings, Part 81 of the CPR applies.

Amendments—Inserted by SI 2014/667.

Parallel rule—CPR 1998, r 81.13.

Permission—The rules in Ch 4 apply only to interference with the administration of justice in connection with family proceedings. (In other cases the CPR apply). Application for permission in such cases must be made to a single judge of the Family Division. Only the High Court has the inherent jurisdiction to deal with this type of contempt. The procedure is in r 37.15.

37.15 Application for permission

(1) The application for permission to make a committal application must be made using the Part 18 procedure, and the application notice must include or be accompanied by –

(a) a detailed statement of the applicant's grounds for making the committal application; and

(b) an affidavit setting out the facts and exhibiting all documents relied upon.

(2) The application notice and the documents referred to in paragraph (1) must be served personally on the respondent unless the court otherwise directs.

(3) Within 14 days of service on the respondent of the application notice, the respondent –

(a) must file and serve an acknowledgment of service; and

(b) may file and serve evidence.

(4) The court will consider the application for permission at an oral hearing, unless it considers that such a hearing is not appropriate.

(5) If the respondent intends to appear at the permission hearing referred to in paragraph (4), the respondent must give 7 days' notice in writing of such intention to the court and any other party and at the same time provide a written summary of the submissions which the respondent proposes to make.

(6) Where permission to proceed is given, the court may give such directions as it thinks fit, and may –

(a) transfer the proceedings to another court; or

(b) direct that the application be listed for hearing before a single judge or a Divisional Court.

Amendments—Inserted by SI 2014/667.

Parallel rule—CPR 1998, r 81.14: see *Cavendish Square Holdings BV v Makdessi* [2013] EWCA Civ 1540 in the commentary thereon.

Chapter 5

Committal for making a false statement of truth (Rule 17.6)

37.16 Scope and interaction with other Chapters of this Part

(1) This Chapter contains rules about committal applications in relation to making, or causing to be made, a false statement in a document verified by a statement of truth, without an honest belief in its truth.

(2) Where the committal application relates only to a false statement of truth, this Chapter applies.

(3) Where the committal application relates to both –

(a) a false statement of truth; and
(b) breach of a judgment, order or undertaking to do or abstain from doing an act,

then Chapter 2 (Committal for breach of a judgment, order or undertaking to do or abstain from doing an act) applies, but subject to paragraph (4).

(4) To the extent that a committal application referred to in paragraph (3) relates to a false statement of truth –

(a) the applicant must obtain the permission of the court in accordance with rule 37.17; or
(b) the court may direct that the matter be referred to the Attorney General with a request that the Attorney General consider whether to bring proceedings for contempt of court.

Amendments—Inserted by SI 2014/667.

Parallel rule—CPR 1998, r 81.17 – see commentary thereon.

False statement of truth—The statement of truth has largely replaced the affidavit. But no statute creates an offence in relation to a false statement of truth. Accordingly a false statement can only be dealt with as a contempt of court under the inherent jurisdiction (see *Brighton and Hove Bus and Coach Co Ltd v Brooks* [2011] EWHC 806).

37.17 Committal application in relation to a false statement of truth

(1) A committal application in relation a false statement of truth in connection with family proceedings in the High Court may be made only –

(a) with the permission of the court dealing with the proceedings in which the false statement was made; or
(b) by the Attorney General.

(2) A committal application in relation to a false statement of truth in connection with proceedings in the family court may be made only –

(a) with the permission of a single judge of the Family Division; or
(b) by the Attorney General.

(3) Where permission is required under paragraph (1)(a) or (2)(a), rule 37.15 applies.

(Under rule 37.15(6)(b), the court granting permission may direct that the application be listed before a single judge or a Divisional Court.)

(4) The court may direct that the matter be referred to the Attorney General with a request that the Attorney General consider whether to bring proceedings for contempt of court.

(5) Where the committal application is made by the Attorney General, the application may be made to a single judge or a Divisional Court.

Amendments—Inserted by SI 2014/667.

Parallel rule—CPR 1998, r 81.18.

Permission—Unless the application is by the Attorney General, only the High Court can deal with this type of committal and permission of a single judge of the Family Division is required. See *Cavendish Square Holdings BV v Makdessi* [2013] EWCA Civ 1540, where the Court of Appeal upheld the judge's decision to grant an application for permission to apply for committal based on a false statement of truth.

Attorney General—The Attorney has an ancient inherent power to bring committal proceedings. Today, the power is rarely used as there is usually an alternative, quicker procedure. The Attorney has stated that he prefers any request to act to come from the court rather than from a party.

PART III

Chapter 6
Writ of sequestration to enforce a judgment, order or undertaking

37.18 Scope

This Chapter contains rules about applications for a writ of sequestration to enforce a judgment, order or undertaking.

Amendments—Inserted by SI 2014/667.

Parallel rule—CPR 1998, r 81.19.

37.19 Writ of sequestration to enforce a judgment, order or undertaking

(1) If –

(a) a person required by a judgment or order to do an act does not do it within the time fixed by the judgment or order; or

(b) a person disobeys judgment or order not to do an act,

then, subject to the provisions of these Rules and if the court permits, the judgment or order may be enforced by a writ of sequestration against the property of that person.

(2) If the time fixed by the judgment or order for doing an act has been varied by a subsequent order, references in paragraph (1)(a) to the time fixed are references to the time fixed by that subsequent order.

(3) If the person referred to in paragraph (1) is a company or other corporation, the writ of sequestration may in addition be issued against the property of any director or other officer of that company or corporation.

(4) So far as applicable, and with the necessary modifications, the Chapter applies to undertakings given by a party as it applies to judgments or orders.

Amendments—Inserted by SI 2014/667.

Parallel rule—CPR 1998, r 81.20.

Sequestration—Sequestration is an ancient procedure of the High Court as a means of enforcing obedience to a judgment or order requiring a person to do an act, e g pay money, deliver up chattels. It is available in appropriate family cases (*Coles v Coles* [1957] P 68). Enforcement in the High Court is now by High Court Enforcement Officers (HCEO). The writ directs the HCEO to take possession of all the contemnor's real and personal property and to collect, receive and get in all rents and profits. It is an expensive remedy to be used where there is no cheaper effective alternative. Permission is required to issue the writ and often the application for permission is sufficient to achieve compliance with the judgment or order.

37.20 Requirement for service of a copy of the judgment or order and time for service

(1) Unless the court dispenses with service under rule 37.23, a judgment or order may not be enforced by writ of sequestration unless a copy of it has been served on the person required to do or not do the act in question, and in the case of a judgment or order requiring a person to act –

(a) the copy has been served before the end of the time fixed for doing the act, together with a copy of any order fixing that time;

(b) where the time for doing the act has been varied by a subsequent order, a copy of that subsequent order has also been served; and

(c) where the judgment or order was made pursuant to an earlier judgment or order requiring the act to be done, a copy of the earlier judgment or order has also been served.

(2) Where the person referred to in paragraph (1) is a company or other corporation, a copy of the judgment or order must also be served on a director or officer of the company or corporation before the end of the time fixed for doing the act.

(3) Copies of the judgment or order and any orders or agreements fixing or varying the time for doing an act must be served in accordance with rule 37.21 or 37.22, or in accordance with an order for alternative service made under rule 37.23(2)(b).

Amendments—Inserted by SI 2014/667.

Parallel rule—CPR 1998, r 81.21.

37.21 Method of service – copies of judgments or orders

Subject to rules 37.22 and 37.23, copies of judgments or order and any orders or agreements fixing or varying the time for doing an act must be served personally.

Amendments—Inserted by SI 2014/667.

Parallel rule—CPR 1998, r 81.22.

37.22 Method of service – copies of undertakings

(1) Subject to paragraph (2) and rule 37.23, a copy of any document recording an undertaking will be delivered by the court to the person who gave the undertaking –

- (a) by handing to that person a copy of the document before that person leaves the court building;
- (b) by posting a copy to that person at the residence or place of business of that person where this is known; or
- (c) by posting a copy to that person's solicitor.

(2) If delivery cannot be effected in accordance with paragraph (1), the court officer will deliver a copy of the document to the party for whose benefit the undertaking was given, and that party must serve it personally on the person who gave the undertaking as soon as practicable.

(3) Where the person referred to in paragraph (1) is a company or other corporation, a copy of the judgment or order must also be served on a director or officer of the company or corporation.

Amendments—Inserted by SI 2014/667.

Parallel rule—CPR 1998, r 81.23.

37.23 Dispensation with personal service

(1) In the case of a judgment or order requiring a person to do or not do an act, the court may dispense with service of a copy of the judgment or order in accordance with rules 37.20 to 37.22 if it is satisfied that the person has had notice of it –

- (a) by being present when the judgment or order was given or made; or
- (b) by being notified of its terms by telephone, email or otherwise.

(2) In the case of any judgment or order the court may –

- (a) dispense with service under rules 37.20 to 37.22 if the court thinks it just to do so; or
- (b) make an order in respect of service by an alternative method or at an alternative place.

Amendments—Inserted by SI 2014/667.

Parallel rule—CPR 1998, r 81.24.

37.24 Requirement for a penal notice on judgments and orders

(1) Subject to paragraph (2), a judgment or order to do or not do an act may not be enforced by a writ of sequestration unless there is prominently displayed, on the front of the copy of the judgment or order served in accordance with this Chapter, a warning to the person required to do or not do the act in question that disobedience to the order would be a contempt of court punishable by imprisonment, a fine or sequestration of assets.

(2) An undertaking to do or not do an act which is contained in a judgment or order may be enforced by a writ of sequestration notwithstanding that the judgment or order does not contain the warning described in paragraph (1).

Amendments—Inserted by SI 2014/667.

Parallel rule—CPR 1998, r 81.25.

37.25 How to make an application for permission to issue a writ of sequestration

(1) An application for permission to issue a writ of sequestration must be made –

- (a) in the High Court, to a single judge of the Family Division; or
- (b) in the family court, to a judge of High Court judge level.

(2) An application for permission to issue a writ of sequestration must be made by filing an application notice using the Part 18 procedure.

PART III

(3) The application notice must –

(a) set out in full the grounds on which the committal application is made and must identify, separately and numerically, each alleged act of contempt including, if known, the date of each of the alleged acts; and

(b) be supported by one or more affidavits containing all the evidence relied upon.

(4) Subject to paragraph (5), the application notice and the evidence in support must be served personally on the respondent.

(5) The court may –

(a) dispense with service under paragraph (4) if it considers it just to do so; or

(b) make an order in respect of service by an alternative method or at an alternative place.

Amendments—Inserted by SI 2014/667.
Parallel rule—CPR 1998, r 81.26.

37.26 Form of writ of sequestration

A writ of sequestration must be in Form No 67 as set out in Practice Direction 5A (or, in the family court, in a form containing corresponding provision).

Amendments—Inserted by SI 2014/667.
Parallel rule—CPR 1998, r 81.27.

Chapter 7
General rules about committal applications, orders for committal and writs of sequestration

37.27 The hearing

(1) Unless the court hearing the committal application or application for sequestration otherwise permits, the applicant may not rely on –

(a) any grounds other than –

(i) those set out in the application notice; or

(ii) in relation to committal application under Chapter 4, the statement of grounds required by rule 37.15(1)(a) (where not included in the application notice);

(b) any evidence unless it has been served in accordance with the relevant Chapter of this Part or the Practice Direction supplementing this Part.

(2) At the hearing, the respondent is entitled –

(a) to give oral evidence, whether or not the respondent has filed or served written evidence, and, if doing so, may be cross-examined; and

(b) with the permission of the court, to call a witness to give evidence whether or not the witness has made an affidavit or witness statement.

(3) The court may require or permit any party or other person (other than the respondent) to give oral evidence at the hearing.

(4) The court may give directions requiring the attendance for cross-examination of a witness who has given written evidence.

(5) The general rule is that a committal application, application for sequestration or application for discharge from custody will be heard, and judgment given, in public, but a hearing, or any part of it, may be in private (but with the matters in paragraph (6) always stated in public) if –

(a) publicity would defeat the object of the hearing;

(b) it involves matters relating to national security;

(c) it involves confidential information (including information relating to personal financial matters) and publication would damage that confidentiality;

(d) a private hearing is necessary to protect the interests of any child or protected party;

(e) it is a hearing of an application made without notice and it would be unjust to any respondent for there to be a public hearing; or

(f) the court considers this to be necessary, in the interests of justice.

(6) If the court hearing an application in private decides to make a committal order against the respondent, it will in public state –

(a) the name of the respondent;

(b) in general terms, the nature of the contempt of court in respect of which the committal order is being made; and

(c) the length of the period of the committal order.

(7) Where a committal order is made in the absence of the respondent, the court may on its own initiative fix a date and time when the respondent is to be brought before the court.

Amendments—Inserted by SI 2014/667.

Parallel rule—CPR 1998, r 81.28.

PD37—Part 37, Ch 7 is supplemented by FPR PD37, paras 7.1–14.5.

Hearing and judgment in public—The modern trend is transparency and this means public hearings as the general rule with hearings in private limited to cases where it is essential. Some matters must always be in public as provided in r 37.27(6).

37.28 Power to suspend execution of a committal order

(1) The court making the committal order may also order that execution of the order will be suspended for such period or on such terms and conditions as the court may specify.

(2) Unless the court otherwise directs, the applicant must serve on the respondent a copy of any order made under paragraph (1).

Amendments—Inserted by SI 2014/667.

Parallel rule—CPR 1998, r 81.29.

Power to suspend—The power of the Family Court to suspend a committal order is now governed by r 37.28 and is quite separate from the power of the criminal court to suspend a sentence. The question of whether to impose a sentence (and if so for how long) and then the question of whether to suspend are separate questions to be asked and answered separately.

Grounds and evidence—It is important that the applicant is clear about the type of committal alleged, eg whether for contempt for breach of a court order and/or contempt in the face of the court. See *Re L (A Child); Re Oddin* [2017] 1 FLR 1135, CA, where lack of clarity contributed to procedural error.

37.29 Warrant of committal

(1) If a committal order is made, the order will be for the issue of a warrant of committal.

(2) Unless the court orders otherwise –

(a) a copy of the committal order must be served on the respondent either before or at the time of the execution of the warrant of committal; or

(b) where the warrant of committal has been signed by the judge, the committal order may be served on the respondent at any time within 36 hours after the execution of the warrant.

(3) Without further order of the court, a warrant of committal must not be enforced more than 2 years after the date on which the warrant is issued.

Amendments—Inserted by SI 2014/667.

Parallel rule—CPR 1998, r 81.30.

37.30 Discharge of a person in custody

(1) A person committed to prison for contempt of court may apply to the court to be discharged.

(2) The application must –

(a) be in writing and attested by the governor of the prison (or any other officer of the prison not below the rank of principal officer);

(b) show that the person committed to prison for contempt has purged, or wishes to purge, the contempt; and

(c) be served on the person (if any) at whose instance the warrant of committal was issued at least one day before the application is made.

(3) Paragraph (2) does not apply to –

(a) a warrant of committal to which CCR Order rule 4 or 14, relates;

PART III

(b) an application made by the Official Solicitor acting with official authority for the discharge of a person in custody.

(4) If the committal order is made in the family court and –

(a) does not direct that any application for discharge must be made to a judge; or
(b) was made by a district judge under section 118 of the County Courts Act 1984;

the application for discharge may be made to a district judge.

(5) If the committal order is made in the High Court, the application for discharge may be made to a single judge of the Family Division.

Amendments—Inserted by SI 2014/667. Amended by SI 2016/355.

Drafting error—The text of rule 37.30(3)(a) is reproduced exactly as it appears in the SI, but there is clearly a number missing after the word 'Order', which must be 28.

Purging of contempt—A person committed for contempt of court has always been able to apply to purge usually involving a belated compliance with the relevant order (and/or promise as to future conduct as appropriate) and an apology. A sentence invariably has two elements i e punitive and coercive. The fact that the coercive element of the sentence no longer has any purpose does not require the sentence to be discharged (*Smith v Doncaster Metropolitan Borough Council* [2014] EWCA Civ 16).

The judge hearing the application to purge has a complete discretion—The judge may grant the application (which means immediate release), order release on a future date (*Yager v Musa* [1961] 2 QB 214, CA, or refuse the application (which leaves the original release date unchanged), but the judge cannot suspend the remainder of the sentence (*Harris v Harris* [2002] 1 FLR 248, CA).

Early release—In any event, the contemnor will serve only half of the imposed sentence and a sentencing judge cannot evade this (*Thomson v Mitchell* [2004] EWCA Civ 1271). Criminal Justice Act 2003, s 258 provides that where a contemnor is sentenced to imprisonment 'it shall be the duty of the Secretary of State to release him unconditionally' as soon as he has served one half of the sentence. As the release is unconditional, the contemnor is not on licence ('parole') and cannot be recalled to prison.

37.31 Discharge of a person in custody where a writ of sequestration has been issued

Where –

(a) a writ of sequestration has been issued to enforce a judgment or order;
(b) the property is in the custody or power of the respondent;
(c) the respondent has been committed for failing to deliver up any property or deposit it in court or elsewhere; and
(d) the commissioners appointed by the writ of sequestration take possession of the property as if it belonged to the respondent;

then, without prejudice to rule 37.30(1) (discharge of a person in custody), the court may discharge the respondent and give such directions for dealing with the property taken by the commissioners as it thinks fit.

Amendments—Inserted by SI 2014/667.
Parallel rule—CPR 1998, r 81.32.

Chapter 8
Penal and disciplinary provisions under the County Courts Act 1984

37.32 Scope

(1) This Chapter applies to the family court only and contains rules in relation to the penal, contempt and disciplinary provisions of the County Courts Act 1984 as they apply to the family court.

(2) In this Chapter, 'the Act' means the County Courts Act 1984.

Amendments—Inserted by SI 2014/667.
Parallel rule—CPR 1998, r 81.33.

37.33 Offences under sections 14, 92 or 118 of the Act

(1) This rule applies where it is alleged that any person has committed an offence –

(a) under section 14 of the Act, by assaulting an officer of the court acting in the execution of the officer's duties;
(b) under section 92 of the Act, by rescuing or attempting to rescue any goods seized in execution; or
(c) under section 118 of the Act, by wilfully insulting a judge, juror, witness or any officer of the court or by wilfully interrupting the proceedings of the family court or otherwise misbehaving in court,

and the alleged offender has not been taken into custody and brought before the court.

(2) The court will issue a summons, which must be served on the alleged offender personally not less than 7 days before the day of the hearing stated in the summons.

(3) Rule 37.29 (warrant of committal) applies, with the necessary modifications, where an order is made under section 14, 92 or 118 of the Act committing a person to prison.

Amendments—Inserted by SI 2014/667.

Parallel rule—CPR 1998, r 81.34: see *Chelmsford County Court v Ramet* [2014] EWHC 56 in commentary thereon.

37.34 Offences under section 124 of the Act

Where a complaint is made against an officer of the court under section 124 of the Act for having lost the opportunity of levying execution, the court will issue a summons, which must be served on the alleged offender personally not less than 7 days before the date of the hearing stated in the summons.

Amendments—Inserted by SI 2014/667.

Parallel rule—CPR 1998, r 81.35.

37.35 Notice to give evidence before or after a fine is imposed under section 31G of the 1984 Act

(1) Before or after imposing a fine on any person under section 31G of the 1984 Act for disobeying a witness summons or refusing to be sworn or give evidence, the court may direct that notice be given to that person in accordance with paragraph (2).

(2) The notice must state that if the recipient of the notice can demonstrate any reason why a fine should not be or should not have been imposed, that person may give evidence –

(a) by witness statement, affidavit or otherwise; and
(b) on a day named in the notice.

Amendments—Inserted by SI 2014/667. Amended by SI 2016/355.

Parallel rule—CPR 1998, r 81.36.

37.36 Non-payment of fine

(1) If a fine is not paid in accordance with the order imposing it, the court officer will, as soon as reasonably possible, report the matter to a judge.

(2) Where by an order imposing a fine –

(a) the amount of the fine is directed to be paid by instalments; and
(b) default is made in the payment of any instalment,

the same proceedings may be taken as if default had been made in respect of the whole of the fine.

Amendments—Inserted by SI 2014/667.

Parallel rule—CPR 1998, r 81.37.

37.37 Repayment of fine

If a person pays a fine and later gives evidence to satisfy the court that, if the evidence had been given earlier, no fine or a smaller fine would have been imposed, the court may order the whole or part of the fine to be repaid.

Amendments—Inserted by SI 2014/667.

Parallel rule—CPR 1998, r 81.38.

37.38 Section 118 of the Act and the tipstaff

For the purposes of section 118 of the Act in its application to the hearing of family proceedings at the Royal Courts of Justice or the principal registry, the tipstaff is deemed to be an officer of the court.

Parallel rule—None. This rule was formerly FPR 2010, r 33.8.
Amendments—Inserted by SI 2014/667.

Practice Direction 37A – Applications and Proceedings in Relation to Contempt of Court

This Practice Direction supplements FPR Part 37.

CHAPTER 2 OF PART 37 – COMMITTAL FOR BREACH OF A JUDGMENT, ORDER OR UNDERTAKING TO DO OR ABSTAIN FROM DOING AN ACT

Requirement for a penal notice on judgments and orders – form of penal notice – Rule 37.9

1.1 A judgment or order which restrains a party from doing an act or requires an act to be done must, if disobedience is to be dealt with by proceedings for contempt of court, have a penal notice endorsed on it as follows (or in words to substantially the same effect) –

> 'If you the within-named [ ] do not comply with this order you may be held to be in contempt of court and imprisoned or fined, or your assets may be seized.'.

1.2 Where an order referred to in rule 37.9(3)(a) or (b) is to be endorsed with or have incorporated in it a penal notice in accordance with rule 37.9(3), the notice must be in the words set out in paragraph 1.1 of the Practice Direction, or words to substantially the same effect.

Requirement for a penal notice on judgments and orders – undertakings – Rule 37.9

2.1 Subject to rule 37.9(2) (which covers the case where the undertaking is contained in an order or judgment), the form of an undertaking to do or abstain from doing any act must be endorsed with a notice setting out the consequences of disobedience as follows (or in words to substantially the same effect) –

> 'You may be held to be in contempt of court and imprisoned or fined, or your assets may be seized, if you break the promises that you have given to the court.'.

2.2 The court may decline to –

(1) accept an undertaking; and
(2) deal with disobedience in respect of an undertaking by contempt of court proceedings,

unless the party giving the undertaking has made a signed statement to the effect that that party understands the terms of the undertaking and the consequences of failure to comply with it, as follows (or in words to substantially the same effect) –

> 'I understand the undertaking that I have given and that if I break any of my promises to the court I may be sent to prison, or fined, or my assets may be seized, for contempt of court.'.

2.3 The statement need not be given before the court in person. It may be endorsed on the court copy of the undertaking or may be filed in a separate document such as a letter.

CHAPTER 3 OF PART 37 – CONTEMPT IN THE FACE OF THE COURT

Committal for contempt in the face of the court – Rule 37.12

3.1 Where the committal proceedings relate to a contempt in the face of the court the matters referred to in paragraph 4.3 should be given particular attention. Normally, it will be appropriate to defer consideration of the respondent's actions and behaviour to allow the respondent time to reflect on what has occurred. The time needed for the following procedures should allow such a period of reflection.

3.2 The use of the Part 18 procedure is not required for contempt falling under Chapter 3 of Part 37, but other provisions of this Practice Direction should be applied, as necessary, or adapted to the circumstances.

3.3 The judge should –

- (1) tell the respondent of the possible penalty that the respondent faces;
- (2) inform the respondent in detail, and preferably in writing, of the actions and behaviour of the respondent which have given rise to the committal application;
- (3) if the judge considers that an apology would remove the need for the committal application, tell the respondent;
- (4) have regard to the need for the respondent to be –
  - (a) allowed a reasonable time for responding to the committal application, including, if necessary, preparing a defence;
  - (b) made aware of the possible availability of criminal legal aid and how to contact the Legal Aid Agency;
  - (c) given the opportunity, if unrepresented, to obtain legal advice;
  - (d) if unable to understand English, allowed to make arrangements, seeking the court's assistance if necessary, for an interpreter to attend the hearing; and
  - (e) brought back before the court for the committal application to be heard within a reasonable time;
- (5) allow the respondent an opportunity to –
  - (a) apologise to the court;
  - (b) explain the respondent's actions and behaviour; and
  - (c) if the contempt is proved, to address the court on the penalty to be imposed on the respondent; and
- (6) where appropriate, nominate a suitable person to give the respondent the information. (It is likely to be appropriate to nominate a person where the effective communication of information by the judge to the respondent was not possible when the incident occurred.)

3.4 If there is a risk of the appearance of bias, the judge should ask another judge to hear the committal application.

3.5 Where the committal application is to be heard by another judge, a written statement by the judge before whom the actions and behaviour of the respondent which have given rise to the committal application took place may be admitted as evidence of those actions and behaviour.

CHAPTER 5 OF PART 37 – COMMITTAL FOR MAKING A FALSE STATEMENT OF TRUTH

Committal application in relation to a false statement of truth – Rule 37.17

4.1 Rules 37.17(1)(b) and 37.17(2)(b) provide that a committal application may be made by the Attorney General. However, the Attorney General prefers a request that comes from the court to one made direct by a party to the proceedings in which the alleged contempt occurred without prior consideration by the court. A request to the Attorney General is not a way of appealing against, or reviewing, the decision of the judge.

4.2 Where the permission of the court is sought under rule 37.17(1)(a) or 37.17(2)(a) so that rule 37.15 is applied by rule 37.17(3), the affidavit evidence in support of the application must –

- (1) identify the statement said to be false;
- (2) explain –
  - (a) why it is false; and
  - (b) why the maker knew the statement to be false at the time it was made; and
- (3) explain why contempt proceedings would be appropriate in the light of the overriding objective in Part 1.

PART III

4.3 The court may –

(1) exercise any of its powers under the rules (including the power to give directions under rule 37.15(6));
(2) initiate steps to consider if there is a contempt of court and, where there is, to punish it; or
(3) as provided by rule 37.17(4), direct that the matter be referred to the Attorney General with a request to consider whether to bring proceedings for contempt of court.

4.4 A request to the Attorney General to consider whether to bring proceedings for contempt of court must be made in writing and sent to the Attorney General's Office at 20 Victoria Street, London, SW1H 0NF.

4.5 A request to the Attorney General must be accompanied by a copy of any order directing that the matter be referred to the Attorney General and must –

(1) identify the statement said to be false;
(2) explain –
    (a) why it is false; and
    (b) why the maker knew the statement to be false at the time it was made; and
(3) explain why contempt proceedings would be appropriate in the light of the overriding objective in Part 1.

4.6 Once the applicant receives the result of the request to the Attorney General, the applicant must send a copy of it to the court that will deal with the committal application, and the court will give such directions as it sees fit.

4.7 The rules do not change the law of contempt or introduce new categories of contempt. A person applying to commence such proceedings should consider whether the incident complained of does amount to contempt of court and whether such proceedings would further the overriding objective in Part 1.

CHAPTER 6 OF PART 37 – WRIT OF SEQUESTRATION TO ENFORCE A JUDGMENT, ORDER OR UNDERTAKING

Requirement for a penal notice on judgments and orders – form of penal notice – Rule 37.24

5 Paragraphs 1 and 2.1 to 2.3 apply to judgments and orders to be enforced by a writ of sequestration.

Levying execution on certain days

6 Unless the court orders otherwise, a writ of sequestration to enforce a judgment, order or undertaking must not be executed on a Sunday, Good Friday or Christmas Day.

CHAPTER 7 OF PART 37 – GENERAL RULES ABOUT COMMITTAL APPLICATIONS, ORDERS FOR COMMITTAL AND WRITS OF SEQUESTRATION

General rules

7.1 Subject to paragraph 7.2, this Section of the Practice Direction applies in relation to all matters covered by Part 37.

7.2 Where there is a conflict between the provisions in this Section of the Practice Direction and specific provisions elsewhere in this Practice Direction or in Part 37, the specific provisions prevail.

Human rights

8 In all cases the Convention rights of those involved should particularly be borne in mind. It should be noted that the standard of proof, having regard to the possibility that a person may be sent to prison, is that the allegation be proved beyond reasonable doubt.

(Section 1 of the Human Rights Act 1998 defines 'the Convention rights'.)

General rules about applications: applications which cannot be made without permission

9 If the committal application is one which cannot be made without permission –

(1) the permission may only be granted by a judge who would have power to hear the committal application if permission were granted;
(2) the date on which and the name of the judge by whom the requisite permission was granted must be stated on the application notice by which the committal application is commenced;
(3) the application notice may not be issued or filed until the requisite permission has been granted; and
(4) Rules 18.10 and 18.11 do not apply.

General rules about applications: using Part 18 procedure

10.1 Where the application is made using the Part 18 procedure in existing proceedings, the application notice must state that the application is made in the proceedings in question, and its title and reference number must correspond with the title and reference number of those proceedings.

10.2 If the application for permission to make a committal application or the committal application is commenced by the filing of an application notice –

(1) Part 18 will apply subject to the provisions of Part 37 and this Practice Direction, in particular sub-paragraphs (2) to (4);
(2) an amendment to the application notice may be made with the permission of the court but not otherwise;
(3) the court may not dispose of the application without a hearing; and
(4) the application notice must contain a prominent notice stating the possible consequences of the court making a committal order and of the respondent not attending the hearing. A form of notice which may be used is annexed to this Practice Direction.

Evidence and information

11.1 Written evidence in support of or in opposition to a committal application must be given by affidavit.

11.2 Written evidence served in support of or in opposition to a committal application must, unless the court otherwise directs, be filed.

11.3 The following rules do not apply to committal applications –

(1) rule 25.11 (Court's power to direct that evidence is to be given by a single joint expert);
(2) rule 25.12 (Instructions to single joint expert); and
(3) rule 25.13 (Power of court to direct a party to provide information).

The hearing – Rule 37.27

12.1 When issuing or filing the application notice for a committal application, the applicant must obtain from the court a date for the hearing of the committal application.

12.2 Unless the court otherwise directs, the hearing date of a committal application must not be less than 14 days after service of the application notice on the respondent. The hearing date must be specified in the application notice or in a Notice of Hearing attached to and served with the application notice.

12.3 The court may on the hearing date –

(1) give case management directions with a view to a hearing of the committal application on a future date; or
(2) if the committal application is ready to be heard, proceed to hear it.

12.4 In dealing with any committal application, the court will have regard to the need for the respondent to have details of the alleged acts of contempt and the opportunity to respond to the committal application.

12.5 The court will also have regard to the need for the respondent to be –

(1) allowed a reasonable time for responding to the committal application including, if necessary, preparing a defence;
(2) made aware of the possible availability of criminal legal aid and how to contact the Legal Aid Agency;
(3) given the opportunity, if unrepresented, to obtain legal advice; and
(4) if unable to understand English, allowed to make arrangements, seeking the assistance of the court if necessary, for an interpreter to attend the hearing.

Striking out, procedural defects and discontinuance

13.1 On application by the respondent or on its own initiative, the court may strike out a committal application if it appears to the court –

(1) that the application and the evidence served in support of it disclose no reasonable ground for alleging that the respondent is guilty of a contempt of court;
(2) that the application is an abuse of the court's process or, if made in existing proceedings, is otherwise likely to obstruct the just disposal of those proceedings; or
(3) that there has been a failure to comply with a rule, practice direction or court order.

13.2 The court may waive any procedural defect in the commencement or conduct of a committal application if satisfied that no injustice has been caused to the respondent by the defect.

13.3 A committal application may not be discontinued without the permission of the court.

ANNEX: PARAGRAPH 10.2(4)

Form of penal notice to be included on committal applications

IMPORTANT NOTICE

The Court has power to send you to prison, to fine you or seize your assets if it finds that any of the allegations made against you are true and amount to a contempt of court. **You must attend court** on the date shown on the front of this form. It is in your own interest to do so. You should bring with you any witnesses and documents which you think will help you put your side of the case. If you consider the allegations are not true you must tell the court why. If it is established that they are true, you must tell the court of any good reason why they do not amount to a contempt of court, or, if they do, why you should not be punished. If you need advice, you should show this document at once to your solicitor or go to a Citizens' Advice Bureau or similar organisation.

PART 38
RECOGNITION AND ENFORCEMENT OF PROTECTION MEASURES

CONTENTS OF THIS PART

Chapter 1

Rule		Page
	Scope and interpretation of this Part	
38.1	Scope and interpretation	2003
	Chapter 2	
	Certificates for outgoing protection measures	
38.2	Application for an Article 5 certificate	2004

38.3 The court to which an application for an Article 5 certificate must be made 2004
38.4 When a request for a translation of an Article 5 certificate may be made 2005
38.5 The court to which a request for translation of an Article 5 certificate must be made 2005
38.6 Service requirements under Article 6 2005
38.7 Notification of the certificate under Article 8 2006
38.8 Rectification of an Article 5 certificate 2006
38.9 Withdrawal of an Article 5 certificate 2006
38.10 When an application for an Article 14 certificate may be made 2007
38.11 The court to which an application for an Article 14 certificate must be made 2007

Chapter 3
Incoming protection measures

38.12 Application for adjustment under Article 11 2008
38.13 Notification of the adjustment under Article 11 2008
38.14 Application for refusal of recognition or enforcement under Article 13 2008
38.15 Application under Article 14(2) 2009

Practice Direction 38A –
Recognition and Enforcement of Protection Measures 2009

Chapter 1
Scope and interpretation of this Part

38.1 Scope and interpretation

(1) This Part contains rules about the mutual recognition and enforcement of protection measures between England and Wales and Member States of the European Union other than the United Kingdom and Denmark.

(2) In this Part –

'Article 5 certificate' means a certificate issued under Article 5 of the Protection Measures Regulation;

'Article 8 notice' means the notification required by Article 8 of the Protection Measures Regulation;

'Article 11 notice' means the notification required by Article 11 of the Protection Measures Regulation;

'Article 14 certificate' means a certificate issued under Article 14 of the Protection Measures Regulation;

'outgoing protection measure' means any protection measure included in any of –

(a) a non-molestation order made under section 42 of the 1996 Act;
(b) an occupation order made under any of sections 33, 35, 36, 37 or 38 of the 1996 Act;
(c) an undertaking accepted by the court under section 46 of the 1996 Act;
(d) an order that has been varied under section 49 of the 1996 Act;
(e) a forced marriage protection order made under section 63A of the 1996 Act;
(f) an undertaking accepted by the court under section 63E of the 1996 Act;
(g) an order that has been varied under section 63G of the 1996 Act;
(h) any other order of the family court or the High Court in family proceedings; or
(i) any other undertaking accepted by the family court or the High Court in family proceedings;

'person causing the risk' has the meaning given to it in the Protection Measures Regulation; and

'protected person' has the meaning given to it in the Protection Measures Regulation.

Amendments—Inserted by SI 2014/3296.

Protection Measures Regulation—This refers to Regulation (EU) No 606/2013 of the European Parliament and of the Council of 12 June 2013 (see Part VI). It applies to all civil and family protection measures. The Civil Jurisdiction and Judgments (Protection of Measures) Regulations 2014 support the implications of the EU

Regulation. They assign the conduct of incoming protection measures to the Family Division of the High Court. They also ensure that the county courts and High Court of Northern Ireland have jurisdiction to deal with protection measures as if they were domestic protection measures. The Civil Procedure (Amendment No 8) Rules 2014 inserted Section VI into CPR 1998, Pt 74 (rr 74.34–74.50), setting out civil protection measures. These rules are in almost identical terms to FPR 1998, Pt 38. The Regulation should not interfere with the functioning of Brussels IIA (see Part VI). Decisions taken under Brussels IIA should continue to be recognised and enforced, but the Regulation does not apply to protection measures falling within the scope of Brussels IIA. The Regulation applies from 11 January 2015 irrespective of when proceedings were issued. Denmark is not bound by or subject to its application. The protection measures ordered for the protection of a person will apply where there exist serious grounds for considering that that person's life, physical or psychological integrity, personal liberty, security or sexual integrity is at risk. By reason of the fact that in some countries protection measures may be made under administrative process, the Regulation includes measures made within the EU of both judicial and administrative authorities. For information about recognition and enforcement of Scottish orders and in Scotland, contact: Simon Stockwell, Family and Property Law, Scottish Government, St Andrew's House, Regent Road, Edinburgh EH1 3DG; email: simon.stockwell@scotland.gsi.gov.uk. For information about Northern Ireland, contact: Naomi Callaghan, Civil Justice Policy Division, Department of Justice, Massey House, Stormont Estate Belfast BT4 3SX; email: Naomi.Callaghan@dojni.x.gsi.gov.uk.

Protection measures—The definition given above and in PD38A, para 1.3 is a repetition of the definition set out in Art 3. FPR 1998, r 38.1 sets out those orders or undertakings that may include a protection measure within the meaning given in the Regulation. In relation to civil matters, this means any protection measures included in (i) an injunction issued under PHA 1997, s 3(3)(a) and (ii) any other injunction order or undertaking accepted by the High Court or the County Court (CPR 1998, r 74.34(f)(i)–(iv)). The effect of recognition of the protection measure is limited to 12 months from the date of issue of the Art 5 certificate (see below), after which the protected person should apply for a protection under the domestic law of the Member State addressed (preamble to the Regulation, para 16) or invoke protection measures of more than 12 months under any other legal act of the EU for providing recognition. It is mandatory for the protected person to have effective access to justice and for legal aid to be provided in accordance with Council Directive 2003/8/EC of 27 January 2003 (preamble, para 34). The Regulation is applied in accordance with the right of defence and fair trial of the person causing the risk (see requirements of service/notification under Arts 6.8 and 11(3) and rights under Art 13).

Chapter 2
Certificates for outgoing protection measures

38.2 Application for an Article 5 certificate

(1) A protected person may apply for an Article 5 certificate –

(a) at the time of application for an order containing an outgoing protection measure; or
(b) at any time after such application, provided either –
 (i) the order or the undertaking containing the outgoing protection measure has not yet been made or accepted, as the case may be; or
 (ii) the outgoing protection measure is still in force.

(2) An application for an Article 5 certificate may be made without notice.

Amendments—Inserted by SI 2014/3296.

The application—Application should be made using the Pt 18 procedure.

Article 5 certificate—In order to provide uniformity, the Regulation introduces a standard multilingual form for the certificate and requires that the certificate is issued in Form 1 in Annex 1 of the Commission Implementing Regulation (EU) No 939/2014 of 2 September 2014 (see *Emergency Remedies in the Family Court*, Family Law). It must contain the information set out in Art 7 (see PD38A, para 2.3). Conditions that apply before a certificate may be issued are set out in Art 6 (see PD38A, paras 2.4 and 2.5). These relate to service of the protection measure on the person causing the harm (see r 38.6). The certificate is effective only after it has been served (see Art 8). Similar provisions are contained in CPR 1998, r 74.38–74.41. To get a protection measure recognised in England and Wales or in another Member State, the protected person must have an Art 5 certificate in addition to the order and where necessary a translation/transliteration of the certificate in accordance with Art 16 (see rr 38.4 and 38.5).

38.3 The court to which an application for an Article 5 certificate must be made

An application for an Article 5 certificate must be made –

(a) where the outgoing protection measure has not yet been ordered or accepted –
 (i) to the family court if the proceedings relating to the outgoing protection measure are before the family court;
 (ii) to the High Court if the proceedings relating to the outgoing protection measure are before the High Court;

(b) where the outgoing protection measure has been ordered or accepted –
  (i) to the family court if that court made the order or accepted the undertaking as the case may be, unless there are proceedings relating to that order or undertaking before the High Court, in which case the application must be made to the High Court;
  (ii) to the High Court if that court made the order or accepted the undertaking as the case may be, unless there are proceedings relating to that order or undertaking before the family court, in which case the application must be made to the family court.

Amendments—Inserted by SI 2014/3296.

Court to which an application should be made—This is the court where the proceedings are pending or where the order was made or undertaking given. FC(CDB)R 2014 have been amended to allocate applications under the Regulation to lay justices in the Family Court, but applying rr 15(2) and 20 of the Rules they may be dealt with by other levels of the judiciary to make effective and efficient use of local judicial resources in cases of emergency and where the factors set out in r 20 are met. In civil proceedings, the application should be made to the appropriate County Court or the High Court, as the case may be (CPR 1998, r 74.37). The application should be made in accordance with FPR 2010, Pt 18 or CPR 1998, Pt 23 (CPR 1998, r 74.35), as the case may be.

38.4 When a request for a translation of an Article 5 certificate may be made

A protected person may request a translation of an Article 5 certificate –

(a) at the time of the application for the Article 5 certificate; or
(b) at any time after such application, provided the Article 5 certificate –
  (i) has not yet been issued; or
  (ii) if issued, is still in force.

Amendments—Inserted by SI 2014/3296.

Request for translation—In relation to civil proceedings, identical provisions are set out in CPR 1998, r 74.38.

38.5 The court to which a request for translation of an Article 5 certificate must be made

A request for a translation of an Article 5 certificate must be made –

(a) if the certificate has not yet been issued, to –
  (i) the family court, if the application for the certificate is before the family court; or
  (ii) he High Court, if the application for the certificate is before the High Court; or
(b) if the certificate has been issued, to –
  (i) the family court, if the family court issued it;
  (ii) the High Court, if the High Court issued it.

Amendments—Inserted by SI 2014/3296.

Court to which request is made—In civil proceedings, the application is made to the County Court or the High Court, as the case may be, where the proceedings are pending or to the court where the certificate was issued (CPR 1998, r 74.39).

Cost of translation—The proposal is for a translation to be provided where necessary without imposing any cost on the protected person by making use of the standard form (Regulation (EU) No 606/2013, paras 23, 24).

38.6 Service requirements under Article 6

(1) Where the outgoing protection measure is included in an order, the court may only issue an Article 5 certificate if satisfied that the order has been served upon the person causing the risk in accordance with the requirements specified in rule 37.5, unless the court has dispensed with service of the order in accordance with the requirements specified in rule 37.8.

(2) Where the protected person is responsible for serving the order on the person causing the risk, any application for an Article 5 certificate must be accompanied by a certificate of service.

Amendments—Inserted by SI 2014/3296.

Service requirements—These requirements comply with Art 6, but it is essential also to comply with rr 37.6, 37.7 and 37.9 and PD37A to ensure that the consequences of a breach are clearly brought to the attention of the person causing the risk. In civil matters, requirements specified in CPR 1998, r 81.5 and 81.8 and PD81 must be complied with.

38.7 Notification of the certificate under Article 8

(1) Subject to paragraph (2), the court officer must give Article 8 notice to the person causing the risk by serving it in accordance with Chapter 3 of Part 6 and the rules in that Chapter shall apply to service of the notice as they apply to any other document served by a court officer.

(2) If the person causing the risk resides in a Member State of the European Union other than the United Kingdom or in a country outside the European Union, the court officer must give Article 8 notice by sending it by registered letter with acknowledgement of receipt or confirmation of delivery or equivalent to the last known place of residence of that person.

Amendments—Inserted by SI 2014/3296.

Notification of the certificate—This is referred to as the Art 8 notice. It is essential for this notice to include an explanation to the person causing the risk that the issue of an Art 5 notice means that the protection measure can be recognised and enforced in another Member State, of the consequences of being punished under the law of that Member State for any breach of the protection measure and of his/her right to challenge the issue of the Art 5 certificate. The requirement of confidentiality referred to in Art 8(3) is set out in PD38A, para 2.6. CPR 1998, r 74.41 contains identical terms.

38.8 Rectification of an Article 5 certificate

(1) An application pursuant to Article 9 of the Protection Measures Regulation for rectification of an Article 5 certificate must be made to –

(a) the family court if the family court issued the certificate;
(b) the High Court if the High Court issued the certificate.

(2) An application for such rectification may be made by –

(a) the protected person; or
(b) the person causing the risk.

(3) An Article 5 certificate may be rectified pursuant to Article 9(1)(a) of the Protection Measures Regulation by the court –

(a) on application under this rule; or
(b) on its own initiative.

Amendments—Inserted by SI 2014/3296.

Grounds for rectification of certificate—Under Art 9, there is only one ground on which a certificate may be rectified on application by either party or on the court's own initiative, i e that due to a clerical error there is a discrepancy between the original protection measure granted by the court of a Member State and the Art 5 certificate (see also PD38A, para 2.8 and CPR 1998, r 74.42). The application for rectification should be made to the appropriate authority of the Member State that issued the Art 5 certificate.

38.9 Withdrawal of an Article 5 certificate

(1) An application pursuant to Article 9 of the Protection Measures Regulation for withdrawal of an Article 5 certificate must be made to –

(a) the family court if the family court issued the certificate; or
(b) the High Court if the High Court issued the certificate.

(2) An application for such withdrawal may be made by –

(a) the protected person; or
(b) the person causing the risk.

(3) An Article 5 certificate may be withdrawn pursuant to Article 9(1)(b) of the Protection Measures Regulation by the court –

(a) on application under this rule; or
(b) on its own initiative.

Amendments—Inserted by SI 2014/3296.

Withdrawal of Art 5 certificate—There is only one ground on which an Art 5 certificate may be withdrawn, i e where it was clearly wrongly granted having regard to the requirements of service of the protection measures set out in Art 6 (Art 9(1)(b)). Similar provisions apply to certificates issued in civil proceedings (see also PD38A, para 2.9).

Effect of withdrawal—The protection measure cannot be recognised or enforced in the state addressed or any other Member State (see PD38A, para 2.9).

38.10 When an application for an Article 14 certificate may be made

A protected person or person causing the risk may apply for an Article 14 certificate –

(a) at the time of application for variation or discharge of the order containing the outgoing protection measure, or for acceptance of a variation or discharge of the undertaking containing the outgoing protection measure, as the case may be;

(b) at any time after the variation or discharge of the order containing the outgoing protection measure has been ordered or the variation or discharge of the undertaking containing the outgoing protection measure has been accepted, as the case may be;

(c) at the time of application under Article 9 of the Protection Measures Regulation for withdrawal of an Article 5 certificate;

(d) at any time after an Article 5 certificate has been withdrawn under Article 9 of the Protection Measures Regulation;

(e) at the time of application for an order staying or suspending enforcement of the order or undertaking containing the outgoing protection measure; or

(f) any time after, the making of an order staying or suspending enforcement of the order or undertaking containing the outgoing protection measure.

Amendments—Inserted by SI 2014/3296.

When an application may be made—CPR 1998, r 74.44 contains similar provisions with one exception, i e whereas in family proceedings the application may be made at the time of making the application or at any time after the order is made withdrawing the protection measure ((c) and (d) above), the equivalent provision in CPR 1998, r 74.44(c) refers only to an application for an Art 14 certificate being made after the Art 5 certificate has been withdrawn. FPR 2010, r 38.10(c) is not reproduced in CPR 1998, r 74.44. However, given that the provisions set out in relation to all other incidents include the right to apply at the time of the application or at any time after the making of an order, it could be argued that it follows that as under r 74.44(a),(d) this must include the right to apply on the making of the order withdrawing the Art 5 certificate.

Article 14 certificate—This must be in Form 2 annexed to the Commission Implementing Regulation (EU) No 939/2014 (see *Emergency Remedies in the Family Court*, Family Law). It must be sent to the Member State addressed so that steps are taken to stop recognition and/or enforcement of the protection measure as required by Art 14(2).

38.11 The court to which an application for an Article 14 certificate must be made

An application for an Article 14 certificate must be made –

(a) if the order containing the outgoing protection measure has not yet been varied or discharged or a variation or discharge of the undertaking containing the protection measure has not yet been accepted, as the case may be, to –

(i) the family court if the application for such variation or discharge is before the family court; or

(ii) the High Court if the application for such variation or discharge is before the High Court;

(b) if there has been an application under Article 9 of the Protection Measures Regulation for withdrawal of the Article 5 certificate, and that application has not yet been decided, to –

(i) the family court if the application for such withdrawal is before the family court; or

(ii) the High Court if the application for such withdrawal is before the High Court;

(c) if the order containing the outgoing protection measure has been varied or discharged or the variation or discharge of the undertaking containing the outgoing protection measure has been accepted, as the case may be, to –

(i) the family court if the family court ordered or accepted such variation or discharge, as the case may be; or

(ii) the High Court if the High Court ordered or accepted such variation or discharge, as the case may be;

(d) if an Article 5 certificate has been withdrawn under Article 9, to –

(i) the family court if the family court ordered such withdrawal; or

(ii) the High Court if the High Court ordered such withdrawal;

(e) where enforcement of the order has been stayed or suspended, to –

PART III

(i) the family court if the family court made the order for the stay or suspension; or
(ii) the High Court if the High Court made the order for the stay or suspension.

Amendments—Inserted by SI 2014/3296.

Which court—In civil matters, it will the County Court or the High Court, as the case may be (CPR 1998, r 74.45 contains similar provisions).

Information/documents to be provided—These are as follows: (i) a copy of the order that included the protection measure; (ii) the Art 5 certificate; and (iii) a copy of the order that varied, stayed, suspended or discharged all or part of the order including the protection measure or notification of the withdrawal of the Art 5 certificate. If neither party is able to provide all or some of these documents, the application can still be made but the court must be provided with the case number so that the orders can be located in the court file (PD38A, para 2.12).

Form of application—Should be in accordance with Pt 18 procedure using Form FP2. In civil cases, the procedure under CPR 1998, Pt 23 should be followed.

Chapter 3
Incoming protection measures

38.12 Application for adjustment under Article 11

A protected person may apply to the court under Article 11 of the Protection Measures Regulation to adjust the factual elements of an incoming protection measure.

Amendments—Inserted by SI 2014/3296.

Adjustments—Since Regulation (EU) No 606/2013 acknowledges in its Preamble that the protection will extend to the place where the protected person lives, works and regularly visits or attends, the court of the Member State addressed is authorised to make factual adjustments to the protection measures where such adjustment is necessary for the recognition and enforcement of the measures to be practically effective in the Member State addressed. The adjustments include amending the address location or the minimum distance that the person causing the risk must keep from the protected person's address or other location, but the type and civil nature of the protection measure may not be affected by any such adjustments (Art 11 and Preamble, paras 19 and 20; PD38A, para 3.3). For civil protection measures, see CPR 1998, r 74.46.

38.13 Notification of the adjustment under Article 11

(1) Subject to paragraph (2), the court officer must give Article 11 notice to the person causing the risk by serving it in accordance with Chapter 3 of Part 6 and the rules in that Chapter apply to service of the notice as they apply to any other document to be served by a court officer.

(2) If the person causing the risk resides in a Member State of the European Union other than the United Kingdom or in a country outside the European Union, the court officer must give Article 11 notice by sending it by registered letter with acknowledgment of receipt or other confirmation of delivery or equivalent to the last known place of residence of that person.

Amendments—Inserted by SI 2014/3296.

Notification—This provision and its equivalent in CPR 1998, r 74.47 meets the requirement of Art 11(2)–(4), but see PD38A, paras 3.3 and 3.4 in relation to disclosure of the protected person's address or location details.

38.14 Application for refusal of recognition or enforcement under Article 13

An application by a person causing the risk for refusal of recognition or enforcement under Article 13 of the Protection Measures Regulation must be made to –

(a) the family court if –
  (i) there are proceedings relating to the same protection measure before the family court; or
  (ii) proceedings relating to the same protection measure were dealt with by the family court;
(b) the High Court if –
  (i) there are proceedings relating to the same protection measure before the High Court; or
  (ii) proceedings relating to the same protection measure were dealt with by the High Court; or
(c) the family court, unless, applying rule 5.4, the application should be made to the High Court.

Amendments—Inserted by SI 2014/3296.

Application for refusal of recognition etc—Rule 38.14 identifies the court to which an application by a person causing the risk for refusal of recognition etc should be made, but does not specifically state that the person has the right to apply to the court. CPR 1998, r 74.49 on the other hand states that a person causing the risk may apply to the court for refusal of recognition and enforcement under Art 13. Similarly, although r 74.49 does not specifically identify the court to which the application should be made, applying the rules as a whole and in line with FPR 2010 this must be either in the County Court or the High Court, as the case may be, where the proceedings relating to the same protection order are pending or have been determined. However, it should be noted that FC(CDB)R 2014 have been amended to provide that where an incoming protection measure is challenged on the grounds set out in Art 13, the application must be heard by the High Court. It is more than likely that an application for recognition and enforcement of the protection measure will be taken by the protected person in the Family Court before any objections to recognition and enforcement are raised, in which case the application if commenced or pending in the Family Court may be transferred to the High Court at that stage. The same principles will apply in relation to civil measures proceeding in the County Court.

Grounds for an application for recognition and enforcement—There are only two grounds on which the person causing the risk may challenge, i e that such recognition is manifestly contrary to public policy in the Member State addressed or irreconcilable with a judgment given or recognised in the Member State addressed (Art 13; c f CACA 1985, Sch 2, Art 10(1)(a)).

Form of application—If an application for recognition has been made, the application for non-recognition should be made using Pt 18 procedure, otherwise Pt 19 procedure should be followed. In civil cases, CPR 1998, Pt 23 should be followed.

Appeals and review of incoming protection measure—No appeal lies against the issuing of an Art 5 certificate and under no circumstances may a protection measure ordered in the Member State of origin be reviewed as to its substance in the Member State addressed (Art 12).

PART III

38.15 Application under Article 14(2)

(1) This rule applies where an Article 14 certificate has been issued in a Member State of the European Union other than the United Kingdom or Denmark.

(2) A protected person or person causing the risk may apply to the court to stay, suspend or withdraw the effects of recognition or, where applicable, the enforcement of the protection measure.

(3) An application under this rule must include a copy of the Article 14 certificate issued in the other Member State.

(4) On an application under this rule, the court must make such orders or give such directions as may be necessary to give effect to the Article 14 certificate.

Amendments—Inserted by SI 2014/3296.

Effect of this rule—See PD38A, para 3.8 below.

Practice Direction 38A – Recognition and Enforcement of Protection Measures

This Practice Direction supplements FPR Part 38.

The Protection Measures Regulation

1.1 The Protection Measures Regulation is an EU law which helps a person who has a 'protection measure' obtained in one Member State to have it recognised and enforced in any other EU Member State (except Denmark). The protection can continue in the other Member State for the length of time the 'protection measure' has been ordered, except it cannot continue for longer than twelve months.

1.2 The Protection Measures Regulation applies across the United Kingdom. Part 38 and this Practice Direction apply in England and Wales only. If you need information about Scotland you should contact the Scottish Government . If you need information about Northern Ireland you should contact the Northern Ireland Department for Justice .

1.3 A 'protection measure' is a decision that says the 'person causing the risk' must comply with one or more of the three kinds of obligation set out below, to protect another person, the 'protected person', from physical or psychological harm.

The obligations are:

- a ban or controls on entering the place where the protected person lives or works, or regularly visits or stays;
- a ban or controls on contact, in any form, with the protected person, including by telephone, post, e-mail, text or social media or any other means;
- a ban or controls on approaching the protected person closer than a stated distance.

1.4 A 'protected person' is the individual who is protected by the obligation in the protection measure. A 'person causing the risk' is the individual on whom the obligation has been imposed.

1.5 In England and Wales in family proceedings a protection measure as set out at paragraph 1.3 above may be included in an order made or undertaking accepted by the family court or the High Court. In this Practice Direction, references to orders made include undertakings accepted.

1.6 Rule 38.1 sets out which orders made in family proceedings in England and Wales could contain a protection measure. In the Protection Measures Regulation, in the Article 5 and Article 14 certificates and in this practice direction the meanings of words are as follows. The family court or the High Court is the 'issuing authority' for the protection measure when it makes the order. The EU Member State where the protection measure is ordered is the 'Member State of origin'. The EU Member State where the protected person can take the protection measure to get it recognised and, where applicable, enforced, is the 'Member State addressed'.

1.7 If the protected person wants to take a protection measure ordered in England and Wales to another EU Member State (except Denmark) to get it recognised and enforced there, it is called an 'outgoing protection measure'. If the protected person is bringing a protection measure from another EU Member State (not from Denmark and not from Scotland or Northern Ireland) to England and Wales to get it recognised and enforced in England and Wales, it is called an 'incoming protection measure'. To get a protection measure recognised and enforced here or in another Member State (except Denmark) it must have a certificate under Article 5 of the Protection Measures Regulation to go with it.

Outgoing protection measures

Application for an Article 5 certificate

2.1 A protected person who wants an outgoing protection measure to be recognised and enforceable in another Member State (except Denmark) can apply under Chapter 2 of Part 38 for an Article 5 certificate. The protected person can apply either at the same time as they are applying for the order which contains a protection measure, or later before the order is made or, provided the order containing the protection measure is still in force, at any time after the order is made.

2.2 The protected person must apply to the court where the proceedings about the order are under way or took place. This will be either the family court or the High Court. At the same time as applying for the certificate, or later, the protected person can ask the court where the proceedings are under way or took place for a translation of the certificate into another EU official language.

2.3 When the protected person applies for an Article 5 certificate they must provide the court with the case number, their full name, date and place of birth and an address to be used for notification purposes. If you are the protected person, you can decide what address to provide and it does not have to be your own home address. THE ADDRESS YOU PROVIDE WILL NOT BE DISCLOSED TO THE PERSON CAUSING THE RISK UNLESS IT IS NECESSARY FOR THE PERSON CAUSING THE RISK TO KNOW IT, TO COMPLY WITH THE PROTECTION MEASURE (see paragraph 2.6 below). If the protected person knows the information, they should provide the court with the following details of the person causing the risk: full name, date and place of birth and an address to be used for notification purposes.

2.4 Before it can issue the Article 5 certificate, the court needs to know that the order containing the protection measure has been made known to ('served on') the person causing the risk. How the court knows depends on when the protected person applies for the certificate. The protected person who is applying for the Article 5 certificate before the order containing the protection measure has been made should use the appropriate form. If the protected person is acting in person and the order is a domestic violence or forced marriage protection order, they can ask the court under rule 10.6(2) or rule 11.7(4), whichever applies, to serve any order made on the person causing the risk. When the court makes and then serves the order and at the same time issues the certificate, the court knows that the person causing the risk has been told about the order.

2.5 If the protected person is applying for a certificate after the order containing the protection measure has been made, the protected person should apply using the appropriate form and provide the certified copy of the order. If the protected person or their legal representative was required to provide a copy of the order made to the person causing the risk, then the protected person must provide a certificate of service with the application for the Article 5 certificate. If the protected person is acting in person and the order is a domestic violence or forced marriage protection order, they can ask the court under rule 10.6(2) or rule 11.7(4), whichever applies, to serve the order on the person causing the risk. If the court has served the order, the protected person does not have to provide a certificate of service.

Notification of the Article 5 certificate

2.6 When the Article 5 certificate has been issued to the protected person, the court officer will notify the person causing the risk of the certificate in accordance with rule 38.7 (Article 8 notice) and provide them with a copy of the Article 5 certificate. The court officer will not tell the person causing the risk the address or contact details of the protected person unless the person causing the risk needs to have this information to comply with the protection measure or the information must be disclosed to get the protection measure enforced. For example, if the person causing the risk must stay away from a specific address, they need to know the address.

2.7 The Article 8 notice will also explain to the person causing the risk that the issue of the Article 5 certificate means the protection measure can now be recognised and is enforceable in other Member States of the European Union (except Denmark). It will explain that if the person causing the risk breaches the protection measure they could be punished under the law of the Member State where enforcement is requested.

'Rectification' of the Article 5 certificate

2.8 The protected person or the person causing the risk can apply for 'rectification' of the Article 5 certificate. 'Rectification' means the correction of a clerical error in which the certificate does not have the same information as the protection measure. The protected person or person causing the risk can apply for rectification under rule 38.8 using the appropriate form to the court which issued the certificate. In addition, if the court notices such a clerical error in an Article 5 certificate, the court will provide to the protected person and to the person causing the risk a corrected certificate on its own initiative.

Withdrawal of the Article 5 certificate

2.9 The protected person or the person causing the risk can apply under rule 38.9 using the appropriate form to the court which issued the Article 5 certificate for it to be withdrawn if it has clearly been wrongly granted under the Protection Measures Regulation. For example, an Article 5 certificate is wrongly granted if the person causing the risk did not know about the protection measure as required by Article 6. The court can also withdraw the Article 5 certificate on its own initiative (without an application) if it has clearly been wrongly granted. If the Article 5 certificate is withdrawn the protection measure cannot be recognised or enforced in any other Member State, including the Member State addressed. The court officer will notify both the protected person and the person causing the risk that the Article 5 certificate has been withdrawn.

2.10 When under Article 10 of the Protection Measures Regulation the protected person asks the court (as the issuing authority) for assistance to obtain information about the authorities in the Member State addressed which can adjust or enforce the protection measure, the court officer will signpost the protected person to the information on the EU website of the European Judicial Network in civil and commercial matters provided by EU Member States (except Denmark).

Changes to protection measure or withdrawal of Article 5 certificate – Article 14 certificate

2.11 If the family court or High Court discharges or stays a protection measure, or makes an order such as a variation that effectively suspends or limits its enforceability, the protected person or person causing the risk can apply for a certificate to be issued under Article 14(1) of the Protection Measures Regulation. Such a certificate can also be applied for if the Article 5 certificate is withdrawn (see paragraph 2.9 above). The application must be made in accordance with rules 38.10 and 38.11. At the same time as applying for the Article 14 certificate, or later, the protected person or the person causing the risk can ask the court where the proceedings are under way or took place for a translation of the Article 14 certificate into another EU official language.

2.12 When applying for an Article 14 certificate, the protected person or the person causing the risk must use the appropriate form and should provide the following documents if available: a certified copy of the court order which included the protection measure, a copy of the Article 5 certificate, a copy of the court order which varied, stayed, suspended or discharged all or part of the order including the protection measure, or the notification of the withdrawal of the Article 5 certificate by the court. The application can also be made if the protected person or the person causing the risk does not have all the documents listed. The applicant should provide the case number so that the court can locate the orders.

2.13 When the Article 14 certificate has been issued to the protected person or the person causing the risk the court will notify the other party. The applicant who has received an Article 14 certificate should send it to the court or other authority in the Member State addressed where the outgoing protection measure has been invoked or enforced so as to stop recognition and enforcement of the protection measure.

Incoming protection measures

3.1 An incoming protection measure for which an Article 5 certificate has been issued in another Member State, is automatically recognised by the court in England and Wales. This section sets out actions the protected person can take in relation to an incoming protection measure, and the points at which the incoming protection measure and Article 5 certificate must be provided to the court. The applications set out below can be made to the family court, the county court and sometimes to the Family Division of the High Court (see rule 5.4 of the Family Procedure Rules 2010). This practice direction and the Family Procedure Rules apply to the family court and Family Division of the High Court only. Applications to the county court are covered by the Civil Procedure Rules.

3.2 The protected person and the person causing the risk can make applications in relation to incoming protection measures using the procedure in Part 18 (or Part 19 if applicable) of the Family Procedure Rules. There is more information in Practice Directions 18A and 19A. These Practice Directions set out the documents the applicant must provide with the application, in addition to any requirements set out in this Practice Direction. When making an application the protected person or the person causing the risk must also provide a copy of the order containing the incoming protection measure and the Article 5 certificate issued in the Member State of origin. (Explanations of the terms used in the Protection Measures Regulation and the certificates are set out in section 1 above.)

Adjustment of 'factual elements' in the protection measure

3.3 The protected person can apply to the court for the adjustment of 'factual elements' in the incoming protection measure to make it effective in England and Wales. 'Factual elements' can, for example, include the address or location the person causing the risk must stay away from, such as the location where the protected person lived or worked in the Member State of origin, or the minimum distance the person causing the risk must keep away from the protected person. To make the protection measure work in England and Wales the protected person can apply for the protection measure to be adjusted to show an address in England or Wales. ANY ADDRESS OR

LOCATION IN THE ADJUSTED PROTECTION MEASURE WILL BE DISCLOSED TO THE PERSON CAUSING THE RISK, BECAUSE THE ADJUSTMENT MUST BE NOTIFIED TO THE PERSON CAUSING THE RISK.

3.4 The protected person can apply to the court under rule 38.12 using the appropriate form for an adjustment to the factual elements to be made. If you are the protected person, you will need to provide an address for notification. You can decide what address to provide and it does not have to be your own home address. IF YOU ARE THE PROTECTED PERSON, AND THE ADDRESS YOU PROVIDE IS ALSO IN THE ADJUSTED PROTECTION MEASURE, THAT ADDRESS WILL BE DISCLOSED TO THE PERSON CAUSING THE RISK, BECAUSE THE PERSON CAUSING THE RISK MUST BE NOTIFIED OF THE ADJUSTMENT TO BE ABLE TO COMPLY WITH IT. When the court adjusts the facts in the protection measure the court officer must notify the person causing the risk of the adjustment in accordance with rule 38.13 (Article 11 notice). A protected person may choose not to apply for an adjustment of a protection measure that contains a specific address or location, and may choose to apply only for adjustments of the factual elements of a protection measure that do not contain such information.

Enforcement of the protection measure

3.5 If the protected person has an incoming protection measure accompanied by an Article 5 certificate from the Member State of origin and they believe the person causing the risk has disobeyed the protection measure, the protected person can apply to the court under rule 10.11 for the issue of a civil warrant for the arrest of the person causing the risk . IF YOU ARE THE PROTECTED PERSON AND YOU BELIEVE THE PERSON CAUSING THE RISK HAS COMMITTED A CRIMINAL OFFENCE UNDER THE LAW OF ENGLAND AND WALES YOU SHOULD CONTACT THE POLICE. If this has happened, the person causing the risk may be subject to criminal punishment under the law of England and Wales.

3.6 Incoming protection measures can be enforced by the family court and the High Court in England and Wales as if they had been ordered by those courts. IF YOU ARE THE PERSON CAUSING THE RISK AND YOU DISOBEY THE PROTECTION MEASURE, YOU MAY BE HELD TO BE IN CONTEMPT OF COURT IN ENGLAND AND WALES AND YOU MAY BE IMPRISONED OR FINED. Part 10 and Part 37 of the FPR provide more information.

Application for refusal to recognise or enforce the protection measure

3.7 The person causing the risk can apply under rule 38.14 using the appropriate form for the court to refuse to recognise an incoming protection measure or to refuse to enforce it against them. Under the Protection Measures Regulation, the court will only refuse to recognise or enforce the protection measure when to do so would be 'manifestly contrary to public policy' or if recognition of the incoming protection measure is 'irreconcilable' with a judgment that has been given or recognised in the United Kingdom.

Suspension or withdrawal of recognition or enforcement

3.8 When a protection measure from another Member State has been suspended, limited or withdrawn in the Member State of origin or an Article 5 certificate has been withdrawn there, and an Article 14 certificate has been issued to confirm this, the protected person or the person causing the risk can apply under rule 38.15 using the appropriate form to the court in England and Wales which dealt or is dealing with the incoming protection measure to ask the court to stay, suspend or withdraw the effects of recognition or enforcement. The applicant must provide a copy of the Article 14 certificate. When the court has made orders or given directions to give effect to the Article 14 certificate the court officer will inform the other party.

Appeals

4.1 All decisions made by the court in England and Wales under the Protection Measures Regulation are subject to ordinary appeal procedures. In most cases permission to appeal will be required, but there is no need to get permission to appeal a decision made by lay justices. (The issue of an Article 5 certificate is separate and cannot be appealed.) Either the protected person or the person causing the risk can seek permission to appeal using the Part 30 procedure.

Appeals/Review of incoming protection order—No appeal lies against the issuing of an Art 5 certificate and under no circumstances may a protection measure be reviewed as to its substance in the Member State addressed (Arts 5(2) and 12).

PART 39
ATTACHMENT OF EARNINGS

CONTENTS OF THIS PART

Chapter I

Rule		Page
	General	
39.1	Application of this Part	2014
39.2	Interpretation of this Part	2015
39.3	Search of court records	2015
	Chapter 2	
	Securing payments under a maintenance order in the family court – attachment of earnings order	
39.4	Where to apply	2015
39.5	Application for an attachment of earnings order	2015
39.6	Service and reply	2016
39.7	Notice to the debtor's employer	2016
39.8	Attachment of earnings order	2016
39.9	Failure by debtor	2016
39.10	Enforcement under section 23(1) of the 1971 Act	2017
39.11	Suspended committal order	2017
39.12	Costs	2018
39.13	Contents and service of the order	2018
39.14	Application to determine whether particular payments are earnings	2018
39.15	Notice that an order has ceased to have effect	2019
39.16	Variation and discharge by the court of its own initiative	2019
39.17	Change of Designated Family Judge area	2019
39.18	Exercise of power to obtain statement of earnings etc.	2019
39.19	Offences	2020
39.20	Permission to enforce arrears	2020
	Chapter 3	
	Securing payments under a maintenance order in the High Court – attachment of earnings order	
39.21		2020

Chapter I
General

39.1 Application of this Part

(1) Chapter 2 of this Part applies where an attachment of earnings order is sought in the family court to secure payments under a family court or High Court maintenance order whether or not arrears have accrued.

(2) Chapter 3 of this Part applies where an attachment of earnings order is sought in the High Court to secure payments under a High Court maintenance order whether or not arrears have accrued.

(Section 1 of the 1971 Act makes provision for when the family court or the High Court may make an attachment of earnings order.)

Amendments—Inserted by SI 2016/355.

39.2 Interpretation of this Part

In this Part –

'the 1971 Act' means the Attachment of Earnings Act 1971 and unless the context otherwise requires or this Part otherwise provides, expressions used in that Act, including the term 'maintenance order', have the same meaning as in that Act;

'creditor' means the person who is entitled to enforce a maintenance order; and

'debtor' means the person against whom a maintenance order was made.

Amendments—Inserted by SI 2016/355.

Scope—This rule deals solely with attachment of earnings applications to enforce maintenance orders. Where the paying party is a member of the armed forces, an application should normally be made instead to the relevant service authorities for a deduction to be made from pay under the Armed Forces (Forfeitures and Deductions) Regulations 2009.

Note that CPR 1998, Pt 89, replacing CCR Ord 27, provides a code, largely delegated to court staff, for attachment of earnings applications to enforce other judgment debts. It is not set out here: see *Civil Court Service* (LexisNexis).

'expressions used' (r 39.2(1))—AEA 1971, ss 2, 24, 25 define the expressions used therein. Note in particular the extended meaning of 'maintenance order' given in s 2(a) (i e order specified in Sch 1 to the Act). As well as orders for periodical maintenance payments, such orders include orders for lump sums and other capital amounts that therefore do not create 'judgment debts' for the purposes of this order. Costs awarded on the making of 'maintenance orders' are treated as part of the maintenance orders (s 25(2)). Orders for costs made, for example, on pronouncement of a decree would not be within Sch 1 and would be 'judgment debts'.

39.3 Search of court records

If requested to do so by any person having a maintenance order against a debtor, the court officer must –

(a) cause a search to be made in the court records to determine whether there is an attachment of earnings order in force in relation to that debtor; and

(b) issue a certificate of the result of the search.

Amendments—Inserted by SI 2016/355.

Forms—Form FE16 has been issued for this purpose.

Chapter 2

Securing payments under a maintenance order in the family court – attachment of earnings order

39.4 Where to apply

An application for an attachment of earnings order to which this Chapter applies must be sent to the family court.

(Her Majesty's Courts and Tribunals Service publishes information to identify the appropriate location to which an application for an attachment of earnings order should be sent.)

Amendments—Inserted by SI 2016/355.

39.5 Application for an attachment of earnings order

(1) Where an application is made for an attachment of earnings order on the making of the maintenance order or of an order varying the maintenance order, the remainder of this rule and rule 39.6 do not apply.

(2) A creditor who wishes to apply for an attachment of earnings order must file –

(a) an application in accordance with rule 33.3(1); and

(b) a copy of the sealed (GL) maintenance order.

(3) When the documents mentioned in paragraph (2) are filed with the court, the court officer must fix a day for the hearing of the application.

Amendments—Inserted by SI 2016/355.

'application in accordance with rule 33.3(1)' (r 39.5(2)(a))—Form FE15 has been prescribed for this purpose. The creditor may seek an order in respect of the ongoing maintenance payments, in respect of the arrears, or in respect of both.

PART III

39.6 Service and reply

(1) Notice of the application and a reply form must be served by the court on the debtor in accordance with Chapter 3 of Part 6.

(2) The notice of application must include an instruction to the debtor to file the reply form within 8 days after service, and that instruction constitutes a requirement imposed under section 14(4) of the 1971 Act.

(3) No proceedings may be brought for an alleged offence under section 23(2)(c) or (f) of the 1971 Act in relation to the requirement to reply unless –

- (a) the notice of application and reply form have been served personally on the debtor; or
- (b) the court is satisfied that those documents came to the debtor's knowledge in sufficient time to comply with the requirement.

(4) The court officer must send to the creditor a copy of any reply form received from the debtor.

Amendments—Inserted by SI 2016/355.

'the reply form' (r 39.6(2))—The debtor replies on Form FE17.

'served personally on the debtor' (r 39.6(3)(a))—If personal service is impractical, the court may order service by another method (r 6.15).

Failure to reply—If the debtor does not return the Form FE17, the court will automatically issue a form endorsed with a penal notice for personal service on the debtor: see r 39.9.

39.7 Notice to the debtor's employer

(1) Without prejudice to the power conferred by section 14(1) of the 1971 Act, a court officer may, at any stage of the proceedings, send to any person appearing to be the debtor's employer a notice requesting that person to give to the court a statement of the debtor's earnings.

(2) The statement of the debtor's earnings must –

- (a) state the debtor's earnings;
- (b) state the debtor's anticipated earnings;
- (c) include such particulars as requested in the notice from the court; and
- (d) be given to the court within such period as is specified in the notice.

Amendments—Inserted by SI 2016/355.

Statement of earnings—The form is N338. A creditor who knows the name of the debtor's employer should always request the issue of Form N338 when applying for attachment of earnings. The court will then have information enabling it to make an order even if the debtor fails to return Form FE17 or fails to attend the hearing.

'notice requesting'—There is no compulsion on the employer to comply with the request but, if he does not do so, the court may decide to make an order under AEA 1971, s 14(1); failure to comply with such an order would be an offence (s 23(2)(c)).

39.8 Attachment of earnings order

An application for an attachment of earnings order to secure payments under a maintenance order must be heard in private, unless the court directs otherwise.

(Rule 39.21 modifies this rule and sets out steps for a court officer of the family court to take when an attachment of earnings order made by the High Court designates the court officer of the family court as the collecting officer.)

Amendments—Inserted by SI 2016/355.

39.9 Failure by debtor

(1) If the debtor has failed to comply with rule 39.6(2) or to make payment to the creditor, the court officer may issue an order under section 14(1) of the 1971 Act which must, in addition to meeting the requirements of rule 39.18(1), direct that any payments made after the date of service of the order must be paid to the court and not direct to the creditor.

(2) Without prejudice to rule 39.19, if the person served with an order referred to in paragraph (1) fails –

- (a) to obey the order;
- (b) to complete and file the form of reply, including the statement of means; or

(c) make payment,

the court officer must issue a notice to the person to attend a hearing at which the court will consider whether an offence has been committed under section 23(2)(c) of the 1971 Act and whether the person should be imprisoned or fined as a result.

(3) A notice of a type referred to in paragraph (2) must be served on the debtor personally not less than 5 days before the hearing.

(4) In this rule, 'statement of means' means a statement given under section 14(1) of the 1971 Act.

Amendments—Inserted by SI 2016/355.

'must be served on the debtor personally' (r 39.9(3))—The wording of this rule differs from that of r 39.11(2) ('unless the court otherwise directs, the creditor must serve on the debtor personally…') and it is accordingly suggested that even if the debtor is deliberately evading service, service by another method is not permissible under this rule.

39.10 Enforcement under section 23(1) of the 1971 Act

(1) An order under section 23(1) of the 1971 Act for the attendance of the debtor at an adjourned hearing for an attachment of earnings order to secure payments under a maintenance order –

(a) must be served on the debtor personally not less than 5 days before the day fixed for the adjourned hearing; and

(b) may direct that any future payments made after the date of service of the order under section 23(1) of the 1971 Act must be paid into the court and not direct to the creditor.

(2) An application by a debtor for the revocation of an order committing the debtor to prison and (if already in custody) for discharge under section 23(7) of the 1971 Act must –

(a) be made to court in writing without notice to any other party, stating the reasons for the debtor's failure to attend the court or refusal to be sworn or to give evidence (as the case may be) and containing an undertaking by the debtor to attend the court or be sworn or to give evidence when required to do so; and

(b) if the debtor has already been lodged in prison, be attested by the governor of the prison (or any other officer of the prison not below rank of principal officer), and in any other case be made in a witness statement or affidavit,

and before dealing with the application the court may, if it thinks fit, cause notice to be given to the creditor that the application has been made and of a date and time when the creditor may attend and be heard.

Amendments—Inserted by SI 2016/355.

'must be served on the debtor personally' (r 39.10(1)(a))—Again, it is suggested that even if the debtor is deliberately evading service, service by another method is not permissible under this rule.

'notice … to the creditor' (r 39.10(2)(b))—The maximum sentence that can be imposed for an offence under the 1971 Act is 14 days' imprisonment, of which the debtor will actually serve 7.

39.11 Suspended committal order

(1) If the debtor fails to attend an adjourned hearing of an application for an attachment of earnings order and a committal order is made, the court making the committal order may direct that its execution be suspended for such period or on such terms or conditions as it may specify.

(2) Unless the court otherwise directs, the creditor must serve on the debtor personally a copy of any order made under paragraph (1).

(3) Where a committal order is suspended under paragraph (1) and the debtor fails to attend at the time and place specified in the committal order, a certificate to that effect given by the court officer is sufficient authority for the issue of a warrant of committal.

(4) If execution of a committal order is suspended under paragraph (1), the debtor may apply for a further suspension.

(5) The debtor may apply for a further suspension by attending at, or writing to, the court office and explaining why they have been unable to comply with the terms of the original suspension.

(6) If the debtor applies for a further suspension in accordance with paragraph (5), the court must –

(a) fix a date for the hearing of the application; and
(b) give the debtor and creditor at least 3 days' notice of the hearing.

(7) The court may suspend execution of the committal order pending the hearing of the application under paragraph (5).

Amendments—Inserted by SI 2016/355.

'a committal order is made' (r 39.11(1))—This is by way of penalty for an offence under AEA 1971, rather than committal for contempt of court, and it was accordingly unnecessary for it to be brought within the scope of the Committal Practice Direction, requiring the judge to be robed and to put a judgment in the public domain. As the objective is ultimately to secure the debtor's cooperation, the more practical approach is that offered by AEA 1971, s 23(1A): 'In any case where the judge has power to make an order of imprisonment under subsection (1) for failure to attend, he may, in lieu of or in addition to making that order, order the debtor to be arrested and brought before the court ...'. That does not involve the making of a committal order and avoids these unnecessary difficulties.

It would have been helpful for the Rule to draw attention to the procedure under s 23(1A).

39.12 Costs

(1) Where costs are allowed to the creditor on an application for an attachment of earnings order, there may be allowed –

(a) a charge of a legal representative for preparing the application, attending the hearing and, if applicable, for serving the application; and
(b) the court fee for issuing the application.

(2) The costs may be fixed and allowed without detailed assessment under CPR Part 47.

Amendments—Inserted by SI 2016/355.

Costs—It is suggested that the use of the expression 'fixed' as opposed to 'summarily assessed' should not be taken to imply that the costs should be the princely £8.50 for each attendance mentioned in CPR 1998, r 45.8.

39.13 Contents and service of the order

(1) An attachment of earnings order must contain such of the following information about the debtor as is known to the court –

(a) the debtor's full name and address;
(b) the debtor's place of work;
(c) the nature of the debtor's work and works number, if any.

(2) That information will be the prescribed particulars for the purposes of section 6(3) of the 1971 Act.

(3) An attachment of earnings order and any order varying or discharging such an order must be served on the parties and on the person to whom the order is directed.

(4) Where –

(a) the order is directed to a corporation; and
(b) that corporation has requested that the court serve on the corporation documents relating to the debtor or to the class of persons to whom the debtor belongs at a particular address, service may be effected on the corporation at that address, if the court thinks fit.

(5) Where an attachment of earnings order is made by the family court to secure payments under a maintenance order made by the High Court, a copy of the attachment of earnings order and of any order discharging or varying it must be sent by the court officer of the family court to the court officer of the High Court.

Amendments—Inserted by SI 2016/355.

39.14 Application to determine whether particular payments are earnings

(1) An application to the court under section 16 of the 1971 Act to determine whether payments to the debtor of a particular class or description are earnings for the purposes of an attachment of earnings order may be made to the court in accordance with Part 18.

(2) If such an application is made, the court officer must fix a date for the hearing of the application by the court and give notice of that hearing to the persons mentioned in section 16(2)(a), (b) and (c) of the 1971 Act.

Amendments—Inserted by SI 2016/355.

39.15 Notice that an order has ceased to have effect

Where an attachment of earnings order made by the family court to secure payments under a maintenance order ceases to have effect under section 8(3) of the 1971 Act and –

(a) the related maintenance order was made by that court; or

(b) the related maintenance order was made by the High Court; and –

(i) the court officer has received notice of the cessation from the court officer of the High Court; or

(ii) a committal order has been made in the family court for the enforcement of the related maintenance order, the court officer of the family court must give notice of the cessation to the person to whom the attachment of earnings order was directed.

Amendments—Inserted by SI 2016/355.

39.16 Variation and discharge by the court of its own initiative

(1) The powers conferred by section 9(1) of the 1971 Act may be exercised by the court of its own initiative in the circumstances specified in this rule.

(2) Where it appears to the court that a person served with an attachment of earnings order does not employ the debtor, the court must discharge the order.

(3) Where an attachment of earnings order which has lapsed under section 9(4) of the 1971 Act is again directed to a person who appears to the court to employ the debtor, the court may make such consequential variations in the order as it thinks fit.

(4) Where the court has made an attachment of earnings order and it appears to the court that the related maintenance order has ceased to have effect (whether by virtue of the terms of the maintenance order or under section 28 of the 1973 Act or otherwise), the court may discharge or vary the attachment of earnings order.

(5) The court may discharge the attachment of earnings order where an attachment of earnings order has been made to secure payments under a maintenance order and –

(a) the court makes an order for another form of enforcement for the recovery of payments under the maintenance order; or

(b) there is no further sum payable under the maintenance order.

(6) Before varying or discharging an attachment of earnings order of its own initiative under any of the paragraphs of this rule, the court must, unless it thinks it unnecessary in the circumstances to do so, give the debtor, and the person on whose application the order was made, an opportunity of being heard on the question of whether the order should be varied or discharged.

(7) The court officer must give those people mentioned in paragraph (6) notice of the date, time and place fixed for the hearing.

Amendments—Inserted by SI 2016/355.

39.17 Change of Designated Family Judge area

If, in the opinion of the family court sitting in a Designated Family Judge area in which an attachment of earnings order has been made, the matter could more conveniently proceed in another Designated Family Judge area (whether by reason of the debtor having become resident in that other Designated Family Judge area or otherwise), the court may order that the matter should proceed in that other area.

Amendments—Inserted by SI 2016/355.

39.18 Exercise of power to obtain statement of earnings etc.

(1) An order under section 14(1) of the 1971 Act must –

(a) be endorsed with or incorporate a notice warning the person to whom it is directed of the consequences of disobeying the order; and

(b) be served on that person personally.

(2) Rule 37.35 applies, with the necessary modifications in relation to any penalty for failure to comply with an order under section 14(1) of the 1971 Act as it applies in relation to a fine under section 31G of the 1984 Act.

Amendments—Inserted by SI 2016/355.

39.19 Offences

(1) Paragraph (2) applies where –

(a) it is alleged that a person has committed any offence mentioned in section 23(2)(a), (b), (d), (e) or (f) of the 1971 Act in relation to proceedings in, or to an attachment of earnings order made by, the family court; and

(b) the alleged offender is not being proceeded against summarily.

(2) The court may issue a notice to the alleged offender to attend a hearing at which the court will consider whether the alleged offence has been committed and whether the alleged offender should be imprisoned or fined as a result.

(3) The notice must be served on the alleged offender personally not less than 14 days before the hearing.

(4) Rules 37.36 and 37.37 apply to proceedings for an offence under section 23(2) of the 1971 Act as they apply to proceedings for offences under the County Courts Act 1984.

(5) Where a person other than a debtor is committed for an offence under section 23(2) of the 1971 Act, rule 37.30 applies to an application by that person to be discharged from custody.

Amendments—Inserted by SI 2016/355.

'any offence' (r 39.19(1)(a))—AEA 1971, s 23(2) gives the exact definitions but the offences may be summarised as follows: employer failing to comply with an attachment of earnings order or variation order (s 23(2)(a)); employer failing to tell the court that the debtor is not in, or has left, his employment (s 23(2)(b)); debtor failing to tell the court of a change in his employment or new employer, who is aware of the order, failing to report the new employment to the court (s 23(2)(c)); giving false information to the court (s 23(2)(e),(f)).

'a person other than a debtor is committed' (r 39.19(5))—This will only arise after the commission of an offence of giving false information. Failure by the employer to comply with an attachment of earnings order is only punishable by a fine.

39.20 Permission to enforce arrears

(1) This rule applies where a creditor applies for an attachment of earnings order to enforce the payment of arrears which became due more than 12 months before the date of the application for an attachment of earnings order.

(2) Where the creditor requires the permission of the court under –

(a) section 32 of the 1973 Act;

(b) section 32(4) of the 1978 Act; or

(c) paragraph 63 of Schedule 5 to the 2004 Act,

to enforce the payment of such arrears, the permission application must be made in the application for the attachment of earnings order.

(3) Notice of the application, together with a form of reply in the appropriate form, must be served on the debtor in the manner set out in rule 6.23 and the notice must be served not less than 14 days before the hearing.

Amendments—Inserted by SI 2016/355.

Chapter 3
Securing payments under a maintenance order in the High Court – attachment of earnings order

39.21 Where an application is made to the High Court under this Chapter, the rules in Chapter 2 apply with the following modifications –

(a) for rule 39.4 there is substituted –

'(1) Subject to paragraph (2), an application for an attachment of earnings order must be sent to the District Registry of the High Court for the district in which the debtor resides.

(2) If the debtor resides outside of England and Wales, or if the debtor's place of residence is not known to the creditor, an application for an attachment of earnings order must be sent to the District Registry of the High Court for the district in which the proceedings which resulted in the maintenance order being made took place.';

(b) for rule 39.8 there is substituted –

'(1) An application for an attachment of earnings order to secure payments under a maintenance order must be heard in private, unless the court directs otherwise.

(2) Where an attachment of earnings order made by the High Court designates the court officer of the family court as the collecting officer, that officer must, on receipt of a certified copy of the order from the court officer of the High Court, send to the person to whom the order is directed a notice as to the mode of payment.';

(c) rule 39.13(5) is omitted;

(d) for rule 39.15 there is substituted –

'Where an attachment of earnings order made by the High Court to secure payments under a High Court maintenance order ceases to have effect under section 8(3) of the 1971 Act, the court officer of the High Court must give notice of the cessation to the person to whom the attachment of earnings order was directed.';

(e) for rule 39.17, including the heading to that rule, there is substituted –

'39.17 Change of District Registry

If, in the opinion of the High Court sitting in a District Registry in which an attachment of earnings order has been made, the matter could more conveniently proceed in another District Registry (whether by reason of the debtor having become resident in the area of that District Registry or otherwise), the court may order that the matter should proceed in that other District Registry.';

(f) in rule 39.19(1)(a), for 'family court' there is substituted 'High Court'; and

(g) in rule 39.20(2), sub-paragraph (b) is omitted.

Amendments—Inserted by SI 2016/355.

PART 40
CHARGING ORDER, STOP ORDER, STOP NOTICE

CONTENTS OF THIS PART

Chapter 1

Rule		Page
	General	
40.1	Application of this Part	2022
40.2	Interpretation of this Part	2022
	Chapter 2 *Charging orders*	
40.3	Scope of this Chapter	2023
40.4	Application for a charging order	2023
40.5	Interim charging order	2023
40.6	Service of an interim charging order	2024
40.7	Effect of interim charging order in relation to securities	2024
40.8	Further consideration of the application	2025
40.9	Discharge or variation of order	2026

PART III

Chapter 3
Stop orders

40.10	Interpretation	2026
40.11	Application for a stop order	2026
40.12	Stop order relating to securities	2026
40.13	Variation or discharge of order	2026

Chapter 4
Stop notices

40.14	General	2027
40.15	Request for a stop notice	2027
40.16	Effect of a stop notice	2027
40.17	Amendment of a stop notice	2028
40.18	Withdrawal of a stop notice	2028
40.19	Discharge or variation of a stop notice	2028
40.20	Practice Direction	2028

Practice Direction 40A –
Charging Orders, Stop Orders and Stop Notices 2028

Chapter 1
General

40.1 Application of this Part

This Part contains rules which provide for a creditor to enforce a judgment or order by obtaining –

(a) a charging order (Chapter 2);
(b) a stop order (Chapter 3); or
(c) a stop notice (Chapter 4),

over or against the debtor's interest in an asset.

Amendments—Inserted by SI 2016/355.

'to enforce a judgment or order' (r 40.1)—The wording is similar, but not identical, to that of CPR 1998, r 73.1, which applies in the civil courts.

Save for CPR 1998, r 73.10C dealing with enforcement of charging orders by way of sale, the provisions of CPR 1998, Pt 73 are not considered in this volume and reference should be made to *Civil Court Service* (LexisNexis)

Procedural Guide—See Procedural Guide C5.

40.2 Interpretation of this Part

In this Part –

'the 1979 Act' means the Charging Orders Act 1979;

'creditor' means the person to whom payment of a sum of money is due under a judgment or order or a person who is entitled to enforce such a judgment or order;

'debtor' means the person against whom a judgment or other order for payment of a sum of money was given, made or ordered, as the case may be;

'interim charging order' means an interim charging order made in accordance with rule 40.5; and

'securities' means securities of any of the kinds specified in section 2(2)(b) of the 1979 Act.

Amendments—Inserted by SI 2016/355.

'payment of a sum of money is due' (r 40.2)—As noted in relation to s 1 of the 1979 Act, there is no power to make a charging order until the sum is ascertained, so an order for costs cannot be secured by a charging order until after assessment (*Magiera v Magiera* [2016] EWCA Civ 1292).

Chapter 2
Charging orders

40.3 Scope of this Chapter

This Chapter applies to an application by a creditor for a charging order under section 1 of the 1979 Act.

Amendments—Inserted by SI 2016/355.

40.4 Application for a charging order

(1) An application for a charging order may be made without notice.

(2) An application must be made to the family court or to the High Court, as appropriate and as specified in section 1 of the 1979 Act.

(Her Majesty's Courts and Tribunals Service publishes information to identify the appropriate location of the family court or High Court to which an application for a charging order should be sent.)

(3) A creditor may apply for a single charging order in respect of more than one judgment or order against the same debtor.

(4) The application must –

(a) be in the form and contain the information required by Practice Direction 40A; and
(b) be verified by a statement of truth.

Amendments—Inserted by SI 2016/355.

'to the High Court' (r 40.4(2))—This refers to the High Court exercising family jurisdiction; if the High Court is exercising its civil jurisdiction, CPR 1998, Pt 73 applies.

'a single charging order in respect of more than one judgment or order' (r 40.4(3))—Issuing separate applications in respect of each of several judgments is likely to be oppressive and the creditor is unlikely to recover more than one set of costs.

40.5 Interim charging order

(1) An application for a charging order will initially be dealt with by the court without a hearing.

(2) The court may make an interim charging order –

(a) imposing a charge over the debtor's interest in the asset to which the application relates; and
(b) fixing a hearing to consider whether to make a final charging order as provided by rule 40.8.

Amendments—Inserted by SI 2016/355.

'the court may make an order' (r 40.5(2))—Lay justices sitting in the Family Court may not make a charging order (FC(CDB)R 2014, r 17, Sch 2).

'may make an order' (r 40.5(2))—An interim order is not granted automatically. It may be refused not only if the application notice fails to comply with PD40A but also if the debt is too small to justify the remedy or the application appears otherwise oppressive.

'an interim charging order' (r 40.5(2))—A charging order is made initially in the form of an interim order, to be confirmed by a final charging order or discharged on the hearing. Any Land Registry notice or restriction or Land Charges Registry entry is properly effected pursuant to COA 1979, s 3(2) or (3) on the making of the interim order, although the arguably defective wording of standard restriction K may require registration to be repeated on the making of a final order in relation to a joint proprietor. Note, however, that the entry of a restriction does not protect the priority of the interest to which it relates for the purpose of LRA 2002, s 29. A charging order affecting only the beneficial interests under a trust is liable to be overreached along with those interests by the operation of LPA 1925, ss 2 and 27. Accordingly, a Form K restriction will usually be cancelled automatically, without application, when a transfer that appears to overreach the beneficial interests is registered. Any such entry should be removed promptly if the interim order is discharged.

'the debtor's interest in the asset' (r 40.5(2)(a))—It is not necessary for the precise extent of that interest to be quantified (*Walton v Allman* [2015] EWHC 3325 (Ch)).

'asset to which the application relates' (r 40.5(2)(a))—More than one asset belonging to the judgment debtor may be included in a single application but a separate interim order will be drawn in respect of each asset (PD40A, para 1.4).

40.6 Service of an interim charging order

(1) Copies of the interim charging order, the application and any documents filed in support of it must, not less than 21 days before the hearing, be served by the creditor on the persons listed in paragraph (3).

(2) The creditor must either –

(a) file a certificate of service in relation to each person served not less than 2 days before the hearing; or

(b) produce a certificate of service at the hearing.

(3) The persons to be served in accordance with paragraph (1) are –

(a) the debtor;

(b) if the order relates to an interest in land, any co-owner;

(c) the debtor's spouse or civil partner (if known);

(d) such other creditors as are identified in the application or as the court directs;

(e) if the order relates to an interest under a trust, on such of the trustees as the court directs; and

(f) if the interest charged is securities, then –

(i) in the case of stock for which the Bank of England keeps the register, the Bank of England;

(ii) in the case of government stock to which sub-paragraph (f)(i) does not apply, the keeper of the register;

(iii) in the case of stock of any body incorporated within England and Wales, that body;

(iv) in the case of stock of any body incorporated outside England and Wales or of any state or territory outside the United Kingdom, which is registered in a register kept in England and Wales, the keeper of that register; and

(v) in the case of units of any unit trust in respect of which a register of the unit holders is kept in England and Wales, the keeper of that register.

Amendments—Inserted by SI 2016/355.

'Service of an interim charging order'—Note that prior to 6 April 2016, the normal procedure was for the interim order to be served by the court by first-class post. Under the new r 40.6(1), the creditor must serve the documents.

'other creditors' (r 40.6(2)(d))—The general rules as to service will apply. The court will usually direct service on all known creditors (see COA 1979, s 1(5)(b)), although service on prior chargees appears not to be necessary for their protection on the basis that they cannot be prejudiced by the making of the order. While the rule has been amended to require service on a spouse or civil partner, former spouses or civil partners are not included. It is suggested that the expression 'creditor' may be given a purposive interpretation to include former spouses or civil partners, where the asset sought to be charged is or was a matrimonial home and an application for financial relief has been registered as a pending action against the property. The form of application notice, Form FE6 or Form FE7, requires all persons interested to be identified. A direction is likely to be given that any such person identified be served (*Harman v Glencross* [1986] 2 FLR 241, CA). Alternatively, such persons may apply after the event under r 40.9 for the final charging order to be varied or discharged.

40.7 Effect of interim charging order in relation to securities

(1) If a debtor disposes of their interest in any securities while they are subject to an interim charging order which has been served on them, that disposition will not, so long as that order remains in force, be valid as against the creditor.

(2) A person served under rule 40.6(3)(f) with an interim charging order relating to securities must not, unless the court gives permission –

(a) permit any transfer of any of the securities; or

(b) pay any dividend, interest or redemption payment relating to them.

(3) If a person acts in breach of paragraph (2), that person will be liable to pay to the creditor –

(a) the value of the securities transferred or the amount of the payment made (as the case may be); or

(b) if less, the amount necessary to satisfy the debt in relation to which the interim charging order was made.

Amendments—Inserted by SI 2016/355.

'order in relation to securities' (r 40.7)—The provisions of CPR 1998, rr 73.5(1)(d)(v) and 73.7 relating to charging orders against funds in court do not appear to have a counterpart in the new Pt 40.

40.8 Further consideration of the application

(1) If any person objects to the court making a final charging order, that person must –

(a) file; and
(b) serve on the creditor,

written evidence stating the grounds of objection, not less than 7 days before the hearing.

(2) At the hearing, the court may –

(a) make a final charging order confirming that the charge imposed by the interim charging order continues, with or without modification;
(b) discharge the interim charging order and dismiss the application;
(c) decide any issues in dispute between the parties, or between any of the parties and any other person who objects to the court making a final charging order;
(d) direct a trial of any such issues, and if necessary give directions; or
(e) make such other order as the court considers appropriate.

(3) If the court makes a final charging order which charges securities, the order must include a stop notice unless the court otherwise orders.

(Chapter 4 of this Part contains provision about stop notices.)

(4) Any order made at the hearing must be served by the creditor on all the persons on whom the interim charging order was served.

Amendments—Inserted by SI 2016/355.

'must file ... written evidence' (r 40.8(1))—This provision is almost invariably honoured in the breach. It remains to be seen whether the procedural changes in relation to charging orders in the County Court, providing that unless the debtor positively objects the court will proceed to consider making a final order on paper, will cause a change in approach.

'the court may' (r 40.8(2))—For the principles on which the court will exercise its discretion, see *Roberts Petroleum Ltd v Bernard Kenny Ltd* [1983] 2 AC 192, at [690] and *British Arab Commercial Bank Plc & Ors v Algosaibi & Ors* [2011] EWHC 2444 (Comm).

'final charging order' (r 40.8(2)(a))—The charge is effective from the day that the interim order is made (*Haley v Barry* (1868) 3 Ch App 452, CA).

'with or without modification' (r 40.8(2)(a))—As there remains only one charging order, it cannot be modified to extend to property that was not included in the interim order. Modifications may include the imposition of conditions on enforcement under COA 1979, s 3(1) (see **Conditions**, below).

'discharge the interim charging order' (r 40.8(2)(b))—All of the factors that are relevant in the exercise of the court's discretion as to whether to grant an interim order under r 40.5(2) apply also in considering whether to make a final charging order or discharge the interim order and dismiss the application. The interim order should be discharged if the debtor had no interest in the property when the interim order was made or if the debtor has since parted with it and passed it on to someone who would not be affected by a mere equitable charge, such as a bona fide purchaser for value without notice (*Howell v Montey* (1990) *The Times*, 17 March, CA).

It is necessary to strike a balance between the normal expectation of a judgment creditor that an order will be made to enforce his judgment and the hardship that such an order may entail to the spouse and children of the debtor: *Harman v Glencross* [1986] 2 FLR 241, CA. There can never be automatic predominance for any claim; each case depends upon striking a fair balance: *Austin-Fell v Austin-Fell and Midland Bank* [1989] 2 FLR 497, FD. Consideration should be given to the factors in FLA 1996, s 33 (*BR v VT (Financial Remedies: Interim)* [2016] 2 FLR 519, FD). In some cases, the balance will be achieved by an order postponing any sale of the property and in a more extreme case it will be achieved by withholding a charging order altogether and transferring the debtor's interest to the spouse free of any encumbrance, as in *Kremen v Agrest* [2013] 2 FLR 187, CA.

Adjournment—The court does have power to adjourn a hearing to another date under FPR 2010, r 4.1(3)(c). Any adjournment should either be to a fixed date or to a particular event, e g the hearing of an application for ancillary relief. It is usual when adjourning to direct specifically that the interim order remain in force.

Conditions—COA 1979, s 3(1) enables the order to be made subject to conditions. Where the order is against the judgment debtor's interest in a family home, conditions delaying execution may now be more frequently used to comply with HRA 1998, Sch 1, Pt I, Art 8.

Costs—Fixed costs of £110 are specified in CPR 1998, r 45.6. Courts may also (and normally will) allow Land Registry fees as disbursements, but it is not appropriate to seek the fee for an advocate attending the hearing – this is included in the fixed costs.

40.9 Discharge or variation of order

(1) Where an application is made to discharge or vary a charging order, the court may direct that –

(a) any interested person be joined as a party to such an application; or
(b) the application be served on any such person.

(2) An order discharging or varying a charging order must be served, by the person who applied for that order, on all the persons on whom the charging order was required to be served.

Amendments—Inserted by SI 2016/355.

'any interested person' (r 40.9(2)(a))—In particular, interested persons who did not receive notice of the making of an interim order may apply under this rule to be joined as parties to the application and for the order to be discharged or varied. Such applications may become inextricably linked with ancillary relief applications under MCA 1973 to the extent that they must be heard together. The competing interests of judgment creditor, judgment debtor and former spouse can then all be decided on a single occasion.

Chapter 3
Stop orders

40.10 Interpretation

In this Chapter, 'stop order' means an order of the High Court not to take, in relation to securities specified in the order, any of the steps listed in section 5(5) of the 1979 Act.

Amendments—Inserted by SI 2016/355.

40.11 Application for a stop order

(1) The High Court may make a stop order relating to securities, on the application of any person claiming to be beneficially entitled to an interest in the securities.

(2) An application for a stop order must be made –

(a) by application in existing proceedings; or
(b) by a Part 19 application if there are no existing proceedings in the High Court.

(3) The application must be served on –

(a) every person whose interest may be affected by the order applied for; and
(b) the person specified in rule 40.6(3)(f).

Amendments—Inserted by SI 2016/355.

40.12 Stop order relating to securities

(1) A stop order relating to securities may prohibit all or any of the following steps –

(a) the registration of any transfer of the securities;
(b) the making of any payment by way of dividend, interest or otherwise in respect of the securities; and
(c) in the case of units of a unit trust, any acquisition of, or other dealing with, the units by any person or body exercising functions under the trust.

(2) The order must specify –

(a) the securities to which it relates;
(b) the name in which the securities stand;
(c) the steps which may not be taken; and
(d) whether the prohibition applies to the securities only or to the dividends or interest as well.

Amendments—Inserted by SI 2016/355.

40.13 Variation or discharge of order

(1) The court may, on the application of any person claiming to have a beneficial interest in the securities to which a stop order relates, make an order discharging or varying the order.

(2) An application seeking the variation or discharge of a stop order must be served on the person who obtained the order.

Amendments—Inserted by SI 2016/355.

Chapter 4
Stop notices

40.14 General

In this Chapter, 'stop notice' means a notice issued by the court which requires a person or body not to take, in relation to securities specified in the notice, any of the steps listed in section 5(5) of the 1979 Act, without first giving notice to the person who obtained the notice.

(Her Majesty's Courts and Tribunals Service publishes information to identify the appropriate court location to which to send a request under rule 40.15 or rule 40.18 or an application under rule 40.19.)

Amendments—Inserted by SI 2016/355.

40.15 Request for a stop notice

(1) The High Court may, on the request of any person claiming to be beneficially entitled to an interest in securities, issue a stop notice.

(A stop notice may also be included in a final charging order, by either the High Court or the family court under rule 40.8(3).)

(2) A request for a stop notice must be made by filing –

- (a) a draft stop notice; and
- (b) written evidence which –
  - (i) identifies the securities in question;
  - (ii) describes the applicant's interest in the securities; and
  - (iii) gives an address for service for the applicant.

(A sample form of stop notice is annexed to Practice Direction 40A.)

(3) If a court officer considers that the request complies with paragraph (2), the court officer must issue a stop notice.

(4) The applicant must serve copies of the stop notice and the applicant's written evidence on the person to whom the stop notice is addressed.

Amendments—Inserted by SI 2016/355.

40.16 Effect of a stop notice

(1) A stop notice –

- (a) takes effect when it is served in accordance with rule 40.15(4); and
- (b) remains in force unless it is withdrawn or discharged in accordance with rule 40.18 or 40.19.

(2) While a stop notice is in force, the person on whom it is served –

- (a) must not –
  - (i) register a transfer of the securities described in the notice; or
  - (ii) take any other step restrained by the notice,

  without first giving 14 days' notice to the person who obtained the stop notice; but
- (b) must not, by reason only of the notice, refuse to register a transfer or to take any other step, after the person has given 14 days' notice under paragraph (2)(a) and that period has expired.

Amendments—Inserted by SI 2016/355.

40.17 Amendment of a stop notice

(1) If any securities are incorrectly described in a stop notice which has been obtained and served in accordance with rule 40.15, the applicant may request an amended stop notice in accordance with that rule.

(2) The amended stop notice takes effect when it is served.

Amendments—Inserted by SI 2016/355.

40.18 Withdrawal of a stop notice

(1) A person who has obtained a stop notice may withdraw it by serving a request for its withdrawal on –

(a) the person or body on whom the stop notice was served; and
(b) the court which issued the stop notice.

(2) The request must be signed by the person who obtained the stop notice, and that person's signature must be witnessed by a practising solicitor.

Amendments—Inserted by SI 2016/355.

40.19 Discharge or variation of a stop notice

(1) The court may, on the application of any person claiming to be beneficially entitled to an interest in the securities to which a stop notice relates, make an order varying or discharging the notice.

(2) An application to discharge or vary a stop notice must be made to the court which issued the notice.

(3) The application must be served on the person who obtained the stop notice.

Amendments—Inserted by SI 2016/355.

40.20 Practice Direction

Practice Direction 40A makes provision for the procedure to be followed when applying for an order under section 23 of the Partnership Act 1890.

Amendments—Inserted by SI 2016/355.

Practice Direction 40A – Charging Orders, Stop Orders and Stop Notices

This Practice Direction supplements FPR Part 40.

Section I – Charging orders

Applicant and application notice – rules 40.2 and 40.4

1.1 A creditor may apply for a charging order. The term 'creditor' is defined in rule 40.2 to mean 'the person to whom payment of a sum of money is due under a judgment or order, or a person who is entitled to enforce such a judgment or order'. A person who is entitled to enforce such a judgment or order would include a court officer who is able to take enforcement proceedings by virtue of rule 32.33.

1.2 An application for a charging order must be made by filing an application in Practice Form N379 if the application relates to land, or N380 if the application relates to securities.

'Practice Form N379 … or N380'—Note that with effect from 6 April 2017, the forms to be used in the Family Court are Form FE6 in relation to land and Form FE7 in relation to securities.

1.3 The application notice must contain the following information –

(1) the name and address of the debtor;
(2) details of the judgment or order sought to be enforced;

(3) the amount of money remaining due under the judgment or order;
(4) if the judgment debt is payable by instalments, the amount of any instalments which have fallen due and remain unpaid;
(5) if the judgment creditor knows of the existence of any other creditors of the judgment debtor, their names and (if known) their addresses;
(6) identification of the asset or assets which it is intended to charge including, where applicable, the title number under which any land upon which it is sought to impose a charge is registered;
(7) details of the debtor's interest in the asset; and
(8) the names and addresses of the persons on whom an interim charging order must be served under rule 40.6.

1.4 A creditor may apply in a single application notice for charging orders over more than one asset, but if the court makes interim charging orders over more than one asset, it will draw up a separate order relating to each asset.

High Court and family court jurisdiction

2.1 The jurisdiction of the High Court and the family court to make charging orders is set out in section 1(2) of the 1979 Act.

Change of location

3.1 The court may, on an application by a debtor who wishes to oppose an application for a charging order, direct that the matter be dealt with in a court building serving the address where the debtor resides or carries on business, or in another location (see rule 29.18 FPR).

Enforcement of charging orders by sale

4.1 The High Court or, subject to the county court limit, the county court can enforce a charging order by an order for sale. Provision in respect of applications for an order for sale is made in rule 73.10C CPR.

Charging Orders made against partnership property

5.1 A charging order or interim charging order may be made against any property, within the jurisdiction, belonging to –
(1) a debtor that is a partnership, or
(2) a debtor who is in a partnership.

5.2 Where paragraph 5.1(1) applies, then for the purposes of rule 40.6 (service of the interim order), the specified documents must be served on –
(1) a member of the partnership within the jurisdiction;
(2) a person authorised by a partner; or
(3) some other person having the control or management of the partnership business.

5.3 Where an order requires a partnership to appear before the court, it will be sufficient for a partner to appear before the court.

Section II – Stop notices

6 A sample form of stop notice is set out in the Appendix to this Practice Direction.

Section III – Applications for orders made under section 23 of the Partnership Act 1890

7.1 This paragraph relates to orders made under section 23 of the Partnership Act 1890 ('Section 23').

7.2 The following applications must be made in accordance with Part 18:
(1) an application for an order under Section 23 of the 1890 Act made by a creditor of a partner;

(2) an application for any order by a partner of the debtor in consequence of any application made by the creditor under Section 23.

7.3 Every application notice filed under this paragraph by a creditor, and every order made following such an application, must be served on the debtor and on any of the other partners that are within the jurisdiction.

7.4 Every application notice filed under this paragraph by a partner of a debtor, and every order made following such an application, must be served –

(1) on the creditor and the debtor; and
(2) on the other partners of the debtor who are not joined in the application and who are within the jurisdiction.

7.5 An application notice or order served under this paragraph on one or more, but not all, of the partners of a partnership is deemed to have been served on all the partners of that partnership.

APPENDIX

STOP NOTICE

To [insert name of person or body to whom the notice is addressed]

TAKE NOTICE that

[insert name and address]

claims to be beneficially entitled to an interest in the following securities –
[specify the securities, giving the name(s) in which they stand]

This Notice requires you to refrain from –

(1) registering a transfer of the securities specified above; or
(2) paying any dividend or interest in respect of the securities [delete if inappropriate];

without first giving 14 days' notice in writing to the said [insert name] of the above address.

GLOSSARY

Scope

This glossary is a guide to the meaning of certain legal expressions as used in these rules, but it does not give the expressions any meaning in the rules which they do not otherwise have in the law.

Expression	*Meaning*
Affidavit	A written, sworn, statement of evidence.
Cross-examination	Questioning of a witness by a party other than the party who called the witness.
Evidence in chief	The evidence given by a witness for the party who called him.
Injunction	A court order prohibiting a person from doing something or requiring a person to do something.
Official copy	A copy of an official document, supplied and marked as such by the office which issued the original.
Pre-action protocol	Statements of best practice about pre-action conduct which have been approved by the President of the Family Division and which are annexed to a Practice Direction.
Privilege	The right of a party to refuse to disclose a document or produce a document or to refuse to answer questions on the ground of some special interest recognised by law.

Expression	*Meaning*
Seal	A seal is a mark which the court puts on document to indicate that the document has been issued by the court.
Service	Steps required by rules of court to bring documents used in court proceedings to a person's attention.
Set aside	Cancelling a judgment or order or a step taken by a party in the proceedings.
Stay	A stay imposes a halt on proceedings, apart from the taking of any steps allowed by the rules or the terms of the stay. Proceedings can be continued if a stay is lifted.
Strike out	Striking out means the court ordering written material to be deleted so that it may no longer be relied upon.
Without prejudice	Negotiations with a view to settlement are usually conducted 'without prejudice' which means that the circumstances in which the content of those negotiations may be revealed to the court are very restricted.

Civil Procedure Rules 1998, SI 1998/3132

PART 1
OVERRIDING OBJECTIVE

CONTENTS OF THIS PART

Rule		Page
1.1	The overriding objective	2031
1.2	Application by the court of the overriding objective	2032
1.3	Duty of the parties	2032
1.4	Court's duty to manage cases	2032

1.1 The overriding objective

(1) These Rules are a new procedural code with the overriding objective of enabling the court to deal with cases justly and at proportionate cost.

(2) Dealing with a case justly and at proportionate cost includes, so far as is practicable –

- (a) ensuring that the parties are on an equal footing;
- (b) saving expense;
- (c) dealing with the case in ways which are proportionate –
  - (i) to the amount of money involved;
  - (ii) to the importance of the case;
  - (iii) to the complexity of the issues; and
  - (iv) to the financial position of each party;
- (d) ensuring that it is dealt with expeditiously and fairly;
- (e) allotting to it an appropriate share of the court's resources, while taking into account the need to allot resources to other cases; and
- (f) enforcing compliance with rules, practice directions and orders.

Amendments—SI 2013/262.

Scope of CPR 1998—The CPR 1998 are a procedural code that replaced both the former RSC 1965 and CCR 1981.

FPR 2010—FPR 2010 are the procedural code for family proceedings and came into force on 6 April 2011. The FPR have their own 'overriding objective', which is not exactly the same as that in the CPR.

1.2 Application by the court of the overriding objective

The court must seek to give effect to the overriding objective when it –

(a) exercises any power given to it by the Rules; or
(b) interprets any rule, subject to rules 76.2, 79.2, 80.2, 82.2 and 88.2.

Amendments—SI 2005/656; SI 2008/3085; SI 2011/2970; SI 2013/1571; SI 2015/406.

'interprets any rule'—The overriding objective applies to every rule. FPR 2010 have a similar, but not identical provision.

1.3 Duty of the parties

The parties are required to help the court to further the overriding objective.

1.4 Court's duty to manage cases

(1) The court must further the overriding objective by actively managing cases.

(2) Active case management includes –

(a) encouraging the parties to co-operate with each other in the conduct of the proceedings;
(b) identifying the issues at an early stage;
(c) deciding promptly which issues need full investigation and trial and accordingly disposing summarily of the others;
(d) deciding the order in which issues are to be resolved;
(e) encouraging the parties to use an alternative dispute resolution[(GL)] procedure if the court considers that appropriate and facilitating the use of such procedure;
(f) helping the parties to settle the whole or part of the case;
(g) fixing timetables or otherwise controlling the progress of the case;
(h) considering whether the likely benefits of taking a particular step justify the cost of taking it;
(i) dealing with as many aspects of the case as it can on the same occasion;
(j) dealing with the case without the parties needing to attend at court;
(k) making use of technology; and
(l) giving directions to ensure that the trial of a case proceeds quickly and efficiently.

PART 2
APPLICATION AND INTERPRETATION OF THE RULES

CONTENTS OF THIS PART

Rule		Page
2.1	Application of the Rules	2032
2.2	The glossary	2033
2.3	Interpretation	2033
2.8	Time	2034

Practice Direction—The Practice Directions that supplement this Part are set out in Section 2 of *Civil Court Service* (LexisNexis).

2.1 Application of the Rules

(1) Subject to paragraph (2), these Rules apply to all proceedings in –

(a) the County Court;
(b) the High Court; and
(c) the Civil Division of the Court of Appeal.

(2) These Rules do not apply to proceedings of the kinds specified in the first column of the following Table (proceedings for which rules may be made under the enactments specified in the second column) except to the extent that they are applied to those proceedings by another enactment –

Proceedings	*Enactments*
1. Insolvency proceedings	Insolvency Act 1986, ss 411 and 412
2. Non-contentious or common form probate proceedings	Senior Courts Act 1981, s 127
3. Proceedings in the High Court when acting as a Prize Court	Prize Courts Act 1894, s 3
4. Proceedings before the Court of Protection	Mental Capacity Act 2005, s 51
5. Family proceedings	Courts Act 2003, s 75
6. Adoption proceedings	Adoption and Children Act 2002, s 141 or Courts Act 2003, s 75
7. Election petitions in the High Court	Representation of the People Act 1983, s 182

Amendments—SI 1999/1008; SI 2003/1242; CRA 2005, Sch 11, para 1(2); SI 2005/3515; SI 2007/2204; SI 2011/1045; SI 2014/407.

Effect of CPR 1998 on family proceedings—Rule 2.1(2) provides that the CPR do not apply to 'family proceedings'. In family proceedings, see FPR 2010, which expressly incorporate certain provisions in the CPR.

2.2 The glossary

(1) The glossary at the end of these Rules is a guide to the meaning of certain legal expressions used in the Rules, but is not to be taken as giving those expressions any meaning in the Rules which they do not have in the law generally.

(2) Subject to paragraph (3), words in these Rules which are included in the glossary are followed by '(GL)'.

(3) The words 'counterclaim', 'damages', 'practice form' and 'service', which appear frequently in the Rules, are included in the glossary but are not followed by '(GL)'.

2.3 Interpretation

(1) In these Rules –

'child' has the meaning given by rule 21.1(2);

'civil restraint order' means an order restraining a party –

(a) from making any further applications in current proceedings (a limited civil restraint order);

(b) from issuing certain claims or making certain applications in specified courts (an extended civil restraint order); or

(c) from issuing any claim or making any application in specified courts (a general civil restraint order).

'claim for personal injuries' means proceedings in which there is a claim for damages in respect of personal injuries to the claimant or any other person or in respect of a person's death, and 'personal injuries' includes any disease and any impairment of a person's physical or mental condition;

'claimant' means a person who makes a claim;

'CCR' is to be interpreted in accordance with Part 50;

'court officer' means a member of the court staff;

'defendant' means a person against whom a claim is made;

'defendant's home court' means –

(a) if a claim is proceeding in the County Court, the County Court hearing centre serving the address where the defendant resides or carries on business; and

(b) if the claim is proceeding in the High Court, the district registry for the district in which the defendant resides or carries on business or, where there is no such district registry, the Royal Courts of Justice;

(Rule 6.23 provides for a party to give an address for service)

…

'filing', in relation to a document, means delivering it, by post or otherwise, to the court office;

'judge' means, unless the context otherwise requires, a judge, Master or District Judge or a person authorised to act as such;

'judge of the County Court' has the meaning given in section 5 of the County Courts Act 1984;

'jurisdiction' means, unless the context requires otherwise, England and Wales and any part of the territorial waters of the United Kingdom adjoining England and Wales;

'legal representative' means a –

(a) barrister;
(b) solicitor;
(c) solicitor's employee;
(d) manager of a body recognised under section 9 of the Administration of Justice Act 1985; or
(e) person who, for the purposes of the Legal Services Act 2007, is an authorised person in relation to an activity which constitutes the conduct of litigation (within the meaning of that Act),

who has been instructed to act for a party in relation to proceedings;

'litigation friend' has the meaning given by Part 21;

'preferred hearing centre' means, if the claim is proceeding in the County Court, the County Court hearing centre the claimant has specified in practice form N1 as the hearing centre to which the proceedings should be sent if necessary;

'protected party' has the meaning given by rule 21.1(2);

'RSC' is to be interpreted in accordance with Part 50;

'statement of case' –

(a) means a claim form, particulars of claim where these are not included in a claim form, defence, Part 20 claim, or reply to defence; and
(b) includes any further information given in relation to them voluntarily or by court order under rule 18.1;

'statement of value' is to be interpreted in accordance with rule 16.3;

'summary judgment' is to be interpreted in accordance with Part 24.

(2) A reference to a 'specialist list' is a reference to a list[(GL)] that has been designated as such by a rule or practice direction.

(3) Where the context requires, a reference to 'the court' means a reference to a the County Court, a District Registry, or the Royal Courts of Justice.

Amendments—SI 2000/2092; SI 2001/4015; SI 2004/2072; SI 2007/2204; SI 2008/2178; SI 2009/3390; SI 2011/3103; SI 2014/407.

****

2.8 Time

(1) This rule shows how to calculate any period of time for doing any act which is specified –

(a) by these Rules;
(b) by a practice direction; or
(c) by a judgment or order of the court.

(2) A period of time expressed as a number of days shall be computed as clear days.

(3) In this rule 'clear days' means that in computing the number of days –

(a) the day on which the period begins; and
(b) if the end of the period is defined by reference to an event, the day on which that event occurs

are not included.

Examples

(i) Notice of an application must be served at least 3 days before the hearing.
An application is to be heard on Friday 20 October.
The last date for service is Monday 16 October.

(ii) The court is to fix a date for a hearing.
The hearing must be at least 28 days after the date of notice.
If the court gives notice of the date of the hearing on 1 October, the earliest date for the hearing is 30 October.

(iii) Particulars of claim must be served within 14 days of service of the claim form.
The claim form is served on 2 October.
The last day for service of the particulars of claim is 16 October.

(4) Where the specified period –

(a) is 5 days or less; and
(b) includes –
 (i) a Saturday or Sunday; or
 (ii) a Bank Holiday, Christmas Day or Good Friday,

that day does not count.

Example

Notice of an application must be served at least 3 days before the hearing.
An application is to be heard on Monday 20 October.
The last date for service is Tuesday 14 October.

(5) Subject to the provisions of Practice Direction 5C, when the period specified –

(a) by these Rules or a practice direction; or
(b) by any judgment or court order,

for doing any act at the court office ends on a day on which the office is closed, that act shall be in time if done on the next day on which the court office is open.

Amendments—SI 2009/3390.

****

PART 3
THE COURT'S CASE AND COSTS MANAGEMENT POWERS

CONTENTS OF THIS PART

Section I

Rule		Page
	Case Management	
3.1	The court's general powers of management	2035
3.3	Court's power to make order of its own initiative	2037

Practice Direction—See *PD (Striking out a Statement of Case)*, *PD (Sanctions for Non-Payment of Fees)* and *PD (Civil Restraint Orders)*, which supplement this Part generally; all three are set out in Section 2 of the *Civil Court Service* (LexisNexis).

Section I
Case Management

3.1 The court's general powers of management

(1) The list of powers in this rule is in addition to any powers given to the court by any other rule or practice direction or by any other enactment or any powers it may otherwise have.

(2) Except where these Rules provide otherwise, the court may –

(a) extend or shorten the time for compliance with any rule, practice direction or court order (even if an application for extension is made after the time for compliance has expired);
(b) adjourn or bring forward a hearing;
(c) require a party or a party's legal representative to attend the court;
(d) hold a hearing and receive evidence by telephone or by using any other method of direct oral communication;
(e) direct that part of any proceedings (such as a counterclaim) be dealt with as separate proceedings;
(f) stay(GL) the whole or part of any proceedings or judgment either generally or until a specified date or event;
(g) consolidate proceedings;
(h) try two or more claims on the same occasion;
(i) direct a separate trial of any issue;
(j) decide the order in which issues are to be tried;
(k) exclude an issue from consideration;
(l) dismiss or give judgment on a claim after a decision on a preliminary issue;
(ll) order any party to file and exchange a costs budget;
(m) take any other step or make any other order for the purpose of managing the case and furthering the overriding objective, including hearing an Early Neutral Evaluation with the aim of helping the parties settle the case.

(3) When the court makes an order, it may –

(a) make it subject to conditions, including a condition to pay a sum of money into court; and
(b) specify the consequence of failure to comply with the order or a condition.

(4) Where the court gives directions it will take into account whether or not a party has complied with the Practice Direction (Pre-Action Conduct) and any relevant pre-action protocol(GL).

(5) The court may order a party to pay a sum of money into court if that party has, without good reason, failed to comply with a rule, practice direction or a relevant pre-action protocol.

(6) When exercising its power under paragraph (5) the court must have regard to –

(a) the amount in dispute; and
(b) the costs which the parties have incurred or which they may incur.

(6A) Where a party pays money into court following an order under paragraph (3) or (5), the money shall be security for any sum payable by that party to any other party in the proceedings.

(7) A power of the court under these Rules to make an order includes a power to vary or revoke the order.

(8) The court may contact the parties from time to time in order to monitor compliance with directions. The parties must respond promptly to any such enquiries from the court.

Amendments—SI 1999/1008; SI 2005/2292; SI 2006/3435; SI 2008/3327; SI 2013/262; SI 2013/1974; SI 2015/1569.

General powers of management—The list of case management powers supplement those in r 1.4. FPR 2010, r 4.1 will provide for case management in family proceedings in similar terms to CPR 1998, r 3.1, although case-law under this rule will be helpful in an understanding of r 4.1.

Case management of parallel family and civil proceedings—Where an application under, for example, CA 1989, s 15 and Sch 1, and a claim under TLATA 1996, s 14, are proceedings in parallel, care is needed to ensure that the CPR 1998, Pt 8 procedure (for s 14 proceedings) and FPR 2010, Pt 9 run in parallel. Typically this occurs where there are proceedings relating to a home owned by an unmarried couple with children (see *W v W (Joinder of Trusts of Land Act and Children Act 1989 Applications)* [2004] 2 FLR 321, CA). The judge had been wrong to try the TLATA application first and separately from the CA 1989 application. The Court of Appeal did not address the question of whether FPR 2010 or CPR 1998 apply. The same question of parallel proceedings under different rules arises; where an issue as to equitable interests arises in respect of specific matrimonial property or where one spouse of civil partner is bankrupt and their interest in the former matrimonial home vests in their trustee in bankruptcy (see case management under FPR 2010, rr 1.4 and 4.1).

Directions—Given the terms of the overriding objective here and in FPR 2010, r 1.4, parties owe a duty to the court and to each other to consider whether preliminary directions, and if so which, should be applied for in any court proceedings, especially where a preliminary issue is identified by one party (see, for example, *TL v ML* above).

Application for order—Where application is made for an order in respect of any of the provisions under r 3.1(2), it is made in accordance with Pt 23 on Form N246 (and see r 3.3 below).

Early Neutral Evaluation (ENE) and matrimonial causes—MCA 1973, s 7 envisages a form of ENE. It remains for the FPR Committee to apply this provision to matrimonial proceedings: only a rule like r 3.1(2)(m) is required.

★★★★

3.3 Court's power to make order of its own initiative

(1) Except where a rule or some other enactment provides otherwise, the court may exercise its powers on an application or of its own initiative.

(Part 23 sets out the procedure for making an application)

(2) Where the court proposes to make an order of its own initiative –

(a) it may give any person likely to be affected by the order an opportunity to make representations; and
(b) where it does so it must specify the time by and the manner in which the representations must be made.

(3) Where the court proposes –

(a) to make an order of its own initiative; and
(b) to hold a hearing to decide whether to make the order,

it must give each party likely to be affected by the order at least 3 days' notice of the hearing.

(4) The court may make an order of its own initiative, without hearing the parties or giving them an opportunity to make representations.

(5) Where the court has made an order under paragraph (4) –

(a) a party affected by the order may apply to have it set aside(GL), varied or stayed(GL); and
(b) the order must contain a statement of the right to make such an application.

(6) An application under paragraph (5)(a) must be made –

(a) within such period as may be specified by the court; or
(b) if the court does not specify a period, not more than 7 days after the date on which the order was served on the party making the application.

(7) If the court of its own initiative strikes out a statement of case or dismisses an application, including an application for permission to appeal or for permission to apply for judicial review) and it considers that the claim or application is totally without merit –

(a) the court's order must record that fact; and
(b) the court must at the same time consider whether it is appropriate to make a civil restraint order.

(CCR Ord 42, in Schedule 2, sets out the circumstances when the court may not make an order of its own initiative against the Crown)

Amendments—SI 2004/2072; SI 2005/2292.

★★★★

PART III

PART 7
HOW TO START PROCEEDINGS – THE CLAIM FORM

CONTENTS OF THIS PART

Rule		Page
7.1	Where to start proceedings	2039
7.2	How to start proceedings	2039
7.2A		2039
7.3	Right to use one claim form to start two or more claims	2040
7.4	Particulars of claim	2040
7.5	Service of a claim form	2040
7.6	Extension of time for serving a claim form	2040
7.7	Application by defendant for service of claim form	2041
7.8	Form for defence etc must be served with particulars of claim	2041
7.9	Fixed date and other claims	2041
7.10	Production Centre for claims	2041
7.11	Human Rights	2042
7.12	Electronic issue of claims	2042
	Practice Direction 7A – How to Start Proceedings	2042

Application of this Part—The provisions of this Part are modified as regards particular kinds of proceedings and care needs to be paid to particular rules or practice directions:

Type of Claim	*CPR Part/Practice Direction*
Consumer Credit Act 1974	Rule 7.9/PD7B
Money Claims Online	PD7E
No substantial dispute of fact	Part 8
Parties and group litigation	Part 19/PD19B
Children or patients	Part 21
Pre-action disclosure of documents	Rule 31.16
Costs-only proceedings	Rule 44.12A
Injunctions and other interim remedies	Part 25
Applications under the Companies Acts 1985–89, the Insurance Companies Act 1982 and Part VII of the Financial Services and Markets Act 2000	PD49B
Appeals	Part 52
Defamation claims	Part 53
Judicial review	Part 54
Claim for possession of land	Part 55
Applications relating to business tenancies	Part 56
Probate claims	Part 57
Claims under the Inheritance (Provision for Family and Dependants) Act 1975	Part 57, Section IV
Commercial Court claims	Part 58
Mercantile court claims	Part 59
Technology and Construction Court claims	Part 60
Admiralty Court claims	Part 61

Type of Claim	*CPR Part/Practice Direction*
Claims or applications under the Arbitration Act 1996	Part 62
Patent claims	Part 63
Claims relating to estates, trusts and charities	Part 64
Proceedings relating to anti-social behaviour and harassment	Part 65
Proceedings relating to solicitors	Part 67
Applications for Writ of Habeas Corpus	Sch 1, RSC Ord 54

7.1 Where to start proceedings

Restrictions on where proceedings may be started are set out in the relevant practice directions supplementing this Part.

Amendments—SI 2009/3390.

7.2 How to start proceedings

(1) Proceedings are started when the court issues a claim form at the request of the claimant.

(2) A claim form is issued on the date entered on the form by the court.

(A person who seeks a remedy from the court before proceedings are started or in relation to proceedings which are taking place, or will take place, in another jurisdiction must make an application under Part 23)

(Part 16 sets out what the claim form must include)

Amendments—SI 2000/1317; SI 2008/2178; SI 2009/3390; SI 2011/88; SI 2013/1974.

Type of Claim	*Claim Form*
Money (which includes a claim for damages)	N1
Consumer Credit Act or similar return of goods claim under r 7.9	N1 (FD)
Claim Production Centre claim form	N1 CPC
Probate claim	N2
Claim for possession by landlord or mortgagor	N5 and N119/N120
Claim for relief from forfeiture	N5A
Applications for accelerated possession of assured tenancies	N5B
Claim for demotion of tenancy	N6
Injunction under Housing Act 1996, s 152	N16A
Claim for possession against trespasser	N5 and N121
Application for possession including application for interim possession order	N5 and N130
Claim where there is no substantial dispute of fact or PD8 has applied the Pt 8 procedure	N208
An additional claim	N211
Time order under Consumer Credit Act 1974	N440
Claims for judicial review	N461

7.2A Practice Direction 7A makes provision for procedures to be followed when claims are brought by or against a partnership within the jurisdiction.

Amendments—Inserted by SI 2006/1689. Amended by SI 2009/3390.

PART III

7.3 Right to use one claim form to start two or more claims

A claimant may use a single claim form to start all claims which can be conveniently disposed of in the same proceedings.

7.4 Particulars of claim

(1) Particulars of claim must –

(a) be contained in or served with the claim form; or
(b) subject to paragraph (2) be served on the defendant by the claimant within 14 days after service of the claim form.

(2) Particulars of claim must be served on the defendant no later than the latest time for serving a claim form.

(Rule 7.5 sets out the latest time for serving a claim form)

(3) Where the claimant serves particulars of claim, then unless a copy of the particulars has already been filed, the claimant must, within 7 days of service on the defendant, file a copy of the particulars except where –

(a) paragraph 5.2(4) of Practice Direction 7C applies; or
(b) paragraph 6.4 of Practice Direction 7E applies.

(Part 16 sets out what the particulars of claim must include)

(Part 22 requires particulars of claim to be verified by a statement of truth)

Amendments—SI 2008/2178; SI 2008/3327; SI 2009/3390; SI 2015/1569.

7.5 Service of a claim form

(1) Where the claim form is served within the jurisdiction, the claimant must complete the step required by the following table in relation to the particular method of service chosen, before 12.00 midnight on the calendar day four months after the date of issue of the claim form.

Method of service	*Step required*
First class post, document exchange or other service which provides for delivery on the next business day	Posting, leaving with, delivering to or collection by the relevant service provider
Delivery of the document to or leaving it at the relevant place	Delivery of the document to or leaving it at the relevant place
Personal service under rule 6.5	Completing the relevant step required by rule 6.5(3)
Fax	Completing the transmission of the fax
Other electronic method	Sending the e-mail or other electronic transmission

(2) Where the claim form is to be served out of the jurisdiction, the claim form must be served in accordance with Section IV of Part 6 within 6 months of the date of issue.

Amendments—Substituted by SI 2008/2178.

7.6 Extension of time for serving a claim form

(1) The claimant may apply for an order extending the period for compliance with rule 7.5.

(2) The general rule is that an application to extend the time for compliance with rule 7.5 must be made –

(a) within the period specified by rule 7.5; or
(b) where an order has been made under this rule, within the period for service specified by that order.

(3) If the claimant applies for an order to extend the time for compliance after the end of the period specified by rule 7.5 or by an order made under this rule, the court may make such an order only if –

(a) the court has failed to serve the claim form; or
(b) the claimant has taken all reasonable steps to comply with rule 7.5 but has been unable to do so; and
(c) in either case, the claimant has acted promptly in making the application.

(4) An application for an order extending the time for compliance with rule 7.5 –

(a) must be supported by evidence; and
(b) may be made without notice.

Amendments—Substituted by SI 2008/2178.

7.7 Application by defendant for service of claim form

(1) Where a claim form has been issued against a defendant, but has not yet been served on him, the defendant may serve a notice on the claimant requiring him to serve the claim form or discontinue the claim within a period specified in the notice.

(2) The period specified in a notice served under paragraph (1) must be at least 14 days after service of the notice.

(3) If the claimant fails to comply with the notice, the court may, on the application of the defendant –

(a) dismiss the claim; or
(b) make any other order it thinks just.

7.8 Form for defence etc must be served with particulars of claim

(1) When particulars of claim are served on a defendant, whether they are contained in the claim form, served with it or served subsequently, they must be accompanied by –

(a) a form for defending the claim;
(b) a form for admitting the claim; and
(c) a form for acknowledging service.

(2) Where the claimant is using the procedure set out in Part 8 (alternative procedure for claims) –

(a) paragraph (1) does not apply; and
(b) a form for acknowledging service must accompany the claim form.

7.9 Fixed date and other claims

A practice direction –

(a) may set out the circumstances in which the court may give a fixed date for a hearing when it issues a claim;
(b) may list claims in respect of which there is a specific claim form for use and set out the claim form in question; and
(c) may disapply or modify these Rules as appropriate in relation to the claims referred to in paragraphs (a) and (b).

7.10 Production Centre for claims

(1) There shall be a Production Centre for the issue of claim forms and other related matters.

(2) Practice Direction 7C makes provision for –

(a) which claimants may use the Production Centre;
(b) the type of claims which the Production Centre may issue;
(c) the functions which are to be discharged by the Production Centre;
(d) the place where the Production Centre is to be located; and
(e) other related matters.

PART III

(3) Practice Direction 7C may disapply or modify these Rules as appropriate in relation to claims issued by the Production Centre.

Amendments—SI 2009/3390.

7.11 Human Rights

(1) A claim under section 7(1)(a) of the Human Rights Act 1998 in respect of a judicial act may be brought only in the High Court.

(2) Any other claim under section 7(1)(a) of that Act may be brought in any court.

Amendments—Inserted by SI 2000/2092.

7.12 Electronic issue of claims

(1) A practice direction may make provision for a claimant to start a claim by requesting the issue of a claim form electronically.

(2) The practice direction may, in particular –

- (a) specify –
  - (i) the types of claim which may be issued electronically; and
  - (ii) the conditions which a claim must meet before it may be issued electronically;
- (b) specify –
  - (i) the court where the claim will be issued; and
  - (ii) the circumstances in which the claim will be transferred to another court;
- (c) provide for the filing of other documents electronically where a claim has been started electronically;
- (d) specify the requirements that must be fulfilled for any document filed electronically; and
- (e) provide how a fee payable on the filing of any document is to be paid where that document is filed electronically.

(3) The practice direction may disapply or modify these Rules as appropriate in relation to claims started electronically.

(Practice Direction 5C deals with electronic issue of claims started or continued under the Electronic Working scheme.)

Amendments—Inserted by SI 2003/3361. Amended by SI 2009/3390.

Practice Direction 7A – How to Start Proceedings

This Practice Direction supplements CPR Part 7

General

1 Subject to the following provisions of this practice direction, proceedings which both the High Court and the County Court have jurisdiction to deal with may be started in the High Court or in the County Court.

Amendments—CPR Update 69.

Where to start proceedings

2.1 Proceedings (whether for damages or for a specified sum) may not be started in the High Court unless the value of the claim is more than £100,000.

2.2 Proceedings which include a claim for damages in respect of personal injuries must not be started in the High Court unless the value of the claim is £50,000 or more (paragraph 9 of the High Court and County Courts Jurisdiction Order 1991 (SI 1991/724 as amended) describes how the value of a claim is to be determined).

2.3 A claim must be issued in the High Court or the County Court if an enactment so requires.

2.4 Subject to paragraphs 2.1 and 2.2 above, a claim should be started in the High Court if by reason of:

(1) the financial value of the claim and the amount in dispute, and/or
(2) the complexity of the facts, legal issues, remedies or procedures involved, and/or
(3) the importance of the outcome of the claim to the public in general,

the claimant believes that the claim ought to be dealt with by a High Court judge.

(CPR Part 30 and Practice Direction 30 contain provisions relating to the transfer to the County Court of proceedings started in the High Court and vice-versa.)

2.4A

(1) A claim in the County Court under Part 7 may be made at any County Court hearing centre, unless any enactment, rule or practice direction provides otherwise.
(2) If a claim which is required to be made at a particular County Court hearing centre is made at the wrong hearing centre, a court officer will send the claim to the correct hearing centre before it is issued.
(3) A claimant should consider the potential delay which may result if a claim is not made at the correct County Court hearing centre in the first instance.

2.5 A claim relating to Chancery business (which includes any of the matters specified in paragraph 1 of Schedule 1 to the Senior Courts Act 1981) may, subject to any enactment, rule or practice direction, be dealt with in the High Court or in the County Court. The claim form should, if issued in the High Court, be marked in the top right hand corner 'Chancery Division' and, if issued in the County Court, be marked 'Chancery Business'.

(For the equity jurisdiction of the County Court, see section 23 of the County Courts Act 1984.)

2.6 A claim relating to any of the matters specified in sub-paragraphs (a) and (b) of paragraph 2 of Schedule 1 to the Senior Courts Act 1981 must be dealt with in the High Court and will be assigned to the Queen's Bench Division.

2.7 Practice directions applying to particular types of proceedings, or to proceedings in particular courts, will contain provisions relating to the commencement and conduct of those proceedings.

2.8 A claim in the High Court for which a jury trial is directed will, if not already being dealt with in the Queen's Bench Division, be transferred to that Division.

2.9 The following proceedings may not be started in the County Court unless the parties have agreed otherwise in writing:

(1) a claim for damages or other remedy for libel or slander, and
(2) a claim in which the title to any toll, fair, market or franchise is in question.

2.10

(1) The normal rules apply in deciding in which court and specialist list a claim that includes issues under the Human Rights Act 1998 should be started. They also apply in deciding which procedure to use to start the claim; this Part or CPR Part 8 or CPR Part 54 (judicial review).
(2) The exception is a claim for damages in respect of a judicial act, which should be commenced in the High Court. If the claim is made in a notice of appeal then it will be dealt with according to the normal rules governing where the appeal is heard.

(The County Court cannot make a declaration of incompatibility in accordance with section 4 of the Human Rights Act 1998. Legislation may direct that such a claim is to be brought before a specified tribunal.)

Amendments—CPR Updates 2, 3, 18, 29, 50, 51, 69.

The claim form

3.1 A claimant must use practice form N1 or practice form N208 (the Part 8 claim form) to start a claim (but see paragraphs 3.2 and 3.4 below).

PART III

3.2 Rule 7.9 deals with fixed date claims and rule 7.10 deals with the Production Centre for the issue of claims; there are separate practice directions supplementing rules 7.9 and 7.10.

3.3 If a claimant wishes the claim to proceed under Part 8, or if the claim is required to proceed under Part 8, the claim form should so state. Otherwise the claim will proceed under Part 7. But note that in respect of claims in specialist proceedings (listed in CPR Part 49) and claims brought under the RSC or CCR set out in the Schedule to the CPR (see CPR Part 50) the CPR will apply only to the extent that they are not inconsistent with the rules and practice directions that expressly apply to those claims.

3.4 Other practice directions may require special practice forms to be used to commence particular types of proceedings, or proceedings in particular courts.

3.5 Where a claim form to be served out of the jurisdiction is one which the court has power to deal with –

(a) under the Civil Jurisdiction and Judgments Act 1982; and
(b) the Judgments Regulation (which has the same meaning as in rule 6.31(d)),

the claim form must, pursuant to rule 6.34, be filed and served with the notice referred to in that rule and paragraph 2.1 of Practice Direction 6B.

3.6 If a claim for damages or for an unspecified sum is started in the High Court, the claim form must:

(1) state that the claimant expects to recover more than £100,000 (or £50,000 or more if the claim is for personal injuries), or
(2) state that some enactment provides that the claim may only be commenced in the High Court and specify that enactment, or
(3) state that the claim is to be in one of the specialist High Court lists (see CPR Parts 49 and 58–62) and specify that list.

3.7 If the contents of a claim form commencing specialist proceedings comply with the requirements of the specialist list in question the claim form will also satisfy paragraph 3.6 above.

3.8 If a claim for damages for personal injuries is started in the County Court, the claim form must state whether or not the claimant expects to recover more than £1000 in respect of pain, suffering and loss of amenity.

3.9 If a claim for housing disrepair which includes a claim for an order requiring repairs or other work to be carried out by the landlord is started in the County Court, the claim form must state:

(1) whether or not the cost of the repairs or other work is estimated to be more than £1000, and
(2) whether or not the claimant expects to recover more than £1000 in respect of any claim for damages[1].

If either of the amounts mentioned in (1) and (2) is more than £1000, the small claims track will not be the normal track for that claim.

1 See rules 16.3(4) and 26.6.

Amendments—CPR Updates 47, 49, 51, 69.

Title of proceedings

4.1 The claim form and every other statement of case, must be headed with the title of the proceedings. The title should state:

(1) the number of proceedings,
(2) the court or Division in which they are proceeding,
(3) the full name of each party,
(4) each party's status in the proceedings (i e claimant/defendant).

(Paragraph 2.6 of Practice Direction 16 sets out what is meant by a full name in respect of each type of claimant.)

4.2 Where there is more than one claimant and/or more than one defendant, the parties should be described in the title as follows:

(1) AB
(2) CD
(3) EF Claimants
and
(1) GH
(2) IJ
(3) KL Defendants

Amendments—CPR Updates 1, 40, 49, 51.

Starting a Part 7 Claim in the County Court

4A.1

(1) Subject to subparagraph (2), if a claim –
  (a) is started in the County Court under Part 7;
  (b) is a claim only for an amount of money, whether specified or unspecified; and
  (c) is not a claim for which special procedures are provided in the Civil Procedure Rules or practice directions,

  practice form N1 must be sent to: County Court Money Claims Centre, PO Box 527, M5 0BY.

(2) For the purpose of this Practice Direction, the procedure in Practice Direction 7D is not a special procedure.

4A.2 In proceedings referred to in paragraph 4A.1, the claimant must specify the preferred hearing centre on practice form N1.

Amendments—CPR Updates 58, 69.

Start of proceedings

5.1 Proceedings are started when the court issues a claim form at the request of the claimant (see rule 7.2) but where the claim form as issued was received in the court office on a date earlier than the date on which it was issued by the court, the claim is 'brought' for the purposes of the Limitation Act 1980 and any other relevant statute on that earlier date.

5.2 The date on which the claim form was received by the court will be recorded by a date stamp either on the claim form held on the court file or on the letter that accompanied the claim form when it was received by the court.

5.3 An enquiry as to the date on which the claim form was received by the court should be directed to a court officer.

5.4 Parties proposing to start a claim which is approaching the expiry of the limitation period should recognise the potential importance of establishing the date the claim form was received by the court and should themselves make arrangements to record the date.

5.5 Where it is sought to start proceedings against the estate of a deceased defendant where probate or letters of administration have not been granted, the claimant should issue the claim against 'the personal representatives of A.B. deceased'. The claimant should then, before the expiry of the period for service of the claim form, apply to the court for the appointment of a person to represent the estate of the deceased.

Amendments—CPR Update 1.

Claims by and against partnerships within the jurisdiction

5A.1 Paragraphs 5A and 5B apply to claims that are brought by or against two or more persons who –

(1) were partners; and
(2) carried on that partnership business within the jurisdiction,

PART III

at the time when the cause of action accrued.

5A.2 For the purposes of this paragraph, 'partners' includes persons claiming to be entitled as partners and persons alleged to be partners.

5A.3 Where that partnership has a name, unless it is inappropriate to do so, claims must be brought in or against the name under which that partnership carried on business at the time the cause of action accrued.

Amendments—CPR Update 42.

Partnership membership statements

5B.1 In this paragraph a 'partnership membership statement' is a written statement of the names and last known places of residence of all the persons who were partners in the partnership at the time when the cause of action accrued, being the date specified for this purpose in accordance with paragraph 5B.3.

5B.2 If the partners are requested to provide a copy of a partnership membership statement by any party to a claim, the partners must do so within 14 days of receipt of the request.

5B.3 In that request the party seeking a copy of a partnership membership statement must specify the date when the relevant cause of action accrued.

(Signing of the acknowledgment of service in the case of a partnership is dealt with in paragraph 4.4 of Practice Direction 10.)

Amendments—CPR Updates 42, 49, 51.

Persons carrying on business in another name

5C.1 This paragraph applies where –

(1) a claim is brought against an individual;
(2) that individual carries on a business within the jurisdiction (even if not personally within the jurisdiction); and
(3) that business is carried on in a name other than that individual's own name ('the business name').

5C.2 The claim may be brought against the business name as if it were the name of a partnership.

Amendments—CPR Updates 42, 49.

Particulars of claim

6.1 Where the claimant does not include the particulars of claim in the claim form, they may be served separately:

(1) either at the same time as the claim form, or
(2) within 14 days after service of the claim form provided that the service of the particulars of claim is within 4 months after the date of issue of the claim form[1] (or 6 months where the claim form is to be served out of the jurisdiction[2]).

1 See rules 7.4(2) and 7.5(1).
2 See rule 7.5(2).

6.2 If the particulars of claim are not included in or have not been served with the claim form, the claim form must contain a statement that particulars of claim will follow[1].

(These paragraphs do not apply where the Part 8 procedure is being used. For information on matters to be included in the claim form or the particulars of claim, see Part 16 (statements of case) and Practice Direction 16.)

1 See rule 16.2(2).

Amendments—CPR Updates 1, 11, 47, 49, 51.

Statement of truth

7.1 Part 22 requires the claim form and, where they are not included in the claim form, the particulars of claim, to be verified by a statement of truth.

7.2 The form of the statement of truth is as follows:

'[I believe][the claimant believes] that the facts stated in [this claim form] [these particulars of claim] are true.'

7.3 Attention is drawn to rule 32.14 which sets out the consequences of verifying a statement of case containing a false statement without an honest belief in its truth.

Amendments—CPR Updates 1, 49.

Extension of time

8.1 An application under rule 7.6 (for an extension of time for serving a claim form under rule 7.6(1)) must be made in accordance with Part 23 and supported by evidence.

8.2 The evidence should state:

(1) all the circumstances relied on,
(2) the date of issue of the claim,
(3) the expiry date of any rule 7.6 extension, and
(4) a full explanation as to why the claim has not been served.

(For information regarding (1) written evidence see Part 32 and Practice Direction 32 and (2) service of the claim form see Part 6 and Practice Directions 6A and 6B.)

Amendments—CPR Updates 1, 51.

★★★★

PART 8
ALTERNATIVE PROCEDURE FOR CLAIMS

CONTENTS OF THIS PART

Rule		Page
8.1	Types of claim in which Part 8 procedure may be followed	2047
8.2	Contents of the claim form	2049
8.2A	Issue of claim form without naming defendants	2050
8.3	Acknowledgment of service	2050
8.4	Consequence of not filing an acknowledgment of service	2050
8.5	Filing and serving written evidence	2050
8.6	Evidence – general	2051
8.7	Part 20 claims	2051
8.8	Procedure where defendant objects to use of the Part 8 procedure	2051
8.9	Modifications to the general rules	2051
	Practice Direction 8A – Alternative Procedure for Claims	2051

8.1 Types of claim in which Part 8 procedure may be followed

(1) The Part 8 procedure is the procedure set out in this Part.

(2) A claimant may use the Part 8 procedure where –

(a) he seeks the court's decision on a question which is unlikely to involve a substantial dispute of fact; or
(b) paragraph (6) applies.

(2A) In the County Court, a claim under the Part 8 procedure may be made at any County Court hearing centre unless an enactment, rule or practice direction provides otherwise.

(Practice Direction 8A includes further direction in respect of claims which are not made at the appropriate County Court hearing centre in the first instance.)

(3) The court may at any stage order the claim to continue as if the claimant had not used the Part 8 procedure and, if it does so, the court may give any directions it considers appropriate.

PART III

(4) Paragraph (2) does not apply if a practice direction provides that the Part 8 procedure may not be used in relation to the type of claim in question.

(5) Where the claimant uses the Part 8 procedure he may not obtain default judgment under Part 12.

(6) A rule or practice direction may, in relation to a specified type of proceedings –

(a) require or permit the use of the Part 8 procedure; and
(b) disapply or modify any of the rules set out in this Part as they apply to those proceedings.

(Rule 8.9 provides for other modifications to the general rules where the Part 8 procedure is being used)

(Part 78 provides procedures for European orders for payment and for the European small claims procedure. It also provides procedures for applications for mediation settlement enforcement orders in relation to certain cross-border disputes.)

Amendments—SI 2000/1317; SI 2008/2178; SI 2011/88; SI 2014/407.

(1) INTRODUCTION

'unlikely to involve a substantial dispute of fact' (r 8.1(2)(a))—This provision encapsulates whether a claim proceeds under Pt 8, or under the more generally used Pt 7. PD to Pt 8, para 3 sets out those claims which may proceed under Pt 8, such as approval of infant settlements (PD8, para 3.1(1)) and (2)); those which must use the Pt 8 procedure: namely a recondite list of forms of proceeding, none of them family proceedings (PD8, para 3.2); and proceedings where the originating summons procedure is prescribed by statute, rule or PD (PD8, para 3.3, eg I(PFD)A 1975, see below). Traditionally, land claims eg under TLATA 1996 and its predecessor, proceeded under Pt 8 because they were issued under the old originating summons procedure. In practice it is likely to be rare that a claim under, eg TLATA 1996, s 14, does not involve a 'substantial dispute of fact', so almost invariably such claims are likely to be issued under Pt 7.

Particular uses of the Pt 8 procedure

(a) *The 'judicial review procedure'* (CPR 1998, r 54.1(2)(e)) prescribes that the procedure for judicial review is the Pt 8 procedure 'as modified' by the detailed provisions of Pt 54 – not always an easy fit, in practice.
(b) *Claims under I(PFD)A 1975, s 1* must be made in accordance with Pt 8.
(c) *Application for a declaration* should in the first instance be issued under Pt 8 (save where other provision is made under statute or rules.

'the claim to continue as if the claimant had not used the Part 8 procedure' (r 8.1(3))—Failure to use the procedure correctly, or where it becomes obvious, for example, that disputed issues of fact will arise, enables the court to switch the claim to the appropriate procedure and give directions accordingly.

Objection to Pt 8 procedure—A defendant who objects to the Pt 8 procedure must so state in his/her acknowledgement of service (rr 8.3 and 8.8(1)).

(2) CLAIMS UNDER HUMAN RIGHTS ACT 1998

Claims under HRA 1998, ss 7 and 8—Claims under HRA 1998 must be in 'civil proceedings' (see commentary under HRA 1998, s 8(2): ie they cannot be in family proceedings). In *Anufrijeva v Southwark LBC* [2004] 1 FLR 8, CA, the Court of Appeal said that procedure for HRA 1998 'maladministration claims' should be by judicial review in the Administrative Court. Judicial review procedure is the Pt 8 procedure as amended by CPR 1998, Pt 54, so whether application is by Pt 8 or by Pt 54 makes relatively little practical difference. Because the claim, in children proceedings, will generally follow existing proceedings, the facts will not be in issue (r 8.1(2)(a); and see **Issue estoppel**, below). If facts are in issue, the Administrative Court, in exceptional cases, can hear contested evidence (*Anufrijeva* was such a case).

Claims under HRA 1998 in children proceedings

(1) *Split issues* Case management rules require that issues be defined by the court (FPR 2010, r 1.4(2)(b)(i)) and that issues, where appropriate, be directed to a separate hearing (FPR 2010, r 4.1(3)(j)). In care proceedings, it is not unusual to separate the CA 1989, s 31(2) threshold from welfare issues (*Re B (Children)* [2008] 2 FLR 141, HL). So too can HRA 1998, s 8 damages issues be separated from other issues of law that arise in children proceedings (and see under LASPOA 2012, s 25 (legal aid statutory charge) where separate proceedings arise).
(2) *Parallel or freestanding claims* In *Re L (Care Proceedings: Human Rights Claims)* [2003] 2 FLR 160, FD, Munby J differentiated between claims parallel to existing CA 1989 proceedings, and later 'freestanding' claims. In *Re V (Care Proceedings: Human Rights Claims)* [2004] 1 FLR 944, CA, the Court said that HRA 1998 claims should be dealt with in care proceedings. Neither case says how 'freestanding' claims should be dealt with. It is submitted that a separately pleaded claim (on analogy with 'chancery' claims per *TL v ML (Ancillary Relief: Claims against Assets of Extended Family)* [2006] 1 FLR 1263, FD) in parallel proceedings under CPR 1998, Pt 8 would not be inconsistent with these 2004 authorities. Careful case management (as with parallel CA 1989, Sch 1 (FPR 2010) and TLATA 1996, s 14 (CPR 1998) cases) would then be needed in case of any parallel factual issues. The hearing of any issue as to liability under HRA 1998, ss 7(1) and 8(1) and of damages can then be adjourned to, or be dealt with by consent in, the appropriate civil court (HRA 1998, s 8(2)).

Claims under HRA 1998 in other family proceedings—Maladministration claims may arise against, for example: the Child Support Agency in parallel with tribunal or other family courts proceedings; HMCTS in cases of delay (contrary to Art 6(1)); and the police or health departments. Each of these will be by judicial review (CPR 1998, Pt 54) with appropriate application in the family courts for disclosure of documents to separate proceedings (CPR 1998, r 5.4C), as need be.

Anonymity—Proceedings under CPR 1998, Pts 8 or 54 are open court (CPR 1998, r 39.2(1)) including any consent order (e g in child settlement cases), so parties will need to include an application for anonymity in their claim form or by separate application under CPR 1998, Pt 23 (along the lines suggested in *Norman v Norman* [2017] EWCA Civ 49 for the Court of Appeal). Children proceedings (but not necessarily for their parents: *Re S (Identification: Restrictions on Publication)* [2005] 1 FLR 591, HL) are among the types of case that are appropriate for anonymity (*X v Dartford and Gravesham NHS Trust (Personal Injury Bar Association and another intervening)* [2015] 1 WLR 3647, CA (child anonymity); *PJS v News Group Newspapers Ltd* [2016] 2 FLR 251, SC (adult anonymity at interim hearing stage); *A v (1) SSWP and (2) G* [2017] UKUT 9).

Claims under HRA 1998, s 8(1)—Claims under HRA 1998, s 8(1) are civil proceedings (s 8(2)) and will be issued under CPR 1998 in parallel with, or subsequently to, CA 1989 proceedings (*H (A Minor) v Northamptonshire County Council & Anor* [2017] EWHC 282 (Fam); *SW & TW (Human Rights Claim: Procedure) (No 1)* [2017] EWHC 450 (Fam)). Issue is in the Queen's Bench Division or the County Court under CPR 1998, Pt 8 (but see *Anufrijeva v Southwark LBC* [2004] 1 FLR 8, CA, which suggests application in judicial review). Such proceedings are likely, in the first instance, to be by the Pt 8 procedure. If the claim is not issued until after conclusion of the care or other family proceedings, it must be by freestanding application (*Re L (Care Proceedings: Human Rights Claims)* [2003] 2 FLR 160, FD).

Guidance for issue of a HRA 1998, s 8 claim 'during the currency of public law proceedings'—In *H (A Minor) v Northamptonshire County Council & Anor* [2017] EWHC 282 (Fam) (at [117]), Keehan J provided guidance (with which Cobb J associated himself in *SW & TW (Human Rights Claim: Procedure) (No 1)* (above)) for the issue of proceedings in parallel with CA 1989, Pts 4 and 5 proceedings:

'(a) *alleged breaches of Convention rights by a local authority must be set out with particularity in a letter before action as soon as ever possible'* – in suitable cases, the Judicial Review Pre-action Protocol Letter with CPR 1998 (*www.justice.gov.uk/courts/procedure-rules/civil/protocol/prot_jrv*) suitably adapted provides a template.

'(b) *every effort should be made by the claimant and the local authority to settle the issues of liability and the quantum of damages before and without the need to issue proceedings'* – if these are civil proceedings, the CPR 1998, Pt 36 procedure applies.

'(c) *where liability and quantum are agreed'* – see **Approval of damages in children cases** (below).

'(d) *the local authority should, save in exceptional circumstances, pay the reasonable costs of the claimant's HRA claim/proceedings*' – see also CPR 1998 r, 44.2(2), which applies in civil proceedings.

Approval of damages in children cases—Where damages are agreed, CPR 1998, Pt 8 and r 21.10 require the court to approve the damages award (*H (A Minor) v Northamptonshire County Council & Anor* [2017] EWHC 282 (Fam), at [117](c)) and see *JXMX v Dartford* (above) for application for anonymity).

8.2 Contents of the claim form

Where the claimant uses the Part 8 procedure the claim form must state –

(a) that this Part applies;

(b) (i) the question which the claimant wants the court to decide; or

(ii) the remedy which the claimant is seeking and the legal basis for the claim to that remedy;

(c) if the claim is being made under an enactment, what that enactment is;

(d) if the claimant is claiming in a representative capacity, what that capacity is; and

(e) if the defendant is sued in a representative capacity, what that capacity is.

(Part 22 provides for the claim form to be verified by a statement of truth)

(Rule 7.5 provides for service of the claim form)

Amendments—SI 2000/1317; SI 2009/3390; SI 2013/1974.

Pleading the claim—The claim is in Form N208 (PD8, para 4.2). The essence of Pt 8 is simplicity and r 8.2 sets out what a Pt 8 claim must include.

Written evidence—Evidence on which the claimant intends to rely must be contained in his/her claim form or served with it (r 8.5(1)). The defendant must file his/her written evidence with his acknowledgement of service (rr 8.3 and 8.5(3)). No evidence can be relied upon unless filed in accordance with r 8.5 (r 8.6), save with permission of the court. A party may apply for time to be extended to file and serve evidence (PD8, para 7.4).

Form of evidence—Evidence will be by affidavit or statement; if a claimant relies on his/her claim form it must be verified by a statement of truth (PD8, para 7.2).

Disposal of the claim—The intention of the Pt 8 procedure is that, where possible, claims should be capable of being disposed of on the documents or with the hearing of only minimal oral evidence.

PART III

8.2A Issue of claim form without naming defendants

(1) A practice direction may set out the circumstances in which a claim form may be issued under this Part without naming a defendant.

(2) The practice direction may set out those cases in which an application for permission must be made by application notice before the claim form is issued.

(3) The application notice for permission –

(a) need not be served on any other person; and
(b) must be accompanied by a copy of the claim form that the applicant proposes to issue.

(4) Where the court gives permission it will give directions about the future management of the claim.

Amendments—Inserted by SI 2000/221. Amended by SI 2001/256.

8.3 Acknowledgment of service

(1) The defendant must –

(a) file an acknowledgment of service in the relevant practice form not more than 14 days after service of the claim form; and
(b) serve the acknowledgment of service on the claimant and any other party.

(2) The acknowledgment of service must state –

(a) whether the defendant contests the claim; and
(b) if the defendant seeks a different remedy from that set out in the claim form, what that remedy is.

(3) The following rules of Part 10 (acknowledgment of service) apply –

(a) rule 10.3(2) (exceptions to the period for filing an acknowledgment of service); and
(b) rule 10.5 (contents of acknowledgment of service).

(4) (*revoked*)

Amendments—SI 2000/1317; SI 2001/4015; SI 2009/3390; SI 2013/1974.

8.4 Consequence of not filing an acknowledgment of service

(1) This rule applies where –

(a) the defendant has failed to file an acknowledgment of service; and
(b) the time period for doing so has expired.

(2) The defendant may attend the hearing of the claim but may not take part in the hearing unless the court gives permission.

8.5 Filing and serving written evidence

(1) The claimant must file any written evidence on which he intends to rely when he files his claim form.

(2) The claimant's evidence must be served on the defendant with the claim form.

(3) A defendant who wishes to rely on written evidence must file it when he files his acknowledgment of service.

(4) If he does so, he must also, at the same time, serve a copy of his evidence on the other parties.

(5) The claimant may, within 14 days of service of the defendant's evidence on him, file further written evidence in reply.

(6) If he does so, he must also, within the same time limit, serve a copy of his evidence on the other parties.

(7) The claimant may rely on the matters set out in his claim form as evidence under this rule if the claim form is verified by a statement of truth.

8.6 Evidence – general

(1) No written evidence may be relied on at the hearing of the claim unless –

- (a) it has been served in accordance with rule 8.5; or
- (b) the court gives permission.

(2) The court may require or permit a party to give oral evidence at the hearing.

(3) The court may give directions requiring the attendance for cross-examination[(GL)] of a witness who has given written evidence.

(Rule 32.1 contains a general power for the court to control evidence)

8.7 Part 20 claims

Where the Part 8 procedure is used, Part 20 (counterclaims and other additional claims) applies except that a party may not make a Part 20 claim (as defined by rule 20.2) without the court's permission.

8.8 Procedure where defendant objects to use of the Part 8 procedure

(1) Where the defendant contends that the Part 8 procedure should not be used because –

- (a) there is a substantial dispute of fact; and
- (b) the use of the Part 8 procedure is not required or permitted by a rule or practice direction,

he must state his reasons when he files his acknowledgment of service.

(Rule 8.5 requires a defendant who wishes to rely on written evidence to file it when he files his acknowledgment of service)

(2) When the court receives the acknowledgment of service and any written evidence it will give directions as to the future management of the case.

(Rule 8.1(3) allows the court to make an order that the claim continue as if the claimant had not used the Part 8 procedure)

8.9 Modifications to the general rules

Where the Part 8 procedure is followed –

- (a) provision is made in this Part for the matters which must be stated in the claim form and the defendant is not required to file a defence and therefore –
  - (i) Part 16 (statements of case) does not apply;
  - (ii) Part 15 (defence and reply) does not apply;
  - (iii) any time limit in these Rules which prevents the parties from taking a step before a defence is filed does not apply;
  - (iv) the requirement under rule 7.8 to serve on the defendant a form for defending the claim does not apply;
- (b) the claimant may not obtain judgment by request on an admission and therefore –
  - (i) rules 14.4 to 14.7 do not apply; and
  - (ii) the requirement under rule 7.8 to serve on the defendant a form for admitting the claim does not apply; and
- (c) the claim shall be treated as allocated to the multi-track and therefore Part 26 does not apply.

Practice Direction 8A – Alternative Procedure for Claims

This Practice Direction supplements CPR Part 8 and Schedule 1 & Schedule 2 to the CPR

Amendments—CPR Update 44.

PART III

Terminology

1.1 In this Practice Direction, 'Schedule rules' means provisions contained in the Schedules to the CPR, which were previously contained in the Rules of the Supreme Court (1965) or the County Court Rules (1981).

Application of this Practice Direction

2.1 Section A contains general provisions about claims and applications to which Part 8 applies. Section B comprises a table listing claims, petitions and applications under various enactments which must be made under Part 8. Section C contains certain additions and modifications to the Part 8 procedure that apply to the particular claims and applications identified.

2.2 Some of the claims and applications listed in the table in Section B are dealt with in the Schedule Rules in the CPR. The table in Section B contains cross-reference to the relevant Schedule Rules.

SECTION A: GENERAL PROVISIONS APPLICABLE TO PART 8 CLAIMS

Types of claim in which the Part 8 procedure may be used

3.1 The types of claim for which the Part 8 procedure may be used include –

(1) a claim by or against a child or protected party, as defined in rule 21.1(2), which has been settled before the commencement of proceedings and the sole purpose of the claim is to obtain the approval of the court to the settlement; or

(2) a claim for provisional damages which has been settled before the commencement of proceedings and the sole purpose of the claim is to obtain a consent judgment.

3.2 (1) The Part 8 procedure must be used for those claims, petitions and applications listed in the table in Section B.

(2) Where a claim is listed in the table in Section B and is identified as a claim to which particular provisions of Section C apply, the Part 8 procedure shall apply subject to the additions and modifications set out in the relevant paragraphs in Section C.

3.3 The Part 8 procedure must also be used for any claim or application in relation to which an Act, rule or practice direction provides that the claim or application is brought by originating summons, originating motion or originating application.

3.4 Where it appears to a court officer that a claimant is using the Part 8 procedure inappropriately, he may refer the claim to a judge for the judge to consider the point.

3.5 The court may at any stage order the claim to continue as if the claimant had not used the Part 8 procedure and, if it does so, the court will allocate the claim to a track and give such directions as it considers appropriate.

Amendments—CPR Update 45.

Issuing the claim

4.1 (1) Part 7 and Practice Direction 7A contain a number of rules and directions applicable to all claims, including those to which Part 8 applies. Those rules and directions should be applied where appropriate.

(2) Subject to the provisions in rule 8.1(2A), in the County Court a claim under the Part 8 procedure may be made in any County Court hearing centre. However, when a claim is given a hearing date the court may direct that proceedings should be transferred to another hearing centre if appropriate to do so. A claimant should consider the potential delay which may result if a claim is not made at the appropriate hearing centre in the first instance.

4.2 Where a claimant uses the Part 8 procedure, the claim form (practice form N208) should be used and must state the matters set out in rule 8.2 and, if rule 8.1(6) applies, must comply with the requirements of the rule or practice direction in question. In particular, the claim form must state that Part 8 applies; a Part 8 claim form means a claim form which so states.

Amendments—CPR Updates 51, 66, 69.

Responding to the claim

5.1 The provisions of Part 15 (defence and reply) do not apply where the claim form is a Part 8 claim form.

5.2 Where a defendant who wishes to respond to a Part 8 claim form is required to file an acknowledgment of service, that acknowledgment of service should be in practice form N210.

5.3 Where a defendant objects to the use of the Part 8 procedure, and his statement of reasons includes matters of evidence, the acknowledgment of service must be verified by a statement of truth.

Managing the claim

6.1 The court may give directions immediately a Part 8 claim form is issued either on the application of a party or on its own initiative. The directions may include fixing a hearing date where –

(1) there is no dispute, such as in child and protected party settlements; or
(2) where there may be a dispute, but a hearing date could conveniently be given.

6.2 Where the court does not fix a hearing date when the claim form is issued, it will give directions for the disposal of the claim as soon as practicable after the defendant has acknowledged service of the claim form or, as the case may be, after the period for acknowledging service has expired.

6.3 Certain applications may not require a hearing.

6.4 The court may convene a directions hearing before giving directions.

Amendments—CPR Updates 45.

Evidence

7.1 A claimant must file the written evidence on which he relies when his Part 8 claim form is issued (unless the evidence is contained in the claim form itself).

7.2 Evidence will normally be in the form of a witness statement or an affidavit but a claimant may rely on the matters set out in his claim form provided that it has been verified by a statement of truth.

(For information about (1) statements of truth see Part 22 and Practice Direction 22, and (2) written evidence see Part 32 and Practice Direction 32.)

7.3 A defendant wishing to rely on written evidence, must file it with his acknowledgment of service.

7.4 A party may apply to the court for an extension of time to serve and file evidence under rule 8.5 or for permission to serve and file additional evidence under rule 8.6(1).

(For information about applications see Part 23 and Practice Direction 23A.)

7.5 (1) The parties may, subject to the following provisions, agree in writing on an extension of time for serving and filing evidence under rule 8.5(3) or rule 8.5(5).

(2) An agreement extending time for a defendant to file evidence under rule 8.5(3) –

(a) must be filed by the defendant at the same time as he files his acknowledgement of service; and

(b) must not extend time by more than 14 days after the defendant files his acknowledgement of service.

(3) An agreement extending time for a claimant to file evidence in reply under rule 8.5(5) must not extend time to more than 28 days after service of the defendant's evidence on the claimant.

Amendments—CPR Update 51.

Hearing

8.1 The court may on the hearing date –

(1) proceed to hear the case and dispose of the claim;
(2) give case management directions.

8.2 Case management directions may include the specific allocation of a case to a track.

8.3 CPR rules 26.5(3) and (4) and rules 26.6 to 26.10 apply to the allocation of a claim under paragraph 8.2.

Amendments—CPR Update 66.

****

PART 18
FURTHER INFORMATION

CONTENTS OF THIS PART

Rule		Page
18.1	Obtaining further information	2054
18.2	Restriction on the use of further information	2054
	Practice Direction 18 – Further Information	2055

18.1 Obtaining further information

(1) The court may at any time order a party to –

(a) clarify any matter which is in dispute in the proceedings; or
(b) give additional information in relation to any such matter,

whether or not the matter is contained or referred to in a statement of case.

(2) Paragraph (1) is subject to any rule of law to the contrary.

(3) Where the court makes an order under paragraph (1), the party against whom it is made must –

(a) file his response; and
(b) serve it on the other parties,

within the time specified by the court.

(Part 22 requires a response to be verified by a statement of truth)

(Part 53 (defamation) restricts requirements for providing further information about sources of information in defamation claims)

Amendments—SI 2000/221.

18.2 Restriction on the use of further information

The court may direct that information provided by a party to another party (whether given voluntarily or following an order made under rule 18.1) must not be used for any purpose except for that of the proceedings in which it is given.

(RSC Order 82, in Schedule 1, provides for circumstances in which further information is not allowed in defamation claims)

Practice Direction 18 – Further Information

This Practice Direction supplements CPR Part 18

Attention is also drawn to Part 22 (Statements of Truth).

Preliminary request for further information or clarification

1.1 Before making an application to the court for an order under Part 18, the party seeking clarification or information (the first party) should first serve on the party from whom it is sought (the second party) a written request for that clarification or information (a Request) stating a date by which the response to the Request should be served. The date must allow the second party a reasonable time to respond.

1.2 A Request should be concise and strictly confined to matters which are reasonably necessary and proportionate to enable the first party to prepare his own case or to understand the case he has to meet.

1.3 Requests must be made as far as possible in a single comprehensive document and not piecemeal.

1.4 A Request may be made by letter if the text of the request is brief and the reply is likely to be brief; otherwise the Request should be made in a separate document.

1.5 If a Request is made in a letter, the letter should, in order to distinguish it from any other that might routinely be written in the course of a case,

(1) state that it contains a Request made under Part 18, and

(2) deal with no matters other than the Request.

1.6 (1) A Request (whether made by letter or in a separate document) must –

(a) be headed with the name of the court and the title and number of the claim,

(b) in its heading state that it is a Request made under Part 18, identify the first party and the second party and state the date on which it is made,

(c) set out in a separate numbered paragraph each request for information or clarification,

(d) where a Request relates to a document, identify that document and (if relevant) the paragraph or words to which it relates,

(e) state the date by which the first party expects a response to the Request,

(2) (a) A Request which is not in the form of a letter may, if convenient, be prepared in such a way that the response may be given on the same document.

(b) To do this the numbered paragraphs of the Request should appear on the left hand half of each sheet so that the paragraphs of the response may then appear on the right.

(c) Where a Request is prepared in this form an extra copy should be served for the use of the second party.

1.7 Subject to the provisions of rule 6.23(5) and (6) and paragraphs 4.1 to 4.3 of Practice Direction 6A, a request should be served by email if reasonably practicable.

Amendments—CPR Updates 35, 47, 51.

Responding to a request

2.1 A response to a Request must be in writing, dated and signed by the second party or his legal representative.

2.2 (1) Where the Request is made in a letter the second party may give his response in a letter or in a formal reply.

(2) Such a letter should identify itself as a response to the Request and deal with no other matters than the response.

PART III

2.3 (1) Unless the Request is in the format described in paragraph 1.6(2) and the second party uses the document supplied for the purpose, a response must:
(a) be headed with the name of the court and the title and number of the claim,
(b) in its heading identify itself as a response to that Request,
(c) repeat the text of each separate paragraph of the Request and set out under each paragraph the response to it,
(d) refer to and have attached to it a copy of any document not already in the possession of the first party which forms part of the response.

(2) A second or supplementary response to a Request must identify itself as such in its heading.

2.4 The second party must when he serves his response on the first party serve on every other party and file with the court a copy of the Request and of his response.

Statements of truth

3 Attention is drawn to Part 22 and to the definition of a statement of case in Part 2 of the rules; a response should be verified by a statement of truth.

General matters

4.1 (1) If the second party objects to complying with the Request or part of it or is unable to do so at all or within the time stated in the Request he must inform the first party promptly and in any event within that time.

(2) He may do so in a letter or in a separate document (a formal response), but in either case he must give reasons and, where relevant, give a date by which he expects to be able to comply.

4.2 (1) There is no need for a second party to apply to the court if he objects to a Request or is unable to comply with it at all or within the stated time. He need only comply with paragraph 4.1(1) above.

(2) Where a second party considers that a Request can only be complied with at disproportionate expense and objects to comply for that reason he should say so in his reply and explain briefly why he has taken that view.

Applications for orders under Part 18

5.1 Attention is drawn to Part 23 (Applications) and to Practice Direction 23A.

5.2 An application notice for an order under Part 18 should set out or have attached to it the text of the order sought and in particular should specify the matter or matters in respect of which the clarification or information is sought.

5.3 (1) If a Request under paragraph 1 for the information or clarification has not been made, the application notice should, in addition, explain why not.

(2) If a Request for clarification or information has been made, the application notice or the evidence in support should describe the response, if any.

5.4 Both the first party and the second party should consider whether evidence in support of or in opposition to the application is required.

5.5 (1) Where the second party has made no response to a Request served on him, the first party need not serve the application notice on the second party, and the court may deal with the application without a hearing.

(2) Subparagraph (1) above only applies if at least 14 days have passed since the Request was served and the time stated in it for a response has expired.

5.6 Unless paragraph 5.5 applies the application notice must be served on the second party and on all other parties to the claim.

5.7 An order made under Part 18 must be served on all parties to the claim.

5.8 Costs:

(1) Attention is drawn to Practice Directions 44 to 48 on costs and, in particular, Subsections 8 and 9 of Practice Direction 44, which relate to the court's power to make a summary assessment of costs.

(2) Attention is also drawn to rule 44.10(1) which provides that if an order does not mention costs no party is entitled to costs relating to that order.

Amendments—CPR Updates 22, 26, 66.

PART 19
PARTIES AND GROUP LITIGATION

CONTENTS OF THIS PART

Rule		Page
19.4A	Human Rights	2057
19.7	Representation of interested persons who cannot be ascertained etc	2058
19.7A	Representation of beneficiaries by trustees etc	2059
19.7B	Postal Services Act 2000	2059

PD—See *PD (Addition and Substitution of Parties)* and *PD (Group Litigation)*, which supplement this Part generally; both are set out in Section 2 of the *Civil Court Service* (LexisNexis).

★★★★

19.4A Human Rights

Section 4 of the Human Rights Act 1998

(1) The court may not make a declaration of incompatibility in accordance with section 4 of the Human Rights Act 1998 unless 21 days' notice, or such other period of notice as the court directs, has been given to the Crown.

(2) Where notice has been given to the Crown a Minister, or other person permitted by that Act, shall be joined as a party on giving notice to the court.

(Only courts specified in section 4 of the Human Rights Act 1998 can make a declaration of incompatibility)

Section 9 of the Human Rights Act 1998

(3) Where a claim is made under that Act for damages in respect of a judicial act –

(a) that claim must be set out in the statement of case or the appeal notice; and

(b) notice must be given to the Crown.

(4) Where paragraph (3) applies and the appropriate person has not applied to be joined as a party within 21 days, or such other period as the court directs, after the notice is served, the court may join the appropriate person as a party.

(Practice Direction 19A makes provision for these notices)

Amendments—Inserted by SI 2000/2092; SI 2009/3390.

Scope—In any proceedings where a human rights point is raised and there is either an issue as to whether a declaration of incompatibility of domestic legislation to ECHR 1950 should be made (as detailed in HRA 1998, s 1) or there has been a potential breach of a provision of ECHR 1950 by virtue of a judicial act, it is necessary to give notice to the Crown with a view to joinder (see also CPR 1998, r 7.11 and FPR 2010, rr 29.5(3)–(5)). The notice given under r 19.4A must be served on the person named in the list published under Crown Proceedings Act 1947, s 17. The list is annexed to CPR PD66 (see PD19, para 6.4(1)).

Declarations of incompatibility—The Home Secretary's scheme to control the right of any person subject to immigration control to marry in the UK was declared unlawful as being inconsistent with ECHR 1950, Art 12 (*R (Baiai) v Secretary of State for the Home Department* [2008] 2 FLR 1462, HL). However, a school's decision to refuse to permit a pupil to wear a 'purity' ring as an expression of her Christian faith and as a sign of her belief of celibacy before marriage did not breach ECHR 1950, Art 9 (*R (Lydia Playfoot) v Millais School Governing Body* [2007] ELR 484, QBD). Further, although a school's decision to refuse to allow a pupil to wear a niqab veil at school engaged her ECHR 1950, Art 9 rights, it did not infringe that right and, even if it had, the decision was objectively justifiable under Art 9(2) (*R (X) v Governors of Y School* [2007] ELR 278, QBD). HFEA 2008, s 54 is incompatible with ECHR, Art 14 on the basis that it discriminates against a single applicant: *Re Z (A Child) (No 2)* [2016] 2 FLR 327, FD.

Injunctions—The court has jurisdiction in appropriate cases to grant an injunction restraining a local authority from, for example, seeking to remove a child from a placement pending a full hearing by the court (*Coventry CC v O (Adoption)* [2011] 2 FLR 936, CA) or to prevent the separation of a mother and child pending a full hearing (*Re H (Care Plan: Human Rights)* [2012] 1 FLR 191, CA).

****

19.7 Representation of interested persons who cannot be ascertained etc

(1) This rule applies to claims about –

- (a) the estate of a deceased person;
- (b) property subject to a trust; or
- (c) the meaning of a document, including a statute.

(2) The court may make an order appointing a person to represent any other person or persons in the claim where the person or persons to be represented –

- (a) are unborn;
- (b) cannot be found;
- (c) cannot easily be ascertained; or
- (d) are a class of persons who have the same interest in a claim and –
  - (i) one or more members of that class are within sub-paragraphs (a), (b) or (c); or
  - (ii) to appoint a representative would further the overriding objective.

(3) An application for an order under paragraph (2) –

- (a) may be made by –
  - (i) any person who seeks to be appointed under the order; or
  - (ii) any party to the claim; and
- (b) may be made at any time before or after the claim has started.

(4) An application notice for an order under paragraph (2) must be served on –

- (a) all parties to the claim, if the claim has started;
- (b) the person sought to be appointed, if that person is not the applicant or a party to the claim; and
- (c) any other person as directed by the court.

(5) The court's approval is required to settle a claim in which a party is acting as a representative under this rule.

(6) The court may approve a settlement where it is satisfied that the settlement is for the benefit of all the represented persons.

(7) Unless the court otherwise directs, any judgment or order given in a claim in which a party is acting as a representative under this rule –

- (a) is binding on all persons represented in the claim; but
- (b) may only be enforced by or against a person who is not a party to the claim with the permission of the court.

Amendments—Inserted by SI 2000/221.

Procedure for making an application—See CPR 1998, Pt 23. The application may be heard in chambers or in open court. The court may direct that it take place by telephone conference. In appropriate cases or where there is agreement the application may be handled without a hearing. The court may also use the hearing to case-manage the proceedings and give directions. A draft of the order sought should be provided to the court. The application notice and any order made must be served unless the court otherwise directs. If the application is made without notice the order should provide for the respondent to the application to apply to have the order set aside or varied within 7 days after the order is served. The court will generally serve such an application but it would be prudent to check with the court that it will effect service. Although the issue of whether to make a representative order is discretionary, the court should have regard to the overriding objective.

19.7A Representation of beneficiaries by trustees etc

(1) A claim may be brought by or against trustees, executors or administrators in that capacity without adding as parties any persons who have a beneficial interest in the trust or estate ('the beneficiaries').

(2) Any judgment or order given or made in the claim is binding on the beneficiaries unless the court orders otherwise in the same or other proceedings.

Amendments—Inserted by SI 2002/2058.

19.7B Postal Services Act 2000

(1) An application under section 92 of the Postal Services Act 2000 for permission to bring proceedings in the name of the sender or addressee of a postal packet or his personal representative is made in accordance with Part 8.

(2) A copy of the application notice must be served on the universal service provider and on the person in whose name the applicant seeks to bring the proceedings.

Amendments—Inserted by SI 2005/2092.

****

PART 21
CHILDREN AND PROTECTED PARTIES

CONTENTS OF THIS PART

Rule		Page
21.1	Scope of this Part	2059
21.2	Requirement for litigation friend in proceedings by or against children and protected parties	2060
21.3	Stage of proceedings at which a litigation friend becomes necessary	2061
21.4	Who may be a litigation friend without a court order	2062
21.5	How a person becomes a litigation friend without a court order	2063
21.6	How a person becomes a litigation friend by court order	2064
21.7	Court's power to change litigation friend and to prevent person acting as litigation friend	2065
21.8	Appointment of litigation friend by court order – supplementary	2065
21.9	Procedure where appointment of litigation friend ceases	2066
21.10	Compromise etc by or on behalf of child or protected party	2067
21.11	Control of money recovered by or on behalf of child or protected party	2068
21.12	Expenses incurred by a litigation friend	2069
21.13	Appointment of guardian of child's estate	2070
	Practice Direction 21 – Children and Protected Parties	2070

Amendments—Part substituted by SI 2007/2204.

Procedural Guide—See Procedural Guide F1(2).

21.1 Scope of this Part

(1) This Part –

- (a) contains special provisions which apply in proceedings involving children and protected parties; and
- (b) sets out how a person becomes a litigation friend; and
- (c) does not apply to –
  - (i) proceedings under Part 75;
  - (ii) enforcement of specified debts by taking control of goods; or
  - (iii) applications in relation to enforcement of specified debts by taking control of goods,

where one of the parties to the proceedings is a child.

(2) In this Part –

(a) 'the 2005 Act' means the Mental Capacity Act 2005;
(b) 'child' means a person under 18;
(c) 'lacks capacity' means lacks capacity within the meaning of the 2005 Act;
(d) 'protected party' means a party, or an intended party, who lacks capacity to conduct the proceedings;
(e) 'protected beneficiary' means a protected party who lacks capacity to manage and control any money recovered by him or on his behalf or for his benefit in the proceedings;
(f) 'specified debts' has the same meaning as in rule 75.1(2)(e); and
(g) 'taking control of goods' means using the procedure to take control of goods contained in Schedule 12 to the Tribunals, Courts and Enforcement Act 2007.

(Rules 6.13 and 6.25 contain provisions about the service of documents on children and protected parties.)

(Rule 46.4 deals with costs where money is payable by or to a child or protected party.)

Amendments—SI 2003/3361; SI 2007/2204; SI 2008/2178; SI 2013/1974; SI 2014/407.

Scope—This Part, which has no application to family proceedings, makes special provision in civil proceedings for those litigants who were previously described as being 'persons under disability'. There are two distinct categories: 'child' and 'protected party' (formerly 'patient') as defined. FPR 2010 will apply instead to family proceedings but there are situations in the family context in which reliance may have to be placed on the CPR (e g an application under the PHA 1997). A representative known as a 'litigation friend' must generally be appointed to conduct the proceedings in the name and on behalf of a child or protected party, and any settlement or compromise must be approved by the court.

'protected party' (r 21.1(2)(d))—Lack of capacity is also defined (see below).

'protected beneficiary' (r 21.1(2)(e))—This definition is necessary because of the decision-specific nature of tests of capacity. A party may lack capacity to conduct the proceedings but nevertheless have the capacity to manage and control his or her money. However, this definition is insufficient for two reasons. First, there is an assumption that only a person who is a protected party may be incapable of financial management. The rule fails to make allowance for the converse, namely that a litigant who has capacity to conduct court proceedings may not have capacity to manage his or her financial affairs. This situation might arise, for example, where a wealthy man with complex financial affairs wished to bring a small claim. Secondly, if the approach of the civil court is to be compatible with that of the Court of Protection it becomes necessary to aggregate the damages recovered with the existing wealth of the protected party and then to decide whether there is capacity to manage the entirety. The Civil Procedure Rules Committee has only looked at this from the perspective of a brain-injured litigant who recovers a substantial sum and did not previously have any personal savings or income of significance.

'child' or 'protected party' (r 21.1(2))—It is possible for a child also to be a protected party and this may be relevant if that condition will continue to subsist on ceasing to be a child (e g in regard to the disposal of money awarded to the child). Thus a child who has severe learning disabilities will continue to be a protected party even after attaining the age of 18.

'litigation friend' (r 21.1(1)(b))—This expression replaces both next friend and guardian ad litem used in previous rules.

Mental Capacity Act 2005—This legislation established from 1 October 2007 a comprehensive new mental capacity jurisdiction. The general principles are to be found in MCA 2005, ss 1-4. They include a new test of 'incapacity' and a 'best interests' approach to any delegated decision-making according to a check list of factors, thus incorporated into CPR 1998, Pt 21. (For an overview of the Act see Part II).

'lacks capacity'—This term is expressly defined as being 'within the meaning of MCA 2005' and therefore the test (and the principles) set out in MCA 2005, Pt 1 apply. Section 2(1) sets out the definition:

> 'a person lacks capacity in relation to a matter if at the material time he is unable to make a decision for himself in relation to the matter because of an impairment of, or a disturbance in the functioning of, the mind or brain.'

A more comprehensive explanation is provided in the annotations to FPR 2010, Pt 15. For an early decision on the test of capacity under the MCA 2005 jurisdiction in regard to a brain injured claimant, see *Saulle v Nouvet* [2007] EWHC 2902 (QB).

21.2 Requirement for litigation friend in proceedings by or against children and protected parties

(1) A protected party must have a litigation friend to conduct proceedings on his behalf.

(2) A child must have a litigation friend to conduct proceedings on his behalf unless the court makes an order under paragraph (3).

(3) The court may make an order permitting a child to conduct proceedings without a litigation friend.

(4) An application for an order under paragraph (3) –

- (a) may be made by the child;
- (b) if the child already has a litigation friend, must be made on notice to the litigation friend; and
- (c) if the child has no litigation friend, may be made without notice.

(5) Where –

- (a) the court has made an order under paragraph (3); and
- (b) it subsequently appears to the court that it is desirable for a litigation friend to conduct the proceedings on behalf of the child,

the court may appoint a person to be the child's litigation friend.

Amendments—SI 2007/2204.

Scope—The general rule is that a child or protected party may only conduct proceedings, whether as claimant or defendant, by a litigation friend. The rule only refers to 'a litigation friend' so this party may not have more than one in any particular proceedings. There is nothing to prevent that party having a different litigation friend in other proceedings of a different nature, except when a deputy (formerly a receiver) has been appointed in which event this person should generally be the only litigation friend for the protected party unless the Court of Protection otherwise orders.

Verification that a party is a child or protected party—Paragraph 2.2 of PD21 requires the litigation friend to state in the 'certificate of suitability' that he consents to act and knows or believes the party to be a child or protected party. The grounds for this belief must be stated and if based upon medical opinion, this document must be attached. It is unlikely to be difficult to ascertain the age of a party, but there may be doubt as to whether a party is a protected party and in that event a preliminary issue as to capacity should be tried with notice being given to that party who may wish to make representations.

Even where the issue does not seem to be contentious, a district judge who is responsible for case management will generally require the assistance of a medical report before being able to be satisfied that incapacity exists. An admission by a person alleged to lack capacity will carry little weight. It may assist for the judge to see the person alleged to lack capacity (*Masterman-Lister v Brutton & Co and Jewell & Home Counties Dairies* [2003] 1 WLR 1511, CA).

Notification to the child or protected party—Neither CPR 1998 nor PDs actually provide that a child or protected party must be given notice of the proceedings, unless (in the case of a protected party) the court is involved in the appointment of the litigation friend, so it is possible for proceedings in the name of a child or protected party to be commenced or defended without the personal knowledge of that party. Reliance is placed on the certificate of suitability (see above) and upon service on the parent or guardian of the child, or the person with whom the protected party resides or in whose care he is (see also PD21, para 2.4). It cannot be assumed that this person will inform the protected party in every situation where this would be prudent.

Child as a party (r 21.2(3))—An all or nothing approach to age is no longer adopted (*Gillick v West Norfolk & Wisbech Area Health Authority* [1986] 1 FLR 224, HL). The court may authorise a child to conduct proceedings, but will only do so when satisfied that the child has the required capacity (ie, is of sufficient maturity and understanding). It is both prudent and good practice for the litigation friend to consult the child once able to make a meaningful contribution and particularly as the child approaches 18, since on attaining that age the appointment of the litigation friend ceases and the child (now an adult) may take over conduct of the proceedings (r 21.9(1)).

Statement of truth—Pt 22 makes provision for certain documents to be verified by a 'statement of truth'. If a party is a child or a protected party it will be the litigation friend (or legal representative on his behalf) who makes and signs this statement (see r 22.1(5),(6)).

Need for a solicitor—There is no requirement in CPR 1998 for a solicitor to act on behalf of a child or protected party whose proceedings are being conducted by a litigation friend. Nevertheless, in a complex or high-value case the court may consider that the litigation friend who acts without a solicitor is not 'suitable' within r 21.4(3) and appoint someone else under r 21.7(1)(c).

21.3 Stage of proceedings at which a litigation friend becomes necessary

(1) This rule does not apply where the court has made an order under rule 21.2(3).

(2) A person may not, without the permission of the court –

- (a) make an application against a child or protected party before proceedings have started; or
- (b) take any step in proceedings except –
  - (i) issuing and serving a claim form; or
  - (ii) applying for the appointment of a litigation friend under rule 21.6,

until the child or protected party has a litigation friend.

(3) If during proceedings a party lacks capacity to continue to conduct proceedings, no party may take any further step in the proceedings without the permission of the court until the protected party has a litigation friend.

(4) Any step taken before a child or protected party has a litigation friend, shall be of no effect unless the court orders otherwise.

Amendments—SI 2007/2204.

Scope—The general principle is that a litigation friend must be appointed before any step is taken in proceedings involving a child or protected party (unless the child has been permitted to conduct those proceedings under r 21.2(3)).

Exceptions—The court has a discretion to permit specified steps to be taken before a litigation friend is appointed ('without the permission of the court' r 21.3(2),(3)) or retrospectively to approve any steps that have been taken without such appointment ('unless the court otherwise orders' (r 21.3(4)). This alleviates the problem under former rules that, where the disability was not identified by the parties or their solicitors or arose during the proceedings without their knowledge, steps taken had no effect and liabilities could arise in respect of abortive costs.

Implications—It is possible to make urgent orders in proceedings involving a child or protected party before the appointment of a litigation friend, but the court should be made fully aware of all relevant circumstances. Where it is realised during the course of proceedings that a party is (and has been) a child or a protected party, then, provided everyone has acted in good faith and there has been no manifest disadvantage to the party subsequently found to have been a protected party, it is likely that the court will regularise the position retrospectively (*Masterman-Lister*, above). This might be the case where the proceedings have effectively been guided throughout by the person being appointed as litigation friend. Proceedings inappropriately conducted by the child or protected party or an unsuitable person on his behalf will be treated as being of no effect and further proceedings may then be commenced in proper form (the Limitation Acts are unlikely to apply). A compromise of the claim of a person who is declared subsequently not to have had capacity at the time of the agreement will be invalidated even where the person's lack of capacity was unknown to anyone acting for either party at that time (*Dunhill (A Protected Party By Her Litigation Friend Tasker) v Burgin (Nos 1 and 2)* [2014] COPLR 199, SC). Although the court has the power to validate retrospectively any step under r 21.3(4), the Supreme Court decided that this must depend upon the particular facts and declined to validate the settlement finally disposing of the claim.

Cessation of appointment of litigation friend upon death of protected party—A litigation friend has no standing to act on behalf of a protected party who has died. Any step taken on behalf of the deceased person is a nullity in the absence of an order pursuant to CPR 1998, r 19.8(1). Furthermore, the grant of letters of administration does not retrospectively validate any step taken between death and the grant (*Hussain & Qutb v Bank of Scotland* [2012] EWCA Civ 264; *Millburn-Snell v Evans* [2012] 1 WLR 41, CA).

21.4 Who may be a litigation friend without a court order

(1) This rule does not apply if the court has appointed a person to be a litigation friend.

(2) A deputy appointed by the Court of Protection under the 2005 Act with power to conduct proceedings on the protected party's behalf, is entitled to be the litigation friend of the protected party in any proceedings to which his power extends.

(3) If nobody has been appointed by the court or, in the case of a protected party, has been appointed as a deputy as set out in paragraph (2), a person may act as a litigation friend if he –

(a) can fairly and competently conduct proceedings on behalf of the child or protected party;

(b) has no interest adverse to that of the child or protected party; and

(c) where the child or protected party is a claimant, undertakes to pay any costs which the child or patient may be ordered to pay in relation to the proceedings, subject to any right he may have to be repaid from the assets of the child or protected party.

Amendments—SI 2007/2204.

Scope—This rule identifies who may act as a litigation friend without an order appointing him.

Authorised person—Any person authorised under MCA 2005 (ie, as a deputy appointed by the Court of Protection) to conduct legal proceedings in the name or on behalf of a protected party is entitled to become the litigation friend in accordance with such authority. An office copy of the order or other authorisation sealed with the official seal of the Court of Protection should be filed. Care should be taken to examine this document because simply being appointed a deputy does not by itself give authority to conduct proceedings. It is not clear if the court has power to appoint someone else (as under the former rules), but this situation is unlikely to arise and conflict between the court dealing with the litigation and the Court of Protection should be avoided.

Attorneys—An attorney under a registered enduring power of attorney (EPA), or donee under a lasting power of attorney for financial affairs (LPA), is not specifically mentioned but would be an obvious person to act as litigation friend because he will control the financial affairs of the protected party (see MCA 2005) and there will, in consequence, be no need for a deputy. An ordinary power of attorney is of no significance because it ceases to have effect upon the incapacity of the donor, but of course the person acting may otherwise be suitable as litigation friend. If an EPA is registered this would normally indicate that the donor is a protected party, but that is not the case for an LPA because registration may take place at an earlier stage.

The court controls its own procedures and principles of agency do not apply. So a power of attorney cannot confer a right to conduct litigation or of audience (*Gregory v Turner; R (Morris) v North Somerset Council* [2003] 1 WLR 1149, CA). A litigation friend does not have to act by a solicitor and can conduct the litigation on behalf of the protected party: *Gregory v Turner*, at [63]. A litigation friend who does not otherwise have a right of audience requires the permission of the court to act as an advocate on behalf of the protected party: *Gregory v Turner*, at [64].

Suitability—There can be no doubt as to the suitability of a person authorised by the Court of Protection (if doubt arises the matter should be referred back to that Court). The rule helpfully sets out the criteria whereby other persons may be regarded as suitable to act as litigation friend (r 21.4(3)), but the court may not waive any of these criteria which the proposed person is unable to satisfy (*R (Hussain) v Birmingham City Council* [2002] EWHC 949 (Admin)). These criteria feature throughout Pt 21, as amplified by PD21, para 2.1, and the court must be satisfied that they are complied with before appointing a litigation friend. They may be relied upon where there is a dispute as to who should be appointed. Apart from this there is no restriction on who may be a litigation friend, save that the person appointed must not be a child or a protected party and (in practice) should normally be within the jurisdiction. The litigation friend should not have any personal involvement in the proceedings, but see *Spurling v Broadhurst* [2012] EWHC 2883 (Ch). If the court becomes aware of the person's unsuitability, it may remove him under r 21.7 and substitute another person as litigation friend, but there is no express duty to monitor the situation. For useful guidance on the interpretation of r 21.4(3)(b), see *Davila v Davila and another* [2016] EWHC B14 (Ch), at [137].

Undertaking as to costs (r 21.4(3)(c))—This undertaking is required from the litigation friend of a claimant (unless appointed by the Court of Protection) but not a defendant (see PD21, para 2.2(e) and 2.3(4)). It is contained in Form N235 *Certificate of Suitability of Litigation Friend*. A mother's undertaking to meet any liability in costs 'if her financial circumstances were to change, enabling her to afford them' did not satisfy the requirement of r 21.4(3)(c) and she was, accordingly, ineligible for appointment as a litigation friend (*R (Hussain) v Birmingham City Council* (above)).

The requirement imposes a severe limitation upon the ability of a child or protected party to bring a claim. Query whether it amounts to discrimination against a person with a mental disability contrary to the Equality Act 2010 or will otherwise be in breach of HRA 1998. The Court of Protection Rules 2007 do not require this undertaking. The litigation friend is, in effect, expected to provide an indemnity so may wish to be protected by a Public Funding certificate or otherwise in control of adequate funds held by the child or protected party. One way of circumventing the undertaking in the case of a protected party is to obtain the authority of the Court of Protection to bring the proceedings. The court has a general discretion as to costs and will take into account the role of the litigation friend but may have power to impose a personal costs liability in case of misconduct quite apart from the undertaking.

21.5 How a person becomes a litigation friend without a court order

(1) If the court has not appointed a litigation friend, a person who wishes to act as a litigation friend must follow the procedure set out in this rule.

(2) A deputy appointed by the Court of Protection under the 2005 Act with power to conduct proceedings on the protected party's behalf must file an official copy(GL) of the order of the Court of Protection which confers his power to act either –

(a) where the deputy is to act as a litigation friend for a claimant, at the time the claim is made; or

(b) where the deputy is to act as a litigation friend for a defendant, at the time when he first takes a step in the proceedings on behalf of the defendant.

(3) Any other person must file a certificate of suitability stating that he satisfies the conditions specified in rule 21.4(3) either –

(a) where the person is to act as a litigation friend for a claimant, at the time when the claim is made; or

(b) where the person is to act as a litigation friend for a defendant, at the time when he first takes a step in the proceedings on behalf of the defendant.

(4) The litigation friend must –

(a) serve the certificate of suitability on every person on whom, in accordance with rule 6.13 (service on parent, guardian etc), the claim form should be served; and

(b) file a certificate of service when filing the certificate of suitability.

(Rules 6.17 and 6.29 set out the details to be contained in a certificate of service.)

Amendments—SI 2007/2204; SI 2008/2178.

Scope—This rule sets out the procedural steps for the appointment of a litigation friend otherwise than by a court order. It will be relied upon in most cases.

No need for court appointment of litigation friend—A litigation friend may be appointed simply by filing the relevant documents. The certificate is a pre-requisite for appointment without a court order, but will not be conclusive in the event of a dispute as to suitability. It is strange that there is no requirement for the child or protected party to be personally notified that proceedings are being brought or defended in his name because he may wish to make representations as to who the litigation friend should be or dispute that he is a protected party (see generally the provisions as to service in CPR 1998, Pt 6). It is good practice for anyone intending to become a litigation friend to serve upon or draw to the attention of the intended protected party the notice of his intention to act as litigation friend and certificate of suitability, unless there is no prospect of a relevant response and the court may require confirmation of this. The Court of Appeal has recommended a change in the rules so that a person cannot become a protected party without knowing what is going on (see *Masterman-Lister*, above).

'certificate of suitability' (r 21.5(3))—This document confirms that the person to be appointed meets the criteria whereby a person may be regarded as suitable for appointment as litigation friend (r 21.4(3)). As to suitability see note to r 21.4. The certificate is not required where the person is a deputy authorised by the Court of Protection to conduct the proceedings (see note to r 21.4).

Form N235 also confirms the maker's consent to act and belief that the party is a protected party (with reasons/medical evidence). There is no specific requirement in the Rules for evidence to be provided notwithstanding that it is fundamental to the appointment.

Deputy appointed by the Court of Protection—An official copy of the order of the Court of Protection, which confers his power to act, must be filed. The rules do not contemplate the Court of Protection authorising a person to conduct proceedings without appointing him to be a deputy, but this could happen. Presumably the court would ensure that this person was appointed and exclude any competing application.

'certificate of service' (r 21.5(6)(b))—Rule 6.13 clarifies the persons on whom the certificate of suitability (when required) must be served in accordance with this rule. The alleged protected party is not included (but see note **No need for court appointment of litigation friend** above).

Forms—Form N235 (Certificate of Suitability of Litigation Friend).

21.6 How a person becomes a litigation friend by court order

(1) The court may make an order appointing a litigation friend.

(2) An application for an order appointing a litigation friend may be made by –

(a) a person who wishes to be the litigation friend; or
(b) a party.

(3) Where –

(a) a person makes a claim against a child or protected party;
(b) the child or protected party has no litigation friend;
(c) the court has not made an order under rule 21.2(3) (order that a child can conduct proceedings without a litigation friend); and
(d) either –
 (i) someone who is not entitled to be a litigation friend files a defence; or
 (ii) the claimant wishes to take some step in the proceedings,

the claimant must apply to the court for an order appointing a litigation friend for the child or protected party.

(4) An application for an order appointing a litigation friend must be supported by evidence.

(5) The court may not appoint a litigation friend under this rule unless it is satisfied that the person to be appointed satisfies the conditions specified in rule 21.4(3).

Amendments—SI 2007/2204.

Scope—This rule sets out the procedural steps for the appointment of a litigation friend by a court order, that is, where it has not been possible to appoint a litigation friend under r 21.5. The court must be satisfied that the person to be appointed is suitable for appointment in accordance with the criteria set out in r 21.4(3). Although the rules do not so provide, the application should be served upon or at least brought to the notice of the party unless there is no prospect of a relevant response (see note **No need for court appointment of litigation friend** under r 21.5).

Official Solicitor—Where the circumstances justify the involvement of the Official Solicitor, a completed questionnaire and a copy of the court file with any order provisionally appointing him should be sent to his office. He will usually consent to act and the case may be allocated within 28 days from invitation, subject to:

(a) satisfactory evidence in the form of an expert's opinion accepted by the party that he or she lacks capacity to conduct the proceedings, OR a finding by the court that the party is a protected party;
(b) confirmation that the Official Solicitor is litigation friend of last resort; and
(c) confirmation that there is security for the costs of legal representation.

Any order making such appointment should be expressed as being subject to the Official Solicitor's consent. Save in the most urgent of cases, it is unlikely that the Official Solicitor will be able to complete his enquiries in less than 3 months. Accordingly, a lengthy adjournment of the proceedings may be necessary and a substantive hearing should not be fixed within such period of his initial appointment without consulting him.

The Official Solicitor to the Senior Courts may be contacted at Victory House, 30–34 Kingsway, London WC2B 6EX, DX 141423 Bloomsbury 7; tel 020 3681 2751 (healthcare and welfare) or 020 3681 2758 (property and affairs); fax 020 3681 2762.

Service—See r 21.8(1) and (2) for the special rules that apply to an application for appointment by the court of a litigation friend. The (alleged) protected party must be served on a first application to appoint a litigation friend unless the court orders otherwise, but there is still no requirement for a child to be notified of proceedings to be conducted in his name and on his behalf even though he may be approaching 18 (see note to r 21.2).

Evidence—Paragraph 3.3 of PD21 clarifies the evidence required. This presumably includes evidence that the party is a child or protected party although this is not expressly stated. Where there is adequate evidence, the requisite consents have been given and there is no suggestion of bad faith, the court should make the order sought and only direct service of the application on the other parties if there are circumstances that make this necessary (*Folks v Faizey* [2006] EWCA Civ 381).

Suitability—See note to r 21.4. The court may appoint the person proposed or any other person who complies with the conditions specified in r 21.4(3) (r 21.8(4)). Thus, the criteria of suitability in r 21.4(3) must be satisfied even though r 21.4(1) expressly states that the rule does not apply if the court has appointed a person to be a litigation friend.

PART III

21.7 Court's power to change litigation friend and to prevent person acting as litigation friend

(1) The court may –

(a) direct that a person may not act as a litigation friend;
(b) terminate a litigation friend's appointment; or
(c) appoint a new litigation friend in substitution for an existing one.

(2) An application for an order under paragraph (1) must be supported by evidence.

(3) The court may not appoint a litigation friend under this rule unless it is satisfied that the person to be appointed satisfies the conditions in rule 21.4(3).

Amendments—SI 2007/2204.

Scope—The court may prevent a person from being a litigation friend or replace a litigation friend during the course of proceedings, whether or not appointed by an order. The court must be satisfied that the person to be appointed is suitable for appointment in accordance with the criteria set out in r 21.4(3).

Service—See r 21.8(1) and (3). See generally note to r 21.6 as to service. Although this does not include the protected party, it is good practice to consult this person as capacity is not an 'all or nothing' concept.

Suitability—See note to r 21.4 above. The court may appoint the person proposed or any other person who complies with the conditions specified in r 21.4(3) (r 21.8(4)). Thus the criteria of suitability in r 21.4(3) must be satisfied even though r 21.4(1) expressly states that the rule does not apply if the court has appointed a person to be a litigation friend.

Applications—This rule contemplates an application by a party or presumably a non-party, such as an alternative representative for the child or protected party. The court may, as part of its case management powers, initiate the process (r 3.3) and has a duty to do so where it is satisfied that an existing litigation friend has become disabled by conflict of interest (*Zarbafi v Zarbafi* [2014] EWCA Civ 1267). Concern as to an actual or potential litigation friend does not necessarily mean that there is someone with an interest in making the application.

Termination—The rules express no limit on the power to terminate the appointment and if the litigation friend acts manifestly contrary to the child's or protected party's best interests the court will remove him, even though neither his good faith nor his diligence is in issue (*Re A (Conjoined Twins: Medical Treatment) (No 2)* [2001] 1 FLR 267, CA). It suggested in this regard that 'best interests' here will now be interpreted by reference to MCA 2005, s 4 (see, by analogy, *Re NRA and Others* [2015] COPLR 690). The court's power to terminate the appointment is not restricted by any requirement to identify a substitute litigation friend and a litigation friend who is unwilling to continue to act would be unlikely to satisfy the condition of being a person who can 'fairly and competently conduct the proceedings on behalf of … the protected party' (*Bradbury and Others v Paterson and Others* [2015] COPLR 425, QBD). The court may not revoke the appointment of a litigation friend retrospectively ab initio (*Davila v Davila and another* [2016] EWHC B14 (Ch). In respect of mentally incapable adults, what are this person's best interests has been clarified by MCA 2005, s 4. For an overview of MCA 2005, see Part II.

21.8 Appointment of litigation friend by court order – supplementary

(1) An application for an order under rule 21.6 or 21.7 must be served on every person on whom, in accordance with rule 6.13 (service on parent, guardian etc), the claim form must be served.

(2) Where an application for an order under rule 21.6 is in respect of a protected party, the application must also be served on the protected party unless the court orders otherwise.

(3) An application for an order under rule 21.7 must also be served on –

(a) the person who is the litigation friend, or who is purporting to act as the litigation friend, when the application is made; and

(b) the person who it is proposed should be the litigation friend, if he is not the applicant.

(4) On an application for an order under rule 21.6 or 21.7, the court may appoint the person proposed or any other person who satisfies the conditions specified in rule 21.4(3).

Amendments—SI 2007/2204; SI 2008/2178.

Scope—This rule makes provision for service where a party is a child or protected party and supplements r 6.13. It also provides that when an application is made to appoint or change a litigation friend the court is not obliged to appoint the person proposed.

Service—Service on the parent or guardian of the child, or the person with whom the protected party resides or in whose care he is, is required in all cases (see r 6.13). Note that the application under r 21.6 must be served on the protected party but this is not a universal provision. Where it is proposed to change the litigation friend both the existing and intended litigation friend must be served. Although the rules do not so provide, the application should be served upon or at least brought to the notice of the protected party unless there is no prospect of a relevant response (see note **No need for court appointment of litigation friend** under r 21.5). There is no requirement to serve a child in any of these situations but see the note to r 21.2.

Who is appointed—The court may decide to appoint any other person who meets the criteria set out in r 21.4(3) and is willing to act.

21.9 Procedure where appointment of litigation friend ceases

(1) When a child who is not a protected party reaches the age of 18, the litigation friend's appointment ceases.

(2) Where a protected party regains or acquires capacity to conduct the proceedings, the litigation friend's appointment continues until it is ended by court order.

(3) An application for an order under paragraph (2) may be made by –

(a) the former protected party;
(b) the litigation friend; or
(c) a party.

(4) The child or protected party in respect of whom the appointment to act has ceased must serve notice on the other parties –

(a) stating that the appointment of his litigation friend to act has ceased;
(b) giving his address for service; and
(c) stating whether or not he intends to carry on the proceedings.

(5) If the child or protected party does not serve the notice required by paragraph (4) within 28 days after the day on which the appointment of the litigation friend ceases the court may, on application, strike out[(GL)] any claim brought by or defence raised by the child or protected party.

(6) The liability of a litigation friend for costs continues until –

(a) the person in respect of whom his appointment to act has ceased serves the notice referred to in paragraph (4); or

(b) the litigation friend serves notice on the parties that his appointment to act has ceased.

Amendments—SI 2007/2204.

Scope—This rule makes provision for a party ceasing to be a child or protected party.

Child—There will be no need for a litigation friend when the child attains 18 (unless the child is also a protected party) and the appointment then ceases automatically. If this party does not then continue the proceedings they may be struck out. There is no express requirement for the child to be notified of the existence of the proceedings up to that point, but notice of an application to strike out under r 21.9(5) must presumably be given to the party formerly a child. The litigation friend will remain liable for costs unless the child gives notice as aforesaid or the litigation friend gives notice under r 21.9(6)(b), which must also be given to the party formerly a child.

Protected party—The position is different in respect of a protected party who recovers capacity. The litigation friend will only be removed by court order following an application under r 21.9(3) and evidence will be required as to capacity. Notice must still be served by the former protected party under r 21.9(4) or the proceedings may be struck out, and the litigation friend will remain liable for costs until that notice is served or he serves his own notice under r 21.9(6)(b).

Liability of litigation friend for costs—The litigation friend of a claimant may have had to give an undertaking as to costs pursuant to r 21.4(3)(c). This liability continues until notice is served on the other parties either by the claimant or the former litigation friend as mentioned above. Presumably the reference in r 21.9(6) to 'The liability of a litigation friend for costs' refers to such undertaking and is not sufficient to create any additional liability. It is not clear whether, when discharged, the litigation friend is released from all liability for costs or only costs incurred from that date, although it is probably the latter.

Relationship between the civil court and the Court of Protection—Doubt may arise in a brain injury claim as to whether the claimant lacks or continues to lack capacity either to litigate or to manage property and affairs. This may be relevant as to the need for a litigation friend and also the quantum of damages to be awarded. In *Saulle v Nouvet* [2007] EWHC 2902 (QB), Mr Andrew Edis QC sitting then as a Deputy Judge of the High Court assumed that the civil court must deal with both assessments of capacity but although that court can make a definitive decision as to capacity to litigate it cannot make a decision as to capacity to manage financial affairs that will be binding on the Court of Protection. Conversely, the Court of Protection has a statutory power to make declarations as to present (but not past) capacity that may relate to both litigation and management of financial affairs and any such declarations are likely to be followed by a civil court. In substantial personal injury claims where the quantum of damages may be affected by the involvement of the Court of Protection there are therefore advantages in the civil court referring both issues of capacity to the Court of Protection for determination. However, where the amount of money involved would not normally trigger the intervention of the Court of Protection, it is proportionate and desirable for the civil court to adjudicate on both aspects of capacity (i e to decide whether the litigant is a protected party and if so whether he is also a protected beneficiary).

Where there is a reference to the Court of Protection in regard to capacity issues, the proceedings should be stayed pending the outcome. It is likely that the defendant will be made a party to the Court of Protection proceedings in view of the financial interest and the advocates in the civil proceedings will thus have a right of audience. The position is different in respect of a dispute as to best welfare interests and in that event the defendants in civil proceedings would not be permitted to become parties to any Court of Protection proceedings. For a full explanation, see the judgment of Bodey J in *Re SK (By his Litigation Friend, the Official Solicitor)* [2012] COPLR 712, COP.

PART III

21.10 Compromise etc by or on behalf of child or protected party

(1) Where a claim is made –

(a) by or on behalf of a child or protected party; or

(b) against a child or protected party,

no settlement, compromise or payment (including any voluntary interim payment) and no acceptance of money paid into court shall be valid, so far as it relates to the claim by, on behalf of or against the child or protected party, without the approval of the court.

(2) Where –

(a) before proceedings in which a claim is made by or on behalf of, or against a child or protected party (whether alone or with any other person) are begun, an agreement is reached for the settlement of the claim; and

(b) the sole purpose of proceedings is to obtain the approval of the court to a settlement or compromise of the claim,

the claim must –

(i) be made using the procedure set out in Part 8 (alternative procedure for claims); and

(ii) include a request to the court for approval of the settlement or compromise.

(3) In proceedings to which Section II or Section III of Part 45 applies, the court shall not make an order for detailed assessment of the costs payable to the child or protected party but will assess the costs in the manner set out in that Section.

(Rule 46.4 contains provisions about costs where money is payable to a child or protected party.)

Amendments—SI 2004/3419; SI 2007/2204; SI 2010/621; SI 2013/262.

Scope—This provision ensures that the approval of the court is obtained to any settlement or compromise on behalf of a child or protected party, and extends to accepting any Pt 36 offer. It applies to claims other than for money and where the claim is made against the child or protected party. Without this approval the settlement, compromise or payment of any claim is wholly invalid and unenforceable, and is made entirely at the risk of the parties and their solicitors. The acceptance by a defendant of a Pt 36 offer to settle made by a litigation friend (including a partial settlement relating to liability) may be withdrawn before court approval is obtained (*Drinkall v Whitwood* [2004] 1 WLR 462, CA).

Setting aside a settlement—Although there is a public interest in the finality of litigation, there is also a public interest in the protection of vulnerable people who lack the mental state to conduct litigation, so a compromise may be set aside many years later where, unknown to the parties, the claimant was a protected party at the time. The test is whether the claimant has capacity to conduct the proceedings, not whether the claimant agrees to the compromise (*Dunhill (A Protected Party By Her Litigation Friend Tasker) v Burgin (Nos 1 and 2)* [2014] COPLR 199, SC). Following *Dietz v Lennin Chemicals Ltd* [1969] 1 AC 170, HL, the Supreme Court held that r 21.10 was intra vires and, in the case of both children and protected parties, prevailed over the general rule that a contract would be binding if the incapacity of a party was not known to the other party. However, even in a case where a claimant has not been declared to lack capacity, the court may consider it appropriate to approve a settlement in the exercise of its inherent jurisdiction, thereby ensuring that the settlement is valid in the event that it is later determined that the claimant lacked capacity (*Coles v Perfect* [2013] EWHC 1955 (QB)).

Test of capacity—Where a compromise is to be negotiated outside court, the Supreme Court in *Dunhill (A Protected Party By Her Litigation Friend Tasker) v Burgin (Nos 1 and 2)* [2014] COPLR 199, SC confirmed that the proper question, as settled by *Masterman-Lister v Brutton & Co and Jewell & Home Counties Dairies* [2003] 1 WLR 1511, CA, was whether the claimant had the necessary capacity to conduct the proceedings (i e to litigate). The test of litigation capacity is the capacity to conduct the claim that the claimant in fact has, rather than to conduct the claim as formulated by the claimant's lawyers.

Varying the settlement—Once the settlement has been approved, it is final and cannot be varied or revoked on the grounds that an unforeseen event has destroyed the assumption on which it was made pursuant to the case-management power of the court under r 3.1(7) (*Roult (by his mother and litigation friend) v North West Strategic Health Authority* [2010] 1 WLR 487, CA).

Need for a public hearing—Although any hearing should normally be held in public to comply with ECHR 1950, Art 6(1) , there are exceptions and hearings involving the interests of a child or protected party may be in private (CPR 1998, r 39.2(3)(d) and PD39A, paras 1.4A, 1.6). Although each application should be considered individually, a limited derogation from the principle of open justice in the form of an anonymity order (namely, an order prohibiting the publication of the claimant's name and address and a restriction on access by non-parties to documents in the court records) will usually provide a reasonable degree of protection both against an unwarranted invasion of privacy and an interference with the right to family life, and against such other risks as there might be, whether of dissipation of assets or otherwise. The following principles should, therefore, apply: (i) the hearing should be listed for hearing in public under the name in which the proceedings had been issued, unless, by the time of the hearing, an anonymity order had already been made; (ii) because the hearing would be held in open court, the press and the public would have a right to be present and to observe the proceedings; (iii) the press would be free to report the proceedings, subject only to any orders restricting publication of the name and address of the claimant, his litigation friend and any anonymity order; (iv) the judge should invite submissions from the parties and the press before making an anonymity order; (v) unless satisfied, after having heard argument, that it was not necessary to do so, the judge should make an anonymity order for the protection of the claimant and his family; (vi) if the judge concluded it was unnecessary to make an anonymity order, he should give a short judgment setting out his reasons; and (vii) the judge should normally give a brief judgment on the application and should make a copy available to the press, on request, as soon as possible after the hearing. (*X v Dartford and Gravesham NHS Trust (Personal Injury Bar Association and another intervening)* [2015] 1 WLR 3647, CA.)

Appeals—A decision not to appeal, where permission has been obtained on the express understanding that the possible appellant needs time to consider the matter, and with no consideration moving from the possible respondents, is not a 'compromise' and does not require the approval of the court (*Re A (Conjoined Twins: Medical Treatment) (No 2)* [2001] 1 FLR 267, CA).

21.11 Control of money recovered by or on behalf of child or protected party

(1) Where in any proceedings –

(a) money is recovered by or on behalf of or for the benefit of a child or protected party; or

(b) money paid into court is accepted by or on behalf of a child or protected party,

the money shall be dealt with in accordance with directions given by the court under this rule and not otherwise.

(2) Directions given under this rule may provide that the money shall be wholly or partly paid into court and invested or otherwise dealt with.

(3) Where money is recovered by or on behalf of a protected party or money paid into court is accepted by or on behalf of a protected party, before giving directions in accordance with this rule, the court will first consider whether the protected party is a protected beneficiary.

Amendments—SI 2007/2204.

Scope—This rule ensures that there is supervision of money awarded to or recovered by a child or protected party who is also a protected beneficiary. Further guidance is to be found in PD21 generally.

Control of money—This subject generally is beyond the scope of this volume. The court will control funds held on behalf of a child, but in the case of a protected beneficiary reference must usually be made to the Court of Protection. If there is a registered attorney under an enduring power or a donee under a lasting power for financial affairs it may be appropriate to release the fund to such attorney or donee. The powers of the litigation friend are restricted to the conduct of the proceedings and do not extend to dealing with the financial affairs of the infant or protected beneficiary.

Additional powers: child—The court will control funds held on behalf of a child, but under r 21.12 (see below) may appoint the Official Solicitor as guardian of that child's estate.

Protected beneficiary—Having approved an award of damages on behalf of a protected party, the court must then consider whether this party is also a protected beneficiary. In that event the fund will either be transferred to the Court of Protection or retained in court and dealt with in like manner to a child's fund, if under £50,000 (or such greater sum as the Court of Protection may authorise) and there are no further financial resources justifying Court of Protection involvement. (See paras 10.2, 10.2A of PD21.)

21.12 Expenses incurred by a litigation friend

(1) Subject to paragraph (1A), in proceedings to which rule 21.11 applies, a litigation friend who incurs costs or expenses on behalf of a child or protected party in any proceedings is entitled on application to recover the amount paid or payable out of any money recovered or paid into court to the extent that it –

(a) has been reasonably incurred; and
(b) is reasonable in amount.

(1A) Costs recoverable under this rule are limited to –

(a) costs incurred by or on behalf of a child and which have been assessed by way of detailed assessment pursuant to rule 46.4(2); or
(b) costs incurred by or on behalf of a child by way of success fee under a conditional fee agreement or sum payable under a damages based agreement in a claim for damages for personal injury where the damages agreed or ordered to be paid do not exceed £25,000, where such costs have been assessed summarily pursuant to rule 46.4(5).

(2) Expenses may include all or part of –

(a) a premium in respect of a costs insurance policy (as defined by section 58C(5) of the Courts and Legal Services Act 1990); or
(b) interest on a loan taken out to pay a premium in respect of a costs insurance policy or other recoverable disbursement.

(3) No application may be made under this rule for costs or expenses that –

(a) are of a type that may be recoverable on an assessment of costs payable by or out of money belonging to a child or protected party; but
(b) are disallowed in whole or in part on such an assessment.

(Costs and expenses which are also 'costs' as defined in rule 44.1(1) are subject to rule 46.4(2) and (3).)

(4) In deciding whether the costs or expenses were reasonably incurred and reasonable in amount, the court will have regard to all the circumstances of the case including the factors set out in rule 44.4(3) and rule 46.9.

(5) When the court is considering the factors to be taken into account in assessing the reasonableness of costs or expenses, it will have regard to the facts and circumstances as they reasonably appeared to the litigation friend or to the child's or protected party's legal representative when the costs or expense was incurred.

(6) Subject to paragraph (7), where the claim is settled or compromised, or judgment is given, on terms that an amount not exceeding £5,000 is paid to the child or protected party, the total amount the litigation friend may recover under paragraph (1) must not exceed 25% of the sum so agreed or awarded, unless the court directs otherwise. Such total amount must not exceed 50% of the sum so agreed or awarded.

(7) The amount which the litigation friend may recover under paragraph (1) in respect of costs must not (in proceedings at first instance) exceed 25% of the amount of the sum agreed or awarded in respect of –

PART III

(a) general damages for pain, suffering and loss of amenity; and
(b) damages for pecuniary loss other than future pecuniary loss,

net of any sums recoverable by the Compensation Recovery Unit of the Department for Work and Pensions.

(8) Except in a case in which the costs payable to a child or protected party are fixed by these rules, no application may be made under this rule for a payment out of the money recovered by the child or protected party until the costs payable to the child or protected party have been assessed or agreed.

Amendments—SI 2005/2292; SI 2007/2204; SI 2013/262; SI 2013/1974; SI 2014/3299 (as amended).

Scope—This rule clarifies the approach to be adopted by the court when a litigation friend seeks approval to deduct from the damages any costs or expenses that are not recoverable from the defendant. For the purposes of this rule, the success fee under a conditional fee agreement and the sum payable under a damages-based agreement are treated as 'costs' but only in personal injury claims by children where the damages recovered do not exceed £25,000. The treatment of such 'costs' does not extend to claims by protected parties. Expenses may include an insurance premium (and interest on a loan to fund the premium) in respect of costs insurance policies permitted by CLSA 1990, s 58C(5) (essentially those in claims for clinical negligence). The rule is silent as to the recoverability of insurance premiums in respect of other insurance policies.

21.13 Appointment of guardian of child's estate

(1) The court may appoint the Official Solicitor to be a guardian of a child's estate where –

(a) money is paid into court on behalf of the child in accordance with directions given under rule 21.11 (control of money received by a child or protected party);
(b) the Criminal Injuries Compensation Authority notifies the court that it has made or intends to make an award to the child;
(c) a court or tribunal outside England and Wales notifies the court that it has ordered or intends to order that money be paid to the child;
(d) the child is absolutely entitled to the proceeds of a pension fund; or
(e) in any other case, such an appointment seems desirable to the court.

(2) The court may not appoint the Official Solicitor under this rule unless –

(a) the persons with parental responsibility (within the meaning of section 3 of the Children Act 1989) agree; or
(b) the court considers that their agreement can be dispensed with.

(3) The Official Solicitor's appointment may continue only until the child reaches 18.

Amendments—SI 2007/2204.

Scope—This rule enables the court to appoint the Official Solicitor to be responsible for the estate of a child in certain defined circumstances.

Official Solicitor—The expression means the Official Solicitor to the Senior Courts provided for by SCA 1981, s 90. The Official Solicitor may be contacted at Victory House, 30–34 Kingsway, London WC2B 6EX, DX 141423 Bloomsbury 7; tel 020 3681 2758; fax 020 3681 2762.

Practice Direction 21 – Children and Protected Parties

This Practice Direction supplements CPR Part 21

General

1.1 In proceedings where one of the parties is a protected party, the protected party should be referred to in the title to the proceedings as 'A.B. (a protected party by C.D. his litigation friend)'.

1.2 In proceedings where one of the parties is a child, where –

(1) the child has a litigation friend, the child should be referred to in the title to the proceedings as 'A.B. (a child by C.D. his litigation friend)'; or

(2) the child is conducting the proceedings on his own behalf, the child should be referred to in the title as 'A.B. (a child)'.

1.3 A settlement of a claim by a child includes an agreement on a sum to be apportioned to a dependent child under the Fatal Accidents Act 1976.

The litigation friend

2.1 A person may become a litigation friend –

(a) without a court order under rule 21.5, or
(b) by a court order under rule 21.6.

2.2 A person who wishes to become a litigation friend without a court order pursuant to rule 21.5(3) must file a certificate of suitability in Practice Form N235 –

(a) stating that he consents to act,
(b) stating that he knows or believes that the [claimant] [defendant] [is a child][lacks capacity to conduct the proceedings],
(c) in the case of a protected party, stating the grounds of his belief and, if his belief is based upon medical opinion or the opinion of another suitably qualified expert, attaching any relevant document to the certificate,
(d) stating that he can fairly and competently conduct proceedings on behalf of the child or protected party and has no interest adverse to that of the child or protected party, and
(e) where the child or protected party is a claimant, undertaking to pay any costs which the child or protected party may be ordered to pay in relation to the proceedings, subject to any right he may have to be repaid from the assets of the child or protected party.

2.3 The certificate of suitability must be verified by a statement of truth.

(Part 22 contains provisions about statements of truth.)

2.4 The litigation friend is not required to serve the document referred to in paragraph 2.2(c) when he serves a certificate of suitability on the person to be served under rule 21.5(4)(a).

Application for a court order appointing a litigation friend

3.1 Rule 21.6 sets out who may apply for an order appointing a litigation friend.

3.2 An application must be made in accordance with Part 23 and must be supported by evidence.

3.3 The evidence in support must satisfy the court that the proposed litigation friend –

(1) consents to act,
(2) can fairly and competently conduct proceedings on behalf of the child or protected party,
(3) has no interest adverse to that of the child or protected party, and
(4) where the child or protected party is a claimant, undertakes to pay any costs which the child or protected party may be ordered to pay in relation to the proceedings, subject to any right he may have to be repaid from the assets of the child or protected party.

3.4 Where it is sought to appoint the Official Solicitor as the litigation friend, provision must be made for payment of his charges.

Procedure where the need for a litigation friend has come to an end

4.1 Rule 21.9 deals with the situation where the need for a litigation friend comes to an end during the proceedings because either –

(1) a child who is not also a protected party reaches the age of 18 (full age) during the proceedings, or
(2) a protected party regains or acquires capacity to conduct the proceedings.

4.2 A child on reaching full age must serve on the other parties to the proceedings and file with the court a notice –

(1) stating that he has reached full age,

PART III

(2) stating that his litigation friend's appointment has ceased,
(3) giving an address for service, and
(4) stating whether or not he intends to carry on with or continue to defend the proceedings.

4.3 If the notice states that the child intends to carry on with or continue to defend the proceedings he must subsequently be described in the proceedings as 'A.B. (formerly a child but now of full age)'.

4.4 Whether or not a child having reached full age serves a notice in accordance with rule 21.9(4) and paragraph 4.2 above, a litigation friend may, at any time after the child has reached full age, serve a notice on the other parties that his appointment has ceased.

4.5 Where a protected party regains or acquires capacity to conduct the proceedings, an application under rule 21.9(3) must be made for an order under rule 21.9(2) that the litigation friend's appointment has ceased.

4.6 The application must be supported by the following evidence –

(1) a medical report or other suitably qualified expert's report indicating that the protected party has regained or acquired capacity to conduct the proceedings,
(2) a copy of any relevant order or declaration of the Court of Protection, and
(3) if the application is made by the protected party, a statement whether or not he intends to carry on with or continue to defend the proceedings.

4.7 An order under rule 21.9(2) must be served on the other parties to the proceedings. The former protected party must file with the court a notice –

(1) stating that his litigation friend's appointment has ceased,
(2) giving an address for service, and
(3) stating whether or not he intends to carry on with or continue to defend the proceedings.

Settlement or compromise by or on behalf of a child or protected party before the issue of proceedings

5.1 Where a claim by or on behalf of a child or protected party has been dealt with by agreement before the issue of proceedings and only the approval of the court to the agreement is sought, the claim must, in addition to containing the details of the claim and satisfying the requirements of rule 21.10(2), include the following –

(1) subject to paragraph 5.3, the terms of the settlement or compromise or have attached to it a draft consent order in Practice Form N292;
(2) details of whether and to what extent the defendant admits liability;
(3) the age and occupation (if any) of the child or protected party;
(4) the litigation friend's approval of the proposed settlement or compromise,
(5) a copy of any financial advice relating to the proposed settlement; and
(6) in a personal injury case arising from an accident –
  (a) details of the circumstances of the accident,
  (b) medical and quantum reports and joint statements material to the opinion required by paragraph 5.2,
  (c) where appropriate, a schedule of any past and future expenses and losses claimed and any other relevant information relating to the personal injury as set out in Practice Direction 16, and
  (d) where considerations of liability are raised –
    (i) any evidence or reports in any criminal proceedings or in an inquest, and
    (ii) details of any prosecution brought.

5.2 (1) An opinion on the merits of the settlement or compromise given by counsel or solicitor acting for the child or protected party must, except in very clear cases, be obtained.
(2) A copy of the opinion and, unless the instructions on which it was given are sufficiently set out in it, a copy of the instructions, must be supplied to the court.

5.3 Where in any personal injury case a claim for damages for future pecuniary loss is settled, the provisions in paragraphs 5.4 and 5.5 must in addition be complied with.

5.4 The court must be satisfied that the parties have considered whether the damages should wholly or partly take the form of periodical payments.

5.5 Where the settlement includes provision for periodical payments, the claim must –

(1) set out the terms of the settlement or compromise; or
(2) have attached to it a draft consent order,

which must satisfy the requirements of rules 41.8 and 41.9 as appropriate.

5.6 Applications for the approval of a settlement or compromise will normally be heard by –

(1) a Master or a District Judge in proceedings involving a child; and
(2) a Master, Designated Civil Judge or his nominee in proceedings involving a protected party.

(For information about provisional damages claims see Part 41 and Practice Direction 41A.)

Amendments—CPR Updates 51, 69, 75.

Settlement or compromise by or on behalf of a child or protected party after proceedings have been issued

6.1 Where in any personal injury case a claim for damages for future pecuniary loss, by or on behalf of a child or protected party, is dealt with by agreement after proceedings have been issued, an application must be made for the court's approval of the agreement.

6.2 The court must be satisfied that the parties have considered whether the damages should wholly or partly take the form of periodical payments.

6.3 Where the settlement includes provision for periodical payments, an application under paragraph 6.1 must –

(1) set out the terms of the settlement or compromise; or
(2) have attached to it a draft consent order,

which must satisfy the requirements of rules 41.8 and 41.9 as appropriate.

6.4 The court must be supplied with –

(1) an opinion on the merits of the settlement or compromise given by counsel or solicitor acting for the child or protected party, except in very clear cases; and
(2) a copy of any financial advice; and
(3) documentary evidence material to the opinion referred to at paragraph 6.4(1).

6.5 Applications for the approval of a settlement or compromise, except at the trial, will normally be heard by –

(1) a Master or a District Judge in proceedings involving a child; and
(2) a Master, Designated Civil Judge or his nominee in proceedings involving a protected party.

Amendments—CPR Update 69, 75.

Apportionment under the Fatal Accidents Act 1976

7.1 A judgment on or settlement in respect of a claim under the Fatal Accidents Act 1976 must be apportioned between the persons by or on whose behalf the claim has been brought.

7.2 Where a claim is brought on behalf of a dependent child or children, any settlement (including an agreement on a sum to be apportioned to a dependent child under the Fatal Accidents Act 1976) must be approved by the court.

7.3 The money apportioned to any dependent child must be invested on the child's behalf in accordance with rules 21.10 and 21.11 and paragraphs 8 and 9 below.

7.4 In order to approve an apportionment of money to a dependent child, the court will require the following information:

PART III

(1) the matters set out in paragraphs 5.1(2) and (3), and
(2) in respect of the deceased –
   (a) where death was caused by an accident, the matters set out in paragraphs 5.1(6)(a), (b) and (c), and
   (b) his future loss of earnings, and
(3) the extent and nature of the dependency.

Control of money recovered by or on behalf of a child or protected party

8.1 When giving directions under rule 21.11, the court –

(1) may direct the money to be paid into court for investment,
(2) may direct that certain sums be paid direct to the child or protected beneficiary, his litigation friend or his legal representative for the immediate benefit of the child or protected beneficiary or for expenses incurred on his behalf, and
(3) may direct that the application in respect of the investment of the money be transferred to a local district registry.

8.2 The court will consider the general aims to be achieved for the money in court (the fund) by investment and will give directions as to the type of investment.

8.3 Where a child also lacks capacity to manage and control any money recovered by him or on his behalf in the proceedings, and is likely to remain so on reaching full age, his fund should be administered as a protected beneficiary's fund.

8.4 Where a child or protected beneficiary is in receipt of publicly funded legal services the fund will be subject to a first charge under section 10 of the Access to Justice Act 1999 (statutory charge) and an order for the investment of money on the child's or protected beneficiary's behalf must contain a direction to that effect.

Investment on behalf of a child

9.1 At the hearing of an application for the approval of a settlement or compromise the litigation friend or his legal representative must provide, in addition to the information required by paragraphs 5 and 6 –

(1) a CFO form 320 (initial application for investment of damages) for completion by the judge hearing the application; and
(2) any evidence or information which the litigation friend wishes the court to consider in relation to the investment of the award for damages.

9.2 Following the hearing in paragraph 9.1, the court will forward to the Court Funds Office a request for investment decision (form 212) and the Court Funds Office will make the appropriate investment.

9.3 Where an award for damages for a child is made at trial, unless paragraph 9.7 applies, the trial judge will –

(1) direct the money to be paid into court and placed into the special investment account until further investment directions have been given by the court;
(2) direct the litigation friend to make an application to a Master or District Judge for further investment directions; and
(3) give such other directions as the trial judge thinks fit, including a direction that the hearing of the application for further investment directions will be fixed for a date within 28 days from the date of the trial.

9.4 The application under paragraph 9.3(2) must be made by filing with the court –

(1) a completed CFO form 320; and
(2) any evidence or information which the litigation friend wishes the court to consider in relation to the investment of the award for damages.

9.5 The application must be sent in proceedings in the Royal Courts of Justice to the Masters' Support Unit (Room E16) at the Royal Courts of Justice.

9.6 If the application required by paragraph 9.3(2) is not made to the court, the money paid into court in accordance with paragraph 9.3(1) will remain in the special investment account subject to any further order of the court or paragraph 9.8.

9.7 If the money to be invested is very small the court may order it to be paid direct to the litigation friend to be put into a building society account (or similar) for the child's use.

9.8 If the money is invested in court, it must be paid out to the child on application when he reaches full age.

Amendments—CPR Updates 66, 69.

Investment on behalf of a protected beneficiary

10.1 The Court of Protection has jurisdiction to make decisions in the best interests of a protected beneficiary. Fees may be charged for the administration of funds and these must be provided for in any settlement.

10.2

(1) Where the sum to be invested for the benefit of the protected beneficiary is £50,000 or more, (save where under paragraph 10.2A the Court of Protection has authorised a sum of £50,000 or more to be dealt with under subparagraph (2) below) unless a person with authority as –
   (a) the attorney under a registered enduring power of attorney;
   (b) the donee of a lasting power of attorney; or
   (c) the deputy appointed by the Court of Protection,

   to administer or manage the protected beneficiary's financial affairs has been appointed, the order approving the settlement will contain a direction to the litigation friend to apply to the Court of Protection for the appointment of a deputy, after which the fund will be dealt with as directed by the Court of Protection; or

(2) Where the sum to be invested for the benefit of the protected party is under £50,000, or such sum as may be authorised by the Court of Protection under paragraph 10.2A, it may be retained in court and invested in the same way as the fund of a child.

10.2A The Court of Protection may authorise a sum of £50,000 or more to be retained in court and invested it the same way as the fund of a child under subparagraph 10.2(2), either of its own initiative or at the request of the judge giving investment directions in respect of the protected beneficiary.

10.3 A form of order transferring the fund to the Court of Protection is set out in practice form N292.

10.4 In order for the Court Funds Office to release a fund which is subject to the statutory charge, the litigation friend or his legal representative or the person with authority referred to in paragraph 10.2(1) must provide the appropriate regional office of the Legal Services Commission with an undertaking in respect of a sum to cover their costs, following which the regional office will advise the Court Funds Office in writing of that sum, enabling them to transfer the balance to the Court of Protection on receipt of a CFO form 200 payment schedule authorised by the court.

10.5 The CFO form 200 should be completed and presented to the court where the settlement or trial took place for authorisation, subject to paragraphs 10.6 and 10.7.

10.6 Where the settlement took place in the Royal Courts of Justice the CFO form 200 must be completed and presented for authorisation –

(1) on behalf of a child, in the Masters' Support Unit, Room E105, and
(2) on behalf of a protected beneficiary, in the Judgment and Orders Section in the Action Department, Room E17.

10.7 Where the trial took place in the Royal Courts of Justice, the CFO form 200 is completed and authorised by the court officer.

Amendments—CPR Update 66.

Note—The Legal Aid Agency replaced the Legal Services Commission on 1 April 2013.

Costs or expenses incurred by a litigation friend

11.1 A litigation friend may make a claim for costs or expenses under rule 21.12(1) –

(1) where the court has ordered an assessment of costs under rule 46.4(2), at the detailed assessment hearing;

(1A) where the court has assessed the costs to be paid by the child by way of summary assessment under rule 46.4(5)(b), at the conclusion of the hearing at which damages to be paid to the child are assessed or at the hearing to approve the compromise or settlement under Part 21, or at any time thereafter;

(2) where the litigation friend's expenses are not of a type which would be recoverable as costs on an assessment of costs between the parties, to the Master or District Judge at the hearing to approve the settlement or compromise under Part 21 (the Master or District Judge may adjourn the matter to the costs judge); or

(3) where an assessment of costs under Part 46.4(2) is not required, and no approval under Part 21 is necessary, by a Part 23 application supported by a witness statement to a Costs Judge or District Judge as appropriate.

11.2 In all circumstances, the litigation friend must support a claim for payment out in relation to costs or expenses by filing a witness statement setting out –

(1) the nature and amount of the costs or expense; and
(2) the reason the costs or expense were incurred.

11.3 Where the application is for payment out of the damages in respect of costs pursuant to rule 21.12(1A) the witness statement must also include (or be accompanied by) –

(1) a copy of the conditional fee agreement or damages based agreement;
(2) the risk assessment by reference to which the success fee was determined;
(3) the reasons why the particular funding model was selected;
(4) the advice given to the litigation friend in relation to funding arrangements;
(5) details of any costs agreed, recovered or fixed costs recoverable by the child; and
(6) confirmation of the amount of the sum agreed or awarded in respect of –
 (a) general damages for pain, suffering and loss of amenity; and
 (b) damages for pecuniary loss other than future pecuniary loss,

net of any sums recoverable by the Compensation Recovery Unit of the Department for Work and Pensions.

Amendments—CPR Updates 60, 69, 78.

Guardian's accounts

12 Paragraph 8 of Practice Direction 40A deals with the approval of the accounts of a guardian of assets of a child.

Amendments—CPR Update 51.

Payment out of funds in court

13.1 Applications to a Master or District Judge –

(1) for payment out of money from the fund for the benefit of the child, or
(2) to vary an investment strategy,

may be dealt with without a hearing unless the court directs otherwise.

13.2 When the child reaches full age –

(1) where his fund in court is a sum of money, it will be paid out to him on application; or
(2) where his fund is in the form of investments other than money (for example shares or unit trusts), the investments will on application be –
 (a) sold and the proceeds of sale paid out to him; or
 (b) transferred into his name.

13.3 Where the fund is administered by the Court of Protection, any payment out of money from that fund must be in accordance with any decision or order of the Court of Protection.

13.4 If an application is required for the payment out of money from a fund administered by the Court of Protection, that application must be made to the Court of Protection.

(For further information on payments out of court, see Practice Direction 37.)

Amendments—CPR Update 69.

★★★★

PART 23
GENERAL RULES ABOUT APPLICATIONS FOR COURT ORDERS

CONTENTS OF THIS PART

Rule		Page
23.1	Meaning of 'application notice' and 'respondent'	2077
23.2	Where to make an application	2077
23.3	Application notice to be filed	2078
23.4	Notice of an application	2078
23.5	Time when an application is made	2078
23.6	What an application notice must include	2078
23.7	Service of a copy of an application notice	2078
23.8	Applications which may be dealt with without a hearing	2079
23.9	Service of application where application made without notice	2079
23.10	Application to set aside or vary order made without notice	2079
23.11	Power of the court to proceed in the absence of a party	2079
23.12	Dismissal of totally without merit applications	2079
	Practice Direction 23A – Applications	2080
	Practice Direction 23B – Applications under Particular Statutes	2085

23.1 Meaning of 'application notice' and 'respondent'

In this Part –

'application notice' means a document in which the applicant states his intention to seek a court order; and

'respondent' means –

(a) the person against whom the order is sought; and
(b) such other person as the court may direct.

23.2 Where to make an application

(1) The general rule is that an application must be made to the court or County Court hearing centre where the claim was started.

(2) If a claim has been transferred to another court, or transferred or sent to another County Court hearing centre since it was started, an application must be made to the court or the County Court hearing centre to which the claim has been transferred or sent, unless there is good reason to make the application to a different court.

(3) If the parties have been notified of a fixed date for the trial, an application must be made to the court where the trial is to take place.

(4) Subject to paragraph (4A), if an application is made before a claim has been started, it must be made to the court where it is likely that the claim to which the application relates will be started unless there is good reason to make the application to a different court.

(4A) An application made in the County Court before a claim has been started may be made at any County Court hearing centre, unless any enactment, rule or practice direction provides otherwise.

(5) If an application is made after proceedings to enforce judgment have begun, it must be made to the court or County Court hearing centre which is dealing with the enforcement of the judgment unless any enactment, rule or practice direction provides otherwise.

Amendments—SI 2011/3103; SI 2014/407.

23.3 Application notice to be filed

(1) The general rule is that an applicant must file an application notice.

(2) An applicant may make an application without filing an application notice if –

(a) this is permitted by a rule or practice direction; or
(b) the court dispenses with the requirement for an application notice.

Filing of an application notice—The applicant should provide certain information (and see r 23.6 below) including in particular:

(a) a summary of the application;
(b) the grounds for the application;
(c) evidence or documents in support of the application; and
(d) a draft of the order applied for.

Interim remedies—Certain defined interim remedies may be claimed under Pt 25 (see remedies listed at r 25.1). Application for such remedies is in accordance with the procedure under Pt 23 (r 25.3).

23.4 Notice of an application

(1) The general rule is that a copy of the application notice must be served on each respondent.

(2) An application may be made without serving a copy of the application notice if this is permitted by –

(a) a rule;
(b) a practice direction; or
(c) a court order.

(Rule 23.7 deals with service of a copy of the application notice)

Not on notice applications—The court has power to make applications 'not on notice' (ex parte) in certain circumstances (and see Pt 25, which deals with interim remedies). If application is made without giving notice the reason for so doing must be stated in the evidence with the application (r 25.3(3)). Rule 23.9 deals with service of a without notice application.

23.5 Time when an application is made

Where an application must be made within a specified time, it is so made if the application notice is received by the court within that time.

23.6 What an application notice must include

An application notice must state –

(a) what order the applicant is seeking; and
(b) briefly, why the applicant is seeking the order.

(Part 22 requires an application notice to be verified by a statement of truth if the applicant wishes to rely on matters set out in his application notice as evidence)

23.7 Service of a copy of an application notice

(1) A copy of the application notice –

(a) must be served as soon as practicable after it is filed; and
(b) except where another time limit is specified in these Rules or a practice direction, must in any event be served at least 3 days before the court is to deal with the application.

(2) If a copy of the application notice is to be served by the court, the applicant must, when he files the application notice, file a copy of any written evidence in support.

(3) When a copy of an application notice is served it must be accompanied by –

(a) a copy of any written evidence in support; and
(b) a copy of any draft order which the applicant has attached to his application.

(4) If –

(a) an application notice is served; but
(b) the period of notice is shorter than the period required by these Rules or a practice direction,

the court may direct that, in the circumstances of the case, sufficient notice has been given and hear the application.

(5) This rule does not require written evidence –

(a) to be filed if it has already been filed; or
(b) to be served on a party on whom it has already been served.

(Part 6 contains the general rules about service of documents including who must serve a copy of the application notice)

23.8 Applications which may be dealt with without a hearing

The court may deal with an application without a hearing if –

(a) the parties agree as to the terms of the order sought;
(b) the parties agree that the court should dispose of the application without a hearing, or
(c) the court does not consider that a hearing would be appropriate.

23.9 Service of application where application made without notice

(1) This rule applies where the court has disposed of an application which it permitted to be made without service of a copy of the application notice.

(2) Where the court makes an order, whether granting or dismissing the application, a copy of the application notice and any evidence in support must, unless the court orders otherwise, be served with the order on any party or other person –

(a) against whom the order was made; and
(b) against whom the order was sought.

(3) The order must contain a statement of the right to make an application to set aside or vary the order under rule 23.10.

23.10 Application to set aside or vary order made without notice

(1) A person who was not served with a copy of the application notice before an order was made under rule 23.9, may apply to have the order set aside(GL) or varied.

(2) An application under this rule must be made within 7 days after the date on which the order was served on the person making the application.

Amendments—SI 2000/221.

23.11 Power of the court to proceed in the absence of a party

(1) Where the applicant or any respondent fails to attend the hearing of an application, the court may proceed in his absence.

(2) Where –

(a) the applicant or any respondent fails to attend the hearing of an application; and
(b) the court makes an order at the hearing,

the court may, on application or of its own initiative, re-list the application.

(Part 40 deals with service of orders)

23.12 Dismissal of totally without merit applications

If the court dismisses an application (including an application for permission to appeal or for permission to apply for judicial review) and it considers that the application is totally without merit –

(a) the court's order must record that fact; and
(b) the court must at the same time consider whether it is appropriate to make a civil restraint order.

Amendments—Inserted by SI 2004/2072. Amended by SI 2005/2292.

Civil restraint orders—Civil restraint orders are dealt with in r 3.11 (from which FPR 2010, r 4.8 is derived) and PD3C.

Practice Direction 23A – Applications

This Practice Direction supplements CPR Part 23

Reference to a judge

1 A Master or District Judge may refer to a judge any matter which he thinks should properly be decided by a judge, and the judge may either dispose of the matter or refer it back to the Master or District Judge.

Amendments—CPR Update 69.

Application notices

2.1 An application notice must, in addition to the matters set out in rule 23.6, be signed and include:

(1) the title of the claim,
(2) the reference number of the claim,
(3) the full name of the applicant,
(4) where the applicant is not already a party, his address for service, including a postcode. Postcode information may be obtained from *www.royalmail.com* or the Royal Mail Address Management Guide, and
(5) either a request for a hearing or a request that the application be dealt with without a hearing.

(Practice Form N244 may be used.)

2.2 On receipt of an application notice containing a request for a hearing the court will notify the applicant of the time and date for the hearing of the application.

2.3 On receipt of an application notice containing a request that the application be dealt with without a hearing, the application notice will be sent to a Master or District Judge so that he may decide whether the application is suitable for consideration without a hearing.

2.4 Where the Master or District Judge agrees that the application is suitable for consideration without a hearing, the court will so inform the applicant and the respondent and may give directions for the filing of evidence. (Rules 23.9 and 23.10 enable a party to apply for an order made without a hearing to be set aside or varied.)

2.5 Where the Master or District Judge does not agree that the application is suitable for consideration without a hearing, the court will notify the applicant and the respondent of the time, date and place for the hearing of the application and may at the same time give directions as to the filing of evidence.

2.6 If the application is intended to be made to a judge, the application notice should so state. In that case, paragraphs 2.3, 2.4 and 2.5 will apply as though references to the Master or District Judge were references to a judge.

2.7 Every application should be made as soon as it becomes apparent that it is necessary or desirable to make it.

2.8 Applications should wherever possible be made so that they can be considered at any other hearing for which a date has already been fixed or for which a date is about to be fixed. This is particularly so in relation to case management conferences, allocation and listing hearings and pre-trial reviews fixed by the court.

2.9 The parties must anticipate that at any hearing the court may wish to review the conduct of the case as a whole and give any necessary case management directions. They should be ready to assist the court in doing so and to answer questions the court may ask for this purpose.

2.10 Where a date for a hearing has been fixed and a party wishes to make an application at that hearing but he does not have sufficient time to serve an application notice he should inform the other party and the court (if possible in writing) as soon as he can of the nature of the application and the reason for it. He should then make the application orally at the hearing.

Amendments—CPR Updates 40, 69.

Applications without service of application notice

3 An application may be made without serving an application notice only:

(1) where there is exceptional urgency,
(2) where the overriding objective is best furthered by doing so,
(3) by consent of all parties,
(4) with the permission of the court,
(5) where paragraph 2.10 above applies, or
(6) where a court order, rule or practice direction permits.

Giving notice of an application

4.1 Unless the court otherwise directs or paragraph 3 or paragraph 4.1A of this practice direction applies the application notice must be served as soon as practicable after it has been issued and, if there is to be a hearing, at least 3 days before the hearing date (rule 23.7(1)(b)).

4.1A Where there is to be a telephone hearing the application notice must be served as soon as practicable after it has been issued and in any event at least 5 days before the date of the hearing.

4.2 Where an application notice should be served but there is not sufficient time to do so, informal notification of the application should be given unless the circumstances of the application require secrecy.

(Rule 2.8 explains how to calculate periods of time expressed in terms of days.)

Amendments—CPR Update 51.

Pre-action applications

5 All applications made before a claim is commenced should be made under Part 23 of the Civil Procedure Rules. Attention is drawn in particular to rule 23.2(4) and (4A).

Amendments—CPR Update 69.

County Court Money Claims Centre

5A.1 If the claim is started in the County Court Money Claims Centre, an application made after a claim has been started must be made to the County Court Money Claims Centre or County Court hearing centre where the claim is being dealt with.

5A.2 A District Judge may –

(a) consider the application without a hearing; or
(b) direct that the application should be transferred to a County Court hearing centre.

Amendments—CPR Update 69.

PART III

Telephone hearings

Interpretation

6.1 In this paragraph –

(a) 'designated legal representative' means the applicant's legal representative (if any), or the legal representative of such other party as the court directs to arrange the telephone hearing; and

(b) 'telephone conference enabled court' means-
  (i) a district registry of the High Court; or
  (ii) a County Court hearing centre,

in which telephone conferencing facilities are available.

When a hearing is to be conducted by telephone

6.2 Subject to paragraph 6.3, at a telephone conference enabled court the following hearings will be conducted by telephone unless the court otherwise orders –

(a) allocation hearings;
(b) listing hearings; and
(c) interim applications, case management conferences and pre-trial reviews with a time estimate of no more than one hour.

6.3 Paragraph 6.2 does not apply where –

(a) the hearing is of an application made without notice to the other party;
(b) all the parties are unrepresented; or
(c) more than four parties wish to make representations at the hearing (for this purpose where two or more parties are represented by the same person, they are to be treated as one party).

6.4 A request for a direction that a hearing under paragraph 6.2 should not be conducted by telephone –

(a) must be made at least 7 days before the hearing or such shorter time as the court may permit; and
(b) may be made by letter,

and the court shall determine such request without requiring the attendance of the parties.

6.5 The court may order that an application, or part of an application, to which paragraph 6.2 does not apply be dealt with by a telephone hearing. The court may make such order –

(a) of its own initiative; or
(b) at the request of the parties.

6.6 The applicant should indicate on his application notice if he seeks a court order under paragraph 6.5. Where he has not done so but nevertheless wishes to seek an order, the request should be made as early as possible.

6.7 An order under paragraph 6.5 will not normally be made unless every party entitled to be given notice of the application and to be heard at the hearing has consented to the order.

6.8 If the court makes an order under paragraph 6.5 it will give any directions necessary for the telephone hearing.

Conduct of the telephone hearing

6.9 No party, or representative of a party, to an application being heard by telephone may attend the judge in person while the application is being heard unless every other party to the application has agreed that he may do so.

6.10 If an application is to be heard by telephone the following directions will apply, subject to any direction to the contrary –

(1) The designated legal representative is responsible for arranging the telephone

conference for precisely the time fixed by the court. The telecommunications provider used must be one on the approved panel of service providers (see Her Majesty's Courts and Tribunals Service website).

(2) The designated legal representative must tell the operator the telephone numbers of all those participating in the conference call and the sequence in which they are to be called.

(3) It is the responsibility of the designated legal representative to ascertain from all the other parties whether they have instructed counsel and, if so, the identity of counsel, and whether the legal representative and counsel will be on the same or different telephone numbers.

(4) The sequence in which they are to be called will be –

(a) the designated legal representative and (if on a different number) his counsel;

(b) the legal representative (and counsel) for all other parties; and

(c) the judge.

(5) Each speaker is to remain on the line after being called by the operator setting up the conference call. The call shall be connected at least ten minutes before the time fixed for the hearing.

(6) When the judge has been connected the designated legal representative (or his counsel) will introduce the parties in the usual way.

(7) If the use of a 'speakerphone' by any party causes the judge or any other party any difficulty in hearing what is said the judge may require that party to use a hand held telephone.

(8) The telephone charges debited to the account of the party initiating the conference call will be treated as part of the costs of the application.

Documents

6.11 Where a document is required to be filed and served the party or the designated legal representative must do so no later than 4pm at least 2 days before the hearing.

6.12 A case summary and draft order must be filed and served in –

(a) multi-track cases; and

(b) small and fast track cases if the court so directs.

6.13 Any other document upon which a party seeks to rely must be filed and served in accordance with the period specified in paragraph 6.11.

(Rule 2.8 explains how to calculate period of time expressed in terms of days.)

Amendments—CPR Updates 45, 51, 58, 69.

Video conferencing

7 Where the parties to a matter wish to use video conferencing facilities, and those facilities are available in the relevant court, they should apply to the Master or District Judge for directions.

Amendments—CPR Updates 38, 69.

Note of proceedings

8 The procedural judge should keep, either by way of a note or a tape recording, brief details of all proceedings before him, including the dates of the proceedings and a short statement of the decision taken at each hearing.

Evidence

9.1 The requirement for evidence in certain types of applications is set out in some of the rules and practice directions. Where there is no specific requirement to provide evidence it should be borne in mind that, as a practical matter, the court will often need to be satisfied by evidence of the facts that are relied on in support of or for opposing the application.

9.2 The court may give directions for the filing of evidence in support of or opposing a particular application. The court may also give directions for the filing of evidence in relation to any hearing that it fixes on its own initiative. The directions may specify the form that evidence is to take and when it is to be served.

9.3 Where it is intended to rely on evidence which is not contained in the application itself, the evidence, if it has not already been served, should be served with the application.

9.4 Where a respondent to an application wishes to rely on evidence which has not yet been served he should serve it as soon as possible and in any event in accordance with any directions the court may have given.

9.5 If it is necessary for the applicant to serve any evidence in reply it should be served as soon as possible and in any event in accordance with any directions the court may have given.

9.6 Evidence must be filed with the court as well as served on the parties. Exhibits should not be filed unless the court otherwise directs.

9.7 The contents of an application notice may be used as evidence (otherwise than at trial) provided the contents have been verified by a statement of truth[1].

1 See Part 22.

Amendments—CPR Update 1.

Consent orders

10.1 Rule 40.6 sets out the circumstances where an agreed judgment or order may be entered and sealed.

10.2 Where all parties affected by an order have written to the court consenting to the making of the order a draft of which has been filed with the court, the court will treat the draft as having been signed in accordance with rule 40.6(7).

10.3 Where a consent order is made by a judge, the order must be drawn so that the judge's name and judicial title can be inserted.

10.4 The parties to an application for a consent order must ensure that they provide the court with any material it needs to be satisfied that it is appropriate to make the order. Subject to any rule or practice direction a letter will generally be acceptable for this purpose.

10.5 Where a judgment or order has been agreed in respect of an application or claim where a hearing date has been fixed, the parties must inform the court immediately. (note that parties are reminded that under rules 28.4 and 29.5 the case management timetable cannot be varied by written agreement of the parties.)

Amendments—CPR Update 88.

Other applications considered without a hearing

11.1 Where rule 23.8(b) applies the parties should so inform the court in writing and each should confirm that all evidence and other material on which he relies has been disclosed to the other parties to the application.

11.2 Where rule 23.8(c) applies the court will treat the application as if it were proposing to make an order on its own initiative.

Applications to stay claim where related criminal proceedings

11A.1 An application for the stay of civil proceedings pending the determination of related criminal proceedings may be made by any party to the civil proceedings or by the prosecutor or any defendant in the criminal proceedings.

11A.2 Every party to the civil proceedings must, unless he is the applicant, be made a respondent to the application.

11A.3 The evidence in support of the application must contain an estimate of the expected duration of the stay and must identify the respects in which the continuance of the civil proceedings may prejudice the criminal trial.

11A.4 In order to make an application under paragraph 11A.1, it is not necessary for the prosecutor or defendant in the criminal proceedings to be joined as a party to the civil proceedings.

Amendments—CPR Update 22.

Miscellaneous

12.1 Except in the most simple application the applicant should bring to any hearing a draft of the order sought. If the case is proceeding in the Royal Courts of Justice and the order is unusually long or complex it should also be supplied on disk for use by the court office.

12.2 Where rule 23.11 applies, the power to re-list the application in rule 23.11(2) is in addition to any other powers of the court with regard to the order (for example to set aside, vary, discharge or suspend the order).

Amendments—CPR Updates 10, 29.

Costs

13.1 Attention is drawn to Practice Directions 44 to 48 on costs and, in particular, to Subsections 8 and 9 of Practice Direction 44 which relate to the court's power to make a summary assessment of costs.

13.2 Attention is also drawn to rule 44.10(1) which provides that if an order makes no mention of costs, none are payable in respect of the proceedings to which it relates.

Amendments—CPR Update 66.

PART III

Practice Direction 23B – Applications under Particular Statutes

This Practice Direction supplements CPR Part 23

Applications under Part III of the Family Law Reform Act 1969 for use of scientific tests to determine parentage

1.1 In this section –

(1) 'the Act' means the Family Law Reform Act 1969;

(2) 'direction' means a direction under section 20(1) of the Act made in any proceedings in which a person's parentage falls to be determined;

(3) 'responsible adult' means –

  (a) in relation to a person under 16 to whom sub-paragraph (b) does not apply, the person having care and control of him;

  (b) in relation to a person who lacks capacity (within the meaning of the Mental Capacity Act 2005) to give his consent to tests –

    (i) a person having power under that Act to give consent on his behalf; or

    (ii) if there is no such person, the person with whom he resides or in whose care he is.

(4) 'samples' means bodily samples within the meaning of section 25 of the Act; and

(5) 'tests' means scientific tests within the meaning of section 25 of the Act.

1.2 Where an application is made for a direction in respect of a person who either –

(a) is under 16; or

(b) lacks capacity (within the meaning of the Mental Capacity Act 2005) to give his consent to the tests,

the application notice must state the name and address of the responsible adult.

1.3 Unless the court orders otherwise –

(1) the court will serve a copy of the application notice on every party to the proceedings other than the applicant; and
(2) the applicant must serve a copy of the application notice personally on any other person who would be directed to give samples and, where paragraph 1.2 applies, on the responsible adult.

1.4 Unless the court orders otherwise, where the court gives a direction –

(1) the court will serve a copy of the direction on every party to the proceedings;
(2) the applicant must serve a copy of the direction personally on any other person directed to give samples and, where paragraph 1.2 applies, on the responsible adult; and
(3) further consideration of the proceedings shall be adjourned until the court receives a report of the tests carried out or samples taken.

1.5 When the court receives the report of the tests carried out or samples taken, the court officer shall send a copy of the report to –

(1) every party to the proceedings;
(2) the responsible adult where paragraph 1.2 applies; and
(3) every other person directed to give samples.

Amendments—CPR Update 45.

★★★★

PART 25
INTERIM REMEDIES AND SECURITY FOR COSTS

CONTENTS OF THIS PART

Rule		Page
25.1	Orders for interim remedies	2086
25.2	Time when an order for an interim remedy may be made	2088
25.3	How to apply for an interim remedy	2088
	Practice Direction 25A – Interim Injunctions	2088

25.1 Orders for interim remedies

(1) The court may grant the following interim remedies –

(a) an interim injunction(GL);
(b) an interim declaration;
(c) an order –
  (i) for the detention, custody or preservation of relevant property;
  (ii) for the inspection of relevant property;
  (iii) for the taking of a sample of relevant property;
  (iv) for the carrying out of an experiment on or with relevant property;
  (v) for the sale of relevant property which is of a perishable nature or which for any other good reason it is desirable to sell quickly; and
  (vi) for the payment of income from relevant property until a claim is decided;
(d) an order authorising a person to enter any land or building in the possession of a party to the proceedings for the purposes of carrying out an order under sub-paragraph (c);
(e) an order under section 4 of the Torts (Interference with Goods) Act 1977 to deliver up goods;
(f) an order (referred to as a 'freezing injunction') –
  (i) restraining a party from removing from the jurisdiction assets located there; or
  (ii) restraining a party from dealing with any assets whether located within the jurisdiction or not;

(g) an order directing a party to provide information about the location of relevant property or assets or to provide information about relevant property or assets which are or may be the subject of an application for a freezing injunction;

(h) an order (referred to as a 'search order') under section 7 of the Civil Procedure Act 1997 (order requiring a party to admit another party to premises for the purpose of preserving evidence etc);

(i) an order under section 33 of the Senior Courts Act 1981 or section 52 of the County Courts Act 1984 (order for disclosure of documents or inspection of property before a claim has been made);

(j) an order under section 34 of the Senior Courts Act 1981 or section 53 of the County Courts Act 1984 (order in certain proceedings for disclosure of documents or inspection of property against a non-party);

(k) an order (referred to as an order for interim payment) under rule 25.6 for payment by a defendant on account of any damages, debt or other sum (except costs) which the court may hold the defendant liable to pay;

(l) an order for a specified fund to be paid into court or otherwise secured, where there is a dispute over a party's right to the fund;

(m) an order permitting a party seeking to recover personal property to pay money into court pending the outcome of the proceedings and directing that, if he does so, the property shall be given up to him;

(n) an order directing a party to prepare and file accounts relating to the dispute;

(o) an order directing any account to be taken or inquiry to be made by the court; and

(p) an order under Article 9 of Council Directive (EC) 2004/48 on the enforcement of intellectual property rights (order in intellectual property proceedings making the continuation of an alleged infringement subject to the lodging of guarantees).

(Rule 34.2 provides for the court to issue a witness summons requiring a witness to produce documents to the court at the hearing or on such date as the court may direct)

(2) In paragraph (1)(c) and (g), 'relevant property' means property (including land) which is the subject of a claim or as to which any question may arise on a claim.

(3) The fact that a particular kind of interim remedy is not listed in paragraph (1) does not affect any power that the court may have to grant that remedy.

(4) The court may grant an interim remedy whether or not there has been a claim for a final remedy of that kind.

Amendments—SI 2002/2058; SI 2005/3515; CRA 2005, Sch 11, para 1(2).

Inherent jurisdiction—The court retains an inherent jurisdiction to grant an injunction (see SCA 1981 and, for example, *Shipman v Shipman* [1991] 1 FLR 250, FD, where the court granted an injunction in the inherent jurisdiction of the High Court. (In family proceedings such an application would be under FPR 2010, r 9.7 or Pt 20 (by the Pt 18 procedure).)

'interim declaration' (r 25.1(1)(b))—Crown Proceedings Act 1947 provides that an injunction does not lie against the Crown. The remedy is by seeking a declaration in the form of order in many judicial review proceedings, or where a government department is the defendant (see discussion of the declaration remedy in *Gillick v West Norfolk and Wisbech AHA* [1986] 1 FLR 224, HL).

'freezing injunction' (r 25.1(1)(f))—The term 'freezing injunction' refers to the *Mareva* order or injunction. This remains an inherent jurisdiction remedy. For further commentary see notes to SCA 1981, s 37.

Issue in High Court—All applications appropriate for issue only in the High Court will be so allocated in accordance with FC(CDB)R 2014, Sch 2, Table 3 (eg for a search order, for an application under HRA 1998 in respect of a judicial act and for a warrant for sequestration).

'search order' (r 25.1(1)(h))—The terminology for the former *Anton Piller* order has been statutorily defined (CPA 1997, s 7(1), set out in the notes under SCA 1981, s 37). This order was considered fully in *Imerman v Tchenguiz and Others* [2010] 2 FLR 814, CA (see further under FPR 2010, r 20.2). Alternatively, it may be appropriate to apply in a breach of confidence damages claim alongside family proceedings for an order to restrain removal of documents. In *L v L* [2007] 2 FLR 171, QBD, the documents comprised the hard drive from the husband's computer.

Impounding a party's passport—To impound a party's passport, application is under Pt 25. The Pt 23 application (on an urgent basis, as need be) is supported by an affidavit (PD25A, para 3.1) (and see further note under SCA 1981, s 19 and FPR 2010, Pt 20).

PART III

25.2 Time when an order for an interim remedy may be made

(1) An order for an interim remedy may be made at any time, including –

(a) before proceedings are started; and
(b) after judgment has been given.

(Rule 7.2 provides that proceedings are started when the court issues a claim form)

(2) However –

(a) paragraph (1) is subject to any rule, practice direction or other enactment which provides otherwise;
(b) the court may grant an interim remedy before a claim has been made only if –
  (i) the matter is urgent; or
  (ii) it is otherwise desirable to do so in the interests of justice; and
(c) unless the court otherwise orders, a defendant may not apply for any of the orders listed in rule 25.1(1) before he has filed either an acknowledgment of service or a defence.

(Part 10 provides for filing an acknowledgment of service and Part 15 for filing a defence)

(3) Where it grants an interim remedy before a claim has been commenced, the court should give directions requiring a claim to be commenced.

(4) In particular, the court need not direct that a claim be commenced where the application is made under section 33 of the Senior Courts Act 1981 or section 52 of the County Courts Act 1984 (order for disclosure, inspection etc before commencement of a claim).

Amendments—SI 2005/3515; CRA 2005, Sch 11, para 1(2).

25.3 How to apply for an interim remedy

(1) The court may grant an interim remedy on an application made without notice if it appears to the court that there are good reasons for not giving notice.

(2) An application for an interim remedy must be supported by evidence, unless the court orders otherwise.

(3) If the applicant makes an application without giving notice, the evidence in support of the application must state the reasons why notice has not been given.

(Part 3 lists general powers of the court)

(Part 23 contains general rules about making an application)

'why notice has not been given' (r 25.3(3))—See consideration of 'without notice applications' under FPR 2010, r 20.2.

★★★★

Practice Direction 25A – Interim Injunctions

This Practice Direction supplements CPR Part 25

Amendments—CPR Update 51.

Jurisdiction

1.1 High Court judges and any other judge duly authorised may grant 'search orders'[1] and 'freezing injunctions'[2].

1 Rule 25.1(1)(h).
2 Rule 25.1(1)(f).

1.2 In a case in the High Court, Masters and District Judges have the power to grant injunctions:

(1) by consent,
(2) in connection with charging orders and appointments of receivers,
(3) in aid of execution of judgments.

1.3 In any other case any judge who has jurisdiction to conduct the trial of the action has the power to grant an injunction in that action.

1.4 A Master or District Judge has the power to vary or discharge an injunction granted by any judge with the consent of all the parties.

Amendments—CPR Updates 22, 69.

Making an application

2.1 The application notice must state:

(1) the order sought, and
(2) the date, time and place of the hearing.

2.2 The application notice and evidence in support must be served as soon as practicable after issue and in any event not less than 3 days before the court is due to hear the application[1].

1 Rule 23.7(1) and (2) and see rule 23.7(4) (short service).

2.3 Where the court is to serve, sufficient copies of the application notice and evidence in support for the court and for each respondent should be filed for issue and service.

2.4 Whenever possible a draft of the order sought should be filed with the application notice and a disk containing the draft should also be available to the court in a format compatible with the word processing software used by the court. This will enable the court officer to arrange for any amendments to be incorporated and for the speedy preparation and sealing of the order.

Amendments—CPR Update 26.

Evidence

3.1 Applications for search orders and freezing injunctions must be supported by affidavit evidence.

3.2 Applications for other interim injunctions must be supported by evidence set out in either:

(1) a witness statement, or
(2) a statement of case provided that it is verified by a statement of truth[1], or
(3) the application provided that it is verified by a statement of truth,

unless the court, an Act, a rule or a practice direction requires evidence by affidavit.

1 See Part 22.

3.3 The evidence must set out the facts on which the applicant relies for the claim being made against the respondent, including all material facts of which the court should be made aware.

3.4 Where an application is made without notice to the respondent, the evidence must also set out why notice was not given.

(See Part 32 and Practice Direction 32 for information about evidence.)

Amendments—CPR Update 51.

Urgent applications and applications without notice

4.1 These fall into two categories:

(1) applications where a claim form has already been issued, and
(2) applications where a claim form has not yet been issued,

and, in both cases, where notice of the application has not been given to the respondent.

4.2 These applications are normally dealt with at a court hearing but cases of extreme urgency may be dealt with by telephone.

4.3 Applications dealt with at a court hearing after issue of a claim form:

(1) the application notice, evidence in support and a draft order (as in 2.4 above) should be filed with the court 2 hours before the hearing wherever possible,
(2) if an application is made before the application notice has been issued, a draft order (as

PART III

in 2.4 above) should be provided at the hearing, and the application notice and evidence in support must be filed with the court on the same or next working day or as ordered by the court, and

(3) except in cases where secrecy is essential, the applicant should take steps to notify the respondent informally of the application.

4.4 Applications made before the issue of a claim form:

(1) in addition to the provisions set out at 4.3 above, unless the court orders otherwise, either the applicant must undertake to the court to issue a claim form immediately or the court will give directions for the commencement of the claim[1],

(2) where possible the claim form should be served with the order for the injunction,

(3) an order made before the issue of a claim form should state in the title after the names of the applicant and respondent 'the Claimant and Defendant in an Intended Action'.

1 Rule 25.2(3).

4.5 Applications made by telephone:

(1) where it is not possible to arrange a hearing, application can be made between 10.00 am and 5.00 pm weekdays by telephoning the Royal Courts of Justice on 020 7947 6000 and asking to be put in contact with a High Court judge of the appropriate Division available to deal with an emergency application in a High Court matter. The appropriate district registry may also be contacted by telephone. In County Court proceedings, the appropriate County Court hearing centre should be contacted,

(2) where an application is made outside those hours the applicant should either –

(a) telephone the Royal Courts of Justice on 020 7947 6000 where he will be put in contact with the clerk to the appropriate Duty judge in the High Court (or the appropriate area Circuit Judge where known), or

(b) the Urgent Court Business Officer of the appropriate Circuit who will contact the local Duty judge,

(3) where the facility is available it is likely that the judge will require a draft order to be faxed to him,

(4) the application notice and evidence in support must be filed with the court on the same or next working day or as ordered, together with two copies of the order for sealing,

(5) injunctions will be heard by telephone only where the applicant is acting by counsel or solicitors.

Amendments—CPR Updates 2, 27, 69.

Orders for injunctions

5.1 Any order for an injunction, unless the court orders otherwise, must contain:

(1) subject to paragraph 5.3, an undertaking by the applicant to the court to pay any damages which the respondent sustains which the court considers the applicant should pay.

(2) if made without notice to any other party, an undertaking by the applicant to the court to serve on the respondent the application notice, evidence in support and any order made as soon as practicable,

(3) if made without notice to any other party, a return date for a further hearing at which the other party can be present,

(4) if made before filing the application notice, an undertaking to file and pay the appropriate fee on the same or next working day, and

(5) if made before issue of a claim form –

(a) an undertaking to issue and pay the appropriate fee on the same or next working day, or

(b) directions for the commencement of the claim.

5.2 Subject to paragraph 5.3, when the court makes an order for an injunction, it should consider whether to require an undertaking by the applicant to pay any damages sustained by a person other than the respondent, including another party to the proceedings or any other person who may suffer loss as a consequence of the order.

5.3 (1) If in an Aarhus Convention claim to which rules 45.43 to 45.45 apply the court is satisfied that an injunction is necessary to prevent significant environmental damage and to preserve the factual basis of the proceedings, the court will, in considering whether to require an undertaking by the applicant to pay any damages which the respondent or any other person may sustain as a result, and the terms of any such undertaking –
  - (a) have particular regard to the need for the terms of the order overall not to be such as would make continuing with the claim prohibitively expensive for the applicant; and
  - (b) make such directions as are necessary to ensure that the case is heard promptly.

(2) In this paragraph
  - (a) 'Aarhus Convention claim' has the same meaning as in rule 45.41(2)(a); and
  - (b) 'member of the public' is to be construed in accordance with rule 45.41(2)(b).

(3) Proceedings are 'prohibitively expensive' if their likely costs, including any court fees payable by the applicant and the amount of any cross-undertaking in damages, and having regard to any limit under Part 45 on a party's maximum costs liability, either –
  - (a) exceed the financial resources of the applicant; or
  - (b) are objectively unreasonable having regard to the factors set out in rule 45.44(3)(b).

(4) When a court considers the financial resources of the applicant, it will have regard to any financial support which any person has provided or is likely to provide to the applicant.

5.4 An order for an injunction made in the presence of all parties to be bound by it or made at a hearing of which they have had notice, may state that it is effective until trial or further order.

5.5 Any order for an injunction must set out clearly what the respondent must do or not do.

Amendments—CPR Updates 42, 60, 88.

Freezing injunctions

Orders to restrain disposal of assets worldwide and within England and Wales

6.1 An example of a Freezing Injunction is annexed to this practice direction.

6.2 This example may be modified as appropriate in any particular case. In particular, the court may, if it considers it appropriate, require the applicant's solicitors, as well as the applicant, to give undertakings.

Amendments—CPR Update 27.

Search orders

Amendments—CPR Update 40.

7.1 The following provisions apply to search orders in addition to those listed above.

7.2 **The Supervising Solicitor**

The supervising solicitor must be experienced in the operation of search orders. A supervising solicitor may be contacted either through the Law Society or, for the London area, through the London Solicitors Litigation Association.

7.3 **Evidence:**

(1) the affidavit must state the name, firm and its address, and experience of the supervising solicitor, also the address of the premises and whether it is a private or business address, and

(2) the affidavit must disclose very fully the reason the order is sought, including the probability that relevant material would disappear if the order were not made.

7.4 **Service:**

(1) the order must be served personally by the supervising solicitor, unless the court otherwise orders, and must be accompanied by the evidence in support and any documents capable of being copied,

(2) confidential exhibits need not be served but they must be made available for inspection by the respondent in the presence of the applicant's solicitors while the order is carried out and afterwards be retained by the respondent's solicitors on their undertaking not to permit the respondent –

(a) to see them or copies of them except in their presence, and

(b) to make or take away any note or record of them,

(3) the supervising solicitor may be accompanied only by the persons mentioned in the order,

(4) the Supervising Solicitor must explain the terms and effect of the order to the respondent in everyday language and advise him –

(a) of his right to take legal advice and to apply to vary or discharge the order; and

(b) that he may be entitled to avail himself of –

(i) legal professional privilege; and

(ii) the privilege against self-incrimination.

(5) where the supervising solicitor is a man and the respondent is likely to be an unaccompanied woman, at least one other person named in the order must be a woman and must accompany the supervising solicitor, and

(6) the order may only be served between 9.30 am and 5.30 pm Monday to Friday unless the court otherwise orders.

7.5 **Search and custody of materials:**

(1) no material shall be removed unless clearly covered by the terms of the order,

(2) the premises must not be searched and no items shall be removed from them except in the presence of the respondent or a person who appears to be a responsible employee of the respondent,

(3) where copies of documents are sought, the documents should be retained for no more than 2 days before return to the owner,

(4) where material in dispute is removed pending trial, the applicant's solicitors should place it in the custody of the respondent's solicitors on their undertaking to retain it in safekeeping and to produce it to the court when required,

(5) in appropriate cases the applicant should insure the material retained in the respondent's solicitors' custody,

(6) the supervising solicitor must make a list of all material removed from the premises and supply a copy of the list to the respondent,

(7) no material shall be removed from the premises until the respondent has had reasonable time to check the list,

(8) if any of the listed items exists only in computer readable form, the respondent must immediately give the applicant's solicitors effective access to the computers, with all necessary passwords, to enable them to be searched, and cause the listed items to be printed out,

(9) the applicant must take all reasonable steps to ensure that no damage is done to any computer or data,

(10) the applicant and his representatives may not themselves search the respondent's computers unless they have sufficient expertise to do so without damaging the respondent's system,

(11) the supervising solicitor shall provide a report on the carrying out of the order to the applicant's solicitors,

(12) as soon as the report is received the applicant's solicitors shall –

(a) serve a copy of it on the respondent, and

(b) file a copy of it with the court, and

(13) where the supervising solicitor is satisfied that full compliance with paragraph 7.5(7) and

(8) above is impracticable, he may permit the search to proceed and items to be removed without compliance with the impracticable requirements.

7.6 The Supervising Solicitor must not be an employee or member of the applicant's firm of solicitors.

7.7 If the court orders that the order need not be served by the Supervising Solicitor, the reason for so ordering must be set out in the order.

7.8 The search order must not be carried out at the same time as a police search warrant.

7.9 There is no privilege against self-incrimination in –

(1) Intellectual Property cases in respect of a 'related offence' or for the recovery of a 'related penalty' as defined in section 72 Senior Courts Act 1981;
(2) proceedings for the recovery or administration of any property, for the execution of a trust or for an account of any property or dealings with property, in relation to –
  (a) an offence under the Theft Act 1968 (see section 31 of the Theft Act 1968); or
  (b) an offence under the Fraud Act 2006 (see section 13 of the Fraud Act 2006) or a related offence within the meaning given by section 13(4) of that Act – that is, conspiracy to defraud or any other offence involving any form of fraudulent conduct or purpose; or
(3) proceedings in which a court is hearing an application for an order under Part IV or Part V of the Children Act 1989 (see section 98 Children Act 1989).

However, the privilege may still be claimed in relation to material or information required to be disclosed by an order, as regards potential criminal proceedings outside those statutory provisions.

7.10 Applications in Intellectual Property cases should be made in the Chancery Division.

7.11 An example of a Search Order is annexed to this practice direction. This example may be modified as appropriate in any particular case.

Amendments—CPR Update 27, 40, 44, 50.

Delivery-up orders

8.1 The following provisions apply to orders, other than search orders, for delivery up or preservation of evidence or property where it is likely that such an order will be executed at the premises of the respondent or a third party.

8.2 In such cases the court shall consider whether to include in the order for the benefit or protection of the parties similar provisions to those specified above in relation to injunctions and search orders.

Injunctions against third parties

9.1 The following provisions apply to orders which will affect a person other than the applicant or respondent, who:

(1) did not attend the hearing at which the order was made; and
(2) is served with the order.

9.2 Where such a person served with the order requests –

(1) a copy of any materials read by the judge, including material prepared after the hearing at the direction of the judge or in compliance with the order; or
(2) a note of the hearing,

the applicant, or his legal representative, must comply promptly with the request, unless the court orders otherwise.

Amendments—CPR Update 40.

ANNEX

FREEZING INJUNCTION **IN THE HIGH COURT OF JUSTICE**

[ ] DIVISION

Before The Honourable Mr Justice [ ]

Claim No

Dated

Applicant

Seal

Respondent

Name, address and reference of respondent

IF YOU [ ][1] DISOBEY THIS ORDER YOU MAY BE HELD TO BE IN CONTEMPT OF COURT AND MAY BE IMPRISONED, FINED OR HAVE YOUR ASSETS SEIZED.

ANY OTHER PERSON WHO KNOWS OF THIS ORDER AND DOES ANYTHING WHICH HELPS OR PERMITS THE RESPONDENT TO BREACH THE TERMS OF THIS ORDER MAY ALSO BE HELD TO BE IN CONTEMPT OF COURT AND MAY BE IMPRISONED, FINED OR HAVE THEIR ASSETS SEIZED.

1 Insert name of Respondent.

This order

1 This is a Freezing Injunction made against [ ] ('the Respondent') on [ ] by Mr Justice [ ] on the application of [ ] ('the Applicant'). The Judge read the Affidavits listed in Schedule A and accepted the undertakings set out in Schedule B at the end of this Order.

2 This order was made at a hearing without notice to the Respondent. The Respondent has a right to apply to the court to vary or discharge the order – see paragraph 13 below.

3 There will be a further hearing in respect of this order on [ ] ('the return date').

4 If there is more than one Respondent –

(a) unless otherwise stated, references in this order to 'the Respondent' mean both or all of them; and

(b) this order is effective against any Respondent on whom it is served or who is given notice of it.

Freezing injunction

[*For injunction limited to assets in England and Wales*]

5 Until the return date or further order of the court, the Respondent must not remove from England and Wales or in any way dispose of, deal with or diminish the value of any of his assets which are in England and Wales up to the value of £ .

[*For worldwide injunction*]

5 Until the return date or further order of the court, the Respondent must not –

(1) remove from England and Wales any of his assets which are in England and Wales up to the value of £ ; or

(2) in any way dispose of, deal with or diminish the value of any of his assets whether they are in or outside England and Wales up to the same value.

[*For either form of injunction*]

6 Paragraph 5 applies to all the Respondent's assets whether or not they are in his own name and whether they are solely or jointly owned. For the purpose of this order the Respondent's assets include any asset which he has the power, directly or indirectly, to dispose of or deal with as if it were his own. The Respondent is to be regarded as having such power if a third party holds or controls the asset in accordance with his direct or indirect instructions.

7 This prohibition includes the following assets in particular –

(a) the property known as [*title/address*] or the net sale money after payment of any mortgages if it has been sold;

(b) the property and assets of the Respondent's business [known as [*name*]] [carried on at [*address*]] or the sale money if any of them have been sold; and

(c) any money standing to the credit of any bank account including the amount of any cheque drawn on such account which has not been cleared.

[*For injunction limited to assets in England and Wales*]

8 If the total value free of charges or other securities ('unencumbered value') of the Respondent's assets in England and Wales exceeds £ , the Respondent may remove any of those assets from England and Wales or may dispose of or deal with them so long as the total unencumbered value of his assets still in England and Wales remains above £ .

[*For worldwide injunction*]

8 (1) If the total value free of charges or other securities ('unencumbered value') of the Respondent's assets in England and Wales exceeds £ , the Respondent may remove any of those assets from England and Wales or may dispose of or deal with them so long as the total unencumbered value of the Respondent's assets still in England and Wales remains above £ .

(2) If the total unencumbered value of the Respondent's assets in England and Wales does not exceed £ , the Respondent must not remove any of those assets from England and Wales and must not dispose of or deal with any of them. If the Respondent has other assets outside England and Wales, he may dispose of or deal with those assets outside England and Wales so long as the total unencumbered value of all his assets whether in or outside England and Wales remains above £ .

Provision of information

9 (1) Unless paragraph (2) applies, the Respondent must [immediately] [within hours of service of this order] and to the best of his ability inform the Applicant's solicitors of all his assets [in England and Wales] [worldwide] [exceeding £ in value] whether in his own name or not and whether solely or jointly owned, giving the value, location and details of all such assets.

(2) If the provision of any of this information is likely to incriminate the Respondent, he may be entitled to refuse to provide it, but is recommended to take legal advice before refusing to provide the information. Wrongful refusal to provide the information is contempt of court and may render the Respondent liable to be imprisoned, fined or have his assets seized.

10 Within [ ] working days after being served with this order, the Respondent must swear and serve on the Applicant's solicitors an affidavit setting out the above information.

Exceptions to this order

11 (1) This order does not prohibit the Respondent from spending £ a week towards his ordinary living expenses and also £ [or a reasonable sum] on legal advice and representation. [But before spending any money the Respondent must tell the Applicant's legal representatives where the money is to come from.]

[(2) This order does not prohibit the Respondent from dealing with or disposing of any of his assets in the ordinary and proper course of business.]

(3) The Respondent may agree with the Applicant's legal representatives that the above

spending limits should be increased or that this order should be varied in any other respect, but any agreement must be in writing.

(4) The order will cease to have effect if the Respondent –

(a) provides security by paying the sum of £ into court, to be held to the order of the court; or

(b) makes provision for security in that sum by another method agreed with the Applicant's legal representatives.

Costs

12 The costs of this application are reserved to the judge hearing the application on the return date.

Variation or discharge of this order

13 Anyone served with or notified of this order may apply to the court at any time to vary or discharge this order (or so much of it as affects that person), but they must first inform the Applicant's solicitors. If any evidence is to be relied upon in support of the application, the substance of it must be communicated in writing to the Applicant's solicitors in advance.

Interpretation of this order

14 A Respondent who is an individual who is ordered not to do something must not do it himself or in any other way. He must not do it through others acting on his behalf or on his instructions or with his encouragement.

15 A Respondent which is not an individual which is ordered not to do something must not do it itself or by its directors, officers, partners, employees or agents or in any other way.

Parties other than the applicant and respondent

16 **Effect of this order**

It is a contempt of court for any person notified of this order knowingly to assist in or permit a breach of this order. Any person doing so may be imprisoned, fined or have their assets seized.

17 **Set off by banks**

This injunction does not prevent any bank from exercising any right of set off it may have in respect of any facility which it gave to the respondent before it was notified of this order.

18 **Withdrawals by the Respondent**

No bank need enquire as to the application or proposed application of any money withdrawn by the Respondent if the withdrawal appears to be permitted by this order.

[*For worldwide injunction*]

19 **Persons outside England and Wales**

(1) Except as provided in paragraph (2) below, the terms of this order do not affect or concern anyone outside the jurisdiction of this court.

(2) The terms of this order will affect the following persons in a country or state outside the jurisdiction of this court –

(a) the Respondent or his officer or agent appointed by power of attorney;

(b) any person who –

(i) is subject to the jurisdiction of this court;

(ii) has been given written notice of this order at his residence or place of business within the jurisdiction of this court; and

(iii) is able to prevent acts or omissions outside the jurisdiction of this court which constitute or assist in a breach of the terms of this order; and

(c) any other person, only to the extent that this order is declared enforceable by or is enforced by a court in that country or state.

[*For worldwide injunction*]

20 **Assets located outside England and Wales**

Nothing in this order shall, in respect of assets located outside England and Wales, prevent any third party from complying with –

(1) what it reasonably believes to be its obligations, contractual or otherwise, under the laws and obligations of the country or state in which those assets are situated or under the proper law of any contract between itself and the Respondent; and

(2) any orders of the courts of that country or state, provided that reasonable notice of any application for such an order is given to the Applicant's solicitors.

Communications with the court

All communications to the court about this order should be sent to –

[*Insert the address and telephone number of the appropriate Court Office*]

If the order is made at the Royal Courts of Justice, communications should be addressed as follows –

Where the order is made in the Chancery Division

Room TM 5.07, Royal Courts of Justice, Strand, London WC2A 2LL quoting the case number. The telephone number is 020 7947 6322.

Where the order is made in the Queen's Bench Division

Room WG034, Royal Courts of Justice, Strand, London WC2A 2LL quoting the case number. The telephone number is 0207 947 6009.

Where the order is made in the Commercial Court

Room E201, Royal Courts of Justice, Strand, London WC2A 2LL quoting the case number. The telephone number is 0207 947 6826.

The offices are open between 10 am and 4.30 pm Monday to Friday.

Amendments—CPR Updates 40, 42, 51.

SCHEDULE A

Affidavits

The Applicant relied on the following affidavits –

[*name*]	[*number of affidavit*]	[*date sworn*]	[*filed on behalf of*]
(1)			
(2)			

SCHEDULE B

Undertakings given to the court by the applicant

(1) If the court later finds that this order has caused loss to the Respondent, and decides that the Respondent should be compensated for that loss, the Applicant will comply with any order the court may make.

[(2) The Applicant will –

(a) on or before [*date*] cause a written guarantee in the sum of £ to be issued from a bank with a place of business within England or Wales, in respect of any order the court may make pursuant to paragraph (1) above; and

(b) immediately upon issue of the guarantee, cause a copy of it to be served on the Respondent.]

(3) As soon as practicable the Applicant will issue and serve a claim form [in the form of the draft produced to the court] [claiming the appropriate relief].

PART III

(4) The Applicant will [swear and file an affidavit] [cause an affidavit to be sworn and filed] [substantially in the terms of the draft affidavit produced to the court] [confirming the substance of what was said to the court by the Applicant's counsel/solicitors].

(5) The Applicant will serve upon the Respondent [together with this order] [as soon as practicable] –

(i) copies of the affidavits and exhibits containing the evidence relied upon by the Applicant, and any other documents provided to the court on the making of the application;
(ii) the claim form; and
(iii) an application notice for continuation of the order.

[(6) Anyone notified of this order will be given a copy of it by the Applicant's legal representatives.]

(7) The Applicant will pay the reasonable costs of anyone other than the Respondent which have been incurred as a result of this order including the costs of finding out whether that person holds any of the Respondent's assets and if the court later finds that this order has caused such person loss, and decides that such person should be compensated for that loss, the Applicant will comply with any order the court may make.

(8) If this order ceases to have effect (for example, if the Respondent provides security or the Applicant does not provide a bank guarantee as provided for above) the Applicant will immediately take all reasonable steps to inform in writing anyone to whom he has given notice of this order, or who he has reasonable grounds for supposing may act upon this order, that it has ceased to have effect.

[(9) The Applicant will not without the permission of the court use any information obtained as a result of this order for the purpose of any civil or criminal proceedings, either in England and Wales or in any other jurisdiction, other than this claim.]

[(10) The Applicant will not without the permission of the court seek to enforce this order in any country outside England and Wales [or seek an order of a similar nature including orders conferring a charge or other security against the Respondent or the Respondent's assets].]

Name and address of applicant's legal representatives

The Applicant's legal representatives are –

[*Name, address, reference, fax and telephone numbers both in and out of office hours and e-mail*]

SEARCH ORDER

IN THE HIGH COURT OF JUSTICE

[ ] DIVISION

Before The Honourable Mr Justice [ ]

Claim No

Dated

Applicant

Seal

Respondent

Name, address and reference of respondent

IF YOU [ ][1] DISOBEY THIS ORDER YOU MAY BE HELD TO BE IN CONTEMPT OF COURT AND MAY BE IMPRISONED, FINED OR HAVE YOUR ASSETS SEIZED.

ANY OTHER PERSON WHO KNOWS OF THIS ORDER AND DOES ANYTHING WHICH HELPS OR PERMITS THE RESPONDENT TO BREACH THE TERMS OF THIS ORDER MAY ALSO BE HELD TO BE IN CONTEMPT OF COURT AND MAY BE IMPRISONED, FINED OR HAVE THEIR ASSETS SEIZED.

1 Insert name of Respondent.

This order

1 This is a Search Order made against [ ] ('the Respondent') on [ ] by Mr Justice [ ] on the application of [ ] ('the Applicant'). The Judge read the Affidavits listed in Schedule F and accepted the undertakings set out in Schedules C, D and E at the end of this order.

2 This order was made at a hearing without notice to the Respondent. The Respondent has a right to apply to the court to vary or discharge the order – see paragraph 27 below.

3 There will be a further hearing in respect of this order on [ ] ('the return date').

4 If there is more than one Respondent –

(a) unless otherwise stated, references in this order to 'the Respondent' mean both or all of them; and
(b) this order is effective against any Respondent on whom it is served or who is given notice of it.

5 This order must be complied with by –

(a) the Respondent;
(b) any director, officer, partner or responsible employee of the Respondent; and
(c) if the Respondent is an individual, any other person having responsible control of the premises to be searched.

The search

6 The Respondent must permit the following persons[1] –

(a) [ ] ('the Supervising Solicitor');
(b) [ ], a solicitor in the firm of [ ], the Applicant's solicitors; and
(c) up to [ ] other persons[2] being [*their identity or capacity*] accompanying them,

(together 'the search party'), to enter the premises mentioned in Schedule A to this order and any other premises of the Respondent disclosed under paragraph 18 below and any vehicles under the Respondent's control on or around the premises ('the premises') so that they can search for, inspect, photograph or photocopy, and deliver into the safekeeping of the Applicant's solicitors all the documents and articles which are listed in Schedule B to this order ('the listed items').

7 Having permitted the search party to enter the premises, the Respondent must allow the search party to remain on the premises until the search is complete. In the event that it becomes necessary for any of those persons to leave the premises before the search is complete, the Respondent must allow them to re-enter the premises immediately upon their seeking re-entry on the same or the following day in order to complete the search.

1 Where the premises are likely to be occupied by an unaccompanied woman and the Supervising Solicitor is a man, at least one of the persons accompanying him should be a woman.
2 None of these persons should be people who could gain personally or commercially from anything they might read or see on the premises, unless their presence is essential.

Restrictions on search

8 This order may not be carried out at the same time as a police search warrant.

9 Before the Respondent allows anybody onto the premises to carry out this order, he is entitled to have the Supervising Solicitor explain to him what it means in everyday language.

PART III

10 The Respondent is entitled to seek legal advice and to ask the court to vary or discharge this order. Whilst doing so, he may ask the Supervising Solicitor to delay starting the search for up to 2 hours or such other longer period as the Supervising Solicitor may permit. However, the Respondent must –

(a) comply with the terms of paragraph 27 below;
(b) not disturb or remove any listed items; and
(c) permit the Supervising Solicitor to enter, but not start to search.

11 (1) Before permitting entry to the premises by any person other than the Supervising Solicitor, the Respondent may, for a short time (not to exceed two hours, unless the Supervising Solicitor agrees to a longer period) –
(a) gather together any documents he believes may be incriminating or privileged; and
(b) hand them to the Supervising Solicitor for him to assess whether they are incriminating or privileged as claimed.

(2) If the Supervising Solicitor decides that the Respondent is entitled to withhold production of any of the documents on the ground that they are privileged or incriminating, he will exclude them from the search, record them in a list for inclusion in his report and return them to the Respondent.

(3) If the Supervising Solicitor believes that the Respondent may be entitled to withhold production of the whole or any part of a document on the ground that it or part of it may be privileged or incriminating, or if the Respondent claims to be entitled to withhold production on those grounds, the Supervising Solicitor will exclude it from the search and retain it in his possession pending further order of the court.

12 If the Respondent wishes to take legal advice and gather documents as permitted, he must first inform the Supervising Solicitor and keep him informed of the steps being taken.

13 No item may be removed from the premises until a list of the items to be removed has been prepared, and a copy of the list has been supplied to the Respondent, and he has been given a reasonable opportunity to check the list.

14 The premises must not be searched, and items must not be removed from them, except in the presence of the Respondent.

15 If the Supervising Solicitor is satisfied that full compliance with paragraphs 13 or 14 is not practicable, he may permit the search to proceed and items to be removed without fully complying with them.

Delivery up of articles/documents

16 The Respondent must immediately hand over to the Applicant's solicitors any of the listed items, which are in his possession or under his control, save for any computer or hard disk integral to any computer. Any items the subject of a dispute as to whether they are listed items must immediately be handed over to the Supervising Solicitor for safe keeping pending resolution of the dispute or further order of the court.

17 The Respondent must immediately give the search party effective access to the computers on the premises, with all necessary passwords, to enable the computers to be searched. If they contain any listed items the Respondent must cause the listed items to be displayed so that they can be read and copied.[1] The Respondent must provide the Applicant's Solicitors with copies of all listed items contained in the computers. All reasonable steps shall be taken by the Applicant and the Applicant's solicitors to ensure that no damage is done to any computer or data. The Applicant and his representatives may not themselves search the Respondent's computers unless they have sufficient expertise to do so without damaging the Respondent's system.

1 If it is envisaged that the Respondent's computers are to be imaged (ie the hard drives are to be copied wholesale, thereby reproducing listed items and other items indiscriminately), special provision needs to be made and independent computer specialists need to be appointed, who should be required to give undertakings to the court.

Provision of information

18 The Respondent must immediately inform the Applicant's Solicitors (in the presence of the Supervising Solicitor) so far as he is aware –

- (a) where all the listed items are;
- (b) the name and address of everyone who has supplied him, or offered to supply him, with listed items;
- (c) the name and address of everyone to whom he has supplied, or offered to supply, listed items; and
- (d) full details of the dates and quantities of every such supply and offer.

19 Within [ ] working days after being served with this order the Respondent must swear and serve an affidavit setting out the above information[1].

1 The period should ordinarily be longer than the period in paragraph (2) of Schedule D, if any of the information is likely to be included in listed items taken away of which the Respondent does not have copies.

Prohibited acts

20 Except for the purpose of obtaining legal advice, the Respondent must not directly or indirectly inform anyone of these proceedings or of the contents of this order, or warn anyone that proceedings have been or may be brought against him by the Applicant until 4.30 p.m. on the return date or further order of the court.

21 Until 4.30 p.m. on the return date the Respondent must not destroy, tamper with, cancel or part with possession, power, custody or control of the listed items otherwise than in accordance with the terms of this order.

22 [Insert any negative injunctions]

23 [Insert any further order]

Costs

24 The costs of this application are reserved to the judge hearing the application on the return date.

Restrictions on service

25 This order may only be served between [ ] am/pm and [ ] am/pm [and on a weekday][1].

26 This order must be served by the Supervising Solicitor, and paragraph 6 of the order must be carried out in his presence and under his supervision.

1 Normally, the order should be served in the morning (not before 9.30 am) and on a weekday to enable the Respondent more readily to obtain legal advice.

Variation and discharge of this order

27 Anyone served with or notified of this order may apply to the court at any time to vary or discharge this order (or so much of it as affects that person), but they must first inform the Applicant's solicitors. If any evidence is to be relied upon in support of the application, the substance of it must be communicated in writing to the Applicant's solicitors in advance.

Interpretation of this order

28 Any requirement that something shall be done to or in the presence of the Respondent means –

- (a) if there is more than one Respondent, to or in the presence of any one of them; and
- (b) if a Respondent is not an individual, to or in the presence of a director, officer, partner or responsible employee.

29 A Respondent who is an individual who is ordered not to do something must not do it himself or in any other way. He must not do it through others acting on his behalf or on his instructions or with his encouragement.

30 A Respondent which is not an individual which is ordered not to do something must not do it itself or by its directors, officers, partners, employees or agents or in any other way.

Communications with the court

All communications to the court about this order should be sent to –

[*Insert the address and telephone number of the appropriate Court Office*]

If the order is made at the Royal Courts of Justice, communications should be addressed as follows –

Where the order is made in the Chancery Division

Room TM 5.07, Royal Courts of Justice, Strand, London WC2A 2LL quoting the case number. The telephone number is 020 7947 6322.

Where the order is made in the Queen's Bench Division

Room WG034, Royal Courts of Justice, Strand, London WC2A 2LL quoting the case number. The telephone number is 0207 947 6009.

Where the order is made in the Commercial Court

Room E201, Royal Courts of Justice, Strand, London WC2A 2LL quoting the case number. The telephone number is 0207 947 6826.

The offices are open between 10 am and 4.30 pm Monday to Friday.

Amendments—CPR Update 42.

SCHEDULE A

THE PREMISES

SCHEDULE B

THE LISTED ITEMS

SCHEDULE C

Undertakings given to the court by the applicant

(1) If the court later finds that this order or carrying it out has caused loss to the Respondent, and decides that the Respondent should be compensated for that loss, the Applicant will comply with any order the court may make. Further if the carrying out of this order has been in breach of the terms of this order or otherwise in a manner inconsistent with the Applicant's solicitors' duties as officers of the court, the Applicant will comply with any order for damages the court may make.

[(2) As soon as practicable the Applicant will issue a claim form [in the form of the draft produced to the court] [claiming the appropriate relief].]

(3) The Applicant will [swear and file an affidavit] [cause an affidavit to be sworn and filed] [substantially in the terms of the draft affidavit produced to the court] [confirming the substance of what was said to the court by the Applicant's counsel/solicitors].

(4) The Applicant will not, without the permission of the court, use any information or documents obtained as a result of carrying out this order nor inform anyone else of these proceedings except for the purposes of these proceedings (including adding further Respondents) or commencing civil proceedings in relation to the same or related subject matter to these proceedings until after the return date.

[(5) The Applicant will maintain pending further order the sum of £ [ ] in an account controlled by the Applicant's solicitors.]

[(6) The Applicant will insure the items removed from the premises.]

SCHEDULE D

Undertakings given by the applicant's solicitors

(1) The Applicant's solicitors will provide to the Supervising Solicitor for service on the Respondent –

(i) a service copy of this order;
(ii) the claim form (with defendant's response pack) or, if not issued, the draft produced to the court;
(iii) an application for hearing on the return date;
(iv) copies of the affidavits [*or draft affidavits*] and exhibits capable of being copied containing the evidence relied upon by the applicant;
(v) a note of any allegation of fact made orally to the court where such allegation is not contained in the affidavits or draft affidavits read by the judge; and
(vi) a copy of the skeleton argument produced to the court by the Applicant's [counsel/solicitors].

(2) The Applicants' solicitors will answer at once to the best of their ability any question whether a particular item is a listed item.

(3) Subject as provided below the Applicant's solicitors will retain in their own safe keeping all items obtained as a result of this order until the court directs otherwise.

(4) The Applicant's solicitors will return the originals of all documents obtained as a result of this order (except original documents which belong to the Applicant) as soon as possible and in any event within [two] working days of their removal.

SCHEDULE E

Undertakings given by the supervising solicitor

(1) The Supervising Solicitor will use his best endeavours to serve this order upon the Respondent and at the same time to serve upon the Respondent the other documents required to be served and referred to in paragraph (1) of Schedule D.

(2) The Supervising Solicitor will offer to explain to the person served with the order its meaning and effect fairly and in everyday language, and to inform him of his right to take legal advice (including an explanation that the Respondent may be entitled to avail himself of the privilege against self-incrimination and legal professional privilege) and to apply to vary or discharge this order as mentioned in paragraph 27 above.

(3) The Supervising Solicitor will retain in the safe keeping of his firm all items retained by him as a result of this order until the court directs otherwise.

(4) Unless and until the court otherwise orders, or unless otherwise necessary to comply with any duty to the court pursuant to this order, the Supervising Solicitor shall not disclose to any person any information relating to those items, and shall keep the existence of such items confidential.

(5) Within [48] hours of completion of the search the Supervising Solicitor will make and provide to the Applicant's solicitors, the Respondent or his solicitors and to the judge who made this order (for the purposes of the court file) a written report on the carrying out of the order.

Amendments—CPR Update 40.

SCHEDULE F

Affidavits

The Applicant relied on the following affidavits –

[*name*]	[*number of affidavit*]	[*date sworn*]	[*filed on behalf of*]
(1)			
(2)			

Name and address of applicant's solicitors

The Applicant's solicitors are –

[Name, address, reference, fax and telephone numbers both in and out of office hours.]

Amendments—CPR Update 27.

★★★★

PART 31
DISCLOSURE AND INSPECTION OF DOCUMENTS

CONTENTS OF THIS PART

Rule		Page
31.1	Scope of this Part	2104
31.2	Meaning of disclosure	2104
31.3	Right of inspection of a disclosed document	2105
31.4	Meaning of document	2106
31.5	Disclosure	2106
31.6	Standard disclosure – what documents are to be disclosed	2107
31.7	Duty of search	2107
31.8	Duty of disclosure limited to documents which are or have been in party's control	2108
31.9	Disclosure of copies	2108
31.10	Procedure for standard disclosure	2108
31.11	Duty of disclosure continues during proceedings	2109
31.12	Specific disclosure or inspection	2109
31.13	Disclosure in stages	2109
31.14	Documents referred to in statements of case etc	2109
31.15	Inspection and copying of documents	2110
31.19	Claim to withhold inspection or disclosure of a document	2110
31.20	Restriction on use of a privileged document inspection of which has been inadvertently allowed	2110
31.21	Consequence of failure to disclose documents or permit inspection	2111
31.22	Subsequent use of disclosed documents and completed Electronic Documents Questionnaires	2111
31.23	False disclosure statements	2111
	Practice Direction 31A – Disclosure and Inspection	2111
	Practice Direction 31B – Disclosure of Electronic Documents	2115

31.1 Scope of this Part

(1) This Part sets out rules about the disclosure and inspection of documents.

(2) This Part applies to all claims except a claim on the small claims track.

Procedure for disclosure under Pt 31—PD31A supplements the rules and explains the steps to be taken on disclosure:

(a) Disclosure is limited to standard disclosure (r 31.5) of certain prescribed documents (r 31.6). Disclosure is predicated upon a duty of 'reasonable search' for documents (r 31.7).

(b) Disclosure should be by list (r 31.10) in Form N265 with documents set out in accordance with PD31A, para 3.2. The list contains a disclosure statement (r 31.10(5) and PD31A, paras 4.1–4.4.

(c) The other party has a right to inspect the documents (r 31.3), normally in practice by receiving copies.

(d) If a party believes that documents have not been disclosed then application can be made for 'specific disclosure' (r 31.12 and PD31A, para 5).

31.2 Meaning of disclosure

A party discloses a document by stating that the document exists or has existed.

Disclosure defined—Disclosure involves only the act of informing a party that a document exists, not the physical act of producing it for inspection. That is a separate concept provided for by r 31.3.

Disclosure and family proceedings—The term disclosure in CPR 1998 is comparable to the equitable remedy of 'discovery'. It applies only to documents (defined by CPR 1998, r 31.4, below). In family proceedings there is a wider duty of relevant (or 'full and frank') disclosure of information and documents (*Livesey (formerly Jenkins) v Jenkins* [1985] FLR 813, HL). It is a duty owed between the parties and to the court (MCA 1973, s 25). See also discussion under FPR 2010, r 21.1 and *Imerman v Tchenguiz and Others* [2010] 2 FLR 814, CA, especially at [27].

31.3 Right of inspection of a disclosed document

(1) A party to whom a document has been disclosed has a right to inspect that document except where –

(a) the document is no longer in the control of the party who disclosed it;
(b) the party disclosing the document has a right or a duty to withhold inspection of it;
(c) paragraph (2) applies; or
(d) rule 78.26 applies.

(Rule 31.8 sets out when a document is in the control of a party)

(Rule 31.19 sets out the procedure for claiming a right or duty to withhold inspection)

(Rule 78.26 contains rules in relation to the disclosure and inspection of evidence arising out of mediation of certain cross-border disputes.)

(2) Where a party considers that it would be disproportionate to the issues in the case to permit inspection of documents within a category or class of document disclosed under rule 31.6(b) –

(a) he is not required to permit inspection of documents within that category or class; but
(b) he must state in his disclosure statement that inspection of those documents will not be permitted on the grounds that to do so would be disproportionate.

(Rule 31.6 provides for standard disclosure)

(Rule 31.10 makes provision for a disclosure statement)

(Rule 31.12 provides for a party to apply for an order for specific inspection of documents)

Amendments—SI 2011/88.

Duty of disclosure—The duty to disclose only arises where the court orders disclosure (r 31.5), although the parties may themselves arrange disclosure and inspection in accordance with their duty to further the overriding objective (eg see rr 1.1(2)(d) and 1.4(2)(a)). Such disclosure will always be subject to further review by the court. Where a party seeks specific disclosure or inspection of documents, application is made under r 31.12, and when he seeks to rely on public interest immunity, application is made under r 31.19.

'duty to withhold inspection' (r 31.3(1)(b))—This expression refers to public interest immunity, for which see r 31.19 below.

'a right or a duty to withhold inspection' (r 31.3(1)(b))—This refers to the doctrine of privilege, defined by the glossary as: 'the right of a party ... recognised by law'; and (the duty to withhold) to public interest immunity. Privilege therefore consists of the right of a party to proceedings to withhold evidence otherwise relevant to an issue before the court, and can be categorised, for present purposes, as falling into three main categories: (1) legal professional privilege; (2) privilege against self-incrimination; (3) 'without prejudice' privilege with its related (a) privilege arising from statements to a conciliator and (b) privilege arising from FDR appointments.

Public interest immunity—See r 31.19 below.

'a party considers that it would be disproportionate to the issues' (r 31.3(2))—First, the disclosing party must take a view on whether inspection of particular documents is disproportionate. Rule 31.12(3) enables the party who seeks inspection of the documents to apply for an order for 'specific inspection'. The court will generally refuse disclosure if to order it would be disproportionate, oppressive for a party required to disclose (see *Hildebrand* below) or it is regarded as irrelevant to the issues before the court.

(1) *Relevance* The question of whether disclosure should be ordered on grounds of relevance is a broader ground than 'proportionality'. It has been applied to family proceedings, for example, to refuse disclosure that was regarded by the court as oppressive (*Hildebrand v Hildebrand* [1992] 1 FLR 244, FD) or to refuse inspection of a third party's documents (formerly a production appointment) against a spouse's cohabitant.
(2) *Standard disclosure* Standard disclosure is defined in rr 31.5 and 31.6. Use of the term 'standard' and the setting out of the specific documents referred to in r 31.6 provide for a more restrictive approach to disclosure than the old rules of discovery. If more than standard disclosure is sought, the court will expect a party to go beyond merely establishing the relevance of the documents required. It is likely that the court will need to be satisfied to a higher standard, namely is the request, and compliance with it, proportionate to the issues before the court?
(3) *Proportionality* At this stage, the party disclosing documents will have in mind the principle of

PART III

'proportionality' within the terms of r 1.1(2)(c); in particular 'the importance of the case', 'the complexity of the issues' involved and the cost to the parties (in the context of the case) of disclosure and inspection of the documents concerned.

31.4 Meaning of document

In this Part –

'document' means anything in which information of any description is recorded; and

'copy', in relation to a document, means anything onto which information recorded in the document has been copied, by whatever means and whether directly or indirectly.

Electronic documents: Practice Direction 31B—PD31B (see *Civil Court Service*; LexisNexis) proposes that the term 'documents' extends to 'Electronic Documents' (para 1). These are defined (para 5(3)) as 'any document held in electronic form' including text messages, email and documents stored on any form of memory device – computer drives, memory sticks and mobile telephones. PD31B, para 2 suggests that the purpose of the practice direction is to help the parties to reach agreement on disclosure of electronic documents 'in a proportionate and cost-effective manner'.

General principles—PD31B, para 6 sets out five general principles where parties 'are considering disclosure': these comprise efficient management of data and communication of the data on inspection by which the discloser provides the same facility of access as he enjoys to the party seeking inspection. Disclosure and inspection must be in accordance with the overriding objective (especially as to what is proportionate to the issues involved) and with a firm eye on what is relevant to the issues for trial.

Discussions between the parties and court directions—The parties (and their legal representatives, if any), before the first case-management conference (for which can be read first directions or other appointments in family cases) must discuss: (1) use of technology as an aid to disclosure (PD31B, para 8); and (2) how to arrange disclosure most effectively to illuminate the case and to present electronic documents to the court (para 9). In some cases an electronic documents questionnaire may help (PD31B, para 10 and Sch). If parties cannot reach agreement as to disclosure of electronic documents they can seek directions from the court (para 17) or the court 'will give written directions in relation to disclosure or order a separate hearing in relation to disclosure' (para 15). Para 20 et seq reminds parties of the requirement of reasonable search and concludes by embedding disclosure of electronic documents into the framework of standard disclosure within the terms of CPR 1998, Pt 31.

31.5 Disclosure

(1) In all claims to which rule 31.5(2) does not apply –

(a) an order to give disclosure is an order to give standard disclosure unless the court directs otherwise;
(b) the court may dispense with or limit standard disclosure; and
(c) the parties may agree in writing to dispense with or to limit standard disclosure.

(2) Unless the court otherwise orders, paragraphs (3) to (8) apply to all multi-track claims, other than those which include a claim for personal injuries.

(3) Not less than 14 days before the first case management conference each party must file and serve a report verified by a statement of truth, which –

(a) describes briefly what documents exist or may exist that are or may be relevant to the matters in issue in the case;
(b) describes where and with whom those documents are or may be located;
(c) in the case of electronic documents, describes how those documents are stored;
(d) estimates the broad range of costs that could be involved in giving standard disclosure in the case, including the costs of searching for and disclosing any electronically stored documents; and
(e) states which of the directions under paragraphs (7) or (8) are to be sought.

(4) In cases where the Electronic Documents Questionnaire has been exchanged, the Questionnaire should be filed with the report required by paragraph (3).

(5) Not less than seven days before the first case management conference, and on any other occasion as the court may direct, the parties must, at a meeting or by telephone, discuss and seek to agree a proposal in relation to disclosure that meets the overriding objective.

(6) If –

(a) the parties agree proposals for the scope of disclosure; and
(b) the court considers that the proposals are appropriate in all the circumstances, the court may approve them without a hearing and give directions in the terms proposed.

(7) At the first or any subsequent case management conference, the court will decide, having regard to the overriding objective and the need to limit disclosure to that which is necessary to deal with the case justly, which of the following orders to make in relation to disclosure –

(a) an order dispensing with disclosure;
(b) an order that a party disclose the documents on which it relies, and at the same time request any specific disclosure it requires from any other party;
(c) an order that directs, where practicable, the disclosure to be given by each party on an issue by issue basis;
(d) an order that each party disclose any documents which it is reasonable to suppose may contain information which enables that party to advance its own case or to damage that of any other party, or which leads to an enquiry which has either of those consequences;
(e) an order that a party give standard disclosure;
(f) any other order in relation to disclosure that the court considers appropriate.

(8) The court may at any point give directions as to how disclosure is to be given, and in particular –

(a) what searches are to be undertaken, of where, for what, in respect of which time periods and by whom and the extent of any search for electronically stored documents;
(b) whether lists of documents are required;
(c) how and when the disclosure statement is to be given;
(d) in what format documents are to be disclosed (and whether any identification is required);
(e) what is required in relation to documents that once existed but no longer exist; and
(f) whether disclosure shall take place in stages.

(9) To the extent that the documents to be disclosed are electronic, the provisions of Practice Direction 31B – Disclosure of Electronic Documents will apply in addition to paragraphs (3) to (8).

Amendments—Substituted by SI 2013/262. Amended by SI 2013/1974.

31.6 Standard disclosure – what documents are to be disclosed

Standard disclosure requires a party to disclose only –

(a) the documents on which he relies; and
(b) the documents which –
 (i) adversely affect his own case;
 (ii) adversely affect another party's case; or
 (iii) support another party's case; and
(c) the documents which he is required to disclose by a relevant practice direction.

31.7 Duty of search

(1) When giving standard disclosure, a party is required to make a reasonable search for documents falling within rule 31.6(b) or (c).

(2) The factors relevant in deciding the reasonableness of a search include the following –

(a) the number of documents involved;
(b) the nature and complexity of the proceedings;
(c) the ease and expense of retrieval of any particular document; and
(d) the significance of any document which is likely to be located during the search.

(3) Where a party has not searched for a category or class of document on the grounds that to do so would be unreasonable, he must state this in his disclosure statement and identify the category or class of document.

(Rule 31.10 makes provision for a disclosure statement)

31.8 Duty of disclosure limited to documents which are or have been in party's control

(1) A party's duty to disclose documents is limited to documents which are or have been in his control.

(2) For this purpose a party has or has had a document in his control if –

(a) it is or was in his physical possession;
(b) he has or has had a right to possession of it; or
(c) he has or has had a right to inspect or take copies of it.

'documents ... in his control' (r 31(1) and (2))—This rule restricts disclosure to those documents that are or have been in a party's control and should be read alongside r 31.6, which defines those documents that should be produced.

31.9 Disclosure of copies

(1) A party need not disclose more than one copy of a document.

(2) A copy of a document that contains a modification, obliteration or other marking or feature –

(a) on which a party intends to rely; or
(b) which adversely affects his own case or another party's case or supports another party's case;

shall be treated as a separate document.

(Rule 31.4 sets out the meaning of a copy of a document)

31.10 Procedure for standard disclosure

(1) The procedure for standard disclosure is as follows.

(2) Each party must make, and serve on every other party, a list of documents in the relevant practice form.

(3) The list must identify the documents in a convenient order and manner and as concisely as possible.

(4) The list must indicate –

(a) those documents in respect of which the party claims a right or duty to withhold inspection; and
(b) (i) those documents which are no longer in the party's control; and
(ii) what has happened to those documents.

(Rule 31.19(3) and (4) require a statement in the list of documents relating to any documents inspection of which a person claims he has a right or duty to withhold)

(5) The list must include a disclosure statement.

(6) A disclosure statement is a statement made by the party disclosing the documents –

(a) setting out the extent of the search that has been made to locate documents which he is required to disclose;
(b) certifying that he understands the duty to disclose documents; and
(c) certifying that to the best of his knowledge he has carried out that duty.

(7) Where the party making the disclosure statement is a company, firm, association or other organisation, the statement must also –

(a) identify the person making the statement; and
(b) explain why he is considered an appropriate person to make the statement.

(8) The parties may agree in writing –

(a) to disclose documents without making a list; and
(b) to disclose documents without the disclosing party making a disclosure statement.

(9) A disclosure statement may be made by a person who is not a party where this is permitted by a relevant practice direction.

Scope—Each party must prepare and serve on other parties (but not file at court) a list in the prescribed form, indicating which documents he has and which he claims the right or duty not to disclose. If necessary, the reasons why documents are no longer in a party's control must be explained. The list must have a signed disclosure statement. Parties may agree to disclose without making a list.

'a list of documents in the relevant practice form' (r 31.10(2))—The relevant form is Form N265.

'right or duty to withhold inspection' (r 31.10(4)(a))—See commentary on this subject under rr 31.3 and 31.19. If a party wishes to claim the right to withhold he must set out the grounds for so doing (*PD (Disclosure and Inspection)*, para 4.5).

'disclosure statement' (r 31.10(5)–(7))—A disclosure statement which complies with r 31.10(6) and (7) is set out in the Annex to PD31) and certain other requirements are set out in paras 4.2–4.6 of the PD.

31.11 Duty of disclosure continues during proceedings

(1) Any duty of disclosure continues until the proceedings are concluded.

(2) If documents to which that duty extends come to a party's notice at any time during the proceedings, he must immediately notify every other party.

'until the proceedings are concluded' (r 31.11(1))—The reference to the conclusion of proceedings includes until the handing down of any reserved judgment (*Vernon v Bosley (No 2)* [1998] 1 FLR 304, CA). For the position as to continuing disclosure in civil (including family) proceedings, see under FPR 2010, Pt 21. Where documents within the terms of this rule come to light a supplemental list must be prepared (PD31, para 3.3) unless such a list can be dispensed with under r 31.10(8).

31.12 Specific disclosure or inspection

(1) The court may make an order for specific disclosure or specific inspection.

(2) An order for specific disclosure is an order that a party must do one or more of the following things –

(a) disclose documents or classes of documents specified in the order;
(b) carry out a search to the extent stated in the order;
(c) disclose any documents located as a result of that search.

(3) An order for specific inspection is an order that a party permit inspection of a document referred to in rule 31.3(2).

(Rule 31.3(2) allows a party to state in his disclosure statement that he will not permit inspection of a document on the grounds that it would be disproportionate to do so)

(Rule 78.26 contains rules in relation to the disclosure and inspection of evidence arising out of mediation of certain cross-border disputes.)

Amendments—SI 2011/88.

Application for specific disclosure or inspection—An application for an order for specific disclosure/inspection is made in accordance with Pt 23. The application should state the order applied for (r 23.6(a) – i e one or more of the orders set out in r 31.12(2) and (3)) and must be supported by a statement of evidence (and see *PD (Applications)*, para 9.1, which reminds parties that 'the court will often need to be satisfied by evidence of the facts that are relied on in support of or for opposing the application'). Grounds for the application may be in the application notice but a statement of evidence should also be filed setting out which documents are sought and why (PD31, para 5.3). In particular, an application for specific inspection will need to deal with the respondent's assertion that inspection is 'disproportionate to the issues' (r 31.3(2)).

Proportionality and relevance—All orders for disclosure are governed by the overriding objective in Pt 1 (PD31, para 5.4). The court should bear in mind the need for 'saving expense' (r 1.1(2)(b)) and that orders for disclosure or inspection should be proportionate 'to the complexity of the issues' in the case (r 1.1(2)(c)(iii)). The court has a discretion as to whether to order disclosure and it retains its equitable jurisdiction to refuse disclosure, akin to its jurisdiction to refuse discovery or inspection on the ground that to order it would be oppressive (*Imerman v Tchenguiz and Others* [2010] 2 FLR 814, CA).

31.13 Disclosure in stages

The parties may agree in writing, or the court may direct, that disclosure or inspection or both shall take place in stages.

31.14 Documents referred to in statements of case etc

(1) A party may inspect a document mentioned in –

(a) a statement of case;
(b) a witness statement;
(c) a witness summary; or

(d) an affidavit(GL).
(e) *(revoked)*

(2) Subject to rule 35.10(4), a party may apply for an order for inspection of any document mentioned in an expert's report which has not already been disclosed in the proceedings.

(Rule 35.10(4) makes provision in relation to instructions referred to in an expert's report)

Amendments—SI 2001/4015.

31.15 Inspection and copying of documents

Where a party has a right to inspect a document –

(a) that party must give the party who disclosed the document written notice of his wish to inspect it;
(b) the party who disclosed the document must permit inspection not more than 7 days after the date on which he received the notice; and
(c) that party may request a copy of the document and, if he also undertakes to pay reasonable copying costs, the party who disclosed the document must supply him with a copy not more than 7 days after the date on which he received the request.

(Rule 31.3 and 31.14 deal with the right of a party to inspect a document)

****

31.19 Claim to withhold inspection or disclosure of a document

(1) A person may apply, without notice, for an order permitting him to withhold disclosure of a document on the ground that disclosure would damage the public interest.

(2) Unless the court orders otherwise, an order of the court under paragraph (1) –

(a) must not be served on any other person; and
(b) must not be open to inspection by any person.

(3) A person who wishes to claim that he has a right or a duty to withhold inspection of a document, or part of a document must state in writing –

(a) that he has such a right or duty; and
(b) the grounds on which he claims that right or duty.

(4) The statement referred to in paragraph (3) must be made –

(a) in the list in which the document is disclosed; or
(b) if there is no list, to the person wishing to inspect the document.

(5) A party may apply to the court to decide whether a claim made under paragraph (3) should be upheld.

(6) For the purpose of deciding an application under paragraph (1) (application to withhold disclosure) or paragraph (3) (claim to withhold inspection) the court may –

(a) require the person seeking to withhold disclosure or inspection of a document to produce that document to the court; and
(b) invite any person, whether or not a party, to make representations.

(7) An application under paragraph (1) or paragraph (5) must be supported by evidence.

(8) This Part does not affect any rule of law which permits or requires a document to be withheld from disclosure or inspection on the ground that its disclosure or inspection would damage the public interest.

31.20 Restriction on use of a privileged document inspection of which has been inadvertently allowed

Where a party inadvertently allows a privileged(GL) document to be inspected, the party who has inspected the document may use it or its contents only with the permission of the court.

31.21 Consequence of failure to disclose documents or permit inspection

A party may not rely on any document which he fails to disclose or in respect of which he fails to permit inspection unless the court gives permission.

31.22 Subsequent use of disclosed documents and completed Electronic Documents Questionnaires

(1) A party to whom a document has been disclosed may use the document only for the purpose of the proceedings in which it is disclosed, except where –

(a) the document has been read to or by the court, or referred to, at a hearing which has been held in public;

(b) the court gives permission; or

(c) the party who disclosed the document and the person to whom the document belongs agree.

(2) The court may make an order restricting or prohibiting the use of a document which has been disclosed, even where the document has been read to or by the court, or referred to, at a hearing which has been held in public.

(3) An application for such an order may be made –

(a) by a party; or

(b) by any person to whom the document belongs.

(4) For the purpose of this rule, an Electronic Documents Questionnaire which has been completed and served by another party pursuant to Practice Direction 31B is to be treated as if it is a document which has been disclosed.

Amendments—SI 2010/1953.

Restriction on use of disclosed documents—Rule 31.22 is the CPR 1998 replacement of the former 'implied undertaking' as to the further production of documents that had been disclosed (discovered) in civil proceedings, as applied in family proceedings by *Clibbery v Allan* [2002] 1 FLR 565, CA. It has no equivalent in family proceedings, although its effect (r 31.22(1)(b)) has been applied in the case of release of disclosed documents to HMRC in *HMRC v Charman and Charman* [2012] 2 FLR 1119, FD.

31.23 False disclosure statements

(1) Proceedings for contempt of court may be brought against a person if he makes, or causes to be made, a false disclosure statement, without an honest belief in its truth.

…

(Section 6 of Part 81 contains provisions in relation to committal for making a false disclosure statement.)

Amendments—Inserted by SI 2000/221. Amended by SI 2012/2208.

Practice Direction 31A – Disclosure and Inspection

This Practice Direction supplements CPR Part 31

Amendments—CPR Update 53.

General

1.1 The normal order for disclosure will be an order that the parties give standard disclosure.

1.2 In order to give standard disclosure the disclosing party must make a reasonable search for documents falling within the paragraphs of rule 31.6.

1.3 Having made the search the disclosing party must (unless rule 31.10(8) applies) make a list of the documents of whose existence the party is aware that fall within those paragraphs and which are or have been in the party's control (see rule 31.8).

PART III

1.4 The obligations imposed by an order for standard disclosure may be dispensed with or limited either by the court or by written agreement between the parties. Any such written agreement should be lodged with the court.

The search

2 The extent of the search which must be made will depend upon the circumstances of the case including, in particular, the factors referred to in rule 31.7(2). The parties should bear in mind the overriding principle of proportionality (see rule 1.1(2)(c)). It may, for example, be reasonable to decide not to search for documents coming into existence before some particular date, or to limit the search to documents in some particular place or places, or to documents falling into particular categories.

Electronic disclosure

2A.1 Rule 31.4 contains a broad definition of a document. This extends to electronic documents, including e-mail and other electronic communications, word processed documents and databases. In addition to documents that are readily accessible from computer systems and other electronic devices and media, the definition covers those documents that are stored on servers and back-up systems and electronic documents that have been 'deleted'. It also extends to additional information stored and associated with electronic documents known as metadata.

2A.2 Practice Direction 31B contains additional provisions in relation to the disclosure of electronic documents in cases that are likely to be allocated to the multi-track.

Amendments—CPR Update 53.

The list

3.1 The list should be in Form N265.

3.2 In order to comply with rule 31.10(3) it will normally be necessary to list the documents in date order, to number them consecutively and to give each a concise description (e g letter, claimant to defendant). Where there is a large number of documents all falling into a particular category the disclosing party may list those documents as a category rather than individually e g 50 bank statements relating to account number at Bank, 20 to 20 ; or, 35 letters passing between and between 20 and 20 .

3.3 The obligations imposed by an order for disclosure will continue until the proceedings come to an end. If, after a list of documents has been prepared and served, the existence of further documents to which the order applies comes to the attention of the disclosing party, the party must prepare and serve a supplemental list.

Amendments—CPR Update 29.

Disclosure statement

4.1 A list of documents must (unless rule 31.10(8)(b) applies) contain a disclosure statement complying with rule 31.10. The form of disclosure statement is set out in Annex A to this practice direction.

4.2 The disclosure statement should:

(1) expressly state that the disclosing party believes the extent of the search to have been reasonable in all the circumstances, and

(2) in setting out the extent of the search (see rule 31.10(6)) draw attention to any particular limitations on the extent of the search which were adopted for proportionality reasons and give the reasons why the limitations were adopted, e g the difficulty or expense that a search not subject to those limitations would have entailed or the marginal relevance of categories of documents omitted from the search.

4.3 Where rule 31.10(7) applies, the details given in the disclosure statement about the person making the statement must include his name and address and the office or position he holds in the disclosing party or the basis upon which he makes the statement on behalf of the party.

4.4 If the disclosing party has a legal representative acting for him, the legal representative must endeavour to ensure that the person making the disclosure statement (whether the disclosing party or, in a case to which rule 31.10(7) applies, some other person) understands the duty of disclosure under Part 31.

4.5 If the disclosing party wishes to claim that he has a right or duty to withhold a document, or part of a document, in his list of documents from inspection (see rule 31.19(3)), he must state in writing:

(1) that he has such a right or duty, and
(2) the grounds on which he claims that right or duty.

4.6 The statement referred to in paragraph 4.5 above should normally be included in the disclosure statement and must identify the document, or part of a document, to which the claim relates.

4.7 An insurer or the Motor Insurers' Bureau may sign a disclosure statement on behalf of party where the insurer or the Motor Insurers' Bureau has a financial interest in the result of proceedings brought wholly or partially by or against that party. Rule 31.10(7) and paragraph 4.3 above shall apply to the insurer or the Motor Insurers' Bureau making such a statement.

Amendments—CPR Updates 7, 22, 26.

Specific disclosure

5.1 If a party believes that the disclosure of documents given by a disclosing party is inadequate he may make an application for an order for specific disclosure (see rule 31.12).

5.2 The application notice must specify the order that the applicant intends to ask the court to make and must be supported by evidence (see rule 31.12(2) which describes the orders the court may make).

5.3 The grounds on which the order is sought may be set out in the application notice itself but if not there set out must be set out in evidence filed in support of the application.

5.4 In deciding whether or not to make an order for specific disclosure the court will take into account all the circumstances of the case and, in particular, the overriding objective described in Part 1. But if the court concludes that the party from whom specific disclosure is sought has failed adequately to comply with the obligations imposed by an order for disclosure (whether by failing to make a sufficient search for documents or otherwise) the court will usually make such order as is necessary to ensure that those obligations are properly complied with.

5.5 An order for specific disclosure may in an appropriate case direct a party to –

(1) carry out a search for any documents which it is reasonable to suppose may contain information which may –
 (a) enable the party applying for disclosure either to advance his own case or to damage that of the party giving disclosure; or
 (b) lead to a train of enquiry which has either of those consequences; and
(2) disclose any documents found as a result of that search.

Amendments—CPR Update 26.

Claims to withhold disclosure or inspection of a document

6.1 A claim to withhold inspection of a document, or part of a document, disclosed in a list of documents does not require an application to the court. Where such a claim has been made, a party who wishes to challenge it must apply to the court (see rule 31.19(5)).

6.2 Rule 31.19(1) and (6) provide a procedure enabling a party to apply for an order permitting disclosure of the existence of a document to be withheld.

PART III

Inspection of documents mentioned in expert's report (Rule 31.14(2))

7.1 If a party wishes to inspect documents referred to in the expert report of another party, before issuing an application he should request inspection of the document informally, and inspection should be provided by agreement unless the request is unreasonable.

7.2 Where an expert report refers to a large number or volume of documents and it would be burdensome to copy or collate them, the court will only order inspection of such documents if it is satisfied that it is necessary for the just disposal of the proceedings and the party cannot reasonably obtain the documents from another source.

Amendments—CPR Updates 1, 26.

False disclosure statement

8 Attention is drawn to rule 31.23 which sets out the consequences of making a false disclosure statement without an honest belief in its truth, and to the procedures set out in rule 81.18 and paragraphs 5.1 to 5.7 of Practice Direction 81 – Applications and proceedings in relation to contempt of court.

Amendments—CPR Updates 21, 26, 59.

ANNEX A

Disclosure statement

I, the above named claimant [or defendant] [if party making disclosure is a company, firm or other organisation identify here who the person making the disclosure statement is and why he is the appropriate person to make it] state that I have carried out a reasonable and proportionate search to locate all the documents which I am required to disclose under the order made by the court on day of . I did not search:

(1) for documents predating ....,
(2) for documents located elsewhere than ....,
(3) for documents in categories other than ....,
(4) for electronic documents

I carried out a search for electronic documents contained on or created by the following: [list what was searched and extent of search]

I did not search for the following:

(1) documents created before … … . . .,
(2) documents contained on or created by the Claimant's/Defendant's PCs/portable data storage media/databases/servers/back-up tapes/off-site storage/mobile phones/laptops/notebooks/handheld devices/PDA devices (delete as appropriate),
(3) documents contained on or created by the Claimant's/Defendant's mail files/document files/calendar files/spreadsheet files/graphic and presentation files/web-based applications (delete as appropriate),
(4) documents other than by reference to the following keyword(s)/concepts … … . . .. (delete if your search was not confined to specific keywords or concepts).

I certify that I understand the duty of disclosure and to the best of my knowledge I have carried out that duty. I certify that the list above is a complete list of all documents which are or have been in my control and which I am obliged under the said order to disclose.

Amendments—CPR Update 40.

Practice Direction 31B – Disclosure of Electronic Documents

This Practice Direction supplements CPR Part 31

Amendments—CPR Update 53.

Note—CPR PD31B is set out in *Civil Court Service* (LexisNexis).

PART 32
EVIDENCE

CONTENTS OF THIS PART

Rule		Page
32.1	Power of court to control evidence	2115
32.2	Evidence of witnesses – general rule	2115
32.3	Evidence by video link or other means	2116
32.4	Requirement to serve witness statements for use at trial	2116
32.18	Notice to admit facts	2116
32.19	Notice to admit or produce documents	2116
	Practice Direction 32 – Evidence	2117

Note—Only CPR 1998, rr 32.1–32.4, 32.18 and 32.19 have been reproduced here. Almost all of the remaining rules are replicated in FPR 2010, Pt 22. For detailed commentary specifically on civil proceedings, see *Civil Court Service* (LexisNexis).

32.1 Power of court to control evidence

(1) The court may control the evidence by giving directions as to –

(a) the issues on which it requires evidence;
(b) the nature of the evidence which it requires to decide those issues; and
(c) the way in which the evidence is to be placed before the court.

(2) The court may use its power under this rule to exclude evidence that would otherwise be admissible.

(3) The court may limit cross-examination[(GL)].

'The court may control the evidence' (r 32.1(1))—This is a helpful description of the powers derived from the overriding objective.

Evidence from third parties—It remains to be seen whether the courts will use powers akin to those assumed by the High Court in *Khanna v Lovell White Durrant (A Firm)* [1995] 1 WLR 121, ChD to require a third party to produce documents in advance of a final hearing.

Bankers' Book Evidence Act 1879—This (or the *Khanna* hearing) is the appropriate procedure to adopt for production of entries in bankers' books. Privilege may be claimed by a third party (*Waterhouse v Barker* [1924] 2 KB 759, CA), but a bank does not breach confidentiality to its customer if it produces his bank statements when ordered so to do (*Robertson v Canadian Imperial Bank of Commerce* [1994] 1 WLR 1493, PC).

32.2 Evidence of witnesses – general rule

(1) The general rule is that any fact which needs to be proved by the evidence of witnesses is to be proved –

(a) at trial, by their oral evidence given in public; and
(b) at any other hearing, by their evidence in writing.

(2) This is subject –

(a) to any provision to the contrary contained in these Rules or elsewhere; or
(b) to any order of the court.

(3) The court may give directions –

(a) identifying or limiting the issues to which factual evidence may be directed;
(b) identifying the witnesses who may be called or whose evidence may be read; or

(c) limiting the length or format of witness statements.

Amendments—SI 2013/262.

Scope—This rule stresses the importance of proving the case by oral evidence in open court at trial and see ECHR 1950, Art 6(1) entitlement to a 'fair and public hearing'. This 'general rule' may be displaced by court order. At other hearings (eg under Pt 23), the general rule is that evidence should be in writing (and see r 32.6 below).

32.3 Evidence by video link or other means

The court may allow a witness to give evidence through a video link or by other means.

Video link and the overriding objective—This rule is consistent with the overriding objective; see r 1.4(2)(k), which provides that case management includes 'making use of technology' and r 3.1(2)(d) which enables the court to 'receive evidence by telephone or by using any other method of direct oral communication'.

32.4 Requirement to serve witness statements for use at trial

(1) A witness statement is a written statement signed by a person which contains the evidence which that person would be allowed to give orally.

(2) The court will order a party to serve on the other parties any witness statement of the oral evidence which the party serving the statement intends to rely on in relation to any issues of fact to be decided at the trial.

(3) The court may give directions as to –

(a) the order in which witness statements are to be served; and
(b) whether or not the witness statements are to be filed.

Witness statements—Witness statements, as stipulated by r 32.8, must comply with the requirements of *PD (Written Evidence)*, paras 17.1–22.2. Hearsay evidence in witness statements is dealt with in r 33.2.

****

32.18 Notice to admit facts

(1) A party may serve notice on another party requiring him to admit the facts, or the part of the case of the serving party, specified in the notice.

(2) A notice to admit facts must be served no later than 21 days before the trial.

(3) Where the other party makes any admission in response to the notice the admission may be used against him only –

(a) in the proceedings in which the notice to admit is served; and
(b) by the party who served the notice.

(4) The court may allow a party to amend or withdraw any admission made by him on such terms as it thinks just.

'notice … to admit the facts … specified' (r 32.18))—Rule 32.18 enables a party to give notice to another to admit facts. Any admission can only be used in the proceedings to which it relates and it can only cause an estoppel if findings are made on the admission to question.

32.19 Notice to admit or produce documents

(1) A party shall be deemed to admit the authenticity of a document disclosed to him under Part 31 (disclosure and inspection of documents) unless he serves notice that he wishes the document to be proved at trial.

(2) A notice to prove a document must be served –

(a) by the latest date for serving witness statements; or
(b) within 7 days of disclosure of the document,

whichever is later.

Notice to prove a document (r 32.19(2))—The heading to this rule is misleading, since the rule provides for a presumption that a party admits that any disclosed document is authentic unless notice is given for the document to be produced at trial within the time limits set out in r 32.19(2).

****

Practice Direction 32 – Evidence

This Practice Direction supplements CPR Part 32

Amendments—CPR Update 40.

Evidence in general

1.1 Rule 32.2 sets out how evidence is to be given and facts are to be proved.

1.2 Evidence at a hearing other than the trial should normally be given by witness statement[1] (see paragraph 17 onwards). However a witness may give evidence by affidavit if he wishes to do so[2] (and see paragraph 1.4 below).

1 See rule 32.6(1).
2 See rule 32.15(2).

1.3 Statements of case (see paragraph 26 onwards) and application notices[1] may also be used as evidence provided that their contents have been verified by a statement of truth[2].

(For information regarding evidence by deposition see Part 34 and Practice Direction 34A.)

1 See Part 23 for information about making an application.
2 Rule 32.6(2) and see Part 22 for information about the statement of truth.

1.4 Affidavits must be used as evidence in the following instances:

(1) where sworn evidence is required by an enactment[1], rule, order or practice direction, and

(2) in any application for a search order, a freezing injunction, or an order requiring an occupier to permit another to enter his land.

(Part 81 – Applications and proceedings in relation to contempt of court, and the Practice Direction accompanying that Part, contain provisions about evidence in relation to contempt of court. Particular attention is drawn to rules 81.10, 81.11, 81.14, 81.15, 81.26 and Practice Direction 81 paragraphs 4.5 and 14.1.).

1 See, eg, s 3(5)(a) of the Protection from Harassment Act 1997.

1.5 If a party believes that sworn evidence is required by a court in another jurisdiction for any purpose connected with the proceedings, he may apply to the court for a direction that evidence shall be given only by affidavit on any pre-trial applications.

1.6 The court may give a direction under rule 32.15 that evidence shall be given by affidavit instead of or in addition to a witness statement or statement of case:

(1) on its own initiative, or

(2) after any party has applied to the court for such a direction.

1.7 An affidavit, where referred to in the Civil Procedure Rules or a practice direction, also means an affirmation unless the context requires otherwise.

Amendments—CPR Updates 22, 29, 51, 59.

AFFIDAVITS

Deponent

2 A deponent is a person who gives evidence by affidavit or affirmation.

Heading

3.1 The affidavit should be headed with the title of the proceedings (see paragraph 4 of Practice Direction 7A and paragraph 7 of Practice Direction 20); where the proceedings are between several parties with the same status it is sufficient to identify the parties as follows:

PART III

Number:
AB (and others) Claimants/Applicants
CD (and others) Defendants/Respondents
(as appropriate)

3.2 At the top right hand corner of the first page (and on the backsheet) there should be clearly written:

(1) the party on whose behalf it is made,
(2) the initials and surname of the deponent,
(3) the number of the affidavit in relation to that deponent,
(4) the identifying initials and number of each exhibit referred to, and
(5) the date sworn.

Amendments—CPR Updates 1, 51.

Body of affidavit

4.1 The affidavit must, if practicable, be in the deponent's own words, the affidavit should be expressed in the first person and the deponent should:

(1) commence 'I (*full name*) of (*address*) state on oath ',
(2) if giving evidence in his professional, business or other occupational capacity, give the address at which he works in (1) above, the position he holds and the name of his firm or employer,
(3) give his occupation or, if he has none, his description, and
(4) state if he is a party to the proceedings or employed by a party to the proceedings, if it be the case.

4.2 An affidavit must indicate:

(1) which of the statements in it are made from the deponent's own knowledge and which are matters of information or belief, and
(2) the source for any matters of information or belief.

4.3 Where a deponent:

(1) refers to an exhibit or exhibits, he should state 'there is now shown to me marked ' ' the (*description of exhibit*),' and
(2) makes more than one affidavit (to which there are exhibits) in the same proceedings, the numbering of the exhibits should run consecutively throughout and not start again with each affidavit.

Jurat

5.1 The jurat of an affidavit is a statement set out at the end of the document which authenticates the affidavit.

5.2 It must:

(1) be signed by all deponents,
(2) be completed and signed by the person before whom the affidavit was sworn whose name and qualification must be printed beneath his signature,
(3) contain the full address of the person before whom the affidavit was sworn, and
(4) follow immediately on from the text and not be put on a separate page.

Format of affidavits

6.1 An affidavit should:

(1) be produced on durable quality A4 paper with a 3.5 cm margin,
(2) be fully legible and should normally be typed on one side of the paper only,
(3) where possible, be bound securely in a manner which would not hamper filing, or otherwise each page should be endorsed with the case number and should bear the initials of the deponent and of the person before whom it was sworn,

(4) have the pages numbered consecutively as a separate document (or as one of several documents contained in a file),
(5) be divided into numbered paragraphs,
(6) have all numbers, including dates, expressed in figures, and
(7) give the reference to any document or documents mentioned either in the margin or in bold text in the body of the affidavit.

6.2 It is usually convenient for an affidavit to follow the chronological sequence of events or matters dealt with; each paragraph of an affidavit should as far as possible be confined to a distinct portion of the subject.

Amendments—CPR Update 15.

Inability of deponent to read or sign affidavit

7.1 Where an affidavit is sworn by a person who is unable to read or sign it, the person before whom the affidavit is sworn must certify in the jurat that:

(1) he read the affidavit to the deponent,
(2) the deponent appeared to understand it, and
(3) the deponent signed or made his mark, in his presence.

7.2 If that certificate is not included in the jurat, the affidavit may not be used in evidence unless the court is satisfied that it was read to the deponent and that he appeared to understand it. Two versions of the form of jurat with the certificate are set out at Annex 1 to this practice direction.

Alterations to affidavits

8.1 Any alteration to an affidavit must be initialled by both the deponent and the person before whom the affidavit was sworn.

8.2 An affidavit which contains an alteration that has not been initialled may be filed or used in evidence only with the permission of the court.

Who may administer oaths and take affidavits

9.1 Only the following may administer oaths and take affidavits –

(1) a commissioner for oaths[1];
(2) (*revoked*)
(3) other persons specified by Statute[2];
(4) certain officials of the Senior Courts[3];
(5) a Circuit Judge or District Judge[4];
(6) any justice of the peace[5]; and
(7) certain officials of the County Court appointed by the judge of that court for the purpose[6].

1 Commissioners for Oaths Acts 1889 and 1891.
2 Sections 12 and 18 of, and Schedules 2 and 4 to, the Legal Services Act 2007.
3 Section 2 of the Commissioners for Oaths Act 1889.
4 Section 58 of the County Courts Act 1984.
5 Section 58 as above.
6 Section 58 as above.

9.2 An affidavit must be sworn before a person independent of the parties or their representatives.

Amendments—CPR Updates 50, 51, 69.

Filing of affidavits

10.1 If the court directs that an affidavit is to be filed[1], it must be filed in the court or Division, or Office or Registry of the court or Division where the action in which it was or is to be used, is proceeding or will proceed.

1 Rules 32.1(3) and 32.4(3)(b).

10.2 Where an affidavit is in a foreign language:

(1) the party wishing to rely on it –
  (a) must have it translated, and
  (b) must file the foreign language affidavit with the court, and
(2) the translator must make and file with the court an affidavit verifying the translation and exhibiting both the translation and a copy of the foreign language affidavit.

EXHIBITS

Manner of exhibiting documents

11.1 A document used in conjunction with an affidavit should be:

(1) produced to and verified by the deponent, and remain separate from the affidavit, and
(2) identified by a declaration of the person before whom the affidavit was sworn.

11.2 The declaration should be headed with the name of the proceedings in the same way as the affidavit.

11.3 The first page of each exhibit should be marked:

(1) as in paragraph 3.2 above, and
(2) with the exhibit mark referred to in the affidavit.

Letters

12.1 Copies of individual letters should be collected together and exhibited in a bundle or bundles. They should be arranged in chronological order with the earliest at the top, and firmly secured.

12.2 When a bundle of correspondence is exhibited, the exhibit should have a front page attached stating that the bundle consists of original letters and copies. They should be arranged and secured as above and numbered consecutively.

Other documents

13.1 Photocopies instead of original documents may be exhibited provided the originals are made available for inspection by the other parties before the hearing and by the judge at the hearing.

13.2 Court documents must not be exhibited (official copies of such documents prove themselves).

13.3 Where an exhibit contains more than one document, a front page should be attached setting out a list of the documents contained in the exhibit; the list should contain the dates of the documents.

Exhibits other than documents

14.1 Items other than documents should be clearly marked with an exhibit number or letter in such a manner that the mark cannot become detached from the exhibit.

14.2 Small items may be placed in a container and the container appropriately marked.

General provisions

15.1 Where an exhibit contains more than one document:

(1) the bundle should not be stapled but should be securely fastened in a way that does not hinder the reading of the documents, and
(2) the pages should be numbered consecutively at bottom centre.

15.2 Every page of an exhibit should be clearly legible; typed copies of illegible documents should be included, paginated with 'a' numbers.

15.3 Where affidavits and exhibits have become numerous, they should be put into separate bundles and the pages numbered consecutively throughout.

15.4 Where on account of their bulk the service of exhibits or copies of exhibits on the other parties would be difficult or impracticable, the directions of the court should be sought as to arrangements for bringing the exhibits to the attention of the other parties and as to their custody pending trial.

Affirmations

16 All provisions in this or any other practice direction relating to affidavits apply to affirmations with the following exceptions:

(1) the deponent should commence 'I (*name*) of (*address*) do solemnly and sincerely affirm ', and
(2) in the jurat the word 'sworn' is replaced by the word 'affirmed'.

WITNESS STATEMENTS

Heading

17.1 The witness statement should be headed with the title of the proceedings (see paragraph 4 of Practice Direction 7A and paragraph 7 of Practice Direction 20); where the proceedings are between several parties with the same status it is sufficient to identify the parties as follows:

	Number:
AB (and others)	Claimants/Applicants
CD (and others)	Defendants/Respondents (as appropriate)

17.2 At the top right hand corner of the first page there should be clearly written:

(1) the party on whose behalf it is made,
(2) the initials and surname of the witness,
(3) the number of the statement in relation to that witness,
(4) the identifying initials and number of each exhibit referred to, and
(5) the date the statement was made.

Amendments—CPR Updates 1, 2, 51.

Body of witness statement

18.1 The witness statement must, if practicable, be in the intended witness's own words, the statement should be expressed in the first person and should also state:

(1) the full name of the witness,
(2) his place of residence or, if he is making the statement in his professional, business or other occupational capacity, the address at which he works, the position he holds and the name of his firm or employer,
(3) his occupation, or if he has none, his description, and
(4) the fact that he is a party to the proceedings or is the employee of such a party if it be the case.

18.2 A witness statement must indicate:

(1) which of the statements in it are made from the witness's own knowledge and which are matters of information or belief, and
(2) the source for any matters of information or belief.

18.3 An exhibit used in conjunction with a witness statement should be verified and identified by the witness and remain separate from the witness statement.

18.4 Where a witness refers to an exhibit or exhibits, he should state 'I refer to the (*description of exhibit*) marked " "'.

18.5 The provisions of paragraphs 11.3 to 15.4 (exhibits) apply similarly to witness statements as they do to affidavits.

PART III

18.6 Where a witness makes more than one witness statement to which there are exhibits, in the same proceedings, the numbering of the exhibits should run consecutively throughout and not start again with each witness statement.

Amendments—CPR Update 1.

Format of witness statement

19.1 A witness statement should:

(1) be produced on durable quality A4 paper with a 3.5 cm margin,
(2) be fully legible and should normally be typed on one side of the paper only,
(3) where possible, be bound securely in a manner which would not hamper filing, or otherwise each page should be endorsed with the case number and should bear the initials of the witness,
(4) have the pages numbered consecutively as a separate statement (or as one of several statements contained in a file),
(5) be divided into numbered paragraphs,
(6) have all numbers, including dates, expressed in figures, and
(7) give the reference to any document or documents mentioned either in the margin or in bold text in the body of the statement.

19.2 It is usually convenient for a witness statement to follow the chronological sequence of the events or matters dealt with, each paragraph of a witness statement should as far as possible be confined to a distinct portion of the subject.

Amendments—CPR Update 15.

Statement of truth

20.1 A witness statement is the equivalent of the oral evidence which that witness would, if called, give in evidence; it must include a statement by the intended witness that he believes the facts in it are true[1].

1 See Part 22 for information about the statement of truth.

20.2 To verify a witness statement the statement of truth is as follows:

'I believe that the facts stated in this witness statement are true'

20.3 Attention is drawn to rule 32.14 which sets out the consequences of verifying a witness statement containing a false statement without an honest belief in its truth.

(Paragraph 3A of Practice Direction 22 sets out the procedure to be followed where the person who should sign a document which is verified by a statement of truth is unable to read or sign the document.)

Amendments—CPR Updates 41, 51.

Alterations to witness statements

22.1 Any alteration to a witness statement must be initialled by the person making the statement or by the authorised person where appropriate (see paragraph 21).

22.2 A witness statement which contains an alteration that has not been initialled may be used in evidence only with the permission of the court.

Filing of witness statements

23.1 If the court directs that a witness statement is to be filed[1], it must be filed in the court or Division, or Office or Registry of the court or Division where the action in which it was or is to be used, is proceeding or will proceed.

1 Rule 32.4(3)(b).

23.2 Where the court has directed that a witness statement in a foreign language is to be filed:

(1) the party wishing to rely on it must –
 (a) have it translated, and

(b) file the foreign language witness statement with the court, and

(2) the translator must make and file with the court an affidavit verifying the translation and exhibiting both the translation and a copy of the foreign language witness statement.

Certificate of court officer

24.1 Where the court has ordered that a witness statement is not to be open to inspection by the public[1] or that words or passages in the statement are not to be open to inspection[2] the court officer will so certify on the statement and make any deletions directed by the court under rule 32.13(4).

1 Rule 32.13(2).
2 Rule 32.13(4).

Amendments—CPR Update 3.

Defects in affidavits, witness statements and exhibits

25.1 Where:

(1) an affidavit,
(2) a witness statement, or
(3) an exhibit to either an affidavit or a witness statement,

does not comply with Part 32 or this practice direction in relation to its form, the court may refuse to admit it as evidence and may refuse to allow the costs arising from its preparation.

25.2 Permission to file a defective affidavit or witness statement or to use a defective exhibit may be obtained from a judge[1] in the court where the case is proceeding.

1 Rule 2.3(1); definition of judge.

Statements of case

26.1 A statement of case may be used as evidence in an interim application provided it is verified by a statement of truth[1].

1 See rule 32.6(2)(a).

26.2 To verify a statement of case the statement of truth should be set out as follows:

'[I believe] [the (*party on whose behalf the statement of case is being signed*) believes] that the facts stated in the statement of case are true'.

26.3 Attention is drawn to rule 32.14 which sets out the consequences of verifying a witness statement containing a false statement without an honest belief in its truth.

(For information regarding statements of truth see Part 22 and Practice Direction 22.)

(Practice Directions 7A and 17 provide further information concerning statements of case.)

Amendments—CPR Update 51.

Agreed bundles for hearings

27.1 The court may give directions requiring the parties to use their best endeavours to agree a bundle or bundles of documents for use at any hearing.

27.2 All documents contained in bundles which have been agreed for use at a hearing shall be admissible at that hearing as evidence of their contents, unless –

(1) the court orders otherwise; or
(2) a party gives written notice of objection to the admissibility of particular documents.

Amendments—CPR Updates 26, 59.

Video conferencing

29.1 Guidance on the use of video conferencing in the civil courts is set out at Annex 3 to this practice direction.

A list of the sites which are available for video conferencing can be found on Her Majesty's Courts and Tribunals Service website.

Amendments—CPR Updates 27, 40, 58.

ANNEX 1

Certificate to be used where a deponent to an affidavit is unable to read or sign it

Sworn at this day of Before me, I having first read over the contents of this affidavit to the deponent [*if there are exhibits, add* 'and explained the nature and effect of the exhibits referred to in it'] who appeared to understand it and approved its content as accurate, and made his mark on the affidavit in my presence.

Or, (after, *Before me*) the witness to the mark of the deponent having been first sworn that he had read over etc (*as above*) and that he saw him make his mark on the affidavit. (*Witness must sign*).

Certificate to be used where a deponent to an affirmation is unable to read or sign it

Affirmed at this day of Before me, I having first read over the contents of this affirmation to the deponent [*if there are exhibits, add* 'and explained the nature and effect of the exhibits referred to in it'] who appeared to understand it and approved its content as accurate, and made his mark on the affirmation in my presence.

Or, (after, *Before me*) the witness to the mark of the deponent having been first sworn that he had read over etc (*as above*) and that he saw him make his mark on the affirmation. (*Witness must sign*).

Amendments—CPR Update 41.

ANNEX 3

Video conferencing guidance

This guidance is for the use of video conferencing (VCF) in civil proceedings. It is in part based, with permission, upon the protocol of the Federal Court of Australia. It is intended to provide a guide to all persons involved in the use of VCF, although it does not attempt to cover all the practical questions which might arise.

Video conferencing generally

1 The guidance covers the use of VCF equipment both (a) in a courtroom, whether via equipment which is permanently placed there or via a mobile unit, and (b) in a separate studio or conference room. In either case, the location at which the judge sits is referred to as the 'local site'. The other site or sites to and from which transmission is made are referred to as 'the remote site' and in any particular case any such site may be another courtroom. The guidance applies to cases where VCF is used for the taking of evidence and also to its use for other parts of any legal proceedings (for example, interim applications, case management conferences, pre-trial reviews).

2 VCF may be a convenient way of dealing with any part of proceedings: it can involve considerable savings in time and cost. Its use for the taking of evidence from overseas witnesses will, in particular, be likely to achieve a material saving of costs, and such savings may also be achieved by its use for taking domestic evidence. It is, however, inevitably not as ideal as having the witness physically present in court. Its convenience should not therefore be allowed to dictate its use. A judgment must be made in every case in which the use of VCF is being considered not only as to whether it will achieve an overall cost saving but as to whether its use will be likely to be beneficial to the efficient, fair and economic disposal of the litigation. In particular, it needs to be recognised that the degree of control a court can exercise over a witness at the remote site is or may be more limited than it can exercise over a witness physically before it.

3 When used for the taking of evidence, the objective should be to make the VCF session as close as possible to the usual practice in a trial court where evidence is taken in open court. To gain the maximum benefit, several differences have to be taken into account. Some matters, which are taken for granted when evidence is taken in the conventional way, take on a different dimension

when it is taken by VCF: for example, the administration of the oath, ensuring that the witness understands who is at the local site and what their various roles are, the raising of any objections to the evidence and the use of documents.

4 It should not be presumed that all foreign governments are willing to allow their nationals or others within their jurisdiction to be examined before a court in England or Wales by means of VCF. If there is any doubt about this, enquiries should be directed to the Foreign and Commonwealth Office (International Legal Matters Unit, Consular Division) with a view to ensuring that the country from which the evidence is to be taken raises no objection to it at diplomatic level. The party who is directed to be responsible for arranging the VCF (see paragraph 8 below) will be required to make all necessary inquiries about this well in advance of the VCF and must be able to inform the court what those inquiries were and of their outcome.

5 Time zone differences need to be considered when a witness abroad is to be examined in England or Wales by VCF. The convenience of the witness, the parties, their representatives and the court must all be taken into account. The cost of the use of a commercial studio is usually greater outside normal business hours.

6 Those involved with VCF need to be aware that, even with the most advanced systems currently available, there are the briefest of delays between the receipt of the picture and that of the accompanying sound. If due allowance is not made for this, there will be a tendency to 'speak over' the witness, whose voice will continue to be heard for a millisecond or so after he or she appears on the screen to have finished speaking.

7 With current technology, picture quality is good, but not as good as a television picture. The quality of the picture is enhanced if those appearing on VCF monitors keep their movements to a minimum.

Preliminary arrangements

8 The court's permission is required for any part of any proceedings to be dealt with by means of VCF. Before seeking a direction, the applicant should notify the listing officer, diary manager or other appropriate court officer of the intention to seek it, and should enquire as to the availability of court VCF equipment for the day or days of the proposed VCF. The application for a direction should be made to the Master, District Judge or judge, as may be appropriate. If all parties consent to a direction, permission can be sought by letter, fax or e-mail, although the court may still require an oral hearing. All parties are entitled to be heard on whether or not such a direction should be given and as to its terms. If a witness at a remote site is to give evidence by an interpreter, consideration should be given at this stage as to whether the interpreter should be at the local site or the remote site. If a VCF direction is given, arrangements for the transmission will then need to be made. The court will ordinarily direct that the party seeking permission to use VCF is to be responsible for this. That party is hereafter referred to as 'the VCF arranging party'.

9 Subject to any order to the contrary, all costs of the transmission, including the costs of hiring equipment and technical personnel to operate it, will initially be the responsibility of, and must be met by, the VCF arranging party. All reasonable efforts should be made to keep the transmission to a minimum and so keep the costs down. All such costs will be considered to be part of the costs of the proceedings and the court will determine at such subsequent time as is convenient or appropriate who, as between the parties, should be responsible for them and (if appropriate) in what proportions.

10 The local site will, if practicable, be a courtroom but it may instead be an appropriate studio or conference room. The VCF arranging party must contact the listing officer, diary manager or other appropriate officer of the court which made the VCF direction and make arrangements for the VCF transmission. Details of the remote site, and of the equipment to be used both at the local site (if not being supplied by the court) and the remote site (including the number of ISDN lines and connection speed), together with all necessary contact names and telephone numbers, will have to be provided to the listing officer, diary manager or other court officer. The court will need to be satisfied that any equipment provided by the parties for use at the local site and also that at the remote site is of sufficient quality for a satisfactory transmission. The VCF arranging party

must ensure that an appropriate person will be present at the local site to supervise the operation of the VCF throughout the transmission in order to deal with any technical problems. That party must also arrange for a technical assistant to be similarly present at the remote site for like purposes.

11 It is recommended that the judge, practitioners and witness should arrive at their respective VCF sites about 20 minutes prior to the scheduled commencement of the transmission.

12 If the local site is not a courtroom, but a conference room or studio, the judge will need to determine who is to sit where. The VCF arranging party must take care to ensure that the number of microphones is adequate for the speakers and that the panning of the camera for the practitioners' table encompasses all legal representatives so that the viewer can see everyone seated there.

13 The proceedings, wherever they may take place, form part of a trial to which the public is entitled to have access (unless the court has determined that they should be heard in private). If the local site is to be a studio or conference room, the VCF arranging party must ensure that it provides sufficient accommodation to enable a reasonable number of members of the public to attend.

14 In cases where the local site is a studio or conference room, the VCF arranging party should make arrangements, if practicable, for the royal coat of arms to be placed above the judge's seat.

15 In cases in which the VCF is to be used for the taking of evidence, the VCF arranging party must arrange for recording equipment to be provided by the court which made the VCF direction so that the evidence can be recorded. An associate will normally be present to operate the recording equipment when the local site is a courtroom. The VCF arranging party should take steps to ensure that an associate is present to do likewise when it is a studio or conference room. The equipment should be set up and tested before the VCF transmission. It will often be a valuable safeguard for the VCF arranging party also to arrange for the provision of recording equipment at the remote site. This will provide a useful back-up if there is any reduction in sound quality during the transmission. A direction from the court for the making of such a back-up recording must, however, be obtained first. This is because the proceedings are court proceedings and, save as directed by the court, no other recording of them must be made. The court will direct what is to happen to the back-up recording.

16 Some countries may require that any oath or affirmation to be taken by a witness accord with local custom rather than the usual form of oath or affirmation used in England and Wales. The VCF arranging party must make all appropriate prior inquiries and put in place all arrangements necessary to enable the oath or affirmation to be taken in accordance with any local custom. That party must be in a position to inform the court what those inquiries were, what their outcome was and what arrangements have been made. If the oath or affirmation can be administered in the manner normal in England and Wales, the VCF arranging party must arrange in advance to have the appropriate holy book at the remote site. The associate will normally administer the oath.

17 Consideration will need to be given in advance to the documents to which the witness is likely to be referred. The parties should endeavour to agree on this. It will usually be most convenient for a bundle of the copy documents to be prepared in advance, which the VCF arranging party should then send to the remote site.

18 Additional documents are sometimes quite properly introduced during the course of a witness's evidence. To cater for this, the VCF arranging party should ensure that equipment is available to enable documents to be transmitted between sites during the course of the VCF transmission. Consideration should be given to whether to use a document camera. If it is decided to use one, arrangements for its use will need to be established in advance. The panel operator will need to know the number and size of documents or objects if their images are to be sent by document camera. In many cases, a simpler and sufficient alternative will be to ensure that there are fax transmission and reception facilities at the participating sites.

The hearing

19 The procedure for conducting the transmission will be determined by the judge. He will determine who is to control the cameras. In cases where the VCF is being used for an application in the course of the proceedings, the judge will ordinarily not enter the local site until both sites are on line. Similarly, at the conclusion of the hearing, he will ordinarily leave the local site while both sites are still on line. The following paragraphs apply primarily to cases where the VCF is being used for the taking of the evidence of a witness at a remote site. In all cases, the judge will need to decide whether court dress is appropriate when using VCF facilities. It might be appropriate when transmitting from courtroom to courtroom. It might not be when a commercial facility is being used.

20 At the beginning of the transmission, the judge will probably wish to introduce himself and the advocates to the witness. He will probably want to know who is at the remote site and will invite the witness to introduce himself and anyone else who is with him. He may wish to give directions as to the seating arrangements at the remote site so that those present are visible at the local site during the taking of the evidence. He will probably wish to explain to the witness the method of taking the oath or of affirming, the manner in which the evidence will be taken, and who will be conducting the examination and cross-examination. He will probably also wish to inform the witness of the matters referred to in paragraphs 6 and 7 above (co-ordination of picture with sound, and picture quality).

21 The examination of the witness at the remote site should follow as closely as possible the practice adopted when a witness is in the courtroom. During examination, cross-examination and re-examination, the witness must be able to see the legal representative asking the question and also any other person (whether another legal representative or the judge) making any statements in regard to the witness's evidence. It will in practice be most convenient if everyone remains seated throughout the transmission.

Amendments—CPR Updates 27, 69.

★★★★

PART 35
EXPERTS AND ASSESSORS

CONTENTS OF THIS PART

Rule		Page
35.1	Duty to restrict expert evidence	2128
35.2	Interpretation and definitions	2128
35.3	Experts – overriding duty to the court	2128
35.4	Court's power to restrict expert evidence	2128
35.5	General requirement for expert evidence to be given in a written report	2128
35.6	Written questions to experts	2128
35.7	Court's power to direct that evidence is to be given by a single joint expert	2129
35.8	Instructions to a single joint expert	2129
35.9	Power of court to direct a party to provide information	2130
35.10	Contents of report	2130
35.11	Use by one party of expert's report disclosed by another	2130
35.12	Discussions between experts	2130
35.13	Consequence of failure to disclose expert's report	2130
35.14	Expert's right to ask court for directions	2130
35.15	Assessors	2131
	Practice Direction 35 – Experts and Assessors	2131

PART III

35.1 Duty to restrict expert evidence

Expert evidence shall be restricted to that which is reasonably required to resolve the proceedings.

35.2 Interpretation and definitions

(1) A reference to an 'expert' in this Part is a reference to an expert who has been instructed to give or prepare evidence for the purpose of proceedings.

(2) 'Single joint expert' means an expert instructed to prepare a report for the court on behalf of two or more of the parties (including the claimant) to the proceedings.

Amendments—Substituted by SI 2009/2092.

Admissibility of 'expert evidence' (r 35.2)—The admissibility of expert evidence depends upon the expert being permitted to be called as a witness so that 'his opinion on any relevant matter on which he is qualified to give expert evidence shall be admissible in evidence' (Civil Evidence Act 1972, s 3(1)) and that other opinion evidence if given as facts 'personally perceived by him, is admissible as evidence of what he perceived' (Civil Evidence Act 1972, s 3(2)).

35.3 Experts – overriding duty to the court

(1) It is the duty of experts to help the court on matters within their expertise.

(2) This duty overrides any obligation to the person from whom experts have received instructions or by whom they are paid.

Amendments—SI 2009/2092.

35.4 Court's power to restrict expert evidence

(1) No party may call an expert or put in evidence an expert's report without the court's permission.

(2) When parties apply for permission they must provide an estimate of the costs of the proposed expert evidence and identify –

- (a) the field in which expert evidence is required and the issues which the expert evidence will address; and
- (b) where practicable, the name of the proposed expert.

(3) If permission is granted it shall be in relation only to the expert named or the field identified under paragraph (2). The order granting permission may specify the issues which the expert evidence should address.

(3A)–(3C) …

(Paragraph 7 of Practice Direction 35 sets out some of the circumstances the court will consider when deciding whether expert evidence should be given by a single joint expert).

(4) The court may limit the amount of a party's expert's fees and expenses that may be recovered from any other party.

Amendments—SI 2009/2092; SI 2009/3390; SI 2013/262; SI 2014/2044.

35.5 General requirement for expert evidence to be given in a written report

(1) Expert evidence is to be given in a written report unless the court directs otherwise.

(2) …

Amendments—SI 2009/2092.

35.6 Written questions to experts

(1) A party may put written questions about an expert's report (which must be proportionate) to –

- (a) an expert instructed by another party; or
- (b) a single joint expert appointed under rule 35.7.

(2) Written questions under paragraph (1) –

- (a) may be put once only;
- (b) must be put within 28 days of service of the expert's report; and
- (c) must be for the purpose only of clarification of the report;

unless in any case,

(i) the court gives permission; or
(ii) the other party agrees.

(3) An expert's answers to questions put in accordance with paragraph (1) shall be treated as part of the expert's report.

(4) Where –

(a) a party has put a written question to an expert instructed by another party; and
(b) the expert does not answer that question,

the court may make one or both of the following orders in relation to the party who instructed the expert –

(i) that the party may not rely on the evidence of that expert; or
(ii) that the party may not recover the fees and expenses of that expert from any other party.

Amendments—SI 2009/2092.

35.7 Court's power to direct that evidence is to be given by a single joint expert

(1) Where two or more parties wish to submit expert evidence on a particular issue, the court may direct that the evidence on that issue is to given by a single joint expert.

(2) Where the parties who wish to submit the evidence ('the relevant parties') cannot agree who should be the single joint expert, the court may –

(a) select the expert from a list prepared or identified by the relevant parties; or
(b) direct that the expert be selected in such other manner as the court may direct.

(3) Where the instructing parties cannot agree who should be the expert, the court may –

(a) select the expert from a list prepared or identified by the instructing parties; or
(b) direct that the expert be selected in such other manner as the court may direct.

Amendments—SI 2009/2092.

Dissatisfaction with joint expert's report for reasons 'not fanciful'—Where a party is dissatisfied with the joint expert's report for reasons 'which are not fanciful', the court has a discretion to order another report (*Daniels v Walker (Practice Note)* [2000] 1 WLR 1382, CA):

(1) Instruction of an expert on jointly agreed instructions.
(2) Failing that, each party can send separate instructions (r 35.8(1)).
(3) If a party is dissatisfied with the report, then within 28 days of service of the report (r 35.6(2)(b)) that party can raise questions of the expert (r 35.6(1); the rules permit this to be done of an expert jointly instructed: r 35.6(1)(b)).
(4) If both parties seek expert evidence and the court agrees, then the experts should discuss their reports before a decision as to whether either, or both, should be called to give evidence is made.
(5) Calling both to be cross-examined should be a 'last resort'.

35.8 Instructions to a single joint expert

(1) Where the court gives a direction under rule 35.7 for a single joint expert to be used, any relevant party may give instructions to the expert.

(2) When a party gives instructions to the expert that party must, at the same time, send a copy to the other relevant parties.

(3) The court may give directions about –

(a) the payment of the expert's fees and expenses; and
(b) any inspection, examination or experiments which the expert wishes to carry out.

(4) The court may, before an expert is instructed –

(a) limit the amount that can be paid by way of fees and expenses to the expert; and
(b) direct that some or all of the relevant parties pay that amount into court.

(5) Unless the court otherwise directs, the relevant parties are jointly and severally liable[(GL)] for the payment of the expert's fees and expenses.

Amendments—SI 2009/2092.

'any relevant party may give instructions to the expert' (r 35.8(1))—Separate instructions may be given to the single joint expert by individual parties (i e there is no need for both or all parties jointly to agree a letter of instruction: c f FPR 2010, r 25.12).

35.9 Power of court to direct a party to provide information

Where a party has access to information which is not reasonably available to another party, the court may direct the party who has access to the information to –

(a) prepare and file a document recording the information; and
(b) serve a copy of that document on the other party.

Amendments—SI 2009/2092.

35.10 Contents of report

(1) An expert's report must comply with the requirements set out in Practice Direction 35.

(2) At the end of an expert's report there must be a statement that the expert understands and has complied with their duty to the court.

(3) The expert's report must state the substance of all material instructions, whether written or oral, on the basis of which the report was written.

(4) The instructions referred to in paragraph (3) shall not be privileged(GL) against disclosure but the court will not, in relation to those instructions –

(a) order disclosure of any specific document; or
(b) permit any questioning in court, other than by the party who instructed the expert,

unless it is satisfied that there are reasonable grounds to consider the statement of instructions given under paragraph (3) to be inaccurate or incomplete.

Amendments—SI 2009/2092; SI 2009/3390.

35.11 Use by one party of expert's report disclosed by another

Where a party has disclosed an expert's report, any party may use that expert's report as evidence at the trial.

35.12 Discussions between experts

(1) The court may, at any stage, direct a discussion between experts for the purpose of requiring the experts to –

(a) identify and discuss the expert issues in the proceedings; and
(b) where possible, reach an agreed opinion on those issues.

(2) The court may specify the issues which the experts must discuss.

(3) The court may direct that following a discussion between the experts they must prepare a statement for the court setting out those issues on which –

(a) they agree; and
(b) they disagree, with a summary of their reasons for disagreeing.

(4) The content of the discussion between the experts shall not be referred to at the trial unless the parties agree.

(5) Where experts reach agreement on an issue during their discussions, the agreement shall not bind the parties unless the parties expressly agree to be bound by the agreement.

Amendments—SI 2001/4015; SI 2009/2092.

35.13 Consequence of failure to disclose expert's report

A party who fails to disclose an expert's report may not use the report at the trial or call the expert to give evidence orally unless the court gives permission.

35.14 Expert's right to ask court for directions

(1) Experts may file written requests for directions for the purpose of assisting them in carrying out their functions.

(2) An expert must, unless the court orders otherwise, provide a copies of the proposed requests for directions under paragraph (1) –

(a) to the party instructing them at least 7 days before they file the requests; and
(b) to all other parties, at least 4 days before they file them.

(3) The court, when it gives directions, may also direct that a party be served with a copy of the directions.

(a), (b) …

Amendments—SI 2001/4015; SI 2009/2092.

35.15 Assessors

This rule applies where the court appoints one or more persons under section 70 of the Senior Courts Act 1981 or section 63 of the County Courts Act 1984 as an assessor.

(2) An assessor will assist the court in dealing with a matter in which the assessor has skill and experience.

(3) An assessor will take such part in the proceedings as the court may direct and in particular the court may direct an assessor to –

(a) prepare a report for the court on any matter at issue in the proceedings; and
(b) attend the whole or any part of the trial to advise the court on any such matter.

(4) If an assessor prepares a report for the court before the trial has begun –

(a) the court will send a copy to each of the parties; and
(b) the parties may use it at trial.

(5) The remuneration to be paid to an assessor is to be determined by the court and will form part of the costs of the proceedings.

(6) The court may order any party to deposit in the court office a specified sum in respect of an assessor's fees and, where it does so, the assessor will not be asked to act until the sum has been deposited.

(7) Paragraphs (5) and (6) do not apply where the remuneration of the assessor is to be paid out of money provided by Parliament.

Amendments—SI 2009/2092.

Practice Direction 35 – Experts and Assessors

This Practice Direction supplements CPR Part 35

Amendments—CPR Update 50.

Introduction

1 Part 35 is intended to limit the use of oral expert evidence to that which is reasonably required. In addition, where possible, matters requiring expert evidence should be dealt with by only one expert. Experts and those instructing them are expected to have regard to the guidance contained in the Guidance for the Instruction of Experts in Civil Claims 2014 (http://www.judiciary.gov.uk).

(Further guidance on experts is contained in Annex C to the Practice Direction (Pre-Action Conduct)).

Amendments—CPR Update 76.

Expert Evidence – General Requirements

2.1 Expert evidence should be the independent product of the expert uninfluenced by the pressures of litigation.

2.2 Experts should assist the court by providing objective, unbiased opinions on matters within their expertise, and should not assume the role of an advocate.

2.3 Experts should consider all material facts, including those which might detract from their opinions.

2.4 Experts should make it clear –

(a) when a question or issue falls outside their expertise; and
(b) when they are not able to reach a definite opinion, for example because they have insufficient information.

2.5 If, after producing a report, an expert's view changes on any material matter, such change of view should be communicated to all the parties without delay, and when appropriate to the court.

2.6 (1) In a soft tissue injury claim, where permission is given for a fixed cost medical report, the first report must be obtained from an accredited medical expert selected via the MedCo Portal (website at: www.medco.org.uk).

(2) The cost of obtaining a further report from an expert not listed in rule 35.4(3C)(a) to (d) is not subject to rules 45.19(2A)(b) or 45.29I(2A)(b), but the use of that expert and the cost must be justified.

(3) 'Accredited medical expert', 'fixed cost medical report', 'MedCo', and 'soft tissue injury claim' have the same meaning as in paragraph 1.1(A1), (10A), (12A) and (16A), respectively, of the RTA Protocol.

Amendments—CPR Update 78. Paragraph 2.6(1) applies only to any soft tissue injury claim for damages which arises from a road traffic accident where the Claim Notification Form is submitted on or after 6 April 2015.

Form and Content of an Expert's Report

3.1 An expert's report should be addressed to the court and not to the party from whom the expert has received instructions.

3.2 An expert's report must:

(1) give details of the expert's qualifications;
(2) give details of any literature or other material which has been relied on in making the report;
(3) contain a statement setting out the substance of all facts and instructions which are material to the opinions expressed in the report or upon which those opinions are based;
(4) make clear which of the facts stated in the report are within the expert's own knowledge;
(5) say who carried out any examination, measurement, test or experiment which the expert has used for the report, give the qualifications of that person, and say whether or not the test or experiment has been carried out under the expert's supervision;
(6) where there is a range of opinion on the matters dealt with in the report –
    (a) summarise the range of opinions; and
    (b) give reasons for the expert's own opinion;
(7) contain a summary of the conclusions reached;
(8) if the expert is not able to give an opinion without qualification, state the qualification; and
(9) contain a statement that the expert –
    (a) understands their duty to the court, and has complied with that duty; and
    (b) is aware of the requirements of Part 35, this practice direction and the Guidance for the Instruction of Experts in Civil Claims 2014.

3.3 An expert's report must be verified by a statement of truth in the following form –

'I confirm that I have made clear which facts and matters referred to in this report are within my own knowledge and which are not. Those that are within my own knowledge I confirm to be true. The opinions I have expressed represent my true and complete professional opinions on the matters to which they refer.

(Part 22 deals with statements of truth. Rule 32.14 sets out the consequences of verifying a document containing a false statement without an honest belief in its truth.)

Amendments—CPR Update 76.

Information

4 Under rule 35.9 the court may direct a party with access to information, which is not reasonably available to another party to serve on that other party a document, which records the information. The document served must include sufficient details of all the facts, tests, experiments and assumptions which underlie any part of the information to enable the party on whom it is served to make, or to obtain, a proper interpretation of the information and an assessment of its significance.

Instructions

5 Cross-examination of experts on the contents of their instructions will not be allowed unless the court permits it (or unless the party who gave the instructions consents). Before it gives permission the court must be satisfied that there are reasonable grounds to consider that the statement in the report of the substance of the instructions is inaccurate or incomplete. If the court is so satisfied, it will allow the cross-examination where it appears to be in the interests of justice.

Questions to Experts

6.1 Where a party sends a written question or questions under rule 35.6 direct to an expert, a copy of the questions must, at the same time, be sent to the other party or parties.

6.2 The party or parties instructing the expert must pay any fees charged by that expert for answering questions put under rule 35.6. This does not affect any decision of the court as to the party who is ultimately to bear the expert's fees.

Single joint expert

7 When considering whether to give permission for the parties to rely on expert evidence and whether that evidence should be from a single joint expert the court will take into account all the circumstances in particular, whether:

(a) it is proportionate to have separate experts for each party on a particular issue with reference to –
 (i) the amount in dispute;
 (ii) the importance to the parties; and
 (iii) the complexity of the issue;

(b) the instruction of a single joint expert is likely to assist the parties and the court to resolve the issue more speedily and in a more cost-effective way than separately instructed experts;

(c) expert evidence is to be given on the issue of liability, causation or quantum;

(d) the expert evidence falls within a substantially established area of knowledge which is unlikely to be in dispute or there is likely to be a range of expert opinion;

(e) a party has already instructed an expert on the issue in question and whether or not that was done in compliance with any practice direction or relevant pre-action protocol;

(f) questions put in accordance with rule 35.6 are likely to remove the need for the other party to instruct an expert if one party has already instructed an expert;

(g) questions put to a single joint expert may not conclusively deal with all issues that may require testing prior to trial;

(h) a conference may be required with the legal representatives, experts and other witnesses which may make instruction of a single joint expert impractical; and

(i) a claim to privilege(GL) makes the instruction of any expert as a single joint expert inappropriate.

PART III

Orders

8 Where an order requires an act to be done by an expert, or otherwise affects an expert, the party instructing that expert must serve a copy of the order on the expert. The claimant must serve the order on a single joint expert.

Discussions between experts

9.1 Unless directed by the court discussions between experts are not mandatory. Parties must consider, with their experts, at an early stage, whether there is likely to be any useful purpose in holding an expert's discussion and if so when.

9.2 The purpose of discussions between experts is not for experts to settle cases but to agree and narrow issues and in particular to identify:

(i) the extent of the agreement between them;

(ii) the points of and short reasons for any disagreement;

(iii) action, if any, which may be taken to resolve any outstanding points of disagreement; and

(iv) any further material issues not raised and the extent to which these issues are agreed.

9.3 Where the experts are to meet, the parties must discuss and if possible agree whether an agenda is necessary, and if so attempt to agree one that helps the experts to focus on the issues which need to be discussed. The agenda must not be in the form of leading questions or hostile in tone.

9.4 Unless ordered by the court, or agreed by all parties, and the experts, neither the parties nor their legal representatives may attend experts discussions.

9.5 If the legal representatives do attend –

(i) they should not normally intervene in the discussion, except to answer questions put to them by the experts or to advise on the law; and

(ii) he experts may if they so wish hold part of their discussions in the absence of the legal representatives.

9.6 A statement must be prepared by the experts dealing with paragraphs 9.2(i)–(iv) above. Individual copies of the statements must be signed by the experts at the conclusion of the discussion, or as soon thereafter as practicable, and in any event within 7 days. Copies of the statements must be provided to the parties no later than 14 days after signing.

9.7 Experts must give their own opinions to assist the court and do not require the authority of the parties to sign a joint statement.

9.8 If an expert significantly alters an opinion, the joint statement must include a note or addendum by that expert explaining the change of opinion.

Assessors

10.1 An assessor may be appointed to assist the court under rule 35.15. Not less than 21 days before making any such appointment, the court will notify each party in writing of the name of the proposed assessor, of the matter in respect of which the assistance of the assessor will be sought and of the qualifications of the assessor to give that assistance.

10.2 Where any person has been proposed for appointment as an assessor, any party may object to that person either personally or in respect of that person's qualification.

10.3 Any such objection must be made in writing and filed with the court within 7 days of receipt of the notification referred to in paragraph 10.1 and will be taken into account by the court in deciding whether or not to make the appointment.

10.4 Copies of any report prepared by the assessor will be sent to each of the parties but the assessor will not give oral evidence or be open to cross-examination or questioning.

****

PART 36
OFFERS TO SETTLE

CONTENTS OF THIS PART

Rule		Page
36.1	Scope of this Part	2135
	Section I *Part 36 Offers to Settle*	
	General	
36.2	Scope of this Section	2136
36.3	Definitions	2136
	Making Offers	
36.5	Form and content of a Part 36 offer	2137
36.6	Part 36 offers – defendant's offer	2137
36.7	Time when a Part 36 offer is made	2137
	Accepting offers	
36.11	Acceptance of a Part 36 offer	2138
36.13	Costs consequences of acceptance of a Part 36 offer	2138
36.14	Other effects of acceptance of a Part 36 offer	2139
	Unaccepted offers	
36.16	Restriction on disclosure of a Part 36 offer	2140
36.17	Costs consequences following judgment	2140

Amendments—Part substituted by SI 2014/3299.

A self-contained costs offer procedure—CPR 1998, Pt 36 replaces the former procedure for payment into court (abolished since 2007) and *Calderbank* letters (*Calderbank v Calderbank* (1975) FLR Rep 113, CA) for civil claims. It provides a procedure that enables the following:

- Offers to settle to be made before issue of proceedings (CPR 1998, r 36.7(1));
- Offers to be made in respect of individual issues; and
- It is intended to encourage claimants to put forward proposals for settlement on similar costs terms as defendants (with the added incentive provided by favourable rates for payment in r 36.17(4)).

Restriction on costs discretion for courts—The effect of Pt 36 is to introduce a regime that reduces the circumstances in which the court is called upon to decide on costs questions. Rules prescribe that acceptance of an offer entitles the claimant to costs (r 36.13(1), save on late acceptance) and the consequences for either party of a judgment at trial being more or less advantageous to the offeror party (r 36.17(3),(4)). The threshold for overriding r 36.17(3),(4) is only whether it would be 'unjust to make [a costs] order'.

Pt 36 proposals—Proposals can be made by claimant or defendant provided they are in the form required by r 36.5. Proposals are then akin to without prejudice or *Calderbank* proposals that cannot be disclosed to the court (r 36.16). Specific costs consequences follow from any acceptance of proposals (r 35.13) or from a judgment and from the fact of beating or failing to beat a Pt 36 proposal (r 36.17).

HRA 1998: damages claims under s 8—Part 36 applies to all CPR 1998 civil proceedings claims (eg I(PFD)A 1975, TLATA 1996), including for HRA 1998, s 8 damages arising alongside care or other children proceedings. In *SW & TW (Human Rights Claim: Procedure) (No 1)* [2017] EWHC 450 (Fam), Cobb J gave guidance as to the issue of HRA 1998 damages claims under CPR 1998, Pt 8 and recalled that the Pt 36 regime applies to such claims (at [3](vi)). Thus, a child or parents (or possibly another relative or carer of the child) will be the claimant in parallel with, or after conclusion of, the children proceedings. The local authority will be the defendant.

Practice direction—Pt 36 is supported by PD36 (see *Civil Court Service*, LexisNexis), which explains the procedure for making and acceptance of an offer, and for its alteration of withdrawal. References to the PD are incorporated into the commentary as need be.

36.1 Scope of this Part

(1) This Part contains a self-contained procedural code about offers to settle made pursuant to the procedure set out in this Part ('Part 36 offers').

…

Amendments—Substituted by SI 2014/3299.

SCA 1981, s 51—SCA 1981, s 51(1) makes decisions as to costs a matter of court discretion, subject 'to rules of court'. CPR 1998, Pt 36 is an example of where rules override the court's general discretion as to award of costs.

Section I

Part 36 Offers to Settle

General

36.2 Scope of this Section

(1) …

(2) Nothing in this Section prevents a party making an offer to settle in whatever way that party chooses, but if the offer is not made in accordance with rule 36.5, it will not have the consequences specified in this Section.

(Rule 44.2 requires the court to consider an offer to settle that does not have the costs consequences set out in this Section in deciding what order to make about costs.)

(3) A Part 36 offer may be made in respect of the whole, or part of, or any issue that arises in –

(a) a claim, counterclaim or other additional claim; or

(b) an appeal or cross-appeal from a decision made at a trial.

…

Amendments—Substituted by SI 2014/3299.

'this Section'—The provisions under review here are in Pt 36, S 1, namely the rules relevant to family and other relevant civil proceedings in rr 36.2 to 36.23.

Calderbank letter and Pt 36 formalities; court's discretion (r 36.2(2))—Rule 36.17 sets out the formal consequences of offers on costs following judgment, but the court still has discretion as to award of costs even where Pt 36 formalities are not complied with (SCA 1981, s 51(3); CPR 1998, r 44.2; *French v Groupama Insurance Company Ltd* [2011] EWCA Civ 1119). For an example of the court holding a defendant to a costs order where she refused pre-proceedings *Calderbank* proposals in what would now be TOLATA 1996 proceedings, see *Butcher v Wolfe and Wolfe* [1999] 1 FLR 334, CA.

Mediation—At [3](x) in *SW & TW* (above), Cobb J stressed the danger that costs can quickly dwarf the damages that can be claimed; and see *Anufrijeva v Southwark LBC* [2004] 1 FLR 8, CA where the Court of Appeal made the same point. Mediation is urged (and see *Cowl & Ors v Plymouth City Council* [2001] EWCA Civ 1935 for use of mediation in public law cases). However, an offer in mediation cannot be a Pt 36 offer: it must be confirmed in writing using the formalities in r 36.5(1).

36.3 Definitions

In this Section –

(a) the party who makes an offer is the 'offeror';

(b) the party to whom an offer is made is the 'offeree';

(c) a 'trial' means any trial in a case whether it is a trial of all issues or a trial of liability, quantum or some other issue in the case;

(d) a trial is 'in progress' from the time when it starts until the time when judgment is given or handed down;

(e) a case is 'decided' when all issues in the case have been determined, whether at one or more trials;

(f) 'trial judge' includes the judge (if any) allocated in advance to conduct a trial; and

(g) 'the relevant period' means –

(i) in the case of an offer made not less than 21 days before a trial, the period specified under rule 36.5(1)(c) or such longer period as the parties agree;

(ii) otherwise, the period up to the end of such trial.

Amendments—Substituted by SI 2014/3299.

****

Making Offers

36.5 Form and content of a Part 36 offer

(1) A Part 36 offer must –

(a) be in writing;
(b) make clear that it is made pursuant to Part 36;
(c) specify a period of not less than 21 days within which the defendant will be liable for the claimant's costs in accordance with rule 36.13 or 36.20 if the offer is accepted;
(d) state whether it relates to the whole of the claim or to part of it or to an issue that arises in it and if so to which part or issue; and
(e) state whether it takes into account any counterclaim.

…

(2) Paragraph (1)(c) does not apply if the offer is made less than 21 days before the start of a trial.

(3) …

(4) A Part 36 offer which offers to pay or offers to accept a sum of money will be treated as inclusive of all interest until –

(a) the date on which the period specified under rule 36.5(1)(c) expires; or
(b) if rule 36.5(2) applies, a date 21 days after the date the offer was made.

Amendments—Substituted by SI 2014/3299.

Formalities - PD36—Para 1.1 draws attention to the fact that an offer or any acceptance can in Form N242A; but this is not obligatory, provided that the formalities in r 36.5(1) are complied with. Where a party is represented, any offer or acceptance must be served on their legal representative (para 1.2). For a Pt 36 offer to have full effect under CPR 1998, Pt 36 (e g under r 36.13), the formalities in r 36.5(1) must be complied with in full. That said, the court can still take into account a deficient offer letter when it exercises discretion.

Claimant's proposals in HRA 1998 damages claims—In *SW & TW* (above), Cobb J stressed the importance of claimants being realistic as to the amounts of their claims (at [41]–[45]); and see HRA 1998, s 8(4): principles of award in European Convention 1950 jurisprudence). Claimants are urged to make offers to settle in a way that, pre-Pt 36, they were under no obligation to do; but in exchange r 36.17(4) provides an extra incentive to claimants to place their settlement cards on the table early.

Offer to settle: legal aid—Civil Legal Aid (Procedure) Regulations 2012, reg 40 requires that any 'offer to settle' should be reported to the Legal Aid Agency and this would include a Pt 36 offer made to a legally aided party.

36.6 Part 36 offers – defendant's offer

(1) Subject to rules 36.18(3) and 36.19(1), a Part 36 offer by a defendant to pay a sum of money in settlement of a claim must be an offer to pay a single sum of money.

(2) A defendant's offer that includes an offer to pay all or part of the sum at a date later than 14 days following the date of acceptance will not be treated as a Part 36 offer unless the offeree accepts the offer.

Amendments—Substituted by SI 2014/3299.

Defendant's offer under HRA 1998—HRA 1998, s 8 empowers the court to award such relief or other remedy within its powers (s 8(1)) and to award damages only where necessary (s 8(3)). Thus, under r 36.6 the form of the offer may not only be monetary: it may also or in the alternative be in the form of an apology or submission to a suitable declaration (as was the case in *Anufrijeva v Southwark LBC* (above)). Thus a defendant's offer may be only of a declaration and apology, but of no monetary element.

36.7 Time when a Part 36 offer is made

(1) A Part 36 offer may be made at any time, including before the commencement of proceedings.

(2) A Part 36 offer is made when it is served on the offeree.

(Part 6 provides detailed rules about service of documents.)

Amendments—Substituted by SI 2014/3299.

'before the commencement of proceedings'—Offers complying with r 36.5(1) formalities are capable of attracting the costs consequences of CPR 1998, r 36.13, including offers if made before the issue of proceedings (for which see also *Butcher v Wolfe* (above)).

****

Accepting offers

36.11 Acceptance of a Part 36 offer

(1) A Part 36 offer is accepted by serving written notice of acceptance on the offeror.

(2) Subject to paragraphs (3) and (4) and to rule 36.12, a Part 36 offer may be accepted at any time (whether or not the offeree has subsequently made a different offer), unless it has already been withdrawn.

…

(3) The court's permission is required to accept a Part 36 offer where –

(a)–(c) …
(d) a trial is in progress.

…

(4) Where the court gives permission under paragraph (3), unless all the parties have agreed costs, the court must make an order dealing with costs, and may order that the costs consequences set out in rule 36.13 apply.

Amendments—Substituted by SI 2014/3299.

Acceptance—Acceptance of an offer can be in Form N242A but this is not obligatory. It must be in writing and (as per PD36, para 3.1) it must be served on:

- the offeror or their legal representative (if represented); and
- the court.

Permission of the court—If permission of the court is required, application is made by CPR 1998, Pt 23 application to a judge other than the trial judge, unless parties agree otherwise (PD36, para 3.2).

****

36.13 Costs consequences of acceptance of a Part 36 offer

(1) Subject to paragraphs (2) and (4) and to rule 36.20, where a Part 36 offer is accepted within the relevant period the claimant will be entitled to the costs of the proceedings (including their recoverable pre-action costs) up to the date on which notice of acceptance was served on the offeror.

…

(2) Where –

(a) a defendant's Part 36 offer relates to part only of the claim; and
(b) at the time of serving notice of acceptance within the relevant period the claimant abandons the balance of the claim,

the claimant will only be entitled to the costs of such part of the claim unless the court orders otherwise.

(3) Except where the recoverable costs are fixed by these Rules, costs under paragraphs (1) and (2) are to be assessed on the standard basis if the amount of costs is not agreed.

(Rule 44.3(2) explains the standard basis for the assessment of costs.)

…

(4) Where –

(a) a Part 36 offer which was made less than 21 days before the start of a trial is accepted; or
(b) a Part 36 offer which relates to the whole of the claim is accepted after expiry of the relevant period; or
(c) subject to paragraph (2), a Part 36 offer which does not relate to the whole of the claim is accepted at any time,

the liability for costs must be determined by the court unless the parties have agreed the costs.

(5) Where paragraph (4)(b) applies but the parties cannot agree the liability for costs, the court must, unless it considers it unjust to do so, order that –

(a) the claimant be awarded costs up to the date on which the relevant period expired; and

(b) the offeree do pay the offeror's costs for the period from the date of expiry of the relevant period to the date of acceptance.

(6) In considering whether it would be unjust to make the orders specified in paragraph (5), the court must take into account all the circumstances of the case including the matters listed in rule 36.17(5).

(7) The claimant's costs include any costs incurred in dealing with the defendant's counterclaim if the Part 36 offer states that it takes it into account.

Amendments—Substituted by SI 2014/3299.

'the costs of the proceedings' (r 36.13(1))—The costs of the proceedings can relate only to the costs of the separate HRA damages proceedings contained in the claim under CPR 1998 and not, for example, the costs of the parallel or earlier care or other children proceedings.

Deemed costs order—CPR 1998, rr 36.13(1) and 44.9(1)(b) deem orders for costs to have been made on acceptance by a claimant of a Pt 36 offer within the relevant period. These costs will be assessed on the standard basis (r 36.13(3)) unless otherwise agreed.

Legal aid statutory charge and costs; separate HRA 1998 proceedings—Any part of a legal aid lawyer's costs not covered by payment by a defendant will be subject to the legal aid statutory charge (LASPOA 2012, s 25(1)) and a retention must be kept by the lawyer to cover this before any payment of damages is made to the client. The costs can only relate to the claim (eg under HRA 1998, s 8) to which the offer relates. The extent to which the charge can apply to any other proceedings (eg under CA 1989, Pts 4 or 5) is considered under LASPOA 2012, s 25.

'determined by the court' (r 36.13(4))—If costs cannot be agreed, application for an order for the periods covered by r 36.13(4) must be made by a costs claimant for a determination:

- In the case of damages where proceedings have already been issued, under the CPR 1998, Pt 23 procedure;
- If a claim has been settled prior to issue of proceedings, by the CPR 1998, Pt 8 procedure.

36.14 Other effects of acceptance of a Part 36 offer

(1) If a Part 36 offer is accepted, the claim will be stayed.

(2) In the case of acceptance of a Part 36 offer which relates to the whole claim, the stay will be upon the terms of the offer.

(3) If a Part 36 offer which relates to part only of the claim is accepted, the claim will be stayed as to that part upon the terms of the offer.

(4) If the approval of the court is required before a settlement can be binding, any stay which would otherwise arise on the acceptance of a Part 36 offer will take effect only when that approval has been given.

(5) Any stay arising under this rule will not affect the power of the court –

(a) to enforce the terms of a Part 36 offer; or

(b) to deal with any question of costs (including interest on costs) relating to the proceedings.

(6) Unless the parties agree otherwise in writing, where a Part 36 offer that is or includes an offer to pay or accept a single sum of money is accepted, that sum must be paid to the claimant within 14 days of the date of –

(a) acceptance; or

(b) the order when the court makes an order under rule 41.2 (order for an award of provisional damages) or rule 41.8 (order for an award of periodical payments), unless the court orders otherwise.

(7) If such sum is not paid within 14 days of acceptance of the offer, or such other period as has been agreed, the claimant may enter judgment for the unpaid sum.

(8) Where –

(a) a Part 36 offer (or part of a Part 36 offer) which is not an offer to which paragraph (6) applies is accepted; and

(b) a party alleges that the other party has not honoured the terms of the offer,

that party may apply to enforce the terms of the offer without the need for a new claim.

Amendments—Substituted by SI 2014/3299.

****

Unaccepted offers

36.16 Restriction on disclosure of a Part 36 offer

(1) A Part 36 offer will be treated as 'without prejudice except as to costs'.

(2) The fact that a Part 36 offer has been made and the terms of such offer must not be communicated to the trial judge until the case has been decided.

(3) Paragraph (2) does not apply –

- (a) where the defence of tender before claim has been raised;
- (b) where the proceedings have been stayed under rule 36.14 following acceptance of a Part 36 offer;
- (c) where the offeror and the offeree agree in writing that it should not apply; or
- (d) where, although the case has not been decided –
  - (i) any part of, or issue in, the case has been decided; and
  - (ii) the Part 36 offer relates only to parts or issues that have been decided.

(4) In a case to which paragraph (3)(d)(i) applies, the trial judge –

- (a) may be told whether or not there are Part 36 offers other than those referred to in paragraph (3)(d)(ii); but
- (b) must not be told the terms of any such other offers unless any of paragraphs (3)(a) to (c) applies.

Amendments—Substituted by SI 2014/3299.

Part 36 and without prejudice proposals—Rule 36.16 puts the Pt 36 offer on a footing equivalent to without prejudice (or *Calderbank*) proposals in terms of not being seen by the court, but with the exceptions set out in r 36.16.

36.17 Costs consequences following judgment

(1) Subject to rule 36.21, this rule applies where upon judgment being entered –

- (a) a claimant fails to obtain a judgment more advantageous than a defendant's Part 36 offer; or
- (b) judgment against the defendant is at least as advantageous to the claimant as the proposals contained in a claimant's Part 36 offer.

…

(2) For the purposes of paragraph (1), in relation to any money claim or money element of a claim, 'more advantageous' means better in money terms by any amount, however small, and 'at least as advantageous' shall be construed accordingly.

(3) Subject to paragraphs (7) and (8), where paragraph (1)(a) applies, the court must, unless it considers it unjust to do so, order that the defendant is entitled to –

- (a) costs (including any recoverable pre-action costs) from the date on which the relevant period expired; and
- (b) interest on those costs.

(4) Subject to paragraph (7), where paragraph (1)(b) applies, the court must, unless it considers it unjust to do so, order that the claimant is entitled to –

- (a) interest on the whole or part of any sum of money (excluding interest) awarded, at a rate not exceeding 10% above base rate for some or all of the period starting with the date on which the relevant period expired;
- (b) costs (including any recoverable pre-action costs) on the indemnity basis from the date on which the relevant period expired;
- (c) interest on those costs at a rate not exceeding 10% above base rate; and
- (d) provided that the case has been decided and there has not been a previous order under this sub-paragraph, an additional amount, which shall not exceed £75,000, calculated by applying the prescribed percentage set out below to an amount which is –

(i) the sum awarded to the claimant by the court; or
(ii) where there is no monetary award, the sum awarded to the claimant by the court in respect of costs –

Amount awarded by the court	*Prescribed percentage*
Up to £500,000	10% of the amount awarded
Above £500,000	10% of the first £500,000 and (subject to the limit of £75,000) 5% of any amount above that figure.

(5) In considering whether it would be unjust to make the orders referred to in paragraphs (3) and (4), the court must take into account all the circumstances of the case including –

(a) the terms of any Part 36 offer;
(b) the stage in the proceedings when any Part 36 offer was made, including in particular how long before the trial started the offer was made;
(c) the information available to the parties at the time when the Part 36 offer was made;
(d) the conduct of the parties with regard to the giving of or refusal to give information for the purposes of enabling the offer to be made or evaluated; and
(e) whether the offer was a genuine attempt to settle the proceedings.

(6) Where the court awards interest under this rule and also awards interest on the same sum and for the same period under any other power, the total rate of interest must not exceed 10% above base rate.

(7) Paragraphs (3) and (4) do not apply to a Part 36 offer –

(a) which has been withdrawn;
(b) which has been changed so that its terms are less advantageous to the offeree where the offeree has beaten the less advantageous offer;
(c) made less than 21 days before trial, unless the court has abridged the relevant period.

(8) Paragraph (3) does not apply to a soft tissue injury claim to which rule 36.21 applies.

(Rule 44.2 requires the court to consider an offer to settle that does not have the costs consequences set out in this Section in deciding what order to make about costs.)

Amendments—Substituted by SI 2014/3299.

Scheme for costs under r 36.17: a Pt 36 offer as or 'more advantageous'—The scheme for award of costs under r 36.17 is designed to cater for offers both by claimants and defendants, and to provide a composite rule for both. In either case, it depends on the judgment made at trial:

- Defendant (e g a local authority in a HRA 1998 damages claim) to pay costs, interest and other payments per r 36.17(4) where a claimant's judgment is 'at least as advantageous' (or better) as a defendant's Pt 36 offer (r 36.17(1)(b)); or
- Claimant to pay costs per r 36.17(3) if s/he does not beat the defendants Pt 36 offer (r 36.17(1)(a)).

Obligatory award of costs—Costs must be awarded where they come within the periods covered by r 36.17(3),(4) unless the court considers this 'unjust' (r 36.17(3)), which is tested by reference to the inclusive list of factors in r 36.17(5).

Costs on indemnity basis (r 36.17(4)(b))—An award of costs on the indemnity basis as part of the costs award is not intended to stigmatise the defendant. It is merely part of the Pt 36 scheme to encourage settlement (*McPhilemy v Times Newspapers Ltd & Ors* [2002] 1 WLR 934, CA).

Failure to engage in mediation—Failure to engage in mediation or to respond to a request to mediate may be among the factors under r 36.17(5) that could persuade a court to find a costs order unjust (*Halsey v Milton Keynes General NHS Trust* [2004] EWCA Civ 576; *PGF II SA v OMFS Company 1 Ltd* [2013] EWCA Civ 1288).

****

PART 39
MISCELLANEOUS PROVISIONS RELATING TO HEARINGS

****

39.2 General rule – hearing to be in public

(1) The general rule is that a hearing is to be in public.

(2) The requirement for a hearing to be in public does not require the court to make special arrangements for accommodating members of the public.

(3) A hearing, or any part of it, may be in private if –

- (a) publicity would defeat the object of the hearing;
- (b) it involves matters relating to national security;
- (c) it involves confidential information (including information relating to personal financial matters) and publicity would damage that confidentiality;
- (d) a private hearing is necessary to protect the interests of any child or protected party;
- (e) it is a hearing of an application made without notice and it would be unjust to any respondent for there to be a public hearing;
- (f) it involves uncontentious matters arising in the administration of trusts or in the administration of a deceased person's estate; or
- (g) the court considers this to be necessary, in the interests of justice.

(4) The court may order that the identity of any party or witness must not be disclosed if it considers non-disclosure necessary in order to protect the interests of that party or witness.

Amendments—Amended by SI 2007/2204.

Open justice principle: 'a hearing is to be in public' (r 39.2(1))—It is a common law principle that all proceedings in civil courts must be in open court (*Scott v Scott* (1913) FLR Rep 657, HL; *A v British Broadcasting Corporation* [2014] UKSC 25). It is confirmed by European Convention 1950, Art 6(1). There are exceptions (summarised in CPR 1998, r 39.2(3)) and all proceedings governed by FPR 2010 are heard in private, save where rules or other enactment provide (FPR 2010, r 27.10). The press and others whom the court permit may be admitted (FPR 2010, r 27.11(2)(f),(g)).

Appeals in family proceedings

(1) Appeals to the Court of Appeal—CPR 1998 apples to appeals to the Court of Appeal and whether they are to be in private or the parties names anonymised will be tested under r 39.2. Open court principles apply save where r 39.2(3) exempts part or all of the hearing or the parties' names from publicity.

(2) Appeals in the family courts—Appeals in the family courts under FPR 2010, Pt 30 are family proceedings covered by FPR 2010: family proceedings privacy and anonymisation principles under FPR 2010, r 27.10 apply.

Anonymisation—The principles in r 39.2(3) apply to anonymisation in the Court of Appeal: the hearing will be in public, the parties named and any judgment in reported, save for cogent reason (*Re Guardian News and Media Ltd* [2010] UKSC 1; *Norman v Norman* [2017] EWCA Civ 49):

(1) *Parties and witnesses in the Court of Appeal* 'It is very rare for [the Court of Appeal] to order anonymisation' in an ancillary relief appeal (*K v L (Non-Matrimonial Property: Special Contribution)* [2011] 2 FLR 980, CA, at [25]). In making any order for anonymisation, the court will be guided by the principles in *JIH v News Group Newspapers* [2011] EWCA Civ 42, at [21], which includes that there is no general exception where private matters are in issue and an order should not necessarily be made merely because the parties consent.

(2) *Children at the centre of an appeal* Anonymisation is more likely in the case of an application that involves, or includes, the European Convention 1950, Art 8 rights of a child (*K v L* (above); *PJS v News Group Newspapers Ltd* [2016] 2 FLR 251, SC, at [72]).

(3) *Proceedings under HRA 1998, ss 7 and 8* Proceedings under HRA 1998 will be under CPR 1998, Pt 8 or 54 and are in open court (CPR 1998, r 39.2(1)) including any consent order (e g in child settlement cases), unless an order is made under r 39.2(3) (e g (c) or (d)). Parties should include any application for anonymity in their claim form or by separate application under CPR 1998, Pt 23. Children proceedings (but not necessarily for their parents: *Re S (Identification: Restrictions on Publication)* [2005] 1 FLR 591, HL) may be apt for anonymity (*X v Dartford and Gravesham NHS Trust (Personal Injury Bar Association and another intervening)* [2015] 1 WLR 3647, CA; *PJS v News Group Newspapers Ltd* [2016] 2 FLR 251, SC (adult anonymity at interim hearing stage)).

Ancillary relief proceedings in the Court of Appeal: application for privacy or anonymisation—In the case of hearings of family proceedings in the Court of Appeal (i e which proceed under CPR 1998, Pt 52, although not for appeals under FPR 2010, Pt 30, which remain family proceedings and therefore covered by FPR 2010, r 27.10), the hearing will be in open court and the parties named unless application is formally made to the court. A 'properly formulated paper application' for anonymity must be made (save where the request is only to leave out information about children, when a letter of request will suffice):

- If made at the time of the appeal application, it can be included in Section 9C in Form N161 (appellant's notice); or
- If made later by CPR 1998, Pt 23, application in the Court of Appeal with grounds set out and appropriate evidence.

Any such application should be served on the Press Association's Copy Direct Service with a copy of the Notice of Appeal and any evidence in support (*Norman v Norman* [2017] EWCA Civ 49, at [34]).

****

PART 44
GENERAL RULES ABOUT COSTS

CONTENTS OF THIS PART

Section I

Rule		Page
	General	
44.1	Interpretation and application	2143
44.2	Court's discretion as to costs	2144
44.3	Basis of assessment	2147
44.4	Factors to be taken into account in deciding the amount of costs	2148
44.5	Amount of costs where costs are payable under a contract	2149
44.6	Procedure for assessing costs	2149
44.7	Time for complying with an order for costs	2149
44.8	Legal representative's duty to notify the party	2149
44.10	Where the court makes no order for costs	2149
44.11	Court's powers in relation to misconduct	2150
44.12	Set Off	2151
	Practice Direction 44 – General Rules About Costs	2151

CPR 1998 costs rules applied to FPR 2010—FPR 2010, Pt 28 incorporates substantial parts of the costs rules in CPR 1998 (as amended by SI 2013/262) into family proceedings. These rules apply to costs orders in all family proceedings, save that certain provisions in CPR 1998, Pt 44 are disapplied and costs orders do not apply in certain financial order proceedings (see FPR 2010, r 28.3).

Section I
General

44.1 Interpretation and application

(1) In Parts 44 to 47, unless the context otherwise requires –

'authorised court officer' means any officer or –

(i) the County Court;
(ii) a district registry;
(iii) the Family Court; or
(iiia) the High Court; or
(iv) the Costs Office,

whom the Lord Chancellor has authorised to assess costs;

'costs' includes fees, charges, disbursements, expenses, remuneration, reimbursement allowed to a litigant in person under rule 46.5 and any fee or reward charged by a lay representative for acting on behalf of a party in proceedings allocated to the small claims track;

'costs judge' means a taxing master of the Senior Courts;

'Costs Office' means the Senior Courts Costs Office;

'costs officer' means –

(i) a costs judge;
(ii) a District Judge; or
(iii) an authorised court officer;

'detailed assessment' means the procedure by which the amount of costs is decided by a costs officer in accordance with Part 47;

'the Director (legal aid)' means the person designated as the Director of Legal Aid Casework pursuant to section 4 of the Legal Aid, Sentencing and Punishment of Offenders Act 2012, or a person entitled to exercise the functions of the Director;

…

PART III

'free of charge' has the same meaning as in section 194(10) of the 2007 Act;

'fund' includes any estate or property held for the benefit of any person or class of person and any fund to which a trustee or personal representative is entitled in that capacity;

'HMRC' means HM Revenue and Customs;

'legal aid' means civil legal services made available under arrangements made for the purposes of Part 1 of the Legal Aid, Sentencing and Punishment of Offenders Act 2012;

'paying party' means a party liable to pay costs;

'the prescribed charity' has the same meaning as in section 194(8) of the 2007 Act;

'pro bono representation' means legal representation provided free of charge;

'receiving party' means a party entitled to be paid costs;

'summary assessment' means the procedure whereby costs are assessed by the judge who has heard the case or application;

'VAT' means Value Added Tax;

'the 2007 Act' means the Legal Services Act 2007.

('Legal representative' has the meaning given in rule 2.3).

(2) The costs to which Parts 44 to 47 apply include –

(a) the following costs where those costs may be assessed by the court –
  (i) costs of proceedings before an arbitrator or umpire;
  (ii) costs of proceedings before a tribunal or other statutory body; and
  (iii) costs payable by a client to their legal representative; and

(b) costs which are payable by one party to another party under the terms of a contract, where the court makes an order for an assessment of those costs.

(3) Where advocacy or litigation services are provided to a client under a conditional fee agreement, costs are recoverable under Parts 44 to 47 notwithstanding that the client is liable to pay the legal representative's fees and expenses only to the extent that sums are recovered in respect of the proceedings, whether by way of costs or otherwise.

Amendments—Inserted by SI 2013/262. Amended by SI 2014/407.

44.2 Court's discretion as to costs

(1) The court has discretion as to –

(a) whether costs are payable by one party to another;
(b) the amount of those costs; and
(c) when they are to be paid.

(2) If the court decides to make an order about costs –

(a) the general rule is that the unsuccessful party will be ordered to pay the costs of the successful party; but
(b) the court may make a different order.

(3) The general rule does not apply to the following proceedings –

(a) proceedings in the Court of Appeal on an application or appeal made in connection with proceedings in the Family Division; or
(b) proceedings in the Court of Appeal from a judgment, direction, decision or order given or made in probate proceedings or family proceedings.

(4) In deciding what order (if any) to make about costs, the court will have regard to all the circumstances, including –

(a) the conduct of all the parties;
(b) whether a party has succeeded on part of its case, even if that party has not been wholly successful; and
(c) any admissible offer to settle made by a party which is drawn to the court's attention, and which is not an offer to which costs consequences under Part 36 apply.

(5) The conduct of the parties includes –

(a) conduct before, as well as during, the proceedings and in particular the extent to which the parties followed the Practice Direction – Pre-Action Conduct or any relevant pre-action protocol;
(b) whether it was reasonable for a party to raise, pursue or contest a particular allegation or issue;
(c) the manner in which a party has pursued or defended the case or a particular allegation or issue; and
(d) whether a claimant who has succeeded in the claim, in whole or in part, exaggerated its claim.

(6) The orders which the court may make under this rule include an order that a party must pay –

(a) a proportion of another party's costs;
(b) a stated amount in respect of another party's costs;
(c) costs from or until a certain date only;
(d) costs incurred before proceedings have begun;
(e) costs relating to particular steps taken in the proceedings;
(f) costs relating only to a distinct part of the proceedings; and
(g) interest on costs from or until a certain date, including a date before judgment.

(7) Before the court considers making an order under paragraph (6)(f), it will consider whether it is practicable to make an order under paragraph (6)(a) or (c) instead.

(8) Where the court orders a party to pay costs subject to detailed assessment, it will order that party to pay a reasonable sum on account of costs, unless there is good reason not to do so.

Amendments—Inserted by SI 2013/262.

Defined terms—'assessment of costs': Pt 47; 'costs': r 44.1(1)); 'Part 36 offer': r 36.5.

Disapplication costs order rules in family proceedings—FPR 2010, r 28.1(1) disapplies r 44.2(2),(3) for proceedings covered by FPR 2010. Thus, there is no rule in family proceedings that costs follow the event, or that a successful party should have his costs (see **'the general rule'** below and r 44.2(2)). In *Gojkovic v Gojkovic (No 2)* [1991] 2 FLR 233, CA, the Court of Appeal suggested that although the rule that 'costs follow the event' did not apply to family proceedings, 'there still remains the necessity for some starting point. That starting point, in my judgment, is that costs prima facie follow the event (see Cumming-Bruce LJ in *Singer (formerly Sharegin) v Sharegin* [1984] FLR 114 [CA] at 119)', per Butler-Sloss LJ.

Discretion on costs (r 44.2(1))—Rule 44.2(1) gives regulatory effect to SCA 1981, s 51(3); namely that costs can only be recovered by order of the court and that orders for costs are in the court's discretion (SCA 1981, s 51(1)). The rule prescribes bases upon which the court is to exercise its discretion.

'In deciding what order … the court must have regard' (r 44.2(4))—It is not a matter of discretion for the court as to whether it considers the factors in r 44.2(4); though having done so it has a discretion as to whether to make an order.

'the amount of those costs' (r 44.2(1)(b))—The court's discretion as to the amount of costs 'includes its discretion to decide whether some or all of the costs awarded should be on a standard or indemnity basis'; and see note under r 44.4 on standard and indemnity costs. In assessing the amount of costs, the court is entitled to take account of whether costs were proportionately and reasonable incurred (eg *K v K* [2016] EWHC 2002 (Fam)).

Practice Direction—Costs Practice Direction (CPR 1998, Pt 44), para 4.2 draws attention to a non-exhaustive list of certain costs orders which the court will commonly make. The following should be particularly noted:

(a) *Respondent's costs* A wholly successful respondent should normally be awarded his costs unless he has brought about the proceedings or has done something in connection with the institution or conduct of the proceedings intended to prolong them or cause unnecessary expense (r 44.2(5)).
(b) *'Costs in the cause' or 'Costs in the application'* Where proceedings are discontinued or withdrawn (eg domestic violence injunction proceedings where applicant does not pursue application beyond initial order) the defendant or respondent does not automatically have an order for costs in his favour where there is an order for 'costs in the cause [or] application': the court retains its discretion as to costs, since no judgment on the issues has yet been given.
(c) *'Costs reserved'* A party in whose favour an order for costs is made will be awarded costs in respect of any 'costs reserved' order, unless some other order is made. Thus, where costs are reserved at an interlocutory hearing and, at the final hearing, costs either (i) are not awarded at all or (ii) are awarded to one or other party, it will be necessary to seek a specific order for the prior hearing, in respect of which costs were reserved, at that final hearing. A party who fails to seek, at the final hearing, an order for the costs which were reserved at an earlier hearing, can cure the omission by making a separate application (*S v S (Reserved Costs Order)* [1995] 1 FLR 739, FD).
(d) *Applicant's costs in the case* (1) If the applicant ('A') is awarded costs at the conclusion of the case, he is entitled to the costs of the application to which the order for costs in the case relates. (2) If another party is awarded costs, he cannot be required to pay A's costs on the part of the proceedings for which costs in the case were awarded.

'the general rule' (r 44.2(2)(a))—This rule replaces the former rule that 'costs should follow the event', unless some other order seems appropriate. The effect of this rule in family proceeding is as follows:

(1) The general rule applies to all family proceedings covered by CPR 1998 (ie I(PFD)A 1975, TLATA 1996, etc).
(2) The general rule does not apply to proceedings covered by FPR 2010 (r 28.1(1)), including appeals to the Court of Appeal and all family proceedings appeals under FPR 2010, Pt 30; but see *Gojkovic v Gojkovic (No 2)* (above).
(3) Financial remedy proceedings (as defined by r 28.3(4) and see the introductory note, above) have their own rules arising from r 28.3(5).

Wide discretion as to by whom costs paid—The court has a wide discretion as to by whom costs should be paid. For example, in *Ben Hashem v Ali Shayif and Radfan Ltd* [2009] 2 FLR 896, FD, in ancillary relief proceedings (1) H was ordered to pay W's costs on an indemnity basis, whereas (2) in parallel Chancery proceedings involving children and a family company W was almost entirely unsuccessful and was required to pay most of their costs. In *Baker v Rowe* [2010] 1 FLR 761, CA (see especially at [24] and [35]), in financial remedy proceedings the real issue on costs was between the interveners: the rule in 28.3(6) that there be no order save by reason of a party's conduct did not apply. The district judge had a 'clean sheet' in relation to the court's costs order but in considering an award of costs the judge could not avoid the fact that one side had succeeded as against the other.

The Act, the Rules, Practice Directions and a Protocol—In *R (Mount Cook Land Limited) v Westminster City Council* [2003] EWCA Civ 1346, CA at [67] Auld LJ examined the interrelationship between statute, CPR 1998 rules and PDs and a protocol (in this instance, judicial review). The costs award hierarchy and the extent to which each can influence the court are as follows:

(1) The court starts from SCA 1981, s 51(1): subject to any contrary enactment or 'rule of court', costs are in the court's discretion;
(2) 'Intrusion' on s 51 can come from r 44.3(2): costs should normally follow the event;
(3) PDs are 'recognised' by CPA 1997, no more. They are guidance as to 'normal practice' of the courts (no more). They are not determinative nor can they be regarded as comprised in an exception to s 51(1);
(4) Any relevant protocol.

'In deciding what order (if any) to make about costs' (r 44.2(4))—The exercise of the court's discretion was considered by Nourse LJ in the Court of Appeal in *Re Elgindata Ltd (No 2)* [1992] 1 WLR 1207, CA (cited with approval as applicable to a financial relief application by Thorpe LJ in *Dart v Dart* [1996] 2 FLR 286, CA). Nourse LJ set out the main principles on which he considered that an order for costs should be awarded:

(a) costs are in the discretion of the court (SCA 1981, s 51(1));
(b) orders for costs should 'follow the event' (ie should be paid to the 'successful party': see r 44.2(2)(a)), unless the court considers that in the circumstances of the case some other order should be made (r 44.2(2)(b));
(c) these general rules do not cease to apply because a party raises issues on which he is not successful, although if, in raising those issues, he substantially lengthens the trial he may lose part or all of his costs;
(d) where a successful party raises issues or makes allegations improperly or unreasonably, the court may deprive him of his costs (and see r 44.2(4)(a) and (5)) and order him to pay the unsuccessful party's costs (SCA 1981, s 51(6)).

'the conduct of all the parties' (r 44.2(4)(a),(5))—In the exercise of its discretion, the court will be required to pay particular attention to the conduct of the parties and r 44.3(5) provides an inclusive check-list of the factors for consideration when assessing conduct. For an example of the balancing exercise required between 'conduct' and success on the event see *McMinn v McMinn (Ancillary Relief: Death of Party to Proceedings: Costs)* [2003] 2 FLR 839, FD (no order for costs in that instance).

'whether a party has succeeded' (r 44.2(4)(b))—This is the terminology used to replace costs following 'the event' as considered by the Court of Appeal in *Gojkovic v Gojkovic (No 2)* [1991] 2 FLR 233, CA; and see *Baker v Rowe* (above), which adopts a similar approach to *Gojkovic* in regarding success in the proceedings as an important factor in determining an order for costs.

Calderbank letters—*Calderbank* letters may be of limited application in financial remedy proceedings but they apply in all other forms of family proceedings. A *Calderbank* letter sets out proposals for settlement of any issue in proceedings (*Calderbank v Calderbank* (1975) FLR Rep 113, CA; and see CPR 1998, r 36.5(2)) 'without prejudice' – i e with privilege attached as with all negotiations; but on terms that, although the privilege is joint, the correspondence can be opened when the question of costs fails to be decided. In *Gojkovic v Gojkovic (No 2)* [1991] 2 FLR 233, CA, at [238F], Butler-Sloss LJ expressed the view that '*Calderbank* offers are required to have teeth in order for them to be effective' and this will remain the position, save in ancillary relief proceedings.

'whether a claimant ... exaggerated his claim' (r 44.2(5)(d))—A party who, though successful on the main issue before the court, has exaggerated a claim and pursued a particular allegation or issue which proves to be of no or only tangential relevance (r 44.3(5)(b) and (c)) may find their costs disallowed or substantially reduced (for an example of exaggeration of claim and cost consequences see e g *A v A (No 2) (Ancillary Relief: Costs)* [2008] 1 FLR 1428, FD).

'an amount to be paid on account' (r 44.2(8))—It is required positively of the court, where costs are awarded, that an amount on account be paid, unless there is some reason not to (similar in principle to *Hadjimilitis (Tsavliris) v Tsavliris* [2003] 1 FLR 81, FD, where the court held that it was appropriate to order a payment on account 'unless there are clear reasons why it would be unfair' (Costs Judgment [4](j)). In the event of an order for costs in ancillary relief proceedings, a payment on account can be requested of the court.

Official Solicitor's costs—The costs of the Official Solicitor are entirely a matter for the discretion of the judge (*B v Croydon Health Authority (No 2)* [1996] 1 FLR 253, CA). It may be appropriate to order a party to pay one half of the Official Solicitor's costs (*Re G (Minors) (Wardship: Costs)* [1982] 1 WLR 438, CA) or, where the Official Solicitor has become involved because of the position the parties find themselves in, he might be expected to bear his own costs (see *Northampton Health Authority v The Official Solicitor and the Governors of St Andrews Hospital* [1994] 1 FLR 162, CA).

Security for costs—In *Charman v Charman (No 3)* [2007] 1 FLR 1237, CA, the wife applied for security to be given by the appellant husband against stay obtained by him in respect of £28m of a £40m lump sum order. This was refused. However, Sir Mark Potter P had no hesitation in ordering security for costs pending the hearing under CPR 1998, r 25.13(2)(a), namely, that the husband is resident out of the jurisdiction and not in a Brussels or Lugano Contracting State. An order under r 25.13 can only be made where CPR 1998 applies to the proceedings. It can only be applied for by a defendant or respondent to an appeal (r 25.12), and will only be ordered where justice demands it and one of the conditions in r 25.13(2) apply, including (a) residence (as above), (d) changes of address to evade the consequences of the litigation and (g) the taking of steps by the claimant/appellant to move assets to make it difficult to enforce any order for costs.

44.3 Basis of assessment

(1) Where the court is to assess the amount of costs (whether by summary or detailed assessment) it will assess those costs –

(a) on the standard basis; or
(b) on the indemnity basis,

but the court will not in either case allow costs which have been unreasonably incurred or are unreasonable in amount.

(Rule 44.5 sets out how the court decides the amount of costs payable under a contract.)

(2) Where the amount of costs is to be assessed on the standard basis, the court will –

(a) only allow costs which are proportionate to the matters in issue. Costs which are disproportionate in amount may be disallowed or reduced even if they were reasonably or necessarily incurred; and
(b) resolve any doubt which it may have as to whether costs were reasonably and proportionately incurred or were reasonable and proportionate in amount in favour of the paying party.

(Factors which the court may take into account are set out in rule 44.4.)

(3) Where the amount of costs is to be assessed on the indemnity basis, the court will resolve any doubt which it may have as to whether costs were reasonably incurred or were reasonable in amount in favour of the receiving party.

(4) Where –

(a) the court makes an order about costs without indicating the basis on which the costs are to be assessed; or
(b) the court makes an order for costs to be assessed on a basis other than the standard basis or the indemnity basis,

the costs will be assessed on the standard basis.

(5) Costs incurred are proportionate if they bear a reasonable relationship to –

(a) the sums in issue in the proceedings;
(b) the value of any non-monetary relief in issue in the proceedings;
(c) the complexity of the litigation;
(d) any additional work generated by the conduct of the paying party; and
(e) any wider factors involved in the proceedings, such as reputation or public importance.

(6) Where the amount of a solicitor's remuneration in respect of non-contentious business is regulated by any general orders made under the Solicitors Act 1974, the amount of the costs to be allowed in respect of any such business which falls to be assessed by the court will be decided in accordance with those general orders rather than this rule and rule 44.4.

(7) Paragraphs (2)(a) and (5) do not apply in relation to –

(a) cases commenced before 1 April 2013; or
(b) costs incurred in respect of work done before 1 April 2013,

PART III

and in relation to such cases or costs, rule 44.4.(2)(a) as it was in force immediately before 1 April 2013 will apply instead.

Amendments—Inserted by SI 2013/262. Amended by SI 2013/515.

Defined terms—'costs': r 44.1(1); 'costs officer': r 44.1(1); 'detailed assessment': r 44.1(1); 'summary assessment': r 44.1(1).

Assessment of costs—Rule 44.3 deals with the basis of the assessment of costs (standard or indemnity) which the court awards; r 44.4 deals with the factors to be taken into account when undertaking that assessment; and r 44.5 deals with the procedure (detailed or summary) by which the assessment is to take place.

Indemnity or standard basis (r 44.3(1))—An award of costs on the indemnity basis is only justified where a paying party has been responsible for conduct which is unreasonable to a high degree: not 'merely wrong or misguided in hindsight' (*Kiam v MGN Ltd (No 2)* [2002] 1 WLR 2810, CA). Where one party makes a sensible attempt at settlement and the other party resists, the latter party puts himself at risk of an indemnity order (*Reid Minty (a firm) v Taylor* [2002] 1 WLR 2800, CA). Implicit disapproval of the way the litigation was conducted may be reflected by such an order.

44.4 Factors to be taken into account in deciding the amount of costs

(1) The court will have regard to all the circumstances in deciding whether costs were –

- (a) if it is assessing costs on the standard basis –
  - (i) proportionately and reasonably incurred; or
  - (ii) proportionate and reasonable in amount, or
- (b) if it is assessing costs on the indemnity basis –
  - (i) unreasonably incurred; or
  - (ii) unreasonable in amount.

(2) In particular, the court will give effect to any orders which have already been made.

(3) The court will also have regard to –

- (a) the conduct of all the parties, including in particular –
  - (i) conduct before, as well as during, the proceedings; and
  - (ii) the efforts made, if any, before and during the proceedings in order to try to resolve the dispute;
- (b) the amount or value of any money or property involved;
- (c) the importance of the matter to all the parties;
- (d) the particular complexity of the matter or the difficulty or novelty of the questions raised;
- (e) the skill, effort, specialised knowledge and responsibility involved;
- (f) the time spent on the case;
- (g) the place where and the circumstances in which work or any part of it was done; and
- (h) the receiving party's last approved or agreed budget.

(Rule 35.4(4) gives the court power to limit the amount that a party may recover with regard to the fees and expenses of an expert.)

Amendments—Inserted by SI 2013/262.

Defined terms—'costs': r 44.1(1); 'indemnity basis': r 44.3(1)(b); 'standard basis': r 44.3(1)(a).

'proportionate and reasonable in amount' (r 44.4(1)(a)(ii))—In assessing what is 'proportionate and reasonable' the court considers, in its assessment on a standard basis, what costs should be awarded if 'the litigation had been appropriately conducted'. A reasonable sum should be awarded for the work which was carried out and was necessary (*Lownds v Home Office (Practice Note)* [2002] 1 WLR 2450, CA; and see *K v K* [2016] EWHC 2002 (Fam)).

'conduct of all the parties' (r 44.4(3)(a))—In assessing one party's costs and their conduct of the dispute, the conduct of the other party is highly relevant. A co-operative opponent can contain costs: by being unco-operative he can increase costs and make work necessary which would otherwise be unnecessary (*Lownds v Home Office* (above)).

'efforts made ... in order to try to resolve the dispute' (r 44.4(3)(a)(ii))—Orders for costs can relate to work done before the issue of proceedings and to proposals for settlement made before issue (*Butcher v Wolfe and Wolfe* [1999] 1 FLR 334, CA).

'the circumstances in which work or any part of it was done' (r 44.4(3)(g))—The court may allow variable rates of remuneration according to the nature of the work done at each stage (*Re Children Act 1989 (Taxation of Costs)* [1994] 2 FLR 934, FD).

44.5 Amount of costs where costs are payable under a contract

(1) Subject to paragraphs (2) and (3), where the court assesses (whether by summary or detailed assessment) costs which are payable by the paying party to the receiving party under the terms of a contract, the costs payable under those terms are, unless the contract expressly provides otherwise, to be presumed to be costs which –

(a) have been reasonably incurred; and
(b) are reasonable in amount,

and the court will assess them accordingly.

(2) The presumptions in paragraph (1) are rebuttable.

Practice Direction 44 – General rules about costs sets out circumstances where the court may order otherwise.

(3) Paragraph (1) does not apply where the contract is between a solicitor and client.

Amendments—Inserted by SI 2013/262. Amended by SI 2016/234.

44.6 Procedure for assessing costs

(1) Where the court orders a party to pay costs to another party (other than fixed costs) it may either –

(a) make a summary assessment of the costs; or
(b) order detailed assessment of the costs by a costs officer,

unless any rule, practice direction or other enactment provides otherwise.

(Practice Direction 44 – General rules about costs sets out the factors which will affect the court's decision under paragraph (1).)

(2) A party may recover the fixed costs specified in Part 45 in accordance with that Part.

Amendments—Inserted by SI 2013/262.

Defined terms—'costs': r 43.2(1)(a); 'costs officer': r 43.2(1)(c); 'detailed assessment': r 43.4; 'summary assessment': r 43.3.

Amount on summary assessment—In determining the amount to be paid on summary assessment, the court is entitled to take account of what is proportionate and reasonable (*K v K* [2016] EWHC 2002 (Fam)).

Summary assessment—PD44, subsection 9 explains the operation of the rules on summary assessment.

44.7 Time for complying with an order for costs

A party must comply with an order for the payment of costs within 14 days of –

(a) the date of the judgment or order if it states the amount of those costs;
(b) if the amount of those costs (or part of them) is decided later in accordance with Part 47, the date of the certificate which states the amount; or
(c) in either case, such other date as the court may specify.

(Part 47 sets out the procedure for detailed assessment of costs.)

Amendments—Inserted by SI 2013/262.

44.8 Legal representative's duty to notify the party

Where –

(a) the court makes a costs order against a legally represented party; and
(b) the party is not present when the order is made,

the party's legal representative must notify that party in writing of the costs order no later than 7 days after the legal representative receives notice of the order.

(Paragraph 10.1 of Practice Direction 44 defines 'party' for the purposes of this rule.)

Amendments—Inserted by SI 2013/262.

****

44.10 Where the court makes no order for costs

(1) Where the court makes an order which does not mention costs –

(a) subject to Paragraphs (2) and (3), the general rule is that no party is entitled –
(i) to costs; or
(ii) to seek an order under section 194(3) of the 2007 Act,

in relation to that order; but

(b) this does not affect any entitlement of a party to recover costs out of a fund held by that party as trustee or personal representative, or under any lease, mortgage or other security.

(2) Where the court makes –

(a) an order granting permission to appeal;
(b) an order granting permission to apply for judicial review; or
(c) any other order or direction sought by a party on an application without notice,

and its order does not mention costs, it will be deemed to include an order for applicant's costs in the case.

(3) Any party affected by a deemed order for costs under paragraph (2) may apply at any time to vary the order.

(4) The court hearing an appeal may, unless it dismisses the appeal, make orders about the costs of the proceedings giving rise to the appeal as well as the costs of the appeal.

(5) Subject to any order made by the transferring court, where proceedings are transferred from one court to another, the court to which they are transferred may deal with all the costs, including the costs before the transfer.

Amendments—Inserted by SI 2013/262.

Deemed orders for costs (r 44.10(2))—Most of the orders referred to are made in the absence of the parties although applications for permission to appeal and to apply for judicial review may be made at contested hearings (rr 52.3(3) and 54.12(3)). In respect of a judicial review permission hearing: if given, costs will not normally awarded against a claimant (PD54A, para 8.6); if refused, then the application for permission is within the terms of 'proceedings' under SCA 1981, s 51(1) and therefore susceptible to an order for costs (see eg *R (Gunn) v Secretary of State for the Home Department* [2001] 1 WLR 1634, CA).

'order for applicant's costs in the case' (r 44.10(2))—See note to r 44.2 above. As an order for costs for a successful defendant or respondent will not include any costs relating to the application covered by r 44.10(2), he will need to apply specifically to vary under r 44.10(3) that an order be deemed under r 44.10(2).

'apply at any time to vary the order' (r 44.10(3)—In principle there would appear to be no reason why such application to vary the order deemed by r 44.10(2) should not be made at the final hearing of the particular claim or application; nor does there seem to be any reason to make formal application under Pt 23 or otherwise to give notice to the receiving party.

The court hearing an appeal (r 44.10(4)))—It will be important, in preparation for an appeal, that the appellate court has information necessary to deal with this provision. Two distinct situations must be borne in mind:

(i) An appeal where costs is one of the issues under appeal. It would be advisable still to appeal against the order for costs, since if the court dismisses the appeal on its merits, it may find that an order for costs below should have been made.
(ii) An appeal where costs is the only issue under appeal.

In the first instance a separate bundle of Pt 36/*Calderbank* correspondence will be necessary (this will remain privileged until the appeal has been heard), with separate submissions and skeleton arguments on the subject. The court will need to have details of the documents considered by the first instance judge and a note of his judgment on costs.

44.11 Court's powers in relation to misconduct

(1) The court may make an order under this rule where –

(a) a party or that party's legal representative, in connection with a summary or detailed assessment, fails to comply with a rule, practice direction or court order; or
(b) it appears to the court that the conduct of a party or that party's legal representative, before or during the proceedings or in the assessment proceedings, was unreasonable or improper.

(2) Where paragraph (1) applies, the court may –

(a) disallow all or part of the costs which are being assessed; or
(b) order the party at fault or that party's legal representative to pay costs which that party or legal representative has caused any other party to incur.

(3) Where –

(a) the court makes an order under paragraph (2) against a legally represented party; and

(b) the party is not present when the order is made,

the party's legal representative must notify that party in writing of the order no later than 7 days after the legal representative receives notice of the order.

Amendments—Inserted by SI 2013/262.

Defined terms—'costs': r 44.1(1); 'costs officer': r 44.1(1); 'detailed assessment': r 42.4.

'unreasonable or improper' (r 44.11(1)(b))—These bases for judging conduct of a party or his representative must be distinguished from the more serious 'wasted costs' criteria set out in SCA 1981, s 51(7) (see further under r 48.7). The purpose of r 44.14 is to enable the court to exercise its discretion to disallow a party's costs and to order him to pay another party's costs (see, for example, *Langley v North West Water Authority* [1991] 1 WLR 697, CA – solicitors ordered to pay costs on their failure to comply with directions; and *R v Nottinghamshire County Council* [1993] Fam Law 625, FD – local authority ordered to pay costs where adjournment was necessary because of their delay).

44.12 Set Off

Where a party entitled to costs is also liable to pay costs, the court may assess the costs which that party is liable to pay and either –

(a) set off the amount assessed against the amount the party is entitled to be paid and direct that party to pay any balance; or

(b) delay the issue of a certificate for the costs to which the party is entitled until the party has paid the amount which that party is liable to pay.

Amendments—Inserted by SI 2013/262.

****

PART III

Practice Direction 44 – General Rules About Costs

This Practice Direction supplements CPR Part 44

Amendments—CPR Update 60.

SECTION 1: GENERAL

Subsection 1 of this Practice Direction – Documents and Forms

Documents and Forms

1.1 In respect of any document which is required by Practice Directions 44 to 47 to be signed by a party or that party's legal representative, the provisions of Practice Direction 22 relating to who may sign apply as if the document in question was a statement of truth. Statements of truth are not required in assessment proceedings unless a rule of Practice Direction so requires or the court so orders.

(Practice Direction 22 makes provision for cases in which a party is a child, a protected party or a company or other corporation and cases in which a document is signed on behalf of a partnership.)

1.2 Form N260 is a model form of Statement of Costs to be used for summary assessments.

(Further details about Statements of Costs are given in paragraph 9.5 below.)

Precedents A, B and C in the Schedule of Costs Precedents annexed to this Practice Direction are model forms of bills of costs to be used for detailed assessments. A party wishing to rely upon a bill which departs from the model forms should include in the background information of the bill an explanation for that departure.

(Further details about bills of costs are given in Practice Direction 47.)

Subsection 2 of this Practice Direction – Special Provisions Relating to VAT

Scope of this subsection

2.1 This subsection deals with claims for VAT) which are made in respect of costs being dealt with by way of summary assessment or detailed assessment.

Subsection on VAT—This subsection can be found in full online at *www.justice.gov.uk/courts/procedure-rules*.

****

Subsection 4 of this Practice Direction – Court's Discretion as to Costs: Rule 44.2

Court's Discretion as to Costs

4.1 The court may make an order about costs at any stage in a case.

4.2 There are certain costs orders which the court will commonly make in proceedings before trial. The following table sets out the general effect of these orders. The table is not an exhaustive list of the orders which the court may make.

Term	Effect
Costs Costs in any event	The party in whose favour the order is made is entitled to the costs in respect of the part of the proceedings to which the order relates, whatever other costs orders are made in the proceedings.
Costs in the case Costs in the application	The party in whose favour the court makes an order for costs at the end of the proceedings is entitled to his costs of the part of the proceedings to which the order relates.
Costs reserved	The decision about costs is deferred to a later occasion, but if no later order is made the costs will be costs in the case.
Claimant's/defendant's costs in the case/application	If the party in whose favour the costs order is made is awarded costs at the end of the proceedings, that party is entitled to his costs of the part of the proceedings to which the order relates. If any other party is awarded costs at the end of the proceedings, the party in whose favour the final costs order is made is not liable to pay the costs of any other party in respect of the part of the proceedings to which the order relates.
Costs thrown away	Where, for example, a judgment or order is set aside, the party in whose favour the costs order is made is entitled to the costs which have been incurred as a consequence. This includes the costs of – (a) preparing for and attending any hearing at which the judgment or order which has been set aside was made; (b) preparing for and attending any hearing to set aside the judgment or order in question; (c) preparing for and attending any hearing at which the court orders the proceedings or the Part In question to be adjourned; (d) any steps taken to enforce a judgment or order which has subsequently been set aside.
Costs of and caused by	Where, for example, the court makes this order on an application to amend a statement of case, the party in whose favour the costs order is made is entitled to the costs of preparing for and attending the application and the costs of any consequential Amendment to his own statement of case.

Term	Effect
Costs here and below	The party in whose favour the costs order is made is entitled not only to his costs in respect of the proceedings in which the court makes the order but also to his costs of the proceedings in any lower court. In the case of an appeal from a Divisional Court the party is not entitled to any costs incurred in any court below the Divisional Court.
No order as to costs Each party to pay his own costs	Each party is to bear his own costs of the part of the proceedings to which the order relates whatever costs order the court makes at the end of the proceedings.

Subsection 5 of this Practice Direction – Fees of Counsel

Fees of Counsel

5.1 (1) When making an order for costs the court may state an opinion as to whether or not the hearing was fit for the attendance of one or more counsel, and, if it does so, the court conducting a detailed assessment of those costs will have regard to the opinion stated.

(2) The court will generally express an opinion only where –

(a) the paying party asks it to do so;

(b) more than one counsel appeared for a party; or

(c) the court wishes to record its opinion that the case was not fit for the attendance of counsel.

5.2 (1) Where the court refers any matter to the conveyancing counsel of the court the fees payable to counsel in respect of the work done or to be done will be assessed by the court in accordance with rule 44.2.

(2) An appeal from a decision of the court in respect of the fees of such counsel will be dealt with under the general rules as to appeals set out in Part 52. If the appeal is against the decision of an authorised court officer, it will be dealt with in accordance with rules 47.22 to 47.24.

Subsection 6 of This Practice Direction – Basis of Assessment: Rule 44.3

Costs on the indemnity basis

6.1 If costs are awarded on the indemnity basis, the court assessing costs will disallow any costs –

(a) which it finds to have been unreasonably incurred; or

(b) which it considers to be unreasonable in amount.

Costs on the standard basis

6.2 If costs are awarded on the standard basis, the court assessing costs will disallow any costs –

(a) which it finds to have been unreasonably incurred;

(b) which it considers to be unreasonable in amount;

(c) which it considers to have been disproportionately incurred or to be disproportionate in amount; or

(d) about which it has doubts as to whether they were reasonably or proportionately incurred, or whether they are reasonable and proportionate in amount.

****

Subsection 8 of This Practice Direction -Procedure for Assessing Costs: Rule 44.6

Procedure for Assessing Costs

8.1 Subject to paragraph 8.3, where the court does not order fixed costs (or no fixed costs are provided for) the amount of costs payable will be assessed by the court. Rule 44.6 allows the court making an order about costs either –

PART III

(a) to make a summary assessment of the amount of the costs; or
(b) to order the amount to be decided in accordance with Part 47 (a detailed assessment).

8.2 An order for costs will be treated as an order for the amount of costs to be decided by a detailed assessment unless the order otherwise provides.

8.3 Where a party is entitled to costs some of which are fixed costs and some of which are not, the court will assess those costs which are not fixed. For example, the court will assess the disbursements payable in accordance with rules 45.12 or 45.19. The decision whether such assessment should be summary or detailed will be made in accordance with paragraphs 9.1 to 9.10 of this Practice Direction.

Subsection 9 of This Practice Direction – Summary Assessment: General Provisions

When the court should consider whether to make a summary assessment

9.1 Whenever a court makes an order about costs which does not provide only for fixed costs to be paid the court should consider whether to make a summary assessment of costs.

Timing of summary assessment

9.2 The general rule is that the court should make a summary assessment of the costs –

(a) …
(b) at the conclusion of any other hearing, which has lasted not more than one day, in which case the order will deal with the costs of the application or matter to which the hearing related. If this hearing disposes of the claim, the order may deal with the costs of the whole claim,

unless there is good reason not to do so, for example where the paying party shows substantial grounds for disputing the sum claimed for costs that cannot be dealt with summarily.

****

Consent orders

9.4 Where an application has been made and the parties to the application agree an order by consent without any party attending, the parties should seek to agree a figure for costs to be inserted in the consent order or agree that there should be no order for costs.

Duty of parties and legal representatives

9.5 (1) It is the duty of the parties and their legal representatives to assist the judge in making a summary assessment of costs in any case to which paragraph 9.2 above applies, in accordance with the following subparagraphs.

(2) Each party who intends to claim costs must prepare a written statement of those costs showing separately in the form of a schedule –
   (a) the number of hours to be claimed;
   (b) the hourly rate to be claimed;
   (c) the grade of fee earner;
   (d) the amount and nature of any disbursement to be claimed, other than counsel's fee for appearing at the hearing;
   (e) the amount of legal representative's costs to be claimed for attending or appearing at the hearing;
   (f) counsel's fees; and
   (g) any VAT to be claimed on these amounts.

(3) The statement of costs should follow as closely as possible Form N260 and must be signed by the party or the party's legal representative. Where a party is –
   (a) an assisted person;
   (b) a LSC funded client;
   (c) a person for who civil legal services (within the meaning of Part 1 of the Legal Aid,

Sentencing and Punishment of Offenders Act 2012) are provided under arrangements made for the purposes of that Part of that Act; or

(d) represented by a person in the party's employment,

the statement of costs need not include the certificate appended at the end of Form N260.

(4) The statement of costs must be filed at court and copies of it must be served on any party against whom an order for payment of those costs is intended to be sought as soon as possible and in any event –

(a) for a fast track trial, not less than 2 days before the trial; and

(b) for all other hearings, not less than 24 hours before the time fixed for the hearing.

9.6 The failure by a party, without reasonable excuse, to comply with paragraph 9.5 will be taken into account by the court in deciding what order to make about the costs of the claim, hearing or application, and about the costs of any further hearing or detailed assessment hearing that may be necessary as a result of that failure.

No summary assessment by a costs officer

9.7 The court awarding costs cannot make an order for a summary assessment of costs by a costs officer. If a summary assessment of costs is appropriate but the court awarding costs is unable to do so on the day, the court may give directions as to a further hearing before the same judge.

Assisted persons

9.8 The court will not make a summary assessment of the costs of a receiving party who is an assisted person or LSC funded client or who is a person for whom civil legal services (within the meaning of Part 1 of the Legal Aid, Sentencing and Punishment of Offenders Act 2012) are provided under arrangements made for the purposes of that Part of that Act.

Children or protected parties

9.9 (1) The court will not make a summary assessment of the costs of a receiving party who is a child or protected party within the meaning of Part 21 unless the legal representative acting for the child or protected party has waived the right to further costs (see Practice Direction 46 paragraph 2.1).

(2) The court may make a summary assessment of costs payable by a child or protected party.

Disproportionate or unreasonable costs

9.10 The court will not give its approval to disproportionate or unreasonable costs. When the amount of the costs to be paid has been agreed between the parties the order for costs must state that the order is by consent.

Subsection 10 of this Practice Direction – Legal Representative's Duty to Notify Party: Rule 44.8

Legal Representative's Duty to Notify Party: Rule 44.8

10.1 For the purposes of rule 44.8 and paragraph 10.2, 'party' includes any person (for example, an insurer, a trade union or the LSC or Lord Chancellor) who has instructed the legal representative to act for the party or who is liable to pay the legal representative's fees.

10.2 A legal representative who notifies a party of an order under rule 44.8 must also explain why the order came to be made.

10.3 Although rule 44.8 does not specify any sanction for breach of the rule the court may, either in the order for costs itself or in a subsequent order, require the legal representative to produce to the court evidence showing that the legal representative took reasonable steps to comply with the rule.

Subsection 11 of this Practice Direction – Court's Powers In Relation To Misconduct: Rule 44.11

Court's Powers In Relation To Misconduct: Rule 44.11

11.1 Before making an order under rule 44.11, the court must give the party or legal representative in question a reasonable opportunity to make written submissions or, if the legal representative so desires, to attend a hearing.

11.2 Conduct which is unreasonable or improper includes steps which are calculated to prevent or inhibit the court from furthering the overriding objective.

11.3 Although rule 44.11(3) does not specify any sanction for breach of the obligation imposed by the rule the court may, either in the order under rule 44.11(2) or in a subsequent order, require the legal representative to produce to the court evidence that the legal representative took reasonable steps to comply with the obligation.

★★★★

PART 46

COSTS – SPECIAL CASES

CONTENTS OF THIS PART

Section I

Rule		Page
	Costs Payable by or to Particular Persons	
46.1	Pre-commencement disclosure and orders for disclosure against a person who is not a party	2156
46.2	Costs orders in favour of or against non-parties	2157
46.3	Limitations on court's power to award costs in favour of trustee or personal representative	2157
46.5	Litigants in person	2158
46.7	Orders in respect of pro bono representation	2159
	Section II	
	Costs Relating to Legal representatives	
46.8	Personal liability of legal representative for costs – wasted costs orders	2159
46.9	Basis of detailed assessment of solicitor and client costs	2161
46.10	Assessment procedure	2161
	Practice Direction 46 – Costs Special Cases	2162

Section I

Costs Payable by or to Particular Persons

46.1 Pre-commencement disclosure and orders for disclosure against a person who is not a party

(1) This paragraph applies where a person applies –

(a) for an order under –

(i) section 33 of the Senior Courts Act 1981[1]; or

(ii) section 52 of the County Courts Act 1984[2],

(which give the court powers exercisable before commencement of proceedings); or

(b) for an order under –

(i) section 34 of the Senior Courts Act 1981[3]; or

(ii) section 53 of the County Courts Act 1984[4],

(which give the court power to make an order against a non-party for disclosure of documents, inspection of property etc.).

(2) The general rule is that the court will award the person against whom the order is sought that person's costs –

(a) of the application; and

(b) of complying with any order made on the application.

(3) The court may however make a different order, having regard to all the circumstances, including –

(a) the extent to which it was reasonable for the person against whom the order was sought to oppose the application; and

(b) whether the parties to the application have complied with any relevant pre-action protocol.

Amendments—Inserted by SI 2013/262.

46.2 Costs orders in favour of or against non-parties

(1) Where the court is considering whether to exercise its power under section 51 of the Senior Courts Act 19815 (costs are in the discretion of the court) to make a costs order in favour of or against a person who is not a party to proceedings, that person must –

(a) be added as a party to the proceedings for the purposes of costs only; and

(b) be given a reasonable opportunity to attend a hearing at which the court will consider the matter further.

(2) This rule does not apply –

(a) where the court is considering whether to –

(i) make an order against the Lord Chancellor in proceedings in which the Lord Chancellor has provided legal aid to a party to the proceedings;

(ii) make a wasted costs order (as defined in rule 46.8); and

(b) in proceedings to which rule 46.1 applies (pre-commencement disclosure and orders for disclosure against a person who is not a party).

Amendments—Inserted by SI 2013/262.

Third party costs orders—SCA 1981, s 51(3) enables a court, in exceptional circumstances, to make an order for costs against a non-party (third party) (eg, see *H (A Minor) v Northamptonshire County Council & Anor* [2017] EWHC 282 (Fam)). This power was considered fully by the Court of Appeal in *Deutsche Bank AG v Sebastian Holdings Inc & Anor* [2016] EWCA Civ 23, which stressed that the guidelines on such orders in *Symphony Group plc v Hodgson* [1994] QB 179, CA (summarised in *Deutsche Bank*, at [15]) are only guidance. For example:

- generally a warning must be given to the third party that an order may be sought;
- the application for costs should normally be decided by the trial judge; and
- procedure for determination should be summary, especially where the third party has had a close connection with the proceedings.

46.3 Limitations on court's power to award costs in favour of trustee or personal representative

(1) This rule applies where –

(a) a person is or has been a party to any proceedings in the capacity of trustee or personal representative; and

(b) rule 44.5 does not apply.

(2) The general rule is that that person is entitled to be paid the costs of those proceedings, insofar as they are not recovered from or paid by any other person, out of the relevant trust fund or estate.

(3) Where that person is entitled to be paid any of those costs out of the fund or estate, those costs will be assessed on the indemnity basis.

Amendments—Inserted by SI 2013/262.

Defined terms—'costs': r 44.1(1); 'indemnity basis': r 44.3.

PART III

Indemnity basis—This rule re-states the general principle that a person acting in a representative capacity should have his costs paid on an indemnity basis and, as seems likely, on the basis that those costs are paid in any event (see r 44.3).

***Beddoe* orders**—Those acting in a fiduciary capacity should be aware of the need, where necessary, to seek a *Beddoe* order (*Re Beddoe* [1893] 1 Ch 547, CA); e g personal representatives in proceedings under I(PFD)A 1975, trustees joined in ancillary relief proceedings, pension fund trustees, trustees in bankruptcy (c f *Albert v Albert* [1996] BPIR 232, CA) and building society (not bank) mortgagees who respond when served in financial remedy proceedings. In many instances, such an application may not be strictly necessary, but in cases of doubt, where a trustee thinks there is any risk of his being criticised by the court for expending the trust, or other (e g pension) fund, application should be made for an order (and see PD46, para 1.1(a)).

Procedure on application for a *Beddoe* order—Application (other than under CPR 1998 proceedings, e g I(PFD)A 1975) will be in the proceedings by FPR 2010, Pt 18 application.

****

46.5 Litigants in person

(1) This rule applies where the court orders (whether by summary assessment or detailed assessment) that the costs of a litigant in person are to be paid by any other person.

(2) The costs allowed under this rule will not exceed, except in the case of a disbursement, two-thirds of the amount which would have been allowed if the litigant in person had been represented by a legal representative.

(3) The litigant in person shall be allowed –

(a) costs for the same categories of –
 (i) work; and
 (ii) disbursements,

which would have been allowed if the work had been done or the disbursements had been made by a legal representative on the litigant in person's behalf;

(b) the payments reasonably made by the litigant in person for legal services relating to the conduct of the proceedings; and

(c) the costs of obtaining expert assistance in assessing the costs claim.

(4) The amount of costs to be allowed to the litigant in person for any item of work claimed will be –

(a) where the litigant can prove financial loss, the amount that the litigant can prove to have been lost for time reasonably spent on doing the work; or

(b) where the litigant cannot prove financial loss, an amount for the time reasonably spent on doing the work at the rate set out in Practice Direction 46.

(5) A litigant who is allowed costs for attending at court to conduct the case is not entitled to a witness allowance in respect of such attendance in addition to those costs.

(6) For the purposes of this rule, a litigant in person includes –

(a) a company or other corporation which is acting without a legal representative; and

(b) any of the following who acts in person (except where any such person is represented by a firm in which that person is a partner) –
 (i) a barrister,
 (ii) a solicitor,
 (iii) a solicitor's employee,
 (iv) a manager of a body recognised under section 9 of the Administration of Justice Act 1985; or
 (v) a person who, for the purposes of the 2007 Act, is an authorised person in relation to an activity which constitutes the conduct of litigation (within the meaning of that Act).

Amendments—Inserted by SI 2013/262.

'legal representative on the litigant in person's behalf' (r 46.5(3))—Costs payable to a legal representative outside the jurisdiction (e g a Jersey advocate) are not payable by an unsuccessful party (*Campbell v Campbell* [2016] EWHC 1828 (Ch)).

Fees of a McKenzie Friend—Fees payable to a McKenzie Friend for assisting a litigant in person with conduct of litigation are not recoverable from another party (*Practice Guidance: McKenzie Friends (Civil and*

Family Courts), para 29 (see Part V)) but where assistance is for exercising a right of audience costs may be recoverable as an expense under r 46.5(3)(a)(ii) (*Practice Guidance*, para 30).

****

46.7 Orders in respect of pro bono representation

(1) Where the court makes an order under section 194(3) of the 2007 Act –

(a) the court may order the payment to the prescribed charity of a sum no greater than the costs specified in Part 45 to which the party with pro bono representation would have been entitled in accordance with that Part and in respect of that representation had it not been provided free of charge; or

(b) where Part 45 does not apply, the court may determine the amount of the payment (other than a sum equivalent to fixed costs) to be made by the paying party to the prescribed charity by –

(i) making a summary assessment; or

(ii) making an order for detailed assessment,

of a sum equivalent to all or part of the costs the paying party would have been ordered to pay to the party with pro bono representation in respect of that representation had it not been provided free of charge.

(2) Where the court makes an order under section 194(3) of the 2007 Act, the order must direct that the payment by the paying party be made to the prescribed charity.

(3) The receiving party must send a copy of the order to the prescribed charity within 7 days of receipt of the order.

(4) Where the court considers making or makes an order under section 194(3) of the 2007 Act, Parts 44 to 47 apply, where appropriate, with the following modifications –

(a) references to 'costs orders', 'orders about costs' or 'orders for the payment of costs' are to be read, unless otherwise stated, as if they refer to an order under section 194(3);

(b) references to 'costs' are to be read, as if they referred to a sum equivalent to the costs that would have been claimed by, incurred by or awarded to the party with pro bono representation in respect of that representation had it not been provided free of charge; and

(c) references to 'receiving party' are to be read, as meaning a party who has pro bono representation and who would have been entitled to be paid costs in respect of that representation had it not been provided free of charge.

Amendments—Inserted by SI 2013/262. Amended by SI 2013/1974.

Section II

Costs Relating to Legal representatives

46.8 Personal liability of legal representative for costs – wasted costs orders

(1) This rule applies where the court is considering whether to make an order under section 51(6) of the Senior Courts Act 1981 (court's power to disallow or (as the case may be) order a legal representative to meet, 'wasted costs').

(2) The court will give the legal representative a reasonable opportunity to make written submissions or, if the legal representative prefers, to attend a hearing before it makes such an order.

(3) When the court makes a wasted costs order, it will –

(a) specify the amount to be disallowed or paid; or

(b) direct a costs judge or a District Judge to decide the amount of costs to be disallowed or paid.

(4) The court may direct that notice must be given to the legal representative's client, in such manner as the court may direct –

(a) of any proceedings under this rule; or

(b) of any order made under it against his legal representative.

Amendments—Inserted by SI 2013/262; SI 2014/407.

Defined terms—'costs': r 43.2(1)(a); 'costs judge': r 43.2(1)(c); 'legal representative': SCA 1981, s 51(13); 'privileged': Glossary; 'wasted costs': SCA 1981, s 51(7).

Jurisdiction—This rule derives from SCA 1981, s 51(6). Where there has been an improper, negligent or unreasonable act by a legal representative, the rule gives the court a discretion to make a wasted costs order against that legal representative personally. The court must give the representative notice of any such application.

Guidance on the court's jurisdiction—In *Ridehalgh v Horsefield, and Watson v Watson (Wasted Costs Order)* [1994] 2 FLR 194, CA, the Court of Appeal fully considered the wasted costs jurisdiction and proposed guidelines as to its exercise. Accordingly, the court must balance two, often conflicting, questions of public interest. On the one hand, lawyers should not be deterred from pursuing their clients' interests for fear of incurring personal liability for costs; on the other hand, other parties to proceedings need to be protected from financial prejudice caused by the unjustifiable conduct of lawyers. The jurisdiction is one which is entirely discretionary.

Meaning of 'improper, unreasonable or negligent'—These words from SCA 1981, s 51(7), were considered fully in *Ridehalgh v Horsefield* (above):

(a) *'Improper'* This word covers conduct which might lead to disbarment, striking off or other serious professional penalty; however, it is not restricted to this and might include other conduct stigmatised by the court in appropriate circumstances.
(b) *'Unreasonable'* This term includes conduct which is vexatious or harasses other parties, but it does not include an approach which merely leads to an unsuccessful result or which a more cautious representative might not have adopted.
(c) *'Negligent'* This term is to be approached in a non-technical way. A legal representative may come within the definition by failing to act with the competence reasonably to be expected of a member of the legal profession (as further explained in *Fisher Meredith v JH and PH (Financial Remedy: Appeal: Wasted Costs)* [2012] 2 FLR 536, FD, at [34]–[37]).

A legal representative is not to be regarded as acting improperly, unreasonably or negligently where pursuing a hopeless case for the client, providing this does not represent an abuse of the court's process. It is the responsibility of a lawyer to present the case and of the court to judge it.

Warnings on unarguable appeals—In *Re G (A Minor) (Role of the Appellate Court)* [1987] 1 FLR 164, CA, at [168], May LJ, firmly echoed by Nourse LJ, issued a warning to legal representatives that the court would not shrink from 'investigating how public money has come to be spent in [unarguable appeals] and to make all appropriate orders to ensure that it has not been wasted'.

Procedure on wasted costs orders—In *Ridehalgh v Horsefield* (above) the Court of Appeal made comments on the procedure for seeking an order.

Procedure after *Ridehalgh*—Any procedure should be as simple and summary as possible, while remaining consistent with fairness to the respondent legal representative. In *Ridehalgh v Horsefield*, Sir Thomas Bingham MR (as he then was) approved the procedure in *Re A Barrister (Wasted Costs Order)* [1993] QB 293, CA, namely:

(a) Where the court intends to exercise the wasted costs jurisdiction it must set out clearly and concisely the complaint and grounds upon which the order is to be made. These measures are draconian and, as with contempt proceedings, the grounds must be clear and particularised.
(b) A three-stage test would apply: (i) Had there been an improper, unreasonable or negligent act or omission? (ii) As a result had any costs been incurred by a party? (iii) If the answers to both questions was 'yes', should the court make an order; and if so what specific sum should be considered?
(c) The court should formally state its complaint, in chambers, and invite comments from the representative. After comments have been heard from any other party, the court should give a formal ruling.
(d) The court must specify the sum to be disallowed.

Procedure—There are two routes to an order (PD46, paras 5.7 and 5.8): (i) the application by a party and (ii) the order by the court of its own initiative. *Re A Barrister (Wasted Costs Order) (No 1 of 1991)* explains a procedure where the court acts or application can be by a party in the proceedings. Now the party seeking a wasted costs order must state a complaint. In either case, it is important for the legal representative to know the case to be met and to have an opportunity (often with assistance from insurers) to answer it.

Application for an order—PD46, para 5.9 requires that the party who wishes to apply for a wasted costs order must give notice of such application in accordance with Pt 23 (or FPR 2010, Pt 18 in family proceedings) or by making an oral application in the course of any hearing. Under CPR 1998, Pt 23 or FPR 2010, Pt 18, the application notice must set out 'what the legal representative is alleged to have done or failed to do', accompanied by details of precisely what costs are sought against him.

'legal representative' (r 46.8(1))—SCA 1981, s 51(13) defines 'legal or other representative' as 'in relation to a party to proceedings, any person exercising a right of audience or right to conduct litigation on his behalf'. Rule 46.8 uses 'legal representative' as synonymous with that definition. CLSA 1990, s 119(1) defines 'right of audience' as 'the right to exercise any of the functions of appearing before and addressing a court including the calling and examining of witnesses'; it defines 'right to conduct litigation' as being the right to issue process and to perform ancillary functions in relation to proceedings.

Wasted costs, proportionality and disclosure of documents—Where a party's solicitors press another party, especially a local authority, for wide-ranging disclosure which may be of dubious relevance to the case, their attention may be drawn to the case of *R v Reading Justices ex parte Berkshire County Council* [1996] 1 FLR 149, QBD, in which disclosure of documents from criminal proceedings was limited to 'material evidence' (MCA 1980, s 97(1)). If the solicitors persist in seeking extensive disclosure, they risk a wasted costs order (*R v M (Wasted Costs Order)* [1996] 1 FLR 750, QBD).

Privilege and wasted costs—Where a paying party has refused to waive advice privilege in respect of documents relevant to assessment of wasted costs, the court cannot make an order against a legal representative who is unable to explain his/her actions by reference to a client's withheld confidential documents (*Medcalf v Weatherhill* [2003] 1 AC 120, HL).

CLS funding (Legal aid)—The court retains its inherent jurisdiction to order solicitors to repay costs to the legal aid fund where there has been a serious dereliction of duty, and presumably now where costs have been wasted, but this applies only where the Legal Aid Agency pursues its remedy promptly (*Clark v Clark (No 2)* [1991] 1 FLR 179, FD).

46.9 Basis of detailed assessment of solicitor and client costs

(1) This rule applies to every assessment of a solicitor's bill to a client except a bill which is to be paid out of the Community Legal Service Fund under the Legal Aid Act 1988 or the Access to Justice Act 1999 or by the Lord Chancellor under Part 1 of the Legal Aid, Sentencing and Punishment of Offenders Act 2012.

(2) Section 74(3) of the Solicitors Act 1974 applies unless the solicitor and client have entered into a written agreement which expressly permits payment to the solicitor of an amount of costs greater than that which the client could have recovered from another party to the proceedings.

(3) Subject to paragraph (2), costs are to be assessed on the indemnity basis but are to be presumed –

(a) to have been reasonably incurred if they were incurred with the express or implied approval of the client;

(b) to be reasonable in amount if their amount was expressly or impliedly approved by the client;

(c) to have been unreasonably incurred if –

(i) they are of an unusual nature or amount; and

(ii) the solicitor did not tell the client that as a result the costs might not be recovered from the other party.

(4) Where the court is considering a percentage increase on the application of the client, the court will have regard to all the relevant factors as they reasonably appeared to the solicitor or counsel when the conditional fee agreement was entered into or varied.

Amendments—Inserted by SI 2013/262. Amended by SI 2013/534.

46.10 Assessment procedure

(1) This rule sets out the procedure to be followed where the court has made an order under Part III of the Solicitors Act 1974 for the assessment of costs payable to solicitor by the solicitor's client.

(2) The solicitor must serve a breakdown of costs within 28 days of the order for costs to be assessed.

(3) The client must serve points of dispute within 14 days after service on him of the breakdown of costs.

(4) The solicitor must serve any reply within 14 days of service on the solicitor of the points of dispute.

(5) Either party may file a request for a hearing date –

(a) after points of dispute have been served; but

(b) no later than 3 months after the date of the order for the costs to be assessed.

(6) This procedure applies subject to any contrary order made by the court.

Amendments—Inserted by SI 2013/262.

****

Practice Direction 46 – Costs Special Cases

This Practice Direction supplements CPR Part 46

Amendments—CPR Update 60.

Awards of Costs in Favour of a Trustee or Personal Representative: Rule 46.3

1.1 A trustee or personal representative is entitled to an indemnity out of the relevant trust fund or estate for costs properly incurred. Whether costs were properly incurred depends on all the circumstances of the case including whether the trustee or personal representative ('the trustee') –

(a) obtained directions from the court before bringing or defending the proceedings;

(b) acted in the interests of the fund or estate or in substance for a benefit other than that of the estate, including the trustee's own; and

(c) acted in some way unreasonably in bringing or defending, or in the conduct of, the proceedings.

1.2 The trustee is not to be taken to have acted for a benefit other than that of the fund by reason only that the trustee has defended a claim in which relief is sought against the trustee personally.

Costs Where Money Is Payable By Or To A Child Or Protected Party: Rule 46.4

2.1 The circumstances in which the court need not order the detailed assessment of costs under rule 46.4(2) are as follows –

(a) where there is no need to do so to protect the interests of the child or protected party or their estate;

(b) where another party has agreed to pay a specified sum in respect of the costs of the child or protected party and the legal representative acting for the child or protected party has waived the right to claim further costs;

(c) where the court has decided the costs payable to the child or protected party by way of summary assessment and the legal representative acting for the child or protected party has waived the right to claim further costs;

(d) where an insurer or other person is liable to discharge the costs which the child or protected party would otherwise be liable to pay to the legal representative and the court is satisfied that the insurer or other person is financially able to discharge those costs; and

(e) where the court has given a direction for summary assessment pursuant to rule 46.4(5).

Amendments—CPR Update 78.

Litigants In Person: Rule 46.5

3.1 In order to qualify as an expert for the purpose of rule 46.5(3)(c) (expert assistance in connection with assessing the claim for costs), the person in question must be a –

(a) barrister;

(b) solicitor;

(c) Fellow of the Institute of Legal Executives;

(d) Fellow of the Association of Costs Lawyers;

(e) law costs draftsman who is a member of the Academy of Experts;

(f) law costs draftsman who is a member of the Expert Witness Institute.

3.2 Where a self-represented litigant wishes to prove that the litigant has suffered financial loss, the litigant should produce to the court any written evidence relied on to support that claim, and serve a copy of that evidence on any party against whom the litigant seeks costs at least 24 hours before the hearing at which the question may be decided.

3.3 A self-represented litigant who commences detailed assessment proceedings under rule 47.5 should serve copies of that written evidence with the notice of commencement.

3.4 The amount, which may be allowed to a self-represented litigant under rule 45.39(5)(b) and rule 46.5(4)(b), is £19 per hour.

Amendments—CPR Update 78.

Orders in Respect of Pro Bono Representation: Rule 46.7

4.1 Where an order is sought under section 194(3) of the Legal Services Act 2007 the party who has pro bono representation must prepare, file and serve a written statement of the sum equivalent to the costs that party would have claimed for that legal representation had it not been provided free of charge.

Personal Liability of Legal Representative for Costs – Wasted Costs Orders: Rule 46.8

5.1 A wasted costs order is an order –

(a) that the legal representative pay a sum (either specified or to be assessed) in respect of costs to a party; or
(b) for costs relating to a specified sum or items of work to be disallowed.

5.2 Rule 46.8 deals with wasted costs orders against legal representatives. Such orders can be made at any stage in the proceedings up to and including the detailed assessment proceedings. In general, applications for wasted costs are best left until after the end of the trial.

5.3 The court may make a wasted costs order against a legal representative on its own initiative.

5.4 A party may apply for a wasted costs order –

(a) by filing an application notice in accordance with Part 23; or
(b) by making an application orally in the course of any hearing.

5.5 It is appropriate for the court to make a wasted costs order against a legal representative, only if –

(a) the legal representative has acted improperly, unreasonably or negligently;
(b) the legal representative's conduct has caused a party to incur unnecessary costs, or has meant that costs incurred by a party prior to the improper, unreasonable or negligent act or omission have been wasted;
(c) it is just in all the circumstances to order the legal representative to compensate that party for the whole or part of those costs.

5.6 The court will give directions about the procedure to be followed in each case in order to ensure that the issues are dealt with in a way which is fair and as simple and summary as the circumstances permit.

5.7 As a general rule the court will consider whether to make a wasted costs order in two stages –

(a) at the first stage the court must be satisfied –
   (i) that it has before it evidence or other material which, if unanswered, would be likely to lead to a wasted costs order being made; and
   (ii) the wasted costs proceedings are justified notwithstanding the likely costs involved;
(b) at the second stage, the court will consider, after giving the legal representative an opportunity to make representations in writing or at a hearing, whether it is appropriate to make a wasted costs order in accordance with paragraph 5.5 above.

5.8 The court may proceed to the second stage described in paragraph 5.7 without first adjourning the hearing if it is satisfied that the legal representative has already had a reasonable opportunity to make representations.

5.9 On an application for a wasted costs order under Part 23 the application notice and any evidence in support must identify –

(a) what the legal representative is alleged to have done or failed to do; and
(b) the costs that the legal representative may be ordered to pay or which are sought against the legal representative.

PART III

Assessment of Solicitor and Client Costs: Rules 46.9 and 46.10

6.1 A client and solicitor may agree whatever terms they consider appropriate about the payment of the solicitor's charges. If however, the costs are of an unusual nature, either in amount or the type of costs incurred, those costs will be presumed to have been unreasonably incurred unless the solicitor satisfies the court that the client was informed that they were unusual and that they might not be allowed on an assessment of costs between the parties. That information must have been given to the client before the costs were incurred.

6.2 Costs as between a solicitor and client are assessed on the indemnity basis. The presumptions in rule 46.9(3) are rebuttable.

6.3 If a party fails to comply with the requirements of rule 46.10 concerning the service of a breakdown of costs or points of dispute, any other party may apply to the court in which the detailed assessment hearing should take place for an order requiring compliance. If the court makes such an order, it may –

(a) make it subject to conditions including a condition to pay a sum of money into court; and

(b) specify the consequence of failure to comply with the order or a condition.

6.4 The procedure for obtaining an order under Part III of the Solicitors Act 1974 is by a Part 8 claim, as modified by rule 67.3 and Practice Direction 67. Precedent J of the Schedule of Costs Precedents is a model form of claim form. The application must be accompanied by the bill or bills in respect of which assessment is sought, and, if the claim concerns a conditional fee agreement, a copy of that agreement. If the original bill is not available a copy will suffice.

6.5 Model forms of order, which the court may make, are set out in Precedents K, L and M of the Schedule of Costs Precedents.

6.6 The breakdown of costs referred to in rule 46.10 is a document which contains the following information –

(a) details of the work done under each of the bills sent for assessment; and

(b) in applications under Section 70 of the Solicitors Act 1974, a cash account showing money received by the solicitor to the credit of the client and sums paid out of that money on behalf of the client but not payments out which were made in satisfaction of the bill or of any items which are claimed in the bill.

6.7 Precedent P of the Schedule of Costs Precedents is a model form of breakdown of costs. A party who is required to serve a breakdown of costs must also serve –

(a) copies of the fee notes of counsel and of any expert in respect of fees claimed in the breakdown, and

(b) written evidence as to any other disbursement which is claimed in the breakdown and which exceeds £250.

6.8 The provisions relating to default costs certificates (rule 47.11) do not apply to cases to which rule 46.10 applies.

6.9 The time for requesting a detailed assessment hearing is within 3 months after the date of the order for the costs to be assessed.

6.10 The form of request for a hearing date must be in Form N258C. The request must be accompanied by copies of –

(a) the order sending the bill or bills for assessment;

(b) the bill or bills sent for assessment;

(c) the solicitor's breakdown of costs and any invoices or accounts served with that breakdown;

(d) a copy of the points of dispute;

(e) a copy of any replies served;

(f) a statement signed by the party filing the request or that party's legal representative giving the names and addresses for service of all parties to the proceedings.

6.11 The request must include the estimated length of hearing.

6.12 On receipt of the request the court will fix a date for the hearing, or will give directions.

6.13 The court will give at least 14 days' notice of the time and place of the detailed assessment hearing.

6.14 Unless the court gives permission, only the solicitor whose bill it is and parties who have served points of dispute may be heard and only items specified in the points of dispute may be raised.

6.15 If a party wishes to vary that party's breakdown of costs, points of dispute or reply, an amended or supplementary document must be filed with the court and copies of it must be served on all other relevant parties. Permission is not required to vary a breakdown of costs, points of dispute or a reply but the court may disallow the variation or permit it only upon conditions, including conditions as to the payment of any costs caused or wasted by the variation.

6.16 Unless the court directs otherwise the solicitor must file with the court the papers in support of the bill not less than 7 days before the date for the detailed assessment hearing and not more than 14 days before that date.

6.17 Once the detailed assessment hearing has ended it is the responsibility of the legal representative appearing for the solicitor or, as the case may be, the solicitor in person to remove the papers filed in support of the bill.

6.18 If, in the course of a detailed assessment hearing of a solicitor's bill to that solicitor's client, it appears to the court that in any event the solicitor will be liable in connection with that bill to pay money to the client, it may issue an interim certificate specifying an amount which in its opinion is payable by the solicitor to the client.

6.19 After the detailed assessment hearing is concluded the court will –

(a) complete the court copy of the bill so as to show the amount allowed;
(b) determine the result of the cash account;
(c) award the costs of the detailed assessment hearing in accordance with Section 70(8) of the Solicitors Act 1974; and
(d) issue a final costs certificate.

****

PART 47
PROCEDURE FOR DETAILED ASSESSMENT OF COSTS AND DEFAULT PROVISIONS

PART III

CONTENTS OF THIS PART

Section I

Rule		Page
	General Rules about Detailed Assessment	
47.1	Time when detailed assessment may be carried out	2166
47.2	No stay of detailed assessment where there is an appeal	2167
47.3	Powers of an authorised court officer	2167
47.4	Venue for detailed assessment proceedings	2167
	Section II	
	Costs Payable by one Party to Another – Commencement of Detailed Assessment Proceedings	
47.5	Application of this Section	2167
47.6	Commencement of detailed assessment proceedings	2168
47.7	Period for commencing detailed assessment proceedings	2168
47.8	Sanction for delay in commencing detailed assessment proceedings	2169
47.9	Points of dispute and consequence of not serving	2169
47.10	Procedure where costs are agreed	2170

Section III
Costs Payable by One Party to Another – Default Provisions

47.11 Default costs certificate 2170
47.12 Setting aside a default costs certificate 2170

Section IV
Costs Payable by One Party to Another – Procedure where Points of Dispute are Served

47.13 Optional Reply 2171
47.14 Detailed assessment hearing 2171
47.15 Provisional Assessment 2172

Section V
Interim Costs Certificate and Final Costs Certificate.

47.16 Power to issue an interim certificate 2173
47.17 Final costs certificate 2173

Section VI
Detailed Assessment Procedure for Costs of a LSC Funded Client, an Assisted Person or Person to Whom Legal Aid is Made Available where Costs are Payable out of the Community Legal Service Fund or by the Lord Chancellor under Part 1 of the Legal Aid, Sentencing and Punishment of Offenders Act 2012

47.18 Detailed assessment procedure where costs are payable out of the Community Legal Services Fund or by the Lord Chancellor under Part 1 of the Legal Aid, Sentencing and Punishment of Offenders Act 2012 2174
47.19 Detailed assessment procedure where costs are payable out of a fund other than the community legal service fund 2174

Section VII
Costs of Detailed Assessment Proceedings

47.20 Liability for costs of detailed assessment proceedings 2175

Section VIII
Appeals from Authorised Court Officers in Detailed Assessment Proceedings

47.21 Right to appeal 2176
47.22 Court to hear appeal 2176
47.23 Appeal procedure 2176
47.24 Powers of the court on appeal 2176

Practice Direction 47 –
Procedure for Detailed Assessment of Costs and Default Provisions 2176

Section I
General Rules about Detailed Assessment

47.1 Time when detailed assessment may be carried out

The general rule is that the costs of any proceedings or any part of the proceedings are not to be assessed by the detailed procedure until the conclusion of the proceedings but the court may order them to be assessed immediately.

(Practice Direction 47 gives further guidance about when proceedings are concluded for the purpose of this rule.)

Amendments—Inserted by SI 2013/262.

Defined terms—'costs': r 44.1(1).

Scope—'Detailed assessment', as distinct from 'summary assessment', is the terminology preferred under CPR 1998 for what was formerly known as taxation of costs under both the old rules governing civil procedure and in legal aid legislation.

Further guidance in the practice direction—PD47, paras 1.2–1.4 provide further guidance as to when detailed assessment may be commenced or when proceedings are concluded, or treated as concluded:

(1) Treated as concluded: The parties may agree or the court order that proceedings be treated as concluded (para 1.2), for example, in long-running children proceedings with successive reviews and an order for costs has been made at some point.
(2) If a notice of commencement is served, a party may question whether the receiving party is entitled to claim at that stage of proceedings (para 1.3).
(3) Where there is no realistic prospect of a claim, continuing detailed assessment may be ordered (para 1.4).

47.2 No stay of detailed assessment where there is an appeal

Detailed assessment is not stayed pending an appeal unless the court so orders.

Amendments—Inserted by SI 2013/262.

No stay pending appeal—This is as with an appeal order. A stay on detailed assessment can be made to the court below or to that court appealed to (PD47, para 2). Application can be included in the appeal notice (which will generally be the most economical way) or must be by FPR 2010, Pt 18 or CPR 1998, Pt 23.

47.3 Powers of an authorised court officer

(1) An authorised court officer has all the powers of the court when making a detailed assessment, except –

(a) power to make a wasted costs order as defined in rule 46.8;
(b) power to make an order under –
  (i) rule 44.11 (powers in relation to misconduct);
  (ii) rule 47.8 (sanction for delay in commencing detailed assessment proceedings);
  (iii) paragraph (2) (objection to detailed assessment by authorised court officer); and
(c) power to make a detailed assessment of costs payable to a solicitor by that solicitor's client, unless the costs are being assessed under rule 46.5 (costs where money is payable to a child or protected party).

(2) Where a party objects to the detailed assessment of costs being made by an authorised court officer, the court may order it to be made by a costs judge or a District Judge.

(Practice Direction 47 sets out the relevant procedure.)

Amendments—Inserted by SI 2013/262. Amended by SI 2014/407.

The relevant procedure—The relevant procedure is set out in PD47, para 3.3.

47.4 Venue for detailed assessment proceedings

(1) All applications and requests in detailed assessment proceedings must be made to or filed at the appropriate office.

(Practice Direction 47 sets out the meaning of 'appropriate office' in any particular case)

(2) The court may direct that the appropriate office is to be the Costs Office.

(3) In the County Court, a court may direct that another County Court hearing centre is to be the appropriate office.

(4) A direction under paragraph (3) may be made without proceedings being transferred to that court.

(Rule 30.2 makes provision for the transfer within the County Court of proceedings for detailed assessment of costs.)

Amendments—Inserted by SI 2013/262.

'appropriate office'—See PD47, para 4.1.

Section II
Costs Payable by one Party to Another – Commencement of Detailed Assessment Proceedings

47.5 Application of this Section

This Section of Part 47 applies where a cost officer is to make a detailed assessment of –

(a) costs which are payable by one party to another; or

(b) the sum which is payable by one party to the prescribed charity pursuant to an order under section 194(3) of the 2007 Act.

Amendments—Inserted by SI 2013/262.

47.6 Commencement of detailed assessment proceedings

(1) Detailed assessment proceedings are commenced by the receiving party serving on the paying party –

(a) notice of commencement in the relevant practice form;
(b) a copy of the bill of costs; and
(c) if a costs management order has been made, a breakdown of the costs claimed for each phase of the proceedings.

(Rule 47.7 sets out the period for commencing detailed assessment proceedings)

(2) The receiving party must also serve a copy of the notice of commencement, the bill and, if a costs management order has been made, the breakdown on any other relevant persons specified in Practice Direction 47.

(3) A person on whom a copy of the notice of commencement is served under paragraph (2) is a party to the detailed assessment proceedings (in addition to the paying party and the receiving party).

(Practice Direction 47 deals with –
other documents which the party must file when requesting detailed assessment;
the court's powers where it considers that a hearing may be necessary;
the form of a bill; and
the length of notice which will be given if a hearing date is fixed.)

(Paragraphs 7B.2 to 7B.7 of the Practice Direction – Civil Recovery Proceedings contain provisions about detailed assessment of costs in relation to civil recovery orders.)

Amendments—Inserted by SI 2013/262. Amended by SI 2013/1695; SI 2015/1569; SI 2016/234.

Defined terms—'costs': r 44.1(1); 'detailed assessment': r 44.3; 'paying party': r 44.1(1)); 'receiving party': r 44.1(1)).

Documents for service—The receiving party must serve a combination of the documents listed in r 47.6(1) and PD47, para 5.2. These include notice of commencement, which is in Form N252.

'any other relevant persons' (r 47.6(2))—PD47, para 5.5 defines a 'relevant person' for the purposes of Pt 47. This definition includes a non-party who may be required to pay costs, a trustee out of whose trust fund costs might, unusually, be paid, but not a legally assisted person (see r 47.17) and probably not a legal representative under a wasted costs order (since costs should be defined by the court at the time of the order: r 48.7(4)).

The client as 'relevant person'—The party in respect of whom the costs are to be paid is not a relevant person, save where application is made by him to be joined as a party to assessment proceedings. A person can apply to be made a party under Pt 19. This will give a legally aided assisted person the right to apply to be heard on assessment of their bill, whereas, in the past, such a person's standing as a party to the taxation process was unclear. These provisions will be of greater significance where costs orders are made for differing amounts, for proportions etc. Practitioners will need to be aware that their interests may be in conflict with those of their client.

47.7 Period for commencing detailed assessment proceedings

The following table shows the period for commencing detailed assessment proceedings.

Source of right to detailed assessment	Time by which detailed assessment proceedings must be commenced
Judgment, direction, order, award or other determination	3 months after the date of the judgment etc. Where detailed assessment is stayed pending an appeal, 3 months after the date of the order lifting the stay
Discontinuance under Part 38	3 months after the date of service of notice of discontinuance under rule 38.3; or 3 months after the date of the dismissal of application to set the notice of discontinuance aside under rule 38.4
Acceptance of an offer to settle under Part 36	3 months after the date when the right to costs arose

Amendments—Inserted by SI 2013/262.

47.8 Sanction for delay in commencing detailed assessment proceedings

(1) Where the receiving party fails to commence detailed assessment proceedings within the period specified –

(a) in rule 47.7; or

(b) by any direction of the court,

the paying party may apply for an order requiring the receiving party to commence detailed assessment proceedings within such time as the court may specify.

(2) On an application under paragraph (1), the court may direct that, unless the receiving party commences detailed assessment proceedings within the time specified by the court, all or part of the costs to which the receiving party would otherwise be entitled will be disallowed.

(3) If –

(a) the paying party has not made an application in accordance with paragraph (1); and

(b) the receiving party commences the proceedings later than the period specified in rule 47.7,

the court may disallow all or part of the interest otherwise payable to the receiving party under –

(i) section 17 of the Judgments Act 1838; or

(ii) section 74 of the County Courts Act 1984,

but will not impose any other sanction except in accordance with rule 44.11 (powers in relation to misconduct).

(4) Where the costs to be assessed in a detailed assessment are payable out of the Community Legal Service Fund, this rule applies as if the receiving party were the solicitor to whom the costs are payable and the paying party were the Legal Services Commission.

(5) Where the costs to be assessed in a detailed assessment are payable by the Lord Chancellor under Part 1 of the Legal Aid, Sentencing and Punishment of Offenders Act 2012, this rule applies as if the receiving party were the solicitor to whom the costs are payable and the paying party were the Lord Chancellor.

Amendments—Inserted by SI 2013/262. Amended by SI 2013/534.

Defined terms—'costs': r 44.1(1); 'detailed assessment': r 44.3; 'paying party': r 44.1(1)); 'receiving party': r 44.1(1).

Delay in commencement of detailed assessment—It is not necessary to obtain court permission to start detailed assessment proceedings out of time but, where proceedings are not commenced, a paying party, including for this purpose the Legal Aid Agency (which replaced the Legal Services Commission on 1 April 2013), can seek an order to require the receiving party to do so. Thereafter, failure to commence proceedings within the requisite period of time may attract an order that all or part of the costs be disallowed. By contrast, failure to commence in accordance with the r 44.7 time-limits may only be penalised by (i) an order that interest be awarded for a shorter period and (ii) an award of costs against the legal representative on the basis of misconduct under r 44.11.

'period specified' (r 47.8(1))—See r 47.7.

'interest otherwise payable to the receiving party' (r 47.8(3))—Rule 44.2(6)(g) provides that an order for payment of interest on costs due can be made by the court at the same time as any order for costs is made.

47.9 Points of dispute and consequence of not serving

(1) The paying party and any other party to the detailed assessment proceedings may dispute any item in the bill of costs by serving points of dispute on –

(a) the receiving party; and

(b) every other party to the detailed assessment proceedings.

(2) The period for serving points of dispute is 21 days after the date of service of the notice of commencement.

(3) If a party serves points of dispute after the period set out in paragraph (2), that party may not be heard further in the detailed assessment proceedings unless the court gives permission.

(Practice Direction 47 sets out requirements about the form of points of dispute)

(4) The receiving party may file a request for a default costs certificate if –

PART III

(a) the period set out in paragraph (2) for serving points of dispute has expired; and
(b) the receiving party has not been served with any points of dispute.

(5) If any party (including the paying party) serves points of dispute before the issue of a default costs certificate the court may not issue the default costs certificate.

(Section IV of this Part sets out the procedure to be followed after points of dispute have been served).

Amendments—Inserted by SI 2013/262.

Defined terms—'costs': r 44.1(1); 'detailed assessment': r 44.3; 'paying party': r 44.1(1)); 'receiving party': r 44.1(1).

Form of points of dispute—PD47, para 8.2 provides that Precedent G from the costs precedents must be used.

Dispute as to items—At this stage in the detailed assessment process the court is still not involved (subject to any order under r 47.8). The paying party who wishes to dispute any item on the detailed assessment bill does so by sending points of dispute, 21 days after service of the bill, to the receiving party and to anyone else interested in the assessment. Failure to send points of dispute within that time (i) prevents the paying party being heard on the detailed assessment except with the court's permission and (ii) enables the receiving party to apply to the court for a default costs certificate.

'points of dispute' (r 47.9(1))—Points of dispute should be briefly set out in accordance with PD47, para 8.2.

'21 days after the date of service of the notice' (r 47.9(2))—See r 6.7 for details of deemed service periods.

47.10 Procedure where costs are agreed

(1) If the paying party and the receiving party agree the amount of costs, either party may apply for a costs certificate (either interim or final) in the amount agreed.

(Rule 47.16 and rule 47.17 contain further provisions about interim and final costs certificates respectively)

(2) An application for a certificate under paragraph (1) must be made to the court which would be the venue for detailed assessment proceedings under rule 47.4.

Amendments—Inserted by SI 2013/262.

Section III
Costs Payable by One Party to Another – Default Provisions

47.11 Default costs certificate

(1) Where the receiving party is permitted by rule 47.9 to obtain a default costs certificate, that party does so by filing a request in the relevant practice form.

(Practice Direction 47 deals with the procedure by which the receiving party may obtain a default costs certificate.)

(2) A default costs certificate will include an order to pay the costs to which it relates.

(3) Where a receiving party obtains a default costs certificate, the costs payable to that party for the commencement of detailed assessment proceedings will be the sum set out in Practice Direction 47.

(4) A receiving party who obtains a default costs certificate in detailed assessment proceedings pursuant to an order under section 194(3) of the 2007 Act must send a copy of the default costs certificate to the prescribed charity.

Amendments—Inserted by SI 2013/262.

Procedure—Practice and procedure governing the application are dealt with in PD47, paras 10.1–10.6.

47.12 Setting aside a default costs certificate

(1) The court will set aside a default costs certificate if the receiving party was not entitled to it.

(2) In any other case, the court may set aside or vary a default costs certificate if it appears to the court that there is some good reason why the detailed assessment proceedings should continue.

(Practice Direction 47 contains further details about the procedure for setting aside a default costs certificate and the matters which the court must take into account)

(3) Where the court sets aside or varies a default costs certificate in detailed assessment proceedings pursuant to an order under section 194(3) of the Legal Services Act 2007, the receiving party must send a copy of the order setting aside or varying the default costs certificate to the prescribed charity.

Amendments—Inserted by SI 2013/262.

Procedure—Practice and procedure for setting aside the certificate are dealt with in PD47, paras 11.1–11.3.

Section IV

Costs Payable by One Party to Another – Procedure where Points of Dispute are Served

47.13 Optional Reply

(1) Where any party to the detailed assessment proceedings serves points of dispute, the receiving party may serve a reply on the other parties to the assessment proceedings.

(2) The receiving party may do so within 21 days after being served with the points of dispute to which the reply relates.

(Practice Direction 47 sets out the meaning of 'reply'.)

Amendments—Inserted by SI 2013/262.

Defined terms—'detailed assessment': r 44.3; 'paying party': r 44.1(1)); 'receiving party': r 44.1(1).

Scope—A receiving party who is served with points of dispute may serve a reply. This is entirely voluntary but if no reply is filed it may be reflected in a later order for costs on the detailed assessment. If a receiving party accepts a point raised in dispute, it might be prudent to indicate this in a reply under r 47.13. However, merely to re-argue points already raised in the bill would seem to be sterile and might risk the receiving party losing the costs so incurred.

'reply'—See PD47, para 12.1.

47.14 Detailed assessment hearing

(1) Where points of dispute are served in accordance with this Part, the receiving party must file a request for a detailed assessment hearing within 3 months of the expiry of the period for commencing detailed assessment proceedings as specified –

(a) in rule 47.7; or
(b) by any direction of the court.

(2) Where the receiving party fails to file a request in accordance with paragraph (1), the paying party may apply for an order requiring the receiving party to file the request within such time as the court may specify.

(3) On an application under paragraph (2), the court may direct that, unless the receiving party requests a detailed assessment hearing within the time specified by the court, all or part of the costs to which the receiving party would otherwise be entitled will be disallowed.

(4) If –

(a) the paying party has not made an application in accordance with paragraph (2); and
(b) the receiving party files a request for a detailed assessment hearing later than the period specified in paragraph (1),

the court may disallow all or part of the interest otherwise payable to the receiving party under –

(i) section 17 of the Judgments Act 1838; or
(ii) section 74 of the County Courts Act 1984,

but will not impose any other sanction except in accordance with rule 44.11 (powers in relation to misconduct).

(5) No party other than –

(a) the receiving party;
(b) the paying party; and
(c) any party who has served points of dispute under rule 47.9,

may be heard at the detailed assessment hearing unless the court gives permission.

PART III

(6) Only items specified in the points of dispute may be raised at the hearing, unless the court gives permission.

(7) If an assessment is carried out at more than one hearing, then for the purposes of rule 52.12 time for appealing shall not start to run until the conclusion of the final hearing, unless the court orders otherwise.

(Practice Direction 47 specifies other documents which must be filed with the request for hearing and the length of notice which the court will give when it fixes a hearing date.)

Amendments—Inserted by SI 2013/262. Amended by SI 2016/788.

Defined terms—'costs': r 44.1(1); 'default costs certificate': 'detailed assessment': r 44.3; 'paying party': r 44.1(1)); 'points of dispute': r 47.9 'receiving party': r 44.1(1)).

Request for detailed assessment—Once points of dispute are served, the receiving party must file a request for a detailed assessment within 3 months. If the receiving party is out of time for filing the request, the paying party can ask the court to specify a date for filing. In default of this requirement, all or part of the costs may be allowed and if both paying and receiving parties delay in applying under this rule, interest on costs due may be disallowed. Only the paying party, the receiving party and any other party who has filed points of dispute may be heard at the detailed assessment hearing(s). Where matters have not been raised in the points of dispute, a party will be estopped from raising them unless the court gives permission.

Practice and procedure—PD47, para 13.2 sets out specific requirements which need to be complied with in the request for a detailed assessment hearing. Applications in the assessment proceedings are made under FPR 2010, Pt 18 or CPR 1998, Pt 23.

Document giving the right to detailed assessment—This document is defined in the practice direction and is crucial to the process of detailed assessment since it underlines the fact that there is a right to proceed with such an assessment.

'request for a detailed assessment hearing' (r 47.14(1))—The request must be in Form N258.

'any party who has served points of dispute under rule 47.9' (r 47.14(6)(c))—Points of dispute may also be served by every other party to the detailed assessment proceedings (r 47.9(1)(b)); only those 'other parties' who have served points of dispute can be heard.

47.15 Provisional Assessment

(1) This rule applies to any detailed assessment proceedings commenced in the High Court or the County Court on or after 1 April 2013 in which the costs claimed are the amount set out in paragraph 14.1 of the practice direction supplementing this Part, or less.

(2) In proceedings to which this rule applies, the parties must comply with the procedure set out in Part 47 as modified by paragraph 14 Practice Direction 47.

(3) The court will undertake a provisional assessment of the receiving party's costs on receipt of Form N258 and the relevant supporting documents specified in Practice Direction 47.

(4) The provisional assessment will be based on the information contained in the bill and supporting papers and the contentions set out in Precedent G (the points of dispute and any reply).

(5) The court will not award more than £1,500 to any party in respect of the costs of the provisional assessment.

(6) The court may at any time decide that the matter is unsuitable for a provisional assessment and may give directions for the matter to be listed for hearing. The matter will then proceed under rule 47.14 without modification.

(7) When a provisional assessment has been carried out, the court will send a copy of the bill, as provisionally assessed, to each party with a notice stating that any party who wishes to challenge any aspect of the provisional assessment must, within 21 days of the receipt of the notice, file and serve on all other parties a written request for an oral hearing. If no such request is filed and served within that period, the provisional assessment shall be binding upon the parties, save in exceptional circumstances.

(8) The written request referred to in paragraph (7) must –

(a) identify the item or items in the court's provisional assessment which are sought to be reviewed at the hearing; and

(b) provide a time estimate for the hearing.

(9) The court then will fix a date for the hearing and give at least 14 days' notice of the time and place of the hearing to all parties.

(10) Any party which has requested an oral hearing, will pay the costs of and incidental to that hearing unless –

(a) it achieves an adjustment in its own favour by 20% or more of the sum provisionally assessed; or

(b) the court otherwise orders.

Amendments—Inserted by SI 2013/262. Amended by SI 2014/407.

Documents in PD47 (r 47.15(2))—See para 14.3.

Section V
Interim Costs Certificate and Final Costs Certificate.

47.16 Power to issue an interim certificate

(1) The court may at any time after the receiving party has filed a request for a detailed assessment hearing –

(a) issue an interim costs certificate for such sum as it considers appropriate or

(b) amend or cancel an interim certificate.

(2) An interim certificate will include an order to pay the costs to which it relates, unless the court orders otherwise.

(3) The court may order the costs certified in an interim certificate to be paid into court.

(4) Where the court –

(a) issues an interim costs certificate; or

(b) amends or cancels an interim certificate,

in detailed assessment proceedings pursuant to an order under section 194(3) of the 2007 Act, the receiving party must send a copy of the interim costs certificate or the order amending or cancelling the interim costs certificate to the prescribed charity.

Amendments—Inserted by SI 2013/262.

Defined terms—'costs': r 44.1(1); 'detailed assessment': r 44.3; 'receiving party': r 44.1(1).

Costs certificates—Once the receiving party has applied under r 47.14 for a detailed assessment hearing, the court may issue an interim certificate or may cancel or amend such a certificate. Costs of the application will normally be included in the certificate and an order may be made that such costs be paid into court.

Procedure for application—In accordance with PD47, para 15 application for a certificate is in accordance with Pt 23 (FPR 2010, Pt 18 in family proceedings).

'issue an interim costs certificate' (r 47.15(1)(a))—This power appears to be additional to the power under r 44.3(8) to order costs to be paid on account before they are assessed, although any payment made under the latter rule will doubtless be taken into account when the amount to be paid under the interim costs certificate is quantified.

47.17 Final costs certificate

(1) In this rule a 'completed bill' means a bill calculated to show the amount due following the detailed assessment of the costs.

(2) The period for filing the completed bill is 14 days after the end of the detailed assessment hearing.

(3) When a completed bill is filed the court will issue a final costs certificate and serve it on the parties to the detailed assessment proceedings.

(4) Paragraph (3) is subject to any order made by the court that a certificate is not to be issued until other costs have been paid.

(5) A final costs certificate will include an order to pay the costs to which it relates, unless the court orders otherwise.

(Practice Direction 47 deals with the form of a final costs certificate)

(6) Where the court issues a final costs certificate in detailed assessment proceedings pursuant to an order under section 194(3) of the 2007 Act, the receiving party must send a copy of the final costs certificate to the prescribed charity.

Amendments—Inserted by SI 2013/262.

Defined terms—'costs': r 44.1(1); 'detailed assessment': r 44.3; 'receiving party': r 44.1(1).

Final costs certificate—Not more than 2 weeks after completion of all detailed assessment hearings, the receiving party should lodge a final bill showing the amount due following such assessment. The court then issues a final costs certificate which includes an order to the paying party to discharge the liability for costs, unless otherwise ordered (eg because the receiving party has an outstanding liability to make payment of a lump sum or costs to the paying party). PD47, paras 16.1–16.8 deal with practice and procedure in relation to obtaining a final costs certificate.

Section VI

Detailed Assessment Procedure for Costs of a LSC Funded Client, an Assisted Person or Person to Whom Legal Aid is Made Available where Costs are Payable out of the Community Legal Service Fund or by the Lord Chancellor under Part 1 of the Legal Aid, Sentencing and Punishment of Offenders Act 2012

Amendments—SI 2013/534.

47.18 Detailed assessment procedure where costs are payable out of the Community Legal Services Fund or by the Lord Chancellor under Part 1 of the Legal Aid, Sentencing and Punishment of Offenders Act 2012

(1) Where the court is to assess costs of a LSC funded client, an assisted person or a person to whom legal aid is provided which are payable out of the Community Legal Services Fund or by the Lord Chancellor under Part 1 of the Legal Aid, Sentencing and Punishment of Offenders Act 2012, that person's solicitor may commence detailed assessment proceedings by filing a request in the relevant practice form.

(2) A request under paragraph (1) must be filed within 3 months after the date when the right to detailed assessment arose.

(3) The solicitor must also serve a copy of the request for detailed assessment on the LSC funded client, the assisted person or the person to whom legal aid is provided, if notice of that person's interest has been given to the court in accordance with community legal service or legal aid regulations.

(4) Where the solicitor has certified that the LSC funded client or that person wishes to attend an assessment hearing, the court will, on receipt of the request for assessment, fix a date for the assessment hearing.

(5) Where paragraph (3) does not apply, the court will, on receipt of the request for assessment provisionally assess the costs without the attendance of the solicitor, unless it considers that a hearing is necessary.

(6) After the court has provisionally assessed the bill, it will return the bill to the solicitor.

(7) The court will fix a date for an assessment hearing if the solicitor informs the court, within 14 days after receiving the provisionally assessed bill, that the solicitor wants the court to hold such a hearing.

Amendments—Inserted by SI 2013/262. Amended by SI 2013/534.

Defined terms—'costs': r 44.1(1); 'detailed assessment': r 43.4; 'request for detailed assessment': r 47.14(1).

47.19 Detailed assessment procedure where costs are payable out of a fund other than the community legal service fund

(1) Where the court is to assess costs which are payable out of a fund other than the Community Legal Service Fund, the receiving party may commence detailed assessment proceedings by filing a request in the relevant practice form.

(2) A request under paragraph (1) must be filed within 3 months after the date when the right to detailed assessment arose.

(3) The court may direct that the party seeking assessment serve a copy of the request on any person who has a financial interest in the outcome of the assessment.

(4) The court will, on receipt of the request for assessment, provisionally assess the costs without the attendance of the receiving party, unless the court considers that a hearing is necessary.

(5) After the court has provisionally assessed the bill, it will return the bill to the receiving party.

(6) The court will fix a date for an assessment hearing if the receiving party informs the court, within 14 days after receiving the provisionally assessed bill, that the receiving party wants the court to hold such a hearing.

Amendments—Inserted by SI 2013/262.

Section VII
Costs of Detailed Assessment Proceedings

47.20 Liability for costs of detailed assessment proceedings

(1) The receiving party is entitled to the costs of the detailed assessment proceedings except where –

- (a) the provisions of any Act, any of these Rules or any relevant practice direction provide otherwise; or
- (b) the court makes some other order in relation to all or part of the costs of the detailed assessment proceedings.

(2) Paragraph (1) does not apply where the receiving party has pro bono representation in the detailed assessment proceedings but that party may apply for an order in respect of that representation under section 194(3) of the 2007 Act.

(3) In deciding whether to make some other order, the court must have regard to all the circumstances, including –

- (a) the conduct of all the parties;
- (b) the amount, if any, by which the bill of costs has been reduced; and
- (c) whether it was reasonable for a party to claim the costs of a particular item or to dispute that item.

(4) The provisions of Part 36 apply to the costs of detailed assessment proceedings with the following modifications –

- (a) 'claimant' refers to 'receiving party' and 'defendant' refers to 'paying party';
- (b) 'trial' refers to 'detailed assessment hearing';
- (c) a detailed assessment hearing is 'in progress' from the time when it starts until the bill of costs has been assessed or agreed;
- (d) for rule 36.14(7) substitute 'If such sum is not paid within 14 days of acceptance of the offer, or such other period as has been agreed, the receiving party may apply for a final costs certificate for the unpaid sum.';
- (e) a reference to 'judgment being entered' is to the completion of the detailed assessment, and references to a 'judgment' being advantageous or otherwise are to the outcome of the detailed assessment.

(5) The court will usually summarily assess the costs of detailed assessment proceedings at the conclusion of those proceedings.

(6) Unless the court otherwise orders, interest on the costs of detailed assessment proceedings will run from the date of default, interim or final costs certificate, as the case may be.

(7) For the purposes of rule 36.17, detailed assessment proceedings are to be regarded as an independent claim.

Amendments—Inserted by SI 2013/262. Under the transitional provisions, r 47.20(1)–(5),(7) do not apply to detailed assessments commenced before 1 April 2013. In respect of such assessments, rr 47.18 and 47.19, which were in force before then, apply instead. Amended by SI 2014/3299.

Section VIII
Appeals from Authorised Court Officers in Detailed Assessment Proceedings

47.21 Right to appeal

(1) Any party to detailed assessment proceedings may appeal against a decision of an authorised court officer in those proceedings.

Amendments—Inserted by SI 2013/262.

47.22 Court to hear appeal

An appeal against a decision of an authorised court officer lies to a costs judge or a District Judge of the High Court.

Amendments—Inserted by SI 2013/262; SI 2014/407.

47.23 Appeal procedure

(1) The appellant must file an appeal notice within 21 days after the date of the decision against which it is sought to appeal.

(2) On receipt of the appeal notice, the court will –

- (a) serve a copy of the notice on the parties to the detailed assessment proceedings; and
- (b) give notice of the appeal hearing to those parties.

Amendments—Inserted by SI 2013/262.

47.24 Powers of the court on appeal

On an appeal from an authorised court officer the court will –

- (a) re-hear the proceedings which gave rise to the decision appealed against; and
- (b) make any order and give any directions as it considers appropriate.

Amendments—Inserted by SI 2013/262.

Practice Direction 47 – Procedure for Detailed Assessment of Costs and Default Provisions

This Practice Direction supplements CPR Part 47

Amendments—CPR Update 60.

Time When Assessment May Be Carried Out: Rule 47.1

1.1 For the purposes of rule 47.1, proceedings are concluded when the court has finally determined the matters in issue in the claim, whether or not there is an appeal, or made an award of provisional damages under Part 41.

1.2 The court may order or the parties may agree in writing that, although the proceedings are continuing, they will nevertheless be treated as concluded.

1.3 A party who is served with a notice of commencement (see paragraph 5.2 below) may apply to a costs judge or a District Judge to determine whether the party who served it is entitled to commence detailed assessment proceedings. On hearing such an application the orders which the court may make include: an order allowing the detailed assessment proceedings to continue, or an order setting aside the notice of commencement.

1.4 A costs judge or a District Judge may make an order allowing detailed assessment proceedings to be commenced where there is no realistic prospect of the claim continuing.

Amendments—CPR Update 69.

No Stay of Detailed Assessment Where There is an Appeal: Rule 47.2

2 An application to stay the detailed assessment of costs pending an appeal may be made to the court whose order is being appealed or to the court which will hear the appeal.

Powers of an Authorised Court Officer: Rule 47.3

3.1 The court officers authorised by the Lord Chancellor to assess costs in the Costs Office and the Principal Registry of the Family Division are authorised to deal with claims where the base costs excluding VAT do not exceed £35,000 in the case of senior executive officers, or their equivalent, and £110,000 in the case of principal officers.

3.2 Where the receiving party, paying party and any other party to the detailed assessment proceedings who has served points of dispute are agreed that the assessment should not be made by an authorised court officer, the receiving party should so inform the court when requesting a hearing date. The court will then list the hearing before a costs judge or a District Judge.

3.3 In any other case a party who objects to the assessment being made by an authorised court officer must make an application to the costs judge or District Judge under Part 23 setting out the reasons for the objection.

Amendments—CPR Update 69.

Venue for Detailed Assessment Proceedings: Rule 47.4

4.1 For the purposes of rule 47.4(1) the 'appropriate office' means –

(a) the district registry or the County Court hearing centre in which the case was being dealt with when the judgment or order was made or the event occurred which gave rise to the right to assessment, or to which it has subsequently been transferred;

(b) where a tribunal, person or other body makes an order for the detailed assessment of costs, a County Court hearing centre (subject to paragraph 4.2); or

(c) in all other cases, including Court of Appeal cases, the Costs Office.

4.2 (1) This paragraph applies where the appropriate office is any of the following County Court hearing centres: Barnet, Brentford, Bromley, Central London, Clerkenwell and Shoreditch, Croydon, Edmonton, Ilford, Kingston, Lambeth, Mayors and City of London, Romford, Uxbridge, Wandsworth, Willesden and Woolwich.

(2) Where this paragraph applies –

(a) the receiving party must file any request for a detailed assessment hearing in the Costs Office and, for all purposes relating to that detailed assessment (other than the issue of default costs certificates and applications to set aside default costs certificates), the Costs Office will be treated as the appropriate office in that case;

(b) default costs certificates should be issued and applications to set aside default costs certificates should be issued and heard in the relevant County Court hearing centre; and

(c) unless an order is made under rule 47.4(2) directing that the Costs Office as part of the High Court shall be the appropriate office, an appeal from any decision made by a costs judge shall lie to the Designated Civil Judge for the London Group of County Court hearing centres or such judge as the Designated Civil Judge shall nominate. The appeal notice and any other relevant papers should be lodged at the Central London Civil Justice Centre.

4.3 (1) A direction under rule 47.4(2) or (3) specifying a particular court, registry or office as the appropriate office may be given on application or on the court's own initiative.

(2) Unless the Costs Office is the appropriate office for the purposes of rule 47.4(1) an order directing that an assessment is to take place at the Costs Office will be made only if it is appropriate to do so having regard to the size of the bill of costs, the difficulty of the issues involved, the likely length of the hearing, the cost to the parties and any other relevant matter.

Amendments—CPR Updates 69, 86, 88.

Modifications—Paras 4.1 and 4.2 are modified for certain purposes by FPR PD28A, para 2.8.

Commencement of Detailed Assessment Proceedings: Rule 47.6

5.1 Precedents A, B, C and D in the Schedule of Costs Precedents annexed to this Practice Direction are model forms of bills of costs for detailed assessment.

5.1A Precedent Q in the Schedule of Costs Precedents annexed to this Practice Direction is a model form of breakdown of the costs claimed for each phase of the proceedings.

5.2 The receiving party must serve on the paying party and all the other relevant persons the following documents –

(a) a notice of commencement in Form N252;
(b) a copy of the bill of costs;
(c) copies of the fee notes of counsel and of any expert in respect of fees claimed in the bill;
(d) written evidence as to any other disbursement which is claimed and which exceeds £500;
(e) a statement giving the name and address for service of any person upon whom the receiving party intends to serve the notice of commencement;
(f) if a costs management order has been made, a breakdown of the costs claimed for each phase of the proceedings.

5.3 The notice of commencement must be completed to show as separate items –

(a) the total amount of the costs claimed in the bill;
(b) the extra sum which will be payable by way of fixed costs and court fees if a default costs certificate is obtained.

5.4 Where the notice of commencement is to be served outside England and Wales the date to be inserted in the notice of commencement for the paying party to send points of dispute is a date (not less than 21 days from the date of service of the notice) which must be calculated by reference to Section IV of Part 6 as if the notice were a claim form and as if the date to be inserted was the date for the filing of a defence.

5.5 (1) For the purposes of rule 47.6(2) a 'relevant person' means –

(a) any person who has taken Part In the proceedings which gave rise to the assessment and who is directly liable under an order for costs made against that person;
(b) any person who has given to the receiving party notice in writing that that person has a financial interest in the outcome of the assessment and wishes to be a party accordingly;
(c) any other person whom the court orders to be treated as such.

(2) Where a party is unsure whether a person is or is not a relevant person, that party may apply to the appropriate office for directions.

(3) The court will generally not make an order that the person in respect of whom the application is made will be treated as a relevant person, unless within a specified time that person applies to the court to be joined as a party to the assessment proceedings in accordance with Part 19 (Parties and Group Litigation).

5.6 Where –

(a) the bill of costs is capable of being copied electronically; and
(b) before the detailed assessment hearing,

a paying party requests an electronic copy of the bill, the receiving party must supply the paying party with a copy in its native format (for example, in Excel or an equivalent) free of charge not more than 7 days after receipt of the request.

Amendments—CPR Update 81.

Form and Contents of Bills of Costs – General

5.7 A bill of costs may consist of such of the following sections as may be appropriate –

(1) title page;
(2) background information;
(3) items of costs claimed under the headings specified in paragraph 5.12;
(4) summary showing the total costs claimed on each page of the bill;
(5) schedules of time spent on non-routine attendances; and
(6) the certificates referred to in paragraph 5.21.

If the only dispute between the parties concerns disbursements, the bill of costs shall be limited to items (1) and (2) above, a list of the disbursements in issue and brief written submissions in respect of those disbursements.

5.8 Where it is necessary or convenient to do so, a bill of costs may be divided into two or more parts, each part containing sections (2), (3) and (4) above. Circumstances in which it will be necessary or convenient to divide a bill into parts include the following –

(1) Where the receiving party acted in person during the course of the proceedings (whether or not that party also had a legal representative at that time) the bill must be divided into different parts so as to distinguish between;
  (a) the costs claimed for work done by the legal representative; and
  (b) the costs claimed for work done by the receiving party in person.
(2) Where the receiving party had pro bono representation for part of the proceedings and an order under section 194(3) of the Legal Services Act 2007 has been made, the bill must be divided into different parts so as to distinguish between –
  (a) the sum equivalent to the costs claimed for work done by the legal representative acting free of charge; and
  (b) the costs claimed for work not done by the legal representative acting free of charge.
(3) Where the receiving party was represented by different legal representatives during the course of the proceedings, the bill must be divided into different parts so as to distinguish between the costs payable in respect of each legal representative.
(4) Where the receiving party obtained legal aid or LSC funding or is a person for whom civil legal services (within the meaning of Part 1 of the Legal Aid, Sentencing and Punishment of Offenders Act 2012) were provided under arrangements made for the purposes of that Part of that Act in respect of all or part of the proceedings the bill must be divided into separate parts so as to distinguish between –
  (a) costs claimed before legal aid or LSC funding was granted or after civil legal services were provided;
  (b) costs claimed after legal aid or LSC funding was granted or after civil legal services were provided; and
  (c) any costs claimed after legal aid or LSC funding ceased or after civil legal services ceased to be provided.
(5) Where the bill covers costs payable under an order or orders under which there are different paying parties the bill must be divided into parts so as to deal separately with the costs payable by each paying party.
(6) Where the bill covers costs payable under an order or orders, in respect of which the receiving party wishes to claim interest from different dates, the bill must be divided to enable such interest to be calculated.
(7) Where the case commenced on or after 1 April 2013, the bill covers costs for work done both before and after that date and the costs are to be assessed on the standard basis, the bill must be divided into parts so as to distinguish between costs shown as incurred for work done before 1 April 2013 and costs shown as incurred for work done on or after 1 April 2013.
(8) Where a costs management order has been made, the costs are to be assessed on the standard basis and the receiving party's budget has been agreed by the paying party or approved by the court, the bill must be divided into separate parts so as to distinguish between the costs claimed for each phase of the last approved or agreed budget, and

within each such part the bill must distinguish between the costs shown as incurred in the last agreed or approved budget and the costs shown as estimated.

(9) Where a costs management order has been made and the receiving party's budget has been agreed by the paying party or approved by the court, (a) the costs of initially completing Precedent H and (b) the other costs of the budgeting and costs management process must be set out in separate parts.

Amendments—CPR Update 83.

5.9 Where a party claims costs against another party and also claims costs against the LSC or Lord Chancellor only for work done in the same period, the costs claimed against the LSC or Lord Chancellor only can be claimed either in a separate part of the bill or in additional columns in the same part of the bill. Precedents B and C in the Schedule of Costs Precedents annexed to this Practice Direction show how bills should be drafted when costs are claimed against the LSC only.

Form and Content of Bills of Costs – Title page

5.10 The title page of the bill of costs must set out –

(1) the full title of the proceedings;
(2) the name of the party whose bill it is and a description of the document showing the right to assessment (as to which see paragraph 13.3 of this Practice Direction);
(3) if VAT is included as part of the claim for costs, the VAT number of the legal representative or other person in respect of whom VAT is claimed;
(4) details of all legal aid certificates, LSC certificates, certificates recording the determinations of the Directions of Legal Aid Casework and relevant amendment certificates in respect of which claims for costs are included in the bill.

Form and Content of Bills of Costs – Background information

5.11 The background information included in the bill of costs should set out –

(1) a brief description of the proceedings up to the date of the notice of commencement;
(2) a statement of the status of the legal representatives' employee in respect of whom costs are claimed and (if those costs are calculated on the basis of hourly rates) the hourly rates claimed for each such person.
(3) a brief explanation of any agreement or arrangement between the receiving party and his legal representatives, which affects the costs claimed in the bill.

Form and Content of Bills of Costs – Heads of costs

5.12 The bill of costs may consist of items under such of the following heads as may be appropriate –

(1) attendances at court and upon counsel up to the date of the notice of commencement;
(2) attendances on and communications with the receiving party;
(3) attendances on and communications with witnesses including any expert witness;
(4) attendances to inspect any property or place for the purposes of the proceedings;
(5) attendances on and communications with other persons, including offices of public records;
(6) communications with the court and with counsel;
(7) work done on documents:
(8) work done in connection with negotiations with a view to settlement if not already covered in the heads listed above;
(9) attendances on and communications with London and other agents and work done by them;
(10) other work done which was of or incidental to the proceedings and which is not already covered in the heads listed above.

5.13 In respect of each of the heads of costs –

(1) 'communications' means letters out e-mails out and telephone calls;

(2) communications, which are not routine communications, must be set out in chronological order;

(3) routine communications must be set out as a single item at the end of each head;

5.14 Routine communications are letters out, e-mails out and telephone calls which because of their simplicity should not be regarded as letters or e-mails of substance or telephone calls which properly amount to an attendance.

5.15 Each item claimed in the bill of costs must be consecutively numbered.

5.16 In each part of the bill of costs which claims items under head (1) in paragraph 5.12 (attendances at court and upon counsel) a note should be made of –

(1) all relevant events, including events which do not constitute chargeable items;

(2) any orders for costs which the court made (whether or not a claim is made in respect of those costs in this bill of costs).

5.17 The numbered items of costs may be set out on paper divided into columns. Precedents A, B and C in the Schedule of Costs Precedents annexed to this Practice Direction illustrate various model forms of bills of costs.

5.18 In respect of heads (2) to (10) in paragraph 5.12 above, if the number of attendances and communications other than routine communications is twenty or more, the claim for the costs of those items in that section of the bill of costs should be for the total only and should refer to a schedule in which the full record of dates and details is set out. If the bill of costs contains more than one schedule each schedule should be numbered consecutively.

5.19 The bill of costs must not contain any claims in respect of costs or court fees which relate solely to the detailed assessment proceedings other than costs claimed for preparing and checking the bill.

5.20 The summary must show the total profit costs and disbursements claimed separately from the total VAT claimed. Where the bill of costs is divided into parts the summary must also give totals for each part. If each page of the bill gives a page total the summary must also set out the page totals for each page.

5.21 The bill of costs must contain such of the certificates, the texts of which are set out in Precedent F of the Schedule of Costs Precedents annexed to this Practice Direction, as are appropriate.

5.22 The following provisions relate to work done by legal representatives –

(1) Routine letters out, routine e-mails out and routine telephone calls will in general be allowed on a unit basis of 6 minutes each, the charge being calculated by reference to the appropriate hourly rate. The unit charge for letters out and e-mails out will include perusing and considering the routine letters in or e-mails in.

(2) The court may, in its discretion, allow an actual time charge for preparation of electronic communications sent by legal representatives, which properly amount to attendances provided that the time taken has been recorded.

(3) Local travelling expenses incurred by legal representatives will not be allowed. The definition of 'local' is a matter for the discretion of the court. As a matter of guidance, 'local' will, in general, be taken to mean within a radius of 10 miles from the court dealing with the case at the relevant time. Where travelling and waiting time is claimed, this should be allowed at the rate agreed with the client unless this is more than the hourly rate on the assessment.

(4) The cost of postage, couriers, out-going telephone calls, fax and telex messages will in general not be allowed but the court may exceptionally in its discretion allow such expenses in unusual circumstances or where the cost is unusually heavy.

(5) The cost of making copies of documents will not in general be allowed but the court may exceptionally in its discretion make an allowance for copying in unusual circumstances or where the documents copied are unusually numerous in relation to the nature of the case. Where this discretion is invoked the number of copies made, their purpose and the costs claimed for them must be set out in the bill.

(6) Agency charges as between principal legal representatives and their agents will be dealt with on the principle that such charges, where appropriate, form part of the principal legal representative's charges. Where these charges relate to head (1) in paragraph 5.12 (attendances at court and on counsel) they must be included in their chronological order in that head. In other cases they must be included in head (9) (attendances on London and other agents).

Period for Commencing Detailed Assessment Proceedings: Rule 47.7

6.1 time for commencing the detailed assessment proceedings may be extended or shortened either by agreement (rule 2.11) or by the court (rule 3.1(2)(a)). Any application is to the appropriate office.

6.2 The detailed assessment proceedings are commenced by service of the documents referred to. Permission to commence assessment proceedings out of time is not required.

Sanction for Delay in Commencing Detailed Assessment Proceedings: Rule 47.8

7 An application for an order under rule 47.8 must be made in writing and be issued in the appropriate office. The application notice must be served at least 7 days before the hearing.

Points of Dispute and Consequences of Not Serving: Rule 47.9

8.1 Time for service of points of dispute may be extended or shortened either by agreement (rule 2.11) or by the court (rule 3.1(2)(a)). Any application is to the appropriate office.

8.2 Points of dispute must be short and to the point. They must follow Precedent G in the Schedule of Costs Precedents annexed to this Practice Direction, so far as practicable. They must:

(a) identify any general points or matters of principle which require decision before the individual items in the bill are addressed; and
(b) identify specific points, stating concisely the nature and grounds of dispute.

Once a point has been made it should not be repeated but the item numbers where the point arises should be inserted in the left hand box as shown in Precedent G.

8.3 The paying party must state in an open letter accompanying the points of dispute what sum, if any, that party offers to pay in settlement of the total costs claimed. The paying party may also make an offer under Part 36.

PROCEDURE WHERE COSTS ARE AGREED AND ON DISCONTINUANCE: RULE 47.10

9.1 Where the parties have agreed terms as to the issue of a costs certificate (either interim or final) they should apply under rule 40.6 (Consent judgments and orders) for an order that a certificate be issued in the terms set out in the application. Such an application may be dealt with by a court officer, who may issue the certificate.

9.2 Where in the course of proceedings the receiving party claims that the paying party has agreed to pay costs but that the paying party will neither pay those costs nor join in a consent application under paragraph 9.1, the receiving party may apply under Part 23 for a certificate either interim or final to be issued.

9.3 Nothing in rule 47.10 prevents parties who seek a judgment or order by consent from including in the draft a term that a party shall pay to another party a specified sum in respect of costs.

9.4 (1) The receiving party may discontinue the detailed assessment proceedings in accordance with Part 38 (Discontinuance).

(2) Where the receiving party discontinues the detailed assessment proceedings before a detailed assessment hearing has been requested, the paying party may apply to the appropriate office for an order about the costs of the detailed assessment proceedings.

(3) Where a detailed assessment hearing has been requested the receiving party may not discontinue unless the court gives permission.

(4) A bill of costs may be withdrawn by consent whether or not a detailed assessment hearing has been requested.

Default Costs Certificate: Rule 47.11

10.1

(1) A request for the issue of a default costs certificate must be made in Form N254 and must be signed by the receiving party or his legal representative.

(2) The request must be accompanied by a copy of the document giving the right to detailed assessment and must be filed at the appropriate office. (Paragraph 13.3 below identifies the appropriate documents).

10.2 A default costs certificate will be in Form N255.

10.3 Attention is drawn to Rules 40.3 (Drawing up and Filing of Judgments and Orders) and 40.4 (Service of Judgments and Orders) which apply to the preparation and service of a default costs certificate. The receiving party will be treated as having permission to draw up a default costs certificate by virtue of this Practice Direction.

10.4 The issue of a default costs certificate does not prohibit, govern or affect any detailed assessment of the same costs which are payable out of the Community Legal Service Fund of by the Lord Chancellor under Part 1 of the Legal Aid, Sentencing and Punishment of Offenders Act 2012.

10.5 An application for an order staying enforcement of a default costs certificate may be made either –

(a) to a costs judge or District Judge of the court office which issued the certificate; or

(b) to the court (if different) which has general jurisdiction to enforce the certificate.

10.6 Proceedings for enforcement of default costs certificates may not be issued in the Costs Office.

Default Costs Certificate: Fixed Costs on the Issue of a Default Costs Certificate

10.7 Unless paragraph 1.2 of Practice Direction 45 (Fixed Costs in Small Claims) applies or unless the court orders otherwise, the fixed costs to be included in a default costs certificate are £80 plus a sum equal to any appropriate court fee payable on the issue of the certificate.

10.8 The fixed costs included in a certificate must not exceed the maximum sum specified for costs and court fee in the notice of commencement.

Setting Aside Default Costs Certificate: Rule 47.12

11.1 A court officer may set aside a default costs certificate at the request of the receiving party under rule 47.12. A costs judge or a District Judge will make any other order or give any directions under this rule.

11.2

(1) An application for an order under rule 47.12(2) to set aside or vary a default costs certificate must be supported by evidence.

(2) In deciding whether to set aside or vary a certificate under rule 47.12(2) the matters to which the court must have regard include whether the party seeking the order made the application promptly.

(3) As a general rule a default costs certificate will be set aside under rule 47.12 only if the applicant shows a good reason for the court to do so and if the applicant files with the application a copy of the bill, a copy of the default costs certificate and a draft of the points of dispute the applicant proposes to serve if the application is granted.

11.3 Attention is drawn to rule 3.1(3) (which enables the court when making an order to make it subject to conditions) and to rule 44.2(8) (which enables the court to order a party whom it has

PART III

ordered to pay costs to pay an amount on account before the costs are assessed). A costs judge or a District Judge may exercise the power of the court to make an order under rule 44.2(8) although he did not make the order about costs which led to the issue of the default costs certificate.

Amendments—CPR Update 69.

Optional Reply: Rule 47.13

12.1 A reply served by the receiving party under Rule 47.13 must be limited to points of principle and concessions only. It must not contain general denials, specific denials or standard form responses.

12.2 Whenever practicable, the reply must be set out in the form of Precedent G.

Detailed Assessment Hearing: Rule 47.14

13.1 The time for requesting a detailed assessment hearing is within 3 months of the expiry of the period for commencing detailed assessment proceedings.

13.2 The request for a detailed assessment hearing must be in Form N258. The request must be accompanied by –

(a) a copy of the notice of commencement of detailed assessment proceedings;

(b) a copy of the bill of costs,

(c) the document giving the right to detailed assessment (see paragraph 13.3 below);

(d) a copy of the points of dispute, annotated as necessary in order to show which items have been agreed and their value and to show which items remain in dispute and their value;

(e) as many copies of the points of dispute so annotated as there are persons who have served points of dispute;

(f) a copy of any replies served;

(g) copies of all orders made by the court relating to the costs which are to be assessed;

(h) copies of the fee notes and other written evidence as served on the paying party in accordance with paragraph 5.2 above;

(i) where there is a dispute as to the receiving party's liability to pay costs to the legal representatives who acted for the receiving party, any agreement, letter or other written information provided by the legal representative to the client explaining how the legal representative's charges are to be calculated;

(j) a statement signed by the receiving party or the legal representative giving the name, address for service, reference and telephone number and fax number, if any, of –

  (i) the receiving party;

  (ii) the paying party;

  (iii) any other person who has served points of dispute or who has given notice to the receiving party under paragraph 5.5(1)(b) above;

and giving an estimate of the length of time the detailed assessment hearing will take;

(k) where the application for a detailed assessment hearing is made by a party other than the receiving party, such of the documents set out in this paragraph as are in the possession of that party;

(l) where the court is to assess the costs of an assisted person or LSC funded client or person to whom civil legal aid services (within the meaning of Part 1 of the Legal Aid, Sentencing and Punishment of Offenders Act 2012) are provided under arrangement made for the purposes of that Part of that Act –

  (i) the legal aid certificate, LSC certificate, the certificate recording the determination of the Direction of Legal Aid Casework and relevant amendment certificates, any authorities and any certificates of discharge or revocation or withdrawal;

  (ii) a certificate, in Precedent F(3) of the Schedule of Costs Precedents;

  (iii) if that person has a financial interest in the detailed assessment hearing and wishes to attend, the postal address of that person to which the court will send notice of any hearing;

(iv) if the rates payable out of the LSC fund or by the Lord Chancellor under Part 1 of the Legal Aid, Sentencing and Punishment of Offenders Act 2012 are prescribed rates, a schedule to the bill of costs setting out all the items in the bill which are claimed against other parties calculated at the legal aid prescribed rates with or without any claim for enhancement: (further information as to this schedule is set out in paragraph 17 of this Practice Direction);

(v) a copy of any default costs certificate in respect of costs claimed in the bill of costs;

(m) if a costs management order has been made, a breakdown of the costs claimed for each phase of the proceedings.

13.3 'The document giving the right to detailed assessment' means such one or more of the following documents as are appropriate to the detailed assessment proceedings –

(a) a copy of the judgment or order of the court or tribunal giving the right to detailed assessment;

(b) a copy of the notice sent by the court under Practice Direction 3B paragraph 1, being notification that a claim has been struck out under rule 3.7 or rule 3.7A1 for non-payment of a fee;

(c) a copy of the notice of acceptance where an offer to settle is accepted under Part 36 (Offers to settle);

(d) a copy of the notice of discontinuance in a case which is discontinued under Part 38 (Discontinuance);

(e) a copy of the award made on an arbitration under any Act or pursuant to an agreement, where no court has made an order for the enforcement of the award;

(f) a copy of the order, award or determination of a statutorily constituted tribunal or body.

13.4 On receipt of the request for a detailed assessment hearing the court will fix a date for the hearing, or, if the costs officer so decides, will give directions or fix a date for a preliminary appointment.

13.5 Unless the court otherwise orders, if the only dispute between the parties concerns disbursements, the hearing shall take place in the absence of the parties on the basis of the documents and the court will issue its decision in writing.

13.6 The court will give at least 14 days' notice of the time and place of the detailed assessment hearing to every person named in the statement referred to in paragraph 13.2(j) above.

13.7 If either party wishes to make an application in the detailed assessment proceedings the provisions of Part 23 apply.

13.8

(1) This paragraph deals with the procedure to be adopted where a date has been given by the court for a detailed assessment hearing and –

(a) the detailed assessment proceedings are settled; or

(b) a party to the detailed assessment proceedings wishes to apply to vary the date which the court has fixed; or

(c) the parties to the detailed assessment proceedings agree about changes they wish to make to any direction given for the management of the detailed assessment proceedings.

(2) If detailed assessment proceedings are settled, the receiving party must give notice of that fact to the court immediately, preferably by fax.

(3) A party who wishes to apply to vary a direction must do so in accordance with Part 23.

(4) If the parties agree about changes they wish to make to any direction given for the management of the detailed assessment proceedings –

(a) they must apply to the court for an order by consent; and

(b) they must file a draft of the directions sought and an agreed statement of the reasons why the variation is sought; and

(c) the court may make an order in the agreed terms or in other terms without a hearing, but it may direct that a hearing is to be listed.

PART III

Note—There is no para 13.9.

13.10

(1) If a party wishes to vary that party's bill of costs, points of dispute or a reply, an amended or supplementary document must be filed with the court and copies of it must be served on all other relevant parties.

(2) Permission is not required to vary a bill of costs, points of dispute or a reply but the court may disallow the variation or permit it only upon conditions, including conditions as to the payment of any costs caused or wasted by the variation.

13.11 Unless the court directs otherwise the receiving party must file with the court the papers in support of the bill not less than 7 days before the date for the detailed assessment hearing and not more than 14 days before that date.

13.12 The papers to be filed in support of the bill and the order in which they are to be arranged are as follows –

(i) instructions and briefs to counsel arranged in chronological order together with all advices, opinions and drafts received and response to such instructions;

(ii) reports and opinions of medical and other experts;

(iii) any other relevant papers;

(iv) a full set of any relevant statements of case

(v) correspondence, file notes and attendance notes;

13.13 The court may direct the receiving party to produce any document which in the opinion of the court is necessary to enable it to reach its decision. These documents will in the first instance be produced to the court, but the court may ask the receiving party to elect whether to disclose the particular document to the paying party in order to rely on the contents of the document, or whether to decline disclosure and instead rely on other evidence.

13.14 Once the detailed assessment hearing has ended it is the responsibility of the receiving party to remove the papers filed in support of the bill.

Amendments—CPR Updates 81, 88.

Provisional Assessment: Rule 47.15

14.1 The amount of costs referred to in rule 47.15(1) is £75,000.

14.2 The following provisions of Part 47 and this Practice Direction will apply to cases falling within rule 47.15 –

(1) rules 47.1, 47.2, 47.4 to 47.13, 47.14 (except Paragraphs (6) and (7)), 47.16, 47.17, 47.20 and 47.21; and

(2) paragraphs 1, 2, 4 to 12, 13 (with the exception of paragraphs 13.4 to 13.7, 13.9, 13.11 and 13.14), 15, and 16, of this Practice Direction.

14.3 In cases falling within rule 47.15, when the receiving party files a request for a detailed assessment hearing, that party must file –

(a) the request in Form N258;

(b) the documents set out at paragraphs 8.3 and 13.2 of this Practice Direction;

(c) an additional copy of the bill, including a statement of the costs claimed in respect of the detailed assessment drawn on the assumption that there will not be an oral hearing following the provisional assessment;

(d) the offers made (those marked 'without prejudice save as to costs' or made under Part 36 must be contained in a sealed envelope, marked 'Part 36 or similar offers', but not indicating which party or parties have made them);

(e) completed Precedent G (points of dispute and any reply).

14.4

(1) On receipt of the request for detailed assessment and the supporting papers, the court will use its best endeavours to undertake a provisional assessment within 6 weeks. No party will be permitted to attend the provisional assessment.

(2) Once the provisional assessment has been carried out the court will return Precedent G (the points of dispute and any reply) with the court's decisions noted upon it. Within 14 days of receipt of Precedent G the parties must agree the total sum due to the receiving party on the basis of the court's decisions. If the parties are unable to agree the arithmetic, they must refer the dispute back to the court for a decision on the basis of written submissions.

14.5 When considering whether to depart from the order indicated by rule 47.15(10) the court will take into account the conduct of the parties and any offers made.

14.6 If a party wishes to be heard only as to the order made in respect of the costs of the initial provisional assessment, the court will invite each side to make written submissions and the matter will be finally determined without a hearing. The court will decide what if any order for costs to make in respect of this procedure.

Power to Issue An Interim Certificate: Rule 47.16

15 A party wishing to apply for an interim certificate may do so by making an application in accordance with Part 23.

Final Costs Certificate: Rule 47.17

16.1 At the detailed assessment hearing the court will indicate any disallowance or reduction in the sums claimed in the bill of costs by making an appropriate note on the bill.

16.2 The receiving party must, in order to complete the bill after the detailed assessment hearing make clear the correct figures agreed or allowed in respect of each item and must re-calculate the summary of the bill appropriately.

16.3 The completed bill of costs must be filed with the court no later than 14 days after the detailed assessment hearing.

16.4 At the same time as filing the completed bill of costs, the party whose bill it is must also produce receipted fee notes and receipted accounts in respect of all disbursements except those covered by a certificate in Precedent F(5) in the Schedule of Costs Precedents annexed to this Practice Direction.

16.5 No final costs certificate will be issued until all relevant court fees payable on the assessment of costs have been paid.

16.6 If the receiving party fails to file a completed bill in accordance with rule 47.17 the paying party may make an application under Part 23 seeking an appropriate order under rule 3.1.

16.7 A final costs certificate will show –

(a) the amount of any costs which have been agreed between the parties or which have been allowed on detailed assessment;

(b) where applicable the amount agreed or allowed in respect of VAT on such costs.

This provision is subject to any contrary statutory provision relating to costs payable out of the Community Legal Service Fund or by the Lord Chancellor under Part 1 of the Legal Aid, Sentencing and Punishment of Offenders Act 2012.

16.8 A final costs certificate will include disbursements in respect of the fees of counsel only if receipted fee notes or accounts in respect of those disbursements have been produced to the court and only to the extent indicated by those receipts.

16.9 Where the certificate relates to costs payable between parties a separate certificate will be issued for each party entitled to costs.

16.10 Form N257 is a model form of interim costs certificate and Form N256 is a model form of final costs certificate.

16.11 An application for an order staying enforcement of an interim costs certificate or final costs certificate may be made either –

(a) to a costs judge or District Judge of the court office which issued the certificate; or

PART III

(b) to the court (if different) which has general jurisdiction to enforce the certificate.

16.12 An interim or final costs certificate may be enforced as if it were a judgment for the payment of an amount of money. However, proceedings for the enforcement of interim costs certificates or final costs certificates may not be issued in the Costs Office.

Amendments—CPR Update 69.

Detailed Assessment Procedure Where Costs are Payable Out of The Community Legal Service Fund or by the Lord Chancellor under Part 1 of the Legal Aid, Sentencing and Punishment of Offenders Act 2012: Rule 47.18

17.1 The time for requesting a detailed assessment under rule 47.18 is within 3 months after the date when the right to detailed assessment arose.

17.2

(1) The request for a detailed assessment of costs must be in Form N258A. The request must be accompanied by –
  (a) a copy of the bill of costs;
  (b) the document giving the right to detailed assessment (see paragraph 13.3 above);
  (c) copies of all orders made by the court relating to the costs which are to be assessed;
  (d) copies of any fee notes of counsel and any expert in respect of fees claimed in the bill;
  (e) written evidence as to any other disbursement which is claimed and which exceeds £500;
  (f) the legal aid certificates, LSC certificates, certificates recording the determinations of the Direction of Legal Aid Casework, any relevant amendment certificates, any authorities and any certificates of discharge, revocation or withdrawal and;
  (g) a statement signed by the legal representative giving the representative's name, address for service, reference, telephone number, fax number, e-mail address where available and, if the assisted person has a financial interest in the detailed assessment and wishes to attend, giving the postal address of that person, to which the court will send notice of any hearing.

(2) The relevant papers in support of the bill as described in paragraph 13.12 must only be lodged if requested by the costs officer.

17.3 Where the court has provisionally assessed a bill of costs it will send to the legal representative a notice, in Form N253 annexed to this practice direction, of the amount of costs which the court proposes to allow together with the bill itself. The legal representative should, if the provisional assessment is to be accepted, then complete the bill.

17.4 If the solicitor whose bill it is, or any other party wishes to make an application in the detailed assessment proceedings, the provisions of Part 23 applies.

17.5 It is the responsibility of the legal representative to complete the bill by entering in the bill the correct figures allowed in respect of each item, recalculating the summary of the bill appropriately and completing the Community Legal Service assessment certificate (Form EX80A).

Costs Payable by the Legal Services Commission or Lord Chancellor at Prescribed Rates

Note—The Legal Aid Agency replaced the Legal Services Commission on 1 April 2013.

17.6 Where the costs of an assisted person or LSC funded client or person to whom civil legal services (within the meaning of Part 1 of the Legal Aid, Sentencing and Punishment of Offenders Act 2012) are provided under arrangements made for the purposes of that Part of that Act are payable by another person but costs can be claimed against the LSC or Lord Chancellor at prescribed rates (with or without enhancement), the solicitor of the assisted person or LSC funded client or person to whom civil legal services are provided must file a legal aid/ LSC schedule in accordance with paragraph 13.2(l) above. The schedule should follow as closely as possible Precedent E of the Schedule of Costs Precedents annexed to this Practice Direction.

17.7 The schedule must set out by reference to the item numbers in the bill of costs, all the costs claimed as payable by another person, but the arithmetic in the schedule should claim those items at prescribed rates only (with or without any claim for enhancement).

17.8 Where there has been a change in the prescribed rates during the period covered by the bill of costs, the schedule (as opposed to the bill) should be divided into separate parts, so as to deal separately with each change of rate. The schedule must also be divided so as to correspond with any divisions in the bill of costs.

17.9 If the bill of costs contains additional columns setting out costs claimed against the LSC or Lord Chancellor only, the schedule may be set out in a separate document or, alternatively, may be included in the additional columns of the bill.

17.10 The detailed assessment of the legal aid/ LSC schedule will take place immediately after the detailed assessment of the bill of costs but on occasions, the court may decide to conduct the detailed assessment of the legal aid/ LSC schedule separately from any detailed assessment of the bill of costs. This will occur, for example, where a default costs certificate is obtained as between the parties but that certificate is not set aside at the time of the detailed assessment of the legal aid costs.

17.11 Where costs have been assessed at prescribed rates it is the responsibility of the legal representative to enter the correct figures allowed in respect of each item and to recalculate the summary of the legal aid/LSC schedule.

Detailed Assessment Procedure Where Costs are Payable Out of a Fund or by the Lord Chancellor under Part 1 of the Legal Aid, Sentencing and Punishment of Offenders Act 2012: Rule 47.19

18.1 Rule 47.19 enables the court to direct under rule 47.19(3) that the receiving party must serve a copy of the request for assessment and copies of the documents which accompany it, on any person who has a financial interest in the outcome of the assessment.

18.2 A person has a financial interest in the outcome of the assessment if the assessment will or may affect the amount of money or property to which that person is or may become entitled out of the fund. Where an interest in the fund is itself held by a trustee for the benefit of some other person, that trustee will be treated as the person having such a financial interest unless it is not appropriate to do so. 'Trustee' includes a personal representative, receiver or any other person acting in a fiduciary capacity.

18.3 The request for a detailed assessment of costs out of the fund should be in Form N258B, be accompanied by the documents set out at paragraph 17.2(1) (a) to (e) and the following –

(a) a statement signed by the receiving party giving his name, address for service, reference, telephone number,

(b) a statement of the postal address of any person who has a financial interest in the outcome of the assessment; and

(c) if a person having a financial interest is a child or protected party, a statement to that effect.

18.4 The court will decide, having regard to the amount of the bill, the size of the fund and the number of persons who have a financial interest, which of those persons should be served and may give directions about service and about the hearing. The court may dispense with service on all or some of those persons.

18.5 Where the court makes an order dispensing with service on all such persons it may proceed at once to make a provisional assessment, or, if it decides that a hearing is necessary, give appropriate directions. Before deciding whether a hearing is necessary, the court may require the receiving party to provide further information relating to the bill.

18.6

(1) The court will send the provisionally assessed bill to the receiving party with a notice in

Form N253. If the receiving party is legally represented the legal representative should, if the provisional assessment is to be accepted, then complete the bill.

(2) The court will fix a date for a detailed assessment hearing, if the receiving party informs the court within 14 days after receiving the notice in Form N253, that the receiving party wants the court to hold such a hearing.

18.7 The court will give at least 14 days' notice of the time and place of the hearing to the receiving party and to any person who has a financial interest and who has been served with a copy of the request for assessment.

18.8 If any party or any person who has a financial interest wishes to make an application in the detailed assessment proceedings, the provisions of Part 23 (General Rules about Applications for Court Orders) apply.

18.9 If the receiving party is legally represented the legal representative must complete the bill by inserting the correct figures in respect of each item and must recalculate the summary of the bill.

Amendments—CPR Update 66.

Costs of Detailed Assessment Proceedings – Rule 47.20: Offers to Settle Under Part 36 or Otherwise

19 Where an offer to settle is made, whether under Part 36 or otherwise, it should specify whether or not it is intended to be inclusive of the cost of preparation of the bill, interest and VAT. Unless the offer states otherwise it will be treated as being inclusive of these.

Appeals from Authorised Court Officers in Detailed Assessment Proceedings: Rules 47.22 To 47.25

20.1 This Section relates only to appeals from authorised court officers in detailed assessment proceedings. All other appeals arising out of detailed assessment proceedings (and arising out of summary assessments) are dealt with in accordance with Part 52 and Practice Directions 52A to 52E. The destination of appeals is dealt with in accordance with the Access to Justice Act 1999 (Destination of Appeals) Order 2016.

20.2 In respect of appeals from authorised court officers, there is no requirement to obtain permission, or to seek written reasons.

20.3 The appellant must file a notice which should be in Form N161 (an appellant's notice).

20.4 The appeal will be heard by a costs judge or a District Judge of the High Court, and is a re-hearing.

20.5 The appellant's notice should, if possible, be accompanied by a suitable record of the judgment appealed against. Where reasons given for the decision have been officially recorded by the court an approved transcript of that record should accompany the notice. Where there is no official record the following documents will be acceptable –

(a) the officer's comments written on the bill;
(b) advocates' notes of the reasons agreed by the respondent if possible and approved by the authorised court officer.

When the appellant was unrepresented before the authorised court officer, it is the duty of any advocate for the respondent to make a note of the reasons promptly available, free of charge to the appellant where there is no official record or if the court so directs. Where the appellant was represented before the authorised court officer, it is the duty of the appellant's own former advocate to make a note available. The appellant should submit the note of the reasons to the costs judge or District Judge hearing the appeal.

20.6 Where the appellant is not able to obtain a suitable record of the authorised court officer's decision within the time in which the appellant's notice must be filed, the appellant's notice must still be completed to the best of the appellant's ability. It may however be amended subsequently with the permission of the costs judge or district.

Amendments—CPR Updates 69, 86.

****

PART 50
APPLICATION OF THE SCHEDULES

50 (1) The Schedules to these Rules set out, with modifications, certain provisions previously contained in the Rules of the Supreme Court 1965 and the County Court Rules 1981.

(2) These Rules apply in relation to the proceedings to which the Schedules apply subject to the provisions in the Schedules and the relevant practice directions.

(3) A provision previously contained in the Rules of the Supreme Court 1965 –

- (a) is headed 'RSC';
- (b) is numbered with the Order and rule numbers it bore as part of the RSC; and
- (c) unless otherwise stated in the Schedules or the relevant practice direction, applies only to proceedings in the High Court.

(4) A provision previously contained in the County Court Rules 1981 –

- (a) is headed 'CCR';
- (b) is numbered with the Order and rule numbers it bore as part of the CCR; and
- (c) unless otherwise stated in the Schedules or the relevant practice direction, applies only to proceedings in the County Court.

(5) A reference in a Schedule to a rule by number alone is a reference to the rule so numbered in the Order in which the reference occurs.

(6) A reference in a Schedule to a rule by number prefixed by 'CPR' is a reference to the rule with that number in these Rules.

(7) In the Schedules, unless otherwise stated, 'the Act' means –

- (a) in a provision headed 'RSC', the Senior Courts Act 1981; and
- (b) in a provision headed 'CCR', the County Courts Act 1984.

Amendments—CRA 2005, Sch 11, para 1(2); SI 2014/407.

****

PART 52
APPEALS

CONTENTS OF THIS PART

Section I

Rule		Page
	Scope and interpretation	
52.1	Scope and interpretation	2192
52.2	Parties to comply with Practice Directions 52A to 52E	2194
	Section II	
	Permission to appeal – General	
52.3	Permission to appeal	2194
52.4	Determination of applications for permission to appeal to the County Court and High Court	2197
52.5	Determination of applications for permission to appeal to the Court of Appeal	2197
52.6	Permission to appeal test – first appeals	2198
52.7	Permission to appeal test – second appeals	2198

PART III

Section III
Permission to appeal – judicial review appeals, planning statutory review appeals and appeals from the Employment Appeal Tribunal

52.8 Judicial review appeals from the High Court 2198
52.9 Judicial review appeals from the Upper Tribunal 2199
52.10 Planning statutory review appeals 2199
52.11 Appeals from the Employment Appeal Tribunal 2199

Section IV
Additional rules

52.12 Appellant's notice 2200
52.13 Respondent's notice 2201
52.14 Transcripts at public expense 2202
52.15 Variation of time 2202
52.16 Stay(GL) 2202
52.17 Amendment of appeal notice 2203
52.18 Striking out(GL) appeal notices and setting aside(GL) or imposing conditions on permission to appeal 2203
52.19 Orders to limit the recoverable costs of an appeal 2203
52.20 Appeal court's powers 2204
52.21 Hearing of appeals 2205
52.22 Non-disclosure of Part 36 offers and payments 2206

Section V
Special provisions relating to the Court of Appeal

52.23 Assignment of appeals to the Court of Appeal 2206
52.24 Who may exercise the powers of the Court of Appeal 2207

Section VII
Reopening final appeals

52.30 Reopening of final appeals 2208

Practice Direction 52A –
Appeals: General Provisions 2208

Practice Direction 52B –
Appeals in the County Court and High Court 2214

Practice Direction 52C –
Appeals to the Court of Appeal 2220

Practice Direction 52D –
Statutory Appeals and Appeals Subject to Special Provision 2233

Practice Direction 52E –
Appeals by way of Case Stated 2251

Amendments—Part substituted by SI 2016/788.

Section I

Scope and interpretation

Note—As from October 2016, appeals in private law children's cases, from circuit judges or recorders, are to be made to the High Court and to be heard by judges of the Family Division and not to the Court of Appeal.

Note—From 1 October 2012, CPR PD52 is replaced by PDs 52A–52E, which shall apply to all appeals where the notice of appeal was filed or permission to appeal was given after that date. The appeal court may direct that the new provisions apply to any appeal, irrespective of the date on which the notice was filed or permission to appeal was given (CPR PD52A, paras 8.1 and 8.2).

52.1 Scope and interpretation

(1) The rules in this Part apply to appeals to –

(a) the civil division of the Court of Appeal;

(b) the High Court; and
(c) the County Court.

(2) This Part does not apply to an appeal in detailed assessment proceedings against a decision of an authorised court officer.

(3) In this Part –

(a) 'appeal' includes an appeal by way of case stated;
(b) 'appeal court' means the court to which an appeal is made;
(c) 'lower court' means the court, tribunal or other person or body from whose decision an appeal is brought;
(d) 'appellant' means a person who brings or seeks to bring an appeal;
(e) 'respondent' means –
    (i) a person other than the appellant who was a party to the proceedings in the lower court and who is affected by the appeal; and
    (ii) a person who is permitted by the appeal court to be a party to the appeal; and
(f) 'appeal notice' means an appellant's or respondent's notice.

(4) This Part is subject to any rule, enactment or practice direction which sets out special provisions with regard to any particular category of appeal.

Amendments—Inserted by SI 2000/221. Last substituted by SI 2016/788.

Scope of Pt 52—This Part applies to all appeals to the Court of Appeal and to appeals to the High Court which are not defined as family proceedings under MFPA 1984, s 40. It applies to non-family appeals to the High Court that were previously covered by RSC Ords 55 and 58. This Part also provides, in addition to appeals to the Court of Appeal, the power of the High Court or the county court on appeal to transfer a case for determination by the Court of Appeal where it is thought that that appeal raises an important point of practice, or there is some other compelling reason (r 52.14).

For the general jurisdiction of the Court of Appeal, see SCA 1981, ss 15–18. For restriction of appeals to the Court of Appeal, see SCA 1981, ss 16, 18.

Compliance with the rules—See notes to CPR 1998, r 30.1.

Appeal—An appeal is an application to set aside or vary a decision of the court below on the ground that it was wrongly made. Baroness Hale has criticised the Court of Appeal's apparent readiness to interfere with the first instance judge's exercise of his discretion: see *Re J (Child Returned Abroad: Convention Rights)* [2005] 2 FLR 802, HL at [12]. An appeal is against the order and not the judgment (*Vaughan v Vaughan* [2008] 1 FLR 1108, CA). Appeals against ex parte orders are discouraged (see **Ex parte orders** under SCA 1981, s 18), as are appeals against interim orders (see *G v G (Interim Custody: Appeal)* (1983) 4 FLR 327, CA; *Edwards v Edwards* [1986] 1 FLR 205, CA). To challenge an order that has been made by consent where the basis of the order has been frustrated by one party, the aggrieved party may appeal or should preferably return to the court which made the order (*Middleton v Middleton* [1998] 2 FLR 821, CA). Where the court has made an order in favour of a party subject to conditions and that party fails to comply, the (most usual) appropriate course is to apply to the first instance judge to set aside the order and not to appeal: see *Walley v Walley* [2005] EWCA Civ 910.

Appeals against case management orders—Such appeals should be dealt with in such a way as to avoid the adjournment of any substantive hearing already listed in the court below. It would be advisable for the Court of Appeal office to be alerted by any party who becomes aware of the possibility of delay and, in particular, the children's guardian has an independent duty to keep the court informed: *Re L (Case Management: Child's Evidence)* [2014] 2 FLR 972, CA.

Finding of fact hearings—Where the lower court refuses to make findings of fact sought by a party, the Court of Appeal has no jurisdiction to entertain an appeal against that decision where the findings of fact sought were not 'pregnant with legal consequences': *Re M (Children)* [2013] EWCA Civ 1170.

Where findings of fact are challenged—The first instance court has no jurisdiction to re-open the findings of fact once an order is sealed and the court has no jurisdiction to permit expert evidence on the point since FPR 2010, r 25.4(3) provides that the court may only give permission to adduce expert evidence if 'the court is of the opinion that the expert evidence is necessary to assist the court to resolve proceedings': *Re G (A Child)* [2014] EWCA Civ 1365.

Interim orders—Where events changed or developed after the making of an interim order, the appropriate course was to seek a variation of the order from the judge, rather than seek to appeal against the order: *Re H (A Child)* [2011] EWCA Civ 762.

Mediation—The Court of Appeal has observed that no family case, even at appellate level, is not potentially open to successful mediation; even if mediation was not attempted or failed at first instance. It was vital there be judicial supervision of the process of mediation: see *Al-Khatib v Masry* [2005] 1 FLR 381, CA. The Court of Appeal has observed that the Court's ADR scheme has a relatively low take up from family appeals but an encouragingly high success rate and 'as a matter of policy it is important that this court should signify that if the parties arrive at a compromise, a clear compromise, within the mediation process, then that compromise will be robustly upheld by this court': *Rothwell v Rothwell* [2009] 2 FLR 96, CA.

Trial judge—The Court of Appeal has emphasised that the appeal court must give great weight to those aspects of the case exclusively within the domain of the trial judge: in particular the judicial assessment of witness credibility and findings of fact (*Re M (Children) (Sexual Abuse)* [2008] EWCA Civ 3).

Reasons—Where a party alleges a judge has failed to deal with an important part of the evidence or has failed to give sufficient or adequate reasons for his decision, the aggrieved party must apply to the trial judge for further reasons: the Court of Appeal will not 'fill that hole' (*Re T (Contact: Alienation: Permission to Appeal)* [2003] 1 FLR 531, CA; *Re M (Children)* [2007] EWCA Civ 177). It is not sufficient for a party to draw attention to an alleged deficiency in a judgment by way of an application for permission to appeal. It is incumbent on the party to point out the deficiency and to request clarification or a supplemental judgment on the issue (*Re A (Child Abuse)* [2008] 1 FLR 1423, CA. The Court of Appeal is losing patience with the failure of practitioners to follow this procedure before seeking permission to appeal: it has recently observed that it is about time the family bar woke up to the fact that the procedure set out in *English v Emery, Reimbold & Strick* [2002] 1 WLR 2409, CA applies to family cases and must be followed (*Re M (Fact-finding Hearing: Burden of Proof)* [2009] 1 FLR 1177, CA)). The Court of Appeal has reiterated the proper course to be taken. Where an alleged lack of reasons in the judgment had not been drawn to the attention of the trial judge or the judge had subsequently failed to elaborate his reasons, the normal procedure was remittal to the judge at first instance with a list of specific questions: *Re A and L (Children)* [2012] 1 FLR 134, CA.

Public funding—The Supreme Court has decided that there must be compelling reasons for withdrawing public funding from a party who had been publicly funded in the court below, had been successful in that court and wished to resist an appeal to a higher court by the unsuccessful party: *R (E) v Governing Body of JFS and the Admissions Appeal Panel of JFS and others* [2009] 1 WLR 2353, SC.

Appeals against decree nisi—CPR PD52D, para 6.1 makes special provision for such appeals.

Contempt appeals—CPR PD52D, para 9.1 makes special provision for such appeals.

52.2 Parties to comply with Practice Directions 52A to 52E

All parties to an appeal must comply with Practice Directions 52A to 52E.

Amendments—Inserted by SI 2000/221. Last substituted by SI 2016/788.

'the relevant practice direction'—See CPR PD52A–PD52E.

Section II

Permission to appeal – General

52.3 Permission to appeal

(1) An appellant or respondent requires permission to appeal –

- (a) where the appeal is from a decision of a judge in the County Court or the High Court, or to the Court of Appeal from a decision of a judge in the family court, except where the appeal is against –
  - (i) a committal order;
  - (ii) a refusal to grant habeas corpus; or
  - (iii) a secure accommodation order made under section 25 of the Children Act 1989; or
- (b) as provided by Practice Directions 52A to 52E.

(Other enactments may provide that permission is required for particular appeals.)

(2) An application for permission to appeal may be made –

- (a) to the lower court at the hearing at which the decision to be appealed was made; or
- (b) to the appeal court in an appeal notice.

(Rule 52.12 sets out the time limits for filing an appellant's notice at the appeal court. Rule 52.13 sets out the time limits for filing a respondent's notice at the appeal court. Any application for permission to appeal to the appeal court must be made in the appeal notice (see rules 52.12(1) and 52.13(3)).)

(3) Where the lower court refuses an application for permission to appeal –

- (a) a further application for permission may be made to the appeal court; and
- (b) the order refusing permission must specify –
  - (i) the court to which any further application for permission should be made; and
  - (ii) the level of judge who should hear the application.

Amendments—Inserted by SI 2000/221. Last substituted by SI 2016/788.

Scope—Save for the limited exceptions contained within r 52.3(1)(a), namely in respect of a committal order, habeas corpus and secure accommodation, permission to appeal is required in all cases (here committal order includes a suspended order – see *Wilkinson v S* [2003] 1 WLR 1254, CA and *Re G (Contempt: Committal)*

[2003] 2 FLR 58, CA). The application should usually be made to the judge whose decision is to be appealed, at the time the decision is made (see CPR PD52A, para 4.1(a)) and, if refused, thereafter to the Court of Appeal. An application directly to the Court of Appeal, while permissible within the terms of the rule (see CPR PD52A, para 4.1(b)), is unusual. If there has been a 'paper' refusal by the Court of Appeal (see CPR PD52C, para 15.1), there may be a renewal of the application before a Lord Justice (see CPR PD52C, para 15.2). It is necessary to show a 'real prospect' of success or 'some other compelling reason' (r 52.3(6)). The Court of Appeal has given guidance on the limited grounds on which the court may grant an application for permission to appeal and to allow an appeal (particularly for the benefit of litigants in person) (*Re W (Permission to Appeal)* [2008] 1 FLR 406, CA). There is no appeal from the decision at the oral hearing. Note, however, the new power of a single judge when refusing permission to appeal on paper: if he considers the application to be wholly without merit he may direct that the application cannot be reconsidered at an oral hearing. It would appear that in appeals from the Family Court made pursuant to CPR 1998, Pt 52 this power is only exercisable by a High Court Judge. By contrast, where an appeal is made pursuant to FPR 2010, Pt 30, the power is exercisable by a High Court or a Designated Family Judge: FPR 2010, r 30.3(5A). Where the appeal to the Court of Appeal is a second appeal (i e an appeal from a decision of the High Court on appeal from the Family Court) there is an additional hurdle to overcome (see r 52.13), namely the requirement to establish an important point of principle or practice or some other compelling reason to grant permission. On a second appeal, the application for permission to appeal must be made to the Court of Appeal (see CPR PD52A, para 4.7). Where the appeal is based in whole or in part on lack of reasons given in the judgment, the first instance judge must be invited to give further reasons for his decision: see *Re T (Contact: Alienation: Permission to Appeal)* [2003] 1 FLR 531, CA. It is not sufficient for a party to draw attention to an alleged deficiency in a judgment by way of an application for permission to appeal and see further **Reasons** under r 52.1.

Application to lower court for permission to appeal—See the commentary to FPR 2010, r 30.3.

Power to change judgment after handing down—In care proceedings a judge is entitled to change his mind – and thus his findings of fact – after delivering judgment, written or oral, at a fact finding hearing even in the absence of an intervening change of circumstances. The Supreme Court held that a court should not be required to make welfare decisions concerning a child on a false factual basis. It declined to offer even a provisional view on whether the power was available after the order made at the conclusion of the fact finding hearing had been perfected (i e sealed by the court): it was said the arguments either way were finely balanced. The power must be exercised 'judicially and not capriciously'. 'The best safeguard against having to do so is a fully and properly reasoned judgment in the first place': *Re L-B (Reversal of Judgment)* [2013] 2 FLR 859, SC.

Abduction appeals—If the obligation to complete proceedings under the Hague Convention and Brussels IIA within 6 weeks was to be met, it was imperative that the Bar ensured draft judgments were returned to the judge within a brief period, the consequential order was then drafted promptly and the approved order sealed immediately thereafter (*Re M (Abduction: Appeals)* [2008] 1 FLR 699, CA).

Appeals against placement orders—The Court of Appeal has set out the mandatory requirements that must be followed in appeals against placement orders: see *Re C (Adoption Proceedings: Change of Circumstances)* [2013] 2 FLR 1393, CA, namely:

(i) The appellant's notice must be filed as soon as possible.
(ii) Those advising the appellant must give careful thought to including in the appellant's notice any appropriate application for a stay or other interim relief.
(iii) If a transcript of the judgment being appealed against is not then available:
    (a) the appellant's notice must be accompanied by whatever note of the judgment (even if unapproved) is available; and
    (b) the transcript must be ordered immediately.
(iv) When an application for a transcript is received, the court from which the appeal is being brought must deal with the application immediately.
(v) Respondents who are parties to any application consequential upon the placement order (eg an application for an adoption order) must immediately inform both the appellant and the Court of Appeal of:
    (a) the fact of the making of the application; and
    (b) the date(s) of any hearing of the application.

Case management appeals—Where an appeal is against a case management decision, the court dealing with the application may take into account whether:

(a) the issue is of sufficient significance to justify the costs of the appeal;
(b) the procedural consequences of an appeal (eg loss of a trial date) outweigh the significance of the case management decision; or
(c) it would be more convenient to determine the issue at or after the trial (CPR PD52A, para 4.6).

See also the President's observations on five basic principles relevant to the approach of the Court of Appeal to appeals against case management decisions in *Re TG (Care Proceedings: Case Management: Expert Evidence)* [2013] 1 FLR 1250, CA, at [24]–[38].

Robust case management—There are limits to robust case management and the judicial voicing of pre-determined views is a step too far: *Re P (A Child)* [2014] EWCA Civ 888.

Committal appeals—CPR 1998, r 52.3(1)(a)(i) could not be construed as restricting the right to appeal as of right to a contemnor and not to an applicant who sought to have a sentence increased and, accordingly, the applicant did not require permission to appeal (*Wood v Collins* [2006] EWCA Civ 743). Any appeal against either a finding of breach or the sentence for a breach must be expedited into court and as a matter of safeguard, should be immediately referred to one of the supervising Lord Justices, so that appropriate directions could be given for an expedited hearing and for whatever else might be needed, as every day that the appeal was delayed might be a day in which the appellant was unjustifiably detained in custody (*G v G* [2007] 2 FLR 1127, CA).

Addendum expert report—When a single Lord Justice wholly exceptionally orders an addendum to an expert report, it is not for the parties to alter the terms of the instruction by agreement between them and without recourse to the court: *Re R (Children)* [2014] EWCA Civ 1110.

Limited permission—It is possible for there to be a grant of permission to appeal in relation to a limited issue (r 52.3(7)). The court should normally refuse permission on the other grounds (see CPR PD52C, para 18) and those issues may then not be raised at the appeal hearing without the court's permission (CPR PD52C, para 18(3)). Where a party has been present at the hearing to determine permission to appeal, he cannot apply to limit the scope of the appeal (see r 52.9).

Observations by Court—Where a single Lord Justice makes observations on Form 269C1, when granting permission to appeal or directing an oral hearing on notice with the appeal to follow immediately if permission was granted, they were to be obeyed. Primary responsibility for a failure to comply will usually lie with the party who brings the appeal/application: *Re M-W (Care Proceedings: Expert Evidence)* [2010] 2 FLR 46, CA.

Consent orders—In relation to a consent order, consideration must be given to whether the matter should be returned to the judge who heard the matter for a rehearing rather than to appeal. This seems to be the preferred course in relation to orders made as a result of fraud, mistake or material non-disclosure, or where there has been a new event to invalidate the basis of the order (see *Re C (Financial Provision: Leave to Appeal)* [1993] 2 FLR 799, FD and *Benson v Benson (Deceased)* [1996] 1 FLR 692, FD). This route is the more appropriate where there are issues of fact to be determined or a substitute order is sought. Bad advice cannot found the basis for an appeal against the making of a consent order (*Tibbs v Dick* [1998] 2 FLR 1118, CA).

Litigants in person—The Court of Appeal has held that the failure to grant a vulnerable litigant in person an adjournment to enable him to obtain alternate legal representation, especially where the delay involved in doing so would be very short, was a breach of his Art 6 rights to a fair trial: *Re L (Application Hearing: Legal Representation)* [2013] 2 FLR 1444, CA. The mere fact that FPR 2010, r 1.1(2)(c) urges the court to establish an equal footing between parties can never be justification of itself for a litigant in person seeking an adjournment or to claim that a failure to grant the same is a breach of Art 6 rights. In each case, a balance has to be struck taking account of the welfare of the child and the fair trial needs of all of the parties. If the court refuses an adjournment, it has the difficult task of ensuring the hearing is conducted in a fashion that seeks to meet the need for all parties to be on an equal footing, albeit that one or more of them is a litigant in person: *Re GB (Children)* [2013] EWCA Civ 164. See also the notes to CPR 1998, r 30.3.

Permission to appeal out of time—When considering an application for permission to appeal out of time, the appellate court may have regard to the underlying merits of the proposed appeal, especially where the grounds of appeal are either very strong or very weak: *Re H (Children) (Application to Extend Time: Merits of Proposed Appeal)* [2016] 1 FLR 952, CA.

Refusal of permission—A refusal of permission to appeal at an oral hearing cannot be renewed: *McHugh v McHugh* [2014] EWCA Civ 1671.

Conditions—The Court of Appeal may impose conditions on the grant of permission if compelling reasons are found to exist (unlike r 52.9, r 52.3(7) does not specify the need for compelling reasons, but the court has held that the latter should be read as if those words were included in the rule). Where a party had attempted to evade enforcement and was in gross breach of court orders, it was appropriate that conditions were attached to the grant of permission to appeal including the transfer of a lump sum into this jurisdiction in a secure environment and a requirement to comply with existing court orders: *Radmacher v Granatino* [2009] 1 FLR 1566, CA.

General observations—Recent decisions of the Court of Appeal highlight the following:

(a) the essential test is: does the judgment sufficiently explain what the judge has found and what he has concluded, as well as the process of reasoning by which he arrived at his findings and then his conclusions? (*Re B (Appeal: Lack of Reasons)* [2003] 2 FLR 1035, CA; *Re A and L (Fact-Finding Hearing: Extempore Judgment)* [2012] 1 FLR 1243, CA);

(b) albeit the course taken by the judge had potential adverse consequences for the child in terms of risk of harm and the delay that could result, he was aware of those consequences and had been entitled to take the approach he did in advancement of the child's welfare: *Re H (Care Proceedings: Foster Care Placement for Mother and Baby)* [2013] 1 FLR 1445, CA;

(c) whatever the allegations, however serious, the balance of probabilities remained the standard of proof. Findings should be made without regard to the gravity of the consequences of the same: *Re D (Children)* [2012] EWCA Civ 1584;

(d) the Court of Appeal is always reluctant to interfere with a judge's assessment of the witnesses who has given evidence before him : *Re A (Removal from Jurisdiction)* [2014] 1 FLR 1, CA;

(e) a trial judge has a wide discretion to accept and deal with the evidence and, fairly, to terminate or permit continuation of a case but there are limits to what is permissible: *Re C (Family Proceedings: Case Management)* [2013] 1 FLR 1089, CA, cf *Re J (Children)* [2012] EWCA Civ 1457;

(f) a trial judge is not entitled to depart from findings made in an extempore judgment delivered at the conclusion of a fact-finding hearing absent further evidence or a significant change in circumstances: *Re L-B (Reversal of Judgment)* [2013] 1 FLR 209, CA;

(g) a trial judge was entitled, however, after reserving judgment, to change his mind about a provisional view he had expressed during the trial about the value of some of the evidence: this was a wholly legitimate aspect of the trial process and could not be characterised as procedurally unfair. The serious procedural irregularity required for an appeal to be allowed is a high hurdle: *Re R (Care Proceedings: Appeal)* [2013] 1 FLR 467, CA;

(h) it was only appropriate to consider inviting a trial judge to provide further reasons for his decision where it might have a bearing on whether to allow the appeal. It was not appropriate to invite a judge to give reasons for his decision on the basis that it would benefit the children: *Re F (Supervised Contact: Disputed Evidence)* [2013] 1 FLR 665, CA;

(i) following a fact-finding hearing before one judge, another judge at the welfare hearing was not entitled to make further findings of fact without giving notice of the possibility of the same to the parties: *Re C (A Child)* [2012] EWCA Civ 535; and

(j) a judge in a fact-finding hearing who is not satisfied that specific allegations in the schedule of findings are not made out is not entitled to make alternative findings that are not set out in the schedule: *Re J-L (Findings of Fact: Schedule of Allegations)* [2013] 1 FLR 1240, CA.

52.4 Determination of applications for permission to appeal to the County Court and High Court

(1) Where an application for permission to appeal is made to an appeal court other than the Court of Appeal, the appeal court will determine the application on paper without an oral hearing, except as provided for under paragraph (2).

(2) Subject to paragraph (3) and except where a rule or practice direction provides otherwise, where the appeal court, without a hearing, refuses permission to appeal, the person seeking permission may request the decision to be reconsidered at an oral hearing.

(3) Where in the appeal court a judge of the High Court, a Designated Civil Judge or a Specialist Circuit Judge refuses permission to appeal without an oral hearing and considers that the application is totally without merit, the judge may make an order that the person seeking permission may not request the decision to be reconsidered at an oral hearing.

(4) For the purposes of paragraph (3), 'Specialist Circuit Judge' means any Circuit Judge in the County Court nominated to hear cases in the Mercantile, Chancery or Technology and Construction Court lists.

(5) Rule 3.3(5) (party able to apply to set aside, etc, a decision made of court's own initiative) does not apply to an order made under paragraph (3) that the person seeking permission may not request the decision to be reconsidered at an oral hearing.

(6) A request under paragraph (2) must be filed within 7 days after service of the notice that permission has been refused.

Amendments—Inserted by SI 2000/221. Last substituted by SI 2016/788.

Oral hearing (r 52.4(2)—This provision permits the applicant for permission to request a reconsideration of a paper refusal of permission by the appeal court. If the appeal court considers the application to be totally without merit, it may order that the applicant may not request an oral hearing (note this provision applies only to appeals to the County Court and to the High Court; for appeals to the Family Court, see FPR 2010, r 30.3(5A),(5B).

Respondent's attendance at permission hearing—The respondent is permitted to attend, but CPR PD52C, para 20 in effect discourages such attendance. In *Livock v Livock* [2012] 1 FLR 776, FD, Coleridge J expressed concern at the lack of notice to a respondent in these circumstances and at his order having been sent back to him for 'review' without it being set aside.

52.5 Determination of applications for permission to appeal to the Court of Appeal

(1) Where an application for permission to appeal is made to the Court of Appeal, the Court of Appeal will determine the application on paper without an oral hearing, except as provided for under paragraph (2).

(2) The judge considering the application on paper may direct that the application be determined at an oral hearing, and must so direct if the judge is of the opinion that the application cannot be fairly determined on paper without an oral hearing.

(3) An oral hearing directed under paragraph (2) must be listed –

(a) no later than 14 days from the date of the direction under that paragraph; and
(b) before the judge who made that direction,

unless the court directs otherwise.

(4) The Court of Appeal may, in any direction under paragraph (2) –

PART III

(a) identify any issue or issues on which the party seeking permission should specifically focus its submissions at the oral hearing in order to assist the court to determine the application; and

(b) direct the respondent to serve and file written submissions and to attend the oral hearing.

Amendments—Inserted by SI 2000/221. Last substituted by SI 2016/788.

Oral hearing—If permission to appeal is refused by the Court of Appeal on paper, the applicant for permission does not now have the right to request that the application be reconsidered at an oral hearing. An oral hearing will only be directed if the judge considers the application cannot fairly be determined on the papers alone.

52.6 Permission to appeal test – first appeals

(1) Except where rule 52.7 applies, permission to appeal may be given only where –

(a) the court considers that the appeal would have a real prospect of success; or

(b) there is some other compelling reason for the appeal to be heard.

(2) An order giving permission under this rule or under rule 52.7 may –

(a) limit the issues to be heard; and

(b) be made subject to conditions.

(Rule 3.1(3) also provides that the court may make an order subject to conditions.)

(Rule 25.15 provides for the court to order security for costs of an appeal.)

Amendments—Inserted by SI 2000/221. Last substituted by SI 2016/788.

52.7 Permission to appeal test – second appeals

(1) Permission is required from the Court of Appeal for any appeal to that court from a decision of the County Court, the family court or the High Court which was itself made on appeal, or a decision of the Upper Tribunal which was made on appeal from a decision of the First-tier Tribunal on a point of law where the Upper Tribunal has refused permission to appeal to the Court of Appeal.

(2) The Court of Appeal will not give permission unless it considers that –

(a) the appeal would –

(i) have a real prospect of success; and

(ii) raise an important point of principle or practice; or

(b) there is some other compelling reason for the Court of Appeal to hear it.

Amendments—Inserted by SI 2000/221. Last substituted by SI 2016/788.

Scope—Where it is proposed to appeal the decision of the County Court, the Family Court or the High Court, which itself was a determination of an appeal, there is an additional hurdle to overcome in obtaining permission to appeal. The proposed appellant must show there is some compelling reason or important point of principle. It is possible that, rather than determining the appeal itself, the lower court, having considered there is some important point of principle or some other compelling reason, may transfer the appeal to be heard by the Court of Appeal (see r 52.23 and CPR PD52A, para 4.7). Permission to appeal may be sought in relation to the substantive order but there can be no appeal in relation to the refusal (of the lower court) to grant permission to appeal (see AJA 1999, s 54; *Bulled v Khayat and Another* [2002] EWCA Civ 804 and *Slot v Isaac* [2002] EWCA Civ 481).

Peremptory orders—The unlawful removal of a child from his usual place of residence calls for a peremptory order to be sought for his return, rather than to seek to challenge the dismissal of an appeal for an interim child arrangements order for living arrangements by way of a second appeal to the Court of Appeal: *Re R (Children: Peremptory Return)* [2011] 2 FLR 863, CA.

Section III

Permission to appeal – judicial review appeals, planning statutory review appeals and appeals from the Employment Appeal Tribunal

52.8 Judicial review appeals from the High Court

(1) Where permission to apply for judicial review has been refused at a hearing in the High Court, an application for permission to appeal may be made to the Court of Appeal.

(2) Where permission to apply for judicial review of a decision of the Upper Tribunal has been refused by the High Court on the papers or where permission to apply for judicial review has been

refused on the papers and recorded as being totally without merit in accordance with rule 23.12, an application for permission to appeal may be made to the Court of Appeal.

(3) An application under paragraph (1) must be made within 7 days of the decision of the High Court to refuse to give permission to apply for judicial review.

(4) An application under paragraph (2) must be made within 7 days of service of the order of the High Court refusing permission to apply for judicial review.

(5) On an application under paragraph (1) or (2), the Court of Appeal may, instead of giving permission to appeal, give permission to apply for judicial review.

(6) Where the Court of Appeal gives permission to apply for judicial review in accordance with paragraph (5), the case will proceed in the High Court unless the Court of Appeal orders otherwise.

Amendments—Inserted by SI 2000/221. Last substituted by SI 2016/788.

52.9 Judicial review appeals from the Upper Tribunal

(1) Where permission to bring judicial review proceedings has been refused by the Upper Tribunal at a hearing and permission to appeal has been refused by the Upper Tribunal, an application for permission to appeal may be made to the Court of Appeal.

(2) Where an application for permission to bring judicial review proceedings has been determined by the Upper Tribunal on the papers and recorded as being totally without merit and permission to appeal has been refused by the Upper Tribunal, an application for permission to appeal may be made to the Court of Appeal.

(3) An application under this rule to the Court of Appeal must be made within 7 days of –

(a) the decision of the Upper Tribunal refusing permission to appeal to the Court of Appeal, where that decision was made at a hearing; or

(b) service of the order of the Upper Tribunal refusing permission to appeal to the Court of Appeal, where the decision to refuse permission was made on the papers.

Amendments—Inserted by SI 2000/221. Last substituted by SI 2016/788.

52.10 Planning statutory review appeals

(1) Where permission to apply for a planning statutory review has been refused at a hearing in the High Court, an application for permission to appeal may be made to the Court of Appeal.

(See Part 8 and Practice Direction 8C.)

(2) Where permission to apply for a planning statutory review has been refused by the High Court on the papers and recorded as totally without merit in accordance with rule 23.12, an application for permission to appeal may be made to the Court of Appeal.

(3) An application under paragraph (1) must be made within 7 days of the decision of the High Court to refuse to give permission to apply for a planning statutory review.

(4) An application under paragraph (2) must be made within 7 days of service of the order of the High Court refusing permission to apply for a planning statutory review.

(5) On an application under paragraph (1) or (2) the Court of Appeal may, instead of giving permission to appeal, give permission to apply for a planning statutory review.

(6) Where the Court of Appeal gives permission to apply for a planning statutory review in accordance with paragraph (5), the case will proceed in the High Court unless the Court of Appeal orders otherwise.

Amendments—Inserted by SI 2000/221. Last substituted by SI 2016/788.

52.11 Appeals from the Employment Appeal Tribunal

(1) Where on an appeal to the Employment Appeal Tribunal either –

(a) the appellant or special advocate has been given notice under rule 3(7) of the Employment Appeal Tribunal Rules 1993 ('the 1993 Rules') and an order has been made under rule 3(7ZA) of those Rules; or

(b) a direction has been made under rule 3(10) of the 1993 Rules that no further action shall be taken on the notice of appeal,

the appellant may apply to the Court of Appeal for permission to appeal.

(2) An application under paragraph (1) must be made within 7 days of the date of –

(a) service of the notice under rule 3(7) of the 1993 Rules; or
(b) the direction made under rule 3(10) of those Rules,

as the case may be.

(3) The Court of Appeal may, instead of giving permission to appeal, direct that the notice under rule 3(7) of the 1993 Rules or (as the case may be) the direction under rule 3(10) of those Rules shall be of no effect so that the appeal shall proceed in the Employment Appeal Tribunal as if the notice or direction had not been given or made, but such a direction shall not be given unless the test for the grant of permission to appeal under rule 52.6(2) is met.

Amendments—Inserted by SI 2000/221. Substituted by SI 2016/788.

Section IV
Additional rules

52.12 Appellant's notice

(1) Where the appellant seeks permission from the appeal court, it must be requested in the appellant's notice.

(2) The appellant must file the appellant's notice at the appeal court within –

(a) such period as may be directed by the lower court (which may be longer or shorter than the period referred to in sub-paragraph (b)); or
(b) where the court makes no such direction, and subject to the specific provision about time limits in rules 52.8 to 52.11 and Practice Direction 52D, 21 days after the date of the decision of the lower court which the appellant wishes to appeal.

(3) Subject to paragraph (4) and unless the appeal court orders otherwise, an appellant's notice must be served on each respondent –

(a) as soon as practicable; and
(b) in any event not later than 7 days,

after it is filed.

(4) Where an appellant seeks permission to appeal against a decision to refuse to grant an interim injunction under section 41 of the Policing and Crime Act 2009, the appellant is not required to serve the appellant's notice on the respondent.

Amendments—Inserted by SI 2000/221. Last substituted by SI 2016/788.

Scope—In children's cases, the Court of Appeal has observed that the period ought generally to be less than 21 days (*Re M-H (Children)* [2006] EWCA Civ 499). Applications for permission to appeal in children's cases, especially those with an international element, have to be brought on for hearing swiftly. First instance judges should, as a matter of routine, establish whether a party wishes to appeal and, whether granting or refusing permission to appeal, give directions to ensure that the inception of the appeal is achieved within the shortest possible period. The period allowed of 21 days is 'over generous' (*Klentzeris v Klentzeris* [2007] 2 FLR 996, CA; *Re EC (Child Abduction: Stayed Proceedings)* [2007] 1 FLR 57, CA). The filing of the notice of appeal should not be delayed until the applicant has received a copy of the approved judgment under appeal (*Re A (Children: Split Hearing)* [2007] 1 FLR 905, CA). The respondent need do nothing until notification of the grant of permission to appeal (CPR PD52C, para 19).

Skeleton arguments—The Notice and a copy of the skeleton argument must be filed at the same time and served as soon as practicable thereafter and in any event not later than 7 days thereafter (CPR PD52C, paras 3, 21, 27 and 31). Practitioners should pay attention to the compulsory directions on the contents of skeleton arguments and the requirements in respect of the citation of authorities (see CPR PD52A, paras 5.1–5.3, CPR PD52C, paras 29 and 31 and the Practice Direction of 24 March 2012: *Citation of Authorities*). The appellant and the respondent(s) may file and serve 'replacement' skeleton arguments to include cross-references to the appeal bundle but must do so no later than 14 days and 7 days, respectively, before the date of the appeal hearing (CPR PD52C, paras 1 and 21). Supplementary skeleton arguments may only be filed where strictly necessary and only with the permission of the Court of Appeal. They must be lodged and served as soon as practicable and be accompanied by a request for permission setting out the reasons why it is necessary and why they could not reasonably have been lodged earlier. Only in exceptional cases will the court allow the use of a supplementary skeleton argument if it is lodged later than 7 days before the hearing (CPR PD52C, para 32(1)–(3)).

Where the appeal is out of time, it seems that a composite application for permission to appeal must be made in order to comply with the general requirement of permission and because the time for appealing has expired. In those circumstances, the Notice of Appeal should seek permission to appeal and an extension of time for filing the Notice of Appeal (see CPR PD52C, para 4). The appellant must file the prescribed documents and an appeal bundle with his Notice of Appeal (see CPR PD52C, para 3).

Procedure following the grant of permission—CPR PD52C, para 3 sets out the documents that the appellant is required to file with the Notice of Appeal. Once permission to appeal has been granted, or the permission application is to be listed with, if granted, the appeal to follow, the appellant must serve a proposed index bundle on each respondent 7 days after the listing window notification and, no later than 42 days before the hearing of the appeal, must file the appropriate number of appeal bundles at the court and serve a copy of the appeal bundle on each of the respondents (CPR PD52C, para 21). The Court of Appeal shall send the parties notification of the period of time in which the appeal is likely to be heard (the 'listing window notification'), together with a questionnaire (CPR PD52C, paras 1, 21 and 23). This requires the appellant to give a time estimate for the hearing of the appeal.

Policing and Crime Act 2009—Section 34 of the Act empowers the court to grant injunctions to prevent gang-related violence. Where the court adjourns a without notice application for an injunction it may grant an interim injunction if it thinks it necessary (s 41). Where the court adjourns a without notice application for an injunction but refuses to grant an interim injunction, the applicant may appeal that decision without giving notice of the appeal to the respondent.

The appeal bundle—CPR PD52C, para 27 sets out the detailed provisions for the preparation of the bundle of documents.

Electronic filing—A party may file a notice by email to the email account specified in the 'Guidelines for filing Appellants' Notices, Respondents' Notices and Application Notices by e-mail' (see *www.civilappeals.gov.uk*), but only where permitted to do so by the guidelines. A party may file notices electronically using the online forms service on the Court of Appeal, Civil Division website where permitted to do so by the 'Guidelines for filing by e-mail'.

52.13 Respondent's notice

(1) A respondent may file and serve a respondent's notice.

(2) A respondent who –

- (a) is seeking permission to appeal from the appeal court; or
- (b) wishes to ask the appeal court to uphold the decision of the lower court for reasons different from or additional to those given by the lower court,

must file a respondent's notice.

(3) Where the respondent seeks permission from the appeal court it must be requested in the respondent's notice.

(4) A respondent's notice must be filed within –

- (a) such period as may be directed by the lower court; or
- (b) where the court makes no such direction, 14 days after the date in paragraph (5).

(5) The date referred to in paragraph (4) is –

- (a) the date the respondent is served with the appellant's notice where –
  - (i) permission to appeal was given by the lower court; or
  - (ii) permission to appeal is not required;
- (b) the date the respondent is served with notification that the appeal court has given the appellant permission to appeal; or
- (c) the date the respondent is served with notification that the application for permission to appeal and the appeal itself are to be heard together.

(6) Unless the appeal court orders otherwise, a respondent's notice must be served on the appellant and any other respondent –

- (a) as soon as practicable; and
- (b) in any event not later than 7 days,

after it is filed.

(7) This rule does not apply where rule 52.12(4) applies.

Amendments—Inserted by SI 2000/221. Last substituted by SI 2016/788.

PART III

Scope—Unless the respondent wishes to cross-appeal or justify the order for different reasons, there is no need to provide a Notice. If the respondent wishes to file a Notice, he must do so within 14 days unless otherwise directed (r 52.13(4)) and serve it as soon as practicable and in any event within 7 days thereafter (r 52.13(6)). An appeal by a respondent will also require permission (CPR PD52C, para 8). A respondent must file and serve a skeleton argument. It must be lodged with the Respondent's Notice and served on each party (CPR PD52C, para 9). If there is no Respondent's Notice, the skeleton argument must be lodged and served 42 days after the date of the listing window notification (CPR PD52C, para 21).

Rule 52.12(4)—Policing and Crime Act 2009, s 34 empowers the court to grant injunctions to prevent gang-related violence. Where the court adjourns a without notice application for an injunction, it may grant an interim injunction if it thinks it necessary (s 41). Where the court adjourns a without notice application for an injunction but refuses to grant an interim injunction, the applicant may appeal that decision without giving notice of the appeal to the respondent.

Respondent's Notices—Respondent's Notices that simply assert their support for the conclusion arrived at by the judge for the reasons he has given are entirely superfluous: *Re S (Care and Placement Orders)* [2013] 1 FLR 354, CA.

52.14 Transcripts at public expense

(1) Subject to paragraph (2), the lower court or the appeal court may direct, on the application of a party to the proceedings, that an official transcript of the judgment of the lower court, or of any part of the evidence or the proceedings in the lower court, be obtained at public expense for the purposes of an appeal.

(2) Before making a direction under paragraph (1), the court must be satisfied that –

(a) the applicant qualifies for fee remission or is otherwise in such poor financial circumstances that the cost of obtaining a transcript would be an excessive burden; and

(b) it is necessary in the interests of justice for such a transcript to be obtained.

Amendments—Inserted by SI 2000/221. Last substituted by SI 2016/788.

Transcripts of the hearing or of the evidence—When considering ordering a transcript of the whole, or part, of the evidence or hearing in the court below, practitioners should bear in mind the following:

(a) The preparation of and authorisation of the payment for a transcript might take time; therefore practitioners should consider whether a transcript is an essential prerequisite before filing of a notice of appeal or before an application for permission to appeal is sought.

(b) Practitioners should consider filing a notice of appeal even though a transcript might not be available.

(c) The judge of the lower court could be contacted if necessary to speed up the process.

(d) Pursuit of a transcript, which might be peripheral, should not affect the consideration of an application for permission to appeal: *Re GB (Children)* [2013] EWCA Civ 164.

The President has observed that too many cases in the Court of Appeal are unnecessarily and quite wrongly delayed by unacceptable delays in obtaining transcripts. The practice and performance in court offices must change: *Re C (Transcripts: Permission to Appeal)* [2014] 2 FLR 147, CA.

52.15 Variation of time

(1) An application to vary the time limit for filing an appeal notice must be made to the appeal court.

(2) The parties may not agree to extend any date or time set by –

(a) these Rules;

(b) Practice Directions 52A to 52E; or

(c) an order of the appeal court or the lower court.

(Rule 3.1(2)(a) provides that the court may extend or shorten the time for compliance with any rule, practice direction or court order (even if an application for extension is made after the time for compliance has expired).)

(Rule 3.1(2)(b) provides that the court may adjourn or bring forward a hearing.)

Amendments—Inserted by SI 2000/221. Last substituted by SI 2016/788.

Appeals—For the ingenuity of the Court of Appeal to rectify a want of jurisdiction to hear an appeal which had been concluded by the court and reported: see *Farley v Secretary of State for Work & Pensions (No 2)* [2005] 2 FLR 1075, CA.

52.16 Stay[(GL)]

Unless –

(a) the appeal court or the lower court orders otherwise; or

(b) the appeal is from the Immigration and Asylum Chamber of the Upper Tribunal, an appeal shall not operate as a stay of any order or decision of the lower court.

Amendments—Inserted by SI 2000/221. Last substituted by SI 2016/788.

Scope—An appeal (meaning an application for permission or following the grant of permission) does not automatically operate to stop the order that is the subject of the appeal taking effect. An application must be made for a stay of the order. A stay should normally be sought at the time of the application for permission to appeal, if not immediately following the decision to be appealed. An application for a stay must be determined by a judge and is usually heard by a single Lord Justice (see r 52.16).

Imposition of conditions to grant of stay—The Supreme Court has criticised the imposition by the Court of Appeal of conditions to the grant of a stay pending determination of an application for permission to appeal by the Supreme Court. Lord Kerr said: 'as a general rule, conditions such as were imposed by the Court of Appeal in this case should not be made where a party seeks permission to appeal, not least because these might be seen as an unwarranted disincentive to the pursuit of what proved in this case to be a fully merited application': *Re B (A Child)* [2010] 1 FLR 551, SC. The Court of Appeal had approved the decision of the court below to transfer residence from the maternal grandmother to the father: in granting a stay of the transfer of residence, the court imposed a provision for extensive overnight staying contact to the father.

Urgent cases—In urgent cases where the judge has refused a stay of the order pending the application for permission to appeal, the prospective appellant may telephone the Court of Appeal to apply for a stay (0207 947 6000 during office hours; out-of-hours contact is made to the security office at the RCJ on 0207 947 6260, who will refer the matter to the duty deputy master; CPR PD52C, para 26). A deputy master will refer the matter to a Lord Justice, who may grant the stay or list the matter urgently for consideration of the application for a stay (*Re S (Child Proceedings: Urgent Appeals)* [2007] 2 FLR 1044, CA). Amended by SI 2003/3361; CRA 2005, Sch 11, para 1(2); SI 2009/2092.

PART III

52.17 Amendment of appeal notice

An appeal notice may not be amended without the permission of the appeal court.

Amendments—Inserted by SI 2003/2113. Last substituted by SI 2016/788.

52.18 Striking out(GL) appeal notices and setting aside(GL) or imposing conditions on permission to appeal

(1) The appeal court may –

- (a) strike out the whole or part of an appeal notice;
- (b) set aside permission to appeal in whole or in part;
- (c) impose or vary conditions upon which an appeal may be brought.

(2) The court will only exercise its powers under paragraph (1) where there is a compelling reason for doing so.

(3) Where a party was present at the hearing at which permission was given, that party may not subsequently apply for an order that the court exercise its powers under subparagraphs (1)(b) or (1)(c).

Amendments—Inserted by SI 2007/2204. Last substituted by SI 2016/788.

Scope—See notes to r 52.3 (above).

Compelling reasons—These are required to impose conditions under this rule and under r 52.3(7). This rule applies where permission to appeal has already been granted on some previous occasion: *Radmacher v Granatino* [2009] 1 FLR 1566, CA.

52.19 Orders to limit the recoverable costs of an appeal

(1) In any proceedings in which costs recovery is normally limited or excluded at first instance, an appeal court may make an order that the recoverable costs of an appeal will be limited to the extent which the court specifies.

(2) In making such an order the court will have regard to –

- (a) the means of both parties;
- (b) all the circumstances of the case; and
- (c) the need to facilitate access to justice.

(3) If the appeal raises an issue of principle or practice upon which substantial sums may turn, it may not be appropriate to make an order under paragraph (1).

(4) An application for such an order must be made as soon as practicable and will be determined without a hearing unless the court orders otherwise.

Amendments—Inserted by SI 2007/2204. Substituted by SI 2016/788.

52.20 Appeal court's powers

(1) In relation to an appeal the appeal court has all the powers of the lower court.

(Rule 52.1(4) provides that this Part is subject to any enactment that sets out special provisions with regard to any particular category of appeal. Where such an enactment gives a statutory power to a tribunal, person or other body, it may be the case that the appeal court may not exercise that power on an appeal.)

(2) The appeal court has power to –

(a) affirm, set aside or vary any order or judgment made or given by the lower court;
(b) refer any claim or issue for determination by the lower court;
(c) order a new trial or hearing;
(d) make orders for the payment of interest;
(e) make a costs order.

(3) In an appeal from a claim tried with a jury the Court of Appeal may, instead of ordering a new trial –

(a) make an order for damages; or
(b) vary an award of damages made by the jury.

(4) The appeal court may exercise its powers in relation to the whole or part of an order of the lower court.

(Part 3 contains general rules about the court's case management powers.)

(5) If the appeal court –

(a) refuses an application for permission to appeal;
(b) strikes out an appellant's notice; or
(c) dismisses an appeal,

and it considers that the application, the appellant's notice or the appeal is totally without merit, the provisions of paragraph (6) must be complied with.

(6) Where paragraph (5) applies –

(a) the court's order must record the fact that it considers the application, the appellant's notice or the appeal to be totally without merit; and
(b) the court must at the same time consider whether it is appropriate to make a civil restraint order.

Amendments—Inserted by SI 2007/2204. Substituted by SI 2016/788.

Scope—Like the High Court, the Court of Appeal is a Superior Court of Record (SCA 1981, s 15) and has all the authority and jurisdiction of the court from which the appeal is brought. Having decided that the decision of the lower court was wrong, the Court of Appeal may set aside the order and order a new trial, substitute an order and make such order as the case may require. This includes a power to make interim orders pending a rehearing (*Re R (Minors) (Custody)* [1986] 1 FLR 6, CA). SCA 1981, s 17 provides that any application for a new trial in the High Court must be made to the Court of Appeal.

'all the powers of the lower court' (r 52.20(1))—See the notes to FPR 2010, r 30.11.

Re-make decision or remit—Once an appeal is allowed, the decision whether to re-make the decision or to remit to the lower court is fact-specific, but the following are relevant considerations:

(i) an appeal court can fill in gaps in the reasoning of the lower court;
(ii) if the error of the lower court is sufficiently discrete, the appeal court can rectify the error;
(iii) if there is a lack of reasoning in the judgment, save for seeking further reasons from the judge in the court below, it is unlikely the same can be rectified on appeal;
(iv) if the key question on which the decision rests has not been answered, it is likely the appeal court will remit the matter for re-hearing: *Re B (A Child)* [2015] 1 FLR 884, CA.

Welfare evaluation on appeal—The appeal court may substitute its own evaluation of the child's welfare for that of the lower court in the event that the appeal is allowed: *Re B (A Child)* [2015] 1 FLR 884, CA.

Fresh evidence—See the notes to FPR 2010, r 30.11.

Reopening an appeal—See the notes to FPR 2010, r 30.11.

Hopeless appeals—Where the Court of Appeal considers the application or appeal is totally without merit, it must record that fact in the court order and consider making a civil restraint order: see CPR 1998, Pt 3.

Civil restraint order—For the power to make a civil restraint order and the procedure to be followed, see CPR 1998, r 3.11 and PD3C.

Wasted costs order—For the appropriate court to determine an appeal against a wasted costs order, see *Gray v Going Places Leisure Travel Ltd* [2005] EWCA Civ 189.

52.21 Hearing of appeals

(1) Every appeal will be limited to a review of the decision of the lower court unless –

- (a) a practice direction makes different provision for a particular category of appeal; or
- (b) the court considers that in the circumstances of an individual appeal it would be in the interests of justice to hold a re-hearing.

(2) Unless it orders otherwise, the appeal court will not receive –

- (a) oral evidence; or
- (b) evidence which was not before the lower court.

(3) The appeal court will allow an appeal where the decision of the lower court was –

- (a) wrong; or
- (b) unjust because of a serious procedural or other irregularity in the proceedings in the lower court.

(4) The appeal court may draw any inference of fact which it considers justified on the evidence.

(5) At the hearing of the appeal, a party may not rely on a matter not contained in that party's appeal notice unless the court gives permission.

Amendments—Inserted by SI 2014/407. Substituted by SI 2016/788.

Listing—Following the grant of permission to appeal, the Court of Appeal will send a questionnaire to the appellant requesting a time estimate and giving the period of time in which the appeal is likely to be heard (CPR PD52C, para 23). An application to expedite or delay a hearing must be made to a Master or single Lord Justice. Applications relating to children must be listed swiftly (*Re A (Children: Split Hearing)* [2007] 1 FLR 905, CA). For the listing of urgent appeals, see CPR PD52C, para 26.

Counsel's convenience—It is a well-recognised principle in the Court of Appeal that a permissions application will not be adjourned for the convenience of counsel. Thus, in *Bracknell Forest Borough Council v N* [2006] *The Times* 6 November, CA, an application should have been made by leading counsel for the Court of Appeal to sit early and the indulgence sought of the trial judge, sitting in the RCJ, for the other case to start late.

Separate representation—The Master of the Rolls has emphasised 'in the strongest possible terms that it is only where it is clear that there is an unavoidable conflict of interest, as a matter of law, between two parties in the same interest that they should have separate legal representation, especially where public money is involved. The fact that the parties may have different factual points, or that one party's case may be seen as stronger than the other's, or that the parties' legal advisers may see the legal arguments or the prospects somewhat differently, are not good reasons for their incurring the expense and the court time of separate representation': *Oxfordshire County Council v X, Y and J* [2011] 1 FLR 272, CA.

Grounds for allowing an appeal—The test is whether the decision was wrong and not whether it was plainly wrong. Whether the threshold criteria of CA 1989, s 31(2) are satisfied and whether the court should make a care order are evaluative exercises and not the exercise of a discretion. Accordingly, the approach set out in *G v G (Minors: Custody Appeal)* [1985] FLR 894, HL is not appropriate: *Re B (Care Proceedings: Appeal)* [2013] 2 FLR 1075, SC; *Re P (A Child)* [2014] 1 FLR 824, CA.

Case management appeals and appeals against discretionary decisions—See *Re W (Relocation: Removal Outside Jurisdiction)* [2011] 2 FLR 409, CA. The President has reiterated that appellate courts should respect brave discretionary decisions made at first instance and must be on 'secure ground' if they are to reverse the exercise of a discretion: *Re W*, at [7]–[12].

Chronology—The Court of Appeal has observed that it would be 'enormously helpful' if a chronology was provided in all family appeals as they are for most first instance hearings: *Re H (Interim Contact: Domestic Violence Allegations)* [2014] 1 FLR 41, CA.

Fresh experts on appeal—The Court of Appeal emphasised that there was an obligation on an applicant seeking permission to appeal, or on an appellant who had obtained permission, to seek the Court of Appeal's leave before instructing a fresh expert and releasing court papers to him. Although the guidelines for instructing medical experts from overseas in family cases had some application to appellate proceedings, they were written for first instance hearings in the course of a trial. However, where an applicant is seeking permission to appeal or an appellant seeks to instruct a fresh expert from some other jurisdiction, regard must be had to those guidelines. In particular, the matters requiring explanation include (a) why a UK expert has not been used; (b) what efforts have been made to identify UK experts; and (c) the financial implications of instructing an overseas expert (*Re McC (Care Proceedings: Fresh Evidence of Foreign Expert)* [2012] 2 FLR 121, CA and the Family Justice Council Guidelines of December 2011, *Instruction of Medical Experts from Overseas in Family Cases* (see Part V)).

Proportionality—The appeal court is not required to determine afresh the proportionality of the decision or order under appeal. The appellate exercise is one of conventional review: *Re B (Care Proceedings: Appeal)* [2013] 2 FLR 1075, SC.

Appeal against findings of fact—See notes to FPR 2010, r 30.12 and *NG v SG (Appeal: Non-Disclosure)* [2012] 1 FLR 1211, FD.

Expediting an appeal—In *Unilever plc v Chefaro Proprietaries Ltd* [1995] 1 FLR 1102, CA, the Court of Appeal set out the approach to applications for expedition of the hearing of an appeal (to be included in the 'expedited list'). It was stated that, in the following cases, justice could be done only if the appeal was heard immediately or within a matter of days:

(a) committal appeals, particularly if there were adverse findings or the sentence was short;
(b) where children were likely to suffer extraordinary prejudice beyond that inevitably involved in the proceedings;
(c) Hague Convention cases;
(d) asylum appeals;
(e) execution of a possession order;
(f) where an irrevocable decision is to be implemented;
(g) publication of allegedly unlawful material;
(h) judicial decisions in the course of proceedings.

Further, the court recognised the need to try to arrange an expedited hearing where otherwise:

(a) a party might lose his livelihood;
(b) the appeal would become futile;
(c) the resolution of other similar cases awaiting the outcome of the appeal would be delayed;
(d) a widespread divergence of practice would continue;
(e) there would be serious detriment to public administration.

Citation of authorities—On 24 March 2012, the Lord Chief Justice issued a practice direction in respect of the citation of authorities: *Citation of Authorities* (see Part V) and see the notes to Procedural Guide E5.

Litigants in person—Where the party seeking to appeal an order in the Court of Appeal in public law proceedings is a litigant in person, the local authority has the responsibility to ensure the appeal court is properly provided with appeal bundles: *Re R (A Child)* [2014] EWCA Civ 597.

Withdrawal of appeal—Once an appeal against a judge's decision in family proceedings had been withdrawn, it is wholly inappropriate for the Court of Appeal to interfere with the order made by the court below other than to add undertakings offered by one party or to update the implementation dates. The appeal court cannot extend the period in which the first instance court has ordered the child to be returned: *Re G (A Child)* [2016] EWCA Civ 297.

52.22 Non-disclosure of Part 36 offers and payments

(1) The fact that a Part 36 offer or payment into court has been made must not be disclosed to any judge of the appeal court who is to hear or determine –

(a) an application for permission to appeal; or
(b) an appeal,

until all questions (other than costs) have been determined.

(2) Paragraph (1) does not apply if the Part 36 offer or payment into court is relevant to the substance of the appeal.

(3) Paragraph (1) does not prevent disclosure in any application in the appeal proceedings if disclosure of the fact that a Part 36 offer or payment into court has been made is properly relevant to the matter to be decided.

(Rule 36.4 has the effect that a Part 36 offer made in proceedings at first instance will not have consequences in any appeal proceedings. Therefore, a fresh Part 36 offer needs to be made in appeal proceedings. However, this rule applies to a Part 36 offer whether made in the original proceedings or in the appeal.)

Amendments—Inserted by SI 2016/788.

Section V
Special provisions relating to the Court of Appeal

52.23 Assignment of appeals to the Court of Appeal

(1) Where the court from or to which an appeal is made or from which permission to appeal is sought ('the relevant court') considers that –

(a) an appeal which is to be heard by the County Court or the High Court would raise an important point of principle or practice; or
(b) there is some other compelling reason for the Court of Appeal to hear it,

the relevant court may order the appeal to be transferred to the Court of Appeal.

(The Master of the Rolls has the separate statutory power to direct that an appeal which would be heard by the County Court or the High Court should be heard instead by the Court of Appeal – see section 57 of the Access to Justice Act 1999.)

(2) The Master of the Rolls or the Court of Appeal may remit an appeal to the court in which the original appeal was or would have been brought.

Amendments—Inserted by SI 2016/788.

Scope—Where an appeal is to be heard in the County Court or the High Court, that court may transfer the appeal to be heard by the Court of Appeal. If that court (the County Court or High Court) hears and determines the appeal, there can be an appeal to the Court of Appeal from that decision only if there is some important point of principle or other compelling reason (see r 52.7).

52.24 Who may exercise the powers of the Court of Appeal

(1) A court officer assigned to the Civil Appeals Office who is –

- (a) a barrister; or
- (b) a solicitor

may exercise the jurisdiction of the Court of Appeal with regard to the matters set out in paragraph (2) with the consent of the Master of the Rolls.

(2) The matters referred to in paragraph (1) are –

- (a) any matter incidental to proceedings in the Court of Appeal;
- (b) any other matter where there is no substantial dispute between the parties; and
- (c) the dismissal of an appeal or application where a party has failed to comply with any order, rule or practice direction.

(3) A court officer may not decide an application for –

- (a) permission to appeal;
- (b) bail pending an appeal;
- (c) an injunction(GL);
- (d) a stay(GL) of execution of any order or decision of the lower court other than a temporary stay over a period when the Court of Appeal is not sitting or cannot conveniently be convened;
- (e) a stay of proceedings in the lower court.

(4) Decisions of a court officer will be made without an oral hearing, unless a court officer directs otherwise.

(5) A party may request any decision of a court officer to be reviewed by a single judge, and –

- (a) the review will be determined on paper without an oral hearing; except that
- (b) the judge determining the review on paper may direct that the review be determined at an oral hearing, and must so direct if the judge is of the opinion that the review cannot be fairly determined on paper without an oral hearing.

(6) A party may request a decision of a single judge made without a hearing (other than a decision made on a review under paragraph (5) and a decision determining an application for permission to appeal) to be reconsidered, and –

- (a) the reconsideration will be determined by the same or another judge on paper without an oral hearing; except that
- (b) the judge determining the reconsideration on paper may direct that the reconsideration be determined at an oral hearing, and must so direct if the judge is of the opinion that the reconsideration cannot be fairly determined on paper without an oral hearing.

(7) A request under paragraph (5) or (6) must be filed within 7 days after the party is served with notice of the decision.

(8) A single judge may refer any matter for a decision by a court consisting of two or more judges.

(Section 54(4) of the Access to Justice Act 1999 provides that there is no appeal from the decision of a single judge on an application for permission to appeal.)

PART III

(Section 58(2) of the Senior Courts Act 1981 provides that there is no appeal to the Supreme Court from decisions of the Court of Appeal that –

(a) are taken by a single judge or any officer or member of staff of that court in proceedings incidental to any cause or matter pending before the civil division of that court; and

(b) do not involve the determination of an appeal or of an application for permission to appeal,

and which may be called into question by rules of court. Paragraphs (5) and (6) of this rule provide the procedure for the calling into question of such decisions.)

Amendments—Inserted by SI 2016/788.

★★★★

Section VII
Reopening final appeals

52.30 Reopening of final appeals

(1) The Court of Appeal or the High Court will not reopen a final determination of any appeal unless –

(a) it is necessary to do so in order to avoid real injustice;

(b) the circumstances are exceptional and make it appropriate to reopen the appeal; and

(c) there is no alternative effective remedy.

(2) In paragraphs (1), (3), (4) and (6), 'appeal' includes an application for permission to appeal.

(3) This rule does not apply to appeals to the County Court.

(4) Permission is needed to make an application under this rule to reopen a final determination of an appeal even in cases where under rule 52.3(1) permission was not needed for the original appeal.

(5) There is no right to an oral hearing of an application for permission unless, exceptionally, the judge so directs.

(6) The judge must not grant permission without directing the application to be served on the other party to the original appeal and giving that party an opportunity to make representations.

(7) There is no right of appeal or review from the decision of the judge on the application for permission, which is final.

(8) The procedure for making an application for permission is set out in Practice Direction 52A.

Amendments—Inserted by SI 2016/788.

Limitations—The jurisdiction to re-open an appeal should only be permitted where the process of justice has been corrupted. It is insufficient for these purposes to establish that there is fresh evidence available that might have had a significant impact on the result: see *Re U (Re-opening of Appeal)* [2005] 2 FLR 444, CA. See CPR PD52A, paras 7.1–7.4.

Practice Direction 52A – Appeals: General Provisions

This Practice Direction supplements CPR Part 52

Amendments—CPR Update 59.

SECTION 1: PRACTICE DIRECTIONS SUPPLEMENTING PART 52

1.1 There are five Practice Directions supplementing Part 52 –

- PD52A – Appeals: general provisions
- PD52B – Appeals in the County Court and the High Court
- PD52C – Appeals to the Court of Appeal

- PD52D – Statutory appeals and appeals subject to special provision
- PD52E – Appeals by way of case stated

Amendments—CPR Update 69.

SECTION 2: INTRODUCTION

2.1 These Practice Directions apply to all appeals to which Part 52 applies.

2.2 Part 52 complements the provisions of sections 54 to 57 of the Access to Justice Act 1999 and provides a uniform procedure for appeals in the County Court and the High Court and a modified procedure for the Civil Division of the Court of Appeal. Part 52 does not apply to –

(a) family proceedings in the High Court or County Court but does apply to appeals to the Court of Appeal from decisions made in family proceedings with such modifications as may be required;

(b) appeals in detailed assessment proceedings against the decision of an authorised court officer.

Amendments—CPR Update 69.

SECTION 3: DESTINATIONS OF APPEAL

3.1 Section 56 of the Access to Justice Act 1999 enables the Lord Chancellor to specify the destinations of appeal in different cases. The Access to Justice Act 1999 (Destinations of Appeal) Order 2016 specifies the general destinations of appeal which apply subject to any statutory provision to the contrary. Appeals in respect of individual insolvency and corporate insolvency proceedings are specified in section 375 of the Insolvency Act 1986 and rule 7.47 of the Insolvency Rules 1986 respectively.

The destinations of appeal provided by these provisions are explained in the following paragraphs of this section of this Practice Direction.

3.2 'Statutory appeals' and 'Appeals by way of case stated' are dealt with in PD52D – refer to those provisions for the appropriate court to which such an appeal may lie.

3.3 The court or judge to which an appeal is to be made (subject to obtaining any necessary permission) is set out in the tables below –

- Table 1 deals with appeals in proceedings other than family and insolvency proceedings;
- Table 2 deals with appeals in insolvency proceedings; and
- Table 3 deals with appeals in family proceedings which may be heard in the Family Division and to which the CPR may apply.

3.4 Definitions of terms and abbreviations used in Tables 1, 2 and 3:

'Destination': the court to which the appeal lies.

…

'DJ': District Judge.

'CJ': Circuit Judge including a recorder or a District Judge who is exercising the jurisdiction of a Circuit Judge with the permission of the Designated Civil Judge in respect of the case.

'CJ (CC)': Circuit Judge in the County Court.

'Master': Master, District Judge sitting in a district registry or any other judge referred to in article 4 of the Destination of Appeals Order.

…

'HC': High Court;

'HCJ': single judge of the High Court.

'HCJ(FD)': single judge of the family Division of the High Court.

'CA': Court of Appeal.

'Companies Acts' means the Companies Act 1985, the Companies Act 1989 and the Companies Act 2006.

…

(Note: Tables 1, 2 and 3 do not include so-called 'leap frog' appeals either to the Court of Appeal pursuant to section 57 of the Access to Justice Act 1999 or to the Supreme Court pursuant to section 13 of the Administration of Justice Act 1969.)

3.5 The destinations in the tables set out below apply in relation to first appeals, whether the decision is interim or final.

(For a second appeal (an appeal from a decision of the County Court or the High Court which was itself made on appeal), the destination is the Court of Appeal (save where the original decision was a decision of an officer authorised to assess costs by the Lord Chancellor: see article 6 of the Access to Justice Act 1999 (Destination of Appeals) Order 2016).)

Table 1: Proceedings other than family or insolvency proceedings

Court	Deciding judge	Decision under appeal	Destination
County	DJ	Any, other than a decision in non-insolvency proceedings brought pursuant to the Companies Acts	CJ (CC)
		A decision in non-insolvency proceedings brought pursuant to the Companies Acts	HC
	CJ	Any	HC
High	Master	Any	HCJ
	HCJ	Any	CA
Intellectual Property Enterprise Court	DJ	Any	Enterprise Judge
	Enterprise Judge	Any	CA

Table 2: Insolvency proceedings

Court	Deciding judge	Proceedings	Destination
County	DJ	Individual insolvency	HCJ
		Corporate insolvency	HCJ or Registrar
	CJ	Any	HCJ
High	Master, Registrar or DJ	Any	HCJ
	HCJ	Any	CA

Table 3: Family proceedings in the Principal Registry of the Family Division and to which the CPR will apply

The proceedings to which this table applies include proceedings under the Inheritance (Provision for Family and Dependants) Act 1975 and proceedings under the Trusts of Land and Appointment of Trustees Act 1996.

Deciding judge	Decision under appeal	Destination
DJ	Any	HCJ (FD)
HCJ (FD)	Any	CA

3.6–3.8 *(omitted)*

Filing appellant's notice in wrong court

3.9 (1) Where a party attempts to file an appellant's notice in a court which does not have jurisdiction to issue the notice, a court officer may notify that party in writing that the appeal court does not have jurisdiction in respect of the notice.

(2) Before notifying a person under paragraph (1) the court officer must confer –

(a) with a judge of the appeal court; or
(b) where the Court of Appeal is the appeal court, with a court officer who exercises the jurisdiction of that Court under rule 52.24.

(3) Where a court officer, in the Court of Appeal, notifies a person under paragraph (1), rule 52.24(5) and (6) shall not apply.

Amendments—CPR Updates 69, 86.

SECTION 4: OBTAINING PERMISSION TO APPEAL

Where to apply for permission

4.1 An application for permission to appeal may be made –

(a) to the lower court at the hearing at which the decision to be appealed against is given (in which case the lower court may adjourn the hearing to give a party an opportunity to apply for permission to appeal); or
(b) where the lower court refuses permission to appeal or where no application is made to the lower court, to the appeal court in accordance with rule 52.12.

Form

4.2 An application for permission to appeal to the appeal court must be made using an appellant's notice (form N161 or N164 (small claims track)).

Appeals from Masters and District Judges of High Court

4.3 In relation to appeals from Masters or District Judges of the High Court: appeals, applications for permission and any other applications in the appeal may be heard and directions in the appeal may be given by a High Court Judge or by any person authorised under section 9 of the Senior Courts Act 1981 to act as a judge of the High Court.

Where the lower court is the County Court

4.4 Where the lower court is the County Court –

(a) subject to sub-paragraph (b), appeals and applications for permission to appeal will be heard by a High Court Judge or by a person authorised under paragraphs (1), (2) or (4) of the Table in section 9(1) of the Senior Courts Act 1981 to act as a judge of the High Court;
(b) an appeal or application for permission to appeal from the decision of a recorder may be heard by a Designated Civil Judge who is authorised under paragraph (5) of the Table in section 9(1) of the Senior Courts Act 1981 to act as a judge of the High Court; and
(c) other applications in the appeal may be heard and directions in the appeal may be given either by a High Court Judge or by any person authorised under section 9 of the Senior Courts Act 1981 to act as a judge of the High Court.

4.5 The Designated Civil Judge in consultation with the Presiding Judge has responsibility for allocating appeals from decisions of District Judges to Circuit Judges.

Appeal in relation to case management decision

4.6 Where the application is for permission to appeal from a case management decision, the court dealing with the application may take into account whether –

(a) the issue is of sufficient significance to justify the costs of an appeal;
(b) the procedural consequences of an appeal (e.g. loss of trial date) outweigh the significance of the case management decision;
(c) it would be more convenient to determine the issue at or after trial.

Case management decisions include decisions made under rule 3.1(2) and decisions about disclosure, filing of witness statements or experts' reports, directions about the timetable of the claim, adding a party to a claim and security for costs.

Second appeal

4.7 An application for permission to appeal from a decision of the High Court or the County Court which was itself made on appeal is a second appeal and must be made to the Court of Appeal. If permission to appeal is granted the appeal will be heard by the Court of Appeal.

Amendments—CPR Updates 60, 69, 86.

SECTION 5: SKELETON ARGUMENTS

5.1 (1) The purpose of a skeleton argument is to assist the court by setting out as concisely as practicable the arguments upon which a party intends to rely.

(2) A skeleton argument must –

- be concise;
- both define and confine the areas of controversy;
- be set out in numbered paragraphs;
- be cross-referenced to any relevant document in the bundle;
- be self-contained and not incorporate by reference material from previous skeleton arguments;
- not include extensive quotations from documents or authorities.

(3) Documents to be relied on must be identified.

(4) Where it is necessary to refer to an authority, a skeleton argument must –

(a) state the proposition of law the authority demonstrates; and
(b) identify the parts of the authority that support the proposition.

If more than one authority is cited in support of a given proposition, the skeleton argument must briefly state why.

(5) The cost of preparing a skeleton argument which –

(a) does not comply with the requirements set out in this paragraph; or
(b) was not filed within the time limits provided by this Practice Direction (or any further time granted by the court),

will not be allowed on assessment except as directed by the court.

5.2 The parties should consider what other information the appeal court will need. This may include a list of persons who feature in the case or glossaries of technical terms. A chronology of relevant events will be necessary in most appeals.

5.3 Any statement of costs must show the amount claimed for the skeleton argument separately.

Amendments—CPR Update 66.

SECTION 6: DISPOSING OF APPLICATIONS AND APPEALS BY CONSENT

Dismissal of applications or appeals by consent

6.1 An appellant who does not wish to pursue an application or appeal may request the appeal court to dismiss the application or the appeal. If such a request is granted it will usually be subject to an order that the appellant pays the costs of the application or appeal.

6.2 If the appellant wishes to have the application or appeal dismissed without costs, his request must be accompanied by a letter signed by the respondent stating that the respondent so consents.

6.3 Where a settlement has been reached disposing of the application or appeal, the parties may make a joint request to the court for the application or appeal to be dismissed by consent. If the request is granted the application or appeal will be dismissed.

Allowing unopposed appeals or applications on paper

6.4 The appeal court will not normally make an order allowing an appeal unless satisfied that the decision of the lower court was wrong or unjust because of a serious procedural or other irregularity. The appeal court may, however, set aside or vary the order of the lower court by consent and without determining the merits of the appeal if it is satisfied that there are good and sufficient reasons for so doing. Where the appeal court is requested by all parties to allow an application or an appeal the court may consider the request on the papers. The request should set out the relevant history of the proceedings and the matters relied on as justifying the order and be accompanied by a draft order.

Disposal of applications and appeals involving children or protected parties

6.5 Where one of the parties is a child or protected party, any disposal of an application or the appeal requires the court's approval. A draft order signed by the parties' solicitors should be sent to the appeal court, together with an opinion from the advocate acting on behalf of the child or protected party and, in the case of a protected party, any relevant documents prepared for the Court of Protection.

SECTION 7: REOPENING APPEALS (RULE 52.30)

7.1 A party applying for permission to reopen an appeal or an application for permission to appeal must apply for such permission from the court whose decision the party wishes to reopen.

7.2 The application for permission must be made by application notice and be supported by written evidence, verified by a statement of truth. A copy of the application for permission must not be served on any other party to the original appeal unless the court so directs.

7.3 Where the court directs that the application for permission is to be served on another party, that party may, within 14 days of the service on him of the copy of the application, file and serve a written statement either supporting or opposing the application.

7.4 The application for permission will be considered on paper by a single judge.

Amendments—CPR Update 86.

SECTION 8: TRANSITIONAL PROVISIONS

8.1 This Practice Direction and Practice Directions 52B, 52C, 52D and 52E shall come into force on 1 October 2012 and shall apply to all appeals where –

(a) the appeal notice was filed; or
(b) permission to appeal was given

on or after that date.

8.2 The appeal court may at any time direct that, in relation to any appeal, one or more of Practice Directions 52A, 52B, 52C, 52D or 52E shall apply irrespective of the date on which the appeal notice was filed or permission to appeal was given.

Practice Direction 52B – Appeals in the County Court and High Court

This Practice Direction supplements CPR Part 52

Amendments—CPR Updates 59, 69.

SECTION 1: APPLICATION

This Practice Direction applies to –

(a) appeals within the County Court (from a District Judge to a Circuit Judge);
(b) appeals from the County Court to the High Court; and
(c) appeals within the High Court (from a Master, a District Judge sitting in a District Registry, a Registrar in Bankruptcy, a Registrar of the Companies Court, a Costs Judge or an officer of the High Court to a judge of the High Court).

Amendments—CPR Update 69.

SECTION 2: VENUE FOR APPEALS AND FILING OF NOTICES AND APPLICATIONS

2.1 Appeals within the County Court, appeals from the County Court and appeals within the High Court to a judge of the High Court must be brought in the appropriate appeal centre and all other notices (including any respondent's notice) and applications must be filed at that appeal centre. The venue for an appeal within the County Court will be determined by the Designated Civil Judge and may be different from the appeal centre.

2.2 The tables at the end of this Practice Direction set out the Appeal Centres for each circuit.

Amendments—CPR Update 69.

SECTION 3: EXTENDING TIME IN WHICH TO APPEAL

3.1 A party may apply to the lower court for an extension of time in which to file an appellant's notice. The application must be made at the same time as the appellant applies to the lower court for permission to appeal.

3.2 Where the time for filing an appellant's notice has expired, the appellant must include an application for an extension of time within the appellant's notice (form N161 or, in respect of a small claim, form N164) stating the reason for the delay and the steps taken prior to making the application.

3.3 The court may make an order granting or refusing an extension of time and may do so with or without a hearing. If an order is made without a hearing, any party seeking to set aside or vary the order may apply, within 14 days of service of the order, for a hearing.

SECTION 4: INITIATING AN APPEAL

4.1 An appellant's notice (Form N161 or, in respect of a small claim, Form N164) must be filed and served in all cases. The appellant's notice must be accompanied by the appropriate fee or, if appropriate, a fee remission application or certificate.

4.2 Documents to be filed with the appellant's notice: The appellant must file with the appellant's notice –

(a) three copies of the appellant's notice and one additional copy for each respondent;
(b) a copy of the sealed order under appeal;
(c) where an application was made to the lower court for permission to appeal, a copy of any order granting or refusing permission to appeal together with a copy of the reasons, if any, for allowing or refusing permission to appeal; and
(d) grounds of appeal, which must be set out on a separate sheet attached to the appellant's notice and must set out, in simple language, clearly and concisely, why the order of the lower court was wrong or unjust because of a serious procedural or other irregularity (Rule 52.21(3)).

4.3 Applications in the appeal: Any application to be made in the appeal (for example, for a stay of the order of the lower court, or for an extension of time) should be included within the appellant's notice. Any application for a transcript at public expense should be made within the appellant's notice.

Amendments—CPR Updates 75, 86.

SECTION 5: CASE MANAGING THE APPEAL; ORDERS OF THE COURT

5.1 The appeal court may make orders for the case management of an appeal.

5.2 When making a case management order, the court may dispense with any requirements of or directions made in this Practice Direction.

SECTION 6: CONDUCT OF THE APPEAL

6.1 Service of appellant's notice on the respondent: The appellant must file a certificate of service of the appellant's notice with the court as soon as practicable after service.

6.2 Transcript of the judgment of the lower court or other record of reasons: Except where the claim has been allocated to the small claims track, the appellant must obtain a transcript or other record of reasons of the lower court as follows –

- (a) where the judgment has been officially recorded, the appellant must apply for an approved transcript as soon as possible and, in any event, within 7 days of the filing of the appellant's notice;
- (b) where the judgment under appeal has been handed down in writing, the appellant must obtain and retain a copy of the written judgment;.
- (c) in any other case, the appellant must cause a note of the judgment under appeal to be made and typed. The parties to the appeal should agree the note, which should then be sent to the judge of the lower court for approval. The parties and their advocates have a duty to make, and to co-operate in agreeing, a note of the judgment.

6.3 Appeal bundle: As soon as practicable, but in any event within 35 days of the filing of the appellant's notice, the appellant must file an appeal bundle which must contain only those documents relevant to the appeal. The appeal bundle must be paginated and indexed.

6.4 Documents relevant to the appeal:

(1) Subject to any order made by the court, the following documents must be included in the appeal bundle –

- (a) a copy of the appellant's notice;
- (b) a copy of any respondent's notice;
- (c) a copy of any appellant's or respondent's skeleton argument;
- (d) a copy of the order under appeal;
- (e) a copy of the order of the lower court granting or refusing permission to appeal together with a copy of the judge's reasons, if any, for granting or refusing permission;
- (f) a copy of any order allocating the case to a track;
- (g) a transcript of the judgment of the lower court or other record of reasons (except in appeals in cases which were allocated to the small claims track and subject to any order of the court).

(2) The following documents should also be considered for inclusion in the appeal bundle but should be included only where relevant to the appeal –

- (a) statements of case;
- (b) application notices;
- (c) other orders made in the case;
- (d) a chronology of relevant events;
- (e) witness statements made in support of any application made in the appellant's notice;
- (f) other witness statements;
- (g) any other documents which any party considers would assist the appeal court.

6.5 Service of the appeal bundle: A copy of the appeal bundle must be served on each respondent –

(a) where permission to appeal was granted by the lower court, at the same time as filing the appeal bundle;

(b) where the appeal court has granted permission to appeal, as soon as practicable after notification and in any event within 14 days of the grant of permission;

(c) where the appeal court directs that the application for permission to appeal is to be heard on the same occasion as the appeal, as soon as practicable and in any event within 14 days after notification of the hearing date.

6.6 Late documents: Any relevant document which is obtained or created after the appeal bundle has been filed (for example a respondent's notice or a skeleton argument) should be added to the appeal bundle as soon as practicable and, in any event, no less than 7 days before the hearing of the appeal or any application.

SECTION 7: DETERMINATION OF APPLICATIONS

7.1 Applications made in the appeal, including applications for permission to appeal under rule 52.3(2)(a) or rule 52.13(3), may be determined with or without a hearing.

7.2 Where the court refuses an application for permission to appeal without a hearing, the appellant (or, where appropriate, the respondent) may request the application to be reconsidered at a hearing.

7.3 Where the court determines any other application without hearing the respondent (including an application for permission to bring the appeal out of time) any party affected by the determination may apply to have the order set aside or varied.

7.4 Any request or application made under this section must be made within 7 days of service of notification of the determination upon the person making the application. Where any such request or application is made –

(a) a copy of the request or application must be served on all other parties at the same time; and

(b) the court will give directions for the determination of the application.

Amendments—CPR Update 86.

SECTION 8: HEARINGS

8.1 Attendance at permission hearings: Where a respondent to an appeal or cross-appeal attends the hearing of an application for permission to appeal, costs will not be awarded to the respondent unless –

(a) the court has ordered or requested attendance by the respondent;

(b) the court has ordered that the application for permission to appeal be listed at the same time as the determination of other applications;

(c) the court has ordered that the hearing of the appeal will follow the hearing of the application if permission is granted; or

(d) the court considers it just, in all the circumstances, to award costs to the respondent.

8.2 Respondent's documents: A respondent who has been served with an appeal bundle and who considers that relevant documents have been omitted may file and serve on all parties a respondent's supplemental appeal bundle containing copies of other relevant documents. The supplemental appeal bundle must be filed and served as soon as practicable after service of the appeal bundle, but in any event not less than 7 days before the hearing.

8.3 Skeleton arguments: Subject to any order of the court, the parties to the appeal should file and serve skeleton arguments only where –

(a) the complexity of the issues of fact or law in the appeal justify them; or

(b) skeleton arguments would assist the court in respects not readily apparent from the papers in the appeal.

Table A: Table of appeal centres for each circuit

Circuit	Court	Appeal Centre
Midland	Birmingham CJC	Birmingham CJC
	Boston	Lincoln
	Burton-upon-Trent	Nottingham
	Chesterfield	Nottingham
	Coventry	Coventry
	Derby	Nottingham
	Dudley	Walsall
	Hereford	Worcester
	Kettering	Northampton
	Kidderminster	Worcester
	Leicester	Leicester
	Lincoln	Lincoln
	Mansfield	Nottingham
	Northampton	Northampton
	Nottingham	Nottingham
	Nuneaton	Coventry
	Redditch	Worcester
	Stafford	Stoke-on-Trent
	Stoke-on-Trent	Stoke-on-Trent
	Telford	Telford
	Walsall	Walsall
	Warwick	Coventry
	Wolverhampton	Walsall
	Worcester	Worcester
North East	Barnsley	Sheffield
	Bradford	Bradford
	Darlington	Teesside
	Doncaster	Sheffield
	Durham	Newcastle-upon-Tyne
	Gateshead	Newcastle-upon-Tyne
	Grimsby	Kingston-upon-Hull
	Harrogate	Leeds
	Huddersfield	Bradford
	Kingston-upon-Hull	Kingston-upon-Hull
	Leeds	Leeds
	Newcastle-upon-Tyne	Newcastle-upon-Tyne
	North Shields	Newcastle-upon-Tyne
	Scarborough	Leeds
	Sheffield	Sheffield
	Skipton	Bradford
	South Shields	Newcastle-upon-Tyne
	Sunderland	Newcastle-upon-Tyne
	Teesside	Teesside
	Wakefield	Leeds
	York	Leeds
Northern	Barrow-in-Furness	Carlisle
	Birkenhead	Liverpool
	Blackburn	Preston
	Blackpool	Preston
	Bolton	Manchester CJC
	Burnley	Preston

PART III

Circuit	Court	Appeal Centre
	Bury	Manchester CJC
	Carlisle	Carlisle
	Chester CJC	Chester CJC
	Crewe	Chester CJC
	Kendal	Carlisle
	Lancaster	Preston
	Liverpool	Liverpool
	Manchester CJC	Manchester CJC
	Oldham	Manchester CJC
	Preston	Preston
	St Helens	Liverpool
	Stockport	Manchester CJC
	West Cumbria	Carlisle
	Wigan	Liverpool
Wales	Aberystwyth	Swansea
	Blackwood	Cardiff CJC
	Caernarfon	Wrexham
	Cardiff	Cardiff CJC
	Carmarthen	Swansea
	Conwy & Colwyn	Wrexham
	Haverfordwest	Swansea
	Llanelli	Swansea
	Llangefni	Wrexham
	Merthyr Tydfil	Cardiff CJC
	Mold	Wrexham
	Newport (Gwent)	Cardiff CJC
	Pontypridd	Cardiff CJC
	Port Talbot	Swansea
	Prestatyn	Wrexham
	Swansea	Swansea
	Welshpool & Newtown	Wrexham
	Wrexham	Wrexham
Western	Aldershot & Farnham	Winchester
	Barnstaple	Barnstaple
	Basingstoke	Winchester
	Bath	Bristol CJC
	Bodmin	Bodmin
	Bournemouth	Bournemouth
	Bristol	Bristol CJC
	Cheltenham	Bristol CJC
	Chippenham	Winchester
	Exeter	Exeter
	Gloucester	Bristol CJC
	Newport (Isle of Wight)	Winchester
	Plymouth	Plymouth
	Portsmouth	Portsmouth
	Salisbury	Winchester
	Southampton	Southampton
	Swindon	Swindon
	Taunton	Bristol CJC
	Torquay & Newton Abbot	Torquay & Newton Abbot
	Trowbridge	Trowbridge

Circuit	Court	Appeal Centre
	Truro	Truro
	Weston-Super-Mare	Bristol CJC
	Weymouth & Dorchester	Winchester
	Winchester	Winchester
	Yeovil	Bristol
South East	Banbury	Oxford
	Barnet	Barnet
	Basildon	Southend
	Bedford	Luton
	Brentford	Brendford
	Brighton	Brighton
	Bromley	Bromley
	Bury St Edmunds	Cambridge
	Cambridge	Cambridge
	Canterbury	Canterbury
	Central London CJC	Central London CJC
	Chelmsford	Southend
	Chichester	Chichester
	Clerkenwell & Shoreditch	Clerkenwell & Shoreditch
	Colchester	Southend
	Croydon	Croydon
	Dartford	Dartford
	Eastbourne	Eastbourne
	Edmonton	Edmonton
	Guildford	Guildford
	Hastings	Hastings
	Hertford	Luton
	High Wycombe	Oxford
	Horsham	Horsham
	Hove	Hove
	Ipswich	Norwich
	Kingston-upon-Thames	Kingston-upon-Thames
	Lambeth	Lambeth
	Lewes	Lewes
	Luton	Luton
	Maidstone	Maidstone
	Mayor's and City	Mayor's and City
	Medway	Medway
	Milton Keynes	Oxford
	Norwich	Norwich
	Oxford	Oxford
	Peterborough	Cambridge
	Reading	Oxford
	Romford	Romford
	Slough	Oxford
	Southend	Southend
	Staines	Staines
	Thanet	Thanet
	Uxbridge	Uxbridge
	Wandsworth	Wandsworth
	Watford	Watford
	Willesden	Willesden
	Woolwich	Woolwich

Circuit	Court	Appeal Centre
	Worthing	Worthing

Table B: Appeals from the County Court or within the High Court: appeal centres for each circuit

Circuit	Appeal Centre
Midland Circuit	Birmingham Nottingham
North Eastern Circuit	Leeds Newcastle Sheffield
Northern Circuit	Manchester Liverpool Preston Chester
Wales Circuit	Cardiff Swansea Mold
Western Circuit	Bristol Exeter Winchester
South Eastern Circuit	Royal Courts of Justice Lewes Luton Norwich Reading Chelmsford Maidstone Oxford

Amendments—CPR Updates 66, 69, 86, 88.

Practice Direction 52C – Appeals to the Court of Appeal

This Practice Direction supplements CPR Part 52

Amendments—CPR Update 59.

Contents of this Practice Direction

This Practice Direction is divided into the following sections:

1 Introduction and interpretation
2 Starting an appeal to the Court of Appeal, Grounds of Appeal and Skeleton Arguments
3 Respondent's notice and respondent's skeleton argument
4 Procedure where permission to appeal is sought from the Court of Appeal
5 Timetable
6 Management of the appeal
7 Bundles, amendment and supplementary skeleton arguments

SECTION 1: INTRODUCTION AND INTERPRETATION

1 In this Practice Direction –

'appeal notice' means either an appellant's notice in form N161 or a respondent's notice in form N162;

'appellant's notice' means an appeal notice filed by an appellant and a 'respondent's notice' means an appeal notice filed by a respondent;

'hearing date' means the date on which the appeal is listed to be heard, including a 'floating' date over two or more days;

'listing window notification' means the letter sent by the Civil Appeals Office in accordance with Section 5: Timetable Part 1 notifying the parties of the window within which the appeal is likely to be heard; and 'date of the listing window notification' means the date of such letter;

'replacement skeleton argument' means a skeleton argument which has been amended in order to include cross references to the appeal bundle and is lodged and served in accordance with the timetable at Section 5 Part 2.

2 The court may make such directions as the case may require and such directions will prevail over any provision of this practice direction.

SECTION 2: STARTING AN APPEAL TO THE COURT OF APPEAL

Filing the Appellant's Notice and accompanying documents

3 (1) An appellant's notice (Form N161) must be filed and served in all cases. The appellant's notice must be accompanied by the appropriate fee or, if appropriate, a fee remission certificate.

(2) The appellant's notice and accompanying documents must be filed in the Civil Appeals Office Registry, Room E307, Royal Courts of Justice, Strand, London, WC2A 2LL.

(3) At the same time as filing an appellant's notice, the appellant must provide for the use of the court three copies of the appellant's notice and one copy of each of the following –

(a) the sealed order or tribunal determination being appealed;

(b) any order granting or refusing permission to appeal, together with a copy of the judge's or tribunal's reasons for granting or refusing permission to appeal;

(c) any witness statements or affidavits relied on in support of any application included in the appellant's notice;

(d) in cases where the decision of the lower court was itself made on appeal, the first order, the reasons given by the judge who made it, and the appellant's notice of appeal against that order;

(e) in a claim for judicial review or a statutory appeal, the original decision which was the subject of the application to the lower court;

(f) the order allocating the case to a track (if any);

(g) the appellant's skeleton argument in support of the appeal;

(h) the approved transcript of the judgment.

(4) The appellant must also provide to the court one copy of the appellant's notice for each respondent for sealing by the court and return to the appellant for service.

(5) Where the appellant applies for permission to appeal, additional documents are required: see Section 4 of this Practice Direction.

(6) Provisions in relation to the skeleton argument are set out in paragraph 31.

Extension of time for filing appellant's notice

4 (1) Where the time for filing an appellant's notice has expired, the appellant must –

(a) file the appellant's notice; and

(b) include in that appellant's notice an application for an extension of time.

(2) The appellant's notice must state the reason for the delay and the steps taken prior to the application being made.

(3) Where the appellant's notice includes an application for an extension of time and permission to appeal has been given or is not required, the respondent has the right to oppose that application and to be heard at any hearing of that application. In respect of any application to extend time –

(a) The respondent must –
  (i) be served with a copy of any evidence filed in support of the application; and
  (ii) inform the court in writing of any objections to the grant of the extension of time within 7 days of being served with the appellant's notice.

(b) A respondent who unreasonably opposes an application for an extension of time may be ordered to pay the costs of the application.

(c) An application for an extension of time will normally be determined without a hearing unless the court directs otherwise.

Grounds of Appeal

5 (1) The grounds of appeal must identify as concisely as possible the respects in which the judgment of the court below is –

(a) wrong; or
(b) unjust because of a serious procedural or other irregularity, as required by rule 52.21(3).

(2) The reasons why the decision under appeal is wrong or unjust must not be included in the grounds of appeal and must be confined to the skeleton argument.

Amendments—CPR Update 86.

Second appeals

5A An application to make a second appeal must identify in the grounds of appeal –

(a) the important point of principle or practice, or
(b) the compelling reason

which is said to justify the grant of permission to appeal.

Amendments—CPR Update 60.

Non-availability of documents

6 (1) If the appellant is unable to provide any of the necessary documents in time, the appellant must complete the appeal notice on the basis of the available documents. The notice may be amended subsequently with the permission of the court (see paragraph 30).

(2) Any application for a transcript at public expense should be made within the appellant's notice.

Amendments—CPR Update 75.

Service on the respondent

7.1 The Civil Appeals Office will not serve documents. Where service is required by the Rules or this Practice Direction, it must be effected by the parties.

7.1A The appellant's skeleton argument in respect of an application for permission to appeal must be served on each respondent at the same time as service of the appellant's notice.

7.2 The evidence in support of any application made in an appellant's notice must be filed and served with the appellant's notice.

7.3 An application for an order to dispense with service of the appellant's notice under rule 6.28 must be made in the appeal notice or, thereafter, by application notice under Part 23.

Amendments—CPR Updates 66, 75.

SECTION 3: RESPONDENT'S NOTICE (RULE 52.13) AND RESPONDENT'S SKELETON ARGUMENT

Amendments—CPR Update 86.

Respondent's notice

8 (1) A respondent who seeks to appeal against any part of the order made by the court below must file an appeal notice.

(2) A respondent who seeks a variation of the order of the lower court must file an appeal notice and must obtain permission to appeal.

(3) A respondent who seeks to contend that the order of the court below should be upheld for reasons other than those given by that court must file a respondent's notice.

(4) The notice may be amended subsequently with the permission of the court (see paragraph 30).

Skeleton argument to be lodged with the respondent's notice

9 A respondent who files a respondent's notice must, within 14 days of filing the notice, lodge a skeleton argument with the court and serve a copy of the skeleton argument on every other party to the appeal.

(Provisions in relation to the skeleton argument are set out in paragraph 31.)

Documents to be filed with respondent's notice

10 The respondent must file the following documents with the respondent's notice –

(a) two additional copies of the respondent's notice for the court; and

(b) one copy each for the appellant and any other respondents.

Applications within respondent's notice

11 (1) A respondent may include an application within a respondent's notice.

(2) The parties must consider whether it would be more convenient for any application to be listed with the appeal or whether the application needs to be considered in advance.

(3) Where parties consider that the time estimate for the appeal will be affected by listing the application with the appeal, they must inform the court without delay.

Time limits: rule 52.13(4) and (5)

12 Where an extension of time is required, the respondent must apply in the respondent's notice and explain the delay.

Amendments—CPR Update 86.

Respondent's skeleton argument (where no respondent's notice filed)

13 (1) In all cases where the respondent is legally represented and proposes to address the court, the respondent must lodge and serve a skeleton argument.

(2) A respondent's skeleton argument must be lodged and served in accordance with Part 1 of the Timetable in Section 5.

(Provisions in relation to the skeleton argument are set out in paragraph 31.)

SECTION 4: PROCEDURE WHERE PERMISSION TO APPEAL IS SOUGHT FROM THE COURT OF APPEAL

Documents for use on an application for permission

14 Within 14 days of filing the appeal notice, the appellant must lodge a core bundle (and, if necessary, a supplementary bundle) for the application for permission to appeal, prepared in accordance with paragraph 27.

Amendments—CPR Update 86.

Determination of applications for permission to appeal

15 (1) Applications for permission to appeal will be determined by the court without a hearing unless the judge considering the application directs that the application be determined at an oral hearing in accordance with rule 52.5(2).

(2) If a judge directs that an oral hearing should take place, the hearing will be listed before the same judge no later than 14 days after the direction was given, unless the court directs otherwise.

(3) When directing that an oral hearing should take place, the judge may also identify any issue or issues on which the applicant should specifically focus its submissions at the oral hearing in order to assist the court to determine the application and may direct the respondent to file and serve written submissions and to attend the oral hearing.

Amendments—CPR Update 86.

Permission hearing

16 (1) The court will notify the respondent of any oral hearing but the respondent is not expected to attend unless the court so directs.

(2) If the court directs the respondent to attend the permission hearing, the appellant must supply the respondent with a copy of the skeleton argument and any documents to which the appellant intends to refer.

Amendments—CPR Update 86.

Appellant in receipt of services funded by the Legal Services Commission applying for permission to appeal

17 Where the appellant is in receipt of services funded by the Legal Services Commission and permission to appeal has been refused by the court without a hearing, the appellant must send a copy of the court's reasons for refusing permission to the Legal Services Commission as soon as it has been received.

Amendments—CPR Update 86.

Note—The Legal Aid Agency replaced the Legal Services Commission on 1 April 2013.

Limited permission: rule 52.6(2)

18 (1) If, under rule 52.6(2), the court grants permission to appeal on some issues only, it will –

- (a) refuse permission on any remaining issues; or
- (b) adjourn the application in respect of those issues to the hearing of the appeal.

(2) If the court adjourns the application under sub-paragraph (1)(b), the appellant must inform the court and the respondent in writing, within 14 days after the date of the court's order, whether the appellant intends to pursue the application. If the appellant intends to pursue the application, the parties must include in any time estimate for the appeal hearing an allowance for the adjourned application.

(3) *(omitted)*

Amendments—CPR Update 86.

Respondents actions when served with the appellant's notice

19 (1)

(a) If the appellant seeks permission to appeal a respondent is permitted, and is encouraged, within 14 days of service of the appellant's notice or skeleton argument if later to file and serve upon the appellant and any other respondent a brief statement of any reasons why permission should be refused, in whole or in part.

(b) The statement should be not more than 3 pages long, and should be directed to the relevant threshold test for the grant of permission to appeal. The statement must also comply with paragraph 31(1)(b).

(c) The statement should identify issues to which the appeal should be limited, and any conditions to which the appeal should be subject (see Rule 52.6(2)).

(2) (a) If the appellant makes any application in addition to an application for permission to appeal (such as a stay of execution, an injunction pending appeal or an extension of time for appeal) a respondent should include in its written statement under paragraph 19(1)(a) any reasons why that application should be refused or granted only on terms.

(b) If, exceptionally, a respondent wishes to rely upon evidence for that purpose its evidence should be included in its written statement, supported by a statement of truth, or filed and served upon the appellant and any other respondent at the same time as its written statement under paragraph 19(1)(a).

(3) Unless the court directs otherwise, a respondent need take no further steps when served with an appellant's notice prior to being notified that permission to appeal has been granted.

Amendments—CPR Updates 79, 86.

Respondent's costs of permission applications

20 (1) There will normally be no order for the recovery of the costs of a respondent's written statement. In most cases an application for permission to appeal will be determined without the need for the respondent to attend a hearing. In such circumstances an order for costs will not normally be made in favour of a respondent who voluntarily attends a hearing.

(2) If the court directs the respondent to file submissions or attend a hearing, it will normally award costs to the respondent if permission is refused.

Amendments—CPR Update 79.

SECTION 5: TIMETABLE

21 Subject to any specific directions that may be given by the court, the timetable for the conduct of an appeal after the date of the listing window notification is set out below:

Timetable Part 1: Listing window notification to lodging bundle

Period within which step is to be taken	Action	Cross reference to relevant provisions in this Practice Direction
Promptly after permission to appeal is granted	**Review case**: parties to review case with a view to resolution or refinement of the issues to be determined at the appeal	Paragraph 27(6) (bundle of documents)

PART III

Period within which step is to be taken	Action	Cross reference to relevant provisions in this Practice Direction
Within 14 days of service of: the appellant's notice if permission has been given by the lower court or is not needed; notification that permission has been granted by the Court of Appeal; or notification that the permission application will be listed with the appeal to follow	**Respondent's notice** (if any) must be filed and served	Paragraph 8 (respondent's notice)
14 days after date of listing window notification	The appellant must file and serve on every respondent the **Appeal Questionnaire**	Paragraph 1 (listing window notification defined) Paragraph 23 (Appeal Questionnaire)
14 days after date of listing window notification	The appellant must serve on every respondent (1) the **appellant's appeal skeleton argument** or confirmation that the appellant intends to rely on the permission to appeal skeleton argument; and (2) **the proposed bundle index for the core appeal bundle and any supplementary bundle**	Paragraph 31 (skeleton argument) Paragraph 27 (bundle of documents)
Within 14 days of filing a respondent's notice	**If respondent has filed a respondent's notice**, respondent must lodge and serve a skeleton argument on every other party	Paragraph 9 (skeleton argument to be lodged with the respondent's notice or within 14 days of filing respondent's notice)
7 days after service of appellant's Appeal Questionnaire	**If a respondent disagrees with appellant's time estimate**, that respondent must file and serve on every other party its own time estimate	Paragraph 24 (time estimate)
35 days after date of listing window notification	**Where Respondent has not filed a respondent's notice**, respondent must lodge skeleton argument and serve on every other party	Paragraph 13 (respondent's skeleton argument where no Respondent's Notice filed) Paragraph 31 (skeleton argument)
49 days after date of listing window notification	**Review case**: parties to have reviewed case with a view to resolution or refinement of the issues to be determined at the appeal	Paragraph 27(6) (bundle of documents)

Period within which step is to be taken	Action	Cross reference to relevant provisions in this Practice Direction
49 days after date of listing window notification	**Agree bundle**: the parties must agree the content of the core appeal bundle and any supplementary bundle for the appeal hearing	Paragraph 27(8) and (9) (bundle of documents) Paragraph 28 (bundle: Appeals from Upper Tribunal Immigration and Asylum Chamber)
63 days after listing window notification	Appellant must serve a **final bundle index** on all the respondents, including page numbers	Paragraph 27 (bundle of documents)
70 days after listing window notification	All respondents must serve on the appellant their **replacement skeleton arguments**	Paragraph 1 (replacement skeleton argument defined) Paragraph 31 (skeleton argument)

PART III

Timetable Part 2: Steps to be taken once hearing date fixed: lodging bundles, supplemental skeletons and bundles of authorities

Time before hearing date when step is to be taken	Action	Cross reference to relevant provisions in this Practice Direction
As soon as practicable and no later than 7 days before the appeal hearing	If a party wishes to rely on a supplementary skeleton argument, the supplementary skeleton argument must be lodged and served together with a request for permission to rely on it. Note – permission will only be granted where strictly necessary.	Paragraph 32 (supplementary skeleton arguments)
No later than 42 days before the appeal hearing	Subject to any direction of the court, the appellant must lodge the appropriate number of **appeal bundles** and serve a copy on all other parties to the appeal. Any unagreed documents bundle must be lodged and served by the party seeking to rely on the unagreed documents.	Paragraph 27 (bundle of documents) Paragraph 28 (bundle: Appeals from Upper Tribunal Immigration and Asylum Chamber)
No later than 7 days before the appeal hearing	Bundles of authorities must be lodged	Paragraph 29 (bundle of authorities)

Amendments—CPR Updates 66, 86.

SECTION 6: MANAGEMENT OF THE APPEAL

Listing and hear-by dates

22 The hear-by date is the last day of the listing window.

Appeal Questionnaire

23 The appellant must complete and file the Appeal Questionnaire and serve it on the respondent within 14 days after the date of the listing window notification.

Time estimates

24 If the respondent disagrees with the appellant's time estimate, the respondent must inform the court within 7 days of service of the Appeal Questionnaire. In the absence of such notification the respondent will be deemed to have accepted the appellant's time estimate.

Multiple Appeals

25 (1) If two or more appeals are pending in the same or related proceedings, the parties must seek directions as to whether they should be heard together or consecutively by the same judges.

(2) Whether appeals are heard together or consecutively, the parties must attempt to agree a single appeal bundle or set of bundles for all the appeals and seek directions if they are unable to do so.

Expedition

26 (1) The court may direct that the hearing of an appeal be expedited.

(2) The court will deal with requests for expedition without a hearing. Requests for expedition must be made by letter setting out succinctly the grounds on which expedition is sought. The letter (or, if time is particularly short, email) must be marked for the immediate attention of the court and copied to the other parties to the appeal.

(3) If an expedited appeal hearing is required as a matter of extreme urgency, the Civil Appeals Office must be informed as soon as possible. If necessary, parties or their legal representatives should call the Royal Courts of Justice switchboard on 020 7947 6000 and ask a member of the security staff to contact the Duty Judge.

(4) An expedited hearing will be listed at the convenience of the court and not according to the availability of counsel.

SECTION 7: BUNDLES, AMENDMENT AND SKELETON ARGUMENTS

Bundle of documents

27 This paragraph of the Practice Direction should be read in conjunction with the Timetable in paragraph 21 above.

(1) **Core bundle for permission to appeal**: Subject to any direction made by the court, the applicant must lodge a core bundle containing only those documents listed in the relevant core bundle index accessible on the Court of Appeal (Civil Division) section of the Justice website (at http://hmctsformfinder.justice.gov.uk/HMCTS/GetForms.do?court_forms_category=Court%20Of%20Appeal%20Civil%20Division) or available from the Civil Appeals Office.

(2) **Supplementary bundle for permission to appeal**: For an application for permission to appeal any additional documents may be included in a supplementary bundle, but only where they are relevant to the grounds of appeal and where it will be necessary for the court to read the document for the purposes of determining whether to grant permission to appeal and any related application. The following documents may be considered for inclusion in a supplementary bundle:

- (a) statements of case
- (b) application notices;
- (c) other orders made in the case;
- (d) witness statements made in support of any application made in the appellant's notice;
- (e) other witness statements relevant to the issues raised in the grounds of appeal;
- (f) key contemporaneous documents.

(3) **Service of indexes for the permission to appeal bundles**: The applicant for permission to appeal must serve on every respondent a copy of the index for the core bundle for permission to appeal and a copy of the index for any supplementary bundle for permission to appeal at the same time as the bundles are lodged with the court (i e within 14 days of the appeal notice: paragraph 14 above).

(4) **Respondent's statement for permission to appeal**: In accordance with paragraph 19, a respondent is encouraged to file and serve a respondent's statement in response to an application for permission to appeal. Any respondent's statement will be copied to the core bundle by the Civil Appeals Office.

(5) **Respondent's Notice**: A respondent who wishes to file a respondent's notice must do so in accordance with the time limits in CPR Part 52.13. If the respondent seeks permission to appeal in their respondent's notice they must on the date when the respondent's skeleton argument is due to be filed lodge a respondent's supplementary permission to appeal bundle. That bundle must contain any documents not included in the appellant's bundle(s) for permission to appeal which are necessary for the court to read for the purpose of determining whether to grant the respondent permission to appeal, including the respondent's notice and the respondent's skeleton argument. On the same date the respondent must serve on every other party a copy of the index for that bundle.

(6) **Reviewing the case after the grant of permission to appeal**: Promptly after permission to appeal is granted to any party and before the appeal skeleton arguments are due to be filed under the Timetable, the parties must review the case with a view to resolution or refinement of the issues to be determined at the appeal hearing.

(7) **Bundles for the appeal hearing**: Subject to any direction made by the court, the appellant must not less than 42 days before the date for the appeal hearing file and serve a core bundle for the appeal hearing and (if required) a supplementary bundle for the appeal hearing. The appellant must seek to agree the contents of the core bundle and the supplementary bundle for the appeal hearing with all other parties in accordance with sub-paragraphs (8) and (9) below.

(8) **Core bundle for the appeal hearing**

(a) In accordance with the Timetable the appellant must serve on every respondent a proposed bundle index for the core bundle for the appeal hearing.

(b) The respondent must either agree the proposed bundle index for the core bundle or notify the appellant of the documents that the respondent considers should be included in, or removed from, the core bundle by sending a revised index. The appellant and respondent must seek to agree the contents of the core bundle.

(c) The core bundle must be lodged by the appellant in accordance with the Timetable and must contain the final form of the skeleton arguments to be relied upon at the hearing, cross-referenced to the pagination in the bundles for the appeal hearing (i e the replacement skeleton arguments).

(d) The core bundle for the appeal hearing must contain only those documents required in the core bundle for permission to appeal, together with copies of the following documents:

(i) any respondent's notice;
(ii) the appellant's replacement skeleton argument;
(iii) the respondent's replacement skeleton argument;
(iv) a copy of any orders made in the Court of Appeal;
(v) if permission to appeal was granted at an oral hearing, a transcript of the judgment giving permission to appeal.

(9) **Supplementary bundle for the appeal hearing**:

(a) In accordance with the Timetable the appellant must serve on every respondent a proposed bundle index for the supplementary bundle for the appeal hearing.

(b) The respondent must either agree the proposed bundle index for the supplementary bundle or notify the appellant of the documents that the respondent considers should be included in, or removed from, the supplementary bundle by sending a revised index. The appellant and respondent must seek to agree the contents of the supplementary bundle.

(c) The supplementary bundle may only contain documents relevant to the grounds of appeal which it will be necessary for the court to read in preparation for or during the appeal hearing. Where a party is represented, this must be certified by the advocate responsible for arguing the case. The following documents may be considered for inclusion in the supplementary bundle:
   (i) statements of case;
   (ii) application notices;
   (iii) other orders made in the case;
   (iv) witness statements relevant to the issues raised in the grounds of appeal;
   (v) key contemporaneous documents.

(10) **Reviewing the case before the appeal hearing**: After the appeal skeleton arguments are filed and served, and in accordance with the Timetable, the parties must review the case with a view to resolution or refinement of the issues to be determined at the appeal hearing.

(11) **Size of supplementary bundle**: No supplementary bundle (whether for permission to appeal or for an appeal hearing) may exceed one lever arch file of 350 pages in size, unless the court gives permission. An application for permission to file a supplementary bundle of more than 350 pages must be made by application notice in accordance with CPR Part 23 and specify exactly what additional documents the party wishes to include; why it is necessary to put the additional documents before the court; and whether there is agreement between the parties as to their inclusion.

(12) **Unagreed documents bundles for the appeal hearing**: If there is no agreement in relation to inclusion of a particular document in the bundles for the appeal hearing, it must be placed in a separate unagreed documents bundle prepared by the party who has proposed its inclusion, and the bundle clearly labelled as such. The permission of the court is required to rely on an unagreed documents bundle. An application for permission must be made by application notice in accordance with CPR Part 23 and include a short statement of not more than three A4 pages explaining why the unagreed documents are relevant and why it is necessary to put them before the court. Any unagreed documents bundle, including at the front the application notice and supporting statement, must be filed and served not less than 42 days before the date for the appeal hearing. Unless the court directs otherwise, the application will be determined by the court at the appeal hearing.

(13) **Bundle format: Core, supplementary and unagreed documents bundles must** –
   (a) be bound and any ring binder folder must be in fully working order;
   (b) be paginated. Page numbering must not reduce the font size of any document below 12 points.
   (c) contain an index at the front referring to relevant page numbers; and
   (d) except for core bundles, be in chronological order.

(14) **Bundles not to include originals**: Unless otherwise directed by the court, no bundle should contain original material such as original documents, photographs or recorded media. Such material should be provided to the court, if necessary, at the hearing. Any copies of photographs included in the bundles must be of good quality and in colour.

(15) **Destruction of bundles**: Bundles lodged with the court will not be returned to the parties but will be destroyed in the confidential waste system at the conclusion of the proceedings and without further notification.

(16) **Timetable**: The Timetable, Parts 1 and 2, at paragraph 21 above sets out the time limits for filing and serving documents referred to in this section.

Amendments—CPR Update 86.

Appeals from the Upper Tribunal Immigration and Asylum Chamber

28 (1) In an appeal from the Immigration and Asylum Chamber of the Upper Tribunal (other than an appeal relating to a claim for judicial review):

- (a) the Immigration and Asylum Chamber of the Upper Tribunal, upon request, shall send to the Civil Appeals Office copies of the documents which were before the relevant Tribunal when it considered the appeal;
- (b) the appellant is not required to file an appeal bundle;
- (c) the appellant must file with the appellant's notice the documents specified in paragraph 3(3)(a) to (e) and (g) of this Practice Direction.

Amendments—CPR Update 81.

Bundle of authorities

29 (1) After consultation with any opposing advocate, the appellant's advocate must file a bundle containing photocopies of the authorities upon which each party will rely at the hearing.

(2) The most authoritative report of each authority must be used in accordance with mandatory requirements set out in paragraphs 5–13 of the Practice Direction on Citation of Authorities [2012] 1 WLR 780 and must have the relevant passages marked by a vertical line in the margin.

(3) Photocopies of authorities should not be in landscape format and the type should not be reduced in size.

(4) The bundle should not –

- (a) include authorities for propositions not in dispute; or
- (b) contain more than 10 authorities unless the issues in the appeal justify more extensive citation.

(5) A bundle of authorities must bear a certificate by the advocates responsible for arguing the case that the requirements of sub-paragraphs (2) to (4) of this paragraph have been complied with in respect of each authority included.

Amendments—CPR Update 86.

Amendment of appeal notice: rule 52.17

30 (1) An appeal notice may not be amended without the permission of the court.

(2) An application for permission to amend made before permission to appeal has been considered will normally be determined without a hearing.

(3) An application for permission to amend (after permission to appeal has been granted) and any submissions in opposition will normally be dealt with at the hearing unless that would cause unnecessary expense or delay, in which case a request should be made for the application to amend to be heard in advance.

(4) Legal representatives must –

- (a) inform the court at the time they make the application if the existing time estimate is affected by the proposed amendment; and
- (b) attempt to agree any revised time estimate no later than 7 days after service of the application.

Amendments—CPR Update 86.

Skeleton argument

31 (1) Any skeleton argument must comply with the provisions of Section 5 of Practice Direction 52A (and in particular must be concise) and must in any event –

- (a) not normally exceed 25 pages (excluding front sheets and back sheets);
- (b) be printed on A4 paper in not less than 12 point font and 1.5 line spacing (including footnotes);

(c) be labelled as applicable (e g appellant's PTA skeleton, appellant's replacement skeleton, respondent's supplementary skeleton), and be dated on its front sheet.

(2) (a) Any skeleton argument that does not comply with the requirements of paragraph 31.1(a), (b) and (c) –
(i) will be returned to its author by the Civil Appeals Office; and
(ii) may not be re-filed unless and until it complies with those requirements; and
(b) if the skeleton argument is re-filed out of time –
(i) it must be served on all other parties to the appeal; but
(ii) the party re-filing it must make an application under Part 23 to obtain the permission of the court in advance of the hearing in order to rely on it.

(3) Where an appellant has filed a skeleton argument in support of an application for permission to appeal, the same skeleton argument may be relied upon in the appeal or the appellant may file an appeal skeleton argument (Timetable Section 5, Part 1).

(4) At the hearing the court may refuse to hear argument on a point not included in a skeleton argument filed within the prescribed time.

(5) The court may disallow the cost of preparing an appeal skeleton argument which does not comply with these requirements or was not filed within the prescribed time.

Amendments—CPR Update 86.

Supplementary skeleton arguments

32 (1) A party may file a supplementary skeleton argument only where strictly necessary and only with the permission of the court

(2) If a party wishes to rely on a supplementary skeleton argument, it must be lodged and served as soon as practicable. It must be accompanied by a request for permission setting out the reasons why a supplementary skeleton argument is necessary and why it could not reasonably have been lodged earlier.

(3) Only exceptionally will the court allow the use of a supplementary skeleton argument if lodged later than 7 days before the hearing.

Documents to be provided to court reporters at the hearing of an appeal

33 (1) Where a party is legally represented at the hearing of an appeal, the legal representative must bring to the hearing two additional copies of the party's skeleton argument (including any supplementary skeleton argument) for provision to accredited law reporters and accredited media reporters in accordance with the following provisions of this paragraph.

(2) In appeals in family proceedings involving a child, the copies of the skeleton argument must be in anonymised form and must omit any detail that might, if reported, lead to the identification of the child.

(3) The additional copies must be supplied before the commencement of the hearing to the usher or other court official present in court.

(4) The usher or other court official to whom the copies are supplied must provide one copy to an accredited law reporter (upon production of their Royal Courts of Justice security pass) and one copy to an accredited media reporter (upon production of their press pass), if so requested by them. Those copies are to be provided only for the purpose of reporting the court proceedings and on the basis that the recipients may remove them from the court and make further copies of them for distribution to other accredited reporters in court, again only for the purpose of reporting the court proceedings.

(5) Any party may apply orally to the court at the commencement of the hearing for a direction lifting or varying the obligations imposed by sub-paragraphs (3) and (4). Where a party intends to make such an application or is notified by another party of the intention to make one, the operation of those sub-paragraphs is suspended pending the ruling of the court.

(6) In deciding whether to make a direction under sub-paragraph (5), the court must take into account all the circumstances of the case and have regard in particular to –

- (a) the interests of justice;
- (b) the public interest;
- (c) the protection of the interests of any child, vulnerable adult or protected party;
- (d) the protection of the identity of any person intended to be protected by an order or direction relating to anonymity; and
- (e) the nature of any private or confidential information (including information relating to personal financial matters) in the document.

A direction may permit a skeleton argument to be supplied in redacted or anonymised form.

(7) For the purposes of this paragraph, 'the hearing of an appeal' includes a hearing listed as an application for permission to appeal with the appeal to follow immediately if permission is granted.

Amendments—CPR Update 83.

Practice Direction 52D – Statutory Appeals and Appeals Subject to Special Provision

This Practice Direction supplements CPR Part 52

Amendments—CPR Update 59.

Contents of this Practice Direction

This Practice Direction is divided into the following sections:

1 Introduction
2 Routes of appeal
3 General provisions about statutory appeals
4 Specific appeals

SECTION 1: INTRODUCTION

1.1 This Practice Direction applies to all statutory appeals, and to other appeals which are subject to special provision, but not to appeals by way of case stated (to which Practice Direction 52E applies).

SECTION 2: ROUTES OF APPEAL

2.1 In this Practice Direction, the court to which an appeal lies is prescribed by statute.

SECTION 3: GENERAL PROVISIONS ABOUT STATUTORY APPEALS

3.1 This Section contains general provisions about statutory appeals (paragraphs 3.2–3.8). For where this Practice Direction or a statute makes additional special provision see also Section 4.

3.2 Where any of the provisions in this Section provide for documents to be filed at the appeal court, those documents are in addition to any documents required under Part 52 or Practice Direction 52B or 52C.

3.3 Subject to rule 52.9 –

Where the appellant wishes to appeal against a decision of the Upper Tribunal, the appellant's notice must be filed within 28 days of the date on which notice of the Upper Tribunal's decision on permission to appeal to the Court of Appeal is sent to the appellant.

3.3A Where a statement of reasons for a decision is given later than the notice of that decision, the period for filing the appellant's notice is calculated from the date on which the statement is sent to the appellant.

Service of appellant's notice: rule 52.12(3)

3.4 (1) The appellant must serve the appellant's notice on the respondent and on the chairman of the tribunal, Minister of State, government department or other person from whose decision the appeal is brought.

(2) In the case of an appeal from the decision of a tribunal that has no chairman or member who acts as a chairman, the appellant's notice must be served on the member (or members if more than one) of the tribunal.

Variation of time: rule 52.15

3.5 Where any statute prescribes a period within which an appeal must be filed then, unless the statute otherwise provides, the appeal court may not extend that period.

Applications by third parties (rule 52.25)

3.6 Where all the parties consent, the court may deal with an application under rule 52.25 without a hearing.

3.7 An application for permission must be made by letter to the relevant court office, identifying the appeal, explaining who the applicant is and indicating why and in what form the applicant wants to participate in the hearing.

3.8 If the applicant is seeking a prospective order as to costs, the letter must say what kind of order and on what grounds.

Amendments—CPR Updates 66, 75, 86.

SECTION 4: SPECIFIC APPEALS

Provisions about specific appeals

4.1 This Section sets out special provisions about the appeals listed in the Table below. This Section is not exhaustive and does not create, amend or remove any right of appeal.

4.2 Part 52 applies to all appeals to which this Section applies subject to any special provisions set out in this Section.

4.3 Where any of the provisions in this Section provide for documents to be filed at the appeal court, these documents are in addition to any documents required under Part 52 or Practice Direction 52B or 52C.

Certain appeals to the High Court to be heard in Chancery Division

5.1 Any appeal to the High Court, and any case stated or question referred for the opinion of that court under any of the following enactments shall be heard in the Chancery Division –

(1) section 38(3) of the Clergy Pensions Measure 1961;
(2) regulation 74 of the European Public Limited-Liability Company Regulations 2004.
(3) the Industrial and Provident Societies Act 1965;
(4) section 222(3) of the Inheritance Tax Act 1984;
(5) the Land Registration Act 2002;
(6) paragraph 16 of Schedule 15 to the Law of Property Act 1922;
(7) section 215 or 217 of the Pensions Act 2003;
(8) section 151 of the Pension Schemes Act 1993;
(9) section 13 and 13B of the Stamp Act 1891;
(10) regulation 8(3) of the Stamp Duty Reserve Tax Regulations 1986.

Table

Statute (or description of appeal)	Appropriate Court	Relevant paragraph in this Practice Direction
Agricultural Land Tribunal	High Court	18.1
Architects Act 1997, s 22	High Court	19.1
Chiropractors Act 1994, s 31	High Court	19.1
Civil Partnership – conditional order for dissolution or nullity	CA	6.1
Clergy Pensions Measure 1961, s 38(3)	High Court	5.1
Competition: Articles 101 and 102 of the Treaty on the Functioning of the European Union and Chapters I and II of Part I of the Competition Act 1998	CA	7.1
Competition Appeal Tribunal	CA	8.1
Contempt of Court	CA	9.1
Court of Protection	CA	10.1
Decree nisi of divorce or nullity of marriage	CA	6.1
Dentists Act 1984, ss 29 and 44	High Court	19.1
Employment Appeal Tribunal	CA	11.1
European Public Limited-Liability Company Regulations 2004, reg 74	High Court	20.1
Extradition Act 2003	High Court	21.1
Friendly Societies Act 1974	High Court	5.1 and 22.1
Friendly Societies Act 1992	High Court	5.1 and 22.1
Health Professions Order 2001, art 38	High Court	19.1
Housing Act 1996, ss 204 and 204A	County Court	28.1
Immigration and Asylum Act 1999, Part II	County Court	29.1
Immigration and Asylum Appeals	CA	12.1
Inheritance Tax Act 1984, s 222	High Court	5.1 and 23.1
Land Registration Act 2002	High Court	5.1 and 24.1
Law of Property Act 1922, para 16 of Sch 15	High Court	5.1
Local Government (Miscellaneous Provisions) Act 1976	County Court	30.1
Medical Act 1983, s 40	High Court	19.1
Medicines Act 1968, ss 82(3) and 83	High Court	19.1
Merchant Shipping Act 1995	High Court	25.1
Nurses, Midwives and Health Visitors Act 1997, s 12	High Court	19.1
Nursing and Midwifery Order 2001 art 38	High Court	19.1
Opticians Act 1989, s 23	High Court	19.1
Osteopaths Act 1993, s 31	High Court	19.1

Statute (or description of appeal)	Appropriate Court	Relevant paragraph in this Practice Direction
Patents Court: on appeal from Comptroller	CA	13.1
Patents: Revocation of patent	CA	14.1
Pensions Act 2004, ss 215 and 217	High Court	5.1
Pension Schemes Act 1993, s 151	High Court	5.1
Pharmacy Act 1954	High Court	19.1
Pharmacy Order 2010, art 58	High Court	19.1
Planning (Listed Buildings and Conservation Areas) Act 1990, s 65	High Court	26.1
Proscribed Organisations Appeal Commission	CA	15.1
Representation of the People Act 1983, s 56	County Court	31.1-31.3
Serious Crime Prevention Orders	CA	16.1
Solicitors Disciplinary Tribunal	High Court	27.1
Special Immigration Appeals Commission	CA	17.1
Stamp Duty Reserve Tax Regulations 1986, reg 8	High Court	5.1 and 23.1
Town and Country Planning Act 1990, s 289	High Court	26.1
UK Borders Act 2007, s 11	County Court	32.1
Welsh statutory appeals	High Court	27A.1–27A.7

Amendments—CPR Update 83.

Appeals to the Court of Appeal

Appeal against decree nisi of divorce or nullity of marriage or conditional dissolution or nullity order in relation to civil partnership

6.1 (1) The appellant must file the appellant's notice at the Court of Appeal within 28 days after the date on which the decree was pronounced or conditional order made.

(2) The appellant must file the following documents with the appellant's notice –

(a) the decree or conditional order; and
(b) a certificate of service of the appellant's notice.

(3) The appellant's notice must be served on the appropriate District Judge (see subparagraph (6)) in addition to the persons to be served under rule 52.12(3) and in accordance with that rule.

(4) The lower court may not alter the time limits for filing of the appeal notices.

(5) Where an appellant intends to apply to the Court of Appeal for an extension of time for serving or filing the appellant's notice the appellant must give notice of that intention to the appropriate District Judge (see sub-paragraph 6) before the application is made.

(6) In this paragraph 'the appropriate District Judge' means, where the lower court is –

(a) the County Court, the District Judge of the County Court hearing centre in question;
(b) a district registry, the District Judge of that registry;
(c) the Principal Registry of the Family Division, the senior District Judge of that division.

Amendments—CPR Updates 69, 86.

Appeals relating to the application of Articles 101 and 102 of the Treaty on the Functioning of the European Union and Chapters I and II of Part I of the Competition Act 1998

7.1 (1) This paragraph applies to any appeal to the Court of Appeal relating to the application of –

(a) Article 101 or Article 102 of the Treaty on the Functioning of the European Union; or
(b) Chapter I or Chapter II of Part I of the Competition Act 1998.

(2) In this paragraph –

(a) 'the Act' means the Competition Act 1998;
(b) 'the Commission' means the European Commission;
(c) 'the Competition Regulation' means Council Regulation (EC) No 1/2003 of 16 December 2002 on the implementation of the rules on competition laid down in Articles 81 and 82 of the Treaty establishing the European Community (as amended in consequence of the Treaty on the Functioning of the European Union);
(d) 'national competition authority' means –
(i) the Office of Fair Trading; and
(ii) any other person or body designated pursuant to Article 5 of the Competition Regulation as a national competition authority of the United Kingdom;
(e) 'the Treaty' means the Treaty on the Functioning of the European Union.

(3) Any party whose appeal notice raises an issue relating to the application of Article 101 or 102 of the Treaty, or Chapter I or II of Part I of the Act, must –

(a) state that fact in the appeal notice; and
(b) serve a copy of the appeal notice on the Office of Fair Trading at the same time as it is served on the other party to the appeal (addressed to the Director of Competition Policy Co-ordination, Office of Fair Trading, Fleetbank House, 2–6 Salisbury Square, London EC4Y 8JX).

(4) Attention is drawn to the provisions of article 15.3 of the Competition Regulation, which entitles competition authorities and the Commission to submit written observations to national courts on issues relating to the application of Article 101 or 102 and, with the permission of the court in question, to submit oral observations to the court.

(5) A national competition authority may also make written observations to the Court of Appeal, or apply for permission to make oral observations, on issues relating to the application of Chapter I or II.

(6) If a national competition authority or the Commission intends to make written observations to the Court of Appeal, it must give notice of its intention to do so by letter to the Civil Appeals Office at the earliest opportunity.

(7) An application by a national competition authority or the Commission for permission to make oral representations at the hearing of an appeal must be made by letter to the Civil Appeals Office at the earliest opportunity, identifying the appeal and indicating why the applicant wishes to make oral representations.

(8) If a national competition authority or the Commission files a notice under subparagraph (6) or an application under sub-paragraph (7), it must at the same time serve a copy of the notice or application on every party to the appeal.

(9) Any request by a national competition authority or the Commission for the court to send it any documents relating to an appeal should be made at the same time as filing a notice under sub-paragraph (6) or an application under sub-paragraph (7).

(10) When the Court of Appeal receives a notice under sub-paragraph (6) it may give case management directions to the national competition authority or the Commission, including directions about the date by which any written observations are to be filed.

(11) The Court of Appeal will serve on every party to the appeal a copy of any directions given or order made –

(a) on an application under sub-paragraph (7); or

(b) under sub-paragraph (10).

(12) Every party to an appeal which raises an issue relating to the application of Article 101 or 102, and any national competition authority which has been served with a copy of a party's appeal notice, is under a duty to notify the Court of Appeal at any stage of the appeal if they are aware that –

(a) the Commission has adopted, or is contemplating adopting, a decision in relation to proceedings which it has initiated; and
(b) the decision referred to in (a) above has or would have legal effects in relation to the particular agreement, decision or practice in issue before the court.

(13) Where the Court of Appeal is aware that the Commission is contemplating adopting a decision as mentioned in sub-paragraph (12)(a), it shall consider whether to stay the appeal pending the Commission's decision.

(14) Where any judgment is given which decides on the application of Article 101 or 102, the court shall direct that a copy of the transcript of the judgment shall be sent to the Commission. Judgments may be sent to the Commission electronically to compamicus@cec.eu.int or by post to the European Commission – DG Competition, B–1049, Brussels.

Appeal from Competition Appeal Tribunal

8.1 (1) Where the appellant applies for permission to appeal at the hearing at which the decision is delivered by the tribunal and –

(a) permission is given; or
(b) permission is refused and the appellant wishes to make an application to the Court of Appeal for permission to appeal,

the appellant's notice must be filed at the Court of Appeal within 14 days after the date of that hearing.

(2) Where the appellant applies in writing to the Registrar of the tribunal for permission to appeal and –

(a) permission is given; or
(b) permission is refused and the appellant wishes to make an application to the Court of Appeal for permission to appeal,

the appellant's notice must be filed at the Court of Appeal within 14 days after the date of receipt of the tribunal's decision on permission.

(3) Where the appellant does not make an application to the tribunal for permission to appeal, but wishes to make an application to the Court of Appeal for permission, the appellant's notice must be filed at the Court of Appeal within 14 days after the end of the period within which the appellant may make a written application to the Registrar of the tribunal.

Appeals in cases of contempt of court (section 13 Administration of Justice Act 1960)

9.1 In an appeal under section 13 of the Administration of Justice Act 1960 (appeals in cases of contempt of court), the appellant must serve the appellant's notice on the court or the Upper Tribunal from whose order or decision the appeal is brought in addition to the persons to be served under rule 52.12(3) and in accordance with that rule.

Amendments—CPR Update 86.

Appeal from the Court of Protection

10.1 (1) In this paragraph –

(a) 'P' means a person who lacks, or who is alleged to lack, capacity within the meaning of the Mental Capacity Act 2005 to make a decision or decisions in relation to any matter that is subject to an order of the Court of Protection;
(b) 'the person effecting notification' means –

(i) the appellant;
(ii) an agent duly appointed by the appellant; or
(iii) such other person as the Court of Protection may direct, who is required to notify P in accordance with this paragraph; and

(c) 'final order' means a decision of the Court of Appeal that finally determines the appeal proceedings before it.

(2) Where P is not a party to the proceedings, unless the Court of Appeal directs otherwise, the person effecting notification must notify P –

(a) that an appellant's notice has been filed with the Court of Appeal and –
   (i) who the appellant is;
   (ii) what final order the appellant is seeking;
   (iii) what will happen if the Court of Appeal makes the final order sought by the appellant; and
   (iv) that P may apply under rule 52.25 (Statutory appeals: court's power to hear any person) by letter for permission to file evidence or make representations at the appeal hearing;

(b) of the final order, the effect of the final order and what steps P can take in relation to it; and

(c) of such other events and documents as the Court of Appeal may direct. (Paragraphs 3.6 to 3.8 of this Practice Direction 52D contain provisions on how a third party can apply for permission to file evidence or make representations at an appeal hearing.)

(3) The person effecting notification must provide P with the information specified in sub-paragraph (2) –

(a) within 14 days of the date on which the appellant's notice was filed with the Court of Appeal;
(b) within 14 days of the date on which the final order was made; or
(c) within such time as the Court of Appeal may direct, as the case may be.

(4) The person effecting notification must provide P in person with the information specified in sub-paragraph (2) in a way that is appropriate to P's circumstances (for example, using simple language, visual aids or any other appropriate means).

(5) Where P is to be notified as to –

(a) the existence or effect of a document other than the appellant's notice or final order; or
(b) the taking place of an event,

the person effecting notification must explain to P –

   (i) in the case of a document, what the document is and what effect, if any, it has; or
   (ii) in the case of an event, what the event is and its relevance to P.

(6) The person effecting notification must, within 7 days of notifying P, file a certificate of notification (form N165) which certifies –

(a) the date on which P was notified; and
(b) that P was notified in accordance with this paragraph.

(7) Where the person effecting notification has not notified P in accordance with this paragraph, a certificate of non-notification (form N165) must be filed with the Court of Appeal stating the reason why notification has not been effected.

(8) Where the person effecting notification must file a certificate of non-notification with the Court of Appeal, the certificate must be filed within the following time limits –

(a) where P is to be notified in accordance with sub-paragraph (2)(a) (appellant's notice), within 21 days of the appellant's notice being filed with the Court of Appeal;
(b) where P is to be notified in accordance with sub-paragraph (2)(b) (final order), within 21 days of the final order being made by the Court of Appeal; or
(c) where P is to be notified of such other events and documents as may be directed by the Court of Appeal, within such time as the Court of Appeal directs.

(9) The appellant or such other person as the Court of Appeal may direct may apply to the Court of Appeal seeking an order –

(a) dispensing with the requirement to comply with the provisions of this paragraph; or
(b) requiring some other person to comply with the provisions of this paragraph.

(10) An application made under sub-paragraph (9) may be made in the appellant's notice or by Part 23 application notice.

(Paragraphs 6.1 to 6.3 of Practice Direction 52A contain provisions about the dismissal of applications or appeals by consent. Paragraph 6.5 of Practice Direction 52A contains provisions about allowing unopposed appeals or applications involving a child or protected party.)

Amendments—CPR Update 86.

Appeal from Employment Appeal Tribunal

11.1 (1) This paragraph applies to an appeal to the Court of Appeal from the Employment Appeal Tribunal (EAT) under section 37 of the Employment Tribunals Act 1996.

(2) If an application for permission to appeal to the Court of Appeal is refused by the EAT or is not made, then such an application must be made to the Court of Appeal within 21 days of the date of the sealed order of the EAT.

(3) An application for extension of time for filing an appellant's notice may be entertained by the EAT but such applications should normally be made to the Court of Appeal.

Immigration and Asylum Appeals

12.1 The provisions of paragraph 28 of Practice Direction 52C (bundle of documents in immigration appeals and asylum appeals) apply to appeals from the Upper Tribunal Immigration and Asylum Chamber.

Appeal from Patents Court on appeal from Comptroller

13.1 Where the appeal is from a decision of the Patents Court which was itself made on an appeal from a decision of the Comptroller-General of Patents, Designs and Trade Marks, the appellant must serve the appellant's notice on the Comptroller in addition to the persons to be served under rule 52.12(3) and in accordance with that rule.

Amendments—CPR Update 86.

Appeal against order for revocation of patent

14.1 (1) This paragraph applies where an appeal lies to the Court of Appeal from an order for the revocation of a patent.

(2) The appellant must serve the appellant's notice on the Comptroller-General of Patents, Designs and Trade Marks (the 'Comptroller') in addition to the persons to be served under rule 52.12(3) and in accordance with that rule.

(3) Where, before the appeal hearing, the respondent decides not to oppose the appeal or not to attend the appeal hearing, the respondent must immediately serve notice of that decision on –

(a) the Comptroller; and
(b) the appellant.

(4) Where the respondent serves a notice in accordance with sub-paragraph (3), copies of the following documents must also be served on the Comptroller with that notice –

(a) the petition;
(b) any statements of claim;
(c) any written evidence filed in the claim.

(5) Within 14 days after receiving the notice in accordance with sub-paragraph (3), the Comptroller must serve on the appellant a notice stating an intention to attend the appeal hearing or otherwise.

(6) The Comptroller may attend the appeal hearing and oppose the appeal –

(a) in any case where notice has been given under paragraph (5) of the intention to attend; and

(b) in any other case (including, in particular, a case where the respondent withdraws his opposition to the appeal during the hearing) if the Court of Appeal so directs or permits.

Amendments—CPR Update 86.

Appeal from Proscribed Organisations Appeal Commission

15.1 The appellant's notice must be filed at the Court of Appeal within 14 days after the date when the Proscribed Organisations Appeal Commission –

(a) granted; or

(b) where section 6(2)(b) of the Terrorism Act 2000 applies, refused permission to appeal.

Appeals in relation to serious crime prevention orders

16.1 (1) This paragraph applies to an appeal under section 23(1) of the Serious Crime Act 2007 or section 16 of the Senior Courts Act 1981 in relation to a serious crime prevention order and is made.

(2) The appellant must serve the appellant's notice on any person who made representations in the proceedings by virtue of section 9(1), (2) or (3) of the Serious Crime Act 2007 in addition to the persons to be served under rule 52.12(3) and in accordance with that rule.

Amendments—CPR Update 86.

Appeal from Special Immigration Appeals Commission

17.1 (1) An application for permission to appeal to the Court of Appeal must first be made to the Special Immigration Appeals Commission pursuant section 7(2) of the Special Immigration Appeals Commission Act 1997 and paragraph 27 of the SIAC (Procedure) Rules 2003 (as amended).

(2) The appellant's notice must be filed at the Court of Appeal within 21 days of the date on which the Special Immigration Appeals Commission's decision granting or refusing permission to appeal to the Court of Appeal is given.

Appeals to the High Court

Reference of question of law by Agricultural Land Tribunal

18.1 (1) A question of law referred to the High Court by an Agricultural Land Tribunal under section 6 of the Agriculture (Miscellaneous Provisions) Act 1954 shall be referred by way of case stated by the Tribunal.

(2) Where the proceedings before the tribunal arose on an application under section 11 of the Agricultural Holdings Act 1986, an –

(a) application notice for an order under section 6 that the tribunal refers a question of law to the court; and

(b) appellant's notice by which an appellant seeks the court's determination on a question of law,

must be served on the authority having power to enforce the statutory requirement specified in the notice in addition to every other party to those proceedings and on the secretary of the tribunal.

(3) Where, in accordance with sub-paragraph (2), a notice is served on the authority mentioned in that paragraph, that authority may attend the appeal hearing and make representations to the court.

PART III

Appeals against decisions affecting the registration of architects and health care professionals

19.1 (1) This paragraph applies to an appeal to the High Court under –

(a) section 22 of the Architects Act 1997;
(b) section 31 of the Chiropractors Act 1994;
(c) section 29 or section 44 of the Dentists Act 1984;
(d) article 38 of the Health Professions Order 2001;
(e) section 40 of the Medical Act 1983;
(f) section 82(3) and 83(2) of the Medicines Act 1968;
(g) section 12 of the Nurses, Midwives and Health Visitors Act 1997;
(h) article 38 of the Nursing and Midwifery Order 2001;
(i) section 23 of the Opticians Act 1989;
(j) section 31 of the Osteopaths Act 1993;
(k) section 10 of the Pharmacy Act 1954;
(l) article 58 of the Pharmacy Order 2010.

(2) Every appeal to which this paragraph applies must be supported by written evidence and, if the court so orders, oral evidence and will be by way of re-hearing.

(3) The appellant must file the appellant's notice within 28 days after the decision that the appellant wishes to appeal.

(4) In the case of an appeal under an enactment specified in column 1 of the following table, the persons to be made respondents are the persons specified in relation to that enactment in column 2 of the table and the person to be served with the appellant's notice is the Registrar of the relevant Council.

1 Enactment	2 Respondent
Architects Act 1997, s 22	The Architects' Registration Council of the United Kingdom
Chiropractors Act 1994, s 31	The General Chiropractic Council
Dentists Act 1984, ss 29 and 44	The General Dental Council
Health Professions Order 2001, art 38	The Health Professions Council
Medical Act 1983, s 40	The General Medical Council
Medicines Act 1968, ss 82(3) and 83(2)	The Pharmaceutical Society of Great Britain
Nurses, Midwives and Health Visitors Act 1997, s 12; Nursing and Midwifery Order 2001, art 38	The Nursing and Midwifery Council
Opticians Act 1989, s 23	The General Optical Council
Osteopaths Act 1993, s 31	The General Osteopathic Council
Pharmacy Act 1954, s 10	The Royal Pharmaceutical Society of Great Britain
Pharmacy Order 2010, art 58	The General Pharmaceutical Council

Appeals under regulation 74 of the European Public Limited-Liability Company Regulations 2004

20.1 (1) In this paragraph –

(a) 'the 2004 Regulations' means the European Public Limited-Liability Company Regulations 2004;
(b) 'the EC Regulation' means Council Regulation (EC) No 2157/2001 of 8 October 2001 on the Statute for a European company (SE);
(c) 'SE' means a European public limited-liability company (Societas Europaea) within the meaning of Article 1 of the EC Regulation.

(2) This paragraph applies to appeals under regulation 74 of the 2004 Regulations against the opposition –

- (a) of the Secretary of State or national financial supervisory authority to the transfer of the registered office of an SE under Article 8(14) of the EC Regulation; and
- (b) of the Secretary of State to the participation by a company in the formation of an SE by merger under Article 19 of the EC Regulation.

(3) Where an SE seeks to appeal against the opposition of the national financial supervisory authority to the transfer of its registered office under Article 8(14) of the EC Regulation, it must serve the appellant's notice on both the national financial supervisory authority and the Secretary of State.

(4) The appellant's notice must contain an application for permission to appeal.

(5) The appeal will be a review of the decision of the Secretary of State and not a re-hearing. The grounds of review are set out in regulation 74(2) of the 2004 Regulations.

(6) The appeal will be heard by a High Court judge.

****

Appeals affecting industrial and provident societies etc.

22.1 (1) This paragraph applies to all appeals under –

- (a) the Friendly Societies Act 1974;
- (b) the Friendly Societies Act 1992 and;
- (c) the Industrial and Provident Societies Act 1965.

(2) At any stage on an appeal, the court may –

- (a) direct that the appellant's notice be served on any person;
- (b) direct that notice be given by advertisement or otherwise of –
  - (i) the bringing of the appeal;
  - (ii) the nature of the appeal; and
  - (iii) the time when the appeal will or is likely to be heard; or
- (c) give such other directions as it thinks proper to enable any person interested in –
  - (i) the society, trade union, alleged trade union or industrial assurance company; or
  - (ii) the subject matter of the appeal, to appear and be heard at the appeal hearing.

Appeals under section 222 of the Inheritance Tax Act 1984 and regulation 8(3) of the Stamp Duty Reserve Tax Regulations 1986

23.1 (1) This paragraph applies to appeals to the High Court under section 222(3) of the Inheritance Tax Act 1984 (the '1984 Act') and regulation 8(3) of the Stamp Duty Reserve Tax Regulations 1986 (the '1986 Regulations').

(2) The appellant's notice must –

- (a) state the date on which the Commissioners for Her Majesty's Revenue and Customs (the 'Board') gave notice to the appellant under section 221 of the 1984 Act or regulation 6 of the 1986 Regulations of the determination that is the subject of the appeal;
- (b) state the date on which the appellant gave to the Board notice of appeal under section 222(1) of the 1984 Act or regulation 8(1) of the 1986 Regulations and, if notice was not given within the time permitted, whether Her Majesty's Revenue and Customs (HMRC) have given their consent or the tribunal has given permission for notice to be given after the time permitted, and where applicable, the date of such consent or permission; and
- (c) either state that the appellant and the Board have agreed that the appeal may be to the High Court or contain an application for permission to appeal to the High Court.

(3) The appellant must file the following documents with the appellant's notice –

- (a) 2 copies of the notice referred to in sub-paragraph 2(a);

PART III

(b) 2 copies of the notice of appeal (under section 222(1) of the 1984 Act or regulation 8(1) of the 1986 Regulations) referred to in paragraph 2(b); and

(c) where the appellant's notice contains an application for permission to appeal, written evidence setting out the grounds on which it is alleged that the matters to be decided on the appeal are likely to be substantially confined to questions of law.

(4) The appellant must –

(a) file the appellant's notice at the court; and

(b) serve the appellant's notice on the Board, within 30 days of the date on which the appellant gave to the Board notice of appeal under section 222(1) of the 1984 Act or regulation 8(1) of the 1986 Regulations or, if HMRC have given consent or the tribunal has given permission for notice to be given after the time permitted, within 30 days of the date on which such consent or permission was given.

(5) The court will set a date for the hearing of not less than 40 days from the date that the appellant's notice was filed.

(6) Where the appellant's notice contains an application for permission to appeal –

(a) a copy of the written evidence filed in accordance with sub-paragraph (3)(c) must be served on the Board with the appellant's notice; and

(b) the Board –

(i) may file written evidence; and

(ii) if it does so, must serve a copy of that evidence on the appellant, within 30 days after service of the written evidence under subparagraph (6)(a).

(7) The appellant may not rely on any grounds of appeal not specified in the notice referred to in sub-paragraph (2)(b) on the hearing of the appeal without the permission of the court.

Appeal against a decision of the adjudicator under section 111 of the Land Registration Act 2002

24.1 (1) A person who is aggrieved by a decision of the adjudicator and who wishes to appeal that decision must obtain permission to appeal.

(2) The appellant must serve on the adjudicator a copy of the appeal court's decision on a request for permission to appeal as soon as reasonably practicable and in any event within 14 days of receipt by the appellant of the decision on permission.

(3) The appellant must serve on the adjudicator and the Chief Land Registrar a copy of any order by the appeal court to stay a decision of the adjudicator pending the outcome of the appeal as soon as reasonably practicable and in any event within 14 days of receipt by the appellant of the appeal court's order to stay.

(4) The appellant must serve on the adjudicator and the Chief Land Registrar a copy of the appeal court's decision on the appeal as soon as reasonably practicable and in any event within 14 days of receipt by the appellant of the appeal court's decision.

Appeals under the Merchant Shipping Act 1995

25.1 (1) This paragraph applies to appeals under the Merchant Shipping Act 1995 and for this purpose a re-hearing and an application under section 61 of the Merchant Shipping Act 1995 are treated as appeals.

(2) The appellant must file any report to the Secretary of State containing the decision from which the appeal is brought with the appellant's notice.

(3) Where a re-hearing by the High Court is ordered under sections 64 or 269 of the Merchant Shipping Act 1995, the Secretary of State must give reasonable notice to the parties whom he considers to be affected by the re-hearing.

Appeals under s 289(6) of the Town and Country Planning Act 1990 and s 65(5) of the Planning (Listed Buildings and Conservation Areas) Act 1990

26.1 (1) An application for permission to appeal to the High Court under section 289 of the Town and Country Planning Act 1990 ('the TCP Act') or section 65 of the Planning (Listed Buildings and Conservation Areas) Act 1990 ('the PLBCA Act') must be made within 28 days after notice of the decision is given to the applicant.

(2) The application –

- (a) must be in writing and must set out the reasons why permission should be granted; and
- (b) if the time for applying has expired, must include an application to extend the time for applying, and must set out the reasons why the application was not made within that time.

(3) The applicant must, before filing the application, serve a copy of it on the persons referred to in sub-paragraph (12) with the draft appellant's notice and a copy of the witness statement or affidavit to be filed with the application.

(4) The applicant must file the application in the Administrative Court Office with –

- (a) a copy of the decision being appealed;
- (b) a draft appellant's notice;
- (c) a witness statement or affidavit verifying any facts relied on; and
- (d) a witness statement or affidavit giving the name and address of, and the place and date of service on, each person who has been served with the application. If any person who ought to be served has not been served, the witness statement or affidavit must state that fact and the reason why the person was not served.

(5) An application will be heard –

- (a) by a single judge; and
- (b) unless the court otherwise orders, not less than 21 days after it was filed at the Administrative Court Office.

(6) Practice direction 54D applies to applications and appeals under this paragraph.

(7) Any person served with the application is entitled to appear and be heard.

(8) Any respondent who intends to use a witness statement or affidavit at the hearing –

- (a) must file it in the Administrative Court Office; and
- (b) must serve a copy on the applicant as soon as is practicable and in any event, unless the court otherwise allows, at least 2 days before the hearing.

(9) The court may allow the applicant to use a further witness statement or affidavit.

(10) Where on the hearing of an application the court is of the opinion that a person who ought to have been served has not been served, the court may adjourn the hearing, on such terms as it directs, in order that the application may be served on that person.

(11) Where the court grants permission –

- (a) it may impose terms as to costs and as to giving security;
- (b) it may give directions; and
- (c) the relevant appellant's notice must be served and filed within 7 days of the grant.

(12) The persons to be served with the appellant's notice are –

- (a) the Secretary of State;
- (b) the local planning authority who served the notice or gave the decision, as the case may be, or, where the appeal is brought by that authority, the appellant or applicant in the proceedings in which the decision appealed against was given;
- (c) in the case of an appeal brought by virtue of section 289(1) of the TCP Act or section 65(1) of the PLBCA Act, any other person having an interest in the land to which the notice relates; and

(d) in the case of an appeal brought by virtue of section 289(2) of the TCP Act, any other person on whom the notice to which those proceedings related was served.

(13) The appeal will be heard and determined by a single judge unless the court directs that the matter be heard and determined by a Divisional Court.

(14) The court may remit the matter to the Secretary of State to the extent necessary to enable the Secretary of State to provide the court with such further information in connection with the matter as the court may direct.

(15) Where the court is of the opinion that the decision appealed against was erroneous in point of law, it will not set aside or vary that decision but will remit the matter to the Secretary of State for re-hearing and determination in accordance with the opinion of the court.

(16) The court may give directions as to the exercise, until an appeal brought by virtue of section 289(1) of the TCP Act is finally concluded and any re-hearing and determination by the Secretary of State has taken place, of the power to serve, and institute proceedings (including criminal proceedings) concerning –

(a) a stop notice under section 183 of that Act; and
(b) a breach of condition notice under section 187A of that Act.

(17) An appeal brought by virtue of sections 289(1) or (2) of the TCP Act or section 65(1) of the PLBCA Act will be treated as if it is a review under statute for the purposes of rules 45.41 to 45.44 and may therefore be an Aarhus Convention claim for the purposes of those rules.

Amendments—CPR Update 88.

Appeals from decisions of the Law Society or the Solicitors Disciplinary Tribunal to the High Court

27.1 (1) This paragraph applies to appeals from the Law Society or the Solicitors Disciplinary Tribunal ('the Tribunal') to the High Court under the Solicitors Act 1974, Administration of Justice Act 1985, the Courts and Legal Services Act 1990, the European Communities (Lawyer's Practice) Regulations 2000 or the European Communities (Recognition of Professional Qualifications) Regulations 2007.

(2) The appellant must file the appellant's notice in the Administrative Court.

(3) Unless the court otherwise orders the appellant must serve the appellant's notice on –

(a) every party to the proceedings before the Tribunal; and
(b) the Law Society.

Appeals from decisions of the Bar Standards Board or Disciplinary Tribunals to the High Court

27.1A (1) This paragraph applies to appeals to the High Court under section 24 of the Crime and Courts Act 2013 –

(a) from decisions of the Bar Standards Board on review under the Bar Training Rules or under Part 3, Section E of its Handbook, relating to the authorisation of bodies to undertake reserved legal activities (including its approval of specific roles within those bodies); or
(b) from decisions of Disciplinary Tribunals of the Council of the Inns of Court.

(2) The appellant must file the appellant's notice in the Administrative Court.

(3) Unless the court otherwise orders, the appellant must serve the appellant's notice on –

(a) every party to the proceedings before the Bar Standards Board or the Disciplinary Tribunal as appropriate; and
(b) the Council of the Inns of Court in the case of appeals from decisions of the Disciplinary Tribunal.

Amendments—CPR Updates 66, 78.

Appeals to the High Court – Wales only

Welsh statutory appeals

INTRODUCTION

27A.1 (1) This paragraph and paragraphs 27A.2 to 27A.7 apply to certain appeals to the High Court under enactments relating to Wales only ('Welsh statutory appeals').

(2) For these purposes, Welsh statutory appeals are appeals under the following enactments –

(a) section 79 of the Local Government Act 2000;
(b) regulation 24 of the General Teaching Council for Wales (Disciplinary Functions) Regulations 2001; and
(c) section 59 of the Welsh Language (Wales) Measure 2011.

Amendments—CPR Update 83.

SERVICE OF DOCUMENTS IN A WELSH STATUTORY APPEAL TO BE BY PARTIES

27A.2 The Administrative Court will not serve documents in a Welsh statutory appeal, and service must be effected by the parties as provided in the following paragraphs.

Amendments—CPR Update 83.

APPELLANT'S NOTICE IN A WELSH STATUTORY APPEAL

27A.3 (1) The appellant must file the appellant's notice in the Administrative Court Office of the High Court at the District Registry in Cardiff.

(2) If the appellant's notice is filed at an Administrative Court Office other than in Cardiff the proceedings will be transferred to Cardiff.

(3) The appellant must file the appellant's notice –

(a) within the time specified in the relevant statutory provision listed in paragraph 27A.1; or
(b) if the relevant statutory provision specifies no time, within 28 days of the date of the decision the appellant wishes to appeal.

(4) The appellant must file with the appellant's notice –

(a) a statement of facts relied on and grounds for bringing the appeal;
(b) a copy of the decision the appellant wishes to appeal;
(c) any written evidence in support of the appeal.

(5) The appellant must –

(a) within 7 days of the date on which the appeal was filed, serve a sealed copy of the appellant's notice and the documents in sub-paragraph (4) on –
    (i) the authority or tribunal which made the decision the appellant wishes to appeal; and
    (ii) the respondent to the appeal, and
(b) file a certificate of service confirming the date of service under sub-paragraph (a).

Amendments—CPR Update 83.

RESPONDENT'S NOTICE IN A WELSH STATUTORY APPEAL

27A.4 If the respondent intends to contest the appeal the respondent must, within 21 days of service under paragraph 27A.3(5)(a), file –

(a) a respondent's notice;
(b) any written evidence in contesting the appeal.

Amendments—CPR Update 83.

TIME OF PERMISSION HEARING IN A WELSH STATUTORY APPEAL

27A.5 Where the relevant statutory provision requires the appellant to obtain the permission of the Court to appeal, a permission hearing will be listed no earlier than 7 days after the expiry of the time limit in paragraph 27A.4.

Amendments—CPR Update 83.

LISTING OF A WELSH STATUTORY APPEAL

27A.6 Unless the Court orders otherwise, the appeal will not be heard earlier than 28 days after the later of –

(a) the expiry of the time limit in paragraph 27A.4; or
(b) if applicable, the date on which permission to appeal is granted.

Amendments—CPR Update 83.

FURTHER DOCUMENTATION FOR HEARING OF A WELSH STATUTORY APPEAL

27A.7 (1) Sub-paragraphs (2) to (4) apply only where permission to appeal has been granted or where permission is not required.

(2) The appellant must, not less than 21 days before the date of the hearing of the appeal, file –

(a) a paginated and indexed bundle of the appellant's and respondent's notices and the documents filed with them; and
(b) a skeleton argument.

(3) The respondent and any other party wishing to make representations at the hearing of the appeal must file a skeleton argument not less than 14 days before the date of the hearing of the appeal.

(4) The appellant must file a paginated and indexed bundle of all statutory materials and case law relied upon by the appellant and the respondent not less than 7 days before the hearing of the appeal.

Amendments—CPR Update 83.

Appeals to the County Court

Appeals under sections 204 and 204A of the Housing Act 1996

28.1 (1) An appellant should include appeals under section 204 and section 204A of the Housing Act 1996 in one appellant's notice.

(2) If it is not possible to do so (for example because an urgent application under section 204A is required) the appeals may be included in separate appellant's notices.

(3) An appeal under section 204A may include an application for an order under section 204A(4)(a) requiring the authority to secure that accommodation is available for the applicant's occupation.

(4) If, exceptionally, the court makes an order under section 204A(4)(a) without notice, the appellant's notice must be served on the authority together with the order. Such an order will normally require the authority to secure that accommodation is available until a hearing date when the authority can make representations as to whether the order under section 204A(4)(a) should be continued.

(5) Unless the court orders otherwise –

(a) the appellant shall file and serve its proposed case management directions for the appeal together with the appellant's notice;
(b) the respondent shall within 14 days thereafter either agree those directions or file and serve alternative proposed directions;
(c) within 14 days after service of the appellant's notice the respondent must disclose any documents relevant to the decision under appeal, in so far as not previously disclosed;

(d) within 14 days after receipt of any documents disclosed under subparagraph (c) the appellant may make any amendments to its grounds of appeal which arise out of those documents.

Appeal under Part II of the Immigration and Asylum Act 1999 (carriers' liability)

29.1 (1) A person appealing to the County Court under section 35A or section 40B of the Immigration and Asylum Act 1999 ('the Act') against a decision by the Secretary of State to impose a penalty under section 32 or a charge under section 40 of the Act must, subject to sub-paragraph (2), file the appellant's notice within 28 days after receiving the penalty notice or charge notice.

(2) Where the appellant has given notice of objection to the Secretary of State under section 35(4) or section 40A(3) of the Act within the time prescribed for doing so, the appellant must file the appellant's notice within 28 days after receiving notice of the Secretary of State's decision in response to the notice of objection.

(3) Sections 35A and 40B of the Act provide that any appeal under those sections shall be a re-hearing of the Secretary of State's decision to impose a penalty or charge, and therefore rule 52.21(1) does not apply.

Amendments—CPR Updates 69, 86.

Local Government (Miscellaneous Provisions) Act 1976

30.1 Where one of the grounds upon which an appeal against a notice under sections 21, 23 or 35 of the Local Government (Miscellaneous Provisions) Act 1976 is brought is that –

(a) it would have been fairer to serve the notice on another person; or
(b) that it would be reasonable for the whole or part of the expenses to which the appeal relates to be paid by some other person,

that person must be made a respondent to the appeal, unless the court, on application of the appellant made without notice, otherwise directs.

Representation of the People Act 1983, National Assembly for Wales (Representation of the People) Order 2007 and Recall of MPs Act 2015 – appeals against decisions of registration officers

31.1 (1) This paragraph applies in relation to an appeal against a decision of a registration officer, being a decision referred to in –

(a) section 56(1) of the Representation of the People Act 1983 ('the Act');
(b) article 5(1) of the National Assembly for Wales (Representation of the People) Order 2007 ('the 2007 Order'); or
(c) regulation 74(1) of the Recall of MPs Act 2015 (Recall Petition) Regulations 2016 ('the 2016 Regulations').

(2) Where a person ('the appellant') has given notice of such an appeal in accordance with the relevant requirements of –

(a) section 56, and the regulations made under section 53 ('the 2001 Regulations') of the Act;
(b) article 5 of, and paragraph 9 of Schedule 1 to, the 2007 Order; or
(c) regulations 74 and 77 of the 2016 Regulations,

the registration officer must, within 7 days after receiving the notice, forward by post to the County Court –

(i) the notice; and
(ii) the statement required by the 2001 Regulations, by paragraph 9 of Schedule 1 to the 2007 Order or by regulation 77 of the 2016 Regulations as the case may be.

(3) The respondents to the appeal will be –

(a) the registration officer; and

(b) if the decision of the registration officer was given in favour of any other person than the appellant, that other person.

(4) On the hearing of the appeal –

(a) the statement forwarded to the court by the registration officer, and any document containing information submitted to the court by the registration officer pursuant to the Regulations, are admissible as evidence of the facts stated in them; and
(b) the court –
(i) may draw any inference of fact that the registration officer might have drawn; and
(ii) may give any decision and make any order that the registration officer ought to have given or made.

(5) A respondent to an appeal (other than the registration officer) is not liable for nor entitled to costs, unless he appears before the court in support of the registration officer's decision.

(6) Rule 52.12(3) (appellant's notice) does not apply to an appeal to which this paragraph applies.

Amendments—CPR Updates 69, 83, 86.

Representation of the People Act 1983 – special provision in relation to anonymous entries in the register

31.2 (1) In this paragraph –

(a) 'anonymous entry' has the meaning given by section 9B(4) of the Representation of the People Act 1983;
(b) 'appeal notice' means the notice required by regulation 32 of the Representation of the People (England and Wales) Regulations 2001.

(2) This paragraph applies to an appeal to the County Court to which paragraph 31.1 (Representation of the People Act 1983 – appeals against decisions of registration officers) applies if a party to the appeal is a person –

(a) whose entry in the register is an anonymous entry; or
(b) who has applied for such an entry.

(3) This paragraph also applies to an appeal to the Court of Appeal from a decision of the County Court in an appeal to which paragraph 31.1 applies.

(4) The appellant may indicate in the appeal notice that an application for an anonymous entry has been applied for, or that the entry in the register is an anonymous entry.

(5) The respondent or any other person who applies to become a party to the proceedings may indicate in a respondent's notice or an application to join the proceedings that the entry in the register is an anonymous entry, or that an application has been made for an anonymous entry.

(6) Where the appellant gives such an indication in the appeal notice, the court will refer the matter to a District Judge for directions about the further conduct of the proceedings, and, in particular, directions about how the matter should be listed in the court list.

(7) Where the court otherwise becomes aware that a party to the appeal is a person referred to in sub-paragraph (2), the court will give notice to the parties that no further step is to be taken until the court has given any necessary directions for the further conduct of the matter.

Representation of the People Act 1983, National Assembly for Wales (Representation of the People) Order 2007 and Recall of MPs Act 2015 – appeals selected as test cases

31.3 (1) Where two or more appeals under –

(a) section 56, and the 2001 Regulations;
(b) article 5 of, and paragraph 9 of Schedule 1 to, the 2007 Order; or
(c) regulations 74 and 77 of the 2016 Regulations,

involve the same point of law, the court may direct that one appeal ('the test-case appeal') is to be heard first as a test case.

(2) The court will send a notice of the direction to each party to all of those appeals.

(3) Where a notice under sub-paragraph (2) is served on any party to an appeal (other than the test-case appeal), that party may (within 7 days after the notice is served on that party) give notice to the court requesting the appeal to be heard and –

- (a) the court will hear that appeal after the test-case appeal is disposed of;
- (b) the court will give the parties to that appeal notice of the day on which it will be heard; and
- (c) the party who gave the notice is not entitled to receive any costs of the separate hearing of that appeal unless the judge otherwise orders.

(4) Where no notice is given under sub-paragraph (3) within the period limited by that paragraph –

- (a) the decision on the test-case appeal binds the parties to each of the other appeals;
- (b) without further hearing, the court will make, in each other appeal, an order similar to the order in the test-case appeal; and
- (c) the party to each other appeal who is in the same interest as the unsuccessful party to the selected appeal is liable for the costs of the test-case appeal in the same manner and to the same extent as the unsuccessful party to that appeal and an order directing the party to pay such costs may be made and enforced accordingly.

(5) Sub-paragraph (4)(a) does not affect the right to appeal to the Court of Appeal of any party to an appeal other than the test-case appeal.

Amendments—CPR Updates 69, 83.

Appeals under section 11 of the UK Borders Act 2007

32.1 (1) A person appealing to the County Court under section 11 of the UK Borders Act 2007 ('the Act') against a decision by the Secretary of State to impose a penalty under section 9(1) of the Act, must, subject to sub-paragraph (2), file the appellant's notice within 28 days after receiving the penalty notice.

(2) Where the appellant has given notice of objection to the Secretary of State under section 10 of the Act within the time prescribed for doing so, the appellant's notice must be filed within 28 days after receiving notice of the Secretary of State's decision in response to the notice of objection.

Amendments—CPR Update 69.

Practice Direction 52E – Appeals by way of Case Stated

This Practice Direction supplements CPR Part 52

Amendments—CPR Update 59.

Note—CPR PD52E is set out in full in *Civil Court Service* (LexisNexis).

****

PART 54
JUDICIAL REVIEW AND STATUTORY REVIEW

CONTENTS OF THIS PART

Section I

Rule		Page
	Judicial Review	
54.1	Scope and interpretation	2252
54.1A	Who may exercise the powers of the High Court	2253
54.2	When this Section must be used	2253

54.3	When this Section may be used	2253
54.4	Permission required	2254
54.5	Time limit for filing claim form	2255
54.6	Claim form	2255
54.7	Service of claim form	2256
54.7A	Judicial review of decisions of the Upper Tribunal	2256
54.8	Acknowledgment of service	2257
54.9	Failure to file acknowledgment of service	2257
54.10	Permission given	2258
54.11	Service of order giving or refusing permission	2258
54.11A	Permission decision where court requires a hearing	2258
54.12	Permission decision without a hearing	2259
54.13	Defendant etc may not apply to set aside(GL)	2259
54.14	Response	2259
54.15	Where claimant seeks to rely on additional grounds	2259
54.16	Evidence	2259
54.17	Court's powers to hear any person	2260
54.18	Judicial review may be decided without a hearing	2260
54.19	Court's powers in respect of quashing orders	2260
54.20	Transfer	2261
	Practice Direction 54A – Judicial Review	2261
	Practice Direction 54C – References by the Legal Services Commission	2266
	Practice Direction 54D – Administrative Court (Venue)	2266

Section I
Judicial Review

54.1 Scope and interpretation

(1) This Section of this Part contains rules about judicial review.

(2) In this Section –

(a) a 'claim for judicial review' means a claim to review the lawfulness of –

(i) an enactment; or

(ii) a decision, action or failure to act in relation to the exercise of a public function.

(b)–(d) (*revoked*)

(e) 'the judicial review procedure' means the Part 8 procedure as modified by this Section;

(f) 'interested party' means any person (other than the claimant and defendant) who is directly affected by the claim; and

(g) 'court' means the High Court, unless otherwise stated.

(Rule 8.1(6)(b) provides that a rule or practice direction may, in relation to a specified type of proceedings, disapply or modify any of the rules set out in Part 8 as they apply to those proceedings)

Amendments—Inserted by SI 2000/2092. Amended by SI 2003/364; SI 2003/3361.

Scope—This rule provides the procedure for an application to the Administrative Court for judicial review. A claim for judicial review means a claim to review the lawfulness of an enactment or a decision, action or failure to act in relation to the exercise of a public function. The procedure must be used where the claimant is seeking a mandatory order (formerly known as an order of mandamus), a prohibiting order (formerly known as an order of prohibition) and a quashing order (formerly known as an order of certiorari) (see r 52.2). The procedure may also be used to obtain a declaration, injunction, order for damages, restitution or the recovery of a sum due (see r 52.3 and SCA 1981, s 31). Note the provisions of the CPR Pre-action Protocol for Judicial Review.

The Administrative Court—All applications for judicial review in England must be made to the Administrative Court, either at The Royal Courts of Justice, The Strand, London WC2A 2LL or at one of the regional centres: Cardiff Civil Justice Centre, 2 Park Street, Cardiff CF10 1ET; Birmingham Civil Justice Centre Priory Courts,

5th Floor, 33 Bull Street, Birmingham B4 6DS; Leeds Combined Court, 1 Oxford Row, Leeds, West Yorkshire LS1 3BG; or Manchester Civil Justice Centre, 12th Floor, 1 Bridge Street West, Manchester M3 3FX. Where a judicial review application is proceeding in Wales (because there is a devolution issue arising out of the Government of Wales Act 1998 or an issue concerning the National Assembly of Wales, the Welsh executive, or any Welsh public body) an application may be lodged at the Royal Courts of Justice in London or at the Cardiff Civil Justice Centre (see also PD54A, para 3.1).

54.1A Who may exercise the powers of the High Court

(1) A court officer assigned to the Administrative Court office who is –

(a) a barrister; or
(b) a solicitor,

may exercise the jurisdiction of the High Court with regard to the matters set out in paragraph (2) with the consent of the President of the Queen's Bench Division.

(2) The matters referred to in paragraph (1) are –

(a) any matter incidental to any proceedings in the High Court;
(b) any other matter where there is no substantial dispute between the parties; and
(c) the dismissal of an appeal or application where a party has failed to comply with any order, rule or practice direction.

(3) A court officer may not decide an application for –

(a) permission to bring judicial review proceedings;
(b) an injunction;
(c) a stay of any proceedings, other than a temporary stay of any order or decision of the lower court over a period when the High Court is not sitting or cannot conveniently be convened, unless the parties seek a stay by consent.

(4) Decisions of a court officer may be made without a hearing.

(5) A party may request any decision of a court officer to be reviewed by a judge of the High Court.

(6) At the request of a party, a hearing will be held to reconsider a decision of a court officer, made without a hearing.

(7) A request under paragraph (5) or (6) must be filed within 7 days after the party is served with notice of the decision.

Amendments—Inserted by SI 2012/2208.

54.2 When this Section must be used

The judicial review procedure must be used in a claim for judicial review where the claimant is seeking –

(a) a mandatory order;
(b) a prohibiting order;
(c) a quashing order; or
(d) an injunction under section 30 of the Senior Courts Act 1981 (restraining a person from acting in any office in which he is not entitled to act).

Amendments—Inserted by SI 2000/2092. Amended by SI 2003/364; CRA 2005, Sch 11, para 1(2).

Scope—Pt 54 provides the only method of seeking the orders set out (see also SCA 1981, ss 29–31; CCA 1984, s 38).

54.3 When this Section may be used

(1) The judicial review procedure may be used in a claim for judicial review where the claimant is seeking –

(a) a declaration; or
(b) an injunction(GL).

(Section 31(2) of the Senior Courts Act 1981 sets out the circumstances in which the court may grant a declaration or injunction in a claim for judicial review)

(Where the claimant is seeking a declaration or injunction in addition to one of the remedies listed in rule 54.2, the judicial review procedure must be used)

(2) A claim for judicial review may include a claim for damages, restitution or the recovery of a sum due but may not seek such a remedy alone.

(Section 31(4) of the Senior Courts Act sets out the circumstances in which the court may award damages, restitution or the recovery of a sum due on a claim for judicial review)

Amendments—Inserted by SI 2000/2092. Amended by SI 2003/364; SI 2003/3361; CRA 2005, Sch 11, para 1(2).

Scope—Pt 54 provides the method of seeking the orders set out (see also SCA 1981, ss 29–31). A declaration or injunction may also be obtained in other proceedings (under the inherent jurisdiction of the High Court; see SCA 1981, s 37 and CCA 1984, s 38 for injunctions). Guidance is given by the Court of Appeal on the approach to damages in judicial review cases where a breach of human rights is alleged: see *Anufrijeva v Southwark LBC* [2004] 1 FLR 8, CA; *Re C (Breach of Human Rights: Damages)* [2007] 1 FLR 1957, CA.

Appeals—Although the Court of Appeal had no original jurisdiction in judicial review cases, it had jurisdiction to consider a new decision within an appeal against an old decision by virtue of SCA 1981, s 9 and of the right to admit fresh evidence as part of an appeal. There could be no latitude on appeal to taking such a pragmatic approach to consider the new decision if that would cause prejudice to either party or because the court would be deprived of any other material required for its decision: *R (O) v London Borough of Hammersmith and Fulham* [2012] 2 FLR 290, CA.

Family proceedings—The normal rule is that claims for alleged breaches of Convention rights should be raised in the family proceedings rather than in separate proceedings for judicial review: *Re V (Care Proceedings: Human Rights Claims)* [2004] 1 FLR 944, CA. Where, however, care proceedings are afoot and a party alleges a breach of his Art 6 and/or Art 8 Convention rights by a local authority, it may be appropriate to institute separate proceedings for judicial review but only where that party has no alternative remedy other than judicial review proceedings to challenge the decision in issue: *R (H) v Kingston upon Hull City Council*, [2014] 1 FLR 1094, QBD.

54.4 Permission required

The court's permission to proceed is required in a claim for judicial review whether started under this Section or transferred to the Administrative Court.

Amendments—Inserted by SI 2000/2092. Amended by SI 2003/364.

Scope—There is a filter process for all applications for judicial review. Permission to apply must be obtained: the application fee is £140: CPFO 2008, fee 1.9(a). This is usually considered, in the first instance without a hearing (see PD54A, para 8.4). The decision of the judge (Form JRJ) will be served upon the claimant, the defendant and any other person named on the claim form. If permission is granted without a hearing the claimant must lodge the fee of £700 with the Administrative Office within 7 days of service of the judge's decision upon him: CPFO 2008, fee 1.9(b). If permission is refused or granted subject to conditions or on certain grounds, the claimant may request an oral hearing. Such a request must be filed within 7 days after service of the notification of the decision (see r 54.12 and PD54A, para 8.5). At the oral hearing the claimant is allocated 30 minutes of court time. If this is considered insufficient, the claimant must file a written estimate and request a special fixture. On an application to request the court to reconsider a decision on permission at a hearing, a fee of £350 is payable. If permission is then granted, the fee payable is £350: CPFO 2008, fee 1.9(b),(c). It is not necessary for the defendant or any interested party to attend, but they may do so (see PD54A, para 8.5). An appeal may be made to the Court of Appeal in respect of the judge's decision, following an oral hearing (see r 52.15).

Documents—The claimant must file a claim form in accordance with CPR 1998, Pt 8 as modified by this rule. The standard form N461 should be used, which may be obtained from the Administrative Office or on the Court Service website (*http://hmctsformfinder.justice.gov.uk/HMCTS/FormFinder.do*). The following documents must be filed with the claim form (PD54A, para 5.6). The claimant must lodge two copies of a paginated and indexed bundle containing the claim form, which must include or be accompanied by:

(1) a detailed statement of the claimant's grounds for bringing the claim for judicial review;
(2) a statement of the facts relied on;
(3) any application to extend the time limit for filing the claim form;
(4) any application for directions; and
(5) a time estimate for the hearing.

In addition, the claim form must be accompanied by:

(i) any written evidence in support of the claim or application to extend time;
(ii) a copy of any order that the claimant seeks to have quashed;
(iii) where the claim for judicial review relates to a decision of a court or tribunal, an approved copy of the reasons for reaching that decision;
(iv) copies of any documents on which the claimant proposes to rely;
(v) copies of any relevant statutory material;
(vi) a list of essential documents for advance reading by the court (with page references to the passages relied on).

Where it is not possible to file all the above documents, the claimant must indicate which documents have not been filed and the reasons why they are not currently available (see PD54A, para 5.6).

Human rights issues—Where the claimant is seeking to raise any human rights issue the claim form must include the information specified in PD16, para 15.1, namely:

(a) give details of the alleged convention right infringed;
(b) specify the relief sought;
(c) state if the relief sought includes a declaration of incompatibility or damages in respect of a judicial act;
(d) where there is a claim for a declaration of incompatibility, give details of the legislative provision;
(e) where the claim relates to unlawfulness by another court or tribunal, give details of the finding;
(f) where the claim relates to a judicial act, provide details of the act complained of and the court or tribunal concerned.

54.5 Time limit for filing claim form

(A1) In this rule –

'the planning acts' has the same meaning as in section 336 of the Town and Country Planning Act 1990;

'decision governed by the Public Contracts Regulations 2015' means any decision the legality of which is or may be affected by a duty owed to an economic operator by virtue of regulations 89 or 90 of those Regulations (and for this purpose it does not matter that the claimant is not an economic operator); and

'economic operator' has the same meaning as in regulation 2(1) of the Public Contracts Regulations 2015.

(1) The claim form must be filed –

(a) promptly; and
(b) in any event not later than 3 months after the grounds to make the claim first arose.

(2) The time limit in this rule may not be extended by agreement between the parties.

(3) This rule does not apply when any other enactment specifies a shorter time limit for making the claim for judicial review.

(4) Paragraph (1) does not apply in the cases specified in paragraphs (5) and (6).

(5) Where the application for judicial review relates to a decision made by the Secretary of State or local planning authority under the planning acts, the claim form must be filed not later than six weeks after the grounds to make the claim first arose.

(6) Where the application for judicial review relates to a decision governed by the Public Contracts Regulations 2015, the claim form must be filed within the time within which an economic operator would have been required by regulation 92(2) of those Regulations (and disregarding the rest of that regulation) to start any proceedings under those Regulations in respect of that decision.

Amendments—Inserted by SI 2000/2092. Amended by SI 2013/1412, subject to savings; SI 2015/102; SI 2016/788.

54.6 Claim form

(1) In addition to the matters set out in rule 8.2 (contents of the claim form) the claimant must also state –

(a) the name and address of any person he considers to be an interested party;
(b) that he is requesting permission to proceed with a claim for judicial review;
(c) any remedy (including any interim remedy) he is claiming; and
(d) where appropriate, the grounds on which it is contended that the claim is an Aarhus Convention claim.

(Rules 45.41 to 45.44 make provision about costs in Aarhus Convention claims)

(Part 25 sets out how to apply for an interim remedy)

(2) The claim form must be accompanied by the documents required by Practice Direction 54A.

Amendments—Inserted by SI 2000/2092. Amended by SI 2009/3390; SI 2013/262.

Scope—See notes to r 54.4 (above).

PART III

54.7 Service of claim form

The claim form must be served on –

(a) the defendant; and
(b) unless the court otherwise directs, any person the claimant considers to be an interested party,

within 7 days after the date of issue.

Amendments—Inserted by SI 2000/2092.

Scope—Within 7 days of the date of issue, the claimant must serve the defendant and any interested party with the claim form and accompanying documents. Once service has been effected, the claimant must lodge a certificate of service in the Administrative Court Office within 7 days of service. The Administrative Court will not effect service save as required by rr 54.11 and 54.12(2) (see PD54A, para 6.1). Thus the court will serve the order giving or refusing permission and any directions given on the claimant, the defendant and on any other person who has filed an acknowledgement of service.

54.7A Judicial review of decisions of the Upper Tribunal

(1) This rule applies where an application is made, following refusal by the Upper Tribunal of permission to appeal against a decision of the First Tier Tribunal, for judicial review –

(a) of the decision of the Upper Tribunal refusing permission to appeal; or
(b) which relates to the decision of the First Tier Tribunal which was the subject of the application for permission to appeal.

(2) Where this rule applies –

(a) the application may not include any other claim, whether against the Upper Tribunal or not; and
(b) any such other claim must be the subject of a separate application.

(3) The claim form and the supporting documents required by paragraph (4) must be filed no later than 16 days after the date on which notice of the Upper Tribunal's decision was sent to the applicant.

(4) The supporting documents are –

(a) the decision of the Upper Tribunal to which the application relates, and any document giving reasons for the decision;
(b) the grounds of appeal to the Upper Tribunal and any documents which were sent with them;
(c) the decision of the First Tier Tribunal, the application to that Tribunal for permission to appeal and its reasons for refusing permission; and
(d) any other documents essential to the claim.

(5) The claim form and supporting documents must be served on the Upper Tribunal and any other interested party no later than 7 days after the date of issue.

(6) The Upper Tribunal and any person served with the claim form who wishes to take part in the proceedings for judicial review must, no later than 21 days after service of the claim form, file and serve on the applicant and any other party an acknowledgment of service in the relevant practice form.

(7) The court will give permission to proceed only if it considers –

(a) that there is an arguable case, which has a reasonable prospect of success, that both the decision of the Upper Tribunal refusing permission to appeal and the decision of the First Tier Tribunal against which permission to appeal was sought are wrong in law; and
(b) that either –
   (i) the claim raises an important point of principle or practice; or
   (ii) there is some other compelling reason to hear it.

(8) If the application for permission is refused on paper without an oral hearing, rule 54.12(3) (request for reconsideration at a hearing) does not apply.

(9) If permission to apply for judicial review is granted –

(a) if the Upper Tribunal or any interested party wishes there to be a hearing of the substantive application, it must make its request for such a hearing no later than 14 days after service of the order granting permission; and

(b) if no request for a hearing is made within that period, the court will make a final order quashing the refusal of permission without a further hearing.

(10) The power to make a final order under paragraph (9)(b) may be exercised by the Master of the Crown Office or a Master of the Administrative Court.

Amendments—Inserted by SI 2012/2208.

Note—Rule 54.7A gives effect to the decision of the Supreme Court in *Cart v The Upper Tribunal* [2012] 1 FLR 997, SC.

54.8 Acknowledgment of service

(1) Any person served with the claim form who wishes to take part in the judicial review must file an acknowledgment of service in the relevant practice form in accordance with the following provisions of this rule.

(2) Any acknowledgment of service must be –

(a) filed not more than 21 days after service of the claim form; and

(b) served on –

(i) the claimant; and

(ii) subject to any direction under rule 54.7(b), any other person named in the claim form,

as soon as practicable and, in any event, not later than 7 days after it is filed.

(3) The time limits under this rule may not be extended by agreement between the parties.

(4) The acknowledgment of service –

(a) must –

(i) where the person filing it intends to contest the claim, set out a summary of his grounds for doing so; and

(ia) where the person filing it intends to contest the application for permission on the basis that it is highly likely that the outcome for the claimant would not have been substantially different if the conduct complained of had not occurred, set out a summary of the grounds for doing so; and

(ii) state the name and address of any person the person filing it considers to be an interested party; and

(b) may include or be accompanied by an application for directions.

(5) Rule 10.3(2) does not apply.

(Section 31(3C) of the Senior Courts Act 1981 requires the court, where it is asked to do so by the defendant, to consider whether the outcome for the claimant would have been substantially different if the conduct complained of had not occurred.)

Amendments—Inserted by SI 2000/2092. Amended by SI 2015/670.

Scope—Any person served with a claim form who wishes to take part in the proceedings must file in the Administrative Court Office an acknowledgment of service on Form N462 (available from the Office or the Court Service website on *http://hmctsformfinder.justice.gov.uk/HMCTS/FormFinder.do* within 21 days of service. The acknowledgment of service must state whether the defendant intends to contest the claim and whether he seeks a different remedy (CPR 1998, r 8.3(2)). The acknowledgment must be served upon the claimant within 7 days of it being filed. The acknowledgment of service may only be amended or withdrawn with permission of the court (see PD10, para 5.4).

54.9 Failure to file acknowledgment of service

(1) Where a person served with the claim form has failed to file an acknowledgment of service in accordance with rule 54.8, he –

(a) may not take part in a hearing to decide whether permission should be given unless the court allows him to do so; but

(b) provided he complies with rule 54.14 or any other direction of the court regarding the filing and service of –

(i) detailed grounds for contesting the claim or supporting it on additional grounds; and

(ii) any written evidence,

may take part in the hearing of the judicial review.

(2) Where that person takes part in the hearing of the judicial review, the court may take his failure to file an acknowledgment of service into account when deciding what order to make about costs.

(3) Rule 8.4 does not apply.

Amendments—Inserted by SI 2000/2092.

54.10 Permission given

(1) Where permission to proceed is given the court may also give directions.

(2) Directions under paragraph (1) may include –

(a) a stay(GL) of proceedings to which the claim relates;

(b) directions requiring the proceedings to be heard by a Divisional Court.

(Rule 3.7 provides a sanction for the non-payment of the fee payable when permission to proceed has been given)

Amendments—Inserted by SI 2000/2092. Amended by SI 2010/2577.

Scope—Upon the granting of permission to proceed, directions may be made about serving the claim form/evidence on any other person and the need for expedition.

Human Rights issues—Where a claim relates to a human rights issue, a direction may be made for giving notice to the Crown or joining it as a party to the proceedings. By virtue of CPR 1998, r 19.4A the court is not entitled to make a declaration of incompatibility in accordance with HRA 1998, s 4 unless 21 days' notice (or such other period as the court may direct) has been given to the Crown. Where notice has been given to the Crown, a Minister or other person permitted by the Act must be joined as a party. There is a similar provision where the claim under HRA 1998, s 9 seeks damages and notice must be given to the Crown. The notice given under r 19.4A must be served on the person named in the list published under Crown Proceedings Act 1947, s 17. The list is annexed to PD66 (see PD19A, para 6.4(1)).

54.11 Service of order giving or refusing permission

The court will serve –

(a) the order giving or refusing permission; and

(ai) any certificate (if not included in the order) that permission has been granted for reasons of exceptional public interest in accordance with section 31(3F) of the Senior Courts Act 1981; and

(b) any directions,

on –

(i) the claimant;

(ii) the defendant; and

(iii) any other person who filed an acknowledgment of service.

Amendments—Inserted by SI 2000/2092. Amended by SI 2015/670.

54.11A Permission decision where court requires a hearing

(1) This rule applies where the court wishes to hear submissions on –

(a) whether it is highly likely that the outcome for the claimant would not have been substantially different if the conduct complained of had not occurred; and if so

(b) whether there are reasons of exceptional public interest which make it nevertheless appropriate to give permission.

(2) The court may direct a hearing to determine whether to give permission.

(3) The claimant, defendant and any other person who has filed an acknowledgment of service must be given at least 2 days' notice of the hearing date.

(4) The court may give directions requiring the proceedings to be heard by a Divisional Court.

(5) The court must give its reasons for giving or refusing permission.

Amendments—Inserted by SI 2015/670.

54.12 Permission decision without a hearing

(1) This rule applies where the court, without a hearing –

(a) refuses permission to proceed; or
(b) gives permission to proceed –
 (i) subject to conditions; or
 (ii) on certain grounds only.

(2) The court will serve its reasons for making the decision when it serves the order giving or refusing permission in accordance with rule 54.11.

(3) Subject to paragraph (7), the claimant may not appeal but may request the decision to be reconsidered at a hearing.

(4) A request under paragraph (3) must be filed within 7 days after service of the reasons under paragraph (2).

(5) The claimant, defendant and any other person who has filed an acknowledgment of service will be given at least 2 days' notice of the hearing date.

(6) The court may give directions requiring the proceedings to be heard by a Divisional Court.

(7) Where the court refuses permission to proceed and records the fact that the application is totally without merit in accordance with rule 23.12, the claimant may not request that decision to be reconsidered at a hearing.

Amendments—Inserted by SI 2000/2092. Amended by SI 2010/2577; SI 2013/1412, subject to savings.

Scope—The court will generally, in the first instance, consider the question of permission without a hearing (PD54A, para 8.4). Where permission has been refused or granted with conditions or on a limited basis, the claimant may seek an oral hearing for reconsideration of the decision (see notes to r 54.4).

54.13 Defendant etc may not apply to set aside[(GL)]

Neither the defendant nor any other person served with the claim form may apply to set aside[(GL)] an order giving permission to proceed.

Amendments—Inserted by SI 2000/2092.

54.14 Response

(1) A defendant and any other person served with the claim form who wishes to contest the claim or support it on additional grounds must file and serve –

(a) detailed grounds for contesting the claim or supporting it on additional grounds; and
(b) any written evidence,

within 35 days after service of the order giving permission.

(2) The following rules do not apply –

(a) rule 8.5(3) and 8.5(4) (defendant to file and serve written evidence at the same time as acknowledgment of service); and
(b) rule 8.5(5) and 8.5(6) (claimant to file and serve any reply within 14 days).

Amendments—Inserted by SI 2000/2092.

Scope—A party who has been served with a claim form may contest the claim. To do so they must, within 35 days of service of the order granting permission, file and serve their grounds and written evidence in a paginated bundle (PD54A, para 10.1).

54.15 Where claimant seeks to rely on additional grounds

The court's permission is required if a claimant seeks to rely on grounds other than those for which he has been given permission to proceed.

Amendments—Inserted by SI 2000/2092.

54.16 Evidence

(1) Rule 8.6(1) does not apply.

PART III

(2) No written evidence may be relied on unless –

(a) it has been served in accordance with any –

(i) rule under this Section; or

(ii) direction of the court; or

(b) the court gives permission.

Amendments—Inserted by SI 2000/2092. Amended by SI 2002/2058; SI 2003/364.

Scope—The provisions for filing evidence in judicial review proceedings are contained within this rule. However, the Pt 8 procedure applies save where expressly disapplied, namely r 8.5(3)–(6) (defendant to file and serve evidence at same time as acknowledgement of service and claimant to file and serve a reply within 14 days) and r 8.6(1) (prohibition on the reliance on evidence unless served in accordance with r 8.5 or with permission of the court): rr 54.14(2) and 54.16(1). When the claim form is lodged, it should be accompanied by written evidence (see notes to r 54.4). If the claimant seeks to rely on further evidence permission must be obtained to do so.

Skeleton arguments—The claimant must file and serve a skeleton argument not less than 21 days before the hearing (or the warned date) (PD54A, para 15.1; for documents to be filed see notes to r 54.4). The skeleton argument must contain:

(1) a time estimate for the complete hearing, including delivery of judgment;
(2) a list of issues;
(3) a list of the legal points to be taken (together with any relevant authorities with page references to the passages relied on);
(4) a chronology of events, with page references to the bundle of documents (see para 16.1);
(5) a list of essential documents for the advance reading of the court, with page references to the passages relied on (if different from that filed with the claim form) and a time estimate for that reading; and
(6) a list of persons referred to.

Any defendant or interested party must file a skeleton argument not less than 14 days before the hearing.

Documents—The claimant must file a paginated and indexed bundle of all relevant documents required for the hearing of the judicial review when he files his skeleton argument. The bundle must also include those documents required by the defendant and any other party who is to make representations at the hearing (PD54A, para 16).

54.17 Court's powers to hear any person

(1) Any person may apply for permission –

(a) to file evidence; or

(b) make representations at the hearing of the judicial review.

(2) An application under paragraph (1) should be made promptly.

Amendments—Inserted by SI 2000/2092.

Scope—Where the parties consent, the court may deal with an application to file evidence without a hearing. Permission to file evidence may be given on conditions or with directions (PD54A, para 13).

54.18 Judicial review may be decided without a hearing

The court may decide the claim for judicial review without a hearing where all the parties agree.

Amendments—Inserted by SI 2000/2092.

54.19 Court's powers in respect of quashing orders

(1) This rule applies where the court makes a quashing order in respect of the decision to which the claim relates.

(2) The court may –

(a)

(i) remit the matter to the decision-maker; and

(ii) direct it to reconsider the matter and reach a decision in accordance with the judgment of the court; or

(b) in so far as any enactment permits, substitute its own decision for the decision to which the claim relates.

(Section 31 of the Senior Courts Act 1981 enables the High Court, subject to certain conditions, to substitute its own decision for the decision in question.)

Amendments—Inserted by SI 2000/2092. Amended by SI 2007/3543; CRA 2005, Sch 11, para 1(2).

Scope—The court is entitled to quash a decision and direct there be a further consideration, or make the decision itself.

54.20 Transfer

The court may –

(a) order a claim to continue as if it had not been started under this Section; and
(b) where it does so, give directions about the future management of the claim.

(Part 30 (transfer) applies to transfers to and from the Administrative Court)

Amendments—Inserted by SI 2000/2092. Amended by SI 2003/364.

Scope—Under CPR 1998, r 30.5 the High Court may transfer proceedings from one Division to another. Any application to transfer should be made to the Judge of the Administrative Court for a matter to proceed in that court. In deciding whether to transfer to the Administrative Court, the court will consider whether the case contains issues of public law (PD54A, para 14.2).

****

Practice Direction 54A – Judicial Review

This Practice Direction supplements CPR Part 54

SECTION I: GENERAL PROVISIONS RELATING TO JUDICIAL REVIEW

1.1 In addition to Part 54 and this practice direction attention is drawn to –

- section 31 of the Senior Courts Act 1981; and
- the Human Rights Act 1998.

Amendments—CPR Update 50.

The court

2.1 Part 54 claims for judicial review are dealt with in the Administrative Court.

(Practice Direction 54D contains provisions about where a claim for judicial review may be started, administered and heard.)

Amendments—CPR Updates 49, 51.

Rule 54.5 – Time limit for filing claim form

4.1 Where the claim is for a quashing order in respect of a judgment, order or conviction, the date when the grounds to make the claim first arose, for the purposes of rule 54.5(1)(b), is the date of that judgment, order or conviction.

Rule 54.6 – Claim form

Interested parties

5.1 Where the claim for judicial review relates to proceedings in a court or tribunal, any other parties to those proceedings must be named in the claim form as interested parties under rule 54.6(1)(a) (and therefore served with the claim form under rule 54.7(b)).

5.2 For example, in a claim by a defendant in a criminal case in the Magistrates' or Crown Court for judicial review of a decision in that case, the prosecution must always be named as an interested party.

Human rights

5.3 Where the claimant is seeking to raise any issue under the Human Rights Act 1998, or seeks a remedy available under that Act, the claim form must include the information required by paragraph 15 of Practice Direction 16.

Devolution issues

5.4 Where the claimant intends to raise a devolution issue, the claim form must –

(1) specify that the applicant wishes to raise a devolution issue and identify the relevant provisions of the Government of Wales Act 2006, the Northern Ireland Act 1998 or the Scotland Act 1998; and

(2) contain a summary of the facts, circumstances and points of law on the basis of which it is alleged that a devolution issue arises.

5.5 In this practice direction 'devolution issue' has the same meaning as in paragraph 1, Schedule 9 to the Government of Wales Act 2006, paragraph 1, Schedule 10 to the Northern Ireland Act 1998; and paragraph 1, Schedule 6 to the Scotland Act 1998.

Claim form

5.6 The claim form must include or be accompanied by –

(1) a detailed statement of the claimant's grounds for bringing the claim for judicial review;
(2) a statement of the facts relied on;
(3) any application to extend the time limit for filing the claim form;
(4) any application for directions.

5.7 In addition, the claim form must be accompanied by –

(1) any written evidence in support of the claim or application to extend time;
(2) a copy of any order that the claimant seeks to have quashed;
(3) where the claim for judicial review relates to a decision of a court or tribunal, an approved copy of the reasons for reaching that decision;
(4) copies of any documents on which the claimant proposes to rely;
(5) copies of any relevant statutory material;
(6) a list of essential documents for advance reading by the court (with page references to the passages relied on); and

5.8 Where it is not possible to file all the above documents, the claimant must indicate which documents have not been filed and the reasons why they are not currently available.

Bundle of documents

5.9 The claimant must file one copy of a paginated and indexed bundle containing all the documents referred to in paragraphs 5.6 and 5.7 unless the case is to be heard before a Divisional Court. For Divisional Court cases the number of bundles required will be one set for each judge hearing the case.

5.10 Attention is drawn to rules 8.5(1) and 8.5(7).

Amendments—CPR Updates 29, 31, 49, 51, 88.

Rule 54.7 – Service of claim form

6.1 Except as required by rules 54.11 or 54.12(2), the Administrative Court will not serve documents and service must be effected by the parties.

6.2 Where the defendant or interested party to the claim for judicial review is –

(a) the Immigration and Asylum Chamber of the First-tier Tribunal, the address for service of the claim form is Official Correspondence Unit, PO Box 6987, Leicester, LE1 6ZX or fax number 0116 249 4240;

(b) the Crown, service of the claim form must be effected on the solicitor acting for the relevant government department as if the proceedings were civil proceedings as defined in the Crown Proceedings Act 1947.

(Practice Direction 66 gives the list published under section 17 of the Crown Proceedings Act 1947 of the solicitors acting in civil proceedings (as defined in that Act) for the different government departments on whom service is to be effected, and of their addresses.)

(Part 6 contains provisions about the service of claim forms.)

Amendments—CPR Updates 19, 51.

Rule 54.8 – Acknowledgment of service

7.1 Attention is drawn to rule 8.3(2) and the relevant practice direction and to rule 10.5.

Rule 54.10 – Permission given

Directions

8.1 Case management directions under rule 54.10(1) may include directions about serving the claim form and any evidence on other persons.

8.2 Where a claim is made under the Human Rights Act 1998, a direction may be made for giving notice to the Crown or joining the Crown as a party. Attention is drawn to rule 19.4A and paragraph 6 of Practice Direction 19A.

Permission without a hearing

8.4 The court will generally, in the first instance, consider the question of permission without a hearing.

Permission hearing

8.5 Neither the defendant nor any other interested party need attend a hearing on the question of permission unless the court directs otherwise.

8.6 Where the defendant or any party does attend a hearing, the court will not generally make an order for costs against the claimant.

Amendments—CPR Updates 49, 51.

Rule 54.11 – Service of order giving or refusing permission

9.1 An order refusing permission or giving it subject to conditions or on certain grounds only must set out or be accompanied by the court's reasons for coming to that decision.

Rule 54.14 – Response

10.1 Where the party filing the detailed grounds intends to rely on documents not already filed, he must file a paginated bundle of those documents when he files the detailed grounds.

Rule 54.15 – Where claimant seeks to rely on additional grounds

11.1 Where the claimant intends to apply to rely on additional grounds at the hearing of the claim for judicial review, he must give notice to the court and to any other person served with the claim form no later than 7 clear days before the hearing (or the warned date where appropriate).

Rule 54.16 – Evidence

12.1 Disclosure is not required unless the court orders otherwise.

Rule 54.17 – Court's powers to hear any person

13.1 Where all the parties consent, the court may deal with an application under rule 54.17 without a hearing.

13.2 Where the court gives permission for a person to file evidence or make representations at the hearing of the claim for judicial review, it may do so on conditions and may give case management directions.

13.3 An application for permission should be made by letter to the Administrative Court office, identifying the claim, explaining who the applicant is and indicating why and in what form the applicant wants to participate in the hearing.

13.4 If the applicant is seeking a prospective order as to costs, the letter should say what kind of order and on what grounds.

13.5 Applications to intervene must be made at the earliest reasonable opportunity, since it will usually be essential not to delay the hearing.

Amendments—CPR Update 29.

Rule 54.20 – Transfer

14.1 Attention is drawn to rule 30.5.

14.2 In deciding whether a claim is suitable for transfer to the Administrative Court, the court will consider whether it raises issues of public law to which Part 54 should apply.

Skeleton arguments

15.1 The claimant must file and serve a skeleton argument not less than 21 working days before the date of the hearing of the judicial review (or the warned date).

15.2 The defendant and any other party wishing to make representations at the hearing of the judicial review must file and serve a skeleton argument not less than 14 working days before the date of the hearing of the judicial review (or the warned date).

15.3 Skeleton arguments must contain –

(1) a time estimate for the complete hearing, including delivery of judgment;
(2) a list of issues;
(3) a list of the legal points to be taken (together with any relevant authorities with page references to the passages relied on);
(4) a chronology of events (with page references to the bundle of documents (see paragraph 16.1);
(5) a list of essential documents for the advance reading of the court (with page references to the passages relied on) (if different from that filed with the claim form) and a time estimate for that reading; and
(6) a list of persons referred to.

Bundle of documents to be filed

16.1 The claimant must file a paginated and indexed bundle of all relevant documents required for the hearing of the judicial review when he files his skeleton argument.

16.2 The bundle must also include those documents required by the defendant and any other party who is to make representations at the hearing.

Agreed final order

17.1 If the parties agree about the final order to be made in a claim for judicial review, the claimant must file at the court a document (with 2 copies) signed by all the parties setting out the terms of the proposed agreed order together with a short statement of the matters relied on as justifying the proposed agreed order and copies of any authorities or statutory provisions relied on.

17.2 The court will consider the documents referred to in paragraph 17.1 and will make the order if satisfied that the order should be made.

17.3 If the court is not satisfied that the order should be made, a hearing date will be set.

17.4 Where the agreement relates to an order for costs only, the parties need only file a document signed by all the parties setting out the terms of the proposed order.

SECTION II: APPLICATIONS FOR PERMISSION TO APPLY FOR JUDICIAL REVIEW IN IMMIGRATION AND ASYLUM CASES – CHALLENGING REMOVAL

18.1

(1) This Section applies where –

(a) a person has been served with a copy of directions for his removal from the United Kingdom by the UK Border Agency of the Home Office and notified that this Section applies; and

(b) that person makes an application for permission to apply for judicial review before his removal takes effect.

(2) This Section does not prevent a person from applying for judicial review after he has been removed.

(3) The requirements contained in this Section of this Practice Direction are additional to those contained elsewhere in the Practice Direction.

18.2

(1) A person who makes an application for permission to apply for judicial review must file a claim form and a copy at court, and the claim form must –

(a) indicate on its face that this Section of the Practice Direction applies; and

(b) be accompanied by –

(i) a copy of the removal directions and the decision to which the application relates; and

(ii) any document served with the removal directions including any document which contains the UK Border Agency's factual summary of the case; and

(c) contain or be accompanied by the detailed statement of the claimant's grounds for bringing the claim for judicial review; or

(d) if the claimant is unable to comply with paragraph (b) or (c), contain or be accompanied by a statement of the reasons why.

(2) The claimant must, immediately upon issue of the claim, send copies of the issued claim form and accompanying documents to the address specified by the UK Border Agency.

(Rule 54.7 also requires the defendant to be served with the claim form within 7 days of the date of issue. Rule 6.10 provides that service on a Government Department must be effected on the solicitor acting for that Department, which in the case of the UK Border Agency is the Treasury Solicitor. The address for the Treasury Solicitor may be found in the Annex to Part 66 of these Rules.)

18.3 Where the claimant has not complied with paragraph 18.2(1)(b) or (c) and has provided reasons why he is unable to comply, and the court has issued the claim form, the Administrative Court –

(a) will refer the matter to a Judge for consideration as soon as practicable; and

(b) will notify the parties that it has done so.

18.4 If, upon a refusal to grant permission to apply for judicial review, the Court indicates that the application is clearly without merit, that indication will be included in the order refusing permission.

Amendments—CPR Updates 44, 47.

SECTION III – APPLICATIONS FOR PERMISSION TO APPLY FOR JUDICIAL REVIEW OF DECISIONS OF THE UPPER TRIBUNAL

19.1 A person who makes an application for permission to apply for judicial review of the decision of the Upper Tribunal refusing permission to appeal must file a claim form which must –

(a) state on its face that the application is made under Rule 54.7A;

(b) set out succinctly the grounds on which it is argued that the criteria in Rule 54.7A(7) are met; and

(c) be accompanied by the supporting documents required under Rule 54.7A(4).

19.2 If the Upper Tribunal or any interested party wishes there to be a hearing of the substantive application under Rule 54.7A(9), it must make its request in writing (by letter copied to the claimant) for such a hearing no later than 14 days after service of the order granting permission.

Practice Direction 54C – References by the Legal Services Commission

This Practice Direction supplements CPR Part 54

Amendments—CPR Update 42.

Note—The Legal Aid Agency replaced the Legal Services Commission on 1 April 2013.

1.1 This Practice Direction applies where the Legal Services Commission ('the Commission') refers to the High Court a question that arises on a review of a decision about an individual's financial eligibility for a representation order in criminal proceedings under the Criminal Defence Service (Financial Eligibility) Regulations 2006.

1.2 A reference of a question by the Legal Services Commission must be made to the Administrative Court.

1.3 Part 52 does not apply to a review under this paragraph.

1.4 The Commission must –

(a) file at the court –

(i) the individual's applications for a representation order and for a review, and any supporting documents;

(ii) a copy of the question on which the court's decision is sought; and

(iii) a statement of the Commission's observations on the question; and

(b) serve a copy of the question and the statement on the individual.

1.5 The individual may file representations on the question at the court within 7 days after service on him of the copy of the question and the statement.

1.6 The question will be decided without a hearing unless the court directs otherwise.

Practice Direction 54D – Administrative Court (Venue)

This Practice Direction supplements CPR Part 54

Amendments—CPR Update 49.

Scope and purpose

1.1 This Practice Direction concerns the place in which a claim before the Administrative Court should be started and administered and the venue at which it will be determined.

1.2 This Practice Direction is intended to facilitate access to justice by enabling cases to be administered and determined in the most appropriate location. To achieve this purpose it provides flexibility in relation to where claims are to be administered and enables claims to be transferred to different venues.

Venue – General provisions

2.1 The claim form in proceedings in the Administrative Court may be issued at the Administrative Court Office of the High Court at –

(1) the Royal Courts of Justice in London; or

(2) at the District Registry of the High Court at Birmingham, Cardiff, Leeds, or Manchester

unless the claim is one of the excepted classes of claim set out in paragraph 3 of this Practice Direction which may only be started and determined at the Royal Courts of Justice in London.

2.2 Any claim started in Birmingham will normally be determined at a court in the Midland region (geographically covering the area of the Midland Circuit); in Cardiff in Wales; in Leeds in the North-Eastern Region (geographically covering the area of the North Eastern Circuit); in London at the Royal Courts of Justice; and in Manchester, in the North-Western Region (geographically covering the Northern Circuit).

Excepted classes of claim

3.1 The excepted classes of claim referred to in paragraph 2.1(2) are –

(1) proceedings to which Part 76 or Part 79 applies, and for the avoidance of doubt –
  (a) proceedings relating to control orders (within the meaning of Part 76);
  (b) financial restrictions proceedings (within the meaning of Part 79);
  (c) proceedings relating to terrorism or alleged terrorists (where that is a relevant feature of the claim); and
  (d) proceedings in which a special advocate is or is to be instructed;
(2) proceedings to which RSC Order 115 applies;
(3) proceedings under the Proceeds of Crime Act 2002;
(4) appeals to the Administrative Court under the Extradition Act 2003;
(5) proceedings which must be heard by a Divisional Court; and
(6) proceedings relating to the discipline of solicitors.

3.2 If a claim form is issued at an Administrative Court office other than in London and includes one of the excepted classes of claim, the proceedings will be transferred to London.

Urgent applications

4.1 During the hours when the court is open, where an urgent application needs to be made to the Administrative Court outside London, the application must be made to the judge designated to deal with such applications in the relevant District Registry.

4.2 Any urgent application to the Administrative Court during the hours when the court is closed, must be made to the duty out of hours High Court judge by telephoning 020 7947 6000.

Assignment to another venue

5.1 The proceedings may be transferred from the office at which the claim form was issued to another office. Such transfer is a judicial act.

5.2 The general expectation is that proceedings will be administered and determined in the region with which the claimant has the closest connection, subject to the following considerations as applicable –

(1) any reason expressed by any party for preferring a particular venue;
(2) the region in which the defendant, or any relevant office or department of the defendant, is based;
(3) the region in which the claimant's legal representatives are based;
(4) the ease and cost of travel to a hearing;
(5) the availability and suitability of alternative means of attending a hearing (for example, by videolink);
(6) the extent and nature of media interest in the proceedings in any particular locality;
(7) the time within which it is appropriate for the proceedings to be determined;
(8) whether it is desirable to administer or determine the claim in another region in the light of the volume of claims issued at, and the capacity, resources and workload of, the court at which it is issued;

(9) whether the claim raises issues sufficiently similar to those in another outstanding claim to make it desirable that it should be determined together with, or immediately following, that other claim; and

(10) whether the claim raises devolution issues and for that reason whether it should more appropriately be determined in London or Cardiff.

5.3 (1) When an urgent application is made under paragraph 4.1 or 4.2, this will not by itself decide the venue for the further administration or determination of the claim.

(2) The court dealing with the urgent application may direct that the case be assigned to a particular venue.

(3) When an urgent application is made under paragraph 4.2, and the court does not make a direction under sub-paragraph (2), the claim will be assigned in the first place to London but may be reassigned to another venue at a later date.

5.4 The court may on an application by a party or of its own initiative direct that the claim be determined in a region other than that of the venue in which the claim is currently assigned. The considerations in paragraph 5.2 apply.

5.5 Once assigned to a venue, the proceedings will be both administered from that venue and determined by a judge of the Administrative Court at a suitable court within that region, or, if the venue is in London, at the Royal Courts of Justice. The choice of which court (of those within the region which are identified by the Presiding Judge of the circuit suitable for such hearing) will be decided, subject to availability, by the considerations in paragraph 5.2.

5.6 When giving directions under rule 54.10, the court may direct that proceedings be reassigned to another region for hearing (applying the considerations in paragraph 5.2). If no such direction is given, the claim will be heard in the same region as that in which the permission application was determined (whether on paper or at a hearing).

****

PART 57
PROBATE, INHERITANCE AND PRESUMPTION OF DEATH

CONTENTS OF THIS PART

Rule		Page
57.1	Scope of this Part and definitions	2269
	Section IV *Claims under the Inheritance (Provision for Family and Dependants) Act 1975*	
57.14	Scope of this Section	2269
57.15	Proceedings in the High Court	2269
57.16	Procedure for claims under section 1 of the Act	2270
	Section V *Proceedings under the Presumption of Death Act 2013*	
57.17	Scope and interpretation	2272
57.18	Proceedings to be in the High Court	2272
57.19	Procedure for claims for a declaration of presumed death or a variation order	2272
57.20	Giving notice of claim	2273
57.21	Advertisement of claim	2273
57.22	Interveners	2274
57.23	Requirement to provide information	2274
	Practice Direction 57A – Probate	2274
	Practice Direction 57B – Proceedings under the Presumption of Death Act 2013	2275

57.1 Scope of this Part and definitions

(1) This Part contains rules about –

(a) probate claims;
(b) claims for the rectification of wills;
(c) claims and applications to –
  (i) substitute another person for a personal representative; or
  (ii) remove a personal representative;
(d) claims under the Inheritance (Provision for Family and Dependants) Act 1975; and
(e) proceedings under the Presumption of Death Act 2013.

(2) In this Part:

(a) 'probate claim' means a claim for –
  (i) the grant of probate of the will, or letters of administration of the estate, of a deceased person;
  (ii) the revocation of such a grant; or
  (iii) a decree pronouncing for or against the validity of an alleged will;

not being a claim which is non-contentious (or common form) probate business;

(Section 128 of the Senior Courts Act 1981 defines non-contentious (or common form) probate business.)

(b) 'relevant office' means –
  (i) in the case of High Court proceedings in a Chancery district registry, that registry;
  (ii) in the case of any other High Court proceedings, Chancery Chambers at the Royal Courts of Justice, Strand, London, WC2A 2LL; and
  (iii) in the case of County Court proceedings, the office of the County Court hearing centre in question;
(c) 'testamentary document' means a will, a draft of a will, written instructions for a will made by or at the request of, or under the instructions of, the testator, and any document purporting to be evidence of the contents, or to be a copy, of a will which is alleged to have been lost or destroyed;
(d) 'will' includes a codicil.

Amendments—Inserted by SI 2001/1388. Amended by SI 2002/2058; CRA 2005, Sch 11, para 1(2); SI 2014/407; SI 2014/2044.

****

Section IV
Claims under the Inheritance (Provision for Family and Dependants) Act 1975

57.14 Scope of this Section

This Section contains rules about claims under the Inheritance (Provision for Family and Dependants) Act 1975 ('the Act').

Amendments—Inserted by SI 2002/2058.

57.15 Proceedings in the High Court

(1) Proceedings in the High Court under the Act shall be issued in either –

(a) the Chancery Division; or
(b) the Family Division.

(2) The Civil Procedure Rules apply to proceedings under the Act which are brought in the Family Division, except that the provisions of the Family Procedure Rules 2010 relating to the drawing up and service of orders apply instead of the provisions in Part 40 and Practice Direction 40B.

Amendments—Inserted by SI 2002/2058. Amended by SI 2009/3390; SI 2011/1045.

Jurisdiction—See **'court'** under I(PFD)A 1975, s 1. The county court has unlimited jurisdiction to hear claims under the Act: CCA 1984, s 25. For transfer of proceedings to a county court and from a county court, see CPR 1998, Pt 30.

Transfer of proceedings—The criteria to which the court must have regard include those set out in CPR 1998, r 30.3(2). Where there are existing related proceedings, these may make transfer appropriate. Where the application involves the taking of complicated accounts, a transfer to the Chancery Division may be considered appropriate as it is better equipped to deal with such issues.

57.16 Procedure for claims under section 1 of the Act

(1) A claim under section 1 of the Act must be made by issuing a claim form in accordance with Part 8.

(2) Rule 8.3 (acknowledgment of service) and rule 8.5 (filing and serving written evidence) apply as modified by paragraphs (3) to (5) of this rule.

(3) The written evidence filed and served by the claimant with the claim form must, except in the circumstances specified in paragraph (3A), have exhibited to it an official copy of –

(a) the grant of probate or letters of administration in respect of the deceased's estate; and
(b) every testamentary document in respect of which probate or letters of administration were granted.

(3A) Where no grant has been obtained, the claimant may make a claim without naming a defendant and may apply for directions as to the representation of the estate. The written evidence must –

(a) explain the reasons why it has not been possible for a grant to be obtained;
(b) be accompanied by the original or a copy (if either is available) of the will or other testamentary document in respect of which probate or letters of administration are to be granted; and
(c) contain the following information, so far as known to the claimant –
    (i) brief details of the property comprised in the estate, with an approximate estimate of its capital value and any income that is received from it;
    (ii) brief details of the liabilities of the estate;
    (iii) the names and addresses of the persons who are in possession of the documents relating to the estate; and
    (iv) the names of the beneficiaries and their respective interests in the estate.

(3B) Where a claim is made in accordance with paragraph (3A), the court may give directions as to the parties to the claim and as to the representation of the estate either on the claimant's application or on its own initiative.

> (Section 4 of the 1975 Act as amended confirms that nothing prevents the making of an application under the Act before representation with respect to the estate of the deceased person is taken out.)

(4) Subject to paragraph (4A), the time within which a defendant must file and serve –

(a) an acknowledgment of service; and
(b) any written evidence,

is not more than 21 days after service of the claim form on him.

(4A) If the claim form is served out of the jurisdiction under rule 6.32 or 6.33, the period for filing an acknowledgment of service and any written evidence is 7 days longer than the relevant period specified in rule 6.35 or Practice Direction 6B.

(5) A defendant who is a personal representative of the deceased must file and serve written evidence, which must include the information required by Practice Direction 57.

Amendments—Inserted by SI 2002/2058. Amended by SI 2004/1306; SI 2008/2178; SI 2009/3390; SI 2014/2044.

Time for application—A claim may now be brought before a grant has been taken out but the time-limit for bringing the claim remains at 6 months after the grant of representation is taken out. Practice Direction of 26 September 1991: *Grants of Representation: Children Act 1989* [1991] 2 FLR 462 sets out the procedure to be followed in relation to grants on behalf of children. An application under I(PFD)A 1975 may not be made after the end of the 6 months from the date on which representation with respect to the estate is first taken out unless the court gives permission to do so (I(PFD)A 1975, s 4). The amendments to CPR 1998, r 57.16 enable a claim to be made without naming the defendant(s) and for an application for direction to be made and for the court to give directions including of its own initiative as to the representation of the estate. The application must be supported by written evidence and the documents specified in the rule. Permission of the court will continue to be required where a claim is proposed to be made out of time. Where an extension of time is sought this must be applied for specifically in the claim form.

Procedure on application—The claim is issued in the case of High Court proceedings either in London (in Chancery Chambers at the Royal Courts of Justice, Strand, London WC2A 2LL or the Central Family Court (formerly the Principal Registry of the Family Division) or in any district registry of the High Court. In the case of county court proceedings, the office of the county court in question. The claimant must file any written statement or an affidavit in support of the claim when he files the claim form and serve a copy on the defendant with the claim form. It should be intituled 'In the matter of [the estate in which the claim arises] and in the matter of the Inheritance (Provision for Family and Dependants) Act 1975'. It must set out concisely the relief or remedy which is claimed in the proceedings. The CPR 1998 apply to service. For service outside the jurisdiction and the court's discretion to grant retrospective permission for service and the application of the overriding objectives, see *Nesheim v Kosa* [2006] EWHC 2710 (Ch).

'claim under section 1' (r 57.16(1))—This is an application for financial provision from a deceased's estate. The relief claimed will generally be that available under ss 2, 5, 10–13, 16 and 17 of the Act.

Subsequent application—Where an order has been made under s 1 of the Act any subsequent applications, eg, under ss 6 and 7 of the Act for variation, discharge or suspension of an order under s 2(1) for periodical payments and a lump sum by instalment, whether by a party to the proceedings or by any other person, should be made by issuing on notice an 'application notice' form in accordance with Pt 23, supported by a witness statement/affidavit. It is submitted that since the application is akin to an application for a variation of an order in matrimonial proceedings the procedure laid down under FPR 2010, Pt 8 should be followed.

Claimants—See PD57, para 17. Where it is discovered that there may be conflicting interests between two or more claimants, e g between mother and a child, the court, on an application for directions, may direct that the claimants be separately represented or that some of the claimants be made defendants, direct that separate applications be issued and then make an order consolidating all the applications.

Witness statement/affidavit in support—This rule and r 8.5 refer to written evidence being filed without referring to the form in which that evidence should be given. It is suggested that the evidence should either take the form of a written statement with the appropriate declaration or an affidavit. This rule does not prescribe the contents of the applicant's witness statement/affidavit but clearly the statement/affidavit must set out facts which establish the right to apply and exhibit to it an official copy of the grant of probate or letters of administration in respect of the deceased's estate and any other testamentary document in respect of which probate or letters of administration was granted. In the case of a spouse the marriage certificate should be exhibited or where a certificate is not available (e g in the case of a customary or religious ceremony) the facts to establish that a ceremony of marriage was performed (see *MA v JA and the Attorney-General* [2013] 2 FLR 68, FD); where there has been a divorce, or a decree of nullity or judicial separation a certified copy of the decree should be exhibited. A certified copy of the death certificate should always be exhibited. Note that it is now possible to seek a declaration of presumed death where a person has been missing for a period of 7 years or more by making an application in the High Court pursuant to the Presumption of Death Act 2013. Such a declaration will be sufficient proof of death (the Act is set out in Part 2; for procedure see below). The applicant should also set out the basis upon which the claim is made. Where a transfer of proceedings is sought between county courts, within the High Court or between the High Court and a county court, it is important to set out particulars of any known proceedings relevant to the application and any other matter referred to in CPR 1998, r 30.3. Such proceedings will often be material to the question whether the application ought to be transferred from the Family Division to the Chancery Division or vice versa. Where the application seeks an order for the avoidance of a disposition, the witness statement/affidavit must show that the conditions set out in ss 10 and 11 are satisfied. In a case where the application seeks the variation of a maintenance agreement, the provisions of FPR 2010, rr 8.6–8.11 should be used as a guide.

Defendants—The personal representatives and the beneficiaries under the will or on intestacy are the defendants to an application under I(PFD)A 1975. Where the defendant is a child or under disability, the usual procedure for the appointment of a litigation friend should be followed. CPR 1998, Sch 1, RSC Ord 99, r 4 provided that the court could direct any person to be added to the proceedings or that notice of the proceedings be served on any person. It also provided that CPR, r 19.7 should apply to proceedings under the Act. CPR, Pt 57 is silent on this issue. However it is submitted that CPR, r 19.7 continues to apply because that rule provides that it applies to 'claims about the estate of a deceased person'. Thus, where there are possible claimants under the deceased's will or intestacy who cannot be ascertained or found, or it appears to the court expedient for the purpose of saving costs, the Official Solicitor can be appointed under this rule to represent the missing beneficiaries or possible claimants. Where the proceedings raise issues of disputed facts, it is not appropriate to order a third party, such as the Official Solicitor, to represent the missing defendant/s (*Cotton v Official Solicitor* [1989] 6 CL 385, ChD). This rule is not however confined to cases of missing claimants or defendants. The court may use its power to join a person, for example a person lacking capacity who may have a possible claim against the estate. In such an instance the person may be joined by his litigation friend and the usual procedure for the appointment of a litigation friend should be followed. If there is a possibility of conflict arising and it is difficult to appoint a suitable person to act for the person lacking capacity it may be more appropriate to invite the Official Solicitor to act.

Acknowledgement of service by personal representative—See PD57, para 15. Where the personal representatives wish to remain neutral, Section A of the acknowledgement of service should be completed with a statement to that effect and agreeing to abide by any decision of the court.

Personal representative's statement/affidavit—For contents of the statement/affidavit see PD57, para 16. It is mandatory for the personal representative to file a statement/affidavit in answer within 21 days of service (including the day of service). The information required to be particularised in the statement/affidavit is that contained in r 5(2). With reference to r 5(2)(d), the facts which might be relevant to the exercise of the court's

PART III

powers depend on the circumstances of each case. I(PFD)A 1975, s 3(1)(g) requires the court to have regard to 'any other matter … which in the circumstances of the case the court may consider relevant'. This provision is wide enough to include, for example, the deceased's reasons for making or not making any provision in his will for the applicant. The deceased's reasons may have been given orally, in writing or otherwise, and may be very relevant. For cases where the deceased's reasons were found to be relevant, see the commentary under I(PFD)A 1975, s 3. The personal representatives must produce the original grant of representation on the hearing of the claim, because if an order is made the court is required to send the original grant together with the order made to the Principal Registry for a memorandum of the order to be endorsed on or permanently annexed to the grant.

Section V

Proceedings under the Presumption of Death Act 2013

57.17 Scope and interpretation

(1) This Section contains rules about proceedings under the Presumption of Death Act 2013.

(2) In this Section, terms used in the Presumption of Death Act 2013 Act have the meaning given by that Act, and –

(a) 'the 2013 Act' means the Presumption of Death Act 2013;

(b) 'a claim for a declaration of presumed death' means a claim under section 1 of the 2013 Act for a declaration that a missing person is presumed to be dead;

(c) 'a claim for a variation order' means a claim for an order under section 5 of the 2013 Act varying or revoking a declaration of presumed death.

Amendments—Inserted by SI 2014/2044.

57.18 Proceedings to be in the High Court

(1) Proceedings under the 2013 Act must be issued in the High Court in either –

(a) the Chancery Division; or

(b) the Family Division.

(2) The Civil Procedure Rules apply to proceedings under the 2013 Act which are brought in the Family Division, except that the provisions of the Family Procedure Rules 2010 relating to the drawing up and service of orders apply instead of the provisions in Part 40 and Practice Direction 40B.

Amendments—Inserted by SI 2014/2044.

57.19 Procedure for claims for a declaration of presumed death or a variation order

(1) A claim for a declaration of presumed death or for a variation order must be made by issuing a claim form in accordance with Part 8.

(2) In addition to the matters set out in rule 8.2 (contents of the claim form), the claim form must also include or be accompanied by the information required by Practice Direction 57B.

(3) Rules 8.2A, 8.3, 8.4 and 8.5 apply as modified by paragraphs (4) to (7) of this rule (and references elsewhere in these Rules to a defendant and to an acknowledgment of service are, where relevant, to be read as references to the substitute terms in rules 8.2A, 8.3, 8.4 and 8.5 as so modified).

(4) Rule 8.2A (issue of claim form without naming defendants) applies as if for 'without naming a defendant' in paragraph (1) there were substituted 'without serving notice on any person'.

(5) Rule 8.3 (acknowledgment of service) applies –

(a) as if, instead of referring to a defendant, it referred to a person giving notice of intention to intervene or applying for permission to intervene, as the case may be;

(b) as if, instead of referring to an acknowledgment of service, it referred to a notice of intention to intervene or an application for permission to intervene, as the case may be; and

(c) subject to paragraph (7), with the substitution of 21 days for 14 days as the time within which the notice of intention to intervene or application for permission to intervene must be filed and served.

(6) Rules 8.4 (consequence of not filing an acknowledgment of service) and 8.5 (filing and serving written evidence) apply –

(a) as if, instead of referring to a defendant, they referred to a person giving notice of intention to intervene or applying for permission to intervene, as the case may be; and

(b) as if, instead of referring to an acknowledgment of service, they referred to a notice of intention to intervene or an application for permission to intervene, as the case may be.

(7) If the claim form is served out of the jurisdiction under rule 6.32 or 6.33, the period for filing notice of intention to intervene or an application for permission to intervene, as the case may be, and any written evidence, is 7 days longer than the relevant period for serving an acknowledgement of service specified in rule 6.35 or Practice Direction 6B.

Amendments—Inserted by SI 2014/2044.

Procedure—The CPR 1998, Pt 8 procedure should be followed with appropriate modification referred to in the rule and PD57B. Rule 6 applies to service generally and specifically to service outside the jurisdiction as set out above on those identified in r 57.20.

57.20 Giving notice of claim

(1) Where the claim is for a declaration of presumed death, the claimant must give notice of the claim by serving a copy of it on the following persons (where not the claimant) –

(a) the spouse or civil partner of the missing person;

(b) any parent of the missing person;

(c) any child of the missing person;

(d) any sibling of the missing person;

(e) if there are no persons within sub-paragraphs (a) to (d), the nearest relative of the missing person known to the claimant; and

(f) any other person (including in particular any insurance company) appearing to the claimant to have an interest in the claim.

(2) Where the claim is for a variation order, the claimant must give notice of the claim by serving a copy of it on the following persons (where not the claimant) –

(a) the person who was the claimant for the declaration of presumed death or (as the case may be) previous variation order which it is sought to have varied or revoked;

(b) the spouse or civil partner of the missing person;

(c) any parent of the missing person;

(d) any child of the missing person;

(e) any sibling of the missing person;

(f) if there are no persons within sub-paragraphs (b) to (e), the nearest relative of the missing person known to the claimant; and

(g) any other person (including in particular any insurance company) appearing to the claimant to have an interest in the claim.

(3) Notice under paragraph (1)(a) to (f) or paragraph (2)(a) to (g) must be given within 7 days after the claim is issued.

Amendments—Inserted by SI 2014/2044.

57.21 Advertisement of claim

(1) The claimant (whether the claim is for a declaration of presumed death or for a variation order) must, within 7 days of issue of the claim, ensure that notice of the claim is published –

(a) in a form which meets the requirements set out in Practice Direction 57B; and

(b) in at least one newspaper circulating in the vicinity of the last known address of the missing person.

(2) The claimant must, at least 5 days before the hearing, file a copy of the page of the newspaper bearing the advertisement of notice of the claim required by paragraph (1) and the date on which it was published.

Amendments—Inserted by SI 2014/2044.

57.22 Interveners

(1) The Attorney General, or a person who is entitled to intervene in proceedings under section 11(1), must first notify the court of the intention to intervene in accordance with the requirements of Practice Direction 57B.

(2) Any other person who wishes to intervene in such proceedings must submit an application for permission to intervene in accordance with the requirements of Practice Direction 57B.

(3) Where the court grants permission to intervene, it may do so on conditions and may give case management directions.

(4) The court may direct that a person who intervenes in proceedings, other than the Attorney General, be joined as a claimant or defendant.

Amendments—Inserted by SI 2014/2044.

57.23 Requirement to provide information

(1) An application for an order under section 12(1) of the 2013 Act must be supported by evidence and must in particular –

(a) specify or describe the information in respect of which the order is sought;

(b) set out the reasons why the person making the application believes that the person against whom the order is sought is likely to have such information; and

(c) include any further details, where known, of the missing person which are likely to assist in providing the information sought.

(2) The person making the application must serve a copy of the application notice on the person against whom the order is sought, and on every other party to the proceedings (within the meaning of section 20(2) of the 2013 Act), at least 14 days before the date fixed for the hearing of the application.

(3) An application for discharge or variation under section 12(6) of an order made under section 12(1) may be made without notice unless the court directs otherwise.

Amendments—Inserted by SI 2014/2044.

Practice Direction 57A – Probate

This Practice Direction supplements CPR Part 57

Amendments—CPR Update 23.

****

IV CLAIMS UNDER THE INHERITANCE (PROVISION FOR FAMILY AND DEPENDANTS) ACT 1975

Acknowledgment of service by personal representative – Rule 57.16(4)

15 Where a defendant who is a personal representative wishes to remain neutral in relation to the claim, and agrees to abide by any decision which the court may make, he should state this in Section A of the acknowledgment of service form.

Amendments—CPR Update 29.

Written evidence of personal representative – Rule 57.16(5)

16 The written evidence filed by a defendant who is a personal representative must state to the best of that person's ability –

(1) full details of the value of the deceased's net estate, as defined in section 25(1) of the Act;

(2) the person or classes of persons beneficially interested in the estate, and –

(a) the names and (unless they are parties to the claim) addresses of all living beneficiaries; and

(b) the value of their interests in the estate so far as they are known.

(3) whether any living beneficiary (and if so, naming him) is a child or a person who lacks capacity (within the meaning of the Mental Capacity Act 2005); and

(4) any facts which might affect the exercise of the court's powers under the Act.

Amendments—CPR Updates 29, 45.

Separate representation of claimants

17 If a claim is made jointly by two or more claimants, and it later appears that any of the claimants have a conflict of interests –

(1) any claimant may choose to be represented at any hearing by separate solicitors or counsel, or may appear in person; and

(2) if the court considers that claimants who are represented by the same solicitors or counsel ought to be separately represented, it may adjourn the application until they are.

Amendments—CPR Update 29.

Production of the grant

18.1 On the hearing of a claim the personal representative must produce to the court the original grant of representation to the deceased's estate.

18.2 If the court makes an order under the Act, the original grant (together with a sealed copy of the order) must be sent to the Principal Registry of the Family Division for a memorandum of the order to be endorsed on or permanently annexed to the grant in accordance with section 19(3) of the Act.

Amendments—CPR Update 29.

****

Practice Direction 57B – Proceedings under the Presumption of Death Act 2013

This Practice Direction supplements CPR Part 57

Amendments—CPR Update 75.

Procedure for claims – Rule 57.19

Claim for declaration of presumed death – claim form

1.1 The claim form for a claim for a declaration of presumed death must include or be accompanied by the following (where known) –

(1) Information about the claimant

(a) the claimant's name and address;

(b) the relationship of the claimant to the missing person; and

(c) if the claimant is not the missing person's spouse, civil partner, parent, child or sibling, details of the claimant's interest in the determination of the application;

(2) Information about the missing person

(a) the missing person's name and surname, and any other names by which the missing person is or has formerly been known;

(b) the missing person's gender;

(c) the missing person's maiden surname (if any);

(d) the missing person's date and place of birth;

(e) the occupation of the missing person;

(f) the occupation, name and surname of—

(i) the missing person's spouse or civil partner (or late spouse or civil partner if the marriage or civil partnership ended on death);

(ii) where the missing person was under 16 years of age, the missing person's parents;

(g) the missing person's National Insurance number;

(h) the date on which missing person is thought to have died, or on which the missing person was last known have been alive;

(i) on which of the grounds in section 1(4) of the 2013 Act the court is considered to have jurisdiction to entertain the claim;

(j) the usual or last known address of the missing person; and

(k) the name and address of the spouse or civil partner, parents, children or siblings of the missing person (if any, and if not the claimant);

(3) Information about steps taken to trace the missing person

(a) details of any enquiries made or other steps taken to trace the missing person or confirm when the missing person was last known to be alive; and

(b) details of the results of such enquiries or other steps;

(4) Information about the missing person's property

(a) an estimate of the total value of the assets of the missing person;

(b) details of property owned by the missing person; and

(c) details of the interest of any other person in the missing person's property which it is sought to have determined by the court; and

(5) Information about advertisement and recipients of notice of the claim

(a) details of the newspaper in which the claimant proposes to advertise the claim; and

(b) details of the persons to whom the claimant is giving notice of the claim and, where notice is being given to a person under rule 57.20(1)(f), the nature of that person's interest in the claim.

Amendments—CPR Update 76.

Claim for variation order

1.2 The claim form for a variation order must include or be accompanied by the following (where known) –

(1) Information about the claimant

(a) the claimant's name and address;

(b) the relationship of the claimant to the missing person; and

(c) details of the claimant's interest in the determination of the application;

(2) Information about previous claim and missing person's property

(a) details of the declaration of presumed death or (as the case may be) previous variation order which it is sought to have varied or revoked;

(b) details of the circumstances which are claimed to justify a variation order, and evidence of the enquiries made and other steps taken to verify them and their outcomes; and

(c) details of any interest in property acquired as a result of the declaration of presumed death or (as the case may be) previous variation order which it is sought to have varied or revoked; and

(3) Information about advertisement and recipients of notice of the claim

(a) details of the newspaper in which the claimant proposes to advertise the claim; and

(b) details of the persons to whom the claimant is giving notice of the claim and, where notice is being given to a person under rule 57.20(2)(g), the nature of that person's interest in the claim.

Issue of claim form without serving notice on any person

1.3 For the purposes of rule 8.2A as modified by rule 57.19, an application for permission to issue a claim form, whether the claim is for a declaration or presumed death or for a variation order, may be made only where the claimant believes there to be no person within paragraph (1)(a) to (f) or paragraph (2)(a) to (g) of rule 57.20. The application must explain why the claimant believes that there is no such person.

Case management – first directions hearing

1.4 A claim (whether for a declaration of presumed death or for a variation order) must be listed for case management directions either –

(a) more than 28 days (but where practicable no more than 56 days) after issue; or
(b) where the claim form has been served outside the jurisdiction, more than 7 days (but where practicable no more than 35 days) after the period for filing provided for by rule 57.19(7),

to allow for time for those served with notice of the claim or who respond to the advertisement of the claim to file notice of intention to intervene or an application for permission to intervene as the case may be.

1.5 The court must notify all those who have filed notice of intention to intervene or an application for permission to intervene of the date of the directions hearing.

Advertisement of claim – Rule 57.21

2.1 The advertisement of the claim required by section 9(2) of the 2013 Act and rule 57.21(1)(a) must be in the form set out below, or contain the equivalent information about the claim and the possibility of applying, and where and by when to apply, to the Court –

IN THE HIGH COURT OF JUSTICE
[CHANCERY] [FAMILY] DIVISION

Case Number ......

IN THE MATTER OF AN APPLICATION FOR A DECLARATION OF THE PRESUMED DEATH OF (INSERT NAME)

A claim has been issued in the High Court of Justice, for a [declaration] [variation of a declaration] that (insert name), whose last known address was (insert address) is presumed to be dead. Any person having an interest may apply to the Court to intervene in the matter.

If you wish to apply to the Court, you should do so at [Court address] as soon as possible, and if possible within 21 days of the date of this notice. Delay may harm your prospects of being able to intervene.

[If the claimant is legally represented]
(Name)
Claimant's Legal Representative
(Address)

[If the claimant is not legally represented]
(Claimant's address for service)

Interveners – Rule 57.22

3.1 The Attorney General, or a person who is entitled to intervene in the proceedings by virtue of section 11(1) (the missing person's spouse, civil partner, parent, child or sibling) should notify the intention to intervene as early as possible by filing, and serving on the claimant, notice in writing, specifying –

(a) the intervener's name and address;
(b) the intervener's relationship to the missing person (where the intervener is not the Attorney General);
(c) the reasons for intervening; and

PART III

(d) particulars of any determination or order sought under section 11(4)(b) or (c) of the 2013 Act.

3.2 An application under rule 57.22(2) for permission to intervene must be served on the claimant and must specify –

(a) the applicant's relationship to the missing person or other interest in the proceedings;
(b) the reasons for seeking to intervene; and
(c) particulars of any determination or order sought under section 11(4)(b) or (c) of the 2013 Act.

PART 65
PROCEEDINGS RELATING TO ANTI-SOCIAL BEHAVIOUR AND HARASSMENT

CONTENTS OF THIS PART

Section V

Rule		Page
	Proceedings under the Protection from Harassment Act 1997	
65.27	Scope of this Section	2278
65.28	Claims under section 3 of the 1997 Act	2278
65.29	Applications for issue of a warrant of arrest under section 3(3) of the 1997 Act	2279
65.30	Proceedings following arrest	2279

Practice Direction—*PD (Anti-Social Behaviour and Harassment)*, which supplements this Part generally, is set out in *Civil Court Service* (LexisNexis).

****

Section V
Proceedings under the Protection from Harassment Act 1997

65.27 Scope of this Section

This Section applies to proceedings under section 3 of the Protection from Harassment Act 1997 ('the 1997 Act').

Amendments—Inserted by SI 2004/1306.

65.28 Claims under section 3 of the 1997 Act

(1) A claim under section 3 of the 1997 Act –

(a) shall be subject to the Part 8 procedure and –
(b)
  (i) in the High Court, must be commenced in the Queen's Bench Division, or
  (ii) in the County Court, may be commenced at any County Court hearing centre.

(2) If the application is commenced at a County Court hearing centre which does not serve the address where –

(a) the defendant resides or carries on business; or
(b) the claimant resides or carries on business,

the claim will be issued by the County Court hearing centre where the claim is commenced and sent to the hearing centre serving the address at (a)(i) or (ii), as appropriate.

(Practice Direction 65 makes further provision in respect of claims which are not commenced at the County Court hearing centre which serves the address where the property is situated.)

Amendments—Inserted by SI 2004/1306. Amended by SI 2014/407.

65.29 Applications for issue of a warrant of arrest under section 3(3) of the 1997 Act

(1) An application for a warrant of arrest under section 3(3) of the 1997 Act –

(a) must be made in accordance with Part 23; and
(b) may be made without notice.

(2) The application notice must be supported by affidavit evidence which must –

(a) set out the grounds for the application;
(b) state whether the claimant has informed the police of the conduct of the defendant as described in the affidavit; and
(c) state whether, to the claimant's knowledge, criminal proceedings are being pursued.

Amendments—Inserted by SI 2004/1306.

65.30 Proceedings following arrest

(1) The judge before whom a person is brought following his arrest may –

(a) deal with the matter; or
(b) adjourn the proceedings.

(2) Where the proceedings are adjourned and the arrested person is released –

(a) the matter must be dealt with (whether by the same or another judge) within 28 days of the date on which the arrested person appears in court; and
(b) the arrested person must be given not less than 2 days' notice of the hearing.

Amendments—Inserted by SI 2004/1306.

****

PART 69
COURT'S POWER TO APPOINT A RECEIVER

****

Note—The appointment of a receiver is a remedy that is occasionally useful (it may enable a judgment creditor to reach interests of the debtor that cannot be taken in execution by other means, such as a right to draw down a lump sum from a pension policy (*(1) Blight (2) Meredith (3) Lewis v Brewster* [2012] BPIR 476, ChD) but the expense means that it is seldom appropriate. See *Civil Court Service* (LexisNexis).

PART 70
GENERAL RULES ABOUT ENFORCEMENT OF JUDGMENTS AND ORDERS

CONTENTS OF THIS PART

Rule		Page
70.1	Scope of this Part and interpretation	2279
70.2	Methods of enforcing judgments or orders	2280
70.2A	Court may order act to be done at expense of disobedient party	2280
70.3	Transfer of proceedings for enforcement	2280
70.4	Enforcement of judgment or order by or against non-party	2281
70.6	Effect of setting aside judgment or order	2281
	Practice Direction 70 – Enforcement of Judgments and Orders	2281

General note—This Part is reproduced as modified for family proceedings by FPR 2010, r 33.2.

70.1 Scope of this Part and interpretation

(1) This Part contains general rules about enforcement of judgments and orders.

(Rules about specific methods of enforcement are contained in Parts 71 to 73, 81, 83, 84 and 89, and Schedule 2 CCR Order 28)

(2) In this Part and in Parts 71 to 73 –

(a) 'judgment creditor' means a person who has obtained or is entitled to enforce a judgment or order;
(b) 'judgment debtor' means a person against whom a judgment or order was given or made;
(c) 'judgment or order' includes an award which the court has –
(i) registered for enforcement;
(ii) ordered to be enforced; or
(iii) given permission to enforce
as if it were a judgment or order of the court, and in relation to such an award, 'the court which made the judgment or order' means the court which registered the award or made such an order; and
(d) 'judgment or order for the payment of money' includes a judgment or order for the payment of costs.

Amendments—Inserted by SI 2001/2792. Amended by SI 2002/2058; SI 2014/407; SI 2016/234.

70.2 Methods of enforcing judgments or orders

(1) Practice Direction 70 sets out methods of enforcing judgments or orders for the payment of money.

(2) A judgment creditor may, except where an enactment, rule or practice direction provides otherwise –

(a) use any method of enforcement which is available; and
(b) use more than one method of enforcement, either at the same time or one after another.

Amendments—Inserted by SI 2001/2792. Amended by SI 2009/3390.

'where an enactment ... provides otherwise' (r 70.2(2))—For example, AEA 1971, s 8(2)(b) provides that where an attachment of earnings order is in force, no execution may issue without leave of the court.

'at the same time' (r 70.2(2)(b))—Although concurrent enforcement by different methods is normally permitted, judgment creditors are obliged by PD70, paras 7.1 and 7.2 to notify in writing either the court or the enforcement officer in the case of a High Court writ of execution, if any payment is made by the judgment debtor in the period between issue and hearing or execution.

70.2A Court may order act to be done at expense of disobedient party

(1) In this rule 'disobedient party' means a party who has not complied with a mandatory order, an injunction or a judgment or order for the specific performance of a contract.

(2) Subject to paragraph (4), if a mandatory order, an injunction or a judgment or order for the specific performance of a contract is not complied with, the court may direct that the act required to be done may, so far as practicable, be done by another person, being –

(a) the party by whom the order or judgment was obtained; or
(b) some other person appointed by the court.

(3) Where paragraph (2) applies –

(a) the costs to another person of doing the act will be borne by the disobedient party;
(b) upon the act being done the expenses incurred may be ascertained in such manner as the court directs; and
(c) execution may issue against the disobedient party for the amount so ascertained and for costs.

(4) Paragraph (2) is without prejudice to –

(a) the court's powers under section 39 of the Senior Courts Act 1981; and
(b) the court's powers to punish the disobedient party for contempt.

Amendments—Inserted by SI 2014/407.

70.3 Transfer of proceedings for enforcement

(1) Subject to rule 83.17, a judgment creditor wishing to enforce a High Court judgment or order in the County Court must apply to the High Court for an order transferring the proceedings.

(2) A practice direction may make provisions about the transfer of proceedings for enforcement.

(Rule 83.19 contains provisions about the transfer of County Court proceedings to the High Court for enforcement)

Amendments—Inserted by SI 2001/2792. Amended by SI 2014/407.

'Subject to rule 83.17' (r 70.3(1))—This rule must be read as referring to the Family Court (FPR 2010, r 33.2(a1)). In the (probably unlikely) event of a creditor wishing to enforce a High Court judgment by issuing a County Court warrant of control or delivery, it is not necessary to transfer the proceedings to the Family Court.

'transfer of proceedings for enforcement' (r 70.3(2))—Note that if it is desired to enforce a Family Court order in the High Court beyond what is permitted by r 33.4, the transfer of the proceedings to the High Court can only be directed by a puisne judge of the High Court (FPR 2010, r 29.17(3)).

70.4 Enforcement of judgment or order by or against non-party

If a judgment or order is given or made in favour of or against a person who is not a party to proceedings, it may be enforced by or against that person by the same methods as if he were a party.

Amendments—Inserted by SI 2001/2792.

****

70.6 Effect of setting aside judgment or order

If a judgment or order is set aside, any enforcement of the judgment or order shall cease to have effect unless the court otherwise orders.

Amendments—Inserted by SI 2001/2792.

'unless the court otherwise orders'—This provision enables the court to preserve the security and priority of a charging order obtained by the judgment creditor as a condition of setting aside a judgment.

Practice Direction 70 – Enforcement of Judgments and Orders

This Practice Direction supplements Parts 70, 71, 72, 73 and 89.

Amendments—CPR Updates 26, 33, 83.

Section I – General

Amendments—CPR Update 58.

Definitions

1A.1 In this Practice Direction –

(1) 'writ of control' is to be construed in accordance with section 62(4) of the Tribunals Courts and Enforcement Act 2007;

(2) 'writ of execution' includes –

(a) a writ of possession;

(b) a writ of delivery;

(c) a writ of sequestration;

(d) a writ of fieri facias de bonis ecclesiasticis,

and any further writ in aid of any such writs, but does not include a writ of control.

Amendments—CPR Update 69.

Methods of Enforcing Money Judgments – Rule 70.2

1.1 A judgment creditor may enforce a judgment or order for the payment of money by any of the following methods:

(1) a writ of control or warrant of control (see Parts 83 and 84);

(2) a third party debt order (see Part 72);

(3) a charging order, stop order or stop notice (see Part 73);

(4) in the County Court, an attachment of earnings order (see Part 89);
(5) the appointment of a receiver (see Part 69).

1.2 In addition the court may make the following orders against a judgment debtor –

(1) an order of committal, but only if permitted by –
(a) a rule; and
(b) the Debtors Acts 1869 and 1878

(See Part 81 – Applications and proceedings in relation to contempt of court, in particular Sections 2 and 8 and the Practice Direction supplementing Part 81, and CCR Order 28); and

(2) in the High Court, a writ of sequestration, but only if permitted by rule 81.20.

Amendments—CPR Updates 29, 59, 69, 83.

'permitted by a rule' (para 1.2(1)(a))—Family proceedings are one of the few situations in which the judgment summons procedure remains available. The procedure is governed by FPR 2010, r 33.9 et seq.

1.3 The enforcement of a judgment or order may be affected by –

(1) the enactments relating to insolvency; and
(2) County Court administration orders.

Proceedings for enforcement in the County Court – rule 70.3

2.1 An application to enforce a judgment in the County Court may be made at any County Court hearing centre, unless an enactment, rule or practice direction provides otherwise.

…

2.3 If for any reason proceedings for the enforcement of a judgment are transferred, the court will give notice of the transfer to all the parties.

2.4 When the proceedings have been transferred, the parties must take any further steps in the proceedings in the court to which they have been transferred, unless a rule or practice direction provides otherwise.

(Part 52 and Practice Directions 52A and 52B provide to which court or judge an appeal against the judgment or order, or an application for permission to appeal, must be made)

Amendments—CPR Updates 59, 69.

Enforcement of High Court Judgment or Order in a County Court – Rule 70.3

3.1 If a judgment creditor wishes to enforce a High Court judgment or order in the County Court, they must file the following documents in the County Court with the application notice or request for enforcement –

(1) a copy of the judgment or order;
(2) a certificate verifying the amount due under the judgment or order;
(3) if a writ of execution or writ of control has previously been issued in the High Court to enforce the judgment or order, a copy of the relevant enforcement officer's return to the writ; and
(4) a copy of the order transferring the proceedings to the County Court.

3.2 In this paragraph and paragraph 7 –

(1) 'enforcement officer' means an individual who is authorised to act as an enforcement officer under the Courts Act 2003; and
(2) 'relevant enforcement officer' means –
(a) in relation to a writ of execution or writ of control which is directed to a single enforcement officer, that officer;
(b) in relation to a writ of execution or writ of control which is directed to two or more enforcement officers, the officer to whom the writ is allocated.

Amendments—CPR Updates 35, 69.

★★★★

Registration of decisions in the High Court for enforcement – rule 70.5(8)

5.1 An application to the High Court under an enactment to register a decision for enforcement must be made in writing to the head clerk of the Action Department at the Royal Courts of Justice, Strand, London WC2A 2LL.

5.2 The application must –

(1) specify the statutory provision under which the application is made;
(2) state the name and address of the person against whom it is sought to enforce the decision;
(3) if the decision requires that person to pay a sum of money, state the amount which remains unpaid.

Amendments—CPR Updates 33, 49.

Interest on Judgment Debts

6 If a judgment creditor is claiming interest on a judgment debt, he must include in his application or request to issue enforcement proceedings in relation to that judgment details of –

(1) the amount of interest claimed and the sum on which it is claimed;
(2) the dates from and to which interest has accrued; and
(3) the rate of interest which has been applied and, where more than one rate of interest has been applied, the relevant dates and rates.

(Interest may be claimed on High Court judgment debts under section 17 of the Judgments Act 1838. The County Courts (Interest on Judgment Debts) Order 1991 specifies when interest may be claimed on County Court judgment debts)

Amendments—CPR Update 69.

'Interest may be claimed'—In the county court, interest may be claimed on relevant 'judgments', see County Courts (Interest on Judgment Debts) Order 1991. The terms of the order are not without difficulty but broadly interest runs at the rate prescribed for the High Court from the date when payment is due under a judgment or order for at least £5000. The judgment rate is currently 8% per annum (Judgment Debts (Rate of Interest) Order 1993). If a lump sum financial provision order is made for less than £5000, any interest ordered to be paid under MCA 1973, s 23(6) will not bring the judgment debt under this rule even though the total due may exceed £5000. Interest will remain payable where a payment on account reduces the balance to less than £5000. No more than 6 years' interest may be recovered (*Lowsley and another v Forbes* [1998] 1 AC 329, HL).

Enforcing a judgment or order against a partnership

6A.1 A judgment or order made against a partnership may be enforced against any property of the partnership within the jurisdiction.

6A.2 Subject to paragraph 6A.3, a judgment or order made against a partnership may be enforced against any person who is not a limited partner and who –

(1) acknowledged service of the claim form as a partner;
(2) having been served as a partner with the claim form, failed to acknowledge service of it;
(3) admitted in his statement of case that he is or was a partner at a material time; or
(4) was found by the court to have been a partner at a material time.

6A.3 A judgment or order made against a partnership may not be enforced against a limited partner or a member of the partnership who was ordinarily resident outside the jurisdiction when the claim form was issued unless that partner or member –

(1) acknowledged service of the claim form as a partner;
(2) was served within the jurisdiction with the claim form as a partner; or
(3) was served out of the jurisdiction with the claim form, as a partner, with the permission of the court given under Section IV of Part 6.

6A.4 A judgment creditor wishing to enforce a judgment or order against a person in circumstances not set out in paragraphs 6A.2 or 6A.3 must apply to the court for permission to enforce the judgment or order.

Amendments—CPR Updates 42, 47.

Payment of Debt after Issue of Enforcement Proceedings

7.1 If a judgment debt or part of it is paid –

(1) after the judgment creditor has issued any application or request to enforce it; but
(2) before –
  (a) any writ or warrant has been executed; or
  (b) in any other case, the date fixed for the hearing of the application;

the judgment creditor must, unless paragraph 7.2 applies, immediately notify the court in writing.

7.2 If a judgment debt or part of it is paid after the judgment creditor has applied to the High Court for a writ of execution or writ of control, paragraph 7.1 does not apply, and the judgment creditor must instead immediately notify the relevant enforcement officer in writing.

Amendments—CPR Updates 35, 69.

****

PART 71
ORDERS TO OBTAIN INFORMATION FROM JUDGMENT DEBTORS

CONTENTS OF THIS PART

Rule		Page
71.1	Scope of this Part	2284
71.2	Order to attend court	2284
71.3	Service of order	2285
71.4	Travelling expenses	2285
71.5	Judgment creditor's affidavit	2286
71.6	Conduct of the hearing	2286
71.7	Adjournment of the hearing	2286
71.8	Failure to comply with order	2286
	Practice Direction 71 – Orders to Obtain Information from Judgment Debtors	2287

71.1 Scope of this Part

This Part contains rules which provide for a judgment debtor to be required to attend court to provide information, for the purpose of enabling a judgment creditor to enforce a judgment or order against him.

Amendments—Inserted by SI 2001/2792.

Procedural guide—See Procedural Guide C11.

71.2 Order to attend court

(1) A judgment creditor may apply for an order requiring –

  (a) a judgment debtor; or
  (b) if a judgment debtor is a company or other corporation, an officer of that body;

to attend court to provide information about –

  (i) the judgment debtor's means; or
  (ii) any other matter about which information is needed to enforce a judgment or order.

(2) An application under paragraph (1) –

  (a) may be made without notice; and
  (b) must be issued in the court or County Court hearing centre which made the judgment or order which it is sought to enforce, except that –
    (i) if the proceedings have since been transferred to a different court or hearing centre, it must be issued in that court; or

(ii) subject to subparagraph (b)(i), if it is to enforce a judgment made in the County Court Money Claims Centre, it must be issued in accordance with section 2 of Practice Direction 70.

(3) The application notice must –

(a) be in the form; and
(b) contain the information

required by Practice Direction 71.

(4) An application under paragraph (1) may be dealt with by a court officer without a hearing.

(5) If the application notice complies with paragraph (3), an order to attend court will be issued in the terms of paragraph (6).

(6) A person served with an order issued under this rule must –

(a) attend court at the time and place specified in the order;
(b) when he does so, produce at court documents in his control which are described in the order; and
(c) answer on oath such questions as the court may require.

(7) An order under this rule will contain a notice in the following terms, or in terms to substantially the same effect –

'If you the within-named [ ] do not comply with this order you may be held to be in contempt of court and imprisoned or fined, or your assets may be seized.'

Amendments—Inserted by SI 2001/2792. Amended by SI 2009/3390; SI 2012/505; SI 2012/2208; SI 2014/407.

Practice Direction—See PD71, para 1.2 (r 71.2(3)).

'to provide information' (r 71.2(1))—The purpose of the rule is to enable the judgment creditor to obtain information as to the best means of satisfying his judgment debt, although the answers to questions may not be relied on in judgment summons proceedings (*Mohan v Mohan* [2014] 1 FLR 717, CA). The judgment debtor is under a duty to make full and frank disclosure of his means.

'a judgment debtor' (r 71.2(1)(a))—There is no jurisdiction to require anyone other than the judgment debtor (or where appropriate an officer of a company judgment debtor) to attend court under this provision (*Watson v Sadiq* [2015] EWHC 3403 (QB)) (son of judgment debtor).

'will be issued' (r 71.2(5))—The judgment creditor will be entitled to an order as of right if any part of a judgment debt remains outstanding. Paragraph (4) merely permits the order to be issued by a court officer rather than a judge but does not confer any discretion on the court.

'answer on oath such questions' (r 71.2(6)(c))—The judgment creditor may cross-examine the debtor vigorously as to his assets (*Republic of Costa Rica v Strousberg* (1880) 16 Ch D 8, CA), including those overseas (*Interpool Ltd v Galani* [1988] QB 738) and as to any means by which the judgment debt may be satisfied, but not for some other purpose (*Watkins v Ross* (1893) 68 LT 423, CA).

The fact that the judgment debtor has obtained a stay of execution does not prevent a judgment creditor from proceeding under this rule, *Sucden Financial v Fluxo-Cane Overseas Ltd* [2009] EWHC 3555 (QB).

71.3 Service of order

(1) An order to attend court must, unless the court otherwise orders, be served personally on the person ordered to attend court not less than 14 days before the hearing.

(2) If the order is to be served by the judgment creditor, he must inform the court not less than 7 days before the date of the hearing if he has been unable to serve it.

Amendments—Inserted by SI 2001/2792.

'unless the court otherwise orders'(r 71.3(1))—Substituted service of an order for questioning, and indeed of a subsequent suspended committal order, may be permitted in an appropriate case (*Ticketus LLP & anor v Whyte*, Lawtel 29 September 2014).

71.4 Travelling expenses

(1) A person ordered to attend court may, within 7 days of being served with the order, ask the judgment creditor to pay him a sum reasonably sufficient to cover his travelling expenses to and from court.

(2) The judgment creditor must pay such a sum if requested.

Amendments—Inserted by SI 2001/2792.

71.5 Judgment creditor's affidavit

(1) The judgment creditor must file an affidavit(GL) or affidavits –

(a) by the person who served the order (unless it was served by the court) giving details of how and when it was served;

(b) stating either that –

(i) the person ordered to attend court has not requested payment of his travelling expenses; or

(ii) the judgment creditor has paid a sum in accordance with such a request; and

(c) stating how much of the judgment debt remains unpaid.

(2) The judgment creditor must either –

(a) file the affidavit(GL) or affidavits not less than 2 days before the hearing; or

(b) produce it or them at the hearing.

Amendments—Inserted by SI 2001/2792.

'unless it was served by the court' (r 71.5(1)(a))—In which case service will be proved by a certificate under CCA 1984, s 133. Such certificate is not conclusive but merely evidence of service (*Maher v Gower (formerly Kubilius)* (1982) 3 FLR 287, FD).

71.6 Conduct of the hearing

(1) The person ordered to attend court will be questioned on oath.

(2) The questioning will be carried out by a court officer unless the court has ordered that the hearing shall be before a judge.

(3) The judgment creditor or his representative –

(a) may attend and ask questions where the questioning takes place before a court officer; and

(b) must attend and conduct the questioning if the hearing is before a judge.

Amendments—Inserted by SI 2001/2792.

'hearing is before a judge' (r 71.6(3)(b))—The hearing will only take place before a judge if there are compelling reasons to make such an order (PD71, para 2.2).

71.7 Adjournment of the hearing

If the hearing is adjourned, the court will give directions as to the manner in which notice of the new hearing is to be served on the judgment debtor.

Amendments—Inserted by SI 2001/2792.

'notice of service of adjourned hearing'—Where the judgment debtor is present and can be given personal notice then and there of the date and time of the new hearing, the court will normally dispense with personal service of notice of the new hearing in accordance with r 1.1(2)(c).

71.8 Failure to comply with order

(1) If a person against whom an order has been made under rule 71.2 –

(a) fails to attend court;

(b) refuses at the hearing to take the oath or to answer any question; or

(c) otherwise fails to comply with the order;

the court will refer the matter to a High Court judge or Circuit Judge.

(2) That judge may, subject to paragraphs (3) and (4), make a committal order against the person.

(3) A committal order for failing to attend court may not be made unless the judgment creditor has complied with rules 71.4 and 71.5.

(4) If a committal order is made, the judge will direct that –

(a) the order shall be suspended provided that the person –

(i) attends court at a time and place specified in the order; and

(ii) complies with all the terms of that order and the original order; and

(b) if the person fails to comply with any term on which the committal order is suspended, he shall be brought before a judge to consider whether the committal order should be discharged.

(Part 81 contains provisions in relation to committal.)

Amendments—Inserted by SI 2001/2792. Amended by SI 2001/4015; SI 2012/2208; SI 2014/407.

'the court will refer the matter to a High Court or circuit judge' (r 71.8(1))—This rule provides a summary or streamlined procedure for use when appropriate. It does not exclude the general power of the court to enforce obedience to its orders by committal in accordance with CPR 1998, r 81.4(1)(a) or its equivalent in the family jurisdiction, FPR 2010, r 37.4(1). 'Where the alleged contempt is simple, such as a failure to attend court, the streamlined process may be appropriate. But where the alleged contempt is more difficult to prove, such as a failure to answer questions honestly, the more detailed process [under Part 81] may be appropriate' (per Teare J in *Deutsche Bank AG v Sebastian Holdings Inc* [2016] EWHC 3222 (Comm)). If the 'more detailed process' is followed, r 81.10 must be carefully observed, and in particular the grounds on which the application is made must be set out and each act of contempt alleged must be identified. Although in the civil jurisdiction such a committal application would be listed before a Circuit Judge or High Court Judge, in the Family Court, any level of judge may deal with it, although Family Court (Contempt of Court) (Powers) Regulations 2014, reg 4 limits the committal power of lay justices to 2 months.

Although suspended committal orders under the 'summary/streamlined' procedure can only be made by Circuit Judges or High Court Judges, the hearing at which the decision is made as to whether the committal order should be discharged may take place before a master or district judge (PD71, para 8.4).

'may ... make a committal order' (r 71.8(2))—The Court of Appeal in *Broomleigh Housing Association Ltd v Okonkwo* [2010] EWCA Civ 1113 was critical of the routine use of suspended committal orders under r 71.8 whenever a judgment debtor had failed to comply with an order to attend court to be questioned about his or her means under CPR, r 71.2. It appeared that a suspended order of committal was being used as little more than a vehicle for fixing a date for an effective adjourned hearing. An order for committal was, it was said, too serious a matter to be used in that way and the Court of Appeal gave guidance to judges on how to exercise their discretion when considering whether to make such an order.

'shall be suspended' (r 71.8(4)(a))—See PD71, para 7.1 for the detailed provisions as to the suspended order. Note that if the procedure under Pt 81 is used, there is no obligation to suspend any committal order; and consider *JSC BTA Bank v Solodchenko & Ors* [2011] EWCA Civ 1241, where in an analogous situation Jackson LJ said that 'Where there is a continuing failure to disclose relevant information, the court should consider imposing a long sentence, possibly even the maximum of two years, in order to encourage future co-operation by the contemnor'. If the matter is of that degree of seriousness, it should not, therefore, be listed before lay justices.

Practice Direction 71 – Orders to Obtain Information from Judgment Debtors

This Practice Direction supplements CPR Part 71

Amendments—CPR Update 26.

Application Notice – Rule 71.2

1.1 An application by a judgment creditor under rule 71.2(1) must be made by filing an application notice in Practice Form N316 if the application is to question an individual judgment debtor, or N316A if the application is to question an officer of a company or other corporation.

1.2 The application notice must –

(1) state the name and address of the judgment debtor;

(2) identify the judgment or order which the judgment creditor is seeking to enforce;

(3) if the application is to enforce a judgment or order for the payment of money, state the amount presently owed by the judgment debtor under the judgment or order;

(4) if the judgment debtor is a company or other corporation, state –

(a) the name and address of the officer of that body whom the judgment creditor wishes to be ordered to attend court; and

(b) his position in the company;

(5) if the judgment creditor wishes the questioning to be conducted before a judge, state this and give his reasons;

(6) if the judgment creditor wishes the judgment debtor (or other person to be questioned) to be ordered to produce specific documents at court, identify those documents; and

PART III

(7) if the application is to enforce a judgment or order which is not for the payment of money, identify the matters about which the judgment creditor wishes the judgment debtor (or officer of the judgment debtor) to be questioned.

1.3 The court officer considering the application notice –

(1) may, in any appropriate case, refer it to a judge (rule 3.2); and
(2) will refer it to a judge for consideration, if the judgment creditor requests the judgment debtor (or officer of the judgment debtor) to be questioned before a judge.

'amount presently owed' (para 1.2(3))—If part of the judgment debt has been paid, the judgment creditor should state the date and amount of the last payment that has been taken into account in arriving at the balance due.

'before a judge' (para 1.2(5))—Note that if the questioning is to take place before a judge, the judgment creditor or his representative must attend the hearing to conduct the questioning (para 5.1).

'give his reasons' (para 1.2(5))—The judgment creditor must show compelling reasons for a hearing before a judge (see para 2.2, below).

Order to Attend Court – Rule 71.2

2.1 The order will provide for the judgment debtor (or other person to be questioned) to attend the County Court hearing centre serving the address where the judgment debtor resides or carries on business, unless a judge decides otherwise.

2.2 The order will provide for questioning to take place before a judge only if the judge considering the request decides that there are compelling reasons to make such an order.

Amendments—CPR Update 69.

Service of Order to Attend Court – Rule 71.3

3 Service of an order to attend court for questioning may be carried out by –

(a) the judgment creditor (or someone acting on the judgment creditor's behalf);
(b) a High Court enforcement officer; or
(c) a County Court bailiff.

Amendments—CPR Updates 47, 69.

'service of an order'—The judgment creditor has four options to effect personal service: (a) he can serve the order himself; (b) he can employ a process server; (c) he can employ a High Court enforcement officer; or (d) he may request a county court bailiff to serve, paying the appropriate fee (£110). If personal service cannot be effected he may then apply for permission to serve by another method under rr 6.15 and 6.27. See in this respect *Ticketus LLP & anor v Whyte*, Lawtel 29 September 2014.

Attendance at Court: Normal Procedure – Rule 71.6

4.1 The court officer will ask a standard series of questions, as set out in the forms in Appendixes A and B to this practice direction. The form in Appendix A will be used if the person being questioned is the judgment debtor, and the form in Appendix B will be used if the person is an officer of a company or other corporation.

4.2 The judgment creditor or his representative may either –

(1) attend court and ask questions himself; or
(2) request the court officer to ask additional questions, by attaching a list of proposed additional questions to his application notice.

4.3 The court officer will –

(1) make a written record of the evidence given, unless the proceedings are tape recorded;
(2) at the end of the questioning, read the record of evidence to the person being questioned and ask him to sign it; and
(3) if the person refuses to sign it, note that refusal on the record of evidence.

'list of proposed additional questions' (para 4.2(2))—The list should allow sufficient space for the answer to each question to be recorded immediately after the question.

'make a written record' (para 4.3(1))—Although both Pt 71 and the PD are silent, the court will send a copy of the record to the judgment creditor.

'unless the proceedings are tape recorded' (para 4.3(1))—Presumably tape-recording is envisaged when the judgment creditor is present or represented and elects to make his own written note of the evidence. Subpara (2) cannot apply when the proceedings have been recorded. It is difficult to see what benefit a recording will be to the judgment creditor until the court is in a position to e-mail the digital recording to the judgment creditor as a file, except as a record in case of subsequent dispute about what was said.

'refuses to sign' (para 4.3(3))—The debtor signs to confirm that his replies have been accurately recorded. There is no sanction for a refusal to sign.

Attendance at Court: Procedure Where the Order is to Attend Before a Judge – Rule 71.6

5.1 Where the hearing takes places before a judge, the questioning will be conducted by the judgment creditor or his representative, and the standard questions in the forms in Appendixes A and B will not be used.

5.2 The proceedings will be tape recorded and the court will not make a written record of the evidence.

'will not be used' (para 5.1)—Some questions in the standard forms may still be relevant and can be asked.

'will be tape recorded' (para 5.2)—The judgment creditor must take a note of the answers given or request a transcript at his (considerable) expense.

Failure to Comply with Order: Reference to Judge – Rule 71.8(1)

6 If a judge or court officer refers to a High Court judge or Circuit Judge the failure of a judgment debtor to comply with an order under rule 71.2, he shall certify in writing the respect in which the judgment debtor failed to comply with the order.

Amendments—CPR Update 69.

'certify in writing'—Surprisingly, the PD makes no provision for a copy of the certificate to be sent to either the judgment creditor or judgment debtor. The failure to provide for the judgment debtor to receive a copy of the certificate at any stage of the proceedings may give rise to challenge to this procedure under HRA 1998, Sch 1, Pt I, Art 6 (*Newman (t/a Mantella Publishing) v Modern Bookbinders Ltd* [2000] 1 WLR 2559, CA). The usual form of suspended committal order (Form N79A) does, however, recite the breach found by the judge in reliance on the certificate and will be served on the debtor.

Suspended Committal Order – Rule 71.8(2) and (4)(a)

7.1 A committal order will be suspended provided that the person attends court at a time and place specified in the order (rule 71.8(4)(a)(i)). The appointment specified will be –

(1) before a judge, if –
  (a) the original order under rule 71.2 was to attend before a judge; or
  (b) the judge making the suspended committal order so directs; and
(2) otherwise, before a court officer.

7.2 Rule 71.3 and paragraph 3 of this practice direction (service of order), and rule 71.5(1)(a) and (2) (affidavit of service), apply with the necessary changes to a suspended committal order as they do to an order to attend court.

'service of order' (para 7.2)—Judgment creditors may wish to serve a copy of the certificate under para 6 with the suspended committal order to reduce the risk of the particular HRA challenge mentioned in the note to para 6, above.

Breach of Terms on which Committal Order is Suspended – Rule 71.8(4)(b)

8.1 If –

(1) the judgment debtor fails to attend court at the time and place specified in the suspended committal order; and
(2) it appears to the judge or court officer that the judgment debtor has been duly served with the order,

the judge or court officer will certify in writing the debtor's failure to attend.

8.2 If the judgment debtor fails to comply with any other term on which the committal order was suspended, the judge or court officer will certify in writing the non-compliance and set out details of it.

8.3 A warrant to bring the judgment debtor before a judge may be issued on the basis of a certificate under paragraph 8.1 or 8.2.

8.4 The hearing under rule 71.8(4)(b) may take place before a Master or District Judge.

8.5 At the hearing the judge will discharge the committal order unless he is satisfied beyond reasonable doubt that –

(1) the judgment debtor has failed to comply with –
  (a) the original order to attend court; and
  (b) the terms on which the committal order was suspended; and
(2) both orders have been duly served on the judgment debtor.

8.6 If the judge decides that the committal order should not be discharged, a warrant of committal shall be issued immediately.

Amendments—CPR Update 69.

'certify in writing' (para 8.2)—See **'certify in writing'** under para 6.

'certificate' (para 8.3)—See **'certify in writing'** under para 6.

'A warrant' (para 8.3)—In a county court, the warrant (Form N40A) authorises the court bailiff to arrest the judgment debtor (and, to be effective, impliedly in so doing to use such force as is necessary) and bring him before a judge.

'At the hearing' (para 8.5)—On its face, this provision bristles with potential HRA pitfalls. In practice, however, if the judgment debtor submits to the original order for questioning, the committal order will be discharged.

'shall be issued immediately' (para 8.6)—Again, if read literally with para 8.5, there are serious HRA problems with this provision. However, the court will in practice do everything possible to obtain the information required without sending the judgment debtor to prison. Thus, a judge before whom a judgment debtor is brought may use the general powers contained in r 3.1(2) and (3) to adjourn the hearing for a short time to allow the judgment debtor a final opportunity to purge his apparent contempt. Paragraph 8.5 should not be interpreted as limiting the judge's power to discharge the order to the matters specified in that paragraph and if the judgment debtor complies the committal order will be discharged. If a full hearing has to take place, the judge will first consider the matters set out in **'At the hearing'** above, if necessary adjourning the hearing on terms as to the judgment debtor's attendance. The judge will further make sure that the judgment debtor is aware of the adjourned hearing before leaving the court building, so that service of the notice of the adjourned hearing can be dispensed with, and warn him that if he fails to attend the court will proceed in his absence. Ultimately, the court retains a discretion whether or not to activate the terms of a suspended committal order (*Re W (B)* [1969] 2 Ch 50, CA).

'duly served' (para 8.5(2))—This may have been by way of substituted service, see *Ticketus LLP & anor v Whyte*, Lawtel 29 September 2014.

Appendices—Appendices A and B to this PD contain Records of Examination EX140 and EX141. These can be accessed on the *Civil Court Service* CD-ROM (LexisNexis).

****

PART 72
THIRD PARTY DEBT ORDERS

CONTENTS OF THIS PART

Rule		Page
72.1	Scope of this Part and interpretation	2291
72.2	Third party debt order	2291
72.3	Application for third party debt order	2291
72.4	Interim third party debt order	2292
72.5	Service of interim order	2292
72.6	Obligations of third parties served with interim order	2293
72.7	Arrangements for debtors in hardship	2293
72.8	Further consideration of the application	2294
72.9	Effect of final third party order	2295
72.11	Costs	2295
	Practice Direction 72 – Third Party Debt Orders	2296

General note—This Part is reproduced as modified for family proceedings by FPR 2010, r 33.24.

Procedural Guide—See Procedural Guide C8.

72.1 Scope of this Part and interpretation

(1) This Part contains rules which provide for a judgment creditor to obtain an order for the payment to him of money which a third party who is within the jurisdiction owes to the judgment debtor.

(2) In this Part, 'bank or building society' includes any person carrying on a business in the course of which he lawfully accepts deposits in the United Kingdom.

Amendments—Inserted by SI 2001/2792. Amended by SI 2001/4015.

72.2 Third party debt order

(1) Upon the application of a judgment creditor, the court may make an order (a 'final third party debt order') requiring a third party to pay to the judgment creditor –

(a) the amount of any debt due or accruing due to the judgment debtor from the third party; or

(b) so much of that debt as is sufficient to satisfy the judgment debt and the judgment creditor's costs of the application.

(2) The court will not make an order under paragraph 1 without first making an order (an 'interim third party debt order') as provided by rule 72.4(2).

(3) In deciding whether money standing to the credit of the judgment debtor in an account to which section 40 of the Senior Courts Act 1981 or section 108 of the County Courts Act 1984 relates may be made the subject of a third party debt order, any condition applying to the account that a receipt for money deposited in the account must be produced before any money is withdrawn will be disregarded.

(Section 40(3) of the Senior Courts Act 1981 and section 108(3) of the County Courts Act 1984 contain a list of other conditions applying to accounts that will also be disregarded)

Amendments—Inserted by SI 2001/2792. Amended by CRA 2005, Sch 11, para 1(2).

'the court may make an order' (r 72.2(1))—Lay justices sitting in the Family Court may not make a third party debt order (FC(CDB)R 2014, r 17, Sch 2).

'any debt' (r 72.2(1)(a))—There must be in existence something recognised in law as a debt, notwithstanding that it may be payable on a future date (*O'Driscoll v Manchester Insurance Committee* [1915] 3 KB 499, CA). Thus, a cause of action in damages is not attachable (*Johnson v Diamond* (1855) 11 Exch 73) until judgment is pronounced (*Holtby v Hodgson* (1889) 24 QBD 103, CA) nor is a right to draw down a lump sum from a pension policy (*(1) Blight (2) Meredith (3) Lewis v Brewster* [2012] BPIR 476, ChD). Once an order is made, a subsequent cross-claim by the third party against the judgment debtor does not reduce the third party's liability under the order (*Wolfe v Marshall and Harding (Garnishee)* [1997] EWCA Civ 1329). In the case of a foreign debt, the court has no jurisdiction to make a third party debt order unless compliance with the order will be recognised as discharging the debt owed by the third party to the judgment debtor under the law that governs that debt (*Société Eram Shipping Co Ltd v Compagnie Internationale de Navigation* [2004] 1 AC 260, HL). If necessary, the court will be prepared to pierce the corporate veil to ascertain the real identity of the person to whom the debt is due. However, this rule is not intended to deal with debts other than those actually owed in the name of the judgment debtor (*Continental Transfert Technique Ltd v Federal Government of Nigeria & ors* [2009] EWHC 2898 (Comm)).

'any condition applying to the account' (r 72.2(3))—If a liability is conditional, there may be no debt if the condition is not satisfied. In the case of balances held for the debtor by banks, building societies and the like, this difficulty is removed by SCA 1981, s 40, and CCA 1984, s 108, which provide that requirements for notice, personal application and production of a passbook are to be disregarded.

The Crown—This procedure is not available against the Crown as third party (CPR 1998, r 66.7(1)(a)). An equivalent procedure is provided by Crown Proceedings Act 1947, s 27 (see CPR 1998, r 66.7(3)). This restriction includes the National Savings Bank and, although SCA 1981, s 139(2) enables the Lord Chancellor to make an order removing the restriction, no such order has been made.

72.3 Application for third party debt order

(1) An application for a third party debt order –

(a) may be made without notice; and

(b) must be issued in the court which made the judgment or order which it is sought to enforce, except that –

PART III

(i) if the proceedings have since been transferred to a different court, it must be issued in that court; or

(ii) subject to subparagraph (b)(i), if it is to enforce a judgment made in the County Court Money Claims Centre, it must be issued in accordance with section 2 of Practice Direction 70.

(2) The application notice must –

(a) (i) be in the form; and

(ii) contain the information

required by Practice Direction 72; and

(b) be verified by a statement of truth.

Amendments—Inserted by SI 2001/2792. Amended by SI 2009/3390; SI 2012/505; SI 2014/407.

72.4 Interim third party debt order

(1) An application for a third party debt order will initially be dealt with by the court without a hearing.

(2) The court may make an interim third party debt order –

(a) fixing a hearing to consider whether to make a final third party debt order; and

(b) directing that until that hearing the third party must not make any payment which reduces the amount he owes the judgment debtor to less than the amount specified in the order.

(3) An interim third party debt order will specify the amount of money which the third party must retain, which will be the total of –

(a) the amount of money remaining due to the judgment creditor under the judgment or order; and

(b) an amount for the judgment creditor's fixed costs of the application, as specified in Practice Direction 72.

(4) An interim third party debt order becomes binding on a third party when it is served on him.

(5) The date of the hearing to consider the application shall be not less than 28 days after the interim third party debt order is made.

Amendments—Inserted by SI 2001/2792. Amended by SI 2009/3390.

Time for making interim order—If the order requires payment by a stated date, then the interim third party debt order will not be made before that date. An interim order is analogous to execution against goods and will not be made where such execution would not issue (*White, Son & Pill v Stennings* [1911] 2 KB 418, CA).

'the judge court may make' (r 72.4(2))—The court has a discretion as to whether to make the interim order and may decline to do so where, for example, the judgment debt is so small that the costs would be disproportionately burdensome.

72.5 Service of interim order

(1) Copies of an interim third party debt order, the application notice and any documents filed in support of it must be served –

(a) on the third party, not less than 21 days before the date fixed for the hearing; and

(b) on the judgment debtor not less than –

(i) 7 days after a copy has been served on the third party; and

(ii) 7 days before the date fixed for the hearing.

(2) If the judgment creditor serves the order, he must either –

(a) file a certificate of service not less than 2 days before the hearing; or

(b) produce a certificate of service at the hearing.

Amendments—Inserted by SI 2001/2792.

Documents to be served—Note that the rule requires the third party to be served not only with the order, but also with the application notice and any documents filed in support.

'must be served' (r 72.5(1))—The general rules as to service set out in Pt 6 apply. Where the third party is a deposit-taking institution, the best practice will be to effect service at the branch where the judgment debtor's account is believed to be held as being a place of business that has a real connection with the claim under r 6.9, as well as at the head office.

72.6 Obligations of third parties served with interim order

(1) A bank or building society served with an interim third party debt order must carry out a search to identify all accounts held with it by the judgment debtor.

(2) The bank or building society must disclose to the court and the creditor within 7 days of being served with the order, in respect of each account held by the judgment debtor –

- (a) the number of the account;
- (b) whether the account is in credit; and
- (c) if the account is in credit –
  - (i) whether the balance of the account is sufficient to cover the amount specified in the order;
  - (ii) the amount of the balance at the date it was served with the order, if it is less than the amount specified in the order; and
  - (iii) whether the bank or building society asserts any right to the money in the account, whether pursuant to a right of set-off or otherwise, and if so giving details of the grounds for that assertion.

(3) If –

- (a) the judgment debtor does not hold an account with the bank or building society; or
- (b) the bank or building society is unable to comply with the order for any other reason (for example, because it has more than one account holder whose details match the information contained in the order, and cannot identify which account the order applies to),

the bank or building society must inform the court and the judgment creditor of that fact within 7 days of being served with the order.

(4) Any third party other than a bank or building society served with an interim third party debt order must notify the court and the judgment creditor in writing within 7 days of being served with the order, if he claims –

- (a) not to owe any money to the judgment debtor; or
- (b) to owe less than the amount specified in the order.

Amendments—Inserted by SI 2001/2792. Amended by SI 2001/4015.

'must disclose to the court and the creditor' (r 72.6(2))—Note that unlike other third parties, banks and building societies are not required to make disclosure in writing, presumably opening the way to allow fax or e-mail communication with the court and judgment creditor.

Effect of interim third party debt order—There seems to be no reason why the relevant law that applied to garnishee orders should not continue to apply to third party debt orders. Thus, the third party's debt to the debtor is not transferred to the judgment creditor, but an equitable charge is created (to the extent stated in the interim order) so that, if a third party who has been served with the interim order makes payment otherwise than to the judgment creditor, he risks having to pay twice (*Galbraith v Grimshaw & Baxter* [1910] AC 508, HL). The judgment creditor can be in no better position against the third party than was the judgment debtor (*Levene v Maton* (1907) 51 SJ 532). If, for example, the judgment debtor assigned the debt to a fourth party before the interim order was served, then there will be no debt due to him for the interim order to attach, even though it was served before the third party had notice of the assignment (*Holt v Heatherfield Trust* [1942] 2 KB 1, KBD). If the third party is aware that a fourth party claims the debt, he must so inform the court, or the fact that he paid the judgment creditor under a third party debt order will not provide a defence to the fourth party's claim (*The Leader* (1868) LR 2 A&E 314, Admlty). The third party is not protected if he pays the judgment creditor upon receipt of the interim order but before it is made final (*Re Webster* [1907] 1 KB 623, KBD).

72.7 Arrangements for debtors in hardship

(1) If –

- (a) a judgment debtor is an individual;
- (b) he is prevented from withdrawing money from his account with a bank or building society as a result of an interim third party debt order; and
- (c) he or his family is suffering hardship in meeting ordinary living expenses as a result,

the court may, on an application by the judgment debtor, make an order permitting the bank or building society to make a payment or payments out of the account ('a hardship payment order').

PART III

(2) An application for a hardship payment order may be made –

(a) in High Court proceedings, at the Royal Courts of Justice, or the principal registry or to any district registry; and

(b) in County Court proceedings, to any County Court hearing centre.

(3) A judgment debtor may only apply to one court for a hardship payment order.

(4) An application notice seeking a hardship payment order must –

(a) include detailed evidence explaining why the judgment debtor needs a payment of the amount requested; and

(b) be verified by a statement of truth.

(5) Unless the court orders otherwise, the application notice –

(a) must be served on the judgment creditor at least 2 days before the hearing; but

(b) does not need to be served on the third party.

(6) A hardship payment order may –

(a) permit the third party to make one or more payments out of the account; and

(b) specify to whom the payments may be made.

Amendments—Inserted by SI 2001/2792. Amended by SI 2014/407.

Scope—This rule, which had no counterpart in the previous rules, was introduced to meet possible challenges to the third party debt order either under HRA 1998, Sch 1, Pt I, Art 8 or Art 1 of the First Protocol. It requires a high degree of communication and co-operation between the court in which the interim order is made and any court that deals with an application for a hardship payment order. Its use is most appropriate when the credit balance that has been frozen by the interim order is one that the judgment debtor reasonably expected would be available to fund essential payments for living expenditure, such as rent or mortgage instalments.

'a bank or building society' (r 72.7(1)b))—A hardship payment order cannot be made in respect of an account with an investment management company that is not a licensed deposit taker (*BM-Bank JSC v Chernyakov & ors*, Lawtel 24 November 2016)

'suffering hardship' (r 72.7(1)(c))—The test is ordinary and not exceptional hardship. A judgment debtor is likely to establish hardship if the interim order prevents him from having sufficient money to cover his rent or mortgage, the cost of travel to work and at least the weekly basic DWP entitlement for himself and his family. A debtor failed to establish hardship where the expenses in question included legal expenses and payments to the captain of his yacht, and he had another available account from which payments could be made (*BM-Bank JSC v Chernyakov & ors*, above).

Venue—Although the application is made in the proceedings, it does not have to be made to the court that made the interim order and will not be transferred to that court for hearing (see PD72, para 5.2).

'must be served' (r 72.7(5)(a))—See PD72, paras 5.4 and 5.5 for the procedure where the application is dealt with without the required notice to the judgment creditor.

72.8 Further consideration of the application

(1) If the judgment debtor or the third party objects to the court making a final third party debt order, he must file and serve written evidence stating the grounds for his objections.

(2) If the judgment debtor or the third party knows or believes that a person other than the judgment debtor has any claim to the money specified in the interim order, he must file and serve written evidence stating his knowledge of that matter.

(3) If –

(a) the third party has given notice under rule 72.6 that he does not owe any money to the judgment debtor, or that the amount which he owes is less than the amount specified in the interim order; and

(b) the judgment creditor wishes to dispute this,

the judgment creditor must file and serve written evidence setting out the grounds on which he disputes the third party's case.

(4) Written evidence under paragraphs (1), (2) or (3) must be filed and served on each other party as soon as possible, and in any event not less than 3 days before the hearing.

(5) If the court is notified that some person other than the judgment debtor may have a claim to the money specified in the interim order, it will serve on that person notice of the application and the hearing.

(6) At the hearing the court may –

(a) make a final third party debt order;

(b) discharge the interim third party debt order and dismiss the application;

(c) decide any issues in dispute between the parties, or between any of the parties and any other person who has a claim to the money specified in the interim order; or

(d) direct a trial of any such issues, and if necessary give directions.

Amendments—Inserted by SI 2001/2792.

'[may] make a final ... order' (r 72.8(6)(a))—There is a general discretion as to whether to make an order. Relevant considerations will include the size of the judgment debt, the existence of an instalment order in respect of that debt, the amount of the debt due from the third party, the existence of an instalment order or agreement in respect of the debt attached and the burden of costs resulting from an order. The interests of any other creditors of the judgment debtor are also material (*Roberts Petroleum Ltd v Bernard Kenny Ltd* [1983] 2 AC 192, CA). However, there is no principle that where a living debtor is insolvent or may be insolvent in the sense of having insufficient assets to pay his judgment creditors, all such creditors should benefit pari passu from the assets found by one such creditor. In *FG Hemisphere Associates LLC v The Republic of Congo* [2005] EWHC 3103 (Comm), Cooke J applied the dictum of Lord Goddard CJ in *James Bibby Ltd v Woods* [1949] 2 KB 449, KBD: 'the person who gets in first gets the fruits of his diligence'. All of the cases where courts have refused to make orders final have concerned statutory insolvency schemes, whether company liquidation or the administration of insolvent estates. The same principles apply to charging orders.

The court will be reluctant to attach the debtor's normal source of the proper living expenses of himself and his family – e g earnings that happened to be passing through the target bank account when the order nisi was served. If there is doubt as to whether the judgment debtor is solvent, the court may order the third party to pay the money into court pending its decision (*George Lee & Sons (Builders) Ltd v Olink* [1972] 1 WLR 214, CA, a case of a questionably solvent estate). If the proceedings concern a 'qualifying periodical maintenance order' within the meaning of MEA 1991, s 1 then the court may of its own motion make a 'means of payment order' under s 1(4)(a) of that Act or an attachment of earnings order by virtue of s 1(4)(b).

'any issues in dispute' (r 72.8(6)(c))—Primarily, the issue is between the judgment creditor and the third party; the judgment debtor is not a party to it. However, if there is a question as to whether another party is interested in or entitled to the fund, that other party may be joined to the proceedings under r 72.8(5). If the judgment creditor prefers not to contest the issue raised, he may abandon his application, but he may be liable in costs (*Wintle v Williams* (1858) 3 H&N 288, Exch).

72.9 Effect of final third party order

(1) A final third party debt order shall be enforceable as an order to pay money.

(2) If –

(a) the third party pays money to the judgment creditor in compliance with a third party debt order; or

(b) the order is enforced against him,

the third party shall, to the extent of the amount paid by him or realised by enforcement against him, be discharged from his debt to the judgment debtor.

(3) Paragraph (2) applies even if the third party debt order, or the original judgment or order against the judgment debtor, is later set aside.

Amendments—Inserted by SI 2001/2792.

****

72.11 Costs

If the judgment creditor is awarded costs on an application for an order under rule 72.2 or 72.10 –

(a) he shall, unless the court otherwise directs, retain those costs out of the money recovered by him under the order; and

(b) the costs shall be deemed to be paid first out of the money he recovers, in priority to the judgment debt.

Amendments—Inserted by SI 2001/2792.

Practice Direction 72 – Third Party Debt Orders

This Practice Direction supplements CPR Part 72

Amendments—CPR Update 26.

Application Notice – Rule 72.3

1.1 An application for a third party debt order must be made by filing an application notice in Practice Form N349.

1.2 The application notice must contain the following information –

(1) the name and address of the judgment debtor;
(2) details of the judgment or order sought to be enforced;
(3) the amount of money remaining due under the judgment or order;
(4) if the judgment debt is payable by instalments, the amount of any instalments which have fallen due and remain unpaid;
(5) the name and address of the third party;
(6) if the third party is a bank or building society –
  (a) its name and the address of the branch at which the judgment debtor's account is believed to be held; and
  (b) the account number;
  or, if the judgment creditor does not know all or part of this information, that fact;
(7) confirmation that to the best of the judgment creditor's knowledge or belief the third party –
  (a) is within the jurisdiction; and
  (b) owes money to or holds money to the credit of the judgment debtor;
(8) if the judgment creditor knows or believes that any person other than the judgment debtor has any claim to the money owed by the third party –
  (a) his name and (if known) his address; and
  (b) such information as is known to the judgment creditor about his claim;
(9) details of any other applications for third party debt orders issued by the judgment creditor in respect of the same judgment debt; and
(10) the sources or grounds of the judgment creditor's knowledge or belief of the matters referred to in (7), (8) and (9).

'the amount of money remaining due under the judgment or order' (para 1.2(3))—While the Practice Direction does not explicitly require this, it is good practice to set out how the amount is arrived at, by analogy with FPR 2010, r 33.3(1)(a).

1.3 The court will not grant speculative applications for third party debt orders, and will only make an interim third party debt order against a bank or building society if the judgment creditor's application notice contains evidence to substantiate his belief that the judgment debtor has an account with the bank or building society in question.

Interim Third Party Debt Order – Rule 72.4

2 An interim third party debt order will specify the amount of money which the third party must retain (rule 72.4(3)). This will include, in respect of the judgment creditor's fixed costs of the application, the amount which would be allowed to the judgment creditor under rule 45.8 if the whole balance of the judgment debt were recovered.

Interim Orders Relating to Bank or Building Society Accounts – Rule 72.6(1)–(3)

3.1 A bank or building society served with an interim third party debt order is only required by rule 72.6, unless the order states otherwise –

(1) to retain money in accounts held solely by the judgment debtor (or, if there are joint judgment debtors, accounts held jointly by them or solely by either or any of them); and
(2) to search for and disclose information about such accounts.

3.2 The bank or building society is not required, for example, to retain money in, or disclose information about –

(1) accounts in the joint names of the judgment debtor and another person; or
(2) if the interim order has been made against a firm, accounts in the names of individual members of that firm.

Attachment of debts owed by a partnership

3A.1 This paragraph relates to debts due or accruing due to a judgment creditor from a partnership.

3A.2 An interim third party debt order under rule 72.4(2) relating to such debts must be served on –

(1) a member of the partnership within the jurisdiction;
(2) a person authorised by a partner; or
(3) some other person having the control or management of the partnership business.

3A.3 Where an order made under rule 72.4(2) requires a partnership to appear before the court, it will be sufficient for a partner to appear before the court.

Amendments—CPR Update 42.

Transfer

4 The court may, on an application by a judgment debtor who wishes to oppose an application for a third party debt order, transfer it to –

(a) in the High Court, the court for the district; or
(b) in the County Court, the County Court hearing centre serving the address,

where the judgment debtor resides carries on business, or to another court.

Amendments—CPR Update 69.

Applications for Hardship Payment Orders – Rule 72.7

5.1 The court will treat an application for a hardship payment order as being made –

(1) in the proceedings in which the interim third party debt order was made; and
(2) under the same claim number,

regardless of where the judgment debtor makes the application.

5.2 An application for a hardship payment order will be dealt with by the court to which it is made.

(Rule 72.7(2) provides that an application may be made –

- in High Court proceedings, in the Royal Courts of Justice or to any district registry; and
- in County Court proceedings, to any County Court hearing centre.)

5.3 If the application is made to a different court from that dealing with the application for a third party debt order –

(1) the application for a third party debt order will not be transferred; but
(2) the court dealing with that application will send copies of –
  (a) the application notice; and
  (b) the interim third party debt order

  to the court hearing the application for a hardship payment order.

5.4 Rule 72.7(3) requires an application for a hardship payment order to be served on the judgment creditor at least 2 days before the court is to deal with the application, unless the court orders otherwise. In cases of exceptional urgency the judgment debtor may apply for a hardship payment order without notice to the judgment creditor and a judge will decide whether to –

(1) deal with the application without it being served on the judgment creditor; or
(2) direct it to be served.

PART III

5.5 If the judge decides to deal with the application without it being served on the judgment creditor, where possible he will normally –

(1) direct that the judgment creditor be informed of the application; and
(2) give him the opportunity to make representations,

by telephone, fax or other appropriate method of communication.

5.6 The evidence filed by a judgment debtor in support of an application for a hardship payment order should include documentary evidence, for example (if appropriate) bank statements, wage slips and mortgage statements, to prove his financial position and need for the payment.

Amendments—CPR Update 69.

Final Orders Relating to Building Society Accounts

6 A final third party debt order will not require a payment which would reduce to less than £1 the amount in a judgment debtor's account with a building society or credit union.

PART 73
CHARGING ORDERS, STOP ORDERS AND STOP NOTICES

Charging orders in civil proceedings—For the provisions of this Part that govern the making of charging orders in civil proceedings, see *Civil Court Service* (LexisNexis). Those provisions changed with effect from 6 April 2016 and differ from those applying in family proceedings.

****

73.10C Enforcement of charging order by sale

(1) Subject to the provisions of any enactment, the court may, upon a claim by a person who has obtained a charging order over an interest in property, order the sale of the property to enforce the charging order.

(2) Where the charging order was made at the County Court Money Claims Centre a claim for an order for sale under this rule must be made to the judgment debtor's home court.

(3) Subject to paragraph (2) a claim for an order for sale under this rule should be made to the court which made the charging order, unless that court does not have jurisdiction to make an order for sale.

(4) The claimant must use the Part 8 procedure.

(5) A copy of the charging order must be filed with the claim form.

Amendments—Inserted by SI 2016/234.

'the court may' (r 73.10C(1))—It sometimes seems to be assumed that a creditor is entitled to an order for sale under this provision as a matter of right, but this is not the case. In the common case where the property concerned is the debtor's home, the debtor's right to respect for his home under ECHR Art 8 must be balanced against the creditor's right to secure payment of his debt, as was emphasised in the ECtHR case of *Zehentner v Austria* [2009] ECHR 1119. The claimant's written evidence should address this issue.

In the case of the debtor's home, it is a draconian step to require a sale to satisfy a simple debt. It is rarely done, except in response to the debtor's contumelious neglect or refusal to pay; even then, the order will often be suspended on terms as to payment. It may be otherwise in the case of investment property. Where the order to be enforced is a maintenance order, the debtor's resources will have been taken into account when it was made and his neglect or refusal may thus be easier to demonstrate.

The fact that the value of the property charged significantly exceeds the judgment debt is not a reason for refusing a sale; it is 'just one of the considerations to be taken into account and not an overriding one'; *Packman Lucas Ltd v (1) Mentmore Towers Ltd (2) Charles Street Holdings Ltd* [2010] EWHC 1037 (TCC).

'interest in property' (r 73.10C(1))—Application under this rule is likely to be useful only where the legal estate of the judgment debtor has been charged. Where the charge has been imposed on the judgment debtor's beneficial interest, sale of that interest alone may be difficult or impossible to achieve and in that case the judgment creditor should take fresh proceedings under TLATA 1996, s 14 using the Pt 8 procedure.

'jurisdiction to make an order for sale' (r 73.10C(3))—The Family Court does not, of course, have such jurisdiction.

The County Court now has jurisdiction to make orders for sale where the amount of the charge at the date of commencement of the proceedings does not exceed £350,000 (CCA 1984, s 23(c), as amended by the County Court Jurisdiction Order 2014) or where the amount exceeds that figure and both parties consent under CCA 1984, s 24. The High Court can transfer an application to the County Court (*National Westminster Bank Plc v King* [2008] Ch 385, ChD) but may now be less ready to do so.

'Part 8 procedure'—That is, the procedure under Pt 8 of the CPR, as to which see *Civil Court Service* (LexisNexis).

★★★★

PART 74
ENFORCEMENT OF JUDGMENTS IN DIFFERENT JURISDICTIONS

★★★★

Scope—Pt 74 and its accompanying PDs set out the procedural rules relating to a number of pieces of legislation allowing foreign judgments to be directly enforced in England and Wales, and English judgments to be directly enforced in foreign courts. The text of Pt 74 with detailed annotation and the PDs are set out in *Civil Court Service* (LexisNexis). The following note is intended as a brief introduction.

General note—A money judgment of a foreign court cannot be directly enforced in England and Wales. However, it can be made the basis of an action in the English courts, in which summary judgment will be granted (see *Colt Industries Inc v Sarlie* (No 2) [1966] 1 WLR 1287, CA) unless the defendant can establish one of a limited number of defences.

Four pieces of legislation, which will be briefly discussed, allow foreign judgments to be registered in the High Court for enforcement, without the claimant needing to bring a fresh action. A fifth, the European Enforcement Order, allows certain judgments from EU countries to be enforced in the High Court or the county court. It is important to realise that unless the case falls within the scope of one of them, there is no power to register a foreign money judgment for enforcement.

Arrears under foreign maintenance orders can generally not be the subject of an action in England (*Harrop v Harrop* [1920] 3 KB 386, KBD) but arrangements have been made for their reciprocal enforcement, for details of which see Procedural Guides C1(1)–C1(15). In *O'Farrell v O'Farrell* [2013] 1 FLR 77, QBD, a European judgment for arrears of maintenance was registered for enforcement in the High Court, but the Court suggested that registration would have been discharged had the payor appealed and references to judgments in Pt 74 should be construed as references to judgments other than maintenance orders.

The Administration of Justice Act 1920 ('the 1920 Act')—This Act provides for reciprocal enforcement of judgments of the superior courts in countries to which the Act had been applied by Order in Council before the 1933 Act came into force. The consolidated list is as follows:

Anguilla, Antigua and Barbuda, Bahamas, Barbados, Belize, Bermuda, Botswana, British Indian Ocean Territory, British Virgin Islands, Cayman Islands, Christmas Island, Cocos (Keeling) Islands, Republic of Cyprus, Dominica, Falkland Islands, Fiji, The Gambia, Ghana, Grenada, Guyana, Jamaica, Kenya, Kiribati, Lesotho, Malawi, Malaysia, Malta, Mauritius, Montserrat, New Zealand, Nigeria, Territory of Norfolk Island, Papua New Guinea, St Christopher and Nevis, St Helena, St Lucia, St Vincent and the Grenadines, Seychelles, Sierra Leone, Singapore, Solomon Islands, Sovereign Base Area of Akrotiri and Dhekelia in Cyprus, Sri Lanka, Swaziland, Tanzania, Tasmania, Trinidad and Tobago, Turks and Caicos Islands, Tuvalu, Uganda, Zambia, Zimbabwe.

The 1920 Act no longer applies to Hong Kong or Gibraltar; Gibraltar is now subject to the Brussels Convention.

See s 9(2) for limitations on the judgments which may be registered.

The Foreign Judgments (Reciprocal Enforcement) Act 1933 ('the 1933 Act')—This Act made further provision for reciprocal enforcement of judgments with a number of countries. The only non-Commonwealth countries to which the 1933 Act is still relevant are Israel, Surinam and Tonga. All of the other countries formerly covered by the Act are now parties to the Brussels or Lugano Conventions or to the various European Regulations and applications should be made under the 1982 Act, the Judgments Regulation or the European Enforcement Order procedure as appropriate. The list of Commonwealth countries to which the Act has been applied is as follows:

Australia including the Australian Capital Territory, the Federal Court of Canada and courts of all provinces except Quebec, Island of Guernsey, Isle of Man, Bailiwick of Jersey, certain territories of the Republic of India named in the Schedule to the Reciprocal Enforcement of Judgments (India) Order 1958 and Pakistan.

A judgment which is capable of being registered under the 1933 Act cannot be made the subject of an action (see s 6 and *Yukon Consolidated Gold Corporation Ltd v Clark* [1938] 2 KB 241, CA).

The Civil Jurisdiction and Judgments Act 1982 ('the 1982 Act')—This Act gave effect to the Brussels Convention (to which the EEC countries were parties) and, as amended, gives effect to the similar Lugano Conventions of 1988 and 2007 signed by Iceland, Switzerland and Norway. Of these, only Norway has ratified the 2007 Convention. As with the 1933 Act, a registrable judgment cannot be made the subject of an action. The grounds on which registration may be set aside are very limited.

Council Regulation (EU) No 1215/2012 ('the Judgments Regulation')—The recast Judgments Regulation, Council Regulation (EU) No 1215/2012, on jurisdiction and the recognition and enforcement of judgments in civil and commercial matters, applies a uniform regime, similar although not identical to that under the Brussels Convention, to the Member States of the European Union. It replaced Regulation (EC) No 44/2001 from 10 January 2015, but only in relation to judgments in proceedings instituted on and after that date. It makes judgments of the courts of Member States directly enforceable without further formality.

The European Enforcement Order (EEO)—Council Regulation (EC) No 805/2004 created an alternative enforcement regime for uncontested claims. It applies to all Member States of the EU other than Denmark. The intention is that a judgment which is certified as an EEO shall be recognised and enforced in the other Member States without the need for a declaration of enforceability and without any possibility of opposing its recognition. Specifically, an application to stay or limit enforcement proceedings under an EEO, must be made to the courts of the Member State of origin. Only then may the courts of the Member State of enforcement stay enforcement to await the outcome of that application. Apart from that, the only power the enforcing court has to refuse to enforce an EEO is that under Art 21 of the Regulation, where the EEO is irreconcilable with an earlier judgment and the irreconcilability was not and could not have been raised as an objection in the court proceedings in the court of origin. Under no circumstances may the judgment, or its certification as an EEO, be reviewed as to their substance in the Member State of enforcement.

It should be noted that a claim may be regarded as 'uncontested' if the debtor has not appeared or been represented at a court hearing regarding it, provided the debtor has been satisfactorily served. The EEO regime applies to any judgment given by a court or tribunal of a Member State, whatever the judgment may be called, and also applies to 'court settlements and authentic instruments'. However, since the coming into force of the Maintenance Regulation (EC) Reg No 4/2009, the EEO procedure no longer applies to maintenance claims.

A judgment creditor is not obliged to use the EEO.

The details of the EEO procedure are to be found in Pt V of Pt 74 comprising rr 74.27–74.33, PD74B and the Regulation itself, which is annexed to the PD.

Protection Measures—Section VI was inserted into Pt 74 with effect from 11 January 2015 to give effect to European Regulation 606/2013 (the 'Protection Measures Regulation'). The Regulation establish rules for 'a simple and rapid mechanism for the recognition of protection measures ordered in a Member State in civil matters', addressing the perceived weakness of such protection measures – that they apply only in the country in which they are granted. (A summary of the Regulation is set out in Part VI.)

Section VI of Pt 74 is drafted in virtually identical terms to FPR 2010, Pt 38. Readers are referred to the discussion of those Rules and PD38A and their compliance with the requirements of the Regulation.

****

PART 81
APPLICATIONS AND PROCEEDINGS IN RELATION TO CONTEMPT OF COURT

CONTENTS OF THIS PART

Section 1

Rule		Page
	Scope and Interpretation	
81.1	Scope	2302
81.2	Saving for other powers	2302
81.3	Interpretation	2302
	Section 2	
	Committal for Breach of a Judgment, Order or Undertaking to Do or Abstain from Doing an Act	
81.4	Enforcement of judgment, order or undertaking to do or abstain from doing an act	2303
81.5	Requirement for service of a copy of the judgment or order and time for service	2303
81.6	Method of service – copies of judgments or orders	2303
81.7	Method of service – copies of undertakings	2304
81.8	Dispensation with personal service	2304
81.9	Requirement for a penal notice on judgments and orders	2304
81.10	How to make the committal application	2304
81.11	Committal for breach of a solicitor's undertaking	2305
	Section 3	
	Committal for Interference with the Due Administration of Justice	
81.12	Scope	2305
81.13	Court to which application for permission under this Section is to be made	2305
81.14	Application for permission (High Court, Divisional Court or Administrative Court)	2306
	Section 4	
	(1) Certifications by Any Court, Tribunal etc to the High Court under any Enactment; and (2) Applications to the High Court under Section 336 of the Charities Act 2011	
81.15	Certifications of conduct, and applications under section 336 of the Charities Act 2011, to the High Court under this Section	2306

Section 5
Contempt in the Face of the Court

81.16 Committal for contempt in the face of the court 2307

Section 6
Committal for Making a False Statement of Truth (rule 32.14) or Disclosure Statement (rule 31.23)

81.17 Scope and interaction with other Sections of this Part 2307
81.18 Committal application in relation to a false statement of truth or disclosure statement 2308

Section 7
Writ of Sequestration to Enforce a Judgment, Order or Undertaking

81.19 Scope 2309
81.20 Writ of sequestration to enforce a judgment, order or undertaking 2309
81.21 Requirement for service of a copy of the judgment or order and time for service 2309
81.22 Method of service – copies of judgments or orders 2309
81.23 Method of service – copies of undertakings 2309
81.24 Dispensation with personal service 2310
81.25 Requirement for a penal notice on judgments and orders 2310
81.26 How to make an application for permission to issue a writ of sequestration 2310
81.27 Form of writ of sequestration 2310

Section 8
General Rules about Committal Applications, Orders for Committal and Writs of Sequestration

81.28 The hearing 2311
81.29 Power to suspend execution of a committal order 2311
81.30 Warrant of committal 2311
81.31 Discharge of a person in custody 2312
81.32 Discharge of a person in custody where a writ of sequestration has been issued 2312

Section 9
Penal, Contempt and Disciplinary Provisions under the County Courts Act 1984

81.33 Scope 2312
81.34 Offences under sections 14, 92 or 118 of the Act 2312
81.35 Offences under section 124 of the Act 2313
81.36 Notice to give evidence before or after a fine is imposed under section 55 of the Act 2313
81.37 Non-payment of fine 2313
81.38 Repayment of fine 2313

Practice Direction 81 –
Applications and Proceedings in relation to Contempt of Court 2314

Scope—CPR Pt 81 came into force on 1 October 2012. It applies only to civil proceedings where the order sought to be enforced by committal was made under the provisions of the CPR (such as an application to commit for breach of an order under the Protection from Harassment Act obtained under Pt 65 or breach of a freezing order obtained under Pt 25). It does not apply to family proceedings, which have their own code under FPR 2010, Pt 37.

Before making any application to commit for contempt, it is necessary to have in mind the relevant law. Rules of procedure do not confer power to commit but merely regulate how the application is made and dealt with. The law on contempt is a complicated mixture of common law, statute and (in the case of the High Court) the inherent jurisdiction.

Pt 81 is divided into Sections, each being structured to deal with a specific type of contempt. This has the disadvantage that the Part is long and repetitive but that is outweighed by the advantage that each of its nine Sections is self-contained and clear. After the necessary 'Scope and interpretation' in Section 1, the most common type of committal, 'Committal for breach of a judgment, order or undertaking to do or abstain from doing an act' is found in Section 2. 'General rules about committal applications, orders for committal and writs of sequestration' are set out in Section 8. These three Sections will need to be referred to more frequently than the others. Pt 81 is supplemented by CPR PD81.

Pt 81 largely replicates the former practice and procedure but does so in a much clearer and more logical fashion. Nowhere is the need for clarity greater than when dealing with the liberty of the subject. One significant change in Pt 81 is in Section 3, 'Committal for interference with the due administration of justice', where a permission stage is introduced.

Section 1
Scope and Interpretation

81.1 Scope

(1) This Part sets out the procedure in respect of –

(a) contempt of court; and
(b) the penal, contempt and disciplinary provisions of the County Courts Act 1984.

(2) So far as applicable, and with the necessary modifications, this Part applies in relation to an order requiring a person –

(a) guilty of contempt of court; or
(b) punishable by virtue of any enactment as if that person had been guilty of contempt of the High Court,

to pay a fine or to give security for good behaviour, as it applies in relation to an order of committal.

(3) Unless otherwise stated, this Part applies to procedure in the Court of Appeal, the High Court and the County Court.

Amendments—SI 2014/407.

81.2 Saving for other powers

(1) This Part is concerned only with procedure and does not itself confer upon the court the power to make an order for –

(a) committal;
(b) sequestration; or
(c) the imposition of a fine in respect of contempt of court.

(2) Nothing in this Part affects the power of the court to make an order requiring a person –

(a) guilty of contempt of court; or
(b) punishable by virtue of any enactment as if that person had been guilty of contempt of the High Court,

to pay a fine or to give security for good behaviour.

(3) Nothing in this Part affects any statutory or inherent power of the court to make a committal order of its own initiative against a person guilty of contempt of court.

81.3 Interpretation

In this Part –

'applicant' means a person making –
(i) an application for permission to make a committal application;
(ii) a committal application; or
(iii) an application for a writ of sequestration;

'committal application' means any application for an order committing a person to prison;

'respondent' means a person –
(i) against whom a committal application is made or is intended to be made; or
(ii) against whose property it is sought to issue a writ of sequestration; and

'undertaking' means an undertaking to the court.

Section 2
Committal for Breach of a Judgment, Order or Undertaking to Do or Abstain from Doing an Act

81.4 Enforcement of judgment, order or undertaking to do or abstain from doing an act

(1) If a person –

- (a) required by a judgment or order to do an act does not do it within the time fixed by the judgment or order; or
- (b) disobeys a judgment or order not to do an act,

then, subject to the Debtors Acts 1869 and 1878 and to the provisions of these Rules, the judgment or order may be enforced by an order for committal.

(2) If the time fixed by the judgment or order for doing an act has been varied by a subsequent order or agreement of the parties under rule 2.11, then references in paragraph (1)(a) to the time fixed are references to the time fixed by that subsequent order or agreement.

(3) If the person referred to in paragraph (1) is a company or other corporation, the committal order may be made against any director or other officer of that company or corporation.

(4) So far as applicable, and with the necessary modifications, this Section applies to undertakings given by a party as it applies to judgments or orders.

(Rules 81.17(3) and (4) make provision for cases in which both this Section and Section 6 (Committal for making a false statement of truth or disclosure statement) may be relevant.)

(5) If a judgment or order requires a person to deliver goods or pay their value –

- (a) the judgment or order may not be enforced by a committal order under paragraph (1);
- (b) the person entitled to enforce the judgment or order may apply to the court for an order requiring that the goods be delivered within a specified time; and
- (c) where the court grants such an order, that order may be enforced under paragraph (1).

81.5 Requirement for service of a copy of the judgment or order and time for service

(1) Unless the court dispenses with service under rule 81.8, a judgment or order may not be enforced under rule 81.4 unless a copy of it has been served on the person required to do or not do the act in question, and in the case of a judgment or order requiring a person to do an act –

- (a) the copy has been served before the end of the time fixed for doing the act, together with a copy of any order fixing that time;
- (b) where the time for doing the act has been varied by a subsequent order or agreement under rule 2.11, a copy of that subsequent order or agreement has also been served; and
- (c) where the judgment or order was made under rule 81.4(5), or was made pursuant to an earlier judgment or order requiring the act to be done, a copy of the earlier judgment or order has also been served.

(2) Where the person referred to in paragraph (1) is a company or other corporation, a copy of the judgment or order must also be served on the respondent before the end of the time fixed for doing the act.

(3) Copies of the judgment or order and any orders or agreements fixing or varying the time for doing an act must be served in accordance with rule 81.6 or 81.7, or in accordance with an order for alternative service made under rule 81.8(2)(b).

81.6 Method of service – copies of judgments or orders

Subject to rules 81.7 and 81.8, copies of judgments or orders and any orders or agreements fixing or varying the time for doing an act must be served personally.

81.7 Method of service – copies of undertakings

(1) Subject to paragraph (2) and rule 81.8, a copy of any document recording an undertaking will be delivered by the court to the person who gave the undertaking –

- (a) by handing to that person a copy of the document before that person leaves the court building;
- (b) by posting a copy to that person at the residence or place of business of that person where this is known; or
- (c) by posting a copy to that person's solicitor.

(2) If delivery cannot be effected in accordance with paragraph (1), the court officer will deliver a copy of the document to the party for whose benefit the undertaking was given and that party must serve it personally on the person who gave the undertaking as soon as practicable.

(3) Where the person referred to in paragraph (1) is a company or other corporation, a copy of the judgment or order must also be served on the respondent.

81.8 Dispensation with personal service

(1) In the case of a judgment or order requiring a person not to do an act, the court may dispense with service of a copy of the judgment or order in accordance with rules 81.5 to 81.7 if it is satisfied that the person has had notice of it –

- (a) by being present when the judgment or order was given or made; or
- (b) by being notified of its terms by telephone, email or otherwise.

(2) In the case of any judgment or order the court may –

- (a) dispense with service under rules 81.5 to 81.7 if the court thinks it just to do so; or
- (b) make an order in respect of service by an alternative method or at an alternative place.

Dispensing with personal service—In *Sports Direct v Rangers Football Club* [2016] EWHC 85 (Ch), where failure to serve personally was not mere oversight, Peter Smith J was not persuaded to exercise discretion to dispense with personal service retrospectively. However, in *JSC Mezhdunarodniy Promyshlenniy Bank v Pugachev* [2016] EWHC 192 (Ch), Rose J held it was in the interests of justice to dispense with personal service (thereby dispensing, retrospectively, with the need for a penal notice). See also *Khawaja v Popat* [2016] EWCA Civ 362.

81.9 Requirement for a penal notice on judgments and orders

(1) Subject to paragraph (2), a judgment or order to do or not do an act may not be enforced under rule 81.4 unless there is prominently displayed, on the front of the copy of the judgment or order served in accordance with this Section, a warning to the person required to do or not do the act in question that disobedience to the order would be a contempt of court punishable by imprisonment, a fine or sequestration of assets.

(2) The following may be enforced under rule 81.4 notwithstanding that they do not contain the warning described in paragraph (1) –

- (a) an undertaking to do or not do an act which is contained in a judgment or order; and
- (b) an incoming protection measure.

(3) In this rule, 'incoming protection measure' has the meaning given to it in rule 74.34(1).

(Paragraphs 2.1 to 2.4 of the Practice Direction supplementing this Part and form N117 contain provisions about penal notices and warnings in relation to undertakings.)

Amendments—SI 2014/3299.

81.10 How to make the committal application

(1) A committal application is made by an application notice under Part 23 in the proceedings in which the judgment or order was made or the undertaking was given.

(2) Where the committal application is made against a person who is not an existing party to the proceedings, it is made against that person by an application notice under Part 23.

(3) The application notice must –

(a) set out in full the grounds on which the committal application is made and must identify, separately and numerically, each alleged act of contempt including, if known, the date of each of the alleged acts; and

(b) be supported by one or more affidavits containing all the evidence relied upon.

(4) Subject to paragraph (5), the application notice and the evidence in support must be served personally on the respondent.

(5) The court may –

(a) dispense with service under paragraph (4) if it considers it just to do so; or

(b) make an order in respect of service by an alternative method or at an alternative place.

81.11 Committal for breach of a solicitor's undertaking

(1) The applicant must obtain permission from the court before making a committal application under this rule.

(2) The application for permission must be made by filing an application notice under Part 23.

(3) The application for permission must be supported by an affidavit setting out –

(a) the name, description and address of the respondent; and

(b) the grounds on which the committal order is sought.

(4) The application for permission may be made without notice.

(5) Rules 23.9 and 23.10 do not apply.

(6) Unless the applicant makes the committal application within 14 days after permission has been granted under this rule, the permission will lapse.

Section 3
Committal for Interference with the Due Administration of Justice

81.12 Scope

(1) This Section regulates committal applications in relation to interference with the due administration of justice in connection with proceedings –

(a) in the High Court;

(b) in a Divisional Court;

(c) in the Court of Appeal;

(d) in an inferior court (which includes the County Court); or

(e) which are criminal proceedings,

except where the contempt is committed in the face of the court or consists of disobedience to an order of the court or a breach of an undertaking to the court.

(2) This Section also regulates committal applications otherwise than in connection with any proceedings.

(3) A committal application under this Section may not be made without the permission of the court.

(The procedure for applying for permission to make a committal application is set out in rule 81.14.)

(Rules 81.17(5) and (6) make provision for cases in which both this Section and Section 6 (Committal for making a false statement of truth or disclosure statement) may be relevant.)

Amendments—SI 2014/407.

81.13 Court to which application for permission under this Section is to be made

(1) Where contempt of court is committed in connection with any proceedings –

(a) in the High Court (other than proceedings in a Divisional Court), the application for

PART III

permission may be made only to a single judge of the Division of the High Court in which the proceedings were commenced or to which they have subsequently been transferred;

(b) in a Divisional Court, the application for permission may be made only to a single judge of the Queen's Bench Division;

(c) in the Court of Appeal, the application for permission may be made only to a Divisional Court of the Queen's Bench Division;

(d) in an inferior court, the application for permission may be made only to a single judge of the High Court; and

(e) which are criminal proceedings, the application for permission may be made only to a Divisional Court of the Queen's Bench Division.

(2) Where contempt of court is committed otherwise than in connection with any proceedings, the application for permission may be made only to the Administrative Court.

Amendments—SI 2014/867.

81.14 Application for permission (High Court, Divisional Court or Administrative Court)

(1) The application for permission to make a committal application must be made by a Part 8 claim form which must include or be accompanied by –

(a) a detailed statement of the applicant's grounds for bringing the committal application; and

(b) an affidavit setting out the facts and exhibiting all documents relied upon.

(2) The claim form and the documents referred to in paragraph (1) must be served personally on the respondent unless the court otherwise directs.

(3) Within 14 days of service on the respondent of the claim form, the respondent –

(a) must file and serve an acknowledgment of service; and

(b) may file and serve evidence.

(4) The court will consider the application for permission at an oral hearing, unless it considers that such a hearing is not appropriate.

(5) If the respondent intends to appear at the permission hearing referred to in paragraph (4), the respondent must give 7 days' notice in writing of such intention to the court and any other party and at the same time provide a written summary of the submissions which the respondent proposes to make.

(6) Where permission to proceed is given, the court may give such directions as it thinks fit, and may –

(a) transfer the proceedings to another court; or

(b) direct that the application be listed for hearing before a single judge or a Divisional Court.

Effect of rule—The circumstances in which an application for permission to make a committal application is required are listed in r 81.13. In *Cavendish Square Holdings BV v Makdessi* [2013] EWCA Civ 1540, D served a defence verified by a statement of truth. He subsequently served an amended defence admitting a matter previously denied and therefore in effect abandoned a denial of breach of fiduciary duty. The Court of Appeal upheld the trial judge's decision to grant C's application for permission to make a committal application based on D having made a false statement in a document verified by a statement of truth.

Section 4

(1) Certifications by Any Court, Tribunal etc to the High Court under any Enactment; and (2) Applications to the High Court under Section 336 of the Charities Act 2011

81.15 Certifications of conduct, and applications under section 336 of the Charities Act 2011, to the High Court under this Section

(1) This Section applies where, by virtue of any enactment, the High Court has power to punish or take steps for the punishment of any person charged with having done or omitted to do

anything in relation to a court, tribunal, body or person which, if it had been an act or omission in relation to the High Court, would have been a contempt of that court.

(2) Subject to paragraph (3), an order under this Section may be made by a single judge of the Administrative Court.

(3) An order made on an application under section 336 of the Charities Act 2011 ('a section 336 application') may be made only by a single judge of the Chancery Division.

(4) The certification or section 336 application, as appropriate, must be in the form annexed to Practice Direction 81 at Annex A, and include or be accompanied by –

- (a) a detailed statement of the grounds for the certification or section 336 application;
- (b) any written evidence relied upon; and
- (c) any other documents required for the disposal of the certification or section 336 application.

(5) Subject to paragraph (6), the certification or section 336 application, accompanied by the other documents referred to in paragraph (4), must be served personally on the respondent.

(6) The court may –

- (a) dispense with service under paragraph (5) if it thinks it just to do so; or
- (b) make an order in respect of service by an alternative method or at an alternative place.

(7) Within 14 days of service on the respondent of the certification or section 336 application, the respondent –

- (a) must file and serve an acknowledgment of service in the form annexed to Practice Direction 81 at Annex B; and
- (b) may file and serve evidence.

Amendments—SI 2014/2044.

Section 5
Contempt in the Face of the Court

81.16 Committal for contempt in the face of the court

(1) Where –

- (a) contempt has occurred in the face of the court; and
- (b) that court has power to commit for contempt,

the court may deal with the matter of its own initiative and give such directions as it thinks fit for the disposal of the matter.

Section 6
Committal for Making a False Statement of Truth (rule 32.14) or Disclosure Statement (rule 31.23)

81.17 Scope and interaction with other Sections of this Part

(1) This Section contains rules about committal applications in relation to making, or causing to be made –

- (a) a false statement in a document verified by a statement of truth; or
- (b) a false disclosure statement,

without an honest belief in its truth.

(2) Where the committal application relates only to a false statement of truth or disclosure statement, this Section applies.

(3) Where the committal application relates to both –

- (a) a false statement of truth or disclosure statement; and
- (b) breach of a judgment, order or undertaking to do or abstain from doing an act,

PART III

Section 2 (Committal for breach of a judgment, order or undertaking to do or abstain from doing an act) applies, but subject to paragraph (4).

(4) To the extent that a committal application referred to in paragraph (3) relates to a false statement of truth or disclosure statement –

(a) the applicant must obtain the permission of the court in accordance with rule 81.18; or
(b) the court may direct that the matter be referred to the Attorney General with a request that the Attorney General consider whether to bring proceedings for contempt of court.

(5) Where the committal application relates to both –

(a) a false statement of truth or disclosure statement; and
(b) other interference with the due administration of justice,

Section 3 (Committal for interference with the due administration of justice) applies, but subject to paragraph (6).

(6) To the extent that a committal application referred to in paragraph (5) relates to a false statement of truth or disclosure statement, the court may direct that the matter be referred to the Attorney General with a request that the Attorney General consider whether to bring proceedings for contempt of court.

Committal for knowingly swearing a false affidavit—Section 6 of Pt 81 deals with contempt in making a false statement of truth, not a false affidavit. Logically, therefore, contempt in making a false statement in an affidavit falls within Section 3 of Pt 81. However, in *International Sports Tours Ltd v Shorey* [2015] EWHC 2040 (QB) it was held that such a case falls outwith the scope of Pt 81 altogether.

81.18 Committal application in relation to a false statement of truth or disclosure statement

(1) A committal application in relation to a false statement of truth or disclosure statement in connection with proceedings in the High Court, a Divisional Court or the Court of Appeal, may be made only –

(a) with the permission of the court dealing with the proceedings in which the false statement or disclosure statement was made; or
(b) by the Attorney General.

(2) Where permission is required under paragraph (1)(a), rule 81.14 applies as if the reference in that rule to a Part 8 claim form were a reference to a Part 23 application notice and the references to the claim form were references to the Part 23 application notice.

(3) A committal application in relation to a false statement of truth or disclosure statement in connection with proceedings in the County Court may be made only –

(a) with the permission of a single judge of the High Court; or
(b) by the Attorney General.

(4) Where permission is required under paragraph (3)(a) rule 81.14 applies without the modifications referred to in paragraph (2).

(Under rule 81.14(6)(b), the court granting permission may direct that the application be listed for hearing before a single judge or a Divisional Court.)

(5) The court may direct that the matter be referred to the Attorney General with a request that the Attorney General consider whether to bring proceedings for contempt of court.

(6) Where the committal application is made by the Attorney General, the application may be made to a single judge or a Divisional Court of the Queen's Bench Division.

Amendments—SI 2014/407; SI 2014/867.

Section 7
Writ of Sequestration to Enforce a Judgment, Order or Undertaking

81.19 Scope

This Section contains rules about applications to the High Court for a writ of sequestration to enforce a judgment, order or undertaking.

81.20 Writ of sequestration to enforce a judgment, order or undertaking

(1) If –

(a) a person required by a judgment or order to do an act does not do it within the time fixed by the judgment or order; or

(b) a person disobeys a judgment or order not to do an act,

then, subject to the provisions of these Rules and if the court permits, the judgment or order may be enforced by a writ of sequestration against the property of that person.

(2) If the time fixed by the judgment or order for doing an act has been varied by a subsequent order or agreement of the parties under rule 2.11, references in paragraph (1)(a) to the time fixed are references to the time fixed by that subsequent order or agreement.

(3) If the person referred to in paragraph (1) is a company or other corporation, the writ of sequestration may in addition be issued against the property of any director or other officer of that company or corporation.

(4) So far as applicable, and with the necessary modifications, this Section applies to undertakings given by a party as it applies to judgments or orders.

81.21 Requirement for service of a copy of the judgment or order and time for service

(1) Unless the court dispenses with service under rule 81.24, a judgment or order may not be enforced by writ of sequestration unless a copy of it has been served on the person required to do or not do the act in question, and in the case of a judgment or order requiring a person to do an act –

(a) the copy has been served before the end of the time fixed for doing the act, together with a copy of any order fixing that time;

(b) where the time for doing the act has been varied by a subsequent order or agreement under rule 2.11, a copy of that subsequent order or agreement has also been served; and

(c) where the judgment or order was made under rule 81.4(5), or was made pursuant to an earlier judgment or order requiring the act to be done, a copy of the earlier judgment or order has also been served.

(2) Where the person referred to in paragraph (1) is a company or other corporation, a copy of the judgment or order must also be served on the respondent before the end of the time fixed for doing the act.

(3) Copies of the judgment or order and any orders or agreements fixing or varying the time for doing an act must be served in accordance with rule 81.22 or 81.23, or in accordance with an order for alternative service made under rule 81.24(2)(b).

81.22 Method of service – copies of judgments or orders

Subject to rules 81.23 and 81.24, copies of judgments or orders and any orders or agreements fixing or varying the time for doing an act must be served personally.

81.23 Method of service – copies of undertakings

(1) Subject to paragraph (2) and rule 81.24, a copy of any document recording an undertaking will be delivered by the court to the person who gave the undertaking –

(a) by handing to that person a copy of the document before that person leaves the court building;

(b) by posting a copy to that person at the residence or place of business of that person where this is known; or

(c) by posting a copy to that person's solicitor.

(2) If delivery cannot be effected in accordance with paragraph (1), the court officer will deliver a copy of the document to the party for whose benefit the undertaking was given and that party must serve it personally on the person who gave the undertaking as soon as practicable.

(3) Where the person referred to in paragraph (1) is a company or other corporation, a copy of the judgment or order must also be served on the respondent.

81.24 Dispensation with personal service

(1) In the case of a judgment or order requiring a person not to do an act, the court may dispense with service of a copy of the judgment or order in accordance with rules 81.21 to 81.23 if it is satisfied that the person has had notice of it –

(a) by being present when the judgment or order was given or made; or

(b) by being notified of its terms by telephone, email or otherwise.

(2) In the case of any judgment or order the court may –

(a) dispense with service under rules 81.21 to 81.23 if the court thinks it just to do so; or

(b) make an order in respect of service by an alternative method or at an alternative place.

81.25 Requirement for a penal notice on judgments and orders

(1) Subject to paragraph (2), a judgment or order to do or not do an act may not be enforced by a writ of sequestration unless there is prominently displayed, on the front of the copy of the judgment or order served in accordance with this Section, a warning to the person required to do or not do the act in question that disobedience to the order would be a contempt of court punishable by imprisonment, a fine or sequestration of assets.

(2) An undertaking to do or not do an act which is contained in a judgment or order may be enforced by a writ of sequestration notwithstanding that the judgment or order does not contain the warning described in paragraph (1).

(Paragraphs 2.1 to 2.4 of the Practice Direction supplementing this Part and form N117 contain provisions about penal notices and warnings in relation to undertakings.)

81.26 How to make an application for permission to issue a writ of sequestration

(1) An application for permission to issue a writ of sequestration must be made –

(a) to a single judge of the Division of the High Court in which the proceedings were commenced or to which they have subsequently been transferred; or

(b) in any other case, to a single judge of the Queen's Bench Division.

(2) An application for permission to issue a writ of sequestration must be made by filing an application notice under Part 23.

(3) The application notice must –

(a) set out in full the grounds on which the application is made and must identify, separately and numerically, each alleged act of contempt including, if known, the date of each of the alleged acts; and

(b) be supported by one or more affidavits containing all the evidence relied upon.

(4) Subject to paragraph (5), the application notice must be served personally on the respondent.

(5) The court may –

(a) dispense with service under paragraph (4) if the court thinks it just to do so; or

(b) make an order in respect of service by an alternative method or at an alternative place.

81.27 Form of writ of sequestration

A writ of sequestration must be in Form No 67 as set out in Practice Direction 4.

Section 8
General Rules about Committal Applications, Orders for Committal and Writs of Sequestration

81.28 The hearing

(1) Unless the court hearing the committal application or application for sequestration otherwise permits, the applicant may not rely on –

(a) any grounds other than –
  (i) those set out in the claim form or application notice; or
  (ii) in relation to a committal application under Section 3 or 4, the statement of grounds required by rule 81.14(1)(a) (where not included in the claim form) or 81.15(4)(a); or

(b) any evidence unless it has been served in accordance with the relevant Section of this Part or the Practice Direction supplementing this Part.

(2) At the hearing, the respondent is entitled –

(a) to give oral evidence, whether or not the respondent has filed or served written evidence, and, if doing so, may be cross-examined; and
(b) with the permission of the court, to call a witness to give oral evidence whether or not the witness has made an affidavit or witness statement.

(3) The court may require or permit any party or other person (other than the respondent) to give oral evidence at the hearing.

(4) The court may give directions requiring the attendance for cross-examination of a witness who has given written evidence.

(5) If the court hearing an application in private decides to make a committal order against the respondent, it will in public state –

(a) the name of the respondent;
(b) in general terms, the nature of the contempt of court in respect of which the committal order is being made; and
(c) the length of the period of the committal order.

(Rule 39.2 contains provisions about hearings in private.)

(6) Where a committal order is made in the absence of the respondent, the court may on its own initiative fix a date and time when the respondent is to be brought before the court.

81.29 Power to suspend execution of a committal order

(1) The court making the committal order may also order that its execution will be suspended for such period or on such terms or conditions as it may specify.

(2) Unless the court otherwise directs, the applicant must serve on the respondent a copy of any order made under paragraph (1).

81.30 Warrant of committal

(1) If a committal order is made, the order will be for the issue of a warrant of committal.

(2) Unless the court orders otherwise –

(a) a copy of the committal order must be served on the respondent either before or at the time of the execution of the warrant of committal; or
(b) where the warrant of committal has been signed by the judge, the committal order may be served on the respondent at any time within 36 hours after the execution of the warrant.

(3) Without further order of the court, a warrant of committal must not be enforced more than 2 years after the date on which the warrant is issued.

81.31 Discharge of a person in custody

(1) A person committed to prison for contempt of court may apply to the court to be discharged.

(2) The application must –

(a) be in writing and attested by the governor of the prison (or any other officer of the prison not below the rank of principal officer);
(b) show that the person committed to prison for contempt has purged, or wishes to purge, the contempt; and
(c) be served on the person (if any) at whose instance the warrant of committal was issued at least one day before the application is made.

(3) Paragraph (2) does not apply to –

(a) a warrant of committal to which CCR Order 27 rule 8, or CCR Order 28 rule 4 or 14 relates; or
(b) an application made by the Official Solicitor acting with official authority for the discharge of a person in custody.

(4) If the committal order is made in the County Court and –

(a) does not direct that any application for discharge must be made to a judge; or
(b) was made by a District Judge under section 118 of the County Courts Act 1984,

the application for discharge may be made to a District Judge.

(5) If the committal order is made in the High Court, the application for discharge may be made to a single judge of the Division in which the committal order was made.

Amendments—SI 2014/407.

Which judge?—An application for discharge should ordinarily be heard by the judge who made the committal order; see *Swindon BC v Webb* [2016] EWCA Civ 152, where the Court of Appeal explains relevant authorities.

81.32 Discharge of a person in custody where a writ of sequestration has been issued

(1) Where –

(a) a writ of sequestration has been issued to enforce a judgment or order;
(b) the property is in the custody or power of the respondent;
(c) the respondent has been committed for failing to deliver up any property or deposit it in court or elsewhere; and
(d) the commissioners appointed by the writ of sequestration take possession of the property as if it belonged to the respondent,

then, without prejudice to rule 81.31(1), the court may discharge the respondent and give such directions for dealing with the property taken by the commissioners as it thinks fit.

Section 9

Penal, Contempt and Disciplinary Provisions under the County Courts Act 1984

81.33 Scope

(1) This Section applies to the County Court only and contains rules in relation to the penal, contempt and disciplinary provisions of the County Courts Act 1984.

(2) In this Section, 'the Act' means the County Courts Act 1984.

Amendments—SI 2014/407.

81.34 Offences under sections 14, 92 or 118 of the Act

(1) This rule applies where it is alleged that any person has committed an offence–

(a) under section 14 of the Act, by assaulting an officer of the court acting in the execution of the officer's duties;

(b) under section 92 of the Act, by rescuing or attempting to rescue any goods seized in execution; or

(c) under section 118 of the Act, by wilfully insulting a judge, juror, witness or any officer of the court or by wilfully interrupting the proceedings of the County Court or otherwise misbehaving in court,

and the alleged offender has not been taken into custody and brought before the court.

(2) The court will issue a summons, which must be served on the alleged offender personally not less than 7 days before the day of the hearing stated in the summons.

(3) Rule 81.30 applies, with the necessary modifications, where an order is made under section 14, 92 or 118 of the Act committing a person to prison.

Amendments—SI 2014/407.

'Double jeopardy'—In *Chelmsford County Court v Ramet* [2014] EWHC 56, a mother and a court officer were assaulted in court by the father. He was prosecuted and sentenced to 20 months imprisonment. On the hearing of summonses under s 118 and s 14(1)(b), Munby P held that the civil court can sentence 'only for such conduct as was not the subject of the criminal proceedings' so no further sentence was imposed.

81.35 Offences under section 124 of the Act

Where a complaint is made against a person under section 124 of the Act for having lost the opportunity of levying execution, the court will issue a summons, which must be served on the alleged offender personally not less than 7 days before the day of the hearing stated in the summons.

Amendments—SI 2014/867.

81.36 Notice to give evidence before or after a fine is imposed under section 55 of the Act

(1) Before or after imposing a fine on any person under section 55 of the Act for disobeying a witness summons or refusing to be sworn or give evidence, the court may direct that notice be given to that person in accordance with paragraph (2).

(2) The notice must state that if the recipient of the notice can demonstrate any reason why a fine should not be or should not have been imposed, that person may give evidence –

(a) by witness statement, affidavit or otherwise; and
(b) on a day named in the notice.

81.37 Non-payment of fine

(1) If a fine is not paid in accordance with the order imposing it, the court officer will, as soon as reasonably possible, report the matter to a judge.

(2) Where by an order imposing a fine –

(a) the amount of the fine is directed to be paid by instalments; and
(b) default is made in the payment of any instalment,

the same proceedings may be taken as if default had been made in payment of the whole of the fine.

(3) If the court makes an order for payment of a fine to be enforced by warrant of control, the order will be treated as an application to the court for the issue of the warrant at the time when the order was made.

Amendments—SI 2014/867.

81.38 Repayment of fine

If a person pays a fine and later gives evidence to satisfy the court that, if the evidence had been given earlier, no fine or a smaller fine would have been imposed, the court may order the whole or part of the fine to be repaid.

Amendments—Inserted by SI 2012/2208.

Practice Direction 81 – Applications and Proceedings in relation to Contempt of Court

This Practice Direction supplements CPR Part 81

Amendments—CPR Update 59.

SECTION 2 OF PART 81 – COMMITTAL FOR BREACH OF A JUDGMENT, ORDER OR UNDERTAKING TO DO OR ABSTAIN FROM DOING AN ACT

1 *Requirement for a penal notice on judgments and orders – form of penal notice – Rule 81.9*

A judgment or order which restrains a party from doing an act or requires an act to be done must, if disobedience is to be dealt with by proceedings for contempt of court, have a penal notice endorsed on it as follows (or in words to substantially the same effect) –

> 'If you the within-named [ ] do not comply with this order you may be held to be in contempt of court and imprisoned or fined, or your assets may be seized.'.

Requirement for a penal notice on judgments and orders – undertakings – Rule 81.9

2.1 The provisions of paragraph 8.1 of Practice Direction 40B – Judgments and orders that supplements Part 40 apply to an order which contains an undertaking by a party to do or not do an act, subject to paragraph 2.2 below.

> (Paragraph 8.1 of Practice Direction 40B contains provisions about specifying the time within which acts must be done.)

2.2 The court may decline to –

(1) accept an undertaking; and

(2) deal with disobedience in respect of an undertaking by contempt of court proceedings,

unless the party giving the undertaking has made a signed statement to the effect that that party understands the terms of the undertaking and the consequences of failure to comply with it.

2.3 The statement may be endorsed on the order containing the undertaking or may be filed in a separate document such as a letter.

2.4 Where the order containing an undertaking is made in the County Court, form N117 may be used.

Amendments—CPR Update 69.

SECTION 4 OF PART 81 – (1) CERTIFICATIONS BY ANY COURT, TRIBUNAL ETC TO THE HIGH COURT UNDER ANY ENACTMENT; (2) APPLICATIONS TO THE HIGH COURT UNDER SECTION 336 OF THE CHARITIES ACT 2011

3 *Scope of Section 4 of Part 81*

Section 4 of Part 81 contains rules in relation to statutory powers of the High Court to commit any person for contempt in respect of anything done or not done in relation to a court, tribunal or person. The statutory powers include –

(1) section 336 of the Charities Act 2011;

(2) sections 436 and 453C of the Companies Act 1985;

(3) paragraph 8 of Schedule 6 to the Data Protection Act 1998; and

(4) sections 18, 161 and 232 of the Financial Services and Markets Act 2000.

SECTION 5 OF PART 81 – CONTEMPT IN THE FACE OF THE COURT

Committal for contempt in the face of the court – Rule 81.16

4.1 Where the committal proceedings relate to a contempt in the face of the court the matters referred to in paragraph 4.3 should be given particular attention. Normally, it will be appropriate to defer consideration of the respondent's actions and behaviour to allow the respondent time to reflect on what has occurred. The time needed for the following procedures should allow such a period of reflection.

4.2 A Part 8 claim form and an application notice are not required for contempt falling under Section 5 of Part 81, but other provisions of this Practice Direction should be applied, as necessary, or adapted to the circumstances.

4.3 The judge should –

(1) tell the respondent of the possible penalty that the respondent faces;
(2) inform the respondent in detail, and preferably in writing, of the actions and behaviour of the respondent which have given rise to the committal application;
(3) if the judge considers that an apology would remove the need for the committal application, tell the respondent;
(4) have regard to the need for the respondent to be –
  (a) allowed a reasonable time for responding to the committal application, including, if necessary, preparing a defence;
  (b) made aware of the possible availability of criminal legal aid and how to contact the Legal Aid Agency;
  (c) given the opportunity, if unrepresented, to obtain legal advice;
  (d) if unable to understand English, allowed to make arrangements, seeking the court's assistance if necessary, for an interpreter to attend the hearing; and
  (e) brought back before the court for the committal application to be heard within a reasonable time;
(5) allow the respondent an opportunity to –
  (a) apologise to the court;
  (b) explain the respondent's actions and behaviour; and
  (c) if the contempt is proved, to address the court on the penalty to be imposed on the respondent; and
(6) where appropriate, nominate a suitable person to give the respondent the information. (It is likely to be appropriate to nominate a person where the effective communication of information by the judge to the respondent was not possible when the incident occurred.)

4.4 If there is a risk of the appearance of bias, the judge should ask another judge to hear the committal application.

4.5 Where the committal application is to be heard by another judge, a written statement by the judge before whom the actions and behaviour of the respondent which have given rise to the committal application took place may be admitted as evidence of those actions and behaviour.

Amendments—CPR Update 69.

SECTION 6 OF PART 81 – COMMITTAL FOR MAKING A FALSE STATEMENT OF TRUTH OR DISCLOSURE STATEMENT

Committal application in relation to a false statement of truth or disclosure statement – Rule 81.18

5.1 Rules 81.18(1)(b) and 81.18(3)(b) provide that a committal application may be made by the Attorney General. However, the Attorney General prefers a request that comes from the court to one made direct by a party to the proceedings in which the alleged contempt occurred without prior consideration by the court. A request to the Attorney General is not a way of appealing against, or reviewing, the decision of the judge.

5.2 Where the permission of the court is sought under rule 81.18(1)(a) or 81.18(3)(a) so that rule 81.14 is applied by rule 81.18(2) or 81.18(4), the affidavit evidence in support of the application must –

(1) identify the statement said to be false;
(2) explain –

(a) why it is false; and
(b) why the maker knew the statement to be false at the time it was made; and
(3) explain why contempt proceedings would be appropriate in the light of the overriding objective in Part 1.

5.3 The court may –

(1) exercise any of its powers under the rules (including the power to give directions under rule 81.14(6));
(2) initiate steps to consider if there is a contempt of court and, where there is, to punish it; or
(3) as provided by rule 81.18(5), direct that the matter be referred to the Attorney General with a request to consider whether to bring proceedings for contempt of court.

5.4 A request to the Attorney General to consider whether to bring proceedings for contempt of court must be made in writing and sent to the Attorney General's Office at 20 Victoria Street, London, SW1H 0NF.

5.5 A request to the Attorney General must be accompanied by a copy of any order directing that the matter be referred to the Attorney General and must –

(1) identify the statement said to be false;
(2) explain –
(a) why it is false; and
(b) why the maker knew the statement to be false at the time it was made; and
(3) explain why contempt proceedings would be appropriate in the light of the overriding objective in Part 1.

5.6 Once the applicant receives the result of the request to the Attorney General, the applicant must send a copy of it to the court that will deal with the committal application, and the court will give such directions as it sees fit.

5.7 The rules do not change the law of contempt or introduce new categories of contempt. A person applying to commence such proceedings should consider whether the incident complained of does amount to contempt of court and whether such proceedings would further the overriding objective in Part 1.

SECTION 7 OF PART 81 – WRIT OF SEQUESTRATION TO ENFORCE A JUDGMENT, ORDER OR UNDERTAKING

6 Requirement for a penal notice on judgments and orders – form of penal notice – Rule 81.25

Paragraphs 1 and 2.1 to 2.4 apply to judgments and orders to be enforced by a writ of sequestration.

Levying execution on certain days

7.1 Unless the court orders otherwise, a writ of sequestration to enforce a judgment, order or undertaking must not be executed on a Sunday, Good Friday or Christmas Day.

7.2 Paragraph 7.1 does not apply to an Admiralty claim in rem.

SECTION 8 OF PART 81 – GENERAL RULES ABOUT COMMITTAL APPLICATIONS, ORDERS FOR COMMITTAL AND WRITS OF SEQUESTRATION

General rules

8.1 Subject to paragraph 8.2, this Section of the Practice Direction applies in relation to all matters covered by Part 81.

8.2 Where there is a conflict between the provisions in this Section of the Practice Direction and specific provisions elsewhere in this Practice Direction or in Part 81, the specific provisions prevail.

9 Human rights

In all cases the Convention rights of those involved should particularly be borne in mind. It should be noted that the standard of proof, having regard to the possibility that a person may be sent to prison, is that the allegation be proved beyond reasonable doubt.

(Section 1 of the Human Rights Act 1998 defines 'the Convention rights'.)

Court to which applications should be made and levels of judiciary

10.1 A committal application or an application for permission to make a committal application –

(1) may be made in the County Court if the alleged contempt is a contempt which the County Court has power to punish; and

(2) must otherwise be made in the High Court.

10.2 Except where under an enactment a Master or District Judge has power to make a committal order, a committal order can only be made –

(1) in High Court proceedings, by a High Court Judge or a person authorised to act as such; or

(2) in County Court proceedings, by a judge of the County Court other than a District Judge of that court, unless they are exercising the jurisdiction of a Circuit Judge with the permission of the Designated Civil Judge.

10.3 Paragraph 10.4 applies in relation to proceedings in any court (the first court) where the judge or judges exercising the jurisdiction of the first court are deemed to constitute a court of the High Court by virtue of an enactment.

10.4 The reference in paragraph 10.2(1) to a High Court Judge will be construed as a reference to a judge of the first court.

Amendments—CPR Update 69.

11 General rules about applications: applications which cannot be made without permission

If the committal application is one which cannot be made without permission –

(1) the permission may only be granted by a judge who would have power to hear the committal application if permission were granted;

(2) the date on which and the name of the judge by whom the requisite permission was granted must be stated on the claim form or application notice by which the committal application is commenced;

(3) the claim form or application notice may not be issued or filed until the requisite permission has been granted; and

(4) Rules 23.9 and 23.10 do not apply.

12 General rules about applications: applications by claim form

If the application for permission to make a committal application or the committal application is commenced by the issue of a claim form –

(1) Part 8 will apply –

(a) subject to the provisions of Part 81 and this Practice Direction, in particular sub-paragraphs (2) to (4);

(b) as though references to 'claimant' were references to the applicant; and

(c) as though references to 'defendant' were references to the respondent;

(2) an amendment to the claim form may be made with the permission of the court but not otherwise;

(3) rule 8.4 does not apply; and

(4) the claim form must contain a prominent notice stating the possible consequences of the court making a committal order and of the respondent not attending the hearing. A form of notice which may be used is annexed to this Practice Direction at Annex 3.

General rules about applications: applications by application notice

13.1 Where the application is made by application notice, the application notice must state that the application is made in the proceedings in question, and its title and reference number must correspond with the title and reference number of those proceedings.

13.2 If the application for permission to make a committal application or the committal application is commenced by the filing of an application notice –

(1) Part 23 will apply subject to the provisions of Part 81 and this Practice Direction, in particular sub-paragraphs (2) to (4);
(2) an amendment to the application notice may be made with the permission of the court but not otherwise;
(3) the court may not dispose of the application without a hearing; and
(4) the application notice must contain a prominent notice stating the possible consequences of the court making a committal order and of the respondent not attending the hearing. A form of notice which may be used is annexed to this Practice Direction at Annex 3.

Evidence and information

14.1 Written evidence in support of or in opposition to a committal application must be given by affidavit.

14.2 Written evidence served in support of or in opposition to a committal application must, unless the court otherwise directs, be filed.

14.3 The following rules do not apply to committal applications –

(1) rule 35.7 (Court's power to direct that evidence is to be given by a single joint expert);
(2) rule 35.8 (Instructions to single joint expert); and
(3) rule 35.9 (Power of court to direct a party to provide information).

14.4 An order under rule 18.1 (Obtaining further information) may not be made against a respondent to a committal application.

The hearing – Rule 81.28

15.1 When issuing or filing the claim form or application notice for a committal application, the applicant must obtain from the court a date for the hearing of the committal application.

15.2 Unless the court otherwise directs, the hearing date of a committal application must not be less than 14 days after service of the claim form or application notice on the respondent. The hearing date must be specified in the claim form or application notice or in a Notice of Hearing attached to and served with the claim form or application notice.

15.3 Paragraphs 15.1 and 15.2 apply to certifications of conduct and applications under section 336 of the Charities Act 2011 ('section 336 application') referred to in Section 4 of Part 81 as if references to the claim form or application notice were references to the certification or section 336 application.

(The definition of 'applicant' in rule 81.3 includes a person who makes a committal application by way of certification or section 336 application.)

15.4 The court may on the hearing date –

(1) give case management directions with a view to a hearing of the committal application on a future date; or
(2) if the committal application is ready to be heard, proceed to hear it.

15.5 In dealing with any committal application, the court will have regard to the need for the respondent to have details of the alleged acts of contempt and the opportunity to respond to the committal application.

15.6 The court will also have regard to the need for the respondent to be –

(1) allowed a reasonable time for responding to the committal application including, if necessary, preparing a defence;
(2) made aware of the possible availability of criminal legal aid and how to contact the Legal Aid Agency;
(3) given the opportunity, if unrepresented, to obtain legal advice; and
(4) if unable to understand English, allowed to make arrangements, seeking the assistance of the court if necessary, for an interpreter to attend the hearing.

Amendments—CPR Update 69.

Striking out, procedural defects and discontinuance

16.1 On application by the respondent or on its own initiative, the court may strike out a committal application if it appears to the court –

(1) that the application and the evidence served in support of it disclose no reasonable ground for alleging that the respondent is guilty of a contempt of court;
(2) that the application is an abuse of the court's process or, if made in existing proceedings, is otherwise likely to obstruct the just disposal of those proceedings; or
(3) that there has been a failure to comply with a rule, practice direction or court order.

16.2 The court may waive any procedural defect in the commencement or conduct of a committal application if satisfied that no injustice has been caused to the respondent by the defect.

16.3 A committal application may not be discontinued without the permission of the court.

****

PART III

PART 83
WRITS AND WARRANTS – GENERAL PROVISIONS

CONTENTS OF THIS PART

Section I

Rule		Page
	Scope and Interpretation	
83.1	Scope and interpretation	2320
	Section II *Writs and Warrants*	
83.2	Writs and warrants of control, writs of execution, warrants of delivery and warrants of possession – permission to issue certain writs or warrants	2321
83.2A	Application for permission to issue a writ of sequestration	2323
83.3	Writs and warrants other than those conferring a power to use the TCG procedure – duration and priority	2323
83.4	Writs and warrants conferring a power to use the TCG procedure – duration and priority	2324
83.5	Writs and warrants – separate enforcement of costs	2324
83.6	Writs and warrants – levying execution on certain days	2325
83.7	Writs of control and warrants – power to stay execution or grant other relief	2325
83.8	Writs and warrants – information about execution of the writ or warrant	2326
	Section III *Writs*	
83.9	Issue of writs of execution and writs of control	2327
83.10	Writs of control and writs of delivery – description of parties	2327
83.11	Writs relating to ecclesiastical property	2327
83.12	Writs other than those conferring a power to use the TCG procedure – order for sale otherwise than by auction	2328

83.13 Enforcement in the High Court of a judgment or order for possession of land 2328
83.14 Enforcement in the High Court of a judgment or order for delivery of goods 2329

Section IV
Warrants

83.15 Application for warrant of control or warrant of delivery 2330
83.16 Warrant of control or warrant of delivery – opposition by debtor and debtor's request for transfer 2331
83.17 Warrant of control or warrant of delivery – execution of High Court judgment 2331
83.18 Warrants of control and warrants of delivery – description of parties 2331
83.19 Creditor's request for transfer to the High Court for enforcement 2331
83.20 Warrants of control – bankruptcy or winding up of debtor 2332
83.21 Warrants where the debtor is a farmer 2332
83.22 Warrants – withdrawal and suspension of warrant at creditor's request 2333
83.23 Warrants of delivery 2333
83.24 Warrants of delivery other than those conferring a power to use the TCG procedure – notice and inventory requirements 2333
83.25 Warrants of delivery conferring a power to use the TCG procedure – notice of enforcement and inventory requirements 2334
83.26 Warrants of possession 2334
83.27 Saving for enforcement by committal 2336
83.28 Suspension of part warrant 2336
83.29 Concurrent warrants 2336

Practice Direction 83 –
Writs and Warrants – General Provisions 2336

General note—Parts 83–86 represent another instalment in the continuing effort to complete the Civil Procedure Rules by doing away with the debris of the old Rules of the Supreme Court and County Court Rules, which survive in Schs 1 and 2. As will especially appear from consideration of Pt 84, modernisation has not meant simplification and has certainly not meant shortening.

Parts 83 and 84 apply with the necessary modifications to an application made in the High Court or the Family Court to enforce an order made in family proceedings – FPR 2010, r 33.1(2).

Part 83 deals with writs and warrants generally (the distinction between enforcement in the High Court and the County Court/Family Court remains). In civil proceedings, an order for payment of £5,000 or more must be enforced in the High Court; an order for payment of less than £600 cannot be (HCCCJO 1991, arts 8(1) and 8(2)). The Family Court is empowered by MFPA 1984, s 31E(2) to issue 'a warrant, directed to an officer of the family court, containing provision corresponding to any that might be contained in' a writ directed to a High Court Enforcement Officer (HCEO), which appears to mean that there is no upper limit on the sum for which a warrant may be issued directed to a court bailiff. However, a HCEO is not an officer of the Family Court and if the issue of a writ of control directed to a HCEO is appropriate, the order of the Family Court must be transferred to the High Court for enforcement under r 33.4.

That rule does not apply to orders for periodical payments and if, exceptionally, it is appropriate to enforce in the High Court such an order made in the Family Court, the proceedings as a whole will need to be transferred to the High Court for the purpose. Note that this can only be authorised by a puisne judge of the High Court (in other words, not a person 'sitting as' a Judge of the High Court under SCA 1981, s 9) (FPR 2010, r 29.17(3)) and the further restrictions on transfer contained in r 29.17(1),(2) appear to apply.

Lay justices sitting in the Family Court may not grant warrants of control or delivery or warrants of possession (FC(CDB)R 2014, r 17, Sch 2).

Part 84 deals with 'enforcement by taking control of goods' and the 'writ of control' (successor to the familiar writ of fieri facias) and 'warrant of control' (successor to the warrant of execution).

Part 85, which deals with claims made against 'controlled or executed' goods (formerly called interpleader proceedings), is not reproduced in this volume and readers are referred to *Civil Court Service* (LexisNexis). It will now be possible for such claims involving County Court warrants to be heard by District Judges following the long-overdue repeal of County Courts Act 1984, s 123.

Section I
Scope and Interpretation

83.1 Scope and interpretation

(1) This Part contains general rules about writs and warrants as follows –

(a) Section II relates to writs and warrants;
(b) Section III relates to writs only; and
(c) Section IV relates to warrants only.

(2) In this Part –

(a) 'the Act' means the Tribunals, Courts and Enforcement Act 2007;
(b) 'the creditor' means a person who has obtained or who is entitled to enforce a judgment or order;
(c) 'the debtor' means a person against whom a judgment or order was given or made;
(d) 'enforcement agent' has the meaning given in paragraph 2(1) of Schedule 12;
(e) 'enforcement officer' means an individual who is authorised to act as an enforcement officer under Schedule 7 to the Courts Act 2003;
(f) 'relevant enforcement officer' means –
  (i) in relation to a writ of execution or a writ of control which is directed to a single enforcement officer, that officer; and
  (ii) in relation to a writ of execution or writ of control which is directed to two or more enforcement officers, the officer to whom the writ is allocated;
(g) 'Schedule 12' means Schedule 12 to the Act;
(h) 'TCG procedure' means the procedure in Schedule 12 to take control of goods and sell them to recover a sum in accordance with that Schedule and regulations made under it;
(i) 'TCG Regulations' means the Taking Control of Goods Regulations 2013;
(j) 'warrant of control' is to be construed in accordance with section 62(4) of the Act;
(k) 'writ of control' is to be construed in accordance with section 62(4) of the Act;
(l) 'writ of execution' includes –
  (i) a writ of possession;
  (ii) a writ of delivery;
  (iii) a writ of sequestration;
  (iv) a writ of fieri facias de bonis ecclesiasticis,

and any further writ in aid of any such writs, but does not include a writ of control.

Amendments—Inserted by SI 2014/407.

Section II
Writs and Warrants

83.2 Writs and warrants of control, writs of execution, warrants of delivery and warrants of possession – permission to issue certain writs or warrants

(1) This rule applies to –

(a) writs and warrants of control;
(b) writs of execution;
(c) warrants of delivery;
(d) warrants of possession.

(2) A writ or warrant to which this rule applies is referred to in this rule as a 'relevant writ or warrant'.

(3) A relevant writ or warrant must not be issued without the permission of the court where –

(a) six years or more have elapsed since the date of the judgment or order;
(b) any change has taken place, whether by death or otherwise, in the parties –
  (i) entitled to enforce the judgment or order; or
  (ii) liable to have it enforced against them;
(c) the judgment or order is against the assets of a deceased person coming into the hands of that person's executors or administrators after the date of the judgment or order, and it is sought to issue execution against such assets;
(d) any goods to be seized under a relevant writ or warrant are in the hands of a receiver appointed by a court or sequestrator;
(e) under the judgment or order, any person is entitled to a remedy subject to the fulfilment of any condition, and it is alleged that the condition has been fulfilled; or
(f) the permission sought is for a writ of control or writ of execution, and that writ is to be in aid of another writ of control or execution.

(4) An application for permission may be made in accordance with Part 23 and must –

(a) identify the judgment or order to which the application relates;
(b) if the judgment or order is for the payment of money, state the amount originally due and, if different, the amount due at the date the application notice is filed;
(c) where the case falls within paragraph (3)(a), state the reasons for the delay in enforcing the judgment or order;
(d) where the case falls within paragraph (3)(b), state the change which has taken place in the parties entitled or liable to execution since the date of the judgment or order;
(e) where the case falls within paragraph (3)(c) or (d), state that a demand to satisfy the judgment or order was made on the person liable to satisfy it and that that person has refused or failed to do so;
(f) give such other information as is necessary to satisfy the court that the applicant is entitled to proceed to execution on the judgment or order, and that the person against whom it is sought to issue execution is liable to execution on it.

(5) An application for permission may be made without notice being served on any other party unless the court directs otherwise.

(6) If because of one event, an applicant seeks permission under paragraph (3)(b) to enforce more than one judgment or order, the applicant need only make one application for permission.

(7) Where paragraph (6) applies –

(a) a schedule must be attached to the application for permission, specifying all the judgments or orders in respect of which the application for permission is made; and
(b) if the application notice is directed to be served on any person, it need set out only such part of the application as affects that person.

(7A) Where –

(a) the court grants permission, under this rule or otherwise, for the issue of a writ of execution or writ of control ('the permission order'); and
(b) the writ is not issued within one year after the date of the permission order,

the permission order will cease to have effect.

(7B) Where a permission order has ceased to have effect, the court may grant a fresh permission order.

(8) Paragraph (3) is without prejudice to section 2 of the Reserve and Auxiliary Forces (Protection of Civil Interests) Act 1951 and any enactment, rule or direction by virtue of which a person is required to obtain the permission of the court for the issue of a warrant or to proceed to execution or otherwise to the enforcement of a judgment or order.

Amendments—Inserted by SI 2014/407. Amended by SI 2014/867.

Insolvency of debtor—Where the debt to be enforced is arrears of periodical payments, leave is not needed merely because a bankruptcy order has been made against the debtor.

'relevant writ' (r 83.2(2))—Note that this expression includes a writ of possession and the other writs mentioned in r 83.1(2)(l).

'6 years or more have elapsed' (r 83.2(3)(a))—The delay should be explained (see r 83.2(4)(c)). The court may be reluctant to allow execution on a stale judgment or order and will not do so if the debtor is prejudiced by the delay.

'any change … in the parties' (r 83.2(3)(b))—The alternative is to apply to change the party under CPR 1998, Pt 19. It is not thought that, following an order under that rule, permission would also be required under this rule. An order under Pt 19 would still be needed before other enforcement proceedings were taken following a (presumably abortive) writ of execution issued with permission under this rule.

'warrants of possession' (r 83.2(3)(d))—Note that the differences between County Court and High Court procedure survive; writs of possession are governed by r 83.13 and notably the continuing requirement in many cases for the permission of the court to be obtained.

'subject to the fulfilment of any condition' (r 83.2(3)(e))—Notwithstanding r 83.2(5), if an order for possession is suspended on terms and it is alleged that those terms have been broken, notice must be given to the defendant (*Fleet Mortgage and Investment Co Ltd v Lower Maisonette, 46 Eaton Place Ltd* [1972] 1 WLR 765, ChD).

83.2A Application for permission to issue a writ of sequestration

Notwithstanding anything in rule 83.2, an application for permission to issue a writ of sequestration must be made in accordance with Part 81 and in particular Section 7 of that Part.

Amendments—Inserted by SI 2014/867.

'writ of sequestration' (r 83.2A)—A warrant of sequestration may not be granted by lay justices, judges of district judge level or judges of circuit judge level (FC(CDB)R 2014, r 17, Sch 2, Table 3).

83.3 Writs and warrants other than those conferring a power to use the TCG procedure – duration and priority

(1) This rule applies to –

- (a) writs of execution;
- (b) warrants of possession; and
- (c) warrants of delivery,

other than writs of execution or warrants that confer a power to use the TCG procedure.

(2) A writ or warrant to which this rule applies is referred to in this rule as a 'relevant writ or warrant', 'relevant writ' or 'relevant warrant' as appropriate.

(3) Subject to paragraph (4), for the purposes of execution, a writ or warrant will be valid for the period of 12 months beginning with the date of its issue.

(4) The court may extend the relevant writ or warrant from time to time for a period of 12 months at any one time.

(5) If the application is made before the expiry of the period of 12 months, the period of extension will begin on the day after the expiry.

(6) If the application is made after the expiry of the period of 12 months, any period of extension will begin on any day after the expiry that the court may allow.

(7) Before a relevant writ that has been extended is executed –

- (a) the court will seal the writ; or
- (b) the applicant for the extension order must serve a notice sealed as described in subparagraph (a) on the relevant enforcement officer informing that officer of the making of the extension order and the date of that order.

(8) In relation to a relevant warrant, the court will endorse the warrant with a note of the renewal or extension.

(9) Irrespective of whether it has been extended under paragraph (4) –

- (a) the priority of a relevant writ will be determined by reference to the time it is originally received by the person who is under a duty to endorse it; and
- (b) the priority of a relevant warrant will be determined by reference to the date on which it was originally issued.

(10) The production of the following will be evidence that the relevant writ or warrant has been extended –

- (a) the writ sealed in accordance with paragraph (7)(a);
- (b) the notice sealed in accordance with paragraph (7)(b);
- (c) the warrant endorsed in accordance with paragraph (8).

(11) If, during the validity of a relevant writ, a person makes an application under Part 85 in relation to an execution under that writ, the validity of the writ will be extended until the expiry of 12 months from the conclusion of the proceedings under Part 85.

Amendments—Inserted by SI 2014/407.

Order to extend validity (r 83.3(4)—The extension is for a period of 12 months at a time. As the order may be made after the expiry of the writ, there may be a gap in the writ's validity unless the court orders otherwise under r 83.3(6).

Procedure on application for extension—The application is initially made by application notice without a hearing under r 23.8(c). The application must be supported by a witness statement or affidavit, which should

PART III

specify the reason for preferring not to proceed by issuing a fresh writ, give the reason why (if applicable) the application is made beyond the writ's expiry and indicate the steps taken to ascertain the views of any other execution creditors, exhibiting their responses.

83.4 Writs and warrants conferring a power to use the TCG procedure – duration and priority

(1) This rule applies to –

(a) a writ of control;
(b) a warrant of control; and
(c) any other writ or warrant that confers power to use the TCG procedure.

(2) A writ or warrant to which this rule applies is referred to in this rule as a 'relevant writ or warrant', 'relevant writ' or 'relevant warrant' as appropriate.

(3) A relevant writ or warrant will be valid for the period in which an enforcement agent may take control of the goods in question, as specified in regulation 9(1) of the TCG Regulations.

(4) If a period in which to take control of goods is extended by the court under regulation 9(3) of the TCG Regulations, the validity of the relevant writ or warrant will be extended for the same period.

(Rule 84.5 contains provisions about applications to the court requesting a time extension.)

(5) Irrespective of whether it has been extended under regulation 9(3) of the TCG Regulations –

(a) the priority of a relevant writ will be determined by reference to the time it is originally received by the person who is under a duty to endorse it; and
(b) the priority of a relevant warrant will be determined by reference to the date on which it was originally issued.

(6) The production of –

(a) the extension order granted under regulation 9(3) of the TCG Regulations, or a copy of it; or
(b) the relevant writ or warrant endorsed in accordance with rule 84.5(3)(b), or a copy of it,

will be evidence that the writ or warrant has been extended.

(7) If, during the validity of a relevant writ or warrant, a person makes an application under Part 85 in relation to goods taken into control under that writ or warrant, the validity of the writ or warrant will be extended until the expiry of 12 months from the conclusion of the proceedings under Part 85.

Amendments—Inserted by SI 2014/407.

Extension of period for taking control of goods (r 83.4(4))—Note that under Taking Control of Goods Regulations 2013, reg 9(3), only one extension of the period may be granted.

83.5 Writs and warrants – separate enforcement of costs

(1) Where –

(a) judgment is given or an order made for –
  (i) payment of a sum otherwise than by instalments ('the sum'); and
  (ii) costs to be assessed; and
(b) default is made in payment of the sum before the costs have been assessed,

a writ of control or warrant of control (as appropriate) may be issued for the recovery of the sum.

(2) If –

(a) paragraph (1) applies;
(b) a writ or warrant is issued for the recovery of the sum;
(c) the costs are assessed; and
(d) default is made in payment of the costs,

a separate writ of control or warrant of control may be issued for the recovery of the costs.

(3) A party entitled to enforce a judgment or order of the High Court for –

(a) the delivery of any property, other than money; or

(b) possession of any property,

may issue a separate writ of control to enforce payment of any damages or costs awarded to that party by that judgment or order.

(4) A party entitled to enforce a judgment or order of the County Court by warrant of delivery may issue a separate warrant of control to enforce payment of any damages or costs awarded to that party by that judgment or order.

Amendments—Inserted by SI 2014/407.

83.6 Writs and warrants – levying execution on certain days

(1) This rule applies to writs and warrants other than –

(a) writs of control;
(b) warrants of control; and
(c) writs or warrants in relation to an Admiralty claim in rem.

(2) Where a writ or warrant is not a writ of control or warrant of control but nevertheless confers the power to use the TCG procedure, this rule applies to the parts of the writ or warrant that do not confer the power to use the TCG Procedure.

(3) Unless the court orders otherwise, a writ or warrant to enforce a judgment or order must not be executed on a Sunday, Good Friday or Christmas Day.

Amendments—Inserted by SI 2014/407. Substituted by SI 2014/2044.

'Unless the court orders otherwise' (r 83.6(3))—As was done, for example, in *Jones & Anor v Persons Unknown & Anor* [2014] EWHC 4691 (Ch).

83.7 Writs of control and warrants – power to stay execution or grant other relief

(1) At the time that a judgment or order for payment of money is made or granted, or at any time thereafter, the debtor or other party liable to execution of a writ of control or a warrant may apply to the court for a stay of execution.

(2) The power of the court to stay execution of a warrant of control may be exercised by a District Judge, or a court officer where paragraph (10) applies, and the power of the court to stay execution of any other warrant or of a writ of control may be exercised by a Master or District Judge.

(3) Where the application for a stay of execution is made on the grounds of the applicant's inability to pay, the witness statement required by paragraph (6)(b) must disclose the debtor's means.

(4) If the court is satisfied that –

(a) there are special circumstances which render it inexpedient to enforce the judgment or order; or
(b) the applicant is unable from any reason to pay the money,

then, notwithstanding anything in paragraph (5) or (6), the court may by order stay the execution of the judgment or order, either absolutely or for such period and subject to such conditions as the court thinks fit.

(5) An application under this rule, if not made at the time the judgment is given or order made –

(a) must be made in accordance with Part 23, as modified by paragraphs (6) to (14); and
(b) may be made even if the party liable to execution did not acknowledge service of the claim form or serve a defence or take any previous part in the proceedings.

(6) The grounds on which an application under this rule is made must –

(a) be set out in the application notice; and
(b) be supported by a witness statement made by or on behalf of the applicant substantiating the grounds.

(7) Paragraphs (8) to (15) apply to applications in the County Court.

(8) Where the debtor makes an application in the County Court, the court will –

PART III

(a) send the creditor a copy of the debtor's application (and statement of means); and
(b) require the creditor to notify the court in writing whether or not the creditor objects to the application, within 14 days of service of the notification, giving reasons for any objection the creditor may have to the granting of the application.

(9) If the creditor does not notify the court of any objection within the time stated, the court officer may make an order suspending the warrant on terms of payment.

(10) Upon receipt of a notice by the creditor under paragraph (8)(b), the court officer may, if the creditor agrees, or objects only to the terms offered, determine the date and rate of payment and make an order suspending the warrant on terms of payment.

(11) Any party affected by an order made under paragraph (10) may, within 14 days of service of the order on that party and giving reasons, apply on notice for the order to be reconsidered.

(12) If a party applies for the order to be reconsidered, the court will –

(a) fix a day for the hearing of the application before the District Judge; and
(b) give to the creditor and the debtor not less than 8 days' notice of the day so fixed.

(13) On hearing an application under paragraph (11), the District Judge may confirm the order or set it aside and make such new order as the court thinks fit.

(14) Where the creditor states in the notice under paragraph (8)(b) that the creditor wishes the enforcement agent to proceed to execute the warrant, the court will –

(a) fix a day for a hearing before the District Judge of the debtor's application; and
(b) give to the creditor and to the debtor not less than 2 days' notice of the day so fixed.

(15) Where an order is made by the District Judge suspending a warrant of execution, the debtor may be ordered to pay the costs of the warrant and any fees or expenses incurred before its suspension and the order may authorise the sale of a sufficient portion of any goods seized to cover such costs, fees and expenses and the expenses of sale.

Amendments—Inserted by SI 2014/407.

'other party liable to execution' (r 83.7(1))—This appears to allow an application by a third party who might be prejudicially affected by the potential execution, for example a person claiming an interest in a chattel apparently the property of the judgment debtor (*Michael Wilson & Partners v Sinclair* [2017] EWCA Civ 55).

'may stay the execution of the judgment or order' (r 83.7(4)—This rule gives the court extremely wide powers to control the execution of a judgment or order if special circumstances make that appropriate or the debtor is 'unable, from any reason, to pay the money'.

The court has a wide discretion that must be exercised from the starting point that there must be good reason to deny the creditor the fruits of his judgment (*Winchester Cigarette Machinery Ltd v Payne* (No 2) (1993) *The Times*, December 15, CA). If the debtor has other assets, such as property, that may provide security for the judgment debt the court may grant a stay conditional upon the debtor agreeing to an immediate charging order over that property without going through the formalities required by CPR 1998, Pt 73 or FPR 2010, Pt 40.

Special circumstances do not include the fact of a pending appeal, as an application for a stay in those circumstances would be made under the rule governing the appeal. They may include a pending application to set aside the judgment or order. For the factors to be considered in an application under this paragraph, see *Burnet v Francis Industries plc* [1987] 1 WLR 802, CA.

The wording of this rule is wider than that of its predecessor in RSC Ord 47, r 1 and is not expressly limited to execution by writ of control. There appears to be no reason why in appropriate circumstances a court should not impose a general stay of execution under this rule (*Michael Wilson & Partners v Sinclair*, above).

83.8 Writs and warrants – information about execution of the writ or warrant

(1) If the creditor or debtor serves notice on the enforcement agent or enforcement officer requiring reasonable information about the execution of a writ or warrant, the enforcement agent or enforcement officer must send such information to the creditor or debtor within 7 days of service of the notice.

(2) If the enforcement agent or enforcement officer fails to comply with the notice, the party who served the notice may apply to the court for an order directing the enforcement agent or enforcement officer to comply with the notice.

Amendments—Inserted by SI 2014/407.

'reasonable information' (r 83.8(1))—It will be borne in mind that time spent answering queries is time that cannot be spent pursuing the debtor.

Section III
Writs

83.9 Issue of writs of execution and writs of control

(1) In this rule 'the appropriate office' means –

- (a) where the proceedings in which execution is to issue are in a District Registry, that Registry;
- (b) where the proceedings are in the Principal Registry of the Family Division, that Registry;
- (c) where the proceedings are Admiralty proceedings or commercial proceedings which are not in a District Registry, the Admiralty and Commercial Registry;
- (ca) where the proceedings are in the Chancery Division, Chancery Chambers;
- (d) in any other case, the Central Office of the Senior Courts.

(2) Issue of a writ of execution or control takes place on its being sealed by a court officer of the appropriate office.

(3) Before a writ is issued a request for its issue must be filed.

(4) The request must be signed –

- (a) by the person entitled to execution, if acting in person; or
- (b) by or on behalf of the solicitor of the person entitled to execution.

(5) The writ will not be sealed unless at the time it is presented for sealing –

- (a) the person presenting the writ produces –
  - (i) the judgment or order on which the writ is to issue, or an office copy of it;
  - (ii) where permission was required for the writ to be issued, the order granting such permission or evidence of the granting of it;
  - (iii) where judgment on failure to acknowledge service has been entered against a State, as defined in section 14 of the State Immunity Act 1978, evidence that the State has been served in accordance with rule 40.10 and that the judgment has taken effect; and
- (b) the court officer authorised to seal it is satisfied that the period, if any, specified in the judgment or order for the payment of any money or the doing of any other act under the judgment or order has expired.

(6) Every writ of execution or control will bear the date of the day on which it is issued.

Amendments—Inserted by SI 2014/407. Amended by SI 2014/2044.

83.10 Writs of control and writs of delivery – description of parties

(1) This rule applies where the name or address of the creditor or debtor as given in the request for the issue of the following differs from that person's name or address in the judgment or order sought to be enforced –

- (a) a writ of control;
- (b) writ of delivery.

(2) If the creditor files a witness statement that satisfies the court officer that the name or address as given in the request is applicable to the person concerned, the creditor or the debtor will be described in the writ as 'CD of [name and address as given in the request] suing [or sued] as AD of [name and address in the judgment or order]'.

Amendments—Inserted by SI 2014/407.

83.11 Writs relating to ecclesiastical property

(1) In this rule, 'a writ relating to ecclesiastical property' means –

- (a) a writ of fieri facias de bonis ecclesiasticis; or
- (b) a writ of sequestrari de bonis ecclesiasticis.

PART III

(2) This rule applies where it appears upon the return of any writ of control that the person against whom the writ was issued –

(a) has no goods or chattels in the district of the relevant enforcement officer; but
(b) is the incumbent of a benefice named in the return.

(3) After the writ and return have been filed, the party by whom the writ of control was issued may issue a writ relating to ecclesiastical property.

(4) Any such writ must be directed and delivered to the bishop of the diocese within which that benefice is, to be executed by that bishop.

(5) The only fees allowed to the bishop or diocesan officer for the execution of the writ are those authorised by or under any enactment, including any measure of the General Synod.

Amendments—Inserted by SI 2014/407.

83.12 Writs other than those conferring a power to use the TCG procedure – order for sale otherwise than by auction

(1) This rule applies in relation to writs that do not confer a power to use the TCG procedure.

(2) A court order under paragraph 10 of Schedule 7 to the Courts Act 2003 that a sale of goods seized under an execution may be made otherwise than by public auction may be made on the application of –

(a) the person at whose instance the writ of execution under which the sale is to be made was issued;
(b) the person against whom that writ was issued (in this rule referred to as 'the judgment debtor'); or
(c) if the writ was directed to one or more enforcement officers, the relevant enforcement officer.

(3) Such an application must be made in accordance with Part 23.

(4) Where the applicant for an order under this rule is not the enforcement officer, the enforcement officer must, on the demand of the applicant, send to the applicant a list, stating –

(a) whether the enforcement officer has notice of the issue of another writ or writs of execution against the goods of the judgment debtor; and
(b) so far as is known to the enforcement officer, the name and address of every creditor who has obtained the issue of another such writ of execution.

(5) Where the enforcement officer is the applicant, the enforcement officer must prepare such a list.

(6) Not less than 3 days before the hearing, the applicant must serve the application notice on each of the other persons by whom the application might have been made and on every person named in the list prepared under paragraph (4) or (5).

(7) Service of the application notice on a person named in the list prepared under paragraph (4) or (5) is notice to that person for the purpose of paragraph 10(3) of Schedule 7 to the Courts Act 2003.

(8) The applicant must produce the list prepared under paragraph (4) or (5) to the court on the hearing of the application.

(9) Every person on whom the application notice was served may attend and be heard on the hearing of the application.

Amendments—Inserted by SI 2014/407.

83.13 Enforcement in the High Court of a judgment or order for possession of land

(1) A judgment or order for the giving of possession of land may be enforced in the High Court by one or more of the following means –

(a) writ of possession;
(b) in a case in which rule 81.4 applies, an order of committal;

(c) in a case in which rule 81.20 applies, writ of sequestration.

(2) Subject to paragraphs (3), (5) and (6), a writ of possession to enforce a judgment or order for the giving of possession of any land will not be issued without the permission of the court.

(3) The court's permission is not required for the issue of a writ of possession in a possession claim against trespassers under Part 55 unless the writ is to be issued after the expiry of three months from the date of the order.

(4) An application for permission under paragraph (3) may be made without notice being served on any other party unless the court orders otherwise.

(5) The courts' permission to issue a writ of restitution in aid of a writ of possession is required whether or not permission was required for the writ of possession.

(6) The court's permission is not required for the issue of a writ of possession to enforce a judgment or order for the giving of possession of any land where the judgment or order was given or made in proceedings in which there is a claim for –

(a) payment of moneys secured by the mortgage;
(b) sale of the mortgaged property;
(c) foreclosure;
(d) delivery of possession (whether before or after foreclosure or without foreclosure) to the mortgagee by the mortgagor or by any other person who is alleged to be in possession of the property;
(e) redemption;
(f) reconveyance of the land or its release from the security; or
(g) delivery of possession by the mortgagee.

(7) In paragraph (6) 'mortgage' includes a legal or equitable mortgage and a legal or equitable charge, and reference to a mortgagor, a mortgagee and mortgaged land is to be interpreted accordingly.

(8) Permission referred to in paragraph (2) will not be granted unless it is shown –

(a) that every person in actual possession of the whole or any part of the land ('the occupant') has received such notice of the proceedings as appears to the court sufficient to enable the occupant to apply to the court for any relief to which the occupant may be entitled; and
(b) if the operation of the judgment or order is suspended by section 16(2) of the Landlord and Tenant Act 1954, that the applicant has not received notice in writing from the tenant that the tenant desires that the provisions of section 16(2)(a) and (b) of that subsection shall have effect.

(9) A writ of possession may include provision for enforcing the payment of any money adjudged or ordered to be paid by the judgment or order which is to be enforced by the writ.

Amendments—Inserted by SI 2014/407.

83.14 Enforcement in the High Court of a judgment or order for delivery of goods

(1) A judgment or order for the delivery of any goods which does not give a person against whom the judgment is given or order made the alternative of paying the assessed value of the goods may be enforced in the High Court by one or more of the following means –

(a) writ of delivery to recover the goods without alternative provision for recovery of the assessed value of those goods ('writ of specific delivery');
(b) in a case in which rule 81.4 applies, an order of committal;
(c) in a case in which rule 81.20 applies, writ of sequestration.

(2) A judgment or order for the delivery of any goods or payment of their assessed value may be enforced by one or more of the following means –

(a) writ of delivery to recover the goods or their assessed value;
(b) by order of the court, writ of specific delivery;
(c) in a case in which rule 81.20 applies, writ of sequestration.

(3) An application for an order under paragraph (2)(b) must be made in accordance with Part 23, and must be served on the defendant against whom the judgment or order sought to be enforced was given or made.

(4) A writ of specific delivery, and a writ of delivery to recover any goods or their assessed value, may include provision for enforcing the payment of any money adjudged or ordered to be paid by the judgment or order which is to be enforced by the writ.

(5) A judgment or order for the payment of the assessed value of any goods may be enforced by the same means as any other judgment or order for the payment of money.

(6) This rule applies to writs in aid of writs of delivery.

Amendments—Inserted by SI 2014/407.

Section IV
Warrants

83.15 Application for warrant of control or warrant of delivery

(1) In this rule, 'instalment order' means an order for payment of a sum of money by instalments.

(2) This rule applies in relation to –

- (a) warrants of control; and
- (b) warrants of delivery.

(3) A creditor may apply for a warrant to be issued by filing a request.

(4) A request for a warrant of control or delivery –

- (a) may be made without notice; and
- (b) must be made to –
  - (i) the County Court hearing centre where the judgment or order which it is sought to enforce was made; or
  - (ii) the County Court hearing centre to which the proceedings have since been transferred.

(5) Subject to paragraph (4)(b)(ii), a request for a warrant of control to enforce a judgment or order made at the County Court Money Claims Centre must be made to that office.

(6) In the request, the creditor must certify –

- (a) the amount remaining due under the judgment or order; and
- (b) where the order made is an instalment order –
  - (i) that the whole or part of any instalment due remains unpaid; and
  - (ii) the amount for which the warrant is to be issued.

(7) The court officer may discharge the functions of the District Judge under section 85(2) of the County Courts Act 1984 of issuing a warrant.

(8) Unless an instalment order has been made and paragraphs (9) and (10) apply, any warrant issued must be issued for the whole of the sum of money and costs remaining unpaid, and may not be issued for part of the sum.

(9) Where the court has made an instalment order and default has been made in payment of an instalment, then subject to paragraph (10), a warrant of control may be issued for –

- (a) the whole of the sum of money and costs then remaining unpaid; or
- (b) for such part of the sum as the creditor may request, which must not be less than the greater of –
  - (i) £50; or
  - (ii) the amount of one monthly instalment or, as the case may be, four weekly instalments.

(10) Where an instalment order has been made, no warrant will be issued unless at the time when it is issued –

- (a) the whole or part of an instalment which has already become due remains unpaid; and

(b) any warrant previously issued for part of the sum of money and costs has expired, been satisfied or abandoned.

Amendments—Inserted by SI 2014/407.

Unless an instalment order has been made (r 83.15(8))—This was understood to be the position under the former rules but is now made explicit. By reason of MFPA 1984, s 31E(2), a warrant of control may be issued in the Family Court even though the amount to be recovered exceeds the £5,000 for which such a warrant could be issued in the County Court.

83.16 Warrant of control or warrant of delivery – opposition by debtor and debtor's request for transfer

The court may, on an application by a debtor who wishes to oppose a request for a warrant of control or warrant of delivery, transfer it to the County Court hearing centre serving the address where the debtor resides or carries on business, or to another court.

Amendments—Inserted by SI 2014/407.

83.17 Warrant of control or warrant of delivery – execution of High Court judgment

(1) Where it is desired to enforce by warrant of control or warrant of delivery –

(a) a judgment or order of the High Court; or

(b) a judgment, order, decree or award which is or has become enforceable as if it were a judgment of the High Court,

the request referred to in rule 83.15(3) may be filed in the County Court hearing centre which serves the address where execution is to be levied.

(2) Subject to paragraph (3), any restriction imposed by these rules on the issue of execution will apply as if the judgment, order, decree or award were a judgment or order of the County Court.

(3) Permission to issue execution will not be required if permission has already been given by the High Court.

(4) Notice of the issue of the warrant will be sent by the County Court to the High Court.

Amendments—Inserted by SI 2014/407.

83.18 Warrants of control and warrants of delivery – description of parties

(1) This rule applies where the name or address of the creditor or debtor as given in the request for the issue of the following differs from that person's name or address in the judgment or order sought to be enforced –

(a) a warrant of control;

(b) a warrant of delivery.

(2) If the creditor files a witness statement that satisfies the court officer that the name or address as given in the request is applicable to the person concerned, the creditor or the debtor will be described in the warrant as 'CD of [name and address as given in the request] suing [or sued] as AD of [name and address in the judgment or order]'.

Amendments—Inserted by SI 2014/407.

83.19 Creditor's request for transfer to the High Court for enforcement

(1) This rule applies where the creditor makes a request for a certificate of judgment under rule 40.14A(1) for the purpose of enforcing the judgment or order in the High Court –

(a) by execution against goods; or

(b) where the judgment or order to be enforced is an order for possession of land made in a possession claim against trespassers.

(2) The grant of a certificate by the court will take effect as an order to transfer the proceedings to the High Court and the transfer will have effect on the grant of that certificate.

(3) On the transfer of proceedings in accordance with paragraph (2), the County Court will –

PART III

(a) give notice to the debtor or the person against whom the possession order was made that the proceedings have been transferred; and

(b) make an entry of the fact of transfer in the court records.

(4) In a case where a request for a certificate of judgment is made under rule 40.14A(1) for the purpose of enforcing a judgment or order in the High Court and any of the following proceedings are pending, the request for the certificate will not be dealt with until those proceedings are determined –

(a) an application for a variation in the date or rate of payment of money due under a judgment or order;

(b) an application under either rule 39.3(3) or rule 13.4;

(c) a request for an administration order; or

(d) an application for a stay of execution under section 88 of the County Courts Act 1984.

Amendments—Inserted by SI 2014/407.

Jurisdiction—This is governed by HCCCJO 1991, art 8. A practice direction relating to the enforcement of County Court judgments in the High Court issued by the Senior Master is set out at [1998] 4 All ER 63.

'a possession claim against trespassers' (r 83.19(1)(b))—This purely administrative procedure is only available to enforce possession orders against trespassers. If it is desired to enforce other possession orders in the High Court, an application must be made to a judge for transfer of the proceedings to the High Court. Simply filing a (false) certificate in such circumstances, which has been known to occur, is quite improper and will usually involve professional misconduct.

'an order to transfer the proceedings to the High Court' (r 83.19(2))—This provision cannot apply to family proceedings because FPR 2010, r 29.17(3) forbids transfer of proceedings from the Family Court to the High Court save by order of a puisne judge of the High Court. Most Family Court orders can be transferred to the High Court for enforcement under r 33.4.

83.20 Warrants of control – bankruptcy or winding up of debtor

(1) This rule applies where the enforcement agent responsible for the execution of a warrant of control is required by any provision of the Insolvency Act 1986 or any other enactment relating to insolvency to retain the proceeds of sale of goods sold under the warrant or money paid in order to avoid a sale.

(2) The enforcement agent will, as soon as practicable after the sale or the receipt of the money, send notice to the creditor and the court.

(3) Where the enforcement agent responsible for the execution of a warrant –

(a) receives notice that –

(i) a bankruptcy order has been made against the debtor; or

(ii) if the debtor is a company –

(aa) a provisional liquidator has been appointed; or

(bb) an order has been made or a resolution passed for the winding up of the company;

(b) withdraws from possession of goods seized; or

(c) pays over to –

(i) the official receiver or trustee in bankruptcy; or

(ii) if the debtor is a company, the liquidator,

the proceeds of sale of goods sold under the warrant or money paid in order to avoid a sale or seized or received in part satisfaction of the warrant,

the enforcement agent must send notice to the creditor and the court.

Amendments—Inserted by SI 2014/407.

83.21 Warrants where the debtor is a farmer

(1) This rule applies if –

(a) any of the following warrants has been issued –

(i) a warrant of control;

(ii) any other warrant conferring the power to use the TCG procedure; or

(iii) a warrant of delivery; and

(b) the enforcement agent has reason to believe that the debtor is a farmer.

(2) If requested to do so by the court or enforcement agent, the creditor must provide the court or enforcement agent with an official certificate, dated not more than three days beforehand, of the result of a search at the Land Registry as to the existence of any charge registered against the debtor under the Agricultural Credits Act 1928.

(3) If the creditor fails to provide the official certificate referred to in paragraph (2) within 7 days of receipt of the request, the court, of its own motion or on the application of the enforcement agent, may order the creditor to provide the certificate.

Amendments—Inserted by SI 2014/407.

83.22 Warrants – withdrawal and suspension of warrant at creditor's request

(1) This rule applies if any of the following warrants has been issued –

(a) a warrant of control;
(b) any other warrant conferring the power to use the TCG procedure; or
(c) a warrant of delivery.

(2) Where a creditor requests the court to withdraw the warrant, subject to the following paragraphs of this rule –

(a) the creditor will be treated as having abandoned the goods; and
(b) the court will mark the warrant as withdrawn by request of the creditor.

(3) Where the request is made in consequence of an application having been made under Part 85, the enforcement power ceases to be exercisable in respect of the goods claimed.

(4) If the court is requested by the creditor to suspend the warrant because of an arrangement with the debtor, the court will mark the warrant as suspended by request of the creditor and the creditor may subsequently apply to the court for it to be re-issued.

(5) Nothing in this rule will prejudice any right of the creditor to apply for the issue of a fresh warrant or will authorise the re-issue of a warrant which has been withdrawn or has expired or has been superseded by the issue of a fresh warrant.

Amendments—Inserted by SI 2014/407.

83.23 Warrants of delivery

(1) In this rule 'warrant of specific delivery' means a warrant to recover goods without alternative provision for recovery of their value.

(2) Except where an act or rule provides otherwise, a judgment or order for the delivery of any goods will be enforceable by warrant of delivery in accordance with this rule.

(3) If the judgment or order does not give the person against whom it was given or made the alternative of paying the value of the goods, it may be enforced by a warrant of specific delivery.

(4) If the judgment or order is for the delivery of the goods or payment of their value, it may be enforced by a warrant of delivery to recover the goods or their value.

(5) Where a warrant of delivery is issued, the creditor will be entitled, by the same or a separate warrant, to execution against the debtor's goods for any money payable under the judgment or order which is to be enforced by the warrant of delivery.

(6) Where –

(a) a judgment or order is given or made for the delivery of goods or payment of their value; and
(b) a warrant is issued to recover the goods or their value,

money paid into court under the warrant will be appropriated first to any sum of money and costs awarded.

Amendments—Inserted by SI 2014/407.

83.24 Warrants of delivery other than those conferring a power to use the TCG procedure – notice and inventory requirements

(1) This rule applies where –

(a) a warrant of delivery has been issued for the whole or part of a sum of money and costs; and

(b) the warrant does not confer power to use the TCG procedure.

(2) Unless the court orders otherwise, the enforcement agent –

(a) must serve the debtor with a notice warning of the warrant; and

(b) must not levy the warrant until at least 7 days after service of the notice.

(3) Upon levying execution of the warrant, the enforcement agent must leave notice of the warrant at the place where it has been executed.

(4) If the enforcement agent removes the goods, the enforcement agent must deliver or send to the debtor an inventory of the goods removed sufficient for the debtor to identify the goods.

(5) The inventory must be delivered or sent to the debtor within 7 days of the goods being seized by –

(a) delivery to the debtor personally;

(b) sending the inventory by post to the debtor's place of residence; or

(c) where the debtor's place of residence is not known, by leaving the inventory for, or sending it to, the debtor at the place from which the goods were removed.

(6) If the enforcement agent fails to supply an inventory in accordance with this rule, the debtor may make an application to the court using the procedure in Part 23, for an order requiring the enforcement agent to do so.

Amendments—Inserted by SI 2014/407.

83.25 Warrants of delivery conferring a power to use the TCG procedure – notice of enforcement and inventory requirements

(1) Where a warrant of delivery confers the power to use the TCG procedure, this rule applies in relation to the parts of the warrant that do not confer that power.

(2) Subject to paragraph (4), the enforcement agent must send a warning notice to the person against whom the warrant is issued not less than 7 clear days before the enforcement agent executes the warrant.

(3) Where the period referred to in paragraph (2) includes a Sunday, bank holiday, Good Friday or Christmas Day, that day does not count in calculating that period.

(4) The court may order that a specified shorter period of notice be given to the debtor.

(5) The enforcement agent may apply for the order by way of application under Part 23 and may make the application as part of an application under rule 84.4.

(6) Upon executing the warrant, the enforcement agent must give to the debtor or leave for the debtor at the place where the warrant is being executed, notice about the execution.

(7) As soon as reasonably practicable, and in any event within 7 days of execution of the warrant, the enforcement agent must provide the debtor with a written inventory of goods taken with a description of the goods to enable the debtor to identify the goods correctly.

(8) If the enforcement agent fails to provide –

(a) notice of execution under paragraph (6); or

(b) an inventory under paragraph (7) within 7 days of execution,

the debtor may make an application to the court under Part 23 for an order requiring the enforcement agent to supply the notice or inventory as appropriate.

(Regulations 6 and 30 to 33 of the TCG Regulations contain notice and inventory requirements that apply in relation to the use of the TCG procedure.)

Amendments—Inserted by SI 2014/407.

83.26 Warrants of possession

(1) A judgment or order for the recovery of land will be enforceable by warrant of possession.

(2) An application for a warrant of possession –

(a) may be made without notice; and
(b) must be made to –
  (i) the County Court hearing centre where the judgment or order which it is sought to enforce was made; or
  (ii) the County Court hearing centre to which the proceedings have since been transferred.

(3) The court may, on an application by a debtor who wishes to oppose an application for a warrant of possession, transfer it to the County Court hearing centre serving the address where the debtor resides or carries on business, or to another court.

(4) Without prejudice to paragraph (7), the person applying for a warrant of possession must file a certificate that the land which is subject of the judgment or order has not been vacated.

(5) When applying for a warrant of possession of a dwelling-house subject to a mortgage, the claimant must certify that notice has been given in accordance with the Dwelling Houses (Execution of Possession Orders by Mortgagees) Regulations 2010.

(6) Where a warrant of possession is issued, the creditor will be entitled, by the same or a separate warrant, to execution against the debtor's goods for any money payable under the judgment or order which is to be enforced by the warrant of possession.

(7) In a case to which paragraph (6) applies or where an order for possession has been suspended on terms as to payment of a sum of money by instalments, the creditor must in the request certify –

(a) the amount of money remaining due under the judgment or order; and
(b) that the whole or part of any instalment due remains unpaid.

(8) A warrant of restitution may be issued, with the permission of the court, in aid of any warrant of possession.

(9) An application for permission under paragraph (8) may be made without notice being served on any other party and must be supported by evidence of –

(a) wrongful re-entry into possession following the execution of the warrant of possession; and
(b) such further facts as would, in the High Court, enable the creditor to have a writ of restitution issued.

(10) A warrant of possession to enforce an order for possession in a possession claim against a trespasser under Part 55 ('a warrant of possession against a trespasser') may be issued at any time after the date on which possession is ordered to be given.

(11) No warrant of possession against a trespasser may be issued after the expiry of 3 months from the date of the order without the permission of the court.

(12) Unless the court otherwise directs, an application for permission under paragraph (11) may be made without notice to any other party.

Amendments—Inserted by SI 2014/407.

Issue—The warrant cannot be issued until the date for possession in the order has passed. However, where the order requires possession 'forthwith', the warrant can be issued immediately. Normal administrative processes mean that several days or weeks may elapse before the eviction takes place. Fixing the actual date is a matter of administrative process, which may be controlled by the court in appropriate cases (*Air Ministry v Harris* [1951] 2 All ER 862, CA). If it is thought necessary, a direction to this effect should be sought from the judge either when the order is made or subsequently.

Effect—When enforcing a warrant of possession, the bailiff need not remove chattels (CCA 1984, s 111(1)) but may evict any person on the premises even though not a party (*R v Wandsworth County Court ex parte London Borough of Wandsworth* [1975] 1 WLR 1314, QBD). An occupier who claims the right to stay may apply to be added as a defendant (r 19.3) in order to apply for the judgment to be set aside.

Warrant of restitution (r 83.26(8))—If after possession has been recovered, the land or premises are re-occupied, application may be made without notice for a warrant of restitution to eject the occupier. There must be a sufficient connection between the original eviction and the re-occupation, but it may be that restitution is effective against someone other than those originally evicted (*Wiltshire County Council v Frazer* [1986] 1 WLR 109, QBD, where, however, there had been a summary order for possession against trespassers).

PART III

83.27 Saving for enforcement by committal

Nothing in rules 83.23 and 83.26 prejudices any power to enforce a judgment or order for the delivery of goods or the recovery of land by any order of committal.

Amendments—Inserted by SI 2014/407.

Enforcement by committal—The court will be reluctant to commit where the order could have been satisfactorily enforced by the less draconian (and much less expensive) option of a warrant (*Danchevsky v Danchevsky* [1975] Fam 17, CA). The applicant for committal should therefore be prepared to show that a warrant has been issued but has proved ineffective or that that method of enforcement is for some reason inappropriate. See generally *Tuohy v Bell* [2003] BPIR 749, CA.

83.28 Suspension of part warrant

(1) This rule applies where a warrant issued for part of a sum of money and costs payable under a judgment or order is suspended on payment of instalments.

(2) Unless the court otherwise directs, the judgment or order will be treated as suspended on those terms as respects the whole of the sum of money and costs then remaining unpaid.

Amendments—Inserted by SI 2014/407.

83.29 Concurrent warrants

Two or more warrants of control may be issued concurrently for execution by two or more different enforcement agents, but –

(a) no more may be levied under all the warrants together than is authorised to be levied under one of them; and

(b) unless the court orders otherwise, the costs of more than one warrant will not be allowed against the debtor.

Amendments—Inserted by SI 2014/407.

Practice Direction 83 – Writs and Warrants – General Provisions

This Practice Direction supplements CPR Part 83

Amendments—CPR Update 69.

PART 83 – SECTION I – SCOPE AND INTERPRETATION

Scope – Rule 83.1

1 In relation to writs and warrants that relate to taking control of goods, Part 83 should be read in conjunction with –

(1) Part 84, which contains rules specifically in relation to taking control of goods; and

(2) the Taking Control of Goods Regulations 2013, which can be found at www.justice.gov.uk/courts/procedure-rules

Writs and warrants other than those conferring a power to use the TCG procedure – duration and priority – Rule 83.3

2 The notice required by rule 83.3(7)(b) should be in Form 71.

PART 83 – SECTION III– WRITS

Forms of writs

3.1 A writ of control must be in Forms 53 to 57 in Practice Direction 4 as appropriate.

3.2 A writ of delivery must be in Form 64 or 65 in Practice Direction 4, whichever is appropriate.

3.3 A writ of possession must be in Form 66 or 66A in Practice Direction 4, whichever is appropriate.

Writs other than those conferring a power to use the TCG procedure– order for sale otherwise than by auction – Rule 83.12

4.1 Rule 83.12 only applies in relation to writs that do not confer a power to use the procedure in Schedule 12. The rule therefore applies in relation to the following writs-

(a) writs of delivery where there is no element of taking control of goods; and
(b) ecclesiastical writs.

4.2 Schedule 7 of the Courts Act 2003 applies in relation to such writs. Paragraph 10(3) of that Schedule provides that if the person who seized the goods has notice of another execution or other executions, the court must not consider an application for leave to sell privately until the notice prescribed by these Rules has been given to the other execution creditor or creditors.

Application for warrant of control – Rule 83.15

5 The request for a warrant of control should be in Form N323.

PART 84
ENFORCEMENT BY TAKING CONTROL OF GOODS

CONTENTS OF THIS PART

Section I

Rule | Page

Scope and Interpretation

84.1 Scope 2338
84.2 Interpretation 2338

Section II
Where and How to Make Applications

84.3 Where and how to make applications 2338

Section III
Taking Control of Goods

84.4 Notice of enforcement prior to taking control of goods – application for notice period of less than the minimum period 2339
84.5 Application to extend the period in which to take control of goods 2339
84.6 Application to take control of goods during prohibited hours 2339
84.7 Application to enter, re-enter or remain on premises otherwise than during permitted hours 2339
84.8 Notice of intention to re-enter premises – application for notice period of less than the minimum period 2340
84.9 Application for a warrant to enter premises – conditions to be satisfied before a warrant may be issued 2340
84.10 Application for a warrant allowing reasonable force in relation to goods on the highway – conditions to be satisfied before a warrant may be issued 2340
84.11 Application for sale otherwise than by public auction 2340
84.12 Application in relation to disposal of abandoned goods 2341
84.13 Application by the debtor for a remedy in relation to goods taken into control 2341
84.14 Application by the enforcement agent for exceptional disbursements 2341
84.15 Application where there is a dispute regarding a co-owner's share of proceeds 2342
84.16 Disputes about the amount of fees or disbursements recoverable under the Fees Regulations 2342

Section IV
Proceedings in relation to certificates under section 64 of the 2007 Act

84.17 Interpretation 2343

84.18 Application for issue of a certificate under section 64 of the 2007 Act 2343
84.19 Issue of replacement certificates and surrender of certificates 2343
84.20 Complaints as to fitness to hold a certificate 2344
Practice Direction 84 –
Enforcement by Taking Control of Goods 2344

General note—This Part cannot be properly understood without reference also to Tribunals, Courts and Enforcement Act 2007, Pt 3 and Sch 12, Taking Control of Goods Regulations 2013, and the Taking Control of Goods (Fees) Regulations 2014, which are not reproduced in this work. Readers are referred to *Civil Court Service* (LexisNexis).

The Taking Control of Goods Regulations 2013 set out in detail which goods are exempt from seizure, and it should be noted that necessary equipment for use in the debtor's business, including computers, is only exempt to a value of £1,350, and not even then in the case of enforcement of council tax and the like. Detailed provisions are set out concerning the powers of enforcement officers.

The fees charged by private bailiffs have been the cause of much controversy and prescribed fees have been introduced by the Taking Control of Goods (Fees) Regulations 2014. Fees are charged according to the stage that enforcement has reached, and if a stage of enforcement begins, the full fee for that stage is payable. Notably, the compliance stage, because it comprises 'all activities from the receipt by the enforcement officer of instructions' (reg 6(1)(a)), attracts a fee of £75 immediately the enforcement officer is instructed.

Section I
Scope and Interpretation

84.1 Scope

This Part contains rules in relation to enforcement by taking control of goods using the procedure in Schedule 12 to the Tribunals, Courts and Enforcement Act 2007.

Amendments—Inserted by SI 2014/407.

84.2 Interpretation

In this Part –

(a) 'the Act' means the Tribunals Courts and Enforcement Act 2007;
(b) 'Schedule 12' means Schedule 12 to the Act;
(c) 'creditor' has the meaning given in paragraph 1(6) of Schedule 12;
(d) 'co-owner' has the meaning given in paragraph 3(1) of Schedule 12;
(e) 'debtor' has the meaning given in paragraph 1(5) of Schedule 12;
(f) 'enforcement agent' has the meaning given in paragraph 2(1) of Schedule 12;
(g) 'Fees Regulations' means the Taking Control of Goods (Fees) Regulations 2014;
(h) 'TCG Regulations' means the Taking Control of Goods Regulations 2013;
(i) 'writ of control' and 'warrant of control' are to be construed in accordance with section 62(4) of the Act.

Amendments—Inserted by SI 2014/407.

Section II
Where and How to Make Applications

84.3 Where and how to make applications

(1) This rule sets out where and how applications referred to in this Part must be made.

(2) Applications referred to in this Part must be made in accordance with the procedure in Part 23 as modified by this Part.

(3) Where there are no pre-existing proceedings, an application referred to in this Part must be made to the County Court.

(4) Where there are pre-existing proceedings, the application must be made to the High Court or the County Court in accordance with rule 23.2.

Amendments—Inserted by SI 2014/407.

Section III

Taking Control of Goods

84.4 Notice of enforcement prior to taking control of goods – application for notice period of less than the minimum period

(1) This rule applies where a person seeks an order under regulation 6(3) of the TCG Regulations that a shorter notice period than the minimum period for taking control of goods set out in regulation 6(1) of those Regulations be given to the debtor.

(2) The person may make an application for the order.

(3) The application –

(a) may be made without notice; and

(b) must be accompanied by evidence demonstrating that if the order is not made, it is likely that goods of the debtor will be moved or otherwise disposed of, in order to avoid the enforcement agent taking control of the goods.

Amendments—Inserted by SI 2014/407.

84.5 Application to extend the period in which to take control of goods

(1) An application under regulation 9(4) of the TCG Regulations (application to extend the period in which to take control of goods) must be accompanied by –

(a) a witness statement made by the person making the application that no previous application under regulation 9(4) has been made to extend that period; and

(b) the applicant's grounds for not taking control of goods of the debtor during the period specified in regulation 9(1).

(2) If –

(a) the application is made before the expiry of the period specified in regulation 9(1); and

(b) the court orders the period of extension,

the period of extension will start on the day after the expiry of the period specified in regulation 9(1), or on such later day as the court may order.

(3) If the court orders the period of extension –

(a) the applicant must serve a copy of the extension order on the debtor, and on the creditor, enforcement agent or enforcement officer as appropriate; and

(b) if the goods are to be taken into control by virtue of a warrant or writ of control, or of any other writ or warrant conferring the power to use the procedure in Schedule 12, the court will endorse on the warrant or writ a note of the extension.

Amendments—Inserted by SI 2014/407.

84.6 Application to take control of goods during prohibited hours

An application by the enforcement agent under regulation 13(2)(a) of the TCG Regulations for an order allowing goods to be taken into control during hours prohibited by regulation 13(1) of those Regulations –

(a) may be made without notice; and

(b) must be accompanied by evidence demonstrating that if the order is not made, it is likely that goods of the debtor will be moved or otherwise disposed of, in order to avoid the enforcement agent taking control of the goods.

Amendments—Inserted by SI 2014/407.

84.7 Application to enter, re-enter or remain on premises otherwise than during permitted hours

An application by the enforcement agent under regulation 22(5) of the TCG Regulations for an order allowing the enforcement agent to enter, re-enter or remain on premises at times other than those permitted by regulation 22(2), (3) or (4) of those Regulations- –

PART III

(a) may be made without notice; and
(b) must be accompanied by evidence demonstrating that if the order is not made, it is likely that goods of the debtor will be moved or otherwise disposed of, in order to avoid the enforcement agent taking control of the goods.

Amendments—Inserted by SI 2014/407.

84.8 Notice of intention to re-enter premises – application for notice period of less than the minimum period

(1) This rule applies where a person seeks an order under regulation 25(3) of the TCG Regulations that a shorter notice period than the minimum period for re-entering premises set out in regulation 25(1) of those Regulations be given to the debtor.

(2) The person may make an application for the order.

(3) The application –
(a) may be made without notice; and
(b) must be accompanied by evidence demonstrating that if the order is not made, it is likely that goods of the debtor will be moved to be disposed of, in order to avoid the enforcement agent inspecting or removing the goods.

Amendments—Inserted by SI 2014/407.

84.9 Application for a warrant to enter premises – conditions to be satisfied before a warrant may be issued

(1) This rule applies to an application by an enforcement agent for –
(a) the issue of a warrant under paragraph 15(1) of Schedule 12;
(b) the issue of a warrant under paragraph 20(2) of Schedule 12 allowing the use of reasonable force to enter premises; or
(c) the inclusion in a warrant power under paragraph 21(2) of Schedule 12 to use reasonable force to enter premises.

(2) Where the application is for the issue of a warrant under paragraph 15(1) of Schedule 12, the enforcement agent must provide the court with sufficient evidence and information to satisfy the court that the conditions in paragraph 15(2) of Schedule 12 are met.

(3) Where the application is for the issue of a warrant under paragraph 20(2) or 21(2) of Schedule 12, the enforcement agent must provide the court with sufficient evidence and information to satisfy the court that the conditions set out in regulation 28(2) of the TCG Regulations have been met.

Amendments—Inserted by SI 2014/407.

84.10 Application for a warrant allowing reasonable force in relation to goods on the highway – conditions to be satisfied before a warrant may be issued

(1) This rule applies to an application by an enforcement agent for the issue of a warrant under paragraph 31(1) of Schedule 12 allowing the use of reasonable force in relation to goods on the highway.

(2) The enforcement agent must provide the court with sufficient evidence and information to satisfy the court that the conditions set out in regulation 29(2) of the TCG Regulations have been met.

Amendments—Inserted by SI 2014/407.

84.11 Application for sale otherwise than by public auction

(1) This rule applies to an application by an enforcement agent for an order for sale otherwise than by public auction under paragraph 41(2) of Schedule 12 ('alternative sale application').

(2) Where the enforcement agent has made a statement to the court under paragraph 41(4) of Schedule 12 (reason to believe that an enforcement power has become exercisable by another creditor against the debtor or co-owner), the alternative sale application must be accompanied by –

(a) a list of the name and address of every other creditor that the enforcement agent has reason to believe has an exercisable enforcement power against the debtor or co-owner and an explanation of why the enforcement agent has such a belief; and
(b) a copy of the notice of application required by paragraph 41(5) of Schedule 12 and proof that the notice has been served on such other creditors not less than 4 days before the day fixed for the hearing of the application.

(3) Every person to whom notice of the application was given may attend and be heard on the hearing of the application.

Amendments—Inserted by SI 2014/407.

Sale otherwise than by public auction—The advantage of seeking a private sale is that a better price may be obtained than at auction, to the benefit of both debtor and creditors. It is preferable for the order to authorise a particular sale and the application should be specific as to the actual sale proposed. The purchaser may be the execution creditor (*Ex parte Villars* (1874) LR 9 Ch 432, CA). If the point is contentious, the applicant must be prepared to compare the proposed sale price with what is likely to be achieved at auction. The procedure may be particularly useful where the creditor has an intimate knowledge of the debtor's leviable assets and, therefore, some idea of the best market for them, or where the goods are of a specialised nature for which there is no ready market.

Note, however, that unlike the situation under the former rules, the application may only be made by the enforcement agent himself.

84.12 Application in relation to disposal of abandoned goods

(1) This rule applies to an application by the enforcement agent under regulation 47(5) of the TCG Regulations for an order for the disposal of goods abandoned by the debtor.

(2) If the enforcement agent applies for an order for disposal by way of donation to a charitable organisation or destruction of goods, the enforcement agent must explain in the application why the enforcement agent does not wish the goods to be made available for a further period of collection.

Amendments—Inserted by SI 2014/407.

84.13 Application by the debtor for a remedy in relation to goods taken into control

(1) This rule applies where the debtor wishes to bring proceedings under paragraph 66 of Schedule 12 for –

(a) breach of a provision of Schedule 12; or
(b) enforcement action taken under a defective instrument.

(2) The debtor may bring proceedings by way of an application.

(3) The application must be accompanied by evidence of how –

(a) the provisions of Schedule 12 are alleged to have been breached; or
(b) the instrument is alleged to be defective.

Amendments—Inserted by SI 2014/407.

84.14 Application by the enforcement agent for exceptional disbursements

(1) This rule applies to an application by an enforcement agent for exceptional disbursements under regulation 10 of the Fees Regulations.

(2) The application must be accompanied by –

(a) evidence of the creditor's consent to the application; and
(b) evidence that the disbursements to which the application relate are necessary for effective enforcement of the sum to be recovered, having regard to all the circumstances including –
    (i) the amount of the sum to be recovered; and
    (ii) the nature and value of the goods which have been taken into control, or which it is sought to take into control.

(3) Where the application is made before the goods are taken into control, it may be made without notice.

Amendments—Inserted by SI 2014/407.

84.15 Application where there is a dispute regarding a co-owner's share of proceeds

(1) This rule applies to an application under regulation 15 of the Fees Regulations to determine the amount of the proceeds payable to a co-owner.

(2) The applicant must file with the application –

- (a) evidence of the enforcement power;
- (b) a copy of the itemised list of goods sold or otherwise disposed of required by regulation 14(1)(a) of the Fees Regulations;
- (c) a copy of the statement of the sum received in relation to each item required by regulation 14(1)(b)(i) of the Fees Regulations;
- (d) a copy of the statement of the proceeds required by regulation 14(1)(b)(ii) of the Fees Regulations;
- (e) a copy of the statement of the application of the proceeds required by regulation 14(1)(b)(iii) of the Fees Regulations;
- (f) evidence that the share of proceeds paid to the co-owner was not proportionate to the co-owner's interest in the goods sold.

(3) The applicant must serve a copy of the application notice in accordance with table 1.

Table 1

Applicant	Those to be served with a copy of the application notice
Co-owner	Any other co-owners; creditor; debtor; enforcement agent
Creditor	Co-owners; debtor; enforcement agent
Debtor	Co-owners; creditor; enforcement agent
Enforcement agent	Co-owners; creditor; debtor

Amendments—Inserted by SI 2014/407.

84.16 Disputes about the amount of fees or disbursements recoverable under the Fees Regulations

(1) This rule applies where –

- (a) there is a dispute about the amount of fees or disbursements, other than exceptional disbursements, recoverable under the Fees Regulations; and
- (b) a party wishes the court to assess the amounts recoverable under regulation 16 of the Fees Regulations.

(2) A party may make an application to the court to assess the amounts.

(3) The application must be accompanied by –

- (a) evidence of the amount of fees or disbursements in dispute;
- (b) evidence that the fees or disbursements in dispute were not applicable, as the debt had been settled before the stage where it would have been necessary to incur those fees or expenses;
- (c) evidence that, because the enforcement agent was instructed to use the TCG procedure in relation to the same debtor but in respect of more than one enforcement power where the enforcement powers could reasonably be exercised at the same time, regulation 11 of the Fees Regulations should have been applied;
- (d) evidence that the fee due and any disbursements for the enforcement stage, first

enforcement stage, or first and second enforcement stage, as appropriate, are not recoverable under regulation 12 of the Fees Regulations; or

(e) where the dispute concerns the amount of the percentage fee, calculated in accordance with regulation 7 of the Fees Regulations, evidence of the amount of the sum to be recovered.

Amendments—Inserted by SI 2014/407.

'amount of fees recoverable' (r 84.16(1))—Note that the fees chargeable by an enforcement officer are now fixed by the Taking Control of Goods (Fees) Regulations 2014 and there is no scope for challenging them on the general ground that they appear disproportionate in a particular case, or on the ground of hardship.

Section IV

Proceedings in relation to certificates under section 64 of the 2007 Act

84.17 Interpretation

In this Section –

(a) 'Certification Regulations' means the Certification of Enforcement Agents Regulations 2014;

(b) 'applicant', 'certificate', 'certificated person' and 'complainant' have the meanings given in regulation 2 of the Certification Regulations.

Amendments—Inserted by SI 2014/482.

PART III

84.18 Application for issue of a certificate under section 64 of the 2007 Act

(1) This rule applies to an application for the issue of a certificate under section 64 of the 2007 Act.

(2) The application must be made to the County Court Business Centre, using the relevant form prescribed in Practice Direction 4.

(3) The application must specify one of the County Court hearing centres listed in Practice Direction 84 as the centre at which the application is to be heard.

(4) The application must, in addition to the matters specified in rule 23.6, provide evidence that the applicant fulfils the requirements of regulation 3(b) of the Certification Regulations, and in particular –

(a) the application must be accompanied by the documents specified in Practice Direction 84; and

(b) the additional documents specified in Practice Direction 84 must be produced to the court on the day of the hearing.

(5) If any reasons have been submitted to the court in response to the notice of the application required by regulation 4(5) of the Certification Regulations, a copy of those reasons must be sent to the applicant at least 7 days before the hearing, and the applicant may respond both in writing and at the hearing.

(6) The applicant must also file such further evidence as the court may direct.

(7) The applicant must attend for examination on the day of the hearing.

(8) Rules 23.2, 23.4, 23.7, 23.8, 23.9 and 23.10 do not apply to an application to which this rule applies.

Amendments—Inserted by SI 2014/482.

84.19 Issue of replacement certificates and surrender of certificates

(1) Where changes are required to be notified and the certificate produced under regulation 8 of the Certification Regulations, the changes must be notified to, and the certificate produced at, the County Court hearing centre at which the certificate was issued.

(2) Where a certificate is required to be surrendered under regulation 12 of the Certification Regulations, the certificate must be surrendered to the County Court hearing centre at which the certificate was issued.

Amendments—Inserted by SI 2014/482.

84.20 Complaints as to fitness to hold a certificate

(1) This rule applies to a complaint under regulation 9(1) of the Certification Regulations.

(2) The complaint must be submitted to the County Court hearing centre at which the certificate was issued, using the relevant form prescribed in Practice Direction 4.

(3) A copy of the complaint must be sent to the applicant at least 14 days before the hearing, and the applicant may respond both in writing and at the hearing.

(4) The complainant is not liable for any costs incurred by the certificated person in responding to the complaint, unless paragraph (5) applies.

(5) The court may order the complainant to pay such costs as it considers reasonable if it is satisfied that the complaint –

(a) discloses no reasonable grounds for considering that the certificated person is not a fit person to hold a certificate; and
(b) amounts to an abuse of the court's process.

Amendments—Inserted by SI 2014/482.

Practice Direction 84 – Enforcement by Taking Control of Goods

This Practice Direction supplements CPR Part 84

Amendments—CPR Update 69.

Interrelationship of rules on taking control of goods with other legislation

1.1 The provisions in this Practice Direction and Part 84 on taking control of goods are closely linked to, and need to be read with –

(1) Part 3 of and Schedule 12 to the Tribunals Courts and Enforcement Act 2007 (The Act), which can be found at www.justice.gov.uk/courts/procedure-rules/;
(2) the Taking Control of Goods Regulations 2013, which can be found at www.justice.gov.uk/courts/procedure-rules; and
(3) the Taking Control of Goods (Fees) Regulations 2013, which can be found at www.justice.gov.uk/courts/procedure-rules.

1.2 Part 83 – Writs and warrants – General provisions, is also relevant and contains provisions relating to writs and warrants of control and also other forms of writ and warrant that confer a power to use the procedure in Schedule 12 to the Act.

1.3 A flow chart providing guidance and setting out the interrelationship between these Rules, the 2007 Act and the Taking Control of Goods Regulations 2013 can be found at www.justice.gov.uk/courts/procedure-rules.

Part 84 – Section IV – Proceedings in relation to certificates under section 64 of the 2007 Act

2.1 Rule 84.18 – Documents to accompany application for issue of a certificate

(1) The application for the issue of a certificate must state the applicant's name (and employer, if any), and be accompanied by the following –

(a) two references, of which –

(i) one may be from the applicant's employer or an approved officer of the Civil Enforcement Association or of the High Court Enforcement Officers' Association; and

(ii) one must deal with the applicant's knowledge of the law and procedure relating to powers of enforcement by taking control of goods and commercial rent arrears recovery, and the applicant's experience of, and conduct in, exercising such powers;

(b) a certified copy of the result of a search (which must be no more than one month old) of the Register of judgments, orders, fines and tribunal decisions against –

(i) the applicant's full name; and

(ii) the applicant's home and business addresses for the last six years;

(c) two passport sized photographs of the applicant (one to be retained on the court file and the other to be affixed to the certificate if issued);

(d) a copy (which must conform to the design and layout prescribed in the Schedule to the Certification Regulations and be on paper of durable quality and in a clear and legible printed or typewritten form with a font size no less than 10 point) of each of the following forms required by the TCG Regulations and intended to be used by the applicant when exercising powers of taking control of goods or commercial rent arrears recovery –

(i) notice of enforcement (required by Regulation 7);

(ii) controlled goods agreement (required by Regulation 15);

(iii) warning of immobilisation (required by Regulation 16(3));

(iv) notice of re-entry (required by Regulation 26);

(v) notice after entry or taking control of goods on a highway and inventory of goods taken into control (required by Regulation 30);

(vi) notice of removal for storage or sale (required by Regulation 32);

(vii) inventory of goods (required by Regulation 33);

(viii) notice of sale (required by Regulation 39);

(ix) notice of abandonment (required by Regulation 47(3));

(e) proof that the applicant –

(i) has achieved at least a qualification on Taking Control of Goods at (or above) Level 2 of the Qualifications and Credit Framework or equivalent as determined by a nationally accredited awarding body; or

(ii) has been authorised to act as an enforcement officer in accordance with the High Court Enforcement Officers Regulations 2004.

(2) In addition, the applicant must produce to the court on the date of the hearing –

(a) a certified copy of a –

(i) criminal conviction certificate;

(ii) criminal record certificate; or

(iii) enhanced criminal record certificate

issued pursuant to Part V of the Police Act 1997 and which is not more than one month old;

(b) written evidence of the lodging by way of bond of the security required by regulation 6 of the Certification Regulations.

2.2 Rule 84.18 – Application for issue of a certificate

The County Court hearing centres referred to in rule 84.18(3) are –

London	Central London
Midlands	Birmingham Northampton Nottingham Worcester
North-East	Gateshead Kingston Upon Hull Middlesbrough York
North-West	Birkenhead Burnley Oldham
South-East	Brighton Chelmsford Dartford Hertford Norwich Oxford
South-West	Bristol Plymouth Southampton
Wales	Caernarfon Cardiff Swansea Wrexham

Amendments—CPR Update 70.

★★★★

PART 87
APPLICATIONS FOR WRIT OF HABEAS CORPUS

CONTENTS OF THIS PART

Section 1

Rule		Page
	Scope and interpretation	
87.1	Scope and interpretation of this Part	2346
	Section 2	
	Applications to the High Court for a writ of habeas corpus for release	
87.2	How to make the application for a writ of habeas corpus for release	2347
87.3	Initial consideration of the application by a single judge	2347
87.4	Initial consideration of the application on paper	2347
87.5	Consideration of the application at a hearing	2348
87.6	Order for release: sufficient authority to release detained person	2348
87.7	Applications involving protected parties	2348
87.8	Form and directions as to the return to the writ	2348
87.9	Service of the writ	2348
87.10	Return to the writ	2349
87.11	Procedure at hearing of the writ	2349
	Section 3	
	Writ of habeas corpus to give evidence or to answer a charge	
87.12	Writ of habeas corpus to give evidence or to answer a charge	2349

Section 1
Scope and interpretation

87.1 Scope and interpretation of this Part

(1) This Part contains rules about applications to the court as follows –

(a) Section 2 relates to applications for a writ of habeas corpus for release; and
(b) Section 3 relates to applications for a writ of habeas corpus to give evidence or a writ of habeas corpus to answer a charge.

(The Family Procedure Rules 2010 contain rules about applications for a writ of habeas corpus for release in relation to a minor.)

(2) In Sections 2 and 3 –

(a) 'judge' means a judge of the High Court; and
(b) 'court' means the High Court,

unless otherwise specified.

Amendments—Inserted by SI 2014/3299.

Applications for the release of a minor—The rules are set out in FPR 2010, r 12.42A

Section 2
Applications to the High Court for a writ of habeas corpus for release

87.2 How to make the application for a writ of habeas corpus for release

(1) The applicant must make the application by filing –

(a) a claim form under Part 8; and
(b) a witness statement or affidavit.

(2) The witness statement or affidavit must –

(a) state that the application is made at the instance of the person being detained;
(b) set out the nature of the detention; and
(c) subject to paragraph (3), be made by the detained person.

(3) If the detained person is unable to make the witness statement or affidavit, the witness statement or affidavit –

(a) may be made by some other person on behalf of the detained person; and
(b) must state the reason why the detained person is unable to make the witness statement or affidavit.

(4) The claim form must be filed in the Administrative Court.

(5) The application may be made without notice.

(6) In cases of urgency, the judge –

(a) may dispense with the requirement that a claim form must be filed; and
(b) must give directions for the conduct of the application.

Amendments—Inserted by SI 2014/3299.

Applications for the release of a minor—The application is made by filing an application notice and is made to the Family Division of the High Court: FPR 2010, r 12.42A(1)(a)(i),(ii).

Procedure—The provisions of FPR 2010, rr 12.5–12.8, 12.12–12.16, 12.21 and 12.39 do not apply to an application for a writ of habeas corpus for the release of a child.

Secure Accommodation Order—There is no provision for a parent or child to apply for the discharge of a SAO: see CA 1989, s 25. It is suggested that the only recourse for a parent or a subject child to secure his/her release from secure accommodation is to make an application for a writ of habeas corpus.

87.3 Initial consideration of the application by a single judge

(1) A judge may consider an application under rule 87.2 initially on paper.

(2) If an application has not been considered initially on paper, it must be considered –

(a) by a judge sitting in court, unless rule 87.7 applies; or
(b) if no judge is sitting in court, by a judge otherwise than in court.

Amendments—Inserted by SI 2014/3299.

87.4 Initial consideration of the application on paper

(1) Where the judge considers the application under rule 87.2 on paper, the judge may –

(a) make an order for the issue of the writ;
(b) adjourn the application to a hearing;

(c) direct that the application be considered by a Divisional Court of the Queen's Bench Division;
(d) direct that the application continues as an application for permission to apply for judicial review;
(e) give such other directions for resolution of the application as may be appropriate; or
(f) dismiss the application.

(2) Where the judge dismisses a paper application, the applicant may request the decision to be reconsidered at a hearing.

(3) A request under paragraph (2) must be filed within 7 days after service of the order dismissing the application.

(4) The applicant and the respondent must be given at least 2 days' notice of the hearing date.

Amendments—Inserted by SI 2014/3299.

87.5 Consideration of the application at a hearing

Where the judge considers the application under rule 87.2 at a hearing, including a hearing ordered under rule 87.4(1)(b) or a hearing requested under rule 87.4(2), the judge may –

(a) make an order for the issue of the writ;
(b) adjourn the application to a further hearing;
(c) direct that the application be considered by a Divisional Court of the Queen's Bench Division;
(d) direct that the application continues as an application for permission to apply for judicial review;
(e) give such other directions for resolution of the application as may be appropriate;
(f) dismiss the application; or
(g) order that the detained person must be released.

Amendments—Inserted by SI 2014/3299.

87.6 Order for release: sufficient authority to release detained person

An order made under rule 87.5(g) is sufficient authorisation for a governor of a prison, police officer or other person to release the detained person.

Amendments—Inserted by SI 2014/3299.

87.7 Applications involving protected parties

Any application made on behalf of a protected party must initially be considered by a judge otherwise than in court.

Amendments—Inserted by SI 2014/3299.

87.8 Form and directions as to the return to the writ

(1) A writ of habeas corpus for release must be in Practice Form No 89 as set out in Practice Direction 4.

(2) A court or judge issuing a writ of habeas corpus for release must give directions as to the court or judge before whom, and the date on which, the writ is returnable.

Amendments—Inserted by SI 2014/3299.

87.9 Service of the writ

(1) Subject to paragraphs (2) and (3), the applicant must serve the writ of habeas corpus for release personally on the respondent.

(2) If it is not practicable to serve the writ personally, or if the respondent is the governor of a prison or other public official, the applicant must serve the writ by leaving it with an employee or agent of the respondent at the place where the detained person is being held.

(3) If there is more than one respondent named in the writ, the original writ must be served according to this rule on the first-named respondent, and copies must be served on the other respondents.

(4) The court must notify all parties –

(a) of the court or judge before whom, and the date on which, the writ is to be returned to the court; and

(b) that in default of obedience, proceedings for committal of the party disobeying may be taken.

Amendments—Inserted by SI 2014/3299.

87.10 Return to the writ

(1) The return to a writ of habeas corpus for release must –

(a) be indorsed on or annexed to the writ; and

(b) state all the causes of the detention of the detained person.

(2) The return may be amended, or another return substituted for it, by permission of the court or judge before whom the writ is returnable.

(3) The return must be filed and served upon the applicant in accordance with the directions of the court issuing the writ.

Amendments—Inserted by SI 2014/3299.

87.11 Procedure at hearing of the writ

At the hearing of the writ an application may be made –

(a) to discharge or remand the detained person; or

(b) to amend or quash the return.

Amendments—Inserted by SI 2014/3299.

Section 3

Writ of habeas corpus to give evidence or to answer a charge

87.12 Writ of habeas corpus to give evidence or to answer a charge

(1) An application for a writ of habeas corpus to give evidence or a writ of habeas corpus to answer a charge must be made to a judge and be supported by a witness statement or affidavit.

(2) A writ of habeas corpus to give evidence must be in Practice Form No 91 as set out in Practice Direction 4.

(3) A writ of habeas corpus to answer a charge must be in Practice Form No 92 as set out in Practice Direction 4.

(4) An application for an order to bring up a prisoner otherwise than by writ of habeas corpus, to give evidence in any criminal or civil proceedings before any court, tribunal or judge, must be –

(a) made to a judge or, in the case of an application for an order under section 57 of the County Courts Act 1984, a judge of the County Court; and

(b) supported by a witness statement or affidavit.

Amendments—Inserted by SI 2014/3299.

****

PART III

Supreme Court Rules 2009, SI 2009/1603

PART 1
INTERPRETATION AND SCOPE

CONTENTS OF THIS PART

Rule		Page
1	Citation and commencement	2350
2	Scope and objective	2350
3	Interpretation	2350
4	Forms	2351
5	Time limits	2351
6	Service	2352
7	Filing	2352
8	Non-compliance with these Rules	2353
9	Procedural decisions	2353

1 Citation and commencement

These Rules may be cited as the Supreme Court Rules 2009 and shall come into force on 1 October 2009.

2 Scope and objective

(1) These Rules apply to civil and criminal appeals to the Court and to appeals and references under the Court's devolution jurisdiction.

(2) The overriding objective of these Rules is to secure that the Court is accessible, fair and efficient.

(3) The Court must interpret and apply these Rules with a view to securing that the Court is accessible, fair and efficient and that unnecessary disputes over procedural matters are discouraged.

The overriding objective (r 2(2))—The SCR follow the example of the CPR in declaring at the outset the 'overriding objective' of the rules. It will be noted that the overriding objective of the SCR is very different from that in Pt 1 of the CPR. There is no statement comparable to the declaration in CPR 1998, r 1.1(1) that these Rules are 'a new procedural code', presumably out of a desire to avoid stating the obvious.

'unnecessary disputes over procedural matters are discouraged' (r 2(3))—Compare CPR 1998, r 1.3.

3 Interpretation

(1) In these Rules –

'the Act' means the Constitutional Reform Act 2005;

'the Court' means the Supreme Court of the United Kingdom;

'Justice' means a judge of the Court and includes its President and Deputy President;

'the Registrar' means the Registrar of the Court;

'the Registry' means the Registry of the Court.

(2) In these Rules except where the context otherwise requires –

'appellant' means a person who files an application for permission to appeal or who files a notice of appeal;

'business day' means any day other than a Saturday, Sunday, Christmas Day, Good Friday or a bank holiday under the Banking and Financial Dealings Act 1971, in England and Wales;

'certificate of service' means a certificate given under rule 6;

'counsel' includes any person with the right to be heard as an advocate at a full hearing before the Court;

'court below' means the court from which an appeal (or application for permission to appeal) is made to the Court;

'court officer' means the Registrar or a member of the court staff;

'devolution jurisdiction' means the jurisdiction transferred to the Court by section 40 of, and Schedule 9 to, the Act;

'electronic means' means CD ROMs, memory sticks, email, fax or other means of electronic communication of the contents of documents;

'filing' means filing in the Registry in accordance with rule 7 and related expressions have corresponding meanings;

'form' and the 'appropriate form' have the meanings given by rule 4;

'panel of Justices' means a panel of at least three Justices;

'party' means an appellant, a respondent and a person who has been given permission to intervene under rule 26;

'the relevant officer' means –

- (a) in relation to proceedings in England and Wales, the Attorney General and, in relation to proceedings that particularly affect Wales, the Counsel General to the Welsh Assembly Government,
- (b) in relation to proceedings in Scotland, the Advocate General for Scotland and the Lord Advocate; and
- (c) in relation to proceedings in Northern Ireland, the Advocate General for Northern Ireland and (when section 22 of the Justice (Northern Ireland) Act 2002 comes into force) the Attorney General for Northern Ireland;

'requisite number of copies' means the number of copies which are to be provided under the relevant practice direction or as directed by the Court;

'respondent' includes a respondent to an application for permission to appeal and means –

- (a) a person other than the appellant who was a party to the proceedings in the court below and who is affected by the appeal; and
- (b) a person who is permitted by the Court to be a party to the appeal;

'service' and related expressions have the meanings given by rule 6;

'solicitor' includes any person authorised to provide legal services other than as counsel in connection with proceedings before the Court.

(3) References in these Rules to a practice direction means a practice direction issued by the President of the Court.

(4) References in these Rules or in any form to a party's signing, filing or serving any document or taking any other procedural step include the signature, filing or service of that document or the taking of such other procedural step by the party's solicitor.

(5) Where any of these Rules or any practice direction requires a document to be signed, that requirement shall be satisfied if the signature is printed by computer or other mechanical means.

(6) Where these Rules require or permit the Court to perform an act of a formal or administrative character, that act may be performed by a court officer.

'a practice direction' (r 3(3))—The *Supreme Court Practice Directions* (referred to below as SCPD) may be found at *www.supremecourt.uk/procedures/practice-directions.html* and are clearly expressed in up-to-date language.

'signature ... printed by computer or other mechanical means' (r 3(5))—Compare para 9 of *PD 5C – Electronic Working Scheme*, which supplements CPR 1998, r 5.5.

4 Forms

(1) In these Rules, a form means a form set out in a practice direction and a reference to the 'appropriate form' means the form provided by the relevant practice direction for any particular case.

(2) The forms shall be used in the cases to which they apply, and in the circumstances for which they are provided by the relevant practice direction, but a form may be varied by the Court or a party if the variation is required by the circumstances of a particular case.

5 Time limits

(1) The Court may extend or shorten any time limit set by these Rules or any relevant practice direction (unless to do so would be contrary to any enactment).

(2) The Court may exercise these powers either on an application by one or more parties or without an application being made.

(3) The Registrar must notify the parties when a time limit is varied under this rule.

(4) An application for an extension of time may be granted after the time limit has expired.

(5) Where a party to a proposed appeal has applied for public funding and the Registrar is informed of the application, the time limits in rules 11 and 19 shall be extended until 28 days after the final determination of the application for public funding.

(6) When the period specified –

- (a) by these Rules or a practice direction, or
- (b) by any judgment or court order,

for doing any act at the Registry ends on a day on which the Registry is closed, that act shall be in time if done on the next day on which the Registry is open.

6 Service

(1) A document may be served by any of the following methods –

- (a) personal service;
- (b) first class post (or an alternative service which provides for delivery on the next working day);
- (c) (with the consent of the party to be served) through a document exchange;
- (d) (with the consent of the party to be served or at the direction of the Registrar) by electronic means in accordance with the relevant practice direction.

(2) Where the address of the person on whom a document is to be served is unknown, the Registrar may direct that service is effected by an alternative method of service.

(3) A document served by first-class post or through a document exchange will be taken to have been served on the second day after it was posted or left at the document exchange, as the case may be (not including days which are not business days).

(4) A certificate of service must give details of the persons served, the method of service used and must state the date on which the document was served personally, posted, delivered to the document exchange or sent electronically, as the case may be.

'the address of the person on whom a document is to be served is unknown' (r 6(2))—Note that this is much more restrictive than the provisions in CPR 1998, r 6.15 for service 'by an alternative method'.

7 Filing

(1) A document may be filed by any of the following methods –

- (a) personal delivery;
- (b) first class post (or an alternative service which provides for delivery on the next working day);
- (c) through a document exchange;
- (d) (with the consent of the Registrar) by electronic means in accordance with the relevant practice direction.

(2) A document filed by first-class post or through a document exchange will be taken to have been filed on the second day after it was posted or left at the document exchange, as the case may be (not including days which are not business days).

(3) Except with the consent of the Registrar, the contents of documents –

- (a) filed in hard copy must also be provided to the Registry by electronic means, and
- (b) filed by electronic means must also be provided to the Registry in hard copy,

in accordance with the relevant practice direction.

(4) A court officer must seal the following documents when they are filed –

- (a) an application for permission to appeal,
- (b) a notice of objection or acknowledgement by the respondent,

(c) a notice of appeal,
(d) an application form,

and may place the seal on the document by hand or by printing a facsimile of the seal on the document whether electronically or otherwise.

(5) A document purporting to bear the Court's seal shall be admissible in evidence without further proof.

'must also be provided to the Registry by electronic means' (r 7(3)(a))—In cases granted permission to appeal before 30 September 2014, material may be submitted electronically either by use of a memory stick or by the use of the eBundle system. In cases granted permission to appeal on or after 1 October 2014, the eBundle system must be used. The Supreme Court's Electronic Bundle Guidelines should be studied carefully.

'the contents of documents ... filed by electronic means must also be provided to the Registry in hard copy' (r 7(3)(b))—Note particularly that the Supreme Court's requirements are diametrically opposite to those meant to prevail in the courts below under para 8.1 of *PD 5B – Electronic Communication and Filing of Documents* (which supplements CPR 1998, r 5.5): 'Where a party files a document electronically, he *must not* send a hard copy of that document to the court'.

8 Non-compliance with these Rules

(1) Any failure by a party to comply with these Rules or any relevant practice direction shall not have the effect of making the proceedings invalid.

(2) Where any provision in these Rules or any relevant practice direction is not complied with, the Court may give whatever directions appear appropriate, having regard to the seriousness of the non-compliance and generally to the circumstances of the case.

(3) In particular, the Registrar may refuse to accept any document which does not comply with any provision in these Rules or any relevant practice direction and may give whatever directions appear appropriate.

(4) Directions given under this rule may include the summary dismissal of an appeal or debarring a respondent from resisting an appeal.

9 Procedural decisions

(1) Subject to paragraph (2), the powers of the Court under the following rules may be exercised by a single Justice or the Registrar without an oral hearing –

(a) rule 5 (time limits),
(b) rule 8 (non-compliance with Rules),
(c) rule 33 (change of interest),
(d) rule 34 (withdrawal of appeal),
(e) rule 35 (advocate to the Court and assessors),
(f) rule 36 (security for costs),
(g) rule 37 (stay of execution) and
(h) rule 41 (devolution jurisdiction).

(2) Any contested application –

(a) alleging contempt of the Court; or
(b) for a direction under rule 8 dismissing an appeal or debarring a respondent from resisting an appeal; or
(c) for security for costs,

shall be referred to a panel of Justices who shall, in a case of alleged contempt, and may, in any other case, hold an oral hearing.

(3) Where under these Rules any matter falls to be decided by a single Justice, that Justice may, where it appears appropriate, direct an oral hearing or may refer the matter to a panel of Justices to be decided with or without an oral hearing.

(4) Where under these Rules any matter falls to be decided by the Registrar, the Registrar may –

(a) direct an oral hearing;
(b) refer the matter to a single Justice (and paragraphs (1) and (3) shall then apply);
(c) refer the matter to a panel of Justices to be decided with or without an oral hearing.

(5) A party may apply for a decision of the Registrar to be reviewed by a single Justice (in which case paragraphs (1) and (3) shall apply) and any application under this rule must be made in the appropriate form and be filed within 14 days of the Registrar's decision.

(6) Subject to rule 27, oral hearings on procedural matters must be heard in open court or in a place to which the public are admitted.

(7) If any procedural question arises which is not dealt with by these Rules, the Court or the Registrar may adopt any procedure that is consistent with the overriding objective, the Act and these Rules.

PART 2
APPLICATION FOR PERMISSION TO APPEAL

CONTENTS OF THIS PART

Rule		Page
10	Form of application	2354
11	Filing of application	2354
12	Service of application	2355
13	Notice of objection by respondent	2355
14	Documents in support of application	2355
15	Interventions in applications	2355
16	Consideration on paper	2356
17	Oral hearing of application	2356

10 Form of application

(1) Every application to the Court for permission to appeal shall be made in the appropriate form.

(2) An application for permission to appeal must be made first to the court below, and an application may be made to the Supreme Court only after the court below has refused to grant permission to appeal.

'the appropriate form' (r 10(1))—This is Form 1 (see SCPD 3, para 3.1.2 and SCPD 7, Annex 1).

11 Filing of application

(1) Subject to any enactment which makes special provision with regard to any particular category of appeal, an application for permission to appeal must be filed within 28 days from the date of the order or decision of the court below.

(2) The Registrar may refuse to accept any application on the ground that –

(a) the Court does not have jurisdiction under section 40 of the Act to issue it;
(b) it contains no reasonable grounds; or
(c) it is an abuse of process,

and may give whatever directions appear appropriate.

(Section 2 of the Administration of Justice Act 1960 provides that an application for permission to appeal to the Supreme Court in a case involving civil contempt of court must be filed within 14 days, beginning with the date on which the application for permission is refused by the court below.)

(Section 13 of the Administration of Justice Act 1969 provides that an application for permission to appeal to the Supreme Court in a 'leapfrog appeal' from the High Court must be filed within one month from the date on which the High Court judge grants a certificate under section 12.)

'an abuse of process' (r 11(2)(c))—Note in particular that under SCPD 3.1.2 grounds of appeal should not normally exceed 10 pages in length and that grounds that 'appear without adequate explanation from counsel to be excessive in length' or 'fail to identify the relevant issues' may be summarily rejected.

'14 days'—AJA 1960, s 2 refers to criminal cases, but is applied to civil contempt by s 13(4). However, since 2005 the time limit for seeking permission is 28 days rather than 14, as a result of Courts Act 2003, s 88(1),(2)(a) and the official note in the Rules is incorrect.

'within one month'—AJA 1969, s 13 in fact allows 1 month *or such extended time as in any particular case the Supreme Court may allow*. It is suggested that it would be unwise to take such an extension of time for granted.

12 Service of application

Before the application is filed, a copy must be served –

(a) on every respondent, and
(b) on any person who was an intervener in the court below,

and, when the application is filed, the appellant must file a certificate of service.

13 Notice of objection by respondent

(1) Each respondent who wishes to object to the application must, within 14 days after service, file notice of objection in the appropriate form together with a certificate of service.

(2) Before the notice is filed, a copy must be served on –

(a) the appellant,
(b) any other respondent, and
(c) any person who was an intervener in the court below.

(3) A respondent who does not file notice under this rule will not be permitted to participate in the application and will not be given notice of its progress.

'respondent who wishes to object to the application' (r 13(1))—A respondent to a prospective appeal to the Supreme Court may file written submissions as to why permission to appeal should be refused. A fee is payable. If permission to appeal is refused, such a respondent will be entitled to costs against the appellant unless the Supreme Court orders otherwise – contrast the position under FPR PD30A, para 4.23.
'the appropriate form' (r 13(1))—This is Form 3 (SCPD 3, para 3.1.8 and SCPD 7, Annex 1).

14 Documents in support of application

(1) The requisite number of copies of the application must be filed together with –

(a) a copy of the order appealed from, and
(b) (if separate) a copy of any order refusing permission to appeal

and, if the order appealed from is not immediately available, the application should be filed without delay and the order filed as soon as it is available.

(2) The appellant must file the further documents required for the use of the Court within 7 days after filing the application.

'requisite number of copies' (r 14(1))—There is a helpful table at SCPD 7, para 7.2.3, setting out the number of copies of various documents required at various stages of the Court's procedures.
'the further documents required' (r 14(2))—See SCPD 3, para 3.2.1.

15 Interventions in applications

(1) Any person and in particular –

(a) any official body or non-governmental organization seeking to make submissions in the public interest or
(b) any person with an interest in proceedings by way of judicial review,

may make written submissions to the Court in support of an application for permission to appeal and request that the Court takes them into account.

(2) Before the submissions are filed, a copy must be served on –

(a) the appellant,
(b) every respondent, and
(c) any person who was an intervener in the court below

and the requisite number of copies of the submissions must be filed together with a certificate of service.

(3) Any submissions which are made shall be referred to the panel of Justices which considers the application for permission to appeal.

PART III

(4) If permission to appeal is granted –

- (a) a person whose submissions were taken into account by the panel will be notified but, if that person wishes to intervene in the appeal, an application must be made under rule 26;
- (b) the appellant must notify any person who was an intervener in the court below whether or not that person made submissions under this rule.

16 Consideration on paper

(1) Every admissible application for permission to appeal (together with any submissions made under rule 15 and any respondent's notice of objection) shall be considered on paper without a hearing by a panel of Justices.

(2) The panel may –

- (a) grant or refuse permission to advance all or any of the grounds of appeal;
- (b) invite the parties to file written submissions within 14 days as to the grant of permission on terms (whether as to costs or otherwise); or
- (c) direct an oral hearing.

(3) Where the panel has invited the parties' submissions as to terms, it shall reconsider the application on paper without a hearing and may refuse permission or grant permission (either unconditionally or on terms) to advance all or any of the grounds of appeal.

(4) Where the panel grants permission to advance limited grounds of appeal it shall (unless it directs otherwise) be taken to have refused permission to advance the other grounds.

(5) An order of the Court shall be prepared and sealed by the Registrar to record any decision made under this rule.

17 Oral hearing of application

(1) Where the panel has directed an oral hearing, the appellant and every respondent who has given notice under rule 13 will be informed of the date of the oral hearing.

(2) An order of the Court shall be prepared and sealed by the Registrar to record any decision made under this rule.

PART 3
COMMENCEMENT AND PREPARATION OF APPEAL

CONTENTS OF THIS PART

Rule		Page
18	Form and filing of notice where permission granted by the Court	2356
19	Form and filing of notice where permission not required	2357
20	Service of notice	2357
21	Acknowledgement by respondent	2357
22	Documents for appeal hearing	2357
23	The core volumes	2358
24	Authorities	2358
25	Cross-appeals	2358
26	Intervention	2358

18 Form and filing of notice where permission granted by the Court

(1) Where the Court grants permission to appeal, rules 19 and 20 shall not apply and

- (a) the application for permission to appeal shall stand as the notice of appeal;
- (b) the grounds of appeal shall be limited to those on which permission has been granted;
- (c) the appellant must, within 14 days of the grant by the Court of permission to appeal, file notice under this rule of an intention to proceed with the appeal.

(2) When notice is filed under rule 18(1)(c), the application for permission to appeal will be resealed and the appellant must then –

(a) serve a copy on each respondent and on any person who was an intervener in the court below or whose submissions were taken into account under rule 15; and
(b) file the requisite number of copies and a certificate of service.

(3) In any other case an appellant must file a notice of appeal under rule 19.

'notice ... of an intention to proceed' (r 18(1)(c))—A further fee is payable, without which this notice will not effectively be given.

19 Form and filing of notice where permission not required

(1) Every notice of appeal shall be made in the appropriate form.

(2) The notice of appeal together with the requisite number of copies must be filed within 42 days of the date of the order or decision of the court below.

(3) The appellant must also file –

(a) a copy of the order appealed from and
(b) (if separate) a copy of the order granting permission to appeal

and, if the order appealed from is not immediately available, the notice of appeal must be filed without delay and the order filed as soon as it is available.

20 Service of notice

(1) Before the notice of appeal is filed, a copy must be served on each respondent and on any person who was an intervener in the court below.

(2) When the notice of appeal is filed, the appellant must file a certificate of service.

21 Acknowledgement by respondent

(1) Each respondent who intends to participate in the appeal must, within 14 days after service under rule 18(2)(a) or 20, file notice in the appropriate form together with a certificate of service.

(2) Before the notice is filed, a copy must be served on –

(a) the appellant,
(b) any other respondent, and
(c) any person who was an intervener in the court below or whose submissions were taken into account under rule 15.

(3) A respondent who does not file notice under this rule will not be permitted to participate in the appeal and will not be given notice of its progress.

22 Documents for appeal hearing

(1) Within 112 days after the filing of the notice under rule 18(1)(c) or the filing of the notice of appeal, the appellant must file –

(a) a statement of the relevant facts and issues; and
(b) an appendix (prepared in accordance with the relevant practice direction) of the essential documents which were in evidence before, or which record the proceedings in, the courts below.

(2) Both the statement and the appendix must be submitted to, and agreed with, every respondent before being filed.

(3) Within 7 days after the filing of the statement and the appendix, every party must –

(a) notify the Registrar that the appeal is ready for listing, and
(b) specify the number of hours that their respective counsel estimate to be necessary for their oral submissions

and the Registrar will subsequently inform the parties of the date fixed for the hearing.

(4) The appellant and every respondent (and any intervener and advocate to the Court) must then sequentially exchange their respective written cases and file them, and every respondent (and any

PART III

intervener and advocate to the Court) must for the purposes of rule 23 provide copies of their respective written cases, in compliance with the relevant practice direction.

23 The core volumes

As soon as the parties' cases have been exchanged and in any event not later than 14 days before the date fixed for the hearing the appellant must file the requisite number of core volumes and, if necessary, additional volumes containing further parts of the appendix, in compliance with the relevant practice direction.

'must file the requisite number of core volumes'—Note that as one would expect from r 7(3), the contents of the core volumes must also be filed electronically. The SCPDs set out detailed provisions as to the preferred format of the electronic copy. It should be noted that if core volumes or other documents exceed 10 megabytes they must be submitted on a memory stick – another respect in which the Supreme Court is breaking new ground.

24 Authorities

The volumes of authorities that may be referred to during the hearing must be prepared in accordance with the relevant practice direction and the requisite number of copies of the volumes of authorities must be filed by the appellant at the same time as the core volumes.

25 Cross-appeals

(1) A respondent who wishes to argue that the order appealed from should be upheld on grounds different from those relied on by the court below, must state that clearly in the respondent's written case (but need not cross-appeal).

(2) Except where –

- (a) leave is required from the Court of Session for an appeal from that court, or
- (b) an appeal lies to the Court as of right, a respondent who wishes to argue that the order appealed from should be varied must obtain permission to cross-appeal from the Court.

(3) Part 2 of these Rules shall apply (with appropriate modifications) to an application to the Court for permission to cross-appeal and (if practicable) applications for permission to appeal and to cross-appeal shall be considered together by the same panel of Justices.

(4) Where there is a cross-appeal, this Part of these Rules shall apply with appropriate modifications and in particular –

- (a) either the application for permission to cross-appeal to the Court shall stand as a notice of cross-appeal, or such a notice (in the appropriate form) shall be filed and served within 42 days of the grant by the Court of permission to appeal or of the filing of the notice of appeal;
- (b) there shall be a single statement of facts and issues, a single appendix of essential documents (divided if necessary into parts) and a single case for each party in respect of the appeal and the cross-appeal (and each case should state clearly that it is in respect of both the appeal and the cross-appeal); and
- (c) the appellant shall remain primarily responsible for the preparation of all the papers for the appeal and for notifying the Registrar under rule 22(3).

26 Intervention

(1) After permission to appeal has been granted by the Court or a notice of appeal has been filed, any person and in particular –

- (a) any official body or non-governmental organization seeking to make submissions in the public interest,
- (b) any person with an interest in proceedings by way of judicial review,
- (c) any person who was an intervener in the court below or whose submissions were taken into account under rule 15,

may apply to the Court for permission to intervene in the appeal.

(2) An application under this rule must be made in the appropriate form and shall be considered on paper by a panel of Justices who may refuse permission to intervene or may permit intervention –

(a) by written submissions only; or
(b) by written submissions and oral submissions

and any oral submissions may be limited to a specified duration.

(3) No permission is required –

(a) for an intervention by the Crown under section 5 of the Human Rights Act 1998, or
(b) for an intervention by the relevant officer in a case where the Court is exercising its devolution jurisdiction.

(For rules relating to Human Rights Act issues and the Court's devolution jurisdiction see rules 40 and 41.)

PART 4
HEARING AND DECISION OF APPEAL

CONTENTS OF THIS PART

Rule		Page
27	Hearing in open court	2359
28	Judgment	2359
29	Orders	2359

27 Hearing in open court

(1) Every contested appeal shall be heard in open court except where it is necessary in the interests of justice or in the public interest to sit in private for part of an appeal hearing.

(2) Where the Court considers it necessary for a party and that party's representative to be excluded from a hearing or part of a hearing in order to secure that information is not disclosed contrary to the public interest, the Court must conduct the hearing, or that part of it from which the party and the representative are excluded, in private but the Court may exclude a party and any representative only if a person who has been appointed as a special advocate to represent the interests of that party is present when the party and the representative are excluded.

(3) Where the Court decides it is necessary for the Court to sit in private, it shall announce its reasons for so doing publicly before the hearing begins.

(4) Hearings shall be conducted in accordance with –

(a) the relevant practice direction, and
(b) any directions given by the Court

and directions given by the Court may limit oral submissions to a specified duration.

'may exclude a party' (r 27(2))—See *Bank Mellat v Her Majesty's Treasury (No 1)* [2013] UKSC 38 (although it is unlikely that this will arise in family proceedings).

'directions given by the Court may limit oral submissions to a specified duration' (r 27(4))—Note that SCPD 6, para 6.2.2 indicates that not more than 2 days will 'normally' be allowed for hearing an appeal.

28 Judgment

A judgment may be –

(a) delivered in open court; or
(b) if the Court so directs, promulgated by the Registrar.

29 Orders

(1) In relation to an appeal or a reference, the Supreme Court has all the powers of the court below and may –

(a) affirm, set aside or vary any order or judgment made or given by that court;

(b) remit any issue for determination by that court;
(c) order a new trial or hearing;
(d) make orders for the payment of interest;
(e) make a costs order.

(2) An order of the Supreme Court may be enforced in the same manner as an order of the court below or of the appropriate superior court.

(3) For the purposes of paragraph (2) 'the appropriate superior court' means –

(a) in the case of an appeal or reference from a court in England and Wales, the High Court;
(b) in the case of an appeal or reference from a court in Scotland –
   (i) where the appeal or reference is in civil proceedings, the Court of Session; and
   (ii) where the appeal or reference is in criminal proceedings, the High Court of Justiciary;
(c) in the case of an appeal or reference from a court in Northern Ireland, the High Court in Northern Ireland.

(4) In the case of references other than those mentioned in paragraph (3) 'the appropriate superior court' in paragraph (2) means –

(a) where the reference is under the Scotland Act 1998, the Court of Session;
(b) where the reference is under the Northern Ireland Act 1998, the High Court in Northern Ireland; and
(c) where the reference is under the Government of Wales Act 2006, the High Court.

(5) Every order of the Court shall be prepared and sealed by the Registrar who may invite written submissions as to the form of the order.

'An order of the Supreme Court may be enforced' (r 29(2))—This provision appears to render redundant para 13.1 of *PD40B – Judgments and Orders* (which supplements CPR 1998, Pt 40), under which an order of the Supreme Court may be made an order of the High Court.

PART 5
FURTHER GENERAL PROVISIONS

CONTENTS OF THIS PART

Rule		Page
30	Procedural applications	2360
31	Requests for expedition	2361
32	Grouping appeals	2361
33	Change of interest	2361
34	Withdrawal etc of application for permission to appeal or of appeal	2361
35	Advocate to the Court and assessors	2361
36	Security for costs	2361
37	Stay of execution	2362
38	Change of solicitor and London agents	2362
39	Disposal of documents	2362

30 Procedural applications

(1) Every procedural application to the Court must be made in the appropriate form for general procedural applications unless a particular form is provided for a specific case.

(2) An application must be made in the appropriate form and must –

(a) set out the reasons for making the application, and
(b) where necessary, be supported by written evidence.

(3) A copy of the application must be served on every other party before it is filed and, when the application is filed, the applicant must file a certificate of service.

(4) A party who wishes to oppose an application must, within 7 days after service, file notice of objection in the appropriate form and must (before filing) serve a copy on the applicant and any other parties.

(5) An application for permission to appeal, a notice of appeal or any other document filed under these Rules may be amended on application under this rule or with the permission of the Registrar on such terms as appear appropriate, and the Registrar may invite the parties' written submissions on any application to amend.

31 Requests for expedition

(1) Any request for urgent consideration of an application for permission to appeal or for an expedited hearing must be made to the Registrar.

(2) Wherever possible the views of all parties should be obtained before such a request is made.

32 Grouping appeals

The Registrar may direct that appeals raising the same or similar issues shall be heard either together or consecutively by the Court constituted by the same Justices and may give any consequential directions that appear appropriate.

33 Change of interest

The Court must be informed promptly of –

- (a) he death or bankruptcy of any individual party;
- (b) the winding up or dissolution of any corporate party;
- (c) any compromise of the subject matter of an appeal;
- (d) any event which does or may deprive an appeal of practical significance to the parties, and the Court may give any consequential directions that appear appropriate.

34 Withdrawal etc of application for permission to appeal or of appeal

(1) An application for permission to appeal or a notice of appeal may be withdrawn with the written consent of all parties or with the permission of the Court on such terms as appear appropriate.

(2) The Court may set aside or vary the order appealed from by consent and without an oral hearing if satisfied that it is appropriate so to do.

(3) In this rule 'a notice of appeal' includes an application for permission to appeal or cross-appeal which (under rule 18 or rule 25) stands as a notice of appeal or cross-appeal.

35 Advocate to the Court and assessors

(1) The Court may request the relevant officer to appoint, or may itself appoint, an advocate to the Court to assist the Court with legal submissions.

(2) In accordance with section 44 of the Act the Court may, at the request of the parties or of its own initiative, appoint one or more independent specially qualified advisers to assist the Court as assessors on any technical matter.

(3) The fees and expenses of any advocate to the Court or assessor shall be costs in the appeal.

36 Security for costs

(1) The Court may on the application of a respondent order an appellant to give security for the costs of the appeal and any order for security shall determine –

- (a) the amount of that security, and
- (b) the manner in which, and the time within which, security must be given.

(2) An order made under this rule may require payment of the judgment debt (and costs) in the court below instead of, or in addition to, the amount ordered by way of security for costs.

37 Stay of execution

Any appellant who wishes to obtain a stay of execution of the order appealed from must seek it from the court below and only in wholly exceptional circumstances will the Court grant a stay.

38 Change of solicitor and London agents

(1) If a party for whom a solicitor is acting wishes to change solicitors, that party or the new solicitor must give the Registrar and the former solicitor written notice of the change.

(2) Until such notices are given the former solicitor shall continue to be treated as the party's solicitor.

(3) Solicitors practising outside London may appoint London agents and additional costs incurred by not appointing London agents may be disallowed.

39 Disposal of documents

(1) All documents filed become the property of the Court and original documents must be retained in the records of the Registry.

(2) Other documents shall be destroyed unless the Registrar (on a written application made within 21 days of the end of the proceedings) directs otherwise.

(3) All documents held by the Court may be inspected by the press or members of the public on application to the Registrar but the Registrar may refuse an application for reasons of commercial confidentiality, national security or in the public interest.

(4) Before allowing an application for inspection under this rule, the Registrar may impose terms or conditions such as the redaction of certain material where such a condition is necessary in the interests of justice or in the public interest.

PART 6
PARTICULAR APPEALS AND REFERENCES

CONTENTS OF THIS PART

Rule		Page
40	Human Rights Act issues	2362
41	Devolution jurisdiction	2362
42	Court of Justice of the European Communities	2363
43	Revocation of patents	2363
44	Criminal appeals	2363

40 Human Rights Act issues

(1) Where an appeal raises a question of incompatibility under section 4 of the Human Rights Act 1998 and the Crown is not already a party to the appeal, the Registrar shall give 21 days' notice of the question to the Crown.

(2) If notice is given that the Crown wishes to be joined, the appropriate Minister or other person shall be joined accordingly.

(3) If such a question arises for the first time during the course of an appeal hearing the Court will if necessary adjourn the proceedings to enable the Registrar to give notice under paragraph (1).

41 Devolution jurisdiction

(1) Appeals or references under the Court's devolution jurisdiction shall in general be dealt with in accordance with these Rules but the Court shall give special directions as and when necessary, and in particular as to –

(a) any question referred under section 33 of the Scotland Act 1998, section 11 of the Northern Ireland Act 1998 or section 96, 99 or 112 of the Government of Wales Act 2006,

(b) any reference of a devolution issue,

(c) any direct references under paragraph 33 or 34 of Schedule 6 to the Scotland Act 1998, paragraph 33 or 34 of Schedule 10 to the Northern Ireland Act 1998 or paragraph 29 or 30 of Schedule 9 to the Government of Wales Act 2006.

(2) A reference made by the relevant officer is made by filing the reference and by serving a copy on any other relevant officer who is not already a party and who has a potential interest in the proceedings.

(3) A reference must state the question or issue to be decided by the Court.

(4) The Registrar shall give notice of the question or issue to the appropriate relevant officer where that officer is not already a party to any proceedings.

42 Court of Justice of the European Communities

(1) Where it is contended on an application for permission to appeal that it raises a question of Community law which should be the subject of a reference under Article 267 of the Treaty on the Functioning of the European Union and permission to appeal is refused, the panel of Justices will give brief reasons for its decision.

(2) Where on an application for permission to appeal a panel of Justices decides to make a reference under Article 267 before determining the application, it will give consequential directions as to the form of the reference and the staying of the application (but it may if it thinks fit dispose of other parts of the application at once).

(3) Where at the hearing of an appeal the Court decides to make a reference under Article 267 it will give consequential directions as to the form of the reference and the staying of the appeal (but it may if it thinks fit dispose of other parts of the appeal at once).

(4) An order of the Court shall be prepared and sealed by the Registrar to record any decision made under this rule.

Amendments—SI 2012/1809.

43 Revocation of patents

(1) On any appeal under sections 12 and 13 of the Administration of Justice Act 1969 from an order for revocation of a patent the appellant must serve notice of the appeal on the Comptroller-General of Patents ('the Comptroller') as well as on every respondent.

(2) A respondent who decides not to oppose the appeal must serve notice of that decision on the Comptroller together with the relevant statements of case.

(3) The Comptroller shall within 14 days serve on the appellant and file a notice stating whether or not the Comptroller intends to appear on the appeal.

(4) Where notice is given under paragraph (3), the Comptroller may appear on the appeal.

44 Criminal appeals

The Court must apply in accordance with the relevant practice direction the code of practice for victims issued under section 32 of the Domestic Violence, Crime and Victims Act 2004.

PART 7
FEES AND COSTS

CONTENTS OF THIS PART

Rule		Page
45	Fees	2364
46	Orders for costs	2364
47	Submissions as to costs	2364
48	Claim for costs	2364
49	Assessment of costs	2364

PART III

50	Basis of assessment	2365
51	The standard basis and the indemnity basis	2365
52	Amount of assessed costs to be specified	2365
53	Appeal from assessment	2365
54	Payment out of security for costs	2365

45 Fees

Where a fee is prescribed by any order made under section 52 of the Act, the Registrar may refuse to accept a document or refuse to allow a party to take any step unless the relevant fee is paid.

46 Orders for costs

(1) The Court may make such orders as it considers just in respect of the costs of any appeal, application for permission to appeal, or other application to or proceeding before the Court.

(2) The Court's powers to make orders for costs may be exercised either at the final determination of an appeal or application for permission to appeal or in the course of the proceedings.

(3) Orders for costs will not normally be made either in favour of or against interveners but such orders may be made if the Court considers it just to do so (in particular if an intervener has in substance acted as the sole or principal appellant or respondent).

47 Submissions as to costs

(1) If a party wishes to defer making submissions as to costs until after judgment, the Court must be informed of this not later than at the close of the oral argument.

(2) If the Court accedes to the request it will give such directions as appear appropriate and it may, in particular, give directions –

(a) for the hearing of oral submissions as to costs immediately after judgment;
(b) for the simultaneous or sequential filing of written submissions as to costs within a specified period after judgment;
(c) for the hearing of oral submissions after the filing of written submissions.

48 Claim for costs

(1) Where the Court has made an order for costs, the claim for costs must be submitted to the Registrar within three months beginning with the date on which the costs order was made.

(2) The form and contents of a claim for costs must comply with the relevant practice direction and the receiving party must supply such further particulars, information and documents as the Registrar may direct.

(3) The receiving party must serve a copy of a claim for costs on the paying party.

(4) Within 21 days beginning with the day on which a claim for costs is served, the paying party may (or, in the circumstances specified in the relevant practice direction, must) file points of dispute and, if so, must serve a copy on the receiving party.

(5) Within 14 days beginning with the day on which points of dispute are served, the receiving party may file a response and, if so, must serve a copy on the paying party.

49 Assessment of costs

(1) Every detailed assessment of costs shall be carried out by two costs officers appointed by the President and –

(a) one costs officer must be a Costs Judge (a Taxing Master of the Senior Courts), and
(b) the second may be the Registrar.

(2) A disputed assessment shall be dealt with at an oral hearing.

(3) An assessment may provide for the costs of the assessment procedure.

(4) The Registrar will give the receiving party and the paying party written notice of the date of the assessment.

(5) Where one of the parties so requests or in the circumstances specified in the relevant practice direction, the Registrar may make a provisional assessment of costs without the attendance of the parties.

(6) The Registrar must inform the parties in writing of the outcome of a provisional assessment and, if a party is dissatisfied with the outcome, or if points of disagreement cannot be resolved in correspondence, the Registrar shall appoint a date for an oral hearing.

(7) Any request for an oral hearing following a provisional assessment of costs must be made within 14 days of the receipt of the Registrar's decision on the assessment.

50 Basis of assessment

(1) Where the Court is to assess the amount of costs it will assess those costs –

(a) on the standard basis, or
(b) on the indemnity basis,

in the manner specified by rule 51 or (where appropriate) on the relevant bases that apply in Scotland or Northern Ireland.

(2) Where –

(a) the Court makes an order about costs without indicating the basis on which the costs are to be assessed, or
(b) the Court makes an order for costs to be assessed on a basis other than one specified in paragraph (1),

the costs will be assessed on the standard basis.

(3) This rule applies subject to any order or direction to the contrary.

51 The standard basis and the indemnity basis

(1) Costs assessed on the standard basis are allowed only if they are proportionate to the matters in issue and are reasonably incurred and reasonable in amount.

(2) Any doubt as to whether costs assessed on the standard basis are reasonably incurred and are reasonable and proportionate in amount will be resolved in favour of the paying party.

(3) Costs assessed on the indemnity basis are allowed only if they are reasonably incurred and reasonable in amount.

(4) Any doubt as to whether costs assessed on the indemnity basis are reasonably incurred and are reasonable in amount will be resolved in favour of the receiving party.

52 Amount of assessed costs to be specified

The amount of any assessed costs will be inserted in the order made under rule 29 but, if that order is drawn up before the assessment has been completed, the amount assessed will be certified by the Registrar.

53 Appeal from assessment

(1) A party who is dissatisfied with the assessment of costs made at an oral hearing may apply for that decision to be reviewed by a single Justice and any application under this rule must be made in the appropriate form and be filed within 14 days of the decision.

(2) The single Justice may (without an oral hearing) affirm the decision made on the assessment or may, where it appears appropriate, refer the matter to a panel of Justices to be decided with or without an oral hearing.

(3) An application may be made under this rule only on a question of principle and not in respect of the amount allowed on any item in the claim for costs.

54 Payment out of security for costs

Any security for costs lodged by an appellant will be dealt with by the Registrar in accordance with the directions of the Court.

PART 8
TRANSITIONAL ARRANGEMENTS

55 Transitional arrangements

(1) Unless the Court or the Registrar directs otherwise, these Rules shall apply, with any necessary modifications, to appeals which were proceeding, and petitions for leave which were lodged, in the House of Lords before 1 October 2009.

(2) The Court or the Registrar may give special directions, as and when necessary, in relation to appeals which were proceeding, and petitions for leave which were lodged, in the House of Lords.

PART IV

Statutory Instruments

PART IV: Statutory Instruments

Contents

All relevant procedural provisions in the following legislation, as amended and fully annotated:

Access to Justice Act 1999 (Destination of Appeals) (Family Proceedings) Order 2011 2371

Access to Justice Act 1999 (Destination of Appeals) (Family Proceedings) Order 2014 2371

Adoptions with a Foreign Element Regulations 2005 2373

Care Planning, Placement and Case Review (England) Regulations 2010 2395

Child Abduction and Custody (Parties to Conventions) Order 1986 2427

Children (Admissibility of Hearsay Evidence) Order 1993 2431

Children (Secure Accommodation) Regulations 1991 2432

Children (Secure Accommodation) (No 2) Regulations 1991 2435

Civil Jurisdiction and Judgments (Maintenance) Regulations 2011 2436

Civil Legal Aid (Remuneration) Regulations 2013 2448

County Court Remedies Regulations 2014 2451

Divorce etc (Pensions) Regulations 2000 2452

Family Court (Composition and Distribution of Business) Rules 2014 2457

Family Court (Contempt of Court) (Powers) Regulations 2014 2468

Family Law Act 1986 (Dependent Territories) Order 1991 2469

Family Proceedings Fees Order 2008 2472

High Court (Distribution of Business) Order 1993 2486

International Recovery of Maintenance (Hague Convention 2007 etc) Regulations 2012 2487

Justices' Clerks and Assistants Rules 2014 2498

Parental Responsibility Agreement Regulations 1991 2503

Parental Responsibility and Measures for the Protection of Children (International Obligations) (England and Wales and Northern Ireland) Regulations 2010 2504

Pensions on Divorce etc (Provision of Information) Regulations 2000 2511

Sharing of State Scheme Rights (Provision of Information and Valuation) (No 2) Regulations 2000 2524

Supreme Court Fees Order 2009 2528

Note—By virtue of Crime and Court Act 2013, s 17, Sch 9, para 11, in relevant legislation: (i) any reference that is or is deemed to be a reference to a county court is to be read as a reference to the County Court; and (ii) any reference that is or is deemed to be a reference to a judge of a county court is, if the context permits, to be read as a reference to the County Court and otherwise is to be read as a reference to a judge of the County Court. Note that (ii) does not apply to a reference to a holder of a particular office (for example, a reference to a Circuit Judge).

Access to Justice Act 1999 (Destination of Appeals) (Family Proceedings) Order 2011, SI 2011/1044

1 Citation, commencement, interpretation and application

(1) This Order may be cited as the Access to Justice Act 1999 (Destination of Appeals) (Family Proceedings) Order 2011 and shall come into force on 6 April 2011.

(2) In this Order –

…

'decision' means a judgment, order or direction of the High Court;

'family proceedings' has the meaning assigned to it by section 32 of the Matrimonial and Family Proceedings Act 1984.

(3) This Order applies to a decision made in family proceedings in the High Court and has effect subject to –

(a) any enactment that provides a different route of appeal (other than section 16(1) of the Senior Courts Act 1981 or section 77(1) of the County Courts Act 1984); and

(b) any requirement to obtain permission to appeal.

Amendments—SI 2014/602.

2 Appeals to a judge of the High Court

(1) An appeal shall lie to a judge of the High Court from a decision in family proceedings made by –

(a) a district judge of the High Court;

(aa) the Senior District Judge of the Family Division;

(b) a district judge of the principal registry of the Family Division;

(c) the Chief Taxing Master;

(cc) a Taxing Master of the Senior Courts; or

(d) a person appointed to act as a deputy for any person holding an office referred to in sub-paragraph (a),(b) or (cc) or to act as a temporary additional officer in any such office.

(2) *(revoked)*

Amendments—SI 2014/602.

3 *(revoked)*

4 Revocation

The Access to Justice Act 1999 (Destination of Appeals) (Family Proceedings) Order 2005 is revoked.

Access to Justice Act 1999 (Destination of Appeals) (Family Proceedings) Order 2014, SI 2014/602

1 Citation, commencement and interpretation

(1) This Order may be cited as the Access to Justice Act 1999 (Destination of Appeals) (Family Proceedings) Order 2014 and comes into force on the date on which section 17(3) of the Crime and Courts Act 2013 is brought fully into force.

PART IV

(2) In this Order –

'the 1984 Act' means the Matrimonial and Family Proceedings Act 1984;

'the 2007 Act' means the Tribunals, Courts and Enforcement Act 2007;

'the 2011 Order' means the Access to Justice Act 1999 (Destination of Appeals) (Family Proceedings) Order 2011;

'authorised court officer' has the meaning assigned to it by rule 44.1 of the Civil Procedure Rules 1998 as applied to family proceedings by rule 28.2(1) of the Family Procedure Rules 2010; and

'justice of the peace' means a justice of the peace who is not a District Judge (Magistrates' Courts).

2 Appeals to the family court

(1) Paragraph (3) applies to an appeal –

- (a) under section 31K(1) of the 1984 Act (appeals from the family court in cases where no other right of appeal exists); or
- (b) under section 13(2A) of the Administration of Justice Act 1960 (appeals in cases of contempt of court) from a decision or order of the family court.

(2) Paragraph (3) does not apply if the person, or any of the persons, who made the decision or order was when making the decision or order deployed in the family court otherwise than as the holder of an office referred to in paragraph (3).

(3) The appeal lies to the family court (instead of to the Court of Appeal) if it is from a decision or order made by –

- (a) the Senior District Judge of the Family Division;
- (b) a district judge of the Principal Registry of the Family Division;
- (c) the Chief Taxing Master;
- (d) a Taxing Master of the Senior Courts;
- (e) a person appointed to act as a deputy for any person holding an office referred to in paragraph (b) or (d), or to act as a temporary additional officer in any such office;
- (f) a district judge;
- (g) a deputy district judge appointed under section 102 of the Senior Courts Act 1981 or section 8 of the County Courts Act 1984;
- (h) a Chamber President, or a Deputy Chamber President, of a chamber of the Upper Tribunal or of a chamber of the First-tier Tribunal;
- (i) a judge of the Upper Tribunal by virtue of appointment under paragraph 1(1) of Schedule 3 to the 2007 Act;
- (j) a transferred-in judge of the Upper Tribunal (see section 31(2) of the 2007 Act);
- (k) a deputy judge of the Upper Tribunal (whether under paragraph 7 of Schedule 3 to, or section 31(2) of, the 2007 Act);
- (l) a judge of the First-tier Tribunal by virtue of appointment under paragraph 1(1) of Schedule 2 to the 2007 Act;
- (m) a transferred-in judge of the First-tier Tribunal (see section 31(2) of the 2007 Act);
- (n) a member of a panel of Employment Judges established for England and Wales or for Scotland;
- (o) a person appointed under section 30(1)(a) or (b) of the Courts-Martial (Appeals) Act 1951 (assistants to the Judge Advocate General);
- (p) a District Judge (Magistrates' Courts);
- (q) two or three justices of the peace;
- (r) a single justice of the peace;
- (s) a justices' clerk or an assistant to a justices' clerk; or
- (t) an authorised court officer.

(4) Paragraph (3) has effect subject to any requirement to obtain permission to appeal.

2A Appeals to the High Court

(1) Paragraph (3) applies to an appeal –

- (a) under section 31K(1) of the 1984 Act (appeals from the family court in cases where no other right of appeal exists); or
- (b) under section 13(2A) of the Administration of Justice Act 1960 (appeals in cases of contempt of court) from a decision or order of the family court.

(2) Paragraph (3) does not apply –

- (a) if the appeal is from a decision or order in proceedings under –
  - (i) Part 4 or 5 of, or paragraph 19(1) of Schedule 2 to, the Children Act 1989; or
  - (ii) the Adoption and Children Act 2002;
- (b) if the appeal is from a decision or order in exercise of the family court's jurisdiction to punish for contempt of court, where that decision or order was made in, or in connection with, proceedings of a type referred to in sub-paragraph (a);
- (c) if the appeal is from a decision or order made on appeal to the family court; or
- (d) if the person who made the decision or order was, when making the decision or order, deployed in the family court otherwise than as the holder of an office referred to in paragraph (3).

(3) The appeal lies to the High Court (instead of to the Court of Appeal) if it is from a decision or order made by –

- (a) a Circuit judge; or
- (b) a Recorder.

(4) Paragraph (3) has effect subject to any requirement to obtain permission to appeal.

Amendments—SI 2016/891.

****

Route of appeal—An appeal from a decision or order of a circuit judge or recorder in private law proceedings now lies to the High Court and not to the Court of Appeal.

Procedure on appeal—For the procedures to be followed on an application for permission to appeal or on the substantive appeal, see the notes to FPR 2010, Pt 30 and Procedural Guides E2, and E5 and E6.

Adoptions with a Foreign Element Regulations 2005, SI 2005/392

ARRANGEMENT OF REGULATIONS

PART I
GENERAL

Regulation		Page
1	Citation, commencement and application	2375
2	Interpretation	2375

PART 2
BRINGING CHILDREN INTO AND OUT OF THE UNITED KINGDOM

Chapter 1
Bringing Children into the United Kingdom

3	Requirements applicable in respect of bringing or causing a child to be brought into the United Kingdom	2376
4	Conditions applicable in respect of a child brought into the United Kingdom	2376
5	Functions imposed on the local authority	2377
6	Application of Chapter 3 of the Act	2379

PART IV

7	Change of name and removal from the United Kingdom	2379
8	Return of the child	2379
9	Child to live with adopters before application	2379

Chapter 2

Taking Children out of the United Kingdom

10	Requirements applicable in respect of giving parental responsibility prior to adoption abroad	2379
11	Application of the Act in respect of orders under section 84	2380

PART 3

ADOPTIONS UNDER THE CONVENTION

Chapter 1

Requirements, Procedure, Recognition and Effect of Adoptions where the United Kingdom is the Receiving State

12	Application of Chapter 1	2381
13	Requirements applicable in respect of eligibility and suitability	2381
14	Counselling and information	2381
15	Procedure in respect of carrying out an assessment	2381
16	Adoption agency decision and notification	2382
17	Review and termination of approval	2382
18	Procedure following decision as to suitability to adopt	2382
19	Procedure following receipt of the Article 16 Information from the CA of the State of origin	2383
20	Procedure where proposed adoption is not to proceed	2384
21	Applicable requirements in respect of prospective adopter entering the United Kingdom with a child	2384
22	Applicable requirements in respect of an adoption agency before the child enters the United Kingdom	2384
23	Applicable provisions following the child's entry into the United Kingdom where no Convention adoption is made	2385
24	Applicable requirements in respect of prospective adopter following child's entry into the United Kingdom	2385
25	Functions imposed on the local authority following the child's entry into the United Kingdom	2385
26	Prospective adopter unable to proceed with adoption	2386
27	Withdrawal of child from prospective adopter	2386
28	Breakdown of placement	2386
29	Convention adoptions subject to a probationary period	2387
30	Report of local authority investigation	2387
31	Convention adoption order	2387
32	Requirements following a Convention adoption order or Convention adoption	2388
33	Refusal of a court in England or Wales to make a Convention adoption order	2388
34	Annulment of a Convention adoption order or a Convention adoption	2388

Chapter 2

Requirements, Procedure, Recognition and Effect of Adoptions in England and Wales where the United Kingdom is the State of Origin

35	Application of Chapter 2	2388
36	Counselling and information for the child	2388
37	Counselling and information for the parent or guardian of the child etc	2388
38	Requirements in respect of the child's permanence report and information for the adoption panel	2389
39	Recommendation of adoption panel	2389
40	Adoption agency decision and notification	2389
41	Convention list	2389
42	Receipt of the Article 15 Report from the CA of the receiving State	2390
43	Proposed placement and referral to adoption panel	2390

44 Consideration by adoption panel 2390
45 Adoption agency's decision in relation to the proposed placement 2391
46 Preparation of the Article 16 Information 2391
47 Requirements to be met before the child is placed for adoption with prospective adopter 2391
48 Requirements in respect of giving parental responsibility prior to a proposed Convention adoption 2392
49 Local authority report 2392
50 Convention adoption order 2392
51 Requirements following a Convention adoption order or Convention adoption 2393

Chapter 3
Miscellaneous Provisions

52 Application, with or without modifications, of the Act 2393
53 Change of name and removal from the United Kingdom 2393
54 Removal of children 2393
55 Modifications of the Act in respect of orders under section 84 where child is to be adopted under the Convention 2393
56 Child to live with adopters before application for a Convention adoption order 2393
57 Notice of intention to adopt 2394
58 Application for Convention adoption order 2394
59 Offences 2394

Schedule 1 – Certificate of Eligibility and Approval 2394
Schedule 2 – Certificate That the Convention Adoption Order Has Been Made In Accordance With the Convention 2395

PART I
GENERAL

1 Citation, commencement and application

(1) These Regulations may be cited as the Adoptions with a Foreign Element Regulations 2005 and shall come into force on 30 December 2005.

(2) These Regulations apply to England and Wales.

2 Interpretation

In these Regulations –

'the Act' means the Adoption and Children Act 2002;

'adoption support services' has the meaning given in section 2(6)(a) of the Act and any regulations made under section 2(6)(b) of the Act;

'adoptive family' has the same meaning as in regulation 31(2)(a) of the Agencies Regulations or corresponding Welsh provision;

'adoption panel' means a panel established in accordance with regulation 3 of the Agencies Regulations or corresponding Welsh provision;

'the Agencies Regulations' means the Adoption Agencies Regulations 2005;

'child's case record' has the same meaning as in regulation 12 of the Agencies Regulations or corresponding Welsh provision;

'CA of the receiving State' means, in relation to a Convention country other than the United Kingdom, the Central Authority of the receiving State;

'CA of the State of origin' means, in relation to a Convention country other than the United Kingdom, the Central Authority of the State of origin;

'Convention adoption' is given a meaning by virtue of section 66(1)(c) of the Act;

'Convention country' has the same meaning as in section 144(1) of the Act;

'Convention list' means –

(a) in relation to a relevant Central Authority, a list of children notified to that Authority in accordance with regulation 40; or

(b) in relation to any other Central Authority within the British Islands, a list of children notified to that Authority in accordance with provisions, which correspond to regulation 40.

'corresponding Welsh provision' in relation to a Part or a regulation of the Agencies Regulations means the provision of regulations made by the Assembly under section 9 of the Act which corresponds to that Part or regulation;

'prospective adopter's case record' has the same meaning as in regulation 23(1) of the Agencies Regulations or corresponding Welsh provision;

'prospective adopter's report' has the same meaning as in regulation 30(2) of the Agencies Regulations or corresponding Welsh provisions;

'receiving State' has the same meaning as in Article 2 of the Convention;

'relevant Central Authority' means –

(a) in Chapter 1 of Part 3, in relation to a prospective adopter who is habitually resident in –
  (i) England, the Secretary of State; and
  (ii) Wales, the National Assembly for Wales; and
(b) in Chapter 2 of Part 3 in relation to a local authority in –
  (i) England, the Secretary of State; and
  (ii) Wales, the National Assembly for Wales;

'relevant local authority' means in relation to a prospective adopter –

(a) the local authority within whose area he has his home; or
(b) in the case where he no longer has a home in England or Wales, the local authority for the area in which he last had his home;

'relevant foreign authority' means a person, outside the British Islands performing functions in the country in which the child is, or in which the prospective adopter is, habitually resident which correspond to the functions of an adoption agency or to the functions of the Secretary of State in respect of adoptions with a foreign element;

'State of origin' has the same meaning as in Article 2 of the Convention.

Amendments—SI 2013/985 (does not apply to Wales).

PART 2
BRINGING CHILDREN INTO AND OUT OF THE UNITED KINGDOM

Chapter 1
Bringing Children into the United Kingdom

3 Requirements applicable in respect of bringing or causing a child to be brought into the United Kingdom

A person intending to bring, or to cause another to bring, a child into the United Kingdom in circumstances where section 83(1) of the Act applies must –

(a) apply in writing to an adoption agency for an assessment of his suitability to adopt a child; and
(b) give the adoption agency any information it may require for the purpose of the assessment.

4 Conditions applicable in respect of a child brought into the United Kingdom

(1) This regulation prescribes the conditions for the purposes of section 83(5) of the Act in respect of a child brought into the United Kingdom in circumstances where section 83 applies.

(2) Prior to the child's entry into the United Kingdom, the prospective adopter must –

(a) receive in writing, notification from the Secretary of State that she has issued a certificate confirming to the relevant foreign authority –
  (i) that the person has been assessed and approved as eligible and suitable to be an adoptive parent in accordance with Part 4 of the Agencies Regulations or corresponding Welsh provision; and

(ii) that if entry clearance and leave to enter and remain, as may be necessary, is granted and not revoked or curtailed, and an adoption order is made or an overseas adoption is effected, the child will be authorised to enter and reside permanently in the United Kingdom;

(b) before visiting the child in the State of origin –

(i) notify the adoption agency of the details of the child to be adopted;

(ii) provide the adoption agency with any information and reports received from the relevant foreign authority; and

(iii) discuss with the adoption agency the proposed adoption and information received from the relevant foreign authority;

(c) visit the child in the State of origin (and where the prospective adopters are a couple each of them); and

(d) after that visit –

(i) confirm in writing to the adoption agency that he has done so and wishes to proceed with the adoption;

(ii) provide the adoption agency with any additional reports and information received on or after that visit; and

(iii) notify the adoption agency of his expected date of entry into the United Kingdom with the child.

(3) The prospective adopter must accompany the child on entering the United Kingdom unless, in the case of a couple, the adoption agency and the relevant foreign authority have agreed that it is necessary for only one of them to do so.

(4) Except where an overseas adoption is or is to be effected, the prospective adopter must within the period of 14 days beginning with the date on which the child is brought into the United Kingdom give notice to the relevant local authority –

(a) of the child's arrival in the United Kingdom; and

(b) of his intention –

(i) to apply for an adoption order in accordance with section 44(2) of the Act; or

(ii) not to give the child a home.

(5) In a case where a prospective adopter has given notice in accordance with paragraph (4) and subsequently moves his home into the area of another local authority, he must within 14 days of that move confirm in writing to that authority, the child's entry into the United Kingdom and that notice of his intention –

(a) to apply for an adoption order in accordance with section 44(2) of the Act has been given to another local authority; or

(b) not to give the child a home,

has been given.

Amendments—SI 2013/985 (does not apply to Wales).

5 Functions imposed on the local authority

(1) Where notice of intention to adopt has been given to the local authority, that authority must –

(a) if it has not already done so, set up a case record in respect of the child and place on it any information received from the –

(i) relevant foreign authority;

(ii) adoption agency, if it is not the local authority;

(iii) prospective adopter;

(iv) entry clearance officer; and

(v) Secretary of State, or as the case may be, the Assembly;

(b) send the prospective adopter's general practitioner written notification of the arrival in England or Wales of the child and send with that notification a written report of the child's health history and current state of health, so far as is known;

(c) send to the clinical commissioning group or Local Health Board (Wales), in whose area the prospective adopter has his home, and to the National Health Service

PART IV

Commissioning Board if the prospective adopter's home is in England, written notification of the arrival in England or Wales of the child;

(d) (*revoked*)

(e) ensure that the child and the prospective adopter are visited within one week of receipt of the notice of intention to adopt and thereafter not less than once a week until the review referred to in sub-paragraph (f) and thereafter at such frequency as the authority may decide;

(f) carry out a review of the child's case not more than 4 weeks after receipt of the notice of intention to adopt and –

(i) visit and, if necessary, review not more than 3 months after that initial review; and

(ii) thereafter not more than 6 months after the date of the previous visit,

unless the child no longer has his home with the prospective adopter or an adoption order is made;

(g) when carrying out a review consider –

(i) the child's needs, welfare and development, and whether any changes need to be made to meet his needs or assist his development;

(ii) the arrangements for the provision of adoption support services and whether there should be any re-assessment of the need for those services; and

(iii) the need for further visits and reviews; and

(h) ensure that –

(i) advice is given as to the child's needs, welfare and development;

(ii) written reports are made of all visits and reviews of the case and placed on the child's case record; and

(iii) on such visits, where appropriate, advice is given as to the availability of adoption support services.

(2) Part 7 of the Agencies Regulations or corresponding Welsh provision (case records) shall apply to the case record set up in respect of the child as a consequence of this regulation as if that record had been set up under the Agencies Regulations or corresponding Welsh provision.

(3) In a case where the prospective adopter fails to make an application under section 50 or 51 of the Act within two years of the receipt by a local authority of the notice of intention to adopt the local authority must review the case.

(4) For the purposes of the review referred to in paragraph (3), the local authority must consider –

(a) the child's needs, welfare and development, and whether any changes need to be made to meet his needs or assist his development;

(b) the arrangements, if any, in relation to the exercise of parental responsibility for the child;

(c) the terms upon which leave to enter the United Kingdom is granted and the immigration status of the child;

(d) the arrangements for the provision of adoption support services for the adoptive family and whether there should be any re-assessment of the need for those services; and

(e) in conjunction with the appropriate agencies, the arrangements for meeting the child's health care and educational needs.

(5) In a case where the local authority to which notice of intention to adopt is given ('the original authority') is notified by the prospective adopter that he intends to move or has moved his home into the area of another local authority, the original authority must notify the local authority into whose area the prospective adopter intends to move or has moved, within 14 days of receiving information in respect of that move, of –

(a) the name, sex, date and place of birth of child;

(b) the prospective adopter's name, sex and date of birth;

(c) the date on which the child entered the United Kingdom;

(d) where the original authority received notification of intention to adopt, the date of receipt of such notification whether an application for an adoption order has been made and the stage of those proceedings; and

(e) any other relevant information.

Amendments—SI 2010/1172; SI 2013/235.

6 Application of Chapter 3 of the Act

In the case of a child brought into the United Kingdom for adoption in circumstances where section 83 of the Act applies –

(a) the modifications in regulations 7 to 9 apply;
(b) section 36(2) and (5) (restrictions on removal) and section 39(3)(a) (partners of parents) of the Act shall not apply.

7 Change of name and removal from the United Kingdom

Section 28(2) of the Act (further consequences of placement) shall apply as if from the words 'is placed' to 'then', there is substituted 'enters the United Kingdom in the circumstances where section 83(1)(a) of this Act applies'.

8 Return of the child

(1) Section 35 of the Act (return of child) shall apply with the following modifications.

(2) Subsections (1), (2) and (3) shall apply as if in each place where –

(a) the words 'is placed for adoption by an adoption agency' occur there were substituted 'enters the United Kingdom in circumstances where section 83(1) applies';
(b) the words 'the agency' occur there were substituted the words 'the local authority'; and
(c) the words 'any parent or guardian of the child' occur there were substituted 'the Secretary of State or, as the case may be, the Assembly'.

(3) Subsection (5) shall apply as if for the words 'an adoption agency' or 'the agency' there were substituted the words 'the local authority'.

PART IV

9 Child to live with adopters before application

(1) In a case where the requirements imposed by section 83(4) of the Act have been complied with and the conditions required by section 83(5) of the Act have been met, section 42 shall apply as if –

(a) subsection (3) is omitted; and
(b) in subsection (5) the words from 'three years' to 'preceding' there were substituted 'six months'.

(2) In a case where the requirements imposed by section 83(4) of the Act have not been complied with or the conditions required by section 83(5) have not been met, section 42 shall apply as if –

(a) subsection (3) is omitted; and
(b) in subsection (5) the words from 'three years' to 'preceding' there were substituted 'twelve months'.

Chapter 2
Taking Children out of the United Kingdom

10 Requirements applicable in respect of giving parental responsibility prior to adoption abroad

The prescribed requirements for the purposes of section 84(3) of the Act (requirements to be satisfied prior to the making of an order) are that –

(a) in the case of a child placed by an adoption agency, that agency has –
  (i) confirmed to the court that it has complied with the requirements imposed in accordance with Part 3 of the Agencies Regulations or corresponding Welsh provision;
  (ii) submitted to the court –
    (aa) the reports and information referred to in regulation 17(2D) and (3), as appropriate of the Agencies Regulations or corresponding Welsh provision;

(bb) the recommendations made by the adoption panel in accordance with regulations 18 (placing child for adoption), where applicable, and 33 (proposed placement) of the Agencies Regulations or corresponding Welsh provision;

(cc) the adoption placement report prepared in accordance with regulation 31(2)(d) of the Agencies Regulations or corresponding Welsh provision;

(dd) the reports of and information obtained in respect of the visits and reviews referred to in regulation 36 of the Agencies Regulations or corresponding Welsh provision; and

(ee) the report referred to in section 43 of the Act as modified by regulation 11;

(b) in the case of a child placed by an adoption agency the relevant foreign authority has –

(i) confirmed in writing to that agency that the prospective adopter has been counselled and the legal implications of adoption have been explained to him;

(ii) prepared a report on the suitability of the prospective adopter to be an adoptive parent;

(iii) determined and confirmed in writing to that agency that he is eligible and suitable to adopt in the country or territory in which the adoption is to be effected; and

(iv) confirmed in writing to that agency that the child is or will be authorised to enter and reside permanently in that foreign country or territory; and

(c) in the case of a child placed by an adoption agency the prospective adopter has confirmed in writing to the adoption agency that he will accompany the child on taking him out of the United Kingdom and entering the country or territory where the adoption is to be effected, or in the case of a couple, the agency and relevant foreign authority have confirmed that it is necessary for only one of them to do so.

Amendments—SI 2012/1410.

11 Application of the Act in respect of orders under section 84

(1) The following provisions of the Act which refer to adoption orders shall apply to orders under section 84 as if in each place where the words 'adoption order' appear there were substituted 'order under section 84' –

(a) section 1(7)(a) (coming to a decision relating to adoption of a child);
(b) section 18(4) (placement for adoption by agencies);
(c) section 21(4)(b) (placement orders);
(d) section 22(5)(a) and (b) (application for placement orders);
(e) section 24(4) (revoking placement orders);
(f) section 28(1) (further consequences of placement);
(g) section 29(4)(a) and (5)(a) (further consequences of placement orders);
(h) section 32(5) (recovery by parent etc where child placed and consent withdrawn);
(i) section 42(7) (sufficient opportunity for adoption agency to see the child);
(j) section 43 (reports where child placed by agency);
(k) section 44(2) (notice of intention to adopt);
(l) section 47(1) to (5), (8) and (9) (conditions for making orders);
(m) section 48(1) (restrictions on making applications);
(n) section 50(1) and (2) (adoption by a couple);
(o) section 51(1) to (4) (adoption by one person);
(p) section 52(1) to (4) (parental etc consent);
(q) section 53(5) (contribution towards maintenance); and
(r) section 141(3) and (4)(c) (rules of procedure).

(2) Section 35(5) of the Act (return of child in other cases) shall apply to orders under section 84 of that Act as if in paragraph (b) of that subsection –

(a) for the first reference to 'adoption order' there were substituted 'order under section 84(1)'; and
(b) the words in brackets were omitted.

PART 3
ADOPTIONS UNDER THE CONVENTION

Chapter 1
Requirements, Procedure, Recognition and Effect of Adoptions where the United Kingdom is the Receiving State

12 Application of Chapter 1

The provisions in this Chapter shall apply where a couple or a person, habitually resident in the British Islands, wishes to adopt a child who is habitually resident in a Convention country outside the British Islands in accordance with the Convention.

13 Requirements applicable in respect of eligibility and suitability

(1) (a) in the case of an adoption agency in Wales, apply in writing to the adoption agency for a determination of eligibility and an assessment of their suitability to adopt, and give the agency any information it may require for the purposes of the assessment, or

(b) in the case of an adoption agency in England, notify the agency that they want to adopt a child, and give the agency any information it may require for the purposes of the pre-assessment process set out in Part 4 of the Agencies Regulations.

(2) An adoption agency in Wales may not consider an application under paragraph (1)(a), and an adoption agency in England may not proceed with the pre-assessment process referred to in paragraph (1)(b), unless at the date of that application or notification (as the case may be) –

(a) in the case of an application by a couple, they have both –
  (i) attained the age of 21 years; and
  (ii) been habitually resident in a part of the British Islands for a period of not less than one year ending with the date of application; and

(b) in the case of an application by one person, he has –
  (i) attained the age of 21 years; and
  (ii) been habitually resident in a part of the British Islands for a period of not less than one year ending with the date of application.

Amendments—SI 2013/985 (does not apply to Wales).

14 Counselling and information

(1) An adoption agency must provide a counselling service in accordance with regulation 24(1)(a) of the Agencies Regulations or corresponding Welsh provision and must –

(a) explain to the prospective adopter the procedure in relation to, and the legal implications of, adopting a child from the State of origin from which the prospective adopter wishes to adopt in accordance with the Convention; and

(b) provide him with written information about the matters referred to in sub-paragraph (a).

(2) Paragraph (1) does not apply if the adoption agency is satisfied that the requirements set out in that paragraph have been carried out in respect of the prospective adopter by another agency.

Amendments—SI 2013/985 (does not apply to Wales).

15 Procedure in respect of carrying out an assessment

(1) Where the adoption agency is satisfied that that the requirements in regulation 14 have been met the agency must consider the suitability of the prospective adopter in accordance with Part 4 of the Agencies Regulations.

(2) *(revoked)*

(3) The adoption agency must place on the prospective adopter's case record any information obtained as a consequence of this Chapter.

(4) The adoption agency must include in the prospective adopter's report –

- (a) the State of origin from which the prospective adopter wishes to adopt a child;
- (b) confirmation that the prospective adopter is eligible to adopt a child under the law of that State;
- (c) any additional information obtained as a consequence of the requirements of that State; and
- (d) the agency's assessment of the prospective adopter's suitability to adopt a child who is habitually resident in that State.

(5) The references to information in regulations 30(2) and 30A(2) of the Agencies Regulations or corresponding Welsh provisions shall include information obtained by the adoption agency or adoption panel as a consequence of this regulation.

Amendments—SI 2013/985 (does not apply to Wales).

16 Adoption agency decision and notification

The adoption agency must make a decision about whether the prospective adopter is suitable to adopt a child in accordance with regulation 30B of the Agencies Regulations and regulations made under section 45 of the Act, or corresponding Welsh provisions.

Amendments—SI 2013/985 (does not apply to Wales).

17 Review and termination of approval

The adoption agency must review the approval of each prospective adopter in accordance with regulation 30D of the Agencies Regulations or corresponding Welsh provision unless the agency has received written notification from the relevant Central Authority that the agreement under Article 17(c) of the Convention has been made.

Amendments—SI 2013/985 (does not apply to Wales).

18 Procedure following decision as to suitability to adopt

(1) Where an adoption agency has made a decision that the prospective adopter is suitable to adopt a child in accordance with regulation 16, it must send to the relevant Central Authority –

- (a) written confirmation of the decision and any recommendation the agency may make in relation to the number of children the prospective adopter may be suitable to adopt, their age range, sex, likely needs and background;
- (b) the enhanced criminal record certificate obtained under regulation 25 of the Agencies Regulations or corresponding Welsh provision;
- (c) all the documents and information which were passed to the adoption panel in accordance with regulations 30(6) or (7) of the Agencies Regulations or corresponding Welsh provision;
- (d) the record of the proceedings of the adoption panel, its recommendation and the reasons for its recommendation; and
- (e) any other information relating to the case as the relevant Central Authority or the CA of the State of origin may require.

(2) If the relevant Central Authority is satisfied that the adoption agency has complied with the duties and procedures imposed by the Agencies Regulations or corresponding Welsh provision, and that all the relevant information has been supplied by that agency, the Authority must send to the CA of the State of origin –

- (a) the prospective adopter's report prepared in accordance with regulation 30 of the Agencies Regulations or corresponding Welsh provision;
- (b) *(revoked)*
- (c) a copy of the adoption agency's decision and the adoption panel's recommendation;
- (d) any other information that the CA of the State of origin may require;
- (da) if the prospective adopter applied to the appropriate Minister for a review under section 12 of the Adoption and Children Act 2002, the record of the proceedings of the panel, its recommendation and the reasons for its recommendation; and
- (e) a certificate in the form set out in Schedule 1 confirming that the –
  - (i) prospective adopter is eligible to adopt;

(ii) prospective adopter has been assessed in accordance with this Chapter;

(iii) prospective adopter has been approved as suitable to adopt a child; and

(iv) child will be authorised to enter and reside permanently in the United Kingdom if entry clearance, and leave to enter or remain as may be necessary, is granted and not revoked or curtailed and a Convention adoption order or Convention adoption is made.

(3) The relevant Central Authority must notify the adoption agency and the prospective adopter in writing that the certificate and the documents referred to in paragraph (2) have been sent to the CA of the State of origin.

Amendments—SI 2005/3482; SI 2013/985 (does not apply to Wales).

19 Procedure following receipt of the Article 16 Information from the CA of the State of origin

(1) Where the relevant Central Authority receives from the CA of the State of origin, the Article 16 Information relating to the child whom the CA of the State of origin considers should be placed for adoption with the prospective adopter, the relevant Central Authority must send that Information to the adoption agency.

(2) The adoption agency must consider the Article 16 Information and –

(a) send that Information to the prospective adopter;

(b) discuss with the prospective adopter –

(i) that Information;

(ii) the proposed placement;

(iii) the availability of adoption support services; and

(c) if appropriate, offer a counselling service and further information as required.

(3) Where –

(a) the procedure in paragraph (2) has been followed; and

(b) the prospective adopter has confirmed in writing to the adoption agency that he wishes to proceed to adopt the child,

the agency must notify the relevant Central Authority in writing that the requirements specified in sub-paragraphs (a) and (b) have been satisfied and at the same time it must confirm that it is content for the adoption to proceed.

(4) Where the relevant Central Authority has received notification from the adoption agency under paragraph (3), the relevant Central Authority shall –

(a) notify the CA of the State of origin that –

(i) the prospective adopter wishes to proceed to adopt the child;

(ii) it is prepared to agree with the CA of the State of origin that the adoption may proceed; and

(b) confirm to the CA of the State of origin that –

(i) in the case where the requirements specified in section 1(5A) of the British Nationality Act 1981 are met that the child will be authorised to enter and reside permanently in the United Kingdom; or

(ii) in any other case, if entry clearance and leave to enter and remain, as may be necessary, is granted and not revoked or curtailed and a Convention adoption order or a Convention adoption is made, the child will be authorised to enter and reside permanently in the United Kingdom.

(5) The relevant Central Authority must inform the adoption agency and the prospective adopter when the agreement under Article 17(c) of the Convention has been made.

(6) For the purposes of this regulation and regulation 20 'the Article 16 Information' means –

(a) the report referred to in Article 16(1) of the Convention including information about the child's identity, adoptability, background, social environment, family history, medical history including that of the child's family and any special needs of the child;

PART IV

(b) proof of confirmation that the consents of the persons, institutions and authorities whose consents are necessary for adoption have been obtained in accordance with Article 4 of the Convention; and

(c) the reasons for the CA of the State of origin's determination on the placement.

Amendments—SI 2009/2563; SI 2013/985 (does not apply to Wales).

20 Procedure where proposed adoption is not to proceed

(1) If, at any stage before the agreement under Article 17(c) of the Convention is made, the CA of the State of origin notifies the relevant Central Authority that it has decided the proposed placement should not proceed –

(a) the relevant Central Authority must inform the adoption agency of the CA of the State of origin's decision;

(b) the agency must then inform the prospective adopter and return the Article 16 Information to the relevant Central Authority; and

(c) the relevant Central Authority must then return those documents to the CA of the State of origin.

(2) Where at any stage before the adoption agency receives notification of the agreement under Article 17(c) of the Convention the approval of the prospective adopter is reviewed under regulation 30D of the Agencies Regulations or corresponding Welsh provision, and as a consequence, the agency determines that the prospective adopter is no longer suitable to adopt a child –

(a) the agency must inform the relevant Central Authority and return the documents referred to in regulation 19(1);

(b) the relevant Central Authority must notify the CA of the State of origin and return those documents.

(3) If, at any stage before any Convention adoption is made and before the child's entry into the United Kingdom, the prospective adopter notifies the adoption agency that he does not wish to proceed with the adoption of the child –

(a) that agency must inform the relevant Central Authority and return the documents to that Authority; and

(b) the relevant Central Authority must notify the CA of the State of origin of the prospective adopter's decision and return the documents to the CA of the State of origin.

Amendments—SI 2009/2563; SI 2013/985 (does not apply to Wales).

21 Applicable requirements in respect of prospective adopter entering the United Kingdom with a child

Following any agreement under Article 17(c) of the Convention, the prospective adopter must –

(a) notify the adoption agency of his expected date of entry into the United Kingdom with the child;

(b) confirm to the adoption agency when the child is placed with him by the competent authority in the State of origin; and

(c) accompany the child on entering the United Kingdom unless, in the case of a couple, the adoption agency and the CA of the State of origin have agreed that it is necessary for only one of them to do so.

22 Applicable requirements in respect of an adoption agency before the child enters the United Kingdom

Where the adoption agency is informed by the relevant Central Authority that the agreement under Article 17(c) of the Convention has been made and the adoption may proceed, before the child enters the United Kingdom that agency must –

(a) send the prospective adopter's general practitioner written notification of the proposed placement and send with that notification a written report of the child's health history and current state of health, so far as it is known; and

(b) send the local authority (if that authority is not the adoption agency) and the clinical commissioning group or Local Health Board (Wales), in whose area the prospective adopter has his home, and to the National Health Service Commissioning Board if the prospective adopter's home is in England, written notification of the proposed arrival of the child into England or Wales; and, where the child is of compulsory school age, include in the notification to the local authority information about the child's educational history and whether the child has been or is likely to be assessed for special educational needs under the Education Act 1996 or the Children and Families Act 2014.

(c) *(revoked)*

Amendments—SI 2010/1172; SI 2013/235; SI 2014/2103.

23 Applicable provisions following the child's entry into the United Kingdom where no Convention adoption is made

Regulations 24 to 27 apply where –

(a) following the agreement between the relevant Central Authority and the CA of the State of origin under Article 17(c) of the Convention that the adoption may proceed, no Convention adoption is made, or applied for, in the State of origin; and

(b) the child is placed with the prospective adopter in the State of origin who then returns to England or Wales with that child.

24 Applicable requirements in respect of prospective adopter following child's entry into the United Kingdom

(1) A prospective adopter must within the period of 14 days beginning with the date on which the child enters the United Kingdom give notice to the relevant local authority –

(a) of the child's arrival in the United Kingdom; and

(b) of his intention –

 (i) to apply for an adoption order in accordance with section 44(2) of the Act; or

 (ii) not to give the child a home.

(2) In a case where a prospective adopter has given notice in accordance with paragraph (1) and he subsequently moves his home into the area of another local authority, he must within 14 days of that move confirm to that authority in writing the child's entry into the United Kingdom and that notice of his intention –

(a) to apply for an adoption order in accordance with section 44(2) of the Act has been given to another local authority; or

(b) not to give the child a home,

has been given.

25 Functions imposed on the local authority following the child's entry into the United Kingdom

(1) Where notice is given to a local authority in accordance with regulation 24, the functions imposed on the local authority by virtue of regulation 5 shall apply subject to the modifications in paragraph (2).

(2) Paragraph (1) of regulation 5 shall apply as if –

(a) in sub-paragraph (a) –

 (i) in head (i) for the words 'relevant foreign authority' there is substituted 'CA of the State of origin and competent foreign authority';

 (ii) in head (v) there is substituted 'the relevant Central Authority'; and

(b) sub-paragraphs (b) to (d) were omitted.

PART IV

26 Prospective adopter unable to proceed with adoption

(1) Where the prospective adopter gives notice to the relevant local authority that he does not wish to proceed with the adoption and no longer wishes to give the child a home, he must return the child to that authority not later than the end of the period of seven days beginning with the date on which notice was given.

(2) Where a relevant local authority have received a notice in accordance with paragraph (1), that authority must give notice to the relevant Central Authority of the decision of the prospective adopter not to proceed with the adoption.

Amendments—SI 2005/3482.

27 Withdrawal of child from prospective adopter

(1) Where the relevant local authority are of the opinion that the continued placement of the child is not in the child's best interests –

(a) that authority must give notice to the prospective adopter of their opinion and request the return of the child to them; and

(b) subject to paragraph (3), the prospective adopter must, not later than the end of the period of seven days beginning with the date on which notice was given, return the child to that authority.

(2) Where the relevant local authority has given notice under paragraph (1), that authority must at the same time notify the relevant Central Authority that they have requested the return of the child.

(3) Where notice is given under paragraph (1) but –

(a) an application for a Convention adoption order was made prior to the giving of that notice; and

(b) the application has not been disposed of,

the prospective adopter is not required by virtue of paragraph (1) to return the child unless the court so orders.

(4) This regulation does not affect the exercise by any local authority or other person of any power conferred by any enactment or the exercise of any power of arrest.

28 Breakdown of placement

(1) This regulation applies where –

(a) notification is given by the prospective adopter under regulation 26 (unable to proceed with adoption);

(b) the child is withdrawn from the prospective adopter under regulation 27 (withdrawal of child from prospective adopter);

(c) an application for a Convention adoption order is refused;

(d) a Convention adoption which is subject to a probationary period cannot be made; or

(e) a Convention adoption order or a Convention adoption is annulled pursuant to section 89(1) of the Act.

(2) Where the relevant local authority are satisfied that it would be in the child's best interests to be placed for adoption with another prospective adopter habitually resident in the United Kingdom they must take the necessary measures to identify a suitable adoptive parent for that child.

(3) Where the relevant local authority have identified and approved another prospective adopter who is eligible, and has been assessed as suitable, to adopt in accordance with these Regulations –

(a) that authority must notify the relevant Central Authority in writing that –

(i) another prospective adopter has been identified; and

(ii) the provisions in regulations 14, 15 and 16 have been complied with; and

(b) the requirements specified in regulations 18 and 19 have been complied with.

(4) Where the relevant Central Authority has been notified in accordance with paragraph (3)(a) –

(a) it shall inform the CA of the State of origin of the proposed placement; and
(b) it shall agree the placement with the CA of the State of origin in accordance with the provisions in this Chapter.

(5) Subject to paragraph (2), where the relevant local authority is not satisfied it would be in the child's best interests to be placed for adoption with another prospective adopter in England or Wales, it must liaise with the relevant Central Authority to arrange for the return of the child to his State of origin.

(6) Before coming to any decision under this regulation, the relevant local authority must have regard to the wishes and feelings of the child, having regard to his age and understanding, and where appropriate, obtain his consent in relation to measures to be taken under this regulation.

29 Convention adoptions subject to a probationary period

(1) This regulation applies where –

(a) the child has been placed with the prospective adopters by the competent authority in the State of origin and a Convention adoption has been applied for by the prospective adopters in the State of origin but the child's placement with the prospective adopter is subject to a probationary period before the Convention adoption is made; and
(b) the prospective adopter returns to England or Wales with the child before that probationary period is completed and the Convention adoption is made in the State of origin.

(2) The relevant local authority must, if requested by the competent authority of the State of origin, submit a report about the placement to that authority and such a report must be prepared within such timescales and contain such information as the competent authority may reasonably require.

30 Report of local authority investigation

The report of the investigation which a local authority must submit to the court in accordance with section 44(5) of the Act must include –

(a) confirmation that the Certificate of eligibility and approval has been sent to the CA of the State of origin in accordance with regulation 18;
(b) the date on which the agreement under Article 17(c) of the Convention was made; and
(c) details of the reports of the visits and reviews made in accordance with regulation 5 as modified by regulation 25.

31 Convention adoption order

An adoption order shall not be made as a Convention adoption order unless –

(a) in the case of –
  (i) an application by a couple, both members of the couple have been habitually resident in any part of the British Islands for a period of not less than one year ending with the date of the application; or
  (ii) an application by one person, the applicant has been habitually resident in any part of the British Islands for a period of not less than one year ending with the date of the application;
(b) the child to be adopted was, on the date on which the agreement under Article 17(c) of the Convention was made, habitually resident in a Convention country outside the British Islands; and
(c) in a case where one member of a couple (in the case of an application by a couple) or the applicant (in the case of an application by one person) is not a British citizen, the Home Office has confirmed that the child is authorised to enter and reside permanently in the United Kingdom.

32 Requirements following a Convention adoption order or Convention adoption

(1) Where the relevant Central Authority receives a copy of a Convention adoption order made by a court in England or Wales that Authority must issue a certificate in the form set out in Schedule 2 certifying that the adoption has been made in accordance with the Convention.

(2) A copy of the certificate issued under paragraph (1) must be sent to the –

(a) CA of the State of origin;

(b) adoptive parent; and

(c) adoption agency and, if different, the relevant local authority.

(3) Where a Convention adoption is made and the relevant Central Authority receives a certificate under Article 23 of the Convention in respect of that Convention adoption, the relevant Central Authority must send a copy of that certificate to the –

(a) adoptive parent; and

(b) adoption agency and, if different, the relevant local authority.

33 Refusal of a court in England or Wales to make a Convention adoption order

Where an application for a Convention adoption order is refused by the court or is withdrawn, the prospective adopter must return the child to the relevant local authority within the period determined by the court.

34 Annulment of a Convention adoption order or a Convention adoption

Where a Convention adoption order or a Convention adoption is annulled under section 89(1) of the Act and the relevant Central Authority receives a copy of the order from the court, it must forward a copy of that order to the CA of the State of origin.

Chapter 2

Requirements, Procedure, Recognition and Effect of Adoptions in England and Wales where the United Kingdom is the State of Origin

35 Application of Chapter 2

The provisions in this Chapter shall apply where a couple or a person habitually resident in a Convention country outside the British Islands, wishes to adopt a child who is habitually resident in the British Islands in accordance with the Convention.

36 Counselling and information for the child

(1) Where an adoption agency is considering whether a child is suitable for an adoption in accordance with the Convention, it must provide a counselling service for and information to that child in accordance with regulation 13 of the Agencies Regulations or corresponding Welsh provision and it must –

(a) explain to the child in an appropriate manner the procedure in relation to, and the legal implications of, adoption under the Convention for that child by a prospective adopter habitually resident in the receiving State; and

(b) provide him with written information about the matters referred to in sub-paragraph (a).

(2) Paragraph (1) does not apply if the adoption agency is satisfied that the requirements set out in that paragraph have been carried out in respect of the prospective adopter by another agency.

37 Counselling and information for the parent or guardian of the child etc

(1) An adoption agency must provide a counselling service and information in accordance with regulation 14 of the Agencies Regulations or corresponding Welsh provision for the parent or guardian of the child and, where regulation 14(4) of the Agencies Regulations or corresponding Welsh provision applies, for the father.

(2) The adoption agency must also –

(a) explain to the parent or guardian, and, where regulation 14(4) of the Agencies Regulations or corresponding Welsh provision applies, the father the procedure in relation to, and the legal implications of, adoption under the Convention by a prospective adopter in a receiving State; and
(b) provide him with written information about the matters referred to in sub-paragraph (a).

(3) Paragraphs (1) and (2) do not apply if the adoption agency is satisfied that the requirements set out in that paragraph have been carried out in respect of the prospective adopter by another agency.

38 Requirements in respect of the child's permanence report and information for the adoption panel

(1) The child's permanence report which the adoption agency is required to prepare in accordance with regulation 17 of the Agencies Regulations or corresponding Welsh provision must include –
(a) a summary of the possibilities for placement of the child within the United Kingdom; and
(b) an assessment of whether an adoption by a person in a particular receiving State is in the child's best interests.

(2) In a case falling within regulation 17(2C) of the Agencies Regulations or the corresponding Welsh provision, the adoption agency must send –
(a) if received, the Article 15 Report; and
(b) their observations on that Report,

together with the reports and information referred to in regulation 17(2D) of the Agencies Regulations or corresponding Welsh provision to the adoption panel.

(3) In a case falling within regulation 17(2) of the Agencies Regulations or the corresponding Welsh provision, the adoption agency must consider –
(a) if received, the Article 15 Report; and
(b) their observations on that Report together with the reports and information referred to in regulation 17(2D) of the Agencies Regulations or the corresponding Welsh provision

in deciding whether the child should be placed for adoption in accordance with the Convention.

Amendments—SI 2012/1410.

39 Recommendation of adoption panel

Where an adoption panel make a recommendation in accordance with regulation 18(1) of the Agencies Regulations or corresponding Welsh provision it must consider and take into account the Article 15 Report, if available, and the observations thereon together with the information passed to it as a consequence of regulation 38.

40 Adoption agency decision and notification

Where the adoption agency decides in accordance with regulation 19 of the Agencies Regulations or corresponding Welsh provision that the child should be placed for an adoption in accordance with the Convention it must notify the relevant Central Authority of –
(a) the name, sex and age of the child;
(b) the reasons why they consider that the child may be suitable for such an adoption;
(c) whether a prospective adopter has been identified and, if so, provide any relevant information; and
(d) any other information that Authority may require.

41 Convention list

(1) The relevant Central Authority is to maintain a Convention list of children who are notified to that Authority under regulation 40 and shall make the contents of that list available for consultation by other Authorities within the British Islands.

(2) Where an adoption agency –

(a) places for adoption a child whose details have been notified to the relevant Central Authority under regulation 40; or

(b) determines that an adoption in accordance with the Convention is no longer in the best interests of the child,

it must notify the relevant Central Authority accordingly and that Authority must remove the details relating to that child from the Convention list.

42 Receipt of the Article 15 Report from the CA of the receiving State

(1) This regulation applies where –

(a) the relevant Central Authority receives a report from the CA of the receiving State which has been prepared for the purposes of Article 15 of the Convention ('the Article 15 Report');

(b) the Article 15 Report relates to a prospective adopter who is habitually resident in that receiving State; and

(c) the prospective adopter named in the Article 15 Report wishes to adopt a child who is habitually resident in the British Islands.

(2) Subject to paragraph (3), if the relevant Central Authority is satisfied the prospective adopter meets the following requirements –

(a) the age requirements as specified in section 50 of the Act in the case of adoption by a couple, or section 51 of the Act in the case of adoption by one person; and

(b) in the case of a couple, both are, or in the case of adoption by one person, that person is habitually resident in a Convention country outside the British Islands,

that Authority must consult the Convention list and may, if the Authority considers it appropriate, consult any Convention list maintained by another Central Authority within the British Islands.

(3) Where a prospective adopter has already been identified in relation to a proposed adoption of a particular child and the relevant Central Authority is satisfied that prospective adopter meets the requirements referred to in paragraph (2)(a) and (b), that Authority –

(a) need not consult the Convention list; and

(b) must send the Article 15 Report to the local authority which referred the child's details to the Authority.

(4) The relevant Central Authority may pass a copy of the Article 15 Report to any other Central Authority within the British Islands for the purposes of enabling that Authority to consult its Convention list.

(5) Where the relevant Central Authority identifies a child on the Convention list who may be suitable for adoption by the prospective adopter, that Authority must send the Article 15 Report to the local authority which referred the child's details to that Authority.

43 Proposed placement and referral to adoption panel

(1) Where the adoption agency is considering whether a proposed placement should proceed in accordance with the procedure provided for in regulation 31 of the Agencies Regulations or corresponding Welsh provision it must take into account the Article 15 Report.

(2) Where the adoption agency refers the proposal to place the child with the particular prospective adopter to the adoption panel in accordance with regulation 31 of the Agencies Regulations or corresponding Welsh provision, it must also send the Article 15 Report to the panel.

44 Consideration by adoption panel

The adoption panel must take into account when considering what recommendation to make in accordance with regulation 32(1) of the Agencies Regulations or corresponding Welsh provision the Article 15 Report and any other information passed to it as a consequence of the provisions in this Chapter.

45 Adoption agency's decision in relation to the proposed placement

(1) Regulation 33 of the Agencies Regulations or corresponding Welsh provision shall apply as if paragraph (3) of that regulation or corresponding Welsh provision was omitted.

(2) As soon as possible after the agency makes its decision, it must notify the relevant Central Authority of its decision.

(3) If the proposed placement is not to proceed –

(a) the adoption agency must return the Article 15 Report and any other documents or information sent to it by the relevant Central Authority to that Authority; and

(b) the relevant Central Authority must then send that Report, any such documents or such information to the CA of the receiving State.

46 Preparation of the Article 16 Information

(1) If the adoption agency decides that the proposed placement should proceed, it must prepare a report for the purposes of Article 16(1) of the Convention which must include –

(a) the information about the child which is specified in Schedule 1 to the Agencies Regulations or corresponding Welsh provision; and

(b) the reasons for their decision.

(2) The adoption agency must send the following to the relevant Central Authority –

(a) the report referred to in paragraph (1);

(b) details of any placement order or other orders, if any, made by the courts; and

(c) confirmation that the parent or guardian consents to the proposed adoption.

(3) The relevant Central Authority must then send the documents referred to in paragraph (2) to the CA of the receiving State.

47 Requirements to be met before the child is placed for adoption with prospective adopter

(1) The relevant Central Authority may notify the CA of the receiving State that it is prepared to agree that the adoption may proceed provided that CA has confirmed that –

(a) the prospective adopter has agreed to adopt the child and has received such counselling as may be necessary;

(b) the prospective adopter has confirmed that he will accompany the child to the receiving State, unless in the case of a couple, the adoption agency and the CA of the receiving State have agreed that it is only necessary for one of them to do so;

(c) it is content for the adoption to proceed;

(d) in the case where a Convention adoption is to be effected, it has explained to the prospective adopter the need to make an application under section 84(1) of the Act; and

(e) the child is or will be authorised to enter and reside permanently in the Convention country if a Convention adoption is effected or a Convention adoption order is made.

(2) The relevant Central Authority may not make an agreement under Article 17(c) of the Convention with the CA of the receiving State unless –

(a) confirmation has been received in respect of the matters referred to in paragraph (1); and

(b) the adoption agency has confirmed to the relevant Central Authority that –

(i) it has met the prospective adopter and explained the requirement to make an application for an order under section 84 of the Act before the child can be removed from the United Kingdom;

(ii) the prospective adopter has visited the child; and

(iii) the prospective adopter is content for the adoption to proceed.

(3) An adoption agency may not place a child for adoption unless the agreement under Article 17(c) of the Convention has been made and the relevant Central Authority must advise that agency when that agreement has been made.

PART IV

(4) In this regulation, the reference to 'prospective adopter' means in the case of a couple, both of them.

48 Requirements in respect of giving parental responsibility prior to a proposed Convention adoption

In the case of a proposed Convention adoption, the prescribed requirements for the purposes of section 84(3) of the Act (requirements to be satisfied prior to making an order) are –

- (a) the competent authorities of the receiving State have –
  - (i) prepared a report for the purposes of Article 15 of the Convention;
  - (ii) determined and confirmed in writing that the prospective adoptive parent is eligible and suitable to adopt;
  - (iii) ensured and confirmed in writing that the prospective adoptive parent has been counselled as may be necessary; and
  - (iv) determined and confirmed in writing that the child is or will be authorised to enter and reside permanently in that State;
- (b) the report required for the purposes of Article 16(1) of the Convention has been prepared by the adoption agency;
- (c) the adoption agency confirms in writing that it has complied with the requirements imposed upon it under Part 3 of the Agencies Regulations or corresponding Welsh provision and this Chapter;
- (d) the adoption agency has obtained and made available to the court –
  - (i) the reports and information referred to in regulation 17(2D) of the Agencies Regulations or corresponding Welsh provision;
  - (ii) the recommendation made by the adoption panel in accordance with regulations 18, where applicable, and 33 of the Agencies Regulations or corresponding Welsh provisions; and
  - (iii) the adoption placement report prepared in accordance with regulation 31(2) of the Agencies Regulations or corresponding Welsh provision;
- (e) the adoption agency includes in their report submitted to the court in accordance with section 43(a) or 44(5) of the Act as modified respectively by regulation 11, details of any reviews and visits carried out as consequence of Part 6 of the Agencies Regulations or corresponding Welsh provision; and
- (f) the prospective adopter has confirmed in writing that he will accompany the child on taking the child out of the United Kingdom to travel to the receiving State or in the case of a couple the agency and competent foreign authority have confirmed that it is necessary for only one of them to do so.

Amendments—SI 2012/1410.

49 Local authority report

In the case of a proposed application for a Convention adoption order, the report which a local authority must submit to the court in accordance with section 43(a) or 44(5) of the Act must include a copy of the –

- (a) Article 15 Report;
- (b) report prepared for the purposes of Article 16(1); and
- (c) written confirmation of the agreement under Article 17(c) of the Convention.

50 Convention adoption order

An adoption order shall not be made as a Convention adoption order unless –

- (a) in the case of –
  - (i) an application by a couple, both members of the couple have been habitually resident in a Convention country outside the British Islands for a period of not less than one year ending with the date of the application; or

(aa) an application by one person, the applicant has been habitually resident in a Convention country outside the British Islands for a period of not less than one year ending with the date of the application;

(b) the child to be adopted was, on the date on which the agreement under Article 17(c) of the Convention was made, habitually resident in any part of the British Islands; and

(c) the competent authority has confirmed that the child is authorised to enter and remain permanently in the Convention country in which the applicant is habitually resident.

51 Requirements following a Convention adoption order or Convention adoption

(1) Where the relevant Central Authority receives a copy of a Convention adoption order made by a court in England or Wales, that Authority must issue a certificate in the form set out in Schedule 2 certifying that the adoption has been made in accordance with the Convention.

(2) A copy of the certificate must be sent to the –

(a) CA of the receiving State; and

(b) the relevant local authority.

(3) Where a Convention adoption is made and the Central Authority receives a certificate under Article 23 in respect of that Convention adoption, the relevant Central Authority must send a copy of that certificate to the relevant local authority.

Chapter 3

Miscellaneous Provisions

52 Application, with or without modifications, of the Act

(1) Subject to the modifications provided for in this Chapter, the provisions of the Act shall apply to adoptions within the scope of the Convention so far as the nature of the provision permits and unless the contrary intention is shown.

53 Change of name and removal from the United Kingdom

In a case falling within Chapter 1 of this Part, section 28(2) of the Act shall apply as if –

(a) at the end of paragraph (a), 'or' was omitted;

(b) at the end of paragraph (b) there were inserted 'or (c) a child is placed by a competent foreign authority for the purposes of an adoption under the Convention,'; and

(c) at the end of subsection (2) there were inserted 'or the competent foreign authority consents to a change of surname.'.

54 Removal of children

(1) In a case falling within Chapter 1 of this Part, sections 36 to 40 of the Act shall not apply.

(2) In a case falling within Chapter 2 of this Part –

(a) section 36 of the Act shall apply, as if –

(i) for the words 'an adoption order' in paragraphs (a) and (c) in subsection (1) there were substituted 'a Convention adoption order'; and

(ii) subsection (2) was omitted; and

(b) section 39 of the Act shall apply as if subsection (3)(a) was omitted.

55 Modifications of the Act in respect of orders under section 84 where child is to be adopted under the Convention

The modifications set out in regulation 11 shall apply in the case where a couple or person habitually resident in a Convention country outside the British Islands intend to adopt a child who is habitually resident in England or Wales in accordance with the Convention.

56 Child to live with adopters before application for a Convention adoption order

Section 42 of the Act shall apply as if –

(a) subsections (1)(b) and (3) to (6) were omitted; and

(b) in subsection (2) from the word 'If' to the end of paragraph (b) there were substituted 'In the case of an adoption under the Convention,'.

57 Notice of intention to adopt

Section 44 of the Act shall apply as if subsection (3) was omitted.

58 Application for Convention adoption order

Section 49 of the Act shall apply as if –

(a) in subsection (1), the words from 'but only' to the end were omitted;
(b) subsections (2) and (3) were omitted.

59 Offences

Any person who contravenes or fails to comply with –

(a) regulation 24 (requirements in respect of prospective adopter following child's entry into the United Kingdom);
(b) regulation 26(1) (return of child to relevant local authority where prospective adopter does not wish to proceed);
(c) regulation 27(1)(b) (return of child to relevant local authority on request of local authority or by order of court); or
(d) regulation 33 (refusal of a court in England or Wales to make a Convention adoption order)

is guilty of an offence and liable on summary conviction to imprisonment for a term not exceeding three months, or a fine not exceeding level 5 on the standard scale, or both.

Amendments—SI 2005/3482.

SCHEDULE 1
CERTIFICATE OF ELIGIBILITY AND APPROVAL

To the Central Authority of the State of origin

Re . . . [*name of applicant*]

In accordance with Article 5 of the Convention, I hereby certify on behalf of the Central Authority for [*England*] [*Wales*] that .... [*name of applicant*] has been counselled, is eligible to adopt and has been assessed and approved as suitable to adopt a child from .... [*State of origin*] by .... [*public authority or accredited body for the purposes of the Convention*].

The attached report has been prepared in accordance with Article 15 of the Convention for presentation to the competent authority in .... [*State of origin*].

This certificate of eligibility and approval and the report under Article 15 of the Convention are provided on the condition that a Convention adoption or Convention adoption order will not be made until the agreement under Article 17(c) of the Convention has been made.

I confirm on behalf of the Central Authority that if following the agreement under Article 17(c) of the Convention that –

[in the case, where the requirements specified in section 1(5A) of the British Nationality Act 1981 are met that the child .... [*name*] will be authorised to enter and reside permanently in the United Kingdom]; or

[in any other case, if entry clearance and leave to enter and remain, as may be necessary, is granted and not revoked, or curtailed and a Convention adoption order or Convention adoption is made, the child .... [*name*] will be authorised to enter and reside permanently in the United Kingdom.]

Name

[*On behalf of the Secretary of State, the Central Authority for England*]

Date

[*the National Assembly for Wales, the Central Authority for Wales*]

SCHEDULE 2
CERTIFICATE THAT THE CONVENTION ADOPTION ORDER HAS BEEN MADE IN ACCORDANCE WITH THE CONVENTION

1 The Central Authority as the competent authority for [*England*] [*Wales*] being the country in which the Convention adoption order was made hereby certifies, in accordance with Article 23(1) of the Convention, that the child:

(a) name .... [name on birth certificate, also known as/now known as ....]
sex: ....
date and place of birth: ....
habitual residence at the time of the adoption: ....
State of origin: ....

(b) was adopted on: ....
by order made by: .... court in [*England*] [*Wales*]

(c) by the following person(s):

(i) family name and first name(s): ....
sex: ....
date and place of birth: ....
Habitual residence at the time adoption order was made: ....

(ii) family name and first name(s): ....
sex: ....
date and place of birth: ....
habitual residence at the time adoption order made: ....

2 The competent authority for [*England*] [*Wales*] in pursuance of Article 23(1) of the Convention hereby certifies that the adoption was made in accordance with the Convention and that the agreement under Article 17(c) was given by:

(a) name and address of the Central Authority in State of origin: ....
date of the agreement: ....

(b) name and address of the Central Authority of receiving State: ....
date of the agreement: ....

Signed

Date

PART IV

Care Planning, Placement and Case Review (England) Regulations 2010, SI 2010/959

ARRANGEMENT OF REGULATIONS

PART 1
GENERAL

Regulation		Page
1	Citation and commencement	2398
2	Interpretation	2398
3		2399

PART 2

ARRANGEMENTS FOR LOOKING AFTER A CHILD

4	Care planning	2400
5	Preparation and content of the care plan	2400
6		2401
7	Health care	2401
8ZA	Contact with a child in care	2402
8	Contact with a child in care	2402

PART 3

PLACEMENTS – GENERAL PROVISIONS

9	Placement plan	2402
10	Avoidance of disruption in education	2403

Placement out of area

11	Placement decision	2403
12	Placements outside England and Wales	2404
13	Notification of placement	2404
14	Termination of placement by the responsible authority	2405

PART 4

PROVISION FOR DIFFERENT TYPES OF PLACEMENT

Chapter 1

Placement of a child in care with P

15	Application	2405
16	Effect of contact order	2406
17	Assessment of P's suitability to care for a child	2406
18	Decision to place a child with P	2406
19	Circumstances in which a child may be placed with P before assessment completed	2406
20	Support for P	2406

Chapter 2

Placement with local authority foster parents

21	Interpretation	2407
22	Conditions to be complied with before placing a child with a local authority foster parent	2407
22A	Placement following consideration in accordance with section 22C(9B)(c) of the Act	2407
22B	Conditions to be complied with before placing C in a long term foster placement	2407
23	Emergency placement with a local authority foster parent	2408
24	Temporary approval of relative, friend or other person connected with C	2408
25	Expiry of temporary approval	2408
25A	Temporary approval of prospective adopter as foster parent	2409
26	Independent fostering agencies – discharge of responsible authority functions	2409

Chapter 3

Other arrangements

27	General duties of the responsible authority when placing a child in other arrangements	2410

PART 5

VISITS BY THE RESPONSIBLE AUTHORITY'S REPRESENTATIVE ETC.

28	Frequency of visits	2410
29	Conduct of visits	2411
30	Consequences of visits	2411
31	Advice, support and assistance for the child	2411

PART 6
REVIEWS OF THE CHILD'S CASE

32	General duty of the responsible authority to review the child's case	2411
33	Timing of reviews	2412
34	Conduct of reviews	2412
35	Considerations to which the responsible authority must have regard	2412
36	The role of the IRO	2412
37	Arrangements for implementing decisions arising out of reviews	2413
38	Records of reviews	2413

PART 7
ARRANGEMENTS MADE BY THE RESPONSIBLE AUTHORITY FOR CEASING TO LOOK AFTER A CHILD

39	Arrangements to be made when the responsible authority is considering ceasing to look after C	2413
40	Eligible children	2414
41	General duties	2414
42	Assessment of needs	2414
43	The pathway plan	2415
44	Functions of the personal adviser	2415

PART 8
INDEPENDENT REVIEWING OFFICERS AND INDEPENDENT VISITORS

45	Additional functions of independent reviewing officers	2415
46	Qualifications and experience of independent reviewing officers	2416
47	Independent visitors	2416

PART 8A
APPLICATION OF THESE REGULATIONS WITH MODIFICATIONS TO CHILDREN ON REMAND

47A	Application of these Regulations with modifications to children on remand	2416
47B		2417
47C		2417
47D		2417
47E		2418
47F		2418

PART 9
MISCELLANEOUS

48	Application of these Regulations with modifications to short breaks	2418
49	Records	2419
50	Retention and confidentiality of records	2419
	Schedule 1 – Care plans	2419
	Schedule 2 – Matters to be dealt with in the placement plan	2420
	Schedule 2A – Matters to be dealt with in the detention placement plan	2422
	Schedule 3 – Matters to be taken into account when assessing the suitability of P to care for C	2423
	Schedule 4 – Matters to be taken into account when assessing the suitability of a connected person to care for C	2424
	Schedule 5 – Agreement with an independent fostering agency relating to the discharge of the responsible authority's functions	2425
	Schedule 6 – Matters to be considered before placing C in accommodation in an unregulated setting under section 22(6)(d)	2425
	Schedule 7 – Considerations to which the responsible authority must have regard when reviewing C's case	2426

Schedule 8 – Matters to be dealt with in the pathway plan 2427

PART 1
GENERAL

1 Citation and commencement

(1) These Regulations may be cited as the Care Planning, Placement and Case Review (England) Regulations 2010 and come into force on 1 April 2011.

(2) These Regulations apply in relation to England only.

2 Interpretation

(1) In these Regulations –

'the 1989 Act' means the Children Act 1989;

'the 2012 Act' means the Legal Aid, Sentencing and Punishment of Offenders Act 2012;

'the Fostering Services Regulations' means the Fostering Services (England) Regulations 2011;

'appropriate person' means –

(a) P, where C is to live, or lives, with P;

(b) F, where C is to be placed, or is placed, with F;

(c) where C is to be placed, or is placed, in a children's home, the person who is registered under Part 2 of the Care Standards Act 2000 in respect of that home; or

(d) where C is to be placed, or is placed, in accordance with other arrangements under section 22C(6)(d), the person who will be responsible for C at the accommodation;

'area authority' means the local authority for the area in which C is placed, or is to be placed, where this is different from the responsible authority;

'C' means a child who is looked after by the responsible authority;

'care plan' means the plan for the future care of C prepared in accordance with Part 2;

'case record' has the meaning given in regulation 49;

'connected person' has the meaning given in regulation 24;

'detention placement plan' has the meaning given in regulation 47C;

'director' means the person in charge of a secure training centre;

'director of children's services' means the officer of the responsible authority appointed for the purposes of section 18 of the Children Act 2004;

'F' means a person who is approved as a local authority foster parent and with whom it is proposed to place C or, as the case may be, with whom C is placed;

'fostering service provider' has the meaning given in regulation 2(1) of the Fostering Services Regulations;

'full assessment process' has the meaning given in regulation 24(2)(c);

'governor' means the person in charge of a young offender institution;

'health plan' has the meaning given in regulation 5(b)(i);

'independent visitor' means the independent person appointed to be C's visitor under section 23ZB;

'IRO' means the independent reviewing officer appointed for C's case under section 25A(1);

'long term foster placement' means an arrangement made by the responsible authority for C to be placed with F where –

(a) C's plan for permanence is foster care,

(b) F has agreed to act as C's foster parent until C ceases to be looked after, and

(c) the responsible authority has confirmed the nature of the arrangement to F, P and C,

and any reference to the responsible authority placing C in such a placement includes, where C is already placed with F, leaving C with F in a long term foster placement;

'nominated officer' means a senior officer of the responsible authority nominated in writing by the director of children's services for the purposes of these Regulations;

'P' means –

(a) a person who is C's parent;

(b) a person who is not C's parent but who has parental responsibility for C; or

(c) where C is in the care of the responsible authority and there was a child arrangements order which regulated C's living arrangements in force immediately before the care order was made, a person named in the child arrangements order as a person with whom C was to live;

'pathway plan' has the meaning given in section 23E(1)(a);

'personal adviser' means the personal adviser arranged for C under paragraph 19C of Schedule 2 to the 1989 Act;

'personal education plan' has the meaning given in regulation 5(b)(ii);

'placement' means –

(i) arrangements made by the responsible authority for C to live with P in accordance with section 22C(2), where C is in the care of the responsible authority, or

(ii) arrangements made by the responsible authority to provide for C's accommodation and maintenance by any of the means specified in section 22C(6);

'placement plan' has the meaning given in regulation 9(1)(a);

'plan for permanence' has the meaning given in regulation 5(1)(a);

'R' means the representative of the responsible authority who is appointed to visit C in accordance with arrangements made by them under section 23ZA;

'registered manager' means the person who is registered under Part 2 of the Care Standards Act 2000 as a manager of a secure children's home;

'remand to local authority accommodation' has the meaning given in section 91(3) of the 2012 Act;

'remand to youth detention accommodation' has the meaning given in section 91(4) of the 2012 Act;

'responsible authority' means the local authority that looks after C;

'secure children's home' has the meaning given in section 102(11) of the 2012 Act;

'secure training centre' has the meaning given in section 43(1)(d) of the Prison Act 1952;

'special educational needs' and 'special educational provision' have the meanings given in section 579 of the Education Act 1996;

'temporary approval' has the meaning given in regulation 24(1); and

'working day' means any day other than –

(a) a Saturday or a Sunday,

(b) Christmas day or Good Friday, or

(c) a bank holiday in England and Wales under the Banking and Financial Dealings Act 1971.

'young offender institution' has the meaning given in section 43(1)(aa) of the Prison Act 1952.

(2) In these Regulations any reference to any document or other record includes any such document or record that is kept or provided in a readily accessible form and includes copies of original documents and electronic methods of recording information.

(3) Save as otherwise appears –

(a) any reference in these Regulations to a numbered section is a reference to that section in the 1989 Act; and

(b) any reference in these Regulations to a numbered regulation, Part or Schedule is a reference to that regulation, Part or Schedule in these Regulations.

Amendments—SI 2011/581; SI 2013/706; SI 2014/852; SI 2014/2103; SI 2015/495.

3 These Regulations do not apply in relation to any child who is looked after by a local authority and who has been placed for adoption under the Adoption and Children Act 2002 unless the child falls within regulation 47A.

Amendments—SI 2013/706.

PART 2
ARRANGEMENTS FOR LOOKING AFTER A CHILD

4 Care planning

(1) Where C is not in the care of the responsible authority and a care plan for C has not already been prepared, the responsible authority must assess C's needs for services to achieve or maintain a reasonable standard of health or development, and prepare such a plan.

(2) Except in the case of a child to whom section 31A (care orders: care plans) applies, or where paragraph (6) applies, the care plan must be prepared before C is first placed by the responsible authority or, if it is not practicable to do so, within ten working days of the start of the first placement.

(3) When assessing C's needs under paragraph (1), the responsible authority must consider whether C's placement meets the requirements of Part 3 of the 1989 Act.

(4) Unless paragraph (5) applies, the care plan should, so far as is reasonably practicable, be agreed by the responsible authority with –

- (a) any parent of C's and any person who is not C's parent but who has parental responsibility for C, or
- (b) if there is no such person, the person who was caring for C immediately before the responsible authority arranged a placement for C.

(5) Where C is aged 16 or over and agrees to be provided with accommodation under section 20, the care plan should be agreed with C by the responsible authority.

(6) Where C was first placed by the responsible authority before 1 April 2011, the care plan must be prepared as soon as reasonably practicable.

5 Preparation and content of the care plan

(1) The care plan must include a record of the following information –

- (a) the long term plan for C's upbringing ('the plan for permanence'),
- (b) the arrangements made by the responsible authority to meet C's needs in relation to –
  - (i) health, including the information set out in paragraph 1 of Schedule 1 ('the health plan'),
  - (ii) education and training, including, so far as reasonably practicable, the information set out in paragraph 2 of Schedule 1 ('the personal education plan'),
  - (iii) emotional and behavioural development,
  - (iv) identity, with particular regard to C's religious persuasion, racial origin and cultural and linguistic background,
  - (v) family and social relationships and in particular the information set out in paragraph 3 of Schedule 1,
  - (vi) social presentation, and
  - (vii) self-care skills,
- (c) except in a case where C is in the care of the responsible authority but is not provided with accommodation by them by any of the means specified in section 22C, the placement plan,
- (d) the name of the IRO, and
- (e) details of the wishes and feelings of the persons listed in section 22(4) about the arrangements referred to in sub-paragraph (b) and the placement plan that have been ascertained and considered in accordance with section 22(4) and (5) and the wishes and feelings of those persons in relation to any change, or proposed change, to the care plan.
- (f) where C is –
  - (i) a victim, or there is reason to believe C may be a victim, of trafficking in human beings within the meaning of the Council of Europe Convention on Action against Trafficking in Human Beings,
  - (ii) an unaccompanied asylum seeking child within the meaning of the Immigration

Rules and has applied, or has indicated to the responsible authority an intention to apply, for asylum and has not been granted indefinite leave to remain,

that fact.

(2) In this regulation 'Immigration Rules' means the rules for the time being laid down by the Secretary of State as mentioned in section 3(2) of the Immigration Act 1971.

Amendments—SI 2014/1917.

6 (1) The responsible authority must keep C's care plan under review in accordance with Part 6 and, if they are of the opinion some change is required, they must revise the care plan or prepare a new care plan accordingly.

(2) Save as otherwise provided in these Regulations, the responsible authority must not make any significant change to the care plan unless the proposed change has first been considered at a review of C's case.

(3) Subject to paragraph (4), the responsible authority must give a copy of the care plan –

- (a) to C, unless it would not be appropriate to do so having regard to C's age and understanding,
- (b) to P,
- (c) to the IRO,
- (d) where C is to be placed, or is placed, with F, to the fostering service provider that approved F in accordance with the Fostering Services Regulations,
- (e) where C is to be placed, or is placed, in a children's home, to the person who is registered under Part 2 of the Care Standards Act 2000 in respect of that home, and
- (f) where C is to be placed, or is placed, in accordance with other arrangements under section 22C(6)(d), to the person who will be responsible for C at the accommodation.

(4) The responsible authority may decide not to give a copy of the care plan, or a full copy of the care plan, to P if to do so would put C at risk of significant harm.

Amendments—SI 2011/581.

7 Health care

(1) Before C is first placed by them or, if that is not reasonably practicable, before the first review of C's case, the responsible authority must make arrangements for a registered medical practitioner to –

- (a) carry out an assessment of C's state of health, and
- (b) provide a written report of the assessment, addressing the matters specified in paragraph 1 of Schedule 1,

as soon as reasonably practicable.

(2) Paragraph (1) does not apply if, within a period of three months immediately preceding the placement, an assessment of C's state of health has been carried out and the responsible authority has obtained a written report that meets the requirements of that paragraph.

(3) The responsible authority must make arrangements for a registered medical practitioner or a registered nurse or registered midwife acting under the supervision of a registered medical practitioner to review C's state of health and provide a written report of each review, addressing the matters specified in paragraph 1 of Schedule 1 –

- (a) at least once in every period of six months before C's fifth birthday, and
- (b) at least once in every period of 12 months after C's fifth birthday.

(4) Paragraphs (1) and (3) do not apply if C refuses consent to the assessment, being of sufficient age and understanding to do so.

(5) The responsible authority must take all reasonable steps to ensure that C is provided with appropriate health care services, in accordance with the health plan, including –

- (a) medical and dental care and treatment, and
- (b) advice and guidance on health, personal care and health promotion issues.

8ZA Contact with a child in care

When considering whether contact between C and any of the persons mentioned in paragraphs (a) to (d) of section 34(1) of the 1989 Act is consistent with safeguarding and promoting C's welfare, the responsible authority must have regard to C's care plan.

Amendments—Inserted by SI 2014/1556.

8 Contact with a child in care

(1) This regulation applies if C is in the care of the responsible authority and they have decided under section 34(6) (refusal of contact as a matter of urgency) to refuse to allow contact that would otherwise be required by virtue of section 34(1) or an order under section 34 (parental contact etc. with children in care).

(2) The responsible authority must immediately give written notification to the following persons of the information specified in paragraph (3) ('the specified information') –

- (a) C, unless it would not be appropriate to do so having regard to C's age and understanding,
- (b) P,
- (c) where, immediately before the care order was made, a person had care of C by virtue of an order made in exercise of the High Court's inherent jurisdiction with respect to children, that person,
- (d) any other person whose wishes and feelings the responsible authority consider to be relevant, and
- (e) the IRO.

(3) The specified information is –

- (a) the responsible authority's decision,
- (b) the date of the decision,
- (c) the reasons for the decision,
- (d) the duration of the decision (if applicable), and
- (e) remedies available in case of dissatisfaction.

(4) The responsible authority may depart from the terms of any order made under section 34 by agreement with the person in relation to whom the order is made, provided that –

- (a) C, being of sufficient age and understanding, also agrees, and
- (b) written notification of the specified information is given within five working days to the persons listed in paragraph (2).

(5) Where the responsible authority has decided to vary or suspend any arrangements made (otherwise than under an order under section 34) with a view to affording any person contact with C, the responsible authority must immediately give written notification containing the specified information to the persons listed in paragraph (2).

(6) The responsible authority must record any decision made under this regulation in C's care plan.

PART 3
PLACEMENTS – GENERAL PROVISIONS

9 Placement plan

(1) Subject to paragraphs (2) and (4), before making arrangements in accordance with section 22C for C's placement, the responsible authority must –

- (a) prepare a plan for the placement ('the placement plan') which –
  - (i) sets out how the placement will contribute to meeting C's needs, and
  - (ii) includes all the matters specified in Schedule 2 as are applicable, having regard to the type of the placement, and
- (b) ensure that –
  - (i) C's wishes and feelings have been ascertained and given due consideration, and

(ii) the IRO has been informed.

(2) If it is not reasonably practicable to prepare the placement plan before making the placement, the placement plan must be prepared within five working days of the start of the placement.

(3) The placement plan must be agreed with, and signed by, the appropriate person.

(4) Where the arrangements for C's placement were made before 1 April 2011, the responsible authority must prepare the placement plan as soon as reasonably practicable.

10 Avoidance of disruption in education

(1) Subject to paragraphs (2) and (3), if C is a registered pupil at a school in the fourth key stage, a decision to make any change to C's placement that would have the effect of disrupting the arrangements made for C's education must not be put into effect until it has been approved by a nominated officer.

(2) Before approving a decision under paragraph (1), the nominated officer must be satisfied that –

(a) the requirements of regulation 9(1)(b)(i) have been complied with,
(b) the educational provision made for C at the placement will promote C's educational achievement and is consistent with C's personal education plan,
(c) the designated teacher at the school has been consulted, and
(d) the IRO has been consulted.

(3) Paragraph (1) does not apply in any case where –

(a) the responsible authority terminates C's placement in accordance with regulation 14(3), or
(b) it is necessary for any other reason to change C's placement in an emergency,

and in such a case the responsible authority must make appropriate arrangements to promote C's educational achievement as soon as reasonably practicable.

(4) In any case not falling within paragraph (1), but where the responsible authority propose making any change to C's placement that would have the effect of disrupting the arrangements made for C's education or training, the responsible authority must ensure that other arrangements are made for C's education or training that meet C's needs and are consistent with C's personal education plan.

(5) In this regulation –

(a) 'registered pupil' has the meaning given in section 20(7) of the Children and Young Persons Act 2008, and
(b) 'school' has the meaning given in section 4 of the Education Act 1996.

Placement out of area

11 Placement decision

(1) Subject to paragraphs (2) to (4), a decision to place C outside the area of the responsible authority (including a placement outside England) –

(a) must not be put into effect until it has been approved by a nominated officer, or
(b) in the case of a proposed placement which is also at a distance, must not be put into effect until it has been approved by the director of children's services.

(2) Before approving a decision under paragraph (1), the nominated officer or, as the case may be, the director of children's services must be satisfied that –

(a) the requirements of regulation 9(1)(b)(i) have been complied with,
(b) the placement is the most appropriate placement available for C and consistent with C's care plan,
(c) C's relatives have been consulted, where appropriate,
(d) in the case of a decision falling within –
   (i) paragraph (1)(a), the area authority have been notified, or

(ii) paragraph (1)(b), the area authority have been consulted and have been provided with a copy of C's care plan, and

(e) the IRO has been consulted.

(3) In the case of a placement made in an emergency, paragraph (2) does not apply and before approving a decision under paragraph (1) the nominated officer must –

(a) be satisfied that regulation 9(1)(b)(i) and the requirements of sub-paragraph (2)(b) have been complied with, and

(b) take steps to ensure that regulation 9(1)(b)(ii) and the requirements set out in sub-paragraphs (2)(c) and (d) are complied with by the responsible authority within five working days of approval of the decision under paragraph (1).

(4) Paragraphs (1) and (2) do not apply to a decision to place C outside the area of the responsible authority with –

(a) F who is a connected person, or

(b) F who is approved as a local authority foster parent by the responsible authority.

(5) In this regulation 'at a distance' means outside the area of the responsible authority and not within the area of any adjoining local authority.

Amendments—SI 2013/3239.

12 Placements outside England and Wales

(1) This regulation applies if –

(a) C is in the care of the responsible authority, and

(b) the responsible authority make arrangements to place C outside England and Wales in accordance with the provisions of paragraph 19 of Schedule 2 to the 1989 Act (placement of a child in care outside England and Wales).

(2) The responsible authority must take steps to ensure that, so far as is reasonably practicable, requirements corresponding with the requirements which would have applied under these Regulations had C been placed in England, are complied with.

(3) The responsible authority must include in the care plan details of the arrangements made by the responsible authority to supervise C's placement.

13 Notification of placement

(1) Subject to paragraph (3), the responsible authority must give written notification to the persons listed in paragraph (2) of the arrangements for C's placement before the placement is made or, if the placement is made in an emergency, within five working days of the start of the placement, unless it is not reasonably practicable to do so.

(2) The persons referred to in paragraph (1) are –

(a) C, unless it would not be appropriate to do so having regard to C's age and understanding,

(b) P,

(c) if C is in the care of the responsible authority, any person who is allowed contact with C under section 34(1) and any person who has contact with C by virtue of an order under section 34,

(d) if C is looked after but is not in the care of the responsible authority, any person who has contact with C pursuant to an order made under section 8 (residence, contact and other orders with respect to children),

(e) any person who was caring for C immediately before the arrangements were made,

(f) the National Health Service Commissioning Board and the clinical commissioning group (or in the case of a child living or to be placed in Wales, the local health board) for the area in which C is living and, if different, for the area in which C is to be placed,

(g) C's registered medical practitioner and, where applicable, the registered medical practitioner with whom C is to be registered during the placement,

(h) any educational institution attended by, or person providing education or training for, C, and

(i) the IRO.

(3) The responsible authority may decide not to give notification to any of the persons listed in sub-paragraphs (b) to (e) if to do so would put C at risk of significant harm.

(4) In the case of a placement outside the area of the responsible authority (including a placement outside England) –

(a) the responsible authority must give written notification to the area authority of the arrangements for C's placement before the placement is made or, if the placement is made in an emergency, within five working days of the start of the placement unless it is not reasonably practicable to do so, and

(b) that notification must include –

(i) details of the responsible authority's assessment of C's needs and the reasons why the placement is the most suitable for responding to these,

(ii) a copy of C's care plan (where this has not already been provided to the area authority by virtue of regulation 11(2)(d)(ii)).

Amendments—SI 2013/235; SI 2013/3239.

14 Termination of placement by the responsible authority

(1) Subject to paragraphs (3) and (5), the responsible authority may only terminate C's placement following a review of C's case in accordance with Part 6.

(2) Subject to paragraphs (3) and (4), before terminating C's placement, the responsible authority must –

(a) make other arrangements for C's accommodation, in accordance with section 22C,

(b) inform the IRO,

(c) so far as is reasonably practicable, give written notification of their intention to terminate the placement to –

(i) all the persons to whom notification of the placement was given under regulation 13,

(ii) the person with whom C is placed,

(iii) where C is placed in the area of another local authority, that authority.

(3) Where there is an immediate risk of significant harm to C, or to protect others from serious injury, the responsible authority must terminate C's placement, and in those circumstances –

(a) paragraph (1) does not apply, and

(b) they must comply with paragraph (2)(a) and (b) as soon as reasonably practicable.

(4) If it is not reasonably practicable to notify any person in accordance with paragraph (2)(c), then the responsible authority must give written notification to that person, within ten working days of the date on which the placement is terminated, of the fact that the placement has been terminated.

(5) This regulation does not apply where C's placement is terminated under regulation 19(c), regulation 23(2) or regulation 25(6), nor where section 22D (review of child's case before making alternative arrangements for accommodation) applies.

PART 4
PROVISION FOR DIFFERENT TYPES OF PLACEMENT

Chapter 1
Placement of a child in care with P

15 Application

(1) This Chapter applies if C is in the care of the responsible authority and they, acting in accordance with section 22C(2), propose to place C with P.

(2) Nothing in this Chapter requires the responsible authority to remove C from P's care if C is living with P before a placement decision is made about C.

16 Effect of contact order

The responsible authority must not place C with P if to do so would be incompatible with any order made by the court under section 34.

17 Assessment of P's suitability to care for a child

Before deciding to place C with P, the responsible authority must –

- (a) assess the suitability of P to care for C, including the suitability of –
  - (i) the proposed accommodation, and
  - (ii) all other persons aged 18 and over who are members of the household in which it is proposed that C will live,
- (b) take into account all the matters set out in Schedule 3 in making their assessment,
- (c) consider whether, in all the circumstances and taking into account the services to be provided by the responsible authority, the placement will safeguard and promote C's welfare and meet C's needs set out in the care plan, and
- (d) review C's case in accordance with Part 6.

18 Decision to place a child with P

(1) The decision to place C with P must not be put into effect until it has been approved by a nominated officer, and the responsible authority have prepared a placement plan for C.

(2) Before approving a decision under paragraph (1), the nominated officer must be satisfied that –

- (a) the requirements of regulation 9(1)(b)(i) have been complied with,
- (b) the requirements of regulation 17 have been complied with,
- (c) the placement will safeguard and promote C's welfare, and
- (d) the IRO has been consulted.

19 Circumstances in which a child may be placed with P before assessment completed

Where the nominated officer considers it to be necessary and consistent with C's welfare, the responsible authority may place C with P before their assessment under regulation 17 ('the assessment') is completed provided that they –

- (a) arrange for P to be interviewed in order to obtain as much of the information specified in Schedule 3 about P and the other persons living in P's household who are aged 18 and over as can be readily ascertained at that interview,
- (b) ensure that the assessment and the review of C's case are completed in accordance with regulation 17 within ten working days of C being placed with P, and
- (c) ensure that a decision in accordance with regulation 18 is made and approved within ten working days after the assessment is completed, and –
  - (i) if the decision is to confirm the placement, review the placement plan and, if appropriate amend it, and
  - (ii) if the decision is not to confirm the placement, terminate the placement.

20 Support for P

Where C is placed, or is to be placed, with P, the responsible authority must provide such services and support to P as appear to them to be necessary to safeguard and promote C's welfare and must record details of such services and support in C's care plan.

Chapter 2
Placement with local authority foster parents

21 Interpretation

(1) In this Chapter 'registered person' has the same meaning as in the Fostering Services Regulations.

(2) Where C is placed jointly with two persons each of whom is approved as a local authority foster parent, any reference in these Regulations to a local authority foster parent is to be interpreted as referring equally to both such persons and any requirement to be satisfied by or relating to a particular local authority foster parent must be satisfied by, or treated as relating to, both of them.

Amendments—SI 2011/581.

22 Conditions to be complied with before placing a child with a local authority foster parent

(1) This regulation applies where the responsible authority propose to place C with F.

(2) The responsible authority may only place C with F if –

- (a) F is approved by –
  - (i) the responsible authority, or
  - (ii) provided that the conditions specified in paragraph (3) are also satisfied, another fostering service provider,
- (b) the terms of F's approval are consistent with the proposed placement, and
- (c) F has entered into a foster care agreement either with the responsible authority or with another fostering service provider in accordance with regulation 27(5)(b) of the Fostering Services Regulations.

(3) The conditions referred to in paragraph (2)(a)(ii) are that –

- (a) the fostering service provider by whom F is approved consents to the proposed placement, and
- (b) where any other local authority currently have a child placed with F, that local authority consents to the proposed placement.

Amendments—SI 2011/581.

22A Placement following consideration in accordance with section 22C(9B)(c) of the Act

(1) This regulation applies where the responsible authority decides to place C in accordance with section 22C of the 1989 Act with a local authority foster parent who is also an approved prospective adopter following consideration in accordance with section 22C(9B)(c) of the 1989 Act.

(2) The decision to place C must not be put into effect until it has been approved by a nominated officer, and the responsible authority have prepared a placement plan for C.

(3) Before approving a decision under paragraph (2), the nominated officer must –

- (a) be satisfied that the placement is the most appropriate placement available for C and will safeguard and promote C's welfare;
- (b) be satisfied that the requirements of regulation 9(1)(b) have been complied with; and
- (c) if their whereabouts are known to the responsible authority, notify the parent or guardian of C of the proposed placement.

Amendments—Inserted by SI 2014/1556.

22B Conditions to be complied with before placing C in a long term foster placement

(1) This regulation applies where the responsible authority propose to place C with F in a long term foster placement.

(2) The responsible authority may only place C with F if –

PART IV

(a) the responsible authority have prepared a placement plan for C,
(b) the requirements of regulation 9(1)(b)(i) have been complied with,
(c) the placement will safeguard and promote C's welfare,
(d) the IRO has been consulted,
(e) C's relatives have been consulted, where appropriate, and
(f) F intends to act as C's foster parent until C ceases to be looked after.

Amendments—Inserted by SI 2015/495.

23 Emergency placement with a local authority foster parent

(1) Where it is necessary to place C in an emergency, the responsible authority may place C with any local authority foster parent who has been approved in accordance with the Fostering Services Regulations, even if the terms of that approval are not consistent with the placement, provided that the placement is for no longer than six working days.

(2) When the period of six working days referred to in paragraph (1) expires, the responsible authority must terminate the placement unless the terms of that person's approval have been amended to be consistent with the placement.

Amendments—SI 2011/581.

24 Temporary approval of relative, friend or other person connected with C

(1) Where the responsible authority is satisfied that –

(a) the most appropriate placement for C is with a connected person, notwithstanding that the connected person is not approved as a local authority foster parent, and
(b) it is necessary for C to be placed with the connected person before the connected person's suitability to be a local authority foster parent has been assessed in accordance with the Fostering Services Regulations,

they may approve that person as a local authority foster parent for a temporary period not exceeding 16 weeks ('temporary approval') provided that they first comply with the requirements of paragraph (2).

(2) Before making a placement under paragraph (1), the responsible authority must –

(a) assess the suitability of the connected person to care for C, including the suitability of –
 (i) the proposed accommodation, and
 (ii) all other persons aged 18 and over who are members of the household in which it is proposed that C will live,

 taking into account all the matters set out in Schedule 4,
(b) consider whether, in all the circumstances and taking into account the services to be provided by the responsible authority, the proposed arrangements will safeguard and promote C's welfare and meet C's needs set out in the care plan, and
(c) make immediate arrangements for the suitability of the connected person to be a local authority foster parent to be assessed in accordance with the Fostering Services Regulations ('the full assessment process') before the temporary approval expires.

(3) In this regulation 'connected person' means a relative, friend or other person connected with C.

Amendments—SI 2011/581.

25 Expiry of temporary approval

(1) Subject to paragraph (4), the responsible authority may extend the temporary approval of a connected person if –

(a) it is likely to expire before the full assessment process is completed, or
(b) the connected person, having undergone the full assessment process, is not approved and seeks a review of the decision in accordance with Regulations made under paragraph 12F(1)(b) of Schedule 2 to the 1989 Act.

(2) In a case falling within paragraph (1)(a), the responsible authority may extend the temporary approval once for a further period of up to eight weeks.

(3) In a case falling within paragraph (1)(b), the responsible authority may extend the temporary approval until the outcome of the review is known.

(4) Before deciding whether to extend the temporary approval in the circumstances set out in paragraph (1), the responsible authority must first –

- (a) consider whether placement with the connected person is still the most appropriate placement available,
- (b) seek the views of the fostering panel established by the fostering service provider in accordance with the Fostering Services Regulations, and
- (c) inform the IRO.

(5) A decision to extend temporary approval must be approved by a nominated officer.

(6) If the period of temporary approval and of any extension to that period expires and the connected person has not been approved as a local authority foster parent in accordance with the Fostering Services Regulations, the responsible authority must terminate the placement after first making other arrangements for C's accommodation.

Amendments—SI 2011/581.

25A Temporary approval of prospective adopter as foster parent

(1) Where the responsible authority is satisfied that –

- (a) the most appropriate placement for C is with a person who is not approved as a local authority foster parent, but who is an approved prospective adopter, and
- (b) it is in C's best interests to be placed with that person,

the responsible authority may approve that person as a local authority foster parent in relation to C for a temporary period ('temporary approval period') provided that the responsible authority first comply with the requirements of paragraph (2).

(2) Before approving an approved prospective adopter as a local authority foster parent under paragraph (1), the responsible authority must –

- (a) assess the suitability of that person to care for C as a foster parent, and
- (b) consider whether, in all the circumstances and taking into account the services to be provided by the responsible authority, the proposed arrangements will safeguard and promote C's welfare and meet C's needs set out in the care plan.

(3) The temporary approval period expires –

- (a) on C's placement with the approved prospective adopter being terminated by the responsible authority,
- (b) on the approved prospective adopter's approval as a prospective adopter being terminated,
- (c) on the approved prospective adopter being approved as a foster parent in accordance with the Fostering Services Regulations,
- (d) if the approved prospective adopter gives written notice to the responsible authority that they no longer wish to be temporarily approved as a foster parent in relation to C, with effect from 28 days from the date on which the notice is received by the responsible authority, or
- (e) on C being placed for adoption with the approved prospective adopter in accordance with the Adoption and Children Act 2002.

(4) In this regulation 'approved prospective adopter' means a person who has been approved as suitable to adopt a child under the Adoption Agencies Regulations 2005 and whose approval has not been terminated.

Amendments—Inserted by SI 2013/984.

26 Independent fostering agencies – discharge of responsible authority functions

(1) A responsible authority may make arrangements in accordance with this regulation for the duties imposed on it as responsible authority by regulation 14(3) and regulation 22 to be discharged on their behalf by a registered person.

(2) No arrangements may be made under this regulation unless the responsible authority has entered into a written agreement with the registered person which includes the information set out in paragraph 1 of Schedule 5, and where the responsible authority proposes to make an arrangement under this regulation in relation to a particular child, the written agreement must also include the matters set out in paragraph 2 of Schedule 5.

(3) The responsible authority must report to the Chief Inspector of Education, Children's Services and Skills any concerns they may have about the services provided by a registered person.

Chapter 3
Other arrangements

27 General duties of the responsible authority when placing a child in other arrangements

Before placing C in accommodation in an unregulated setting under section 22C(6)(d), the responsible authority must –

- (a) be satisfied that the accommodation is suitable for C, having regard to the matters set out in Schedule 6,
- (b) unless it is not reasonably practicable, arrange for C to visit the accommodation, and
- (c) inform the IRO.

PART 5
VISITS BY THE RESPONSIBLE AUTHORITY'S REPRESENTATIVE ETC.

28 Frequency of visits

(1) As part of their arrangements for supervising C's welfare, the responsible authority must ensure that their representative ('R') visits C in accordance with this regulation, wherever C is living.

(2) Subject to paragraphs (3) to (6), the responsible authority must ensure that R visits C –

- (a) within one week of the start of any placement,
- (b) at intervals of not more than six weeks for the first year of any placement, and
- (c) thereafter –
  - (i) where the placement is intended to last until C is aged 18, at intervals of not more than three months,
  - (ii) and in any other case, at intervals of not more than six weeks.

(3) Where regulation 19 applies, the responsible authority must ensure that R visits C –

- (a) at least once a week until the first review carried out in accordance with Part 6, and
- (b) thereafter at intervals of not more than six weeks.

(3A) Where –

- (a) C is in a long term foster placement and has been in that placement for at least one year, and
- (b) C, being of sufficient age and understanding, agrees to be visited less frequently than required by paragraph (2)(c),

the responsible authority must ensure that R visits C at intervals of no more than 6 months.

(4) Where regulation 24 applies, or where an interim care order has been made in relation to C under section 38 (interim orders) and C is living with P, the responsible authority must ensure that R visits C –

- (a) at least once a week until the first review carried out in accordance with Part 6, and
- (b) thereafter at intervals of not more than four weeks.

(5) Where a care order has been made in relation to C under section 31 (care and supervision orders) and C is living with P, the responsible authority must ensure that R visits C –

- (a) within one week of the making of the care order, and

(b) thereafter at intervals of not more than six weeks.

(6) Where C is in the care of the responsible authority but another person is responsible for the arrangements under which C is living for the time being ('C's living arrangements'), the responsible authority must ensure that R visits C –

(a) within one week of the start of C's living arrangements and within one week of any change to C's living arrangements,

(b) at intervals of not more than six weeks for the first year thereafter, and

(c) at intervals of not more than three months in any subsequent year.

(7) In addition to visits in accordance with paragraphs (2) to (6), the responsible authority must ensure that R visits C –

(a) whenever reasonably requested to do so by –

(i) C,

(ii) where paragraphs (2), (3), (3A) or (4) apply, the appropriate person, or

(iii) where paragraph (5) applies, the person responsible for C's living arrangements,

(b) within one week of first receiving notification under section 30A of the Care Standards Act 2000 (notification of matters relating to persons carrying on or managing certain establishments or agencies), where the children's home in which C is placed for the time being is referred to in that notification.

Amendments—SI 2015/495.

29 Conduct of visits

On each visit, R must speak to C in private unless –

(a) C, being of sufficient age and understanding to do so, refuses,

(b) R considers it inappropriate to do so, having regard to C's age and understanding, or

(c) R is unable to do so.

30 Consequences of visits

Where, as the result of a visit carried out in accordance with this Part, R's assessment is that C's welfare is not adequately safeguarded and promoted by the placement, the responsible authority must review C's case in accordance with Part 6.

31 Advice, support and assistance for the child

When making arrangements in accordance with section 23ZA(2)(b) for advice, support and assistance to be available to C between R's visits, the responsible authority must ensure that –

(a) the arrangements –

(i) are appropriate having regard to C's age and understanding, and

(ii) give due consideration to C's religious persuasion, racial origin, cultural and linguistic background and to any disability C may have, and

(b) so far as is reasonably practicable having regard to C's age and understanding, C knows how to seek appropriate advice, support and assistance from them.

PART 6
REVIEWS OF THE CHILD'S CASE

32 General duty of the responsible authority to review the child's case

(1) The responsible authority must review C's case in accordance with this Part.

(2) The responsible authority must not make any significant change to C's care plan unless the proposed change has first been considered at a review of C's case, unless this is not reasonably practicable.

(3) Nothing in this Part prevents any review of C's case being carried out at the same time as any other review assessment or consideration of C's case under any other provision.

33 Timing of reviews

(1) The responsible authority must first review C's case within 20 working days of the date on which C becomes looked after.

(2) The second review must be carried out not more than three months after the first, and subsequent reviews must be carried out at intervals of not more than six months.

(3) The responsible authority must carry out a review before the time specified in paragraph (1) or (2) if –

(aa) the responsible authority considers that C is, or has been, persistently absent from a placement,

(ab) the responsible authority is notified that the appropriate person, P, or the area authority is concerned that C is at risk of harm,

(ac) subject to paragraph (4), C so requests,

(a) the IRO so requests,

(b) regulation 30 applies,

(c) C is provided with accommodation under section 21(2)(b) or (c) and a review would not otherwise occur before C ceases to be so provided with accommodation,

(d) C is in the care of the responsible authority and is detained in a secure training centre or a young offenders institution, and a review would not otherwise occur before C ceases to be so detained, or

(e) C is looked after but is not in the care of the responsible authority and

(i) the responsible authority propose to cease to provide accommodation for C, and

(ii) accommodation will not subsequently be provided for C by C's parents (or one of them) or any person who is not C's parent but who has parental responsibility for C.

(4) The responsible authority is not required to carry out a review pursuant to sub-paragraph (3)(ac) if the IRO considers that a review before the time specified in paragraph (1) or (2) is not justified.

Amendments—SI 2013/3239.

34 Conduct of reviews

Local authority's policy on reviews

(1) The responsible authority must prepare and implement a written policy regarding the manner in which they will review cases in accordance with this Part.

(2) The responsible authority must provide a copy of their policy to –

(a) C, unless it would not be appropriate to do so having regard to C's age and understanding,

(b) C's parents, or any person who is not C's parent but who has parental responsibility for C, and

(c) any other person whose views the responsible authority consider to be relevant.

35 Considerations to which the responsible authority must have regard

The considerations to which the responsible authority must have regard in reviewing each case are set out in Schedule 7.

36 The role of the IRO

(1) The IRO must –

(a) so far as reasonably practicable, attend any meeting held as part of the review ('the review meeting') and, if attending the review meeting, chair it,

(b) speak to C in private about the matters to be considered at the review unless C, being of sufficient understanding to do so, refuses or the IRO considers it inappropriate having regard to C's age and understanding,

(c) ensure that, so far as reasonably practicable, the wishes and feelings of C's parents, or any person who is not C's parent but who has parental responsibility for C, and the views of the appropriate person, have been ascertained and taken into account, and

(d) ensure that the review is conducted in accordance with this Part and in particular –

(i) that the persons responsible for implementing any decision taken in consequence of the review are identified, and

(ii) that any failure to review the case in accordance with this Part or to take proper steps to implement decisions taken in consequence of the review are brought to the attention of an officer at an appropriate level of seniority within the responsible authority.

(2) The IRO may, if not satisfied that sufficient information has been provided by the responsible authority to enable proper consideration of any of the matters in Schedule 7, adjourn the review meeting once for not more than 20 working days, and no proposal considered in the course of the review may be implemented until the review has been completed.

Amendments—SI 2015/495.

37 Arrangements for implementing decisions arising out of reviews

The responsible authority must –

(a) make arrangements to implement decisions made in the course, or as a result, of the review, and

(b) inform the IRO of any significant failure to make such arrangements, or any significant change of circumstances occurring after the review that affects those arrangements.

38 Records of reviews

The responsible authority must ensure that a written record of the review is prepared, and that the information obtained in the course of the review, details of proceedings at the review meeting, and any decisions made in the course, or as a result, of the review are included in C's case record.

PART 7

ARRANGEMENTS MADE BY THE RESPONSIBLE AUTHORITY FOR CEASING TO LOOK AFTER A CHILD

39 Arrangements to be made when the responsible authority is considering ceasing to look after C

(1) This regulation applies where the responsible authority are considering ceasing to look after C.

(2) Before deciding to cease to look after C the responsible authority must –

(a) carry out an assessment of the suitability of the proposed arrangements for C's accommodation and maintenance when C ceases to be looked after by them,

(b) carry out an assessment of the services and support that C and, where applicable P, might need when the responsible authority ceases to look after C,

(c) ensure that C's wishes and feelings have been ascertained and given due consideration, and

(d) consider whether, in all the circumstances and taking into account any services or support the responsible authority intend to provide, that ceasing to look after C will safeguard and promote C's welfare.

(3) The responsible authority must include in C's care plan (or where regulation 47B(4) applies, the detention placement plan) details of the advice, assistance and support that the responsible authority intend to provide for C when C ceases to be looked after by them.

(4) Subject to paragraph (5), where C has been a looked after child for at least 20 working days, any decision to cease to look after C must not be put into effect until it has been approved by a nominated officer.

(5) In any case where C is aged 16 or 17 and is not in the care of the local authority, the decision to cease to look after C must not be put into effect until it has been approved by the responsible authority's director of children's services.

(6) Before approving a decision under paragraph (4) or (5), the nominated officer or director of children's services must be satisfied that –

(a) the requirements of regulation 9(1)(b)(i) have been complied with,
(b) ceasing to look after C will safeguard and promote C's welfare,
(c) the support the responsible authority intend to provide will safeguard and promote C's welfare,
(d) C's relatives have been consulted, where appropriate,
(e) the IRO has been consulted, and
(f) where appropriate, regulations 40 to 43 have been complied with.

Amendments—Last substituted by SI 2015/495.

40 Eligible children

Meaning of eligible child

(1) For the purposes of paragraph 19B(2)(b) of Schedule 2 to the 1989 Act (meaning of eligible child), the prescribed period is 13 weeks and the prescribed age is 14.

(2) For the purposes of paragraph 19B(3)(b) of that Schedule, if C is a child to whom regulation 48 applies, C is not an eligible child despite falling within paragraph 19B(2) of that Schedule.

41 General duties

If C is an eligible child, the responsible authority must –

(a) assess C's needs in accordance with regulation 42, and
(b) prepare C's pathway plan, in accordance with regulation 43.

42 Assessment of needs

(1) The responsible authority must complete the assessment of C's needs in accordance with paragraph 19B(4) of Schedule 2 to the 1989 Act not more than three months after the date on which C reaches the age of 16 or becomes an eligible child after that age.

(2) In carrying out their assessment of C's likely needs when C ceases to be looked after, the responsible authority must take account of the following considerations –

(a) C's state of health (including physical, emotional and mental health) and development,
(b) C's continuing need for education, training or employment,
(ba) where C falls within regulation 5(1)(f), any needs C has as a result of that status,
(c) the support that will be available to C from C's parents and other connected persons,
(d) C's actual and anticipated financial resources and capacity to manage personal finances independently,
(e) the extent to which C possesses the practical and other skills necessary for independent living,
(f) C's need for continuing care, support and accommodation,
(g) the wishes and feelings of –
   (i) C,
   (ii) any parent of C's and any person who is not C's parent but who has parental responsibility for C,
   (iii) the appropriate person,
(h) the views of –
   (i) any person or educational institution that provides C with education or training and, if C has a statement of special educational needs, the local authority who maintain the statement (if different),
   (ii) the IRO,
   (iii) any person providing health (whether physical, emotional or mental health) or dental care or treatment to C,
   (iv) the personal adviser appointed for C, and

(v) any other person whose views the responsible authority, or C, consider may be relevant.

Amendments—SI 2014/1917.

43 The pathway plan

(1) The pathway plan must be prepared as soon as possible after the assessment of C's needs and must include, in particular –

(a) C's care plan, and
(b) the information referred to in Schedule 8.

(2) The pathway plan must, in relation to each of the matters referred to in paragraphs 2 to 10 of Schedule 8, set out –

(a) the manner in which the responsible authority propose to meet C's needs, and
(b) the date by which, and by whom, any action required to implement any aspect of the plan will be carried out.

44 Functions of the personal adviser

The personal adviser's functions in relation to C are to –

(a) provide advice (including practical advice) and support,
(b) participate in reviews of C's case carried out under Part 6,
(c) liaise with the responsible authority in the implementation of the pathway plan,
(d) co-ordinate the provision of services and take reasonable steps to ensure C makes use of such services,
(e) remain informed about C's progress and wellbeing, and
(f) maintain a written record of their contacts with C.

PART 8
INDEPENDENT REVIEWING OFFICERS AND INDEPENDENT VISITORS

45 Additional functions of independent reviewing officers

(1) The IRO must ensure that, having regard to C's age and understanding, C has been informed by the responsible authority of the steps C may take under the 1989 Act and in particular, where appropriate, of –

(a) C's rights to apply, with leave, for a section 8 order (residence, contact and other orders with respect to children) and, where C is in the care of the responsible authority, to apply for the discharge of the care order, and
(b) the availability of the procedure established by them under section 26(3) for considering any representations (including complaints) C may wish to make about the discharge by the responsible authority of their functions, including the availability of assistance to make such representations under section 26A (advocacy services).

(2) If C wishes to take legal proceedings under the 1989 Act, the IRO must –

(a) establish whether an appropriate adult is able and willing to assist C to obtain legal advice or bring proceedings on C's behalf, and
(b) if there is no such person, assist C to obtain such advice.

(3) In the following circumstances the IRO must consider whether it would be appropriate to refer C's case to an officer of the Children and Family Court Advisory and Support Service –

(a) in the opinion of the IRO, the responsible authority have failed in any significant respect to –
(i) prepare C's care plan in accordance with these Regulations,
(ii) review C's case in accordance with these Regulations, or effectively implement any decision taken in consequence of a review,
or are otherwise in breach of their duties to C in any material respect, and
(b) having drawn the failure or breach to the attention of persons at an appropriate level of

seniority within the responsible authority, it has not been addressed to the satisfaction of the IRO within a reasonable period of time.

(4) When consulted by the responsible authority about any matter concerning C, or when informed of any matter relating to C in accordance with these Regulations, the IRO must –

- (a) ensure that the responsible authority have ascertained and, subject to C's age and understanding, given due consideration to, C's wishes and feelings concerning the matter in question, and
- (b) consider whether to request a review of C's case.

46 Qualifications and experience of independent reviewing officers

(1) The IRO must be registered as a social worker in Part 16 of the register maintained by the Health and Care Professions Council under article 5 of the Health and Social Work Professions Order 2001, in the register maintained by Social Care Wales under section 80 of the Regulation and Inspection of Social Care (Wales) Act 2016, or in a corresponding register maintained under the law of Scotland or Northern Ireland.

(2) The IRO must have sufficient relevant social work experience with children and families to perform the functions of an independent reviewing officer set out in section 25B(1) and under these Regulations in an independent manner and having regard to C's best interests.

(3) The responsible authority must not appoint any of the following as the IRO –

- (a) a person involved in preparing C's care plan or the management of C's case,
- (b) R,
- (c) C's personal adviser,
- (d) a person with management responsibilities in relation to a person mentioned in sub-paragraphs (a) to (c), or
- (e) a person with control over the resources allocated to the case.

Amendments—SI 2012/1479; SI 2017/52.

47 Independent visitors

A person appointed by the responsible authority as an independent visitor under section 23ZB(1) is to be regarded as independent of that authority where the person appointed is not connected with the responsible authority by virtue of being –

- (a) a member of the responsible authority or any of their committees or sub-committees, whether elected or co-opted,
- (b) an officer of the responsible authority employed in relation to the exercise of the functions referred to in section 18(2) of the Children Act 2004, or
- (c) a spouse, civil partner or other person (whether of different sex or the same sex) living in the same household as the partner of a person falling within sub-paragraph (a) or (b).

PART 8A

APPLICATION OF THESE REGULATIONS WITH MODIFICATIONS TO CHILDREN ON REMAND

47A Application of these Regulations with modifications to children on remand

(1) These Regulations apply with the modifications set out in this Part while C is –

- (a) remanded to local authority accommodation, or
- (b) remanded to youth detention accommodation ('YDA').

(2) In these Regulations –

- (a) where C is remanded to local authority accommodation, or to YDA, references to 'the responsible authority' are to be read as if they were references to the local authority designated by the court under section 92(2) or section 102(6), as the case may be, of the 2012 Act,

(b) where C is remanded to YDA, references to C being 'placed' are to be read as if they were references to C being so remanded,

(c) where C is remanded to YDA, references to the 'placement plan' (and where C is a looked after child only by reason of being so remanded, references to the 'care plan') are to be read as if they were references to the 'detention placement plan'.

Amendments—Inserted by SI 2013/706.

47B (1) Part 2 (arrangements for looking after a child) applies with the following modifications.

(2) Where C is a looked after child only by reason of being remanded to local authority accommodation –

(a) in regulation 4(2), the care plan must be prepared within five working days of C being so remanded, and

(b) regulation 5(a) does not apply.

(3) Where C is remanded to YDA and was a looked after child immediately before being so remanded –

(a) regulation 5(c) does not apply, and instead the care plan must include a detention placement plan,

(b) in regulation 6(3), the responsible authority must also give a copy of the care plan to the director, governor or registered manager (as the case may be) of the YDA,

(c) regulation 7(1) to (4) does not apply.

(4) Where C is a looked after child only by reason of being remanded to YDA –

(a) regulation 5 does not apply, and instead the responsible authority must prepare a detention placement plan, which also includes details of the wishes and feelings of the persons listed in section 22(4) about the detention placement plan that have been ascertained and considered in accordance with section 22(4) and (5), and the wishes and feelings of those persons in relation to any change, or proposed change, to the detention placement plan,

(b) regulation 7(1) to (4) does not apply, and regulation 7(5) applies with the modification that for 'health plan' there is substituted 'detention placement plan'.

Amendments—Inserted by SI 2013/706.

47C (1) Part 3 (placements) applies with the following modifications.

(2) Where C is remanded to YDA, regulations 9, 10, 11 and 14 do not apply, and instead –

(a) the responsible authority must prepare a plan for the remand ('the detention placement plan') within ten working days of C's remand to YDA which –

(i) sets out how the YDA will meet C's needs, and

(ii) includes the address of the YDA and all the matters specified in Schedule 2A,

(b) the responsible authority must ensure –

(i) that C's wishes and feelings have been ascertained and given due consideration,

(ii) where C was looked after immediately before being so remanded, that the IRO has been informed of the remand,

(c) the detention placement plan must be agreed with, and signed by, the director, governor or registered manager (as the case may be) of the YDA.

(3) Where C is remanded to local authority accommodation, regulation 9(1) applies with the modification that the placement plan must be prepared within five working days of C being so remanded.

47D Part 4 (provision for different types of placement) does not apply where C is remanded to YDA.

Amendments—Inserted by SI 2013/706.

PART IV

47E Part 5 (visits by the responsible authority's representative etc.) applies with the modification that in regulation 28(7)(a), the responsible authority must also ensure that R visits C, where C is remanded to YDA, whenever reasonably requested to do so by the director, governor or registered manager (as the case may be) of the YDA.

Amendments—Inserted by SI 2013/706.

47F Part 6 (reviews) applies with the modification that in regulation 35, the considerations to which the responsible authority must have regard in reviewing C's case where C is remanded to YDA, are set out in paragraphs 1, 4, and 6 to 13, of Schedule 7 (considerations to which the responsible authority must have regard when reviewing C's case).

Amendments—Inserted by SI 2013/706.

PART 9
MISCELLANEOUS

48 Application of these Regulations with modifications to short breaks

(1) In the circumstances set out in paragraph (2) these Regulations apply with the modifications set out in paragraph (3).

(2) The circumstances are that –

- (a) C is not in the care of the responsible authority,
- (b) the responsible authority have arranged to place C in a series of short-term placements with the same person or in the same accommodation ('short breaks'), and
- (c) the arrangement is such that –
  - (i) no single placement is intended to last for longer than 17 days,
  - (ii) at the end of each such placement, C returns to the care of C's parent or a person who is not C's parent but who has parental responsibility for C, and
  - (iii) the short breaks do not exceed 75 days in total in any period of 12 months.

(3) The modifications are that –

- (a) regulations 5 and 9 do not apply, but instead the care plan must set out the arrangements made to meet C's needs with particular regard to –
  - (i) C's health and emotional and behavioural development, in particular in relation to any disability C may have,
  - (ii) promoting contact between C and C's parents and any other person who is not C's parent but who has parental responsibility for C, during any period when C is placed,
  - (iii) C's leisure interests, and
  - (iv) promoting C's educational achievement,

  and must include the name and address of C's registered medical practitioner, and the information set out in paragraph 3 of Schedule 2, where appropriate,
- (b) regulations 7, 13 and 49(2)(b) do not apply,
- (c) regulation 28(2) does not apply, but instead the responsible authority must ensure that R visits C on days when C is in fact placed, at regular intervals to be agreed with the IRO and C's parents (or any person who is not C's parent but who has parental responsibility for C) and recorded in the care plan before the start of the first placement, and in any event –
  - (i) the first visit must take place within three months of the start of the first placement, or as soon as practicable thereafter, and
  - (ii) subsequent visits must take place at intervals of not more than six months, for as long as the short breaks continue,
- (d) regulation 33 does not apply, but instead –
  - (i) the responsible authority must first review C's case within three months of the start of the first placement, and
  - (ii) the second and subsequent reviews must be carried out at intervals of not more than six months.

49 Records

Establishment of records

(1) The responsible authority must establish and maintain a written case record for C ('C's case record'), if one is not already in existence.

(2) The case record must include –

(a) C's care plan, including any changes made to the care plan and any subsequent plans,
(b) reports obtained under regulation 7,
(c) any other document created or considered as part of any assessment of C's needs, or of any review of C's case,
(d) any court order relating to C,
(e) details of any arrangements that have been made by the responsible authority with any other local authority or with an independent fostering agency under regulation 26 and Schedule 5, or with a provider of social work services, under which any of the responsible authority's functions in relation to C are discharged by that local authority or independent fostering agency or provider of social work services.

50 Retention and confidentiality of records

(1) The responsible authority must retain C's case record either –

(a) until the seventy-fifth anniversary of C's birth, or
(b) if C dies before attaining the age of 18, for fifteen years beginning with the date of C's death.

(2) The responsible authority must secure the safe keeping of C's case record and take any necessary steps to ensure that information contained in it is treated as confidential subject only to –

(a) any provision of, or made under or by virtue of, a statute under which access to such a record or information may be obtained or given,
(b) any court order under which access to such a record or information may be obtained or given.

****

SCHEDULE 1
CARE PLANS

1 Information to be included in the health plan

(1) C's state of health including C's physical, emotional and mental health.

(2) C's health history including, so far as practicable, C's family's health history.

(3) The effect of C's health and health history on C's development.

(4) Existing arrangements for C's medical and dental care including –

(a) routine checks of C's general state of health, including dental health,
(b) treatment for, and monitoring of, identified health (including physical, emotional and mental health) or dental care needs,
(c) preventive measures such as vaccination and immunisation,
(d) screening for defects of vision or hearing, and
(e) advice and guidance on promoting health and effective personal care.

(5) Any planned changes to existing arrangements.

(6) The role of the appropriate person, and of any other person who cares for C, in promoting C's health.

PART IV

2 Information to be included in the personal education plan

(1) C's educational and training history, including information about educational institutions attended and C's attendance and conduct record, C's academic and other achievements, and C's special educational needs, if any.

(2) Existing arrangements for C's education and training, including details of any special educational provision and any other provision made to meet C's particular educational or training needs, and to promote C's educational achievement, and including the name and contact details of the person appointed under section 22(3B) of the 1989 Act for the purpose of discharging the responsible authority's duty under section 22(3A) (duty to promote the educational achievement of children looked after by the authority).

(3) Any planned changes to existing arrangements for C's education or training and, where any changes to the arrangements are necessary, provision made to minimise disruption to that education or training.

(4) C's leisure interests.

(5) The role of the appropriate person, and of any other person who cares for C, in promoting C's educational achievements and leisure interests.

Amendments—SI 2013/706; SI 2014/1556.

3 Family and social relationships

(1) If C has a sibling for whom the responsible authority or another authority are providing accommodation, and the children have not been placed together, the arrangements made to promote contact between them, so far as is consistent with C's welfare.

(2) If C is looked after by, but is not in the care of, the responsible authority, details of any order relating to C made under section 8.

(3) If C is in the care of the responsible authority, details of any order relating to C made under section 34 (parental contact etc with children in care).

(4) Any other arrangements made to promote and maintain contact in accordance with paragraph 15 of Schedule 2 of the 1989 Act, so far as is reasonably practicable and consistent with C's welfare, between C and –

(a) any parent of C's and any person who is not C's parent but who has parental responsibility for C, and

(b) any other connected person.

(5) Where section 23ZB(1) applies, the arrangements made to appoint an independent visitor for C or, if section 23ZB(6) applies (appointment of independent visitor not made where child objects), that fact.

SCHEDULE 2
MATTERS TO BE DEALT WITH IN THE PLACEMENT PLAN

1 Information to be included in C's placement plan

(1) How on a day to day basis C will be cared for and C's welfare will be safeguarded and promoted by the appropriate person.

(2) Any arrangements made for contact between C and any parent of C's and any person who is not C's parent but who has parental responsibility for C, and between C and any other connected person including, if appropriate –

(a) the reasons why contact with any such person would not be reasonably practicable or would not be consistent with C's welfare,

(b) if C is not in the care of the responsible authority, details of any order made under section 8,

(c) if C is in the care of the responsible authority, details of any order relating to C made under section 34,

(d) the arrangements for notifying any changes in the arrangements for contact.

(3) The arrangements made for C's health (including physical, emotional and mental health) and dental care including –

(a) the name and address of C's registered medical and dental practitioners and, where applicable, any registered medical or dental practitioner with whom C is to be registered following the placement,
(b) any arrangements for the giving or withholding of consent to medical or dental examination or treatment for C.

(4) The arrangements made for C's education and training including –

(a) the name and address of any school at which C is a registered pupil,
(b) the name of the designated teacher at the school (if applicable),
(c) the name and address of any other educational institution that C attends, or of any other person who provides C with education or training,
(d) where C has a statement of special educational needs, details of the local authority that maintains the statement.

(5) The arrangements made for R to visit C in accordance with Part 5, the frequency of visits and the arrangements made for advice, support and assistance to be available to C between visits in accordance with regulation 31.

(6) If an independent visitor is appointed, the arrangements made for them to visit C.

(7) The circumstances in which the placement may be terminated and C removed from the appropriate person's care in accordance with regulation 14.

(8) The name and contact details of –

(a) the IRO,
(b) C's independent visitor (if one is appointed),
(c) R, and
(d) if C is an eligible child, the personal adviser appointed for C.

2 Additional information to be included where C is placed with P

(1) Details of support and services to be provided to P during the placement.

(2) The obligation on P to notify the responsible authority of any relevant change in circumstances, including any intention to change address, any changes in the household in which C lives, and of any serious incident involving C.

(3) The obligation on P to ensure that any information relating to C or C's family or any other person given in confidence to P in connection with the placement is kept confidential, and that such information is not disclosed to any person without the consent of the responsible authority.

(4) The circumstances in which it is necessary to obtain the prior approval of the responsible authority for C to live in a household other than P's household.

(5) The arrangements for requesting a change to the placement plan.

(6) The circumstances in which the placement will be terminated in accordance with regulation 19(c)(ii).

3 Additional information to be included where C is placed with F, in a children's home or in other arrangements

(1) The type of accommodation to be provided, the address and, where C is placed under section 22C(6)(d), the name of the person who will be responsible for C at that accommodation on behalf of the responsible authority (if any).

(1ZA) Where C is placed with F in a long term foster placement, that fact.

(1A) Where –

(a) the responsible authority has, or is notified of, child protection concerns relating to C, or
(b) C has gone missing from the placement or from any previous placement,

the day to day arrangements put in place by the appropriate person to keep C safe.

(2) C's personal history, religious persuasion, cultural and linguistic background, and racial origin.

(3) Where C is not in the care of the responsible authority –

(a), (b) *(revoked)*

(c) the expected duration of the arrangements and the steps which should be taken to bring the arrangements to an end, including arrangements for C to return to live with C's parents, or any person who is not C's parent but who has parental responsibility for C, and

(d) where C is aged 16 or over and agrees to being provided with accommodation under section 20, that fact.

(4) The respective responsibilities of the responsible authority, C's parents, and any person who is not C's parent but who has parental responsibility for C.

(4A) Any delegation of authority to make decisions about C's care and upbringing by the persons mentioned in paragraph (4) (as appropriate) to –

(a) the responsible authority,

(b) F, and

(c) where C is placed in a children's home, the appropriate person,

in relation to the matters set out in paragraph (4B), and identifying any matters about which the persons mentioned in paragraph (4) consider that C may make a decision.

(4B) The matters referred to in paragraph (4A) are –

(a) medical and dental treatment,

(b) education,

(c) leisure and home life,

(d) faith and religious observance,

(e) use of social media,

(f) any other matters which the persons mentioned in paragraph (4) consider appropriate.

(5) The responsible authority's arrangements for the financial support of C during the placement.

(6) Where C is placed with F, the obligation on F to comply with the terms of the foster care agreement made under regulation 27(5)(b) of the Fostering Services Regulations.

Amendments—SI 2011/581; SI 2013/984; SI 2013/3239; SI 2015/495.

SCHEDULE 2A

MATTERS TO BE DEALT WITH IN THE DETENTION PLACEMENT PLAN

1 How on a day to day basis C will be cared for and C's welfare will be safeguarded and promoted by the staff of the YDA.

2 Any arrangements made for contact between C and any parent of C's and any person who is not C's parent but who has parental responsibility for C, and between C and any other connected person including, if appropriate –

(a) the reasons why contact with any such person would not be reasonably practicable or would not be consistent with C's welfare,

(b) if C is not in the care of the responsible authority, details of any order made under section 8,

(c) if C is in the care of the responsible authority, details of any order relating to C made under section 34,

(d) the arrangements for notifying any changes in the arrangements for contact.

3 The arrangements made for R to visit C in accordance with Part 5, the frequency of visits and the arrangements made for advice, support and assistance to be available to C between visits in accordance with regulation 31.

4 If an independent visitor is appointed, the arrangements made for them to visit C.

5 The arrangements made by the staff of the YDA for C's health (including physical, emotional and mental health) and dental care.

6 The arrangements made by staff of the YDA for C's education and training including –

(a) the name and address of any educational or training institution C was attending, or any other person providing C with education or training, immediately before his detention,

(b) where C has a statement of special educational needs, details of the local authority that maintains the statement.

7 C's personal history, religious persuasion, cultural and linguistic background, and racial origin, and the arrangement put in place by the staff of the YDA for meeting C's religious, cultural or linguistic needs.

8 The arrangements put in place by the staff of the YDA for supporting C to develop self-care skills.

9 The name and contact details of –

(a) the IRO,

(b) C's independent visitor (if one is appointed),

(c) R,

(d) if C is an eligible child, the personal adviser appointed for C,

(e) the person appointed under section 22(3B) of the 1989 Act for the purpose of discharging the responsible authority's duty under section 22(3A) (duty to promote the educational achievement of children looked after by the authority).

Amendments—SI 2014/1556.

10 Details of how C's welfare should be adequately safeguarded and promoted when C ceases to be remanded to YDA, in particular –

(a) whether C will be provided with accommodation by the responsible authority or another local authority, and

(b) whether any other services should be provided by the responsible authority or another local authority in the exercise of their duties under the 1989 Act.

Amendments—Inserted by SI 2013/706.

SCHEDULE 3
MATTERS TO BE TAKEN INTO ACCOUNT WHEN ASSESSING THE SUITABILITY OF P TO CARE FOR C

1 In respect of P –

(a) P's capacity to care for children and in particular in relation to C to –

(i) provide for C's physical needs and appropriate medical and dental care,

(ii) protect C adequately from harm or danger, including from any person who presents a risk of harm to C,

(iii) ensure that the home environment is safe for C,

(iv) ensure that C's emotional needs are met and C is provided with a positive sense of self, including any particular needs arising from C's religious persuasion, racial origin and cultural and linguistic background, and any disability C may have,

(v) promote C's learning and intellectual development through encouragement, cognitive stimulation and the promotion of educational success and social opportunities,

(vi) enable C to regulate C's emotions and behaviour, including by modelling appropriate behaviour and interactions with others, and

PART IV

(vii) provide a stable family environment to enable C to develop and maintain secure attachments to P and other persons who provide care for C,

(b) P's state of health including P's physical, emotional and mental health and medical history including any current or past issues of domestic violence, substance misuse or mental health problems,

(c) P's family relationships and the composition of P's household, including particulars of –

(i) the identity of all other members of the household, including their age and the nature of their relationship with P and with each other, including any sexual relationship,

(ii) any relationship with any person who is a parent of C,

(iii) other adults not being members of the household who are likely to have regular contact with C, and

(iv) any current or previous domestic violence between members of the household, including P,

(d) P's family history, including –

(i) particulars of P's childhood and upbringing including the strengths and difficulties of P's parents or other persons who cared for P,

(ii) P's relationships with P's parents and siblings, and their relationships with each other,

(iii) P's educational achievement and any specific learning difficulty or disability,

(iv) a chronology of significant life events, and

(v) particulars of other relatives and their relationships with C and P,

(e) particulars of any criminal offences of which P has been convicted or in respect of which P has been cautioned,

(f) P's past and present employment and other sources of income, and

(g) the nature of the neighbourhood in which P's home is situated and resources available in the community to support C and P.

2 In respect of members of P's household aged 18 and over, so far as is practicable, all the particulars specified in paragraph 1 except sub-paragraphs (d), (f) and (g).

SCHEDULE 4
MATTERS TO BE TAKEN INTO ACCOUNT WHEN ASSESSING THE SUITABILITY OF A CONNECTED PERSON TO CARE FOR C

1 In respect of the connected person –

(a) the nature and quality of any existing relationship with C,

(b) their capacity to care for children and in particular in relation to C to –

(i) provide for C's physical needs and appropriate medical and dental care,

(ii) protect C adequately from harm or danger including from any person who presents a risk of harm to C,

(iii) ensure that the accommodation and home environment is suitable with regard to the age and developmental stage of C,

(iv) promote C's learning and development, and

(v) provide a stable family environment which will promote secure attachments for C, including promoting positive contact with P and other connected persons, unless to do this is not consistent with the duty to safeguard and promote C's welfare,

(c) their state of health including their physical, emotional and mental health and medical history including any current or past issues of domestic violence, substance misuse or mental health problems,

(d) their family relationships and the composition of their household, including particulars of –

(i) the identity of all other members of the household, including their age and the nature of their relationship with the connected person and with each other, including any sexual relationship,

(ii) any relationship with any person who is a parent of C,
(iii) any relationship between C and other members of the household
(iv) other adults not being members of the household who are likely to have regular contact with C, and
(v) any current or previous domestic violence between members of the household, including the connected person,

(e) their family history, including –
(i) particulars of their childhood and upbringing including the strengths and difficulties of their parents or other persons who cared for them,
(ii) their relationships with their parents and siblings, and their relationships with each other,
(iii) their educational achievement and any specific learning difficulty or disability,
(iv) a chronology of significant life events, and
(v) particulars of other relatives and their relationships with C and the connected person,

(f) particulars of any criminal offences of which they have been convicted or in respect of which they have been cautioned,
(g) their past and present employment and other sources of income, and
(h) the nature of the neighbourhood in which their home is situated and resources available in the community to support C and the connected person.

SCHEDULE 5
AGREEMENT WITH AN INDEPENDENT FOSTERING AGENCY RELATING TO THE DISCHARGE OF THE RESPONSIBLE AUTHORITY'S FUNCTIONS

1 The agreement must contain the following information –

(1) the services to be provided to the responsible authority by the registered person,
(2) the arrangements for the selection by the responsible authority of F from those approved by the registered person,
(3) a requirement for the registered person to submit reports to the responsible authority on any placements as may be required by the responsible authority, and
(4) the arrangements for the termination of the agreement.

2 Where the agreement relates to a particular child, it must also contain the following information –

(1) F's details,
(2) details of any services that C is to receive and whether the services are to be provided by the responsible authority or by the registered person,
(3) the terms (including as to payment) of the proposed placement agreement,
(4) the arrangements for record keeping about C and for the return of records at the end of the placement,
(5) a requirement for the registered person to notify the responsible authority immediately in the event of any concerns about the placement, and
(6) whether, and on what basis, other children may be placed with F.

SCHEDULE 6
MATTERS TO BE CONSIDERED BEFORE PLACING C IN ACCOMMODATION IN AN UNREGULATED SETTING UNDER SECTION 22(6)(D)

1 In respect of the accommodation, the –

(a) facilities and services provided,
(b) state of repair,
(c) safety,
(d) location,

(e) support,
(f) tenancy status, and
(g) the financial commitments involved for C and their affordability.

2 In respect of C, C's –

(a) views about the accommodation,
(b) understanding of their rights and responsibilities in relation to the accommodation, and
(c) understanding of funding arrangements.

SCHEDULE 7
CONSIDERATIONS TO WHICH THE RESPONSIBLE AUTHORITY MUST HAVE REGARD WHEN REVIEWING C'S CASE

1 The effect of any change in C's circumstances since the last review, in particular of any change made by the responsible authority to C's care plan, whether decisions taken at the last review have been successfully implemented, and if not, the reasons for that.

2 Whether the responsible authority should seek any change in C's legal status.

3 Whether there is a plan for permanence for C.

4 The arrangements for contact and whether there is any need for changes to the arrangements in order to promote contact between C and P, or between C and other connected persons.

5 Whether C's placement continues to be the most appropriate available, and whether any change to the placement plan or any other aspects of the arrangements made to provide C with accommodation is, or is likely to become, necessary or desirable before the next review of C's case.

5A Whether C's placement safeguards and promotes C's welfare, and whether any safeguarding concerns have been raised.

Amendments—Inserted by SI 2013/3239.

6 C's educational needs, progress and development and whether any change to the arrangements for C's education or training is, or is likely to become, necessary or desirable to meet C's particular needs and to promote C's educational achievement before the next review of C's case, having regard to the advice of any person who provides C with education or training, in particular the designated teacher of any school at which C is a registered pupil.

7 C's leisure interests.

8 The report of the most recent assessment of C's state of health obtained in accordance with regulation 8 and whether any change to the arrangements for C's health care is, or is likely to become, necessary or desirable before the next review of C's case, having regard to the advice of any health care professional received since the date of that report, in particular C's registered medical practitioner.

9 Whether C's needs related to C's identity are being met and whether any particular change is required, having regard to C's religious persuasion, racial origin and cultural background.

10 Whether the arrangements made in accordance with regulation 31 continue to be appropriate and understood by C.

11 Whether any arrangements need to be made for the time when C will no longer be looked after by the responsible authority.

12 C's wishes and feelings, and the views of the IRO, about any aspect of the case and in particular about any changes the responsible authority has made since the last review or proposes to make to the C's care plan.

13 Where regulation 28(3) applies, the frequency of R's visits.

Amendments—SI 2011/581.

14 Where C falls within regulation 5(1)(f), whether C's needs as a result of that status are being met.

Amendments—Inserted by SI 2014/1917.

15 Whether the delegation of authority to make decisions about C's care and upbringing, if any, recorded in C's care plan by virtue of paragraph 3(4A) of Schedule 2, continues to be appropriate and in C's best interests.

Amendments—Inserted by SI 2015/495.

SCHEDULE 8

MATTERS TO BE DEALT WITH IN THE PATHWAY PLAN

1 The name of C's personal adviser.

2 The nature and level of contact and personal support to be provided to C, and by whom.

3 Details of the accommodation C is to occupy when C ceases to be looked after.

4 The plan for C's continuing education or training when C ceases to be looked after.

5 How the responsible authority will assist C in obtaining employment or other purposeful activity or occupation.

6 The support to be provided to enable C to develop and sustain appropriate family and social relationships.

7 A programme to develop the practical and other skills C needs to live independently.

8 The financial support to be provided to enable C to meet accommodation and maintenance costs.

9 C's health care needs, including any physical, emotional or mental health needs and how they are to be met when C ceases to be looked after.

10 The responsible authority's contingency plans for action to be taken in the event that the pathway plan ceases to be effective for any reason.

****

Child Abduction and Custody (Parties to Conventions) Order 1986, SI 1986/1159

1 This Order may be cited as the Child Abduction and Custody (Parties to Conventions) Order 1986, and shall come into operation on 1 August 1986.

2 (1) In this Article of, and in Schedule 1 to, this Order 'the Convention' means the Convention on the Civil Aspects of International Child Abduction which was signed at The Hague on 25 October 1980.

(2) (a) The Contracting States to the Convention shall be as specified in the first column of Schedule 1 to this Order.

(b) Where the Convention applies, or applies only, to a particular territory or particular territories specified in a declaration made by a Contracting State under Article 39 or 40 of the Convention, the territory or territories in question shall be as specified in the second column of Schedule 1 to this Order.

PART IV

(c) The date of the coming into force of the Convention as between the United Kingdom and any State or territory so specified shall be as specified in the third column of Schedule 1 to this Order.

3 (1) In this Article of, and in Schedule 2 to, this Order 'the Convention' means the European Convention on Recognition and Enforcement of Decisions concerning Custody of Children and on the Restoration of Custody of Children which was signed in Luxembourg on 20 May 1980.

(2) (a) The Contracting States to the Convention shall be as specified in the first column of Schedule 2 to this Order.

(b) Where the Convention applies, or applies only, to a particular territory or particular territories specified by a Contracting State under Article 24 or 25 of the Convention, the territory or territories in question shall be as specified in the second column of Schedule 2 to this Order.

(c) The date of the coming into force of the Convention as between the United Kingdom and any State or territory so specified shall be as specified in the third column of Schedule 2 to this Order.

SCHEDULE 1
CONVENTION ON THE CIVIL ASPECTS OF INTERNATIONAL CHILD ABDUCTION, THE HAGUE, 25 OCTOBER 1980

Contracting States to the Convention	*Territories specified in Declarations under Article 39 or 40 of the Convention*	*Date of Coming into Force of Convention as between the United Kingdom and the State or Territory*
Argentina	—	1 June 1991
Australia	Australian States and mainland Territories	1 January 1987
Austria	—	1 October 1988
The Bahamas	—	1 January 1994
Belarus	—	1 October 2003
Belgium	—	1 May 1999
Belize	—	1 October 1989
Bosnia and Herzegovina	—	1 December 1991
Brazil	—	1 March 2005
Bulgaria	—	1 May 2009
Burkina Faso	—	1 November 1992
Canada	Ontario	1 August 1986
	New Brunswick	1 August 1986
	British Columbia	1 August 1986
	Manitoba	1 August 1986
	Nova Scotia	1 August 1986
	Newfoundland and Labrador	1 August 1986
	Prince Edward Island	1 August 1986
	Quebec	1 August 1986
	Yukon Territory	1 August 1986
	Saskatchewan	1 November 1986
	Alberta	1 February 1987
	Northwest Territories	1 April 1988
	Nunavut	1 January 2001
Chile	—	1 May 1994
China	Hong Kong Special Administrative Region	1 September 1997
	Macau Special Administrative Region	1 March 1999
Columbia	—	1 March 1996

Contracting States to the Convention	Territories specified in Declarations under Article 39 or 40 of the Convention	Date of Coming into Force of Convention as between the United Kingdom and the State or Territory
Costa Rica	—	1 May 2009
Croatia	—	1 December 1991
Cyprus	—	1 February 1995
Czech Republic	—	1 March 1998
Denmark	—	1 July 1991
Ecuador	—	1 June 1992
El Salvador	—	1 May 2009
Estonia	—	1 October 2003
Fiji	—	1 October 2003
Finland	—	1 August 1994
France	—	1 August 1986
Georgia	—	1 October 1997
Germany	—	1 December 1990
Greece	—	1 June 1993
Honduras	—	1 March 1994
Hungary	—	1 September 1986
Iceland	—	1 November 1996
Ireland	—	1 October 1991
Israel	—	1 December 1991
Italy	—	1 May 1995
Japan	—	1 April 2014
Latvia	—	1 October 2003
Lithuania	—	1 March 2005
Luxembourg	—	1 January 1987
Macedonia	—	1 December 1991
Malta	—	1 March 2002
Mauritius	—	1 June 1993
Mexico	—	1 October 1991
Monaco	—	1 February 1993
Montenegro	—	1 December 1991
Netherlands	—	1 September 1990
New Zealand	—	1 October 1991
Norway	—	1 April 1989
Panama	—	1 May 1994
Peru	—	1 October 2003
Poland	—	1 November 1992
Portugal	—	1 August 1986
Romania	—	1 February 1993
St Kitts and Nevis	—	1 August 1994
San Marino	—	1 June 2011
Serbia	—	1 December 1991
Slovakia	—	1 February 2001
Slovenia	—	1 June 1994
South Africa	—	1 October 1997
Spain	—	1 September 1987
Sweden	—	1 June 1989
Switzerland	—	1 August 1986
Turkey	—	1 August 2000
Turkmenistan	—	1 March 1998
Ukraine	—	1 June 2011
United States of America	—	1 July 1988
Uruguay	—	1 October 2003

PART IV

Contracting States to the Convention	*Territories specified in Declarations under Article 39 or 40 of the Convention*	*Date of Coming into Force of Convention as between the United Kingdom and the State or Territory*
Uzbekistan	—	1 October 2003
Venezuela	—	1 January 1997
Zimbabwe	—	1 July 1995

Amendments—Schedule last substituted by SI 2011/1081.

SCHEDULE 2
EUROPEAN CONVENTION ON RECOGNITION AND ENFORCEMENT OF DECISIONS CONCERNING CUSTODY OF CHILDREN AND ON THE RESTORATION OF CUSTODY OF CHILDREN, LUXEMBOURG, 20TH MAY 1980

Contracting States to the Convention	*Territories specified in Declarations under Article 24 or 25 of the Convention*	*Date of Coming into Force of Convention as between the United Kingdom and the State or Territory*
Austria	—	1 August 1986
Belgium	—	1 August 1986
Bulgaria	—	1 October 2003
Cyprus	—	1 October 1986
Czech Republic	—	1 July 2000
Denmark	—	1 August 1991
Estonia	—	1 September 2001
Finland	—	1 August 1994
France	—	1 August 1986
Germany	—	1 February 1991
Greece	—	1 July 1993
Hungary	—	1 June 2004
Iceland	—	1 November 1996
Ireland	—	1 October 1991
Italy	—	1 June 1995
Latvia	—	1 August 2002
Liechtenstein	—	1 August 1997
Lithuania	—	1 May 2003
Luxembourg	—	1 August 1986
Macedonia	—	1 March 2003
Malta	—	1 February 2000
Moldova	—	1 May 2004
Montenegro	—	6 June 2006
Netherlands	—	1 September 1990
Norway	—	1 May 1989
Poland	—	1 March 1996
Portugal	—	1 August 1986
Romania	—	1 September 2004
Serbia	—	1 May 2002
Slovakia	—	1 September 2001
Spain	—	1 August 1986
Sweden	—	1 July 1989
Switzerland	—	1 August 1986
Turkey	—	1 June 2000

Amendments—Schedule last substituted by SI 2009/702.

Children (Admissibility of Hearsay Evidence) Order 1993, SI 1993/621

1 Citation and commencement

This Order may be cited as the Children (Admissibility of Hearsay Evidence) Order 1993 and shall come into force on 5 April 1993.

2 Admissibility of hearsay evidence

In –

(a) civil proceedings before the High Court or a county court; and
(b) (i) family proceedings, and
(ii) civil proceedings under the Child Support Act 1991 in a magistrates' court,

evidence given in connection with the upbringing, maintenance or welfare of a child shall be admissible notwithstanding any rule of law relating to hearsay.

Defined terms—'child': CA 1989, s 105(1).

'civil proceedings'—This term is not defined for the purposes of the Order but will not usually cause any difficulty. The Civil Evidence Act 1968 contains a definition of civil proceedings but only for the purpose of clarifying the position of proceedings before tribunals and arbitrations, which do not arise in relation to the scope of this Order, and excluding certain proceedings from the strict rules of evidence, which is immaterial for the purposes of this Order as it imposes no preconditions for admissibility.

'civil proceedings under the Child Support Act 1991'—The relevant proceedings in a magistrates' court are under s 20 (appeals from a child support officer where made in accordance with the Child Support Appeals (Jurisdiction of Courts) Order 2002, i e on an issue of parentage), s 26 (reference to court for declaration of parentage), and certain proceedings on enforcement under ss 33–40.

'in connection with the upbringing, maintenance or welfare of a child'—This is a flexible form of words which will need to be applied in relation to each individual case. The concept of a question with respect to the upbringing of a child is also one of the triggers for activating the principle that the court should treat the child's welfare as its paramount consideration (CA 1989, s 1(1)). 'In connection with' leaves some uncertainty about what it is that should relate to the 'upbringing etc'. It is submitted that if the proceedings are about the child's upbringing, maintenance or welfare, e g s 8 proceedings, it is not necessary to determine whether particular things that are sought to be proved in those proceedings so relate; if the proceedings so relate, every piece of evidence allowed to be adduced will necessarily be relevant to the outcome and thus within the scope of the Order, even though the evidence itself may not directly relate to any of the three things specified in the Order. For example, in proceedings for child maintenance the respondent's income is clearly relevant and, although his wage slips do not relate directly to the maintenance of the child, they are relevant to the issue of how much child maintenance should be ordered and are therefore admissible under the Order. Where proceedings consist of more than one aspect not all of which relate to any of the three issues, it will be necessary to analyse whether the fact sought to be admitted by virtue of the Order relates to any of those issues.

The Order clearly applies to contempt proceedings which take place as part of 'family proceedings'. For hearsay evidence to be admissible under the Order, the onus lies on the applicant seeking to rely on the hearsay evidence to show that the evidence has a 'substantial connection with the upbringing, maintenance or welfare of a child'. If the injunctive relief is being granted to protect a child, evidence from the child of any breach of the injunction is likely to have a 'substantial connection' with his welfare. However, if the injunction was granted in a parental dispute to protect one parent, the evidence of a child as to a breach of that injunction, where he himself was not directly affected by it, would be unlikely to show a 'substantial connection' with his welfare (*C v C (Contempt: Evidence)* [1993] 1 FLR 220, CA). The decision as to admissibility will be for the judge to consider on the particular facts of each case. Where this Order does not apply, hearsay evidence may nevertheless be admissible following the ruling in *Savings and Investment Bank Ltd v Gasco Investments (Netherlands) BV (No 2)* [1988] Ch 422, CA.

'shall be admissible'—The effect of this Order is to render hearsay evidence admissible. Thus, a local authority is entitled to adduce in evidence the written and videotaped record of a child's interview in which allegations of sexual abuse are made, and can decline to call her to give oral evidence. In *Re P (Witness Summons)* [1997] 2 FLR 447, CA it was observed that the only way in which another party could secure the child's attendance to give evidence was to issue a witness summons against the child under CCR Ord 20, r 12 (now FPR 2010, r 24.2), and that the judge had a discretion whether to issue such a summons. In *Re P* it was held that the question of whether to issue a witness summons against a child was not a question with respect to upbringing and therefore CA 1989, s 1(1) did not apply (though the case provides useful guidance on the factors to be considered in the exercise of the discretion).

As to the right approach to hearsay evidence in care proceedings see *Re H (Care: Change in Care Plan)* [1998] 1 FLR 193, CA where the Court of Appeal accepted that even an unsworn allegation was capable of constituting a very serious cause for concern which a court could accept provided it was evaluated against testimony on oath. What weight should be attached to the particular piece of hearsay evidence is a question for the court to decide (*F v Child Support Agency* [1999] 2 FLR 244, QBD; *Re W (Fact Finding: Hearsay Evidence)* [2014] 2 FLR 703, CA.

'rule of law relating to hearsay'—Hearsay evidence is, at common law, inadmissible save in certain circumstances. The number of exceptions to the rule against hearsay has been increased by or under statute over the years. This Order may be relied on in preference to other exceptions which may also apply and which are less attractive because they have preconditions; for example, if evidence is admissible under the Order, no notice need be served in accordance with the exception created by the Civil Evidence Act 1995.

****

Children (Secure Accommodation) Regulations 1991, SI 1991/1505

****

1A Disapplication to Wales

(1) These regulations do not apply in relation to –

(a) the provider of a children's home in Wales;

(b) an application to court for authority to place a child in secure accommodation in Wales.

(2) Regulations 4, 14, 15 and 16 do not apply to a local authority in Wales in respect of a placement in secure accommodation under section 25 of the Act.

(3) Where paragraphs (1) and (2) apply, refer to section 119 of the Social Services and Well-being (Wales) Act 2014 and the Children (Secure Accommodation) (Wales) Regulations 2015.

Amendments—Inserted by SI 2015/1988. Substituted by SI 2016/211.

****

3 Approval by Secretary of State of secure accommodation in a children's home

Accommodation in a children's home shall not be used as secure accommodation unless it has been approved by the Secretary of State for such use and approval shall be subject to such terms and conditions as he sees fit.

Amendments—SI 1995/1398.

Note—None of these provisions applies to Wales as from April 2016.

4 Placement of a child aged under 13 in secure accommodation in a children's home

A child under the age of 13 years shall not be placed in secure accommodation in a children's home without the prior approval of the Secretary of State to the placement of that child and such approval shall be subject to such terms and conditions as he sees fit.

Amendments—SI 1992/2117; SI 1995/1398.

5 Children to whom section 25 of the Act shall not apply

(1) Section 25 of the Act shall not apply to a child who is detained under any provision of the Mental Health Act 1983 or in respect of whom an order has been made under section 90 or 91 of the Powers of the Criminal Courts (Sentencing) Act 2000 (detention at Her Majesty's pleasure or for specified period).

(2) Section 25 of the Act shall not apply to a child –

(a) to whom section 20(5) of the Act (accommodation of persons over 16 but under 21) applies and who is being accommodated under that section,

(b) in respect of whom an order has been made under section 43 of the Act (child assessment order) and who is kept away from home pursuant to that order.

Amendments—SI 2002/546.

5A Section 25 of the Act shall not apply to a child who is remanded to youth detention accommodation and who is to be treated as looked after by virtue of section 104(1) of the Legal Aid, Sentencing and Punishment of Offenders Act 2012.

Amendments—Inserted by SI 2012/2813.

6 Detained and remanded children to whom section 25 of the Act shall have effect subject to modifications

(1) Subject to regulation 5, section 25 of the Act shall have effect subject to the modification specified in paragraph (2) in relation to children who are being looked after by a local authority and are of the following descriptions –

(a) children aged 12 or over but under the age of 18 detained under section 38(6) of the Police and Criminal Evidence Act 1984 (detained children),

(b) *(revoked)*

(2) The modification referred to in paragraph (1) is that, for the words 'unless it appears' to the end of subsection (1), there shall be substituted the following words –

'unless it appears that any accommodation other than that provided for the purpose of restricting liberty is inappropriate because –

(a) the child is likely to abscond from such other accommodation, or

(b) the child is likely to injure himself or other people if he is kept in any such other accommodation'.

Amendments—SI 1992/2117; SI 2012/3134; SI 2015/1883.

Regulation 5A—By virtue of LASPOA 2012, s 104, any child who is remanded to youth detention accommodation is to be treated as 'looked after' by the designated authority.

Regulation 6(1)(a)—The age range is increased from under 17 to under 18 (SI 2015/1883).

Regulation 6(1)(b)—Where a child is detained under Police and Criminal Evidence Act 1984, s 38(6), the Youth Court has power to make a secure accommodation order even if the s 25 criteria are not met, provided that the criteria in reg 6(2) are met.

7 Children to whom section 25 of the Act shall apply and have effect subject to modifications

(1) Subject to regulation 5 and paragraphs (2) and (3) of this regulation section 25 of the Act shall apply (in addition to children looked after by a local authority) –

(a) to children, other than those looked after by a local authority, who are accommodated by health authorities, National Health Service trusts established under section 5 of the National Health Service and Community Care Act 1990, NHS foundation trusts or local authorities in the exercise of education functions or who are accommodated pursuant to arrangements made by the Secretary of State, the National Health Service Commissioning Board or a clinical commissioning group under the National Health Service Act 2006, and

(b) to children, other than those looked after by a local authority, who are accommodated in care homes or independent hospitals.

(2) In relation to the children of a description specified in paragraph (1)(a) section 25 of the Act shall have effect subject to the following modifications –

(a) for the words 'who is being looked after by a local authority' in subsection (1) there shall be substituted the words 'who is being provided with accommodation by a health authority, a National Health Service trust established under section 5 of the National Health Service and Community Care Act 1990, an NHS foundation trust or a local authority in the exercise of education functions or who is being provided with accommodation pursuant to arrangements made by the Secretary of State, the National Health Service Commissioning Board or a clinical commissioning group under the National Health Service Act 2006'.

(b) for the words 'local authorities' in subsection (2)(c) there shall be substituted the words

PART IV

'health authorities, National Health Service trusts, NHS foundation trusts, local authorities, the Secretary of State, the National Health Service Commissioning Board or clinical commissioning groups'.

(3) In relation to the children of a description specified in paragraph (1)(b), section 25 of the Act shall have effect subject to the following modifications –

(a) for the words 'who is being looked after by a local authority' in subsection (1) there shall be substituted the words 'who is being provided with accommodation in a care home or an independent hospital'; and

(b) for the words 'local authorities' in subsection (2)(c) there shall be substituted the words 'persons carrying on care homes or independent hospitals'.

Amendments—SI 2000/694; SI 2002/546; SI 2004/696; SI 2010/1172; SI 2013/235.

8 Applications to court

Subject to section 101 of the Local Government Act 1972 or to provisions in or under sections 14 to 20 of the Local Government Act 2000, applications to a court under section 25 of the Act in respect of a child shall be made only by the local authority or local authority in Wales which are looking after that child.

Amendments—SI 2001/2237; SI 2016/211.

'local authority which are looking after that child'—See CA 1989, s 22(1) and *Re W (A Child)* [2016] EWCA Civ 804 and, as to a child who is bailed with a condition of residence to the local authority, see *Re C (Secure Accommodation: Bail)* [1994] 2 FLR 922, FD.

****

10 Maximum period in secure accommodation without court authority

(1) Subject to paragraphs (2) and (3), the maximum period beyond which a child to whom section 25 of the Act applies may not be kept in secure accommodation without the authority of a court is an aggregate of 72 hours (whether or not consecutive) in any period of 28 consecutive days.

(2) Where authority of a court to keep a child in secure accommodation has been given, any period during which the child has been kept in such accommodation before the giving of that authority shall be disregarded for the purposes of calculating the maximum period in relation to any subsequent occasion on which the child is placed in such accommodation after the period authorised by court has expired.

(3) Where a child is in secure accommodation at any time between 12 midday on the day before and 12 midday on the day after a public holiday or a Sunday, and

(a) during that period the maximum period specified in paragraph (1) expires, and

(b) the child had, in the 27 days before the day on which he was placed in secure accommodation, been placed and kept in such accommodation for an aggregate of more than 48 hours,

the maximum period does not expire until 12 midday on the first day, which is not itself a public holiday or a Sunday, after the public holiday or Sunday.

Period—A freestanding application for an interim secure accommodation order cannot be made. Where the court was satisfied it had all the information needed to determine the issues raised by the application and that it would be procedurally fair to proceed, it is unlikely there would be grounds upon which the court could properly adjourn the application. Prolonging secure accommodation proceedings simply in order to keep a children's guardian involved for the purposes of assisting the child or overseeing the performance of the local authority's statutory duties, was not a proper use of the court's power (*Birmingham City Council v M* [2008] 2 FLR 542, FD).

11 Maximum initial period of authorisation by a court

Subject to regulations 12 and 13 the maximum period for which a court may authorise a child to whom section 25 of the Act applies to be kept in secure accommodation is three months.

12 Further periods of authorisation by a court

Subject to regulation 13 a court may from time to time authorise a child to whom section 25 of the Act applies to be kept in secure accommodation for a further period not exceeding six months at any one time.

****

14 Duty to inform parents and others in relation to children in secure accommodation in a children's home

Where a child to whom section 25 of the Act applies is kept in secure accommodation in a children's home and it is intended that an application will be made to a court to keep the child in that accommodation, the local authority which are looking after the child shall if practicable inform of that intention as soon as possible –

(a) his parents,
(b) any person who is not a parent of his but who has parental responsibility for him,
(c) the child's independent visitor, if one has been appointed, and
(d) any other person who that local authority consider should be informed.

Amendments—SI 1995/1398.

****

Children (Secure Accommodation) (No 2) Regulations 1991, SI 1991/2034

Disapplication to Wales—By virtue of SI 2015/1988, these Regulations are disapplied in relation to Wales as from April 2016.

1 Citation and commencement

(1) These Regulations may be cited as the Children (Secure Accommodation) (No 2) Regulations 1991 and shall come into force on 14 October 1991 immediately after the Children (Secure Accommodation) Regulations 1991.

2 Applications to court – special cases

(1) Applications to a court under section 25 of the Children Act 1989 in respect of a child provided with accommodation by a health authority, a National Health Service trust established under section 5 of the National Health Service and Community Care Act 1990, an NHS foundation trust or a local authority in the exercise of education functions or provided with accommodation pursuant to arrangements made by the Secretary of State, the National Health Service Commissioning Board or a clinical commissioning group under the National Health Service Act 2006 shall, unless the child is looked after by a local authority, be made only by the health authority, National Health Service trust, NHS foundation trust or local authority providing accommodation for the child or by the person (namely, the Secretary of State, the National Health Service Commissioning Board or a clinical commissioning group) who has made arrangements for the provision of accommodation for the child.

(2) Applications to a court under section 25 of the Children Act 1989 in respect of a child provided with accommodation in a care home or independent hospital shall, unless the child is looked after by a local authority, be made only by the person carrying on the home in which accommodation is provided for the child.

Amendments—SI 2000/694; SI 2002/546; SI 2004/696; SI 2010/1172; SI 2013/235.

'looked after by a local authority'—See CA 1989, s 22(1) and *Re W (A Child)* [2016] EWCA Civ 804, and as to a child who is bailed with a condition of residence to the local authority, see *Re C (Secure Accommodation: Bail)* [1994] 2 FLR 922, FD.

Civil Jurisdiction and Judgments (Maintenance) Regulations 2011, SI 2011/1484

ARRANGEMENT OF REGULATIONS

Regulation		Page
1	Citation, commencement and extent	2436
2	Interpretation	2437
3	The Maintenance Regulation	2437
4	Provisions relating to information	2437
5	Provisions relating to authentic instruments and court settlements	2437
8	Allocation of jurisdiction within the United Kingdom	2437
10	Review	2437
	Schedule 1 – The Maintenance Regulation	2438
	Part 1 – Introductory	2438
	Part 2 – Recognition and enforcement of maintenance decisions made by courts in Maintenance Regulation States other than Denmark	2438
	Part 3 – Recognition and enforcement of maintenance decisions made by courts in Denmark etc	2440
	Part 4 – Recognition and enforcement of maintenance decisions – general	2441
	Part 5 – Establishment and modification of maintenance under the Maintenance Regulation	2442
	Schedule 2 – Provisions relating to information	2444
	Schedule 3 – Provisions Relating to Authentic Instruments and Court Settlements	2445
	Schedule 6 – Allocation within the United Kingdom of Jurisdiction Relating to Maintenance Matters	2446

Scope—These Regulations facilitate the application of Council Regulation (EC) No 4/2009 ('the Maintenance Regulation') in the UK from 18 June 2011. Reference should be made to the annotations to the Maintenance Regulation and to FPR 2010, Pt 34, Ch 3. FPR PD34C also makes provision for the application of the Maintenance Regulation.

The Regulations are structured by division into schedules:

Reg 3 and Sch 1	Provisions relating to the recognition and enforcement in the UK jurisdictions of maintenance decisions from other Member States
Reg 4 and Sch 2	Provisions regarding the sharing of information between the designated central authorities of the UK and certain designated public bodies under Arts 61–62 of the Maintenance Regulation
Reg 5 and Sch 3	Provisions relating to the recognition and enforcement in the UK jurisdictions of authentic instruments and court settlements from other Member States as required by Art 48 of the Maintenance Regulation
Reg 6 and Sch 4	Amendments to CJJA 1982 arising from the application of the Maintenance Regulation
Reg 7 and Sch 5	Amendments to the Civil Jurisdiction and Judgments Order 2001 arising from the application of the Maintenance Regulation
Reg 8 and Sch 6	Provisions relating to the allocation of jurisdiction to hear maintenance matters as between the courts of the different parts of the UK (England and Wales, Scotland and Northern Ireland) adapting the jurisdictional rules of the Maintenance Regulation
Reg 9 and Sch 7	Consequential amendments

1 Citation, commencement and extent

(1) These Regulations may be cited as the Civil Jurisdiction and Judgments (Maintenance) Regulations 2011, and shall come into force on 18 June 2011.

(2) These Regulations extend to England and Wales, Scotland and Northern Ireland.

(3) An amendment, repeal or revocation made by these Regulations has the same extent as the enactment amended, repealed or revoked.

2 Interpretation

In these Regulations –

'the Act' means the Civil Jurisdiction and Judgments Act 1982;

'the Order' means the Civil Jurisdiction and Judgments Order 2001;

'the Maintenance Regulation' means Council Regulation (EC) No 4/2009 including as applied in relation to Denmark by virtue of the Agreement made on 19 October 2005 between the European Community and the Kingdom of Denmark;

'Maintenance Regulation State' in any provision, in the application of that provision in relation to the Maintenance Regulation, refers to any of the Member States.

3 The Maintenance Regulation

Schedule 1 (which contains provisions relating to the enforcement of maintenance decisions pursuant to the Maintenance Regulation) has effect.

4 Provisions relating to information

Schedule 2 (which contains provisions relating to access to, and the transmission and use of, information) has effect.

5 Provisions relating to authentic instruments and court settlements

Schedule 3 (which contains provisions relating to authentic instruments and court settlements) has effect.

****

8 Allocation of jurisdiction within the United Kingdom

Schedule 6 (which contains rules for the allocation of jurisdiction within the United Kingdom in relation to maintenance) has effect.

****

10 Review

(1) Before the end of each review period, the Secretary of State must –

(a) carry out a review of the provisions of these Regulations,

(b) set out the conclusions of the review in a report, and

(c) publish the report.

(2) The review shall relate to the operation of these Regulations as they affect England and Wales only.

(3) In carrying out the review the Secretary of State must, so far as is reasonable, have regard to how the Maintenance Regulation has been given effect in other Member States.

(4) The report must in particular –

(a) set out the objectives intended to be achieved by the provisions of these Regulations,

(b) assess the extent to which those objectives are achieved, and

(c) assess whether those objectives remain appropriate, and, if so, the extent to which they could be achieved in a manner that imposes less regulation.

(5) 'Review period' means –

(a) the period of five years beginning with the day on which these Regulations come into force, and

(b) subject to paragraph (6), each successive period of five years.

(6) If a report under this regulation is published before the last day of the review period to which it relates, the following review period is to begin with the day on which that report is published.

PART IV

SCHEDULE 1
THE MAINTENANCE REGULATION

Scope—Sch 1 is divided into five parts: Pts 1, 4 and 5 being of general application, Pt 2 applying to decisions made by courts in Member States other than Denmark (to which the procedures in Ch 4, S 1 of the Maintenance Regulation apply) and Pt 3 applying to decisions made by courts in Denmark, and in transitional cases (Art 75) (to which Ch 4, S 2 of the Maintenance Regulation applies).

PART 1
INTRODUCTORY

1 Interpretation

(1) In this Schedule –

'court' includes a tribunal, and any administrative authority which is a court for the purposes of the Maintenance Regulation by virtue of Article 2(2) of that Regulation;

'debtor', in relation to a maintenance decision, means the person liable, or alleged to be liable, to make the payments for which that decision provides;

'maintenance decision' has the meaning given to 'decision' by Article 2 of the Maintenance Regulation.

(2) In this Schedule –

(a) any reference to a numbered Article is a reference to the Article so numbered in the Maintenance Regulation and any reference to a sub-division of a numbered Article shall be construed accordingly;

(b) references to a registered decision include, to the extent of its registration, references to a decision so registered to a limited extent only.

(3) Anything authorised or required by the Maintenance Regulation or by this Schedule to be done by, to or before a particular magistrates' court may be done by, to or before any magistrates' court acting for the same petty sessions district in Northern Ireland as that court.

Amendments—SI 2014/879.

2 Central authorities

(1) The following are designated as Central Authorities under Article 49 of the Maintenance Regulation –

(a) in relation to England and Wales, the Lord Chancellor;

(b) in relation to Scotland, the Scottish Ministers;

(c) in relation to Northern Ireland, the Department of Justice.

(2) If a person outside the United Kingdom does not know to which Central Authority in the United Kingdom a communication should be addressed, the person may address it to the Lord Chancellor.

PART 2
RECOGNITION AND ENFORCEMENT OF MAINTENANCE DECISIONS MADE BY COURTS IN MAINTENANCE REGULATION STATES OTHER THAN DENMARK

3 Application of Part 2

This Part shall apply to maintenance decisions made by courts in Maintenance Regulation States other than Denmark.

4 Enforcement of maintenance decisions

(1) Subject to sub-paragraph (2), where a maintenance decision falls to be enforced in the United Kingdom under Section 1 of Chapter IV of the Maintenance Regulation, the court to which an application for enforcement is to be made is –

(a) in England and Wales, the family court,

(b) in Scotland, a sheriff court, and
(c) in Northern Ireland, a magistrates' court.

(2) An application for enforcement is to be transmitted to the family court, the magistrates' court or sheriff court designated for these purposes by rules of court ('the enforcing court') –

(a) in England and Wales, by the Lord Chancellor,
(b) in Scotland, by the Scottish Ministers, and
(c) in Northern Ireland, by the Department of Justice.

(3) Jurisdiction in relation to applications for enforcement of such maintenance decisions lies with the courts for the part of the United Kingdom in which –

(a) the person against whom enforcement is sought is resident,
(b) assets belonging to that person and which are susceptible to enforcement are situated or held.

(4) For the purposes of the enforcement of a maintenance decision –

(a) the decision shall be of the same force and effect,
(b) the enforcing court shall have in relation to its enforcement the same powers, and
(c) proceedings for or with respect to its enforcement may be taken, as if the decision had originally been made by the enforcing court.

(5) Sub-paragraph (4) is subject to sub-paragraphs (6) and (7).

(6) (a) A maintenance decision which is enforceable in England and Wales by virtue of Section 1 of Chapter IV of the Maintenance Regulation and these Regulations shall be enforceable in the family court in the same manner as a maintenance order made by that court.
(b) In this sub-paragraph 'maintenance order' has the meaning given by section 1(10) of the Maintenance Enforcement Act 1991.

(7) A maintenance decision which is enforceable in Northern Ireland by virtue of Section 1 of Chapter IV of the Maintenance Regulation and these Regulations shall be enforceable in a magistrates' court in Northern Ireland in the same manner as an order made by that court, save that Article 98 of the Magistrates' Courts (Northern Ireland) Order 1981 has effect as modified by section 5(6A) of the Act.

(8) Sub-paragraph (4) is also subject to –

(a) Article 21 (application by debtor for refusal or suspension of enforcement);
(b) paragraph 8 below;
(c) any provision made by rules of court as to the procedure for the enforcement of maintenance decisions given in another Maintenance Regulation State.

(9) (a) The debtor under a maintenance decision which is or has been the subject of enforcement proceedings in England and Wales or Northern Ireland by virtue of Section 1 of Chapter IV of the Maintenance Regulation and these Regulations must give notice of any change of address to the court officer, or in Northern Ireland, the clerk, of the court in which enforcement proceedings have been, or are being, taken.
(b) A person who without reasonable excuse fails to comply with this sub-paragraph shall be guilty of an offence and liable on summary conviction to a fine not exceeding level 2 on the standard scale.

(10) An application for refusal or suspension of enforcement under Article 21(2) or (3) of the Maintenance Regulation shall be made –

(aa) in England and Wales, to the family court by way of application notice,
(a) in Northern Ireland, to a magistrates' court by way of complaint, and
(b) in Scotland, to a sheriff court by way of summary application.

Amendments—SI 2012/2814; SI 2014/879.

'transmitted to the Family Court' (para 4(2))—An applicant is not required to approach the Family Court via the Central Authority, although he/she may do so. If the applicant wishes, an application may be made directly

PART IV

to the Family Court (*MS v PS* (Case C-283/16) [2017] 1 FLR 1163, CJEU following *EDG v RR (Enforcement of Foreign Maintenance Order)* [2015] 1 FLR 270, FD; and disapproving *AB v JJB* [2015] 2 FLR 1143, FD).

PART 3
RECOGNITION AND ENFORCEMENT OF MAINTENANCE DECISIONS MADE BY COURTS IN DENMARK ETC

5 Application of Part 3

This Part applies in relation to –

(a) maintenance decisions made by courts in Denmark, and

(b) maintenance decisions to which Sections 2 and 3 of Chapter IV of the Maintenance Regulation apply by virtue of Article 75(2)(a) or (b).

6 Recognition and enforcement of maintenance orders

(1) Subject to sub-paragraph (2), the court to which an application for registration of a maintenance decision under Section 2 of Chapter IV of the Maintenance Regulation is to be made is –

(a) in England and Wales, the family court,

(b) in Scotland, a sheriff court, and

(c) in Northern Ireland, a magistrates' court.

(2) An application for registration is to be transmitted to the family court, the magistrates' court or sheriff court designated for these purposes by rules of court ('the registering court') –

(a) in England and Wales, by the Lord Chancellor,

(b) in Scotland, by the Scottish Ministers, and

(c) in Northern Ireland, by the Department of Justice.

(3) Where an application for registration of a maintenance decision is transmitted to a court –

(a) the decision may be registered for enforcement by the court, and

(b) if so registered, the decision shall be treated as having been declared enforceable for the purposes of Section 2 of Chapter IV of the Maintenance Regulation.

(4) (a) An application for registration shall be determined in the first instance by the prescribed officer of the registering court.

(b) In this sub-paragraph, 'prescribed' means prescribed by rules of court.

(5) For the purposes of the enforcement of a registered maintenance decision –

(a) the decision shall be of the same force and effect,

(b) the registering court shall have in relation to its enforcement the same powers, and

(c) proceedings for or with respect to its enforcement may be taken, as if the decision had originally been made by the registering court.

(6) Sub-paragraph (5) is subject to sub-paragraphs (7) and (8).

(7) (a) A maintenance decision which is enforceable in England and Wales by virtue of Section 2 of Chapter IV of the Maintenance Regulation and these Regulations shall be enforceable in the family court in the same manner as a maintenance order made by that court.

(b) In this sub-paragraph 'maintenance order' has the meaning given by section 1(10) of the Maintenance Enforcement Act 1991.

(8) A maintenance decision which is enforceable in Northern Ireland by virtue of Section 2 of Chapter IV of the Maintenance Regulation and these Regulations shall be enforceable in a magistrates' court in Northern Ireland in the same manner as an order made by that court, save that Article 98 of the Magistrates' Courts (Northern Ireland) Order 1981 has effect as modified by section 5(6A) of the Act.

(9) Sub-paragraph (5) is also subject to –

(a) Article 36(3) (restriction on enforcement where appeal pending or time for appeal unexpired);
(b) paragraph 8 below;
(c) any provision made by rules of court as to the procedure for the enforcement of maintenance decisions registered under the Maintenance Regulation and these Regulations.

(10)
(a) The debtor under a maintenance decision registered in accordance with this paragraph in the family court or, in Northern Ireland, a magistrates' court must give notice of any change of address to the court officer, or in Northern Ireland, the clerk of that court.
(b) A person who without reasonable excuse fails to comply with this sub-paragraph shall be guilty of an offence and liable on summary conviction to a fine not exceeding level 2 on the standard scale.

Amendments—SI 2014/879.

7 Proceedings to contest decisions given on appeal in connection with applications for registration

An appeal under Article 33 may only be on a point of law and lies –
(a) in England and Wales, to the family court in accordance with section 111A of the Magistrates' Courts Act 1980;
(b) in Scotland, to the Inner House of the Court of Session;
(c) in Northern Ireland, to the Court of Appeal.

Amendments—SI 2014/879.

PART 4
RECOGNITION AND ENFORCEMENT OF MAINTENANCE DECISIONS – GENERAL

8 Interest on judgments

(1) Subject to sub-paragraphs (2) and (3) and rules of court as to the payment of interest under this paragraph, where a person applying for registration or enforcement of a maintenance decision shows that –
(a) the decision provides for the payment of a sum of money, and
(b) in accordance with the law of the Maintenance Regulation State in which the maintenance decision was given and the terms of the decision, interest on that sum is recoverable at a particular rate and from a particular date or time, the debt resulting from registration or enforcement of the decision is to carry interest at that rate and from that date or time.

(2) In the case of an application for registration of a maintenance decision, interest is not recoverable unless the rate of interest and the date or time referred to in sub-paragraph (1)(b) are registered with the decision.

(3) (a) Interest on arrears of sums payable under a maintenance decision which falls to be enforced in the family court, or a magistrates' court in Northern Ireland by virtue of the Maintenance Regulation and these Regulations shall not be recoverable in that court.
(b) But this sub-paragraph does not affect the operation in relation to any such maintenance decision of section 11A of the Maintenance and Affiliation Orders Act (Northern Ireland) 1966 (which enables interest to be recovered if the decision is registered for enforcement in the High Court).

(4) Except as mentioned in sub-paragraph (3), debts under maintenance decisions enforceable in the United Kingdom by virtue of the Maintenance Regulation shall carry interest only as provided by this paragraph.

Amendments—SI 2014/879.

9 Currency of payments under maintenance decisions

(1) Sums payable under a maintenance decision enforceable in the United Kingdom by virtue of the Maintenance Regulation, including any arrears so payable, shall be paid in sterling where an order is made on an application for enforcement in England and Wales, Scotland or Northern Ireland.

(2) Where the maintenance decision is expressed in any other currency, the amount shall be converted on the basis of the exchange rate prevailing on the date on which the application for enforcement or registration of the decision was received by a Central Authority in the United Kingdom for transmission to a court.

(3) For the purposes of this paragraph, a written certificate purporting to be signed by an officer of any bank in the United Kingdom and stating the exchange rate prevailing on a specified date shall be evidence of the facts stated (and in Scotland, sufficient evidence of those facts).

10 Proof and admissibility of certain maintenance decisions and related documents

(1) For the purposes of proceedings relating to the Maintenance Regulation –

(a) a document, duly authenticated, which purports to be a copy of a maintenance decision given by a court in a Maintenance Regulation State shall without further proof be deemed to be a true copy, unless the contrary is shown; and

(b) an extract from a maintenance decision issued by a court in a Maintenance Regulation State in accordance with Article 20 or Article 28 (as the case may be) shall be evidence that that decision is enforceable there.

(2) A document purporting to be a copy of a maintenance decision given by a court mentioned in sub-paragraph (1)(a) is duly authenticated for the purposes of this paragraph if it purports –

(a) to bear the seal of that court; or

(b) to be certified by any person in his capacity as a judge or officer of that court to be a true copy of a maintenance decision given by that court.

(3) Nothing in this paragraph shall prejudice the admission in evidence of any document which is admissible apart from this paragraph.

PART 5
ESTABLISHMENT AND MODIFICATION OF MAINTENANCE UNDER THE MAINTENANCE REGULATION

11 (1) This paragraph applies to an application submitted under Article 56 for establishment or modification of a decision to the Lord Chancellor, in relation to England and Wales, or to the Department of Justice in relation to Northern Ireland.

(2) Upon receipt of an application submitted under Article 56 for establishment or modification of a decision in England and Wales, the Lord Chancellor shall send that application to the court officer of the family court in the Maintenance Enforcement Business Centre for the area in which the respondent is residing.

(3) Upon receipt of the application under sub-paragraph (2), the court officer of that court shall decide –

(a) whether the courts of England and Wales have jurisdiction to determine the application by virtue of the Maintenance Regulation and Schedule 6 to these Regulations; and

(b) if so, whether the family court has power to make the decision or modification sought under the law in force in England and Wales.

(4) Where the court officer decides under sub-paragraph (3)(a) that the courts of England and Wales do not have jurisdiction to determine the application, the officer shall return the application to the Lord Chancellor with a written explanation of the reasons for that decision.

(5) *(revoked)*

(6) Subject to sub-paragraph (7), if the court officer decides under sub-paragraph (3)(b) that the family court has power to make the decision or modification sought, the court officer shall issue the application and serve it on the respondent.

(7) If the respondent does not reside in the area covered by the Maintenance Enforcement Business Centre to which the application has been sent, the court officer shall –

(a) if satisfied that the respondent is residing within the area covered by another Maintenance Enforcement Business Centre, send the application to the court officer of the family court in the Maintenance Enforcement Business Centre for that other area and inform the Lord Chancellor that it has been so sent; or

(b) if unable to establish where the respondent is residing, return the application to the Lord Chancellor.

(8) A court officer who receives an application by virtue of sub-paragraph (7)(a) shall proceed under sub-paragraph (6) as if that court officer had decided that the family court has power to make the decision or modification sought.

(9) Where the court officer has determined in accordance with sub-paragraph (3)(b) that the family court has power to make the decision or modification sought, the application shall be treated for the purpose of establishment or modification of a decision under the Maintenance Regulation as an application under the law in force in England and Wales.

(10) Sub-paragraphs (2) to (9) apply to an application submitted under Article 56 for establishment or modification of a decision in Northern Ireland to the Department of Justice in relation to Northern Ireland as if –

(a) references to England and Wales were references to Northern Ireland;

(b) references to the Lord Chancellor were references to the Department of Justice;

(c) for 'court officer' were substituted 'clerk of petty sessions';

(d) …

(e) references to the courts of England and Wales or to the family court were references to the courts of Northern Ireland;

(ea) in sub-paragraph (2), for 'the Maintenance Enforcement Business Centre for the area' there were substituted 'the petty sessions district';

(f) for sub-paragraph (3)(b) there were substituted –

'(b) if so, whether the magistrates' court has power to make the decision or modification sought under –

(i) the Domestic Proceedings (Northern Ireland) Order 1980; or

(ii) Article 15 of and Schedule 1 to the Children (Northern Ireland) Order 1995.'

(g) after paragraph (4) there were inserted –

'(5) Where the clerk of petty sessions decides under sub-paragraph (3)(b) that the magistrates' court does not have power to make the decision or modification sought, the clerk of petty sessions shall send the application to –

(a) the High Court of Judicature; or

(b) a county court,

as appears to the clerk of petty sessions to be appropriate.';

(ga) in sub-paragraph (7) –

(i) for 'the area covered by the Maintenance Enforcement Business Centre' there were substituted 'the petty sessions district'; and

(ii) in paragraph (a) –

(aa) for 'the area covered by another Maintenance Enforcement Business Centre' there were substituted 'another petty sessions district'; and

(bb) 'in the Maintenance Enforcement Business Centre for' were omitted; and

(h) in sub-paragraph (9) for 'the law in force in England and Wales' there were substituted 'the Domestic Proceedings (Northern Ireland) Order 1980 or Article 15 of and Schedule 1 to the Children (Northern Ireland) Order 1995'.

(11) In this paragraph –

'respondent' means the person who is alleged in an application for establishment of a decision under Article 56 to owe maintenance, or where the application is for modification of a decision, the person against whom the modification is sought;

and a reference to an application is a reference to an application together with any documents which accompany it.

Amendments—Inserted by SI 2012/2814. Amended by SI 2014/879; SI 2015/1489.

Modification—From 31 July 2015, the administration of reciprocal maintenance enforcement is handled in three Maintenance Enforcement Business Centres. Reciprocal enforcement in Wales will be handled in Bridgend and in England in Bury St Edmunds, except that London reciprocal enforcements are handled by the London Maintenance Enforcement Business Centre.

SCHEDULE 2
PROVISIONS RELATING TO INFORMATION

Scope—Sch 2 makes necessary provision for the sharing of information between public bodies designated for the task and designated central authorities. Para 1 lists the public bodies designated by the UK to share the information identified in Art 61(2) of the Maintenance Regulation with the three UK central authorities (Sch 1, para 2). The giving of access to specific information held by public bodies is intended to facilitate the collection of maintenance. Information may only be withheld for national security or public safety reasons (Maintenance Regulation, Art 61). The information must be information already held by the relevant public body. There is no requirement to seek out, compile and maintain additional information not already held on databases in the public domain. The information sought must be adequate, relevant and not excessive and must relate to (a) the address of the debtor or of the creditor; (b) the debtor's income; (c) the identification of the debtor's employer and/or of the debtor's bank account(s); (d) the debtor's assets (Maintenance Regulation, Art 61.2). Information may only be used for recovery of maintenance claims (Maintenance Regulation, Arts 62.1 and 62.2).

1 (1) The following are designated for the purposes of Article 61(1) of the Maintenance Regulation to provide the information referred to in Article 61(2) to the Central Authorities designated under paragraph 2 of Schedule 1 –

(a) the Secretary of State;
(b) *(revoked)*
(c) the Revenue and Customs officers;
(d) the Department for Employment and Learning in Northern Ireland;
(e) the Department of the Environment in Northern Ireland;
(f) the Department of Finance and Personnel in Northern Ireland;
(g) the Department for Social Development in Northern Ireland.

(2) The information to be supplied by the Secretary of State is limited to information held for functions relating to social security, child support or employment or training.

(3) In sub-paragraph (2), 'functions relating to social security' includes functions relating to statutory payments as defined in section 4C(11) of the Social Security Contributions and Benefits Act 1992 and maternity allowance under section 35 of that Act.

(4) In this Schedule, references to the Secretary of State include a person providing services to the Secretary of State in connection with the functions mentioned in sub-paragraph (2).

Amendments—SI 2012/2814.

'the Child Maintenance and Enforcement Commission' (para 1(1)(b))—By virtue of SI 2012/2007, art 5(3), this should be read as 'the Secretary of State'.

2 Subject to the provisions of Chapter VII of the Maintenance Regulation, the persons and authorities to whom the Central Authorities transmit information in accordance with Article 62(1) of that Regulation may process that information in any manner necessary to facilitate the adjudication and recovery of maintenance claims.

3 (1) Information referred to in Article 61(2) of the Maintenance Regulation which is received by a Central Authority, or by a person supplying services to a Central Authority, from a body or person designated under paragraph 1 cannot be disclosed to another person unless the disclosure is in connection with a function of the Central Authority under, and is in accordance with, Chapter VII of the Maintenance Regulation.

(2) Sub-paragraph (1) does not apply to –

(a) the disclosure of information which is in the form of a summary or collection of information so framed as not to enable identification of any person from the information;

(b) disclosure which is made in pursuance of an order of a court;

(c) disclosure which is required by any other enactment.

4 (1) Subject to sub-paragraph (3), a person who –

(a) is or has been employed by a Central Authority designated under paragraph 2 of Schedule 1; or

(b) provides or has provided services to such a Central Authority,

is guilty of an offence if he or she discloses, otherwise than in accordance with paragraph 3, information referred to in Article 61(2) of the Maintenance Regulation which has been obtained from a person or body designated under paragraph 1 and which relates to a person whose identity is specified in the information disclosed or can be deduced from it.

(2) It is a defence to prove that, at the time of the alleged offence, the person believed that he or she was making the disclosure lawfully in accordance with this Schedule and the Maintenance Regulation, and had no reasonable cause to believe otherwise.

(3) Sub-paragraph (1) does not apply to disclosure of information received by such a person –

(a) from the Department for Employment and Learning in Northern Ireland, the Department of the Environment in Northern Ireland, or the Department of Finance and Personnel in Northern Ireland;

(b) from the Secretary of State where the information so disclosed is held by the Secretary of State for the purposes of employment and training only.

5 A person found guilty of an offence under this Schedule shall be liable –

(a) on conviction on indictment, to imprisonment for a term not exceeding two years, to a fine or to both;

(b) on summary conviction, to imprisonment for a term not exceeding 3 months or to a fine not exceeding the statutory maximum or to both.

SCHEDULE 3
PROVISIONS RELATING TO AUTHENTIC INSTRUMENTS AND COURT SETTLEMENTS

Scope—Sch 3 makes provision relating to authentic instruments and court settlements that are sent to the UK for enforcement from other Member States. The purpose of the Schedule is to modify the application of Sch 1 to these instruments, as appropriate, so as to respect the obligation in Art 48 of the Maintenance Regulation to recognise and enforce such instruments in the same way as decisions.

1 References in this Schedule to authentic instruments and court settlements are references to those authentic instruments and court settlements (as defined in Article 2 of the Maintenance Regulation) which are to be recognised and enforceable in the same way as maintenance decisions by virtue of Article 48 of that Regulation.

2 (1) In relation to an authentic instrument or court settlement which is enforceable in the Maintenance Regulation State of origin, Schedule 1 applies, subject to the modifications in subparagraphs (2), (3) and (4), as if that authentic instrument or court settlement was a maintenance decision given by a court in that Maintenance Regulation State.

(2) Paragraphs 4(4) and 6(5) of Schedule 1 apply in relation to authentic instruments and court settlements as if, for the words 'as if the decision had been originally made' there were substituted 'as if it was a decision which had originally been made'.

(3) Paragraph 10 of Schedule 1 applies to authentic instruments as if –

(a) in sub-paragraph (1)(a), for the words 'given by a court' there were substituted 'drawn up by, registered by, authenticated by or concluded before a competent authority';

PART IV

(b) for sub-paragraph (1)(b) there were substituted –

'(b) an extract from an authentic instrument issued by a competent authority in a Maintenance Regulation State in accordance with Article 48 shall be evidence that that instrument is enforceable there.';

(c) for sub-paragraph (2) there were substituted –

'(2) A document purporting to be a copy of an authentic instrument drawn up by, registered by, authenticated by or concluded before a competent authority in a Maintenance Regulation State is duly authenticated for the purposes of this paragraph if it purports to be certified to be a true copy of such an instrument by a person duly authorised in that State to do so.'

(4) Paragraph 10(1)(b) of Schedule 1 applies to court settlements as if, for the words 'Article 20 or Article 28 (as the case may be)' there were substituted 'Article 48'.

3 Section 18(7) of the Act (disapplication of section 18) has effect to disapply section 18 in relation to an authentic instrument or court settlement to which Article 48 applies.

****

SCHEDULE 6
ALLOCATION WITHIN THE UNITED KINGDOM OF JURISDICTION RELATING TO MAINTENANCE MATTERS

Scope—'Maintenance' has been excluded by Sch 4 from the regime contained in CJJA 1982 ('the 1982 Act'), s 16 and Sch 4 and s 20 and Sch 8 (Scotland) regarding the allocation of jurisdiction as between the different parts of the UK. Sch 6 establishes a replacement regime relating to maintenance within the UK previously contained in Sch 4 of the 1982 Act based on the Maintenance Regulation. See, further, *Re V (European Maintenance Regulation)* [2017] 1 FLR 1083, FD. Sch 6, para 16 lists the matters and proceedings in which the rules in the Schedule do not apply, in particular, the jurisdiction of the CSA on behalf of the Department for Work and Pensions following the abolition of CMEC to make child support calculations in the UK is not subject to the Schedule.

1 The provisions of this Schedule have effect for determining, as between the parts of the United Kingdom, whether the courts of a particular part of the United Kingdom, or any particular court in that part, have or has jurisdiction in proceedings where the subject-matter of the proceedings is within the scope of the Maintenance Regulation as determined by Article 1 of that Regulation.

2 In this Schedule, a reference to an Article by number alone is a reference to the Article so numbered in the Maintenance Regulation.

3 The provisions of Chapter II of the Maintenance Regulation apply to the determination of jurisdiction in the circumstances mentioned in paragraph 1, subject to the modifications specified in the following provisions of this Schedule.

4 Article 3 applies as if –

(a) the references in Article 3(a) and (b) to the court for the place where the defendant or the creditor is habitually resident were references to the court for the part of the United Kingdom in which the defendant, or the creditor, as the case may be, is habitually resident;

(b) the references to a person's nationality were references to a person's domicile.

5 Article 4(1) to (3) applies as if –

(a) for 'Member State', wherever it occurs, there were substituted 'part of the United Kingdom';

(b) the reference to a person's nationality was a reference to a person's domicile.

6 Article 5 applies as if –

(a) after 'this Regulation' there were inserted 'as modified by Schedule 6 to the Civil Jurisdiction and Judgments (Maintenance) Regulations 2011';

(b) for 'Member State' there were substituted 'part of the United Kingdom'.

7 Where Article 6, as read with the second paragraph of Article 2(3), indicates that the courts of the United Kingdom have jurisdiction under the Maintenance Regulation, and the parties are domiciled in different parts of the United Kingdom, the courts of either part may exercise jurisdiction (subject to Article 12 as it has effect by virtue of this Schedule).

8 Article 7 applies as if for the second sentence there were substituted –

'The dispute must have a sufficient connection with the part of the United Kingdom in which the court seised is located.'.

9 (1) Sub-paragraphs (2) and (3) have effect in addition to Article 8.

(2) Where a decision is given in a part of the United Kingdom where the creditor is habitually resident, proceedings to modify the decision or to have a new decision given cannot be brought by the debtor in any other part of the United Kingdom as long as the creditor remains habitually resident in the part of the United Kingdom in which the decision was given.

(3) Sub-paragraph (2) does not apply where –

- (a) the parties have agreed that the courts of that other part of the United Kingdom are to have jurisdiction in accordance with Article 4 as applied by paragraph 5 of this Schedule, or
- (b) the creditor submits to the jurisdiction of the courts of that other part of the United Kingdom pursuant to Article 5 as applied by paragraph 6 of this Schedule.

10 Article 9 does not apply.

11 (1) Sub-paragraphs (2) and (3) have effect instead of Articles 10 and 11.

(2) Where a defendant habitually resident in one part of the United Kingdom is sued in a court of another part of the United Kingdom and does not enter an appearance, the court will declare of its own initiative that it has no jurisdiction unless its jurisdiction is derived from the provisions of this Schedule.

(3) The court will stay the proceedings so long as it is not shown that the defendant has been able to receive the document instituting the proceedings or an equivalent document in sufficient time to enable him to arrange for his defence, or that all necessary steps have been taken to this end.

12 Article 12 applies as if after 'different Member States' there were inserted 'or different parts of the United Kingdom'.

13 Article 13 applies as if after 'different Member States' there were inserted 'or different parts of the United Kingdom'.

14 Article 14 applies as if –

- (a) for 'a Member State' there were substituted 'a part of the United Kingdom';
- (b) after 'another Member State' there were inserted 'or another part of the United Kingdom'.

15 Notwithstanding the preceding provisions of this Schedule, the exercise of jurisdiction in any proceedings in a court in the United Kingdom is subject to –

- (a) the Maintenance Regulation;
- (b) the Convention on jurisdiction and the recognition and enforcement of judgments in civil and commercial matters, between the European Community and the Republic of Iceland, the Kingdom of Norway, the Swiss Confederation and the Kingdom of Denmark signed on behalf of the European Community on 30 October 2007;
- (c) the Convention on jurisdiction and the enforcement of judgments in civil and commercial matters signed at Brussels on the 27 September 1968; and
- (d) the Convention on jurisdiction and the enforcement of judgments in civil and commercial matters concluded at Lugano on the 16 September 1988.

16 This Schedule does not apply to –

(a) matters in relation to which –

(i) the Secretary of State has jurisdiction to make a maintenance calculation by virtue of section 44 of the Child Support Act 1991;

(ii) the Department for Social Development in Northern Ireland has jurisdiction to make a maintenance calculation by virtue of Article 41 of the Child Support (Northern Ireland) Order 1991;

(b) proceedings for, or otherwise relating to, an order under any of the following Provisions –

(i) paragraph 23 of Schedule 2 to the Children Act 1989 (contribution orders);

(ii) section 106 of the Social Security Administration Act 1992 (recovery of expenditure on benefit from person liable for maintenance);

(iii) section 80 of the Social Work (Scotland) Act 1968 (enforcement of duty to make contributions);

(iv) section 81 of the Social Work (Scotland) Act 1968 (provisions as to decrees for aliment);

(v) Article 101 of the Health and Personal Social Services (Northern Ireland) Order 1972 (recovery of cost of accommodation for persons in need);

(vi) section 101 of the Social Security Administration (Northern Ireland) Act 1992 (recovery of expenditure on benefit from person liable for maintenance);

(vii) Article 41 of the Children (Northern Ireland) Order 1995 (contribution orders).

Amendments—SI 2012/2814.

****

Civil Legal Aid (Remuneration) Regulations 2013, SI 2013/422

****

SCHEDULE 5
EXPERTS' FEES AND RATES

1 Subject to paragraph 2, where the expert service is of a type listed in the Table, the Lord Chancellor must pay remuneration to the provider for the expert service at the fixed fees or at rates not exceeding the rates set out in the Table.

Table

Expert	*Non-London – hourly rate unless stated to be a fixed fee*	*London – hourly rate unless stated to be a fixed fee*
A&E consultant	£100.80	£108
Accident reconstruction	£72	£54.40
Accountant	£64	£64
Accountant (general staff)	£40	£40
Accountant (manager)	£86.40	£86.40
Accountant (partner)	£108	£115.20
Anaesthetist	£108	£108
Architect	£79.20	£72
Cardiologist	£115.20	£115.20
Cell telephone site analysis	£72	£72
Child psychiatrist	£108	£108

Expert	*Non-London – hourly rate unless stated to be a fixed fee*	*London – hourly rate unless stated to be a fixed fee*
Child psychologist	£100.80	£100.80
Computer expert	£72	£72
Consultant engineer	£72	£54.40
Dentist	£93.60	£93.60
Dermatologist	£86.40	£86.40
Disability consultant	£54.40	£54.40
DNA (testing of sample)	£252 per test	£252 per test
DNA (preparation of report)	£72	£72
Doctor (GP)	£79.20	£72
Employment consultant	£54.40	£54.40
Enquiry agent	£25.60	£18.40
ENT surgeon	£100.80	£100.80
General surgeon	£108	£72
Geneticist	£86.40	£86.40
GP (records report)	£50.40 fixed fee	£72 fixed fee
Gynaecologist	£108	£72
Haematologist	£97.60	£72
Handwriting expert	£72	£72
Interpreter	£28	£25
Lip reader/Signer	£57.60	£32.80
Mediator	£100.80	£100.80
Medical consultant	£108	£72
Medical microbiologist	£108	£108
Meteorologist	£100.80	£144 fixed fee
Midwife	£72	£72
Neonatologist (non-clinical negligence cerebral palsy case	£108	£108
Neonatologist (clinical negligence cerebral palsy case)	£180	£180
Neurologist (non-clinical negligence cerebral palsy case)	£122.40	£72
Neurologist (clinical negligence cerebral palsy case)	£200	£200
Neuropsychiatrist	£126.40	£72
Neuroradiologist (non-clinical negligence cerebral palsy case)	£136.80	£136.80
Neuroradiologist (clinical negligence cerebral palsy case)	£180	£180
Neurosurgeon	£136.80	£72
Nursing expert	£64.80	£64.80
Obstetrician	£108	£108
Occupational therapist	£54.50	£54.40
Oncologist	£112	£112
Orthopaedic surgeon	£115.20	£115.20
Paediatrician	£108	£72
Pathologist	£122.40	£432 fixed fee
Pharmacologist	£97.60	£97.60
Photographer	£25.60	£18.40
Physiotherapist	£64.80	£64.80
Plastic surgeon	£108	£108
Process server	£25.60	£18.40
Psychiatrist	£108	£108
Psychologist	£93.60	£93.60

PART IV

Expert	*Non-London – hourly rate unless stated to be a fixed fee*	*London – hourly rate unless stated to be a fixed fee*
Radiologist	£108	£108
Rheumatologist	£108	£108
Risk assessment expert	£50.40	£50.40
Speech therapist	£79.20	£79.20
Surveyor (housing disrepair)	£85	£115
Surveyor (non-housing disrepair)	£40	£40
Telecoms expert	£72	£72
Toxicologist	£108	£108
Urologist	£108	£108
Vet	£72	£72
Voice recognition	£93.60	£72

Amendments—Table substituted by SI 2013/2877.

2 Exceptional circumstances

(1) The Lord Chancellor may increase the fixed fees or rates set out in the Table after paragraph 1 if the Lord Chancellor considers it reasonable to do so due to exceptional circumstances.

(2) In sub-paragraph (1), 'exceptional circumstances' mean that the expert's evidence is key to the client's case and either –

(a) the complexity of the material is such that an expert with a high level of seniority is required; or

(b) the material is of such a specialised and unusual nature that only very few experts are available to provide the necessary evidence.

3 Payment of expert services of a type not listed in the Table after Part 1

Where the expert service is of a type not listed in the Table after paragraph 1, in considering the rate at which to fund the expert service the Lord Chancellor –

(a) must have regard to the rates set out in the Table after paragraph 1; and

(b) may require a number of quotes for provision of the service to be submitted to the Lord Chancellor.

4 General provisions relating to experts

(1) The costs and expenses relating to experts listed at sub-paragraph (2) are not payable by the Lord Chancellor.

(2) The costs and expenses are –

(a) any administration fee charged by an expert, including (but not limited to) –
   (i) a fee in respect of office space or provision of a consultation room;
   (ii) a fee in respect of administrative support services, such as typing services;
   (iii) a fee in respect of courier services;
   (iv) a subsistence fee; and

(b) any cancellation fee charged by an expert, where the notice of cancellation was given to the expert more than 72 hours before the relevant hearing or appointment.

5

The maximum amount that the Lord Chancellor may pay as a disbursement in respect of an expert's vehicle mileage is £0.45 per mile.

6

The maximum amount that the Lord Chancellor may pay as a disbursement in respect of an expert's travel time is £40 per hour.

County Court Remedies Regulations 2014, SI 2014/982

General note—These Regulations were necessitated by the creation of the single County Court and the Family Court and by the general increase in the powers of the County Court. They have repealed and replaced the 1991 Regulations and, unlike the former Regulations, impose no limit on the powers of the County Court to grant a 'freezing order' in an appropriate case. The 2014 Regulations are concerned solely with 'search orders'. The Regulations are clear and generally prevent the County Court granting a 'search order' and describe what to do where such an order is required in a County Court case.

Procedure—In a civil case, see CPR 1998, Pt 25 and PD25 and in a family case see FPR 2010, Pt 20 and PD20A.

1 Citation, commencement and interpretation

(1) These Regulations may be cited as the County Court Remedies Regulations 2014 and come into force on 22 April 2014 or, if made on or after that date, on the day after the day on which they are made.

(2) In these Regulations –

'judge of the County Court' is to be construed in accordance with section 5 of the County Courts Act 1984 Act; and

'search order' means an order under section 7 of the Civil Procedure Act 1997 (order requiring a party to admit another party to premises for the purpose of preserving evidence, etc.).

2 Revocation of the 1991 Regulations

The County Court Remedies Regulations 1991 ('the 1991 Regulations') are revoked.

3 The County Court's jurisdiction to make search orders

(1) Subject to the following provisions of this regulation, the County Court shall not grant a search order or vary or revoke a search order made by the High Court.

(2) Paragraph (1) shall not apply to a judge of the Court of Appeal or a High Court Judge sitting as a judge of the County Court.

(3) Paragraph (1) shall not –

(a) affect or modify powers expressly conferred on the County Court by or under any enactment other than section 38 of the County Courts Act 1984; or

(b) prevent the County Court from varying a search order where all the parties are agreed on the terms of the variation.

4 Applications for search orders in County Court proceedings

An application to the High Court for a search order in County Court proceedings shall be deemed to include an application for transfer of the proceedings to the High Court.

5 Transfer of proceedings to the County Court

(1) After an application for a search order has been disposed of by the High Court, the proceedings shall, unless the High Court orders otherwise, be transferred to the County Court if –

(a) they were transferred to the High Court; or

(b) apart from these Regulations, they should have been commenced in the County Court.

(2) Where a search order is made on an application made without notice, the application shall not be treated as disposed of for the purposes of paragraph (1) until any application to set aside or vary the order has been heard, or until the expiry of 28 days (or such other period as the Court may specify) during which no such application has been made.

PART IV

Divorce etc (Pensions) Regulations 2000, SI 2000/1123

ARRANGEMENT OF REGULATIONS

Regulation		Page
1	Citation, commencement and transitional provisions	2452
2	Interpretation	2452
3	Valuation	2452
4	Pension attachment: notices	2453
5	Pension attachment: reduction in benefits	2454
6	Pension attachment: change of circumstances	2454
7	Pension attachment: transfer of rights	2455
7A	Pension attachment: discharge of liability of the Board	2456
8	Service	2456
9	Pension sharing order not to take effect pending appeal	2457

General note—These regulations relate in the main to pension attachment (regs 4–8). However, reg 3 sets out the valuation methodology for the purposes of both pension sharing and attachment and reg 9 makes provision as to when a pension sharing order takes effect. These regulations apply only to pension arrangements (MCA 1973, ss 21A(2)(a) and 25D(3)). The corresponding regulations in relation to PPF compensation are the Divorce and Dissolution etc (Pension Protection Fund) Regulations 2011, which came into effect on 6 April 2011. The 2011 Regulations follow the scheme of the 2000 Regulations as to valuation, change in circumstances, service and the date when a pension compensation sharing order takes effect.

1 Citation, commencement and transitional provisions

(1) These Regulations may be cited as the Divorce etc (Pensions) Regulations 2000 and shall come into force on 1 December 2000.

(2) These Regulations shall apply to any proceedings for divorce, judicial separation or nullity of marriage commenced on or after 1 December 2000, and any such proceedings commenced before that date shall be treated as if these Regulations had not come into force.

2 Interpretation

In these Regulations –

(a) a reference to a section by number alone means the section so numbered in the Matrimonial Causes Act 1973;

(b) 'the 1984 Act' means the Matrimonial and Family Proceedings Act 1984;

(c) expressions defined in sections 21A and 25D(3) have the meanings assigned by those sections;

(d) every reference to a rule by number alone means the rule so numbered in the Family Procedure Rules 2010.

Amendments—SI 2011/1045.

3 Valuation

(1) For the purposes of the court's functions in connection with the exercise of any of its powers under Part II of the Matrimonial Causes Act 1973, benefits under a pension arrangement shall be calculated and verified in the manner set out in regulation 3 of the Pensions on Divorce etc (Provision of Information) Regulations 2000, and –

(a) the benefits shall be valued as at a date to be specified by the court (being not earlier than one year before the date of the petition and not later than the date on which the court is exercising its power);

(b) in determining that value the court may have regard to information furnished by the person responsible for the pension arrangement pursuant to any of the provisions set out in paragraph (2); and

(c) in specifying a date under sub-paragraph (a) above the court may have regard to the date specified in any information furnished as mentioned in sub-paragraph (b) above.

(2) The relevant provisions for the purposes of paragraph (1)(b) above are –

(a) the Pensions on Divorce etc (Provision of Information) Regulations 2000;
(b) regulation 5 of and Schedule 2 to the Occupational Pension Schemes (Disclosure of Information) Regulations 1996 and regulation 11 of and Schedule 1 to the Occupational Pension Schemes (Transfer Value) Regulations 1996;
(c) sections 93A and 94(1) of the Pension Schemes Act 1993;
(d) section 94(2) of the Pension Schemes Act 1993 or paragraph 2(a) (or, where applicable, 2(b)) of Schedule 2 to the Personal Pension Schemes (Disclosure of Information) Regulations 1987.

Amendments—SI 2016/289.

Scope—This regulation provides the valuation methodology for pension sharing and attachment by cross-referencing to the Pensions on Divorce etc (Provision of Information) Regulations 2000, reg 3, (i e the Cash Equivalent (CE)); reference should be made to the annotations to this regulation. The date of valuation referred to in this regulation is the date of the CE put before the court as valuation evidence. The CE used for this purpose may range from not earlier than 1 year before the date of the petition up to the date on which the court makes an order. The valuation may be furnished specifically for the purpose of family proceedings under the Pensions on Divorce etc (Provision of Information) Regulations 2000 or may be one supplied in the ordinary course of events under the provisions referred to in reg 3(2)(b)–(d). It should be noted that the Occupational Pension Schemes (Disclosure of Information) Regulations 1996 and the Personal Pension Schemes (Disclosure of Information) Regulations 1987 were revoked and replaced by the Occupational and Personal Pension Schemes (Disclosure of Information) Regulations 2013 with effect from 6 April 2014: see Pensions on Divorce etc (Provision of Information) Regulations 2000, reg 11.

4 Pension attachment: notices

(1) This regulation applies in the circumstances set out in section 25D(1)(a) (transfers of pension rights).

(2) Where this regulation applies, the person responsible for the first arrangement shall give notice in accordance with the following paragraphs of this regulation to –

(a) the person responsible for the new arrangement, and
(b) the other party.

(3) The notice to the person responsible for the new arrangement shall include copies of the following documents –

(a) every order made under section 23 imposing any requirement on the person responsible for the first arrangement in relation to the rights transferred;
(b) any order varying such an order;
(c) all information or particulars which the other party has been required to supply under any provision of rule 9.33 or 9.34 for the purpose of enabling the person responsible for the first arrangement –
  (i) to provide information, documents or representations to the court to enable it to decide what if any requirement should be imposed on that person; or
  (ii) to comply with any order imposing such a requirement;
(d) any notice given by the other party to the person responsible for the first arrangement under regulation 6;
(e) where the pension rights under the first arrangement were derived wholly or partly from rights held under a previous pension arrangement, any notice given to the person responsible for the previous arrangement under paragraph (2) of this regulation on the occasion of that acquisition of rights.

(4) The notice to the other party shall contain the following particulars –

(a) the fact that the pension rights have been transferred;
(b) the date on which the transfer takes effect;
(c) the name and address of the person responsible for the new arrangement;
(d) the fact that the order made under section 23 is to have effect as if it had been made in respect of the person responsible for the new arrangement.

(5) Both notices shall be given –

(a) within the period provided by section 99 of the Pension Schemes Act 1993 for the person responsible for the first arrangement to carry out what the member requires; and

PART IV

(b) before the expiry of 21 days after the person responsible for the first arrangement has made all required payments to the person responsible for the new arrangement.

Amendments—SI 2011/1045.

Scope—This regulation provides for the situation where a scheme member transfers the whole of his pension rights which are the subject of a pension attachment order into another pension arrangement, for example, on a change of employment. Providing the notices referred to in this regulation have been given, the pension attachment order will have effect as if it had been made in respect of the new pension arrangement (MCA 1973, s 25D(1)). This may be of particular importance where the scheme member transfers to a money purchase pension arrangement so as to take advantage of the flexibilities created by the Taxation of Pensions Act 2014. An application for a variation of the pension attachment order or an injunction under MCA 1973, s 37 may be appropriate.

5 Pension attachment: reduction in benefits

(1) This regulation applies where –

(a) an order under section 23 or under section 17 of the 1984 Act has been made by virtue of section 25B or 25C imposing any requirement on the person responsible for a pension arrangement;

(b) an event has occurred which is likely to result in a significant reduction in the benefits payable under the arrangement, other than:

(i) the transfer from the arrangement off all the rights of the party with pension rights in the circumstances set out in section 25D(1)(a), or

(ii) a reduction in the value of assets held for the purposes of the arrangement by reason of a change in interest rates or other market conditions.

(2) Where this regulation applies, the person responsible for the arrangement shall, within 14 days of the occurrence of the event mentioned in paragraph (1)(b), give notice to the other party of –

(a) that event;

(b) the likely extent of the reduction in the benefits payable under the arrangement.

(3) Where the event mentioned in paragraph (1)(b) consists of a transfer of some but not all of the rights of the party with pension rights from the arrangement, the person responsible for the first arrangement shall, within 14 days of the transfer, give notice to the other party of the name and address of the person responsible for any pension arrangement under which the party with pension rights has acquired rights as a result of that event.

Scope—This regulation applies where the scheme member transfers some, but not all, of his accrued rights in a pension arrangement against which a pension attachment order has been made into a new arrangement, or some other event occurs which is likely to result in a significant reduction in the benefits payable (apart from a transfer of all of the accrued rights or a reduction in the value of the assets of the arrangement by reason of a change in interest rates or other market condition). In these circumstances, the pension arrangement against which the pension attachment order was made must give notice under this regulation to the party with the benefit of the pension attachment order enabling that party to apply for a variation of the pension attachment order or an order under MCA 1973, s 37.

6 Pension attachment: change of circumstances

(1) This regulation applies where –

(a) an order under section 23 or under section 17 of the 1984 Act has been made by virtue of section 25B or 25C imposing any requirement on the person responsible for a pension arrangement; and

(b) any of the events set out in paragraph (2) has occurred.

(2) Those events are –

(a) any of the particulars supplied by the other party under rule 9.33 or 9.34 for any purpose mentioned in regulation 4(3)(c) has ceased to be accurate; or

(b) by reason of the remarriage of the other party, or his having formed a subsequent civil partnership, or otherwise, the order has ceased to have effect.

(3) Where this regulation applies, the other party shall, within 14 days of the event, give notice of it to the person responsible for the pension arrangement.

(4) Where, because of the inaccuracy of the particulars supplied by the other party under rule 9.33 or 9.34 or because the other party has failed to give notice of their having ceased to be

accurate, it is not reasonably practicable for the person responsible for the pension arrangement to make a payment to the other party as required by the order:

(a) it may instead make that payment to the party with pension rights, and
(b) it shall then be discharged of liability to the other party to the extent of that payment.

(5) Where an event set out in paragraph (2)(b) has occurred and, because the other party has failed to give notice in accordance with paragraph (3), the person responsible for the pension arrangement makes a payment to the other party as required by the order –

(a) its liability to the party with pension rights shall be discharged to the extent of that payment, and
(b) the other party shall, within 14 days of the payment being made, make a payment to the party with pension rights to the extent of that payment.

Amendments—SI 2005/2114, art 2(1), Sch 1, para 8; SI 2011/1045.

Scope—This regulation provides for the person with the benefit of a pension attachment order to give notice to the pension arrangement against which the order has been made of a specified change of circumstances (eg of address, remarriage or formation of a subsequent civil partnership). Where, because of the inaccuracy of the information held by the pension arrangement, it is not reasonably practicable for the pension arrangement to make payment to the party with the benefit of the pension attachment order, it may discharge its liability by making payment to the party with pension rights.

7 Pension attachment: transfer of rights

(1) This regulation applies where –

(a) a transfer of rights has taken place in the circumstances set out in section 25D(1)(a);
(b) notice has been given in accordance with regulation 4(2)(a) and (b);
(c) any of the events set out in regulation 6(2) has occurred; and
(d) the other party has not, before receiving notice under regulation 4(2)(b), given notice of that event to the person responsible for the first arrangement under regulation 6(3).

(2) Where this regulation applies, the other party shall, within 14 days of the event, give notice of it to the person responsible for the new arrangement.

(3) Where, because of the inaccuracy of the particulars supplied by the other party under rule 9.33 or 9.34 for any purpose mentioned in regulation 4(3)(c) or because the other party has failed to give notice of their having ceased to be accurate, it is not reasonably practicable for the person responsible for the new arrangement to make a payment to the other party as required by the order –

(a) it may instead make that payment to the party with pension rights, and
(b) it shall then be discharged of liability to the other party to the extent of that payment.

(4) Subject to paragraph (5), where this regulation applies and the other party, within one year from the transfer, gives to the person responsible for the first arrangement notice of the event set out in regulation 6(2) in purported compliance with regulation 7(2), the person responsible for the first arrangement shall –

(a) send that notice to the person responsible for the new arrangement, and
(b) give the other party a second notice under regulation 4(2)(b);

and the other party shall be deemed to have given notice under regulation 7(2) to the person responsible for the new arrangement.

(5) Upon complying with paragraph (4) above, the person responsible for the first arrangement shall be discharged from any further obligation under regulation 4 or 7(4), whether in relation to the event in question or any further event set out in regulation 6(2) which may be notified to it by the other party.

Amendments—SI 2011/1045.

Scope—This regulation deals with the situation which arises where there has been a transfer of all of the accrued pension rights subject to a pension attachment order, in relation to which notice has been given under reg 4(2)(a),(b), and a change of circumstances as provided for by reg 6(2) occurs, but the person with the benefit of the pension attachment order ('the other party') has not been able to give notice of the change of circumstances to the first pension arrangement.

PART IV

7A Pension attachment: discharge of liability of the Board

(1) This regulation applies where –

(a) the Board has assumed responsibility for a pension arrangement as mentioned in section 25E(2)(a); and

(b) the Board has given notice that it has so assumed responsibility to members and beneficiaries of the pension arrangement in compliance with regulation 3(6) of the Pension Protection Fund (Provision of Information) Regulations 2005.

(2) Where –

(a) any of the events set out in regulation 6(2) have occurred; and

(b) the other party has not, before receiving the notice referred to in (1)(b) above, given notice of that event to the person responsible for the pension arrangement in accordance with regulation 6(3),

the other party shall, within 14 days of the event, give notice of it to the Board.

(3) Paragraph (4) applies where it is not reasonably practicable for the Board to make a payment to the other party as required by the order because –

(a) of the inaccuracy of the particulars supplied by the other party under rule 9.33 or 9.34 for any purpose mentioned in regulation 4(3)(c); or

(b) the other party has failed to give notice that the particulars have ceased to be accurate.

(4) Where this paragraph applies, the Board –

(a) may instead make the payment due to the other party to the party entitled to PPF compensation; and

(b) shall then be discharged of liability to the other party to the extent of that payment.

(5) Where an event set out in regulation 6(2)(b) has occurred and, because the other party has failed to give notice in accordance with paragraph (2), the Board makes a payment to the other party as required by the order –

(a) its liability to the party entitled to PPF compensation shall be discharged to the extent of that payment; and

(b) the other party shall, within 14 days of the payment being made, make a payment to the party entitled to PPF compensation to the extent of that payment.

(6) In this regulation 'the Board' and 'PPF compensation' have the meanings given in section 25E(9).

Amendments—SI 2011/1045.

Modification—By virtue of SI 2006/1932, in relation to modified pension attachment orders, the Divorce etc (Pensions) Regulations 2000 are modified with effect from 8 August 2006 so as to apply as if the above reg 7A were inserted.

Scope—This regulation deals with the situation which arises where the Pension Protection Fund (PPF) has assumed responsibility for a pension arrangement. It provides for the person with the benefit of a pension attachment order ('the other party') to give notice to the PPF, rather than to the pension arrangement against which the order has been made, of specified changes in circumstances, enabling the PPF to discharge its liability by making payment to the party entitled to PPF compensation where it is not practicable to make a payment to the other party. Alternatively, where the PPF makes a payment in error to the other party because of a failure by that party to notify the PPF of the change of circumstances, the liability of the PPF is discharged to the extent of the payment and the other party is required, within 14 days of the payment being made, to make a payment to the party entitled to the PPF compensation.

As to the PPF generally, reference should be made to the annotations to MCA 1973, ss 21B and 25E and FPR 2010, r 9.37.

8 Service

A notice under regulation 4, 5, 6 *or 7* [, 7 or 7A] may be sent by fax or by ordinary first class post to the last known address of the intended recipient and shall be deemed to have been received on the seventh day after the day on which it was sent.

Modification—By virtue of SI 2006/1932, in relation to modified pension attachment orders, the Divorce etc (Pensions) Regulations 2000 are modified with effect from 8 August 2006 so that they apply as if in reg 8 for the words in italics 'or 7' there were substituted the words ', 7 or 7A' in brackets.

9 Pension sharing order not to take effect pending appeal

(1) No pension sharing order under section 24B or variation of a pension sharing order under section 31 shall take effect earlier than 7 days after the end of the period for filing notice of appeal against the order.

(2) The filing of a notice of appeal within the time allowed for doing so prevents the order taking effect before the appeal has been dealt with.

Notice of appeal—Time for filing notice of appeal is 21 days (FPR 2010, r 30.4). See also MCA 1973, s 24C.

****

Family Court (Composition and Distribution of Business) Rules 2014, SI 2014/840

ARRANGEMENT OF RULES

PART 1
INTRODUCTORY PROVISIONS

Rule		Page
1	Citation, commencement and interpretation	2458
2		2458

PART 2
COMPOSITION OF THE FAMILY COURT

3	Composition: general	2459
4	Composition: allocation decision	2459
5	Composition: appeals heard by a judge of district judge level	2459
6	Composition: appeals heard by a judge of circuit judge level or a judge of High Court level	2460
7	Composition: appeals heard by a judge of High Court level	2460
8	Composition: matters part heard	2460

PART 3
AUTHORISATIONS

9	Powers to grant authorisations	2461

PART 4
LAY JUSTICES: CHAIRMANSHIP OF THE FAMILY COURT

10	Interpretation of this Part	2461
11	Chairman	2461
12	Absence of authorised lay justice entitled to preside	2461

PART 5
DISTRIBUTION OF BUSINESS OF THE FAMILY COURT

12A	Interpretation of this Part	2461
13	General	2462
14	Persons who may exercise jurisdiction of the family court	2462
15	Allocation of proceedings in Schedule 1	2462
16	Allocation of emergency applications	2462
17	Allocation: applications in existing proceedings or in connection with proceedings that have concluded	2463
18	Allocation: costs	2464

PART IV

19	Allocation: appeals	2464
20	Allocation: all other proceedings	2464
	PART 6 GUIDANCE	
21	Guidance on distribution of business of the family court	2464
	Schedule 1 – Allocation	2465
	Schedule 2 – Remedies	2467

Note—These Rules replaced the Allocation and Transfer of Proceedings Order 2008 from 22 April 2014.

Scope—The Rules provide detailed provisions relating to: the composition of a court when a case is allocated for decision and in relation to certain appeals; the need for a judge of district judge or circuit judge level to conduct certain business only if authorised to do so (para 9); and the distribution of business among the judges of the Family Court. They set out to which level of judiciary (provided authorised) specified emergency cases should be allocated. The Rules make it clear that lay justices are not permitted to undertake cases under FLA 1996, Pt 4 where the applicant is under 18 years of age or an application is made under s 33 of that Act that requires determination of question of property ownership and FMPO. The two Schedules list in Table form the jurisdiction of lay justices and other levels of the judiciary and the remedies that each are not permitted to grant.

Remedies—Note the extension of the Family Court's jurisdiction (lay justices excluded) set out in Sch 2, Table 2, which includes jurisdiction to grant freezing injunctions in relation to assets whether located in the jurisdiction or not. Similar powers are given to County Court judges under the CCRR 2014 as from 22 April 2014.

PART 1
INTRODUCTORY PROVISIONS

1 Citation, commencement and interpretation

These Rules may be cited as the Family Court (Composition and Distribution of Business) Rules 2014 and come into force on 22 April 2014.

2 (1) In these Rules –

'the 1991 Act' means the Child Support Act 1991;

'appeal' includes an application seeking permission to appeal and an application in the course of the appeal proceedings;

'assistant to a justices' clerk' has the meaning given in section 27(5) of the Courts Act 2003;

'authorised', except in the context of references to an authorised court officer, means authorised by the President of the Family Division or nominated by or on behalf of the Lord Chief Justice to conduct particular business in the family court, in accordance with Part 3;

'authorised court officer' has the meaning assigned to it by rule 44.1 of the Civil Procedure Rules 1998 as applied to family proceedings by rule 28.2(1) of the Family Procedure Rules 2010;

'costs judge' means –

(a) the Chief Taxing Master;

(b) a taxing master of the Senior Courts; or

(c) a person appointed to act as deputy for the person holding office referred to in paragraph (b) or to act as a temporary additional officer for any such office;

'financial remedy' has the meaning assigned to it by rule 2.3 of the Family Procedure Rules 2010;

'judge of circuit judge level' means –

(a) a circuit judge who, where applicable, is authorised;

(b) a Recorder who, where applicable, is authorised;

(c) any other judge of the family court authorised to sit as a judge of circuit judge level in the family court;

'judge of district judge level' means –

(a) the Senior District Judge of the Family Division;

(b) a district judge of the Principal Registry of the Family Division;

(c) a person appointed to act as deputy for the person holding office referred to in paragraph (b) or to act as a temporary additional officer for any such office;
(d) a district judge who, where applicable, is authorised;
(e) a deputy district judge appointed under section 102 of the Senior Courts Act 1981 or section 8 of the County Courts Act 1984 who, where applicable, is authorised;
(f) an authorised District Judge (Magistrates' Courts);
(g) any other judge of the family court authorised to sit as a judge of district judge level in the family court.

'judge of High Court judge level' means –
(a) a deputy judge of the High Court;
(b) a puisne judge of the High Court;
(c) a person who has been a judge of the Court of Appeal or a puisne judge of the High Court who may act as a judge of the family court by virtue of section 9 of the Senior Courts Act 1981;
(d) the Senior President of Tribunals;
(e) the Chancellor of the High Court;
(f) an ordinary judge of the Court of Appeal (including the vice-president, if any, of either division of that court);
(g) the President of the Queen's Bench Division;
(h) the President of the Family Division;
(i) the Master of the Rolls;
(j) the Lord Chief Justice;

'judge of the family court' means a judge referred to in section 31C(1) of the Matrimonial and Family Proceedings Act 1984;

'justices' clerk' has the meaning given in section 27(1) of the Courts Act 2003; and

'lay justice' means an authorised justice of the peace who is not a District Judge (Magistrates' Courts).

(2) In these Rules, references to provisions of the Adoption and Children Act 2002 include, as applicable, references to those provisions as modified by the Human Fertilisation and Embryology (Parental Orders) Regulations 2010.

PART 2
COMPOSITION OF THE FAMILY COURT

3 Composition: general

(1) Subject to rules in this Part, the family court shall be composed of –

(a) one of the following –
  (i) a judge of district judge level;
  (ii) a judge of circuit judge level; or
  (iii) a judge of High Court judge level; or
(b) two or three lay justices.

(2) Where paragraph (1)(b) applies, the court shall include, so far as is practicable, both a man and a woman.

4 Composition: allocation decision

When making a decision on allocation to which rule 20 applies, the family court shall be composed of one or more of the following –

(a) a judge of district judge level;
(b) a judge of circuit judge level.

5 Composition: appeals heard by a judge of district judge level

(1) Subject to rule 7, the family court shall be composed of a judge of district judge level when hearing an appeal from the decision of the Secretary of State where an appeal is brought under –

PART IV

(a) regulation 25AB(1) of the Child Support (Collection and Enforcement) Regulations 1992 (Appeals);
(b) section 20(1) (a) or (b) of the 1991 Act to a court by virtue of article 3 of the Child Support Appeals (Jurisdiction of Courts) Order 2002 (Parentage appeals to be made to courts).

(2) The family court may be composed of a judge of district judge level when hearing applications in the course of appeal proceedings against decisions of persons referred to in rule 6(2)(b) to (d) or decisions of the court referred to in rule 6(3).

(3) The family court shall be composed of a costs judge or a district judge of the High Court when hearing an appeal against the decision of an authorised court officer.

6 Composition: appeals heard by a judge of circuit judge level or a judge of High Court level

(1) Subject to rule 7, when hearing an appeal from the decisions of persons referred to in paragraph (2) or the court referred to in paragraph (3), the family court shall be composed of –

(a) a judge of circuit judge level; or
(b) a judge of High Court level where there is a need for such a level of judge to hear the appeal to make most effective and efficient use of local judicial resource and the resource of the High Court bench.

(2) The persons referred to in paragraph (1) are –

(a) a judge of district judge level;
(b) two or three lay justices;
(c) a lay justice; or
(d) a justices' clerk or an assistant to a justices' clerk.

(3) The court referred to in paragraph (1) is a magistrates' court where an appeal is brought under section 111A of the Magistrates' Courts Act 1980 (appeals on ground of error of law in child support proceedings).

7 Composition: appeals heard by a judge of High Court level

(1) The family court shall be composed of a judge of High Court level when hearing an appeal from the decision of –

(a) the Senior District Judge of the Family Division in financial remedy proceedings;
(b) a district judge of the Principal Registry of the Family Division in financial remedy proceedings or a person appointed to act as deputy or as a temporary additional officer for such a district judge in these proceedings;
(c) a costs judge; or
(d) the Gender Recognition Panel where an appeal is brought under section 8(1) of the Gender Recognition Act 2004 (Appeals etc.).

(2) The family court shall be composed of a judge of High Court level (instead of a judge of district judge level or a judge of circuit judge level) where there is –

(a) an appeal against a decision referred to in rules 5 and 6; and
(b) the Designated Family Judge or a judge of High Court level considers that the appeal would raise an important point of principle or practice.

8 Composition: matters part heard

(1) Paragraph (2) applies where a hearing –

(a) was before two or three lay justices; and
(b) was part heard.

(2) The court which resumes the hearing shall, wherever possible, be composed of the same lay justices as dealt with the previous part of the hearing.

PART 3
AUTHORISATIONS

9 Powers to grant authorisations

(1) Paragraph (2) applies to business in such categories as may be specified from time to time by the President of the Family Division.

(2) A judge of district judge level or a judge of circuit judge level may conduct business to which this paragraph applies in the family court only if authorised by the President of the Family Division to do so.

(3) The President of the Family Division may specify the matters referred to in paragraph (1) in directions, after consulting the Lord Chancellor.

(4) A lay justice may conduct business in the family court only if authorised by the Lord Chief Justice to do so.

PART 4
LAY JUSTICES: CHAIRMANSHIP OF THE FAMILY COURT

10 Interpretation of this Part

In this Part, '2016 Rules' means the Justices of the Peace Rules 2016.

Amendments—SI 2016/709.

11 Chairman

(1) When the family court is composed of two or three lay justices, it shall sit under the chairmanship of a lay justice who has been approved to preside in accordance with the 2016 Rules.

(2) A lay justice may preside before being approved to preside in accordance with the 2016 Rules only if that lay justice is –

(a) under the supervision of another authorised lay justice who is approved to preside in accordance with the 2016 Rules; and

(b) has completed the training course required by rule 19 of the 2016 Rules.

(3) *(revoked)*

(4) This rule and rule 12 are subject to sections 18(1) and (2) of the Courts Act 2003.

Amendments—SI 2016/709.

12 Absence of authorised lay justice entitled to preside

(1) The lay justices present may appoint one of their number to preside in the family court to deal with any case in the absence of a lay justice entitled to preside under rule 11 if –

(a) before making such appointment the lay justices present are satisfied as to the suitability for this purpose of the lay justice proposed; and

(b) expect as mentioned in paragraph (2), the lay justice proposed has completed or is undergoing a chairman training course in accordance with rule 19(f) of the 2016 Rules.

(2) The condition in paragraph (1)(b) does not apply if by reason of illness, circumstances unforeseen when the lay justices to sit were chosen, or other emergency, no lay justice who complies with that condition is present.

Amendments—SI 2016/709.

PART 5
DISTRIBUTION OF BUSINESS OF THE FAMILY COURT

12A Interpretation of this Part

In this Part –

'incoming protection measure' means a protection measure that has been ordered in a Member State of the European Union other than the United Kingdom or Denmark;

'protection measure' has the meaning given to it in the Protection Measures Regulation;

'Protection Measures Regulation' means Regulation (EU) No 606/2013 of the European Parliament and of the Council of 12 June 2013 on mutual recognition of protection measures in civil matters.

Amendments—Inserted by SI 2014/3297.

13 General

(1) This Part makes provision for the distribution of business of the family court among the judges of the family court.

(2) Rules 15 and 20 are subject to rule 17.

(3) Rules 15, 16, 17, 18, 19 and 20 make provision regarding the level of judge of the family court to which a matter is to be allocated initially.

(Rule 29.19 of the Family Procedure Rules 2010 makes provision for a judge of the family court to determine that a matter should be heard by a different level of judge of the family court.)

14 Persons who may exercise jurisdiction of the family court

Subject to the provisions of this Part or of any other enactment, any jurisdiction and powers conferred by any enactment on the family court, or on a judge of the family court, may be exercised by any judge of the family court.

15 Allocation of proceedings in Schedule 1

(1) An application in a type of proceedings listed in the first column of the table in Schedule 1 shall be allocated to be heard by a judge of the level listed in the second column of that table.

(2) Paragraph (1) and the provisions of Schedule 1 are subject to the need to take into account the need to make the most effective and efficient use of local judicial resource and the resource of the High Court bench that is appropriate given the nature and type of the application.

16 Allocation of emergency applications

(1) In this rule –

'the 1986 Act' means the Family Law Act 1986;
'the 1989 Act' means the Children Act 1989; and
'the 1996 Act' means the Family Law Act 1996.

(2) An application of a type referred to in paragraph (3) shall be allocated to the first available judge of the family court who –

(a) where applicable, is authorised to conduct the type of business to which the application relates; and
(b) would not be precluded by Schedule 2 from dealing with the application.

(3) The types of applications are those –

(a) under –
 (i) section 33 of the 1986 Act (disclosure of information as to the whereabouts of a child);
 (ii) section 34 of the 1986 Act (order authorising the taking charge and delivery of a child);
 (iii) section 44(1) of the 1989 Act (emergency protection order);
 (iv) section 44(9)(b) of the 1989 Act (varying a direction in an emergency protection order given under section 44(6) of the 1989 Act);
 (v) section 45(4) of the 1989 Act (extending the period during which an emergency protection order is to have effect);
 (vi) section 45(8) of the 1989 Act (to discharge an emergency protection order);
 (vii) section 45(8A) of the 1989 Act (to vary or discharge an emergency protection order in so far as it imposes an exclusion requirement on a person who is not entitled to apply for the order to be discharged);

(viii) section 45(8B) of the 1989 Act (to vary or discharge an emergency protection order in so far as it confers powers of arrest attached to an exclusion requirement);

(ix) section 48(9) of the 1989 Act (warrant to assist in discovery of children who may be in need of emergency protection);

(x) section 50 of the 1989 Act (recovery of abducted children);

(xi) section 102(1) of the 1989 Act (warrant for a constable to assist in the exercise of certain powers to search for children or inspect premises);

(xii) Part 4 of the 1996 Act which are made without notice, except where the applicant is under 18 or where an application for an occupation order under section 33 of that Act requires a determination of a question of property ownership;

(xiii) section 41 of the Adoption and Children Act 2002 (recovery order);

(xiv) section 79 of the Childcare Act 2006 (warrant for a constable to assist in the exercise of powers of entry);

(xv) the Protection Measures Regulation made within or in connection with an application under sub-paragraph (xii); or

(xvi) Article 11 of the Protection Measures Regulation for adjustment of an incoming protection measure except where the applicant is aged under 18; or

(b) which are not referred to in paragraph (a) but which require the immediate attention of the court;

(c) the Protection Measures Regulation made within or in connection with an application under sub-paragraph (a) or (b);

(d) Article 11 of the Protection Measures Regulation for adjustment of an incoming protection measure where the applicant is aged under 18.

(4) An application of a type listed in paragraph (5) shall be allocated to the first available judge of the family court, other than lay justices, who, where applicable, is authorised to conduct the type of business to which the application relates.

(5) The types of application are those under –

(a) Part 4 of the 1996 Act which are made without notice and where the applicant is aged under 18 or where an application for an occupation order under section 33 of that Act requires a determination of a question of property ownership;

(b) Part 4A of the 1996 Act which are made without notice;

(c) the Protection Measures Regulation made within or in connection with an application under sub-paragraph (a) or (b);

(d) Article 11 of the Protection Measures Regulation for adjustment of an incoming protection measure where the applicant is aged under 18;

(e) Part 1 of Schedule 2 to the Female Genital Mutilation Act 2003 which are made without notice.

Amendments—SI 2014/3297; SI 2015/1421.

17 Allocation: applications in existing proceedings or in connection with proceedings that have concluded

(1) Subject to paragraphs (3) to (5), an application made within existing proceedings in the family court shall be allocated to the level of judge who is dealing with the existing proceedings to which the application relates.

(2) Subject to paragraphs (3) to (5), an application made in connection with proceedings in the family court that have concluded shall be allocated to the level of judge who last dealt with those proceedings.

(3) In Schedule 2 –

(a) the remedies listed in tables 1, 2 and 3 may not be granted by lay justices;

(b) the remedies listed in tables 2 and 3 may not be granted by a judge of district judge level;

(c) the remedies listed in table 3 may not be granted by a judge of circuit judge level, subject to any exception stated in that table.

(4) Where the effect of Schedule 2 is that an application for a particular remedy may not be granted by the level of judge referred to in paragraph (1) or (2), then that application shall be allocated to a level of judge who is able to grant that remedy.

(5) Any power of the family court to make an order for committal in respect of a breach of a judgment, order or undertaking to do or abstain from doing an act may only be made by a judge of the same level as, or of a higher level than, the judge who make the judgment or order, or who accepted the undertaking, as the case may be.

Allocation to s 9 judge where relief is sought under the inherent jurisdiction—See the President's Guidance of December 2016: *Allocation of Work to Section 9 Judges* (set out in Part V).

18 Allocation: costs

Subject to any direction of the court, an application for detailed assessment of a bill of costs shall be allocated to an authorised court officer, a district judge or a costs judge.

19 Allocation: appeals

An appeal shall be allocated to a judge in accordance with rules 5 to 7.

20 Allocation: all other proceedings

(1) An application of a type not referred to in other rules in this Part or in Schedule 1 or Schedule 2 shall be allocated by one or more of the persons referred to in rule 4.

(2) When deciding which level of judge to allocate such an application to, the decision must be based on consideration of the relative significance of the following factors –

(a) the need to make the most effective and efficient use of the local judicial resource and the resource of the High Court bench that is appropriate, given the nature and type of application;
(b) the need to avoid delay;
(c) the need for judicial continuity;
(d) the location of the parties or of any child relevant to the proceedings; and
(e) complexity.

Allocation—Before allocating proceedings to be heard by a High Court Judge to a s 9 judge, advance authorisation must be sought, as required under the President's Guidance of December 2016: *Allocation of Work to Section 9 Judges* (set out in Part V).)

PART 6
GUIDANCE

21 Guidance on distribution of business of the family court

(1) The President of the Family Division may, after consulting the Lord Chancellor, issue guidance on the application or interpretation of Part 5.

(2) Where the Lord Chancellor determines that the guidance has significant implications for resources, it may only be issued with the agreement of the Lord Chancellor.

(3) If the Lord Chancellor does not agree the guidance, the Lord Chancellor must provide the President of the Family Division with written reasons why the Lord Chancellor does not agree the guidance.

Guidance on allocation—See further the President's Guidance of December 2016: *Allocation of Work to Section 9 Judges* (set out in Part V).

SCHEDULE 1
ALLOCATION

Type of proceedings	*Level of judge*
1. Proceedings under – (a) the Maintenance Orders (Facilities for Enforcement) Act 1920; (b) the Marriage Act 1949; (c) the Maintenance Orders Act 1950; (d) the Maintenance Orders Act 1958; (e) the Maintenance Orders (Reciprocal Enforcement) Act 1972; (f) the Domestic Proceedings and Magistrates' Courts Act 1978; (g) the Civil Jurisdiction and Judgments Act 1982; (h) the Family Law Act 1986, section 55A (declarations of parentage); (i) the Child Support Act 1991, except section 32L or appeals; (j) the Crime and Disorder Act 1998, section 11 (child safety order); (k) Council Regulation (EC) No 44/2001 (known as the Judgments Regulation); (l) section 34 of the Children and Families (Wales) Measure 2010; (m) Schedule 6 to the Civil Partnership Act 2004; (n) the Childcare Act 2006, except section 79; (o) the Human Fertilisation and Embryology Act 2008, section 54, where the child's place of birth was in England and Wales and where all respondents agree to the making of the order; (p) Council Regulation (EC) No 4/2009 (known as the Maintenance Regulation); (q) the Protection Measures Regulation for enforcement of an incoming protection measure.	Lay justices
2. Proceedings under – (a) the Married Women's Property Act 1882; (b) the Matrimonial Causes Act 1973; (c) the Matrimonial and Family Proceedings Act 1984 sections 13 and 12 (permission and substantive application) where the parties consent to permission being granted and to the substantive order sought; (d) the Children Act 1989, Schedule 1; (e) the Gender Recognition Act 2004, except appeals under section 8(1) and referrals to the court under section 8(5); (f) the Civil Partnership Act 2004, except under – (i) Schedule 6 (financial provision corresponding to provision made by the Domestic Proceedings and Magistrates' Courts Act 1978); or (ii) Schedule 7 (financial relief after overseas dissolution), unless the parties consent to permission being granted and to the substantive order sought.	Judge of district judge level
3. Proceedings under – (a) the Family Law Act 1986 section 55 (declarations as to marital status), 56 (declarations as to legitimacy or legitimation) or 57 (declarations as to adoptions effected overseas); (b) the Child Support Act 1991 under section 32L (orders preventing avoidance); (c) the Human Fertilisation and Embryology Act 2008, section 54, where the child's place of birth was in England and Wales but where not all respondents agree to the making of the order.	Judge of circuit judge level

Type of proceedings	*Level of judge*
4. Proceedings under – (a) the Matrimonial and Family Proceedings Act 1984, sections 13 and 12 (permission and substantive application) where – (i) the parties do not consent to permission being granted; or (ii) the parties consent to permission being granted but do not consent to the substantive order sought; (b) the Adoption and Children Act 2002, section 60(3) (order to disclose or to prevent disclosure of information to an adopted person); (c) the Adoption and Children Act 2002, section 79(4) (order for Registrar General to give information); (d) the Civil Partnership Act 2004, paragraphs 4 and 9 of Schedule 7 (permission and substantive application) where – (i) the parties do not consent to permission being granted; or (ii) the parties consent to permission being granted but do not consent to the substantive order sought; (e) referrals to the court under section 8(5) of the Gender Recognition Act 2004; (f) the Human Fertilisation and Embryology Act 2008, section 54, where the child's place of birth was outside of England and Wales; (g) Article 13 of the Protection Measures Regulation.	Judge of High Court judge level
5. Proceedings under the Adoption and Children Act 2002 under – (a) section 21 (placement order); (b) section 23 (order varying a placement order); (c) section 24 (order revoking a placement order); (d) section 26 (contact order); (e) section 27 (order varying or revoking a contact order); (f) section 28(2) or (3) (order permitting the child's name to be changed or the removal of the child from the United Kingdom); (g) section 46(c) (adoption order) except where – (i) a local authority is a party to the application; (ii) the application is for an overseas adoption within the meaning given in section 87 of the Adoption and Children Act 2002; or (iii) the application is for a Convention adoption within the meaning given in section 66(1)(c) of the Adoption and Children Act 2002; (h) section 51A(2)(a) or (b)(d) (post adoption contact); (i) section 55(e) (revocation of adoption on legitimation); (j) paragraph 4 of Schedule 1 (amendment of orders).	Level of judge who is dealing with, or has dealt with, proceedings relating to the same child or, if there are or were no such proceedings, to lay justices.
6. Proceedings under the Adoption and Children Act 2002 under section 46 (adoption order) where – (a) a local authority is a party to the application; (b) the application is for an overseas adoption within the meaning given in section 87 of the Adoption and Children Act 2002; or (c) the application is for a Convention adoption within the meaning given in section 66(1)(c) of the Adoption and Children Act 2002.	Level of judge who is dealing with, or dealt with, proceedings relating to the same child or, if there are or were no such proceedings, to a judge of district judge level

Amendments—SI 2014/3297.

Allocation of proceedings—See also the Schedules to the Public and Private law *Allocation and Gatekeeping* Guidances of 22 April 2014 and the President's Guidance of December 2016: *Allocation of Work to Section 9 Judges* (all set out in Part V).

SCHEDULE 2
REMEDIES

Table 1

Remedies which may not be granted by lay justices in the family court
1. Charging order.
2. Order (known as a 'freezing injunction') restraining a party from:
(a) removing from the jurisdiction assets located there;
(b) dealing with any assets whether located in the jurisdiction or not.
3. Interim injunction.
4. Interim declaration.
5. Order under section 34 Senior Courts Act 1981 or section 53 County Courts Act 1984, as applied to the family court under section 31E Matrimonial and Family Proceedings Act 1984, for disclosure of documents or inspection of property against a non-party.
6. Order for a specified fund to be paid into court where there is a dispute over a party's right to the fund.
7. Order permitting a party seeking to recover personal property to pay money into court pending the outcome of the proceedings and directing that, if money is paid into court, the property must be given to that party.
8. Order directing a party to provide information about the location of relevant property or assets or to provide information about relevant property or assets, which are or may be the subject of an application for a freezing injunction.
9. Order directing a party to prepare and file accounts relating to the dispute.
10. Order directing an account to be taken or enquiry to be made by the court.
11. Third party debt order.
12. Order for –
(a) detention, custody or preservation of relevant property;
(b) inspection of relevant property;
(c) taking of a sample of relevant property;
(d) carrying out an experiment on or with relevant property;
(e) sale of relevant property which is of a perishable nature or which for any other good reason it is desirable to sell quickly;
(f) the payment of income from relevant property until an application is decided.
13. Order authorising a person to enter any land or building in the possession of a party for the purposes of carrying out an order referred to in paragraph 12.
14. Warrant of delivery.
15. Warrant of control.
16. Warrant for the possession of land.
17. Order to deliver up goods under section 4 of the Torts (Interference with Goods) Act 1977.

Table 2

Remedies which may not be granted by lay justices or judges of district judge level in the family court
1. Civil restraint order (limited).

PART IV

Table 3

Remedies which may not be granted by lay justices, judges of district judge level or judges of circuit judge level in the family court

1. Civil restraint order (extended or general), except that such orders may be granted by a Designated Family Judge or a deputy Designated Family Judge.
2. Search order requiring a party to admit another party to premises for the purposes of preserving evidence etc (section 7 Civil Procedure Act 1997).
3. Claims in respect of a judicial act under the Human Rights Act 1998.
4. Action in respect of the interference with the due administration of justice.
5. Warrants of sequestration to enforce a judgment, order or undertaking in the family court.
6. Order under Article 13 of the Protection Measures Regulation refusing to recognise or enforce an incoming protection measure.

Amendments—SI 2014/3297.

Family Court (Contempt of Court) (Powers) Regulations 2014, SI 2014/833

General note—These regulations clearly set out the powers of the different levels of the Family Court to punish for a contempt of court. Note that by s 14(4B) of CCA 1981, ss 14(1)–(4A) of that Act do not apply to the Family Court, save for the limited exceptions mentioned.

Powers of Family Court Judges—These Regulations need to be read in conjunction with ss 31A–31P inserted into MFPA 1984 by CCA 2013, s 17 and Sch 10. The Family Court has the powers of the High Court, subject to Regulations made by the Lord Chancellor under s 31H. These Regulations are made under that section and do impose limitations. The effect of the Act and Regulations is set out in the following Table.

Level of Judge	Breach of Judgment/Order	Contempt in the face of the Court
Lay Magistrate	2 months/up to Level 5 fine	1 month/up to Level 5 fine
District Judge (Magistrates' Court)	2 years/up to Level 5 fine	1 month/up to Level 5 fine
District Judge	2 years/up to Level 5 fine	1 month/up to Level 5 fine
Circuit Judge	2 years/up to Level 5 fine	2 years/up to Level 5 fine
High Court Judge	2 years/unlimited fine	2 years/unlimited fine

1 Citation, commencement and interpretation

These Regulations may be cited as the Family Court (Contempt of Court) (Powers) Regulations 2014 and come into force on 22 April 2014

2 In these Regulations –

'judge of district judge level' means –

(a) the Senior District Judge of the Family Division;

(b) a district judge of the Principal Registry of the Family Division;

(c) a person appointed to act as deputy for the person holding office referred to in paragraph (b) or to act as a temporary additional officer for any such office;

(d) is a district judge (which by virtue of section 8(1C) of the Country Courts Act 1984, here includes a deputy district judge appointed under section 8 of that Act);

(e) a deputy district judge appointed under section 102 of the Senior Courts Act 1981;

(f) a District Judge (Magistrates' Courts); or

(g) any other judge of the family court authorised to sit as a judge of district judge level in the family court;

'lay justice' means a justice of the peace who is not a District Judge (Magistrates' Courts);

'judge of the family court' means a judge referred to in section 31C(1) of the Matrimonial and Family Proceedings Act 1984; and 'judge of High Court judge level' means –

(a) a deputy judge of the High Court;
(b) a puisne judge of the High Court;
(c) a person who has been a judge of the Court of Appeal or a puisne judge of the High Court who may act as a judge of the family court by virtue of section 9 of the Senior Courts Act 1981;
(d) the Senior President of Tribunals;
(e) the Chancellor of the High Court;
(f) an ordinary judge of the Court of Appeal (including the vice-president, if any, of either division of that court);
(g) the President of the Queen's Bench Division;
(h) the President of the Family Division;
(i) the Master of the Rolls; or
(j) the Lord Chief Justice.

3 Limits on committal powers exercisable by judges of district judge level for contempt in the face of the court in the family court

The committal powers exercisable by a judge of district judge level in the family court when dealing with an individual for –

(a) wilfully insulting a judge of the family court, or any witness, or any officer of the court during his or her sitting or attendance in court, or in going to or returning from the court; or
(b) wilfully interrupting the proceedings of the family court or otherwise misbehaving in court,

are limited to a period not exceeding one month.

4 Limits on committal powers exercisable by lay justices for certain types of contempt of court in the family court

The committal powers exercisable by a lay justice in the family court when dealing with an individual for contempt of court in the family court are limited to a period not exceeding –

(a) two months where any individual disobeys a judgement or an order of, or an undertaking given to, the family court that requires that individual to do anything other than the payment of money or to abstain from doing anything; and
(b) one month where any individual –
    (i) wilfully insults a judge of the family court, or any witness, or any officer of the court during his or her sitting or attendance in court, or in going to or returning from the court; or
    (ii) wilfully interrupts the proceedings of the family court or otherwise misbehaves in court.

5 Limits on fines for contempt of court in the family court

In any case where a judge of the family court, except a judge of High Court judge level, has the power to impose a fine when dealing with a person for contempt of court in the family court, the fine must not exceed level 5 on the standard scale.

'level 5 on the standard scale'—The amount is £5000.00.

Family Law Act 1986 (Dependent Territories) Order 1991, SI 1991/1723

1 This Order may be cited as the Family Law Act 1986 (Dependent Territories) Order 1991 and shall come into force on 14 October 1991.

PART IV

2 In this Order –

'the Act' means the Family Law Act 1986;

'specified dependent territory' means a dependent territory specified in column 1 of Schedule 1 to this Order;

'Part I order' has the meaning given by section 1(1) of the Act;

'part of the United Kingdom' has the meaning given by section 42(1) of the Act.

3 (1) This Order applies in relation to a specified dependent territory from the date specified opposite the name of that territory in column 2 of Schedule 1 to this Order.

(2) Part I of the Act shall apply, for the purpose of regulating, as between any specified dependent territory and any part of the United Kingdom, the jurisdiction of courts to make Part I orders, and the recognition and enforcement of orders corresponding to such orders, with the modifications specified in Schedule 2 to this Order.

(3) Each Part of Schedule 3 to this Order shall have effect for the construction of Part I of the Act as modified by this Order in relation to the specified dependent territory named in the heading to that Part of that Schedule.

4 This Order does not extend to any territory outside the United Kingdom.

SCHEDULE 1
SPECIFIED DEPENDENT TERRITORIES

Dependent Territory	*Date from which this Order applies*
The Isle of Man	14 October 1991
Jersey	10 July 2006

Amendments—SI 2006/1456.

****

SCHEDULE 3
INTERPRETATION OF CERTAIN EXPRESSIONS IN PART I OF THE FAMILY LAW ACT 1986 AS MODIFIED BY SCHEDULE 2 TO THIS ORDER

PART I
THE ISLE OF MAN

1 In section 1(1)(f) 'an order made by the court in a specified dependent territory corresponding to an order within paragraphs (a) to (e) above' means –

(a) an order under section 9 of the Family Law Act 1991 (an Act of Tynwald) or any of the following enactments (being enactments repealed by that Act) –
  (i) section 3(5) of the Guardianship of Infants Act 1953 (an Act of Tynwald), so far as it relates to the custody of infants;
  (ii) section 4(1) of that Act, except so far as it relates to costs, but including that section as applied by section 3(1) of the Legitimacy Act 1962 (an Act of Tynwald);
  (iii) section 42(1) or (2) of the Judicature (Matrimonial Causes) Act 1976 (an Act of Tynwald);
  (iv) section 8(2) or 18(1)(ii) of the Domestic Proceedings Act 1983 (an Act of Tynwald);
  (v) section 34(1) of that Act;
  (vi) section 49(1) of that Act, so far as it relates to the custody of or access to a child;

(b) an order made by the High Court of Justice of the Isle of Man in the exercise of its jurisdiction relating to wardship or its inherent jurisdiction with respect to children –
  (i) so far as it gives care of a child to any person or provides for contact with or access to, or the education of, a child but

(ii) excluding an order varying or revoking such an order, or an order relating to a child of whom care or control is (immediately after the making of the order) vested in a public authority in the Isle of Man.

2 In each of sections 2A(3), 3(3), 6(4), 11(2), 13(5), 20(3), 21(4) and 23(4) –

(a) in paragraph (a) 'corresponding dependent territory order' means an order under section 3(3) of the Child Custody Act 1987 (an Act of Tynwald);
(b) in paragraph (b) 'corresponding dependent territory order' means an order under section 4(2) of that Act.

3 In section 13(6)(a)(ii), 'corresponding dependent territory provision' means section 2(2) or 5(3) of the Child Custody Act 1987 (an Act of Tynwald).

4 (1) In section 27(1) 'corresponding provision' means section 7 of the Child Custody Act 1987 (an Act of Tynwald).

(2) In section 27(4) 'corresponding dependent territory provision' means section 12(3) of that Act.

5 (1) In section 32(1) 'the corresponding court' means the High Court of Justice of the Isle of Man.

(2) In section 32(1) and (3)(a) 'the corresponding dependent territory provisions' means Part I of the Child Custody Act 1987 (an Act of Tynwald).

6 In section 42(6)(e) 'corresponding dependent territory provision' means –

(a) section 42(6) or (7) of the Judicature (Matrimonial Causes) Act 1976 (an Act of Tynwald);
(b) section 18(6) of the Domestic Proceedings Act 1983 (an Act of Tynwald).

PART II
JERSEY

7 In section 1(1)(f), 'an order made by the court in a specified dependent territory corresponding to an order within paragraphs (a) to (e) above' means –

(a) an order under Article 10 of the Children (Jersey) Law 2002;
(b) an order referred to in paragraph 2(1) of Schedule 5 to the Children (Jersey) Law 2002;
(c) an order made by the Royal Court in the exercise of its inherent jurisdiction with respect to children –
   (i) so far as it gives care of the child to any person or provides for contact with or access to, or the education of, a child; but
   (ii) excluding an order varying or revoking such an order, or an order relating to a child of whom care or control is (immediately after the making of the order) vested in a public authority in Jersey.

8 In each of sections 2A(3), 3(3), 6(4), 11(2), 13(5), 20(3), 21(4) and 23(4) –

(a) in paragraph (a), 'corresponding dependent territory order' means an order under Article 7(3) of the Child Custody (Jurisdiction) (Jersey) Law 2005;
(b) in paragraph (b), 'corresponding dependent territory order' means an order under Article 8(2) of that Law.

9 In section 13(6)(a)(ii), 'corresponding dependent territory provision' means Article 6(2) or 9(3) of the Child Custody (Jurisdiction) (Jersey) Law 2005.

10 (1) In section 27(1), 'corresponding provision' means Article 11 of the Child Custody (Jurisdiction) (Jersey) Law 2005.

(2) In section 27(4), 'corresponding dependent territory provision' means Article 16(3) of that Law.

11 (1) In section 32(1), 'the corresponding court' means the Royal Court of Jersey.

PART IV

(2) In section 32(1) and (3)(a), 'the corresponding dependent territory provisions' means the Child Custody (Jurisdiction) (Jersey) Law 2005.

Amendments—SI 2006/1456.

Family Proceedings Fees Order 2008, SI 2008/1054

1 Citation and commencement

(1) This Order may be cited as the Family Proceedings Fees Order 2008 and shall come into force on 1 May 2008.

(2) In this Order –

- (a) 'LSC' means the Legal Services Commission established under section 1 of the Access to Justice Act 1999;
- (b) 'the FPR 2010' means the Family Procedure Rules 2010; and
- (c) expressions also used in the FPR 2010 have the same meaning as in the FPR 2010;
- (d) 'EU Regulation 606/2013' means Regulation (EU) No 606/2013 of the European Parliament and of the Council of June 2013 on mutual recognition of protection measures in civil matters; and
- (e) 'protection measure' and 'protected person' have the same meaning as in EU Regulation 606/2013.

Amendments—SI 2011/1045; SI 2015/687.

Note—The Legal Aid Agency replaced the Legal Services Commission on 1 April 2013.

2 Fees payable

The fees set out in column 2 of Schedule 1 are payable in family proceedings in the High Court and in the family court in respect of the items described in column 1 in accordance with and subject to the directions specified in that column.

Amendments—SI 2014/877.

3 Where by any convention entered into by Her Majesty with any foreign power it is provided that no fee is required to be paid in respect of any proceedings, the fees specified in this Order are not payable in respect of those proceedings.

3A Fees 1.1, 5.1 and 5.3 in Schedule 1 (fees to be taken) are not payable –

- (a) in any proceedings relating to protection measures under EU Regulation 606/2013 if the person who would otherwise be liable to pay the fee is the protected person;
- (b) in proceedings for –
  - (i) a non-molestation order;
  - (ii) an occupation order; or
  - (iii) a forced marriage protection order,

  under Part 4 or 4A of the Family Law Act 1996; or
- (bb) in proceedings for a female genital mutilation protection order under Part 1 of Schedule 2 to the Female Genital Mutilation Act 2003; or
- (c) in proceedings issued by the person who commenced proceedings referred to in sub-paragraphs (b) or (bb), where that person applies to vary or discharge an order made in those proceedings.

Amendments—Inserted by SI 2015/687. Amended by SI 2015/1419.

4 Remissions and part remissions

Schedule 2 applies for the purpose of ascertaining whether a party is entitled to a remission or part remission of a fee prescribed by this Order.

5 Revocations

The instruments listed in column 1 of the table in Schedule 3 (which have the references listed in column 2) are revoked.

6 Transitional provision

Fees 2.2(b) and (c) are not payable in respect of an issues resolution hearing, pre-hearing review or final hearing which has been listed on any day between 1 May 2008 and 14 May 2008 inclusive.

SCHEDULE 1
FEES TO BE TAKEN

Column 1 *Number and description of fee*	*Column 2* *Amount of fee*
1 Commencement of proceedings	
1.1 On filing an application to start proceedings where no other fee is specified.	£245
1.2 On presenting an application for –	£550
(a) a decree of divorce made under section 1 of the Matrimonial Causes Act 1973;	
(b) a decree of nullity made under sections 11 or 12 of the Matrimonial Causes Act 1973;	
(c) a dissolution order or nullity order made under section 37 of the Civil Partnership Act 2004.	
1.3 On presenting an application for –	£365
(a) a matrimonial or civil partnership order, other than an application for a decree of divorce, a decree of nullity, a dissolution order, nullity order or to which rule 7.7(1)(b) of the Family Procedure Rules 2010 applies, or	
(b) a declaration to which Chapter 5 of Part 8 of the Family Procedure Rules 2010 applies.	
Note: Fee 1.3 is payable only once for each declaration to which Chapter 5 of Part 8 of the Family Procedure Rules 2010 applies.	
1.4 (*revoked*)	
1.5 On amending an application for a matrimonial or civil partnership order, amending an application for a declaration to which Chapter 5 of Part 8 of the Family Procedure Rules 2010 applies, or making an application to which rule 7.7(1)(b) of the Family Procedure Rules 2010 applies.	£95
1.6 On filing an answer to an application for a matrimonial or civil partnership order.	£245
1.7 On applying for an order under Part 3 of the Solicitors Act 1974 for the assessment of costs payable to a solicitor by a client; or on the commencement of costs-only proceedings.	£50
1.8 On an application under section 54 (parental order) of the Human Fertilisation and Embryology Act 2008.	£215
2 Proceedings under the Children Act 1989 or, where specified, the Social Services and Well-being (Wales) Act 2014	
2.1 On an application for an order under the following provisions of the Children Act 1989 or, where specified, the Social Services and Well-being (Wales) Act 2014 –	
(a) section 4(1)(c) or (3), 4A(1)(b) or (3)(h) (parental responsibility);	£215
(b) section 4ZA(1)(c) or (6)(i) (parental responsibility);	£215
(c) section 5(1) or 6(7) (guardians);	£215
(d) section 10(1) or (2) (section 8 orders);	£215
(e) section 11J(2)(j) (enforcement orders);	£215

PART IV

Column 1 Number and description of fee		Column 2 Amount of fee
(f)	section 11O(2)(k) (compensation for financial loss);	£215
(g)	section 13(1) (change of child's surname or removal from jurisdiction while child arrangements order in force);	£215
(h)	section 14A(3) or (6)(a), 14C(3) or 14D(1)(l) (special guardianship orders);	£215
(i)	section 25 (secure accommodation order);	£215
(ia)	section 119 of the Social Services and Well-being (Wales) Act 2014 (secure accommodation order);	£215
(j)	section 33(7) (change of child's surname or removal from jurisdiction while care order in force);	£215
(k)	section 34(2), (3), (4) or (9) (contact with child in care);	£215
(l)	section 36(1) (education supervision order);	£215
(m)	section 39 (variation or discharge etc of care and supervision orders);	£215
(n)	section 43(1) (child assessment order);	£215
(o)	sections 44, 45 and 46 (emergency protection orders);	£215
(p)	section 48 (warrant to assist person exercising powers under emergency protection order);	£215
(q)	section 50 (recovery order);	£215
(r)	section 79K (cancellation, variation or removal or imposition of condition of registration of child minder or day carer);	£215
(s)	section 102 (warrant to assist person exercising powers to search for children or inspect premises);	£215
(t)	paragraph 4(2), 6(2), 7(2) or 9(2) of Schedule A1(m) (applications in respect of enforcement orders);	£95
(u)	paragraph 5(2) of Schedule A1 (amendment of enforcement order by reason of change of address);	£95
(v)	paragraph 1(1) or (4), 2(1) or (5), 5(6), 6(5), (7) or (8), 8(2), 10(2), 11 or 14(1) of Schedule 1 (financial provision for children);	£215
(w)	paragraph 19(1) of Schedule 2 (approval of court for child in care of local authority to live abroad);	£215
(wa)	section 124(1) of the Social Services and Well-being (Wales) Act 2014 (approval of court for child in care of local authority to live abroad);	£215
(x)	paragraph 6 of Schedule 3 (extension of supervision order);	£215
(y)	paragraph 15(2) or 17(1) of Schedule 3 (extension or discharge of education supervision order).	£215
(z)	paragraph 8(1) of Schedule 8 (appeals concerning foster parenting).	£215
2.2 On an application under section 31 of the Children Act 1989 (care and supervision orders).		£2,055
Notes to fees 2.1 and 2.2 Where an application requires the permission of the court, the relevant fee is payable when permission is sought but no further fee will be charged if permission is granted and the application is made. Where an application is made, permission is sought or an appeal is commenced under or relating to provisions of the Children Act 1989 or, where specified, the Social Services and Well-being (Wales) Act 2014 which are listed in two or more different numbered fees, or require two or more different numbered forms, only one fee is payable, and if those fees are different, only the highest fee is payable.		

Column 1 *Number and description of fee*	*Column 2* *Amount of fee*
Where an application is made, permission is sought or an appeal is commenced under or relating to two or more provisions of the Children Act 1989 or, where specified, the Social Services and Well-being (Wales) Act 2014 which are listed in the same numbered fee, that fee is payable only once. Where the same application is made, permission is sought or an appeal is commenced in respect of two or more children, who are siblings or children of the family, at the same time, only one fee is payable in respect of each numbered fee. Note to fee 2.2 only Where proceedings are consolidated with other proceedings, any fee which falls to be paid after the date on which the proceedings are consolidated is payable only once.	
2.3 On commencing an appeal in relation to proceedings to which the fees listed as 2.1(a) to (s), (v) to (y) and 2.2 apply.	£215
2.4 On commencing an appeal under paragraph 23(11) of Schedule 2 to the Children Act 1989 (appeal against contribution order).	£215
2.5 On commencing appeal under paragraph 3(11) of Schedule 1 to the Social Services and Well-being (Wales) Act 2014 (appeal against contribution order)	£215
3 Adoption and wardship applications	
3.1 On applying or requesting permission to apply under any provision in Part 1 of the Adoption and Children Act 2002, other than an application under section 22 of that Act.	£170
3.2 On applying under section 22 of the Adoption and Children Act 2002 (placement order).	£455
3.3 On applying for the exercise by the High Court of its inherent jurisdiction with respect to children.	£170
Notes to fees 3.1, 3.2 and 3.3 Fee 3.1 is payable where an application requires the permission of the court when permission is sought, but no further fee will be charged if permission is granted and the application is made. Where an application is made or permission is sought at the same time under or relating to two or more provisions in Part 1 of the Adoption and Children Act 2002, other than an application under section 22 of that Act, fee 3.1 is payable only once. In relation to fees 3.1 and 3.2, where an application is made or permission is sought at the same time under or relating to provisions of the Adoption and Children Act 2002, only one fee is payable and, if those fees are different, the higher fee 3.2 is payable. In relation to fees 3.1, 3.2 and 3.3, where the same application is made or permission is sought at the same time in respect of two or more children who are siblings or children of the same family, only one fee is payable in respect of each numbered fee.	
4 Proceedings under the Children and Adoption Act 2006	
4.1 On an application for a warning notice to be attached to a contact order.	£50
Notes: Where an application is made or permission is sought under or relating to provisions of the Children Act 1989 or, where specified, the Social Services and Well-being (Wales) Act 2014 and the Children and Adoption Act 2006 which are listed in two or more different numbered fees, only one fee is payable.	

PART IV

Column 1 *Number and description of fee*	*Column 2* *Amount of fee*
Where the same application is made or permission is sought in respect of two or more children at the same time, and those children are siblings or children of the family, only one fee is payable in respect of each numbered fee.	
5 Applications in existing proceedings	
5.1 On an application in existing proceedings without notice or by consent, except where separately listed in this Schedule.	£50
Notes: Fee 5.1 is not payable in relation to an application by consent for an adjournment of a hearing where the application is received by the court at least 14 days before the date set for that hearing. Fee 5.1 is not payable on an application to make a decree or order absolute or final, as the case may be, where the applicant has paid fee 1.2. Fee 5.1 is payable in proceedings under the Children Act 1989 or, where specified, the Social Services and Well-being (Wales) Act 2014 to which the fees listed at 2.1 apply.	
5.2 On an application under rule 7.19 of the Family Procedure Rules 2010 for the court to consider the making of a decree nisi, conditional order, a decree of judicial separation or a separation order (other than in an undefended case where no fee is payable).	£50
5.3 On an application in existing proceedings on notice, except where separately listed in this Schedule.	£155
Note: Fee 5.3 is payable in proceedings under the Children Act 1989 or, where specified, the Social Services and Well-being (Wales) Act 2014 to which the fees listed at 2.1 apply, except for those at 2.1(t) and (u), where the application fee of £95 is payable.	
5.4 On the filing of – (a) a notice of intention to proceed with an application for a financial order to which rule 9.4(a) of the Family Procedure Rules 2010 applies; or (b) an application for a financial order to which rule 9.4(b) of the Family Procedure Rules 2010 applies, other than an application for a consent order.	£255
6 Appeal	
6.1 On filing an appeal notice from a district judge, one or more lay justices, a justices' clerk or an assistant to a justices' clerk.	£125
6.2 On commencing an appeal under section 20 in proceedings under the Child Support Act 1991	£165
7 Searches	
7.1 On making a search in the central index of decrees absolute or of final orders kept at the Principal Registry of the Family Division for any specified period of ten calendar years or, if no such period is specified, for the ten most recent years, and, if appropriate, providing a certificate of decree absolute or of final order, as the case may be	£65
7.2 On making a search in the central index of parental responsibility agreements kept at the Principal Registry of the Family Division in accordance with regulations made under section 4(2) of the Children Act 1989 and, if appropriate, providing a copy of the agreement.	£45
7.3 On making a search in the index of decrees absolute or of final orders kept at any designated family court or district registry for any specified period of ten calendar years or, if no period is specified, for the ten most recent years, and if appropriate, providing a certificate of decree absolute or of final order, as the case may be.	£45

Column 1 *Number and description of fee*	*Column 2* *Amount of fee*
8 Copy documents	
8.1 On a request for a copy document (other than where fee 8.2 applies) –	
(a) for ten pages or less; and	£10
(b) for each subsequent page.	50p
Note: The fee payable under fee 9.1 includes – – where the court allows a party to fax to the court for the use of that party a document that has not been requested by the court and is not intended to be placed on the court file. – where a party requests that the court fax a copy of a document from the court file. – where the court provides a subsequent copy of a document which it has previously provided.	
8.2 On a request for a copy of a document on a computer disk or in other electronic form, for each such copy.	£10
9 Determination of costs	
9.1 On filing a request for detailed assessment where the party filing the request is legally aided, is funded by the Legal Services Commission or is a person for whom civil legal services have been made available under arrangements made by the Lord Chancellor under Part of the Legal Aid, Sentencing and Punishment of Offenders Act 2012 and no other party is ordered to pay the costs of the proceedings.	£200
9.2 On filing a request for detailed assessment in any case where fee 9.1 does not apply; or on filing a request for a hearing date for the assessment of costs payable to a solicitor by a client pursuant to an order under Part 3 of the Solicitors Act 1974 where the amount of the costs claimed –	
(a) does not exceed £15,000;	£335
(b) exceeds £15,000 but does not exceed £50,000;	£675
(c) exceeds £50,000 but does not exceed £100,000;	£1,005
(d) exceeds £100,000 but does not exceed £150,000;	£1,345
(e) exceeds £150,000 but does not exceed £200,000;	£1,680
(f) exceeds £200,000 but does not exceed £300,000;	£2,520
(g) exceeds £300,000 but does not exceed £500,000;	£4,200
(h) exceeds £500,000.	£5,600
Where there is a combined standard basis and legal aid, or a combined standard basis and Legal Services Commission, or a combined standard basis and Lord Chancellor, or a combined standard basis, and one or more of legal aid, Legal Services Commission or Lord Chancellor determination of costs, fee 9.2 will be attributed proportionately to the standard basis, legal aid, Legal Services Commission or Lord Chancellor (as the case may be) portions of the bill on the basis of the amount allowed.	
9.3 On a request for the issue of a default costs certificate.	£60
9.4 On commencing an appeal against a decision made in detailed assessment proceedings.	£210
9.5 On an application to set aside a default costs certificate.	£110
10 Registration of maintenance orders	
10.1 (*revoked*)	
10.2 On an application for a maintenance order to be registered under the Maintenance Orders Act 1950 or the Maintenance Orders Act 1958.	£50

Column 1 *Number and description of fee*	*Column 2* *Amount of fee*
11 Financial Provision 11.1 Proceedings under the Domestic Proceedings and Magistrates' Courts Act 1978 or Schedule 6 to the Civil Partnership Act 2004 on an application for an order for financial provision (other than an application to vary or revoke such an order, or an application for an order for financial provision made for the benefit of, or against, a person residing outside the United Kingdom).	£215
12 Enforcement 12.1 On an application to question a judgment debtor or other person on oath in connection with enforcement of a judgment, or on an application to which rule 33.3(2)(b) of the Family Procedure Rules 2010 applies.	£50
12.2 On an application for a third party debt order or the appointment of a receiver by way of equitable execution.	£100
Note: Fee 12.2 is payable in respect of each third party against whom the order is sought.	
12.3 On an application for a charging order.	£100
Note: Fee 12.3 is payable in respect of each charging order applied for.	
12.4 On an application for a judgment summons.	£100
12.5 On an application for an attachment of earnings order to secure money due under an order made in family proceedings.	£100
Fee 12.5 is payable in respect of each defendant against whom an order is sought. Fee 12.5 is not payable where the attachment of earnings order is made on the hearing of a judgment summons.	
13 Enforcement in the family court 13.1 On an application for or in relation to enforcement of a judgment or order by the issue of a warrant of control against goods except a warrant to enforce payment of a fine.	£100
13.2 On a request for further attempt at execution of a warrant at a new address where the warrant has been returned to the court not executed (except where the warrant has been returned after it has been suspended by the court).	£30
13.3 On the issue of a warrant of possession or a warrant of delivery.	£110
Note on fee 13.3: Where the recovery of a sum of money is sought in addition, no further fee is payable.	
14 Enforcement in the High Court 14.1 On sealing a writ of control/possession/delivery.	£60
Note on fee 14.1: Where the recovery of a sum of money is sought in addition to a writ of possession and delivery, no further fee is payable.	
14.2 On a request or application to register a judgment or order; or for permission to enforce an arbitration award; or for a certified copy of a judgment or order for use abroad.	£60
15 Service 15.1 On a request for service by bailiff of any document except –	£110
(a) an order for a debtor to attend the adjourned hearing of a judgment summons;	
(b) a claim to controlled, executed or exempt goods;	
(c) an order made under section 23 of the Attachment of Earnings Act 1971 (enforcement provisions);	
(d) an order for a debtor to attend an adjourned oral examination of means; or	

Column 1 Number and description of fee	Column 2 Amount of fee
(e) an application for (and accompanying documentation), or an order for, or an application to vary, extend or discharge – (i) a non-molestation order; (ii) an occupation order; or (iii) a forced marriage protection order, under Part 4 or Part 4A of the Family Law Act 1996; or (f) an application for (and accompanying documentation), or an order for, or an application to vary or discharge a female genital mutilation protection order under Part 1 of Schedule 2 to the Female Genital Mutilation Act 2003.	
16 Sale	
16.1 For removing or taking steps to remove goods to a place of deposit.	The reasonable expenses incurred.
Fee 16.1 is to include the reasonable expenses of feeding and caring for animals.	
16.2 For the appraisement of goods.	5p in the £1 or part of a £1 of the appraised value.
16.3 For the sale of goods (including advertisements, catalogues, sale and commission and delivery of goods).	15p in the £1 or part of a £1 on the amount realised by the sale or such other sum as the district judge may consider to be justified in the circumstances.
16.4 Where no sale takes place by reason of an execution being withdrawn, satisfied or stopped.	(a) 10p in the £1 or part of a £1 on the value of the goods seized, the value to be the appraised value where the goods have been appraised or such other sum as the district judge may consider to be justified in the circumstances; and in addition (b) any sum payable under fee 16.1 and 16.2.
17 Affidavits in the High Court only	
17.1 On taking an affidavit or an affirmation or attestation upon honour in lieu of an affidavit or a declaration.	£11
17.2 For each exhibit referred to and required to be marked.	£2

Amendments—Schedule last substituted by SI 2014/877. Amended by SI 2015/687; SI 2015/1419; SI 2016/211; SI 2016/402.

Note—The Legal Aid Agency replaced the Legal Services Commission on 1 April 2013.

SCHEDULE 2
REMISSIONS AND PART REMISSIONS

1 Interpretation

(1) In this Schedule –

'child' means a person –

(a) whose main residence is with a party and who is aged –

(i) under 16 years; or

(ii) 16 to 19 years; and is –

(aa) not married or in a civil partnership; and

(bb) enrolled or accepted in full-time education that is not advanced education, or approved training; or

(b) in respect of whom a party or their partner pays child support maintenance or periodic payments in accordance with a maintenance agreement,

and 'full-time education', 'advanced education' and 'approved training' have the meaning given by the Child Benefit (General) Regulations 2006;

'child support maintenance' has the meaning given in section 3(6) of the Child Support Act 1991;

'couple' has the meaning given in section 3(5A) of the Tax Credits Act 2002;

'disposable capital' has the meaning given in paragraph 5;

'excluded benefits' means any of the following –

(a) any of the following benefits payable under the Social Security Contributions and Benefits Act 1992 or the corresponding provisions of the Social Security Contributions and Benefits (Northern Ireland) Act 1992 –

(i) attendance allowance under section 64;

(ii) severe disablement allowance;

(iii) carer's allowance;

(iv) disability living allowance;

(v) constant attendance allowance under section 104 as an increase to a disablement pension;

(vi) any payment made out of the social fund;

(vii) housing benefit;

(viii) widowed parents allowance;

(b) any of the following benefit payable under the Tax Credits Act 2002 –

(i) any disabled child element or severely disabled child element of the child tax credit;

(ii) any childcare element of the working tax credit;

(c) any direct payment made under the Community Care, Services for Carers and Children's Services (Direct Payments) (England) Regulations 2009, the Carers and Direct Payments Act (Northern Ireland) 2002, section 12B(1) of the Social Work (Scotland) Act 1968, the Social Care (Self-directed Support) (Scotland) Act 2013 or under regulations made under sections 50 to 53 of the Social Services and Well-being (Wales) Act 2014;

(d) a back to work bonus payable under section 26 of the Jobseekers Act 1995, or article 28 of the Jobseekers (Northern Ireland) Order 1995;

(e) any exceptionally severe disablement allowance paid under the Personal Injuries (Civilians) Scheme 1983;

(f) any payments from the Industrial Injuries Disablement Benefit;

(g) any pension paid under the Naval, Military and Air Forces etc. (Disablement and Death) Service Pension Order 2006;

(h) any payment made from the Independent Living Funds;

(i) any payment of bereavement support payment under section 30 of the Pensions Act 2014;

(j) any financial support paid under an agreement for the care of a foster child;

(k) any housing credit element of pension credit;

(l) any armed forces independence payment;

(m) any personal independence payment payable under the Welfare Reform Act 2012;

(n) any payment on account of benefit as defined in the Social Security (Payments on Account of Benefit) Regulations 2013;

(o) any of the following amounts, as defined by the Universal Credit Regulations 2013, that make up an award of universal credit –

(i) an additional amount to the child element in respect of a disabled child;

(ii) a housing costs element;

(iii) a childcare costs element;

(iv) a carer element;
(v) a limited capability for work or limited capacity for work and work -related activity element.

'family help (higher)' has the meaning given in paragraph 15(3) of the Civil Legal Aid (Merits Criteria) Regulations 2013;

'family help (lower)' has the meaning given in paragraph 15(2) of the Civil Legal Aid (Merits Criteria) Regulations 2013;

'gross monthly income' has the meaning given in paragraph 13;

'Independent Living Funds' means the funds listed at regulation 20(2)(b) of the Criminal Legal Aid (Financial Resources) Regulations 2013;

'legal representation' has the meaning given in paragraph 18(2) of the Civil Legal Aid (Merits Criteria) Regulations 2013;

'maintenance agreement' has the meaning given in subsection 9(1) of the Child Support Act 1991;

'partner' means a person with whom the party lives as a couple and includes a person with whom the party is not currently living but from whom the party is not living separate and apart;

'party' means the individual who would, but for this Schedule, be liable to pay a fee under this Order;

'restraint order' means –

(a) an order under section 42(1A) of the Senior Courts Act 1981;
(b) an order under section 33 of the Employment Tribunals Act 1996;
(c) a civil restraint order made under rule 3.11 of the Civil Procedure Rules 1998, or a practice direction made under that rule; or
(d) a civil restraint order under rule 4.8 of the Family Procedure Rules 2010, or the practice direction referred to in that rule.

(2) References to remission of a fee are to be read as including references to a part remission of a fee as appropriate and remit and remitted shall be construed accordingly.

Amendments—SI 2015/687; SI 2016/402; SI 2017/422.

Modifications—Para 1(1) modified for certain purposes by SI 2014/513.

2 Fee remission

If a party satisfies the disposable capital test, the amount of any fee remission is calculated by applying the gross monthly income test.

Disposable capital test

3 Disposable capital test

(1) Subject to paragraph 4, a party satisfies the disposable capital test if –

(a) the fee payable by the party and for which an application for remission is made, falls within a fee band set out in column 1 of Table 1; and
(b) the party's disposable capital is less than the amount in the corresponding row of column 2.

Table 1

Column 1 (*fee band*)	*Column 2* (*disposable capital*)
Up to and including £1,000	£3,000
£1,001 to £1,335	£4,000
£1,336 to £1,665	£5,000
£1,666 to £2,000	£6,000
£2,001 to £2,330	£7,000
£2,331 to £4,000	£8,000

PART IV

Column 1	Column 2
£4,001 to £5,000	£10,000
£5,001 to £6,000	£12,000
£6,001 to £7,000	£14,000
£7,001 or more	£16,000

4 Subject to paragraph 14, if a party or their partner is aged 61 or over, that party satisfies the disposable capital test if that party's disposable capital is less than £16,000.

5 Disposable capital

Subject to paragraph 14, disposable capital is the value of every resource of a capital nature belonging to the party on the date on which the application for remission is made, unless it is treated as income by this Order, or it is disregarded as excluded disposable capital.

6 Disposable capital – non-money resources

The value of a resource of a capital nature that does not consist of money is calculated as the amount which that resource would realise if sold, less –

(a) 10% of the sale value; and

(b) the amount of any borrowing secured against that resource that would be repayable on sale.

7 Disposable capital – resources held outside the United Kingdom

(1) Capital resources in a country outside the United Kingdom count towards disposable capital.

(2) If there is no prohibition in that country against the transfer of a resource into the United Kingdom, the value of that resource is the amount which that resource would realise if sold in that country, in accordance with paragraph 6.

(3) If there is a prohibition in that country against the transfer of a resource into the United Kingdom, the value of that resource is the amount that resource would realise if sold to a buyer in the United Kingdom.

8 Disposable capital – foreign currency resources

Where disposable capital is held in currency other than sterling, the cost of any banking charge or commission that would be payable if that amount were converted into sterling, is deducted from its value.

9 Disposable capital – jointly owned resources

Where any resource of a capital nature is owned jointly or in common, there is a presumption that the resource is owned in equal shares, unless evidence to the contrary is produced.

10 Excluded disposable capital

The following things are excluded disposable capital –

(a) a property which is the main or only dwelling occupied by the party;

(b) the household furniture and effects of the main or only dwelling occupied by the party;

(c) articles of personal clothing;

(d) any vehicle, the sale of which would leave the party, or their partner, without motor transport;

(e) tools and implements of trade, including vehicles used for business purposes;

(f) the capital value of the party's or their partner's business, where the party or their partner is self-employed;

(g) the capital value of any funds or other assets held in trust, where the party or their partner is a beneficiary without entitlement to advances of any trust capital;

(h) a jobseeker's back to work bonus;

(i) a payment made as a result of a determination of unfair dismissal by a court or tribunal, or by way of settlement of a claim for unfair dismissal;

(j) any compensation paid as a result of a determination of medical negligence or in respect of any personal injury by a court, or by way of settlement of a claim for medical negligence or personal injury;
(k) the capital held in any personal or occupational pension scheme;
(l) any cash value payable on surrender of a contract of insurance;
(m) any capital payment made out of the Independent Living Funds;
(n) any bereavement support payment in respect of the rate set out in regulation 3(2) or (5) of the Bereavement Support Payment Regulations 2017 (rate of bereavement support payment);
(o) any capital insurance or endowment lump sum payments that have been paid as a result of illness, disability or death;
(p) any student loan or student grant;
(q) any payments under the criminal injuries compensation scheme.

Amendments—SI 2017/422.

Gross monthly income test

11 Remission of fees – gross monthly income

(1) If a party satisfies the disposable capital test, no fee is payable under this Order if, at the time when the fee would otherwise be payable, the party or their partner has the number of children specified in column 1 of Table 2 and –

(a) if the party is single, their gross monthly income does not exceed the amount set out in the appropriate row of column 2; or
(b) if the party is one of a couple, the gross monthly income of that couple does not exceed the amount set out in the appropriate row of column 3.

Table 2

Column 1 *Number of children of party*	*Column 2* *Single*	*Column 3* *Couple*
no children	£1,085	£1,245
1 child	£1,330	£1,490
2 children	£1,735	£1,735

(2) If a party or their partner has more than 2 children, the relevant amount of gross monthly income is the appropriate amount specified in Table 2 for 2 children, plus the sum of £245 for each additional child.

(3) For every £10 of gross monthly income received above the appropriate amount in Table 2, including any additional amount added under sub-paragraph (2), the party must pay £5 towards the fee payable, up to the maximum amount of the fee payable.

(4) This paragraph is subject to paragraph 12.

12 Gross monthly income cap

(1) No remission is available if a party or their partner has the number of children specified in column 1 of Table 3 and –

(a) if the party is single, their gross monthly income exceeds the amount set out in the appropriate row of column 2 of Table 3; or
(b) if the party is one of a couple, the gross monthly income of that couple exceeds the amount set out in the appropriate row of column 3 of Table 3.

Table 3

Column 1	*Column 2*	*Column 3*
Number of children of party	*Single*	*Couple*
no children	£5,085	£5,245
1 child	£5,330	£5,490
2 children	£5,575	£5,735

(2) If a party or their partner has more than 2 children, the relevant amount of gross monthly income is the appropriate amount specified in Table 3 for 2 children, plus the sum of £245 for each additional child.

13 Gross monthly income

(1) Subject to paragraph 14, gross monthly income means the total monthly income, for the month preceding that in which the application for remission is made, from all sources, other than receipt of any of the excluded benefits.

(2) Income from a trade, business or gainful occupation other than an occupation at a wage or salary is calculated as –

- (a) the profits which have accrued or will accrue to the party; and
- (b) the drawings of the party;

in the month preceding that in which the application for remission is made.

(3) In calculating profits under sub-paragraph (2)(a), all sums necessarily expended to earn those profits are deducted.

General

14 Resources and income treated as the party's resources and income

(1) Subject to sub-paragraph (2), the disposable capital and gross monthly income of a partner of a party is to be treated as disposable capital and gross monthly income of the party.

(2) Where the partner of a party has a contrary interest to the party in the matter to which the fee relates, the disposable capital and gross monthly income of that partner, if any, is not treated as the disposable capital and gross monthly income of the party.

15 Application for remission of a fee

(1) An application for remission of a fee must be made at the time when the fee would otherwise be payable.

(2) Where an application for remission of a fee is made, the party must –

- (a) indicate the fee to which the application relates;
- (b) declare the amount of their disposable capital; and
- (c) provide documentary evidence of their gross monthly income and the number of children relevant for the purposes of paragraphs 11 and 12.

(3) Where an application for remission of a fee is made on or before the date on which a fee is payable, the date for payment of the fee is disapplied.

(4) Where an application for remission is refused, or if part remission of a fee is granted, the amount of the fee which remains unremitted must be paid within the period notified in writing to the party.

16 Remission in exceptional circumstances

A fee specified in this Order may be remitted where the Lord Chancellor is satisfied that there are exceptional circumstances which justify doing so.

17 Refunds

(1) Subject to sub-paragraph (3), where a party pays a fee at a time when that party would have been entitled to a remission if they had provided the documentary evidence required by paragraph 15, the fee, or the amount by which the fee would have been reduced as the case may be, must be refunded if documentary evidence relating to the time when the fee became payable is provided at a later date.

(2) Subject to sub-paragraph (3), where a fee has been paid at a time when the Lord Chancellor, if all the circumstances had been known, would have remitted the fee under paragraph 15, the fee or the amount by which the fee would have been reduced, as the case may be, must be refunded to the party.

(3) No refund shall be made under this paragraph unless the party who paid the fee applies within 3 months of the date on which the fee was paid.

(4) The Lord Chancellor may extend the period of 3 months mentioned in sub-paragraph (3) if the Lord Chancellor considers that there is a good reason for a refund being made after the end of the period of 3 months.

18 Legal Aid

A party is not entitled to a fee remission if, under Part 1 of the Legal Aid, Sentencing and Punishment of Offenders Act 2012, they are in receipt of the following civil legal services –

(a) Legal representation; or
(b) Family help (higher); or
(c) Family help (lower) in respect of applying for a consent order.

PART IV

19 Vexatious litigants

(1) This paragraph applies where –

(a) a restraint order is in force against a party; and
(b) that party makes an application for permission to –
   (i) issue proceedings or take a step in proceedings as required by the restraint order;
   (ii) apply for amendment or discharge of the order; or
   (iii) appeal the order.

(2) The fee prescribed by this Order for the application is payable in full.

(3) If the party is granted permission, they are to be refunded the difference between –

(a) the fee paid; and
(b) the fee that would have been payable if this Schedule had been applied without reference to this paragraph.

20 Exceptions

No remissions or refunds are available in respect of the fee payable for –

(a) copy or duplicate documents;
(b) searches.

Amendments—Schedule last substituted by SI 2013/2302. Amended by SI 2014/590.

'full-time education' of a 'child' (para 1(1))—'Full-time education' is a component of 'advanced' education and (per Child Benefit (General) Regulations 2006, reg 1(3)) the following:

- education undertaken in pursuit of a course, where the average time spent during term time in receiving tuition, engaging in practical work or supervised study, or taking examinations exceeds 12 hours a week; and
- in calculating the time spent in pursuit of the course, no account shall be taken of time occupied by meal breaks or spent on unsupervised study.

'advanced education' (para 1(1))—Child Benefit (General) Regulations 2006, reg 1(3) provides that:

'"advanced education" means full-time education for the purposes of –

(a) a course in preparation for a degree, a diploma of higher education, a higher national certificate, a higher national diploma, or a teaching qualification; or

(b) any other course which is of a standard above ordinary national diploma, a national diploma or national certificate of Edexcel, a general certificate of education (advanced level), or Scottish national qualifications at higher or advanced higher level;'

'approved training' (para 1(1))—Child Benefit (General) Regulations 2006, reg 1(3) provides that:

'"approved training" means arrangements made by the Government—

(a) in relation to England, known as "Foundation Learning" or "Access to Apprenticeships";

(b) in relation to Wales, known as "Skillbuild", "Skillbuild+" or "Traineeships" or "Foundation Apprenticeships"; ...'

'Child support Act 1991, s 3(6)' (para 1(1))—The fees exempt applicant will need to know that there are two versions of s 3(6) (according to whether the applicant is CS1 or CS2/CS3 (see CSA 1991, s 4). The most recent version is as s 4 (above). The old version is on the government website at *www.legislation.gov.uk/ukpga/1991/48/section/3/enacted* (CSA 1991 remains on that site unamended).

Couple—Tax Credits Act 2002, s 3(5A) provides as follows:

'(5A) In this Part "couple" means –

(a) a man and woman who are married to each other and are neither –
    (i) separated under a court order, nor
    (ii) separated in circumstances in which the separation is likely to be permanent,

(b) a man and woman who are not married to each other but are living together as husband and wife,

(c) two people of the same sex who are civil partners of each other and are neither –
    (i) separated under a court order, nor
    (ii) separated in circumstances in which the separation is likely to be permanent, or

(d) two people of the same sex who are not civil partners of each other but are living together as if they were civil partners.'

'Civil Legal Aid (Merits Criteria) Regulations 2013, reg 15'—This provides as follows:

'(1) Family help may be provided in a family dispute as either family help (lower) or family help (higher).

(2) "Family help (lower)" means—

(a) civil legal services provided in relation to the negotiation of a family dispute before the issuing of proceedings; or

(b) civil legal services provided in relation to the issuing of proceedings in order to obtain a consent order following the settlement of a family dispute.

(3) 'Family help (higher)' means such civil legal services as are available under legal representation but does not include preparation for, or representation at, a contested final hearing or appeal.'

'20(2)(b) of the Criminal Legal Aid (Financial Resources) Regulations 2013'—This provides as follows:

'(b) any payments paid out of—
    (i) the Independent Living Fund;
    (ii) the Independent Living (Extension) Fund;
    (iii) the Independent Living (1993) Fund; or
    (iv) the Independent Living Fund (2006);'

The Funds are defined in Criminal Defence Service (Financial Eligibility) Regulations 2006, reg 2.

'Civil Legal Aid (Merits Criteria) Regulations 2013, reg 18(2)'—This provides as follows:

'(2) 'Legal representation' means the provision of civil legal services, other than acting as a mediator or arbitrator, to an individual or legal person in particular proceedings where that individual or legal person –

(a) is a party to those proceedings;

(b) wishes to be joined as a party to those proceedings; or

(c) is contemplating issuing those proceedings.'

****

High Court (Distribution of Business) Order 1993,

SI 1993/622

1 This order may be cited as the High Court (Distribution of Business) Order 1993 and shall come into force on 5 April 1993.

2 There shall be assigned to the Family Division all proceedings in the High Court under the Child Support Act 1991.

****

'all proceedings'—Such proceedings will be rare (eg declarations of parentage under CSA 1991, s 27 and transferred upwards) and may include judicial review applications brought as a result of the Act.

International Recovery of Maintenance (Hague Convention 2007 etc) Regulations 2012, SI 2012/2814

ARRANGEMENT OF REGULATIONS

Regulation		Page
1	Citation, commencement and extent	2487
2		2487
3	Interpretation	2487
4	Central Authority for England and Wales	2488
5	The Convention	2488
6	Enforcement	2488
7	Provisions relating to information	2488
	Schedule 1 – Recognition and Enforcement of Non-EU Maintenance Decisions, and Establishment and Modification of Maintenance Obligations under the Convention	2488
	Schedule 2 – Enforcement of International Maintenance Orders Driving Disqualification Orders	2492
	Schedule 3 – Provisions Relating to Information	2496

Scope—These Regulations support the application of the Convention on the International Recovery of Child Support and other forms of Family Maintenance of 23 November 2007 ('the 2007 Convention'; see Part VI) in England and Wales primarily. The 2007 Convention came into force in the EU on 1 August 2014. Certain statutes with UK application (e g Maintenance Orders (Facilities for Enforcement) Act 1920) have been amended by these Regulations, which have been made under the European Communities Act 1972, of which Act s 2(2) permits the amendment to primary legislation to remove inconsistencies with the 2007 Convention.

Reg 4 designates the Lord Chancellor as the Central Authority for England and Wales, as required by the 2007 Convention, Art 4.

Reg 5 and Sch 1 make provision for the enforcement of maintenance decisions and maintenance arrangements made in Contracting States to the 2007 Convention by the courts of England and Wales.

Reg 6 and Sch 2 enable courts to which an application is made to enforce a maintenance decision under certain international instruments by way of a driving disqualification order. These provisions apply to England, Wales and Scotland.

Reg 7 and Sch 3 make provision for the sharing of information by certain government departments to facilitate the establishment and enforcement of maintenance decisions to which the 2007 Convention applies. These provisions apply to England, Wales, Scotland and Northern Ireland.

Reg 8 and Sch 4 provide for consequential statutory amendments.

Reg 9 and Sch 5 make provision for consequential statutory amendments relating to the Maintenance Regulation.

1 Citation, commencement and extent

(1) These Regulations may be cited as the International Recovery of Maintenance (Hague Convention 2007 etc) Regulations 2012, and, subject as follows, shall come into force on the day on which the Convention enters into force in respect of the European Union, which day will be notified in the London, Edinburgh and Belfast Gazettes.

(2) Regulations 1, 2, 3 and 9, and Schedule 5 come into force on 7 December 2012.

(3) Regulation 6 and Schedule 2 come into force on 1 April 2013, except in so far as they apply to the enforcement of a maintenance decision registered under the Convention.

2 (1) Subject as follows, these Regulations extend only to England and Wales.

(2) Regulations 1 to 3, 4(2), 6, 7 and 10 and Schedules 2 and 3 also extend to Scotland.

(3) Regulations 1 to 3, 4(2), 7 and 10 and Schedule 3 also extend to Northern Ireland.

(4) Any amendment, repeal or revocation made by these Regulations has the same extent as the enactment to which it relates.

3 Interpretation

In these Regulations –

'the Convention' means the Convention on the International Recovery of Child Support and other forms of Family Maintenance done at The Hague on 23 November 2007; and

'the Maintenance Regulation' means Council Regulation (EC) No 4/2009 on jurisdiction, applicable law, recognition and enforcement of decisions and cooperation in matters relating to maintenance obligations, including as applied in relation to Denmark by virtue of the Agreement made on 19 October 2005 between the European Community and the Kingdom of Denmark.

4 Central Authority for England and Wales

(1) The Lord Chancellor is designated under Article 4 of the Convention as the Central Authority in relation to England and Wales.

(2) If a person outside the United Kingdom does not know to which Central Authority in the United Kingdom a communication should be addressed, the person may address it to the Lord Chancellor.

5 The Convention

Schedule 1 (which contains provisions relating to the establishment, modification, recognition and enforcement in England and Wales pursuant to the Convention of maintenance decisions made in States bound by the Convention which are not European Union Member States) has effect.

6 Enforcement

Schedule 2 (which contains provisions for the enforcement in England and Wales and Scotland of certain international maintenance obligations in relation to children by way of driving disqualification orders) has effect.

7 Provisions relating to information

Schedule 3 (which contains provisions relating to access to, and the transmission and use of, information) has effect.

****

SCHEDULE 1
RECOGNITION AND ENFORCEMENT OF NON-EU MAINTENANCE DECISIONS, AND ESTABLISHMENT AND MODIFICATION OF MAINTENANCE OBLIGATIONS UNDER THE CONVENTION

1 Interpretation

(1) In this Schedule –

'Contracting State' means a State bound by the Convention other than an EU Member State;

'court', in relation to a maintenance decision given in a Contracting State, includes a tribunal, and any administrative authority (within the meaning of Article 19(3)) with competence to make a decision in respect of a maintenance obligation;

'maintenance decision' means a decision, or part of a decision, made by a court in a Contracting State, to which Chapter V of the Convention applies by virtue of Article 19(1).

(2) In this Schedule, any reference to a numbered Article is a reference to the Article so numbered in the Convention and any reference to a sub-division of a numbered Article shall be construed accordingly.

(3) *(revoked)*

Amendments—SI 2014/879.

2 Recognition and enforcement of maintenance decisions made by courts in Contracting States

(1) Subject to sub-paragraph (2), the court in England and Wales to which an application for registration of a maintenance decision under the Convention is to be made is the family court.

(2) An application for registration is to be transmitted by the Lord Chancellor to the family court ('the registering court').

(3) Jurisdiction in relation to applications for registration of maintenance decisions lies with the courts of England and Wales if –

- (a) the person against whom enforcement is sought is resident in England and Wales, or
- (b) assets belonging to that person and which are susceptible to enforcement are situated or held in England and Wales.

(4) An application for registration shall be determined in the first instance by the prescribed officer of the registering court. In this sub-paragraph and in sub-paragraph (5), 'prescribed' means prescribed by rules of court.

(5) The decision of the prescribed officer may be appealed to the registering court in accordance with rules of court.

(6) For the purposes of the enforcement of a maintenance decision registered under the Convention in the registering court –

- (a) the decision shall be of the same force and effect,
- (b) the registering court shall have in relation to its enforcement the same powers, and
- (c) proceedings for or with respect to its enforcement may be taken, as if the decision had originally been made by the registering court.

(7) Sub-paragraph (6) is subject to sub-paragraph (8).

(8) A maintenance decision which is so registered shall be enforceable in the family court in the same manner as a maintenance order made by that court.

In this sub-paragraph 'maintenance order' has the meaning given by section 1(10) of the Maintenance Enforcement Act 1991.

(9) Sub-paragraph (6) is also subject to –

- (a) paragraph 3;
- (b) any provision made by rules of court as to the procedure for the enforcement of maintenance decisions registered in accordance with this paragraph.

(10) The debtor under a maintenance decision registered in accordance with this paragraph in the family court must give notice of any change of address to the court officer of the family court in the Designated Family Judge area in which the maintenance decision is registered.

In this sub-paragraph, 'debtor' has the meaning given by Article 3.

(11) A person who without reasonable excuse fails to comply with sub-paragraph (10) shall be guilty of an offence and liable on summary conviction to a fine not exceeding level 2 on the standard scale.

Amendments—SI 2014/879.

3 Interest on judgments

(1) Subject to sub-paragraph (2) and rules of court as to the payment of interest under this paragraph, where a person applying for registration of a maintenance decision shows that –

- (a) the decision provides for the payment of money, and
- (b) in accordance with the law of the Contracting State in which the maintenance decision was given and the terms of the decision, interest on that sum is recoverable at a particular rate and from a particular date or time,

the debt resulting from registration of the decision is to carry interest at that rate and from that date or time.

(2) Interest is not recoverable under sub-paragraph (1) unless the rate of interest and the date or time referred to in sub-paragraph (1)(b) are registered with the decision.

(3), (4) (*revoked*)

Amendments—SI 2014/879.

4 Currency of payments under a maintenance decision

(1) Sums payable under a maintenance decision registered in England and Wales under the Convention, including any arrears so payable, shall be paid in sterling.

(2) Where the maintenance decision is expressed in any other currency, the amounts shall be converted on the basis of the exchange rate prevailing on the date on which the application for registration was received by the Lord Chancellor for transmission to a court.

(3) For the purposes of this paragraph, a written certificate purporting to be signed by an officer of any bank in England and Wales and stating the exchange rate prevailing on a specified date shall be evidence of the facts stated.

5 Proof and admissibility of certain maintenance decisions and related documents

(1) For the purposes of proceedings relating to the Convention a document, duly authenticated, which purports to be a copy of a maintenance decision given by a court in a Contracting State shall without further proof be deemed to be a true copy, unless the contrary is shown.

(2) A document purporting to be a copy of a maintenance decision given by a court in a Contracting State is duly authenticated for the purposes of this paragraph if it purports –

(a) to bear the seal of that court; or

(b) to be certified by any person in that person's capacity as a judge or officer of that court to be a true copy of a maintenance decision given by that court.

(3) Nothing in this paragraph shall prejudice the admission in evidence of any document which is admissible apart from this paragraph.

6 Maintenance arrangements

(1) References in this paragraph to maintenance arrangements are to those maintenance arrangements (as defined in Article 3(e)) which are to be recognised and enforceable in the same way as maintenance decisions by virtue of Article 30.

(2) In relation to a maintenance arrangement which is enforceable as a maintenance decision in the Contracting State of origin, this Schedule applies, subject to the modifications in subparagraphs (3), (4) and (5), as if that maintenance arrangement was a maintenance decision given by a court of that State.

(3) Paragraph 2 applies to maintenance arrangements as if –

(a) in sub-paragraph (6), for 'as if the decision had originally' there were substituted 'as if it were a decision which had originally';

(b) after sub-paragraph (9)(b) there were inserted –

'(c) Article 30(6) (restriction on enforcement where there is a challenge to a maintenance arrangement in the Contracting State of origin).'.

(4) Paragraph 3 applies to maintenance arrangements as if in sub-paragraph (1)(b), for the word 'given' there were substituted 'concluded'.

(5) Paragraph 5 applies to maintenance arrangements as if –

(a) in sub-paragraph (1), for 'given by a court' there were substituted 'formally drawn up or registered as an authentic instrument by, or authenticated by, or concluded, registered or filed with a competent authority';

(b) for sub-paragraph (2) there were substituted –

'(2) A document purporting to be a copy of a maintenance arrangement drawn up or registered as an authentic instrument by, or authenticated by, or concluded, registered or filed with a competent authority in a Contracting State is duly authenticated for the purposes of this paragraph if it purports to be certified to be a true copy of such an arrangement by a person duly authorised in that State to do so.'.

(6) Section 18 of the Civil Jurisdiction and Judgments Act 1982 does not apply to maintenance arrangements.

7 Applications for establishment or modification of maintenance in England and Wales

(1) Upon receipt of an application submitted under Article 10 for establishment or modification of a decision, the Lord Chancellor shall send that application to the court officer of the family court in the Maintenance Enforcement Business Centre for the area in which the respondent is residing.

(2) Upon receipt of the application under sub-paragraph (1), the court officer of that court shall decide –

- (a) whether the courts of England and Wales have jurisdiction to determine the application by virtue of the Maintenance Regulation and Schedule 6 to the Civil Jurisdiction and Judgments (Maintenance) Regulations 2011; and
- (b) if so, whether the family court has the power to make the decision or modification sought under the law in force in England and Wales.

(3) Where the court officer decides under sub-paragraph (2)(a) that the courts of England and Wales do not have jurisdiction to determine the application, the court officer shall return the application to the Lord Chancellor with a written explanation of the reasons for that decision.

(4) (*revoked*)

(5) Subject to sub-paragraph (6), if the court officer decides under sub-paragraph (2)(b) that the family court has power to make the decision or modification sought, the court officer shall issue the application and serve it on the respondent.

(6) If the respondent does not reside in the area covered by the Maintenance Enforcement Business Centre to which the application has been sent, the court officer shall –

- (a) if satisfied that the respondent is residing within the area covered by another Maintenance Enforcement Business Centre, send the application to the court officer of the family court in the Maintenance Enforcement Business Centre for that other area and inform the Lord Chancellor that it has been so sent; or
- (b) if unable to establish where the respondent is residing, return the application to the Lord Chancellor.

(7) A court officer who receives an application by virtue of sub-paragraph (6)(a) shall proceed under sub-paragraph (5) as if that court officer had decided that the family court has power to make the decision or modification sought.

(8) Where the court officer has determined in accordance with sub-paragraph (2)(b) that the family court has power to make the decision or modification sought, the application shall be treated for the purpose of establishment or modification of a decision under the law in force in England and Wales.

(9) In this paragraph –

'respondent' means the person who is alleged in an application for establishment of a decision under Article 10 to owe maintenance, or where the application is for modification of a decision, the applicant for the original decision; and

a reference to an application is a reference to an application together with any documents which accompany it.

Amendments—SI 2014/879; SI 2015/1489.

Modification—'Maintenance Enforcement Business Centre': see commentary to CJJ(M)R 2011, Sch 1, Pt 5.

PART IV

SCHEDULE 2
ENFORCEMENT OF INTERNATIONAL MAINTENANCE ORDERS DRIVING DISQUALIFICATION ORDERS

Scope—Sch 2 applies to child maintenance decisions enforceable under the instruments, including the 2007 Convention, listed in para 1. The 2007 Convention, Art 33 requires that the same range of enforcement methods is made available to cases under the 2007 Convention as is available in domestic cases. Although driving disqualification orders are not available for cases of spousal maintenance or in relation to child maintenance orders made by a court, they are available under CSA 1991 for domestic cases and therefore an equivalent enforcement method is required for cases under the 2007 Convention. Under domestic law, driving disqualification orders may be made under CSA 1991, ss 39A and 40B and CS(CE)R 1992, Pt IV. A driving disqualification order may be used to enforce a 'maintenance decision' as defined by Sch 2, para 2. The definition requires that the maintenance obligation being enforced has to be both an obligation to which an international agreement listed in Sch 2, para 1 applies and a maintenance order enforceable in the Family Court. Para 3 sets out the preconditions for an application for a driving disqualification order in England and Wales, making it clear that it is viewed as an enforcement measure of last resort.

1 Application

The provisions of this Schedule apply in relation to the enforcement of a maintenance decision relating to a child where that maintenance decision is registered for enforcement, or enforceable, by virtue of –

(a) the Council Regulation;
(b) the Lugano Convention;
(c) the Maintenance Regulation; or
(d) the Convention.

2 Interpretation

(1) In this Schedule –

'the 1980 Act' means the Magistrates' Courts Act 1980;

'the Council Regulation' means Council Regulation (EC) No 44/2001 on jurisdiction and the recognition and enforcement of judgments in civil and commercial matters;

'the Lugano Convention' means the Convention on jurisdiction and the recognition and enforcement of judgments in civil and commercial matters signed on behalf of the European Community on 30 October 2007;

'arrears' means a sum or sums payable to the creditor from the debtor which have fallen due under the terms of a maintenance decision and which the debtor has not paid;

'the court' means –

in England and Wales, a magistrates' court;

in Scotland, the sheriff court;

'the creditor' means a person to whom a sum or sums of maintenance are owed by the debtor under the terms of a maintenance decision in relation to which an application under this Schedule is made, and includes –

a public body acting in place of an individual to whom maintenance is owed or to which reimbursement is owed for benefits provided in place of maintenance, to the extent that such a body may seek enforcement of a maintenance decision under the terms of an international agreement referred to in paragraph 1; and

an officer of the family court, where the sum or sums of maintenance must be paid to the family court;

'the debtor' means the person who is liable to pay a sum or sums to the creditor under the terms of the maintenance decision in relation to which a complaint referred to in paragraph 3(2) or an application referred to in paragraph 4(1) of this Schedule is made;

'driving disqualification order' means an order under paragraph 5(1)(a) of this Schedule;

'maintenance decision' means a maintenance obligation to which an international agreement mentioned in paragraph 1 applies and which is –

in England and Wales, a maintenance order enforceable in the family court;

in Scotland, a maintenance order within the meaning of section 106 of the Debtors (Scotland) Act 1987.

(2) In this Schedule –

(a) 'child' means a person who –
  (i) either –
    (aa) has not attained the age of 16, or
    (bb) has not attained the age of 20, and is receiving full time education or vocational training; and
  (ii) is not or has not been party to a marriage, to a civil partnership or to an overseas relationship treated as a civil partnership under section 215 of the Civil Partnership Act 2004,

  and for the purposes of sub-paragraph (ii) 'marriage' and 'civil partnership' include a void marriage and a void civil partnership respectively;

(b)
  (i) 'driving licence' means a licence to drive a motor vehicle granted under Part III of the Road Traffic Act 1988;
  (ii) …

(c) *(revoked)*

Amendments—SI 2014/879; SI 2015/583; SI 2015/1489.

3 Application for a driving disqualification order – England and Wales

(1) This paragraph applies to England and Wales only.

(2) Where payment under a maintenance decision is in arrears, the court may make a driving disqualification order on complaint made by a creditor.

(2A) A complaint under sub-paragraph (2) shall not be made earlier than the fifteenth day after the making of the maintenance decision to which it relates, but subject to this such a complaint may be made at any time.

(2B) Section 55 of the 1980 Act shall not apply in relation to a complaint under sub-paragraph (2).

(2C) Section 56 of the 1980 Act shall have effect in relation to a complaint under sub-paragraph (2) as if the words 'if evidence has been received on a previous occasion' were omitted.

(2D) Sub-paragraph (2E) applies where, at the time and place appointed for the hearing or adjourned hearing of a complaint under sub-paragraph (2), the complainant appears but the defendant does not.

(2E) The court may proceed in the absence of the defendant if –

(a) it is proved to the satisfaction of the court, on oath or in such other manner as may be prescribed in rules of court, that the summons was served on the defendant within what appears to the court to be a reasonable time before the hearing or adjourned hearing; or

(b) the defendant has appeared on a previous occasion to answer the complaint.

(2F) If a complaint under sub-paragraph (2) is substantiated on oath, any justice of the peace acting in the same local justice area as a court having jurisdiction to hear the complaint may issue a warrant for the defendant's arrest, whether or not a summons has been issued previously.

(3) The court shall not make a driving disqualification order –

(a) in the absence of the debtor;

(b) if it considers that, in a case in which it has power to do so, it is appropriate to –
  (i) make an attachment of earnings order;
  (ii) make an order under section 59(4) of the 1980 Act; or
  (iii) issue a warrant of control for the purpose of recovering the arrears under section 76(1) of that Act;

(c) unless either –
  (i) the creditor has sought to obtain a charging order or a third party debt order in respect of the arrears and the arrears or any portion of them remain unpaid; or
  (ii) the debtor has no assets in England and Wales which are susceptible to such methods of enforcement.

PART IV

(4) Pending the entry into force of section 62 of, and Schedule 12 to, the Tribunals, Courts and Enforcement Act 2007, the reference in sub-paragraph (b)(iii) to obtaining a warrant of control is to be read as a reference to obtaining a warrant of distress.

Amendments—SI 2014/879.

4 Application for a driving disqualification order – Scotland

(1) In Scotland, the creditor may, by summary application, apply to the court for a driving disqualification order where the conditions mentioned in sub-paragraphs (2), (3) and (4) are met.

(2) The first condition is that arrears have arisen under the maintenance decision.

(3) The second condition is that –

- (a) a diligence against earnings listed in section 46(1) of the Debtors (Scotland) Act 1987 has been executed or made under Part 3 of that Act to secure the payment of sums due under the maintenance decision and it has proved ineffective as a means of securing that payments are made in accordance with the maintenance decision; or
- (b) such diligence against earnings is inappropriate because the debtor is unemployed or otherwise has no earnings which could be the subject of a diligence against earnings.

(4) The third condition is that the creditor has sought to recover the arrears by –

- (a) an attachment;
- (b) an arrestment; or
- (c) an inhibition,

and the arrears or any portion of them remain unpaid or the debtor has no assets in Scotland which are susceptible to the methods of enforcement mentioned in this sub-paragraph.

5 Making of a driving disqualification order

(1) If, but only if, the court is of the opinion that the failure to pay the arrears is due to wilful refusal or culpable neglect on the part of the debtor, it may –

- (a) make an order (a driving disqualification order) disqualifying the debtor from holding or obtaining a driving licence for such period specified in the order, not exceeding two years, as it thinks fit; or
- (b) make a driving disqualification order but suspend its operation until such time and on such conditions (if any) as it thinks just.

(2) The court shall not make a driving disqualification order unless it has enquired, in the presence of the debtor, as to –

- (a) the debtor's means;
- (b) whether the debtor needs a driving licence to earn his or her living; and
- (c) whether the failure to pay the arrears is due to wilful refusal or culpable neglect on the part of the debtor.

6 A driving disqualification order must state the amount of arrears in respect of which it is made and the period to which they relate and the amount may not exceed the arrears owing under the maintenance decision at the date on which the complaint referred to in paragraph 3 or the application under paragraph 4 was made.

7 A court which makes a driving disqualification order shall require the person to whom it relates to produce any driving licence held by that person.

8 (1) The court shall not, in relation to arrears –

- (a) make a driving disqualification order during the currency of a warrant committing the debtor to prison in respect of the same arrears;
- (b) issue a warrant committing the debtor to prison where a driving disqualification order has been made in respect of the same arrears but the period of disqualification specified in the driving disqualification order has not expired.

(2) In sub-paragraph (1) –

(a) references to a warrant committing the debtor to prison include such a warrant which has been postponed;

(b) references to a driving disqualification order include such an order which has been suspended in accordance with paragraph 5(1)(b); and

(c) references to the currency of a warrant, or to the period of disqualification specified in a driving disqualification order, are to be read as including references to the period of postponement of a warrant or suspension of disqualification respectively.

9 Variation, revocation and expiry of driving disqualification order

(1) On application by the creditor or the debtor, the court –

(a) may, if part of the amount in respect of which the order is made is paid to any person authorised to receive it, make an order substituting a shorter period of disqualification, or revoking the driving disqualification order; and

(b) must, if the whole of the amount is so paid, make an order revoking the driving disqualification order.

(2) An application under sub-paragraph (1) shall be made –

(a) in England and Wales, by complaint;

(b) in Scotland, by summary application.

10 Upon the making of a further complaint under paragraph 3(2) of this Schedule or application under paragraph 4 of this Schedule, the court may make a further driving disqualification order if the arrears in respect of which the driving disqualification order was made have not been paid in full when the period of disqualification specified in that order expires.

Amendments—SI 2014/879.

11 Notification to the Secretary of State

Where a court –

(a) makes a driving disqualification order; or

(b) makes an order varying or revoking a driving disqualification order,

it shall send notice of that fact and any driving licence produced to the court to the Secretary of State.

12 Production of driving licence in England and Wales

In England and Wales, a justice of the peace may issue a summons to the debtor to produce to a magistrates' court any driving licence held by the debtor, and issue a warrant for the debtor's arrest if the debtor does not comply.

13 Procedure on an application for a driving disqualification order in Scotland

In Scotland, the power of the Court of Session by Act of Sederunt to regulate the procedure and practice in civil proceedings in the sheriff court includes the power to make, in relation to driving disqualification orders made under this Schedule, provision –

(a) as to the form of any order issued under this Schedule;

(b) allowing an application under this Schedule to be renewed where no order is issued;

(c) that a statement in writing to the effect that wages of any amount have been paid to the debtor during any period, purported to be signed by or on behalf of the debtor's employer, is sufficient evidence of the facts stated;

(d) that, for the purposes of enabling an inquiry to be made as to the debtor's conduct and means, the sheriff may issue a citation to the debtor to appear before the sheriff and (if the debtor does not obey) may issue a warrant for the debtor's arrest;

(e) that, for the purposes of enabling such an inquiry, the sheriff may issue a warrant for the debtor's arrest without issuing a citation;

(f) as to the execution of a warrant of arrest.

PART IV

SCHEDULE 3
PROVISIONS RELATING TO INFORMATION

Scope—To help the Central Authority fulfil its obligations under Arts 6 and 7 of 2007 Convention as to the location of the creditor or the debtor, and obtaining financial information on the debtor to assist in enforcement applications, Sch 3 provides a regime for data-sharing to the Central Authority from the Department for Work and Pensions and HMRC. There are restrictions on the circumstances in which information can be shared. The information is not available, unless the application is made under Art 10 of the 2007 Convention, through a Central Authority, and must be relevant to the recovery of maintenance under the 2007 Convention. Although information may be sought in relation to the debtor's financial circumstances, such information is available only in enforcement cases; information on the creditor's financial circumstances is not available under Sch 3 (para 3(2)). A request for information may be made by the Central Authority in relation to a specific measures request under Art 7 of the 2007 Convention, where no application under the 2007 Convention, Art 10 is pending. However, the details of the debtor's financial circumstances are not available at this stage, but only an indication that the debtor does or does not have an income or assets in this country (para 6).

1 (1) Subject to the provisions of this Schedule, the Secretary of State, and Revenue and Customs officials, shall provide to the Central Authority such information mentioned at paragraph 3 as they hold in the course of their ordinary activities and which is necessary to facilitate establishment, modification, recognition, registration or enforcement of a maintenance obligation to which the Convention applies, except that provision of information may be refused where it would pose a threat to public safety or national security.

(2) The information to be supplied by the Secretary of State is limited to information held for functions relating to social security, child support, employment or training.

(3) In this Schedule, references to the Secretary of State include a person providing services to the Secretary of State in connection with the functions mentioned at sub-paragraph (2).

2 (1) The information shall be provided to the Central Authority upon its request.

(2) The Central Authority may not request the information unless the following conditions are met –

(a) the application to which the request relates has been made under Chapter III of the Convention (applications through Central Authorities) or is an application for a specific measure under Article 7 relating to the location of the debtor or creditor, or to obtaining the information in Article 6(2)(c) (relevant financial circumstances);

(b) the request is limited to information which is relevant for the establishment, modification, recognition, registration or enforcement (as the case may be) of the maintenance obligation in question.

3 (1) Subject to sub-paragraphs (2) to (4), the information to be supplied under paragraph 1 is –

(a) the address of the debtor or of the creditor;

(b) details of the debtor's income;

(c) the identity and contact details of the debtor's employer;

(d) details of any deposit account or withdrawable share account that the debtor holds with a deposit-taker;

(e) details of the debtor's assets.

(2) Where the application to which the request relates is for establishment or modification of a maintenance obligation, the Central Authority may only request the address of the debtor or of the creditor.

(3) The information at sub-paragraph (1)(e) may not be requested unless the information at subparagraphs (1)(b) to (d) is insufficient to enable enforcement of the maintenance obligation.

(4) Where the application to which the request relates is for a specific measure in accordance with paragraph 2(2)(a), the information in sub-paragraph (1)(b), (d) and (e) –

(a) shall consist only of an indication as to whether the debtor has income or assets in England and Wales, Scotland or Northern Ireland (as the case may be); and

(b) shall be supplied only if the creditor produces to the Central Authority a copy of the maintenance obligation or an abstract from it together with the document required by Article 25(1)(b) or Article 30(3)(b), as appropriate, stating that it is enforceable in the

Contracting State in which it was made, and no information may be supplied in relation to the identity and contact details of the debtor's employer.

4 (1) The Central Authority shall transmit the information received in accordance with this Schedule to

(a) the relevant court in England and Wales, or Scotland or Northern Ireland (as the case may be) seised of the application referred to in paragraph 2(2)(a);
(b) where necessary, the requesting Central Authority,

as appropriate.

5 Subject to the provisions of the Convention and of this Schedule, the persons and authorities to whom the Central Authority transmits information in accordance with this Schedule and the requirements of Articles 6 and 7 may process that information in any manner necessary to facilitate the adjudication and recovery of the maintenance obligation to which the request relates.

6 The Central Authority, any court to which it transmits information in accordance with paragraph 4, and any person or authority within the United Kingdom to whom that information is transmitted (whether by a court or by the Central Authority) –

(a) may use information provided under this Schedule only for the purpose of facilitating recovery of maintenance in accordance with this Schedule and the Convention;
(b) may not disclose to the applicant the information so provided, except that –
  (i) the existence, or not as the case may be, of an address, income or assets in England and Wales, or Scotland or Northern Ireland (as relevant) may be so disclosed;
  (ii) the information may be disclosed if required by rules of court;
(c) may not store the information beyond the period necessary for the purpose it was provided to it.

7 (1) Subject to paragraph 6(b), information referred to in paragraph 3(1) which is received by a Central Authority from a person or an authority listed in paragraph 1 cannot be disclosed to another person unless the disclosure is in connection with a function of the Central Authority under Articles 6 and 7, and Chapter III.

(2) Sub-paragraph (1) does not apply to –

(a) the disclosure of information which is in the form of a summary or collection of information so framed as not to enable identification of any person from the information;
(b) disclosure which is made in pursuance of an order of a court;
(c) disclosure which is required by any other enactment.

8 (1) Subject to sub-paragraph (3), a person who –

(a) is or has been employed by the Central Authority; or
(b) provides or has provided services to the Central Authority,

is guilty of an offence if that person makes disclosure, otherwise than in accordance with this Schedule, of information referred to in paragraph 3 which has been obtained from a person or authority listed in paragraph 1 and which relates to a person whose identity is specified in the information disclosed or can be deduced from it.

(2) It is a defence to prove that, at the time of the alleged offence, the person making the disclosure believed that the person was making the disclosure lawfully in accordance with this Schedule and the Convention, and had no reasonable cause to believe otherwise.

(3) Sub-paragraph (1) does not apply to disclosure of information received by such a person from the Secretary of State where the information so disclosed is held by the Secretary of State for the purposes of employment or training only.

9 A person found guilty of an offence under this Schedule shall be liable –

(a) on conviction on indictment, to imprisonment for a term not exceeding 2 years, to a fine or to both;

(b) on summary conviction, to imprisonment for a term not exceeding 3 months or to a fine not exceeding the statutory maximum or to both.

10 (1) In this Schedule –

'Central Authority' means –

(a) in relation to England and Wales, the Lord Chancellor;

(b) in relation to Scotland, the Scottish Ministers; and

(c) in relation to Northern Ireland, the Department of Justice,

and references to 'Central Authority' include persons employed by or supplying services to that Central Authority;

'deposit-taker' means any person who may, in the course of their business, lawfully accept deposits in the United Kingdom;

'maintenance obligation' means any maintenance obligation to which the Convention (as applied by the United Kingdom) applies, and includes maintenance arrangements as defined in Article 3(e);

'requesting Central Authority' means the Central Authority of another Contracting State to the Convention which has made the request for information or sent the application under Article 10, or the specific measures request under Article 7;

'Revenue and Customs officials' has the meaning given by section 18 of the Commissioners for Revenue and Customs Act 2005;

'functions relating to social security' includes functions relating to statutory payments as defined in section 4C(11) of the Social Security Contributions and Benefits Act 1992 and maternity allowance under section 35 of that Act.

(2) In this Schedule any reference to a numbered Article or Chapter is to the Article or Chapter so numbered in the Convention and any reference to a sub-division of a numbered Article shall be construed accordingly.

****

Justices' Clerks and Assistants Rules 2014, SI 2014/603

1 Citation, commencement and interpretation

(1) These Rules may be cited as the Justices' Clerks and Assistants Rules 2014 and shall come into force on the day on which section 17(3) of the Crime and Courts Act 2013 comes fully into force.

(2) In these Rules –

'the Act' means the Matrimonial and Family Proceedings Act 1984;

'assistant justices' clerk' is an assistant to a justices' clerk within the meaning of section 27(5) of the Courts Act 2003;

'CPA' means the Civil Partnership Act 2004;

'FPR' means the Family Procedure Rules 2010;

'MCA' means the Matrimonial Causes Act 1973;

'undefended case' has the meaning given in FPR rule 7.1(3);

2 Functions which may be carried out by a justices' clerk

The functions of the family court or of a judge of the court that may be carried out by a justices' clerk are the functions of the family court or of a judge of the court specified in the provisions listed in the first column of the table in the Schedule subject to the exceptions or restrictions specified in the second column in relation to particular functions.

3 Functions which may be carried out by an assistant justices' clerk

(1) An assistant justices' clerk may carry out any function that a justices' clerk may carry out pursuant to rule 2, provided that that assistant justices' clerk has been authorised by a justices' clerk to carry out that function.

(2) The functions specified in section 31O(2) of the Act may be carried out by an assistant justices' clerk.

(3) An authorisation by a justices' clerk under paragraph (1) above must be recorded in writing at the time the authorisation is given or as soon as practicable thereafter.

4 Duty to refer if inappropriate to carry out function

(1) When considering carrying out a function specified in the Schedule, a justices' clerk must consider whether in the particular circumstances it would be inappropriate to carry out the function.

(2) If a justices' clerk determines that it would be inappropriate to carry out a function specified in the Schedule, the justices' clerk must refer the matter to the court.

(3) References in this rule to a justices' clerk include a person authorised in accordance with rule 3.

SCHEDULE

FPR rule 3.3	
FPR rule 3.4	
FPR rule 3.10	
FPR rule 4.1(3)(a)	Except any extensions in public law proceedings that would have the effect that disposal of the application would occur later than the end of twenty-six weeks beginning with the day on which the application was issued.
FPR rule 4.1(3)(b), (c), (d), (f), (h), (j), (k), (n), (o)	
FPR rule 4.3(2)	
FPR rule 4.3(5)	
FPR rule 4.7(a) and (b)	
FPR rule 6.24(2)	
FPR rule 6.26(5)	
FPR rule 6.32	
FPR rule 6.36	
MCA, section 1(3)	Only in undefended cases
MCA, sections 1(4) and 1(5)	Only in undefended cases, and only the making 'absolute' of decrees of divorce
MCA, section 6(2)	Only where the parties consent to the adjournment
MCA, sections 10A(2) and (3)	Only in an application under section 10A(2) to which the other party consents
MCA, section 17(2)	Only in undefended cases
CPA, section 37(1)(a) and (d)	Only in undefended cases, and only the making 'final' of such orders
CPA, section 42(3)	Only where the parties consent to the adjournment
CPA, sections 44(2) and (4)	Only in undefended cases
FPR rule 7.13(5)(b)	Only in undefended cases
FPR rule 7.13(7)	Only in undefended cases
FPR rule 7.13(8)	Only in undefended cases
FPR rule 7.14(1)	Only if the parties consent to the court giving such permission
FPR rule 7.20(2)	
FPR rule 7.20(3)	
FPR rule 7.20(5)	
FPR rule 7.21(3)	
FPR rule 7.30(1)(d)(ii) and (3)	Only where the application under section 10A(2) was made on consent
FPR 7.32(2)	
FPR rule 8.20(4)	Only where the parties consent to the person being made a respondent and where the person is not a child
FPR rule 9.18	
FPR rule 9.20	
FPR rule 9.26	
FPR rule 10.3(1)	

PART IV

FPR rule 10.6(2)	
FPR rule 10.7	
FPR rule 12.3(2)	Only where the parties consent to the person being made a respondent and where the person is not a child
FPR rule 12.3(3)	Only where the parties consent to the person being made a respondent and where the person is not a child
FPR rule 12.3(4)	Only where otherwise authorised to add or remove the person as a party
FPR rule 12.4(5)	Only where the parties consent to the person being made a respondent and where the person is not a child
FPR rule 12.5(1)	
Children Act 1989, section 32(1)	
Children Act 1989, section 32(4)	Except that the carrying out of such function must not have the direct or indirect effect of extending the timetable for the proceedings with the effect that the disposal of the application would occur later than the end of twenty-six weeks beginning with the day on which the application was issued
FPR rule 12.5(2)	Except at an Issues Resolution Hearing for which Practice Direction 12A makes provision, and except the carrying out of any function that has the direct or indirect effect of extending the timetable for the proceedings with the effect that the disposal of the application would occur later than the end of twenty-six weeks beginning with the day on which the application was issued
FPR rule 12.6(a)–(c)	
Children Act 1989, section 7(1) and FPR rule 12.6(d)	
FPR rule 12.12	Except at an Issues Resolution Hearing for which Practice Direction 12A makes provision, and except any direction in public law proceedings that has the direct or indirect effect of extending the timetable for the proceedings with the effect that the disposal of the application would occur later than the end of twenty-six weeks beginning with the day on which the application was issued
FPR rule 12.13	Except that in any public law proceedings, the carrying out of such function must not have the direct or indirect effect of extending the timetable for the proceedings with the effect that the disposal of the application would occur later than the end of twenty-six weeks beginning with the day on which the application was issued
FPR rule 12.14(3) and (4)	
FPR rule 12.15	Except any direction in a public law proceeding that has the direct or indirect effect of extending the timetable for the proceedings with the effect that the disposal of the application would occur later than the end of twenty-six weeks beginning with the day on which the application was issued
FPR rule 12.16(6)	
FPR rule 12.16(7)	
FPR rule 12.19(2) and (3)	
FPR rule 12.21(1)	
FPR rule 12.22	
FPR rule 12.73(1)(b)	
Practice Direction 12G, paragraph 1.2	
Practice Direction 12J, paragraph 6, first three bullet points only	
Practice Direction 12J, paragraph 8	
Practice Direction 12J, paragraph 15	
Practice Direction 12J, paragraph 21	
FPR rule 12.24	
FPR rule 12.25(1), (2) and (5)	
FPR rule 12.26	
FPR rule 12.29	
FPR rule 12.30	

Children Act 1989, section 41	
Children Act 1989, sections 10(1) and (2)	Only where – (a) a previous such order has been made in the same proceedings; (b) the terms of the order sought are the same as those of the last such order made; (c) the order is an order in the course of proceedings and does not dispose finally of the proceedings; and (d) a written request for such an order has been made and – (i) the other parties and any children's guardian consent to the request and they or their legal representatives have signed the request; or (ii) at least one of the other parties and any children's guardian consent to the request and they or their legal representatives have signed the request, and the remaining parties have not indicated that they either consent to or oppose the making of the order.
Children Act 1989, section 38(1)	Only where – (a) a previous such order has been made in the same proceedings; (b) the terms of the order sought are the same as those of the last such order made; and (c) a written request for such an order has been made and – (i) the other parties and any children's guardian consent to the request and they or their legal representatives have signed the request; or (ii) at least one of the other parties and any children's guardian consent to the request and they or their legal representatives have signed the request, and the remaining parties have not indicated that they either consent to or oppose the making of the order.
FPR rule 12.31	
FPR rule 13.3(3)	
FPR rule 13.3(4)	
FPR rule 13.3(5)	
FPR rule 13.5	
FPR rule 13.8	
FPR rule 13.9(1)	Except 13.9(1)(e) and (f)
FPR rule 13.9(3)	
FPR rule 13.9(6)	
FPR rule 13.9(8)	
FPR rule 13.9(9)	
FPR rule 13.11(1)	
FPR rule 13.14	
FPR rule 13.16	
FPR rule 13.17	
FPR rule 13.21(1)	
FPR rule 13.21(4)	
FPR rule 13.22(4)	
FPR rule 14.2(3)	Only where the applicant consents to the removal
FPR rule 14.3(2)	Only where the parties consent to the child being made a respondent
FPR rule 14.3(3)	Only where the parties consent to the person or body being made a respondent or to a party being removed, as the case may be, and only where the person being made a respondent or being removed as a party is not a child
FPR rule 14.3(4)	Only where such directions are consequential on directions made under FPR rule 14.3(2) or (3)
FPR rule 14.5(2)(b) and (3)	
FPR rule 14.6(1)	
FPR rule 14.6(2)(a)	
FPR rule 14.6(2)(b)	
FPR rule 14.6(3)(b)	
FPR rule 14.6(4)	
FPR rule 14.7	
Adoption and Children Act 2002, section 51B(3)	
FPR rule 14.8(1)	Except 14.8(1)(d)
FPR rule 14.8(4)	
FPR rule 14.8(6)	
FPR rule 14.8(7)	
FPR rule 14.9(4)(b)	
FPR rule 14.10(2)	
FPR rule 14.14	
FPR rule 14.16(4) and (7)	
FPR rule 14.18	
FPR rule 14.20	

FPR rule 14.26(1)	
FPR rule 14.27(2)	
Practice Direction 14E, paragraph 1.2	
FPR rule 15.6(3)	
FPR rule 15.6(5)	
FPR rule 15.8(1)(b)	
FPR rule 15.9	
Practice Direction 15B	
FPR rule 16.3(1)	
FPR rule 16.3(2), (3) and (4)	Only in relation to specified proceedings as defined in the Children Act 1989, section 41(6)
FPR rule 16.4	
FPR rule 16.11(3)	
FPR rule 16.11(5) and (6)	
FPR rule 16.21	
FPR rule 16.24	
FPR rule 16.30	
FPR rule 16.33	
FPR rule 16.34	
FPR rule 17.3(2)	
FPR rule 17.4	
FPR rule 17.5	
FPR rule 18.3(1)(c)	Only where the parties consent to the person being made a respondent and where the person being made a respondent is not a child
FPR rule 18.4(2)(b)	
FPR rule 18.5(2)(c)	
FPR rule 18.8(4)	
FPR rule 18.9(1)	Only where authorised by these Rules to deal with the application with a hearing
Practice Direction 18A, paragraph 8.1	
Practice Direction 18A, paragraph 10.1	
Practice Direction 18A, paragraph 11.2	

FPR rule 19.1(3)	
FPR rule 19.4(4)	
FPR rule 19.6(2)	
FPR rule 19.8(1)(b)	
FPR rule 19.8(3)	
FPR rule 19.9(2)	
Practice Direction 19A, paragraphs 4.1 and 4.4	
FPR rule 21.2(3)	Only where the parties consent to the application for disclosure
Practice Direction 21A, paragraph 2.4	
FPR rule 22.1(1)	
FPR rule 22.3	
FPR rule 22.5	
FPR rule 22.7(1)	
FPR rule 22.9	
FPR rule 22.10	
Practice Direction 22A, paragraph 5.3	
FPR rule 23.4(1)	
FPR rule 23.6(8)	
The Act, section 31G(2)	
FPR rule 23.9	
FPR rule 24.3	
FPR rule 24.4(2)	
FPR rule 24.7	
FPR rule 24.8	
FPR rule 24.9	
FPR rule 24.10	
FPR rule 24.11(3)	
FPR rule 24.13	
Children and Families Act 2014, section 13	
FPR rule 25.4	
FPR rule 25.8	
FPR rule 25.9	
FPR rule 25.10(2)	

FPR rule 25.10(3)	
FPR rule 25.10(4)	
FPR rule 25.11	
FPR rule 25.12	
FPR rule 25.13	
FPR rule 25.16	
FPR rule 25.17	
FPR rule 25.18	
FPR rule 25.19	
Practice Direction 25A, paragraph 2.1	
Practice Direction 25B, paragraphs 10.1 and 10.2	
Practice Direction 25E, paragraph 4.1	
FPR rule 26.3	
FPR rule 26.4	
FPR rule 27.3	
FPR rule 27.4	
FPR rule 27.7	
FPR rule 29.1	
FPR rule 29.4	
FPR rule 29.11	
FPR rule 29.14	
FPR rule 29.15	Only where the order in question is one which the justices' clerk or assistant justices' clerk made
FPR rule 29.16	Only where the order in question is one which a justices' clerk or assistant justices' clerk made
FPR rule 29.19(5)	
FPR rule 37.9(3)	
The Family Court (Composition and Distribution of Business) Rules 2014, rule 20	

Amendments—SI 2014/841; SI 2015/890.

Parental Responsibility Agreement Regulations 1991, SI 1991/1478

1 Citation, commencement and interpretation

(1) These regulations may be cited as the Parental Responsibility Agreement Regulations 1991 and shall come into force on 14 October 1991.

(2) In these Regulations, 'the Principal Registry' means the principal registry of the Family Division of the High Court.

2 Form of parental responsibility agreement

A parental responsibility agreement –

(a) under section 4(1)(b) of the Children Act 1989 (acquisition of parental responsibility by father), shall be made in form C(PRA1) set out in the Schedule to these Regulations;

(b) under section 4A(1)(a) of that Act (acquisition of parental responsibility by step-parent), shall be made in form C(PRA2) set out in that Schedule; and

(c) under section 4ZA(1)(b) of that Act (acquisition of parental responsibility by second female parent) shall be made in Form C(PRA3) set out in that Schedule.

Amendments—SI 2005/2808; SI 2009/2026.

Form of agreement—The prescribed form for the acquisition of parental responsibility by a father is C(PRA1), by a step-parent is C(PRA2) and by a second female parent is C(PRA3); they come with explanatory notes. As to evidence of identity, see further *Court Business* (June 1995), referred to at [1995] Fam Law 385, which also points out that, while the person who witnesses the signatures on Forms C(PRA1), C(PRA2) and C(PRA3) (who must be a justice of the peace, a justices' clerk or a court official who is authorised by the judge to administer oaths) need not be attached to a court *with family jurisdiction*, solicitors cannot witness the signatures because they are not officers of the Family Court.

3 Recording of parental responsibility agreement

(1) A parental responsibility agreement shall be recorded by the filing of the agreement, together with sufficient copies for each person with parental responsibility for the child, in the Principal Registry.

(2) Upon the filing of documents under paragraph (1), an officer of the Principal Registry shall seal the copies and send one to each person with parental responsibility for the child.

(3) The record of an agreement under paragraph (1) shall be made available, during office hours, for inspection by any person upon –

(a) written request to an officer of the Principal Registry, and

(b) payment of such fee as may be prescribed in an Order under section 92 of the Courts Act 2003 (Fees).

Amendments—SI 2004/3123; SI 2005/2808.

Defined terms—'parental responsibility agreement': CA 1989, s 4(1)(b).

Scope—This regulation prescribes the method by which a parental responsibility agreement must be recorded. CA 1989, s 4(2) provides that, unless the regulations are complied with, the agreement is not valid for the purposes of CA 1989.

'payment of such fee as may be prescribed' (reg 3(3)(b))—The fee is prescribed by FPFO 2008, Sch 1, fee 6.2 and includes the cost of providing a copy of the agreement, if appropriate.

****

Parental Responsibility and Measures for the Protection of Children (International Obligations) (England and Wales and Northern Ireland) Regulations 2010, SI 2010/1898

ARRANGEMENT OF REGULATIONS

Regulation		Page
1	Citation, commencement and extent	2505
2	Interpretation	2505
3	Power of court to remove stay under Article 8	2505
4	Local authorities and Northern Ireland authorities: application to court to make request under Article 9	2505
5	Local authorities: application for interim care order or supervision order	2506
6	Northern Ireland authorities: application for interim care order or supervision order	2507
7	Application of Article 15	2507
8	Judicial authorities	2507
9	Central authorities	2508
10	Requests for information by Central Authority where request received under Article 31(c)	2508
11	Requests for information under Council Regulation	2509
12	Power to request report on child's situation	2509
13	Local authorities and Northern Ireland authorities: requirement to provide a report	2510
14	Power to respond to a request under Article 34	2510
15	Northern Ireland: power of court to authorise disclosure	2510
16	Services under Article 35	2510
17	Amendments to other enactments	2511

1 Citation, commencement and extent

(1) These Regulations may be cited as the Parental Responsibility and Measures for the Protection of Children (International Obligations) (England and Wales and Northern Ireland) Regulations 2010.

(2) These Regulations come into force on the day on which the Convention enters into force for the United Kingdom, which date will be notified in the London, Edinburgh and Belfast Gazettes.

(3) These Regulations extend to England and Wales and Northern Ireland.

2 Interpretation

In these Regulations –

'Central Authority' has the meaning given by regulation 9(1);

'Contracting State' means a state party to the Convention;

'the Convention' means the Convention on Jurisdiction, Applicable Law, Recognition, Enforcement and Co-Operation in respect of Parental Responsibility and Measures for the Protection of Children that was signed at The Hague on 19 October 1996;

'the Council Regulation' means Council Regulation (EC) No 2201/2003 concerning jurisdiction and the recognition and enforcement of judgments in matrimonial matters and the matters of parental responsibility;

'Department of Justice' means the Department of Justice in Northern Ireland;

'local authority' means –

(a) in relation to England, the council of a county, a metropolitan district, the Council of the Isles of Scilly, a London borough or the Common Council of the City of London, and

(b) in relation to Wales, the council of a county or a county borough;

'member State' means a member State of the European Union which is bound by the Council Regulation;

'Northern Ireland authority' means an authority within the meaning given by Article 2(2) of the Children (Northern Ireland) Order 1995;

'public authority' means a body whose functions are wholly or mainly of a public nature;

'Welsh family proceedings officer' has the meaning given by section 35 of the Children Act 2004.

PART IV

3 Power of court to remove stay under Article 8

(1) This regulation applies where –

(a) a court has exercised its power under Article 8 of the Convention to request an authority of another Contracting State to assume jurisdiction in relation to an application,

(b) the court has stayed proceedings on the application, and.

(c) Part 1 of the Family Law Act 1986 does not apply in relation to the application.

(2) The court may remove a stay granted in order for it to exercise its powers under Article 8 of the Convention, and withdraw any request made by it under that Article to an authority in another Contracting State to assume jurisdiction, if –

(a) the authority in the other Contracting State does not assume jurisdiction within the period for which the court granted the stay, or

(b) the parties do not, within the period specified by the court, request the authority in the other Contracting State to assume jurisdiction.

4 Local authorities and Northern Ireland authorities: application to court to make request under Article 9

(1) This regulation applies where –

(a) either –

(i) a local authority in England and Wales wishes to make an application in respect of a child under section 31 of the Children Act 1989 (care and supervision orders), or

(ii) a Northern Ireland authority wishes to make an application in respect of a child under Article 50 of the Children (Northern Ireland) Order 1995 (care and supervision orders), and

(b) the authorities of another Contracting State have jurisdiction in respect of the child under the Convention.

(2) The local authority or Northern Ireland authority must make an application to the High Court, requesting the court to exercise its power under Article 9 of the Convention (request to competent authority of the Contracting State of the habitual residence of the child for authorisation to exercise jurisdiction).

5 Local authorities: application for interim care order or supervision order

(1) This regulation applies where –

(a) a local authority in England and Wales thinks that the conditions in section 31(2)(a) and (b) of the Children Act 1989 (threshold for care and supervision orders) apply in relation to a child, and.

(b) one of the following applies in relation to the child –

(i) Article 11 of the Convention (measures of protection in cases of urgency),

(ii) Article 12 of the Convention (measures of a provisional character), or

(iii) Article 20 of the Council Regulation (provisional and protective measures).

(2) Where this regulation applies, section 38 of the Children Act 1989 (interim orders) has effect as if –

(a) for subsection (1)(a) and (b) there were substituted –

'(a) a local authority makes an application for an interim care order or interim supervision order in relation to a child, and.

(b) one of the following applies in relation to the child –

(i) Article 11 of the Convention on Jurisdiction, Applicable Law, Recognition, Enforcement and Co-Operation in respect of Parental Responsibility and Measures for the Protection of Children that was signed at The Hague on 19 October 1996 (measures of protection in cases of urgency) ('the Convention'),

(ii) Article 12 of the Convention (measures of a provisional character'), or

(iii) Article 20 of Council Regulation (EC) No 2201/2003 concerning jurisdiction and the recognition and enforcement of judgments in matrimonial matters and the matters of parental responsibility (provisional and protective measures) ('the Council Regulation'),',

(b) subsection (3) were omitted,

(c) in subsection (4)(b) the words 'in the same proceedings' were omitted, and

(d) for subsection (4)(c) to (e) there were substituted –

'(c) in a case which falls within subsection (1)(b)(i) or (ii), when –

(i) the authorities in another Contracting State with jurisdiction under the Convention have taken the measures required by the situation, or

(ii) measures taken by the authorities of another State are recognised in England and Wales;

(d) in a case which falls within subsection (1)(b)(iii), when the court of the member State with jurisdiction under the Council Regulation has taken the measures it considers appropriate.'.

(3) Where this regulation applies –

(a) section 31 of the Children Act 1989 (care and supervision orders) has effect as if, in section 31(3A), after 'care order' there were inserted the words ', other than an interim care order,'

(b) section 31A of that Act (care plans) has effect as if subsection (5) were omitted, and

(c) section 41 of that Act (representation of child's interests) has effect as if in subsection (6) there were included a reference to an application for an interim care order or interim supervision order by virtue of this regulation.

6 Northern Ireland authorities: application for interim care order or supervision order

(1) This regulation applies where –

(a) a Northern Ireland authority thinks that the conditions in Article 50(2)(a) and (b) of the Children (Northern Ireland) Order 1995 (threshold for care and supervision orders) are met, and

(b) one of the following applies in relation to the child –

(i) Article 11 of the Convention (measures of protection in cases of urgency),

(ii) Article 12 of the Convention (measures of a provisional character), or

(iii) Article 20 of the Council Regulation (provisional and protective measures).

(2) Where this regulation applies, Article 57 of the Children (Northern Ireland) Order 1995 has effect as if –

(a) for paragraph (1)(a) and (b) there were substituted –

'(a) an authority makes an application for an interim care order or interim supervision order in relation to a child, and

(b) one of the following applies in relation to the child –

(i) Article 11 of the Convention on Jurisdiction, Applicable Law, Recognition, Enforcement and Co-Operation in respect of Parental Responsibility and Measures for the Protection of Children that was signed at The Hague on 19 October 1996 (measures of protection in cases of urgency) ('the Convention'),

(ii) Article 12 of the Convention (measures of a provisional character), or

(iii) Article 20 of Council Regulation (EC) No. 2201/2003 concerning jurisdiction and the recognition and enforcement of judgments in matrimonial matters and the matters of parental responsibility (provisional and protective measures) ('the Council Regulation'),',

(b) paragraph (3) were omitted,

(c) in paragraph (4)(b) the words 'in the same proceedings' were omitted, and

(d) for paragraph (4)(c) to (e) there were substituted –

'(c) in a case which falls within subsection (1)(b)(i) or (ii), when –

(i) the authorities in another Contracting State with jurisdiction under the Convention have taken the measures required by the situation, or

(ii) measures taken by the authorities of another State are recognised in Northern Ireland;

(d) in a case which falls within subsection (1)(b)(iii), when the court of the member State with jurisdiction under the Council Regulation has taken the measures it considers appropriate.'.

(3) Where this regulation applies, Article 60 of the Children (Northern Ireland) Order 1995 (representation of child's interests) has effect as if in paragraph (6) there were included a reference to an application for an interim care order or interim supervision order by virtue of this regulation.

7 Application of Article 15

The reference to Chapter II of the Convention in Article 15(1) of the Convention is to be read as including a reference to Chapter II of the Council Regulation.

8 Judicial authorities

(1) The High Court has jurisdiction to entertain an application under Article 24 of the Convention for recognition, or non-recognition, of a measure taken in another Contracting State.

(2) But where the recognition or non-recognition of a measure is raised as an incidental question in another court, that court may determine the issue.

(3) The High Court is also to have jurisdiction –

(a) to register a measure taken in another Contracting State for enforcement under Article 26 of the Convention, and
(b) to entertain an application for a declaration –
   (i) that a person has, or does not have, parental responsibility for a child by virtue of Article 16 of the Convention, or
   (ii) as to the extent of a person's parental responsibility for a child by virtue of that Article.

9 Central authorities

(1) The functions under the Convention of a Central Authority are to be discharged –

(a) in England, by the Lord Chancellor,
(b) in Wales, by the Welsh Ministers, and
(c) in Northern Ireland, by the Department of Justice,

and a reference in these Regulations to a 'Central Authority' means any of the Lord Chancellor, the Welsh Ministers or the Department of Justice in so far as they have functions under this regulation.

(2) If a person outside the United Kingdom does not know to which Central Authority in the United Kingdom a communication should be addressed, the person may address it to the Lord Chancellor.

10 Requests for information by Central Authority where request received under Article 31(c)

(1) Paragraphs (2), (3) and (4) apply if a Central Authority receives a request for assistance under Article 31(c) of the Convention (either directly or via another Central Authority in the United Kingdom).

(2) The Lord Chancellor may request information about the whereabouts of a child from –

(a) a local authority in England, or
(b) the Secretary of State.

(3) The Welsh Ministers may request information about the whereabouts of a child from –

(a) a local authority in Wales,
(b) a Local Health Board (within the meaning given by section 11 of the National Health Service (Wales) Act 2006), or
(c) an NHS Trust (within the meaning given by section 18 of that Act).

(4) The Department of Justice may request information about the whereabouts of a child from a public authority in Northern Ireland, but may do so only in circumstances where a requirement to provide information could be imposed on the public authority by an Act of the Northern Ireland Assembly without the consent of the Secretary of State (see sections 6 to 8 of the Northern Ireland Act 1998).

(5) A person (other than a court in Northern Ireland) who receives a request for information under this regulation must comply with the request as soon as reasonably practicable (but this is subject to paragraph (6)).

(6) Nothing in this regulation requires a person to disclose information if –

(a) Article 37 of the Convention applies, or
(b) the disclosure would constitute contempt of court or a criminal offence.

(7) If a person who receives a request under this regulation thinks that it is desirable, in responding to the request, to refer to information the disclosure of which would constitute contempt of court, the person must notify the court.

(8) If a person who receives a request under this regulation thinks that it is desirable, in responding to the request, to refer to information the disclosure of which would constitute a criminal offence unless the disclosure were authorised by a court, the person must notify the court.

11 Requests for information under Council Regulation

(1) This regulation applies if the designated Central Authority in England and Wales under Article 53 of the Council Regulation receives a request for information from another member State under Article 55(a)(i) of the Council Regulation.

(2) The designated Central Authority in England and Wales may request information about the whereabouts of a child from –

- (a) a local authority in England,
- (b) a local authority in Wales,
- (c) the Secretary of State,
- (d) an officer of the Children and Family Court Advisory and Support Service,
- (e) a Welsh family proceedings officer,
- (f) a Local Health Board (within the meaning given by section 11 of the National Health Service (Wales) Act 2006), or
- (g) an NHS Trust (within the meaning given by section 18 of that Act).

(3) The designated Central Authority in England and Wales may request a report on the situation of a child from –

- (a) a local authority in England,
- (b) a local authority in Wales,
- (c) an officer of the Children and Family Court Advisory and Support Service, or
- (d) a Welsh family proceedings officer.

(4) A person who receives a request for information under this regulation must comply with the request as soon as reasonably practicable (but this is subject to paragraph (5)).

(5) Nothing in this regulation requires a person to disclose information if the disclosure would constitute contempt of court or a criminal offence.

(6) If a person who receives a request under this regulation thinks that it is desirable, in responding to the request, to refer to information the disclosure of which would constitute contempt of court, the person must notify the court.

(7) If a person who receives a request under this regulation thinks that it is desirable, in responding to the request, to refer to information the disclosure of which would constitute a criminal offence unless the disclosure were authorised by a court, the person must notify the court.

12 Power to request report on child's situation

(1) This regulation applies where a Central Authority thinks it appropriate to provide a report on the situation of a child under Article 32(a) of the Convention.

(2) The Lord Chancellor may request a written report on the situation of the child from –

- (a) a local authority in England, or
- (b) an officer of the Children and Family Court Advisory and Support Service.

(3) The Welsh Ministers may request a written report on the situation of the child from –

- (a) a local authority in Wales, or
- (b) a Welsh family proceedings officer.

(4) The Department of Justice may request a written report on the situation of the child from a public authority or other person in Northern Ireland, but may do so only in circumstances where a requirement to provide information could be imposed on the public authority or other person by an Act of the Northern Ireland Assembly without the consent of the Secretary of State (see sections 6 to 8 of the Northern Ireland Act 1998).

(5) A person in England and Wales or any public authority, other than a court, in Northern Ireland who receives a request for a report under this regulation must comply with the request as soon as reasonably practicable (but this is subject to paragraph (6)).

(6) Nothing in this regulation requires a person to disclose information if –

(a) Article 37 of the Convention applies, or
(b) the disclosure would constitute contempt of court or a criminal offence.

(7) If a person who receives a request under this regulation thinks that it is desirable, in responding to the request, to refer to information the disclosure of which would constitute contempt of court, the person must notify the court.

(8) If a person who receives a request under this regulation thinks that it is desirable, in responding to the request, to refer to information the disclosure of which would constitute a criminal offence unless the disclosure were authorised by a court, the person must notify the court.

13 Local authorities and Northern Ireland authorities: requirement to provide a report

(1) This regulation applies if a local authority in England and Wales or a Northern Ireland authority is contemplating –

(a) placing a child in another Contracting State, within the meaning given by Article 33 of the Convention, or
(b) placing a child in another member State, within the meaning given by Article 56 of the Council Regulation.

(2) Either the court or the local authority or Northern Ireland authority, whichever has jurisdiction under Articles 5 to 10 of the Convention or Articles 8 to 14 of the Council Regulation, as the case may be ('the authority') –

(a) must provide a report to the Central Authority, or other competent authority, of the other Contracting State in accordance with Article 33(1) of the Convention, if the authority is exercising jurisdiction under the Convention, or
(b) must consult the Central Authority, or other competent authority, of the other member State in accordance with Article 56 of the Council Regulation, if the authority is exercising jurisdiction under the Council Regulation.

14 Power to respond to a request under Article 34

A public authority in England and Wales or Northern Ireland may provide information in response to a request communicated to it by the Central Authority under Article 34 of the Convention.

15 Northern Ireland: power of court to authorise disclosure

If a court in Northern Ireland is satisfied that a disclosure of information relating to proceedings before a court sitting in private is for the purpose of enabling the Central Authority in Northern Ireland to exercise a function under the Convention –

(a) the court may authorise the disclosure of the information, and.
(b) a disclosure authorised under paragraph (a) is not punishable as contempt of court.

16 Services under Article 35

(1) The Secretary of State may charge a reasonable fee in respect of the provision of a service under Article 35 (1) or (2) of the Convention.

(2) The Welsh Ministers may charge a reasonable fee in respect of the provision of a service under Article 35(1) or (2) of the Convention.

(3) The Department of Justice may charge a reasonable fee in respect of the provision of a service under Article 35(1) or (2) of the Convention.

(4) A request under Article 35(2) of the Convention is to be made –

(a) if the parent making the request resides in England and Wales, to the local authority in whose area the parent resides, and.
(b) if the parent making the request resides in Northern Ireland, to the Department of Justice.

(5) A local authority in England may charge a reasonable fee in respect of the provision of a service under Article 35(1) or (2) of the Convention.

(6) A local authority in Wales may charge a reasonable fee in respect of the provision of a service under Article 35(1) or (2) of the Convention.

(7) A fee is 'reasonable' for the purposes of this regulation if the income from fees of that kind equates as nearly as possible to the costs of providing the service to which the fees relate (including a reasonable share of expenditure which is referable only partly or only indirectly to the provision of that service).

17 Amendments to other enactments

The Schedule contains amendments to other enactments consequential on the entry into force of the Convention for the United Kingdom.

****

Pensions on Divorce etc (Provision of Information) Regulations 2000, SI 2000/1048

ARRANGEMENT OF REGULATIONS

Regulation		Page
1	Citation, commencement and interpretation	2512
2	Basic information about pensions and divorce or dissolution of a civil partnership	2513
3	Information about pensions and divorce and dissolution of a civil partnership: valuation of pension benefits	2514
4	Provision of information in response to a notification that a pension sharing order or provision may be made	2517
5	Information required by the person responsible for the pension arrangement before the implementation period may begin	2518
6	Provision of information after the death of the person entitled to the pension credit before liability in respect of the pension credit has been discharged	2519
7	Provision of information after receiving a pension sharing order or provision	2520
8	Provision of information after the implementation of a pension sharing order or provision	2521
9	Penalties	2523
10	Provision of information after receipt of an earmarking order	2523
11	Provision of information	2524

General Note—These regulations provide for the information that the pension arrangement must disclose (reg 2), specify the methodology for the valuation of pension benefits (reg 3), specify the information that the pension arrangement must provide once given notice that a pension sharing order may be made (reg 4), specify the information that both parties must give to a pension arrangement after a pension sharing order has been made before the four month implementation period can begin (reg 5) and the information that the pension arrangement must give after notice of a pension sharing or attachment order and after it has implemented the order (regs 7, 8 and 10).

When the Pension Protection Fund assumes responsibility for a pension scheme, reference should be made to the Pension Protection Fund (Provision of Information) Regulations 2005. See, further, annotations to MCA 1973, s 25E.

Where a pension compensation sharing order or a pension compensation attachment order is to be made against a pension arrangement for which the Pension Protection Fund has already assumed responsibility, the relevant corresponding regulations are the Pension Protection Fund (Pension Compensation Sharing and Attachment on Divorce etc) Regulations 2011.

Provision of information and valuation of shareable state scheme rights (see annotations to MCA 1973, s 21A) are dealt with in the Sharing of State Scheme Rights (Provision of Information and Valuation) (No 2) Regulations 2000 below.

1 Citation, commencement and interpretation

(1) These Regulations may be cited as the Pensions on Divorce etc (Provision of Information) Regulations 2000 and shall come into force on 1 December 2000.

(2) In these Regulations –

'the 1993 Act' means the Pension Schemes Act 1993;

'the 1995 Act' means the Pensions Act 1995;

'the 1999 Act' means the Welfare Reform and Pensions Act 1999;

'the Charging Regulations' means the Pensions on Divorce etc (Charging) Regulations 2000;

'the Implementation and Discharge of Liability Regulations' means the Pension Sharing (Implementation and Discharge of Liability) Regulations 2000;

'the Valuation Regulations' means the Pension Sharing (Valuation) Regulations 2000;

'active member' has the meaning given by section 124(1) of the 1995 Act;

'day' means any day other than –

(a) Christmas Day or Good Friday; or

(b) a bank holiday, that is to say, a day which is, or is to be observed as, a bank holiday or a holiday under Schedule 1 to the Banking and Financial Dealings Act 1971;

'deferred member' has the meaning given by section 124(1) of the 1995 Act;

'implementation period' has the meaning given by section 34(1) of the 1999 Act;

'member' means a person who has rights to future benefits, or has rights to benefits payable, under a pension arrangement;

'money purchase benefits' has the meaning given by section 181(1) of the 1993 Act;

'normal benefit age' has the meaning given by section 101B of the 1993 Act;

'normal pension age' has the meaning given in section 180 of the 1993 Act (normal pension age);

'notice of discharge of liability' means a notice issued to the member and his former spouse or former civil partner by the person responsible for a pension arrangement when that person has discharged his liability in respect of a pension credit in accordance with Schedule 5 to the 1999 Act;

'notice of implementation' means a notice issued by the person responsible for a pension arrangement to the member and his former spouse or former civil partner at the beginning of the implementation period notifying them of the day on which the implementation period for the pension credit begins;

'occupational pension scheme' has the meaning given by section 1 of the 1993 Act;

'the party with pension rights' and 'the other party' have the meanings given by section 25D(3) of the Matrimonial Causes Act 1973;

'pension arrangement' has the meaning given in section 46(1) of the 1999 Act;

'pension credit' means a credit under section 29(1)(b) of the 1999 Act;

'pension credit benefit' means the benefits payable under a pension arrangement or a qualifying arrangement to or in respect of a person by virtue of rights under the arrangement in question which are attributable (directly or indirectly) to a pension credit;

'pension credit rights' means rights to future benefits under a pension arrangement or a qualifying arrangement which are attributable (directly or indirectly) to a pension credit;

'pension sharing order or provision' means an order or provision which is mentioned in section 28(1) of the 1999 Act;

'pensionable service' has the meaning given by section 124(1) of the 1995 Act;

'pensioner member' has the meaning given by section 124(1) of the 1995 Act;

'person responsible for a pension arrangement' has the meaning given by section 46(2) of the 1999 Act;

'personal pension scheme' has the meaning given by section 1 of the 1993 Act;

'qualifying arrangement' has the meaning given by paragraph 6 of Schedule 5 to the 1999 Act;

'retirement annuity contract' means a contract or scheme approved under Chapter III of Part XIV of the Income and Corporation Taxes Act 1988;

'salary related occupational pension scheme' has the meaning given by regulation 1A of the Transfer Values Regulations;

'transfer day' has the meaning given by section 29(8) of the 1999 Act;

'the Transfer Values Regulations' means the Occupational Pension Schemes (Transfer Values) Regulations 1996;

'transferee' has the meaning given by section 29(8) of the 1999 Act;

'transferor' has the meaning given by section 29(8) of the 1999 Act.

'trustees or managers' has the meaning given by section 46(1) of the 1999 Act.

Amendments—SI 2000/2691; SI 2005/2877; SI 2007/60; SI 2008/1050; SI 2009/615; SI 2016/289.

2 Basic information about pensions and divorce or dissolution of a civil partnership

(1) The requirements imposed on a person responsible for a pension arrangement for the purposes of section 23(1)(a) of the 1999 Act (supply of pension information in connection with divorce etc) are that he shall furnish –

(a) on request from a member, the information referred to in paragraphs (2) and (3)(b) to (f);

(b) on request from the spouse or civil partner of a member, the information referred to in paragraph (3); or

(c) pursuant to an order of the court, the information referred to in paragraph (2), (3) or (4),

to the member, the spouse or civil partner of the member, or, as the case may be, to the court.

(2) The information in this paragraph is a valuation of pension rights or benefits accrued under that member's pension arrangement.

(3) The information in this paragraph is –

(a) a statement that on request from the member, or pursuant to an order of the court, a valuation of pension .rights or benefits accrued under that member's pension arrangement, will be provided to the member, or, as the case may be, to the court;

(b) a statement summarising the way in which the valuation referred to in paragraph (2) and sub-paragraph (a) is calculated;

(c) the pension benefits which are included in a valuation referred to in paragraph (2) and sub-paragraph (a);

(d) whether the person responsible for the pension arrangement offers membership to a person entitled to a pension credit, and if so, the types of benefits available to pension credit members under that arrangement;

(e) whether the person responsible for the pension arrangements intends to discharge his liability for a pension credit other than by offering membership to a person entitled to a pension credit; and

(f) the schedule of charges which the person responsible for the pension arrangement will levy in accordance with regulation 2(2) of the Charging Regulations (general requirements as to charges).

(4) The information in this paragraph is any other information relevant to any power with respect to the matters specified in section 23(1)(a) of the 1999 Act and which is not specified in Schedules 2 to 5 (basic information; information to be given on request; summary funding statements; statements of benefits: non money purchase benefits) and Schedule 6 (statements of benefits: money purchase benefits and cash balance benefits) or 7 (information to be given by schemes that relates to accessing benefits) (whichever is relevant) to the Occupational and Personal Pension Schemes (Disclosure of Information) Regulations 2013, in a case where those Regulations apply.

(5) Where the member's request for, or the court order for the provision of, information includes a request for, or an order for the provision of, a valuation under paragraph (2), the person responsible for the pension arrangement shall furnish all the information requested, or ordered, to the member –

PART IV

(a) within 3 months beginning with the date the person responsible for the pension arrangement receives that request or order for the provision of the information;

(b) within 6 weeks beginning with the date the person responsible for the pension arrangement receives the request, or order, for the provision of the information, if the member has notified that person on the date of the request or order that the information is needed in connection with proceedings commenced under any of the provisions referred to in section 23(1)(a) of the 1999 Act; or

(c) within such shorter period specified by the court in an order requiring the person responsible for the pension arrangement to provide a valuation in accordance with paragraph (2).

(6) Where –

(a) the member's request for, or the court order for the provision of, information does not include a request or an order for a valuation under paragraph (2); or

(b) the member's spouse or civil partner requests the information specified in paragraph (3),

the person responsible for the pension arrangement shall furnish that information to the member, his spouse, civil partner, or the court, as the case may be, within one month beginning with the date that person responsible for the pension arrangement receives the request for, or the court order for the provision of, the information.

(7) At the same time as furnishing the information referred to in paragraph (1), the person responsible for a pension arrangement may furnish the information specified in regulation 4(2) (provision of information in response to a notification that a pension sharing order or provision may be made).

Amendments—SI 2005/2877; SI 2016/289.

Scope—This regulation specifies the information to be furnished by a pension arrangement on request from a member or the spouse/civil partner of a member or pursuant to a court order. All requests for information as to valuation must be made by the member, but the court may intervene to order the provision of a valuation to the non-member spouse/civil partner and may order a pension arrangement to supply 'any other information relevant to any power with respect to the matters specified in WRPA 1999, s 23(1)(a) [financial relief under MCA 1973, Pt II]' subject to certain exceptions (reg 2(4)). Regulation 2(5) and (6) sets out the time limits for provision of the requested or ordered information.

A charge may be made for the basic information requested or ordered under reg 2 (Pensions on Divorce etc (Charging) Regulations 2000, reg 3(1)). However, a charge will not be made for basic information under reg 2(2) and (3), including a valuation where there has been no valuation supplied within the previous 12 months (unless the information is required in less than 3 months of the date of request/order or the member has reached normal retirement age on or before the date of the request or the court order for the provision of the information or is due to reach normal retirement age within 12 months of such date) (Pensions on Divorce etc (Charging) Regulations 2000, reg 3(2)). A pension arrangement is not able to recover charges when a pension sharing order is made, unless a schedule of charges is provided as part of the basic information under reg 2 (Pensions on Divorce etc (Charging) Regulations 2000, reg 2). It is permissible for a pension arrangement to postpone implementation until its charges have been paid (WRPA 1999, s 41(2)(a); Pensions on Divorce etc (Charging) Regulations 2000, reg 7). In certain circumstances, a pension arrangement is allowed to deduct the costs directly from the pension credit (or, on an internal transfer, from the transferee's pension credit benefits), from the accrued rights of the member, from the calculation of a transfer value or, if the pension is in payment, from the member's pension benefits (WRPA 1999, s 38(2)(c); Pensions on Divorce etc (Charging) Regulations 2000, reg 9). Alternatively, the parties may pay in cash if they prefer. Pension arrangements are permitted to insist on payment before providing certain information for which a charge may be made, unless the information is sought pursuant to a court order (Pensions on Divorce etc (Charging) Regulations 2000, reg 4(1)(b)).

3 Information about pensions and divorce and dissolution of a civil partnership: valuation of pension benefits

(1) Where an application for financial relief under any of the provisions referred to in section 23(a)(i),(ia),(iii) or (iv) of the 1999 Act (supply of pension information in connection with domestic and overseas divorce etc in England and Wales and corresponding Northern Ireland powers) has been made or is in contemplation, the valuation of benefits under a pension arrangement shall be calculated and verified for the purposes of regulation 2 of these Regulations in accordance with –

(a) paragraphs (3) and (4), if the person with pension rights is an active member, a deferred member or a pensioner member of an occupational pension scheme;

(b) *(revoked)*
(c) paragraphs (5) and (6), if –
 (i) the person with pension rights is a member of a personal pension scheme; or
 (ii) those pension rights are contained in a retirement annuity contract; or
(d) paragraphs (7) and (8) if –
 (i) the pension of the person with pension rights is in payment;
 (ii) the rights of the person with pension rights are contained in an insurance policy or annuity contract other than a retirement annuity contract;
 (iii) the rights of the person with pension rights are contained in a deferred annuity contract other than a retirement annuity contract; or
 (iv) the pension of the person with pension rights is not in payment and the person has attained normal pension age.

(2) Where an application for financial provision under any of the provisions referred to in section 23(1)(a)(ii) of the 1999 Act (corresponding Scottish powers) has been made, or is in contemplation, the valuation of benefits under a pension arrangement shall be calculated and verified for the purposes of regulation 2 of these Regulations in accordance with regulation 3 of the Divorce etc (Pensions) (Scotland) Regulations 2000 (valuation).

(3) Where a person with pension rights is an active member, a deferred member or a pensioner member of an occupational pension scheme, the value of those rights in relation to a category of benefits referred to in section 93(6) of the 1993 Act (category of benefits) must be calculated and verified in accordance with regulations 7 to 7C and 7E(1) to (3) of the Transfer Values Regulations (calculation and verification of cash equivalent), as if –

(a) in the case of benefits other than money purchase benefits, the member has made an application for a statement of entitlement under section 93A of the 1993 Act (right to statement of entitlement: benefits other than money purchase) on the date that the request for the valuation was received; or
(b) in the case of money purchase benefits, the member has made an application under section 95 of the 1993 Act (ways of taking right to cash equivalent) to take the cash equivalent of those benefits on the date that the request for the valuation was received.

(4) Where the person with pension rights is continuing to accrue rights to benefits in the category of benefits to be valued, paragraph (3) applies as if the person had ceased to accrue rights in that category of benefits on the date that the request for the valuation was received.

(5) Where the person with pension rights is a member of a personal pension scheme, or those rights are contained in a retirement annuity contract, the value of the benefits which he has under that scheme or contract shall be taken to be the cash equivalent to which he would have acquired a right under section 94 of the 1993 Act (right to cash equivalent), if he had made an application under section 95(1) of that Act on the date on which the request for the valuation was received.

(6) In relation to a personal pension scheme which is comprised in a retirement annuity contract made before 4 January 1988, paragraph (5) shall apply as if such a scheme were not excluded from the scope of Chapter 1 of Part 4ZA of the 1993 Act by section 93(5)(b) of that Act (scope of Chapter 1).

(7) Cash equivalents are to be calculated and verified in accordance with regulations 7 to 7C and 7E(1) to (3) of the Transfer Values Regulations as appropriate.

(8) When calculating and verifying a cash equivalent, regulations 7 to 7C and 7E(1) to (3) of the Transfer Values Regulations are to be read as if –

(a) in regulation 7 –
 (i) in paragraph (1)(a), the words 'and then making any reductions in accordance with regulation 7D' do not appear;
 (ii) in paragraph (1)(b), the words 'regulation 7E' are replaced with 'regulation 7E(1) to (3)';
 (iii) in paragraphs (2) and (4), the word 'trustees' is replaced with 'person responsible for the pension arrangement';

PART IV

(iv) in paragraph (3), the words 'trustees are' are replaced with 'person responsible for the pension arrangement is';

(v) in paragraph (5), the words 'trustees of the scheme in question have' are replaced with 'person responsible for the pension arrangement has';

(b) in regulations 7A and 7B, in each place where it appears, the word 'trustees' is replaced with 'person responsible for the pension arrangement';

(c) in regulation 7C –

(i) in paragraph (3), in both places where it appears, the word 'trustees' is replaced with 'person responsible for the pension arrangement';

(ii) in paragraph (4)(b)(iv), the words 'trustees determine' are replaced with 'person responsible for the pension arrangement determines';

(d) in regulation 7E –

(i) in paragraph (1), the words 'trustees have' are replaced with 'person responsible for the pension arrangement has';

(ii) in paragraph (2), the word 'trustees' is replaced with 'person responsible for the pension arrangement'.

Amendments—SI 2005/2877; SI 2007/60; SI 2008/1050; SI 2016/289.

Scope—By a combination of this regulation and the Divorce (Pensions) Regulations 2000, reg 3, the valuation methodology prescribed is the Cash Equivalent (CE) in all cases (except pension schemes administered overseas), adopting the highly technical formulae of this regulation. All these technical formulae have in common the fact that they are founded on taking the value of the pension rights in today's terms on the basis that the member left service at the time the valuation request was received. Thus, no account is taken of future service. This regulation was significantly amended by the Occupational Pension Schemes (Transfer Values) (Amendment) Regulations 2008 ('the Amendment Regulations') with effect from 1 October 2008 and the Pension Sharing (Miscellaneous Amendments) Regulations 2016 (the 2016 Regulations) with effect from 6 April 2016. As a result of the Amendment Regulations, the term Cash Equivalent Transfer Value (CETV) was abandoned and there is no longer a separate valuation methodology for pensions in payment (formerly the Cash Equivalent of Benefits (CEB) as discussed in *Martin-Dye v Martin-Dye* [2006] 2 FLR 901, CA). Further, the Amendment Regulations introduced a new valuation category, namely, the pension rights not in payment of a person who has attained normal pension age (reg 3(1)(d)(iv)). The 2016 Regulations make amendments consequent upon the Pension Schemes Act 2015.

The CE is a calculation of the transfer value at the current time of the total of the following elements in a pension scheme:

(i) the member's pension at retirement;
(ii) the lump sum benefit payable on death after leaving active membership of the scheme, but before retirement;
(iii) the lump sum payable on retirement;
(iv) the lump sum payable on death after retirement; and
(v) the spouse's pension payable either on the member's death after leaving active membership of the scheme but before retirement or after the member's retirement.

The CE therefore does *not* include:

(i) any lump sum payable if the member died in service (which in many public service and company pension schemes is substantial);
(ii) the spouse's pension payable if the member died in service; and
(iii) future expectations based upon future salary increases and future pensionable service.

The CE may or may not include discretionary benefits, which usually relate to generous early retirement terms or increases in pensions in payment.

Case-law provides guidance on pensions valuation:

(1) It is necessary to have regard when valuing a pension to the special characteristics of pension funds: present capital should not be confused with financial benefits on retirement, only part of which can be taken as a tax-free lump sum (*Cowan v Cowan* [2001] 2 FLR 192, CA; *Maskell v Maskell* [2003] 1 FLR 1138, CA; *Martin-Dye v Martin-Dye* (above); *Vaughan v Vaughan* [2008] 1 FLR 1108, CA).
(2) It is a convenient practice to include in a spreadsheet, underneath the total value of other capital, the capital value of pension rights, then arriving at a grand total (*Vaughan v Vaughan* (above), at [25]).
(3) Where the parties' assets exceed their needs, a capital approach (as opposed to valuation by reference to a projected income stream at a particular age) may be adopted (*SJ v RA* [2014] EWHC 4054 (Fam)). This will particularly be the case in relation to money purchase schemes, where the member is aged 55 or over. However, due regard must be had to the impact of taxation on the withdrawn funds. In such a case, actuarial advice may not be necessary, but taxation advice may be.
(4) Where an application is to be approached by reference to needs (by reference to a projected income stream) or in an application concerning a defined benefits scheme, actuarial advice may still be proportionate and necessary. This will enable factors such as pre-marital accruals and age difference to be factored into account (*SJ v RA* (above); *B v B (Assessment of Assets: Pre-Marital Property)* [2012] 2 FLR 22, FD).

(5) Where a capital approach is adopted, it should not be calculated by reference to the cost of a replacement annuity (*BJ v MJ (Financial Order: Overseas Trust)* [2012] 1 FLR 667, FD; *JL v SL (No 3) (Post-Judgment Amplification)* [2015] 2 FLR 1220, FD). However, utilising annuity rates remains the standard practice in actuarial reports for projecting future income streams regardless of how a party may wish to generate pension benefits (e g by means of income drawdown).

(6) The correct approach to pensions offsetting should be based upon *Duxbury* calculations as opposed to the sum required to purchase an annuity to generate an equivalent pension income (*WS v WS* [2015] EWHC 3941 (Fam)).

(7) Where a claim is based on sharing/entitlement rather than needs, it may be appropriate to cross-check a division of CEs by reference to the resulting income effect, adjusting as necessary for fairness by reference particularly to needs (*M v M* [2015] EWFC B63).

(8) A number of factors may lead to a CE not providing an adequate indication of value. These include scheme under-funding, the impact of market value adjusters and guaranteed annuity rates, the member's health and the fact that the member is close to retirement. Furthermore, there are particular valuation issues affecting several public sector pension schemes. All of these issues point to the need to obtain expert actuarial advice, where it is proportionate to do so. An adequate indication of value in a CE is to be distinguished from an actuarial or computer error in its calculation (*Clark v Cabinet Office and Paymaster* (1836) Limited (2007) 19 November, ref R00408, Pensions Ombudsman; *Brown v British Airways Pension Trustees Limited* (2012), 13 January, ref 83320/1, Deputy Pensions Ombudsman; *McNicholas v Scottish Widows* (2013) 11 April, ref PO408, Pensions Ombudsman; *Adams v Innovene Trustees Ltd* (2013) 18 September, ref PO823, Pensions Ombudsman). For a consideration of the effect of early retirement on the calculation of a CE, see *Slattery v Cabinet Office (Civil Service Pensions) and another* [2009] 1 FLR 1365, ChD.

(9) Whichever valuation test is applied, it must be appreciated that different currencies are in operation when comparing one party's public sector pension with another party's private sector pension or a final salary pension as against a money purchase pension.

4 Provision of information in response to a notification that a pension sharing order or provision may be made

(1) A person responsible for a pension arrangement shall furnish the information specified in paragraph (2) to the member or to the court, as the case may be –

(a) within 21 days beginning with the date that the person responsible for the pension arrangement received the notification that a pension sharing order or provision may be made; or

(b) if the court has specified a date which is outside the 21 days referred to in sub-paragraph (a), by that date.

(2) The information referred to in paragraph (1) is –

(a) the full name of the pension arrangement and address to which any order or provision referred to in section 28(1) of the 1999 Act (activation of pension sharing) should be sent;

(b) in the case of an occupational pension scheme, whether the scheme is winding up, and, if so, –

(i) the date on which the winding up commenced;

(ii) the name and address of the trustees who are dealing with the winding up; and

(iii) whether the member's rights to benefit are to be or are likely to be reduced in accordance with sections 73 to 74 of the 1995 Act (winding up provisions);

(c) in the case of an occupational pension scheme, whether a cash equivalent of the member's pension rights, if calculated on the date the notification referred to in paragraph (1)(a) was received by the trustees or managers of that scheme, would be reduced in accordance with the provisions of paragraphs 2,3 and 12 of Schedule 1A to the Transfer Values Regulations (reductions in initial cash equivalents) if the member were to transfer the cash equivalent of those rights out of the scheme;

(d) whether the person responsible for the pension arrangement is aware that the member's rights under the pension arrangement are subject to any, and if so, to specify which, of the following –

(i) any order or provision specified in section 28(1) of the 1999 Act;

(ii) an order under section 23 of the Matrimonial Causes Act 1973 (financial provision orders in connection with divorce etc.), so far as it includes provision made by virtue of section 25B or 25C of that Act (powers to include provisions about pensions);

(iii) an order under section 12A(2) or (3) of the Family Law (Scotland) Act 1985 (powers in relation to pensions lump sums when making a capital sum order) which relates to benefits or future benefits to which the member is entitled under the pension arrangement;

(iv) an order under Article 25 of the Matrimonial Causes (Northern Ireland) Order 1978, so far as it includes provision made by virtue of Article 27B or 27C of that Order (Northern Ireland powers corresponding to those mentioned in paragraph (2)(d)(ii));

(v) a forfeiture order;

(vi) a bankruptcy order;

(vii) an award of sequestration on a member's estate or the making of the appointment on his estate of a judicial factor under section 41 of the Solicitors (Scotland) Act 1980 (appointment of judicial factor);

(e) whether the member's rights under the pension arrangement include rights specified in regulation 2 of the Valuation Regulations (rights under a pension arrangement which are not shareable);

(f) if the person responsible for the pension arrangement has not at an earlier stage provided the following information, whether that person requires the charges specified in regulation 3 (charges recoverable in respect of the provision of basic information), 5 (charges in respect of pension sharing activity), or 6 (additional amounts recoverable in respect of pension sharing activity) of the Charging Regulations to be paid before the commencement of the implementation period, and if so –

(i) whether that person requires those charges to be paid in full; or

(ii) the proportion of those charges which he requires to be paid;

(g) whether the person responsible for the pension arrangement may levy additional charges specified in regulation 6 of the Charging Regulations, and if so, the scale of the additional charges which are likely to be made;

(h) whether the member is a trustee of the pension arrangement;

(i) whether the person responsible for the pension arrangement may request information about the member's state of health from the member if a pension sharing order or provision were to be made;

(j) …

(k) whether the person responsible for the pension arrangement requires information additional to that specified in regulation 5 (information required by the person responsible for the pension arrangement before the implementation period may begin) in order to implement the pension sharing order or provision.

Amendments—SI 2000/2691; SI 2003/1727; SI 2008/1050; SI 2016/289.

Scope—This regulation sets out the information which a pension arrangement must furnish following notification that a pension sharing order may be made, which will indicate whether the pension arrangement is one in relation to which pension sharing is possible. It should be noted that the pension sharing annex (Form P1) Pt E incorporates a certificate that the parties have received this information attached to Form P (Pension Inquiry Form) and that it appears from that information that there is power to make a pension sharing order (FPR 2010, r 9.35).

'notification that a pension sharing order … may be made' (reg 4(1)(a))—It is submitted that 'notification' includes either formal service of Form A or prior informal notification by letter. In many instances, Form A will not specify the terms of the order requested because the requisite information will not be available at the time of issue. In such circumstances, this information will need to be added to Form A at the First Appointment as suggested by FPR 2010, r 9.31, when a direction may be made for the completion of Form P, Pt C of which seeks the information required by this regulation.

5 Information required by the person responsible for the pension arrangement before the implementation period may begin

The information prescribed for the purposes of section 34(1)(b) of the 1999 Act (information relating to the transferor and the transferee which the person responsible for the pension arrangement must receive) is –

(a) in relation to the transferor –

(i) all names by which the transferor has been known;

(ii) date of birth;
(iii) address;
(iv) National Insurance number;
(v) the name of the pension arrangement to which the pension sharing order or provision relates; and
(vi) the transferor's membership or policy number in that pension arrangement;

(b) in relation to the transferee –
(i) all names by which the transferee has been known;
(ii) date of birth;
(iii) address;
(iv) National Insurance number; and
(v) if the transferee is a member of the pension arrangement from which the pension credit is derived, his membership or policy number in that pension arrangement;

(c) where the transferee has given his consent in accordance with paragraph 1(3)(c), 3(3)(c) or 4(2)(c) of Schedule 5 to the 1999 Act (mode of discharge of liability for a pension credit) to the payment of the pension credit to the person responsible for a qualifying arrangement –
(i) the full name of that qualifying arrangement;
(ii) its address;
(iii) if known, the transferee's membership number or policy number in that arrangement; and
(iv) the name or title, business address, business telephone number, and, where available, the business facsimile number and electronic mail address of a person who may be contacted in respect of the discharge of liability for the pension credit;

(d) where the rights from which the pension credit is derived are held in an occupational pension scheme which is being wound up, whether the transferee has given an indication whether he wishes to transfer his pension credit rights which may have been reduced in accordance with the provisions of regulation 16(1) of the Implementation and Discharge of Liability Regulations (adjustments to the amount of the pension credit – occupational pension schemes which are underfunded on the valuation day) to a qualifying arrangement; and

(e) any information requested by the person responsible for the pension arrangement in accordance with regulation 4(2)(i) or (k).

Scope—This regulation sets out the specific information required by a pension arrangement in order to implement a pension sharing order about the parties and the destination arrangement for the pension credit. The 4-month implementation period will only begin on the later of the day on which the pension sharing order takes effect (MCA 1973, ss 24B(2), 24C(1)) and the day on which the pension arrangement receives the pension sharing order and decree absolute as well as the information under this regulation (WRPA 1999, s 34(1)). The 4-month implementation period is a maximum period; unnecessary delays within that period by a pension arrangement may give rise to an award of compensation by the Pensions Ombudsman (*Boughton v Punter Southall* (2009) 22 September, ref 74851/1, Pensions Ombudsman). See, also, annotations to MCA 1973, s 24B.

6 Provision of information after the death of the person entitled to the pension credit before liability in respect of the pension credit has been discharged

(1) Where the person entitled to the pension credit dies before the person responsible for the pension arrangement has discharged his liability in respect of the pension credit, the person responsible for the pension arrangement shall, within 21 days of the date of receipt of the notification of the death of the person entitled to the pension credit, notify in writing any person whom the person responsible for the pension arrangement considers should be notified of the matters specified in paragraph (2).

(2) The matters specified in this paragraph are –

(a) how the person responsible for the pension arrangement intends to discharge his liability in respect of the pension credit;

(b) whether the person responsible for the pension arrangement intends to recover charges from the person nominated to receive pension credit benefits, in accordance with

PART IV

regulations 2 to 9 of the Charging Regulations, and if so, a copy of the schedule of charges issued to the parties to pension sharing in accordance with regulation 2(2)(b) of the Charging Regulations (general requirements as to charges); and

(c) a list of any further information which the person responsible for the pension arrangement requires in order to discharge his liability in respect of the pension credit.

Amendments—SI 2000/2691.

Scope—A pension sharing order is not affected by the death of either party, although an application for permission to appeal out of time might be made. If an application for leave is successful, one course might be an appeal under MCA 1973, s 40A or 40B. This assumes that the original pension sharing order has been implemented in full. If, however, it has not and the person entitled to the pension credit dies before the liability for the pension credit has been discharged, WRPA 1999, s 35(2) and the Pension Sharing (Implementation and Discharge of Liability) Regulations 2000, reg 6 prescribes how the liability is to be discharged. The Finance Act 2006, Sch 23, para 2 provides that, if a person dies having become entitled to pension credits, but without having rights attributable to them, the person is to be treated as having acquired, immediately before the death, the rights by virtue of which the liability in respect of the pension credits is subsequently discharged. In this rare situation, the pension arrangement has full discretion to discharge its liability in accordance with appropriately drafted scheme rules subject to HMRC limits in favour of 'one or more persons'. Arguably, this expression could include the pension scheme member. In some cases, the discharge of liability will be effected by a lump sum payment; in others, by payment of a pension or both a pension and a lump sum. Pension arrangements may discharge their liability by entering into an annuity contract and/or an insurance contract to provide benefits for survivors. If the scheme rules do not make provision for payments of the type mentioned, the pension credit will be retained by the pension arrangement from which it was derived (Pension Sharing (Implementation and Discharge of Liability) Regulations 2000, reg 6(4)). If the transferee would have become entitled to a personal pension, the amount of the pension credit may be paid into the deceased transferee's estate. For all of these reasons, the pension sharing order could be expressed only to take effect in the event of the transferee not predeceasing the transferor, where this is considered appropriate.

7 Provision of information after receiving a pension sharing order or provision

(1) A person responsible for a pension arrangement who is in receipt of a pension sharing order or provision relating to that arrangement shall provide in writing to the transferor and transferee, or, where regulation 6(1) applies, to the person other than the person entitled to the pension credit referred to in regulation 6 of the Implementation and Discharge of Liability Regulations (discharge of liability in respect of a pension credit following the death of the person entitled to the pension credit), as the case may be –

(a) a notice in accordance with the provisions of regulation 7(1) of the Charging Regulations (charges in respect of pension sharing activity – postponement of implementation period);

(b) a list of information relating to the transferor or the transferee, or, where regulation 6(1) applies, the person other than the person entitled to the pension credit referred to in regulation 6 of the Implementation and Discharge of Liability Regulations, as the case may be, which –

(i) has been requested in accordance with regulation 4(2)(i) and (k), or, where appropriate, 6(2)(c), or should have been provided in accordance with regulation 5;

(ii) the person responsible for the pension arrangement considers he needs in order to begin to implement the pension sharing order or provision; and

(iii) remains outstanding;

(c) a notice of implementation; or

(d) a statement by the person responsible for the pension arrangement explaining why he is unable to implement the pension sharing order or agreement.

(2) The information specified in paragraph (1) shall be furnished in accordance with that paragraph within 21 days beginning with –

(a) in the case of sub-paragraph (a), (b) or (d) of that paragraph, the day on which the person responsible for the pension arrangement receives the pension sharing order or provision; or

(b) in the case of sub-paragraph (c) of that paragraph, the later of the days specified in section 34(1)(a) and (b) of the 1999 Act (implementation period).

Scope—This regulation sets out the information which the pension arrangement must provide to the parties after a pension sharing order has been made, but before implementation commences.

8 Provision of information after the implementation of a pension sharing order or provision

(1) The person responsible for the pension arrangement shall issue a notice of discharge of liability to the transferor and the transferee, or, as the case may be, the person entitled to the pension credit by virtue of regulation 6 of the Implementation and Discharge of Liability Regulations no later than the end of the period of 21 days beginning with the day on which the discharge of liability in respect of the pension credit is completed.

(2) In the case of a transferor whose pension is not in payment, the notice of discharge of liability shall include the following details –

(a) the value of the transferor's accrued rights as determined by reference to the cash equivalent value of those rights calculated and verified in accordance with regulation 3 of the Valuation Regulations (calculation and verification of cash equivalents for the purposes of the creation of pension debits and credits);

(b) the value of the pension debit;

(c) any amount deducted from the value of the pension rights in accordance with regulation 9(2)(c) of the Charging Regulations (charges in respect of pension sharing activity – method of recovery);

(d) the value of the transferor's rights after the amounts referred to in sub-paragraphs (b) and (c) have been deducted; and

(e) the transfer day.

(3) In the case of a transferor whose pension is in payment, the notice of discharge of liability shall include the following details –

(a) the value of the transferor's benefits under the pension arrangement as determined by reference to the cash equivalent value of those rights calculated and verified in accordance with regulation 3 of the Valuation Regulations;

(b) the value of the pension debit;

(c) the amount of the pension which was in payment before liability in respect of the pension credit was discharged;

(d) the amount of pension which is payable following the deduction of the pension debit from the transferor's pension benefits;

(e) the transfer day;

(f) if the person responsible for the pension arrangement intends to recover charges, the amount of any unpaid charges –

(i) not prohibited by regulation 2 of the Charging Regulations (general requirements as to charges); and

(ii) specified in regulations 3 and 6 of those Regulations;

(g) how the person responsible for the pension arrangement will recover the charges referred to in sub-paragraph (f), including –

(i) whether the method of recovery specified in regulation 9(2)(d) of the Charging Regulations will be used;

(ii) the date when payment of those charges in whole or in part is required; and

(iii) the sum which will be payable by the transferor, or which will be deducted from his pension benefits, on that date.

(4) In the case of a transferee –

(a) whose pension is not in payment; and

(b) who will become a member of the pension arrangement from which the pension credit rights were derived,

the notice of discharge of liability to the transferee shall include the following details –

(i) the value of the pension credit;

(ii) any amount deducted from the value of the pension credit in accordance with regulation 9(2)(b) of the Charging Regulations;

(iii) the value of the pension credit after the amount referred to in sub-paragraph (b)(ii) has been deducted;

PART IV

(iv) the transfer day;
(v) any periodical charges the person responsible for the pension arrangement intends to make, including how and when those charges will be recovered from the transferee; and
(vi) information concerning membership of the pension arrangement which is relevant to the transferee as a pension credit member.

(5) In the case of a transferee who is transferring his pension credit rights out of the pension arrangement from which those rights were derived, the notice of discharge of liability to the transferee shall include the following details –

(a) the value of the pension credit;
(b) any amount deducted from the value of the pension credit in accordance with regulation 9(2)(b) of the Charging Regulations;
(c) the value of the pension credit after the amount referred to in sub-paragraph (b) has been deducted;
(d) the transfer day; and
(e) details of the pension arrangement, including its name, address, reference number, telephone number, and, where available, the business facsimile number and electronic mail address, to which the pension credit has been transferred.

(6) In the case of a transferee, who has reached normal benefit age on the transfer day, and in respect of whose pension credit liability has been discharged in accordance with paragraph 1(2), 2(2), 3(2) or 4(4) of Schedule 5 to the 1999 Act (pension credits: mode of discharge – funded pension schemes, unfunded public service pension schemes, other unfunded pension schemes, or other pension arrangements), the notice of discharge of liability to the transferee shall include the following details –

(a) the amount of pension credit benefit which is to be paid to the transferee;
(b) the date when the pension credit benefit is to be paid to the transferee;
(c) the transfer day;
(d) if the person responsible for the pension arrangement intends to recover charges, the amount of any unpaid charges –
  (i) not prohibited by regulation 2 of the Charging Regulations; and
  (ii) specified in regulations 3 and 6 of those Regulations; and
(e) how the person responsible for the pension arrangement will recover the charges referred to in sub-paragraph (d), including –
  (i) whether the method of recovery specified in regulation 9(2)(e) of the Charging Regulations will be used;
  (ii) the date when payment of those charges in whole or in part is required; and
  (iii) the sum which will be payable by the transferee, or which will be deducted from his pension credit benefits, on that date.

(7) In the case of a person entitled to the pension credit by virtue of regulation 6 of the Implementation and Discharge of Liability Regulations, the notice of discharge of liability shall include the following details –

(a) the value of the pension credit rights as determined in accordance with regulation 10 of the Implementation and Discharge of Liability Regulations (calculation of the value of appropriate rights);
(b) any amount deducted from the value of the pension credit in accordance with regulation 9(2)(b) of the Charging Regulations;
(c) the value of the pension credit;
(d) the transfer day; and
(e) any periodical charges the person responsible for the pension arrangement intends to make, including how and when those charges will be recovered from the payments made to the person entitled to the pension credit by virtue of regulation 6 of the Implementation and Discharge of Liability Regulations.

Scope—After the pension sharing order has been implemented, the pension arrangement must issue a notice of discharge of liability to the parties within 21 days of completing discharge of the liability in respect of the pension credit. The information required in the notice differs depending on whether, for example, the pension is in payment.

9 Penalties

Where any trustee or manager of an occupational pension scheme fails, without reasonable excuse, to comply with any requirement imposed under regulation 6, 7 or 8, the Regulatory Authority may by notice in writing require that trustee or manager to pay within 28 days from the date of its imposition, a penalty which shall not exceed –

(a) £200 in the case of an individual, and
(b) £1,000 in any other case.

Amendments—SI 2009/615.

10 Provision of information after receipt of an earmarking order

(1) The person responsible for the pension arrangement shall, within 21 days beginning with the day that he receives –

(a) an order under section 23 of the Matrimonial Causes Act 1973, so far as it includes provision made by virtue of section 25B or 25C of that Act (powers to include provision about pensions);
(b) an order under section 12A(2) or (3) of the Family Law (Scotland) Act 1985; or
(c) an order under Article 25 of the Matrimonial Causes (Northern Ireland) Order 1978, so far as it includes provision made by virtue of Article 27B or 27C of that Order (Northern Ireland powers corresponding to those mentioned in sub-paragraph (a)),

issue to the party with pension rights and the other party a notice which includes the information specified in paragraphs (2) and (5), or (3), (4) and (5), as the case may be.

(2) Where an order referred to in paragraph (1)(a), (b) or (c) is made in respect of the pension rights or benefits of a party with pension rights whose pension is not in payment, the notice issued by the person responsible for a pension arrangement to the party with pension rights and the other party shall include a list of the circumstances in respect of any changes of which the party with pension rights or the other party must notify the person responsible for the pension arrangement.

(3) Where an order referred to in paragraph (1)(a) or (c) is made in respect of the pension rights or benefits of a party with pension rights whose pension is in payment, the notice issued by the person responsible for a pension arrangement to the party with pension rights and the other party shall include –

(a) the value of the pension rights or benefits of the party with pension rights;
(b) the amount of the pension of the party with pension rights after the order has been implemented;
(c) the first date when a payment pursuant to the order is to be made; and
(d) a list of the circumstances, in respect of any changes of which the party with pension rights or the other party must notify the person responsible for the pension arrangement.

(4) Where an order referred to in paragraph (1)(a) or (c) is made in respect of the pension rights of a party with pension rights whose pension is in payment, the notice issued by the person responsible for a pension arrangement to the party with pension rights shall, in addition to the items specified in paragraph (3), include –

(a) the amount of the pension of the party with pension rights which is currently in payment; and
(b) the amount of pension which will be payable to the party with pension rights after the order has been implemented.

(5) Where an order referred to in paragraph (1)(a), (b) or (c) is made the notice issued by the person responsible for a pension arrangement to the party with pension rights and the other party shall include –

(a) the amount of any charges which remain unpaid by –

(i) the party with pension rights; or

(ii) the other party,

in respect of the provision by the person responsible for the pension arrangement of information about pensions and divorce or dissolution of a civil partnership pursuant to regulation 3 of the Charging Regulations, and in respect of complying with an order referred to in paragraph (1)(a), (b) or (c); and

(b) information as to the manner in which the person responsible for the pension arrangement will recover the charges referred to in sub-paragraph (a), including –

(i) the date when payment of those charges in whole or in part is required;

(ii) the sum which will be payable by the party with pension rights or the other party, as the case may be; and

(iii) whether the sum will be deducted from payments of pension to the party with pension rights, or, as the case may be, from payments to be made to the other party pursuant to an order referred to in paragraph (1)(a), (b) or (c).

Amendments—SI 2005/2877.

Scope—This regulation provides for the information to be provided to or by a pension arrangement where a pension attachment (formerly earmarking) order has been made.

11 Provision of information

(1) Subject to paragraph (2) a person required to provide information under regulation 2, 4, 6, 7, 8 or 10 must provide that information in accordance with regulations 26 to 28 of the Occupational and Personal Pension Schemes (Disclosure of Information) Regulations 2013 (giving information and documents).

(2) Information may be provided to the court by means of an electronic communication only where the court has given its permission.

(3) In this regulation 'electronic communication' has the meaning given by the Electronic Communications Act 2000.

Amendments—Inserted by SI 2013/2734.

Sharing of State Scheme Rights (Provision of Information and Valuation) (No 2) Regulations 2000,

SI 2000/2914

General note—These Regulations set out the information which must be given by the Secretary of State and the method of valuation of shareable old state scheme rights and shareable new state scheme rights. As to state pension reform and the single-tier pension applicable from 6 April 2016 under the Pensions Act 2014, see annotations to MCA 1973, s 21A. As of 6 April 2016, these Regulations have been amended by the State Pension Regulations 2015, reg 14 and Schedule (the amendments are set out below). The 2015 Regulations distinguish between shareable old state scheme rights (i e the ASP and a 'shared additional pension' (i e an ASP resulting from a pension credit derived from a spouse's ASP in previous family proceedings)) and shareable new state scheme rights (i e the 'protected payment') (see below).

The ASP was the collective term for the State Earnings Related Pension Scheme (SERPS) and the State Second Pension (S2P). S2P came into effect on 6 April 2002 replacing SERPS. Pension sharing was not available in relation to the basic state retirement pension (where the substitution rules applied). Pension sharing was, however, available in relation to ASP, including ASP in payment or a 'shared additional pension'. No charge was made for the implementation of a pension sharing order in relation to ASP.

The Pensions Act 2014 does not affect the validity of a pension sharing order made before 6 April 2016 in respect of the ASP of an individual who falls within the single-tier pension. The Pensions Act 2014 allows for pension sharing of new state scheme rights in certain limited circumstances. It is possible to obtain a pension sharing order in respect of the 'protected payment', i e in relation to the excess amount by which an individual's rate of pension exceeds the full rate of the single-tier pension (WRPA 1999, s 47(3),(4)). A pension sharing order that takes effect on or after 6 April 2016 is implemented under the regime applicable to shareable new scheme rights subject to transitional rules contained in the Pensions Act 2014 (Pension Sharing on Divorce etc) (Transitional Provision) Order 2016, which provide that where the proceedings (i e the date of the petition) are commenced before 6 April 2016, the previous regime in relation to pension sharing of state scheme rights will continue to apply. Where a state pension is in payment before 6 April 2016, the ASP will be shareable even if divorce proceedings commence after 6 April 2016 (WRPA 1999, s 49). WRPA 1999, s 49 also applies where an individual reaches state retirement age before 6 April 2016, but defers taking payment. The system for the creation of pension debits and credits in relation to shareable new scheme rights contained in WRPA 1999, s 49A do not apply in either of these situations.

The legislative background to the Regulations is found in WRPA 1999, ss 23, 47–51, the Social Security Contributions and Benefits Act 1992, ss 55A–55C and 175 and the Pensions Act 2014, ss 2, 4, 8, 16–19, 22, 54, Sch 8, para 4 and Sch 10, para 4. Consequential amendments were made on the introduction of civil partnership by the Civil Partnership (Pensions, Social Security and Child Support) (Consequential, etc Provisions) Order 2005.

PART 1
GENERAL

Amendments—Part number and title inserted by SI 2015/173.

1 Citation, commencement and interpretation

(1) These Regulations may be cited as the Sharing of State Scheme Rights (Provision of Information and Valuation) (No 2) Regulations 2000 and shall come into force on 1 December 2000.

(2) In these Regulations –

'the 1992 Act' means the Social Security Contributions and Benefits Act 1992;
'the 1999 Act' means the Welfare Reform and Pensions Act 1999;
'new state scheme pension credit' is a credit under section 49A(2)(b) of the 1999 Act;
'old state scheme pension credit' is a credit under section 49(1)(b) of the 1999 Act;
'relevant date' has the meaning given by section 10(3) of the Family Law (Scotland) Act 1985;
'shareable new state scheme rights' has the meaning given by section 47(3) of the 1999 Act;
'shareable old state scheme rights' has the meaning given by section 47(2) of the 1999 Act.

Amendments—SI 2015/173.

PART 2
OLD STATE SCHEME PENSION CREDITS AND DEBITS

Amendments—Part number and title inserted by SI 2015/173.

2 Basic information about the sharing of state scheme rights and divorce or the dissolution of a civil partnership

(1) The requirements imposed on the Secretary of State for the purposes of section 23(1)(a) of the 1999 Act (supply of pension information in connection with divorce etc) are that he shall furnish –

(a) the information specified in paragraphs (2) and (3) –
  (i) to a person who has shareable old state scheme rights on request from that person; or
  (ii) to the court, pursuant to an order of the court; or

(b) the information specified in paragraph (3) to the spouse or civil partner of a person who has shareable old state scheme rights, on request from that spouse or civil partner.

(2) The information specified in this paragraph is a valuation of the person's shareable old state scheme rights.

(3) The information in this paragraph is an explanation of –

(a) the shareable old state scheme rights;

(b) how a pension sharing order or provision will affect a person's shareable old state scheme rights; and

(c) how a pension sharing order or provision in respect of a person's shareable old state scheme rights will result in the spouse or civil partner of the person who has shareable old state scheme rights becoming entitled to a shared additional pension because of an old state scheme pension credit.

(4) The Secretary of State shall furnish the information specified in paragraphs (2) and (3) to the court or, as the case may be, to the person who has shareable old state scheme rights within –

PART IV

(a) 3 months beginning with the date the Secretary of State receives the request or, as the case may be, the order for the provision of that information;

(b) 6 weeks beginning with the date the Secretary of State receives the request or, as the case may be, the order for the provision of the information, if the person who has shareable old state scheme rights has notified the Secretary of State on the date of the request or order that the information is needed in connection with proceedings commenced under any of the provisions referred to in section 23(1)(a) of the 1999 Act; or

(c) such shorter period specified by the court in an order requiring the Secretary of State to provide a valuation in accordance with paragraph (2).

(5) Where –

(a) the request made by the person with shareable old state scheme rights for, or the court order requiring, the provision of information does not include a request or, as the case may be, an order for a valuation under paragraph (2); or

(b) the spouse or civil partner of the person with shareable old state scheme rights requests the information specified in paragraph (3),

the Secretary of State shall furnish that information to the person who has shareable old state scheme rights, his spouse, civil partner, or the court, as the case may be, within one month beginning with the date the Secretary of State receives the request or the court order for the provision of that information.

Amendments—SI 2005/2877; SI 2015/173.

Scope—This regulation specifies the information which the Secretary of State must supply to the parties to a marriage/civil partnership or the court in relation to the sharing of old state scheme rights as well as the time limits within which that information must be furnished.

3 Information about the sharing of state scheme rights and divorce or dissolution of a civil partnership: valuation of shareable old state scheme rights

Where an application for financial relief or financial provision under any of the provisions referred to in section 23(1)(a) of the 1999 Act has been made or is in contemplation, the valuation of shareable old state scheme rights shall be calculated and verified for the purposes of regulation 2(2) of these Regulations in such manner as may be approved by or on behalf of the Government Actuary.

Amendments—SI 2005/2877; SI 2015/173.

Scope—This regulation sets out how the value of old state scheme rights must be calculated and verified when a valuation of those rights is requested in connection with pension sharing.

4 Calculation and verification of cash equivalents for the purposes of the creation of state scheme pension debits and credits

For the purposes of –

(a) section 49 of the 1999 Act (creation of state scheme pension debits and credits: transferor in old state pension system or pension sharing activated before 6 April 2016);

(b) section 45B of the 1992 Act (reduction of additional pension in Category A retirement pension: pension sharing);

(c) section 55A of the 1992 Act (shared additional pension because of an old state scheme pension credit); and

(d) section 55B of the 1992 Act (reduction of shared additional pension: pension sharing);

(e) paragraph 2 of Schedule 8 to the Pensions Act 2014; and .

(f) paragraph 2 of Schedule 10 to the Pensions Act 2014,

cash equivalents or notional rates shall be calculated and verified in such manner as may be approved by or on behalf of the Government Actuary.

Amendments—SI 2015/173.

Scope—This regulation provides for how cash equivalents are to be calculated and verified for the purposes of the creation of state scheme pension debits and credits, the reduction of the additional pension, the creation of the shared additional pension and the reduction of the shared additional pension as a result of pension sharing.

5 Revocation

The Sharing of State Scheme Rights (Provision of Information and Valuation) Regulations 2000 are revoked.

PART 3
NEW STATE SCHEME PENSION CREDITS AND DEBITS

Amendments—Part number and title inserted by SI 2015/173.

6 Basic information about the sharing of state scheme rights and divorce or the dissolution of a civil partnership

(1) The requirements imposed on the Secretary of State for the purposes of section 23(1)(a) of the 1999 Act (supply of pension information in connection with divorce etc.) are that he shall furnish –

(a) the information specified in paragraphs (2) to (6) –
  (i) to a person who has shareable new state scheme rights on request from that person; or
  (ii) to the court, pursuant to an order of the court; or

(b) the information specified in paragraph (6) to the spouse or civil partner of a person who has shareable new state scheme rights, on request from that spouse or civil partner.

(2) Except where paragraphs (3) or (4) apply, the information specified in this paragraph is a valuation of the person's shareable new state scheme rights as at the date of receipt of a request for such a valuation.

(3) The information specified in this paragraph is a valuation of the person's shareable new state scheme rights as at the relevant date, where the relevant date is on or after 6 April 2016.

(4) The information specified in this paragraph is a valuation of the person's previous shareable old state scheme rights as at the relevant date, where the relevant date is before 6 April 2016 and the request for a valuation is received on or after 6 April 2016.

(5) The information specified in this paragraph is the amount of the person's former entitlement to a category A retirement pension by virtue of section 44(3)(b) of the 1992 Act as at the relevant date and immediately before 6 April 2016, where the relevant date is before 6 April 2016 and the request for information about that amount is received on or after 6 April 2016.

(6) The information in this paragraph is an explanation of –

(a) the shareable new state scheme rights;

(b) how a pension sharing order or provision will affect a person's shareable new state scheme rights;

(c) how a pension sharing order or provision in respect of a person's shareable new state scheme rights will result in the spouse or civil partner of the person who has shareable new state scheme rights becoming entitled to an amount because of a new state scheme pension credit; and

(d) how any amount in sub-paragraph (c) differs from an amount of shared additional pension because of an old state scheme pension credit.

(7) The Secretary of State shall furnish the information specified in paragraphs (2) to (6) to the court, or, as the case may be, to the person who has shareable new state scheme rights within –

(a) three months beginning with the date the Secretary of State receives the request or, as the case may be, the order for the provision of that information;

(b) six weeks beginning with the date the Secretary of State receives the request or, as the case may be, the order for the provision of the information, if the person who has shareable new state scheme rights has notified the Secretary of State by the date the Secretary of State receives the request or order that the information is needed in connection with proceedings commenced under any of the provisions referred to in section 23(1)(a) of the 1999 Act; or

PART IV

(c) such shorter period specified by the court in an order requiring the Secretary of State to provide a valuation in accordance with paragraphs (2), (3) or (4) or an amount in accordance with paragraph (5).

(8) Where –

(a) the request made by the person with shareable new state scheme rights for, or the court order requiring, the provision of information does not include a request or, as the case may be, an order for a valuation under paragraphs (2), (3) or (4) or an amount under paragraph (5); or

(b) the spouse or civil partner of the person with shareable new state scheme rights requests the information specified in paragraph (6),

the Secretary of State shall furnish that information to the person who has shareable new state scheme rights, that person's spouse or civil partner, or the court, as the case may be, within one month beginning with the date the Secretary of State receives the request or the court order for the provision of that information.

Amendments—Inserted by SI 2015/173.

7 Information about the sharing of state scheme rights and divorce or dissolution of a civil partnership: valuation of shareable old or new state scheme rights

Where an application for financial relief or financial provision under any of the provisions referred to in section 23(1)(a) of the 1999 Act has been made or is in contemplation, the valuation of shareable old or new state scheme rights shall be calculated and verified for the purposes of regulation 6(2) to (4) of these Regulations in accordance with guidance from time to time prepared by the Government Actuary.

Amendments—Inserted by SI 2015/173.

Supreme Court Fees Order 2009, SI 2009/2131

1 Citation, commencement and interpretation

(1) This Order may be cited as the Supreme Court Fees Order 2009 and comes into force on 1 October 2009.

(2) In this Order –

'the 2009 Rules' means the Supreme Court Rules 2009;

'devolution jurisdiction' means proceedings under the Scotland Act 1998, the Government of Wales Act 2006 or the Northern Ireland Act 1998.

(3) Subject to paragraph (2), expressions used in this Order which are also used in the 2009 Rules have the same meaning as in those Rules.

2 Fees payable

(1) Subject to the following paragraphs, the fees set out in column (2) of the table in Schedule 1 are payable in the Supreme Court in respect of the items described in column (1) of that table.

(2) No fee in column (2) is payable in respect of criminal proceedings, other than the fee payable on submitting a claim for costs.

(3) In relation to its devolution jurisdiction the fees set out in column (3) of that table are payable in the Supreme Court in respect of the items described in column (1) of that table.

3 Remissions and part remissions

Schedule 2 applies for the purpose of ascertaining whether a party is entitled to a remission or part remission of a fee prescribed by this Order.

SCHEDULE 1
FEES PAYABLE IN THE SUPREME COURT

(1) *Number and description of fee*	*(2)* *Amount of fee*	*(3)* *Amount of fee*
1 *Application for permission to appeal*		
1.1 On filing an application for permission to appeal.	£1000	£400
1.2 On filing notice of objection to an application for permission to appeal.	£160	£160
2 *Appeals etc*		
2.1 On filing notice under rule 18(1)(c) of the 2009 Rules of an intention to proceed with an appeal.	£800	£400
2.2 On filing a notice of appeal.	£1600	£400
2.3 On filing a reference under the Supreme Court's devolution jurisdiction. No fee is payable where the reference is made by a court.	n/a	£200
2.4 On filing notice under rule 21(1) of the 2009 Rules (acknowledgement by respondent).	£320	£160
2.5 On filing a statement of relevant facts and issues and an appendix of essential documents.	£4820	£800
3 *Procedural applications*		
3.1 On filing an application for a decision of the Registrar to be reviewed.	£1500	£200
3.2 On filing an application for permission to intervene in an appeal.	£800	£200
3.3 On filing any other procedural application.	£350	£200
3.4 On filing notice of objection to a procedural application.	£150	£150
4 *Costs*		
4.1 On submitting a claim for costs.	2.5% of the sum claimed	2.5% of the sum claimed
4.2 On certification by the Registrar under rule 52 of the 2009 Rules of the amount of assessed costs, or on receipt of an order showing the amount.	2.5% of the sum allowed	2.5% of the sum allowed
5 *Copying*		
5.1 On a request for a copy of a document (other than where fee 5.2 or 5.3 applies) –		
(a) for ten pages or less;	£5	£5
(b) for each subsequent page	50p	50p
5.2 On a request for a copy of a document to be provided on a computer disk or in other electronic form, for each such copy.	£5	£5
5.3 On a request for a certified copy of a document.	£20	£20

Amendments—SI 2011/1737.

SCHEDULE 2
REMISSIONS AND PART REMISSIONS

Amendments—Schedule last substituted by SI 2013/2302. Amended by SI 2014/590; SI 2017/422.

Note—This Schedule is not set out here because it is identical to FPFO 2008, Sch 2 (set out earlier in this Part), save for the following amendments (by virtue of SI 2013/2302):

- In paras 16 and 17, for 'Lord Chancellor', in each place, substitute 'Chief Executive of the Supreme Court'.
- For para 18, substitute:

'**18** A party is not entitled to a remission of a fee if, for the purpose of the proceedings to which the fee relates –

(a) they are in receipt of the following services under Part 1 of the Legal Aid, Sentencing and Punishment of Offenders Act 2012:

(i) Legal representation; or

(ii) Family help (higher);

(b) they are in receipt of legal aid under Part 2 of the Legal Aid, Advice and Assistance (Northern Ireland) Order 1981; or

(c) they are living in Scotland and are in receipt of legal aid.'.

– At the end of Sch 2, add:

'21 Remission for charitable or not-for-profit organisations

Where an application for permission to intervene in an appeal is filed by a charitable or not-for-profit organisation which seeks to make submissions in the public interest, the Chief Executive of the Supreme Court may reduce or remit the fee in that case.'.

****

PART V

Practice Guidance

PART V: Practice Guidance

Contents

Since 6 April 2011, a number of practice directions supplement the Family Procedure Rules 2010 and are set out in Part III of this work, following their respective FPR 2010 Parts. These replace, in many cases, the previous judicial practice directions. The remaining judicial practice directions set out in Part V of this work are still in force. For any other of the previous practice directions, reference should be made to the 2010 edition of The Family Court Practice.

The Practice Directions in Part V are arranged in date order.

1991

19 August	Practice Direction (Statutory Charge: Form of the Order of the Court)	2539

1997

June	Best Practice Guidance (Handbook of Best Practice in Children Act Cases)	2539

1998

22 April	Practice Statement (Supreme Court: Judgments)	2552
25 November	Practice Statement (Supreme Court: Judgments (No 2))	2555

2000

24 July	President's Direction (Human Rights Act 1998)	2556
2 October	Practice Direction (Justices: Clerk to Court)	2557

2001

11 January	Practice Direction (Judgments: Form and Citation)	2559
9 April	Practice Direction (Citation of Authorities)	2560
19 December	Attorney-General's Memorandum (Requests for the Appointment of an Advocate to the Court)	2562

2003

January	Protocol (Child Abduction Cases between the UK and Pakistan)	2564

2004

21 January	President's Guidance (UK Passport Applications on Behalf of Children in the Absence of the Signature of a Person with Parental Responsibility)	2566

PART V

2005
17 January Cairo Declaration (Resulting from Anglo-Egyptian Meetings on Judicial Co-operation in International Child Abduction Matters between Egypt and the UK) 2567
18 March Cafcass Practice Note (Applications for Reporting Restriction Orders) 2567
December Protocol (Protocol between the National Youth Advocacy Service and the Children and Family Court Advisory and Support Service) 2573

2006
28 July Practice Note (Official Solicitor: Declaratory Proceedings: Medical and Welfare Decisions for Adults who Lack Capacity) 2576
28 July Practice Note (Official Solicitor, CAFCASS and the National Assembly for Wales: Urgent and Out of Hours Cases in the Family Division of the High Court) 2576

2007
December Guidance (JSB's Equal Treatment Advisory Committee (ETAC) Guidance on Religious Dress) 2578

2008
3 October President's Guidance (Listing Final Hearings in Adoption Cases) 2582
6 November Practice Direction (Enforcement of Children Act 1989 Contact Orders: Disclosure of Information to Officers of the National Probation Service (High Court and County Court)) 2584
6 November Practice Direction (Enforcement of Children Act 1989 Contact Orders: Disclosure of Information to Officers of the National Probation Service (Magistrates' Court)) 2584

2009
22 April President's Guidance (Applications Consequent upon the Attendance of the Media in Family Proceedings) 2585
August Best Practice Guide (Preparing for Care and Supervision Proceedings) 2588

2010
April Practice Note (Guidelines for Judges Meeting Children who are Subject to Family Proceedings) 2611
May President's Guidance (Split Hearings (Bulletin Number 1)) 2612
June Practice Guidance (Re S (Wardship) Guidance in Cases of Stranded Spouses) 2614
2 July Revised Protocol (Referrals of Families to Supported Child Contact Centres by Judges and Magistrates) 2615

12 July	Practice Guidance (McKenzie Friends (Civil and Family Courts)) 2618
18 November	President's Guidance (Out of Hours Hearings) 2621
December	President's Joint Guidance (Cases Involving Protected Parties in which the Official Solicitor is being invited to Act as Guardian Ad Litem or Litigation Friend) 2622

2011
April	Cafcass Practice Note (Cafcass and the Work of Independent Reviewing Officers) 2623
16 June	Guidance Note (In-Court Family Mediation Services) 2628
29 July	President's Joint Message (Joint Message from Sir Nicholas Wall, President of the Family Division and Anthony Douglas CBE, the Chief Executive of Cafcass) 2629
November	Domestic Abuse Committee of the Family Justice Council Protocol (Process Servers: Non-Molestation Orders) 2631
December	Working Party of the Family Justice Council Guidelines (Children Giving Evidence in Family Proceedings) 2632
December	Working Party of the Family Justice Council Guidance (MARACs and Disclosure into Court Proceedings) 2636
December	Experts Committee of the Family Justice Council Guidelines (Instruction of Medical Experts from Overseas in Family Cases) 2638

2012
24 March	Practice Direction (Citation of Authorities) 2641

2013
March	Practice Guidance (Terminology for Litigants in Person) 2643
19 July	Protocol (Communications Between Judges of the Family Court and Immigration and Asylum Chambers of the First-tier Tribunal and Upper Tribunal) 2643
October	Protocol and Good Practice Model (Disclosure of Information in Cases of Alleged Child Abuse and Linked Criminal and Care Directions Hearings) 2645

2014
16 January	Practice Guidance (Transparency in the Family Courts: Publication of Judgments) 2656
March	Justices' Clerks' Society and Magistrates' Association Revised Guidance (Provision of Justices' Reasons in Uncontested Cases) 2659
22 April	President's Guidance (Allocation and Gatekeeping for Care, Supervision and other Proceedings under Part IV of the Children Act 1989 (Public Law)) 2661
22 April	President's Guidance (Continuity and Deployment (Public Law)) 2666

PART V

22 April	President's Guidance (Use of Prescribed Documents (Public Law))	2669
22 April	President's Guidance (Allocation and Gatekeeping for Proceedings under Part II of the Children Act 1989 (Private Law))	2670
22 April	President's Guidance (Continuity and Deployment (Private Law))	2676
22 April	President's Guidance (Use of Prescribed Documents (Private Law))	2677
10 November	President's Guidance (The International Child Abduction and Contact Unit (ICACU))	2679
2015		
26 March	President's Guidance (The Role of the Attorney General in Appointing Advocates to the Court or Special Advocates in Family Cases)	2686
26 March	Practice Direction (Committal for Contempt of Court – Open Court)	2687
April	Practice Guidance (Tagging or Electronic Monitoring in Family Cases)	2690
June	Guidance Note (Financial Remedies Unit at the Central Family Court)	2692
24 June	Practice Guidance (Committal for Contempt of Court – Open Court)	2693
8 October	President's Guidance (Radicalisation Cases in the Family Courts)	2695
23 November	President's Practice Guidance (Arbitration in the Family Court)	2697
2016		
1 February	Mr Justice Mostyn's Statement (Statement on the Efficient Conduct of Financial Remedy Hearings Allocated to a High Court Judge Whether Sitting at the Royal Courts of Justice or Elsewhere)	2702
April	Guidance from the President's Office (Liaison between Courts in England and Wales and British Embassies and High Commissions Abroad)	2706
April	Guidance for the Judiciary (Transfer of proceedings under Article 15 of Brussels IIa and Articles 8 and/or 9 of the 1996 Hague Convention)	2709
17 October	Local Direction (Electronic Filing at the Central Family Court: Pilot Scheme)	2712
December	President's Guidance (Allocation of Work to Section 9 Judges)	2714

2017

January	Practice Note (The Official Solicitor to the Senior Courts: Appointment in Family Proceedings and Proceedings under the Inherent Jurisdiction in Relation to Adults)	2716
18 January	Practice Guidance (Family Court – Duration of Ex Parte (Without Notice) Orders)	2721

Practice Direction 19 August 1991

Citations: [1991] 1 WLR 955; [1991] 2 FLR 384

Statutory Charge: Form of the Order of the Court

Regulation 90(3) of the Civil Legal Aid (General) Regulations 1989, SI 1989/339, directs that where, in proceedings under the Married Women's Property Act 1882, the Matrimonial Causes Act 1973 or the Inheritance (Provision for Family and Dependants) Act 1975 [or Sch 1 to the Children Act 1989], property is recovered or preserved for an assisted person, which by order of the court is to be used as a home or a sum of money is to be used to purchase a home for the assisted person or his dependants, the assisted person's solicitor shall inform the Area Director.

In such a case, by virtue of regs 96 and 97, the Legal Aid Board may, subject to conditions, agree to defer enforcing the statutory charge on the property recovered or preserved imposed by s 16(6) of the Legal Aid Act 1988.

To avoid any doubt whether the order of the court must expressly state that the property is to be used as a home or to purchase a home, the Legal Aid Board has agreed that a certificate incorporated in the body of the order in the following form will be regarded as a sufficient compliance with the Regulations:

> 'And it is certified for the purpose of the Civil Legal Aid (General) Regulations 1989 [that the lump sum of £x has been ordered to be paid to enable the petitioner/respondent to purchase a home for himself/herself (or his/her dependants)] [that the property (*address*) has been preserved/recovered for the petitioner/respondent for use as a home for himself/herself (or his/her dependants)].'

Issued [in its original form] with the concurrence of the Lord Chancellor.

G. Angel
Senior District Judge

LASPOA 2012, s 25—This provides that where civil legal aid services are made available to an individual, such amounts are to be recovered as the first charge upon (a) property recovered or preserved in proceedings in connection with which services are provided and (b) any costs payable to an individual by another person in connection with the proceedings.

Best Practice Guidance June 1997

Note—The following material is taken from the *Children Act Advisory Committee Handbook of Best Practice in Children Act Cases*, and is reproduced with the kind permission of the President of the Family Division.

Public Law Outline (PLO)—The PLO is contained in FPR PD12A. It applies to all courts hearing applications issued by local authorities under CA 1989, Pt IV (care and supervision orders). As a result of the significant revisions to the PLO during 2013 resulting in the new FPR PD12A, some terminology has changed, and as a result of the creation of a single Family Court there have been radical changes to the way family courts are organised; readers are asked to bear these changes in mind when considering the material below. See further **Case management hearing** and **Issues resolution hearing** under FPR 2010, r 12.25 and notes on the timetable for proceedings under FPR 2010, r 12.12.

CFA 2014—CA 1989 has been amended by CFA 2014 with effect from 22 April 2014. Residence and contact orders have been removed from CA 1989, s 8 and replaced with child arrangements orders, which regulate the arrangements relating to (a) with whom a child is to live, spend time or otherwise have contact, and (b) when a child is to live, spend time or otherwise have contact with any person (cl 12(3)). See further under CA 1989, s 8.

Child Arrangements Programme (CAP)—The CAP is contained in FPR PD12B. It applies in all courts hearing family proceedings. See further under FPR 2010, rr 12.31, 12.32. It is respectfully submitted that where the *Best Practice Guidance* below conflicts with the CAP, the latter is to be preferred.

Form C100—In CA 1989, s 8 applications for child arrangements, specific issue and prohibited steps orders, Form C100 must be used in place of Form C1. Any references in the *Best Practice Guidance* below to Form C1 should therefore be read with this in mind. The forms to be used for applications in family proceedings are set out in FPR 2010, PD5A.

Handbook of Best Practice in Children Act Cases

Introduction

When writing its final report, the Committee thought it might be helpful to gather together in a separate document the guidance available on best practice in Children Act proceedings with a view to providing a useful tool for the conscientious but busy practitioner. Some of this material is newly written and some is a compendium of guidance from our earlier reports updated both by experience and authoritative reported decisions. It follows that some of this guidance is firmly authoritative (deriving from binding decisions or practice directions) whilst much remains advisory, but based on accumulated experience of what works best.

The basic message of this Handbook is that the earlier matters are considered and acted upon by the parties and their advisers, and the more that can be done jointly with other parties, the better the court process can serve the interests of children. Work done in preparation, and in liaison with other parties, is rarely wasted and indeed is almost always productive in terms of avoiding, or at least reducing, the trial process which is after all both the most costly and certainly the most stressful part of the whole proceedings.

We hope that all practitioners (and not just the lawyers) will find this Handbook useful as we try to translate into practice in each case the obligation to promote the welfare of the children with whom we are dealing. We have set out this Handbook with a view primarily to ease of reference in the hope that it will find widespread use in practice.

Section 1 – Preparation for court in care proceedings

Local authority solicitors

1 At the earliest stage, when first consulted, focus on:

- (a) the issues;
- (b) the legal framework;
- (c) the evidence needed to support an application;
- (d) the proposed care plan;
- (e) the appropriate level of court; and
- (f) the likely time scale for concluding the court case in the light of:
  - (i) the complexities involved, and
  - (ii) the ages and needs of the children.

2 If counsel is to be instructed, do so at an early stage. Consider together the preparation for trial and whether transfer to the care centre is appropriate.

All parties and their legal advisers

3 By the first directions hearing, consider whether the issues of fact are stark enough to justify a split hearing, with an early resolution of factual disputes to enable a definitive care plan to be formulated and to enable the guardian ad litem to make recommended actions as to outcome. For example, this is likely to arise in cases of alleged non-accidental injury where different persons are in the frame as possible perpetrators and/or accomplices, and in cases of sexual abuse.

4 Use directions hearings imaginatively. Anticipate problems and address them in advance.

- (a) Ensure strict compliance with timetables for filing evidence and documents.
- (b) Inform the court, as a matter of urgency, if the timetable cannot be met for any reason.
- (c) Be prepared in advance with dates and availability of witnesses and time needed to adduce evidence.
- (d) Liaise with other parties to ensure that all issues are addressed at an early stage, for example:
  - (i) whether transfer to the care centre would be appropriate;
  - (ii) which other persons are seeking party status;
  - (iii) issues of disclosure and confidentiality; or
  - (iv) any assessments or experts' reports sought by any party.

(e) Fix the final hearing, even if only provisionally.

5 All parties, and in particular the guardian ad litem, have a duty to:

(a) advise the court on the timetable appropriate to the issues and timescale of the child concerned;

(b) keep the timetable under constant review throughout the preparation for the hearing; and

(c) bring to the attention of the court promptly any significant developments and seek further directions.

Instruction of experts

6 See **Section 5** below.

The care plan

7 Ensure that the issues raised by the local authority are clearly set out with a fully researched care plan, to enable the parties to know what case they have to meet.

8 If permanent placement in an alternative family is the plan, prepare the ground as far as possible without pre-empting the court's decision.

9 If the plan is for an adoptive placement, the court will be handicapped in assessing the plan and the timescale, unless the child concerned has already been considered and approved by the adoption and fostering panel, and potential suitable adoptive families have been identified. It is not good practice to await the making of a care order before obtaining such information, because the court is deprived of important background information and significant delay can occur in placing the child in the event of the court approving the plan.

10 If the plan involves a specialist placement with therapy and/or further assessment, identify the placement and any professionals involved, together with the timescale and the availability of appropriate funding.

11 If the plan depends upon the finding of facts or determination of particular issues by the court, state why and set out clear alternative proposals.

12 If no firm proposal can be made, that should be made clear and explained.

****

Note—Paragraphs 13–20: 'Preparing the Evidence'; paragraph 21: 'The Court'; paragraphs 22–32: 'Section 2 – Renewal of Interim Care Orders'; and paragraphs 33–35: 'Section 3 – First Appointments in Public Law Cases in the County Courts: The Role of the Court' have been removed on the basis that their substance has in part been superseded by FPR PD12A.

Section 4 – Private law cases

Note—See annotations **Child Arrangements Programme (CAP)** and **Form C100** at the start of this Guidance.

Introduction

36 The following is a brief guide to best practice in applications made under section 8 of the Children Act. This guidance may need to be tailored to deal with cases involving unrepresented litigants.

37 Specific good practice for cases involving allegations of sexual abuse is set out in the Annex to this section.

Before proceedings

38 Consider whether the dispute between the parties could be resolved in any way other than litigation. Most areas have a mediation service which would be able to attempt to deal with disputes by way of negotiation and agreement. There is rarely anything to be lost, and normally much to be gained, by mediation.

39 At the earliest stage, if it becomes clear that negotiated or mediated settlement will not be possible, focus on:

PART V

(a) the issues, including the question of how crucial facts are to be proved;
(b) the legal framework; and
(c) the evidence needed to support the case to be put forward.

Issue of proceedings

40 Ensure that form C1 contains all relevant information, including a brief outline of the case (but not a detailed statement by the applicant).

41 To prevent unnecessary delay at the first directions appointment, prepare at least draft statements by:

(a) the applicant, and
(b) any witnesses who it is known will have to give evidence.

The first directions appointment

THE ROLE OF THE COURT

42 The court will fix a first directions appointment when an application is issued. The task of the court at the first appointment is to:

(a) investigate the issues;
(b) inquire into the possibility of settlement; and
(c) give directions in any case which has to proceed.

43 When giving directions, the court will normally:

(a) consider the appropriate tier of court;
(b) order the filing of witness statements;
(c) consider whether there are circumstances justifying sequential rather than simultaneous exchange;
(d) express times for filing (for example, of witness statements or the court welfare officer's report) by fixing a date, e g 'by 28 April 1997' and not 'within 14 days'; and
(e) include in the order the date for the next appointment and, even if only provisionally, the final hearing.

44 An order should not provide for an application to be adjourned generally unless the parties consider that it will not be necessary to return to court. In that event the order should also provide for the application to stand dismissed if not restored by a certain date.

45 The order should provide that any letter of instructions to experts (to be joint instructions wherever possible) is to be filed at court.

46 A paginated bundle of documents and chronology should be normal practice except in the simplest case.

THE ROLE OF THE PARTIES

47 Parties and their legal representatives must attend directions appointments unless specifically excused.

48 A party's legal representative must have both sufficient knowledge and authority to take any necessary decisions.

49 Use the first appointment imaginatively, anticipating problems and addressing them in advance, and dealing with questions of expert evidence. (See **Section 5**)

50 When it is to be suggested that there should be contact at a contact centre or supervised contact by an individual, make enquiries to ensure that the centre or individual will be available to provide the service.

Welfare reports

51 Parties should have access to a court welfare officer, or other person qualified to assist them, at or before the first appointment. Some courts achieve this by requiring a court welfare officer to attend the first appointment, others by referring the parties to the welfare officer before the date of the first appointment. Ask about the practice of the local court if you are in any doubt.

52 If a welfare officer has attempted to mediate between the parties, he should not be involved in the case in any other way.

53 When ordering a welfare report, the guidance as to best practice under 'Welfare Reports' at *Best Practice Note of January 1995* should be followed. In particular:

(a) the request for a report should state the issue giving rise to the request;
(b) addendum reports should not normally be ordered, and should not be necessary for the hearing if timetabling has been effective;
(c) any request for the court welfare officer to attend the final hearing should be examined carefully, and not granted as a matter of course;
(d) when a court requires the court welfare officer to attend a hearing, enquiry should be made to ensure that he is available; and
(e) the court hearing the case should allow the officer to give evidence first and then to be released.

Final directions appointments or pre-trial reviews

54 The final directions appointment, or pre-trial review, should be timetabled to take place when any welfare report and all evidence has been filed.

55 The applicant's solicitor must prepare an agreed and paginated bundle of documents, containing an index and a chronology, not less than 24 hours before the hearing.

56 The court will expect the parties' advisers to have addressed the question of what evidence can be agreed and what is in dispute. An order will be made accordingly.

57 The counsel or solicitor who will attend the final hearing should attend the pre-trial review. If this is not possible, the person attending must be thoroughly conversant with the case and competent to make any necessary concessions or admissions and to advise the lay client in respect of settlement.

The final hearing

58 Except by direction of the court, children should not attend a hearing.

59 Consider how the decision of the court is to be communicated to the children. In some cases, particularly where the court's decision is contrary to the reported wishes of the child, it may be appropriate for the court welfare officer to see the child to explain what has happened.

ANNEX – FLAWED SEXUAL ABUSE INVESTIGATION

Despite the guidance in *B v B (Sexual Abuse: Procedural Delay)* [1994] 1 FLR 323 and *Re A and B (Minors) (No 2)* [1995] 1 FLR 351, problems continue to occur in private law cases where allegations of sexual abuse of a child are investigated by the police and/or social services. Frequently the cases involve an application for contact with a child, where the primary carer has refused contact on the ground that the child has been sexually abused by the applicant. Such cases cause particular difficulties where the applicant denies the allegation, and alleges that the other parent has either invented the sexual abuse or has brainwashed the child into believing that sexual abuse has occurred. The parent opposing contact may be obstructive and use delaying tactics in order to prevent contact taking place, even under supervision. If such cases are not strictly timetabled, resulting delays can achieve the object of frustrating resumption of contact, even if the court finds that sexual abuse is not proved. Good practice requires as follows:

(a) The legal representatives have a duty, irrespective of whether or not delay might be tactically of advantage to their client, to ensure that a case does not drift and is resolved with the minimum of delay.
(b) The timetable must be strictly controlled by the court and must never be left to the parties. As in public law cases, the court must monitor the procedural steps ordered, building in reviews of progress and setting stringent time limits and return dates.
(c) When the local authority is involved with a concurrent, but independent investigation, the principal co-ordinating agency for the determination of issues is the court, using section 7 of the Children Act 1989 which enables the court to require the local authority

PART V

to report to the court on the nature, progress and outcome of the child protection investigation. Section 7 should be used to keep the parties informed of progress and material available.

(d) The local authority should make available a social worker to give evidence on the report and to be cross examined if so required.

(e) Any joint child abuse interview conducted by police and social services must follow the memorandum of good practice. Otherwise not only is the resulting interview of no forensic value, but it may impede or contaminate any further assessment of the child ordered by the court.

(f) The court has power to compel discovery of documents held by local authorities or the police, e g videos of interview with the child. If any arguments arise as to confidentiality, or public interest immunity, they should be determined at an early stage at a directions hearing.

(g) Although the court cannot compel a prosecuting authority to reach decisions speedily, the court can and should bring to the attention of the authority the need for a timely decision on criminal prosecution.

(h) Even when there is a police investigation, there is no good legal or social work reason why the social worker should not make contact with the parent under investigation, so that information can be given and exchanged which is relevant to the welfare of the child. The social worker should make it clear that until the police investigation is complete, the specific allegation cannot be discussed. Many parents under police investigation suffer a sense of grievance when no reason is given for denial of contact, with the result that the parent perceives the local authority as pursuing investigations with a closed mind and a presumption of guilt.

(i) The issue whether or not a child has been sexually abused is for decision by the court and it is essential that other agencies await that decision before introducing management, counselling or therapy that pre-judges the issue. Therefore, the welfare of the child demands speedy resolution of issues.

(j) If leave is sought to instruct an expert, it is essential to define the issues, to establish the area of expertise required and the proposed timetable, to consider joint instruction and to follow the guidance in **Section 5**. In deciding whether to grant leave for a child to be assessed the court should consider carefully the issues, and whether the court is likely to be assisted in determining whether sexual abuse has been established, as opposed to outcome, by the contribution from an expert in the field of psychological medicine.

(k) There is often a tension between a positive clinical finding of sexual abuse, and judicial findings that abuse has not occurred. In contested cases clinical methods will inevitably be subjected to scrutiny. Any investigation which focuses attention on the statements of the child runs the risk of producing a false result if what the child says is unreliable or if the child's primary caretaker is unreliable, particularly where the allegation emerges in bitterly contested section 8 proceedings. The dangers of a false conclusion are enhanced if the alleged perpetrator is excluded from clinical investigation. It is vital to approach a child abuse investigation with an open mind.

(l) Where possible directions appointments should be heard by the judge who is likely to determine the substantive issues.

(m) In cases in which there is a stark factual issue to be determined the court will need to consider carefully whether it is appropriate to obtain a section 7 report clarifying the issues before ordering a welfare report, whether factual issues need to be determined by the court before a welfare report is ordered as to outcome, or whether a report should be ordered at an early stage in the proceedings. Each case needs to be considered on its merits, and the court welfare service should be invited to make representations.

Section 5 – Experts and the courts

PLO – instructing and calling experts—In all public law proceedings under CA 1989, Pt IV, the PLO must be followed. It is contained in FPR PD12A and is designed to streamline care proceedings by emphasising good case preparation by the parties and their legal representatives and promoting active case management by the court. The PLO must be read in conjunction with FPR PD25A–PD25F. See further **Case management hearing** and **Issues resolution hearing** under FPR 2010, r 12.25.

****

86 Further information about the Expert Witness Group and the Expert Witness Pack may be obtained from: Dr Eileen Vizard, Consultant Child and Adolescent Psychiatrist, Camden and Islington Community Health Services NHS Trust, Simmons House Adolescent Unit, St. Luke's-Woodside Hospital, Woodside Avenue, London N10 3HU (Telephone: 0181 219 1883).

Section 6 – Appeals from the Family Proceedings Courts under Section 94 of the Children Act 1989

****

Note—Section 6 has been overtaken by procedural rules. As a result of the creation of the single Family Court, references to the 'family proceedings court' are now obsolete. All appeals from lay justices under CA 1989, s 94 are now governed by FPR 2010, Pt 30. The routes of appeal are set out in FPR PD30A, para 2.1. See Procedural Guide E2.

Section 7 – Disclosure of local authority documents

Early consideration

93 Crown Prosecution Service and defence solicitors should give early consideration whether disclosure of records held in the possession of a local authority may be required. The appropriate time for such consideration will be at the commencement of the 4 weeks period (custody cases) or 6 weeks period (bail cases) between committal or transfer and the plea and directions hearing.

94 The parties should inform the judge of the steps that have been taken so that, if necessary, directions may be given and noted on the questionnaire.

95 Requests by the Crown Prosecution Service or the defence solicitor for disclosure should:

- (a) be made in writing to the legal services department of the local authority who will nominate a lawyer to deal with the matter;
- (b) provide specific details of the information required and an explanation as to why it is relevant to the proceedings, identifying as precisely as possible the category and nature of the documents for which disclosure is sought and
- (c) be accompanied by a copy of the indictment or of the schedule of charges upon committal.

96 If the defence solicitors request information, they should notify the Crown Prosecution Service of the request and vice versa.

97 Case records will be examined by legal services and the appropriate officer to identify whether they contain the information which is sought.

98 Information which is disclosed to the defence solicitors will also be disclosed to the Crown Prosecution Service and vice versa.

99 If the case records do *not* contain the requested information, the requester will be so informed by legal services which, subject to relevance and the principle of confidentiality, may be able (but is not bound) to provide a summary of the type of information which is on file.

100 If the requester is not satisfied with the response, legal services, after appropriate consultation, will provide the name of a person to be witness summonsed to attend court with the records.

101 Where the case records do contain the information requested, legal services will disclose it so long as it is not protected by public interest immunity, legal privilege or statutory confidentiality.

102 If the local authority wishes to assert protection from disclosure for the records requested or any of them, legal services, after appropriate consultation, will provide the name of a person to be witness summonsed to attend court with the records.

103 If the local authority wishes to make representations as to why the records requested should not be disclosed, it will inform:

(a) the requester;
(b) the opposing party's representative and
(c) the court listing officer,

and a convenient date for listing, before a judge will be set.

104 The local authority should provide a skeleton argument and serve it on the parties and the court.

105 At the hearing:

(a) the witness must produce the records to the judge;
(b) files must be flagged to identify the documents for which immunity from disclosure is sought;
(c) representations will be made on behalf of the parties; and
(d) the judge will give appropriate directions.

106 Whenever possible, the hearing will be before the judge who will be conducting the trial. If the trial judge has not been nominated, then the hearing judge may determine the issue of disclosure.

107 The judge will give his decision in court or chambers, in the presence of the parties' representatives.

108 The judge may also give direction as to the custody of the records pending trial and as to any copies to be obtained on behalf of the parties.

109 The hearing referred to above should take place not less than 4 weeks before trial.

110 Where the requester has reasonable grounds to believe that a witness or a defendant has been involved with social services, information may be obtained by writing to the relevant department stating the witness's or defendant's name, date of birth and address.

Confidentiality of records

111 The court will normally conduct the hearing at which public interest immunity is claimed in chambers, where the local authority may be represented by a solicitor.

112 When records are disclosed to the parties by order of the court, it is on the undertaking that:

(a) they will only be used for the purpose of the criminal proceedings before the court; and
(b) their contents are revealed only to the parties and their legal representatives. (Leave of the court must be obtained for wider disclosure, e g to an expert witness.)

Costs

113 An officer of the local authority who necessarily attends court for the purpose of the proceedings otherwise than as a witness may be allowed expenses (Regulation 18(2) within Costs in Criminal Cases (General) Regulations 1986).

114 The court has no power to order payment from central funds of the cost of a search or legal costs.

115 If the court rules that the application for disclosure is frivolous or by way of a fishing expedition, it may order that costs be paid by the applicant or his legal advisers.

APPENDIX A
GUIDANCE, BEST PRACTICE NOTES AND PRO FORMAS FROM THE COMMITTEE'S PREVIOUS ANNUAL REPORTS

I Best Practice Guidance on section 37(1) directions

Set out in the notes to CA 1989, s 37(1).

II Urgent hearings on Circuit before Family Division judges: standby procedure

[*see following page for Questionnaire on guardian ad litem performance*]

Note—See FPR PD12E.

III Questionnaire on guardian ad litem performance

Name of Guardian

Name of case: No:

Part one *(To be completed by the staff)*

1. Did the GAL appoint a solicitor for the first hearing? Yes/No
2. Did the GAL attend all directions and interim hearings as appropriate? Yes/No
3. Did the GAL adhere to the court timetable? Yes/No
4. Did the GAL respond to telephone calls and letters satisfactorily? Yes/No

Part two *(To be completed by the Judge/Magistrates)*

5.Did you consider the report to be *(Tick as appropriate)*

Good

Adequate

Poor

6. Did the GAL give oral evidence *(Tick as appropriate)*

Well

Adequately

Inadequately

7. Did the GAL's argument / evidence justify the recommendation made? *(Tick as appropriate)*

Well

Adequately

Inadequately

8. If you have any further comments as to any aspects of the GAL's work please state them:

Name of court:

Date:

Signed:

Name:

Please return to:

IV Local authority assessments

Special considerations arise where the local authority wish to carry out an assessment eg a Section 37 assessment or family assessment.

In such cases the court should:

(i) Identify the purpose of the assessment.
(ii) Specify the time in which the assessment is to be carried out and direct that evidence of the outcome of the assessment be filed by a given date.
(iii) Fix a directions hearing for a date immediately after the date fixed for the completion of the assessment.
(iv) At the directions hearing the court should consider what evidence is needed to bring the case speedily and fairly to final or substantive hearing.
(v) Where the court exercises its discretion to grant leave for the papers to be shown to a particular expert, the court should go on to give directions.

These should:

- State the timescale in which the evidence in question should be produced.
- Provide for the disclosure of any written expert report both to all parties and to the other experts in the case. When a report is disclosed it should include a copy of the letter of instruction.
- Provide for discussion between experts following mutual disclosure of reports and for the filing of further evidence by the experts stating the areas of agreement and disagreement between the experts. Parties should only instruct experts who are willing to meet in advance of the hearing. When granting leave, the court must make this a condition of the appointment.

Where it proves impracticable to give such directions at the time when leave to disclose the report is granted, the court must set a date for a further directions hearing at which such directions can be given.

V Bundles of documents

Note—See FPR PD27A and r 12.12.

VI Best practice note for the judiciary and family proceedings courts when ordering a court welfare officer's report

Note—See FPR PD12B, which governs the procedure in private law cases.

VII Best practice note to court staff when welfare reports have been ordered

Note—See FPR PD12B, which governs the procedure in private law cases.

VIII Welfare report referral form

[*see following page for Receipt and undertaking for video recordings*]

Note—See FPR PD12B, which governs the procedure in private law cases.

IX Receipt and undertaking for video recordings

Name of solicitor Name of firm

Address

Telephone Solicitor's reference

I, the above named solicitor, hereby confirm that I am acting for (insert name of client):

who is a party to the proceedings currently before the court concerning (insert name of child or children):

I acknowledge receipt of the recording marked "Evidence of "

I acknowledge that this recording is and will remain the property of the Chief Constable of .... Police notwithstanding the fact that I agree to pay the reasonable expenses incurred by .... Police in providing me with this recording on loan.

I undertake that whilst the recording is in my possession I shall:

(a) not make or permit any other person to make a copy of the recording;
(b) not make or permit any disclosure of the recording or its contents to any person except when in my opinion it is strictly necessary in the interests of the child and / or the interests of justice;
(c) not part with possession of the recording to anyone other than to counsel instructed by me or to an expert witness authorised by the court, and in particular
(d) NOT PART WITH POSSESSION OF THE RECORDING TO *(insert name of client)*

(e) at all times (except whilst being played) keep the recording in a locked, secure container and not leave it unattended in vehicles or otherwise unprotected;
(f) record details of the name of any person allowed access to the recording and produce such record to an officer of .... Police upon request;
(g) ensure that any person who takes possession of the recording under paragraph (c) above is supplied with a copy of this undertaking and agrees to be bound by its terms;
(h) return the recording to .... Police immediately upon the conclusion of the proceedings or when I am no longer professionally instructed in the matter whichever is sooner;
(i) give notice to .... Police of any application to the court which may result in the variation of the terms set out in this undertaking.

Signed:
Dated:

PART V

X Guidance as to preparation of the justices' written findings and reasons – The Honourable Mr Justice Cazalet

GENERAL

1 The obligations placed upon justices and their clerks are set out succinctly in Rules 21(5) and (6) of the Family Proceedings Courts (Children Act 1989) Rules 1991. Stated summarily these require that before the court makes an order or refuses an application or request, the justices' clerk shall record in writing, in consultation with the justices, the reason for the court's decision and any finding of fact. Furthermore, when justices make an order or refuse an application, the court, or one of the justices constituting the court by which the decision is made, shall state any finding of fact or reasons for the court's decision. These provisions are straightforward and are expressed in terminology which is unequivocal. They must be interpreted literally and strictly.

2 The justices and their clerks must ensure that the reasons and findings of fact are stated at the time the order is made. They cannot be added to subsequently. The written reasons and findings of fact must accord with what is stated in court. Justices cannot make an order and then reserve judgment (a luxury which the Court of Appeal is permitted). Justices must give their reasons, and any findings made, each time they make an order or decline to make an order.

3 There can be no 'back door' process. That is to say that if, on appeal, a point is taken which the justices did consider in their deliberations but omitted to put in their reasons, they cannot formally make a subsequent addendum to those reasons and supply them to the appeal court.

4 Even when the parties are agreed, there is, none the less, an overriding duty in the court to investigate the proposals advanced by the parties. However, the extent of the investigation must reflect reality and so, when an agreed order is sought, the investigation of the evidence need not and should not be dealt with in full detail unless there are concerns as to the propriety of the order. Nevertheless, it is particularly important that in cases where a care order is made by consent the basis upon which the care order is made is clearly stated, for example because of a failure to protect from an abusive spouse or an agreed non-accidental injury as set out in some statement identified in the proceedings. If this step is taken it will avoid a long and perhaps inconclusive later trawl through the evidence in the earlier case in an attempt to establish what the actual finding then was and its relevance to a different child or new family situation. Also, justices must bear in mind that it will always be important for the child's wishes (given that the child is of sufficient age and maturity for those wishes to be relevant) to be taken into consideration. A consent order sought by the parents may not always properly reflect this.

5 The Children Act has brought two fundamental changes in the way that justices conduct hearings. First they must read all the papers before coming to court (that is to say they must come into court 'hot'); second they must give their reasons and findings of fact in writing. It is essential that justices are fully conversant with the written documents before the case starts. This will have one advantage in particular. The justices will know when to intervene to stop evidence being led which simply repeats what has already been stated, usually in a statement of evidence in chief. This unnecessary repetition can be extremely time wasting.

6 It is vital to remember that the findings of fact and reasons will form the basis of any appeal accordingly they must be clearly stated. In order to avoid pressure of time when reasons are being prepared it may be appropriate to release the parties for a period or to require them to come back the next day. In this event only one of the justices concerned need attend and read out the written reasons and findings.

7 Clarity in findings and reasons is important not only so that the appeal court knows the basis on which the decision has been made but also so that the losing party knows why the decision has gone against him. It is worth remembering that decisions in family cases, unlike most other decisions in the courts, concern the future. If the losing party leaves court without understanding properly why the order has been made against him because the court has not clearly explained the reason for its decision then this will not augur well for later hearings and may well give rise to a sense of grievance which impedes the working of the order.

8 Do not be afraid to raise points with advocates during their speeches. This should help to clarify difficult points.

9 When justices make an order which differs from the advice or conclusion reached in the report of the court welfare officer or guardian ad litem it is imperative for them to set out in clear terms why they have done so. This need not be stated at great length but it must be possible for the parties (and if there is an appeal, for the appellate court) to follow the process whereby the different conclusion was reached.

10 When the arguments of the losing party are being dealt with in the findings state these first before the arguments of the party in whose favour the decision is to be made.

11 When you intervene because an advocate is being too long winded, repetitious or adversarial you will carry much more authority if you have read and fully understood the papers in the case. When you do intervene be firm, courteous and controlled.

12 When you are dealing with a care case it is usually helpful to require the advocate when opening the case for the local authority to state specifically the facts upon which he relies as establishing that the threshold criteria apply. This will enable the court to direct its mind to the material evidence as it emerges and should help to clarify at an early stage the findings which will have to be made to support a care order.

MORE SPECIFIC GUIDELINES IN SETTING OUT REASONS AND FINDINGS OF FACT

There are a number of different proformas used by different justices for the purposes of setting out their reasons and findings of fact. Once a particular system which works satisfactorily has evolved then it would be a mistake to interfere with it in any fundamental way. I accordingly set out below some guidelines which may be of assistance in formulating reasons and findings.

1 At the start state brief details about the child, parents and any other party (this includes dealing with family, siblings and where the child makes his/her home etc).

2 State, in concise form, the competing applications (i e the orders which each party is seeking). PART V

3 State the relevant facts not in dispute, including appropriate background details (this will include stating physical injuries, emotional or educational problems from which the child may have suffered and which are not in dispute. This will *not* deal with the cause of such injuries unless that also is not in dispute). Keep this short.

4 Set out in general form the facts in dispute (for example the cause of a non-accidental injury). This will normally involve a short statement of the competing assertions by the parties concerned.

5 State your findings of fact including in particular, where appropriate, whose evidence was preferred. In general terms you should state the reasons for preferring one witness to another (for example because he or she was more convincing, because there was corroboration, or because one witness clearly had a better recollection than another and so forth). Be careful before you call a witness a liar. We are not infallible!

6 An appellate court cannot write into justices' reasons inference and findings working backwards from their conclusions. The material findings of fact must be stated so be as firm as you feel you can be when stating your findings.

7 State concisely any relevant law, and refer to the threshold criteria. Refer to any *relevant* passage of legal authority cited.

8 State your conclusions from the facts found. In particular, if you are dealing with a care case you should state why you consider the threshold criteria to apply.

9 State your decision and reasons for it, making clear that you have taken into account the welfare checklist by going through the relevant provisions.

CONCLUSION

The sequence stated above is the one that I usually follow. It matters not if you vary it somewhat or if your proforma follows a somewhat different sequence. The importance is that you should deal with all those particular headings.

The clerk is under a legal duty to record your findings and reasons in consultation with you. Once you have completed your deliberations you should call in the clerk and go through the record of your findings of fact and reasons. On the back of the proforma your clerk will enter the details of all the documentary evidence which was considered by the court.

Provided you follow these various heads you should cover all essential matters. The important thing is to get a system a sequence of headings under which you deal with the evidence and any submissions made by the advocates which lead on to your decision. Once you have learned to work within a particular framework, the preparation of the written findings and reasons will come much more easily.

APPENDIX B
THE OFFICIAL SOLICITOR: APPOINTMENT IN FAMILY PROCEEDINGS (PRACTICE NOTE)

Appointment as guardian ad litem of child subject of proceedings

Note—See FPR PD16A.

APPENDIX C
PRACTICE DIRECTIONS BY THE PRESIDENT OF THE FAMILY DIVISION

I Applications by children

Note—See FC(CDB)R 2014, Sch 1, para 5, the President's Guidance on Allocation and Gatekeeping and the Schedule thereto.

II Case management

Note—See FPR PD12A, which applies to all courts hearing applications issued by local authorities under CA 1989, Pt IV (care and supervision orders). See further **Case management hearing** and **Issues resolution hearing** under FPR 2010, r 12.25 and notes on the timetable for proceedings under FPR 2010, r 12.12.

Practice Statement
22 April 1998

Citations: [1998] 1 WLR 825; [1998] 1 FLR 1102

Supreme Court: Judgments

New arrangements for the delivery of judgments in all divisions of the High Court and in the Court of Appeal would be introduced to facilitate the availability and speedy publication of the approved text of judgments and to prevent the dissemination of unapproved texts.

The arrangements, made in agreement with Lord Woolf MR, Sir Richard Scott V-C, and Sir Stephen Brown, President of the Family Division, were to be regarded as experimental and would apply forthwith.

Lord Bingham of Cornhill CJ: Unless the court otherwise ordered, for example, if a judgment contained price-sensitive information, copies of the written judgment would be made available to the parties' legal advisers at about 4pm on the second working day before judgment was due to be pronounced on condition that the contents were not communicated to the parties themselves until one hour before the listed time for pronouncement of judgment.

Delivery to legal advisers was made primarily to enable them to consider the judgment and decide what consequential orders they should seek. The condition was imposed to prevent the outcome of the case being publicly reported before judgment was given, since the judgment was confidential until then.

Some judges might decide to allow the parties' legal advisers to communicate the contents of the judgment to their clients 2 hours before the listed time, in order that they might be able to submit minutes of the proposed order, agreed by their clients, to the judge before the judge came into court, and it would be open to judges to permit more information about the result of a case to be communicated on a confidential basis to the client at an earlier stage if good reason were shown for making such a direction.

If, for any reason, a party's legal advisers had special grounds for seeking a relaxation of the usual condition restricting disclosure to the party itself, a request for relaxation of the condition might be made informally through the judge's clerk, or through the associate, if the judge had no clerk.

A copy of the written judgment would be made available to any party who was not legally represented at the same time as to legal advisers. It had to be treated as confidential until judgment was given.

Every page of every judgment which was made available in that way would be marked 'Unapproved judgment: No permission is granted to copy or use in court'. These words would carry the authority of the judge and would mean what they said.

The time at which copies of the judgment were being made available to the parties' legal advisers was being brought forward 24 hours in order to enable them to submit any written suggestions to the judge about typing errors, wrong references and other minor corrections of that kind in good time, so that, if the judge thought fit, the judgment could be corrected before it was handed down formally in court.

The parties' legal advisers were therefore requested to submit a written list of corrections of that kind to the judge's clerk, or to the associate, if the judge had no clerk, by 3pm on the day before judgment was handed down.

In divisions of the court which had two or more judges, the list should be submitted in each case to the judge who was to deliver the judgment in question.

Lawyers were not being asked to carry out proofreading for the judiciary, but a significant cause of the present delays was the fact that minor corrections of that type were being mentioned to the judge for the first time in court, when there was no time to make any necessary corrections to the text.

Availability of approved versions of handed-down judgments: new arrangements

That course would make it very much easier for the judge to make any necessary corrections and to hand down the judgment formally as the approved judgment of the court without any need for the delay involved in requiring the court shorthand writer, in courts which had an official shorthand writer, to resubmit the judgment to the judge for approval.

It would always be open to the judge to direct the shorthand writer at the time of the hearing in court to include in the text of the judgment any last-minute corrections which were mentioned for the first time in court, or which it had proved impractical to incorporate in the judgments handed down.

In such an event the judge would make it clear whether the shorthand writer could publish the judgment, as corrected, as the approved judgment of the court without any further reference to the judge, or whether it should be resubmitted to the judge for approval.

It would be open to judges, if they wished, to decline to approve their judgments at the time they were delivered, in which case the existing practice of submitting the judgment for their approval would continue.

Handing down judgment in court: availability of uncorrected copies

When the court handed down its written judgment, it would pronounce judgment in open court. Copies of the written judgment would then be made available to accredited representatives of the media, and to accredited law reporters who were willing to comply with restrictions on copying, who identified themselves as such.

In cases of particular interest to the media, it would be helpful if requests for copies could be intimated to the judge's clerk, or the presiding Lord Justice's clerk, in advance of judgment, so that the likely demand for copies could be accurately estimated.

Because there would usually be insufficient time for the judge's clerk to prepare the necessary number of copies of the corrected judgment in advance, in most cases these uncorrected copies would similarly bear the warning 'Unapproved Judgment: No permission is granted to copy or use in court'.

The purpose of those arrangements was to place no barrier in the way of accredited representatives of the media who wished to report the judgments of the court immediately in the usual way, or to accredited law reporters who wished to prepare a summary or digest of the judgment or to read it for the purpose of deciding whether to obtain an approved version for reporting purposes.

Its purpose was to put a stop to the dissemination of unapproved, uncorrected, judgments for other purposes, while seeking to ensure that everyone who was interested in the judgment, other than the immediate parties, might be able to buy a copy of the approved judgment in most cases much more quickly than was possible at present.

If any member of the public, other than a party to the case, or any law reporter who was not willing to comply with the restrictions on copying, wished to read the written judgment of the court on the occasion when it was handed down, a copy would be made available for him or her to read and note in court on request made to the associate or to the clerk to the judge or the presiding Lord Justice.

The copy could not be removed from the court and had to be handed back after reading. The object was to ensure that such a person was in no worse a position than if the judgment had been read aloud in full.

Availability of approved judgments

In courts without an official shorthand writer, the approved judgment should contain on its frontispiece the rubric: 'This is the official judgment of the court and I direct that no further note or transcript be made'.

That would cover the requirements of Ord 68, r 1 of the Rules of the Supreme Court, in the cases to which that rule applied, and would provide for certainty in all other cases.

In future, all judgments delivered at the Royal Courts of Justice would be published in a common format.

For cases decided in the two divisions of the Court of Appeal and in the Crown Office List, copies of the approved judgment could be ordered from the official shorthand writers, on payment of the appropriate fee.

In the other courts in the Royal Courts of Justice, copies of the approved judgment could be ordered from the Mechanical Recording Department, on payment of the fee prescribed for copy documents. Disks containing the judgment would also be available from the official shorthand writers, and the Mechanical Recording Department, where relevant, on payment of an appropriate charge.

It was hoped that in most cases copies of the approved judgment would be available from these sources on the same day as the judgment was handed down: they should no longer be sought from judges' clerks.

Restrictions on disclosure or reporting

Anyone who was supplied with a copy of the handed-down judgment, or who read it in court, would be bound by any direction which the court might have given in a child case under s 39 of the Children and Young Persons Act 1933, or any other form of restriction on disclosure, or reporting of information in the judgment.

Availability of approved versions of ex tempore judgments

Delays had also been experienced in the publication of approved versions of ex tempore judgments, whether they were produced by the official shorthand writers or by contractors transcribing the tapes which had been mechanically recorded.

Sometimes the delay was caused in courts without an official shorthand writer because a transcript was bespoken by one of the parties a long time after the judgment was delivered. If a transcribed copy of such a judgment was to be required, in connection with an appeal, for example, it should be ordered as soon as practicable after judgment was delivered.

Delays were also sometimes caused in those cases because judgments were delivered to a judge for approval without supplying the judge with copies of the material quoted in the judgment.

In future no judge should be invited to approve any such transcript unless the transcriber had been provided by the party ordering the transcript with copies of all the material from which the judge had quoted.

If the transcript was ordered by a person who was not a party to the case, such as a law reporter, that person should make arrangements with one of the parties to ensure that the transcriber, and the judge, would have access to all the material quoted in the judgment.

From time to time delays were also caused because judges had been slow in returning approved transcripts to the transcribers. His Lordship and the other heads of division had recently asked judges, as a general rule, that they should endeavour to return approved transcripts to the transcribers within 2 weeks of their being delivered to them for approval. If anyone encountered serious delay on that account, the relevant head of division should be informed.

****

Conclusion

The purpose of these changes, which were being made on an experimental basis after full consultation with the Court Service, was to improve the quality of service rendered by the judges to those who used the courts.

Any comments on those changes, or suggestions about further improvements in relation to the matters set out in the statement, should be addressed to Brooke LJ at the Royal Courts of Justice.

They would be taken fully into account when the time came to decide whether these arrangements should be formalised, with or without amendment, in a Practice Direction.

Bingham of Cornhill LCJ

PART V

Practice Statement
25 November 1998

Citations: [1999] 1 WLR 1; [1999] 1 FLR 314

Supreme Court: Judgments (No 2)

I am making this further statement with the agreement of Lord Woolf MR, Sir Richard Scott V-C, and Sir Stephen Brown P. Like the earlier statement I made on 22 April 1998 *(Practice Statement (Supreme Court: Judgments)* [1998] 1 FLR 1102), this statement applies to judgments delivered in all Divisions of the High Court and the Court of Appeal.

In my earlier statement I said that the arrangements I was announcing should be regarded as experimental, and that they would be kept under review. Experience since that time has shown that in general the new arrangements are working well, but that there is scope for some fine tuning. In particular, for a number of reasons it has not proved possible for the official shorthand writers to publish the official transcripts of approved, handed down, judgments quite as quickly as we had hoped, and there has been some uncertainty as to the status of the judgment given by the court to the shorthand writers.

We have decided to retain the embargo on copying the draft judgment which is sent to the parties 2 days before a judgment is handed down. An approved judgment, when handed down in court, will now be entitled 'Judgment: Approved by the court for handing down (subject to editorial corrections)', and every page of a judgment which is handed down in this form will be marked in a similar manner. There will be no embargo on copying a judgment handed down in this form, so long as its status is made clear, and at present no charge will be made for permission to copy it.

In order to make it possible for approved judgments to be handed down in this way, the parties' legal advisers will be requested to submit their written list of suggested corrections by 12 noon, not 3pm, on the day before judgment is handed down. If it is not possible to comply with this deadline, any later corrections approved by the judge will be included in the final text which the official shorthand writer (or the judge's clerk, in courts which lack an official shorthand writer) will incorporate into the approved official text of the judgment as soon as practicable.

Where a reserved written judgment has not been reported, reference must still be made in court to the approved official transcript (if this is available) and not to the approved transcript which is handed down, since this may have been subject to late revision after the text was prepared for handing down.

We will continue to keep these experimental arrangements under review. Comments or suggestions about any aspect of the arrangements should, once again, be addressed to Brooke LJ.

Bingham of Cornhill LCJ

President's Direction 24 July 2000

Citations: [2000] 1 WLR 1782; [2000] 2 FLR 429

Human Rights Act 1998

1 It is directed that the following practice shall apply as from 2 October 2000 in all family proceedings:

Citation of authorities

2 When an authority referred to in s 2 of the Human Rights Act 1998 ('the Act') is to be cited at a hearing:

(a) the authority to be cited shall be an authoritative and complete report;

(b) the court must be provided with a list of authorities it is intended to cite and copies of the reports:

(i) in cases to which *Practice Direction (Family Proceedings: Court Bundles)* (10 March 2000) [2000] 1 FLR 536 applies, as part of the bundle;

(ii) otherwise, not less than 2 clear days before the hearing; and

(c) copies of the complete original texts issued by the European Court and Commission, either paper based or from the Court's judgment database (HUDOC) which is available on the internet, may be used.

Note—In place of *Practice Direction (Family Proceedings: Court Bundles)* (10 March 2000) [2000] 1 FLR 536, see FPR PD27A, as amended with effect from 31 July 2014, especially para 4.3.

Allocation to judges

3 (1) The hearing and determination of the following will be confined to a High Court judge:

(a) a claim for a declaration of incompatibility under s 4 of the Act; or

(b) an issue which may lead to the court considering making such a declaration.

(2) The hearing and determination of a claim made under the Act in respect of a judicial act shall be confined in the High Court to a High Court judge and in county courts to a circuit judge.

Issued with the concurrence and approval of the Lord Chancellor.

Dame Elizabeth Butler-Sloss
President

Practice Direction 2 October 2000

Citations: [2000] 1 WLR 1886

Justices: Clerk to Court

1 A justices' clerk is responsible for:

(a) the legal advice tendered to the justices within the area;
(b) the performance of any of the functions set out below by any member of his/her staff acting as legal adviser;
(c) ensuring that competent advice is available to justices when the justices' clerk is not personally present in court;
(d) the effective delivery of case management and the reduction of unnecessary delay.

2 Where a person other than the justices' clerk, a legal adviser who is authorised to do so, performs any of the functions referred to in this direction s/he will have the same responsibilities as the justices' clerk.

The legal adviser can consult the justices' clerk or other person authorised by the justices' clerk for that purpose before tendering advice to the bench. If the justices' clerk or that person gives any advice directly to the bench, s/he shall give the parties or their advocates an opportunity of repeating any relevant submissions prior to the advice being given.

3 It will be the responsibility of the legal adviser to provide the justices with any advice they require to properly perform their functions, whether or not the justices have requested that advice, on:

(i) questions of law, including European Court of Human Rights jurisprudence and those matters set out in section 2(1) of the Human Rights Act 1998;
(ii) questions of mixed law and fact;
(iii) matters of practice and procedure;
(iv) the range of penalties available;
(v) any relevant decisions of the superior courts or other guidelines;
(vi) other issues relevant to the matter before the court;
(vii) the appropriate decision-making structure to be applied in any given case.

In addition to advising the justices it will be the legal adviser's responsibility to assist the court, where appropriate, as to the formulation of reasons and the recording of those reasons.

4 A justices' clerk or legal adviser must not play any part in making findings of fact but can assist the bench by reminding them of the evidence, using any notes of the proceedings for that purpose.

5 A justices' clerk or legal adviser can ask questions of witnesses and the parties in order to clarify the evidence and any issues in the case.

6 A legal adviser has a duty to ensure that every case is conducted fairly.

7 When advising the justices the justices' clerk or legal adviser, whether or not previously in court, shall:

(i) ensure that s/he is aware of the relevant facts;
(ii) provide the parties with the information necessary to enable the parties to make any representations they wish as to the advice before it is given.

8 At any time, justices are entitled to receive advice to assist them in discharging their responsibilities.

If they are in any doubt as to the evidence which has been given, they should seek the aid of their legal adviser, referring to his/her notes as appropriate. That should ordinarily be done in open court. Where the justices request their adviser to join them in the retiring room, that request should be made in the presence of the parties in court.

Any legal advice given to the justices other than in open court should be clearly stated to be provisional and the adviser should subsequently repeat the substance of the advice in open court and give the parties an opportunity to make any representations they wish on that provisional advice.

The legal adviser should then state in open court whether the provisional advice is confirmed or, if it is varied, the nature of the variation.

9 The performance of a legal adviser can be appraised by a person authorised by the magistrates' courts committee to do so.

For that purpose the appraiser can be present in the justices' retiring room. The content of the appraisal is confidential, but the fact that an appraisal has taken place, and the presence of the appraiser in the retiring room, should be briefly explained in open court.

10 The legal adviser is under a duty to assist unrepresented parties to present their case, but must do so without appearing to become an advocate for the party concerned.

11 The role of legal advisers in fine default proceedings or any other proceedings for the enforcement of financial orders, obligations or penalties is to assist the court. They must not act in an adversarial or partisan manner.

With the agreement of the justices a legal adviser can ask questions of the defaulter to elicit information which the justices will require to make an adjudication, for example to facilitate his or her explanation for the default.

A legal adviser can also advise the justices in the normal way as to the options open to them in dealing with the case. It will be inappropriate for the legal adviser to set out to establish wilful refusal or neglect or any other type of culpable behaviour, to offer an opinion on the facts, or to urge a particular course of action upon the justices.

The duty of impartiality is the paramount consideration for the legal adviser at all times, and that takes precedence over any role s/he may have as a collecting officer.

The appointment of other staff to 'prosecute' the case for the collecting officer is not essential to ensure compliance with the law, including the Human Rights Act 1998. Whether to make such appointments is a matter for the justices' chief executive.

12 *Practice Direction (Justices: Clerk to Court)* ([1981] 1 WLR 1163) is revoked. *Practice Note (Justices' Clerks)* ([1954] 1 WLR 213) remains in force.

Lord Woolf
Lord Chief Justice

Practice Direction
11 January 2001

Citations: [2001] 1 WLR 194

Judgments: Form and Citation

Lord Woolf CJ: gave the following direction at the sitting of the court.

This practice direction is made with the concurrence of the Master of the Rolls, the Vice-Chancellor and the President of the Family Division. It represents the next stage in the process of modernising the arrangements for the preparation, distribution and citation of judgments given in every division of the High Court, whether in London or in courts outside London.

Form of judgments

1.1 With effect from 11 January 2001, all judgments in every division of the High Court and the Court of Appeal will be prepared for delivery, or issued as approved judgments, with single spacing, paragraph numbering (in the margins) but no page numbers. In courts with more than one judge, the paragraph numbering will continue sequentially through each judgment, and will not start again at the beginning of the second judgment. Indented paragraphs will not be given a number.

1.2 The main reason of these changes is to facilitate the publication of judgments on the World Wide Web and their subsequent use by the increasing numbers of those who had access to the Web. The changes should also assist those who used and wish to search judgments stored on electronic databases.

1.3 It is desirable in the interests of consistency that all judgments prepared for delivery (or issued as approved judgments) in county courts, should also contain paragraph numbering (in the margins).

Neutral citation of judgments

2.1 With effect from 11 January 2001 a form of neutral citation will be introduced in both divisions of the Court of Appeal and in the Administrative Court. A unique number will be given by the official shorthand writers to each approved judgment issued out of these courts. The judgments will be numbered in the following way:

Court of Appeal (Civil Division) [2000] EWCA Civ 1, 2, 3 etc
Court of Appeal (Criminal Division) [2000] EWCA Crim 1, 2, 3 etc
High Court (Administrative Court) [2000] EWHC Admin 1, 2, 3 etc

2.2 Under these new arrangements, paragraph 59 in *Smith v Jones*, the tenth numbered judgment of the year in the Civil Division of the Court of Appeal, would be cited: *Smith v Jones* [2001] EWCA Civ 10 at [59].

2.3 The neutral citation will be the official number attributed to the judgment by the court and must always be used on at least one occasion when the judgment was cited in a later judgment. Once the judgment is reported, the neutral citation will appear in front of the familiar citation from the law report series: thus *Smith v Jones* [2001] EWCA Civ 10 at [30], [2001] QB 124, [2001] 2 All ER 364, etc. The paragraph number must be the number allotted by the court in all future versions of the judgment.

2.4 If a judgment is cited on more than one occasion in a later judgment, it will be of the greatest assistance if only one abbreviation, if desired, is used. Thus *Smith v Jones* [2001] EWCA Civ 10 could be abbreviated on subsequent occasions to *Smith v Jones*, or *Smith's* case, but preferably not both in the same judgment.

PART V

2.5 If it is desired to cite more than one paragraph of a judgment each numbered paragraph should be enclosed with a square bracket: thus *Smith v Jones* [2001] EWCA Civ 10 at [30]–[35], or *Smith v Jones* [2001] EWCA Civ 10 at [30], [35], and [40]–[43].

2.6 The neutral citation arrangements will be extended to include other parts of the High Court as soon as the necessary administrative arrangements can be made.

2.7 The Administrative Court citation will be given to all judgments in the Administrative Court, whether they are delivered by a Divisional court or by a single judge.

Citation of judgments in court

(*revoked*)

Note—See PD of 24 March 2012: *Citation of Authorities*.

Concluding comments

4.1 The changes described in this practice direction follow what is becoming accepted international practice. They are intended to make it easier to distribute, store and search judgments, and less expensive and time-consuming to reproduce them for use in court. Lord Justice Brooke is still responsible for advising the Judges' Council on these matters, and any comments on these new arrangements, or suggestions about ways in which they could be improved still further, should be addressed to him at the Royal Courts of Justice, WC2A 2LL.

Lord Woolf

Lord Chief Justice

Practice Direction
9 April 2001

Citations: [2001] 1 WLR 1001

Citation of Authorities

Introduction

1 In recent years, there has been a substantial growth in the number of readily available reports of judgments in this and other jurisdictions, such reports being available either in published reports or in transcript form. Widespread knowledge of the work and decisions of the courts is to be welcomed. At the same time, however, the current weight of available material causes problems both for advocates and for courts in properly limiting the nature and amount of material that is used in the preparation and argument of subsequent cases.

2 The latter issue is a matter of rapidly increasing importance. Recent and continuing efforts to increase the efficiency, and thus reduce the costs, of litigation, whilst maintaining the interests of justice, will be threatened if courts are burdened with a weight of inappropriate and unnecessary authority, and if advocates are uncertain as to the extent to which it is necessary to deploy authorities in the argument of any given case.

3 With a view to limiting the citation of previous authority to cases that are relevant and useful to the court, this Practice Direction lays down a number of rules as to what material may be cited, and the manner in which that cited material should be handled by advocates. These rules are in large part such as many courts already follow in pursuit of their general discretion in the management of litigation. However, it is now desirable to promote uniformity of practice by the same rules being followed by all courts.

4 It will remain the duty of advocates to draw the attention of the court to any authority not cited by an opponent which is adverse to the case being advanced.

5 This Direction applies to all courts apart from criminal courts, including within that latter category the Court of Appeal (Criminal Division).

Categories of judgments that may only be cited if they fulfil specified requirements

6.1 A judgment falling into one of the categories referred to in paragraph 6.2 below may not in future be cited before any court unless it clearly indicates that it purports to establish a new principle or to extend the present law. In respect of judgments delivered after the date of this Direction, that indication must take the form of an express statement to that effect. In respect of judgments delivered before the date of this Direction that indication must be present in or clearly deducible from the language used in the judgment.

6.2 Paragraph 6.1 applies to the following categories of judgment:

Applications attended by one party only;
Applications for permission to appeal;
Decisions on applications that only decide that the application is arguable;
county court cases, unless:

(a) cited in order to illustrate the conventional measure of damages in a personal injury case; or
(b) cited in a county court in order to demonstrate current authority at that level on an issue in respect of which no decision at a higher level of authority is available.

6.3 These categories will be kept under review, such review to include consideration of adding to the categories.

Citation of other categories of judgment

7.1 Courts will in future pay particular attention, when it is sought to cite other categories of judgment, to any indication given by the court delivering the judgment that it was seen by that court as only applying decided law to the facts of the particular case; or otherwise as not extending or adding to the existing law.

7.2 Advocates who seek to cite a judgment that contains indications of the type referred to in paragraph 7.1 will be required to justify their decision to cite the case.

Methods of citation

8.1 Advocates will in future be required to state, in respect of each authority that they wish to cite, the proposition of law that the authority demonstrates, and the parts of the judgment that support that proposition. If it is sought to cite more than one authority in support of a given proposition, advocates must state the reason for taking that course.

8.2 The demonstration referred to in paragraph 8.1 will be required to be contained in any skeleton argument and in any appellant's or respondent's notice in respect of each authority referred to in that skeleton or notice.

8.3 Any bundle or list of authorities prepared for the use of any court must in future bear a certification by the advocate responsible for arguing the case that the requirements of this paragraph have been complied with in respect of each authority included.

8.4 The statements referred to in paragraph 8.1 should not materially add to the length of submissions or of skeleton arguments, but should be sufficient to demonstrate, in the context of the advocate's argument, the relevance of the authority or authorities to that argument and that the citation is necessary for a proper presentation of that argument.

Authorities decided in other jurisdictions

9.1 Cases decided in other jurisdictions can, if properly used, be a valuable source of law in this jurisdiction. At the same time, however, such authority should not be cited without proper consideration of whether it does indeed add to the existing body of law.

9.2 In future, therefore, any advocate who seeks to cite an authority from another jurisdiction must:

(i) comply in respect of that authority, with the rules set out in paragraph 8 above;
(ii) indicate in respect of each authority what that authority adds that is not to be found in authority in this jurisdiction; or, if there is said to be justification for adding to domestic authority, what that justification is; and
(iii) certify that there is no authority in this jurisdiction that precludes the acceptance by the court of the proposition that the foreign authority is said to establish.

9.3 For the avoidance of doubt, paragraphs 9.1 and 9.2 do not apply to cases decided in either the European Court of Justice or the organs of the European Convention of Human Rights. Because of the status in English law of such authority, as provided by, respectively, section 3 of the European Communities Act 1972 and section 2(1) of the Human Rights Act 1998, such cases are covered by the earlier paragraphs of this Direction.

Note—See also PD of 24 March 2012: *Citation of Authorities*.

Lord Woolf
Lord Chief Justice

Attorney-General's Memorandum 19 December 2001

Citations: [2002] Fam Law 229

Requests for the Appointment of an Advocate to the Court

Practice Guidance of 26 March 2015—The President has issued guidance on appointments by the Attorney-General of advocates to the court or special advocates in family proceedings. This distinguishes between three separate categories of appointment:

(1) Advocate to the court in cases where points of law may arise;
(2) Special advocate where public interest immunity may arise; and
(3) Instructions in children proceedings where the Official Solicitor or Cafcass (legal) are instructed.

1 The memorandum has been agreed between the Attorney-General and the Lord Chief Justice. It gives guidance about making a request for the appointment of an advocate to the court (formerly called an amicus curiae).

2 In most cases, an advocate to the court is appointed by the Attorney-General, following a request by the court. In some cases, an advocate to the court will be appointed by the Official Solicitor or the Children and Family Court Advisory and Support Service (CAFCASS) (see paras 11 and 12 below).

The role of an advocate to the court

3 A court may properly seek the assistance of an advocate to the court when there is a danger of an important and difficult point of law being decided without the court hearing relevant argument. In those circumstances the Attorney-General may decide to appoint an advocate to the court.

4 It is important to bear in mind that an advocate to the court represents no one. His or her function is to give to the court such assistance as he or she is able on the relevant law and its application to the facts of the case. An advocate to the court will not normally be instructed to lead evidence, cross-examine witnesses, or investigate the facts. In particular, it is not appropriate for the court to seek assistance from an advocate to the court simply because a defendant in criminal proceedings refuses representation.

Circumstances of instruction—An advocate to the court may only be appointed by the Attorney-General in family proceedings where the court has asked for assistance either generally or through the Official Solicitor. Official Solicitor instructions are dealt with at paras 11 and 12. The 26 March 2015 *Guidance* draws attention to the fact that criteria for appointment are likely to be limited to:

- cases where 'there is a danger of an important and difficult point of law being decided' (the guidance stresses the point must be both 'important and difficult'; and
- cases where a 'difficult' point requires decision: this is not confined to cases where there are litigants in person.

Application by the court—Application for an advocate is made by the court (i e not by a party to the proceedings) at case management stage, direct to the Attorney-General (addresses below). The contents of the request are referred to at para 9.

Advocate retained by Attorney-General—The advocate is retained by the Attorney-General and 'represents no one' (for an example in children proceedings, see *H v L and R* (below)).

Examination of vulnerable witnesses; MFPA 1984, s 31G(6)—In *H v L and R* [2007] 2 FLR 162, FD, an advocate to the court was appointed to examine a vulnerable witness, but the appropriateness of this appointment was doubted in *Re K and H (Private Law: Public Funding)* [2016] 1 FLR 754, CA; (sub nom *Re K and H (Children)* (and see under MFPA 1984, s 31(6).

Special advocate—Appointment by the Attorney-General of a special advocate is a separate procedure (as the 26 March 2015 *Guidance* stresses): see **Special advocate to the court** under FPR 2010, r 21.3.

5 The following circumstances are to be distinguished from those where it will be appropriate for the court to seek the assistance of an advocate to the court:

(i) where a point of law which affects a government department is being argued in a case where the department is not represented and where the court believes that the department may wish to be represented;

(ii) where the Attorney believes it is necessary for him to intervene as a party in his capacity as guardian of the public interest;

(iii) where the court believes it is appropriate for a litigant in person to seek free (pro bono) assistance;

(iv), (v) *(applies to criminal proceedings only)*

6 In the first of these five cases, the court may invite the Attorney to make arrangements for the advocate to be instructed on behalf of the department. In the second, the court may grant the Attorney permission to intervene, in which case the advocate instructed represents the Attorney. In neither case is the advocate an advocate to the court.

7 In the third case the court may grant a litigant in person an adjournment to enable him or her to seek free (pro bono) assistance. In doing so, the court should bear in mind that it is likely to take longer to obtain free (pro bono) representation than funded representation. In contrast to an advocate to the court, a free (pro bono) legal representative will obtain his or her instructions from the litigant and will represent the interests of that party. His or her role before the court and duty to the court will be identical to that of any other representative of the parties. Accordingly it will not be appropriate for the court to take such a course where the type of assistance required is that provided by an advocate to the court.

8 *(applies to criminal proceedings only)*

Making a request to the Attorney-General

9 A request for an advocate to the court should be made by the court as soon as convenient after it is made aware of the point of law which requires the assistance of an advocate to the court. The request should set out the circumstances which have occurred, identifying the point of law upon which assistance is sought and the nature of the assistance required. The court should consider whether it would be sufficient for such assistance to be in writing in the form of submissions as to the law, or whether the assistance should include oral submissions at the hearing. The request should ordinarily be made in writing and be accompanied by the papers necessary to enable the Attorney to reach a decision on the basis of a proper understanding of the case.

10 The Attorney will decide whether it is appropriate to provide such assistance and, if so, the form such assistance should take. Before reaching a decision he may seek further information or assistance from the court. The Attorney will also ask the court to keep under review the need for such assistance. Where the circumstances which gave rise to the original request have changed, such that the court may now anticipate hearing all relevant argument on the point of law without the presence of an advocate to the court, either the court or the Attorney may ask the advocate to the court to withdraw.

Requests to the Official Solicitor or CAFCASS

11 A request for an advocate to the court may be made to the Official Solicitor or CAFCASS (Legal Services and Special Casework) where the issue is one in which their experience of representing children and adults under disability gives rise to special experience. The division of responsibility between them is outlined in Practice Notes reported at [2001] 2 FLR 151 and [2001] 2 FLR 155.

12 The procedure and circumstances for requesting an advocate to the court to be appointed by the Official Solicitor or CAFCASS are the same as those applying to requests to the Attorney-General. In cases of extreme urgency, telephone requests may be made. In some cases, the Official Solicitor himself will be appointed as advocate to the court. He may be given directions by the court authorising him to obtain documents, conduct investigations and enquiries and to advise the court. He may appear by counsel or an in-house advocate.

Lord Goldsmith QC
Attorney-General

Lord Woolf
Lord Chief Justice

Requests for an advocate to the court should be addressed as follows:

The Legal Secretary,
The Legal Secretariat to the Law Officers,
Attorney-General's Chambers,
9 Buckingham Gate,
London SW1E 6JP,
tel 020 7271 2417 (criminal), 020 7271 2413 (civil),
fax 020 7271 2434.

Official Solicitor to the Supreme Court,
81 Chancery Lane,
London WC2A 1DD,
tel 020 7911 7127, fax 020 7911 7105.

CAFCASS (Legal Services and Special Casework),
Newspaper House,
8–16 Great New Street,
London EC4A 3BN,
tel 020 7904 0867, fax 020 7904 0868/9.

For information about free (pro bono) services: Bar Pro Bono Unit, 7 Gray's Inn Square, London WC1R 5AZ, tel 020 7831 9711, fax 020 7831 9733, email enquiries@barprobonounit.f9.co.uk.

Note—The address for the Official Solicitor is: Victory House, 30–34 Kingsway, London WC2B 6EX, DX 141423 Bloomsbury 7; email enquiries@offsol.gsi.gov.uk. The address for Cafcass is: 3rd Floor, 21 Bloomsbury Street, London WC1 3HF; tel: 07776 470065.

Protocol January 2003

Citations: [2003] Fam Law 199

Child Abduction Cases between the UK and Pakistan

The President of the Family Division and the Hon Chief Justice of Pakistan in consultation with senior members of the family judiciary of the United Kingdom ('the UK') and the Islamic Republic of Pakistan ('Pakistan'), having met on 15–17 January 2003 in the Royal Courts of Justice in London, reach the following consensus:

WHEREAS:

(a) Desiring to protect the children of the UK and Pakistan from the harmful effects of wrongful removal or retention from one country to the other;

(b) Mindful that the UK and Pakistan share a common heritage of law and a commitment to the welfare of children;

(c) Desirous of promoting judicial cooperation, enhanced relations and the free flow of information between the judiciaries of the UK and Pakistan; and

(d) Recognising the importance of negotiation, mediation and conciliation in the resolution of family disputes;

IT IS AGREED THAT:

1 In normal circumstances the welfare of a child is best determined by the courts of the country of the child's habitual/ordinary residence.

2 If a child is removed from the UK to Pakistan, or from Pakistan to the UK, without the consent of the parent with a custody/residence order or a restraint/interdict order from the court of the child's habitual/ordinary residence, the judge of the court of the country to which the child has been removed shall not ordinarily exercise jurisdiction over the child, save in so far as it is necessary for the court to order the return of the child to the country of the child's habitual/ordinary residence.

3 If a child is taken from the UK to Pakistan, or from Pakistan to the UK, by a parent with visitation/access/contact rights with the consent of the parent with a custody/residence order or a restraint/interdict order from the court of the child's habitual/ordinary residence or in consequence of an order from that court permitting the visit, and the child is retained in that country after the end of the visit without consent or in breach of the court order, the judge of the court of the country in which the child has been retained shall not ordinarily exercise jurisdiction over the child, save in so far as it is necessary for the court to order the return of the child to the country of the child's habitual/ordinary residence.

4 The above principles shall apply without regard to the nationality, culture or religion of the parents or either parent and shall apply to children of mixed marriages.

5 In cases where the habitual/ordinary residence of the child is in dispute the court to which an application is made should decide the issue of habitual/ordinary residence before making any decision on the return or on the general welfare of the child, and upon determination of the preliminary issue as to habitual/ordinary residence should then apply the general principles set out above.

6 These applications should be lodged by the applicant, listed by the court and decided expeditiously.

7 It is recommended that the respective governments of the UK and Pakistan give urgent consideration to identifying or establishing an administrative service to facilitate or oversee the resolution of child abduction cases (not covered by the 1980 Hague Convention on the Civil Aspects of International Child Abduction).

8 It is further recommended that the judiciaries, the legal practitioners and the non-governmental organisations in the UK and Pakistan use their best endeavours to advance the objects of this protocol.

9 It is agreed that the UK and Pakistan shall each nominate a judge of the superior court to work in liaison with each other to advance the objects of this protocol.

SIGNED BY: Dame Elizabeth Butler-Sloss, DBE, President of the Family Division of the High Court of England and Wales and The Hon Mr Justice Sh Riaz Ahmad, Chief Justice of the Supreme Court of Pakistan

Dame Elizabeth Butler-Sloss
President

President's Guidance 21 January 2004

Citations: [2004] 1 FLR 746

UK Passport Applications on Behalf of Children in the Absence of the Signature of a Person with Parental Responsibility

1 This guidance deals with situations in which the court has decided that it is in a child's best interests that s/he be issued with a passport, but the adult/s with parental responsibility have refused to sign the passport application form.

2 This kind of situation might arise where a child is voluntarily accommodated by a local authority and, for example, wishes to go on holiday independently or with his/her carers.

3 The UK Passport Application form is in a standard form which will not be entirely suitable in these kinds of circumstances.

4 The UK Passport Service has therefore agreed that it will be acceptable to complete the form in the following manner:

Sections 1–6

5 These sections must be completed.

Section 7 (Relevant only re: Children aged 16 or 17)

6 If no person with parental responsibility is prepared to sign section 7, and the court has decided that it is in the best interests of the child that a passport be issued to the child, then the section may be left blank provided that the application is accompanied by an order of the court that:

(a) the parent/s (as appropriate) should not use their parental responsibility to veto the application; and
(b) that the court considers it to be in the best interests of the child that a passport be issued.

Section 8

7 This question should be completed if relevant to the application.

Section 9

8 *Where a child is aged 16 or 17*: the child may personally sign this section.

9 *Where a child is aged under 16*: it is imperative that an adult sign this section. In the absence of a person holding parental responsibility, there will presumably be another adult in a position to sign the form (eg the adult with whom the child is going on holiday). It would not be necessary or proper for the judge to sign the form personally.

10 If the adult signing the form is not a parent or guardian with parental responsibility for the child, the section can be manually altered as follows:

(a) Clauses 2, 3, 4 and 6 may be deleted, if any of them causes any concern or difficulty for the adult signing the form.
(b) Clauses 1, 5, 7 and 8 must not be deleted: they are mandatory declarations without which the application will not be processed.

11 If any clauses are deleted in accordance with para 10 above, then the application form must be accompanied by:

(a) An order of the court that:
    (i) the parent/s (as appropriate) should not use their parental responsibility to veto the application; and

(ii) that the court considers it to be in the best interests of the child that a passport be issued; plus

(b) A statement from the adult signing s 9 setting out a written explanation as to why they are making the application on the child's behalf, what their relationship is to the child, and in the case of a child being accommodated by a local authority an explanation from that authority.

12 Additionally, if cl 3 is deleted, then the adult signing the form must instead enter at s 8 a statement in the following terms: 'The person named at s 2 is, to the best of my knowledge and belief, a British national and has not lost or renounced his/her national status'.

Ananda Hall
Family Division Lawyer

Cairo Declaration
17 January 2005

Resulting from Anglo-Egyptian Meetings on Judicial Co-operation in International Child Abduction Matters between Egypt and the UK

Note—The Declaration can be found at *www.reunite.org/edit/files/Library%20-%20International%20 Regulations/Cairo%20Declaration.pdf* and in *Emergency Remedies in the Family Courts* (Family Law).

Cafcass Practice Note
18 March 2005

Citations: [2005] 2 FLR 111

(*amended 25 March 2015*)

Applications for Reporting Restriction Orders

1 *Introduction*

This Note sets out recommended practice in relation to any application in the Family Division founded on Convention rights for an order which restricts freedom of expression and is subject to decisions of the courts.

2 *Statutory provisions*

An application founded on Convention rights need only be made where statutory provisions cannot provide adequate protection. Relevant provisions are Administration of Justice Act 1960, s 12(1); Children and Young Persons Act 1933, s 39; Contempt of Court Act 1981, s 11; Children Act 1989, s 8 (prohibited steps order preventing disclosure of information by parental figure) and s 97(2). While the President's Practice Direction is not aimed at applications under these provisions, s 12(2) of the Human Rights Act 1998 applies to any application for relief which might affect the exercise of the Convention right to freedom of expression and the procedures set out in this Note, including the arrangements for advance notification, can be used to secure compliance with this section in relation to any such application under these provisions.

An order founded on Convention rights may be required, for example, because:

– the need for protection is not linked to particular court proceedings
– the statutory provisions do not prevent publication of all kinds of information
– an injunction is needed to prevent approaches to family, doctors or carers.

3 *Application and evidence*

The application may be a freestanding claim brought under the Part 8 procedure in the Civil Procedure Rules 1998 or it may be made within existing proceedings to which either the CPR or Family Proceedings Rules 1991 apply. It may be appropriate to seek a direction under CPR 39.2(4), where it applies, that the identity of a party or witness should not be disclosed, and for documents to be drafted identifying individuals by initials.

The applicant should prepare (a) the application/claim form (b) a witness statement justifying the need for an order (c) any legal submissions (d) a draft order and (e) an explanatory note.

Model Forms of Order and an example of an explanatory note are attached to this Practice Note.

In the rare event that it is not possible to draft such documentation in the time available before the hearing, the court is likely to require the applicant to file a statement at the earliest opportunity, setting out the information placed orally before the Court.

Subject to any contrary direction of the court, this material should be made available on request to any person who is affected by the order. See *W v H (Family Division: Without Notice Orders)* [2001] 2 WLR 253; [2001] 2 FLR 927.

4 *Service of application*

As required by the Practice Direction, advance notice should normally be given to the national media via the Press Association's CopyDirect service. CopyDirect will be responsible for notifying the individual media organisations who participate in the service. The website: *http://www.medialawyer.press.net/courtapplications* gives details of the organisations represented and instructions for service of the application and sets out the President' Practice Direction on Applications for Reporting Restrictions Orders of 18 March 2005. Unless there is a particular reason not to do so, copies of all the documents referred to above should be served. If there is a reason for not serving some or all of the documents (or parts of them), the applicant should ensure sufficient detail is given to enable the media to make an informed decision as to whether it wishes to attend or be legally represented.

The CopyDirect service does not extend to local or regional media or magazines. If service of the application on any specific organisation or person not covered is required it should be effected directly.

Note—The *Financial Times* and *Sky News* do not participate in the CopyDirect service. These two companies need to be served directly with the notice of application. Similarly, local and regional newspapers or magazines are not served with notice of an application by the CopyDirect service. Note also the judgment of the President in *Re P (Enforced Caesarean: Reporting Restrictions)* [2014] 2 FLR 410, FD, at [46], where he makes observations on the use of the Press Association's CopyDirect Injunctions Alert Service:

> 'Shortly before the hearing a question arose about the operation of the Press Association's CopyDirect Injunctions Alerts Service, use of which is required by PD 12I. In the circumstances it may be useful for me to set out for the attention of a wider audience a most helpful note which was sent to my office on 12 December 2013 by Mike Dodd, legal editor of the Press Association. Having said that he was unable to attend the hearing the following day, and explained that he is the individual with responsibility for oversight of the Press Association's Injunctions Alerts Service, Mr Dodd continued:
>
> "There is a page on the Injunctions Alerts Service website http://www.medialawyer.press.net/courtapplications/mediaorganisations.jsp – which lists the media organisations served, and the relevant telephone numbers, and which states at the top:
>
> 'The notification system serves all the national media (newspapers and broadcasters) with the exception of the Financial Times and Sky News. If notice has to be served on these two companies it needs to be served on them directly.'
>
> The service was also established on the basis that subscribing organisations would be taken to have been served with an application if notification was sent via the service. The system works as follows: Would-be applicants are supposed to call a number, given in the Practice Note, and speak to the Customer Services staff who deal with the service. They then send the documents, electronically (which is easier) or by fax, to the service. These documents are, if necessary, scanned to be put into electronic form, and are then distributed via e-mail alerts to the national media. Distribution is followed up by calls to each of the subscribing organisations to check that service has been received. The service does not:
>
> 1: Serve regional and local newspapers, or magazines
>
> 2: Serve orders which have been obtained from the courts (despite the continuing efforts by some law firms to use it for this purpose).
>
> The website's Home page, and the pages for the Practice Direction, Practice Note and for the Notification system all contain a red-bordered box detailing what it does and not do. The box is the same on all

pages. It will be updated in the New Year, due to increasing use of the service by applicants seeking injunctions in the QBD who are also being required to notify the media of their applications. These mostly are cases involving settlements of medical negligence cases involving children."'

5 The hearing

Any application invoking Convention rights will involve a balancing of rights under Article 8 (right to respect for private and family life) and Article 10 (freedom of expression). There is no automatic precedence as between these Articles, and both are subject to qualification where (among other considerations) the rights of others are engaged. Section 12(4) of the Act requires the court to have particular regard to the importance of freedom of expression. It must also have regard to the extent to which material has or is about to become available to the public, the extent of the public interest in such material being published and the terms of any relevant privacy code or regulation.

6 Scope of order

Persons protected

The aim should be to protect the child or incapacitated adult, rather than to confer anonymity on other individuals or organisations. However, the order may include restrictions on identifying or approaching specified family members, carers, doctors or organisations in cases where the absence of such restriction is likely to prejudice their ability to care for the child or patient, or where identification of such persons might lead to identification of the child or patient and defeat the purpose of the order. In cases where the court receives expert evidence the identity of the experts (as opposed to treating clinicians) is not normally subject to restriction.

Identifying persons protected

Once an order has been made, the details of those protected by the order should normally be contained in the Schedule. In exceptional cases (for example *Leeds NHS Trust-v-A & B* [2003] 1 FLR 1091) where it is not appropriate for details to be given, a description by reference to the facts of the case should be contained in the Schedule to enable those reading the order to identify whether a person is likely to be the subject of the order.

Information already in the public domain

Orders will not usually prohibit publication of material which is already in the public domain, other than in exceptional cases such as *Venables and Thompson-v-News Group Newspapers Ltd* [2001] Fam 430.

Duration of order

Orders should last for no longer than is necessary to achieve the purpose for which they are made. The maximum extent of an order in a child case will usually be the child's 18th birthday.

In some cases a later date may be necessary, to protect safety or welfare, or the anonymity of other children who are named in the order and who are still under age, or to maintain the anonymity of doctors or carers after the death of a patient. See for example:

Re C (Adult Patient: Publicity [1996] 2 FLR 251; *Venables and Thompson-v-News Group Newspapers Ltd* [2001] Fam 430; *X (formerly known as Mary Bell)-v-Y and others* [2003] EWHC QB 1101.

7 Service of orders

Service of orders should be effected in the usual way, in accordance with the Rules. Contact details for the national press and broadcasters can be found at *http://www.medialawyer.press.net/courtapplications*.

Note—The CopyDirect service is not to be used to serve court orders.

PART V

8 *Undertakings in damages*

The court will consider whether it is appropriate to require an applicant to give such an undertaking in an individual case, particularly when an order is made without notice, and will bear in mind the applicant's capacity to fulfil any such undertaking.

9 *Explanatory notes*

It is helpful if applications and orders are accompanied by an explanatory note, from which persons served can readily understand the nature of the case. In any case where notice of an application has not been given, the explanatory note should explain why it cannot be provided. The order should also include a schedule of the names and addresses of those who are covered by the order.

(1) MODEL ORDER

IN THE HIGH COURT OF JUSTICE **Case Number:**
FAMILY DIVISION
[PRINCIPAL REGISTRY]

BEFORE [*JUDGE*] IN PRIVATE

IN THE MATTER OF THE COURT'S INHERENT JURISDICTION

BETWEEN

[ ]

and

[ ]

REPORTING RESTRICTION ORDER

IMPORTANT

If you disobey this order you may be found guilty of contempt of court and may be sent to prison or be fined or have your assets seized. You should read the order carefully and are advised to consult a solicitor as soon as possible. You have the right to ask the Court to vary or discharge the order.

EXPLANATION

A On [*date*] the Court considered an application for a reporting restriction order.

B The following persons and/or organisations were represented before the Court: [*describe parties and their advocates*]

C The Court read the following documents: [*list the documents*]
and/or
The Court directed the [Applicant/Claimant] to file a statement no later than [*date*] setting out the information presented to the court at the hearing.
and/or
The Court directed that copies of the attached Explanatory Note and [*list any other documents*] be made available by the [Applicant/Claimant] to any person affected by this Order.

[D *In a case where an undertaking in damages is required by the Court:*
The Applicant gave an undertaking that if the Court later finds that this Order was obtained as a result of any deliberate or careless misrepresentation by the Applicant, and that this has caused loss to any person served with the Order, and that that person should be compensated, the Applicant will comply with any order the Court may make.]

E *In the case of an order made without notice:*
This order was made without notice to those affected by it, the Court having considered section 12(2) Human Rights Act 1998 and being satisfied (i) that the [Applicant/Claimant] has taken all practicable steps to notify persons affected and/or (ii) that there are compelling reasons for notice not being given, namely: [*set out the Court's reasons for making the order without notice*]

[F *In the case of an application by a local authority:*

The Court granted permission to the Applicant to apply for the exercise of the Court's inherent jurisdiction]

ORDER

1 Duration

Subject to any different order made in the meantime, this order shall have effect

[*in the case of an adult*] during the lifetime of the [Defendant], whose details are set out in Schedule 1 to this order.

[*in the case of a child]* until [*date*], the 18th birthday of the child whose details are set out in Schedule 1 to this order ('the Child').

2 Who is bound

This order binds all persons and all companies (whether acting by their directors, employees or agents or in any other way) who know that the order has been made.

3 Publishing restrictions

This order prohibits the publishing or broadcasting in any newspaper, magazine, public computer network, internet website, sound or television broadcast or cable or satellite programme service of:

(a) the name and address of
  (i) the [Defendant/Child];
  (ii) [*in the case of a child*] the Child's parents ('the parents'), whose details are set out in Schedule 2 to this order;
  (iii) any individual having day-to-day care of or medical responsibility for the [Defendant/Child] ('a carer'), whose details are set out in Schedule 3 to this Order;
  (iv) any residential home or hospital, or other establishment in which the [Defendant/Child] is residing or being treated ('an establishment');
(b) any picture being or including a picture of either the [Defendant/Child], a carer or an establishment;
(c) any other particulars or information relating to the [Defendant/Child];

IF, BUT ONLY IF, such publication is likely to lead to the identification of the [Defendant/Child] as being [*set out the feature of the situation which has led to the granting of the order*].

4 No publication of the text or a summary of this order (except for service of the order under paragraph 7 below) shall include any of the matters referred to in paragraph 3 above.

[5 Restriction on seeking information

This Order prohibits any person from seeking any information relating to the [Defendant/Child] [or the parents] or a carer from any of the following:

(a) the [Defendant/Child];
[(b) the parents];
(c) a carer;
(d) the staff or residents of an establishment.]

6 What is not restricted by this Order

Nothing in this Order shall prevent any person from:

(a) publishing information relating to any part of a hearing in a court in England and Wales (including a coroner's court) in which the court was sitting in public and did not itself make any order restricting publication.
(b) seeking or publishing information which is not restricted by Paragraph 3 above.
(c) inquiring whether a person or place falls within paragraph 3(a) above.
(d) seeking information relating to the [Defendant/Child] while acting in a manner authorised by statute or by any court in England and Wales.

PART V

(e) seeking information from the responsible solicitor acting for any of the parties or any appointed press officer, whose details are set out in Schedule 4 to this order.

(f) seeking or receiving information from anyone who before the making of this order had previously approached that person with the purpose of volunteering information (but this paragraph will not make lawful the provision or receipt of private information which would otherwise be unlawful).

(g) publishing information which before the service on that person of this order was already in the public domain in England and Wales as a result of publication by another person in any newspaper, magazine, sound or television broadcast or cable or satellite programme service, or on the internet website of a media organisation operating within England and Wales.

7 Service

Copies of this Order endorsed with a notice warning of the consequences of disobedience shall be served by the [Applicant/Claimant] (and may be served by any other party to the proceedings)

(a) by service on such newspaper and sound or television broadcasting or cable or satellite or programme services as they think fit, by fax or first class post addressed to the editor (in the case of a newspaper) or senior news editor (in the case of a broadcasting or cable or satellite programme service) or website administrator (in the case of an internet website) and/or to their respective legal departments; and/or

(b) on such other persons as the parties may think fit, by personal service.

8 Further applications about this Order

The parties and any person affected by any of the restrictions in paragraphs 3–5 above may make application to vary or discharge it to a Judge of the High Court on not less than [48 hours] notice to the parties.

SCHEDULE 1

[*The [Defendant/Child]'s Full Name:*

Born:

Address:]

or

[*Information enabling those affected by order to identify the Defendant/Child*]

SCHEDULE 2

[*Similar details of parents*]

SCHEDULE 3

[*Similar details of carers or other persons protected*]

SCHEDULE 4

[*Contact details of responsible solicitor and/or press officer*]

Date of Order: [ ]

(2) EXAMPLE OF EXPLANATORY NOTE

NHS TRUST X v AB

Application for a Reporting Restriction Order

DRAFT EXPLANATORY NOTE

1 AB is a child who suffers from a degenerative disease. An application has been made by the NHS Hospital Trust responsible for his care for the Court's approval of the withdrawal of ventilation. This course is opposed by AB's family.

2 On [date] the application will be heard by the President of the Family Division, who will give judgment in open court.

3 A Reporting Restriction Order has been [made/applied for] to protect AB's right to confidentiality in respect of his medical treatment. This does not restrict publication of information or discussion about the treatment of patients with similar conditions, provided that such publication is not likely to lead to the identification of AB, those caring for him, the NHS Trust concerned or the establishment at which he is being cared for.

Protocol December 2005

Protocol between the National Youth Advocacy Service and the Children and Family Court Advisory and Support Service

This protocol aims to clarify the roles of both agencies representing children in private law proceedings in order to meet, in the best possible way, the needs of all children and families.

General note—The purpose of the Protocol is to facilitate the exchange of information between Cafcass and NYAS when a case passes from one organisation to the other after a judge decides on an appointment.

FPR 1991, r 9.5—References in this Protocol to FPR 1991, r 9.5 should be read as references to FPR 2010, Pt 16, specifically rr 16.2, 16.4, 16.24 and 16.27.

Shared commitments

- Compliance with article 12 of the United Nations Convention on the Rights of the Child
- Improved Services for Children in family proceedings
- A co-ordinated response to changing practice and regional needs

National Youth Advocacy Service

1 NYAS is a UK charity offering socio-legal information, advice and legal representation to children and young people up to the age of 25. NYAS has developed a strong identity as a leading Children's Rights organisation with provision of advocacy services. NYAS has advocates across England and Wales, supported by a Legal Team and a free phone helpline and advice service for children and young people. NYAS also provides separate representation for children and young people where the court considers that such representation is necessary under Rule 9.5 of the Family Proceedings Rules and in line with the Practice Direction of The President of the Family Division of April 2004.[1]

1 [2004] 1 FLR 1188

2 NYAS is committed to Article 12 of the UN Convention of the Rights of the Child. The object of NYAS representing young people is, wherever possible, to protect the young person from the damaging effects of being caught up in legal proceedings. It is a common misconception that children as parties to the proceedings would always give instructions, although they may do so with leave of the court or if they if they are competent to instruct a solicitor directly. A child who is capable of forming his or her own views has the right to express those views in the proceedings with the views being given due weight in accordance with the age and maturity of the child. The child's true wishes and feelings should be put before the court as part of an holistic approach in terms of assessing the whole background and dynamics of the situation. The child should have the opportunity to have their situation represented separately from that of any of the adults.

3 The suitability of NYAS to act as guardian in appropriate cases was approved by Dame Elizabeth Butler-Sloss in the case of *Re A (Separate Representation)*[2]. There are a number of accepted situations in which separate representation of children in private law proceedings is either appropriate or acceptable and NYAS has also been involved in the recent cases *A v A (Shared Residence)*[3] and *Re S (Unco-operative Mother)*[4].

2 [2001] 1 FLR 715; 3 [2004] EWHC 142 Fam; 4 [2004] EWCA Civ 597

PART V

4 It is the policy of NYAS to appoint a caseworker who is an independent social worker and usually a children's guardian in the public law sense. The lawyer and caseworker work in tandem to provide representation for children and young people.

Children and Family Court Advisory and Support Service (CAFCASS)

5 CAFCASS is a Non-Departmental Public Body. The service was established to combine the functions previously carried out by the Family Court Welfare Service provided by the Probation Service, the Children's Branch of the Official Solicitor's Department and the GALRO Service provided by local authorities. Its function is to safeguard the interests of children who are the subject of family proceedings. Social workers employed by CAFCASS are appointed as Family Court Advisers (FCAs) and carry out a number of roles according to the nature of the proceedings in which the child is involved.

CAFCASS duties are to:

– Safeguard and promote the welfare of the child
– Give advice to the court about any application made to it in such proceedings
– Make provision for children to be represented in such proceedings
– Provide information, advice and support for children and their families[5]

5 Criminal Justice and Court Services Act 2000, section 12

Safeguarding and promoting the interests of children

6 CAFCASS' responsibility is to safeguard and promote the interests of individual children who are the subject of family proceedings by providing independent social work advice to the court. In addition to its general duties it meets these responsibilities in some private law Children Act cases where an officer of CAFCASS accepts appointment as guardian under r 9.5 of the Family Proceedings Rules 1991. In these cases the child will always have the benefit of legal representation and the FCA acting as guardian will instruct the solicitor.

7 Certain specialist High Court appointments for children are handled by the CAFCASS High Court Team based at National Office in London. They are responsible for medical treatment cases and cases with particularly complex features.

Children made a party in private law proceedings

8 Rule 9.5 of the Family Proceedings Rules 1991 states:

> '(1) …if in any family proceedings it appears to the court that it is in the best interests of any child to be made a party to the proceedings, the court may appoint –
> (a) an officer of the service
> (b) (if he consents) the Official Solicitor[6]; or
> (c) (if he consents) some other proper person,
>
> to be the guardian ad litem of the child with authority to take part in the proceedings on the child's behalf.'

6 For the Official Solicitor's functions in family cases see Practice Note dated 2 April 2001 [2001] 2 FLR 155. He acts as guardian ad litem of minors who are not subject of the proceedings such as respondent minor parents and child applicants.

Note—Practice Note of 2 April 2001: see now Practice Note of January 2017 (*The Official Solicitor to the Senior Courts: Appointment in Family Proceedings and Proceedings under the Inherent Jurisdiction in Relation to Adults*).

9 The President's Practice Direction makes it clear that the child should only be made a party in a minority of cases featuring issues of significant difficulty. Such decisions are only made by a Circuit Judge, High Court Judge or District Judge in the Principal Registry of the Family Division (unless there are exceptional circumstances when a District Judge can make an order).

10 CAFCASS should be approached first to provide a guardian. The provision of a guardian when requested by the court is a significant and core task for CAFCASS and CAFCASS has a duty to

appoint a guardian and cannot refuse appointment. Guidance has been issued to clarify that where a judge has decided that an appointment under Rule 9.5 is necessary that Service Managers must prioritise the allocation of the case.

National Youth Advocacy Service and CAFCASS working together

11 The National Youth Advocacy Service often provided a guardian in private law proceedings before the inception of CAFCASS when there was limited provision for guardians to be appointed. NYAS has continued to provide such a service particularly where judges have previous experience of their effective work in this area. This is part of NYAS' broader commitment to provide information and advice to children and young people.

12 Since 2001 when CAFCASS was created to provide a service in both public and private law proceedings there has been a considerable growth in rule 9.5 appointments undertaken by CAFCASS. As clarified in the President's Direction it is recognised that in many cases the child will benefit from representation by a guardian who has already met them in their capacity as children and family reporter in the case.

When NYAS may be appointed guardian:

13 The Practice Direction of April 2004 states;

> '5 When a child is made a party and a guardian is to be appointed:
>
> 5.1 Consideration should first be given to appointing an officer of CAFCASS as guardian …
>
> 5.2 If CAFCASS is unable to provide a guardian without delay, or if for some other reason the appointment of a CAFCASS officer is not appropriate, FPR rule 9.5(1) makes further provision for the appointment of a guardian'

14 CAFCASS should be approached first and will usually provide a guardian. However, NYAS may, for example, be asked by the court to provide a guardian in any matter (likely to be long standing) where, despite the best efforts of CAFCASS staff, one or more members of the family can no longer work with the organisation.

General principles

15 Both agencies are committed to effective communication in the best interests of the child in accordance with the law. The normal points of contact should be the CAFCASS service manager and the nominated NYAS lawyer. If any case moves between the two agencies, it is particularly important to pass on information which may assist the work with the child and family, e g aspects of risk management, conflict of interest issues and any particular needs of the child. If NYAS is invited to provide r 9.5 representation where CAFCASS has not been approached, NYAS will discuss the matter with CAFCASS and will be responsible for notifying the court in the first instance.

16 CAFCASS and NYAS will work together to advise the court whenever there appears to be good reason for a guardian not to be appointed e g when there is an alternative preferable route such as a section 37 report from the local authority.

This Protocol will be reviewed in twelve months' time.

Elena Fowler
Chief Executive, NYAS
Anthony Douglas
Chief Executive, CAFCASS

Practice Note
28 July 2006

Citations: [2006] 2 FLR 373

Official Solicitor: Declaratory Proceedings: Medical and Welfare Decisions for Adults who Lack Capacity

****

Explanatory note—This *Practice Note* related to the inherent jurisdiction of the High Court (Family Division) which has been replaced by the jurisdiction of the Court of Protection under MCA 2005. The inherent jurisdiction may still be exercised in respect of vulnerable adults who do not lack capacity but who require protective measures to be put in place: *A Local Authority v DL & Ors* [2012] COPLR 504, CA. There is, however, uncertainty as to the extent or limit of the use of the inherent jurisdiction and the definition of a 'vulnerable adult'.

Practice Note
28 July 2006

Citations: [2006] 2 FLR 354

Official Solicitor, CAFCASS and the National Assembly for Wales: Urgent and Out of Hours Cases in the Family Division of the High Court

1 This Practice Note is issued jointly by the Official Solicitor, the Chief Executive of CAFCASS, and the Chief Executive of CAFCASS Cymru on behalf of the National Assembly for Wales. It describes the procedure to be followed in respect of urgent and out of hours cases in which a decision is sought by a judge of the Family Division of the High Court. It is issued with the approval of the President of the Family Division.

2 In some cases, urgent or out of hours applications become necessary because applications to the court have not been pursued sufficiently promptly. This is undesirable, in particular because urgent applications may be founded on incomplete evidence, inquiries and under-prepared advocacy, and should be avoided where possible. A judge who has concerns that the urgent or out of hours facilities may have been abused may require a representative of the claimant to attend at a subsequent directions hearing to provide an explanation.

3 Whenever possible, urgent applications should be made within court hours. The earliest possible liaison is required with the Clerk of the Rules. It will usually be possible to accommodate a genuinely urgent application (at least for initial directions) in the Family Division applications court, from which the matter may, if necessary and possible, be referred to another judge.

4 When it is not possible to apply within court hours, contact should be made with the security office at the Royal Courts of Justice (020 7947 6000) who will refer the matter to the urgent business officer. The urgent business officer can contact the duty judge. The judge may agree to hold a hearing, either convened at court or elsewhere, or by telephone. When the hearing is to take place by telephone it should be by tape-recorded conference call arranged (and paid for in the first instance) by the claimant's solicitors. Solicitors acting for NHS Trusts or other potential claimants should have standing arrangements with their telephone service providers under which such conference calls can be arranged. All parties (especially the judge) should be informed that the call is being recorded by the service provider. The claimant should order a transcript of the hearing from the service provider.

Adult medical treatment and welfare cases

5 The Official Solicitor will act in urgent cases under the inherent jurisdiction concerning medical treatment to, or the welfare of, an adult who lacks capacity to make decisions for himself or

herself. His office should be contacted at the earliest possible opportunity if an urgent application is envisaged. Where cases arise out of hours the urgent business officer will be able to contact him or his representative. As with cases dealt with on a less urgent basis, evidence is required of incapacity and as to best interests. When written evidence is not available, oral evidence of incapacity must be available. When there is a telephone hearing, oral evidence must be given as part of the conference call.

6 When final evidence either as to capacity or best interests is not available, the court may be willing to grant an interim declaration (r 25.1(1)(b) of the Civil Procedure Rules 1998 (CPR) – *NHS Trust v T (Adult Patient: Refusal of Medical Treatment)* [2004] EWHC 1279 (Fam), [2005] 1 All ER 387). Evidence establishing on the balance of probability that the patient is under incapacity and that the treatment proposed is in his or her best interest must be adduced. An interim injunction to restrain treatment may be granted *Re C (Adult) (Refusal of Treatment)* [1994] 1 WLR 290, [1994] 1 FLR 31.

7 An adult patient must be a party and must be represented through a litigation friend (r 21.3 of the CPR). Notice of an application must be given to the patient (or his or her litigation friend). The claimant may be an NHS Trust, local authority, relative, carer, or the patient. The Official Solicitor stands ready to accept appointment as litigation friend (usually for the patient as defendant) if the conditions for his appointment are shown (either on an interim or final basis) to exist. Should a declaration be made without notice, it is of no effect and may be set aside – *St George's Healthcare NHS Trust v S; R (S) v Collins and Others* [1999] Fam 26, [1998] 2 FLR 728.

Children medical treatment and welfare cases

8 It may be desirable for a child who is the subject of such proceedings to be made a party and represented through a guardian ad litem (usually an officer of CAFCASS or a Welsh Family Proceedings Officer). CAFCASS and CAFCASS Cymru stand ready to arrange for an officer to accept appointment as guardian ad litem. They should be contacted at the earliest opportunity where an urgent application is envisaged. For urgent out of hours applications, the urgent business officer is able to contact a representative of CAFCASS. CAFCASS Cymru is not able to deal with cases that arise out of office hours and those cases should be referred to CAFCASS who will deal with the matter on behalf of CAFCASS Cymru until the next working day. A child of sufficient understanding to instruct his or her own solicitor should be made a party and given notice of any application.

9 Interim declarations/orders under the wardship jurisdiction (or the Children Act 1989) may be made on application either by an NHS trust, a local authority, an interested adult (where necessary with the leave of the court) or by the child if he or she has sufficient understanding to make the application.

General issues

10 Parents, carers or other necessary respondents should be given the opportunity to have independent legal advice or at least to have access to support or counselling.

11 In suitable cases, application may be made for direction providing for anonymity of the parties and others involved in the matter in any order or subsequent listing of the case. Exceptionally, a reporting restriction order may be sought – see the *President's Practice Direction (Applications for Reporting Restriction Orders)* [2005] 2 FLR 120 issued on 18 March 2005.

12 Either the Official Solicitor or CAFCASS, as the case may be, may be appointed by the court as advocate to the court – see Memorandum from the Lord Chief Justice and the Attorney-General reproduced in *The White Book Service 2006, Civil Procedure* (Sweet & Maxwell, 2006) at 39.8.2, especially at 39.8.5.

13 Draft standard form orders for use in urgent and out of hours medical treatment cases are annexed to this note. They should be adapted to suit the individual circumstances of each case.

Consultation with CAFCASS, CAFCASS CYMRU and Official Solicitor

14 Members of the Official Solicitor's legal staff, CAFCASS, and CAFCASS Cymru are prepared to discuss medical cases before proceedings are issued. In all cases in which the urgent and out of hours procedures are to be used it would be helpful if the Official Solicitor, CAFCASS or CAFCASS Cymru have had some advance notice of the application and its circumstances. Inquiries about adult medical and welfare cases should be addressed to a family and medical litigation lawyer at the office of the Official Solicitor, 81 Chancery Lane, London, WC2A, telephone 0207 911 7127, fax number: 0207 911 7105, email: inquiries@offsol.gsi.gov.uk. Inquiries about children medical cases should be directed to the duty lawyer at CAFCASS, 8th Floor, South Quay Plaza 3, 189 Marsh Wall, London, E14 9SH, telephone: 0207 510 7000, fax number: 0207 510 7104. Inquiries about children medical cases in Wales should be directed to the Social Care Team, Legal Services, National Assembly for Wales, Cathays Park, Cardiff, CF10 3NQ, telephone: 02920 826813, fax no: 02920 823834.

Note—The address for the Official Solicitor is: Victory House, 30–34 Kingsway, London WC2B 6EX, DX 141423 Bloomsbury 7; email: enquiries@offsol.gsi.gov.uk. The address for Cafcass is: 3rd Floor, 21 Bloomsbury Street, London WC1 3HF; tel: 07776 470065. This number operates 9–5. The Family Division High Court Judges have access to an out-of-hours number for Cafcass Legal.

Laurence Oates
Official Solicitor
Anthony Douglas
Chief Executive
CAFCASS

Dafydd Ifans
Chief Executive
CAFCASS CYMRU
National Assembly for Wales

ANNEX

OUT OF HOURS ADULT INTERIM DECLARATION AND DIRECTIONS

****

Guidance December 2007

JSB's Equal Treatment Advisory Committee (ETAC) Guidance on Religious Dress

General note—See FPR 2010, r 12.21, **Wearing of veils in court**.

A person's religion or belief can influence the way they dress and present themselves in public. In most instances, such clothing will present few, if any, issues for judges. In practice, there are very few real clashes between the court process and different cultural practices within the UK. There is room for diversity, and there should be willingness to accommodate different practices and approaches to religious and cultural observance.

While there are other examples of religious items of clothing (the Jewish skullcap – the kippahor yarmulke- is one; the Sikh turban another), the issue of religious dress is one that is most likely to arise in relation to the niqab, or full veil, sometimes worn by Muslim women. As the niqab involves the full covering of the face, the judge may have to consider if any steps are required to ensure effective participation and a fair hearing, both for the woman wearing the niqab and other participants in the proceedings. Some useful guidance on the background to and religious significance of the wearing of different styles of Muslim headscarf can be found at *http://news.bbc.co.uk/1/hi/world/middle_east/5411320.stm*.

The following general guidance is designed to assist judges in relation to the matters that should be borne in mind if presented with this issue in courts and tribunals. While there are a range of different possible approaches, depending on the circumstances of the particular case and the individual concerned, the interests of justice remain paramount. In essence, it is for the judge, in any set of circumstances, to consider what difference, if any, would be made to those interests by the niqab being worn. It may well be, that after consideration, there is no necessity to take any steps at all.

A number of judges have provided helpful accounts as to how they have dealt with such situations themselves, and to which we have had regard in formulating the following guidance. It is not possible to give advice here on any specific situation. It is possible, however, to give some indication of the factors to be taken into account in different types of case, and where the woman concerned is fulfilling different roles in the proceedings. It is worth re-emphasising that on this issue, as in so many areas of courtroom practice, there are rarely 'model answers' in terms of a response to a given set of circumstances. Judges may find it helpful to contact Circuit Community Liaison Judges or the judicial members of ETAC if they wish to discuss further any of the issues raised.

It is important to acknowledge from the outset that for Muslim women who do choose to wear the niqab, it is an important element of their religious and cultural identity. To force a choice between that identity (or cultural acceptability), and the woman's involvement in the criminal, civil justice, or tribunal system (as a witness, party, member of court staff or legal office-holder) may well have a significant impact on that woman's sense of dignity and would likely serve to exclude and marginalise further women with limited visibility in courts and tribunals. This is of particular concern for a system of justice that must be, and must be seen to be, inclusive and representative of the whole community. While there may be a diversity of opinions and debates between Muslims about the nature of dress required, for the judicial system the starting point should be respect for the choice made, and for each woman to decide on the extent and nature of the dress she adopts.

Different roles

As in all walks of life, the justice system should encourage practices which will enable as many people as possible to participate and engage with judicial processes as effectively as possible in whatever position, whether as witnesses, complainants, jurors, judicial office-holders, advocates or court staff. Each situation should be considered individually in order to find the best solution in each case.

Essentially, any consideration concerning the wearing of the niqab should be functional; that is, on the basis that the niqab prevents a person from seeing a woman's face. The primary question that needs to be asked by any judicial office holder before coming to a decision is: What is the significance of seeing this woman's face to the judicial task that I have to fulfil? How does being capable of observing her facial expressions impact on the court's decision-making, given her particular role in the proceedings? A distinction can be made, therefore, between situations where this may be useful or important (for example, when assessing the evidence of a witness, particularly whose evidence is in dispute), situations where it is essential (for example, for purposes of identification), and other situations where it may not be of any relevance (for example, arguably, for court clerks or ushers).

As a judge. It is where the woman concerned is providing the 'face' of justice – as a judge, magistrate or tribunal member – that the question of the 'transparency of justice' might be said most obviously to come into play. Is the constituency which is served by the courts entitled to see the person dispensing justice? In reality, it will be rare for a set of circumstances to arise in which another judicial office-holder is called upon to make a decision on this point. Questions relating to the appointment of judges and the terms under which they hold office are matters for the Lord Chief Justice or other appropriate members of the senior judiciary, to whom the matter should be referred if the question arises.

As a juror. There may be circumstances where a judge has to hear a challenge for cause on the inclusion of a woman wearing the full veil as a member of a jury. The judge may feel the challenge justified and excuse her from serving on that jury, with the proviso that she may serve on another where no such challenge is made. Here, the decision must depend to a degree on the view of the parties to the particular case. But caution needs to be exercised, as in all such challenges, that there is a genuine and legitimate basis for such a challenge, based on the particular circumstances of the case. There may well be situations in which such a juror would be welcomed by the parties, or one party at least, as having some insight which may be relevant to the task of the jury in the case.

Steps are under way to enable the JSB to give guidance on what judges should say in summing up to a jury, where one of the witnesses or the defendant is wearing a niqab.

As a victim or complainant. The primary aim is, as stated before, to ensure a fair hearing. What needs to be considered, therefore, is: What is required to enable a woman wearing a niqab to participate in the legal process, to facilitate her ability to give her best evidence and to ensure, so far as practicable, a fair hearing for both sides? It should not automatically be assumed that any difficulty is created by a woman in court, in whatever capacity, who chooses to wear a niqab. Nor should it ever be assumed without good reason that it is inappropriate for a woman to give evidence in court wearing the full veil. Where, for example, the case involves domestic abuse or the possible abuse of her children, the judge may consider it contrary to the interests of justice to make her choose between giving evidence to secure a conviction and wearing the full veil.

Generally speaking, a woman who wears a niqab would do so because it enables her to participate in a public space, such as a court. In situations where a fair hearing may require a woman to remove her niqab, or where she feels she may be able to participate more effectively without her niqab, however, there are a whole variety of special measures available to the court (e.g. live link, screens, clearing the public gallery) that may be considered. The most appropriate course will depend on the issues in the case. As with any consideration of the permitted special measures in a criminal or family case, this is a point on which a decision should ideally be reached after discussion at a preparatory or preliminary hearing, rather than at a final hearing in open court.

As with all practices, the response must be thoughtful and sensitive. If having considered the nature of the case, the nature of the evidence and the prevailing circumstances, it is the view of the judicial office holder that he or she cannot properly ensure fairness or record the evidence fully in a way that will do justice to the case, then careful consideration will need to be given to asking the woman concerned whether she would remove simply that part of the veil that covers the main part of her face. It should be fully explained what the difficulty is, and why the judge considers that he or she will be in difficulty in properly fulfilling the judicial decision-making task and in ensuring fairness to all sides. Having given that explanation, one option might be to allow a short adjournment to enable the woman concerned to seek guidance or advice or possibly to enable her to attend court differently attired, or perhaps for the court to be cleared of anyone other than those directly involved with the case.

As a witness or defendant. For a witness or defendant, similarly, a sensitive request to remove a veil, with no sense of obligation or pressure, maybe appropriate, but careful thought must be given to such a request. The very fact of appearing in a court or tribunal will be quite traumatic for many, and additional pressure may well have an adverse impact on the quality of evidence given. Any request to remove a veil should be accompanied by an explanation by the judge of their concern that, where there are crucial issues of credit, the woman might be at a disadvantage if the judge or jury is not able to assess her demeanour or facial expressions when responding to questions. The witness or party may wish to discuss the matter with her legal representative or witness support worker.

It is worth emphasising that while it may be more difficult in some cases to assess the evidence of a woman wearing a niqab, the experiences of judges in other cases have shown that it is often possible to do so, depending on all the circumstances – hence the need to give careful thought to whether the veil presents a true obstacle to the judicial task. Responses, behaviour and manner in which a person delivers evidence can be affected anyway by a range of matters, including social and cultural background and ethnicity or the effects of injury or disability. It will always be necessary to have regard to these factors in assessing the extent to which a person's demeanour or the way in which they give evidence otherwise assists in weighing or evaluating their evidence. Can it be said, in the circumstances of the particular case, that any assessment will be different where the judge is able to see the witness's face? In a criminal case, the position should be explained in the absence of the jury and the possibility considered of offering the use of permitted special measures, for example a TV link.

Where identification is an issue, then it must be dealt with appropriately, and may require the witness to make a choice between giving evidence in the case whilst showing her face, and not being able to be a witness.

Whilst not exact analogies, there are, of course, other circumstances in which a judge will take evidence without being able to see the face of the witness – for example, where evidence is taken on the phone, or where the judge is visually-impaired.

Sitting as a magistrate, or on other judicial tribunals of more than one member. Sitting as a magistrate, and therefore as one of a panel of three, can raise its own issues. The aim is, of course, the same – that is, to weigh and accurately evaluate the evidence of every witness appearing in the magistrates' court. As in the Crown Court, that assessment is based upon a number of different factors, and the degree to which it is relevant or necessary to that assessment to see a woman's face may depend on the type of case, and the nature of the evidence that the witness gives.

Taking all this into account (and the effect that a range of matters may have on the manner in which a person delivers their evidence, as acknowledged above), there may still be a concern about hearing and weighing the evidence from a woman whose face is veiled and whose expression is invisible.

It is possible that not all the panel will agree on the best way of proceeding. If any one of the magistrates is of the view that he or she may be disadvantaged in assessing the witness, then the magistrates should retire and discuss the most appropriate course of action. This is not to be decided on a majority decision because each magistrate must be faithful to his or her oath. If, following discussion, the question of a veil remains a matter for concern, such a course of action may well include asking the defendant or witness to remove that part of the veil which covers her face and to consider what might be done to facilitate a resolution to the difficulty.

If the court does decide to ask a defendant or witness to remove that part of the veil which covers the face, it should be fully explained that the reason for the request is that the role of the magistrates is to weigh and evaluate the evidence presented in court and that, in order to make that evaluation, magistrates draw on the full range of information available to them. This includes the oral evidence of witnesses whether called by the prosecution or the defence. In relation to witnesses (and the defendant generally), that evaluation also involves, to some extent, an assessment of the way in which the person gives that evidence, how each responds or reacts to questions to even to other people in court. In every case, magistrates will always try their best to do justice in the case before them and while the way in which evidence is given may only be part of the assessment, in certain cases they may feel that they cannot be assured that they can provide a fair and just assessment of all the evidence without seeing the defendant/witness's face during the course of the hearing, thereby potentially creating disadvantage. This is because the magistrate will not have had the benefit of what they consider to be the best evidence and as a result they may feel that their ability to ensure fairness to all sides is affected. It would need to be made clear that, whilst demeanour and facial expressions will not be allowed to over-influence the consideration given to any case, these features may be able to assist magistrates when weighing up the evidence.

As an advocate. In the case of those who wish to practise as an advocate different considerations should be borne in mind. A general policy enabling the judiciary to decide whether the wearing of the niqab should be permitted or refused on a case by case basis would place Muslim women advocates, and their clients, at a disadvantage where the woman concerned felt unable to appear in a court or tribunal without her veil. This is because she would be unable to say in advance of any hearing whether the judge would allow her to appear in her niqab. The starting point should therefore be that she is entitled to appear as an advocate when wearing it.

Once again the interests of justice will be paramount and the judge may need to consider whether, in any particular circumstances which arise, the interests of justice are being impeded by the fact that the advocate's face cannot be seen. In reality, in the absence of any question relating to identification, there are few instances where an advocate or representative appearing in a niqab would be likely to present any real issue. Such concerns would be likely to centre round the fact that the woman could not be heard, rather than seen. So long as the advocate can be heard reasonably clearly it is unlikely that the interests of justice will be impeded. Just as in any case where a judge might have difficulty in hearing any party, witness or advocate, sensitively enquiring whether they can speak any louder or providing other means of amplification should suffice and such measures should be considered with the advocate before asking her to remove her veil.

Judge craft

As with so much guidance in this bench book, the best way of proceeding comes down to basic good judge craft. There is room for diversity in our system of justice, and there should be willingness to accommodate different practices and approaches to religious and cultural observance. A good understanding of the special measures that may be of use in the particular case, and of the need to identify the need for such adaptations at a preliminary hearing, are key.

When an issue relating to the wearing of the niqab does arise, the judicial office-holder must reach a decision on how to proceed having regard to the interests of justice in the particular case. This will include combining sensitivity to any expressed wish not to remove the niqab with a clear explanation, where appropriate, of the reasons for any request for its removal, and the disadvantages for the judge of not removing it. In many cases, there will be no need for a woman to remove her niqab, provided that the judge is of the view that justice can be properly served.

President's Guidance
3 October 2008

Listing Final Hearings in Adoption Cases

1 This Guidance is issued with the purpose of clarifying the legal requirements and practical arrangements for final hearings in adoption applications.

2 This Guidance does not apply to any case where the child has been freed for adoption under the provisions of the Adoption Act 1976 or where the parent or guardian of the child cannot be found.

3 In this Guidance:

(a) 'the 2002 Act' means the Adoption and Children Act 2002;

(b) any reference to a rule by number is a reference to the rule so numbered in the Family Procedure (Adoption) Rules 2005.

4 Section 141(3) of the 2002 Act and rule 31 place an obligation on the court officer to give to the persons listed in rule 31, including birth parent(s) with parental responsibility, notice of the date and place of the final hearing of an adoption application.

5 The requirement to give notice is mandatory. Notice of the final hearing must be given to any person listed in rule 31 who can be found and there is no discretion to dispense with such notice. The provisions of rule 39 (power of court to dispense with service) do not apply to notice of the final hearing. By rule 32(1) any person who has been given notice under rule 31 has the right to attend the final hearing and, except where rule 32(2) applies, to be heard on the question of whether an adoption order should be made.

6 In some cases the welfare of the child will require arrangements to be made to ensure that the birth parent(s) and the applicant(s) or the child do not meet at or in the vicinity of the court. This will apply particularly to proceedings in which a serial number has been assigned to the applicant

under rule 20(2); rule 20(4)(b) provides that, in such a case, the proceedings will be conducted with a view to securing that the applicant is not seen by or made known to any party who is not already aware of his identity except with his consent.

7 Rule 32(6) provides that the court cannot make an adoption order unless the applicant and the child personally attend the final hearing. However, rule 32(6) is subject to rule 32(7), which gives the court a discretion to direct that the applicant or the child need not attend the final hearing; this provision permits the court, where appropriate, to direct that the attendance of the applicant or the child or both of them at the final hearing is not required.

8 When giving directions for the conduct of the final hearing of an adoption application, the court should consider in particular: whether to give a direction under r 32(7) that the applicant or the child need not attend the hearing; whether to give a direction under r 32(4) that any person must attend the hearing; whether arrangements need to be made to ensure that the birth parent(s) and the applicant or the child do not meet at or in the vicinity of the court; the arrangements for ensuring that the ascertainable wishes and feelings of the child regarding the adoption decision are placed before the court; the facilities at the place where the final hearing is to take place, including the availability of suitable accommodation and the use of any electronic information exchange and video or telephone conferencing links.

9 In proceedings in which a serial number has been assigned to the applicant under rule 20(2), it will generally be appropriate to excuse the attendance of the child at the final hearing. It may also be appropriate to excuse the attendance of the applicant, if necessary to ensure that confidentiality is preserved. Where in such a case the attendance of the applicant is required, arrangements must be made to ensure that the applicant is not seen by or made known to any party who is not already aware of his identity.

10 In any case in which a direction is given that the applicant or the child need not attend the final hearing, the order and any notice of hearing issued by the court must state clearly that the applicant or the child, as the case may be, should not attend.

11 Each Adoption Centre and each magistrates' court which hears family proceedings must have arrangements in place to provide information to the relevant parties about any special arrangements made for their attendance at and the conduct of the final hearing.

12 The application for an adoption order should be determined at the hearing of which notice has been given under rule 31. If the application is not determined at that hearing, notice of the adjourned final hearing should be given under rule 31 and this Guidance shall apply equally to the adjourned hearing.

13 Where an adoption order is made in the absence of the applicant or the child, the court should consider making facilities available for a celebratory event. The event should not normally be held before the expiry of the appeal period (generally 14 days). Except in exceptional circumstances, the judge or, in the magistrates' court at least one of the magistrates, who made the adoption order should host the celebratory event. Arrangements for the celebratory event should be made with the applicant(s) by the court.

Note—In *Re W (Adoption Order: Leave to Oppose); Re H (Adoption Order: Application for Permission for Leave to Oppose)* [2014] 1 FLR 1266, CA, this *Guidance* was modified to the effect that at the conclusion of the final hearing, if the court has determined that an adoption order should be made then there is no harm in announcing that that is the outcome; however, the actual adoption order should not be made (and no celebratory hearing with the child should occur) until the parent's time for applying for permission to appeal has expired. See also *Re W (Adoption: Procedure: Conditions)* [2016] 1 FLR 454, CA.

Practice Direction 6 November 2008

Citation: [2009] 1 FLR 373

Enforcement of Children Act 1989 Contact Orders: Disclosure of Information to Officers of the National Probation Service (High Court and County Court)

This Practice Direction is issued by the President of the Family Division with the agreement of the Lord Chancellor.

1 This Practice Direction applies to proceedings in the High Court or a county court where:

(a) the court is considering an application for an enforcement order[1] or for an order following an alleged breach of an enforcement order[2] and asks an officer of the Service or a Welsh family proceedings officer to provide information to the court in accordance with section 11L(5) of the Children Act 1989; or

1 Under section 11J of the Children Act 1989.
2 Under paragraph 9 of Schedule A1 to the Children Act 1989.

(b) the court makes an enforcement order or an order following an alleged breach of an enforcement order and asks an officer of the Service or a Welsh family proceedings officer to monitor compliance with that order and to report to the court in accordance with section 11M of the Children Act 1989.

2 In all cases in which paragraph 1 applies, the officer of the Service or Welsh family proceedings officer will need to discuss aspects of the court case with an officer of the National Probation Service.

3 In order to ensure that the officer of the Service or Welsh family proceedings officer will not potentially be in contempt of court by virtue of such discussions, the court should, when making a request under section 11L(5) or section 11M of the Children Act 1989, give leave to that officer to disclose to the National Probation Service such information (whether or not contained in a document filed with the court) in relation to the proceedings as is necessary.

4 This Practice Direction comes into force on 8 December 2008.

The Right Honourable Sir Mark Potter
President of the Family Division and Head of Family Justice

Practice Direction 6 November 2008

Enforcement of Children Act 1989 Contact Orders: Disclosure of Information to Officers of the National Probation Service (Magistrates' Court)

This Practice Direction is issued by the Lord Chief Justice with the agreement of the Lord Chancellor.

1 This Practice Direction applies to proceedings in the magistrates' court where:

(a) the court is considering an application for an enforcement order[1] or for an order following an alleged breach of an enforcement order[2] and asks an officer of the Service or a Welsh family proceedings officer to provide information to the court in accordance with section 11L(5) of the Children Act 1989; or

1 Under section 11J of the Children Act 1989.
2 Under paragraph 9 of Schedule A1 to the Children Act 1989.

(b) the court makes an enforcement order or an order following an alleged breach of an enforcement order and asks an officer of the Service or a Welsh family proceedings officer to monitor compliance with that order and to report to the court in accordance with section 11M of the Children Act 1989.

2 In all cases in which paragraph 1 applies, the officer of the Service or Welsh family proceedings officer will need to discuss aspects of the court case with an officer of the National Probation Service.

3 In order to ensure that the officer of the Service or Welsh family proceedings officer will not potentially be in contempt of court by virtue of such discussions, the court should, when making a request under section 11L(5) or section 11M of the Children Act 1989, give leave to that officer to disclose to the National Probation Service such information (whether or not contained in a document filed with the court) in relation to the proceedings as is necessary.

4 This Practice Direction comes into force on 8 December 2008.

Lord Chief Justice

'officer of the service'—See CJCSA 2000, s 11(3).

President's Guidance 22 April 2009

Citation: [2009] 2 FLR 167

Applications Consequent upon the Attendance of the Media in Family Proceedings

1 The Government's announcement about the attendance of the media at hearings in family proceedings (see *Family Justice in View* Cm 7502, December 2008) has been implemented by a change to the Family Proceedings Rules made by *The Family Proceedings (Amendment) (No 2) Rules 2009* SI 2009 No 857 (county court and High Court) and *The Family Proceedings Courts (Miscellaneous Amendments) Rules 2009* SI 2009 No 858 (magistrates' courts) and two Practice Directions *Attendance of Media Representatives at Hearings in Family Proceedings* dated 20th April 2009 made by the President to support the rule changes in the respective courts.

2 In the county court and High Court media attendance is implemented by the change to FPR Rule 10.28. (to which the Practice Direction applies). Change regarding media attendance in the family proceedings courts is introduced through amendment to the Family Proceedings Courts (Children Act 1989) Rules 1991, with the insertion of rule 16A.

3 In broad terms the changes for the county court and the High Court relating to media attendance permit duly accredited representatives of news gathering and reporting organisations, and any other unaccredited person whom the court permits, to be present at hearings of all family proceedings (defined by s 32 Matrimonial and Family Proceedings Act 1984) except hearings conducted for the purposes of judicially assisted conciliation or negotiation. They also provide that the court can exclude media representatives

4 For the county court and the High Court, the change relates to most of the proceedings which are for the time being heard in private. It therefore covers a wide range of proceedings including for example public and private law proceedings under the Children Act 1989 and claims for ancillary relief under the Matrimonial Causes Act 1973.

5 Representatives of newspapers or news agencies are admitted to the family proceedings courts under section 69 (2) Magistrates' Courts Act 1980. Media attendance will now be regulated by the insertion of rule '16A Restrictions on presence of persons at directions appointment and hearing'. Duly accredited representatives of news gathering and reporting organisations are not entitled to be present at hearings conducted for the purposes of judicially assisted conciliation or negotiation. They may also be excluded for reasons set out in rule 16A(3).

PART V

6 In respect of the county court and the High Court the new Part 11 of the FPR, and in respect of the family proceedings court the new Part 11C of the Family Proceedings Courts (Children Act 1989) Rules 1991 as amended, regarding communication of information only apply to proceedings concerning children. In particular, they do not apply to proceedings for ancillary relief. Nor do they expressly cover communication of information to representatives of the media.

7 As appears from the Practice Direction governing the county court and High Court, it is a premise of the change for these courts that the proceedings remain proceedings held in private and that therefore the existing position relating to the publication of matters relating to proceedings which are so heard continues to apply, both whilst the proceedings continue and when they have ended (see the Practice Direction paras 2.4 and 2.5)

8 Useful summaries of the position relating to the publication of matters relating to proceedings heard in private can be found in: *Clayton v Clayton* [2006] EWCA Civ 878 [2007] 1 FLR 11 (in particular at paragraphs 23 to 60, 82 to 85, 92 to 104 and 118 to 136 and *Re B (A Child) (Disclosure)* [2004] EWHC 411 (Fam), [2004] 2 FLR 142 (in particular at paragraphs 62 to 82 (on s 12 AJA 1960) and 83 to 107 (on the jurisdiction to relax or increase the statutory restrictions on publication). Other useful cases are listed in the footnote to this paragraph.[1]

1 *Re S (A Child) (Identification: Restrictions on Publication)* [2004] UKHL 47, [2005] 1 AC 593; *Pelling v Bruce-Williams (Secretary of State for Constitutional Affairs Intervening)* [2004] EWCA Civ 845, [2004] Fam 155, [2004] 2 FLR 823; *Re Webster; Norfolk County Council v Webster and Others (No 1)* [2006] EWHC 2733 (Fam), [2007] 1 FLR 1146; *Re Webster; Norfolk County Council v Webster and Others (No 2)* [2006] EWHC 2898 (Fam), [2007] 2 FLR 415; *Re B; X Council v B* [2007] EWHC 1622 (Fam), [2008] 1 FLR 482; *Re B; X Council v B (No 2)* [2008] EWHC 270 (Fam), [2008] 1 FLR 1460; *BBC v Cafcass* [2007] EWHC 616 (Fam), [2007] 2 FLR 765; *Oldham Metropolitan Borough Council v GW & PW* [2007] EWHC 136 (Fam), [2007] 2 FLR 597.

9 It is to be noted that the above decisions all concern the interests and welfare of children and that the approach in ancillary relief proceedings (which are also likely to be productive of media applications) has not been the subject of similar judicial consideration and guidance.

10 The new Rules and the Practice Directions include provisions relating to the exclusion of media representatives but are silent on the approach to be taken by the courts to the exercise of their discretion in respect of other issues which may well arise as a consequence of the attendance of media representatives at hearings in family proceedings. In this respect the Government declined to adopt the recommendation of the High Court judges to address the detail of such issues when introducing the change. It is therefore left to the courts to determine how such issues are to be approached and decided. It is clear that a principled approach to such issues should be applied by the courts and that this can only properly be developed by the courts with the benefit of full argument from the interested parties.

Note—The reference to a 'discretion' to exclude the media is a misnomer: see *Re Child X (Residence and Contact: Rights of Media Attendance – FPR r 10.28(4)* [2009] 2 FLR 1467, FD.

11 The change to admit media representatives to hearings in family proceedings in county courts and the High Court is likely to give rise to a number of issues relating to the exercise of discretion by all levels of court. In particular it is likely that courts will quickly be faced with applications for the provision of documents to media representatives present in court to enable them the better to follow the substance of the proceedings. If minded to grant such application, the court will need to consider the terms of any restriction relating to the use (and in particular the publication) of information contained in any such documents provided to media representatives as a condition of their being so provided.

12 In cases involving children, applications, whether by the media or the parties, are also likely to raise issues as to

(i) The proper application of the existing statutory provisions restricting the publication of the identity of children and information relating to proceedings heard in private;
(ii) the adequacy of the protection afforded in children cases by Section 12 of the Administration of Justice Act 1960 ('AJA 1960') which, inter alia, does not extend to the identity of the parties or witnesses;
(iii) the effect of the publication of any anonymised judgment;

and whether or not injunctive relief may be required upon a wider basis.

13 In relation to the need for injunctive relief in cases affecting children, particularly in local courts, it may be necessary to consider how far it is appropriate to protect from identification not only the children and the parties, but also witnesses and others whose identities will be known locally as associated with the child or his family.

14 Finally, there will be issues over the need on child welfare grounds for protection to extend beyond the end of the hearing (see paragraph 2.5 of the respective Practice Directions).

15 No doubt the basic opposing arguments in relation to the question of access to documents will be, on the one hand, that the Government has sought to retain the basic structure and rationale of the long standing policy of privacy in relation to children proceedings, while at the same time admitting the press, to avoid charges of 'secret justice' and to promote better understanding of the working of the family courts. For these purposes, however, access to court documents is not generally necessary or desirable having regard to their confidential nature.

16 On the other hand, the media may argue that, particularly in those cases where there is not a formal oral opening, they should be enabled to see statements and documents filed in order fully to understand the nature and progress of the proceedings, and so as to be able to publish articles, within appropriate reporting constraints, about the cases which they attend. In this connection, it is likely, if not inevitable, that in individual cases of high interest to the media, courts at all levels and all over the country will be faced with detailed legal argument relating to rival Convention Rights, public and private interests, the welfare of children, and the construction and application of the primary and secondary legislation.

17 Inconsistency of approach in children cases as to the principles to be applied to the determination of such issues on the part of the courts, parties, witnesses, other persons involved in the relevant events (eg social workers and doctors) and the media could well give rise to justified criticism on grounds of uncertainty. It would not promote the public interest in the proper administration of justice and could be damaging to children.

18 So far as ancillary relief proceedings are concerned, policy, privacy and Convention issues may also arise for decision, albeit the interests of children may not be engaged.

19 The purpose of this guidance is therefore to try to avoid, or at least to minimise, inconsistency by providing that decisions are made by the High Court (and the Appellate Courts) as soon as possible as to the principled approach to be taken. Its purpose is also to provide that, until that is done, delay in decision making in individual cases, (particularly those concerning children) should be avoided. It is to be hoped that the media will co-operate in these aims.

20 Pending the availability of formal judicial guidance from the High Court or Court of Appeal as to the principled approach to be adopted, all County Courts and Magistrates' Courts hearing family proceedings should carefully consider adopting the following course:

(i) The court should deal in accordance with the Rules and Practice Directions with any application made for exclusion of the media from the proceedings or any part of them on any of the grounds set out in the Practice Directions.

(ii) Where a representative of the media in attendance at the proceedings applies to be shown court documents, the court should seek the consent of the parties to such representative being permitted (subject to appropriate conditions as to anonymity and restrictions upon onward disclosure) to see such summaries, position statements and other documents as appear reasonably necessary to a broad understanding of the issues in the case.

(iii) If the objection of any of the parties is maintained, then in any case where the objecting party demonstrates reasonably arguable grounds for resisting disclosure of the document or documents sought, no order for disclosure should be made, but the following course of action should be considered.

(iv) If considered necessary or appropriate the court should transfer (or, in the case of a

PART V

family proceedings court, take the first step to bring about an urgent transfer of) the proceedings to the High Court for the determination of any disclosure and/or reporting issues.

(v) Alternatively, in order to avoid delay in decision making on the substantive issues in the case, the court should adjourn determination of any disclosure and/or reporting issues pending a decision by the High Court (or the Appellate Courts) on the principled approach to be taken to them and should make any necessary interim orders in accordance with the argument mentioned in paragraph 15 above in order to secure the position meanwhile.

(vi) Similarly, if a representative of the media applies for reporting restrictions to be lifted during the currency of a case, in the absence of agreement between the parties the court should consider following one or the other of the alternative steps set out in sub-paragraphs (iv)–(v) above.

(vii) If injunctive relief is sought restraining publication based on Convention rights rather than statutory provisions, the matter should in any event be transferred to the High Court to be dealt with under the *President's Practice Direction (Applications for Reporting Restriction Orders)* 18 March 2005 and the *Practice Note (Official Solicitor: Deputy Director of Legal Services CAFCASS: Applications for Reporting Restriction Orders* [2005] 2 FLR 111 and, if interim injunctive relief appears necessary under threat of publication before such application can be dealt with by a High Court judge, the county court should comply with s 12(2) of Human Rights Act 1998.

Note—The President has given guidance on the approach to be adopted when considering whether to exclude the media from hearings in *Re Child X* (above).

21 The underlying aim of this guidance is to seek to ensure that the principled approach to be taken is determined by the High Court (and the Appellate Courts) as soon as possible and that in the interim changes of practice do not take place which may not accord with that principled approach. Though this may result in delayed rulings on some early contested applications involving arguments such as those mentioned in paragraphs 15 and 16 above, it may be considered desirable, in the absence of legislative guidance, that such rulings should only be made on the basis of authoritative judicial guidance following proper determination, with the benefit of full argument, of the relevant principled approach for the longer term.

22 To assist in the early determination of the principled approach:

(i) Arrangements will be made in the High Court to identify appropriate test cases and for their early determination, and

(ii) Arrangements will be made to seek to ensure that directions are given as soon as is practicable in any proceedings that are transferred to the High Court because they raise substantial issues arising from the attendance of media representatives

(iii) Proceedings which are transferred to the High Court other than in the PRFD should be put before a family High Court Judge on circuit or, failing the presence on circuit of a High Court Judge, before the Family Division Liaison Judge as an urgent application for directions.

Sir Mark Potter
President of the Family Division

Best Practice Guide August 2009

Note—Applications for care and supervision orders under CA 1989, s 31 are Pt IV proceedings for the purpose of FPR PD36C, para 6.1 and as such are subject to the provisions of FPR 2010, Pt 12 and the revised Public Law Outline (PLO) contained in the Annex to FPR PD36C. See in particular Case management hearing, Further case management hearing and Issues resolution hearing in FPR PD36C.

Preparing for Care and Supervision Proceedings

A best practice guide for use by all professionals involved with children and families pre-proceedings and in preparation for applications made under section 31 of the Children Act 1989.

Produced by the Care Proceedings Programme, Ministry of Justice, August 2009.

Foreword

This comprehensive best practice guide is based on the findings of inter-agency workshops and has been extensively peer reviewed. It sets out examples and puts forward suggestions as to how we can all work together, valuing and understanding the work and roles of colleagues, and puts the needs of the child firmly back at the heart of care proceedings.

The guide will complement the Statutory Guidance and Public Law Outline but it is not intended to be prescriptive. However, it describes the processes involved; the respective roles of those involved; tackles some of the most difficult and frequently raised areas of uncertainty; and provides examples of good practice. It also acts as a sign post towards the regulations and Statutory Guidance on specific issues and is one of a range of measures aimed at developing a consistent and practical approach to care proceedings.

The publication of this guide is particularly timely in view of the recommendations in Lord Laming's report 'The Protection of Children in England: A progress report', published in March 2009. The UK Government has accepted all 58 of Lord Laming's recommendations, and published an action plan on 6 May 2009, setting out the detailed response to the recommendations. The action plan is available at: *www.everychildmatters.gov.uk/laming*.

Note—The action plan can be found at *www.education.gov.uk/publications/eOrderingDownload/DCSF-Laming.pdf*.

The Welsh Assembly Government has put in place a programme of measures to strengthen arrangements to safeguard children. These include new arrangements to establish teams to provide intensive support to families whose children may be subject of a care order.

The guide has the full support of the National Family Justice Board. We would like to express our thanks to all those practitioners who have co-operated and contributed to this publication and in particular to the Family Law Bar Association and the Law Society for their endorsement.

PART V

Contents

Abbreviations

Chapter 1 – Introduction

1.1	Background to the reforms	
1.2	The status of this best practice guide	
1.3	Who should read this guide	
1.4	How to use this guide	
Chapter 2 – Pre-proceedings stages		Who should read*
2.1	Introduction	all
2.2	Social work	sw
2.3	The Legal Gateway/Planning Meeting	sw, lfLA
2.4	The Letter before Proceedings (LbP)	sw, lfLA, lfp
2.4.1	Ownership	sw, lfLA
2.4.2	Timing	sw, lfLA
2.4.3	Contents	sw, lfLA
2.4.4	Plans and Agreements	sw, lfLA
2.4.5	Communicating messages	sw, lfLA
2.5	The Pre-proceedings Meeting (PPM)	sw, lfLA, lfc, lfp
2.5.1	Timing	sw, lfLA, lfc, lfp
2.5.2	Organisation and co-ordination	sw, lfLA, lfc, lfp
2.5.3	Participants	sw, lfLA, lfc, lfp
2.5.4	Attendees with special circumstances	sw, lfLA, lfc, lfp
2.5.5	Reviewing plans	sw, lfLA, lfc, lfp

Abbreviations

2.5.6	The role of the child/voice of the child	sw, lfLA, lfc, lfp
2.5.7	The role of lawyers	sw, lfLA, lfc, lfp
2.5.8	Lawyer for the parent	sw, lfLA, lfc, lfp
2.6	Public Funding (Legal Help & Legal Aid)	
2.6.1	Legal Help – public law	sw, lfLA, lfc, lfp
2.6.2	Importance of the LbP	sw, lfLA, lfc, lfp
2.6.3	Family Help Lower	sw, lfLA, lfc, lfp
2.6.4	Exceptional cases	sw, lfLA, lfc, lfp
2.6.5	Further information	sw, lfLA, lfc, lfp
2.7	Assessments	sw, lfLA, lfc, lfp
2.7.1	Adapting to change	sw, lfLA, lfc, lfp
2.7.2	Change of circumstances	sw, lfLA, lfc, lfp
2.7.3	Specialist assessments (pre-proceedings)	sw, lfLA, lfc, lfp
2.8	Alternative care for children – Section 20 Children Act 1989	sw, lfLA, lfc, lfp, cg
2.9	Safeguarding and Child Protection	sw, lfLA, lfc, lfp, cg
2.9.1	Threshold	sw, lfLA, lfc, lfp, cg
2.9.2	Managing significant harm	sw, lfLA, lfc, lfp, cg
2.10	Working with partner organisations and agencies	sw, lfLA, lfc, lfp, cg
2.10.1	Sharing information	sw, lfLA, lfc, lfp, cg
Chapter 3 – Making a section 31 Children Act 1989 application		
3.1	Preparing an application for court	sw, lfLA, hmcs
3.1.1	The forms	sw, lfLA, hmcs
3.1.2	The documentation	sw, lfLA, hmcs
3.2	Parties with special circumstances	sw, lfLA, lfc, lfp, cg
3.3	Advocates' Meetings	sw, lfLA, lfc, lfp, cg, hmc
3.3.1	Attendees	sw, lfLA, lfc, lfp, cg, hmc
3.3.2	Preparation	sw, lfLA, lfc, lfp, cg, hmc
3.3.3	Drafting the Case Management Order	sw, lfLA, lfc, lfp, cg, hmc
3.4	Care planning	sw, lfLA, lfc, lfp, cg
3.5	Role of the Children's Guardian and the Independent Reviewing Officer	sw, lfLA, lfc, lfp, cg
3.6	Issues Resolution Hearings and Final Hearings	all
3.7	Collective participation and co-operation	all
3.8	The nature of the Public Law Outline	all
Annexes		
Annex A	Immediate Issue Letter (template)	
Annex B	Letter notifying a child about a pre-proceedings meeting (template)	
Annex C	List of potential agenda items for a PPM	

*sw	Social work professionals
lfc	lawyers for children
lfp	lawyers for parents or those with PR
lfLA	lawyers for the Local Authority
hmcs	court staff and magistrates' legal advisers
cg	Children's Guardians
j	Judiciary

Abbreviations

ACA 2002	Adoption and Children Act 2002
ALDT/CLDT	Adults with Learning Difficulties Team/Community Learning Disability Team or LA equivalent
CA 1989	Children Act 1989
CA 2004	Children Act 2004
Cafcass	Child and Family Court Advisory Service
CAFCASS CYMRU	The Welsh Assembly Government Service in Wales
CMC	Case Management Conference
Experts PD	Practice Direction: Experts in Family Proceedings Relating to Children (President of the Family Division, April 2008)

FA	First Appointment
FGC	Family Group Conference
FH	Final Hearing
Framework	Framework for the Assessment of Children in Need and their Families, 2000, Department of Health. Framework for the Assessment of Children in Need and their Families, 2001, Welsh Assembly Government
HMCS	Her Majesty's Court Service
IRH	Issues Resolution Hearing
IRO	Independent Reviewing Officer
LA	Local Authority
LbP	Letter before Proceedings
LSCB	Local Safeguarding Children's Board
LSC	Legal Services Commission
Parent	The term 'parent' is used throughout but should be read to include 'parent(s) or other person(s) with PR'
PD	Practice Direction: Guide to Case Management in Public Law Cases (Judiciary of England & Wales and Ministry of Justice, April 2008)
PLO	Public Law Outline (this is contained in the PD and replaces the previous 2003 protocol)
PPM	Pre-Proceedings Meeting
PR	Parental responsibility, defined in section 3 of the Children Act 1989
SG	Statutory Guidance The Children Act 1989 Guidance and Regulations, Volume 1: Court Orders (Department for Children, Schools and Families, April 2008) and the Welsh equivalent, The Children Act 1989 Guidance and Regulations, Volume 1: Court Orders (Wales)
Working Together	Working Together under the Children Act 2004 to Safeguard Children: Every Child matters. A guide to inter-agency working to safeguard and promote the welfare of children, 2006, HM Government Wales – Safeguarding Children – Working Together under the Children Act 2004

Note—The Legal Aid Agency replaced the Legal Services Commission on 1 April 2013.

Chapter 1 – Introduction

1.1 Background to the reforms

Following the *Review of the Child Care Proceedings System in England and Wales*[1], reforms to s 31 CA 1989 proceedings were brought into effect in April 2008 by two key documents:

1. The Practice Direction: Guide to Case Management in Public Law Cases[2]; and
2. The Children Act 1989 Guidance and Regulations, Volume 1: Court Orders[3] in England, and The Children Act 1989 Guidance and Regulations, Volume 1: Court Orders (Wales)[4] in Wales.

The aim of the reforms can be broadly stated as an intention to make the system for s 31 CA 1989 proceedings more efficient by reducing delay and to improve the outcomes for children and families who may become the subject of court proceedings. The Statutory Guidance focuses on social work undertaken pre-proceedings for two principal reasons. In many cases there will still be an opportunity for the social worker to work with the child and family with a view to avoiding the need for court proceedings. Secondly, work done at these stages can impact on the proceedings (if proceedings are later initiated) and the ability for the proceedings to be conducted as smoothly and expeditiously as possible providing the best possible outcome for the child and his/her family.

1 Review of the Child Care Proceedings System in England and Wales, Department of Constitutional Affairs, Department for Education and Skills and Welsh Assembly Government (May 2006). Accessible at: http://www.dca.gov.uk/publications/reports_reviews/childcare_ps.pdf

2 The Practice Direction: Guide to Case Management in Public Law Cases, Judiciary of England & Wales and Ministry of Justice (April 2008). Accessible at: http://www.judiciary.gov.uk/docs/public_law_outline.pdf

3 The Children Act 1989 Guidance and Regulations, Volume 1: Court Orders, Department for Children, Schools and Families (April 2008). Accessible at: http://www.dcsf.gov.uk/localauthorities/_documents/content/childrensactguidance.pdf

4 The Children Act 1989 Guidance and Regulations, Volume 1: Court Orders, Welsh Assembly Government and NHS Wales (March 2008). Accessible at: http://new.wales.gov.uk/dhss/publications/children/guidance/actguidance/courtorderse.pdf?lang=en

Note—For the *Review of the Child Care Proceedings System in England and Wales*, see *www.familieslink.co.uk/download/june07/Review%20of%20child%20care.pdf*; for the *Guide to Case Management in Public Law Cases*, see FPR PD12A; for the Children Act 1989 Guidance and Regulations, Volume 1: Court Orders (Department for Children, Schools and Families), see *https://www.gov.uk/government/publications/children-act-1989-court-orders–2*; for the Children Act 1989 Guidance and Regulations, Volume 1: Court Orders (Welsh Assembly Government and NHS Wales), see *http://wales.gov.uk/topics/health/publications/socialcare/guidance1/orders/?lang=en*.

1.2 *The status of this best practice guide*

Ten initiative areas[1] tested elements of the PLO prior to it being finalised. Professionals from those areas were well placed to share information about how their areas were dealing with the reforms 'on the ground'. The Ministry of Justice's Care Proceedings Programme Office[2] held two workshops in July 2008 (Reading and Liverpool). The 'Moving Forward Workshops' brought together professionals from all fields of expertise (HMCS, legal, social work and Cafcass/CAFCASS CYMRU) from the initiative areas. A wealth of information came out of the workshops. We learned about the many examples of good practice, which some areas had already implemented and were working to; many of those ideas have been incorporated into this guide. We also learned of challenges, which some professionals were experiencing. We have sought to bring all that information into this one comprehensive guide to both share the ideas of good practice already operating but also to address and assist with some of the perceived problems.

The guide is not Statutory Guidance: it has no legal status. We have taken careful steps to ensure that various experts in their respective fields reviewed this guide before it was finalised. We hope practitioners may find it a useful additional source of information and explanation but it is no substitute for acting within the statutory framework set out in the Children Act 1989 and the regulations made under Part 3 of the Act and the Statutory Guidance on it.

1 Birmingham, London, Liverpool, Warrington/Chester, Newcastle/Sunderland, Exeter/Plymouth, Leicester, Milton Keynes/Oxford, Swansea, Portsmouth.

2 An inter-agency group set up to deliver the recommendations arising from the 2006 Care Review at: *http://www.justice.gov.uk/guidance/careproceedings.htm*

Note—See *http://webarchive.nationalarchives.gov.uk/20130128112038/http://www.justice.gov.uk/downloads/protecting-the-vulnerable/official-solicitor/childrens-cases/prepcarenadsupervisionprocs.pdf*.

1.3 *Who should read this guide*

This guide is written for all professionals who work with or for children and families where s 31 CA 1989 care proceedings are being considered or applied for. In the main those who we hope will find the guide of most use to their work are: LA social workers, LA managers, lawyers for the LA and for parents, Children's Guardians, lawyers for children, HMCS court staff and legal advisers, the judiciary and expert assessors who may be instructed pre-proceedings and within proceedings.

1.4 *How to use this guide*

This guide is separated into two parts. Chapter 2 covers the pre-proceedings stages up to the point that a s 31 CA 1989 application is issued at court. Chapter 3 looks at the stages from the point that the LA issues a s 31 CA 1989 application through to disposal of the application and conclusion of the proceedings.

Some of the aspects discussed in this guide will be connected or relate to other aspects. We have used cross-referencing where this is the case. The intention of the guide is that it should act as a quick-reference tool to good practice. As the guide has been written to cater for all parties involved in care proceedings readers should gain a better understanding of the roles and responsibilities of other professionals involved. To make the guide as user-friendly as possible the contents identify the paragraphs which are recommended reading for the various professionals involved in s 31 CA 1989 proceedings.

Chapter 2 – Pre-proceedings stages

2.1 *Introduction*

In this document the term pre-proceedings is used to indicate the several stages of interaction between the child, family and the LA which occur prior to a court application being issued for a s 31 CA 1989 order. It is straightforward to ascertain the 'end' of pre-proceedings because this will be the date that the application to court is issued. Where the pre-proceedings stages 'begin' however, is less well defined. On the one hand all stages of involvement prior to an application being made could be termed 'pre-proceedings' but for the purposes of the recent reforms the use of the term pre-proceedings is rather precise. It denotes the stages from the point that the LA is considering making an application to court to protect the child but the risk of harm to the child is manageable if an application is not made immediately. Effectively, the LA's approach will be to further attempt to engage with the parent in order to put an agreement in place which reduces the risk of significant harm to the child to a manageable level at that stage.

The point at which pre-proceedings stages nominally commence in view of the recent reforms is where the legal gateway/planning meeting (section 2.3) has been held and the LA makes the decision to send a Letter before Proceedings (LbP) (section 2.4).

2.2 Social work

Volume 1 of the Children Act Guidance and Regulations is issued under section 7 of the Local Authority Social Services Act 1970. Local Authorities must, in exercising their social services functions, act under this guidance.

The Children Act 1989, the Adoption and Children Act 2002, and the Children Act 2004 combined with Regulations made under those statutes and the Statutory Guidance set out the statutory framework within which social workers should perform functions on behalf of the LA. The Statutory Guidance seeks to provide advice to the LA on relevant matters. In relation to care proceedings the Guidance stipulates the 'matters to be considered by the LA before making an application for a care or supervision order'[1]. The LA has many duties and obligations with which it must comply. The most relevant (at this stage) is the general duty to safeguard and promote the welfare of children in need and 'so far as is consistent with that duty, to promote the upbringing of such children by their families by providing a range and level of services appropriate to those children's needs' (s 17(1) CA 1989).

The original version of Volume 1 was published in 1991. The revised Guidance gives updated advice to LAs on how they should meet their duties. Some key points from the Guidance are:

- That voluntary arrangements for the provision of services should be fully explored together with consideration of potential alternative carers
- That prior to proceedings, work should be undertaken to explore alternative care solutions for the child, assess the suitability of those arrangements and consider the legal status of those arrangements.

1 Statutory Guidance, paras 3.22–3.33.

2.3 The legal gateway/planning meeting

The purpose of a legal gateway or planning meeting is for the LA to seek legal advice about a particular case. These meetings should be attended by the child's social worker and managers together with the lawyer advising the LA. The social work team will usually set out the facts of the case, their concerns and explain what has been done to work with the child and family. The ultimate question will be 'is the threshold criteria met and are court proceedings necessary at this stage?'

In those cases where it is agreed that it will be necessary to initiate Care Proceedings the LA will consider if it is appropriate to write to the parent to inform him or her that an application to court will be made shortly and to explain that he or she should seek legal advice. A template letter can be found at Annex A. There are two important points to note about sending such a letter to the parent:

- This letter is not intended to be a 'LbP' and therefore may not act as the trigger letter for Family Help Lower (level 2) publicly funded advice and assistance (section 2.6.3). However, the parent may still be eligible for means-tested advice under Legal Help (level 1) from a solicitor. Parents should be advised to seek further guidance from a solicitor on this point; and

PART V

- It will not be appropriate to send this letter in all cases where immediate issue of proceedings is decided. Whether or not to send the letter requires very careful assessment by the LA. For example, there may be concerns that if a parent knows that the LA is going to apply to court for an order allowing it to remove the child from his or her care, the parent and their children may leave the area.

2.4 *The Letter before Proceedings (LbP)*

If following a legal gateway/planning meeting it is decided that there is time to work with the family to avoid proceedings, and the short term safety and welfare of the child permits, a LbP should be issued. The LbP allows social workers to structure their work with the child and family and to consider alternative options and services which could be provided to the family. Once the LbP inviting a parent to a Pre Proceedings Meeting (PPM) is sent out, the LA has an opportunity to work with the family and to explore all options prior to making an application to court. Some LAs have indicated that the use of the LbP has helped to stop the drift in more long-standing cases. We found that many LAs have given lots of time and effort to adjusting the template LbP contained in the Statutory Guidance to their particular areas and we have been informed that generally parents have found the LbP useful as it sets out in one place the LA's concerns.

2.4.1 Ownership

As the LbP is a new stage in the process introduced by the revised Statutory Guidance (SG) we are aware that LAs have varying experiences of its use. The template LbP which is annexed to the SG envisages that the signature carried on the LbP will be that of the social worker's team manager. The LA should request that their legal department check the contents of this letter to ensure that it includes all information relevant to the grounds for proceedings.

2.4.2 Timing

In deciding the timing about when best to send the LbP, the LA will have first considered and sought legal advice about whether it should make an application to the court (section 2.3). If it makes an 'in principle' decision that it would be appropriate to apply for an order but also concludes that the risk can be managed without an immediate application, the LA is effectively concluding that it can see a window of opportunity to try to continue to work with the family to maintain their children safely with their parents. The LbP should be sent at this point.

Once the LbP is sent the LA should utilise this opportunity to secure a plan or agreement to protect the child safely at home and work towards reducing the risk of significant harm to the child.

Where a local authority judges that there is not a window of opportunity to work with the family to continue to maintain the child at home, given its assessment of the safeguarding concerns in the case, the LA will need to apply immediately to court even on short notice for a s 31 CA 1989 order. Where this is the case LAs should consider using the immediate issue template letter at Annex A.

2.4.3 Contents

The Letter before Proceedings (LbP) is an important letter and should be carefully drafted. It is the trigger for non-means, non-merits tested publicly funded legal advice and assistance under 'Family Help Lower' (also referred to as Level 2 advice) (sections 2.6.2 & 2.6.3). It will be filed with the court, and it needs to be concise, clear and focused. For this reason the template LbP in the Statutory Guidance should be used as the basis for the letter.

It is important that the LbP is understood by the recipient. The template LbP in the Statutory Guidance uses very simple English and is jargon free so that it can be understood by recipients. If applicable it should be translated into the language used by the parent or carer. It is important that there should be no surprises in the LbP. Although the parent should already have had notice or knowledge of the LA's concerns, the purpose of the LbP is to be clear (in one place) about the concerns and what the LA needs to change or improve in order to reduce those concerns. Finally, it acts as formal notification that the parent should seek legal advice, together with a final warning that court proceedings may follow if the situation fails to improve.

The LbP also invites the parent to a Pre Proceedings Meeting (PPM) to discuss matters and hopefully finalise a plan or agreement. There needs to be sufficient time balanced against risk to the child to allow the recipient of the LbP to actually receive the letter, consider it and to seek advice from a lawyer in advance. Social workers will need to consider these factors when proposing the date and time of the PPM in the LbP.

2.4.4 Plans and agreements

The Letter before Proceedings will state what concerns need to be addressed by the parent and what support will be provided by the LA to help. These issues will be reflected in the existing child in need/child protection or care plan. The plan may be one of the following formats:

(a) a care plan because the child is looked-after by the LA pursuant to a s 20 CA 1989 agreement; a looked after child's plan can only be amended at a Statutory review at which the parents will (hopefully) be present;

(b) a child protection plan if the child is already the subject of child protection measures;

(c) a Child in Need plan if the child is not looked-after but is deemed to be 'in need' of services pursuant to s 17 CA 1989.

It follows that the LA should update the plan and send it to the parent as a draft plan (ideally with the LbP) which he or she will be asked to agree at the PPM.

The Pre Proceedings Meeting (PPM) will work best where both the LA and the parent have had a good opportunity to prepare. For the parent this will mean considering the LbP and understanding the plan which he or she is being asked to agree to. The LbP must actively encourage the parent to see a solicitor for advice; ideally he or she will have given instructions and at least sought some brief advice before coming to the PPM with the solicitor. Parents should understand the details of the concerns about the child's developmental needs, including the need for safeguarding and the plan to meet them in order to know what is required of them and how they can fulfil the requirements or discuss the issues if they feel unable to make a meaningful change. Alternatively, they will be in a position to suggest factual corrections or amendments to the proposed plan through the negotiation that will take place during the PPM.

2.4.5 Communicating messages

It is important to be sensitive and careful in communicating messages from the LbP. Nothing in the proposed plan should be new or a surprise to the parent. The concerns will have continuously been referred to during meetings, case conferences, documents or correspondence between the LA and the parent.

- The LA should consider hand delivering the LbP (taking into account if it is safe to do so) so that the social worker can be sure that the LbP was actually delivered.
- The social worker may wish to ask the parent to sign a 'receipt' to evidence delivery of the LbP. Feedback informs us that parents are more likely to attend the PPM where the LA has met the parent to deliver the LbP to reinforce its meaning and purpose.
- If communication is difficult it will be even more important to record on the LA file the methods attempted by the social worker to deliver the letter.
- Where the LbP is being posted then use recorded delivery.

The expectation is that the parents will seek legal advice and take the LbP to their solicitor.

The Ministry of Justice's Care Proceedings Programme Office will be issuing in 2009 a written pack for parents to encourage better engagement during the pre-proceedings stages. The material's target audience will be parents who are involved with the LA at the pre-proceedings stages. It is hoped that social workers and lawyers for parents will be able to refer parents to the material to aid their understanding of the pre-proceedings stages. It is intended that the material will be made more widely available within voluntary sector agencies/organisations whose service-user groups include parents involved with the LA in relation to their children.

PART V

2.5 The Pre Proceedings Meeting (PPM)

2.5.1 TIMING

The Letter before Proceedings will have stated a date, time and venue for the PPM. Consideration should be given to re-scheduling when requested by the parents so long as this not does affect the child's safety and welfare.

2.5.2 ORGANISATION AND CO-ORDINATION

Ethos: The aim of the PPM is to reach an agreement on the proposed plan between the family and the LA. Although agreement may not be able to be reached in all cases or about all areas of the plan, a conciliatory approach is encouraged of the participants and their lawyers. It should be noted that the PPM is not intended to be adversarial in nature and therefore it would be unhelpful for any participant to take such an approach. It must be borne in mind that the PPM is a social work led meeting and not a court or tribunal where a judge or arbiter listens to evidence, argument and makes decisions. Neither is the PPM a forum for disputed facts to be determined, such as in a fact finding hearing. If there are disputed facts or issues, the participants can through negotiation agree facts or narrow issues down voluntarily. The PPM will not however, decide on anything which fundamentally remains contested or disputed. No participant should feel pressured to agree to anything that he or she does not want to. Legal advice during the meeting will assist the parent with this. It is vital for the parent to understand that the proposed plan being put forward by the LA warrants careful thought so that the parent is aware of what is likely to happen in the event that an agreement to the plan or amended plan cannot be secured.

Venue of the PPM: We know that in certain familial situations the issue of where the PPM takes place can be 'make or break' in terms of whether the parent will attend and engage in the PPM. The decision regarding venue will be taken by the social worker in conjunction with his or her manager and the person who will chair the PPM. The social worker will be key in influencing this decision – having the most detailed knowledge of the circumstances of the family.

Agenda for the PPM: Many LAs have formulated an outline agenda for use at the PPM. They have found that this is helpful as it formalises the meeting, ensures that everything is covered and demonstrates to the participants that the PPM is of a more serious nature than perhaps other routine meetings between a parent and the LA. Annex C is a list of points/agenda items which may be considered for inclusion in any agenda for such meetings. It remains, of course, for each LA to decide how it wishes to conduct the meetings and whether it chooses to create its own agenda using some or all of the suggestions contained in Annex C.

Engaging the parent: There may be times when a parent will either refuse to attend the PPM or disagree with the proposed plan. This can be a difficult process but there may still be an opportunity to narrow some of the issues. A brief case example is given at the bottom of Annex C.

Minutes of the PPM: It is good practice for minutes to be taken of the PPM and then for those to be approved by the LA and circulated to the parent as quickly as possible. The parent will then have the opportunity to suggest corrections or additions which the LA can then consider. We suggest that the LA adopt a similar practice regarding minutes of the PPM as they will have in place for child protection case/review conferences. Minutes are important for any formal meeting and it is preferable that they are provided in relation to all PPMs.

Communicating plans: The plan and any agreement which has been reached during the meeting will be a material document and it is important that it is accurate, and comprehensive.

2.5.3 PARTICIPANTS

Legal: If parents attend with their lawyer the LA lawyer should also attend.

Wider family members: Should a parent wish to bring a person in a supportive role it is in the discretion of the LA to allow this.

One possible tool that the LA might re-consider at this point is the use of a Family Group Conference/Family meeting which might assist identification of wider family support. However, it must be remembered that the child's welfare is paramount and also that the parents should be central to this process and their agreement obtained at the outset and throughout the process.

Other agencies/organisations: The PPM is not a multi-disciplinary meeting or forum and it is not appropriate for other agencies to attend.

Chairing the PPM: Some LAs have stated that they have not found it helpful for the child's social worker or manager to chair the PPM. Some suggestions on people who might be better suited to chair the PPM are:

- A senior manager from the LA; or
- A contracted person who is suitably qualified akin to an Independent Reviewing Officer.

In either case, it is preferable that the person who does chair should be someone with no prior direct involvement with the child and family and where practicable that this person should chair all the PPMs in that LA. LAs who are operating a system of one nominated person as chair for all meetings are finding this is beneficial to the outcome.

If this person has no prior involvement the chances of a productive meeting increase as the parent will hopefully look to the chair as someone who is fresh to the case, less likely to have preconceived ideas about the child or family, perhaps be more impartial than the child's social worker, and is sufficiently distanced to have a wider perspective on the issues. If the chair is able to gain the trust of the participants in the meeting, the meeting will proceed more effectively.

2.5.4 ATTENDEES WITH PARTICULAR NEEDS

Given the nature, sensitivity and seriousness of the issues which fall to be discussed at the PPM it is crucial that the participants understand and are able to follow the discussions.

Some of the issues which come within the remit of the pre-proceedings stages are just as important as some of those that arise within proceedings. Where a person lacks the capacity to follow the litigation within proceedings, it is likely that he or she would also find it difficult to understand everything that is being said and asked of him or her pre-proceedings. Where an informal assessment suggests a parent may struggle to follow the pre-proceedings discussions or otherwise may have a learning disability or mental health problems which affect the parent's ability to follow the issues, then an immediate and urgent referral must be made to the Adults with Learning Disability Team/Community Learning Disability Team (ALDT/CLDT) or LA equivalent. Lord Justice Wall's comments in a recent case have clarified the Court's expectations in this instance:

> 'It is, I think, inevitable that in its pre-proceedings work with a child's family, the local authority will gain information about the capacity of the child's parents. The critical question is what it does with that information, particularly in a case where the social workers form the view that the parent in question may have learning difficulties.' (para 175).
>
> 'At this point, in many cases, the local authority will be working with the child's parents in an attempt to keep the family together. In my judgment, the practical answer in these circumstances is likely to be that the parent in question should be referred to the local authority's adult learning disability team (or its equivalent) for help and advice. If that team thinks that further investigations are required, it can undertake them: it should, moreover, have the necessary contacts and resources to commission a report so that as soon as the pre-proceedings letter is written, and proceedings are issued, the legal advisers for the parent can be in a position, with public funding, to address the question of a litigation friend. It is, I think, important that judgments on capacity are not made by the social workers from the child protection team.' (para 176).
>
> 'In the pre-proceedings phase local authorities should feel free to do whatever is necessary in social work terms to assist parents who may become protected parties. My view, however, is that this is best achieved by members of the adult learning disabilities team who do not have responsibility for the children concerned.' (para 181).
>
> *P v. Nottingham City Council and the Official Solicitor* [2008] EWCA Civ 462.

PART V

On a practical level ALDT/CLDT must be asked to assess the parent and to make recommendations as to capacity to understand the information being discussed and shared at the pre-proceedings meetings. It may be that the parent can properly engage during pre-proceedings if supported by a social worker from the ALDT/CLDT. Alternatively, a voluntary sector organisation may be able to provide an advocate who is experienced in working with those with learning disability. If those options fail then the LA may wish to consider inviting a close family member or friend to support the parent during the PPM. That however is not ideal. Ultimately, if the social worker or the lawyer for the parent believes that the parent is unable to understand and follow the subject matter properly in order to then give considered instructions to the solicitor, it may be the case that the LA will have to issue an application to court so that the Official Solicitor can be invited to act for the parent within the proceedings.

Language barriers must also be considered where a parent's capacity to understand is clearly limited and the LA should make arrangements for a suitable independent interpreter and not rely on a family member or friend.

2.5.5 Reviewing plans

The objective of the PPM is to:

- Agree a plan; and
- Track and monitor progress to implementing the plan.

The plan for the child might be that the child will be accommodated by the local authority. This is a key option for the child even if only as a temporary measure (section 2.8). If it is agreed that the child should be looked-after under s 20 1989 the LA must comply with all statutory duties in relation to looked after children.

Where the child is not a looked-after child because he or she will remain in the care of the family or be subject to a private fostering arrangement between the parent and a third person (such as a family friend or more distant relative) it is likely that the child will remain a child in need for the requisite period. The LA will however be responsible for checking and supervising any private fostering arrangements. If the arrangements are brokered by the LA then the child becomes a looked-after child under a s 23 placement.

2.5.6 Children's participation and the participation of the child

So far as it is reasonably practicable and consistent with the child's welfare, every child should be notified in age appropriate language by the LA that a PPM is to be held, with an explanation that the purpose is to help parents to keep them safe. The child should then be given the chance to make written representations to the PPM. The social worker has an ongoing duty to ascertain the wishes and feelings of the child[1]. The social worker should be in a position to feed those wishes and feelings into the PPM. Acting in the best interests of the child will be the responsibility which pervades everything the social worker does in a particular case. The social worker is therefore in a position to make clear the child's views at the PPM.

Additionally, the LA must decide in each individual case whether to invite the child to the PPM. In considering the matter, there will be a variety of factors which will be taken into account including:

- The child's age;
- The child's level of understanding as to what is involved;
- The child's coping skills; and
- Whether it is appropriate for the child to be present for all or for part of the PPM.

If the child is invited and attends the meeting, the LA should review agenda items, as there may be information that could be difficult for a child to manage within this forum. The social worker should also inform the chair of the PPM that the child will be attending.

If it is felt inappropriate to invite the child to attend the PPM or the child rejects the invitation, the social worker must consider how the child's wishes and feelings could be heard at the PPM.

The LA should ascertain the parent's views towards the child's attendance at the meeting. If the parents oppose the child's attendance at the meeting it must be remembered that the LA does not have parental responsibility at this stage.

If parents do not wish the child to attend, the child should be informed about the LAs complaints procedure. In these circumstances the LA should consider other methods of ensuring that the child's voice is heard, such as:

- the child making written representations for the meeting;
- the social worker having a meeting with the child;
- the child being referred to a local advocacy service able to support the child.

A template letter to the child can be found at Annex B. This should be tailored and adapted where the LA decide to notify a child about the PPM in writing. If the child does not attend the meeting the social worker will explain the plan to the child and take account of their wishes and feelings. As in all issues pre, during and after proceedings there must be a child focused timetable.

1 Amendments were made by s 53 CA 2004 to the following sections of CA 1989: s 17(4A), s 47(5A) and s 20(6) (all of which relate to ascertaining wishes and feelings of the child).

2.5.7 The role of lawyers

The role of lawyers in PPMs is to provide impartial legal advice in private to a client if appropriate.

If the lawyer is able to familiarise himself or herself with the relevant papers at the outset this will aid his or her ability to properly advise the client when needed. Lawyers for LAs are likely to first hear about a particular case during the legal gateway/planning meeting. It may however, be some time later when the LA come back to the lawyer for further advice or to ask that the lawyer be present at the PPM. Reading updated social work documents is useful at this point. In relation to lawyers for parents, in some circumstances the lawyer will have been instructed even prior to the LbP being sent (section 2.6.1). Where this is the case, the lawyer may have already seen documents or will have sought disclosure from the LA. Otherwise the first involvement for the lawyer for the parent will be where the parent brings in the LbP to the first attendance with the solicitor. There may be very little time between instruction of lawyers and the PPM taking place.

PART V

2.5.8 Lawyer for the parent

If the PPM is to have the best possible chance of resolving issues or identifying an alternative care solution it is vital that both the LA and the parent have appropriate advice from their qualified legal advisors.

2.6 Public funding (Legal Help and Legal Aid)

2.6.1 Legal Help – public law

Some parents may have had a lawyer during other stages of their involvement with the LA. In those cases the lawyer will have assessed the client's eligibility for Legal Help (referred to as 'Level 1 Advice'). Unlike Family Help Lower this level of service is means-tested and therefore not all parents will be financially eligible. There is also a merits-test which has a low threshold ('the sufficient benefit test'). This is payable by way of a fixed fee.

2.6.2 Importance of the LbP

Each local authority will have sent the parent a Letter before Proceedings (LbP) inviting the recipient of the letter to a meeting to discuss concerns and plans for the child and family. From the moment that the letter is received, the person to whom it is addressed automatically becomes eligible for advice and assistance. It is vital that the LA ensure that the parent receives the LbP (section 2.4). Only then will he or she be able to secure non-means, non-merits tested advice and assistance from a solicitor on this basis; the LbP acting as the trigger for eligibility. The LA are encouraged to enclose with the LbP a list of firms/organisations who do such work and in particular those that have staff who are members of the Solicitors Regulation Authority's (formerly the Law Society) Children Panel.

2.6.3 FAMILY HELP LOWER

Advice and assistance is provided by the legal advisor under a scheme called Family Help Lower (also referred to as 'Level 2 Advice'). This is a form of Controlled Work and therefore it is for the lawyer to assess whether the person seeking assistance is eligible for this level of service. Any parent or person with Parental Responsibility (PR) who receives a LbP is entitled to this level of service; it is non-means and non-merits tested. The parent is free to instruct any firm or organisation which does public funded family work.

The level of service (Family Help Lower) is remunerated as a standard fee. The LSC has calculated this fee based upon Controlled Legal Representation rates, which are higher than Legal Help and are similarly used in mental health and immigration cases involving priority clients. The LSC has increased the fee so that it currently represents over 7 hours of work.

2.6.4 EXCEPTIONAL CASES

There may be cases where the issues are very complex or great in numbers. For example there may be several persons with PR or the LA has had long-standing involvement and so there are many historic but relevant issues and documents or the assisted person (client) has significant learning difficulties or mental health problems. Those circumstances may make taking instructions, advising the client or negotiation on behalf of the client difficult and complicated. Work done under either Legal Help, Family Help Lower (or both levels of service) when compared to hourly rates may exceed the fixed fee. Where the work was justified and the time spent (based on applicable hourly rates) amounts to three times or over the fixed fee the firm/organisation will be able to claim their costs on a full hourly rates basis rather than being restricted to the fixed fee.

2.6.5 FURTHER INFORMATION

Further information about publicly funded family services can be found on the Legal Service Commission's website: *www.legalservices.gov.uk*[1]. A list of LSC family regional contacts can be found at: *http://www.legalservices.gov.uk/civil/civil_justice_system_initiatives.asp*.

1 A Q&A document is also helpful reading and is accessible at: *http://www.legalservices.gov.uk/docs/cls_main/QandAPublicLawCareProceedings050308.pdf*

Note—The Legal Services Commission is now the Legal Aid Agency, see *www.gov.uk/government/organisations/legal-aid-agency*.

2.7 Assessments

2.7.1 ADAPTING TO CHANGE

The assessment of children and their families is a key task for social work professionals. What the reforms do is to focus on purposeful, analytical and evidence based assessments and their importance. The child's allocated social worker is responsible for coordinating the work on that child's case with support from team/service managers and possibly other agencies. The assessment process is discussed in the Statutory Guidance[1] and in Working Together[2]. Assessments, both Initial and Core should be undertaken in accordance with these documents and the detailed guidance set out in the Framework for the Assessment of Children in Need and their Families (DH et al (2000)). The LA must not work in isolation and it is imperative that the appropriate sharing of information between the professional network continues to take place to ensure that the child's safety and welfare is kept central to the process.

Where cases rely on specialist assessments to inform the assessment which may not be completed within the target time frame, the core assessment should still be completed and should note any timescales agreed with partners who may be undertaking specialist assessments documented[3]. Planning, intervention and urgent work to safeguard the child's welfare will need to continue not withstanding an incomplete or outstanding core assessment.

The core assessment is the means by which LAs gather and analyse information about the child and family as it undertakes its s 47 CA 1989 enquires[4]. It is the process by which evidence is gathered which is important to the LA's case when it applies to court[5]; the LA will file the core assessment record with the court as its primary piece of evidence to support its application. As it is a live document it will continue to be updated during the LA's involvement with the child and it may well evolve as circumstances change and new information about the family is obtained. Assessment is a continuing process and not a single event.

1 Statutory Guidance, paras 3.12–3.18.
2 *Working Together*, paras 5.60–5.67.
3 Statutory Guidance, para 3.16.
4 Statutory Guidance, para 3.15.
5 Statutory Guidance, para 3.16.

2.7.2 Change of circumstances

It is essential that the extent to which a child is suffering, or is likely to suffer, harm is kept under constant review and that if necessary the matter proceeds immediately to court irrespective of whether or not the LA has completed its preparation or documentation.

Where the LA decides (usually having taken legal advice) that it needs to take steps to protect a child who it considers to be suffering or likely to suffer significant harm, the LA may take immediate protective measures which could include requesting police protection or an application at court for an order. This may be for an emergency protection order (EPO)[1] because the LA believes the child is in imminent danger, or for an interim care or supervision order[2] in order to safeguard the child. It is recognised that in some cases a core assessment will not have been completed or even started at the point that an application is made to the court. Where however, the LA has been involved with a family for some time and/or has already commenced enquiries pursuant to s 47 CA 1989 it should be conducting the enquiries via a core assessment and documenting findings from the assessment process in a core assessment record. Where the core assessment is not available or completed at the time of issue, the LA will inform the court of the reason why it has not been filed and of the expected date of filing. That information should be given at column (d) of Part 1 ('Pre-proceedings checklist') of the Supplementary PLO1 form. See the Practice Direction 10.2 and 10.3 for guidance on compliance with the pre-proceedings checklist.

1 Statutory Guidance, paras 4.25–4.63.
2 Statutory Guidance, paras 3.44–3.47.

2.7.3 Specialist assessments (pre-proceedings)

The key question for the LA to ask itself is 'is there an element or aspect of the core assessment process which cannot be completed because specialist expertise is required'.

Specialist assessments are those assessments which the LA believe are required when for example there is a particular aspect of the child's or family's circumstances which require a specialist assessment from a professional other than a social worker such as an adult mental health assessment. The specialist assessment will only address that specific aspect and it will feed into the core assessment.

Where a specialist assessment is thought to be required, the decision to commission such an assessment must be made as soon as possible to avoid introducing unnecessary delay into resolution of the proceedings. Consideration should also be given to the joint instruction of experts. The PPM can be used for this purpose.

Any specialist assessments commissioned pre proceedings should be presented by the LA in any proceedings, and for that reason it is suggested that the LA consider the requirements of the Experts PD[1], particularly those that relate to pre-proceedings assessments.

1 *http://www.hmcourts-service.gov.uk/cms/files/Experts-PD-flagB-final-version-14-01-08.pdf*

Note—For the Experts PD, see FPR PD25B.

2.8 Alternative care for children

Section 20 Children Act 1989 and the function of the Independent Reviewing Officer (IRO)

There will be some circumstances where it will be appropriate for children to be looked after by the local authority following agreement with those who have parental responsibility that this arrangement would be the best way to meet the child's needs. Where the authority provides

PART V

accommodation for a child under a voluntary agreement, then the LA does not share parental responsibility for the child and the parents may remove the child from the arrangement at any time. The parents' wishes regarding the care of their child must be respected, unless they are putting the child at risk of significant harm, and the parents and the child must be consulted before any decisions are taking that affect their child. Providing services to children in this way will not be appropriate where there are continuing concerns about significant harm to the child.

Children accommodated under s 20. like every other looked after child, must have a care plan based on a comprehensive assessment of their needs, setting out how the authority intends to meet those needs in partnership with the child's parents. This will include detail about how the authority intends to establish legally secure care arrangements for the child (e.g. permanency options might include making arrangements to reunite the child with their birth family or planning for the child to be placed in a permanent substitute family or long term foster care). The care plan must be regularly reviewed. Review meetings must be held at minimum statutory intervals – within 28 days of placement, then within 3 months and six monthly thereafter. Reviews must involve the child, their carers and representatives of the local authority responsible for their care, most reviews will also involve other appropriate professionals. The LA must appoint an Independent Reviewing Officer (IRO) to chair reviews.

The IRO's functions are to

(a) Participate in the review of the case of each looked after child
(b) Monitor the authority's functions in respect of the review
(c) Refer a case to Cafcass/CAFCASS CYMRU if the failure to implement the care plan might be considered to breach the child's human rights

Regulations require IROs to fulfil the following responsibilities

(a) To ensure that the views of children and young people are understood and taken into account (in care planning);
(b) that the person's responsible for implementing any decision taken in consequence of the review are identified; and
(c) that any failure to review the case or to take proper steps (to implement review recommendations) is brought to the attention of person's at an appropriate level of seniority within the responsible authority.

The review meeting is one of the key components within the core processes of working with children and families. The purpose of the review meeting is to consider the plan for the welfare of the child and then to monitor the progress of the plan and make decisions to amend the plan as necessary in light of changed knowledge and circumstances. The appropriate legal status for the child's care must be considered at every review meeting and the review should make recommendations to senior managers in children's services if the child's legal status no longer seems appropriate to the child's needs. For example, where the circumstances of a child accommodated under s 20 have changed such that it may be necessary for the authority to consider making application for a care order to make legally secure plans to meet the child's future needs.

DCSF are currently re-writing all the Children Act 1989 regulations and guidance and the NMS for fostering and adoption services. In addition DCSF will be issuing Strategic Guidance for consultation in October 2009 on a new framework for family and friends care which will contain a model for assessing relative carers.

2.9 *Safeguarding and child protection*

2.9.1 THRESHOLD

S 31 (2) Children Act 1989 sets out the threshold criteria. A court has no power to make a care or supervision order in favour of a local authority unless, as a matter of fact, it is satisfied that:

(a) the child concerned is suffering, or is likely to suffer, significant harm, and
(b) that the harm or likelihood of harm is attributable to either (i) the care given to a child

or likely to be given to him if the order were not made not being what it would be reasonable to expect a parent to give him or (ii) the child is beyond parental control.

Harm includes impairment from seeing or hearing the ill treatment of another.

The court will only act on evidence and will make findings of fact about whether the child is suffering significant harm. If the LA have reasonable cause to suspect that a child is suffering significant harm they will make, or cause to be made, such enquiries as they consider necessary to enable them to decide whether they should take any action to safeguard or promote a child's welfare. The court has to establish that it is more probable that the fact(s) in question occurred than they did not. Mere suspicions are not sufficient. It has to be shown that the child is or is likely to suffer significant harm, with significant being the key word. The harm has to be due to unreasonable parenting i.e. parents not giving the care it would be reasonable for a parent to give that child.

The threshold is established as a matter of fact on the evidence at the point when protective measures are implemented.

Only once the court is satisfied that this threshold has been established does the court have the power to make a care or supervision order.

Finding that threshold is proven does not mean that the court must automatically make a care order. Once threshold is established, the court will then go on to hear argument and evidence to determine what order is in the best interests of the child having regard to the welfare checklist set out in section 1 of the Children Act 1989. This might be a care or supervision order or, for example where a suitable kinship carer has been identified, it might be a residence order. The final outcome may also be an order of 'No Order' where the court believes that the interests of the child would be best served by no order being made.

The Public Law Outline usually needs to be considered in the context of whether or not there is a need for an order at that stage and the focus should be upon whether the risk is manageable without an order.

2.9.2 Managing significant harm

Managing possible harm to the child whilst working with families is a delicate task which demands careful social work judgement in discussion with line managers. The Statutory Guidance emphasises the importance of taking pre-proceedings steps such as the Pre Proceedings Meeting which follows the Letter before Proceedings (LbP) and investigating alternative care solutions, it also recognises that there will be some cases where an immediate application to court will be required. The LA may consider that a case may fit into this category and that certain pre-proceedings steps e.g. dispatch of the LbP cannot be complied with because it might place the child at increased risk of harm or fail to stop the child suffering harm. A typical example might be where the social worker considers there is a real risk of a parent absconding with the child if he or she were to become aware that that the LA is considering applying to court. This is entirely a decision for the LA, making a judgement based on its professional experience of child protection and its knowledge of the child and the family.

When the court application is prepared there may be some information or documentation which cannot be submitted with the application such as the LbP or kinship assessments which may not yet be completed. It is again essential to emphasise that if the child is suffering or likely to suffer significant harm and s 31 threshold has been established following legal advice, the matter must proceed to court. The supplementary form PLO1 lists the documentation, which should accompany the application form itself. Column (d) on that form allows the Applicant Authority to state any reason why it has not filed any document. In an emergency LAs are not required to provide pre-proceedings documentation on issue but will be required to file it later.

2.10 Working with partner organisations and agencies

2.10.1 Sharing information

Sharing information arising from the PPM is subject to the usual guidance and practice which governs the LA sharing of information. The general position is that 'the consent of children, young people and their parents or caregivers should be obtained when sharing information, unless to do so would place the child at risk of significant harm. Decisions should also be made with their agreement, whenever possible, unless to do so would place the child at risk of significant harm'[1].

Where consent to sharing information cannot be secured it will generally be safe to share information where this is justified in the public interest. For example, where there is a clear risk of significant harm to a child or adult it will usually be justified to share information so long as sharing that information is in the best interest of the child's safety and welfare. Detailed guidance can be found in 'Information sharing: Practitioners' guide'[2].

1 *Working Together* p 101.
2 'Information sharing: Practitioners' guide', HM Government 920020. Accessible at: *http://www.everychildmatters.gov.uk_files/ACB1BA35C20D4C42A1FE6F9133A7C614.pdf*

Note—See *www.gov.uk/government/publications/safeguarding-practitioners-information-sharing-advice*.

Chapter 3 – Making a section 31 CA 1989 application

3.1 Preparing an application for court

3.1.1 THE FORMS

Set out below is a list of some of the forms available at the present time with advice on their completion:

- **PLO1 – Application for a care order or supervision order: Supplementary form:** To be filed by the LA with its application. Part 1 is a checklist of the necessary documents. Part 2 is the Record of Case Management Documents filed and to record which case management documents are filed as the case progresses.
- **PLO2 – Local Authority Case Summary**: This standard form should be filed by the LA setting out its position, before the First Appointment (FA), Case Management Conference (CMC) and Issues Resolution Hearing (IRH) and will include details of: proceedings relating to the child, living arrangements, summary of incidents/concerns, key issues in the case and directions for the court to consider.
- **PLO3 – Case Management Order:** This contains standard provisions designed to help the parties, their legal representatives and the court, and has three sections: 1) Preliminary, 2) Order and 3) Recitals. The LA should prepare an initial draft in advance of each advocates' discussion/meeting and share this with all advocates involved in the case, as this document forms the basis of discussions at the advocates' meeting. Following each advocates' discussion/meeting, it is the responsibility of the local authority advocate to file the draft order with the court at least one working day before either the CMC or IRH.
- **PLO4 – Allocation Record and Timetable for the Child**: To be filed by the LA with its application. It sets out an allocation proposal regarding the appropriate tier of court. It will also be used to record the court's allocation decision and reasons. The LA also uses it to provide important dates in the child's life to assist the court set a suitable Timetable for the Child.
- **PLO5 – Standard Directions and allocation on issue of proceedings**
- **PLO6 – Standard Directions and allocation at First Appointment**: Forms PLO 5 and 6 are completed by a judge or legal adviser once an application is lodged at court and at the First Appointment. The court will consider giving standard directions appropriate to each case at Issue and First Appointment stages using these forms.

3.1.2 THE DOCUMENTATION

All pre-proceedings checklist documents should be filed with the application where available.

The documents which the LA are called upon to create specifically for filing with the application are:

1 The Schedule of Proposed Findings;
2 Initial Social Work Statement;
3 Care Plan for each child;

4 The Allocation Record; and
5 Timetable for the Child.

The Public Law Outline is explicit about the required documents that should be filed and issued by the court.

LAs should file and serve under the category of the 'Other relevant reports and records' (see item 7 on form PLO1, Part 1) the child's full birth certificate or relevant ID as this is likely to be required by the court at some stage and therefore would be useful to be filed at the outset.

3.2 Parties with particular needs

In s 31 CA 1989 proceedings where the social worker or any party believes that a parent may not have capacity to conduct the litigation the court can be asked to make a direction inviting the Official Solicitor to act on that person's behalf. It must be considered that appropriate social work expertise within the local authority disability team can be used pre or post proceedings to inform a decision on their client's capacity. The Official Solicitor is a 'litigation friend of last resort' and will only accept that invitation if there is no one else who is willing and suitable to conduct the litigation on the parent's behalf. Invariably in family proceedings it will be difficult to say with any certainty that another family member is suitable because he or she may have a view which is in conflict with the parent or otherwise because he or she is very close to the subject of the litigation so will not be able to present the parent's views properly. It is important that the Official Solicitor is approached as soon as possible if required to assist:

> 'if all the professionals involved with the proceedings and with the parents, including the judges, solicitors, barristers, advocates, and court staff, are aware of the need from the start of the proceedings to take time to consider the parent and whether the proceedings are proving too much for the parent to fully understand. If at any time there is a genuine concern about the parent's capacity to understand the proceedings and to instruct their solicitor, the parent should be able to ask for, and to receive assistance without being made to feel stigmatised by their disability.'
>
> *http://www.officialsolicitor.gov.uk/docs/parentsnetworkarticle.doc*

Note—The article is no longer available online.

3.3 Advocates' meetings

3.3.1 ATTENDEES

A Children's Guardian (CG) is a social work professional appointed by a court to independently represent a child subject a care or adoption procedures. They are officers of Cafcass/CAFCASS CYMRU. Children's Guardians and social workers must not attend Advocates' Meetings but they should be notified of the time and date of the meeting and they should be contactable throughout so that counsel may take instructions as necessary.

The Advocates' Meeting should not take place on the morning of the hearing but in accordance with the requirements of the PLO. It is advisable to book the meeting promptly following any previous meeting. When advocates are considering timetabling a meeting, due consideration should be given to utilising telephone or video conferencing where attendance in person is impractical.

It is recognised that it is sometimes unhelpful to a party to have a different advocates representing him or her at various hearings. At times, this can have a bearing on the smooth running of the proceedings. Any client should be free of constraints to choose who he or she wishes to instruct as his or her representative and therefore the Practice Direction (PD) cannot be prescriptive on the issue. Nevertheless the PD does acknowledge the concern and provides a reminder to advocates (for all parties) that the advocate who represents at the final hearing should be the same advocate representing the client at the CMC and IRH. Where this is not possible the PD suggests that an advocate who is familiar with the issues in the case should attend[1].

1 PD, para 16.

3.3.2 Preparation

The aim of the Advocates' Meeting is to facilitate agreement between the parties and narrow the issues in dispute[1]. In order to save valuable court time the Advocates' Meeting also acts as a forum where the draft Case Management Order is discussed and prepared[2]. Meetings will only be productive if all the advocates have prepared what is the background to and the issues in the case, what their respective client seeks to achieve from the proceedings, and up to date instructions from their clients in advance but as close to the Advocates' Meeting as possible.

To aid the smooth running of the Advocates' Meeting the draft Case Management Order should be prepared as an initial draft by the LA in advance of the Advocates' Meeting itself. If this is circulated to the other parties even a day before the Advocates' Meeting is scheduled to take place, it will act as a working document which all can come to the meeting armed with comments on. It will also act as the agenda for the meeting which would be helpful.

If proceedings are to run smoothly and with as little delay as possible, it will be important that all parties comply with the filing of evidence and in time. Where compliance with a particular direction is not looking possible, the relevant party's representative must seek agreement from all the parties for an extension of time or draw the non-compliance to the attention of the court.

1 PD, para 3.11.
2 PD, paras 13.1–13.7.

3.3.3 Drafting the Case Management Order

During the Advocates' Meeting there will be a discussion about the Case Management Order and the Applicant's advocate (usually the LA) will take the lead in preparing or drafting that document together with the other advocates. Ideally matters can be agreed and the Case Management Order can be filed as a single agreed case management tool to assist the judge at the hearing. Where that is not possible the advocates will specify on the Case Management Order (or on a separate document if necessary) the provisions which they agree and disagree1. There must be a clear narrative detailing what the LA is asking the court to do, with the CMO fully completed. Detailed standard variable directions are available from the HMCS website to provide assistance on the full and appropriate wording to be used when considering the required directions for the draft case management order.

1 PD, para 13.5.

3.4 Care planning

The plan for the care of the child should be based on findings from the initial and core assessments. It should set out the aims of the plan and intended outcomes for the child, informed by the findings from the assessments ie. The identified developmental needs of the child and the capacity of the parents to respond to the child's needs in the context of their wide family and environmental factors. It will set out clearly what the plan for the child if the Court makes a care order.

In those relatively few cases where the identified permanence option, at the point of the commencement of proceedings, is for the adoption of the child, and where the decision that the child should be placed for adoption has been taken in accordance with the Adoption Agencies Regulations 2005 (SI 2005/389), the local authority must apply for a placement order issued simultaneously with, or as soon as possible after, the issue of the care proceedings.

3.5 Role of the Children's Guardian and the Independent Reviewing Officer

Where possible the Children's Guardian (CG) should meet with the child, where age appropriate, and with other parties in advance of the First Appointment (FA). The Guardian must have read the court papers and provided the required analysis.

The Practice Direction defines Case Analysis & Recommendation (A&R) as being a 'written or oral outline of the case from the child's perspective prepared by the Children's Guardian or other officer…'[1]. A list follows that paragraph of the PD setting out the particular points that the Case A&R should address. It is anticipated that the CG may not always be in a position to file a written Case A&R and this is why the definition allows for an oral outline to be provided by the CG at the

FA. Where an oral report is given it is suggested that the child's solicitor takes a note of the oral report and then files it as an agreed note. However, in Wales practice guidance requires that the CG provides an initial analysis in written form at the earliest stage and if feasible by the FA.

In subsequent hearings, the CG should be up to speed and in a position to provide written Case A&R that will be filed by the child's solicitor as per the court's directions.

The child's care plan must be maintained by the local authority and kept under review at the statutory intervals and whenever significant changes are proposed to the plan throughout proceedings. It will be good practice for the Children's Guardian and the IRO to maintain a constructive working relationship throughout proceedings. Both the Children's Guardian and the IRO should be properly informed about the local authority's plans for the child so they are able to scrutinise these plans to make sure that they are based on good quality assessment so that the plan demonstrates how the child's needs will be met, with the child being provided with the opportunity to be meaningfully involved in planning for their care. The local authority will need to take the views of the IRO on the quality of planning into account in formulating the final care plan to be put to the Court[2].

Where a child is accommodated by the LA upon issue of proceedings e.g. under s 20 of the CA 1989, it is good practice for the LA to serve a copy of the LA Case Summary (form PLO2) together with a copy of the Initial Social Work Statement, Schedule of Proposed Findings, Care Plan and Allocation Record and timetable for the child on the IRO. Additionally the LA should provide the parties and the Children's Guardian with the name and contact details of the IRO together with the dates of any statutory reviews which have been arranged.

At the conclusion of proceedings IROs may well have an important role in ensuring that the implications of the agreed care plan are understood by all professionals, cares and family members, as there will no longer be any oversight by the Court of the care planning process. In particular, the IRO will have a role in enabling the child to understand their plan and to participate in future care planning.

1 PD, para 25(8).
2 The Children and Young Person Act includes provision which significantly strengthens the IRO function. In future each looked after child must have their own personal named IRO; the IRO will be responsible for monitoring the quality of the local authority's care planning function; and ensure that in every care plan due consideration has been given to the child's wishes and feelings.

PART V

3.6 *Issues Resolution Hearings and Final Hearings*

The purpose of the Issues Resolution Hearing (IRH) is to narrow the issues in so far as to conclude proceedings if possible.

There is some concern amongst professionals that a final hearing is only listed by the court at the IRH. This seems to have given rise to some anxiety about the List Office's ability to secure a date in the court diary for a final hearing soon after the IRH. Where the court is able to do this, some are worried that there will not be an opportunity to give adequate notice to experts and that this may also cause difficulty for the consistency of advocates.

The Practice Direction itself does not require final hearings to only be listed at the IRH. The PD states that at the Case Management Conference (CMC) the court will set a date for the IRH and 'if necessary, specify a period within which the Final Hearing of the application is to take place unless a date has already been set'[1]. Rather than taking a prescriptive approach the PD is flexible about the listing of final hearings leaving it for the court to decide when it lists the final hearing and in accordance with its case management functions. The Timetable for the Child will greatly influence how the court manages its case especially in regard to the listing of hearings.

1 PD, para 14.5(2).

3.7 *Collective participation and co-operation*

All professionals involved in public law proceedings will work together with the court to assist achievement of the overriding objective. The parties have a duty to do this, which is enshrined in the PD[1].

It is also emphasised[2] that the parties and their representatives should co-operate with the court in case management. Furthermore, the parties and representatives should monitor compliance (generally) with the Court's directions and inform the court or court officer about any failure to comply with a direction of the court or any other delay within the proceedings[3]. A number of courts have a case progression officer (CPO) who should be the first point of contact with regard to Public Law cases.

1 PD, para 2.3.
2 PD, para 5.4.
3 PD, para 5.5.

3.8 The nature of the Public Law Outline

The purpose of the PLO is to reduce delay in these important proceedings concerning the short and long-term placement future of children. It has had to be robust in order to achieve its objectives and to secure outcomes for children and families involved within the target timeframe set by the Timetable for the Child (which is one of the case management tools)[1]. It should be borne in mind that the PD does acknowledge that the court has flexible powers. At any stage in the proceedings the court may exercise those powers[2].

The expectations[3] are that the proceedings should be conducted using the Case Management Tools and Documentation and determined in accordance with the stages in the Timetable for the Child (together with the timeframes indicated for the various stages within the PLO). It is however, acknowledged that the child's welfare in some cases may require a more tailored approach; possibly one that does not fall firmly within the stages and expectations of the PLO. In those cases it will be for the court to determine the appropriate case management directions and timetable[4] but the court must record on the face of any order its reasons for departing from the PLO's general approach. This aids the parties' understanding of why the court is managing its case in the way it is and it also protects the court itself from any potential criticism for departing from the PLO's expectations.

1 PD, paras 3.2–3.4.
2 PD, paras 17.1–17.3.
3 PD, para 4.1.
4 PD, para 4.2.

ANNEX A – IMMEDIATE ISSUE LETTER (TEMPLATE)

SENT BY [RECORDED DELIVERY/BY HAND]

Office Address

Contact

Direct line

My ref

Fax

E-mail

Date

Dear [parent and/or full name(s) of all people with parental responsibility]

Re: [insert name of Local Authority] CONCERNS ABOUT [insert name(s) of child]

I am writing as you were told I would, when you spoke to [name of social worker] on [insert date of last interaction]. As you are aware [name of Local Authority] is extremely worried about your care of [name(s) of child/ren]. We told you about these main concerns in [reference to the Letter before Proceedings/PPM/child protection case conference/any social work meetings].

We have tried to work with you to help you improve your care of [name(s) of child/ren] but unfortunately things have not changed. We are writing to tell you again that we will be going to court to try and make sure [name of child] is safe. You will soon receive a copy of our application to the court and other important documents, which set out the key issues.

We would urge you, if you have not done so already, to get advice from a solicitor. We have sent with this letter a list of local solicitors who specialise in work with children and families. They are not part of Children's Services (Social Services).

Yours sincerely

[name]
Team Manager
Local office/service
cc. Social Worker [name]
Local Authority in house Legal Team
Enc. List of Law Society Children Panel Solicitors

ANNEX B – LETTER NOTIFYING A CHILD ABOUT A PRE-PROCEEDINGS MEETING (TEMPLATE)

Delivered by Hand
Office Address
Contact
Direct line
My ref
Fax
E-mail

Dear [name]

As you know, there have been some concerns about how your parents/carers [delete as appropriate and/or name] have been looking after you.

Although we have been trying hard to sort out these problems, unfortunately, at the moment, we are still worried that you may be at risk of harm.

Our next step therefore is to hold a 'pre-proceedings meeting'. At that meeting we will try to agree a plan with your parents/carers about what needs to be done to deal with our worries about you. If we cannot sort things with your parents/carers at this meeting, it may mean that our only option is to go to court. Hopefully this will not happen but if it does, you will be given plenty of information about what happens and your role in it all.

I am now writing to invite you to attend the pre-proceedings meeting which is being held on [date] at [time] at [venue]. This will give you the chance to tell the meeting about your thoughts, wishes and feelings. If you would rather not attend the meeting, that is fine. You can always put your thoughts in writing if that is easier.

I shall be present at the meeting, with my manager, [name] and our legal advisor. Your parents have of course been invited and may have their lawyer with them.

I shall call you soon to check if you would like to attend all or part of the meeting. It may be that you would like an adult (who should be unconnected to the family) to support you during the meeting.

Alternatively, I may be able to arrange for an advocate to attend the meeting with you. An advocate's job is to make sure that a young person's views are heard, either through speaking for a young person or helping a young person speak for him or herself. Please let me know if you would like any more information on this and you can telephone me on [..........].

If you have any questions or worries please contact me on the above number.

Yours sincerely

Social Worker [name]
Local office/service

ANNEX C – LIST OF POTENTIAL AGENDA ITEMS FOR A PRE-PROCEEDINGS MEETING

- Introductions
- Setting out any special requirements (interpreter, sign language interpreter, presence of an advocate)
- Outline the purpose of the meeting and establish ground rules and specify roles
- Outline duty of the LA to protect children, duty (where possible) to promote the child living with the family, balance of that against need to protect and promote welfare of the child. Explaining why it may be that a court application is necessary but that the LA hopes that the meeting may avoid the need for that
- Explain the concerns of the LA and referencing the LbP
- Initial views and opinions of the parent and specifying or clarifying any areas of agreement and disagreement
- Discuss what can be done to help improve the child's situation on the part of the parent including any assessment outcomes and gaps identified
- Discuss what services have been be provided to the family by the LA and can be provided to help i.e. promoting the idea of collaborative working between family and the LA in the best interests of the child
- Discuss the outcome of the Family Group Conference/Family meeting
- Identification of alternative carers (this will be a revisit to the concept as it will have been discussed previously within the assessment process)
- Lead into a discussion of the proposed plan for the child including the need for any further assessments (the auspices of that plan i.e. Child in Need plan or Child Protection Plan)
- Break away for both parent and the LA to take advice from their respective lawyers
- Initial views from parent as to their thoughts on the plan/agreement
- Reconvene for focused discussion on the plan. Can an agreement be reached on the plan/agreement as it stands in draft or can revisions/amendments be agreed now to avoid proceedings
- If no agreement can be reached such that the LA believes it will have to issue an application with the court consider scope for discussion as to any issues which may be resolved now.

Brief case example: mother abuses alcohol and her partner is abusive to her. Both elements raise safeguarding concerns. At the PPM the plan is that mother should (1) agree to cease excessive drinking and agree to attend a community drugs and alcohol programme; and (2) agree to her partner moving out of the family home and to seek assistance from domestic abuse support group/project to support mother with skills/knowledge to leave a violent relationship and to avoid entering into similar relationships in the future. Mother agrees to do (1) but not to do (2). Mother provides details for the first time of alternative carers but refuses to agree to information being disclosed to those persons. The LA decides that it will need to seek an interim care order to safeguard the child. Although proceedings have not been avoided, one crucial issue has (potentially) been resolved and the LA will now be able to press ahead with consideration of alternative carers whilst not disclosing information which the mother has not consented to.

Practice Note
April 2010

Citation: [2010] 2 FLR 1872

Guidelines for Judges Meeting Children who are Subject to Family Proceedings

Produced by the Family Justice Council and approved by the President of the Family Division. April 2010

In these Guidelines –

– All references to 'child or 'children' are intended to include a young person or young people the subject of proceedings under the Children Act 1989.
– 'Family proceedings' includes both public and private law cases.
– 'Judge' includes magistrates.
– Cafcass includes CAFCASS CYMRU.

Purpose

The purpose of these Guidelines is to encourage Judges to enable children to feel more involved and connected with proceedings in which important decisions are made in their lives and to give them an opportunity to satisfy themselves that the Judge has understood their wishes and feelings and to understand the nature of the Judge's task.

Preamble

– In England and Wales in most cases a child's needs, wishes and feelings are brought to the court in written form by a Cafcass officer. Nothing in this guidance document is intended to replace or undermine that responsibility.

– It is Cafcass practice to discuss with a child in a manner appropriate to their developmental understanding whether their participation in the process includes a wish to meet the Judge. If the child does not wish to meet the Judge discussions can centre on other ways of enabling the child to feel a part of the process. If the child wishes to meet the Judge, that wish should be conveyed to the Judge where appropriate.

– The primary purpose of the meeting is to benefit the child. However, it may also benefit the Judge and other family members.

Guidelines

1 The Judge is entitled to expect the lawyer for the child and/or the Cafcass officer:

(i) to advise whether the child wishes to meet the Judge;
(ii) if so, to explain from the child's perspective, the purpose of the meeting;
(iii) to advise whether it accords with the welfare interests of the child for such a meeting take place; and
(iv) to identify the purpose of the proposed meeting as perceived by the child's professional representative/s.

2 The other parties shall be entitled to make representations as to any proposed meeting with the Judge before the Judge decides whether or not it shall take place.

3 In deciding whether or not a meeting shall take place and, if so, in what circumstances, the child's chronological age is relevant but not determinative. Some children of 7 or even younger have a clear understanding of their circumstances and very clear views which they may wish to express.

4 If the child wishes to meet the Judge but the Judge decides that a meeting would be inappropriate, the Judge should consider providing a brief explanation in writing for the child.

5 If a Judge decides to meet a child, it is a matter for the discretion of the Judge, having considered representations from the parties –

(i) the purpose and proposed content of the meeting;
(ii) at what stage during the proceedings, or after they have concluded, the meeting should take place;
(iii) where the meeting will take place;
(iv) who will bring the child to the meeting;
(v) who will prepare the child for the meeting (this should usually be the Cafcass officer);
(vi) who shall attend during the meeting – although a Judge should never see a child alone;
(vii) by whom a minute of the meeting shall be taken, how that minute is to be approved by the Judge, and how it is to be communicated to the other parties.

It cannot be stressed too often that the child's meeting with the judge is not for the purpose of gathering evidence. That is the responsibility of the Cafcass officer. The purpose is to enable the child to gain some understanding of what is going on, and to be reassured that the judge has understood him/her.

6 If the meeting takes place prior to the conclusion of the proceedings –

(i) The Judge should explain to the child at an early stage that a Judge cannot hold secrets. What is said by the child will, other than in exceptional circumstances, be communicated to his/her parents and other parties.
(ii) The Judge should also explain that decisions in the case are the responsibility of the Judge, who will have to weigh a number of factors, and that the outcome is never the responsibility of the child.
(iii) The Judge should discuss with the child how his or her decisions will be communicated to the child.
(iv) The parties or their representatives shall have the opportunity to respond to the content of the meeting, whether by way of oral evidence or submissions.

Sir Nicholas Wall
President of the Family Division and Head of Family Justice

President's Guidance May 2010

Citations: [2010] 2 FLR 1897

Note—FPR PD12J incorporates and supersedes this Guidance as it applies to proceedings for child arrangements orders.

From time to time issues will arise with which magistrates and judges at every level will have to grapple and which will cause difficulties. Against this background I intend from time to time to issue what I propose to call 'Guidance' designed to help colleagues make difficult decisions. Self-evidently such Guidance is not designed to tell courts what to decide: the objective is to assist them in the process of going about the decision making progress. Plainly, it will be appropriate not to follow the Guidance in some circumstances: what I hope is that in a sufficiently large number of instances the Guidance will be of use and will help magistrates and judges in the decision making process.

Split Hearings (Bulletin Number 1)

Introduction

1 Over recent months and years it has become apparent to me that split hearings are: (1) taking place when they need not do so; and (2) are taking up a disproportionate amount of the court's time and resources.

2 I have therefore decided to issue the following Guidance in an attempt to assist judges and magistrates who are invited to direct split hearings.

3 Like all Guidance, what follows is not binding on the judiciary at any level. It is an attempt to identify good practice. Moreover, it is designed to apply in both private and public law proceedings.

4 In this Guidance, I propose to use the following terminology –

A 'split hearing' is a hearing divided into two parts, during the first of which the court makes findings of fact on issues either identified by the parties or the court, and during the second part of which the court, based on the findings which it has made, decides the case.

A 'fact finding hearing' is the first limb of a split hearing.

Guidance

5 Judges and magistrates should always remember that the decision to direct a split hearing or to conduct a fact finding hearing is a *judicial* decision. It is not a decision for *Cafcass* or for the parties. It is a decision to be taken by the court. Thus the court should not direct a fact finding hearing simply because the parties agree that one is necessary or because *Cafcass* says that it cannot report without one. Such considerations are, of course, to be taken into account, but they are not conclusive. In any event, the focus of any report is a matter for the court.

6 Judges and magistrates should always remember that a fact finding hearing is a working tool designed to assist them to decide the case. Thus a fact finding hearing should only be ordered if the court takes the view that the case cannot properly be decided without such a hearing.

7 Even when the court comes to the conclusion that a fact finding hearing is necessary, it by no means follows that such a hearing needs to be separate from the substantive hearing. In nearly every case, the court's findings of fact inform its conclusions. In my judgment it will be a rare case in which a separate fact finding hearing is necessary.

8 Thus, for example, the fact that domestic abuse is put forward by the residential parent of a child as a reason for denying the non-residential parent contact with the child is not automatically as reason for a split hearing with a preliminary fact finding hearing. As the President's *Practice Direction: Residence and Contact order: Domestic Violence and Harm* of 14 January 2009 [2009] 2 FLR 1400 makes clear, the court must consider the nature of any allegations, and the extent to which those allegations, if admitted or proved '*would be relevant in deciding whether to make an order about residence or contact and, if so, in what terms*' – see para [3] (emphasis supplied). In para [11] the court is again instructed to '*consider the likely impact of that issue (domestic abuse) on the outcome of the proceedings*' (emphasis supplied) and whether or not the decision of the court is likely to be affected by findings of domestic abuse. Plainly, if the allegations are unlikely to have any impact on the court's order, there is no need for a separate fact finding hearing.

9 In addition, in cases in which the court concludes that a fact-finding hearing is necessary, the *Practice Direction* requires the court to give directions designed to ensure that '*the matters in issue are determined expeditiously and fairly*' (emphasis supplied).

10 None of the foregoing is designed to minimise or trivialise domestic abuse or its effects on children and upon its other victims, or to discourage victims from coming forward with abuse allegations. I repeat that the aim of the Guidance is to enable magistrates and judges fully to address their minds to the need for a separate fact finding hearing.

11 The rationale for split hearings in care proceedings was enunciated by Bracewell J in *Re S (Care Proceedings: Split Hearing)* [1996] 2 FLR 773 when, voicing the views of the Children Act Advisory Committee, she stated that consideration could usefully be given to whether or not there were questions of fact within a case which needed to be determined at an early stage. The advantages of doing so, she said were that early resolution of such facts 'would enable the substantive hearing to proceed more speedily' and would enable the court to 'focus on the child's welfare with greater clarity'. Cases suitable for split hearings, she commented 'would be likely to be cases in which there is a clear and stark issue, such as sexual abuse or physical abuse'. Once again, the object was 'to prevent delay and the ill-focused use of scarce expert resources'. These factors should be borne in mind by the court when deciding whether or not to order a split hearing.

12 Magistrates and judges are reminded of the decision of the Court of Appeal in *Re C* [2009] EWCA Civ 994. They might also care to look at paragraphs 27 to 35 of my recent judgment in the case of *W (Children)* [2009] EWCA Civ 644, now also reported at [2009] 3 FCR 1.

13 Courts are also reminded of the provisions of the *Practice Direction: The Revised Private Law Programme* which came into effect from 1 April 2010.

Nicholas Wall

Practice Guidance June 2010

Citations: [2011] 1 FLR 319

Re S (Wardship) Guidance in Cases of Stranded Spouses

Having given Judgment in respect of the fact-finding hearing and as there have been a number of similar cases, some of which have been reported, and counsel and solicitor for the mother are aware of other current cases where it is alleged that a parent has been left stranded abroad by the other parent, it was suggested that it would be helpful to practitioners and other Judges if I could provide some guidance and assistance with the issues that such cases raise, and which may need to be considered by the Court at an early stage in proceedings.

The suggestions I make are designed inter alia to ensure that the 'stranded spouse's' and indeed the other parties' Article 6 and 8 ECHR rights are upheld; to ensure that there is a fair trial of the factual allegations and to enable the child/children to have contact with both parents pending a final welfare based determination on issues of residence and contact.

1 Given the international element and the experience of the Judges of the Family Division in dealing with cases of this type, child abduction and other international cases, the best vehicle for these types of cases is wardship. Such proceedings should be managed, if possible, and heard by a Judge of the Family Division.

2 At the first hearing (on an ex parte basis) the making of a Tipstaff Passport order should be considered (amended where necessary) to include that the tipstaff shall search for and seize the mother's passport where it is alleged that the father has taken it. Location Orders are also suitable in these cases but Collections orders should only be employed in the most exceptional of cases.

3 There should be a Court request for disclosure from the Home Office in form EX660 at the ex parte stage to ascertain the spouses' immigration status so that s/he can immediately make arrangements to obtain an expedited visa/transfer of an existing valid visa to a new passport. This information may also assist the stranded parent in knowing which immigration application should be made. That parent's solicitor may also wish to consider whether expert immigration advice might assist, and if so seek the appropriate direction at an early date.

4 At an early stage the Court should consider whether there should be an urgent fact-finding hearing to investigate and ascertain the circumstances in which the parent and child/children came to be stranded internationally. Consideration should be given to any disputed allegations made by the stranded parent, as to the gravity of such allegation and if proved, the impact it may have upon the Court's determining the welfare issues and future upbringing of the child/children concerned. If a fact-finding hearing is thought to be appropriate, directions should be given for an early hearing, and thereafter the judgment to be disclosed to CAFCASS, and such other agencies including the Local Authority and local police as may be deemed appropriate.

5 If the Court considers that the stranded parent's presence in this jurisdiction is necessary to the Court's determination of the child's/children's welfare appropriate recitals in directions orders may assist with that parent's application for a visa to enter/re-enter the jurisdiction. Such directions could include:

(a) the mother must attend the hearing at .... on ....

(b) the Court indicating that the mother needs to be here to determine issues as to ………………;

(c) the court expressing the view that the mother's evidence be best given in person in this jurisdiction.6 The Court could consider allowing semi-anonymised publicity in the media to highlight the stranded parent's circumstances, particularly if other efforts to secure that parent's return to participate in the proceedings have been unsuccessful. It would be appropriate to canvass the views of any CAFCASS officer/Guardian ad Litem in relation to publicity as CAFCASS would be concerned about publishing any information that would lead to identification of the child or potentially put the child at risk of harm.

7 The Court should consider whether to invite/order any members of the family to assist with funding flight costs to enable the stranded parent to return to participate in the proceedings. If they refuse such invitation or disobey an order the Court could consider making an order for costs at the conclusion of the fact-finding hearing/welfare hearing.

8 The Court should consider whether to request the relevant British High Commission/Embassy and/or FCO to assist by provision of information or otherwise as may be appropriate.

9 The Court should consider whether the Local Authority in which the child is living should be directed to investigate the child's/children's circumstances and report pursuant to S37 of the Children Act 1989. Such a direction will be dependent on whether the evidence filed indicates that the child/children may be suffering, or at risk of suffering significant harm.

10 In such cases, it would be appropriate to consider whether the child should be joined as a party and a Guardian ad Litem appointed. Given the expertise of the CAFCASS High Court Team the Court should consider referring the case to the manager of the team to consider the papers and the Courts invitation to appoint a Guardian. Until the stranded parent is able to return to the jurisdiction the Guardian's role may be limited and it may not be appropriate to expect the Guardian and lawyer to attend frequent review hearings during the fact-finding process. However, their assistance will be of importance when the Court deals with the issues of interim care and control, and interim contact issues that might arise particularly on the stranded parent's return to the jurisdiction and with safeguarding checks.

11 The Court may, and the stranded parent's solicitor should, consider that assistance may be provided by the various agencies to the stranded spouse upon the return to the jurisdiction, and what monetary or other applications should be made against the other parent.

12 Upon the return of the stranded parent there should be an urgent interlocutory hearing to consider further directions and the interim welfare arrangements for the child/children and the Court's managed reunification of the stranded parent and his/her child, which will probably require the input of the CAFCASS High Court Team Guardian.

Justice Hogg
Family Division

Revised Protocol 2 July 2010

Referrals of Families to Supported Child Contact Centres by Judges and Magistrates

The protocol for referrals of families to Child Contact Centres, designed to assist judges and magistrates who are proposing to make orders for contact involving the use of a Child Contact Centre, was originally introduced in 2000 following widespread consultation and had the endorsement of the President of the Family Division, Dame Elizabeth Butler-Sloss, and subsequently that of the former President, Sir Mark Potter.

Following recent changes in arrangements regarding referrals to supervised contact centres this protocol now governs only referrals to Supported Child Contact Centres. Consultation on practical matters affecting Supported Child Contact centres has shown the need to address some matters in more detail and has led to this revised Protocol, which has the support of Sir Nicholas Wall, President of the Family Division and Patron of The National Association of Child Contact Centres (NACCC) who said:

> 'Supported Child Contact Centres are integral to the better working of the wider family justice system, offering a most valuable resource to courts dealing with difficult and often acrimonious family disputes over contact. They also provide safe, comfortable and pleasant surroundings for children meeting the non-resident parents.
>
> It is crucial that Supported Child Contact Centres are used appropriately. This means that the safety of the children being referred, the other families using the centre as well as the staff and volunteers must be considered before an order is made. Supported Child Contact Centres offer a voluntary service and must be able to decide whether to accept or refuse a referral.
>
> Furthermore, Courts recognise that Supported Contact Centres are charities and nearly all the staff are volunteers. They can only undertake their work if free of any risk of being drawn into individual cases or disputes. Accordingly, courts and parties will not require or seek their involvement in resolving disputes, writing reports, noting events or attending, in any capacity, any family court hearing.
>
> This admirable protocol will be of the greatest help to judges and magistrates to ensure that Supported Child Contact Centres are used to their best advantage for children needing this valuable and scarce resource.'

Sir Nicholas Wall
President of the Family Division

Referrals to supported contact centres

Supported Child Contact Centres do not offer Supervised Contact. The provision offered by Supported Child Contact Centres is described in the Manual of Guidance produced by the National Association of Child Contact Centres as follows:

> 'Supported contact takes place in a variety of neutral community venues where there are safe facilities to enable children to develop and maintain positive relationships with non-resident parents and other family members. Supported Child Contact Centres are suitable for families when no risk to the child or those around the child, unmanageable by the centre, has been identified during an intake procedure.'

It is a requirement that the parents and children attend a pre-contact meeting or equivalent (for example a telephone discussion). Parents are seen or spoken to separately so that the Centres can follow their own risk assessment procedure. A number of children's story books about visiting a Child Contact Centre are available via the NACCC website www.naccc.org.uk.

The basic elements of supported contact are as follows:

- Impartiality.
- Staff and volunteers are available for practical assistance (for example calming a tearful child) and keeping a watchful eye. They do not monitor or evaluate individual contact/conversations.
- Several families are usually together in one or a number of rooms.
- Families are encouraged to develop mutual trust and consider more satisfactory family venues.
- Apart from confirmation of attendance dates and times, no report will be made to a referrer, CAFCASS, a party's solicitor or court.
- Supported Child Contact Centre staff and volunteers are not available to be called as witnesses unless it is a criminal matter.
- It is acknowledged that the Supported Child Contact Centre is a temporary arrangement, to be reviewed after an agreed period of time.

THINGS TO CHECK

Before making an Order for Contact at a Supported Child Contact Centre (whether interim or final) please check that the matters set out below have been addressed.

1 If you are considering making an Order for contact at a Supported Child Contact Centre, please ensure that you have addressed whether referral to a Supported as opposed to a Supervised Contact Centre is appropriate where any one or a combination of the following are present
   (a) Domestic Violence
   (b) Drug or substance misuse
   (c) Alcohol misuse
   (d) Mental illness.

2 That the Child Contact Centre Co-ordinator has been contacted and has confirmed that:
   (a) The centre is an accredited member of NACCC.
   (b) The referral appears to be suitable for that particular Centre, subject to a satisfactory pre-visit or equivalent. (In line with its Safeguarding Policy a Supported Child Contact Centre can refuse to accept families if the circumstances appear to them to be inappropriate for the Centre.)
   (c) The intended day and times are available at the particular Centre concerned.
   (d) A vacancy is available or a place on a waiting list has been allocated.

3 That you have directed that a copy of the Order is provided to the Centre by one or other of the parties within a specified time together with any other injunctive or relevant Orders on the court file.

4 That it has been agreed who will have responsibility for completing and returning the Centre's referral form. Solicitors for both parties should agree the contents and it should be forwarded to the Child Contact Centre within 24 hours of the court hearing.

5 That the parties understand that the Child Contact Centre offers supported contact only; and that parties and their solicitors are aware that apart from attendance dates and times, no report will be made to a referrer, CAFCASS, a party's solicitor or court; and that the parties understand that the centre staff and volunteers are not available to be called as witnesses unless it is a criminal matter.

6 That if contact is to be observed at the Child Contact Centre by a CAFCASS officer or other third party that this is a facility offered by that Centre and that the Centre has agreed to this course of action. Many do not permit such attendance.

7 That where there may be a communication problem related to language, arrangements have been made for the provision of an independent interpreter. This is not the responsibility of the Supported Child Contact Centre.

8 That the Order clearly defines whether or not any other family members are to be a part of the Contact visit.

9 That it is agreed who is going to tell the children where and when they will see their non-Resident parent.

10 That it has been agreed who will be responsible for informing the Centre when the place is no longer required.

11 That a date has been set for a review of contact, including the use of the Supported Child Contact Centre and of any other steps parties have been ordered or undertaken to take which are relevant to contact and for further directions if necessary. Only in exceptional circumstances should an order be made allowing for the open-ended use of a Supported Child Contact Centre.

PLEASE ALSO NOTE

1 The order should be worded 'Subject to the parties attendance at a pre-contact meeting or equivalent, the availability of a place and the parties abiding by the rules of the centre ....'

PART V

2 The Centre or Centres at which you direct contact should take place will very much welcome a visit from you and your colleagues. Volunteer staff greatly appreciate the Judiciary taking a positive interest in their local Centres. Such visits will also help you to understand the facilities available locally and thus the type of case that is most suited to contact at the Supported Child Contact Centre.

National Association of Child Contact Centres (NACCC), 1 Heritage Mews, High Pavement, Nottingham NG1 1HN; Tel: 0845 4500 280; Fax: 0845 4500 420; email: contact@naccc.org.uk; website: www.naccc.org.uk

Practice Guidance
12 July 2010

Citation: [2010] 2 FLR 962

McKenzie Friends (Civil and Family Courts)

1 This Guidance applies to civil and family proceedings in the Court of Appeal (Civil Division), the High Court of Justice, the County Courts and the Family Proceedings Court in the Magistrates' Courts.[1] It is issued as guidance (**not** as a Practice Direction) by the Master of the Rolls, as Head of Civil Justice, and the President of the Family Division, as Head of Family Justice. It is intended to remind courts and litigants of the principles set out in the authorities and supersedes the guidance contained in *Practice Note (Family Courts: McKenzie Friends) (No 2)* [2008] 1 WLR 2757, which is now withdrawn.[2] It is issued in light of the increase in litigants-in-person (litigants) in all levels of the civil and family courts.

1 References to the judge or court should be read consistently with the provisions of FPR 2010, rr 2.5–2.7 and FPR PD2A.

2 *R v Leicester City Justices, ex parte Barrow* [1991] 260, *Chauhan v Chauhan* [1997] FCR 206, *R v Bow County Court, ex parte Pelling* [1999] 1 WLR 1807, *Attorney-General v Purvis* [2003] EWHC 3190 (Admin), *Clarkson v Gilbert* [2000] CP Rep 58, *United Building and Plumbing Contractors v Kajla* [2002] EWCA Civ 628, *Re O (Children) (Hearing in Private: Assistance)* [2005] 3 WLR 1191, *Westland Helicopters Ltd v Sheikh Salah Al-Hejailan (No 2)* [2004] 2 Lloyd's Rep 535. *Agassi v Robinson (Inspector of Taxes) (No 2)* [2006] 1 WLR 2126, *Re N (A Child) (McKenzie Friend: Rights of Audience) Practice Note* [2008] 1 WLR 2743.

The Right to Reasonable Assistance

2 Litigants have the right to have reasonable assistance from a layperson, sometimes called a McKenzie Friend (MF). Litigants assisted by MFs remain litigants-in-person. MFs have no independent right to provide assistance. They have no right to act as advocates or to carry out the conduct of litigation.

What McKenzie Friends may do

3 MFs may: i) provide moral support for litigants; ii) take notes; iii) help with case papers; iv) quietly give advice on any aspect of the conduct of the case.

What McKenzie Friends may not do

4 MFs may not: i) act as the litigants' agent in relation to the proceedings; ii) manage litigants' cases outside court, for example by signing court documents; or iii) address the court, make oral submissions or examine witnesses.

Exercising the Right to Reasonable Assistance

5 While litigants ordinarily have a right to receive reasonable assistance from MFs the court retains the power to refuse to permit such assistance. The court may do so where it is satisfied that, in that case, the interests of justice and fairness do not require the litigant to receive such assistance.

6 A litigant who wishes to exercise this right should inform the judge as soon as possible indicating who the MF will be. The proposed MF should produce a short curriculum vitae or other statement setting out relevant experience, confirming that he or she has no interest in the case and understands the MF's role and the duty of confidentiality.

7 If the court considers that there might be grounds for circumscribing the right to receive such assistance, or a party objects to the presence of, or assistance given by a MF, it is not for the litigant to justify the exercise of the right. It is for the court or the objecting party to provide sufficient reasons why the litigant should not receive such assistance.

8 When considering whether to circumscribe the right to assistance or refuse a MF permission to attend the right to a fair trial is engaged. The matter should be considered carefully. The litigant should be given a reasonable opportunity to argue the point. The proposed MF should not be excluded from that hearing and should normally be allowed to help the litigant.

9 Where proceedings are in *closed court*, i.e. the hearing is in chambers, is in private, or the proceedings relate to a child, the litigant is required to justify the MF's presence in court. The presumption in favour of permitting a MF to attend such hearings, and thereby enable litigants to exercise the right to assistance, is a strong one.

10 The court may refuse to allow a litigant to exercise the right to receive assistance at the start of a hearing. The court can also circumscribe the right during the course of a hearing. It may be refused at the start of a hearing or later circumscribed where the court forms the view that a MF may give, has given, or is giving, assistance which impedes the efficient administration of justice. However, the court should also consider whether a firm and unequivocal warning to the litigant and/or MF might suffice in the first instance.

11 A decision by the court not to curtail assistance from a MF should be regarded as final, save on the ground of subsequent misconduct by the MF or on the ground that the MF's continuing presence will impede the efficient administration of justice. In such event the court should give a short judgment setting out the reasons why it has curtailed the right to assistance. Litigants may appeal such decisions. MFs have no standing to do so.

12 The following factors should not be taken to justify the court refusing to permit a litigant receiving such assistance:

(i) The case or application is simple or straightforward, or is, for instance, a directions or case management hearing;
(ii) The litigant appears capable of conducting the case without assistance;
(iii) The litigant is unrepresented through choice;
(iv) The other party is not represented;
(v) The proposed MF belongs to an organisation that promotes a particular cause;
(vi) The proceedings are confidential and the court papers contain sensitive information relating to a family's affairs.

13 A litigant may be denied the assistance of a MF because its provision might undermine or has undermined the efficient administration of justice. Examples of circumstances where this might arise are: i) the assistance is being provided for an improper purpose; ii) the assistance is unreasonable in nature or degree; iii) the MF is subject to a civil proceedings order or a civil restraint order; iv) the MF is using the litigant as a puppet; v) the MF is directly or indirectly conducting the litigation; vi) the court is not satisfied that the MF fully understands the duty of confidentiality.

14 Where a litigant is receiving assistance from a MF in care proceedings, the court should consider the MF's attendance at any advocates' meetings directed by the court, and, with regard to cases commenced after 1.4.08, consider directions in accordance with paragraph 13.2 of the Practice Direction Guide to Case Management in Public Law Proceedings.

15 Litigants are permitted to communicate any information, including filed evidence, relating to the proceedings to MFs for the purpose of obtaining advice or assistance in relation to the proceedings.

16 Legal representatives should ensure that documents are served on litigants in good time to enable them to seek assistance regarding their content from MFs in advance of any hearing or advocates' meeting.

17 The High Court can, under its inherent jurisdiction, impose a civil restraint order on MFs who repeatedly act in ways that undermine the efficient administration of justice.

Rights of audience and rights to conduct litigation

18 MFs do **not** have a right of audience or a right to conduct litigation. It is a criminal offence to exercise rights of audience or to conduct litigation unless properly qualified and authorised to do so by an appropriate regulatory body or, in the case of an otherwise unqualified or unauthorised individual (i.e., a lay individual including a MF), the court grants such rights on a case-by-case basis.[3]

3 Legal Services Act 2007 s 12–19 and Schedule 3.

19 Courts should be slow to grant any application from a litigant for a right of audience or a right to conduct litigation to any lay person, including a MF. This is because a person exercising such rights must ordinarily be properly trained, be under professional discipline (including an obligation to insure against liability for negligence) and be subject to an overriding duty to the court. These requirements are necessary for the protection of all parties to litigation and are essential to the proper administration of justice.

20 Any application for a right of audience or a right to conduct litigation to be granted to any lay person should therefore be considered very carefully. The court should only be prepared to grant such rights where there is good reason to do so taking into account all the circumstances of the case, which are likely to vary greatly. Such grants should not be extended to lay persons automatically or without due consideration. They should not be granted for mere convenience.

21 Examples of the type of special circumstances which have been held to justify the grant of a right of audience to a lay person, including a MF, are: i) that person is a close relative of the litigant; ii) health problems preclude the litigant from addressing the court, or conducting litigation, and the litigant cannot afford to pay for a qualified legal representative; iii) the litigant is relatively inarticulate and prompting by that person may unnecessarily prolong the proceedings.

22 It is for the litigant to persuade the court that the circumstances of the case are such that it is in the interests of justice for the court to grant a lay person a right of audience or a right to conduct litigation.

23 The grant of a right of audience or a right to conduct litigation to lay persons who hold themselves out as professional advocates or professional MFs or who seek to exercise such rights on a regular basis, whether for reward or not, will however only be granted in exceptional circumstances. To do otherwise would tend to subvert the will of Parliament.

24 If a litigant wants a lay person to be granted a right of audience, an application must be made at the start of the hearing. If a right to conduct litigation is sought such an application must be made at the earliest possible time and must be made, in any event, before the lay person does anything which amounts to the conduct of litigation. It is for litigants to persuade the court, on a case-by-case basis, that the grant of such rights is justified.

25 Rights of audience and the right to conduct litigation are separate rights. The grant of one right to a lay person does not mean that a grant of the other right has been made. If both rights are sought their grant must be applied for individually and justified separately.

26 Having granted either a right of audience or a right to conduct litigation, the court has the power to remove either right. The grant of such rights in one set of proceedings cannot be relied on as a precedent supporting their grant in future proceedings.

Remuneration

27 Litigants can enter into lawful agreements to pay fees to MFs for the provision of reasonable assistance in court or out of court by, for instance, carrying out clerical or mechanical activities,

such as photocopying documents, preparing bundles, delivering documents to opposing parties or the court, or the provision of legal advice in connection with court proceedings. Such fees cannot be lawfully recovered from the opposing party.

28 Fees said to be incurred by MFs for carrying out the conduct of litigation, where the court has not granted such a right, cannot lawfully be recovered from either the litigant for whom they carry out such work or the opposing party.

29 Fees said to be incurred by MFs for carrying out the conduct of litigation after the court has granted such a right are in principle recoverable from the litigant for whom the work is carried out. Such fees cannot be lawfully recovered from the opposing party.

30 Fees said to be incurred by MFs for exercising a right of audience following the grant of such a right by the court are in principle recoverable from the litigant on whose behalf the right is exercised. Such fees are also recoverable, in principle, from the opposing party as a recoverable disbursement: CPR 48.6(2) and 48(6)(3)(ii).

Note—For CPR 1998, r 48.6, see CPR 1998, r 46.5.

Personal Support Unit & Citizen's Advice Bureau

31 Litigants should also be aware of the services provided by local Personal Support Units and Citizens' Advice Bureaux. The PSU at the Royal Courts of Justice in London can be contacted on 020 7947 7701, by email at cbps@bello.co.uk or at the enquiry desk. The CAB at the Royal Courts of Justice in London can be contacted on 020 7947 6564 or at the enquiry desk.

Lord Neuberger of Abbotsbury
Master of the Rolls

Sir Nicholas Wall
President of the Family Division

PART V

President's Guidance
18 November 2010

Citations: [2011] 1 FLR 303

Out of Hours Hearings

1 It is perhaps not sufficiently appreciated by the general public that there is always a High Court judge of the Family Division on duty 'out of hours' – that is to say every day of the year including all holiday periods either: (1) between 16.15 on day one and 10.30 am on day two of a normal court sitting; or (2) between 16.15 on any given Friday and 10.30 the following Monday. In vacations, when the court is not sitting, a similar service is provided at any time of the day or night.

2 It is of the utmost importance that this service is used for its intended purposes and is not abused. It is designed for urgent cases. In this context 'urgent' has a specific meaning. It means cases in which an order of the court is required to regulate the position between the moment the order is made and the next available sitting of the court in conventional court hours – that is, usually, 10.30 on the following morning.

3 Judges of the Family Division have no complaint, for example, if, in the middle of the night, they are asked to sanction lifesaving medical treatment, or if they have to visit a hospital at such a time in order to decide whether a given individual should undergo urgent and specific treatment.

4 Any application that is 'urgent' within the definition set out in paragraph 2 above must be capable of being reduced to a faxed sheet of A4 (or its email equivalent), or a short telephone conversation. Whether or not a case is 'urgent' will always be a matter for the judge.

5 What is unacceptable is an application which can plainly wait until the normal sitting of the court and/or which involves a substantial amount of documentation. A judge cannot and should not be expected either to receive or to assimilate a substantial volume of documentation in an urgent, out of hours application unless both are absolutely essential to a proper understanding of the order which the judge is being asked to make. Equally, judges who are on duty out of hours should not be expected to make arrangements to sit in court unless such a sitting is strictly necessary to enable an order to be made. The profession should also remember that the judge on duty, whilst always available on the telephone, will be at home, and that 'home' may not be in London.

6 Lawyers who abuse the system, particularly those who seek to take advantage of an order not made on notice and out of hours with a speedy return date in hours may not only be the subject of orders for wasted costs, but may find themselves reported to their professional bodies for serious professional misconduct. The profession is thus reminded of the definition of 'urgent' set out in paragraph 2 of this note.

7 Nothing in this note supersedes any previous Guidance or Practice Note relating to out of hours applications.

Sir Nicholas Wall
President of the Family Division

President's Joint Guidance December 2010

Citations: [2011] 1 FLR 943

Cases Involving Protected Parties in which the Official Solicitor is being invited to Act as Guardian Ad Litem or Litigation Friend

Public and private law children's cases

1 Many practitioners and judges will know of the Official Solicitor's recent difficulties in accepting requests to act as guardian ad litem/litigation friend for protected parties in proceedings relating to children. Although, currently, there are unallocated cases, the backlog has reduced significantly in recent months.

2 The Official Solicitor is subject to severe budgetary constraints – a situation which is unlikely to ameliorate in the medium term.

3 In all cases, the Official Solicitor will need to be satisfied of the following criteria before accepting a case, and parties may need reminding of the need to provide confirmation of these matters immediately on approaching the Official Solicitor's office:

- satisfactory evidence or a finding by the court that the party lacks capacity to conduct the proceedings and is therefore a protected party;
- confirmation that there is security for the costs of legal representation;
- there is no other person who is suitable and willing to act as guardian ad litem/litigation friend.

4 In order to assist the Official Solicitor in the decisions he makes about allocating case workers, in certain cases, judges should consider whether it may be appropriate to indicate with as much particularity as possible the relative urgency of the proceedings and the likely effect upon the child (and family) of delay. The Official Solicitor will very carefully consider giving priority to such cases.

5 It is and remains the judge's duty in children's cases, so far as he is able, to eradicate delay.

Court of Protection welfare cases (including medical cases)

6 The number of welfare cases brought under the provisions of the Mental Capacity Act 2005 is rising exponentially with concomitant resource implications for the Official Solicitor.

7 Judges should be alert to the problems the Official Solicitor may have in attending at each and every preliminary hearing. Consideration should be given, in appropriate cases, to dispensing with the requirement that he should be present at a time when he is unable to contribute meaningfully to the process. In circumstances where his position has been/will be communicated in writing it may be particularly appropriate for the judge to indicate that the Official Solicitor's attendance at the next directions' hearing is unnecessary.

8 The Court of Protection Rules make clear that the judge is under a duty to restrict expert evidence to that which is reasonably required to resolve the proceedings. The explanatory note to r 121 states that the court will consider what 'added value' expert evidence will give to the case. Unnecessary expert assessments must be avoided. It will be rare indeed for the court to sanction the instruction of more than one expert to advise in relation to the same issue.

9 The Practice Direction – *Experts in Family Proceedings Relating to Children*, 1 April 2008 specifies that the expert should assist by 'providing objective, unbiased opinion on matters within his expertise, and should not assume the role of advocate'. The form and content of the expert's report are prescribed, in detail, by paragraph 9 of the Practice Direction. It is no part of the expert's function to analyse or summarise the evidence. Focused brevity in report writing is to be preferred over discussion.

Note—PD of 1 April 2008: *Experts in Family Proceedings Relating to Children* was superseded by FPR PD25A (now FPR PDs 25A–25F) as of 6 April 2011.

Mrs Justice Pauffley

Cafcass Practice Note April 2011

Cafcass and the Work of Independent Reviewing Officers

(*amended 1 March 2017*)

1 Introduction

1.1 The purpose of this Practice Note is to explain the functions and duties of Cafcass in relation to cases which involve Independent Reviewing Officers ('IROs'). There are two instances when Cafcass practitioners[1] come into contact with IROs: as part of family proceedings when a child is looked after or when a referral is made in accordance with section 25B(3)(a) Children Act 1989. Guidance on what to do in the former is detailed in section 2 and for the latter in section 3 below.

1 In this practice note, 'Cafcass practitioner' is used to represent the statutory roles of 'officer of the Service' as defined in the Criminal Justice and Court Services Act 2000 and 'officer of the Children and Family Court Advisory and Support Service' as referred to in the Review of Children's Cases (Amendment) (England) Regulations 2004.

1.2 This replaces the previous Cafcass Practice Note, dated May 2007.

1.3 This Practice Note applies to Cafcass in England. It is issued for Cafcass personnel (including self-employed contractors). It will be of interest to IROs, local authorities and other relevant professionals but does not replace or contradict in any way the DfE guidance. It will be reviewed annually.

1.4 Separate arrangements apply in Wales. Enquiries relating to Wales should be directed to: the Social Care Team, Legal Services, National Assembly for Wales, Cathays Park, Cardiff CF10 3NQ, telephone 02920 826813.

REFERENCES

1.5 The key regulations and guidance are:

- a The Children and Family Court Advisory and Support Service (Reviewed Case Referral) Regulations 2004 ('the Cafcass Regulations')
- b Statutory guidance for IROs and Local Authorities on their functions in relation to care management and review for looked after children (known as the IRO Handbook). *https://www.gov.uk*
- c Care Planning, Placement and Case Review (England) Regulations 2010
- d The Arrangements for Placement of Children by Voluntary Organisations and others (England) Regulations 2011

2 IROs and Cafcass in Care Proceedings

2.1 IROs monitor the performance by local authorities of their functions in relation to children who are looked after by them. The regulations in 'd' (above) confirm that voluntary organisations and private children's homes will also have to appoint IROs to monitor their functions in relation children placed with them. Because IROs work with all looked after children, some of their work will be with children who are the subject of current care proceedings or placement proceedings. These children will also have a Cafcass practitioner, appointed to act as children's guardian. In these cases, both the children's guardian and the IRO will need to consider what communication is necessary in order to promote the best possible care planning process for this individual child. As a minimum, the children's guardian will:

- a identify who is the named IRO within the local authority, with responsibility for the child;
- b contact the IRO and provide the IRO with the children's guardian's name and contact details;
- c read copies of all review documentation;
- d consult with the IRO as part of the ongoing analysis and ascertain whether the IRO has any concerns about the care planning process in this case. For example: where one exists, have any stages of the local dispute resolution process been triggered, or have any complaints or representations been received about the child's case?
- e ensure they are informed of review meetings and be aware of any planning meeting that take place and liaise with the IRO following such meetings to discuss any decisions that are made. The IRO will alert the children's guardian to any issues that arise in planning and review meetings
- f liaise with the IRO if appropriate on the wishes of child, the care plan, and issues which may have been raised at court and ensure that there is an independent assessment of the child's best interests.

2.2 In all cases where the child is expected to remain looked after following proceedings, the children's guardian should confirm that all the relevant documents have been forwarded to the IRO.

2.3 In all cases where the child remains looked after following proceedings, the children's guardian should have a final discussion with the IRO about the case with a view to identifying any outstanding issues on particular matters that should be kept under review. It will be important that this is part of the closing of cases by the children's guardian and not a drift into extended involvement.

3 Referrals to CAFCASS

3.1 Section 25B(3)(a) of the Children Act 1989 and the IRO handbook states that the IRO should refer the case of any looked after child to Cafcass where the IRO considers it appropriate to do so. The IRO must consider the impact on the child of a referral and make a decision based on the timetable for the child. There will be some cases where there will be time available to pursue the full dispute resolution process but this may not always be the case.

3.2 A Cafcass lawyer is on duty every working day and is available to give guidance (but not legal advice) to IROs about the matters dealt with in this Practice Note. (See paragraph 5.1 below for contact details). Unless there are overriding child protection concerns, Cafcass Legal will instigate no action on the basis of informal telephone discussions unless requested to do so by the IRO. Any record will remain confidential unless and until the IRO makes a formal referral to Cafcass. If a formal referral is made, the record will be shared with the relevant Cafcass practitioner as part of the case.

3.3 A Cafcass practitioner is only authorised to bring judicial review proceedings or free standing applications under the Human Rights Act 1998 by virtue of section 25B(3)(a) of the Children Act 1989 and the supporting regulations referred to above.

3.4 Cafcass may only take such action against local authorities on referral from an IRO in accordance with the Cafcass Regulations and the IRO Regulations, or the Adoption Agencies Regulations. Other interested parties concerned about the actions of local authorities should continue to use the established procedures to make their concerns known to the local authority. They cannot refer cases directly to Cafcass.

RESPONSIBILITY FOR CASES IN CAFCASS

3.5 All cases referred in accordance with this Practice Note should be sent to Cafcass Legal whose contact details can be found in paragraph 5.1 below. Some examples of the types of cases which may be suitable for referral can be found in the Annex to this Practice Note.

3.6 On receipt of a referral, Cafcass Legal will immediately refer the case either to the local Cafcass manager for allocation to a practitioner who has previously been involved or to the Cafcass High Court Team for allocation. Cafcass Legal will also notify the Local Authority Legal Department.

DOCUMENTATION

3.7 The documents to be sent to Cafcass Legal are set out in paragraph 8.15 of the IRO Handbook.

3.8 It is not necessary to obtain permission of the court to disclose documents to Cafcass. Cafcass will need the court's permission to disclose any documents filed in family proceedings in connection with judicial review or freestanding Human Rights proceedings.

3.9 Where the documentation is for any reason not complete, the referral should still be made without further delay so that the Cafcass practitioner can begin his or her enquiries, but the IRO should stipulate a date when the documentation will be provided.

3.10 It is critically important that where the child is of sufficient age and understanding, the IRO conveys the child's wishes and feelings, including his or her views in relation to potential court proceedings.

3.11 In addition to the documentation listed at paragraph 8.15 of the IRO Handbook, the following documentation should be sent to Cafcass:

- a names of relevant staff and contact details in relation to any other agencies involved such as the local education authority or an NHS Trust.
- b relevant information about diversity issues for this child and family, including whether the child or family members will need additional assistance to aid communication.

PROCEDURE

3.12 The Cafcass practitioner will gather information through the following processes, which are not set out in any order of timescale or importance.

- a reading the documentation provided by the IRO, any information held by Cafcass, and any further documentation that may be requested by the practitioner;
- b meeting the child if appropriate;
- c discussing the case with the IRO;

PART V

- d discussions with any relevant person including staff from the local authority. If such discussions are to take place with persons who were not party to any previous family proceedings, the lawyer from Cafcass Legal will advise whether permission of the court is required;
- e discussion with the previous children's guardian, where he or she is not the same person now allocated to the case;
- f discussion with people with parental responsibility and wider family members (where appropriate). Again, if such discussions are to take place with persons who were not party to any previous family proceedings, the lawyer from Cafcass Legal will advise the practitioner on whether permission of the court is required

3.13 Whether or not proceedings have been issued, Cafcass may seek to settle the case with use of negotiation or mediation. The aim is to ensure that the local authority or other responsible authority (as defined in The Arrangements for Placement of Children by Voluntary Organisations and others (England) Regulations 2011) makes good any breach of its duties towards the child and/or any defects in the implementation of the care plan.

3.14 In consultation with his or her manager and with Cafcass Legal, the Cafcass practitioner will seek, within two weeks of the referral, to make decisions about the most appropriate action to take, based on the following questions:

- a is there evidence that the child's human rights are being compromised by the actions (or inaction) of the local authority or the responsible authority?
- b if so, are there further opportunities for dispute resolution? By whom should this be initiated? By the IRO, by the family or by Cafcass?
- c could the problem be solved by other proceedings (for example an application under the Children Act for contact) and, if so, should Cafcass initiate these? Should the child be encouraged to initiate court proceedings?
- d are judicial review proceedings necessary or should there be a free-standing human rights application?
- e What are the ascertainable wishes and feelings of the child

3.16 Where it is not possible to submit a written report with a decision on the action to be taken within the two week period, the Cafcass practitioner will write to the persons included in the list at paragraph 3.22 below explaining the reasons for delay. A report will be provided as soon as reasonably practicable thereafter.

3.17 If further action is needed, Cafcass will decide who should take that action. The following questions should be considered: where there is a need for court proceedings, is the child able and willing to instruct lawyers to start proceedings? Or is there an adult able and willing to initiate proceedings? Only if neither of these applies will the Cafcass practitioner initiate proceedings.

INVOLVING THE CHILD

3.18 The Cafcass practitioner will involve the child in the case to the extent that is appropriate in the light of his or her age, understanding, needs and circumstances and if appropriate will:

- a meet with the child to ascertain his or her views about his or her case, the role of the local authority (or 'responsible authority') and the referral to Cafcass.
- b provide information to ensure that he or she knows how to contact Cafcass.
- c respond promptly to any representations from the child. If at any time the child wants to take over the conduct of the case from Cafcass and is competent to do so, the Cafcass practitioner will give as much help as possible including supplying a list of solicitors whom the child might wish to instruct.

LEGAL PROCEEDINGS

3.19 If, on referral from an IRO and having consulted with his or her manager and taken legal advice, the Cafcass practitioner decides it is necessary to bring civil proceedings such as judicial review, or a free-standing application under the Human Rights Act 1998, he or she will take steps to secure appointment as the child's litigation friend.

3.20 The Cafcass practitioner must seek to start any such civil proceedings within six weeks of receipt of the referral. In some cases, the timetable will need to be much shorter due to the urgent nature of the concern. Even after proceedings have been issued, the Cafcass practitioner will continue to try to settle the case.

TIMETABLING AND SHARING INFORMATION

3.21 The Cafcass practitioner will at all times have in mind the principle that delay may be harmful to the child and will have regard to relevant limitation periods. He or she will write a report detailing with reasons the course of action to be taken in the case including, where appropriate, reasons for not taking any action requested by the IRO. The practitioner will seek to prepare the report within two weeks of the referral. At the conclusion of the case whether by judgment of the court or after the case has been settled, the practitioner will provide a further report within six weeks of judgment or settlement. That report will include the reasons for the decision to bring proceedings to an end, the reason for any delay in the time limits, the detail of any settlement and any other comments or recommendations

3.22 The reports will be sent to the following people:

a the child, depending on his or her level of understanding.
b the IRO.
c the Chief Executive of the local authority and the Director of Children's Services or equivalent.
d the Chief Executive or equivalent of the voluntary organisation of private children's home
e the social worker and their team manager with day-to-day responsibility for the case.
f any other person the officer of the Service considers should be informed. The officer of the Service will take advice from Cafcass Legal for instance in relation to persons with parental responsibility.

PART V

4 *Cases which are not appropriate for a referral to Cafcass*

4.1 The following are situations where a referral to Cafcass will not be appropriate:

a where the child is of sufficient age and understanding to bring proceedings himself or herself without the need for an adult to act on his or her behalf. In such cases the IRO should ensure that the child has access to a suitably experienced solicitor and an explanation about legal aid.
b where a suitable adult is able and willing to bring the proceedings on behalf of a child.
c Where the timescales for the child permit the full dispute resolution procedures to be exhausted. This will depend on the particular circumstances of the case. For example, an immediate placement issue might require curtailment of the process while a dispute about an educational placement provision planned for the following school year would not. Some situations (for example, an issue about sibling contact) could be resolved by proceedings under the Children Act. It is not appropriate to pursue non-family litigation such as a judicial review if a remedy may be available in current or new Children Act proceedings.

4.2 Cafcass will not deal with compensation claims, which will continue to be the responsibility of the Official Solicitor.

4.3 The Official Solicitor conducts a wide range of civil litigation on behalf of children. Cafcass Legal will pass on to the Official Solicitor any cases that are felt more appropriate for him. (See the Annex to this Practice Note.) IROs should therefore refer any suitable cases directly to the Official Solicitor whose contact details can be found in paragraph 5.2 below. In any case where it is anticipated that such a referral may be warranted, the IRO should ask for the permission of the court to disclose papers to the Official Solicitor.

4.4 In some cases it may be unclear which course of action to take. Lawyers in Cafcass Legal and the Official Solicitor's Office are available for discussion or to give guidance to IROs about potential referrals.

5 Useful contact details

5.1 Cafcass Legal's address is:

Cafcass, 3rd Floor, 21 Bloomsbury Street, London, WC1B 3HF

Tel: 07776 470065

5.2 The Official Solicitor's address is:

Office of the Official Solicitor and Public Trustee

Victory House, 30–34 Kingsway, London WC2B 6EX
DX 141423 Bloomsbury 7

Anthony Douglas
Chief Executive, CAFCASS

Official Solicitor—The preferred email address is enquiries@offsol.gsi.gov.uk.

ANNEX

A Examples of cases to be referred by IROs to Cafcass. In each example, the child could be either accommodated or subject of a care order or placement order This is not intended as an exhaustive list:

(i) Unreasonable failure by a local authority to meet the statutory requirements for the looked after child – for example, lengthy delays in allocating a social worker; failure to make timely visits to the child.
(ii) Unreasonable failure by a local authority to implement an important element of a care plan – for example sibling contact, or a foster placement for an asylum seeking child.
(iii) Unreasonable failure by a local authority to implement an important element of a care plan due to conflicts in decision making outside of the review process – for example, funding of a specialist placement or therapy.
(iv) Unreasonable decision to move a child to a placement

B Examples of cases more suitable for the Official Solicitor:

(i) A personal injury claim against a local authority
(ii) A claim for the harm a child has suffered through a local authority's negligence in failing to bring care proceedings.
(iii) Dispute in the case of a 17 year old young person who is incapable of managing his or her affairs due to mental disability, and likely to remain so after attaining his or her majority.

Guidance Note
16 June 2011

In-Court Family Mediation Services

Note—As from 22 April 2014, the protocol mentioned below has now become a statutory requirement. This means that in certain family proceedings applicants must first attend a mediation information and assessment meeting (unless they fall within one of the exemptions) before making an application to court. See FPR 2010, PD3A and the CAP in PD12B.

Introduction

The pre-application protocol for family Mediation Information and Assessment Meetings (MIAM) came into effect on 6 April 2011. This aims to help the public become aware of mediation and understand how it could support them going through separation and divorce. Those individuals wishing to make an application to court, whether publicly funded or otherwise, will have to first consider, as appropriate, alternative means of resolving their disputes.

From April 2011, all potential applicants for a court order in relevant family proceedings are expected, before making their application, to have followed the steps set out in the Protocol. This requires a potential applicant, except in certain specified circumstances, to consider with a mediator whether the dispute may be capable of being resolved through mediation. The court will expect all applicants to have complied with the Protocol before commencing proceedings and (except where exceptional circumstances apply) will expect any respondent to have attended a MIAM, if invited to do so.

If court proceedings are taken, the court will wish to know at the first hearing whether mediation has been considered by the parties. In considering the conduct of any relevant family proceedings, the court will take into account any failure to comply with the Protocol and may refer the parties to a meeting with a mediator before the proceedings continue further.

New guidance for in-court mediation

There will be instances where self-funding individuals will attend court and be unaware of the need to have MIAM. Or they may be referred to a MIAM at the first hearing. It has been agreed by the Justice Minister Jonathan Djanogly MP that mediators ought to be able to charge those that are self-funded for the MIAM or Mediation Sessions within the court precinct.

This is comes into effect immediately and will help to provide improve access to mediation services and prevent delays.

What you need to do

The majority of courts already know their local family mediation services and will have mediators who come into court on a regular basis. However, with this new guidance, courts may be approached by new mediation services. You should make sure:

– the mediation service is recognised by the Family Mediation Council, who ensure that mediators are trained to an appropriate standard
– consider whether you have suitable accommodation for a consulting room
– advise your judges of the arrangements you have made with the local mediation services

If you have any questions regarding this guidance, please contact:
Atul Sharda (Head of Family ADR Branch) Ministry of Justice;

Tel: 0203 334 4273; e-mail: atul.sharda@justice.gsi.gov.uk

PART V

President's Joint Message 29 July 2011

Joint Message from Sir Nicholas Wall, President of the Family Division and Anthony Douglas CBE, the Chief Executive of Cafcass

Note—The Agreement between the President of the Family Division and the Chief Executive of Cafcass dated 1 October 2010 expired on 30 September 2011. It was felt that the good practice generated by it is now so well established that it would continue without the need for any formal agreement. The expired Agreement is set out in *The Family Court Practice 2011*. It was to be read alongside the Public Law Outline (FPR PD12A) and set out guidelines that aimed to improve inter-agency working, reduce the backlog in the allocation of public law guardians, assist guardians to make the best use of their time and minimise the use of Cafcass 'duty advisers'.

On 1 October 2009 and again on 1 April 2010 Sir Mark Potter P and the Chief Executives of HMCS (as it then was) and Cafcass entered into agreements for what were described as 'short-term measures' and which became known as his 'Interim Guidance' (PIG1 and PIG2). Each was designed initially to last six months.

On the Expiry of PIG2 on 1 October 2010, we came to an Agreement to assist Cafcass to manage constantly increasing demand for its services pending implementation of the Family Justice Review.

The Agreement was to last until 30 September 2011 and contained provision for the Ministry of Justice, HMC(T)S, and the Department for Education to monitor its effect. The Ministry of Justice and the Department for Education have sent the Local Performance Improvement Groups the results of their 'Review of local arrangements between Cafcass and Designated Family Judges.' This review document concludes that the Agreement, 'has been successful in achieving its aims, which is demonstrably clear from the statistical evidence, supported by concurring opinion from frontline practitioners collected through an online survey.'

The success of the Agreement has been as a result of two main factors –

1 Cooperative working between the courts, Cafcass and other agencies with strong information-sharing across the system being used to identify ways of improving the system locally.

2 Improved good practice in observing the detailed case management provisions of the Public Law Outline Practice Direction.

While we accept the recommendation in the review document that, 'with the continued high levels of s 31 applications being forecast and the consequent continuation of high demand for Cafcass services, there is strong evidence that the successful working practices adopted by local areas to manage current workloads should be maintained', we are confident that the arrangements for good communication and working relations which were already in existence in some areas, but which were formalised by the Designated Family Judges and Cafcass Heads of Service under the PIGs and restated at paragraph 4 of the Agreement will be maintained.

In these circumstances, we have come to the conclusion, after consulting the Designated Family Judges and local Cafcass managers, that it would not be right formally to renew the Agreement and that in any event it is unnecessary to do so.

We are both of the view that the good practice generated by the PIGs and by the Agreement is now well established and should continue without the need for any formal agreement between us. Thus the spirit of the Agreement will continue to operate: local discussions and initiatives will continue and local agreements or protocols will remain in place or new ones be drawn up as the need arises. We are confident that Judges and magistrates hearing cases under the Children Act will continue to manage according to the Public Law Outline and the Private Law Programme and will continue to assist guardians in the manner envisaged in paragraphs 9 to 11 of the Agreement and set out in the final paragraph of the joint message which we sent with the Agreement on 1 October 2010.

Sir Nicholas Wall
President of the Family Division

Anthony Douglas, CBE
Chief Executive, Cafcass

Domestic Abuse Committee of the Family Justice Council Protocol November 2011

Citations: [2012] 1 FLR 1226

Process Servers: Non-Molestation Orders

Introduction

This is to set out clearly an agreed protocol for the service of non-molestation orders and injunctions made by the courts to protect people from violence and harassment.

Without these orders being correctly served on the person against whom they are made, and proper proof of that service, the courts cannot enforce the orders or punish any breach or the breaking of any term of the order.

All process servers must ensure that the rules of service are followed carefully or the order served will not be enforceable; **orders that are not enforceable do not protect.**

Steps to take

These are the steps which should be taken with orders from both the Family Proceedings Courts (Magistrates' Court) and the County Court to put them in force.

1 **Service on the respondent against whom the order was made.** When the court makes a non-molestation order and/or any other order/s to which a power of arrest is attached the orders are to be set out in Form FL406 or Form FL404a. That form (and any other order of the court made at the same time) must be served directly and personally on the respondent (or he must have been present when the order was made or be told by telephone or told directly in some other way).The respondent does not need to take the form or orders in his hand but some attempt must be made to hand them to him and tell him of their contents.

2 **Statement or proof of service.** As soon as the respondent has been handed the forms or orders (or told of the details of the order/s and power of arrest by telephone or otherwise) the process server (or person who has told him of the details of the order) must prepare a statement of service which will be served on the relevant police station. This statement will be used as proof that the respondent knew that there were orders made by the court that he had to obey. This statement should be made under oath or affirmation so that it can be relied on in the civil and the criminal courts.

3 **Statement requirement for the Criminal Courts.** In addition, so as to comply with legal requirements in the Criminal Courts, all statements must include the following words at the beginning –

> 'Criminal Justice Act 1967, s 9; Magistrates' Courts Act 1980, ss 5A(3)(a) & 5B; Magistrates' Courts Rules 1981, Rule 70.
>
> This statement consisting of __ pages each signed by me, is true to the best of my knowledge and belief and I make it knowing that if it is tendered in evidence I shall be liable to prosecution if I have wilfully stated anything which I know to be false or do not believe to be true.
>
> Signed ......'

This should avoid the need for attendance at the criminal courts as statements in this form can be accepted as evidence: without these words they cannot. Therefore, **all** statements should start with these words. **Proof of service means that orders can be enforced.**

4 **Identification.** The statement must include details of how the respondent was identified as the person to be served. Identification is important and how it took place must be clearly set out in the sworn statement. Ideally, identification should be from a photograph given to the process server but it can be from a description given to the process server by someone who knows the respondent

well. The respondent admitting his identity is not enough on its own, but can be part of the identification. Identification can also be because he was identified by someone else. The statement must contain a description of the respondent, as seen by the process server and a detailed description of service or the attempt at service on him.

5 **Service on the Police**. Without delay, the Form FL404a or FL406, and a copy of the statement showing that the respondent has been served with a copy of the order and/or informed of its terms, must be delivered to the officer in charge at that time at the police station for the applicant's address or the police station which has been named (or specified) by the court.

Proper service means proper protection.

Working Party of the Family Justice Council Guidelines December 2011

Citations: [2012] Fam Law 79

These guidelines on the issue of children giving evidence in family proceedings, have been produced by the Family Justice Council Working Party on Children Giving Evidence, chaired by the Rt Hon. Lord Justice Thorpe. They have been approved by the Council and I wish to add my endorsement.

The working party was set up following a referral from the Court of Appeal in *Re W* [2010] EWCA Civ 57. The Supreme Court in *Re W* [2010] UKSC 12 subsequently held that there was no longer a presumption or even a starting point against children giving evidence in such cases.

I am sure that these guidelines will be of benefit to members of the judiciary, lawyers and professionals, who have to deal with applications for children to give evidence in family proceedings.

May I take this opportunity to express my gratitude to all the members of the working party, and in particular to Alex Verdan QC, for the final version of these guidelines.

Sir Nicholas Wall
President of the Family Division

Children Giving Evidence in Family Proceedings

1 These Guidelines have been produced by Lord Justice Thorpe's Working Party.

2 This Working Party was set up following a request to the President of the Family Division by the Court of Appeal in *Re W* [2010] EWCA Civ 57, a case which considered the issue of children giving evidence in family proceedings.

3 That same case then went to the Supreme Court and is reported as *Re W* [2010] UKSC 12. It is now the leading authority on this issue. The Supreme Court held that there was no longer a presumption or even a starting point against children giving evidence in such cases.

4 Enquiries by this Working Party suggests that the number of applications for children giving evidence since this decision may be increasing.

5 The aim of these Guidelines is to provide those involved in family proceedings with advice as to what matters should be taken into account in such situations.

6 Hearsay evidence is of course admissible in family proceedings: Children (Admissibility of Hearsay Evidence) Order 1993, SI 1993/621.

7 The issue of whether a child should be further questioned or give evidence in family proceedings should be considered at the earliest possible opportunity by the court and all the parties and not left to the party intending to so apply.

Legal considerations

8 In light of *Re W*, in deciding whether a child should give evidence, the court's principal objective should be achieving a fair trial.

9 With that objective the court should carry out a balancing exercise between the following primary considerations:

(i) the possible advantages that the child being called will bring to the determination of truth balanced against;
(ii) the possible damage to the child's welfare from giving evidence i.e. the risk of harm to the child from giving evidence;

having regard to:

(a) the child's wishes and feelings, in particular their willingness to give evidence, as an unwilling child should rarely if ever be obliged to give evidence;
(b) the child's particular needs and abilities;
(c) the issues that need to be determined;
(d) the nature and gravity of the allegations;
(e) the source of the allegations;
(f) whether the case depends on the child's allegations alone;
(g) corroborative evidence;
(h) the quality and reliability of the existing evidence;
(i) the quality and reliability of any ABE interview;
(j) whether the child has retracted allegations;
(k) the nature of any challenge a party wishes to make;
(l) the age of the child; generally the older the child the better;
(m) the maturity, vulnerability and understanding, capacity and competence of the child; this may be apparent from the ABE or from professionals' discussions with the child;
(n) the length of time since the events in question;
(o) the support or lack of support the child has;
(p) the quality and importance of the child's evidence;
(q) the right to challenge evidence;
(r) whether justice can be done without further questioning;
(s) the risk of further delay;
(t) the views of the guardian who is expected to have discussed the issue with the child concerned if appropriate and those with parental responsibility;
(u) specific risks arising from the possibility of the child giving evidence twice in criminal or other and family proceedings taking into account that normally the family proceedings will be heard before the criminal; and
(v) the serious consequences of the allegations i.e. whether the findings impact upon care and contact decisions.

10 The Court must always take into account the risk of harm which giving evidence may do to children and how to minimise that harm, although that may vary from case to case but the Court does not necessarily need expert evidence in order to assess the risk.

11 Where there are concurrent or linked criminal proceedings there should be close liaison between the respective parties and the allocated judges and ideally linked directions hearings. The Police/CPS should be informed of any proposal that a child give evidence in family proceedings and their views obtained before any such decision is made.

Alternatives to child giving live evidence at a hearing

12 The Court needs to consider seriously the possibility of further questions being put to the child on an occasion distinct from the substantive hearing so as to avoid oral examination. This option would have significant advantages to the child and should be considered at the earliest opportunity and in any event before that substantive hearing. Such further questioning should be carried out as soon as possible after the incident in question.

PART V

The Court will need to take into account practical and procedural issues including:

(a) giving the child the opportunity to refresh his memory;
(b) the appropriate identity of the questioner;
(c) matching the skills of the questioner to the communication needs of the child;
(d) where the questioning should take place;
(e) the type and nature of the questions;
(f) advance judicial approval of any questions proposed to be put to the child;
(g) the need for ground rules to be discussed ahead of time by the judge, lawyers (and intermediary, if applicable) about the examination; and
(h) how the interview should be recorded.

Practical considerations pre-hearing

13 Once a decision has been made that a child should give evidence at a hearing and be questioned at court, the Court must factor in steps to improve the quality of the child's evidence and minimise the risk of harm to the child.

14 At the earliest opportunity and in any event before the hearing at which the child's evidence is taken, the following matters need to be considered:

(a) if 'live' cross examination is appropriate, the need for and use of a registered intermediary (subject to their availability) or other communication specialist to facilitate the communication of others with the child or relay questions directly, if indicated by the needs of the child;
(b) the use of other 'special measures' in particular live video link and screens;
(c) the full range of special measures in light of the child's wishes and needs;
(d) advance judicial approval of any questions proposed to be put to the child;
(e) the need for ground rules to be discussed ahead of time by the judge, lawyers (and intermediary, if applicable) about the examination;
(f) information about the child's communication skills, length of concentration span and level of understanding e.g. from an expert or an intermediary or other communication specialist;
(g) the need for breaks;
(h) the involvement and identity of a supporter for the child;
(i) the timetable for children's evidence to minimise time at court and give them a fresh clear start in the morning;
(j) the child's dates to avoid attending court;
(k) the length of any ABE recording, the best time for the child and the Court to view it (the best time for the child may not be when the recording is viewed by the court);
(l) admissions of as much of the child's evidence as possible in advance; including locations, times, and lay-outs;
(m) save in exceptional circumstances, agreement as to (i) the proper form and limit of questioning and (ii) the identity of the questioner.

15 If a child is to give oral evidence at the hearing the following should occur:

(a) a familiarisation visit by the child to the court before the hearing with a demonstration of special measures, so that the child can make an informed view about their use;
(b) the child should be accompanied and have a known neutral supporter, not directly involved in the case, present during their evidence;
(c) the child should see their ABE interview and/or their existing evidence before giving evidence for the purpose of memory refreshing;
(d) consideration of the child's secure access to the building and suitability of waiting/eating areas so as to ensure there is no possibility of any confrontation with anyone which might cause distress to the child (where facilities are inadequate, use of a remote link from another court or non-court location);
(e) identification of where the child will be located at court and the need for privacy.

16 Where possible the children's solicitor/Cafcass should be deputed to organise these matters.

17 A child should never be questioned directly by a litigant in person who is an alleged perpetrator.

Practical considerations at hearing

18 If the decision has been made that the child should give oral evidence at the hearing the following should occur:

(a) advocates should introduce themselves to the child;
(b) judges and magistrates should ask if the child would like to meet them, to help to establish rapport and reinforce advice;
(c) children should be encouraged to let the court know if they have a problem or want a break but cannot be relied upon to do so;
(d) professionals should be vigilant to identify potential miscommunication;
(e) the child should be told how the live video link works and who can see who;
(f) a check should be made (before the child is seated in the TV link room) to ensure that the equipment is working, recordings can be played and that camera angles will not permit the witness to see the Respondents;
(g) the parties should agree which documents the child will be referred to and ensure they are in the room where the child is situated for ease of access.

Examination of children

19 If the Court decides a child should give oral evidence, the Court and all parties should take into account the Good Practice Guidance in managing young witness cases and questioning children (part of the NSPCC/Nuffield Foundation research 'Measuring Up' July 2009 by Joyce Plotnikoff and Richard Woolfson) and the subsequent Progress Report which Guidance has been endorsed by the Judicial Studies Board, the Director of Public Prosecutions, the Criminal Bar Association and the Law Society: http://www.nspcc.org.uk/Inform/research/findings/measuring_up_guidance_wdf66581.pdf.

20 Examination of the child should take into account the Court of Appeal judgment in *R v Barker* [2010] EWCA Crim 4, para [42], which called for the advocacy to be adapted 'to enable the child to give the best evidence of which he or she is capable' and which questioning should:

(a) be at the child's pace and consistent with their understanding;
(b) use simple common words and phrases;
(c) repeat names and places frequently;
(d) ask one short question (one idea) at a time;
(e) let the child know the subject of the question;
(f) follow a structured approach, signposting the subject;
(g) avoid negatives;
(h) avoid repetition;
(i) avoid suggestion or leading, including 'tag' questions;
(j) avoid a criminal or 'Old Bailey' style cross examination;
(k) avoid 'do you remember' questions;
(l) avoid restricted choice questions;
(m) be slow and allow enough time to answer;
(n) check child's understanding;
(o) test the evidence not trick the witness;
(p) take into account and check the child's level of understanding;
(q) not assume the child understands;
(r) be alert to literal interpretation;
(s) take care with times, numbers and frequency;
(t) avoid asking the child to demonstrate intimate touching on his or her own body (if such a question is essential, an alternative method, such as pointing to a body outline, should be agreed beforehand).

Court's overriding duty

21 All advocates have a responsibility to manage the questioning of a child witness fairly. However, the ultimate responsibility for ensuring that the child gives the best possible evidence in order to inform the court's decision rests with the tribunal. It should set out its expectations of the advocates and make it clear to the child witness that they can indicate to the court if they feel they are not saying what they want to say or do not understand what is being said to them.

The court must be scrupulous in the attention it gives to the case management and control of the questioning process and should be prepared to intervene if the questioning is inappropriate or unnecessary.

22 These Guidelines will be reviewed periodically. Those involved in family proceedings are invited to contact the Family Justice Council with any relevant comments.

Working Party of the Family Justice Council

Working Party of the Family Justice Council Guidance December 2011

Citations: [2012] 1 FLR 980

MARACs and Disclosure into Court Proceedings

1 Multi-agency risk assessment conferences (MARACs) are a recent development in addressing the highest risk cases of domestic abuse. There are regular MARAC meetings held in most local authority areas in England and Wales that collate information about high risk cases of domestic abuse with a view to creating a co-ordinated safety plan for the victim and children (if any). The work is case specific and all relevant agencies (both statutory and voluntary) will attend at or contribute to the conference. MARACs can therefore appear a valuable source of information in court proceedings where domestic abuse may be an issue.

2 Normally, if it is a matter of public record that domestic abuse has occurred (e.g. through Police involvement), the victim is aware that a MARAC is taking place and should be offered support through an Independent Domestic Violence Advisor (IDVA). However, the alleged perpetrator will not have been so informed but may sometimes be aware of it e.g. through the victim.

3 The essential purposes of a MARAC are:

- (a) To share information about risk;
- (b) To devise a co-ordinated safety plan for the adult victim;
- (c) To liaise with appropriate agencies to address safety of children and include as needed safety actions in the plan;
- (d) To address the behaviour of the alleged perpetrator;
- (e) To address the safety of staff working with the family.

Clearly it is of importance that generally the details of the MARAC safety plan are kept confidential if it is to be effective for to do otherwise would be to increase risk. Hence the tension between the potential existence of relevant information and the need for confidentiality.

4 MARAC staff members are neither lawyers nor paralegals. Thus they will have no inherent appreciation of what may be 'disclosable material'. Moreover, minute-taking may not be seen as a primary skill and thus minutes may be neither full nor entirely reliable.

5 Accordingly it is thought helpful to offer some guidance both to legal practitioners and to MARACs where consideration is being given to seeking disclosure of documents or other information. Such a request is most likely to come from the one whose conduct is under scrutiny at the MARAC.

6 Three key principles underpin this guidance –

(a) A MARAC is not a legal entity and therefore the owner of information shared at a MARAC is the original supplying agency;
(b) MARACs should only be required to disclose information by an order of the court;
(c) Any request for information must be an informed request setting out the nature of the information sought i.e. there must be no 'fishing expedition'.

7 The question of disclosure should always be considered well in advance of a contested hearing and be dealt with by an order for directions. Notice should ordinarily be given to the Chair of the MARAC; if that is not practicable, the order should allow a MARAC representative to appear and object before compliance is required. Any order should be addressed to the Chair of the MARAC.

8 When any such order for disclosure is made and served on a MARAC, the Chair of the MARAC is under a duty to raise formal objection if any disclosure will interfere significantly with a safety plan or may cause harm to any relevant child. If, however, a decision is made not to make a formal objection –

(a) The MARAC Chair should identify the documents currently held (which in practice will usually only be the minutes);
(b) If the minutes refer to information supplied and held by another organisation, the court should be invited to make an order directed to that organisation (if necessary) unless the Chair has that organisation's consent to disclose;
(c) This approach should apply both to statutory and voluntary organisations;
(d) If any document ordered to be disclosed is believed by the Chair to be potentially unreliable (e.g. the minutes), the court should be so informed;
(e) If a MARAC is in doubt whether to disclose they may make disclosure to the court setting out their concerns and reservations (e.g. any potential impact on safety) but, in so doing, they accept that the court may nevertheless order disclosure;
(f) The MARAC Chair may also draw to the attention of the court, the parties or the relevant organisation (as the case may be) that the significance of any information held depends upon other information held by a participating organisation and identify that organisation.

9 It will sometimes happen that MARACs hold information that they believe would be useful to a court but which they do not want to disclose to all parties. In those circumstances they should disclose the information to the relevant statutory body (local authority, Police, Cafcass) for them to use as appropriate in court proceedings.

10 As with supported contact centres, MARAC workers and IDVAs (as opposed to professional representatives of organisations attending a MARAC) should not ordinarily be called as a witness in court proceedings.

Working Party of the Family Justice Council

ANNEX – WHAT IS A MARAC?

More detailed information is available from the CAADA website[1]. In brief:

A MARAC is a meeting where information is shared on the highest risk domestic abuse cases between representatives of local police, health, child protection, housing practitioners, Independent Domestic Violence Advisors (IDVAs) and other specialists from the statutory and voluntary sectors. After sharing all relevant information they have about a victim, the representatives discuss options for increasing the safety of the victim and turn these into a co-ordinated action plan. The primary focus of the MARAC is to safeguard the adult victim. The MARAC will also make links with other fora to safeguard children and manage the behaviour of the perpetrator.

1 http://www.caada.org.uk/News/FAQs.htm#whatismarac

At the heart of a MARAC is the working assumption that no single agency or individual can see the complete picture of the life of a victim, but all may have insights that are crucial to their safety. The victim does not attend the meeting but is represented by an IDVA who speaks on their behalf and whose work has been found to make a significant positive difference for the non-abusive adult and children[2].

PART V

2 Safety in Numbers research 2009: http://www.caada.org.uk/research/research.html

Any frontline agency representative that undertakes a risk assessment with a victim, and thereby determines that their case meets the high risk threshold, can refer a victim's case to a local MARAC. IDVAs, police and health professionals commonly refer high risk victims to MARAC. This represents about 10% of the most serious domestic violence cases, including honour-based violence.

MARACs operate at a local level and are now in almost every area of England and Wales with 250 operational. The meeting takes place either fortnightly or monthly. All agencies contribute what is known about a family, and the agreed actions are noted for the follow-up safety plan. In the 12 months to June 2011, MARACs considered over 47,000 cases, which involved almost 64,000 children.

The membership of MARACs is taken from statutory and voluntary agencies. They have become the broadest multi-agency fora for considering the safety of adults and children affected by domestic abuse. The role of a dedicated caseworker or IDVA and the contribution of agencies that have been traditionally harder to engage – e.g. women's refuges, health professionals, housing – are important reasons for their perceived success.

Note—For information on MARACs, see *www.safelives.org.uk/practice-support/resources-marac-meetings*. A summary of the 2009 Safety in Numbers research is available at *www.safelives.org.uk/sites/default/files/resources/Safety%20In%20Numbers%202pp%20October%202010.pdf*.

Experts Committee of the Family Justice Council Guidelines December 2011

Citations: [2012] 1 FLR 889

Instruction of Medical Experts from Overseas in Family Cases

Foreword by the President of the Family Division

These guidelines for the instruction of medical experts from overseas in family cases have been produced by the Experts Committee of the Family Justice Council. They have been approved by the Council and I wish to add my endorsement.

We live in an age where people and ideas are much more mobile than hitherto and it is, perhaps, not surprising that the use of experts from overseas has grown in recent years. The welfare of the child demands that the best quality evidence should be available to the court, and specific expertise unavailable in the UK may be found elsewhere. In addition, given the problems that family courts experience with the supply of appropriately qualified experts, any enlargement of the pool of expertise is to be welcomed.

However, there are a number of issues relating to the regulation of overseas experts and to the need to have a clear understanding of their qualifications and credentials, as well as the applicability of their expertise to the UK context, which are addressed in this guidance.

Ultimately, it is for the court to be satisfied that it is appropriate for a suitably qualified overseas expert to be instructed to provide evidence on the issues identified by the court. I believe that this guidance will be of benefit to the judges, barristers, solicitors and experts dealing with family proceedings where expert evidence is required.

The Rt Hon. Sir Nicholas Wall

Background

Cases that come before the family courts involving issues of potential physical or psychological abuse and/or neglect and where there is a requirement for expert evidence are, by their very nature, complex.

The cases and the expert opinion which may be required cover the entire spectrum of child maltreatment and neglect. For the efficient delivery of justice in the Family Division, the courts require timely access to expert evidence and need to have confidence in the quality and validity of the expert advice and opinion given.

Whilst the initial draft discussion document was initially produced by a number of doctors who sit on the Expert Committee of the Family Justice Council, it is acknowledged that the principles discussed apply equally to non-medical experts working in the Family Justice system and indeed all experts in the jurisdiction. We are extremely grateful for the very helpful comments on earlier drafts of this document by the General Medical Council (GMC) and, particularly, by the Safeguarding Committee of the FJC and the Family Subcommittee of the Council of Circuit Judges.

Availability of experts

Many different aspects of medical expert evidence may be called for by the courts but in cases of child maltreatment there are usually relatively small numbers of individuals who are willing to act as experts, a problem which is acknowledged to have been exacerbated by the publicity that a small number of high profile cases has attracted over recent years.

Although in the main these high-profile cases have related to cases before the criminal courts, the implications for expert evidence as a whole have been all too apparent in the courts of the Family Division.

Advantages and disadvantages of the use of experts from overseas

Experts from overseas represent a valuable resource for the family justice system but it is recognised that there are potential advantages and disadvantages to their use.

(I) POTENTIAL ADVANTAGES

(a) May create a greater pool of expertise available to the courts.

(b) May make available to the courts expertise from very small super specialist areas where similar expertise is simply not available in the UK (but the number of cases where this is likely to be an issue would be very small).

(c) Allows the availability of a further opinion from outwith the jurisdiction which may occasionally be of use to the court in arbitrating between opposing views.

(d) Use of an expert with genuinely new evidence and opinion can help promote discussion and dissemination of information.

(II) POTENTIAL DISADVANTAGES

(a) UK medical experts are almost invariably involved in active clinical practice appropriate to their expertise and are usually current NHS employees. The clinical practice of overseas experts may be organised in an entirely different way and the reason they may become known to advocates is as a result of 'headline' publications. There may be difficulties for the courts in obtaining appropriate information about an overseas expert's practice and/or experience.

(b) Experts chosen because they are known to hold opinions which are acknowledged to be consistently outwith the range of mainstream or reasonable range of opinion runs the risk of returning to a 'hired gun' mentality that the reforms of expert evidence over the past few years have sought to prevent.

(c) Need for the courts to ensure that overseas experts are familiar with UK court process.

(d) Cost.

(e) Possible need to ensure a regulatory system in place which is (i) applicable to all experts and (ii) has ability to impose sanctions on overseas experts who fail in their duties to UK courts.

PART V

Recommendations regarding the instruction of experts from overseas

We believe that there are sufficient safeguards currently available regarding the instruction of experts provided those safeguards are rigorously and consistently applied by the courts.

It is critical that all experts are properly instructed in accordance with the 2008 Practice Direction 'Experts in Family Proceedings Relating to Children' and any subsequent relevant Practice Direction issued by the President. It is for the court and not the parties to determine whether a particular expert is instructed and, if so, on what terms. Strict compliance with the terms of the Practice Direction by both advocates and Judges should obviate the potential disadvantages of the use of overseas experts addressed above. The court will no doubt wish to consider whether the instruction of an expert from overseas is justified according to the welfare needs of the child or children concerned and/or the Article 6 rights of any of the parties.

An application to instruct an expert from overseas should set out in writing:

(a) Why a UK-based expert is not to be used;
(b) What efforts have been made to identify a suitable UK expert;
(c) The financial implications of the instruction of the overseas expert and
(d) What consideration has been given as to the practical arrangements required to allow the foreign expert to contribute fully to experts meetings and for giving evidence to the court?

Prior to the instruction of an expert from outside the jurisdiction that expert should provide information that fulfils the recommendations outlined in Baroness Kennedy's report into *Sudden Unexpected Death in Infancy*[1]. This details the characteristics of the expert which are of equal importance to all experts instructed by the courts in England and Wales and is a position recently endorsed in a decision of the Court of Appeal (Criminal Division)[2].

1 *Sudden Unexpected Death in Infancy: The Report of a Working Group by the Royal College of Pathologists and the Royal College of Paediatrics and Child Health* (2004). Royal College of Pathologists and the Royal College of Paediatrics and Child Health.

2 *Henderson v R* [2010] EWCA Crim 1269.

Therefore, before an expert is instructed, the trial judge should in all cases establish:

- What is the expert's area of practice in terms of the relevance to the issues upon which the court requires guidance? Does the expert have something genuinely exceptional to offer in terms of his/her expertise?

This should be detailed in the curriculum vitae.

- Whether the expert is still in active clinical practice?

This has been modified by the CMO's report (Bearing Good Witness) to accept clinicians who are recently retired, within two years of active NHS equivalent practice.

- To what extent is the prospective witness an expert in the subject in which he or she will be required to give an opinion in written or oral evidence?

This should be apparent from the CV.

- When did he/she last see a case relevant to the instant case in their own clinical practice?

This is important and should differentiate those experts who offer an opinion in a clinical area in which they do not practise.

- Whether the prospective witness is in good standing with their Medical Royal College or overseas equivalent? Is he/she up-to-date with Continuing Professional Development? Is their current practice regulated by a Statutory Body? If so what is that body?

This should be apparent from the CV which should list membership of the appropriate professional organisation and make comment upon maintaining CPD.

- Has he/she received training in the role of the Expert Witness within the last five years? What experience does the expert have in providing reports for and giving evidence to the Courts in this and other jurisdictions over a similar period of time?

Expert Witness training is discussed in Baroness Kennedy's report, but is aspirational in the CMO's report.

- To what extent is his/her view widely held in terms of accepted mainstream views and the spectrum of opinion overall?

This information may be more readily available for UK based experts but should be sought as assiduously for experts from overseas.

- That the expert has confirmed his/her familiarity with the Practice Direction, is willing to comply with all its requirements and acknowledges the potential consequences of failure to so comply. These consequences would include:
  - that any judgment arising from the case is likely to be made available to the GMC (or any other equivalent regulatory body) should a complaint be made about the experts conduct within the proceedings and
  - that judgments in which criticisms are made of experts who are judged to be partial are likely to be made in the public domain.
- The Judge should also direct the means by which feedback regarding the outcome of the case should be provided to all of the experts instructed.

This should in most cases be by means of provision of a copy of the Judgment or those aspects of it of direct relevance to the Court's assessment of the relevant expert's evidence.

Conclusions

We believe that the above principles regarding the instruction of all experts, whether UK-based or from overseas, should be considered a Guide to Best Practice and that their universal and consistent application will go as far as is reasonably possible to ensure that appropriate expert evidence is available to the courts of the Family Division and that, when required, such evidence is given by individuals with the appropriate expertise and experience.

Experts Committee of the Family Justice Council

Practice Direction 24 March 2012

Citation of Authorities

Preamble

1 This Practice Direction is issued in order to clarify the practice and procedure governing the citation of authorities and applies throughout the Senior Courts of England and Wales, including the Crown Court, in county courts and in magistrates' courts.

Repeal

2 Practice Direction (Court of Appeal: Citation of Authority) [1995] 1 WLR 1096 of 22 June 1995, Practice Statement (Court of Appeal: Authorities) [1996] 1 WLR 854 of 15 May 1996, paragraph 8 of Practice Statement (Supreme Court: Judgments) [1998] 1 WLR 825 of 22 April 1998, paragraph 3 of Practice Direction (Judgments: Form and Citation) [2001] 1 WLR 194 of 11 January 2001, and, in so far as they remain in force, paragraphs 10.1 and 10.2 of Practice Direction ((Court of Appeal (Civil Division)) [1999] 1 WLR 1027 of 19 April 1999 are hereby revoked.

Variation

3 Practice Direction (Criminal Proceedings: Consolidation) [2002] 1 WLR 2870 of 8 July 2002 (as amended) is varied so that all references to paragraph 10.1 of Practice Direction (Court of Appeal (Civil Division)) [1999] 1 WLR 1027; [1999] 2 All ER 490 are to read as references to paragraphs 5–13 of this Practice Direction.

4 Practice Direction 52 supplementing CPR Pt 52 is varied so that paragraph 15.11(2) reads as follows:

'(2) The bundle of authorities should comply with the requirements of Practice Direction: Citation of Authorities (2012) and in general –

(a) have the relevant passages of the authorities marked;
(b) not include authorities for propositions not in dispute; and
(c) not contain more than 10 authorities unless the scale of the appeal warrants more extensive citation.'

Citation of Authority

5 When authority is cited, whether in written or oral submissions, the following practice should be followed.

6 Where a judgment is reported in the Official Law Reports (AC, QB, Ch, Fam) published by the Incorporated Council of Law Reporting for England and Wales, that report must be cited. These are the most authoritative reports; they contain a summary of the argument. Other series of reports and official transcripts of judgment may only be used when a case is not reported in the Official Law Reports.

7 If a judgment is not (or not yet) reported in the Official Law Reports but it is reported in the Weekly Law Reports (WLR) or the All England Law Reports (All ER) that report should be cited. If the case is reported in both the WLR and the All ER either report may properly be cited.

8 If a judgment is not reported in the Official Law Reports, the WLR, or the All ER, but it is reported in any of the authoritative specialist series of reports which contain a headnote and are made by individuals holding a Senior Courts qualification (for the purposes of section 115 of the Courts and Legal Services Act 1990), the specialist report should be cited.

9 Where a judgment is not reported in any of the reports referred to in paragraphs [6] to [8] above, but is reported in other reports, they may be cited.

10 Where a judgment has not been reported, reference may be made to the official transcript if that is available, not the handed-down text of the judgment, as this may have been subject to late revision after the text was handed down. Official transcripts may be obtained from, for instance, BAILLI (http://www.bailii.org/). An unreported case should not usually be cited unless it contains a relevant statement of legal principle not found in reported authority.

11 Occasions arise when one report is fuller than another, or when there are discrepancies between reports. On such occasions, the practice outlined above need not be followed, but the court should be given a brief explanation why this course is being taken, and the alternative references should be given.

12 If a judgment under appeal has been reported before the hearing but after skeleton arguments have been filed with the court, and counsel wish to argue from the published report rather than from the official transcript, the court should be provided with photocopies of the report for the use of the court.

13 Judgments reported in any series of reports, including those of the Incorporated Council of Law Reporting, should be provided either by way of a photocopy of the published report or by way of a copy of a reproduction of the judgment in electronic form that has been authorised by the publisher of the relevant series, but in any event (1) the report must be presented to the court in an easily legible form (a 12-point font is preferred but a 10- or 11-point font is acceptable) and (2) the advocate presenting the report is satisfied that it has not been reproduced in a garbled form from the data source. In any case of doubt the court will rely on the printed text of the report (unless the editor of the report has certified that an electronic version is more accurate because it corrects an error contained in an earlier printed text of the report).

14 This Direction is made by the Lord Chief Justice with the agreement of the Master of the Rolls and the President of the Family Division. It is issued in accordance with the procedure laid down in Part 1 of Schedule 2 to the Constitutional Reform Act 2005.

The Right Honourable
The Lord Judge
The Lord Chief Justice of England and Wales

Practice Guidance
March 2013

Terminology for Litigants in Person

1 In its Report of November 2011 the Civil Justice Council (CJC) recommended that in future individuals who conduct legal proceedings on their own behalf, and have traditionally been referred to as Litigants in Person (LiPs), should in future be referred to as self-represented litigants (SRLs). Subsequently the term SRL has gained some currency. LiP has however also continued to be used. The use of two terms to refer to the same thing is less than ideal. It is confusing both for individual litigants and the courts.

2 The Judges' Council (including the Lord Chief Justice and President of the Family Division) has consequently considered the CJC's recommendation, and authorised me as Master of the Rolls and Head of Civil Justice, to issue Guidance, to promote clarity, certainty and simplicity, on the term to be used in future.

3 I have considered all the circumstances, including the fact that the term LiP: is used in statute (eg, The Litigants in Person (Costs and Expenses) Act 1975); is and will continue to be used by Government; is commonly understood and well-known both by the legal profession and individuals generally; the term SRL is unclear in its scope, as it can variously be understood to suggest that individuals are conducting the entirety of legal proceedings on their own behalf, that they are only conducting court advocacy on their own behalf or, that they have themselves obtained representation i.e., secured the service of an advocate.

4 In the light of these factors I have therefore determined, with the unanimous agreement of the Judges' Council, that the term SRL should not be adopted or used in future.

5 The term 'Litigant in Person' (LiP) should continue to be the sole term used to describe individuals who exercise their right to conduct legal proceedings on their own behalf.

6 This Guidance applies to all proceedings in all criminal, civil and family courts.

Lord Dyson MR

Judicial response to litigants in person—The Judicial Working Group on Litigants in Person: report (Judiciary of England and Wales, July 2013) contains a number of recommendations for judges and the parties where one or more parties are in person in civil and family proceedings. Adjustment towards a more inquisitorial approach to case management and to assist litigants in person is recommended and the working group urges training for the judiciary and an approach that spans all forms of civil proceedings. The role of lay assistants (McKenzie friends) is considered fully.

Protocol
19 July 2013

Communications Between Judges of the Family Court and Immigration and Asylum Chambers of the First-tier Tribunal and Upper Tribunal

Introduction

1 This protocol has been issued by the Senior President of Tribunals and the President of the Family Division and Head of Family Justice

PART V

2 This protocol applies where an immigration appeal is pending before the Tribunal and the welfare of a child in the United Kingdom is likely to be affected by the decision in those proceedings and there are family proceedings in existence relating to that child. It applies to all family proceedings in the High Court, a County Court or a Family Proceedings Court and (once the Family Court has been established) in the High Court or the Family Court. For ease of reference, these courts are all referred to hereafter as the Family Court.

3 It is anticipated that judges in the Tribunal and the Family Court will be assisted by knowing of the existence of the proceedings in the other jurisdiction, the issues arising, the procedure and time scale for determining them and any information disclosed in the other jurisdiction that may be of relevance to the respective immigration or family court decision.

4 This protocol is designed to enable judges in each jurisdiction to communicate in order to obtain information about proceedings in their respective jurisdictions which may affect the outcome of the proceedings before them and to make better informed decisions.

5 The timeline of the respective proceedings is likely to be of assistance to each jurisdiction. Regard should be had to the guidance in *Re M and N (Parallel Family and Immigration Proceedings)* [2008] EWHC Fam 2281, [2008] 2 FLR 2030.

6 It is not the role of the judges in either jurisdiction to predict the outcome of the proceedings in the other jurisdiction. Where the decision in the Family Court is likely to be a weighty consideration in the immigration decision, it is anticipated that it will normally be necessary for the Tribunal to wait until the Family Court judge has reached a decision on the issue relevant to the immigration appeal. If so, either the appeal will be allowed by the Tribunal in anticipation of a short period of leave being granted or the hearing will be adjourned, depending on the anticipated timescale of the family proceedings.

Disclosure of documents and directions

A DIRECTIONS

7 Documents in family proceedings cannot be disclosed to third parties including judges in the Tribunal without an order of the Family Court Judge. There are no formal constraints on disclosure of material supplied for the purpose of an appeal in the Tribunal; a direction is sufficient to respond to a request from the Family Court. The First-tier Tribunal's powers to give directions do not include the power to direct disclosure from the parties or third parties although it may issue a witness summons but the Upper Tribunal has such a power where necessary for the fair hearing of the appeal.

8 Where it appears to a judge that there are or may be relevant proceedings pending in another court or Tribunal directions may be issued at case management stage requiring disclosure by the relevant party of the court reference numbers of any past or current immigration proceedings or any past or current family proceedings that have involved any of the parties.

9 The kind of information likely to be relevant that may be held by either jurisdiction is indicated at Annex 1 to this Protocol.

B COMMUNICATION

10 A request for disclosure of documents in the immigration proceedings may be sought at the instigation of the family judge using the form of order set out in Annex 2 part 1.

11 An application for disclosure of documents in family proceedings should be directed to the Designated Family Judge and should state clearly the date by which such information is to be needed which should ideally be no longer than four weeks.

12 A request for disclosure of information or documents in the family proceedings may be sought either by one of the parties direct or at the instigation of the Tribunal judge using the form set out in Annex 2 part 3.

13 A request for the supply of information or documents from the Tribunal should be directed to the Resident Judge of the relevant Tribunal Chamber.

C SUPPLY OF INFORMATION

14 A draft direction of the Tribunal judge responding to the application of the Family judge is set out in Annex 2 part 2.

15 Where a judge of the family court decides that information can be supplied to a judge in the Tribunal, the judge shall inform the Resident Judge of this fact and at the same time indicate any conditions on the use of the material that are necessary in the circumstances. A draft order is set out in Annex 2 part 4.

16 Directions providing for the anonymity of children and where necessary other parties in both family and immigration proceedings will be considered by the judge in accordance with the joint guidance issued by the President of the Family Division, the Judicial College and the Society of Editors in July 2011 (see 17) and Anonymity Directions in the First-tier Tribunal (IAC) Presidential Guidance Note No 2 of February 2011 (see 18).

17 http://www.judiciary.gov.uk/publications-and-reports/guidance/2011/family-courts-media-access-reporting

Note—See *www.familylaw.co.uk/system/uploads/attachments/0002/9373/family-courts-media-july2011.pdf*.

18 http://www.justice.gov.uk/downloads/tribunals/immigration-and-asylum/lower/guidance-2-2011-.pdf

Sir James Munby
President of the Family Division and Head of Family Justice

Sir Jeremy Sullivan
Senior President of Tribunals

****

Note—The Annexes are available to download at *www.familylaw.co.uk*.

PART V

Protocol and Good Practice Model October 2013

Disclosure of Information in Cases of Alleged Child Abuse and Linked Criminal and Care Directions Hearings

1 PARTIES

1.1 The signatories to the 2013 Protocol and Good Practice Model (hereinafter the '2013 protocol') with the exception of the paragraphs listed at 1.4 below are the Senior Presiding Judge, the President of the Family Division, and the Director of Public Prosecutions on behalf of the Crown Prosecution Service (CPS).

1.2 This 2013 protocol is issued with the support of the Association of Chief Police Officers (ACPO), HM Courts & Tribunals Service and the Association of Independent Local Safeguarding Children Board (LSCB) Chairs.

1.3 The Department for Education (DfE), the Welsh Government (WG), Local Government Association (LGA) and Association of Directors of Children Services (ADCS) are not signatories to the 2013 protocol and the content of this document is not, nor does it seek to be binding on Local Authorities. However, the DfE, WG, LGA and ADCS support the content of this document and consider it to be a Good Practice Model, offered by way of assistance, and therefore urge all Local Authorities to adopt the disclosure practices described within the document, observance of which will improve timeliness and therefore achieve better outcomes for children and young people who are subject to the relevant proceedings.

1.4 Paragraphs 7.1, 11.5, 11.7, 11.8, 16.1 to 16.7, 16.9, 16.10, 16.15 and all of 17 of this 2013 protocol are directed at the judiciary. The signatories to those paragraphs are the President of the Family Division and the Senior Presiding Judge.

2 SCOPE

2.1 This 2013 protocol will apply to cases involving criminal investigations into alleged child abuse[1] (child victims who were aged 17 and under at the time of the alleged offending) and/or Family Court[2] proceedings concerning a child (aged 17 and under).

1 Child abuse includes both sexual abuse and non-sexual abuse
2 Family Court means for the time being the Family Proceedings Court, the County Court (when exercising its family jurisdiction) and the Family Division of the High Court. Once the Family Court comes into existence it means the Family Court and the Family Division of the High Court

2.2 This 2013 protocol will come into force on 1 January 2014.

3 AIMS AND OBJECTIVES

3.1 To provide early notification to the Local Authority and to the Family Court that a criminal investigation has been commenced.

3.2 To provide timely early notification to the Local Authority and to the Family Court of the details and timescale of criminal prosecution.

3.3 To facilitate timely and consistent disclosure of information and documents from the police, and the CPS, into the Family Justice System.

3.4 To provide notification to the police and the CPS of an application to the Family Court for an order for the disclosure of prosecution material into the Family Justice System.

3.5 Subject to the Family Procedure Rules 2010 (and relevant Practice Directions[3]) the Criminal Procedure Rules 2013 and the common law duty of confidentiality, to facilitate timely and consistent disclosure of information and documents from the Family Justice System to the police and/or the CPS.

3 In particular, Practice Direction 12G

3.6 To provide a timely expeditious process for the Local Authority to respond to a request from the police for material held by the Local Authority which would assist a criminal investigation.

3.7 To provide for timely consultation between the CPS and the Local Authority where Local Authority material satisfies the test in Criminal Procedure and Investigations Act 1996 for disclosure to the defence.

3.8 To provide a streamlined and standard process for applications by the police and/or the CPS for the permission of the Family Court for disclosure of material relating to Family Court Proceedings.

3.9 To specify a procedure for linked directions hearings in concurrent criminal and care proceedings.

Part A: Disclosure into the Family Justice System

LOCAL AUTHORITY REQUEST TO THE POLICE FOR DISCLOSURE

4.1 As soon as reasonably practicable and in any event on issue of proceedings, the Local Authority will provide notice to the police of the contemplation or existence of Family Proceedings using the form at Annex D to this agreement. The form at Annex D also acts as a request for disclosure from the police (to include a reasonable timescale[4] not exceeding 14 days for the disclosure of the material). The form at Annex D will be sent to the police single point of contact (SPOC) attached at Annex A; (see paragraph 19.2 below).

4 In setting the appropriate reasonable timescale, the Local Authority will take account of the timetable of the Family Court proceedings, the requirement that care proceedings must be completed within 26 weeks of the date on which the application was issued, and the requirements of the revised Public Law Outline (PLO)

4.2 Where criminal proceedings have been commenced (or are contemplated), the police will immediately forward a copy of the form at Annex D to the CPS. The CPS will give due priority to making charging decisions in cases involving Family Court Proceedings.

4.3 Where the information or documents sought does not relate to a child abuse investigation, the police SPOC will forward the form at Annex D to the unit or units holding the information or documents and will take responsibility for liaison with those units and to ensure the provision of information to the Local Authority.

4.4 It is to be understood by all Parties that the 2013 protocol should be used proportionately and is designed to facilitate only requests for material held by the police relevant to the central issues in the case. Requests for disclosure should not be drawn any wider than is absolutely necessary and only relevant material should be disclosed. The disclosure request to the police must be focussed identifying the documents which are really needed[5].

5 *Re H-L (A child)* [2013] EWCA Civ 655

5 NOTIFICATION BY THE POLICE TO THE LOCAL AUTHORITY OF THE EXISTENCE AND STATUS OF CRIMINAL INVESTIGATION

5.1 Within 5 working days of the commencement of the investigation, the police will provide to the Local Authority SPOC details of the criminal investigation using the form at Annex C to this Protocol (contact details for Local Authority SPOCs are listed at Annex B, see paragraph 19.3 below).

5.2 The police will contact the Local Authority SPOC at the point of charge, providing details of offences, custody status of defendants, bail conditions and court timescales. The police will also provide to the Local Authority contact details for the CPS.

5.3 In the event that the suspect(s) is/are not charged, the police in consultation with the CPS will provide the Local Authority with reasons why there will be no prosecution[6].

6 Decisions to prosecute are made in accordance with the Code for Crown Prosecutors (section 10 Prosecution of Offences Act 1985)

5.4 Within 5 working days of each Case Management Hearing[7] in the Crown Court, the CPS will provide to the Local Authority SPOC (or Local Authority lawyer if known) details of the future timetable of the criminal proceedings and details of any directions relevant to the Local Authority or to concurrent Family Proceedings.

7 Case management hearings in the Crown Court will include Preliminary Hearings and Plea and Case Management Hearings

5.5 Within 2 working days of receipt, the Local Authority will forward the details at paragraphs 5.1 to 5.4 above to the Family Court.

6 VOLUNTARY DISCLOSURE BY POLICE/CPS TO LOCAL AUTHORITY AND INTO THE FAMILY JUSTICE SYSTEM

6.1 Where criminal proceedings have been commenced (or are contemplated), the police should consult with the CPS before a decision is made on whether to disclose police material to the Local Authority. The timing of such consultation must take into account any reasonable timescale specified by the Local Authority at paragraph 4.1 above.

6.2 Within the timescale specified by the Local Authority in Annex D (paragraph 4.1 above), the police will provide (via secure means, e.g. secure email) the requested material to the Local Authority. The police will complete and return the second part of the form at Annex D. The Local Authority agrees that the police material will only be disclosed to the professionals and Parties in the Family Proceedings (unless the permission of the court is obtained to disclose material to others).

6.3 Visually recorded interviews (Achieving Best Evidence interviews) will not be released to the Local Authority except against a written undertaking from the Local Authority in order to prevent the unauthorised use of the evidence. The form of undertaking at Annex G should be used for this purpose.

6.4 Unless disclosure is required to ensure the immediate safety of a child, the police will not disclose material where to do so might prejudice the investigation and/or prosecution (or where on the grounds of confidentiality it is necessary to obtain the consent of persons providing statements). However, redacted disclosure should be made wherever possible. The police will indicate on the form at Annex D the approximate date on which disclosure can be made. The police (in consultation with the CPS) must provide detailed reasons on Annex D as to why any material is being withheld.

6.5 Alternatively, the police can indicate that disclosure will be made in the event that the Local Authority obtains a Family Court order stating that the material is not to be disclosed to named individual(s) (typically, suspects and/or witnesses in the criminal proceedings). Such a court order should also be obtained where possible in the event that disclosure is made (as at paragraph 6.4 above) to ensure the immediate safety of a child.

6.6 The Family Court may request disclosure from the Local Authority of material held by them and relating to the criminal case. Again, the Local Authority will notify the CPS (or the police if criminal proceedings have not commenced) as soon as reasonably practicable. Where the police and/or the CPS object to disclosure, they will make appropriate and timely representations to the Family Court explaining why such disclosure might be capable of prejudicing the criminal proceedings.

7 FAMILY COURT PROCEEDINGS: ORDERS FOR DISCLOSURE AGAINST THE POLICE AND/OR THE CPS

7.1 The Local Authority shall notify (within 2 working days of the application being made) the police and the CPS of any application to the Family Court (whether by the Local Authority or any other party) for disclosure of prosecution material. The Local Authority shall notify the police and/or the CPS of the date and time of the Family Court hearing at which disclosure will be determined[8]. Any order by the Family Court for disclosure will be in the form at Annex H to this protocol (use of which by the Family Court is mandatory). Where appropriate, the police and/or the CPS will assist the Local Authority in drafting Directions.

8 The Standard Directions Order, which is made by the Family Court in accordance with the PLO within 24 hours of care proceedings being issued, provides for any application for disclosure from any agency to be filed and served by a specified date prior to the Case Management Hearing (CMH) in the Family Court. Note that the PLO requires the CMH to be no later than 12 working days after the commencement of the care proceedings

7.2 Where directed, the police and/or the CPS shall attend the Family Court hearing to explain the implications for a criminal trial when orders for disclosure are being considered by the court. In any event, the police and/or the CPS shall provide written representations to the Family Court and the Local Authority where disclosure is opposed (explaining why disclosure might reasonably be considered capable of prejudicing the investigation and/or prosecution).

7.3 The Local Authority will ensure that any Order against the police and/or the CPS is served as soon as reasonably practicable (and in any event within 2 working days of the date of the order) on the police and/or the CPS.

7.4 The police and the CPS will comply with any court order.

Part B: Disclosure from the Local Authority/ Family Justice System into the Criminal Justice System

8 NOTIFICATION BY LOCAL AUTHORITY TO THE POLICE OF THE EXISTENCE AND STATUS OF FAMILY PROCEEDINGS

8.1 As soon as reasonably practicable and in any event on issue of proceedings, the Local Authority will provide notice to the police of the contemplation or existence of Family Proceedings using the form at Annex D to this 2013 protocol. Where Family Proceedings have commenced, details of all parties (and legal representatives) will be provided. Details of the allocated Local Authority lawyer will be provided. The form at Annex D will be sent to the police single point of contact (SPOC) attached at Annex A.

8.2 Where the form at Annex D is sent to the police at a stage before details of all parties to the Family Proceedings are known, the Local Authority will notify the police recipient of Annex D of the details of all parties (and legal representatives) to the Family Proceedings. The Local Authority will also provide details of the future timetable of the Family Proceedings. The police will forward the information to the CPS.

8.3 Where criminal proceedings have been commenced (or are contemplated), the police will forward a copy of the form at Annex D to the CPS. The CPS will give due priority to making charging decisions in cases involving Family Court Proceedings.

9 POLICE REQUEST TO LOCAL AUTHORITY FOR DISCLOSURE

9.1 Following the commencement of the investigation, the police will provide to the Local Authority SPOC the form at Annex C to this 2013 protocol. Details of the SPOC for each Local Authority are set out at Annex B (see paragraph 19.3 below).

9 Paragraph 3.6 Code of Practice Criminal Procedure and Investigations Act 1996

9.2 The Annex C form will include details of the investigation and prosecution if commenced (see paragraph 5.1 above). Requests for material must be as prescriptive and detailed as possible and necessary for the pursuit of reasonable lines of enquiry[9]. The form at Annex C will include reasonable timescales for the police to be given access to relevant material, but the presumption will be that the Local Authority will deal with any request from the police as expeditiously as possible so as to not to jeopardise the criminal investigation. Timescales will be case specific taking account of the stage/nature of the investigation and/or prosecution.

10 DISCLOSURE BY THE LOCAL AUTHORITY TO THE POLICE

10.1 Upon receipt of the form at Annex C from the police, the Local Authority SPOC (or delegated officer) will identify and collate relevant material from the Children's Services or other files as appropriate, the SPOC (or delegated officer) will liaise with relevant departments within the Local Authority in the collation of such material for the police to assist the criminal investigation.

10.2 The Local Authority will identify for the police the school(s) attended by the child/children subject to the investigation. This will enable the police to approach the school directly. Alternatively, if it is practicable to do so, the Local Authority will obtain and collate relevant educational files for police examination.

PART V

10.3 Subject to paragraphs 10.4 and 10.5 below, the Local Authority will ensure that documents relating to Family Court proceedings[10] are not included in the files to be examined by the police. Where there are documents relating to Family Court proceedings, the Local Authority will provide a list (e.g. by providing a copy of redacted court index) of that material without describing what it is, in order for the police and/or the CPS, if appropriate, to apply to the Family Court for disclosure.

10 Section 12(1) Administration of Justice Act 1960 prohibits such communication

10.4 Importantly, the Local Authority can disclose to the police documents which are lodged at court, or used in the proceedings, which already existed[11] (e.g. pre-existing medical reports). Similarly, the text or summary of a judgment given in the Family Court proceedings can be included in the files to be examined by the police[12].

11 *Re Ward (A Child)* [2010] EWHC 16 (Fam); [2010] 1 FLR 1497

12 Rule 12.73(1)(c) Family Procedure Rules 2010 and Practice Direction 12G

10.5 Paragraph 10.3 above does not prevent the Local Authority providing to the police documents or information relating to Family Court proceedings where (a) the police officer to whom disclosure is made is carrying out duties under section 46 Children Act 1989 or serving in a child protection or paedophile unit and (b) disclosure is for the purposes of child protection and not for the purposes of the criminal investigation[13].

13 Rule 12.73(1)(a)(viii) Family Procedure Rules 2010

10.6 Where material is disclosed in accordance with paragraph 10.5 above, the police cannot make onward disclosure of any documentation or information contained therein for the purpose of the investigation or prosecution without the express permission of the Family Court[14] (for the avoidance of doubt, this will include disclosure to the CPS).

14 A District Council (Applicant) v M (Respondent) & West Yorkshire Police (Interveners) [2007] EWHC 3471 (Fam); [2008] 2 FLR 390

10.7 Where, in exceptional circumstances[15], the Local Authority is not able to include other material (not relating to Family Court proceedings) in the files to be examined by the police, the Local Authority will notify the police in writing of the existence of this material; indicating the reason why the material is not being made available to the police. Such a course should be exceptional because the Local Authority recognises that the material will be regarded as sensitive by the police and the CPS. It will not be disclosed to the defence without further consultation with the Local Authority or order of the court (see paragraph 13.9 to 14.3 below).

15 The law permits the disclosure of confidential information where a countervailing public interest can be identified. Such a public interest will include the administration of justice, the prevention of wrongdoing and enabling another public body to perform its public duty (*R v Chief Constable of North Wales Police ex parte Thorpe* [1996] QB 396). In these circumstances, the exchange of relevant material with the police and CPS is not restricted under Data Protection Act 1998

10.8 Within the timescales set out in the Annex C request (or otherwise agreed between the Local Authority and the police), the police will examine and review the material collated by the Local Authority. The review will usually take place on Local Authority premises but may be elsewhere by agreement. The police may make notes and/or take copies of the material. The material will not be disclosed to the defence without further consultation with the Local Authority or order of the court (see paragraph 13.9 to 14.3 below).

10.9 Where further relevant Local Authority material comes to light after the police examination of the material at paragraph 10.8 above, the Local Authority will contact the police and/or the CPS to arrange an examination of the new material by the police.

10.10 Similarly, where new issues arise in the criminal case (e.g. following the receipt of the defence case statement), the police will submit a further Annex C form requesting access to material not previously examined.

11 APPLICATIONS BY POLICE AND THE CPS TO THE FAMILY COURT FOR DISCLOSURE OF MATERIAL RELATING TO FAMILY PROCEEDINGS

11.1 At the stage prior to service of prosecution papers pursuant to section 51 of the Crime and Disorder Act 1998, applications will be generally made by the police. After this stage, applications will generally be made by the CPS.

11.2 Applications by the police for disclosure must contain details of the named officer to whom release is sought[16] and must specify the purpose and use to which the material is intended to be put. Applications should seek leave (where appropriate) to disclose the material to the CPS, to disclose the material to the criminal defence solicitors[17] and (subject to section 98(2) of the Children Act 1989[18]) to use the material in evidence at the criminal proceedings.

16 *Re H (Children)* [2009] EWCA Civ. 704; [2009] 2 FLR 1531

17 Where required under section 3 or section 7A Criminal Procedure and Investigations Act 1996

18 Section 98(2) provides that statements and admissions in Family Court proceedings are not admissible in criminal proceeding

11.3 Applications by the CPS must specify the purpose and use to which the material is intended to be put and should seek leave to share the material with the police and with the defence and (subject to section 98(2) Children Act 1989) to use the material in evidence at the criminal proceedings.

11.4 Applications shall be made on Form C2. The application must be served by police or the CPS on all Parties to the Family Proceedings (The Local Authority having informed the police of details of all parties to Family Proceedings as per paragraphs 8.1 and 8.2 of this protocol).

11.5 The application will be determined at a hearing at the Family Court. Police and the CPS will not attend the hearing unless directed to do so by the Family Court.

11.6 Where it is practicable to seek prior written consent to disclosure from all Parties to the Family Proceedings, the police or the CPS should do so. Application should then be made in writing to the Family Court seeking a consent order.

11.7 Alternatively (and whenever this is possible), the police and/or the CPS will ask the Local Authority allocated lawyer (or SPOC if details of allocated lawyer are not known) to request that the Family Court considers the issue of disclosure to the police and/or the CPS at the next hearing. In this way, the Family Court will be in a position to make any orders as appear appropriate without the need for police and/or the CPS to make application to the Family Court. When requesting the Family Court to make an order in accordance with this paragraph, the Local Authority will put the other parties to the proceedings on notice; and will provide the court with details of the officer to whom disclosure is to be made and the purpose for which it is to be made.

11.8 In rare cases, where it considers it appropriate to do so, the Family Court should make orders for disclosure to the police and/or the CPS without application having been made by the police or the CPS.

12 TEXT OR SUMMARY OF JUDGMENT IN FAMILY PROCEEDINGS[19]

19 Rule 12.73(1)(c) Family Procedure Rules 2010 and Practice Direction 12G permits the disclosure of the text or summary of the whole or part of a judgement given in family proceedings to a police officer or a member of the CPS for the purpose of a criminal investigation or to enable the CPS to discharge its functions. The Police Officer or CPS lawyer may only communicate the information for the purpose for which he/she received the information.

12.1 The Local Authority will forward to the CPS copies of relevant Family Court judgments (and summaries thereof) in the possession of the Local Authority. The judgments may be appropriately redacted.

12.2 Where the Local Authority is not in possession of a judgment which appears to be relevant to the concurrent criminal proceedings (e.g. fact-finding judgment), it will notify the CPS in order that the CPS can obtain the judgment directly from the Family Court. In these circumstances it will not be necessary to make formal application for disclosure on Form C2; the CPS will request release of the judgment under Practice Direction 12G above.

12.3 Where it appears to the Local Authority that the judgment will be relevant to the criminal proceedings, the Local Authority will request that the Family Court expedites the preparation of the judgment for release to the CPS (and if possible at public expense). Alternatively, the issue of disclosure of the judgment to the CPS under Practice Direction 12G can be considered at a linked directions hearing.

13 DISCLOSURE BY THE CPS TO THE CRIMINAL DEFENCE

13.1 The Criminal Procedure and Investigations Act 1996[20] requires the prosecution to disclose to the defence any material (including sensitive material) that could reasonably be considered capable of undermining the prosecution case against the accused or of assisting the case for the accused (the 'disclosure test'). Where appropriate, application can be made to the criminal court to withhold sensitive material which satisfies the disclosure test on the grounds of public interest immunity (PII application).

20 Section 3 and section 7A

13.2 PII applications to the criminal court for the withholding of sensitive material should be rare. Fairness ordinarily requires that all material which weakens the prosecution case or strengthens that of the defence should be disclosed. There is no basis for making a PII application except where the prosecutor has identified material that fulfils the disclosure test, disclosure of which would create a real risk of serious prejudice to an important public interest[21].

21 *R v H and C* [2004] 2 AC 134

13.3 All material obtained from the Local Authority will be listed by the police on the sensitive disclosure schedule MG6D. The lists of material not disclosed by the Local Authority to the police will also be included on the MG6D (see paragraph 10.3 above: material relating to Family Proceedings; and paragraph 10.7 above: material withheld on the ground of confidentiality).

PART V

13.4 Material obtained by the police in accordance with Rule 12.73(1)(a)(viii) Family Procedure Rules 2010 (see paragraphs 10.5 and 10.6 above) must not be disclosed to the CPS. The police will reveal the existence of the material on the MG6D (without describing it). As appropriate, the CPS will seek the permission of the Family Court to access the material.

13.5 Where the material has been obtained following an application by the police to the Family Court, the police must indicate to the CPS whether the Family Court has given permission for the material to be shared with the CPS and with the defence. Further application to the Family Court may be required by the police and/or the CPS as appropriate.

13.6 The CPS will review the material in accordance with its statutory duties[22] and under the Attorney General's Guidelines on Disclosure. Only material which might undermine the prosecution case or might reasonably assist the defence case will fall to be disclosed. There will in no circumstances be 'blanket' disclosure to the defence.

22 Under Criminal Procedure and Investigations Act 1996

13.7 Where in accordance with paragraph 10.7 above a Local Authority document is not made available to the police on the basis of confidentiality (e.g. consent has not been obtained from the person to whom the document relates), the CPS will consider whether it is appropriate to seek access to such material by means of a witness summons in the criminal court[23].

23 Section 2 Criminal Procedure (Attendance of Witnesses) Act 1965

13.8 Where in these circumstances application is made by the CPS for a witness summons, the CPS will serve the application on the criminal court and the Local Authority, identifying the Local Authority SPOC as the person who is required to produce the document(s)[24]. In addition, where the Crown Court so directs[25], the CPS will, in accordance with the Criminal Procedure Rules, serve the application on the person to whom the confidential document relates.

24 Rule 28.5(3)(a) Criminal Procedure Rules 2013
25 Rule 28.5(3)(b)(i) Criminal Procedure Rules 2013

13.9 Where any Local Authority material reviewed by the CPS falls within the statutory disclosure test under the CPIA, the CPS will write to the Local Authority SPOC, within 2 working days of review whenever possible, setting out the reasons why the material falls to be disclosed and informing them of that decision. The form at Annex E to this 2013 protocol will be used by the CPS. The CPS will provide to the Local Authority proposals for the editing or summarising of the material for the purposes of disclosure to the defence. Where no material falls for disclosure, the CPS will inform the Local Authority that this is the case.

13.10 Within 5 working days of receipt of that notification, the Local Authority shall be given an opportunity to make any representations in writing to the CPS on the issues of disclosure. This will include objections to disclosure on the basis that the person to whom the material relates has not consented. Note that disclosure of documentation which has been created under the auspices, and for the purposes, of the LSCB, can only be made with the prior consent of the LSCB Chair[26].

26 For example, reports or documentation related to a Serious Case Review belong to the LSCB, rather than the Local Authority or other member agency of the LSCB

13.11 The form at Annex F to this 2013 protocol will be used for this purpose. Where, exceptionally, the Local Authority is unable to meet the 5 working day timescale, the Local Authority will contact the CPS to discuss whether the timescale can be extended in the particular circumstances of the case.

14 PUBLIC INTEREST IMMUNITY (PII) APPLICATION

14.1 If the Local Authority does not agree to disclosure of Local Authority material to the defence, the CPS must negotiate with the Local Authority to explore whether disclosure can be made in edited form or by summarising in another document the issues arising in the material[27]. Whilst recognising that the prosecution must always comply with its statutory duty of disclosure, the sensitivity can often be removed in this way. PII applications in the criminal court will be rare. Local Authority material relating to a child is no longer a 'class' of material to which PII applies. Depending on the sensitivity of the material, the Local Authority may itself agree that the public interest in the prosecution of crime overrides the interests of confidentiality[28]. In highly exceptional cases, the CPS may need to make disclosure to the defence of the edited/summarised document without the consent of the Local Authority.

27 *R v H and C* [2004] 2 AC 134
28 *R v Chief Constable of West Midlands ex parte Wiley* [1995] 1 AC 274

14.2 If a PII application is appropriate, the CPS will make a PII application to the criminal court as soon as reasonably practicable. The CPS will notify the Local Authority of the date and venue of the PII application and inform the Local Authority of their right to make representations to the criminal court[29].

29 Rule 22.3(b)(ii) Criminal Procedure Rules 2013

14.3 Where PII is sought on the basis of lack of consent from the person to whom the confidential document relates, CPS must in accordance with the Criminal Procedure Rules notify the person to whom the document relates[30] (as above, notification of date and venue of PII application and the interested person's right to make representations to the court).

30 Rule 22.3(b)(ii) Criminal Procedure Rules 2013

Part C: Linked Directions Hearings

15 Linked criminal and care directions hearings- criteria

15.1 This 2013 protocol will apply where a person connected with the child who is the subject of the care proceedings or the child himself is to be tried at the Crown Court for any violent or sexual offence or for an offence of child cruelty against the child, or any other child or any person connected with the child; and either:

(i) The Local Authority, CPS, or any party to the care proceedings (including the child's guardian) considers that the care and criminal proceedings do, or may, impinge on one another; or

(ii) In any public law proceedings in the High Court or County Court or in any proceedings in the Crown Court, a judge is satisfied that the protocol does, or may, apply.

PART V

16 ARRANGEMENTS FOR LINKED DIRECTIONS HEARINGS

16.1 The allocated case management judge in the Family Court (ACMJ)[31] will consider whether or not there is likely to be a need for a linked directions hearing in respect of the criminal and family cases. If the ACMJ considers that a linked directions hearing is likely to be appropriate he/she shall liaise with the relevant Resident Judge to invite him to nominate a judge to be responsible for the management of the criminal case.

31 In the Family Proceedings Court this will be the legal adviser

16.2 In the care proceedings it is expected that the ACMJ will issue directions for the linked hearing which will spell out the respective parties' obligations, and which may include, but will not be limited to, recordings and, orders in the form at Annex I to this protocol (use of which by the Family Court is mandatory). At the same time, the ACMJ will consider giving permission to the Local Authority to serve its case summary on the CPS and the Crown Court (in accordance with paragraph 16.6 below).

16.3 Once a judge has been identified to manage the criminal proceedings, the Resident Judge shall direct the listing officers to liaise with family listing to agree the listing of the criminal and care cases for a linked directions hearing before the nominated criminal judge and the ACMJ. In an appropriate case the Resident Judge may agree to the ACMJ undertaking the responsibility for the management of the criminal case if he/she is authorised to try criminal cases, and, where appropriate, serious sexual offence cases.

16.4 If on receipt of criminal proceedings sent from the Magistrates' Courts and consideration of that case by the Resident Judge, or if during a Case Management hearing[32] or other pre-trial hearing listed before the Crown Court, the Resident Judge or judge (as the case may be) is satisfied that this Protocol does or may apply but that no reference has yet been made to the ACMJ for consideration in accordance with paragraph 16.1 above, the judge shall notify the Designated Family Judge accordingly who shall consider with the relevant Resident Judge and the ACMJ, whether a linked directions hearing is required. If there is agreement on the need for a linked directions hearing, the Resident Judge shall nominate a judge to be responsible for the management of the criminal case and arrangements shall then be made for the criminal and care cases to be listed for a linked directions hearing in accordance with paragraph 16.3 above.

32 Case management hearings in the Crown Court will include Preliminary Hearings and Plea and Case Management Hearings

16.5 The criminal case shall be listed before the judge at the Crown Court in public with the linked directions appointment in the care proceedings listed for hearing in private immediately thereafter. Subject to any specific objections raised by the parties, the advocates appearing in the criminal case may be invited to remain during the directions appointment in the care proceedings.

16.6 In every case involving a linked directions hearing the Local Authority's legal representative, by no later than 4.00pm not less than 5 working days prior to the linked directions hearing, shall with the permission of the family court prepare and serve on the CPS and the Crown Court a case summary setting out the basis of the Local Authority's application, its contentions in respect of findings sought in relation to the 'threshold criteria' (Local Authority's 'threshold document'), the current position in respect of the child, details of the proposed assessments and/or expert(s) assessments being undertaken and the timescales for the same and the timetable (if any) set for the proceedings within the Family Court.

16.7 The Local Authority's legal representative and the CPS shall agree a schedule of issues identifying those matters which are likely to be considered at the linked directions hearing. The Local Authority shall circulate the Schedule to the solicitors for the other parties in the criminal and care proceedings by no later than 4.00pm not less than 2 working days prior to the linked directions hearing.

16.8 On the day of the linked directions hearing the advocates in the criminal and care proceedings shall meet no later than one hour prior to the time fixed for the hearing to discuss the schedule of issues with a view to identifying what directions may be required with particular reference to the trial timetable, disclosure and expert evidence and such other matters as may be identified by this Protocol.

16.9 The respective court files in the criminal and care proceedings shall be cross referenced and shall be clearly marked as 'linked' cases.

16.10 The directions hearing will be linked but not wholly combined because of the different parties and different procedural rules (such as with regard to privacy and rights of audience) which apply. The judge shall determine whether it is appropriate for some or all of the directions to be issued at a joint hearing or separately and the order of any directions to be issued.

16.11 At the conclusion of the hearing in the criminal case, counsel for the Crown will be invited to draw the minute of order, to be agreed with the defence, which will be submitted to the judge on the day of the hearing, for his/her approval.

16.12 The approved minute of order made in the criminal proceedings will be copied to the parties in the care proceedings by the CPS.

16.13 With the permission of the family court, the order made in the care proceedings will be copied by the Local Authority to the CPS and defence lawyers in the criminal proceedings.

16.14 The timing of the proceedings in a linked care and criminal case should appear in the Timetable for the Child[33].

33 In accordance with the Public Law Outline

16.15 Judicial continuity: Any adjourned linked directions hearing shall be listed before the same judge (unless the judge otherwise directs) but the judge who is the ACMJ shall not preside over the trial in the criminal proceedings, or pass sentence if there is a guilty plea, nor shall the judge give a 'Goodyear indication'. The judge in the criminal trial or who passes sentence if there is a guilty plea shall notify the ACMJ of the outcome.

17 Matters to be considered at the linked directions hearing

17.1 The timetabling[34] of both the criminal and care proceedings (with a view to such timetabling being coordinated to ensure the most appropriate order of trial and that each case is heard as expeditiously as possible).

34 *Re TB* [1995] 2 FLR 801 makes it clear beyond peradventure that the starting point is that the existence of criminal proceedings is not a reason to adjourn the care proceedings. For an exception see: *Re L* [2010] 1 FLR 790: in the particular circumstances, the welfare stage of Family Proceedings should have been delayed until after the criminal proceedings

17.2 Disclosure of evidence with particular reference to disclosure of evidence from one set of proceedings into the other with such permission as may be required by the relevant procedural rules.

17.3 Expert evidence with particular reference to the identification of expert witnesses, their willingness to act within the court timetable and the requirements of the Practice Direction concerning the instruction of Experts, their availability and role in the criminal and care hearings.

17.4 Any directions to be given in relation to issues of public interest immunity and for any witness summonses required for third party disclosure (Rule 28 Criminal Procedure Rules 2013).

17.5 Arrangements for the interviewing of children in care for the purpose of the criminal proceedings and any arrangements for the child to give evidence at any criminal or family hearing.

17.6 To ensure where appropriate that a transcript of relevant evidence or judgment in the trial heard first in time is available in the subsequent proceedings.

17.7 Issues relating to any question of assessment or therapeutic input required by any child involved in the proceedings.

17.8 Issues in relation to restrictions on publicity which it is considered may be required.

17.9 Issues in relation to any relevant material which may be pertinent to the issue of bad character (in respect of previous convictions or other alleged 'reprehensible behaviour'), whether of defendants or nondefendants.

17.10 Other legal or social work related steps in the Family Court proceedings.

18 REVIEW

18.1 The parties to this 2013 protocol and Good Practice Model and the organisations at paragraphs 1.1 and 1.2 above supporting the 2013 protocol will continuously review and monitor the operation of the provisions. The protocol will be subject to a formal review 12 months after the date of implementation.

19 LOCAL PROTOCOLS

19.1 Local agencies should agree and adopt a local protocol to give effect to this 2013 protocol signed by the Crown Court Resident Judges, Designated Family Judges, Police Forces, CPS and Local Authorities in each CPS Area. A local protocol must not depart from the requirements of the PLO and must require that orders used are in the form of Annex H and Annex I.

19.2 Each Police Force signatory to the local protocol will provide on the form at Annex A details of a suitable single point of contact (SPOC) for the receipt by secure email of the Annex D disclosure request from the Local Authority.

19.3 Each Local Authority signatory to the local protocol will provide on the form at Annex B details of a suitable single point of contact (SPOC) for the receipt by secure email of the Annex C disclosure request from the police.

20 SIGNATORIES

20.1 The following are signatories to the protocol: Date of agreement: **17 October 2013**

Senior Presiding Judge for England and Wales
Lord Justice Gross

President of the Family Division
The Rt. Hon Sir James Munby

Director of Public Prosecutions, Crown Prosecution Service
Keir Starmer QC

The following support the protocol: Association of Chief Police Officers, Association of Directors of Children Services, Association of Independent Local Safeguarding Children Board Chairs, Department for Education, HM Courts & Tribunals Service, Local Government Association, Welsh Government.

****

Note—The Annexes are available to download at *www.familylaw.co.uk*.

Practice Guidance 16 January 2014

Transparency in the Family Courts: Publication of Judgments

Application of practice guidance—The application of this guidance was considered in *H v A (No 2)* [2016] 2 FLR 723, FD.

The purpose of this Guidance

1 This Guidance (together with similar Guidance issued at the same time for the Court of Protection) is intended to bring about an immediate and significant change in practice in relation to the publication of judgments in family courts and the Court of Protection.

2 In both courts there is a need for greater transparency in order to improve public understanding of the court process and confidence in the court system. At present too few judgments are made available to the public, which has a legitimate interest in being able to read what is being done by the judges in its name. The Guidance will have the effect of increasing the number of judgments available for publication (even if they will often need to be published in appropriately anonymised form).

3 In July 2011 Sir Nicholas Wall P issued, jointly with Bob Satchwell, Executive Director of the Society of Editors, a paper, *The Family Courts: Media Access & Reporting* (Media Access & Reporting), setting out a statement of the current state of the law. In their preface they recognised that the debate on increased transparency and public confidence in the family courts would move forward and that future consideration of this difficult and sensitive area would need to include the questions of access to and reporting of proceedings by the media, whilst maintaining the privacy of the families involved. The paper is to be found at:

http://www.judiciary.gov.uk/Resources/JCO/Documents/Guidance/family-courts-media-july2011.pdf

Note—See *www.familylaw.co.uk/system/uploads/attachments/0002/9373/family-courts-media-july2011.pdf*.

4 In April 2013 I issued a statement, *View from the President's Chambers: the Process of Reform*, [2013] Fam Law 548, in which I identified transparency as one of the three strands in the reforms which the family justice system is currently undergoing. I said:

> 'I am determined to take steps to improve access to and reporting of family proceedings. I am determined that the new Family Court should not be saddled, as the family courts are at present, with the charge that we are a system of secret and unaccountable justice. Work, commenced by my predecessor, is well underway. I hope to be in a position to make important announcements in the near future.'

5 That applies just as much to the issue of transparency in the Court of Protection.

6 Very similar issues arise in both the Family Court (as it will be from April 2014) and the Court of Protection in relation to the need to protect the personal privacy of children and vulnerable adults. The applicable rules differ, however, and this is something that needs attention. My starting point is that so far as possible the same rules and principles should apply in both the family courts (in due course the Family Court) and the Court of Protection.

7 I propose to adopt an incremental approach. Initially I am issuing this Guidance. This will be followed by further Guidance and in due course more formal Practice Directions and changes to the Rules (the Court of Protection Rules 2007 and the Family Procedure Rules 2010). Changes to primary legislation are unlikely in the near future.

8 As provided in paragraph 14 below, this Guidance applies only to judgments delivered by certain judges. In due course, following the introduction of the Family Court, consideration will be given to extending it to judgments delivered by other judges (including lay justices).

The legal framework

9 The effect of section 12 of the Administration of Justice Act 1960 is that it is a contempt of court to publish a judgment in a family court case involving children unless either the judgment has been delivered in public or, where delivered in private, the judge has authorised publication. In the latter case, the judge normally gives permission for the judgment to be published on condition that the published version protects the anonymity of the children and members of their family.

10 In every case the terms on which publication is permitted are a matter for the judge and will be set out by the judge in a rubric at the start of the judgment.

11 The normal terms as described in paragraph 9 may be appropriate in a case where no-one wishes to discuss the proceedings otherwise than anonymously. But they may be inappropriate, for example, where parents who have been exonerated in care proceedings wish to discuss their experiences in public, identifying themselves and making use of the judgment. Equally, they may be inappropriate in cases where findings have been made against a person and someone else contends and/or the judge concludes that it is in the public interest for that person to be identified in any published version of the judgment.

12 If any party wishes to identify himself or herself, or any other party or person, as being a person referred to in any published version of the judgment, their remedy is to seek an order of the court and a suitable modification of the rubric: Media Access & Reporting, para 82; *Re RB (Adult) (No 4)* [2011] EWHC 3017 (Fam), [2012] 1 FLR 466, paras [17], [19].

13 Nothing in this Guidance affects the exercise by the judge in any particular case of whatever powers would otherwise be available to regulate the publication of material relating to the proceedings. For example, where a judgment is likely to be used in a way that would defeat the purpose of any anonymisation, it is open to the judge to refuse to publish the judgment or to make an order restricting its use.

Guidance

14 This Guidance takes effect from 3 February 2014. It applies

(i) in the family courts (and in due course in the Family Court), to judgments delivered by Circuit Judges, High Court Judges and persons sitting as judges of the High Court; and
(ii) to all judgments delivered by High Court Judges (and persons sitting as judges of the High Court) exercising the inherent jurisdiction to make orders in respect of children and incapacitated or vulnerable adults.

15 The following paragraphs of this Guidance distinguish between two classes of judgment:

(i) those that the judge *must* ordinarily allow to be published (paragraphs 16 and 17); and
(ii) those that *may* be published (paragraph 18).

16 Permission to publish a judgment should always be given whenever the judge concludes that publication would be in the public interest and whether or not a request has been made by a party or the media.

17 Where a judgment relates to matters set out in Schedule 1 or 2 below and a written judgment already exists in a publishable form or the judge has already ordered that the judgment be transcribed, the starting point is that permission should be given for the judgment to be published unless there are compelling reasons why the judgment should not be published.

Schedule 1

In the family courts (and in due course in the Family Court), including in proceedings under the inherent jurisdiction of the High Court relating to children, judgments arising from:

(i) a substantial contested fact-finding hearing at which serious allegations, for example allegations of significant physical, emotional or sexual harm, have been determined;
(ii) the making or refusal of a final care order or supervision order under Part 4 of the Children Act 1989, or any order for the discharge of any such order, except where the order is made with the consent of all participating parties;
(iii) the making or refusal of a placement order or adoption order under the Adoption and Children Act 2002, or any order for the discharge of any such order, except where the order is made with the consent of all participating parties;
(iv) the making or refusal of any declaration or order authorising a deprivation of liberty, including an order for a secure accommodation order under section 25 of the Children Act 1989;
(v) any application for an order involving the giving or withholding of serious medical treatment;
(vi) any application for an order involving a restraint on publication of information relating to the proceedings.

Schedule 2

In proceedings under the inherent jurisdiction of the High Court relating to incapacitated or vulnerable adults, judgments arising from:

(i) any application for a declaration or order involving a deprivation or possible deprivation of liberty;
(ii) any application for an order involving the giving or withholding of serious medical treatment;
(iii) any application for an order that an incapacitated or vulnerable adult be moved into or out of a residential establishment or other institution;
(iv) any application for a declaration as to capacity to marry or to consent to sexual relations;
(v) any application for an order involving a restraint on publication of information relating to the proceedings.

18 In all other cases, the starting point is that permission may be given for the judgment to be published whenever a party or an accredited member of the media applies for an order permitting publication, and the judge concludes that permission for the judgment to be published should be given.

19 In deciding whether and if so when to publish a judgment, the judge shall have regard to all the circumstances, the rights arising under any relevant provision of the European Convention on Human Rights, including Articles 6 (right to a fair hearing), 8 (respect for private and family life) and 10 (freedom of expression), and the effect of publication upon any current or potential criminal proceedings.

20 In all cases where a judge gives permission for a judgment to be published:

(i) public authorities and expert witnesses should be named in the judgment approved for publication, unless there are compelling reasons why they should not be so named;
(ii) the children who are the subject of the proceedings in the family courts, and other members of their family, and the person who is the subject of proceedings under the inherent jurisdiction of the High Court relating to incapacitated or vulnerable adults,

and other members of their family, should not normally be named in the judgment approved for publication unless the judge otherwise orders;

(iii) anonymity in the judgment as published should not normally extend beyond protecting the privacy of the children and adults who are the subject of the proceedings and other members of their families, unless there are compelling reasons to do so.

21 Unless the judgment is already in anonymised form or the judge otherwise orders, any necessary anonymisation of the judgment shall be carried out, in the case of judgments being published pursuant to paragraphs 16 and 17 above, by the solicitor for the applicant in the proceedings and, in the case of a judgment being published pursuant to paragraph 18 above, by the solicitor for the party or person applying for publication of the judgment. The anonymised version of the judgment must be submitted to the judge within a period specified by the judge for approval. The version approved for publication will contain such rubric as the judge specifies. Unless the rubric specified by the judge provides expressly to the contrary every published judgment shall be deemed to contain the following rubric:

> 'This judgment was delivered in private. The judge has given leave for this version of the judgment to be published on condition that (irrespective of what is contained in the judgment) in any published version of the judgment the anonymity of the children and members of their family must be strictly preserved. All persons, including representatives of the media, must ensure that this condition is strictly complied with. Failure to do so will be a contempt of court.'

22 The judge will need to consider who should be ordered to bear the cost of transcribing the judgment. Unless the judge otherwise orders:

(i) in cases falling under paragraph 16 the cost of transcribing the judgment is to be at public expense;

(ii) subject to (i), in cases falling under paragraph 17 the cost of transcribing the judgment shall be borne equally by the parties to the proceedings;

(iii) in cases falling under paragraph 18, the cost of transcribing the judgment shall be borne by the party or person applying for publication of the judgment.

23 In all cases where permission is given for a judgment to be published, the version of the judgment approved for publication shall be made available, upon payment of any appropriate charge that may be required, to any person who requests a copy. Where a judgment to which paragraph 16 or 17 applies is approved for publication, it shall as soon as reasonably practicable be placed by the court on the BAILII website. Where a judgment to which paragraph 18 applies is approved for publication, the judge shall consider whether it should be placed on the BAILII website and, if so, it shall as soon as reasonably practicable be placed by the court on the BAILII website.

Sir James Munby
President of the Family Division

PART V

Justices' Clerks' Society and Magistrates' Association Revised Guidance
March 2014

Note—This guidance was issued with the approval of the President of the Family Division following comments made by Pauffley J in *Re NL (Appeal: Interim Care Order: Facts and Reasons)* [2014] 1 FLR 1384, FD. It supersedes the section of the November 2007 Joint Guidance entitled *Good Practice in Relation to Uncontested Cases* and prohibits the use by magistrates of suggested draft reasons supplied by the parties, whether in agreed cases or cases where there is no active opposition in either public or private law proceedings.

Provision of Justices' Reasons in Uncontested Cases

Following the decision in *Re NL (A Child) (Appeal: Interim Care Order: Facts and Reasons)* [2014] EWHC 270, there is a need to revise part of the November 2007 Joint Guidance in relation to

Justices' Reasons in the Family Proceedings Court. The section entitled 'Good Practice in Relation to Uncontested Cases' as reproduced on page 248 of the Family Proceedings Court Bench Book is no longer sustainable and should be discarded.

The updated guidance is detailed below:

(A) Public Law

- Under no circumstances should the local authority or any other party to the proceedings be involved in drafting Justices' written Reasons. This prohibition applies irrespective of whether orders are said to be agreed or 'not opposed.'
- Henceforth, the court should never ask any party to supply draft Reasons or suggest that a draft be circulated amongst or consulted upon by the parties.
- The practice of inviting parties to submit their own position statements in which they may set out analyses of the facts as well as their contentions in relation to resulting orders is unobjectionable.
- It is entirely permissible for Justices' Reasons to include references to documents filed by the parties – for example position statements, case summaries and chronologies. As appropriate, parts may be adopted e.g. 'The background facts of the case are as set out in the case summary supplied by Miss A on behalf of X County Council'.
- In all cases, as part of the case management process, the parties should provide written details of the agreed issues as well as those which are in dispute. It is acceptable and often helpful to record that information in the Justices' Reasons.
- Templates and / or pro forma Facts and Reasons documents may be used so long as they are created by the Justices in consultation with their Legal Adviser. If a template or pro forma is employed, the Justices must ensure that (a) case specific detail is incorporated to explain the key aspects of their decision and (b) they alone determine the content. Examples of key decisions recorded upon a template will be, how, if at all, the threshold criteria are established; and whether upon consideration of a child's welfare interests, he should remain with or be separated from his parents at any stage of the proceedings.
- The detail and length of the Reasons document will vary according to the complexity of the case; the stage reached in the proceedings and whether any of the facts, or the order sought, are disputed. Where all or some aspects of the case are contested, the competing arguments and the reasons for preferring a particular course should be given.
- In every case, even where the order is said to be agreed or where there is no active opposition, there is still a judicial task to perform. Justices must ensure not only that justice is done but also that it is seen to be done.

(B) Private law

- Whilst the decision in *Re NL* related to public law, the key principles applicable to the compilation of Reasons apply equally in private law. A distinction should be drawn between agreements reached between the parties and Justices' Reasons for their decisions.
- Current and future practice in private law cases emphasises the benefit in parties reaching agreements between themselves, with the active assistance and encouragement of the court and other agencies. The advice that courts should not 'go behind' such agreements without good cause remains valid.
- Where an order is imposed by the court, Reasons should be prepared by the Justices and no one else. Neither party should be invited to supply a draft of suggested Reasons.
- Where orders are agreed, it is highly likely that Reasons will be brief. Nonetheless, the Justices should demonstrate that they have applied the key principles of the Children Act 1989 in coming to their decision, if it be the case, of approving the draft consent order.

The President of the Family Division has approved this Guidance.

President's Guidance 22 April 2014

Allocation and Gatekeeping for Care, Supervision and other Proceedings under Part IV of the Children Act 1989 (Public Law)

Issued in accordance with rule 21 of the Family Court (Composition and Distribution of Business) Rules 2014

Introduction

1 This Guidance is issued by the President of the Family Division and applies to all care, supervision and other Part IV proceedings commencing on and after 22 April 2014. It is issued following consultation with, and where applicable the agreement of, the Lord Chancellor, in accordance with rule 21 of the Family Court (Composition and Distribution of Business) Rules 2014, and is to be read with those Rules and PD12A (PLO 2014).

2 This Guidance applies to the allocation of all relevant proceedings to judges of the Family Court, including allocation to lay justices working with Justices' Clerks or Assistant Justices' Clerks (referred to in this guidance as 'legal advisers'). The purpose of the Guidance is to ensure that all new care, supervision and other Part IV proceedings are allocated to the appropriate level of judge and, where appropriate, to a named case management judge (or case manager) who shall provide continuity for the proceedings in accordance with the President's Guidance on Judicial Continuity and Deployment (Public Law).

Gatekeeping teams

3 Each Designated Family Judge (DFJ) will lead a gatekeeping team in each Designated Family Centre. A gatekeeping team will consist of the Designated Family Judge, his nominated deputy, the Justices' Clerk (or his nominated legal adviser) and an equal number of District Judges nominated by the Designated Family Judge, and legal advisers who will be identified by the Justices' Clerk in agreement with the Designated Family Judge. The number of legal advisers and District Judges is to be consistent with the needs of the business and the expertise of those who are available. Members of the gatekeeping team are referred to in this guidance as 'gatekeepers'.

4 All applications for care, supervision and other Part IV orders which are received for issue by 4.00 pm will be issued by HMCTS and placed before gatekeepers for their joint consideration on the next working day. Applications that are considered urgent will be allocated to the first available judge of the Family Court (in accordance with rule 16 of the Family Court (Composition and Distribution of Business) Rules 2014).

5 Local Authority applicants are to complete the Allocation Proposal section of the C110A application form when issuing proceedings. The Allocation Proposal section is to be used by the gatekeepers to record their allocation decision.

6 Members of the gatekeeping team are to be available at fixed times on each weekday to allocate jointly all relevant proceedings that have been issued. It is recommended that if they do not sit together at a fixed time in a court list for this purpose, they have a listed time for discussion between each other, for example, an hour at the beginning of the day. The gatekeepers will have access to information about existing allocated case volumes in the family court to help inform allocation decisions, as well as information about when and where Case Management Hearings can be listed. They will consider the file in each new application that has been issued on the preceding day and any outstanding applications and determine, in accordance with the Family Court (Composition and Distribution of Business) Rules 2014 and this guidance, the level of judge, and where possible the identity of the judge to which the proceedings are to be allocated. They will record their allocation decision on the Allocation Proposal section of the C110A application form.

7 When the allocation decision has been made, the case management judge or case manager will issue the Standard Directions on Issue and Allocation (SDO) in accordance with PD12A (PLO 2014) together with any appropriate Notice of Hearing. Court staff will notify by e-mail the relevant local authority of the date, time, location and identity of the allocated case management judge (or case manager) for the case management hearing and will list the case management hearing before an identified case management judge or case manager in accordance with the guidance of the DFJ and the allocation decision that has been made.

8 If the gatekeepers cannot agree on an allocation decision or they require further guidance, they must refer the allocation decision to the Designated Family Judge or his nominated deputy.

9 An allocation decision made by the gatekeepers does not prevent the possibility of a party to the proceedings making a subsequent application for a review of the decision.

10 If a care or supervision application is issued by a local authority as 'urgent' with a request for an early hearing to authorise the removal of a child and permission to abridge time to serve the parties, the application for expedition and any consequential directions will be considered by the gatekeepers. These are exceptional cases which may include newborn babies who are about to be discharged from hospital where the issue of care and supervision order applications is part of planned pre-proceedings involvement with the family. In all other cases where there is an identified real and immediate safety risk to the child, the expectation is that an application will be made for an Emergency Protection Order. This Guidance does not affect the existing procedures for dealing with Emergency Protection Order applications.

11 The Designated Family Judge shall monitor the allocation and gatekeeping process with a consultation group comprising: a Circuit Judge, a District Judge, a District Judge (Magistrates Court), the Justices' Clerk or his nominated deputy, a legal adviser and two members of the administration in the Designated Family Centre. The consultation group will meet at least once a month to identify any allocation questions upon which the advice of the Designated Family Judge or the Family Division Liaison Judge is required to ensure that there is consistency of allocation, effective use of resources and the identification of specific questions, the answers to which will be used as local guidance by the gatekeepers.

Principles

12 Allocation decisions must be made in accordance with the Family Court (Composition and Distribution of Business) Rules 2014.

13 This Guidance is consistent with those Rules, the guidance issued by the President of the Family Division in accordance with PD12A (PLO 2014), and decisions of the superior courts. It is intended to reflect the wide variation in the level of experience and expertise in the Family Court. Cases should be allocated to judges (including lay justices) and case managers with the appropriate level of experience to ensure that judicial resources are used most effectively.

14 In determining allocation, the gatekeepers shall consider each application having regard to the information provided on and with the C110A application form and shall determine the appropriate level of judge of the Family Court, in accordance with the requirements of rule 20 of the Family Court (Composition and Distribution of Business) Rules 2014:

(a) the need to make the most effective and efficient use of the local judicial resources that is appropriate, given the nature and type of application;
(b) the need to avoid delay;
(c) the need for judicial continuity;
(d) the location of the parties or of any child relevant to the proceedings; and
(e) complexity.

15 In the Family Court, no distinction is to be drawn between proceedings which may be heard by District Judges and District Judges (Magistrates Courts) (judges of 'district judge level'). There is an expectation that judges of district judge level will assume personal responsibility for all case management hearings in proceedings allocated to them, in accordance with the President's Guidance on Judicial Continuity and Deployment (Public Law).

Allocation Guidance

16 The factors set out at paragraph (14) above, include at (a) the judicial and HMCTS resources available in each court location, at (b) the needs of the parties to ensure that cases are listed before the appropriate level of judge with the minimum of delay, so that all proceedings are heard within the Timetable for the Child and within a maximum of 26 weeks or any extended Timetable for the Proceedings, as directed by the case management judge, at (c) the President's Guidance on Judicial Continuity and Deployment (Public Law) and at (d) a location that is suitable for the parties, particularly if special requirements or circumstances exist.

17 The schedule to this Guidance sets out matters which are likely to be relevant to the consideration of the 'complexity' factor referred to at paragraph (14)(e) above.

18 Subject to the guidance given below, all care, supervision and other Part IV proceedings may be heard by any judge of the Family Court (including lay justices) who has been authorised or nominated to conduct care and supervision proceedings and may be case managed by any judge or legal adviser who has likewise been authorised or nominated.

19 It is not expected that proceedings described in the schedule to this Guidance will be allocated to lay justices or the legal adviser acting as their case manager unless specifically approved by the Justices' Clerk (or his nominated deputy) in consultation with the Designated Family Judge. There is also an expectation that magistrates will not hear any contested hearing where the ELH is in excess of 3 days without the same having been approved from time to time by the Justices' Clerk (or his nominated deputy) in consultation with the Designated Family Judge.

20 It is expected that proceedings described in column 1 of the schedule to this Guidance will be allocated to a judge of district judge level.

21 It is expected that proceedings described in column 2 of the schedule to this Guidance will be allocated to a judge of circuit judge level or a judge of High Court judge level and will not be allocated to a judge of district judge level unless specifically released by the Designated Family Judge or one of his nominated deputies.

22 Proceedings described in paragraph H of column 2 of the schedule to this Guidance are to be issued in the Family Division of the High Court of Justice.

Schedule to the Allocation and Gatekeeping Guidance

Column 1	Column 2
A) Risk assessment issues	**A) Risk assessment issues**
(1) Allegations or risk of a) serious physical or sexual abuse causing or likely to cause significant injury to the relevant children, and/or b) serious sexual abuse of the relevant children	(1) Allegations of physical or sexual abuse which involve any of the following features: • Exceptional gravity in relation to the acts alleged or the nature of the harm suffered • Where there is, or is likely to be, conflicting expert opinion from more than two expert witnesses on any key issue • Shaking injuries involving retinal haemorrhage/ brain injury/ fractures • Complex medical questions involving novel issues or the determination of causation
(2) Allegations of serious domestic violence eg. causing significant injury particularly if witnessed by the child	(2) Allegations of extremely serious domestic violence or rape, particularly if witnessed by the child

PART V

	(3) Risk of serious physical or emotional harm arising from – • Death of another child in family, a parent or other significant person • A parent or other significant person who may have committed a grave crime e.g. murder, manslaughter or rape
(4) Significant disputed issues relating to psychiatric illness of a parent and/or a child	
	(5) History of suspicious death of a child in the family
(6) Significant disputed medical issues relating to the relevant child	(6) Complex medical issues, including medical causation issues and medical treatment issues including where any of the parties suffer from psychiatric illness or psychological issues or any significant disability such as profound deafness, blindness or learning disability, or which will require specialist knowledge and services in respect of parenting capacity or the needs of the children
B) Unusual/Complex issues relating to ethnicity or religion None	**B) Unusual/Complex issues relating to ethnicity or religion** (7) Significant contested issues in respect of religion, culture or ethnicity or involving medical treatment relating to the same
C) Non-subject child as a party (particularly if under 16) (8) Where a child may be required to give evidence.	**C) Non-subject child as a party (particularly if under 16)** (8) Where children (including parents who are under the age of 18) are, or may be, required to give evidence and be joined as a party
D) Capacity issues (9) Where there is a need for the Official Solicitor or another litigation friend to represent the interests of an incapacitated adult	**D) Capacity issues** (9) Where there is a need for the Official Solicitor or another litigation friend to represent the interests of more than one incapacitated party
E) Real possibility of conflict of expert evidence or difficulty in resolving conflict in the evidence of witnesses (10) Where there is an identified need for no more than two expert witnesses to report on the same key issue(s)	**E) Real possibility of conflict of expert evidence or difficulty in resolving conflict in the evidence of witnesses** (10) Where there is an identified need for more than two expert witnesses to report on the same key issue(s)

F) Novel or difficult point of law	**F) Novel or difficult point of law**
None	(11) Where the case involves a difficult point of law, issues of public policy or unusually complex or sensitive issues
	(12) Allegations of serious abuse where there are, or are likely to be, criminal proceedings and consideration of issues regarding disclosure of information or public interest immunity
	(13) Complex issues as to disclosure – where a party seeks leave to withhold information from another party, or where there is an issue about the release of confidential information involving a difficult point of law, or where disclosure of documentation involves a difficult or sensitive exercise of discretion or public policy issues
	(14) Where there are concurrent criminal proceedings in the Crown Court relevant to the issues between the parties and joint directions hearing(s) may be required.
	(15) Cases not in category H below, but which have significant immigration/status issues.
G) Existing proceedings relating to the child or a sibling which are proceeding before another court or have been recently completed before another court	**G) Existing proceedings relating to the child or a sibling which are proceeding before another court or have been recently completed before another court**
(16) Consideration must be given to listing the current proceedings before the judge who heard or is hearing the proceedings relating to the child or sibling in order to provide continuity.	(16) Consideration must be given to listing the current proceedings before the judge who heard or is hearing the proceedings relating to the child or sibling in order to provide continuity.
International Proceedings	**H) High Court Reserved Jurisdictions** **International Issues**
	(17) There is an issue concerning placement for adoption of the child outside the jurisdiction
(18) Cases to which Brussels II revised applies	(18) Proceedings with an international element relating to recognition or enforcement of orders, conflict or comity of laws or which have exceptional immigration / asylum status issues
(19) Cases in which placement is limited to temporary removal to a Hague Convention country.	(19) Cases in which an application is made for (a) permanent placement or (b) temporary removal from the jurisdiction to a non-Hague convention country;

	20) Cases in which a child has been brought to this jurisdiction in circumstances which might constitute a wrongful removal or retention either from a EC Member State, a Hague Convention country (a contracting State to the 1980 Hague Child Abduction Convention and/or a contracting State to the 1996 Hague Child Protection Convention) or a non-Convention country; (21) Cases in which a child is alleged to have been abducted overseas and applications have been made in this jurisdiction such as for a declaration that the child was habitually resident in this country prior to the abduction or for an order that the child be returned with a request for assistance etc; and (22) Cases in which Tipstaff Orders are applied for.
	Inherent Jurisdiction (23) Injunctions invoking the inherent jurisdiction of the court (24) Interim or substantive relief which requires the inherent jurisdiction of the High Court to be invoked.
	Other (25) Applications for Declaratory Relief (26) Applications which require the jurisdiction of the Administrative Court to be invoked (27) Issues as to publicity (identification of a child or restriction on publication or injunctions seeking to restrict the freedom of the media) (28) Applications in medical treatment cases e.g. for novel medical treatment or lifesaving procedures
I) Other case management issues (29) Where a 'split hearing' or finding of fact hearing is necessary and judicial continuity cannot otherwise be ensured	**I) Other case management issues** (29) Where a 'split hearing' or finding of fact hearing is necessary and judicial continuity before a District Judge cannot be ensured (30) Where possible local authority failures to progress plans to protect the child(ren) in the case are likely to be addressed critically by the court because it is alleged that there has been systemic failure in the proceedings and other proceedings

President's Guidance 22 April 2014

Continuity and Deployment (Public Law)

Introduction

1 This Guidance is issued by the President of the Family Division under PD12A (PLO 2014).

2 This Guidance applies to all care and supervision proceedings and other Part IV Proceedings heard in the Family Court.

3 Deployment is a judicial function which includes the patterning of judges and lay justices, the management of the workload of the court, allocation and listing.

4 The purpose of this Guidance is to ensure that family proceedings are accorded the appropriate level of priority in their listing and that they are case managed and heard by judges, lay justices, Justices' Clerks and assistant Justices' Clerks (legal advisers) who provide continuity of the conduct of the proceedings.

Continuity and Docketing

5 In accordance with the guidance given by HMCTS on the introduction of a system for the docketing of cases (which is annexed to this Guidance) all public law proceedings are to be allocated to a case management judge or a case manager who will be responsible for case management hearings in the proceedings.

6 For lay justices, the case manager is the Justices' Clerk or Assistant Justices' Clerk (legal adviser) where the functions of the court are delegated to a Justices' Clerk or an Assistant Justices' Clerk under the Justices' Clerks and Assistants Rules 2014. Continuity of the case manager is as essential as continuity of the case management judge.

7 On the issue of a care, supervision or other part IV order application, the court must nominate a case management judge or case manager(s) to be responsible for the management of the case throughout its hearings. The name of the case management judge or case manager(s) must be recorded on the outside of the court file.

8 Where possible, the case management judge or lay justices assisted by the case manager are to conduct any contested hearing, including the final hearing in all proceedings allocated to them.

9 No hearing at any stage of the proceedings should conclude without a date for the next hearing having been fixed for the earliest possible date.

10 It is not good practice for proceedings to have to wait until the case manager or the case management judge is available. Discussions must take place during case management hearings and with HMCTS to ensure that one of the two case managers or the case management judge is available to hear the proceedings on the date fixed for the next appointment. Legal advisers and judges must fit their availability around the case, not the other way around. Continuity of representation is also important, and lawyers will be expected to organise their diaries to ensure that cases are heard without delay.

11 The allocation of care, supervision and other Part IV proceedings is to be undertaken in accordance with the President's Guidance on Allocation and Gatekeeping for Care, Supervision and Other Proceedings under Part IV of the Children Act 1989 (Public Law).

12 The allocation of private law proceedings is the subject of separate guidance issued by the President.

Deployment

13 Circuit judges authorised to conduct public law children proceedings should be patterned to sit not less than 40% of their time on public law proceedings unless for reasons for example of geography that is not possible and the Family Division Liaison Judge (FDLJ) has granted an exemption in consultation with the President. Public law circuit judges must be patterned so as to be able to sit in public law proceedings with a gap of no more than a month so as to provide continuity for their allocated proceedings.

14 District judges authorised to conduct public law proceedings should be patterned to sit not less than 40% of their time in both public and private law proceedings. Public law district judges must be patterned so as to be able to sit in public and private law proceedings with a gap of no more than a month so as to provide continuity for their allocated proceedings.

15 District judges (magistrates' court) who sit on private and public law proceedings are identified by the Chief Magistrate and authorised by the President. The deployment of DJsMC is determined by the Chief Magistrate in consultation with Presiding Judges and the FDLJ on each Circuit.

16 Legal advisers are generally to be patterned so that they are available to the Family Court for not less than 40% of their time. Those sitting as case managers must sit for 40% or more of their time in public and private law proceedings. Each care or supervision application which is allocated to the lay justices must have one and not more than two allocated case managers who are legal advisers.

17 Justices' Clerks will be expected to agree the deployment of their lay justices with Designated Family Judges (DFJs) and this should be done in direct meetings between the DFJ and the Justices' Clerk and his/her tier 4 specialists. Any disagreements are to be referred immediately to the FDLJ and the Regional Delivery Director through the regional Head of Civil, Family and Tribunals.

18 The deployment of circuit judges and district judges (i.e. their patterns and itineraries) is decided by the Presiding Judges in consultation with and on the advice of the FDLJ, and the Designated and Resident Judges. DFJs are encouraged to agree a protocol with Resident Judges for the patterning of mixed ticket judges and their availability to provide judicial continuity.

19 The following arrangements will apply to proceedings which are allocated to lay justices and their legal adviser for case management and hearing.

20 Lay justices are patterned to sit by their Justices' Clerk. Continuity should be provided for in the individual case where a decision of fact has been made which renders a case theoretically or actually part heard, in accordance with *Re B (Children)* [2008] UKHL 35, and rule 8 of the Family Court (Composition and Distribution of Business) Rules 2014. Wherever possible, the court which resumes the hearing shall be composed of the same lay justices as dealt with the previous part of the hearing; alternatively, continuity is to be provided by at least one of the lay justices (preferably the Chairman) as well as the legal adviser who is the case manager for the proceedings. Most interim care orders do not involve decisions of fact but rather are an analysis of whether a prima facie case exists. Lay justices who have undertaken merits based decision such as the removal of a child may need to hear subsequent contested proceedings.

21 Lay justices will not normally hear a Case Management Hearing or a Further Case Management Hearing unless there are difficult or contentious issues to be resolved or where there is repeated non-compliance. The Case Management Hearings and Further Case Management Hearings will normally be conducted by the case manager. Lay justices assisted by the case manager should hear Issues Resolution Hearings and the Final Hearing which may follow on.

22 Any decision concerning rehabilitation or placement of a child (or children) with extended family members or friends following assessment within the proceedings should be approved by lay justices assisted by the case manager.

23 Any decision concerning proposed rehabilitation of a child (or children) consequent upon the need for a parent to undergo any therapeutic programme or process in accordance with recommendations made by an expert following assessment within the proceedings should be approved by lay justices assisted by the case manager.

Appeals

24 Appeals within the Family Court are to be allocated to judges in accordance with the Family Court (Composition and Distribution of Business) Rules 2014. Circuit judges who hear appeals in the Family Court are allocated by the DFJ in consultation with the FDLJ. Appeals from judges of the Family Court at circuit judge level and second appeals will continue to be heard by the Court of Appeal.

****

President's Guidance 22 April 2014

Use of Prescribed Documents (Public Law)

1 This guidance is issued by the President of the Family Division in accordance with PD12A (PLO 2014).

2 The President will identify documents that are to be in prescribed form from time to time with the object of ensuring that documents filed by the parties and their lawyers comply with the content and standards set out in any prescribed form. The identification of prescribed forms is additional to and not in place of the forms which are referred to in PD5A which supports FPR 5.1.

3 The documents referred to below support PD12A (PLO 2014): Care, Supervision and other Part IV Proceedings: Guide to Case Management.

Standard Directions on Issue and Allocation (SDO)

4 The gatekeeper(s) as defined in the President's Guidance on Allocation and Gatekeeping for Care, Supervision and other Proceedings under Part IV of the Children Act 1989 (Public Law) will give standard directions which shall include all those matters set out in the prescribed form of Standard Directions on Issue and Allocation Order (SDO).

Local Authority Case Summary

5 The legal representative for the local authority applicant shall file and serve a case summary in the form agreed from time to time with their local Designated Family Judge.

Case Management Order (CMO)

6 The court will give directions at an urgent preliminary Case Management Hearing (where one is held), the Case Management Hearing (CMH) and Further Case Management Hearing (FCMH) (where one is held) and at the Issues Resolution Hearing (IRH) in the prescribed form of Case Management Order (CMO) which includes the information that is to be recorded by the court on the Care Monitoring System (CMS).

7 At the CMH, and no later than at the FCMH (where one is held), the court will identify and record on the face of the CMO the Timetable for the Child and the Timetable for Proceedings for that child, which shall be a maximum of 26 weeks unless extended.

8 The recitals to the CMO shall contain the following, which will be announced in court:

(a) The main reason for the grant or refusal of any adjournment and for the grant or refusal of permission for an expert to be appointed together with a short explanation of the reason for the same and the impact which the decision will have on the welfare of the child.

(b) The reasons for the Timetable for the Proceedings being extended beyond 26 weeks and the reasons for any decision which has the effect of varying or extending the Timetable (for example, a request for an adjournment, or an additional assessment or expert report which is granted) and a short explanation of the impact which the decision will have on the welfare of the child

9 The recitals to the CMO shall also contain

(a) the key issues to be determined; and
(b) the positions of the parties, including the child.

10 The court will give and enforce directions in a form which ensures compliance by the parties with PD12A (PLO 2014) and the directions given previously by the court in the proceedings, for example, identifying by name on the face of the CMO the lawyer, social worker, children's guardian, expert or party who is to undertake the work in accordance with each direction of the court and the timetable for the same.

PART V

President's Guidance
22 April 2014

Allocation and Gatekeeping for Proceedings under Part II of the Children Act 1989 (Private Law)

Issued in accordance with rule 21 of the Family Court (Composition and Distribution of Business) Rules 2014

Introduction

1 This Guidance is issued by the President of the Family Division and applies to all private law proceedings under Part II of the Children Act 1989 (hereinafter referred to as 'private law proceedings') from 22 April 2014. It is issued following consultation with, and where applicable with the agreement of, the Lord Chancellor, in accordance with rule 21 of the Family Court (Composition and Distribution of Business) Rules 2014, and is to be read with those Rules and PD12B FPR (CAP 2014)).

2 The purpose of the Guidance is to ensure that all new private law proceedings are allocated to the appropriate level of judge and, where appropriate to a named case management judge (or case manager in those cases allocated to lay justices) who shall provide continuity for the proceedings in accordance with the President's Guidance on Judicial Continuity and Deployment (Private Law).

3 This Guidance applies to the allocation of all relevant proceedings to all judges of the Family Court (including lay justices sitting with assistant justices' clerks (referred to in this Guidance as legal advisers). During the implementation and consolidation of arrangements for the Family Court, this includes allocation to legal advisers conducting FHDRAs in court centres where:

(i) there is agreement between the Designated Family Judge ('DFJ'), HMCTS Head of CFT, the justices' clerk and the relevant Panel Chair(s) that available judicial resources locally require that FHDRAs continue to be listed before the legal advisers; or

(ii) in areas where the practice does not currently take place, where there is agreement between the DFJ, HMCTS Head of CFT, the justices' clerk and the relevant Panel Chair(s), and specific permission granted from the President of the Family Division and the HMCTS Director for Civil Family and Tribunals, that it be extended to facilitate the appropriate allocation of cases;

And in any event

(iii) provided that such allocation does not restrict the court's ability to make substantive orders on the day of the hearing (i.e. by using parallel or back-to-back lists, so that lay justices or judges are available to consider the case and, where appropriate, make a substantive order).

Allocation and Resources

4 In some DFJ's areas, full implementation of this guidance may result in a significant shift of caseload between levels of the judiciary. Before implementation it will therefore be necessary for the DFJ in consultation with the local judiciary, the justices' clerk, and HMCTS to review the available resources, in terms of courtrooms, court staff and judiciary including lay justices and legal advisers. The extent and timescale of implementation of the guidance should take these factors into account alongside any shift in allocation of public law cases following the implementation of the President's Guidance on Allocation Gatekeeping for Care Supervision and other Proceedings under Part IV of the Children Act 1989 (Public Law). The overarching intention should be to avoid delay in all children's proceedings wherever possible.

Allocation and listing schedules

5 The DFJ in consultation with the judiciary, the justices' clerk and HMCTS should review the family listing schedules in place within the DFJ's area taking into account the plans for the implementation of the Family Court. Where feasible and practical, consideration should be given

to arranging listing schedules so that First Hearing Dispute Resolution Appointments (FHDRAs) are taking place in parallel lists (i.e. on the same day and ideally in the same building) before District Judges and lay justices (sitting with a legal adviser), or where appropriate (in accordance with paragraph 3 above) before legal advisers sitting alone. This will allow for re-allocation to be considered up to and including the date of the hearing of the case, so that an alternative judicial level to that selected by the Gatekeeper(s) (see paragraph 6 below) can be arranged if necessary (in particular, should receipt of the Cafcass Safeguarding checks or interview with the parties raise matters of particular significance which justify a revised allocation decision).

Gatekeeping teams

6 Each DFJ will lead a gatekeeping team responsible for private law gatekeeping in each of the Family Hearing Centres that are nominated by the President to be Designated Family Centres. The team will consist of the DFJ and the justices' clerk with as many legal advisers and District Judges as the DFJ considers necessary to carry out the gatekeeping role depending on local demand and conditions. The DFJ in consultation with the District Judges and the justices' clerk will determine whether gatekeeping decisions are to be made by the District Judges or legal advisers acting alone, or together. The District Judge and legal advisers when making gatekeeping and allocation decisions are referred to as 'the Gatekeeper(s)' in this guidance.

7 All applications for private law orders which are received by 4.00 pm will be issued by HMCTS and placed before the Gatekeeper(s) for their consideration on the next working day, except where they are (or have been) dealt with as an urgent application. The Gatekeeper(s) should consider the application on the basis of the information provided in the application, and shall determine the appropriate level of judiciary in accordance with this guidance, and the requirements of the Family Court (Composition and Distribution of Business) Rules 2014, based on consideration of the relative significance of:

(a) The need to make the most effective and efficient use of the local judicial resources that is appropriate, given the nature and type of application;
(b) The need to avoid delay;
(c) The need for judicial continuity;
(d) The location of the parties or of any child relevant to the proceedings; and
(e) Complexity.

8 The judiciary including lay justices and legal advisers have an ongoing duty to keep allocation decisions under review particularly:

(a) when any response to the application is received;
(b) the safeguarding checks are received; and
(c) at the FHDRA when further information has been ascertained from the parties and Cafcass or CAFCASS Cymru at court.

9 When making an allocation decision the Gatekeepers will enquire into whether a MIAM exemption has been validly claimed, to the extent possible at this stage. If the MIAM exemption has not been validly claimed, the Gatekeepers shall give directions in accordance with rule 3.10(2)/(3) FPR 2010.

10 Prior to making an allocation decision the Gatekeeper(s) shall consider whether to allocate the application to a different location for hearing within the DFJ area, or to transfer the application to another DFJ area, where it appears that the parties, and/or the child(ren) who are the subject of the application, reside(s) in an area other than that covered by the DFJ.

11 Gatekeeper(s) are to be made available for a period of time on each weekday to allocate all private law proceedings which have been issued. Gatekeeper(s) will consider the file in each new application which has been issued on the preceding day and any urgent applications which are outstanding, and determine to which level of judge the proceedings should be allocated, i.e. to lay justices, a judge at District Judge level, a judge at Circuit Judge level or judge at High Court level sitting in the Family Court:

PART V

(a) Based on consideration of the relative significance of the matters set out in paragraph 7(a)–(e) (above),

and

(b) When considering complexity, by reference to the schedule to this guidance.

The Gatekeeper(s) will record their allocation decision and reasons on the case papers and make any appropriate arrangements for transfer (between courts) as necessary. In addition, where it appears that a case needs an urgent listing, the Gatekeeper(s) will ensure that the case is listed as a matter of urgency, and will give directions to abridge time for service if necessary.

12 The DFJ shall make arrangements to ensure the swift allocation of all cases within the Family Court to a named case manager so that it can be listed (in accordance with this Guidance and the Family Court (Composition and Distribution of Business) Rules 2014) in week 5 or 6 after issue, for an FHDRA, or sooner if an FHDRA is not appropriate.

13 If any Gatekeeper requires further guidance on a particular case, they should refer the allocation decision to the DFJ or his nominated deputy.

14 An allocation decision made by the Gatekeepers does not prevent a party to the proceedings applying for a review of the decision

15 The DFJ shall monitor the allocation and gatekeeping practices in the DFJ area to ensure that there is consistency of allocation, effective use of resources and the capacity to list cases at the earliest opportunity to avoid delay. He/she may issue local guidance to the Gatekeepers from time to time to reflect local circumstances and ensure the best use of resources. The allocation of work between the Circuit Bench, the District Bench, the lay justices and, where appropriate and agreed, the legal advisers may be subject to local directions by the DFJ .

Directions on Issue

16 Gatekeepers shall be able to issue Directions on Issue on Form CAP01 in the following circumstances:

(a) where the Gatekeeper finds on the basis of the information provided that the exemption from attending a MIAM has not validly been claimed, the Gatekeeper will direct the applicant, or will direct the parties, to attend a MIAM before the FHDRA, unless the Gatekeeper considers that in all the circumstances of the case the MIAM requirement should not apply to the application in question; the Gatekeeper will have regard to the matters set out in rule 3.10(3) FPR when making this decision;

(b) where it appears that an urgent issue requires determination, the Gatekeeper may give directions for an accelerated hearing;

(c) exceptionally, where it appears that directions need to be given for the service and filing of evidence, he/she may give directions for the filing of evidence.

Principles of Allocation

17 Allocation decisions must be made in accordance with the Family Court (Composition and Distribution of Business) Rules 2014.

18 This Guidance identifies criteria which are intended to be consistent with the Family Court (Composition and Distribution of Business) Rules 2014, and the decisions of superior courts.

19 In determining allocation, judicial continuity is an important consideration and the President's Guidance on Judicial Continuity and Deployment (Private Law) is to be followed.

20 In determining allocation consideration must be given to the matters set out in paragraph 7(a)–(e) above, in particular the need to avoid delay and provide the earliest possible hearing dates consistent with the welfare of the subject child(ren).

21 No distinction is to be drawn between proceedings which may be heard by District Judges and District Judges (Magistrates' Courts). There is an expectation that District Judges will assume personal responsibility for all case management hearings in proceedings allocated to them in accordance with the President's Guidance on Judicial Continuity and Deployment (Private Law).

Allocation Guidance

22 Subject to the guidance given below, all private law proceedings may be heard by any judge who has been authorised or nominated to conduct such proceedings, and may be case managed by the same judge or legal adviser.

23 When considering specifically the complexity of a case (see paragraph 7(e) above), it is envisaged that all relevant family applications (as defined in CAP paragraph 23) will be heard by lay justices (or at the FHDRA by legal advisers) unless they are of the type set out in the Schedule to this Guidance (see paragraphs 25 and 26 below). Additionally, a relevant family application may:

(a) be allocated to be heard by lay justices where specifically approved by the justices' clerk (or his nominated deputy) in consultation with the DFJ, or

(b) be re-allocated to be heard by lay justices where, at FHDRA or other hearing, it appears to the judge that the case does not fall, or no longer falls, within the Schedule.

24 There is an expectation that lay justices will not hear any contested private law application where the estimated length of the hearing is in excess of 3 days without the same having been approved by the justices' clerk in consultation with the DFJ.

25 When considering specifically the complexity of a case (see paragraph 7(e) above), it is envisaged that:

(c) proceedings described in Part 1 of the schedule to this Guidance will be allocated to a District Judge, or a District Judge (Magistrates' Court). If, on allocation it appears to the District Judge that the particular circumstances of the individual case justify allocation to a Circuit Judge, the District Judge shall so allocate it.

(d) subject to paragraph 27 (below), proceedings described in Part 2 of the schedule to this Guidance will be allocated to either a District Judge, District Judge (Magistrates' Court) or to a Circuit Judge or a High Court Judge.

26 Where the Gatekeeper allocates proceedings described in Part 2 of the schedule to a Circuit Judge or to a High Court Judge sitting in the Family Court, the FHDRA for that case shall be listed before a District Judge or District Judge (Magistrates' Court) unless the Gatekeeper considers (in discussion with the DFJ) that the FHDRA should be conducted by the Circuit Judge or High Court Judge (as appropriate).

27 Proceedings described in Part 3 of the schedule to this Guidance are to be issued in the High Court, not the Family Court. If they are received in the Family Court, then they must be identified and transferred to the Family Division of the High Court.

28 Where it appears to a Court that the issues in a case have developed from the point of initial allocation in such a way as to justify re-allocation, the court shall consider re-allocation in accordance with this Guidance and Schedule, having regard to the matters set out in paragraph 7(a)–(e) above, and taking account to the extent appropriate the principle of judicial continuity, and the need to avoid delay.

Urgent hearings

29 Urgent applications are those in which the applicant for a private law family order invites the court by application C2 either to (a) list the application for a hearing without notice to the respondent, or (b) reduce the normal (14 days) time-limit for service of an application and list a hearing at short notice.

30 If the application is considered by the Gatekeeper(s), they are to have regard generally to the guidance in paragraph 12.1–12.5 of the CAP in relation to the making of without notice orders when considering how to allocate an application that is presented for allocation as 'urgent'.

31 When presented with an application said to be urgent, the Gatekeeper(s) shall upon receipt:

(a) allocate the application to the appropriate level of judiciary in accordance with rule 16 of the Family Court (Composition and Distribution of Business) Rules 2014, and

(b) determine whether the application requires

  (i) a hearing on that day, or

(ii) requires an early hearing in advance of the FHDRA, with a reduced time for service of the application.

If an application for an urgent hearing is refused, reasons shall be given in writing and the application listed for FHDRA; the Gatekeeper may issue further directions in accordance with paragraph 16 above.

Schedule to the Allocation and Gatekeeping Guidance – Private Law

NOTE THAT

When, on allocation, Gatekeepers are considering specifically the issue of complexity, it is envisaged that they will allocate all relevant family applications (as defined in the Child Arrangements Programme paragraph 23) to the lay justices (or at the FHDRA by legal advisers) UNLESS they are of the type set out in this Schedule (below) (See paragraph 23 Guidance on Allocation & Gatekeeping for Proceedings under Part II of the Children Act 1989 (Private Law Proceedings))

Part 1 – District Judge (unless in the opinion of the allocated District Judge, the particular characteristics of the individual case justify transfer to a Circuit Judge)	*Part 2 – District Judge but may be by Circuit Judge (or at most serious level by High Court Judge)*	*Part 3 – High Court and Inherent Jurisdiction*
Allegations of significant physical, emotional or sexual abuse, or behaviours which have caused, or are at risk of causing, significant harm to the relevant child.	Cases involving significant factual disputes (including allegations of abuse, violence, alleged or proven criminal activity, gravely inappropriate behaviours, sexual abuse, complex physical and/or mental health issues in relation to relevant adults or children) particularly where a fact finding hearing of 3 days or more is a real possibility and/or where it is likely that more than one expert (not including CAFCASS and/or social worker) will be involved.	Inherent jurisdiction of the court relating to minors Application to make a child a ward of court, or to bring such an order to an end. Proceedings under the Child Abduction & Custody Act 1985, and other international abduction cases Proceedings with an international element relating to or enforcement of Orders, conflict or comity of laws which have exceptional immigration/asylum status issues. Declarations of incompatibility under the Human Rights Act 1998
Cases where significant factual matters are in issue (including substance misuse, domestic abuse, paternity, physical and/or mental health of relevant adults or children) such that a fact-finding hearing lasting more than one day is likely and the necessity for expert evidence (i.e. beyond the expertise of CAFCASS and/or social worker) is likely to arise.	Cases where there are particularly difficult and unusual immigration or jurisdictional issues. Cases involving leave to remove (permanently or temporarily) from the jurisdiction to Hague Convention and/or EU countries which are factually or legally complex. Cases which appear to involve, or have the potential to involve, intractable opposition to contact.	Applications for Declaratory Relief Registration of foreign judgments under Part 1 of the Foreign Judgments (Reciprocal Enforcement) Act 1920 Registration of judgments given in a different part of the UK under Part 2 of the Civil Jurisdiction and Judgments Act 1982
Cases where the capacity of one of the parents is, or is likely to be, raised as an issue. Cases where there is a real possibility that the child will have to be joined as a party (see guidelines under rule 16.4 FPR 2010) &/or may be called to give evidence.	Cases seeking enforcement of existing Orders made by a Circuit Judge or Recorder or in cases where a Circuit Judge or Recorder has previously made orders in relation to the same parties. Allocation should be to the same Circuit Judge or Recorder where practicable.	Registration of custody (Part 1) orders made in a court in another part of the UK under the Family Law Act 1986, section 32(1) Parental Responsibility order prior to adoption abroad (Adoption and Children Act 2002, section 84(1))

Part 1 – District Judge (unless in the opinion of the allocated District Judge, the particular characteristics of the individual case justify transfer to a Circuit Judge)	*Part 2 – District Judge but may be by Circuit Judge (or at most serious level by High Court Judge)*	*Part 3 – High Court and Inherent Jurisdiction*
Cases where there is, or is likely to be, a significant issue in relation to disclosure of documents to or from third parties or outside agencies. Cases where immigration issues are likely to be relevant and significant	Circuit Judge (not District Judge): Cases seeking leave to remove from the jurisdiction [permanently or temporarily] outside of the Hague Convention/ the EU. Where there are particular factual or legal complexities, the cases should ordinarily be allocated to the High Court following consultation with the DFJ.	Application for direction that section 67(3) of the Adoption and Children Act 2002 (status conferred by adoption) does not apply. Application for annulment of overseas or Convention adoption under Adoption and Children Act 2002, section 89
Cases involving leave to remove children (permanently or temporarily) from the jurisdiction to Hague Convention and/ or EU countries.		Issuance of letter of request for person to be examined out of the jurisdiction. Applications under Article 15 of the 2201/ 2003 Council Regulation and Article 9 of the 1996 Hague Convention (request for transfer of jurisdiction).
Cases which involve significant issues to be determined in relation to the disclosure of information to one or other of the parties (e.g. where the Cafcass officer seeks to withhold information contained in a Safeguarding letter).		Applications under Article 16 of the 1996 Hague Convention for a declaration as to the extent or existence of parental responsibility. Applications under Part 31 of the FPR (registration of orders under the 2201/ 2003 Council Regulation, the 1996 Hague Convention and the Civil Partnership (Jurisdiction and Recognition of Judgments) Regulations 2005).
Cases involving the enforcement of existing orders made by a District Judge or cases where a District Judge has previously made orders in relation to the same parties. Allocation should be to the same District Judge where practicable. Cases where there is a real possibility that Public Law Orders will be required, where the issues arising are of a type described in Part 1 or Part 2 of the Schedule to the President's Guidance on Allocation and Gatekeeping for Care, Supervision and other Part 4 proceedings.		Cases which require the jurisdiction of the Administrative Court to be invoked

Allocation of work to section 9 judges—See the commentary under the President's Guidance of December 2016.

PART V

President's Guidance 22 April 2014

Continuity and Deployment (Private Law)

Introduction

1 This Guidance is issued by the President of the Family Division.

2 This Guidance applies to all private law proceedings under Part II of the Children Act 1989 (private children proceedings) heard in the Family Court.

3 Deployment is a judicial function which includes the patterning of judges and lay justices, the management of the workload of the court, allocation and listing.

4 The purpose of this Guidance is to ensure that family proceedings are accorded the appropriate level of priority in their listing and that they are case managed and heard by judges (including lay justices) and legal advisers who provide continuity of the conduct of the proceedings.

Continuity and Docketing

5 In accordance with the Guidance given by HMCTS on the introduction of a system for the docketing of cases (which is annexed to this Guidance) all private children proceedings are to be allocated to a case management judge in the Family Court who will be responsible for any case management hearings in the proceedings.

6 For the lay justices, the case manager is the justices' clerk or assistant justices' clerk (legal adviser) who manages the case. Continuity of the case manager for hearings before lay justices is as essential as continuity of the case management judge for other judges of the Family Court.

7 The name of the case manager(s) or case management judge must be recorded on the outside of the court file by the court staff immediately after the FHDRA or other first hearing.

8 Where possible, the case management judge or the case manager sitting with lay justices is to conduct any contested hearing including the final hearing in all proceedings allocated to them

9 No hearing at any stage of the proceedings should conclude without a date for the next hearing having been fixed for the earliest possible date, and communicated to the parties at court.

10 It is not good practice for proceedings to have to wait until the case manager or the case management judge is available. Discussions must take place during the FHDRA, DRA or other hearings (and with HMCTS) to ensure that one of the two case managers or the case management judge is available to hear the proceedings on the date fixed for the next appointment. Legal advisers and judges must fit their availability around the case, not the other way around. Although continuity of representation is important, lawyers will be expected to organise their diaries to ensure that cases are heard without delay.

11 The allocation of private children proceedings is to be undertaken in accordance with the President's Guidance on Allocation and Gatekeeping (Private Law), and the Family Court (Composition and Distribution of Business) Rules 2014.

Deployment

12 Circuit Judges and District Judges hearing private children proceedings should be patterned so as to be able to sit in private children proceedings with a gap of no more than a month so as to provide continuity for their allocated proceedings.

13 District Judges (Magistrates' Court) who sit on private children proceedings are identified by the Chief Magistrate and authorised by the President. The deployment of DJsMC is determined by the Chief Magistrate in consultation with Presiding Judges and the Family Division Liaison Judge (FDLJ) on each Circuit.

14 Legal advisers are generally to be patterned so that they are available to the Family Court for not less than 40% of their time. Those sitting as case managers must sit for 40% or more of their

time in public and private law. Each private law application which is allocated to the lay justices must have one and not more than two allocated case managers who are legal advisers.

15 Justices' clerks will be expected to agree the deployment of their lay justices with Designated Family Judges (DFJs) and this should be done in direct meetings between the DFJ and the justices' clerk and his/her tier 4 specialists. Any disagreements are to be referred immediately to the FDLJ and the Regional Delivery Director through his/her Head of Civil, Family and Tribunals

16 The deployment of Circuit Judges and District Judges in the Family Court (i.e. their patterns and itineraries) is decided by the Presiding Judges in consultation with and on the advice of the FDLJ, and the Designated and Resident Judges. DFJs are encouraged to agree a protocol with Resident Judges for the patterning of mixed ticketed judges and their availability to provide judicial continuity.

Continuity by Lay Justices

17 The following arrangements will apply to proceedings heard by lay justices in the Family Court for case management and hearing.

18 Lay justices are patterned to sit by their justices' clerk. Continuity should be provided for in the individual case, where a decision of fact has been made which renders a case theoretically or actually part heard, in accordance with the guidance in Re B (Children) [2008] UKHL 35, and rule 8 of the Family Court (Composition and Distribution of Business) Rules 2014. Wherever possible, the court which resumes a hearing shall be composed of the same lay justices as dealt with the previous part of the hearing; alternatively, continuity is to be provided by at least one of the lay justices (preferably the Chairman) as well as the legal adviser who is the case manager for the proceedings.

Appeals

19 Appeals within the Family Court are to be allocated to judges in accordance with the Family Court (Composition and Distribution of Business) Rules 2014. Appeals from Circuit Judges and second appeals will continue to be heard by the Court of Appeal.

President's Guidance
22 April 2014

Use of Prescribed Documents (Private Law)

1 This Guidance is issued by the President of the Family Division.

2 The President will identify documents that are to be in prescribed form from time to time with the object of ensuring that documents filed by the parties and their lawyers comply with the content and standards set out in any prescribed form. The identification of prescribed forms is additional to and not in place of the forms which are referred to in Practice Direction 5A which supports FPR 5.1.

3 The documents referred to below support the 'Child Arrangements Programme' under Part II of the Children Act 1989.

Directions on Allocation [CAP01]

4 The Gatekeeper (as defined in the President's Guidance on Allocation and Gatekeeping (Private Law)) may give directions on allocation, in the following circumstances:

a where the Gatekeeper finds that the exemption from attending a MIAM has not validly been claimed, the Gatekeeper will direct the applicant, or will direct the parties, to attend a MIAM before the FHDRA, unless the Gatekeeper considers that in all the circumstances of the case the MIAM requirement should not apply to the application in question; the Gatekeeper will have regard to the matters set out in rule 3.10(3) FPR when making this decision;

b where it appears that an urgent issue requires determination, the Gatekeeper may give directions for an accelerated hearing;

c exceptionally, where it appears that directions need to be given for the service and filing of evidence, the Gatekeeper may give directions for the filing of evidence.

5 The Directions on Allocation will be given on form CAP01.

Order at FHDRA [CAP02]

6 If the proceedings do not conclude with agreement or final order at the FHDRA, the court will give directions on form CAP02.

7 In the Order CAP02, the court will identify and record on the face of the Order

a compliance with the requirement for MIAM;

b where the court finds that the exemption from attending a MIAM has not been validly been claimed, the court will direct the applicant, or will direct the parties to attend a MIAM (and will if necessary adjourn the proceedings to enable a MIAM to take place), unless the court considers that in all the circumstances of the case the MIAM requirement should not apply to the application in question; the court will have regard to the matters set out in rule 3.10(3) FPR when making this decision;

c that non-court dispute resolution has been considered and/or directed;

d the timetable for the proceedings for that child, including the listing of a DRA (Dispute Resolution Appointment);

e recitals setting out the issues in the case which require to be determined, and the respective positions of the parties;

f reason(s) for any decision in summary, including where a section 7 report has been ordered, or permission granted for an expert to be instructed, by reference to the benefits and detriments to the welfare of the child identified by the court;

g the date, time and venue of the next hearing.

Order at DRA [CAP03]

8 If the proceedings do not conclude with agreement or final order at the DRA, the court will give directions on form CAP03.

9 In the Order CAP03, the court will identify and record on the face of the Order

a What, if any, issues have been resolved;

b What, if any, issues it remains necessary to decide in order to determine the applications;

c The interim arrangements for the child[ren];

d Directions for any further hearing, including the requirement for the attendance of the section 7 reporter, and the attendance of the parties;

e The date, time and venue of the next hearing.

Final Order [CAP04]

10 Form CAP04 will be used when the court makes a final order.

11 In the Order CAP04, the court will identify and record on the face of the Order:

a Any agreements reached between the parties;

b Any undertakings offered to the court;

c Any child arrangements orders made;

d Any orders made in relation to parental responsibility, activity conditions, prohibited steps, specific issue, contact centre directions, monitoring contact orders, or Family Assistance Orders.

President's Guidance 10 November 2014

The International Child Abduction and Contact Unit (ICACU)

I am aware that an increasing number of children cases have an international element and that courts often require information from other jurisdictions before being able to proceed. It is not always easy to know how to obtain this information.

While it may not always be possible to obtain the information sufficiently quickly to enable the court to hear these cases within 26 weeks, I am very grateful to the International Child Abduction and Contact Unit (ICACU) for providing the following, which will help practitioners to follow the correct route to obtain information to help the court when necessary. It has been approved by Lady Justice Black and the Senior Master.

Practitioners will also need to be alive to Chapter VI of Part 12 of the Family Procedure Rules 2010 as amended, and to The Parental Responsibility and Measures for the Protection of Children (International Obligations) (England and Wales and Northern Ireland) Regulations 2010.

Sir James Munby

President of the Family Division

The ICACU

The ICACU is the operational Central Authority for England and Wales for Council Regulation (EC) 2201/2003 ('Brussels IIA' or 'the Revised Brussels II Regulation') and for England only for the 1996 Hague Convention on Jurisdiction, Applicable Law, Recognition, Enforcement and Co-operation in Respect of Parental Responsibility and Measures for the Protection of Children ('the 1996 Hague Convention')[1].

The ICACU provides a standard response to enquiries about requests for co-operation from local authorities explaining about other sources of assistance including where to find information and contact details of other bodies which may be able to assist. A copy of that standard response is attached as it is a helpful resource.

1 The ICACU is also the operational Central Authority for the 1980 Hague Convention on the Civil Aspects of International Child Abduction and the 1980 Hague European Convention on Recognition and Enforcement of Decisions Concerning Custody of Children and Restoration of Custody of Children.

Can the ICACU help?

The ICACU is a small administrative unit. Its staff are not lawyers or social workers. The ICACU cannot give legal advice.

The ICACU may however be able to help by making a request for co-operation to another country, in particular for the collection and exchange of information if the other country is:

(a) either a Member State of the European Union (other than Denmark); or
(b) a State Party to the 1996 Hague Convention; and
(c) the request for co-operation is in scope of the Revised Brussels II Regulation or of the 1996 Hague Convention

To decide if the proposed request for co-operation is in scope consider Articles 1, 53–57 of the Revised Brussels II Regulation and Articles 1, 3, 4, 30–37 of the 1996 Hague Convention.

ICACU can have a role in relation to transfers between courts under Article 15 of the Revised Brussels II Regulation or authorities under Articles 8 and 9 the 1996 Hague Convention; this role is not covered by this 'view'.

Requests for co-operation involving the collection and exchange of information under Article 55 of the Revised Brussels II Regulation or under Article 34 of the 1996 Hague Convention must be distinguished from requests for evidence.

If making a request under the 1996 Hague Convention consideration should be given to Article 37 of the 1996 Hague Convention before deciding to contact the ICACU.

If considering placement of a child in another country:

- for an EU Member State you should consider Article 56 of the Revised Brussels II Regulation and the decision of the Court of Justice of the European Union (CJEU) on the operation of Article 56 in case C 92/12 PPU;
- for a 1996 Hague Convention country you should consider Article 33 of the Convention.

Whether or not placement of a child in another country is considered to be placement in institutional care or with a foster family, is a question for the requested country not for the requesting country. A placement which from a domestic perspective is a private law placement may be regarded as a public law placement by the requested country. A request for co-operation can be made to establish if, in principle, the consent of the other country would be required for placement even if the care plan for the child is not yet fully informed.

The ICACU may have practical knowledge and experience of the processes and procedures in the other country which it can usefully share in response to an enquiry. However before relying on information formerly provided by the ICACU in another case you should bear in mind that the other country's processes and procedures may have changed since you last contacted the ICACU.

If your request is not in scope of the Revised Brussels II Regulation or of the 1996 Hague Convention, it may be in scope of another European Regulation or international Convention and another central authority or body may be able to assist.

For example, in England and Wales:

The **Senior Master** is

(a) the transmitting agency under Article 2 of Council Regulation (EC) No 1393/2007 of 13 November 2007 on the service in the Member States of judicial and extrajudicial documents in civil or commercial matters, ('the Service Regulation')

(b) the central authority under Article 3 of the 1965 Hague Convention on the Service Abroad of Judicial and Extrajudicial Documents in Civil or Commercial Matters ('the 1965 Hague Convention')

(c) the central body under Article 3 of Council Regulation (EC) No 1206/2001 of 28 May 2001 on cooperation between the courts of the Member States in the taking of evidence in civil or commercial matters ('the Taking of Evidence Regulation')

(d) the central authority under Article 2 of the 1970 Hague Convention on the Taking of Evidence Abroad in Civil or Commercial Matters ('the 1970 Hague Convention').

The administrative unit which supports the Senior Master is the Foreign Process Section based in the Royal Courts of Justice.

Member States have differing views as to what comes within scope of the Revised Brussels II Regulation and what comes within scope of the Taking of Evidence Regulation. If you are in doubt this may be where the ICACU's practical knowledge and experience of the other country's processes and procedures can be of assistance. In such cases you should make an early enquiry to avoid delay at the point the formal request needs to be made.

The **UKCA-ECR** is the central authority for the exchange of criminal records between Member States of the European Union.

What the ICACU does not do

As the ICACU has no role to play in the operation of:

- the Service Regulation, or of
- the 1965 Hague Convention,

the ICACU will not serve or arrange service of court documents and nor will its counterpart in the other country.

As the mechanism for the taking of evidence abroad is in the Taking of Evidence Regulation or the 1970 Hague Convention, the ICACU will not assist in acquiring evidence.

Please note that the ICACU does not forward requests for co-operation on to other domestic central authorities or bodies when it receives a request which is outside the scope of the Revised Brussels II Regulation or of the 1996 Hague Convention.

The ICACU does not notify consular authorities about proceedings concerning a child of a foreign nationality either pursuant to *Re E (A Child)* [2014] EWHC 6 (Fam) or at all as that is not a central authority duty or function. Consular authorities, not the ICACU, should also be contacted about passports and other travel documents such as visas.

A request for an opinion on jurisdiction is not a question for central authorities. The ICACU will not offer an opinion on jurisdiction and nor should a question about jurisdiction form part of a request for the collection and exchange of information.

The ICACU will not transmit a request for formal criminal record checks as that is a request properly directed to the UKCA-ECR.

The ICACU does not become directly involved in the court proceedings. Central authorities are not under any obligation to engage in proceedings and do not require a court order before discharging their duties and responsibilities under the Revised Brussels II Regulation or the 1996 Hague Convention.

Contacting the ICACU

The ICACU's general office telephone number is 0203 681 2608 and can be used by parties seeking 'in principle' advice based on the ICACU's experience of the other country. However the ICACU prefers contact to be made by email using the email address: icacu@offsol.gsi.gov.uk.

Email contact allows the ICACU to manage their busy workload and to collate information about the types of requests and countries. If an enquiry is made by telephone the ICACU will usually ask that the enquiry also be put in writing but understands that if a matter is urgent a telephone enquiry may first be necessary.

Making a request for co-operation

Requests for co-operation need to be **relevant**, **focused**, **timely** and **practical**.

You should specify whether the request is being made under the Revised Brussels II Regulation or under the 1996 Hague Convention. You should identify in your request the Article(s) relied on by you for the purpose of making the request. Remember that the request needs to be in scope of the Revised Brussels II Regulation or the 1996 Hague Convention.

Requests for co-operation should be made as early as practicably possible. There is nothing in the Revised Brussels II Regulation or the 1996 Hague Convention which requires a requested State to respond to a request for co-operation within a particular timescale. The ICACU cannot compel the requested central authority or foreign competent authorities to respond within a specific timetable but their counterparts are more likely to be able to offer assistance if the request is focused and made on a timely basis. The ICACU therefore asks that any request for co-operation is made as early as practicable in the proceedings and that it is informed about the court timetable including the date of any listed hearing.

When fixing the court timetable the timescale for a response from the other jurisdiction needs to be realistic having regard to the number of steps involved in a request for co-operation. In a public law case those steps may involve:

- the decision to make a request for co-operation by the local authority whether following the court's direction or otherwise;
- request received by the ICACU;
- the ICACU requesting any necessary translations;
- the request being transmitted by the ICACU to the requested central authority;
- the requested central authority making any enquiries directly or of its competent authorities to enable it to respond;
- the requested central authority or the ICACU arranging any necessary translations of the response;

- the ICACU transmitting the response to the local authority here;
- the initial response from the requested central authority may include a request for additional information and documents in order to enable a more detailed response to be provided.

A sealed copy of any relevant court order should be provided to the ICACU promptly (to assist in avoiding delay).

In formulating the request for co-operation you should give consideration to what information practically the requested central authority and their competent authorities may require in order to respond to the request. A clear background case summary will assist. You should always provide the full name and date(s) of birth of the child(ren) and of any relevant adult and an explanation of the family relationship(s). If the case involves a more complex family structure (full, half or step siblings, different generations in the same household etc) then a genogram is likely to be of assistance. Additionally:

- for the benefit of the requested central authority you should explain technical language (for example what is meant by section 20 consent) and acronyms;
- for kinship care assessments it may be useful to explain what the local authority or court would find helpful for the assessment to cover but it is unlikely to be appropriate to ask foreign authorities to complete domestic forms;
- for requests to identify potential kinship carers provide as much information as possible to assist the requested State to trace the individuals concerned; if current contact details are not known, then the last known address in the requested country (or as much information as possible as to where the family is from in that country), social security details or passport/foreign identity document details may also assist;
- only the documents relevant to the request should be sent; it is not usually necessary for the whole court bundle to be provided;
- if the court's permission is required to disclose information or documents to the ICACU and to the requested central authority the permission application should be made promptly.

The ICACU has a limited budget for translations. It will arrange translation of the request for co-operation but the parties to the court proceedings will need to agree who is to prepare translations of any supporting documents.

If the welfare plan for the child is for placement in the other country you should check if that country's consent to the placement is required under either Article 56 of the Revised Brussels II Regulation or under Article 33 of the 1996 Hague Convention. Whether or not consent is required is a question for the other country. If there is any doubt about whether the consent of the other country will be required a request for co-operation can be made in order to clarify the position.

The ICACU does not require a court order in order to discharge its duties and functions as the operational central authority but it may be helpful if the court directs one party to the proceedings to make the request for co-operation to the ICACU and to do so within a particular time frame. The parties may of course consult with each other as to the content of the request for co-operation.

In public law children cases the ICACU prefers that the local authority (rather than any other party) contact the ICACU about a request for co-operation (or any other request – for example, assistance with an Article 15 transfer request). The ICACU's experience is that a request for co-operation to the other country may be followed by a request from that country about the same child. If the ICACU receives a request from the other country it will transmit it to the local authority and it is administratively more efficient and less likely to give rise to miscommunication if the ICACU is in contact with one party only.

Although the court may request or invite assistance from foreign authorities orders should not be made against foreign authorities including central authorities, consular authorities or other public bodies in another country.

APPENDIX

General Information about the ICACU and its role

This leaflet provides some general information about the ICACU and its role which you may find helpful to read in the first instance when you are considering making a request for co-operation to the ICACU.

The ICACU is the operational Central Authority:

(1) in England and Wales for **Council Regulation (EC) No 2201/2003** also known as 'Brussels IIA' or 'the Revised Brussels II Regulation' ('the Regulation')

(2) in England for the **1996 Hague Convention on Jurisdiction, Applicable Law, Recognition, Enforcement and Co-operation in Respect of Parental Responsibility and Measures for the Protection of Children** ('the 1996 Hague Convention') (the Welsh Government is the Central Authority in Wales for the Convention).

The ICACU is also the operational central authority for England and Wales for the 1980 Hague Convention on the Civil Aspects of International Child Abduction, and the European Convention on Recognition and Enforcement of Decisions Concerning Custody of Children and on Restoration of Custody of Children but this standard email response focuses on the Regulation and the 1996 Hague Convention.

Both the Regulation and the 1996 Hague Convention provide for co-operation between central authorities. The ICACU handles co-operation requests both into and out of this jurisdiction.

Chapter IV of the Regulation and Chapter V of the 1996 Hague Convention are the co-operation chapters. Please see in particular Articles 55 and 56 of the Regulation and Articles 30, 33 and 34 of the 1996 Hague Convention. The ICACU may also be able to assist under Article 15(6) of the Regulation and Articles 8(1) or 9(1) of the 1996 Hague Convention.

Can the ICACU help you?

Is the other country

- a Member State of the European Union (other than Denmark); or
- a State Party to the 1996 Hague Convention?

Is the request for co-operation in scope of the Regulation or 1996 Hague Convention?

See:

- Article 1 of the Regulation, or
- Articles 1, 3 and 4 of the 1996 Hague Convention

Please note that notification to consular authorities pursuant to the President of the Family Division's decision in *Re E (A Child)* [2014] EWHC 6 (Fam) is not a request for co-operation. Consular authorities are based in a country's Embassy or High Commission. If you are need to give notice to consular authorities you should contact the other country's Embassy or High Commission.

Can you help to avoid delay in obtaining a response to your request?

There are no time requirements in either the Regulation or in the 1996 Hague Convention for responding to a request for co-operation and communication may involve both the need for translations and for the requested central authority to liaise with their own competent authorities in order to respond to the request. It is therefore all the more important that your request is:

- **Relevant**

Please specify the Article or Articles you are relying on in the Regulation or the 1996 Hague Convention.

- **Focused**

Be clear about the information you are asking for.

PART V

- **Timely**

If there are court proceedings your request should be made as early as possible. Please make it clear if there is a listed court hearing and tell the ICACU what week it is in the court timetable.

- **Practical**

Check you have provided enough information and/or supporting documents and/or reasons to enable the other central authority to be able to respond to your request. But do not simply provide all the documents in the case.

Helpful sources of information

Please see below. Helpful sources include:

– a 2012 decision of the Court of Justice of the European Union (CJEU) on the operation of Article 56 (Placement of a child in another Member State) of the Regulation. This is because the ICACU's experience has been that an Article 55 request for co-operation may be followed, or accompanied by, a request for consent to placement of a child in the other country;

– domestic cases which consider and provide guidance about the differing roles of the Judicial Network, central authorities, consular authorities and the court.

- The text of **Council Regulation (EC) No 2201/2003** is available on the website:

http://eur-lex.europa.eu/

- The European Commission publishes a **Practice Guide for the application of the new Brussels II Regulation** which is available on the website:

http://ec.europa.eu/civiljustice/

- A list of **EU Member States** is available at:

http://europa.eu/about-eu/countries/member-countries/index_en.htm

- The CJEU decision in case **C-92/12 PPU** about operation of Article 56 of the Regulation is available from the website:

http://curia.europa.eu/juris/recherche.jsf

- The text of the **1996 Hague Convention, the Explanatory Report on the 1996 Hague Convention, the Practical Handbook on the operation of the 1996 Hague Convention**, and information about 1996 Hague Convention countries are all available from the website of the Hague Conference on Private International Law:

http://www.hcch.net/

- The Department for Education published guidance for local authorities: **Placement of looked-after children in EU Member States** is available at:

https://www.gov.uk/government/uploads/system/uploads/attachment_data/file/351145/Working_with_Foreign_Authorities_-_Child_Protection_and_Court_Orders.pdf

- The following domestic case law is available from the website for the British and Irish Legal Information Institute: http://www.bailii.org/

Re B (A Child) **[2013] EWCA Civ 1434**

Leicester City Council v S **[2014] EWHC 1575 (Fam)**

The following European legislation may also be relevant to your enquiry:

Council Regulation (EC) No 1393/2007 of 13 November 2007 on the service in the Member States of judicial and extrajudicial documents in civil or commercial matters ('**the Service Regulation**')

Council Regulation (EC) No 1206/2001 of 28 May 2001 on cooperation between the courts of the Member States in the taking of evidence in civil or commercial matters ('**the Taking of Evidence Regulation**')

The text of the Regulations is available from the website:

http://eur-lex.europa.eu/

Please note that the **transmitting agency** in England and Wales under Article 2 of the Service Regulation is the Senior Master. The central body under Article 3 of the Taking of Evidence Regulation is also the Senior Master. The administrative unit is the **Foreign Process Section** whose contact details are:

The Senior Master	Tel: +44 20 7947 6691
For the attention of the Foreign Process Section	+44 20 7947 7786
Room E16	+44 20 7947 6488
Royal Courts of Justice	+44 20 7947 6327
Strand	+44 20 7947 1741
London WC2A 2LL	Fax: +44 870 324 0025
United Kingdom	@: foreignprocess.rcj@hmcts.gsi.gov.uk

Note—The Foreign Process Section switchboard number is 0207 947 7772; please select option 6 from the menu.

The **UK Central Authority for the Exchange of Criminal Records** (UKCA-ECR) is the UK's central authority for **Council Framework Decision 2009/315/JHA** of 26 February 2009 on the organisation and content of the exchange of information extracted from the criminal record between Member States' is the relevant framework for requests for criminal records from other Member States. You should contact the UKCA-ECR direct for information about the process.

The UKCA-ECR's contact details are:

UKCA-ECR
PO Box 481
Fareham
PO14 9FS
Tel: 01962 871 609
@: UKCA@acro.pnn.police.uk

The ICACU will contact you about your own request shortly. If having read this you send any further correspondence or information before we have responded to you, please make sure you refer to your earlier correspondence when doing so.

Note—Up-to-date contact details for the UKCA-ECR are: tel: 02380 479920; email: customer.services@acro.pnn.police.uk.

26 January 2016

Care cases with an international element: New ICACU form for requests for co-operation under Brussels IIa and the 1996 Hague Child Protection Convention and guidance notes

The International Child Abduction and Contact Unit ('ICACU') discharges the day-to-day duties of the central authority in England and Wales for Council Regulation (EC) No 2201/2003 ('Brussels IIa') and in England for the 1996 Hague Child Protection Convention. It acts as a contact point for requests for co-operation into and out of this jurisdiction made under either Brussels IIa or under the 1996 Hague Convention.

A request for co-operation can be made where the issues are covered by Brussels IIa or the 1996 Hague Convention and the other country is a Member State of the European Union and/or the 1996 Hague Convention is in force between the other country and the UK including, for example, if:

- a local authority needs information to assist it in developing a care plan for a child either because the child or their family are originally from the other country or because they have family in the other country who may be able to care for the child; or
- because the local authority needs to share information about a child with the authorities in the other country.

The ICACU has published **a form and guidance notes** (*https://www.gov.uk/government/publications/international-child-abduction-unit-request-for-co-operation-form*) for local authorities to use in child protection cases to make a request for co-operation to another country. The form is intended to help local authorities check their request is covered by the Regulation or Convention and to ensure that they include enough information to enable the ICACU to process their request. The form can be completed by a local authority lawyer or social worker.

The aim of the form is to:

- to reduce delay and improve care planning for the child where the case has an international element and
- to help local authorities make better formulated requests for information or assistance to the other country and
- to improve communication when sharing information about the child with the other country.

The form should be read in conjunction with:

1. the guidance published by the President of the Family Division about the ICACU's role in these cases: *http://www.judiciary.gov.uk/publications/presidents-guidance-on-the-international-child-abduction-and-contact-unit-icacu-and-its-role/*
2. Departmental advice published by the Department for Education for local authorities where a case has a cross-border element:
   a. **October 2012**: Cross-border child protection cases: the 1996 Hague Convention: *https://www.gov.uk/government/publications/cross-border-child-protection-cases-the-1996-hague-convention*
   b. **January 2013**: Advice on Placement of Looked After Children across Member States of the European Union: *https://www.gov.uk/government/publications/placement-of-looked-after-children-in-eu-member-states*
   c. **July 2014**: Working with foreign authorities: child protection cases and care orders: Departmental advice for local authorities, social workers, service managers and children's services lawyers: *https://www.gov.uk/government/publications/child-protection-working-with-foreign-authorities*

President's Guidance 26 March 2015

The Role of the Attorney General in Appointing Advocates to the Court or Special Advocates in Family Cases

Note—This Guidance should be read in conjunction with the Attorney General's Memorandum of 19 December 2001: *Requests for the Appointment of an Advocate to the Court*, which remains in force.

I have updated guidance first circulated by Mr Justice Holman, when he was Acting President, on 21 November 2012. The roles of Advocate to the Court, and Special Advocate are, of course, quite separate and distinct but each is potentially a burden on the limited public interest funds of the Attorney General.

Advocates to the Court

The Memorandum agreed between Lord Goldsmith and Lord Woolf on 19 December 2001 remains in effect and applies in family as in other cases. It is reproduced in the annual *The Family Court Practice*, in the 2015 edition at page 2923. The test or criterion for seeking the assistance of an advocate to the court is at paragraph 3, namely 'when there is a danger of an important and difficult point of law being decided without the court hearing relevant argument'. This requires that the point is both 'important' and 'difficult'. It also requires that there is a danger of the point 'being decided'. This is different and distinct from the point having been decided, but the court being unclear what the decided law is. The Memorandum is very clear, and the Attorney General is clear, that an Advocate to the Court ought not to be requested simply because there are self-represented litigants and the court does not know what the decided law is. We must be very sparing in requests for Advocates to the Court, and ensure that the request does properly fall within the test in the Memorandum.

There may of course be cases (particularly as Litigants in Person are now more common since most private law cases were taken out of scope of Legal Aid in April 2013) in which a judge genuinely perceives that an important and difficult point of law requires to be decided, but he is unaware that the point has already been decided. I have agreed with the Attorney General that in such a case, when responding to the court's request, his office may bring to the court's attention the relevant decided law.

Special Advocates

These are not the subject of the above, or any, Memorandum. Usually a Special Advocate is required because a public body that is party to the litigation, often a local authority or the police, resist disclosure of sensitive documents. The Attorney General has asked that at the point of requesting him to instruct a Special Advocate the court should specifically consider and make provision (after, of course, hearing submissions from the parties) as to which party should pay the costs of the Special Advocate. The essential point is that this is not a service which the Attorney General will normally cover. I can see no reason why he should be expected to do so, and no reason why the court should not fix in advance which party will pay the costs of the Special Advocate. Please, therefore, do this.

It is rare that an Advocate to the Court or Special Advocate is requested by judges below that of the High Court Bench in the Family Court. If these issues arise below the level of the High Court Bench it would be prudent to seek the views of the Family Division Liaison Judge before considering any request.

Sir James Munby
President of the Family Division

PART V

Practice Direction
26 March 2015

Committal for Contempt of Court – Open Court

Note—For answers to various questions that have arisen on the application and interpretation of this Practice Direction, see the Practice Guidance of 24 June 2015, which is set out below.

Preamble

1 This Practice Direction applies to all proceedings for committal for contempt of court, including contempt in the face of the court, whether arising under any statutory or inherent jurisdiction and, particularly, supplements the provisions relating to contempt of court in the Civil Procedure Rules 1998, the Family Procedure Rules 2010, the Court of Protection Rules 2007, and the Criminal Procedure Rules 2014 and any related Practice Directions supplementing those various provisions. It applies in all courts in England and Wales, including the Court of Protection, and supersedes the *Practice Guidance: Committal for Contempt* [2013] 1 WLR 1326, dated 3 May 2013; *Practice Guidance (Committal Proceedings: Open Court) (No 2)* [2013] 1 WLR 1753, dated 4 June 2013; and *President's Circular: Committals* (*The Family Court Practice 2014* at p 2976), dated 2 August 2013.

2 Any reference in this Practice Direction to a judgment includes reference to written reasons provided in accordance with rule 27.2 of the Family Procedure Rules 2010.

Open Justice

3 Open justice is a fundamental principle. The general rule is that hearings are carried out in, and judgments and orders are made in, public. This rule applies to all hearings, whether on application or otherwise, for committal for contempt irrespective of the court in which they are heard or of the proceedings in which they arise.

4 Derogations from the general principle can only be justified in exceptional circumstances, when they are strictly necessary as measures to secure the proper administration of justice. Derogations shall, where justified, be no more than strictly necessary to achieve their purpose.

Committal Hearings – in Public

5 (1) All committal hearings, whether on application or otherwise and whether for contempt in the face of the court or any other form of contempt, shall be listed and heard in public.

(2) They shall, except where paragraph 5(3) applies, be listed in the public court list as follows:

FOR HEARING IN OPEN COURT
Application by (*full name of applicant*) for
the Committal to prison of
(*full name of the person alleged to be in contempt*)

(3) In those cases where the person alleged to be in contempt is subject to arrest for an alleged breach of an order, including a location or collection order or an order made under the Family Law Act 1996, the hearing shall be listed in the public court list as follows:

FOR HEARING IN OPEN COURT [*add, where there has been a remand in custody:* in accordance with the order of (name of judge) dated (*date*)]
Proceedings for the Committal to prison of
(*full name of the person alleged to be in contempt*)
who was arrested on (*date*) in accordance with and for alleged breach of a [location/collection/Family Law Act 1996/other] order made by (*name of judge*) on (*date*).

6 Where it is not possible to publish the details required by paragraph 5(3) in the public court list in the usual way the day before the hearing ie, in such circumstances where the alleged contemnor is produced at court by the Tipstaff or a constable on the morning of the hearing, having been arrested over night, the following steps should be taken:

(1) Where, as in the Royal Courts of Justice, the public court list is prepared and accessible in electronic form, it should be updated with the appropriate entry as soon as the court becomes aware that the matter is coming before it;

(2) Notice of the hearing should at the same time be placed outside the door of the court in which the matter is being, or is to be heard, and at whatever central location in the building the various court lists are displayed;

(3) Notice should be given to the national print and broadcast media, via the Press Association's CopyDirect service, of the fact that the hearing is taking or is shortly due to take place.

If an alleged contemnor is produced at court, having been arrested overnight, the person shall immediately be produced before a judge who shall sit in public.

7 Where the committal hearing is brought by way of application notice, the court may authorise any person who is not a party to proceedings to obtain a copy of the application notice, upon request and subject to payment of any appropriate fee. Authorisation shall be granted in all but exceptional circumstances. Where authorisation is refused, the reasons for that refusal shall be set out in writing by the judge and supplied to the person who made the request.

Committal Hearings – in Private

8 Where the court, either on application or otherwise, is considering derogating from the general rule and holding a committal hearing in private, or imposing any other such derogation from the principle of open justice:

(1) it shall in all cases before the hearing takes place, notify the national print and broadcast media, via the Press Association's CopyDirect service, of the fact of the committal hearing (whether it is brought on application or otherwise) when and where it is listed for hearing, and the nature of the proposed derogation; and

(2) at the outset of the committal hearing the court shall hear submissions from the parties and/or the media on the question whether to impose the proposed derogation.

9 In considering the question whether there are exceptional circumstances justifying a derogation from the general rule, and whether that derogation is no more than strictly necessary the fact that the committal hearing is made in the Court of Protection or in any proceedings relating to a child does not of itself justify the matter being heard in private. Moreover the fact that the hearing may involve the disclosure of material which ought not to be published does not of itself justify hearing the application in private if such publication can be restrained by an appropriate order.

10 Where the court decides to exercise its discretion to derogate from the general rule, and particularly where it decides to hold a committal hearing in private, it shall, before it continues to do so, sit in public in order to give a reasoned public judgment setting out why it is doing so.

11 Where, having decided to exercise its discretion to hold a committal hearing in private, the court further decides that the substantive committal application is to be adjourned to a future date, the adjourned hearing shall be listed in the public court list as follows:

FOR HEARING IN PRIVATE
In accordance with the order of (*name of judge*) dated (*date*)
[On the application of (*full name of applicant*)]
Proceedings for the Committal to prison of
(*full name of the person alleged to be in contempt*)

12 Orders directing a committal hearing be heard in private or of other such derogations from the principle of open justice shall not be granted by consent of the parties: see *JIH v News Group Newspapers* [2011] EWCA Civ 42, [2011] 1 WLR 1645 at [21].

Judgments

13 (1) In all cases, irrespective of whether the court has conducted the hearing in public or in private, and the court finds that a person has committed a contempt of court, the court shall at the conclusion of that hearing sit in public and state:

(i) the name of that person;

(ii) in general terms the nature of the contempt of court in respect of which the committal order, which for this purpose includes a suspended committal order, is being made;

(iii) the punishment being imposed; and

(iv) provide the details required by (i) to (iii) to the national media, via the CopyDirect service, and to the Judicial Office, at *judicialwebupdates@judiciary.gsi.gov.uk*, for publication on the website of the Judiciary of England and Wales.

(2) There are no exceptions to these requirements. There are never any circumstances in which any one may be committed to custody or made subject to a suspended committal order without these matters being stated by the court sitting in public.

14 In addition to the requirements at paragraph 13, the court shall, in respect of all committal decisions, also either produce a written judgment setting out its reasons or ensure that any oral judgment is transcribed, such transcription to be ordered the same day as the judgment is given and prepared on an expedited basis. It shall do so irrespective of its practice prior to this Practice Direction coming into force and irrespective of whether or not anyone has requested this.

15 Copies of the written judgment or transcript of judgment shall then be provided to the parties and the national media via the CopyDirect service. Copies shall also be supplied to BAILII and to the Judicial Office at *judicialwebupdates@judiciary.gsi.gov.uk* for publication on their websites as soon as reasonably practicable.

16 Advocates and the judge (except judges and justices of the peace in the Magistrates' courts) shall be robed for all committal hearings.

This Direction is made by the Lord Chief Justice, following consultation with the Master of the Rolls, President of the Queen's Bench Division, President of the Family Division and of the Court of Protection, and Chancellor of the High Court. It is issued in accordance with the procedure laid down in Part 1 of Schedule 2 to the Constitutional Reform Act 2005.

Lord Thomas LCJ

Practice Guidance April 2015

Tagging or Electronic Monitoring in Family Cases

Note—This revised Practice Guidance was issued by Her Majesty's Courts and Tribunals Service (HMCTS) in 2015 and was set out by Sir James Munby, President of the Family Division, as an annex to *Re X (Children) and Y (Children) (No 1)* [2015] 2 FLR 1487, FD.

Occasionally a judge will request a parent or party to the proceedings to be electronically tagged. This is a device that is fitted on the leg and allows the Electronic Monitoring contractor to monitor compliance against a curfew. It is normally referred to as a curfew or tagging order in family proceedings and is only available in High Court matters.

It is usually ordered in children's cases when there is a real risk of one of the parents' abducting the child. These matters clearly need to be dealt with as a PRIORITY and should be processed on day of receipt.

The National Offender Management Service (NOMS) is responsible for the electronic monitoring contract and there is a contract in place with Capita, operating as Electronic Monitoring Services (EMS), who monitors these orders on behalf of agencies. If possible EMS need to be contacted by 15.00 hrs to ensure that the tag can be fitted the same day but if they receive the order after this time then they will endeavour to install that same day but they are permitted, under the contract, to install the tag the following day.

This guidance shows you how to deal with such a request once an order has been made.

1 Q: Have family courts the legal power to make such orders?

The judgment of Parker J from March 2009 makes clear that electronic monitoring is available in High Court matters.

2 Q: Is there a specific protocol/contract in place to deal with tagging requests in family proceedings?

Due to the relatively low number of such requests there is not a specific contract in place to provide this service. NOMS have a contract in place with two providers for tagging orders in the criminal courts and we operate within this to get family orders actioned.

3 Q: What are the requirements for the order?

The order or an attachment to the order must contain:

- Full name of the person to be tagged.
- Date of birth of the person to be tagged.
- Full address of the place of curfew.
- Date and time which the electronically tagged person agrees to be present at the address to allow the device to be fitted.

NOTE: usually the provider will fit the device anytime prior to midnight (22:00 for young people) the day that the curfew is due to start, or the following day.

- A schedule of the times at which the court expects the person to be at home (or any other relevant place), so that the service provider can monitor compliance.
  - (a) the start date of the curfew, and if known,
  - (b) the end date of the curfew
  - (c) the days on which the curfew operates
  - (d) the curfew hours each day.

The name and contact details of the relevant officer/solicitor whom the service provider should report to if there is any breach of the above schedule or if the person appears to have removed, or attempted to remove the tag. NOTE: a named contact must be given – usually the solicitor in the case.

4 Q: Who do I need to contact and by when?

Once an order has been made you should contact the service provider directly.

Due the rarity of these orders it is best practice to call the providers initially so they can prepare for the incoming order. EMS can be contacted on 0161 862 1200.

Be sure to contact the solicitors in the case, if appropriate, to confirm that the order has been received and has been processed by the provider.

5 Q: What if a tagging order is subsequently extended?

Occasionally, the judge will extend the time of the curfew that is already in place.

REQUIREMENTS:

- Sealed Order giving further leave to extend the time of the curfew – note any new instructions there may be.
- New schedule, setting out the information as stated above.

Repeat all the actions at point 4.

6 Q: What happens once a curfew has expired?

Unless the provider receives instructions to the contrary once a curfew order has expired the service provider will automatically remove the electronic monitoring device without any further contact from the court.

7 Q: What happens if a curfew is breached?

Depending on the contents of the order the service provider will normally contact the named person on the order to notify them of the breach. This is why it should usually be a solicitor to the case as they will be able to take immediate action. If the named contact is a member of court staff you should notify a member of the judiciary immediately to get further directions.

At annex A there is an example of what a tagging or curfew order may look like.

The annexed form of order is as follows:

'IN THE HIGH COURT OF JUSTICE

FAMILY DIVISION

PRINCIPAL REGISTRY

BEFORE xxxx SITTING IN CHAMBERS AT xxxx ON xxxx.

IN THE MATTER OF xxxx (BORN ON xxxx) (A CHILD)

AND IN THE MATTER OF AN APPLICATION UNDER THE INHERENT JURISDICTION OF THE HIGH COURT

AND IN THE MATTER OF AN APPLICATION UNDER THE SENIOR COURTS ACT 1981

BETWEEN:

xxxx

Applicant

PART V

and

xxxx

Respondent

UPON HEARING xxx

BY CONSENT

IT IS ORDERED THAT:

1 EMS is requested to take such steps as are necessary to effect and to continue the electronic tagging of the respondent xxxx, xxxx (D.O.B. xxxx) in accordance with the schedule of information provided below.

Schedule of information provided for the purposes of effecting and continuing the electronic tagging of a person

Name and date of birth of person to be electronically tagged	xxxx (D.O.B. xxxx)
Address of the place of curfew	xxxx
Date and time at which the electronically tagged person agrees to be present at the address of the place of curfew for the purposes of the installation of the monitoring device	xxxx
State date of curfew	xxxx
End date of curfew	xxxx (include time curfew ends)
Days on which curfew is in place	xxxx
Curfew hours	xxxx
Name and contact details of relevant person whom should be contacted if there is a breach of the curfew or if the tag is removed or otherwise interfered with	xxxx

DATED xxxx'

Guidance Note June 2015

Financial Remedies Unit at the Central Family Court

The Financial Remedies Unit (FRU) is a specialist unit within the Central Family Court. It currently comprises seven full time courts conducted by specialist financial judges. It is headed by His Honour Judge Martin O'Dwyer.

1 Administratively it is supported by dedicated FRU staff and clerks who deal with all issuing, listing and drawing orders in Financial Matters.

2 The purpose is the efficient handling of complex financial cases.

3 The overriding criterion for a case being retained in FRU is complexity, ie is a case of such complexity that it is appropriately dealt with in a specialist financial unit.

4 The FRU has a number of internal procedures for the efficient managing of financial cases and an Enforcement Unit headed by DJ Robinson in cooperation with the Legal Advisers.

5 The contact email address is cfc.fru@hmcts.gsi.gov.uk.

Bury St Edmunds Divorce Centre

6 All Forms A subject to the following should will be issued at Bury St Edmunds (BSE) Divorce Centre or other Divorce Centre and allocated to the appropriate Family Court centre on a local court basis.

Issuing at CFC

7 Forms A may be issued directly in FRU at the Central Family Court upon completion of the Certificate identifying the appropriate level of complexity.

8 If it appears on the face of the Certificate that the criterion of complexity is or may not be met the matter will be referred to a judge of FRU who may decide to return the application or to refer the Form A to BSE for allocation on the appropriate local court criteria or to list the matter up to First Appointment in FRU.

9 Cases inappropriately issued in FRU which have to be referred to BSE may be subject to delay as the matter is transferred between courts. Similarly those whose first appointment is listed in FRU when the matter is not appropriately retained may suffer delay as the matter is then transferred to the appropriate local family court.

10 Transfers between courts

- (a) To FRU. Any family court may transfer cases to FRU where by reason of complexity or other good reason it is not convenient to retain the hearing in the local family court.
- (b) From FRU. Nothing in these procedures is intended to restrict the judicial decision as to appropriate venue and FRU will liaise with other family courts for the efficient conduct of judicial business.

11 Petitions and Forms A may be issued at the CFC and other Family Court Centres in addition where

- (a) There is a jurisdictional 'race' between issues between competing jurisdictions
- (b) Urgent relief is required e g freezing orders

Such applications once issued and the urgent matters dealt with, the normal test of rules of complexity or locality should determine venue.

HHJ Altman, Senior Designated Family Judge for London

Rachel Jones, Operations Manager, Central Family Court

Note—The Certificate of Financial Complexity can be downloaded at *www.familylaw.co.uk/news_and_comment/how-to-refer-cases-to-the-financial-remedies-unit*.

PART V

Practice Guidance
24 June 2015

Committal for Contempt of Court – Open Court

Preamble

1 This Practice Guidance answers various questions which have arisen on the application and interpretation of the Practice Direction: *Committal for Contempt – Open Court*, dated 26 March 2015 (the Committal PD).

Press Notification – Hearings

2 The Committal PD only requires the press to be notified before a committal hearing in two circumstances:

- (1) where it is not possible to list the committal hearing in the public court list in the usual way the day before the hearing is to take place, see paragraph 6 of the Committal PD; and

(2) where, in advance of a hearing, the court, either on application or of its own initiative, is considering holding the committal hearing in private, see paragraph 8 of the Committal PD.

3 Press notification of a committal hearing is not therefore required in respect of all committal hearings.

Judgments

4 Paragraph 13 of the Committal PD only applies where the court finds that a person has committed a contempt of court and makes either an order for committal or a suspended committal order, see specifically paragraph 13(1)(ii). It does not apply where the court makes any other order having found a person has committed a contempt of court.

5 Where paragraph 13 applies, the following format for providing the required information should be used:

'Pursuant to paragraph 13 of Practice Direction: Committal for Contempt of Court – Open Court

In relation to [*insert case number*] on [*insert date*], at [*insert court*] I, [*insert title and name of judge*] sentence [*insert name of individual subject to the committal or suspended committal order*], to [*an immediate/suspended custodial sentence*] of [*insert term of sentence*] for contempt of court. The basis of that sentence was that [*short, general reasons*].'

6 For the purposes of paragraph 14 of the Committal PD, where it is not the usual practice of a court to give reasoned judgments because, for instance, it is not a court of record, the judgment, should set out the information required by paragraph 13(1)(i)–(iii) of the PD with short, written, reasons why the court arrived at its decision. Annex 1 to this Guidance contains a judgment pro forma for this purpose. This may be of particular assistance in the County Court and Magistrates' courts.

Application to proceedings under CPR r 71 and CCR O 27 and FPR rr 33.19, 33.19A and 33.23

7 The Committal PD applies to committal hearings, see paragraph 5(1) of the Committal PD.

8 The Committal PD does not apply to orders made on a written reference to a High Court judge or Circuit judge under the procedure set out in CPR r 71.8(1) and r 71.8(2) and CPR PD71, paragraph 6 and 7. It does not as CPR r 71 provides a process whereby any committal order made on such a written reference must be suspended on terms, amongst other things, that the person subject to the order attend court and is therefore capable of challenge before enforcement: see CPR r 71.8(3) and r 71.8(4) and *Broomleigh Housing Association Ltd v Okonkwo* [2010] EWCA Civ 1113 at [22]. The Committal PD does, as a consequence, apply to any hearing under CPR r 71.8(4)(b)).

9 The Committal PD applies to the attachment of earnings procedure under CCR O 27 r 7 and O 27 r 7A as it does to CPR r 71. It therefore only applies to the adjourned hearing referred to in CCR O 27 r 7B and to any further hearing to deal with a suspended committal order made under that provision.

10 Paragraphs 7–9 apply to FPR rr 33.19, 33.19A and 33.23 in so far as they apply the procedure in CCR O 27 and CPR r 71 to proceedings to which the Family Procedure Rules 2010 apply.

CCR Ord 27 and FPR 2010, r 33.19A—Both of these are revoked but the Guidance has not yet been amended.

Applications to proceedings under the Policing and Crime Act 2009 and the Anti-Social Behaviour, Crime and Policing Act 2014

11 The Policing and Crime Act 2009 makes provision for civil injunctions to be made in respect of gang-related violence. The Anti-Social Behaviour, Crime and Policing Act 2014 makes provision for civil injunctions to be made in respect of certain types of anti-social behaviour.

12 The Committal PD applies to committal hearings in respect of adults who are alleged to have breached injunctions made under the 2009 Act and the 2014 Act. It does not however apply to hearings arising from alleged breaches of injunctions made under either the 2009 Act or the 2014 Act by individuals under the age of 18 as they are not applications for committal to prison for contempt, but are rather applications for a supervision or detention order under the statutory procedure set out in schedule 5A of the 2009 Act and schedule 2 of the 2014 Act.

13 In certain circumstances section 43 of the 2009 Act and section 9 of 2014 Act may require breach of an injunction to be dealt with by a judge outside the court's normal opening hours, ie, in the evening, at a weekend or on a bank holiday.

14 Where an 'out of hours' court is open and available, such matters should be listed and heard at that court 'out of hours'. Paragraph 6(3) of the Committal PD applies to such listings.

15 Where no 'out of hours' court is open and available, the judge should consider whether the matter can properly be dealt with, at a location other than an open court, through exercise of the power to remand on bail or in custody, provided under section 43(5) and schedule 5 of the 2009 or section 9(5) and schedule 1 of the 2014 Act. Use of the remand power does not engage the notification requirements of paragraphs 5, 6, 13 or 15 of the Committal PD. Those requirements will be met when the matter comes back before the court as specified below.

16 Where breach of an injunction is dealt with by way of remand on bail, the committal hearing should be listed, in accordance with the provisions of the Committal PD, at the first convenient date when the court is sitting.

17 Where breach of an injunction is dealt with by way of remand in custody, the committal hearing should be listed for hearing, within any applicable statutory time limit and in accordance with the provisions of the Committal PD, in the nearest appropriate court to the place of custody on the first convenient date when the court is sitting.

Review

18 The operation of the Committal PD will be subject to review in October 2015.

Lord Thomas LCJ

★★★★

President's Guidance
8 October 2015

Radicalisation Cases in the Family Courts

Note—To read the Guidance in full (including cited cases), see *www.familylaw.co.uk/news_and_comment/president-s-guidance-on-radicalisation-cases-in-the-family-courts*.

1 Recent months have seen increasing numbers of children cases coming before the Family Division and the Family Court where there are allegations or suspicions: that children, with their parents or on their own, are planning or attempting or being groomed with a view to travel to parts of Syria controlled by the so-called Islamic State; that children have been or are at risk of being radicalised; or that children have been or at are at risk of being involved in terrorist activities either in this country or abroad.

2 Most of these cases have been brought under the inherent jurisdiction, where the children have been made wards of court. Such cases are necessarily in the High Court. Others have been care cases commenced in the Family Court. Some cases have started out under the inherent jurisdiction but then become care cases.

3 Only a local authority can start care proceedings (see section 31(1) of the Children Act 1989 – the police powers are set out in section 46). However, *any* person with a proper interest in the welfare of a child can start proceedings under the inherent jurisdiction or apply to make a child a ward of court. Usually, in cases falling within the description in paragraph 1 above, it will be the

local authority which starts proceedings under the inherent jurisdiction or applies to make a child a ward of court, and the court would not expect the police (who have other priorities and responsibilities) to do so. There is, however, no reason why in a case where it seems to the police to be necessary to do so, the police should not start such proceedings for the purposes, for example, of making a child a ward of court, obtaining an injunction to prevent the child travelling abroad, obtaining a passport order, or obtaining a Tipstaff location or collection order.

4 Given the complexities of these cases, I have decided that, for the time being at least, *all* cases falling within the description in paragraph 1 above are to be heard by High Court Judges of the Family Division. For the purpose of this Guidance the expression High Court Judge of the Family Division does *not* include a judge or other person authorised to sit as a High Court Judge under section 9 of the Senior Courts Act 1981.

5 Where a case falling within the description in paragraph 1 above is issued in the Family Court, or where a case issued in the Family Court becomes a case falling within the description in paragraph 1 above, then:

(a) the Designated Family Judge must be notified immediately;
(b) the Designated Family Judge must immediately notify the Family Division Liaison Judge (who should liaise with the President of the Family Division); and
(c) urgent steps must be taken, in consultation with the Family Division Liaison Judge, to allocate the case to a High Court Judge of the Family Division.

6 In exceptional circumstances a case falling within the description in paragraph 1 above may be heard by a Designated Family Judge, or a judge authorised to sit as a High Court Judge under section 9 of the Senior Courts Act 1981, but only if this has previously been authorised *in relation to that particular case* by the President of the Family Division or the Family Division Liaison Judge. Such permission will not normally be given in any case:

(a) raising PII issues;
(b) requiring a closed hearing or use of a special advocate; or
(c) where electronic tagging is proposed.

7 Judges hearing cases falling within the description in paragraph 1 above will wish to be alert to:

(a) the need to protect the Article 6 rights of all the parties;
(b) the fact that much of the information gathered by the police and other agencies will not be relevant to the issues before the court;
(c) the fact that some of the information gathered by the police and other agencies is highly sensitive and such that its disclosure may damage the public interest or even put lives at risk;
(d) the need to avoid inappropriately wide or inadequately defined requests for disclosure of information or documents by the police or other agencies;
(e) the need to avoid seeking disclosure from the police or other agencies of information or material which may be subject to PII, or the disclosure of which might compromise ongoing investigations, damage the public interest or put lives at risk, unless the judge is satisfied that such disclosure is '*necessary to enable the court to resolve the proceedings justly*' within the meaning given to those words when used in, for example, sections 32(5) and 38(7A) of the Children Act 1989 and section 13(6) of the Children and Families Act 2014;
(f) the need to safeguard the custody of, and in appropriate cases limit access to, any sensitive materials provided to the court by the police or other agencies;
(g) the need to consider any PII issues and whether there is a need for a closed hearing or use of a special advocate;
(h) the need to safeguard the custody of, and in appropriate cases limit access to, (i) the tape or digital recordings of the proceedings or (ii) any transcripts;
(i) the need to ensure that the operational requirements of the police and other agencies are not inadvertently compromised or inhibited either because a child is a ward of court or because of any order made by the court;
(j) the assistance that may be gained if the police or other agencies are represented in court, including, in appropriate cases, by suitably expert counsel.

8 Judges hearing cases falling within the description in paragraph 1 above will also wish to consider whether in any particular case there is a need (i) to exclude the media, or (ii) to make a reporting restriction order, or (iii) to make an 'anti-tipping-off' order (for instance when making an order for disclosure against a third party). The media should be excluded only as a last resort and if there is reason to believe that the situation cannot be adequately protected by a reporting restriction order or 'anti-tipping-off' order.

9 Advocates appearing in cases falling within the description in paragraph 1 above need to be alert to and be prepared to argue the issues that may arise, including those referred to in paragraphs 7 and 8 above.

10 I draw attention to what Hayden J has said about 'The importance of coordinated strategy, predicated on open and respectful cooperation between all the safeguarding agencies involved' and the need for 'open dialogue, appropriate sharing of information, mutual respect for the differing roles involved and inter-agency cooperation' if children in such cases are to be provided with the kind of protection they require.

11 This is a two-way process. The court can expect to continue to receive the assistance it has hitherto been given in these cases by the police and by other agencies. But there must be reciprocity.

12 The police and other agencies recognise the point made by Hayden J that 'in this particular process it is the interest of the individual child that is paramount. This cannot be eclipsed by wider considerations of counter terrorism policy or operations.' The police and other agencies also recognise the point made by Bodey J that 'it is no part of the functions of the Courts to act as investigators, or otherwise, on behalf of prosecuting authorities … or other public bodies.' But subject to those qualifications, it is important that the family justice system works together in cooperation with the criminal justice system to achieve the proper administration of justice in both jurisdictions, for the interests of the child are not the sole consideration. So the family courts should extend all proper assistance to those involved in the criminal justice system, for example, by disclosing materials from the family court proceedings into the criminal process.

13 In the same way, the police and other agencies will wish to be alert to the need of the court for early access to information, for example, information derived from examination of seized electronic equipment, *so far as such information is relevant to the issues in the family proceedings*. Accordingly, the court should be careful to identify with as much precision as possible in any order directed to the police or other agencies: the issues which arise in the family proceedings; the types of information it seeks; and the timetable set by the court for the family proceedings.

****

James Munby

President of the Family Division

PART V

President's Practice Guidance
23 November 2015

Arbitration in the Family Court

1 This Guidance concerns the interface between the Family Court and Arbitrations conducted in accordance with the provisions of the Arbitration Act 1996 (AA96) where the parties to a post-relationship breakdown financial dispute have agreed to submit issues for decision by an arbitrator whose award is to be binding upon them.

2 It is a fundamental requirement of this Guidance that the arbitrator will decide the substance of the dispute only in accordance with the law of England and Wales. This Guidance does not apply to, or sanction, any arbitral process based on a different system of law nor, in particular, one where there is reason to believe that, whatever system of law is purportedly being applied, there may have been gender-based discrimination.

3 To avoid unnecessary complication this Guidance is directed towards what may well be the most common form of arbitration with which the Family Court will become concerned, where the issues between the parties involve relief or an award by way of one or more of the financial remedies listed in rule 2.3 of the Family Procedure Rules 2010 (FPR).

4 In order to be effective, elements of some arbitral awards (by comprehensive dismissal of claims to create a clean break, or so as to bind the provider to a pension split, for example) will require their terms to be reflected in a Family Court order. If enforcement of the award becomes necessary, doing so via Family Court processes will be available only if orders reflecting the award are obtained. (Paragraph 30 below describes an alternative route which may be available via section 66 of AA96 in the county court or in the Family Division of the High Court.)

5 But it should be borne in mind that not every award need be brought before the Family Court for a financial order to be made, and that it may be more appropriate for some to be brought (if necessary) before a court which does not exercise family jurisdiction. Thus, for instance, where an arbitrator has decided upon the title to or possession of property under the Married Women's Property Act 1882, or has determined the respective beneficial interests of the disputants in a property or fund, the parties may simply choose to operate in accordance with the award and thus have no need for a court order to reflect it. Or a Trustees of Land and Appointment of Trustees Act 1996 ('TOLATA') award might more appropriately be made the subject of an order in the County Court if it simply declares the interests of the parties and does not involve any financial remedy element. It should be noted, however, that (pending any statutory changes to facilitate the Family Court hearing them) only the High Court and county court have jurisdiction to determine applications made under TOLATA or the Inheritance (Provision for Family and Dependants) Act 1975.

6 Taking the most common example of an arbitration where the agreed issues are what periodical payments, lump sum and adjustment of property awards should be received by a claimant spouse, it is important first to establish whether or not financial remedy proceedings have already been instituted and a Form A issued.

A Where there are subsisting proceedings seeking the same relief as is in issue in the arbitration

STAY OF PROCEEDINGS:

7 The court should be invited to stay the financial remedy proceedings pending delivery of the award. The arbitration agreement (in the case of an IFLA Scheme arbitration, the Form ARB1) will in most instances only recently have been signed by both parties, and thus contested applications for a stay will likely be rare. CPR rule 62.3(2) provides that such an application 'must be made by application notice to the court dealing with those proceedings'.

8 The Family Court has an obligation under FPR 3.3(1)(b) 'where the parties agree, to enable non-court dispute resolution to take place.' Section 9(4) of AA96 requires that the court 'shall grant a stay unless satisfied that the arbitration agreement is null and void, inoperative, or incapable of being performed' and makes it clear that a stay application should be made to the court where the subsisting proceedings are pending. By paragraph 6.2 of Form ARB1 the parties will have agreed that they 'will apply for or consent to a stay of any existing court proceedings, as necessary.'

9 In such circumstances where the application to stay is by consent or unopposed it should be dealt with on paper and (absent any unusual circumstances indicating a need) without listing or hearing.

10 Parties seeking such a stay should (in person or through their solicitors, who need not for this purpose be on the court record in the financial remedy proceedings) lodge in the place where the proceedings have been commenced, and within those proceedings, clear evidence of their agreement (or lack of opposition) to the stay order, together with a copy of their signed arbitration agreement (such as the IFLA Form ARB1). One of the standard orders approved for use in conjunction with arbitrations provides for a stay, and a copy completed with the details of the case, and signed by both parties or their representatives to signify approval, should be lodged with

the other documents. The file will then be placed before a judge for approval, or for queries to be raised and dealt with by correspondence, and/or (if necessary) a hearing listed. The suite of arbitration-specific standard orders are Annexed to this Guidance: see below.

APPLYING FOR AN ORDER TO REFLECT THE AWARD: BY CONSENT

11 The terms of the proposed consent order will be drafted to reflect the decisions and directions contained in the award. Insofar as financial remedy orders are involved, their form should follow the relevant paragraphs of the standard orders, which contain recitals apt for an arbitration award case. Together with a signed copy of the proposed order in the terms agreed, the parties, in order to take advantage of this accelerated procedure, should at the same time lodge their Forms A and D81, a copy of the arbitrator's award and (unless already on the court file) their Form ARB1. There is no reason in principle why unopposed applications for a consent order should not be dealt with on paper by a District Judge, although the court will always retain the ability to raise questions in correspondence or to call for a hearing.

12 Attention is drawn to my observations in *S v S (Financial Remedies: Arbitral Award)* [2014] EWHC 7 (Fam), [2014] 1 FLR 1257, about the attitude likely to be adopted by the court in such cases: 'where the parties are putting the matter before the court by consent, ... it can only be in the rarest of cases that it will be appropriate for the judge to do other than approve the order.'

13 Draft orders submitted which invite the court to make orders it has no jurisdiction to make (or which are otherwise in unacceptable form) will, like any other defective consent order submitted, be returned for reconsideration. There is of course no objection to recitals which express the parties' agreement to provisions which fall outside the scope of the available statutory relief. Nor indeed is there anything to prevent parties agreeing to change the terms of an award if they are agreed upon a revised formulation. In that event, though, it would be sensible for the covering correspondence to make it clear which provisions of the award have been overtaken by what subsequent arrangement arrived at by the parties.

14 Parties anxious to preserve the privacy and to maintain the confidentiality of the award should lodge that document in a sealed envelope, clearly marked with the name and number of the case and the words '**Arbitration Award: Confidential**'. The award will remain on the court file but should be placed in an envelope clearly marked as above, plus '**not to be opened without the permission of a judge of the Family Court**.' The request for the award to be sealed once the order has been approved should be made prominently in the covering letter.

PART V

APPLYING FOR AN ORDER TO REFLECT THE AWARD: OPPOSED

15 The party seeking to have the award reflected in a court order will need to proceed adopting what at para [25] of *S v S* was described as the 'notice to show cause' procedure. An alternative formulation of the Arbitration recital for such a situation is contained in each standard order.

16 Similar documentation should be submitted with the application, except of course that the order proposed is likely to have been unilaterally drafted on behalf of the party seeking to obtain the order. An application of this sort will ordinarily be listed for a hearing before a judge of Circuit Judge or High Court Judge level.

17 Attention is drawn to my observations in *S v S* concerning the attitude likely to be adopted by the court in opposed cases:

> 'The court will no doubt adopt an appropriately robust approach, both to the procedure it adopts in dealing with such a challenge and to the test it applies in deciding the outcome. ... The parties will almost invariably forfeit the right to anything other than a most abbreviated hearing; only in highly exceptional circumstances is the court likely to permit anything more than a very abbreviated hearing.'

18 Applications for consent orders are specifically placed outside the scope of the MIAMs requirement by Practice Direction 3A, para 13(2). So, by virtue of the same provision, are proceedings 'for enforcement of any order made in proceedings for a financial remedy or of any agreement made in or in contemplation of proceedings for a financial remedy.' Parties who have

agreed to arbitrate but have become engaged in any post-arbitral award dispute, as for instance a contested 'show cause' application, should not be required to deviate into a MIAM.

B Arbitration claims

19 An 'arbitration claim' is a term of art, and its scope for the purposes of its application to arbitrations conducted under AA96 is defined by CPR rule 62.2(1) in these terms:

> [*In relation to AA96*] 'arbitration claim' means –
>
> (a) any application to the court under the 1996 Act;
> (b) a claim to determine –
> (i) whether there is a valid arbitration agreement;
> (ii) whether an arbitration tribunal is properly constituted; or
>
> what matters have been submitted to arbitration in accordance with an arbitration agreement;
>
> (c) a claim to declare that an award by an arbitral tribunal is not binding on a party; and
> (d) any other application affecting –
> (i) arbitration proceedings (whether started or not); or
> (ii) an arbitration agreement.

20 The court where 'arbitration claims' as so defined are to be commenced is governed by CPR PD62 para 2 and the High Court and County Courts (Allocation of Arbitration Proceedings) Order 1996 (SI 1996/3215) as amended (the 1996 Order), which do not currently cater for such claims to be launched in the Family Court. Pending changes made to CPR PD62 and/or the 1996 Order, an applicant for an 'arbitration claim' should issue the requisite Form (see *below*) in the Commercial Court and should at the time of issue seek transfer to the Family Division. Para [6] of the 1996 Order does not as yet permit the transfer of any such application to the Family Court – the transfer must therefore be to the Family Division of the High Court.

21 The Form N8 initiating such a claim should be prominently marked '**Family business: direction sought for transfer to the Family Division of the High Court**' and should detail (where there are subsisting Family Court proceedings, albeit stayed) the case title and number.

22 Attention is drawn to sections 42 (enforcement of peremptory orders of the arbitrator) and 43 (securing the attendance of witnesses) of AA96 which are the provisions in relation to which an 'arbitration claim' is most likely to be sought in the course of an ongoing post-separation financial arbitration. Attention is also drawn to the provisions of section 44 (court powers exercisable in support of arbitral proceedings). Standard Orders have been issued to meet each of these contingencies: see Annex A, below.

23 As these are all within the CPR definition of 'arbitration claims,' pending changes to para [2] of CPR PD62 such applications should (as described *above*) be issued in the Commercial Court and bear prominently upon them a request for speedy transfer to the Family Division (or, in the case of, for instance, a TOLATA claim which does not also invoke the family court jurisdiction, to the relevant county court).

24 In relation to applications under sections 42 and 43 the standard orders are self-explanatory. Such applications should be heard by a judge of High Court level.

C Arbitrations conducted when there are no subsisting proceedings seeking relevant relief

STAY OF PROCEEDINGS:

25 An application to stay legal proceedings under section 9 of AA96 is in effect excluded from the definition of and procedural requirements for 'arbitration claims' by CPR rule 62.3(2), which provides that such an application 'must be made by application notice to the court dealing with those proceedings'.

26 In the case of an IFLA Scheme arbitration the parties will have agreed (by paragraph 6.2 of their Form ARB1) that they 'will not commence court proceedings ... in relation to the same subject matter'. If however such proceedings are thereafter initiated then it is open to either party to apply for a stay pursuant to section 9 of AA96 in the court where the proceedings have been

commenced, and within those proceedings. If a stay remains opposed an early hearing will obviously be required to determine the application.

APPLYING FOR AN ORDER TO REFLECT THE AWARD: BY CONSENT

27 The principles discussed in Part A apply, but if the relief awarded and sought to be reflected in an order includes one or more financial remedies only capable of being made on or after pronouncement of a decree, then it will be necessary for 'status proceedings' seeking divorce, judicial separation, nullity or (in the case of civil partners) dissolution to have been instituted, the relevant financial remedies applied for, and the stage in the proceedings reached when it will be appropriate for the court to make an order. In the case of divorce proceedings that would normally predicate a decree nisi having been pronounced, but see *JP v NP* [2014] EWHC 1101 (Fam), [2015] 1 FLR 659.

APPLYING FOR AN ORDER TO REFLECT THE AWARD: OPPOSED

28 The section of Part A describing the 'show cause' procedure applies, and again it would be necessary to have the necessary status proceedings in being for financial remedy orders to be made.

29 Where the aid of the Court is needed in support of a family financial arbitration in relation to which status proceedings have not yet been commenced, then the route suggested in paragraph 20 *et seq above* must be followed, and transfer from the Commercial Court sought. It will however be necessary for the FPR Part 18 procedure to be adopted in order to bring the arbitration claim (for instance, under section 42 or section 43 of AA96) before the Family Division.

D Enforcement

30 Section 3 of CPR Part 62 (rules 62.17 and 62.18) make provision for the direct enforcement of awards. In some situations it may be possible to pray section 66 of AA96 in aid to enforce an award. Para 4 of the 1996 Order authorises the commencement in any county court of section 66 proceedings under which awards can, with the court's permission, be enforced in the same way as a judgment or order of the court to the same effect. This may prove effective in the case of a TOLATA award but is not appropriate in the case of a financial remedy award.

E Challenging the Award under sections 67 to 71 of the Arbitration Act

31 Some very specific bases for challenging arbitrations are contained in these sections of AA96. They are hedged about with preconditions and limitations, and the commercial experience in arbitration is that they are relatively rarely successful. In relation to an arbitration dealing with family financial issues, however, it would ordinarily be appropriate for a High Court Judge of the Family Division to hear them, and thus it is to be expected that applications commenced pursuant to these provisions will by the same route be transferred to that court.

F Arbitration-specific standard court orders

32 This suite now consists of three orders for use in conjunction with arbitrations. They are reproduced in their approved form within Annex A to this Guidance and comprise orders to:

- Stay pursuant to Arbitration Act 1996 section 9 and/or under the court's case management powers
- Enforce an arbitrator's peremptory order under section 42, Arbitration Act 1996
- Secure the attendance of witnesses under section 43, Arbitration Act 1996

33 The forms of 'omnibus' orders already commonly in use for both Financial Remedy and Children Act Schedule 1 Final Orders each contain a recital to be completed where the order sought was to reflect an arbitral award. A slightly revised form for such recital is included in Annex B.

34 Pending any new or revised Practice Direction to accompany Part 5, these formulations should be adopted for use, subject always to the proviso that their provisions may be varied by the court or a party if the variation is required by the circumstances of a particular case.

James Munby

President of the Family Division

****

Note—This Guidance applies to arbitration in financial remedy matters, as defined in FPR 2010, r 2.3, which include CA 1989, Sch 1 proceedings as well as the traditional list of financial orders upon divorce or civil partnership dissolution. The dispute must be decided by the arbitrator in accordance with the law of England and Wales. Care must be taken to choose the appropriate court when applying for an arbitral award to be made an order of the court, i e a standalone award in a TLATA 1996 dispute will be more appropriately placed before a judge of the County Court.

If the parties agree to the arbitration process, any court proceedings should be stayed: a consensual application for a stay will normally be dealt with on paper. Similarly, if the parties submit a draft consent order to the court reflecting the arbitrator's decision – and with the appropriate documentation – the court may deal with the matter without a hearing, if appropriate. If one party seeks an order of the court to reflect an arbitrator's award but the other party opposes such an order, it is appropriate to issue a 'notice to show cause' application.

The full Guidance (see *www.jordanpublishing.co.uk/system/froala_assets/documents/341/Arbitration_in_the_Family_Court.pdf*) includes a selection of annex materials, including model orders and useful recitals.

Mr Justice Mostyn's Statement 1 February 2016

Statement on the Efficient Conduct of Financial Remedy Hearings Allocated to a High Court Judge Whether Sitting at the Royal Courts of Justice or Elsewhere

1 I am authorised by the President to release this statement.

2 In order to enhance efficiency in the disposal of financial remedy cases allocated to be heard by a High Court Judge, and to ensure that such cases are allotted an appropriate share of the court's resources, the following standards and procedures must be observed.

3 **Principles of allocation.**

The governing principle is that a case should only be allocated for hearing by a High Court judge if it is exceptionally complex or there is another substantial ground for the case being heard at that level and that allocation to that level is proportionate. Such allocation is rarely likely to be proportionate unless the net assets exceed £7.5m.

In determining whether the governing principle is satisfied the following are relevant considerations:

(1) The overall net assets exceed £15m; and/or
(2) The overall net earned annual income exceeds £1m.

In a case falling within (1) or (2) the governing principle will likely, but not necessarily, be satisfied. There will be some relatively straightforward cases falling within (1) or (2) where a transfer to High Court judge level will nevertheless not be proportionate.

In a case not falling within (1) or (2) above but where the net assets are said to exceed £7.5m:

(3) There is a serious case advanced of non-disclosure of assets.
(4) Substantial assets are held offshore either directly or through the medium of trust or corporate entities and there may be issues as to the enforceability of any award.
(5) Substantial assets are held in trusts which are said to be variable nuptial settlements.
(6) Substantial assets are held through the medium of unquoted corporate entities and detailed expert valuation evidence will be required.
(7) A serious, carefully considered and potentially influential argument is being advanced of:
 (a) compensation,

(b) non-matrimonial property, or
(c) conduct.

(8) There are serious, substantial third party claims to the assets otherwise subject to the dispositive powers of the court.

(9) There is a serious, carefully considered and potentially influential issue as to the effect of a nuptial agreement.

(10) The application involves a novel and important point of law.

Where, on any view, the net assets do not exceed £7.5m allocation to a High Court Judge is only likely to be proportionate where the application involves a novel and important point of law.

4 Every case will be allocated to an individual High Court Judge at the earliest opportunity. He or she will, unless this is completely impracticable, conduct all future hearings, including the final hearing, apart from the FDR. Early allocation is essential to achieve judicial continuity which is to be regarded as a critically important objective.

5 Allocation will be undertaken as follows:

(a) If the case is at High Court Judge level by virtue of the self-certification procedure (see para 20 below) then the allocated judge will be determined by the judge in charge of the money list (presently Mostyn J) when granting the certificate. For this purpose it is vital that the available dates of counsel for the First Appointment are stated on the certificate.

(b) If the case has been transferred to High Court Judge level by a district or circuit judge sitting in the Family Court in London or elsewhere on the South-Eastern Circuit the order for transfer, together with available dates of counsel for the next hearing, must be emailed to the judge in charge of the money list (c/o his clerk) who will determine the allocated judge.

(c) If the case has been transferred to High Court Judge level by a district or circuit judge sitting in the Family Court on circuit (other than the South-Eastern Circuit) the order for transfer, together with available dates of counsel for the next hearing, must be emailed to the relevant FDLJ (c/o his or her clerk) who will determine the allocated judge.

(d) If the case has been transferred to High Court Judge level by a High Court Judge (for example on or following an early application for a freezing injunction) that judge will normally allocate the case to himself or herself. If he or she does not do so the procedure in (b) or (c) should apply depending on whether the case was heard in London or on circuit.

6 If the allocated Judge deems it appropriate, the date for the final hearing may be fixed at the First Appointment.

7 The FDR will be listed with a time estimate of 1 day unless (i) the parties certify, giving written reasons, that a lesser period is sufficient and (ii) obtain the written permission of the FDR Judge (before whom the case is listed for hearing) for the reduced time estimate.

8 Any interlocutory application in the course of the proceedings must be made to the allocated Judge, unless to do so would be impracticable or would cause undue delay.

9 Every case allocated to a High Court Judge must be the subject of a Pre-Trial Review before that judge held approximately 4 weeks before the final hearing. If the case is to be heard on circuit the Pre-Trial Review may be heard before the allocated judge sitting in London by video-link.

10 At the Pre-Trial Review a final hearing template must be prepared. This should:

(a) allow a reasonable and realistic time for judicial reading and judgment writing;
(b) not normally allow longer than one hour for opening; and
(c) not allow for any evidence-in-chief unless the court has expressly authorised this at the Pre-Trial Review within the terms of FPR rules 22.6(2)–(4). Pursuant to rule 22.6(2) the parties' section 25 statements will almost invariably stand as their evidence-in-chief.

11 The parties' section 25 statements must only contain evidence. By virtue of FPR PD22A para 4.3(b) the statement must indicate the source for any matters of information and belief. On no account should a section 25 statement contain argument or other rhetoric.

PART V

12 If a direction for a discussion between experts has not previously been made pursuant to FPR rule 25.16 and PD25E then that matter must be raised at the Pre-Trial Review. There would have to be very good reasons why such a direction should not be made at the Pre-Trial Review.

13 At the Pre-Trial Review a direction should be made which ensures compliance with the indispensable requirement in FPR PD27A para 4.3(b) of provision of an agreed statement of the issues to be determined at the final hearing. To the statement of issues must be attached:

(a) an agreed schedule of assets on which any un-agreed items must be clearly denoted; and
(b) an agreed chronology on which any un-agreed events must be clearly denoted.

It is absolutely unacceptable for the court to be presented at the final hearing with competing asset schedules and chronologies.

14 The court bundle for the final hearing must scrupulously comply with FPR PD27A. This limits the size of the bundle to a single file containing no more than 350 pages: a specific prior direction from the court must be obtained at the Pre-Trial Review if the bundle is to exceed that limit (PD27A para 5.1). The limit of 350 pages includes the skeleton arguments (see para 15 below) and the agreed documents under para 13 above. Only those documents which are relevant to the hearing and which it is necessary for the court to read, or which will actually be referred to during the hearing, may be included: correspondence (including with experts), bank or credit card statements and other financial records must not be included unless a specific prior direction of the court at the Pre-Trial Review has been obtained (PD27A para 4.1). A separate bundle of all authorities relied on must be prepared and this must be agreed between the advocates (PD27A para 4.3). That bundle should not contain more than an absolute maximum of 10 authorities. Practitioners are specifically referred to the decision of the President in *Re L (A Child)* [2015] EWFC 15, paras 9–25, and to the earlier pronouncements referred to there, all of which apply fully to financial hearings.

15 Skeleton arguments must:

(a) be concise and not exceed:
   (i) for the first appointment, or any other interim hearing, 10 pages (including any attached schedules);
   (ii) for the FDR, 15 pages (excluding agreed documents but including any other appended schedules);
   (iii) for the final hearing, 20 pages (excluding agreed documents under para 13 above, but including any other appended schedules);
(b) be printed on A4 paper in not less than 12 point font and 1.5 line spacing;
(c) both define and confine the areas of controversy;
(d) be set out in numbered paragraphs;
(e) be cross-referenced to any relevant documents in the bundle;
(f) be self-contained and not incorporate by reference material from previous skeleton arguments; and
(g) not include extensive quotations from documents.

Where it is necessary to refer to an authority, a skeleton argument must first state the proposition of law the authority demonstrates; and then identify the parts of the authority that support the proposition, but without extensive quotation from it.

16 If a skeleton argument for the final hearing is intended to exceed the limit of 20 pages a direction to that effect should be sought at the Pre-Trial Review. Very good reasons would have to be shown for such a direction to be made. A skeleton argument which breaches the limit will be returned unread for abridgement.

17 At the final hearing the parties' advocates will be expected to adhere to the hearing template. Slippage will not be tolerated unless there are very good reasons. When conducting cross-examination advocates must have in mind the strictures of Lord Judge LCJ in *R v Farooqi & Ors* [2013] EWCA Crim 1649 at para 113, where he stated 'what ought to be avoided is the increasing modern habit of assertion, (often in tendentious terms or incorporating comment), which is not true cross-examination'.

18 If advocates unreasonably fail to comply with paras 13 (provision of agreed statement of issues, schedule of assets and chronology), 15 (length and content of skeleton argument) or 17 (adherence to hearing template) they will risk an order being made disallowing a proportion of their fees pursuant to CPR 44.11(1)(b) and/or section 51(6) Senior Courts Act 1981. In this regard attention is drawn to the comparable warning in CPR PD52C para 31(4).

19 If, following receipt of a draft written judgment either party wishes to seek permission to appeal, grounds of appeal must be filed at court and served on the other party at least one clear business day before the hearing of the application for permission.

20 The self-certification procedure concerning the allocation of financial remedy cases to a High Court Judge is set out below.

Guidance: Financial Proceedings: cases to be allocated to a judge of the High Court by self-certification

1 This Guidance takes effect from 1 July 2015 and applies, as far as practicable, to cases commenced before, as well as those commenced on or after, that date. It applies to financial remedy applications pending in the Family Court where the parties seek allocation to a judge of the High Court. It is no longer confined to cases proceeding in the CFC.

2 An application for a financial remedy will normally only be considered suitable for hearing by a High Court judge if it is exceptionally complex or there is another substantial ground for the case being heard by a High Court judge.

3 Where the parties seek the allocation of the proceedings to a High Court judge before an allocation direction has been made both counsel or, if counsel are not instructed, solicitor(s) for the parties must complete and file a certificate in the form annexed to this Guidance, stating concisely the reasons for certifying that the application is suitable for determination by a Judge of the Family Division. The completed certificate must be filed with the Clerk of the Rules not less than 21 days before the date fixed for the First Appointment in the Family Court.

4 The completed certificate will be referred to and considered by the Judge of the Family Division in charge of the money list who will determine whether the certificate indicates that the case is suitable for hearing by a High Court judge. If so determined, the case will be allocated to a Judge of the Family Division. A date will be fixed for the First Appointment before the allocated Judge and the merits of the certification will be further considered at that appointment.

5 If, at the First Appointment, the allocated Judge considers that the certification was not appropriate, the proceedings will be re-allocated within the Family Court and the allocated Judge may give directions as to case management, including the level of judiciary before whom the case should be listed. The allocated Judge may make such orders as to costs as considered appropriate.

6 Where proceedings are allocated to a High Court judge under paragraph 3, it is the responsibility of the solicitor for the applicant to ensure that the First Appointment fixed in the Family Court is vacated.

****

Note—The certificate is available at *www.familylaw.co.uk/news_and_comment/length-of-high-court-financial-remedy-case-skeleton-arguments-to-be-reduced*.

Guidance from the President's Office April 2016

Liaison between Courts in England and Wales and British Embassies and High Commissions Abroad

(1) This guidance note describes procedures which are to be followed when a court in England and Wales exercising family jurisdiction seeks to invoke diplomatic assistance. The procedures have been agreed between the President of the Family Division and the Foreign and Commonwealth Office (FCO).

(2) Courts exercising family jurisdiction in England and Wales regularly deal with cases where children have been wrongfully removed to a foreign country or have been retained there wrongfully, most commonly by a parent or relative. Such cases may involve abduction or removal by one or both parents with a view to forced marriage abroad, in which case a Forced Marriage Protection Order (FMPO) may be appropriate.

(3) When the court is exercising family jurisdiction in such circumstances, diplomatic assistance may be sought, via the FCO in London, from the relevant British Embassies and High Commissions abroad.

(4) Where the country to which the child has been taken is a party to the Convention on the Civil Aspects of International Child Abduction signed at The Hague on 25 October 1980 (Hague Convention), established procedures apply for the making of applications for the return of the child, via the central authority (which for England and Wales is The International Child Abduction and Contact Unit (ICACU), situated in the Office of the Official Solicitor and Public Trustee at Victory House, 30–34 Kingsway, London, WC2B 6EX, telephone 020 3681 2608, email ICACU@offsol.gsi.gov.uk.

(5) Where the country to which the child has been taken is a party to either of the following Conventions, the court will need to consider the Convention when deciding what steps to take:

- 1980 European Convention on Recognition and Enforcement of Decisions concerning Custody of Children and on Restoration of Custody of Children
- 1996 Hague Convention on Jurisdiction, applicable law, recognition, enforcement and cooperation in respect of parental responsibility and measures for the protection of children. Please note that for the 1996 Hague Convention, ICACU is the (operational) central authority for England and the Welsh Government is separately the central authority for Wales (Tel: 44 (29) 2082 5512. Email: WalesCAHague1996@wales.gsi.gov.uk)

(6) ICACU has published guidance on the assistance which can be provided in respect of the above named Conventions: *https://www.gov.uk/government/publications/international-child-abduction-and-contact-unit-application-form*

(7) Where however, the country concerned is not a party to any of the above Conventions, consideration will need to be given in each case as to what orders if any should be made to secure the return of the child to England and Wales.

(8) It may be possible in appropriate cases for representatives from the relevant British Embassy, High Commission or Consulate to work with local authorities to assist in ascertaining the whereabouts of child[ren], to conduct consular checks, and to facilitate travel arrangements for the return of the child[ren] to England and Wales. Such activities will however always be subject to the requirements of the domestic law of the country in question. The FCO has sole discretion in deciding how to conduct international affairs, and the Court cannot order them to exercise consular assistance.

(9) Before the court requests assistance from the FCO, contact should be made by telephone or email with the Child Protection Unit at the FCO, or the Forced Marriage Unit if the case involves forced marriage. This is to provide the FCO with an opportunity to clarify what level of assistance

it is in a position to offer in the country concerned. The FCO will be able to identify the relevant Embassy, High Commission or Consulate to which any order or request for assistance should be directed, and to forward documents.

(10) The FCO provides a facilitative role in relation to the return of the child but is not able to care for, take control of, or assist in procuring the return of the child. The naming of specific officials (for example Ambassadors, High Commissioners or other FCO officials) must be avoided. Instead reference should be made to 'The Consular Department of the Foreign and Commonwealth Office'.

(11) Consular staff are not trained to assess the welfare of a child as a professional social worker would be. Accordingly, the FCO cannot conduct welfare visits. However, in some exceptional circumstances, and with the consent of both parents, a consular visit to the child can be conducted. This would result in a brief factual summary of any discussion and observations from the visit.

(12) The FCO is keen to co-operate in any way which is appropriate but courts and practitioners should be aware of the limited efficacy of orders which provide for the deposit of passports at an Embassy, High Commission or Consulate. It should be noted that:

(a) The FCO is dependent upon the co-operation of the person with parental responsibility to comply with such an order and there is nothing the FCO can do to guarantee compliance.

(b) If at any time the person with parental responsibility requests the return of the passports it would be inappropriate for the FCO to retain them.

(c) On return of the passports no further responsibility lies with the FCO in relation to the parties' future movements.

(13) The FCO can work with local authorities and NGOs in the relevant country to assist in locating the child[ren], and to assist a local authority to return the child[ren]. However UK Social Services are not authorised to work outside of the UK and as such the primary work of returning the child should fall to in-country teams.

(14) The FCO can grant Emergency Travel Documents (ETDs), although FCO policy states that ETDs can only be issued where all those with parental responsibility have given consent. This policy is deviated from only in exceptional circumstances. It is helpful to the FCO if the court can make it clear when an ETD may be issued with the consent of only one person with parental responsibility or, where necessary, without the consent of anyone with parental responsibility.

(15) The FCO cannot be required to provide any financial assistance for the repatriation of a child. What can be achieved will depend on the particular circumstances of each case.

(16) In a case where assistance can be given by the FCO, the order should provide for disclosure of relevant documents to the FCO and its representatives. A copy of all such orders should be sent to the Child Protection Unit, Foreign and Commonwealth Office, King Charles Street, London, SW1A 2AH; Consular.ChildrensPolicyOfficer@fco.gov.uk. Telephone contact may also be made via the FCO Switchboard: 020 7008 1500.

(17) If the order relates to the 2003 UK–Pakistan Protocol on Child Contact and Abduction, a copy should in addition be sent by email to Karen.Wheller@judiciary.gsi.gov.uk. Telephone enquiries regarding the operation of the Protocol may be made of Karen Wheller on 0207 947 7225.

(18) Attached is a Schedule of specimen provisions which may be included in orders principally directed to cases where a child has been wrongfully removed to/retained in a foreign country.

The Rt Hon Sir James Munby

President of the Family Division

Schedule

SPECIMEN PROVISIONS FOR ORDERS

AND WHEREAS [AB] is a Ward of this Honourable Court and is a British citizen; born in and domiciled in the United Kingdom; and currently [believed to be] travelling outside England and Wales with a United Kingdom passport

AND WHEREAS in consequence of the fact that this Court has ordered that [AB] remain a Ward of this Court while (until [s]he attains the age of 18 years on [date]) [s]he remains a minor, this Court is empowered and required to exercise its custodial jurisdiction over him/her and to ascertain his/her best interests and to facilitate and protect those best interests

AND WHEREAS it appears from an order made in [details of proceedings] on [date] (of which a copy is attached) that [AB] was habitually resident in England and Wales [on [date]/at the time [s]he was removed from this jurisdiction]

AND WHEREAS this Honourable Court is anxious to protect and secure his/her wellbeing and best interests and to ensure that [s]he may freely express his/her wishes concerning his/her country and place of residence

AND WHEREAS this Honourable Court is anxious to ensure that [s]he is not induced or coerced into contracting any marriage or betrothal against his/her will

AND WHEREAS this Honourable Court is satisfied that all interested parties are before the Court including CAFCASS (the Child and Family Court Advisory and Support Services) appointed by the Court to represent the Ward

AND WHEREAS this Honourable Court having heard oral evidence from [ ] is of the view that serious grounds exist in the present circumstances to question whether this Honourable Court's Ward [AB] is able freely to express his/her views and wishes and in particular with regard to his/her country of residence

AND WHEREAS this Honourable Court has in the interests of [AB] determined that [s]he should so soon as practicable return/be returned to England and Wales IT IS ORDERED that every person within the jurisdiction of this Court who is in a position to do so shall co-operate in assisting and securing the immediate return to England and Wales of [AB], a Ward of this Honourable Court

AND NOW THEREFORE THIS COURT RESPECTFULLY REQUESTS any person not within the jurisdiction of this Court who is in a position to do so to co-operate in assisting and securing the immediate return to England and Wales of the Ward [AB]

AND THIS COURT RESPECTFULLY INVITES all judicial and administrative bodies in the State of [ ] to render assistance in establishing the whereabouts of the Ward of this Honourable Court and in arranging for him/her to be placed in contact with and facilitating his/her travel to the British Embassy/High Commission/Consulate at [ ] with a view to his/her immediate return to the United Kingdom

AND IN THE EVENT that the said [AB] discloses to the British Embassy/High Commission/Consul (or their authorised representative) at [ ] that [s]he wishes unequivocally to return to England and Wales, [s]he do so return; and that in that event the judicial and administrative authorities of the State of [ ] be respectfully invited to take all such actions as may facilitate such return

AND NOW THEREFORE THIS COURT RESPECTFULLY REQUESTS all judicial, administrative and law enforcement authorities of the Islamic Republic of Pakistan to use their best endeavours to assist in taking any steps which may to them appear necessary and appropriate in locating, safeguarding and facilitating the return to England and Wales of the said minor child[ren] pursuant to the laws of the Islamic Republic of Pakistan and in accordance with the Protocol made on 17 January 2003 in London and signed by the Honourable Chief Justice of the Supreme Court of Pakistan and by the Right Honourable The President of the Family Division of the High Court of Justice of England and Wales

OTHER EXAMPLES OF HELPFUL WORDING

FOR THE AVOIDANCE OF DOUBT the Foreign and Commonwealth Office and/or Her Majesty's Passport Office may grant a passport, travel document or emergency travel document to [names of child/ren] without the consent of [name of parent/mother/father]

PERMISSION IS HEREBY GIVEN to the Foreign and Commonwealth Office of the United Kingdom to share the information disclosed to them in accordance with paragraph [X] above with [named bodies/persons] [and any other relevant agency]

Note—See also the Guidance for the Judiciary of April 2016 on *Transfer of proceedings under Article 15 of Brussels IIa and Articles 8 and/or 9 of the 1996 Hague Convention* (below) and the frequently asked questions on practical issues arising in family cases with an international aspect, which is available at: *www.familylaw.co.uk/news_and_comment/president-issues-guidance-on-international-family-law*.

Guidance for the Judiciary April 2016

Transfer of proceedings under Article 15 of Brussels IIa and Articles 8 and/or 9 of the 1996 Hague Convention

Introduction

This Guidance is being provided along with Guidance to HMCTS staff. Its principal purpose is to deal with the process for the registration of all applications and requests for transfer of jurisdiction as required by FPR 2010, r 12.61(5).

The Guidance provides an administrative/procedural context for the registration process and is not intended to provide guidance on legal issues arising from Articles 15, 8 or 9 or more generally.

1 Background

BRUSSELS IIA

1.1 Council Regulation (EC) No 2201/2003 (**BIIa**) governs jurisdiction and recognition of judgments in matrimonial matters and matters of parental responsibility. The Regulation applies to all EU members states with the exception of Denmark. In matters of parental responsibility, the Regulation gives primary jurisdiction to the courts of the State in which the child is habitually resident at the time the court becomes involved, but there are exceptions to this.

1.2 In particular, Article 15 provides a procedure for the 'transfer' of proceedings from a court having substantive jurisdiction to the court of another Member State if certain conditions are fulfilled.

The court may take the steps set out in Article 15(1)(a) or (b) (see para 1.3 below) if:

(i) the child has a particular connection with that State, as described in Art 15(3); and
(ii) the court considers that a court of that State would be better placed to hear the case, or a specific part of it; and
(iii) the court considers that it is in the best interests of the child to do so.

1.3 Where these criteria are satisfied the court may:

(a) stay the proceedings (or part of them) and invite the parties to introduce a request before the other court to assume jurisdiction; or
(b) request the other court to assume jurisdiction.

Where the court invites the parties to take the necessary steps, it must set a time limit by which the parties should introduce the request to the other court. If the other court is not thereby seised within that time, jurisdiction will remain with the original court.

PART V

1.4 The court to which the request is made (either by the parties or by the court) may accept jurisdiction within 6 weeks from its 'seisure' – which would seem to mean from receipt of the request. If it does so, the original court must decline jurisdiction; otherwise the original court retains jurisdiction.

1.5 The court's powers under Article 15 may be exercised on the application of a party or on the court's own initiative or on application from a court of another Member State with which the child has a particular connection.

1.6 Court has a broad definition: Article 2(1).

1996 HAGUE CONVENTION

1.7 Articles 8 and 9 of the **1996 Hague Convention** provide for the transfer of jurisdiction to or from another Hague Convention State in broadly similar terms to Article 15 of BIIa.

PROCEEDINGS NOT WITHIN BIIA OR 1996 CONVENTION

1.8 Note that the provisions for transfer do not apply to matrimonial proceedings or to the establishment of the parent-child relationship, to decisions about or preparatory to adoption or to maintenance obligations: Article 1(3) of BIIa and Article 4 of the 1996 Convention.

2 Procedure

2.1 The procedure on an application for transfer of proceedings under Article 15 of Brussels IIa or Articles 8 or 9 of the 1996 Hague Convention is governed by the Family Procedure Rules 2010, rr 12.61–12.67.

There is a specific form available for an application for transfer (Form C68), which is intended for use by a person who is or would be a party to the proceedings. It is expected that an application or request from the court of another State will be made informally.

2.2 An application/request for transfer of jurisdiction **from** England and Wales under Article 15 of BIIa or under Article 8/9 of the 1996 Hague Convention is known as an 'outgoing request'. An application/request for transfer of jurisdiction **to** England and Wales is known as an 'incoming request'.

OUTGOING REQUESTS

2.3 An application by a party to transfer proceedings from a court in England and Wales to the court of another Member State or Contracting State must be made to the court in which the proceedings are continuing and it is that court which may exercise powers under Article 15 or Article 8, as appropriate.

2.4 Where the court is considering exercising its powers under Article 15 or Article 8 on its own initiative, the court must fix a hearing and give the parties as least 5 days' notice (r 12.64)

2.5 Where a request is received from another State by a court in which proceedings are continuing in England and Wales, the court must fix a hearing and notify the parties **and** the Central Authority (ICACU in England and Wales) not less than 5 days before the hearing (r 12.63).

2.6 In any of these cases the court may give directions for the filing of evidence or representations.

2.7 When the court is considering whether to make an outgoing request under Article 15 or Article 8, in the absence of a party having already made the appropriate enquiries, early consideration should be given to directing a nominated party to obtain information through ICACU (i) of the process by which such a request would need to be made and (ii) of how arrangements might be made for the child/children to move/to be cared for in the other State if the request is accepted.

2.8 When the court has made a request under Article 15 or Article 8, the request should be sent by a nominated party to ICACU for onward transmission to the other State unless the court has been notified that it should be sent otherwise.

INCOMING REQUESTS

2.9 An application for the court in England and Wales to request transfer of jurisdiction from a court of another Member State or Contracting State to a court in England and Wales under Article 15 or Article 9 must be made to the High Court (PRFD) (r 12.65).

2.10 Any request by the court of another Member State or Contracting State for a court in England and Wales to assume jurisdiction must be considered by the High Court. Where a request is received by a court other than the High Court, it must be referred to a Judge of the High Court for a decision on acceptance (r 12.66).

2.11 If, as a result of a request made by the High Court or by a court in another State, jurisdiction is transferred to a court in England and Wales, the proceedings may be allocated to the Family Court or High Court as appropriate, in the same manner as proceedings commenced in England and Wales.

3 *Register for incoming and outgoing requests under Article 15 of Brussels IIa and Articles 8 and/or 9 of the 1996 Hague Convention*

3.1 There is a requirement that the details of all applications and requests for transfer of jurisdiction to or from another Member State or Contracting State must be entered in a Register kept by the High Court (PRFD): see FPR 2010, r 12.61(5).

3.2 The guidance below sets out the information which is required for inclusion in the Register. This guidance has also been provided to HMCTS staff.

THE REGISTER FOR OUTGOING REQUESTS

3.3 An outgoing request will be considered by the relevant court in England and Wales. If granted, it is then for the other state to accept or refuse the transfer request.

3.4 Once the court in England and Wales has determined an application/request for a transfer of jurisdiction under Article 15 or under Articles 8 and/or 9 (either by making a request or by staying the proceedings or by not making a request or by refusing a request) the information set out below must be sent by a member of HMCTS staff to the National Family Team, who will keep the register on behalf of the PRFD.

3.5 The Central Register will be updated and maintained by the National Family Team in the Courts and Tribunals Development Directorate. Courts are instructed to provide the National Family Team with the relevant information via email to update the register.

INFORMATION REQUIRED BY THE COURT

3.6 The National Family Team will require a copy of the order and the following information:

- Whether it relates to Article 15 or Article 8 and/or 9
- Case Number
- Name of Applicant
- Name of Respondent
- Name of children
- The other country / state involved
- Date of order and whether the request was granted
- Confirmation of whether the request was made by a party, of the court's own motion or from another state /country
- Whether the transfer has been accepted by the other state

3.7 This information should be included in the order, but if any information is omitted it should be contained in the body of the email to the National Family Team. Court staff should send the email with the order attached to civil&familybusinesssupport@hmcts.gsi.gov.uk with 'Central Register entry' in the subject box.

3.8 The core information required for the register should be provided as soon as possible after the order is made. It is not necessary to wait until a response is received from the court in the other State.

3.9 However, the register must also record whether the transfer request has been accepted or refused. It is recommended that once an order has been made a diary entry be noted 6 weeks ahead to check the position. The court order should direct the applicant, or, in public law children proceedings, the Local Authority to inform the court of the decision made by the other State. Once this information is received by the court, it must be sent to the National Family Team by email as above.

INCOMING REQUESTS

3.10 Applications to the court in England and Wales for transfer from another State must be made to the High Court (PRFD) at the Royal Courts of Justice. These applications will be entered onto the register maintained by the team at the PRFD.

3.11 If the request is accepted, the court officer will notify the parties to the proceedings and the case will be allocated as if the application had been made in England and Wales. Allocation will normally be to the relevant Family Court centre, unless a direction has been made for the case to proceed in the High Court.

REQUESTS FOR INFORMATION

3.12 If the court receives a request for information as to whether a case has been transferred out under Article 15 or Article 8 the enquirer will be advised by court staff to email civil&familybusinesssupport@hmcts.gsi.gov.uk who will be able to deal with their request.

3.13 For information on whether a transfer in was accepted a request can be emailed to the team at the PRFD – rcj.familyhighcourt@hmcts.gsi.gov.uk

The Rt Hon Sir James Munby

President of the Family Division

Note—See also the President's Guidance of April 2016 on *Liaison between Courts in England and Wales and British Embassies and High Commissions abroad* (above) and the frequently asked questions on practical issues arising in family cases with an international aspect, which is available at: *www.familylaw.co.uk/news_and_comment/president-issues-guidance-on-international-family-law*.

Local Direction 17 October 2016

Electronic Filing at the Central Family Court: Pilot Scheme

The Financial Remedies Unit at the Central Family Court issues the following Local Direction in relation to all applications for Financial Remedies and Financial Orders (as defined under Rule 2.3 of the Family Procedure Rules 2010).

The Direction supplements, and does not derogate from, the operation of FPR 5.5 and PD5B within the Financial Remedies Unit.

The operation of the Pilot Scheme will be reviewed in April 2017.

The directions are given under the Court's powers and duty to manage cases actively making use of technology under Rule 1.4 of the Family Procedure Rules 2010.

No part of this direction applies to:

(i) The Petition for Divorce, Nullity or Dissolution of Civil Partnership or proceedings thereunder;

(ii) Any contempt proceedings; or

(iii) Children Proceedings (save for Financial Remedies or Financial Orders).

1 All applications for the issue of financial proceedings, or applications made within financial remedy proceedings that were issued since 1 January 2016, may be made by email to the Financial Remedies Unit at the Central Family Court at cfc.efiling.fru@hmcts.gsi.gov.uk.

General requirements

2 The following requirements apply to such applications:

(a) All documents filed in connection with the application should not exceed 10MB in size collectively;
(b) PDF format is memory efficient and should be used wherever possible;
(c) PDF copies of signatures supporting such application will be required at time of the receipt of the application, together with confirmation that the original document with the original signature will be available for inspection at any time if required by the court.

Fees

3 No application will be processed without payment of the court fee. Payment can be made as stated below:

(a) cheque/cash/postal order;
(b) debit or credit card at the public counter;
(c) debit or credit card over the telephone on 020 7421 8606*;
(d) fee remission, see https://www.gov.uk/get-help-with-court-fees.

* you must state in your email that you wish to pay over the telephone and the court will advise accordingly.

Service

4 Upon issuing the application the court will return the sealed application in duplicate, one of which the applicant or their solicitors must serve on the respondent. The applicant must serve the application on the respondent in accordance with Part 6 of the Family Procedure Rules 2010 unless the respondent agrees to accept service of proceedings by email to a specified email address or the court directs such service.

Filing of documents with the court.

5 Each party may file their Form E (but not the attached documents) with the court by email provided that:

(a) The Form E does not exceed 10MB in size;
(b) The Form E and the required supporting documents have been exchanged between the parties (whether in hard copy or, if agreed between the parties, electronically);
(c) There is confirmation to the court that:
  (i) the Form E and the supporting documents have been supplied to the other party; and
  (ii) all the required supporting documentation is held by the party for inspection by the court if required.

6 The documents required to be served and filed under Rule 9.14(5) and 9.14(6) may be filed with the court and, if both parties agree, served on the other party by email.

7 At the First Appointment the court will make a direction for the filing and serving of all documents (save for the court bundle) by email if reasonably possible. Such a direction may also be made at any urgent hearing before the First Appointment.

8 Currently the court bundle needs to be lodged in hard copy for every hearing in the Financial Remedies Unit in strict compliance with PD27A of the Family Procedure Rules 2010. This provision may be revised once secure cloud facilities are available.

Orders

9 From 31 October 2016 all draft orders from the outcome of a hearing within the Financial Remedies Unit should be emailed to the court at cfc.frucourtorders@hmcts.gsi.gov.uk

Issued by:

HHJ Tolson QC, *Designated Family Judge for Central London*

HHJ Martin O'Dwyer, *Judicial Head of FRU*

This Local Practice Direction is approved as a Pilot Scheme by:

Mostyn J, *Family Division Judge with responsibility for the Money List*

Moor J, *Family Division Liaison Judge for the Financial Remedies Unit*

All queries regarding this e-filing protocol should be sent to ryan.gallagher@hmcts.gsi.gov.uk

President's Guidance December 2016

Allocation of Work to Section 9 Judges

1 Where proceedings are issued in the Family Court but are allocated at the Gatekeeping stage to be heard by a High Court Judge (particularly if they are proceedings described in *Paragraph H* of *Part 2* of the *Schedule to Public Law Allocation and Gatekeeping Guidance 2013*[1], or *Part 3* of the *Schedule to the Allocation and Gatekeeping Guidance – Private Law 2014*[2]), the DFJ must obtain the agreement of the FDLJ (or in a case of urgency from the Urgent Applications Judge of the Family Division, or other Judge of the Family Division) before any hearing in proceedings allocated to High Court level is conducted by a section 9 Judge[3].

1 Public law Guidance: *https://www.judiciary.gov.uk/wp-content/uploads/JCO/Documents/family-court-guide/pfd-guidance-on-allocation-and-gatekeeping.pdf*, and Public law Schedule, see *https://www.judiciary.gov.uk/wp-content/uploads/JCO/Documents/family-court-guide/schedule-to-the-allocation-and-gatekeeping-guidance.pdf*

2 Private law Guidance: *https://www.justice.gov.uk/downloads/family-justice-reform/allocation-and-gatekeeping-guidance.pdf*, and Private law schedule, see *http://www.justice.gov.uk/downloads/family-justice-reform/schedule-to-allocation-and-gatekeeping-guidance.pdf*

3 This Guidance refers to 'section 9 Judges' as those appointed under **Section 9(1)** ('Judge of the High Court') and **Section 9(4)** ('Deputy Judge of the High Court') of the **Senior Courts Act 1981**

'Public Law Allocation and Gatekeeping Guidance 2013'—It is believed this should refer to the 2014 Guidance.

2 Where free-standing proceedings are issued in the Family Division of the High Court on circuit[4], the DFJ must obtain the agreement of the FDLJ (or in a case of urgency from the Urgent Applications Judge of the Family Division, or other Judge of the Family Division) before any hearing in such proceedings is conducted by a section 9 Judge.

4 This phrase 'on circuit' means in any court centre in England and Wales other than the Principal Registry of the Family Division, London.

3 Where an application is made in the High Court, in the context of and during proceedings which are before the Family Court (e g where relief is sought under the inherent jurisdiction ancillary to an application for a public law order before the Family Court), advance authorisation must be sought from the FDLJ (or in a case of urgency from the Urgent Applications Judge of the Family Division, or other Judge of the Family Division) for the High Court application to be heard by the judge (who must be suitably authorised) sitting as a section 9 judge[5].

5 This addresses the points considered in *RE v North Yorkshire* [2015] at §23 and *Redcar & Cleveland v B* [2013] at §7.

4 If proceedings are issued in the Family Court but an issue arises as to *transfer* of the proceedings to the High Court, except as provided for in paragraph [5] below, the DFJ shall refer the case to the FDLJ under *rule 29.17(3)/(4) FPR 2010* for decision.

5 A section 9 judge may make a decision to transfer proceedings from the Family Court to the High Court solely for the purpose of making an order under the inherent jurisdiction of the High Court to require a Government Department or agency to disclose an address to the court (*PD29C FPR 2010 at §2*).

6 If at any time a judge who is conducting proceedings considers that they should be re-allocated to High Court level for hearing by a High Court Judge or a section 9 judge, the judge shall, before re-allocating the case, discuss the matter with the DFJ, who shall if necessary consult the FDLJ.

7 All orders made by section 9 judges in family proceedings, whether in the Family Court or the High Court, shall specifically state that the order was made by a section 9 judge. The destination for any appeal is affected by the tier of judiciary dealing with the application at first instance.

8 No Tipstaff Orders may be made by a section 9 judge without prior authorisation from the FDLJ (or in a case of urgency from the Urgent Applications Judge of the Family Division, or other Judge of the Family Division).

9 Proceedings under the Mental Capacity Act 2005 in the Court of Protection shall not be allocated or transferred to a section 9 judge[6] without prior authorisation from the FDLJ (or in a case of urgency from the Urgent Applications Judge of the Family Division, or other Judge of the Family Division).

6 Tier 3 Judge: see PD3B CoPR 2007 para 3(viii)

President of the Family Division

Section 9 judge—The opening paragraph to the Guidance states that this refers to those who are appointed under s 9(1) (Judge of the High Court) and s 9(4) (Deputy Judge of the High Court). These provisions authorise the appointment of circuit judges, Recorders and other judges to sit as deputy judges of the High Court if it is expedient as a temporary measure in order to facilitate the disposal of business in the High Court.

Scope—This guidance formalises the practice and procedure that has been in existence to ensure compliance with the statutory requirements set out in SCA 1981, s 9 and to avoid the procedure being overlooked or over-stepped and orders being made that lack jurisdictional basis. It is clearly designed to address the concern raised by the Court of Appeal in *Re B* [2014] 1 FLR 277, CA, where Black LJ observed that 'where a circuit judge is to sit as a High Court judge, it seems to me that this needs to be arranged deliberately, with the proceedings commenced in or transferred to the High Court. The mere fact that the judge who has heard the case happens to be authorised to sit as a High Court judge or to try Administrative Court cases might not redeem a failure to observe proper practice', at [7] and in *RE v North Yorkshire County Council, LO and A (A Child)* [2015] EWCA Civ 1169, where declaration could not be made pursuant to the inherent jurisdiction of the High Court by a circuit judge without first obtaining authorisation.

The Guidance supplements the allocation provisions set out in FC(CDB)R 2014, the Allocation and Gatekeeping Guidances of 22 April 2014 in relation to both public and private law proceedings and FPR 2010, r 29.17(3),(4) and PD29C and therefore must be considered alongside these provisions when consideration is being given to allocate or transfer a family case to a High Court judge (and therefore by implication to a judge or Recorder permitted pursuant to s 9 as a deputy High Court Judge). The cases to which the guidance applies include: (a) proceedings issued in the Family Court but allocated to be heard by a High Court Judge and in particular those listed in the Allocation Guidances of 22 April 2014 relating to both public and private law proceedings (set out in this Part); (b) where a freestanding application is issued in a Family Court Centre other than the PRFD; (c) where, during any proceedings before the Family Court, relief is sought that can only be granted by the High Court, e g in the exercise of its inherent jurisdiction; (d) where a transfer of proceedings to the High Court or reallocation of the proceedings to the High Court is being considered pursuant to FPR 2010, r 29.17(3),(4) and PD29C, save in relation to orders for disclosure of address from a Government department or agency; and (e) Tipstaff orders. In all these instances, the Designated Family Judge must be informed and agreement must be obtained from the Family Division Liaison Judge or, in the case of urgency, from the Urgent Applications Judge of the Family Division or other judge of the Family Division before any hearing in such proceedings is conducted by a s 9 judge. Finally, it confirms the practice that all orders made by a s 9 judge in family proceedings must specifically state that the order was made by a s 9 judge.

Practice Note January 2017

The Official Solicitor to the Senior Courts: Appointment in Family Proceedings and Proceedings under the Inherent Jurisdiction in Relation to Adults

Introduction

1 This Practice Note replaces the Practice Note dated March 2013 issued by the Official Solicitor.

2 It concerns:

(a) the appointment of the Official Solicitor as 'litigation friend' of a 'protected party' or child in family proceedings, where the Family Division of the High Court is being invited to exercise its inherent jurisdiction in relation to a vulnerable adult[1] or where proceedings in relation to a child aged 16 or 17 are transferred into the Court of Protection;

(b) requests by the court to the Official Solicitor to conduct *Harbin v Masterman*[2] enquiries; and

(c) requests by the court to the Official Solicitor to act as, or appoint counsel to act as, an advocate to the court[3].

The Note is intended to be helpful guidance, but is always subject to legislation including the Rules of Court, to Practice Directions, and to case law.

In this Note 'FPR 2010' means Family Procedure Rules 2010, 'CPR 1998' means Civil Procedure Rules 1998 and 'CoPR 2007' means Court of Protection Rules 2007.

1 In this context a 'vulnerable adult' is a person who has mental capacity in respect of the decisions in question but who lacks litigation capacity.

2 [1896] 1 Ch 351.

3 See the Attorney-General's Memorandum of 19 December 2001: 'Requests for the appointment of an advocate to the court'.[2002] Fam Law 229

3 For the avoidance of doubt, the Children and Family Court Advisory and Support Service (CAFCASS) has responsibilities in relation to a child in family proceedings in which their welfare is or may be in question (Criminal Justice and Court Services Act 2000, section 12). Since 1 April 2001 the Official Solicitor has not represented a child who is the subject of family proceedings (other than in very exceptional circumstances). In cases of doubt or difficulty, staff of the Official Solicitor's office will liaise with staff of CAFCASS Legal Services to avoid duplication and ensure the most suitable arrangements are made.

Appointment of a litigation friend for a protected party

4 A 'protected party' requires a litigation friend. In family proceedings this requirement appears in Part 15 of the FPR 2010, in proceedings in the Family Division of the High Court of Justice under the court's inherent jurisdiction it appears in Part 21 of the CPR 1998 and in proceedings in the Court of Protection it appears in Part 17 of the CoPR 2007.

5 In family proceedings, a 'protected party' means a party, or an intended party, who lacks capacity (within the meaning of the Mental Capacity Act 2005) to conduct the proceedings: FPR 2010, rule 2.3; and in proceedings under the inherent jurisdiction the expression has the same meaning: CPR 1998, rule 21.2. The following should be noted:

(a) there must be undisputed evidence the party, or intended party, lacks capacity to conduct the proceedings;

(b) that evidence, and what flows from the party, or intended party, being a protected party, should have been disclosed to, and carefully explained to, the party or intended party;

(c) the party, or intended party, is entitled to dispute an opinion that they lack capacity to conduct the proceedings; there may be cases where the party's, or intended party's, capacity to conduct the proceedings is the subject of dispute between competent experts. In either case a formal finding by the court under FPR 2010, rule 2.3, or CPR 1998, rule 21.2 is required.

Vulnerable adult

6 Applications made under the inherent jurisdiction in respect of a 'vulnerable' adult are made to the Family Division of the High Court but are not family proceedings; the CPR 1998 apply to proceedings under the inherent jurisdiction in respect of adults and the application should be made on a Part 8 claim form using the Part 8 alternative procedure.

7 Difficult questions may arise if the 'vulnerable' adult despite having capacity to make the decision or decisions in question nonetheless lacks capacity to conduct the proceedings.

8 A litigation friend is only required if the 'vulnerable' adult does lack capacity to conduct the proceedings and is therefore a protected party as defined in CPR 1998, rule 21.2.

Court of Protection

9 The Court of Protection was established by section 45 Mental Capacity Act 2005. Court of Protection proceedings are not family proceedings. 'P' in Court of Protection proceedings is any person (other than a protected party) who lacks or, so far as consistent with the context, is alleged to lack capacity to make a decision or decisions in relation to any matter that is the subject of an application to the Court of Protection (CoPR 2007, rule 6).

10 A 'protected party' is a party or an intended party (other than P or a child) who lacks capacity to conduct the proceedings (CoPR 2007, rule 6).

Children who require a litigation friend in proceedings

11 Non-subject child: a child who is not the subject of family proceedings may nevertheless be a party and subject to FPR 2010 rule 16.6 (see paragraph 7), requires a litigation friend in family proceedings. The most common examples are:

(a) a child who is also the parent of a child, and who is a respondent to a Children Act 1989 or Adoption and Children Act 2002 application;
(b) a child who wishes to make an application for a Children Act 1989 order naming another child (typically a child arrangements order for contact with a sibling);
(c) a child who has been joined as an intervener in a public law children case to respond to allegations;
(d) a child intervenor in financial remedy proceedings;
(e) a child party to applications for declarations of status under Part III Family Law Act 1986 other than section 55A applications;
(f) a child applicant for, or respondent to, an application for an order under Part IV (Family Homes and Domestic Violence) or Part 4A (Forced Marriage) of the Family Law Act 1996;

12 Child parties to applications for declarations of parentage under section 55A Family Law Act 1986: subject to FPR 2010 rule 16.6, in section 55A cases

(a) any child whose parentage is in dispute and who has been joined as party under FPR 2010 rule 16.2 would have a children's guardian appointed under rule 16.4;
(b) a child party whose parentage is not in dispute requires a litigation friend.

13 FPR 2010 Part 16 makes provision for the representation of children.

(a) Rule 16.6 sets out the circumstances in which a child does not need a children's guardian or litigation friend. A child party to proceedings under the Children Act 1989, section 55A Family Law Act 1986, Part 4A Family Law Act 1996, applications in adoption, placement and related proceedings, or proceedings relating to the exercise of the court's inherent jurisdiction with respect to children, may rely on the provisions of rule 16.6.

PART V

(b) However this rule does not apply to those children who are the subject of and party to specified proceedings or proceedings to which Part 14 applies.

14 Children aged 16–17 years: the Mental Capacity Act 2005 (Transfer of Proceedings) Order 2007 (SI 2007/1899) makes provision for the transfer of proceedings from the Court of Protection to a court having jurisdiction under the Children Act 1989. The Order also makes provision for the transfer of the whole or part of the proceedings from a court having jurisdiction under the Children Act 1989 to the Court of Protection where it considers that in all circumstances, it is just and convenient to transfer the proceedings:

(a) Article 3(3) of the Order lists those factors to which the court must have regard when making a determination about transfer to the Court of Protection either on an application or of its own initiative;
(b) proceedings transferred under Article 3 are to be treated for all purposes as if they were proceedings under the Mental Capacity Act 2005 which had been started in the Court of Protection;
(c) as Court of Protection proceedings are not family proceedings transfer of proceedings into the Court of Protection means any involvement by CAFCASS in those proceedings will end;
(d) there should be reason to believe that the child lacks capacity (within the meaning of the Mental Capacity Act 2005) in relation to a matter or matters concerning their own welfare and that it is likely that they will still lack capacity to make decisions in respect of that matter when they reach 18.

15 Rules 141(4)–(5) of the CoPR 2007 make provision for a child to be permitted to conduct proceedings in the Court of Protection without a litigation friend. However if the child is 'P' within the meaning of rule 6 of the CoPR 2007 reference should be made to rule 141(1) and rule 147 of those Rules in relation to the appointment of a litigation friend.

The role of a litigation friend

16 The case law and the Rules provide that a litigation friend must fairly and competently conduct the proceedings in the protected party's or child's best interests[4], and must have no interest in the proceedings adverse to that of the protected party or child. The procedure and basis for the appointment of a litigation friend and the duty of a litigation friend are contained in Part 15 (Representation of Protected Parties) FPR 2010 and Part 16 (Representation of Children and Reports in Proceedings Involving Children) FPR 2010 and the associated Practice Directions.

4 Sir Robert Megarry V-C said in *Re E (mental health patient)* [1984] 1 All ER 309 at pages 312–3 'The main function of a [litigation] friend appears to be to carry on the litigation on behalf of the plaintiff and in his best interests. For this purpose the [litigation] friend must make all the decisions that the plaintiff would have made, had he been able… the [litigation] friend … is responsible to the court for the propriety and the progress of the proceedings. The [litigation] friend does not, however, become a litigant himself…'

The Official Solicitor's criteria for consenting to act as litigation friend

17 The Official Solicitor is the litigation friend of last resort. No person, including the Official Solicitor, can be appointed to act as litigation friend without their consent. The Official Solicitor will not accept appointment where there is another person who is suitable and willing to act as litigation friend. The Official Solicitor's criteria for consenting to act as litigation friend are:

(a) in the case of an adult that the party or intended party is a protected party[5];
(b) there is security for the costs of legal representation of the protected party which the Official Solicitor considers satisfactory. Sources of security may be:
  (i) the Legal Aid Agency where the protected party or child is eligible for legal aid;
  (ii) the protected party's or child's own funds where they have financial capacity or where they do not where the Court of Protection has given him authority to recover the costs from the adult's or child's funds;
  (iii) an undertaking from another party to pay his costs;
(c) the case is a last resort case.

5 The Official Solicitor is able to provide a pro forma certificate of capacity to conduct proceedings and guidance notes. The pro forma is also available on www.gov.uk.

Invitations to the Official Solicitor: new cases

18 Solicitors who have been consulted by a child or a protected party (or by someone acting on their behalf, or concerned about their interests) should write to the Official Solicitor setting out the background to the proposed case and explaining the basis on which the Official Solicitor's criteria for acting are met.

Invitations to the Official Solicitor: pending proceedings

19 Where a case is already before the court, an order inviting the Official Solicitor to act should be expressed as being made subject to his consent. The Official Solicitor cannot consent to act unless and until he is satisfied that his criteria are met.

20 If so satisfied, he will allocate public law children cases to a case manager within 2 working days of his criteria being met; all other cases will be allocated within 5 working days. The position in relation to allocation may be subject to change from time to time

Public law children cases

21 Allocation to a case manager does not preclude the need for the case manager to be given sufficient time to become familiar with the facts of, and issues in the case before the Official Solicitor, as litigation friend of the protected party or child, is able to give instructions. The case manager will have existing cases and must make decisions about priorities. Allocation to a case manager in close proximity to a hearing may require that the hearing be re-listed.

22 To enable the Official Solicitor promptly to consider the invitation to him to act, he should be sent as soon as possible the completed referral form for public law children cases (available at www.gov.uk[6]) and the documents that form refers to.

6 https://www.gov.uk/government/publications/official-solicitor-referral-form-for-children-act-public-law-proceedings

All other cases

23 In all other cases the Official Solicitor should be provided with the following as soon as possible:

- (a) the sealed court order inviting him to act as litigation friend (with a note of the reasons approved by the Judge if appropriate);
- (b) (adult party):
  - (i) a copy of the letter of instruction to the expert by which an opinion was sought as to the party's capacity to conduct the proceedings;
  - (ii) the opinion on capacity (the Official Solicitor's pro forma certificate of capacity to conduct proceedings may be requested from his office for the purpose of obtaining an opinion and is available on www.gov.uk[7]);
- (c) a full explanation as to how the costs of legal representation are to be paid (including any relevant supporting documents) – it is a matter for the Official Solicitor whether the proposed security for costs is satisfactory;
- (d) confirmation that there is no other person suitable and willing to act as litigation friend (including enquiries made about this);
- (e) the court file (provision of the court file may not be necessary if the court directs a party to provide a full indexed copy of the bundle to the Official Solicitor on a timely basis).

7 https://www.gov.uk/government/publications/certificate-as-to-capacity-to-conduct-proceedings

Litigants in person

24 If one or more of the parties is or are litigants in person, and there is reason to believe that a litigant in person may lack capacity to conduct the proceedings, the court will need to consider, and if necessary give directions as to:

(a) who is to arrange for assessment of their capacity to conduct the proceedings;
(b) how the cost of that assessment is to be funded;
(c) how any invitation to act as litigation friend is to be made either to any suitable and willing person or to the Official Solicitor so as to provide the proposed litigation friend with the documents and relevant information (including information to enable enquiries necessary to establish whether or not funding for legal costs is available);
(d) any resulting timetabling: where the Official Solicitor is being invited to be litigation friend regard should be had to the Official Solicitor's need to investigate whether his acceptance criteria are met including the possibility that an application to the Court of Protection (for authority to pay the costs out of the protected party's or child's funds) may be necessary.

25 The Official Solicitor will notify the court in the event he expects a delay in accepting appointment either because it is not evident that his criteria are met or for any other reason. The court may wish to consider:

(a) making enquiries of the parties as to the steps being taken by them to establish that the Official Solicitor's criteria for acting are met;
(b) whether directions should be made to ensure that the parties progress such enquiries on a timely basis;
(c) fixing a further directions appointment.

26 If, at any time, another litigation friend is appointed before the Official Solicitor is in a position to accept the invitation to him to act, the Official Solicitor should be notified without delay.

Where the Official Solicitor has accepted appointment as litigation friend

27 Once the Official Solicitor is able to accept appointment as litigation friend he will need time to prepare the case on behalf of the protected party or child and may wish to make submissions about any substantive hearing date.

28 In all cases to avoid unnecessary delay in progression of the case, he requires from the solicitors he appoints for the protected party or child:

(a) a reading list identifying the material documents;
(b) identification of the issues including those which require consideration on behalf of the protected party or child;
(c) a summary of the background to, and major steps in the proceedings;
(d) advice as to the steps the Official Solicitor, as litigation friend, should now take in the proceedings on behalf of the protected party or child;
(e) copies of all notes of attendance on the protected party or child (so that the Official Solicitor is properly informed as to the views and wishes expressed by the protected party or child to date);
(f) confirmation of the protected party's or child's ascertainable present views and wishes in relation to the proceedings.

Advising the court: Harbin v Masterman enquiries and Advocate to the Court

29 Where the Official Solicitor is invited, with his consent, to conduct enquiries under *Harbin v Masterman* and it appears to the Official Solicitor that any public body wishes to seek the assistance of the court but is unwilling to carry out the enquiries itself, the Official Solicitor may seek an undertaking from that public body to indemnify him in respect of his costs of carrying out those enquiries.

30 The Official Solicitor may be invited by the court to act or instruct counsel as a friend of the court (advocate to the court) if it appears to the court that such an invitation is more appropriately addressed to him rather than (or in addition to) CAFCASS Legal Services or to the Attorney-General. It is a matter for him whether he accepts that invitation.

Contacting the Official Solicitor

31 It may be helpful to discuss the question of appointment with the Official Solicitor or one of his staff by telephoning 020 3681 2755 (General enquiries: public law family cases) 020 3681 2754 (General enquiries: private law family cases including divorce), or 020 3681 2751 (General enquiries: Court of Protection healthcare & welfare). In particular:

(a) if in doubt about whether the Official Solicitor's acceptance criteria are met, or

(b) to request a copy of the Official Solicitor's pro forma certificate of capacity to conduct proceedings and guidance notes .

32 Enquiries about the appointment of the Official Solicitor as litigation friend in family proceedings should be addressed:

(a) (in private law family cases) to the Team Leader, Family Litigation (Private Law);

(b) (in public law family ca

All other enquiries should be addressed to a family lawyer.

The contact details are:

Office of the Official Solicitor to the Senior Courts
Victory House
30–34 Kingsway
London WC2B 6EX
DX 141423 Bloomsbury 7
Fax: 020 3681 2762
E-mail: enquiries@offsol.gsi.gov.uk

Alastair Pitblado
Official Solicitor

PART V

Practice Guidance 18 January 2017

Family Court – Duration of Ex Parte (Without Notice) Orders

This Guidance was originally issued on 13 October 2014. This revised Guidance, issued on 18 January 2017, supersedes the previous Guidance.

1 The Magistrates' Association and the National Bench Chairs' Forum have raised with me the question of whether it is proper to grant an ex parte non-molestation injunction for an unlimited period. They suggest that practice varies. They express the view that to grant such an order for an unlimited time is wrong in principle.

2 In expressing that view, the Magistrates' Association and the National Bench Chairs' Forum are entirely correct. To grant an ex parte (without notice) injunction for an unlimited time is wrong in principle. The practice of granting such orders for an unlimited time, if this is still occurring, must stop.

3 Subject only to paragraph 8, the same principles, as set out below, apply to all ex parte (without notice) injunctive orders made by the Family Court or by the Family Division, irrespective of the subject matter of the proceedings or the terms of the order.

4 The law is to be found in *Horgan v Horgan* [2002] EWCA Civ 1371, paras 5–6 (Ward LJ), *R (Casey) v Restormel Borough Council* [2007] EWHC 2554 (Admin), paras 37–41 (Munby J), *In re C (A Child) (Family Proceedings: Practice)* [2013] EWCA Civ 1412, [2014] 1 WLR 2182, [2014] 1 FLR 1239, para 15 (Ryder LJ), and *Re A (A Child)* [2016] EWCA Civ 572, [2016] 4 WLR 111, paras 49–61, esp paras 59–61 (Munby P).

5 The relevant principles, compliance with which is essential, are as follows:

(i) An ex parte (without notice) injunctive order must never be made without limit of time.

There must be a fixed end date. It is not sufficient merely to specify a return day. The order must specify on its face and in clear terms precisely when it expires (eg, 12 noon on 20 March 2017).

(ii) The order must also fix a return day. The order must specify the date, time and place of the hearing on the return day. The return day should normally be no more than 14 days after the date when the order was made. How long the hearing on the return day should be listed for must be a matter for the discretion of the judge. However, having regard to paragraph 6, often a very short listing may well be appropriate.

(iii) Careful consideration needs to be given to the duration of any order made ex parte (without notice). Many orders will be of short duration, typically no more than 14 days. But in appropriate cases involving personal protection, such as non-molestation injunctions granted in accordance with Part IV of the Family Law Act 1996, the order itself can be for a longer period, such as 6 or even 12 months, provided that the order specifies a return day within no more than 14 days. This must be a matter for the discretion of the judge, but a period longer than 6 months is likely to be appropriate only where the allegation is of long term abuse or where some other good reason is shown. Conversely, a period shorter than 6 months may be appropriate in a case where there appears to be a one-off problem that may subside in weeks rather than months.

(iv) The order must make it clear that (a) it was made in the absence of the respondent and that the court has considered only the evidence of the applicant and (b) the court has made no finding of fact. Where the evidence is written, it must be identified in the order. Where, exceptionally, the court has received oral or other evidence (eg, a photograph) that evidence should be recorded on the face of the order or reduced to writing and served with the order.

(v) Where the order has been made in accordance with Part IV of the Family Law Act 1996 it must recite that the court has had regard to sections 45(1) and (2) of the Act.

(vi) The order (see FPR 18.10(3)) 'must contain a statement of the right to make an application to set aside or vary the order under rule 18.11.' The phrase 'liberty to apply' is not sufficient for this purpose. The order must spell out that the respondent is entitled, without waiting for the return day, to apply to set aside or vary the order.

(vii) If the respondent does apply to set aside or vary the order the court must list the application as a matter of urgency, within a matter of days at most.

6 Experience suggests that in certain types of case, for example, non-molestation or other orders granted in accordance with Part IV of the Family Law Act 1996, the respondent frequently neither applies to set aside or vary the order nor attends the hearing on the return day.

(i) When, in such cases, there is no attendance by the respondent and the order, having been served, does not require amendment there is no need for re-service. The order made on the return should however record that the respondent, although afforded the opportunity to be heard, has neither attended nor sought to be heard.

(ii) If, however, variation of the original order is sought by the applicant (e g by extending the ambit or the duration of the order) then:

  (a) Paragraphs 5(i), (iii)–(v) must be complied with in relation to the new order and the new order will need to be served.

  (b) Unless, before the return day, the respondent was given proper notice of the proposed amendments, either in the application or in the initial order, (a) the new order must specify a new return day, and (b) paragraph 5(ii) must be complied with in relation to the new order.

7 I remind all practitioners and judges of the principle, which applies to all ex parte (without notice) injunctive orders made by the Family Court or by the Family Division, irrespective of the subject matter of the proceedings or the terms of the order, that a without notice application will normally be appropriate only if:

(a) there is an emergency or other great urgency, so that it is impossible to give any notice, however short or informal, or

(b) there is a real risk that, if alerted to what is proposed, if 'tipped off', the respondent will take steps in advance of the hearing to thwart the court's order or otherwise to defeat the ends of justice. In an appropriate case this can justify the grant of a non-molestation injunction without notice, lest the respondent, having been served with an application, further molests his (or her) victim or exerts pressure on her (him) to abandon the proceedings.

8 Nothing in this Guidance derogates from, or otherwise modifies, the principles and safeguards to be observed on an application for an ex parte (without notice) freezing or search order: see *L v K (Freezing Orders: Principles and Safeguards)* [2013] EWHC 1735 (Fam), [2014] Fam 35.

Sir James Munby

President of the Family Division

take steps in advance of the hearing to thwart the court's order or otherwise to defeat the ends of justice. In an appropriate case this can justify the grant of a non-molestation injunction without notice, lest the respondent, having been served with an application, further molests his (or her) victim or exerts pressure on her (him) to abandon the proceedings.

Nothing in this Guidance derogates from, or otherwise modifies, the principles and safeguards to be observed on an application for an ex parte (without notice) freezing or search order: see *L v K (Freezing Orders: Principles and Safeguards)* [2013] EWHC 1735 (Fam), [2014] Fam 35.

Sir James Munby

President of the Family Division

PART VI

European Material

PART VI: European Material

Contents

Convention on Jurisdiction, Applicable Law, Recognition, Enforcement and Co-Operation in Respect of Parental Responsibility and Measures for the Protection of Children 2729

Council Regulation (EC) No 1206/2001 2753

Council Regulation (EC) No 2201/2003 2770

Council Regulation (EC) No 805/2004 2810

Council Regulation (EC) No 1393/2007 2822

Convention on the International Recovery of Child Support and Other Forms of Family Maintenance 2833

Council Regulation (EC) No 4/2009 2857

Regulation (EU) No 606/2013 of the European Parliament and of the Council 2890

Convention on Jurisdiction, Applicable Law, Recognition, Enforcement and Co-Operation in Respect of Parental Responsibility and Measures for the Protection of Children

Scope—This is also referred to as the 1996 Hague Convention on the Protection of Children, the 1996 Hague Child Protection Convention, the Hague Convention 1996 or the 1996 Convention. It was signed on 19 October 1996, but pursuant to Art 61 it could only come into force on the first day of the month following the expiration of 3 months after three states had ratified the Convention. The first three states to ratify it were Monaco in May 1997, the Czech Republic in March 2000 and Slovakia in 2001 and thus it came into force in January 2002. It was ratified by the UK on 27 July 2012 and came into force on 1 November 2012.

The aim of the Convention is to provide a uniform system to improve cross-border protection of children, to avoid conflict between the legal systems in respect of jurisdiction, applicable law, recognition and enforcement of measures and to provide co-operation and collaboration between states, with the best interests of the child as the primary consideration.

The Convention is divided into seven Chapters:

Chapter 1 (Arts 1–4) deals with the scope of the Convention. It sets out the objectives of the Convention, a non-exhaustive list of measures that may be covered by the Convention, a list of those matters that are excluded and to which the Convention does not apply and affirms that it applies to children from the moment of birth until they reach the age of 18 years.

Chapter 2 (Arts 5–14) deals with jurisdiction and makes the child's habitual residence the basis on which a state has jurisdiction to take measures to protect the child and his property. It makes provisions for jurisdiction in respect of refugee children and those children who are internationally displaced to be based on presence. It deals with jurisdiction in respect of abducted children and the transfer by agreement of jurisdiction between states when it is considered that another Contracting State would be better placed in the particular case to assess the best interest of the child. It provides for a Contracting State dealing with the parents' divorce, legal separation or nullity to deal also with matters in relation to the child, notwithstanding the fact the child is habitually resident in another Contracting State, providing that certain conditions set out in Art 10 are met. It also makes provisions in all cases of urgency for a Contracting State in whose territory the child or the property of the child is present to have jurisdiction to take any necessary measures for the protection of the child and his property. Provision is also made for provisional protective (not urgent) measures to be taken by the state in whose territory the child or his property is, provided it is not incompatible with measures already taken by authorities that have jurisdiction.

Chapter 3 (Arts 15–22) deals with the applicable law and lays down the principle that in exercising jurisdiction the authorities of the Contracting States should apply their own domestic law save in exceptional circumstances. Issues relating to attribution and extinction of parental responsibility are also covered.

Chapter 4 (Arts 23–28) deals with recognition, non-recognition, registration and enforcement of measures taken across all Contracting States. It sets out the principle that measures taken by the authorities of a Contracting State shall be recognised by operation of law in all other Contracting States without the need to take proceedings for registration. Where there is non-compliance or opposition, recognition may only be refused on the specified grounds.

Chapter 5 (Arts 29–39) deals with co-operation and collaboration through the Central Authorities, with specific and obligatory provisions for the sharing and exchange of information and cross-border placement of children.

Chapter 6 (Arts 40–56) sets out general provisions, such as the issuing of certificates of parental responsibility, confidentiality and the interplay between various international instruments, specifically the 1980 Hague Convention and Brussels IIA.

Chapter 7 (Arts 57–63) contain the final provisions, which deal with the process of ratification and accession to the Convention.

The Explanatory Report prepared by Professor Paul Lagarde ('the *Lagarde Report*') provides useful material for interpreting the Convention. The *Practical Handbook on the Operation of the 1996 Hague Child Protection Convention* was published on 22 April 2014. It is a useful guide on the operation of the Convention and provides many examples. Both are available on The Hague Conference website (*www.hcch.net*). Practitioners may also find the Ministry of Justice *1996 Hague Convention Practice Guide* (published on 8 February 2013) useful as a quick guide. It is available on the MOJ website.

PART VI

Table of 1996 Convention Contracting States

Country	Ratified date	Entry into force
Albania A*	18 May 2006	1 April 2007
Australia	29 April 2003	1 August 2003
Austria	22 December 2010	1 April 2011

Country	Ratified date	Entry into force
Armenia A*	1 March 2007	1 May 2008
Belgium	28 May 2014	1 September 2014
Bulgaria	8 March 2006	1 February 2007
Croatia	4 September 2009	1 January 2010
Cyprus	21 July 2010	1 November 2010
Czech Republic	13 March 2000	1 January 2002
Denmark	30 June 2011	1 October 2011
Dominican Republic A*	14 December 2009	1 October 2010
Ecuador A*	5 November 2002	1 September 2003
Estonia	6 August 2002	1 June 2003
Finland	19 November 2010	1 March 2011
France	15 October 2010	1 February 2011
Georgia A*	1 April 2014	1 March 2015
Germany	17 September 2010	1 January 2011
Greece	7 February 2012	1 June 2012
Hungary	13 January 2006	1 May 2006
Ireland	30 September 2010	1 January 2011
Italy	30 September 2015	1 January 2016
Latvia	12 December 2002	1 April 2003
Lesotho A	18 June 2012	1 June 2013
Lithuania	29 October 2003	1 September 2004
Luxembourg	5 August 2010	1 December 2010
Malta A	24 February 2011	1 January 2012
Monaco	14 May 1997	1 January 2002
Montenegro A	14 February 2012	1 January 2013
Morocco	22 August 2002	1 December 2002
Netherlands	31 January 2011	1 May 2011
Norway	30 April 2016	1 July 2016
Poland	27 July 2010	1 November 2010
Portugal	14 April 2011	1 August 2011
Romania	8 September 2010	1 January 2011
Russian Federation A	20 August 2012	1 June 2013
Serbia A	15 January 2016	1 November 2016
Slovakia	21 September 2001	1 January 2002
Slovenia	11 October 2004	1 February 2005

Country	Ratified date	Entry into force
Spain	6 September 2010	1 January 2011
Sweden	26 September 2012	1 January 2013
Switzerland	27 March 2009	1 July 2009
Turkey	7 October 2016	1 February 2017
Ukraine A*	3 April 2007	1 February 2008
United Kingdom of Great Britain and Northern Ireland	27 July 2012	1 November 2012
Uruguay	17 November 2009	1 March 2010

A—Accession: see Arts 58(1) and 61(1).

A*—Accession giving rise to an acceptance procedure. Denmark has raised objections against these countries. Therefore, the Convention will not enter into force between these countries and Denmark (see Art 58(3)).

Contracting States—The above table sets out the full list of Contracting States to the 1996 Convention on Jurisdiction, Applicable Law, Recognition, Enforcement and Co-operation in Respect of Parental Responsibility and Measures for the Protection of Children. The Hague Conference on Private International Law (HccH) may publish, from time to time, updates on states' accession to the Convention on the relevant part of its website (*www.hcch.net*), which also contains information on any declarations/reservations that particular states may have recorded (e g under Arts 29, 54, 55 or 59).

(Concluded 19 October 1996)

The States signatory to the present Convention,

Considering the need to improve the protection of children in international situations,

Wishing to avoid conflicts between their legal systems in respect of jurisdiction, applicable law, recognition and enforcement of measures for the protection of children,

Recalling the importance of international co-operation for the protection of children,

Confirming that the best interests of the child are to be a primary consideration,

Noting that the Convention of 5 October 1961 concerning the powers of authorities and the law applicable in respect of the protection of minors is in need of revision,

Desiring to establish common provisions to this effect, taking into account the United Nations Convention on the Rights of the Child of 20 November 1989,

Have agreed on the following provisions –

PART VI

CHAPTER I
SCOPE OF THE CONVENTION

Article 1

(1) The objects of the present Convention are –

(a) to determine the State whose authorities have jurisdiction to take measures directed to the protection of the person or property of the child;

(b) to determine which law is to be applied by such authorities in exercising their jurisdiction;

(c) to determine the law applicable to parental responsibility;

(d) to provide for the recognition and enforcement of such measures of protection in all Contracting States;

(e) to establish such co-operation between the authorities of the Contracting States as may be necessary in order to achieve the purposes of this Convention.

(2) For the purposes of this Convention, the term 'parental responsibility' includes parental authority, or any analogous relationship of authority determining the rights, powers and responsibilities of parents, guardians or other legal representatives in relation to the person or the property of the child.

Contracting States—This means states that are party to the Convention (see above). For an up-to-date list of Contracting States, see *www.hcch.net*.

'parental responsibility' (Art 1(2))—The definition is intended to have an autonomous wide international meaning (see the *Lagarde Report*, para 14), so it does not follow that it will necessarily have the same meaning as that which applies under CA 1989.

Article 2

The Convention applies to children from the moment of their birth until they reach the age of 18 years.

Age—Unlike the Hague Convention 1980, the 1996 Convention applies to a child 'from the moment of birth' until the child attains the age of 18, irrespective of the age of majority under the law of a Contracting State. Thus it may in appropriate cases be relied on to obtain relief when the 1980 Convention does not apply. For other instances where the Convention may be useful, see the *Practical Handbook on the Operation of the 1996 Hague Child Protection Convention*. The Convention continues to apply to a person who is married but under the age of 18. For children beyond the age of 18 and whose capacity is impaired and who are not in a position to protect their interests, the Hague Convention of 13 January 2000 on the International Protection of Adults will apply if the relevant states are Contracting States to that Convention (see further the *Handbook*, para 3.10–3.13 and the examples therein)

'from the moment of their birth'—The Convention thus does not apply to an unborn child.

Article 3

The measures referred to in Article 1 may deal in particular with –

(a) the attribution, exercise, termination or restriction of parental responsibility, as well as its delegation;

(b) rights of custody, including rights relating to the care of the person of the child and, in particular, the right to determine the child's place of residence, as well as rights of access including the right to take a child for a limited period of time to a place other than the child's habitual residence;

(c) guardianship, curatorship and analogous institutions;

(d) the designation and functions of any person or body having charge of the child's person or property, representing or assisting the child;

(e) the placement of the child in a foster family or in institutional care, or the provision of care by kafala or an analogous institution;

(f) the supervision by a public authority of the care of a child by any person having charge of the child;

(g) the administration, conservation or disposal of the child's property.

The issues listed in (a) to (f)—This list is not exhaustive but is set out to identify some of the issues that may be covered by the Convention. See further the *Lagarde Report*, paras 18–36.

Measures—No definition is provided but since it refers to Art 1 it must be confined to decisions made and actions taken by the judicial or administrative authorities of the Contracting States and that can be enforced.

'rights of custody' (Art 3(b))—The definition is similar to that in Art 5 of the Hague Convention 1980. See further CACA 1985, Sch 1 and *Re K (Abduction: Incohate Rights)* [2014] 2 FLR 629, SC. See also para 3.22 of the *Handbook* for situations that may be covered under this definition.

Guardianship etc—This will cover situations such as a guardianship order under CA 1989 or guardianship that may arise on the death of a parent where parental responsibility for a child is exercised by a person other than a parent.

'designation and functions of any person or body' (Art 3(d))—This could include any person who has the care and responsibility for a child temporarily or for a defined period, for example when a child is on a school or holiday outing.

Supervision by a public authority—See further, the *Handbook*, para 3.28 and generally paras 3.15–3.30.

'the administration, conservation or disposal of the child's property' (Art 3(g))—This would include the authority of a person to represent the child in order to authorise or approve a sale or purchase of property, but it does not seek to interfere with substantive rules of property or trusts law (see the *Lagarde Report*, paras 25 and 32). See also Art 55, which permits Contracting States to reserve jurisdiction to its authorities to take measures directed to the protection of a child's property that is situated on its territory and the right not to recognise any parental responsibility or measures insofar as they are incompatible with any measures taken by its authorities in relation to that property. Armenia, for instance, has reserved this right.

Article 4

The Convention does not apply to –

(a) the establishment or contesting of a parent-child relationship;
(b) decisions on adoption, measures preparatory to adoption, or the annulment or revocation of adoption;
(c) the name and forenames of the child;
(d) emancipation;
(e) maintenance obligations;
(f) trusts or succession;
(g) social security;
(h) public measures of a general nature in matters of education or health;
(i) measures taken as a result of penal offences committed by children;
(j) decisions on the right of asylum and on immigration.

Matters not covered by the Convention—This list is exhaustive and it is apparent that some of the matters set out are not concerned with the protection of a child and others (such as maintenance obligations) will be covered by other international instruments. (For further information on why and how far the above matters are excluded, see the *Handbook*, paras 3.31–3.51.)

CHAPTER II
JURISDICTION

Article 5

(1) The judicial or administrative authorities of the Contracting State of the habitual residence of the child have jurisdiction to take measures directed to the protection of the child's person or property.

(2) Subject to Article 7, in case of a change of the child's habitual residence to another Contracting State, the authorities of the State of the new habitual residence have jurisdiction.

Jurisdiction—The Convention determines only the Contracting States whose authorities have jurisdiction to take measures directed at the protection of the child's person or property, but not the authority within the Contracting State that is competent to do so, which question is left to the national procedural law. The Convention rules apply where a child is habitually resident in a Contracting State that is not a Brussels IIA State (see Council Regulation (EC) No 2201/2003, Art 61(a)). Thus, in what will be the vast majority of cases, where the child is habitually resident in the European Union, in respect of matters falling within its scope Brussels IIA must be applied. Where, however, the child is habitually resident in a Contracting State that is not subject to Brussels IIA, the Convention will apply.

Judicial or administrative authorities—The use of the words 'judicial or administrative authorities' means that the Convention is intended to cover decisions made not only by the courts but also by other public bodies who have responsibility for child protection and are authorised to take measures to protect a child. Thus, in England and Wales the Convention will apply both to child protection measures within the scope of the Convention taken by the courts and to those taken by the local authority that do not require court intervention.

Habitual residence—Whereas the term 'habitual residence' is not defined, it is the key connecting factor in the Convention and central to the determination of which state has jurisdiction to take measures directed to the protection of the child's person or property. The *Convention Handbook* stipulates that habitual residence is a factual concept to be determined by the relevant authorities on the basis of factual elements. The large number of cases under the Hague Convention 1980 and Brussels IIA may be of some relevance when dealing with the determination of habitual residence under the Convention (see **Habitual residence** under CACA 1985, Sch 1, Art 4 and under Council Regulation (EC) No 2201/2003, Art 3), but since habitual residence is a factual concept it is important to remember that there may be different considerations to be taken into account when determining the habitual residence of the child for the purposes of the Convention. In particular, it is important to note that whereas under the Hague Convention 1980 and Brussels IIA the determination of habitual residence is a prerequisite for remedies to apply and is part of the wider enquiry as to whether there has been a wrongful retention of the child, the role of habitual residence under the Convention is generally to assess which Contracting State's authorities have jurisdiction to take measures of protection and whether their decisions should be recognised and enforced in other Contracting States. Accordingly, under the Convention, habitual residence is an autonomous concept and should be interpreted in light of the objectives of the Convention rather than according to the constraints of domestic law. This would appear to suggest that the European cases concerned with the question of jurisdiction, and the concept of a degree of integration in a societal and family environment, will be central in determining whether, as a matter of fact, a child is habitually resident in a particular Contracting State for the purposes of the Convention (*Re A (Area of Freedom, Security* *and Justice)* [2009] 2 FLR 1, ECJ; *Mercredi v Chaffe* [2011] 1 FLR 1293, CJEU). Note that where a child is habitually resident in the European Union, jurisdiction must be exercised under Brussels IIA in respect of matters falling within its scope rather than Art 5 of the Convention (see Council Regulation (EC) No 2201/2003, Art 61(a)).

A change of the child's habitual residence—Jurisdiction moves with the child. Accordingly, where a child's habitual residence changes to another Contracting State, that State will have jurisdiction. Note, however, that in some cases the principal of perpetuation fori may apply under Brussels IIA (see Council Regulation (EC) No 2201/2003, Art 12 and *Re A; HA v MB (Brussels II Revised: Article 11(7) Application)* [2008] 1 FLR 289, FD). For the situation where there has been a wrongful removal or retention, see the commentary under Art 7 below. The change of habitual residence does not act to terminate any measures already taken (see Art 14). Authorities of a Contracting State must abstain from exercising jurisdiction (other than under the emergency and temporary jurisdiction provisions of Arts 11 and 12) if, at the time of commencement of proceedings, corresponding measures have been requested from the authorities of another Contracting State having jurisdiction under Art 5 and those proceedings are still pending, save where the authority first seised declines jurisdiction (see Art 13(2)). Where a child's habitual residence changes from a Contracting State to a non-Contracting State, Art 5 will cease to apply from the time of the change of the child's habitual residence, although the Contracting State of the child's former habitual residence may still be able to take measures of protection under the Convention if Arts 11 or 12 apply.

Article 6

(1) For refugee children and children who, due to disturbances occurring in their country, are internationally displaced, the authorities of the Contracting State on the territory of which these children are present as a result of their displacement have the jurisdiction provided for in paragraph 1 of Article 5.

(2) The provisions of the preceding paragraph also apply to children whose habitual residence cannot be established.

Internationally displaced children—This term is intended to be sufficiently broad to surmount the limits that individual states may place on the definition of 'refugee' (see the *Handbook*, para 4.13). The *Lagarde Report* (para 44) suggests that these are likely to be 'limited to those who have left their countries because of conditions which were arising there, and who often are not accompanied and, in any case, are temporarily or definitively deprived of their parents'.

Jurisdiction—The jurisdiction in cases of refugee children or children internationally displaced due to disturbances occurring in their country is based on the presence of those children in a Contracting State. The concept of 'presence' denotes mere physical presence in the territory of the Contracting State concerned. Note that where a child is a refugee or internationally displaced, both Brussels IIA and the Convention will apply.

Children whose habitual residence cannot be established—Where the habitual residence of a child cannot be established, jurisdiction is based on the presence of the child in the territory of the Contracting State. Where the habitual residence of the child becomes established, the jurisdiction under Art 6(2) will cease and the jurisdiction of the Contracting State will become limited to taking necessary urgent or provisional protective measures under Arts 11 and 12. It should not be lightly concluded that a child's habitual residence cannot be established. Note that where a child has no habitual residence, both Brussels IIA and the Convention will apply.

Article 7

(1) In case of wrongful removal or retention of the child, the authorities of the Contracting State in which the child was habitually resident immediately before the removal or retention keep their jurisdiction until the child has acquired a habitual residence in another State, and

- (a) each person, institution or other body having rights of custody has acquiesced in the removal or retention; or
- (b) the child has resided in that other State for a period of at least one year after the person, institution or other body having rights of custody has or should have had knowledge of the whereabouts of the child, no request for return lodged within that period is still pending, and the child is settled in his or her new environment.

(2) The removal or the retention of a child is to be considered wrongful where –

- (a) it is in breach of rights of custody attributed to a person, an institution or any other body, either jointly or alone, under the law of the State in which the child was habitually resident immediately before the removal or retention; and
- (b) at the time of removal or retention those rights were actually exercised, either jointly or alone, or would have been so exercised but for the removal or retention.

The rights of custody mentioned in sub-paragraph (a) above, may arise in particular by operation of law or by reason of a judicial or administrative decision, or by reason of an agreement having legal effect under the law of that State.

(3) So long as the authorities first mentioned in paragraph 1 keep their jurisdiction, the authorities of the Contracting State to which the child has been removed or in which he or she has been retained can take only such urgent measures under Article 11 as are necessary for the protection of the person or property of the child.

Scope—Art 7 deals with an important jurisdictional ground in cases concerning international child abduction. The state of the child's habitual residence immediately before the wrongful removal or retention will retain its jurisdiction until the child acquires habitual residence in another state provided that either there has been acquiescence or the child has resided in the new Contracting State for at least 1 year after those having rights of custody have or should have had knowledge of the whereabouts of the child and no request for return lodged within that period is pending and the child is settled in his/her new environment (i e the child has become settled). The Supreme Court in *Re J (Jurisdiction: Abduction)* [2016] 1 FLR 170, SC) ruled that since the focus of the 1996 Convention is on care and upbringing of the child, a return order to the country of the child's habitual residence is a measure of protection that falls within the scope of the Convention; jurisdiction in abduction cases remains with the authorities of the child's habitual residence immediately before the removal (Art 7). Article 11 supplies the additional jurisdiction to the court where the child is present in cases of urgency. The court should therefore consider whether it is appropriate to exercise jurisdiction under Art 11 on the basis that the country where the child is present is best placed to make the appropriate orders. The machinery for obtaining and enforcing an order made by the court of the child's habitual residence may be slow and cumbersome and may thus result in the child's interests being compromised if the country where the child is present fails to take effective action in support of a return.

Habitual residence—This is not defined but, as with the Hague Convention 1980 and Brussels IIA, it is central to the determination of which state has jurisdiction (see under Art 5 and the 1980 Hague Convention under CACA 1985, Sch 1, where this is discussed in detail). Some insight on how those drafting the Convention intended it be determined may be obtained from the *Handbook*, where at para 4.5 it is stated that habitual residence is fact-specific and has to be determined on the basis of 'factual elements' and that it is an autonomous concept and should be interpreted in the light of the objective of the Convention rather than under domestic law constraints.

'acquiesced' (Art 1(a))—This is not defined. Consent or acquiescence is one of the grounds of opposing a return order under the 1980 Hague Convention so the case-law that has developed under that Convention may provide some guidance (see the 1980 Hague Convention under CACA 1985, Sch 1).

'the child has resided in that other State' (Art 1(b))—Contrast this provision with that under Art 12 of the 1980 Convention, where the period of 1 year begins from the date of the wrongful removal or retention. Under the 1996 Convention, it will be necessary first to establish that the child has acquired a habitual residence in the new state (State B) and then to establish that the child has lived in State B for at least 1 year after the person, institution or other body having 'rights of custody' has or should have had knowledge of the child's whereabouts. It must also be shown that no request for return lodged within that period is still pending and that the child is settled in his or her new environment. However, where there is a need to take urgent measures to protect a child, the state where the child or his property is present may exercise jurisdiction under Art 11, or provisional measures under Art 12 where applicable, notwithstanding that it does not have jurisdiction under Art 7, but such measures will lapse as soon as a Contracting State that has jurisdiction under Arts 5-10 has taken appropriate protective measures. (See further under Art 11.)

PART VI

Article 8

(1) By way of exception, the authority of a Contracting State having jurisdiction under Article 5 or 6, if it considers that the authority of another Contracting State would be better placed in the particular case to assess the best interests of the child, may either

– request that other authority, directly or with the assistance of the Central Authority of its State, to assume jurisdiction to take such measures of protection as it considers to be necessary, or
– suspend consideration of the case and invite the parties to introduce such a request before the authority of that other State.

(2) The Contracting States whose authorities may be addressed as provided in the preceding paragraph are

(a) a State of which the child is a national,
(b) a State in which property of the child is located,
(c) a State whose authorities are seised of an application for divorce or legal separation of the child's parents, or for annulment of their marriage,
(d) a State with which the child has a substantial connection.

(3) The authorities concerned may proceed to an exchange of views.

(4) The authority addressed as provided in paragraph 1 may assume jurisdiction, in place of the authority having jurisdiction under Article 5 or 6, if it considers that this is in the child's best interests.

Scope—This Article (along with Art 9) applies to cases where a state does not have jurisdiction but is better placed to assess the best interests of the child. The Contracting State that does have jurisdiction may transfer jurisdiction for the purposes of protective measures being taken (provided that a connection between that state and the child is established on the basis of the criteria set out in Art 8(2)). Both the requesting state and the requested state must be satisfied that the transfer would allow a better assessment of the child's best interests (i e both states must agree to the transfer). The assumption of jurisdiction on such a transfer would not be permanent. The transfer may involve a transfer of a specific issue. The *Handbook* provides further guidance on this. See also the terms under Brussels IIA, Art 15 and **Request for another Member State to assume jurisdiction** under CA 1989, s 31 for a discussion of the relevant case-law.

'request that other authority' (Art 8(1))—The request may be made directly or with the assistance of the Central Authority or the proceedings may be stayed for a specified period to enable the parties to make the request before the authority of the other state. The PRMPC(IO)(EWNI)R 2010, reg 3(2) enables the court in England and Wales to remove a stay granted for these purposes if jurisdiction is not assumed within the period for which the stay was granted or the parties do not within the time limit specified by the court make a request to the authority in the other Contracting State to assume jurisdiction.

'The authorities concerned may proceed to an exchange of views' (Art 8(3))—This provision implies that there will be liaison between the liaison judges and Central Authorities of the respective states as there is in international child abduction and under the Hague Convention 1980. See the guidance in *N v K (Jurisdiction: International Liaison (No 2)* [2014] 2 FLR 1147, FD on the principles that apply when judicial liaison is pursued. The President's Guidance of 10 November 2014 on the International Child Abduction and Contact Unit (see Part V) should also be referred to.

Central Authority—In England, this is the Lord Chancellor but the functions will be discharged by the International Child Abduction Unit; in Wales, by the Welsh Ministers; in Scotland, by the Scottish Ministers; and in Northern Ireland, by the Department of Justice.

Article 9

(1) If the authorities of a Contracting State referred to in Article 8, paragraph 2, consider that they are better placed in the particular case to assess the child's best interests, they may either

– request the competent authority of the Contracting State of the habitual residence of the child, directly or with the assistance of the Central Authority of that State, that they be authorised to exercise jurisdiction to take the measures of protection which they consider to be necessary, or

– invite the parties to introduce such a request before the authority of the Contracting State of the habitual residence of the child.

(2) The authorities concerned may proceed to an exchange of views.

(3) The authority initiating the request may exercise jurisdiction in place of the authority of the Contracting State of the habitual residence of the child only if the latter authority has accepted the request.

Scope—This Article should be read alongside Art 8, which permits transfers to be made from authorities with jurisdiction under Arts 5 and 6. Art 9 permits requests to be made to the competent authority of the child's habitual residence (i e having jurisdiction under Art 5). An Art 9 request may only be made to the Contracting State of the child's habitual residence and it is thus narrower than the provisions under Art 8. The jurisdiction may only be exercised by the state that does not have jurisdiction if the Contracting State of the child's habitual residence agrees and accepts the request. The procedure for a transfer of jurisdiction is the same as that provided for Brussels IIA, Art 15. FPR 2010, rr 12.60–12.66 apply to such applications. See also under Art 8. *JA v TH* [2016] EWHC 2535 (Fam) is the first decision where reliance has been placed on a request for a transfer to this jurisdiction because, with Norway not being a Member State of the EU, BIIA, Art 15 did not apply. Baker J considered that the English court was better placed to exercise jurisdiction because the child living with the mother in Norway was a British national and he had been habitually resident in England until 2015 and his father and brother were both habitually resident in England where contact between the siblings occurred. This may be the route that will be used after Brexit.

Article 10

(1) Without prejudice to Articles 5 to 9, the authorities of a Contracting State exercising jurisdiction to decide upon an application for divorce or legal separation of the parents of a child

habitually resident in another Contracting State, or for annulment of their marriage, may, if the law of their State so provides, take measures directed to the protection of the person or property of such child if

(a) at the time of commencement of the proceedings, one of his or her parents habitually resides in that State and one of them has parental responsibility in relation to the child, and

(b) the jurisdiction of these authorities to take such measures has been accepted by the parents, as well as by any other person who has parental responsibility in relation to the child, and is in the best interests of the child.

(2) The jurisdiction provided for by paragraph 1 to take measures for the protection of the child ceases as soon as the decision allowing or refusing the application for divorce, legal separation or annulment of the marriage has become final, or the proceedings have come to an end for another reason.

Scope—Art 10 is one of the exceptions to the general rule that measures of protection in relation to children should be taken by the judicial/administrative authorities of the Contracting State (CS) in which the child is habitually resident. It is possible for the authorities of a CS exercising jurisdiction in an application for divorce, legal separation or annulment of the marriage of the parents of a child habitually resident in another Contracting State to take measures relating to the person and property of the child if the cumulative conditions set out in Art 10(1)(a),(b) are met. Such a situation may occur, for example, where a parent lawfully relocates with a child from one CS to another following the breakdown of the marriage and the other parent remains in the first CS and issues proceedings for divorce there. It would, of course, be a matter for the law of the CS where the proceedings were issued to determine whether it had jurisdiction to hear them and to determine whether its law permits it to take such measures relating to the person and/or property of the child in such circumstances (see the *Handbook*, para 4.26, note 131). This jurisdiction ceases when the divorce proceedings come to an end. This might be when the proceedings have resulted in a decision that has become final, granting or refusing the request for divorce, or for another reason such as the withdrawal or lapsing of the request or the death of a party (*Handbook*, para 4.27). The date on which the divorce proceedings come to an end is a matter for determination by the law of the Contracting State in which they take place (*Handbook*, para 4.28). See also the example at 4(e) of the *Handbook*.

Article 11

(1) In all cases of urgency, the authorities of any Contracting State in whose territory the child or property belonging to the child is present have jurisdiction to take any necessary measures of protection.

(2) The measures taken under the preceding paragraph with regard to a child habitually resident in a Contracting State shall lapse as soon as the authorities which have jurisdiction under Article 5 to 10 have taken the measures required by the situation.

(3) The measures taken under paragraph 1 with regard to a child who is habitually resident in a non-Contracting State shall lapse in each Contracting State as soon as measures required by the situation and taken by the authorities of another State are recognised in the Contracting State in question.

Jurisdiction—The jurisdiction to take necessary measures of protection in cases of urgency is based on the child being present in the territory of the relevant Contracting State. The concept of 'presence' denotes mere physical presence in the territory of the Contracting State concerned. The jurisdiction of a Contracting State based on urgency is a jurisdiction concurrent with the general jurisdiction under Arts 5–10 and subordinate to the latter jurisdiction. Art 11(2),(3) provides that necessary measures taken under Art 11(1) will lapse either once the authorities of the Contracting State that has general jurisdiction under Arts 5–10 has taken measures required by the situation or, where the child is habitually resident in a non-Contracting State, once the measures required by the situation and taken by the authorities of another State are recognised by the Contracting State in question. Note that Art 13 of the Convention does not apply where necessary measures of protection are taken under Art 11. Art 11 may be relied on for necessary protective measures in cases of wrongful removal (see Art 7(3)). An abduction case governed solely by the 1996 Convention is not invariably one 'of urgency' but the Supreme Court observed in *Re J (Jurisdiction: Abduction)* [2016] 1 FLR 170, SC that it is difficult to envisage a case in which the court should not consider it to be so and go on to consider whether it is appropriate to exercise the Art 11 jurisdiction. An order made under Art 11 can have extra-territorial effect and the jurisdiction is not limited to cases of wrongful removal but also extends to safeguarding children who are lawfully present in another country. As such, it can secure a valuable 'soft landing' for children whose return to their home country is ordered under the 1980 Hague Convention. Art 11 should not however be used to interfere in issues that are more properly dealt with by the home country (*Re J (A Child)*). The PRMPC(IO)(EWNI)R 2010, r 5 amends CA 1989, s 38 where Art 11 applies to permit an interim care or interim supervision order to be made to provide temporary protection, notwithstanding that the court has no international jurisdiction to make a final care or supervision order.

Urgency—The Convention does not define 'urgency' and it will be for the judicial or administrative authorities of the Contracting State in question to determine whether a particular situation is one of urgency. The *Handbook* to the Convention suggests that a useful approach to establishing whether a given situation is one of urgency is to ask 'whether the child is likely to suffer irreparable harm or to have his or her protection or interests compromised if a measure is not taken to protect him/her in the period that is likely to elapse before the authorities with general jurisdiction under Arts 5 to 10 can take the necessary measures of protection' (*Handbook*, para 6.2 and the examples in para 6.4).

Necessary measures of protection—The measures of protection available under Art 11 will be materially the same as those that can be taken under Arts 5–10 in accordance with the provisions of Arts 3 and 4. However, the Convention does not define 'necessary' and it will be a matter for the judicial or administrative authorities in each Contracting State to determine, based upon the facts of the particular case, what measures within the scope of the Convention are necessary to deal with a situation of urgency (*Handbook*, para 6.5).

Recognition and enforcement of measures taken under Art 11—Measures of protection taken in cases of urgency under Art 11 are entitled to recognition and enforcement in accordance with Ch IV of the Convention (see Art 23 et seq). The grounds of non-recognition are limited in cases of urgency (see Art 23(2)(b) and (c)).

Article 12

(1) Subject to Article 7, the authorities of a Contracting State in whose territory the child or property belonging to the child is present have jurisdiction to take measures of a provisional character for the protection of the person or property of the child which have a territorial effect limited to the State in question, in so far as such measures are not incompatible with measures already taken by authorities which have jurisdiction under Articles 5 to 10.

(2) The measures taken under the preceding paragraph with regard to a child habitually resident in a Contracting State shall lapse as soon as the authorities which have jurisdiction under Articles 5 to 10 have taken a decision in respect of the measures of protection which may be required by the situation.

(3) The measures taken under paragraph 1 with regard to a child who is habitually resident in a non-Contracting State shall lapse in the Contracting State where the measures were taken as soon as measures required by the situation and taken by the authorities of another State are recognised in the Contracting State in question.

Scope—This Article relates to states that are Contracting States and situations where one state is a Contracting State and the state of habitual residence is not. It authorises a Contracting State to exercise jurisdiction to take 'provisional measures' in non-urgent situations to protect the child or his property, provided the child or his property is present within that state (although it does not have jurisdiction under the provisions of Arts 5–10). However, the measures taken will only have effect within the territory of the state in question and provided that the measures taken are not incompatible with any measures already taken by a state with jurisdiction under Arts 5–10. Any measure taken will also lapse as soon as the Contracting State with jurisdiction takes protective measures. Where the child is habitually resident in a non-Contracting State, any provisional measures taken in the Contracting State in relation to the child or his property will lapse on measures being taken by the authorities of another state being recognised in the Contracting State. The provisions in this Article are aimed at dealing with situations that could arise when a child is on holiday or attending an educational establishment. Although there may appear to be similarities between this Article and Art 11, there are subtle differences. The effects of Art 12 orders are limited in that they will only have effect within the territory of the state in question. Art 12 does not apply to a child who has been abducted (see Art 7(3)) and it specifically provides that the measures taken must not be incompatible with measures taken by an authority of competent jurisdiction. However, subject to them not being incompatible, the measures can be taken even if there is no urgency. There is no equivalent provision within Brussels IIA, which only provides for measures to be taken if the situation is urgent.

Provisional measures—This is not defined but an example is suggested by the *Handbook* where there is a need for a child to be placed in alternative care under state supervision or where the child's placement has broken down and an alternative placement is needed in the best interests of the child. Where provisional measures are taken under this Article by a Contracting State, that state should inform the authorities of the state in which the child is habitually resident of the measures taken. (See the *Handbook* para 7.49 and generally Ch 7.) Undertakings given by a parent or party in the proceedings are classed as 'measures' for the purposes of all relevant Articles and do not have to be expressed in the form of an order (*Re Y (Abduction: Undertakings Given for Return of Child)* [2013] 2 FLR 649, CA). Mostyn J, however, issued an injunction and made interim orders rather than accept undertakings in *B v B* [2014] EWHC 1804 (Fam) and *RB v DB* [2015] EWHC 1817 (Fam).

Article 13

(1) The authorities of a Contracting State which have jurisdiction under Articles 5 to 10 to take measures for the protection of the person or property of the child must abstain from exercising this jurisdiction if, at the time of the commencement of the proceedings, corresponding measures

have been requested from the authorities of another Contracting State having jurisdiction under Articles 5 to 10 at the time of the request and are still under consideration.

(2) The provisions of the preceding paragraph shall not apply if the authorities before whom the request for measures was initially introduced have declined jurisdiction.

Scope—Art 13 provides for the resolution of possible conflicts of jurisdiction in cases where the authorities of more than one Contracting State (CS) have jurisdiction to take measures of protection in respect of a child. The authorities of a CS that has jurisdiction under Arts 5–10 must abstain from exercising it if, at the time of the commencement of the proceedings, 'corresponding measures' have been requested from the authorities of another CS having jurisdiction under Arts 5–10 at the time of the request and those measures are still under consideration. 'Corresponding measures' is not defined in the Convention but it appears that, for Art 13 to apply, the requests before both the CSs must be the same or similar in substance (*Handbook*, para 4.31, and *Lagarde Report*, para 79). For example, if one CS is seised of custody proceedings in respect of a child and another CS is requested to take measures of protection in relation to his property, the latter CS may decide that 'corresponding measures' have not been requested from the first CS and it can therefore hear the request regarding the child's property. Art 13 applies for as long as the proceedings in respect of the 'corresponding measures' in the other CS are still under consideration. However, it does not apply if the authorities of the CS initially seised have declined jurisdiction (Art 13(2)). The *Lagarde Report* states that the ability of the authorities of the first CS to decline or renounce their jurisdiction enables that CS to give precedence to the CS second seised, despite Art 13(1), if it is considered a more appropriate forum. However, to ensure the protection of the child where a CS is considering declining jurisdiction it will usually be good practice for communication to take place between the two CSs involved (through Central Authorities or direct judicial communications) to ensure that no gap in the protection of the child results. See the examples at 4(f) and (g) in the *Handbook*.

Article 14

The measures taken in application of Articles 5 to 10 remain in force according to their terms, even if a change of circumstances has eliminated the basis upon which jurisdiction was founded, so long as the authorities which have jurisdiction under the Convention have not modified, replaced or terminated such measures.

The measures taken remain in force—The provisions of Art 14 ensure that measures taken by an authority having jurisdiction under Arts 5–10 to protect a child continue, where for instance the child subsequently moves and establishes habitual residence in another Contracting State, until the authorities in the new state modify, replace or terminate those measures. The measures taken will, however, continue only for the duration of the term specified. If the term refers to the occurrence of an event, the measures will lapse when the event occurs. For examples of instances to which Art 14 applies, see the *Handbook*, Ch 8. When provisional measures are taken, the order should specify either the period for which such measures are to remain in force or the occurrence or termination of an event.

'change of circumstances'—This will depend on the basis on which jurisdiction was based within Arts 5–10. If the jurisdiction was based on Arts 8 and 9, the change will be the conclusion of the proceedings.

CHAPTER III

APPLICABLE LAW

Article 15

(1) In exercising their jurisdiction under the provisions of Chapter II, the authorities of the Contracting States shall apply their own law.

(2) However, in so far as the protection of the person or the property of the child requires, they may exceptionally apply or take into consideration the law of another State with which the situation has a substantial connection.

(3) If the child's habitual residence changes to another Contracting State, the law of that other State governs, from the time of the change, the conditions of application of the measures taken in the State of the former habitual residence.

Modifications—Art 15(1) modified for certain purposes by SI 2010/1898, reg 7.

Scope—Art 15(1) applies the basic principle that the Contracting State should apply its own law when exercising jurisdiction, but Art 15(2) makes it clear that this principle may be departed from in exceptional circumstances and the law of another state with which the situation has a substantial connection may be applied or taken into consideration. Note that Art 15(2) refers to the 'the law of another State', and not a Contracting State, and thus the law applied in such circumstances may be that of a non-Contracting State. The Handbook suggests that the authorities should be satisfied that the application of the foreign law under this provision is in the best interests of the child. (See the *Handbook* for examples of instances where the law of another state may be applied and see also the *Lagarde Report*, para 89.)

'In exercising ... jurisdiction under the provision of Chapter II' (Art 15(1)—This provision should be read with the provisions set out in PRMPC(IO)(EWNI)R 2010, reg 7, which provides that the reference to Ch II of the Convention in Art 15(1) is to be read as including a reference to Ch II of the Council Regulations (ie Brussels IIA).

'If the child's habitual residence changes to another Contracting State' (Art 15(3))—The provisions of Art 15(3) thus do not apply to non-Contracting States. In such a case, the *Handbook* (para 9.8) suggests that the international private law rules of the non-Contracting State would apply to determine if the measures of protection could be recognised in that state and the conditions under which it could be applied. Where there is a change in the child's habitual residence, the law of that state will govern from the time of the change. If measures to protect the child have been taken to provide continuity pursuant to Art 14, those measures will remain in force until they have been modified, replaced or terminated.

'the conditions of application of the measures' (Art 15(3))—This is not defined. The *Handbook* suggests that the term relates to the way the measure is to be exercised in the 'other State' (State B) but it also makes reference to the difficulty in distinguishing between the subsistence of a measure taken under Art 14 by State A that is to continue and applying 'the conditions of application of that measure' (ie the manner of its application) under the law of State B. (See the *Handbook* for further guidance.) When considering this Article, reference should also be made to Art 22, which allows the application of the measure to be refused if this would be manifestly contrary to the public policy, taking into account the best interests of the child.

Article 16

(1) The attribution or extinction of parental responsibility by operation of law, without the intervention of a judicial or administrative authority, is governed by the law of the State of the habitual residence of the child.

(2) The attribution or extinction of parental responsibility by an agreement or a unilateral act, without intervention of a judicial or administrative authority, is governed by the law of the State of the child's habitual residence at the time when the agreement or unilateral act takes effect.

(3) Parental responsibility which exists under the law of the State of the child's habitual residence subsists after a change of that habitual residence to another State.

(4) If the child's habitual residence changes, the attribution of parental responsibility by operation of law to a person who does not already have such responsibility is governed by the law of the State of the new habitual residence.

Scope—Art 16 stipulates the law applicable to the attribution or extinction of parental responsibility without intervention by judicial or administrative authority (Art 16(1),(2)) and what happens to the attribution (but not extinction) of parental responsibility when the habitual residence of a child changes (Art 16(3)). Note that Art 22 of the Convention provides a general release from applying these provisions where to do so would be manifestly contrary to the public policy of the state, taking into account the child's best interests. Specific provision is made by FPR 2010, r 12.4 for notice of proceedings to be given to a person with parental responsibility conferred by the law of another state. Pursuant to FPR 2010, r 12.71(1)(b), an application may be made for declaration as to the extent, or existence, of parental responsibility in relation to a child under Art 16.

Parental responsibility—Art 1(2) of the Convention defines the term 'parental responsibility' as including 'parental authority, or any analogous relationship of authority determining the rights, powers and responsibilities of parents, guardians or other legal representatives in relation to the person or the property of the child'.

Agreement—Under the law of England and Wales, the 'agreement' will be a parental responsibility agreement under CA 1989, s 4(1)(b).

Article 17

The exercise of parental responsibility is governed by the law of the State of the child's habitual residence. If the child's habitual residence changes, it is governed by the law of the State of the new habitual residence.

Scope—Art 17 stipulates the law governing the exercise of parental responsibility, namely its exercise is always governed by the law of the state of the child's current habitual residence.

Article 18

The parental responsibility referred to in Article 16 may be terminated, or the conditions of its exercise modified, by measures taken under this Convention.

Scope—Art 18 provides for measures of protection to be taken under the Convention, which have the effect of terminating or modifying parental responsibility subject to the Convention rules on jurisdiction and applicable law.

Article 19

(1) The validity of a transaction entered into between a third party and another person who would be entitled to act as the child's legal representative under the law of the State where the transaction was concluded cannot be contested, and the third party cannot be held liable, on the sole ground that the other person was not entitled to act as the child's legal representative under the law designated by the provisions of this Chapter, unless the third party knew or should have known that the parental responsibility was governed by the latter law.

(2) The preceding paragraph applies only if the transaction was entered into between persons present on the territory of the same State.

Scope—Art 19 stipulates the circumstances in which a third party will be held liable if they enter into a contract with a person whom they believe to be the holder of parental responsibility but who in fact is not. Such a third party may not be held liable on the ground that the other person was not entitled to act as the child's legal representative under the law designated by the rules of the Convention unless that third party knew, or should have known, that the parental responsibility was governed by that law (see also Art 40). The protection is not entirely absolute because the requirement 'should have known' suggests that the third party has a duty to exercise due diligence. The protection thus will only apply if the third party acted in good faith. Note also that this protection is only available 'if the transaction was entered into between persons present on the territory of the same State' (Art 19(2)).

Article 20

The provisions of this Chapter apply even if the law designated by them is the law of a non-Contracting State.

Article 21

(1) In this Chapter the term 'law' means the law in force in a State other than its choice of law rules.

(2) However, if the law applicable according to Article 16 is that of a non-Contracting State and if the choice of law rules of that State designate the law of another non-Contracting State which would apply its own law, the law of the latter State applies. If that other non-Contracting State would not apply its own law, the applicable law is that designated by Article 16.

Scope—This Article excludes the choice of law rules save for the exceptions in Arts 15(2) and 21(2). Art 21(2) is designed so as not to interfere with the private international law rules that apply between non-Contracting States (*Handbook*, para 9.24).

Article 22

The application of the law designated by the provisions of this Chapter can be refused only if this application would be manifestly contrary to public policy, taking into account the best interests of the child.

Taking account of the best interests of the child—In applying this exception, one must not lose sight of what is in the best interests of the child. Article 22 clearly indicates that the best interests of the child remains the focal point of any decision. The *Handbook* (para 9.26) suggests that the 'use of public policy' to refuse the application of the designated law can only occur when the best interests of child are taken into account. Therefore, the emphasis is more on what is in the best interests of the child.

CHAPTER IV
RECOGNITION AND ENFORCEMENT

Article 23

(1) The measures taken by the authorities of a Contracting State shall be recognised by operation of law in all other Contracting States.

(2) Recognition may however be refused –

(a) if the measure was taken by an authority whose jurisdiction was not based on one of the grounds provided for in Chapter II;

(b) if the measure was taken, except in a case of urgency, in the context of a judicial or administrative proceeding, without the child having been provided the opportunity to be heard, in violation of fundamental principles of procedure of the requested State;

(c) on the request of any person claiming that the measure infringes his or her parental responsibility, if such measure was taken, except in a case of urgency, without such person having been given an opportunity to be heard;

(d) if such recognition is manifestly contrary to public policy of the requested State, taking into account the best interests of the child;

(e) if the measure is incompatible with a later measure taken in the non-Contracting State of the habitual residence of the child, where this later measure fulfils the requirements for recognition in the requested State;

(f) if the procedure provided in Article 33 has not been complied with.

Scope—The aim of the Convention is to create a unified approach to the recognition of measures taken in a Contracting State (CS) in all other CSs so as to reduce the need to issue fresh proceedings in relation to cases that have already been adjudicated upon by another CS. Art 23(1) confirms this position, save for the exceptions set out in Art 23(2). The *Handbook* also suggests that recognition of the measure by operation of law will be sufficient where the measure is voluntarily complied with or where there is no opposition (*Handbook*, para 10.3 and see also the examples given). Thus, an order is recognised automatically in England and Wales without any steps having to be taken by any party but one party may seek to challenge recognition under Art 23(2) without any time limit. The Convention does not set out any formal procedure but it would be good practice for written confirmation to be provided and in an emergency a telephone call may suffice (see the *Handbook*, para 10.2). Where there is non-compliance or where there is opposition to the measures, it may be necessary to commence enforcement proceedings under Art 26. The procedure for registration etc is governed by FPR 2010, Pt 31 and PD31A. However, in *Re P (Recognition and Registration of Orders under the Hague Child Protection Convention)* [2014] EWHC 2845 (Fam) Moylan J observed that the procedural requirements set out in Pt 31 and PD31 appear 'to challenge the concept of simple' (see para 25). He concluded that 'given the increasing number of litigants in person and given the need for our process to be simple and rapid these requirements need to be applied with a light touch', as suggested by Thorpe LJ with reference to Brussels IIA in *Re S (Foreign Contact Order)* [2010] 1 FLR 982, CA. The judge has discretion under FPR 2010, r 31.5(c) to dispense with production of the required documents and information where he has sufficient information, particularly when a mirror order is being sought and when the application follows a direct request for assistance from a judge of the International Hague Network of Judges. The unsatisfactory nature of the procedure for registering and enforcing a foreign order and that any challenge to the enforceability of a foreign order is not required to be addressed when the application for registration is made has also been criticised in the Australian case *Merrick & Wellington* [2014] Fam CA 514, referred to in Moylan J's judgment.

'Recognition may however be refused' (Art 23(2))—Recognition may only be refused on the limited grounds set out in Art 23(2). The power to refuse is not mandatory and therefore there is a discretion to recognise the measures taken even if the conditions are met. These provisions are not unlike those under Brussels IIA, Art 23 and case-law, for example guidance given on substantive and procedural requirements: see *Re D (Recognition and enforcement of Romanian Order); sub nom MD v AA* [2015] 1 FLR 1272, FD and *MD v CT (Parental Responsibility Order: Recognition and Enforcement)* [2015] 1 FLR 213, FD where father's application for recognition and enforcement of an order made in France under Brussels IIA was refused because the mother had not been served in time for her to prepare her defence as required under Brussels IIA, Art 23(1)(c). See also *Re N (Abduction: Brussels II Revised)* [2015] 1 FLR 227, FD.

Child being given an opportunity to be heard—See under CACA 1985 regarding the importance of the child's participation in proceedings and of the child's voice being heard. In *NG v OG* [2014] EWHC 4182 (Fam), the application for registration of a Russian order was refused under Art 23(2)(b) because it was made in respect of one of two children without any steps taken to ascertain the children's wishes and feelings. In the English hearing, Cafcass was directed to obtain the views of the child in respect of whom the order in Russia was made. The court also declared that the children had become habitually resident in England (see Art 5(2)).

'manifestly contrary to public policy' (Art 23(2)(d))—See *Re L (Brussels II Revised: Appeal)* [2013] 1 FLR 430, CA. Cases listed under Brussels IIA, Art 23 suggest that this refusal on public policy grounds will apply only in exceptional circumstances.

Jurisdiction not based on the grounds under the Convention—This may occur where State A has taken measures under its own domestic law of jurisdiction that does not accord with the jurisdictional grounds under the Convention (eg where jurisdiction was based on nationality or presence, State B may verify what the ground of jurisdiction was, but pursuant to Art 25 it is bound by the findings of fact on which the authority of State A based its jurisdiction).

Article 24

Without prejudice to Article 23, paragraph 1, any interested person may request from the competent authorities of a Contracting State that they decide on the recognition or non-recognition of a measure taken in another Contracting State. The procedure is governed by the law of the requested State.

Scope—This Article permits any interested party to seek a declaration from the authorities of a Contracting State (CS) whether or not an order in their favour (eg for contact) will be recognised in another CS (ie an advanced recognition of the order). There is no time limit within which a decision must be given, neither is there any requirement as under Art 26 for a simple and rapid procedure.

The procedure is governed by the law of the requested state—The procedure to be followed in England and Wales is set out in FPR 2010, Pt 31 and PD31A.

Article 25

The authority of the requested State is bound by the findings of fact on which the authority of the State where the measure was taken based its jurisdiction.

Article 26

(1) If measures taken in one Contracting State and enforceable there require enforcement in another Contracting State, they shall, upon request by an interested party, be declared enforceable or registered for the purpose of enforcement in that other State according to the procedure provided in the law of the latter State.

(2) Each Contracting State shall apply to the declaration of enforceability or registration a simple and rapid procedure.

(3) The declaration of enforceability or registration may be refused only for one of the reasons set out in Article 23, paragraph 2.

'procedure provided in the law of the latter State' (Art 26(1))—The procedure for applying for enforcement will be that provided by the domestic law of the requested state. This recognises that the internal laws of enforcement of Contracting States may differ. It will be of interest to see how orders for contact made in a Contracting State (CS) that are not drafted in an injunctive form will be enforced in the UK or how the matter will be dealt with if a *Gillick*-competent child refuses to attend for contact, particularly when this Article clearly envisages that if the measures taken in the CS of origin are enforceable there and require enforcement in another CS, that measure 'shall be declared enforceable in that other State'. Also note that the application may be refused only on the grounds set out in Art 23(2). It is likely that this will be applied strictly, as occurs in cases under the Hague Convention 1980. These grounds mirror those in Brussels IIA. As regards the effect of a declaration of enforcement, see Art 28. The procedure for making an application is set out in FPR 2010, Pt 31 and PD31A.

'an interested party' (Art 26(1))—There is a mandatory duty to make the declaration on the application of an interested party. Contrast this with Art 24 in relation to recognition or non-recognition, under which any interested party has merely a right to apply.

'simple and rapid procedure' (Art 26(2))—Unlike the Hague Convention 1980 and Brussels IIA (although the Article provides for a rapid disposal) there is no time limit set within which such proceedings should be completed. The *Handbook* does not provide any guidance. As an analogy, applying the decisions under the Hague Convention 1980 it could be argued that failure to provide an effective speedy procedure and to enforce the measures is a breach of the rights of the person in whose favour the order was made and that of the child under Art 8 of the European Convention on Human Rights. See also the observations of Moylan J in *Re P (Recognition and Registration of Orders under the Hague Child Protection Convention)* (see under Art 23) on the unsatisfactory procedure under the rules, and guidance given by him on procedure to be adopted and on how the court's discretion should be exercised.

Article 27

Without prejudice to such review as is necessary in the application of the preceding Articles, there shall be no review of the merits of the measure taken.

'there shall be no review of the merits of the measure taken'—This is a mandatory provision. As with an application under the Hague Convention 1980, in determining an application for a declaration of recognition, non-recognition registration and enforcement, the authorities of the Contracting State to whom the application is made must not review the merits of the measures taken and thus reopen the case (see also Art 25). Similar restrictions apply under Brussels IIA, Art 26.

Article 28

Measures taken in one Contracting State and declared enforceable, or registered for the purpose of enforcement, in another Contracting State shall be enforced in the latter State as if they had been taken by the authorities of that State. Enforcement takes place in accordance with the law of the requested State to the extent provided by such law, taking into consideration the best interests of the child.

'taking into consideration the best interests of the child'—The reference to 'the best interests of the child' in Art 28 should not be interpreted as an invitation to a further enquiry on the merits (see *Handbook*, para 10.17). In any event, any review of the merits is prohibited under the mandatory provisions of Art 27.

CHAPTER V
CO-OPERATION

Article 29

(1) A Contracting State shall designate a Central Authority to discharge the duties which are imposed by the Convention on such authorities.

(2) Federal States, States with more than one system of law or States having autonomous territorial units shall be free to appoint more than one Central Authority and to specify the territorial or personal extent of their functions. Where a State has appointed more than one Central Authority, it shall designate the Central Authority to which any communication may be addressed for transmission to the appropriate Central Authority within that State.

Central Authority—See under Art 8 and note that the Central Authority for Wales under this Convention is not the same as under the Hague Convention 1980 and Brussels IIR and therefore it will be necessary to ensure that there is an effective and efficient level of communication and collaboration between them where there is an interplay between these three international instruments.

Article 30

(1) Central Authorities shall co-operate with each other and promote co-operation amongst the competent authorities in their States to achieve the purposes of the Convention.

(2) They shall, in connection with the application of the Convention, take appropriate steps to provide information as to the laws of, and services available in, their States relating to the protection of children.

Scope—There are two situations in which there is an obligation to cooperate, consult and share information, namely when an authority with jurisdiction under Arts 5–10 is contemplating the placement of a child in another Contracting State (see Art 33) and in any case where a child is exposed to serious danger and the competent authorities of the Contracting State where measures for the protection of the child have been taken or are under consideration are informed that the child's residence has changed to, or that the child is present in, another state (see Arts 36).

Article 31

The Central Authority of a Contracting State, either directly or through public authorities or other bodies, shall take all appropriate steps to –

(a) facilitate the communications and offer the assistance provided for in Articles 8 and 9 and in this Chapter;

(b) facilitate, by mediation, conciliation or similar means, agreed solutions for the protection of the person or property of the child in situations to which the Convention applies;

(c) provide, on the request of a competent authority of another Contracting State, assistance in discovering the whereabouts of a child where it appears that the child may be present and in need of protection within the territory of the requested State.

Regulations—The PRMPC(IO)(EWNI)R 2010, reg 10 prescribes the domestic rules that apply and identifies the 'public bodies and other bodies' to whom request for assistance and information may be made where a Central Authority receives a request for assistance under Art 31(c) of the Convention, either directly or via another Central Authority in the United Kingdom.

Article 32

On a request made with supporting reasons by the Central Authority or other competent authority of any Contracting State with which the child has a substantial connection, the Central Authority of the Contracting State in which the child is habitually resident and present may, directly or through public authorities or other bodies,

(a) provide a report on the situation of the child;

(b) request the competent authority of its State to consider the need to take measures for the protection of the person or property of the child.

Scope—The provision of a report on the situation of the child and/or a request that a Contracting State consider the need to take protective measures for the child is not mandatory. The request must be accompanied by 'supporting reasons'. For what is meant by 'substantial connection', see the *Handbook*, para 13.82.

Regulations—The PRMPC(IO)(EWNI)R 2010, reg 12 prescribes the domestic rules that apply and identifies the bodies to whom a request for a written report may be made where a Central Authority thinks it appropriate to provide a report on the situation of the child under Art 32(a) of the Convention.

Article 33

(1) If an authority having jurisdiction under Articles 5 to 10 contemplates the placement of the child in a foster family or institutional care, or the provision of care by kafala or an analogous institution, and if such placement or such provision of care is to take place in another Contracting State, it shall first consult with the Central Authority or other competent authority of the latter State. To that effect it shall transmit a report on the child together with the reasons for the proposed placement or provision of care.

(2) The decision on the placement or provision of care may be made in the requesting State only if the Central Authority or other competent authority of the requested State has consented to the placement or provision of care, taking into account the child's best interests.

Failure to comply with consultation and consent provisions—Where the procedure under Art 33(1) is not followed, the measure can be refused recognition under the Convention (see Art 23(2)(f)). See *Re AB (BIIR: Care Proceedings)* [2013] 1 FLR 168, CA, dealing with the similar provisions of Council Regulation (EC) No 2201/2003, Art 56(1),(2). See also *HSE Ireland v SF (A Minor)* [2012] 2 FLR 1131, FD.

Regulations—The PRMPC(IO)(EWNI)R 2010, reg 13 prescribes the domestic rules that apply to the transmission of a report on the child under Art 33(1) where a local authority is contemplating placing a child in another Contracting State within the meaning of Art 33.

Article 34

(1) Where a measure of protection is contemplated, the competent authorities under the Convention, if the situation of the child so requires, may request any authority of another Contracting State which has information relevant to the protection of the child to communicate such information.

(2) A Contracting State may declare that requests under paragraph 1 shall be communicated to its authorities only through its Central Authority.

Grounds for request—The request for information may only be made where the competent authority is contemplating taking a measure of protection in respect of the child and the situation of the child requires a request to be made.

Regulations—The PRMPC(IO)(EWNI)R 2010, reg 14 permits a public authority in England and Wales to provide information in response to a request communicated to it by the Central Authority under Art 34 of the Convention.

'Contracting State may declare' (Art 34(2))—Art 34(1) provides for the request for information to be made to 'any authority' of another Contracting State unless a declaration has been made that such requests may only be made through its Central Authority. Art 63(d) requires the declaration under this Article to be made to the Government of the Kingdom of Netherlands in its capacity as the depository of the Convention (to establish whether a Contracting State has made such a declaration, see the Status table for the Convention at *www.hcch.net*). Therefore, if a request is to be made by a competent authority in England to another Contracting State, it will be necessary to ascertain whether that state has opted to have all communication (including under Art 34) to be made through its Central Authority. The UK has made such a declaration, hence the provision contained in reg 14 above.

Article 35

(1) The competent authorities of a Contracting State may request the authorities of another Contracting State to assist in the implementation of measures of protection taken under this Convention, especially in securing the effective exercise of rights of access as well as of the right to maintain direct contacts on a regular basis.

(2) The authorities of a Contracting State in which the child does not habitually reside may, on the request of a parent residing in that State who is seeking to obtain or to maintain access to the

PART VI

child, gather information or evidence and may make a finding on the suitability of that parent to exercise access and on the conditions under which access is to be exercised. An authority exercising jurisdiction under Articles 5 to 10 to determine an application concerning access to the child, shall admit and consider such information, evidence and finding before reaching its decision.

(3) An authority having jurisdiction under Articles 5 to 10 to decide on access may adjourn a proceeding pending the outcome of a request made under paragraph 2, in particular, when it is considering an application to restrict or terminate access rights granted in the State of the child's former habitual residence.

(4) Nothing in this Article shall prevent an authority having jurisdiction under Articles 5 to 10 from taking provisional measures pending the outcome of the request made under paragraph 2.

Scope—The provisions of Art 35 are clearly aimed on the one hand at providing child protection measures and on the other at safeguarding rights of access to a child as well as the right to maintain direct contact on a regular basis in another Contracting State.

Regulations—The PRMPC(IO)(EWNI)R 2010, reg 16 prescribes the domestic rules that will apply in respect of Art 35 of the Convention.

Securing the effective exercise of rights of access—Art 35 specifically seeks to secure effective rights of access, as well as the right to maintain direct contact on a regular basis. See also Art 10 of the United Nations Convention on the Rights of the Child.

Duty to consider information—Art 35(2) permits the authorities of a Contracting State in which the child is not habitually resident but in which a parent resides to gather information or evidence and make a finding on the suitability of that parent to exercise access and on the conditions under which that access is to be exercised. Where the authorities of a Contracting State in which the child does not habitually reside have gathered such information or made a finding, an authority exercising jurisdiction under Arts 5–10 must admit and consider that information, evidence and finding before reaching a decision.

Adjournment—Where an authority having jurisdiction under Arts 5–10 is waiting for the receipt of the information, evidence and finding requested pursuant to Art 35(2), it may adjourn proceedings, in particular if the proceedings concern an application to restrict or terminate rights of access granted in the state of the child's former habitual residence.

Article 36

In any case where the child is exposed to a serious danger, the competent authorities of the Contracting State where measures for the protection of the child have been taken or are under consideration, if they are informed that the child's residence has changed to, or that the child is present in another State, shall inform the authorities of that other State about the danger involved and the measures taken or under consideration.

Scope—Art 36 compels the competent authorities of a Contracting State where measures of protection have been taken or are under consideration in respect of a child who is exposed to serious danger to inform the authorities of the state to which the child's residence has changed or in which the child is present about the danger involved and the measures taken or under consideration. The information, however, should not be requested or transmitted if the conditions in Art 37 apply (see below). For examples on how this Article operates, see the *Handbook*, examples 11(c)–11(f).

Non-Contracting States—The words 'another State' in Art 36 mean that the obligation to provide information about the danger to the child and the measures taken or under consideration by the Contracting State extends to children who have become resident in or are present in a non-Contracting State.

Location of a child exposed to serious danger—Where the competent authorities suspect that a child may have become resident in or is present in another Contracting State, those authorities may use Art 31(c) to ascertain the whereabouts of the child so that information can be provided pursuant to Art 36.

Article 37

An authority shall not request or transmit any information under this Chapter if to do so would, in its opinion, be likely to place the child's person or property in danger, or constitute a serious threat to the liberty or life of a member of the child's family.

Scope—The restrictions imposed by this Article apply to all authorities, which includes courts local authorities and other public bodies. It may be desirable to undertake a risk assessment regarding those who are directly connected with the child and his or her family before information is transmitted. See also the provisions of Arts 41 and 42 regarding the restriction on personal data and the need to ensure confidentiality.

Article 38

(1) Without prejudice to the possibility of imposing reasonable charges for the provision of services, Central Authorities and other public authorities of Contracting States shall bear their own costs in applying the provisions of this Chapter.

(2) Any Contracting State may enter into agreements with one or more other Contracting States concerning the allocation of charges.

'Without prejudice to the possibility of imposing reasonable charges for the provision of services' (Art 38(1))—The PRMPC(IO)(EWNI)R 2010, reg 16 authorises a reasonable fee to be charged for services provided under Art 35.

'public authorities'—This term in Art 38 refers to the administrative authorities of the Contracting States and not to the courts. Court costs and the cost of proceedings and lawyers do not fall within the ambit of Art 38.

Article 39

Any Contracting State may enter into agreements with one or more other Contracting States with a view to improving the application of this Chapter in their mutual relations. The States which have concluded such an agreement shall transmit a copy to the depositary of the Convention.

'The States which have concluded such an agreement'—To establish which Contracting States have concluded agreements, see the table in the notes at the beginning of this Convention.

CHAPTER VI
GENERAL PROVISIONS

Article 40

(1) The authorities of the Contracting State of the child's habitual residence, or of the Contracting State where a measure of protection has been taken, may deliver to the person having parental responsibility or to the person entrusted with protection of the child's person or property, at his or her request, a certificate indicating the capacity in which that person is entitled to act and the powers conferred upon him or her.

(2) The capacity and powers indicated in the certificate are presumed to be vested in that person, in the absence of proof to the contrary.

(3) Each Contracting State shall designate the authorities competent to draw up the certificate.

'a certificate indicating the capacity in which that person is entitled to act' (Art 40(1)—Note that this provision is not mandatory.

'shall designate the authorities competent to draw up the certificate' (Art 40(3))—This is a mandatory provision. The Contracting State competent to deliver a certificate is the Contracting State of the child's habitual residence or the Contracting State of origin of the measure. The designated authorities can be found at: *www.hcch.net*.

Content of the certificate—The certificate should usually indicate: (i) who is the holder of parental responsibility; (ii) whether this results by operation of law (from the law that is applicable under Art 16) or from a measure of protection taken by a competent authority according to Ch II of the Convention; (iii) the powers of the person having parental responsibility; and (iv) where appropriate, the powers that the person does not have.

The capacity and powers indicated in the certificate are presumed to be vested in that person in the absence of proof to the contrary. It will therefore be possible for any interested party to contest the correctness of the indications appearing on the certificate, but in the absence of a contest, a third party may act on a certificate provided it is within the limits of the powers mentioned in the certificate.

Article 41

Personal data gathered or transmitted under the Convention shall be used only for the purposes for which they were gathered or transmitted.

Scope—The information gathered under the Convention must be treated confidentially and the authorities to whom the information is given must ensure its confidentiality in accordance with the law of their state (see Art 42).

Article 42

The authorities to whom information is transmitted shall ensure its confidentiality, in accordance with the law of their State.

Article 43

All documents forwarded or delivered under this Convention shall be exempt from legalisation or any analogous formality.

Article 44

Each Contracting State may designate the authorities to which requests under Articles 8, 9 and 33 are to be addressed.

Designated authorities—See under Art 8.

Article 45

(1) The designations referred to in Articles 29 and 44 shall be communicated to the Permanent Bureau of the Hague Conference on Private International Law.

(2) The declaration referred to in Article 34, paragraph 2, shall be made to the depositary of the Convention.

Article 46

A Contracting State in which different systems of law or sets of rules of law apply to the protection of the child and his or her property shall not be bound to apply the rules of the Convention to conflicts solely between such different systems or sets of rules of law.

Article 47

In relation to a State in which two or more systems of law or sets of rules of law with regard to any matter dealt with in this Convention apply in different territorial units –

(1) any reference to habitual residence in that State shall be construed as referring to habitual residence in a territorial unit;

(2) any reference to the presence of the child in that State shall be construed as referring to presence in a territorial unit;

(3) any reference to the location of property of the child in that State shall be construed as referring to location of property of the child in a territorial unit;

(4) any reference to the State of which the child is a national shall be construed as referring to the territorial unit designated by the law of that State or, in the absence of relevant rules, to the territorial unit with which the child has the closest connection;

(5) any reference to the State whose authorities are seised of an application for divorce or legal separation of the child's parents, or for annulment of their marriage, shall be construed as referring to the territorial unit whose authorities are seised of such application;

(6) any reference to the State with which the child has a substantial connection shall be construed as referring to the territorial unit with which the child has such connection;

(7) any reference to the State to which the child has been removed or in which he or she has been retained shall be construed as referring to the relevant territorial unit to which the child has been removed or in which he or she has been retained;

(8) any reference to bodies or authorities of that State, other than Central Authorities, shall be construed as referring to those authorised to act in the relevant territorial unit;

(9) any reference to the law or procedure or authority of the State in which a measure has been taken shall be construed as referring to the law or procedure or authority of the territorial unit in which such measure was taken;

(10) any reference to the law or procedure or authority of the requested State shall be construed as referring to the law or procedure or authority of the territorial unit in which recognition or enforcement is sought.

Article 48

For the purpose of identifying the applicable law under Chapter III, in relation to a State which comprises two or more territorial units each of which has its own system of law or set of rules of law in respect of matters covered by this Convention, the following rules apply –

(a) if there are rules in force in such a State identifying which territorial unit's law is applicable, the law of that unit applies;

(b) in the absence of such rules, the law of the relevant territorial unit as defined in Article 47 applies.

Article 49

For the purpose of identifying the applicable law under Chapter III, in relation to a State which has two or more systems of law or sets of rules of law applicable to different categories of persons in respect of matters covered by this Convention, the following rules apply –

(a) if there are rules in force in such a State identifying which among such laws applies, that law applies;

(b) in the absence of such rules, the law of the system or the set of rules of law with which the child has the closest connection applies.

Article 50

This Convention shall not affect the application of the Convention of 25 October 1980 on the Civil Aspects of International Child Abduction, as between Parties to both Conventions. Nothing, however, precludes provisions of this Convention from being invoked for the purposes of obtaining the return of a child who has been wrongfully removed or retained or of organising access rights.

The impact of the Convention on child abduction cases—Art 50 acknowledges the primacy of the 1980 Convention but, by also stating that nothing precludes its provisions 'from being invoked for the purposes of obtaining the return of a child who has been wrongfully removed or retained or of organising access rights' and providing for the recognition and enforcement of custody and access orders, it provides an alternative means of dealing with child abduction, especially in situations where neither the 1980 Convention nor Brussels IIA applies.

The 1996 Convention will apply where a state is a Contracting State under the 1996 Convention but not under the 1980 Convention or where a state has acceded to the Convention but that accession is not recognised by the other state as occurred in *Re J (A Child) (1996 Hague Convention) (Morocco)* [2015] 2 FLR 513, CA (see *www.hcch.net* for a list of ratifying states and acceding states). There may also be instances, for example, where the child is over 16 years of age where although the relevant states are parties to the 1980 Convention, the remedies available under that Convention cannot be pursued or where the lapse of time or delay may prove to be a hurdle. In such instances, consideration should be given to whether the matter can be pursued under the 1996 Convention.

Even where the 1980 Convention applies, consideration would have to be given to the provisions set out in Arts 5–14 on the issue of jurisdiction and in Arts 15–22, which deal with the applicable law that would be particularly relevant on the issue of attribution and extinction of parental responsibility and more specially in relation to an unmarried father. The power given to the courts to take necessary measures in an emergency for the protection of the child under the 1996 Convention (see Art 7(3) or in the best interest of the child (Arts 5–10) may also prove useful in a case under the 1980 Convention.

Art 7(2) of the 1996 Hague Convention provides an identical basis for determining whether removal or retention is wrongful to that set out in Art 3 of the 1980 Convention. It also provides that rights of custody may arise in three different ways: (a) by operation of law; (b) by reason of a judicial or administrative decision (eg when a court makes an order concerning living arrangements or grants parental responsibility); or (c) by reason of an agreement (ie without intervention by the court) having legal effect under the law of that state. Art 7(1) confirms the retention of jurisdiction by the state of the child's habitual residence in child abduction cases until the child has acquired a habitual residence in another state and each person, institution or other body having rights of custody has acquiesced in the removal or retention or the child has resided in that other state for a period of 1 year after that person, institution or other body has or should have had knowledge of the whereabouts of the child and no request for the return of the child has been lodged and the child is settled in his or her new environment. This provision is clearly aimed at indicating that abductors cannot assume that they will achieve an advantage by their wrongful action. The exception of acquiescence echoes the position that applies under Art 13(a) of the 1980 Convention and the second exception is similar to the provision of Art 12 of the 1980 Convention but with the difference that the period of 1 year starts after 'knowledge of the whereabouts of the child', whereas under the 1980 Convention it starts with the wrongful removal or retention. Since the Convention is intended to provide protection of children, provision is also made that in the case of urgency the state to which the child has been removed or in which the child is retained may take such urgent measures under Art 11 as are necessary for the protection of the child or property of the child (Art 7(3)), for example by way of an injunction or, in an extreme case, the placement of a child in the care of a local authority.

The provision in Art 7(1) of the 1996 Convention that the state in which the child was habitually resident before the wrongful removal or retention retains jurisdiction also reasserts the provisions of Brussels IIA, Arts 10 and 17 that where there has been a wrongful detention, the court must of its own motion decline to entertain an application that offends the primary responsibility of another European Court. It also echoes the provision that the abductor is prevented from asserting a change of residence in such a case, bar the two exceptions. *Re AJ (Brussels II Revised)* [2012] 2 FLR 689, FD and *Re H (Child Abduction)* [2012] EWCA Civ 913 are examples of how the provisions in Brussels IIA and the 1996 Convention (which are identical) operate, so that despite a non-return order (in the former case) or delay (in the latter case) the state of origin retains jurisdiction unless the conditions set out in Art 10 of Brussels IIA and Art 7 of the 1996 Convention are met. See also *JRG v EB (Abduction: Brussels II Revised)* [2013] 1 FLR 203, FD, where the court declined to adjudicate on the application under the 1980 Hague Convention because there was in existence a French residence and contact order and therefore Brussels IIA had precedence over the Hague Convention. In such cases, application should be made for recognition and enforcement of the order of the state of origin. This is the correct route in respect of cases that fall under either Brussels IIA or the 1996 Convention. However, Brussels IIA applies only to Member States within the European Union and makes its own provisions of how matters should be dealt with following a decision under the 1980 Convention, especially if a non-return order is made. It also has its own regulations for recognition and enforcement of the order of the state of origin. The 1996 Convention has its own provision for the recognition and enforcement of orders.

The applicable law provision in the 1996 Convention will also be relevant on the issue of 'rights of custody and access' and parental responsibility, especially in relation to unmarried fathers who do not acquire parental responsibility unless they are registered on the child's birth certificate or are granted parental responsibility by a court order or acquire it by agreement. Under the 1996 Convention:

- the attribution and extinction of parental responsibility by operation of law without the intervention of a judicial or administrative authority is governed by the law of the state of the child's habitual residence;
- the attribution and extinction of parental responsibility by agreement or a unilateral act without intervention of a judicial or administrative authority is governed by the law of the state of the child's habitual residence at the time when the agreement or unilateral act takes effect;
- parental responsibility that exists under the law of the state of the child's habitual residence subsists after a change of the habitual residence to another state (Art 16);
- The above provisions will apply even if the law designated by them is the law of a non-Contracting State (Art 21).

The application of these provisions may be refused only if it would be manifestly contrary to public policy of the state to which the family has moved, taking into account the best interests of the child (Art 22). The *Handbook* gives an example of a same-sex female couple where both have parental responsibility under the law of the original state but under the law of Contracting State B, where the family has become habitually resident, that is considered to be contrary to public policy. It suggests that State B should give careful consideration as to whether it would be in the best interests of the children to refuse to do so. Morocco is a good example of a Contracting State where such a situation might occur.

Article 51

In relations between the Contracting States this Convention replaces the Convention of 5 October 1961 concerning the powers of authorities and the law applicable in respect of the protection of minors, and the Convention governing the guardianship of minors, signed at The Hague 12 June 1902, without prejudice to the recognition of measures taken under the Convention of 5 October 1961 mentioned above.

Article 52

(1) This Convention does not affect any international instrument to which Contracting States are Parties and which contains provisions on matters governed by the Convention, unless a contrary declaration is made by the States Parties to such instrument.

(2) This Convention does not affect the possibility for one or more Contracting States to conclude agreements which contain, in respect of children habitually resident in any of the States Parties to such agreements, provisions on matters governed by this Convention.

(3) Agreements to be concluded by one or more Contracting States on matters within the scope of this Convention do not affect, in the relationship of such States with other Contracting States, the application of the provisions of this Convention.

(4) The preceding paragraphs also apply to uniform laws based on special ties of a regional or other nature between the States concerned.

Article 53

(1) The Convention shall apply to measures only if they are taken in a State after the Convention has entered into force for that State.

(2) The Convention shall apply to the recognition and enforcement of measures taken after its entry into force as between the State where the measures have been taken and the requested State.

Scope—Note that the Convention is not retrospective. This ensures reciprocity. It will therefore be necessary to ascertain whether the Convention has come into force in a state and on what date it did so. As between states, it will be necessary to establish if the Convention has come into force between the two states and if so on what date.

Article 54

(1) Any communication sent to the Central Authority or to another authority of a Contracting State shall be in the original language, and shall be accompanied by a translation into the official language or one of the official languages of the other State or, where that is not feasible, a translation into French or English.

(2) However, a Contracting State may, by making a reservation in accordance with Article 60, object to the use of either French or English, but not both.

Article 55

(1) A Contracting State may, in accordance with Article 60,

(a) reserve the jurisdiction of its authorities to take measures directed to the protection of property of a child situated on its territory;

(b) reserve the right not to recognise any parental responsibility or measure in so far as it is incompatible with any measure taken by its authorities in relation to that property.

(2) The reservation may be restricted to certain categories of property.

Article 56

The Secretary General of the Hague Conference on Private International Law shall at regular intervals convoke a Special Commission in order to review the practical operation of the Convention.

CHAPTER VII
FINAL CLAUSES

Scope—The Articles under this Chapter provide for the process that must be used for ratification of the Convention and any reservations that a Contracting State wishes to make. For example, where the state consists of several territorial units that apply their own laws, the Contracting State may identify to which territorial units within its state the Convention is to apply (see Art 59).

Article 57

(1) The Convention shall be open for signature by the States which were Members of the Hague Conference on Private International Law at the time of its Eighteenth Session.

(2) It shall be ratified, accepted or approved and the instruments of ratification, acceptance or approval shall be deposited with the Ministry of Foreign Affairs of the Kingdom of the Netherlands, depositary of the Convention.

Scope—The rules regarding whether the Convention has come into force in a state differ depending on whether the state has ratified or acceded to the Convention. Ratification is only open to those states that were already members of the 18th Session of the Hague Conference on Private International Law (19 October 1996). All other states may only accede to the Convention (see Art 58).

Article 58

(1) Any other State may accede to the Convention after it has entered into force in accordance with Article 61, paragraph 1.

(2) The instrument of accession shall be deposited with the depositary.

(3) Such accession shall have effect only as regards the relations between the acceding State and those Contracting States which have not raised an objection to its accession in the six months after the receipt of the notification referred to in sub-paragraph b of Article 63. Such an objection may also be raised by States at the time when they ratify, accept or approve the Convention after an accession. Any such objection shall be notified to the depositary.

Scope—For those states that can only accede to the Convention, it takes 9 months for the process of accession to be completed. During the first 6 months, Contracting States have the opportunity to raise objections and then it will take another 3 months for the accession to be completed. Accession will take effect only between those states that have not raised any objections in the 6-month period. Where a state ratifies the Convention after another state has already acceded to it, it can raise objections at the time of ratification.

Article 59

(1) If a State has two or more territorial units in which different systems of law are applicable in relation to matters dealt with in this Convention, it may at the time of signature, ratification, acceptance, approval or accession declare that the Convention shall extend to all its territorial units or only to one or more of them and may modify this declaration by submitting another declaration at any time.

(2) Any such declaration shall be notified to the depositary and shall state expressly the territorial units to which the Convention applies.

(3) If a State makes no declaration under this Article, the Convention is to extend to all territorial units of that State.

Article 60

(1) Any State may, not later than the time of ratification, acceptance, approval or accession, or at the time of making a declaration in terms of Article 59, make one or both of the reservations provided for in Articles 54, paragraph 2, and 55. No other reservation shall be permitted.

(2) Any State may at any time withdraw a reservation it has made. The withdrawal shall be notified to the depositary.

(3) The reservation shall cease to have effect on the first day of the third calendar month after the notification referred to in the preceding paragraph.

Scope—This Article sets the time limit within which any reservations under the preceding Articles must be made.

Article 61

(1) The Convention shall enter into force on the first day of the month following the expiration of three months after the deposit of the third instrument of ratification, acceptance or approval referred to in Article 57.

(2) Thereafter the Convention shall enter into force –

- (a) for each State ratifying, accepting or approving it subsequently, on the first day of the month following the expiration of three months after the deposit of its instrument of ratification, acceptance, approval or accession;
- (b) for each State acceding, on the first day of the month following the expiration of three months after the expiration of the period of six months provided in Article 58, paragraph 3;
- (c) for a territorial unit to which the Convention has been extended in conformity with Article 59, on the first day of the month following the expiration of three months after the notification referred to in that Article.

Scope—See notes under Arts 57 and 58.

Article 62

(1) A State Party to the Convention may denounce it by a notification in writing addressed to the depositary. The denunciation may be limited to certain territorial units to which the Convention applies.

(2) The denunciation takes effect on the first day of the month following the expiration of twelve months after the notification is received by the depositary. Where a longer period for the denunciation to take effect is specified in the notification, the denunciation takes effect upon the expiration of such longer period.

Article 63

The depositary shall notify the States Members of the Hague Conference on Private International Law and the States which have acceded in accordance with Article 58 of the following –

(a) the signatures, ratifications, acceptances and approvals referred to in Article 57;
(b) the accessions and objections raised to accessions referred to in Article 58;
(c) the date on which the Convention enters into force in accordance with Article 61;
(d) the declarations referred to in Articles 34, paragraph 2, and 59;
(e) the agreements referred to in Article 39;
(f) the reservations referred to in Articles 54, paragraph 2, and 55 and the withdrawals referred to in Article 60, paragraph 2;
(g) the denunciations referred to in Article 62.

Council Regulation (EC) No 1206/2001

of 28 May 2001

on cooperation between the courts of the Member States in the taking of evidence in civil or commercial matters

Scope—This Regulation (the EU Evidence Regulation) came into force on 1 January 2004. The Regulation applies to all EU Member States except Denmark. It allows the taking of evidence from one Member State to another without recourse to consular and diplomatic channels by allowing direct contact between the courts in Member States.

Prior to 1 January 2004, the taking of evidence was carried out either under the Hague Convention on the Taking of Evidence Abroad in Civil and Commercial Matters of 18 March 1970 (the Hague Evidence Convention), which was introduced into English law by the Evidence (Proceedings in Other Jurisdictions) Act 1975, or by letters of request (letters rogatory). The Hague Evidence Convention operates through Central Authorities. Outside the EU, these methods (depending upon whether the jurisdiction concerned is a signatory to the Hague Evidence Convention) remain applicable. In relation to the USA, s 1782 (Assistance to foreign and international tribunals and to litigants before such tribunals) of Title 28 of the US Code allows a party to proceedings outside the USA to apply to an American court to obtain evidence for use in the non-USA proceedings. The procedure in relation to jurisdictions not covered by the EU Evidence Regulation is contained in FPR 2010, r 24.12 and PD24A, para 5.

The EU Evidence Regulation creates a simplified system for the direct transmission between courts of Member States of requests for the taking of evidence (Art 2). Each Member State must designate a Central Body responsible for the operation of the Regulation, which in the UK is the Senior Master of the QBD (Art 3 and FPR PD24A, para 8). Each Member State has prepared a list of 'designated courts' competent to take evidence under the Regulation. The designated courts in England and Wales are the RCJ (QBD) and the Family Court at Birmingham, Bristol, Cardiff, Manchester and Leeds (Art 3 and FPR PD24A, para 7 and Annex C).

The Regulation lays down precise criteria as to the form and content of the request (Art 4). The request must be lodged using the form specified in the Annex to the Regulation and must be drafted in the official language of the requested Member State or in any other language that the requested Member State has indicated it can accept (Art 5).

An acknowledgment of receipt must be sent to the requesting court within 7 days of receipt of the request (Art 7). The request must be executed without delay and, at the latest, within 90 days of receipt of the request (Art 10.1). If the requested court is unable to execute the request within 90 days of receipt, it must inform the requesting court giving grounds as well as an estimated time that will be needed to execute the request (Art 15). Requests are executed in accordance with local law (Art 10.2), but can take account of any requests for execution by any special procedure (Art 10.3). The requesting court may ask for the use of communications technology, for example, video conferencing or teleconferencing (Art 10.4).

The execution of a request may be refused only if:

(a) the request does not fall within the scope of the Regulation (e g it concerns criminal rather than civil or commercial proceedings) (Art 14.2(a));
(b) the execution of the request does not fall within the functions of the judiciary (Art 14.2(b));
(c) the request is incomplete (Arts 8, 9 and 14.2(c));

PART VI

(d) a person from whom evidence has been requested claims a right to refuse, or a prohibition, from giving evidence (Art 14.1);
(e) a deposit or advance relating to the costs of consulting an expert has not been made (Arts 14.2(b) and 18.3).

Where a request is refused, the requested court must notify the requesting court within 60 days of receipt of the request (Art 14.4).

If it is permitted by the law of the Member State of the requesting court, the parties and their legal representatives have the right to be present in court at the taking of evidence, although this may be by use of video conferencing or teleconferencing (Arts 10.4 and 11). Representatives of the requesting court also have the right to be present, if it is compatible with the law of the requesting court (Art 12).

The Regulation provides for the use of coercive measures in the Member State where the evidence is to be taken in accordance with local law (Art 13).

The relevant procedure is set out in FPR 2010, r 24.16 and PD24A, paras 6–9, adopting the FPR 2010, Pt 18 procedure. The Forms are annexed to the Regulation.

The Regulation is of particular assistance in relation to requests under Brussels IIA, Art 15: see, for example, *Southampton City Council v IB* [2014] EWFC 16, at [27]; *Re A and B (Children: Brussels II Revised: Article 15)* [2014] EWFC 40, at [42] and [43]; and *Leicester City Council v S* [2015] 1 FLR 1182, FD, at [14(e)].

Chapter I (Arts 1–3) contains general provisions.

Chapter II (Arts 4–18) contains five Sections and deals with the transmission and execution of requests. Section 1 (Arts 4–6) deals with the transmission of the request. Section 2 (Arts 7–9) deals with the receipt of the request. Section 3 (Arts 10–16) deals with the taking of evidence by the requested court. Section 4 (Art 17) deals with the direct taking of evidence by the requesting court and Section 5 (Art 18) deals with costs.

Chapter III (Arts 19–24) contains final provisions.

Evidence of criminal convictions—The Council Framework Decision 2009/315/JHA of 26 February 2009 introduced a system for Member States to exchange information on criminal records with one another. The Council Decision 209/316/JHA of 6 April 2009 establishes the European Criminal Records Information System (ECRIS). Each Member State is required to designate a central authority for the purposes of exchange of information on convictions. The UK Central Authority for the Exchange of Criminal Records may be contacted at PO Box 481, Fareham PO14 9FS (01962 871609; ukca@acro.pnn.police.uk; *www.acro.police.uk*). Requests for information on convictions may be made under the Council Framework Decision, Art 6.1 for purposes other than that of criminal proceedings, a response to which should be given in accordance with Art 7.2.

THE COUNCIL OF THE EUROPEAN UNION,

Having regard to the Treaty establishing the European Community, and in particular Article 61(c) and Article 67(1) thereof,

Having regard to the initiative of the Federal Republic of Germany,

Having regard to the opinion of the European Parliament,

Having regard to the opinion of the Economic and Social Committee,

Whereas:

(1) The European Union has set itself the objective of maintaining and developing the European Union as an area of freedom, security and justice in which the free movement of persons is ensured. For the gradual establishment of such an area, the Community is to adopt, among others, the measures relating to judicial cooperation in civil matters needed for the proper functioning of the internal market.

(2) For the purpose of the proper functioning of the internal market, cooperation between courts in the taking of evidence should be improved, and in particular simplified and accelerated.

(3) At its meeting in Tampere on 15 and 16 October 1999, the European Council recalled that new procedural legislation in cross-border cases, in particular on the taking of evidence, should be prepared.

(4) This area falls within the scope of Article 65 of the Treaty.

(5) The objectives of the proposed action, namely the improvement of cooperation between the courts on the taking of evidence in civil or commercial matters, cannot be sufficiently achieved by the Member States and can therefore be better achieved at Community level. The Community may adopt measures in accordance with the principle of subsidiarity as set out in Article 5 of the Treaty. In accordance with the principle of proportionality, as set out in that Article, this Regulation does not go beyond what is necessary to achieve those objectives.

(6) To date, there is no binding instrument between all the Member States concerning the taking of evidence. The Hague Convention of 18 March 1970 on the taking of evidence abroad in civil or commercial matters applies between only 11 Member States of the European Union.

(7) As it is often essential for a decision in a civil or commercial matter pending before a court in a Member State to take evidence in another Member State, the Community's activity cannot be limited to the field of transmission of judicial and extrajudicial documents in civil or commercial matters which falls within the scope of Council Regulation (EC) No 1348/2000 of 29 May 2000 on the serving in the Member States of judicial and extrajudicial documents in civil or commercial matters. It is therefore necessary to continue the improvement of cooperation between courts of Member States in the field of taking of evidence.

(8) The efficiency of judicial procedures in civil or commercial matters requires that the transmission and execution of requests for the performance of taking of evidence is to be made directly and by the most rapid means possible between Member States' courts.

(9) Speed in transmission of requests for the performance of taking of evidence warrants the use of all appropriate means, provided that certain conditions as to the legibility and reliability of the document received are observed. So as to ensure the utmost clarity and legal certainty the request for the performance of taking of evidence must be transmitted on a form to be completed in the language of the Member State of the requested court or in another language accepted by that State. For the same reasons, forms should also be used as far as possible for further communication between the relevant courts.

(10) A request for the performance of the taking of evidence should be executed expeditiously. If it is not possible for the request to be executed within 90 days of receipt by the requested court, the latter should inform the requesting court accordingly, stating the reasons which prevent the request from being executed swiftly.

(11) To secure the effectiveness of this Regulation, the possibility of refusing to execute the request for the performance of taking of evidence should be confined to strictly limited exceptional situations.

(12) The requested court should execute the request in accordance with the law of its Member State.

(13) The parties and, if any, their representatives, should be able to be present at the performance of the taking of evidence, if that is provided for by the law of the Member State of the requesting court, in order to be able to follow the proceedings in a comparable way as if evidence were taken in the Member State of the requesting court. They should also have the right to request to participate in order to have a more active role in the performance of the taking of evidence. However, the conditions under which they may participate should be determined by the requested court in accordance with the law of its Member State.

(14) The representatives of the requesting court should be able to be present at the performance of the taking of evidence, if that is compatible with the law of the Member State of the requesting court, in order to have an improved possibility of evaluation of evidence. They should also have the right to request to parti-cipate, under the conditions laid down by the requested court in accordance with the law of its Member State, in order to have a more active role in the performance of the taking of evidence.

(15) In order to facilitate the taking of evidence it should be possible for a court in a Member State, in accordance with the law of its Member State, to take evidence directly in another Member State, if accepted by the latter, and under the conditions determined by the central body or competent authority of the requested Member State.

(16) The execution of the request, according to Article 10, should not give rise to a claim for any reimbursement of taxes or costs. Nevertheless, if the requested court requires reimbursement, the fees paid to experts and interpreters, as well as the costs occa-sioned by the application of Article 10(3) and (4), should not be borne by that court. In such a case, the requesting court is to take the necessary measures to ensure reimbursement without delay. Where the opinion of an expert is required, the requested court may, before executing the request, ask the requesting court for an adequate deposit or advance towards the costs.

(17) This Regulation should prevail over the provisions applying to its field of application, contained in international conventions concluded by the Member States. Member States should be free to adopt agreements or arrangements to further facilitate cooperation in the taking of evidence.

(18) The information transmitted pursuant to this Regulation should enjoy protection. Since Directive 95/46/EC of the European Parliament and of the Council of 24 October 1995 on the protection of individuals with regard to the processing of personal data and on the free movement of such data, and Directive 97/66/EC of the European Parliament and of the Council of 15 December 1997 concerning the processing of personal data and the protection of privacy in the telecommunications sector, are applicable, there is no need for specific provisions on data protection in this Regulation.

(19) The measures necessary for the implementation of this Regulation should be adopted in accordance with Council Decision 1999/468/EC of 28 June 1999 laying down the procedures for the exercise of implementing powers conferred on the Commission.

(20) For the proper functioning of this Regulation, the Commission should review its application and propose such amendments as may appear necessary.

(21) The United Kingdom and Ireland, in accordance with Article 3 of the Protocol on the position of the United Kingdom and Ireland annexed to the Treaty on the European Union and to the Treaty establishing the European Community, have given notice of their wish to take part in the adoption and application of this Regu-lation.

(22) Denmark, in accordance with Articles 1 and 2 of the Protocol on the position of Denmark annexed to the Treaty on European Union and to the Treaty establishing the European Community, is not participating in the adoption of this Regulation, and is therefore not bound by it nor subject to its application,

HAS ADOPTED THIS REGULATION:

CHAPTER I
GENERAL PROVISIONS

Article 1
Scope

1 This Regulation shall apply in civil or commercial matters where the court of a Member State, in accordance with the provisions of the law of that State, requests:

(a) the competent court of another Member State to take evidence; or
(b) to take evidence directly in another Member State.

2 A request shall not be made to obtain evidence which is not intended for use in judicial proceedings, commenced or contemplated.

3 In this Regulation, the term 'Member State' shall mean Member States with the exception of Denmark.

Article 2
Direct transmission between the courts

1 Requests pursuant to Article 1(1)(a), hereinafter referred to as 'requests', shall be transmitted by the court before which the proceedings are commenced or contemplated, hereinafter referred to as the 'requesting court', directly to the competent court of another Member State, hereinafter referred to as the 'requested court', for the performance of the taking of evidence.

2 Each Member State shall draw up a list of the courts competent for the performance of taking of evidence according to this Regulation. The list shall also indicate the territorial and, where appropriate, the special jurisdiction of those courts.

Article 3
Central body

1 Each Member State shall designate a central body responsible for:

(a) supplying information to the courts;
(b) seeking solutions to any difficulties which may arise in respect of a request;
(c) forwarding, in exceptional cases, at the request of a requesting court, a request to the competent court.

2 A federal State, a State in which several legal systems apply or a State with autonomous territorial entities shall be free to designate more than one central body.

3 Each Member State shall also designate the central body referred to in paragraph 1 or one or several competent authority(ies) to be responsible for taking decisions on requests pursuant to Article 17.

CHAPTER II
TRANSMISSION AND EXECUTION OF REQUESTS

Section 1
Transmission of the request

Article 4
Form and content of the request

1 The request shall be made using form A or, where appropriate, form I in the Annex. It shall contain the following details:

(a) the requesting and, where appropriate, the requested court;
(b) the names and addresses of the parties to the proceedings and their representatives, if any;
(c) the nature and subject matter of the case and a brief statement of the facts;
(d) a description of the taking of evidence to be performed;
(e) where the request is for the examination of a person:
  – the name(s) and address(es) of the person(s) to be examined,
  – the questions to be put to the person(s) to be examined or a statement of the facts about which he is (they are) to be examined,
  – where appropriate, a reference to a right to refuse to testify under the law of the Member State of the requesting court,
  – any requirement that the examination is to be carried out under oath or affirmation in lieu thereof, and any special form to be used,
  – where appropriate, any other information that the requesting court deems necessary;
(f) where the request is for any other form of taking of evidence, the documents or other objects to be inspected;
(g) where appropriate, any request pursuant to Article 10(3) and (4), and Articles 11 and 12 and any information necessary for the appli-cation thereof.

2 The request and all documents accompanying the request shall be exempted from authentication or any equivalent formality.

3 Documents which the requesting court deems it necessary to enclose for the execution of the request shall be accompanied by a translation into the language in which the request was written.

Article 5
Language

The request and communications pursuant to this Regulation shall be drawn up in the official language of the requested Member State or, if there are several official languages in that Member State, in the official language or one of the official languages of the place where the requested taking of evidence is to be performed, or in another language which the requested Member State has indicated it can accept. Each Member State shall indicate the official language or languages of the institutions of the European Community other than its own which is or are acceptable to it for completion of the forms.

Article 6
Transmission of requests and other communications

Requests and communications pursuant to this Regulation shall be transmitted by the swiftest possible means, which the requested Member State has indicated it can accept. The transmission may be carried out by any appropriate means, provided that the document received accurately reflects the content of the document forwarded and that all information in it is legible.

Section 2
Receipt of request

Article 7
Receipt of request

1 Within seven days of receipt of the request, the requested competent court shall send an acknowledgement of receipt to the requesting court using form B in the Annex. Where the request does not comply with the conditions laid down in Articles 5 and 6, the requested court shall enter a note to that effect in the acknowledgement of receipt.

2 Where the execution of a request made using form A in the Annex, which complies with the conditions laid down in Article 5, does not fall within the jurisdiction of the court to which it was trans-mitted, the latter shall forward the request to the competent court of its Member State and shall inform the requesting court thereof using form A in the Annex.

Article 8
Incomplete request

1 If a request cannot be executed because it does not contain all of the necessary information pursuant to Article 4, the requested court shall inform the requesting court thereof without delay and, at the latest, within 30 days of receipt of the request using form C in the Annex, and shall request it to send the missing information, which should be indicated as precisely as possible.

2 If a request cannot be executed because a deposit or advance is necessary in accordance with Article 18(3), the requested court shall inform the requesting court thereof without delay and, at the latest, within 30 days of receipt of the request using form C in the Annex and inform the requesting court how the deposit or advance should be made. The requested Court shall acknowledge receipt of the deposit or advance without delay, at the latest within 10 days of receipt of the deposit or the advance using form D.

Article 9
Completion of the request

1 If the requested court has noted on the acknowledgement of receipt pursuant to Article 7(1) that the request does not comply with the conditions laid down in Articles 5 and 6 or has informed the requesting court pursuant to Article 8 that the request cannot be executed because it does not contain all of the necessary information pursuant to Article 4, the time limit pursuant to Article 10 shall begin to run when the requested court received the request duly completed.

2 Where the requested court has asked for a deposit or advance in accordance with Article 18(3), this time limit shall begin to run when the deposit or the advance is made.

Section 3
Taking of evidence by the requested court

Article 10
General provisions on the execution of the request

1 The requested court shall execute the request without delay and, at the latest, within 90 days of receipt of the request.

2 The requested court shall execute the request in accordance with the law of its Member State.

3 The requesting court may call for the request to be executed in accordance with a special procedure provided for by the law of its Member State, using form A in the Annex. The requested court shall comply with such a requirement unless this procedure is incompatible with the law of the Member State of the requested court or by reason of major practical difficulties. If the requested court does not comply with the requirement for one of these reasons it shall inform the requesting court using form E in the Annex.

4 The requesting court may ask the requested court to use communications technology at the performance of the taking of evidence, in particular by using videoconference and teleconference.

The requested court shall comply with such a requirement unless this is incompatible with the law of the Member State of the requested court or by reason of major practical difficulties.
If the requested court does not comply with the requirement for one of these reasons, it shall inform the requesting court, using form E in the Annex.

If there is no access to the technical means referred to above in the requesting or in the requested court, such means may be made available by the courts by mutual agreement.

Article 11
Performance with the presence and participation of the parties

1 If it is provided for by the law of the Member State of the requesting court, the parties and, if any, their representatives, have the right to be present at the performance of the taking of evidence by the requested court.

2 The requesting court shall, in its request, inform the requested court that the parties and, if any, their representatives, will be present and, where appropriate, that their participation is requested, using form A in the Annex. This information may also be given at any other appropriate time.

3 If the participation of the parties and, if any, their representatives, is requested at the performance of the taking of evidence, the requested court shall determine, in accordance with Article 10, the conditions under which they may participate.

4 The requested court shall notify the parties and, if any, their representatives, of the time when, the place where, the proceedings will take place, and, where appropriate, the conditions under which they may participate, using form F in the Annex.

5 Paragraphs 1 to 4 shall not affect the possibility for the requested court of asking the parties and, if any their representatives, to be present at or to participate in the performance of the taking of evidence if that possibility is provided for by the law of its Member State.

Article 12
Performance with the presence and participation of representatives of the requesting court

1 If it is compatible with the law of the Member State of the requesting court, representatives of the requesting court have the right to be present in the performance of the taking of evidence by the requested court.

2 For the purpose of this Article, the term 'representative' shall include members of the judicial personnel designated by the requesting court, in accordance with the law of its Member State. The requesting court may also designate, in accordance with the law of its Member State, any other person, such as an expert.

3 The requesting court shall, in its request, inform the requested court that its representatives will be present and, where appropriate, that their participation is requested, using form A in the Annex. This information may also be given at any other appropriate time.

4 If the participation of the representatives of the requesting court is requested in the performance of the taking of evidence, the requested court shall determine, in accordance with Article 10, the conditions under which they may participate.

5 The requested court shall notify the requesting court, of the time when, and the place where, the proceedings will take place, and, where appropriate, the conditions under which the representatives may parti-cipate, using form F in the Annex.

Article 13
Coercive measures

Where necessary, in executing a request the requested court shall apply the appropriate coercive measures in the instances and to the extent as are provided for by the law of the Member State of the requested court for the execution of a request made for the same purpose by its national authorities or one of the parties concerned.

Article 14
Refusal to execute

1 A request for the hearing of a person shall not be executed when the person concerned claims the right to refuse to give evidence or to be prohibited from giving evidence,

(a) under the law of the Member State of the requested court; or

(b) under the law of the Member State of the requesting court, and such right has been specified in the request, or, if need be, at the instance of the requested court, has been confirmed by the requesting court.

2 In addition to the grounds referred to in paragraph 1, the execution of a request may be refused only if:

(a) the request does not fall within the scope of this Regulation as set out in Article 1; or

(b) the execution of the request under the law of the Member State of the requested court does not fall within the functions of the judiciary; or

(c) the requesting court does not comply with the request of the requested court to complete the request pursuant to Article 8 within 30 days after the requested court asked it to do so; or

(d) a deposit or advance asked for in accordance with Article 18(3) is not made within 60 days after the requested court asked for such a deposit or advance.

3 Execution may not be refused by the requested court solely on the ground that under the law of its Member State a court of that Member State has exclusive jurisdiction over the subject matter of the action or that the law of that Member State would not admit the right of action on it.

4 If execution of the request is refused on one of the grounds referred to in paragraph 2, the requested court shall notify the requesting court thereof within 60 days of receipt of the request by the requested court using form H in the Annex.

Article 15
Notification of delay

If the requested court is not in a position to execute the request within 90 days of receipt, it shall inform the requesting court thereof, using form G in the Annex. When it does so, the grounds for the delay shall be given as well as the estimated time that the requested court expects it will need to execute the request.

Article 16
Procedure after execution of the request

The requested court shall send without delay to the requesting court the documents establishing the execution of the request and, where appro-priate, return the documents received from the requesting court. The documents shall be accompanied by a confirmation of execution using form H in the Annex.

Section 4
Direct taking of evidence by the requesting court

Article 17

1 Where a court requests to take evidence directly in another Member State, it shall submit a request to the central body or the competent authority referred to in Article 3(3) in that State, using form I in the Annex.

2 Direct taking of evidence may only take place if it can be performed on a voluntary basis without the need for coercive measures.

Where the direct taking of evidence implies that a person shall be heard, the requesting court shall inform that person that the performance shall take place on a voluntary basis.

3 The taking of evidence shall be performed by a member of the judicial personnel or by any other person such as an expert, who will be designated, in accordance with the law of the Member State of the requesting court.

4 Within 30 days of receiving the request, the central body or the competent authority of the requested Member State shall inform the requesting court if the request is accepted and, if necessary, under what conditions according to the law of its Member State such performance is to be carried out, using form J.

In particular, the central body or the competent authority may assign a court of its Member State to take part in the performance of the taking of evidence in order to ensure the proper application of this Article and the conditions that have been set out.

The central body or the competent authority shall encourage the use of communications technology, such as videoconferences and telecon-ferences.

5 The central body or the competent authority may refuse direct taking of evidence only if:

(a) the request does not fall within the scope of this Regulation as set out in Article 1;
(b) the request does not contain all of the necessary information pursuant to Article 4; or
(c) the direct taking of evidence requested is contrary to fundamental principles of law in its Member State.

6 Without prejudice to the conditions laid down in accordance with paragraph 4, the requesting court shall execute the request in accordance with the law of its Member State.

Section 5
Costs

Article 18

1 The execution of the request, in accordance with Article 10, shall not give rise to a claim for any reimbursement of taxes or costs.

PART VI

2 Nevertheless, if the requested court so requires, the requesting court shall ensure the reimbursement, without delay, of:

– the fees paid to experts and interpreters, and
– the costs occasioned by the application of Article 10(3) and(4).

The duty for the parties to bear these fees or costs shall be governed by the law of the Member State of the requesting court.

3 Where the opinion of an expert is required, the requested court may, before executing the request, ask the requesting court for an adequate deposit or advance towards the requested costs. In all other cases, a deposit or advance shall not be a condition for the execution of a request.

The deposit or advance shall be made by the parties if that is provided for by the law of the Member State of the requesting court.

CHAPTER III
FINAL PROVISIONS

Article 19
Implementing rules

1 The Commission shall draw up and regularly update a manual, which shall also be available electronically, containing the information provided by the Member States in accordance with Article 22 and the agreements or arrangements in force, according to Article 21.

2 The updating or making of technical amendments to the standard forms set out in the Annex shall be carried out by the Commission. Those measures, designed to amend non-essential elements of this Regulation, shall be adopted in accordance with the regulatory procedure with scrutiny referred to in Article 20(2).

Article 20

1 The Commission shall be assisted by a committee.

2 Where reference is made to this paragraph, Article 5a(1) to (4) and Article 7 of Decision 1999/468/EC shall apply, having regard to the provisions of Article 8 thereof.

Article 21
Relationship with existing or future agreements or arrangements between Member States

1 This Regulation shall, in relation to matters to which it applies, prevail over other provisions contained in bilateral or multilateral agreements or arrangements concluded by the Member States and in particular the Hague Convention of 1 March 1954 on Civil Procedure and the Hague Convention of 18 March 1970 on the Taking of Evidence Abroad in Civil or Commercial Matters, in relations between the Member States party thereto.

2 This Regulation shall not preclude Member States from maintaining or concluding agreements or arrangements between two or more of them to further facilitate the taking of evidence, provided that they are compatible with this Regulation.

3 Member States shall send to the Commission:

(a) by 1 July 2003, a copy of the agreements or arrangements main-tained between the Member States referred to in paragraph 2;
(b) a copy of the agreements or arrangements concluded between the Member States referred to in paragraph 2 as well as drafts of such agreements or arrangements which they intend to adopt; and
(c) any denunciation of, or amendments to, these agreements or arrangements.

Article 22
Communication

By 1 July 2003 each Member State shall communicate to the Commission the following:

(a) the list pursuant to Article 2(2) indicating the territorial and, where appropriate, the special jurisdiction of the courts;
(b) the names and addresses of the central bodies and competent autho-rities pursuant to Article 3, indicating their territorial jurisdiction;
(c) the technical means for the receipt of requests available to the courts on the list pursuant to Article 2(2);
(d) the languages accepted for the requests as referred to in Article 5.

Member States shall inform the Commission of any subsequent changes to this information.

Article 23
Review

No later than 1 January 2007, and every five years thereafter, the Commission shall present to the European Parliament, the Council and the Economic and Social Committee a report on the application of this Regulation, paying special attention to the practical application of Article 3(1)(c) and 3, and Articles 17 and 18.

Article 24
Entry into force

1 This Regulation shall enter into force on 1 July 2001.

2 This Regulation shall apply from 1 January 2004, except for Articles 19, 21 and 22, which shall apply from 1 July 2001.

This Regulation shall be binding in its entirety and directly applicable in the Member States in accordance with the Treaty establishing the European Community.

Done at Brussels, 28 May 2001.

For the Council

The President

T. BODSTRÖM

ANNEX

FORM A

Request for the taking of evidence
(Article 4 of Council Regulation (EC) No 1206/2001 of 28 May 2001 on cooperation between the courts of the Member States in the taking of evidence in civil or commercial matters (OJ L 174, 27.6.2001, p. 1))

1 Reference of the requesting court:
2 Reference of the requested court:
3 Requesting court:
3.1 Name:
3.2 Address:
3.2.1 Street and No/PO box:
3.2.2 Place and postcode:
3.2.3 Country:
3.3 Tel.
3.4 Fax
3.5 E-mail:
4 Requested court:
4.1 Name:

PART VI

4.2 Address:
4.2.1 Street and No/PO box:
4.2.2 Place and postcode:
4.2.3 Country:
4.3 Tel.
4.4 Fax
4.5 E-mail:

5 In the case brought by the claimant/petitioner:
5.1 Name:
5.2 Address:
5.2.1 Street and No/PO box:
5.2.2 Place and postcode:
5.2.3 Country:
5.3 Tel.
5.4 Fax
5.5 E-mail:

6 Representatives of the claimant/petitioner:
6.1 Name:
6.2 Address:
6.2.1 Street and No/PO box:
6.2.2 Place and postcode:
6.2.3 Country:
6.3 Tel.
6.4 Fax
6.5 E-mail:

7 Against the defendant/respondent:
7.1 Name:
7.2 Address:
7.2.1 Street and No/PO box:
7.2.3 Place and postcode:
7.2.3 Country:
7.3 Tel.
7.4 Fax
7.5 E-mail:

8 Representatives of defendant/respondent:
8.1 Name:
8.2 Address:
8.2.1 Street and No/PO box:
8.2.2 Place and postcode:
8.2.3 Country:
8.3 Tel:
8.4 Fax:
8.5 E-mail:

9 Presence and participation of the parties:
9.1 Parties and, if any, their representatives will be present at the taking of evidence: ☐
9.2 Participation of the parties and, if any, their representatives is requested: ☐

10 Presence and participation of the representatives of the requesting court:
10.1 Representatives will be present at the taking of evidence: ☐
10.2 Participation of the representatives is requested: ☐
10.2.1 Name:
10.2.2 Title:
10.2.3 Function:
10.2.4 Task:

11 Nature and subject matter of the case and a brief statement of the facts (in annex, where appropriate):

12 Taking of evidence to be performed
12.1 Description of the taking of evidence to be performed (in annex, where appropriate):
12.2 Examination of witnesses:
12.2.1 Name and surname:
12.2.2 Address:
12.2.3 Tel.
12.2.4 Fax

12.2.5 E-mail:

12.2.6 Questions to be put to the witness or a statement of the facts about which they are to be examined (in annex, where appropriate):

12.2.7 Right to refuse to testify under the law of the Member State of the requesting court (in annex, where appropriate):

12.2.8 Please examine the witness:

12.2.8.1 under oath: ☐

12.2.8.2 on affirmation: ☐

12.2.9 Any other information that the requesting court deems necessary (in annex, where appropriate):

12.3 Other taking of evidence:

12.3.1 Documents to be inspected and a description of the requested taking of evidence (in annex, where appropriate):

12.3.2 Objects to be inspected and a description of the requested taking of evidence (in annex, where appropriate):

13 Please execute the request

13.1 In accordance with a special procedure (Article 10(3)) provided for by the law of the Member State of the requesting court and/or by the use of communications technology (Article 10(4)) described in annex:

13.2 Following information is necessary for the application thereof:

Done at:

Date:

Notification of forwarding the request
Article 7(2) of Council Regulation (EC) No 1206/2001 of 28 May 2001 on cooperation between the courts of the Member States in the taking of evidence in

14 The request does not fall within the jurisdiction of the court indicated in point 4 above and was forwarded to

14.1 Name of the competent court:

14.2 Address:

14.2.1 Street and No/PO box:

14.2.2 Place and postcode:

14.2.3 Country:

14.3 Tel.

14.4 Fax

14.5 E-mail:

Done at:

Date:

FORM B

Acknowledgement of receipt of a request for the taking of evidence
(Article 7(1) of Council Regulation (EC) No 1206/2001 of 28 May 2001 on cooperation between the courts of the Member States in the taking of evidence in civil or commercial matters (OJ L 174, 27.6.2001, p. 1))

1 Reference of the requesting court:

2 Reference of the requested court:

3 Name of the requesting court:

4 Requested court:

4.1 Name:

4.2 Address:

4.2.1 Street and No/PO box:

4.2.2 Place and postcode:

4.2.3 Country:

4.3 Tel.

4.4 Fax

4.5 Email:

5 The request was received on ... (date of receipt) by the court indicated in point 4 above.

6 The request cannot be dealt with because:

6.1 The language used to complete the form is not acceptable (Article 5): ☐

6.1.1 Please use one the following languages:

6.2 The document is not legible (Article 6): ☐

Done at:

Date:

FORM C

Request for additional information for the taking of evidence
(Article 8 of Council Regulation (EC) No 1206/2001 of 28 May 2001 on cooperation between the courts of the Member States in the taking of evidence in civil or commercial matters (OJ L 174, 27.6.2001, p. 1))

1 Reference of the requested court:
2 Reference of the requesting court:
3 Name of the requesting court:
4 Name of the requested court:
5 The request cannot be executed without the following additional information:
6 The request cannot be executed before a deposit or advance is made in accordance with Article 18(3). The deposit or advance should be made in the following way:

Done at:

Date:

FORM D

Acknowledgement of receipt of the deposit or advance
(Article 8(2) of Council Regulation (EC) No 1206/2001 of 28 May 2001 on cooperation between the courts of the Member States in the taking of evidence in civil or commercial matters (OJ L 174, 27.6.2001, p. 1))

1 Reference of the requesting court:
2 Reference of the requested court:
3 Name of the requesting court:
4 Name of the requested court:
5 The deposit or advance was received on … (date of receipt) by the court indicated in point 4 above.

Done at:

Date:

FORM E

Notification concerning the request for special procedures and/or for the use of communications technologies
(Article 10(3) and (4) of Council Regulation (EC) No 1206/2001 of 28 May 2001 on cooperation between the courts of the Member States in the taking of evidence in civil or commercial matters (OJ L 174, 27.6.2001, p. 1))

1 Reference of the requested court:
2 Reference of the requesting court:
3 Name of the requesting court:
4 Name of the requested court:
5 The requirement for execution of the request according to the special procedure indicated in point 13.1 of the request (Form A) could not be complied with because:
5.1 the required procedure is incompatible with the law of the Member State of the requested court: ☐
5.2 the performance of the requested procedure is not possible by reason of major practical difficulties: ☐
6 The requirement for execution of the request for the use of communications technologies indicated in point 13.1 of the request (Form A) could not be complied with because:
6.1 The use of communications technology is incompatible with the law of the Member State of the requested court ☐
6.2 The use of the communications technology is not possible by reason of major practical difficulties ☐

Done at:

Date:

FORM F

Notification of the date, time, place of performance of the taking of evidence and the conditions for participation
(Articles 11(4) and 12(5) of Council Regulation (EC) No 1206/2001 of 28 May 2001 on cooperation between the courts of the Member States in the taking of evidence in civil or commercial matters (OJ L 174, 27.6.2001, p. 1))

1 Reference of the requesting court:
2 Reference of the requested court:
3 Requesting court
 3.1 Name:
 3.2 Address:
  3.2.1 Street and No/PO box:
  3.2.2 Place and postcode:
  3.2.3 Country:
 3.3 Tel.
 3.4 Fax
 3.5 E-mail:
4 Requested court
 4.1 Name:
 4.2 Address:
  4.2.1 Street and No/PO box:
  4.2.2 Place and postcode:
  4.2.3 Country:
 4.3 Tel.
 4.4 Fax
 4.5 E-mail:
5 Date and time of the performance of the taking of evidence:
6 Place of the performance of the taking of evidence, if different from that referred to in point 4 above:
7 Where appropriate, conditions under which the parties and, if any, their representatives may participate:
8 Where appropriate, conditions under which the representatives of the requesting court may participate:

Done at:
Date:

FORM G

Notification of delay
(Article 15 of Council Regulation (EC) No 1206/2001 of 28 May 2001 on cooperation between the courts of the Member States in the taking of evidence in civil or commercial matters (OJ L 174, 27.6.2001, p. 1))

1 Reference of the requested court:
2 Reference of the requesting court:
3 Name of the requesting court:
4 Name of the requested court:
5 The request can not be executed within 90 days of receipt for the following reasons:
6 It is estimated that the request will be executed by … (indicate an estimated date)

Done at:
Date:

FORM H

Information on the outcome of the request
(Articles 14 and 16 of Council Regulation (EC) No 1206/2001 of 28 May 2001 on cooperation between the courts of the Member States in the taking of evidence in civil or commercial matters (OJ L 174, 27.6.2001, p. 1))

1 Reference of the requested court:
2 Reference of the requesting court:
3 Name of the requesting court:
4 Name of the requested court:

5 The request has been executed. ☐
The documents establishing execution of the request are attached:
6 Execution of the request has been refused because:
6.1 the person to be examined has claimed the right to refuse to give evidence or has claimed to be prohibited from giving evidence:
6.1.1 under the law of the Member State of the requested court: ☐
6.1.2 under the law of the Member State of the requesting court: ☐
6.2 The request does not fall within the scope of this Regulation ☐
6.3 Under the law of the Member State of the requested court, the execution of the request does not fall within the functions of the judiciary: ☐
6.4 The requesting court has not complied with the request for additional information from the requested court dated … (date of the request): ☐
6.5 A deposit or advance asked for in accordance with Article 18(3) has not been made: ☐

Done at:
Date:

FORM I

Request for direct taking of evidence
(Article 17 of Council Regulation (EC) No 1206/2001 of 28 May 2001 on cooperation between the courts of the Member States in the taking of evidence in civil or commercial matters (OJ L 174, 27.6.2001, p 1))

1 Reference of the requesting court:
2 Reference of the central body/competent authority:
3 Requesting court:
3.1 Name:
3.2 Address:
3.2.1 Street and No/PO box:
3.2.2 Place and postcode:
3.2.3 Country:
3.3 Tel.
3.4 Fax
3.5 E-mail:
4 Central body/competent authority of the requested State:
4.1 Name:
4.2 Address:
4.2.1 Street and No/PO box:
4.2.2 Place and postcode:
4.2.3 Country:
4.3 Tel.
4.4 Fax
4.5 E-mail:
5 In the case brought by the claimant/petitioner:
5.1 Name:
5.2 Address:
5.2.1 Street and No/PO box:
5.2.2 Place and postcode:
5.2.3 Country:
Tel
Fax
E-mail:
6 Representatives of the claimant/petitioner:
6.1 Name:
6.2 Address:
6.2.1 Street and No/PO box:
6.2.2 Place and postcode:
6.2.3 Country:
6.3 Tel.
6.4 Fax
6.5 E-mail:

7 Against the defendant/respondent:
 7.1 Name:
 7.2 Address:
  7.2.1 Street and No/PO box:
  7.2.2 Place and postcode:
  7.2.3 Country:
 7.3 Tel.
 7.4 Fax
 7.5 E-mail:
8 Representatives of defendant/respondent:
 8.1 Name:
 8.2 Address:
  8.2.1 Street and No/PO box:
  8.2.2 Place and postcode:
  8.2.3 Country:
 8.3 Tel.
 8.4 Fax
 8.5 E-mail:
9 The taking of evidence shall be performed by:
 9.1 Name:
 9.2 Title:
 9.3 Function:
 9.4 Task:
10 Nature and subject matter of the case and a brief statement of the facts (in annex, where appropriate):
11 Taking of evidence to be performed:
 11.1 Description of the taking of evidence to be performed (in annex, where appropriate):
 11.2 Examination of witnesses:
  11.2.1 First names and surname:
  11.2.2 Address:
  11.2.3 Tel.
  11.2.4 Fax
  11.2.5 E-mail:
  11.2.6 Questions to be put to the witness or a statement of the facts about which they are to be examined (in the annex, where appropriate):
  11.2.7 Right to refuse to testify under the law of the Member State of the requesting court (in annex, where appropriate):
 11.3 Other taking of evidence (in annex, where appropriate):
12 The requesting court requests to take evidence directly by use of the following communications technology (in annex, where appropriate):

Done at:

Date:

FORM J

Information from the central body/competent authority

(Article 17 of Council Regulation (EC) No 1206/2001 of 28 May 2001 on cooperation between the courts of the Member States in the taking of evidence in civil or commercial matters (OJ L 174, 27.6.2001, p. 1))

1 Reference of the requesting court:
2 Reference of the central body/competent authority:
3 Name of the requesting court:
4 Central body/competent authority:
 4.1 Name:
 4.2 Address:
  4.2.1 Street and No/PO box:
  4.2.2 Place and postcode:
  4.2.3 Country:
 4.3 Tel.
 4.4 Fax
 4.5 E-mail:

PART VI

5 Information from the central body/competent authority:

5.1 Direct taking of evidence in accordance with the request is accepted: ☐

5.2 Direct taking of evidence in accordance with the request is accepted under the following conditions (in annex, where appropriate): ☐

5.3 Direct taking of evidence in accordance with the request is refused for the following reasons:

5.3.1 The request does not fall within the scope of this Regulation: ☐

5.3.2 The request does not contain all of the necessary information pursuant to Article 4: ☐

5.3.3 The direct taking of evidence requested for is contrary to fundamental principles of law of the Member State of the central body/competent authority: ☐

Done at:

Date:

Council Regulation (EC) No 2201/2003

of 27 November 2003

concerning jurisdiction and the recognition and enforcement of judgments in matrimonial matters and the matters of parental responsibility, repealing Regulation (EC) No 1347/2000

Scope—Brussels IIA (variously otherwise referred to as Brussels II bis, Brussels IIA or the Council Regulation) came into force on 1 March 2005 in all 28 Member States of the European Union (EU) other than Denmark. Brussels IIA replaced Brussels II (Council Regulation (EC) No 1347/1000) concerning jurisdiction and the recognition and enforcement of judgments and matrimonial matters and in matters of parental responsibility for children of both spouses, which came into force on 1 March 2001. Consultation is underway for Brussels IIA Recast, which will repeal Brussels IIA. Brussels IIA is an EU Regulation (and not a Directive) and is therefore directly applicable in Member States. It does not need implementation through UK legislation and prevails over domestic law. For the purposes of Brussels IIA, the UK includes Gibraltar (Treaty on the Functioning of the European Union, Art 349), but not the Isle of Man nor the Channel Islands. Although a member of the EU, Denmark has opted out of Brussels IIA. Forum disputes involving Denmark must therefore be treated in the same way as forum disputes involving non-EU countries in Europe and the rest of the world.

Council Regulation (EU) No 1259/2010 of 20 December 2010 implementing enhanced cooperation in the area of the law applicable to divorce and legal separation (Rome III) enables parties to agree in advance which law would apply in the event of divorce or legal separation or, in the absence of agreement, stipulates which country's law will apply. The UK is not a participating Member State.

Council Regulations (EU) Nos 2016/1103 and 2016/1104 of 24 June 2016 implementing enhanced cooperation in the area of jurisdiction, applicable law and the recognition and enforcement of decisions in matters of matrimonial property regimes and of the property consequences of registered partnerships (Rome IVa and IVb) determine which court has jurisdiction and which law applies in proceedings concerning the property of international couples. The UK is not a participating Member State.

Chapter I (Arts 1 and 2) deals with scope and definitions. Chapter II (Arts 3–20) deals with jurisdiction. Section 1 of Chapter II (Arts 3–7) deals with jurisdiction in relation to divorce, legal separation and marriage annulment. The provisions of Brussels II in this context remain unchanged (subject to changes to Article numbering). Cases decided under Brussels II retain their force. It establishes the principle of lis pendens or 'the first to issue secures jurisdiction'. Section 2 of Chapter I (Arts 8–15) relates to jurisdiction in the context of parental responsibility and brings about changes to Brussels II, creating a scheme for jurisdiction in matters of parental responsibility which is much closer to the scheme for jurisdiction for divorce etc in Section 1 than was the case under Brussels II. Section 3 of Chapter II (Arts 16–20) contains provisions which are common to both divorce etc and parental responsibility.

Chapter III (Arts 21–52) deals with recognition and enforcement. Section 1 of Chapter III (Arts 21–27) provides for recognition of judgments covered by Brussels IIA without any special procedure subject to specific grounds for non-recognition. Section 2 of Chapter III (Arts 28–36) deals with an application for a declaration of enforceability. Section 3 of Chapter III (Arts 37–39) contains provisions common to recognition and enforcement. Many of the provisions are common to divorce etc and questions of parental responsibility, and are derived from Brussels I. Section 4 of Chapter III (Arts 40–45) deals with the enforceability of judgments concerning rights of access and the return of a child. Section 5 of Chapter III (Art 46) provides for authentic instruments and agreements enforceable in one Member State to be recognised and enforceable in the same way as judgments. Section 6 of Chapter III (Arts 47–52) contains other provisions dealing with practical enforcement arrangements, the exercise of the rights of access, costs and legal aid.

Chapter IV (Arts 53–58) deals with the cooperation between Central Authorities in matters of parental responsibility.

Chapter V (Arts 59–63) deals with the relationship of Brussels IIA with other instruments (eg the Hague Conventions).

Chapter VI (Art 64) contains transitional provisions and Chapter VII (Arts 65–72) final provisions which provide (Art 65) for a review of Brussels IIA on 1 January 2012 and every 5 years thereafter, and for Member States (eg the UK) with two or more legal systems (Art 66).

The recitals to Brussels IIA set out areas that are not intended to be covered including the grounds for divorce, property consequences of the marriage and other ancillary measures (recital 8) and maintenance obligations (recital 11).

THE COUNCIL OF THE EUROPEAN UNION,

Having regard to the Treaty establishing the European Community, and in particular Article 61(c) and Article 67(1) thereof,

Having regard to the proposal from the Commission,

Having regard to the opinion of the European Parliament,

Having regard to the opinion of the European Economic and Social Committee,

Whereas:

(1) The European Community has set the objective of creating an area of freedom, security and justice, in which the free movement of persons is ensured. To this end, the Community is to adopt, among others, measures in the field of judicial cooperation in civil matters that are necessary for the proper functioning of the internal market.

(2) The Tampere European Council endorsed the principle of mutual recognition of judicial decisions as the cornerstone for the creation of a genuine judicial area, and identified visiting rights as a priority.

(3) Council Regulation (EC) No 1347/2000 sets out rules on jurisdiction, recognition and enforcement of judgments in matrimonial matters and matters of parental responsibility for the children of both spouses rendered on the occasion of the matrimonial proceedings. The content of this Regulation was substantially taken over from the Convention of 28 May 1998 on the same subject matter.

(4) On 3 July 2000 France presented an initiative for a Council Regulation on the mutual enforcement of judgments on rights of access to children.

(5) In order to ensure equality for all children, this Regulation covers all decisions on parental responsibility, including measures for the protection of the child, independently of any link with a matrimonial proceeding.

(6) Since the application of the rules on parental responsibility often arises in the context of matrimonial proceedings, it is more appropriate to have a single instrument for matters of divorce and parental responsibility.

(7) The scope of this Regulation covers civil matters, whatever the nature of the court or tribunal.

(8) As regards judgments on divorce, legal separation or marriage annulment, this Regulation should apply only to the dissolution of matrimonial ties and should not deal with issues such as the grounds for divorce, property consequences of the marriage or any other ancillary measures.

(9) As regards the property of the child, this Regulation should apply only to measures for the protection of the child, i.e. (i) the designation and functions of a person or body having charge of the child's property, representing or assisting the child, and (ii) the administration, conservation or disposal of the child's property. In this context, this Regulation should, for instance, apply in cases where the parents are in dispute as regards the administration of the child's property. Measures relating to the child's property which do not concern the protection of the child should continue to be governed by Council Regulation (EC) No 44/2001 of 22 December 2000 on jurisdiction and the recognition and enforcement of judgments in civil and commercial matters.

(10) This Regulation is not intended to apply to matters relating to social security, public measures of a general nature in matters of education or health or to decisions on the right of asylum and on immigration. In addition it does not apply to the establishment of parenthood, since this is a different matter from the attribution of parental responsibility, nor to other questions linked to the status of persons. Moreover, it does not apply to measures taken as a result of criminal offences committed by children.

(11) Maintenance obligations are excluded from the scope of this Regulation as these are already covered by Council Regulation No 44/2001. The courts having jurisdiction under this Regulation will generally have jurisdiction to rule on maintenance obligations by application of Article 5(2) of Council Regulation No 44/2001.

(12) The grounds of jurisdiction in matters of parental responsibility established in the present Regulation are shaped in the light of the best interests of the child, in particular on the criterion of proximity. This means that jurisdiction should lie in the first place with the Member State of the child's habitual residence, except for certain cases of a change in the child's residence or pursuant to an agreement between the holders of parental responsibility.

(13) In the interest of the child, this Regulation allows, by way of exception and under certain conditions, that the court having jurisdiction may transfer a case to a court of another Member State if this court is better placed to hear the case. However, in this case the second court should not be allowed to transfer the case to a third court.

(14) This Regulation should have effect without prejudice to the application of public international law concerning diplomatic immunities. Where jurisdiction under this Regulation cannot be exercised by reason of the existence of diplomatic immunity in accordance with international law, jurisdiction should be exercised in accordance with national law in a Member State in which the person concerned does not enjoy such immunity.

(15) Council Regulation (EC) No 1348/2000 of 29 May 2000 on the service in the Member States of judicial and extrajudicial documents in civil or commercial matters should apply to the service of documents in proceedings instituted pursuant to this Regulation.

(16) This Regulation should not prevent the courts of a Member State from taking provisional, including protective measures, in urgent cases, with regard to persons or property situated in that State.

(17) In cases of wrongful removal or retention of a child, the return of the child should be obtained without delay, and to this end the Hague Convention of 25 October 1980 would continue to apply as complemented by the provisions of this Regulation, in particular Article 11. The courts of the Member State to or in which the child has been wrongfully removed or retained should be able to oppose his or her return in specific, duly justified cases. However, such a decision could be replaced by a subsequent decision by the court of the Member State of habitual residence of the child prior to the wrongful removal or retention. Should that judgment entail the return of the child, the return should take place without any special procedure being required for recognition and enforcement of that judgment in the Member State to or in which the child has been removed or retained.

(18) Where a court has decided not to return a child on the basis of Article 13 of the 1980 Hague Convention, it should inform the court having jurisdiction or central authority in the Member State where the child was habitually resident prior to the wrongful removal or retention. Unless the court in the latter Member State has been seised, this court or the central authority should notify the parties. This obligation should not prevent the central authority from also notifying the relevant public authorities in accordance with national law.

(19) The hearing of the child plays an important role in the application of this Regulation, although this instrument is not intended to modify national procedures applicable.

(20) The hearing of a child in another Member State may take place under the arrangements laid down in Council Regulation (EC) No 1206/2001 of 28 May 2001 on cooperation between the courts of the Member States in the taking of evidence in civil or commercial matters.

(21) The recognition and enforcement of judgments given in a Member State should be based on the principle of mutual trust and the grounds for non-recognition should be kept to the minimum required.

(22) Authentic instruments and agreements between parties that are enforceable in one Member State should be treated as equivalent to 'judgments' for the purpose of the application of the rules on recognition and enforcement.

(23) The Tampere European Council considered in its conclusions (point 34) that judgments in the field of family litigation should be 'automatically recognised throughout the Union without any intermediate proceedings or grounds for refusal of enforcement'. This is why judgments on rights of access and judgments on return that have been certified in the Member State of origin in accordance with the provisions of this Regulation should be recognised and enforceable in all other Member States without any further procedure being required. Arrangements for the enforcement of such judgments continue to be governed by national law.

(24) The certificate issued to facilitate enforcement of the judgment should not be subject to appeal. It should be rectified only where there is a material error, i.e. where it does not correctly reflect the judgment.

(25) Central authorities should cooperate both in general matter and in specific cases, including for purposes of promoting the amicable resolution of family disputes, in matters of parental responsibility. To this end central authorities shall participate in the European Judicial Network in civil and commercial matters created by Council Decision 2001/470/EC of 28 May 2001 establishing a European Judicial Network in civil and commercial matters.

(26) The Commission should make publicly available and update the lists of courts and redress procedures communicated by the Member States.

(27) The measures necessary for the implementation of this Regulation should be adopted in accordance with Council Decision 1999/468/EC of 28 June 1999 laying down the procedures for the exercise of implementing powers conferred on the Commission.

(28) This Regulation replaces Regulation (EC) No 1347/2000 which is consequently repealed.

(29) For the proper functioning of this Regulation, the Commission should review its application and propose such amendments as may appear necessary.

(30) The United Kingdom and Ireland, in accordance with Article 3 of the Protocol on the position of the United Kingdom and Ireland annexed to the Treaty on European Union and the Treaty establishing the European Community, have given notice of their wish to take part in the adoption and application of this Regulation.

(31) Denmark, in accordance with Articles 1 and 2 of the Protocol on the position of Denmark annexed to the Treaty on European Union and the Treaty establishing the European Community, is not participating in the adoption of this Regulation and is therefore not bound by it nor subject to its application.

(32) Since the objectives of this Regulation cannot be sufficiently achieved by the Member States and can therefore be better achieved at Community level, the Community may adopt measures, in accordance with the principle of subsidiarity as set out in Article 5 of the Treaty. In accordance with the principle of proportionality, as set out in that Article, this Regulation does not go beyond what is necessary in order to achieve those objectives.

(33) This Regulation recognises the fundamental rights and observes the principles of the Charter of Fundamental Rights of the European Union. In particular, it seeks to ensure respect for the fundamental rights of the child as set out in Article 24 of the Charter of Fundamental Rights of the European Union,

HAS ADOPTED THE PRESENT REGULATION:

Note—The EC Treaty has become the Treaty on the Functioning of the European Union (TFEU) and the Articles have been re-numbered: Art 5 is replaced, in substance, by Art 5 of the Treaty on the European Union; Art 61 is Art 67 TFEU; and Art 67 is repealed.

CHAPTER I

SCOPE AND DEFINITIONS

Article 1
Scope

1 This Regulation shall apply, whatever the nature of the court or tribunal, in civil matters relating to:

PART VI

(a) divorce, legal separation or marriage annulment;
(b) the attribution, exercise, delegation, restriction or termination of parental responsibility.

2 The matters referred to in paragraph 1(b) may, in particular, deal with:

(a) rights of custody and rights of access;
(b) guardianship, curatorship and similar institutions;
(c) the designation and functions of any person or body having charge of the child's person or property, representing or assisting the child;
(d) the placement of the child in a foster family or in institutional care;
(e) measures for the protection of the child relating to the administration, conservation or disposal of the child's property.

3 This Regulation shall not apply to:

(a) the establishment or contesting of a parent-child relationship;
(b) decisions on adoption, measures preparatory to adoption, or the annulment or revocation of adoption;
(c) the name and forenames of the child;
(d) emancipation;
(e) maintenance obligations;
(f) trusts or succession;
(g) measures taken as a result of criminal offences committed by children.

'Civil matters' (Art 1.1)—This term encompasses public law care proceedings (*Re C* (Case C–435/06) [2008] 1 FLR 490, ECJ; *Re A (Area of Freedom, Security and Justice)* [2009] 2 FLR 1, ECJ).

'Rights of custody and rights of access' (Art 1.2(a))—This term includes penalty payments imposed to ensure compliance with access rights, but only when the amount has been finally determined (*Bohez v Wiertz* (Case C-4/14) [2016] 1 FLR 1159, CJEU).

Article 2
Definitions

For the purposes of this Regulation:

1 the term 'court' shall cover all the authorities in the Member States with jurisdiction in the matters falling within the scope of this Regulation pursuant to Article 1;

2 the term 'judge' shall mean the judge or an official having powers equivalent to those of a judge in the matters falling within the scope of the Regulation;

3 the term 'Member State' shall mean all Member States with the exception of Denmark;

4 the term 'judgment' shall mean a divorce, legal separation or marriage annulment, as well as a judgment relating to parental responsibility, pronounced by a court of a Member State, whatever the judgment may be called, including a decree, order or decision;

5 the term 'Member State of origin' shall mean the Member State where the judgment to be enforced was issued;

6 the term 'Member State of enforcement' shall mean the Member State where enforcement of the judgment is sought;

7 the term 'parental responsibility' shall mean all rights and duties relating to the person or the property of a child which are given to a natural or legal person by judgment, by operation of law or by an agreement having legal effect. The term shall include rights of custody and rights of access;

8 the term 'holder of parental responsibility' shall mean any person having parental responsibility over a child;

9 the term 'rights of custody' shall include rights and duties relating to the care of the person of a child, and in particular the right to determine the child's place of residence;

10 the term 'rights of access' shall include in particular the right to take a child to a place other than his or her habitual residence for a limited period of time;

11 the term 'wrongful removal or retention' shall mean a child's removal or retention where:

(a) it is in breach of rights of custody acquired by judgment or by operation of law or by an agreement having legal effect under the law of the Member State where the child was habitually resident immediately before the removal or retention; and

(b) provided that, at the time of removal or retention, the rights of custody were actually exercised, either jointly or alone, or would have been so exercised but for the removal or retention. Custody shall be considered to be exercised jointly when, pursuant to a judgment or by operation of law, one holder of parental responsibility cannot decide on the child's place of residence without the consent of another holder of parental responsibility.

'Parental responsibility' (Art 2.7)—A child's need to obtain a passport and a parent's right to apply for a passport and travel abroad with a child without the other parent's agreement is within the scope of 'parental responsibility' for the purposes of Brussels IIA (*Gogova v Iliev* [2016] 1 FLR 158, CJEU).

'Rights of custody' (Arts 2.9, 2.11)—'Rights of custody' is an autonomous concept independent of the law of Member States. It is a separate matter from the identity of the person who has rights of custody and it is for the Member State to determine who has rights of custody at the relevant time (*JMcB v Le* (Case C-400/10) [2011] 1 FLR 518, ECJ). 'Rights of custody' include informal rights ('inchoate rights') (*Re K (A Child) (Northern Ireland)* [2014] 2 FLR 629, SC).

'Wrongful removal or retention' (Art 2.11)—Where the removal of a child has taken place in accordance with a judgment that is provisionally enforceable and that was overturned subsequently by a judgment that fixed the residence of the child at the home of the parent living in the Member State of origin, the court of the Member State to which the child was removed, seised of an application for the return of the child, had to determine, by undertaking an assessment of all the circumstances of facts specific to the individual case, whether the child was still habitually resident in the Member State of origin immediately before the alleged wrongful retention. A failure to return the child to the Member State of origin following the subsequent judgment is wrongful since it constitutes a breach of rights of custody. Brussels IIA, Art 11 will be applicable if it is held that the child was still habitually resident in the Member State of origin immediately before the detention (*C v M* (Case C-376/14 PPU) [2015] 1 FLR 1, CJEU).

CHAPTER II
JURISDICTION

Section 1
Divorce, legal separation and marriage annulment

Article 3
General jurisdiction

1 In matters relating to divorce, legal separation or marriage annulment, jurisdiction shall lie with the courts of the Member State

(a) in whose territory:
- the spouses are habitually resident, or
- the spouses were last habitually resident, insofar as one of them still resides there, or
- the respondent is habitually resident, or
- in the event of a joint application, either of the spouses is habitually resident, or
- the applicant is habitually resident if he or she resided there for at least a year immediately before the application was made, or
- the applicant is habitually resident if he or she resided there for at least six months immediately before the application was made and is either a national of the Member State in question or, in the case of the United Kingdom and Ireland, has his or her 'domicile' there;

(b) of the nationality of both spouses or, in the case of the United Kingdom and Ireland, of the 'domicile' of both spouses.

2 For the purpose of this Regulation, 'domicile' shall have the same meaning as it has under the legal systems of the United Kingdom and Ireland.

Defined terms—'court': Art 2.1; 'Member State': Art 2.3.

Scope—In respect of proceedings for divorce or judicial separation commenced on or after 1 March 2005, the court has jurisdiction to entertain proceedings only if the court has jurisdiction under Art 3 or no court of a Contracting State has jurisdiction under Art 3 and either of the parties to the marriage is domiciled in England

and Wales on the date when the proceedings are begun (DMPA 1973, s 5(2)). In respect of proceedings for nullity commenced on or after 1 March 2005, the position is the same save that, where no court of a Contracting State has jurisdiction under Art 3, jurisdiction may alternatively be established where either of the parties to the marriage died before the date when proceedings are begun and either was at death domiciled in England and Wales or had been habitually resident in England and Wales throughout the period of 1 year ending with the date of death (DMPA 1973, s 5(3)). Jurisdiction under Art 3.1(a) is founded on habitual residence and applies whether or not the parties are nationals of another EU Member State (*Sulaiman v Juffali* [2002] 1 FLR 479, FD). A person's presence in England for the purpose of receiving medical treatment, which prevented him from leaving the jurisdiction, did not enable a divorce petition to be based upon habitual residence in England (*Breuning v Breuning* [2002] 1 FLR 888, FD). Jurisdiction may only be based on the domicile of *either* party in England and Wales on the date when proceedings are begun if no Member State has jurisdiction under Arts 3, 4 or 5 (Art 7 and DMPA 1973, s 5(2)(b)).

Where a court has jurisdiction under Art 3, it will also have jurisdiction to examine a counterclaim (eg an application for divorce by a respondent) (Art 4). Where a court has given a judgment on a legal separation, it will also have jurisdiction to convert that judgment into a divorce (Art 5). Articles 3, 4 and 5 provide an exclusive jurisdictional code (Art 6).

The court's jurisdiction under Art 3 should not be exercised by analogy with the decision in *Owusu v Jackson* [2005] QB 801, ECJ, ECJ under Brussels I. Where a state has jurisdiction under Brussels IIA, there remains a jurisdiction to grant a stay of English proceedings under DMPA 1973, Sch 1, para 9 on the ground of forum non conveniens (*JKN v JCN (Divorce: Forum)* [2011] 1 FLR 826, FD; *M v M (sub nom Mittal v Mittal)* [2014] 1 FLR 1514, CA; *Tan v Choy* [2015] 1 FLR 492, CA).

The court may permit amendment to the pleaded grounds for jurisdiction in a petition that is first in time, even though the original grounds were open to serious challenge and proceedings had been issued in a second Member State which would become first seised in the event of the first in time petition being dismissed unamended (*Rogers-Headicar v Headicar* [2005] 2 FCR 1, CA; *R v R (Divorce: Jurisdiction: Domicile)* [2006] 1 FLR 389, FD). Despite the court's obligation to conduct an examination as to jurisdiction (Art 17), it is advisable to plead jurisdiction under as many cases as possible under Art 3.1 (see, for example, *CC v NC (Maintenance Pending Suit)* [2015] 1 FLR 404, FD; *Chai v Peng* [2015] 2 FLR 424, FD and [2015] 2 FLR 412, FD, confirmed on appeal: *Peng v Chai* [2017] 1 FLR 318, CA). Exceptionally, the court may dismiss a first petition without adjudication on the merits so as to permit a fresh one to be issued to eliminate unnecessary argument about the habitual residence and domicile of the petitioner as at the date of the original petition (*Peng v Chai* [2015] EWCA Civ 1312).

In the UK and Ireland, joint domicile provides jurisdictional basis under Art 3.1(b); in all other Member States, joint nationality must be shown to establish jurisdiction under Art 3.1(b). It is not necessary in the UK and Ireland to demonstrate joint domicile as well as joint nationality (*Re N (Jurisdiction)* [2007] 2 FLR 1196, FD).

Brussels IIA does not apply to jurisdiction in relation to civil partnerships which are regulated by CPA 2004, s 221 and the Civil Partnership (Jurisdiction and Recognition of Judgments) Regulations 2005; jurisdiction in relation to same sex marriages is regulated by the DMPA 1973, s 5(5A), Sch A1 and the Marriage (Same Sex Couples) (Jurisdiction and Recognition of Judgments) Regulations 2014.

'Habitual residence' (Art 3.1(a))—Habitual residence is 'the place where the person had established, on a fixed basis, his permanent or habitual centre of interests, with all the relevant facts being taken into account for the purpose of determining such residence' (*L-K v K (No 2)* [2007] 2 FLR 729, FD). This approach evolved in the European Court of Justice rather than under English domestic law is the applicable test (*L-K v K (No 2)* [2007] 2 FLR 729, FD; *Marinos v Marinos* [2007] 2 FLR 1018, FD); *Z v Z (Divorce: Jurisdiction)* [2010] 1 FLR 694, FD). Habitual residence is interpreted differently in the context of Art 8 (parental responsibility). There is no requirement that the centre of interests must be permanent; it need only be habitual. However, it must have a stable character. A person can only have one habitual residence at a given date (*Z v Z (Divorce: Jurisdiction)*. Although the test for habitual residence is objective, when considering a party's centre of interests, the party's intention forms part of the court's overall assessment. This enables the court objectively to assess the mental element in concepts such as 'permanent', 'habitual', 'residence' and 'home'. Intention in this context means the reasons for the parties' actions and is not synonymous with the subjective capricious wish-fulfilment of one party (*V v V (Divorce: Jurisdiction)* [2011] 2 FLR 778, FD). Three tests were identified in *Tan v Choy* [2015] 1 FLR 492, CA in order to establish 'habitual residence':

(i) there must be a permanence or stability in the residence of the person concerned in the relevant territory (rather than residence that is temporary or intermittent);
(ii) the location was the centre of the person's interests; and
(iii) the person had, at the time, no other 'habitual residence'.

As to whether there is any distinction between 'habitual residence' and 'residence' for the purposes of cases 2, 5 and 6 of Art 3(1)(a), Munby J held in *Marinos v Marinos* [2007] 2 FLR 1018, FD that mere residence would suffice, whereas Bennett J took an opposing view in *Munro v Munro* [2008] 1 FLR 1613, FD. See, also, *Olafisoye v Olafisoye* [2011] 2 FLR 553, FD and *Tan v Choy* [2015] 1 FLR 492, CA. *Marinos* was followed in preference to *Munro* in *V v V* (above). It is possible to be habitually resident in one country and resident (but not habitually) in another. It is also possible to be resident in more than one country (*V v V* (above) applying *Marinos*).

See also, *Saward v Saward* [2013] EWCA Civ 1060. As to the evidence required to establish habitual residence, see *BE v DE* [2014] EWHC 2318 (Fam) (wife/petitioner permitted to rely upon an agreement, referring to her living in London, as this was not privileged).

'Domicile' (Art 3.1(b))—In deciding a person's domicile for the purposes of jurisdiction, the applicable law is the lex fori, namely, the law of England and Wales (*Chandler v Chandler* [2011] EWCA Civ 143). The relevant principles were considered in *Sekhri v Ray* [2014] 1 FLR 612, FD applying the principles summarised by Arden LJ in *Barlow Clowes International Limited v Henwood* [2008] BPIR 778, CA.

Article 4
Counterclaim

The court in which proceedings are pending on the basis of Article 3 shall also have jurisdiction to examine a counterclaim, insofar as the latter comes within the scope of this Regulation.

Defined terms—'court': Art 2.1.

Article 5
Conversion of legal separation into divorce

Without prejudice to Article 3, a court of a Member State that has given a judgment on a legal separation shall also have jurisdiction for converting that judgment into a divorce, if the law of that Member State so provides.

Defined terms—'court': Art 2.1; 'Member State': Art 2.3; 'judgment': Art 2.4.

Article 6
Exclusive nature of jurisdiction under Articles 3, 4 and 5

A spouse who:

(a) is habitually resident in the territory of a Member State; or
(b) is a national of a Member State, or, in the case of the United Kingdom and Ireland, has his or her 'domicile' in the territory of one of the latter Member States,

may be sued in another Member State only in accordance with Articles 3, 4 and 5.

Defined terms—'Member State': Art 2.3.

Scope—This Article sets out the exclusive nature of jurisdiction under Arts 3, 4 and 5. As to the interrelationship between this exclusive jurisdiction and the residual jurisdiction under Art 7, see *Sundelind Lopez v Lopez Lizazo* [2008] 1 FLR 582, ECJ.

Article 7
Residual jurisdiction

1 Where no court of a Member State has jurisdiction pursuant to Articles 3, 4 and 5, jurisdiction shall be determined, in each Member State, by the laws of that State.

2 As against a respondent who is not habitually resident and is not either a national of a Member State or, in the case of the United Kingdom and Ireland, does not have his 'domicile' within the territory of one of the latter Member States, any national of a Member State who is habitually resident within the territory of another Member State may, like the nationals of that State, avail himself of the rules of jurisdiction applicable in that State.

Defined terms—'court': Art 2.1; 'Member State': Art 2.3.

Scope—This Article provides for a residual jurisdiction where no court of a Member State has jurisdiction under the exclusive jurisdictional code of Arts 3–5 to be determined by domestic law, i e on the sole domicile of one party under DMPA 1973, s 5(2)(b) (e g *F v F (Divorce: Jurisdiction)* [2009] 2 FLR 1496, FD). This does not enable a spouse who is neither a national of nor habitually resident in a Member State to be sued under Art 7, even if another Member State has jurisdiction under Art 3 (*Sundelind Lopez v Lopez Lizazo* [2008] 1 FLR 582, ECJ). The relevant principles were considered in *Sekhri v Ray* [2014] 1 FLR 612, FD and *Divall v Divall* [2014] 2 FLR 1104, FD, each applying the principles summarised by Arden LJ in *Barlow Clowes International Limited v Henwood* [2008] BPIR 778, CA.

Section 2
Parental responsibility

Article 8
General jurisdiction

1 The courts of a Member State shall have jurisdiction in matters of parental responsibility over a child who is habitually resident in that Member State at the time the court is seised.

PART VI

2 Paragraph 1 shall be subject to the provisions of Articles 9, 10 and 12.

Defined terms—'court': Art 2.1; 'Member State': Art 2.3; 'parental responsibility': Art 2.7; 'seised': Art 16.

Scope—The scope of matters covered by Brussels IIA in relation to parental responsibility are set out in Art 1.2. However, Brussels IIA does not apply to those matters of parental responsibility set out in Art 1.3. Article 8 sets out the general rule as to jurisdiction that jurisdiction lies with the courts of the Member State in which the child is habitually resident at the time the court is seised. Articles 9–15 set out the exceptions to this general rule. The jurisdictional scheme in Brussels IIA is not geographically limited to the EU (*Re I (A Child) (Contact Application: Jurisdiction)* [2010] 1 FLR 361, SC; *Re A (Jurisdiction: Return of Child)* [2014] 1 FLR 111, SC, at [33]).

The starting point in any case where there is a foreign dimension is an inquiry as to where the child is habitually resident. The issue must be addressed at the outset of the proceedings. Good practice requires that in every such case the court sets out explicitly, both in its judgment and in its order, the basis upon which it has either accepted or rejected jurisdiction under Art 8 (*Re F (A Child)* [2014] EWCA Civ 789; *Re E (Brussels II Revised: Vienna Convention: Reporting Restrictions)* [2014] 2 FLR 151, FD).

Where a court in a Member State has delivered a judgment that has become final concerning rights of custody, rights of access and maintenance obligations with regard to a minor child, that court no longer has jurisdiction to rule on an application to vary that judgment if the child's habitual residence is not in that Member State (*W and V v X* (2017) (Case C-499/15), CJEU).

'Habitually resident'—'Habitual residence' under Brussels IIA, Arts 8 and 10 must be given an independent and uniform interpretation throughout the EU, having regard to the context in Brussels IIA. Brussels IIA, Arts 8 and 10 do not make express reference to the law of the Member States for the purpose of determining the meaning and scope of 'habitual residence', which is to be interpreted for the purposes of Arts 8 and 10 as corresponding to the place that reflected some degree of integration by a child in a social and family environment (*Mercredi v Chaffe* [2011] 1 FLR 1293, CJEU at [56]; see also *Re A (Area of Freedom, Security and Justice)* [2009] 2 FLR 1, ECJ).

Habitual residence is a question of fact and not a legal concept such as domicile. There is no longer a supposed 'rule' that, where two parents have parental responsibility for a child, neither can unilaterally change the child's habitual residence. What is required is a factual inquiry tailored to the circumstances of the individual case (*Re H (Jurisdiction)* [2015] 1 FLR 1132, CA). Any challenge to a child's habitual residence should be by way of seeking permission to appeal rather than an application to set aside (*Re SJ (A Child) (Habitual Residence: Application to Set Aside)* [2014] EWHC 58 (Fam)). The test for habitual residence is the same for the purposes of FLA 1986, the Hague Convention 1980 and Brussels IIA, namely, that adopted by the CJEU in *Mercredi v Chaffe* and *Re A*, rather than the domestic test established by *R v Barnet Borough Council ex parte Shah* [1983] 2 AC 309, HL and the line of authority following it. The CJEU test of habitual residence reflecting some degree of integration by a child in a social family environment depends upon numerous factors, including the reasons for the family's stay in the country in question (*Re A (Jurisdiction: Return of Child)* [2014] 1 FLR 111, SC, specifically at [54]). See, also, *N v K* [2013] EWHC 2774 (Fam) and *West Sussex CC v H* [2014] EWHC 2550 (Fam). Parental intention plays a part in establishing or changing the habitual residence of a child, but is one of many factors relevant to whether there is a sufficient degree of stability to amount to a change of habitual residence (*Re KL (A Child)* [2014] 1 FLR 772, SC). Where an adolescent child has resided with a parent in a particular place (especially if only for a short period), it could be appropriate for the court to have regard to the child's state of mind during the period of residence when determining whether the child shared the parent's habitual residence in that place (*Re LC (Reunite: International Child Abduction Centre Intervening)* [2014] 1 FLR 1486, SC). See, also, *AR v RN (Scotland) (Habitual Residence)* [2015] 2 FLR 503, SC and *Re B (A Child) (Habitual Residence: Inherent Jurisdiction)* [2016] 1 FLR 561, SC (the modern concept of a child's habitual residence operates so that it is unlikely that a child will be left without a habitual residence; it is to be expected that, when a child gains a new habitual residence, he/she loses their old one). As to case preparation involving habitual residence of a child, see *Re B (A Minor) (Habitual Residence)* [2016] EWHC 2174 (Fam), at [18].

It would appear as a matter of fact that presence is a necessary precursor to habitual residence on the basis that a child could not be integrated into the social environment of a place to which his primary carer had never taken him (*Re A* at [55]).

See also, the annotations to CACA 1985, Sch 1, Art 4.

Habitual residence is interpreted differently in the context of Art 3 (divorce, legal separation and annulment).

Liaison judge—In [2008] Fam Law 105, Thorpe LJ offered the following information as to the role of the Head of International Family Justice:

> 'In trans-national cases there is a high chance of contemporaneous proceedings in both the involved jurisdictions. Unless the two responsible judges communicate, there is an obvious risk of conflict, legal complexity, delay and wasted costs. Each jurisdiction needs a co-ordinator, a liaison judge available to facilitate the essential communication. In this jurisdiction I am responsible for that service. My office is well equipped to initiate the process that results in judge communicating with judge.'

The route for contacting the International Liaison Judge or the Office of the Head of International Family Justice (Black LJ) is tel: 020 7947 7197; email: IFJOffice@hmcts.gsi.gov.uk.

However, the European Judicial Network should not be used to obtain an authoritative determination from the court of a network judge where there are no proceedings pending relating to a child (*Re B (Care Order: Jurisdiction)* [2014] 1 FLR 900, CA). International judicial communication is not intended to be a substitute for obtaining legal advice or obtaining expert evidence as to foreign law or procedure. It could not be deployed as a mechanism for judges to settle welfare disputes nor as a means of making submissions to a foreign court (*N v K (Jurisdiction: International Liaison) (No 2)* [2014] 2 FLR 1147, FD).

See, also, Art 55 in relation to obtaining information from other Member States.

Article 9

Continuing jurisdiction of the child's former habitual residence

1 Where a child moves lawfully from one Member State to another and acquires a new habitual residence there, the courts of the Member State of the child's former habitual residence shall, by way of exception to Article 8, retain jurisdiction during a three-month period following the move for the purpose of modifying a judgment on access rights issued in that Member State before the child moved, where the holder of access rights pursuant to the judgment on access rights continues to have his or her habitual residence in the Member State of the child's former habitual residence.

2 Paragraph 1 shall not apply if the holder of access rights referred to in paragraph 1 has accepted the jurisdiction of the courts of the Member State of the child's new habitual residence by participating in proceedings before those courts without contesting their jurisdiction.

Defined terms—'Member State': Art 2.3; 'judgment': Art 2.4.

Scope—Article 9 provides, by way of exception to the general rule in Art 8, that, where a child has moved lawfully from one Member State to another and becomes habitually resident there, the courts of the original Member State may continue in specified circumstances to have jurisdiction for 3 months only (*Re J (A Child) (Finland) (Habitual Residence)* [2017] EWCA Civ 80) after the move for limited purposes in relation to access (contact).

'Date of service'—Issues as to the timing and regularity of service are determined by reference to the Second Service Regulation and not the law of the Member State addressed (*Tavoulareas v Tsavliris* [2004] EWCA Civ 48).

Article 10

Jurisdiction in cases of child abduction

In case of wrongful removal or retention of the child, the courts of the Member State where the child was habitually resident immediately before the wrongful removal or retention shall retain their jurisdiction until the child has acquired a habitual residence in another Member State and:

(a) each person, institution or other body having rights of custody has acquiesced in the removal or retention; or

(b) the child has resided in that other Member State for a period of at least one year after the person, institution or other body having rights of custody has had or should have had knowledge of the whereabouts of the child and the child is settled in his or her new environment and at least one of the following conditions is met:

  (i) within one year after the holder of rights of custody has had or should have had knowledge of the whereabouts of the child, no request for return has been lodged before the competent authorities of the Member State where the child has been removed or is being retained;

  (ii) a request for return lodged by the holder of rights of custody has been withdrawn and no new request has been lodged within the time limit set in paragraph (i);

  (iii) a case before the court in the Member State where the child was habitually resident immediately before the wrongful removal or retention has been closed pursuant to Article 11(7);

  (iv) a judgment on custody that does not entail the return of the child has been issued by the courts of the Member State where the child was habitually resident immediately before the wrongful removal or retention.

Defined terms—'court': Art 2.1; 'Member State': Art 2.3; 'rights of custody': Art 2.9; 'judgment': Art 2.4; 'wrongful removal or retention': Art 2.11.

Scope—Article 10 provides that, in cases of child abduction, again by way of exception to the general rule in Art 8, the courts of the Member State from which the child was wrongfully removed/retained retain jurisdiction subject to certain conditions (*Re A; HA v MB (Brussels II Revised: Article 11(7) Application)* [2008] 1 FLR 289, FD). Art 10 ensures that an abductor is prevented from successfully asserting a change of habitual residence as a consequence of wrongful retention (*Re H (Child Abduction)* [2012] EWCA Civ 913). Where there is a wrongful removal or retention, an application may either be made for an order under the Hague Convention 1980 (see Art 11) in the Member State where the child is resident or an application may be made under this Article in the Member State from which the child has been removed/retained, in which event such an order will be automatically enforceable in the Member State in which the child is now resident. Where two remedies are available in different courts in different jurisdictions, Hague Convention proceedings do not take automatic precedence (*B v D (Abduction: Inherent Jurisdiction)* [2009] 1 FLR 1015, FD). A child can be

PART VI

habitually resident in only one country at a time (*Re A; HA v MB (Brussels II Revised: Article 11(7) Application)* (above)). Where two children had been abducted from Poland and accommodated by the local authority, the English court had jurisdiction to make care orders under Art 10 either by acquiescence or because the children had been in the jurisdiction with the knowledge of all concerned for over a year, were settled and no request for a return had been made (*Tower Hamlets London Borough Council v MK and Others* [2012] 2 FLR 762, FD). See also **Liaison judge** under Art 8.

Habitual residence—See annotations to Art 8.

'acquired a habitual residence in another Member State'—The retained jurisdiction is not brought to an end where the child's new habitual residence is in a non-Member State, even though the jurisdictional scheme in Brussels IIA is not geographically limited to the EU (*Re H (Jurisdiction)* [2015] 1 FLR 1132, CA; *Re K and D (Wardship Without Notice Return Order)* [2017] EWHC 153 (Fam)).

'Knowledge of whereabouts' (Art 10(b)–(c))—*M v M (Abduction: Settlement)* [2008] 2 FLR 1884, FD.

'Judgment on custody that does not entail the return of the child' (Art 10(b)(iv))—A provisional measure does not constitute a 'judgment on custody that does not entail the return of the child' and cannot be the basis of a transfer of jurisdiction to the courts of the country to which a child has been unlawfully removed (*Povse v Alpago* [2010] 2 FLR 1343, ECJ). See also *Re AJ (Brussels II Revised)* [2012] 2 FLR 689, FD and *Re AJ (Contact: Brussels II Revised)* [2012] 2 FLR 1065, FD.

Article 11
Return of the child

1 Where a person, institution or other body having rights of custody applies to the competent authorities in a Member State to deliver a judgment on the basis of the Hague Convention of 25 October 1980 on the Civil Aspects of International Child Abduction (hereinafter 'the 1980 Hague Convention'), in order to obtain the return of a child that has been wrongfully removed or retained in a Member State other than the Member State where the child was habitually resident immediately before the wrongful removal or retention, paragraphs 2 to 8 shall apply.

2 When applying Articles 12 and 13 of the 1980 Hague Convention, it shall be ensured that the child is given the opportunity to be heard during the proceedings unless this appears inappropriate having regard to his or her age or degree of maturity.

3 A court to which an application for return of a child is made as mentioned in paragraph 1 shall act expeditiously in proceedings on the application, using the most expeditious procedures available in national law.

Without prejudice to the first subparagraph, the court shall, except where exceptional circumstances make this impossible, issue its judgment no later than six weeks after the application is lodged.

4 A court cannot refuse to return a child on the basis of Article 13b of the 1980 Hague Convention if it is established that adequate arrangements have been made to secure the protection of the child after his or her return.

5 A court cannot refuse to return a child unless the person who requested the return of the child has been given an opportunity to be heard.

6 If a court has issued an order on non-return pursuant to Article 13 of the 1980 Hague Convention, the court must immediately either directly or through its central authority, transmit a copy of the court order on non-return and of the relevant documents, in particular a transcript of the hearings before the court, to the court with jurisdiction or central authority in the Member State where the child was habitually resident immediately before the wrongful removal or retention, as determined by national law. The court shall receive all the mentioned documents within one month of the date of the non-return order.

7 Unless the courts in the Member State where the child was habitually resident immediately before the wrongful removal or retention have already been seised by one of the parties, the court or central authority that receives the information mentioned in paragraph 6 must notify it to the parties and invite them to make submissions to the court, in accordance with national law, within three months of the date of notification so that the court can examine the question of custody of the child.

Without prejudice to the rules on jurisdiction contained in this Regulation, the court shall close the case if no submissions have been received by the court within the time limit.

8 Notwithstanding a judgment of non-return pursuant to Article 13 of the 1980 Hague Convention, any subsequent judgment which requires the return of the child issued by a court having jurisdiction under this Regulation shall be enforceable in accordance with Section 4 of Chapter III below in order to secure the return of the child.

Defined terms—'rights of custody': Art 2.9; 'Member State': Art 2.3; 'wrongful removal or retention': Art 2.11; 'court': Art 2.1.

Scope—The Hague Convention 1980 (incorporated in CACA 1985) continues to apply but is supplemented by Brussels IIA, which complements the Convention (recital 17). However, Brussels IIA takes precedence over the Hague Convention 1980 (Art 60; *JRG v EB (Abduction: Brussels II Revised)* [2013] 1 FLR 203, FD). Art 11 only applies to return applications in cases of wrongful removal/retention (as defined by Art 2.11) made under the Hague Convention 1980 by one Member State (excluding Denmark: Art 2.3) to another. Reference should also be made to the annotations to Arts 10, 40 and 42. Where a parent has failed to obtain a summary return order under the Hague Convention 1980, Art 12, it may be wiser to pursue the procedure provided by Art 11 to obtain an order that would be automatically enforced in the requested state rather than to pursue the appellate process in the requested state (*Re F (Abduction: Refusal to Return)* [2009] 2 FLR 1023, CA). Only if a child's non-return is pursuant to the Hague Convention 1980, Art 13, is the court or Central Authority of the home state competent to examine the question of the custody of a child under Art 11.7 (*Re RC and BC (Child Abduction) (Brussels II Revised: Article 11(7))* [2009] 1 FLR 574, FD; *Re RD (Child Abduction) (Brussels II Revised: Arts 11(7) and 19)* [2009] 1 FLR 586, FD). The overreaching procedure in Arts 11.6–11.8 is only available where a defence has been established under the Hague Convention 1980, Art 13b. Art 11 is not available where the defence is under the Hague Convention 1980, Art 3 (no breach of rights of custody, or child not habitually resident in home country), Art 12 (settlement) or Art 20 (violation of human rights) (*SP v EB and KP* [2016] 1 FLR 228, FD).

'Opportunity to be heard' (Art 11.2)—Ensuring that a child is given the opportunity to be heard will normally be through a Cafcass report (*Re D (Abduction: Rights of Custody)* [2007] 1 FLR 961, HL; *Re F (Abduction: Child's Wishes)* [2007] 2 FLR 697, CA; *K v K* [2006] EWHC 2685 (Fam)), although it may lead to the child being given separate party status (*Re D* (above); *Re F (Abduction: Joinder of Child as Party)* [2007] 2 FLR 313, CA; *Re M (Abduction: Zimbabwe)* [2008] 1 FLR 251, HL; *Re C (Abduction: Separate Representation of Children)* [2008] 2 FLR 6, FD; *M v T (Abduction: Brussels II Revised, Art 11(7))* [2010] 2 FLR 1685, FD). It may be appropriate to take into account the objections of younger children, although the objections of an older child will deserve greater weight (*Re R (Child Abduction: Acquiescence*) [1995] 1 FLR 716, CA; *Re D* (above); *Re W (Abduction: Child's Objections)* [2010] 2 FLR 1165, CA). There must be a clear distinction between a child's objections and a child's wishes and feelings (*Re K (Abduction: Case Management)* [2011] 1 FLR 1268, CA; *LCG v RL (Abduction: Habitual Residence and Child's Objections)* [2014] 1 FLR 307, FD).

'Expeditiously' (Art 11.3)—Guidance has been given by the Court of Appeal in *Vigreux v Michel* [2006] 2 FLR 1180, CA, at [33].

'Adequate arrangements ... to secure the protection of the child' (Art 11.4)—See *F v M (Abduction: Grave Risk of Harm)* [2008] 2 FLR 1263, FD; *WF v FJ, BF and RF (Abduction: Child's Objections)* [2011] 1 FLR 1153, FD; *Re K (Abduction: Case Management)*, above; *B v B* [2014] EWHC 1804 (Fam). The focus of Art 11.4 is to design arrangements to protect a child from being exposed on return to a grave risk of harm or placed in an intolerable situation so as to give rise to a defence under Art 13b of the Hague Convention 1980 (*WF v FJ, BF and RF (Abduction: Child's Objections)* [2011] 1 FLR 1153, FD). If the court is able to make protective measures under the Hague Convention 1996, Art 11 (as to the scope of which, see *Re J (Jurisdiction: Abduction)* [2016] 1 FLR 170, SC) or Brussels IIA, Art 20, it will not be possible to advance a case under the Hague Convention 1980, Art 13b. Art 11.4 does not apply to the defence of a child's objections under the Hague Convention 1980, Art 13. However, if protective measures are made under the Hague Convention 1996, Art 11, those protective measures will overreach a child's objections, even if they are validly expressed. Therefore, where the court makes protective measures under either Brussels IIA, Art 20 or the Hague Convention 1996, Art 11, Art 11.4 will make it impossible to advance the defence in the Hague Convention 1980, Art 13b (*RB v DB* [2015] EWHC 1817 (Fam)).

'Examine the question of custody of the child' (Art 11.7)—In exercising jurisdiction under Art 11.7, the court is neither carrying out an appeal process in respect of a decision by a foreign court nor applying Hague Convention 1980, Art 13. Rather, it is exercising its jurisdiction under Art 10 (which is a welfare jurisdiction). In exercising its welfare jurisdiction, the court has the power to make a summary order under Art 11.7 in an appropriate case. This will not involve a full welfare enquiry, even though a welfare approach is to be applied (*M v T (Abduction: Brussels II Revised, Art 11(7))* [2010] 2 FLR 1685, FD). The foundation for this welfare jurisdiction is based on Art 11.7 and need not be categorised as deriving from the inherent jurisdiction (*D v N and D (by her Guardian Ad Litem)* [2011] 2 FLR 464, FD). See also, *AF v T and Another (Brussels II Revised: Art 11(7) Application)* [2011] 2 FLR 891, FD, *Re H (Jurisdiction)* [2010] 1 FLR 598, FD and *WF v FJ, BF and RF*, above. The decision of the European Court of Human Rights in *Neulinger and Shuruk v Switzerland* [2011] 1 FLR 122, ECHR (where it was held that to enforce an order under the Hague Convention 1980 to return a child to Israel would be in breach of the right to respect for the private and family lives of mother and child under ECHR, Art 8, the mother's defence under Art 13b of the Hague Convention having been rejected) does not require a departure from the normal summary process, provided that the decision is not arbitrary or mechanical (*Re E (Children) (Abduction: Custody Appeal)* [2011] 2 FLR 758, SC).

'Judgment which requires the return of the child' (Art 11.8)—Neither an order concerning contact nor an order for shared living arrangements amounts to such a judgment (*Re A; HA v MB (Brussels II Revised: Article 11(7) Application)* [2008] 1 FLR 289, FD). A judgment of the court with jurisdiction ordering the return of a child fell within the scope of Art 11.8, even if not preceded by a final judgment of that court relating to rights

PART VI

of custody concerning the child (*Povse v Alpago* [2010] 2 FLR 1343, ECJ). See also, *Re SJ (A Child) (Habitual Residence: Application to Set Aside)* [2014] EWHC 58 (Fam).

'Shall be enforceable' (Art 11.8)—See *WF v FJ, BF and RF (Abduction: Child's Objections)* [2011] 1 FLR 1153, FD; *SP v EB and KP* [2016] 1 FLR 228, FD (cf where the Hague Convention 1980, Art 20 defence is relied upon).

Article 12

Prorogation of jurisdiction

1 The courts of a Member State exercising jurisdiction by virtue of Article 3 on an application for divorce, legal separation or marriage annulment shall have jurisdiction in any matter relating to parental responsibility connected with that application where:

(a) at least one of the spouses has parental responsibility in relation to the child; and

(b) the jurisdiction of the courts has been accepted expressly or otherwise in an unequivocal manner by the spouses and by the holders of parental responsibility, at the time the court is seised, and is in the superior interests of the child.

2 The jurisdiction conferred in paragraph 1 shall cease as soon as:

(a) the judgment allowing or refusing the application for divorce, legal separation or marriage annulment has become final;

(b) in those cases where proceedings in relation to parental responsibility are still pending on the date referred to in (a), a judgment in these proceedings has become final;

(c) the proceedings referred to in (a) and (b) have come to an end for another reason.

3 The courts of a Member State shall also have jurisdiction in relation to parental responsibility in proceedings other than those referred to in paragraph 1 where:

(a) the child has a substantial connection with that Member State, in particular by virtue of the fact that one of the holders of parental responsibility is habitually resident in that Member State or that the child is a national of that Member State; and

(b) the jurisdiction of the courts has been accepted expressly or otherwise in an unequivocal manner by all the parties to the proceedings at the time the court is seised and is in the best interests of the child.

4 Where the child has his or her habitual residence in the territory of a third State which is not a contracting party to the Hague Convention of 19 October 1996 on jurisdiction, applicable law, recognition, enforcement and cooperation in respect of parental responsibility and measures for the protection of children, jurisdiction under this Article shall be deemed to be in the child's interest, in particular if it is found impossible to hold proceedings in the third State in question.

Defined terms—'court': Art 2.1; 'Member State': Art 2.3; 'parental responsibility': Art 2.7; 'holder of parental responsibility': Art 2.8; 'seised': Art 16.

Scope—The combined effect of Arts 3 and 8 is that the courts of one Member State may be seised with jurisdiction for divorce etc and the courts of another Member State seised with jurisdiction in relation to parental responsibility. Article 12 permits parties in certain circumstances to confer a time-limited parental responsibility jurisdiction on the court dealing with the divorce etc. Prorogation of jurisdiction under Art 12 does not endure beyond the final order (*Re S (Jurisdiction: Prorogation); sub nom PB v SE* [2013] 2 FLR 1584, FD). Article 12 can apply to cases where a child is lawfully resident outside the jurisdiction (*Re I (A Child) (Contact Application: Jurisdiction)* [2010] 1 FLR 361, SC, at [17]; *X v Y and Another* [2015] 1 FLR 1463, FD). The filing of a statement of arrangements in answer in relation to children in English divorce proceedings does not amount to unequivocal acceptance of the parental responsibility jurisdiction of the English court (*Bush v Bush* [2008] 2 FLR 1437, CA). The fact that the question of the residence of children was in issue would prevent there being 'unequivocal' acceptance of jurisdiction (*Re A (Removal Outside Jurisdiction: Habitual Residence)* [2011] 1 FLR 2025, CA). The acceptance of jurisdiction does not have to be in writing and subsequent acts and contact can illuminate the quality of the acceptance at the time the court was seised (*VC v GC (Jurisdiction: Brussels II Revised Art 12)* [2013] 1 FLR 244, FD, applying *Re I* (above)).See also, *T v T (Jurisdiction)* [2013] 1 FLR 1419, FD; *Re LR (A Child)* [2015] 2 FLR 1066, FD; *L v M (R Intervening)* (Case C-656/13) [2015] Fam 173, CJEU. Where Member State 1 acquires jurisdiction under Art 12 for issues of parental responsibility concerning a child who subsequently becomes habitually resident in Member State 2, the retention of jurisdiction by Member State 1 is not conditional upon the courts of Member State 2 finding that that was in the superior interests of the child, nor could the jurisdiction of the courts of Member State 1 be terminated by a decision of the courts of Member State 2 (*Re S-R (Jurisdiction: Contact)* [2008] 2 FLR 1741, FD; *AP v TD (Relocation: Retention of Jurisdiction)* [2011] 1 FLR 1851, FD).

Article 12 will apply regardless of whether the other country or countries concerned were themselves subject to Brussels IIA (*Re I* (above)).

Where there are no matrimonial proceedings, Art 12.3 additionally provides that the courts of a Member State will have jurisdiction in relation to parental responsibility in specified circumstances including a substantial connection between the child and the Member State (*B v B (Brussels II Revised: Jurisdiction) sub nom Butt v Butt* [2011] 1 FLR 54, FD). See also, *H v H (Jurisdiction to Grant Wardship)* [2012] 1 FLR 23, CA, *Re A*, above, and *B v B (Relinquishment of Jurisdiction: Brussels II Revised Art 12)* [2013] 2 FLR 1145, FD.

'Superior interests of the child' (Art 12.1(b))—This is to be determined on forum conveniens principles as between competing Member States (on the balance of fairness including convenience): *Bush v Bush* [2008] 2 FLR 1437, CA.

'Final' (Arts 12.2(a) and (b))—See *Re A (Foreign Contact Order: Jurisdiction)* [2004] 1 FLR 641, FD; *A v L (Jurisdiction: Brussels II)* [2002] 1 FLR 1042, FD (judgment has not become final where there is an outstanding appeal); *Re G (Jurisdiction: Art 19, BIIR)* [2015] 1 FLR 276, CA (judgment final, even if executory).

'Jurisdiction in relation to parental responsibility' (Art 12.3)—Both limbs of Art 12.3 must be satisfied to establish jurisdiction (*Re LR (A Child)* [2015] 2 FLR 1066, CA). Jurisdiction prorogued under Art 12.3 ceases following a final judgment in those proceedings (*E v B* (Case C-436/13) [2015] 1 FLR 64, CJEU). See, also, *Re S (Jurisdiction: Prorogation); sub nom PB v SE* [2013] 2 FLR 1584, CJEU.

'Accepted expressly or otherwise in an unequivocal manner' (Art 12.3(b))—This provision must be interpreted strictly. At least, the defendant must be aware of the proceedings taking place. Jurisdiction will not have been accepted for the purposes of Art 12.3(b) where a legal representative appointed by the court of its own initiative, because of the impossibility of serving a defendant, has not pleaded lack of jurisdiction (*Gogova v Iliev* (Case C-215/15) [2016] 1 FLR 158, CJEU).

'Best interests of the child' (Art 12.3(b))—See *B v B (Brussels II Revised: Jurisdiction) sub nom Butt v Butt* [2011] 1 FLR 54, FD (jurisdiction not established despite a substantial connection and acceptance of jurisdiction where acceptance of jurisdiction is not in the best interests of the child); cf *T v T (Jurisdiction)* [2013] 1 FLR 1419, FD. See also, *B v B (Relinquishment of Jurisdiction: Brussels II Revised Art 12)* [2013] 2 FLR 1145, FD. The evaluation of a child's best interests is limited in its extent to the issue of forum and not best interests overall (*Re I (A Child) (Contact Application: Jurisdiction)* [2010] 1 FLR 361, SC). The principle of paramountcy does not apply in the best interests analysis (*Re K (A Child); sub nom Re T (A Child: Article 15 of Brussels II Revised)* [2014] 1 FLR 749, CA at [25] and [26]; *Re M (Brussels II Revised: Art 15)* [2014] 2 FLR 1372, CA).

'Third State' (Art 12.4)—Art 12 could apply to a child who is lawfully resident outside the EU (*Re I (A Child) (Contact Application: Jurisdiction)* [2010] 1 FLR 361, SC).

Article 13
Jurisdiction based on the child's presence

1 Where a child's habitual residence cannot be established and jurisdiction cannot be determined on the basis of Article 12, the courts of the Member State where the child is present shall have jurisdiction.

2 Paragraph 1 shall also apply to refugee children or children internationally displaced because of disturbances occurring in their country.

Defined terms—'court': Art 2.1; 'Member State': Art 2.3.

Scope—Where Arts 8–12 are not engaged because a child's habitual residence cannot be established and jurisdiction cannot be established by prorogation of jurisdiction under Art 12, the courts of the Member State where the child is present will have jurisdiction. See *Mercredi v Chaffe* [2011] 1 FLR 1293, CJEU at [57], *Re F (Habitual Residence)* [2015] 1 FLR 1303, FD (English court had jurisdiction in care proceedings under Art 13 as the child was not habitually resident anywhere), *Lambeth LBC v JO* [2014] EWHC 3597 (Fam) (jurisdiction assumed under Art 13 where court unable to determine habitual residence of two children integrated into family and social life in both England and Nigeria) and *London Borough of Barking and Dagenham v SS* [2015] 2 FLR 181, FD.

Article 14
Residual jurisdiction

Where no court of a Member State has jurisdiction pursuant to Articles 8 to 13, jurisdiction shall be determined, in each Member State, by the laws of that State.

Defined terms—'court': Art 2.1; 'Member State': Art 2.3.

Scope—Article 14 provides for residual jurisdiction where no courts of a Member State have jurisdiction under Arts 8–13, which jurisdiction is to be determined in each Member State according to its own domestic law. Therefore, the common law rules as to the inherent jurisdiction of the High Court will continue to apply if a child is not habitually resident in a Member State. The Crown retains an exceptional protective (parens patriae) jurisdiction over a child of British nationality wherever he is. For most types of order, this jurisdiction was removed by FLA 1986 (*Re A (Jurisdiction: Return of Child)* [2014] 1 FLR 111, SC). As to the exceptional nature of this jurisdiction, see *Re B; RB v FB and MA (Forced Marriage: Wardship: Jurisdiction)* [2008] 2 FLR 1624, FD and *Re N (Abduction: Appeal)* [2013] 1 FLR 457, CA.

Article 15

Transfer to a court better placed to hear the case

1 By way of exception, the courts of a Member State having jurisdiction as to the substance of the matter may, if they consider that a court of another Member State, with which the child has a particular connection, would be better placed to hear the case, or a specific part thereof, and where this is in the best interests of the child:

(a) stay the case or the part thereof in question and invite the parties to introduce a request before the court of that other Member State in accordance with paragraph 4; or

(b) request a court of another Member State to assume jurisdiction in accordance with paragraph 5.

2 Paragraph 1 shall apply:

(a) upon application from a party; or

(b) of the court's own motion; or

(c) upon application from a court of another Member State with which the child has a particular connection, in accordance with paragraph 3.

A transfer made of the court's own motion or by application of a court of another Member State must be accepted by at least one of the parties.

3 The child shall be considered to have a particular connection to a Member State as mentioned in paragraph 1, if that Member State:

(a) has become the habitual residence of the child after the court referred to in paragraph 1 was seised; or

(b) is the former habitual residence of the child; or

(c) is the place of the child's nationality; or

(d) is the habitual residence of a holder of parental responsibility; or

(e) is the place where property of the child is located and the case concerns measures for the protection of the child relating to the administration, conservation or disposal of this property.

4 The court of the Member State having jurisdiction as to the substance of the matter shall set a time limit by which the courts of that other Member State shall be seised in accordance with paragraph 1.

If the courts are not seised by that time, the court which has been seised shall continue to exercise jurisdiction in accordance with Articles 8 to 14.

5 The courts of that other Member State may, where due to the specific circumstances of the case, this is in the best interests of the child, accept jurisdiction within six weeks of their seisure in accordance with paragraph 1(a) or 1(b). In this case, the court first seised shall decline jurisdiction. Otherwise, the court first seised shall continue to exercise jurisdiction in accordance with Articles 8 to 14.

6 The courts shall cooperate for the purposes of this Article, either directly or through the central authorities designated pursuant to Article 53.

Defined terms—'court': Art 2.1; 'Member State': Art 2.3; 'parental responsibility': Art 2.7; 'holder of parental responsibility': Art 2.8; 'particular connection': Art 15.3.

Scope—Article 15 provides an exceptional mechanism to transfer a (specific part of a) case to another Member State with which the child has a particular connection if that court is better placed to hear the case and it is in the best interests of the child. Art 15 applies only to questions of parental responsibility dealt with in Brussels IIA, Section 2; thus, a request by the court of another Member State to take over divorce proceedings and a child maintenance application was ineffective (maintenance obligations being excluded under the scope of Brussels IIA by Art 1.3(e)) (*T v T (Brussels II Revised: Art 15)* [2013] 2 FLR 1326, FD; *S v S (Brussels II Revised: Art 19(1) and (3): Reference to CJEU)* [2015] 2 FLR 364, FD, at [17]). See FPR 2010, rr 12.61–12.67. Guidance for the judiciary on the transfer of proceedings under Art 15 was issued by the President of the Family Division in April 2016 (see Part V).

See **Request for another Member State to assume jurisdiction** under CA 1989, s 31 for a detailed discussion of the relevant case-law.

Section 3
Common provisions

Article 16
Seising of a Court

1 A court shall be deemed to be seised:

(a) at the time when the document instituting the proceedings or an equivalent document is lodged with the court, provided that the applicant has not subsequently failed to take the steps he was required to take to have service effected on the respondent; or

(b) if the document has to be served before being lodged with the court, at the time when it is received by the authority responsible for service, provided that the applicant has not subsequently failed to take the steps he was required to take to have the document lodged with the court.

Defined terms—'court': Art 2.1.

Scope—A court is deemed to be seised only where a document instituting proceedings or its equivalent is lodged with the court subject to taking steps to effect service (see below). A court will not therefore be seised by the making of a telephone application (*Mercredi v Chaffe* [2011] 1 FLR 1293, CJEU). To ensure that a court is seised, proceedings must not simply be issued but the process of service must be started. However, there is no time limit for service of divorce proceedings in England and Wales. Furthermore, irregular service (eg on a Sunday) will not necessarily nullify the proceedings (*W v W (Divorce Proceedings)* [2011] 1 FLR 372, FD). Issuing proceedings as a precautionary measure, but not then effecting service, will not gain priority under Brussels IIA (*R v R (Divorce: Stay of Proceedings)* [1994] 2 FLR 1036, FD). See also, *C v S (Divorce: Jurisdiction)* [2011] 2 FLR 19, FD. Actual service need not be effected to establish jurisdiction. The International Committee of Resolution (*International Aspects of Family Law* (3rd edn 2009), p 359) expressed the view that the required steps to effect service will have been taken when documents have been sent to the transmitting agency, eg the Foreign Process Section of the RCJ. The issue of when a court is seised is not affected by the lis pendens provisions of Art 19 (*E v E (BIIA: Arts 16 and 19)* [2017] 1 FLR 658, FD). Time differences do not affect the operation of Art 16, which is based upon chronological precedence (*A v B* (Case C-489/14) [2016] 1 FLR 31, CJEU).

Service is available through formal channels: see the EU Service Regulation 1393/2007 of 13 November 2007 (set out below) on the service in the Member States of judicial and extra-judicial documents in civil or commercial matters, which applies from 13 November 2008. It provides a procedure for the service of documents through designated 'transmitting agencies' and 'receiving agencies' in Member States without recourse to consular and diplomatic channels. The Regulation applies to all EU Member States including Denmark.

'Lodged'—Lodged means that a document is filed with the court in a manner which is accepted by the court and which leads to the institution of proceedings by the court. There is no sanction for failing to file a marriage certificate as required by FPR PD7A, para 3 (*L-K v K (No 3)* [2007] 2 FLR 741, FD). See, also, *MH v MH* (Case C-173/16) (2016) 22 June, CJEU (the time when the document instituting the proceedings is lodged with the court is the time when that document is lodged with the court concerned, even if under national law lodging that document does not in itself immediately institute proceedings). Such a failure is a minor procedural irregularity and not fatal to England being seised with jurisdiction. The requirement is administrative rather than substantive and the court may dispense with the requirement retrospectively (*L-K v K (Brussels II Revised: Maintenance Pending Suit)* [2006] 2 FLR 1113, FD). Article 16.1 does not say that a court is seised when a document has been lodged and the applicant has effected (or taken the required step to effect) service, but that the court is seised when the document is lodged, subject to the proviso that there has not been a subsequent failure to take required steps (*W v W (Divorce Proceedings)* [2011] 1 FLR 372, FD; *L v C (Applications by Non-Biological Mother)* [2015] 1 FLR 674, FD). See also **'establish'** under Art 19.

Article 17
Examination as to jurisdiction

Where a court of a Member State is seised of a case over which it has no jurisdiction under this Regulation and over which a court of another Member State has jurisdiction by virtue of this Regulation, it shall declare of its own motion that it has no jurisdiction.

Defined terms—'court': Art 2.1; 'Member State': Art 2.3.

Scope—Article 17 places a duty upon the courts of Member States to conduct an examination as to jurisdiction. See also FPR 2010, r 7.27(4); *Re H (Child Abduction)* [2012] EWCA Civ 913; *Re E (Brussels II Revised: Vienna Convention: Reporting Restrictions)* [2014] 2 FLR 151, FD; *Re B (Care Order: Jurisdiction)* [2014] 1 FLR 900, CA.

PART VI

Article 18

Examination as to admissibility

1 Where a respondent habitually resident in a State other than the Member State where the action was brought does not enter an appearance, the court with jurisdiction shall stay the proceedings so long as it is not shown that the respondent has been able to receive the document instituting the proceedings or an equivalent document in sufficient time to enable him to arrange for his defence, or that all necessary steps have been taken to this end.

2 Article 19 of Regulation (EC) No 1348/2000 shall apply instead of the provisions of paragraph 1 of this Article if the document instituting the proceedings or an equivalent document had to be transmitted from one Member State to another pursuant to that Regulation.

3 Where the provisions of Regulation (EC) No 1348/2000 are not applicable, Article 15 of the Hague Convention of 15 November 1965 on the service abroad of judicial and extrajudicial documents in civil or commercial matters shall apply if the document instituting the proceedings or an equivalent document had to be transmitted abroad pursuant to that Convention.

Defined terms—'Member State': Art 2.3; 'court': Art 2.1.

Scope—Comparable with the duty imposed by Art 17 to conduct an examination as to the court's jurisdiction is the duty imposed by this Article to stay proceedings until it can be shown that a respondent, habitually resident in a Member State other than that in which the proceedings are taking place and who has not entered an appearance (eg an acknowledgment of service), has been able to receive the relevant documents in sufficient time to enable him to arrange for his defence, or that all necessary steps have been taken to this end. This duty does not apply if service was in accordance with the EU Service Regulation (EC) 1393/2007 of 13 November 2007 (set out below): see annotations to Art 16.

Article 19

Lis pendens and dependent actions

1 Where proceedings relating to divorce, legal separation or marriage annulment between the same parties are brought before courts of different Member States, the court second seised shall of its own motion stay its proceedings until such time as the jurisdiction of the court first seised is established.

2 Where proceedings relating to parental responsibility relating to the same child and involving the same cause of action are brought before courts of different Member States, the court second seised shall of its own motion stay its proceedings until such time as the jurisdiction of the court first seised is established.

3 Where the jurisdiction of the court first seised is established, the court second seised shall decline jurisdiction in favour of that court.

In that case, the party who brought the relevant action before the court second seised may bring that action before the court first seised.

Defined terms—'court': Art 2.1; 'Member State': Art 2.3; 'seised': Art 16; 'parental responsibility': Art 2.7.

Scope—Where there are concurrent proceedings relating to either divorce, legal separation or marriage annulment or parental responsibility between the same parties before courts of different Member States, the court second seised must, of its own motion, stay its proceedings until such time as the jurisdiction of the court first seised is established (eg *Re RD (Child Abduction) (Brussels II Revised: Arts 11(7) and (19))* [2009] 1 FLR 586, FD; *A v B (Jurisdiction)* [2012] 1 FLR 768, FD). There is no provision to decline jurisdiction on the basis that another jurisdiction is the forum conveniens (*Wermuth v Wermuth (No 1)* [2003] 1 FLR 1022, FD; *Wermuth v Wermuth (No 2)* [2003] 1 FLR 1029, CA). However, determination of which of the competing jurisdictions is first seised may be left to the court of another Member State in an appropriate case (*Chorley v Chorley* [2005] 2 FLR 38, CA). Where proceedings in the court first seised have been brought to an end, that court will no longer be seised for the purposes of Art 19, unless and until an application for revival is made, and accordingly a court second seised could correctly assume jurisdiction (*C v S (Divorce: Jurisdiction)* [2011] 2 FLR 19, FD; *Ville de Bauge v China* [2015] 2 FLR 873, FD; *A v B* [2016] 1 FLR 31, CJEU (eg where the jurisdiction of the court first seised lapsed as a result of which the court second seised became the court first seised on the date of lapse)). The issue of when a court is seised as provided by Art 16 is not affected by Art 19. The lis pendens provisions of Art 19 require two extant sets of proceedings in different member states (*E v E (BIIA: Arts 16 and 19)* [2017] 1 FLR 658, FD). Art 19.2 is not applicable where a court of a Member State first seised for the purposes of obtaining measures in matters of parental responsibility is seised only for the purposes of it granting provisional measures under Art 20 (*Purrucker v Vallés Pérez (No 2)* (Case C-296/10) [2012] 1 FLR 925, CJEU). A court is not first seised where a final order has already been made (*Re G (Jurisdiction: Art 19, BIIR)* [2015] 1 FLR 276, CA). The system established by Art 19 applies without exception and cannot be overridden by estoppel or agreement (*Jefferson v O'Connor* [2014] 2 FLR 759, CA).

'stay' (Art 19.1); **'decline'** (Art 19.3)—Where jurisdiction in the court of a Member State first seised has been confirmed, jurisdiction in the other state does not remain deferred: declining and deferring (and thus imposing a stay) are two very different concepts. Once the court first seised has confirmed its jurisdiction, the declining of jurisdiction by the court second seised is mandatory and must be absolute (*Ville de Bauge v China* [2015] 2 FLR 873, FD).

'establish' (Art 19.3)—A party's failure to progress proceedings is not relevant in determining whether the jurisdiction of a court first seised has been established. The time difference between Member States is not capable of frustrating the application of the lis pendens rules in Art 19, which taken in conjunction with Art 16, are based on chronological precedence (*S v S (Brussels II Revised: Art 19(1) and (3): Reference to CJEU)* [2015] 2 FLR 364, FD; *A v B* [2016] 1 FLR 31, CJEU).

For the procedure for an application for a stay under Art 19, see FPR 2010, r 7.27.

Article 20
Provisional, including protective, measures

1 In urgent cases, the provisions of this Regulation shall not prevent the courts of a Member State from taking such provisional, including protective, measures in respect of persons or assets in that State as may be available under the law of that Member State, even if, under this Regulation, the court of another Member State has jurisdiction as to the substance of the matter.

2 The measures referred to in paragraph 1 shall cease to apply when the court of the Member State having jurisdiction under this Regulation as to the substance of the matter has taken the measures it considers appropriate.

Defined terms—'court': Art 2.1; 'Member State': Art 2.3.

Scope—In urgent cases, Art 20 enables the courts of a Member State to take such provisional, including protective, measures even if the courts of another Member State have jurisdiction as to the substance of the matter. Art 20.1 entitles the courts of a Member State to take provisional or other protective measures only if three cumulative conditions are satisfied: the measures concerned must be urgent, must be taken in respect of persons or assets in the Member State and must be provisional (*Detiček v Sgueglia* [2010] 1 FLR 1381, ECJ). A measure under Art 20 may prevail over an earlier judgment adopted by the court of another Member State that has substantive jurisdiction. However, the system of recognition and enforcement provided for by Brussels IIA is not applicable to measures that fall within Art 20 (*Purrucker v Vallés Pérez (No 1)* (Case C-256/09) [2012] 1 FLR 903, CJEU). Measures under Art 20 include the power to make interim orders, including care orders in public law proceedings in respect of a child who is habitually resident in another Member State where the child is currently living in the Member State making the interim order (*Re A (Area of Freedom, Security and Justice)* [2009] 2 FLR 1, ECJ; *Re S (Care: Jurisdiction)* [2009] 2 FLR 550, FD) and an order requiring a parent to take a child to another jurisdiction by a certain date (*Re G (Jurisdiction: Art 19, BIIR)* [2015] 1 FLR 276, CA). In such a context, Art 20 has been held to contemplate 'short-term holding arrangements' (*Re B (Care Order: Jurisdiction)* [2014] 1 FLR 900, CA). Article 20 should not be used to secure an order for the return of a child where Hague Convention 1980 proceedings are pending (*Re A (A Child)* [2016] EWCA Civ 572). Article 20 refers to measures intended to preserve the factual or legal situation so as to safeguard rights, the recognition of which is being sought elsewhere in litigation in the court which has jurisdiction as to the substance of the matter. In contrast to the Hague Convention 1996, Art 11, where an order can have extra territorial effect, an order under Art 20 is purely an ancillary power (*Re J (Jurisdiction: Abduction)* [2016] 1 FLR 170, SC). Maintenance pending suit does not fall within Art 20 (*Wermuth v Wermuth (No 2)* [2003] 1 FLR 1029, CA; *N v N (Stay of Maintenance Proceedings)* [2014] 1 FLR 1399, FD). However, where there are concurrent proceedings and the other Member State has declined jurisdiction at first instance on the basis that it was not first seised, but its appeal process is not completed, there is jurisdiction to make an order for maintenance pending suit so long as the decision of the court at first instance in the other Member State remains in force (*L-K v K (Brussels II Revised: Maintenance Pending Suit)* [2006] 2 FLR 1113, FD). It was held in *Moses-Taiga v Taiga* [2006] 1 FLR 1074, CA that an order for maintenance pending suit could be made even when the divorce jurisdiction was subject to challenge. See, also, *MET v HAT* [2015] 1 FLR 576, FD; *MET v HAT (No 2)* [2015] 1 FLR 576, FD; *CC v NC (Maintenance Pending Suit)* [2015] 1 FLR 404, FD. See, further, the notes to Art 56 and the Maintenance Regulation, Art 14.

CHAPTER III
RECOGNITION AND ENFORCEMENT

Section 1
Recognition

Article 21
Recognition of a judgment

1 A judgment given in a Member State shall be recognised in the other Member States without any special procedure being required.

2 In particular, and without prejudice to paragraph 3, no special procedure shall be required for updating the civil-status records of a Member State on the basis of a judgment relating to divorce, legal separation or marriage annulment given in another Member State, and against which no further appeal lies under the law of that Member State.

3 Without prejudice to Section 4 of this Chapter, any interested party may, in accordance with the procedures provided for in Section 2 of this Chapter, apply for a decision that the judgment be or not be recognised.

The local jurisdiction of the court appearing in the list notified by each Member State to the Commission pursuant to Article 68 shall be determined by the internal law of the Member State in which proceedings for recognition or non-recognition are brought.

4 Where the recognition of a judgment is raised as an incidental question in a court of a Member State, that court may determine that issue.

Defined terms—'judgment': Art 2.4; 'Member State': Art 2.3; 'court': Art 2.1.

Scope—Article 21 establishes the principle of automatic recognition in all Member States of orders covered by Brussels IIA made in one Member State without any special procedure, although some Member States insist on the filing of a certificate under Art 34. The general rule established in Art 21 is subject to the exceptions contained in Arts 22 (divorce, legal separation and marriage annulment) and 23 (parental responsibility) as well as the stay provisions of Art 27.

For a discussion of the relationship between ss 1 (recognition) and 2 (enforceability) of Chapter III, see annotations to Art 28. Registration of a judgment under FPR 2010, r 31.1 serves for the purposes of Art 21.3 as a decision that the judgment is recognised (FPR 2010, r 31.12).

Article 22
Grounds of non-recognition for judgments relating to divorce, legal separation or marriage annulment

A judgment relating to a divorce, legal separation or marriage annulment shall not be recognised:

(a) if such recognition is manifestly contrary to the public policy of the Member State in which recognition is sought;

(b) where it was given in default of appearance, if the respondent was not served with the document which instituted the proceedings or with an equivalent document in sufficient time and in such a way as to enable the respondent to arrange for his or her defence unless it is determined that the respondent has accepted the judgment unequivocally;

(c) if it is irreconcilable with a judgment given in proceedings between the same parties in the Member State in which recognition is sought; or

(d) if it is irreconcilable with an earlier judgment given in another Member State or in a non-Member State between the same parties, provided that the earlier judgment fulfils the conditions necessary for its recognition in the Member State in which recognition is sought.

Defined terms—'judgment': Art 2.4; 'Member State': Art 2.3.

'Public policy'—See annotations to Art 23.

Article 23
Grounds of non-recognition for judgments relating to parental responsibility

A judgment relating to parental responsibility shall not be recognised:

(a) if such recognition is manifestly contrary to the public policy of the Member State in which recognition is sought taking into account the best interests of the child;

(b) if it was given, except in case of urgency, without the child having been given an opportunity to be heard, in violation of fundamental principles of procedure of the Member State in which recognition is sought;

(c) where it was given in default of appearance if the person in default was not served with the document which instituted the proceedings or with an equivalent document in sufficient time and in such a way as to enable that person to arrange for his or her defence unless it is determined that such person has accepted the judgment unequivocally;

(d) on the request of any person claiming that the judgment infringes his or her parental responsibility, if it was given without such person having been given an opportunity to be heard;

(e) if it is irreconcilable with a later judgment relating to parental responsibility given in the Member State in which recognition is sought;

(f) if it is irreconcilable with a later judgment relating to parental responsibility given in another Member State or in the non-Member State of the habitual residence of the child provided that the later judgment fulfils the conditions necessary for its recognition in the Member State in which recognition is sought; or

(g) if the procedure laid down in Article 56 has not been complied with.

Defined terms—'judgment': Art 2.4; 'parental responsibility': Art 2.7; 'Member State': Art 2.3.

Scope—Art 23 sets out the grounds on which a judgment relating to parental responsibility will not be recognised. Only in the most exceptional circumstances would the policy of Brussels IIA be allowed to be subverted by non-recognition and/or non-enforcement (*Re S (Brussels II: Recognition: Best Interests of the Child) (No 1)* [2004] 1 FLR 571, FD; *W v W (Residence: Enforcement of Order)* [2005] EWHC 1811 (Fam); *Re D (Brussels II Revised: Contact)* [2008] 1 FLR 516, FD; *LAB v KB (Abduction: Brussels II Revised)* [2010] 2 FLR 1664, FD). The passage of time is not, without substantially more, sufficient to avoid recognition (*LAB v KB (Abduction: Brussels II Revised)*). As to the three stages involved in establishing non-recognition under Art 23(c), see *MD v CT (Parental Responsibility Order: Recognition and Enforcement)* [2015] 1 FLR 213, FD. See, also, *Re D (A Child) (International Recognition)* [2016] 2 FLR 347, CA. (The Supreme Court subsequently held in *Re D (A Child) (Supreme Court: Jurisdiction)* [2016] 2 FLR 379, SC that it did not have jurisdiction to hear an appeal from the Court of Appeal's decision.)

'Public policy'—There is no definition of 'public policy' in Brussels IIA. A refusal to recognise a judgment based on public policy (Art 23(a)) should operate only in exceptional circumstances (*Hoffman v Krieg* (No 145/86) [1988] ECR 645, ECJ) in relation to Brussels I; *Re S (Brussels II: Recognition: Best interests of the child) (No 1)* [2004] 1 FLR 571, FD; *LAB v KB (Abduction: Brussels II Revised)* [2010] 2 FLR 1664, FD; *Re L (Brussels II Revised: Appeal)* [2013] 1 FLR 430, CA; *JRG v EB (Abduction: Brussels II Revised)* [2013] 1 FLR 203, FD; *ET v TZ (Recognition and Enforcement of Foreign Residence Order)* [2014] 2 FLR 373, FD). However, there might be extremely rare cases in which the order of a foreign court was so contrary to the welfare of the child that its recognition was manifestly contrary to English public policy (*LAB v KB (Abduction: Brussels II Revised)*). See also, *Re N (Abduction: Brussels II Revised)* [2015] 1 FLR 227, FD (test is public policy not welfare, still less then paramountcy of welfare). Article 23(a) does not allow a court of a Member State that considered it had jurisdiction to rule on the custody of a child to refuse to recognise the judgment of a court of another Member State that had ruled on the custody of that child in the absence of a manifest breach (having regard to the best interests of the child) of a rule of law regarded as essential in the legal order of a Member State or of a right recognised as being fundamental within that legal order; a mere error of law will not suffice to establish that a judgment is contrary to public policy (*Re P* [2016] 1 FLR 337, CJEU).

'Default of appearance ... not served ... accepted the judgment unequivocally' (Art 23(c))—The three stages involved in establishing grounds for non-recognition under Art 23(c) are discussed by Mostyn J in *MD v CT (Parental Responsibility Order: Recognition and Enforcement)* [2015] 1 FLR 213, FD.

PART VI

Article 24
Prohibition of review of jurisdiction of the court of origin

The jurisdiction of the court of the Member State of origin may not be reviewed. The test of public policy referred to in Articles 22(a) and 23(a) may not be applied to the rules relating to jurisdiction set out in Articles 3 to 14.

Defined terms—'court': Art 2.1; 'Member State': Art 2.3.

'Public policy'—See annotations to Art 23.

Article 25
Differences in applicable law

The recognition of a judgment may not be refused because the law of the Member State in which such recognition is sought would not allow divorce, legal separation or marriage annulment on the same facts.

Defined terms—'judgment': Art 2.4; 'Member State': Art 2.3.

Article 26
Non-review as to substance

Under no circumstances may a judgment be reviewed as to its substance.

Defined terms—'judgment': Art 2.4.

Article 27
Stay of proceedings

1 A court of a Member State in which recognition is sought of a judgment given in another Member State may stay the proceedings if an ordinary appeal against the judgment has been lodged.

2 A court of a Member State in which recognition is sought of a judgment given in Ireland or the United Kingdom may stay the proceedings if enforcement is suspended in the Member State of origin by reason of an appeal.

Defined terms—'court': Art 2.1; 'Member State': Art 2.3; 'judgment': Art 2.4.

Scope—Recognition proceedings of an order made in another Member State may be stayed if the order is under appeal or, in the case of an order given in Ireland or the UK, if enforcement is suspended by reason of an appeal.

Section 2

Application for a declaration of enforceability

Article 28
Enforceable judgments

1 A judgment on the exercise of parental responsibility in respect of a child given in a Member State which is enforceable in that Member State and has been served shall be enforced in another Member State when, on the application of any interested party, it has been declared enforceable there.

2 However, in the United Kingdom, such a judgment shall be enforced in England and Wales, in Scotland or in Northern Ireland only when, on the application of any interested party, it has been registered for enforcement in that part of the United Kingdom.

Defined terms—'judgment': Art 2.4; 'parental responsibility': Art 2.7; 'Member State': Art 2.3.

Scope—Section 2 of Chapter III (Arts 28–36) provides for an application for a declaration of enforceability in the Member State where it is sought to enforce the judgment. Recognition (Section 1 of Chapter III) is dealt with separately from enforceability (Section 2 of Chapter III) in Brussels IIA. Nonetheless, an application for a declaration of enforceability (in the rest of Europe) or for registration (in the UK) and applying for a judgment to be recognised are one and the same thing. Similarly, an appeal against the registration of a judgment is the means by which an application is made for a judgment not to be recognised (*Re D (Brussels II Revised: Contact)* [2008] 1 FLR 516, FD). The clear route for recognition and enforcement contained in Brussels IIA takes precedence over the Hague Convention 1980 (*JRG v EB (Abduction: Brussels II Revised)* [2013] 1 FLR 203, FD: application under the Hague Convention 1980 adjourned without adjudication to permit an application to be issued under Art 28.1).

Article 28.2 provides that in the UK a judgment on parental responsibility given in another Member State is only enforceable when, on the application of any interested party, it has been registered for enforcement in the relevant part of the UK. References to a 'declaration of enforceability' in the UK are references to a notice of registration of the judgment under FPR 2010, r 31.11 (*Re D (Brussels II Revised: Contact)* [2008] 1 FLR 516, FD).

The procedure for registration of incoming orders from another Member State under Brussels IIA is to be found in FPR 2010, Pt 31 and PD31A.

Article 29
Jurisdiction of local courts

1 An application for a declaration of enforceability shall be submitted to the court appearing in the list notified by each Member State to the Commission pursuant to Article 68.

2 The local jurisdiction shall be determined by reference to the place of habitual residence of the person against whom enforcement is sought or by reference to the habitual residence of any child to whom the application relates.

Where neither of the places referred to in the first subparagraph can be found in the Member State of enforcement, the local jurisdiction shall be determined by reference to the place of enforcement.

Defined terms—'Member State': Art 2.3: 'Member State of enforcement': Art 2.6.

Scope—An application for permission under Art 29 should be submitted to the Principal Registry of the Family Division and is essentially administrative, falling within the province of a district judge (*Re S (Foreign Contact Order)* [2010] 1 FLR 982, CA).

Article 30
Procedure

1 The procedure for making the application shall be governed by the law of the Member State of enforcement.

2 The applicant must give an address for service within the area of jurisdiction of the court applied to. However, if the law of the Member State of enforcement does not provide for the furnishing of such an address, the applicant shall appoint a representative ad litem.

3 The documents referred to in Articles 37 and 39 shall be attached to the application.

Defined terms—'Member State of enforcement': Art 2.3; 'court': Art 2.1.

Article 31
Decision of the court

1 The court applied to shall give its decision without delay. Neither the person against whom enforcement is sought, nor the child shall, at this stage of the proceedings, be entitled to make any submissions on the application.

2 The application may be refused only for one of the reasons specified in Articles 22, 23 and 24.

3 Under no circumstances may a judgment be reviewed as to its substance.

Defined terms—'court': Art 2.1; 'judgment': Art 2.4.

'Submissions' (Art 31.1)—Art 31.1 does not apply to proceedings for non-recognition of a judicial decision (*Re Rinau* [2008] 2 FLR 1495, ECJ).

Article 32
Notice of the decision

The appropriate officer of the court shall without delay bring to the notice of the applicant the decision given on the application in accordance with the procedure laid down by the law of the Member State of enforcement.

Defined terms—'court': Art 21; 'Member State of enforcement': Art 2.6.

Article 33
Appeal against the decision

1 The decision on the application for a declaration of enforceability may be appealed against by either party.

2 The appeal shall be lodged with the court appearing in the list notified by each Member State to the Commission pursuant to Article 68.

3 The appeal shall be dealt with in accordance with the rules governing procedure in contradictory matters.

4 If the appeal is brought by the applicant for a declaration of enforceability, the party against whom enforcement is sought shall be summoned to appear before the appellate court. If such person fails to appear, the provisions of Article 18 shall apply.

5 An appeal against a declaration of enforceability must be lodged within one month of service thereof. If the party against whom enforcement is sought is habitually resident in a Member State other than that in which the declaration of enforceability was given, the time for appealing shall be two months and shall run from the date of service, either on him or at his residence. No extension of time may be granted on account of distance.

Defined terms—'court': Art 2.1; 'Member State': Art 2.3.

Scope—An appeal under Art 33 against registration is directed to the Principal Registry of the Family Division of the High Court to be heard by a Family Division judge. No permission to appeal is required. A second appeal lies under Art 34 to the Court of Appeal and permission to appeal is required (*Re S (Foreign Contact Order)* [2010] 1 FLR 982, CA).

Article 34
Courts of appeal and means of contest

The judgment given on appeal may be contested only by the proceedings referred to in the list notified by each Member State to the Commission pursuant to Article 68.

Defined terms—'judgment': Art 2.4; 'Member State': Art 2.3.

Case-law—*Re D (A Child) (Supreme Court: Jurisdiction)* [2016] 2 FLR 379, SC.

Article 35
Stay of proceedings

1 The court with which the appeal is lodged under Articles 33 or 34 may, on the application of the party against whom enforcement is sought, stay the proceedings if an ordinary appeal has been lodged in the Member State of origin, or if the time for such appeal has not yet expired. In the latter case, the court may specify the time within which an appeal is to be lodged.

2 Where the judgment was given in Ireland or the United Kingdom, any form of appeal available in the Member State of origin shall be treated as an ordinary appeal for the purposes of paragraph 1.

Defined terms—'court': Art 2.1; 'Member State of origin': Art 2.5; 'judgment': Art 2.4.

Article 36
Partial enforcement

1 Where a judgment has been given in respect of several matters and enforcement cannot be authorised for all of them, the court shall authorise enforcement for one or more of them.

2 An applicant may request partial enforcement of a judgment.

Defined terms—'judgment': Art 2.4; 'court': Art 2.1.

Section 3
Provisions common to Sections 1 and 2

Article 37
Documents

1 A party seeking or contesting recognition or applying for a declaration of enforceability shall produce:

(a) a copy of the judgment which satisfies the conditions necessary to establish its authenticity; and

(b) the certificate referred to in Article 39.

2 In addition, in the case of a judgment given in default, the party seeking recognition or applying for a declaration of enforceability shall produce:

(a) the original or certified true copy of the document which establishes that the defaulting party was served with the document instituting the proceedings or with an equivalent document; or

(b) any document indicating that the defendant has accepted the judgment unequivocally.

Defined terms—'judgment': Art 2.4.

Article 38
Absence of documents

1 If the documents specified in Article 37(1)(b) or (2) are not produced, the court may specify a time for their production, accept equivalent documents or, if it considers that it has sufficient information before it, dispense with their production.

2 If the court so requires, a translation of such documents shall be furnished. The translation shall be certified by a person qualified to do so in one of the Member States.

Defined terms—'court': Art 2.1; 'Member State': Art 2.3.

Article 39
Certificate concerning judgments in matrimonial matters and certificate concerning judgments on parental responsibility

The competent court or authority of a Member State of origin shall, at the request of any interested party, issue a certificate using the standard form set out in Annex I (judgments in matrimonial matters) or in Annex II (judgments on parental responsibility).

Defined terms—'court': Art 2.1; 'Member State of origin': Art 2.5.

Scope—The Art 39 procedure, which is available as of right, should not be circumvented, although the domestic enforcement armoury remains the same (*Cambra v Jones* [2014] 1 FLR 5, FD, at [56]).

'Certificate'—See *MA v DB (Inherent Jurisdiction)* [2011] 1 FLR 724, FD.

Section 4

Enforceability of certain judgments concerning rights of access and of certain judgments which require the return of the child

Article 40
Scope

1 This Section shall apply to:

(a) rights of access; and

(b) the return of a child entailed by a judgment given pursuant to Article 11(8).

2 The provisions of this Section shall not prevent a holder of parental responsibility from seeking recognition and enforcement of a judgment in accordance with the provisions in Sections 1 and 2 of this Chapter.

Defined terms—'right of access': Art 2.10; 'judgment': Art 2.4; 'holder of parental responsibility': Art 2.8.

Scope—Section 4 of Chapter 3 makes special provision for the enforceability of judgments relating to rights of access (Art 41) and the return of a child (Art 42). In these two categories the requirement to obtain the declaration of enforceability is substituted by a certificate granted by the court in the Member State where the order was made.

Article 41
Rights of access

1 The rights of access referred to in Article 40(1)(a) granted in an enforceable judgment given in a Member State shall be recognised and enforceable in another Member State without the need for a declaration of enforceability and without any possibility of opposing its recognition if the judgment has been certified in the Member State of origin in accordance with paragraph 2.

Even if national law does not provide for enforceability by operation of law of a judgment granting access rights, the court of origin may declare that the judgment shall be enforceable, notwithstanding any appeal.

2 The judge of origin shall issue the certificate referred to in paragraph 1 using the standard form in Annex III (certificate concerning rights of access) only if:

(a) where the judgment was given in default, the person defaulting was served with the document which instituted the proceedings or with an equivalent document in sufficient time and in such a way as to enable that person to arrange for his or her defense, or, the

PART VI

person has been served with the document but not in compliance with these conditions, it is nevertheless established that he or she accepted the decision unequivocally;

(b) all parties concerned were given an opportunity to be heard; and

(c) the child was given an opportunity to be heard, unless a hearing was considered inappropriate having regard to his or her age or degree of maturity.

The certificate shall be completed in the language of the judgment.

3 Where the rights of access involve a cross-border situation at the time of the delivery of the judgment, the certificate shall be issued ex officio when the judgment becomes enforceable, even if only provisionally. If the situation subsequently acquires a cross-border character, the certificate shall be issued at the request of one of the parties.

Defined terms—'rights of access': Art 2.10; 'judgment': Art 2.4; 'Member State': Art 2.3; 'Member State of origin': Art 2.5.

'Certificate'—See *Re C (Costs: Enforcement of Foreign Contact Order)* [2008] 1 FLR 619, FD; *AD v CD and AD* [2008] 1 FLR 1003, CA; *Re S (Brussels II Revised: Enforcement of Contact Order)* [2008] 2 FLR 1358, FD; *MA v DB (Inherent Jurisdiction)* [2011] 1 FLR 724, FD.

Article 42
Return of the child

1 The return of a child referred to in Article 40(1)(b) entailed by an enforceable judgment given in a Member State shall be recognised and enforceable in another Member State without the need for a declaration of enforceability and without any possibility of opposing its recognition if the judgment has been certified in the Member State of origin in accordance with paragraph 2.

Even if national law does not provide for enforceability by operation of law, notwithstanding any appeal, of a judgment requiring the return of the child mentioned in Article 11(b)(8), the court of origin may declare the judgment enforceable.

2 The judge of origin who delivered the judgment referred to in Article 40(1)(b) shall issue the certificate referred to in paragraph 1 only if:

(a) the child was given an opportunity to be heard, unless a hearing was considered inappropriate having regard to his or her age or degree of maturity;

(b) the parties were given an opportunity to be heard; and

(c) the court has taken into account in issuing its judgment the reasons for and evidence underlying the order issued pursuant to Article 13 of the 1980 Hague Convention.

In the event that the court or any other authority takes measures to ensure the protection of the child after its return to the State of habitual residence, the certificate shall contain details of such measures.

The judge of origin shall of his or her own motion issue that certificate using the standard form in Annex IV (certificate concerning return of the child(ren)).

The certificate shall be completed in the language of the judgment.

Defined terms—'judgment': Art 2.4; 'Member State': Art 2.3; 'Member State of origin': Art 2.5; 'court': Art 2.1; 'judge': Art 2.2.

Certificate—See *Re Rinau* [2008] 2 FLR 1495, ECJ (a certificate under Art 42 cannot be issued unless a judgment of non-return has been issued beforehand, even if that decision has been challenged). Enforcement of a certified judgment could not be refused in the enforcement state because of welfare concerns, which must be pleaded in the Member State of origin and which should also hear any application to suspend enforcement of its judgment.

'Opportunity to be heard'—The requirement to give the child and the parties an opportunity to be heard does not impose an obligation to do nothing until the child and/or the parents have been heard (*Re A (Custody Decision after Maltese Non-Return Order)* [2007] 1 FLR 1923, FD).

Article 43
Rectification of the certificate

1 The law of the Member State of origin shall be applicable to any rectification of the certificate.

2 No appeal shall lie against the issuing of a certificate pursuant to Articles 41(1) or 42(1).

Defined terms—'Member State of origin': Art 2.5.

Article 44
Effects of the certificate

The certificate shall take effect only within the limits of the enforceability of the judgment.

Defined terms—'judgment': Art 2.4.

Article 45
Documents

1 A party seeking enforcement of a judgment shall produce:

(a) a copy of the judgment which satisfies the conditions necessary to establish its authenticity; and

(b) the certificate referred to in Article 41(1) or Article 42(1).

2 For the purposes of this Article,

– the certificate referred to in Article 41(1) shall be accompanied by a translation of point 12 relating to the arrangements for exercising right of access,

– the certificate referred to in Article 42(1) shall be accompanied by a translation of its point 14 relating to the arrangements for implementing the measures taken to ensure the child's return.

The translation shall be into the official language or one of the official languages of the Member State of enforcement or any other language that the Member State of enforcement expressly accepts. The translation shall be certified by a person qualified to do so in one of the Member States.

Defined terms—'judgment': Art 2.4; rights of access': Art 2.10; 'Member State of enforcement': Art 2.6; 'Member State': Art 2.3.

Section 5
Authentic instruments and agreements

Article 46

Documents which have been formally drawn up or registered as authentic instruments and are enforceable in one Member State and also agreements between the parties that are enforceable in the Member State in which they were concluded shall be recognised and declared enforceable under the same conditions as judgments.

Defined terms—'Member State': Art 2.3; 'judgment': Art 2.4.

Section 6
Other provisions

Article 47
Enforcement procedure

1 The enforcement procedure is governed by the law of the Member State of enforcement.

2 Any judgment delivered by a court of another Member State and declared to be enforceable in accordance with Section 2 or certified in accordance with Article 41(1) or Article 42(1) shall be enforced in the Member State of enforcement in the same conditions as if it had been delivered in that Member State.

In particular, a judgment which has been certified according to Article 41(1) or Article 42(1) cannot be enforced if it is irreconcilable with a subsequent enforceable judgment.

Defined terms—'Member State': Art 2.3; 'judgment': Art 2.4; 'Member State of enforcement': Art 2.6.

'Subsequent enforceable judgment' (Art 47.2)—Art 47.2 is to be interpreted as meaning that a judgment delivered subsequently by a court in the enforcement state, awarding provisional custody rights, and deemed to be enforceable under the law of that state, could not preclude enforcement of a certified judgment delivered previously by the court with jurisdiction in the Member State of origin, ordering the return of the child (*Povse v Alpago* [2010] 2 FLR 1343, ECJ).

Article 48

Practical arrangements for the exercise of rights of access

1 The courts of the Member State of enforcement may make practical arrangements for organising the exercise of rights of access, if the necessary arrangements have not or have not sufficiently been made in the judgment delivered by the courts of the Member State having jurisdiction as to the substance of the matter and provided the essential elements of this judgment are respected.

2 The practical arrangements made pursuant to paragraph 1 shall cease to apply pursuant to a later judgment by the courts of the Member State having jurisdiction as to the substance of the matter.

Defined terms—'court': Art 2.1; 'Member State of enforcement': Art 2.6; 'Member State': Art 2.3; 'rights of access': Art 2.10; 'judgment': Art 2.4.

Scope—Article 48 provides that the courts of a Member State where access is to be enforced may make practical arrangements for organising access if not set out sufficiently or at all in the original order. Any arrangements made under Art 48 cease to apply if the courts of the Member State having jurisdiction as to the substance of the matter make a further order.

Article 49

Costs

The provisions of this Chapter, with the exception of Section 4, shall also apply to the determination of the amount of costs and expenses of proceedings under this Regulation and to the enforcement of any order concerning such costs and expenses.

Article 50

Legal aid

An applicant who, in the Member State of origin, has benefited from complete or partial legal aid or exemption from costs or expenses shall be entitled, in the procedures provided for in Articles 21, 28, 41, 42 and 48 to benefit from the most favourable legal aid or the most extensive exemption from costs and expenses provided for by the law of the Member State of enforcement.

Defined terms—'Member State of origin': Art 2.5; 'Member State of enforcement': Art 2.6.

Article 51

Security, bond or deposit

No security, bond or deposit, however described, shall be required of a party who in one Member State applies for enforcement of a judgment given in another Member State on the following grounds:

(a) that he or she is not habitually resident in the Member State in which enforcement is sought; or

(b) that he or she is either a foreign national or, where enforcement is sought in either the United Kingdom or Ireland, does not have his or her 'domicile' in either of those Member States.

Defined terms—'Member State': Art 2.3; 'judgment': Art 2.4.

Article 52

Legalisation or other similar formality

No legalisation or other similar formality shall be required in respect of the documents referred to in Articles 37, 38 and 45 or in respect of a document appointing a representative ad litem.

CHAPTER IV
COOPERATION BETWEEN CENTRAL AUTHORITIES IN MATTERS OF PARENTAL RESPONSIBILITY

Article 53
Designation

Each Member State shall designate one or more central authorities to assist with the application of this Regulation and shall specify the geographical or functional jurisdiction of each. Where a Member State has designated more than one central authority, communications shall normally be sent direct to the relevant central authority with jurisdiction. Where a communication is sent to a central authority without jurisdiction, the latter shall be responsible for forwarding it to the central authority with jurisdiction and informing the sender accordingly.

Defined terms—'Member State': Art 2.3.

Scope—Chapter IV (Arts 53–58) places the responsibility on Central Authorities in Member States to communicate requests for assistance by holders of parental responsibility and to facilitate international cooperation under Brussels IIA in the context of comity, information, child welfare and child protection. The International Child Abduction and Contact Unit (ICACU) is the Central Authority for England and Wales.

Article 54
General functions

The central authorities shall communicate information on national laws and procedures and take measures to improve the application of this Regulation and strengthening their cooperation. For this purpose the European Judicial Network in civil and commercial matters created by Decision No 2001/470/EC shall be used.

Article 55
Cooperation on cases specific to parental responsibility

The central authorities shall, upon request from a central authority of another Member State or from a holder of parental responsibility, cooperate on specific cases to achieve the purposes of this Regulation. To this end, they shall, acting directly or through public authorities or other bodies, take all appropriate steps in accordance with the law of that Member State in matters of personal data protection to:

- (a) collect and exchange information:
  - (i) on the situation of the child;
  - (ii) on any procedures under way; or
  - (iii) on decisions taken concerning the child;
- (b) provide information and assistance to holders of parental responsibility seeking the recognition and enforcement of decisions on their territory, in particular concerning rights of access and the return of the child;
- (c) facilitate communications between courts, in particular for the application of Article 11(6) and (7) and Article 15;
- (d) provide such information and assistance as is needed by courts to apply Article 56; and
- (e) facilitate agreement between holders of parental responsibility through mediation or other means, and facilitate cross-border cooperation to this end.

Defined terms—'Member State': Art 2.3; 'holder of parental responsibility': Art 2.8.

Scope—This Article contains important provisions for requests for information from Central Authorities in relation to parental responsibility. The Art 55 process is intended to work both ways (*Re E (Brussels II Revised: Vienna Convention: Reporting Restrictions)* [2014] 2 FLR 151, FD).

Article 56
Placement of a child in another Member State

1 Where a court having jurisdiction under Articles 8 to 15 contemplates the placement of a child in institutional care or with a foster family and where such placement is to take place in another

PART VI

Member State, it shall first consult the central authority or other authority having jurisdiction in the latter State where public authority intervention in that Member State is required for domestic cases of child placement.

2 The judgment on placement referred to in paragraph 1 may be made in the requesting State only if the competent authority of the requested State has consented to the placement.

3 The procedures for consultation or consent referred to in paragraphs 1 and 2 shall be governed by the national law of the requested State.

4 Where the authority having jurisdiction under Articles 8 to 15 decides to place the child in a foster family, and where such placement is to take place in another Member State and where no public authority intervention is required in the latter Member State for domestic cases of child placement, it shall so inform the central authority or other authority having jurisdiction in the latter State.

Defined terms—'court': Art 2.1; 'Member State': Art 2.3; 'judgment': Art 2.4.

Scope—This article permits the placement of a child in institutional care or with a foster family in another Member State following consultation with, and the consent of, the competent authority in the requested state. FPR 2010, r 31.17 provides that the court has a discretion to permit urgent enforcement where necessary to secure a child's welfare, notwithstanding the general position that enforcement is suspended pending expiry of the relevant appeal period. The amendment ensures compliance with the judgment of the CJEU in *Health Service Executive v SC and AC* [2012] 2 FLR 1040, CJEU, which determined that the possibility of appeals against a decision on registration of an order from another Member State under Brussels IIA should not result in automatic suspension of enforcement of a registered order during the time limit for appealing where the best interests of the child require enforcement as a matter of urgency. The amendment obviates the need to resort to Art 20 (provisional, including protective, measures). See also, *HSE Ireland v SF (A Minor)* [2012] 2 FLR 1131, FD.

'Placement of a child in institutional care or with a foster family' (Art 56.1)—The purpose of Art 56 is to require a court that is considering placing a child in institutional or foster care in another Member State to consult any authority responsible for child placements in that Member State and not to decide on any such placement without that authority's consent. Art 56 does not give a Member State an entitlement to call for the placement of a child within its jurisdiction (*Re AB (BIIR: Care Proceedings)* [2013] 1 FLR 168, CA; *Kent County Council v IS and others* [2014] 1 FLR 787, FD; *Re J and S (Children)* [2015] 1 FLR 850, FD).

'Institutional care' (Art 56.1)—Institutional care includes a placement in a secure care institution (*Health Service Executive v SC and AC* [2012] 2 FLR 1040, CJEU).

'Consented to the placement' (Art 56.2)—The consent must be given before the making of the judgment on the placement of the child by the competent authority and not merely by the institution where the child is to be placed (*Health Service Executive v SC and AC* [2012] 2 FLR 1040, CJEU). Where consent to the placement is given for a specified period of time, that consent does not apply to orders that are intended to extend the duration of the placement. In such circumstances, an application for a new consent must be made, together with a new declaration of enforceability under Art 28 (*Health Service Executive v SC and AC*, above).

Article 57
Working method

1 Any holder of parental responsibility may submit, to the central authority of the Member State of his or her habitual residence or to the central authority of the Member State where the child is habitually resident or present, a request for assistance as mentioned in Article 55. In general, the request shall include all available information of relevance to its enforcement. Where the request for assistance concerns the recognition or enforcement of a judgment on parental responsibility that falls within the scope of this Regulation, the holder of parental responsibility shall attach the relevant certificates provided for in Articles 39, 41(1) or 42(1).

2 Member States shall communicate to the Commission the official language or languages of the Community institutions other than their own in which communications to the central authorities can be accepted.

3 The assistance provided by the central authorities pursuant to Article 55 shall be free of charge.

4 Each central authority shall bear its own costs.

Defined terms—'holder of parental responsibility': Art 2.8; 'Member State': Art 2.3.

Article 58
Meetings

1 In order to facilitate the application of this Regulation, central authorities shall meet regularly.
2 These meetings shall be convened in compliance with Decision No 2001/470/EC establishing a European Judicial Network in civil and commercial matters.

CHAPTER V
RELATIONS WITH OTHER INSTRUMENTS

Article 59
Relation with other instruments

1 Subject to the provisions of Articles 60, 63, 64 and paragraph 2 of this Article, this Regulation shall, for the Member States, supersede conventions existing at the time of entry into force of this Regulation which have been concluded between two or more Member States and relate to matters governed by this Regulation.

2 (a) Finland and Sweden shall have the option of declaring that the Convention of 6 February 1931 between Denmark, Finland, Iceland, Norway and Sweden comprising international private law provisions on marriage, adoption and guardianship, together with the Final Protocol thereto, will apply, in whole or in part, in their mutual relations, in place of the rules of this Regulation. Such declarations shall be annexed to this Regulation and published in the Official Journal of the European Union. They may be withdrawn, in whole or in part, at any moment by the said Member States.
(b) The principle of non-discrimination on the grounds of nationality between citizens of the Union shall be respected.
(c) The rules of jurisdiction in any future agreement to be concluded between the Member States referred to in subparagraph (a) which relate to matters governed by this Regulation shall be in line with those laid down in this Regulation.
(d) Judgments handed down in any of the Nordic States which have made the declaration provided for in subparagraph (a) under a forum of jurisdiction corresponding to one of those laid down in Chapter II of this Regulation, shall be recognised and enforced in the other Member States under the rules laid down in Chapter III of this Regulation.

3 Member States shall send to the Commission:

(a) a copy of the agreements and uniform laws implementing these agreements referred to in paragraph 2(a) and (c);
(b) any denunciations of, or amendments to, those agreements or uniform laws.

Defined terms—'Member State': Art 2.3; 'judgment': Art 2.4.

Article 60
Relations with certain multilateral conventions

In relations between Member States, this Regulation shall take precedence over the following Conventions in so far as they concern matters governed by this Regulation:

(a) the Hague Convention of 5 October 1961 concerning the Powers of Authorities and the Law Applicable in respect of the Protection of Minors;
(b) the Luxembourg Convention of 8 September 1967 on the Recognition of Decisions Relating to the Validity of Marriages;
(c) the Hague Convention of 1 June 1970 on the Recognition of Divorces and Legal Separations;
(d) the European Convention of 20 May 1980 on Recognition and Enforcement of Decisions concerning Custody of Children and on Restoration of Custody of Children; and

(e) the Hague Convention of 25 October 1980 on the Civil Aspects of International Child Abduction.

Defined terms—'Member State': Art 2.3.
'Precedence'—For an example of the precedence accorded to Brussels IIA over the Hague Convention, see *ET v TZ (Recognition and Enforcement of Foreign Residence Order)* [2014] 2 FLR 373, FD. See, further, *Re A (A Child)* [2016] EWCA Civ 572, at [30].

Article 61

Relation with the Hague Convention of 19 October 1996 on Jurisdiction, Applicable law, Recognition, Enforcement and Cooperation in Respect of Parental Responsibility and Measures for the Protection of Children

As concerns the relation with the Hague Convention of 19 October 1996 on Jurisdiction, Applicable law, Recognition, Enforcement and Cooperation in Respect of Parental Responsibility and Measures for the Protection of Children, this Regulation shall apply:

(a) where the child concerned has his or her habitual residence on the territory of a Member State;

(b) as concerns the recognition and enforcement of a judgment given in a court of a Member State on the territory of another Member State, even if the child concerned has his or her habitual residence on the territory of a third State which is a contracting Party to the said Convention.

Defined terms—'Member State': Art 2.3.

Article 62
Scope of effects

1 The agreements and conventions referred to in Articles 59(1), 60 and 61 shall continue to have effect in relation to matters not governed by this Regulation.
2 The conventions mentioned in Article 60, in particular the 1980 Hague Convention, continue to produce effects between the Member States which are party thereto, in compliance with Article 60.

Defined terms—'Member State': Art 2.3.
Case-law—See *Re A (A Child)* [2016] EWCA Civ 572, at [30].

Article 63
Treaties with the Holy See

1 This Regulation shall apply without prejudice to the International Treaty (Concordat) between the Holy See and Portugal, signed at the Vatican City on 7 May 1940.

2 Any decision as to the invalidity of a marriage taken under the Treaty referred to in paragraph 1 shall be recognised in the Member States on the conditions laid down in Chapter III, Section 1.

3 The provisions laid down in paragraphs 1 and 2 shall also apply to the following international treaties (Concordats) with the Holy See:

(a) 'Concordato lateranense' of 11 February 1929 between Italy and the Holy See, modified by the agreement, with additional Protocol signed in Rome on 18 February 1984;
(b) Agreement between the Holy See and Spain on legal affairs of 3 January 1979.
(c) Agreement between the Holy See and Malta on the recognition of civil effects to canonical marriages and to decisions of ecclesiastical authorities and tribunals on those marriages of 3 February 1993, including the Protocol of application of the same date, with the second Additional Protocol of 6 January 1995.

4 Recognition of the decisions provided for in paragraph 2 may, in Spain, Italy or Malta, be subject to the same procedures and the same checks as are applicable to decisions of the ecclesiastical courts handed down in accordance with the international treaties concluded with the Holy See referred to in paragraph 3.

5 Member States shall send to the Commission:

(a) a copy of the Treaties referred to in paragraphs 1 and 3;
(b) any denunciations of or amendments to those Treaties.

Defined terms—'Member State': Art 2.3.

CHAPTER VI
TRANSITIONAL PROVISIONS

Article 64

1 The provisions of this Regulation shall apply only to legal proceedings instituted, to documents formally drawn up or registered as authentic instruments and to agreements concluded between the parties after its date of application in accordance with Article 72.

2 Judgments given after the date of application of this Regulation in proceedings instituted before that date but after the date of entry into force of Regulation (EC) No 1347/2000 shall be recognised and enforced in accordance with the provisions of Chapter III of this Regulation if jurisdiction was founded on rules which accorded with those provided for either in Chapter II or in Regulation (EC) No 1347/2000 or in a convention concluded between the Member State of origin and the Member State addressed which was in force when the proceedings were instituted.

3 Judgments given before the date of application of this Regulation in proceedings instituted after the entry into force of Regulation (EC) No 1347/2000 shall be recognised and enforced in accordance with the provisions of Chapter III of this Regulation provided they relate to divorce, legal separation or marriage annulment or parental responsibility for the children of both spouses on the occasion of these matrimonial proceedings.

4 Judgments given before the date of application of this Regulation but after the date of entry into force of Regulation (EC) No 1347/2000 in proceedings instituted before the date of entry into force of Regulation (EC) No 1347/2000 shall be recognised and enforced in accordance with the provisions of Chapter III of this Regulation provided they relate to divorce, legal separation or marriage annulment or parental responsibility for the children of both spouses on the occasion of these matrimonial proceedings and that jurisdiction was founded on rules which accorded with those provided for either in Chapter II of this Regulation or in Regulation (EC) No 1347/2000 or in a convention concluded between the Member State of origin and the Member State addressed which was in force when the proceedings were instituted.

Defined terms—'judgment': Art 2.4; 'Member State of origin': Art 2.5; 'Member State': Art 2.3; 'parental responsibility': Art 2.7.

CHAPTER VII
FINAL PROVISIONS

Article 65
Review

No later than 1 January 2012, and every five years thereafter, the Commission shall present to the European Parliament, to the Council and to the European Economic and Social Committee a report on the application of this Regulation on the basis of information supplied by the Member States. The report shall be accompanied if need be by proposals for adaptations.

Defined terms—'Member State': Art 2.3.

Article 66
Member States with two or more legal systems

With regard to a Member State in which two or more systems of law or sets of rules concerning matters governed by this Regulation apply in different territorial units:

(a) any reference to habitual residence in that Member State shall refer to habitual residence in a territorial unit;

(b) any reference to nationality, or in the case of the United Kingdom 'domicile', shall refer to the territorial unit designated by the law of that State;
(c) any reference to the authority of a Member State shall refer to the authority of a territorial unit within that State which is concerned;
(d) any reference to the rules of the requested Member State shall refer to the rules of the territorial unit in which jurisdiction, recognition or enforcement is invoked.

Defined terms—'Member State': Art 2.3.

Article 67
Information on central authorities and languages accepted

The Member States shall communicate to the Commission within three months following the entry into force of this Regulation:

(a) the names, addresses and means of communication for the central authorities designated pursuant to Article 53;
(b) the languages accepted for communications to central authorities pursuant to Article 57(2); and
(c) the languages accepted for the certificate concerning rights of access pursuant to Article 45(2).

The Member States shall communicate to the Commission any changes to this information.

The Commission shall make this information publicly available.

Defined terms—'Member State': Art 2.3.

Article 68
Information relating to courts and redress procedures

The Member States shall notify to the Commission the lists of courts and redress procedures referred to in Articles 21, 29, 33 and 34 and any amendments thereto.

The Commission shall update this information and make it publicly available through the publication in the Official Journal of the European Union and any other appropriate means.

Defined terms—'Member State': Art 2.3.

'Lists of courts'—It is not open to an English court to depart from the court designations incorporated within the lists attached to Art 68 (*Re S (Foreign Contact Order)* [2010] 1 FLR 982, CA). See, also, *Re D (A Child) (Supreme Court: Jurisdiction)* [2016] 2 FLR 379, SC.

Article 69
Amendments to the Annexes

Any amendments to the standard forms in Annexes I to IV shall be adopted in accordance with the consultative procedure set out in Article 70(2).

Article 70
Committee

1 The Commission shall be assisted by a committee (committee).

2 Where reference is made to this paragraph, Articles 3 and 7 of Decision 1999/468/EC shall apply.

3 The committee shall adopt its rules of procedure.

Article 71
Repeal of Regulation (EC) No 1347/2000

1 Regulation (EC) No 1347/2000 shall be repealed as from the date of application of this Regulation.

2 Any reference to Regulation (EC) No 1347/2000 shall be construed as a reference to this Regulation according to the comparative table in Annex V.

Article 72
Entry into force

This Regulation shall enter into force on 1 August 2004.

The Regulation shall apply from 1 March 2005, with the exception of Articles 67, 68, 69 and 70, which shall apply from 1 August 2004.

This Regulation shall be binding in its entirety and directly applicable in the Member States in accordance with the Treaty establishing the European Community.

Done at Brussels, 27 November 2003.

For the Council

The President

R. CASTELLI

ANNEX I
CERTIFICATE REFERRED TO IN ARTICLE 39 CONCERNING JUDGMENTS IN MATRIMONIAL MATTERS[1]

1 Member State of origin

2 Court or authority issuing the certificate

- 2.1 Name
- 2.2 Address
- 2.3 Tel./fax/e-mail

3 Marriage

- 3.1 Wife
  - 3.1.1 Full name
  - 3.1.2 Address
  - 3.1.3 Country and place of birth
  - 3.1.4 Date of birth
- 3.2 Husband
  - 3.2.1 Full name
  - 3.2.2 Address
  - 3.2.3 Country and place of birth
  - 3.2.4 Date of birth
- 3.3 Country, place (where available) and date of marriage
  - 3.3.1 Country of marriage
  - 3.3.2 Place of marriage (where available)
  - 3.3.3 Date of marriage

4 Court which delivered the judgment

- 4.1 Name of Court
- 4.2 Place of Court

5 Judgment

- 5.1 Date
- 5.2 Reference number
- 5.3 Type of judgment
  - 5.3.1 Divorce
  - 5.3.2 Marriage annulment
  - 5.3.3 Legal separation
- 5.4 Was the judgment given in default of appearance?
  - 5.4.1 No
  - 5.4.2 Yes[2]

6 Names of parties to whom legal aid has been granted

PART VI

7 Is the judgment subject to further appeal under the law of the Member State of origin?

7.1 No
7.2 Yes

8 Date of legal effect in the Member State where the judgment was given

8.1 Divorce
8.2 Legal separation

Done at . . ., date . . .

Signature and/or stamp

1 Council Regulation (EC) No 2201/2003 of 27 November 2003 concerning jurisdiction and the recognition and enforcement of judgments in matrimonial matters and the matters of parental responsibility, repealing Regulation (EC) No 1347/2000.
2 Documents referred to in Article 37(2) must be attached.

ANNEX II

CERTIFICATE REFERRED TO IN ARTICLE 39 CONCERNING JUDGMENTS ON PARENTAL RESPONSIBILITY[1]

1 Member State of origin

2 Court or authority issuing the certificate

2.1 Name
2.2 Address
2.3 Tel./Fax/e-mail

3 Person(s) with rights of access

3.1 Full name
3.2 Address
3.3 Date and place of birth (where available)

4 Holders of parental responsibility other than those mentioned under 3[2]

4.1 4.1.1 Full name
4.1.2 Address
4.1.3 Date and place of birth (where available)
4.2 4.2.1 Full Name
4.2.2 Address
4.2.3 Date and place of birth (where available)
4.3 4.3.1 Full name
4.3.2 Address
4.3.3 Date and place of birth (where available)

5 Court which delivered the judgment

5.1 Name of Court
5.2 Place of Court

6 Judgment

6.1 Date
6.2 Reference number
6.3 Was the judgment given in default of appearance?
6.3.1 No
6.3.2 Yes[3]

7 Children who are covered by the judgment[4]

7.1 Full name and date of birth
7.2 Full name and date of birth
7.3 Full name and date of birth
7.4 Full name and date of birth

8 Names of parties to whom legal aid has been granted

9 Attestation of enforceability and service

9.1 Is the judgment enforceable according to the law of the Member State of origin?
 9.1.1 Yes
 9.1.2 No
9.2 Has the judgment been served on the party against whom enforcement is sought?
 9.2.1 Yes
  9.2.1.1 Full name of the party
  9.2.1.2 Address
  9.2.1.3 Date of service
 9.2.2 No

10 Specific information on judgments on rights of access where 'exequatur' is requested under Article 28. This possibility is foreseen in Article 40(2).

10.1 Practical arrangements for exercise of rights of access (to the extent stated in the judgment)
 10.1.1 Date and time
  10.1.1.1 Start
  10.1.1.2 End
 10.1.2 Place
 10.1.3 Specific obligations on holders of parental responsibility
 10.1.4 Specific obligations on the person with right of access
 10.1.5 Any restrictions attached to the exercise of rights of access

11 Specific information for judgments on the return of the child in cases where the 'exequatur' procedure is requested under Article 28. This possibility is foreseen under Article 40(2).

11.1 The judgment entails the return of the child
11.2 Person to whom the child is to be returned (to the extent stated in the judgment)
 11.2.1 Full name
 11.2.2 Address

Done at . . ., date . . ..

Signature and/or stamp

1 Council Regulation (EC) No 2201/2003 of 27 November 2003 concerning jurisdiction and the recognition and enforcement of judgments in matrimonial matters and the matters of parental responsibility, repealing Regulation (EC) No 1347/2000.
2 In cases of joint custody, a person already mentioned under item 3 may also be mentioned under item 4.
3 Documents referred to in Article 37(2) must be attached.
4 If more than four children are covered, use a second form.

ANNEX III

CERTIFICATE REFERRED TO IN ARTICLE 41(1) CONCERNING JUDGMENTS ON RIGHTS OF ACCESS[1]

1 Member State of origin

2 Court or authority issuing the certificate

2.1 Name
2.2 Address
2.3 Tel./fax/e-mail

3 Person(s) with rights of access

3.1 Full name
3.2 Address
3.3 Date and place of birth (where available)

4 Holders of parental responsibility other than those mentioned under 3[2,3]

4.1 4.1.1 Full name
4.1.2 Address
4.1.3 Date and place of birth (where available)

4.2 4.2.1 Full name
4.2.2 Address
4.2.3 Date and place of birth (where available)

4.3 Other
4.3.1 Full name
4.3.2 Address
4.3.3 Date and place of birth (where available)

5 Court which delivered the judgment

5.1 Name of Court
5.2 Place of Court

6 Judgment

6.1 Date
6.2 Reference number

7 Children who are covered by the judgment[4]

7.1 Full name and date of birth
7.2 Full name and date of birth
7.3 Full name and date of birth
7.4 Full name and date of birth

8 Is the judgment enforceable in the Member State of origin?

8.1 Yes
8.2 No

9 Where the judgment was given in default of appearance, the person defaulting was served with the document which instituted the proceedings or with an equivalent document in sufficient time and in such a way as to enable that person to arrange for his or her defence, or the person has been served with the document but not in compliance with these conditions, it is nevertheless established that he or she accepted the decision unequivocally

10 All parties concerned were given an opportunity to be heard

11 The children were given an opportunity to be heard, unless a hearing was considered inappropriate having regard to their age or degree of maturity

12 Practical arrangements for exercise of rights of access (to the extent stated in the judgment)

12.1 Date and time
12.1.1 Start
12.1.2 End
12.2 Place
12.3 Specific obligations on holders of parental responsibility
12.4 Specific obligations on the person with right of access
12.5 Any restrictions attached to the exercise of rights of access

13 Names of parties to whom legal aid has been granted

Done at . . ., date . . ..

Signature and/or stamp

1 Council Regulation (EC) No 2201/2003 of 27 November 2003 concerning jurisdiction and the recognition and enforcement of judgments in matrimonial matters and the matters of parental responsibility, repealing Regulation (EC) No 1347/2000.
2 In cases of joint custody, a person already mentioned under item 3 may also be mentioned in item 4.
3 Please put a cross in the box corresponding to the person against whom the judgment should be enforced.
4 If more than four children are concerned, use a second form.

ANNEX IV
CERTIFICATE REFERRED TO IN ARTICLE 42(1) CONCERNING THE RETURN OF THE CHILD[1]

1 Member State of origin

2 Court or authority issuing the certificate

2.1 Name
2.2 Address
2.3 Tel./fax/e-mail

3 Person to whom the child has to be returned (to the extent stated in the judgment)

3.1 Full name
3.2 Address
3.3 Date and place of birth (where available)

4 Holders of parental responsibility[2]

4.1 Mother
4.1.1 Full name
4.1.2 Address (where available)
4.1.3 Date and place of birth (where available)
4.2 Father
4.2.1 Full name
4.2.2 Address (where available)
4.2.3 Date and place of birth (where available)
4.3 Other
4.3.1 Full name
4.3.2 Address (where available)
4.3.3 Date and place of birth (where available)

5 Respondent (where available)

5.1 Full name
5.2 Address (where available)

6 Court which delivered the judgment

6.1 Name of Court
6.2 Place of Court

7 Judgment

7.1 Date
7.2 Reference number

8 Children who are covered by the judgment[3]

8.1 Full name and date of birth
8.2 Full name and date of birth
8.3 Full name and date of birth
8.4 Full name and date of birth

9 The judgment entails the return of the child

10 Is the judgment enforceable in the Member State of origin?

10.1 Yes
10.2 No

11 The children were given an opportunity to be heard, unless a hearing was considered inappropriate having regard to their age or degree of maturity

12 The parties were given an opportunity to be heard

PART VI

13 The judgment entails the return of the children and the court has taken into account in issuing its judgment the reasons for and evidence underlying the decision issued pursuant to Article 13 of the Hague Convention of 25 October 1980 on the Civil Aspects of International Child Abduction

14 Where applicable, details of measures taken by courts or authorities to ensure the protection of the child after its return to the Member State of habitual residence

15 Names of parties to whom legal aid has been granted

Done at . . ., date . . ..

Signature and/or stamp

1 Council Regulation (EC) No 2201 of 27 November 2003 concerning jurisdiction and the recognition and enforcement of judgments in matrimonial matters and the matters of parental responsibility, repealing Regulation (EC) No 1347/2000.

2 This item is optional.

3 If more than four children are covered, use a second form.

ANNEX V
COMPARATIVE TABLE WITH REGULATION (EC) NO 1347/2000

Articles repealed	Corresponding Articles of new text	Articles repealed	Corresponding Articles of new text
1	1, 2	27	34
2	3	28	35
3	12	29	36
4		30	50
5	4	31	51
6	5	32	37
7	6	33	39
8	7	34	38
9	17	35	52
10	18	36	59
11	16, 19	37	60, 61
12	20	38	62
13	2, 49, 46	39	
14	21	40	63
15	22, 23	41	66
16		42	64
17	24	43	65
18	25	44	68, 69
19	26	45	70
20	27	46	72
21	28	Annex I	68
22	21, 29	Annex II	68
23	30	Annex III	68
24	31	Annex IV	Annex I
25	32	Annex V	Annex II
26	33		

ANNEX VI

DECLARATIONS BY SWEDEN AND FINLAND PURSUANT TO ARTICLE 59(2)(A) OF THE COUNCIL REGULATION CONCERNING JURISDICTION AND THE RECOGNITION AND ENFORCEMENT OF JUDGMENTS IN MATRIMONIAL MATTERS AND MATTERS OF PARENTAL RESPONSIBILITY, REPEALING REGULATION (EC) NO 1347/2000.

Declaration by Sweden:

Pursuant to Article 59(2)(a) of the Council Regulation concerning jurisdiction and the recognition and enforcement of judgments in matrimonial matters and matters of parental responsibility, repealing Regulation (EC) No 1347/2000, Sweden hereby declares that the Convention of 6 February 1931 between Denmark, Finland, Iceland, Norway and Sweden comprising international private law provisions on marriage, adoption and guardianship, together with the Final Protocol thereto, will apply in full in relations between Sweden and Finland, in place of the rules of the Regulation.

Declaration by Finland:

Pursuant to Article 59(2)(a) of the Council Regulation concerning jurisdiction and the recognition and enforcement of judgments in matrimonial matters and matters of parental responsibility, repealing Regulation (EC) No 1347/2000, Finland hereby declares that the Convention of 6 February 1931 between Finland, Denmark, Iceland, Norway and Sweden comprising international private law provisions on marriage, adoption and guardianship, together with the Final Protocol thereto, will apply in full in relations between Finland and Sweden, in place of the rules of the Regulation.

Date:

Signature and/or stamp:

Council Regulation (EC) No 805/2004

of 21 April 2004

creating a European Enforcement Order for uncontested claims

Scope—The European Enforcement Order (EEO) came into force on 21 October 2005 and applies to uncontested judgments, court settlements and authentic instruments made after 21 January 2005. The EEO is not concerned exclusively with family law obligations. The EEO has been replaced by the Maintenance Regulation, except where the maintenance obligations arise in a Member State not bound by the 2007 Hague Protocol (i e the UK and Denmark) (Maintenance Regulation, Art 68.2). (See, further, the annotations to the Maintenance Regulation, Art 68.2.) However, the EEO does not apply to Denmark (Recital 25 and Art 2.3). Subject to these limitations, the EEO provides a simpler method of reciprocal enforcement than the Maintenance Regulation for English outgoing consent maintenance orders, which require registration to become enforceable under the simplified exequatur procedure for Member States not bound by the 2007 Hague Protocol.

The recipient of an uncontested maintenance obligation in the Member State of origin may apply for an EEO certificate from their domestic court, which allows the judgment to be transferred to another Member State for enforcement. It is unnecessary to obtain a declaration of enforceability under the exequatur procedure (Art 5). Art 6 sets out the conditions required for certification. Disputes regarding the EEO certificate are dealt with in the court of origin and not the enforcing jurisdiction (Art 10). However, the maintenance creditor is limited to the methods of enforcement available in the enforcing jurisdiction (Art 20.1). The definition of 'uncontested' is found in Art 3. Where the maintenance claim is contested, the Maintenance Regulation applies as between Member States. A 'claim' is defined by Art 4.2 as a claim for payment of a specific sum of money that has fallen due or for which the due date is indicated in the judgment. A claim therefore could encompass not only a maintenance order but also lump sum orders or property adjustment orders by way of capitalised maintenance (see annotations to the Maintenance Regulation). The EEO does not apply to rights in property arising out of a matrimonial relationship (Art 2.2(a)). It does apply to orders for costs (Art 7), claims under CA 1989, Sch 1 and child maintenance calculations by the CMS. Owing to different procedural requirements between Member States (particularly in relation to service), Chapter III of the EEO lays down minimum standards for uncontested claims procedure.

The Annexes to the EEO, which contain a series of standard forms, were replaced by the Commission Regulation (EC) No 1869/2005 of 16 November 2005.

Chapter I (Arts 1–4) deals with subject matter, scope and definitions.
Chapter II (Arts 5–11) sets out the requirements for an EEO.
Chapter III (Arts 12–19) deals with the minimum standards for uncontested claims procedures.
Chapter IV (Arts 20–23) deals with enforcement.
Chapter V (Arts 24–25) deals with court settlements and authentic instruments.
Chapter VI (Art 26) deals with transitional provision.
Chapter VII (Arts 27–28) deals with the relationship with other community instruments.

Chapter VIII (Arts 29–33) contains general and final provisions.

The procedural requirements are regulated by CPR 1998, rr 74.27–74.33 and PD74B. See Procedural Guide C1(15).

THE EUROPEAN PARLIAMENT AND THE COUNCIL OF THE EUROPEAN UNION,

Having regard to the Treaty establishing the European Community, and in particular Articles 61(c) and the second indent of Article 67(5) thereof,

Having regard to the proposal from the Commission,

Having regard to the Opinion of the European Economic and Social Committee,

Acting in accordance with the procedure laid down in Article 251 of the Treaty,

Whereas:

(1) The Community has set itself the objective of maintaining and developing an area of freedom, security and justice, in which the free movement of persons is ensured. To this end, the Community is to adopt, inter alia, measures in the field of judicial cooperation in civil matters that are necessary for the proper functioning of the internal market.

(2) On 3 December 1998, the Council adopted an Action Plan of the Council and the Commission on how best to implement the provisions of the Treaty of Amsterdam on an area of freedom, security and justice (the Vienna Action Plan).

(3) The European Council meeting in Tampere on 15 and 16 October 1999 endorsed the principle of mutual recognition of judicial decisions as the cornerstone for the creation of a genuine judicial area.

(4) On 30 November 2000, the Council adopted a programme of measures for implementation of the principle of mutual recognition of decisions in civil and commercial matters. This programme includes in its first stage the abolition of exequatur, that is to say, the creation of a European Enforcement Order for uncontested claims.

(5) The concept of 'uncontested claims' should cover all situations in which a creditor, given the verified absence of any dispute by the debtor as to the nature or extent of a pecuniary claim, has obtained either a court decision against that debtor or an enforceable document that requires the debtor's express consent, be it a court settlement or an authentic instrument.

(6) The absence of objections from the debtor as stipulated in Article 3(1)(b) can take the shape of default of appearance at a court hearing or of failure to comply with an invitation by the court to give written notice of an intention to defend the case.

(7) This Regulation should apply to judgments, court settlements and authentic instruments on uncontested claims and to decisions delivered following challenges to judgments, court settlements and authentic instruments certified as European Enforcement Orders.

(8) In its Tampere conclusions, the European Council considered that access to enforcement in a Member State other than that in which the judgment has been given should be accelerated and simplified by dispensing with any intermediate measures to be taken prior to enforcement in the Member State in which enforcement is sought. A judgment that has been certified as a European Enforcement Order by the court of origin should, for enforcement purposes, be treated as if it had been delivered in the Member State in which enforcement is sought. In the United Kingdom, for example, the registration of a certified foreign judgment will therefore follow the same rules as the registration of a judgment from another part of the United Kingdom and is not to imply a review as to the substance of the foreign judgment. Arrangements for the enforcement of judgments should continue to be governed by national law.

PART VI

(9) Such a procedure should offer significant advantages as compared with the exequatur procedure provided for in Council Regulation (EC) No 44/2001 of 22 December 2000 on jurisdiction and the recognition and enforcement of judgments in civil and commercial matters, in that there is no need for approval by the judiciary in a second Member State with the delays and expenses that this entails.

(10) Where a court in a Member State has given judgment on an uncontested claim in the absence of participation of the debtor in the proceedings, the abolition of any checks in the Member State of enforcement is inextricably linked to and dependent upon the existence of a sufficient guarantee of observance of the rights of the defence.

(11) This Regulation seeks to promote the fundamental rights and takes into account the principles recognised in particular by the Charter of Fundamental Rights of the European Union. In particular, it seeks to ensure full respect for the right to a fair trial as recognised in Article 47 of the Charter.

(12) Minimum standards should be established for the proceedings leading to the judgment in order to ensure that the debtor is informed about the court action against him, the requirements for his active participation in the proceedings to contest the claim and the consequences of his non-participation in sufficient time and in such a way as to enable him to arrange for his defence.

(13) Due to differences between the Member States as regards the rules of civil procedure and especially those governing the service of documents, it is necessary to lay down a specific and detailed definition of those minimum standards. In particular, any method of service that is based on a legal fiction as regards the fulfilment of those minimum standards cannot be considered sufficient for the certification of a judgment as a European Enforcement Order.

(14) All the methods of service listed in Articles 13 and 14 are characterised by either full certainty (Article 13) or a very high degree of likelihood (Article 14) that the document served has reached its addressee. In the second category, a judgment should only be certified as a European Enforcement Order if the Member State of origin has an appropriate mechanism in place enabling the debtor to apply for a full review of the judgment under the conditions set out in Article 19 in those exceptional cases where, in spite of compliance with Article 14, the document has not reached the addressee.

(15) Personal service on certain persons other than the debtor himself pursuant to Article 14(1)(a) and (b) should be understood to meet the requirements of those provisions only if those persons actually accepted/received the document in question.

(16) Article 15 should apply to situations where the debtor cannot represent himself in court, as in the case of a legal person, and where a person to represent him is determined by law as well as situations where the debtor has authorised another person, in particular a lawyer, to represent him in the specific court proceedings at issue.

(17) The courts competent for scrutinising full compliance with the minimum procedural standards should, if satisfied, issue a standardised European Enforcement Order certificate that makes that scrutiny and its result transparent.

(18) Mutual trust in the administration of justice in the Member States justifies the assessment by the court of one Member State that all conditions for certification as a European Enforcement Order are fulfilled to enable a judgment to be enforced in all other Member States without judicial review of the proper application of the minimum procedural standards in the Member State where the judgment is to be enforced.

(19) This Regulation does not imply an obligation for the Member States to adapt their national legislation to the minimum procedural standards set out herein. It provides an incentive to that end by making available a more efficient and rapid enforceability of judgments in other Member States only if those minimum standards are met.

(20) Application for certification as a European Enforcement Order for uncontested claims should be optional for the creditor, who may instead choose the system of recognition and enforcement under Regulation (EC) No 44/2001 or other Community instruments.

(21) When a document has to be sent from one Member State to another for service there, this Regulation and in particular the rules on service set out herein should apply together with Council Regulation (EC) No 1348/2000 of 29 May 2000 on the service in the Member States of judicial and extrajudicial documents in civil or commercial matters, and in particular Article 14 thereof in conjunction with Member States declarations made under Article 23 thereof.

(22) Since the objectives of the proposed action cannot be sufficiently achieved by the Member States and can therefore, by reason of the scale or effects of the action, be better achieved at Community level, the Community may adopt measures, in accordance with the principle of subsidiarity as set out in Article 5 of the Treaty. In accordance with the principle of proportionality, as set out in that Article, this Regulation does not go beyond what is necessary in order to achieve those objectives.

(23) The measures necessary for the implementation of this Regulation should be adopted in accordance with Council Decision 1999/468/EC of 28 June 1999 laying down the procedures for the exercise of implementing powers conferred on the Commission.

(24) In accordance with Article 3 of the Protocol on the position of the United Kingdom and Ireland annexed to the Treaty on European Union and the Treaty establishing the European Community, the United Kingdom and Ireland have notified their wish to take part in the adoption and application of this Regulation.

(25) In accordance with Articles 1 and 2 of the Protocol on the position of Denmark annexed to the Treaty on European Union and the Treaty establishing the European Community, Denmark does not take part in the adoption of this Regulation, and is therefore not bound by it or subject to its application.

(26) Pursuant to the second indent of Article 67(5) of the Treaty, the codecision procedure is applicable from 1 February 2003 for the measures laid down in this Regulation,

HAVE ADOPTED THIS REGULATION:

Note—The EC Treaty has become the Treaty on the Functioning of the European Union (TFEU) and the Articles have been re-numbered: Art 251 is now Art 294 TFEU.

CHAPTER I
SUBJECT MATTER, SCOPE AND DEFINITIONS

Article 1
Subject matter

The purpose of this Regulation is to create a European Enforcement Order for uncontested claims to permit, by laying down minimum standards, the free circulation of judgments, court settlements and authentic instruments throughout all Member States without any intermediate proceedings needing to be brought in the Member State of enforcement prior to recognition and enforcement.

Article 2
Scope

1 This Regulation shall apply in civil and commercial matters, whatever the nature of the court or tribunal. It shall not extend, in particular, to revenue, customs or administrative matters or the liability of the State for acts and omissions in the exercise of State authority ('acta iure imperii').

2 This Regulation shall not apply to:

(a) the status or legal capacity of natural persons, rights in property arising out of a matrimonial relationship, wills and succession;
(b) bankruptcy, proceedings relating to the winding-up of insolvent companies or other legal persons, judicial arrangements, compositions and analogous proceedings;
(c) social security;
(d) arbitration.

3 In this Regulation, the term 'Member State' shall mean Member States with the exception of Denmark.

Article 3
Enforcement titles to be certified as a European Enforcement Order

1 This Regulation shall apply to judgments, court settlements and authentic instruments on uncontested claims.

A claim shall be regarded as uncontested if:

(a) the debtor has expressly agreed to it by admission or by means of a settlement which has been approved by a court or concluded before a court in the course of proceedings; or

(b) the debtor has never objected to it, in compliance with the relevant procedural requirements under the law of the Member State of origin, in the course of the court proceedings; or

(c) the debtor has not appeared or been represented at a court hearing regarding that claim after having initially objected to the claim in the course of the court proceedings, provided that such conduct amounts to a tacit admission of the claim or of the facts alleged by the creditor under the law of the Member State of origin; or

(d) the debtor has expressly agreed to it in an authentic instrument.

2 This Regulation shall also apply to decisions delivered following challenges to judgments, court settlements or authentic instruments certified as European Enforcement Orders.

Article 4
Definitions

For the purposes of this Regulation, the following definitions shall apply:

1 'judgment': any judgment given by a court or tribunal of a Member State, whatever the judgment may be called, including a decree, order, decision or writ of execution, as well as the determination of costs or expenses by an officer of the court;

2 'claim': a claim for payment of a specific sum of money that has fallen due or for which the due date is indicated in the judgment, court settlement or authentic instrument;

3 'authentic instrument':

(a) a document which has been formally drawn up or registered as an authentic instrument, and the authenticity of which:

(i) relates to the signature and the content of the instrument; and

(ii) has been established by a public authority or other authority empowered for that purpose by the Member State in which it originates;

or

(b) an arrangement relating to maintenance obligations concluded with administrative authorities or authenticated by them;

4 'Member State of origin': the Member State in which the judgment has been given, the court settlement has been approved or concluded or the authentic instrument has been drawn up or registered, and is to be certified as a European Enforcement Order;

5 'Member State of enforcement': the Member State in which enforcement of the judgment, court settlement or authentic instrument certified as a European Enforcement Order is sought;

6 'court of origin': the court or tribunal seised of the proceedings at the time of fulfilment of the conditions set out in Article 3(1)(a), (b) or (c);

7 in Sweden, in summary proceedings concerning orders to pay (*betalningsföreläggande*), the expression 'court' includes the Swedish enforcement service (*kronofogdemyndighet*).

CHAPTER II
EUROPEAN ENFORCEMENT ORDER

Article 5
Abolition of exequatur

A judgment which has been certified as a European Enforcement Order in the Member State of origin shall be recognised and enforced in the other Member States without the need for a declaration of enforceability and without any possibility of opposing its recognition.

Article 6
Requirements for certification as a European Enforcement Order

1 A judgment on an uncontested claim delivered in a Member State shall, upon application at any time to the court of origin, be certified as a European Enforcement Order if:

(a) the judgment is enforceable in the Member State of origin; and
(b) the judgment does not conflict with the rules on jurisdiction as laid down in sections 3 and 6 of Chapter II of Regulation (EC) No 44/2001; and
(c) the court proceedings in the Member State of origin met the requirements as set out in Chapter III where a claim is uncontested within the meaning of Article 3(1)(b) or (c); and
(d) the judgment was given in the Member State of the debtor's domicile within the meaning of Article 59 of Regulation (EC) No 44/2001, in cases where
- a claim is uncontested within the meaning of Article 3(1)(b) or (c); and
- it relates to a contract concluded by a person, the consumer, for a purpose which can be regarded as being outside his trade or profession; and
- the debtor is the consumer.

2 Where a judgment certified as a European Enforcement Order has ceased to be enforceable or its enforceability has been suspended or limited, a certificate indicating the lack or limitation of enforceability shall, upon application at any time to the court of origin, be issued, using the standard form in Annex IV.

3 Without prejudice to Article 12(2), where a decision has been delivered following a challenge to a judgment certified as a European Enforcement Order in accordance with paragraph 1 of this Article, a replacement certificate shall, upon application at any time, be issued, using the standard form in Annex V, if that decision on the challenge is enforceable in the Member State of origin.

Article 7
Costs related to court proceedings

Where a judgment includes an enforceable decision on the amount of costs related to the court proceedings, including the interest rates, it shall be certified as a European Enforcement Order also with regard to the costs unless the debtor has specifically objected to his obligation to bear such costs in the course of the court proceedings, in accordance with the law of the Member State of origin.

Article 8
Partial European Enforcement Order certificate

If only parts of the judgment meet the requirements of this Regulation, a partial European Enforcement Order certificate shall be issued for those parts.

Article 9
Issue of the European Enforcement Order certificate

1 The European Enforcement Order certificate shall be issued using the standard form in Annex I.

2 The European Enforcement Order certificate shall be issued in the language of the judgment.

Article 10
Rectification or withdrawal of the European Enforcement Order certificate

1 The European Enforcement Order certificate shall, upon application to the court of origin, be

(a) rectified where, due to a material error, there is a discrepancy between the judgment and the certificate;

(b) withdrawn where it was clearly wrongly granted, having regard to the requirements laid down in this Regulation.

2 The law of the Member State of origin shall apply to the rectification or withdrawal of the European Enforcement Order certificate.

3 An application for the rectification or withdrawal of a European Enforcement Order certificate may be made using the standard form in Annex VI.

4 No appeal shall lie against the issuing of a European Enforcement Order certificate.

Note—A miscalculation of arrears was corrected under Art 10 in a European Enforcement Order certificate based on an authentic instrument (*Vogel v Lothschütz* [2012] EWHC 3411 (QB)).

Article 11
Effect of the European Enforcement Order certificate

The European Enforcement Order certificate shall take effect only within the limits of the enforceability of the judgment.

CHAPTER III
MINIMUM STANDARDS FOR UNCONTESTED CLAIMS PROCEDURES

Article 12
Scope of application of minimum standards

1 A judgment on a claim that is uncontested within the meaning of Article 3(1)(b) or (c) can be certified as a European Enforcement Order only if the court proceedings in the Member State of origin met the procedural requirements as set out in this Chapter.

2 The same requirements shall apply to the issuing of a European Enforcement Order certificate or a replacement certificate within the meaning of Article 6(3) for a decision following a challenge to a judgment where, at the time of that decision, the conditions of Article 3(1)(b) or (c) are fulfilled.

Article 13
Service with proof of receipt by the debtor

1 The document instituting the proceedings or an equivalent document may have been served on the debtor by one of the following methods;

(a) personal service attested by an acknowledgement of receipt, including the date of receipt, which is signed by the debtor;

(b) personal service attested by a document signed by the competent person who effected the service stating that the debtor has received the document or refused to receive it without any legal justification, and the date of the service;

(c) postal service attested by an acknowledgement of receipt including the date of receipt, which is signed and returned by the debtor;

(d) service by electronic means such as fax or e-mail, attested by an acknowledgement of receipt including the date of receipt, which is signed and returned by the debtor.

2 Any summons to a court hearing may have been served on the debtor in compliance with paragraph 1 or orally in a previous court hearing on the same claim and stated in the minutes of that previous court hearing.

Article 14

Service without proof of receipt by the debtor

1 Service of the document instituting the proceedings or an equivalent document and any summons to a court hearing on the debtor may also have been effected by one of the following methods:

(a) personal service at the debtor's personal address on persons who are living in the same household as the debtor or are employed there;
(b) in the case of a self-employed debtor or a legal person, personal service at the debtor's business premises on persons who are employed by the debtor;
(c) deposit of the document in the debtor's mailbox;
(d) deposit of the document at a post office or with competent public authorities and the placing in the debtor's mailbox of written notification of that deposit, provided that the written notification clearly states the character of the document as a court document or the legal effect of the notification as effecting service and setting in motion the running of time for the purposes of time limits;
(e) postal service without proof pursuant to paragraph 3 where the debtor has his address in the Member State of origin;
(f) electronic means attested by an automatic confirmation of delivery, provided that the debtor has expressly accepted this method of service in advance.

2 For the purposes of this Regulation, service under paragraph 1 is not admissible if the debtor's address is not known with certainty.

3 Service pursuant to paragraph 1, (a) to (d), shall be attested by:

(a) a document signed by the competent person who effected the service, indicating:
   (i) the method of service used; and
   (ii) the date of service; and
   (iii) where the document has been served on a person other than the debtor, the name of that person and his relation to the debtor,

   or
(b) an acknowledgement of receipt by the person served, for the purposes of paragraphs 1(a) and (b).

Scope—Service under Art 14 is narrowly drafted, eg service by an electronic method has to have been accepted by the debtor in advance (Art 14.1(f)) and service under Art 14.1 is not admissible if the debtor's address is not known with certainty (Art 14.2). However, it may be possible to rely on Art 18 to cure non-compliance (*Chachani Misti v Hostplanet Limited and Finn Grimpe* [2016] EWHC 983 (Ch)).

Article 15

Service on the debtor's representatives

Service pursuant to Articles 13 or 14 may also have been effected on a debtor's representative.

Article 16

Provision to the debtor of due information about the claim

In order to ensure that the debtor was provided with due information about the claim, the document instituting the proceedings or the equivalent document must have contained the following:

(a) the names and the addresses of the parties;
(b) the amount of the claim;
(c) if interest on the claim is sought, the interest rate and the period for which interest is sought unless statutory interest is automatically added to the principal under the law of the Member State of origin;
(d) a statement of the reason for the claim.

Article 17

Provision to the debtor of due information about the procedural steps necessary to contest the claim

The following must have been clearly stated in or together with the document instituting the proceedings, the equivalent document or any summons to a court hearing:

(a) the procedural requirements for contesting the claim, including the time limit for contesting the claim in writing or the time for the court hearing, as applicable, the name and the address of the institution to which to respond or before which to appear, as applicable, and whether it is mandatory to be represented by a lawyer;

(b) the consequences of an absence of objection or default of appearance, in particular, where applicable, the possibility that a judgment may be given or enforced against the debtor and the liability for costs related to the court proceedings.

Article 18

Cure of non-compliance with minimum standards

1 If the proceedings in the Member State of origin did not meet the procedural requirements as set out in Articles 13 to 17, such non-compliance shall be cured and a judgment may be certified as a European Enforcement Order if:

(a) the judgment has been served on the debtor in compliance with the requirements pursuant to Article 13 or Article 14; and

(b) it was possible for the debtor to challenge the judgment by means of a full review and the debtor has been duly informed in or together with the judgment about the procedural requirements for such a challenge, including the name and address of the institution with which it must be lodged and, where applicable, the time limit for so doing; and

(c) the debtor has failed to challenge the judgment in compliance with the relevant procedural requirements.

2 If the proceedings in the Member State of origin did not comply with the procedural requirements as set out in Article 13 or Article 14, such non-compliance shall be cured if it is proved by the conduct of the debtor in the court proceedings that he has personally received the document to be served in sufficient time to arrange for his defence.

'conduct of the debtor' (Art 18.2)—Such conduct goes wider than formal steps taken in the proceedings and extends to steps that are informal or not procedurally required (eg an email) (*Chachani Misti v Hostplanet Limited and Finn Grimpe* [2016] EWHC 983 (Ch)).

Article 19

Minimum standards for review in exceptional cases

1 Further to Articles 13 to 18, a judgment can only be certified as a European Enforcement Order if the debtor is entitled, under the law of the Member State of origin, to apply for a review of the judgment where:

(a) (i) the document instituting the proceedings or an equivalent document or, where applicable, the summons to a court hearing, was served by one of the methods provided for in Article 14; and

(ii) service was not effected in sufficient time to enable him to arrange for his defence, without any fault on his part;

or

(b) the debtor was prevented from objecting to the claim by reason of force majeure, or due to extraordinary circumstances without any fault on his part,

provided in either case that he acts promptly.

2 This Article is without prejudice to the possibility for Member States to grant access to a review of the judgment under more generous conditions than those mentioned in paragraph 1.

CHAPTER IV
ENFORCEMENT

Article 20
Enforcement procedure

1 Without prejudice to the provisions of this Chapter, the enforcement procedures shall be governed by the law of the Member State of enforcement.

A judgment certified as a European Enforcement Order shall be enforced under the same conditions as a judgment handed down in the Member State of enforcement.

2 The creditor shall be required to provide the competent enforcement authorities of the Member State of enforcement with:

(a) a copy of the judgment which satisfies the conditions necessary to establish its authenticity; and

(b) a copy of the European Enforcement Order certificate which satisfies the conditions necessary to establish its authenticity; and

(c) where necessary, a transcription of the European Enforcement Order certificate or a translation thereof into the official language of the Member State of enforcement or, if there are several official languages in that Member State, the official language or one of the official languages of court proceedings of the place where enforcement is sought, in conformity with the law of that Member State, or into another language that the Member State of enforcement has indicated it can accept. Each Member State may indicate the official language or languages of the institutions of the European Community other than its own which it can accept for the completion of the certificate. The translation shall be certified by a person qualified to do so in one of the Member States.

3 No security, bond or deposit, however described, shall be required of a party who in one Member State applies for enforcement of a judgment certified as a European Enforcement Order in another Member State on the ground that he is a foreign national or that he is not domiciled or resident in the Member State of enforcement.

Article 21
Refusal of enforcement

1 Enforcement shall, upon application by the debtor, be refused by the competent court in the Member State of enforcement if the judgment certified as a European Enforcement Order is irreconcilable with an earlier judgment given in any Member State or in a third country, provided that:

(a) the earlier judgment involved the same cause of action and was between the same parties; and

(b) the earlier judgment was given in the Member State of enforcement or fulfils the conditions necessary for its recognition in the Member State of enforcement; and

(c) the irreconcilability was not and could not have been raised as an objection in the court proceedings in the Member State of origin.

2 Under no circumstances may the judgment or its certification as a European Enforcement Order be reviewed as to their substance in the Member State of enforcement.

Article 22
Agreements with third countries

This Regulation shall not affect agreements by which Member States undertook, prior to the entry into force of Regulation (EC) No 44/2001, pursuant to Article 59 of the Brussels Convention on jurisdiction and the enforcement of judgments in civil and commercial matters, not to recognise judgments given, in particular in other Contracting States to that Convention, against defendants domiciled or habitually resident in a third country where, in cases provided for in Article 4 of that

Convention, the judgment could only be founded on a ground of jurisdiction specified in the second paragraph of Article 3 of that Convention.

Article 23
Stay or limitation of enforcement

Where the debtor has

- challenged a judgment certified as a European Enforcement Order, including an application for review within the meaning of Article 19, or
- applied for the rectification or withdrawal of a European Enforcement Order certificate in accordance with Article 10,

the competent court or authority in the Member State of enforcement may, upon application by the debtor:

(a) limit the enforcement proceedings to protective measures; or
(b) make enforcement conditional on the provision of such security as it shall determine; or
(c) under exceptional circumstances, stay the enforcement proceedings.

CHAPTER V
COURT SETTLEMENTS AND AUTHENTIC INSTRUMENTS

Article 24
Court settlements

1 A settlement concerning a claim within the meaning of Article 4(2) which has been approved by a court or concluded before a court in the course of proceedings and is enforceable in the Member State in which it was approved or concluded shall, upon application to the court that approved it or before which it was concluded, be certified as a European Enforcement Order using the standard form in Annex II.

2 A settlement which has been certified as a European Enforcement Order in the Member State of origin shall be enforced in the other Member States without the need for a declaration of enforceability and without any possibility of opposing its enforceability.

3 The provisions of Chapter II, with the exception of Articles 5, 6(1) and 9(1), and of Chapter IV, with the exception of Articles 21(1) and 22, shall apply as appropriate.

Article 25
Authentic instruments

1 An authentic instrument concerning a claim within the meaning of Article 4(2) which is enforceable in one Member State shall, upon application to the authority designated by the Member State of origin, be certified as a European Enforcement Order, using the standard form in Annex III.

2 An authentic instrument which has been certified as a European Enforcement Order in the Member State of origin shall be enforced in the other Member States without the need for a declaration of enforceability and without any possibility of opposing its enforceability.

3 The provisions of Chapter II, with the exception of Articles 5, 6(1) and 9(1), and of Chapter IV, with the exception of Articles 21(1) and 22, shall apply as appropriate.

CHAPTER VI
TRANSITIONAL PROVISION

Article 26

Transitional provision

This Regulation shall apply only to judgments given, to court settlements approved or concluded and to documents formally drawn up or registered as authentic instruments after the entry into force of this Regulation.

CHAPTER VII
RELATIONSHIP WITH OTHER COMMUNITY INSTRUMENTS

Article 27
Relationship with Regulation (EC) No 44/2001

This Regulation shall not affect the possibility of seeking recognition and enforcement, in accordance with Regulation (EC) No 44/2001, of a judgment, a court settlement or an authentic instrument on an uncontested claim.

Article 28
Relationship with Regulation (EC) No 1348/2000

This Regulation shall not affect the application of Regulation (EC) No 1348/2000.

CHAPTER VIII
GENERAL AND FINAL PROVISIONS

Article 29
Information on enforcement procedures and authorities

The Member States shall cooperate to provide the general public and professional circles with information on:

(a) the methods and procedures of enforcement in the Member States; and
(b) the competent authorities for enforcement in the Member States,

in particular via the European Judicial Network in civil and commercial matters established in accordance with Decision 2001/470/EC.

Article 30
Information relating to redress procedures, languages and authorities

1 The Member States shall notify the Commission of:

(a) the procedures for rectification and withdrawal referred to in Article 10(2) and for review referred to in Article 19(1);
(b) the languages accepted pursuant to Article 20(2)(c);
(c) the lists of the authorities referred to in Article 25;

and any subsequent changes thereof.

2 The Commission shall make the information notified in accordance with paragraph 1 publicly available through publication in the *Official Journal of the European Union* and through any other appropriate means.

Article 31
Amendments to the Annexes

The Commission shall amend the standard forms set out in the Annexes. Those measures, designed to amend nonessential elements of this Regulation, shall be adopted in accordance with the regulatory procedure with scrutiny referred to in Article 32(2).

Article 32
Committee

1 The Commission shall be assisted by the committee provided for by Article 75 of Regulation (EC) No 44/2001.

2 Where reference is made to this paragraph, Articles 3 and 7 of Decision 1999/468/EC shall apply, having regard to the provisions of Article 8 thereof.

Article 33
Entry into force

This Regulation shall enter into force on 21 January 2005.

It shall apply from 21 October 2005, with the exception of Articles 30, 31 and 32, which shall apply from 21 January 2005.

This Regulation shall be binding in its entirety and directly applicable in the Member States in accordance with the Treaty establishing the European Community.

Done at Strasbourg, 21 April 2004.

For the European Parliament

The President

P. COX

For the Council

The President

D. ROCHE

****

Council Regulation (EC) No 1393/2007

of 13 November 2007

on the service in the Member States of judicial and extrajudicial documents in civil or commercial matters (service of documents), and repealing Council Regulation (EC) No 1348/2000

Scope—This Regulation (the Second Service Regulation) repeals Council Regulation (EC) No 1348/2000 of 29 May 2000 (the First Service Regulation). The Second Service Regulation came into effect on 13 November 2008. However, the First Service Regulation is still applicable in relation to issues of service before 13 November 2008. The Second Service Regulation applies to all EU Member States including Denmark, to which the provisions of the First Service Regulation were extended from 1 July 2007. Outside of the EU, reference should be made to the Hague Service Convention (the Hague Convention on the Service Abroad of Judicial and Extra-Judicial Documents in Civil or Commercial Matters 1965).

The Second Service Regulation provides an official system of service within the EU (Arts 4–11). Its scope extends beyond family proceedings (Art 1). It is not mandatory – other means of service are permitted: transmission by consular or diplomatic channels (Art 12); service by diplomatic or consular agents (Art 13); service by post (Art 14); and direct service (Art 15). See, however, restrictions on other methods of service discussed below under Ch 11. The Second Service Regulation does not establish any hierarchy between the methods of service referred to in it (*Plumex v Young Sports NV* [2006] ECR I-1417, ECJ). See, further, annotations to Art 7. The official system of service provided by the Second Service Regulation may be more persuasive in some EU jurisdictions than other methods of service, which is an important factor to be taken into account when establishing which EU member is first seised for the purposes of Brussels IIA.

The Regulations must be read in conjunction with the information that Member States must communicate in accordance with Art 23, which may be found at *http://ec.europa.eu/justice_home/judicialatlascivil/html/pdf/vers_consolide_en_1348.pdf*.

The structure of the Second Service Regulation is broadly similar to that of the First.

Chapter I (Arts 1–3) contains general provisions. Art 2 provides for the designation of 'transmitting agencies' and 'receiving agencies' for each Member State, which for England and Wales is the Senior Master, Queen's Bench Division, Foreign Process Section, Room E16, Royal Courts of Justice, Strand, London WC2A 2LL, DX 44450 Strand (tel 0207 947 6691/6327/6488/7786; fax 0870 324 0025; email: foreignprocess.rcj@hmcts.gsi.gov.uk).

Chapter II (Arts 4–15) deals with judicial documents. Section 1 (Arts 4–11) provides for the transmission and service of judicial documents. Art 4 governs the means by which documents requiring to be served are transmitted between Member States (i e between transmitting agencies and receiving agencies). Art 5 sets out the requirement for translations and Art 6 the obligations upon the receiving agency upon receipt of documents for service. Art 7 provides for the service of documents by the receiving agency as soon as possible and in any event within 1 month of receipt. Art 8 contains provisions as to circumstances in which a respondent may refuse to accept service. Art 9 provides that the date of service is the date on which the documents are served in accordance with the law of the receiving Member State. Art 10 provides for certificates of service and Art 11 for the costs of service. Section 2 (Arts 12–16) provides for means of transmission and service of judicial documents other than through transmitting and receiving agencies. Arts 12 and 13 deal with transmission and service by diplomatic or consular channels or agents. Art 14 provides for postal service by Member States on persons residing in another Member State by registered letter with acknowledgment of receipt or equivalent. Art 15 provides for direct service by any person through judicial offices or other competent persons of the Member State addressed, where such direct service is permitted under the law of the Member State. The Second Service Regulation envisages methods of service other than through transmitting and receiving agencies (Chapter II, section 2). However, such service must be effected by the transmitting Member State rather than by the applicant attempting to serve an addressee in another Member State by direct postal service, unless the provisions of Art 15 apply.

Chapter III (Art 16) provides for the transmission of extra-judicial documents for service in the same way as judicial documents.

Chapter IV (Arts 17–26) contains final provisions.

Issues as to the timing and validity of service in this context should be determined by reference to the Second Service Regulation and not the law of the receiving Member State (*Tavoulareas v Tsavliris* [2004] EWCA Civ 48).

The procedure for service out of England and Wales is governed by FPR 2010, Pt 6, Ch 4. For those proceedings to which the FPR do not apply (e g I(PFD)A 1975, TLATA 1996 and PHA 1997), reference should be made to CPR 1998, rr 6.17–6.31.

As to the service in England and Wales of foreign proceedings, where the Second Service Regulation applies, the transmitting agency of the other Member State should be used.

When an application is served out of the jurisdiction, the time limit for serving an acknowledgment of service or answer to the application is longer (FPR 2010, r 6.42 and PD6B). The procedure for service in accordance with the Second Service Regulation is contained in FPR 2010, r 6.44 and PD6B, para 2.

To ensure that a court is seised, proceedings must simply not be issued but the process of service must be started (Brussels IIA, Art 16). Issuing proceedings as a precautionary measure, but not then effecting service, will not gain priority under Brussels IIA (*R v R (Divorce: Stay of Proceedings)* [1994] 2 FLR 1036, FD). Actual service does not need to have been effected to establish jurisdiction: see annotations to Brussels IIA, Art 16.

The Annexes to the Second Service Regulation contain the standard forms that should be used: Annex I – request for service of documents; Annex II – information to the addressee about the right to refuse to accept a document; Annex III – correlation table [as between the First Service Regulation and the Second Service Regulation].

THE EUROPEAN PARLIAMENT AND THE COUNCIL OF THE EUROPEAN UNION,

Having regard to the Treaty establishing the European Community, and in particular Article 61(c) and Article 67(5), second indent, thereof,

Having regard to the proposal from the Commission,

Having regard to the opinion of the European Economic and Social Committee,

Acting in accordance with the procedure laid down in Article 251 of the Treaty,

Whereas:

(1) The Union has set itself the objective of maintaining and developing the Union as an area of freedom, security and justice, in which the free movement of persons is assured. To establish such an area, the Community is to adopt, among others, the measures relating to judicial cooperation in civil matters needed for the proper functioning of the internal market.

(2) The proper functioning of the internal market entails the need to improve and expedite the transmission of judicial and extrajudicial documents in civil or commercial matters for service between the Member States.

(3) The Council, by an Act dated 26 May 1997, drew up a Convention on the service in the Member States of the European Union of judicial and extrajudicial documents in civil or commercial matters and recommended it for adoption by the Member States in accordance with their respective constitutional rules. That Convention has not entered into force. Continuity in the results of the negotiations for conclusion of the Convention should be ensured.

(4) On 29 May 2000 the Council adopted Regulation (EC) No 1348/2000 on the service in the Member States of judicial and extrajudicial documents in civil or commercial matters. The main content of that Regulation is based on the Convention.

(5) On 1 October 2004 the Commission adopted a report on the application of Regulation (EC) No 1348/2000. The report concludes that the application of Regulation (EC) No 1348/2000 has generally improved and expedited the transmission and the service of documents between Member States since its entry into force in 2001, but that nevertheless the application of certain provisions is not fully satisfactory.

(6) Efficiency and speed in judicial procedures in civil matters require that judicial and extrajudicial documents be transmitted directly and by rapid means between local bodies designated by the Member States. Member States may indicate their intention to designate only one transmitting or receiving agency or one agency to perform both functions, for a period of five years. This designation may, however, be renewed every five years.

(7) Speed in transmission warrants the use of all appropriate means, provided that certain conditions as to the legibility and reliability of the document received are observed. Security in transmission requires that the document to be transmitted be accompanied by a standard form, to be completed in the official language or one of the official languages of the place where service is to be effected, or in another language accepted by the Member State in question.

(8) This Regulation should not apply to service of a document on the party's authorised representative in the Member State where the proceedings are taking place regardless of the place of residence of that party.

(9) The service of a document should be effected as soon as possible, and in any event within one month of receipt by the receiving agency.

(10) To secure the effectiveness of this Regulation, the possibility of refusing service of documents should be confined to exceptional situations.

(11) In order to facilitate the transmission and service of documents between Member States, the standard forms set out in the Annexes to this Regulation should be used.

(12) The receiving agency should inform the addressee in writing using the standard from that he may refuse to accept the document to be served at the time of service or by returning the document to the receiving agency within one week if it is not either in a language which he understands or in the official language or one of the official languages of the place of service. This rule should also apply to the subsequent service once the addressee has exercised his right of refusal. These rules on refusal should also apply to service by diplomatic or consular agents, service by postal services and direct service. It should be established that the service of the refused document can be remedied through the service on the addressee of a translation of the document.

(13) Speed in transmission warrants documents being served within days of receipt of the document. However, if service has not been effected after one month has elapsed, the receiving agency should inform the transmitting agency. The expiry of this period should not imply that the request be returned to the transmitting agency where it is clear that service is feasible within a reasonable period.

(14) The receiving agency should continue to take all necessary steps to effect the service of the documents also in cases where it has not been possible to effect service within the month, for example, because the defendant has been away from his home on holiday or away from his office on business. However, in order to avoid an open-ended obligation for the receiving agency to take steps to effect the service of a document, the transmitting agency should be able to specify a time limit in the standard form after which service is no longer required.

(15) Given the differences between the Member States as regards their rules of procedure, the material date for the purposes of service varies from one Member State to another. Having regard to such situations and the possible difficulties that may arise, this Regulation should provide for a system where it is the law of the Member State addressed which determines the date of service. However, where according to the law of a Member State a document has to be served within a particular period, the date to be taken into account with respect to the applicant should be that determined by the law of that Member State. This double date system exists only in a limited number of Member States. Those Member States which apply this system should communicate this to the Commission, which should publish the information in the *Official Journal of the European Union* and make it available through the European Judicial Network in Civil and Commercial Matters established by Council Decision 2001/470/EC.

(16) In order to facilitate access to justice, costs occasioned by recourse to a judicial officer or a person competent under the law of the Member State addressed should correspond to a single fixed fee laid down by that Member State in advance which respects the principles of proportionality and non-discrimination. The requirement of a single fixed fee should not preclude the possibility for Member States to set different fees for different types of service as long as they respect these principles.

(17) Each Member State should be free to effect service of documents directly by postal services on persons residing in another Member State by registered letter with acknowledgement of receipt or equivalent.

(18) It should be possible for any person interested in a judicial proceeding to effect service of documents directly through the judicial officers, officials or other competent persons of the Member State addressed, where such direct service is permitted under the law of that Member State.

(19) The Commission should draw up a manual containing information relevant for the proper application of this Regulation, which should be made available through the European Judicial Network in Civil and Commercial Matters. The Commission and the Member States should do their utmost to ensure that this information is up to date and complete especially as regards contact details of receiving and transmitting agencies.

(20) In calculating the periods and time limits provided for in this Regulation, Regulation (EEC, Euratom) No 1182/71 of the Council of 3 June 1971 determining the rules applicable to periods, dates and time limits should apply.

(21) The measures necessary for the implementation of this Regulation should be adopted in accordance with Council Decision 1999/468/EC of 28 June 1999 laying down the procedures for the exercise of implementing powers conferred on the Commission.

(22) In particular, power should be conferred on the Commission to update or make technical amendments to the standard forms set out in the Annexes. Since those measures are of general scope and are designed to amend/delete non-essential elements of this Regulation, they must be adopted in accordance with the regulatory procedure with scrutiny provided for in Article 5a of Decision 1999/468/EC.

(23) This Regulation prevails over the provisions contained in bilateral or multilateral agreements or arrangements having the same scope, concluded by the Member States, and in particular the Protocol annexed to the Brussels Convention of 27 September 1968 and the Hague Convention of 15 November 1965 in relations between the Member States party thereto. This Regulation does not preclude Member States from maintaining or concluding agreements or arrangements to expedite or simplify the transmission of documents, provided that they are compatible with this Regulation.

(24) The information transmitted pursuant to this Regulation should enjoy suitable protection. This matter falls within the scope of Directive 95/46/EC of the European Parliament and of the Council of 24 October 1995 on the protection of individuals with regard to the processing of personal data and on the free movement of such data, and of Directive 2002/58/EC of the

European Parliament and of the Council of 12 July 2002 concerning the processing of personal data and the protection of privacy in the electronic communications sector (Directive on privacy and electronic communications).

(25) No later than 1 June 2011 and every five years thereafter, the Commission should review the application of this Regulation and propose such amendments as may appear necessary.

(26) Since the objectives of this Regulation cannot be sufficiently achieved by the Member States and can therefore, by reason of the scale or effects of the action, be better achieved at Community level, the Community may adopt measures, in accordance with the principle of subsidiarity as set out in Article 5 of the Treaty. In accordance with the principle of proportionality, as set out in that Article, this Regulation does not go beyond what is necessary in order to achieve those objectives.

(27) In order to make the provisions more easily accessible and readable, Regulation (EC) No 1348/2000 should be repealed and replaced by this Regulation.

(28) In accordance with Article 3 of the Protocol on the position of the United Kingdom and Ireland, annexed to the Treaty on European Union and to the Treaty establishing the European Community, the United Kingdom and Ireland are taking part in the adoption and application of this Regulation.

(29) In accordance with Articles 1 and 2 of the Protocol on the position of Denmark, annexed to the Treaty on European Union and to the Treaty establishing the European Community, Denmark does not take part in the adoption of this Regulation and is not bound by it or subject to its application,

HAVE ADOPTED THIS REGULATION:

Note—The EC Treaty has become the Treaty on the Functioning of the European Union (TFEU) and the Articles have been re-numbered: Art 5 is replaced, in substance, by Art 5 of the Treaty on the European Union; Art 61 is now Art 67 TFEU; Art 67 is repealed; and Art 251 is now Art 294 TFEU.

CHAPTER I
GENERAL PROVISIONS

Article 1
Scope

1 This Regulation shall apply in civil and commercial matters where a judicial or extrajudicial document has to be transmitted from one Member State to another for service there. It shall not extend in particular to revenue, customs or administrative matters or to liability of the State for actions or omissions in the exercise of state authority (*acta iure imperii*).

2 This Regulation shall not apply where the address of the person to be served with the document is not known.

3 In this Regulation, the term 'Member State' shall mean the Member States with the exception of Denmark.

Article 2
Transmitting and receiving agencies

1 Each Member State shall designate the public officers, authorities or other persons, hereinafter referred to as 'transmitting agencies', competent for the transmission of judicial or extra-judicial documents to be served in another Member State.

2 Each Member State shall designate the public officers, authorities or other persons, hereinafter referred to as 'receiving agencies', competent for the receipt of judicial or extrajudicial documents from another Member State.

3 A Member State may designate one transmitting agency and one receiving agency, or one agency to perform both functions. A federal State, a State in which several legal systems apply or a State with autonomous territorial units shall be free to designate more than one such agency. The designation shall have effect for a period of five years and may be renewed at five-year intervals.

4 Each Member State shall provide the Commission with the following information:

(a) the names and addresses of the receiving agencies referred to in paragraphs 2 and 3;
(b) the geographical areas in which they have jurisdiction;
(c) the means of receipt of documents available to them; and
(d) the languages that may be used for the completion of the standard form set out in Annex I.

Member States shall notify the Commission of any subsequent modification of such information.

Article 3
Central body

Each Member State shall designate a central body responsible for:

(a) supplying information to the transmitting agencies;
(b) seeking solutions to any difficulties which may arise during transmission of documents for service;
(c) forwarding, in exceptional cases, at the request of a transmitting agency, a request for service to the competent receiving agency.

A federal State, a State in which several legal systems apply or a State with autonomous territorial units shall be free to designate more than one central body.

CHAPTER II
JUDICIAL DOCUMENTS

Section 1
Transmission and service of judicial documents

Article 4
Transmission of documents

1 Judicial documents shall be transmitted directly and as soon as possible between the agencies designated pursuant to Article 2.

2 The transmission of documents, requests, confirmations, receipts, certificates and any other papers between transmitting agencies and receiving agencies may be carried out by any appropriate means, provided that the content of the document received is true and faithful to that of the document forwarded and that all information in it is easily legible.

3 The document to be transmitted shall be accompanied by a request drawn up using the standard form set out in Annex I. The form shall be completed in the official language of the Member State addressed or, if there are several official languages in that Member State, the official language or one of the official languages of the place where service is to be effected, or in another language which that Member State has indicated it can accept. Each Member State shall indicate the official language or languages of the institutions of the European Union other than its own which is or are acceptable to it for completion of the form.

4 The documents and all papers that are transmitted shall be exempted from legalisation or any equivalent formality.

5 When the transmitting agency wishes a copy of the document to be returned together with the certificate referred to in Article 10, it shall send the document in duplicate.

Scope—Art 4 governs the means by which documents requiring to be served are transmitted between Member States. Documents are to be transmitted directly and as soon as possible between the designated agencies by 'any appropriate means', provided that the content of the document received is 'true and faithful' and all information is 'easily legible', encompassing the possible use of fax or email. The document(s) to be transmitted must be accompanied by a request drawn up using the form set out in Annex I (not reproduced here) completed in the official language (or one of them) of the Member State addressed. Translations of the documents to be served are required (Arts 5 and 8).

Article 5
Translation of documents

1 The applicant shall be advised by the transmitting agency to which he forwards the document for transmission that the addressee may refuse to accept it if it is not in one of the languages provided for in Article 8.

2 The applicant shall bear any costs of translation prior to the transmission of the document, without prejudice to any possible subsequent decision by the court or competent authority on liability for such costs.

Article 6
Receipt of documents by receiving agency

1 On receipt of a document, a receiving agency shall, as soon as possible and in any event within seven days of receipt, send a receipt to the transmitting agency by the swiftest possible means of transmission using the standard form set out in Annex I.

2 Where the request for service cannot be fulfilled on the basis of the information or documents transmitted, the receiving agency shall contact the transmitting agency by the swiftest possible means in order to secure the missing information or documents.

3 If the request for service is manifestly outside the scope of this Regulation or if non-compliance with the formal conditions required makes service impossible, the request and the documents transmitted shall be returned, on receipt, to the transmitting agency, together with the notice of return using the standard form set out in Annex I.

4 A receiving agency receiving a document for service but not having territorial jurisdiction to serve it shall forward it, as well as the request, to the receiving agency having territorial jurisdiction in the same Member State if the request complies with the conditions laid down in Article 4(3) and shall inform the transmitting agency accordingly using the standard form set out in Annex I. That receiving agency shall inform the transmitting agency when it receives the document, in the manner provided for in paragraph 1.

Article 7
Service of documents

1 The receiving agency shall itself serve the document or have it served, either in accordance with the law of the Member State addressed or by a particular method requested by the transmitting agency, unless that method is incompatible with the law of that Member State.

2 The receiving agency shall take all necessary steps to effect the service of the document as soon as possible, and in any event within one month of receipt. If it has not been possible to effect service within one month of receipt, the receiving agency shall:

(a) immediately inform the transmitting agency by means of the certificate in the standard form set out in Annex I, which shall be drawn up under the conditions referred to in Article 10(2); and

(b) continue to take all necessary steps to effect the service of the document, unless indicated otherwise by the transmitting agency, where service seems to be possible within a reasonable period of time.

Scope—The receiving agency must serve the documents or have them served either in accordance with the receiving Member State's internal law or by any particular method requested by the transmitting agency (unless the method requested is incompatible with the law of the receiving Member State). All necessary steps must be taken to effect service as soon as possible and in any event within 1 month of receipt. If that is not possible, the receiving agency must inform the transmitting agency of the delay and must continue to take all necessary steps to effect service. Issues as to the timing and validity of service are to be determined by reference to the Second Service Regulation and not the law of the receiving Member State (*Tavoulareas v Tsavliris* [2004] EWCA Civ 48). The methods of service stipulated in the Second Service Regulation are not hierarchical. It is therefore possible to attempt service by two or more methods simultaneously so that time will begin to run from the date on which service was first validly effected in compliance with the Second Service Regulation (*Plumex v Young Sports NV* (Case C-473/04) [2006] ECR I-1417, ECJ). Being aware of proceedings does not amount to service within the meaning of the Second Service Regulation (*Tavoulareas v Tsavliris*, above).

Article 8
Refusal to accept a document

1 The receiving agency shall inform the addressee, using the standard form set out in Annex II, that he may refuse to accept the document to be served at the time of service or by returning the document to the receiving agency within one week if it is not written in, or accompanied by a translation into, either of the following languages:

(a) a language which the addressee understands; or
(b) the official language of the Member State addressed or, if there are several official languages in that Member State, the official language or one of the official languages of the place where service is to be effected.

2 Where the receiving agency is informed that the addressee refuses to accept the document in accordance with paragraph 1, it shall immediately inform the transmitting agency by means of the certificate provided for in Article 10 and return the request and the documents of which a translation is requested.

3 If the addressee has refused to accept the document pursuant to paragraph 1, the service of the document can be remedied through the service on the addressee in accordance with the provisions of this Regulation of the document accompanied by a translation into a language provided for in paragraph 1. In that case, the date of service of the document shall be the date on which the document accompanied by the translation is served in accordance with the law of the Member State addressed. However, where according to the law of a Member State, a document has to be served within a particular period, the date to be taken into account with respect to the applicant shall be the date of the service of the initial document determined pursuant to Article 9(2).

4 Paragraphs 1, 2 and 3 shall also apply to the means of transmission and service of judicial documents provided for in Section 2.

5 For the purposes of paragraph 1, the diplomatic or consular agents, where service is effected in accordance with Article 13, or the authority or person, where service is effected in accordance with Article 14, shall inform the addressee that he may refuse to accept the document and that any document refused must be sent to those agents or to that authority or person respectively.

Scope—An addressee may refuse to accept service of documents that are not in a language that the addressee understands or that are not in the official language of the Member State addressed. An initial invalid attempt to serve without a translation may be rectified by commissioning a translation and then re-serving (Art 8.3; *Leffler v Berlin Chemie AG* (Case C-443/03) [2005] ECR I-9611, ECJ).

PART VI

Article 9
Date of service

1 Without prejudice to Article 8, the date of service of a document pursuant to Article 7 shall be the date on which it is served in accordance with the law of the Member State addressed.

2 However, where according to the law of a Member State a document has to be served within a particular period, the date to be taken into account with respect to the applicant shall be that determined by the law of that Member State.

3 Paragraphs 1 and 2 shall also apply to the means of transmission and service of judicial documents provided for in Section 2.

Article 10
Certificate of service and copy of the document served

1 When the formalities concerning the service of the document have been completed, a certificate of completion of those formalities shall be drawn up in the standard form set out in Annex I and addressed to the transmitting agency, together with, where Article 4(5) applies, a copy of the document served.

2 The certificate shall be completed in the official language or one of the official languages of the Member State of origin or in another language which the Member State of origin has indicated

that it can accept. Each Member State shall indicate the official language or languages of the institutions of the European Union other than its own which is or are acceptable to it for completion of the form.

Article 11
Costs of service

1 The service of judicial documents coming from a Member State shall not give rise to any payment or reimbursement of taxes or costs for services rendered by the Member State addressed.

2 However, the applicant shall pay or reimburse the costs occasioned by:

(a) recourse to a judicial officer or to a person competent under the law of the Member State addressed;
(b) the use of a particular method of service.

Costs occasioned by recourse to a judicial officer or to a person competent under the law of the Member State addressed shall correspond to a single fixed fee laid down by that Member State in advance which respects the principles of proportionality and non-discrimination. Member States shall communicate such fixed fees to the Commission.

Section 2
Other means of transmission and service of judicial documents

Article 12
Transmission by consular or diplomatic channels

Each Member State shall be free, in exceptional circumstances, to use consular or diplomatic channels to forward judicial documents, for the purpose of service, to those agencies of another Member State which are designated pursuant to Articles 2 or 3.

Article 13
Service by diplomatic or consular agents

1 Each Member State shall be free to effect service of judicial documents on persons residing in another Member State, without application of any compulsion, directly through its diplomatic or consular agents.

2 Any Member State may make it known, in accordance with Article 23(1), that it is opposed to such service within its territory, unless the documents are to be served on nationals of the Member State in which the documents originate.

Article 14
Service by postal services

Each Member State shall be free to effect service of judicial documents directly by postal services on persons residing in another Member State by registered letter with acknowledgement of receipt or equivalent.

Article 15
Direct service

Any person interested in a judicial proceeding may effect service of judicial documents directly through the judicial officers, officials or other competent persons of the Member State addressed, where such direct service is permitted under the law of that Member State.

CHAPTER III
EXTRAJUDICIAL DOCUMENTS

Article 16
Transmission

Extrajudicial documents may be transmitted for service in another Member State in accordance with the provisions of this Regulation.

CHAPTER IV
FINAL PROVISIONS

Article 17
Implementing rules

Measures designed to amend non-essential elements of this Regulation relating to the updating or to the making of technical amendments to the standard forms set out in Annexes I and II shall be adopted in accordance with the regulatory procedure with scrutiny referred to in Article 18(2).

Article 18
Committee

1 The Commission shall be assisted by a committee.

2 Where reference is made to this paragraph, Article 5a(1) to (4), and Article 7 of Decision 1999/468/EC shall apply, having regard to the provisions of Article 8 thereof.

Article 19
Defendant not entering an appearance

1 Where a writ of summons or an equivalent document has had to be transmitted to another Member State for the purpose of service under the provisions of this Regulation and the defendant has not appeared, judgment shall not be given until it is established that:

(a) the document was served by a method prescribed by the internal law of the Member State addressed for the service of documents in domestic actions upon persons who are within its territory; or

(b) the document was actually delivered to the defendant or to his residence by another method provided for by this Regulation; and that in either of these cases the service or the delivery was effected in sufficient time to enable the defendant to defend.

2 Each Member State may make it known, in accordance with Article 23(1), that the judge, notwithstanding the provisions of paragraph 1, may give judgment even if no certificate of service or delivery has been received, if all the following conditions are fulfilled:

(a) the document was transmitted by one of the methods provided for in this Regulation;

(b) a period of time of not less than six months, considered adequate by the judge in the particular case, has elapsed since the date of the transmission of the document;

(c) no certificate of any kind has been received, even though every reasonable effort has been made to obtain it through the competent authorities or bodies of the Member State addressed.

3 Notwithstanding paragraphs 1 and 2, the judge may order, in case of urgency, any provisional or protective measures.

4 When a writ of summons or an equivalent document has had to be transmitted to another Member State for the purpose of service under the provisions of this Regulation and a judgment has been entered against a defendant who has not appeared, the judge shall have the power to relieve the defendant from the effects of the expiry of the time for appeal from the judgment if the following conditions are fulfilled:

(a) the defendant, without any fault on his part, did not have knowledge of the document in sufficient time to defend, or knowledge of the judgment in sufficient time to appeal; and
(b) the defendant has disclosed a *prima facie* defence to the action on the merits.

An application for relief may be filed only within a reasonable time after the defendant has knowledge of the judgment.

Each Member State may make it known, in accordance with Article 23(1), that such application will not be entertained if it is filed after the expiry of a time to be stated by it in that communication, but which shall in no case be less than one year following the date of the judgment.

5 Paragraph 4 shall not apply to judgments concerning the status or capacity of persons.

'Defendant not entering an appearance'—This will include, in the context of an English divorce petition, not completing an acknowledgment of service.

Article 20
Relationship with agreements or arrangements to which Member States are party

1 This Regulation shall, in relation to matters to which it applies, prevail over other provisions contained in bilateral or multilateral agreements or arrangements concluded by the Member States, and in particular Article IV of the Protocol to the Brussels Convention of 1968 and the Hague Convention of 15 November 1965.

2 This Regulation shall not preclude individual Member States from maintaining or concluding agreements or arrangements to expedite further or simplify the transmission of documents, provided that they are compatible with this Regulation.

3 Member States shall send to the Commission:

(a) a copy of the agreements or arrangements referred to in paragraph 2 concluded between the Member States as well as drafts of such agreements or arrangements which they intend to adopt; and
(b) any denunciation of, or amendments to, these agreements or arrangements.

Article 21
Legal aid

This Regulation shall not affect the application of Article 23 of the Convention on civil procedure of 17 July 1905, Article 24 of the Convention on civil procedure of 1 March 1954 or Article 13 of the Convention on international access to justice of 25 October 1980 between the Member States party to those Conventions.

Article 22
Protection of information transmitted

1 Information, including in particular personal data, transmitted under this Regulation shall be used by the receiving agency only for the purpose for which it was transmitted.

2 Receiving agencies shall ensure the confidentiality of such information, in accordance with their national law.

3 Paragraphs 1 and 2 shall not affect national laws enabling data subjects to be informed of the use made of information transmitted under this Regulation.

4 This Regulation shall be without prejudice to Directives 95/46/EC and 2002/58/EC.

Article 23
Communication and publication

1 Member States shall communicate to the Commission the information referred to in Articles 2, 3, 4, 10, 11, 13, 15 and 19. Member States shall communicate to the Commission if, according to their law, a document has to be served within a particular period as referred to in Articles 8(3) and 9(2).

2 The Commission shall publish the information communicated in accordance with paragraph 1 in the *Official Journal of the European Union* with the exception of the addresses and other contact details of the agencies and of the central bodies and the geographical areas in which they have jurisdiction.

3 The Commission shall draw up and update regularly a manual containing the information referred to in paragraph 1, which shall be available electronically, in particular through the European Judicial Network in Civil and Commercial Matters.

Article 24
Review

No later than 1 June 2011, and every five years thereafter, the Commission shall present to the European Parliament, the Council and the European Economic and Social Committee a report on the application of this Regulation, paying special attention to the effectiveness of the agencies designated pursuant to Article 2 and to the practical application of Article 3(c) and Article 9. The report shall be accompanied if need be by proposals for adaptations of this Regulation in line with the evolution of notification systems.

Article 25
Repeal

1 Regulation (EC) No 1348/2000 shall be repealed as from the date of application of this Regulation.

2 References made to the repealed Regulation shall be construed as being made to this Regulation and should be read in accordance with the correlation table in Annex III.

Article 26
Entry into force

This Regulation shall enter into force on the 20th day following its publication in the *Official Journal of the European Union.*

It shall apply from 13 November 2008 with the exception of Article 23 which shall apply from 13 August 2008.

This Regulation shall be binding in its entirety and directly applicable in the Member States in accordance with the Treaty establishing the European Community.

Done at Strasbourg, 13 November 2007.

For the European Parliament

The President

H.-G. PÖTTERING

For the Council

The President

M. LOBO ANTUNES

****

PART VI

Convention on the International Recovery of Child Support and Other Forms of Family Maintenance

Scope—The Hague Convention on the International Recovery of Child Support and other forms of Family Maintenance of 23 November 2007 (the 2007 Convention) was negotiated by the Hague Conference on Private International Law at the same time as the Maintenance Regulation was under negotiation by EU Member States. The EU is a party to the 2007 Convention, thus binding all EU Member States. However, the

2007 Convention does not apply within the EU, as the Maintenance Regulation takes precedence. The EU ratified the 2007 Convention on 9 April 2014 and it came into force in the EU on 1 August 2014. Other parties to the Convention may be identified at *www.hcch.net/index_en.php?act=conventions.status&cid=131*.

The 2007 Convention is intended to provide a simpler, quicker and more efficient global system for the reciprocal enforcement of family maintenance. EU Member States will use the 2007 Convention with non-EU Contracting States only; the Maintenance Regulation will be used as between Member States.

Most of the 2007 Convention is directly applicable in European law and therefore under the law of England and Wales. Although no specific legislation is required in England and Wales to implement the 2007 Convention, it is supported by the International Recovery of Maintenance (Hague Convention 2007 etc) Regulations 2012 (set out in Part V (which provide inter alia that a magistrates' court may impose a driving disqualification order)), the International Recovery of Maintenance (Hague Convention 2007) (Rules of Court) Regulations 2012, SI 2012/1770, which amends MCA 1980 and CJJA 1982, and the Family Procedure (Amendment No 4) Rules 2012, which amend principally FPR 2010, Pts 9 and 34 (in particular rr 34.28A–34.36C) and insert PD34A and PD34E.

Administrative cooperation is carried out by the designated Central Authority for each Contracting State (Art 4). The Central Authority for England and Wales is the Lord Chancellor, whose functions are carried out by the Reciprocal Enforcement of Maintenance Unit (REMO) in the Office of the Official Solicitor and Public Trustee, Victory House, 30–34 Kingsway, London WC2B 6EX, DX 141423 Bloomsbury 7; tel: 020 3681 2757; fax: 020 3681 2762; email: remo@offsol.gsi.gov.uk.

The 2007 Convention replaces the Convention of 2 October 1973 on the Recognition and Enforcement of Decisions relating to Maintenance Obligations (the 1973 Convention) (Art 48) and the EU Convention on the Recovery Abroad of Maintenance 1956 (the New York Convention) (Art 49) as between Contracting States to each except where there is a difference in the scope applied by one or both states.

Chapter I provides for the object (Art 1), scope (Art 2) and definitions (Art 3).

Chapters II and III contain administrative cooperation provisions. Chapter II (Arts 4–8) deals with the designation and functions of Central Authorities. Chapter III (Arts 9–17) deals with the process of applying through Central Authorities.

Chapter IV (Art 18) provides for restrictions on bringing proceedings in jurisdictional terms.

Chapter V (Arts 19–31) deals with recognition and enforcement.

Chapter VI (Arts 32-35) makes provision as to how a decision, once recognised and declared enforceable, is enforced in the requested Contracting State.

Chapter VII (Art 36) provides for the position of public bodies as applicants.

Chapter VIII (Arts 37–57) contains general provisions.

Chapter IX (Arts 58–65) contains final provisions.

Forms are contained in the Annexes:

Annex 1: Transmittal form under Art 12(2).

Annex 2: Acknowledgment form under Art 12(3).

(Concluded 23 November 2007)

The States signatory to the present Convention,

Desiring to improve co-operation among States for the international recovery of child support and other forms of family maintenance,

Aware of the need for procedures which produce results and are accessible, prompt, efficient, cost-effective, responsive and fair,

Wishing to build upon the best features of existing Hague Conventions and other international instruments, in particular the United Nations Convention on the Recovery Abroad of Maintenance of 20 June 1956,

Seeking to take advantage of advances in technologies and to create a flexible system which can continue to evolve as needs change and further advances in technology create new opportunities,

Recalling that, in accordance with Articles 3 and 27 of the United Nations Convention on the Rights of the Child of 20 November 1989,

- in all actions concerning children the best interests of the child shall be a primary consideration,
- every child has a right to a standard of living adequate for the child's physical, mental, spiritual, moral and social development,
- the parent(s) or others responsible for the child have the primary responsibility to secure, within their abilities and financial capacities, the conditions of living necessary for the child's development, and
- States Parties should take all appropriate measures, including the conclusion of international agreements, to secure the recovery of maintenance for the child from the parent(s) or other responsible persons, in particular where such persons live in a State different from that of the child,

Have resolved to conclude this Convention and have agreed upon the following provisions –

CHAPTER I
OBJECT, SCOPE AND DEFINITIONS

Article 1
Object

The object of the present Convention is to ensure the effective international recovery of child support and other forms of family maintenance, in particular by –

(a) establishing a comprehensive system of co-operation between the authorities of the Contracting States;
(b) making available applications for the establishment of maintenance decisions;
(c) providing for the recognition and enforcement of maintenance decisions; and
(d) requiring effective measures for the prompt enforcement of maintenance decisions.

Article 2
Scope

(1) This Convention shall apply –

(a) to maintenance obligations arising from a parent-child relationship towards a person under the age of 21 years;
(b) to recognition and enforcement or enforcement of a decision for spousal support when the application is made with a claim within the scope of sub-paragraph (a); and
(c) with the exception of Chapters II and III, to spousal support.

(2) Any Contracting State may reserve, in accordance with Article 62, the right to limit the application of the Convention under sub-paragraph (1)(a), to persons who have not attained the age of 18 years. A Contracting State which makes this reservation shall not be entitled to claim the application of the Convention to persons of the age excluded by its reservation.

(3) Any Contracting State may declare in accordance with Article 63 that it will extend the application of the whole or any part of the Convention to any maintenance obligation arising from a family relationship, parentage, marriage or affinity, including in particular obligations in respect of vulnerable persons. Any such declaration shall give rise to obligations between two Contracting States only in so far as their declarations cover the same maintenance obligations and parts of the Convention.

(4) The provisions of this Convention shall apply to children regardless of the marital status of the parents.

Scope—Art 2(1) provides for the core scope of the 2007 Convention. The core scope is: maintenance owed by a parent to a child under the age of 21 (regardless of the marital status of the parents, but not by non-parents); recognition and enforcement of spousal maintenance where the claim is made together with a child maintenance claim; and spousal support where no child claim is made, but in such cases Chs II and III (the administrative cooperation provisions) do not apply. It is possible to limit or extend the core scope. By Art 2(2), a Contracting State may reserve the right to limit the scope of child maintenance to persons under 18 years, but will not then be able to use the 2007 Convention for its own children between the ages of 18 and 21. By Art 2(3), a Contracting State may declare that it will extend the provisions of the 2007 Convention to wider forms of family maintenance (eg affinity cases, such as support by a person to his/her parent). The effect of such a declaration is that the relevant Contracting State will give, and receive, such extended assistance only to and from other Contracting States whose declarations as to scope match. By the Council Decision of 9 June 2011 (2011/432/EU), the EU has extended the scope of the 2007 Convention by applying Chs II and III on administrative cooperation to all cases of spousal support, regardless of whether or not they accompany a child maintenance claim.

Article 3
Definitions

For the purposes of this Convention –

(a) 'creditor' means an individual to whom maintenance is owed or is alleged to be owed;
(b) 'debtor' means an individual who owes or who is alleged to owe maintenance;

(c) 'legal assistance' means the assistance necessary to enable applicants to know and assert their rights and to ensure that applications are fully and effectively dealt with in the requested State. The means of providing such assistance may include as necessary legal advice, assistance in bringing a case before an authority, legal representation and exemption from costs of proceedings;

(d) 'agreement in writing' means an agreement recorded in any medium, the information contained in which is accessible so as to be usable for subsequent reference;

(e) 'maintenance arrangement' means an agreement in writing relating to the payment of maintenance which –

  (i) has been formally drawn up or registered as an authentic instrument by a competent authority; or

  (ii) has been authenticated by, or concluded, registered or filed with a competent authority, and may be the subject of review and modification by a competent authority;

(f) 'vulnerable person' means a person who, by reason of an impairment or insufficiency of his or her personal faculties, is not able to support him or herself.

CHAPTER II
ADMINISTRATIVE CO-OPERATION

Article 4
Designation of Central Authorities

(1) A Contracting State shall designate a Central Authority to discharge the duties that are imposed by the Convention on such an authority.

(2) Federal States, States with more than one system of law or States having autonomous territorial units shall be free to appoint more than one Central Authority and shall specify the territorial or personal extent of their functions. Where a State has appointed more than one Central Authority, it shall designate the Central Authority to which any communication may be addressed for transmission to the appropriate Central Authority within that State.

(3) The designation of the Central Authority or Central Authorities, their contact details, and where appropriate the extent of their functions as specified in paragraph 2, shall be communicated by a Contracting State to the Permanent Bureau of the Hague Conference on Private International Law at the time when the instrument of ratification or accession is deposited or when a declaration is submitted in accordance with Article 61. Contracting States shall promptly inform the Permanent Bureau of any changes.

'Federal states'—Because the UK has more than one system of law, there are separate Central Authorities for England and Wales, Scotland and Northern Ireland. The Central Authority for England and Wales acts as the 'lead' Central Authority under Art 4(2).

Article 5
General functions of Central Authorities

Central Authorities shall –

(a) co-operate with each other and promote co-operation amongst the competent authorities in their States to achieve the purposes of the Convention;

(b) seek as far as possible solutions to difficulties which arise in the application of the Convention.

Article 6

Specific functions of Central Authorities

(1) Central Authorities shall provide assistance in relation to applications under Chapter III. In particular they shall –

(a) transmit and receive such applications;

(b) initiate or facilitate the institution of proceedings in respect of such applications.

(2) In relation to such applications they shall take all appropriate measures –

(a) where the circumstances require, to provide or facilitate the provision of legal assistance;
(b) to help locate the debtor or the creditor;
(c) to help obtain relevant information concerning the income and, if necessary, other financial circumstances of the debtor or creditor, including the location of assets;
(d) to encourage amicable solutions with a view to obtaining voluntary payment of maintenance, where suitable by use of mediation, conciliation or similar processes;
(e) to facilitate the ongoing enforcement of maintenance decisions, including any arrears;
(f) to facilitate the collection and expeditious transfer of maintenance payments;
(g) to facilitate the obtaining of documentary or other evidence;
(h) to provide assistance in establishing parentage where necessary for the recovery of maintenance;
(i) to initiate or facilitate the institution of proceedings to obtain any necessary provisional measures that are territorial in nature and the purpose of which is to secure the outcome of a pending maintenance application;
(j) to facilitate service of documents.

(3) The functions of the Central Authority under this Article may, to the extent permitted under the law of its State, be performed by public bodies, or other bodies subject to the supervision of the competent authorities of that State. The designation of any such public bodies or other bodies, as well as their contact details and the extent of their functions, shall be communicated by a Contracting State to the Permanent Bureau of the Hague Conference on Private International Law. Contracting States shall promptly inform the Permanent Bureau of any changes.

(4) Nothing in this Article or Article 7 shall be interpreted as imposing an obligation on a Central Authority to exercise powers that can be exercised only by judicial authorities under the law of the requested State.

Article 7
Requests for specific measures

(1) A Central Authority may make a request, supported by reasons, to another Central Authority to take appropriate specific measures under Article 6(2)(b), (c), (g), (h), (i) and (j) when no application under Article 10 is pending. The requested Central Authority shall take such measures as are appropriate if satisfied that they are necessary to assist a potential applicant in making an application under Article 10 or in determining whether such an application should be initiated.

(2) A Central Authority may also take specific measures on the request of another Central Authority in relation to a case having an international element concerning the recovery of maintenance pending in the requesting State.

Scope—Art 7(1) permits pre-application investigation and imposes a duty on the receiving Central Authority to take the requested specific measure if it is satisfied that it is necessary to assist a potential applicant in making an application or in determining whether such an application should be initiated. Art 7(2) also gives a discretion to a receiving Central Authority to take a specific measure in a case pending in the requesting Contracting State having an international element (eg where it would be relevant to have information on the debtor's assets).

Article 8
Central Authority costs

(1) Each Central Authority shall bear its own costs in applying this Convention.

(2) Central Authorities may not impose any charge on an applicant for the provision of their services under the Convention save for exceptional costs arising from a request for a specific measure under Article 7.

(3) The requested Central Authority may not recover the costs of the services referred to in paragraph 2 without the prior consent of the applicant to the provision of those services at such cost.

CHAPTER III
APPLICATIONS THROUGH CENTRAL AUTHORITIES

Scope—Chapter III deals with applications that may be made to a Central Authority and the processes involved. Art 10 permits applications for the establishment of a maintenance decision in the territory of the requested Contracting State, recognition and enforcement in maintenance decisions from another Contracting State and modification of decisions. The law to be applied is that of the requesting Contracting State and establishment decisions are subject to the relevant jurisdictional provisions of that Contracting State, which in the case of the UK is the Maintenance Regulation (Art 10). Art 11 provides for the minimum contents of an application and Art 12 makes provisions for the methods by which Central Authorities must process applications, with only limited scope for refusal (Art 12.8). Arts 14–17 make provision for legal aid. The general principle is that entitlement to legal aid should not be less than in equivalent domestic cases (Art 14(4)). The general rule for child support cases is free legal aid for all applications concerning a child (Art 15). The EU has decided not to make a declaration for use of the child-centred means test in Art 16 and therefore Art 15 is the applicable system for the UK. However, for any application except for recognition and enforcement, a Contracting State may refuse legal aid if the application crosses the high threshold of being manifestly unfounded (Art 15(2)). In consequence, the vast majority of child cases will be dealt with on the basis of free legal aid under Chs II and III. For non-child cases, Art 17 provides the basic rule that, for all applications, provision of legal aid may be subject to means and merit testing in accordance with national law. For recognition and enforcement cases, there is a special rule so that, where the applicant received legal aid in the proceedings in the Contracting State of origin, he/she will receive legal aid to at least the same extent in the recognition and enforcement proceedings.

Article 9
Application through Central Authorities

An application under this Chapter shall be made through the Central Authority of the Contracting State in which the applicant resides to the Central Authority of the requested State. For the purpose of this provision, residence excludes mere presence.

Article 10
Available applications

(1) The following categories of application shall be available to a creditor in a requesting State seeking to recover maintenance under this Convention –

(a) recognition or recognition and enforcement of a decision;
(b) enforcement of a decision made or recognised in the requested State;
(c) establishment of a decision in the requested State where there is no existing decision, including where necessary the establishment of parentage;
(d) establishment of a decision in the requested State where recognition and enforcement of a decision is not possible, or is refused, because of the lack of a basis for recognition and enforcement under Article 20, or on the grounds specified in Article 22(b) or (e);
(e) modification of a decision made in the requested State;
(f) modification of a decision made in a State other than the requested State.

(2) The following categories of application shall be available to a debtor in a requesting State against whom there is an existing maintenance decision –

(a) recognition of a decision, or an equivalent procedure leading to the suspension, or limiting the enforcement, of a previous decision in the requested State;
(b) modification of a decision made in the requested State;
(c) modification of a decision made in a State other than the requested State.

(3) Save as otherwise provided in this Convention, the applications in paragraphs 1 and 2 shall be determined under the law of the requested State, and applications in paragraphs 1(c) to (f) and 2(b) and (c) shall be subject to the jurisdictional rules applicable in the requested State.

Article 11
Application contents

(1) All applications under Article 10 shall as a minimum include –

(a) a statement of the nature of the application or applications;
(b) the name and contact details, including the address and date of birth of the applicant;

(c) the name and, if known, address and date of birth of the respondent;
(d) the name and date of birth of any person for whom maintenance is sought;
(e) the grounds upon which the application is based;
(f) in an application by a creditor, information concerning where the maintenance payment should be sent or electronically transmitted;
(g) save in an application under Article 10(1)(a) and (2)(a), any information or document specified by declaration in accordance with Article 63 by the requested State;
(h) the name and contact details of the person or unit from the Central Authority of the requesting State responsible for processing the application.

(2) As appropriate, and to the extent known, the application shall in addition in particular include –

(a) the financial circumstances of the creditor;
(b) the financial circumstances of the debtor, including the name and address of the employer of the debtor and the nature and location of the assets of the debtor;
(c) any other information that may assist with the location of the respondent.

(3) The application shall be accompanied by any necessary supporting information or documentation including documentation concerning the entitlement of the applicant to free legal assistance. In the case of applications under Article 10(1)(a) and (2)(a), the application shall be accompanied only by the documents listed in Article 25.

(4) An application under Article 10 may be made in the form recommended and published by the Hague Conference on Private International Law.

Article 12
Transmission, receipt and processing of applications and cases through Central Authorities

(1) The Central Authority of the requesting State shall assist the applicant in ensuring that the application is accompanied by all the information and documents known by it to be necessary for consideration of the application.

(2) The Central Authority of the requesting State shall, when satisfied that the application complies with the requirements of the Convention, transmit the application on behalf of and with the consent of the applicant to the Central Authority of the requested State. The application shall be accompanied by the transmittal form set out in Annex 1. The Central Authority of the requesting State shall, when requested by the Central Authority of the requested State, provide a complete copy certified by the competent authority in the State of origin of any document specified under Articles 16(3), 25(1)(a), (b) and (d) and (3)(b) and 30(3).

(3) The requested Central Authority shall, within six weeks from the date of receipt of the application, acknowledge receipt in the form set out in Annex 2, and inform the Central Authority of the requesting State what initial steps have been or will be taken to deal with the application, and may request any further necessary documents and information. Within the same six-week period, the requested Central Authority shall provide to the requesting Central Authority the name and contact details of the person or unit responsible for responding to inquiries regarding the progress of the application.

(4) Within three months after the acknowledgement, the requested Central Authority shall inform the requesting Central Authority of the status of the application.

(5) Requesting and requested Central Authorities shall keep each other informed of –

(a) the person or unit responsible for a particular case;
(b) the progress of the case, and shall provide timely responses to enquiries.

(6) Central Authorities shall process a case as quickly as a proper consideration of the issues will allow.

(7) Central Authorities shall employ the most rapid and efficient means of communication at their disposal.

(8) A requested Central Authority may refuse to process an application only if it is manifest that the requirements of the Convention are not fulfilled. In such case, that Central Authority shall promptly inform the requesting Central Authority of its reasons for refusal.

(9) The requested Central Authority may not reject an application solely on the basis that additional documents or information are needed. However, the requested Central Authority may ask the requesting Central Authority to provide these additional documents or information. If the requesting Central Authority does not do so within three months or a longer period specified by the requested Central Authority, the requested Central Authority may decide that it will no longer process the application. In this case, it shall inform the requesting Central Authority of this decision.

Article 13
Means of communication

Any application made through Central Authorities of the Contracting States in accordance with this Chapter, and any document or information appended thereto or provided by a Central Authority, may not be challenged by the respondent by reason only of the medium or means of communication employed between the Central Authorities concerned.

Article 14
Effective access to procedures

(1) The requested State shall provide applicants with effective access to procedures, including enforcement and appeal procedures, arising from applications under this Chapter.

(2) To provide such effective access, the requested State shall provide free legal assistance in accordance with Articles 14 to 17 unless paragraph 3 applies.

(3) The requested State shall not be obliged to provide such free legal assistance if and to the extent that the procedures of that State enable the applicant to make the case without the need for such assistance, and the Central Authority provides such services as are necessary free of charge.

(4) Entitlements to free legal assistance shall not be less than those available in equivalent domestic cases.

(5) No security, bond or deposit, however described, shall be required to guarantee the payment of costs and expenses in proceedings under the Convention.

Article 15
Free legal assistance for child support applications

(1) The requested State shall provide free legal assistance in respect of all applications by a creditor under this Chapter concerning maintenance obligations arising from a parent-child relationship towards a person under the age of 21 years.

(2) Notwithstanding paragraph 1, the requested State may, in relation to applications other than those under Article 10(1)(a) and (b) and the cases covered by Article 20(4), refuse free legal assistance if it considers that, on the merits, the application or any appeal is manifestly unfounded.

Article 16
Declaration to permit use of child-centred means test

(1) Notwithstanding Article 15(1), a State may declare, in accordance with Article 63, that it will provide free legal assistance in respect of applications other than under Article 10(1)(a) and (b) and the cases covered by Article 20(4), subject to a test based on an assessment of the means of the child.

(2) A State shall, at the time of making such a declaration, provide information to the Permanent Bureau of the Hague Conference on Private International Law concerning the manner in which the assessment of the child's means will be carried out, including the financial criteria which would need to be met to satisfy the test.

(3) An application referred to in paragraph 1, addressed to a State which has made the declaration referred to in that paragraph, shall include a formal attestation by the applicant stating that the child's means meet the criteria referred to in paragraph 2. The requested State may only request further evidence of the child's means if it has reasonable grounds to believe that the information provided by the applicant is inaccurate.

(4) If the most favourable legal assistance provided for by the law of the requested State in respect of applications under this Chapter concerning maintenance obligations arising from a parent-child relationship towards a child is more favourable than that provided for under paragraphs 1 to 3, the most favourable legal assistance shall be provided.

Article 17
Applications not qualifying under Article 15 or Article 16

In the case of all applications under this Convention other than those under Article 15 or Article 16 –

- (a) the provision of free legal assistance may be made subject to a means or a merits test;
- (b) an applicant, who in the State of origin has benefited from free legal assistance, shall be entitled, in any proceedings for recognition or enforcement, to benefit, at least to the same extent, from free legal assistance as provided for by the law of the State addressed under the same circumstances.

CHAPTER IV
RESTRICTIONS ON BRINGING PROCEEDINGS

Article 18
Limit on proceedings

(1) Where a decision is made in a Contracting State where the creditor is habitually resident, proceedings to modify the decision or to make a new decision cannot be brought by the debtor in any other Contracting State as long as the creditor remains habitually resident in the State where the decision was made.

(2) Paragraph 1 shall not apply –

- (a) where, except in disputes relating to maintenance obligations in respect of children, there is agreement in writing between the parties to the jurisdiction of that other Contracting State;
- (b) where the creditor submits to the jurisdiction of that other Contracting State either expressly or by defending on the merits of the case without objecting to the jurisdiction at the first available opportunity;
- (c) where the competent authority in the State of origin cannot, or refuses to, exercise jurisdiction to modify the decision or make a new decision; or
- (d) where the decision made in the State of origin cannot be recognised or declared enforceable in the Contracting State where proceedings to modify the decision or make a new decision are contemplated.

Scope—Art 18 contains the only direct rule of jurisdiction in the 2007 Convention, in contrast to the Maintenance Regulation, which contains a comprehensive jurisdictional code. This rule of jurisdiction was incorporated in the Maintenance Regulation and is therefore already part of UK law. It reflects a deliberate policy choice in the 2007 Convention to favour the creditor.

CHAPTER V
RECOGNITION AND ENFORCEMENT

Article 19
Scope of the Chapter

(1) This Chapter shall apply to a decision rendered by a judicial or administrative authority in respect of a maintenance obligation. The term 'decision' also includes a settlement or agreement

concluded before or approved by such an authority. A decision may include automatic adjustment by indexation and a requirement to pay arrears, retroactive maintenance or interest and a determination of costs or expenses.

(2) If a decision does not relate solely to a maintenance obligation, the effect of this Chapter is limited to the parts of the decision which concern maintenance obligations.

(3) For the purpose of paragraph 1, 'administrative authority' means a public body whose decisions, under the law of the State where it is established –

- (a) may be made the subject of an appeal to or review by a judicial authority; and
- (b) have a similar force and effect to a decision of a judicial authority on the same matter.

(4) This Chapter also applies to maintenance arrangements in accordance with Article 30.

(5) The provisions of this Chapter shall apply to a request for recognition and enforcement made directly to a competent authority of the State addressed in accordance with Article 37.

Scope—The scope of the recognition and enforcement provisions is defined in wide terms to include decisions of administrative authorities (eg the CSA; Art 19(1),(3)) and maintenance arrangements (Arts 3 and 30). Partial enforcement of a decision is possible where the decision is not enforceable as a whole (Arts 19(2) and 21).

Defined term—'maintenance arrangement': Art 3(e).

Article 20
Bases for recognition and enforcement

(1) A decision made in one Contracting State ('the State of origin') shall be recognised and enforced in other Contracting States if –

- (a) the respondent was habitually resident in the State of origin at the time proceedings were instituted;
- (b) the respondent has submitted to the jurisdiction either expressly or by defending on the merits of the case without objecting to the jurisdiction at the first available opportunity;
- (c) the creditor was habitually resident in the State of origin at the time proceedings were instituted;
- (d) the child for whom maintenance was ordered was habitually resident in the State of origin at the time proceedings were instituted, provided that the respondent has lived with the child in that State or has resided in that State and provided support for the child there;
- (e) except in disputes relating to maintenance obligations in respect of children, there has been agreement to the jurisdiction in writing by the parties; or
- (f) the decision was made by an authority exercising jurisdiction on a matter of personal status or parental responsibility, unless that jurisdiction was based solely on the nationality of one of the parties.

(2) A Contracting State may make a reservation, in accordance with Article 62, in respect of paragraph 1(c), (e) or (f).

(3) A Contracting State making a reservation under paragraph 2 shall recognise and enforce a decision if its law would in similar factual circumstances confer or would have conferred jurisdiction on its authorities to make such a decision.

(4) A Contracting State shall, if recognition of a decision is not possible as a result of a reservation under paragraph 2, and if the debtor is habitually resident in that State, take all appropriate measures to establish a decision for the benefit of the creditor. The preceding sentence shall not apply to direct requests for recognition and enforcement under Article 19(5) or to claims for support referred to in Article 2(1)(b).

(5) A decision in favour of a child under the age of 18 years which cannot be recognised by virtue only of a reservation in respect of paragraph 1(c), (e) or (f) shall be accepted as establishing the eligibility of that child for maintenance in the State addressed.

(6) A decision shall be recognised only if it has effect in the State of origin, and shall be enforced only if it is enforceable in the State of origin.

Scope—Because the 2007 Convention contains no rules as to jurisdiction (apart from Art 18), a mechanism is provided by Art 20, which stipulates that recognition and enforcement occurs in another Contracting State where the decision in the state of origin (as defined in Art 20(1)) complies with one of the jurisdictional bases in Art 20(1). The authorities of the Contracting State addressed are bound by any findings of fact on which the requesting Contracting State based jurisdiction (Art 27). A decision must first be enforceable in the state of origin to qualify for recognition and enforcement in another Contracting State (Art 20(6)).

'Reservation'—Whereas reservations under Art 62 are possible as the basis of providing alternative means of obtaining maintenance, no such reservations have been made by the EU.

Article 21
Severability and partial recognition and enforcement

(1) If the State addressed is unable to recognise or enforce the whole of the decision, it shall recognise or enforce any severable part of the decision which can be so recognised or enforced.

(2) Partial recognition or enforcement of a decision can always be applied for.

Article 22
Grounds for refusing recognition and enforcement

Recognition and enforcement of a decision may be refused if –

- (a) recognition and enforcement of the decision is manifestly incompatible with the public policy ('*ordre public*') of the State addressed;
- (b) the decision was obtained by fraud in connection with a matter of procedure;
- (c) proceedings between the same parties and having the same purpose are pending before an authority of the State addressed and those proceedings were the first to be instituted;
- (d) the decision is incompatible with a decision rendered between the same parties and having the same purpose, either in the State addressed or in another State, provided that this latter decision fulfils the conditions necessary for its recognition and enforcement in the State addressed;
- (e) in a case where the respondent has neither appeared nor was represented in proceedings in the State of origin –
  - (i) when the law of the State of origin provides for notice of proceedings, the respondent did not have proper notice of the proceedings and an opportunity to be heard; or
  - (ii) when the law of the State of origin does not provide for notice of the proceedings, the respondent did not have proper notice of the decision and an opportunity to challenge or appeal it on fact and law; or
- (f) the decision was made in violation of Article 18.

Scope—Art 22 provides for the discretionary grounds for refusal of recognition and enforcement. Art 22(c) is a necessary accommodation of the fact that there are no direct rules of jurisdiction in the 2007 Convention.

Article 23
Procedure on an application for recognition and enforcement

(1) Subject to the provisions of the Convention, the procedures for recognition and enforcement shall be governed by the law of the State addressed.

(2) Where an application for recognition and enforcement of a decision has been made through Central Authorities in accordance with Chapter III, the requested Central Authority shall promptly either –

- (a) refer the application to the competent authority which shall without delay declare the decision enforceable or register the decision for enforcement; or
- (b) if it is the competent authority take such steps itself.

(3) Where the request is made directly to a competent authority in the State addressed in accordance with Article 19(5), that authority shall without delay declare the decision enforceable or register the decision for enforcement.

(4) A declaration or registration may be refused only on the ground set out in Article 22(a). At this stage neither the applicant nor the respondent is entitled to make any submissions.

(5) The applicant and the respondent shall be promptly notified of the declaration or registration, made under paragraphs 2 and 3, or the refusal thereof in accordance with paragraph 4, and may bring a challenge or appeal on fact and on a point of law.

(6) A challenge or an appeal is to be lodged within 30 days of notification under paragraph 5. If the contesting party is not resident in the Contracting State in which the declaration or registration was made or refused, the challenge or appeal shall be lodged within 60 days of notification.

(7) A challenge or appeal may be founded only on the following –

- (a) the grounds for refusing recognition and enforcement set out in Article 22;
- (b) the bases for recognition and enforcement under Article 20;
- (c) the authenticity or integrity of any document transmitted in accordance with Article 25(1)(a), (b) or (d) or (3)(b).

(8) A challenge or an appeal by a respondent may also be founded on the fulfilment of the debt to the extent that the recognition and enforcement relates to payments that fell due in the past.

(9) The applicant and the respondent shall be promptly notified of the decision following the challenge or the appeal.

(10) A further appeal, if permitted by the law of the State addressed, shall not have the effect of staying the enforcement of the decision unless there are exceptional circumstances.

(11) In taking any decision on recognition and enforcement, including any appeal, the competent authority shall act expeditiously.

Scope—Art 23 describes the procedure on an application for recognition and enforcement, which applies both to applications made through Central Authorities (Art 23(2)) and those made directly (Art 23(3)). The procedure is in two stages, with the possibility of an appeal against the second stage. First, the application is considered without submissions from either party and will be recognised unless Art 22(a) (recognition manifestly incompatible with the public policy of the Contracting State addressed) applies. At the second stage, the parties are notified of the decision and either may appeal (Art 23(5)). The bases of appeal are limited to the grounds set out in Art 23(7),(8).

'Further appeal' (Art 23(10))—A further appeal from the second stage of the procedure is provided for in England and Wales by MCA 1980, s 111A.

Article 24

Alternative procedure on an application for recognition and enforcement

(1) Notwithstanding Article 23(2) to (11), a State may declare, in accordance with Article 63, that it will apply the procedure for recognition and enforcement set out in this Article.

(2) Where an application for recognition and enforcement of a decision has been made through Central Authorities in accordance with Chapter III, the requested Central Authority shall promptly either –

- (a) refer the application to the competent authority which shall decide on the application for recognition and enforcement; or
- (b) if it is the competent authority, take such a decision itself.

(3) A decision on recognition and enforcement shall be given by the competent authority after the respondent has been duly and promptly notified of the proceedings and both parties have been given an adequate opportunity to be heard.

(4) The competent authority may review the grounds for refusing recognition and enforcement set out in Article 22(a), (c) and (d) of its own motion. It may review any grounds listed in Articles 20, 22 and 23(7)(c) if raised by the respondent or if concerns relating to those grounds arise from the face of the documents submitted in accordance with Article 25.

(5) A refusal of recognition and enforcement may also be founded on the fulfilment of the debt to the extent that the recognition and enforcement relates to payments that fell due in the past.

(6) Any appeal, if permitted by the law of the State addressed, shall not have the effect of staying the enforcement of the decision unless there are exceptional circumstances.

(7) In taking any decision on recognition and enforcement, including any appeal, the competent authority shall act expeditiously.

Article 25
Documents

(1) An application for recognition and enforcement under Article 23 or Article 24 shall be accompanied by the following –

- (a) a complete text of the decision;
- (b) a document stating that the decision is enforceable in the State of origin and, in the case of a decision by an administrative authority, a document stating that the requirements of Article 19(3) are met unless that State has specified in accordance with Article 57 that decisions of its administrative authorities always meet those requirements;
- (c) if the respondent did not appear and was not represented in the proceedings in the State of origin, a document or documents attesting, as appropriate, either that the respondent had proper notice of the proceedings and an opportunity to be heard, or that the respondent had proper notice of the decision and the opportunity to challenge or appeal it on fact and law;
- (d) where necessary, a document showing the amount of any arrears and the date such amount was calculated;
- (e) where necessary, in the case of a decision providing for automatic adjustment by indexation, a document providing the information necessary to make the appropriate calculations;
- (f) where necessary, documentation showing the extent to which the applicant received free legal assistance in the State of origin.

(2) Upon a challenge or appeal under Article 23(7)(c) or upon request by the competent authority in the State addressed, a complete copy of the document concerned, certified by the competent authority in the State of origin, shall be provided promptly –

- (a) by the Central Authority of the requesting State, where the application has been made in accordance with Chapter III;
- (b) by the applicant, where the request has been made directly to a competent authority of the State addressed.

(3) A Contracting State may specify in accordance with Article 57 –

- (a) that a complete copy of the decision certified by the competent authority in the State of origin must accompany the application;
- (b) circumstances in which it will accept, in lieu of a complete text of the decision, an abstract or extract of the decision drawn up by the competent authority of the State of origin, which may be made in the form recommended and published by the Hague Conference on Private International Law; or
- (c) that it does not require a document stating that the requirements of Article 19(3) are met.

Article 26
Procedure on an application for recognition

This Chapter shall apply mutatis mutandis to an application for recognition of a decision, save that the requirement of enforceability is replaced by the requirement that the decision has effect in the State of origin.

Article 27
Findings of fact

Any competent authority of the State addressed shall be bound by the findings of fact on which the authority of the State of origin based its jurisdiction.

Article 28
No review of the merits

There shall be no review by any competent authority of the State addressed of the merits of a decision.

Article 29
Physical presence of the child or the applicant not required

The physical presence of the child or the applicant shall not be required in any proceedings in the State addressed under this Chapter.

Article 30
Maintenance arrangements

(1) A maintenance arrangement made in a Contracting State shall be entitled to recognition and enforcement as a decision under this Chapter provided that it is enforceable as a decision in the State of origin.

(2) For the purpose of Article 10(1)(a) and (b) and (2)(a), the term 'decision' includes a maintenance arrangement.

(3) An application for recognition and enforcement of a maintenance arrangement shall be accompanied by the following –

- (a) a complete text of the maintenance arrangement; and
- (b) a document stating that the particular maintenance arrangement is enforceable as a decision in the State of origin.

(4) Recognition and enforcement of a maintenance arrangement may be refused if –

- (a) the recognition and enforcement is manifestly incompatible with the public policy of the State addressed;
- (b) the maintenance arrangement was obtained by fraud or falsification;
- (c) the maintenance arrangement is incompatible with a decision rendered between the same parties and having the same purpose, either in the State addressed or in another State, provided that this latter decision fulfils the conditions necessary for its recognition and enforcement in the State addressed.

(5) The provisions of this Chapter, with the exception of Articles 20, 22, 23(7) and 25(1) and (3), shall apply mutatis mutandis to the recognition and enforcement of a maintenance arrangement save that –

- (a) a declaration or registration in accordance with Article 23(2) and (3) may be refused only on the ground set out in paragraph 4(a);
- (b) a challenge or appeal as referred to in Article 23(6) may be founded only on the following –
  - (i) the grounds for refusing recognition and enforcement set out in paragraph 4;
  - (ii) the authenticity or integrity of any document transmitted in accordance with paragraph 3;
- (c) as regards the procedure under Article 24(4), the competent authority may review of its own motion the ground for refusing recognition and enforcement set out in paragraph 4(a) of this Article. It may review all grounds listed in paragraph 4 of this Article and the authenticity or integrity of any document transmitted in accordance with paragraph 3 if raised by the respondent or if concerns relating to those grounds arise from the face of those documents.

(6) Proceedings for recognition and enforcement of a maintenance arrangement shall be suspended if a challenge concerning the arrangement is pending before a competent authority of a Contracting State.

(7) A State may declare, in accordance with Article 63, that applications for recognition and enforcement of a maintenance arrangement shall only be made through Central Authorities.

(8) A Contracting State may, in accordance with Article 62, reserve the right not to recognise and enforce a maintenance arrangement.

Scope—Art 30 sets out the circumstances in which a maintenance arrangement may be recognised and enforced under the 2007 Convention. Recognition and enforcement of a maintenance arrangement may be sought through a Central Authority under the administrative cooperation procedures because it will be treated as a 'decision' under Art 10(1)(a),(b) and (2)(a) (Art 30(2)). The accompanying documentation required for an application for recognition and enforcement of a maintenance arrangement differs from other decisions (Art 30(3)) and the grounds for refusal of recognition and enforcement are more restricted, owing to the nature of maintenance arrangements (Art 30(4)). Art 30(5) makes necessary modifications to the Ch IV procedure. The EU has not chosen to reserve a right not to recognise and enforce maintenance arrangements in accordance with Art 62 (Art 30(8)).

Defined term—'maintenance arrangement': Art 3(e).

Article 31
Decisions produced by the combined effect of provisional and confirmation orders

Where a decision is produced by the combined effect of a provisional order made in one State and an order by an authority in another State ('the confirming State') confirming the provisional order –

(a) each of those States shall be deemed for the purposes of this Chapter to be a State of origin;

(b) the requirements of Article 22(e) shall be met if the respondent had proper notice of the proceedings in the confirming State and an opportunity to oppose the confirmation of the provisional order;

(c) the requirement of Article 20(6) that a decision be enforceable in the State of origin shall be met if the decision is enforceable in the confirming State; and

(d) Article 18 shall not prevent proceedings for the modification of the decision being commenced in either State.

Scope—Art 31 refers to the process of provisional and confirmation orders, which, as far as the UK is concerned, is in use primarily for Commonwealth jurisdictions, the relevant domestic legislation being MO(RE)A 1972, Pt I and MO(FE)A 1920. Art 31 provides for the application of the 2007 Convention to such procedures.

CHAPTER VI
ENFORCEMENT BY THE STATE ADDRESSED

Article 32
Enforcement under internal law

(1) Subject to the provisions of this Chapter, enforcement shall take place in accordance with the law of the State addressed.

(2) Enforcement shall be prompt.

(3) In the case of applications through Central Authorities, where a decision has been declared enforceable or registered for enforcement under Chapter V, enforcement shall proceed without the need for further action by the applicant.

(4) Effect shall be given to any rules applicable in the State of origin of the decision relating to the duration of the maintenance obligation.

(5) Any limitation on the period for which arrears may be enforced shall be determined either by the law of the State of origin of the decision or by the law of the State addressed, whichever provides for the longer limitation period.

Scope—Enforcement is, under domestic law, subject to the provisions of the 2007 Convention.

Article 33
Non-discrimination

The State addressed shall provide at least the same range of enforcement methods for cases under the Convention as are available in domestic cases.

Note—See annotations to the International Recovery of Maintenance (Hague Convention 2007 etc) Regulations 2012, Sch 2.

Article 34
Enforcement measures

(1) Contracting States shall make available in internal law effective measures to enforce decisions under this Convention.

(2) Such measures may include –

(a) wage withholding;
(b) garnishment from bank accounts and other sources;
(c) deductions from social security payments;
(d) lien on or forced sale of property;
(e) tax refund withholding;
(f) withholding or attachment of pension benefits;
(g) credit bureau reporting;
(h) denial, suspension or revocation of various licenses (for example, driving licenses);
(i) the use of mediation, conciliation or similar processes to bring about voluntary compliance.

Scope—Art 34 requires the provision of effective enforcement measures. However, the list in Art 34(2) is illustrative and not exhaustive.

Article 35
Transfer of funds

(1) Contracting States are encouraged to promote, including by means of international agreements, the use of the most cost-effective and efficient methods available to transfer funds payable as maintenance.

(2) A Contracting State, under whose law the transfer of funds is restricted, shall accord the highest priority to the transfer of funds payable under this Convention.

CHAPTER VII
PUBLIC BODIES

Article 36
Public bodies as applicants

(1) For the purposes of applications for recognition and enforcement under Article 10(1)(a) and (b) and cases covered by Article 20(4), 'creditor' includes a public body acting in place of an individual to whom maintenance is owed or one to which reimbursement is owed for benefits provided in place of maintenance.

(2) The right of a public body to act in place of an individual to whom maintenance is owed or to seek reimbursement of benefits provided to the creditor in place of maintenance shall be governed by the law to which the body is subject.

(3) A public body may seek recognition or claim enforcement of –

(a) a decision rendered against a debtor on the application of a public body which claims payment of benefits provided in place of maintenance;
(b) a decision rendered between a creditor and debtor to the extent of the benefits provided to the creditor in place of maintenance.

(4) The public body seeking recognition or claiming enforcement of a decision shall upon request furnish any document necessary to establish its right under paragraph 2 and that benefits have been provided to the creditor.

Scope—Art 36 provides for the position of public bodies (eg the CMS) as applicants and permits a public body to obtain recognition or enforcement of a decision against a debtor where the public body seeks reimbursement of benefits paid to the creditor in lieu of maintenance.

CHAPTER VIII
GENERAL PROVISIONS

Article 37
Direct requests to competent authorities

(1) The Convention shall not exclude the possibility of recourse to such procedures as may be available under the internal law of a Contracting State allowing a person (an applicant) to seise directly a competent authority of that State in a matter governed by the Convention including, subject to Article 18, for the purpose of having a maintenance decision established or modified.

(2) Articles 14(5) and 17(b) and the provisions of Chapters V, VI, VII and this Chapter, with the exception of Articles 40(2), 42, 43(3), 44(3), 45 and 55, shall apply in relation to a request for recognition and enforcement made directly to a competent authority in a Contracting State.

(3) For the purpose of paragraph 2, Article 2(1)(a) shall apply to a decision granting maintenance to a vulnerable person over the age specified in that sub-paragraph where such decision was rendered before the person reached that age and provided for maintenance beyond that age by reason of the impairment.

Scope—The 2007 Convention does not exclude the possibility of a direct request to competent authorities (in the UK, the court), even though an application through the Central Authority would be available. However, in relation to applications for registration and enforcement, all such applications must be made through the Lord Chancellor as the Central Authority for England and Wales (International Recovery of Maintenance (Hague Convention 2007 etc) Regulations 2012).

Article 38
Protection of personal data

Personal data gathered or transmitted under the Convention shall be used only for the purposes for which they were gathered or transmitted.

Article 39
Confidentiality

Any authority processing information shall ensure its confidentiality in accordance with the law of its State.

Article 40
Non-disclosure of information

(1) An authority shall not disclose or confirm information gathered or transmitted in application of this Convention if it determines that to do so could jeopardise the health, safety or liberty of a person.

(2) A determination to this effect made by one Central Authority shall be taken into account by another Central Authority, in particular in cases of family violence.

(3) Nothing in this Article shall impede the gathering and transmitting of information by and between authorities in so far as necessary to carry out the obligations under the Convention.

Article 41
No legalisation

No legalisation or similar formality may be required in the context of this Convention.

'Under the same conditions' (Art 41.1)—In consequence of this provision, driving disqualification orders have been extended to the Maintenance Regulation by the International Recovery of Maintenance (Hague Convention 2007 etc) Regulations 2012, Sch 2.

Article 42
Power of attorney

The Central Authority of the requested State may require a power of attorney from the applicant only if it acts on his or her behalf in judicial proceedings or before other authorities, or in order to designate a representative so to act.

Article 43
Recovery of costs

(1) Recovery of any costs incurred in the application of this Convention shall not take precedence over the recovery of maintenance.

(2) A State may recover costs from an unsuccessful party.

(3) For the purposes of an application under Article 10(1)(b) to recover costs from an unsuccessful party in accordance with paragraph 2, the term 'creditor' in Article 10(1) shall include a State.

(4) This Article shall be without prejudice to Article 8.

Article 44
Language requirements

(1) Any application and related documents shall be in the original language, and shall be accompanied by a translation into an official language of the requested State or another language which the requested State has indicated, by way of declaration in accordance with Article 63, it will accept, unless the competent authority of that State dispenses with translation.

(2) A Contracting State which has more than one official language and cannot, for reasons of internal law, accept for the whole of its territory documents in one of those languages shall, by declaration in accordance with Article 63, specify the language in which such documents or translations thereof shall be drawn up for submission in the specified parts of its territory.

(3) Unless otherwise agreed by the Central Authorities, any other communications between such Authorities shall be in an official language of the requested State or in either English or French. However, a Contracting State may, by making a reservation in accordance with Article 62, object to the use of either English or French.

Article 45
Means and costs of translation

(1) In the case of applications under Chapter III, the Central Authorities may agree in an individual case or generally that the translation into an official language of the requested State may be made in the requested State from the original language or from any other agreed language. If there is no agreement and it is not possible for the requesting Central Authority to comply with the requirements of Article 44(1) and (2), then the application and related documents may be transmitted with translation into English or French for further translation into an official language of the requested State.

(2) The cost of translation arising from the application of paragraph 1 shall be borne by the requesting State unless otherwise agreed by Central Authorities of the States concerned.

(3) Notwithstanding Article 8, the requesting Central Authority may charge an applicant for the costs of translation of an application and related documents, except in so far as those costs may be covered by its system of legal assistance.

Article 46
Non-unified legal systems – interpretation

(1) In relation to a State in which two or more systems of law or sets of rules of law with regard to any matter dealt with in this Convention apply in different territorial units –

(a) any reference to the law or procedure of a State shall be construed as referring, where appropriate, to the law or procedure in force in the relevant territorial unit;

(b) any reference to a decision established, recognised, recognised and enforced, enforced or modified in that State shall be construed as referring, where appropriate, to a decision established, recognised, recognised and enforced, enforced or modified in the relevant territorial unit;

(c) any reference to a judicial or administrative authority in that State shall be construed as referring, where appropriate, to a judicial or administrative authority in the relevant territorial unit;

(d) any reference to competent authorities, public bodies, and other bodies of that State, other than Central Authorities, shall be construed as referring, where appropriate, to those authorised to act in the relevant territorial unit;

(e) any reference to residence or habitual residence in that State shall be construed as referring, where appropriate, to residence or habitual residence in the relevant territorial unit;

(f) any reference to location of assets in that State shall be construed as referring, where appropriate, to the location of assets in the relevant territorial unit;

(g) any reference to a reciprocity arrangement in force in a State shall be construed as referring, where appropriate, to a reciprocity arrangement in force in the relevant territorial unit;

(h) any reference to free legal assistance in that State shall be construed as referring, where appropriate, to free legal assistance in the relevant territorial unit;

(i) any reference to a maintenance arrangement made in a State shall be construed as referring, where appropriate, to a maintenance arrangement made in the relevant territorial unit;

(j) any reference to recovery of costs by a State shall be construed as referring, where appropriate, to the recovery of costs by the relevant territorial unit.

(2) This Article shall not apply to a Regional Economic Integration Organisation.

Article 47
Non-unified legal systems – substantive rules

(1) A Contracting State with two or more territorial units in which different systems of law apply shall not be bound to apply this Convention to situations which involve solely such different territorial units.

(2) A competent authority in a territorial unit of a Contracting State with two or more territorial units in which different systems of law apply shall not be bound to recognise or enforce a decision from another Contracting State solely because the decision has been recognised or enforced in another territorial unit of the same Contracting State under this Convention.

(3) This Article shall not apply to a Regional Economic Integration Organisation.

Article 48
Co-ordination with prior Hague Maintenance Conventions

In relations between the Contracting States, this Convention replaces, subject to Article 56(2), the Hague Convention of 2 October 1973 on the Recognition and Enforcement of Decisions Relating to Maintenance Obligations and the Hague Convention of 15 April 1958 concerning the recognition and enforcement of decisions relating to maintenance obligations towards children in so far as their scope of application as between such States coincides with the scope of application of this Convention.

Article 49
Co-ordination with the 1956 New York Convention

In relations between the Contracting States, this Convention replaces the United Nations Convention on the Recovery Abroad of Maintenance of 20 June 1956, in so far as its scope of application as between such States coincides with the scope of application of this Convention.

Article 50
Relationship with prior Hague Conventions on service of documents and taking of evidence

This Convention does not affect the Hague Convention of 1 March 1954 on civil procedure, the Hague Convention of 15 November 1965 on the Service Abroad of Judicial and Extrajudicial Documents in Civil or Commercial Matters and the Hague Convention of 18 March 1970 on the Taking of Evidence Abroad in Civil or Commercial Matters.

Article 51
Co-ordination of instruments and supplementary agreements

(1) This Convention does not affect any international instrument concluded before this Convention to which Contracting States are Parties and which contains provisions on matters governed by this Convention.

(2) Any Contracting State may conclude with one or more Contracting States agreements, which contain provisions on matters governed by the Convention, with a view to improving the application of the Convention between or among themselves, provided that such agreements are consistent with the objects and purpose of the Convention and do not affect, in the relationship of such States with other Contracting States, the application of the provisions of the Convention. The States which have concluded such an agreement shall transmit a copy to the depositary of the Convention.

(3) Paragraphs 1 and 2 shall also apply to reciprocity arrangements and to uniform laws based on special ties between the States concerned.

(4) This Convention shall not affect the application of instruments of a Regional Economic Integration Organisation that is a Party to this Convention, adopted after the conclusion of the Convention, on matters governed by the Convention provided that such instruments do not affect, in the relationship of Member States of the Regional Economic Integration Organisation with other Contracting States, the application of the provisions of the Convention. As concerns the recognition or enforcement of decisions as between Member States of the Regional Economic Integration Organisation, the Convention shall not affect the rules of the Regional Economic Integration Organisation, whether adopted before or after the conclusion of the Convention.

Scope—Art 51 enables EU Member States to continue to operate the Maintenance Regulation, giving it precedence over the 2007 Convention as between EU Member States, whereas EU Member States will have to apply the 2007 Convention in their relations with non-EU Contracting States that are Contracting States to the 2007 Convention.

Article 52
Most effective rule

(1) This Convention shall not prevent the application of an agreement, arrangement or international instrument in force between the requesting State and the requested State, or a reciprocity arrangement in force in the requested State that provides for –

(a) broader bases for recognition of maintenance decisions, without prejudice to Article 22(f) of the Convention;
(b) simplified, more expeditious procedures on an application for recognition or recognition and enforcement of maintenance decisions;
(c) more beneficial legal assistance than that provided for under Articles 14 to 17; or
(d) procedures permitting an applicant from a requesting State to make a request directly to the Central Authority of the requested State.

(2) This Convention shall not prevent the application of a law in force in the requested State that provides for more effective rules as referred to in paragraph 1(a) to (c). However, as regards simplified, more expeditious procedures referred to in paragraph 1(b), they must be compatible with the protection offered to the parties under Articles 23 and 24, in particular as regards the rights of the parties to be duly notified of the proceedings and be given adequate opportunity to be heard and as regards the effects of any challenge or appeal.

Article 53
Uniform interpretation

In the interpretation of this Convention, regard shall be had to its international character and to the need to promote uniformity in its application.

Article 54
Review of practical operation of the Convention

(1) The Secretary General of the Hague Conference on Private International Law shall at regular intervals convene a Special Commission in order to review the practical operation of the Convention and to encourage the development of good practices under the Convention.

(2) For the purpose of such review, Contracting States shall co-operate with the Permanent Bureau of the Hague Conference on Private International Law in the gathering of information, including statistics and case law, concerning the practical operation of the Convention.

Article 55
Amendment of forms

(1) The forms annexed to this Convention may be amended by a decision of a Special Commission convened by the Secretary General of the Hague Conference on Private International Law to which all Contracting States and all Members shall be invited. Notice of the proposal to amend the forms shall be included in the agenda for the meeting.

(2) Amendments adopted by the Contracting States present at the Special Commission shall come into force for all Contracting States on the first day of the seventh calendar month after the date of their communication by the depositary to all Contracting States.

(3) During the period provided for in paragraph 2 any Contracting State may by notification in writing to the depositary make a reservation, in accordance with Article 62, with respect to the amendment. The State making such reservation shall, until the reservation is withdrawn, be treated as a State not Party to the present Convention with respect to that amendment.

Article 56
Transitional provisions

(1) The Convention shall apply in every case where –

- (a) a request pursuant to Article 7 or an application pursuant to Chapter III has been received by the Central Authority of the requested State after the Convention has entered into force between the requesting State and the requested State;
- (b) a direct request for recognition and enforcement has been received by the competent authority of the State addressed after the Convention has entered into force between the State of origin and the State addressed.

(2) With regard to the recognition and enforcement of decisions between Contracting States to this Convention that are also Parties to either of the Hague Maintenance Conventions mentioned in Article 48, if the conditions for the recognition and enforcement under this Convention prevent the recognition and enforcement of a decision given in the State of origin before the entry into force of this Convention for that State, that would otherwise have been recognised and enforced under the terms of the Convention that was in effect at the time the decision was rendered, the conditions of that Convention shall apply.

(3) The State addressed shall not be bound under this Convention to enforce a decision or a maintenance arrangement, in respect of payments falling due prior to the entry into force of the Convention between the State of origin and the State addressed, except for maintenance obligations arising from a parent-child relationship towards a person under the age of 21 years.

Article 57

Provision of information concerning laws, procedures and services

(1) A Contracting State, by the time its instrument of ratification or accession is deposited or a declaration is submitted in accordance with Article 61 of the Convention, shall provide the Permanent Bureau of the Hague Conference on Private International Law with –

(a) a description of its laws and procedures concerning maintenance obligations;
(b) a description of the measures it will take to meet the obligations under Article 6;
(c) a description of how it will provide applicants with effective access to procedures, as required under Article 14;
(d) a description of its enforcement rules and procedures, including any limitations on enforcement, in particular debtor protection rules and limitation periods;
(e) any specification referred to in Article 25(1)(b) and (3).

(2) Contracting States may, in fulfilling their obligations under paragraph 1, utilise a country profile form recommended and published by the Hague Conference on Private International Law.

(3) Information shall be kept up to date by the Contracting States.

CHAPTER IX
FINAL PROVISIONS

Article 58

Signature, ratification and accession

(1) The Convention shall be open for signature by the States which were Members of the Hague Conference on Private International Law at the time of its Twenty-First Session and by the other States which participated in that Session.

(2) It shall be ratified, accepted or approved and the instruments of ratification, acceptance or approval shall be deposited with the Ministry of Foreign Affairs of the Kingdom of the Netherlands, depositary of the Convention.

(3) Any other State or Regional Economic Integration Organisation may accede to the Convention after it has entered into force in accordance with Article 60(1).

(4) The instrument of accession shall be deposited with the depositary.

(5) Such accession shall have effect only as regards the relations between the acceding State and those Contracting States which have not raised an objection to its accession in the 12 months after the date of the notification referred to in Article 65. Such an objection may also be raised by States at the time when they ratify, accept or approve the Convention after an accession. Any such objection shall be notified to the depositary.

Article 59

Regional Economic Integration Organisations

(1) A Regional Economic Integration Organisation which is constituted solely by sovereign States and has competence over some or all of the matters governed by this Convention may similarly sign, accept, approve or accede to this Convention. The Regional Economic Integration Organisation shall in that case have the rights and obligations of a Contracting State, to the extent that the Organisation has competence over matters governed by the Convention.

(2) The Regional Economic Integration Organisation shall, at the time of signature, acceptance, approval or accession, notify the depositary in writing of the matters governed by this Convention in respect of which competence has been transferred to that Organisation by its Member States. The Organisation shall promptly notify the depositary in writing of any changes to its competence as specified in the most recent notice given under this paragraph.

(3) At the time of signature, acceptance, approval or accession, a Regional Economic Integration Organisation may declare in accordance with Article 63 that it exercises competence over all the matters governed by this Convention and that the Member States which have transferred

competence to the Regional Economic Integration Organisation in respect of the matter in question shall be bound by this Convention by virtue of the signature, acceptance, approval or accession of the Organisation.

(4) For the purposes of the entry into force of this Convention, any instrument deposited by a Regional Economic Integration Organisation shall not be counted unless the Regional Economic Integration Organisation makes a declaration in accordance with paragraph 3.

(5) Any reference to a 'Contracting State' or 'State' in this Convention shall apply equally to a Regional Economic Integration Organisation that is a Party to it, where appropriate. In the event that a declaration is made by a Regional Economic Integration Organisation in accordance with paragraph 3, any reference to a 'Contracting State' or 'State' in this Convention shall apply equally to the relevant Member States of the Organisation, where appropriate.

Article 60
Entry into force

(1) The Convention shall enter into force on the first day of the month following the expiration of three months after the deposit of the second instrument of ratification, acceptance or approval referred to in Article 58.

(2) Thereafter the Convention shall enter into force –

(a) for each State or Regional Economic Integration Organisation referred to in Article 59(1) subsequently ratifying, accepting or approving it, on the first day of the month following the expiration of three months after the deposit of its instrument of ratification, acceptance or approval;

(b) for each State or Regional Economic Integration Organisation referred to in Article 58(3) on the day after the end of the period during which objections may be raised in accordance with Article 58(5);

(c) for a territorial unit to which the Convention has been extended in accordance with Article 61, on the first day of the month following the expiration of three months after the notification referred to in that Article.

Article 61
Declarations with respect to non-unified legal systems

(1) If a State has two or more territorial units in which different systems of law are applicable in relation to matters dealt with in the Convention, it may at the time of signature, ratification, acceptance, approval or accession declare in accordance with Article 63 that this Convention shall extend to all its territorial units or only to one or more of them and may modify this declaration by submitting another declaration at any time.

(2) Any such declaration shall be notified to the depositary and shall state expressly the territorial units to which the Convention applies.

(3) If a State makes no declaration under this Article, the Convention shall extend to all territorial units of that State.

(4) This Article shall not apply to a Regional Economic Integration Organisation.

Article 62
Reservations

(1) Any Contracting State may, not later than the time of ratification, acceptance, approval or accession, or at the time of making a declaration in terms of Article 61, make one or more of the reservations provided for in Articles 2(2), 20(2), 30(8), 44(3) and 55(3). No other reservation shall be permitted.

(2) Any State may at any time withdraw a reservation it has made. The withdrawal shall be notified to the depositary.

(3) The reservation shall cease to have effect on the first day of the third calendar month after the notification referred to in paragraph 2.

(4) Reservations under this Article shall have no reciprocal effect with the exception of the reservation provided for in Article 2(2).

Article 63
Declarations

(1) Declarations referred to in Articles 2(3), 11(1)(g), 16(1), 24(1), 30(7), 44(1) and (2), 59(3) and 61(1), may be made upon signature, ratification, acceptance, approval or accession or at any time thereafter, and may be modified or withdrawn at any time.

(2) Declarations, modifications and withdrawals shall be notified to the depositary.

(3) A declaration made at the time of signature, ratification, acceptance, approval or accession shall take effect simultaneously with the entry into force of this Convention for the State concerned.

(4) A declaration made at a subsequent time, and any modification or withdrawal of a declaration, shall take effect on the first day of the month following the expiration of three months after the date on which the notification is received by the depositary.

Article 64
Denunciation

(1) A Contracting State to the Convention may denounce it by a notification in writing addressed to the depositary. The denunciation may be limited to certain territorial units of a multi-unit State to which the Convention applies.

(2) The denunciation shall take effect on the first day of the month following the expiration of 12 months after the date on which the notification is received by the depositary. Where a longer period for the denunciation to take effect is specified in the notification, the denunciation shall take effect upon the expiration of such longer period after the date on which the notification is received by the depositary.

Article 65
Notification

The depositary shall notify the Members of the Hague Conference on Private International Law, and other States and Regional Economic Integration Organisations which have signed, ratified, accepted, approved or acceded in accordance with Articles 58 and 59 of the following –

(a) the signatures, ratifications, acceptances and approvals referred to in Articles 58 and 59;
(b) the accessions and objections raised to accessions referred to in Articles 58(3) and (5) and 59;
(c) the date on which the Convention enters into force in accordance with Article 60;
(d) the declarations referred to in Articles 2(3), 11(1)(g), 16(1), 24(1), 30(7), 44(1) and (2), 59(3) and 61(1);
(e) the agreements referred to in Article 51(2);
(f) the reservations referred to in Articles 2(2), 20(2), 30(8), 44(3) and 55(3), and the withdrawals referred to in Article 62(2);
(g) the denunciations referred to in Article 64.

In witness whereof the undersigned, being duly authorised thereto, have signed this Convention.

Done at The Hague, on the 23rd day of November 2007, in the English and French languages, both texts being equally authentic, in a single copy which shall be deposited in the archives of the Government of the Kingdom of the Netherlands, and of which a certified copy shall be sent, through diplomatic channels, to each of the Members of the Hague Conference on Private International Law at the date of its Twenty-First Session and to each of the other States which have participated in that Session.

★★★★

Council Regulation (EC) No 4/2009

of 18 December 2008

on jurisdiction, applicable law, recognition and enforcement of decisions and cooperation in matters relating to maintenance obligations

Scope—The Regulation (known as the Maintenance Regulation) came into force in the UK on 18 June 2011. It replaced Brussels I (Council Regulation (EC) No 44/2001 of 22 December 2000; now with effect from 10 January 2015, the Brussels I Regulation Recast or the Judgments Regulation (Regulation (EU) No 1215/2012)) in relation to maintenance obligations except in relation to procedures underway on 18 June 2011 (Art 75). As to Brussels I, see *The Family Court Practice 2011*. The Brussels I Regulation Recast is still of relevance, for example, to proceedings under TLATA 1996 (eg *Webb v Webb* (Case C-294/92) [1994] QB 696, ECJ; *Prazic v Prazic* [2006] 2 FLR 1128, CA; *G v G* [2015] EWHC 2101 (Fam)).

The Regulation does not as such provide for rules of applicable law, but instead refers (Art 15) to the Hague Protocol on the Law Applicable to Maintenance Obligations of 23 November 2007 (the Hague Protocol). Denmark (see, however, below) and the UK are not bound by the Hague Protocol (see annotations to Art 15). The CJJ(M)R 2011 (set out in Part IV), Sch 6 applies the Maintenance Regulation within the UK, for which purpose Scotland and Northern Ireland are in effect treated as separate Member States (see *Re V (European Maintenance Regulation)* [2017] 1 FLR 1083, FD).

The Regulation is designed to offer greater certainty and predictability to creditors and debtors of maintenance obligations and establishes common procedural rules in relation to cross-border disputes by permitting maintenance decisions, court settlements and authentic instruments (Art 2) made in one Member State to be recognised and enforced in another Member State without further formality (Recital 9). However, because of the position of the UK and Denmark, the Maintenance Regulation establishes two parallel recognition and enforcement regimes, described below. It has not as yet been decided whether a decision under the Maintenance Regulation would prevent the court from exercising its jurisdiction under MFPA 1984, Pt III (see *Agbaje v Agabje* [2010] 1 FLR 1813, SC, at [55]).

'Maintenance obligation' is not defined. However, the Regulation applies to maintenance obligations arising from a family relationship, parentage, marriage or affinity and is to be interpreted autonomously (Recital (11)). Furthermore, it applies to administratively made decisions (eg the CMS), not just court orders (Recital (12) and Art 2.2). See also, *Van den Boogaard v Laumen* [1997] 2 FLR 399, ECJ; *Moore v Moore* [2007] 2 FLR 339, CA; *T v T (Occupation Orders)* [2013] 1 FLR 364, FD; *Traversa v Freddi* [2011] 2 FLR 272, CA: 'maintenance' includes payment of a lump sum or a transfer of property in the nature of maintenance by way of spousal support (but not for the purpose of division of property or assets or compensation).

The Maintenance Regulation is used between Member States. Where non-EU Contracting States are concerned, Member States must use the Hague Convention 2007 on the International Recovery of Child Support and other forms of Family Maintenance.

To enable a maintenance creditor to obtain a decision easily in a Member State that will be automatically enforceable in another Member State without further formalities, the Regulation brings together provisions on jurisdiction, conflict of laws, recognition and enforceability, enforcement, legal aid and co-operation between Central Authorities. The available applications that can be made pursuant to the Regulation are set out at Art 56.

A decision given in a Member State bound by the Hague Protocol is recognised in another Member State without any special procedure being required and without any possibility of its recognition being opposed. Further, a decision that is enforceable in the originating Member State is enforceable in another Member State without the need for a declaration of enforceability (Art 17). Thus, the Regulation abolishes the exequatur procedure for decisions given by a Member State bound by the Hague Protocol.

For those Member States not bound by the Hague Protocol (the UK and Denmark), a decision will still be recognised without any special procedure being required. However, if the recognition of a decision is contested, it will be necessary for any interested party to apply for a decision that the decision be recognised (Art 23). Art 24 provides for when a decision is not to be recognised. Further, for a decision in a Member State not bound by the Hague Protocol to be enforceable in another Member State, it is necessary for it first to be declared enforceable in that Member State (Art 26). Art 28 deals with the procedure to follow for such a declaration of enforceability. The decision on the application for a declaration of enforceability may be appealed by either party (Art 32).

For Member States, whether or not bound by the Hague Protocol, the procedure for the enforcement of decisions given in another Member State is governed by the law of the Member State of enforcement (Art 41).

The Regulation does not in any way imply recognition of the family relationship, parentage, marriage or affinity underlying the maintenance obligation (Art 22).

As to procedure under the Regulation, see CJJ(M)R 2011 (in Part IV of this work) and FPR 2010, Pt 34, Ch 3 and PD34C.

Denmark is in a special position so far as the Maintenance Regulation is concerned. Recital 48 records Denmark's non-participation in the Regulation. However, Denmark subsequently entered into a side agreement with the European Community to apply the Regulation in part by notification under Art 3.2 of the Agreement of 19 October 2005 between the European Community and the Kingdom of Denmark on jurisdiction and the recognition and enforcement of judgments in civil and commercial matters (Council Decision 2006/325/EC). On 14 January 2009, Denmark gave notice of its intention to implement the Maintenance Regulation to the extent to which it modified Brussels I. The Maintenance Regulation applies to Denmark to this extent:

- Ch III (applicable law) and Ch VII (cooperation between Central Authorities) do not apply;
- Art 2 (definitions) and Ch IX (final provisions) apply only to the extent relevant to Denmark's participation.
- Ch II (jurisdiction) applies, as does Ch IV, S 2 (recognition and enforcement as a non-Hague Protocol Member State) and the provisions relating to legal aid (limited by Denmark's non-participation in Ch VII) and as to public bodies as creditors, authentic instruments and court settlements.

The Forms prescribed by the Maintenance Regulation are contained in its Annexes (not reproduced in this work), updates to which may be accessed at *https://e-justice.europa.eu/content_maintenance_obligations_forms-274-en.do*.

THE COUNCIL OF THE EUROPEAN UNION,

Having regard to the Treaty establishing the European Community,

and in particular Article 61(c) and Article 67(2) thereof,

Having regard to the proposal from the Commission,

Having regard to the opinion of the European Parliament,

Having regard to the opinion of the European Economic and

Social Committee,

Whereas:

(1) The Community has set itself the objective of maintaining and developing an area of freedom, security and justice, in which the free movement of persons is ensured. For the gradual establishment of such an area, the Community is to adopt, among others, measures relating to judicial cooperation in civil matters having cross-border implications, in so far as necessary for the proper functioning of the internal market.

(2) In accordance with Article 65(b) of the Treaty, these measures must aim, inter alia, to promote the compatibility of the rules applicable in the Member States concerning the conflict of laws and of jurisdiction.

(3) In this respect, the Community has among other measures already adopted Council Regulation (EC) No 44/2001 of 22 December 2000 on jurisdiction and the recognition and enforcement of judgments in civil and commercial matters, Council Decision 2001/470/EC of 28 May 2001 establishing a European Judicial Network in civil and commercial matters, Council Regulation (EC) No 1206/2001 of 28 May 2001 on cooperation between the courts of the Member States in the taking of evidence in civil or commercial matters, Council Directive 2003/8/EC of 27 January 2003 to improve access to justice in cross-border disputes by establishing minimum common rules relating to legal aid for such disputes, Council Regulation (EC) No 2201/2003 of 27 November 2003 on jurisdiction and the recognition and enforcement of judgments in matrimonial matters and in matters of parental responsibility, Regulation (EC) No 805/2004 of the European Parliament and of the Council of 21 April 2004 creating a European Enforcement Order for uncontested claims, and Regulation (EC) No 1393/2007 of the European Parliament and of the Council of 13 November 2007 on the service in the Member States of judicial and extrajudicial documents in civil or commercial matters (service of documents).

(4) The European Council in Tampere on 15 and 16 October 1999 invited the Council and the Commission to establish special common procedural rules to simplify and accelerate the

settlement of cross-border disputes concerning, inter alia, maintenance claims. It also called for the abolition of intermediate measures required for the recognition and enforcement in the requested State of a decision given in another Member State, particularly a decision relating to a maintenance claim.

(5) A programme of measures for the enforcement of the principle of mutual recognition of decisions in civil and commercial matters, common to the Commission and to the Council, was adopted on 30 November 2000. That programme provides for the abolition of the exequatur procedure for maintenance claims in order to boost the effectiveness of the means by which maintenance creditors safeguard their rights.

(6) The European Council meeting in Brussels on 4 and 5 November 2004 adopted a new programme called 'The Hague Programme: strengthening freedom, security and justice in the European Union' (hereinafter referred to as The Hague Programme).

(7) At its meeting on 2 and 3 June 2005, the Council adopted a Council and Commission Action Plan which implements The Hague Programme in concrete actions and which mentions the necessity of adopting proposals on maintenance obligations.

(8) In the framework of The Hague Conference on Private International Law, the Community and its Member States took part in negotiations which led to the adoption on 23 November 2007 of the Convention on the International Recovery of Child Support and other Forms of Family Maintenance (hereinafter referred to as the 2007 Hague Convention) and the Protocol on the Law Applicable to Maintenance Obligations (hereinafter referred to as the 2007 Hague Protocol). Both those instruments should therefore be taken into account in this Regulation.

(9) A maintenance creditor should be able to obtain easily, in a Member State, a decision which will be automatically enforceable in another Member State without further formalities.

(10) In order to achieve this goal, it is advisable to create a Community instrument in matters relating to maintenance obligations bringing together provisions on jurisdiction, conflict of laws, recognition and enforceability, enforcement, legal aid and cooperation between Central Authorities.

(11) The scope of this Regulation should cover all maintenance obligations arising from a family relationship, parentage, marriage or affinity, in order to guarantee equal treatment of all maintenance creditors. For the purposes of this Regulation, the term 'maintenance obligation' should be interpreted autonomously.

(12) In order to take account of the various ways of resolving maintenance obligation issues in the Member States, this Regulation should apply both to court decisions and to decisions given by administrative authorities, provided that the latter offer guarantees with regard to, in particular, their impartiality and the right of all parties to be heard. Those authorities should therefore apply all the rules of this Regulation.

(13) For the reasons set out above, this Regulation should also ensure the recognition and enforcement of court settlements and authentic instruments without affecting the right of either party to such a settlement or instrument to challenge the settlement or instrument before the courts of the Member State of origin.

(14) It should be provided in this Regulation that for the purposes of an application for the recognition and enforcement of a decision relating to maintenance obligations the term 'creditor' includes public bodies which are entitled to act in place of a person to whom maintenance is owed or to claim reimbursement of benefits provided to the creditor in place of maintenance. Where a public body acts in this capacity, it should be entitled to the same services and the same legal aid as a creditor.

(15) In order to preserve the interests of maintenance creditors and to promote the proper administration of justice within the European Union, the rules on jurisdiction as they result from Regulation (EC) No 44/2001 should be adapted. The circumstance that the defendant is habitually resident in a third State should no longer entail the non-application of Community rules on

jurisdiction, and there should no longer be any referral to national law. This Regulation should therefore determine the cases in which a court in a Member State may exercise subsidiary jurisdiction.

(16) In order to remedy, in particular, situations of denial of justice this Regulation should provide a forum necessitates allowing a court of a Member State, on an exceptional basis, to hear a case which is closely connected with a third State. Such an exceptional basis may be deemed to exist when proceedings prove impossible in the third State in question, for example because of civil war, or when an applicant cannot reasonably be expected to initiate or conduct proceedings in that State. Jurisdiction based on the forum necessitatis should, however, be exercised only if the dispute has a sufficient connection with the Member State of the court seised, for instance the nationality of one of the parties.

(17) An additional rule of jurisdiction should provide that, except under specific conditions, proceedings to modify an existing maintenance decision or to have a new decision given can be brought by the debtor only in the State in which the creditor was habitually resident at the time the decision was given and in which he remains habitually resident. To ensure proper symmetry between the 2007 Hague Convention and this Regulation, this rule should also apply as regards decisions given in a third State which is party to the said Convention in so far as that Convention is in force between that State and the Community and covers the same maintenance obligations in that State and in the Community.

(18) For the purposes of this Regulation, it should be provided that in Ireland the concept of 'domicile' replaces the concept of 'nationality' which is also the case in the United Kingdom, subject to this Regulation being applicable in the latter Member State in accordance with Article 4 of the Protocol on the position of the United Kingdom and Ireland annexed to the Treaty on European Union and the Treaty establishing the European Community.

(19) In order to increase legal certainty, predictability and the autonomy of the parties, this Regulation should enable the parties to choose the competent court by agreement on the basis of specific connecting factors. To protect the weaker party, such a choice of court should not be allowed in the case of maintenance obligations towards a child under the age of 18.

(20) It should be provided in this Regulation that, for Member States bound by the 2007 Hague Protocol, the rules on conflict of laws in respect of maintenance obligations will be those set out in that Protocol. To that end, a provision referring to the said Protocol should be inserted. The 2007 Hague Protocol will be concluded by the Community in time to enable this Regulation to apply. To take account of a scenario in which the 2007 Hague Protocol does not apply to all the Member States a distinction for the purposes of recognition, enforceability and enforcement of decisions needs to be made in this Regulation between the Member States bound by the 2007 Hague Protocol and those not bound by it.

(21) It needs to be made clear in this Regulation that these rules on conflict of laws determine only the law applicable to maintenance obligations and do not determine the law applicable to the establishment of the family relationships on which the maintenance obligations are based. The establishment of family relationships continues to be covered by the national law of the Member States, including their rules of private international law.

(22) In order to ensure swift and efficient recovery of a maintenance obligation and to prevent delaying actions, decisions in matters relating to maintenance obligations given in a Member State should in principle be provisionally enforceable. This Regulation should therefore provide that the court of origin should be able to declare the decision provisionally enforceable even if the national law does not provide for enforceability by operation of law and even if an appeal has been or could still be lodged against the decision under national law.

(23) To limit the costs of proceedings subject to this Regulation, the greatest possible use of modern communications technologies, particularly for hearing parties, would be helpful.

(24) The guarantees provided by the application of rules on conflict of laws should provide the justification for having decisions relating to maintenance obligations given in a Member State

bound by the 2007 Hague Protocol recognised and regarded as enforceable in all the other Member States without any procedure being necessary and without any form of control on the substance in the Member State of enforcement.

(25) Recognition in a Member State of a decision relating to maintenance obligations has as its only object to allow the recovery of the maintenance claim determined in the decision. It does not imply the recognition by that Member State of the family relationship, parentage, marriage or affinity underlying the maintenance obligations which gave rise to the decision.

(26) For decisions on maintenance obligations given in a Member State not bound by the 2007 Hague Protocol, there should be provision in this Regulation for a procedure for recognition and declaration of enforceability. That procedure should be modelled on the procedure and the grounds for refusing recognition set out in Regulation (EC) No 44/2001. To accelerate proceedings and enable the creditor to recover his claim quickly, the court seised should be required to give its decision within a set time, unless there are exceptional circumstances.

(27) It would also be appropriate to limit as far as possible the formal enforcement requirements likely to increase the costs to be borne by the maintenance creditor. To that end, this Regulation should provide that a maintenance creditor ought not to be required to have a postal address or an authorised representative in the Member State of enforcement, without this otherwise affecting the internal organisation of the Member States in matters relating to enforcement proceedings.

(28) In order to limit the costs of enforcement proceedings, no translation should be required unless enforcement is contested, and without prejudice to the rules applicable to service of documents.

(29) In order to guarantee compliance with the requirements of a fair trial, this Regulation should provide for the right of a defendant who did not enter an appearance in the court of origin of a Member State bound by the 2007 Hague Protocol to apply for a review of the decision given against him at the stage of enforcement. However, the defendant must apply for this review within a set period which should start no later than the day on which, in the enforcement proceedings, his property was first made non-disposable in whole or in part. That right to apply for a review should be an extraordinary remedy granted to the defendant in default and not affecting the application of any extraordinary remedies laid down in the law of the Member State of origin provided that those remedies are not incompatible with the right to a review under this Regulation.

(30) In order to speed up the enforcement in another Member State of a decision given in a Member State bound by the 2007 Hague Protocol it is necessary to limit the grounds of refusal or of suspension of enforcement which may be invoked by the debtor on account of the cross-border nature of the maintenance claim. This limitation should not affect the grounds of refusal or of suspension laid down in national law which are not incompatible with those listed in this Regulation, such as the debtor's discharge of his debt at the time of enforcement or the unattachable nature of certain assets.

(31) To facilitate cross-border recovery of maintenance claims, provision should be made for a system of cooperation between Central Authorities designated by the Member States. These Authorities should assist maintenance creditors and debtors in asserting their rights in another Member State by submitting applications for recognition, enforceability and enforcement of existing decisions, for the modification of such decisions or for the establishment of a decision. They should also exchange information in order to locate debtors and creditors, and identify their income and assets, as necessary. Lastly, they should cooperate with each other by exchanging general information and promoting cooperation amongst the competent authorities in their Member States.

(32) A Central Authority designated under this Regulation should bear its own costs, except in specifically determined cases, and should provide assistance for all applicants residing in its Member State. The criterion for determining a person's right to request assistance from a Central Authority should be less strict than the connecting factor of 'habitual residence' used elsewhere in this Regulation. However, the 'residence' criterion should exclude mere presence.

(33) In order to provide full assistance to maintenance creditors and debtors and to facilitate as much as possible crossborder recovery of maintenance, the Central Authorities should be able to obtain a certain amount of personal information. This Regulation should therefore oblige the Member States to ensure that their Central Authorities have access to such information through the public authorities or administrations which hold the information concerned in the course of their ordinary activities. It should however be left to each Member State to decide on the arrangements for such access. Accordingly, a Member State should be able to designate the public authorities or administrations which will be required to supply the information to the Central Authority in accordance with this Regulation, including, if appropriate, public authorities or administrations already designated in the context of other systems for access to information. Where a Member State designates public authorities or administrations, it should ensure that its Central Authority is able to access the requisite information held by those bodies as provided for in this Regulation. A Member State should also be able to allow its Central Authority to access requisite information from any other legal person which holds it and controls its processing.

(34) In the context of access to personal data and the use and transmission thereof, the requirements of Directive 95/46/EC of the European Parliament and of the Council of 24 October 1995 on the protection of individuals with regard to the processing of personal data and on the free movement of such data, as transposed into the national law of the Member States, should be complied with.

(35) For the purposes of the application of this Regulation it is however necessary to define the specific conditions of access to personal data and of the use and transmission of such data. In this context, the opinion of the European Data Protection Supervisor has been taken into consideration. Notification of the data subject should take place in accordance with national law. It should however be possible to defer the notification to prevent the debtor from transferring his assets and thus jeopardising the recovery of the maintenance claim.

(36) On account of the costs of proceedings it is appropriate to provide for a very favourable legal aid scheme, that is, full coverage of the costs relating to proceedings concerning maintenance obligations in respect of children under the age of 21 initiated via the Central Authorities. Specific rules should therefore be added to the current rules on legal aid in the European Union which exist by virtue of Directive 2003/8/EC thus setting up a special legal aid scheme for maintenance obligations. In this context, the competent authority of the requested Member State should be able, exceptionally, to recover costs from an applicant having received free legal aid and lost the case, provided that the person's financial situation so permits. This would apply, in particular, where someone well-off had acted in bad faith.

(37) In addition, for maintenance obligations other than those referred to in the preceding recital, all parties should be guaranteed the same treatment in terms of legal aid at the time of enforcement of a decision in another Member State. Accordingly, the provisions of this Regulation on continuity of legal aid should be understood as also granting such aid to a party who, while not having received legal aid in the proceedings to obtain or amend a decision in the Member State of origin, did then benefit from such aid in that State in the context of an application for enforcement of the decision. Similarly, a party who benefited from free proceedings before an administrative authority listed in Annex X should, in the Member State of enforcement, benefit from the most favourable legal aid or the most extensive exemption from costs or expenses, provided that he shows that he would have so benefited in the Member State of origin.

(38) In order to minimise the costs of translating supporting documents the court seised should only require a translation of such documents when this is necessary, without prejudice to the rights of the defence and the rules applicable concerning service of documents.

(39) To facilitate the application of this Regulation, Member States should be obliged to provide the Commission with the names and contact details of their Central Authorities and with other information. That information should be made available to practitioners and to the public through publication in the Official Journal of the European Union or through electronic access to the European Judicial Network in civil and commercial matters established by Decision 2001/470/EC.

Furthermore, the use of forms provided for in this Regulation should facilitate and speed up communication between the Central Authorities and make it possible to submit applications electronically.

(40) The relationship between this Regulation and the bilateral or multilateral conventions and agreements on maintenance obligations to which the Member States are party should be specified. In this context it should be stipulated that Member States which are party to the Convention of 23 March 1962 between Sweden, Denmark, Finland, Iceland and Norway on the recovery of maintenance by the Member States may continue to apply that Convention since it contains more favourable rules on recognition and enforcement than those in this Regulation. As regards the conclusion of future bilateral agreements on maintenance obligations with third States, the procedures and conditions under which Member States would be authorised to negotiate and conclude such agreements on their own behalf should be determined in the course of discussions relating to a Commission proposal on the subject.

(41) In calculating the periods and time limits provided for in this Regulation, Regulation (EEC, Euratom) No 1182/71 of the Council of 3 June 1971 determining the rules applicable to periods, dates and time limits should apply.

(42) The measures necessary for the implementation of this Regulation should be adopted in accordance with Council Decision 1999/468/EC of 28 June 1999 laying down the procedures for the exercise of implementing powers conferred on the Commission.

(43) In particular, the Commission should be empowered to adopt any amendments to the forms provided for in this Regulation in accordance with the advisory procedure provided for in Article 3 of Decision 1999/468/EC. For the establishment of the list of the administrative authorities falling within the scope of this Regulation, and the list of authorities competent to certify the right to legal aid, the Commission should be empowered to act in accordance with the management procedure provided for in Article 4 of that Decision.

(44) This Regulation should amend Regulation (EC) No 44/2001 by replacing the provisions of that Regulation applicable to maintenance obligations. Subject to the transitional provisions of this Regulation, Member States should, in matters relating to maintenance obligations, apply the provisions of this Regulation on jurisdiction, recognition, enforceability and enforcement of decisions and on legal aid instead of those of Regulation (EC) No 44/2001 as from the date on which this Regulation becomes applicable.

(45) Since the objectives of this Regulation, namely the introduction of a series of measures to ensure the effective recovery of maintenance claims in cross-border situations and thus to facilitate the free movement of persons within the European Union, cannot be sufficiently achieved by the Member States and can therefore, by reason of the scale and effects of this Regulation, be better achieved at Community level, the Community may adopt measures in accordance with the principle of subsidiarity as set out in Article 5 of the Treaty. In accordance with the principle of proportionality as set out in that Article this Regulation does not go beyond what is necessary to achieve those objectives.

(46) In accordance with Article 3 of the Protocol on the position of the United Kingdom and Ireland, annexed to the Treaty on European Union and to the Treaty establishing the European Community, Ireland has given notice of its wish to take part in the adoption and application of this Regulation.

(47) In accordance with Articles 1 and 2 of the Protocol on the position of the United Kingdom and Ireland, annexed to the Treaty on European Union and to the Treaty establishing the European Community, the United Kingdom is not taking part in the adoption of this Regulation and is not bound by it or subject to its application. This is, however, without prejudice to the possibility for the United Kingdom of notifying its intention of accepting this Regulation after its adoption in accordance with Article 4 of the said Protocol.

(48) In accordance with Articles 1 and 2 of the Protocol on the position of Denmark annexed to the Treaty on European Union and the Treaty establishing the European Community, Denmark is not taking part in the adoption of this Regulation and is not bound by it or subject to its

application, without prejudice to the possibility for Denmark of applying the amendments made here to Regulation (EC) No 44/2001 pursuant to Article 3 of the Agreement of 19 October 2005 between the European Community and the Kingdom of Denmark on jurisdiction and the recognition and enforcement of judgments in civil and commercial matters,

HAS ADOPTED THIS REGULATION:

CHAPTER I
SCOPE AND DEFINITIONS

Article 1
Scope of application

1 This Regulation shall apply to maintenance obligations arising from a family relationship, parentage, marriage or affinity.

2 In this Regulation, the term 'Member State' shall mean Member States to which this Regulation applies.

Scope—The scope of the Regulation is wide and could cover, for example, maintenance obligations arising from overseas relationships entitled to be treated as civil partnerships.

Article 2
Definitions

1 For the purposes of this Regulation:

1 the term 'decision' shall mean a decision in matters relating to maintenance obligations given by a court of a Member State, whatever the decision may be called, including a decree, order, judgment or writ of execution, as well as a decision by an officer of the court determining the costs or expenses. For the purposes of Chapters VII and VIII, the term 'decision' shall also mean a decision in matters relating to maintenance obligations given in a third State;

2 the term 'court settlement' shall mean a settlement in matters relating to maintenance obligations which has been approved by a court or concluded before a court in the course of proceedings;

3 the term 'authentic instrument' shall mean:

(a) a document in matters relating to maintenance obligations which has been formally drawn up or registered as an authentic instrument in the Member State of origin and the authenticity of which:

(i) relates to the signature and the content of the instrument, and

(ii) has been established by a public authority or other authority empowered for that purpose; or,

(b) an arrangement relating to maintenance obligations concluded with administrative authorities of the Member State of origin or authenticated by them;

4 the term 'Member State of origin' shall mean the Member State in which, as the case may be, the decision has been given, the court settlement has been approved or concluded, or the authentic instrument has been established;

5 the term 'Member State of enforcement' shall mean the Member State in which the enforcement of the decision, the court settlement or the authentic instrument is sought;

6 the term 'requesting Member State' shall mean the Member State whose Central Authority transmits an application pursuant to Chapter VII;

7 the term 'requested Member State' shall mean the Member State whose Central Authority receives an application pursuant to Chapter VII;

8 the term '2007 Hague Convention Contracting State' shall mean a State which is a contracting party to the Hague Convention of 23 November 2007 on the International Recovery of Child Support and other Forms of Family Maintenance (hereinafter referred to as the 2007 Hague Convention) to the extent that the said Convention applies between the Community and that State;

9 the term 'court of origin' shall mean the court which has given the decision to be enforced;

10 the term 'creditor' shall mean any individual to whom maintenance is owed or is alleged to be owed;

11 the term 'debtor' shall mean any individual who owes or who is alleged to owe maintenance.

2 For the purposes of this Regulation, the term 'court' shall include administrative authorities of the Member States with competence in matters relating to maintenance obligations provided that such authorities offer guarantees with regard to impartiality and the right of all parties to be heard and provided that their decisions under the law of the Member State where they are established:

(i) may be made the subject of an appeal to or review by a judicial authority; and

(ii) have a similar force and effect as a decision of a judicial authority on the same matter.

These administrative authorities shall be listed in Annex X. That Annex shall be established and amended in accordance with the management procedure referred to in Article 73(2) at the request of the Member State in which the administrative authority concerned is established.

3 For the purposes of Articles 3, 4 and 6, the concept of 'domicile' shall replace that of 'nationality' in those Member States which use this concept as a connecting factor in family matters.

For the purposes of Article 6, parties which have their 'domicile' in different territorial units of the same Member State shall be deemed to have their common 'domicile' in that Member State.

'decision', 'court settlement'—A decision by a wife to withdraw a maintenance claim in a Member State does not amount to a 'court decision' or a 'court settlement' (*Ramadani v Ramadani* [2015] EWCA Civ 1138).

'court settlement'—This term would cover a consent order made by a court in England or Wales: see further, Art 48.

'authentic instrument'—This is not a concept explicitly recognised by English law, but is a form of agreement between the parties formally notarised or converted into a deed in those Member States whose law provides for it: see Art 48.

CHAPTER II
JURISDICTION

Scope—Chapter 2 sets out an exhaustive code as to the international jurisdiction of Member States with regard to maintenance obligations.

Article 3
General provisions

In matters relating to maintenance obligations in Member States, jurisdiction shall lie with:

(a) the court for the place where the defendant is habitually resident, or

(b) the court for the place where the creditor is habitually resident, or

(c) the court which, according to its own law, has jurisdiction to entertain proceedings concerning the status of a person if the matter relating to maintenance is ancillary to those proceedings, unless that jurisdiction is based solely on the nationality of one of the parties, or

(d) the court which, according to its own law, has jurisdiction to entertain proceedings concerning parental responsibility if the matter relating to maintenance is ancillary to those proceedings, unless that jurisdiction is based solely on the nationality of one of the parties.

Scope—The Maintenance Regulation contains a comprehensive system of jurisdictional rules that governs all maintenance applications in EU Member States, regardless of whether or not the other jurisdiction involved is an EU Member State. There is no jurisdictional hierarchy under Art 3; each basis of jurisdiction is available in the alternative. Art 3(c) in conjunction with Art 2.3 confers jurisdiction where the maintenance matter is ancillary to divorce proceedings, unless the jurisdictional basis of the divorce is the sole domicile of one party. Therefore, in the case of a divorce petition issued after 18 June 2011 on the basis of the sole domicile of one party, the English court will not have jurisdiction to hear a claim for spousal maintenance, unless Art 3(a) or (b) can be relied on (eg under MCA 1973, s 27, where the applicant's habitual residence is not of sufficient length to meet the requirements of Brussels IIA, Art 3.1(a)). Article 3(d) was not found in Brussels I and allows the court to take jurisdiction on the basis that the maintenance matter is ancillary to parental responsibility proceedings where it has jurisdiction under its own law, unless the jurisdictional basis for the proceedings is the sole domicile of one party. In the case of the UK and Ireland, 'domicile' should be substituted for 'nationality' (Art 2.3). While the aim of the Maintenance Regulation is to provide a protective regime for maintenance creditors by the automatic recognition of decisions made by courts of other Member States, this does not override the jurisdictional requirements (*EA v AP* [2013] EWHC 2344 (Fam)). Where a court in a Member State has delivered a judgment that has become final concerning rights of custody, rights of access and maintenance obligations with regard to a minor child, that court no longer has jurisdiction to rule on an application to vary that judgment if the child's habitual residence is not in that Member State (*W and V v X* (2017) (Case C-499/15), CJEU).

'Ancillary to'—Where a court of a Member State is seised of proceedings concerning the status of a person (e g dissolution or separation) involving the parents of a minor child and a court of another Member State is seised of proceedings relating to parental responsibility involving the same child, an application relating to maintenance concerning that child is ancillary only to the proceedings concerning parental responsibility (*A v B* (Case C-184/14) [2015] 2 FLR 637, CJEU).

'Defendant'—If the maintenance debtor (i e the paying party) wishes to commence proceedings, he/she will not be the defendant: see, also, the limit on proceedings contained in Art 8.

'Creditor'—This term means any individual to whom maintenance is owed or is alleged to be owed (Art 2.1.10). It includes an applicant in the sense of a potential creditor (*Farrell v Long* [1998] 1 FLR 559, ECJ; *M v W (Application after New Zealand Financial Agreement)* [2015] 1 FLR 465, FD).

Article 4
Choice of court

1 The parties may agree that the following court or courts of a Member State shall have jurisdiction to settle any disputes in matters relating to a maintenance obligation which have arisen or may arise between them:

(a) a court or the courts of a Member State in which one of the parties is habitually resident;

(b) a court or the courts of a Member State of which one of the parties has the nationality;

(c) in the case of maintenance obligations between spouses or former spouses:

  (i) the court which has jurisdiction to settle their dispute in matrimonial matters; or

  (ii) a court or the courts of the Member State which was the Member State of the spouses' last common habitual residence for a period of at least one year.

The conditions referred to in points (a), (b) or (c) have to be met at the time the choice of court agreement is concluded or at the time the court is seised.

The jurisdiction conferred by agreement shall be exclusive unless the parties have agreed otherwise.

2 A choice of court agreement shall be in writing. Any communication by electronic means which provides a durable record of the agreement shall be equivalent to 'writing'.

3 This Article shall not apply to a dispute relating to a maintenance obligation towards a child under the age of 18.

4 If the parties have agreed to attribute exclusive jurisdiction to a court or courts of a State party to the Convention on jurisdiction and the recognition and enforcement of judgments in civil and commercial matters, signed on 30 October 2007 in Lugano (hereinafter referred to as the Lugano Convention), where that State is not a Member State, the said Convention shall apply except in the case of the disputes referred to in paragraph 3.

Scope—Article 4 (derived from Brussels I, Art 23) permits the parties a certain degree of autonomy to designate a court to have jurisdiction to settle a maintenance dispute. Such a court will have exclusive jurisdiction, unless otherwise agreed, precluding recourse to alternative grounds for jurisdiction under the Regulation, even if another Member State is validly seised of jurisdiction for divorce under Brussels IIA. Such a choice may be made in advance of proceedings or at the time that the court is seised. Such an agreement may be informal (as Art 4.2 indicates), for example in solicitors' correspondence (*Baldwin v Baldwin* [2014] EWHC 4857 (Fam)). Most commonly, such an agreement will be found in a premarital agreement. An agreement as to choice of court may not be applied to maintenance for a child under 18 (Art 4.3) (see also, Recital 19). Article 4 applies to agreements entered into before 18 June 2011, providing that the proceedings are instituted after that date (Art 75). A choice of court agreement is treated as waived if an unconditional appearance is entered to the proceedings (Art 5). There is no requirement in Art 4 that the parties should obtain independent legal advice or formal disclosure before making such an agreement. In the case of the UK and Ireland, 'domicile' should be substituted for 'nationality' (Art 2.3).

Article 5
Jurisdiction based on the appearance of the defendant

Apart from jurisdiction derived from other provisions of this Regulation, a court of a Member State before which a defendant enters an appearance shall have jurisdiction. This rule shall not apply where appearance was entered to contest the jurisdiction.

Scope—Article 5 bases jurisdiction on submission, i e the rule that, if a defendant appears before the court that does not have jurisdiction under the Regulation, that court will have jurisdiction, unless the defendant did so simply to contest jurisdiction (as under Brussels I, Art 24). A mere acknowledgment of service to a divorce petition does not give the court jurisdiction under Art 5. However, the acceptance of an order for directions in maintenance pending suit proceedings requiring a party to file a statement of means would do so (*Baldwin v Baldwin* [2014] EWHC 4857 (Fam)).

Article 6
Subsidiary jurisdiction

Where no court of a Member State has jurisdiction pursuant to Articles 3, 4 and 5 and no court of a State party to the Lugano Convention which is not a Member State has jurisdiction pursuant to the provisions of that Convention, the courts of the Member State of the common nationality of the parties shall have jurisdiction.

Scope—Article 6 provides a new subsidiary jurisdiction, providing common nationality as a basis for jurisdiction where no court of a Member State has jurisdiction under Arts 3, 4 or 5. It is therefore no longer left to national law to determine jurisdiction, as was the case under Brussels I, Art 4. In the case of the UK and Ireland, 'domicile' should be substituted for 'nationality' (Art 2.3).

Article 7
Forum necessitatis

Where no court of a Member State has jurisdiction pursuant to Articles 3, 4, 5 and 6, the courts of a Member State may, on an exceptional basis, hear the case if proceedings cannot reasonably be brought or conducted or would be impossible in a third State with which the dispute is closely connected. The dispute must have a sufficient connection with the Member State of the court seised.

Scope—Article 7 is another novel concept introducing a forum necessitatis, which provides jurisdiction for the courts of a Member State on an exceptional basis so that it may hear the case if proceedings cannot reasonably be brought or conducted, or would be impossible, in a third State with which the dispute is closely connected. Recital 16 suggests that this might be, for example, where there is civil war in that third state. The dispute must still have a sufficient connection with the forum necessitatis.

Art 7 might provide a jurisdictional basis for obtaining a pension sharing order under the MFPA 1984, Pt III, where the pension in question is administered in England and Wales, but neither of the parties fulfil the primary jurisdictional qualifications of s 15(1) of the 1984 Act or Arts 3–6 (s 15(1A) of the 1984 Act).

'Reasonably'—Part of the reasonableness evaluation in Art 7 relates to the extent to which a party has committed himself to the proceedings, having been induced into a belief by the other party that the court was to deal with maintenance (*Baldwin v Baldwin* [2014] EWHC 4857 (Fam)).

Article 8
Limit on proceedings

1 Where a decision is given in a Member State or a 2007 Hague Convention Contracting State where the creditor is habitually resident, proceedings to modify the decision or to have a new decision given cannot be brought by the debtor in any other Member State as long as the creditor remains habitually resident in the State in which the decision was given.

2 Paragraph 1 shall not apply:

(a) where the parties have agreed in accordance with Article 4 to the jurisdiction of the courts of that other Member State;

(b) where the creditor submits to the jurisdiction of the courts of that other Member State pursuant to Article 5;

(c) where the competent authority in the 2007 Hague Convention Contracting State of origin cannot, or refuses to, exercise jurisdiction to modify the decision or give a new decision; or

(d) where the decision given in the 2007 Hague Convention Contracting State of origin

PART VI

cannot be recognised or declared enforceable in the Member State where proceedings to modify the decision or to have a new decision given are contemplated.

Scope—Article 8 provides a restrictive jurisdiction for applications to vary, reflecting the philosophy of protection of the creditor. It is in effect an anti-forum-shopping provision. If an order has been made in the Member State where the creditor is habitually resident, the debtor cannot apply to vary that order or apply for a new order in any other Member State so long as the debtor remains resident in the state where the order was made. However, Art 8 forms part of the overall jurisdictional scheme of the Maintenance Regulation (see *AB v JJB* [2015] 2 FLR 1143, FD, at [37]), while not creating any separate or additional basis of jurisdiction. Article 42 provides that under no circumstances may a decision given in a Member State be reviewed as to its substance in the Member State in which recognition, enforceability or enforcement is sought, although there are some limited exceptions to this bar. Article 24 provides that a decision that has the effect of modifying an earlier decision on maintenance on the basis of changed circumstances is not to be considered an irreconcilable decision constituting grounds for refusal of recognition.

Article 9
Seising of a court

For the purposes of this Chapter, a court shall be deemed to be seised:

(a) at the time when the document instituting the proceedings or an equivalent document is lodged with the court, provided that the claimant has not subsequently failed to take the steps he was required to take to have service effected on the defendant; or

(b) if the document has to be served before being lodged with the court, at the time when it is received by the authority responsible for service, provided that the claimant has not subsequently failed to take the steps he was required to take to have the document lodged with the court.

Scope—Articles 9–13 make provision for determining when a court is seised, when a court may accept jurisdiction and/or when it must stay proceedings. The aim is to ensure that there are not parallel proceedings in Member States. Where there is more than one basis upon which jurisdiction may be accepted under the Regulation, it is necessary to make provision to ensure that only one court is able to proceed.

Article 10
Examination as to jurisdiction

Where a court of a Member State is seised of a case over which it has no jurisdiction under this Regulation it shall declare of its own motion that it has no jurisdiction.

Article 11
Examination as to admissibility

1 Where a defendant habitually resident in a State other than the Member State where the action was brought does not enter an appearance, the court with jurisdiction shall stay the proceedings so long as it is not shown that the defendant has been able to receive the document instituting the proceedings or an equivalent document in sufficient time to enable him to arrange for his defence, or that all necessary steps have been taken to this end.

2 Article 19 of Regulation (EC) No 1393/2007 shall apply instead of the provisions of paragraph 1 of this Article if the document instituting the proceedings or an equivalent document had to be transmitted from one Member State to another pursuant to that Regulation.

3 Where the provisions of Regulation (EC) No 1393/2007 are not applicable, Article 15 of the Hague Convention of 15 November 1965 on the service abroad of judicial and extrajudicial documents in civil or commercial matters shall apply if the document instituting the proceedings or an equivalent document had to be transmitted abroad pursuant to that Convention.

Scope—Article 11 protects the rights of defendants by ensuring that proceedings cannot proceed against them in a Member State other than that of their habitual residence, unless they have properly been made aware of the proceedings.

Article 12
Lis pendens

1 Where proceedings involving the same cause of action and between the same parties are brought in the courts of different Member States, any court other than the court first seised shall of its own motion stay its proceedings until such time as the jurisdiction of the court first seised is established.

2 Where the jurisdiction of the court first seised is established, any court other than the court first seised shall decline jurisdiction in favour of that court.

Scope—Article 12 (cf Brussels I, Art 27) provides that, for proceedings with the same cause of action (lis pendens), the court of any Member State other than that first seised must stay the proceedings of its own initiative, until the jurisdiction of the Member State first seised is established. If it is so established, the other court(s) must decline jurisdiction, even if this causes hardship and injustice. See, for example, *EA v AP* [2013] EWHC 2344 (Fam). It should be noted that Art 12 deals with the same cause of action and imposes an obligatory stay, whereas Art 13 deals with connected but different issues and imposes only a discretionary stay. For a discussion of the interrelation between the counterpart provisions of Brussels I (Arts 27 and 28), see *Re PJ (Adoption: Practice on Appeal)* [1998] 2 FLR 252, CA; *Moore v Moore* [2007] 2 FLR 339, CA, at [103]; *J v P* [2007] EWHC 704 (Fam); *B v R* [2010] 1 FLR 563, FD; *Traversa v Freddi* [2011] 2 FLR 272, CA; *T v T (Occupation Orders)* [2013] 1 FLR 364, FD. A Scottish writ of divorce issued before an English maintenance application under MCA 1973, s 27 did not secure maintenance jurisdiction where it did not include a claim for financial provision (*Re V (European Maintenance Regulation)* [2017] 1 FLR 1083, FD).

Article 13
Related actions

1 Where related actions are pending in the courts of different Member States, any court other than the court first seised may stay its proceedings.

2 Where these actions are pending at first instance, any court other than the court first seised may also, on the application of one of the parties, decline jurisdiction if the court first seised has jurisdiction over the actions in question and its law permits the consolidation thereof.

3 For the purposes of this Article, actions are deemed to be related where they are so closely connected that it is expedient to hear and determine them together to avoid the risk of irreconcilable judgments resulting from separate proceedings.

Scope—Article 13 (cf Brussels I, Art 28) makes provision for related actions, under which the court of the Member State other than that first seised may stay proceedings and may, on the application of one of the parties, decline jurisdiction if the court first seised has jurisdiction over the related action and can consolidate those actions.

'Declined jurisdiction' (Art 13.2)—See *N v N (Stay of Maintenance Proceedings)* [2014] 1 FLR 1399, FD (where the court declined jurisdiction pursuant to Art 13.2 on a wife's application for interim periodical payments pursuant to MCA 1973, s 27, when it was accepted that an application for maintenance pending suit did not fall within the terms of Brussels IIA, Art 12; if the court were to assume jurisdiction and entertain the application, it would in effect be overturning *Wermuth v Wermuth (No 2)* [2003] 1 FLR 1029, CA).

'Irreconcilable judgments' (Art 13.3)—See *Prazic v Prazic* [2006] 2 FLR 1128, CA (in relation to Brussels I, Art 28, in which English proceedings under TLATA 1996 were struck out where there were prior French divorce proceedings).

'related actions'—See Art 13.3.

Article 14
Provisional, including protective, measures

Application may be made to the courts of a Member State for such provisional, including protective, measures as may be available under the law of that State, even if, under this Regulation, the courts of another Member State have jurisdiction as to the substance of the matter.

Scope—Article 14 ensures that, notwithstanding that a court does not have jurisdiction under the Regulation, it can still make interim protective orders in relation to the matter, provided that the national law permits this (i e the Regulation does not provide jurisdiction as such, but will not prevent such jurisdiction being accepted on the limited basis provided for by Art 14). See, also, annotations to Brussels IIA, Art 20. It has been held (in relation to the equivalent provisions in Brussels IIA) that three conditions need to be satisfied: (i) the measure needs to be urgent; (ii) the measure must be for persons or assets in the Member State concerned; and (iii) the measure must be provisional (*Re A (Area of Freedom, Security and Justice)* [2009] 2 FLR 1, ECJ). The urgency must relate to the situation itself and the impossibility of bringing proceedings in the Member State seised with

PART VI

the matter. Once provisional measures have been exercised in the Member State with jurisdiction, further provisional measures cannot be sought in another jurisdiction (*Detiček v Sgueglia* [2010] 1 FLR 1381, ECJ).

'Provisional'—This would not include an application for interim maintenance/maintenance pending suit: *Wermuth v Wermuth (No 2)* [2003] 1 FLR 1029, CA (Brussels I, Art 31); *Moore v Moore* [2007] 2 FLR 339, CA; *EA v AP* [2013] EWHC 2344 (Fam); cf *L-K v K (Brussels II Revised: Maintenance Pending Suit)* [2006] 2 FLR 1113, FD).

'Protective'—This would include an application for a freezing order to protect assets. An application for an occupation order was held to fall within the definition of 'provisional, including protective measures' (in the context of Brussels I) in *T v T (Occupation Orders)* [2013] 1 FLR 364, FD.

CHAPTER III
APPLICABLE LAW

Article 15
Determination of the applicable law

The law applicable to maintenance obligations shall be determined in accordance with the Hague Protocol of 23 November 2007 on the law applicable to maintenance obligations (hereinafter referred to as the 2007 Hague Protocol) in the Member States bound by that instrument.

Scope—Chapter III, Art 15 of the Regulation deals with the law applicable to maintenance obligations, stating that the applicable law is to be determined in accordance with the Hague Protocol of 23 November 2007 in those Member States bound by the Protocol. The UK and Denmark (see introductory annotations) have not ratified the Protocol and therefore the law applied to maintenance obligations in England is English law. The applicable law provisions apply in other Member States with the result that they must apply English law in appropriate circumstances, for example where the parties have so agreed (Art 8 of the Protocol). The general rule under the Protocol is that the law governing the dispute is that of the state of the creditor's habitual residence, save where the Protocol provides otherwise (Art 3 of the Protocol). This gives rise to the two different systems for enforcement under Ch IV. Where a Member State applies the Hague Protocol, the decisions of its court are not subject to the exequatur system requiring a declaration of enforceability (or in the UK and Ireland, registration) of that decision before the decision being enforceable in another Member State.

CHAPTER IV
RECOGNITION, ENFORCEABILITY AND ENFORCEMENT OF DECISIONS

Scope—Under Brussels I, a declaration of enforceability (exequatur) was required. The aim of the Regulation is automatic enforcement in one Member State of a decision relating to maintenance made in another. Accordingly, the process of exequatur (or 'registration' for the UK: Art 38.2 of Brussels I) has been abolished in relation to decisions made in those Member States bound by the Hague Protocol (all Member States except the UK and Denmark). Where a decision by a Member State bound by the Protocol is enforceable in that State, it is enforceable in another Member State (including England) without the need for registration (Art 17). For non-Hague Protocol Member States (the UK and Denmark: see introductory annotations), Ch IV, S 2 applies.

Article 16
Scope of application of this Chapter

1 This Chapter shall govern the recognition, enforceability and enforcement of decisions falling within the scope of this Regulation.

2 Section 1 shall apply to decisions given in a Member State bound by the 2007 Hague Protocol.

3 Section 2 shall apply to decisions given in a Member State not bound by the 2007 Hague Protocol.

4 Section 3 shall apply to all decisions.

Section 1
Decisions given in a Member State bound by the 2007 Hague Protocol

Article 17
Abolition of exequatur

1 A decision given in a Member State bound by the 2007 Hague Protocol shall be recognised in another Member State without any special procedure being required and without any possibility of opposing its recognition.

2 A decision given in a Member State bound by the 2007 Hague Protocol which is enforceable in that State shall be enforceable in another Member State without the need for a declaration of enforceability.

Scope—Article 17 allows the Hague Protocol Member State decision to be immediately enforceable in another Member State without more. The procedure is governed by the Maintenance Regulation, Ch IV, SS 1 and 3 and CJJ(M)R 2011, reg 3 and Sch 1, Pt 2. See *EDG v RR (Enforcement of Foreign Maintenance Order)* [2015] 1 FLR 270, FD.

'exequatur'—This Latin term approximates to 'let it be executed' and is the 'declaration of enforceability' referred to in Art 17(2). Compare Art 38(1) of Council Regulation (EC) No 44/2001 (Brussels I) (see *The Family Court Practice 2011*).

'a Member State bound by the 2007 Hague Protocol' (Art 17.1)—At present this includes all Member States other than Denmark and the UK.

'recognised' (Art 17.1)—See *Hoffman v Krieg* (No 145/86) [1988] ECR 645, ECJ.

Article 18
Protective measures

An enforceable decision shall carry with it by operation of law the power to proceed to any protective measures which exist under the law of the Member State of enforcement.

Scope—Article 18 allows automatic access to any protective measures available under the requested Member State's law.

Article 19
Right to apply for a review

1 A defendant who did not enter an appearance in the Member State of origin shall have the right to apply for a review of the decision before the competent court of that Member State where:

(a) he was not served with the document instituting the proceedings or an equivalent document in sufficient time and in such a way as to enable him to arrange for his defence; or

(b) he was prevented from contesting the maintenance claim by reason of force majeure or due to extraordinary circumstances without any fault on his part;

unless he failed to challenge the decision when it was possible for him to do so.

2 The time limit for applying for a review shall run from the day the defendant was effectively acquainted with the contents of the decision and was able to react, at the latest from the date of the first enforcement measure having the effect of making his property non-disposable in whole or in part. The defendant shall react promptly, in any event within 45 days. No extension may be granted on account of distance.

3 If the court rejects the application for a review referred to in paragraph 1 on the basis that none of the grounds for a review set out in that paragraph apply, the decision shall remain in force.

If the court decides that a review is justified for one of the reasons laid down in paragraph 1, the decision shall be null and void. However, the creditor shall not lose the benefits of the interruption of prescription or limitation periods, or the right to claim retroactive maintenance acquired in the initial proceedings.

Scope—Article 19 gives a defendant who did not enter an appearance (in the circumstances set out in Art 19.1) to the original decision the right to obtain a review in the Member State of origin with appropriate protection for the creditor relating to limitation periods. The right to a review is subject to strict time limits (Art 19.2) and should be considered an extraordinary remedy (Recital 29). The right to apply for a review under Art 19 is a limited exception to the general principle contained in Art 42.

Article 20
Documents for the purposes of enforcement

1 For the purposes of enforcement of a decision in another Member State, the claimant shall provide the competent enforcement authorities with:

(a) a copy of the decision which satisfies the conditions necessary to establish its authenticity;

PART VI

(b) the extract from the decision issued by the court of origin using the form set out in Annex I;

(c) where appropriate, a document showing the amount of any arrears and the date such amount was calculated;

(d) where necessary, a transliteration or a translation of the content of the form referred to in point (b) into the official language of the Member State of enforcement or, where there are several official languages in that Member State, into the official language or one of the official languages of court proceedings of the place where the application is made, in accordance with the law of that Member State, or into another language that the Member State concerned has indicated it can accept. Each Member State may indicate the official language or languages of the institutions of the European Union other than its own which it can accept for the completion of the form.

2 The competent authorities of the Member State of enforcement may not require the claimant to provide a translation of the decision. However, a translation may be required if the enforcement of the decision is challenged.

3 Any translation under this Article must be done by a person qualified to do translations in one of the Member States.

Scope—Article 20 explains that documents must be provided for the purposes of enforcement in the requested Member State. See also, the Family Procedure (Amendment) Rules 2011.

'may not require the claimant to provide a translation of the decision' (Art 20(2))—Compare Art 55(2) of Brussels I (see *The Family Court Practice 2011*). If, exceptionally, a translation is called for, see Article 45(f).

Article 21
Refusal or suspension of enforcement

1 The grounds of refusal or suspension of enforcement under the law of the Member State of enforcement shall apply in so far as they are not incompatible with the application of paragraphs 2 and 3.

2 The competent authority in the Member State of enforcement shall, on application by the debtor, refuse, either wholly or in part, the enforcement of the decision of the court of origin if the right to enforce the decision of the court of origin is extinguished by the effect of prescription or the limitation of action, either under the law of the Member State of origin or under the law of the Member State of enforcement, whichever provides for the longer limitation period.

Furthermore, the competent authority in the Member State of enforcement may, on application by the debtor, refuse, either wholly or in part, the enforcement of the decision of the court of origin if it is irreconcilable with a decision given in the Member State of enforcement or with a decision given in another Member State or in a third State which fulfils the conditions necessary for its recognition in the Member State of enforcement.

A decision which has the effect of modifying an earlier decision on maintenance on the basis of changed circumstances shall not be considered an irreconcilable decision within the meaning of the second subparagraph.

3 The competent authority in the Member State of enforcement may, on application by the debtor, suspend, either wholly or in part, the enforcement of the decision of the court of origin if the competent court of the Member State of origin has been seised of an application for a review of the decision of the court of origin pursuant to Article 19.

Furthermore, the competent authority of the Member State of enforcement shall, on application by the debtor, suspend the enforcement of the decision of the court of origin where the enforceability of that decision is suspended in the Member State of origin.

Scope—Whereas there are no grounds for refusing to recognise a decision on maintenance to which Ch IV, S 1 applies, Art 21 provides a basis for refusing or suspending enforcement in the requested Member State in restricted circumstances (based on limitation, or irreconcilability with another decision enforceable in that requested Member State).

Article 22
No effect on the existence of family relationships

The recognition and enforcement of a decision on maintenance under this Regulation shall not in any way imply the recognition of the family relationship, parentage, marriage or affinity underlying the maintenance obligation which gave rise to the decision.

Section 2
Decisions given in a Member State not bound by the 2007 Hague Protocol

Scope—Section 2 makes provision for the enforcement of decisions in non-Hague Protocol Member States (the UK and Denmark (see introductory annotations)) and follows the model of registration before enforcement. Following recognition, a maintenance decision of a non-Hague Protocol Member State requires a declaration of enforceability (Art 26). In effect, S 2 contains a simplified exequatur procedure.

Article 23
Recognition

1 A decision given in a Member State not bound by the 2007 Hague Protocol shall be recognised in the other Member States without any special procedure being required.

2 Any interested party who raises the recognition of a decision as the principal issue in a dispute may, in accordance with the procedures provided for in this Section, apply for a decision that the decision be recognised.

3 If the outcome of proceedings in a court of a Member State depends on the determination of an incidental question of recognition, that court shall have jurisdiction over that question.

Scope—Article 23 provides that recognition of the maintenance decision is automatic, but an interested party can apply for a specific decision on the point. Article 23.3 enables a court of a Member State to deal with the question of recognition where it arises incidentally in other proceedings.

'a Member State not bound by the 2007 Hague Protocol'—Currently, this refers to Denmark (see introductory annotations) and the UK.

Article 24
Grounds of refusal of recognition

A decision shall not be recognised:

(a) if such recognition is manifestly contrary to public policy in the Member State in which recognition is sought. The test of public policy may not be applied to the rules relating to jurisdiction;

(b) where it was given in default of appearance, if the defendant was not served with the document which instituted the proceedings or with an equivalent document in sufficient time and in such a way as to enable him to arrange for his defence, unless the defendant failed to commence proceedings to challenge the decision when it was possible for him to do so;

(c) if it is irreconcilable with a decision given in a dispute between the same parties in the Member State in which recognition is sought;

(d) if it is irreconcilable with an earlier decision given in another Member State or in a third State in a dispute involving the same cause of action and between the same parties, provided that the earlier decision fulfils the conditions necessary for its recognition in the Member State in which recognition is sought.

A decision which has the effect of modifying an earlier decision on maintenance on the basis of changed circumstances shall not be considered an irreconcilable decision within the meaning of points (c) or (d).

Scope—Article 24 contains grounds for non-recognition, including public policy (Art 24(a)), rights of the defendant (Art 24(b)) and irreconcilability with other maintenance decisions of the Member State in which enforcement is sought, or which are susceptible to recognition in that state (Art 24(c) and (d)).

'Public policy' (Art 24(a))—Refusal of recognition on public policy grounds is only available in limited circumstances: see, by analogy, *Krombach v Bamberski* (Case C–7-98) [2000] ECR I-1935, ECJ (Brussels I); *Smith v Huertas* [2015] EWHC 3745 (Comm) (Brussels I); *Superior Composite Structures LLC v Parrish* [2015] EWHC 3688 (Admin) (common law).

PART VI

Article 25
Staying of recognition proceedings

A court of a Member State in which recognition is sought of a decision given in a Member State not bound by the 2007 Hague Protocol shall stay the proceedings if the enforceability of the decision is suspended in the Member State of origin by reason of an appeal.

Article 26
Enforceability

A decision given in a Member State not bound by the 2007 Hague Protocol and enforceable in that State shall be enforceable in another Member State when, on the application of any interested party, it has been declared enforceable there.

'Declared enforceable'—See Art 30.

Article 27
Jurisdiction of local courts

1 The application for a declaration of enforceability shall be submitted to the court or competent authority of the Member State of enforcement notified by that Member State to the Commission in accordance with Article 71.

2 The local jurisdiction shall be determined by reference to the place of habitual residence of the party against whom enforcement is sought, or to the place of enforcement.

Article 28
Procedure

1 The application for a declaration of enforceability shall be accompanied by the following documents:

(a) a copy of the decision which satisfies the conditions necessary to establish its authenticity;

(b) an extract from the decision issued by the court of origin using the form set out in Annex II, without prejudice to Article 29;

(c) where necessary, a transliteration or a translation of the content of the form referred to in point (b) into the official language of the Member State of enforcement or, where there are several official languages in that Member State, into the official language or one of the official languages of court proceedings of the place where the application is made, in accordance with the law of that Member State, or into another language that the Member State concerned has indicated it can accept. Each Member State may indicate the official language or languages of the institutions of the European Union other than its own which it can accept for the completion of the form.

2 The court or competent authority seised of the application may not require the claimant to provide a translation of the decision. However, a translation may be required in connection with an appeal under Articles 32 or 33.

3 Any translation under this Article must be done by a person qualified to do translations in one of the Member States.

Procedure—See FPR 2010, rr 34.39, 34.40.

Article 29
Non-production of the extract

1 If the extract referred to in Article 28(1)(b) is not produced, the competent court or authority may specify a time for its production or accept an equivalent document or, if it considers that it has sufficient information before it, dispense with its production.

2 In the situation referred to in paragraph 1, if the competent court or authority so requires, a translation of the documents shall be produced. The translation shall be done by a person qualified to do translations in one of the Member States.

Article 30
Declaration of enforceability

The decision shall be declared enforceable without any review under Article 24 immediately on completion of the formalities in Article 28 and at the latest within 30 days of the completion of those formalities, except where exceptional circumstances make this impossible. The party against whom enforcement is sought shall not at this stage of the proceedings be entitled to make any submissions on the application.

Procedure—A declaration of enforceability is obtained by means of registration of the order in the magistrates' court (CJJ(M)R 2011, reg 3 and Sch 1, Pt 3 and FPR 2010, Pt 34 and PD34A, paras 1.1–2.3.

Article 31
Notice of the decision on the application for a declaration

1 The decision on the application for a declaration of enforceability shall forthwith be brought to the notice of the applicant in accordance with the procedure laid down by the law of the Member State of enforcement.

2 The declaration of enforceability shall be served on the party against whom enforcement is sought, accompanied by the decision, if not already served on that party.

Article 32
Appeal against the decision on the application for a declaration

1 The decision on the application for a declaration of enforceability may be appealed against by either party.

2 The appeal shall be lodged with the court notified by the Member State concerned to the Commission in accordance with Article 71.

3 The appeal shall be dealt with in accordance with the rules governing procedure in contradictory matters.

4 If the party against whom enforcement is sought fails to appear before the appellate court in proceedings concerning an appeal brought by the applicant, Article 11 shall apply even where the party against whom enforcement is sought is not habitually resident in any of the Member States.

5 An appeal against the declaration of enforceability shall be lodged within 30 days of service thereof. If the party against whom enforcement is sought has his habitual residence in a Member State other than that in which the declaration of enforceability was given, the time for appealing shall be 45 days and shall run from the date of service, either on him in person or at his residence. No extension may be granted on account of distance.

Article 33
Proceedings to contest the decision given on appeal

The decision given on appeal may be contested only by the procedure notified by the Member State concerned to the Commission in accordance with Article 71.

Article 34
Refusal or revocation of a declaration of enforceability

1 The court with which an appeal is lodged under Articles 32 or 33 shall refuse or revoke a declaration of enforceability only on one of the grounds specified in Article 24.

2 Subject to Article 32(4), the court seised of an appeal under Article 32 shall give its decision within 90 days from the date it was seised, except where exceptional circumstances make this impossible.

3 The court seised of an appeal under Article 33 shall give its decision without delay.

Article 35
Staying of proceedings

The court with which an appeal is lodged under Articles 32 or 33 shall, on the application of the party against whom enforcement is sought, stay the proceedings if the enforceability of the decision is suspended in the Member State of origin by reason of an appeal.

Article 36
Provisional, including protective measures

1 When a decision must be recognised in accordance with this Section, nothing shall prevent the applicant from availing himself of provisional, including protective, measures in accordance with the law of the Member State of enforcement without a declaration of enforceability under Article 30 being required.

2 The declaration of enforceability shall carry with it by operation of law the power to proceed to any protective measures.

3 During the time specified for an appeal pursuant to Article 32(5) against the declaration of enforceability and until any such appeal has been determined, no measures of enforcement may be taken other than protective measures against the property of the party against whom enforcement is sought.

Article 37
Partial enforceability

1 Where a decision has been given in respect of several matters and the declaration of enforceability cannot be given for all of them, the competent court or authority shall give it for one or more of them.

2 An applicant may request a declaration of enforceability limited to parts of a decision.

Article 38
No charge, duty or fee

In proceedings for the issue of a declaration of enforceability, no charge, duty or fee calculated by reference to the value of the matter at issue may be levied in the Member State of enforcement.

Section 3
Common provisions

Scope—Section 3 sets out common provisions for recognition and enforcement whether or not the decision was given in a Member State bound by the 2007 Hague Protocol. The procedure for enforcement is governed by the law of the Member State of enforcement (Art 41).

Article 39
Provisional enforceability

The court of origin may declare the decision provisionally enforceable, notwithstanding any appeal, even if national law does not provide for enforceability by operation of law.

'provisionally enforceable, notwithstanding any appeal'—Compare FPR 2010, r 30.8.

Article 40
Invoking a recognised decision

1 A party who wishes to invoke in another Member State a decision recognised within the meaning of Article 17(1) or recognised pursuant to Section 2 shall produce a copy of the decision which satisfies the conditions necessary to establish its authenticity.

2 If necessary, the court before which the recognised decision is invoked may ask the party invoking the recognised decision to produce an extract issued by the court of origin using the form set out in Annex I or in Annex II, as the case may be.

The court of origin shall also issue such an extract at the request of any interested party.

3 Where necessary, the party invoking the recognised decision shall provide a transliteration or a translation of the content of the form referred to in paragraph 2 into the official language of the Member State concerned or, where there are several official languages in that Member State, into the official language or one of the official languages of court proceedings of the place where the recognised decision is invoked, in accordance with the law of that Member State, or into another language that the Member State concerned has indicated it can accept. Each Member State may indicate the official language or languages of the institutions of the European Union other than its own which it can accept for the completion of the form.

4 Any translation under this Article must be done by a person qualified to do translations in one of the Member States.

Procedure—See FPR 2010, rr 34.39, 34.40.

Article 41
Proceedings and conditions for enforcement

1 Subject to the provisions of this Regulation, the procedure for the enforcement of decisions given in another Member State shall be governed by the law of the Member State of enforcement. A decision given in a Member State which is enforceable in the Member State of enforcement shall be enforced there under the same conditions as a decision given in that Member State of enforcement.

2 The party seeking the enforcement of a decision given in another Member State shall not be required to have a postal address or an authorised representative in the Member State of enforcement, without prejudice to persons with competence in matters relating to enforcement proceedings.

'under the same conditions as a decision given in that Member State' (Art 41.1)—A maintenance creditor who has obtained an order in another Member State is entitled to make an application for enforcement directly to the Family Court and is not obliged to proceed through the Central Authority (*MS v PS* (Case C-283/16) [2017] 1 FLR 1163, CJEU).

Article 42
No review as to substance

Under no circumstances may a decision given in a Member State be reviewed as to its substance in the Member State in which recognition, enforceability or enforcement is sought.

Article 43
No precedence for the recovery of costs

Recovery of any costs incurred in the application of this Regulation shall not take precedence over the recovery of maintenance.

CHAPTER V
ACCESS TO JUSTICE

Article 44
Right to legal aid

1 Parties who are involved in a dispute covered by this Regulation shall have effective access to justice in another Member State, including enforcement and appeal or review procedures, in accordance with the conditions laid down in this Chapter. In cases covered by Chapter VII, effective access to justice shall be provided by the requested Member State to any applicant who is resident in the requesting Member State.

2 To ensure such effective access, Member States shall provide legal aid in accordance with this Chapter, unless paragraph 3 applies.

3 In cases covered by Chapter VII, a Member State shall not be obliged to provide legal aid if and to the extent that the procedures of that Member State enable the parties to make the case without the need for legal aid, and the Central Authority provides such services as are necessary free of charge.

4 Entitlements to legal aid shall not be less than those available in equivalent domestic cases.

5 No security, bond or deposit, however described, shall be required to guarantee the payment of costs and expenses in proceedings concerning maintenance obligations.

'Member States shall provide legal aid' (Art 44.2)—Save in respect of child maintenance, such legal aid may be means-tested or subject to a merits test (Art 47.1), but the entitlements to it 'shall not be less than those available in equivalent domestic proceedings' (Art 44.4). Legal aid is envisaged as enabling parties to *assert* their rights and to *bring a case before* the court; as Art 56.2 specifically refers to applications by the paying party, the principle of equality of arms ought to allow legal aid to a paying party in an appropriate case.

Article 45
Content of legal aid

Legal aid granted under this Chapter shall mean the assistance necessary to enable parties to know and assert their rights and to ensure that their applications, lodged through the Central Authorities or directly with the competent authorities, are fully and effectively dealt with. It shall cover as necessary the following:

(a) pre-litigation advice with a view to reaching a settlement prior to bringing judicial proceedings;

(b) legal assistance in bringing a case before an authority or a court and representation in court;

(c) exemption from or assistance with the costs of proceedings and the fees to persons mandated to perform acts during the proceedings;

(d) in Member States in which an unsuccessful party is liable for the costs of the opposing party, if the recipient of legal aid loses the case, the costs incurred by the opposing party, if such costs would have been covered had the recipient been habitually resident in the Member State of the court seised;

(e) interpretation;

(f) translation of the documents required by the court or by the competent authority and presented by the recipient of legal aid which are necessary for the resolution of the case;

(g) travel costs to be borne by the recipient of legal aid where the physical presence of the persons concerned with the presentation of the recipient's case is required in court by the law or by the court of the Member State concerned and the court decides that the persons concerned cannot be heard to the satisfaction of the court by any other means.

Article 46
Free legal aid for applications through central authorities concerning maintenance to children

1 The requested Member State shall provide free legal aid in respect of all applications by a creditor under Article 56 concerning maintenance obligations arising from a parent-child relationship towards a person under the age of 21.

2 Notwithstanding paragraph 1, the competent authority of the requested Member State may, in relation to applications other than those under Article 56(1)(a) and (b), refuse free legal aid if it considers that, on the merits, the application or any appeal or review is manifestly unfounded.

'The requested Member State shall provide free legal aid' (Art 46(1))—In relation to child maintenance, free legal aid must be provided in respect of all applications by the receiving party unless (save in the case of recognition or enforcement of an existing decision) the application, or any appeal or review, is 'manifestly unfounded'. This requirement does not extend to applications by the paying party.

Article 47

Cases not covered by Article 46

1 Subject to Articles 44 and 45, in cases not covered by Article 46, legal aid may be granted in accordance with national law, particularly as regards the conditions for the means test or the merits test.

2 Notwithstanding paragraph 1, a party who, in the Member State of origin, has benefited from complete or partial legal aid or exemption from costs or expenses, shall be entitled, in any proceedings for recognition, enforceability or enforcement, to benefit from the most favourable legal aid or the most extensive exemption from costs or expenses provided for by the law of the Member State of enforcement.

3 Notwithstanding paragraph 1, a party who, in the Member State of origin, has benefited from free proceedings before an administrative authority listed in Annex X, shall be entitled, in any proceedings for recognition, enforceability or enforcement, to benefit from legal aid in accordance with paragraph 2. To that end, he shall present a statement from the competent authority in the Member State of origin to the effect that he fulfils the financial requirements to qualify for the grant of complete or partial legal aid or exemption from costs or expenses. Competent authorities for the purposes of this paragraph shall be listed in Annex XI. That Annex shall be established and amended in accordance with the management procedure referred to in Article 73(2).

CHAPTER VI

COURT SETTLEMENTS AND AUTHENTIC INSTRUMENTS

Article 48

Application of this Regulation to court settlements and authentic instruments

1 Court settlements and authentic instruments which are enforceable in the Member State of origin shall be recognised in another Member State and be enforceable there in the same way as decisions, in accordance with Chapter IV.

2 The provisions of this Regulation shall apply as necessary to court settlements and authentic instruments.

3 The competent authority of the Member State of origin shall issue, at the request of any interested party, an extract from the court settlement or the authentic instrument using the forms set out in Annexes I and II or in Annexes III and IV as the case may be.

CHAPTER VII

COOPERATION BETWEEN CENTRAL AUTHORITIES

Scope—Chapter 7 provides for cooperation between and assistance from Central Authorities, both in relation to making applications (transmission and processing) and obtaining information about a creditor or debtor and their respective financial circumstances.

'Central Authority'—The Lord Chancellor has been designated as the Central Authority in relation to England and Wales (CJJ(M)R 2011, reg 2(1)(a)). The Lord Chancellor's powers are exercised by the Reciprocal Enforcement of Maintenance Unit (REMO), Office of the Official Solicitor and Public Trustee, Victory House, 30–34 Kingsway, London WC2B 6EX, DX 141423 Bloomsbury 7; tel: 020 3681 2757; fax: 020 3681 2762.

Article 49

Designation of Central Authorities

1 Each Member State shall designate a Central Authority to discharge the duties which are imposed by this Regulation on such an authority.

2 Federal Member States, Member States with more than one system of law or Member States having autonomous territorial units shall be free to appoint more than one Central Authority and shall specify the territorial or personal extent of their functions. Where a Member State has appointed more than one Central Authority, it shall designate the Central Authority to which any communication may be addressed for transmission to the appropriate Central Authority within

that Member State. If a communication is sent to a Central Authority which is not competent, the latter shall be responsible for forwarding it to the competent Central Authority and for informing the sender accordingly.

3 The designation of the Central Authority or Central Authorities, their contact details, and where appropriate the extent of their functions as specified in paragraph 2, shall be communicated by each Member State to the Commission in accordance with Article 71.

Scope—Article 49 creates the obligation to establish a Central Authority. It also provides that Member States with more than one system of law or having autonomous territorial units must establish more than one Central Authority. Accordingly, there are three Central Authorities within the UK, one for each of England and Wales, Scotland and Northern Ireland.

'Central Authority'—See annotations to Art 48.

Article 50
General functions of Central Authorities

1 Central Authorities shall:

(a) cooperate with each other, including by exchanging information, and promote cooperation amongst the competent authorities in their Member States to achieve the purposes of this Regulation;

(b) seek as far as possible solutions to difficulties which arise in the application of this Regulation.

2 Central Authorities shall take measures to facilitate the application of this Regulation and to strengthen their cooperation. For this purpose the European Judicial Network in civil and commercial matters established by Decision 2001/470/EC shall be used.

'Central Authority'—See annotations to Art 48.

Article 51
Specific functions of Central Authorities

1 Central Authorities shall provide assistance in relation to applications under Article 56 and shall in particular:

(a) transmit and receive such applications;

(b) initiate or facilitate the institution of proceedings in respect of such applications.

2 In relation to such applications Central Authorities shall take all appropriate measures:

(a) where the circumstances require, to provide or facilitate the provision of legal aid;

(b) to help locate the debtor or the creditor, in particular pursuant to Articles 61, 62 and 63;

(c) to help obtain relevant information concerning the income and, if necessary, other financial circumstances of the debtor or creditor, including the location of assets, in particular pursuant to Articles 61, 62 and 63;

(d) to encourage amicable solutions with a view to obtaining voluntary payment of maintenance, where suitable by use of mediation, conciliation or similar processes;

(e) to facilitate the ongoing enforcement of maintenance decisions, including any arrears;

(f) to facilitate the collection and expeditious transfer of maintenance payments;

(g) to facilitate the obtaining of documentary or other evidence, without prejudice to Regulation (EC) No 1206/2001;

(h) to provide assistance in establishing parentage where necessary for the recovery of maintenance;

(i) to initiate or facilitate the institution of proceedings to obtain any necessary provisional measures which are territorial in nature and the purpose of which is to secure the outcome of a pending maintenance application;

(j) to facilitate the service of documents, without prejudice to Regulation (EC) No 1393/2007.

3 The functions of the Central Authority under this Article may, to the extent permitted under the law of the Member State concerned, be performed by public bodies, or other bodies subject to the supervision of the competent authorities of that Member State. The designation of any such

public bodies or other bodies, as well as their contact details and the extent of their functions, shall be communicated by each Member State to the Commission in accordance with Article 71.

4 Nothing in this Article or in Article 53 shall impose an obligation on a Central Authority to exercise powers that can be exercised only by judicial authorities under the law of the requested Member State.

'Central Authority'—See annotations to Art 48.

Article 52
Power of attorney

The Central Authority of the requested Member State may require a power of attorney from the applicant only if it acts on his behalf in judicial proceedings or before other authorities, or in order to designate a representative so to act.

'Central Authority'—See annotations to Art 48.

Article 53
Requests for specific measures

1 A Central Authority may make a request, supported by reasons, to another Central Authority to take appropriate specific measures under points (b), (c), (g), (h), (i) and (j) of Article 51(2) when no application under Article 56 is pending. The requested Central Authority shall take such measures as are appropriate if satisfied that they are necessary to assist a potential applicant in making an application under Article 56 or in determining whether such an application should be initiated.

2 Where a request for measures under Article 51(2)(b) and (c) is made, the requested Central Authority shall seek the information requested, if necessary pursuant to Article 61. However, the information referred to in points (b), (c) and (d) of Article 61(2) may be sought only when the creditor produces a copy of the decision, court settlement or authentic instrument to be enforced, accompanied by the extract provided for in Articles 20, 28 or 48, as appropriate.

The requested Central Authority shall communicate the information obtained to the requesting Central Authority. Where that information was obtained pursuant to Article 61, this communication shall specify only the address of the potential defendant in the requested Member State. In the case of a request with a view to recognition, declaration of enforceability or enforcement, the communication shall, in addition, specify merely whether the debtor has income or assets in that State.

If the requested Central Authority is not able to provide the information requested it shall inform the requesting Central Authority without delay and specify the grounds for this impossibility.

3 A Central Authority may also take specific measures at the request of another Central Authority in relation to a case having an international element concerning the recovery of maintenance pending in the requesting Member State.

4 For requests under this Article, the Central Authorities shall use the form set out in Annex V.

Scope—The purpose of 'specific measures' under Art 53 may be, for example, to establish before making an application whether the intended defendant is in the requested Member State or, in enforcement proceedings whether the defendant is in receipt of an income in that Member State.

'Central Authority'—See annotations to Art 48.

Article 54
Central Authority costs

1 Each Central Authority shall bear its own costs in applying this Regulation.

2 Central Authorities may not impose any charge on an applicant for the provision of their services under this Regulation save for exceptional costs arising from a request for a specific measure under Article 53.

For the purposes of this paragraph, costs relating to locating the debtor shall not be regarded as exceptional.

3 The requested Central Authority may not recover the costs of the services referred to in paragraph 2 without the prior consent of the applicant to the provision of those services at such cost.

'Central Authority'—See annotations to Art 48.

Article 55
Application through Central Authorities

An application under this Chapter shall be made through the Central Authority of the Member State in which the applicant resides to the Central Authority of the requested Member State.

'Central Authority'—See annotations to Art 48.

Article 56
Available applications

1 A creditor seeking to recover maintenance under this Regulation may make applications for the following:

(a) recognition or recognition and declaration of enforceability of a decision;
(b) enforcement of a decision given or recognised in the requested Member State;
(c) establishment of a decision in the requested Member State where there is no existing decision, including where necessary the establishment of parentage;
(d) establishment of a decision in the requested Member State where the recognition and declaration of enforceability of a decision given in a State other than the requested Member State is not possible;
(e) modification of a decision given in the requested Member State;
(f) modification of a decision given in a State other than the requested Member State.

2 A debtor against whom there is an existing maintenance decision may make applications for the following:

(a) recognition of a decision leading to the suspension, or limiting the enforcement, of a previous decision in the requested Member State;
(b) modification of a decision given in the requested Member State;
(c) modification of a decision given in a State other than the requested Member State.

3 For applications under this Article, the assistance and representation referred to in Article 45(b) shall be provided by the Central Authority of the requested Member State directly or through public authorities or other bodies or persons.

4 Save as otherwise provided in this Regulation, the applications referred to in paragraphs 1 and 2 shall be determined under the law of the requested Member State and shall be subject to the rules of jurisdiction applicable in that Member State.

Scope—As an alternative to direct enforcement under Ch IV, Art 56 provides a separate procedure allowing parties to make application for new orders or for enforcement of existing orders through Central Authorities (*EDG v RR (Enforcement of Foreign Maintenance Order)* [2015] 1 FLR 270, FD; cf *AB v JJB* [2015] 2 FLR 1143, FD (variation application)). The issue was referred to the CJEU (*MS v PS (Enforcement Procedure Under the Maintenance Regulation: Reference to CJEU)* [2017] 1 FLR 394, FD), which gave a preliminary ruling that a maintenance creditor could apply directly to the competent authority and did not need to submit an application through the Central Authority. Member States are required to give effects to Art 41.1 by amending rules procedure where appropriate (*MS v PS* (Case C-283/16) [2017] 1 FLR 1163, CJEU). The applications available to a creditor are set out in Art 56.1; those available to a debtor are in Art 56.2. Under the alternative Art 56 procedure, it is for the Central Authority of the requested Member State to provide the assistance and representation referred to in Art 45(b) (Art 56.3). Applications under Art 56 are determined under the law of the requested Member State and are subject to the rules of jurisdiction applicable in that Member State (Art 56.4). Article 56 does not of itself confer jurisdiction. The procedure under Art 56 is contained in FPR 2010, PD34E, para 7.3.

'establishment of a decision in the requested Member State where there is no existing decision, including where necessary the establishment of parentage' (Art 56.1(c))—The ability of a court in England and Wales to make such a decision (for example, to establish paternity) will depend on whether it otherwise has jurisdiction under the Maintenance Regulation. Article 56 does not of itself confer jurisdiction.

Article 57
Application contents

1 An application under Article 56 shall be made using the form set out in Annex VI or in Annex VII.

2 An application under Article 56 shall as a minimum include:

(a) a statement of the nature of the application or applications;
(b) the name and contact details, including the address, and date of birth of the applicant;
(c) the name and, if known, address and date of birth of the defendant;
(d) the name and the date of birth of any person for whom maintenance is sought;
(e) the grounds upon which the application is based;
(f) in an application by a creditor, information concerning where the maintenance payment should be sent or electronically transmitted;
(g) the name and contact details of the person or unit from the Central Authority of the requesting Member State responsible for processing the application.

3 For the purposes of paragraph 2(b), the applicant's personal address may be replaced by another address in cases of family violence, if the national law of the requested Member State does not require the applicant to supply his or her personal address for the purposes of proceedings to be brought.

4 As appropriate, and to the extent known, the application shall in addition in particular include:

(a) the financial circumstances of the creditor;
(b) the financial circumstances of the debtor, including the name and address of the employer of the debtor and the nature and location of the assets of the debtor;
(c) any other information that may assist with the location of the defendant.

5 The application shall be accompanied by any necessary supporting information or documentation including, where appropriate, documentation concerning the entitlement of the applicant to legal aid. Applications under Article 56(1)(a) and (b) and under Article 56(2)(a) shall be accompanied, as appropriate, only by the documents listed in Articles 20, 28 and 48, or in Article 25 of the 2007 Hague Convention.

'Central Authority'—See annotations to Art 48.

Article 58
Transmission, receipt and processing of applications and cases through Central Authorities

1 The Central Authority of the requesting Member State shall assist the applicant in ensuring that the application is accompanied by all the information and documents known by it to be necessary for consideration of the application.

2 The Central Authority of the requesting Member State shall, when satisfied that the application complies with the requirements of this Regulation, transmit the application to the Central Authority of the requested Member State.

3 The requested Central Authority shall, within 30 days from the date of receipt of the application, acknowledge receipt using the form set out in Annex VIII, and inform the Central Authority of the requesting Member State what initial steps have been or will be taken to deal with the application, and may request any further necessary documents and information. Within the same 30-day period, the requested Central Authority shall provide to the requesting Central Authority the name and contact details of the person or unit responsible for responding to inquiries regarding the progress of the application.

4 Within 60 days from the date of acknowledgement, the requested Central Authority shall inform the requesting Central Authority of the status of the application.

5 Requesting and requested Central Authorities shall keep each other informed of:

(a) the person or unit responsible for a particular case;
(b) the progress of the case;

and shall provide timely responses to enquiries.

6 Central Authorities shall process a case as quickly as a proper consideration of the issues will allow.

7 Central Authorities shall employ the most rapid and efficient means of communication at their disposal.

8 A requested Central Authority may refuse to process an application only if it is manifest that the requirements of this Regulation are not fulfilled. In such a case, that Central Authority shall promptly inform the requesting Central Authority of its reasons for refusal using the form set out in Annex IX.

9 The requested Central Authority may not reject an application solely on the basis that additional documents or information are needed. However, the requested Central Authority may ask the requesting Central Authority to provide these additional documents or this information. If the requesting Central Authority does not do so within 90 days or a longer period specified by the requested Central Authority, the requested Central Authority may decide that it will no longer process the application. In this case, it shall promptly notify the requesting Central Authority using the form set out in Annex IX.

'Central Authority'—See annotations to Art 48.

Article 59
Languages

1 The request or application form shall be completed in the official language of the requested Member State or, if there are several official languages in that Member State, in the official language or one of the official languages of the place of the Central Authority concerned, or in any other official language of the institutions of the European Union which that Member State has indicated it can accept, unless the Central Authority of that Member State dispenses with translation.

2 The documents accompanying the request or application form shall not be translated into the language determined in accordance with paragraph 1 unless a translation is necessary in order to provide the assistance requested, without prejudice to Articles 20, 28, 40 and 66.

3 Any other communication between Central Authorities shall be in the language determined in accordance with paragraph 1 unless the Central Authorities agree otherwise.

'Central Authority'—See annotations to Art 48.

Article 60
Meetings

1 In order to facilitate the application of this Regulation, Central Authorities shall meet regularly.

2 These meetings shall be convened in compliance with Decision 2001/470/EC.

'Central Authority'—See annotations to Art 48.

Article 61
Access to information for Central Authorities

1 Under the conditions laid down in this Chapter and by way of exception to Article 51(4), the requested Central Authority shall use all appropriate and reasonable means to obtain the information referred to in paragraph 2 necessary to facilitate, in a given case, the establishment, the modification, the recognition, the declaration of enforceability or the enforcement of a decision.

The public authorities or administrations which, in the course of their ordinary activities, hold, within the requested State, the information referred to in paragraph 2 and which control the processing thereof within the meaning of Directive 95/46/EC shall, subject to limitations justified on grounds of national security or public safety, provide the information to the requested Central Authority at its request in cases where the requested Central Authority does not have direct access to it.

Member States may designate the public authorities or administrations able to provide the requested Central Authority with the information referred to in paragraph 2. Where a Member State makes such a designation, it shall ensure that its choice of authorities and administrations permits its Central Authority to have access, in accordance with this Article, to the information requested.

Any other legal person which holds within the requested Member State the information referred to in paragraph 2 and controls the processing thereof within the meaning of Directive 95/46/EC shall provide the information to the requested Central Authority at the latter's request if it is authorised to do so by the law of the requested Member State.

The requested Central Authority shall, as necessary, transmit the information thus obtained to the requesting Central Authority.

2 The information referred to in this Article shall be the information already held by the authorities, administrations or persons referred to in paragraph 1. It shall be adequate, relevant and not excessive and shall relate to:

- (a) the address of the debtor or of the creditor;
- (b) the debtor's income;
- (c) the identification of the debtor's employer and/or of the debtor's bank account(s);
- (d) the debtor's assets.

For the purpose of obtaining or modifying a decision, only the information listed in point (a) may be requested by the requested Central Authority.

For the purpose of having a decision recognised, declared enforceable or enforced, all the information listed in the first subparagraph may be requested by the requested Central Authority. However, the information listed in point (d) may be requested only if the information listed in points (b) and (c) is insufficient to allow enforcement of the decision.

'Central Authority'—See annotations to Art 48.

Article 62
Transmission and use of information

1 The Central Authorities shall, within their Member State, transmit the information referred to in Article 61(2) to the competent courts, the competent authorities responsible for service of documents and the competent authorities responsible for enforcement of a decision, as the case may be.

2 Any authority or court to which information has been transmitted pursuant to Article 61 may use this only to facilitate the recovery of maintenance claims.

Except for information merely indicating the existence of an address, income or assets in the requested Member State, the information referred to in Article 61(2) may not be disclosed to the person having applied to the requesting Central Authority, subject to the application of procedural rules before a court.

3 Any authority processing information transmitted to it pursuant to Article 61 may not store such information beyond the period necessary for the purposes for which it was transmitted.

4 Any authority processing information communicated to it pursuant to Article 61 shall ensure the confidentiality of such information, in accordance with its national law.

'Central Authority'—See annotations to Art 48.

Article 63
Notification of the data subject

1 Notification of the data subject of the communication of all or part of the information collected on him shall take place in accordance with the national law of the requested Member State.

2 Where there is a risk that it may prejudice the effective recovery of the maintenance claim, such notification may be deferred for a period which shall not exceed 90 days from the date on which the information was provided to the requested Central Authority.

'Central Authority'—See annotations to Art 48.

CHAPTER VIII
PUBLIC BODIES

Scope—Chapter VIII makes provision for recovery of maintenance by public bodies that have been obliged to pay benefits to the maintenance creditor due to the debtor's failure to pay what is owed. Article 64 enables such a public body effectively to recover maintenance in lieu of benefits paid by it under the recognition and enforcement provisions of the Maintenance Regulation, subject to certain conditions.

Article 64
Public bodies as applicants

1 For the purposes of an application for recognition and declaration of enforceability of decisions or for the purposes of enforcement of decisions, the term 'creditor' shall include a public body acting in place of an individual to whom maintenance is owed or one to which reimbursement is owed for benefits provided in place of maintenance.

2 The right of a public body to act in place of an individual to whom maintenance is owed or to seek reimbursement of benefits provided to the creditor in place of maintenance shall be governed by the law to which the body is subject.

3 A public body may seek recognition and a declaration of enforceability or claim enforcement of:

(a) a decision given against a debtor on the application of a public body which claims payment of benefits provided in place of maintenance;

(b) a decision given between a creditor and a debtor to the extent of the benefits provided to the creditor in place of maintenance.

4 The public body seeking recognition and a declaration of enforceability or claiming enforcement of a decision shall upon request provide any document necessary to establish its right under paragraph 2 and to establish that benefits have been provided to the creditor.

CHAPTER IX
GENERAL AND FINAL PROVISIONS

Article 65
Legalisation or other similar formality

No legalisation or other similar formality shall be required in the context of this Regulation.

Article 66
Translation of supporting documents

Without prejudice to Articles 20, 28 and 40, the court seised may require the parties to provide a translation of supporting documents which are not in the language of proceedings only if it deems a translation necessary in order to give a decision or to respect the rights of the defence.

Article 67
Recovery of costs

Without prejudice to Article 54, the competent authority of the requested Member State may recover costs from an unsuccessful party having received free legal aid pursuant to Article 46, on an exceptional basis and if his financial circumstances so allow.

Article 68
Relations with other Community instruments

1 Subject to Article 75(2), this Regulation shall modify Regulation (EC) No 44/2001 by replacing the provisions of that Regulation applicable to matters relating to maintenance obligations.

2 This Regulation shall replace, in matters relating to maintenance obligations, Regulation (EC) No 805/2004, except with regard to European Enforcement Orders on maintenance obligations issued in a Member State not bound by the 2007 Hague Protocol.

3 In matters relating to maintenance obligations, this Regulation shall be without prejudice to the application of Directive 2003/8/EC, subject to Chapter V.

4 This Regulation shall be without prejudice to the application of Directive 95/46/EC.

'Regulation (EC) No 805/2004'—This is the European Enforcement Order (EEO) for uncontested claims (see above). Under Art 68.2, the Maintenance Regulation replaces the EEO in matters relating to maintenance obligations except with regard to EEOs on maintenance obligations issued in Member States not bound by the 2007 Hague Protocol, i e the UK and Denmark. The rationale behind this provision is that the EEO provided a speedy means of enforcing an uncontested claim in another Member State because it did not require the exequatur procedure of Brussels I. Where a Member State is bound by the Hague Protocol, the Maintenance Regulation itself provides for such a speedy enforcement procedure without the former exequatur procedure. In consequence of this, uncontested claims from such Member States no longer need to apply the EEO. However, S 2 of Ch IV still maintains a simplified exequatur procedure for Member States not bound by the 2007 Hague Protocol, which States do therefore still require a EEO for uncontested claims.

Article 69
Relations with existing international conventions and agreements

1 This Regulation shall not affect the application of bilateral or multilateral conventions and agreements to which one or more Member States are party at the time of adoption of this Regulation and which concern matters governed by this Regulation, without prejudice to the obligations of Member States under Article 307 of the Treaty.

2 Notwithstanding paragraph 1, and without prejudice to paragraph 3, this Regulation shall, in relations between Member States, take precedence over the conventions and agreements which concern matters governed by this Regulation and to which Member States are party.

3 This Regulation shall not preclude the application of the Convention of 23 March 1962 between Sweden, Denmark, Finland, Iceland and Norway on the recovery of maintenance by the Member States which are party thereto, since, with regard to the recognition, enforceability and enforcement of decisions, that Convention provides for:

(a) simplified and more expeditious procedures for the enforcement of decisions relating to maintenance obligations, and
(b) legal aid which is more favourable than that provided for in Chapter V of this Regulation.

However, the application of the said Convention may not have the effect of depriving the defendant of his protection under Articles 19 and 21 of this Regulation.

Scope—The Maintenance Regulation takes precedence over all instruments concerning matters governed by it. Because of the comprehensive coverage contained in the Maintenance Regulation, there will be no scope for the application of other instruments (for example, the 2007 Lugano Convention) as between Member States. However, Member States will continue to apply other international instruments as they relate to other states. The rules as to jurisdiction contained in Ch II will bind Member States regardless of whether the issue relates to a third state or a Member State.

Article 70
Information made available to the public

The Member States shall provide within the framework of the European Judicial Network in civil and commercial matters established by Decision 2001/470/EC the following information with a view to making it available to the public:

(a) a description of the national laws and procedures concerning maintenance obligations;
(b) a description of the measures taken to meet the obligations under Article 51;

(c) a description of how effective access to justice is guaranteed, as required under Article 44, and

(d) a description of national enforcement rules and procedures, including information on any limitations on enforcement, in particular debtor protection rules and limitation or prescription periods.

Member States shall keep this information permanently updated.

Article 71
Information on contact details and languages

1 By 18 September 2010, the Member States shall communicate to the Commission:

(a) the names and contact details of the courts or authorities with competence to deal with applications for a declaration of enforceability in accordance with Article 27(1) and with appeals against decisions on such applications in accordance with Article 32(2);

(b) the redress procedures referred to in Article 33;

(c) the review procedure for the purposes of Article 19 and the names and contact details of the courts having jurisdiction;

(d) the names and contact details of their Central Authorities and, where appropriate, the extent of their functions, in accordance with Article 49(3);

(e) the names and contact details of the public bodies or other bodies and, where appropriate, the extent of their functions, in accordance with Article 51(3);

(f) the names and contact details of the authorities with competence in matters of enforcement for the purposes of Article 21;

(g) the languages accepted for translations of the documents referred to in Articles 20, 28 and 40;

(h) the languages accepted by their Central Authorities for communication with other Central Authorities referred to in Article 59.

The Member States shall apprise the Commission of any subsequent changes to this information.

2 The Commission shall publish the information communicated in accordance with paragraph 1 in the Official Journal of the European Union, with the exception of the addresses and other contact details of the courts and authorities referred to in points (a), (c) and (f).

3 The Commission shall make all information communicated in accordance with paragraph 1 publicly available through any other appropriate means, in particular through the European Judicial Network in civil and commercial matters established by Decision 2001/470/EC.

Article 72
Amendments to the forms

Any amendment to the forms provided for in this Regulation shall be adopted in accordance with the advisory procedure referred to in Article 73(3).

Article 73
Committee

1 The Commission shall be assisted by the committee established by Article 70 of Regulation (EC) No 2201/2003.

2 Where reference is made to this paragraph, Articles 4 and 7 of Decision 1999/468/EC shall apply.

The period laid down in Article 4(3) of Decision 1999/468/EC shall be set at three months.

3 Where reference is made to this paragraph, Articles 3 and 7 of Decision 1999/468/EC shall apply.

Article 74
Review clause

By five years from the date of application determined in the third subparagraph of Article 76 at the latest, the Commission shall submit to the European Parliament, the Council and the European Economic and Social Committee a report on the application of this Regulation, including an evaluation of the practical experiences relating to the cooperation between Central Authorities, in particular regarding those Authorities' access to the information held by public authorities and administrations, and an evaluation of the functioning of the procedure for recognition, declaration of enforceability and enforcement applicable to decisions given in a Member State not bound by the 2007 Hague Protocol. If necessary the report shall be accompanied by proposals for adaptation.

Article 75
Transitional provisions

1 This Regulation shall apply only to proceedings instituted, to court settlements approved or concluded, and to authentic instruments established as from its date of application, subject to paragraphs 2 and 3.

2 Sections 2 and 3 of Chapter IV shall apply:

(a) to decisions given in the Member States before the date of application of this Regulation for which recognition and the declaration of enforceability are requested as from that date;

(b) to decisions given as from the date of application of this Regulation following proceedings begun before that date,

in so far as those decisions fall with the scope of Regulation (EC) No 44/2001 for the purposes of recognition and enforcement.

Regulation (EC) No 44/2001 shall continue to apply to procedures for recognition and enforcement under way on the date of application of this Regulation.

The first and second subparagraphs shall apply mutatis mutandis to court settlements approved or concluded and to authentic instruments established in the Member States.

3 Chapter VII on cooperation between Central Authorities shall apply to requests and applications received by the Central Authority as from the date of application of this Regulation.

Scope—Sections 2 and 3 of Ch IV apply to decisions given in Member States before 18 June 2011, where the request for recognition or enforceability is made after that date, as well as to decisions given in Member States after 18 June 2011 where the application was made before that date, provided that the decision is within the scope of Brussels I. Therefore, where the decision or application pre-dates 18 June 2011, it can be recognised and enforced under the regime applying to non-Hague Protocol Member States contained in Sections 2 and 3 of Ch IV, regardless of whether it comes from a Hague Protocol Member State. However, Brussels I will continue to apply where the recognition and enforcement procedure was in train at 18 June 2011. The provisions as to the cooperation between Central Authorities contained in Ch VII only apply as from 18 June 2011.

'as from' (Arts 75.1 and 75.2)—'after' was used in the original version of Art 75 rather than 'as from', meaning that it was arguable that the transitional provisions only applied from 19 June 2011.

Article 76
Entry into force

This Regulation shall enter into force on the 20th day following its publication in the Official Journal of the European Union.

Articles 2(2), 47(3), 71, 72 and 73 shall apply from 18 September 2010.

Except for the provisions referred to in the second paragraph, this Regulation shall apply from 18 June 2011, subject to the 2007 Hague Protocol being applicable in the Community by that date. Failing that, this Regulation shall apply from the date of application of that Protocol in the Community.

PART VI

This Regulation shall be binding in its entirety and directly applicable in the Member States in accordance with the Treaty establishing the European Community.

Done at Brussels, 18 December 2008.

For the Council
The President
M. BARNIER

****

Regulation (EU) No 606/2013 of the European Parliament and of the Council

of 12 June 2013

on mutual recognition of protection measures in civil matters

Note—This Regulation is not set out, but is summarised below. The full text of the Regulation is available at *http://eur-lex.europa.eu*.

Subject matter and scope of the provisions

The EU Regulation on Mutual Recognition of Protection Measures in Civil Matters (European Civil Protection Regulation (606/2013) of 12 June 2013) establishes rules for a simple, rapid and less-costly mechanism within the Union for cross-border recognition of protection measures in civil matters without any special procedure being required (Art 1). It came into effect on 11 January 2015 and applies to protection measures ordered on or after that date, irrespective of when proceedings were instituted. It is binding in its entirety and directly applicable (Art 22). It does not apply to (a) criminal matters covered by Directive 2011/99; (b) matters that fall within the scope of Brussels IIA (Art 2; preamble, paras 9, 11).

Application—The Regulation applies to protective measures within the EU of both judicial and administrative authorities (but not, in any circumstances, police authorities), provided that the latter offer guarantees with regard in particular to their impartiality and the right of the parties to judicial review (preamble, para 13).

Nature, definition and extent of 'protection measures' to which it applies—The Regulation applies to protection measures ordered for the protection of a person where there exist serious grounds for considering that the person's life, physical or psychological integrity, personal liberty, security or sexual integrity is at risk, e g physical violence, harassment, sexual aggression, stalking, intimidation or other forms of indirect coercion (preamble, para (6)). 'Protection measure' is defined as meaning any decision that imposes one or more of the following obligations on the person causing the risk (respondent) with a view to protecting the victim when the latter's physical or psychological integrity is at risk, namely a prohibition or regulation: (a) on entering the place where the protected person (PP) resides, works or regularly visits or stays; (b) of contact in any form with the PP, including by telephone, electronic or ordinary mail, fax or any other means; or (c) on approaching the PP closer than a prescribed distance (Art 3). The protection measures are not limited to a specific address or circumscribed area and will thus extend to the place of residence, place of work or a place that the PP visits on a regular basis, such as the residence of relatives or the school or educational establishment attended by his/her child (Art 21; preamble, para 19). Hence the competent authority of the Member State (MS) addressed is given powers to adjust the factual elements of the protection measures where and to the extent necessary to give effect to the measures (Art 11(1)). Any adjustments made will be governed by the law of the MS but must be brought to the notice of the respondent in accordance with the law of that State. Where the respondent resides in a MS other than the MS addressed or in a third country, the notice should be served by registered post with the acknowledgement of receipt or equivalent (Art 11(2),(3)). Where the respondent's whereabouts are unknown or the person is evading service, the mode of alternative or substituted service is to be governed by the law of the MS addressed (Art 11(4)). Both the PP and the respondent have the right of appeal against any adjustments made. The appeal procedure is to be governed by the law of the MS but the appeal will not result in a suspension of the protective measures (Art 11(5)).

Recognition and enforcement—It is mandatory for the protective measures to be recognised automatically without any procedure being required and enforceable without a need for declaration of enforceability, so that a protection measure ordered in one MS is treated as if it had been ordered in the MS where recognition is sought (preamble, para 4).

Review—Under no circumstances may a protection measure be reviewed as to its substance in the MS addressed (Art 12; c f 1996 Convention, Art 25 and Brussels IIA, Art 24).

Introduction of uniform model form of certificate—A new multilingual form is introduced. The PP will need to obtain the appropriate certificate to invoke the protection measure in another MS, translation and transliteration of which will be provided without any cost to the PP. Translation and transliteration beyond the text will be allocated as provided under the law of the MS of origin. Where a certificate contains free text, it will be for the MS addressed to determine whether any translation or transliteration is required. In any event, the PP is given the right to provide a translation or transliteration on his/her own initiative. There is no appeal against the issuing of the certificate (Art 5; preamble, paras 22–24). In the event of any variation or suspension or discharge of the protection measure, a certificate indicating the change using the multilingual standard form should be issued upon the request by the PP or the respondent. On receipt of such a certificate, the MS must suspend or withdraw the effects of the recognition or the enforcement of the protection measure (Art 14).

Condition of issue of certificate—The certificate may only be issued if the protection measure has been brought to the notice of the respondent in accordance with the law of the MS of origin. Where the order is made in default of appearance, a certificate may only be issued if the respondent was served with notice of the application or otherwise informed of the proceedings in sufficient time and in such a way as to enable him/her to arrange for his/her defence. Where the order was obtained on a without notice application, the certificate may only be issued if the respondent had the right to challenge the protection measure under the law of the MS of origin (Art 6; preamble, para 25).

Contents of the certificate—To be valid and effective, the certificate must contain the information set out in Art 7. It must also indicate whether the address specified in the protection measure constitutes the place of residence, the place of work or a place that the PP visits on a regular basis. Where relevant, the circumscribed areas (an approximate radius from the specific address) imposed by the protection measure should also be indicated in the certificate (preamble, para 21).

Service on the respondent—It is the responsibility of the issuing authority of the MS of origin to bring to the notice of the respondent that a certificate has been issued and that it is recognised and enforceable in all MS, pursuant to Art 4 of the Regulation (Art 4(1)). Where the respondent resides in another MS or another country, notice of the issue of the certificate and its effect must be effected by registered post with acknowledgement of receipt or other proof of delivery. Where the respondent's whereabouts are not known or he/she refuses to accept service (avoid service) the issue will be governed by the law of the MS of origin. However, on no account must the PP's contact details be disclosed to the respondent unless the disclosure is necessary for compliance with, or enforcement of, the protection measure (Art 8(2),(3); preamble, para 27).

Rectification or withdrawal of the certificate—Although Art 5(2) provides that no appeal shall lie against the issuing of the certificate, the PP or the respondent may request the issuing authority of the MS of origin to rectify discrepancy between the protection measure and the certificate due to clerical error, eg typing error, error of transcription or copying, or where the certificate does not correctly reflect the protection measure. The certificate may also be rectified on the authority's own initiative. Similarly, the certificate must be withdrawn where it was clearly wrongly granted, eg where it falls outside the scope of the Regulation or where it was issued in breach of the requirements for its issue. The procedure, including any appeal with regard to rectification or withdrawal, is to be governed by the law of the MS of origin (Arts 9, 5(2); preamble, para 29).

Duration of protection measures—The effect of recognition of the protection measures will be limited to 12 months from the date of issue of the certificate, irrespective of whether the order lasts for longer (Art 4(4); preamble, para 15). Where the duration of the protection measure is longer than 12 months, the PP has a right to invoke protection measures under any legal act of the Union for recognition or to apply for a national protection measure in the MS addressed (preamble, para 16).

Defences—Recognition or enforcement may be refused on the grounds that it is (a) contrary to public policy or (b) irreconcilable with the judgment given or recognised in the MS addressed (cf the 1996 Hague Convention, Art 23 and Brussels IIA, Arts 22, 23 and the commentaries thereunder). But recognition may not be refused on the ground that the law of the MS addressed does not allow for such a measure based on the facts (Art 13).

Legal aid—It is mandatory for the PP to have effective access to justice, which requires legal aid to be provided in accordance with Council Directive 2003/8/EC of 27 January 2003 (preamble, para 34).

Protection of human rights—The fundamental rights and principles under Arts 47 and 48 of the Charter of Fundamental Rights of the European Union, which seek to ensure the right of defence and fair trial, are respected (para 38), hence the provisions in relation to service of notice of the proceedings and of the grant of the certificate.

The Regulation deals only with the recognition of the obligation imposed by the protection measure. It does not regulate the procedures for implementation or enforcement of the protection measure nor should it cover any potential sanctions that might be imposed if the obligation ordered by the protection measure is infringed in the MS addressed. Those matters are left to the law of that MS. However, in accordance with the general principles of Union law and of mutual recognition, MS are to ensure that protection measures recognised under the Regulation can take effect in the MS addressed.

In order to facilitate the application of the Regulation, MS are required to provide certain information regarding national rules and procedure concerning protection measures in civil matters through the European Judicial Network and access to the information provided through the European e-Justice Portal (Art 17; preamble, para 34).

Denmark—Note that Denmark is not a party to the Regulation and is not bound by it or subject to its application (preamble, para 41).

be for the MS addressed to determine whether any translation or transliteration is required. In any event, the PP is given the right to provide a translation or transliteration on his/her own initiative. There is no appeal against the issuing of the certificate (Art 5; preamble, paras 22–24). In the event of any variation or suspension or discharge of the protection measure, a certificate indicating the change using the multilingual standard form should be issued upon the request by the PP or the respondent. On receipt of such a certificate, the MS must suspend or withdraw the effects of the recognition or the enforcement of the protection measure (Art 14).

Condition of issue of certificate—The certificate may only be issued if the protection measure has been brought to the notice of the respondent in accordance with the law of the MS of origin. Where the order is made in default of appearance, a certificate may only be issued if the respondent was served with notice of the application or otherwise informed of the proceedings in sufficient time and in such a way as to enable him/her to arrange for his/her defence. Where the order was obtained on a without notice application, the certificate may only be issued if the respondent had the right to challenge the protection measure under the law of the MS of origin (Art 6; preamble, para 25).

Contents of the certificate—To be valid and effective, the certificate must contain the information set out in Art 7. It must also indicate whether the address specified in the protection measure constitutes the place of residence, the place of work or a place that the PP visits on a regular basis. Where relevant, the circumscribed areas (an approximate radius from the specific address) imposed by the protection measures should also be indicated in the certificate (preamble, para 21).

Service on the respondent—It is the responsibility of the issuing authority of the MS of origin to bring to the notice of the respondent that a certificate has been issued and that it is recognised and enforceable in all MS pursuant to Art 4 of the Regulation (Art 8(1)). Where the respondent resides in another MS or another country notice of the issue of the certificate and its effect must be effected by registered post with acknowledgement of receipt or other proof of delivery. Where the respondent's whereabouts are not known or he/she refuses to accept service (avoid service) the issue will be governed by the law of the MS of origin. However, on no account must the PP's contact details be disclosed to the respondent unless the disclosure is necessary for compliance with, or enforcement of, the protection measure (Art 8(3); preamble, para 27).

Rectification or withdrawal of the certificate—Although Art 5(2) provides that no appeal shall lie against the issuing of the certificate, the PP or the respondent may request the issuing authority of the MS of origin to rectify discrepancy between the protection measure and the certificate due to clerical error, eg typing error, error of transcription or copying, or where the certificate does not correctly reflect the protection measure. The certificate may also be rectified on the authority's own initiative. Similarly, the certificate must be withdrawn where it was clearly wrongly granted, eg where it falls outside the scope of the Regulation or where it was issued in breach of the requirements for its issue. The procedure, including any appeal with regard to rectification or withdrawal, is to be governed by the law of the MS of origin (Arts 9, 9(2); preamble, para 29).

Duration of protection measures—The effect of recognition of the protection measures will be limited to 12 months from the date of issue of the certificate, irrespective of whether the order lasts for longer (Art 4(4); preamble, para 13). Where the duration of the protection measure is longer than 12 months, the PP has a right to invoke protection measures under any legal act of the Union for recognition or to apply for a national protection measure in the MS addressed (preamble, para 18).

Defences—Recognition or enforcement may be refused on the grounds that it is (a) contrary to public policy or (b) irreconcilable with the judgment given or recognised in the MS addressed (cf the 1996 Hague Convention, Art 23 and Brussels IIA, Arts 22, 23 and the commentaries thereunder). But recognition may not be refused on the ground that the law of the MS addressed does not allow for such a measure based on the facts (Art 13).

Legal aid—It is mandatory for the PP to have effective access to justice, which requires legal aid to be provided in accordance with Council Directive 2003/8/EC of 27 January 2003 (preamble, para 34).

Protection of human rights—The fundamental rights and principles under Arts 47 and 48 of the Charter of Fundamental Rights of the European Union which seek to ensure the right of defence and fair trial, are respected (para 38). Hence the provisions in relation to service of notice of the proceedings and of the grant of the certificate.

The Regulation deals only with the recognition of the obligation imposed by the protection measure. It does not regulate the procedures for implementation or enforcement of the protection measure nor should it cover any potential sanctions that might be imposed if the obligation ordered by the protection measure is infringed in the MS addressed. Those matters are left to the law of that MS. However, in accordance with the general principles of Union law and of mutual recognition, MS are to ensure that protection measures recognised under the Regulation can take effect in the MS addressed.

In order to facilitate the application of the Regulation, MS are required to provide certain information regarding national rules and procedure concerning protection measures in civil matters through the European Judicial Network and access to the information provided through the European e-Justice Portal (Art 17; preamble, para 34).

Denmark—Note that Denmark is not a party to the Regulation, and is not bound by it, or subject to its application (preamble, para 41).

Index

References are to page numbers.

Abduction *see also* Hague Abduction Convention 1980; Removal of child
- acquiescence *see* 'consent or acquiescence' *below*
- appeals 2195
- application in respect of abducted child *see also* Custody (of child); Hague Convention 176, 180, 853
- asylum, and claim for 391
- Brussels IIA 2779
- child in care, police protection etc, of 583
- child's objections 390
- consent or acquiescence 388
- grave risk 389
- Hague Convention 1996 2749
- international, Practice Direction 1606
- intolerable situation 391
- Isle of Man 365
- liaison judge 375, 2778
- MIAM exemption 1311
- non-Convention cases 179, 1611
- parental responsibility judgment, recognition and enforcement of 2777
- recovery order *see* Recovery order
- return of child *see* Return of child
- tracing 1373
- UK/Pakistan Protocol 1616, 2564, 2707

ABE (achieving best evidence) interviews 542, 624

Abroad *see also* England and Wales
- assistance from authorities abroad 526
- assistance to child to live 664
- embassies, liaison between courts and 2706
- enforcement
  - custody etc order *see* Custody (of child)
  - maintenance order *see* Maintenance order enforcement; Maintenance order registration
  - recovery of maintenance *see* Maintenance order enforcement
  - registration of order *see* Registration of orders
- High Commissions, liaison between courts and 2706
- relocation
  - shared living arrangements 442

Abuse
- care proceedings 2645
- criminal investigations, notification to local authority of 2647
- criminal proceedings 2645
- Crown Prosecution Service
  - disclosure 2647
- information 2645
- police
  - disclosure 2647
- prevention of 658

Abuse—*continued*
- public interest immunity 2652

Access *see also* Contact
- habitual residence 2778
- order, recognition 396, 852
- rights 381
  - Hague Convention 1996 2746

Accidental injuries
- burden of proof 535
- causation 536

Accommodation, provision of
- adoption agency, by, inspection 607
- alternative, for person living with child 658
- boarding school/college, by, meaning 613
- care home or hospital, child in 612
- ceasing to provide 2413
- child between 16 and 21, for 492
- child ceasing to be looked after, for 503
- child in care 498
  - Wales 498
- child in need, for 492
  - wishes and feelings of child 493
- children eligible 493
- consent 494
- documentation 495
- family centre, at 659
- information on change of authority 662
- inspection 607
- local authority duty 492
  - accommodated children 659
  - child in police protection etc 495
- local authority power 493
- looked after child 498
  - general duty 500
  - review before change 500
- notification requirements 611, 612
  - visits to child after 613
- parental responsibility, and *see* Parental responsibility: child is accommodated by local authority, where
- police protection, etc, during 495
- private fostering *see* Private fostering
- removal from 493
  - exceptions 493
- secure *see* Secure accommodation
- services for accommodated child 659
- transfer of child 493
- voluntary organisation, by 590
- welfare of child, and 492

Accounts
- order for preparation and filing 2087

Acknowledgment of service 2050
- appeal, for 2357
- filing
  - failure, consequences 2050
  - period for 1384

Acknowledgment of service—*continued*
filing—*continued*
period for, service out of jurisdiction 1358
service deemed on 1351
Supreme Court 2357
Part 8 claim 2050
Acquiescence
Hague Convention 1996 2735
Acting in person *see* Litigant in person
Actions done by court/court officer 1306
Activity condition 461
factors to be taken into account when making 461
financial assistance with charges 461
monitoring by Cafcass officer 462
monitoring compliance with 462
provision for 460
Activity direction 461
child arrangements order 458
discharge
care order, by 618
factors to be taken into account when making 461
financial assistance with charges 461
monitoring by Cafcass officer 462
monitoring compliance with 462
provision for 147, 459
Activity order
suspension on stay of Part I order (FLA) 842
Address
child, of, information on 662
education supervision order, under 675
supervision order, under 673
disclosure
attachment of earnings order 106
charging order 109
committal by way of judgment summons 119
execution of goods, for 113
Government Department, by 1373
means of payment order 120
non-disclosure application 1852
enquiries as to respondent's 1349
notification of change, Family Court maintenance order 656
proper 637
service, for 637
matrimonial/civil partnership order application 1348, 1349
not matrimonial etc application 1354
unknown 2352
usual or last known residence 1349
Adjournment
court's case management powers 1320
Family Procedure Rules 1308
Hague Convention 1996 2746
Administration of estate
civil partnerships 702
Administration order
attachment of earnings *see also* County Court: attachment of earnings order in 356
County Court powers 347
Administrative authorities 2733
Administrative Court 2252
urgent applications 2267
Admission
notice to admit facts, in response to 2116
'only in the proceedings' 1767
Adopted Children Register 296
birth register, connection with 297
cancellation of entry 323
General Register Office 296
High Court power to restrict disclosure from records 297
interpretation 299
rectification 322
search 297
Adoption *see also* Convention adoption order; Hague Adoption Convention 1993
abroad
arrangements to assist child to live abroad 664
parental responsibility 2379
provisions applying to 2380, 2393
removal of child for 302
adopted adult, disclosure rights 1679
adopted child *see also* 'child' *below*
change of name 322
information rights 323
information rights (transitional) 309
legitimation of 1057, 1058
status of 292, 326
advertisements 261, 313, 314
agency *see* Adoption agency
applicant for
child to have home with 277
civil partner 285, 318
couple 187, 284, 318
domicile/habitual residence 187, 284
removal of child from 274
single person 187, 284, 285
application 186
confidentiality 187
form 187
pending (transitional provision) 326
persons to receive copy 1663
respondents 187
withdrawal 1853
arrangements
offence 307
attendance
prerequisite for order 189
baby 257, 266, 270
becoming an adopted person 256
birth records of adopted child 323
birth registration, re-registration 323
bringing a child into the UK 300
adopted child, bringing in a 301
'restricted country', from a 300
statutory requirements 300
Brussels IIA 280, 522
Cafcass officer
access to records 311
appointment of 310
ceasing to be member of original family 256
Channel Islands 312
Channel Islands, registration in 321

Adoption—*continued*
child
disclosure of whereabouts 276
foreign 2375, 2379
orphan 260
who may be adopted 187
child in care 260
children and family reporter
report 188
children's guardian
appointment 188
commencement and extent (ACA 2002) 319, 320
communicating information relating to proceedings 1657
conditions precedent to making application 284
confidentiality of reports 1657
consent to 185, 188, 260, 281
advance 260
care proceedings, in 259
condition for making order 281
consequences 258, 1656
dispensing with 188, 256, 288, 289
evidence of 311
father without parental responsibility 283
forms 259, 283, 1653, 1656
guardian, and 281
meaning 259
placement for adoption 259
placement with parental consent 258
procedure for dispensing with 290
proof 283
request to dispense with 263
requirement 280
welfare of child, and 281, 289
withdrawal of 259, 271
contact, and 266, 267
adoption agency is authorised to place child for adoption, where 266
adoption agency power to refuse to allow 267
application for, when placement for adoption authorised 267
arrangements for 280
habitual residence /presence condition 838
Part I order 837
post-adoption 286, 287
transitional 309
Convention *see also* Convention adoption order 292
certificate 2393
that are not 'full' adoptions 293
court 1644
declaration, adoption effected overseas 871
delay, reducing 255, 312
directions
first directions hearing 1664
disclosure of information 291, 1675
adopted adult, rights to 1679
permitted 1675
prospective adopters, information concerning 553
dispensing with consent *see* 'consent to: dispensing with' *above*

Adoption—*continued*
effect 280
expenses of Crown 319
father without parental responsibility 1650
notice to 283
first directions hearing 188, 1654
foreign child 1664
adoption agency report 1666
foreign order in relation to, immigration clearance 301
parental responsibility order 1664, 1665
foreign element 296, 302, 303, 2375
bringing child into UK 2376
fees 305
restrictions 299
change of name consent 2379
child to have home with applicant 2379
definitions 2375
first directions appointment 1664
local authority functions 2377
parental responsibility order 301
practice direction 1664
procedural rules (FPR) 1644
provisions applying 2393
registration 321
return of child 2379
former parent of child freed for adoption 1650
foster parents (local authority)
removal of child from 274
foster parent's partner
removal of child from 275
freeing for *see* Freeing for adoption
guardian, consent to 281
home with applicant 277, 301
insurance, effect on 296
intercountry *see also* 'foreign element' *above*; Convention adoption order 283, 329, 1654
central authorities 329, 331
Hague Adoption Convention 1993 text 330
liaison judge 328
procedural requirements 331, 333
recognition 335
interpretation provisions 317
Isle of Man 312
Isle of Man, registration in 321
jurisdiction of Family Division 1250
leave to oppose 282
legitimation, revocation on 291
registration cancellation 323
listing final hearings, President's Guidance 2582
local authority good practice where adoption is best option 530
matters for court 255
meaning 291
modification of CA 1989 290
Northern Ireland 282, 312
registration in 321
notice of intention to adopt
appropriate local authority 279
local authority, to 279
notice to respondents 1650
notification of applications 326

Adoption—*continued*
offences 307
consent to proceedings 309
corporate /unincorporated body 316
removal of child 270, 272, 274
one person, by 286
order
amendment 322
meaning 279
preconditions 277, 278, 280
registration of 320, 321
Scotland 321
restrictions 284
revocation 291
overseas *see* Overseas adoption
panel 1676, 1678
parent, by 286
parental consent *see* 'consent to' *above*
parental responsibility
during placement 265
order gives 189, 279
payment
excepted 308
interpretation 308
prohibition 307, 336
pension entitlement 296
permission to refuse *see* Parent: permission to oppose adoption
person aged over 18 years 284
placement for *see* Placement
pre-30 December 2005 291
private proceedings 310
procedure for 280, 530, 1643
property, and
disposition, meaning 295
disposition, rules 294, 295
peerage, devolving with 295
personal representative /trustee, protection 295
proportionality 538
prospective adopter(s)
notice of intention to adopt 278
return of child
duty 271, 272, 273
voluntary 273
suitability of 279
recognised by law of England and Wales 292
recognition of judgments and orders 282
records 571
recovery of child by parent 270, 271, 272
recovery order 276
register *see* Adopted Children Register
registers to be kept 320
foreign adoption 321
Scotland 321
registration 326
relationship child has with relatives 256
relative
meaning 293, 299, 317
religious persuasion *see* Religious persuasion: adoption, and
removal of child
restrictions on 270, 272, 274, 275
breach of 276

Adoption—*continued*
reporting officer
appointment 1710
duties 1718
restrictions on appointment 1711
reports 278
agency 278
interpretation 308
restrictions 307
welfare 188
research into 610
respondents 187
restriction on arranging 306
restriction on reports 307
restrictions on advertisements 306
return of child in emergency 273
Scotland 281, 282, 312
serial number case 1658
Service *see* Adoption agency
service (of documents), postal 313
service on parent 1651
solicitor for child 188
special guardianship and, choice between 256
statement of facts 1655
status conferred by 293
status of adopted child 292
application to court for declaration as to 292
subordinate legislation 314
procedural rules 315
sufficient opportunities to see child in home environment 278
surrogacy 989
transitional (ACA 2002) 325
Wales 319
ward of court, of 1549
welfare of child, and 255
consent, dispensing with, and 281
'welfare throughout his life' 256
Adoption agency
applicant in freeing application *see* Freeing for adoption
Convention adoption of child
decision 2391
information provision duties 2388, 2389
referral to panel 2390
report 2391
Convention adoption of foreign child
approval review 2382
decision 2382
entry into UK, requirements 2384
information provision duties 2381, 2382
placement not proceeding 2384
procedure 2383
definition 634
matters for 255
parental responsibility 265
placement for adoption 257
authorisation circumstances 258
parental consent, with 258
removal of child prohibitions 270
report by 278
content 1665
practice direction 1665

Adoption Contact Register 298, 299
Adoption order
child under 6 weeks 283
conditions for making 281
not available over age of 19 years 283
respect for private and family life, and 1008
revocation
procedure 291
Adoption Service *see* Adoption agency
Adoption society
accredited body for intercountry adoption 329
approved 329
registered 329
ADR *see* Alternative dispute resolution
Adultery
divorce etc cause 1147, 1149
Advanced education 2485
Advertisements
adoption, relating to 261, 313, 314
private fostering, for 681
surrogacy arrangement, about proposed 1258
Advice *see also* Advice and assistance
Cafcass function to provide 807
child being looked after, for
cessation of care, on 503, 506, 666
child in need, for 659
family centre, at 659
supervisor, by 553
education supervision order, under 673
Advice and assistance *see also* Befriending; Family assistance order
children's home, in 593
conditions 508
person qualifying for 507
representations, advocacy services 517
supervisor, by 553
voluntary organisation, by 591
Advocate
continuing duty 1529
judge seeing *see* Judge: seeing advocates
Advocate to the court 1530
appointment and role 2562
request to Attorney-General 2563, 2686
request to Official Solicitor / Cafcass 2564
Official Solicitor as *see* Official Solicitor: amicus curiae, as
Aeroplane
return of child by 1633
Affidavit *see also* Evidence
alteration 2119
committal application 1989
court order, under 1766
defect 2123
deponent unable to sign 2119, 2124
deponent, meaning of 2117
exhibit 2120
family provision 2271
filing 2119
form of (CPR) 2118
form of (FPR) 1766
format 2117
inspection of documents referred to 2109
made outside jurisdiction 1766
mandatory use of 2117
Affidavit—*continued*
signed documents distinguished, and 1722
swearing 2119
use of (CPR) 2117
use of (FPR) 1766
when required 2117
Affiliation order *see also* Maintenance order
meaning 1102
reciprocal enforcement, and 1085, 1102
Affirmation 1766
evidence 2121
Age
'attained the age of' 285, 286
child 1285
assessment of child's needs 658
child support 416
court to consider 422
financial provision, and 813, 1197
Hague Abduction Convention 1980 application 376
Hague Convention 1996 2732
local authority to consider 497
section 8 order, and 450
voluntary organisation to consider 592
contemnor 793
majority, of 917
time of attainment 919
Agreement
Hague Convention 1996 2740
Agricultural tenancy
transfer of, on divorce etc
FLA 1996 provisions 914
Alien
political activity of 1011
Allocation of proceedings 1859, 1881
care orders 522
emergency applications 1743
judge 2714
maintenance jurisdiction within UK 2446
Part 8 claim 2051
procedure 1860, 2464, 2715
supervision orders 522
Allocation questionnaire *see* Case management
Alternative (Part 8) procedure for claim *see also* Claim form (alternative Part 8 procedure)
Alternative dispute resolution *see also* Non-court dispute resolution
matrimonial / civil partnership proceedings 1396
Amendment
matrimonial / civil partnership application, to (FPR) 1387
Amicus curiae *see* Advocate to the court
Ancillary relief *see* Financial provision
Annuity *see* Pension
Annulment *see* Nullity
Anonymity
Court of Appeal 2142
financial provision 2142
freedom of expression, and 1010
human rights 2049
party 2142
principles 2068, 2142
social workers 544
waiver 248

Anonymity—*continued*
witness 2142
Answer 1286
defence or reply to an application form 1722
defended case
amendment to 1387
period for filing 49, 1385
service 49
Form C7 1541
matrimonial and civil partnership proceedings 1380
defended proceedings 1387
written 1541
Antenuptial agreement *see also* Prenuptial agreement 1153
Anton Piller order *see* Search order
Appeal 2193
appellant's notice
permission request in 1866
applications 1863
attachment of earnings 352
Brussels and Lugano Conventions, under 690
case management 2215
case stated, by way of
High Court 2234
child support 412, 1468
chronology 1870
citation of authorities *see* Citation of authorities
committal order 793
compromise on behalf of child or protected party, and 2068
contempt of court 249, 352
court for 249
costs
against 1235, 2150
detailed assessment 2176
County Court
FPR 1862
from 798
judge's note 799
court bundle 1865, 1881, 1882
Court of Appeal, to *see also* Court of Appeal 1863
declarations 1422
decree nisi or conditional order 1395
destination of appeal 2209
disclosure *see* Disclosure: appellate process, and the
discretionary decisions, against 1866
district judge, from *see* District judge: appeal from
duties of solicitor acting for child 1710
emergency protection order 132
evidence for
judge's note 799
extension of time 1235, 1869
Family Court, from 1140, 2545
Court of Appeal, to 202
High Court, to 193
Family Court, to judge of 193
family proceedings court, from 2545
final decision
reopening, procedure 213
findings of fact, against 1871, 2193

Appeal—*continued*
fresh evidence 1753, 1870
fresh experts on 1871
further
Hague Convention on the International Recovery of Child Support 2007, under 2844
general observations 2196
grounds for allowing 1871
hearing 2216
High Court 2373
High Court, to or from *see* High Court
hopeless 1871
identification of child 1516
Immigration and Asylum Chamber 2231
information, communication of 1468
interim care or supervision order 566
interlocutory injunction 1243
judge 209, 1888
judicial review 2198
judicial review cases 2254
litigant in person 206, 1865
magistrates' child support proceedings 198, 1059
material omission 1865
matrimonial / civil partnership proceedings 1399
new evidence *see* 'fresh evidence' *above*
new trial application 1234
observations by court 2196
parentage 411, 870
permission *see* Permission: appeal, to 1877
litigant in person 1865
power to change judgment after handing down 1865, 2195
powers of lower court 1870
Practice Direction 1872
Court of Appeal 2221
general 2208
High Court / County Court 2214
statutory appeal 2233
presumption of death 1224
private sitting, power 808
procedure 209, 1863, 2373
proportionality 1870
protection measures 2009, 2014
real prospect of success 1866
rectification of want of jurisdiction to hear 2202
refusal of permission 244
reopening 1871
final appeals 1235, 2208
procedure 213
respondent, by
Court of Appeal 2223
role of appellate court 1871
scope of Pt 52 2193
second 1870
skeleton arguments 1867, 1868
special provisions 1863
statutory appeal 2233
stay, imposition of conditions to grant of 1869
Supreme Court, to *see also* Supreme Court
certificate for 198
contempt of court case 249

Appeal—*continued*
Supreme Court, to—*continued*
Court of Appeal, from 199, 249
permission for 199
time-limit *see* Time-limit 2196
transcripts *see* Transcript: appeals
trial judge 2194
urgent 566
Applicant
duties to court and other parties
full and fair disclosure 1746
hearing in absence of 1520
proceedings in absence of 1833
Application
abducted child, relating to
European Convention, under 177
FLA, under 180, 853
Hague Abduction Convention 1980, under 177
adoption *see also* Adoption 186
alternative procedure 1736
Practice Direction 1739
amendment to (FPR) 1387
attachment of earnings order 105
care order *see* Care order
child arrangements order 452
child assessment order 571
child support, for 402
child, by *see also* Child 453
committal, for *see* Committal order
consent, by 2084
contact with child in care, for order 166
contribution order, for 668
court for (CPR) 2077
declaration for *see* Declaration
decree of divorce etc *see* Divorce
dismissal 2079
education supervision order 553
discharge 675
extension 675
emergency protection order 132, 572
discharge 134, 577
extension 137
evidence 2083
family provision from deceased's estate
procedure generally 22
financial relief for child (CA) 12
form
date of 1331
issue of 1331
meaning 1285
other than in accordance with Part 18 procedure 1285
guardian, appointment of *see* Guardian
Hague Convention 176
hearing, dealt with without 2079
interim remedies 2078, 2088
issue
date of 1331
start of proceedings on 1331
lump sum order, for 644
maintenance agreement, variation 20
matrimonial / civil partnership
High Court / County Court 1379

Application—*continued*
matrimonial / civil partnership—*continued*
Practice Direction 1406
means of payment order *see* Means of payment order
miscellaneous, FPR 1418
not on notice 2078
note of proceedings 2083
notice
made without, interim remedy 2088
parentage declaration 2085
parental responsibility order 142, 426
Part 18 procedure (FPR) 1728
general provision, Practice Direction 1732
Part 19 procedure (FPR) 1736
Practice Direction 1739
periodical payments order, for 644
permission for start proceedings 1728
pre-action 2081
procedure (FPR) 1732
prohibited steps order 150
proprietary rights enforcement, for 14
recovery order 140
reference to a judge 2080
restriction on 618, 1381
secure accommodation order 171
specific issue order 150
stamping and sealing 1855
start of proceedings 1331
supervision order *see* Supervision order
telephone hearing 2082
time for *see* Time-limit
totally without merit 1731
vexatious 1245
video conferencing 2083
withdrawal 1382, 1853
without hearing 2084
related criminal proceedings 2084
without merit 2079
without notice *see* Without notice application
Application notice 2080
address details 2080
application made without notice, service 2079
application without service of 2081
contents 2078
filing 2078
meaning 1285, 2077
Part 18 procedure, under, form for 1332
service 2078, 2081
out of jurisdiction 1358
time application made, and 2078
use as evidence 2117
verification of 2084
written evidence, filing with 2078
Approved training 2486
Arbitral award 1153
consent order 1153
mistake 1308
Arbitration *see also* Arbitration agreement 366, 1307, 1308, 1448, 2478
advantages 1448
challenging awards 2701
claims, definition of 2700
consent orders 1448

Arbitration—*continued*
consent orders and, relationship between 1448
enforcement of awards 2701
Family Court 2697
Family Law Arbitration Scheme 440
standard court orders 2701
stay of proceedings 2700
Arbitration agreement
meaning (SCA) 1249
Armed forces member
deduction from pay 105
Arrears
child support maintenance *see* Child support
maintenance payments *see* Maintenance order enforcement
Arrest *see also* Committal order; Warrant of arrest
occupation order, court powers 30, 127, 891
power 1538
Artificial insemination *see* Fertility services; Surrogacy
Assault on court officer, etc 795
Assembly and association, freedom of 1010
Assessment *see also* Child assessment order; MIAMs
children proceedings 685
child's needs 485
provision of services, for 657
Guidance 2548
interim care /supervision order, for 557
Assessor 1801
appointment of 1825
court appointment 2131
Practice Direction 2131
Assets
disposal of, order restraining or setting aside 55, 1208
interim injunction restraining dealings 1240
Assistance *see also* Advice and assistance; Befriending
cash *see* Cash
investigation of circumstances, and 554
local authority duty 507, 509
child in need 485, 657
provision of accommodation to protect child, for 658
supervisor, by 553
education supervision order, under 673
Assisted reproduction *see* Fertility services
Attachment of debt *see also* Garnishee order
County Court jurisdiction 802
High Court jurisdiction 1244
Attachment of earnings order 106, 2014
administration order 356
application for 105, 341, 2015
application of sums collected 347
attendance of debtor 348
availability 105
armed forces member 105
cessation 344, 346, 347, 349, 2019
collecting officer of the court 342, 345, 347
application for determination of earnings by 348
committal proceedings, and 344
suspended order 2017
conditions of court's power to make 341
contents 342, 2018
Attachment of earnings order—*continued*
costs 2018
County Court, in 1060
offences 2020
procedure 105
courts with power to order 339
Crown employees 350
debtor
address 106
application for order by 341
definition 340
employee, as 342
employment by Crown 350
failure to reply if no payment 2016
obligations 348
particulars of 342
reply by 2016
statement of earnings by 347
deductions 343, 356
definitions 340, 353
disablement or disability, pension or allowances payable in respect of 353
earnings
determination of 348, 349, 2018
meaning 352
effect 342
employer 343
fee for deductions 343
meaning 342, 353
notice 2016
obligations of 343, 346, 348
scheme of deductions 356
enforcement provisions 350
execution proceedings, and 344
expressions used 2015
Family Court, in
special provisions 349
fines officer making 342, 344, 357
form 106, 343
Her Majesty's forces 353
High Court, in 1060
procedure 105
holiday pay 353
income tax 347
insolvency 343
judgment debt, to secure 341, 344, 347, 356
lapse 345
leave, when required 105
maintenance order, and 339, 340, 342, 344, 345, 346, 347, 354
meaning 342
means of payment order 1060
normal deduction rate 342, 343, 348
reduction 345
variation 346
offences 350, 352, 2020
officer designated by Lord Chancellor 343
orders to which Act applies 340
own motion powers 342
penal notice on 2017, 2019
penalties 350, 352
pension 353
prescribed deduction 344
prescribed particulars 343

Attachment of earnings order—*continued*
priority 343, 344, 357
protected earnings rate 342, 343
provisions applying 340
registration/cancellation of registration of maintenance order 346
resources and needs 348
restriction on 341
right or liability of debtor to deduct income tax 343
service 2018
service and reply 2016
statement of earnings 347
transfer 2019
variation 344, 347, 2019
Attendance
child 1519, 1706
adoption proceedings 1658
children proceedings 1514
court order for 622
section 8 order hearing 2543
secure accommodation proceedings 512
children's proceedings, at (FPR) 1517
committal order 1932
debtor *see* Attachment of earnings order: attendance of debtor
directions appointment 1832
emergency protection order hearing, at 578
evidence, to give *see* Evidence: compelling attendance of party to give
failure in, power to proceed in absence of party 1832, 2079
judgment debtor, order for 2284
media *see* Media: attendance
neither applicant nor respondent attends 1521
private hearing 1836
seeking a direction dispensing with 1519
setting aside judgment given in party's absence 1834
Attorney-General
committal proceedings 1991
declaration application to, copy of 1424
declaration of status under FLA, role 872
Audience, rights of 1046, 1529, 2620
Cafcass officer 808
conduct of litigation, for
exempt person 1054
meaning 1052
exempt person 1053
meaning 1052
'reserved legal activity' 1046
Authentic instrument
Regulation (EC) No 4/2009, under 2865
Authorities
citation *see* Citation of authorities
judicial or administrative 2733
Avoidance of disposition order *see also* Prevention of disposition order
application for (FPR) 1432
family provision on death application 1029, 1030
financial relief application 55, 1208
application procedure 56, 1432
meaning (FPR) 1429

Avoidance of disposition order—*continued*
overseas proceedings 57, 1132
Babies
relinquished/abandoned babies 533
Bailiff
service by 1348
failure notification 1353, 1357
Bank account etc
attachment of debts, and 802, 1244
order to open, for payment of maintenance 119, 1061
third party debt order, and debtor's account 2298
Bank holiday
definition 634
Bankruptcy *see also* Insolvency
financial provision (ancillary relief) and, relationship between 1173
financial provision in connection with divorce 1170
MIAMs 1316
property adjustment order, and 1211
rights of trustees in 1173
trustee in *see* Trust of land: trustee in bankruptcy, application by
Barrister *see* Counsel
***Beddoe* order** 2158
procedure on application for 2158
Befriending
children's home, in 593
family assistance order, under 481
supervisor, by 553
education supervision order, under 673
voluntary organisation, by 591
Beneficiary
protected
meaning 2060
money recovered, control of 2068
representation of 2059
trust of land
application to court for order 1261
occupation right 1260
Benefits
child support maintenance, and *see* Child support
Best interests of child
arrangements to assist child to live abroad 664
Hague Convention 1996 525, 2741, 2744
natural parents 441
Regulation (EC) No 2201/2003, under 2783
Best interests of the child
care order 539
litigant in person 542
supervision order 539
Birth, registration of
acquired gender recognition 954
adopted child 297, 323
fertility services, and 986
legitimated child, and 1058
transsexual parents 448
Birth, removal of baby at *see* Removal of child: removal of babies at birth
Blood test
proof of legitimacy 924

Bodily sample
definition 924
Body corporate
offences 633
representation of 1835
Brexit 2736
British Overseas Territory
service in 1360
Brussels Convention 1968
assets, interim relief 695
Contracting State 688
definition 688
force of law 689
foreign judgment recognition
admissibility 693
appeals 691
copies of UK judgment 694
interest on 692
implementation 688
interpretation 688
maintenance order enforcement 689, 694, 1953
Brussels IIA 384, 838, 2299
abduction 2779
adoption 280, 522
Brexit 2736
care proceedings 525
civil partnership dissolution, etc 1897
Practice Direction (FPR) 1905
dependent actions 2786
enforcement 2790
habitual residence 522
of children 2779
International Child Abduction and Contact Unit (ICACU) 2685
jurisdiction 2775
lis pendens 2786
parental responsibility 2777
provisional and protective measures 2787
recognition of judgments and orders 2787
seising of a court 2785
text 2771
transfer of proceedings 2709
UK, jurisdictions within the 526
Brussels IIR
domicile 46
habitual residence 46
Bundle *see* Court bundle
Burden of proof 1761
accidental injuries 535
committal 413
domicile 828
reversal 535
Business (individual) *see also* Family business
claim against 2046

Cafcass 435, 514, 2623
advocate to court, request to appoint 2564
appointment of children's guardian 1697, 1707
duty to provide guardian as soon as practicable 808
establishment 806
functions 807
officer of the Service 436, 823
Cafcass—*continued*
President's Interim Guidance to address backlog of work for 435
Protocol with National Youth Advocacy Service 2573
referral by independent reviewing officer 514
status 807
Cafcass officer
access to records 570
activity direction or condition, monitoring compliance 462
adoption
access to records 311
appointment in 310
foreign, directions as to need 1665
appointment in family proceedings 2716
children's guardian appointment *see also* Children's guardian
care /supervision order 162
discharge etc 165
contact with child in care 168
conduct of litigation and right of audience 808
contact order, monitoring compliance 149, 463
cross-examination of 808
duties 1720
enforcement order, monitoring compliance 467
family assistance order, named in 481
independent reviewing officer's reference to 515
investigations by 1721
meaning 806
report, rules of evidence 568
reporting restrictions, Practice Note 2567
risk assessment 483
Practice Direction 1631
service 1542
welfare checklist, regard to 1712
welfare report 435
Calculators
errors 12
HM Courts and Tribunals Service (HMCTS) 12
setting aside or variation of orders due to errors 12
CAP *see* Child arrangements programme
Capacity *see also* Mental disorder; Protected party 1216
ability to rely upon advice 1682
assessment 1682
best interests 1221
child *see* Child: capacity to refuse to be examined etc
Child Arrangements Programme 1590
consent to marriage 338
decision-making 1221
default orders 1683
'incapacity', meaning of 1221
issues as to 1683
'lacks capacity' 1681, 2060
litigate, assessment of capacity to 541
medical and welfare decisions for adults lacking capacity 2576
medical evidence 224, 1683
Mental Capacity Act 2005 2060
person lacking
best interests determination 1217

Capacity—*continued*
person lacking—*continued*
consent to bodily sampling 922
declarations 1424
deprivation of liberty
life sustaining treatment, for 1219
restrictions 1218
inability to make decisions 1217
inherent jurisdiction 1547
meaning 1131, 1217
medical treatment 1219
payments under MCA 1973 1212
principles 1216
respect for private and family life, and 1008
persons who lack 1680
presumptions as to 1681
recovery 1685
scientific tests 922
tests 1682, 2068
'unable to make a decision' 1681
uncertainty, resolving 223
Court of Protection involvement 225
Capital order
no repayment in respect of 1205
Capitalisation of income order 1169
Care home *see* Residential care home
Care monitoring system 531, 1534
Care order
adoption, and 260, 549
agency placement prohibited 258
interaction with 269
age limit 520
agreed orders 540
application for 159, 520
answer 162
appeal 163
applicant 160
authorised person 160, 521
court 160
directions 162
fee 161
joinder 162
notice to non-parties 1601
order 162
respondents 161
restrictions 521
service 161
best interests of the child 539
Best Practice Guide 2589
care plan (s 31A care plan), prerequisite for 544
case management, Public Law Outline 161
child arrangements order, and 550
children's guardian 162
concessions 540
court's powers 520
criminal 617
definition 635
delay, avoidance of 546, 547
directions in proceedings for 1533
discharge 163, 563
answer 165
appeal 166
applicant 164
application 163
Care order—*continued*
discharge—*continued*
children's guardian 165
court 164
directions 165
form 166
joinder 165
pre-proceedings checklist 164
respondents 165
service 165
duration 618
effect 548, 617
emergency protection order, and 618
human rights issues 528
interim 162, 557
abolition of requirement to renew order 558
duration 557
exclusion requirement *see also* Exclusion requirement 163, 562
Hague Convention 1996 provisions 2506
interim or full order 559
medical examination etc 557
nature of interim order 558
power of arrest 563
removal under an order 558
split hearings, and 560
undertaking on 563
intervention of court after making of 530
local authority
designated for 521
investigation prior to 554
meaning 522
parental responsibility, and *see* Parental responsibility: care order is in place, where
parties 1493
pending appeal 565
removal of child from UK 549
residence order's effect on 617
respect for private and family life, and 1008
review of case 554
section 8 order, discharges 619
supervision order in substitution 564
supervision order, or 539
threshold criteria 520
respect for private and family life, and 1008
timetable 546
start 161
wardship, effect on 618, 619
Care order, 'interim'
short stays 205
Care orders
agreed orders 540
allocation of proceedings 522
Care plan 2398
care order prerequisite (s 31A care plan) 544
child ceasing to be looked after 2413
contents 2400
matters to be included 2419
duty to prepare 515, 2400
cases other than s 31A care plan cases 2400
education 2400
file, need to 545

Care plan—*continued*
  Guidance 2541
  health care 2401
  health plan 2400, 2419
  meaning 2398
  modification where short break placements 2418
  need to file 1508
  review 515, 2401
    significant change, prior to 2411
  scrutiny 529
Care proceedings *see also* Care order; Children proceedings
  abuse 2645
  attribution of harm to care that is not reasonable 532
  Basic Guidance to Good Practice 531
  Best Practice Guide 2589
    status of 2592
  Brussels IIA 525
  burden and standard of proof 535
  children's guardian, appointment for child 154
  concurrent criminal proceedings 249, 543, 1762, 2645
  concurrent immigration proceedings 543
  consent to adoption, and *see* Adoption: consent to: care proceedings, in
  control of evidence 1762
  costs 544
  evidence in
    parents can be compelled to give 541
  extended definition of 'harm' 533
  hearings 1532
  involvement of parents in planning process 529
  jurisdiction, assumption of 525
  more than one local authority involved 1509
  placement order application consolidated with *see* Placement order: application: consolidated with care proceedings
  preparation for court 2540
  radicalisation 2696
  reduction of need for, local authority duty 659
  representation of protected parties 1683
  significant harm
    degree to be proved 532
  'suffering' and 'is likely to suffer' 532
  summary disposal 540
  terrorism
    disclosure of involvement of parents in 1510
  threshold test
    objective nature 532
  withdrawal 544
    human rights issues 1853
    oral hearing in presence of parties 1853
    written request for permission 1853
  written directions in difficult cases 1515
Carer *see also* Day carer
  certificate of suitability (Wales) 606
  welfare of child, promotion of 425
Carers
  fabricated or induced illness 534
Case management 1525, 1526
  active 2032
    list 1278
  appeals 1866, 2193, 2195, 2215
  application for order 2037
  care and supervision orders 526
  children proceedings 1506, 1507
  court duty 2032
  declarations 1422
  decree nisi or conditional order 1394
  directions 2037
  exclusion of issue from consideration 1321
  financial dispute resolution appointment 1442
  forced marriage protection order *see* Forced marriage protection order: case management
  general powers 1319, 1507, 2035, 2036
  hearing 1535
  matrimonial/civil partnership proceedings 1395, 1402
  overriding objective 1277, 2031
    active management 1278
    parties' duty to help 1278
  parallel family and civil proceedings 2036
  public law proceedings, in 1534
  robust 2195
  separate trial of any issue 1320
Case management conference
  care and supervision proceedings 1534
Cash
  provision of, by local authority 485, 503, 658
Causation
  accidental injuries 536
Central Authority
  Hague Convention 1996 2736, 2744
  Hague Convention 2007, under 2836
  Regulation (EC) No 4/2009, under 2879
Central Council for Education and Training in Social Work 610
Central Family Court (Financial Remedies Unit)
  Certificates of Financial Complexity 51
  complex cases 51
  judges 2692
Certificate
  appeal to Supreme Court, for 198
  legal aid
    revocation or discharge 1827
  Regulation (EC) No 2201/2003, under 2793, 2794
  Regulation (EU) No 606/2013, under 2890
  suitability to care for child (Wales) 606
Certificates of Financial Complexity
  Central Family Court (Financial Remedies Unit) 51
Certiorari, order of *see also* Judicial review
  application for 1237
    claim procedure 2253
    leave for, as stay of proceedings 800
    reconsideration of 1238
  court power 192, 2260
  High Court jurisdiction 1236
Chambers
  contempt of court and proceedings in 244
  family proceedings 809

Chambers—*continued*
publication of text and transcripts 244
Change of circumstances
Hague Convention 1996 2739
Channel Islands
adoption 312
registration of 321
application of CA 1989 to 638
effect of orders 632
service in 1360
Charge
legal services, for 1042
rights of occupation of home, as 875
cancellation of registration 907
registration of 876, 907
Charging order 2023
adjournment 2025
anti-evasion provisions 1255
appeal 110
application 109, 2023
court for 2023
procedure 108
asset to which application relates 2023
availability 108
charge, the 1255
child support maintenance, to enforce 412
conditions 2025
County Court limit 359
court for 108, 358
declaration of a charge 1255
definitions 362
discharge 360
interim order 2025
disclosure of debtor's address 109
effect, general 360
enforcement by way of order for sale 361
final 110, 2025
date for 109, 2023
objections to 110
financial thresholds 361
hearing 110
interest in property 2298
interested persons 2026
interests which may be charged 359
interim 109, 2023
procedure 108
service 109
jurisdiction for 358
jurisdiction to make order for sale 2298
Land Registry entry 110, 360
leave, circumstances for 108, 1203
maintenance order, to enforce 108
modification 2025
origin of the charge 1255
Part 8 procedure 2299
partnerships 360
power to make 2023
prescribed securities 361
procedure 1255
property which may be charged 359
receiver, enforcement by 802
sale, enforcement by 110, 2298
securities, meaning 361, 362

Charging order—*continued*
service 109
interim order 2024
single order in respect of several judgments 2023
Solicitors Act 1974, s 73, under 1255
stock, meaning for 362
stop notice 361, 2027
stop order 361, 2026
terms of order 360
unit trust, meaning for 362
written evidence, filing of 2025
Charging orders
reform proposals 108
Child
adequate arrangements to secure protection of 2781
adopted *see* Adoption
age *see* Age: child
attaining 18, end of lack of capacity *see also* Age 2066, 2071
attainment of majority 1700
attendance *see* Attendance: child
best interests *see* Best interests of child
capacity to refuse to be examined etc 1705
care of local authority, in *see also* Child in care 451, 454
circumstances of
change in, effect, consideration for court 422
investigation of, by court 554
communication to 1351
compromise for 2067
confidentiality and *see* Confidentiality: children, and
definition 1285
CA 1989 635
child support 401
CPR 219, 2033, 2039
CSA 416
European Convention 393
financial relief order, for 656
FLRA 1969 217
MCA 1214
detention *see* Detention: child or vulnerable adult
divorce etc, arrangements on *see* Child of the family
evidence by *see* Evidence: child, by
exposed to serious danger, location of child 2746
family proceedings involving 217, 1488, 1503
family provision, and *see* Family provision: child of the deceased
family, of the *see* Child of the family
financial provision *see also* Financial relief order (for child) 767
guardian for *see* Guardian
guardian of estate, appointment of 2070
habitual residence 2779
in need *see* Child in need
inspection of, by Secretary of State 607
internationally displaced 2734
joinder *see* Joinder of party: child
judge seeing *see* Judge: seeing child

Child—*continued*
jurisdiction for proceedings concerning 1250
legal representation of *see* Legal representative; Official Solicitor; Solicitor
maintenance *see also* Child support; Financial relief order (for child); Maintenance 2431
variation application 1195, 1198
marriage, consent to
application to court 131
procedure (FPR) 1426
MIAMs 1313
money recovered, control of 2068, 2074
investment 2074
payment out of funds in court 2076
needs *see* Needs of child
non-family proceedings involving 219
opportunity to be heard 2781
party, as *see also* Party 1530, 1695, 2061
conduct of proceedings with court permission 1698
guidance 1716
joinder, direction for 1506
litigation friend requirement 1697
privacy 626
proceedings in absence of party 1834
property of 2732
protected party, as *see also* Protected party 2060
qualifying, for child support *see* Child support
recovery *see* Removal of child
removal *see* Removal of child
representation *see* Children's guardian; Representation: child
representations by *see* Representations: child, by
resident outside EU *see* Jurisdiction: child resident outside EU
responsible adult 1350
revealing fact of existence of 448
service of documents on *see* Service
settlement for *see* Settlement
sufficient understanding 1699
sum to be paid to 1142
superior interests of 2783
surname, change of 470
understanding 1285
assessment, and refusal to submit 572
conduct of proceedings, for 1698
medical etc examination or treatment, under supervision order 671, 672
undesirable association 1546
upbringing 2431
welfare *see* Welfare of child
whereabouts *see* Disclosure: child's whereabouts, of
wishes and feelings *see* Wishes of child
witness, as *see* Evidence: child, by
Child abduction *see* Abduction; Removal of child
Child arrangements order
activity condition 460, 461
activity direction 147, 458, 459, 461
adult 'child', for 440
application 144
appeal 147
applicant 145, 452
Child arrangements order—*continued*
application—*continued*
court and judge for 146
directions 147
form 147
joinder 146
order 147
relative, by 452
respondents 146
restrictions on court's powers 147
service 146
time-limits 146
withdrawal 147
without notice 146
breach 149
attendance at activity 150
committal 150
enforcement order *see also* Enforcement: child arrangements order 148, 150, 465, 1632, 2584
financial compensation order 148, 150, 468, 469
change of surname 470
leave required 470
child in care, for 550
consequences of failing to comply with 464
contact activity condition 147
contact, for
determining with whom child lives 442
court power 438
definition 438
discharge application 144
enforcement *see* Enforcement: child arrangements order
family assistance order, interaction with 482
family proceedings, in 550
financial relief order, court's powers 645, 653
force, in 454
'interim' 847
interim application in pending care proceedings, on 560
jurisdiction 836
living arrangements, concerning
events develop following making or interim order 458
proceedings in which court is considering whether to make order 570
local authority, no application by 451
maintenance, local authority contributions 656
monitoring by Cafcass officer 149, 463
monitoring compliance with 463
more than one person, for 456
no order
child in care, notification duty 2402
parental responsibility, and 469
parents living together, and 456
placement of child *see* Placement: discharge of child arrangements order
procedural rules (FPR) 1644
removal of child 470
section 8 order 439
shared living arrangements, for 441
variation application 144
procedural rules (FPR) 1644

Child arrangements order—*continued*
warning notices on 147, 148, 149, 443, 464
care required when drafting order 443, 464
procedure for applying for 464
transitional orders 464
Child Arrangements Programme 423, 440, 1504, 1507, 1525, 1541, 2539
allocation 1582
capacity of litigants 1590
children's guardian 1590
court applications 1581
enforcement 1591
evidence 1590
First Hearing Dispute Resolution Appointment 1585
gatekeeping 1582
judicial continuity 1583
legal aid 1577
Local Good Practice 1581
non-court dispute resolution 1579
orders, format of 1527
parenting plans 1577
President's Guidance to support 1504
safeguarding 1585
signposting services 1577
timetable 1589, 1592
urgent application 1584
welfare of child 1579, 1583
without notice applications 1584
Child assessment order
application for 571
authorised person 521, 572
notice of 572
notice to non-parties 1601
conditions for 571
definition 635
development of child, assessment of 571
duration 571
harm to child, suspicion of 571
health of child, assessment of 571
meaning 571
parties 1494
persons to be given notice of application 572
significant harm 571
Child at risk
refuge for 585
risk assessment *see* Cafcass officer; Multi-agency risk assessment conference
Child being looked after *see also* Child in care
accommodation for
alternative arrangements, review before 500
general duty 500
inspection of premises 607
ways of providing 498, 500
arrangements for 2400
ceasing to be looked after 502
advice and assistance 507, 508
assessment of needs 506
care plan details 2413
complaint or representation 510
duties to 503, 504, 665, 2414
duty to carry out assessment 503
eligible child 665, 2414
former relevant child 504
Child being looked after—*continued*
ceasing to be looked after—*continued*
maintenance, accommodation, etc 503
pathway plan *see* Pathway plan
personal adviser 503, 504, 506, 666, 2415
relevant child 502, 503
responsible authority 502
'suitable accommodation' meaning of 503
visits and support, local authority duty 501
contact, duty of authority to promote 662
death of 666
deprivation of liberty 494
duty to ascertain wishes and feelings
any other person, of 498
parents, of 498
former relevant child
education or training, assistance 505
higher education, payment for 504
'other assistance', meaning of 505
guarantee of apprenticeship deeds etc 663
independent reviewing officer
appointment 513
functions 513, 514
local authority duty to 496, 498, 662
contact, as to 662
maintenance 498
local authority looking after child 2434, 2435
maintenance of 663
contributions to *see also* Contribution order 666
duty of local authority 498
meaning 496, 497
placement *see* Placement
records 2419
review of cases 514, 517
secure accommodation for *see also* Secure accommodation 510
visits and support
expenses 663
independent visitor 501
local authority duty 501
Child care training
definition 609
expenses of 609
review of 610
Child Contact Centres
referral to, Protocol (revised) 2615
Child in care *see also* Care order; Child being looked after
abduction of 583
accommodation for, local authority duty 498
adoption order 260
child being looked after, as 496
contact with *see* Contact: child in care, with
living with parent, etc 667
local authority duty to 496
maintenance of, contributions to *see also* Contribution order 666
placement *see* Placement
section 8 order, and 450
Child in need
accommodation provision for 492
advice, guidance etc 659
assessing age of child 486

Child in need—*continued*
contact with family 660
extent of local authorities' duties 485
failed asylum seekers, children of 486
family home, maintenance for 660
holiday 659
home help 659
identification of 657
living with family, services for 659
local authority duty to 484, 659
meaning 485
occupational etc activities 659
recreational activities 659
services for 484, 659
wishes and feelings of child 484
travel, help with 659
'within their area' 486
Child maintenance order *see* Maintenance order: child
Child minder
appeals (Wales) 604
application to be *see* 'registration' *below*
certificate of suitability, child 8 to 14 (Wales) 606
definition and exclusions (Wales) 598
emergency protection of children (Wales) 603
exemptions from regulation (Wales) 681, 682
foster parent not (Wales) 598
inspection of children, premises etc 607
cooperation between authorities (Wales) 684
entry etc powers (Wales) 605
power of constable to assist 633
local authority functions 606
offences 600
(Wales) 602, 606
certificate of suitability 606
proceedings 607
premises
inspection 607
suitability (Wales) 599
registration
application 601
cancellation (Wales) 602, 603, 604
certificate (Wales) 684
conditions (Wales) 602, 603, 604
definitions (Wales) 599
disqualification from (Wales) 682
fees 684
grant (Wales) 602
notice of intention to take steps (Wales) 604
qualification (Wales) 599
refusal (Wales) 602, 604
requirement (Wales) 601
resignation (Wales) 603
suspension (Wales) 603
Wales 601
requirements / regulation 600
significant harm, risk of (Wales) 603
Child of the family
civil partnership
meaning 778
welfare of child, court duty 777

Child of the family—*continued*
maintenance for 811, 813, 816, 1107
Children Act, and 817
divorce etc, on *see also* Divorce 1160
overseas divorce etc, after 1128
recovery by person in Convention country 1106
meaning 825, 1016, 1160, 1214, 1285
Child periodical payments order *see* Periodical payments order: child, for
Child protection *see* Hague Convention 1996
Child safety order
curfew notice contravention, after 580
Child support *see also* Hague Convention on the International Recovery of Child Support 2007; Maintenance
absent parent
application for maintenance calculation *see also* 'maintenance calculation' *below* 402
benefit, on *see* 'benefit, person with care on' *below*
meaning 401
tracing 402
appeal 1468
application for *see also* 'maintenance calculation' *below* 402
arrears 411, 412
backdating of orders 407
benefit, person with care on 403
calculation *see* 'maintenance calculation' *below*
child support maintenance
calculation *see* 'maintenance calculation' *below*
meaning 402
child support officer 401, 404
'child', meaning for 416
civil partnerships 751, 756
cohabitation 406
consent order, and 404
County Court, enforcement in 412
declaration of parentage 410
deduction from earnings order
alternative where inappropriate 411
definitions 415
disclosure of information or evidence (FPR) 1852
divorce, interaction with periodical payments order on 1197
duty to maintain 400
effective date 404
enforcement 402, 411, 412
discretion of Secretary of State 412
driving disqualification 413
driving disqualification (international) 2492
international (Hague Convention 2007) 2488, 2835
involvement of Family Court 411
non-EU states, between 2835
regulations 2488
payments in question 412
Family Court hearsay evidence in 2431
father *see* 'parentage' *below*

Child support—*continued*
financial relief order, interaction with 647, 814, 1197
flat rate 403
FPR 2010 407
freezing injunctions *see* Freezing injunction: enforcement of assessments under CSA 1991
High Court proceedings, assigned to Family Division 2486
information, communication of 1468
interim applications 407
judicial review 401, 411
jurisdiction provisions 414
liability order 411
enforcement 412
maintenance agreement, and 407
application prevented 408
meaning for 407
variation 408, 819, 1855
maintenance calculation 402
deferral 403
effect 409
effective date 407
jurisdiction exclusion 414
jurisdiction to make 406, 414
magistrates 'shall not question' 412
meaning 415, 657
outline 403
relationship with court orders 408, 819
restriction on right to apply for 408
maintenance order and, court's powers 403, 404, 406
application procedure (FPR) 1855
officer *see* 'child support officer' *above*
order(s)
periodical payments 647, 1197
relationship with maintenance calculation 408, 819
restriction on 404
parent
absent *see* 'absent parent' *above*
meaning 415
parentage
declaration of 410
dispute on 410
periodical payments order, and 648, 814, 1197
person with care
application for maintenance calculation *see also* 'maintenance calculation' *above* 402
meaning 401
person with care or non-resident parent may apply 404
procedural and practice rules 400
procedural overview 400
qualifying child 401
recovery of maintenance *see* 'enforcement' *above*
reduced rate 403
relevant other children 404
request to Secretary of State to 'cease acting' 404
top-up order, application for 407
date for 407

Child support—*continued*
voluntary payments 407
welfare of child, principle 401
written agreements 407, 408
Children and Family Court Advisory and Support Service (Cafcass) *see* Cafcass
Children and family reporter *see also* Cafcass officer
appointment, restrictions 1711
duties 1719
report 1710
Children proceedings
agreement between parties as to management of proceedings 1514
assessment 685
communication of information *see* Communication: children proceedings
consolidation with other proceedings 1515
court 1513
definition 1795, 1803
directions for conduct of proceedings 1513
directions of court's own initiative
notice of intention 1515
dismissal of proceedings at directions stage 1514
expert evidence 685, 1795, 1797
standards for expert witnesses 1807
fixing a new date 1517
forms 1504
repeated applications 1514
service of documents 1515
start of proceedings 1504
without prejudice rule and *see* Without prejudice rule: children proceedings, and
Children's guardian *see also* Cafcass officer
adoption proceedings 1653
inspection of records 1653
involvement in decision-making 1653
advising the court 1705
appointment 1505, 1514
care order /proceedings, child subject of 154, 1696
contact with child in care, for 168
court, by 1504, 1707, 1708
duration 1704
emergency protection order
application 134
discharge 136
extension 139
not necessary 1505
other than specified proceedings 1696, 1706, 1717, 1718, 1719
reasons for terminating 1709
recovery order application 141
refusal 1696
restrictions on 1711
secure accommodation order, with 172
specific issue order application 170
specified proceedings, in 567, 1536, 1696
termination 1704, 1708
who may be appointed 1703
without court order 1717
attendance 1715
care order, no continuing role after making of 543

Children's guardian—*continued*
change of 1707
Child Arrangements Programme 1590
child instructing solicitor/conducting proceedings 1706
communication of court decision to child 1716
continuing role
'specified' proceedings cease to be 'specified' 1697
contribution order 12
detached from child 1705
duties 1505, 1704, 1717
interests of child, and 567
not required, circumstances 1698
panel 568
placement order, and *see* Placement order: children's guardian, and
powers 1704
Practice Direction 1715
questioning 1530
report 1716
representation by *see* Representation: children's guardian or solicitor, by
role 568
rules for (FPR) 1703
section 37 order, and 556
secure accommodation proceedings, role in 512
service etc of documents for child 1716
specified proceedings, suitability 1717
status 1696
steps to be taken by, court approval 1521
tandem model 1705
welfare report where children's guardian acting 436
where child and children's guardian part company 1530
where court differs from advice of 1706
where interests of children conflict 1505, 1696
written report by 1706
Children's home
national authority provision of 500
secure accommodation in
approval 2432
child under 13 2432
Children's home (registered)
advice and assistance 593
after leaving 507
befriending of child 593
disqualification from carrying on 594
appeal against refusal of consent 594, 595
consent of appropriate authority 594
employment of disqualified person 594
appeal against refusal of consent 594, 595
fostering
when is 677
when not 593, 677, 678
inspection 593, 594, 607
local authority duties 592, 594
offence 594
records 594
refuge, as 585
registration 593
secure accommodation in 510
notification duty 2435
Children's home (registered)—*continued*
services, use of 593
visits to child 592, 594
welfare of child 593
wishes of child etc 593
CICA *see* Criminal Injuries Compensation Authority
Citation of authorities 1513, 1867
in court 2716
neutral 2559
Practice Direction 2559, 2560, 2641, 2642
Civil debt
charges for services etc recoverable as 519
Civil partnership
adoption
by civil partner 285, 318
of civil partner, prohibition 281
agreement 718
termination 718
application procedure 1379
Practice Direction 1406
assurance policy for benefit of partner 717
case management hearing 1395
child in
consent for (FPR) 1426
not a 'child' for child support 416
child of family 635
financial provision
Family Court 764, 766, 771
High Court/County Court 731, 732, 738, 739, 750
legitimacy, principles 924
legitimation 1056
conditional order *see* Decree nisi or conditional order
costs in proceedings 1395
declaration application 714
intervention 714
jurisdiction 725
supplementary 715
defended case 1380
defended proceedings 49, 1385, 1392
disclosure and inspection 1410
dissolution order 703
agreement or arrangement 706
appeal 2236
restriction 1234
application procedure 45, 46
conditional 703, 705
application for 1391
application to make final 1400, 1402, 1404
intervention to show cause after 1401
rescission 705, 709
documents with application 46
filing application without certificate 47
final 703, 704, 1402, 1404
gender recognition certificate issue 951
ground and facts 706, 707
interaction with other orders 708
intervention 704
joinder of parties 715
jurisdiction 724, 725
pension orders 734
procedure 46

Civil partnership—*continued*
dissolution order—*continued*
recognition of overseas 726, 727, 728
recognition within UK 725, 729
reconciliation attempts 705
reconciliation statement 1381
records of final orders 1406
refusal, five-year separation 708
registration under Council Regulation 1897
relief for respondent 715
rescission of 1399
section 8 order, jurisdiction 839
service of application 47
tenancy transfer, court power 784
time bar 705
undefended cause 46
validity within UK 866
DPMCA 1978 provisions applying 777
end of 703
joinder of parties 715
evidence by partner, rules for 719
failure to maintain
child of family (High Court/County Court) 747, 748
factors for court (High Court/County Court) 748
High Court/County Court 747
interim order (High Court/County Court) 747
orders available 747
variation of order (High Court/County Court) 753
family provision on death 22, 702, 1013, 1015
cessation of order 1037
court powers 1036
definitions 1038
factors for court 1021
former civil partner 1013, 1037, 1038
maintenance agreement variation 1036
orders possible 1019
fertility services, parenthood where two women 982, 984
financial provision after divorce, effect of formation on 1173, 1196, 1207, 1210
financial relief
arrears
Family Court 776
High Court/County Court 752, 756
attachment of earnings 355
avoidance of transactions to prevent
High Court/County Court 761
child over 18, for 647
child, for 657
consent order
Family Court 766
High Court/County Court 758
duration of order
Family Court 770
High Court/County Court 749
enforcement 105
Family Court 718, 764
High Court/County Court 718, 730
interim order
Family Court 769

Civil partnership—*continued*
financial relief—*continued*
interim order—*continued*
High Court/County Court 747
lay justices' powers 25
living apart by agreement, Family Court's powers 768
lump sum 730
Family Court 765
High Court/County Court 731
maintenance agreement
High Court/County Court 758
maintenance order 251
matters for court
Family Court 765
High Court/County Court 738, 740, 742
orders, court powers 781
overseas dissolution, after 778
periodical payments 647
Family Court 764
High Court/County Court 730
repayment order
Family Court 776
High Court/County Court 756, 757
settlement
High Court/County Court 762
variation or discharge of orders
Family Court 773
High Court/County Court 751
gender, change in 955
hearing of application 1390
heterosexual couples 701
home rights 874
charge, as, priority 875
Isle of Man 701
jurisdiction 46, 722, 724, 725
court 723
domicile of civil partners 780
EU cases 777, 780
limitation on applications 1381
maintenance agreement 758
alteration 759
validity 759
maintenance pending suit 50
High Court/County Court 745
marriage converted from
grounds on which void or voidable 1157
Married Women's Property Act 1882, application of 1123
meaning 703
non-molestation order 27, 886
Northern Ireland
ineligibility in 722
residence in 712
notice of hearing 1391
nullity order 703
appeal restriction 1234
appeal to Court of Appeal 2236
application procedure 1383
bars 710
conditional 703, 705
final 703, 704
gender recognition certificate issue 951

Civil partnership—*continued*
nullity order—*continued*
grounds 710
intervention 704
jurisdiction 724, 725
recognition of overseas 726, 727, 728
recognition within UK 725, 729
registration under Council Regulation 1897
occupation order 877
application 27
'order' 1281, 1380
overseas orders
domicile issues 728
recognition 726
recognition refusal 727
registration under Council Regulation 1897
overseas relationship treated as 719, 720, 722, 787
general rule 721
public policy exception 722
same-sex requirement 721
parental order 42
parental responsibility as step-parent 142, 430
Part I order (FLA) provisions 839, 841, 843, 844, 849, 862
ward of court removal 860
parties to proceedings 1382
pension
attachment order 734, 2523
compensation order 734
information supply 2513, 2517, 2518, 2519, 2525
loss of benefit, court regard to 740
loss of PPF compensation, court regard to (High Court/County Court) 742
pension compensation sharing order 734, 736, 743, 751, 763, 781
sharing order 734, 781, 2518, 2519, 2520, 2521
High Court/County Court 735
variation (High Court/County Court) 753
valuation 2514
presumption of death order 703, 713
conditional 703, 705
final 703, 704
intervention 704
jurisdiction 724
procedure for proceedings (FPR) 1379
proceedings
cease to be party, direction to 1389
consent
notice of 1386
withdrawal 1386
co-respondents 1383
dismissal of party from suit 1383
'proceedings'
FLA 844, 852
FPR 1281
property adjustment order (High Court/County Court) 732
variation 753
property rights, declaration and enforcement 14

Civil partnership—*continued*
property/financial arrangements
contributions 715
disputes 716
disputes after dissolution 717
tort actions 717
publicity and reporting restrictions 1039
reconciliation statement, filing of 1381
registration 701
registration and recognition of judgments relating to 1897
Practice Direction (FPR) 1905
sale of property order (High Court/County Court) 733
same-sex marriage, conversion to 1119
Scotland
ineligibility in 722
residence in 712
section 8 order application 452
separation cases, protection for respondent 1400
separation order 703
agreement or arrangement 706
death of partner during 713
ground and facts 713
jurisdiction 724, 725
recognition of overseas 726, 727, 728
recognition within UK 725, 729
reconciliation attempts 705
reconciliation statement 1381
registration under Council Regulation 1897
service of application 1382
special guardianship, and 433
stay of proceedings *see* Stay of proceedings: civil partnership proceedings
tenancy transfer of home 41
undefended proceedings 46, 1392
validity 285, 710, 711, 712, 714
void 710, 1215
legitimacy of child 925
voidable 710, 1215
withdrawal of application 1382, 1853
Civil partnership proceedings *see* Matrimonial and civil partnership proceedings
Civil Procedure Rules
application 2032
costs in proceedings, application to 1846
definitions 2033
effect on family proceedings 2033
RSC and CCR provisions 2191
Schedules 1 and 2 1928
scope 2031
terms 2033
Civil proceedings
meaning 920, 1778, 2431
Civil restraint order 1246, 1323, 2037, 2079, 2080
definition (CPR) 2033
power of court to make 1324, 1326, 1731
Claim
striking out *see* Striking out
Claim form 2038
form for defence 2041
issue
electronic 2042

Claim form—*continued*
issue—*continued*
Production Centre for 2041
money claim *see* Money claim
particulars of claim *see* Particulars of claim
practice direction 2043
service 2040
single form for two or more claims 2040
statement of case
inspection of documents mentioned 2109
title of proceedings 2044
type of claim 2039
Claim form (alternative Part 8 procedure) *see also* Part 8 procedure 2054
contents 2049
evidence 2053
issue 2052
management 2053
practice direction 2043
response 2053
types of claim 2052
use for settlement etc for child/protected party 2067
Claimant
meaning (Social Security Administration Act) 1254
Clean break
divorce etc, on 54, 1184
Closed material procedure 1754
CMS *see* Care monitoring system
Cohabitant
beneficial ownership of land, declaration of 1261
definition 27
family provision, and *see* Family provision: cohabitant of the deceased
occupation/non-molestation order application 27, 881, 884
parental order applicant 42
resource, cohabitation as a 1183
same-sex *see* Civil partnership
tenancy transfer by court 41, 911
Collection order 353
College *see* School
Comity
Hague Convention 1996 525
Commencement of proceedings
CPR 2039
financial remedy (ancillary relief) (FPR) 1432
forms (FPR) 1330
interim remedy, after 2088
issue of application form, on 1331
Practice Direction (CPR) 2042
pre-action application 2077, 2081
Committal *see also* Sentencing
appeals 2195
application 1728, 1988
burden of proof 413
contempt, for *see also* Contempt of court 466
criminal proceedings pending, hearing while 1984
evidence 413
false statement of truth 1991
Committal—*continued*
forced marriage protection order, breach of 36, 1483
hearing and judgment in public 1995
hearing procedure 1984
inability to pay 805
judgment summons 1934
continued default after committal 1934
procedure 250
summons procedure 805
type committed 1995
wardship proceedings 1549
Committal order *see also* Contempt of court
application 2304
contempt in face of court 2307, 2314
hearing 2311
interference with administration of justice 2305
Practice Direction 2316
attendance 1932
breach of judgment or order, for 125, 2303
appeal 131
application procedure 125
court 127
discharge 131
disposal powers 130
hearing 129
service 131
breach of undertaking, for 125, 2303
child support maintenance arrears, for *see* Child support
contempt of court 2693
County Court powers 804
dispensing with personal service 2304
disposal proportionate 130
double jeopardy 2313
enforcement of order by *see* 'breach of judgment or order, for' *above*
evidence *see* Evidence: committal application, in support of
judgment or order enforced by 125
judgment summons, and *see also* Judgment summons 803, 1930
maintenance arrears, and 1078
power to suspend 1995
practice direction 1631
suspended 2018, 2311
human rights issues 2290
service of order 2289
warrant to bring judgment debtor before judge 2290
tape recording of proceedings 2289
warrant of commitment *see* Warrant of committal
Committal proceedings *see* Committal order; Contempt of court; Warrant of committal
Communication
children proceedings 1563
Practice Direction 1618
when permitted in 1563, 1564
difficulties 1681
facilitated *see* Facilitated communication
safeguards 1564

Community home
assisted 587
disputes 587
child in 493
closure by local authority 588
compensation on cessation 589
controlled 587
disputes 587
discontinuance 588
notice of, by voluntary organisation 588
grants 609, 638
local authority duty to provide 586
management of 586
secure accommodation in 587, 609
Company/corporation *see* Body corporate
Compensation
child arrangements order breach, for financial loss from 148, 468, 469
Complaint
local authority, to 510, 516
advocacy services 517
qualifying functions within scope 516
Complex cases
Central Family Court (Financial Remedies Unit) 51
Certificates of Financial Complexity 51
determination of complexity 51
Compromise *see* Protected party; Settlement
Concurrent planning 531
Conditional order *see* Decree nisi or conditional order
Conduct
financial provision application, and 812
harassment 1232
Confidentiality *see also* Disclosure; Privacy 1753
adoption proceedings, in *see* Adoption: confidentiality of reports
attendance at private hearings 1837
children proceedings 626
children, and 1754
children's guardian 1705
Egdell and overriding 1754
non-court dispute resolution *see* Non-court dispute resolution: confidentiality of statements by parties
privacy and *see* Privacy: confidentiality, and
public interest immunity 2546
welfare report 438
Consent
Children Act, for, notification 1539
marriage, to
application 131
court 131
procedure (FPR) 1426
respondents 131
service 132
medical examination, to 572
Consent order 1129, 2084
appeals 1235, 2196
arbitration 1448
child support 407, 408
drafting 1449
financial remedy (ancillary relief) 1446
property adjustment, on 1205
Consent order—*continued*
interpretation 1205
negligence 1449
setting aside 1448
Consolidated proceedings
court power 2036
Constable *see also* Police protection
power to assist person to search or inspect 633
Consular advice
hearings 248
Contact
adoption, and *see* Adoption: contact, and; Adoption Contact Register
arrangements 553
child arrangements order for *see* Child arrangements order: contact, for
child in care, with 549, 570, 662, 2402
application for order 166, 167
court for application 167
local authority's promotion of contact 663
pre-proceedings checklist 167
refusal, notification duty 2402
discharge of s 34(4) 'no contact' order 552
discretion of local authority, at 552
disputes
separate representation *see* Separate representation: contact disputes
disturbance to child or parent 446
domestic violence cases 444, 552
father, importance of contact with 552
human rights issues 443, 552
implacable hostility to 443
interim
hearing 551
pending assessments 445
intractable opposition by children to 443
looked after child, promotion for 662
no order as to 552
order *see* Child arrangements order; Contact order
refusal 445
reasons for 446
review by the court 551
supervision 553
supported contact centre, Protocol (revised) 2615
views and wishes of the child 424
Contact activity condition
provision for 147
Contact activity direction *see* Activity direction
Contact order *see also* Child arrangements order
child in care, for
application 166
children's guardian 168, 170
discharge or variation of order 169
joinder or removal of party 168
respondents 168
timetable, Public Law Outline 167
Contempt of court 910
appeals 249, 352, 2194
court for 249
attachment of earnings 352
attendance centre, power to compel attendance at 793

Contempt of court—*continued*
- attendance of victim 1983
- breach of judgment, order or undertaking 1986
- committal order *see* Committal order 2693
  - open court (PD) 125, 2687, 2693
- communication of information 1564
- County Court powers 804
- discharge of person committed 131
- disclosure of information
  - when permitted, children's proceedings 1563, 1564, 1618
- earlier discharge, power of court to order 792
- early release 1996
- enforcement of orders or undertakings to pay money 1983
- evidence *see* Evidence: contempt of court hearing
- face of the court, contempt in the 791, 792, 1989
  - procedure by judge 804
- false statement
  - disclosure statement 2111
- Family Court 2468
- fines 791, 793, 1985
- fixed-term committal 791
- FLA 1996 provisions 896
- forced marriage protection order, and 906
- freezing order, disobedience of 1243
- importance of abiding by correct procedure 1984
- legal aid *see* Legal aid: contempt of court hearing
- meaning 896
- mental illness, and 791, 793
- money, breach of order to pay 118
- non-molestation order, breach of 1473
- non-payment 792
- occupation order, breach of 1473
- parent who releases 'required' information 1852
- power to limit court's powers 1138
- powers of inferior courts 792
- procedure 2302, 2314
- proceedings for, general 791
- production in court of person arrested 1983
  - procedural powers of court 1984
- publication of information, private sittings 244
- purging of contempt 792, 1996
  - judge's discretion 1996
- relevant judicial authority 1473
- service *see* Service: contempt of court
- superior court, meaning 791
- time on remand 793
- treatment of contempt prisoners 793
- unrepresented contemnors 1984
- witnesses *see* Witness: contempt of court hearing

Contract
- engagement to marry not effective as 1041

Contracting State
- meaning 688

Contribution
- contribution notice 667
- local authority considerations 669
- maintenance of child, to 666, 668

Contribution order
- appeal 12, 668

Contribution order—*continued*
- application for 11, 668
- children's guardian 12
- court for 11
- directions 12
- discharge 11
- due regard to contributor's means 669
- effect 668
- enforcement 669
- evidence, admissibility on enforcement 669
- joinder etc 11
- notice 11
- parties 1496
- power to make 12
- Practice Direction 1623
- respondents 11, 1496
- service 11
- variation 11, 668

Contributor
- definition 666

Convention
- Brussels *see also* 'foreign judgment recognition' *below*
  - text (Brussels IIA) 2771
- European *see* European Convention (recognition and enforcement of custody decisions)

Convention adoption *see* Adoption: Convention

Convention adoption order
- applicants 2394
- child from outside British Islands
  - annulment of order 2388
  - breakdown of placement 2386
  - certificate 2395
  - change of name/removal after placement 2393
  - counselling 2381
  - eligibility 2382, 2394
  - eligibility to adopt 2387
  - entry into UK, requirements 2384, 2385
  - habitual residence of adopter(s) 2387
  - local authority functions 2385
  - no order made after entry 2385
  - placement not proceeding 2384
  - probationary period 2387
  - procedure 2381, 2383
  - prospective adopter not proceeding 2386
  - refusal to make order 2388
  - requirements following 2388
  - withdrawal of child from prospective adopter 2386
- child from UK
  - consideration of proposed placement 2390
  - Convention list 2389
  - counselling 2388
  - habitual residence of adopter(s) 2392
  - local authority report 2392
  - panel recommendation 2389
  - parental responsibility requirements 2392
  - permanence report 2389
  - procedure 2388, 2390
  - provisions applying 2393
  - requirements prior to placement 2391
- child to live with applicants 2393
- notice of intention to adopt 2394

Convention adoption order—*continued*
offences 2394
practice direction 1664
status after, declaration of 871
Co-respondent 1383, 1386
matrimonial and civil partnership proceedings 1383
intervener co-respondent 1383
Corporation *see* Body corporate
Costs
allowances 1165
Sch 1 applications, in 646
amount, discretion as to 2145
appeals against *see* Appeal: costs, against
applicant's costs, order for 2150
assessment 2148
attachment of earnings 2018
avoidance of transactions intended to prevent or reduce financial relief 1210
basis of assessment 230
indemnity basis 230
standard basis 230
Best Practice Guidance 2546
bill of costs
form and content 2178
bundles 1513
by whom paid, discretion as to 2146
Calderbank letters 2146
care proceedings 544
charging orders 2026
circumstances in which work done 2148
civil proceedings, in
reasonableness 1044
conduct 229, 1847, 1849, 2146, 2148
'unreasonable or improper' 2151
County Court, in 1247
Court of Appeal, in 1247
CPR rules applied to FPR 2143
default costs certificates 2183
detailed assessment 232
appeal 2176
certificates 2173
client as 'relevant person' 2168
commencement 2168
default costs certificate 233, 2170
delay in 2169, 2182
dispute as to items 2170
document giving right to 2172
documents for service 2168
final costs certificate 2173, 2174
form of points of dispute 2170
hearing 233, 234, 2184
interim certificate 2173
meaning 1285
no stay pending appeal 2167
optional reply 2171
other parties, points of dispute served by 2172
points of dispute 233, 2170
procedure 232
application 2173
relevant persons 2168
request for 2172
time for 232

Costs—*continued*
detailed assessment—*continued*
venue for proceedings 2167
disapplication costs order rules in family proceedings 2145
discretion on 2145
efforts made to resolve dispute 2148
equal footing 1277
estimates 2036
exaggeration of claim 2146
expert witness, and 1795
factors court must have regard to 2145
failure to admit facts, on 1767
Family Court, in 228
family proceedings, in 228, 1846
final costs certificates 2187
financial dispute resolution appointment stage, at 1443
financial provision in case of neglect to maintain 1196
financial relief after overseas divorce 1125
financial relief order for child 481
financial remedy (ancillary relief) proceedings 1286, 1452, 1847, 1848
Practice Direction 1850
general rule 2146
financial order 229
head of costs 2180
High Court, in 228, 1247
indemnity basis 2148, 2158
inherent jurisdiction *see* Inherent jurisdiction: costs, order for
interim certificates 2187
legal aid 2188
legal representative, personal liability *see* Wasted costs order
legal representatives from outside the jurisdiction 2158
liability for
litigation friend *see* Litigation friend: liability for costs
litigation friend 2076
local authority officer's expenses 2546
maintenance pending suit 50, 1163
on civil partnership breakdown (High Court /County Court) 745
matrimonial/civil partnership proceedings 1386, 1395
offer to settle, account of 229
Official Solicitor's 1847, 2147
order 229
children cases, in 450
common types 2145
deciding what order to make 2146
deemed 2150
family provision 1021
financial remedy (ancillary relief) proceedings 1440
maintenance pending suit hearing, following 1164
payment 1140
Sch 1 applications, in 646
variation 2150

Costs—*continued*
payment into court, or offer of, and *see* Payment into court
payment on account 230, 2146
Practice Direction 1849
'proportionate and reasonable' 2148
provisional assessment 2186
public funding *see* Community Legal Service
recoupment of, by local authority 518
relationship between Act, Rules, Practice Directions and Protocol 2146
relief from sanctions 1323
representation of protected parties 1684
sanctions
bundle 1513
saving expense 1277
search for a starting point 1849
security for *see* Security for costs
Senior Courts, in 1247
discretion as to 1247
wasted costs order 1247
setting aside 1849
single joint expert 1799
standard basis 2148
success in proceedings, effect of 2146
summary assessment 231, 2149
application 232
court power 232
meaning 1285
procedure 231
Supreme Court 2364
taxation *see* 'detailed assessment' *above*
third party 2157
third party costs order 2157
transfer of tenancy 911
translation 1511
trust of land 1264
undertakings as to
litigation friends 1686, 1701, 2063
VAT, claims for 2152
wasted *see* Wasted costs order
Costs judge
appeal, permission for 194
Counsel *see also* Legal services
barrister's fees
charging orders, and 1255
conveyancing, use of 656, 1198
Counselling
child in need, for 659
family centre, at 659
Counterclaim
permission of court 2051
County Court *see also* Divorce County Court
appeal from 798
agreement not to appeal 799
contempt of court case 249
judge's note 799
private sitting 808
restrictions 244
appeal to
special appeals 2248
appeal within/from, practice direction 2214
attachment of debts 802

County Court—*continued*
attachment of earnings order in *see also* Attachment of earnings order 339, 341, 344
charging order in *see* Charging order
Children Act proceedings *see* High Court
confidentiality 626
costs *see also* Costs 1247
definitions 805
delivery order, enforcement *see* Warrant of delivery
discharge, order for 805
divorce in *see* Matrimonial and civil partnership proceedings
enforcement of orders *see* 'judgment summons' *below*
execution of instrument *see also* Execution of instrument; Warrant of execution 1243
family proceedings in *see also* 'judgment summons' *below*; Matrimonial and civil partnership proceedings
transfer from High Court to 1144
transfer to High Court 1145
family provision on death application *see* Family provision
financial provision orders, powers 823
garnishee proceedings in *see also* Garnishee order 802
hearsay evidence 2431
injunction
harassment, restraining 36, 1230
non-molestation 36
instalments, execution of order 801
judgment creditor *see* Judgment creditor
judgment debtor *see* Judgment debtor
judgment or order *see also* Judgment 796, 798
enforcement in 801
judgment summons
meaning 806
penalty for non-attendance 803
procedure 118
maintenance order enforcement *see also* Attachment of earnings order; Maintenance order enforcement 1060, 1080
maintenance order registration, in Family Court *see also* Maintenance order registration 1075
matrimonial proceedings in *see* Matrimonial and civil partnership proceedings
meaning 805
officer, assault of 795
orders in *see* 'judgment or order' *above*
possession order, enforcement *see* Warrant of possession
receiver, appointment in 802
regulations restricting powers of 797
remedies available 796, 2451
search orders 2451
stay of execution 802
stay of proceedings 800
transfer of proceedings from *see also* Transfer of proceedings

County Court—*continued*
warrant of execution *see also* Warrant of execution 801
Couple
meaning 285, 318, 2486
Court *see also* HM Courts and Tribunals Service (HMCTS)
actions done by 1306
definition (CA 1989) 621
designations
Regulation (EC) No 2201/2003, under 2802
duty of parties to 1278
family provision 1016
public authority for human rights 997
judicial act, proceedings for 1001
resources 1277
venue, discretion as to 1290
Court bundle
admissibility of documents as evidence 2123
agreed 2123
appeal 1865, 1881, 1882
permission 2224
certificates of compliance 1838
children proceedings 1513
core volumes (SCR) 2358
costs sanctions 1513
Family Court (FPR) 1834, 1881
financial dispute resolution appointment 1442
format 2230
High Court 1882
index, service of 2229
Practice directions 2228
translation 205
unagreed documents 2230
Court of Appeal *see also* Appeal
anonymity 2142
appeal from, to Supreme Court 209
contempt of court, on 249
leave application 199
procedure 198
respondents 200
who may appeal 199
appeal to
Family Court, from 202
High Court, from 198
meaning 1249
new trial 1234
power to hear 1234
practice direction 2221
procedure 207
restrictions 1234
second appeals 244
skeleton argument 207
special appeals 2236
assignment to 244, 2206
bundle of documents 2228
citation 2559
civil division 1233
costs in *see also* Costs 1247
criminal division 1233
divorce and nullity 2236
documents to be lodged 208
expedited hearings 2228
jurisdiction 1233
Court of Appeal—*continued*
multiple appeals 2228
new trial 1234
permission for appeal 207, 243, 808
Practice Direction 2224
powers 209
appeal from County Court 799
private sitting 808
questionnaires 2228
respondent 208
respondent's notice 2223
second appeals 2222
skeleton argument 2223
superior court of record 1233
timetable 2225
urgent hearing before *see* Urgent hearing: Court of Appeal, before
who may exercise powers 2207
Court of Protection 1221
media, and the 248
freedom of expression 1009
need for involvement 1684
payments under order, role regarding 1212
powers 225
relationship between civil court and 2067
Court officer
action in children's proceedings, in 1505
actions done by 1306
assault of, offence 795
attachment of earnings, for *see* Attachment of earnings order
conditional order made final, action on 1406
court documents, stamping and sealing of 1855
decree nisi made absolute, action on 1405
enforcement proceedings 1923
reference to court, power 1321
Court settlement
Regulation (EC) No 4/2009, under 2865
Creditor
Regulation (EC) No 4/2009, under 2866
Criminal appeal
Supreme Court, to 2363
Criminal care order 617
Criminal compensation order
financial proceedings, and *see* Financial proceedings: criminal compensation orders, relationship with
Criminal contempt
appeal 249
Criminal convictions
evidence 2754
Criminal Injuries Compensation Authority (CICA)
application to 1543
Criminal offences
forced marriage 337
Criminal proceedings *see also* Crown court
abuse 2645
concurrent care proceedings *see* Care proceedings: concurrent criminal proceedings
custody *see* Prison
declarations of incompatibility 996
delay and *see* Delay: criminal proceedings, and pending

Criminal proceedings—*continued*
investigations, notification of
abuse 2647
reduction of, local authority duty 659
standard of proof 1762
ward and *see* Ward of court: criminal proceedings, and
Criminal supervision order 617
Cross-border disputes
maintenance, EU Maintenance Regulation 689, 2857
implementation 2436
respondent outside UK 1445
Mediation Directive
FPR 1976
Practice Direction (FPR) 1979
Cross-examination *see also* Witness
application 1779
Cafcass officer 808
debtor 121
legal aid 439
limits on 1761
litigant in person, in interests of 1765
Crown
declarations of incompatibility 996
joinder as party
human rights case 1860
Crown agent
for overseas governments and administrations 1946
Crown court
appeal from
contempt of court case 249
private sitting 808
Crown Prosecution Service (CPS)
abuse 2647
Cruelty *see* Ill-treatment
Culpable neglect
meaning 413
Curfew notice
contravention, investigation by local authority 580
Currency
registered (foreign) maintenance order, and 693, 1099
Custody (detention in) *see* Committal; Prison
Custody (of child) *see also* Hague Convention on the International Recovery of Child Support 2007
disclosure of whereabouts 155, 856
examination of question of 2781
habitual residence 2778
judgment on, that does not entail return of child 2780
Northern Ireland, jurisdiction in 848
order for
duration 843
enforcement 854, 855
jurisdiction 838
meaning 397, 856
recognition of 852
registration etc, UK 180, 853, 1919
Part I order, meaning 836, 860

Custody (of child)—*continued*
recognition and enforcement of custody decisions *see* European Convention (recognition and enforcement of custody decisions)
recovery, power to order 157, 857
rights of custody 375, 379
Hague Convention 1996 2732
Regulation (EC) No 2201/2003, under 2775
unmarried fathers, and 380, 1610
Damages
court approval 2049
harassment, for 1230
human rights violation 999
judicial review, on 1238
Day care
charges for 518
contributions to cost of 518
meaning (Wales) 598
racial origins, and 660
unincorporated association providing, offences by (Wales) 684
Day carer
appeals (Wales) 604
definition (Wales) 598
emergency protection of children (Wales) 603
exemptions from regulation (Wales) 681, 682
inspection of children, premises etc 607
cooperation between authorities (Wales) 684
entry etc powers (Wales) 605
power of constable to assist 633
offences 600
(Wales) 602, 606
premises
inspection 607
suitability (Wales) 599
registration
application 601
cancellation (Wales) 602, 603, 604
certificate (Wales) 684
conditions (Wales) 602, 603, 604
disqualification from (Wales) 682
fees 684
grant (Wales) 602
notice of intention to take steps (Wales) 604
qualification (Wales) 599
refusal (Wales) 602, 604
requirement (Wales) 601
resignation (Wales) 603
separate premises, for 601
suspension (Wales) 603
requirements/regulation 600
Death
child being looked after, of 666
estate of deceased, representation of interested person 2058
family provision claim *see* Family provision
parent paying secured periodical payments, of 652
party, of, maintenance agreement alteration 1207
presumption *see* Presumption of death

Death penalty 1004
Debt
attachment *see* Attachment of debt
civil *see* Civil debt
garnished *see* Garnishee order
judgment *see* Judgment debt
Debtor(s) *see also* Attachment of earnings order; Judgment debtor
charge on interest *see* Charging order
cross-examination of 121
discharge order, County Court power 805
enforcement against, order for appropriate method 120
judgment summons *see also* Judgment summons
attendance 119
means of payment order *see* Means of payment order
Deceased person
provision from estate *see* Family provision
Decision *see also* Judgment; Order
announcing 1832
appeal from *see* Appeal
establishment of, where no existing decision 2882
provisionally enforceable 2876
reasons for *see* Reasons: decision, for
translation 2872
Declaration
adding parties to application 1423
application for 1237
answer to 1422
form 1422
beneficial ownership of land, of 1261
directions as to who should be made a respondent 1423
incompatibility 995, 996, 1854, 2057
effective remedy 996
hopeless applications 996
lacuna in legislation 996
making a declaration 995
notice to Crown 2057
procedure 995
rectification 996
inherent jurisdiction, and the 1421
interim 1742, 2086, 2087
judicial review, in 2253
parentage *see* Parentage: declaration
Part 19 requirements 1421
procedure 1421
progress of application 1421
proprietary rights of spouses, of 14, 1122, 1215, 1216
respondent considers should be made a party 1423
respondent's acknowledgement of service 1422
status, of 45, 869
adoption effected overseas 871, 1421
Attorney-General's role 872
general provisions 871
legitimacy 870, 871
marital 45, 869, 1421
parentage 869
restriction of publicity 809
Decree
divorce *see* Decree absolute or final order; Decree nisi or conditional order; Divorce: decree
Decree absolute or final order 49
appeal pending 1235
application for 1154, 1404
discretion 1405
expedited decree 1403
original applicant, application by 1405
postponement 1155
records 1406
service on the Queen's Proctor 1405
stay 48, 1402, 1404
time for application for 1148
Decree nisi or conditional order 47, 1148
appeals 2194
application for 1389, 1391, 1392
statement, and 1392
application to make final 1400, 1404
application to set aside a certificate 1394
certificate of entitlement to 1393
consideration statement 1392
court not satisfied 1394
directions 1397
court officer action on making final 1406
court satisfied that applicant entitled to 1394
court's duties on application for consideration 1393
defended cases 1394
determination of proceedings 1393
evidence for *see* Evidence: decree nisi or conditional order, for
grounds for setting aside a certificate 1394
hearing of application 1394
intervention to show cause after 1154, 1401
notice lodged more than 12 months after 1404
Pounds procedure 1395
procedure for setting aside 1395
religious marriage, procedure after 1156
rescission 709, 1149
application 1155
procedure for application for 1155
setting aside *see* Setting aside: decree nisi or conditional order
Defence
allocation questionnaire on filing *see* Case management
Regulation (EU) No 606/2013, under 2891
Defendant *see also* Party
definition (CPR) 2033
not entering an appearance 2832
Regulation (EC) No 4/2009, under 2866
service on *see* Claim form; Service
Delay
care or supervision order *see* Care order: delay, avoidance of; Supervision order: delay, avoidance of
costs 2182
criminal proceedings, and pending 423
judgments 548
matrimonial/civil partnership proceedings 1404
section 8 order *see* Section 8 order: delay, avoidance of

Delay—*continued*
secure accommodation order 1540
welfare of child, and 422, 423
welfare report, occasioned by obtaining 437
Delivery up order 1742, 2086, 2093
Denmark
maintenance decision made in, recognition and enforcement 91, 1114, 1953, 2440
non-party to Regulation (EU) No 606/2013 2891
Dental treatment
consent to 918
Dependent actions
Brussels IIA 2786
Dependent territory 863, 868
specified
custody order made in 837, 2469
territory specified 2469, 2470
Deponent
meaning 2117
Deposition
examination of deponent out of jurisdiction 1785
FPR (general provisions) 1782, 1783
use at hearing 1785
Deprivation of liberty *see also* Detention
liberty and security, right to 1006, 1547
looked after children 494
principles 487
Deputy *see also* Litigation friend
definition 1686
Desertion
financial provision application *see* Financial provision
spouse, by 1147, 1149, 1150
Detailed assessment *see* Costs: detailed assessment
Detention *see also* Deprivation of liberty; Hospital order; Prison
accommodation for child in 495
secure accommodation 2433
child or vulnerable adult
inherent jurisdiction 1547
Detention (property) *see* Property
Development
assessment *see* Child assessment order
meaning
care/supervision order, for 521
child in need, of 485
Devolution
appeal to Supreme Court 2362
Die, right to 1004
Directions *see also* Practice directions
appointment, attendance at 1832
children's proceedings, in 1506
commencement of claim after interim remedy (CPR) 2088
education supervision order, for 673
emergency protection order, for 572
failure to comply 423, 1517
interim 854
local authority investigation 675
section 8 order, for 456, 2542
section 37(1), under 555, 569
section 38(6), under 560
Director
liability for offence by company 633
Disabilities, parents with
discrimination 541
participation in proceedings 541
Disabilities, persons with *see* Disabilities, parents with; Disability, person under; Disabled child
Disability working allowance
maintenance contributions to local authority, where parent receiving 667
services provided by local authority, repayment 485, 518
Disability, person under *see also* Child; Protected party
family provision 1023
physical disability *see* Physical disabilities
reporting restriction order for 2569
Disabled child
carer suitability (Wales) 606
congenital disability, disclosure of donor parent 972
local authority duty 658
meaning (child in need) 485
privately fostered, age 595
register of 657
Discharge application 1539
Disclosure *see also* Legal professional privilege
address *see* Address
Adopted Children Register *see* Adopted Children Register: High Court power to restrict disclosure from records
adoption information *see* Adoption: disclosure of information
appellate process, and the 1753
applicant's duty *see* Applicant: duty to court and other parties: full and fair disclosure
artificial insemination, parentage 971
care and supervision orders 527
care proceedings
terrorism, parent's involvement in 1510
child support, information relating to 1852
children proceedings 1509, 1563
communication of information 1563, 1564
Practice Direction 1618
child's whereabouts, of 184, 1549
European Convention, under 373
FLA, under 181, 856
Hague Abduction Convention 1980, under 178, 373
parties 1498
procedure 155
recovery order 584
Regulation (EC) No 2201/2003, under 2780
civil proceedings, in (CPR) 2104
documents in his control 2108
claim to withhold 2113
continuing duty 2109
copies 2108
copying 2110
court adoption records 1661
court directions 2106
disclosure statement 2112, 2114
false 2111
meaning 2108

Disclosure—*continued*
discussions between parties 2106
disproportionate to the issues 2105
documents 2106
party's control, in 2108
duty 2105
continuing 1752
general 1752
when arises 1752
withhold inspection, to 2105
electronic 2111, 2112
enforcement of order 1440
exception, rather than rule, as 1757
expert's report *see* Expert's report: routine disclosure 2114
failure, effect 2111
false, committal application 2308, 2315
family proceedings, in 1754, 2105
procedure 1755
first appointment *see* Financial remedy: first appointment: ongoing duty of disclosure
forced marriage protection orders 899
FPR 2010 and *see* Family Procedure Rules: disclosure, and
general principles 2106
High Court, powers of
before commencement of proceedings 1139
power to order disclosure 1139
human rights issues 1513
Imerman documents 1755
inherent jurisdiction 247
inspection
specific 2109
withholding 2105, 2109
inspection (CPR)
documents referred to in statement of case, etc 2109
failure to permit 2111
procedure 2110
right of 2105
withholding 2110
joint investigations 1755
limitations 1756
local authority documents, of 2545
matrimonial and civil partnership proceedings 1390
meaning 1753, 1756, 2104, 2115
media 1756
medical records 247
millionaire's defence 1440
non-party, by 1510
non-party, order against (FPR) 1742, 1756
order for (CPR) 2087, 2109
Part 36 offers and payments 2206
personal details, non-disclosure application 1852
police 1510
possession or control 1753
power of court to allow 247
Practice Direction (FPR) 1759
pre-application protocol 1467
privileged document 2110
procedure for 1758, 2104, 2106
relevant practice form 2109
restraint jurisdiction, and 246

Disclosure—*continued*
restriction on use of disclosed documents 2111
search order application *see* Search order: duty of disclosure
Security Services, to 527
self-help 1440
specific 1755, 2113
application for 2109
CPR 2109
order for 2113
proportionality and relevance 2109
stages, in 2109
standard 2106
dispensing with or limiting 2106
documents to be disclosed 2107
meaning 2111
procedure 2108
search 2112
search duty 2107
standard disclosure (CPR)
list 2112
statement 2109
subsequent use 2111
surrogacy, parentage 971
terrorism
parent's involvement in 1510
third parties, against 1440, 1755
wardship proceedings 1543
wasted costs orders 2161
whereabouts of child 1757
withholding 1758
procedure 1755
public interest, in 1757, 2110
procedure 1758
Discovery of documents *see also* Disclosure
Discretion
litigation friend 1700
Discrimination, prohibition 1010
disabilities, parents with 541
Disposition *see also* Avoidance of disposition order; Prevention of disposition order
future, order restraining 55, 1208
legitimacy, and 926
Dissolution of civil partnership *see* Civil partnership
Dissolution of marriage *see also* Divorce; Nullity
presumption of death, on 1160
District judge
appeal from 193, 1866
permission, circumstances for 194
attachment of earnings 352
court functions under FPR, power to perform 1288
Divorce *see also* Pilot scheme for online divorce
adultery 1147, 1149
agreement of parties, referral to court 1152
answer *see* Answer
appeal against decree nisi
Court of Appeal, to 2236
application procedure 45, 46, 1379
amended petition 47
avoidance of disposition order *see* Avoidance of disposition order
bar within one year of marriage 1149

Divorce—*continued*
behaviour of respondent 1147, 1149
financial provision application *see* Financial provision
breakdown of marriage, ground for 1147
Bury St Edmunds Divorce Centre 2693
change in circumstances
maintenance agreement alteration 1206, 1207
repayment 1204
child of family
meaning 1214
orders for 54, 1160, 1163, 1167, 1171, 1177
child, meaning 1214
clean break 1184
direction 54
conditional order 47
consent order 1205
consent to decree 1149
rescission where misled 1155
costs 48, 50
County Court
rules for (FPR) *see* Matrimonial and civil partnership proceedings
decree *see also* Decree nisi or conditional order; Decree absolute or final order 49, 1148
appeal 1234
financial provision on, jurisdiction 1167, 1171
defended 49
answer 49
jurisdiction to hear 49, 2465
procedure 49
definitions 1214
desertion 1147, 1149, 1150
discharge of financial relief orders 1198
documents with application 46
no marriage certificate 47, 1408
duty of court to inquire into facts alleged 1148, 1159
early neutral evaluation (ENE) 1153
evidence
marriage breakdown, of 1147
facts alleged by petitioner / respondent 1148
family provision, and
application restrictions 1033
no financial relief granted 1033
financial provision orders *see also* Financial remedy 1160
arrears 1203
child support maintenance, and 1197
duration 1196, 1197
matters for court 1177, 1184, 1190
pension scheme benefits *see* Pension
person lacking capacity 1212
procedure 50
variation and discharge 1198
financial relief *see also* Financial remedy 1198
avoidance of transactions to defeat 1132, 1208
overseas divorce etc, after 57, 1124
five-year separation 1147, 1149
financial provision 50
procedure 1400

Divorce—*continued*
five-year separation—*continued*
refusal, grounds 1151
foreign *see* Foreign divorce
grave financial or other hardship 1151
ground for 1147
High Court, rules for (FPR) *see* Matrimonial and civil partnership proceedings
intention to defeat financial relief, orders 1132
interim maintenance order *see also* Maintenance: pending suit 1125, 1195, 1198, 1204
judicial separation, after 1159
judicial separation, interaction with 1150
jurisdiction 46, 827
lump sum orders 1160, 1167
age limit 1197
variation of instalments 1198
maintenance agreement 1205
alteration 1206, 1207
maintenance pending suit *see* Maintenance: pending suit
marriage, proof of, where no marriage certificate 1408
matrimonial home, occupation of *see* Matrimonial home
matters which occurred before 1150
no decree 'without receiving evidence from the petitioner' 1151
online divorce, pilot scheme for 1406
overseas *see* Overseas divorce etc, financial relief after
parties named and not named 1148
periodical payments order 1160, 1163, 1167, 1177
age limit 1197
child support maintenance, and 1197, 1201
duration 1196, 1197
pending suit 50, 1163, 1198
repayment 1204
variation etc 1198
periodical payments orders *see* Periodical payments order
petition for 1285
procedure 1148
property adjustment order 1160, 1171, 1198
procedure 50
proprietary rights order 1122, 1215, 1216
Queen's Proctor, action by 1154
recognition in UK 863
granted in Britain 863
granted overseas 863
refusal of 866
remarriage and 866
transitional 867
reconciliation 1152
statement, filing of 46
religious marriage, procedure 1400
remarriage / civil partnership formation
effect on financial relief 1196, 1210
repayment of sums 1210
rescission 212
rescission of decree nisi
respondent misled 1155

Divorce—*continued*
respondent 47, 49
relief for 1160
Rome III Regulation 2770
sale of property order 54, 1173, 1177
variation etc 1198
secured payments 1160, 1196, 1197, 1198
conveyancing counsel, instruction of 1198
repayment 1204
variation, etc 1198
separation *see* 'five-year separation' *above*; 'two-year separation' *below*
service 47
settlement 1160
bankruptcy of settlor 1211
variation 1198
stay of proceedings 48
tenancy, transfer of, on *see also* Tenancy 41, 894, 911, 1132
compensation 915
transfer of property order 1160
bankruptcy of settlor 1211
duration / age limit 1197
transnational 864
two-year separation 1147, 1149
financial provision 50
rescission of decree 1155
written record 1400
undefended cause
application 45
procedure 45, 46, 47
unreasonable behaviour 1147, 1149
variation etc of financial relief orders 1198
Divorce Centres
Forms A, issuing 51
Divorce County Court *see also* Divorce
jurisdiction 1144
Document *see also* Evidence; Report; Service
accommodation, provision of 495
appeals 1867, 1868
bundle *see* Court bundle
copy 2106, 2108
court
attendance at private hearings 1837
stamping and sealing 1855
disclosure *see* Confidentiality; Disclosure
electronic *see* Electronic document
electronic exchange *see* Electronic exchange of documents
electronic questionnaire, as disclosed document 2111
execution of 1243
exhibit 2120
filing
Family Court (FPR) 1834
High Court / County Court 2083
Supreme Court 2352
foreign judgment, proof of 693, 694
hard copy 2353
impounded 1835
order, by 1835
inspection and access, court retained 1858
judicial review 2254, 2260

Document—*continued*
lodging
Regulation (EC) No 2201 /2003, under 2785
meaning
disclosure, for (CPR) 2106
representation of interested person in claim 2058
media, disclosure to 1756
necessary, evidence as to why 1757
notice to admit or produce 1767, 2116
proof of
European Convention, and 372
Hague Abduction Convention 1980, and 366
maintenance order, and 1073
retained in court, access and inspection 1858
secure editing 1526
service *see* Service
signed
affidavit distinguished *see* Affidavit: signed documents distinguished, and
third party, release of court document to 1755
verification *see* Verification
Domestic violence *see also* Injunction; Non-molestation order 887
contact, and *see* Contact: domestic violence cases
evidence 1311
fact-finding hearing *see* Fact-finding hearing: domestic violence
financial abuse 440
High Court / County Court discharge of Family Court order 823
injunction application *see* Injunction; Non-molestation order
legal aid 440
24-month rule 440
MIAMs 1315
Domicile 826, 828
adoption applications 284
Brussels IIR 46
burden of proof 828
child, of, where parents apart 826
civil partners, and court jurisdiction 780
dependent 826
family provision 1014
independent 826
jurisdiction (matrimonial), and 827
origin, of 828
parental orders 990
Regulation (EC) No 2201 /2003, under 2776
wife's, dependent, abolition of 826
Domicile, choice of 828
Donatio mortis cause 1028
Driving disqualification
child support enforcement power 413
international orders 2492
Dwelling house *see also* Matrimonial home
meaning (CA 1989) 635
Early neutral evaluation (ENE)
divorce 1153
Earnings
attachment of earnings, and
determination of 348

Earnings—*continued*
attachment of earnings, and—*continued*
meaning 352
statement of, by debtor 347
Education
advanced 2485
after leaving care, etc
assistance to former relevant child 505
assistance with 509
payment for higher education, former relevant child 504
care plan, personal plan in 2400
child being looked after, local authority duty 496
child's needs 422
full-time 2485
human right 1011
Education authority *see* Local education authority
Education supervision order
applicant 1497
application 553
authority in whose favour order was made 675
child in care, and 553
consultation provision 554
directions 673
offences 676
discharge 675
duration 675
effect 673
extension 675
investigation by local authority 675, 676
local education authority for 553
meaning 553
parent, definition 676
properly educated 553
child not being, circumstances for assumption of 553
regulations, provision for 676
respondents 1497
school attendance order, and 674
supervision order, and 674
supervisor
contact 675
duties 673
information to 675
Education, health and care plan *see* EHC
EEO *see* European enforcement order
EFTA *see* European Free Trade Association
EHC (education, health and care plan) 491
Electronic communications *see also* Electronic filing
divorce 1406
service 2817
Electronic document 2106
claim form 2042
disclosure 2112
filing 2353
questionnaire as disclosed document 2111
Electronic exchange of documents 1509
Electronic filing *see also* Pilot scheme for online divorce
Family Court 2712
financial remedy 51
Electronic tagging 446
practice direction 2690
Electronic tagging—*continued*
radicalisation 859
Email
practice direction 1342
service 1362
specified organisations 1342
statements of truth 1345
technical specifications 1343
Embassies
courts in England and Wales, liaison with 2706
Embryo
germ cell use 963
human admixed
meaning 964
prohibitions 964
storage 969
licence for activities 962, 966, 967, 973
supplementary conditions, human application 975
woman from whom taken 968
meaning 960
permitted, meaning 963
'placing in a woman a human embryo' 963
primitive streak 963
prohibitions as to use 962
storage 961
conditions 969
period 970
suitable condition 974
testing 974, 975
use of an 963
Emergency placement
local authority foster parents, with 2408
Emergency proceedings for child
meaning (FPR) 1489
Emergency protection order
abduction of child under *see also* Recovery order 583
appeal 132, 577
applicant 132, 1537
application for 132, 572
appeal 134
authorised person 573
children's guardian 134
court 133
directions 134
discharge 134, 577
ex parte 133
order 134
procedure 132
respondents 133
service 133
without notice 1521
child assessment order application treated as 571
conditions for 572
contact and 573
directions 573
discharge 134, 577
answer 136
appeal 136
applicant 135
application 134
children's guardian 136

Emergency protection order—*continued*
discharge—*continued*
court 135
directions 136
respondents 135
service 136
special requirements 136
without notice 136
disclosure of information, provision for 582
doctor, nurse, etc
accompanying applicant 577
accompanying constable with warrant 583
duration 576
entry into premises, provision for 582
offence 582
evidence admissible 577
exclusion requirement 134, 575
cessation of 576
conditions 575
meaning 575
power of arrest 575, 577
rules 1537
variation or discharge 136, 577
extension 137, 576
answer 139
appeal 139
application 137
children's guardian 139
court 137
directions 139
order 139
respondents 138
service 138
without notice 139
investigation by local authority 580
meaning 573
medical etc examination 573
name of child in 574
notice to non-parties 1601
offence 574
parties 1494
police officer's application 579
power of arrest 578
powers of court to ensure effect 582
procedure for application of 574
prohibition on appeal relating to direction 578
removal of child where order is in force 580
restrictions on appeal 578
service 134
significant harm, likelihood of 572
supplemental provisions 576
undertaking with 576
variation *see* 'discharge' *above*
variation/discharge of exclusion requirement 578
warrant authorising assistance 583
name of child in 583
procedure 137
warrants, issue of 583
Emotional harm
radicalisation 533
Employment
after leaving care, etc, assistance with 509

Employment—*continued*
'reserved legal activity'
carried out by employee 1047
offence 1048
Enduring power of attorney 1685
payments under order 1212
Enforcement
Brussels IIA 2790
child arrangements order 149, 442, 458, 553
child does not wish to go 466
Practice Direction (disclosure of information) 2584
Child Arrangements Programme 1591
child support *see* Child support: enforcement
committal, by *see also* Committal 2336
disclosure of child's whereabouts 857
European Enforcement Order (text) 2811
family assistance order 483
Family Court orders 1142
Family Court, in 1141
financial order 1928
forced marriage protection order *see* Forced marriage protection order: enforcement of orders and undertakings
Hague Convention 1996 2738
information or documents, order to provide *see* Disclosure: enforcement of order
injunctions 797
order made in civil proceedings (CPR), general rules 2279
order made in family proceedings, general rules (FPR) 1927
Practice Direction (disclosure of information) 2584
'proceed for recovery of any sum' 1142
protection measures 2003, 2890
reciprocal *see* Judgment; Maintenance order enforcement
sale of property 1174
section 8 order 450
s 11(7) direction and conditions 458
settlement 1442
Supreme Court order 2360
two or more orders 1142
undertakings 797
do or abstain from act 1936
payment of money 1936
form of 1937
Enforcement order
amendment 641, 644
breach 642, 643
child arrangements order breach, on 148, 465, 466
amendment application procedure 1541
conditions for making 466
monitoring compliance 467
service 1542
warning notice 468
notification of application, duties on 1713
Practice Direction (disclosure of information) 1632
revocation power 641
stay of matrimonial proceedings, effect on 834
suspension on stay of Part I order (FLA) 842

Enforcement order—*continued*
unpaid work requirement 640
warning and report 642
Engagement *see* Marriage: engagements
England and Wales
child resident outside, financial provision 656
child to live outside, court approval 664
effect of orders 632
enforcement abroad of judgment made in *see also* Judgment 83, 86
enforcement of foreign judgment in 87
placement of child in care outside 2404
notice of order for 1601
Entry into premises, etc *see also* Emergency protection order; Recovery order
order for
CPR 2086
FPR 1742
search for evidence, for 789
Equal marriage *see* Same-sex marriage
Equality of arms
legal aid 440
Error
arbitral award 1308
Calculators 12
order or judgment in, 'slip rule' 1859
procedural, court power to rectify 1324
ESO *see* Education supervision order
Estate, administration of *see* Administration of estate
Estoppel *see* Issue estoppel
European Community
Court of Justice reference, and appeal to Supreme Court 2363
enforcement in, civil partnership 722
European Convention (human rights)
Convention rights *see* Human rights
European Convention (recognition and enforcement of custody decisions) 368, 1550
abducted child, application under in respect of 177
application under 393
central authorities 369
child, definition of 393
child's whereabouts, disclosure 373
contracting state
cost of enquiries in 397
meaning 369
two or more law systems in 397
custody order, termination of existing 374
decision of UK court 372
decision relating to custody 370, 371, 372, 374, 393, 394
enforcement/recognition of 396
subsequent decision 396
decision relating to rights of access 374, 396
declaration of unlawful removal 372, 396
determination of application 394
discharge of functions in UK 369
discretion to fix condition 396
documents, provision of by court 372
effects of original decision 395
European Convention (recognition and enforcement of custody decisions)—*continued*
enforcement of decisions 372, 393
powers 371
evidence 372
force of law in UK 368
improper removal 370, 393
incompatibility with decision enforceable in State addressed 394
incompatibility with fundamental principles of family law 395
interim powers 371
issues to be determined 395
object 369
parties to 2430
proceedings under *see* Hague Convention: proceedings under Hague Convention or European Convention
proof of documents 372
recognition and enforcement 394
recognition of decisions 369, 393, 394
conditions 396
refusal of 394, 396
registration of decisions 370
report on child 372
review of foreign decision 394
revocation of decision abroad 370
Rules, power to make 373
suspension of court's powers 371
variation of decision abroad 370
views of child 397
European enforcement order 2299
court for enforcement 101
enforcement in England 101
registration of English judgment as 100
text 2811
European Free Trade Association
enforcement in
maintenance order 89
Lugano Convention *see* Convention: Lugano
European Union
European Certificate of Succession 1023
reciprocal enforcement of judgments *see also* Judgment 94
reciprocal enforcement of maintenance orders *see also* Maintenance order
enforcement 89, 91, 1971
English order 1971
Service Regulation 1358
service within 1359
transfer of proceedings 525
Evidence *see also* Affidavit; Burden of proof; Standard of proof; Witness: statement 2051
admissibility 623, 1760
copy local authority records 570
affirmation 2121
'allowed to give' 1763
alternative Part 8 claim 2053
appeal, for *see* Appeal
banker's books, production of entries in 2115
capacity, as to *see also* Capacity: medical evidence 224
Child Arrangements Programme 1590

Evidence—*continued*
child, by 623
child as witness in family proceedings 624
child's understanding of nature of oath 625
guidelines 2632
children's proceedings, order in 1506, 1526
civil partnership proceedings, in 1767
civil proceedings (CPR) 2115
general rule 2115
witness cross-examination, limiting 2115
committal 413
committal application, in support of 1988
compelling attendance of party to give 626
contempt of court hearing 1985
cooperation between courts of Member States 2753
court's control 2115
covert 624
criminal convictions 2754
cross-examination, on *see* Witness
decree nisi or conditional order, for 1393
standard or detail of evidence 1394
defining issues for trial 1762
delivery up /preservation order 2093
deposition 1783
deponent 1769
examination of deponent out of jurisdiction 1785
use at hearing 1785
disclosure of child's whereabouts 857
documentary, filing with application notice (CPR) 2078
domestic violence 1311
European Convention, under 372
exceptions to general rule 1763
exclusion power of court
CPR 2115
FPR 1761
exhibit 2120
defect 2123
expert *see* Expert evidence
facts, of
admission (CPR) 2116
proof, general rule (FPR) 1762
Family Court, in the 1760
family proceedings (FPR) 1761
filing of 2050
final hearing, at 1764
financial provision 767, 816
forced marriage protection orders 899
foreign law, on question of 1780
Hague Abduction Convention 1980, under 366
hearings, at 1760
hearsay *see* Hearsay evidence
husband and wife, of, as to sexual intercourse 1214
interim hearing, at 1724
interim remedy *see* Interim remedy: evidence in support
judgment summons 1931, 1932
debtor may not be compelled to give evidence 1933
judgment, of any 993
litigation friend 2065

Evidence—*continued*
local authority investigation 1525
maintenance order, and 1069, 1098
matrimonial /civil partnership proceedings 1767
'matters set out as' 1724
medical *see* Medical evidence
modification of rules of 1331
notarial act or instrument as 1767
notice to admit facts
CPR 2116
FPR 1767
notice to admit or produce document 1767, 2116
oral 1763, 2051
general principle 2115
order made 'without taking evidence' 1136
other than final hearing, at 1765
overriding statement, and
identification of issues 1760
party not legally represented 1762
pilot scheme for online divorce 1408
plans, photos etc, use of 1779
Practice Direction (written evidence FPR) 1768
preliminary issues 1762
preservation, court power to make order 789
prosecuted parent 1762
recovery of child 858
relevance 1760, 1761
relief from sanctions 1324
requirements 2051
rules of 1760
section 8 cases 1526
self-incrimination 629
service 2050
special guardianship cases 1526
statement
separate 1538
statement of case as *see* Statement of case: evidence, as
submission
children proceedings 1509
surveillance 624
third parties, from 2115
unsworn
given by child 625
video link
CPR 2116
FPR 1763
weight 1778
withholding inspection or disclosure 1758
without notice application *see* Without notice application: evidence in support, and

Ex parte order *see also* Without notice application
appeals against 1235
'ex parte' 890

Examination *see also* Assessment; Cross-examination; Medical examination; Psychiatric examination
permission requirement 1804

Examiner
appointment 1786
fees 1786

Exclusion of party 1519
reasons for *see* Reasons: exclusion, for

Exclusion order/injunction
occupation order, exclusion under *see* Occupation order
Exclusion requirement
emergency protection order, with 134, 575, 577
rules 1537
variation etc 136
interim care order, with 163, 562
cessation of 562
conditions 562
consent 562
meaning 562
power of arrest 562, 564
rules 1537
variation or discharge 564
Execution *see also* Money judgment; Warrant of execution; Writ of fieri facias
goods *see* Goods
stay *see* Stay of execution
Execution of instrument
nominated person, by 1243
Exequatur 2871
Expenses
conduct money 1933
Expert
agreement between experts 1800
attendance at court 1807
Best Practice Guidance 2544
child(ren), for 1817
children proceedings 1797
confidentiality 1814
standards 1807
copies of orders and documents 1800
court directed meetings, public law children cases 1824
departure from opinion 1532, 1832
directions from court, right to 1800, 2130
discussions between experts 1799, 2130
duties 1795, 1803
emergency or urgent case, in 1802
first appointment, direction as to 1438
function and role of 2544
impartiality 1795
information from party to, court power to direct 1799, 2130
instruction of
letter of instruction 1816
pre-application 1802
protected party, for 1816
psychiatrist or psychologist 1818
separate experts 1813
single joint expert 1816
joint instruction 1438
meaning 1803, 2128
medical examiner as *see* Medical examiner: expert, as
overriding duty to court 1795
overseas medical expert, guidelines on instruction of 2638
party to inform of determination of case, etc 1800
permission to instruct
children proceedings 1813
draft order 1815, 1821
Expert—*continued*
permission to instruct—*continued*
timing of application 1814, 1820
permission to instruct, requirement for 1796, 1804, 2128
application notice 1797
grant 1797
non-children proceedings 1819
Practice Direction
CPR 2131
Public Law Outline 2544
report *see* Expert's report
separate instructions by individual parties 2130
single joint 1800, 2129
children proceedings 1812
court direction for use 1798
instruction of 1816
instructions to 1799, 2129
non-children proceedings 1819
valuation of assets 1438
written questions to 1798, 2128
Expert evidence 1506, 1793
admissibility 2128
arrangements for 1806
children proceedings 685, 686, 1812
codes for 1793
common law 1794
control 1794
family proceedings, in all 1795
disclosure
restrictions 1795
form of 1797, 2128
given by expert 1794
impartiality of opinion 1794
judge differing from expert's opinion 1794
'necessary to assist the court' 686
non-children proceedings 1818
overriding duty to court 1803, 2128
permission
application notice 1797
circumstances for 1796, 1804, 2128
costs estimate with application 2128
grant of 1797, 2128
whether to give 687
restriction by court 2128
single joint expert 1798
veracity or validity of children's evidence, assessment of 624
Expert Witness Group 2545
Experts
fees and rates 2448
legal aid 2448
Expert's report *see also* Evidence: documentary; Expert; Expert evidence
addendum 2196
contents 1799, 1805, 2130
disclosure
failure 2130
use after 1799, 2130
dissatisfaction with joint expert's report 2129
form 1797
inspection of documents referred to 2109
routine disclosure 246, 1563
verification by statement of truth 1724

Extradition
respect for private and family life, and 1008
Extra-territoriality
same-sex marriage 1121
Fabricated or induced illness (FII)
carers 534
Facilitated communication 1528
Fact-finding hearing *see also* Finding of fact 445, 1508
domestic violence 1508
harm 1508
Facts and reasons *see also* Reasons 1279
Fair trial, right to a
civil rights and obligations 1006
duty to protect 997
legal representation at hearing 1529
provision of legal assistance 1007
public hearing 2142
radicalisation 533
reporting restrictions 627
rights protected 1007
text 1006
Witnesses, findings against professional 204
Family assistance order
consultation, Practice Direction 1632
court power to make 481
duration 482
section 8 order, interaction with 482
Family business 1144
Family centre
facilities at 659
meaning 659
provision of, local authority duty 659
Family Court
appeal from 1140, 2545
Court of Appeal, to 202
High Court, to 193
appeal to judge of 193
arrears, of periodical payments *see also* Maintenance order enforcement 1068
prohibition of committal more than once 1078
attachment of earnings order in *see also* Attachment of earnings order 341
restrictions on designated officer's power 349
authorisations 2461
clerk *see* Justices' clerk
composition 2458
confidentiality 626
contempt of court 2468
costs in 228
County Court powers 1135
court bundle 1881
court of record, as a 1134
designated officer
information to Secretary of State 610
distribution of business 2458, 2461
electronic filing 2712
enforcement 1141
evidence
hearsay 2431
family proceedings in 1279
Family Court—*continued*
financial provision, application for 811
age of child 813
agreed payments 815
conduct 812
death of payer 814
definitions 825
duration of order 813
enforcement 823
grounds for application 811
interim order 818
jurisdiction 823
matters to which court to have regard 812
orders 811, 815, 1107
parties living apart 816
parties living together 822
powers 811
reconciliation prospects 822
remarriage 1215
welfare of child 817
hearings (FPR) 1830
attendance at 1832
High Court, powers of 1135, 1139
income support, complaint for recovery of 1252
claimant 1254
interim order 818
judge 2459
powers 2468
judgment summons
maintenance order enforcement 118
jurisdiction 621
EU cases 823
justices' clerk *see* Justices' clerk
justices' clerk and assistants 2498
functions of 1142
lump sum order *see also* Lump sum order 811
maintenance agreement, alteration of 654
maintenance failure, application for 811
maintenance order *see also* 'financial provision, application for' *above*; 'periodical payments order' *below*
arrears *see* 'arrears, of periodical payments' *above*
committal, provisions on 1078
Convention country, reciprocal enforcement 1105, 1106, 1111, 1113
discharge and variation 1069, 1071
enforcement *see also* Maintenance order enforcement 656, 823, 1066, 1068, 1078
lay justice's powers 102
interim 818
Northern Ireland, in *see* Northern Ireland
reciprocal enforcement, rules 1101
reciprocating country, provisional order against payer in 1088
registration of *see also* Maintenance order registration 104, 1066, 1074, 1075, 1079
remarriage of party 1215
Republic of Ireland, and *see* Republic of Ireland
Scotland, in *see* Scotland
variation 1089, 1100, 1111, 1113

Family Court—*continued*
maintenance, liability for and benefit recovery 1252
means of payment order 1075, 1111
'officer of the court' 858
order
domestic violence, for *see* Non-molestation order; Occupation order
enforceable as maintenance order *see* 'maintenance order' *above*
variation or revocation 819
periodical payments order *see also* 'financial provision, application for' *above*; Periodical payments order 811
arrears *see* 'arrears, of periodical payments' *above*
variation 652, 819
powers 1139
privacy for child 626
private hearing 1835
attendance 1836
proceedings and decisions 1135
publication of judgment 2656
radicalisation 2695
reasons 1830, 2660
Guidance 2550
remedies 2458
shorthand note of proceedings 1835
sittings 1134
transparency 2656
warrant of committal 1078
maintenance order enforced by 1078

Family credit
maintenance contributions to local authority, where parent receiving 667
services provided by local authority, repayment 485, 518

Family Division
child support proceedings, assignment to 2486
proceedings for 1250

Family home *see also* Exclusion requirement; Matrimonial home; Occupation order; Tenancy
child in need, maintenance for 660
home rights 874
charge, as 875, 879
charge, as, priority of 875, 876, 909
civil partner 874
death of spouse /civil partner 876
end of 875, 876
one spouse no estate 874
release of 908
party permitted to enter
leave of court 874
tenancy, transfer of 894

Family life, right to respect for *see* Human rights: private and family life, right to respect for

Family mediation information and assessment meetings *see* MIAMs

Family Procedure Rules 2031
court functions under, power to perform 1288
disclosure, and 1752
glossary 1279
interpretation 1279, 1285

Family Procedure Rules—*continued*
new procedural code 1277

Family proceedings
alternative procedure 236
application of FPR to 1279
children, relating to (FPR 2010) 1488
court action after application issue 1503
costs in 1846
definition of 439
existing Practice Directions, continued application of 1292
Family Court, in 1279
fees 2472
remissions 2479
meaning 1279
parental responsibility 429, 432
powers of court in 554
transfer from High Court to County Court 1144
transfer to High Court 1145

Family provision
acknowledgement of service by personal representative 2271
affidavit in answer 24
answer 24
appeal 24
applicants 22, 1013
cohabitant 22
cohabitant not maintained by deceased 1013, 1022
disability of 1021
financial resources and needs of 1021, 1022
representation of 2275
application out of time 1025
avoidance of dispositions etc 1029, 1030, 1031, 1032
beneficiary of estate
application to vary periodical payments order 1027
meaning 1037
resources and needs 1021
child of the deceased 22, 1015
child, meaning 1038
civil partnership of the deceased *see* Civil partnership: family provision on death
claimants 2271
cohabitant of the deceased 22, 1013, 1016, 1022
conduct 1023
contract to leave money by will 1030
County Court application 22
answer 24
form 22
jurisdiction 796
deceased, obligations of 1021
deceased's reason 1023
deductions out of the estate 1039
defendants 23, 2271
definitions 1037
disability, and *see* Disability, person under: family provision
dispositions to defeat 1029
divorce etc
no financial relief granted 1033
overseas, restriction on application 1034

Family provision—*continued*
divorce etc—*continued*
restriction on application 1033
documents on application 23
European Certificate of Succession 1023
financial needs 1022
forfeiture rule 1024
former spouse of the deceased 1015
former wife and former husband 1038
High Court application 22, 2269
affidavit in answer 24
form 22
parties 23
husband, meaning 1038
interim order 24, 1025
joint tenancy 1028
jurisdiction *see* Jurisdiction: family provision
listing questionnaire, completion of 24
lump sum order 24, 1019, 1026
variation of instalments 1027
maintained by deceased 1013, 1014
maintenance agreement, variation etc of 24, 1035
matters to which the court must have regard 1021
net estate 1020, 1023, 1027, 1038
obligations and responsibilities 1023
orders 24, 1019
effect of 1037
filing of copies 1037
periodical payments order 24, 1019, 1026, 1035
discharge 1026
remarriage, and 1037
secured, deceased payer 1035, 1036
variation 1026
personal representative
neutral, remaining 23
production of grant 2275
statement /affidavit 2271
written evidence 2274
procedure for claim 22, 2269, 2270, 2271, 2274
proof of death 1014
property, meaning 1038
provision spouse might have expected to receive on divorce 1024
reasonable financial provision 1017, 1022
service 23
settlement, order for 24
spouse of the deceased 1014
standing searches 1025
subsequent application 2271
time-limit 1024, 2270
trustee, dispositions to, avoidance 1032
Family, right to found a 1010
Fatal accident
apportionment, practice direction 2073
Father
assisted reproduction
agreed fatherhood conditions 979
death of husband, etc, not sperm provider 981
meaning for 978, 981, 982
use of sperm after death of provider 980

Father—*continued*
child support, denial that is father *see* Child support
contact, and *see* Contact: father, importance of contact with
fertility services, consent to 979
meaning 285
parental responsibility of *see also* Parental responsibility 424
parental responsibility, without
consent to adoption *see* Adoption: consent to: father without parental responsibility
revealing identity of 448
unmarried *see* Unmarried father
Fax
service by 1362
FDR *see* Financial dispute resolution appointment
Feelings of child *see* Wishes of child
Fees *see also* Costs
civil restraint orders 1324
family proceedings, in 2472
remissions 2479
McKenzie friend 2159
occupation order or non-molestation order, applications for 1470
Supreme Court 2364, 2528
Female genital mutilation (FGM) 927
inherent jurisdiction 938
injunctions 631
medical examination 534
protection orders
permission to apply 1478
significant harm 539
Fertility services *see also* Surrogacy 959
basic partner treatment 961, 966, 967
consent 979
counselling required as condition of licence 967
definitions 959
embryo use etc *see* Embryo
father, consent of 979
fees 972
gamete use etc *see* Gamete
Human Fertilisation and Embryology Authority 965, 967
legitimacy of child, principles 924
legitimation of child
extraneous law, by 1056
subsequent civil partnership 1056
licensing 962, 964, 973
conditions 966, 967
embryo testing 974, 975
human application 970, 975
non-medical services 969, 975
records 966
scope 966
sex selection 974, 975
meaning 964
mitochondrial donation 972
non-human genetic material, prohibitions 964
opportunity to receive counselling 969
parental order 1634
parental responsibility, two female parents 424, 429

Fertility services—*continued*
parenthood 978, 985
agreed fatherhood conditions 979
agreed female parenthood conditions 983
consent 983
death of one of two female parents 984
father 978, 980, 981, 982
mother 978
parties to a civil partnership 986
parties to a marriage 986
rights/status of biological mother 978
status of biological father 984
two women in civil partnership 982, 985
use of sperm after death of provider 980
woman to be treated as parent of child 985
permitted eggs, embryo and sperm 963
provision of relevant information 969
register 971
schedule 3 compliance 967
storage licence, conditions 969, 970
succession on intestacy, two female parents 925
treatment for purpose of assisting women to carry children 962
FGM *see* Female genital mutilation (FGM)
FII *see* Fabricated or induced illness
Filing *see also* Document; Evidence
Supreme Court 2352
Final hearing
children proceedings 1535
Financial circumstances form
meaning 1430
Financial compensation order 469
child arrangements order breach 148, 468, 469
notification of application, duties on 1713
Part I order (FLA) enforcement, interaction with 855
parties 1492
Financial dispute resolution appointment 1441
Financial order 50, 1285, 1286
definition 50, 1281
enforcement 1928
interim order 1432
meaning 1285
MWPA 1882 order application in proceedings for 1420
offer to settle
costs orders, factors for court 229
procedure 1161, 1194
Financial proceedings
criminal compensation orders, relationship with 1161
Financial provision *see also* Financial relief order (for child); Financial remedy; Lump sum order; Periodical payments order
age of the parties 1183
anonymity 2142
applicant 51, 811
application
commencement of proceedings 1193
grounds (within marriage) 811, 1194
High Court/County Court, in 51
behaviour of respondent ground 811
child 767
child of family to whom application relates 812

Financial provision—*continued*
conduct 1184
contribution 1184
duration of the marriage 1183
enforcement
attachment of earnings 105
charging order 108
writ of fieri facias 112
evidence 767
failure to maintain, on 1194
civil partnership 747
interim order 1195
order 1195
warrant of execution, permission for 1935
Family Court, in
age of child 813
agreed payments 815
application 811, 815, 816
conduct 812
death of payer 814
definitions 825
duration of order 813
enforcement 823
grounds for application 811
interim order 818
jurisdiction 823
matters to which court to have regard 812
orders 811, 815
parties living apart 816
parties living together 822
powers 811
reconciliation prospects 822
remarriage 1215
repayment on 824
variation of orders 819
welfare of child 817
financial resources 1181
form of application 816
form of order 812
High Court/County Court, in
orders 54
procedure 53
lay justices' powers
appeals 26
applicant 25
directions 26
order, form of 26
procedure 25
respondent 25
revival of order 26
service 26
variation of order 26
lump sums 812, 816
magistrates' court, in
application 25
procedure 50
maintenance failure (within marriage) 811
matrimonial property 1180
method of payment 812
needs and obligations 1183
orders available 812, 1160
overseas divorce etc, after *see also* Overseas divorce etc, financial relief after 1124
orders 1127

Financial provision—*continued*
personal injury awards 1181
post-separation accruals 1182, 1183
pre-acquired assets 1182
procedure on application 811
prohibition on application after remarriage 1197
reasonable financial provision 1013, 1038
respondent 53
revival of orders 813, 815
settlement, order for 1019
share schemes 1183
standard of living 1184
transfer of property order 1019
valuable consideration 1038
variation of order 821
wife, meaning 1038
Financial provision order
meaning 1204
Financial relief *see also* Financial relief order (for child)
judge, allocation to 2705
meaning 1165
setting aside orders 212
settlement 1442
Financial relief order (for child) *see also* Financial provision; Lump sum order; Maintenance agreement; Maintenance order; Periodical payments order; Settlement; Transfer of property order
appeals 14
application for 12, 644
child
meaning for 656
resident outside England and Wales, for 656
child arrangements order, and 645, 653
child support maintenance, interaction with 647, 651
conveyancing counsel, use of 656
directions 13
discharge 644
divorce etc, in connection with *see* Divorce
duration 647
exercise of discretion 648
further orders 644
interim 13, 653
lump sum order 12
lump sum, power to order 645
matters for court 648
orders 14, 644
parent 656
parents, against 481
periodical payments order 12
persons aged over 18, order for 481, 646
powers of court 480, 644
procedure 481
respondents 13
review, power to order a 646
service 13
setting aside procedure 213
transfer of property order 12
transfer property, power to 645
types of order 14, 644
variation 644
Financial relief order (for child)—*continued*
ward of court, for 645
Financial Remedies Unit *see* Central Family Court (Financial Remedies Unit)
Financial remedy
Central Family Court (Financial Remedies Unit) 51
consent order application *see* Consent order: financial remedy
costs *see* Financial dispute resolution appointment
disclosure *see also* Disclosure
efficiency 2702
electronic filing 51
financial dispute resolution appointment *see* Costs: financial remedy proceedings
hearing 51, 2702
High Court, hearings in the 51
information, communication of 1461, 1468
interim orders *see* Interim order: financial remedy
meaning 1281
setting aside 1465
setting aside orders 1433
Financial remedy (ancillary relief)
adding or removing parties 1450
application for order 1163
court for 1432
Practice Direction 1466
procedure (FPR) 1429, 1432
procedure in Family Court 1443
procedure in High Court/County Court 1435
time for 1432
avoidance of disposition order 56
child, in respect of 12, 1434
separate representation, circumstances for 1435
clean break 1447
court for application 12
definition 50
disclosure 1467
enforcement 1142
expert evidence (Practice Direction) 1818
Family Court
procedure after filing 1443
financial provision and property adjustment orders 1160
financial statement 26
EU cases 1431
exchange 1436
requirements 1437
first appointment 1438
attendance of media representatives at 1439
directions at 1439
documents to be exchanged and filed before 1438
fixing the next stage 1439
no further production of documents without permission 1441
ongoing duty of disclosure 1439
procedure after 1441
procedure before 1436
'for' or 'about' a 1849

Financial remedy (ancillary relief)—*continued*
hearing
court for 1446
High Court/County Court procedure after filing 1435
jurisdictional issues, application for maintenance 1449
maintenance agreement variation 1855
meaning 1286
orders 1429
MIAMs 1314
open proposals 1452
overseas proceedings, permission application 1424
application 1424
application without notice 1425
draft order 1425
hearing of application 1425
notification of hearing 1425
opposed substantive applications 1425
pensions, orders relating to 1455
periodical payments
civil partnership proceedings 1433
matrimonial proceedings 1433
pre-application protocol 1431, 1462
principles 1467
scope 1466
preliminary oral hearing 1439
procedure 51, 1431, 1443
Family Court 1443
respondents 1445
revival or revocation application 819
respondents 1445
sale of property order 1446
service of application 1436
trustee's consent to act, evidence of 1780
variation application 1935
lay justices' powers 26
Financial remedy (ancillary relief) proceedings
meaning 1165, 1285, 1286, 1848
Part 28, in 1286
Financial statement 26
European cases 1443, 1444
alternative terms under 1431
requirements 1437
verification 26
European cases 1437
Finding of fact
appeal against *see* Appeal: findings of fact, against
Finding of fact hearing *see also* Fact-finding hearing
appeals 1235
First appointment
care and supervision proceedings 1534
First court seised
lis pendens 2785
First hearing dispute resolution appointment
Child Arrangements Programme 1585
date for 1541
FMPO *see* Forced marriage protection order
Foetus *see* Embryo; Gamete; Surrogacy
Forced marriage 899
criminal offences 337
Forced marriage—*continued*
inherent jurisdiction and *see* Inherent jurisdiction: forced marriages, and
offence 338
remand 905
respect for private and family life 1008
Forced marriage protection order 899
applicant 32
application 901, 1477
breach 902
case management 1480
circumstances for 900
committal for breach *see* Committal: forced marriage protection order, breach of
consequential directions 1480
contempt of court 906
contents 900
court for 906
court's own initiative, made on 1481
criminal offence, breach as 35
definitions 906
delivery to the police 1482
disclosure *see* Disclosure: forced marriage protection orders
duration 904
enforcement 36, 127
enforcement of orders and undertakings 1484
evidence *see* Evidence: forced marriage protection orders
ex parte 902
form of 34
forms 1477
guidance 906
hearing of application 34, 1480
interaction with other protection 906
legal aid 33
order 901
parties, joinder or removal 1479
permission to apply 32, 1478
application 1478
person to be protected lacks capacity 1479
power of arrest, attachment of
remand for medical examination 905
power to adjourn 1484
power to grant bail 1483
power to remand for medical examination and report 1483
power to remand in custody 1483
procedure 32, 1477
proceedings following arrest 1483
release on bail 905
relevant third party 901
representations 1482
rules applying to proceedings 1477
service of application 33, 1479
notice, on 1479
service of order 1478, 1480
evidence 1479
on any other person named in order 1481
without notice 33
statement in support 1477
undertaking alternative 35, 903
variation or discharge 35, 904, 1482
warrant, application for 904, 1483

Forced marriage protection order—*continued*
who may apply 901
withholding of submissions etc 1481
without notice 33
Foreign adoption *see* Adoption: foreign element
Foreign divorce *see also* Overseas divorce etc, financial relief after
permission to apply for financial remedy (ancillary relief) after
maintenance pending suit where 1164
Foreign law
evidence on question of 1780
marriage governed by 1158
Forms
alternative procedure for applications 1736
Divorce Centres 51
Form C7 *see* Answer: Form C7
Form C100 2539
FPR 1330
documents to be attached 1331
index to 1333
list 1334
Practice Direction 1332
Maintenance Regulation 89
procedure for other applications in proceedings 1728
section 8 cases 1526
special guardianship cases 1526
Supreme Court 2351
Foster allowance
payment 498
Foster parent
freedom of thought, conscience and religion, and 1009
local authority *see* Local authority foster parent
number of children, limits 676
placement of child with
Regulation (EC) No 2201/2003, under 2798
provision of refuge by 585
racial origins, and 660
voluntary organisation's placement with 590
Fostering
adopt, to *see* Concurrent planning
private arrangements for *see* Private fostering
siblings 677
usual fostering limit 676
complaints 677
exceeding, effect 677
exemption 677
voluntary organisation, by 676
Freedom of press
proceedings restraining 247
Freedoms under European Convention of Human Rights *see* Human rights
Freeing for adoption *see also* Adoption
consent to *see also* Adoption: consent to 281
order continuing in effect 325
pending applications 325
Freezing injunction 797, 1241
assets outside the jurisdiction 1242
contempt of court *see* Contempt of court: freezing order, disobedience of
court power 55, 1208, 1240, 2086
FPR 1742
Freezing injunction—*continued*
enforcement of assessments under CSA 1991 1243
form 1242
limitations 1242
matrimonial disputes 1241
matrimonial financial order proceedings, and 1744
meaning 2087
notice 1242
principles on which injunction is made 1241
procedure for 1241
respondent's access to assets 1242
specimen 2091, 2094
Full-time education 2485
Funding *see also* Legal aid 439
HMCTS, by 1138
Further information
application to court 2056
obtaining 2054
request 2055, 2056
response 2055, 2056
restrictions on use 2054
statement of truth 2056
Gamete
licence for activities 964, 966, 967, 973
person providing gametes 968
supplementary conditions, human application 975
prohibitions 964
storage 961, 964
conditions 969
period 970
third party agreement, activities pursuant to 964
Gatekeeping 1859, 1881
Gender recognition
birth registration 448
private and family life, right to respect for 946
Gender recognition certificate 1412
administration of estate issues 955, 956
application procedure 944, 952
determination rules 945
evidence 945
civil partnership 955
commencement of legislation 958
correction procedure 1418
disclosure of information prohibition 957
documents in proceedings 1855
error in 952
foreign marriage, issue after 956
full 948, 949, 950
civil partner applicant 951
correction application procedure 1418
effect of 953
interim 948, 1384
civil partnership, effect on 710
full certificate, issue of 949
interpretation 958
issue 948
marriage, party to a 954
parenthood, effect on 955
refusal, appeal 945, 952

General public *see* Public
Gift
engaged couple, between 1041
Glossary
FPR 2030
Goods *see also* Warrant of delivery; Warrant of execution; Warrant of distress; Writ of fieri facias
delivery up, order for 2086
sale under execution, County Court 801
Grants
Secretary of State, by 609, 638
Grooming
Islamic State 1544
radicalisation 533, 1544
Guardian *see also* Children's guardian; Parent 283
adoption, consent for 281
appointment 431
court, by 431
disclaimer 433
duration 618
end 433
joint 432
notice of application 1600
parent etc, by 431
revocation 433
child in care, contact with 549
parental responsibility of 432
section 8 order 454
Guardian ad litem *see also* Children's guardian
Questionnaire on performance 2547
Guardianship
Hague Convention 1996 2732
Guardianship order
court officer's duty on 1474, 1484

Habeas corpus *see* Writ of habeas corpus
Habitual residence 376, 828, 2778
adoption applications 284
Brussels IIA 522, 2779
Brussels IIR 46
child support 415
children 2779
custody 2778
Hague Convention 1996 2733, 2734, 2735, 2740
jurisdiction for order in matrimonial/civil partnership proceedings 840
maintenance 2778
meaning 841
Northern Ireland, in, Part I order application 849
reciprocal enforcement of maintenance order 1088
Regulation (EC) No 2201/2003, under 2776, 2778, 2780
removal from jurisdiction, after 860
Scotland, in, Part I order application 845
views and wishes of the child 2742
Hague Abduction 1980
Convention
proceedings under Hague Convention or European Convention 1550
Hague Abduction Convention 1980
access, rights of 379

Hague Abduction Convention 1980—*continued*
application under 365, 392
appeal 179
applicant 177
conditions 177
court 365
documents 177
orders 178
procedure in England 177
respondents 178
service of answer 178
without notice 178
appointment of children's guardian 1697, 1707
central authorities 364, 1608
child
objection to being returned 388
settled in new environment 382
to whom Convention applies 376
whereabouts of, disclosure 373
consent to removal etc 388
contracting states, meaning 364
custody
rights of, meaning 379
discharge of functions in UK 364
evidence 366
force of law in UK 363
grave risk of harm 388
interim powers 365
lodging of application within reasonable time 393
notice 392
object 364
Practice Direction 1607
procedural steps to be taken by court 393
proceedings under Hague Convention or European Convention
adjournment 1554
answer 1553
application 1551
central index of decisions 1557
directions 1552
disclosure of information in proceedings under European Convention 1557
evidence in support of application 1551
filing and serving written evidence 1553
revocation and variation of registered decisions 1556
stay of proceedings 1555
transfer of proceedings 1556
where to start proceedings 1551
without notice applications 1551
proof of documents 366
protective measures 2781
report on child 366
request by judicial or administrative authorities of Contracting State 392
return of child 382, 388, 392
Contracting States to act expeditiously 381
delay over decision, applicant's rights 381
non-return order 1558
non-return order made in another Member State 1558

Hague Abduction Convention 1980—*continued*
return orders
variation, suspension, revocation or rescission 384
service 178
urgent application 382
wrongful removal or detention 392
declaration of 367
Hague Adoption Convention 1993 1664
adoption order 329
text of Convention 330
annulment 304
conditions 304
copy order, applicant entitlement to 1858
objects of Convention 330
overseas determinations and orders 305
Hague Choice of Court Convention 2005
judgments, proof and admissibility 694
Hague Convention *see also* Abduction
application under 176
statement verification 178
contracting states, meaning 2427
International Child Abduction and Contact Unit (ICACU) 2685
parties to 2428
Hague Convention 1996 173, 433, 450, 476, 1550, 2729, 2731
applicable law 2739
applicant 173
application 393, 1557
declaration as to, for 1562, 2740
form 1898, 1904
application under
costs of 368
Article 15 test 525
assumption of jurisdiction by another member state 525
best interests of child 525
Central Authority 1904
certified copy, application for 1904
comity 525
cooperation 525
cooperation between states 2744
custody
merits of rights of, meaning 367
expenses 368
High Court jurisdiction 2507
judicial discretion 525
jurisdiction 2733
declining 1561
request from another Member State to assume 1561
service of order or request 1561
parental responsibility 426
definition of 2732
Part I order (FLA), interaction with 842
Northern Ireland 850
procedure 173
protection of child 2736
recognition and enforcement provisions 2741
recognition/enforcement of order, application in relation to 1904
regulations under 2505
Hague Convention 1996—*continued*
rules of court
power to make 367
sealed copy of court order, effect of 1902
stay of proceedings 525
jurisdiction question, for 1561
supporting documents 1904
suspension of court's powers 367
text of 2731
transfer of proceedings 525, 1559, 2709
wrongful removal or detention 375
Hague Convention 2007
Central Authority
information provision to 2496
meaning 2498
regulations 2488
Hague Convention adoption
procedure
child from outside British Islands 2381
child from UK 2388
provisions applying 2393
Hague Convention on the International Recovery of Child Support 2007 1444, 2835
application
Central Authority, through 2838
public body applicant 2848
application under
court 177
Central Authority
application through 2838
costs 2837
designation 2836
functions, general 2836
functions, specific 2836
co-ordination with other Conventions 2851
countries 1943
entry into force 2855
magistrates
court rules, reciprocal maintenance enforcement
cancellation of registration 1096
evidence 1098
FPR provisions 1946
registration of order in UK 1091
transmission of order made in UK 1088
Maintenance Regulation 89
registration of orders 77
United States 78
Hague Service Convention 1965 1358, 1360
Handbook of Best Practice 2540
pro formas, etc 2546
Harassment
ambit of injunction 1231
apprehended breach 1231
concurrent proceedings 1231
conduct 1232
course of conduct 1229, 1230, 1232
damages claim 1230
procedure 2278
injunction restraining 37
applicant 37
breach 39
committal for breach 128
interim injunction 38

Harassment—*continued*
- injunction restraining—*continued*
  - procedure 36, 37
  - service 40
  - warrant for arrest 40, 1230, 2279
  - without notice 38, 39
- meaning 1230, 1232
- offence 1230
  - contempt of court, relation with 1230
  - penalties 1230, 1231
- procedure 1231
- statutory tort and crime 1229
- two or more persons, involving 1229
  - injunction for victim 1231
- undertaking restraining 40

Harm
- child suffering or at risk of 585
  - court to consider 422
- fact-finding hearing *see* Fact-finding hearing: harm
- female genital mutilation 539
- meaning (CA 1989) 521, 635
- police protection *see* Police protection
- relinquished/abandoned babies 533
- risk assessment by Cafcass officer 483
- significant
  - care/supervision order 520, 521
  - child minder, etc, from (Wales) 603
  - investigation by local authority 580
  - suspicion that child suffering etc *see* Child assessment order; Emergency protection order; Police protection

Health
- assessment of child's *see* Child assessment order
- meaning
  - care/supervision order, for 521
  - child in need, of 485

Health authority
- accommodation by
  - inspection 607
  - notification of local authority 611
- secure accommodation 2433, 2435

Health plan 2398, 2419
- care plan, in 2400

Health reports
- practice direction 1673

Hearing
- agreed bundles 2123
- alternative Part 8 procedure 2054
- appeal 2216
- attendance *see* Attendance
- care proceedings *see* Care proceedings: hearings
- case management *see* Case management: hearing
- costs, detailed assessment of 2184
- date, children's proceedings 1517
- directions, court power 1526
- discretion as to whether held in open court or in chambers 1248
- evidence at *see* Evidence: hearings, at
- Family Court (FPR) 1830
- final *see* Final hearing
- financial remedy 51, 2702

Hearing—*continued*
- forced marriage protection order *see* Forced marriage protection order: hearing of application
- full hearing not always appropriate 1527
- issues resolution *see* Issues resolution hearing
- matrimonial and civil partnership proceedings 1391
- meaning 1290
- none (CPR) 2079
- notice of 1391
- out-of-hours *see* Out of hours application
- place court considers appropriate 1290
- private *see* Private hearing
- public
  - general rule 1390
  - matrimonial/civil partnership application 1390
- split *see* Split hearing
- telephone 2082
- urgent (High Court)
  - inherent jurisdiction, under 184
  - Practice Direction 2576
- venue, court's discretion as to 1290

Hearings
- consular advice 248
- permission
  - appeal, to 2224

Hearsay evidence
- admissibility, civil proceedings 2431
- credibility 1779
- cross-examination of witness on 1778
- definition 1778
- FPR 1777
- judicial findings on 1779
- notice of intention to rely on 1777, 1778
  - not required, circumstances 1778
- order for cross-examination 1765
- rule of law relating to 2432
- secure accommodation order 1540
- weight 1779

High Commissions
- courts in England and Wales, liaison with 2706

High Court
- adoption proceedings 1644
- appeal 2373
- appeal from
  - contempt of court case 249
  - Court of Appeal, to 1234
  - new trial, and 1234
  - private sitting 808
  - restrictions 244, 1234
- appeal to
  - Chancery Division, to be heard in 2234
  - contempt of court case 249
  - Family Court, from 193, 2545
  - FPR 1862
  - special appeals 2241
- appeal within/from, practice direction 2214
- application to *see* Claim form; Application
- attachment of debts 1244
- attachment of earnings order in 339, 341
- certiorari, leave for, effect 800

High Court—*continued*
Children Act proceedings in (FPR)
children's guardian *see* Children's guardian
solicitor for child *see* Solicitor
confidentiality 626
costs in *see also* Costs 1247
court bundle 1882
declaration, Hague Abduction Convention 1980 application 367
disclosure, powers of *see* Disclosure: High Court, powers of
domestic violence, application for *see* Non-molestation order; Occupation order
enforcement of orders *see* Judgment summons
execution of instruments, order for 1243
Family Court, powers in respect of 1139
family proceedings in *see also* Matrimonial and civil partnership proceedings
transfer of proceedings 1144
financial provision
powers 823
financial relief order for child *see* Financial relief order (for child)
financial remedy hearings 51
general principles of practice in 1137
hearsay evidence 2431
inherent jurisdiction *see* Inherent jurisdiction
injunction, power to grant *see* Injunction: High Court power to grant
issue in 2087
judge, meaning (SCA) 1249
judgment *see also* Judgment
delivery of (PD) 2552, 2555
judgment summons *see* Judgment summons
judicial review *see* Judicial review
jurisdiction 1235
maintenance order enforcement *see also* Maintenance order enforcement 1060, 1080, 1103
maintenance order registration *see also* Maintenance order registration 104, 1074, 1075, 1080, 1081
matrimonial causes in *see* Matrimonial and civil partnership proceedings
meaning 1279
new trial, in Court of Appeal 1234
prize court, as, appeal from 1234
prohibition, leave for, effect 800
radicalisation 1544, 1859
receiver, power to appoint 1240
registered order, enforcement 854
section 89 order 1661
single judge 1236
transfer of proceedings *see also* Transfer of proceedings
urgent application, Practice Direction 1605
vexatious proceedings, power 1245
ward of court, jurisdiction *see also* Ward of court 1245
HM Chief Inspector of Education, Children's Services and Skills 595, 614
HM Courts and Tribunals Service (HMCTS)
automatic calculators
errors 12
HMCTS *see* Funding: HMCTS, by
HMRC *see* Inland Revenue
Holiday *see also* Abduction; Removal of child
child in need, for 659
Home help
child in need, for 659
Home Office
request for order against 1515
Homicide
where one parent has been killed by the other 534
Honour-based violence 445
Hospital (independent)
accommodation in, notification of local authority 612
Hospital order 1474
court officer's duty on 1474, 1484
Human Fertilisation and Embryology Authority *see* Fertility services
Human rights *see also* Declaration: incompatibility; Fair trial, right to a 992
abuse of, prohibition of 1011
act or proposed act 1000
allocation to judges 2556
anonymity 2049
appeal
Supreme Court, to 2362
appellant's notice 1867
award of damages 1000
care orders, and *see* Care order: human rights issues
citation of authorities 2556
competing Convention rights 994
contact, and *see* Contact: human rights issues
Convention rights 1004
interpretation by court 993
meaning 992
reliance on in proceedings 998
text of 1004
Crown, joinder as party 1860
definitions 1002
disclosure, and *see* Disclosure: human rights issues
domestic legislation, interpretation of 994
education, right to 1011
embryo and 960
expression, freedom of 1001, 1009
failure to legislate or make remedial order, exclusion of 998
fair trial
radicalisation 533
findings of breach of Convention rights 1000
functions of a public/private nature 997
granting of relief or remedy 1000
judicial act 1855
claim for damages 2057
meaning 1001
proceedings for 1001
judicial review 2048
judicial review cases 2255, 2258
just satisfaction 1000

Human rights—*continued*
no punishment without law 1007
orders, court powers 236
parallel or free-standing claims 2048
parental responsibility, and *see* Parental responsibility: human rights issues
Parliament, and 998
power to exclude evidence 1761
Practice Direction (FPR) 1861
precedent 994
primary legislation 1004
defence 997
private and family life, right to respect for 1007
balancing of rights 1008
fairness 1008
'family life', meaning of 1008
'home', meaning of 1008
'private life', meaning of 1007
procedure 235, 999, 1854, 2042
court 235
raising issues under HRA 1998 529
property, protection of 1011
protection of
Regulation (EU) No 606/2013, under 2891
public authority 997, 999
public authority act 997
proceedings for 998
remedies 999
quantum of damages 1001
religion, etc, freedom of 1009
representation of protected parties 1684
restriction on, limitation on use of 1011
return of child 383
split issues 2048
subordinate legislation 1004
victim 995, 999
applicant, to be 235
withdrawal of care proceedings, and *see* Care proceedings: withdrawal: human rights issues

Husband and wife *see also* Marriage; Wife
contributions to property improvement 1215
evidence as to sexual intercourse 1214
meaning 1635
money and property from housekeeping 1123
property rights, declaration and enforcement 14, 1122, 1215, 1216
application 14
court 14
procedure 14

ICACU *see* International Child Abduction and Contact Unit
Ill-treatment *see also* Accidental injuries
Illegitimacy *see also* Legitimacy
proof of, civil proceedings 924
subsequent marriage, effect 1056
Illness *see also* Health; Medical treatment
fabricated or induced *see* Fabricated or induced illness
Ill-treatment
alternative accommodation for ill-treater 658
meaning for care/supervision order 521
prevention of 658

Immigration
concurrent care proceedings *see* Care proceedings: concurrent immigration proceedings
respect for private and family life, and 1008
Immigration and Asylum Chamber
appeal 2231
judicial review of decision
address for service 2262
permission application (removal challenge) 2265
Protocol between judges of Family Court and 1516
Immunisation *see* Vaccination 559
Immunity
blanket
rejection 1754
public interest *see* Public interest immunity
without prejudice rule *see* Without prejudice rule: immunity
Imprisonment *see* Prison
In camera
family proceedings hearing 809
publication of text and transcripts 244
Income
financial provision application, and 812
financial relief order, and 648
Income support
attachment of earnings order, payee on 106
liability for maintenance, and 1252
maintenance contributions to local authority, where parent receiving 667
maintenance order enforcement, and 1252
recovery from person liable for maintenance 1251, 1252
services provided by local authority, repayment 485, 518
Incompatibility, declaration of *see* Declaration: incompatibility
Independent reviewing officer 2398, 2623
additional functions 2415
appointment 513, 515
care plan, name in 2400
communication to (children proceedings) 1563
copy of care plan to 2401
functions 513, 514, 515
notification of alternative arrangements to 2410
qualification 2416
role in review of case 2412
Independent school
inspection 607, 633
Information *see also* Disclosure; Document; MIAMs; Publicity
abuse 2645
child being looked after, on 662
communication *see* Communication
debtor, from 121
disclosure *see* Disclosure
duty to consider
Hague Convention 1996 2746
duty to share information 1756
further *see* Further information
local authority duty, child no longer looked after 509

Information—*continued*
- matrimonial and civil partnership proceedings 1390
- presumption of death 1227
- publication of, on private proceedings 244
- release 248, 1563
- supervisor, to 633, 673

Inherent jurisdiction 450, 551, 1235, 1236, 1741, 2087
- applicant 182
- application under 181
- costs, order for 1548
- declarations and *see* Declaration: inherent jurisdiction, and the
- disclosure 247
- discretionary exercise of court's powers 1548
- female genital mutilation 938
- forced marriages, and 632
- jurisdiction under 1545
- nature 1543
- Official Solicitor 2716
- Part I order 837
- powers of court 1545
- Practice Direction 1602
- proceedings under 839
- publication, use to prohibit 246
- restraining disposal 55
- restrictions on 630
- transfer of proceedings 1544, 1862
- urgent/out of hours application 181, 184
- wardship application 181
- wardship distinguished *see* Wardship: distinguishing characteristics
- where to start proceedings 1542
- without notice application 1521

Inheritance claim *see* Family provision

In-house expertise 1799

Injunction *see also* Interim remedy
- application for 1237
- avoidance of disposition order application, on 56, 1208
- breach 125
- care proceedings 543
- conditions on 1137
- contra mundum 1009
- enforcement *see also* Committal order; Warrant of arrest 127
- female genital mutilation 631
- freezing *see* Freezing injunction
- harassment, restraining 1230, 1231
- High Court power to grant 1237, 1240, 1743
  - harassment, restraining 1230
- Human Rights Act 1998, under 1855, 2058
- interim (CPR) 2086, 2088
- interim (FPR) 1742
- interlocutory 1240
- judicial review, in 1237, 2253
- jurisdiction *see* Jurisdiction: injunctions
- matrimonial *see* Non-molestation order; Occupation order
- MCA 1973, under 797
- MWPA 1882, under 797
- personal protection 37, 797
  - application 37

Injunction—*continued*
- personal protection—*continued*
  - urgent application 37
- power of arrest 797
- publication, preventing 1010
- receiver's appointment ancillary to 1240
- restraining person from acting in office 1237
  - claim procedure 2253
- section 37
  - breach 1210
- service 127
- third party, against 2093
- undertaking in lieu *see* Undertaking: injunction, in lieu of

Injunctions
- contents of orders 2090

Injuries *see* Accidental injuries; Ill-treatment

Inland Revenue
- disclosure of addresses by 1377

Insolvency *see also* Bankruptcy
- writs and warrants 2322

Inspection 1753
- accommodation, of 607
- child minder, premises, etc 607
- child, of (Secretary of State's power) 608
- children proceedings 1509
- children's home 593, 594, 607
- day carer premises, etc 607
- directions as to 1511
- documents *see* Disclosure
- independent school, of 607
- meaning (FPR) 1756
- power of constable to assist in 633
- private fostering, of 596, 607
- property, of, interim order 1742, 2086
- records, of (Secretary of State's power) 607, 608
- school (boarding), of 614, 615
  - duties of inspectors 616
  - fee 617
  - quality assurance 616
- specific 1755
- voluntary organisation, premises, children etc 593, 607
- withholding 1758

Instalment
- default, and power to make charging order 360
  - no default 358
- lump sum
  - payable by 650
  - variation 1027
- order for payment by, execution of 801

Institutional care 2798

Intercountry adoption *see* Adoption: foreign element; Adoption: intercountry; Convention adoption order

Interest
- financial provision in connection with divorce 1170
- judgment debts, on 2283
- order for payment of interest on costs 2169
- registered judgment, on 692

Interests of justice
- expert evidence 1797

Interim care order
applicant 1537
listing subsequent applications 575
Interim contact *see* Contact: interim
Interim gender recognition certificate 1384
Interim hearing 1526
evidence at *see* Evidence: interim hearing, at
Interim order 1136
adoption *see* Adoption
appeals 1863, 2193
application without notice (CPR) 2088
care or supervision, for *see* Care order: interim; Supervision order: interim
court power (CPR) 2086, 2088
court power (FPR) 1742
evidence in support (CPR) 2088
family provision from deceased's estate, for 1025
financial order (FPR) 50, 54, 1432
financial provision in case of neglect to maintain 1196
financial provision in connection with divorce 1170
financial provision, for 653, 818
financial relief for child 646
financial remedy (ancillary relief) 1136
further applications 619
maintenance, for 1125, 1163, 1195, 1198, 1203
court powers 818
enforcement 1204
secure accommodation order *see* Secure accommodation order: interim
supervision order 557
Interim payment
order for (CPR) 2087
Interim remedy
application procedure (CPR) 2089
application procedure (FPR) 1746
directions before application has been started 1745
evidence in support 1746, 2088
freezing injunction 1742, 2091
interim injunction 1742
Aarhus Convention claim 2091
contents of order 2090
evidence 2089
jurisdiction 2088
setting aside on stay of application 1746
urgent applications 2089
judicial review, on 191
meaning 1742
other interim remedies 1741
Practice Direction (FPR) 1748
procedure
urgent applications 1745
search order 1742, 2091
service of application 1745
terminology 1741
time for 1745
when proceedings are started 1745
Intermediary 625
appointment and funding of 1684
International Child Abduction and Contact Unit (ICACU) 365, 2679
Brussels IIA 2685
International social services 435
Internationally displaced children 2734
Intervener
appeal, in (SCR) 2358
permission to appeal application to Supreme Court, in 2355
presumption of death 1227
Intestacy
succession on, legitimacy and 925
Investigation
Cafcass officer, by 1721
local authority, by *see* Local authority: investigation by
Ireland, Republic of *see* Republic of Ireland
IRH *see* Issues resolution hearing
IRO *see* Independent reviewing officer
ISIS *see* Islamic State
Islamic State
grooming 1544
radicalisation 1544
removal of child from UK 1544
travel to 533, 2695
Isle of Man
abduction 365
adoption 312
adoption, registration of 321
civil partnership 701
custody etc order made in *see* Dependent territory: specified
effect of orders 632
service in 1360
specified dependent territory 2470
order made in 2470
Isles of Scilly
application of CA to 639
Issue of proceedings 1286
Issues Resolution Hearing 1535
care /supervision proceedings 1534
Jersey
specified dependent territory 2470
order made in 2471
Jewish marriage
procedure for dissolution 1156
Joinder of party
child 1502
children's proceedings 1506
civil partnership dissolution etc 715
Crown, human rights 1860
declarations 1424
factors in decision 1500
forced marriage protection order application 1479
granting request without hearing 1503
parental orders 1636
request to be joined 1502
Joint lives order 1168, 1169
Joint tenancy
family provision, and 1028
Judge
allocation of proceedings 2714

Judge—*continued*
allocation of proceedings to
human rights proceedings 2556
appeal 1888
appeal from decision
circuit judge to High Court 209
Court of Appeal *see* Court of Appeal
High Court *see* High Court
change of mind prior to order being perfected 1533
Child Arrangements Programme 1583
court functions under FPR, power to perform 1288
District *see* District judge
Family Court 2459
powers 2468
judicial act as human rights violation *see also* Human rights 1001
liaison *see* Adoption: intercountry: liaison judge
meeting the child 623, 1530
note made by 1141
recusing himself from case 1532
section 9 judges 2714
seeing advocates 1532
seeing child 1530, 1700
Senior Courts, of (RSC) 1249
senior, meaning (SCA) 1249
unannounced visits 1528

Judges
Central Family Court (Financial Remedies Unit) 2692

Judgment *see also* Order
appeal, on (SCR) 2359
citation, neutral (PD) 2559
Commonwealth country, made in, enforcement of 84
County Court *see* County Court: judgment or order
date effective 1858
drawing up and filing 1857
enforcement
Commonwealth countries 83, 84
European Community /EFTA, and 689
European Union /EFTA, in 94
goods, delivery of *see* Writ of fieri facias
money payment *see* Judgment debt
order made in civil proceedings (CPR), general rules 2279
sequestration, by *see* Writ of sequestration
service of copy 2303, 2309
error or omission, correction of 1859
European Union /EFTA, enforcement within 94, 95, 689
evidence *see* Evidence: judgment, of any
Family Court 2656
final and conclusive between the parties 1136
foreign, recognition etc, Brussels Convention
appeals 691
proof of admissibility 693
foreign, recognition etc, Brussels /Lugano Convention
interest on 692
meaning 695

Judgment—*continued*
foreign, recognition etc, Lugano Convention
appeals 692
proof of admissibility 694
High Court
delivery (PD) 2552, 2555
enforcement in Commonwealth country 83
instalments, and power to make charging order 358
instalments, payment by *see* Instalment
irreconcilable 2869
'judgment or order', meaning of 1234
maintenance, for *see* Maintenance order enforcement
material omission 194
meaning (SCA) 1249
money *see* Money judgment
name and judicial title of person who made it 1857
reasons 539
service 1858, 2303
setting aside for non-attendance of party 1834
standard requirements (FPR) 1857
subsequent enforceable 2795
summary or streamlined procedure
failure to comply 2287
Supreme Court (PD) 2552, 2555
UK
copy of, for enforcement abroad 694
enforcement within other parts of UK 97, 98

Judgment (or order)
delay 548
Hague Choice of Court Convention 2005
proof and admissibility 694

Judgment debt *see also* Judgment summons; Money judgment 340
attachment of earnings 356
venue *see* Attachment of earnings order
County Court powers to secure payment 341, 344, 347
definition (attachment of earnings) 340

Judgment debtor *see also* Debtor(s)
attendance at court, order for 2284
judgment creditor's affidavit 2286
list of proposed additional questions 2288
non-compliance sanctions 2289
procedure 2288
refusal to sign 2289
service of order 2288
tape recording of proceedings 2289
written record 2288
cross-examination of 121
amount presently owed 2288
answer on oath 2285
attendance at court for 2284
certificate 2289
circuit judge 2287
discretion to make order 2287
hearing before judge 2286
High Court judge 2287
issue of order 2285
non-compliance sanctions 2289
notice of service of adjourned hearing 2286

Judgment debtor—*continued*
cross-examination of—*continued*
oath, on 2286
Practice Direction 2287
provision of information 2285
questioning before judge 2288
reasons for hearing before judge 2288
service by court 2286
substituted service 2285
suspended order 2287
enforcement against, order for appropriate method 120
service 2290
Judgment summons
appeal 119
application 118
attendance of debtor 803
committal *see* Committal: judgment summons
committal order 119, 803
debtor's address 119
FPR 1930
maintenance order enforcement 118
evidence *see* Evidence: judgment summons
form 119
multiple 1933
new order 1934
order 119
permission, circumstances 118, 1203
procedure 118
service 119
venue 1931
Judgments Regulation
financial relief after foreign divorce jurisdiction 1126
meaning 688
Judicial act
human rights violation
claim for damages 2057
Judicial authorities 2733
Judicial continuity 1541
private law proceedings, in 1507
public law proceedings, in 1507
Judicial office holder 406, 435, 626, 651, 778, 811, 1156
Judicial reasoning 1533
Judicial review 1000
acknowledgment of service 2263
agreed final order 2264
appeal 192, 2198
application for 189, 1237
claim form 191, 2255, 2261, 2262
court 2261
directions by the court 2263
directions/stay 191, 2258
documents 192
evidence 2259, 2263
orders 192
permission *see* 'permission to apply' *below*
procedure 189, 2252, 2261
response 191, 2259, 2263
service 191
skeleton arguments 192, 2264
time limit 2261

Judicial review—*continued*
child support, and *see* Child support: judicial review
claim form, contents of 2262
court bundle 2262, 2263, 2264
court officer for exercise of High Court powers 2253
court's powers 2263
damages 1238, 2254
court power 192
declaration 191, 192
delay 1238
devolution issues 2262
family proceedings 2254
hearing 192
none 2260
representations at 2260
High Court jurisdiction 1236, 1237
quashing decision, additional powers on 1238
human rights 2048, 2261
violation proceedings 998, 1001
Immigration and Asylum Chamber of First-tier Tribunal decision 2262
permission application (removal challenge) 2265
injunction, court power 191, 192
interested parties 2261
mandamus, order of *see* Mandamus, order of
permission to apply 2254, 2258, 2263
additional grounds 2263
claim form 189
grant 2263
hearing 2263
order giving or refusing 2263
refusal 2258, 2263
without hearing 2263
prohibition *see* Prohibition, order of
response
additional grounds 2263
detailed grounds 2263
restraint from acting in office 1237
service 191, 2256, 2262
acknowledgment of 191, 2257
skeleton arguments 2260
sufficient interest 1239
time-limit 2255
transfer 2261, 2264
conditions for 1239
Upper Tribunal, to 1239
undue delay in making application 1239
Upper Tribunal decision 2256
permission application 2265
Judicial separation *see also* Divorce; Matrimonial and civil partnership proceedings; Separation 1161
agreement of parties, referral to court 1152, 1159
amendment of petition or application 1382
application procedure 1159, 1379
defended 49
undefended 45
bar on petitions for divorce within one year of marriage, and 1150

Judicial separation—*continued*
decree 1159
divorce not precluded 1150
effect of decree 1159
family provision from deceased's estate, and 1033
financial provision on 1160
commencement of proceedings 1193
matters for court 1177
grounds for 1147, 1159
intestacy and 1159
jurisdiction 827
section 8 order 839
overseas, financial relief after 1124
application for leave 58, 1125
procedure 57
petition for 1159
petition for divorce after decree of 1151
proprietary rights declaration, and 14, 1122, 1215, 1216
recognition in UK 863
granted in Britain 863
granted overseas 863
refusal of 866
transitional 867
reconciliation 1152, 1159
statement, filing of 1381
Rome III Regulation 2770
sale of property order 1173, 1177
transfer of tenancy on *see* Tenancy
undefended cause procedure 47
Jurisdiction *see also* Proceedings
Brussels IIA 2775
CA 1989, under 621
care and supervision orders 522
case management 523
interim protective measure pending determination of jurisdiction 523
request for another Member State to assume jurisdiction 524
child resident outside EU 839
civil partnership 46
contribution orders 669
Convention on (Brussels) *see* Convention
Convention rights 992
deal with matter, to 1332
declined 2869
'dependent territory' 840
divorce 46
enforcement of judgments in High Court 2332
family provision 2269
financial provision orders in connection with divorce 1168
FLA 1996 provisions 896
Hague Convention 1996 1898, 2733, 2734, 2737
High Court 1236
inherent *see* Inherent jurisdiction
injunctions 1240, 1241
law and equity, of courts 1246
maintenance pending suit 1163
matrimonial proceedings, in 827
EC Council Regulation 827, 2771
meaning 1283
Mental Capacity Act 2005, under 1220, 1222
Jurisdiction—*continued*
parental orders 990
parental responsibility order 428
Part I order (FLA 1986), for 838
Part 18 1741
private law proceedings 453, 1503
proceedings are continuing 840, 841
relevant date 844
removal from *see* Removal from jurisdiction
residual 840
same-sex couple 829
same-sex marriage 46, 1121
section 8 order 839, 840
Service
impossibility 2783
service out of 1358
transfer of proceedings, and 796
wasted costs orders 2160
Justice(s)
single, powers 1289
Practice Direction 1297
Justices' chief executive *see* Justices' clerk
Justices' clerk
Family Court 1142, 2498
power 1290
responsibilities (PD) 2557

Land *see also* Charging order; Property
beneficial ownership declaration, application procedure 1261
entry, order for *see* Entry into premises, etc
equitable execution, and 802
proprietary rights to, between spouses 14, 1122, 1216
receiver, and 802
writ or warrant of possession *see* Warrant of possession
Land Registry
charging order entry in 360
Landlord
occupation order, service of 1470
Lasting power of attorney 1685
payments under order 1212
Lawyer *see* Counsel; Legal representative; Legal services; Official Solicitor; Solicitor
Lay justice
appeals 1863
reasons for decision by 1533
Lease
contract for grant, cancellation of occupation rights 907
Leave *see also* Permission
certiorari order, for, effect 800
child applicant, for 452
child, for non-molestation /occupation order application 888
local authority foster parent, for section 8 order 450
orders under s 91(14) 619, 621
overseas divorce, for financial relief on 1125
parental contact with child in care 551
parental contact, for 619
payment of arrears 1204
prohibition order, for, effect 800

Leave—*continued*
revocation
children's guardian or litigation friend not required 1700
section 8 order application, for 451
Legal advice privilege 1753
Legal aid
appeals 2194
certificate *see also* Certificate: legal aid
Child Arrangements Programme practice direction 1577
contempt of court hearing 1985
contempt proceedings 796
costs 2188
cross-examination 439
domestic violence 440
equality of arms 440
experts' fees and rates 2448
Member State, provision by 2878, 2891
paternity 440
statutory charge 1042
wasted costs orders 2161
Legal Aid Agency
costs
detailed assessment procedure 2174
replacement of Legal Services Commission 1254
statutory charge 2539
Legal proceedings *see* Proceedings
Legal professional privilege 542, 1753
waiver 1510
Legal representation *see* Representation
Legal representative *see also* Counsel; Official Solicitor; Solicitor
certificate of discussion of reconciliation by 1381
disclosure in child support cases 1853
discussion between advocates, care and supervision proceedings
direction for 1535
meaning 806, 907, 1283, 2034, 2160
regulatory framework *see* Legal services
Legal services
authorised person 1047, 1049
charge on property 1042
costs in civil proceedings 1044
employees 1048
exempt person 1047, 1053
alteration of categories 1054
European lawyer 1054
meaning 1050
'legal activity' 1046
orders for payment in respect of 1165
regulators 1050
provisional designation 1051
regulatory arrangements 1050
'reserved legal activity' 1046
activity ceasing to be 1052
alteration power 1051
employees 1047, 1048
entitlement to carry out 1047
offence if not entitled 1047
offence to pretend to be entitled 1049
provisions 1052
Legal services—*continued*
rights of audience *see also* Audience, rights of 1052
scope 1165
transitional authorisation 1051
Legal services payment order
principles to be considered in application for 1166
Legitimacy
declaration of 870, 871
procedure 1421
dispositions, and 926
Family Division jurisdiction 1250
intestacy, and 925
principles of 924
probate entitlement, and 926
proof of, civil proceedings 924
void marriage, of child of 1055, 1059
Legitimation
adopted child, of 1057
disposition of property to 1058
civil partnership of parents, on subsequent 1056
declaration of 870, 871
procedure 1421
extraneous law, by 1056
meaning of legitimated person 1059
property rights, effect on 1057, 1058
re-registration of birth after, duty 1058
rights and obligations after 1058
subsequent marriage, by 1056
Liability order *see* Child support
Liaison judge *see* Adoption: intercountry: liaison judge
Liberty and security of person, right to 1005
deprivation of liberty 1547
deprivation restrictions, person lacking capacity 1218
life sustaining treatment exception 1219
Liberty and security, right to
deprivation of liberty 1006
Life, right to 1004
LIP *see* Litigant in person
Lis pendens
Brussels IIA 2786
first court seised 2785
Litigant in person 1138, 1529
appeal 206
permission to 1865
appeals 1871, 2196
best interests of the child 542
Citizens' Advice Bureaux, use of 2621
compliance with rules 1863
cross-examination in interests of *see* Cross-examination: litigant in person, in interests of
divorce
financial guide 1171
judicial response to 2643
orders under s 91(14), and 620
Personal Support Units for service 1838
stay of proceedings 793
terminology, Practice Direction 2643

Litigation friend 2059
administration of funds 1684, 1703
adoption proceedings, in *see* Adoption
adult medical treatment or welfare cases 2577
applications 2065
appointment 1515
court order, by 1687, 2064
application procedure 2071
child, for 1702
service of application 2065
suitability 2064, 2065
who is appointed 2066
other than by court order 1685, 2062
child, for 1701
procedure 2063
suitability 2062
supplementary 1688
attorneys 2062
authorised person 2062
certificate of service 2064
certificate of suitability 2064
cessation of appointment 2066
death of protected party, upon 2062
Practice Direction 2071
change of 221
court power 1688, 1702
change /preventing acting, court power 2065
child acting without
order appointing litigation friend 2061
order permitting 2061
child attains 18 2066
child, for 1700
appointment by court 1702
appointment by order 1702
appointment without court order 1701
end of appointment 1703
not required 1698
powers and duties 1703
Practice Direction 1714, 2070
requirement for 1697
stage of proceedings for 1700
costs 2076
deputy appointed by Court of Protection 2064
documents to be filed 1687, 1701
duties 1703
duty 1686, 1701
evidence *see* Evidence: litigation friend
expenses 2069, 2076
forms 2064
liability for costs 1689, 1703, 2067
meaning 1684, 1700, 2034, 2060
no need for court appointment 2064
notice to child 1701
notice to protected party 1687
Official Solicitor 2716
Official Solicitor as *see* Official Solicitor: litigation friend, as
person appointed 1687, 1702
persons to be served 1687, 1701, 1703
powers 1703
Practice Direction 1689, 2071
protected party recovers capacity 2066
protected party, for 216, 1684

Litigation friend—*continued*
requirement for 2060
exceptions 2062
implications 2062
time for 2061
service *see* Service: litigation friend
solicitor, need for 1685, 1700
status 1684
suitability 1686, 1701, 2063, 2065
certificate 1687, 1701
termination of appointment 2065
time for filing 1687, 1701
undertakings as to costs *see* Costs: undertakings as to: litigation friends
who is appointed 1686, 2066
Litigation privilege 1753
materials for 1753
Litigation, conduct of *see also* Audience, rights of; Legal services
'reserved legal activity' 1046
Living arrangements *see* Child arrangements order: living arrangements, concerning; Residence: transfer of living arrangements; Shared living arrangements
Local authority *see also* Adoption; Care proceedings; Social worker
accommodation, provision 492
child in police protection etc 495
inspection 607
adoption placement order 185, 260, 272
change of local authority 264
effects 269
mandatory application 261
optional application 261
advice and assistance *see* Advice and assistance
application by, procedure *see* Public Law Outline
appropriate authority 580, 1524
assessment, Guidance 2548
befriending of child, by officer 481
care plan (s 31A care plan), statutory duty to prepare 544
child ceasing to be looked after by *see* Child being looked after
children's home, duties 592, 594
complaint to
advocacy services 517
procedure 516
scope of complaints procedure 517
cooperation with other authorities 518
declaration absolving from duty to consult and provide information 611
default, order declaring 611
designated 160, 520, 540
designation 540
disabled child, duty 658
disclosure of records 2545
duty to consult with children's guardian 1706
education supervision order application *see* Education supervision order
family centre, provision duty 660
forced marriage protection order applicant 32
foster parent *see* Local authority foster parent
High Court's inherent jurisdiction, application 630

Local authority—*continued*
- 'in care of' 554
- information to other authority, child no longer looked after 509
- information to Secretary of State 610
- investigation by 1524
  - joint investigations 1755
  - time for filing statements and documents 1525
- investigation of child's circumstances 554, 580
  - wishes and feelings of child 581
- looked after child *see* Child being looked after
- maintenance contributions where residence order in force 656
- meaning 635, 675
- party, as 556
- private fostering, duties 595
- provision of services by 484, 657
- public authority for human rights 997
- reduction of need for care proceedings etc 659
- representations to, procedure 516
- research by 610
- review of cases by 514
- section 8 orders, restrictions 450
- section 37 direction, and 556
- secure accommodation *see also* Secure accommodation
  - application by 2434
  - duty to inform parents etc 2434
- services by *see* Services, provision of
- special guardian
  - assessment of need for support 479
  - investigation and report on applicant 474
  - support services 479
- voluntary organisation's accommodation, duties *see also* Voluntary organisation 592
- wardship etc application, leave required 630
- welfare of child, duty
  - accommodation by health authority etc 612
  - accommodation by residential care home etc 612
  - general 496
- welfare report from, court's power 434

Local authority foster parent 451
- number of children, limits 676
- placement with 660, 2407
- refuge, provision by 585
- section 8 order application 452
- section 8 order, leave to apply 450

Local education authority
- accommodation
  - inspection 607
  - notification of local authority 611
- cooperation with other authorities 518
- education supervision order
  - application for 553
  - designated in 553
- secure accommodation 2433, 2435

Local Health Board
- accommodation, notification of local authority 611
- cooperation with other authorities 518
- meaning 636

Local housing authority
- cooperation with other authorities 518

Local Safeguarding Children Boards
- research into functions or performance of 610

Location orders 178, 181, 184, 365, 630, 1549, 1551, 2614

Looked after child *see* Child being looked after

Lord Chancellor
- attachment of earnings, officer designated by 343

***Lucas* direction** 543

Lugano Convention 1988
- admissibility and proof 694
- appeal on point of law 692
- assets, interim relief 695
- definition 688
- foreign judgment recognition
  - meaning of judgment 695
- maintenance order enforcement 689, 694, 1953
- recognition and enforcement of maintenance orders under 690
- State bound by the 689

Lump sum order
- application for 644
- civil partnership, applied to
  - Family Court 764, 765
  - High Court / County Court 730, 731
- discharge etc of periodical payments order, on 650
- divorce, on 54, 1160, 1167
  - age limit 1197
  - court power 1200
  - matters for court to regard 1177
- failure to maintain, for 1195
- Family Court, in 650, 811, 1107
  - age of child 813
  - agreed payments 815
  - interim order 818
  - periodical payments order variation etc, on 819
- family provision from deceased's estate, for 1019, 1020, 1026, 1027
- financial relief for child
  - power to enforce order 646
- financial relief order (for child) 12
- instalments 650, 1167, 1199
- number of applications for 1169
- person over 18, for 646, 656
- provisions for 650
- qualifying periodical maintenance orders, and 1062

Magistrates' court
- appeal from
  - Child Support Act 1991, under 198
- maintenance order
  - reciprocating country, provisional order against payer in 74
  - registration 1916

Maintenance *see also* Child support; Financial provision; Financial relief order (for child); Maintenance agreement; Maintenance order; Periodical payments order
- application for, Family Court 811

Maintenance—*continued*
child of family, for 811, 812, 816, 1106, 1107
Children Act, and 817
divorce, etc, on *see also* Divorce 50, 1160
child support maintenance *see* Child support
child, of, liability for 1251
contributions to cost of 519, 666
local authority, by, where residence order 656
duty to maintain *see also* Child support 400
failure to provide
civil partnership
High Court / County Court 747, 748
jurisdiction 747
Family Court
ground 811
interim order 1195, 1198, 1203
jurisdiction 1194
lay justices' powers 25
marriage, during 811
orders on 1194
warrant of execution, permission for 1935
habitual residence 2778
income support, and 1251
liability for 1251
meaning 401
pending suit 1163, 1198, 1199
application 50
arrears 1203
civil partnership breakdown (High Court / County Court) 745
commencement of proceedings 1193
conversion to final order 1163
divorce, etc, on 1151, 1163, 1198
procedure 51
repayment 1204
reasonableness 2867
recovery of contributions towards child's maintenance 498
Scotland 2869
wife or husband, of, liability for 1251
Maintenance agreement
alteration 408
child support, and 403, 407
civil partnership 758
alteration 759
validity 759
divorce, etc, on 1205, 1207
alteration 1206
financial provision for child, containing
alteration 481
meaning 408, 1206
variation of 654
after death of one party 20, 655, 1207
applicant 20
application 14, 20
court powers (FPR) 1855
death of one party 1419
during parents' lives 20, 654, 1206
EU cases, jurisdiction 1206
Family Court's power 654, 1206
High Court / County Court procedure 21
jurisdiction 654
order 21, 1206, 1207
Maintenance Enforcement Business Centre (MEBC)
reciprocal enforcement 1955, 1973
Maintenance order *see also* Periodical payments order 340, 359
abroad, confirmation of order made, in England *see also* 'foreign' *below* 1091
application by interested party 1062
arrears *see also* Maintenance order enforcement
committal for 1078, 1079
leave for enforcement 1203
registered order 1068
attachment of earnings order, and *see also* Attachment of earnings order 339, 342, 344, 345, 346, 347, 2015, 2020
cessation of 346
County Court rules *see* Attachment of earnings order: County Court, in
definition 340, 353
Family Court, special provisions 349
child
power to vary order 1202
child support, and *see* Child support
confirmation of order made outside UK 67, 1082, 1083
Convention country, and 689, 694, 1104
currency for foreign order 693, 1099
discharge and variation 70, 1069, 1071, 1083
procedure 70
divorce, on *see* Divorce
enforcement *see* 'arrears' *above*; Maintenance order enforcement
evidence
admissibility of, given in Convention country 1114
admissibility of, given in reciprocating country 1098
obtaining for proceedings in UK 1115
transmission between courts 1069
Family Court *see* Family Court: maintenance order
foreign *see also* Maintenance order enforcement: reciprocal
central authority, communication with 1449
confirmation of order in England 76
judgment, decision, etc enforceable by magistrates 251, 355
reciprocal arrangements *see* Maintenance order enforcement: reciprocal
recognition of, under Conventions 89, 689, 690, 694
interim order 1125, 1163, 1195, 1198, 1203, 1204
court powers 818
jurisdictional issues 1449
made on or after date prescribed 404
meaning 250, 340, 1074, 1254
reciprocal enforcement, for 1952
means of payment order 1060, 1075, 1111
methods of payment 1062
opportunity to make representations 1062
periodical, meaning 1060
power to prohibit extension of term 1196
prohibition of any restriction on right to apply 1206

Maintenance order—*continued*
proof
documents, of 1073
provisional (payer resident out of UK) 66, 1081, 1083, 1088
qualifying periodical maintenance order 1062
reciprocal enforcement *see* Maintenance order enforcement: reciprocal
registered foreign judgment 251, 355
registration *see* Maintenance order registration
remarriage of party 1215
revocation, variation etc, Family Court 1083
Maintenance order enforcement
abroad 78
admissibility of evidence 1114
appropriate method, order for 120
attachment of earnings *see also* Attachment of earnings order 105
Brussels/Lugano/2007 Hague, and
jurisdictional issues 1449
respondent not appearing 1445
charging order *see* Charging order
collecting officer 1068
committal 1078
Commonwealth countries, and 64, 1080, 1940
Convention country, claim for recovery 1104
application by UK resident 81, 1105
claim against UK resident 81, 1105, 1106
evidence, provisions as to 1116
Family Court powers 1105, 1106, 1111, 1113, 1116
former spouse, application by 1107
means of payment order 1106
Northern Ireland, in 1108, 1109, 1114
payer resident outside England and Wales 1113
transfer, variation etc of orders 1109, 1111
Convention, Brussels/Lugano/2007 Hague, and 89, 689, 1953
Denmark, made by court in 91, 2440
England and Wales, within, of foreign order 72, 91
court for 91
EU Member State 1970
jurisdiction 91
Family Court order abroad 1958
Family Court powers as to foreign order 1082, 1083, 1084, 1110, 1111, 1113
Family Court, in
authority for 1066
Children Act, of order made under 656
collecting officer's powers 1068
DPMCA money order, and 823
High Court/County Court order registered in 1075, 1076, 1077, 1079
lay justice's powers 102
Practice Direction (FPR) 1959
foreign order 1084, 1110
confirmation application 67, 1082
decision under Maintenance Regulation 2443
jurisdiction issues 2442
procedure 68
provisional 67, 1082

Maintenance order enforcement—*continued*
foreign order—*continued*
registration application 65, 72
variation and revocation 82
FPR 1910
High Court/County Court order 1959
High Court/County Court, in 1060, 1076, 1079, 1080
income support recipient 1252
interest 693, 1066, 1076
judgment summons 118, 1203
leave for, circumstances 1203
magistrates' court powers as to foreign order 67, 68
means of payment order 119, 1075, 1111
methods of payment 1094
Northern Ireland *see* Northern Ireland: maintenance order enforcement
payment of monies collected 1094
power to enforce 1080
proof of documents 1084
provisional order 66, 1081
publicity restrictions 809
reciprocal 1087, 1093
admissibility of documents 1957
admissibility of foreign evidence 1098, 1114
alteration of order 1093
appeals 1097
application for transmission to reciprocating country 71, 1087, 1088, 1943
confirmation of provisional order made abroad 1091, 1943
Convention country *see* 'Convention country, claim for recovery' *above*
countries, table of 59
currency conversion 1099
declaration under EU Maintenance Regulation 2874
declaration under Hague Convention 2007 2835
definitions 1102, 1118
discharge of UK order 78
discharge, meaning 1103
enforcement provisions 1110
English order 694, 1957, 1971
EU Maintenance Regulation *see* Maintenance Regulation
EU, within 1449, 1970, 1971, 2865
evidence 1098, 1115, 1116, 1118
evidence request 1957
extension to other countries 1117
Family Court jurisdiction 1088, 1100
Family Court rules 1101
foreign order, jurisdiction issues 2442
FPR provisions 1939, 1942
Hague Convention on international recovery 2488
Hague Convention on the International Recovery of Child Support 2007 2835
jurisdictional issues 1449
magistrates' court jurisdiction 74
magistrates' court rules
FPR provisions 1940

Maintenance order enforcement—*continued*
reciprocal—*continued*
magistrates' court rules—*continued*
variation etc of UK order 1100
meaning 1952
methods of payment 1093
non-appearance of defendant living abroad 1100
non-EU states, between 2835
obtaining evidence for UK proceedings 1115
payer not in UK 1088, 1097
periodical payments in arrears 1946
Practice Direction (FPR) 1959
proof of order made abroad 1099
provisional order by magistrates 75, 1088, 1118
reciprocating countries 1087, 1103, 1104
registration in UK 1066, 1091
regulations, list 2436
remarriage, effect 1118
Republic of Ireland, with *see* Republic of Ireland
Scotland, restrictions 1101
Secretary of State power 1253
statement of possible grounds of opposition 1093
tracing payer 1969
transfer of orders 1109
transitional provisions 1103, 1104, 1971
transmission of UK order 71, 1088
USA, with *see* United States of America: maintenance order, reciprocal enforcement
variation and revocation of UK order 78, 1089, 1100, 1943
Republic of Ireland, and 1080
transmission of UK order 71
UK, in, of foreign order *see also* 'reciprocal' *above* 689, 1080, 1091
FPR provisions 1940
UK, within *see also* Attachment of earnings order 1066
jurisdiction allocation 2446
writ of fieri facias 112, 1203
Maintenance order registration
application 1066, 1075
cancellation 1071, 1077, 1096
Commonwealth countries, and 64, 1080, 1087, 1940
Convention, Brussels/Lugano/2007 Hague, and 89, 689, 1953
countries, table of 59
date from which order takes effect 1080
directions, court power 1957
discharge of registered order 70, 1069, 1071, 1917
duty to keep the register 1073
English order 71
provisional, respondent abroad 66, 1081
EU Maintenance Regulation, effect of 1970, 1971
European Union/EFTA, and 689, 694
court directions 1956
Maintenance order registration—*continued*
Family Court orders, of, in High Court 1074, 1075
cancellation 1077
notices by designated officer, form 1075
variation of 1077, 1111
Family Court, in 104
foreign order, registration in England 72
Commonwealth countries 65, 1080
provisional order, confirmation 67, 1082
FPR 1910
grounds supporting application 1916
High Court/County Court orders, of, in Family Court 104, 1074, 1075
application 1916
cancellation 1077
discharge 1917
FPR 1916
notices by designated officer, form 1075
variation 1076, 1917
magistrates' court rules 1073
magistrates' court orders, of, in High Court
interest on sums recoverable 1076
method 1916
Northern Ireland *see* Northern Ireland: maintenance order registration
notice of variation etc 1071
periodical payments arrears 1954, 1955
person entitled to receive payments 1076
procedure 78
proof of documents 1073
provisional order from reciprocating country, confirmation 76, 1091
Maintenance Regulation not applicable 77
reciprocal enforcement, for 68, 72, 1066, 1091
cancellation 1096
enforcement 72
transfer of orders 1109
Republic of Ireland *see* Republic of Ireland
Scotland 68, 1066
County Court order 1912
FPR 1911
High Court order 1911
Scottish order 1913
'shall be registered' 1080
sheriff court, in 1066
summary court, in 1066, 1067, 1073
UK, in different parts of 1064, 1066
variation of registered order 82, 1069, 1071, 1076, 1077, 1094, 1111, 1113, 1917, 1955
Maintenance Regulation 251, 355, 406, 689, 1285, 1444, 1970, 1971, 2857, 2865
applications available under 2882
procedure in England and Wales 2442
forms 89
Hague Child Support Convention 2007 89
Northern Ireland 2857
regulations 2438
Scotland 2857
Manager
liability for offence by company 633

Mandamus, order of
application for 1237
claim procedure 2253
default order on local authority, enforceable by 611
High Court jurisdiction 192, 1236
MARAC *see* Multi-agency risk assessment conference
***Mareva* injunction** *see* Freezing injunction
Marital status
declaration of 869
application 45
court for 45
order 45
procedure 45, 1421
Marriage *see also* Cohabitant; Forced marriage; Remarriage
breakdown of, as ground for divorce 45, 1147
child in, not a 'child' for child support 416
civil partnership, converted from
grounds on which void or voidable 1157
consent to
application 131
court 131
procedure (FPR) 1426
respondents 131
service 132
dissolution on presumption of death 1160
jurisdiction of courts 827
end *see* Divorce; Judicial separation; Nullity
engagements
enforceability 1041
gifts 1041
Married Women's Property Act 1882, application of 1123
property rights on termination 1041
foreign gender change 956
gender, change in 954
legitimation by *see* Legitimation
maintenance failure, etc, financial provision application *see* Financial provision
nullity application 1383
polygamous 1123, 1157
FLA relief applies 898
matrimonial relief for 1213
same-sex *see* Civil partnership; Same-sex marriage
validity 285
declaration 45, 869
void 1156
child of 1055, 1059
voidable 1157, 1159
Married woman
housekeeping money, share in 1123
property rights, declaration and enforcement of 14, 1122, 1216
financial order proceedings, in 1420
Marry, right to 1010
Matrimonial and civil partnership proceedings 839, 1379, 1380
amended petitions 1382, 1389
amendment of answer 1389
appeal *see* Appeal: matrimonial / civil partnership proceedings

Matrimonial and civil partnership proceedings—*continued*
application by respondent
permission not required 1382
application for information 1390
application in the same proceedings 1389
application procedure 1379
Practice Direction 1406
application to amend 1389
applications and orders 1399
case management *see* Case management: matrimonial / civil partnership proceedings
cease to be party, direction to 1389
consent to decree 1382
co-respondent 1383
costs *see also* Costs 1395
costs of amendment 1389
death, decree of presumption of 1285
declarations of status etc *see* Declaration
decree absolute 1402
application 1404
decree nisi
application 1391
final, making 1402
intervention to show cause after 1154, 1401
rescission application 1155
defended 1380, 1385, 1392, 1410
defended and undefended 1386
dismissal of party from suit 1383
evidence *see* Evidence: decree nisi or conditional order, for; Evidence: matrimonial / civil partnership proceedings
Family Division, assigned to 1250
financial provision order *see also* Divorce; Financial remedy 1167
forms of court determination under Part 7 1399
freezing order and *see* Freezing injunction: matrimonial financial order proceedings, and
further applications 1381
further evidence 1382
further information, order for 1390
hearing 1390
hearing in public 1391
right to transcript 1391
how respondent can make application 1389
improper association 1383
interests of child or protected party 1391
jurisdiction 827
reciprocal enforcement 2771
limitation on applications 1381
maintenance pending suit 1163
maintenance, failure to provide *see* Financial provision; Maintenance
matrimonial and non-matrimonial property distinguished 1182
'matrimonial cause', meaning (FPR) 1283
meaning (FPR) 1285
notice of consent 1386
notice of hearing 1391
order that hearing be in private 1391
overriding objective 1396
parties 1382

Matrimonial and civil partnership proceedings—*continued*
permission for second application 1382
permission out of time to file answer 1387
permission under r 7.7 1382
permission where r 7.20 certificate signed 1387
personal financial matters 1391
procedural guides 1390
procedure 1379
procedure for permission application 1387
publicity and reporting restrictions 1039
Queen's Proctor, action by 1154
reconciliation statement, filing of 1381
re-hearing 1399
religious marriage 1400
representation of protected parties 1688
rescission of decree nisi
respondent misled 1155
rescission of order 1399
review or re-hearing of orders and certificates 1399
rules of pleading 1386
section 8 order jurisdiction 839
semantics 1379
separation cases 1400
service of application 1382, 1703
simplification 1379
statutory provision 1379
stay of 827, 831, 1386, 1398
child arrangements order enforcement, effect on 834
structure of Part 7 and its PD 1379
supplemental petitions 1389
terminology 1380
test for permission application 1387
time for filing answer 1387
undefended 1392
withdrawal of application 1382, 1853
withdrawal of consent 1386
r 7.20 certificate signed, after 1386
Matrimonial home *see also* Exclusion requirement; Family home; Occupation order; Tenancy
criminal liability 877
duration of rights 875
meaning 875, 1126
taxation of costs *see* Costs
tenancy, transfer of 41, 1132
transfer *see* Property adjustment order
treatment of one spouse's rights and obligations as those of the other spouse 875
Matrimonial order
definition (FPR) 1283
pilot scheme for online divorce 1379
McKenzie friend 1529
fees 2159
Practice Guidance 2618
Means of payment order
appeal 120
application 119
attachment of earnings, and 1060
availability 119, 1060
disclosure of debtor's address 120
Family Court, in 1075, 1111
procedure 119
Media *see also* Freedom of press; Reporting restriction order
attendance 248, 1516, 1843
financial dispute resolution appointment, at 1442
first appointment *see* Financial remedy: first appointment: attendance of media representatives at
Court of Protection and the *see* Court of Protection: media, and the
disclosure of court documents 1756
discretion to exclude 1844
'duly accredited' representatives 1836
privacy, balancing exercise with regard to 628
publication of information, restrictions 244
Mediation *see also* Alternative dispute resolution; Non-court dispute resolution
appeals 2193
authorised family mediator 1311
in-court family, Guidance 2628
issues, and 1762
Mediation Directive
FPR 1976
Practice Direction 1979
Mediation information and assessment meetings *see* MIAMs
Medical evidence
capacity *see* Capacity: medical evidence
non-attendance, to justify 1519
Medical examination
child assessment order, under 571
consent to 572
emergency protection order, under 573
consent to 573
female genital mutilation 534
interim care /supervision order, and 557
nullity proceedings 1397
occupation /non-molestation order, adjournment for 893
supervision order, under 671
consent to 671
Medical examiner
appointment 1397
expert, as 1397
Medical records
disclosure 247
parents, disclosure of 247
private and family life, right to respect for 247
Medical treatment
adult lacking capacity
deprivation of liberty for life sustaining treatment 1219
urgent application 2576
child nearly 16 years old 918
consent to 918
experimental 1548
inherent jurisdiction 1546
supervision order, under 671
withdrawal of, persistent vegetative state etc cases 227
Mental capacity *see* Capacity
Mental disorder *see also* Capacity 1681
contempt of court, and *see* Contempt of court: mental illness, and

Mental disorder—*continued*
family provision 1020
meaning 407, 487, 1157, 1158
remand for report 893
Mental nursing home
accommodation in, inspection 607
research on 610
secure accommodation 2433, 2435
MF *see* McKenzie friend
MIAMs 12, 13, 20, 50, 52, 153, 811, 1312, 1317, 1443, 2628
applications 1309, 1314
attendance 1317
authorised family mediator, finding a 1316
bankruptcy 1316
child
private law proceedings 1313
conduct of meetings 1311
direction to attend 1312
domestic violence 1315
exemptions 1309, 1311, 1314
financial remedy (ancillary relief), proceedings for 1314
funding attendance 1317
inquiries by the court 1317
legal aid 1317
practice direction 1312
Millionaire's defence *see* Disclosure: millionaire's defence
Mingling of property 1182
Minor *see also* Child
consent to marriage *see* Marriage
disabled *see* Disabled child
Family Division jurisdiction 1250
ward of court *see* Ward of court; Wardship
Molestation *see* Non-molestation order
Money *see* Cash; Money claim; Money judgment; Payment
recovered for child/patient *see* Settlement
Money claim
claim form 2039
designated
enforcement procedure 2023
Money judgment *see also* Judgment debt; Judgment summons
enforcement
Commonwealth countries 83
European enforcement order 100, 101
execution 801
FPR 1928
means of enforcement court considers appropriate 1928
order to attend court 1929
reciprocal 86, 87
registration in High Court 98
rule or practice direction otherwise requires 1928
transfer of orders 1929
within UK 97
Money order
payment by instalments 1137
Mortgage *see also* Land
dwelling house, of
mortgagee's action, joinder of parties 895
Mortgage—*continued*
dwelling house, of—*continued*
mortgagee's action, service of notice 895
mortgagee's rights 29, 894
payments made by non-owner spouse 874, 881
proprietary rights of spouses, application details 1122, 1216
rights of occupation
priority of charge 876
Mortgagee
occupation order, service of 1470
Mother *see also* Parent
assisted reproduction, meaning for 978
parental responsibility of 424
surrogate 1256
teenage mothers and their children 531
Multi-agency risk assessment conference 543, 552, 888, 900, 1481, 1513
Guidance 2636

Name
care/supervision order, no change during 549
change of forename 448
change of surname 446, 470, 549
allocation of application for permission 549
leave to change 470
method of application for leave 471
procedural rules (FPR) 1644
child arrangements order, and 470
publication *see* Publicity
National Health Service trust
accommodation
inspection 607
notification of local authority 611
cooperation with other authorities 518
secure accommodation 2433
application by 2435
National Youth Advocacy Service 435
Protocol with Cafcass 2573
role 1530
Natural parents
best interests of the child 441
Needs of child
assessment of 657
court to have regard to 422
financial, financial provision order 812
Neglect
prevention of 658
Negligence
consent orders, drafting 1449
New Zealand
payments under New Zealand court order 1941
Niqab *see* Veil
Nominal order 1168
Non-Contracting States
Hague Convention 1996 2746
Non-Convention country
return of child application 179, 1611
Non-court dispute resolution *see also* Alternative dispute resolution; MIAMs 1507
Child Arrangements Programme 1579
confidentiality of statements by parties 1513
court's duty and powers 1308

Non-court dispute resolution—*continued*
court's duty to consider 1309
encouragement to use 1308
facilitation 1308
privilege for *see* Privilege: non-court dispute resolution, for
Non-molestation order *see also* Guardianship order; Hospital order 886
agreement to marry/form civil partnership, and
evidence of 889
termination, effect 886
applicant 886
application 27
procedure 1469
withdrawal of 1853
arrest
no power attachable 30, 888
power of 888, 892, 1471
warrant of 892
associated persons 886, 896, 897
breach
criminal offence 30, 128, 888
person under 18 130
child applicant 888
child, protection of 886, 896
civil partners 886
contempt proceedings 896
court power 29, 886
criteria 887
definitions 27, 897
delivery to police station 893
duration 30, 887, 888, 889
enforcement *see* 'breach' *above*
ex parte, court power 889
form of injunction 797
forms 888
hearing 29
meaning 886
medical examination, remand for 893
'molesting', meaning of 887
power to adjourn hearing for consideration of penalty 1474
proceedings following arrest 1472
scope 29, 887
service of application 888
certificate of service 1470
notice, on 1470
service of order 31, 888
agreed protocol 163, 2631
personal service 1471
service on the police 1472
undertaking 30, 890
enforcement 31, 890
variation and discharge 893
violence threatened or used 890
without notice, court power 28
wording 887
Non-party
notice of application to 1600
Northern Ireland
adoption 312
recognition of judgments and orders 282
registration of 321
Northern Ireland—*continued*
attachment of earnings, Family Court jurisdiction 349
Children Act, application to 639
civil partnership 712
custody order, meaning 399
effect of orders 632
enforcement
judgment of High Court/County Court, of 97, 98
maintenance order *see* 'maintenance order enforcement' *below*
European Convention, central authority for 369
Hague Abduction Convention 1980
central authority for 364
court for application 365
maintenance order enforcement *see also* 'maintenance order registration' *below* 1066, 1068, 1069, 1071, 1089, 1094, 1111
Convention country, and 1108, 1109, 1114
means of payment order 1112
provisional order confirmation 1092
maintenance order registration 68, 696, 1066, 1073, 1913
cancellation 70, 697, 1072
County Court order 1912
FPR 1911
payments 697, 698
procedural table 68
rules for procedure 1073, 1101, 1117
variation or discharge 698, 1069, 1094, 1100, 1112
Maintenance Regulation 2857
parental responsibility, recognition and enforcement of judgments 2505
Part I order
duration 851
enforcement 854
jurisdiction 848, 849, 852
meaning 837
refusal of application 850
registration 853
registration variation or cancellation 853
social security benefit recovery from person in 1063
Note
judge, of, for appeal 799
Notice
application *see* Application notice
change of solicitor 1827
date of hearing 1520
family proceedings, methods (FPR) 1853
hearing, of (matrimonial/civil partnership application) 1391
'notify' and 'notification' 1706
order made without 2079
penal *see* Penal notice
Notice of appeal
Supreme Court 2356
form and filing 2357
service 2357
NSPCC
care order application by 520

NSPCC—*continued*
child assessment order application by 571
emergency protection order application by 572
supervision order application by 520
Nullity
appeal 2236
application procedure
defended cause 49
undefended cause 45
civil partnership 703
application procedure 1379, 1383
medical examination 1397
clean break 1184
consent to marriage, and 1157
decree nisi 1148, 1154, 1159
family provision from deceased's estate, and 1033
financial provision on 1160
commencement of proceedings 1193
matters for court 1177
pension sharing 1174
foreign law, marriage governed by 1158
general powers of court after proceedings 1154
grounds for 1156, 1157
incapacity to consummate 1157, 1214
medical examination 1411
interim gender recognition certificate ground 950
intervention of Queen's Proctor 1154
jurisdiction 827
marriage 1379, 1383
medical examination 1397
mental disorder, and 1157
non-consummation 1157, 1214
overseas, financial relief after 1124
application for leave 58, 1125
procedure 57
pregnancy of respondent by another 1157
proprietary rights declaration, and 14, 1122, 1216
recognition 863
granted in Britain 863
granted overseas 863
meaning of annulment for 868
transitional 867
sale of property order 1173, 1177
transfer of tenancy *see* Tenancy
undefended cause procedure 47
venereal disease, and 1157
void marriage, grounds for 1156
voidable marriage
effect of decree 1159
grounds for 1157
Nuptial agreement *see also* Antenuptial agreement; Prenuptial agreement 1179
need 1180
Nursing home
accommodation
inspection 607, 633
research on 610
secure accommodation 2433
application for 2435
NYAS *see* National Youth Advocacy Service

Occupation
cessation of rights 877
right of *see also* Matrimonial home
prohibition or restriction of *see also* Occupation order 29
Occupation order *see also* Guardianship order; Hospital order 877, 879, 881, 883
additional provisions, court power 885
agreement to marry /form civil partnership 889
termination, effect 877
applicant has estate /interest 29, 877, 894
applicant with no right to occupy 30, 879, 881, 883, 884
application 28, 885
procedure 1469
withdrawal of 1853
arrest
power of 30, 891, 892, 894, 1471
warrant of 892
associated persons 897
'balance of harm' test 879, 881, 883, 884, 885
breach
contempt proceedings 896
remand 909
child applicant 888
child, protection of 878, 880, 882, 883, 884, 896, 898
civil partners 877
cohabitants 881, 882, 884
meaning 896
connected person 895
definition 894
contempt proceedings 896
court's powers 879, 884, 885
criteria 879, 881, 884
death of spouse /civil partner 878, 881, 882, 908
definitions 896, 897
delivery to police station 893
duration 30, 889
cohabitants 882, 884
spouses 878, 881, 883
enforcement *see* 'breach' *above*
ex parte, court power 889
exclusion from area 29
extension of home rights 879
furniture /contents obligation 885
hearing 29
home rights as charge, effect 879
matters for court 878, 880, 882, 884
meaning 885
medical examination, remand for 893
mortgagee's action
joinder of parties 895
service of notice 895
mortgagee's rights 29, 894
neither cohabitant right to occupy 884
neither spouse /civil partner right to occupy 883
non-molestation order, court to consider making 886
outgoings /regular payments obligation 885
penal notice, when mandatory 30
power to adjourn hearing for consideration of penalty 1474
proceedings following arrest 1472

Occupation order—*continued*
rent/mortgage payment obligation 885
repair and maintenance 885
scope of orders 29
service of application
certificate of service 1470
notice, on 1470
service of order 31
personal service 1471
Protocol terms 31
service on the police 1472
undertaking 30, 890
enforcement 31, 890
variation and discharge 893
without notice, court power 28
Offer to settle *see also* Part 36 offers and payments; Payment into court
financial order 229
Office
public, restraint from acting 1237
Officer of the service *see* Cafcass officer
Official Solicitor
advocate to court, request to appoint 2564
amicus curiae, as 568
appointment 568, 1515, 2716
appointment of children's guardian 1697, 1707
children's guardian, as
appointment, Guidance 2552
costs *see* Costs: Official Solicitor's
guardian of child's estate, as 2070
inherent jurisdiction 2716
litigation friend 2716
litigation friend, as 1686, 1687, 1688, 1701, 1702, 2064
representation of protected parties 1683
vulnerable adult 2716
Opinion evidence *see* Expert evidence
Oral evidence *see* Evidence
Oral examination *see* Examination
Order *see also* Judgment; Recognition of judgments and orders
absence of party, made in 1834, 2079
age of child, and 618
agreed 1527
applications, repeated 618
breach of, committal for 125
Channel Islands, effect 632
Child Arrangements Programme (CAP) 1527
committal *see* Committal order
conditions on 1137
copy 1832
court power, own initiative 1321, 1507, 2037
setting aside, etc 2037
court's considerations on making etc 422
court's powers to make 854
custody *see* Custody (of child)
date effective 1858
default of local authority, of 611
drawing up and filing 1857
duration 617
effect 617
between parts of UK 632

Order—*continued*
enforcement
maintenance order *see* Maintenance order enforcement
order made in civil proceedings (CPR), general rules 2279
order made in family proceedings (FPR), general rules 1927
error or omission, correction of 1859
Family Court *see* Family Court: order 1136
final and conclusive between the parties 1136
garnishee *see* Garnishee order
interim *see* Interim order
Isle of Man, effect 632
'judgment or order', meaning of 1234
judgment summons *see* Judgment summons
jurisdiction (CA 1989) 621
location *see* Location order
maintenance *see* Maintenance order; Periodical payments order
mandamus *see* Mandamus, order of
means of payment order *see* Means of payment order
money payment, for, enforcement *see also* Judgment summons 823
name and judicial title of person who made it 1857
'no order' principle 424
non-parties 1757
Northern Ireland, effect 632
pending appeal 565
power to vary or revoke 1321
power to vary, suspend, rescind or revive 1137
recognition, custody etc 369, 393
registration
European Convention, under 370
maintenance order *see* Maintenance order registration
Northern Ireland, in 696
restrictions on applications 618
sale of property, for
on divorce etc 1173
sealing 1136
service *see* Service
service out of jurisdiction 1358
setting aside 212
CPR, under 2079
stamping and sealing 1855
standard requirements (FPR) 1857
Orders
penal warnings 1527
Out of hours application
High Court, Practice Direction 1605
inherent jurisdiction, under 181
medical and welfare decisions for adults lacking capacity 2576
President's Guidance 1522, 2621
Overseas adoption 292, 303, 305
annulment 304, 1664
declaration on 871, 1421
practice direction 1664
Overseas divorce etc, financial relief after 1124
appeal 59
application 57, 1124, 1129

Overseas divorce etc, financial relief after—*continued*
application for leave 58, 1125, 1127
avoidance of transactions 1132
child of family, welfare of 1128
consent order 58, 1129
definitions 1134
interim order 1125
jurisdiction 1126, 1129
matrimonial home, and 1125, 1129
matters for court 1128
orders 59, 1127, 1128, 1129
pension benefits, court regard to 1128
pension compensation sharing order 1127, 1130
pension sharing 1127, 1130
permission application 1424
powers of court 1132
procedure 57
remarriage, and 1124
restraint of anticipated dealings 1133
tenancy transfer 1132
venue 1127
Overseas medical expert, guidelines on instruction of 2638

Parent *see also* Father; Mother
adoption by *see* Adoption: parent, by
capability of, court to consider 422
duty to work to put aside differences 440
fertility services, meaning for *see* Fertility services
financial relief order against 644
income etc, court to consider 648
homicide of one parent by the other 534
maintenance, duty of *see also* Child support; Maintenance 400
meaning 259, 282, 401, 454, 675, 870, 1540
medical records, disclosure of 247
permission to oppose adoption 281, 282
presumption of involvement of both parents 423
wishes of
local authority to ascertain 496
voluntary organisation to ascertain 592
Parentage *see also* Blood test; Paternity; Scientific test
applications 411
declaration 869, 1698
application for 1422
applications in proceedings 1422
child support 410
delay in registration 1424
notification to Registrar General 870
parentage and parenthood in issue 1422
parties to application 1422
procedure 1421, 2085
statutory 428
sufficient personal interest 411
denial 410
disputed (child support) 410
establishment of 2882
inference 410
Parental contact
leave of court for 619

Parental order
agreement 1639
form 1639
mother and any other parent of child, of 990
not required 1638
person who cannot be found, of 991
amendment and revocation 1642
application 1635
applicants 42, 988
parties 1635
two people, made by 990
child's home with the applicants 990
civil partners 42
consent of woman who carried child 1639
directions 1638
without a hearing 1636
expenses reasonably incurred 991
first directions hearing 1636
timing 1636
unless court otherwise directs 1637
Practice Direction 1634
service 1637, 1638
duty for 1637
time for 1637
tracing other parent or person who carried child 1638
Parental order reporter 1711
appointment 1636
powers and duties 1639, 1711, 1720
report 1637
disclosure 1639, 1640
Parental responsibility *see also* Hague Convention 1996
acquisition 564, 572
acts not to be incompatible with orders 425
agreement *see* Parental responsibility agreement
'any other person with' 1635
arrangement for another to have 425
Brussels IIA 2777
care order is in place, where 428, 548
child is accommodated by local authority, where 428
civil partner 701
conditions, subject to 428
declaration under Hague Convention 1562
definition 1503
duty on parents to work to put aside differences 426
father and mother not married to each other at time of child's birth 426
father without
consent to adoption *see* Adoption: consent to: father without parental responsibility
father, of *see* Parental responsibility order; Unmarried father
fertility services, two female parents 424, 429
foreign, child habitually resident in UK
notice of proceedings 1503, 1635
Hague Convention 1996 2740
human rights issues 428
meaning 425
mother, of 424

Parental responsibility—*continued*
non-parent, for
automatic order 431
order *see* Parental responsibility order
passport 2775
person with 424, 578, 585
recognition and enforcement of judgments on
see also Hague Convention 1996 2777
Hague Convention 1996 application 1557, 2505, 2731
High Court jurisdiction 2507
Northern Ireland 2505
Regulation (EC) No 2201/2003, under 2783
same-sex families 427
step-parent, for
automatic order 431
surrender or transfer 425
unmarried father *see* Unmarried father: parental responsibility
Parental responsibility agreement
application to terminate 429
discharge application procedure 142
duration 618
effect of 426
form of 2503
formalities of 426, 2504
prescribed form 429
record and copies 2504
recording in prescribed manner 429
step-parent 430
Parental responsibility order 426, 618
appeal 144
applicant 142
application for 142, 426, 429
application to terminate 429
court and judge 142
directions 143
discharge
application procedure 142
permission to seek
child's understanding 429
procedure where leave is given 429
duration 426
father, on application of 427
form 143
joinder 143
jurisdiction *see* Jurisdiction: parental responsibility order
order 144
parties 1491
procedure 142
respondents 143
second female parent, for
automatic order 430
service 143
step-parent 430
suspension, not susceptible to 428
Parenthood
declarations *see* Parentage: declaration: parentage and parenthood in issue
Parenting plan
Child Arrangements Programme 1577
Part I order (FLA)
definitions 860, 861
Part I order (FLA)—*continued*
disclosure of whereabouts of child, court power 856
enforcement 854
dismissal of proceedings 855
stay of proceedings 855
interaction with orders outside jurisdiction 841, 843, 851
jurisdiction 838, 840
meaning 836, 856, 860
particulars of other proceedings, duty to give 860
recognition within UK 852
recovery of child, court power 857
refusal/stay of proceedings 841
registration 853
FPR 1919
inspection of register 1922
Scotland, jurisdiction in 845
Part 8 procedure
allocation 2051
claim form 2043
contents 2049
defendant not named 2050
issue 2052
disposal of claim 2049
evidence 2050
form of evidence 2049
objection to 2048, 2051
pleading the claim 2049
postal packet, claim relating to 2059
Rules not applying 2051
service 2050
switching of claim to appropriate procedure 2048
types of claim 2047, 2052
'unlikely to involve a substantial dispute of fact' 2048
written evidence 2049
Part 18 procedure 1728
form for application by application notice 1332
Practice Direction 1732
Part 19 procedure 1736
Practice Direction 1739
Part 36 offers and payments
disclosure 2206
Particulars of claim 2040, 2046
form for defence to be served with 2041
Partner, civil *see* Civil partnership
Partnership
charging order, and *see* Charging order: partnerships
claim by or against 2045
Party *see also* Respondent
anonymity 2142
attendance *see* Attendance
child as *see* Child: party, as
children, proceedings relating to 1490
death *see* Death
discharge 1500
exclusion 2359
financial remedy (ancillary relief) proceedings, adding or removing 1450

Party—*continued*
forced marriage protection order application 1479
joinder *see* Joinder of party
loss of self-control 620
matrimonial and civil partnership proceedings 1383
statutory provision 1383
meaning 1249, 1382, 1525, 1530
overriding objective of court, duty to help 1278
personal details, non-disclosure application 1852
proceedings, to 1539
steps to be taken by, court approval 1521
Passport
child for, without adult signature 2566
impounding 57, 1210, 1236, 1243, 1744, 2087
issue of, ward of court 1633
parental responsibility 2775
surrender of 859
Patent
revocation appeal to Supreme Court 2363
Paternity *see also* Blood test; Parentage; Scientific test
legal aid 440
tests to establish 919
funding 920
Pathway plan 503, 504, 665, 2399, 2414
child ceasing to be looked after 665
preparation 2415
matters to be dealt with in 2427
meaning 506
Patient *see* Protected party
Payment
child/protected party, for, approval of court 2067
instalments, by *see* Instalment
interim 2087
means of payment order *see* Means of payment order
written offer *see* Payment into court
Payment into court *see also* Recognizance
child/protected party, for
approval of court 2067
control of 2068
condition of order 2036
order, in dispute 2087
Penal notice *see also* Committal order 118, 797, 892, 1473
occupation order, with 30
requirement for 2304
undertaking, requirement for 2314
wording 1988
Pension
attachment of earnings *see* Attachment of earnings order: pension
attachment order 54, 1186, 1457
application under FPR 2010 1456
consent order application under FPR 2010 1456
court powers 1187
information 2523
meaning (FPR) 1430
PPF compensation, and 1192
supplementary provisions 1188

Pension—*continued*
cash equivalent 2452, 2514
civil partnership dissolution, etc, orders 702, 734
compensation attachment order *see* Pension compensation attachment order
compensation sharing order *see* Pension compensation sharing order
earmarking
changed circumstances 2454, 2455
discharge of liability by Board 2456
notices 2453, 2455
reduction in benefits 2454
service of notices 2456
valuation 2452
valuation date 2452
financial remedy (ancillary relief) 51, 1455, 2452
additional state pension 2524
court to have regard to 1186
information 2512, 2513, 2517, 2518, 2519, 2523, 2524
lump sums 1187
splitting 1186
supplementary provisions 1188
transfer credits, and 1188
valuation 2514, 2524
variation of order 1199
person responsible for pension arrangement
meaning 1189
notification duty 2454
resource, as a 1182
service personnel, assignment by 1170, 1210
Pension compensation attachment order 55
application for
copy to PPF Board 1460
consent order 1460
court duty 1461
meaning (FPR) 1430
rules 1460
Pension compensation sharing order 54, 55
appeal against 1213
application for
copy to PPF Board 1460
civil partners 734, 736, 751, 763, 781
restrictions 736
consent order 1460
court duty 1461
court power on divorce or nullity 1176
meaning 1162, 1430
overseas divorce 1130
prohibition if other orders made 1176
rules 1460
valuation 1177
Pension protection fund 741
attachment of PPF compensation, civil partners 743
compensation 1459
meaning 1431
court regard to 1190
civil partners 742
involvement of 1458
pension attachment orders, court power 1192
pension compensation sharing order
appeal 1213

Pension protection fund—*continued*
pension compensation sharing order—*continued*
civil partners, and 736
Pension sharing order 51, 54, 55, 1457
appeal after order effective 1212
appeal, effect of 2457
application under FPR 2010 1455
apportionment of charges 735, 1175
attachment not possible with 1187, 1188
cash equivalent 54
civil partners 734, 781
High Court/County Court 735
consent order application under FPR 2010 1455
court powers 1174, 1200
debits and credits 1264
duty to stay 1175
first appointment, duties of court at 1440
form 1454
implementation 1454
information 2518, 2519, 2520, 2521
meaning (FPR) 1430
notification that order may be made 2518
outline of procedural framework 1453
overseas divorce 1127, 1130
pensions in payment 1175
percentage value 1162
prohibition if other orders made 1175
provision of information 1454
restrictions 735, 1187, 1188, 1201
service 1454
service and objection by pension provider 1454
shareable rights under a specified pension arrangement 1161
shareable state scheme rights 1161
valuation 1175, 2452
valuation date 1265, 2452
value transferred 1264
variation 1199
Periodical payments order *see also* Child support; Financial relief order (for child); Financial remedy; Maintenance order
application for 644
application included in composite financial remedy (ancillary relief) application 1857
arrears
registered foreign order 1954
attachment of earnings *see* Attachment of earnings order
capitalisation on application for clean break 1202
child outside England and Wales, for 656
child support maintenance, interaction with 647, 651, 814, 1197
court powers (FPR) 1855
child, for *see also* Financial relief order (for child) 480, 644
duration and form 1170
maintenance assessment, and 814
civil partnership, applied to
Family Court 764
FPR 1433
High Court/County Court 730
Periodical payments order—*continued*
death, on 754
discharge 644, 651
divorce, on 1160
age limit 1197
child support maintenance, and 1197, 1201
child, for 54
duration 1196
matters for court to regard 1177
pending suit 1163, 1198
repayment 1204
spouse, for 54
variation 1198
duration 647, 1168
failure to maintain, for 1195
interim order 1195
Family Court 811
agreed payments 815
child, for 811, 813, 816
death of payer 814
discharge 823
duration 813
interim 818
parties living apart 816
parties living together 822
recovery by person in Convention country 1105, 1106
revival 821
revocation 819
variation 652, 819, 821
family provision from deceased's estate, for 1019, 1020, 1026
financial relief order (for child) 12
form 1168
interim order 50, 653
joint lives order 1168
magistrates' court 82
'maintenance order' 251
maintenance pending suit 50, 1163
on civil partnership breakdown (High Court/County Court) 745
matrimonial proceedings (FPR) 1433
maximum term 1196
meaning 647
number of applications 1168
'periodical payments', meaning of 401
person over 18, for 646, 651, 656
power to extend term 1202
remarriage, and 1196, 1210
secured 1196
conveyancing counsel, instruction of 1198
discharge, etc 1198
divorce, etc on 1160, 1196, 1198
duration 1169
failure to maintain, for 1194
form 1169
maximum term 1196
meaning 653
number of applications for 1169
power to vary due to death 1202
variation 404, 644, 651
secured, on death of parent 652
Perishable property
sale, order for 2086

Permission
adoption, to oppose *see* Parent: permission to oppose adoption
appeal, to 243, 799, 1235, 1865
conditions 1869, 2196
court bundle 2224
court for application 1864
hearings 2224
limited permission 1866, 2196
magistrates' child support proceedings 1060
no requirement for 1864
once permission is granted 1866
permission not required 1865
procedure for listing applications 1866
refused as without merits application 1864
request for oral hearing 1865
requirement for 1864
respondent's attendance at hearing 1866
without a hearing 1865
application procedure (FPR) 1728, 1732
children's guardian or litigation friend not required 1699
committal for breach of solicitor's undertaking 1989
committal for interference with due administration of justice 1990
committal for making false statement of truth 1991
setting aside or varying witness summons 1783
Perpetrators, children as 625
Persistent vegetative state etc cases
withdrawal of treatment 227
Person with care
meaning 402
Personal protection
emergency protection order *see* Emergency protection order
injunction scope *see also* Harassment 36
police protection *see* Police protection
Personal representative
adoption, and protection of 1058
family provision proceedings, neutrality in 23
legitimation, and protection of 1058
maintenance agreement variation 655
periodical payments order, variation 652
substitution or removal 2269
Petition
judicial separation *see* Judicial separation
nullity *see* Nullity
Physical disabilities 1681
PII *see* Public interest immunity
Pilot Scheme for Online Divorce 46
applications 1379
controlled access 1980
interpretation 1980
matrimonial order
use of term 1379
Practice Direction 1980
proof of marriage 1408, 1981
purpose 1980
Placement *see also* Adoption; Local authority:
adoption placement order 257
agency, by 258
consequences 268

Placement—*continued*
change of surname, limit on 259
child under 6 weeks old 259
connected person
expiry of temporary approval 2408
meaning 2408
suitability as carer 2424
temporary approval as carer 2408
discharge of child arrangements orders 259
embargo on, where revocation application pending 265
foster family, with 2798
Hague Convention or Council Regulation, request under
England or Wales, for placement in 1561
English court, for placement in another Member State 1562
health care 2401
independent fostering agency, delegation to 2409
agreement for 2425
institutional care, in 2798
local authority foster parents *see also* Local authority foster parent 2407
connected person, expiry of temporary approval 2408
connected person, temporary approval as 2408
emergency, in 2408
placement following consideration 2407
pre-conditions 2407
local authority, by 498, 660
general duties where not local authority fostering 2410
general provisions 2402
meaning 499, 2399
notification duty 2404
outside England and Wales 2404
notice of order for 1601
parent, etc, with 2405
child arrangements order, effect 2406
decision 2406
suitability assessment 2406, 2423
support services 2406
'placed for adoption' 265
'placement for adoption' 258
placement plan 2402
matters to be dealt with in 2420
meaning 2399
private foster parent *see* Private foster parent
removal of child
application in pending placement proceedings 270
limit on 259
short breaks 2418
siblings 499
contact between where separated 2420
termination 2405
two routes to 258
unregulated setting, in
duties of local authority 2410
matters for consideration 2425
visits after, local authority duty 2410
voluntary organisation, by 590

Placement order *see also* Adoption; Local authority:
- adoption placement order 185, 260
- adoption agency report 1670
- appeals against 2195
- application 185, 261
  - change of local authority, for 264
  - consolidated with care proceedings 263
  - court that made, to 269
- care order, interaction with 269
- change in circumstances 265
- children's guardian, and 263
- conditions for making 260
- consequences 261
- duration 260, 264
- effect of 269
- final hearing 263
- first directions hearing 263
- form 264
- grant of leave to apply to revoke 265
- local authority required to apply for 262
- preliminary steps to be taken by court 263
- procedural rules 1643
- procedure 263
- removal of child prohibitions 272
- revocation 264
  - procedure 265
- specified proceedings, application is 567
- substitution of local authority 264

Plan
- care *see* Care plan
- placement *see* Placement

PLO *see* Public Law Outline

Police *see* Constable
- abuse
  - disclosure 2647
- disclosure 1510
- radicalisation 2697
- search warrant under CA 1989 633

Police protection 578
- abduction of child in *see also* Recovery order 583
- accommodation for child in 495
- contact 579
- Court of Appeal guidance 580
- designated officer 580, 585
- duration 579
- duties of constable 578
- emergency protection application during 579
- guidance 496, 578
- local authority investigation 580
- meaning 578
- recovery order, application by officer for 584
- significant harm, removal etc to prevent 578
- welfare of child, promotion of under 579

Port alert *see also* Removal of child 179, 181, 184, 859, 1545, 1613

Postal packet
- claim relating to 2059

Power of attorney *see* Enduring power of attorney; Lasting power of attorney

Practice directions
- court bundle 2228
- electronic tagging 2690
- email, communication and filing by 1342

Practice directions—*continued*
- pilot scheme for online divorce 1980

Pre-action protocols 1321

Precedence
- Regulation (EC) No 2201/2003, under 2800

Premises
- entry, order for *see* Entry into premises, etc

Prenuptial agreement *see also* Antenuptial agreement
- maintenance pending suit where 1163

Pre-nuptial agreement
- need 1180

Preservation of property *see* Freezing injunction; Property

Press *see* Media

Presumption of death
- civil partnership 703, 713
- declarations
  - application 1222
  - effect 1223
  - making 1223
  - variation 1224
- information 1227
- intervene, right to 1227
- jurisdiction of courts 827
- marriage, dissolution of 1160
- notice of application 1226
- other determinations 1228
- Presumption of Death Act 2013 1222
  - proceedings under 2272, 2275
- procedure 2273
- revocation of declaration 1224
- variation of declarations 1224

Prevention of disposition order *see also* Avoidance of disposition order
- family proceedings where order unavailable 1744

Prison *see also* Arrest; Committal order; Sentencing; Warrant of committal
- discharge order, County Court 805
- maintenance arrears, for 1078

Privacy *see also* Confidentiality; Private and family life, right to respect for; Private hearing 626
- media, balancing exercise with regard to 628
- right to 1008

Private and family life, respect for *see also* Human rights: private and family life, right to respect for
- gender recognition 946
- medical records 247

Private foster parent
- advice from local authority 595
- disqualification 596
- number of children, limits 676, 678
- prohibition 597
  - appeal 597, 680
- requirement 597, 678
- unsuitability 597

Private fostering
- accommodation in own home 595
- advertisements for 681
- appeals 680
- consent of local authority to 597
  - appeal 680

Private fostering—*continued*
definition 595, 678
disabled child 595
exemptions 678
child subject of proposed adoption 678
foster parent *see* Private foster parent
inspection 596, 607
power of constable to assist 633
insurance, and 681
local authority duties 595
after end of 507
notification requirements 679
public awareness, local authority duty 680
offences 598
power to prohibit 597
privately fostered child 595
requirements, power to impose 597, 678
appeal 680
schools, extension to 681
unsuitable premises 597
visits to child 595, 598
welfare of child 595, 597
monitoring of 596
Private hearing 1527
appeal to Supreme Court, interests of justice 202
appeal, for 808
attendance at 1836
circumstances for 1390
defended matrimonial case 49
Family Court 1835
forced marriage protection order 34, 1481
'in private' 1470, 1837
occupation/non-molestation order 29
publication, information relating to 244
taking charge of child 159
whereabouts of child 157
Private law proceedings
judicial continuity in *see* Judicial continuity: private law proceedings, in
jurisdiction 453, 1503
meaning (FPR) 1490
Privilege *see also* Disclosure 1753
legal advice *see* Legal advice privilege
legal professional *see* Legal professional privilege
litigation *see* Litigation privilege
non-court dispute resolution, for 1754
self-incrimination *see* Self-incrimination privilege
waiver 1754
Probate
entitlement to, legitimacy and 926
procedural rules 2269
Procedural code *see also* Case management
overriding objective 1277, 2031
duty of parties 2032
Procedure Rules
Civil *see* Civil Procedure Rules
Family *see* Family Procedure Rules
Proceedings
allocation *see* Allocation of proceedings
commencement *see* Claim form; Commencement of proceedings
family *see* Family proceedings
publicity, restrictions on 809
Proceedings—*continued*
specified, meaning 567
stay *see* Stay of proceedings
title *see* Title of proceedings
transfer *see* Transfer of proceedings
vexatious/persistent institution of 1245
withdrawal *see* Withdrawal of proceedings
Production 1753
children proceedings 1509
directions as to 1511
Production Centre
issue of claim form 2041
Professional legal adviser
meaning 1563
Professional negligence
consent orders 1449
solicitors 1449
Prohibited steps order 448
application 150
court and judge for 151
definition 438
directions 152
discharge application 150
ex parte application 150
form 152
joinder 151
notice to non-party 151, 1600
respondents 151
restrictions on 450, 451
section 8 order 439
service 151
time-limits 151
variation application 150
without notice procedure 151
Prohibition, order of
application for 800, 1237
claim procedure 2253
leave for, as stay of proceedings 800
court power 192
High Court jurisdiction 1236
Proof *see* Burden of proof; Evidence; Standard of proof
Property *see also* Assets
beneficial ownership, application for declaration of 1261
charge on *see* Charge; Charging order
charging orders 1256
child, of 2732
detention, preservation etc, of *see also* Search order 1742, 2086
court power to make order 789
divorce, order for sale on 1173
engaged couples, rights 1041
human rights, peaceful enjoyment of 1011
husband and wife, of, enforcement etc of rights 1122, 1216
appeals 15
housekeeping, derived from 1123
improvements, contributions to 1215
respondents 15
interim order, court power
CPR 2086
FPR 1742

Property—*continued*
legitimated person, rights to take interest in 1057, 1058
meaning 1028, 1122, 1171
mingling 1182
non-matrimonial property 1182
perishable, sale, order for 2086
settlement, for child, order for 644
transfer of, order for 644
trust, in *see* Trust
Property adjustment order *see also* Settlement; Transfer of property order
civil partnership, applied to
High Court / County Court 732
divorce, on 1160, 1171
conveyancing counsel, use of 1198
court power 1200
procedure 50
remarriage, effect 1196
no power to make interim order 1172
number of applications 1172
overseas divorce etc, after 1127
protective charges 1172
timing of application 1172
Proportionality
adoption 538
Proprietary estoppel 1023
Protected beneficiary
control of money 2068, 2069
meaning 2060
Protected child
inspection of premises 607, 633
Protected party *see also* Capacity
capacity issues 223
medical evidence 224
child as 2060
communication to 1351
compromise by
after issue of proceedings 2073
approval of court 2067
before issue of proceedings 2072
CPR 2059
end of lack of capacity 2066, 2071
evidence, ability to give 1691
expert evidence 1794
expert for 1816
expert, instruction for 1692
family proceedings involving 215
litigation friend 216, 1684
costs 2076
expenses 2076
stage in proceedings for 1685
suitability 216
meaning 215, 219, 1680, 2034, 2060
money recovered, control of 2068, 2074
need for public hearing 2068
non-family proceedings involving 219
notification to 2061
Official Solicitor for
President's Joint Guidance 2622
power to pay monies to another person 1685
Practice Direction 1689, 2070
representation *see* Representation: protected party

Protected party—*continued*
responsible adult 1350
service on
matrimonial / civil partnership order application 1349
non-matrimonial etc application 1354
verification 2061
withdrawal of application involving 1853
Protection measures 2004, 2300
adjustments 2008
notification 2008
appeals *see* Appeal: protection measures
application 2004
application for refusal of recognition etc 2009
form of application 2009
grounds for application 2009
Article 5 certificate 2004
Article 14 certificate 2007
court to which application must be made 2008
form of application 2008
information / documents to be provided 2008
when an application may be made 2007
court to which application should be made 2005
grounds for rectification of certificate 2006
notification of certificate 2006
recognition and enforcement 2003, 2890
request for translation 2005
cost of translation 2005
court to which request is made 2005
review of incoming protection measure 2009, 2014
service *see* Service: protection measures
withdrawal of Art 5 certificate 2006
effect of withdrawal 2006
Protection Measures Regulation 2003
Protection of child *see* Hague Convention 1996
Rules and regulations power 586
Protective measures
Hague Abduction Convention 1980 2781
Provisional and protective measures
Brussels IIA 2787
Regulation (EC) No 4 /2009, under 2870
Provisional measures
Hague Convention 1996 2738
PSO *see* Prohibited steps order
Psychiatric examination
interim care / supervision order, for 557
permission for *see* Expert
supervision order, under 671
Psychiatric treatment
supervision order, under 671
Public
attendance at private hearings 1837
protection of, from serious injury 497
Public authority
Hague Convention 1996 2747
Public funding *see also* Community Legal Service; Legal aid; Legal Aid Agency
Public hearing
directions by court to protect position of witnesses and other parties in 790
fair trial, right to a 1007, 2142

Public hearing—*continued*
general rule 1390, 2142
Public interest
disclosure, withholding in 2110
protection of property, and 1011
Public interest immunity 570, 1511, 1754, 2546
abuse 2652
application for 1512
applications 2652
blanket
rejection 1511
effect 1754
special advocate, and 1758
Public law cases
flexible powers of court to give directions 1507
preparation 1507
timetable for *see* Timetable: public law cases, for
Public Law Outline 423, 1507, 1524, 1533, 2539
care and supervision orders 526
timetable 161
contact order (child in care) timetable 167
emergency protection orders 575
experts, instructing and calling 2544
interim care and supervision orders 558
who the parties are 1500
Public law proceedings
case management in *see* Case management: public law proceedings, in
judicial continuity in *see* Judicial continuity: public law proceedings, in
meaning (FPR) 1490
Public policy
discretion to refuse recognition of divorce 867
recognition of judgments and orders 2873
Regulation (EC) No 2201/2003, under 2789
Publication *see also* Reporting restrictions 246
court order and judgment 248
duration of prohibition on 248
information relating to proceedings in private
matters to be considered 247
inherent jurisdiction *see* Inherent jurisdiction: publication, use to prohibit
injunction preventing *see* Injunction: publication, preventing
material intended or likely to identify child 627
'publish', meaning of 626
statutory restrictions on 1837
Publicity *see also* Disclosure
appeals, private sittings 809
declarations of status 809
identity of ward in criminal proceedings
power of court to restrict publicity 247
judicial proceedings, regulation of reports 1039
maintenance proceedings 809
proceedings, publication of information relating to 244
restrictions on *see* Reporting restrictions
wardship proceedings 1543

Racial origin
adoption, consideration for 255
children's home accommodation, regard for 594
day care, and 660
foster parents, and 660
Racial origin—*continued*
local authority to consider 497
voluntary organisation to consider 592
Radicalisation
alleged 533, 2695
care proceedings 2696
electronic tagging 859
emotional harm 533
fair trial, right to a 533
Family Court 2695
grooming 533, 1544
High Court 1544, 1859
Islamic State 1544
travel to 533, 2695
police 2697
removal of child from UK 859
terrorism 2695
Reasons *see also* Judicial reasoning; Lay justice: reasons for decision by
appeals 2194
contact, denial of 446
decision, for 1831
preparation guidance 2550
exclusion, for 1837
Family Court 2660
guidance for justices on preparation 2550
judgment 539
not attending, for 1834
uncontested cases 2660
Receiver
appointment of
County Court, application in 802
CPR applied 1935
equitable execution, permission for 1203
High Court power 1240
court's power to appoint 2279
Reciprocal enforcement
judgment or order *see* Judgment
Maintenance Enforcement Business Centre (MEBC) 1955, 1973
maintenance order *see* Maintenance order enforcement
table of countries 59
Recognition of judgments and orders *see also* Judgment
adoption 282
Brussels IIA 2787
civil partnership dissolution, etc 725, 729
custody 369, 393, 852
custody of child *see* European Convention (recognition and enforcement of custody decisions)
divorces, etc 863
Hague Convention 1996 2738, 2742
maintenance *see* Maintenance order
parental responsibility, etc *see* Hague Convention 1996
protection measures 2003, 2890
public policy 2873
Recognizance
High Court/County Court, in 1474
Reconciliation
divorce proceedings, certification of discussion of 1152

Reconciliation—*continued*
judicial separation, provisions apply on 1159
magistrates to consider, financial provision orders 822
statement, filing of 46, 1381
Records *see also* Disclosure
adoption *see* Adopted Children Register; Adoption: records
direction to undertake local authority investigation 1524
inspection *see also* Children's guardian: adoption proceedings: inspection of records
children's guardian, by 1706
Secretary of State, by 607
inspection by Secretary of State 608
looked after child 2419
search of, in matrimonial and civil partnership proceedings 1404
Recovery of child *see also* Abduction; Removal of child; Retention of child
execution of order 858
form of order 858
procedure on application for s 34 order 858
Recovery order
adoption process, power during 276
applicants for 140, 584, 1498
application 140
appeal 141
children's guardian 141, 162, 165, 166, 168, 170, 171
court 140
order 141
procedure 1641
respondents 140
service 141
without notice 141
conditions for 583
disclosure of child's whereabouts 584
entry of premises 584
meaning 583
offence 584
procedure 585
removal or production of child 584
respondents 1498
Recreational activities
child in need, for 659
family centre, at 660
Refuge
child at risk, provision for 585
Registration of orders
application 853
appropriate court 853
countries, table of 59
custody etc 853
cancellation 853
variation 853
documents 853
European Convention, under 370
family proceedings, in (High Court/County Court) 853
Hague Convention 77
maintenance order *see also* Maintenance order registration 1080
FPR 1953

Registration of orders—*continued*
maintenance order—*continued*
Northern Ireland, in *see also* Northern Ireland 696
prescribed manner 853
reciprocal enforcement of maintenance order, and *see also* Maintenance order enforcement
registration in UK of foreign order 1066, 1091
registration in UK of foreign order 72
Relative
child arrangements order applicant 452
contact, promotion of 662
meaning 318, 636
special guardianship order applicant 474
Release of a minor *see* Writ of habeas corpus
Religious dress 1529, 2578
Religious marriage
procedure for dissolution 1156, 1400
Religious persuasion
adoption, and 255, 256
care/supervision order, and 548, 549
children's home, and 594
local authority duty to consider 497
voluntary organisation to consider 592
Relocation
shared living arrangements, and *see* Shared living arrangements: relocation
within the UK 472
Relocation abroad
shared living arrangements 442
Remand 893, 1984
breach of undertaking 128
child on, accommodation for 495
secure accommodation 2433
disobedience of injunctive order 128
forced marriage 905
re-remand 910
Remarriage
family provision, effect on 1037
financial provision orders
effect on 1196
repayment of sums paid 824, 1210
repayment order 824
maintenance order, and 1215
reciprocal arrangements, and 1118
meaning (MCA 1973) 1215
non-recognition of decree, and 866
overseas divorce etc, financial relief and 1124
Remedial order 1004
Remedy
defines procedure 1741
interim *see* Interim remedy
Removal from jurisdiction 471
Removal of child *see also* Abduction; Port alert; Recovery of child; Retention of child
care/supervision order, and 549
child arrangements order, and 470
foreign adoption, for 302
habitual residence after 860
improper 370, 395
orders made after 381
orders restricting, reciprocal effect 858

Removal of child—*continued*
placement proceedings pending *see* Placement: removal of child
recovery, power of 157, 857
remedies for prevention of 859
removal of babies at birth 529
surrender of passport 859
unlawful
declaration 396
usual place of residence, removal from 1522
ward of court
modification of restrictions 859
Practice Direction 1633
wrongful 376
Hague Abduction Convention 1980
application 367
application of 363
Removal of child from UK 1544
radicalisation 859
temporary removal 473
welfare of child 471
wrongful removal or retention 2775
Report
adoption proceedings, in *see* Adoption
Cafcass officer *see* Cafcass officer
European Convention, for purposes of 372
expert *see* Expert's report
Hague Abduction Convention 1980, for purposes of 366
Reporting officer 1710
adoption application, in *see* Adoption
freeing for adoption application *see* Freeing for adoption
Reporting restriction order 247, 1002, 1563
application for
CAFCASS Practice Note 2567
freedom of expression right, regard to 1001
President's Direction 1623
applications for 1002
Reporting restrictions *see also* Publicity 627, 1039
adoption, and *see* Adoption: restriction on reports
fair trial, right to a 627
matrimonial proceedings 1039
power to dispense with restrictions on publicity 628
prejudice, risk of 628
Representation *see also* Children's guardian; Legal representative
child 1695
child acting without 1698
declarations 1422
Practice Direction 1713
children's guardian or solicitor, by 567, 1520, 1833
company/corporation, of 1835
fair trial *see* Human rights: fair hearing: legal representation at hearing
interested person, of 2058
protected party 1680
separate *see* Separate representation
Representations
attendance at private hearings 1837
child, by 1520, 1833
Representations—*continued*
local authority, to 516
advocacy services 517
duty to consider representations made by parent 517
qualifying functions within scope 516
opportunity to make 1520
Republic of Ireland
maintenance order enforcement, and 1080
Rescission
divorce 212
matrimonial/civil partnership order 1399
Reservation
Hague Convention on the International Recovery of Child Support 2007, under 2843
Residence
determination of 520
ordinary 637, 638
person with whom child has lived 454
transfer of living arrangements 444
suspended 444
usual or last known 1349
Residence order *see* Child arrangements order
Residential care home
accommodation
advice and assistance after leaving 507
inspection 607, 633
research on 610
secure accommodation 2433
applicant 2435
Resources *see also* Case management; Costs
parents, of 520
Respect for private and family life *see* Human rights: private and family life, right to respect for
Respondent
children, proceedings relating to 1490
co-respondent *see* Co-respondent
divorce, etc, petition, to 1382
answer by 49
financial remedy (ancillary relief) proceedings 1445
hearing in absence of 1520
matrimonial and civil partnership proceedings 1383
meaning
CPR 2077
FPR 1381
non-attendance, Family Court 1832
proceedings in absence of 1833
service on 1347
address for 1349
Response 2056
Restraint jurisdiction *see* Disclosure: restraint jurisdiction, and
Restraint of disposition *see* Disposition
Restrictions on publicity *see* Reporting restrictions
Retention of child *see also* Abduction; Recovery of child; Removal of child 376
Return of child
duty to order 383
expiration of 12 months, after 386
duty to return in non-Convention cases 385

Return of child—*continued*
enforcement of order 388
Hague Abduction Convention 1980 384
judgment which requires 2781
opportunity to be heard 2794
Returns of information
Secretary of State, to 610
Review
care plan 515, 2401, 2411
considerations 2412, 2426
timing 2412
implementation of decisions following 2413
IRO role 2412
local authority, by, of cases 514
maintenance calculation decision *see* Child support
policy for 2412
protection measures 2890
records 2413
Rights of access *see* Access: rights
Rights of audience *see* Audience, rights of
Rights of custody *see* Custody (of child): rights of custody
Risk assessment *see also* Cafcass officer 445, 483
duty arising even where no pending proceedings 483
Practice Direction 483, 1631
Rome III Regulation
divorce 2770
judicial separation 2770
Rome IVa Regulation 2770
Rome IVb Regulation 2770
RRO *see* Reporting restriction order
Rules *see also* Civil Procedure Rules; Family Procedure Rules
non-compliance sanctions
apply unless relief obtained 1323
relief from 1323
power under CA 1989
procedure 634
protection of children 586
rules of court 621
Wales 634

Sale of property order
civil partnership, High Court / County Court 733
divorce, etc, on 54, 1173, 1198
procedure (FPR) 1446
Same-sex couple *see also* Civil partnership; Same-sex marriage
declarations as to marital status 869
jurisdiction 829
parental responsibility and *see* Parental responsibility: same-sex families, and
parenting 441
Same-sex families
parental responsibility 427
Same-sex marriage
civil partnerships, conversion of 1119
effect of extension of marriage 1121
extra-territoriality 1121
introduction 1119
jurisdiction 46, 1121
Same-sex marriage—*continued*
right to marry, and 1010
Sample
bodily or blood sample *see* Blood test; Scientific test
property, of, order for 1742, 2086
School *see also* Education
boarding, welfare of child 613
entry powers 614
inspection 615, 616
'provision of accommodation' 613
independent *see* Independent school
private fostering, and 681
School attendance order
care order discharges 618
education supervision order discharges 674
School fees 1170
Scientific test 411, 870, 1422
application procedure 226
child's best interests for sample to be taken 922
consent to bodily sample 921, 923
person lacking capacity 922
costs 920
definition 924
direction 921
discretion to direct 921
fees for 411
inference 923
interests of justice 921
parentage, to determine 919
application procedure 922
bodily samples 919
personation offence 923
persons to give bodily samples 919
party to the proceedings 921
presumption of law 923
procedure 921
refusal 923
responsible adult 921
two or more putative fathers 921
Scotland
adoption 312
recognition of judgments and orders 282
registration in 321
adoption, permanence orders for 281
aliment payments, child support maintenance and 407
attachment of earnings, Family Court jurisdiction 349
Children Act, application 639
civil partnership 712
custody order, meaning 398
custody rights *see* 'Hague Convention, and' *below*
delivery of child, order for 848
enforcement
judgment of High Court / County Court, of 97, 98
maintenance order 1066, 1068, 1069, 1071
English maintenance 2869
European Convention, central authority for 369
guardianship order 837, 847
Hague Abduction Convention 1980, and
central authority for 364
court for application 365

Scotland—*continued*
maintenance
English maintenance 2869
maintenance order registration 1066
cancellation 70, 1072
discharge and variation of registered order 1069
enforcement 1066
FPR 1911
restrictions on enforcement 1101
Maintenance Regulation 2857
parental responsibilities or rights order
enforcement in 856
meaning 861
Part I order
duration 847
emergency jurisdiction 846
enforcement 854
jurisdiction 845, 846, 848
meaning 837, 856
refusal of application 847
registration 853
variation or cancellation 854
social security benefit, recovery from person in 1063
Seal
court 1855
Search
child, for
authority for, under FLA 157, 857
constable's power to assist 633
custody order, under 857
search of premises *see* Search order
Search order 1240, 2091
County Court 2451
court power
CPR 2087
FPR 1742
discharge 1241
duty of disclosure 1240
effect 1240
meaning 2087
procedure for 1240
restrictions on search under 2099
safeguards for interests of defendant 1241
search and seizure of documents and articles 1241
self-incrimination privilege 2093, 2103
specimen 2098
supervising solicitor 2091, 2103
Search warrant
assistance for inspection of premises or search for child 633
emergency protection order, and 583
***Sears Tooth* assignment** 1255
Secretary (company)
liability for offence by company 633
Secretary of State 2444
child support maintenance calculation, jurisdiction 414
grant by 609, 638
homes provided by 609
income support recipient, maintenance order enforcement for 1252
Secretary of State—*continued*
information to be given to 610
inspection of premises etc 607
research 610
supervisory functions 607
Section 8 order *see also* Child arrangements order; Prohibited steps order; Specific issue order
age of child, and 450
applicant's connection with child 456
application for 451, 453
child, by 453
leave for 451
person requiring leave 454
person who may make 452
without notice 1521
application for leave
child, by 454
person other than child concerned, by 455
procedure on 456
Best Practice Guidance 2541
care order discharges *see* Care order: section 8 order, discharges
child in care, and 450
conditions 456
consent of authority 451
definition 439
delay, avoidance of 456, 457
directions 456, 2542
duration 457, 618
enforcement *see* Enforcement: section 8 order
evidence, additional 1525
final disposal of proceedings, making order before 457
form of consent 454
hearing 2543
incidental etc provision in 457
jurisdiction 838, 839
leave to apply 451
notice to non-party 1600
Part I order, as 836
parties 1491
person entitled to apply for 453
power of court to make 451, 456
proceedings in which question of making order arises 457
restrictions 450
rules of court entitling persons to apply for 454
variation or discharge 452
persons not otherwise entitled to apply for 454
procedure on application for 454
welfare of child, and 422
welfare report, and 2542
when the court may make a 453
Secure accommodation 496
age under 13 2432
appropriate court 513
avoidance of need for, local authority duty 659
child who is not legally represented 512
children's home, in, approval 2432
community home, in 587, 609
detained/remanded child, use for 2433
duration 510
further periods 2435

Secure accommodation—*continued*
duration—*continued*
maximum periods 511
maximum with court authority 2434
maximum without court authority 2434
duty to inform parents, etc 2435
expenses of, grants 609, 610, 638
legal representation, and 511
meaning 511, 610
overseas placements 513
removal of child, parent's right 511
restrictions on use 2432
youth detention accommodation, child in 2433
specified placements 512
use of
child being accommodated by health authority etc 2433
child being looked after 510
Wales 2432
Youth Court 171
Secure accommodation order 510, 2347
application for 171
answer 172
appeals 173
applicant 171
children's guardian 172
court 171
directions 172
form 172, 1540
joinder 172
local authority, by 2435
respondents 172
service 172
special cases, in 2435
copies of reports 1540
criteria for 511
duration 512
interim 1540
parties 1493
persons entitled to notice of hearing 1540
refusal of bail and, relationship between 513
Secured periodical payments order *see* Periodical payments order: secured
Securities
charging order, and
effect 2024
service 2024
stop notice 361, 2027
stop order 361, 2026
Security for costs 1746, 2096, 2147
application 1747
family proceedings, in 1747
order for 1747
Segal order 1164, 1168
Self-incrimination 629
search order 2093
Self-incrimination privilege 1753
Sentencing 792
contempt proceedings 796, 805
County Court to be treated as superior court 792
early release 792
fixed term, sentence must be for 792
Sentencing—*continued*
imprisonment not exceeding two years 792
Separate representation 1502, 1871
children as parties where 1502
contact disputes 446
Hague Abduction Convention 1980
application 386
Separate trial of issue
court power 2036
Separation *see also* Judicial separation
leaflet CB7 1504
Separation order
application procedure 1379
court power to make 703
registration and recognition under Council Regulation 1897
Sequestration *see* Writ of sequestration
Serious injury
protection of public from 497
Service
acknowledgment *see* Acknowledgment of service; Hague Service Convention 1965
address for 637, 1354
adoption proceedings, in *see* Adoption
alternative method / place 1352
application notice 2078
application made without notice 2079
bailiff, by 1348
failure notification 1353, 1357
certificate of service 1357
child, on
matrimonial / civil partnership order application 1349
non-matrimonial etc application 1354
children proceedings 1505
Practice Direction 1598
civil or commercial matters, documents in, EC Council Regulation 2823
claim form 2040
contempt of court 1987
dispensation with service 1987
court, by 1348, 1353
failure notification 1353
record as proof 1352
date
Regulation (EC) No 2201 / 2003, under 2779
deemed 1351
matrimonial / civil partnership order application 1351
defendant's application for 2041
dispensing with 1352
non-matrimonial etc application 1357
documents (not matrimonial etc application) 1353
electronic communications 2817
electronic means 1362
email 1362
EU, within 1359
extension of time *see* Time-limit
failure in, setting aside for (CPR) 2079
fax, by *see* Fax
financial remedy (ancillary relief) application
lay justices' powers 26
mortgagees, trustees, etc, on 1436

Service—*continued*
  Foreign Office, through 1361
  FPR 1346
  impossibility 2783
  judgment, of (FPR) 1858
    party as well as solicitor 1858
  jurisdiction
    impossibility of service 2783
  litigant in person 1838
  litigation friend 1688, 1702, 2065, 2066
  matrimonial / civil partnership order
      application 1347, 1365
    address for 1348, 1349
    bailiff, by 1348, 1353
    court, by 1348
    methods 1347
    person to serve 1347
    personal service 1347, 1351
    Practice Direction 1362
    respondent, on 1347, 1382
    solicitor, on 1348
  method for 637
    CPR, under 2040
    FPR, under 1347, 1353
    Supreme Court Rules, under 2352
  notice 1351
  notice of appeal, Supreme Court 2357
  order, of (FPR) 1858
    party as well as solicitor 1858
  out of England and Wales 1357
    acknowledgment, period for 1358
    Hague Convention country 1360
    method for 1359
    permitted by law of country 1359
    Practice Direction 1368
    Service Regulation 1359
    translation 1361
  Part 8 claim 2050
  person to be served 1350
  personal service 1347, 1354
    proof, no acknowledgment filed 1351
  proof of 1351, 1352
  protection from harassment 1231
  protection measures 2005
  Regulation (EU) No 606 / 2013, under 2891
  relevant person, on 1538
  Service Regulation 1358
    under 1359, 1373
  solicitor, on
    authorised person, term includes 1347
    matrimonial / civil partnership order
        application 1348
  Supreme Court 2352
  time-limit for claim form 2040
    extension of time 2040
Service Regulation 1359
Services
  use of available
    by children's home 593
    by voluntary organisation 591
Services, provision of
  accommodated child, for 659
  adoption, on *see* Adoption agency

Services, provision of—*continued*
  charges for 518, 2747
    exceptions 518
  child in need, identification of 657
    living with family, for 659
  conditions 485
  contributions to cost of *see also* Contribution
      order 518, 666
  disabled child register 657
  disabled child, for 658
  investigation of circumstances, and 554
  local authority duty 484, 657, 659
  needs of child, assessment 657
  prevention of neglect, etc, duty 658
Setting aside
  agreement of parties 1153
  asset disposal *see* Assets
  costs 1849
  decree nisi or conditional order 1399
    setting aside district judge's certificate 1394
    setting aside for vitiating factor 1394
  financial relief order (for child) 213
  financial remedy 1433, 1465
  judgment *see* Judgment
  matrimonial / civil partnership order 1399
  order *see* Order
  settlements 2068
  witness summons 1783
Settlement
  approval 1684, 1700
  child, for
    after issue of proceedings 2073
    alternative (Part 8) procedure claim, use
        of 2067
    approval of court 2067
    before issue of proceedings 2072
    order for 644
  divorce, on, order for 1160
    bankruptcy of settlor, avoidance on 1211
    variation 1198
  enforceability 1442
  family provision order for, from deceased's
      estate 1019
  financial relief 1442
  legitimated person, and 1057
  meaning 1172
  protected party, for 2067
    after issue of proceedings 2073
    alternative (Part 8) procedure claim, use
        of 2067
    before issue of proceedings 2072
  setting aside *see* Setting aside: settlements
  variation application 2068
    representation of child 1435
    service of application 1436
Sex
  child, of, consideration for court 422
Sexual abuse
  investigations, guidance 2543
Sexual offence
  child charged with, secure accommodation
      for 2433
Sexual orientation *see* Same sex families
SGO *see* Special guardianship order

Share schemes
financial provision 1183
Shared living arrangements
child arrangements order for *see* Child arrangements order: shared living arrangements, for
relocation 442
abroad 442
Short stays
care order, 'interim' 205
Shorthand note
Family Court proceedings, of 1835
Sibling
fostering of 677
placement of
apart, contact between 2420
siblings together 499
Signature
printed by computer/other mechanical means 2351
verification by statement of truth 1724
Signposting services
Child Arrangements Programme 1577
Single joint expert *see* Expert
SIO *see* Specific issue order
Sisting of proceedings
custody order enforcement, of 855
Skeleton argument *see* Appeal: skeleton arguments; Judicial review: skeleton arguments
Skype, use of 1636, 1639
Slavery and forced labour prohibition 1005
Slip rule 1859
Social security benefit
income support *see* Income support
parent of child receiving, child support and *see* Child support
recovery of 1063, 1252
repayment from person liable to maintain 1252
Social work practice 531
Social worker *see also* Local authority
expert evidence from 687
Solicitor *see also* Legal services; Official Solicitor
acceptance of instructions
children's guardian or litigation friend not required 1699
appointment 569
section 41(3), under 1515
authorised person, term includes (FPR) 1347
ceasing to act 1827
change of (FPR) 1825
Practice Direction 1828
child, for 567
appointment 1504
attendance 1715
duties 1708
tandem model 1705
children's guardian 1705
disclosure, guidance 1467
litigation friend, for *see* Litigation friend: solicitor, need for
power to appoint 568
protected party, for 2061
removal 1828
Solicitor—*continued*
representation by *see* Representation: children's guardian or solicitor, by
service by/on *see* Service
tandem model 1705
undertaking given by *see* Undertaking: solicitor, given by
Special advocate 1512
appointment
request to Attorney-General 2686
public interest immunity and *see* Public interest immunity: special advocate, and
Special guardian
appointment 153, 431, 473, 476
death, replacement on 431
procedure 153
revocation of 433
child arrangements order 452
contact 476
child in care 550
eligibility 473
family assistance order, named in 481
financial support for 480
local authority
investigation and report 474
support services 479
parental responsibility, child in care 548
section 8 order application 452
suitability assessments 476
Special guardianship
adoption and, choice between *see* Adoption: special guardianship and, choice between
Guidance 475
kinship cases, not confined to 475
support services
more than one local authority involved 480
Special guardianship order *see* Special guardianship order 153, 473
additional evidence 1525
advice and assistance for older child 509
applicants 473
conditions or directions in 155, 478
considerations for court 155, 476
court's own motion 475
effect 153, 477
financial relief, powers of court 645, 653
guidance on making 474
habitual residence/presence condition 838
leave to apply 475
leave to apply to discharge 478
local authority report, need for 476
more than one local authority involved 475
notice to non-party 1601
orders discharged by 618
Part I order 837
parties 1492
report disclosure 1525
report prerequisite 474
rules power 478
variation/discharge 155, 477, 478, 1492
Specific issue order 449
court and judge for 151
definition 438
directions 152

Specific issue order—*continued*
discharge / variation application 150
ex parte application 150
form 152
joinder 151
notice to non-party 151, 1600
respondents 151
restrictions on 451
restrictions on power to make 450
service 151
time-limits 151
without notice procedure 151
Specified proceedings 567, 569, 1536
children's guardian, appointment of 1536
Speeches
order 1529
Sperm *see also* Fertility services
known sperm donor 428, 441
permitted, meaning 963
Split hearing 423, 445, 534, 548, 1507, 1528, 1658, 2540
Guidance 2612
interim orders and *see* Care order: interim: split hearings, and; Supervision order: interim: split hearings, and
Spouse *see* Husband and wife
stranded *see* Stranded spouse
Stamp
court 1855
Standard of proof 1761
contempt proceedings 795
criminal standard 1762
presumption as to legitimacy and illegitimacy 924
State benefit *see* Social security benefit
Statement of case *see also* Claim form
evidence, as 1765
failure to verify
effective unless struck out 1724
family proceedings, in 1722
meaning 1721
use as evidence 2117, 2123
verification 1722
Statement of truth 1722, 2046
email 1345
facts, as to 1724
false, committal application 2308, 2315
financial remedy (ancillary relief) proceedings 1444
form of 1725
Practice Direction 1725
protected parties 2061
requirement for 1722
response 2056
signature 1726
verification by 1765
'verified by' 1723
Statutory appeal *see* Appeal
Statutory charge
avoidance or evasion 1044
operation 1042
regulations 1044
rollover 1169, 1172
Statutory tenancy
transfer
divorce etc, after *see* Tenancy
overseas divorce etc, after 1132
Stay of execution 2326
County Court powers 802
Stay of proceedings 828
applications for stay
procedure 829
arbitration 2700
care or supervision 566
imposition of conditions to grant of stay 566
certiorari or prohibition, in case of 800
civil partnership proceedings 831
court power (CPR) 2036
custody order enforcement, and 855
Hague Convention 1996 525
litigant in person 793
matrimonial / civil partnership proceedings 827, 831, 1398
Part I order (FLA), where foreign proceedings 841
Step-down order 1168
Step-parent 285
contact with child in care 550
parental responsibility 142, 430
child in care 548
section 8 order application 452
Stop notice
amended 2028
effect 2027
meaning 361
request for 2027
Stop order
court power 2026
meaning 361
Stranded spouse
guidance in cases 1516
Striking out
claim 2037
civil restraint order, circumstances for 2037
matrimonial / civil partnership proceedings 1397
statement of case
power 1322
Practice Direction 1325
Subpoena *see* Witness: summons
Summary assessment *see* Costs: summary assessment
Summons
High Court *see* Application
judgment *see* Judgment summons
witness *see* Witness
Supervision *see also* Supervision order; Supervisor
contact 553
Supervision order
age limit 520
application for 159, 520
answer 162
appeal 163
applicant 160
authorised person 160, 521
court 160
directions 162

Supervision order—*continued*
application for—*continued*
joinder 162
notice to non-parties 1601
order 162
respondents 161
restrictions 521
service 161
best interests of the child 539
Best Practice Guide 2589
status of 2592
care order, or 539
care order's effect on 618
children's guardian 162, 165
concessions 540
court cannot specify directions to be given 670
court's powers 520
criminal 617
delay, avoidance of 546, 547
directions 670, 1533
discharge 163, 563
answer 165
appeal 166
applicant 164
application 163
court 164
directions 165
form 166
joinder 165
pre-proceedings checklist 164
respondent 165
service 165
supervisor's duty to consider 553
duration 672
education supervision order, and 674
effect 553
earlier orders, on 673
examination, medical or psychiatric 671
extension 163, 672
alternative applications 673
test on extension application 672
imperative requirements 620
interim 162, 557, 565
abolition of requirement to renew order 558
duration 557
Hague Convention 1996 provisions 2506
medical examination etc 557
nature of interim order 558
removal under an order 558
split hearings, and 560
local authority
designated for 521
functions 673
investigation, prior to 554
meaning 522
parties 1493
pending appeal 565
requirement, imposing a 564
responsible person 670
obligations on 670
review of case 554
substitution of, for care order 163, 564
supervisor *see* Supervisor

Supervision order—*continued*
threshold criteria 520
timetable 546
start 161
treatment, medical or psychiatric 671
variation 163, 563
Supervision orders
allocation of proceedings 522
Supervisor
assistance etc to child 553
contact with child 673
definition 636
directions 670
duties 553
education supervision order, under 673
information to 673
local authority as 673
selection of 673
Supported Child Contact Centres
referral to, Protocol (revised) 2615
Supreme Court
acknowledgement of service 2357
appeal to 199
certificate for 198
contempt of court case 249
Court of Appeal, from 199
High Court from 199
permission for 199
authorities, preparation of 2358
core volumes 2358
costs 2364
criminal appeal 2363
cross-appeal 2358
devolution appeal 2362
documents for hearing 2357
European Community issue 2363
exclusion of party from hearing 2359
expedition request 2361
fees 2364, 2528
filing 2352
forms 2351
grouping of appeals 2361
hearing 2359
human rights appeal 2362
information to court on death or bankruptcy, etc 2361
intervention 2358
judgment 2359
notice of appeal 2356
form and filing 2357
service 2357
orders 2359
patent revocation appeal 2363
permission to appeal
application 2354
documents in support 2355
filing of application 2354
intervention in application 2355
not required 2357
notice of objection 2355
objection to application by respondent 2355
oral hearing 2356
paper consideration 2356
service of application 2355

Supreme Court—*continued*
procedural applications 2360
procedural decisions, persons who may take 2353
respondent
acknowledgement by 2357
cross-appeal 2358
notice of objection 2361
Rules 2350
non-compliance 2353
security for costs 2362
service 2352
stay of execution 2362
time-limit 2351
withdrawal of application 2361
Surname *see* Name: change of surname
Surrogacy
adoption 989
definitions 959, 960, 1256
Directives 960
disclosure provisions 971
embryo, storage of 961
gamete, storage of 961
mother 1256
parental order *see* Parental order
surrogacy arrangement
advertisements 1258
commercial negotiation of 1256
meaning 1256
non-profit making body 1257
offences 1257, 1258, 1259
unenforceability 1256
surrogate mother 1256
third party agreement
embryo kept pursuant to 962
meaning 962
Surveillance 624

Tagging *see* Electronic tagging
Taking control of goods
amount of fees recoverable 2343
extension of period for 2324
sale otherwise than by public auction 2341
Taxation *see* Costs
Telephone conferencing 1509
Telephone hearing 1320, 2082
Tenancy
joint *see* Joint tenancy
prevention of unilateral termination of 875, 894
restraining surrender of 1210
transfer on divorce etc 41, 894, 911
civil partnership dissolution 784
compensation 915
'dwelling-house' 912
liabilities of spouses 915
MCA 1973 s 24, interrelation with 914
overseas divorce etc, after 1132
procedure 911, 1426
undertaking not to surrender 41
Terrorism
disclosure 1510
radicalisation 2695
Third party
attacks on property transfers 1173
Third party—*continued*
avoidance of transactions intended to prevent or reduce financial relief 1210
costs 2157
disclosure against *see* Disclosure: third parties, against
document, release of court 1755
evidence from *see* Evidence: third parties, from
injunction against 2093
property jointly owned with 1174
property rights 1172
Third party debt order
amount of money remaining due 2296
application 114, 2291
court for 114, 2291
bank account, etc, and 1244, 2298
child support maintenance, to enforce 412
conditions applying to account 2291
costs 2295
CPR 113, 2291
Crown as third party 2291
debt, existence of 2291
disclosure 2293
discretion to make order 2295
expenses of 803, 1244
final order 2291
effect of 117, 2291, 2295
hearing 117, 2295
objection to 116, 2294
FPR provisions applying CPR 1936
hardship 2294
hardship payment order 116, 2293
hearing 114
interim 114, 2291, 2292
discretion to make 2292
effect 2293
obligations of persons served 2293
service 115, 2292
time for making 2292
issues in dispute 2295
lay justices not permitted to make 2291
Practice Direction (CPR) 2296
procedure 113
service 2292, 2294
venue 2294
Time estimates 1508
Time-limit *see also* Delay
alteration of maintenance agreement 1208
appeals 2196
care proceedings
extension of time 548
judgments
delay 548
computation of time 1291, 2034
extension of time 1865, 2196
appeal restrictions 1234
practice direction 2047
failure to observe 1517
family provision application, for 1024, 2270
magistrates' child support proceedings 1060
Married Women's Property Act 1882, application under 1123
parental orders 989

Time-limit—*continued*
service of claim form 2040
extension of time 2040
Supreme Court 2351
variation 1517
Timetable
proceedings, for the 1508
public law cases, for 1508, 1534
extension of time 548
Tipstaff 1549
contact details 1605
role 1545
Title of proceedings 1700
representation of protected parties 1684
Tort *see also* Harassment
harassment, statutory prohibition 1229
personal protection injunction 36
Torture, etc, prohibition 1005
Tracing
Practice Direction 1373
Practice Note 1969
Training
after leaving care, etc
assistance with 509
approved 2486
Transcript
appeals 799, 1867
Transfer of living arrangements *see* Residence: transfer of living arrangements
Transfer of proceedings 1515
adoption *see* Adoption
Brussels IIA 2709
enforcement, for 2281, 2332
family proceedings (High Court/County Court) 1144, 1145
family provision 2270
freedom of movement 525
Hague Convention 1996 525, 2709
inherent jurisdiction *see* Inherent jurisdiction: transfer of proceedings 1862
judicial review, of application for 1239, 2264
jurisdiction and *see* Jurisdiction: transfer of proceedings, and
Transfer of property order 644
divorce, order on 1160, 1171
bankruptcy of settlor, avoidance on 1211
duration/age limit 1197
family provision from deceased's estate, for 1019
financial relief for child
power to enforce order 646
financial relief order (for child) 12
Transgender persons *see* Gender recognition
Translation
bundles 205
costs 1511
Transparency
Family Court 2656
Travel
help with, child in need 659
Treatment *see* Dental treatment; Medical treatment
Trespassers
possession claim against 2332
Trial *see* Hearing
bundle *see* Court bundle
Trust
claim by or against trustees 2059
property in
representation of interested person 2058
Trust of land
application to court for order 1261
application to court, matters for court 1261
beneficial ownership declaration, application procedure 1261
cohabitees or family members, application by 1262
exclusion of beneficiary from occupation 1260
MCA 1973, relationship with 1262
occupation right of beneficiary 1260
principle of land law apply 1262
registration in a sole name 1263
registration in joint names 1262
trustee in bankruptcy, application by 1264
Trustee
adoption, and protection of 1058
bankruptcy, in *see* Trust of land: trustee in bankruptcy, application by
consent to act, evidence of 1780
home rights of non-beneficiary spouse/civil partner 874, 876, 879
legitimation, and protection of 1058
UN Convention on the Rights of the Child
views and wishes of the child 386, 1531, 1697
Understanding of child *see* Child: understanding
Undertaking 797, 1473
breach of, committal for 125
care proceedings 543
consent order containing 1447
contempt of court 1986, 1988
copy of undertaking 1987
emergency protection order, with 576
enforcement *see* Enforcement: undertakings
forced marriage protection order, as alternative to 903
harassment protection, for 40
injunction, in lieu of 1242
interim care order, with 563
occupation/non-molestation order application, in 30, 890
penal notice, requirement for 2314
procedure 891
restriction on 891
solicitor, given by 1137
enforcement, permission 2305
warrant of arrest 891
Unit trust
charging order on, meaning for 362
United Kingdom
adoption of child from outside UK *see* Convention adoption order
maintenance order
reciprocal enforcement 2446
reciprocal enforcement outside 1087
United States
Hague Child Support Convention 2007 78

United States of America
maintenance order, reciprocal enforcement 1949
FPR provisions 1948
procedure 72
registration 74
variation etc of UK order 80
Unmarried father
custody rights and *see* Custody (of child): unmarried fathers, and
parental responsibility *see also* Parental responsibility order
acquisition of 426, 427
automatic order 429
Birth Register not signed, where 428
duration 618
end of 426
registration as father 426
Unpaid work requirement
enforcement order 640
Upbringing
child in need, promotion of 484
Urgency
orders for interim remedies 1743
Urgent application
Administrative Court 2267
Child Arrangements Programme 1584
expert evidence 1802
Hague Abduction Convention 1980 382
Hague Convention 1996 2738
inherent jurisdiction, under 184
interim remedy *see* Interim remedy: procedure: urgent applications
personal protection injunction 37
President's Guidance 2621
Urgent hearing *see also* Emergency protection order; Hearing
Court of Appeal, before 1522
Vaccination
child subject to interim care order 559
Variation application 1539
Variation order
meaning (FPR) 1431
Vehicle
'premises', as 790
Veil
Muslim niqab, guidance 1529, 2578
Venue
court discretion as to 1290
Verification 1724
application 1724
power of court 1724
Vexatious proceedings
restriction 1245
Video conferencing 1509, 1879
directions application for use 2083
guidance
CPR 2124
FPR 1774
procedure 2123
use 1773
Video link
child witness 1763
Video link—*continued*
expert evidence 1798
overriding objective, and the 2116
use of
CPR 2116
FPR 1763
vulnerable witness 1763
Views and wishes of child
children's home, and 593
court to have regard to 422
local authority to ascertain 496
voluntary organisation to ascertain 592
welfare of child, and 424
Views and wishes of the child
contact 424
habitual residence 2742
objections 390
UN Convention on the Rights of the Child 386, 1531, 1697
Violence
child charged with violent offence, secure accommodation 2433
domestic *see* Domestic violence
honour-based *see* Honour-based violence
Visit
children's home, child in 592, 594
expense of (child being looked after) 663
placement, after, local authority duty 2410
private fostering, child in 595, 598
voluntary organisation, to child accommodated by 592
Visitor
child in specified accommodation, local authority duty 613
independent
looked after child, local authority duty 501
meaning of independent 2416
Void/voidable marriage *see* Marriage
Voluntary home
definition 591
refuge, as 585
registration of 591
regulation of 591
Voluntary organisation *see also* Voluntary home
accommodation, provision by 590, 592
community home *see* Community home
computer records 593
definition 636
duties 591
fostering, number of children 676
grants to 609, 638
information to Secretary of State 610
inspection of children, premises etc 593, 607
power of constable to assist 633
local authority duties 592
records 593
services, use of 591
visits to child 592
welfare of child 592
wishes of child etc 592
Vulnerable adult
detention *see* Detention: child or vulnerable adult

Vulnerable adult—*continued*
- forced marriage protection order *see* Forced marriage protection order: person to be protected lacks capacity
- inherent jurisdiction 1547
- Official Solicitor 2716

Vulnerable witness
- cross-examination by unrepresented party 1762
- video link 1763

Wales *see also* England and Wales; Local Health Board
- accommodation provision for child in care 498
- child minder in *see* Child minder
- day care in schools, exemptions from regulation 681
- devolution issues 2262
- English law, divergence from 484
- family proceedings officer, risk assessment duty 483
- local authority, meaning of 635

Ward of court
- adoption of 1549
- ceasing to be 1549
- criminal proceedings, and 1543
- financial relief order 645
- High Court jurisdiction 1245
- party to proceedings, as 1548
- register of wards 1548
- removal from jurisdiction, and 859
  - passport 1633
  - Practice Direction 1633

Wardship
- application 181
  - affidavit 183
  - appeal 184
  - applicant 182
  - court 182
  - directions 183
  - orders 184
  - service 183
- care order brings to an end *see* Care order: wardship, effect on
- care order, effect on 618
- child subject of, permission to be party 1548
- commencement of application 1544
- confirmation 1549
- disclosure *see* Disclosure: wardship proceedings
- distinguishing characteristics 1543
- enforcement of orders by tipstaff 1549
- local authority, leave required 630
- Practice Guidance 2614
- proceedings that should be dealt with in High Court 1544
- publicity *see* Publicity: wardship proceedings
- restrictions on 630
- restrictions under CA 1989 1544
- stranded spouse cases, Guidance 2614
- whereabouts of child, notice as to 1548

Warning notice
- child arrangements order, for 147, 148, 149
  - application procedure 1541
  - parties to application 1500
- contact order, for 464

Warning notice—*continued*
- enforcement order 468

Warrant
- forced marriage protection order *see* Forced marriage protection order: warrant, application for
- search *see* Search warrant

Warrant of arrest
- courts' power 127
- occupation /non-molestation order breach 127, 892
- protection from harassment 1231

Warrant of committal 2311
- child support enforcement 413
- immediate issue 2290
- maintenance order enforced by 1078

Warrant of control
- instalment order 2331

Warrant of delivery *see also* Writ of delivery
- appeal 111
- application 111
- availability 111
- composition of court 111
- form of 111
- issue 111
- permission 111

Warrant of execution *see also* Execution of instrument; Goods
- appeal 113
- application for, County Court 801
- availability 112
- form 113
- FPR provisions 1935
- issue 112
- payment, execution superseded by 801
- sale of goods 801
- stay of, County Court powers 802
- variation of existing order pending, permission required 1935

Warrant of possession 2322
- appeal 125
- availability 124
- effect 2335
- enforcement of judgment by
  - form 125
- issue 124, 2335
- procedure 124

Warrant of restitution 2335

Wasted costs order 1247
- application for 2160
- disclosure *see* Disclosure: wasted costs orders
- 'improper, unreasonable or negligent', meaning of 2160
- jurisdiction *see* Jurisdiction: wasted costs orders
- legal aid *see* Legal aid: wasted costs orders
- notice of application 231
- privilege and 2161
- procedure 231, 2160
- procedure after *Ridehalgh* 2160
- proportionality 2161
- warnings on unarguable appeals 2160

Welfare of child
- adoption, and *see* Adoption: consent to: welfare of child, and

Welfare of child—*continued*
- boarding school/college, child in 613, 615
  - entry powers 614
  - inspection 616
  - national minimum standards 617
  - 'provision of accommodation' 613
- Cafcass function to safeguard and promote 807, 1712
- checklist factors 423
- Child Arrangements Programme 1579, 1583
- child in need, promotion of 484, 657
- child support, principle of 401
- children's home, and 593
- court's approach to application 1853
- delay, and 422
- enforcement of child support 411
- European Convention (recognition and enforcement of custody decisions) application 396
- fertility services 969
- financial provision, Family Court 817
- Hague Abduction Convention 1980 application 392
- health authority accommodation, in 612
- local authority duty
  - accommodation by health authority etc 612
  - accommodation by residential care home etc 612
  - general 496
- local education authority accommodation, in 612
- principle for courts 422, 2431
  - circumstances for 422
  - factors for 422
- private fostering, and 595
- proportionality, and 538
- removal of child from UK 471
- voluntary organisation, and 591

Welfare officer
- meaning 1711

Welfare report
- conciliation as an alternative 436
- court differing with recommendation in 438
- court's power to call for 434, 1505, 1710
- duties of officer preparing 1719
- duty to comply 437
- form of 434
- independent 438
- preparation 1515
- section 8 order application 2542
- statements and evidence otherwise inadmissible 437

Whereabouts of child *see also* Disclosure: child's whereabouts, of
- disclosure 1757

Wife *see also* Husband and wife; Stranded spouse
- domicile, dependent, abolition of 826

Wilful refusal
- meaning 413

Will
- civil partnerships 702
- mutual 1024
- rectification 2269

Wishes of the child *see* Views and wishes of the child

Withdrawal of application 1853
- matrimonial/civil partnership, of 1382

Withdrawal of proceedings 1700
- representation of protected parties 1684

Withdrawal of treatment
- persistent vegetative state etc cases 227

Without notice application
- application on short notice as alternative to 1523
- Child Arrangements Programme 1584
- child, proceedings relating to 1521
- evidence in support, and 1746
- Hague Convention or European Convention, proceedings under *see* Hague Convention: proceedings under Hague Convention or European Convention: without notice applications
- meaning 1289
- notice, on 1523
- occupation order or non-molestation order, applications for 1469
- order desirable in interests of justice 1746
- protection of child in emergency (regulations governing child minders and day care providers) 603
- recovery of child 858
- service 2079
- wards of court 1245
- 'without notice' 890

Without notice order
- application to set aside 1524
- avoidance of transactions intended to prevent or reduce financial relief 1210
- duration 1744, 2721
- forced marriage protection order 903
- power of arrest 892
  - duration 892
- power to make 1522
- procedure for 1522
- refusal of application for 1524
- reporting restrictions 1002
- service 1523

Without prejudice rule
- agreement in correspondence covered by 1153
- children proceedings, and 1754
- immunity 1753
- waiver 1754

Witness *see also* Evidence
- affidavit evidence *see* Affidavit
- anonymity 1530, 2142
- attendance, enforcing 1784
- Cafcass officer 808
- child
  - oral evidence 542
  - summons 1138
  - veracity or validity of evidence 624
  - video link 1763
- child as *see* Evidence: child, by
- contempt of court hearing 1985
- court calling 1530
- cross-examination
  - limits (CPR) 2115

Witness—*continued*
cross-examination—*continued*
order for 1765
witness statement, on 1766
examination 1760, 1784
expenses 1783
expert *see* Expert; Expert evidence
fair trial, right to a 204
family proceedings, in 1761
FPR (general provisions) 1782
money to be paid to 1783
oral evidence 1762, 1764
party, by 2051
production of documents by 1511
professional witnesses, findings against 204
representation of protected parties 1684
statement *see also* Evidence 2116
failure to verify 1724
family provision 2271
final hearing, use at 1764, 1767
foreign and translated 1764
format 1760
hearsay evidence in *see* Hearsay evidence
inspection of documents mentioned in 2109
meaning 1763, 2116
occupation order or non-molestation order, applications for 1469
open to inspection 1768
oral evidence on 1764
other than final hearing, use at 1765
service and filing 1764, 2116
use in specific proceedings 1767, 1768
verification of 2122
summary 1766
failure to serve 1766
summons 626, 1138, 1783, 1985, 2431
child 1138
court officer, by 1138
FPR 1782
Practice Direction (FPR) 1787
video link 1763
written evidence 1762
Witness statement
alteration 2122
certificate of court officer 2123

Witness statement—*continued*
defect 2123
filing 2122
format 2121
statement of truth 2122
when required 2117
World Wide Web
publication of judgments on 2559
Writ ne exeat regno *see also* Passport: impounding 1236, 1243, 1744
Writ of delivery *see also* Warrant of delivery
procedure 111
Writ of fieri facias *see also* Goods; Warrant of execution
appeal 113
availability 112
composition of court 113
disclosure of debtor's address 113
form 113
issue 112
money judgment enforced by 801
permission 112
writ of execution, as 801
Writ of habeas corpus 1250, 1550, 1865
applications for 1550, 2346
Writ of possession *see also* Warrant of possession
procedure 124
Writ of sequestration 1992, 2323
judgment enforced by
penal notice requirement 2316
procedure
CPR 2309
Writ of subpoena *see* Witness: summons
Written statement *see* Document; Statement of case; Statement of truth; Witness
Wrongful removal or retention *see* Abduction; Hague Convention: wrongful removal or retention; Removal of child: wrongful

Youth Court
secure accommodation 171
Youth rehabilitation order
care supervision order, interaction with 521
education supervision order, interaction with 674
private fostering incompatible with 678

SUMMARY OF FEES

This non-exhaustive list sets out the fees relating to applications most frequently made by family law practitioners.

FAMILY PROCEEDINGS

			£
A	*Family Court*		£
1	Issue of application to start proceedings not mentioned below		245
2	Matrimonial causes		
	(a)	Any application for a decree of nullity, divorce or dissolution of a civil partnership	550
	(b)	Amending an application for a matrimonial or civil partnership order	95
	(c)	Filing an answer to an application for a matrimonial or civil partnership order	245
	(d)	Application for financial relief (except consent application)	255
	(e)	Application for consent order for financial relief	50
	(f)	Any other application on notice	155
3	Children Act 1989 proceedings		
	Commencement application or requesting permission for:		
	(i)	parental responsibility order (ss 4–4ZA)	215
	(ii)	section 8 order (s 10)	215
	(iii)	leave to take child out of jurisdiction or change surname (s 13)	215
	(iv)	financial provision for children (Sch 1)	215
	(v)	variation, revocation or discharge of financial provision order (Sch 1)	215
	(vi)	care or supervision order (s 31)	2055
	(vii)	discharge or variation of care or supervision order (s 39)	215
	(viii)	contact with child in care (s 34)	215
	(ix)	child assessment order (s 43)	215
	(x)	emergency protection order (s 44)	215
	(xi)	recovery order (s 50)	215
	(xii)	secure accommodation order (s 25)	215
	(xiii)	special guardianship order (ss 14A–14F)	215